The Harper American Literature

Volume 2

▶ Donald McQuade
University of California, Berkeley
General Editor

▶ Robert Atwan
Seton Hall University

▶ Martha Banta
University of California at Los Angeles

▶ Justin Kaplan

▶ David Minter
Emory University

▶ Cecelia Tichi
Boston University

▶ Helen Vendler
Harvard University

Harper & Row, Publishers, New York
Cambridge, Philadelphia, San Francisco, Washington,
London, Mexico City, São Paulo, Singapore, Sydney

Cover and Frontispiece Photo
Charles Sheeler, *Classic Landscape*,
1931.
Courtesy of Barney A. Ebsworth.

Sponsoring Editor
Phillip Leininger

Coordinating Editor
Jonathan Haber

Development Editor
Nat LaMar

Project Editor
Lenore Bonnie Biller

Text and Cover Design
Karen Salsgiver

Text Art
Vantage Art, Inc.

Production Manager
Jeanie Berke

Production Assistant
Brenda DeMartini

Compositor
*ComCom Division of Haddon
Craftsmen, Inc.*

Printer and Binder
R. R. Donnelley & Sons, Company

For permission to use copyrighted
material, grateful acknowledgment
is made to the copyright holders
listed on pp. 2881–2890, which
are hereby made part of this copyright page.

The Harper American Literature,
Volume 2

Copyright © 1987 by Harper &
Row, Publishers, Inc.

Library of Congress Cataloging in
Publication Data

The Harper American literature.

   Includes bibliographies and
indexes.
    I. American literature.
I. McQuade, Donald.
II. Harper & Row, Publishers.
PS507.H227 1987 810'.8 86-19412
ISBN 0-06-044372-3 (v. 1)
ISBN 0-06-044367-7 (pbk.: v. 1)
ISBN 0-06-044373-1 (v. 2)
ISBN 0-06-044368-5 (pbk.: v. 2)
ISBN 0-06-044374-x (Compact
Edition)
ISBN 0-06-044371-5 (pbk.: Com-
pact Edition)

86 87 88 89 9 8 7 6 5 4 3 2 1

Contents

Adventures of Huckleberry Finn—*A centennial edition,
edited by Hamlin Hill, is published with this volume*

1489 # The Literature of Modernism: Poetry / 1912–1940

1745 # The Literature of Postwar America: Prose / 1940–1973

2243 # The Literature of Postwar America: Poetry / 1940–1973

2571 The Literature of Contemporary America: Prose

2737 # The Literature of Contemporary America: Poetry

Preface

The Harper American Literature reaffirms and invigorates what is now a nearly 150-year-old tradition of multivolume collections of American literature. From the publication in 1855 of Evert A. and George L. Duyckinck's two-volume *Cyclopaedia of American Literature,* readers wanting to explore what the Duyckincks called "the literary biography of America" have had ready access to what each succeeding generation judged the literature most worthy of its collective attention. But *The Harper American Literature* realizes for the first time a goal announced in the Duyckinck's preface and subsequently endorsed by the editors of virtually every collection of American literature—"to bring together in one book convenient for perusal and reference . . . memorials and records of the writers of the country and their works, from the earliest period to the present day." What distinguishes *The Harper American Literature* from its predecessors is its commitment to presenting fully the richness of American literature, its thematic and stylistic range as well as its geographical and ethnic diversity. To this end, we have worked to extend the conventional boundaries of the American literary tradition.

Virtually all collections of American literature now in print begin either with a generous selection of Puritan writings or, in fewer instances, with Captain John Smith and his engaging account of the early years of the Virginia colony. Yet such beginnings ignore a great deal of compelling literature written in and about America long before the first settlements at either Roanoke Island or Plymouth Plantation—from Cabeza de Vaca's harrowing sixteenth century narrative of his struggles to survive along the southeast coast of what is now Texas to the compelling creation myths of Native Americans. To supplant the narrow, northeastern, Puritan bias of currently available texts, we begin with a wealth of presettlement writing. "The Literature of the New World, 1492–1620," maps out new approaches to the important cultural forces that have helped shape American life.

The Harper American Literature extends America's literary tradition in another significant direction. Its final section, "The Literature of Contemporary America, 1973–Present," gives unprecedented attention to our most recent—and eloquent—

writers of fiction, poetry, and drama, far beyond the mid-1960s boundaries set by editors of nearly all other collections. Sampling the work of such important contemporary writers of fiction as Raymond Carver and Bobbie Ann Mason, poets Louise Glück and Robert Pinsky, and playwright David Mamet—to name but a few of these many fresh and already celebrated voices—will enable readers to explore unexpected dimensions of American literature.

These unique sections, "The Literature of the New World" and "The Literature of Contemporary America," enlarge our presentation of the American literary scene. The earliest of our texts dates from 1492, the latest from 1986. We also reprint important but neglected works by classic writers, as well as important works by such neglected writers as Abigail Adams and Harriet Beecher Stowe. Throughout *The Harper American Literature,* the seven contributing editors aim to present the most comprehensive regathering and reassessment ever of America's literary tradition, including but extending beyond classic works. For example, we reprint as a separately bound supplement the centennial edition of *Adventures of Huckleberry Finn,* with a reconsideration of the novel's significance by the distinguished critic Hamlin Hill. At the same time, we include extensive portions of Twain's *Roughing It* as well as several of his tales, essays, and letters. Along with the most familiar sections of Washington Irving's *Sketch Book,* we include a representative chapter from his *History of the Life and Voyages of Christopher Columbus,* a rarely reprinted work that underscores both the continuity of American literature and the fascination of early nineteenth-century American writers with their distant past. To highlight the dramatic changes in Walt Whitman's poetic vision and accomplishments, we end our first volume with the 1855 edition of *Leaves of Grass,* reprinted in its entirety, and begin Volume Two with generous selections from the 1891 "Deathbed Edition" of his poems. Later in Volume Two, we give unprecedented attention to Gertrude Stein's role in the emergence of American modernism. By offering fresh perspectives on the work of America's literary masters, we provide evidence of the ways in which American literature helped shape, and in turn was influenced by, American culture during each period in its history. Throughout, we have taken special care to provide readers with ready access to unexpected and inviting selections without overburdening overcrowded reading schedules. We hope that inquisitive readers will be prompted to explore further the works, careers, and interconnections that give American literature its inexhaustible richness.

Committed to offering a broader range in the characteristic modes of America's most prominent literary figures, we established the following criteria to guide us in presenting the work of each writer: the literary merits of a particular selection, its significance in American literary history, its reflection of the range and depth of the writer's accomplishments, its connections to other themes and styles, and its power to document the literary values of the cultural context within which the writer works. Most often, we represent American writers by their most important work and by a sampling of other literary performances that show them engaging significant cultural issues.

A perennial problem of any collection of American literature is a structure that appears to isolate careers and periods without adequate attention to the interactions of these lives, works, and times. *The Harper American Literature* represents a concerted effort to weave selections, footnotes, author headnotes, and period introductions into a unified approach to American literature and the culture that informs it. In these two volumes, we seek not only to celebrate the classics of American literature and to locate neglected works of special literary merit, but also to suggest the many ways in which these works are enmeshed in a particular social and cultural context. We have designed the eleven period introductions to *The Harper American Literature* to show how major American writers were shaped by, how they were influential in, how they were responsive to their times—to offer a memorable view of the cultural immediacy of a period, what Gertrude Stein calls "the continuous present."

Each introduction focuses on the prevailing circumstances and competitions American writers faced in each period. What was it like for writers to work at different moments in American cultural history? Were writers peripheral or central figures in examining the major issues and crises of their eras? What major developments occurred in the related arts? What was the taste of the reading public in each period? What, more generally, was the state of language, literacy, and public discourse? The answers to these and similar questions create vivid images of what it was like for writers to live and work in their times.

Each period introduction highlights relevant American literary issues, cultural materials, and personalities. Brief "boxed inserts" include (but are not restricted to) selections from writers who otherwise may not warrant full representation, as well as literary and cultural documents. These literary and folk pieces, philosophical and historical statements, and illustrations add texture to the introductions. A short list of suggested further reading, arranged chronologically, follows each introduction.

A brief informative essay introduces each writer represented in *The Harper American Literature*. These headnote essays provide biographical details and the specific literary context for each writer's work. One major purpose of these headnotes is to show writers writing. In them, we trace the shape of an author's career and address the question of that writer's place in American literary history. We also consider how each writer feeds on, recoils from, or is in conflict with a particular literary, social, political, or cultural environment. At once biographical, contextual, and analytical, these essays counter the tendency to view writers in isolation from one another—by placing their contributions in the context of the main thematic and stylistic traditions of American literature. We designed the headnote essays to be informative enough to free our readers from the need to surround themselves with additional secondary sources before they read, but suggestions for further reading assist those who want to explore further the life and work of a particular author.

The Harper American Literature reprints virtually every recognized American literary classic. Yet we want these classics to reflect more than an attenuated literary tradition, one too often dismissed as elitist. We believe that America's literary classics can—and should—exemplify what the scholar Nathan Huggins calls a "pluralistic realism." No collection of American literature can be complete unless it includes a wide range of distinctive voices, including those of women, blacks, Asian-Americans, Mexican-Americans, and Native Americans. In our selections, headnote essays, and section introductions, we blend these works of literary and cultural merit with other, more traditional, selections so that these new voices can be heard as more than simply statistical responses or intellectual concessions to contemporary propriety.

The Harper American Literature broadens the restrictive notion of what constitutes an American classic. We include, for example, a representative selection of Native American oral and written literatures, stretching from the oral poetry of the sixteenth century to the fiction of such contemporary writers as N. Scott Momaday and Leslie Silko. In doing so, we seek to show how celebrated and less-heralded works of literature illumine each other and enable us to appreciate the diverse achievements that have shaped a distinctively American culture. For "major" and "minor" figures alike, our consistent editorial aim has been to preserve the writer's living complexity, his or her verbal struggles with the challenges of shaping a self, modifying a genre, extending a literary tradition, or enriching a cultural context—as these are reflected in individual acts of composition.

The Harper American Literature follows a simple chronological organization, established by the author's date of birth yet remaining responsive to such instructional clusters as "The Fiction of the Early Republic." We set no guidelines for the length of our selections, which vary from short poems to full-length novels (The Scarlet Letter and Adventures of Huckleberry Finn) and novellas—including Melville's Benito Cereno and Billy Budd, Henry James's Daisy Miller and The Turn of the Screw, Edith Wharton's Summer, Gertrude Stein's The Gentle Lena, and Saul Bellow's Seize the Day—as well as such extended works of nonfiction as Thoreau's Walden. We avoid excerpting whenever possible, but when a writer's most important work is principally in extended prose forms, we reprint self-contained chapters or passages. James Fenimore Cooper, for example, is represented by a chapter from each of The Leather-Stocking Tales, featuring the life and death of Natty Bumppo. Other selections, as in the case of Nabokov's Lolita, are justified by its author's having previously supervised publication of the material in an abbreviated format. Several authors, including Max Apple, Harold Brodkey, David Mamet, and Robert Stone, offered recommendations on which of their works to include.

We have taken great care to provide reliable and readable texts, editing or modernizing only as needed (principally in spelling and punctuation). We have aimed to maintain the flavor of the original while making it accessible to contemporary readers. We note special textual problems and give the date of first publication at the end of each selection, preceded by the date of composition, if known. Footnotes, which are kept to a judicious minimum, explain obscure references, biblical and classical allusions, foreign words, and phrases having special or archaic meanings. We avoid interpretive footnotes. We have tried in every way possible to create conditions for reading that will enable students to discover and develop the integrity of their own responses with the support of their instructors.

We present The Harper American Literature as the most comprehensive collection ever assembled for the purpose of understanding—and reconstructing—American literary history. But we also intend it to be a flexible instructional resource. Because it contains virtually all the primary and supporting material required for instructional use and leisurely reading, *The Harper American Literature* enables instructors and students to concentrate on the literary merits of major American writing. Readers will find in these pages new forms, subjects, themes, and styles—each the product of a distinctive American literary imagination.

Projects with the scope and complexity of *The Harper American Literature* are by interest and necessity collaborative intellectual enterprises. The seven contributing editors of this project met for extended periods to plan the project—to articulate the principles and procedures that would guide its development, decide on the features that would distinguish it from its predecessors, and agree on the authors and selections to be included. Within this collaborative context, several of the editors made selections and wrote headnote essays for writers in periods outside their areas of primary responsibility. And while the eleven period introductions are unified by common principles and purposes, each essay in *The Harper American Literature* remains an extended individual critical statement summarizing the literary and cultural distinctiveness of each period in American literary history. Robert Atwan is the author of the introduction to "The Literature of the New World, 1492–1620"; Cecelia Tichi of "The Literature of Colonial America, 1620–1776"; Donald McQuade of "The Literature of the New Republic, 1776–1836"; and Justin Kaplan of "The Literature of the American Renaissance, 1836–1865." For "The Literature of an Expanding Nation, 1865–1912," Justin Kaplan treated the decade following the Civil War, Martha Banta the next thirty years. David Minter wrote the introductions to "The Literature of Modernism: Prose, 1912–1940"; "The Literature of Postwar America: Prose, 1940–1973"; and "The Literature of Contemporary America: Prose, 1973–Present." Helen Vendler is the author of the introductions to "The Literature of Modernism: Poetry, 1912–1940"; "The Literature of Postwar America: Poetry, 1940–1973"; and "The Literature of Contemporary America: Poetry, 1973–Present."

Donald McQuade,
General Editor

Acknowledgments

The publication of *The Harper American Literature* represents the collaborative efforts of numerous professionals. In many ways its final shape challenges the accuracy of a century-old American adage, first recorded in Henry Ward Beecher's *Proverbs from Plymouth Pulpit* (1887): "It is not the going out of port, but the coming in, that determines the success of a voyage." As *The Harper American Literature* comes to completion, its seven contributing editors would like to acknowledge those who contributed to this ambitious undertaking at both ends.

   The Harper American Literature could not have been launched without the intelligence and vision of John J. McDermott, Distinguished Professor of Philosophy at Texas A & M University, who helped articulate the need for a substantially different collection of American writing. His generous advice and rich understanding of American culture have proven invaluable throughout the project's development. Helene Brewer, Queens College, CUNY, served as a limitless resource during the early phases of shaping this collection. John Frederick Nims, University of Illinois at Chicago Circle, and Joseph F. Trimmer, Ball State University, made significant contributions to the project's development, especially during the first several rounds of extended conversations about its distinctive features. We are grateful for their continued support.

During the several years that the contributing editors developed *The Harper American Literature,* many of our colleagues across the country offered incisive readings of various drafts of the manuscript. For their thoughtful critiques and helpful suggestions, we would like to thank the following reviewers: Daniel Aaron, Harvard University; Maurice Bassan, San Francisco State University; Calvin Bedient, University of California at Los Angeles; Frank Bergon, Vassar College; Dennis Berthold, Texas A & M University; Lynn Z. Bloom, Virginia Commonwealth University; Virginia W. Brumbach, Eastfield College; Louis J. Budd, Duke University; Lawrence Buell, Oberlin College; Robert P. Burke, Joliet Junior College; Edwin H. Cady, Duke University; Bonnie Costello, Radcliffe College; Michael Dunne, Middle Tennessee State University; Kathy Early, Middlesex County College; Emory Elliott, Princeton University; Suzanne Ferguson, Ohio State University; Steven Fink, Ohio State University; Benjamin Franklin Fisher IV, University of Mississippi; Michael T. Gilmore, Brandeis University; James Goodwin, University of California at Los Angeles; Robert C. Grayson, Southeast Missouri State University; Malcolm Griffith, University of Washington; Phillip F. Gura, University of Colorado, Boulder; William Howarth, Princeton University; J. G. Jannsen, Arizona State University; Donald Kartiganer, University of Washington; Merrill Lewis, Western Washington University; John S. Mann, Western Illinois University; Terence Martin, Indiana University; Lee Mitchell, Princeton University; James Moore, Mount San Antonio College; Elsa Nettels, College of William and Mary; Sarah Emily Newton, California State University, Chico; John Frederick Nims, University of Illinois at Chicago Circle; Thornton H. Parsons, Syracuse University; David Perkins, Harvard University; Marjorie Perloff, University of Southern California; Robert L. Phillips, Mississippi State University; Donald Pizer, Tulane University; Joel Porte, Harvard University; Carolyn Porter, University of California, Berkeley; John Reardon, Miami University, Ohio; Louis D. Rubin, University of North Carolina at Chapel Hill; Henry M. Sayre, Oregon State University; Richard Schramm, University of Utah; Dorothy U. Seyler, Northern Virginia Community College; Frank Shuffelton, University of Rochester; Ellen Hurt Smith, Stetson University; Haskell Springer, University of Kansas; William T. Stafford, Purdue University; Eric J. Sundquist, University of California, Berkeley; David O. Tomlinson, U. S. Naval Academy; Darwin T. Turner, University of Iowa; Emily S. Watts, University of Illinois at Urbana—Champaign; Robert P. Weeks, University of Michigan; Michael West, University of Pittsburgh; Ann Woodlief, Virginia Commonwealth University; Larzer Ziff, Johns Hopkins University.

We are especially grateful to the following colleagues and friends for their many helpful suggestions and generous encouragement: Daniel Aaron, Harvard University; Max Apple, Rice University; Helene Atwan; Anne Bernays; Joe Cuomo, Queens College, CUNY; Joan Feinberg; Joseph A. Finder; Steven Fink, Ohio State University; Sally Fitzgerald; Bruce Forer, Queens College; William Howarth, Princeton University; Dennis Huston, Rice University; Walter Isle, Rice University; Betsy B. Kaufman, Queens College; Bridget Gellert Lyons, Rutgers University; Robert B. Lyons, Queens College; Rosemary Magee, Emory University; Wendy Martin, Queens College; Larry McMurtry; Susanne B. McQuade; Caroline Minter; Marie Ponsot, Queens College; Carolyn Porter, University of California, Berkeley; Edward Quinn, City College, CUNY; Harold Schechter, Queens College; Nancy Sommers, Rutgers University; Donald Stone, Queens College; Robert Towers, Columbia University; William Vesterman, Rutgers University; William P. Wilson, Queens College; and Thomas Wortham, University of California at Los Angeles. We are also indebted to Frederick Buell, Queens College, CUNY; his imaginative intelligence, critical acumen, and patient understanding made this a far more solid book than it otherwise would have been. William P. Kelly, Queens College, generously and repeatedly made his knowledge of American literature and culture available. Elissa Weaver, University of Chicago, provided what are at once highly reliable and readable new translations of materials relating to Columbus's voyages. Wallace Chafe, University of California at Santa Barbara; Russ Hall, Harper & Row; and William C. Sturtevant, Smithsonian Institution, helped strengthen our representation of Native American literature, as did the work of Paula Gunn Allen, University of California, Berkeley, and her colleagues on the Modern Language Association's Commission on the Languages and Literature of America. Sally McLendon, Hunter College, CUNY, contributed immeasurably to our efforts to call greater attention to the eloquence and significance of Native American oral and written literatures. H. Barbara Weinberg, Queens College, CUNY, served as an extraordinary resource for exploring the interrelations of American literature and art. Her command of American art history has made each volume of *The Harper American Literature* more attractive as well as more responsive to the interplay of artistic forces in our culture. We are grateful for her assistance.

We would like to acknowledge the first-rate research and editorial assistance of Dianne Armstrong, University of California at Los Angeles; Stephanie Bobo, Boston University; Ruth Burke, University of California at Los Angeles; Carolyn Denard, Kennesaw College; JoEllen Fisherkeller, University of California, Berkeley; Ken Houghton, University of California at San Diego; Karen Johnson, Indiana University—Purdue University, Indianapolis; Laura Parkington, Seton Hall University; John Pearson, Boston University; and David Wheeler. Virginia, Marise, and Tara McDermott ingeniously prepared a chart of American literature that helped clarify our work. We would also like to acknowledge the special contributions of Trudy Baltz, who devoted great intelligence and energy to the project long before it took final shape, as well as of Michael Arnold and James Barszcz, both of Rutgers University, who offered incisive readings and excellent advice as the project neared completion. The preparation of this manuscript benefited greatly from the skillful and genial assistance of Nora Elias and

Jeannette Gilkison at the University of California at Los Angeles, as well as Sandy Qualls and Jo Taylor at Emory University.

We would also like to express our appreciation to the staffs at the libraries of Boston, Columbia, Emory, Harvard, Indiana, Princeton, and Seton Hall Universities; the University of California, Berkeley; the University of California at San Diego; Queens College; and the Maplewood and South Orange public libraries. In addition, we often relied on the expertise of Anthony Shipps, Indiana University; Elizabeth Smith, slide collection manager of the art history program, CUNY Graduate Center; and Errol Somay, New York Public Library.

Our continuing thanks go to the skillful and gracious professionals at Harper & Row. This project could not have been published without the support of Neale Sweet, vice-president and publisher. His commitment to *The Harper American Literature* and the principles underlying it has been exemplary. Lauren Bahr, director of development, kept the project on course with a masterful blend of energy, intelligence, and good will. Nat LaMar, development editor, quickly became an indispensable intellectual presence. His editorial insights and his knowledge of American literature are everywhere apparent to the contributing editors. We are also indebted to Jonathan Haber, who deftly coordinated the in-house editorial process with rare intelligence and excellent literary taste. Bonnie Biller, project editor, managed the flow of several thousand pages of manuscript and page proof with intelligent exactness and irrepressible good cheer. For the elegant look of these volumes, we would like to thank Karen Salsgiver. Claudia Kohner successfully guided the manuscript through its early development. Cara Tate proved to be an inexhaustible resource for solving every conceivable editorial and administrative problem; she helped make *The Harper American Literature* a better book to work on and read. George Blaine and Kathy Vuignier quietly contributed to the project with daily examples of efficiency. We would also like to thank Barbara Cinquegrani, Peter Coveney, Carole Knoeller, and Mira Schachne for their fine work.

Our greatest debt is to Phil Leininger, sponsoring editor. His expansive and detailed knowledge of American literature as well as his understanding and appreciation of this project's purpose made him a constant source of imaginative recommendations and useful advice. He helped us in every way to refine and realize our vision. Quite simply, *The Harper American Literature* would not exist without his having cultivated the commitment he shared with us to reexamine— and reconstruct—America's distinctive literary heritage.

We trust that all those who contributed to putting *The Harper American Literature* in print will endorse Ralph Waldo Emerson's notion that "the reward of a thing well done is to have it done."

The
Harper
American
Literature

Volume 2

Alfred Stieglitz,
The Steerage,
photograph, 1907.
International Museum
of Photography
at George Eastman House.

Julius J. Stewart,
*The Yacht Namouna
in Venetian Waters,*
oil on canvas, 1890.
Courtesy, Wadsworth Atheneum,
Hartford.
The Ella Gallup Sumner and
Mary Catlin Sumner Collection.

The Literature of an Expanding Nation 1865–1912

Reconciliation

 At a cost of over 600,000 lives, the Civil War put an end to chattel slavery, but not its heritage of social injustice, and vindicated the principle of Union. *United States* became a singular collective noun in postwar usage, instead of a plural one as before. The name now denoted a powerful young nation supposedly at peace with itself and dedicated to binding up its wounds. Whitman's image for the advent of peace was "Reconciliation . . . word over all, beautiful as the sky." But such sentiments, reflecting hopes rather than realities, belonged to what Emerson called "the optative mood" of American literature and spiritual history and found little support in the events of the period. Lincoln's martyrdom and "ascension" were followed in 1868 by impeachment proceedings against President Andrew Johnson for "high crimes and misdemeanors." Reconstruction politics tended to be a continuation of war by other means. For Whitman the democratic vistas of 1871 were marked by abandonment of principle, "hollowness of heart," "hypocrisy," "depravity," "robbery and scoundrelism": "What penetrating eye does not everywhere see through the mask? The spectacle is appalling." James Russell Lowell scanned "the festering news . . . of public scandal, private fraud" in "the Land of Broken Promise."

"There's millions in it," says Mark Twain's Colonel Beriah Sellers *(The Gilded Age)*. "I've got the biggest scheme on earth—and I'll take you in; I've taken in every friend I've got that's ever stood by me, for there's enough for all, and to spare." A dealer in schemes involving mules, corn, bottled eyewash, and an illusory rail line serving Slouchburg, Hallelujah, and Corruptionville, the fictional Sellers typifies the promoter, a distinctive occupation of the period. The joining of the Union Pacific and Central Pacific rail lines at Promontory Point, Utah, in 1869 was a promoter's triumph. It fulfilled vision, purpose, engineering genius, and venture capitalism; passengers and goods traveled in less than a week across a nation whose separate parts were now bound to each other by three thousand miles of steel. The promoters of the transcontinental railroad, it was soon learned, had set up a construction company, Crédit Mobilier, that bilked the investing public of more than $20 million and, to avoid exposure, bribed the vice-president of the United States, Schuyler Colfax, along with members of the House and Senate. The Crédit Mobilier affair, which unraveled just before the general election of 1872, was the Watergate of its day but not an isolated instance. On "Black Friday" in September 1869, the market collapsed after two sharpers, Jim Fisk and Jay Gould, tried to make a corner in gold. On "Black Friday" in 1873, an economy built on wildcat speculations fell on its face, ushering in the worst depression the United States had yet known. Crédit Mobilier was part of a cycle of abuses and reverses that darkened nearly every corner of national life.

The Reconstruction era had more than its share of memorably representative figures, among them Ulysses Grant, the North's supreme military hero. Men like General William Tecumseh Sherman had fought under Grant with "the faith a Christian has in his Savior." Grant's two terms in the White House, however, were notable for corruption, neglect, incompetence, and cronyism. (America had "reverted to the stone age," Henry Adams lamented. "The progress of evolution from President Washington to President Grant was alone evidence enough to upset Darwin.") In New York "Boss" William Tweed and his Tammany ring made off with somewhere between $30 million and $100 million in public funds.

The Revised Catechism

What is the chief end of man?—to get rich. In what way?—dishonestly if we must; honestly if we can. Who is God, the one only and true? Money is God. Gold and Greenbacks and Stock—father, son, and the ghost of same—three persons in one; these are the true and only God, mighty and supreme: and William Tweed is his prophet.

Mark Twain, in the *New York Tribune* (September 27, 1871)

Victoria Woodhull and her sister Tennessee Celeste Claflin, reformers and leaders in the suffragist movement, set themselves up as financial wizards on Wall Street and in 1872 precipitated what Victoria called "one of the most stupendous scandals which has ever occurred in any community." They accused Harriet Beecher Stowe's brother, Henry Ward Beecher, the most popular Protestant divine of his day, of carrying on an adulterous relationship with a parishioner. The charge was never proved, but "the Beecher horror," as Lowell called it, dragged on in the press and courts through the summer of 1875. By then Beecher's guilt was more or less taken for granted and accepted as further evidence, if any were needed, of wickedness in high places.

The tutelary spirit of the Reconstruction era was not Lincoln but Benjamin Franklin, stripped for the most part of his irony, sense of play, heterodoxy, and free-ranging intellectual curiosity. In 1864 one of his biographers, the popular historian James Parton, counted 136 American towns named after Franklin; Ohio alone had nineteen. "I think I adequately appreciate the greatness of Washington," said Horace Greeley, the powerful editor of the *New York Tribune*, "yet I must place Franklin above him as the consummate type and flowering of human nature under the skies of colonial America." But it was not until 1868 that Franklin's *Autobiography*, long established as obligatory reading for his compatriots, was first published from a complete and authentic manuscript instead of a corrupt, partial source. This prompted a rediscovery and consequently a reinterpretation of the man in line with some of the dominant values of the era. His humble origins, dedication to self-improvement, and genius for business set an example for "Self-Made Men" (the title of Greeley's popular lecture) determined to acquire what the master showman P. T. Barnum called "The Art of Money-Getting." Barnum's best-selling autobiography, *Struggles and Triumphs*, suggests not only that his chief model was Franklin but that he regarded himself as the Franklin of humbug, harnessing credulity instead of lightning. If there was "a sucker born every minute," as Barnum is supposed to have said, credulity was never in short supply.

"A Bread-Winner in the Family"

The eldest son of parents who were themselves poor, I had, fortunately, to begin to perform some useful work in the world while still very young in order to earn an honest livelihood, and was thus shown even in early boyhood that my duty was to assist my parents and like them become, as soon as possible, a bread-winner in the family. . . . It seems, nowadays, a matter of universal desire that poverty should be abolished. We should be quite willing to abolish luxury, but to abolish honest, industrious, self-denying poverty would be to destroy the soil upon which mankind produces the virtues which enable our race to reach a still higher civilization than it now possesses.

Andrew Carnegie, "How I Served My Apprenticeship," *Youth's Companion* (April 23, 1896)

Franklin's gospel of getting on in the world, as it was then interpreted at face value, merged with practical Christianity, Emersonian self-reliance, and social Darwinism, an application of evolutionary theories of natural selection and the survival of the fittest to the daily race for bread, money, and status. The results of the merger could be seen in Horatio Alger's Ragged Dick books (1867 and after), lecture performances such as Henry Ward Beecher's "The Ministry of Wealth" and Thomas Wentworth Higginson's "The Natural Aristocracy of the Dollar," and Acres of Diamonds, an inspirational address that Philadelphia Baptist clergyman Russell Conwell, founder of Temple University, delivered about six thousand times. "Opportunity is in your own backyard," Conwell said. "Money is power. Every good man and woman ought to strive for power, to do good with it when obtained."

The Gilded Age

The most enduring label for the period that followed Lee's surrender at Appomattox and Lincoln's death comes from the novel Mark Twain wrote in 1873 with his Hartford neighbor, Charles Dudley Warner: The Gilded Age. It connotes vulgarity, boom times, specious glitter, and superficial glow. Since then historians of the period have generated many other phrases that tend to scant the vitality and significant achievements of the times. A synoptic account compiled from book titles and verbal tags might read something like this: During a "tragic era" that was also an "age of negation," an "age of excess," and an "awkward age" and spanned several "brown decades," the American people, traveling "the road to reunion," were lured into "pragmatic acquiescence" and sedated by a bloodless "genteel tradition"; they created a cheap "chromo civilization" and watched complacently as "robber barons" devoured the nation's resources in a "great barbecue."

Labels aside, however, this was a dynamic era out of which emerged cultural and industrial maturity together with other lineaments of the United States in the coming century. Corruption and abuse brought on investigation and exposure; the beginnings of a reform, protest, and labor movement; and searching structural critiques such as Whitman's Democratic Vistas and Henry George's Progress and Poverty in the 1870s and, at the turn of the century, the economist and social theorist Thorstein Veblen's The Theory of the Leisure Class. Warring profiteers wasted money and labor, but the railroads were built all the same. During 1872 more miles of track (7,500) were put down than in any other year before or after; the combined systems grew from 35,000 miles in 1865 to 93,000 in 1880, by which time the refrigerator car had enabled Chicago to become Carl Sandburg's "Hog Butcher for the World." Parvenus and vulgarians set a pattern for what Veblen called the "conspicuous consumption of valuable goods," but they did so by virtue of a social and economic mobility that made everyone a potential tycoon. The tycoons amassed enormous fortunes, but some of them—Andrew Carnegie and John D. Rockefeller, for example—endowed universities and libraries and set up great private foundations dedicated to education, research, and public welfare.

"The Reaction Must Come"

In the United States it is clear that squalor and misery, and the vices and crimes that spring from them, everywhere increase as the village grows to the city, and the march of development brings the advantages of the improved methods of production and exchange. It is in the older and richer sections of the Union that pauperism and distress among the working classes are becoming most painfully apparent. . . . So long as all the increased wealth which modern progress brings goes but to build up great fortunes and make sharper the contrast between the House of Have and the House of Want, progress is not real and cannot be permanent. The reaction must come.

Henry George, *Progress and Poverty* (1879)

The year 1876, the hundredth anniversary of the Declaration of Independence, offers a fair sampling of the varieties and vicissitudes of American life in the Gilded Age. At Little Bighorn, Montana, Sioux Indians led by Chiefs Sitting Bull and Crazy Horse annihilated Lieutenant Colonel George Armstrong Custer and his expeditionary force. Jesse James, the American Robin Hood, reached the zenith of his career by robbing a stagecoach in Texas, a train in Missouri, and a bank in Minnesota. Evangelists Dwight Moody and Ira Sankey led a nationwide crusade to eradicate sin and reduce the future population of hell. President Grant's secretary of war and private secretary stood accused, respectively, of bribery and tax fraud. In a bitterly contested presidential election—its outcome was tainted at the polls and nearly decided at bayonet point—Rutherford B. Hayes of Ohio defeated Samuel J. Tilden of New York. Thomas Edison established his "invention factory" at Menlo Park, New Jersey. J. W. Draper took the first photographs of the solar spectrum. Alexander Graham Bell patented the telephone. Daniel Coit Gilman reorganized Johns Hopkins University and set national standards for graduate studies and advanced research. William James, then an instructor in physiology at Harvard, established the first American psychological laboratory. Professor Willard Gibbs of Yale published a paper on thermodynamics, "On the Equilibrium of Heterogeneous Substances," that remains one of the great creative achievements of nineteenth-century science. Mark Twain published *The Adventures of Tom Sawyer*.

Nearly eight million visitors, equal to a sixth of the national population, passed through the turnstiles of the Centennial Exhibition at Philadelphia. Most of them were impressed by how far the United States had come during its first one hundred years toward fulfilling its mission to be the driving force as well as the light of the world. Dominating the exhibition was a forty-foot-high Corliss steam engine, which supplied power to the eight thousand presses, pumps, gins, mills, and lathes chugging away in Machinery Hall. "Yes, it is still in these things of iron and steel," said William Dean Howells, "that the national genius most freely speaks." But the national genius also spoke, if perhaps less freely, in other things and with a degree of distinction and purpose that should have won over English skeptics such as Darwin's champion, T. H. Huxley, and the poet-critic

Matthew Arnold. Architect H. H. Richardson, painters Thomas Eakins, Winslow Homer, and Albert Pinkham Ryder, motion photography pioneer Eadweard Muybridge, and the Roeblings, father and son engineers and bridge builders, to name only a few, did their part in making what Lewis Mumford has called a "Buried Renaissance," "buried" because "the laval flow of industrialism after the war had swept over all the cities of the spirit, leaving here and there only an ashen ruin, standing erect in the crumbled landscape."

Labor unrest, on the rise since the Panic of 1873, peaked in 1877, a year of violence marked by riots and the use of federal troops to put down railroad strikes in West Virginia, Maryland, and Pennsylvania. In response, armories multiplied in cities all over America. Their crenellations, embrasures, and iron-studded sally ports suggested that the enemies of an economic society founded on steam, electricity, and dynamite were going to be repelled with crossbow, harquebus, and boiling oil. The age produced other public buildings that were anachronisms, eyesores, or swindles from their footings up. The Philadelphia city hall carried ornamentation about as far and as high as it could go. Tweed's Manhattan County Courthouse, a three-story iron-and-marble Palladian villa, cost taxpayers almost twice what Seward had paid for Alaska. Yet out of the same era came the Brooklyn Bridge, a structure of such purity and aspiration that it seemed to leap out of its century while fulfilling, at the same time, that century's passion for force and quantification. From the bridge's two majestic towers, together containing 85,159 cubic yards of masonry, hung four cables, each woven of 3,515 miles of wire and capable of supporting 24,621,780 pounds. The entire structure added up to an incomparably moving presence. "No one who has ever been upon it can ever forget it," said Mayor Seth Low of New York when the bridge was opened to traffic in 1883, thirteen years after construction began. "Not one shall see it and not feel prouder to be a man." In Hart Crane's epic celebration it was to be, quite simply, *The Bridge.*

"Civilization in the United States"

I cannot say that I am in the slightest degree impressed by your bigness, or your material resources, as such. Size is not grandeur, and territory does not make a nation. The great issue, about which hangs a true sublimity, and the terror of overhanging fate, is what are you going to do with all these things? What is to be the end to which these are to be the means?

T. H. Huxley, *American Addresses* (1877)

In truth, everything is against distinction in America, and against the sense of elevation to be gained through admiring and respecting it. The glorification of "the average man," who is quite a religion with statesmen and publicists there, is against it. The addiction to "the funny man," who is a national misfortune there, is against it. Above all, the newspapers are against it.

Matthew Arnold, "Civilization in the United States," *The Nineteenth Century* (April 1888)

The Old Order

"If the tone of the American world is in some respects provincial, it is in none more so than in this matter of the exaggerated homage rendered to authorship," Henry James wrote in *Hawthorne* (1879). "In the United States at present authorship is a pedestal and literature is the fashion." These were signs of waning vitality, even stagnation, and of the need once again for those fresh currents of life and thought Margaret Fuller had called for thirty years earlier. ("Instead of mighty and vital breezes," Whitman said of "the existing condition of poetry," "I find a few little silly fans languidly moved by shrunken fingers.")

By the centennial year, Whitman, Melville, and Lowell, all born in 1819, were lapsing, respectively, into self-imitation, silence, and public service. Emily Dickinson, with Whitman the most important American poet of the century, was active during the 1860s, 1870s, and 1880s but remained a largely invisible literary presence (only half a dozen fugitive verses appeared in print) until the 1890s, when three volumes of her work were published posthumously. Of the older writers, Poe, Hawthorne, and Thoreau were dead. Whittier, Holmes, Longfellow, and Emerson, the last slipping into senility, were figures in a pantheon, objects of quasi-religious veneration. What Emerson once called "the Movement" and "the party of the Future" had become "the Establishment" and "the party of the Past" and now served as guardians and high priests of an official culture. The critic Tony Tanner has described this as a "culture of forms, frozen on the surface, hollow within; prohibitant rather than enabling; a series of habits adhered to by the imaginatively somnolent."

Local colorists were already celebrating the regional ambience and folkways of the Maine forests, Louisiana bayous, and Western mining camps. Realism asserted itself in frontier tales and the novels of William Dean Howells and Henry James. Naturalist writers such as Frank Norris and Stephen Crane would portray characters who were victims of circumstance and natural law instead of the free creatures of the Romantic tradition. And a literature of social protest and of America's oppressed races was about to emerge. Meanwhile, during the late 1870s Mark Twain and Henry James figured separately in two public controversies that illuminate the conflict between representatives of the old literary order and the new.

Written almost thirty years after the event it describes, "The Story of a Speech" is Mark Twain's still-divided account of his performance at Whittier's seventieth-birthday dinner, sponsored by the *Atlantic Monthly,* in December 1877. He had recently published *Tom Sawyer* and begun the long composition of *Adventures of Huckleberry Finn,* a task that occupied him, intermittently, for nearly eight years. His tribute to Emerson ("a seedy little bit of a chap"), Holmes ("fat as a balloon"), and Longfellow ("built like a prize-fighter") asserted a spirit of travesty then considered alien to the occasion. He insinuated, although perhaps only in a subintentional way, that the three "gracious singers" might themselves be "impostors." Howells, the *Atlantic* editor in chief, a pilgrim from Ohio who had come to New England to worship at the feet of her great men, recalled his friend's after-dinner speech as an "amazing mistake," a "bewildering blunder," a "cruel catastrophe" that left Mark Twain "standing solitary amid his appalled and appalling listeners, with his joke dead on his hands." "Literary men in America, where so much is tolerated," one newspaper letter concluded, "ought to aim higher than the gutter, no matter what they have of talent, or even genius." Other published responses and reports agreed that "a wild Californian bull" in the "China shop" of polite letters had committed an unpardonable breach of taste, decorum, and morals. This was the same charge soon to be brought against *Huckleberry Finn,* a revolutionary work of realism and social satire that opened up new possibilities for the American writer.

Henry James's offense against official culture came from a different vantage and raised once again the question of whether America could nurture artists. James had taken up residence in England and consolidated his reputation there by seeing through the press, in the course of one year, 1879, no fewer than seven volumes of his work, including *The American, Daisy Miller,* and *Hawthorne,* the first book-length critical study of an American writer. The alleged condescension and European bias of James's *Hawthorne,* along with its comments on the narrowness of American experience and materials, stirred up a controversy that he tried to dismiss as "a very big tempest in a very small teapot," "the clucking of a brood of prairie hens." His outraged critics cast "a lurid light upon the state of American 'culture,'" he said, and supplied him further "evidence for calling American taste 'provincial.'" Issued in London, *Hawthorne* was also the first American subject among the twenty-nine volumes of John Morley's English Men of Letters series; in loyal response, Charles Dudley Warner and the publishing house of Houghton Mifflin launched their American Men of Letters series in 1881. Two related developments also suggest the degree (excessive, in James's understanding) to which the country had become aware of its home-grown writers: Princeton offered a college course on American literature as early as 1872; six years later Moses Coit Tyler published his scholarly, durable *History of American Literature During the Colonial Time.*

"Exquisitely and Consistently Provincial"

When I say inexperience, I mean that Hawthorne's experience had been narrow. His fifty years had been spent, for much the larger part, in small American towns—Salem, the Boston of forty years ago, Concord, Lenox, West Newton —and he had led exclusively what one may call a village life. . . . In other words, and to call things by their names, he was exquisitely and consistently provincial.

Henry James, *Hawthorne* (1879)

The Writer's Profession

Seemingly opposed figures except in their rejection of New England, James looked toward Europe and high art, while Mark Twain spoke for the vernacular West and what he called "the mighty mass of the uncultivated." It was clear in many other ways that the sources of continuing vitality were no longer located in and around Boston. A new class of professional writers, diverse in geographic and social origins and working under new professional conditions, emerged to make the nation's literature, a significant part of it regional in program and nature. Indicatively, William Dean Howells, the adoptive New Englander from the Midwest, was to leave the *Atlantic* to write for the *Century* and *Harper's*, both published in New York, where he eventually settled. But although this city became the nation's book and magazine publishing center, it was not necessarily where other writers chose to live and work. "Death to the spirit," Whitman said of New York, "a good market for the harvest but a bad place for farming." Among writers born during the three decades before the Civil War, George Washington Cable and Kate Chopin flourished in New Orleans; Joel Chandler Harris wrote his Uncle Remus stories in Atlanta; Ambrose Bierce, a midwesterner like Howells and Hamlin Garland, lived and worked for fifty years in San Francisco, a literary frontier that counted Mark Twain, Bret Harte, and Joaquin Miller among its celebrities. This dispersal of centers of literary creation from the eastern seaboard augured a later generation of writers of the Midwest (Willa Cather, Sherwood Anderson, Sinclair Lewis, F. Scott Fitzgerald, Ernest Hemingway) and of the South (Katherine Anne Porter, William Faulkner, Thomas Wolfe, Zora Neale Hurston, Richard Wright).

Post–Civil War book publishing had become a two-tiered, two-culture system that reached overlapping but distinguishable classes of readers. "Trade" publishers —centered in New York, Boston, and Philadelphia—sold their books in bookstores to a primarily urban and educated audience, enjoyed prestige, and in turn conferred it on their authors. "Subscription" publishers, on the other hand, were merchandisers who employed door-to-door salesmen, armed with alluring prospectuses and binders' dummies, to work the towns and country districts; a broad, nonliterary audience—often tradesmen, farmers, and their families— ordered in advance of publication works of history, moral philosophy, patriotism, medical advice, and occasionally humor and fiction. "Anything but subscription publishing is printing for private circulation," Mark Twain said. He showed fellow writers like Howells, Thomas Bailey Aldrich, and Cable yet other avenues to income: the lecture circuit (later, public "readings"), the magazines, and the theater, with dramatizations of his novels. The career of letters had become a matter of business as well as craft and during the 1880s began to require the professional services of literary agents.

But if the rewards for American writers were now greater than they had been before the war, so were the risks and pitfalls of celebrity, the star system, and the box office. Transplanted from Albany to San Francisco, for a brief period in the early 1870s Bret Harte may have been the most famous writer in America. A pioneering local colorist, he helped create, in "The Luck of Roaring Camp" and other popular stories, the literary West, an imaginary region populated by sentimental gamblers, gallant badmen, and whores with middle-class hearts of gold, many of them speaking what Mel Brooks (in his western parody film, *Blazing Saddles*) was to call "frontier gibberish." At thirty-five Harte traveled east like a conqueror and signed a $10,000 contract with the *Atlantic Monthly,* only to begin a long slide into debt, disenchantment, mediocrity, and finally self-imposed exile in Europe and England. His career was a cautionary tale for writers. As F. Scott Fitzgerald was later to say of his own early fame and its crushing sequel, "There were no second acts in American lives."

In other ways, too, the post–Civil War era opened up vistas of regret as well as opportunity for American writers. The world they inhabited, said Henry James, "was a more complicated place than it had hitherto seemed, the future more treacherous, success more difficult." Henry Adams, who lived into the twentieth century but thought of himself as a child of the eighteenth, felt like a ghost or revenant. Mark Twain's Connecticut Yankee mourns a "lost land . . . so fresh and new, so virgin" that progress and the industrial revolution had destroyed. Similarly, a significant number of writers attempted to preserve in fiction or memoir what seemed the idyllic simplicities of village life before the war and helped create a literary cult of childhood and innocence. Harriet Beecher Stowe's *Oldtown Folks,* Louisa May Alcott's *Little Women,* and Thomas Bailey Aldrich's *The Story of a Bad Boy* were all published in 1868 or 1869; *Tom Sawyer* was their counterpart for the 1870s and a likely model for Howells's *A Boy's Town* (1890). Looking to the present, however, many writers discovered that the union of art and realism sparked literary controversies that opened up broader opportunities than their predecessors had known.

The Outcasts of Poker Flat

At the head of the gulch, on one of the largest pine-trees, they found the deuce of clubs pinned to the bark with a bowie-knife. It bore the following, written in pencil in a firm hand:

BENEATH THIS TREE

LIES THE BODY

OF

JOHN OAKHURST

WHO STRUCK A STREAK OF BAD LUCK

ON THE 23D OF NOVEMBER 1850,

AND

HANDED IN HIS CHECKS

ON THE 7TH DECEMBER, 1850.

†

Bret Harte (1869)

Realism, Naturalism, and Idealism

The Civil War had ended in the spring of 1865, but the consequences of that brutal struggle continued to send shocks throughout the nation's cultural life. As the year 1900 drew nearer, a civil war of sorts continued between the literary camps of the Realists and the Romanticists. Leading writers and arbiters of taste like William Dean Howells were convinced that Realism was the only honest way to record what it was actually like to live the everyday American life. Howells and his friends (Mark Twain and Henry James) and protégés (Hamlin Garland, Stephen Crane, and Sarah Orne Jewett) viewed Romanticism as an adversary of truth and common humanity, with its soft-focused views that preferred sentimental, pretty, happy emotions and denied the less pleasant facts cast up by late-nineteenth-century existence. Of course, there were writers—such as Ambrose "Bitter" Bierce—who disagreed with Howells. Realism, Bierce wrote in *The Devil's Dictionary,* is "the art of depicting nature as it is seen by toads, the charm suffusing a landscape painted by a mole, or a story written by a measuring-worm."

The honor roll of the Realists includes Mark Twain, Henry James, Hamlin Garland, and Edith Wharton, together with Howells, but even these champions of the cause of honesty allowed certain kinds of romanticism to infiltrate and energize their works. In his later years especially, Howells realized that the Realism versus Romanticism standoff was not quite as simple as he, or Bierce, sometimes pictured it, and he began to explore the darker reaches of the psyche, which had been the favorite stalking ground for the great American Romantics in the years prior to the war.

Just as "idealism" (the belief that the universe is run according to the principles of absolute and eternal goodness) could mean either a profound examination of important human concerns or become the slovenly basis for whatever people desired to think life ought to be like, "romanticism" also cut two ways—either toward an escapism that twisted facts past recognition (what the Realists detested) or toward a responsible reexploration of areas dismissed by the literal-minded (areas the Realists dared not ignore).

Becoming a Realist, then, could mean being expansive and exploratory or being merely a self-limiting advocate of small home truths; a Romanticist might be a student of complex reality or just one of those who glossed over unpleasantness. But American writers had more to choose between than these schools: A writer could decide to follow the lead of the literary school of Naturalism that spilled over from the Continent in the 1890s. Stephen Crane, Frank Norris, Jack London, and Theodore Dreiser each responded differently to the precepts of objective, scientific reporting set down in France by Émile Zola in *Le Roman Expérimental* in 1880. There was no single "Naturalism," just as there was no one "Realism" or "Romanticism," but one distinctive trait separates these several ways of seeing the world and the role taken by the individual. This difference is not a matter of setting or theme; ugly, sordid events were as much the property of the writers of Romance and of Realism as of the Naturalists. Nor is the crucial distinction based on who lays claim to being true to life; the best writers in any one of these literary groupings were confident they were doing just that. The differences among them depend, rather, on the relative amount of individual choice allowed the characters whose lives are portrayed by Naturalists, Romanticists, and Realists.

Generally speaking (for even here there must be notable exceptions), the writers in the Romantic tradition emphasized the possible triumph of the human will; the Realists qualified freedom of choice with large provisos concerning the power of outside forces; the Naturalists tended to reduce to nil all human chances of winning on their own terms. The Romanticists liked to view man as a god; the Realists said man is just that—a man; the Naturalists admitted that in the end man is not much more than a physical object, subject to forces of biology and environment well beyond his control.

This, then, was the situation American writers had to confront. From the start, they all had careers to make, and all had private needs to answer: to feel accepted, earn a living, express what had to be told, and satisfy the demands of their imaginations. During the 1890s and after, many writers also began to assume a definite sense of social obligation to their readers, even those who paid great mind to matters of style and form and went with "the art for art's sake" crowd. To write clearly and effectively about important personal and public issues might help save American society from the enemies who lay within and without. Their stories could not directly bring about changes in the social attitudes of their readers, but still these writers wanted *to have an effect.*

Some shook up their readers by writing humor (Mark Twain and Joel Chandler Harris). Some acted as chroniclers of regional "local color" (Sarah Orne Jewett, Kate Chopin, Bret Harte). Others took old formalities of poetic versification and introduced surprises with new words, topics, and realignments of sounds (Emily Dickinson, Walt Whitman). Still others put the strengths of the native tongue and an interest in native themes to extensive use in their novels (William Dean Howells, Hamlin Garland).

The country's writers had also to contend with the many Americans who preferred to be entertained, instructed, and (sometimes) saved by what they read. On occasion, the public seemed stupidly reluctant to face the realities the writers singled out for its attention. There were times when the public was more interested in being indulged than in being startled into emotional and intellectual life. But a marvelous thing happened. The writers whom we now think of as having contributed the best and most interesting literature of the fifty years between 1865 and 1915 got themselves published, read, and to some extent or another recognized.

The careers of some (Dreiser, Cable, Chopin, Chesnutt, Whitman) were often troubled and filled with disappointments. The writing life of Kate Chopin, for example, came to an abrupt halt when her novel *The Awakening* took liberties concerning a woman's capacity for sensuality that the general public was not willing to allow. But an exceptional number of American writers found appreciative readers, both early and late—not as many, perhaps, as the writers might have liked; not as many as Twain and Howells could regularly count on; but enough. The American literary innovators were heard then and continue to be heard now. They expressed what it meant to them and to their contemporaries to be buffeted by the changes all Americans experienced as they moved rapidly into a future that had largely discarded the past in the process of somewhat crudely creating the present. The writers were creatures of their time, but they were also capable, at their best, of transcending those times. They reflected the boundlessness and the limits of the age. Sometimes they tried to make that age better; they seldom left it worse.

What is entailed by social and technological progress and whether wars are necessary were but two of the questions to which Americans had to respond during the late 1800s and the early 1900s. They also had to ask what it meant *to do good* and *to be good* in a world where *making good* seemed to have replaced the old moral notion of "goodness." The necessity to assess society and to reexamine the literary means for expressing what it meant to live in the decades after the close of the Civil War fell with particular weight upon American writers. Sometimes they wrote from deep within the silence of their hearts, as did Emily Dickinson. Sometimes they wrote directly from the public square because of their awareness of grave social issues, as did William Dean Howells, Frank Norris, and Mark Twain. Writers and readers alike were part of a period that pushed inquiries about whether the United States was—or could become—any better as a nation than the world at large. Everyone was living through many changes taking place very fast over an immense area of American life. The one thing the writers *could* do was to express, in imaginative terms, their responses to the thickness of the surrounding facts. They realized that those facts would have no human meaning unless they as writers had the skill to reveal those facts through the stories they told about America.

Fictional narrative reflected in various ways the often squalid yet humanly inspiring facts of lives as actually experienced in the shock of the times. A record kept by a young woman worker in the New York City sweatshops preserves in diary form just one of the tales that American writers had to tell.

The Diary of a Shirtwaist Striker

I've come to believe that this strike business is something like a catching sickness—measles or chicken-pox. Once you get it it sticks to you until it's all over.

And then again, one can't really help standing up for the girls. I went down to see Minnie; she's down in bed; some hoodlum hit her last night. God! how these people do live! I don't see how she can afford to stop for a single day.

Her brother Mack is out of work, her father never works, Minnie and her sister, Sarah, are out on strike. Talk about nerve, I really think them Jew girls have it all. I'd like a share of it myself, but somehow I aint of the brave kind. Ray said she'd rather starve to death than be a scab and take some one else's bread out of their mouths. I'm sure I couldn't have that much courage, but I'd hate to go back on the girls.

Theresa Serber Malkiel (1910)

Redefinitions and New Vocabularies

With changes marking almost every corner of American existence, it was inevitable that old words had new meanings forced upon them and that new phrases spun into being. The forty years between 1888 and 1928 witnessed the introduction of one new word out of every ten. As Mark Sullivan pointed out in his six-volume study *Our Times*, three thousand new words received official recognition between 1909 and 1927 alone. Most of these words reflected the discoveries taking place continually in physics, chemistry, and medicine and in the widening use of technology. But along with *X-ray, dynamo, telephone,* and *aeroplane* were words like *flivver, Kodak, movies, skyscraper,* and *el*—slangier references to the new entities filling everyday lives.

Going west in the 1860s as a greenhorn, Samuel Clemens dragged along a massive dictionary in the stagecoach he took out of St. Joseph, Missouri. But Clemens found out that many of the words acceptable back east were of little use beyond the Mississippi. Words like *coyote* and *blind lead* were more to the point in his new life. The 1884 edition of *The Adventures of Huckleberry Finn* was drummed off the shelf of the public library in Concord, Massachusetts, because it contained the ungrammatical sentences and lower-class language of a vagabond boy without genteel schooling. Yet Mark Twain's use of the vernacular proved one of the strongest elements of the thrust toward literary independence that was well under way by the 1890s.

Mark Twain, William Dean Howells, and Henry James introduced the flavor of colloquial speech into their fiction. Frank Norris's dentist MacTeague and Stephen Crane's infantryman Henry Fleming talked like such people might talk. Sarah Orne Jewett and Mary Wilkins Freeman accurately noted the linguistic mannerisms of rural characters from New England. Hamlin Garland did the same for his farmers from Wisconsin and the Dakotas, just as Joel Chandler Harris provided dialect stories of the Georgia blacks, and Kate Chopin and George Washington Cable emphasized the southern phrasings characteristic of the Creoles and Cajuns of Louisiana. As one result, the reading public was exposed to *American* speech distinctively unlike that of a "proper" literature derived from Boston or Great Britain.

The Devil's Dictionary

Conservative: A statesman who is enamored of existing evils, as distinguished from the Liberal, who wishes to replace them with others.

Vote: The instrument and symbol of a freeman's power to make a fool of himself and a wreck of his country.

Presidency: The greased pig in the field game of American politics.

Ambrose Bierce (1906)

So many new words! *Teddy bear* (inspired by the popular image of President Theodore Roosevelt), *she's a daisy,* and *ragtime* represented the simple pleasures of the nursery, the holiday outing, and the music hall. Still other words were less innocent records of current social upheavals and maladies: *Jim Crow, carpetbagger, skid row, the Four Hundred, nabobs, the Pinkertons, sweatshop,* and *the Molly Maguires.* The influx of immigrants meant the incorporation of words from Yiddish, Polish, Gaelic, and Italian into the basic pool of Yankee speech. They also kicked up new terms of insult: *Yid, Polack, Mick, Dago.* American life was turning inside out, and the good and the bad found the vocabularies needed to express their cruder emotions and deepest needs.

Older words were also redefined. On the battlefield in *The Red Badge of Courage,* Crane's Henry Fleming is forced to test accepted meanings for *heroism, glory,* and *patriotism.* Blacks in the South and the North and the slum dwellers in the cities had to reassess what it meant to live with the way words such as *values, equality,* and *freedom* were actually being used. Businessmen had to relearn what *individualism* and *business* signified in an economy where corporate organizations and new marketing techniques made the small, family-run company an anachronism. Faithful believers in American democracy had one set of definitions for *conservative, vote,* and *presidency;* Ambrose Bierce, dipping into his cynicism for *The Devil's Dictionary,* had others.

Home and the words that traditionally cluster around its values *(mother, wife, family, breadwinner)* were placed under the stress of still newer terms: *apartment, the working woman,* and *divorce. West, East, North,* and *South* were reassessed in light of what such labels meant to politicians dickering for votes, to bankers packaging far-flung mergers, to arbiters of culture attempting to create a national taste, to agronomists and economists trying to bring supply and demand into line, and to all those people piling onto the trains and wagons that moved them from one place to another in their search for a better life and true-blue American values.

Everywhere Strangers

Even the word *America* underwent severe testing. Questions arose over what constituted a *real* citizen of the United States. The religious preferences, cultural habits, racial and national antecedents of "the others" were probed to determine whether Catholics, Jews, Indians, Slavs, Slovenes, Asians, blacks, and Mexicans could ever be considered "one of us." The melting pot theory promised a massive process of national assimilation. The nativists insisted that such types would remain forever "aliens."

The debate over who would be permitted to claim the proud name "American" (native Anglo-Saxon stock only, or latecomers as well?) was complicated by the sense of national mission that reached its peak during the Spanish-American War and the takeover of the Philippines in 1898 and 1899. After all, so the argument went, it was precisely *as* Americans that the people of the United States had the duty to see to it that others became Americanized, whatever the contradictions involved in this transformation.

"Th' White Civilization"

"Ye see, Hinnissy, th' Indyun is bound f'r to give way to th' onward march iv white civilization. You an' me, Hinnissy, is th' white civilization."

"Mr. Dooley" (Finley Peter Dunne)

The strong stomach of American civilization may, and doubtless will, digest and assimilate ultimately this unsavory and repellent throng. . . . In time they catch the spirit of the country and form an element of decided worth.

The Philadelphia Press (1888)

Just as cross-fertilization is beneficial to plant life, the intermingling of peoples in this country must produce the most beautiful, most intellectual, and most powerful race of the world. . . . *[The] American, even to-day, presents the highest type of beauty which ever adorned the earth.*

Professor W. J. McGee (1906)

The members of the newly formed Anti-Imperalist League stepped in to say nay to this mood of expansionism. They stated the objections that found confirmation in Mark Twain's satiric essay "To a Person Sitting in Darkness" and in William James's "The Moral Equivalent of War." But it became increasingly difficult to interpret the words used to define America's proper role at home and abroad, just as it had been puzzling from the first to know exactly how to "read" the features of the colossal Statue of Liberty that stood at the nation's gates.

"Civilize and Christianize Them"

I walked the floor of the White House night after night until midnight; and I am not ashamed to tell you, gentlemen, that I went down on my knees and prayed Almighty God for light and guidance more than one night. And one night it came to me late this way—I don't know how it was, but it came . . . that there was nothing left for us to do but to take them all, and to educate the Filipinos, and uplift and civilize and Christianize them, and by God's grace do the very best we could for them, as our fellow-men for whom Christ also died.

President William McKinley (1899)

"Whin we plant what Hogan calls th' starry banner iv Freedom in th' Ph'lippeens," said Mr. Dooley, "an' give th' sacred blessin' iv liberty to th' poor, down-trodden people iv thim unfortunate isles—dam thim!—we'll larn thim a lesson."

"Mr. Dooley" (Finley Peter Dunne)

The New Colossus

Not like the brazen giant of Greek fame,
With conquering limbs astride from land to land;
Here at our sea-washed, sunset gates shall stand
A mighty woman with a torch, whose flame
Is the imprisoned lightning, and her name
Mother of Exiles. From her beacon-hand
Glows world-wide welcome; her mild eyes command
The air-bridged harbor that twice cities frame.
"Keep, ancient lands, your storied pomp!" cries she
With silent lips. "Give me your tired, your poor,
Your huddled masses yearning to breathe free,
The wretched refuse of your teeming shore.
Send these, the homeless, tempest-tossed to me:
I lift my lamp beside the golden door!"

Emma Lazarus (1886)

More than racial and ethnic labels were readjusted; class structures were also shifted. A sizable middle-class bloc emerged. At the high end of the spectrum lay what the newspapers liked to call "the plutocrats," while at the bottom of the heap huddled "the other half." (Reliable statistics gathered by 1915 indicate that the poor totaled sixty-five percent of the population, the lower and middle classes together made up thirty-three percent, and the wealthy constituted only two percent of the whole.)

How was one to know who was who in a society in which the signs of recognition were changing overnight? Could one distinguish friends from strangers—in class terms, at least—by the houses they lived in? Andrew Carnegie thought so. As he expounded in his 1889 essay "Wealth": "It is well, nay, essential, for the progress of the race that the houses of some should be homes for all that is highest and best in literature and the arts, and for all the refinements of civilization, rather than that none should be so. Much better this great irregularity than universal squalor."

Edith Wharton and Henry James certainly knew how to make clear the distinctions between "new" and "old" money—the differences between those who make a great show of their wealth and those who carefully keep their possessions under wraps. These were the same distinctions Thorstein Veblen made famous in his study of 1899, *The Theory of the Leisure Class.* He analyzed the look of affluence that places a successful man's possessions (wife and house) on public display. "The more reputable, 'presentable' portion of middle-class household paraphernalia are, on the one hand, items of conspicuous consumption, and on the other hand, apparatus for putting in the vicarious leisure rendered by the housewife."

In 1890 Jacob Riis attempted to do for the poor of the New York City slums what Wharton, James, and Veblen did for the well-to-do. In Riis's book of words and photographs, *How the Other Half Lives,* he analyzed the tonal differences between the families herded into Jewtown and the free-lance hoodlums who made the neighborhood of "the Bend" a synonym for crime. Willa Cather's memories of farm and village life in Nebraska also caught the distinctions between ethnic and class structures; she vividly portrayed the special vitality each immigrant servant girl (whether Bohemian, Swede, or German) brought to the Saturday night dances that threw the pallid, native-born town girls into the shade.

Transformations

If there were problems in knowing whether other people were friends or potential enemies in a world full of change, there was also the possible terror of inner transformations. William James lets it be known that the green-faced idiot he once saw sitting on a bench in an insane asylum is essentially what he, and we all, might yet become. Horatio Alger's Ragged Dick is transformed into a respectable wage-earning citizen. Dreiser's George Hurstwood, on the other hand, is plucked from the midst of health and well-being and cast down into degradation and death. Frank Norris's novels furnish many unsettling examples of characters who go through reversions to the most primitive stages. Perhaps one of the saddest, and most hilarious, of all lines from American literature comes in Norris's novel *Vandover and the Brute.* The main protagonist, Vandover, after dropping to all fours to howl at the moon, contrasts the wolfish brute he is turning into with what he had formerly been. "My God! to think I was a Harvard man once!"

Not all the transformations were as sensational as those insisted upon by Norris, Dreiser, and Jack London—writers who endorsed the current scientific and philosophical theories concerning the determining forces of heredity and environment. But even the metamorphoses taking place within the species "young American woman" proved disturbing to many who witnessed new types of the female rushing into existence. Henry James (with Daisy Miller and Isabel Archer) and William Dean Howells (with Kitty Ellison, Florida Vervain, and Lydia Blood) initiated the type of the American girl in the 1870s and 1880s. By the 1890s two of the most talked-about versions (favorites of the popular magazines and the Sunday newspaper supplements) were "the American heiress" and "the new woman."

Women as a sexual and social subclass were, by tradition, supposedly the most stable of all elements of American nineteenth-century life, fixed firmly within their sphere of home and hearth. In 1880 one of the many popular books of etiquette that taught Americans the proper "code of manners" stated flatly, "The power of a woman is in her refinement, gentleness and elegance; it is she who makes etiquette, and it is she who preserves the order and decency of society. Without women, men soon resume the savage state, and the comfort and the graces of the home are exchanged for the misery of the mining camp." But should a woman slip loose from the restraining influences of the home, she was transformed into that ancient aspect of Eve feared by "good society" and beloved of the tabloids.

The American heiress and the new woman. Left: Howard Chandler Christy, in *Our Girls, Poems in Praise of the American Girl* (1907). Right: The cover of *The Evolution of Woman* by Harry Whitney McVickar (1896).

There was no finer instance of the type of the femme fatale at the turn of the century than Evelyn Nesbit, over whose tarnished innocence one man (her husband, Harry Thaw) shot to death another man (her lover, the well-known architect Stanford White). The reporter for the *New York Evening World* covering the sensational murder trial of 1907 was agog over Nesbit's beauty— dangerous because it seemed so innocent. Hers was "the slim, quick grace of a fawn, a head that sat on the faultless throat as a lily on its stem, eyes that were the color of blue-brown pansies and the size of half-dollars, a mouth made of rumpled rose petals."

"Why Don't All These Ladies Do Something?"

And in the midst of the mild little tumult a certain Rose Lipschowsky got upon a soap-box in Union Square to say violently: "Why don't all these ladies do something to help the Garment Workers' Union instead of saying how good and refined they are?" She was much applauded, got down from her soap-box and vanished altogether, an unconscious symbol of what suffrage in the '90's omitted from its speeches and programs.

Thomas Beer, *The Mauve Decade* (1926)

It was a shock (of delight for some, of dismay for many) to realize that there were still other forms of female behavior coming into play by the 1870s and after than those of "the Eternal Evelyn." New occupations brought women (before and after marriage) into the work place. Enhanced college programs for women led them toward an education in new ideas, as well as in professional skills hitherto relegated to men alone. The *New York Journal* of March 22, 1896, headlined its alarm: "Are We Destroying Woman's Beauty? The Startling Warning of a Great English Physician Against Higher Education of Women. How Intellectual Work Destroys Beauty."

Women also pushed their way into politics. The suffrage movement made a widely publicized comeback in the 1880s after a relatively quiescent period in the years following the Civil War. The suffragists had no clear sailing, however. The right-to-vote advocates were criticized from without and within the movement. From outside their ranks, women as well as men feared the damage that social radicalism might do to the sanctity of the home. From inside the world of political activism, working-class women charged the middle-class members of the movement with elitism and ineffectual action, as in the confrontation in 1893, reported by Thomas Beer.

To the dizzying effect of the political and economic transformations taking place in the woman's world in America, add the burst of international marriages that allied the new wealth of young American girls with the old titles held by European noblemen who were not always noble in character. "The American heiress" as a type especially piqued the interest of readers of the Hearst and Pulitzer papers and such newly flourishing women's magazines as the *Ladies' Home Journal, Cosmopolitan,* and *Good Housekeeping.* Headed for a sumptuous life abroad, the heiress was a particular pet of the public when her romantic adventures were supplemented by the illustrations of Charles Dana Gibson, Howard Chandler Christy, Albert Beck Wenzell, and others. Some, like Christy, saw the heiress going from triumph to triumph. In *The American Girl as Seen and Portrayed by Howard Chandler Christy,* Christy extolled the type as proof of Darwinistic theories of evolution, sanctified as an icon enfolded in Old Glory. "She is the culmination of mankind's long struggle upward from his barbarism into civilization. To make her all that she is countless millions have lived and died." Others, however, expressed apprehension over the buying and selling of the American girl. James and Wharton did this in their novels and stories, as did Charles Dana Gibson in satiric exposés. Commentators on the American scene decided that "one is inclined to believe that a 'palatial' residence is sometimes the rich American girl's compensation for the absence of a 'palatial' husband."

Many of the fears and aspirations released during this period of change and transformation, affecting males and females alike, focused on the image of the American girl. What happened to her represented what was going on in every area of American society. In 1895 the *New York World* featured "a Scathing Rebuke of the Unfettered Female, Her Mannish Ways, Hatred of Children, Chewing Gum, and Erotic Novels." As the *New York Journal* warned in 1896, the show of energy embodied by the girl might bring to her and to society at large a massive "disorganization of the nervous system," leading to "loss of graceful outlines, loss of appetite, lines in the face, bad teeth, bad complexion, short sight and possibly hysteria, epilepsy and insanity!" No wonder that Henry

The ambitious mother and the obliging clergyman. Charles Dana Gibson, from The Gibson Book in Two Volumes *(1906)*.

Adams (at a higher intellectual level than the Hearst or Pulitzer papers offered) was studying with fascination the kinds of force represented by "the dynamo" and "the virgin." The male machine (symbolized by the Corliss engine, which dominated the American imagination after its presentation at the 1876 Philadelphia Centennial Exposition) was in power at the moment, but Adams had the premonition that female energy, hitherto frustrated and wasted, was about to force its way upon the American scene. As pupil and historian of modern times, Adams was eager to see what the outcome of such an explosion might be.

Making Contact

New people, new places, new objects, new ideas, new types—all located in new patterns of interchange and communication. There were no guarantees, however, that the newest inventions would not result in shocks and confusions rather than in clarity of meaning and the enhancement of personal and social life.

The Pullman car, the transcontinental railway, the electric trolley car, the transoceanic steamship, the bicycle, and the automobile were made possible by major advances in the technology of transportation. The telegraph, the Atlantic cable, and the telephone speeded the transport of messages. But it was in the world of the printed page that many of the most startling innovations took place. Dozens of new magazines and newspapers appeared so quickly that it was hard to keep up with the blur of words and images. Advances in printing techniques increased the amount, the kind, and the quality of illustrations that could be included in books, journals, and newspapers. Photographs were in common use for public purposes by the late 1890s. More words and pictures could be printed faster, for the viewing of more people, than ever before.

Certain Dangerous Tendencies in American Life

The young people of the mills generally read the story papers, published (most of them) in New York city, and devoted to interminably "continued" narratives, of which there are always three or four in process of publication in each paper. . . . They have usually no very distinct educational quality of tendency, good or bad. They are simply stories,—vapid, silly, turgid, and incoherent. As the robber-heroes are mostly grand-looking fellows, and all the ladies have white hands and splendid attire, it may be that some of the readers find hard work more distasteful because of their acquaintance with the gorgeous idlers and thieves, who, in these fictions are always so much more fortunate than the people who are honest and industrious. But usually . . . the only effect of this kind of reading is that it serves "to pass away the time," by supplying a kind of entertainment, a stimulus or opiate for the mind, and that these people resort to it and feel a necessity for it in much the same way that others feel they must have a whisky or opium. The reading is a narcotic, but it is less pernicious than those just named.

Jonathan Baxter Harrison (1880)

Improved print and picture meant spreading contact through all layers of society. Farmers, factory workers, city dwellers (whether in the tenements, the big houses, or the new apartment complexes), ethnic groups, and people from every geographic region now had a newspaper or a magazine addressed expressly to them. At the same time special audiences were being singled out, methods for the standardization of production and consumption were also under way. A great deal of what went into print was couched in broadly nationalistic terms. The jarring headlines or the newest best-sellers that intrigued readers on one coast aroused the interest of audiences on the opposite coast and just about everyone in between.

Together with the widening of the general readership (aided by an increased access to public schools, land-grant colleges, and special-training courses) came a vertical thrust down through the layers of class. The so-called genteel readership that had once centered in Boston and radiated out from other established eastern communities had always possessed a selection of magazines that suited its particular tastes in the arts and in politics. Now brash new publications were supplying things to read all the way down the cultural slope to the shop girls and foreign-born mechanics.

Upper- and middle-class magazines prided themselves on being responsible to the intellectual and spiritual values of their readers. Sometimes this sense of social obligation defined itself as smug support of traditional views and as fear of change. In 1889 Thomas DeWitt Talmage wrote *Social Dynamite; or, The Wickedness of Modern Society.* Talmage was certain that "poison" would replace "truth" if the unwary allowed popular romances into their homes. On other occasions, Clarence S. Darrow criticized the literature of moral evasion and urged reforms in the direction of reality. Darrow, no less than Talmage, sought the truth, but each found what he praised in the writings the other man condemned.

Social Dynamite

Look through your library, and then, having looked through your library, look on the stand where you keep your pictorials and newspapers, and apply the Christian principles I have laid down. If there is anything in your home that can not stand the test, do not give it away, for it might spoil an immortal soul; do not sell it, for the money you get would be the price of blood; but rather kindle a fire on your kitchen hearth, or in your back yard, and then drop the poison in it, and keep stirring the blaze until from preface to appendix there shall not be a single paragraph left, and the bonfire in your city shall be as consuming as that one in the streets of Ephesus.

Thomas DeWitt Talmage, *Social Dynamite; or, The Wickedness of Modern Society* (1889)

The popular press was somewhat more cheerfully cynical about its role as critic of social ills and upholder of sacred truths. Editors of the large-circulation papers and magazines directed toward the working classes were diligent enough in exposing national corruptions and local connivings since just such stories (done up in bold headlines) both did society some good and sold like hotcakes. By the 1890s Hearst and Pulitzer refined the formulas that brought their readers news that went to the extremes of sensationalism. Available facts were keyed up to make the stories splashier, or facts were invented to bring stories—even wars—into existence.

Entertainment, instruction, and reform made the interconnecting worlds of journalism, magazine publication, and book sales go; but there continued to be a deep split in tastes between one segment of the American population and another. Van Wyck Brooks, the man who helped popularize the terms *highbrow* and *lowbrow,* drove home the point that America was in the midst of a cultural civil war. Brooks saw the nation as divided: "on the one hand a quite unclouded, quite unhypocritical assumption of transcendent theory ('high ideals'); on the other a simultaneous acceptance of catchpenny realities. Between university ethic and business ethics, between American culture and American humor, between Good Government and Tammany, between academic pedantry and pavement slang, there is no community, no genial middle ground."

Along with all the other "strangers" (by virtue of race, heritage, economic status, region, and gender) American society had to contend with, those who lived by ideals were estranged from those who abided by the way things were. This cultural division made itself felt in the way American writers and artists viewed their chances at success and effectiveness in a nation where the business of being an American seemed mainly to be just that: *business.*

The Intellectual and Aesthetic Life

By the 1890s and 1900s the new professionals of the advertising and promotion world were using the picture and print industry to the utmost. New products were featured in entirely new areas of merchandising: big department stores, mail-order catalogs, national and international fairs and expositions. New approaches to the marketing of sports, theaters, and museums disclosed different ways to place entertainment on display and to "sell" the pleasures of culture. There was a riot of new things in America to desire. It was up to everyone to take advantage of the chances to make, to sell, and to buy.

Not all the new in American life came in the form of material objects or tangible events. Ideas were important too, even the more abstract, unsellable kind. The final decades of the nineteenth century were marked by a distinguished group of thinkers who tried out new intellectual methods for resolving both age-old philosophical questions and the brand-new difficulties that rushed into existence. A great deal of hard thinking went on, especially from the 1880s onwards, over matters of social justice and humanistic concerns.

PUCK.

LET THE ADVERTISING AGENTS TAKE CHARGE OF THE BARTHOLDI BUSINESS, AND THE MONEY WILL BE RAISED WITHOUT DELAY

The back cover of Puck *(April 1, 1885).*

> ## "The World Asks for Facts"
>
> The world has grown tired of preachers and sermons; to-day it asks for facts. It has grown tired of fairies and angels, and asks for flesh and blood. It looks on life as it exists to-day—both in its beauty and its horror, its joy and its sorrow. It wishes to see all; not only the prince and the millionaire, but the laborer and the beggar, the master and the slave. We see the beautiful and the ugly, and know what the world is and what it ought to be, and the true picture which the author saw and painted stirs the heart to holier feelings and to grander thoughts.
>
> Clarence S. Darrow, "Realism in Literature and Art" (1892)

Josiah Royce, George Santayana, William James, Charles Sanders Peirce, and John Dewey as philosophers; Justice Oliver Wendell Holmes as an authority on the law; Thorstein Veblen, Herbert Croly, Lester Frank Ward, and Henry George as economists and political scientists—all countered the slipshod notions and vicious ideologies, the *bad* thinking, that crowded the mental spaces of American life. The men named here, as well as many others (women, too), argued vigorously about such sharp-edged issues as how best to educate the young, to put equitable laws into practice, to assure racial and economic fairness, to encourage ethical behavior, to initiate tax reforms, and to reshape democratic principles to fit the times. These overtly social questions battled for public attention alongside equally vital questions concerning freedom of choice, the existence of God or goodness, the ways by which complex minds work and the bodily instincts function, and—above all—the nature of truths in an ambiguous universe and the means by which to signify them in language and in deeds.

The new school of American philosophers and psychologists saw to it that seemingly abstruse queries about materialism (emphasis on things), idealism (concentration on ideas and principles), determinism (what you cannot control), and free will (the choices you can make) received recognition among thoughtful Americans as matters that concretely affected everyone's life. They wanted to prevent what many feared might take place: the loss of one's sense of humanity in a torrent of sensual impressions or the chance of that humanity being locked into grids by massive mechanistic forces.

In 1890 William James graphically imaged the mind's environment. It was precisely *that* environment out of which turn-of-the-century Americans had to make something good for themselves and their fellow citizens or go down in defeat. Somehow the life of the mind, as well as that of the body, had to be conducted under imperfect conditions. The soul was also important, at least to idealists like Josiah Royce who still held a toehold in a world of contingencies and materiality. Mind, body, or soul, the sense of *being human* had to make itself felt as an experienced fact; otherwise, it would all signify nothing. In *The Principles of Psychology,* William James hit it right on the mark: "Millions of items of the outward order are present to my senses which never properly enter into my experience. Why? Because they have no *interest for me. My experience is what I agree to attend to.*"

The Stream of Thought

Out of what is in itself an undistinguishable, swarming *continuum,* devoid of distinction or emphasis, our senses make for us, by attending to this motion and ignoring that, a world full of contrasts, of sharp accents, of abrupt changes of picturesque light and shade.

William James, *The Principles of Psychology* (1890)

Science received the kind of rapt attention of which William James spoke. In his sixties, Henry Adams, for example, tried to make up for the botched education he had received as a Harvard undergraduate in the 1850s by teaching himself the essentials of the new mathematics and physics. Speculation about thermodynamics, X-rays, and "the supersensual chaos" of the universe occupied Adams's busy mind until his death in 1918, just after Albert Einstein's momentous discoveries about cosmic time, space, and energy.

From the 1860s onward Darwinism and its permutations affected the way Americans came to view their economic system (competitiveness versus regulation in the marketplace), their religious beliefs (God versus chance as the master of the universe), their bodies (theirs to direct versus control by inherited "tendencies"), and their physical surroundings (a thing of spirit versus a conglomeration of geologic earth-masses). Herbert Spencer (champion of Social Darwinism) and Pierre and Marie Curie (discovers of radium) were names that caught the interest of the public as much as those of Thomas Edison, George Pullman, and the builders of Chicago's skyscrapers and Brooklyn's bridge. The age became known as the Age of Energy. The forces set loose by the new science heartened some and dismayed others, but no one escaped its impact.

For many Americans, *being human* meant paying attention to the aesthetic side of life in order to offset the jars of science, technology, and the business of buying and selling. The worth of literature, painting, music, architecture, the theater, and the decorative arts was reexamined (along with everything else) by the rising generation of young writers and artists, who often felt they had to fight for attention in a society that seemed more interested in the Corliss engine, the Bessemer steel-processing method, and Standard Oil takeovers than in what artists had to express or how they expressed it.

The problems that nagged the more radical among the writers and artists of the late nineteenth century were not as much caused by lack of interest in the arts on the part of the general American public as they were affected by the questionable kind and quality of art that found quickest acceptance around the country. There is an ingrained contradiction here, since admirable, often outstanding advances were made in the fine and applied arts and architecture of the period, fully commensurate with the striking triumphs achieved in literature. The paintings of Thomas Eakins, John Singer Sargent, Winslow Homer, James Abbott McNeill Whistler, and Mary Cassatt, the sculpture of Augustus Saint-Gaudens and Daniel Chester French, the architectural plans of Henry

Hobson Richardson, Stanford White, and Louis Sullivan, and the decorative designs of Louis Tiffany and John La Farge can hardly be dismissed. Photography as a skilled art form had its champions in Frances Benjamin Johnston, Gertrude Käsebier, F. Holland Day, and Clarence White, and the display poster achieved an enviable peak with the work of Will Bradley, Louis Rhead, and Edward Penfield.

Nor could anyone suggest that the American public was not avidly interested in the artistic side of life. The arts exhibits at the Centennial Exposition held in Philadelphia in 1876 and (together with a number of writers' congresses) at the Columbian Exposition in Chicago in 1893 drew large audiences. So did the expositions in St. Louis and San Francisco in subsequent years. *The Book of the Fair,* compiled by Hubert Howe Bancroft after the Columbian Exposition, proudly declared that "the Fair has been to the world a revelation, to Americans an inspiration. It has shown, as no written or spoken words could show, the power and progress of a nation where all are free to strive for the highest rewards that energy and talent can win." The museums that first opened their neo-Renaissance portals to the public during the 1890s and 1900s also stirred wide interest. The many salon showings of contemporary paintings (both American and European), the ample inclusion of fine arts reproductions in the magazines, the commissions given to muralists and sculptors to decorate the stately new municipal buildings, and the widespread practice of placing copies of famous works of art in the classrooms of the public schools indicate that there was much interest in art (and the moral values it was meant to represent) at one level of American taste or another.

What irritated the artists was that the views on "taste" sponsored by the academies and the official showplaces of aesthetic wares encouraged the public to respond negatively to themes that were demonstrably American and to techniques that were experimentally modern. And the artists' problem was shared with the writers of the period. No one could accuse the American public of not wanting to read stories, poetry, and novels; there was an insatiable appetite for almost everything in print. But what most people said they liked did not often coincide with what those who opposed traditional literary values upheld as true art.

"Sentimental Romance to Bitter Realism"

Owen Wister and Alfred Henry Lewis were busy with [the] past. . . . Kirk Munro told tales for boys. Mary Hallock Foote varied from sentimental romance to a sudden passage or two of bitter realism. . . . Stephen Crane flashed his short string of Western sketches through *McClure's* and the *Century,* refutations of melodrama in melodrama's terms. . . . The stencilled characters of Bret Harte returned thinly masked in the *Argonaut,* the *Wave* and the *Overland Monthly.* So in 1898 Harry Thurston Peck mourned: "I would have given ten Mrs. Humphrey Wards for one good realistic novel about Denver and Seattle."

Thomas Beer, *The Mauve Decade* (1926)

Artists and writers in America of an independent turn of the imagination had enemies aplenty. H. H. Boyesen named one of the worst as "the Iron Madonna," the female reader "who strangles in her fond embrace the American novelist; the Moloch upon whose altar he sacrifices, willingly or unwillingly, his chances of greatness." Thomas Beer went even further when he blamed the namby-pamby conservatism of the general imagination.

Americans who wanted to say something real, strong, and earnest usually received small encouragement from the people at the top. President Grover Cleveland put it nicely: "When I come [to the theater] I want to see something to make me laugh." But even the most shallow or timid consumers of the written word sooner or later learned that there was something more that had to be said. When Mary Roberts Coolidge examined "why women are so," she described the shock that occurs when fantasies of evasion—such as those concerning love's young dream about getting married—are jolted by the realities.

The best of the writers who rode out the storms of late-nineteenth-century American life took on the task of dealing with just these "puzzling and inevitable facts of nature." They did it in many different ways. Henry James's *Daisy Miller* does not read like Theodore Dreiser's *Sister Carrie* or Edith Wharton's *Summer*. Walt Whitman's *Leaves of Grass* makes use of other poetic means than those of Emily Dickinson's "A Narrow Fellow in the Grass." William Dean Howells and Henry Adams shake up the imagination of their readers by means of indirection. Ambrose Bierce, Stephen Crane, and Upton Sinclair pounce on the emotions straight on. Mark Twain is a realist through slam-bang humor. Frank Norris goes in for all-out horror.

Such pluralism of literary approaches was all to the good at the turn of the century since the reality of American life the writers tried to record was "the buzzing booming chaos" described by William James. Faced by a world like this, American writers needed complex minds and hearts to do it justice. Fortunately, among the best "products" coming out of late-nineteenth-century America were precisely the minds and hearts Henry James said "the complex fate" of being an American required.

Further Reading:

P. Buck, *The Road to Reunion*, 1937.
V. Brooks, *New England: Indian Summer*, 1940.
L. Mumford, *The Brown Decades*, 1941.
D. Wecter, *The Hero in America*, 1941.
R. E. Spiller et al., *Literary History of the United States*, 1948 (and supplements).
E. Wilson, *Patriotic Gore*, 1962.
T. Tanner, *The Reign of Wonder*, 1965.
L. Ziff, *The American 1890s*, 1966.
J. Martin, *Harvests of Change*, 1967.
Popular Culture and Industrialism, ed. H. Smith, 1967.

Democratic Vistas: 1860–1880, ed. A. Trachtenberg, 1970.
H. M. Jones, *The Age of Energy*, 1971.
D. McCullough, *The Great Bridge*, 1972.
D. Aaron, *The Unwritten War*, 1973.
N. Harris, *Humbug: The Art of P. T. Barnum*, 1973.
D. Boorstin, *The Americans: The Democratic Experience*, 1974.
W. S. McFeely, *Grant*, 1981.
A. Kazin, *An American Procession*, 1984.

Walt Whitman
1819–1892

Whitman is the great bridge figure of nineteenth-century American literature. He links the era of Hawthorne and Thoreau to that of Mark Twain and Henry James. He fulfilled the promise of romanticism while pointing to the open road of modernist form, vision, and experiment. His powerful, imperial presence continues to assert itself in the work of Wallace Stevens, William Carlos Williams, Ezra Pound, Hart Crane, and the generation of Allen Ginsberg. Whitman once said that his leading trait was caution and that there was "something in my nature *furtive* like an old hen." Still, he worshiped boldness, contradiction, and change, shocked contemporaries with his candor about sexuality, and created a radical poetry voicing a radical consciousness: "For I confront peace, security, and all the settled laws, to unsettle them." He was the most ardent of nationalists and said that his book "could not possibly have emerged or been fashion'd or completed, from any other era than the latter half of the Nineteenth Century, nor from any other land than democratic America." Yet he was also America's chief poet of international standing, with followers in the British Isles, Europe, and Scandinavia. Today his work is read in Chinese, Japanese, Russian, and every other major tongue.

When Whitman was born in 1819, in a farmhouse on eastern Long Island, New York, the United States was rural and relatively isolated. The President, James Monroe, had fought in the Revolution and still wore knee breeches. When Whitman died in 1892, in a working-class neighborhood of Camden, New Jersey, a corporation lawyer, Benjamin Harrison, occupied the White House and the United States was a world power.

During the poet's early years, the Whitmans, descendants of early Dutch and English settlers, fell on hard times and moved from the country districts to Brooklyn, then a thriving, independent city. They were in psychic as well as economic disarray. A failure at farming and business, Walter Whitman, Sr., was "addicted to alcohol," according to his son, and frequently depressed. Of his eight children who survived infancy, four were disturbed or incompetent, but one went on to celebrate "physiology from top to toe . . . Life immense in passion, pulse, and power."

Walt Whitman's dependent childhood, along with all the formal schooling he was ever to have, came to an end when he was about twelve. Like Benjamin Franklin, Mark Twain, and William Dean Howells, he learned the printing trade and in the printing office, the poor-boy's college for many Americans, began to acquire a miscellaneous literary and intellectual culture. He worked in Brooklyn and New York and on Long Island as a typesetter, schoolteacher, newspaper editor, free-lance journalist, storekeeper, and housebuilder. During the 1840s he published a novel, *Franklin Evans,* about the evils of drink, at least sixteen conventional poems, and about two dozen stories and sketches, most of them imitative or hackwork, that nevertheless anticipate many of the themes and images of his mature work.

The poet, Whitman was to say, "must flood himself with the immediate age as with vast oceanic tides." He absorbed the Emersonian gospel of self-trust and the infinitude of the private man; oratory; the writings of George Sand and Thomas Carlyle; science, art, and philosophy; the Free-Soil movement; the vibrant life of Broadway and "million-footed Manhattan." He studied linguistics and the American vernacular, believing that "a perfect writer would make words sing, dance, kiss, do the male and female act, bear children . . . or do any thing that man or woman or the natural powers can do." Whitman's discovery of grand opera, which was then enjoying its first vogue in the United States, released his emotions, suggested poetic equivalents for recitative and aria, and helped free him from conventional forms and meters. Although he may have reasoned his way to the right conclusions by using the wrong data, phrenology and other pseudosciences and improving regimens revealed a creative potential within himself that he believed was as large as the American continent. He saw the continent itself and democratic vistas of city and wilderness in a five-thousand-mile journey he took in 1848 from New York to New Orleans and back. Egyptology and Eastern wisdom-writing opened up other vistas of time and space.

"I was simmering, simmering, simmering." In his early thirties Whitman at last found a supreme purpose, to be "a master after my own kind, making the poems of emotions, as they pass or stay, the poems of freedom, and the exposé of personality—singing in high tones democracy and the New World of it through These States." He intended *Leaves of Grass* to be nothing less than a "new Bible" for the new age of democracy and science. A pre-1855 verse fragment suggests the inner drama of Whitman's transformation: "I cannot be awake, for nothing looks to me as it did before, / Or else I am awake for the first time, and all before has been a mean sleep."

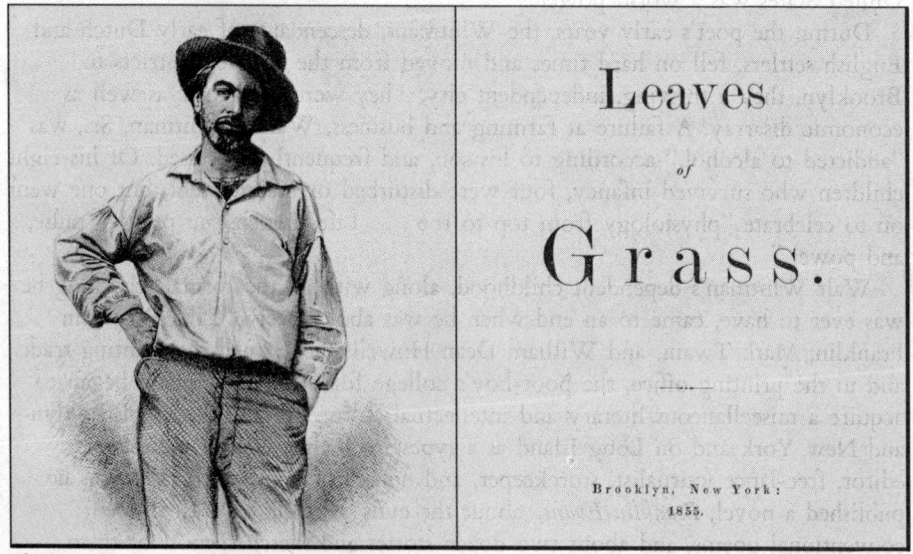

Photograph courtesy of the Library of Congress

In July 1855, "after many MS. doings and undoings—(I had great trouble in leaving out the stock 'poetical' touches—but succeeded at last)," Whitman issued the first edition of *Leaves of Grass*. A slim volume, with its title stamped on the cloth cover in tendriled letters, Whitman's ninety-six-page book opened with an uncaptioned frontispiece portrait of a bearded man wearing a broad-brimmed hat and an open-necked shirt. The facing title page did not give the author's name. An eccentrically punctuated prose preface, the most decisive of Whitman's critical manifestos, introduced twelve as yet untitled poems, at first glance clusters of prose sentences set up like Bible verses. Not until page twenty-nine did the author declare his identity: "Walt Whitman, An American, one of the roughs, a kosmos, / Disorderly, fleshy and sensual."

Leaves of Grass came into a largely indifferent world in 1855 not as a trial venture, not as a greatly "promising" book, but as a stylistically and substantively achieved masterpiece. "I find it the most extraordinary piece of wit and wisdom that America has yet contributed," Emerson wrote to the new poet. "I give you joy of your free and brave thought. I have great joy in it. I find incomparable things said incomparably well, as they must be. I find the courage of treatment which so delights us, and which large perception only can inspire. I greet you at the beginning of a great career, which yet must have had a long foreground somewhere, for such a start." Emerson's celebrated letter remains unequaled for the generosity, force, and simple justice of its understanding.

Leaves of Grass changed and grew over the next four decades. Whitman wished to endow it with the scope and structure of something monumental, a great tree with many growth rings, a cathedral, a modern city like his million-footed Manhattan. His second edition (1856) added twenty new poems, among them "Crossing Brooklyn Ferry"; his third (1860) added 146, including "Out of the Cradle Endlessly Rocking" and two cycles, or "clusters," "Calamus" (treating "manly love," or "the love of comrades") and "Children of Adam" (treating heterosexual love); his fourth (1867) added the Civil War cycle "Drum-Taps" and the majestic poem of mourning for Abraham Lincoln, "When Lilacs Last in the Dooryard Bloom'd." By the time Whitman issued his final ("deathbed") edition of 1891–1892, the original ninety-six printed pages of 1855 had grown to 438. After the late 1850s, a markedly tragic element tempered his early, lyric celebrations. Still later, his diction, once assertively American and vernacular, tended to become somewhat denatured, even transatlantic, and he vacillated between a poetry of precise observation and a poetry of ideas and large declarations.

"The proof of a poet," Whitman declared in his preface, "is that his country absorbs him as affectionately as he has absorbed it." Years later he was to concede, "I have not gain'd the acceptance of my time." While he lived, his most fervent readers as a group turned out to be not the working-class American men and women—the democratic leaven—he had hoped to reach but another class altogether, even another nationality: highly cultivated foreign writers and intellectuals like William Michael Rossetti, Oscar Wilde, Algernon Charles Swinburne, Robert Louis Stevenson, Gerard Manley Hopkins, poet laureate

Alfred Tennyson, John Addington Symonds, and Professor Edward Dowden of Trinity College, Dublin. One English admirer, Anne Gilchrist, wrote an important appreciation, fell in love with Whitman, and came to America with the hope of marrying him. But aside from his attachments to semiliterate younger men, it was Whitman's book that remained his sole heart's companion, the center of his life. He was willing to go to any length to preserve, protect, and defend it.

Whitman's effective exploitation of Emerson's private letter (he circulated it without permission and used it as promotional material) distressed the Concord sage and his friends. But this episode only marked the beginning of Whitman's unremitting campaign to assure *Leaves of Grass* a breathing space in the world. Like Mark Twain a brilliant publicist, he reviewed his own book on several occasions, planted newspaper stories about his doings and whereabouts, interviewed himself, collaborated with the authors of biographies, polemics, and encomiums, and eagerly sat for hundreds of photographs and portraits that called attention to his trademark flowing beard and open-necked shirts. One unsigned article by Whitman, published in a Camden paper in 1876, touched off a noisy Anglo-American controversy over the extent to which he was allegedly neglected by his compatriots.

For a few years after 1855, Whitman made a living as a newspaper editor and free-lance journalist. During the Civil War, having vowed to live a "purged" and "cleansed" life, he turned his back on New York's literary and artistic bohemia and moved to beleaguered Washington. There, supporting himself by part-time clerking in the army paymaster's office, he served as volunteer nurse and comforter—"wound-dresser"—in the military hospitals. This caring for the sick, wounded, and dying may have been the most intense emotional experience of his middle and later years. In 1865 he was appointed to a full-time government clerkship, a job that paid him about $1,600 a year until 1874. By then he was an invalid, having suffered a paralytic stroke the year before, and had moved, permanently, from Washington to Camden. With the major exceptions of trips to Colorado and Canada in 1879 and 1880, he spent the rest of his life in Camden, first as a paying guest in his brother's house and finally as the owner of 328 Mickle Street, "a little old shanty of my own" that he bought for $1,750. Whitman managed to live in frugal comfort, and even build an imposing tomb, on money derived from royalties, direct sales of books, fees and honoraria, and gifts from admirers. His average annual income from 1876 to 1892 was $1,270. During those years, as for most of his career, he mainly isolated himself from professional literary people in New York, Philadelphia, and Boston, preferring the company of the small band of disciples that had formed around him and celebrated his birthdays with eucharistic feasts.

An important prose writer as well as a poet, Whitman published *Democratic Vistas* (1871), a searching essay on American society and ideals, and *Specimen Days* (1882), a loosely structured autobiography focusing on the Civil War period. His history after 1855, however, is largely the history of *Leaves of Grass* in its successive editions and collisions with guardians of public taste and morals. Despite Emerson's endorsement, early reviewers called Whitman's poetry "a mass of stupid filth" and its author a pig rooting "among a rotten garbage of licentious thoughts." In 1865 the secretary of the Interior fired Whitman from his clerkship on the grounds that *Leaves of Grass* violated "the rules of decorum and propriety prescribed by a Christian Civilization." Whitman was quickly transferred to an equivalent post in the attorney general's office, but in the hands of supporters like William Douglas O'Connor, Whitman's dismissal became a cause célèbre and served an important purpose in his developing reputation: No longer "one of the roughs," he was now, in O'Connor's words, "The Good Gray Poet," sage, martyr, and redeemer. Fifteen years later a district attorney in Boston found *Leaves of Grass* actionable under "the Public Statutes respecting obscene literature" and in effect forced Whitman's publishers there to withdraw the book. *Leaves of Grass* moved to Philadelphia for its final editions. Such "bruises" and "buffetings" did not discourage its author. Whitman believed that his book was "a candidate for the future" and that its value would be "decided by time."

Further Reading:
H. Traubel, *With Walt Whitman in Camden*, 6 vols., 1906–1982.
N. Arvin, *Whitman*, 1938.
H. S. Canby, *Walt Whitman, An American*, 1943.
R. D. Faner, *Walt Whitman and Opera*, 1951.
R. Chase, *Walt Whitman Reconsidered*, 1955.
Leaves of Grass One Hundred Years After, ed. M. Hindus, 1955.
J. E. Miller, Jr., *A Critical Guide to Leaves of Grass*, 1957.
R. Asselineau, *The Evolution of Walt Whitman*,

2 vols., 1960, 1962.
Whitman: A Collection of Critical Essays, ed. R. H. Pierce, 1962.
G. W. Allen, *The Solitary Singer*, 1967.
E. H. Miller, *Walt Whitman's Poetry: A Psychological Journey*, 1968.
G. W. Allen, *The New Walt Whitman Handbook*, 1975.
S. Black, *Whitman's Journey into Chaos*, 1975.
J. Kaplan, *Walt Whitman: A Life*, 1980.
P. Zweig, *Walt Whitman: The Making of the Poet*, 1984.

Texts:
Leaves of Grass, 1891–1892.
Collected Prose Works, 1892.

See also *The Collected Writings of Walt Whitman*, ed. G. W. Allen and S. Bradley, 1963–.

from Leaves of Grass [1891–1892]

from Inscriptions

One's-Self I Sing

One's-Self I sing, a simple separate person,
Yet utter the word Democratic, the word En-Masse.

Of physiology from top to toe I sing,
Not physiognomy alone nor brain alone is worthy for the Muse, I say the
   Form complete is worthier far,
The Female equally with the Male I sing.

5

Of Life immense in passion, pulse, and power,
Cheerful, for freest action form'd under the laws divine,
The Modern Man I sing.
1867

When I Read the Book

When I read the book, the biography famous,
And is this then (said I) what the author calls a man's life?
And so will some one when I am dead and gone write my life?
(As if any man really knew aught of my life,
Why even I myself I often think know little or nothing of my real life,   5
Only a few hints, a few diffused faint clews and indirections
I seek for my own use to trace out here.)
1867

Beginning My Studies

Beginning my studies the first step pleas'd me so much,
The mere fact consciousness, these forms, the power of motion,
The least insect or animal, the senses, eyesight, love,
The first step I say awed me and pleas'd me so much,
I have hardly gone and hardly wish'd to go any farther,   5
But stop and loiter all the time to sing it in ecstatic songs.
1865

I Hear America Singing

I hear America singing, the varied carols I hear,
Those of mechanics, each one singing his as it should be blithe and strong,
The carpenter singing his as he measures his plank or beam,
The mason singing his as he makes ready for work, or leaves off work,
The boatman singing what belongs to him in his boat, the deckhand singing on
      the steamboat deck,   5
The shoemaker singing as he sits on his bench, the hatter singing as he stands,
The wood-cutter's song, the ploughboy's on his way in the morning, or at noon
      intermission or at sundown,
The delicious singing of the mother, or of the young wife at work, or of the
      girl sewing or washing,
Each singing what belongs to him or her and to none else,
The day what belongs to the day—at night the party of young fellows, robust,
      friendly,   10
Singing with open mouths their strong melodious songs.
1860

*Song of Myself**

1

I celebrate myself, and sing myself,
And what I assume you shall assume,
For every atom belonging to me as good belongs to you.

I loafe and invite my soul,
I lean and loafe at my ease observing a spear of summer grass.   5

My tongue, every atom of my blood, form'd from this soil, this air,
Born here of parents born here from parents the same, and their parents the
     same,
I, now thirty-seven years old in perfect health begin,
Hoping to cease not till death.

Creeds and schools in abeyance,   10
Retiring back a while sufficed at what they are, but never forgotten,
I harbor for good or bad, I permit to speak at every hazard,
Nature without check with original energy.

2

Houses and rooms are full of perfumes, the shelves are crowded with perfumes,
I breathe the fragrance myself and know it and like it,   15
The distillation would intoxicate me also, but I shall not let it.

The atmosphere is not a perfume, it has no taste of the distillation, it is
     odorless,
It is for my mouth forever, I am in love with it,
I will go to the bank by the wood and become undisguised and naked,
I am mad for it to be in contact with me.   20

The smoke of my own breath,
Echoes, ripples, buzz'd whispers, love-root, silk-thread, crotch and vine,
My respiration and inspiration, the beating of my heart, the passing of blood
     and air through my lungs,
The sniff of green leaves and dry leaves, and of the shore and dark-color'd
     sea-rocks, and of hay in the barn,
The sound of the belch'd words of my voice loos'd to the eddies of the wind,   25
A few light kisses, a few embraces, a reaching around of arms,
The play of shine and shade on the trees as the supple boughs wag,
The delight alone or in the rush of the streets, or along the fields and hill-sides,

---

* Untitled when first published in the 1855
edition of *Leaves of Grass,* "Song of Myself"
became "Poem of Walt Whitman, an

American" and then "Walt Whitman" before
being given its final title in 1881.

The feeling of health, the full-noon trill, the song of me rising from bed and
    meeting the sun.

Have you reckon'd a thousand acres much? have you reckon'd the earth much? 30
Have you practis'd so long to learn to read?
Have you felt so proud to get at the meaning of poems?

Stop this day and night with me and you shall possess the origin of all poems,
You shall possess the good of the earth and sun, (there are millions of suns left,)
You shall no longer take things at second or third hand, nor look through the
    eyes of the dead, nor feed on the spectres in books, 35
You shall not look through my eyes either, nor take things from me,
You shall listen to all sides and filter them from your self.

3

I have heard what the talkers were talking, the talk of the beginning and the
    end,
But I do not talk of the beginning or the end.

There was never any more inception than there is now, 40
Nor any more youth or age than there is now,
And will never be any more perfection than there is now,
Nor any more heaven or hell than there is now.

Urge and urge and urge,
Always the procreant urge of the world. 45

Out of the dimness opposite equals advance, always substance and increase,
    always sex,
Always a knit of identity, always distinction, always a breed of life.

To elaborate is no avail, learn'd and unlearn'd feeling that it is so.

Sure as the most certain sure, plumb in the uprights, well entretied,[1] braced in
    the beams,
Stout as a horse, affectionate, haughty, electrical, 50
I and this mystery here we stand.

Clear and sweet is my soul, and clear and sweet is all that is not my soul.

Lack one lacks both, and the unseen is proved by the seen,
Till that becomes unseen and receives proof in its turn.

---

[1] Cross-braced.

Showing the best and dividing it from the worst age vexes age,   55
Knowing the perfect fitness and equanimity of things, while they discuss I am
   silent, and go bathe and admire myself.

Welcome is every organ and attribute of me, and of any man hearty and clean,
Not an inch nor a particle of an inch is vile, and none shall be less familiar
   than the rest.

I am satisfied—I see, dance, laugh, sing;
As the hugging and loving bed-fellow sleeps at my side through the night, and
   withdraws at the peep of the day with stealthy tread,   60
Leaving me baskets cover'd with white towels swelling the house with their
   plenty,
Shall I postpone my acceptation and realization and scream at my eyes,
That they turn from gazing after and down the road,
And forthwith cipher and show me to a cent,
Exactly the value of one and exactly the value of two, and which is ahead?   65

4

Trippers and askers surround me,
People I meet, the effect upon me of my early life or the ward and city I live
   in, or the nation,
The latest dates, discoveries, inventions, societies, authors old and new,
My dinner, dress, associates, looks, compliments, dues,
The real or fancied indifference of some man or woman I love,   70
The sickness of one of my folks or of myself, or ill-doing or loss or lack of
   money, or depressions or exaltations,
Battles, the horrors of fratricidal war, the fever of doubtful news, the fitful
   events;
These come to me days and nights and go from me again,
But they are not the Me myself.

Apart from the pulling and hauling stands what I am,   75
Stands amused, complacent, compassionating, idle, unitary,
Looks down, is erect, or bends an arm on an impalpable certain rest,
Looking with side-curved head curious what will come next,
Both in and out of the game and watching and wondering at it.
Backward I see in my own days where I sweated through fog with linguists
   and contenders,   80
I have no mockings or arguments, I witness and wait.

5

I believe in you my soul, the other I am must not abase itself to you,
And you must not be abased to the other.

Loafe with me on the grass, loose the stop from your throat,
Not words, not music or rhyme I want, not custom or lecture, not even the
    best,   85
Only the lull I like, the hum of your valvèd voice.

I mind how once we lay such a transparent summer morning,
How you settled your head athwart my hips and gently turn'd over upon me,
And parted the shirt from my bosom-bone, and plunged your tongue to my
    bare-stript heart,
And reach'd till you felt my beard, and reach'd till you held my feet.   90

Swiftly arose and spread around me the peace and knowledge that pass all the
    argument of the earth,
And I know that the hand of God is the promise of my own,
And I know that the spirit of God is the brother of my own,
And that all the men ever born are also my brothers, and the women my sisters
    and lovers,
And that a kelson[2] of the creation is love,   95
And limitless are leaves stiff or drooping in the fields,
And brown ants in the little wells beneath them,
And mossy scabs of the worm fence, heap'd stones, elder, mullein and
    poke-weed.

6

A child said *What is the grass?* fetching it to me with full hands;
How could I answer the child? I do not know what it is any more than he.   100
I guess it must be the flag of my disposition, out of hopeful green stuff woven.

Or I guess it is the handkerchief of the Lord,
A scented gift and remembrancer designedly dropt,
Bearing the owner's name someway in the corners, that we may see and remark,
    and say *Whose?*

Or I guess the grass is itself a child, the produced babe of the vegetation.   105

Or I guess it is a uniform hieroglyphic,
And it means, Sprouting alike in broad zones and narrow zones,
Growing among black folks as among white,
Kanuck,[3] Tuckahoe,[4] Congressman, Cuff,[5] I give them the same, I receive them
    the same.

And now it seems to me the beautiful uncut hair of graves.   110

---

[2] Superstructure of a ship's keel.   [4] Native of tidewater Virginia.
[3] French Canadian.   [5] Black.

Tenderly will I use you curling grass,
It may be you transpire from the breasts of young men,
It may be if I had known them I would have loved them,
It may be you are from old people, or from offspring taken soon out of their
    mothers' laps,
And here you are the mothers' laps.   115

This grass is very dark to be from the white heads of old mothers,
Darker than the colorless beards of old men,
Dark to come from under the faint red roofs of mouths.

O I perceive after all so many uttering tongues,
And I perceive they do not come from the roofs of mouths for nothing.   120

I wish I could translate the hints about the dead young men and women,
And the hints about old men and mothers, and the offspring taken soon out of
    their laps.
What do you think has become of the young and old men?
And what do you think has become of the women and children?

They are alive and well somewhere,   125
The smallest sprout shows there is really no death,
And if ever there was it led forward life, and does not wait at the end to arrest
    it,
And ceas'd the moment life appear'd.

All goes onward and outward, nothing collapses,
And to die is different from what any one supposed, and luckier.   130

7

Has any one supposed it lucky to be born?
I hasten to inform him or her it is just as lucky to die, and I know it.

I pass death with the dying and birth with the new-wash'd babe, and am not
    contain'd between my hat and boots,
And peruse manifold objects, no two alike and every one good,
The earth good and the stars good, and their adjuncts all good.   135

I am not an earth nor an adjunct of an earth,
I am the mate and companion of people, all just as immortal and fathomless as
    myself,
(They do not know how immortal, but I know.)

Every kind for itself and its own, for me mine male and female,
For me those that have been boys and that love women,   140
For me the man that is proud and feels how it stings to be slighted,

For me the sweet-heart and the old maid, for me mothers and the mothers of
    mothers,
For me lips that have smiled, eyes that have shed tears,
For me children and the begetters of children.
Undrape! you are not guilty to me, nor stale nor discarded,   145
I see through the broadcloth and gingham whether or no,
And am around, tenacious, acquisitive, tireless, and cannot be shaken away.

8

The little one sleeps in its cradle,
I lift the gauze and look a long time, and silently brush away flies with my
    hand.

The youngster and the red-faced girl turn aside up the bushy hill,   150
I peeringly view them from the top.

The suicide sprawls on the bloody floor of the bedroom,
I witness the corpse with its dabbled hair, I note where the pistol has fallen.

The blab of the pave, tires of carts, sluff of boot-soles, talk of the promenaders,
The heavy omnibus, the driver with his interrogating thumb, the clank of the
    shod horses on the granite floor,   155
The snow-sleighs, clinking, shouted jokes, pelts of snow-balls,
The hurrahs for popular favorites, the fury of rous'd mobs,
The flap of the curtain'd litter, a sick man inside borne to the hospital,
The meeting of enemies, the sudden oath, the blows and fall,
The excited crowd, the policeman with his star quickly working his passage to
    the centre of the crowd,   160
The impassive stones that receive and return so many echoes,
What groans of over-fed or half-starv'd who fall sunstruck or in fits,
What exclamations of women taken suddenly who hurry home and give birth
    to babes,
What living and buried speech is always vibrating here, what howls restrain'd
    by decorum,
Arrests of criminals, slights, adulterous offers made, acceptances, rejections with
    convex lips,   165
I mind them or the show or resonance of them—I come and I depart.

9

The big doors of the country barn stand open and ready,
The dried grass of the harvest-time loads the slow-drawn wagon,
The clear light plays on the brown gray and green intertinged,
The armfuls are pack'd to the sagging mow.   170

I am there, I help, I came stretch'd atop of the load,
I felt its soft jolts, one leg reclined on the other,
I jump from the cross-beams and seize the clover and timothy,
And roll head over heels and tangle my hair full of wisps.

10

Alone far in the wilds and mountains I hunt,   175
Wandering amazed at my own lightness and glee,
In the late afternoon choosing a safe spot to pass the night,
Kindling a fire and broiling the fresh-kill'd game,
Falling asleep on the gather'd leaves with my dog and gun by my side.

The Yankee clipper is under her sky-sails, she cuts the sparkle and scud,   180
My eyes settle the land, I bend at her prow or shout joyously from the deck.

The boatmen and clam-diggers arose early and stopt for me,
I tuck'd my trowser-ends in my boots and went and had a good time;
You should have been with us that day round the chowder-kettle.

I saw the marriage of the trapper in the open air in the far west, the bride was
    a red girl,   185
Her father and his friends sat near cross-legged and dumbly smoking, they had
    moccasins to their feet and large thick blankets hanging from their shoulders,
On a bank lounged the trapper, he was drest mostly in skins, his luxuriant
    beard and curls protected his neck, he held his bride by the hand,
She had long eyelashes, her head was bare, her coarse straight locks descended
    upon her voluptuous limbs and reach'd to her feet.

The runaway slave came to my house and stopt outside,
I heard his motions crackling the twigs of the woodpile,   190
Through the swung half-door of the kitchen I saw him limpsy and weak,
And went where he sat on a log and led him in and assured him,
And brought water and fill'd a tub for his sweated body and bruis'd feet,
And gave him a room that enter'd from my own, and gave him some coarse
    clean clothes,
And remember perfectly well his revolving eyes and his awkwardness,   195
And remember putting plasters on the galls of his neck and ankles;
He staid with me a week before he was recuperated and pass'd north,
I had him sit next me at table, my fire-lock lean'd in the corner.

11

Twenty-eight young men bathe by the shore,
Twenty-eight young men and all so friendly;
Twenty-eight years of womanly life and all so lonesome.   200

She owns the fine house by the rise of the bank,
She hides handsome and richly drest aft the blinds of the window.

Which of the young men does she like the best?
Ah the homeliest of them is beautiful to her.   205

Where are you off to, lady? for I see you,
You splash in the water there, yet stay stock still in your room.

Dancing and laughing along the beach came the twenty-ninth bather,
The rest did not see her, but she saw them and loved them.
The beards of the young men glisten'd with wet, it ran from their long hair,   210
Little streams pass'd all over their bodies.

An unseen hand also pass'd over their bodies,
It descended tremblingly from their temples and ribs.

The young men float on their backs, their white bellies bulge to the sun, they
    do not ask who seizes fast to them,
They do not know who puffs and declines with pendant and bending arch,   215
They do not think whom they souse with spray.

12

The butcher-boy puts off his killing-clothes, or sharpens his knife at the stall in
    the market,
I loiter enjoying his repartee and his shuffle[6] and break-down.[7]

Blacksmiths with grimed and hairy chests environ the anvil,
Each has his main-sledge, they are all out, there is a great heat in the fire.   220

From the cinder-strew'd threshold I follow their movements,
The lithe sheer of their waists plays even with their massive arms,
Overhand the hammers swing, overhand so slow, overhand so sure,
They do not hasten, each man hits in his place.

13

The negro holds firmly the reins of his four horses, the block swags underneath
    on its tied-over chain,   225
The negro that drives the long dray of the stone-yard, steady and tall he stands
    pois'd on one leg on the string-piece,[8]
His blue shirt exposes his ample neck and breast and loosens over his hip-band,

---

[6] Slow dance.
[7] Rollicking dance.
[8] Connective or supporting timber.

His glance is calm and commanding, he tosses the slouch of his hat away from
    his forehead,
The sun falls on his crispy hair and mustache, falls on the black of his polish'd
    and perfect limbs.
I behold the picturesque giant and love him, and I do not stop there,   230
I go with the team also.

In me the caresser of life wherever moving, backward as well as forward sluing,
To niches aside and junior bending, not a person or object missing,
Absorbing all to myself and for this song.

Oxen that rattle the yoke and chain or halt in the leafy shade, what is that you
    express in your eyes?   235
It seems to me more than all the print I have read in my life.

My tread scares the wood-drake and wood-duck on my distant and day-long
    ramble,
They rise together, they slowly circle around.

I believe in those wing'd purposes,
And acknowledge red, yellow, white, playing within me,   240
And consider green and violet and the tufted crown intentional,
And do not call the tortoise unworthy because she is not something else,
And the jay in the woods never studied the gamut, yet trills pretty well to me,
And the look of the bay mare shames silliness out of me.

14

The wild gander leads his flock through the cool night,   245
Ya-honk he says, and sounds it down to me like an invitation,
The pert may suppose it meaningless, but I listening close,
Find its purpose and place up there toward the wintry sky.

The sharp-hoof'd moose of the north, the cat on the house-sill, the chickadee,
    the prairie-dog,
The litter of the grunting sow as they tug at her teats,   250
The brood of the turkey-hen and she with her half-spread wings,
I see in them and myself the same old law.
The press of my foot to the earth springs a hundred affections,
They scorn the best I can do to relate them.

I am enamour'd of growing out-doors,   255
Of men that live among cattle or taste of the ocean or woods,
Of the builders and steerers of ships and the wielders of axes and mauls, and the
    drivers of horses,
I can eat and sleep with them week in and week out.

What is commonest, cheapest, nearest, easiest, is Me,
Me going in for my chances, spending for vast returns,   260
Adorning myself to bestow myself on the first that will take me,
Not asking the sky to come down to my good will,
Scattering it freely forever.

15

The pure contralto sings in the organ loft,
The carpenter dresses his plank, the tongue of his foreplane whistles its wild
    ascending lisp,   265
The married and unmarried children ride home to their Thanksgiving dinner,
The pilot seizes the king-pin, he heaves down with a strong arm,
The mate stands braced in the whale-boat, lance and harpoon are ready,
The duck-shooter walks by silent and cautious stretches,
The deacons are ordain'd with cross'd hands at the altar,   270
The spinning-girl retreats and advances to the hum of the big wheel,
The farmer stops by the bars as he walks on a First-day loafe and looks at the
    oats and rye,
The lunatic is carried at last to the asylum a confirm'd case,
(He will never sleep any more as he did in the cot in his mother's bed-room;)
The jour printer[9] with gray head and gaunt jaws works at his case,   275
He turns his quid of tobacco while his eyes blurr with the manuscript;
The malform'd limbs are tied to the surgeon's table,
What is removed drops horribly in a pail;
The quadroon girl is sold at the auction-stand, the drunkard nods by the
    bar-room stove,
The machinist rolls up his sleeves, the policeman travels his beat, the gate-keeper
    marks who pass,   280
The young fellow drives the express-wagon, (I love him, though I do not
    know him;)
The half-breed straps on his light boots to compete in the race,
The western turkey-shooting draws old and young, some lean on their rifles,
    some sit on logs,
Out from the crowd steps the marksman, takes his position, levels his piece;
The groups of newly-come immigrants cover the wharf or levee,   285
As the woolly-pates hoe in the sugar-field, the overseer views them from his
    saddle,
The bugle calls in the ball-room, the gentlemen run for their partners, the
    dancers bow to each other,
The youth lies awake in the cedar-roof'd garret and harks to the musical rain,
The Wolverine[10] sets traps on the creek that helps fill the Huron,
The squaw wrapt in her yellow-hemm'd cloth is offering moccasins and
    bead-bags for sale,   290

[9] Journeyman or working printer (from French   [10] Native of Michigan.
jour: "day").

The connoisseur peers along the exhibition-gallery with half-shut eyes bent
   sideways,
As the deck-hands make fast the steamboat the plank is thrown for the
   shore-going passengers,
The young sister holds out the skein while the elder sister winds it off in a ball,
   and stops now and then for the knots,
The one-year wife is recovering and happy having a week ago borne her first
   child,
The clean-hair'd Yankee girl works with her sewing-machine or in the factory
   or mill,   295
The paving-man leans on his two-handed rammer, the reporter's lead flies
   swiftly over the note-book, the sign-painter is lettering with blue and gold,
The canal boy trots on the tow-path, the book-keeper counts at his desk, the
   shoemaker waxes his thread,
The conductor beats time for the band and all the performers follow him,
The child is baptized, the convert is making his first professions,
The regatta is spread on the bay, the race is begun, (how the white sails
   sparkle!)   300
The drover watching his drove sings out to them that would stray,
The pedler sweats with his pack on his back, (the purchaser higgling about the
   odd cent;)
The bride unrumples her white dress, the minute-hand of the clock moves
   slowly,
The opium-eater reclines with rigid head and just-open'd lips,
The prostitute draggles her shawl, her bonnet bobs on her tipsy and pimpled
   neck,   305
The crowd laugh at her blackguard oaths, the men jeer and wink to each
   other,
(Miserable! I do not laugh at your oaths nor jeer you;)
The President holding a cabinet council is surrounded by the great Secretaries,
On the piazza walk three matrons stately and friendly with twined arms,
The crew of the fish-smack pack repeated layers of halibut in the hold,   310
The Missourian crosses the plains toting his wares and his cattle,
As the fare-collector goes through the train he gives notice by the jingling of
   loose change,
The floor-men are laying the floor, the tinners are tinning the roof, the masons
   are calling for mortar,
In single file each shouldering his hod pass onward the laborers;
Seasons pursuing each other the indescribable crowd is gather'd, it is the fourth
   of Seventh-month, (what salutes of cannon and small arms!)   315
Seasons pursuing each other the plougher ploughs, the mower mows, and the
   winter-grain falls in the ground;
Off on the lakes the pike-fisher watches and waits by the hole in the frozen
   surface,
The stumps stand thick round the clearing, the squatter strikes deep with his
   axe,
Flatboatmen make fast towards dusk near the cotton-wood or pecan-trees,

Coon-seekers go through the regions of the Red river or through those drain'd
    by the Tennessee, or through those of the Arkansas,   320
Torches shine in the dark that hangs on the Chattahooche or Altamahaw,
Patriarchs sit at supper with sons and grandsons and great-grandsons around
    them,
In walls of adobie, in canvas tents, rest hunters and trappers after their day's
    sport,
The city sleeps and the country sleeps,
The living sleep for their time, the dead sleep for their time,   325
The old husband sleeps by his wife and the young husband sleeps by his wife;
And these tend inward to me, and I tend outward to them,
And such as it is to be of these more or less I am,
And of these one and all I weave the song of myself.

16

I am of old and young, of the foolish as much as the wise,   330
Regardless of others, ever regardful of others,
Maternal as well as paternal, a child as well as a man,
Stuff'd with the stuff that is coarse and stuff'd with the stuff that is fine,
One of the Nation of many nations, the smallest the same and the largest the
    same,
A Southerner soon as a Northerner, a planter nonchalant and hospitable down
    by the Oconee I live,   335
A Yankee bound my own way ready for trade, my joints the limberest joints
    on earth and the sternest joints on earth,
A Kentuckian walking the vale of the Elkhorn in my deerskin leggings, a
    Louisianian or Georgian,
A boatman over lakes or bays or along coasts, a Hoosier, Badger, Buckeye;[11]
At home on Kanadian snow-shoes or up in the bush, or with fishermen off
    Newfoundland,
At home in the fleet of ice-boats, sailing with the rest and tacking,   340
At home on the hills of Vermont or in the woods of Maine, or the Texan
    ranch,
Comrade of Californians, comrade of free North-Westerners, (loving their big
    proportions,)
Comrade of raftsmen and coalmen, comrade of all who shake hands and
    welcome to drink and meat,
A learner with the simplest, a teacher of the thoughtfullest,
A novice beginning yet experient of myriads of seasons,   345
Of every hue and caste am I, of every rank and religion,
A farmer, mechanic, artist, gentleman, sailor, quaker,
Prisoner, fancy-man, rowdy, lawyer, physician, priest.

---

[11] Hoosier; Badger; Buckeye: natives, respectively,
of Indiana, Wisconsin, and Ohio.

I resist any thing better than my own diversity,
Breathe the air but leave plenty after me,   350
And am not stuck up, and am in my place.

(The moth and the fish-eggs are in their place,
The bright suns I see and the dark suns I cannot see are in their place,
The palpable is in its place and the impalpable is in its place.)

17

These are really the thoughts of all men in all ages and lands, they are not
    original with me,   355
If they are not yours as much as mine they are nothing, or next to nothing,
If they are not the riddle and the untying of the riddle they are nothing,
If they are not just as close as they are distant they are nothing.

This is the grass that grows wherever the land is and the water is,
This the common air that bathes the globe.   360

18

With music strong I come, with my cornets and my drums,
I play not marches for accepted victors only, I play marches for conquer'd and
    slain persons.
Have you heard that it was good to gain the day?
I also say it is good to fall, battles are lost in the same spirit in which they are
    won.

I beat and pound for the dead,   365
I blow through my embouchures[12] my loudest and gayest for them.

Vivas to those who have fail'd!
And to those whose war-vessels sank in the sea!
And to those themselves who sank in the sea!
And to all generals that lost engagements, and all overcome heroes!   370
And the numberless unknown heroes equal to the greatest heroes known!

19

This is the meal equally set, this the meat for natural hunger,
It is for the wicked just the same as the righteous, I make appointments with
    all,
I will not have a single person slighted or left away,
The kept-woman, sponger, thief, are hereby invited,   375

[12] Mouthpieces of wind instruments.

The heavy-lipp'd slave is invited, the venerealee is invited;
There shall be no difference between them and the rest.

This is the press of a bashful hand, this the float and odor of hair,
This the touch of my lips to yours, this the murmur of yearning,
This the far-off depth and height reflecting my own face,   380
This the thoughtful merge of myself, and the outlet again.

Do you guess I have some intricate purpose?
Well I have, for the Fourth-month showers have, and the mica on the side of a
    rock has.

Do you take it I would astonish?
Does the daylight astonish? does the early redstart twittering through the
    woods?   385
Do I astonish more than they?
This hour I tell things in confidence,
I might not tell everybody, but I will tell you.

20

Who goes there? hankering, gross, mystical, nude;
How is it I extract strength from the beef I eat?   390

What is a man anyhow? what am I? what are you?

All I mark as my own you shall offset it with your own,
Else it were time lost listening to me.

I do not snivel that snivel the world over,
That months are vacuums and the ground but wallow and filth.   395

Whimpering and truckling fold with powders for invalids, conformity goes to
    the fourth-remov'd,
I wear my hat as I please indoors or out.

Why should I pray? why should I venerate and be ceremonious?

Having pried through the strata, analyzed to a hair, counsel'd with doctors and
    calculated close,
I find no sweeter fat than sticks to my own bones.   400

In all people I see myself, none more and not one a barley-corn less,
And the good or bad I say of myself I say of them.

I know I am solid and sound,
To me the converging objects of the universe perpetually flow,
All are written to me, and I must get what the writing means.   405

I know I am deathless,
I know this orbit of mine cannot be swept by a carpenter's compass,
I know I shall not pass like a child's carlacue[13] cut with a burnt stick at night.
I know I am august,
I do not trouble my spirit to vindicate itself or be understood,   410
I see that the elementary laws never apologize,
(I reckon I behave no prouder than the level I plant my house by, after all.)

I exist as I am, that is enough,
If no other in the world be aware I sit content,
And if each and all be aware I sit content.   415

One world is aware and by far the largest to me, and that is myself,
And whether I come to my own to-day or in ten thousand or ten million
    years,
I can cheerfully take it now, or with equal cheerfulness I can wait.

My foothold is tenon'd and mortis'd in granite,
I laugh at what you call dissolution,   420
And I know the amplitude of time.

21

I am the poet of the Body and I am the poet of the Soul,
The pleasures of heaven are with me and the pains of hell are with me,
The first I graft and increase upon myself, the latter I translate into a new
    tongue.

I am the poet of the woman the same as the man,   425
And I say it is as great to be a woman as to be a man,
And I say there is nothing greater than the mother of men.

I chant the chant of dilation or pride,
We have had ducking and deprecating about enough,
I show that size is only development.   430

Have you outstript the rest? are you the President?
It is a trifle, they will more than arrive there every one, and still pass on.

I am he that walks with the tender and growing night,
I call to the earth and sea half-held by the night.

Press close bare-bosom'd night—press close magnetic nourishing night!   435
Night of south winds—night of the large few stars!
Still nodding night—mad naked summer night.

[13] Curlicue.

Smile O voluptuous cool-breath'd earth!
Earth of the slumbering and liquid trees!
Earth of departed sunset—earth of the mountains misty-topt!   440
Earth of the vitreous pour of the full moon just tinged with blue!
Earth of shine and dark mottling the tide of the river!
Earth of the limpid gray of clouds brighter and clearer for my sake!
Far-swooping elbow'd earth—rich apple-blossom'd earth!
Smile, for your lover comes.   445

Prodigal, you have given me love—therefore I to you give love!
O unspeakable passionate love.

22

You sea! I resign myself to you also—I guess what you mean,
I behold from the beach your crooked inviting fingers,
I believe you refuse to go back without feeling of me,   450
We must have a turn together, I undress, hurry me out of sight of the land,
Cushion me soft, rock me in billowy drowse,
Dash me with amorous wet, I can repay you.

Sea of stretch'd ground-swells,
Sea breathing broad and convulsive breaths,   455
Sea of the brine of life and of unshovell'd yet always-ready graves,
Howler and scooper of storms, capricious and dainty sea,
I am integral with you, I too am of one phase and of all phases.
Partaker of influx and efflux I, extoller of hate and conciliation,
Extoller of amies and those that sleep in each others' arms.   460

I am he attesting sympathy,
(Shall I make my list of things in the house and skip the house that supports
   them?)

I am not the poet of goodness only, I do not decline to be the poet of
   wickedness also.

What blurt is this about virtue and about vice?
Evil propels me and reform of evil propels me, I stand indifferent,   465
My gait is no fault-finder's or rejecter's gait,
I moisten the roots of all that has grown.

Did you fear some scrofula out of the unflagging pregnancy?
Did you guess the celestial laws are yet to be work'd over and rectified?

I find one side a balance and the antipodal side a balance,   470
Soft doctrine as steady help as stable doctrine,
Thoughts and deeds of the present our rouse and early start.

This minute that comes to me over the past decillions,
There is no better than it and now.

What behaved well in the past or behaves well to-day is not such a wonder,   475
The wonder is always and always how there can be a mean man or an infidel.

23

Endless unfolding of words of ages!
And mine a word of the modern, the word En-Masse.

A word of the faith that never balks,
Here or henceforward it is all the same to me, I accept Time absolutely.   480
It alone is without flaw, it alone rounds and completes all,
That mystic baffling wonder alone completes all.

I accept Reality and dare not question it,
Materialism first and last imbuing.

Hurrah for positive science! long live exact demonstration!   485
Fetch stonecrop mixt with cedar and branches of lilac,
This is the lexicographer, this the chemist, this made a grammar of the old
    cartouches,
These mariners put the ship through dangerous unknown seas.
This is the geologist, this works with the scalpel, and this is a mathematician.

Gentlemen, to you the first honors always!   490
Your facts are useful, and yet they are not my dwelling,
I but enter by them to an area of my dwelling.

Less the reminders of properties told my words,
And more the reminders they of life untold, and of freedom and extrication,
And make short account of neuters and geldings, and favor men and women
    fully equipt,   495
And beat the gong of revolt, and stop with fugitives and them that plot and
    conspire.

24

Walt Whitman, a kosmos, of Manhattan the son,
Turbulent, fleshy, sensual, eating, drinking and breeding,
No sentimentalist, no stander above men and women or apart from them,
No more modest than immodest.   500

Unscrew the locks from the doors!
Unscrew the doors themselves from their jambs!

Whoever degrades another degrades me,
And whatever is done or said returns at last to me.
Through me the afflatus surging and surging, through me the current and index. 505

I speak the pass-word primeval, I give the sign of democracy,
By God! I will accept nothing which all cannot have their counterpart of on
    the same terms.

Through me many long dumb voices,
Voices of the interminable generations of prisoners and slaves,
Voices of the diseas'd and despairing and of thieves and dwarfs, 510
Voices of cycles of preparation and accretion,
And of the threads that connect the stars, and of wombs and of the father-stuff,
And of the rights of them the others are down upon,
Of the deform'd, trivial, flat, foolish, despised,
Fog in the air, beetles rolling balls of dung. 515

Through me forbidden voices,
Voices of sexes and lusts, voices veil'd and I remove the veil,
Voices indecent by me clarified and transfigur'd.

I do not press my fingers across my mouth,
I keep as delicate around the bowels as around the head and heart, 520
Copulation is no more rank to me than death is.

I believe in the flesh and the appetites,
Seeing, hearing, feeling, are miracles, and each part and tag of me is a miracle.

Divine am I inside and out, and I make holy whatever I touch or am touch'd
    from,
The scent of these arm-pits aroma finer than prayer, 525
This head more than churches, bibles, and all the creeds.

If I worship one thing more than another it shall be the spread of my own
    body, or any part of it,
Translucent mould of me it shall be you!
Shaded ledges and rests it shall be you!
Firm masculine colter it shall be you! 530
Whatever goes to the tilth of me it shall be you!
You my rich blood! your milky stream pale strippings of my life!
Breast that presses against other breasts it shall be you!
My brain it shall be your occult convolutions!
Root of wash'd sweet-flag! timorous pond-snipe! nest of guarded duplicate
    eggs! it shall be you! 535
Mix'd tussled hay of head, beard, brawn, it shall be you!
Trickling sap of maple, fibre of manly wheat, it shall be you!
Sun so generous it shall be you!

Vapors lighting and shading my face it shall be you!
You sweaty brooks and dews it shall be you!   540
Winds whose soft-tickling genitals rub against me it shall be you!
Broad muscular fields, branches of live oak, loving lounger in my winding
     paths, it shall be you!
Hands I have taken, face I have kiss'd, mortal I have ever touch'd, it shall be
     you.

I dote on myself, there is that lot of me and all so luscious,
Each moment and whatever happens thrills me with joy,   545
I cannot tell how my ankles bend, nor whence the cause of my faintest wish,
Nor the cause of the friendship I emit, nor the cause of the friendship I take
     again.

That I walk up my stoop, I pause to consider if it really be,
A morning-glory at my window satisfies me more than the metaphysics of
     books.

To behold the day-break!   550
The little light fades the immense and diaphanous shadows,
The air tastes good to my palate.

Hefts of the moving world at innocent gambols silently rising freshly exuding,
Scooting obliquely high and low.

Something I cannot see puts upward libidinous prongs,   555
Seas of bright juice suffuse heaven.
The earth by the sky staid with, the daily close of their junction,
The heav'd challenge from the east that moment over my head,
The mocking taunt. See then whether you shall be master!

25

Dazzling and tremendous how quick the sun-rise would kill me,   560
If I could not now and always send sun-rise out of me.

We also ascend dazzling and tremendous as the sun,
We found our own O my soul in the calm and cool of the day-break.

My voice goes after what my eyes cannot reach,
With the twirl of my tongue I encompass worlds and volumes of worlds.   565

Speech is the twin of my vision, it is unequal to measure itself,
It provokes me forever, it says sarcastically,
Walt you contain enough, why don't you let it out then?

Come now I will not be tantalized, you conceive too much of articulation,
Do you not know O speech how the buds beneath you are folded? 570
Waiting in gloom, protected by frost,
The dirt receding before my prophetical screams,
I underlying causes to balance them at last,
My knowledge my live parts, it keeping tally with the meaning of all things,
Happiness, (which whoever hears me let him or her set out in search of this
    day.) 575

My final merit I refuse you, I refuse putting from me what I really am,
Encompass worlds, but never try to encompass me,
I crowd your sleekest and best by simply looking toward you.
Writing and talk do not prove me,
I carry the plenum of proof and every thing else in my face, 580
With the hush of my lips I wholly confound the skeptic.

26

Now I will do nothing but listen,
To accrue what I hear into this song, to let sounds contribute toward it.

I hear bravuras of birds, bustle of growing wheat, gossip of flames, clack of
    sticks cooking my meals,
I hear the sound I love, the sound of the human voice, 585
I hear all sounds running together, combined, fused or following,
Sounds of the city and sounds out of the city, sounds of the day and night,
Talkative young ones to those that like them, the loud laugh of work-people at
    their meals,
The angry base of disjointed friendship, the faint tones of the sick,
The judge with hands tight to the desk, his pallid lips pronouncing a
    death-sentence, 590
The heave'e'yo of stevedores unlading ships by the wharves, the refrain of the
    anchor-lifters,
The ring of alarm-bells, the cry of fire, the whirr of swift-streaking engines and
    hose-carts with premonitory tinkles and color'd lights,
The steam-whistle, the solid roll of the train of approaching cars,
The slow march play'd at the head of the association marching two and two,
(They go to guard some corpse, the flag-tops are draped with black muslin.) 595

I hear the violoncello, ('tis the young man's heart's complaint,)
I hear the key'd cornet, it glides quickly in through my ears,
It shakes mad-sweet pangs through my belly and breast.

I hear the chorus, it is a grand opera,
Ah this indeed is music—this suits me. 600
A tenor large and fresh as the creation fills me,
The orbic flex of his mouth is pouring and filling me full.

I hear the train'd soprano (what work with hers is this?)
The orchestra whirls me wider than Uranus flies,
It wrenches such ardors from me I did not know I possess'd them, 605
It sails me, I dab with bare feet, they are lick'd by the indolent waves,
I am cut by bitter and angry hail, I lose my breath,
Steep'd amid honey'd morphine, my windpipe throttled in fakes of death,
At length let up again to feel the puzzle of puzzles,
And that we call Being. 610

27

To be in any form, what is that?
(Round and round we go, all of us, and ever come back thither,)
If nothing lay more develop'd the quahaug in its callous shell were enough.

Mine is no callous shell,
I have instant conductors all over me whether I pass or stop, 615
They seize every object and lead it harmlessly through me.

I merely stir, press, feel with my fingers, and am happy,
To touch my person to some one else's is about as much as I can stand.

28

Is this then a touch? quivering me to a new identity,
Flames and ether making a rush for my veins, 620
Treacherous tip of me reaching and crowding to help them,
My flesh and blood playing out lightning to strike what is hardly different
    from myself,
On all sides prurient provokers stiffening my limbs,
Straining the udder of my heart for its withheld drip,
Behaving licentious toward me, taking no denial, 625
Depriving me of my best as for a purpose,
Unbuttoning my clothes, holding me by the bare waist,
Deluding my confusion with the calm of the sunlight and pasture-fields,
Immodestly sliding the fellow-senses away,
They bribed to swap off with touch and go and graze at the edges of me, 630
No consideration, no regard for my draining strength or my anger,
Fetching the rest of the herd around to enjoy them a while,
Then all uniting to stand on a headland and worry me.

The sentries desert every other part of me,
They have left me helpless to a red marauder, 635
They all come to the headland to witness and assist against me.

I am given up by traitors,
I talk wildly, I have lost my wits, I and nobody else am the greatest traitor,
I went myself first to the headland, my own hands carried me there.

You villain touch! what are you doing? my breath is tight in its throat,   640
Unclench your floodgates, you are too much for me.

29

Blind loving wrestling touch, sheath'd hooded sharp-tooth'd touch!
Did it make you ache so, leaving me?

Parting track'd by arriving, perpetual payment of perpetual loan,
Rich showering rain, and recompense richer afterward.   645

Sprouts take and accumulate, stand by the curb prolific and vital,
Landscapes projected masculine, full-sized and golden.

30

All truths wait in all things,
They neither hasten their own delivery nor resist it,
They do not need the obstetric forceps of the surgeon,   650
The insignificant is as big to me as any,
(What is less or more than a touch?)

Logic and sermons never convince,
The damp of the night drives deeper into my soul.

(Only what proves itself to every man and woman is so,   655
Only what nobody denies is so.)

A minute and a drop of me settle my brain,
I believe the soggy clods shall become lovers and lamps,
And a compend of compends is the meat of a man or woman,
And a summit and flower there is the feeling they have for each other,   660
And they are to branch boundlessly out of that lesson until it becomes omnific,
And until one and all shall delight us, and we them.

31

I believe a leaf of grass is no less than the journey-work of the stars,
And the pismire is equally perfect, and a grain of sand, and the egg of the
     wren,
And the tree-toad is a chef-d'œuvre for the highest,   665
And the running blackberry would adorn the parlors of heaven,
And the narrowest hinge in my hand puts to scorn all machinery,

And the cow crunching with depress'd head surpasses any statue,
And a mouse is miracle enough to stagger sextillions of infidels.

I find I incorporate gneiss, coal, long-threaded moss, fruits, grains, esculent
    roots,   670
And am stucco'd with quadrupeds and birds all over,
And have distanced what is behind me for good reasons,
But call any thing back again when I desire it.
In vain the speeding or shyness,
In vain the plutonic rocks send their old heat against my approach,   675
In vain the mastodon retreats beneath its own powder'd bones,
In vain objects stand leagues off and assume manifold shapes,
In vain the ocean settling in hollows and the great monsters lying low,
In vain the buzzard houses herself with the sky,
In vain the snake slides through the creepers and logs,   680
In vain the elk takes to the inner passes of the woods,
In vain the razor-bill'd auk sails far north to Labrador,
I follow quickly, I ascend to the nest in the fissure of the cliff.

32

I think I could turn and live with animals, they are so placid and self-contain'd,
I stand and look at them long and long.   685

They do not sweat and whine about their condition,
They do not lie awake in the dark and weep for their sins,
They do not make me sick discussing their duty to God,
Not one is dissatisfied, not one is demented with the mania of owning things,
Not one kneels to another, nor to his kind that lived thousands of years ago,   690
Not one is respectable or unhappy over the whole earth.

So they show their relations to me and I accept them,
They bring me tokens of myself, they evince them plainly in their possession.

I wonder where they get those tokens,
Did I pass that way huge times ago and negligently drop them?   695

Myself moving forward then and now and forever,
Gathering and showing more always and with velocity,
Infinite and omnigenous,[14] and the like of these among them,
Not too exclusive toward the reachers of my remembrancers,
Picking out here one that I love, and now go with him on brotherly terms.   700

A gigantic beauty of a stallion, fresh and responsive to my caresses,
Head high in the forehead, wide between the ears,

---

[14] Of all kinds.

Limbs glossy and supple, tail dusting the ground,
Eyes full of sparkling wickedness, ears finely cut, flexibly moving.

His nostrils dilate as my heels embrace him,   705
His well-built limbs tremble with pleasure as we race around and return.

I but use you a minute, then I resign you, stallion,
Why do I need your paces when I myself out-gallop them?
Even as I stand or sit passing faster than you.

33

Space and Time! now I see it is true, what I guess'd at,   710
What I guess'd when I loaf'd on the grass,
What I guess'd while I lay alone in my bed,
And again as I walk'd the beach under the paling stars of the morning.

My ties and ballasts leave me, my elbows rest in sea-gaps,
I skirt sierras, my palms cover continents,   715
I am afoot with my vision.

By the city's quadrangular houses—in log huts, camping with lumbermen,
Along the ruts of the turnpike, along the dry gulch and rivulet bed,
Weeding my onion-patch or hoeing rows of carrots and parsnips, crossing
    savannas, trailing in forests,
Prospecting, gold-digging, girdling the trees of a new purchase,   720
Scorch'd ankle-deep by the hot sand, hauling my boat down the shallow river,
Where the panther walks to and fro on a limb overhead, where the buck turns
    furiously at the hunter,
Where the rattlesnake suns his flabby length on a rock, where the otter is
    feeding on fish,
Where the alligator in his tough pimples sleeps by the bayou,
Where the black bear is searching for roots or honey, where the beaver pats the
    mud with his paddle-shaped tail;   725
Over the growing sugar, over the yellow-flower'd cotton plant, over the rice in
    its low moist field,
Over the sharp-peak'd farm house, with its scallop'd scum and slender shoots
    from the gutters,
Over the western persimmon, over the long-leav'd corn, over the delicate
    blue-flower flax,
Over the white and brown buckwheat, a hummer and buzzer there with the
    rest,
Over the dusky green of the rye as it ripples and shades in the breeze;   730
Scaling mountains, pulling myself cautiously up, holding on by low scragged
    limbs,
Walking the path worn in the grass and beat through the leaves of the brush,
Where the quail is whistling betwixt the woods and the wheat-lot,

Where the bat flies in the Seventh-month eve, where the great goldbug drops
    through the dark,
Where the brook puts out of the roots of the old tree and flows to the
    meadow,   735
Where cattle stand and shake away flies with the tremulous shuddering of their
    hides,
Where the cheese-cloth hangs in the kitchen, where andirons straddle the
    hearth-slab, where cobwebs fall in festoons from the rafters;
Where trip-hammers crash, where the press is whirling its cylinders,
Wherever the human heart beats with terrible throes under its ribs,
Where the pear-shaped balloon is floating aloft, (floating in it myself and
    looking composedly down,)   740
Where the life-car is drawn on the slip-noose, where the heat hatches pale-green
    eggs in the dented sand,
Where the she-whale swims with her calf and never forsakes it,
Where the steam-ship trails hind-ways its long pennant of smoke,
Where the fin of the shark cuts like a black chip out of the water,
Where the half-burn'd brig is riding on unknown currents,   745
Where shells grow to her slimy deck, where the dead are corrupting below;
Where the dense-starr'd flag is borne at the head of the regiments,
Approaching Manhattan up by the long-stretching island,
Under Niagara, the cataract falling like a veil over my countenance,
Upon a door-step, upon the horse-block of hard wood outside,   750
Upon the race-course, or enjoying picnics or jigs or a good game of base-ball,
At he-festivals, with blackguard gibes, ironical license, bull-dances, drinking,
    laughter,
At the cider-mill tasting the sweets of the brown mash, sucking the juice
    through a straw,
At apple-peelings wanting kisses for all the red fruit I find,
At musters, beach-parties, friendly bees, huskings, house-raisings;   755
Where the mocking-bird sounds his delicious gurgles, cackles, screams, weeps,
Where the hay-rick stands in the barn-yard, where the dry-stalks are scatter'd,
    where the brood-cow waits in the hovel,
Where the bull advances to do his masculine work, where the stud to the mare,
    where the cock is treading the hen,
Where the heifers browse, where geese nip their food with short jerks,
Where sun-down shadows lengthen over the limitless and lonesome prairie,   760
Where herds of buffalo make a crawling spread of the square miles far and
    near,
Where the humming-bird shimmers, where the neck of the long-lived swan is
    curving and winding,
Where the laughing-gull scoots by the shore, where she laughs her near-human
    laugh,
Where bee-hives range on a gray bench in the garden half hid by the high
    weeds,
Where band-neck'd partridges roost in a ring on the ground with their heads
    out,   765

Where burial coaches enter the arch'd gates of a cemetery,
Where winter wolves bark amid wastes of snow and icicled trees,
Where the yellow-crown'd heron comes to the edge of the marsh at night and
    feeds upon small crabs,
Where the splash of swimmers and divers cools the warm noon,
Where the katy-did works her chromatic reed on the walnut-tree over the
    well,   770
Through patches of citrons and cucumbers with silver-wired leaves,
Through the salt-lick or orange glade, or under conical firs,
Through the gymnasium, through the curtain'd saloon, through the office or
    public hall;
Pleas'd with the native and pleas'd with the foreign, pleas'd with the new and
    old,
Pleas'd with the homely woman as well as the handsome,   775
Pleas'd with the quakeress as she puts off her bonnet and talks melodiously,
Pleas'd with the tune of the choir of the whitewash'd church,
Pleas'd with the earnest words of the sweating Methodist preacher, impress'd
    seriously at the camp-meeting;
Looking in at the shop-windows of Broadway the whole forenoon, flatting the
    flesh of my nose on the thick plate glass,
Wandering the same afternoon with my face turn'd up to the clouds, or down
    a lane or along the beach,   780
My right and left arms round the sides of two friends, and I in the middle;
Coming home with the silent and dark-cheek'd bush-boy, (behind me he rides
    at the drape of the day,)
Far from the settlements studying the print of animals' feet, or the moccasin
    print,
By the cot in the hospital reaching lemonade to a feverish patient,
Nigh the coffin'd corpse when all is still, examining with a candle;   785
Voyaging to every port to dicker and adventure,
Hurrying with the modern crowd as eager and fickle as any,
Hot toward one I hate, ready in my madness to knife him,
Solitary at midnight in my back yard, my thoughts gone from me a long
    while,
Walking the old hills of Judæa with the beautiful gentle God by my side,   790
Speeding through space, speeding through heaven and the stars,
Speeding amid the seven satellites and the broad ring, and the diameter of
    eighty thousand miles,
Speeding with tail'd meteors, throwing fire-balls like the rest,
Carrying the crescent child that carries its own full mother in its belly,
Storming, enjoying, planning, loving, cautioning,   795
Backing and filling, appearing and disappearing,
I tread day and night such roads.

I visit the orchards of spheres and look at the product,
And look at quintillions ripen'd and look at quintillions green.

I fly those flights of a fluid and swallowing soul,   800
My course runs below the soundings of plummets.

I help myself to material and immaterial,
No guard can shut me off, no law prevent me.

I anchor my ship for a little while only,
My messengers continually cruise away or bring their returns to me.   805

I go hunting polar furs and the seal, leaping chasms with a pike-pointed staff,
    clinging to topples of brittle and blue.

I ascend to the foretruck,
I take my place late at night in the crow's-nest,
We sail the arctic sea, it is plenty light enough,
Through the clear atmosphere I stretch around on the wonderful beauty,   810
The enormous masses of ice pass me and I pass them, the scenery is plain in all
    directions,
The white-topt mountains show in the distance, I fling out my fancies toward
    them,
We are approaching some great battle-field in which we are soon to be
    engaged,
We pass the colossal outposts of the encampment, we pass with still feet and
    caution,
Or we are entering by the suburbs some vast and ruin'd city,   815
The blocks and fallen architecture more than all the living cities of the globe.

I am a free companion, I bivouac by invading watchfires,
I turn the bridegroom out of bed and stay with the bride myself,
I tighten her all night to my thighs and lips.

My voice is the wife's voice, the screech by the rail of the stairs,   820
They fetch my man's body up dripping and drown'd.

I understand the large hearts of heroes,
The courage of present times and all times,
How the skipper saw the crowded and rudderless wreck of the steam-ship, and
    Death chasing it up and down the storm,
How he knuckled tight and gave not back an inch, and was faithful of days
    and faithful of nights,   825
And chalk'd in large letters on a board, *Be of good cheer, we will not desert you;*
How he follow'd with them and tack'd with them three days and would not
    give it up,
How he saved the drifting company at last,
How the lank loose-gown'd women look'd when boated from the side of their
    prepared graves,

How the silent old-faced infants and the lifted sick, and the sharp-lipp'd
    unshaved men;   830
All this I swallow, it tastes good, I like it well, it becomes mine,
I am the man, I suffer'd, I was there.

The disdain and calmness of martyrs,
The mother of old, condemn'd for a witch, burnt with dry wood, her children
    gazing on,
The hounded slave that flags in the race, leans by the fence, blowing, cover'd
    with sweat,   835
The twinges that sting like needles his legs and neck, the murderous buckshot
    and the bullets,
All these I feel or am.

I am the hounded slave, I wince at the bite of the dogs,
Hell and despair are upon me, crack and again crack the marksmen,
I clutch the rails of the fence, my gore dribs, thinn'd with the ooze of my skin, 840
I fall on the weeds and stones,
The riders spur their unwilling horses, haul close,
Taunt my dizzy ears and beat me violently over the head with whip-stocks.

Agonies are one of my changes of garments,
I do not ask the wounded person how he feels, I myself become the wounded
    person,   845
My hurts turn livid upon me as I lean on a cane and observe.

I am the mash'd fireman with breast-bone broken,
Tumbling walls buried me in their debris,
Heat and smoke I inspired, I heard the yelling shouts of my comrades,
I heard the distant click of their picks and shovels,   850
They have clear'd the beams away, they tenderly lift me forth.

I lie in the night air in my red shirt, the pervading hush is for my sake,
Painless after all I lie exhausted but not so unhappy,
White and beautiful are the faces around me, the heads are bared of their
    fire-caps,
The kneeling crowd fades with the light of the torches.   855

Distant and dead resuscitate,
They show as the dial or move as the hands of me, I am the clock myself.

I am an old artillerist, I tell of my fort's bombardment,
I am there again.

Again the long roll of the drummers,   860
Again the attacking cannon, mortars,
Again to my listening ears the cannon responsive.

I take part, I see and hear the whole,
The cries, curses, roar, the plaudits for well-aim'd shots,
The ambulanza[15] slowly passing trailing its red drip,   865
Workmen searching after damages, making indispensable repairs,
The fall of grenades through the rent roof, the fan-shaped explosion,
The whizz of limbs, heads, stone, wood, iron, high in the air.

Again gurgles the mouth of my dying general, he furiously waves with his
    hand,
He gasps through the clot *Mind not me—mind—the entrenchments.*   870

34

Now I tell what I knew in Texas in my early youth,
(I tell not the fall of Alamo,
Not one escaped to tell the fall of Alamo,
The hundred and fifty are dumb yet at Alamo,)
'Tis the tale of the murder in cold blood of four hundred and twelve young
    men.   875

Retreating they had form'd in a hollow square with their baggage for
    breastworks,
Nine hundred lives out of the surrounding enemy's, nine times their number,
    was the price they took in advance,
Their colonel was wounded and their ammunition gone,
They treated for an honorable capitulation, receiv'd writing and seal, gave up
    their arms and march'd back prisoners of war.

They were the glory of the race of rangers,   880
Matchless with horse, rifle, song, supper, courtship,
Large, turbulent, generous, handsome, proud, and affectionate,
Bearded, sunburnt, drest in the free costume of hunters,
Not a single one over thirty years of age.

The second First-day morning they were brought out in squads and massacred,
    it was beautiful early summer,   885
The work commenced about five o'clock and was over by eight.

None obey'd the command to kneel,
Some made a mad and helpless rush, some stood stark and straight,
A few fell at once, shot in the temple or heart, the living and dead lay
    together,
The maim'd and mangled dug in the dirt, the new-comers saw them there,   890
Some half-kill'd attempted to crawl away,
These were despatch'd with bayonets or batter'd with the blunts of muskets,

[15] Italian: "ambulance."

A youth not seventeen years old seiz'd his assassin till two more came to release
   him,
The three were all torn and cover'd with the boy's blood.

At eleven o'clock began the burning of the bodies;   895
That is the tale of the murder of the four hundred and twelve young men.

35

Would you hear of an old-time sea-fight?
Would you learn who won by the light of the moon and stars?
List to the yarn, as my grandmother's father the sailor told it to me.

Our foe was no skulk in his ship I tell you, (said he,)   900
His was the surly English pluck, and there is no tougher or truer, and never
   was, and never will be;
Along the lower'd eve he came horribly raking us.

We closed with him, the yards entangled, the cannon touch'd,
My captain lash'd fast with his own hands.

We had receiv'd some eighteen pound shots under the water,   905
On our lower-gun-deck two large pieces had burst at the first fire, killing all
   around and blowing up overhead.

Fighting at sun-down, fighting at dark,
Ten o'clock at night, the full moon well up, our leaks on the gain, and five
   feet of water reported,
The master-at-arms loosing the prisoners confined in the after-hold to give them
   a chance for themselves.

The transit to and from the magazine is now stopt by the sentinels,   910
They see so many strange faces they do not know whom to trust.

Our frigate takes fire,
The other asks if we demand quarter?
If our colors are struck and the fighting done?

Now I laugh content, for I hear the voice of my little captain,   915
We have not struck, he composedly cries, *we have just begun our part of the
   fighting.*

Only three guns are in use,
One is directed by the captain himself against the enemy's mainmast,
Two well serv'd with grape and canister silence his musketry and clear his
   decks.

The tops alone second the fire of this little battery, especially the main-top,   920
They hold out bravely during the whole of the action.

Not a moment's cease,
The leaks gain fast on the pumps, the fire eats toward the powder-magazine.

One of the pumps has been shot away, it is generally thought we are sinking.

Serene stands the little captain,   925
He is not hurried, his voice is neither high nor low,
His eyes give more light to us than our battle-lanterns.

Toward twelve there in the beams of the moon they surrender to us.

36

Stretch'd and still lies the midnight,
Two great hulls motionless on the breast of the darkness,   930
Our vessel riddled and slowly sinking, preparations to pass to the one we have
    conquer'd,
The captain on the quarter-deck coldly giving his orders through a countenance
    white as a sheet,
Near by the corpse of the child that serv'd in the cabin,
The dead face of an old salt with long white hair and carefully curl'd whiskers,
The flames spite of all that can be done flickering aloft and below,   935
The husky voices of the two or three officers yet fit for duty,
Formless stacks of bodies and bodies by themselves, dabs of flesh upon the masts
    and spars,
Cut of cordage, dangle of rigging, slight shock of the soothe of waves,
Black and impassive guns, litter of powder-parcels, strong scent,
A few large stars overhead, silent and mournful shining,   940
Delicate sniffs of sea-breeze, smells of sedgy grass and fields by the shore,
    death-messages given in charge to survivors,
The hiss of the surgeon's knife, the gnawing teeth of his saw,
Wheeze, cluck, swash of falling blood, short wild scream, and long, dull,
    tapering groan,
These so, these irretrievable.

37

You laggards there on guard! look to your arms!   945
In at the conquer'd doors they crowd! I am possess'd!
Embody all presences outlaw'd or suffering,
See myself in prison shaped like another man,
And feel the dull unintermitted pain.

For me the keepers of convicts shoulder their carbines and keep watch, 950
It is I let out in the morning and barr'd at night.

Not a mutineer walks handcuff'd to jail but I am handcuff'd to him and walk
    by his side,
(I am less the jolly one there, and more the silent one with sweat on my
    twitching lips.)

Not a youngster is taken for larceny but I go up too, and am tried and
    sentenced.

Not a cholera patient lies at the last gasp but I also lie at the last gasp, 955
My face is ash-color'd, my sinews gnarl, away from me people retreat.

Askers embody themselves in me and I am embodied in them,
I project my hat, sit shame-faced, and beg.

38

Enough! enough! enough!
Somehow I have been stunn'd. Stand back! 960
Give me a little time beyond my cuff'd head, slumbers, dreams, gaping,
I discover myself on the verge of a usual mistake.
That I could forget the mockers and insults!
That I could forget the trickling tears and the blows of the bludgeons and
    hammers!
That I could look with a separate look on my own crucifixion and bloody
    crowning. 965

I remember now,
I resume the overstaid fraction,
The grave of rock multiplies what has been confided to it, or to any graves,
Corpses rise, gashes heal, fastenings roll from me.

I troop forth replenish'd with supreme power, one of an average unending
    procession, 970
Inland and sea-coast we go, and pass all boundary lines,
Our swift ordinances on their way over the whole earth,
The blossoms we wear in our hats the growth of thousands of years.

Eleves,[16] I salute you! come forward!
Continue your annotations, continue your questionings. 975

[16] Pupils or disciples (from French *élève:*
    "student").

39

The friendly and flowing savage, who is he?
Is he waiting for civilization, or past it and mastering it?

Is he some Southwesterner rais'd out-doors? is he Kanadian?
Is he from the Mississippi country? Iowa, Oregon, California?
The mountains? prairie-life, bush-life? or sailor from the sea?   980

Wherever he goes men and women accept and desire him,
They desire he should like them, touch them, speak to them, stay with them.

Behavior lawless as snow-flakes, words simple as grass, uncomb'd head, laughter,
    and naivetè,
Slow-stepping feet, common features, common modes and emanations,
They descend in new forms from the tips of his fingers,   985
They are wafted with the odor of his body or breath, they fly out of the
    glance of his eyes.

40

Flaunt of the sunshine I need not your bask—lie over!
You light surfaces only, I force surfaces and depths also.

Earth! you seem to look for something at my hands,
Say, old top-knot,[17] what do you want?   990

Man or woman, I might tell how I like you, but cannot,
And might tell what it is in me and what it is in you, but cannot,
And might tell that pining I have, that pulse of my nights and days.

Behold, I do not give lectures or a little charity,
When I give I give myself.   995

You there, impotent, loose in the knees,
Open your scarf'd chops till I blow grit within you,
Spread your palms and lift the flaps of your pockets,
I am not to be denied, I compel, I have stores plenty and to spare,
And any thing I have I bestow.   1000

I do not ask who you are, that is not important to me,
You can do nothing and be nothing but what I will infold you.

[17] An Indian.

To cotton-field drudge or cleaner of privies I lean,
On his right cheek I put the family kiss,
And in my soul I swear I never will deny him.   1005

On women fit for conception I start bigger and nimbler babes,
(This day I am jetting the stuff of far more arrogant republics.)

To any one dying, thither I speed and twist the knob of the door,
Turn the bed-clothes toward the foot of the bed,
Let the physician and the priest go home.   1010
I seize the descending man and raise him with resistless will,
O despairer, here is my neck,
By God, you shall not go down! hang your whole weight upon me.

I dilate you with tremendous breath, I buoy you up,
Every room of the house do I fill with an arm'd force,   1015
Lovers of me, bafflers of graves.

Sleep—I and they keep guard all night,
Not doubt, not decease shall dare to lay finger upon you,
I have embraced you, and henceforth possess you to myself,
And when you rise in the morning you will find what I tell you is so.   1020

41

I am he bringing help for the sick as they pant on their backs,
And for strong upright men I bring yet more needed help.

I heard what was said of the universe,
Heard it and heard it of several thousand years;
It is middling well as far as it goes—but is that all?   1025

Magnifying and applying come I,
Outbidding at the start the old cautious hucksters,
Taking myself the exact dimensions of Jehovah,
Lithographing Kronos, Zeus his son, and Hercules[18] his grandson,
Buying drafts of Osiris, Isis,[19] Belus, Brahma,[20] Buddha,[21]   1030
In my portfolio placing Manito[22] loose, Allah[23] on a leaf, the crucifix engraved,
With Odin[24] and the hideous-faced Mexitli[25] and every idol and image,
Taking them all for what they are worth and not a cent more,
Admitting they were alive and did the work of their days,

[18] Kronos; Zeus; Hercules: divinities in Greek
   mythology.
[19] Osiris; Isis: Egyptian deities.
[20] Belus; Brahma: Hindu gods.
[21] Indian religious leader ("the Enlightened One").
[22] Algonquin Indian nature spirit.
[23] Moslem supreme being.
[24] Norse god of war.
[25] Aztec god of war.

(They bore mites as for unfledg'd birds who have now to rise and fly and sing
    for themselves,)   1035
Accepting the rough deific sketches to fill out better in myself, bestowing them
    freely on each man and woman I see,
Discovering as much or more in a framer framing a house,
Putting higher claims for him there with his roll'd-up sleeves driving the mallet
    and chisel,
Not objecting to special revelations, considering a curl of smoke or a hair on
    the back of my hand just as curious as any revelation,
Lads ahold of fire-engines and hook-and-ladder ropes no less to me than the
    gods of the antique wars,   1040
Minding their voices peal through the crash of destruction,
Their brawny limbs passing safe over charr'd laths, their white foreheads whole
    and unhurt out of the flames;
By the mechanic's wife with her babe at her nipple interceding for every person
    born,
Three scythes at harvest whizzing in a row from three lusty angels with shirts
    bagg'd out at their waists,
The snag-tooth'd hostler with red hair redeeming sins past and to come,   1045
Selling all he possesses, traveling on foot to fee lawyers for his brother and sit
    by him while he is tried for forgery;
What was strewn in the amplest strewing the square rod about me, and not
    filling the square rod then,
The bull and the bug never worshipp'd half enough,
Dung and dirt more admirable than was dream'd,
The supernatural of no account, myself waiting my time to be one of the
    supremes,   1050
The day getting ready for me when I shall do as much good as the best, and be
    as prodigious;
By my life-lumps! becoming already a creator,
Putting myself here and now to the ambush'd womb of the shadows.

42

A call in the midst of the crowd,
My own voice, orotund sweeping and final.   1055

Come my children,
Come my boys and girls, my women, household and intimates,
Now the performer launches his nerve, he has pass'd his prelude on the reeds
    within.
Easily written loose-finger'd chords—I feel the thrum of your climax and close.

My head slues round on my neck,   1060
Music rolls, but not from the organ,
Folks are around me, but they are no household of mine.

Ever the hard unsunk ground,
Ever the eaters and drinkers, ever the upward and downward sun, ever the air
    and the ceaseless tides,
Ever myself and my neighbors, refreshing, wicked, real,   1065
Ever the old inexplicable query, ever that thorn'd thumb, that breath of itches
    and thirsts,
Ever the vexer's *hoot! hoot!* till we find where the sly one hides and bring him
    forth,
Ever love, ever the sobbing liquid of life,
Ever the bandage under the chin, ever the trestles of death.

Here and there with dimes on the eyes walking,   1070
To feed the greed of the belly the brains liberally spooning,
Tickets buying, taking, selling, but in to the feast never once going.
Many sweating, ploughing, thrashing, and then the chaff for payment receiving,
A few idly owning, and they the wheat continually claiming.

This is the city and I am one of the citizens,   1075
Whatever interests the rest interests me, politics, wars, markets, newspapers,
    schools,
The mayor and councils, banks, tariffs, steamships, factories, stocks, stores, real
    estate and personal estate.

The little plentiful manikins skipping around in collars and tail'd coats,
I am aware who they are, (they are positively not worms or fleas,)
I acknowledge the duplicates of myself, the weakest and shallowest is deathless
    with me,   1080
What I do and say the same waits for them,
Every thought that flounders in me the same flounders in them.
I know perfectly well my own egotism,
Know my omnivorous lines and must not write any less,
And would fetch you whoever you are flush with myself.   1085

Not words of routine this song of mine,
But abruptly to question, to leap beyond yet nearer bring;
This printed and bound book—but the printer and the printing-office boy?
The well-taken photographs—but your wife or friend close and solid in your
    arms?
The black ship mail'd with iron, her mighty guns in her turrets—but the pluck
    of the captain and engineers?   1090
In the houses the dishes and fare and furniture—but the host and hostess, and
    the look out of their eyes?
The sky up there—yet here or next door, or across the way?
The saints and sages in history—but you yourself?
Sermons, creeds, theology—but the fathomless human brain,
And what is reason? and what is love? and what is life?   1095

43

I do not despise you priests, all time, the world over,
My faith is the greatest of faiths and the least of faiths,
Enclosing worship ancient and modern and all between ancient and modern,
Believing I shall come again upon the earth after five thousand years,
Waiting responses from oracles, honoring the gods, saluting the sun,   1100
Making a fetich of the first rock or stump, powowing with sticks in the circle
  of obis,[26]
Helping the llama[27] or brahmin as he trims the lamps of the idols,
Dancing yet through the streets in a phallic procession, rapt and austere in the
  woods a gymnosophist,[28]
Drinking mead from the skull-cup, to Shastas[29] and Vedas admirant, minding
  the Koran,
Walking the teokallis,[30] spotted with gore from the stone and knife, beating the
  serpent-skin drum,   1105
Accepting the Gospels, accepting him that was crucified, knowing assuredly that
  he is divine,
To the mass kneeling or the puritan's prayer rising, or sitting patiently in a
  pew,
Ranting and frothing in my insane crisis, or waiting deadlike till my spirit
  arouses me,
Looking forth on pavement and land, or outside of pavement and land,
Belonging to the winders of the circuit of circuits.   1110

One of that centripetal and centrifugal gang I turn and talk like a man leaving
  charges before a journey.

Down-hearted doubters dull and excluded,
Frivolous, sullen, moping, angry, affected, dishearten'd, atheistical,
I know every one of you, I know the sea of torment, doubt, despair and
  unbelief.

How the flukes splash!   1115
How they contort rapid as lightning, with spasms and spouts of blood!

Be at peace bloody flukes of doubters and sullen mopers,
I take my place among you as much as among any,
The past is the push of you, me, all, precisely the same,
And what is yet untried and afterward is for you, me, all, precisely the same. 1120

I do not know what is untried and afterward,
But I know it will in its turn prove sufficient, and cannot fail.

---

[26] I.e., obeah, referring to West African witchcraft and sorcery.
[27] I.e., lama, a Buddhist monk.
[28] Hindu ascetic.
[29] I.e., Shastras, Hindu sacred writings (cf. the Vedas).
[30] Aztec temples.

Each who passes is consider'd, each who stops is consider'd, not a single one can it fail.

It cannot fail the young man who died and was buried,
Nor the young woman who died and was put by his side,   1125
Nor the little child that peep'd in at the door, and then drew back and was never seen again,
Nor the old man who has lived without purpose, and feels it with bitterness worse than gall,
Nor him in the poor house tubercled by rum and the bad disorder,
Nor the numberless slaughter'd and wreck'd, nor the brutish koboo[31] call'd the ordure of humanity,
Nor the sacs merely floating with open mouths for food to slip in,   1130
Nor any thing in the earth, or down in the oldest graves of the earth,
Nor any thing in the myriads of spheres, nor the myriads of myriads that inhabit them,
Nor the present, nor the least wisp that is known.

44

It is time to explain myself—let us stand up.

What is known I strip away,   1135
I launch all men and women forward with me into the Unknown.

The clock indicates the moment—but what does eternity indicate?

We have thus far exhausted trillions of winters and summers,
There are trillions ahead, and trillions ahead of them.

Births have brought us richness and variety,   1140
And other births will bring us richness and variety.

I do not call one greater and one smaller,
That which fills its period and place is equal to any.

Were mankind murderous or jealous upon you, my brother, my sister?
I am sorry for you, they are not murderous or jealous upon me,   1145
All has been gentle with me, I keep no account with lamentation,
(What have I to do with lamentation?)
I am an acme of things accomplish'd, and I an encloser of things to be.

My feet strike an apex of the apices of the stairs,
On every step bunches of ages, and larger bunches between the steps,   1150
All below duly travel'd, and still I mount and mount.

---

[31] Sumatran savage.

Rise after rise bow the phantoms behind me,
Afar down I see the huge first Nothing, I know I was even there,
I waited unseen and always, and slept through the lethargic mist,
And took my time, and took no hurt from the fetid carbon.   1155

Long I was hugg'd close—long and long.

Immense have been the preparations for me,
Faithful and friendly the arms that have help'd me.

Cycles ferried my cradle, rowing and rowing like cheerful boatmen,
For room to me stars kept aside in their own rings,   1160
They sent influences to look after what was to hold me.

Before I was born out of my mother generations guided me,
My embryo has never been torpid, nothing could overlay it.

For it the nebula cohered to an orb,
The long slow strata piled to rest it on,   1165
Vast vegetables gave it sustenance,
Monstrous sauroids[32] transported it in their mouths and deposited it with care.

All forces have been steadily employ'd to complete and delight me,
Now on this spot I stand with my robust soul.

45

O span of youth! ever-push'd elasticity!   1170
O manhood, balanced, florid and full.
My lovers suffocate me,
Crowding my lips, thick in the pores of my skin,
Jostling me through streets and public halls, coming naked to me at night,
Crying by day *Ahoy!* from the rocks of the river, swinging and chirping over
    my head,   1175
Calling my name from flower-beds, vines, tangled underbrush.
Lighting on every moment of my life,
Bussing my body with soft balsamic busses,
Noiselessly passing handfuls out of their hearts and giving them to be mine.

Old age superbly rising! O welcome, ineffable grace of dying days!   1180

Every condition promulges not only itself, it promulges[33] what grows after and
    out of itself,
And the dark hush promulges as much as any.

---

[32] Prehistoric reptiles.   [33] Promulgates.

I open my scuttle at night and see the far-sprinkled systems,
And all I see multiplied as high as I can cipher edge but the rim of the farther
   systems.

Wider and wider they spread, expanding, always expanding,   1185
Outward and outward and forever outward.

My sun has his sun and round him obediently wheels,
He joins with his partners a group of superior circuit,
And greater sets follow, making specks of the greatest inside them.

There is no stoppage and never can be stoppage,   1190
If I, you, and the worlds, and all beneath or upon their surfaces, were this
   moment reduced back to a pallid float, it would not avail in the long run,
We should surely bring up again where we now stand,
And surely go as much farther, and then farther and farther.

A few quadrillions of eras, a few octillions of cubic leagues, do not hazard the
   span or make it impatient,   1195
They are but parts, any thing is but a part.
See ever so far, there is limitless space outside of that,
Count ever so much, there is limitless time around that.

My rendezvous is appointed, it is certain,
The Lord will be there and wait till I come on perfect terms,   1200
The great Camerado, the lover true for whom I pine will be there.

46

I know I have the best of time and space, and was never measured and never
   will be measured.

I tramp a perpetual journey, (come listen all!)
My signs are a rain-proof coat, good shoes, and a staff cut from the woods,
No friend of mine takes his ease in my chair,   1205
I have no chair, no church, no philosophy,
I lead no man to a dinner-table, library, exchange,
But each man and each woman of you I lead upon a knoll,
My left hand hooking you round the waist,
My right hand pointing to landscapes of continents and the public road.   1210

Not I, not any one else can travel that road for you,
You must travel it for yourself.

It is not far, it is within reach,
Perhaps you have been on it since you were born and did not know,
Perhaps it is everywhere on water and on land.   1215

Shoulder your duds dear son, and I will mine, and let us hasten forth,
Wonderful cities and free nations we shall fetch as we go.

If you tire, give me both burdens, and rest the chuff[34] of your hand on my hip,
And in due time you shall repay the same service to me,
For after we start we never lie by again.   1220
This day before dawn I ascended a hill and look'd at the crowded heaven,
And I said to my spirit *When we become the enfolders of those orbs, and the*
   pleasure and knowledge of every thing in them, shall we be fill'd and satisfied then?
And my spirit said *No, we but level that lift to pass and continue beyond.*

You are also asking me questions and I hear you,
I answer that I cannot answer, you must find out for yourself.   1225

Sit a while dear son,
Here are biscuits to eat and here is milk to drink,
But as soon as you sleep and renew yourself in sweet clothes, I kiss you with a
   good-by kiss and open the gate for your egress hence.

Long enough have you dream'd contemptible dreams,
Now I wash the gum from your eyes,   1230
You must habit yourself to the dazzle of the light and of every moment of
   your life.

Long have you timidly waded holding a plank by the shore,
Now I will you to be a bold swimmer,
To jump off in the midst of the sea, rise again, nod to me, shout, and
   laughingly dash with your hair.

47

I am the teacher of athletes,   1235
He that by me spreads a wider breast than my own proves the width of my
   own,
He most honors my style who learns under it to destroy the teacher.

The boy I love, the same becomes a man not through derived power, but in his
   own right,
Wicked rather than virtuous out of conformity or fear,
Fond of his sweetheart, relishing well his steak,   1240
Unrequited love or a slight cutting him worse than sharp steel cuts,
First-rate to ride, to fight, to hit the bull's eye, to sail a skiff, to sing a song or
   play on the banjo,
Preferring scars and the beard and faces pitted with smallpox over all latherers,
And those well-tann'd to those that keep out of the sun.

[34] Heel.

I teach straying from me, yet who can stray from me?   1245
I follow you whoever you are from the present hour
My words itch at your ears till you understand them.

I do not say these things for a dollar or to fill up the time while I wait for a
     boat,
(It is you talking just as much as myself, I act as the tongue of you,
Tied in your mouth, in mine it begins to be loosen'd.)   1250

I swear I will never again mention love or death inside a house,
And I swear I will never translate myself at all, only to him or her who
     privately stays with me in the open air.

If you would understand me go to the heights or water-shore,
The nearest gnat is an explanation, and a drop or motion of waves a key,
The maul, the oar, the hand-saw, second my words.   1255

No shutter'd room or school can commune with me,
But roughs and little children better than they.

The young mechanic is closest to me, he knows me well,
The woodman that takes his axe and jug with him shall take me with him all
     day,
The farm-boy ploughing in the field feels good at the sound of my voice,   1260
In vessels that sail my words sail, I go with fishermen and seamen and love
     them.

The soldier camp'd or upon the march is mine,
On the night ere the pending battle many seek me, and I do not fail them,
On that solemn night (it may be their last) those that know me seek me.
My face rubs to the hunter's face when he lies down alone in his blanket,   1265
The driver thinking of me does not mind the jolt of his wagon,
The young mother and old mother comprehend me,
The girl and the wife rest the needle a moment and forget where they are,
They and all would resume what I have told them.

48

I have said that the soul is not more than the body,   1270
And I have said that the body is not more than the soul,
And nothing, not God, is greater to one than one's self is,
And whoever walks a furlong without sympathy walks to his own funeral drest
     in his shroud,
And I or you pocketless of a dime may purchase the pick of the earth,
And to glance with an eye or show a bean in its pod confounds the learning of
     all times,   1275

And there is no trade or employment but the young man following it may
   become a hero,
And there is no object so soft but it makes a hub for the wheel'd universe,
And I say to any man or woman, Let your soul stand cool and composed
   before a million universes.

And I say to mankind, Be not curious about God,
For I who am curious about each am not curious about God,   1280
(No array of terms can say how much I am at peace about God and about
   death.)

I hear and behold God in every object, yet understand God not in the least,
Nor do I understand who there can be more wonderful than myself.

Why should I wish to see God better than this day?
I see something of God each hour of the twenty-four, and each moment then,   1285
In the faces of men and women I see God, and in my own face in the glass,
I find letters from God dropt in the street, and every one is sign'd by God's
   name,
And I leave them where they are, for I know that wheresoe'er I go,
Others will punctually come for ever and ever.

49

And as to you Death, and you bitter hug of mortality, it is idle to try to alarm
   me.   1290

To his work without flinching the accoucheur[35] comes,
I see the elder-hand pressing receiving supporting,
I recline by the sills of the exquisite flexible doors,
And mark the outlet, and mark the relief and escape.

And as to you Corpse I think you are good manure, but that does not offend
   me,   1295
I smell the white roses sweet-scented and growing,
I reach to the leafy lips, I reach to the polish'd breasts of melons.

And as to you Life I reckon you are the leavings of many deaths,
(No doubt I have died myself ten thousand times before.)

I hear you whispering there O stars of heaven,   1300
O suns—O grass of graves—O perpetual transfers and promotions,
If you do not say any thing how can I say any thing?

---

[35] Midwife.

Of the turbid pool that lies in the autumn forest,
Of the moon that descends the steeps of the soughing twilight,
Toss, sparkles of day and dusk—toss on the black stems that decay in the muck,
Toss to the moaning gibberish of the dry limbs.
I ascend from the moon, I ascend from the night,   1305
I perceive that the ghastly glimmer is noonday sunbeams reflected,
And debouch to the steady and central from the offspring great or small.

50

There is that in me—I do not know what it is—but I know it is in me.   1310

Wrench'd and sweaty—calm and cool then my body becomes,
I sleep—I sleep long.

I do not know it—it is without name—it is a word unsaid,
It is not in any dictionary, utterance, symbol.

Something it swings on more than the earth I swing on,   1315
To it the creation is the friend whose embracing awakes me.

Perhaps I might tell more. Outlines! I plead for my brothers and sisters.

Do you see O my brothers and sisters?
It is not chaos or death—it is form, union, plan—it is eternal life—it is
   Happiness.

51

The past and present wilt—I have fill'd them, emptied them,   1320
And proceed to fill my next fold of the future.

Listener up there! what have you to confide to me?
Look in my face while I snuff the sidle of evening,
(Talk honestly, no one else hears you, and I stay only a minute longer.)

Do I contradict myself?   1325
Very well then I contradict myself,
(I am large, I contain multitudes.)
I concentrate toward them that are nigh, I wait on the door-slab.

Who has done his day's work? who will soonest be through with his supper?
Who wishes to walk with me?   1330

Will you speak before I am gone? will you prove already too late?

52

The spotted hawk swoops by and accuses me, he complains of my gab and my
    loitering.

I too am not a bit tamed, I too am untranslatable,
I sound my barbaric yawp over the roofs of the world.

The last scud of day holds back for me,   1335
It flings my likeness after the rest and true as any on the shadow'd wilds,
It coaxes me to the vapor and the dusk.

I depart as air, I shake my white locks at the runaway sun,
I effuse my flesh in eddies, and drift it in lacy jags.

I bequeath myself to the dirt to grow from the grass I love,   1340
If you want me again look for me under your boot-soles.

You will hardly know who I am or what I mean,
But I shall be good health to you nevertheless,
And filter and fibre your blood.

Failing to fetch me at first keep encouraged,   1345
Missing me one place search another,
I stop somewhere waiting for you.
1855

from **Children of Adam**
I Sing the Body Electric

1

I sing the body electric,
The armies of those I love engirth me and I engirth them,
They will not let me off till I go with them, respond to them,
And discorrupt them, and charge them full with the charge of the soul.

Was it doubted that those who corrupt their own bodies conceal themselves?   5
And if those who defile the living are as bad as they who defile the dead?
And if the body does not do fully as much as the soul?
And if the body were not the soul, what is the soul?

2

The love of the body of man or woman balks account, the body itself balks
    account,
That of the male is perfect, and that of the female is perfect.   10

The expression of the face balks account,
But the expression of a well-made man appears not only in his face,
It is in his limbs and joints also, it is curiously in the joints of his hips and
    wrists,
It is in his walk, the carriage of his neck, the flex of his waist and knees, dress
    does not hide him,
The strong sweet quality he has strikes through the cotton and broadcloth,   15
To see him pass conveys as much as the best poem, perhaps more,
You linger to see his back, and the back of his neck and shoulder-side.

The sprawl and fulness of babes, the bosoms and heads of women, the folds of
    their dress, their style as we pass in the street, the contour of their shape
    downwards,
The swimmer naked in the swimming-bath, seen as he swims through the
    transparent green-shine, or lies with his face up and rolls silently to and fro
    in the heave of the water,
The bending forward and backward of rowers in row-boats, the horseman in his
    saddle,   20
Girls, mothers, house-keepers, in all their performances,
The group of laborers seated at noon-time with their open dinner-kettles, and
    their wives waiting,
The female soothing a child, the farmer's daughter in the garden or cow-yard,
The young fellow hoeing corn, the sleigh-driver driving his six horses through
    the crowd,
The wrestle of wrestlers, two apprentice-boys, quite grown, lusty, good-natured,
    native-born, out on the vacant lot at sundown after work,   25
The coats and caps thrown down, the embrace of love and resistance,
The upper-hold and under-hold, the hair rumpled over and blinding the eyes;
The march of firemen in their own costumes, the play of masculine muscle
    through clean-setting trowsers and waist-straps,
The slow return from the fire, the pause when the bell strikes suddenly again,
    and the listening on the alert,
The natural, perfect, varied attitudes, the bent head, the curv'd neck and the
    counting;   30
Such-like I love—I loosen myself, pass freely, am at the mother's breast with
    the little child,
Swim with the swimmers, wrestle with wrestlers, march in line with the
    firemen, and pause, listen, count.

3

I knew a man, a common farmer, the father of five sons,
And in them the fathers of sons, and in them the fathers of sons.
This man was of wonderful vigor, calmness, beauty of person,   35
The shape of his head, the pale yellow and white of his hair and beard, the

immeasurable meaning of his black eyes, the richness and breadth of his
 manners,
These I used to go and visit him to see, he was wise also,
He was six feet tall, he was over eighty years old, his sons were massive, clean,
 bearded, tan-faced, handsome,
They and his daughters loved him, all who saw him loved him,
They did not love him by allowance, they loved him with personal love,   40
He drank water only, the blood show'd like scarlet through the clear-brown
 skin of his face,
He was a frequent gunner and fisher, he sail'd his boat himself, he had a fine
 one presented to him by a ship-joiner, he had fowling-pieces presented to
 him by men that loved him,
When he went with his five sons and many grand-sons to hunt or fish, you
 would pick him out as the most beautiful and vigorous of the gang,
You would wish long and long to be with him, you would wish to sit by him
 in the boat that you and he might touch each other.

4

I have perceiv'd that to be with those I like is enough,   45
To stop in company with the rest at evening is enough,
To be surrounded by beautiful, curious, breathing, laughing flesh is enough,
To pass among them or touch any one, or rest my arm ever so lightly round
 his or her neck for a moment, what is this then?
I do not ask any more delight, I swim in it as in a sea.

There is something in staying close to men and women and looking on them,
 and in the contact and odor of them, that pleases the soul well,   50
All things please the soul, but these please the soul well.

5

This is the female form,
A divine nimbus exhales from it from head to foot,
It attracts with fierce undeniable attraction,
I am drawn by its breath as if I were no more than a helpless vapor, all falls
 aside but myself and it,   55
Books, art, religion, time, the visible and solid earth, and what was expected of
 heaven or fear'd of hell, are now consumed,
Mad filaments, ungovernable shoots play out of it, the response likewise
 ungovernable,
Hair, bosom, hips, bend of legs, negligent falling hands all diffused, mine too
 diffused,
Ebb stung by the flow and flow stung by the ebb, love-flesh swelling and
 deliciously aching,
Limitless limpid jets of love hot and enormous, quivering jelly of love,
 white-blow and delirious juice,   60

Bridegroom night of love working surely and softly into the prostrate dawn,
Undulating into the willing and yielding day,
Lost in the cleave of the clasping and sweet-flesh'd day.
This the nucleus—after the child is born of woman, man is born of woman,
This the bath of birth, this the merge of small and large, and the outlet again.   65

Be not ashamed women, your privilege encloses the rest, and is the exit of the
     rest,
You are the gates of the body, and you are the gates of the soul.

The female contains all qualities and tempers them,
She is in her place and moves with perfect balance,
She is all things duly veil'd, she is both passive and active,   70
She is to conceive daughters as well as sons, and sons as well as daughters.

As I see my soul reflected in Nature,
As I see through a mist, One with inexpressible completeness, sanity, beauty,
See the bent head and arms folded over the breast, the Female I see.

6

The male is not less the soul nor more, he too is in his place,   75
He too is all qualities, he is action and power,
The flush of the known universe is in him,
Scorn becomes him well, and appetite and defiance become him well,
The wildest largest passions, bliss that is utmost, sorrow that is utmost become
     him well, pride is for him,
The full-spread pride of man is calming and excellent to the soul,   80
Knowledge becomes him, he likes it always, he brings every thing to the test of
     himself,
Whatever the survey, whatever the sea and the sail he strikes soundings at last
     only here,
(Where else does he strike soundings except here?)

The man's body is sacred and the woman's body is sacred,
No matter who it is, it is sacred—is it the meanest one in the laborers' gang?   85
Is it one of the dull-faced immigrants just landed on the wharf?
Each belongs here or anywhere just as much as the well-off, just as much as
     you,
Each has his or her place in the procession.

(All is a procession,
The universe is a procession with measured and perfect motion.)   90

Do you know so much yourself that you call the meanest ignorant?
Do you suppose you have a right to a good sight, and he or she has no right
     to a sight?

Do you think matter has cohered together from its diffuse float, and the soil is
   on the surface, and water runs and vegetation sprouts,
For you only, and not for him and her?

7

A man's body at auction,   95
(For before the war I often go to the slave-mart and watch the sale,)
I help the auctioneer, the sloven does not half know his business.

Gentlemen look on this wonder,
Whatever the bids of the bidders they cannot be high enough for it,
For it the globe lay preparing quintillions of years without one animal or plant, 100
For it the revolving cycles truly and steadily roll'd.

In this head the all-baffling brain,
In it and below it the makings of heroes.

Examine these limbs, red, black, or white, they are cunning in tendon and
   nerve,
They shall be stript that you may see them.   105
Exquisite senses, life-lit eyes, pluck, volition,
Flakes of breast-muscle, pliant backbone and neck, flesh not flabby, good-sized
   arms and legs,
And wonders within there yet.

Within there runs blood,
The same old blood! the same red-running blood!   110
There swells and jets a heart, there all passions, desires, reachings, aspirations,
(Do you think they are not there because they are not express'd in parlors and
   lecture-rooms?)

This is not only one man, this the father of those who shall be fathers in their
   turns,
In him the start of populous states and rich republics,
Of him countless immortal lives with countless embodiments and enjoyments. 115

How do you know who shall come from the offspring of his offspring through
   the centuries?
(Who might you find you have come from yourself, if you could trace back
   through the centuries?)

8

A woman's body at auction,
She too is not only herself, she is the teeming mother of mothers,
She is the bearer of them that shall grow and be mates to the mothers.   120

Have you ever loved the body of a woman?
Have you ever loved the body of a man?
Do you not see that these are exactly the same to all in all nations and times all
    over the earth?

If any thing is sacred the human body is sacred,
And the glory and sweet of a man is the token of manhood untainted,   125
And in man or woman a clean, strong, firm-fibred body, is more beautiful than
    the most beautiful face.
Have you seen the fool that corrupted his own live body? or the fool that
    corrupted her own live body?
For they do not conceal themselves, and cannot conceal themselves.

9

O my body! I dare not desert the likes of you in other men and women, nor
    the likes of the parts of you,
I believe the likes of you are to stand or fall with the likes of the soul, (and
    that they are the soul,)   130
I believe the likes of you shall stand or fall with my poems, and that they are
    my poems,
Man's, woman's, child's, youth's, wife's, husband's, mother's, father's, young
    man's, young woman's poems,
Head, neck, hair, ears, drop and tympan of the ears,
Eyes, eye-fringes, iris of the eye, eyebrows, and the waking or sleeping of the
    lids,
Mouth, tongue, lips, teeth, roof of the mouth, jaws, and the jaw-hinges,   135
Nose, nostrils of the nose, and the partition,
Cheeks, temples, forehead, chin, throat, back of the neck, neck-slue,
Strong shoulders, manly beard, scapula, hind-shoulders, and the ample
    side-round of the chest,
Upper-arm, armpit, elbow-socket, lower-arm, arm-sinews, arm-bones,
Wrist and wrist-joints, hand, palm, knuckles, thumb, forefinger, finger-joints,
    finger-nails,   140
Broad breast-front, curling hair of the breast, breast-bone, breast-side,
Ribs, belly, backbone, joints of the backbone,
Hips, hip-sockets, hip-strength, inward and outward round, man-balls, man-root,
Strong set of thighs, well carrying the trunk above,
Leg-fibres, knee, knee-pan, upper-leg, under-leg,   145
Ankles, instep, foot-ball, toes, toe-joints, the heel;
All attitudes, all the shapeliness, all the belongings of my or your body or of
    any one's body, male or female,
The lung-sponges, the stomach-sac, the bowels sweet and clean,
The brain in its folds inside the skull-frame,
Sympathies, heart-valves, palate-valves, sexuality, maternity,   150
Womanhood, and all that is a woman, and the man that comes from woman,

The womb, the teats, nipples, breast-milk, tears, laughter, weeping, love-looks,
    love-perturbations and risings,
The voice, articulation, language, whispering, shouting aloud,
Food, drink, pulse, digestion, sweat, sleep, walking, swimming,
Poise on the hips, leaping, reclining, embracing, arm-curving and tightening,   155
The continual changes of the flex of the mouth, and around the eyes,
The skin, the sunburnt shade, freckles, hair,
The curious sympathy one feels when feeling with the hand the naked meat of
    the body,
The circling rivers the breath, and breathing it in and out,
The beauty of the waist, and thence of the hips, and thence downward toward
    the knees,   160
The thin red jellies within you or within me, the bones and the marrow in the
    bones,
The exquisite realization of health;
O I say these are not the parts and poems of the body only, but of the soul,
O I say now these are the soul!

1855

A Woman Waits for Me

A woman waits for me, she contains all, nothing is lacking,
Yet all were lacking if sex were lacking, or if the moisture of the right man
    were lacking.

Sex contains all, bodies, souls,
Meanings, proofs, purities, delicacies, results, promulgations,
Songs, commands, health, pride, the maternal mystery, the seminal milk,   5
All hopes, benefactions, bestowals, all the passions, loves, beauties, delights of
    the earth,
All the governments, judges, gods, follow'd persons of the earth,
These are contain'd in sex as parts of itself and justifications of itself.

Without shame the man I like knows and avows the deliciousness of his sex,
Without shame the woman I like knows and avows hers.   10

Now I will dismiss myself from impassive women,
I will go stay with her who waits for me, and with those women that are
    warm-blooded and sufficient for me,
I see that they understand me and do not deny me,
I see that they are worthy of me, I will be the robust husband of those women.

They are not one jot less than I am,   15
They are tann'd in the face by shining suns and blowing winds,
Their flesh has the old divine suppleness and strength,
They know how to swim, row, ride, wrestle, shoot, run, strike, retreat, advance,
    resist, defend themselves,

They are ultimate in their own right—they are calm, clear, well-possess'd of
    themselves.

I draw you close to me, you women,   20
I cannot let you go, I would do you good,
I am for you, and you are for me, not only for our own sake, but for others'
    sakes,
Envelop'd in you sleep greater heroes and bards,
They refuse to awake at the touch of any man but me.

It is I, you women, I make my way,   25
I am stern, acrid, large, undissuadable, but I love you,
I do not hurt you any more than is necessary for you,
I pour the stuff to start sons and daughters fit for these States, I press with slow
    rude muscle,
I brace myself effectually, I listen to no entreaties,
I dare not withdraw till I deposit what has so long accumulated within me.   30
Through you I drain the pent-up rivers of myself,
In you I wrap a thousand onward years,
On you I graft the grafts of the best-beloved of me and America,
The drops I distil upon you shall grow fierce and athletic girls, new artists,
    musicians, and singers,
The babes I beget upon you are to beget babes in their turn,   35
I shall demand perfect men and women out of my love-spendings,
I shall expect them to interpenetrate with others, as I and you interpenetrate
    now,
I shall count on the fruits of the gushing showers of them, as I count on the
    fruits of the gushing showers I give now,
I shall look for loving crops from the birth, life, death, immortality, I plant so
    lovingly now.
1856

Once I Pass'd Through a Populous City

Once I pass'd through a populous city imprinting my brain for future use with
    its shows, architecture, customs, traditions,
Yet now of all that city I remember only a woman I casually met there who
    detain'd me for love of me,
Day by day and night by night we were together—all else has long been
    forgotten by me,
I remember I say only that woman who passionately clung to me,
Again we wander, we love, we separate again,   5
Again she holds me by the hand, I must not go,
I see her close beside me with silent lips sad and tremulous.
1860

Facing West from California's Shores

Facing west from California's shores,
Inquiring, tireless, seeking what is yet unfound,
I, a child, very old, over waves, towards the house of maternity, the land of
    migrations, look afar,
Look off the shores of my Western sea, the circle almost circled;
For starting westward from Hindustan, from the vales of Kashmere,   5
From Asia, from the north, from the God, the sage, and the hero,
From the south, from the flowery peninsulas and the spice islands,
Long having wander'd since, round the earth having wander'd,
Now I face home again, very pleas'd and joyous,
(But where is what I started for so long ago?   10
And why is it yet unfound?)
1860

As Adam Early in the Morning

As Adam early in the morning,
Walking forth from the bower refresh'd with sleep,
Behold me where I pass, hear my voice, approach,
Touch me, touch the palm of your hand to my body as I pass,
Be not afraid of my body.   5
1861

from **Calamus**

Scented Herbage of My Breast

Scented herbage of my breast,
Leaves from you I glean, I write, to be perused best afterwards,
Tomb-leaves, body-leaves growing up above me above death,
Perennial roots, tall leaves, O the winter shall not freeze you delicate leaves,
Every year shall you bloom again, out from where you retired you shall
    emerge again;   5
O I do not know whether many passing by will discover you or inhale your
    faint odor, but I believe a few will;
O slender leaves! O blossoms of my blood! I permit you to tell in your own
    way of the heart that is under you,
O I do not know what you mean there underneath yourselves, you are not
    happiness,
You are often more bitter than I can bear, you burn and sting me,
Yet you are beautiful to me you faint tinged roots, you make me think of
    death,   10
Death is beautiful from you, (what indeed is finally beautiful except death and
    love?)
O I think it is not for life I am chanting here my chant of lovers, I think it
    must be for death,

For how calm, how solemn it grows to ascend to the atmosphere of lovers,
Death or life I am then indifferent, my soul declines to prefer,
(I am not sure but the high soul of lovers welcomes death most,) 15
Indeed O death, I think now these leaves mean precisely the same as you mean,
Grow up taller sweet leaves that I may see! grow up out of my breast!
Spring away from the conceal'd heart there!
Do not fold yourself so in your pink-tinged roots timid leaves!
Do not remain down there so ashamed, herbage of my breast! 20
Come I am determin'd to unbare this broad breast of mine, I have long enough
    stifled and choked;
Emblematic and capricious blades I leave you, now you serve me not,
I will say what I have to say by itself,
I will sound myself and comrades only, I will never again utter a call only
    their call,
I will raise with it immortal reverberations through the States, 25
I will give an example to lovers to take permanent shape and will through the
    States,
Through me shall the words be said to make death exhilarating,
Give me your tone therefore O death, that I may accord with it,
Give me yourself, for I see that you belong to me now above all, and are
    folded inseparably together, you love and death are,
Nor will I allow you to balk me any more with what I was calling life, 30
For now it is convey'd to me that you are the purports essential,
That you hide in these shifting forms of life, for reasons, and that they are
    mainly for you,
That you beyond them come forth to remain, the real reality,
That behind the mask of materials you patiently wait, no matter how long,
That you will one day perhaps take control of all, 35
That you will perhaps dissipate this entire show of appearance,
That may-be you are what it is all for, but it does not last so very long,
But you will last very long.

1860

Recorders Ages Hence

Recorders ages hence,
Come, I will take you down underneath this impassive exterior, I will tell you
    what to say of me,
Publish my name and hang up my picture as that of the tenderest lover,
The friend the lover's portrait, of whom his friend his lover was fondest,
Who was not proud of his songs, but of the measureless ocean of love within
    him, and freely pour'd it forth, 5
Who often walk'd lonesome walks thinking of his dear friends, his lovers,
Who pensive away from one he lov'd often lay sleepless and dissatisfied at
    night,
Who knew too well the sick, sick dread lest the one he lov'd might secretly be
    indifferent to him,

Whose happiest days were far away through fields, in woods, on hills, he and
    another wandering hand in hand, they twain apart from other men,
Who oft as he saunter'd the streets curv'd with his arm the shoulder of his
    friend, while the arm of his friend rested upon him also.   10
1860

When I Heard at the Close of the Day

When I heard at the close of the day how my name had been receiv'd with
    plaudits in the capitol, still it was not a happy night for me that follow'd,
And else when I carous'd, or when my plans were accomplish'd, still I was not
    happy,
But the day when I rose at dawn from the bed of perfect health, refresh'd,
    singing, inhaling the ripe breath of autumn,
When I saw the full moon in the west grow pale and disappear in the morning
    light,
When I wander'd alone over the beach, and undressing bathed, laughing with
    the cool waters, and saw the sun rise,   5
And when I thought how my dear friend my lover was on his way coming, O
    then I was happy,
O then each breath tasted sweeter, and all that day my food nourish'd me more,
    and the beautiful day pass'd well,
And the next came with equal joy, and with the next at evening came my
    friend,
And that night while all was still I heard the waters roll slowly continually up
    the shores,
I heard the hissing rustle of the liquid and sands as directed to me whispering to
    congratulate me,   10
For the one I love most lay sleeping by me under the same cover in the cool
    night,
In the stillness in the autumn moonbeams his face was inclined toward me,
And his arm lay lightly around my breast—and that night I was happy.
1860

I Saw in Louisiana a Live-Oak Growing

I saw in Louisiana a live-oak growing,
All alone stood it and the moss hung down from the branches,
Without any companion it grew there uttering joyous leaves of dark green,
And its look, rude, unbending, lusty, made me think of myself,
But I wonder'd how it could utter joyous leaves standing alone there without
    its friend near, for I knew I could not,   5
And I broke off a twig with a certain number of leaves upon it, and twined
    around it a little moss,
And brought it away, and I have placed it in sight in my room,
It is not needed to remind me as of my own dear friends,
(For I believe lately I think of little else than of them,)

Yet it remains to me a curious token, it makes me think of manly love;   10
For all that, and though the live-oak glistens there in Louisiana solitary in a
    wide flat space,
Uttering joyous leaves all its life without a friend a lover near,
I know very well I could not.

1860

Here the Frailest Leaves of Me

Here the frailest leaves of me and yet my strongest lasting,
Here I shade and expose my thoughts, I myself do not expose them,
And yet they expose me more than all my other poems.

1860

Crossing Brooklyn Ferry[*]

1

Flood-tide below me! I see you face to face!
Clouds of the west—sun there half an hour high—I see you also face to face.

Crowds of men and women attired in the usual costumes, how curious you are
    to me!
On the ferry-boats the hundreds and hundreds that cross, returning home, are
    more curious to me than you suppose,
And you that shall cross from shore to shore years hence are more to me, and
    more in my meditations, than you might suppose.   5

2

The impalpable sustenance of me from all things at all hours of the day,
The simple, compact, well-join'd scheme, myself disintegrated, every one
    disintegrated yet part of the scheme,
The similitudes of the past and those of the future,
The glories strung like beads on my smallest sights and hearings, on the walk in
    the street and the passage over the river,
The current rushing so swiftly and swimming with me far away,
The others that are to follow me, the ties between me and them,   10
The certainty of others, the life, love, sight, hearing of others.

Others will enter the gates of the ferry and cross from shore to shore,
Others will watch the run of the flood-tide,

[*] Titled "Sun-Down Poem" when first published
in 1856.

Others will see the shipping of Manhattan north and west, and the heights of
    Brooklyn to the south and east,   15
Others will see the islands large and small;
Fifty years hence, others will see them as they cross, the sun half an hour high,
A hundred years hence, or ever so many hundred years hence, others will see
    them,
Will enjoy the sunset, the pouring-in of the flood-tide, the falling-back to the
    sea of the ebb-tide.

3

It avails not, time nor place—distance avails not,   20
I am with you, you men and women of a generation, or ever so many
    generations hence,
Just as you feel when you look on the river and sky, so I felt,
Just as any of you is one of a living crowd, I was one of a crowd,
Just as you are refresh'd by the gladness of the river and the bright flow, I was
    refresh'd,
Just as you stand and lean on the rail, yet hurry with the swift current, I stood
    yet was hurried,   25
Just as you look on the numberless masts of ships and the thick-stemm'd pipes
    of steamboats, I look'd.

I too many and many a time cross'd the river of old,
Watched the Twelfth-month[36] sea-gulls, saw them high in the air floating with
    motionless wings, oscillating their bodies,
Saw how the glistening yellow lit up parts of their bodies and left the rest in
    strong shadow,
Saw the slow-wheeling circles and the gradual edging toward the south,   30
Saw the reflection of the summer sky in the water,
Had my eyes dazzled by the shimmering track of beams,
Look'd at the fine centrifugal spokes of light round the shape of my head in the
    sunlit water,
Look'd on the haze on the hills southward and southwestward,
Look'd on the vapor as it flew in fleeces tinged with violet,   35
Look'd toward the lower bay to notice the vessels arriving,
Saw their approach, saw aboard those that were near me,
Saw the white sails of schooners and sloops, saw the ships at anchor,
The sailors at work in the rigging or out astride the spars,
The round masts, the swinging motion of the hulls, the slender serpentine
    pennants,   40
The large and small steamers in motion, the pilots in their pilot-houses,
The white wake left by the passage, the quick tremulous whirl of the wheels,
The flags of all nations, the falling of them at sunset,

[36] December (Quaker style).

The scallop-edged waves in the twilight, the ladled cups, the frolicsome crests
    and glistening,
The stretch afar growing dimmer and dimmer, the gray walls of the granite
    storehouses by the docks,
On the river the shadowy group, the big steam-tug closely flank'd on each side   45
    by the barges, the hay-boat, the belated lighter,
On the neighboring shore the fires from the foundry chimneys burning high
    and glaringly into the night,
Casting their flicker of black contrasted with wild red and yellow light over
    the tops of houses, and down into the clefts of streets.

4

These and all else were to me the same as they are to you,
I loved well those cities, loved well the stately and rapid river,
The men and women I saw were all near to me,   50
Others the same—others who look back on me because I look'd forward to
    them,
(The time will come, though I stop here to-day and to-night.)

5

What is it then between us?
What is the count of the scores or hundreds of years between us?   55

Whatever it is, it avails not—distance avails not, and place avails not,
I too lived, Brooklyn of ample hills was mine,
I too walk'd the streets of Manhattan island, and bathed in the waters around it,
I too felt the curious abrupt questionings stir within me,
In the day among crowds of people sometimes they came upon me,   60
In my walks home late at night or as I lay in my bed they came upon me,
I too had been struck from the float forever held in solution,
I too had receiv'd identity by my body,
That I was I knew was of my body, and what I should be I knew I should be
    of my body.

6

It is not upon you alone the dark patches fall,
The dark threw its patches down upon me also,   65
The best I had done seem'd to me blank and suspicious,
My great thoughts as I supposed them, were they not in reality meagre?
Nor is it you alone who know what it is to be evil,
I am he who knew what it was to be evil,
I too knotted the old knot of contrariety,   70
Blabb'd, blush'd, resented, lied, stole, grudg'd,
Had guile, anger, lust, hot wishes I dared not speak,

Was wayward, vain, greedy, shallow, sly, cowardly, malignant,
The wolf, the snake, the hog, not wanting in me,   75
The cheating look, the frivolous word, the adulterous wish, not wanting,
Refusals, hates, postponements, meanness, laziness, none of these wanting,
Was one with the rest, the days and haps of the rest,
Was call'd by my nighest name by clear loud voices of young men as they saw
    me approaching or passing,
Felt their arms on my neck as I stood, or the negligent leaning of their flesh
    against me as I sat,   80
Saw many I loved in the street or ferry-boat or public assembly, yet never told
    them a word,
Lived the same life with the rest, the same old laughing, gnawing, sleeping,
Play'd the part that still looks back on the actor or actress,
The same old role, the role that is what we make it, as great as we like,
Or as small as we like, or both great and small.   85

7

Closer yet I approach you,
What thought you have of me now, I had as much of you—I laid in my stores
    in advance,
I consider'd long and seriously of you before you were born.

Who was to know what should come home to me?
Who knows but I am enjoying this?   90
Who knows, for all the distance, but I am as good as looking at you now, for
    all you cannot see me?

8

Ah, what can ever be more stately and admirable to me than mast-hemm'd
    Manhattan?
River and sunset and scallop-edg'd waves of flood-tide?
The sea-gulls oscillating their bodies, the hat-boat in the twilight, and the
    belated lighter?
What gods can exceed these that clasp me by the hand, and with voices I love
    call me promptly and loudly by my nighest name as I approach?   95
What is more subtle than this which ties me to the woman or man that looks
    in my face?
Which fuses me into you now, and pours my meaning into you?

We understand then do we not?
What I promis'd without mentioning it, have you not accepted?
What the study could not teach—what the preaching could not accomplish is
    accomplish'd, is it not?   100

9

Flow on, river! flow with the flood-tide, and ebb with the ebb-tide!
Frolic on, crested and scallop-edg'd waves!
Gorgeous clouds of the sunset! drench with your splendor me, or the men and
    women generations after me!
Cross from shore to shore, countless crowds of passengers!
Stand up, tall masts of Mannahatta! stand up, beautiful hills of Brooklyn!   105
Throb, baffled and curious brain! throw out questions and answers!
Suspend here and everywhere, eternal float of solution!
Gaze, loving and thirsting eyes, in the house or street or public assembly!
Sound out, voices of young men! loudly and musically call me by my nighest
    name!
Live, old life! play the part that looks back on the actor or actress!   110
Play the old role, the role that is great or small according as one makes it!
Consider, you who peruse me, whether I may not in unknown ways be looking
    upon you;
Be firm, rail over the river, to support those who lean idly, yet haste with the
    hasting current;
Fly on, sea-birds! fly sideways, or wheel in large circles high in the air;
Receive the summer sky, you water, and faithfully hold it till all downcast eyes
    have time to take it from you!   115
Diverge, fine spokes of light, from the shape of my head, or any one's head, in
    the sunlit water!
Come on, ships from the lower bay! pass up or down, white-sail'd schooners,
    sloops, lighters!
Flaunt away, flags of all nations! be duly lower'd at sunset!
Burn high your fires, foundry chimneys! cast black shadows at nightfall! cast
    red and yellow light over the tops of the houses!
Appearances, now or henceforth, indicate what you are,   120
You necessary film, continue to envelop the soul,
About my body for me, and your body for you, be hung out divinest aromas,
Thrive, cities—bring your freight, bring your shows, ample and sufficient
    rivers,
Expand, being than which none else is perhaps more spiritual,
Keep your places, objects than which none else is more lasting.   125

You have waited, you always wait, you dumb, beautiful ministers,
We receive you with free sense at last, and are insatiate henceforward,
Not you any more shall be able to foil us, or withhold yourselves from us,
We use you, and do not cast you aside—we plant you permanently within us,
We fathom you not—we love you—there is perfection in you also,   130
You furnish your parts toward eternity,
Great or small, you furnish your parts toward the soul.
1856

from **Song of the Exposition**

Come Muse migrate from Greece and Ionia,
Cross out please those immensely overpaid accounts,
That matter of Troy and Achilles' wrath, and Æneas', Odysseus' wanderings,[37]
Placard "Removed" and "To Let" on the rocks of your snowy Parnassus,[38]
Repeat at Jerusalem, place the notice high on Jaffa's gate and on Mount
    Moriah,[39]   5
The same on the walls of your German, French and Spanish castles, and Italian
    collections,
For know a better, fresher, busier sphere, a wide, untried domain awaits,
    demands you.

1871

from **Sea-Drift**

*Out of the Cradle Endlessly Rocking**

Out of the cradle endlessly rocking,
Out of the mocking-bird's throat, the musical shuttle,
Out of the Ninth-month[40] midnight,
Over the sterile sands and the fields beyond, where the child leaving his bed
    wander'd alone, bareheaded, barefoot,
Down from the shower'd halo,   5
Up from the mystic play of shadows twining and twisting as if they were alive,
Out from the patches of briers and blackberries,
From the memories of the bird that chanted to me,
From your memories sad brother, from the fitful risings and fallings I heard,
From under that yellow half-moon late-risen and swollen as if with tears,   10
From those beginning notes of yearning and love there in the mist,
From the thousand responses of my heart never to cease,
From the myriad thence-arous'd words,
From the word stronger and more delicious than any,
From such as now they start the scene revisiting,   15
As a flock, twittering, rising, or overhead passing,
Borne hither, ere all eludes me, hurriedly,
A man, yet by these tears a little boy again,
Throwing myself on the sand, confronting the waves,
I, chanter of pains and joys, uniter of here and hereafter,   20
Taking all hints to use them, but swiftly leaping beyond them,
A reminiscence sing.

---

[37] Here and in the following line Whitman refers
to the Homeric epics.
[38] Dwelling place of the classical muses.
[39] Jaffa: seaport in Israel; Mount Moriah: in
Jerusalem, the site of King Solomon's temple.

* Titled "A Child's Reminiscence" when first
published in *Saturday Press* (New York),
December 24, 1859.
[40] September (Quaker style).

Once Paumanok,[41]
When the lilac-scent was in the air and Fifth-month[42] grass was growing,
Up this seashore in some briers,   25
Two feather'd guests from Alabama, two together,
And their nest, and four light-green eggs spotted with brown,
And every day the he-bird to and fro near at hand,
And every day the she-bird crouch'd on her nest, silent, with bright eyes,
And every day I, a curious boy, never too close, never disturbing them,   30
Cautiously peering, absorbing, translating.

Shine! shine! shine!
Pour down your warmth, great sun!
While we bask, we two together.

Two together!   35
Winds blow south, or winds blow north,
Day come white, or night come black,
Home, or rivers and mountains from home,
Singing all time, minding no time,
While we two keep together.   40

Till of a sudden,
May-be kill'd, unknown to her mate,
One forenoon the she-bird crouch'd not on the nest,
Nor return'd that afternoon, nor the next,
Nor ever appear'd again.   45

And thenceforward all summer in the sound of the sea,
And at night under the full of the moon in calmer weather,
Over the hoarse surging of the sea,
Or flitting from brier to brier by day,
I saw, I heard at intervals the remaining one, the he-bird,   50
The solitary guest from Alabama.

Blow! blow! blow!
Blow up sea-winds along Paumanok's shore;
I wait and I wait till you blow my mate to me.

Yes, when the stars glisten'd,   55
All night long on the prong of a moss-scallop'd stake,
Down almost amid the slapping waves,
Sat the lone singer wonderful causing tears.

He call'd on his mate,
He pour'd forth the meanings which I of all men know.   60

[41] Indian name for Long Island.   [42] May (Quaker style).

Yes my brother I know,
The rest might not, but I have treasur'd every note,
For more than once dimly down to the beach gliding,
Silent, avoiding the moonbeams, blending myself with the shadows,
Recalling now the obscure shapes, the echoes, the sounds and sights after their
    sorts,   65
The white arms out in the breakers tirelessly tossing,
I, with bare feet, a child, the wind wafting my hair,
Listen'd long and long.

Listen'd to keep, to sing, now translating the notes,
Following you my brother.   70

Soothe! soothe! soothe!
Close on its wave soothes the wave behind,
And again another behind embracing and lapping, every one close,
But my love soothes not me, not me.

Low hangs the moon, it rose late,   75
It is lagging—O I think it is heavy with love, with love.

O madly the sea pushes upon the land,
With love, with love.

O night! do I not see my love fluttering out among the breakers?
What is that little black thing I see there in the white?   80

Loud! loud! loud!
Loud I call to you, my love!

High and clear I shoot my voice over the waves,
Surely you must know who is here, is here,
You must know who I am, my love.   85

Low-hanging moon!
What is that dusky spot in your brown yellow?
O it is the shape, the shape of my mate!
O moon do not keep her from me any longer.
Land! land! O land!   90
Whichever way I turn, O I think you could give me my mate back again if you only
    would,
For I am almost sure I see her dimly whichever way I look.

O rising stars!
Perhaps the one I want so much will rise, will rise with some of you.

O throat! O trembling throat!   95
Sound clearer through the atmosphere!
Pierce the woods, the earth,
Somewhere listening to catch you must be the one I want.

Shake out carols!
Solitary here, the night's carols!   100
Carols of lonesome love! death's carols!
Carols under that lagging, yellow, waning moon!
O under that moon where she droops almost down into the sea!
O reckless despairing carols.

But soft! sink low!   105
Soft! let me just murmur,
And do you wait a moment you husky-nois'd sea,
For somewhere I believe I heard my mate responding to me,
So faint, I must be still, be still to listen,
But not altogether still, for then she might not come immediately to me.   110

Hither my love!
Here I am! here!
With this just-sustain'd note I announce myself to you,
This gentle call is for you my love, for you.

Do not be decoy'd elsewhere,   115
That is the whistle of the wind, it is not my voice,
That is the fluttering, the fluttering of the spray,
Those are the shadows of leaves.

O darkness! O in vain!
O I am very sick and sorrowful.   120
O brown halo in the sky near the moon, drooping upon the sea!
O troubled reflection in the sea!
O throat! O throbbing heart!
And I singing uselessly, uselessly all the night.

O past! O happy life! O songs of joy!   125
In the air, in the woods, over fields,
Loved! loved! loved! loved! loved!
But my mate no more, no more with me!
We two together no more.

The aria sinking,   130
All else continuing, the stars shining,
The winds blowing, the notes of the bird continuous echoing,
With angry moans the fierce old mother incessantly moaning,
On the sands of Paumanok's shore gray and rustling,

The yellow half-moon enlarged, sagging down, drooping, the face of the sea
    almost touching,   135
The boy ecstatic, with his bare feet the waves, with his hair the atmosphere
    dallying,
The love in the heart long pent, now loose, now at last tumultuously bursting,
The aria's meaning, the ears, the soul, swiftly depositing,
The strange tears down the cheeks coursing,
The colloquy there, the trio, each uttering,   140
The undertone, the savage old mother incessantly crying,
To the boy's soul's questions sullenly timing, some drown'd secret hissing,
To the outsetting bard.

Demon or bird! (said the boy's soul,)
Is it indeed toward your mate you sing? or is it really to me?   145
For I, that was a child, my tongue's use sleeping, now I have heard you,
Now in a moment I know what I am for, I awake,
And already a thousand singers, a thousand songs, clearer, louder and more
    sorrowful than yours,
A thousand warbling echoes have started to life within me, never to die.
O you singer solitary, singing by yourself, projecting me,   150
O solitary me listening, never more shall I cease perpetuating you,
Never more shall I escape, never more the reverberations,
Never more the cries of unsatisfied love be absent from me,
Never again leave me to be the peaceful child I was before what there in the
    night,
By the sea under the yellow and sagging moon,   155
The messenger there arous'd, the fire, the sweet hell within,
The unknown want, the destiny of me.

O give me the clew! (it lurks in the night here somewhere,)
O if I am to have so much, let me have more!

A word then, (for I will conquer it,)   160
The word final, superior to all,
Subtle, sent up—what is it?—I listen;
Are you whispering it, and have been all the time, you seawaves?
Is that it from your liquid rims and wet sands?

Whereto answering, the sea,   165
Delaying not, hurrying not,
Whisper'd me through the night, and very plainly before daybreak,
Lisp'd to me the low and delicious word death,
And again death, death, death, death,
Hissing melodious, neither like the bird nor like my arous'd child's heart,   170
But edging near as privately for me rustling at my feet,
Creeping thence steadily up to my ears and laving me softly all over,
Death, death, death, death, death.

Which I do not forget,
But fuse the song of my dusky demon and brother,   175
That he sang to me in the moonlight on Paumanok's gray beach,
With the thousand responsive songs at random,
My own songs awaked from that hour,
And with them the key, the word up from the waves,
The word of the sweetest song and all songs,   180
That strong and delicious word which, creeping to my feet,
(Or like some old crone rocking the cradle, swathed in sweet garments, bending
    aside,)
The sea whisper'd me.

1859

As I Ebb'd with the Ocean of Life*

1

As I ebb'd with the ocean of life,
As I wended the shores I know,
As I walk'd where the ripples continually wash you Paumanok,
Where they rustle up hoarse and sibilant,
Where the fierce old mother endlessly cries for her castaways,   5
I musing late in the autumn day, gazing off southward,
Held by this electric self out of the pride of which I utter poems,
Was seiz'd by the spirit that trails in the lines underfoot,
The rim, the sediment that stands for all the water and all the land of the
    globe.

Fascinated, my eyes reverting from the south, dropt, to follow those slender
    windrows,   10
Chaff, straw, splinters of wood, weeds, and the sea-gluten,
Scum, scales from shining rocks, leaves of salt-lettuce, left by the tide,
Miles walking, the sound of breaking waves the other side of me,
Paumanok there and then as I thought the old thought of likenesses,
These you presented to me you fish-shaped island,   15
As I wended the shores I know,
As I walk'd with that electric self seeking types.

2

As I wend to the shores I know not,
As I list to the dirge, the voices of men and women wreck'd,
As I inhale the impalpable breezes that set in upon me,   20
As the ocean so mysterious rolls toward me closer and closer,

* First published with the title "Bardic Symbols"
in the *Atlantic Monthly,* April 1860.

I too but signify at the utmost a little wash'd-up drift,
A few sands and dead leaves to gather,
Gather, and merge myself as part of the sands and drift.

O baffled, balk'd, bent to the very earth,   25
Oppress'd with myself that I have dared to open my mouth,
Aware now that amid all that blab whose echoes recoil upon me I have not
 once had the least idea who or what I am,
But that before all my arrogant poems the real Me stands yet untouch'd, untold,
 altogether unreach'd,
Withdrawn far, mocking me with mock-congratulatory signs and bows,
With peals of distant ironical laughter at every word I have written,   30
Pointing in silence to these songs, and then to the sand beneath.

I perceive I have not really understood any thing, not a single object, and that
 no man ever can,
Nature here in sight of the sea taking advantage of me to dart upon me and
 sting me,
Because I have dared to open my mouth to sing at all.

3

You oceans both, I close with you,   35
We murmur alike reproachfully rolling sands and drift, knowing not why,
These little shreds indeed standing for you and me and all.

You friable shore with trails of debris,
You fish-shaped island, I take what is underfoot,
What is yours is mine my father.   40

I too Paumanok,
I too have bubbled up, floated the measureless float, and been wash'd on your
 shores,
I too am but a trail of drift and debris,
I too leave little wrecks upon you, you fish-shaped island.
I throw myself upon your breast my father,   45
I cling to you so that you cannot unloose me,
I hold you so firm till you answer me something.

Kiss me my father,
Touch me with your lips as I touch those I love,
Breathe to me while I hold you close the secret of the murmuring I envy.   50

4

Ebb, ocean of life, (the flow will return,)
Cease not your moaning you fierce old mother,

Endlessly cry for your castaways, but fear not, deny not me,
Rustle not up so hoarse and angry against my feet as I touch you or gather
    from you.

I mean tenderly by you and all,   55
I gather for myself and for this phantom looking down where we lead, and
    following me and mine.

Me and mine, loose windrows, little corpses,
Froth, snowy white, and bubbles,
(See, from my dead lips the ooze exuding at last,   60
See, the prismatic colors glistening and rolling,)
Tufts of straw, sands, fragments,
Buoy'd hither from many moods, one contradicting another,
From the storm, the long calm, the darkness, the swell,
Musing, pondering, a breath, a briny tear, a dab of liquid or soil,   65
Up just as much out of fathomless workings fermented and thrown,
A limp blossom or two, torn, just as much over waves floating, drifted at
    random,
Just as much for us that sobbing dirge of Nature,
Just as much whence we come that blare of the cloud-trumpets,
We, capricious, brought hither we know not whence, spread out before you,
You up there walking or sitting,   70
Whoever you are, we too lie in drifts at your feet.
1860

On the Beach at Night Alone

On the beach at night alone,
As the old mother sways her to and fro singing her husky song,
As I watch the bright stars shining, I think a thought of the clef of the
    universes and of the future.

A vast similitude interlocks all,
All spheres, grown, ungrown, small, large, suns, moons, planets,   5
All distances of place however wide,
All distances of time, all inanimate forms,
All souls, all living bodies though they be ever so different, or in different
    worlds,
All gaseous, watery, vegetable, mineral processes, the fishes, the brutes,
All nations, colors, barbarisms, civilizations, languages,   10
All identities that have existed or may exist on this globe, or any globe,
All lives and deaths, all of the past, present, future,
This vast similitude spans them, and always has spann'd,
And shall forever span them and compactly hold and enclose them.
1856

from **By the Roadside**

When I Heard the Learn'd Astronomer

When I heard the learn'd astronomer,
When the proofs, the figures, were ranged in columns before me,
When I was shown the charts and diagrams, to add, divide, and measure them,
When I sitting heard the astronomer where he lectured with much applause in
    the lecture-room,
How soon unaccountable I became tired and sick,   5
Till rising and gliding out I wander'd off by myself,
In the mystical moist night-air, and from time to time,
Look'd up in perfect silence at the stars.

1865

The Dalliance of the Eagles

Skirting the river road, (my forenoon walk, my rest,)
Skyward in air a sudden muffled sound, the dalliance of the eagles,
The rushing amorous contact high in space together,
The clinching interlocking claws, a living, fierce, gyrating wheel,
Four beating wings, two beaks, a swirling mass tight grappling,   5
In tumbling turning clustering loops, straight downward falling,
Till o'er the river pois'd, the twain yet one, a moment's lull,
A motionless still balance in the air, then parting, talons loosing,
Upward again on slow-firm pinions slanting, their separate diverse flight,
She hers, he his, pursuing.   10

1880

from **Drum-Taps**

Beat! Beat! Drums!

Beat! beat! drums!—blow! bugles! blow!
Through the windows—through doors—burst like a ruthless force,
Into the solemn church, and scatter the congregation,
Into the school where the scholar is studying;
Leave not the bridegroom quiet—no happiness must he have now with his
    bride,   5
Nor the peaceful farmer any peace, ploughing his field or gathering his grain,
So fierce you whirr and pound you drums—so shrill you bugles blow.

Beat! beat! drums!—blow! bugles! blow!
Over the traffic of cities—over the rumble of wheels in the streets;
Are beds prepared for sleepers at night in the houses? no sleepers must sleep in
    those beds,   10
No bargainers' bargains by day—no brokers or speculators—would they
    continue?

Would the talkers be talking? would the singer attempt to sing?
Would the lawyer rise in the court to state his case before the judge?
Then rattle quicker, heavier drums—you bugles wilder blow.

Beat! beat! drums!—blow! bugles! blow!   15
Make no parley—stop for no expostulation,
Mind not the timid—mind not the weeper or prayer,
Mind not the old man beseeching the young man,
Let not the child's voice be heard, nor the mother's entreaties,
Make even the trestles to shake the dead where they lie awaiting the hearses,   20
So strong you thump O terrible drums—so loud you bugles blow.

1861

Cavalry Crossing a Ford

A line in long array where they wind betwixt green islands,
They take a serpentine course, their arms flash in the sun—hark to the musical
    clank,
Behold the silvery river, in it the splashing horses loitering stop to drink,
Behold the brown-faced men, each group, each person a picture, the negligent
    rest on the saddles,
Some emerge on the opposite bank, others are just entering the ford—while,   5
Scarlet and blue and snowy white,
The guidon flags flutter gayly in the wind.

1865

Bivouac on a Mountain Side

I see before me now a traveling army halting,
Below a fertile valley spread, with barns and the orchards of summer,
Behind, the terraced sides of a mountain, abrupt, in places rising high,
Broken, with rocks, with clinging cedars, with tall shapes dingily seen,
The numerous camp-fires scatter'd near and far, some away up on the mountain,   5
The shadowy forms of men and horses, looming, large-sized, flickering,
And over all the sky—the sky! far, far out of reach, studded, breaking out, the
    eternal stars.

1865

Vigil Strange I Kept on the Field One Night

Vigil strange I kept on the field one night;
When you my son and my comrade dropt at my side that day,
One look I but gave which your dear eyes return'd with a look I shall never
    forget,
One touch of your hand to mine O boy, reach'd up as you lay on the ground,
Then onward I sped in the battle, the even-contested battle,   5
Till late in the night reliev'd to the place at last again I made my way,

Found you in death so cold dear comrade, found your body son of responding
    kisses, (never again on earth responding,)
Bared your face in the starlight, curious the scene, cool blew the moderate
    night-wind,
Long there and then in vigil I stood, dimly around me the battle-field
    spreading,
Vigil wondrous and vigil sweet there in the fragrant silent night,   10
But not a tear fell, not even a long-drawn sigh, long, long I gazed,
Then on the earth partially reclining sat by your side leaning my chin in my
    hands,
Passing sweet hours, immortal and mystic hours with you dearest comrade—not
    a tear, not a word,
Vigil of silence, love and death, vigil for you my son and my soldier,
As onward silently stars aloft, eastward new ones upward stole,   15
Vigil final for you brave boy, (I could not save you, swift was your death,
I faithfully loved you and cared for you living, I think we shall surely meet
    again,)
Till at latest lingering of the night, indeed just as the dawn appear'd,
My comrade I wrapt in his blanket, envelop'd well his form,
Folded the blanket well, tucking it carefully over head and carefully under feet, 20
And there and then and bathed by the rising sun, my son in his grave, in his
    rude-dug grave I deposited,
Ending my vigil strange with that, vigil of night and battlefield dim,
Vigil for boy of responding kisses, (never again on earth responding,)
Vigil for comrade swiftly slain, vigil I never forget, how as day brighten'd,
I rose from the chill ground and folded my soldier well in his blanket,   25
And buried him where he fell.

1865

A March in the Ranks Hard-Prest, and the Road Unknown

A march in the ranks hard-prest, and the road unknown,
A route through a heavy wood with muffled steps in the darkness,
Our army foil'd with loss severe, and the sullen remnant retreating,
Till after midnight glimmer upon us the lights of a dim-lighted building,
We come to an open space in the woods, and halt by the dim-lighted building, 5
'Tis a large old church at the crossing roads, now an impromptu hospital,
Entering but for a minute I see a sight beyond all the pictures and poems ever
    made,
Shadows of deepest, deepest black, just lit by moving candles and lamps,
And by one great pitchy torch stationary with wild red flame and clouds of
    smoke,
By these, crowds, groups of forms vaguely I see on the floor, some in the pews
    laid down,   10
At my feet more distinctly a soldier, a mere lad, in danger of bleeding to death,
    (he is shot in the abdomen,)

I stanch the blood temporarily, (the youngster's face is white as a lily,)
Then before I depart I sweep my eyes o'er the scene fain to absorb it all,
Faces, varieties, postures beyond description, most in obscurity, some of them dead,
Surgeons operating, attendants holding lights, the smell of ether, the odor of blood,   15
The crowd, O the crowd of the bloody forms, the yard outside also fill'd,
Some on the bare ground, some on planks or stretchers, some in the death-spasm sweating,
An occasional scream or cry, the doctor's shouted orders or calls,
The glisten of the little steel instruments catching the glint of the torches,
These I resume as I chant, I see again the forms, I smell the odor,   20
Then hear outside the orders given, *Fall in, my men, fall in;*
But first I bend to the dying lad, his eyes open, a half-smile gives he me,
Then the eyes close, calmly close, and I speed forth to the darkness,
Resuming, marching, ever in darkness marching, on in the ranks,
The unknown road still marching.   25
1865

A Sight in Camp in the Daybreak
Gray and Dim

A sight in camp in the daybreak gray and dim,
As from my tent I emerge so early sleepless,
As slow I walk in the cool fresh air the path near by the hospital tent,
Three forms I see on stretchers lying, brought out there untended lying,
Over each the blanket spread, ample brownish woolen blanket,   5
Gray and heavy blanket, folding, covering all.

Curious I halt and silent stand,
Then with light fingers I from the face of the nearest the first just lift the blanket;
Who are you elderly man so gaunt and grim, with well-gray'd hair, and flesh all sunken about the eyes?
Who are you my dear comrade?   10

Then to the second I step—and who are you my child and darling?
Who are you sweet boy with cheeks yet blooming?

Then to the third—a face nor child nor old, very calm, as of beautiful yellow-white ivory;
Young man I think I know you—I think this face is the face of the Christ himself,
Dead and divine and brother of all, and here again he lies.   15
1865

The Wound-Dresser

1

An old man bending I come among new faces,
Years looking backward resuming in answer to children,
Come tell us old man, as from young men and maidens that love me,
(Arous'd and angry, I'd thought to beat the alarum, and urge relentless war,
But soon my fingers fail'd me, my face droop'd and I resign'd myself,   5
To sit by the wounded and soothe them, or silently watch the dead;)
Years hence of these scenes, of these furious passions, these chances,
Of unsurpass'd heroes, (was one side so brave? the other was equally brave;)
Now be witness again, paint the mightiest armies of earth,
Of those armies so rapid so wondrous what saw you to tell us?   10
What stays with you latest and deepest? of curious panics,
Of hard-fought engagements or sieges tremendous what deepest remains?

2

O maidens and young men I love and that love me,
What you ask of my days those the strangest and sudden your talking recalls,
Soldier alert I arrive after a long march cover'd with sweat and dust,   15
In the nick of time I come, plunge in the fight, loudly shout in the rush of
    successful charge,
Enter the captur'd works—yet lo, like a swift-running river they fade,
Pass and are gone they fade—I dwell not on soldiers' perils or soldier's joys,
(Both I remember well—many the hardships, few the joys, yet I was content.)

But in silence, in dreams' projections,   20
While the world of gain and appearance and mirth goes on,
So soon what is over forgotten, and waves wash the imprints off the sand,
With hinged knees returning I enter the doors, (while for you up there,
Whoever you are, follow without noise and be of strong heart.)

Bearing the bandages, water and sponge,   25
Straight and swift to my wounded I go,
Where they lie on the ground after the battle brought in,
Where their priceless blood reddens the grass the ground,
Or to the rows of the hospital tent, or under the roof'd hospital,
To the long rows of cots up and down each side I return,   30
To each and all one after another I draw near, not one do I miss,
An attendant follows holding a tray, he carries a refuse pail,
Soon to be fill'd with clotted rags and blood, emptied, and fill'd again.

I onward go, I stop,
With hinged knees and steady hand to dress wounds,   35

I am firm with each, the pangs are sharp yet unavoidable,
One turns to me his appealing eyes—poor boy! I never knew you,
Yet I think I could not refuse this moment to die for you, if that would save
   you.

3

On, and I go, (open doors of time! open hospital doors!)
The crush'd head I dress, (poor crazed hand tear not the bandage away,)   40
The neck of the cavalry-man with the bullet through and through I examine,
Hard the breathing rattles, quite glazed already the eye, yet life struggles hard,
(Come sweet death! be persuaded O beautiful death!
In mercy come quickly.)

From the stump of the arm, the amputated hand,   45
I undo the clotted lint, remove the slough, wash off the matter and blood,
Back on his pillow the soldier bends with curv'd neck and side-falling head,
His eyes are closed, his face is pale, he dares not look on the bloody stump,
And has not yet look'd on it.
I dress a wound in the side, deep, deep,   50
But a day or two more, for see the frame all wasted and sinking,
And the yellow-blue countenance see.

I dress the perforated shoulder, the foot with the bullet-wound,
Cleanse the one with a gnawing and putrid gangrene, so sickening, so offensive,
While the attendant stands behind aside me holding the tray and pail.   55

I am faithful, I do not give out,
The fractur'd thigh, the knee, the wound in the abdomen,
These and more I dress with impassive hand, (yet deep in my breast a fire, a
   burning flame.)

4

Thus in silence in dreams' projections,
Returning, resuming, I thread my way through the hospitals,   60
The hurt and wounded I pacify with soothing hand,
I sit by the restless all the dark night, some are so young,
Some suffer so much, I recall the experience sweet and sad,
(Many a soldier's loving arms about this neck have cross'd and rested,
Many a soldier's kiss dwells on these bearded lips.)   65
1865

Reconciliation

Word over all, beautiful as the sky,
Beautiful that war and all its deeds of carnage must in time be utterly lost,
That the hands of the sisters Death and Night incessantly softly wash again, and
    ever again, this soil'd world;
For my enemy is dead, a man divine as myself is dead,
I look where he lies white-faced and still in the coffin—I draw near,   5
Bend down and touch lightly with my lips the white face in the coffin.

1865–1866

from **Memories of President Lincoln**

When Lilacs Last in the Dooryard Bloom'd

1

When lilacs last in the dooryard bloom'd,
And the great star[43] early droop'd in the western sky in the night,
I mourn'd, and yet shall mourn with ever-returning spring.

Ever-returning spring, trinity sure to me you bring,
Lilac blooming perennial and drooping star in the west,   5
And thought of him I love.

2

O powerful western fallen star!
O shades of night—O moody, tearful night!
O great star disappear'd—O the black murk that hides the star!
O cruel hands that hold me powerless—O helpless soul of me!   10
O harsh surrounding cloud that will not free my soul.

3

In the dooryard fronting an old farm-house near the white-wash'd palings,
Stands the lilac-bush tall-growing with heart-shaped leaves of rich green,
With many a pointed blossom rising delicate, with the perfume strong I love,
With every leaf a miracle—and from this bush in the dooryard,   15
With delicate-color'd blossoms and heart-shaped leaves of rich green,
A sprig with its flower I break.

[43] I.e., the planet Venus.

4

In the swamp in secluded recesses,
A shy and hidden bird is warbling a song.

Solitary the thrush,   20
The hermit withdrawn to himself, avoiding the settlements,
Sings by himself a song.
Song of the bleeding throat,
Death's outlet song of life, (for well dear brother I know,
If thou wast not granted to sing thou would'st surely die.)   25

5

Over the breast of the spring, the land, amid cities,
Amid lanes and through old woods, where lately the violets peep'd from the
    ground, spotting the gray debris,
Amid the grass in the fields each side of the lanes, passing the endless grass,
Passing the yellow-spear'd wheat, every grain from its shroud in the
    dark-brown fields uprisen,
Passing the apple-tree blows of white and pink in the orchards,   30
Carrying a corpse to where it shall rest in the grave,
Night and day journeys a coffin.

6

Coffin that passes through lanes and streets,
Through day and night with the great cloud darkening the land,
With the pomp of the inloop'd flags with the cities draped in black,   35
With the show of the States themselves as of crape-veil'd women standing,
With processions long and winding and the flambeaus of the night,
With the countless torches lit, with the silent sea of faces and the unbared
    heads,
With the waiting depot, the arriving coffin, and the sombre faces,
With dirges through the night, with the thousand voices rising strong and
    solemn,
                                                                                                  40
With all the mournful voices of the dirges pour'd around the coffin,
The dim-lit churches and the shuddering organs—where amid these you
    journey,
With the tolling tolling bells' perpetual clang,
Here, coffin that slowly passes,
I give you my sprig of lilac.   45

7

(Nor for you, for one alone,
Blossoms and branches green to coffins all I bring,

For fresh as the morning, thus would I chant a song for you O sane and sacred
    death.

All over bouquets of roses,
O death, I cover you over with roses and early lilies,   50
But mostly and now the lilac that blooms the first,
Copious I break, I break the sprigs from the bushes,
With loaded arms I come, pouring for you,
For you and the coffins all of you O death.)

8

O western orb sailing the heaven,   55
Now I know what you must have meant as a month since I walk'd,
As I walk'd in silence the transparent shadowy night,
As I saw you had something to tell as you bent to me night after night,
As you droop'd from the sky low down as if to my side, (while the other stars
    all look'd on,)
As we wander'd together the solemn night, (for something I know not what
    kept me from sleep,)   60
As the night advanced, and I saw on the rim of the west how full you were of
    woe,
As I stood on the rising ground in the breeze in the cool transparent night,
As I watch'd where you pass'd and was lost in the netherward black of the
    night,
As my soul in its trouble dissatisfied sank, as where you sad orb,
Concluded, dropt in the night, and was gone.   65

9

Sing on there in the swamp,
O singer bashful and tender, I hear your notes, I hear your call,
I hear, I come presently, I understand you,
But a moment I linger, for the lustrous star has detain'd me,
The star my departing comrade holds and detains me.   70

10

O how shall I warble myself for the dead one there I loved?
And how shall I deck my song for the large sweet soul that has gone?
And what shall my perfume be for the grave of him I love?

Sea-winds blown from east and west,
Blown from the Eastern sea and blown from the Western sea, till there on the
    prairies meeting,   75
These and with these and the breath of my chant,
I'll perfume the grave of him I love.

11

O what shall I hang on the chamber walls?
And what shall the pictures be that I hang on the walls,
To adorn the burial-house of him I love?   80

Pictures of growing spring and farms and homes,
With the Fourth-month eve at sundown, and the gray smoke lucid and bright,
With floods of the yellow gold of the gorgeous, indolent, sinking sun, burning,
  expanding the air,
With the fresh sweet herbage under foot, and the pale green leaves of the trees
  prolific,
In the distance the flowing glaze, the breast of the river, with a wind-dapple
  here and there,   85
With ranging hills on the banks, with many a line against the sky, and
  shadows,
And the city at hand with dwellings so dense, and stacks of chimneys,
And all the scenes of life and the workshops, and the workmen homeward
  returning.

12

Lo, body and soul—this land,
My own Manhattan with spires, and the sparkling and hurrying tides, and the
  ships,   90
The varied and ample land, the South and the North in the light, Ohio's shores
  and flashing Missouri,
And ever the far-spreading prairies cover'd with grass and corn.

Lo, the most excellent sun so calm and haughty,
The violet and purple morn with just-felt breezes,
The gentle soft-born measureless light,   95
The miracle spreading bathing all, the fulfill'd noon,
The coming eve delicious, the welcome night and the stars,
Over my cities shining all, enveloping man and land.

13

Sing on, sing on you gray-brown bird,
Sing from the swamps, the recesses, pour your chant from the bushes,   100
Limitless out of the dusk, out of the cedars and pines.

Sing on dearest brother, warble your reedy song,
Loud human song, with voice of uttermost woe.

O liquid and free and tender!
O wild and loose to my soul—O wondrous singer!   105

You only I hear—yet the star holds me, (but will soon depart,)
Yet the lilac with mastering odor holds me.

14

Now while I sat in the day and look'd forth,
In the close of the day with its light and the fields of spring, and the farmers
    preparing their crops,
In the large unconscious scenery of my land with its lakes and forests,   110
In the heavenly aerial beauty, (after the perturb'd winds and the storms,)
Under the arching heavens of the afternoon swift passing, and the voices of
    children and women,
The many-moving sea-tides, and I saw the ships how they sail'd,
And the summer approaching with richness, and the fields all busy with labor,
And the infinite separate houses, how they all went on, each with its meals and
    minutia of daily usages,   115
And the streets how their throbbings throbb'd, and the cities pent—lo, then and
    there,
Falling upon them all and among them all, enveloping me with the rest,
Appear'd the cloud, appear'd the long black trail,
And I knew death, its thought, and the sacred knowledge of death.

Then with the knowledge of death as walking one side of me,   120
And the thought of death close-walking the other side of me,
And I in the middle as with companions, and as holding the hands of
    companions,
I fled forth to the hiding receiving night that talks not,
Down to the shores of the water, the path by the swamp in the dimness,
To the solemn shadowy cedars and ghostly pines so still.   125

And the singer so shy to the rest receiv'd me,
The gray-brown bird I know receiv'd us comrades three,
And he sang the carol of death, and a verse for him I love.

From deep secluded recesses,
From the fragrant cedars and the ghostly pines so still,   130
Came the carol of the bird.

And the charm of the carol rapt me,
As I held as if by their hands my comrades in the night,
And the voice of my spirit tallied the song of the bird.

Come lovely and soothing death,   135
Undulate round the world, serenely arriving, arriving,
In the day, in the night, to all, to each,
Sooner or later delicate death.

Prais'd be the fathomless universe,
For life and joy, and for objects and knowledge curious,   140
And for love, sweet love—but praise! praise! praise!
For the sure-enwinding arms of cool-enfolding death.

Dark mother always gliding near with soft feet,
Have none chanted for thee a chant of fullest welcome?
Then I chant it for thee, I glorify thee above all,   145
I bring thee a song that when thou must indeed come, come unfalteringly.

Approach strong deliveress,
When it is so, when thou hast taken them I joyously sing the dead,
Lost in the loving floating ocean of thee,
Laved in the flood of thy bliss O death.   150

From me to thee glad serenades,
Dances for thee I propose saluting thee, adornments and feastings for thee,
And the sights of the open landscape and the high-spread sky are fitting,
And life and the fields, and the huge and thoughtful night.

The night in silence under many a star,   155
The ocean shore and the husky whispering wave whose voice I know,
And the soul turning to thee O vast and well-veil'd death,
And the body gratefully nestling close to thee.

Over the tree-tops I float thee a song,
Over the rising and sinking waves, over the myriad fields and the prairies wide,   160
Over the dense-pack'd cities all and the teeming wharves and ways,
I float this carol with joy, with joy to thee O death.

15

To the tally of my soul,
Loud and strong kept up the gray-brown bird,
With pure deliberate notes spreading filling the night.   165

Loud in the pines and cedars dim,
Clear in the freshness moist and the swamp-perfume,
And I with my comrades there in the night.

While my sight that was bound in my eyes unclosed,
As to long panoramas of visions.   170
And I saw askant the armies,
I saw as in noiseless dreams hundreds of battle-flags,
Borne through the smoke of the battles and pierc'd with missiles I saw them,
And carried hither and yon through the smoke, and torn and bloody,

And at last but a few shreds left on the staffs, (and all in silence,)   175
And the staffs all splinter'd and broken.

I saw battle-corpses, myriads of them,
And the white skeletons of young men, I saw them,
I saw the debris and debris of all the slain soldiers of the war,
But I saw they were not as was thought,   180
They themselves were fully at rest, they suffer'd not,
The living remain'd and suffer'd, the mother suffer'd,
And the wife and the child and the musing comrade suffer'd,
And the armies that remain'd suffer'd.

16

Passing the visions, passing the night,   185
Passing, unloosing the hold of my comrades' hands,
Passing the song of the hermit bird and the tallying song of my soul,
Victorious song, death's outlet song, yet varying ever-altering song,
As low and wailing, yet clear the notes, rising and falling, flooding the night,
Sadly sinking and fainting, as warning and warning, and yet again bursting
        with joy,   190
Covering the earth and filling the spread of the heaven,
As that powerful psalm in the night I heard from recesses,
Passing, I leave thee lilac with heart-shaped leaves,
I leave thee there in the door-yard, blooming, returning with spring.

I cease from my song for thee,   195
From my gaze on thee in the west, fronting the west, communing with thee,
O comrade lustrous with silver face in the night.
Yet each to keep and all, retrievements out of the night,
The song, the wondrous chant of the gray-brown bird,
And the tallying chant, the echo arous'd in my soul,   200
With the lustrous and drooping star with the countenance full of woe,
With the holders holding my hand nearing the call of the bird,
Comrades mine and I in the midst, and their memory ever to keep, for the
        dead I loved so well,
For the sweetest, wisest soul of all my days and lands—and this for his dear
        sake,
Lilac and star and bird twined with the chant of my soul,   205
There in the fragrant pines and the cedars dusk and dim.

1865–1866

O Captain! My Captain!

O Captain! my Captain! our fearful trip is done,
The ship has weather'd every rack, the prize we sought is won,
The port is near, the bells I hear, the people all exulting,

While follow eyes the steady keel, the vessel grim and daring;
    But O heart! heart! heart!
        O the bleeding drops of red,   5
            Where on the deck my Captain lies,
            Fallen cold and dead.

O Captain! my Captain! rise up and hear the bells;
Rise up—for you the flag is flung—for you the bugle trills,   10
For you bouquets and ribbon'd wreaths—for you the shores a-crowding,
For you they call, the swaying mass, their eager faces turning;
    Here Captain! dear father!
        This arm beneath your head!
            It is some dream that on the deck,   15
            You've fallen cold and dead.

My Captain does not answer, his lips are pale and still,
My father does not feel my arm, he has no pulse nor will,
The ship is anchor'd safe and sound, its voyage closed and done,
From fearful trip the victor ship comes in with object won;   20
    Exult O shores, and ring O bells!
        But I with mournful tread,
            Walk the deck my Captain lies,
            Fallen cold and dead.

1865–1866

from Autumn Rivulets

There Was a Child Went Forth

There was a child went forth every day,
And the first object he look'd upon, that object he became,
And that object became part of him for the day or a certain part of the day,
Or for many years or stretching cycles of years.

The early lilacs became part of this child,   5
And grass and white and red morning-glories, and white and red clover, and
    the song of the phœbe-bird,
And the Third-month lambs and the sow's pink-faint litter, and the mare's foal
    and the cow's calf,
And the noisy brood of the barnyard or by the mire of the pond-side,
And the fish suspending themselves so curiously below there, and the beautiful
    curious liquid,
And the water-plants with their graceful flat heads, all became part of him.   10

The field-sprouts of Fourth-month and Fifth-month became part of him,
Winter-grain sprouts and those of the light-yellow corn, and the esculent roots
    of the garden,

And the apple-trees cover'd with blossoms and the fruit afterward, and
    wood-berries, and the commonest weeds by the road,
And the old drunkard staggering home from the outhouse of the tavern whence
    he had lately risen,
And the schoolmistress that pass'd on her way to the school,   15
And the friendly boys that pass'd, and the quarrelsome boys,
And the tidy and fresh-cheek'd girls, and the barefoot negro boy and girl,
And all the changes of city and country wherever he went.

His own parents, he that had father'd him and she that had conceiv'd him in
    her womb and birth'd him,
They gave this child more of themselves than that,   20
They gave him afterward every day, they became part of him.

The mother at home quietly placing the dishes on the supper-table,
The mother with mild words, clean her cap and gown, a wholesome odor
    falling off her person and clothes as she walks by,
The father, strong, self-sufficient, manly, mean, anger'd, unjust,
The blow, the quick loud word, the tight bargain, the crafty lure,   25
The family usages, the language, the company, the furniture, the yearning and
    swelling heart,
Affection that will not be gainsay'd, the sense of what is real, the thought if
    after all it should prove unreal,
The doubts of day-time and the doubts of night-time, the curious whether and
    how,
Whether that which appears so is so, or is it all flashes and specks?
Men and women crowding fast in the streets, if they are not flashes and specks
    what are they?   30
The streets themselves and the façades of houses, and goods in the windows,
Vehicles, teams, the heavy-plank'd wharves, the huge crossing at the ferries,
The village on the highland seen from afar at sunset, the river between,
Shadows, aureola and mist, the light falling on roofs and gables of white or
    brown two miles off,
The schooner near by sleepily dropping down the tide, the little boat
    slack-tow'd astern,   35
The hurrying tumbling waves, quick-broken crests, slapping,
The strata of color'd clouds, the long bar of maroon-tint away solitary by itself,
    the spread of purity it lies motionless in,
The horizon's edge, the flying sea-crow, the fragrance of salt marsh and shore
    mud,
These became part of that child who went forth every day, and who now goes,
    and will always go forth every day.

1855

This Compost

1

Something startles me where I thought I was safest,
I withdraw from the still woods I loved,
I will not go now on the pastures to walk,
I will not strip the clothes from my body to meet my lover the sea,
I will not touch my flesh to the earth as to other flesh to renew me.   5

O how can it be that the ground itself does not sicken?
How can you be alive you growths of spring?
How can you furnish health you blood of herbs, roots, orchards, grain?
Are they not continually putting distemper'd corpses within you?
Is not every continent work'd over and over with sour dead?   10

Where have you disposed of their carcasses?
Those drunkards and gluttons of so many generations?
Where have you drawn off all the foul liquid and meat?
I do not see any of it upon you to-day, or perhaps I am deceiv'd,
I will run a furrow with my plough, I will press my spade through the sod and
    turn it up underneath,   15
I am sure I shall expose some of the foul meat.

2

Behold this compost! behold it well!
Perhaps every mite has once form'd part of a sick person—yet behold!
The grass of spring covers the prairies,
The bean bursts noiselessly through the mould in the garden,   20
The delicate spear of the onion pierces upward,
The apple-buds cluster together on the apple-branches,
The resurrection of the wheat appears with pale visage out of its graves,
The tinge awakes over the willow-tree and the mulberry-tree,
The he-birds carol mornings and evenings while the she-birds sit on their nests,   25
The young of poultry break through the hatch'd eggs,
The new-born of animals appear, the calf is dropt from the cow, the colt from
    the mare,
Out of its little hill faithfully rise the potato's dark green leaves,
Out of its hill rises the yellow maize-stalk, the lilacs bloom in the dooryards,
The summer growth is innocent and disdainful above all those strata of sour
    dead.   30

What chemistry!
That the winds are really not infectious,
That this is no cheat, this transparent green-wash of the sea which is so amorous
    after me,

That it is safe to allow it to lick my naked body all over with its tongues,
That it will not endanger me with the fevers that have deposited themselves in
    it,   35
That all is clean forever and forever,
That the cool drink from the well tastes so good,
That blackberries are so flavorous and juicy,
That the fruits of the apple-orchard and the orange-orchard, that melons, grapes,
    peaches, plums, will none of them poison me,
That when I recline on the grass I do not catch any disease,   40
Though probably every spear of grass rises out of what was once a catching
    disease.

Now I am terrified at the Earth, it is that calm and patient,
It grows such sweet things out of such corruptions,
It turns harmless and stainless on its axis, with such endless successions of
    diseas'd corpses,
It distills such exquisite winds out of such infused fetor,   45
It renews with such unwitting looks its prodigal, annual, sumptuous crops,
It gives such divine materials to men, and accepts such leavings from them at
    last.

1856

Passage to India

1

Singing my days,
Singing the great achievements of the present,
Singing the strong light works of engineers,
Our modern wonders, (the antique ponderous Seven outvied,)
In the Old World the east the Suez canal,[44]   5
The New by its mighty railroad spann'd,
The seas inlaid with eloquent gentle wires;[45]
Yet first to sound, and ever sound, the cry with thee O soul,
The Past! the Past! the Past!

The Past—the dark unfathom'd retrospect!   10
The teeming gulf—the sleepers and the shadows!
The past—the infinite greatness of the past!
For what is the present after all but a growth out of the past?
(As a projectile form'd, impell'd, passing a certain line, still keeps on,
So the present, utterly form'd, impell'd by the past.)   15

[44] Opened in 1869.
[45] The transcontinental railroad link was   completed in 1869 and the Atlantic Cable successfully completed in 1866.

2

Passage O soul to India!
Eclaircise[46] the myths Asiatic, the primitive fables.

Not you alone proud truths of the world,
Nor you alone ye facts of modern science,
But myths and fables of eld, Asia's, Africa's fables,   20
The far-darting beams of the spirit, the unloos'd dreams,
The deep diving bibles and legends,
The daring plots of the poets, the elder religions;
O you temples fairer than lilies pour'd over by the rising sun!
O you fables spurning the known, eluding the hold of the known, mounting to
     heaven!   25
You lofty and dazzling towers, pinnacled, red as roses, burnish'd with gold!
Towers of fables immortal fashion'd from mortal dreams!
You too I welcome and fully the same as the rest!
You too with joy I sing.
Passage to India!   30
Lo, soul, seest thou not God's purpose from the first?
The earth to be spann'd, connected by network,
The races, neighbors, to marry and be given in marriage,
The oceans to be cross'd, the distant brought near,
The lands to be welded together.   35

A worship new I sing,
You captains, voyagers, explorers, yours,
You engineers, you architects, machinists, yours,
You, not for trade or transportation only,
But in God's name, and for thy sake O soul.   40

3

Passage to India!
Lo soul for thee of tableaus twain,
I see in one the Suez canal initiated, open'd,
I see the procession of steamships, the Empress Eugenie's[47] leading the van,
I mark from on deck the strange landscape, the pure sky, the level sand in the
     distance,   45
I pass swiftly the picturesque groups, the workmen gather'd,
The gigantic dredging machines.

In one again, different, (yet thine, all thine, O soul, the same,)
I see over my own continent the Pacific railroad surmounting every barrier,

---

[46] French: "clarify."   [47] Empress Eugenie was the wife of Napoleon III.

I see continual trains of cars winding along the Platte carrying freight and
    passengers,   50
I hear the locomotives rushing and roaring, and the shrill steam-whistle,
I hear the echoes reverberate through the grandest scenery in the world,
I cross the Laramie plains, I note the rocks in grotesque shapes, the buttes,
I see the plentiful larkspur and wild onions, the barren, colorless, sage-deserts,
I see in glimpses afar or towering immediately above me the great mountains, I
    see the Wind river and the Wahsatch mountains,   55
I see the Monument mountain and the Eagle's Nest, I pass the Promontory, I
    ascend the Nevadas,
I scan the noble Elk mountain and wind around its base,
I see the Humboldt range, I thread the valley and cross the river,
I see the clear waters of lake Tahoe, I see forests of majestic pines,
Or crossing the great desert, the alkaline plains, I behold enchanting mirages of
    waters and meadows,   60
Marking through these and after all, in duplicate slender lines,
Bridging the three or four thousand miles of land travel,
Tying the Eastern to the Western sea,
The road between Europe and Asia.

(Ah Genoese[48] thy dream! thy dream!   65
Centuries after thou art laid in thy grave,
The shore thou foundest verifies thy dream.)

4

Passage to India!
Struggles of many a captain, tales of many a sailor dead,
Over my mood stealing and spreading they come,   70
Like clouds and cloudlets in the unreach'd sky.

Along all history, down the slopes,
As a rivulet running, sinking now, and now again to the surface rising,
A ceaseless thought, a varied train—lo, soul, to thee, thy sight, they rise,
The plans, the voyages again, the expeditions;   75
Again Vasco de Gama sails forth,
Again the knowledge gain'd, the mariner's compass,
Lands found and nations born, thou born America,
For purpose vast, man's long probation fill'd,
Thou rondure of the world at last accomplish'd.   80

5

O vast Rondure, swimming in space,
Cover'd all over with visible power and beauty,

[48] I.e., Christopher Columbus.

Alternate light and day and the teeming spiritual darkness,
Unspeakable high processions of sun and moon and countless stars above,
Below, the manifold grass and waters, animals, mountains, trees,   85
With inscrutable purpose, some hidden prophetic intention,
Now first it seems my thought begins to span thee.

Down from the gardens of Asia descending radiating,
Adam and Eve appear, then their myriad progeny after them,
Wandering, yearning, curious, with restless explorations,   90
With questionings, baffled, formless, feverish, with never-happy hearts,
With that sad incessant refrain, *Wherefore unsatisfied soul?* and *Whither O
    mocking life?*

Ah who shall soothe these feverish children?
Who justify these restless explorations?
Who speak the secret of impassive earth?   95
Who bind it to us? what is this separate Nature so unnatural?
What is this earth to our affections? (unloving earth, without a throb to answer
    ours,
Cold earth, the place of graves.)

Yet soul be sure the first intent remains, and shall be carried out,
Perhaps even now the time has arrived.   100

After the seas are all cross'd, (as they seem already cross'd,)
After the great captains and engineers have accomplish'd their work,
After the noble inventors, after the scientists, the chemist, the geologist,
    ethnologist,
Finally shall come the poet worthy that name,
The true son of God shall come singing his songs.   105

Then not your deeds only O voyagers, O scientists and inventors, shall be
    justified,
All these hearts as of fretted children shall be sooth'd,
All affection shall be fully responded to, the secret shall be told,
All these separations and gaps shall be taken up and hook'd and link'd together,
The whole earth, this cold, impassive, voiceless earth, shall be completely
    justified,   110
Trinitas divine shall be gloriously accomplish'd and compacted by the true son
    of God, the poet,
(He shall indeed pass the straits and conquer the mountains,
He shall double the cape of Good Hope to some purpose,)
Nature and Man shall be disjoin'd and diffused no more,
The true son of God shall absolutely fuse them.   115

6

Year at whose wide-flung door I sing!
Year of the purpose accomplish'd!
Year of the marriage of continents, climates and oceans!
(No mere doge of Venice now wedding the Adriatic,)
I see O year in you the vast terraqueous globe given and giving all,   120
Europe to Asia, Africa join'd, and they to the New World,
The lands, geographies, dancing before you, holding a festival garland,
As brides and bridegrooms hand in hand.

Passage to India!
Cooling airs from Caucasus far, soothing cradle of man,   125
The river Euphrates flowing, the past lit up again.

Lo soul, the retrospect brought forward,
The old, most populous, wealthiest of earth's lands,
The streams of the Indus and the Ganges and their many affluents,
(I my shores of America walking to-day behold, resuming all,)   130
The tale of Alexander[49] on his warlike marches suddenly dying,
On one side China and on the other side Persia and Arabia,
To the south the great seas and the bay of Bengal,
The flowing literatures, tremendous epics, religions, castes,
Old occult Brahma interminably far back, the tender and junior Buddha,   135
Central and southern empires and all their belongings, possessors,
The wars of Tamerlane, the reign of Aurungzebe,
The traders, rulers, explorers, Moslems, Venetians, Byzantium, the Arabs,
    Portuguese,
The first travelers famous yet, Marco Polo, Batouta the Moor,
Doubts to be solv'd, the map incognita, blanks to be fill'd,   140
The foot of man unstay'd, the hands never at rest,
Thyself O soul that will not brook a challenge.

The mediæval navigators rise before me,
The world of 1492, with its awaken'd enterprise,
Something swelling in humanity now like the sap of the earth in spring,   145
The sunset splendor of chivalry declining.

And who art thou sad shade?
Gigantic, visionary, thyself a visionary,
With majestic limbs and pious beaming eyes,
Spreading around with every look of thine a golden world,   150
Enhuing it with gorgeous hues.

---

[49] Alexander the Great (356–323 B.C.)

As the chief histrion,
Down to the footlights walks in some great scena,
Dominating the rest I see the Admiral himself,
(History's type of courage, action, faith,)
Behold him sail from Palos leading his little fleet,   155
His voyage behold, his return, his great fame,
His misfortunes, calumniators, behold him a prisoner, chain'd,
Behold his dejection, poverty, death.

(Curious in time I stand, noting the efforts of heroes,   160
Is the deferment long? bitter the slander, poverty, death?
Lies the seed unreck'd for centuries in the ground? lo, to God's due occasion,
Uprising in the night, it sprouts, blooms,
And fills the earth with use and beauty.)

7.

Passage indeed O soul to primal thought,   165
Not lands and seas alone, thy own clear freshness,
The young maturity of brood and bloom,
To realms of budding bibles.

O soul, repressless, I with thee and thou with me,
Thy circumnavigation of the world begin,   170
Of man, the voyage of his mind's return,
To reason's early paradise,
Back, back to wisdom's birth, to innocent intuitions,
Again with fair creation.

8.

O we can wait no longer,   175
We too take ship O soul,
Joyous we too launch out on trackless seas,
Fearless for unknown shores on waves of ecstasy to sail,
Amid the wafting winds, (thou pressing me to thee, I thee to me, O soul,)
Caroling free, singing our song of God,   180
Chanting our chant of pleasant exploration.

With laugh and many a kiss,
(Let others deprecate, let others weep for sin, remorse, humiliation,)
O soul thou pleasest me, I thee.

Ah more than any priest O soul we too believe in God,   185
But with the mystery of God we dare not dally.

O soul thou pleasest me, I thee,
Sailing these seas or on the hills, or waking in the night,
Thoughts, silent thoughts, of Time and Space and Death, like waters flowing,
Bear me indeed as through the regions infinite,   190
Whose air I breathe, whose ripples hear, lave me all over,
Bathe me O God in thee, mounting to thee,
I and my soul to range in range of thee.
O Thou transcendent,
Nameless, the fibre and the breath,   195
Light of the light, shedding forth universes, thou centre of them,
Thou mightier centre of the true, the good, the loving,
Thou moral, spiritual fountain—affection's source—thou reservoir,
(O pensive soul of me—O thirst unsatisfied—waitest not there?
Waitest not haply for us somewhere there the Comrade perfect?)   200
Thou pulse—thou motive of the stars, suns, systems,
That, circling, move in order, safe, harmonious,
Athwart the shapeless vastnesses of space,
How should I think, how breathe a single breath, how speak, if, out of myself,
I could not launch, to those, superior universes?   205

Swiftly I shrivel at the thought of God,
At Nature and its wonders, Time and Space and Death,
But that I, turning, call to thee O soul, thou actual Me,
And lo, thou gently masterest the orbs,
Thou matest Time, smilest content at Death,   210
And fillest, swellest full the vastnesses of Space.

Greater than stars or suns,
Bounding O soul thou journeyest forth;
What love than thine and ours could wider amplify?
What aspirations, wishes, outvie thine and ours O soul?   215
What dreams of the ideal? What plans of purity, perfection, strength?
What cheerful willingness for others' sake to give up all?
For others' sake to suffer all?

Reckoning ahead O soul, when thou, the time achiev'd,
The seas all cross'd, weather'd the capes, the voyage done,   220
Surrounded, copest, frontest God, yieldest, the aim attain'd,
As fill'd with friendship, love complete, the Elder Brother found,
The Younger melts in fondness in his arms.

9

Passage to more than India!
Are thy wings plumed indeed for such far flights?   225
O soul, voyagest thou indeed on voyages like those?
Disportest thou on waters such as those?

Soundest below the Sanscrit and the Vedas?
Then have thy bent unleash'd.

Passage to you, your shores, ye aged fierce enigmas!   230
Passage to you, to mastership of you, ye strangling problems!
You, strew'd with the wrecks of skeletons, that, living, never reach'd you.

Passage to more than India!
O secret of the earth and sky!
Of you O waters of the sea! O winding creeks and rivers!   235
Of you O woods and fields! of you strong mountains of my land!
Of you O prairies! of you gray rocks!
O morning red! O clouds! O rain and snows!
O day and night, passage to you!

O sun and moon and all you stars! Sirius and Jupiter!   240
Passage to you!

Passage, immediate passage! the blood burns in my veins!
Away O soul! hoist instantly the anchor!
Cut the hawsers—haul out—shake out every sail!
Have we not stood here like trees in the ground long enough?   245
Have we not grovel'd here long enough, eating and drinking like mere brutes?
Have we not darken'd and dazed ourselves with books long enough?

Sail forth—steer for the deep waters only,
Reckless O soul, exploring, I with thee, and thou with me,
For we are bound where mariner has not yet dared to go,   250
And we will risk the ship, ourselves and all.
O my brave soul!
O farther farther sail!
O daring joy, but safe! are they not all the seas of God?
O farther, farther, farther sail!   255
1871

The Sleepers

1

I wander all night in my vision,
Stepping with light feet, swiftly and noiselessly stepping and stopping,
Bending with open eyes over the shut eyes of sleepers,
Wandering and confused, lost to myself, ill-assorted, contradictory,
Pausing, gazing, bending, and stopping.   5

How solemn they look there, stretch'd and still,
How quiet they breathe, the little children in their cradles.

The wretched features of ennuyés,[50] the white features of corpses, the livid faces
    of drunkards, the sick-gray faces of onanists,
The gash'd bodies on battle-fields, the insane in their strong-door'd rooms, the
    sacred idiots, the new-born emerging from gates, and the dying emerging
    from gates,
The night pervades them and infolds them.   10
The married couple sleep calmly in their bed, he with his palm on the hip of
    the wife, and she with her palm on the hip of the husband,
The sisters sleep lovingly side by side in their bed,
The men sleep lovingly side by side in theirs,
And the mother sleeps with her little child carefully wrapt.

The blind sleep, and the deaf and dumb sleep,   15
The prisoner sleeps well in the prison, the runaway son sleeps,
The murderer that is to be hung next day, how does he sleep?
And the murder'd person, how does he sleep?

The female that loves unrequited sleeps,
And the male that loves unrequited sleeps,   20
The head of the money-maker that plotted all day sleeps,
And the enraged and treacherous dispositions, all, all sleep.

I stand in the dark with drooping eyes by the worst-suffering and the most
    restless,
I pass my hands soothingly to and fro a few inches from them,
The restless sink in their beds, they fitfully sleep.   25

Now I pierce the darkness, new beings appear,
The earth recedes from me into the night,
I saw that it was beautiful, and I see that what is not the earth is beautiful.

I go from bedside to bedside, I sleep close with the other sleepers each in turn,
I dream in my dream all the dreams of the other dreamers,   30
And I become the other dreamers.

I am a dance—play up there! the fit is whirling me fast!

I am the ever-laughing—it is new moon and twilight,
I see the hiding of douceurs,[51] I see nimble ghosts whichever way I look,
Cache[52] and cache again deep in the ground and sea, and where it is neither
    ground nor sea.   35
Well do they do their jobs those journeymen divine,
Only from me can they hide nothing, and would not if they could,
I reckon I am their boss and they make me a pet besides,

---

[50] French: "bored persons."
[51] French: "delights."
[52] Hide (from French *cacher*: "to hide").

And surround me and lead me and run ahead when I walk,
To lift their cunning covers to signify me with stretch'd arms, and resume the
    way;   40
Onward we move, a gay gang of blackguards! with mirth-shouting music and
    wild-flapping pennants of joy!

I am the actor, the actress, the voter, the politician,
The emigrant and the exile, the criminal that stood in the box,
He who has been famous and he who shall be famous after to-day,
The stammerer, the well-form'd person, the wasted or feeble person.   45

I am she who adorn'd herself and folded her hair expectantly,
My truant lover has come, and it is dark.

Double yourself and receive me darkness,
Receive me and my lover too, he will not let me go without him.

I roll myself upon you as upon a bed, I resign myself to the dusk.   50

He whom I call answers me and takes the place of my lover,
He rises with me silently from the bed.

Darkness, you are gentler than my lover, his flesh was sweaty and panting,
I feel the hot moisture yet that he left me.

My hands are spread forth, I pass them in all directions,   55
I would sound up the shadowy shore to which you are journeying.

Be careful darkness! already what was it touch'd me?
I thought my lover had gone, else darkness and he are one,
I hear the heart-beat, I follow, I fade away.

2

I descend my western course, my sinews are flaccid,   60
Perfume and youth course through me and I am their wake.

It is my face yellow and wrinkled instead of the old woman's,
I sit low in a straw-bottom chair and carefully darn my grandson's stockings.

It is I too, the sleepless widow looking out on the winter midnight,
I see the sparkles of starshine on the icy and pallid earth.   65

A shroud I see and I am the shroud, I wrap a body and lie in the coffin,
It is dark here under ground, it is not evil or pain here, it is blank here, for
    reasons.

(It seems to me that every thing in the light and air ought to be happy,
Whoever is not in his coffin and the dark grave let him know he has enough.)

3

I see a beautiful gigantic swimmer swimming naked through the eddies of the
    sea,   70
His brown hair lies close and even to his head, he strikes out with courageous
    arms, he urges himself with his legs,
I see his white body, I see his undaunted eyes,
I hate the swift-running eddies that would dash him head-foremost on the
    rocks.

What are you doing you ruffianly red-trickled waves?
Will you kill the courageous giant? will you kill him in the prime of his
    middle age?   75

Steady and long he struggles,
He is baffled, bang'd, bruis'd, he holds out while his strength holds out,
The slapping eddies are spotted with his blood, they bear him away, they roll
    him, swing him, turn him,
His beautiful body is borne in the circling eddies, it is continually bruis'd on
    rocks,
Swiftly and out of sight is borne the brave corpse.   80

4

I turn but do not extricate myself,
Confused, a past-reading, another, but with darkness yet.

The beach is cut by the razory ice-wind, the wreck-guns sound,
The tempest lulls, the moon comes floundering through the drifts.

I look where the ship helplessly heads end on, I hear the burst as she strikes, I
    hear the howls of dismay, they grow fainter and fainter.   85

I cannot aid with my wringing fingers,
I can but rush to the surf and let it drench me and freeze upon me.

I search with the crowd, not one of the company is wash'd to us alive,
In the morning I help pick up the dead and lay them in rows in a barn.

5

Now of the older war-days, the defeat at Brooklyn,[53]   90
Washington stands inside the lines, he stands on the intrench'd hills amid a
   crowd of officers,
His face is cold and damp, he cannot repress the weeping drops,
He lifts the glass perpetually to his eyes, the color is blanch'd from his cheeks,
He sees the slaughter of the southern braves confided to him by their parents.

The same at last and at last when peace is declared,   95
He stands in the room of the old tavern,[54] the well-belov'd soldiers all pass
   through,
The officers speechless and slow draw near in their turns,
The chief encircles their necks with his arm and kisses them on the cheek,
He kisses lightly the wet cheeks one after another, he shakes hands and bids
   good-by to the army.

6

Now what my mother told me one day as we sat at dinner together,   100
Of when she was a nearly grown girl living home with her parents on the old
   homestead.

A red squaw came one breakfast-time to the old homestead,
On her back she carried a bundle of rushes for rush-bottoming chairs,
Her hair, straight, shiny, coarse, black, profuse, half-envelop'd her face,
Her step was free and elastic, and her voice sounded exquisitely as she spoke.   105

My mother look'd in delight and amazement at the stranger,
She look'd at the freshness of her tall-borne face and full and pliant limbs,
The more she look'd upon her she loved her,
Never before had she seen such wonderful beauty and purity,
She made her sit on a bench by the jamb of the fireplace, she cook'd food for
   her,   110
She had no work to give her, but she gave her remembrance and fondness.

The red squaw staid all the forenoon, and toward the middle of the afternoon
   she went away,
O my mother was loth to have her go away,
All the week she thought of her, she watch'd for her many a month,
She remember'd her many a winter and many a summer,   115
But the red squaw never came nor was heard of there again.

<hr>

[53] In the battle of Long Island, August 1776.   [54] Fraunces Tavern in New York City.

7

A show of the summer softness—a contact of something unseen—an amour of
  the light and air,
I am jealous and overwhelm'd with friendliness,
And will go gallivant with the light and air myself.

O love and summer, you are in the dreams and in me,   120
Autumn and winter are in the dreams, the farmer goes with his thrift,
The droves and crops increase, the barns are well-fill'd.

Elements merge in the night, ships make tacks in the dreams,
The sailor sails, the exile returns home,
The fugitive returns unharm'd, the immigrant is back beyond months and years, 125
The poor Irishman lives in the simple house of his childhood with the
  well-known neighbors and faces,
They warmly welcome him, he is barefoot again, he forgets he is well off,
The Dutchman voyages home, and the Scotchman and Welshman voyage home,
  and the native of the Mediterranean voyages home,
To every port of England, France, Spain, enter well-fill'd ships,
The Swiss foots it toward his hills, the Prussian goes his way, the Hungarian his
  way, and the Pole his way,   130
The Swede returns, and the Dane and Norwegian return.

The homeward bound and the outward bound,
The beautiful lost swimmer, the ennuyé, the onanist, the female that loves
  unrequited, the money-maker,
The actor and actress, those through with their parts and those waiting to
  commence,
The affectionate boy, the husband and wife, the voter, the nominee that is
  chosen and the nominee that has fail'd,   135
The great already known and the great any time after to-day,
The stammerer, the sick, the perfect-form'd, the homely,
The criminal that stood in the box, the judge that sat and sentenced him, the
  fluent lawyers, the jury, the audience,
The laugher and weeper, the dancer, the midnight widow, the red squaw,
The consumptive, the erysipalite, the idiot, he that is wrong'd,   140
The antipodes, and every one between this and them in the dark,
I swear they are averaged now—one is no better than the other,
The night and sleep have liken'd them and restored them.

I swear they are all beautiful,
Every one that sleeps is beautiful, every thing in the dim light is beautiful,   145
The wildest and bloodiest is over, and all is peace.

Peace is always beautiful,
The myth of heaven indicates peace and night.

The myth of heaven indicates the soul,
The soul is always beautiful, it appears more or it appears less, it comes or it
    lags behind,   150
It comes from its embower'd garden and looks pleasantly on itself and encloses
    the world,
Perfect and clean the genitals previously jetting, and perfect and clean the
    womb cohering,
The head well-grown proportion'd and plumb, and the bowels and joints
    proportion'd and plumb.

The soul is always beautiful,
The universe is duly in order, every thing is in its place,   155
What has arrived is in its place and what waits shall be in its place,
The twisted skull waits, the watery or rotten blood waits,
The child of the glutton or venerealee waits long, and the child of the
    drunkard waits long, and the drunkard himself waits long,
The sleepers that lived and died wait, the far advanced are to go on in their
    turns, and the far behind are to come on in their turns,
The diverse shall be no less diverse, but they shall flow and unite—they unite
    now.   160

8

The sleepers are very beautiful as they lie unclothed,
They flow hand in hand over the whole earth from east to west as they lie
    unclothed,
The Asiatic and African are hand in hand, the European and American are hand
    in hand,
Learn'd and unlearn'd are hand in hand, and male and female are hand in hand,
The bare arm of the girl crosses the bare breast of her lover, they press close
    without lust, his lips press her neck,   165
The father holds his grown or ungrown son in his arms with measureless love,
    and the son holds the father in his arms with measureless love,
The white hair of the mother shines on the white wrist of the daughter,
The breath of the boy goes with the breath of the man, friend is inarm'd by
    friend,
The scholar kisses the teacher and the teacher kisses the scholar, the wrong'd is
    made right,
The call of the slave is one with the master's call, and the master salutes the
    slave,   170
The felon steps forth from the prison, the insane becomes sane, the suffering of
    sick persons is reliev'd,
The sweatings and fevers stop, the throat that was unsound is sound, the lungs
    of the consumptive are resumed, the poor distress'd head is free,
The joints of the rheumatic move as smoothly as ever, and smoother than ever,
Stiflings and passages open, the paralyzed become supple,
The swell'd and convuls'd and congested awake to themselves in condition, 175

They pass the invigoration of the night and the chemistry of the night, and
    awake.

I too pass from the night,
I stay a while away O night, but I return to you again and love you.

Why should I be afraid to trust myself to you?
I am not afraid, I have been well brought forward by you,   180
I love the rich running day, but I do not desert her in whom I lay so long,
I know not how I came of you and I know not where I go with you, but I
    know I came well and shall go well.

I will stop only a time with the night, and rise betimes,
I will duly pass the day O my mother, and duly return to you.

1855

from **Whispers of Heavenly Death**
A Noiseless Patient Spider

A noiseless patient spider,
I mark'd where on a little promontory it stood isolated,
Mark'd how to explore the vacant vast surrounding,
It launch'd forth filament, filament, filament, out of itself,
Ever unreeling them, ever tirelessly speeding them.   5

And you O my soul where you stand,
Surrounded, detached, in measureless oceans of space,
Ceaselessly musing, venturing, throwing, seeking the spheres to connect them,
Till the bridge you will need be form'd, till the ductile anchor hold,
Till the gossamer thread you fling catch somewhere, O my soul.   10

1868

from **From Noon to Starry Night**
To a Locomotive in Winter

Thee for my recitative,
Thee in the driving storm even as now, the snow, the winter-day declining,
Thee in thy panoply, thy measur'd dual throbbing and thy beat convulsive,
Thy black cylindric body, golden brass and silvery steel,
Thy ponderous side-bars, parallel and connecting rods, gyrating, shuttling at thy
    sides,   5
Thy metrical, now swelling pant and roar, now tapering in the distance,
Thy great protruding head-light fix'd in front,
Thy long, pale, floating vapor-pennants, tinged with delicate purple,

The dense and murky clouds out-belching from thy smokestack,
Thy knitted frame, thy springs and valves, the tremulous twinkle of thy wheels,   10
Thy train of cars behind, obedient, merrily following,
Through gale or calm, now swift, now slack, yet steadily careering;
Type of the modern—emblem of motion and power—pulse of the continent,
For once come serve the Muse and merge in verse, even as here I see thee,
With storm and buffeting gusts of wind and falling snow,   15
By day thy warning ringing bell to sound its notes,
By night thy silent signal lamps to swing.

Fierce-throated beauty!
Roll through my chant with all thy lawless music, thy swinging lamps at night,
Thy madly-whistled laughter, echoing, rumbling like an earth-quake, rousing
    all,   20
Law of thyself complete, thine own track firmly holding,
(No sweetness debonair of tearful harp or glib piano thine,)
Thy trills of shrieks by rocks and hills return'd,
Launch'd o'er the prairies wide, across the lakes,
To the free skies unpent and glad and strong.   25
1876

from **Songs of Parting**

Joy, Shipmate, Joy!

Joy, shipmate, joy!
(Pleas'd to my soul at death I cry,)
Our life is closed, our life begins,
The long, long anchorage we leave,
The ship is clear at last, she leaps!   5
She swiftly courses from the shore,
Joy, shipmate, joy!
1871

So Long!

To conclude, I announce what comes after me.

I remember I said before my leaves sprang at all,
I would raise my voice jocund and strong with reference to consummations.

When America does what was promis'd,
When through these States walk a hundred millions of superb persons,   5
When the rest part away for superb persons and contribute to them,
When breeds of the most perfect mothers denote America,
Then to me and mine our due fruition.

I have press'd through in my own right,
I have sung the body and the soul, war and peace have I sung, and the songs of
    life and death,   10
And the songs of birth, and shown that there are many births.

I have offer'd my style to every one, I have journey'd with confident step;
While my pleasure is yet at the full I whisper *So long!*
And take the young woman's hand and the young man's hand for the last time.

I announce natural persons to arise,   15
I announce justice triumphant,
I announce uncompromising liberty and equality,
I announce the justification of candor and the justification of pride.
I announce that the identity of these States is a single identity only,
I announce the Union more and more compact, indissoluble,   20
I announce splendors and majesties to make all the previous politics of the earth
    insignificant.

I announce adhesiveness,[55] I say it shall be limitless, unloosen'd,
I say you shall yet find the friend you were looking for.

I announce a man or woman coming, perhaps you are the one, (*So long!*)
I announce the great individual, fluid as Nature, chaste, affectionate,
    compassionate, fully arm'd.   25

I announce a life that shall be copious, vehement, spiritual, bold,
I announce an end that shall lightly and joyfully meet its translation.

I announce myriads of youths, beautiful, gigantic, sweetblooded,
I announce a race of splendid and savage old men.

O thicker and faster—(*So long!*)   30
O crowding too close upon me,
I foresee too much, it means more than I thought,
It appears to me I am dying.

Hasten throat and sound your last,
Salute me—salute the days once more. Peal the old cry once more.   35

Screaming electric, the atmosphere using,
At random glancing, each as I notice absorbing,
Swiftly on, but a little while alighting,
Curious envelop'd messages delivering,

[55] In phrenology, friendship, or the love of
comrades, as distinguished from amativeness, or
sexual love.

Sparkles hot, seed ethereal down in the dirt dropping,   40
Myself unknowing, my commission obeying, to question it never daring,
To ages and ages yet the growth of the seed leaving,
To troops out of the war arising, they the tasks I have set promulging,
To women certain whispers of myself bequeathing, their affection me more
    clearly explaining,
To young men my problems offering—no dallier I—I the muscle of their
    brains trying,   45
So I pass, a little time vocal, visible, contrary,
Afterward a melodious echo, passionately bent for, (death making me really
    undying,)
The best of me then when no longer visible, for toward that I have been
    incessantly preparing.

What is there more, that I lag and pause and crouch extended with unshut
    mouth?
Is there a single final farewell?   50

My songs cease, I abandon them,
From behind the screen where I hid I advance personally solely to you.

Camerado, this is no book,
Who touches this touches a man,
(Is it night? are we here together alone?)   55
It is I you hold and who holds you,
I spring from the pages into your arms—decease calls me forth.

O how your fingers drowse me,
Your breath falls around me like dew, your pulse lulls the tympans of my ears,
I feel immerged from head to foot,   60
Delicious, enough.

Enough, O deed impromptu and secret,
Enough O gliding present—enough O summ'd-up past.

Dear friend whoever you are take this kiss,
I give it especially to you, do not forget me,   65
I feel like one who has done work for the day to retire awhile,
I receive now again of my many translations, from my avataras[56] ascending,
    while others doubtless await me,
An unknown sphere more real than I dream'd, more direct, darts awakening
    rays about me, *So long!*
Remember my words, I may again return,
I love you, I depart from materials,
I am as one disembodied, triumphant, dead.   70

1860

[56] I.e., avatars: incarnations or manifestations.

from **First Annex: Sands at Seventy**
Yonnondio

(The sense of the word is *Lament for the Aborigines.*
It is an Iroquois term; and has been used for a
personal name.)

A song, a poem of itself—the word itself a dirge,
Amid the wilds, the rocks, the storm and wintry night,
To me such misty, strange tableaux the syllables calling up;
Yonnondio—I see, far in the west or north, a limitless ravine, with plains and
    mountains dark,
I see swarms of stalwart chieftains, medicine-men, and warriors,   5
As flitting by like clouds of ghosts, they pass and are gone in the twilight,
(Race of the woods, the landscapes free, and the falls!
No picture, poem, statement, passing them to the future:)
Yonnondio! Yonnondio!—unlimn'd they disappear;
To-day gives place, and fades—the cities, farms, factories fade;   10
A muffled sonorous sound, a wailing word is borne through the air for a
    moment,
Then blank and gone and still, and utterly lost.
1887

A Prairie Sunset

Shot gold, maroon and violet, dazzling silver, emerald, fawn,
The earth's whole amplitude and Nature's multiform power consign'd for once
    to colors;
The light, the general air possess'd by them—colors till now unknown,
No limit, confine—not the Western sky alone—the high meridian—North,
    South, all,
Pure luminous color fighting the silent shadows to the last.   5
1888

After the Supper and Talk

After the supper and talk—after the day is done,
As a friend from friends his final withdrawal prolonging,
Good-bye and Good-bye with emotional lips repeating,
(So hard for his hand to release those hands—no more will they meet,
No more for communion of sorrow and joy, of old and young,   5
A far-stretching journey awaits him, to return no more,)
Shunning, postponing severance—seeking to ward off the last word ever so
    little,
E'en at the exit-door turning—charges superfluous calling back—e'en as he
    descends the steps,
Something to eke out a minute additional—shadows of nightfall deepening,

Farewells, messages lessening—dimmer the forthgoer's visage and form, 10
Soon to be lost for aye in the darkness—loth, O so loth to depart!
Garrulous to the very last.

1887

from Specimen Days

Down at the Front

FALMOUTH, VA., *opposite Fredericksburgh, December 21, 1862.* —Begin my visits among the camp hospitals in the army of the Potomac. Spend a good part of the day in a large brick mansion on the banks of the Rappahannock, used as a hospital since the battle—seems to have receiv'd only the worst cases. Our doors, at the foot of a tree, within ten yards of the front of the house, I notice a heap of amputated feet, legs, arms, hands, &c., a full load for a one-horse cart. Several dead bodies lie near, each cover'd with its brown woolen blanket. In the door-yard, towards the river, are fresh graves, mostly of officers, their names on pieces of barrel-staves or broken boards, stuck in the dirt. (Most of these bodies were subsequently taken up and transported north to their friends.) The large mansion is quite crowded upstairs and down, everything impromptu, no system, all bad enough, but I have no doubt the best that can be done; all the wounds pretty bad, some frightful, the men in their old clothes, unclean and bloody. Some of the wounded are rebel soldiers and officers, prisoners. One, a Mississippian, a captain, hit badly in leg, I talk'd with some time; he ask'd me for papers, which I gave him. (I saw him three months afterward in Washington, with his leg amputated, doing well.) I went through the rooms, downstairs and up. Some of the men were dying. I had nothing to give at that visit, but wrote a few letters to folks home, mothers, &c. Also talk'd to three or four, who seem'd most susceptible to it, and needing it.

After First Fredericksburg

December 23 to 31. —The results of the late battle[1] are exhibited everywhere about here in thousands of cases, (hundreds die every day,) in the camp, brigade, and division hospitals. These are merely tents, and sometimes very poor ones, the wounded lying on the ground, lucky if their blankets are spread on layers of pine or hemlock twigs, or small leaves. No cots; seldom even a mattress. It is pretty cold. The ground is frozen hard, and there is occasional snow. I go around from one case to another. I do not see that I do much good to these wounded and dying; but I cannot leave them. Once in a while some youngster holds on to me convulsively, and I do what I can for him; at any rate, stop with him and sit near him for hours, if he wishes it.

---

[1] Fought at Fredericksburg, Virginia, December 13, 1862. The Union army suffered about 12,600 casualties.

Besides the hospitals, I also go occasionally on long tours through the camps, talking with the men, &c. Sometimes at night among the groups around the fires, in their shebang² enclosures of bushes. These are curious shows, full of characters and groups. I soon get acquainted anywhere in camp, with officers or men, and am always well used. Sometimes I go down on picket with the regiments I know best. As to rations, the army here at present seems to be tolerably well supplied, and the men have enough, such as it is, mainly salt pork and hard tack. Most of the regiments lodge in the flimsy little shelter-tents. A few have built themselves huts of logs and mud, with fire-places.

Back to Washington

January, '63. —Left camp at Falmouth, with some wounded, a few days since, and came here by Aquia creek railroad, and so on government steamer up the Potomac. Many wounded were with us on the cars and boat. The cars were just common platform ones. The railroad journey of ten or twelve miles was made mostly before sunrise. The soldiers guarding the road came out from their tents or shebangs of bushes with rumpled hair and half-awake look. Those on duty were walking their posts, some on banks over us, others down far below the level of the track. I saw large cavalry camps off the road. At Aquia creek landing were numbers of wounded going north. While I waited some three hours, I went around among them. Several wanted word sent home to parents, brothers, wives, &c., which I did for them, (by mail the next day from Washington.) On the boat I had my hands full. One poor fellow died going up.

I am now remaining in and around Washington, daily visiting the hospitals. Am much in Patent-office, Eighth street, H street, Armory-square, and others. Am now able to do a little good, having money, (as almoner of others home,) and getting experience. To-day, Sunday afternoon and till nine in the evening, visited Campbell hospital; attended specially to one case in ward 1, very sick with pleurisy and typhoid fever, young man, farmer's son, D. F. Russell, company E, 60th New York, down-hearted and feeble; a long time before he would take any interest; wrote a letter home to his mother, in Malone, Franklin county, N. Y., at his request; gave him some fruit and one or two other gifts; envelop'd and directed his letter, &c. Then went thoroughly through ward 6, observ'd every case in the ward, without, I think, missing one; gave perhaps from twenty to thirty persons, each one some little gift, such as oranges, apples, sweet crackers, figs, &c.

Thursday, Jan. 21. —Devoted the main part of the day to Armory-square hospital; went pretty thoroughly through wards F, G, H, and I; some fifty cases in each ward. In ward F supplied the men throughout with writing paper and stamp'd envelope each; distributed in small portions, to proper subjects, a large jar of first-rate preserv'd berries, which had been donated to me by a lady—her own cooking. Found several cases I thought good subjects for small sums of money, which I furnish'd. (The wounded men often come up broke, and it helps their spirits to have even the small sum I give them.) My paper and envelopes all gone, but distributed a good lot of amusing reading matter; also, as I thought judicious, tobacco, oranges, apples, &c.

² Crude shelter

Interesting cases in ward one; Charles Miller, bed 19, company D, 53d Pennsylvania, is only sixteen years of age, very bright, courageous boy, left leg amputated below the knee; next bed to him, another young lad very sick; gave each appropriate gifts. In the bed above, also, amputation of the left leg; gave him a little jar of raspberries; bed 1 this ward, gave a small sum; also to a soldier on crutches, sitting on his bed near. . . . (I am more and more surprised at the very great proportion of youngsters from fifteen to twenty-one in the army. I afterwards found a still greater proportion among the southerners.)

Evening, same day, went to see D. F. R., before alluded to; found him remarkably changed for the better; up and dress'd—quite a triumph; he afterwards got well, and went back to his regiment. Distributed in the wards a quantity of note-paper, and forty or fifty stamp'd envelopes, of which I had recruited my stock, and the men were much in need.

Fifty Hours Left Wounded on the Field

Here is a case of a soldier I found among the crowded cots in the Patent-office. He likes to have some one to talk to, and we will listen to him. He got badly hit in his leg and side at Fredericksburgh that eventful Saturday, 13th of December. He lay the succeeding two days and nights helpless on the field, between the city and those grim terraces of batteries; his company and regiment had been compell'd to leave him to his fate. To make matters worse, it happen'd he lay with his head slightly down hill, and could not help himself. At the end of some fifty hours he was brought off, with other wounded, under a flag of truce. I ask him how the rebels treated him as he lay during those two days and nights within reach of them—whether they came to him —whether they abused him? He answers that several of the rebels, soldiers and others, came to him at one time and another. A couple of them, who were together, spoke roughly and sarcastically, but nothing worse. One middle-aged man, however, who seem'd to be moving around the field, among the dead and wounded, for benevolent purposes, came to him in a way he will never forget; treated our soldier kindly, bound up his wounds, cheer'd him, gave him a couple of biscuits and a drink of whiskey and water; asked him if he could eat some beef. This good secesh, however, did not change our soldier's position, for it might have caused the blood to burst from the wounds, clotted and stagnated. Our soldier is from Pennsylvania; has had a pretty severe time; the wounds proved to be bad ones. But he retains a good heart, and is at present on the gain. (It is not uncommon for the men to remain on the field this way, one, two, or even four or five days.)

Hospital Scenes and Persons

Letter Writing.—When eligible, I encourage the men to write, and myself, when called upon, write all sorts of letters for them, (including love letters, very tender ones.) Almost as I reel off these memoranda, I write for a new patient to his wife. M. de F., of the 17th Connecticut, company H, has just come up (February 17th) from Windmill point, and is received in ward H, Armory-square. He is an intelligent looking man, has a foreign accent, black-eyed and hair'd, a Hebraic appearance. Wants a telegraphic message sent to his wife, New Canaan, Conn. I agree to send the message—but to make things sure I also sit down and write the wife a letter, and despatch it to the post-office immediately, as he fears she will come on, and he does not wish her to, as he will surely get well.

Saturday, January 30th.—Afternoon, visited Campbell hospital. Scene of cleaning up the ward, and giving the men all clean clothes—through the ward (6) the patients dressing or being dress'd—the naked upper half of the bodies—the good-humor and fun—the shirts, drawers, sheets of beds, &c., and the general fixing up for Sunday. Gave J.L. 50 cents.

Wednesday, February 4th.—Visited Armory-square hospital, went pretty thoroughly through wards E and D. Supplied paper and envelopes to all who wish'd —as usual, found plenty of men who needed those articles. Wrote letters. Saw and talk'd with two or three members of the Brooklyn 14th regt. A poor fellow in ward D, with a fearful wound in a fearful condition, was having some loose splinters of bone taken from the neighborhood of the wound. The operation was long, and one of great pain—yet, after it was well commenced, the soldier bore it in silence. He sat up, propp'd—was much wasted—had lain a long time quiet in one position (not for days only but weeks,) a bloodless, brown-skinn'd face, with eyes full of determination—belong'd to a New York regiment. There was an unusual cluster of surgeons, medical cadets, nurses, &c., around his bed—I thought the whole thing was done with tenderness, and done well. In one case, the wife sat by the side of her husband, his sickness typhoid fever, pretty bad. In another, by the side of her son, a mother—she told me she had seven children, and this was the youngest. (A fine, kind, healthy, gentle mother, good-looking, not very old, with a cap on her head, and dress'd like home—what a charm it gave to the whole ward.) I liked the woman nurse in ward E—I noticed how she sat a long time by a poor fellow who just had, that morning, in addition to his other sickness, bad hemorrhage—she gently assisted him, reliev'd him of the blood, holding a cloth to his mouth, as he coughed it up—he was so weak he could only just turn his head over on the pillow.

One young New York man, with a bright, handsome face, had been lying several months from a most disagreeable wound, receiv'd at Bull Run. A bullet had shot him right through the bladder, hitting him front, low in the belly, and coming out back. He had suffer'd much—the water came out of the wound, by slow but steady quantities, for many weeks—so that he lay almost constantly in a sort of puddle— and there were other disagreeable circumstances. He was of good heart, however. At present comparatively comfortable, had a bad throat, was delighted with a stick of horehound candy I gave him, with one or two other trifles.

Patent-Office Hospital

February 23.—I must not let the great hospital at the Patent-office pass away without some mention. A few weeks ago the vast area of the second story of that noblest of Washington buildings was crowded close with rows of sick, badly wounded and dying soldiers. They were placed in three very large apartments. I went there many times. It was a strange, solemn, and, with all its features of suffering and death, a sort of fascinating sight. I go sometimes at night to soothe and relieve particular cases. Two of the immense apartments are fill'd with high and ponderous glass cases, crowded with models in miniature of every kind of utensil, machine or invention, it ever enter'd into the mind of man to conceive; and with curiosities and foreign presents. Between these cases are lateral openings, perhaps eight feet wide and quite deep, and in these were placed the sick, besides a great long double row of them up and down through the middle of the hall. Many of them were very bad cases, wounds and amputations. Then there was a gallery running above the hall in which there were beds also. It was, indeed, a curious scene, especially at night when lit up. The glass cases, the beds, the forms lying there, the gallery above, and the marble pavement under foot—the suffering, and the fortitude to bear it in various degrees—occasionally, from some, the groan that could not be repress'd—sometimes a poor fellow dying, with emaciated face and glassy eye, the nurse by his side, the doctor also there, but no friend, no relative—such were the sights but lately in the Patent-office. (The wounded have since been removed from there, and it is now vacant again.)

The Wounded from Chancellorsville

May, '63. —As I write this, the wounded have begun to arrive from Hooker's command from bloody Chancellorsville.[3] I was down among the first arrivals. The men in charge told me the bad cases were yet to come. If that is so I pity them, for these are bad enough. You ought to see the scene of the wounded arriving at the landing here at the foot of Sixth street, at night. Two boat loads came about half-past seven last night. A little after eight it rain'd a long and violent shower. The pale, helpless soldiers had been debark'd, and lay around on the wharf and neighborhood anywhere. The rain was, probably, grateful to them; at any rate they were exposed to it. The few torches light up the spectacle. All around—on the wharf, on the ground, out on side places—the men are lying on blankets, old quilts, &c., with bloody rags bound round heads, arms, and legs. The attendants are few, and at night few outsiders also —only a few hard-work'd transportation men and drivers. (The wounded are getting to be common, and people grow callous.) The men, whatever their condition, lie there, and patiently wait till their turn comes to be taken up. Near by, the ambulances are now arriving in clusters, and one after another is call'd to back up and take its load. Extreme cases are sent off on stretchers. The men generally make little or no ado, whatever their sufferings. A few groans that cannot be suppress'd, and occasionally a scream of pain as they lift a man into the ambulance. To-day, as I write, hundreds more are expected, and to-morrow and the next day more, and so on for many days. Quite often they arrive at the rate of 1000 a day.

A Night Battle, Over a Week Since

May 12. —There was part of the late battle at Chancellorsville, (second Fredericksburgh,) a little over a week ago, Saturday, Saturday night and Sunday, under Gen. Joe Hooker, I would like to give just a glimpse of—(a moment's look in a terrible storm at sea—of which a few suggestions are enough, and full details impossible.) The fighting had been very hot during the day, and after an intermission the latter part, was resumed at night, and kept up with furious energy till 3 o'clock in the morning.

[3] The Battle of Chancellorsville (May 2–4, 1863) was one of the major engagements of the war.

That afternoon (Saturday) an attack sudden and strong by Stonewall Jackson had gain'd a great advantage to the southern army, and broken our lines, entering us like a wedge, and leaving things in that position at dark. But Hooker at 11 at night made a desperate push, drove the secesh forces back, restored his original lines, and resumed his plans. This night scrimmage was very exciting, and afforded countless strange and fearful pictures. The fighting had been general both at Chancellorsville and northeast at Fredericksburgh. (We heard of some poor fighting, episodes, skedaddling on our part. I think not of it. I think of the fierce bravery, the general rule.) One corps, the 6th, Sedgewick's, fights four dashing and bloody battles in thirty-six hours, retreating in great jeopardy, losing largely but maintaining itself, fighting with the sternest desperation under all circumstances, getting over the Rappahannock only by the skin of its teeth, yet getting over. It lost many, many brave men, yet it took vengeance, ample vengeance.

But it was the tug of Saturday evening, and through the night and Sunday morning, I wanted to make a special note of. It was largely in the woods, and quite a general engagement. The night was very pleasant, at times the moon shining out full and clear, all Nature so calm in itself, the early summer grass so rich, and foliage of the trees—yet there the battle raging, and many good fellows lying helpless, with new accessions to them, and every minute amid the rattle of muskets and crash of cannon, (for there was an artillery contest too,) the red life-blood oozing out from heads or trunks or limbs upon that green and dew-cool grass. Patches of the woods take fire, and several of the wounded, unable to move, are consumed—quite large spaces are swept over, burning the dead also—some of the men have their hair and beards singed—some, burns on their faces and hands—others holes burnt in their clothing. The flashes of fire from the cannon, the quick flaring flames and smoke, and the immense roar—the musketry so general, the light nearly bright enough for each side to see the other—the crashing, tramping of men—the yelling—close quarters— we hear the secesh yells—our men cheer loudly back, especially if Hooker is in sight —hand to hand conflicts, each side stands up to it, brave, determin'd as demons, they often charge upon us—a thousand deeds are done worth to write newer greater poems on—and still the woods on fire—still many are not only scorch'd—too many, unable to move, are burn'd to death.

Then the camps of the wounded—O heavens, what scene is this?—is this indeed *humanity*—these butchers' shambles? There are several of them. There they lie, in the largest, in an open space in the woods, from 200 to 300 poor fellows—the groans and screams—the odor of blood, mixed with the fresh scent of the night, the grass, the trees—that slaughter-house! O well is it their mothers, their sisters cannot see them —cannot conceive, and never conceiv'd, these things. One man is shot by a shell, both in the arm and leg—both are amputated—there lie the rejected members. Some have their legs blown off—some bullets through the breast—some indescribably horrid wounds in the face or head, all mutilated, sickening, torn, gouged out—some in the abdomen—some mere boys—many rebels, badly hurt—they take their regular turns with the rest, just the same as any—the surgeons use them just the same. Such is the camp of the wounded—such a fragment, a reflection afar off of the bloody scene— while over all the clear, large moon comes out at times softly, quietly shining. Amid the woods, that scene of flitting souls—amid the crack and crash and yelling sounds —the impalpable perfume of the woods—and yet the pungent, stifling smoke—the

radiance of the moon, looking from heaven at intervals so placid—the sky so heavenly
—the clear-obscure up there, those buoyant upper oceans—a few large placid stars
beyond, coming silently and languidly out, and then disappearing—the melancholy,
draperied night above, around. And there, upon the roads, the fields, and in those
woods, that contest, never one more desperate in any age or land—both parties now
in force—masses—no fancy battle, no semi-play, but fierce and savage demons
fighting there—courage and scorn of death the rule, exceptions almost none.

What history, I say, can ever give—for who can know—the mad, determin'd tussle
of the armies, in all their separate large and little squads—as this—each steep'd from
crown to toe in desperate, mortal purports? Who know the conflict, hand-to-
hand—the many conflicts in the dark, those shadowy-tangled, flashing moonbeam'd
woods—the writhing groups and squads—the cries, the din, the cracking guns
and pistols—the distant cannon—the cheers and calls and threats and awful music
of the oaths—the indescribable mix—the officers' orders, persuasions, encourage-
ments—the devils fully rous'd in human hearts—the strong shout, *Charge, men,
charge*—the flash of the naked sword, and rolling flame and smoke? And still the
broken, clear and clouded heaven—and still again the moonlight pouring silvery
soft its radiant patches over all. Who paint the scene, the sudden partial panic of
the afternoon, at dusk? Who paint the irrepressible advance of the second division
of the Third corps, under Hooker himself, suddenly order'd up—those rapid-filing
phantoms through the woods? Who show what moves there in the shadows, fluid
and firm—to save, (and it did save,) the army's name, perhaps the nation? as there
the veterans hold the field. (Brave Berry[4] falls not yet—but death has mark'd
him—soon he falls.)

Abraham Lincoln

August 12th. —I see the President almost every day, as I happen to live where he passes
to or from his lodgings out of town. He never sleeps at the White House during the
hot season, but has quarters at a healthy location some three miles north of the city,
the Soldiers' home, a United States military establishment. I saw him this morning
about 8 1/2 coming in to business, riding on Vermont avenue, near L street. He always
has a company of twenty-five or thirty cavalry, with sabres drawn and held upright
over their shoulders. They say this guard was against his personal wish, but he let his
counselors have their way. The party makes no great show in uniform or horses. Mr.
Lincoln on the saddle generally rides a good-sized, easy-going gray horse, is dress'd
in plain black, somewhat rusty and dusty, wears a black stiff hat, and looks about as
ordinary in attire, &c., as the commonest man. A lieutenant, with yellow straps, rides
at his left, and following behind, two by two, come the cavalry men, in their
yellow-striped jackets. They are generally going at a slow trot, as that is the pace set
them by the one they wait upon. The sabres and accoutrements clank, and the entirely
unornamental *cortège* as it trots towards Lafayette square arouses no sensation, only
some curious stranger stops and gazes. I see very plainly ABRAHAM LINCOLN's dark

[4] General Hiram G. Berry of the Union army,
killed at Chancellorsville.

brown face, with the deep-cut lines, the eyes, always to me with a deep latent sadness in the expression. We have got so that we exchange bows, and very cordial ones. Sometimes the President goes and comes in an open barouche. The cavalry always accompany him, with drawn sabres. Often I notice as he goes out evenings—and sometimes in the morning, when he returns early—he turns off and halts at the large and handsome residence of the Secretary of War, on K street, and holds conference there. If in his barouche, I can see from my window he does not alight, but sits in his vehicle, and Mr. Stanton comes out to attend him. Sometimes one of his sons, a boy of ten or twelve, accompanies him, riding at his right on a pony. Earlier in the summer I occasionally saw the President and his wife, toward the latter part of the afternoon, out in a barouche, on a pleasure ride through the city. Mrs. Lincoln was dress'd in complete black, with a long crape veil. The equipage is of the plainest kind, only two horses, and they nothing extra. They pass'd me once very close, and I saw the President in the face fully, as they were moving slowly, and his look, though abstracted, happen'd to be directed steadily in my eye. He bow'd and smiled, but far beneath his smile I noticed well the expression I have alluded to. None of the artists or pictures has caught the deep, though subtle and indirect expression of this man's face. There is something else there. One of the great portrait painters of two or three centuries ago is needed.

Three Years Summ'd Up

During those three years in hospital, camp or field, I made over six hundred visits or tours, and went, as I estimate, counting all, among from eighty thousand to a hundred thousand of the wounded and sick, as sustainer of spirit and body in some degree, in time of need. These visits varied from an hour or two, to all day or night; for with dear or critical cases I generally watch'd all night. Sometimes I took up my quarters in the hospital, and slept or watch'd there several nights in succession. Those three years I consider the greatest privilege and satisfaction, (with all their feverish excitements and physical deprivations and lamentable sights,) and, of course, the most profound lesson of my life. I can say that in my ministerings I comprehended all, whoever came in my way, northern or southern, and slighted none. It arous'd and brought out and decided undream'd-of depths of emotion. It has given me my most fervent views of the true *ensemble* and extent of the States. While I was with wounded and sick in thousands of cases from the New England States, and from New York, New Jersey, and Pennsylvania, and from Michigan, Wisconsin, Ohio, Indiana, Illinois, and all the Western States, I was with more or less from all the States, North and South, without exception. I was with many from the border States, especially from Maryland and Virginia, and found, during those lurid years 1862–63, far more Union southerners, especially Tennesseans, than is supposed. I was with many rebel officers and men among our wounded, and gave them always what I had, and tried to cheer them the same as any. I was among the army teamsters considerably, and, indeed, always found myself drawn to them. Among the black soldiers, wounded or sick, and in the contraband camps, I also took my way whenever in their neighborhood, and did what I could for them.

The Million Dead, Too, Summ'd Up

The dead in this war—there they lie, strewing the fields and woods and valleys and battle-fields of the south—Virginia, the Peninsula—Malvern hill and Fair Oaks—the banks of the Chickahominy—the terraces of Fredericksburgh—Antietam bridge—the grisly ravines of Manassas—the bloody promenade of the Wilderness—the varieties of the *strayed* dead, (the estimate of the War department is 25,000 national soldiers kill'd in battle and never buried at all, 5,000 drown'd—15,000 inhumed by strangers, or on the march in haste, in hitherto unfound localities—2,000 graves cover'd by sand and mud by Mississippi freshets, 3,000 carried away by caving-in of banks, &c.,)— Gettysburgh, the West, Southwest—Vicksburgh—Chattanooga—the trenches of Petersburgh—the numberless battles, camps, hospitals everywhere—the crop reap'd by the mighty reapers, typhoid, dysentery, inflammations—and blackest and loathesomest of all, the dead and living burial-pits, the prison-pens of Andersonville, Salisbury, Belle-Isle, &c., (not Dante's pictured hell and all its woes, its degradations, filthy torments, excell'd those prisons)—the dead, the dead, the dead—*our* dead—or South or North, ours all, (all, all, all, finally dear to me)—or East or West—Atlantic coast or Mississippi valley—somewhere they crawl'd to die, alone, in bushes, low gullies, or on the sides of hills—(there, in secluded spots, their skeletons, bleach'd bones, tufts of hair, buttons, fragments of clothing, are occasionally found yet)—our young men once so handsome and so joyous, taken from us—the son from the mother, the husband from the wife, the dear friend from the dear friend—the clusters of camp graves, in Georgia, the Carolinas, and in Tennessee—the single graves left in the woods or by the road-side, (hundreds, thousands, obliterated)—the corpses floated down the rivers, and caught and lodged, (dozens, scores, floated down the upper Potomac, after the cavalry engagements, the pursuit of Lee, following Gettysburgh) —some lie at the bottom of the sea—the general million, and the special cemeteries in almost all the States—the infinite dead—(the land entire saturated, perfumed with their impalpable ashes' exhalation in Nature's chemistry distill'd, and shall be so forever, in every future grain of wheat and ear of corn, and every flower that grows, and every breath we draw)—not only Northern dead leavening Southern soil— thousands, aye tens of thousands, of Southerners, crumble today in Northern earth.

And everywhere among these countless graves—everywhere in the many soldier Cemeteries of the Nation, (there are now, I believe, over seventy of them)—as at the time in the vast trenches, the depositories of slain, Northern and Southern, after the great battles—not only where the scathing trail passed those years, but radiating since in all the peaceful quarters of the land—we see, and ages yet may see, on monuments and gravestones, singly or in masses, to thousands or tens of thousands, the significant word Unknown.

(In some of the cemeteries nearly *all* the dead are unknown. At Salisbury, N. C., for instance, the known are only 85, while the unknown are 12,027, and 11,700 of these are buried in trenches. A national monument has been put up here, by order of Congress, to mark the spot—but what visible, material monument can ever fittingly commemorate that spot?)

from **The Real War Will Never Get in the Books**

And so good-bye to the war. I know not how it may have been, or may be, to others
—to me the main interest I found, (and still, on recollection, find,) in the rank and
file of the armies, both sides, and in those specimens amid the hospitals, and even the
dead on the field. To me the points illustrating the latent personal character and
eligibilities of these States, in the two or three millions of American young and
middle-aged men, North and South, embodied in those armies—and especially the
one-third or one-fourth of their number, stricken by wounds or disease at some time
in the course of the contest—were of more significance even than the political interests
involved. (As so much of a race depends on how it faces death, and how it stands
personal anguish and sickness. As, in the glints of emotions under emergencies, and
the indirect traits and asides in Plutarch, we get far profounder clues to the antique
world than all its more formal history.)

Future years will never know the seething hell and the black infernal background
of countless minor scenes and interiors, (not the official surface-courteousness of the
Generals, not the few great battles) of the Secession war; and it is best they should
not—the real war will never get in the books. In the mushy influences of current
times, too, the fervid atmosphere and typical events of those years are in danger of
being totally forgotten. I have at night watch'd by the side of a sick man in the
hospital, one who could not live many hours. I have seen his eyes flash and burn as
he raised himself and recurr'd to the cruelties of his surrender'd brother, and mutila-
tions of the corpse afterward. . . .

Such was the war. It was not a quadrille in a ball-room. Its interior history will
not only never be written—its practicality, minutiæ of deeds and passions, will never
be even suggested. The actual soldier of 1862–'65, North and South, with all his ways,
his incredible dauntlessness, habits, practices, tastes, language, his fierce friendship, his
appetite, rankness, his superb strength and animality, lawless gait, and a hundred
unnamed lights and shades of camp, I say, will never be written—perhaps must not
and should not be.

The preceding notes may furnish a few stray glimpses into that life, and into those
lurid interiors, never to be fully convey'd to the future. The hospital part of the drama
from '61 to '65, deserves indeed to be recorded. Of that many-threaded drama, with
its sudden and strange surprises, its confounding of prophecies, its moments of despair,
the dread of foreign interference, the interminable campaigns, the bloody battles, the
mighty and cumbrous and green armies, the drafts and bounties—the immense money
expenditure, like a heavy-pouring constant rain—with, over the whole land, the last
three years of the struggle, an unending, universal mourning-wail of women, parents,
orphans—the marrow of the tragedy concentrated in those Army Hospitals—(it
seem'd sometimes as if the whole interest of the land, North and South, was one vast
central hospital, and all the rest of the affair but flanges)—those forming the untold
and unwritten history of the war—infinitely greater (like life's) than the few scraps
and distortions that are ever told or written. Think how much, and of importance,
will be—how much, civic and military, has already been—buried in the grave, in
eternal darkness.

1875–1876

from Democratic Vistas

[*from* **Democracy in America**]

I say that democracy can never prove itself beyond cavil, until it founds and luxuriantly grows its own forms of art, poems, schools, theology, displacing all that exists,
or that has been produced anywhere in the past, under opposite influences. It is curious
to me that while so many voices, pens, minds, in the press, lecture-rooms, in our
Congress, &c., are discussing intellectual topics, pecuniary dangers, legislative problems, the suffrage, tariff and labor questions, and the various business and benevolent
needs of America, with propositions, remedies, often worth deep attention, there is
one need, a hiatus the profoundest, that no eye seems to perceive, no voice to state.
Our fundamental want to-day in the United States, with closest, amplest reference
to present conditions, and to the future, is of a class, and the clear idea of a class, of
native authors, literatures, far different, far higher in grade than any yet known,
sacerdotal, modern, fit to cope with our occasions, lands, permeating the whole mass
of American mentality, taste, belief, breathing into it a new breath of life, giving it
decision, affecting politics far more than the popular superficial suffrage, with results
inside and underneath the elections of Presidents or Congresses—radiating, begetting
appropriate teachers, schools, manners, and, as its grandest result, accomplishing, (what
neither the schools nor the churches and their clergy have hitherto accomplish'd, and
without which this nation will no more stand, permanently, soundly, than a house
will stand without a substratum,) a religious and moral character beneath the political
and productive and intellectual bases of the States. For know you not, dear, earnest
reader, that the people of our land may all read and write, and may all possess the
right to vote—and yet the main things may be entirely lacking?—(and this to suggest
them.)

View'd, to-day, from a point of view sufficiently over-arching, the problem of
humanity all over the civilized world is social and religious, and is to be finally met
and treated by literature. The priest departs, the divine literatus comes. Never was
anything more wanted than, to-day, and here in the States, the poet of the modern
is wanted, or the great literatus of the modern. At all times, perhaps, the central point
in any nation, and that whence it is itself really sway'd the most, and whence it sways
others, is its national literature, especially its archetypal poems. Above all previous
lands, a great original literature is surely to become the justification and reliance, (in
some respects the sole reliance,) of American democracy.

Few are aware how the great literature penetrates all, gives hue to all, shapes
aggregates and individuals, and, after subtle ways, with irresistible power, constructs,
sustains, demolishes at will. Why tower, in reminiscence, above all the nations of the
earth, two special lands, petty in themselves, yet inexpressibly gigantic, beautiful,
columnar? Immortal Judah lives, and Greece immortal lives, in a couple of poems.

Nearer than this. It is not generally realized, but it is true, as the genius of Greece,
and all the sociology, personality, politics and religion of those wonderful states,
resided in their literature or esthetics, that what was afterwards the main support of
European chivalry, the feudal, ecclesiastical, dynastic world over there—forming its
osseous structure, holding it together for hundreds, thousands of years, preserving its

flesh and bloom, giving it form, decision, rounding it out, and so saturating it in the conscious and unconscious blood, breed, and belief, and intuitions of men, that it still prevails powerful to this day, in defiance of the mighty changes of time—was its literature, permeating to the very marrow, especially that major part, its enchanting songs, ballads, and poems.[1]

To the ostent of the senses and eyes, I know, the influences which stamp the world's history are wars, uprisings or downfalls of dynasties, changeful movements of trade, important inventions, navigation, military or civil governments, advent of powerful personalities, conquerors, &c. These of course play their part; yet, it may be, a single new thought, imagination, abstract principle, even literary style, fit for the time, put in shape by some great literatus, and projected among mankind, may duly cause changes, growths, removals, greater than the longest and bloodiest war, or the most stupendous merely political, dynastic, or commercial overturn.

In short, as, though it may not be realized, it is strictly true, that a few first-class poets, philosophs, and authors, have substantially settled and given status to the entire religion, education, law, sociology, &c., of the hitherto civilized world, by tinging and often creating the atmospheres out of which they have arisen, such also must stamp, and more than ever stamp, the interior and real democratic construction of this American continent, to-day, and days to come. Remember also this fact of difference, that, while through the antique and through the mediæval ages, highest thoughts and ideals realized themselves, and their expression made its way by other arts, as much as, or even more than by, technical literature, (not open to the mass of persons, or even to the majority of eminent persons,) such literature in our day and for current purposes, is not only more eligible than all the other arts put together, but has become the only general means of morally influencing the world. Painting, sculpture, and the dramatic theatre, it would seem, no longer play an indispensable or even important part in the workings and mediumship of intellect, utility, or even high esthetics. Architecture remains, doubtless with capacities, and a real future. Then music, the combiner, nothing more spiritual, nothing more sensuous, a god, yet completely human, advances, prevails, holds highest place; supplying in certain wants and quarters what nothing else could supply. Yet in the civilization of to-day it is undeniable that, over all the arts, literature dominates, serves beyond all—shapes the character of church and school—or, at any rate, is capable of doing so. Including the literature of science, its scope is indeed unparallel'd.

Before proceeding further, it were perhaps well to discriminate on certain points. Literature tills its crops in many fields, and some may flourish, while others lag. What I say in these Vistas has its main bearing on imaginative literature, especially poetry, the stock of all. In the department of science, and the specialty of journalism, there appear, in these States, promises, perhaps fulfilments, of highest earnestness, reality, and

[1] Whitman's note: "See, for hereditaments, specimens, Walter Scott's Border Minstrelsy, Percy's collection, Ellis's early English Metrical Romances, the European continental poems of Walter of Aquitania, and the Nibelungen, of pagan stock, but monkish-feudal redaction; the history of the Troubadours, by Fauriel; even the far-back cumbrous old Hindu epics, as indicating the Asian eggs out of which European chivalry was hatch'd; Ticknor's chapters on the Cid, and on the Spanish poems and poets of Calderon's time. Then always, and, of course, as the superbest poetic culmination-expression of feudalism, the Shaksperean dramas, in the attitudes, dialogue, characters, &c., of the princes, lords and gentlemen, the pervading atmosphere, the implied and express'd standard of manners, the high port and proud stomach, the regal embroidery of style, &c."

life. These, of course, are modern. But in the region of imaginative, spinal and essential attributes, something equivalent to creation is, for our age and lands, imperatively demanded. For not only is it not enough that the new blood, new frame of democracy shall be vivified and held together merely by political means, superficial suffrage, legislation, &c., but it is clear to me that, unless it goes deeper, gets at least as firm and as warm a hold in men's hearts, emotions and belief, as, in their days, feudalism or ecclesiasticism, and inaugurates its own perennial sources, welling from the centre forever, its strength will be defective, its growth doubtful, and its main charm wanting. I suggest, therefore, the possibility, should some two or three really original American poets, (perhaps artists or lecturers,) arise, mounting the horizon like planets, stars of the first magnitude, that, from their eminence, fusing contributions, races, far localities, &c., together they would give more compaction and more moral identity, (the quality to-day most needed,) to these States, than all its Constitutions, legislative and judicial ties, and all its hitherto political, warlike, or materialistic experiences. As, for instance, there could hardly happen anything that would more serve the States, with all their variety of origins, their diverse climes, cities, standards, &c., than possessing an aggregate of heroes, characters, exploits, sufferings, prosperity or misfortune, glory or disgrace, common to all, typical of all—no less, but even greater would it be to possess the aggregation of a cluster of mighty poets, artists, teachers, fit for us, national expressers, comprehending and effusing for the men and women of the States, what is universal, native, common to all, inland and seaboard, northern and southern. The historians say of ancient Greece, with her ever-jealous autonomies, cities, and states, that the only positive unity she ever own'd or receiv'd, was the sad unity of a common subjection, at the last, to foreign conquerors. Subjection, aggregation of that sort, is impossible to America; but the fear of conflicting and irreconcilable interiors, and the lack of a common skeleton, knitting all close, continually haunts me. Or, if it does not, nothing is plainer than the need, a long period to come, of a fusion of the States into the only reliable identity, the moral and artistic one. For, I say, the true nationality of the States, the genuine union, when we come to a mortal crisis, is, and is to be, after all, neither the written law, nor, (as is generally supposed,) either self-interest, or common pecuniary or material objects—but the fervid and tremendous IDEA, melting everything else with resistless heat, and solving all lesser and definite distinctions in vast, indefinite, spiritual, emotional power.

It may be claim'd, (and I admit the weight of the claim,) that common and general worldly prosperity, and a populace well-to-do, and with all life's material comforts, is the main thing, and is enough. It may be argued that our republic is, in performance, really enacting to-day the grandest arts, poems, &c., by beating up the wilderness into fertile farms, and in her railroads, ships, machinery, &c. And it may be ask'd, Are these not better, indeed, for America, than any utterances even of greatest rhapsode, artist, or literatus?

I too hail those achievements with pride and joy: then answer that the soul of man will not with such only—nay, not with such at all—be finally satisfied; but needs what, (standing on these and on all things, as the feet stand on the ground,) is address'd to the loftiest, to itself alone.

Out of such considerations, such truths, arises for treatment in these Vistas the important question of character, of an American stock-personality, with literatures and arts for outlets and return-expressions, and, of course, to correspond, within outlines common to all. To these, the main affair, the thinkers of the United States, in general so acute, have either given feeblest attention, or have remain'd, and remain, in a state of somnolence.

For my part, I would alarm and caution even the political and business reader, and to the utmost extent, against the prevailing delusion that the establishment of free political institutions, and plentiful intellectual smartness, with general good order, physical plenty, industry, &c., (desirable and precious advantages as they all are,) do, of themselves, determine and yield to our experiment of democracy the fruitage of success. With such advantages at present fully, or almost fully, possess'd—the Union just issued, victorious, from the struggle with the only foes it need ever fear, (namely, those within itself, the interior ones,) and with unprecedented materialistic advancement—society, in these States, is canker'd, crude, superstitious, and rotten. Political, or law-made society is, and private, or voluntary society, is also. In any vigor, the element of the moral conscience, the most important, the verteber to State or man, seems to me either entirely lacking, or seriously enfeebled or ungrown.

I say we had best look our times and lands searchingly in the face, like a physician diagnosing some deep disease. Never was there, perhaps, more hollowness at heart than at present, and here in the United States. Genuine belief seems to have left us. The underlying principles of the States are not honestly believ'd in, (for all this hectic glow, and these melo-dramatic screamings,) nor is humanity itself believ'd in. What penetrating eye does not everywhere see through the mask? The spectacle is appaling. We live in an atmosphere of hypocrisy throughout. The men believe not in the women, nor the women in the men. A scornful superciliousness rules in literature. The aim of all the *littérateurs* is to find something to make fun of. A lot of churches, sects, &c., the most dismal phantasms I know, usurp the name of religion. Conversation is a mass of badinage. From deceit in the spirit, the mother of all false deeds, the offspring is already incalculable. An acute and candid person, in the revenue department in Washington, who is led by the course of his employment to regularly visit the cities, north, south and west, to investigate frauds, has talk'd much with me about his discoveries. The depravity of the business classes of our country is not less than has been supposed, but infinitely greater. The official services of America, national, state, and municipal, in all their branches and departments, except the judiciary, are saturated in corruption, bribery, falsehood, mal-administration; and the judiciary is tainted. The great cities reek with respectable as much as non-respectable robbery and scoundrelism. In fashionable life, flippancy, tepid amours, weak infidelism, small aims, or no aims at all, only to kill time. In business, (this all-devouring modern word, business,) the one sole object is, by any means, pecuniary gain. The magician's serpent in the fable ate up all the other serpents; and money-making is our magician's serpent, remaining to-day sole master of the field. The best class we show, is but a mob of fashionably dress'd speculators and vulgarians. True, indeed, behind this fantastic farce, enacted on the visible stage of society, solid things and stupendous labors are to be discover'd, existing crudely and going on in the background, to advance and tell themselves in time. Yet the truths are none the less terrible. I say that our New World democracy, however great a success in uplifting the masses out of their sloughs, in materialistic development, products, and in a certain highly-deceptive superficial popular intellectuality, is, so far, an almost complete failure in its social aspects, and in really grand religious, moral, literary, and esthetic results. In vain do we march with unprecedented strides to empire so colossal, outvying the antique, beyond Alexander's, beyond the proudest sway of Rome. In vain have we annex'd Texas, California, Alaska, and reach north for Canada and south for Cuba. It is as if we were somehow being endow'd with a vast and more and more thoroughly-appointed body, and then left with little or no soul.

Let me illustrate further, as I write, with current observations, localities, &c. The subject is important, and will bear repetition. After an absence, I am now again (September, 1870) in New York city and Brooklyn, on a few weeks' vacation. The splendor, picturesqueness, and oceanic amplitude and rush of these great cities, the unsurpass'd situation, rivers and bay, sparkling sea-tides, costly and lofty new buildings, facades of marble and iron, of original grandeur and elegance of design, with the masses of gay color, the preponderance of white and blue, the flags flying, the endless ships, the tumultuous streets, Broadway, the heavy, low, musical roar, hardly ever intermitted, even at night; the jobbers' houses, the rich shops, the wharves, the great Central Park, and the Brooklyn Park of hills, (as I wander among them this beautiful fall weather, musing, watching, absorbing)—the assemblages of the citizens in their groups, conversations, trades, evening amusements, or along the by-quarters —these, I say, and the like of these, completely satisfy my senses of power, fulness, motion, &c., and give me, through such senses and appetites, and through my esthetic conscience, a continued exaltation and absolute fulfilment. Always and more and more, as I cross the East and North rivers, the ferries, or with the pilots in their pilot-houses, or pass an hour in Wall street, or the gold exchange, I realize, (if we must admit such partialisms,) that not Nature alone is great in her fields of freedom and the open air, in her storms, the shows of night and day, the mountains, forests, seas—but in the artificial, the work of man too is equally great—in this profusion of teeming humanity—in these ingenuities, streets, goods, houses, ships—these hurrying, feverish, electric crowds of men, their complicated business genius, (not least among the geniuses,) and all this mighty, many-threaded wealth and industry concentrated here.

But sternly discarding, shutting our eyes to the glow and grandeur of the general superficial effect, coming down to what is of the only real importance, Personalities, and examining minutely, we question, we ask, Are there, indeed, *men* here worthy the name? Are there athletes? Are there perfect women, to match the generous material luxuriance? Is there a pervading atmosphere of beautiful manners? Are there crops of fine youths, and majestic old persons? Are there arts worthy freedom and a rich people? Is there a great moral and religious civilization—the only justification of a great material one? Confess that to severe eyes, using the moral microscope upon humanity, a sort of dry and flat Sahara appears, these cities, crowded with petty grotesques, malformations, phantoms, playing meaningless antics. Confess that everywhere, in shop, street, church, theatre, bar-room, official chair, are pervading flippancy and vulgarity, low cunning, infidelity—everywhere the youth puny, impudent, foppish, prematurely ripe—everywhere an abnormal libidinousness, unhealthy forms, male, female, painted, padded, dyed, chignon'd, muddy complexions, bad blood, the capacity for good motherhood decreasing or decreas'd, shallow notions of beauty, with a range of manners, or rather lack of manners, (considering the advantages enjoy'd,) probably the meanest to be seen in the world.[2]

Of all this, and these lamentable conditions, to breathe into them the breath recuperative of sane and heroic life, I say a new founded literature, not merely to copy and reflect existing surfaces, or pander to what is called taste—not only to amuse, pass away time, celebrate the beautiful, the refined, the past, or exhibit technical, rhythmic, or grammatical dexterity—but a literature underlying life, religious, consistent with science, handling the elements and forces with competent power, teaching and training men—and, as perhaps the most precious of its results, achieving the entire redemption of woman out of these incredible holds and webs of silliness, millinery, and every kind of dyspeptic depletion—and thus insuring to the States a strong and sweet Female Race, a race of perfect Mothers—is what is needed.

And now, in the full conception of these facts and points, and all that they infer, pro and con—with yet unshaken faith in the elements of the American masses, the composites, of both sexes, and even consider'd as individuals—and ever recognizing in them the broadest bases of the best literary and esthetic appreciation—I proceed with my speculations, Vistas.

First, let us see what we can make out of a brief, general, sentimental consideration of political democracy, and whence it has arisen, with regard to some of its current features, as an aggregate, and as the basic structure of our future literature and authorship. We shall, it is true, quickly and continually find the origin-idea of the singleness of man, individualism, asserting itself, and cropping forth, even from the opposite ideas. But the mass, or lump character, for imperative reasons, is to be ever carefully weigh'd, borne in mind, and provided for. Only from it, and from its proper regulation and potency, comes the other, comes the chance of individualism. The two are contradictory, but our task is to reconcile them.[3]

The political history of the past may be summ'd up as having grown out of what underlies the words, order, safety, caste, and especially out of the need of some prompt deciding authority, and of cohesion at all cost. Leaping time, we come to the period within the memory of people now living, when, as from some lair where they had

---

[2] Whitman's note: "Of these rapidly-sketch'd hiatuses, the two which seem to me most serious are, for one, the condition, absence, or perhaps the singular abeyance, of moral conscientious fibre all through American society; and, for another, the appaling depletion of women in their powers of sane athletic maternity, their crowning attribute, and ever making the woman, in loftiest spheres, superior to the man.

I have sometimes thought, indeed, that the sole avenue and means of a reconstructed sociology depended, primarily, on a new birth, elevation, expansion, invigoration of woman, affording, for races to come, (as the conditions that antedate birth are indispensable,) a perfect motherhood. Great, great, indeed, far greater than they know, is the sphere of women. But doubtless the question of such new sociology all goes together, includes many varied and complex influences and premises, and the man as well as the woman, and the woman as well as the man."

[3] Whitman's note: "The question hinted here is one which time only can answer. Must not the virtue of modern Individualism, continually enlarging, usurping all, seriously affect, perhaps keep down entirely, in America, the like of the ancient virtue of Patriotism, the fervid and absorbing love of general country? I have no doubt myself that the two will merge, and will mutually profit and brace each other, and that from them a greater product, a third, will arise. But I feel that at present they and their oppositions form a serious problem and paradox in the United States."

slumber'd long, accumulating wrath, sprang up and are yet active, (1790, and on even to the present, 1870,) those noisy eructations, destructive iconoclasms, a fierce sense of wrongs, amid which moves the form, well known in modern history, in the old world, stain'd with much blood, and mark'd by savage reactionary clamors and demands. These bear, mostly, as on one inclosing point of need.

For after the rest is said—after the many time-honor'd and really true things for subordination, experience, rights of property, &c., have been listen'd to and acquiesced in—after the valuable and well-settled statement of our duties and relations in society is thoroughly conn'd over and exhausted—it remains to bring forward and modify everything else with the idea of that Something a man is, (last precious consolation of the drudging poor,) standing apart from all else, divine in his own right, and a woman in hers, sole and untouchable by any canons of authority, or any rule derived from precedent, state-safety, the acts of legislatures, or even from what is called religion, modesty, or art. The radiation of this truth is the key of the most significant doings of our immediately preceding three centuries, and has been the political genesis and life of America. Advancing visibly, it still more advances invisibly. Underneath the fluctuations of the expressions of society, as well as the movements of the politics of the leading nations of the world, we see steadily pressing ahead and strengthening itself, even in the midst of immense tendencies toward aggregation, this image of completeness in separatism, of individual personal dignity, of a single person, either male or female, characterized in the main, not from extrinsic acquirements or position, but in the pride of himself or herself alone; and, as an eventual conclusion and summing up, (or else the entire scheme of things is aimless, a cheat, a crash,) the simple idea that the last, best dependence is to be upon humanity itself, and its own inherent, normal, full-grown qualities, without any superstitious support whatever. This idea of perfect individualism it is indeed that deepest tinges and gives character to the idea of the aggregate. For it is mainly or altogether to serve independent separatism that we favor a strong generalization, consolidation. As it is to give the best vitality and freedom to the rights of the States, (every bit as important as the right of nationality, the union,) that we insist on the identity of the Union at all hazards.

The purpose of democracy—supplanting old belief in the necessary absoluteness of establish'd dynastic rulership, temporal, ecclesiastical, and scholastic, as furnishing the only security against chaos, crime, and ignorance—is, through many transmigrations, and amid endless ridicules, arguments, and ostensible failures, to illustrate, at all hazards, this doctrine or theory that man, properly train'd in sanest, highest freedom, may and must become a law, and series of laws, unto himself, surrounding and providing for, not only his own personal control, but all his relations to other individuals, and to the State; and that, while other theories, as in the past histories of nations, have proved wise enough, and indispensable perhaps for their conditions, *this,* as matters now stand in our civilized world, is the only scheme worth working from, as warranting results like those of Nature's laws, reliable, when once establish'd, to carry on themselves.

The argument of the matter is extensive, and, we admit, by no means all on one side. What we shall offer will be far, far from sufficient. But while leaving unsaid much that should properly even prepare the way for the treatment of this many-sided question of political liberty, equality, or republicanism—leaving the whole history and consideration of the feudal plan and its products, embodying humanity, its politics and civilization, through the retrospect of past time, (which plan and products, indeed, make up all of the past, and a large part of the present)—leaving unanswer'd, at least by any specific and local answer, many a well-wrought argument and instance, and many a conscientious declamatory cry and warning—as, very lately, from an eminent and venerable person abroad[4]—things, problems, full of doubt, dread, suspense, (not new to me, but old occupiers of many an anxious hour in city's din, or night's silence,) we still may give a page or so, whose drift is opportune. Time alone can finally answer these things. But as a substitute in passing, let us, even if fragmentarily, throw forth a short direct or indirect suggestion of the premises of that other plan, in the new spirit, under the new forms, started here in our America.

As to the political section of Democracy, which introduces and breaks ground for further and vaster sections, few probably are the minds, even in these republican States, that fully comprehend the aptness of that phrase, "THE GOVERNMENT OF THE PEOPLE, BY THE PEOPLE, FOR THE PEOPLE," which we inherit from the lips of Abraham Lincoln; a formula whose verbal shape is homely wit, but whose scope includes both the totality and all minutiæ of the lesson.

The People! Like our huge earth itself, which, to ordinary scansion, is full of vulgar contradictions and offence, man, viewed in the lump, displeases, and is a constant puzzle and affront to the merely educated classes. The rare, cosmical, artist-mind, lit with the Infinite, alone confronts his manifold and oceanic qualities—but taste, intelligence and culture, (so-called,) have been against the masses, and remain so. There is plenty of glamour about the most damnable crimes and hoggish meannesses, special and general, of the feudal and dynastic world over there, with its *personnel* of lords and queens and courts, so well-dress'd and so handsome. But the People are ungrammatical, untidy, and their sins gaunt and ill-bred.

Literature, strictly consider'd, has never recognized the People, and, whatever may be said, does not to-day. Speaking generally, the tendencies of literature, as hitherto pursued, have been to make mostly critical and querulous men. It seems as if, so far, there were some natural repugnance between a literary and professional life, and the rude rank spirit of the democracies. There is, in later literature, a treatment of benevolence, a charity business, rife enough it is true; but I know nothing more rare, even in this country, than a fit scientific estimate and reverent appreciation of the People—of their measureless wealth of latent power and capacity, their vast, artistic contrasts of lights and shades—with, in America, their entire reliability in emergencies, and a certain breadth of historic grandeur, of peace or war, far surpassing all the vaunted samples of book-heroes, or any *haut-ton* coteries, in all the records of the world. . . .

[4] The English essayist and historian Thomas Carlyle (1795–1881) attacked democratic ideology and institutions in "Shooting Niagara" (1867). Whitman's note follows. " 'SHOOTING NIAGARA.'—I was at first roused to much anger and abuse by this essay from Mr. Carlyle, so insulting to the theory of America—but happening to think afterwards how I had more than once been in the like mood, during which his essay was evidently cast, and seen persons and things in the same light, (indeed some might say there are signs of the same feeling in these Vistas)—I have since read it again, not only as a study, expressing as it does certain judgments from the highest feudal point of view, but have read it with respect as coming from an earnest soul, and as contributing certain sharp-cutting metallic grains, which, if not gold or silver, may be good hard, honest iron."

[from A National Character]

So much contributed, to be conn'd well, to help prepare and brace our edifice, our plann'd Idea—we still proceed to give it in another of its aspects—perhaps the main, the high façade of all. For to democracy, the leveler, the unyielding principle of the average, is surely join'd another principle, equally unyielding, closely tracking the first, indispensable to it, opposite, (as the sexes are opposite,) and whose existence, confronting and ever modifying the other, often clashing, paradoxical, yet neither of highest avail without the other, plainly supplies to these grand cosmic politics of ours, and to the launch'd forth mortal dangers of republicanism, to-day or any day, the counterpart and offset whereby Nature restrains the deadly original relentlessness of all her first-class laws. This second principle is individuality, the pride and centripetal isolation of a human being in himself—identity—personalism. Whatever the name, its acceptance and thorough infusion through the organizations of political common-alty now shooting Aurora-like about the world, are of utmost importance, as the principle itself is needed for very life's sake. It forms, in a sort, or is to form, the compensating balance-wheel of the successful working machinery of aggregate America.

And, if we think of it, what does civilization itself rest upon—and what object has it, with its religions, arts, schools, &c., but rich, luxuriant, varied personalism? To that, all bends; and it is because toward such result democracy alone, on anything like Nature's scale, breaks up the limitless fallows of humankind, and plants the seed, and gives fair play, that its claims now precede the rest. The literature, songs, esthetics, &c., of a country are of importance principally because they furnish the materials and suggestions of personality for the women and men of that country, and enforce them in a thousand effective ways.[5] As the top-most claim of a strong consolidating of the nationality of these States, is, that only by such powerful compaction can the separate States secure that full and free swing within their spheres, which is becoming to them,

---

[5] Whitman's note: "After the rest is satiated, all interest culminates in the field of persons, and never flags there. Accordingly in this field have the great poets and literatuses signally toil'd. They too, in all ages, all lands, have been creators, fashioning, making types of men and women, as Adam and Eve are made in the divine fable. Behold, shaped, bred by orientalism, feudalism, through their long growth and culmination, and breeding back in return—(when shall we have an equal series, typical of democracy?)—behold, commencing in primal Asia, (apparently formulated, in what beginning we know, in the gods of the mythologies, and coming down thence,) a few samples out of the countless product, bequeath'd to the moderns, bequeath'd to America as studies. For the men, Yudishtura, Rama, Arjuna, Solomon, most of the Old and New Testament characters; Achilles, Ulysses, Theseus, Prometheus, Hercules, Æneas, Plutarch's heroes; the Merlin of Celtic bards; the Cid, Arthur and his knights, Siegfried and Hagen in the Nibelungen; Roland and Oliver; Roustam in the Shah-Nemah; and so on to Milton's Satan, Cervantes' Don Quixote, Shakspere's Hamlet, Richard II., Lear, Marc Antony, &c., and the modern Faust. These, I say, are models, combined, adjusted to other standards than America's, but of priceless value to her and hers.

Among women, the goddesses of the Egyptian, Indian and Greek mythologies, certain Bible characters, especially the Holy Mother; Cleopatra, Penelope; the portraits of Brunhelde and Chriemhilde in the Nibelungen; Oriana, Una, &c.; the modern Consuelo, Walter Scott's Jeanie and Effie Deans, &c., &c. (Yet woman portray'd or outlin'd at her best, or as perfect human mother, does not hitherto, it seems to me, fully appear in literature.)"

each after its kind, so will individuality, with unimpeded branchings, flourish best under imperial republican forms.

Assuming Democracy to be at present in its embryo condition, and that the only large and satisfactory justification of it resides in the future, mainly through the copious production of perfect characters among the people, and through the advent of a sane and pervading religiousness, it is with regard to the atmosphere and spaciousness fit for such characters, and of certain nutriment and cartoon-draftings proper for them, and indicating them for New World purposes, that I continue the present state-ment—an exploration, as of new ground, wherein, like other primitive surveyors, I must do the best I can, leaving it to those who come after me to do much better. (The service, in fact, if any, must be to break a sort of first path or track, no matter how rude and ungeometrical.)

   We have frequently printed the word Democracy. Yet I cannot too often repeat that it is a word the real gist of which still sleeps, quite unawaken'd, notwithstanding the resonance and the many angry tempests out of which its syllables have come, from pen or tongue. It is a great word, whose history, I suppose, remains unwritten, because that history has yet to be enacted. It is, in some sort, younger brother of another great and often-used word, Nature, whose history also waits unwritten. As I perceive, the tendencies of our day, in the States, (and I entirely respect them,) are toward those vast and sweeping movements, influences, moral and physical, of humanity, now and always current over the planet, on the scale of the impulses of the elements. Then it is also good to reduce the whole matter to the consideration of a single self, a man, a woman, on permanent grounds. Even for the treatment of the universal, in politics, metaphysics, or anything, sooner or later we come down to one single, solitary soul.

There is, in sanest hours, a consciousness, a thought that rises, independent, lifted out from all else, calm, like the stars, shining eternal. This is the thought of identity—yours for you, whoever you are, as mine for me. Miracle of miracles, beyond statement, most spiritual and vaguest of earth's dreams, yet hardest basic fact, and only entrance to all facts. In such devout hours, in the midst of the significant wonders of heaven and earth, (significant only because of the Me in the centre,) creeds, conven-tions, fall away and become of no account before this simple idea. Under the luminousness of real vision, it alone takes possession, takes value. Like the shadowy dwarf in the fable, once liberated and look'd upon, it expands over the whole earth, and spreads to the roof of heaven.

   The quality of BEING, in the object's self, according to its own central idea and purpose, and of growing therefrom and thereto—not criticism by other standards, and adjustments thereto—is the lesson of Nature. True, the full man wisely gathers, culls, absorbs; but if, engaged disproportionately in that, he slights or overlays the precious idiocrasy and special nativity and intention that he is, the man's self, the main thing, is a failure, however wide his general cultivation. Thus, in our times, refinement and delicatesse are not only attended to sufficiently, but threaten to eat us up, like a cancer. Already, the democratic genius watches, ill-pleased, these tendencies. Provision for a little healthy rudeness, savage virtue, justification of what one has in one's self, whatever it is, is demanded. Negative qualities, even deficiencies, would be a relief. Singleness and normal simplicity and separation, amid this more and more complex, more and more artificialized state of society—how pensively we yearn for them! how we would welcome their return!

In some such direction, then—at any rate enough to preserve the balance—we feel called upon to throw what weight we can, not for absolute reasons, but current ones. To prune, gather, trim, conform, and ever cram and stuff, and be genteel and proper, is the pressure of our days. While aware that much can be said even in behalf of all this, we perceive that we have not now to consider the question of what is demanded to serve a half-starved and barbarous nation, or set of nations, but what is most applicable, most pertinent, for numerous congeries of conventional, over-corpulent societies, already becoming stifled and rotten with flatulent, infidelistic literature, and polite conformity and art. In addition to establish'd sciences, we suggest a science as it were of healthy average personalism, on original-universal grounds, the object of which should be to raise up and supply through the States a copious race of superb American men and women, cheerful, religious, ahead of any yet known.

America has yet morally and artistically originated nothing. She seems singularly unaware that the models of persons, books, manners, &c., appropriate for former conditions and for European lands, are but exiles and exotics here. No current of her life, as shown on the surfaces of what is authoritatively called her society, accepts or runs into social or esthetic democracy; but all the currents set squarely against it. Never, in the Old World, was thoroughly upholster'd exterior appearance and show, mental and other, built entirely on the idea of caste, and on the sufficiency of mere outside acquisition—never were glibness, verbal intellect, more the test, the emula-tion—more loftily elevated as head and sample—than they are on the surface of our republican States this day. The writers of a time hint the mottoes of its gods. The word of the modern, say these voices, is the word Culture.

We find ourselves abruptly in close quarters with the enemy. This word Culture, or what it has come to represent, involves, by contrast, our whole theme, and has been, indeed, the spur, urging us to engagement. Certain questions arise. As now taught, accepted and carried out, are not the processes of culture rapidly creating a class of supercilious infidels, who believe in nothing? Shall a man lose himself in countless masses of adjustments, and be so shaped with reference to this, that, and the other, that the simply good and healthy and brave parts of him are reduced and clipp'd away, like the bordering of box in a garden? You can cultivate corn and roses and orchards—but who shall cultivate the mountain peaks, the ocean, and the tumbling gorgeousness of the clouds? Lastly—is the readily-given reply that culture only seeks to help, systematize, and put in attitude, the elements of fertility and power, a conclusive reply?

I do not so much object to the name, or word, but I should certainly insist, for the purposes of these States, on a radical change of category, in the distribution of precedence. I should demand a programme of culture, drawn out, not for a single class alone, or for the parlors or lecture-rooms, but with an eye to practical life, the west, the working-men, the facts of farms and jack-planes and engineers, and of the broad range of the women also of the middle and working strata, and with reference to the perfect equality of women, and of a grand and powerful motherhood. I should demand of this programme or theory a scope generous enough to include the widest human area. It must have for its spinal meaning the formation of a typical personality of character, eligible to the uses of the high average of men—and *not* restricted by conditions ineligible to the masses. The best culture will always be that of the manly and courageous instincts, and loving perceptions, and of self-respect—aiming to form, over this continent, an idiocrasy of universalism, which, true child of America, will bring joy to its mother, returning to her in her own spirit, recruiting myriads of offspring, able, natural, perceptive, tolerant, devout believers in her, America, and with some definite instinct why and for what she has arisen, most vast, most formidable of historic births, and is, now and here, with wonderful step, journeying through Time.

The problem, as it seems to me, presented to the New World, is, under permanent law and order, and after preserving cohesion, (ensemble-Individuality,) at all hazards, to vitalize man's free play of special Personalism, recognizing in it something that calls ever more to be consider'd, fed, and adopted as the substratum for the best that belongs to us, (government indeed is for it,) including the new esthetics of our future.

To formulate beyond this present vagueness—to help line and put before us the species, or a specimen of the species, of the democratic ethnology of the future, is a work toward which the genius of our land, with peculiar encouragement, invites her well-wishers. Already certain limnings, more or less grotesque, more or less fading and watery, have appear'd. We too, (repressing doubts and qualms,) will try our hand.

Attempting, then, however crudely, a basic model or portrait of personality for general use for the manliness of the States, (and doubtless that is most useful which is most simple and comprehensive for all, and toned low enough,) we should prepare the canvas well beforehand. Parentage must consider itself in advance. (Will the time hasten when fatherhood and motherhood shall become a science—and the noblest science?) To our model, a clear-blooded, strong-fibred physique, is indispensable; the questions of food, drink, air, exercise, assimilation, digestion, can never be intermitted. Out of these we descry a well-begotten selfhood—in youth, fresh, ardent, emotional, aspiring, full of adventure; at maturity, brave, perceptive, under control, neither too talkative nor too reticent, neither flippant nor sombre; of the bodily figure, the movements easy, the complexion showing the best blood, somewhat flush'd, breast expanded, an erect attitude, a voice whose sound outvies music, eyes of calm and steady gaze, yet capable also of flashing—and a general presence that holds its own in the company of the highest. (For it is native personality, and that alone, that endows a man to stand before presidents or generals, or in any distinguish'd collection, with *aplomb*—and *not* culture, or any knowledge or intellect whatever.)

With regard to the mental-educational part of our model, enlargement of intellect, stores of cephalic knowledge, &c., the concentration thitherward of all the customs of our age, especially in America, is so overweening, and provides so fully for that part, that, important and necessary as it is, it really needs nothing from us here—except, indeed, a phrase of warning and restraint. Manners, costumes, too, though important, we need not dwell upon here. Like beauty, grace of motion, &c., they are results. Causes, original things, being attended to, the right manners unerringly follow. Much is said, among artists, of "the grand style," as if it were a thing by itself. When a man, artist or whoever, has health, pride, acuteness, noble aspirations, he has the motive-elements of the grandest style. The rest is but manipulation, (yet that is no small matter.)

Leaving still unspecified several sterling parts of any model fit for the future personality of America, I must not fail, again and ever, to pronounce myself on one, probably the least attended to in modern times—a hiatus, indeed, threatening its gloomiest consequences after us. I mean the simple, unsophisticated Conscience, the primary moral element. If I were asked to specify in what quarter lie the grounds of darkest dread, respecting the America of our hopes, I should have to point to this particular. I should demand the invariable application to individuality, this day and any day, of that old, ever-true plumb-rule of persons, eras, nations. Our triumphant modern civilizee, with his all-schooling and his wondrous appliances, will still show himself but an amputation while this deficiency remains. Beyond, (assuming a more hopeful tone,) the vertebration of the manly and womanly personalism of our western world, can only be, and is, indeed, to be, (I hope,) its all penetrating Religiousness.

The ripeness of Religion is doubtless to be looked for in this field of individuality, and is a result that no organization or church can ever achieve. As history is poorly retain'd by what the technists call history, and is not given out from their pages, except the learner has in himself the sense of the well-wrapt, never yet written, perhaps impossible to be written, history—so Religion, although casually arrested, and, after a fashion, preserv'd in the churches and creeds, does not depend at all upon them, but is a part of the identified soul, which, when greatest, knows not bibles in the old way, but in new ways—the identified soul, which can really confront Religion when it extricates itself entirely from the churches, and not before.

Personalism fuses this, and favors it. I should say, indeed, that only in the perfect uncontamination and solitariness of individuality may the spirituality of religion positively come forth at all. Only here, and on such terms, the meditation, the devout ecstasy, the soaring flight. Only here, communion with the mysteries, the eternal problems, whence? whither? Alone, and identity, and the mood—and the soul emerges, and all statements, churches, sermons, melt away like vapors. Alone, and silent thought and awe, and aspiration—and then the interior consciousness, like a hitherto unseen inscription, in magic ink, beams out its wondrous lines to the sense. Bibles may convey, and priests expound, but it is exclusively for the noiseless operation of one's isolated Self, to enter the pure ether of veneration, reach the divine levels, and commune with the unutterable.

To practically enter into politics is an important part of American personalism. To every young man, north and south, earnestly studying these things, I should here, as an offset to what I have said in former pages, now also say, that may-be to views of very largest scope, after all, perhaps the political, (perhaps the literary and sociological,) America goes best about its development its own way—sometimes, to temporary sight, appaling enough. It is the fashion among dillettants and fops (perhaps I myself am not guiltless,) to decry the whole formulation of the active politics of America, as beyond redemption, and to be carefully kept away from. See you that you do not fall into this error. America, it may be, is doing very well upon the whole, notwithstanding these antics of the parties and their leaders, these half-brain'd nominees, the many ignorant ballots, and many elected failures and blatherers. It is the dillettants, and all who shirk their duty, who are not doing well. As for you, I advise you to enter more strongly yet into politics. I advise every young man to do so. Always inform yourself; always do the best you can; always vote. Disengage yourself from parties. They have been useful, and to some extent remain so; but the floating, uncommitted electors, farmers, clerks, mechanics, the masters of parties—watching aloof, including victory this side or that side—such are the ones most needed, present and future. For America, if eligible at all to downfall and ruin, is eligible within herself, not without; for I see clearly that the combined foreign world could not beat her down. But these savage, wolfish parties alarm me. Owning no law but their own will, more and more combative, less and less tolerant of the idea of ensemble and of equal brotherhood, the perfect equality of the States, the ever-overarching American ideas, it behooves you to convey yourself implicitly to no party, nor submit blindly to their dictators, but steadily hold yourself judge and master over all of them.

So much, (hastily toss'd together, and leaving far more unsaid,) for an ideal, or intimations of an ideal, toward American manhood. But the other sex, in our land, requires at least a basis of suggestion.

I have seen a young American woman, one of a large family of daughters, who, some years since, migrated from her meagre country home to one of the northern cities, to gain her own support. She soon became an expert seamstress, but finding the employment too confining for health and comfort, she went boldly to work for others, to house-keep, cook, clean, &c. After trying several places, she fell upon one where she was suited. She has told me that she finds nothing degrading in her position; it is not inconsistent with personal dignity, self-respect, and the respect of others. She confers benefits and receives them. She has good health; her presence itself is healthy and bracing; her character is unstain'd; she has made herself understood, and preserves her independence, and has been able to help her parents, and educate and get places for her sisters; and her course of life is not without opportunities for mental improvement, and of much quiet, uncosting happiness and love.

I have seen another woman who, from taste and necessity conjoin'd, has gone into practical affairs, carries on a mechanical business, partly works at it herself, dashes out more and more into real hardy life, is not abash'd by the coarseness of the contact, knows how to be firm and silent at the same time, holds her own with unvarying coolness and decorum, and will compare, any day, with superior carpenters, farmers, and even boatmen and drivers. For all that, she has not lost the charm of the womanly nature, but preserves and bears it fully, though through such rugged presentation.

Then there is the wife of a mechanic, mother of two children, a woman of merely passable English education, but of fine wit, with all her sex's grace and intuitions, who exhibits, indeed, such a noble female personality, that I am fain to record it here. Never abnegating her own proper independence, but always genially preserving it, and what belongs to it—cooking, washing, child-nursing, house-tending—she beams sunshine out of all these duties, and makes them illustrious. Physiologically sweet and sound, loving work, practical, she yet knows that there are intervals, however few, devoted to recreation, music, leisure, hospitality—and affords such intervals. Whatever she does, and wherever she is, that charm, that indescribable perfume of genuine womanhood attends her, goes with her, exhales from her, which belongs of right to all the sex, and is, or ought to be, the invariable atmosphere and common aureola of old as well as young.

My dear mother once described to me a resplendent person, down on Long Island, whom she knew in early days. She was known by the name of the Peacemaker. She was well toward eighty years old, of happy and sunny temperament, had always lived on a farm, and was very neighborly, sensible and discreet, an invariable and welcom'd favorite, especially with young married women. She had numerous children and grandchildren. She was uneducated, but possess'd a native dignity. She had come to be a tacitly agreed upon domestic regulator, judge, settler of difficulties, shepherdess, and reconciler in the land. She was a sight to draw near and look upon, with her large figure, her profuse snow-white hair, (uncoif'd by any head-dress or cap,) dark eyes, clear complexion, sweet breath, and peculiar personal magnetism.

The foregoing portraits, I admit, are frightfully out of line from these imported models of womanly personality—the stock feminine characters of the current novelists, or of the foreign court poems, (Ophelias, Enids, princesses, or ladies of one thing or another,) which fill the envying dreams of so many poor girls, and are accepted by our men, too, as supreme ideals of feminine excellence to be sought after. But I present mine just for a change.

Then there are mutterings, (we will not now stop to heed them here, but they must be heeded,) of something more revolutionary. The day is coming when the deep questions of woman's entrance amid the arenas of practical life, politics, the suffrage, &c., will not only be argued all around us, but may be put to decision, and real experiment.

Of course, in these States, for both man and woman, we must entirely recast the types of highest personality from what the oriental, feudal, ecclesiastical worlds bequeath us, and which yet possess the imaginative and esthetic fields of the United States, pictorial and melodramatic, not without use as studies, but making sad work, and forming a strange anachronism upon the scenes and exigencies around us. Of course, the old undying elements remain. The task is, to successfully adjust them to new combinations, our own days. Nor is this so incredible. I can conceive a community, to-day and here, in which, on a sufficient scale, the perfect personalities, without noise meet; say in some pleasant western settlement or town, where a couple of hundred best men and women, of ordinary worldly status, have by luck been drawn together, with nothing extra of genius or wealth, but virtuous, chaste, industrious, cheerful, resolute, friendly and devout. I can conceive such a community organized in running order, powers judiciously delegated—farming, building, trade, courts, mails, schools, elections, all attended to; and then the rest of life, the main thing, freely branching and blossoming in each individual, and bearing golden fruit. I can see there, in every young and old man, after his kind, and in every woman after hers, a true personality, develop'd, exercised proportionately in body, mind, and spirit. I can imagine this case as one not necessarily rare or difficult, but in buoyant accordance with the municipal and general requirements of our times. And I can realize in it the culmination of something better than any stereotyped *eclat* of history or poems. Perhaps, unsung, undramatized, unput in essays or biographies—perhaps even some such community already exists, in Ohio, Illinois, Missouri, or somewhere, practically fulfilling itself, and thus outvying, in cheapest vulgar life, all that has been hitherto shown in best ideal pictures.

In short, and to sum up, America, betaking herself to formative action, (as it is about time for more solid achievement, and less windy promise,) must, for her purposes, cease to recognize a theory of character grown of feudal aristocracies, or form'd by merely literary standards, or from any ultramarine, full-dress formulas of culture, polish, caste, &c., and must sternly promulgate her own new standard, yet old enough, and accepting the old, the perennial elements, and combining them into groups, unities, appropriate to the modern, the democratic, the west, and to the practical occasions and needs of our own cities, and of the agricultural regions. Ever the most precious in the common. Ever the fresh breeze of field, or hill, or lake, is more than any palpitation of fans, though of ivory, and redolent with perfume; and the air is more than the costliest perfumes. . . .

[*from* **A National Literature**]

Compared with the past, our modern science soars, and our journals serve—but ideal and even ordinary romantic literature, does not, I think, substantially advance. Behold the prolific brood of the contemporary novel, magazine-tale, theatre-play, &c. The same endless thread of tangled and superlative love-story, inherited, apparently from the Amadises and Palmerins of the 13th, 14th, and 15th centuries over there in Europe. The costumes and associations brought down to date, the seasoning hotter and more varied, the dragons and ogres left out—but the *thing,* I should say, has not advanced—is just as sensational, just as strain'd—remains about the same, nor more, nor less.

What is the reason our time, our lands, that we see no fresh local courage, sanity, of our own—the Mississippi, stalwart Western men, real mental and physical facts, Southerners, &c., in the body of our literature? especially the poetic part of it. But always, instead, a parcel of dandies and ennuyees, dapper little gentlemen from abroad, who flood us with their thin sentiment of parlors, parasols, piano-songs, tinkling rhymes, the five-hundredth importation—or whimpering and crying about something, chasing one aborted conceit after another, and forever occupied in dyspeptic amours with dyspeptic women. While, current and novel, the grandest events and revolutions, and stormiest passions of history, are crossing to-day with unparallel'd rapidity and magnificence over the stages of our own and all the continents, offering new materials, opening new vistas, with largest needs, inviting the daring launching forth of conceptions in literature, inspired by them, soaring in highest regions, serving art in its highest, (which is only the other name for serving God, and serving humanity,) where is the man of letters, where is the book, with any nobler aim than to follow in the old track, repeat what has been said before—and, as its utmost triumph, sell well, and be erudite or elegant?

Mark the roads, the processes, through which these States have arrived, standing easy, henceforth ever-equal, ever-compact, in their range to-day. European adventures? the most antique? Asiatic or African? old history—miracles—romances? Rather, our own unquestion'd facts. They hasten, incredible, blazing bright as fire. From the deeds and days of Columbus down to the present, and including the present—and especially the late Secession war—when I con them, I feel, every leaf, like stopping to see if I have not made a mistake, and fall'n on the splendid figments of some dream. But it is no dream. We stand, live, move, in the huge flow of our age's materialism—in its spirituality. We have had founded for us the most positive of lands. The founders have pass'd to other spheres—but what are these terrible duties they have left us?

Their politics the United States have, in my opinion, with all their faults, already substantially establish'd, for good, on their own native, sound, long-vista'd principles, never to be overturn'd, offering a sure basis for all the rest. With that, their future religious forms, sociology, literature, teachers, schools, costumes, &c., are of course to make a compact whole, uniform, on tallying principles. For how can we remain, divided, contradicting ourselves, this way?[6] I say we can only attain harmony and stability by consulting ensemble and the ethic purports, and faithfully building upon them. For the New World, indeed, after two grand stages of preparation-strata, I perceive that now a third stage, being ready for, (and without which the other two were useless,) with unmistakable signs appears. The First stage was the planning and putting on record the political foundation rights of immense masses of people—indeed all people—in the organization of republican National, State, and municipal governments, all constructed with reference to each, and each to all. This is the American programme, not for classes, but for universal man, and is embodied in the compacts of the Declaration of Independence and, as it began and has now grown, with its amendments, the Federal Constitution—and in the State governments, with all their interiors, and with general suffrage; those having the sense not only of what is in themselves, but that their certain several things started, planted, hundreds of others in the same direction duly arise and follow. The Second stage relates to material prosperity, wealth, produce, labor-saving machines, iron, cotton, local, State and continental railways, intercommunication and trade with all lands, steamships, mining, general employment, organization of great cities, cheap appliances for comfort, numberless technical schools, books, newspapers, a currency for money circulation, &c. The Third stage, rising out of the previous ones, to make them and all illustrious, I, now, for one, promulge, announcing a native expression-spirit, getting into form, adult, and through mentality, for these States, self-contain'd, different from others, more expansive, more rich and free, to be evidenced by original authors and poets to come, by American personalities, plenty of them, male and female, traversing the States, none excepted—and by native superber tableaux and growths of language, songs, operas, orations, lectures, architecture—and by a sublime and serious Religious Democracy sternly taking command, dissolving the old, sloughing off surfaces, and from its own interior and vital principles, reconstructing, democratizing society.

[6] Whitman's note: "Note, to-day, an instructive, curious spectacle and conflict. Science, (twin, in its fields, of Democracy in its)—Science, testing absolutely all thoughts, all works, has already burst well upon the world—a sun, mounting, most illuminating, most glorious—surely never again to set. But against it, deeply entrench'd, holding possession, yet remains, (not only through the churches and schools, but by imaginative literature, and unregenerate poetry,) the fossil theology of the mythic-materialistic, superstitious, untaught and credulous, fable-loving, primitive ages of humanity."

For America, type of progress, and of essential faith in man, above all his errors and wickedness—few suspect how deep, how deep it really strikes. The world evidently supposes, and we have evidently supposed so too, that the States are merely to achieve the equal franchise, an elective government—to inaugurate the respectability of labor, and become a nation of practical operatives, law-abiding, orderly and well off. Yes, those are indeed parts of the task of America; but they not only do not exhaust the progressive conception, but rather arise, teeming with it, as the mediums of deeper, higher progress. Daughter of a physical revolution—mother of the true revolutions, which are of the interior life, and of the arts. For so long as the spirit is not changed, any change of appearance is of no avail.

The old men, I remember as a boy, were always talking of American independence. What is independence? Freedom from all laws or bonds except those of one's own being, control'd by the universal ones. To lands, to man, to woman, what is there at last to each, but the inherent soul, nativity, idiocrasy, free, highest-poised, soaring its own flight, following out itself?

At present, these States, in their theology and social standards, (of greater importance than their political institutions,) are entirely held possession of by foreign lands. We see the sons and daughters of the New World, ignorant of its genius, not yet inaugurating the native, the universal, and the near, still importing the distant, the partial, and the dead. We see London, Paris, Italy—not original, superb, as where they belong—but second-hand here, where they do not belong. We see the shreds of Hebrews, Romans, Greeks; but where, on her own soil, do we see, in any faithful, highest, proud expression, America herself? I sometimes question whether she has a corner in her own house.

Not but that in one sense, and a very grand one, good theology, good art, or good literature, has certain features shared in common. The combination fraternizes, ties the races—is, in many particulars, under laws applicable indifferently to all, irrespective of climate or date, and, from whatever source, appeals to emotions, pride, love, spirituality, common to humankind. Nevertheless, they touch a man closest, (perhaps only actually touch him,) even in these, in their expression through autochthonic lights and shades, flavors, fondnesses, aversions, specific incidents, illustrations, out of his own nationality, geography, surroundings, antecedents, &c. The spirit and the form are one, and depend far more on association, identity and place, than is supposed. Subtly interwoven with the materiality and personality of a land, a race—Teuton, Turk, Californian, or what not—there is always something—I can hardly tell what it is—history but describes the results of it—it is the same as the untellable look of some human faces. Nature, too, in her stolid forms, is full of it—but to most it is there a secret. This something is rooted in the invisible roots, the profoundest meanings of that place, race, or nationality; and to absorb and again effuse it, uttering words and products as from its midst, and carrying it into highest regions, is the work, or a main part of the work, of any country's true author, poet, historian, lecturer, and perhaps even priest and philosoph. Here, and here only, are the foundations for our really valuable and permanent verse, drama, &c.

But at present, (judged by any higher scale than that which finds the chief ends of existence to be to feverishly make money during one-half of it, and by some "amusement," or perhaps foreign travel, flippantly kill time, the other half,) and consider'd with reference to purposes of patriotism, health, a noble personality, religion, and the democratic adjustments, all these swarms of poems, literary magazines, dramatic plays, resultant so far from American intellect, and the formation of our best ideas, are useless and a mockery. They strengthen and nourish no one, express nothing characteristic, give decision and purpose to no one, and suffice only the lowest level of vacant minds.

Of what is called the drama, or dramatic presentation in the United States, as now put forth at the theatres, I should say it deserves to be treated with the same gravity, and on a par with the questions of ornamental confectionery at public dinners, or the arrangement of curtains and hangings in a ball-room—nor more, nor less. Of the other, I will not insult the reader's intelligence, (once really entering into the atmosphere of these Vistas,) by supposing it necessary to show, in detail, why the copious dribble, either of our little or well-known rhymesters, does not fulfil, in any respect, the needs and august occasions of this land. America demands a poetry that is bold, modern, and all-surrounding and kosmical, as she is herself. It must in no respect ignore science or the modern, but inspire itself with science and the modern. It must bend its vision toward the future, more than the past. Like America, it must extricate itself from even the greatest models of the past, and, while courteous to them, must have entire faith in itself, and the products of its own democratic spirit only. Like her, it must place in the van, and hold up at all hazards, the banner of the divine pride of man in himself, (the radical foundation of the new religion.) Long enough have the People been listening to poems in which common humanity, deferential, bends low, humiliated, acknowledging superiors. But America listens to no such poems. Erect, inflated, and fully self-esteeming be the chant; and then America will listen with pleased ears.

Nor may the genuine gold, the gems, when brought to light at last, be probably usher'd forth from any of the quarters currently counted on. To-day, doubtless, the infant genius of American poetic expression, (eluding those highly-refined imported and gilt-edged themes, and sentimental and butterfly flights, pleasant to orthodox publishers—causing tender spasms in the coteries, and warranted not to chafe the sensitive cuticle of the most exquisitely artificial gossamer delicacy,) lies sleeping far away, happily unrecognized and uninjur'd by the coteries, the art-writers, the talkers and critics of the saloons, or the lecturers in the colleges—lies sleeping, aside, unrecking itself, in some western idiom, or native Michigan or Tennessee repartee, or stump-speech—or in Kentucky or Georgia, or the Carolinas—or in some slang or local song or allusion of the Manhattan, Boston, Philadelphia or Baltimore mechanic —or up in the Maine woods—or off in the hut of the California miner, or crossing the Rocky mountains, or along the Pacific railroad—or on the breasts of the young farmers of the northwest, or Canada, or boatmen of the lakes. Rude and coarse nursing-beds, these; but only from such beginnings and stocks, indigenous here, may haply arrive, be grafted, and sprout, in time, flowers of genuine American aroma, and fruits truly and fully our own.

I say it were a standing disgrace to these States—I say it were a disgrace to any nation, distinguish'd above others by the variety and vastness of its territories, its materials, its inventive activity, and the splendid practicality of its people, not to rise and soar above others also in its original styles in literature and art, and its own supply of intellectual and esthetic masterpieces, archetypal, and consistent with itself. I know not a land except ours that has not, to some extent, however small, made its title clear. The Scotch have their born ballads, subtly expressing their past and present, and expressing character. The Irish have theirs. England, Italy, France, Spain, theirs. What has America? With exhaustless mines of the richest ore of epic, lyric, tale, tune, picture, &c., in the Four Years' War; with, indeed, I sometimes think, the richest masses of material ever afforded a nation, more variegated, and on a larger scale—the first sign of proportionate, native, imaginative Soul, and first-class works to match, is, (I cannot too often repeat), so far wanting.

Long ere the second centennial arrives, there will be some forty to fifty great States, among them Canada and Cuba. When the present century closes, our population will be sixty or seventy millions. The Pacific will be ours, and the Atlantic mainly ours. There will be daily electric communication with every part of the globe. What an age! What a land! Where, elsewhere, one so great? The individuality of one nation must then, as always, lead the world. Can there be any doubt who the leader ought to be? Bear in mind, though, that nothing less than the mightiest original non-subordinated SOUL has ever really, gloriously led, or ever can lead. (This Soul—its other name, in these Vistas, is LITERATURE.)

In fond fancy leaping those hundred years ahead, let us survey America's works, poems, philosophies, fulfilling prophecies, and giving form and decision to best ideals. Much that is now undream'd of, we might then perhaps see establish'd, luxuriantly cropping forth, richness, vigor of letters and of artistic expression, in whose products character will be a main requirement, and not merely erudition or elegance.

Intense and loving comradeship, the personal and passionate attachment of man to man—which, hard to define, underlies the lessons and ideals of the profound saviours of every land and age, and which seems to promise, when thoroughly develop'd, cultivated and recognized in manners and literature, the most substantial hope and safety of the future of these States, will then be fully express'd.[7]

A strong-fibred joyousness and faith, and the sense of health *al fresco,* may well enter into the preparation of future noble American authorship. Part of the test of

[7] Whitman's note: "It is to the development, identification, and general prevalence of that fervid comradeship, (the adhesive love, at least rivaling the amative love hitherto possessing imaginative literature, if not going beyond it,) that I look for the counterbalance and offset of our materialistic and vulgar American democracy, and for the spiritualization thereof. Many will say it is a dream, and will not follow my inferences: but I confidently expect a time when there will be seen, running like a half-hid warp through all the myriad audible and visible worldly interests of America, threads of manly friendship, fond and loving, pure and sweet, strong and life-long, carried to degrees hitherto unknown—not only giving tone to individual character, and making it unprecedently emotional, muscular, heroic, and refined, but having the deepest relations to general politics. I say democracy infers such loving comradeship, as its most inevitable twin or counterpart, without which it will be incomplete, in vain, and incapable of perpetuating itself."

a great literatus shall be the absence in him of the idea of the covert, the lurid, the maleficent, the devil, the grim estimates inherited from the Puritans, hell, natural depravity, and the like. The great literatus will be known, among the rest, by his cheerful simplicity, his adherence to natural standards, his limitless faith in God, his reverence, and by the absence in him of doubt, ennui, burlesque, persiflage, or any strain'd and temporary fashion.

Nor must I fail, again and yet again, to clinch, reiterate more plainly still, (O that indeed such survey as we fancy, may show in time this part completed also!) the lofty aim, surely the proudest and the purest, in whose service the future literatus, of whatever field, may gladly labor. As we have intimated, offsetting the material civilization of our race, our nationality, its wealth, territories, factories, population, products, trade, and military and naval strength, and breathing breath of life into all these, and more, must be its moral civilization—the formulation, expression, and aidancy whereof, is the very highest height of literature. The climax of this loftiest range of civilization, rising above all the gorgeous shows and results of wealth, intellect, power, and art, as such—above even theology and religious fervor—is to be its development, from the eternal bases, and the fit expression, of absolute Conscience, moral soundness, Justice. Even in religious fervor there is a touch of animal heat. But moral conscientiousness, crystalline, without flaw, not Godlike only, entirely human, awes and enchants forever. Great is emotional love, even in the order of the rational universe. But, if we must make gradations, I am clear there is something greater. Power, love, veneration, products, genius, esthetics, tried by subtlest comparisons, analyses, and in serenest moods, somewhere fail, somehow become vain. Then noiseless, with flowing steps, the lord, the sun, the last ideal comes. By the names right, justice, truth, we suggest, but do not describe it. To the world of men it remains a dream, an idea as they call it. But no dream is it to the wise—but the proudest, almost only solid lasting thing of all. Its analogy in the material universe is what holds together this world, and every object upon it, and carries its dynamics on forever sure and safe. Its lack, and the persistent shirking of it, as in life, sociology, literature, politics, business, and even sermonizing, these times, or any times, still leaves the abysm, the mortal flaw and smutch, mocking civilization to-day, with all its unquestion'd triumphs, and all the civilization so far known.[8]

Present literature, while magnificently fulfilling certain popular demands, with

[8] Whitman's note: "I am reminded as I write that out of this very conscience, or idea of conscience, of intense moral right, and in its name and strain'd construction, the worst fanaticisms, wars, persecutions, murders, &c., have yet, in all lands, in the past, been broach'd, and have come to their devilish fruition. Much is to be said—but I may say here, and in response, that side by side with the unflagging stimulation of the elements of religion and conscience must henceforth move with equal sway, science, absolute reason, and the general proportionate development of the whole man. These scientific facts, deductions, are divine too —precious counted parts of moral civilization, and, with physical health, indispensable to it, to prevent fanaticism. For abstract religion, I perceive, is easily led astray, ever credulous, and is capable of devouring, remorseless, like fire and flame. Conscience, too, isolated from all else, and from the emotional nature, may but attain the beauty and purity of glacial, snowy ice. We want, for these States, for the general character, a cheerful, religious fervor, endued with the ever-present modifications of the human emotions, friendship, benevolence, with a fair field for scientific inquiry, the right of individual judgment, and always the cooling influences of material Nature."

plenteous knowledge and verbal smartness, is profoundly sophisticated, insane, and its very joy is morbid. It needs tally and express Nature, and the spirit of Nature, and to know and obey the standards. I say the question of Nature, largely consider'd, involves the questions of the esthetic, the emotional, and the religious—and involves happiness. A fitly born and bred race, growing up in right conditions of out-door as much as in-door harmony, activity and development, would probably, from and in those conditions, find it enough merely *to live*—and would, in their relations to the sky, air, water, trees, &c., and to the countless common shows, and in the fact of life itself, discover and achieve happiness—with Being suffused night and day by wholesome extasy, surpassing all the pleasures that wealth, amusement, and even gratified intellect, erudition, or the sense of art, can give.

In the prophetic literature of these States (the reader of my speculations will miss their principal stress unless he allows well for the point that a new Literature, perhaps a new Metaphysics, certainly a new Poetry, are to be, in my opinion, the only sure and worthy supports and expressions of the American Democracy,) Nature, true Nature, and the true idea of Nature, long absent, must, above all, become fully restored, enlarged, and must furnish the pervading atmosphere to poems, and the test of all high literary and esthetic compositions. I do not mean the smooth walks, trimm'd hedges, poseys and nightingales of the English poets, but the whole orb, with its geologic history, the kosmos, carrying fire and snow, that rolls through the illimitable areas, light as a feather, though weighing billions of tons. Furthermore, as by what we now partially call Nature is intended, at most, only what is entertainable by the physical conscience, the sense of matter, and of good animal health—on these it must be distinctly accumulated, incorporated, that man, comprehending these, has, in towering superaddition, the moral and spiritual consciences, indicating his destination beyond the ostensible, the mortal.

To the heights of such estimate of Nature indeed ascending, we proceed to make observations for our Vistas, breathing rarest air. What is I believe called Idealism seems to me to suggest, (guarding against extravagance, and ever modified even by its opposite,) the course of inquiry and desert of favor for our New World metaphysics, their foundation of and in literature, giving hue to all.[9]

[9] Whitman's note: "The culmination and fruit of literary artistic expression, and its final fields of pleasure for the human soul, are in metaphysics, including the mysteries of the spiritual world, the soul itself, and the question of the immortal continuation of our identity. In all ages, the mind of man has brought up here—and always will. Here, at least, of whatever race or era, we stand on common ground. Applause, too, is unanimous, antique or modern. Those authors who work well in this field—though their reward, instead of a handsome percentage, or royalty, may be but simply the laurel-crown of the victors in the great Olympic games—will be dearest to humanity, and their works, however esthetically defective, will be treasur'd forever. The altitude of literature and poetry has always been religion—and always will be. The Indian Vedas, the Nackas of Zoroaster, the Talmud of the Jews, the Old Testament, the Gospel of Christ and his disciples, Plato's works, the Koran of Mohammed, the Edda of Snorro, and so on toward our own day, to Swedenborg, and to the invaluable contributions of Leibnitz, Kant and Hegel—these, with such poems only in which, (while singing well of persons and events, of the passions of man, and the shows of the material universe,) the religious tone, the consciousness of mystery, the recognition of the future, of the unknown, of Deity over and under all, and of the divine purpose, are never absent, but indirectly give tone to all—exhibit literature's real heights and elevations, towering up like the great mountains of the earth.

Standing on this ground—the last, the highest, only permanent ground—and sternly criticising, from it, all works, either of the

(continued)

The elevating and etherealizing ideas of the unknown and of unreality must be brought forward with authority, as they are the legitimate heirs of the known, and of reality, and at least as great as their parents. Fearless of scoffing, and of the ostent, let us take our stand, our ground, and never desert it, to confront the growing excess and arrogance of realism. To the cry, now victorious—the cry of sense, science, flesh, incomes, farms, merchandise, logic, intellect, demonstrations, solid perpetuities, buildings of brick and iron, or even the facts of the shows of trees, earth, rocks, &c., fear not, my brethren, my sisters, to sound out with equally determin'd voice, that conviction brooding within the recesses of every envision'd soul—illusions! apparitions! figments all! True, we must not condemn the show, neither absolutely deny it, for the indispensability of its meanings; but how clearly we see that, migrate in soul to what we can already conceive of superior and spiritual points of view, and, palpable as it seems under present relations, it all and several might, nay certainly would, fall apart and vanish.

I hail with joy the oceanic, variegated, intense practical energy, the demand for facts, even the business materialism of the current age, our States. But wo to the age or land in which these things, movements, stopping at themselves, do not tend to ideas. As fuel to flame, and flame to the heavens, so must wealth, science, materialism—even this democracy of which we make so much—unerringly feed the highest mind, the soul. Infinitude the flight: fathomless the mystery. Man, so diminutive, dilates beyond the sensible universe, competes with, outcopes space and time, meditating even one great idea. Thus, and thus only, does a human being, his spirit, ascend above, and justify, objective Nature, which, probably nothing in itself, is incredibly and divinely serviceable, indispensable, real, here. And as the purport of objective Nature is doubtless folded, hidden, somewhere here—as somewhere here is what this globe and its manifold forms, and the light of day, and night's darkness, and life itself, with all its experiences, are for—it is here the great literature, especially verse, must get its inspiration and throbbing blood. Then may we attain to a poetry worthy the immortal soul of man, and which, while absorbing materials, and, in their own sense, the shows

literary, or any art, we have peremptorily to dismiss every pretensive production, however fine its esthetic or intellectual points, which violates or ignores, or even does not celebrate, the central divine idea of All, suffusing universe, of eternal trains of purpose, in the development, by however slow degrees, of the physical, moral, and spiritual kosmos. I say he has studied, meditated to no profit, whatever may be his mere erudition, who has not absorb'd this simple consciousness and faith. It is not entirely new—but it is for Democracy to elaborate it, and look to build upon and expand from it, with uncompromising reliance. Above the doors of teaching the inscription is to appear, Though little or nothing can be absolutely known, perceiv'd, except from a point of view which is evanescent, yet we know at least one permanency, that Time and Space, in the will of God, furnish successive chains, completions of material births and beginnings, solve all discrepancies, fears and doubts, and eventually fulfil happiness—and that the prophecy of those births, namely spiritual results, throws the true arch over all teaching, all science. The local considerations of sin, disease, deformity, ignorance, death, &c., and their measurement by the superficial mind, and ordinary legislation and theology, are to be met by science, boldly accepting, promulging this faith, and planting the seeds of superber laws—of the explication of the physical universe through the spiritual—and clearing the way for a religion, sweet and unimpugnable alike to little child or great savan."

of Nature, will, above all, have, both directly and indirectly, a freeing, fluidizing, expanding, religious character, exulting with science, fructifying the moral elements, and stimulating aspirations, and meditations on the unknown. . . .
1871

Elizabeth Barstow Stoddard
1823–1902

Elizabeth Barstow Stoddard resisted the conventional in nearly every aspect of her life and work. She rarely felt comfortable growing up in what was essentially a traditional middle-class New England village or studying in what were some of the most refined educational circumstances then available to young women. Her intellectual brilliance, when recognized, was often overlooked by those who found her personally overbearing and disputatious. ("My father said once he never saw any human being with such a talent for the disagreeable," she admitted.) And in a period when sentimental "women's fiction" had cornered the literary marketplace, Stoddard wrote assertive, incisive, often satirical essays on virtually every serious issue of her time. She experimented boldly in her short stories and novels with several narrative techniques that other writers would later turn into hallmarks of twentieth-century literature. Yet most of her writing remained unread during her own life, her career hardly noticed.

Elizabeth Barstow was born in 1823 in Mattapoisett, a small fishing village on Massachusetts's Buzzard's Bay. Her mother was the daughter of the local tailor, her father a shipbuilder whose company built the sloop that Herman Melville sailed to the South Seas. The Barstow family's financial and social standing depended on the uncertainties of the father's business, and young Elizabeth seemed at once envious and resentful of the local gentility. As a child, she read, with the guidance of the local Congregational minister, virtually everything she could locate. She studied at nearby Wheaton College, where she cultivated her interest in literature and resisted the evangelical fervor surrounding her.

At the age of twenty-nine, she married Richard Stoddard, a poet with at best a minor reputation, and moved to New York, where he worked at a customhouse job arranged by Nathaniel Hawthorne. (Several years later, Richard Stoddard would do the same for Herman Melville.) In 1854 Elizabeth Barstow Stoddard began writing a semimonthly column of news and reviews for the *Daily Alta California*. Despite her identity as the eastern "Lady Correspondent" for that San Francisco newspaper, she steadfastly avoided the subjects women writers were conventionally expected to cover: domestic issues addressed to female readers. Instead, she tackled the leading literary and political controversies of the time, wrote entertaining—and often acerbic—sketches of the most prominent figures in those circles, defended her own literary preferences, and repeatedly reminded her audience (and would soon demonstrate herself) that women writers of that period were quite capable of producing more than second-rate popular fiction. The seventy-five columns of sophisticated cultural and social commentary she wrote for that paper read more like journal entries than essays. Their intelligence and wit are matched only by the reports Margaret Fuller filed with the *New York Tribune* some ten years before. Stoddard took great pleasure in what would be her only literary success and delighted in what she called "the artful self-dramatizations" she created in both her life and her writing.

Elizabeth Barstow Stoddard's fiction spans the periods from Hawthorne's romances to the late-nineteenth-century regional realism of Sarah Orne Jewett and Mary Wilkins Freeman. Yet Stoddard's is at once a more intense—and far more elliptical—psychological portrait of character and a more gothic rendition of women's daily routines and social relations. As such, her work stands as a reminder of the limitations of dividing nineteenth-century fiction into "romantic" (antebellum) and "realistic" (post–Civil War) periods.

Her first novel, *The Morgesons,* is a largely autobiographical account of a middle-class individual's quest to overcome the resistance of her family, friends, and acquaintances to her efforts to express a still half-articulated sense of her own sexual and social power. Stoddard's treatment of female psychological complexity cut against the grain of the stereotypes promoted by the popular women's fiction of the time—the works of those widely read writers whom Hawthorne branded a "damned mob of scribbling women." Her psychological portraits may at first recall his work, but Stoddard created in Cassandra Morgeson a stronger, more wide-ranging woman than Hawthorne seemed ready to allow in his fiction. This remarkably unconventional figure more appropriately can be said to complement in specific terms the general definition of "true womanhood" Margaret Fuller offered in *Woman in the Nineteenth Century.*

The Morgesons was published in 1862, ten days after the Battle of Bull Run, and received favorable notices. Yet the public, caught up in the events of the Civil War, paid it scant attention. "*The Morgesons* was my Bull Run," Stoddard sardonically explained years later. Her next novels, *Two Men* (1865) and *Temple House* (1867), elicited similar responses. Although each novel deals generally with the same subject in a similar style, each is narrated from a male's perspective, and each responds more consciously to the prevailing popular taste in fiction. Her last major book-length publication was *Lolly Dink's Doings* (1874), a curious blend of family sketches and portraits published initially as a children's book but clearly with adults in mind. It too slipped past the public eye. Except for a brief flurry of interest in the 1880s, Stoddard's books remained essentially unread by the American public.

The slight public recognition Elizabeth Barstow Stoddard enjoyed in her own lifetime came primarily from her newspaper columns and short stories. She found both a willing publisher and adequate compensation for her stories at *Harper's New Monthly Magazine,* and in short fiction she found a more manageable structure to work with. In "Lemorne *versus* Huell" (1863), for example, Stoddard skillfully combined first-person narrative techniques with social satire to produce playful variations on the formulas for writing romance promulgated by such magazines as *Harper's.* At her best, Elizabeth Barstow Stoddard succeeded admirably, to quote Lawrence Buell and Sandra Zagarell, the scholars most responsible for reclaiming her work for modern readers, in "dramatizing the idiosyncratic behavior of people and communities where deep, strong, passionate instinct is locked in a perpetual struggle with habit, family allegiances, social taboos, and traditional New England restraint."

Although Elizabeth and Richard Stoddard had made the acquaintance of many celebrated American and British writers (including Bryant, Hawthorne, Melville, Whitman, and Lowell), they chose to remain at the center of a small literary circle of nondescript writers, many of whom offered less than judicious responses to their writing and poor advice about their careers. Richard eventually turned to scattered, relatively insignificant, literary enterprises; and Elizabeth's life sank steadily into personal rancor, her writing deeper into obscurity.

One regrettable fact of Elizabeth Barstow Stoddard's literary life, then, was that she was read well neither by the general book-buying public nor by her close literary friends and supporters. Yet despite her unsuccessful efforts to earn a broader audience for her work, Stoddard's writing merits both a more secure place in American literary history and the following praise from her distinguished contemporary William Dean Howells: "In a time when most of us had to write like Tennyson, or Longfellow, or Browning, she would never write like anyone but herself."

Further Reading:
William Dean Howells, *Literary Friends and Acquaintances,* 1900.
J. H. Matlack, "The Literary Career of Elizabeth Barstow Stoddard" (Ph.D. dissertation, Yale University), 1967.
R. Foster, "Introduction," *The Morgesons,* 1971.

Text:
L. Buell and S. A. Zagarell, *The Morgesons and Other Writings, Published and Unpublished,* 1984.

Lemorne *Versus* Huell

The two months I spent at Newport[1] with Aunt Eliza Huell, who had been ordered to the sea-side for the benefit of her health, were the months that created all that is dramatic in my destiny. My aunt was troublesome, for she was not only out of health, but in a lawsuit. She wrote to me, for we lived apart, asking me to accompany her—not because she was fond of me, or wished to give me pleasure, but because I was useful in various ways. Mother insisted upon my accepting her invitation, not because she loved her late husband's sister, but because she thought it wise to cotton to her in every particular, for Aunt Eliza was rich, and we—two lone women—were poor.

[1] Newport, Rhode Island, one of
nineteenth-century America's most popular
summer resorts.

I gave my music-pupils a longer and earlier vacation than usual, took a week to arrange my wardrobe—for I made my own dresses—and then started for New York, with the five dollars which Aunt Eliza had sent for my fare thither. I arrived at her house in Bond Street at 7 a.m., and found her man James in conversation with the milkman. He informed me that Miss Huell was very bad, and that the housekeeper was still in bed. I supposed that Aunt Eliza was in bed also, but I had hardly entered the house when I heard her bell ring as she only could ring it—with an impatient jerk.

"She wants hot milk," said James, "and the man has just come."

I laid my bonnet down, and went to the kitchen. Saluting the cook, who was an old acquaintance, and who told me that the "divil" had been in the range that morning, I took a pan, into which I poured some milk, and held it over the gaslight till it was hot; then I carried it up to Aunt Eliza.

"Here is your milk, Aunt Eliza. You have sent for me to help you, and I begin with the earliest opportunity."

"I looked for you an hour ago. Ring the bell."

I rang it.

"Your mother is well, I suppose. She would have sent you, though, had she been sick in bed."

"She has done so. She thinks better of my coming than I do."

The housekeeper, Mrs. Roll, came in, and Aunt Eliza politely requested her to have breakfast for her niece as soon as possible.

"I do not go down of mornings yet," said Aunt Eliza, "but Mrs. Roll presides. See that the coffee is good, Roll."

"It is good generally, Miss Huell."

"You see that Margaret brought me my milk."

"Ahem!" said Mrs. Roll, marching out.

At the beginning of each visit to Aunt Eliza I was in the habit of dwelling on the contrast between her way of living and ours. We lived from "hand to mouth." Every thing about her wore a hereditary air; for she lived in my grandfather's house, and it was the same as in his day. If I was at home when these contrasts occurred to me I should have felt angry; as it was, I felt them as in a dream—the china, the silver, the old furniture, and the excellent fare soothed me.

In the middle of the day Aunt Eliza came down stairs, and after she had received a visit from her doctor, decided to go to Newport on Saturday. It was Wednesday; and I could, if I chose, make any addition to my wardrobe. I had none to make, I informed her. What were my dresses?—had I a black silk? she asked. I had no black silk, and thought one would be unnecessary for hot weather.

"Who ever heard of a girl of twenty-four having no black silk! You have slimsy[2] muslins, I dare say?"

"Yes."

"And you like them?"

"For present wear."

That afternoon she sent Mrs. Roll out, who returned with a splendid heavy silk for me, which Aunt Eliza said should be made before Saturday, and it was. I went

[2] Flimsy.

to a fashionable dress-maker of her recommending, and on Friday it came home, beautifully made and trimmed with real lace.

"Even the Pushers could find no fault with this," said Aunt Eliza, turning over the sleeves and smoothing the lace. Somehow she smuggled into the house a white straw-bonnet, with white roses; also a handsome mantilla. She held the bonnet before me with a nod, and deposited it again in the box, which made a part of the luggage for Newport.

On Sunday morning we arrived in Newport, and went to a quiet hotel in the town. James was with us, but Mrs. Roll was left in Bond Street, in charge of the household. Monday was spent in an endeavor to make an arrangement regarding the hire of a coach and coachman. Several livery-stable keepers were in attendance, but nothing was settled, till I suggested that Aunt Eliza should send for her own carriage. James was sent back the next day, and returned on Thursday with coach, horses, and William her coachman. That matter being finished, and the trunks being unpacked, she decided to take her first bath in the sea, expecting me to support her through the trying ordeal of the surf. As we were returning from the beach we met a carriage containing a number of persons with a family resemblance.

When Aunt Eliza saw them she angrily exclaimed, "Am I to see those Uxbridges every day?"

Of the Uxbridges this much I knew—that the two brothers Uxbridge were the lawyers of her opponents in the lawsuit which had existed three or four years. I had never felt any interest in it, though I knew that it was concerning a tract of ground in the city which had belonged to my grandfather, and which had, since his day, become very valuable. Litigation was a habit of the Huell family. So the sight of the Uxbridge family did not agitate me as it did Aunt Eliza.

"The sly, methodical dogs! but I shall beat Lemorne yet!"

"How will you amuse yourself then, aunt?"

"I'll adopt some boys to inherit what I shall save from his clutches."

The bath fatigued her so she remained in her room for the rest of the day; but she kept me busy with a hundred trifles. I wrote for her, computed interest, studied out bills of fare, till four o'clock came, and with it a fog. Nevertheless I must ride on the Avenue, and the carriage was ordered.

"Wear your silk, Margaret; it will just about last your visit through—the fog will use it up."

"I am glad of it," I answered.

"You will ride every day. Wear the bonnet I bought for you also."

"Certainly; but won't that go quicker in the fog than the dress?"

"Maybe; but wear it."

I rode every day afterward, from four to six, in the black silk, the mantilla, and the white straw. When Aunt Eliza went she was so on the alert for the Uxbridge family carriage that she could have had little enjoyment of the ride. Rocks never were a passion with her, she said, nor promontories, chasms, or sand. She came to Newport to be washed with salt-water; when she had washed up to the doctor's prescription she should leave, as ignorant of the peculiar pleasures of Newport as when she arrived. She had no fancy for its conglomerate societies, its literary cottages, its parvenue suits of rooms, its saloon habits, and its bathing herds.

I considered the rides a part of the contract of what was expected in my two months' performance. I did not dream that I was enjoying them, any more than I supposed myself to be enjoying a sea-bath while pulling Aunt Eliza to and fro in the surf. Nothing in the life around me stirred me, nothing in nature attracted me. I liked the fog; somehow it seemed to emanate from me instead of rolling up from the ocean, and to represent me. Whether I went alone or not, the coachman was ordered to drive a certain round; after that I could extend the ride in whatever direction I pleased, but I always said, "Any where, William." One afternoon, which happened to be a bright one, I was riding on the road which led to the glen, when I heard the screaming of a flock of geese which were waddling across the path in front of the horses. I started, for I was asleep probably, and, looking forward, saw the Uxbridge carriage, filled with ladies and children, coming toward me; and by it rode a gentleman on horseback. His horse was rearing among the hissing geese, but neither horse nor geese appeared to engage him; his eyes were fixed upon me. The horse swerved so near that its long mane almost brushed against me. By an irresistible impulse I laid my ungloved hand upon it, but did not look at the rider. Carriage and horseman passed on, and William resumed his pace. A vague idea took possession of me that I had seen the horseman before on my various drives. I had a vision of a man galloping on a black horse out of the fog, and into it again. I was very sure, however, that I had never seen him on so pleasant a day as this! William did not bring his horses to time; it was after six when I went into Aunt Eliza's parlor, and found her impatient for her tea and toast. She was crosser than the occasion warranted; but I understood it when she gave me the outlines of a letter she desired me to write to her lawyer in New York. Something had turned up, he had written her; the Uxbridges believed that they had ferreted out what would go against her. I told her that I had met the Uxbridge carriage.

"One of them is in New York; how else could they be giving me trouble just now?"

"There was a gentleman on horseback beside the carriage."

"Did he look mean and cunning?"

"He did not wear his legal beaver[3] up, I think; but he rode a fine horse and sat it well."

"A lawyer on horseback should, like the beggar of the adage, ride to the devil."

"Your business now is the 'Lemorne?'"

"You know it is."

"I did not know but that you had found something besides to litigate."

"It must have been Edward Uxbridge that you saw. He is the brain of the firm."

"You expect Mr. Van Horn?"

"Oh, he must come; I can not be writing letters."

We had been in Newport two weeks when Mr. Van Horn, Aunt Eliza's lawyer, came. He said that he would see Mr. Edward Uxbridge. Between them they might delay a term, which he thought would be best. "Would Miss Huell ever be ready for a compromise?" he jestingly asked.

"Are you suspicious?" she inquired.

---

[3] Hinged portion, protecting the face, on the helmet of a suit of armor. When the beaver is raised, the face is exposed. Thus, Margaret is saying that Uxbridge's personality was concealed behind his legal persona.

"No; but the Uxbridge chaps are clever."

He dined with us; and at four o'clock Aunt Eliza graciously asked him to take a seat in the carriage with me, making some excuse for not going herself.

"Hullo!" said Mr. Van Horn when we had reached the country road; "there's Uxbridge now." And he waved his hand to him.

It was indeed the black horse and the same rider that I had met. He reined up beside us, and shook hands with Mr. Van Horn.

"We are required to answer this new complaint?" said Mr. Van Horn.

Mr. Uxbridge nodded.

"And after that the judgment?"

Mr. Uxbridge laughed.

"I wish that certain gore of land had been sunk instead of being mapped in 1835."

"The surveyor did his business well enough, I am sure."

They talked together in a low voice for a few minutes, and then Mr. Van Horn leaned back in his seat again. "Allow me," he said, "to introduce you, Uxbridge, to Miss Margaret Huell, Miss Huell's niece. Huell *vs.* Brown, you know," he added, in an explanatory tone; for I was Huell *vs.* Brown's daughter.

"Oh!" said Mr. Uxbridge bowing, and looking at me gravely. I looked at him also; he was a pale, stern-looking man, and forty years old certainly. I derived the impression at once that he had a domineering disposition, perhaps from the way in which he controlled his horse.

"Nice beast that," said Mr. Van Horn.

"Yes," he answered, laying his hand on its mane, so that the action brought immediately to my mind the recollection that I had done so too. I would not meet his eye again, however.

"How long shall you remain, Uxbridge?"

"I don't know. You are not interested in the lawsuit, Miss Huell?" he said, putting on his hat.

"Not in the least; nothing of mine is involved."

"We'll gain it for your portion yet, Miss Margaret," said Mr. Van Horn, nodding to Mr. Uxbridge, and bidding William drive on. He returned the next day, and we settled into the routine of hotel life. A few mornings after, she sent me to a matinée, which was given by some of the Opera people, who were in Newport strengthening the larynx with applications of brine. When the concert was half over, and the audience were making the usual hum and stir, I saw Mr. Uxbridge against a pillar, with his hands incased in pearl-colored gloves, and holding a shiny hat. He turned half away when he caught my eye, and then darted toward me.

"You have not been much more interested in the music than you are in the lawsuit," he said, seating himself beside me.

"The *tutoyer*[4] of the Italian voice is agreeable, however."

"It makes one dreamy."

"A child."

"Yes, a child; not a man nor a woman."

---

[4] French: literally, "to speak familiarly to"; used here as a casual musical term to characterize the singer's voice.

"I teach music. I can not dream over 'one, two, three.'"

"*You*—a music teacher!"

"For six years."

I was aware that he looked at me from head to foot, and I picked at the lace of my invariable black silk; but what did it matter whether I owned that I was a genteel pauper, representing my aunt's position for two months, or not?

"Where?"

"In Waterbury."

"Waterbury differs from Newport."

"I suppose so."

"You suppose!"

A young gentleman sauntered by us, and Mr. Uxbridge called to him to look up the Misses Uxbridge, his nieces, on the other side of the hall.

"Paterfamilias Uxbridge has left his brood in my charge," he said. "I try to do my duty," and he held out a twisted pearl-colored glove, which he pulled off while talking. What white nervous fingers he had! I thought they might pinch like steel.

"You suppose," he repeated.

"I do not look at Newport."

"Have you observed Waterbury?"

"I observe what is in my sphere."

"Oh!"

He was silent then. The second part of the concert began; but I could not compose myself to appreciation. Either the music or I grew chaotic. So many tumultuous sounds I heard—of hope, doubt, inquiry, melancholy, and desire; or did I feel the emotions which these words express? Or was there magnetism stealing into me from the quiet man beside me? He left me with a bow before the concert was over, and I saw him making his way out of the hall when it was finished.

I had been sent in the carriage, of course; but several carriages were in advance of it before the walk, and I waited there for William to drive up. When he did so, I saw by the oscillatory motion of his head, though his arms and whiphand were perfectly correct, that he was inebriated. It was his first occasion of meeting fellow-coachman in full dress, and the occasion had proved too much for him. My hand, however, was on the coach door, when I heard Mr. Uxbridge say, at my elbow.

"It is not safe for you."

"Oh, Sir, it is in the programme that I ride home from the concert." And I prepared to step in.

"I shall sit on the box, then."

"But your nieces?"

"They are walking home, squired by a younger knight."

Aunt Eliza would say, I thought, "Needs must when a lawyer drives"; and I concluded to allow him to have his way, telling him that he was taking a great deal of trouble. He thought it would be less if he were allowed to sit inside; both ways were unsafe.

Nothing happened. William drove well from habit; but James was obliged to assist him to dismount. Mr. Uxbridge waited a moment at the door, and so there was quite a little sensation, which spread its ripples till Aunt Eliza was reached. She sent for William, whose only excuse was "dampness."

"Uxbridge knew my carriage, of course," she said, with a complacent voice.

"He knew me," I replied.

"You do not look like the Huells."

"I look precisely like the young woman to whom he was introduced by Mr. Van Horn."

"Oh ho!"

"He thought it unsafe for me to come alone under William's charge."

"Ah ha!"

No more was said on the subject of his coming home with me. Aunt Eliza had several fits of musing in the course of the evening while I read aloud to her, which had no connection with the subject of the book. As I put it down she said that it would be well for me to go to church the next day. I acquiesced, but remarked that my piety would not require the carriage, and that I preferred to walk. Besides, it would be well for William and James to attend divine service. She could not spare James, and thought William had better clean the harness, by way of penance.

The morning proved to be warm and sunny. I donned a muslin dress of home manufacture and my own bonnet, and started for church. I had walked but a few paces when the consciousness of being *free* and *alone* struck me. I halted, looked about me, and concluded that I would not go to church, but walk into the fields. I had no knowledge of the whereabouts of the fields; but I walked straight forward, and after a while came upon some barren fields, cropping with coarse rocks, along which ran a narrow road. I turned into it, and soon saw beyond the rough coast the blue ring of the ocean—vast, silent, and splendid in the sunshine. I found a seat on the ruins of an old stone-wall, among some tangled bushes and briers. There being no Aunt Eliza to pull through the surf, and no animated bathers near, I discovered the beauty of the sea, and that I loved it.

Presently I heard the steps of a horse, and, to my astonishment, Mr. Uxbridge rode past. I was glad he did not know me. I watched him as he rode slowly down the road, deep in thought. He let drop the bridle, and the horse stopped, as if accustomed to the circumstance, and pawed the ground gently, or yawed his neck for pastime. Mr. Uxbridge folded his arms and raised his head to look seaward. It seemed to me as if he were about to address the jury. I had dropped so entirely from my observance of the landscape that I jumped when he resumed the bridle and turned his horse to come back. I slipped from my seat to look among the bushes, determined that he should not recognize me; but my attempt was a failure—he did not ride by the second time.

"Miss Huell!" And he jumped from his saddle, slipping his arm through the bridle.

"I am a runaway. What do you think of the Fugitive Slave Bill?"[5]

"I approve of returning property to its owners."

"The sea must have been God's temple first, instead of the groves."[6]

"I believe the Saurians were an Orthodox tribe."

"Did you stop yonder to ponder the sea?"

"I was pondering 'Lemorne vs. Huell.'"

---

[5] The Fugitive Slave Bill (1850) made it a crime to assist slaves trying to escape from bondage.

[6] Adaptation of the opening line of William Cullen Bryant's poem "A Forest Hymn" (1825): "The groves were God's first temples."

He looked at me earnestly, and then gave a tug at the bridle, for his steed was inclined to make a crude repast from the bushes.

"How was it that I did not detect you at once?" he continued.

"My apparel is Waterbury apparel."

"Ah!"

We walked up the road slowly till we came to the end of it; then I stopped for him to understand that I thought it time for him to leave me. He sprang into the saddle.

"Give us good-by!" he said, bringing his horse close to me.

"We are not on equal terms; I feel too humble afoot to salute you."

"Put your foot on the stirrup then."

A leaf stuck in the horse's forelock, and I pulled it off and waved it in token of farewell. A powerful light shot into his eyes when he saw my hand close on the leaf.

"May I come and see you?" he asked, abruptly. "I will."

"I shall say neither 'No' nor 'Yes.'"

He rode on at a quick pace, and I walked homeward forgetting the sense of liberty I had started with, and proceeded straightway to Aunt Eliza.

"I have not been to church, aunt, but to walk beyond the town; it was not so nominated in the bond, but I went. The taste of freedom was so pleasant that I warn you there is danger of my 'striking.' When will you have done with Newport?"

"I am pleased with Newport now," she answered, with a curious intonation. "I like it."

"I do also."

Her keen eyes sparkled.

"Did you ever like anything when you were with me before?"

"Never. I will tell you why I like it: because I have met, and shall probably meet, Mr. Uxbridge. I saw him to-day. He asked permission to visit me."

"Let him come."

"He will come."

But we did not see him either at the hotel or when we went abroad. Aunt Eliza rode with me each afternoon, and each morning we went to the beach. She engaged me every moment when at home, and I faithfully performed all my tasks. I clapped to[7] the door on self-investigation—locked it against any analysis or reasoning upon any circumstance connected with Mr. Uxbridge. The only piece of treachery to my code that I was guilty of was the putting of the leaf which I brought home on Sunday between the leaves of that poem whose motto is,

"Mariana in the moated grange."[8]

On Saturday morning, nearly a week after I saw him on my walk, Aunt Eliza proposed that we should go to Turo Street on a shopping excursion; she wanted a cap, and various articles besides. As we went into a large shop I saw Mr. Uxbridge at a counter buying gloves; her quick eye caught sight of him, and she edged away,

[7] Closed; shut.
[8] The poem is Alfred Tennyson's "Mariana" (1830), whose motto is drawn from Shakespeare's *Measure for Measure*.

saying she would look at some goods on the other side; I might wait where I was. As he turned to go out he saw me and stopped.

"I have been in New York since I saw you," he said. "Mr. Lemorne sent for me."

"There is my aunt," I said.

He shrugged his shoulders.

"I shall not go away soon again," he remarked. "I missed Newport greatly."

I made some foolish reply, and kept my eyes on Aunt Eliza, who dawdled unaccountably. He appeared amused, and after a little talk went away.

Aunt Eliza's purchase was a rose-colored moire antique,[9] which she said was to be made for me; for Mrs. Bliss, one of our hotel acquaintances, had offered to chaperon me to the great ball which would come off in a few days, and she had accepted the offer for me.

"There will be no chance for you to take a walk instead," she finished with.

"I can not dance, you know."

"But you will be *there*."

I was sent to a dress-maker of Mrs. Bliss's recommending; but I ordered the dress to be made after my own design, long plain sleeves, and high plain corsage,[10] and requested that it should not be sent home till the evening of the ball. Before it came off Mr. Uxbridge called, and was graciously received by Aunt Eliza, who could be gracious to all except her relatives. I could not but perceive, however, that they watched each other in spite of their lively conversation. To me he was deferential, but went over the ground of our acquaintance as if it had been the most natural thing in the world. But for my life-long habit of never calling in question the behavior of those I came in contact with, and of never expecting any thing different from that I received, I might have wondered over his visit. Every person's individuality was sacred to me, from the fact, perhaps, that my own individuality had never been respected by any person with whom I had any relation—not even by my own mother.

After Mr. Uxbridge went, I asked Aunt Eliza if she thought he looked mean and cunning? She laughed, and replied that she was bound to think that Mr. Lemorne's lawyer could not look otherwise.

When, on the night of the ball, I presented myself in the rose-colored moire antique for her inspection, she raised her eyebrows, but said nothing about it.

"I need not be careful of it, I suppose, aunt?"

"Spill as much wine and ice-cream on it as you like."

In the dressing room Mrs. Bliss surveyed me.

"I think I like this mass of rose-color," she said. "Your hair comes out in contrast so brilliantly. Why, you have not a single ornament on!"

"It is so easy to dress without."

This was all the conversation we had together during the evening, except when she introduced some acquaintance to fulfill her matronizing duties. As I was no dancer I was left alone most of the time, and amused myself by gliding from window to window along the wall, that it might not be observed that I was a

---

[9] Type of dress fabric.   [10] Waist or bodice.

fixed flower. Still I suffered the annoyance of being stared at by wandering squads of young gentlemen, the "curled darlings" of the ballroom. I borrowed Mrs. Bliss's fan in one of her visits for a protection. With that, and the embrasure of a remote window where I finally stationed myself, I hoped to escape further notice. The music of the celebrated band which played between the dances recalled the chorus of spirits which charmed Faust:

"And the fluttering
Ribbons of drapery
Cover the plains,
Cover the bowers,
Where lovers,
Deep in thought,
Give themselves for life."[11]

The voice of Mrs. Bliss broke its spell.
"I bring an old friend, Miss Huell, and he tells me an acquaintance of yours."
It was Mr. Uxbridge.
"I had no thought of meeting you, Miss Huell."
And he coolly took the seat beside me in the window, leaving to Mrs. Bliss the alternative of standing or of going away; she chose the latter.
"I saw you as soon as I came in," he said, "gliding from window to window, like a vessel hugging the shore in a storm."
"With colors at half-mast; I have no dancing partner."
"How many have observed you?"
"Several young gentlemen."
"Moths."
"Oh no, butterflies."
"They must keep away now."
"Are you Rhadamanthus?"[12]
"And Charon,[13] too. I would have you row in the same boat with me."
"Now you are fishing."
"Won't you compliment me. Did I ever look better?"
His evening costume *was* becoming, but he looked pale, and weary, and disturbed. But if we were engaged for a tournament, as his behavior indicated, I must do my best at telling. So I told him that he never looked better, and asked him how I looked. He would look at me presently, he said, and decide. Mrs. Bliss skimmed by us with nods and smiles; as she vanished our eyes followed her, and we talked vaguely on various matters, sounding ourselves and each other. When a furious redowa[14] set in which cut our conversation into rhythm he pushed up the window and said, "Look out."
I turned my face to him to do so, and saw the moon at the full, riding through

---

[11] From Johann Wolfgang von Goethe's *Faust* (1808), Part I, ll 1463–1469.
[12] Judge of the underworld in Greek mythology.
[13] In Greek mythology, the person who ferries the dead to Hades across the river Styx.
[14] Waltz of Bohemian origin.

the strip of sky which our vision commanded. From the moon our eyes fell on each other. After a moment's silence, during which I returned his steadfast gaze, for I could not help it, he said:

"If we understand the impression we make upon each other, what must be said?"

I made no reply, but fanned myself, neither looking at the moon, nor upon the redowa, nor upon any thing.

He took the fan from me.

"Speak of yourself," he said.

"Speak you."

"I am what I seem, a man within your sphere. By all the accidents of position and circumstance suited to it. Have you not learned it?"

"I am not what I seem. I never wore so splendid a dress as this till tonight, and shall not again."

He gave the fan such a twirl that its slender sticks snapped, and it dropped like the broken wing of a bird.

"Mr. Uxbridge, that fan belongs to Mrs. Bliss."

He threw it out of the window.

"You have courage, fidelity, and patience—this character with a passionate soul. I am sure that you have such a soul?"

"I do not know."

"I have fallen in love with you. It happened on the very day when I passed you on the way to the Glen. I never got away from the remembrance of seeing your hand on the mane of my horse."

He waited for me to speak, but I could not; the balance of my mind was gone. Why should this have happened to me—a slave? As it had happened, why did I not feel exultant in the sense of power which the chance for freedom with him should give?

"What is it, Margaret? your face is as sad as death."

"How do you call me 'Margaret?' "

"As I would call my wife—Margaret."

He rose and stood before me to screen my face from observation. I supposed so, and endeavored to stifle my agitation.

"You are better," he said, presently. "Come go with me and get some refreshment." And he beckoned to Mrs. Bliss, who was down the hall with an unwieldy gentleman.

"Will you go to supper now?" she asked.

"We are only waiting for you," Mr. Uxbridge answered, offering me his arm.

When we emerged into the blaze and glitter of the supper-room I sought refuge in the shadow of Mrs. Bliss's companion, for it seemed to me that I had lost my own.

"Drink this Champagne," said Mr. Uxbridge. "Pay no attention to the Colonel on your left; he won't expect it."

"Neither must you."

"Drink."

The Champagne did not prevent me from reflecting on the fact that he had not yet asked whether I loved him.

The spirit chorus again floated through my mind:

"Where lovers,
Deep in thought,
Give themselves for life."

I was not allowed to *give* myself—I was *taken*.
"No heel-taps," he whispered, "to the bottom quaff."[15]
"Take me home, will you?"
"Mrs. Bliss is not ready."
"Tell her that I must go."
He went behind her chair and whispered something, and she nodded to me to go without her.

When her carriage came up, I think he gave the coachman an order to drive home in a round-about way, for we were a long time reaching it. I kept my face to the window, and he made no effort to divert my attention. When we came to a street whose thick rows of trees shut out the moonlight my eager soul longed to leap out into the dark and demand of him his heart, soul, life, for *me*.

I struck him lightly on the shoulder; he seized my hand.
"Oh, I know you, Margaret; you are mine!"
"We are at the hotel."
He sent the carriage back, and said that he would leave me at my aunt's door. He wished that he could see her then. Was it magic that made her open the door before I reached it?

"Have you come on legal business?" she asked him.
"You have divined what I come for."
"Step in, step in; it's very late. I should have been in bed but for neuralgia.[16] Did Mr. Uxbridge come home with you, Margaret?"
"Yes, in Mrs. Bliss's carriage; I wished to come before she was ready to leave."
"Well, Mr. Uxbridge is old enough for your protector, certainly."
"I *am* forty, ma'am."
"Do you want Margaret?"
"I do."
"You know exactly how much is involved in your client's suit?"
"Exactly."
"You also know that his claim is an unjust one."
"Do I?"
"I shall not be poor if I lose; if I gain, Margaret will be rich."
" 'Margaret will be rich,' " he repeated, absently.
"What! have you changed your mind respecting the orphans, aunt?"
"She has, and is—nothing," she went on, not heeding my remark. "Her father

---

[15] Heel-tap: small amount of drink left in a glass; to the bottom quaff: drink heartily and completely what is in one's glass.
[16] Painful disorder of the nerve ends in various parts of the body, but also used historically to refer to a wide variety of ailments for which no cause could be identified.

married below his station; when he died his wife fell back to her place—for he spent his fortune—and there she and Margaret must remain, unless Lemorne is defeated."

"Aunt, for your succinct biography of my position many thanks."

"Sixty thousand dollars," she continued. "Van Horn tells me that, as yet, the firm of Uxbridge Brothers have only an income—no capital."

"It is true," he answered, musingly.

The clock on the mantle struck two.

"A thousand dollars for every year of my life," she said. "You and I, Uxbridge, know the value and beauty of money."

"Yes, there is beauty in money, and"—looking at me—"beauty without it."

"The striking of the clock," I soliloquized, "proves that this scene is not a phantasm."[17]

"Margaret is fatigued," he said, rising. "May I come to-morrow?"

"It is my part only," replied Aunt Eliza, "to see that she is, or is not, Cinderella."

"If you have ever thought of me, aunt, as an individual, you must have seen that I am not averse to ashes."

He held my hand a moment, and then kissed me with a kiss of appropriation.

"He is in love with you," she said, after he had gone. "I think I know him. He has found beauty ignorant of itself; he will teach you to develop it."

The next morning Mr. Uxbridge had an interview with Aunt Eliza before he saw me.

When we were alone I asked him how her eccentricities affected him; he could not but consider her violent, prejudiced, warped, and whimsical. I told him that I had been taught to accept all that she did on this basis. Would this explain to him my silence in regard to her?

"Can you endure to live with her in Bond Street for the present, or would you rather return to Waterbury?"

"She desires my company while she is in Newport only. I have never been with her so long before."

"I understand her. Law is a game, in her estimation, in which cheating can as easily be carried on as at cards."

"Her soul is in this case."

"Her soul is not too large for it. Will you ride this afternoon?"

I promised, of course. From that time till he left Newport we saw each other every day, and though I found little opportunity to express my own peculiar feelings, he comprehended many of my wishes, and all my tastes. I grew fond of him hourly. Had I not reason? Never was friend so considerate, never was lover more devoted.

When he had been gone a few days, Aunt Eliza declared that she was ready to depart from Newport. The rose-colored days were ended! In two days we were on the Sound,[18] coach, horses, servants, and ourselves.

It was the 1st of September when we arrived in Bond Street. A week from that date Samuel Uxbridge, the senior partner of Uxbridge Brothers, went to Europe with his family, and I went to Waterbury, accompanied by Mr. Uxbridge. He consulted mother in regard to our marriage, and appointed it in November. In October Aunt Eliza sent for me to come back to Bond Street and spend a week. She had some fine

---

[17] Unreal happening or fantasy. [18] Long Island Sound.

marking to do, she wrote. While there I noticed a restlessness in her which I had never before observed, and conferred with Mrs. Roll on the matter. "She do be awake nights a deal, and that's the reason," Mrs. Roll said. Her manner was the same in other respects. She said she would not give me any thing for my wedding outfit, but she paid my fare from Waterbury and back.

She could not spare me to go out, she told Mr. Uxbridge, and in consequence I saw little of him while there.

In November we were married. Aunt Eliza was not at the wedding, which was a quiet one. Mr. Uxbridge desired me to remain in Waterbury till spring. He would not decide about taking a house in New York till then; by that time his brother might return, and if possible we would go to Europe for a few months. I acquiesced in all his plans. Indeed I was not consulted; but I was happy—happy in him, and happy in every thing.

The winter passed in waiting for him to come to Waterbury every Saturday; and in the enjoyment of the two days he passed with me. In March Aunt Eliza wrote me that Lemorne was beaten! Van Horn had taken up the whole contents of his snuff-box in her house the evening before in amazement at the turn things had taken.

That night I dreamed of the scene in the hotel at Newport. I heard Aunt Eliza saying, "If I gain, Margaret will be rich." And I heard also the clock strike two. As it struck I said, "*My husband is a scoundrel*," and woke with a start.

1863

Emily Dickinson
1830–1886

Walt Whitman and Emily Dickinson are America's nineteenth-century poetic geniuses; separately, they resisted the Anglophilia that had hobbled American verse in genteel forms. Whitman invented American free verse unrhymed and unmeasured; Dickinson invented a free form of England's most common poem, the hymn. Except for a very few early experiments, Dickinson wrote in hymn meters all her life, shaping her single form till it responded effortlessly to her intensity of perception and expression.

Dickinson, brought up in conventional Protestantism, never abandoned the metaphysical questions of her upbringing—questions of mortality, renunciation, perfection, existential meaning. But she emptied them of specifically Christian import, though she continued to employ Christian symbols, especially those of damnation, salvation, crucifixion, and heaven. "Some keep the Sabbath going to Church— / I keep it, staying at Home—" she wrote. Her poetry is frequently blasphemous, as when she indicts God as the torturer who "scalps your naked Soul." She does not evade her Puritan and Emersonian inheritance of personal ethical responsibility, but she wrenches it powerfully to her own uses.

A second Dickinson, as powerful as the metaphysical one, is the observer of nature, watching a bird eat a worm raw or coming upon a snake and feeling "Zero at the Bone—" This Dickinson hears the "unobtrusive Mass" of the crickets and perceives "a Druidic Difference" on the face of the world. She notices "a certain Slant of light, / Winter Afternoons"—a light that makes "Shadows—hold their breath." The New England seasons ("I see—New Englandly—," she said) are memorialized in her work in all their variety.

The third, and greatest, Dickinson is the psychological analyst. Herself subject to extremes of anxiety and depression, she never flinched from interrogating her own mental states, taming them (at least to some degree) by her fine-drawn descriptions of the horrors she experienced. When "a Plank in Reason, broke," or when "the Nerves sit ceremonious, like Tombs—," or when "Chaos—Stopless— cool" besets the soul, Dickinson watches, then reports. Though she concealed herself, in life, from others, she was nakedly exposed to herself.

There are other Dickinsons—the love poet, the social satirist, the observer of people, the poet of aesthetic reflection—each of them a considerable talent. The almost two thousand poems in the Dickinson canon can scarcely be fully present even to Dickinson critics, let alone to the common reader. A search through Dickinson's *Complete Poems* never fails to turn up new poems of great value.

And yet this great poet published only a dozen poems in her lifetime. It was not until 1955 that all her known poetry was published, and this was the first collection to reproduce Dickinson's texts as she wrote them, without many editorial changes; it was not until 1982 that her own arrangement of many of her poems in little books, or "fascicles," was made known in facsimile publication. Dickinson was perhaps discouraged by the criticism her poems received from Thomas Wentworth Higginson, an editor of the *Atlantic Monthly,* to whom she sent poems in 1862; but her friend Helen Hunt Jackson, a well-known author, could have helped to ensure that more poems were published had Dickinson been willing. Dickinson's personal reclusiveness forbade self-promotion, however, and she allowed her poems to accumulate instead in her bureau drawers.

Dickinson grew up in a well-to-do household and had the run of her father's library. Her father was the treasurer of Amherst College, and her grandfather had been one of its founders. She spent a single year at the South Hadley Female Seminary (later to become Mount Holyoke College) but did not remain; she experienced there the inability to believe in institutional religion that caused her to abandon attendance at the Congregational Church. After leaving school, Dickinson became increasingly unwilling to engage in social interchange outside her own house. Though she made brief visits to Boston, Philadelphia, and Washington, D.C., she spent her entire life in her father's house, eventually seeing no visitors. Her brother Austin, after his marriage, lived next door with his wife, the difficult "Sister Sue" to whom many of Dickinson's poems were addressed. Dickinson wrote hundreds of letters and poems yearly (366 poems in the single year 1862). Her neighbors, noting her elusiveness and her constant wearing of white, considered her eccentric. They had no idea of the practical purpose served by her withdrawal, which permitted her to escape the enormous labors usually required of single women, who were freely called on to attend the young, the sick, and the dying. Dickinson reserved her energies for her genius.

Dickinson's early poetry, when it is weak, displays hysteria, self-absorption, and a coy whimsicality. To watch her develop as a poet is to see the whimsicality relax, the hysteria become disciplined by intellectual analysis, and the self-absorption strengthen itself into meditation on the human lot. Her irony turns on herself as well as on the universe; her love of paradox deepens to an examination of the laws of necessity, creative and destructive at once. In manuscript, the smallest Dickinson poem spreads, in her enlarged handwriting, to fill the whole page on which it is written, as though each blank piece of paper were the brain, or the world, filled to the margins with a single mood or insight. Dickinson's bold calligraphy and her composition by phrase—each marked off by a dash with space before and after—puts emphasis on each stamp or impress of the mind in its analysis of experience. Slant rhymes and an oblique form of expression ensure the oddness of surface in Dickinson's poems; the resonant forms of her language stand for her conviction of the baffling eccentricity of life and thought. Though her poetry reflects her reading of many English poets (Shakespeare, Keats, Mrs. Browning) and of Emerson, she is the least imitative of American poets, turning the discursive certainties of writers and philosophers alike into her own preferred thematic form, the riddle. Enigma is her genre, and pain her topic; her anatomy of psychic skepticism remains one of the great documents of American nineteenth-century attitudes. The best measure of her success in verse is the way in which her poems make themselves remembered. Without any effort on our part to memorize them, we find we cannot forget her lines. Her fame has continued to grow. Her poems, once rewritten by others for public acceptability, are now known in their full power and self-assertion.

Further Reading:

G. F. Whicher, *This Was a Poet: A Critical Biography of Emily Dickinson*, 1939.
R. Chase, *Emily Dickinson*, 1951.
C. R. Anderson, *Emily Dickinson's Poetry*, 1960.
A. J. Gelpi, *Emily Dickinson: The Mind of the Poet*, 1965.
B. Lindberg-Seyersted, *The Voice of the Poet: Aspects of Style in the Poetry of Emily Dickinson*, 1968.
R. B. Sewall, *The Life of Emily Dickinson*, 1974.

S. Cameron, *Lyric Time: Dickinson & the Limits of Genre*, 1979.
K. Keller, *The Only Kangaroo Among the Beauty: Emily Dickinson and America*, 1979.
J. F. Diehl, *Dickinson and the Romantic Imagination*, 1981.
R. W. Franklin, *The Manuscript Books of Emily Dickinson*, 1981.
R. Porter, *Dickinson, the Modern Idiom*, 1981.
S. Juhasz, *The Undiscovered Continent: Emily Dickinson and the Space of the Mind*, 1983.

Text:

The Poems of Emily Dickinson, ed. T. H. Johnson, 3 vols., 1953.

See also *The Letters of Emily Dickinson*, ed. T. H. Johnson and T. Ward, 1958.

185

"Faith" is a fine invention
When Gentlemen can *see*—
But *Microscopes* are prudent
In an Emergency.

1951

213

Did the Harebell loose her girdle
To the lover Bee
Would the Bee the Harebell *hallow*
Much as formerly?

Did the "Paradise"—persuaded—   5
Yield her moat of pearl—
Would the Eden *be* an Eden,
Or the Earl—an *Earl?*

1951

216

[Draft 1]

Safe in their Alabaster Chambers—
Untouched by Morning
And untouched by Noon—
Sleep the meek members of the Resurrection—
Rafter of satin,   5
And Roof of stone.

Light laughs the breeze
In her Castle above them—

Babbles the Bee in a stolid Ear,
Pipe the Sweet Birds in ignorant cadence—
Ah, what sagacity perished here!
1859/1951

[Draft 2]

Safe in their Alabaster Chambers—
Untouched by Morning—
And untouched by Noon—
Lie the meek members of the Resurrection—
Rafter of Satin—and Roof of Stone!

Grand go the Years—in the Crescent—above
    them—
Worlds scoop their Arcs—
And Firmaments—row—
Diadems—drop—and Doges'—surrender—
Soundless as dots—on a Disc of Snow—
1861/1951

241

I like a look of Agony,
Because I know it's true—
Men do not sham Convulsion,
Nor simulate, a Throe—

The Eyes glaze once—and that is Death—
Impossible to feign
The Beads upon the Forehead
By homely Anguish strung.
1951

' Early chief magistrates of the Italian republics
 of Venice and Genoa; in this context, rulers.

254

"Hope" is the thing with feathers—
That perches in the soul—
And sings the tune without the words—
And never stops—at all—

And sweetest—in the Gale—is heard—   5
And sore must be the storm—
That could abash the little Bird
That kept so many warm—

I've heard it in the chillest land—
And on the strangest Sea—   10
Yet, never, in Extremity,
It asked a crumb—of Me.

1951

258

There's a certain Slant of light,
Winter Afternoons—
That oppresses, like the Heft
Of Cathedral Tunes—

Heavenly Hurt, it gives us—   5
We can find no scar,
But internal difference,
Where the Meanings, are—

None may teach it—Any—
'Tis the Seal Despair—   10
An imperial affliction
Sent us of the Air—

When it comes, the Landscape listens—
Shadows—hold their breath—
When it goes, 'tis like the Distance   15
On the look of Death—

1951

280

I felt a Funeral, in my Brain,
And Mourners to and fro
Kept treading—treading—till it seemed
That Sense was breaking through—

And when they all were seated,   5
A Service, like a Drum—
Kept beating—beating—till I thought
My Mind was going numb—

And then I heard them lift a Box
And creak across my Soul   10
With those same Boots of Lead, again,
Then Space—began to toll,

As all the Heavens were a Bell,
And Being, but an Ear,
And I, and Silence, some strange Race   15
Wrecked, solitary, here—

And then a Plank in Reason, broke,
And I dropped down, and down—
And hit a World, at every plunge,
And Finished knowing—then—   20
1951

290

Of Bronze—and Blaze—
The North—Tonight—
So adequate—it forms—
So preconcerted with itself
So distant—to alarms—   5
An Unconcern so sovreign
To Universe, or me—
Infects my simple spirit
With Taints of Majesty—

Till I take vaster attitudes—   10
And strut upon my stem—
Disdaining Men, and Oxygen,
For Arrogance of them—

My Splendors, are Menagerie—
But their Competeless Show   15
Will entertain the Centuries
When I, am long ago,
An Island in dishonored Grass—
Whom none but Daisies, know.

1951

303

The Soul selects her own Society—
Then—shuts the Door—
To her divine Majority—
Present no more—

Unmoved—she notes the Chariots—pausing—   5
At her low Gate—
Unmoved—an Emperor be kneeling
Upon her Mat—

I've known her—from an ample nation—
Choose One—   10
Then—close the Valves of her attention—
Like Stone—

1951

324

Some keep the Sabbath going to Church—
I keep it, staying at Home—
With a Bobolink for a Chorister—
And an Orchard, for a Dome—

Some keep the Sabbath in Surplice— 5
I just wear my Wings—
And instead of tolling the Bell, for Church,
Our little Sexton—sings.

God preaches, a noted Clergyman—
And the sermon is never long, 10
So instead of getting to Heaven at last—
I'm going, all along.

1951

327

Before I got my eye put out
I liked as well to see—
As other Creatures, that have Eyes
And know no other way—

But were it told to me—Today— 5
That I might have the sky
For mine—I tell you that my Heart
Would split, for size of me—

The Meadows—mine—
The Mountains—mine— 10
All Forests—Stintless Stars—
As much of Noon as I could take
Between my finite eyes—

The Motions of the Dipping Birds—
The Morning's Amber Road— 15
For mine—to look at when I liked—
The News would strike me dead—

So safer—guess—with just my soul
Upon the Window pane—
Where other Creatures put their eyes— 20
Incautious—of the Sun—

1951

332

There are two Ripenings—one—of sight—
Whose forces Spheric wind
Until the Velvet product
Drop spicy to the ground—
A homelier maturing—   5
A process in the Bur—
That teeth of Frosts alone disclose
In far October Air.
1951

338

I know that He exists.
Somewhere—in Silence—
He has hid his rare life
From our gross eyes.

'Tis an instant's play.   5
'Tis a fond Ambush—
Just to make Bliss
Earn her own surprise!

But—should the play
Prove piercing earnest—   10
Should the glee—glaze—
In Death's—stiff—stare—

Would not the fun
Look too expensive!
Would not the jest—   15
Have crawled too far!
1951

341

After great pain, a formal feeling comes—
The Nerves sit ceremonious, like Tombs—
The stiff Heart questions was it He, that bore,
And Yesterday, or Centuries before?

The Feet, mechanical, go round—   5
Of Ground, or Air, or Ought—
A Wooden way
Regardless grown,
A Quartz contentment, like a stone—

This is the Hour of Lead—   10
Remembered, if outlived,
As Freezing persons, recollect the Snow—
First—Chill—then Stupor—then the letting go—
1951

379

Rehearsal to Ourselves
Of a Withdrawn Delight—
Affords a Bliss like Murder—
Omnipotent—Acute—

We will not drop the Dirk¹—   5
Because We love the Wound
The Dirk Commemorate—Itself
Remind Us that we died.
1951

---

¹ Dagger

401

What Soft—Cherubic Creatures—
These Gentlewomen are—
One would as soon assault a Plush—
Or violate a Star—

Such Dimity Convictions—   5
A Horror so refined
Of freckled Human Nature—
Of Deity—ashamed—

It's such a common—Glory—
A Fisherman's—Degree—   10
Redemption—Brittle Lady—
Be so—ashamed of Thee—

1951

414

'Twas like a Maelstrom, with a notch,
That nearer, every Day,
Kept narrowing its boiling Wheel
Until the Agony

Toyed coolly with the final inch   5
Of your delirious Hem—
And you dropt, lost,
When something broke—
And let you from a Dream—

As if a Goblin with a Gauge—   10
Kept measuring the Hours—
Until you felt your Second
Weigh, helpless, in his Paws—

And not a Sinew—stirred—could help,
And sense was setting numb—   15
When God—remembered—and the Fiend
Let go, then, Overcome—

As if your Sentence stood—pronounced—
And you were frozen led
From Dungeon's luxury of Doubt   20
To Gibbets, and the Dead—

And when the Film had stitched your eyes
A Creature gasped "Reprieve"!
Which Anguish was the utterest—then—
To perish, or to live?
1951   25

435

Much Madness is divinest Sense—
To a discerning Eye—
Much Sense—the starkest Madness—
'Tis the Majority
In this, as All, prevail—   5
Assent—and you are sane—
Demur—you're straightway dangerous—
And handled with a Chain—
1951

441

This is my letter to the World
That never wrote to Me—
The simple News that Nature told—
With tender Majesty

Her Message is committed   5
To Hands I cannot see—
For love of Her—Sweet—countrymen—
Judge tenderly—of Me
1951

448

This was a Poet—It is That
Distills amazing sense
From ordinary Meanings—
And Attar[1] so immense

From the familiar species   5
That perished by the Door—
We wonder it was not Ourselves
Arrested it—before—

Of Pictures, the Discloser—
The Poet—it is He—   10
Entitles Us—by Contrast—
To ceaseless Poverty—

Of Portion—so unconscious—
The Robbing—could not harm—
Himself—to Him—a Fortune—   15
Exterior—to Time—

1951

449

I died for Beauty—but was scarce
Adjusted in the Tomb
When One who died for Truth, was lain
In an adjoining Room—

He questioned softly "Why I failed"?   5
"For Beauty", I replied—
"And I—for Truth—Themself are One—
We Brethren, are", He said—

[1] Distilled fragrance, usually concentrated and intense.

And so, as Kinsmen, met a Night—
We talked between the Rooms—   10
Until the Moss had reached our lips—
And covered up—our names—
1951

465

I heard a Fly buzz—when I died—
The Stillness in the Room
Was like the Stillness in the Air—
Between the Heaves of Storm—

The Eyes around—had wrung them dry—   5
And Breaths were gathering firm
For that last Onset—when the King
Be witnessed—in the Room—

I willed my Keepsakes—Signed away
What portion of me be   10
Assignable—and then it was
There interposed a Fly—

With Blue—uncertain stumbling Buzz—
Between the light—and me—
And then the Windows failed—and then   15
I could not see to see—
1951

510

It was not Death, for I stood up,
And all the Dead, lie down—
It was not Night, for all the Bells
Put out their Tongues, for Noon.

It was not Frost, for on my Flesh   5
I felt Siroccos'—crawl—
Nor Fire—for just my Marble feet
Could keep a Chancel, cool—

And yet, it tasted, like them all,
The Figures I have seen   10
Set orderly, for Burial,
Reminded me, of mine—

As if my life were shaven,
And fitted to a frame,
And could not breathe without a key,   15
And 'twas like Midnight, some—

When everything that ticked—has stopped—
And Space stares all around—
Or Grisly frosts—first Autumn morns,
Repeal the Beating Ground—   20

But, most, like Chaos—Stopless—cool—
Without a Chance, or Spar—
Or even a Report of Land—
To justify—Despair.

1951

536

The Heart asks Pleasure—first—
And then—Excuse from Pain—
And then—those little Anodynes
That deaden suffering—

And then—to go to sleep—   5
And then—if it should be
The will of its Inquisitor
The privilege to die—

1951

<hr>

¹ Sirocco (Italian origin): hot, dry wind.

561

I measure every Grief I meet
With narrow, probing, Eyes—
I wonder if It weighs like Mine—
Or has an Easier size.

I wonder if They bore it long—   5
Or did it just begin—
I could not tell the Date of Mine—
It feels so old a pain—

I wonder if it hurts to live—
And if They have to try—   10
And whether—could They choose between—
It would not be—to die—

I note that Some—gone patient long—
At length, renew their smile—
An imitation of a Light   15
That has so little Oil—

I wonder if when Years have piled—
Some Thousands—on the Harm—
That hurt them early—such a lapse
Could give them any Balm—   20

Or would they go on aching still
Through Centuries of Nerve—
Enlightened to a larger Pain—
In Contrast with the Love—

The Grieved—are many—I am told—   25
There is the various Cause—
Death—is but one—and comes but once—
And only nails the eyes—

There's Grief of Want—and Grief of Cold—
A sort they call "Despair"—   30
There's Banishment from native Eyes—
In sight of Native Air—

And though I may not guess the kind—
Correctly—yet to me

A piercing Comfort it affords   35
In passing Calvary¹—

To note the fashions—of the Cross—
And how they're mostly worn—
Still fascinated to presume
That Some—are like My Own—   40

1951

569

I reckon—when I count at all—
First—Poets—Then the Sun—
Then Summer—Then the Heaven of God—
And then—the List is done—

But, looking back—the First so seems   5
To Comprehend the Whole—
The Others look a needless Show—
So I write—Poets—All—

Their Summer—lasts a Solid Year—
They can afford a Sun   10
The East—would deem extravagant—
And if the Further Heaven—

Be Beautiful as they prepare
For Those who worship Them—
It is too difficult a Grace—   15
To justify the Dream—

1951

¹ The hill on which Jesus was crucified.

632

The Brain—is wider than the Sky—
For—put them side by side—
The one the other will contain
With ease—and You—beside—

The Brain is deeper than the sea—   5
For—hold them—Blue to Blue—
The one the other will absorb—
As Sponges—Buckets—do—

The Brain is just the weight of God—
For—Heft them—Pound for Pound—   10
And they will differ—if they do—
As Syllable from Sound—
1951

640

I cannot live with You—
It would be Life—
And Life is over there—
Behind the Shelf

The Sexton keeps the Key to—   5
Putting up
Our Life—His Porcelain—
Like a Cup—

Discarded of the Housewife—
Quaint—or Broke—   10
A newer Sevres' pleases—
Old Ones crack—

I could not die—with You—
For One must wait

---

[1] Porcelain made in the town of Sèvres, France.

To shut the Other's Gaze down—   15
You—could not—

And I—Could I stand by
And see You—freeze—
Without my Right of Frost—
Death's privilege?   20

Nor could I rise—with You—
Because Your Face
Would put out Jesus'—
That New Grace

Glow plain—and foreign   25
On my homesick Eye—
Except that You than He
Shone closer by—

They'd judge Us—How—
For You—served Heaven—You know,   30
Or sought to—
I could not—

Because You saturated Sight—
And I had no more Eyes
For sordid excellence   35
As Paradise

And were You lost, I would be—
Though My Name
Rang loudest
On the Heavenly fame—   40

And were You—saved—
And I—condemned to be
Where You were not—
That self—were Hell to Me—

So We must meet apart—   45
You there—I—here—
With just the Door ajar
That Oceans are—and Prayer—
And that White Sustenance—
Despair—   50

1951

650

Pain—has an Element of Blank—
It cannot recollect
When it begun—or if there were
A time when it was not—

It has no Future—but itself—   5
Its Infinite contain
Its Past—enlightened to perceive
New Periods—of Pain.
1951

657

I dwell in Possibility—
A fairer House than Prose—
More numerous of Windows—
Superior—for Doors—

Of Chambers as the Cedars—   5
Impregnable of Eye—
And for an Everlasting Roof
The Gambrels of the Sky—

Of Visitors—the fairest—
For Occupation—This—   10
The spreading wide my narrow Hands
To gather Paradise—
1951

664

Of all the Souls that stand create—
I have elected—One—
When Sense from Spirit—files away—
And Subterfuge—is done—
When that which is—and that which was—   5
Apart—instrinsic—stand—
And this brief Drama in the flesh—
Is shifted—like a Sand—
When Figures show their royal Front—
And Mists—are carved away,   10
Behold the Atom—I preferred—
To all the lists of Clay!

1951

670

One need not be a Chamber—to be Haunted—
One need not be a House—
The Brain has Corridors—surpassing
Material Place—

Far safer, of a Midnight Meeting   5
External Ghost
Than its interior Confronting—
That Cooler Host.

Far safer, through an Abbey gallop,
The Stones a'chase—   10
Than Unarmed, one's a'self encounter—
In lonesome Place—

Ourself behind ourself, concealed—
Should startle most—
Assassin hid in our Apartment   15
Be Horror's least.

The Body—borrows a Revolver—
He bolts the Door—
O'erlooking a superior spectre—
Or More—   20
1951

675

Essential Oils—are wrung—
The Attar¹ from the Rose
Be not expressed by Suns—alone—
It is the gift of Screws—

The General Rose—decay—   5
But this—in Lady's Drawer
Make Summer—When the Lady lie
In Ceaseless Rosemary—
1951

712

Because I could not stop for Death—
He kindly stopped for me—
The Carriage held but just Ourselves—
And Immortality.

We slowly drove—He knew no haste   5
And I had put away
My labor and my leisure too,
For His Civility—

We passed the School, where Children strove
At Recess—in the Ring—   10
We passed the Fields of Gazing Grain—
We passed the Setting Sun—

¹ Distilled fragrance, usually concentrated and
intense; perfume.

Or rather—He passed Us—
The Dews drew quivering and chill—
For only Gossamer, my Gown—   15
My Tippet¹—only Tulle—

We paused before a House that seemed
A Swelling of the Ground—
The Roof was scarcely visible—
The Cornice—in the Ground—   20

Since then—'tis Centuries—and yet
Feels shorter than the Day
I first surmised the Horses' Heads
Were toward Eternity—

1951

721

Behind Me—dips Eternity—
Before Me—Immortality—
Myself—the Term between—
Death but the Drift of Eastern Gray,
Dissolving into Dawn away,   5
Before the West begin—

'Tis Kingdoms—afterward—they say—
In perfect—pauseless Monarchy—
Whose Prince—is Son of None—
Himself—His Dateless Dynasty—   10
Himself—Himself diversify—
In Duplicate divine¹—

'Tis Miracle before Me—then—
'Tis Miracle behind—between—
A Crescent in the Sea—   15
With Midnight to the North of Her—
And Midnight to the South of Her—
And Maelstrom—in the Sky—

1951

---

¹ Short shoulder cape or scarf.
¹ Reference to the Christian doctrine of the
Trinity, which states that the Son issues from
the Father, and the Holy Spirit from the union
of Father and Son.

745

Renunciation—is a piercing Virtue—
The letting go
A Presence—for an Expectation—
Not now—
The putting out of Eyes—   5
Just Sunrise—
Lest Day—
Day's Great Progenitor—
Outvie—
Renunciation—is the Choosing   10
Against itself—
Itself to justify
Unto itself—
When larger function—
Make that appear—   15
Smaller—that Covered Vision—Here—

1951

754

My Life had stood—a Loaded Gun—
In Corners—till a Day
The Owner passed—identified—
And carried Me away—

And now We roam in Sovereign Woods—   5
And now We hunt the Doe—
And every time I speak for Him—
The Mountains straight reply—

And do I smile, such cordial light
Upon the Valley glow—
It is as a Vesuvian[1] face   10
Had let its pleasure through—

---

[1] Reference to Mount Vesuvius, the famous
volcano on the Bay of Naples.

And when at Night—Our good Day done—
I guard My Master's Head—
'Tis better than the Eider-Duck's   15
Deep Pillow²—to have shared—

To foe of His—I'm deadly foe—
None stir the second time—
On whom I lay a Yellow Eye—
Or an emphatic Thumb—   20

Though I than He—may longer live
He longer must—than I—
For I have but the power to kill,
Without—the power to die—

1951

764

Presentiment—is that long Shadow—on the Lawn—
Indicative that Suns go down—

The Notice to the startled Grass
That Darkness—is about to pass—

1951

812

A Light exists in Spring
Not present on the Year
At any other period—
When March is scarcely here

A Color stands abroad   5
On Solitary Fields

² I.e., filled with soft feathers.

That Science cannot overtake
But Human Nature feels.

It waits upon the Lawn,
It shows the furthest Tree   10
Upon the furthest Slope you know
It almost speaks to you.

Then as Horizons step
Or Noons report away
Without the Formula of sound   15
It passes and we stay—

A quality of loss
Affecting our Content
As Trade had suddenly encroached
Upon a Sacrament.   20
1951

910

Experience is the Angled Road
Preferred against the Mind
By—Paradox—the Mind itself—
Presuming it to lead

Quite Opposite—How Complicate   5
The Discipline of Man—
Compelling Him to Choose Himself
His Preappointed Pain—
1951

986

A narrow Fellow in the Grass
Occasionally rides—
You may have met Him—did you not
His notice sudden is—

The Grass divides as with a Comb—   5
A spotted shaft is seen—
And then it closes at your feet
And opens further on—

He likes a Boggy Acre
A Floor too cool for Corn—   10
Yet when a Boy, and Barefoot—
I more than once at Noon
Have passed, I thought, a Whip lash
Unbraiding in the Sun
When stooping to secure it   15
It wrinkled, and was gone—

Several of Nature's People
I know, and they know me—
I feel for them a transport
Of cordiality—   20

But never met this Fellow
Attended, or alone
Without a tighter breathing
And Zero at the Bone—
1951

997

Crumbling is not an instant's Act
A fundamental pause
Dilapidation's processes
Are organized Decays.

'Tis first a Cobweb on the Soul   5
A Cuticle of Dust
A Borer in the Axis
An Elemental Rust—

Ruin is formal—Devil's work
Consecutive and slow—   10
Fail in an instant, no man did
Slipping—is Crash's law.
1951

1052

I never saw a Moor—
I never saw the Sea—
Yet know I how the Heather looks
And what a Billow be.

I never spoke with God   5
Nor visited in Heaven—
Yet certain am I of the spot
As if the Checks[1] were given—

1951

1062

He scanned it—staggered—
Dropped the Loop
To Past or Period—
Caught helpless at a sense as if
His Mind were going blind—   5

Groped up, to see if God was there—
Groped backward at Himself
Caressed a Trigger absently
And wandered out of Life.

1951

1068

Further in Summer than the Birds
Pathetic from the Grass
A minor Nation celebrates
Its unobtrusive Mass.

[1] Railway tickets.

No Ordinance be seen 5
So gradual the Grace
A pensive Custom it becomes
Enlarging Loneliness.

Antiquest felt at Noon
When August burning low 10
Arise this spectral Canticle
Repose to typify

Remit as yet no Grace
No Furrow on the Glow
Yet a Druidic Difference 15
Enhances Nature now

1951

1071

Perception of an object costs
Precise the Object's loss—
Perception in itself a Gain
Replying to its Price—

The Object Absolute—is nought— 5
Perception sets it fair
And then upbraids a Perfectness
That situates so far—

1951

1100

The last Night that She lived
It was a Common Night
Except the Dying—this to Us
Made Nature different

We noticed smallest things—   5
Things overlooked before
By this great light upon our Minds
Italicized—as 'twere.

As We went out and in
Between Her final Room   10
And Rooms where Those to be alive
Tomorrow were, a Blame

That Others could exist
While She must finish quite
A Jealousy for Her arose   15
So nearly infinite—

We waited while She passed—
It was a narrow time—
Too jostled were Our Souls to speak
At length the notice came.   20

She mentioned, and forgot—
Then lightly as a Reed
Bent to the Water, struggled scarce—
Consented, and was dead—

And We—We placed the Hair—   25
And drew the Head erect—
And then an awful leisure was
Belief to regulate—

1951

1126

Shall I take thee, the Poet said
To the propounded word?
Be stationed with the Candidates
Till I have finer tried—

The Poet searched Philology   5
And when about to ring
For the suspended Candidate
There came unsummoned in—

That portion of the Vision
The Word applied to fill   10
Not unto nomination
The Cherubim[1] reveal—
1951

1129

Tell all the Truth but tell it slant—
Success in Circuit lies
Too bright for our infirm Delight
The Truth's superb surprise

As Lightning to the Children eased   5
With explanation kind
The Truth must dazzle gradually
Or every man be blind—
1951

1177

A prompt—executive Bird is the Jay—
Bold as a Bailiff's Hymn—
Brittle and Brief in quality—
Warrant in every line—

Sitting a Bough like a Brigadier   5
Confident and straight—
Much is the mien of him in March
As a Magistrate—
1951

[1] The angels who guard the throne of God.

1212

A word is dead
When it is said,
Some say.
I say it just
Begins to live   5
That day.
1951

1282

[Draft 1]

Art thou the thing I wanted?
Begone—my Tooth has grown—
Supply the minor Palate
That has not starved so long—
I tell thee while I waited   5
The mystery of Food
Increased till I abjured it
And dine without Like God—
1873?/1951

[Draft 2]

Art thou the thing I wanted?
Begone—my Tooth has grown—
Affront a minor palate
Thou could'st not goad so long—

I tell thee while I waited—   5
The mystery of Food
Increased till I abjured it
Subsisting now like God—
1873?/1951

1393

Lay this Laurel[1] on the One
Too intrinsic for Renown—
Laurel—veil your deathless tree—
Him you chasten, that is He!

1951

1540

As imperceptibly as Grief
The Summer lapsed away—
Too imperceptible at last
To seem like Perfidy—
A Quietness distilled   5
As Twilight long begun,
Or Nature spending with herself
Sequestered Afternoon—
The Dusk drew earlier in—
The Morning foreign shone—   10
A courteous, yet harrowing Grace,
As Guest, that would be gone—
And thus, without a Wing
Or service of a Keel
Our Summer made her light escape   15
Into the Beautiful.

1951

---

[1] Traditionally, a laurel wreath signified honor
and immortality.

1545

The Bible is an antique Volume—
Written by faded Men
At the suggestion of Holy Spectres[1]—
Subjects—Bethlehem—
Eden—the ancient Homestead—   5
Satan—the Brigadier—
Judas—the Great Defaulter—
David—the Troubadour[2]—
Sin—a distinguished Precipice
Others must resist—   10
Boys that "believe" are very lonesome—
Other Boys are "lost"—
Had but the Tale a warbling Teller—
All the Boys would come—
Orpheus' Sermon captivated[3]—   15
It did not condemn—

1951

1593

There came a Wind like a Bugle—
It quivered through the Grass
And a Green Chill upon the Heat
So ominous did pass
We barred the Windows and the Doors   5
As from an Emerald Ghost—
The Doom's electric Moccasin[1]
That very instant passed—
On a strange Mob of panting Trees
And Fences fled away   10
And Rivers where the Houses ran

---

[1] The Holy Spirit is said to be the inspirer of the authors of the Bible.
[2] Beginning in line 4 Dickinson enumerates, out of order, the fall of Satan and his rebel angels, the creation of Man in Eden, Original Sin and the Fall, the composition of the Psalms by King David, the birth of Jesus in Bethlehem, and the betrayal of Jesus by Judas.
[3] In mythology, when Orpheus played his lyre and sang, trees and rocks danced, and all the animals came to listen.
[1] Soft leather shoe worn by American Indians.

Those looked that lived—that Day—
The Bell within the steeple wild
The flying tidings told—
How much can come   15
And much can go,
And yet abide the World!

1951

1624

Apparently with no surprise
To any happy Flower
The Frost beheads it at its play—
In accidental power—
The blonde Assassin passes on—   5
The Sun proceeds unmoved
To measure off another Day
For an Approving God.

1951

1651

A Word made Flesh[1] is seldom
And tremblingly partook[2]
Nor then perhaps reported
But have I not mistook
Each one of us has tasted   5
With ecstasies of stealth
The very food debated[3]
To our specific strength—

---

[1] "And the Word was made flesh and dwelt among us," are St. John's words for the Incarnation of Christ. (See John 1:14.)
[2] In the Christian rite of Holy Communion, believers "partake" of the bread and wine, symbols of Jesus' body and blood, respectively.
[3] Determined by discussion to be accurate.

A Word that breathes distinctly
Has not the power to die   10
Cohesive as the Spirit
It may expire if He—
"Made Flesh and dwelt among us"
Could condescension[4] be
Like this consent of Language   15
This loved Philology.

1951

1670

In Winter in my Room
I came upon a Worm—
Pink, lank and warm—
But as he was a worm
And worms presume   5
Not quite with him at home—
Secured him by a string
To something neighboring
And went along.

A Trifle afterward   10
A thing occurred
I'd not believe it if I heard
But state with creeping blood—
A snake with mottles rare
Surveyed my chamber floor   15
In feature as the worm before
But ringed with power—
The very string with which
I tied him—too
When he was mean and new   20
That string was there—

I shrank—"How fair you are"!
Propitiation's claw—
"Afraid," he hissed
"Of me"?   25

---

[4] Used theologically to signify Christ's descent
from the Godhead into flesh.

"No cordiality"—
He fathomed me—
Then to a Rhythm *Slim*
Secreted in his Form
As Patterns swim   30
Projected him.

That time I flew
Both eyes his way
Lest he pursue
Nor ever ceased to run   35
Till in a distant Town
Towns on from mine
I set me down
This was a dream.
1951

1732

My life closed twice before its close—
It yet remains to see
If Immortality unveil
A third event to me

So huge, so hopeless to conceive   5
As these that twice befell.
Parting is all we know of heaven,
And all we need of hell.
1951

1755

To make a prairie it takes a clover and one bee,
One clover, and a bee,
And revery.
The revery alone will do,
If bees are few.   5
1951

1760

Elysium[1] is as far as to
The very nearest Room
If in that Room a Friend await
Felicity or Doom—

What fortitude the Soul contains, 5
That it can so endure
The accent of a coming Foot—
The opening of a Door—

1951

Native American Literature: Assimilation and a Reemerging Tradition

Some races of men seem molded in wax, soft and melting, at once plastic and feeble. Some races, like some metals, combine the greatest flexibility with the greatest strength. But the Indian is hewn out of rock. You cannot change the form without destruction of the substance. Such, at least, has too often proved the case. Races of inferior energy have possessed a power of expansion and assimilation to which he is a stranger; and it is this fixed and rigid quality which has proved his ruin. He will not learn the arts of civilization, and he and his forest must perish together. The stern, unchanging features of his mind excite our admiration, from their very immutability; and we look with deep interest on the fate of this irreclaimable son of the wilderness, the child who will not be weaned from the breast of his rugged mother. And our interest increases when we discern in the unhappy wanderer, mingled among his vices, the germs of heroic virtues—a hand bountiful to bestow, as it is rapacious to receive, and, even in extreme famine, imparting its last morsel to a fellow-sufferer; a heart which, strong in friendship as in hate, thinks it not too much to lay down life for its chosen comrade; a soul true to its own idea of honor, and burning with an unquenchable thirst for greatness and renown.

Francis Parkman, *The Conspiracy of Pontiac* (1851)

[1] Mythological equivalent to the Christian heaven.

If the savage resists, civilization, with the ten commandments in one hand and the sword in the other, demands his immediate extermination.

President Andrew Johnson, Message to Congress (1867)

The idea that a handful of wild, half-naked, thieving, plundering, murdering savages should be dignified with the sovereign attributes of nations, enter into solemn treaties, and claim a country five hundred miles wide by one thousand miles long as theirs in fee simple, because they hunted buffalo and antelope over it, might do for beautiful reading in Cooper's novels or Longfellow's *Hiawatha*, but is unsuited to the intelligence and justice of this age, or the natural rights of mankind.

United States v. *Lucero* (1869)

So intimately has the Indian become associated with the government as ward of the nation, and so prominent a place among the questions of national policy does the much mooted "Indian question" occupy, that it behooves us no longer to study this problem from works of fiction, but to deal with it as it exists in reality. Stripped of the beautiful romance with which we have been so long willing to envelope him, transferred from the inviting pages of the novelist to the localities where we are compelled to meet with him, in his native village, on the war path, and when raiding upon our frontier settlements and lines of travel, the Indian forfeits his claim to the appellation of the "noble red man." We see him as he is, and, so far as all knowledge goes, as he ever has been, a savage in every sense of the word; not worse, perhaps, than his white brother would be similarly born and bred, but one whose cruel and ferocious nature far exceeds that of any wild beast of the contact with the wild tribes will deny. Perhaps there are some who, as members of peace commissions or as wandering agents of some benevolent society, may have visited these tribes or attended with them at councils held for some pacific purpose, and who, by passing through the villages of the Indian while at peace, may imagine their opportunities for judging of the Indian nature all that could be desired. But the Indian, while he can seldom be accused of indulging in a great variety of wardrobe, can be said to have character capable of adapting itself to almost every occasion. He has one character, perhaps his most serviceable one, which he preserves carefully, and only airs it when making his appeal to the government or its agents for arms, ammunition, and license to employ them. This character is invariably paraded, and often with telling effect, when the motive is a peaceful one. Prominent chiefs invited to visit Washington invariably don this character, and in their "talks" with the "Great Father" and other less prominent personages they successfully contrive to exhibit but this one phase. Seeing under these or similar circumstances only, it is not surprising that by many the Indian is looked upon as a simple-minded "son of nature," desiring nothing beyond the privilege of roaming and hunting over the vast unsettled wilds of the West, inheriting and asserting but few native rights, and erroneous with that which regards the Indian as a creature possessing the human form but divested of all other attributes of humanity, and whose traits of character, habits, modes of life, disposition, and savage customs disqualify him from the exercise of all rights and privileges, even those pertaining to life itself.

General George Armstrong Custer, *My Life on the Plains* (1872)

As to our aboriginal or Indian population—the Aztec in the South, and many a tribe in the North and West—I know it seems to be agreed that they must gradually dwindle as time rolls on, and in a few generations more leave only a reminiscence, a blank. But I am not at all clear about that. As America, from its many far-back sources and current supplies, develops, adapts, entwines, faithfully identifies its own—are we to see it cheerfully accepting and using all the contributions of foreign lands from the whole outside globe—and then rejecting the only ones distinctively its own—the autochthonic ones?

Walt Whitman, letter to the city officials at Santa Fe, New Mexico (1883)

The allotment of lands in severalty, which began in land lust and is being carried to the bitter end by those who believe a Stone Age man can be developed into a citizen of the United States in single generation, is in violent antagonism to every wish and innate desire of the red man, and has failed of expected results, even among the Southern Cheyennes, where the land is rich and climate mild, because it presents a somber phase of civilized life.

The attempt to make the Sioux a greedy landowner, content to live the lonely life of the poor Western rancher, cut off from daily association with his fellows, is to me uselessly painful. If we would convert the primitive man to our ways, we must make our ways alluring.

Hamlin Garland, *The North American Review* (April 1902)

"Relinquish," McCaslin said. "Relinquish. You, the direct male descendant of him who saw the opportunity and took it, bought the land, took the land, got the land no matter how, out of the old grant, the first patent, when it was a wilderness of wild beasts and wilder men, and cleared it, translated it into something to bequeath to his children, worthy of bequeathment for his descendants' ease and security and pride, and to perpetuate his name and accomplishments. . . .

"I can't repudiate it. It was never mine to repudiate. It was never Father's and Uncle Buddy's to bequeath me to repudiate, because it was never Grandfather's to bequeath them to bequeath me to repudiate, because it was never old Ikkemotubbe's to sell to Grandfather for bequeathment and repudiation. Because it was never Ikkemotubbe's fathers' fathers' to bequeath Ikkemotubbe to sell to Grandfather or any man because on the instant when Ikkemotubbe discovered, realized, that he could sell it for money, on that instant it ceased ever to have been his forever, father to father to father, and the man who bought it bought nothing."

William Faulkner, *The Bear* (1942)

Seattle
1786–1866

Few Native Americans have had as enduring a presence in ordinary American life as Seattle, chief of the Suquamish and Dewamish tribes. The Pacific Northwest's largest city is named in his honor. He and his predecessors maintained amiable relations with white settlers and traders for several generations—relations that were strengthened by Seattle's conversion to Christianity in the 1830s. Intent on minimizing the possible conflicts between his people and the American government, Seattle was the first Native American to sign the Treaty of Port Elliott in 1855. That agreement provided Seattle's tribe with a reservation in what is now Washington State. In many respects, Seattle's public identity encapsulated the cumulative image white Americans had found it useful to cultivate—a trustworthy, noble "savage" who had been "civilized" by Christianity and the American government's "generosity."

In 1853 the Washington Territory was organized, and a plan for the city of Seattle was prepared. Two years later, Isaac Stevens, the governor of the territory, visited the city, seeking a pledge of cooperation from the Native Americans. Seattle willingly offered that, but his response to Stevens, printed here, sought assurances that his people would be treated humanely and that their cultural differences with the white settlers would be recognized and respected. The speech was recorded by Henry Smith, a physician fluent in the tribal languages. But the existing text appears to be corrupt; white American interpolations ("pale-face," "Happy Hunting Ground," and the like) suggest that Seattle's speech has been edited to make it conform to the settlers' highly romanticized, stereotypical view of Native Americans.

Further Reading:
E. G. Anderson, *Chief Seattle*, 1943.
W. C. Vanderwerth, *Indian Oratory*, 1971.
A. Rosenteil, *Red and White: Indian Views of the White Man*, 1983.

Text:
The Washington Historical Quarterly, 1931.

"Our People Are Ebbing Away Like a Rapidly Receding Tide"*

Yonder sky that has wept tears of compassion upon my people for centuries untold, and which to us appears changeless and eternal, may change. Today is fair. Tomorrow it may be overcast with clouds. My words are like the stars that never change.

---

* Speech delivered to Governor Isaac Stevens of the Oregon Territory, 1855.

Whatever Seattle says the great chief at Washington[1] can rely upon with as much certainty as he can upon the return of the sun or the seasons. The White Chief says that Big Chief at Washington sends us greetings of friendship and good will. This is kind of him for we know he has little need of our friendship in return. His people are many. They are like the grass that covers vast prairies. My people are few. They resemble the scattering trees of a storm-swept plain. The Great—and I presume—good White Chief sends us word that he wishes to buy our lands but is willing to allow us enough to live comfortably. This indeed appears just, even generous, for the Red Man no longer has rights that he need respect, and the offer may be wise also, as we are no longer in need of an extensive country.

There was a time when our people covered the land as the waves of a wind-ruffled sea cover its shell-paved floor, but that time long since passed away with the greatness of tribes that are now but a mournful memory. I will not dwell on, nor mourn over, our untimely decay, nor reproach my pale face brothers with hastening it as we too may have been somewhat to blame.

Youth is impulsive. When our young men grow angry at some real or imaginary wrong, and disfigure their faces with black paint, it denotes that their hearts are black —and then they are often cruel and relentless, and our old men and old women are unable to restrain them. Thus it has ever been. Thus it was when the white man first began to push our forefathers westward. But let us hope that the hostilities between us may never return. We would have everything to lose and nothing to gain. Revenge by young braves is considered gain, even at the cost of their own lives, but old men who stay at home in times of war, and mothers who have sons to lose, know better.

Our good father at Washington—for I presume he is now our father as well as yours, since King George[2] has moved his boundaries further north—our great and good father, I say, sends us word that if we do as he desires he will protect us. His brave warriors will be to us a bristling wall of strength, and his wonderful ships of war will fill our harbors so that our ancient enemies far to the northward—the Hidas and Timpsions,[3] will cease to frighten our women, children and old men. Then in reality will he be our father and we his children. But can that ever be? Your God is not our God! Your God loves your people and hates mine. He folds his strong protecting arms lovingly about the pale face and leads him by the hand as a father leads his infant son—but He has forsaken His red children—if they are really His. Our God, the Great Spirit, seems also to have forsaken us. Your God makes your people wax strong every day. Soon they will fill all the land. Our people are ebbing away like a rapidly receding tide that will never return. The white man's God can not love our people or He would protect them. They seem to be orphans who can look nowhere for help. How then can we be brothers? How can your God become our God and renew our prosperity and awaken in us dreams of returning greatness. If we have a common Heavenly Father He must be partial—for He came to His pale-face[4] children. We never saw Him. He gave you laws but had no word for His red children whose teeming multitudes once filled this vast continent as stars fill the

---

[1] President Franklin Pierce.
[2] King of England during the American Revolution.
[3] I.e., the Haidas and Tsimshian, two Northwest Coast Indian groups living in what is now British Columbia, Canada.
[4] This and terms that follow, such as "Happy Hunting Ground" and "a few more moons," suggest that the text has been heavily edited by white Americans to conform to stereotypes of Indian speech.

firmament. No. We are two distinct races with separate origins and separate destinies. There is little in common between us.

To us the ashes of our ancestors are sacred and their resting place is hallowed ground. You wander far from the graves of your ancestors and seemingly without regret. Your religion was written on tables of stone by the iron finger of your God so that you could not forget. The Red Man could never comprehend nor remember it. Our religion is the traditions of our ancestors—the dreams of our old men, given them in the solemn hours of night by the Great Spirit; and the visions of our sachems, and is written in the hearts of our people.

Your dead cease to love you and the land of their nativity as soon as they pass the portals of the tomb and wander away beyond the stars. They are soon forgotten and never return. Our dead never forget the beautiful world that gave them being. They still love its verdant valleys, its murmuring rivers, its magnificent mountains, sequestered vales and verdant-lined lakes and bays, and ever yearn in tender, fond affection over the lonely hearted living, and often return from the Happy Hunting Ground to visit, guide, console and comfort them.

Day and night can not dwell together. The Red Man has ever fled the approach of the White Man as the morning mist flees before the rising sun.

However, your proposition seems fair, and I think that my folks will accept it and will retire to the reservation you offer them. Then we will dwell apart in peace for the words of the Great White Chief seem to be the voice of Nature speaking to my people out of dense darkness.

It matters little where we pass the remnant of our days. They will not be many. The Indian's night promises to be dark. Not a single star of hope hovers above his horizon. Sad-voiced winds moan in the distance. Grim Nemesis[5] seems to be on the Red Man's trail, and wherever he goes he will hear the approaching footsteps of his fell destroyer and prepare to stolidly meet his doom, as does the wounded doe that hears the approaching footsteps of the hunter.

A few more moons. A few more winters—and not one of the descendants of the mighty hosts that once moved over this broad land or lived in happy homes, protected by the Great Spirit, will remain to mourn over the graves of a people—once more powerful and hopeful than yours. But why should I mourn at the untimely fate of my people? Tribe follows tribe, and nation follows nation, like the waves of the sea. It is the order of nature, and regret is useless. Your time of decay may be distant—but it will surely come, for even the White Man whose God walked and talked with him as friend with friend, can not be exempt from the common destiny. We may be brothers after all. We will see.

We will ponder your proposition and when we decide we will let you know. But should we accept it, I here and now make this condition—that we will not be denied the privilege without molestation, of visiting at any time the tombs of our ancestors, friends and children. Every part of this soil is sacred, in the estimation of my people. Every hillside, every valley, every plain and grove, has been hallowed by some sad or happy event in days long vanished. Even the rocks, which seem to be dumb and dead as they swelter in the sun along the silent shore thrill with memories of stirring events connected with the lives of my people, and the very dust upon which you now stand responds more lovingly to their footsteps than to yours, because it is rich with

[5] Retribution.

the dust of our ancestors and our bare feet are conscious of the sympathetic touch. Our departed braves, fond mothers, glad, happy-hearted maidens, and even the little children who lived here and rejoiced here for a brief season, still love these sombre solitudes and at eventide they grow shadowy of returning spirits. And when the last Red Man shall have perished, and the memory of my tribe shall have become a myth among the white man, these shores will swarm with the invisible dead of my tribe, and when your children's children think themselves alone in the field, the store, the shop, upon the highway, or in the silence of the pathless woods, they will not be alone. In all the earth there is no place dedicated to solitude. At night when the streets of your cities and villages are silent and you think them deserted, they will throng with the returning hosts that once filled them and still love this beautiful land. The White Man will never be alone.

Let him be just and deal kindly with my people, for the dead are not powerless. Dead—I say? There is no death. Only a change of worlds.

1855/1931

Sarah Winnemucca Hopkins
1844–1891

Native American women helped for centuries to preserve and enrich their tribes' splendid traditions of oral literature. Yet as *writers* using English to chronicle their own lives as well as Native American history and culture, Indian women began to appear in print, albeit sporadically, only in the second half of the nineteenth century. Because they wrote primarily for white audiences interested in the "savage" world, these Native American women writers often adopted the styles prevalent in the popular literature of the time—romantic, sentimental, and often fictional renditions of their lives, their tribes, and their contacts with white settlers and the American government. Sarah Winnemucca Hopkins's *Life Among the Piutes* (1883) is one of the most engaging examples of this relatively recent development in Native American literature.

Sarah Winnemucca Hopkins was born in northwestern Nevada, the granddaughter of Truckee and the daughter of Old Winnemucca, successive chiefs of the Paiute tribes. Because she was fluent in English at an early age, Hopkins was for much of her youth a liaison between her people and the white settlers in Nevada and later in Oregon, where many Paiutes had moved in response to the westward surge of frontier settlers. Increasing disenchantment with federal Indian policies prompted Hopkins to seek a broader public forum for the concerns of her people. In 1879 she began an extensive tour in the East that included more than three hundred lectures detailing the plight of the Paiutes and other Native Americans. After these heralded efforts and the publication of her book did not produce the results she had hoped for, she resettled in Nevada and opened a school for Paiute children on her brother's farm. Her poor health and inadequate finances could sustain the school only until 1887. She died in 1891.

Life Among the Piutes skillfully blends personal and tribal narrative to create an informative and at times harrowing account of the terrifying extremes the Paiutes were forced to undertake to preserve their families and culture.

Further Reading:

M. E. Gridley, *American Indian Women,* 1974.
W. F. Smith, Jr., "American Indian Autobiographies," *American Indian Quarterly,* 1975.
C. S. Fowler, "Sarah Winnemucca," in

American Indian Intellectuals, ed. M. Liberty, 1976.
A. Krupat, "American Indian Autobiographies: Origins, Type, and Function," *American Literature,* 1981.

Text:

Life Among the Piutes: Their Wrongs and Claims, 1883.

---

from Life Among the Piutes[1]

from Chapter I: First Meeting of Piutes and Whites

I was born somewhere near 1844, but am not sure of the precise time. I was a very small child when the first white people came into our country. They came like a lion, yes, like a roaring lion, and have continued so ever since, and I have never forgotten their first coming. My people were scattered at that time over nearly all the territory now known as Nevada. My grandfather was chief of the entire Piute nation, and was camped near Humboldt Lake,[2] with a small portion of his tribe, when a party travelling eastward from California was seen coming. When the news was brought to my grandfather, he asked what they looked like? When told that they had hair on their faces, and were white, he jumped up and clasped his hands together, and cried aloud,—

"My white brothers,—my long-looked for white brothers have come at last!"

He immediately gathered some of his leading men, and went to the place where the party had gone into camp. Arriving near them, he was commanded to halt in a manner that was readily understood without an interpreter. Grandpa at once made signs of friendship by throwing down his robe and throwing up his arms to show them he had no weapons; but in vain,—they kept him at a distance. He knew not what to do. He had expected so much pleasure in welcoming his white brothers to the best in the land, that after looking at them sorrowfully for a little while, he came away quite unhappy. But he would not give them up so easily. He took some of his most trustworthy men and followed them day after day, camping near them at night, and travelling in sight of them by day, hoping in this way to gain their confidence. But he was disappointed, poor dear old soul!

---

[1] I.e., Paiutes, two subroups of the Shoshone-language Indians. The Southern Paiutes lived in southern Utah, Arizona, southern Nevada, and southeastern California. Hopkins was a member of the Northern Paiutes, who lived in western Nevada, eastern Oregon, and east-central California.
[2] Lake in northwestern Nevada, also known as Humboldt Sink.

I can imagine his feelings, for I have drank deeply from the same cup. When I think of my past life, and the bitter trials I have endured, I can scarcely believe I live, and yet I do; and, with the help of Him who notes the sparrow's fall, I mean to fight for my down-trodden race while life lasts.

Seeing they would not trust him, my grandfather left them, saying, "Perhaps they will come again next year." Then he summoned his whole people, and told them this tradition:—

"In the beginning of the world there were only four, two girls and two boys. Our forefather and mother were only two, and we are their children. You all know that a great while ago there was a happy family in this world. One girl and one boy were dark and the others were white. For a time they got along together without quarelling, but soon they disagreed, and there was trouble. They were cross to one another and fought, and our parents were very much grieved. They prayed that their children might learn better, but it did not do any good; and afterwards the whole household was made so unhappy that the father and mother saw that they must separate their children; and then our father took the dark boy and girl, and the white boy and girl, and asked them, 'Why are you so cruel to each other?' They hung down their heads, and would not speak. They were ashamed. He said to them, 'Have I not been kind to you all, and given you everything your hearts wished for? You do not have to hunt and kill your own game to live upon. You see, my dear children, I have power to call whatsoever kind of game we want to eat; and I also have the power to separate my dear children, if they are not good to each other.' So he separated his children by a word. He said, 'Depart from each other, you cruel children;—go across the mighty ocean and do not seek each other's lives.'

"So the light girl and boy disappeared by that one word, and their parents saw them no more, and they were grieved, although they knew their children were happy. And by-and-by the dark children grew into a large nation; and we believe it is the one we belong to, and that the nation that sprung from the white children will some time send some one to meet us and heal all the old trouble. Now, the white people we saw a few days ago must certainly be our white brothers, and I want to welcome them. I want to love them as I love all of you. But they would not let me; they were afraid. But they will come again, and I want you one and all to promise that, should I not live to welcome them myself, you will not hurt a hair on their heads, but welcome them as I tried to do." . . .

The following spring, before my grandfather returned home, there was a great excitement among my people on account of fearful news coming from different tribes, that the people whom they called their white brothers were killing everybody that came in their way, and all the Indian tribes had gone into the mountains to save their lives. So my father told all his people to go into the mountains and hunt and lay up food for the coming winter. Then we all went into the mountains. There was a fearful story they told us children. Our mothers told us that the whites were killing everybody and eating them. So we were all afraid of them. Every dust that we could see blowing in the valleys we would say it was the white people. In the late fall my father told his people to go to the rivers and fish, and we all went to Humboldt River,[3] and the women went to work gathering wild seed, which they grind between the

[3] River flowing southwest into Humboldt Lake; it was an important route for immigrants traveling from Salt Lake City to central California.

rocks. The stones are round, big enough to hold in the hands. The women did this when they got back, and when they had gathered all they could they put it in one place and covered it with grass, and then over the grass mud. After it is covered it looks like an Indian wigwam.

Oh, what a fright we all got one morning to hear some white people were coming. Every one ran as best they could. My poor mother was left with my little sister and me. Oh, I never can forget it. My poor mother was carrying my little sister on her back, and trying to make me run; but I was so frightened I could not move my feet, and while my poor mother was trying to get me along my aunt overtook us, and she said to my mother: "Let us bury our girls, or we shall all be killed and eaten up." So they went to work and buried us, and told us if we heard any noise not to cry out, for if we did they would surely kill us and eat us. So our mothers buried me and my cousin, planted sage bushes over our faces to keep the sun from burning them, and there we were left all day.

Oh, can any one imagine my feelings *buried alive,* thinking every minute that I was to be unburied and eaten up by the people that my grandfather loved so much? With my heart throbbing, and not daring to breathe, we lay there all day. It seemed that the night would never come. Thanks be to God! the night came at last. Oh, how I cried and said: "Oh, father, have you forgotten me? Are you never coming for me?" I cried so I thought my very heartstrings would break.

At last we heard some whispering. We did not dare to whisper to each other, so we lay still. I could hear their footsteps coming nearer and nearer. I thought my heart was coming right out of my mouth. Then I heard my mother say, " 'T is right here!" Oh, can any one in this world ever imagine what were my feelings when I was dug up by my poor mother and father? My cousin and I were once more happy in our mothers' and fathers' care, and we were taken to where all the rest were.

I was once buried alive; but my second burial shall be for ever, where no father or mother will come and dig me up. It shall not be with throbbing heart that I shall listen for coming footsteps. I shall be in the sweet rest of peace,—I, the chieftain's weary daughter. . . .

1883

Charles Alexander Eastman
1858–1939

The youngest of five children, Charles Alexander Eastman was named Hakadah ("the pitiful last") at his birth in Redwood Falls, Minnesota, to a Sioux father and a half-blooded mother who died soon after his birth. At the age of four he was renamed Ohiyesa ("the winner") and would go on to distinguish himself as perhaps the best-known Native American in the late nineteenth and early twentieth centuries. A renowned writer, lecturer, and physician, Eastman's life and career were heralded by the nation at large as an example of what Native Americans could accomplish if only they would adopt the values and life-styles of white America.

Raised by his paternal grandmother and uncle, Ohiyesa fled with them to Canada after the 1862 Sioux uprising in Minnesota. He did not encounter a white person until a teenager. Then he was reclaimed by his father, who had converted to Christianity and accepted the traditional forms of white civilization and who brought him to the Santee Sioux farming community in Flandreau, South Dakota. Renamed Charles Alexander Eastman, the young Native American attended the mission school at Santee, Nebraska, where his unusually quick progress prompted school officials to send him to Beloit College in Wisconsin. After several brief stops at other colleges, Eastman headed for Dartmouth College, where so many Native Americans had previously found an intellectual haven and from which he graduated in 1887. Three years later he received an M.D. degree from the Boston University School of Medicine.

Eastman first worked as the federal government's physician at the Pine Ridge Agency in South Dakota. He served there for nearly three years, including the period of disturbances that erupted in the 1890 massacre at Wounded Knee. During this time Eastman met and married Elaine Goodale, a poet and teacher from Massachusetts working on the Sioux reservation. In 1893 the Eastmans moved to St. Paul, Minnesota, where he practiced medicine and served as the traveling secretary of the Young Men's Christian Association among the Indian people. Eastman spent much of the next two decades working on behalf of Native Americans, serving for a time as the Sioux's official representative in the nation's capital. One of the founders and the first president of the Society of American Indians, Eastman also helped the federal government revise the Sioux allotment roles, selected permanent family names for them, and collected cultural data on their behalf. He represented the Native Americans at the First Universal Races Congress in London in 1911. During World War I the Eastmans moved to New Hampshire, where they owned a summer camp. There they struggled to maintain their marriage through financial difficulties, differing political and social views, and a daughter's death. After their separation in the early 1920s, Eastman eventually settled in a cabin in a small wooded area near Desbarats, Ontario, and depended on the generosity of friends for survival. He died in January 1939, a victim of smoke inhalation during a fire in his cabin.

Eastman's first published work was an autobiographical sketch in 1893. In each of the nine books that followed—including *The Soul of the Indians* (1911); *The Indian Today* (1915); the second installment of his autobiography, *From the Deep Woods to Civilization* (1916); and *Indian Heroes and Great Chieftains* (1918)— Eastman collaborated with his wife, whose "devoted cooperation" he acknowledged. His first book, *Indian Boyhood* (1902), was written for his children. Blending personal experiences with tribal history and lore, as well as character sketches and ethnological data, Eastman recounts the most instructive episodes of his early life to underscore the simple proposition announced in its early pages: "What boy would not be an Indian for a while when he thinks of the freest life in the world? This life was mine. Every day there was a real hunt. There was real game." In the episode printed here, the young Eastman is initiated into the philosophy of Sioux life in the woods. The writing links the Native American tradition with its cultural counterpart expressed in the classic American literature of such writers as Twain and Faulkner.

Further Reading:
R. Wilson, "The Writings of Ohiyesa—
Alexander Eastman, M.D., Santee Sioux," *South
Dakota History* 1975.
D. R. Miller, "Charles Alexander Eastman, the
'Winner': From Deep Woods to Civilization,"

in *American Indian Intellectuals,* ed. M. Liberty,
1976.
A. L. Stensland, "Charles Alexander Eastman:
Sioux Storyteller and Historian," *American
Indian Quarterly,* 1977.

Text:
Indian Boyhood, 1902.

from Indian Boyhood

Chapter III: The Boy Hunter

It will be no exaggeration to say that the life of the Indian hunter was a life of
fascination. From the moment that he lost sight of his rude home in the midst of the
forest, his untutored mind lost itself in the myriad beauties and forces of nature. Yet
he never forgot his personal danger from some lurking foe or savage beast, however
absorbing was his passion for the chase.

The Indian youth was a born hunter. Every motion, every step expressed an inborn
dignity and, at the same time, a depth of native caution. His moccasined foot fell like
the velvet paw of a cat—noiselessly; his glittering black eyes scanned every object that
appeared within their view. Not a bird, not even a chipmunk, escaped their piercing
glance.

I was scarcely over three years old when I stood one morning just outside our
buffalo-skin teepee, with my little bow and arrows in my hand, and gazed up among
the trees. Suddenly the instinct to chase and kill seized me powerfully. Just then a bird
flew over my head and then another caught my eye, as it balanced itself upon a
swaying bough. Everything else was forgotten and in that moment I had taken my
first step as a hunter.

There was almost as much difference between the Indian boys who were brought
up on the open prairies and those of the woods, as between city and country boys.
The hunting of the prairie boys was limited and their knowledge of natural history
imperfect. They were, as a rule, good riders, but in all-round physical development
much inferior to the red men of the forest.

Our hunting varied with the season of the year, and the nature of the country
which was for the time our home. Our chief weapon was the bow and arrows, and
perhaps, if we were lucky, a knife was possessed by some one in the crowd. In the
olden times, knives and hatchets were made from bone and sharp stones.

For fire we used a flint with a spongy piece of dry wood and a stone to strike with.
Another way of starting fire was for several of the boys to sit down in a circle and
rub two pieces of dry, spongy wood together, one after another, until the wood took
fire.

We hunted in company a great deal, though it was a common thing for a boy to
set out for the woods quite alone, and he usually enjoyed himself fully as much. Our

game consisted mainly of small birds, rabbits, squirrels and grouse. Fishing, too, occupied much of our time. We hardly ever passed a creek or a pond without searching for some signs of fish. When fish were present, we always managed to get some. Fish-lines were made of wild hemp, sinew or horse-hair. We either caught fish with lines, snared or speared them, or shot them with bow and arrows. In the fall we charmed them up to the surface by gently tickling them with a stick and quickly threw them out. We have sometimes dammed the brooks and driven the larger fish into a willow basket made for that purpose.

It was part of our hunting to find new and strange things in the woods. We examined the slightest sign of life; and if a bird had scratched the leaves off the ground, or a bear dragged up a root for his morning meal, we stopped to speculate on the time it was done. If we saw a large old tree with some scratches on its bark, we concluded that a bear or some raccoons must be living there. In that case we did not go any nearer than was necessary, but later reported the incident at home. An old deer-track would at once bring on a warm discussion as to whether it was the track of a buck or a doe. Generally, at noon, we met and compared our game, noting at the same time the peculiar characteristics of everything we had killed. It was not merely a hunt, for we combined with it the study of animal life. We also kept strict accounts of our game, and thus learned who were the best shots among the boys.

I am sorry to say that we were merciless toward the birds. We often took their eggs and their young ones. My brother Chatanna and I once had a disagreeable adventure while bird-hunting. We were accustomed to catch in our hands young ducks and geese during the summer, and while doing this we happened to find a crane's nest. Of course, we were delighted with our good luck. But, as it was already midsummer, the young cranes—two in number—were rather large and they were a little way from the nest; we also observed that the two old cranes were in a swampy place near by; but, as it was moulting-time, we did not suppose that they would venture on dry land. So we proceeded to chase the young birds; but they were fleet runners and it took us some time to come up with them.

Meanwhile, the parent birds had heard the cries of their little ones and come to their rescue. They were chasing us, while we followed the birds. It was really a perilous encounter! Our strong bows finally gained the victory in a hand-to-hand struggle with the angry cranes; but after that we hardly ever hunted a crane's nest. Almost all birds make some resistance when their eggs or young are taken, but they will seldom attack man fearlessly.

We used to climb large trees for birds of all kinds; but we never undertook to get young owls unless they were on the ground. The hooting owl especially is a dangerous bird to attack under these circumstances.

I was once trying to catch a yellow-winged woodpecker in its nest when my arm became twisted and lodged in the deep hole so that I could not get it out without the aid of a knife; but we were a long way from home and my only companion was a deaf mute cousin of mine. I was about fifty feet up in the tree, in a very uncomfortable position, but I had to wait there for more than an hour before he brought me the knife with which I finally released myself.

Our devices for trapping small animals were rude, but they were often successful. For instance, we used to gather up a peck or so of large, sharp-pointed burrs and scatter them in the rabbit's furrow-like path. In the morning, we would find the little fellow sitting quietly in his tracks, unable to move, for the burrs stuck to his feet.

Another way of snaring rabbits and grouse was the following: We made nooses of twisted horsehair, which we tied very firmly to the top of a limber young tree, then bent the latter down to the track and fastened the whole with a slip-knot, after adjusting the noose. When the rabbit runs his head through the noose, he pulls the slip-knot and is quickly carried up by the spring of the young tree. This is a good plan, for the rabbit is out of harm's way as he swings high in the air.

Perhaps the most enjoyable of all was the chipmunk hunt. We killed these animals at any time of year, but the special time to hunt them was in March. After the first thaw, the chipmunks burrow a hole through the snow crust and make their first appearance for the season. Sometimes as many as fifty will come together and hold a social reunion. These gatherings occur early in the morning, from daybreak to about nine o'clock.

We boys learned this, among other secrets of nature, and got our blunt-headed arrows together in good season for the chipmunk expedition.

We generally went in groups of six to a dozen or fifteen, to see which would get the most. On the evening before, we selected several boys who could imitate the chipmunk's call with wild oat-straws and each of these provided himself with a supply of straws.

The crust will hold the boys nicely at this time of the year. Bright and early, they all come together at the appointed place, from which each group starts out in a different direction, agreeing to meet somewhere at a given position of the sun.

My first experience of this kind is still well remembered. It was a fine crisp March morning, and the sun had not yet shown himself among the distant tree-tops as we hurried along through the ghostly wood. Presently we arrived at a place where there were many signs of the animals. Then each of us selected a tree and took up his position behind it. The chipmunk caller sat upon a log as motionless as he could, and began to call.

Soon we heard the patter of little feet on the hard snow; then we saw the chipmunks approaching from all directions. Some stopped and ran experimentally up a tree or a log, as if uncertain of the exact direction of the call; others chased one another about.

In a few minutes, the chipmunk-caller was besieged with them. Some ran all over his person, others under him and still others ran up the tree against which he was sitting. Each boy remained immovable until their leader gave the signal; then a great shout arose, and the chipmunks in their flight all ran up the different trees.

Now the shooting-match began. The little creatures seemed to realize their hopeless position; they would try again and again to come down the trees and flee away from the deadly aim of the youthful hunters. But they were shot down very fast; and whenever several of them rushed toward the ground, the little red-skin hugged the tree and yelled frantically to scare them up again.

Each boy shoots always against the trunk of the tree, so that the arrow may bound back to him every time; otherwise, when he had shot away all of them, he would be helpless, and another, who had cleared his own tree, would come and take away his game, so there was warm competition. Sometimes a desperate chipmunk would jump from the top of the tree in order to escape, which was considered a joke on the boy who lost it and a triumph for the brave little animal. At last all were killed or gone, and then we went on to another place, keeping up the sport until the sun came out and the chipmunks refused to answer the call.

When we went out on the prairies we had a different and less lively kind of sport.

We used to snare with horse-hair and bow-strings all the small ground animals, including the prairie-dog. We both snared and shot them. Once a little boy set a snare for one, and lay flat on the ground a little way from the hole, holding the end of the string. Presently he felt something move and pulled in a huge rattlesnake; and to this day, his name is "Caught-the-Rattlesnake." Very often a boy got a new name in some such manner. At another time, we were playing in the woods and found a fawn's track. We followed and caught it while asleep; but in the struggle to get away, it kicked one boy, who is still called "Kicked-by-the-Fawn."

It became a necessary part of our education to learn to prepare a meal while out hunting. It is a fact that most Indians will eat the liver and some other portions of large animals raw, but they do not eat fish or birds uncooked. Neither will they eat a frog, or an eel. On our boyish hunts, we often went on until we found ourselves a long way from our camp, when we would kindle a fire and roast a part of our game.

Generally we broiled our meat over the coals on a stick. We roasted some of it over the open fire. But the best way to cook fish and birds is in the ashes, under a big fire. We take the fish fresh from the creek or lake, have a good fire on the sand, dig in the sandy ashes and bury it deep. The same thing is done in case of a bird, only we wet the feathers first. When it is done, the scales or feathers and skin are stripped off whole, and the delicious meat retains all its juices and flavor. We pulled it off as we ate, leaving the bones undisturbed.

Our people had also a method of boiling without pots or kettles. A large piece of tripe was thoroughly washed and the ends tied, then suspended between four stakes driven into the ground and filled with cold water. The meat was then placed in this novel receptacle and boiled by means of the addition of red-hot stones.

Chatanna was a good hunter. He called the doe and fawn beautifully by using a thin leaf of birchbark between two flattened sticks. One morning we found the tracks of a doe and fawn who had passed within the hour, for the light dew was brushed from the grass.

"What shall we do?" I asked. "Shall we go back to the teepee and tell uncle to bring his gun?"

"No, no!" exclaimed Chatanna. "Did not our people kill deer and buffalo long ago without guns? We will entice her into this open space, and, while she stands bewildered, I can throw my lasso line over her head."

He had called only a few seconds when the fawn emerged from the thick woods and stood before us, prettier than a picture. Then I uttered the call, and she threw her tobacco-leaf-like ears toward me, while Chatanna threw his lasso. She gave one scream and launched forth into the air, almost throwing the boy hunter to the ground. Again and again she flung herself desperately into the air, but at last we led her to the nearest tree and tied her securely.

"Now," said he, "go and get our pets and see what they will do."

At that time he had a good-sized black bear partly tamed, while I had a young red fox and my faithful Ohitika or Brave. I untied Chagoo, the bear, and Wanahon, the fox, while Ohitika got up and welcomed me by wagging his tail in a dignified way.

"Come," I said, "all three of you. I think we have something you would all like to see."

They seemed to understand me, for Chagoo began to pull his rope with both paws, while Wanahon undertook the task of digging up by the roots the sapling to which I had tied him.

Before we got to the open spot, we already heard Ohitika's joyous bark, and the two wild pets began to run, and pulled me along through the underbrush. Chagoo soon assumed the utmost precaution and walked as if he had splinters in his soles, while Wanahon kept his nose down low and sneaked through the trees.

Out into the open glade we came, and there, before the three rogues, stood the little innocent fawn. She visibly trembled at the sight of the motley group. The two human rogues looked to her, I presume, just as bad as the other three. Chagoo regarded her with a mixture of curiosity and defiance, while Wanahon stood as if rooted to the ground, evidently planning how to get at her. But Ohitika (Brave), generous Ohitika, his occasional barking was only in jest. He did not care to touch the helpless thing.

Suddenly the fawn sprang high into the air and then dropped her pretty head on the ground.

"Ohiyesa, the fawn is dead," cried Chatanna. "I wanted to keep her."

"It is a shame," I chimed in.

We five guilty ones came and stood around her helpless form. We all looked very sorry; even Chagoo's eyes showed repentance and regret. As for Ohitika, he gave two great sighs and then betook himself to a respectful distance. Chatanna had two big tears gradually swamping his long, black eye-lashes; and I thought it was time to hide my face, for I did not want him to look at me.

1902

Chona
ca. 1841–1935

"I was born there, on the Land," the elderly woman reported, pointing to what is now the Papago reservation in southwestern Arizona, situated between Tucson and the Mexican border. The Papago Indians call themselves the Desert People, after their circumstances, or the Bean People, after their principal crop. They belong to the Piman-Sonoran language group, which they share with the Pima, who are known as the River People.

According to Ruth M. Underhill, the Columbia anthropologist who recorded the following autobiography, "Chona is a corruption of the Spanish name Encarnación, with which the old woman had been baptized on a childhood visit to Mexico." The daughter of a prominent village chief, and the sister and wife of shamans, Chona was ninety years old in 1931 when she related the description printed here of the centuries-old tribal lore and rituals that determine behavior before, during, and after battle. The adversary is the Papago's longtime enemy and persecutor, the Apache, whom the Papago and the Pima helped U.S. troops subdue in 1887.

As a woman, Chona was prohibited from taking part in many tribal ceremonies, principally because women were regarded as impure. Yet, as this episode suggests, male Papago rituals of war and purification depended on the biological clocks of women, a reality Chona noted somewhat matter-of-factly: "You see we *have* power. Men have to dream to get power from the spirits and they think of everything they can—songs and speeches and marching around, hoping that the spirits will notice them and give them some power. But we *have* power. . . . Don't you see that without us, there would be no men? Why should we envy men? We *made* the men."

Further Reading:

R. M. Underhill, *Singing for Power: The Song Magic of the Papago Indians of Southwestern Arizona*, 1938.
R. M. Underhill, *The Papago Indians of Southwestern Arizona and Their Relatives, the*

Pimas, U.S. Office of Indian Affairs, Sherman Pamphlets No. 3, 1940.
D. Saxton and L. Saxton, *O'othham Hoho'ok A'agitha: Legends and Lore of the Papago Indians*, 1973.

Text:

Memoir 46 of the American Anthropological Association, 1936.

---

from The Autobiography of Chona, a Papago Woman

[The Powers of Enemy Slayers]

My father told my mother, "There is going to be a big war party. We have sent men to run to the Place of the Burnt Seeds and the Buffalo Head and Where the Willows Grow and Where the Owls Hoot and to Hackberry Pond. They are to meet us in ten days at the foot of the hills where the Apaches live."

My mother was frightened. It was near her time to menstruate and she was afraid it would not be over before my father wanted to go. Then he would have to stay home, because a menstruating wife would weaken him so he would be killed. My mother was careful about that. She went out of the house as soon as it began; she never waited a minute. She never touched my father's arrows nor even looked at them when she could hurt them. So she told him. Then she went straight out to the Little House so it would be safe for my father to mend his arrows and twist a new bow string. I took her food to her, and every day I would ask, "Has it come?" And on the second day she said, "Yes." So it passed and my father could go.

The men went early in the morning before light, and they were gone eight days. All that time we girls and women kept very quiet. When the older girls came home with a load of wood, they never threw it down hard; they placed it softly. We did not laugh nor talk loud. Old Leaf Buds came to see us. Her husband was going to take care of my father if he was a Killer. And Leaf Buds was going to take care of my mother. So my mother tried to finish the mat she was making, because if my father was a Killer, she would have to be purified and then she could not work at all.

She talked to us while she was finishing her work and told us what to do, because she would be gone four times four days. I was little then and I thought it would be good to stop work for so many days. But some of the women did not like it. They asked their husbands not to be Killers. There was once a woman who was making a big basket and she wanted to get it done. But the men made up a war party. So she told her husband she was menstruating and he had to stay home. They say that woman never menstruated again.

The men were gone eight days. I know how that fight was because my father told me. We were not women who were afraid of war power. We were Killers' women.

The men from all the villages met at Basket Cap Mountain, and there my father made them speeches, sitting with his arms folded and talking low as all great men do. Then they sang the war songs:

> Oh, bitter wind, keep blowing
> That therewith my enemy
> Staggering forward
>   Shall fall.

> Oh, bitter wind, keep blowing
> That therewith my enemy
> Staggering sideways
>   Shall fall.

Many, many songs they sang but I, a woman, cannot tell you all. I know that they made the enemy blind and dizzy with their singing and that they told the gopher to gnaw their arrows. And I know that they called on our dead warriors who have turned into owls and live in the Apache country to come and tell them where the enemy were. Facing the enemy they sat, while they sang, that they might bring darkness upon him.

All that time the medicine man sat alone on a little hill waiting for the owl-dead to come to him. He had dreamed of owls himself and so he could speak with them. They always took an Owl-Meeter[1] on to war with them to call the dead who are our spies.

Soon that medicine man came back to the others and said, "Has anyone some of our old, wild tobacco?" They gave him some. Then he went back and they saw lights when he made two cigarettes. They saw those lights move as cigarettes do when two people are smoking. They heard the medicine man talking, very low, and then saw both cigarettes thrown away. The medicine man came back and said, "The enemy are at Smooth Ground. We will come up with them at noon tomorrow."

So they did. They jumped on the enemy and fought. When our men go toward an Apache, they do not just walk. They leap. My father got separated from the others, he and one Apache. There was a giant cactus between them. You know a cactus trunk is as wide as a thin man. Each shot at the other, and the other dodged behind the cactus till it was stuck full of arrows to the height of a man.

They could both talk a little Spanish, so they shouted at each other. The Apache said, "I am a *man.*" My father: "I, also, a *man!*" They threw down their bows and

---

[1] Medicine-man.

arrows and started wrestling. My father was down. Far away, his brother saw that and came running. He clubbed the Apache from behind. My father got up and clubbed, too. So he was dead and my father and his brother were Enemy Slayers.

They stopped fighting right away because an enemy's death lets power loose. You must take care of yourself until you have tamed that power or it will kill you. You could not stand against arrows with such power around you. You would be like a sick man. You would fall. So they painted their faces black to show what had happened. They carried black paint for that in little deerskin bags. They stood away from the others, and other men who had killed came to join them.

The leader of the fight saw and he sent an old man who had killed, himself, so that he was not in danger. That man kept them away from the other men the way you keep away people who have a sickness. He made them walk behind the others and camp away from them all the way home. They never mixed their cornmeal for themselves. He mixed it for them—oh, so very little. Brave men do not want to eat when they are getting power. He spoke to them, telling them how they would dream. I do not know what he said to them. Old men know that—old Killers. Even a Slayer's woman like me is not told. But my father told me the end of every speech he made because it was always the same:

> Verily, who desires this thing?
> Do not you desire it?
> Then learn to endure hardship

One morning we heard shouting. It was the messengers from the war party, two men who had been sent ahead on the fastest horses. They were far outside the village, standing up in their stirrups and yelling:

> One Ear—has killed!
> Ridge Face—has killed!
> The Gambler—has killed!

The last one was my father. They called the name of his brother too, but it was words you white people do not like to say, about peoples' bodies.

We heard them far off, over and over again in a loud sing-song, and everyone came outside to listen to know if we now belonged to the families of Enemy Slayers.

My mother had a basket of corn kernels in her hand; she was going to grind flour. But when she heard the shout she set it down and just stood there. Then Leaf Buds came running to our house. She just motioned to my mother to come with her. My mother did not speak to us, and she did not take anything with her; just her cotton blanket to put over her head, because the wife of a man who is being purified must not see the sun. The husband of Leaf Buds was building a shelter for my mother, out away from the houses. He had to run to do it as soon as he heard the shouts. Until it was done, my mother went to Leaf Buds' house and sat there with her blanket over her head, not speaking. They did not make us children do anything, because children cannot stand the suffering of being purified. But my grandmother called us into the house and told us to stay quietly there. She gave us sticks to scratch our heads with so we would not use our hands and make our hair fall out. She told us not to speak much and never to go near the fire.

So we could not go out to see the men come in. The young girls whose men were not Enemy Slayers ran out to meet the fighters, far into the mountains. Ah, that is a good dance. I did it myself, at other times when there was no Power in the family. The girls stand across the warriors' path and take their weapons from them. They take arrows and quivers and bows, yes, clubs and shields. And they dance with them in front of the men. They dance and they sing with those weapons, and they will not give them back until the men have paid them.

We heard those girls run out, the girls who could run far. And when the men came near we saw the old woman go dancing out; the woman who takes the scalps. Foamy Water was her name; a woman who could not menstruate and hurt those powerful things. She took it when she was old enough from her mother who was called Painted Girl, because Painted Girl was so old she could not dance any more.

But Foamy Water danced hard. They gave her the hair of the Apache, not scalps, just long hairs from the temples, and they gave her his beaded buckskin shoe. They had tied those things on a pole, and she came dancing with it into the village, dancing at every house. She came outside our house making the pole go up and down. She sang:

Here I stand, singing for my prisoner
Come and see, Oh, women!
I dreamed that I saw light
At the tips of the warriors' feathers.

Then she stuck the pole in front of the council house and all the people went there to hear about the fight. It is the two messengers who tell that story before the fighters come, and sometimes after they tell about the killing, they end up, "But they got some of our men." Then they tell how they made a fire and burned up the dead men with everything they had. Because we dare not bury a man who died in the enemy country. We must have fire to take away the power of the Apache.

We thought if anyone was dead we would hear the crying. So my grandmother listened; she knew the women's voices. But there was no crying. So my grandmother cooked us our food, and she did not put any salt in it, because we were being purified. I sat by the house wall away from the fire and I was cold. I heard the men who had not killed come into the village, yelling and whipping their horses, and I heard everybody singing at the council house, stamping up and down:

Poor crow. There it hangs. Poor crow.

They sang that way every night for all the days of purifying. It is a good thing to have the enemy's hair raised on a pole above our houses. It calls the clouds to it and brings rain on our land, and then the corn comes up. But those who have brought the blessing cannot dance. Not they and not their families. Leaf Buds' husband went out to meet my father and led him to a mesquite tree far away so that his power would not come near us. He hung his bow and arrows on that tree, and my father sat down under it. So! Do you see? With legs under him and his head on his breast.

So our powerful men always sit waiting for a vision. And visions always came to my father.

> I did not know
> I did not know
> And then I knew.

That was what he sang, all alone in the night.

> Alas!
> Something I know
> Clearly I know
> I killed an Apache woman
> She was crying.

> And now light has come to me.

That is the song the Killers have sung since the first one killed an enemy woman. It says that the light has come and told them how to purify themselves.

We did not go near my father. That would have made us sick. And we could not go near my mother in her shelter of branches. But we used to run behind the house and watch when she came out once or twice a day with the sheet over her head so the sun should not see her.

We saw Leaf Buds working all the time making pots. She was a good potter. That was one reason my father had chosen her husband to take care of him, for many bowls are used while a person is being purified. Leaf Buds made new clay bowls, and in one of them she took pinole to my mother, and her husband took another to my father. Every four days the bowl had to be thrown away because it had too much of the power, and she had to have a new one ready. That was the woman who worked hard! She had to make two great jars, new so that they would keep the water cool, and in them she and her husband had to bathe my mother and father every four days. They poured that water over their heads while they sat still, arms folded. It takes a great deal to wash off that power and make it fit to use.

My grandmother bathed us children. She came with the jar at dawn and I ran away around the house. It was cold. She caught me and made me sit facing the west with my arms folded, just like my father. Then she poured it over my head and said, "Now you'll be early rising and industrious. You'll go early for water and wood." She poured it over my brothers too, and said to them, "Now you'll be a good runner, a hunter, able to stand cold and hunger. A Killer!" Those are the things that come to us, the families of the powerful.

The rest of our family were getting ready for the dance. All the old Enemy Slayers were going to sing for my father to take him back again when the four times four days were over. My grandmother boiled big pots of dried corn and dried squash and succotash, to give those singers food. All my father's sisters and the wives of his brothers made tortillas. The young women of our family brought wood for the dance fire. My father's brothers counted how many cows and horses they could give to the dancers. Our family did not have much because our men were always fighting. They were brave.

At sunset, when the four times four days were over, the people came to the dance place. Then they brought my father and the Enemy Slayers and us, too. They did not take us to the fire. Far away in the cold they dug four little holes and there the Slayers sat, facing east. Behind them there were holes for their wives. They must sit up all night, straight and not move. They had stakes driven into the ground behind them so they could lean back a little when they were too tired. My grandmother sat with us children far away in the dark.

The people went around the fire singing:

Kill the Apache, kill the Apache!
Dry the skin, dry the skin!
Soften it, soften it!
Hang it up, hang it up!
A-a-a-a-a-a-h!
There are still some Apaches left.

I could not hear the songs that night when my father was a Slayer but I know them now, for I learn well. I learn everything that the men sing.

The people stopped going around, and a man came into the middle to dance the warrior's dance. Only a young man can do that dance. He holds the shield and a club, and first he leaps to one side and then to the other as though the enemy's arrows were flying at him. Then he leaps up and lets them pass under him. Behind him, other young men, or maybe women, if they are strong and wild, take bows and arrows and leap as he does. The singers sing for them.

Sitting with my back against the dawn
I got drunk, my younger brothers.
I met the white wind and it drove me mad.

Four young men danced. To each, one of my father's brothers came up and put a piece of manure into his hand. First it was from a cow and then another cow, and then a horse and another horse. That was what my family gave to men who leaped in the war dance. It made them (my family) poor.

Then the old warriors began to sing for the Slayers, because the Pleiades[2] had come to the top of the sky and it was midnight. They sang very secret songs that had come to them when they themselves were purified. Then they lit a long cane cigarette, such as our people used to use, and went and blew the smoke over the new Slayers. They spoke to them as relatives, taking them back again. "Hail, my younger brother. Hail, my nephew. Thus I do to you. You will be like me. You will be a great Killer. You will always find the enemy. You will be hunger-enduring, cold-enduring, thirst-enduring. Thus you will live well." I could not see all this. They made me stay in the dark with my grandmother. But my father told me afterward, for I am a woman to whom a man can tell solemn words and she will remember them well.

Then they took my father out in the dark before the morning came and bathed

[2] A cluster of stars in the constellation Taurus,
consisting of several hundred stars, of which six
are visible to the naked eye.

him again, and they bathed us, too. Then we were purified and we could have the Apache scalp in our family to work for us like a relative. All the time that my father was being purified a woman had been making a basket, the kind that we use only for scalps and other sacred things. My father's guardian had taken the Apache hair and made it into a little man. He could touch Apache hair because he was a Slayer and it would not make him sick.

That little man had a buckskin shirt with fringe, like an Apache, and a feather in its hair and little moccasins. The guardian brought it to my father in the basket. My father was not afraid of that enemy's hair. He said to it, "My child." Then he gave it to my mother and she took it in her arms and said, "My child." He gave it to my brothers and my sisters and me. We held it and said, "My younger brother." Then it was in our family and it would always help us. My father laid it in the basket and all around it he put eagle feathers which are powerful. He put in tobacco and he said, "This is your house, my child." Then he wrapped that basket in deerskins and hung it in the thatch and we had Power. . . .

1936

John Rollin Ridge
1827–1867

The California territory in the early years of the gold rush lacked a folk hero comparable to those in other regions of the United States who wrestled alligators, laid steel rail, or logged the tall timber of the backwoods. Precious little heroic action suggested itself in discovering instant wealth or in falling into abject poverty while panning for gold. Yet the Cherokee writer John Rollin Ridge recognized in these circumstances the dramatic potential for a western version of Robin Hood. And in Joaquín Murieta, the legendary Mexican bandit, Ridge found a figure whom he could convert into a dashing, good-looking, and good-hearted outlaw who stole from the rich to give to the poor.

A few years before John Rollin Ridge published *The Life and Adventures of Joaquín Murieta, the Celebrated California Bandit* (1854), the California legislature had posted a sizable reward for "Joaquín, dead or alive." Local newspapers in northern California regularly published reported sightings of the bandit as well as editorials debunking claims that he had been captured or killed. Ridge's *Life and Adventures of Joaquín Murieta* created a fictional biography that featured virtually every element of what became the traditional western tall tale, including deadly shoot-outs, hairbreadth escapes, and harrowing exploits. Ridge portrayed Murieta as a man of "generous and noble nature . . . gracefully built and active as a young tiger." Ridge decided that his outlaw, "beloved by all with whom he came into contact," was forced into a life of charitable crime by the American miners who had beaten him, raped his loved ones, and hanged his half-brother on spurious charges: "It was then that the character of Joaquín changed, suddenly and irrevocably. Wanton cruelty, and the tyranny of prejudice had reached their climax . . . He would henceforth live for revenge, and . . . his path should be marked with blood." The episode printed here illustrates the thrilling pace of the bandit's adventurous life.

The details of John Rollin Ridge's own life suggest that he was something of an outlaw himself. He was born in the Cherokee Nation east of the Mississippi in 1827, the eldest son of John Ridge (see his "Essay on Cherokee Civilization" in Volume 1 of the *Harper American Literature*), one of the signers of the Treaty of Echoton (1835), which agreed to the Cherokee removal to what is now Arkansas and Oklahoma. Like his father and uncles, John Rollin Ridge attended school in New England. In 1839 he witnessed the murder of his father, grandfather, and uncle, ingraining in him what he later described as "a deep-seated principle of revenge" from which he never fully freed himself. Ridge eventually became embroiled in tribal politics, and he consistently and forcefully defended the Cherokee removal to the western frontier. In 1849 Ridge was charged with the death of a fellow Cherokee, Judge David Kell. The precise details of their encounter are unclear, but most reports indicate that Ridge acted in self-defense. Certain that he would not be tried fairly in the Cherokee Nation, Ridge fled first to Missouri and then set out for California, where he worked at odd jobs as a trader and miner before establishing himself as a frontier poet under his Cherokee name, which means "yellow bird." His collected poems were published posthumously in 1868.

The Life and Adventures of Joaquín Murieta was Ridge's only novel. It inspired scores of imitations in Europe and South America. In his two decades in California, Ridge wrote for and edited many newspapers, including the *California Express,* the *Sacramento Bee,* the *Daily National Democrat,* and the *San Francisco Herald.* Yet he always sought to return to the Cherokee Nation. In an 1854 letter to Stand Watie, one of the Cherokee leaders, Ridge announced his ambition "to do some good":

> I want to write the history of the Cherokee Nation as it *Should* be written and not as white men will write it and as they will tell the tale, to screen and justify themselves. . . . Don't you see how much precious time I am wasting in California? Instead of writing for my living here I should be using my pen in behalf of my own people and in rescuing from oblivion the proud names of our race.

John Rollin Ridge died in 1867 without having realized that goal.

Further Reading:
A. Debo, "John Rollin Ridge," *Southwest Review,* 1932.
C. T. Foreman, "Edward W. Bushyhead and John Rollin Ridge, Cherokee Editors in California," *Chronicles of Oklahoma,* 1936.
F. Walker, *San Francisco Literary Frontier,* 1939, 1969.
E. E. Dale and G. Litton, *Cherokee Cavaliers:*

Forty Years of Cherokee History as Told in the Correspondence of the Ridge-Watie-Boudinot Family, 1969.
T. Wilkins, *Cherokee Tragedy: The Story of the Ridge Family and the Decimation of a People,* 1970.
R. Nadeau, *The Real Joaquín Murieta: Robin Hood Hero or Gold Rush Gangster?,* 1974.

Text:
The Life and Adventures of Joaquín Murieta, the Celebrated California Bandit, 1854.

from The Life and Adventures of Joaquín Murieta

I sit down to write somewhat concerning the life and character of *Joaquín Murieta,* a man as remarkable in the annals of crime as any of the renowned robbers of the Old or New World, who have preceded him; and I do this, not for the purpose of ministering to any depraved taste for the dark and horrible in human action, but rather to contribute my mite to those materials out of which the early history of California shall one day be composed. The character of this truly wonderful man was nothing more than a natural production of the social and moral condition of the country in which he lived, acting upon certain peculiar circumstances favorable to such a result, and, consequently, his individual history is a part of the most valuable history of the State.

There were two Joaquíns, bearing the various surnames of Murieta, O'Comorenia, Valenzuela, Botellier, and Carillo—so that it was supposed there were no less than five sanguinary devils ranging the country at one and the same time. It is now fully ascertained that there were only two, whose proper names were Joaquín Murieta and Joaquín Valenzuela, the latter being nothing more than a distinguished subordinate to the first, who is the Rinaldo Rinaldini[1] of California.

Joaquín Murieta was a Mexican, born in the province of Sonora[2] of respectable parents and educated in the schools of Mexico. While growing up, he was remarkable for a very mild and peaceable disposition, and gave no sign of that indomitable and daring spirit which afterwards characterized him. Those who knew him in his school-boy days speak affectionately of his generous and noble nature at that period of his life and can scarcely credit the fact that the renowned and bloody bandit of California was one and the same being. At an early age of his manhood—indeed, while he was yet scarcely more than a boy—he became tired of the uncertain state of affairs in his own country, the usurpations and revolutions which were of such common occurrence, and resolved to try his fortunes among the American people, of whom he had formed the most favorable opinion from an acquaintance with the few whom he had met in his own native land. The war with Mexico[3] had been fought, and California belonged to the United States. Disgusted with the conduct of his degenerate country-men and fired with enthusiastic admiration of the American character, the youthful Joaquín left his home with a buoyant heart and full of the exhilarating spirit of adventure. The first that we hear of him in the Golden State is that, in the spring of 1850, he is engaged in the honest occupation of a miner in the Stanislaus placers,[4] then reckoned among the richest portions of the mines. He was then eighteen years of age, a little over the medium height, slenderly but gracefully built, and active as a young

---

[1] Presumably, a celebrated mid-nineteenth century bandit.

[2] Province in northwest Mexico bounded on the north by the United States and on the west by Baja and the Gulf of California.

[3] Fought between Mexico and the United States, 1846–1848.

[4] Glacial deposits of sand gravel containing eroded particles of valuable minerals; Stanislaus is located in central California.

tiger. His complexion was neither very dark or very light, but clear and brilliant, and his countenance is pronounced to have been, at that time, exceedingly handsome and attractive. His large black eyes, kindling with the enthusiasm of his earnest nature, his firm and well-formed mouth, his well-shaped head from which the long, glossy, black hair hung down over his shoulders, his silvery voice full of generous utterance, and the frank and cordial bearing which distinguished him made him beloved by all with whom he came in contact. He had the confidence and respect of the whole community around him, and was fast amassing a fortune from his rich mining claim. He had built him a comfortable mining residence in which he had domiciled his heart's treasure—a beautiful Sonorian girl, who had followed the young adventurer in all his wanderings with that devotedness of passion which belongs to the dark-eyed damsels of Mexico. It was at this moment of peace and felicity that a blight came over the young man's prospects. The country was then full of lawless and desperate men, who bore the name of Americans but failed to support the honor and dignity of that title. A feeling was prevalent among this class of contempt for any and all Mexicans, whom they looked upon as no better than conquered subjects of the United States, having no rights which could stand before a haughtier and superior race. They made no exceptions. If the proud blood of the Castilians[5] mounted to the cheek of a partial descendant of the Mexiques, showing that he had inherited the old chivalrous spirit of his Spanish ancestry, they looked upon it as a saucy presumption in one so inferior to them. The prejudice of color, the antipathy of races, which are always stronger and bitterer with the ignorant and unlettered, they could not overcome, or if they could, would not, because it afforded them a convenient excuse for their unmanly cruelty and oppression. A band of these lawless men, having the brute power to do as they pleased, visited Joaquín's house and peremptorily bade him leave his claim, as they would allow no Mexicans to work in that region. Upon his remonstrating against such outrageous conduct, they struck him violently over the face, and, being physically superior, compelled him to swallow his wrath. Not content with this, they tied him hand and foot and ravished his mistress before his eyes. They left him, but the soul of the young man was from that moment darkened. It was the first injury he had ever received at the hands of the Americans, whom he had always hitherto respected, and it wrung him to the soul as a deeper and deadlier wrong from that very circumstance. He departed with his weeping and almost heart-broken mistress for a more northern portion of the mines; and the next we hear of him, he is cultivating a little farm on the banks of a beautiful stream that watered a fertile valley, far out in the seclusion of the mountains. Here he might hope for peace—here he might forget the past, and again be happy. But his dream was not destined to last. A company of unprincipled Americans—shame that there should be such bearing the name!—saw his retreat, coveted his little home surrounded by its fertile tract of land, and drove him from it, with no other excuse than that he was "an infernal Mexican intruder!" Joaquín's blood boiled in his veins, but his spirit was still unbroken, nor had the iron so far entered his soul as to sear up the innate sensitiveness to honor and right which reigned in his bosom. Twice broken up in his honest pursuit of fortune, he resolved still to labor on with unflinching brow and with that true *moral* bravery, which throws its redeeming light forward upon his subsequently dark and criminal career. How deep

[5] Here, the Spanish.

must have been the anguish of that young heart and how strongly rooted the native honesty of his soul, none can know or imagine but they who have been tried in a like manner. He bundled up his little movable property, still accompanied by his faithful bosom-friend, and again started forth to strike once more, like a brave and honest man, for fortune and for happiness. He arrived at "Murphy's Diggings" in Calaveras County,[6] in the month of April, and went again to mining, but, meeting with nothing like his former success, he soon abandoned that business and devoted his time to dealing "monte,"[7] a game which is common in Mexico, and has been almost universally adopted by gamblers in California. It is considered by the Mexican in no manner a disreputable employment, and many well-raised young men from the Atlantic States have resorted to it as a profession in this land of luck and chances. It was then in much better odor than it is now, although it is at present a game which may be played on very fair and honest principles; provided, anything can be strictly honest or fair which allows the taking of money without a valuable consideration. It was therefore looked upon as no departure from rectitude on the part of Joaquín, when he commenced the business of dealing "monte." Having a very pleasing exterior and being, despite of all his sorrows, very gay and lively in disposition, he attracted many persons to his table, and won their money with such skill and grace, or lost his own with such perfect good humor that he was considered by all the very beau ideal of a gambler and the prince of clever fellows. His sky seemed clear and his prospects bright, but Fate was weaving her mysterious web around him, and fitting him to be by the force of circumstances what nature never intended to make him.

He had gone a short distance from Murphy's Diggings to see a half-brother, who had been located in that vicinity for several months, and returned to Murphy's upon a horse which his brother had lent him. The animal proved to have been stolen, and being recognized by a number of individuals in town, an excitement was raised on the subject. Joaquín suddenly found himself surrounded by a furious mob and charged with the crime of theft. He told them how it happened that he was riding the horse and in what manner his half-brother had come in possession of it. They listened to no explanation, but bound him to a tree, and publicly disgraced him with the lash. They then proceeded to the house of his half-brother and hung him without judge or jury. It was then that the character of Joaquín changed, suddenly and irrevocably. Wanton cruelty and the tyranny of prejudice had reached their climax. His soul swelled beyond its former boundaries, and the barriers of honor, rocked into atoms by the strong passion which shook his heart like an earthquake, crumbled around him. Then it was that he declared to a friend that he would live henceforth for revenge and that his path should be marked with blood. Fearfully did he keep his promise, as the following pages will show.

It was not long after this unfortunate affair that an American was found dead in the vicinity of Murphy's Diggings, having been cut to pieces with a knife. Though horribly mangled, he was recognized as one of the mob engaged in whipping Joaquín. A doctor, passing in the neighborhood of this murder, was met, shortly afterward, by two men on horseback, who fired their revolvers at him, but, owing to his speed on foot, and the unevenness of the ground, he succeeded in escaping with no further

---

[6] In central California.
[7] Game of Spanish origin in which players bet which of two cards will be matched by the dealer; also called "three-card monte."

injury than having a bullet shot through his hat within an inch of the top of his head! A panic spread among the rash individuals who had composed that mob, and they were afraid to stir out on their ordinary business. Whenever any one of them strayed out of sight of his camp or ventured to travel on the highway, he was shot down suddenly and mysteriously. Report after report came into the villages that Americans had been found dead on the highways, having been either shot or stabbed, and it was invariably discovered, for many weeks, that the murdered men belonged to the mob who publicly whipped Joaquín. It was fearful and it was strange to see how swiftly and mysteriously those men disappeared. "Murieta's revenge was very nearly complete," said an eyewitness of these events, in reply to an inquiry which I addressed him. "I am inclined to think he *wiped out* the most of those prominently engaged in whipping him."

Thus far, who can blame him? But the iron had entered too deeply in his soul for him to stop here. He had contracted a hatred to the whole American race, and was determined to shed their blood, whenever and wherever an opportunity occurred. It was no time now for him to retrace his steps. He had committed deeds which made him amenable to the law, and his only safety lay in a persistence in the unlawful course which he had begun. It was necessary that he should have horses and that he should have money. These he could not obtain except by robbery and murder, and thus he became an outlaw and a bandit on the verge of his nineteenth year.

The year 1850 rolled away, marked with the eventful history of this young man's wrongs and trials, his bitter revenge on those who had perpetrated the crowning act of his deep injury and disgrace; and, as it closed, it shut him away forever from his peace of mind and purity of heart. He walked forth into the future a dark, determined criminal, and his proud nobility of soul existed only in memory.

It became generally known in 1851 that an organized banditti was ranging the country; but it was not yet ascertained who was the leader. Travelers, laden with the produce of the mines, were met upon the roads by well-dressed men who politely invited them to "stand and deliver"; persons riding alone in the many wild and lonesome regions, which form a large portion of this country, were skillfully noosed with the lasso (which the Mexicans throw with great accuracy, being able thus to capture wild cattle, elk, and sometimes even grizzly bears, upon the plains), dragged from their saddles, and murdered in the adjacent thickets. Horses of the finest mettle were stolen from the ranches, and, being tracked up, were found in the possession of a determined band of men, ready to retain them at all hazards and fully able to stand their ground. The scenes of murder and robbery shifted with the rapidity of lightning. At one time, the northern countries would be suffering slaughters and depredations, at another the southern, and, before one would have imagined it possible, the east and the west, and every point of the compass would be in trouble. There had never been before this, either in '49 or '50, any such as an organized banditti, and it had been a matter of surprise to every one, since the country was so well adapted to a business of this kind—the houses scattered at such distances along the roads, the plains so level and open in which to ride with speed, and the mountains so rugged with their ten thousand fastnesses in which to hide. Grass was abundant in the far-off valleys which lay hidden in the rocky gorges, cool, delicious streams made music at the feet of the towering peaks, or came leaping down in gladness from their sides—game abounded on every hand, and nine unclouded months of the year made a climate so salubrious that nothing could be sweeter than a day's rest under the tall pines or a night's repose under the open canopy of heaven. Joaquín knew his advantages. His superior intelligence and education gave him the respect of his comrades, and, appealing to the prejudice against the "Yankees," which the disastrous results of the Mexican war had not tended to lessen in their minds, he soon assembled around him a powerful band of his countrymen. . . .

Among the many thrilling instances of the daring and recklessness of spirit which belonged to Joaquín, there is one which I do not feel at liberty to omit—especially as it comes naturally and properly in this connection. Shortly after he parted from Reis and Luis Vulvia, he went up into the extreme north of the country. There, at the head of a branch of the South Fork of the Mokelumne River,[8] in a wild and desolate region near the boundary line of Calaveras and El Dorado Counties,[9] were located a company of miners, consisting of twenty-five men. They were at a long distance from any neighbors, having gone there well armed on a prospecting tour which resulted in their finding diggings so rich that they were persuaded to pitch their tents and remain. One morning while they were eating their breakfast on a flat rock —a natural table which stood in front of their tents—armed as usual with their revolvers, a young fellow with very dark hair and eyes rode up and saluted them. He spoke very good English and they could scarcely make out whether he was a Mexican or an American. They requested him to get down and eat with them, but he politely declined. He sat with one leg crossed over his horse's neck very much at his ease, conversing very freely on various subjects, until Jim Boyce, one of the partners who had been to the spring after water, appeared in sight. At the first glance on him, the young horseman flung his reclining leg back over the saddle and spurred his horse. Boyce roared out:

"Boys, that fellow is *Joaquín;* d——n it, shoot him!" At the same instant, he himself fired but without effect.

Joaquín dashed down to the creek below with headlong speed and crossed with the intention, no doubt, to escape over the hills which ran parallel with the stream, but his way was blocked up by perpendicular rocks, and his only practicable path was a narrow digger-trail which led along the side of a huge mountain, directly over a ledge of rocks a hundred yards in length, which hung beatling over the rushing stream beneath in a direct line with the hill upon which the miners had pitched their tents, and not more than forty yards distant. It was a fearful gauntlet for any man to run. Not only was there danger of falling a hundred feet from the rocks, but he must run in a parallel line with his enemies, and in pistol-range, for a hundred yards. In fair view of him stood the whole company with their revolvers drawn. He dashed along that fearful trail as if he had been mounted upon a spirit-steed, shouting as he passed: "I am Joaquín! kill me if you can!"

Shot after shot came clanging around his head, and bullet after bullet flattened on the wall of slate at his right. In the midst of the first firing, his hat was knocked from his head, and left his long black hair streaming behind him. He had no time to use his own pistol, but, knowing that his only chance lay in the swiftness of his sure-footed animal, he drew his keenly polished bowie-knife in proud defiance of the danger and

---

[8] River in central California, in the foothills of the Sierras.   [9] In central California.

waved it in scorn as he rode on. It was perfectly sublime to see such super-human daring and recklessness. At each report, which came fast and thick, he kissed the flashing blade and waved it at his foes. He passed the ordeal, as awful and harrowing to a man's nerves as can be conceived, untouched by a ball and otherwise unharmed. In a few moments, a loud whoop rang out in the woods a quarter of a mile distant, and the bold rider was safe!

Joaquín, knowing well the determined character of Jim Boyce, and, deeming it more than probable that he had heard of the different large rewards offered for his capture or death amounting in the aggregate to $15,000 or $20,000, he made up his mind speedily that an attack would be made upon him by the whole party of miners if he remained at his encampment, which was some five miles distant from their tents. Concluding that they could not collect their horses together and prepare their arms and ammunition in a proper manner for an attack or pursuit before night, he conceived a plan, the most brilliant and ingenious that ever entered an outlaw's brain, by which to defeat their purposes and carry out his own original intention of robbing them. Knowing that a trail could very well be made in the night but that it could only be followed in the day-time, he ordered his men, numbering fifteen, to saddle up and make ready for a ride. They obeyed with alacrity and without question, and in a few moments were on their horses and ready to move forward. The chief led the way in silence, proceeding over the pin ridges in an easterly direction. He rode on vigorously until night over very rough ground, having traversed a distance of twenty miles; but, wishing to place a still greater distance between him and the encampment which he had left, he did not come to final halt until a late hour. Building a huge fire and hitching their animals near by, the wearied bandits hastily threw their blankets down and stretched their limbs upon them for repose. Sentinels alternately sat up until day-light, so that at the first touch of dawn the whole band arose and again started, having lost only four hours in sleep. They journeyed on in the same course as briskly as possible until noon, when, having reached a nice little valley, covered with grass and wild clover, and watered by a beautiful spring which bubbled up from the roots of a clump of evergreen oaks, distant about twenty miles from their last encampment, they stopped for two hours to let their horses graze and to refresh their own rather empty stomachs with the sardines and crackers which they generally carried with them. Here they left strong indications that they had spent the night but established the contrary fact by riding on for the remainder of the day, whose close found them at another distance of twenty miles. Building fires as before and eating a hasty supper, they again mounted, and, having made a circle of five miles in their course, suddenly turned to the westward and encamped about three o'clock, A.M., at a spot distant another common day's journey from the last starting point. Thus traveling and resting, after the lapse of a few days they found themselves in the original trail upon which they had started.

Jim Boyce and company had struck the path of the robbers on the next morning after their departure and had camped each night at the fires which they had left, expecting, as was natural, that they would come to a final stopping-place when they had proceeded as far as they liked. Joaquín smiled with exquisite satisfaction when he perceived that Boyce was certainly ahead of him and, from every indication, unsuspecting in the remotest degree that his arch-enemy was at that moment in his rear.

At night, after a long day's ride over rugged mountains and deep gulches, Jim Boyce and his company, numbering twenty-five men including himself, were seated around one of Joaquín's late fires, which they had rekindled, quietly enjoying their pipes and laughing over the numerous stereotyped jokes, which had descended, like Shakspeare, from one gentleman to another, and are too good ever to be worn out. The Heavens were cloudy, and a boundary of solid darkness lay around the lighted ring in which they sat. In the ragged clouds a few stars dimly struggled, and the lonesome scream of the cougar, like the wail of a lost spirit benighted in the infinity of darkness, gave a wild terror to the surrounding woods.

Suddenly and startlingly, the simultaneous reports of fifteen pistols rent the air, the dark outer-wall of the fire-circle blazed, as if a cloud had unbosomed its lightnings, and the astonished survivors of the company bounded up to see fifteen of their number stretched upon the earth and to meet with the deadly repetition of the fifteen revolvers. Panic-stricken and bewildered, the survivors of the second discharge, numbering three men among whom was Jim Boyce, fled head-long into the darkness, and, taking no time to choose their ground, hurried madly and distractedly away from the horrible scene. Joaquín stepped quietly into the circle to see if Jim Boyce was killed, but Three-Fingered Jack leaped in like a demon with his huge knife in his mutilated hand, which had lost none of its strength, but did its three-fingered work far better than many other whole hands could do it, and soon quenched the last spark of beating life in the pale forms around him. Every one must know that death from a bullet flings a sudden and extreme paleness over the countenance, and thus the light from the fire, falling upon the ghastly faces around, displayed a sight so hideous and harrowing that Joaquín exclaimed with a shudder:

"Let's leave here, we will camp tonight, somewhere else."

Searching the bundles upon which the company had been seated, he found in different buckskin purses a sum amounting to not less than thirty thousand dollars. He also added fifteen excellent horses and ten powerful mules to his live-stock.

Jim Boyce and his surviving companions wandered to the distant settlements, which, after many hardships, they reached in safety, and it is pleasant to add that in a short time they raised another company with whom they went back to their rich diggings, and, in spite of their immense loss by Joaquín's robbery, made for themselves ample fortunes, with which they returned to the States. Should Jim Boyce chance to read this humble narrative of mine, I beg him to receive my warmest congratulations. . . .

1854

Emily Pauline Johnson
1861–1913

As a child, Emily Pauline Johnson compensated for her two years of formal schooling with a seemingly insatiable interest in reading early-nineteenth-century English and American literature, especially Byron, Shelley, Scott, and Longfellow. Her poetry, suffused with the romantic diction and melodramatic action of the writers she admired most, earned her the largest audience of any Native American woman writer in the late nineteenth and early twentieth centuries. By the time of her death from cancer in 1913, her importance as a Native American writer had transcended the American and southeastern Canadian borders that had divided her ancestral tribe, the Mohawk.

Emily Pauline Johnson was born in 1861 to G. H. M. Johnson (Onwanonsyshon), the one-time chief of the Six Nations, and Emily S. Howells, his English wife. Emily Johnson first drew widespread attention in the early 1890s for public recitations of her poetry. She enjoyed a successful two-decades-long career performing her poetry in the United States, Canada, and England—always dressed in native garb and billed with her Indian name, Tehakionwake. Her enthusiastic reception in England spurred interest in her first volume of poems, *The White Wampum* (1895), from which the poems printed here—two of her most popular—were drawn. In 1912 she collected her verse in *Flint and Feather.*

Johnson also published *Legends of Vancouver* in 1911 and, in 1913, two collections of stories, *The Shagganappi* (which means "buckskin Cayuse" in the Cree language) and *The Moccasin Maker,* both of which feature engaging renditions of mixed-blood characters and relationships. In these volumes, Johnson drew heavily on her parents' experience with the widespread prejudice against mixed-blood marriages, a theme she handles with considerable skill. As the following poems suggest, Johnson's treatment of Indian lore, frontier landscape, and Native American–white relations is often more romantic than accurate, yet she succeeds in creating appealing poetic reinterpretations of the oral literature of her Native American predecessors.

Further Reading:
W. McCraye, *The Town Hall Tonight,* 1929.
G. Foster, *The Mohawk Princess,* 1931.
W. McCraye, *Pauline Johnson and Her Friends,* 1947.
M. Van Steen, *Pauline Johnson: Her Life and Work,* 1965.
M. E. Gridley, *American Indian Women,* 1974.

Text:
The White Wampum, 1895.

As Red Men Die

Captive! Is there a hell to him like this?
A taunt more galling than the Huron's[1] hiss?
He—proud and scornful, he—who laughed at law,
He—scion of the deadly Iroquois,

[1] Huron: confederation of four tribes of Iroquoian-speaking Indians formerly inhabiting the region east of Lake Huron and the St. Lawrence Valley.

He—the bloodthirsty, he—the Mohawk[2] chief,   5
He—who despises pain and sneers at grief,
Here in the hated Huron's vicious clutch,
That even captive he disdains to touch!

Captive! But *never* conquered; Mohawk brave
Stoops not to be to *any* man a slave;   10
Least, to the puny tribe his soul abhors,
The tribe whose wigwams sprinkle Simcoe's[3] shores.
With scowling brow he stands and courage high,
Watching with haughty and defiant eye
His captors, as they council o'er his fate,   15
Or strive his boldness to intimidate.
Then fling they unto him the choice;

                    "Wilt thou
Walk o'er the bed of fire[4] that waits thee now—
Walk with uncovered feet upon the coals   20
Until thou reach the ghostly Land of Souls,
And, with thy Mohawk death-song[5] please our ear?
Or wilt thou with the women rest thee here?"[6]
His eyes flash like an eagle's, and his hands
Clench at the insult. Like a god he stands.   25
"Prepare the fire!" he scornfully demands.

He knoweth not that this same jeering band
Will bite the dust—will lick the Mohawk's hand;
Will kneel and cower at the Mohawk's feet;
Will shrink when Mohawk war-drums wildly beat.   30

His death will be avenged with hideous hate
By Iroquois, swift to annihilate
His vile detested captors, that now flaunt
Their war clubs in his face with sneer and taunt,

[2] Most easterly tribe of the Iroquoian-speaking Indians, inhabiting the territory from the Mohawk River to the St. Lawrence.

[3] Simcoe lake, in southern Ontario, Canada.

[4] Johnson presents the ethnographic details inaccurately. Mohawk and Huron Indians are not known to have made prisoners walk on beds of fire. They either tied prisoners to a stake and then tortured them by burning or else forced prisoners to run a gauntlet composed of the village's adults.

[5] Iroquois men had each their own death song that they were prepared to sing while being tortured, and showing no emotion, in the event of their capture.

[6] No such choice is known to have been given to the captives of Iroquois groups. All northern Iroquois groups were matrilineal (i.e., reckoned descent through the mother), and it was the right of the women of a clan to initiate an attack to revenge the death of a male member of their clan; the woman who initiated the attack decided whether prisoners would be adopted to take the place of their dead kinsman or tortured to death. (See "The Unseen Helpers" from Senecan oral history for an example of Cherokee women being asked to make such a decision.)

Not thinking, soon that reeking, red, and raw,   35
Their scalps will deck the belts of Iroquois.

The path of coals outstretches, white with heat,
A forest fir's length—ready for his feet.
Unflinching as a rock he steps along
The burning mass, and sings his wild war song;   40
Sings, as he sang when once he used to roam
Throughout the forests of his southern home,
Where, down the Genesee,[7] the water roars,
Where gentle Mohawk purls between its shores,
Songs, that of exploit and of prowess tell;   45
Songs of the Iroquois invincible.

Up the long trail of fire he boasting goes,
Dancing a war dance to defy his foes.
His flesh is scorched, his muscles burn and shrink,
But still he dances to death's awful brink.   50
The eagle plume that crests his haughty head
Will *never* droop until his heart be dead.
Slower and slower yet his footstep swings,
Wilder and wilder still his death-song rings,
Fiercer and fiercer thro' the forest bounds   55
His voice that leaps to Happier Hunting Grounds.
One savage yell—

                         Then loyal to his race,
He bends to death—but *never* to disgrace.
1895

The Song My Paddle Sings

       West wind blow from your prairie nest?
       Blow from the mountains, blow from the west.
       The sail is idle, the sailor too;
       O! wind of the west, we wait for you.
       Blow, blow!   5
       I have wooed you so,
       But never a favour you bestow.

[7] River rising in the Alleghenies in northern
Pennsylvania and New York State.

You rock your cradle the hills between,
But scorn to notice my white lateen.

I stow the sail, unship the mast: 10
I wooed you long but my wooing's past;
My paddle will lull you into rest.
O! drowsy wind of the drowsy west,
Sleep, sleep,
By your mountain steep,   15
Or down where the prairie grasses sweep!
Now fold in slumber your laggard wings,
For soft is the song my paddle sings.
August is laughing across the sky,
Laughing while paddle, canoe and I,   20
Drift, drift,
Where the hills uplift
On either side of the current swift.

The river rolls in its rocky bed;
My paddle is plying its way ahead;   25
Dip, dip,
While the waters flip
In foam as over their breast we slip.

And oh, the river runs swifter now;
The eddies circle about my bow.   30
Swirl, swirl!
How the ripples curl
In many a dangerous pool awhirl!

And forward far the rapids roar,
Fretting their margin for evermore.   35
Dash, dash,
With a mighty crash,
They seethe, and boil, and bound, and splash.

Be strong, O paddle! be brave, canoe!
The reckless waves you must plunge into.   40
Reel, reel,
On your trembling keel,
But never a fear my craft will feel.

We've raced the rapid, we're far ahead!
The river slips through its silent bed.   45
Sway, sway,
As the bubbles spray
And fall in tinkling tunes away.

And up on the hills against the sky,
A fir tree rocking its lullaby,   50
Swings, swings,
Its emerald wings,
Swelling the song that my paddle sings.
1895

Alexander Lawrence Posey
1873–1908

One of the best-known Native American humorists and journalists, Alexander
Posey also wrote some of the most compelling Native American poetry in the
late nineteenth and early twentieth centuries. Alexander Posey was born in what
is now McIntosh County, Oklahoma, on August 3, 1873, the son of a Creek
mother and a part-Creek, part–Scots-Irish father. Alexander Posey learned English
at the age of twelve from a private teacher whom he later described as "a
dried-up, hard-up, weazen-faced, irritable fellow." Posey began publishing essays
on Indian affairs while studying at the Indian University in what was then the
Oklahoma Territory. He entered public life in 1895 when he was elected to the
Creek Nation's House of Warriors. His fluency in both Creek and English as
well as his honesty and sense of responsibility earned him membership on
virtually every important tribal council until his death in 1908 from drowning.

In 1896 Posey served as superintendent of the Creek Orphan Asylum and,
beginning in 1897, as superintendent of public instruction for the Creek Nation.
In 1902 Posey started a two-year stint as editor of the still-publishing *Indian
Journal,* where he printed a series of political satires under the heading "Fus
Fixico Letters" (meaning "bird with no heart") and became a strong advocate of
statehood for Oklahoma, which he proposed calling Sequoyah. During this same
period Posey also wrote a great deal of poetry, much of which was printed over
the pseudonym "Chinnubbie Harjo," an evil genius in Creek myth. "All of my
people are poets," Posey proclaimed, "natural-born poets, gifted with wonderful
imaginative power and the ability to express in sonorous, musical phrases their
impressions of life and nature." In the poems printed here, Posey applies those
skills to commemorating two Creeks who articulated and defended their nation's
rights.

Further Reading:
D. Challacombe, "Alexander Lawrence Posey,"
Chronicles of Oklahoma, 1933.
L. G. Barnett, "Este Cate Emunkv: Red Man
Always," *Chronicles of Oklahoma,* 1968.

Text:
The Poems of Alexander Lawrence Posey, ed.
with "Memoir" by W. E. Connelly, 1910.
See also "Journal of Alexander Lawrence Posey
with Annotations, January 1–September 4,
1897," ed. E. E. Dale, *Chronicles of Oklahoma,*
1967–1968.

Ode to Sequoyah[1]

The names of Waitie and Boudinot[2]—
 The valiant warrior and gifted sage—
And other Cherokees, may be forgot,
 But thy name shall descend to every age;
The mysteries enshrouding Cadmus'[3] name   5
Cannot obscure thy claim to fame.

The people's language cannot perish—nay,
 When from the face of this great continent
Inevitable doom hath swept away
 The last memorial—the last fragment   10
Of tribes,—some scholar learned shall pore
Upon thy letters, seeking ancient lore.

Some bard shall lift a voice in praise of thee,
 In moving numbers tell the world how men
Scoffed thee, hissed thee, charged with lunacy! 15
 And who could not give 'nough honor when
At length, in spite of jeers, of want and need,
Thy genius shaped a dream into a deed.

By cloud-capped summits in the boundless west,[4]
 Or mighty river rolling to the sea,   20
Where'er thy footsteps led thee on that quest,
 Unknown, rest thee, illustrious Cherokee!

1910

---

[1] Posey's note: "SEQUOYAH—The Cherokee who invented the Cherokee alphabet."

[2] Elias Boudinot, founder of the *Cherokee Phoenix* newspaper and advocate of Cherokee culture and human rights.

[3] Cadmus: perhaps the Phoenician prince who killed a dragon and sowed its teeth, from which sprang up an army of men who fought one another until only five survived; with these Cadmus founded the city of Thebes.

[4] Posey's note: "Sequoyah wandered away from his tribe, and died somewhere in the southwest part of the United States or in Mexico."

On the Capture and Imprisonment of Crazy Snake[1]

January, 1900

Down with him! chain him! bind him fast!
Slam to the iron door and turn the key!
The one true Creek, perhaps the last
To dare declare, "You have wronged me!"
Defiant, stoical, silent,   5
Suffers imprisonment!

Such coarse black hair! such eagle eye!
Such stately mien!—how arrow-straight!
Such will! such courage to defy
The powerful makers of his fate!   10
A traitor, outlaw,—what you will,
He is the noble red man still.

Condemn him and his kind to shame!
I bow to him, exalt his name!   15

1910

Mark Twain
1835–1910

Mark Twain (born Samuel Longhorne Clemens) looked back with longing to
what he recalled as the innocence, simplicity, and rectitude of pre–Gold Rush
America. Yet no other writer partook so hungrily of the wealth, status, fame,
and other rewards that the Gilded Age offered. A divided sensibility who
alternately craved attention and solitude, he lived on the scale of a prince of
industry or banking in New York, Hartford, and the great cities of Europe while
his imagination remained tied to the drowsing villages of the Mississippi River
valley. The words "when I was a boy" were his mantra, with magical power to
unlock memory and emotion. "The part of him that was Western in his
Southwestern origin Clemens kept to the end," recalled William Dean Howells,
his friend for over forty years, "but he was the most desouthernized Southerner I
ever knew." Out of such oppositions came one of the dominating prose styles of

---

[1] Posey's note: "CRAZY SNAKE—Chitto Harjo.
The leader of a band of Creeks who oppose the
abolishment of their tribal rights. Several times
Harjo has been imprisoned because of his
defying the United States authorities."

American literature, half a dozen of its classics, and an incomparably attractive public voice and personality.

Caught up in the westward tide of expansion, Samuel Clemens's parents, poor but blood-proud Virginia gentry, settled along what was then the southwestern frontier, first in the crossroads hamlet of Florida, Missouri, where he was born in 1835, and four years later in Hannibal. His father, a justice of the peace, failed in the law, shopkeeping, land speculation, and ventures in slave trading. The boy left school at twelve to earn his living; he worked in a printing office and wrote occasional newspaper items, burlesques, and humorous sketches. "One isn't a printer ten years," he was to recall, "without setting up acres of good and bad literature, and learning—unconsciously at first, consciously later—to discriminate between the two, within his mental limitations; and meanwhile he is consciously acquiring what is called a 'style.' " But he also realized the boyhood ambition he was to write about in *Old Times on the Mississippi:* In 1859, after two years of "cubbing," he earned a pilot's license and stood in princely grandeur in the wheelhouse of a river steamboat.

The coming of the Civil War put an end to this occupation and to commercial traffic on the river. Young Clemens spent a few grim weeks in the field as a Confederate irregular (an experience considerably embroidered in "The Private History of a Campaign That Failed") before going West to try his hand at prospecting in the Nevada Territory and California. While working as reporter on the *Virginia City Territorial Enterprise,* he settled finally on his vocation: "seriously scribbling to excite the *laughter* of God's creatures." He was to learn that the punishing thing about laughter is that people refuse to take it seriously, even though, as he argued time and again, laughter was a supreme moral weapon. All his life he felt compelled to defend his profession, to segregate the noun *humorist* from the adjective *mere* and the synonym *clown.* Reciprocally, Americans of his time tended to cherish him as entertainer alone and, as soon as the smiles faded from their faces, trivialize his genius and irony, his moral passion and assaults on conventional wisdom.

In 1865, two years after Samuel Clemens's pseudonym "Mark Twain" appeared in print for the first time, he published "The Notorious Jumping Frog of Calaveras County." Although he once dismissed it as "a villainous backwoods sketch," the "Jumping Frog" is a brilliant experiment in narrative technique, point of view, and language. It points the way to the tales that make up much of *Roughing It* (1872), Mark Twain's account of his life in the West, and to *Adventures of Huckleberry Finn* (1885).

With *The Innocents Abroad* (1869), a humorous travel narrative that held Europe and the Holy Land up to American standards but was equally unsparing about America, Mark Twain first established himself as a popular author. His books, sold by door-to-door salesmen taking orders in advance of publication, reached a broad, nonliterary audience, typically the families of tradesmen, farmers, and small-town professionals. His royalties (he figured that *The Innocents Abroad* sold some 100,000 copies in two years) were supplemented by his earnings as one of the rising stars of the lecture circuit, successor to Artemus Ward. He owned and edited a daily newspaper in Buffalo, New York, and married Olivia Langdon, heiress to a coal fortune, after a courtship that he made part of the folklore of love in America: "I saw her first in the form of an ivory miniature. . . ."

In 1871 they moved to Hartford, midway in values as well as distance between two literary capitals in transition, New York and Boston. They rented, and soon built, a house at Nook Farm, a tightly knit, high-minded enclave of writers and intellectuals that included Harriet Beecher Stowe and Charles Dudley Warner. *The Gilded Age* (1873), a novel Mark Twain wrote in collaboration with Warner, fed rather than exorcised his growing anger at American society and institutions. In time he would be regarded as a spokesman for American democracy, for what he called "the mighty mass of the uncultivated" instead of "the thin top crust of humanity." But during the 1870s, believing that the American system had broken down, he raged against universal suffrage, the jury system, and what he saw as an "era of incredible rottenness." He crossed the Atlantic to "breathe the free air of Europe," indulge his worship of all things English (the English, in turn, lionized him), and write another travel book, *A Tramp Abroad* (1880). *The Gilded Age,* subtitled "A Tale of Today," helped turn his mind toward the more malleable yesterdays of *Old Times on the Mississippi* (1875), *The Adventures of Tom Sawyer* (1876), and *The Prince and the Pauper* (1882), the last a concession to genteel taste.

In 1884, after eight years of intermittent struggles with plot problems, Mark Twain completed his masterpiece, *Adventures of Huckleberry Finn.* He wrote this realistic, satiric, yet lyrical novel in the southwestern vernacular from the first-person point of view of an unlettered boy at the bottom of the white social order. "It's the best book we've had," Ernest Hemingway wrote in 1935. T. S. Eliot said Mark Twain discovered "a new way of writing" that brought literary language "up to date." But though it has now been read in millions of copies and become a fixture in world literature, *Huckleberry Finn,* like *Leaves of Grass,* entered the world under a cloud of disapproval. Demanding refined language, exemplary heroes, and elevating morals, guardians of the genteel tradition inevitably found Mark Twain's book coarse, vulgar, and immoral. In 1885 the trustees of the Concord (Massachusetts) Public Library expelled the book from their shelves as "trash and suitable only for the slums." Today, *Huckleberry Finn,* a passionately humanitarian and antiracist book, often comes under fire because readers misunderstand Mark Twain's language, his portrayal of the fugitive slave Jim, and the irony framing and shaping the entire narrative.

At fifty it seemed that Mark Twain was blessed with everything: overflowing creative energies, as *Huckleberry Finn* demonstrated; domestic happiness; world fame and social eminence; friendships with Howells and other writers; wealth; and an eye-catching brick-and-brownstone mansion—part steamboat, part medieval stronghold, part cuckoo clock—that was one of Hartford's curiosities. The house at 351 Farmington Avenue, now maintained as a memorial to its owner, served as a reminder of how far he had traveled from a clapboard dwelling "the size of a birdhouse" in Hannibal. He invested heavily in speculative business ventures. One was a New York subscription publishing house, Charles L. Webster & Company, which, in addition to Mark Twain's own books, issued *Personal Memoirs of U. S. Grant* (1885), a huge commercial success. It earned the general's widow about half a million dollars in royalties but misled Mark Twain into expecting even bigger bonanzas. Over the course of about fifteen years he also poured steadily increasing amounts of money and faith into James W. Paige's automatic typesetting machine, a device timely in concept but committed to impossibly expensive standards of perfection and hopeless competition with Ottmar Mergenthaler's superior Linotype.

The anarchic impulses unleashed in *A Connecticut Yankee in King Arthur's Court* (1889)—the book ends with a massacre and a rejection of new and old values alike—reflect Mark Twain's anguish and frustration during this period. After the final collapse of both typesetter and publishing house in 1894, he filed for bankruptcy. He copyrighted his new novel, *Pudd'nhead Wilson,* in his wife's name to keep it out of the hands of creditors. To pay off his debts he traveled to Australia, New Zealand, India, and South Africa on a yearlong lecture tour. He was the most famous American author in the world. People in India knew only three things about the United States, he noted—"George Washington, Mark Twain, and the Chicago Fair." He had settled in England to write a book about his journey around the world, *Following the Equator* (1897), when he learned by cable from Hartford that his favorite daughter had died of meningitis.

"It is one of the mysteries of our nature," Mark Twain was to reflect, "that a man, all unprepared, can receive a thunder-stroke like that and live." For a while he walked the edge of madness in a self-induced dream state that he hoped would reveal to him where and why he had gone wrong. He worked on a series of unfinished and perhaps unfinishable symbolic stories, voyage and dream narratives characterized by dislocations of time, place, and scale. These stories of the "Great Dark" (collected and published in 1967 as *Which Was the Dream?*) deal with guilt, responsibility, and identity. They are reminders that this humorist and realist, so anchored in the particularities and textures of day-to-day existence, also sailed the spectral seas of Poe, Hawthorne, and Melville. ("Everyone is a moon," he said, "and has a dark side which he never shows to anybody.") He survived the crisis narrowly enough to give unintended irony to the statement he released to the press from London in 1897, "The report of my death was an exaggeration."

To the end of his days Mark Twain argued that personality was merely a machine driven by self-interest and the craving for approval, a doctrine he elaborated in his "bible," *What Is Man?* (first published, anonymously, in 1906). Like "The Man That Corrupted Hadleyburg" (1899), much of his late work is marked by moral and logical clarity instead of a rich sprawl of incident and anecdote. To get his juices flowing he relied on progressively larger jolts of indignation directed at God, orthodox Christianity, Mary Baker Eddy (founder of Christian Science), imperialism, racism, lynching, the martial spirit, and "corn-pone opinions" in general. His preferred forms were polemics, satire, and, above all, personal reminiscence. Mark Twain's free-form autobiography, in manuscript a million words or more of written and dictated prose, is the major work of his last years. Its chief unifying principle is the accent and rhythm and attack of his voice. (Ostensibly an integral work of Twain's last years, *The Mysterious Stranger,* published after his death, has proved to be a textual pastiche put together by his editor and his literary executor.)

Restored to financial health, Mark Twain moved back to the United States in 1900. (He had lived abroad for approximately half of the previous twenty-two

years.) The ovation that welcomed him continued until his death in 1910. "The
Hero as Man of Letters," newspaper editorials said, had emerged from bankruptcy
with "unsullied honor." "The most conspicuous person on the planet," he was the
idol of New York society and of plutocrats like the steelmaster Andrew Carnegie
and Henry H. Rogers of the Standard Oil Trust; a spellbinding after-dinner
speaker; a leading voice in the anti-imperialist movement; the most quotable
public personality of his time; a master showman who wore white suits winter
and summer, flaunted his shock of white hair, and made it a rule "never to
smoke when asleep, and never to refrain when awake." In 1902 he revisited
Missouri, "a great and beautiful country," for the last time and imagined Tom
and Huck coming home to Hannibal old and withered. Five years later he
journeyed to England to receive the degree of Doctor of Letters from Oxford
University. For this honor, to himself and to the profession of humor, he said he
would have been willing to "journey to Mars." He died in 1910 at Stormfield,
his Italianate villa perched on a hilltop in Redding, Connecticut. He had built
this last home with the proceeds from his serialized autobiography.

"Emerson, Longfellow, Lowell, Holmes—" Howells wrote in his memoir, *My
Mark Twain*, "I knew them all and all the rest of our sages, poets, seers, critics,
humorists; they were like one another and like other literary men; but Clemens
was sole, incomparable, the Lincoln of our literature."

Further Reading:
W. D. Howells, *My Mark Twain*, 1910.
A. B. Paine, *Mark Twain: A Biography*, 3 vols., 1912.
V. Brooks, *The Ordeal of Mark Twain*, 1920.
B. DeVoto, *Mark Twain's America*, 1932.
K. Andrews, *Nook Farm: Mark Twain's Hartford Circle*, 1950.
E. Branch, *The Literary Apprenticeship of Mark Twain*, 1950.
D. Wecter, *Sam Clemens of Hannibal*, 1952.
E. H. Long, *Mark Twain Handbook*, 1957.
P. Fatout, *Mark Twain on the Lecture Circuit*, 1960.
W. Blair, *Mark Twain and Huck Finn*, 1960.
H. N. Smith, *Mark Twain: The Development of a Writer*, 1962.
J. M. Cox, *Mark Twain: The Fate of Humor*, 1966.
J. Kaplan, *Mr. Clemens and Mark Twain*, 1966.
H. Hill, *Mark Twain, God's Fool*, 1973.
L. J. Budd, *Our Mark Twain: The Making of His Public Personality*, 1983.

Texts:
"The Notorious Jumping Frog of Calaveras County," *Mark Twain's Sketches*, 1875.
Roughing It, 1872.
Old Times on the Mississippi, in the *Atlantic Monthly*, 1875.
"The Story of a Speech," "The Private History of a Campaign That Failed," "Fenimore Cooper's Literary Offenses," "The War Prayer," "Corn-Pone Opinions," and letter to William Dean Howells from *The Writings of Mark Twain*, 37 vols., ed. A. B. Paine, 1922–1925.
A Tramp Abroad, 1880.
Letter to Orion and Mollie Clemens, *My Dear Bro*, 1961.
Letter to Will Bowen, *Mark Twain's Letters to Will Bowen*, 1941.
See also *The Mark Twain Papers*, ed. F. Anderson et al., 1967–.
The Works of Mark Twain, ed. J. Gerber et al., 1972–.

The Notorious Jumping Frog
of Calaveras County

In compliance with the request of a friend of mine, who wrote me from the East, I called on good-natured, garrulous old Simon Wheeler, and inquired after my friend's friend, Leonidas W. Smiley, as requested to do, and I hereunto append the result. I have a lurking suspicion that *Leonidas W.* Smiley is a myth; that my friend never knew such a personage; and that he only conjectured that if I asked old Wheeler about him, it would remind him of his infamous *Jim* Smiley, and he would go to work and bore me to death with some exasperating reminiscence of him as long and as tedious as it should be useless to me. If that was the design, it succeeded.

I found Simon Wheeler dozing comfortably by the bar-room stove of the dilapidated tavern in the decayed mining camp of Angel's, and I noticed that he was fat and bald-headed, and had an expression of winning gentleness and simplicity upon his tranquil countenance. He roused up, and gave me good-day. I told him a friend of mine had commissioned me to make some inquiries about a cherished companion of his boyhood named *Leondias W.* Smiley—*Rev. Leondias W.* Smiley, a young minister of the Gospel, who he had heard was at one time a resident of Angel's Camp. I added that if Mr. Wheeler could tell me anything about this Rev. Leonidas W. Smiley, I would feel under many obligations to him.

Simon Wheeler backed me into a corner and blockaded me there with his chair, and then sat down and reeled off the monotonous narrative which follows this paragraph. He never smiled, he never frowned, he never changed his voice from the gentle-flowing key to which he tuned his initial sentence, he never betrayed the slightest suspicion of enthusiasm; but all through the interminable narrative there ran a vein of impressive earnestness and sincerity, which showed me plainly that, so far from his imagining that there was anything ridiculous or funny about his story, he regarded it as a really important matter, and admired its two heroes as men of transcendent genius in *finesse.* I let him go on in his own way, and never interrupted him once.

"Rev. Leonidas W. H'm, Reverend Le—well, there was a feller here once by the name of *Jim* Smiley, in the winter of '49—or may be it was the spring of '50—I don't recollect exactly, somehow, though what makes me think it was one or the other is because I remember the big flume warn't finished when he first come to the camp; but any way, he was the curiosest man about always betting on anything that turned up you ever see, if he could get anybody to bet on the other side; and if he couldn't he'd change sides. Any way that suited the other man would suit *him* —any way just so's he got a bet, *he* was satisfied. But still he was lucky, uncommon lucky; he most always come out winner. He was always ready and laying for a chance; there couldn't be no solit'ry thing mentioned but that feller'd offer to bet on it, and take ary side you please, as I was just telling you. If there was a horse-race, you'd find him flush or you'd find him busted at the end of it; if there was a dog-fight, he'd bet on it; if there was a cat-fight, he'd bet on it; if there was a chicken-fight, he'd bet on it; why, if there was two birds setting on a fence, he would bet you which one would fly first; or if there was a camp-meeting, he would be there reg'lar to bet on Parson Walker, which he judged to be the best exhorter about here, and so he was too, and a good man. If he even see a straddle-bug start to go anywheres, he would bet you how long it would take him to get to—to wherever he was going to, and if you took him up, he would foller that straddle-bug to Mexico but what he would find out where he was bound for and how long he was on the road. Lots of the boys here has seen that Smiley, and can tell you about him. Why, it never made no difference to *him*—he'd bet on *any* thing—the dangdest feller. Parson Walker's wife laid very sick once, for a good while, and it seemed as if they warn't going to save her; but one morning he come in, and Smiley up and asked him how she was, and he said she was considable better—thank the Lord for his inf'nit mercy—and coming on so smart that with the blessing of Prov'dence she'd get well yet; and Smiley, before he thought says, "Well, I'll resk two-and-a-half she don't anyway."

Thish-yer Smiley had a mare—the boys called her the fifteen-minute nag, but that was only in fun, you know, because of course she was faster than that—and he used to win money on that horse, for all she was so slow and always had the asthma, or the distemper, or the consumption, or something of that kind. They used to give her two or three hundred yards' start, and then pass her under way; but always at the fag-end of the race she'd get excited and desperate-like, and come cavorting and straddling up, and scattering her legs around limber, sometimes in the air, and sometimes out to one side amongst the fences, and kicking up m-o-r-e dust and raising m-o-r-e racket with her coughing and sneezing and blowing her nose— and *always* fetch up at the stand just about a neck ahead, as near as you could cipher it down.

And he had a little small bull-pup, that to look at him you'd think he warn't worth a cent but to set around and look ornery and lay for a chance to steal something. But as soon as money was up on him he was a different dog; his under-jaw'd begin to stick out like the fo'castle of a steamboat, and his teeth would uncover and shine like the furnaces. And a dog might tackle him and bully-rag him, and bite him, and throw him over his shoulder two or three times, and Andrew Jackson—which was the name of the pup—Andrew Jackson would never let on but what *he* was satisfied, and hadn't expected nothing else—and the bets being doubled and doubled on the other side all the time, till the money was all up; and then all of a sudden he would grab that other dog jest by the j'int of his hind leg and freeze to it—not chaw, you understand, but only just grip and hang on till they throwed up the sponge, if it was a year. Smiley always come out winner on that pup, till he harnessed a dog once that didn't have no hind legs, because they'd been sawed off in a circular saw, and when the thing had gone along far enough, and the money was all up, and he come to make a snatch for his pet holt, he see in a minute how he'd been imposed on, and how the other dog had him in the door, so to speak, and he 'peared surprised, and then he looked sorter discouraged-like, and didn't try no more to win the fight, and so he got shucked out bad. He give Smiley a look, as much as to say his heart was broke, and it was *his* fault, for putting up a dog that hadn't no hind legs for him to take holt of, which was his main dependence in a fight, and then he limped off a piece and laid down and died. It was a good pup, was that Andrew Jackson, and would have made a name for hisself if he'd lived, for the stuff was in him and he had genius—I know it, because he hadn't no opportunities to speak of, and it don't stand to reason that a dog could make such a fight as he could under them circumstances if he hadn't no talent. It always makes me feel sorry when I think of that last fight of his'n, and the way it turned out.

Well, thish-yer Smiley had rat-tarriers, and chicken cocks, and tom-cats and all them kind of things, till you couldn't rest, and you couldn't fetch nothing for him to bet on but he'd match you. He ketched a frog one day, and took him home, and said he cal'lated to educate him; and so he never done nothing for three months but set in his back-yard and learn that frog to jump. And you bet you he *did* learn him, too. He'd give him a little punch behind, and the next minute you'd see that frog whirling in the air like a doughnut—see him turn one summerset, or may be a couple, if he got a good start, and come down flat-footed and all right, like a cat. He got him up so in the ma'ter of ketching flies, and kep' him in practice so constant, that he'd nail a fly every time as fur as he could see him. Smiley said all a frog wanted was education, and he could do 'most anything—and I believe him. Why, I've seen him set Dan'l Webster down here on this floor—Dan'l Webster was the name of the frog—and sing out, "Flies, Dan'l, flies!" and quicker'n you could wink he'd spring straight up and snake a fly off'n the counter there, and flop down on the floor ag'in as solid as a gob of mud, and fall to scratching the side of his head with his hind foot as indifferent as if he hadn't no idea he'd been doin' any more'n any frog might do. You never see a frog so modest and straightfor'ard as he was, for all he was so gifted. And when it come to fair and square jumping on a dead level, he could get over more ground at one straddle than any animal of his breed you ever see. Jumping on a dead level was his strong suit, you understand; and when it come to that, Smiley would ante up money on him as long as he had a red. Smiley was monstrous proud of his frog, and well he might be, for fellers that had traveled and been everywheres, all said he laid over any frog that ever *they* see.

Well, Smiley kep' the beast in a little lattice box, and he used to fetch him down town sometimes and lay for a bet. One day a feller—a stranger in the camp, he was—come acrost him with his box, and says:

"What might it be that you've got in the box?"

And Smiley says, sorter indifferent-like, "It might be a parrot, or it might be a canary, maybe, but it ain't—it's only just a frog."

And the feller took it, and looked at it careful, and turned it round this way and that, and says, "H'm—so 'tis. Well, what's *he* good for?"

"Well," Smiley, says, easy and careless, "he's good enough for *one* thing, I should judge—he can outjump any frog in Calaveras county."

The feller took the box again, and took another long, particular look, and give it back to Smiley, and says, very deliberate, "Well," he says, "I don't see no p'ints about that frog that's any better'n any other frog."

"Maybe you don't," Smiley says. "Maybe you understand frogs and maybe you don't understand 'em; maybe you've had experience, and maybe you ain't only a amature, as it were. Anyways, I've got *my* opinion and I'll resk forty dollars that he can outjump any frog in Calaveras county."

And the feller studied a minute, and then says, kinder sad like, "Well, I'm only a stranger here, and I ain't got no frog; but if I had a frog, I'd bet you."

And then Smiley says, "That's all right—that's all right—if you'll hold my box a minute, I'll go and get you a frog." And so the feller took the box, and put up his forty dollars along with Smiley's, and set down to wait.

So he set there a good while thinking and thinking to hisself, and then he got the frog out and prized his mouth open and took a teaspoon and filled him full of quail shot—filled him pretty near up to his chin—and set him on the floor. Smiley he went to the swamp and slopped around in the mud for a long time, and finally he ketched a frog, and fetched him in, and give him to this feller, and says:

"Now, if you're ready, set him alongside of Dan'l, with his fore-paws just even with Dan'l's, and I'll give the word." Then he says, "One—two—three—*git!*" and him and the feller touched up the frogs from behind, and the new frog hopped off lively, but Dan'l give a heave, and hysted up his shoulders—so—like a Frenchman, but it warn't no use—he couldn't budge; he was planted as solid as a church, and he couldn't no more stir than if he was anchored out. Smiley was a good deal surprised, and he was disgusted too, but he didn't have no idea what the matter was, of course.

The feller took the money and started away; and when he was going out at the door, he sorter jerked his thumb over his shoulder—so—at Dan'l, and says again, very deliberate, "Well," he says "*I* don't see no p'ints about that frog that's any better'n any other frog."

Smiley he stood scratching his head and looking down at Dan'l a long time, and at last he says, "I do wonder what in the nation that frog throw'd off for—I wonder if there ain't something the matter with him—he 'pears to look mighty baggy, somehow." And he ketched Dan'l by the nap of the neck, and hefted him, and says, "Why blame my cats if he don't weigh five pound!" and turned him upside down and he belched out a double handful of shot. And then he see how it was, and he was the maddest man—he set the frog down and took out after that feller, but he never ketched him. And—"

(Here Simon Wheeler heard his name called from the front yard, and got up to see what was wanted.) And turning to me as he moved away, he said: "Just set where you are, stranger, and rest easy—I ain't going to be gone a second."

But, by your leave, I did not think that a continuation of the history of the enterprising vagabond *Jim* Smiley would be likely to afford me much information concerning the Rev. *Leonidas W.* Smiley, and so I started away.

At the door I met the sociable Wheeler returning, and he button-holed me and re-commenced:

"Well, thish-yer Smiley had a yaller one-eyed cow that didn't have no tail, only jest a short stump like a bannanner, and—"

However, lacking both time and inclination, I did not wait to hear about the afflicted cow, but took my leave.

1865

---

from Roughing It

Chapter 1: [St. Louis to "St. Jo"[1]]

My brother had just been appointed Secretary of Nevada Territory—an office of such majesty that it concentrated in itself the duties and dignities of Treasurer, Comptroller, Secretary of State, and Acting Governor in the Governor's absence. A salary of

---

[1] I.e., St. Joseph, Missouri

eighteen hundred dollars a year and the title of "Mr. Secretary," gave to the great position an air of wild and imposing grandeur. I was young and ignorant, and I envied my brother. I coveted his distinction and his financial splendor, but particularly and especially the long, strange journey he was going to make, and the curious new world he was going to explore. He was going to travel! I never had been away from home, and that word "travel" had a seductive charm for me. Pretty soon he would be hundreds and hundreds of miles away on the great plains and deserts, and among the mountains of the Far West, and would see buffaloes and Indians, and prairie dogs, and antelopes, and have all kinds of adventures, and may be get hanged or scalped, and have ever such a fine time, and write home and tell us all about it, and be a hero. And he would see the gold mines and the silver mines, and maybe go about of an afternoon when his work was done, and pick up two or three pailfuls of shining slugs, and nuggets of gold and silver on the hillside. And by and by he would become very rich, and return home by sea, and be able to talk as calmly about San Francisco and the ocean, and "the isthmus" as if it was nothing of any consequence to have seen those marvels face to face. What I suffered in contemplating his happiness, pen cannot describe. And so, when he offered me, in cold blood, the sublime position of private secretary under him, it appeared to me that the heavens and the earth passed away, and the firmament was rolled together as a scroll! I had nothing more to desire. My contentment was complete. At the end of an hour or two I was ready for the journey. Not much packing up was necessary, because we were going in the overland stage from the Missouri frontier to Nevada, and passengers were only allowed a small quantity of baggage apiece. There was no Pacific railroad in those fine times of ten or twelve years ago—not a single rail of it.

I only proposed to stay in Nevada three months—I had no thought of staying longer than that. I meant to see all I could that was new and strange, and then hurry home to business. I little thought that I would not see the end of that three-month pleasure excursion for six or seven uncommonly long years!

I dreamed all night about Indians, deserts, and silver bars, and in due time, next day, we took shipping at the St. Louis wharf on board a steamboat bound up the Missouri River.

We were six days going from St. Louis to "St. Jo."—a trip that was so dull, and sleepy, and eventless that it has left no more impression on my memory than if its duration had been six minutes instead of that many days. No record is left in my mind, now, concerning it, but a confused jumble of savage-looking snags, which we deliberately walked over with one wheel or the other; and of reefs which we butted and butted, and then retired from and climbed over in some softer place; and of sand-bars which we roosted on occasionally, and rested, and then got out our crutches and sparred over. In fact, the boat might almost as well have gone to St. Jo. by land, for she was walking most of the time, anyhow—climbing over reefs and clambering over snags patiently and laboriously all day long. The captain said she was a "bully" boat, and all she wanted was more "shear" and a bigger wheel. I thought she wanted a pair of stilts, but I had the deep sagacity not to say so.

Chapter 2: [An Imposing Cradle on Wheels]

The first thing we did on that glad evening that landed us at St. Joseph was to hunt up the stage-office, and pay a hundred and fifty dollars apiece for tickets per overland coach to Carson City, Nevada.

The next morning, bright and early, we took a hasty breakfast, and hurried to the starting-place. Then an inconvenience presented itself which we had not properly appreciated before, namely, that one cannot make a heavy traveling trunk stand for twenty-five pounds of baggage—because it weighs a good deal more. But that was all we could take—twenty-five pounds each. So we had to snatch our trunks open, and make a selection in a good deal of a hurry. We put our lawful twenty-five pounds apiece all in one valise, and shipped the trunks back to St. Louis again. It was a sad parting, for now we had no swallow-tail coats and white kid gloves to wear at Pawnee receptions in the Rocky Mountains, and no stovepipe hats nor patent-leather boots, nor anything else necessary to make life calm and peaceful. We were reduced to a war-footing. Each of us put on a rough, heavy suit of clothing, woolen army shirt and "stogy" boots included; and into the valise we crowded a few white shirts, some under-clothing and such things. My brother, the Secretary, took along about four pounds of United States statutes and six pounds of Unabridged Dictionary; for we did not know—poor innocents—that such things could be bought in San Francisco on one day and received in Carson City the next. I was armed to the teeth with a pitiful little Smith & Wesson's seven-shooter, which carried a ball like a homœopathic pill, and it took the whole seven to make a dose for an adult. But I thought it was grand. It appeared to me to be a dangerous weapon. It only had one fault—you could not hit anything with it. One of our "conductors" practiced awhile on a cow with it, and as long as she stood still and behaved herself she was safe; but as soon as she went to moving about, and he got to shooting at other things, she came to grief. The Secretary had a small-sized Colt's revolver strapped around him for protection against the Indians, and to guard against accidents he carried it uncapped. Mr. George Bemis was dismally formidable. George Bemis was our fellow-traveler. We had never seen him before. He wore in his belt an old original "Allen" revolver, such as irreverent people called a "pepperbox." Simply drawing the trigger back, cocked and fired the pistol. As the trigger came back, the hammer would begin to rise and the barrel to turn over, and presently down would drop the hammer, and away would speed the ball. To aim along the turning barrel and hit the thing aimed at was a feat which was probably never done with an "Allen" in the world. But George's was a reliable weapon, nevertheless, because, as one of the stage-drivers afterward said, "If she didn't get what she went after, she would fetch something else." And so she did. She went after a deuce of spades nailed against a tree, once, and fetched a mule standing about thirty yards to the left of it. Bemis did not want the mule; but the owner came out with a double-barreled shotgun and persuaded him to buy it, anyhow. It was a cheerful weapon—the "Allen." Sometimes all its six barrels would go off at once, and then there was no safe place in all the region round about, but behind it.

We took two or three blankets for protection against frosty weather in the mountains. In the matter of luxuries we were modest—we took none along but some pipes and five pounds of smoking tobacco. We had two large canteens to carry water in, between stations on the Plains, and we also took with us a little shot-bag of silver coin for daily expenses in the way of breakfasts and dinners.

By eight o'clock everything was ready, and we were on the other side of the river. We jumped into the stage, the driver cracked his whip, and we bowled away and left "the States" behind us. It was a superb summer morning, and all the landscape was brilliant with sunshine. There was a freshness and breeziness, too, and an exhilarating sense of emancipation from all sorts of cares and responsibilities, that almost made us feel that the years we had spent in the close, hot city, toiling and slaving, had been wasted and thrown away. We were spinning along through Kansas, and in the course of an hour and a half we were fairly abroad on the great Plains. Just here the land was rolling—a grand sweep of regular elevations and depressions as far as the eye could reach—like the stately heave and swell of the ocean's bosom after a storm. And everywhere were cornfields, accenting with squares of deeper green, this limitless expanse of grassy land. But presently this sea upon dry ground was to lose its "rolling" character and stretch away for seven hundred miles as level as a floor!

Our coach was a great swinging and swaying stage, of the most sumptuous description—an imposing cradle on wheels. It was drawn by six handsome horses, and by the side of the driver sat the "conductor," the legitimate captain of the craft; for it was his business to take charge and care of the mails, baggage, express matter, and passengers. We three were the only passengers, this trip. We sat on the back seat, inside. About all the rest of the coach was full of mail bags—for we had three days' delayed mails with us. Almost touching our knees, a perpendicular wall of mail matter rose up to the roof. There was a great pile of it strapped on top of the stage, and both the fore and hind boots were full. We had twenty-seven hundred pounds of it aboard, the driver said—"a little for Brigham, and Carson, and 'Frisco, but the heft of it for the Injuns, which is powerful troublesome 'thout they get plenty of truck to read." But as he just then got up a fearful convulsion of his countenance which was suggestive of a wink being swallowed by an earthquake, we guessed that his remark was intended to be facetious, and to mean that we would unload the most of our mail matter somewhere on the Plains and leave it to the Indians, or whosoever wanted it.

We changed horses every ten miles, all day long, and fairly flew over the hard, level road. We jumped out and stretched our legs every time the coach stopped, and so the night found us still vivacious and unfatigued.

After supper a woman got in, who lived about fifty miles further on, and we three had to take turns at sitting outside with the driver and conductor. Apparently she was not a talkative woman. She would sit there in the gathering twilight and fasten her steadfast eyes on a mosquito rooting into her arm, and slowly she would raise her other hand till she had got his range, and then she would launch a slap at him that would have jolted a cow; and after that she would sit and contemplate the corpse with tranquil satisfaction—for she never missed her mosquito; she was a dead shot at short range. She never removed a carcase, but left them there for bait. I sat by this grim Sphynx and watched her kill thirty or forty mosquitoes—watched her, and waited for her to say something, but she never did. So I finally opened the conversation myself. I said:

"The mosquitoes are pretty bad, about here, madam."

"You bet!"

"What did I understand you to say, madam?"

"You BET!"

Then she cheered up, and faced around and said:

"Danged if I didn't begin to think you fellers was deef and dumb. I did, b' gosh. Here I've sot, and sot, and sot, a-bust'n muskeeters and wonderin' what was ailin' ye. Fust I thot you was deef and dumb, then I thot you was sick or crazy, or suthin', and then by and by I begin to reckon you was a passel of sickly fools that couldn't think of nothing to say. Wher'd ye come from?"

The Sphynx was a Sphynx no more! The fountains of her great deep were broken up, and she rained the nine parts of speech forty days and forty nights, metaphorically speaking, and buried us under a desolating deluge of trivial gossip that left not a crag or pinnacle of rejoinder projecting above the tossing waste of dislocated grammar and decomposed pronunciation!

How we suffered, suffered, suffered! She went on, hour after hour, till I was sorry I ever opened the mosquito question and gave her a start. She never did stop again until she got to her journey's end toward daylight; and then she stirred us up as she was leaving the stage (for we were nodding, by that time), and said:

"Now you git out at Cottonwood, you fellers, and lay over a couple o' days, and I'll be along some time to-night, and if I can do ye any good by edgin' in a word now and then, I'm right thar. Folks'll tell you't I've always ben kind o' offish and partic'lar for a gal that's raised in the woods, and I *am,* with the rag-tag and bob-tail, and a gal *has* to be, if she wants to *be* anything, but when people comes along which is my equals, I reckon I'm a pretty sociable heifer after all."

We resolved not to "lay by at Cottonwood."

Chapter 3: ["The Thoroughbrace Is Broke!"]

About an hour and a half before daylight we were bowling along smoothly over the road—so smoothly that our cradle only rocked in a gentle, lulling way, that was gradually soothing us to sleep, and dulling our consciousness—when something gave away under us! We were dimly aware of it, but indifferent to it. The coach stopped. We heard the driver and conductor talking together outside, and rummaging for a lantern, and swearing because they could not find it—but we had no interest in whatever had happened, and it only added to our comfort to think of those people out there at work in the murky night, and we snug in our nest with the curtains drawn. But presently, by the sounds, there seemed to be an examination going on, and then the driver's voice said:

"By George, the thoroughbrace is broke!"

This startled me broad awake—as an undefined sense of calamity is always apt to do. I said to myself: "Now, a thoroughbrace is probably part of a horse; and doubtless a vital part, too, from the dismay in the driver's voice. Leg, maybe—and yet how could he break his leg waltzing along such a road as this? No, it can't be his leg. That is impossible, unless he was reaching for the driver. Now, what can be the thoroughbrace of a horse, I wonder? Well, whatever comes, I shall not air my ignorance in this crowd, anyway."

Just then the conductor's face appeared at a lifted curtain, and his lantern glared in on us and our wall of mail matter. He said:

"Gents, you'll have to turn out a spell. Thoroughbrace is broke."

We climbed out into a chill drizzle, and felt ever so homeless and dreary. When I found that the thing they called a "thoroughbrace" was the massive combination of belts and springs which the coach rocks itself in, I said to the driver:

"I never saw a thoroughbrace used up like that, before, that I can remember. How did it happen?"

"Why, it happened by trying to make one coach carry three days' mail—that's how it happened," said he. "And right here is the very direction which is wrote on all the newspaper-bags which was to be put out for the Injuns for to keep 'em quiet. It's most uncommon lucky, becuz it's so nation dark I should 'a' gone by unbeknowns if that air thoroughbrace hadn't broke."

I knew that he was in labor with another of those winks of his, though I could not see his face, because he was bent down at work; and wishing him a safe delivery, I turned to and helped the rest get out the mail-sacks. It made a great pyramid by the roadside when it was all out. When they had mended the thoroughbrace we filled the two boots again, but put no mail on top, and only half as much inside as there was before. The conductor bent all the seat-backs down, and then filled the coach just half full of mail-bags from end to end. We objected loudly to this, for it left us no seats. But the conductor was wiser than we, and said a bed was better than seats, and moreover, this plan would protect his thoroughbraces. We never wanted any seats after that. The lazy bed was infinitely preferable. I had many an exciting day, subsequently, lying on it reading the statutes and the dictionary, and wondering how the characters would turn out.

The conductor said he would send back a guard from the next station to take charge of the abandoned mail-bags, and we drove on.

It was now just dawn; and as we stretched our cramped legs full length on the mail sacks, and gazed out through the windows across the wide wastes of greensward clad in cool, powdery mist, to where there was an expectant look in the eastern horizon, our perfect enjoyment took the form of a tranquil and contented ecstasy. The stage whirled along at a spanking gait, the breeze flapping curtains and suspended coats in a most exhilarating way; the cradle swayed and swung luxuriously, the pattering of the horses' hoofs, the cracking of the driver's whip, and his "Hi-yi! g'lang!" were music; the spinning ground and the waltzing trees appeared to give us a mute hurrah as we went by, and then slack up and look after us with interest, or envy, or something; and as we lay and smoked the pipe of peace and compared all this luxury with the years of tiresome city life that had gone before it, we felt that there was only one complete and satisfying happiness in the world, and we had found it.

After breakfast, at some station whose name I have forgotten, we three climbed up on the seat behind the driver, and let the conductor have our bed for a nap. And by and by, when the sun made me drowsy, I lay down on my face on top of the coach, grasping the slender iron railing, and slept for an hour or more. That will give one an appreciable idea of those matchless roads. Instinct will make a sleeping man grip a fast hold of the railing when the stage jolts, but when it only swings and sways, no grip is necessary. Overland drivers and conductors used to sit in their places and sleep thirty or forty minutes at a time, on good roads, while spinning along at the rate of eight or ten miles an hour. I saw them do it, often. There was no danger about it; a sleeping man *will* seize the irons in time when the coach jolts. These men were hard worked, and it was not possible for them to stay awake all the time.

By and by we passed through Marysville, and over the Big Blue and Little Sandy; thence about a mile, and entered Nebraska. About a mile further on, we came to the Big Sandy—one hundred and eighty miles from St. Joseph.

As the sun was going down, we saw the first specimen of an animal known familiarly over two thousand miles of mountain and desert—from Kansas clear to the Pacific Ocean—as the "jackass rabbit." He is well named. He is just like any other rabbit, except that he is from one third to twice as large, has longer legs in proportion to his size, and has the most preposterous ears that ever were mounted on any creature *but* a jackass. When he is sitting quiet, thinking about his sins, or is absent-minded or unapprehensive of danger, his majestic ears project above him conspicuously; but the breaking of a twig will scare him nearly to death, and then he tilts his ears back gently and starts for home. All you can see, then, for the next minute, is his long gray form stretched out straight and "streaking it" through the low sage-brush, head erect, eyes right, and ears just canted a little to the rear, but showing you where the animal is, all the time, the same as if he carried a jib. Now and then he makes a marvelous spring with his long legs, high over the stunted sage-brush, and scores a leap that would make a horse envious. Presently he comes down to a long, graceful "lope," and shortly he mysteriously disappears. He has crouched behind a sage-bush, and will sit there and listen and tremble until you get within six feet of him, when he will get under way again. But one must shoot at this creature once, if he wishes to see him throw his heart into his heels, and do the best he knows how. He is frightened clear through, now, and he lays his long ears down on his back, straightens himself out like a yard-stick every spring he makes, and scatters miles behind him with an easy indifference that is enchanting.

Our party made this specimen "hump himself," as the conductor said. The secretary started him with a shot from the Colt; I commenced spitting at him with my weapon; and all in the same instant the old "Allen's" whole broadside let go with a rattling crash, and it is not putting it too strong to say that the rabbit was frantic! He dropped his ears, set up his tail, and left for San Francisco at a speed which can only be described as a flash and a vanish! Long after he was out of sight we could hear him whiz.

I do not remember where we first came across "sage-brush," but as I have been speaking of it I may as well describe it. This is easily done, for if the reader can imagine a gnarled and venerable live oak-tree reduced to a little shrub two feet high, with its rough bark, its foliage, its twisted boughs, all complete, he can picture the "sage-brush" exactly. Often, on lazy afternoons in the mountains, I have lain on the ground with my face under a sage-bush, and entertained myself with fancying that the gnats among its foliage were liliputian birds, and that the ants marching and countermarching about its base were liliputian flocks and herds, and myself some vast loafer from Brobdignag waiting to catch a little citizen and eat him.

It is an imposing monarch of the forest in exquisite miniature, is the "sage-brush." Its foliage is a grayish green, and gives that tint to desert and mountain. It smells like our domestic sage, and "sage-tea" made from it tastes like the sage-tea which all boys are so well acquainted with. The sage-brush is a singularly hardy plant, and grows right in the midst of deep sand, and among barren rocks, where nothing else in the vegetable world would try to grow, except "bunch-grass."[2] The sage-bushes grow from three to six or seven feet apart, all over the mountains and deserts of the Far West, clear to the borders of California. There is not a tree of any kind in the deserts, for hundreds of miles—there is no vegetation at all in a regular desert, except the sage-brush and its cousin the "greasewood," which is so much like the sage-brush that the difference amounts to little. Camp-fires and hot suppers in the deserts would be impossible but for the friendly sage-brush. Its trunk is as large as a boy's wrist (and from that up to a man's arm), and its crooked branches are half as large as its trunk—all good, sound, hard wood, very like oak.

When a party camps, the first thing to be done is to cut sage-brush; and in a few minutes there is an opulent pile of it ready for use. A hole a foot wide, two feet deep, and two feet long, is dug, and sage-brush chopped up and burned in it till it is full to the brim with glowing coals. Then the cooking begins, and there is no smoke, and consequently no swearing. Such a fire will keep all night, with very little replenishing; and it makes a very sociable camp-fire, and one around which the most impossible reminiscences sound plausible, instructive, and profoundly entertaining.

Sage-brush is very fair fuel, but as a vegetable it is a distinguished failure. Nothing can abide the taste of it but the jackass and his illegitimate child the mule. But their testimony to its nutritiousness is worth nothing, for they will eat pine knots, or anthracite coal, or brass filings, or lead pipe, or old bottles, or anything that comes handy, and then go off looking as grateful as if they had had oysters for dinner. Mules and donkeys and camels have appetites that anything will relieve temporarily, but nothing satisfy. In Syria, once, at the head-waters of the Jordan, a camel took charge of my overcoat while the tents were being pitched, and examined it with a critical eye, all over, with as much interest as if he had an idea of getting one made like it; and then, after he was done figuring on it as an article of apparel, he began to contemplate it as an article of diet. He put his foot on it, and lifted one of the sleeves out with his teeth, and chewed and chewed at it, gradually taking it in, and all the while opening and closing his eyes in a kind of religious ecstasy, as if he had never tasted anything as good as an overcoat before, in his life. Then he smacked his lips once or twice, and reached after the other sleeve. Next he tried the velvet collar, and smiled a smile of such contentment that it was plain to see that he regarded that as the daintiest thing about an overcoat. The tails went next, along with some percussion caps and cough candy, and some fig-paste from Constantinople. And then my newspaper correspondence dropped out, and he took a chance in that—manuscript letters written for the home papers. But he was treading on dangerous ground, now. He began to come across solid wisdom in those documents that was rather weighty on his stomach; and occasionally he would take a joke that would shake him up till it loosened his teeth; it was getting to be perilous times with him, but he held his grip with good courage and hopefully, till at last he began to stumble on statements that

[2] Twain's note: " 'Bunch-grass' grows on the bleak mountain-sides of Nevada and neighboring territories, and offers excellent feed for stock, even in the dead of winter, wherever the snow is blown aside and exposes it; notwithstanding its unpromising home, bunch-grass is a better and more nutritious diet for cattle and horses than almost any other hay or grass that is known—so stock-men say."

not even a camel could swallow with impunity. He began to gag and gasp, and his eyes to stand out, and his forelegs to spread, and in about a quarter of a minute he fell over as stiff as a carpenter's work-bench, and died a death of indescribable agony. I went and pulled the manuscript out of his mouth, and found that the sensitive creature had choked to death on one of the mildest and gentlest statements of fact that I ever laid before a trusting public.

I was about to say, when diverted from my subject, that occasionally one finds sage-brushes five or six feet high, and with a spread of branch and foliage in proportion, but two or two and a half feet is the usual height.

from **Chapter 4: [Old Overland Stage-Coaching]**

As the sun went down and the evening chill came on, we made preparation for bed. We stirred up the hard leather letter-sacks, and the knotty canvas bags of printed matter (knotty and uneven because of projecting ends and corners of magazines, boxes and books). We stirred them up and redisposed them in such a way as to make our bed as level as possible. And we *did* improve it, too, though after all our work it had an upheaved and billowy look about it, like a little piece of a stormy sea. Next we hunted up our boots from odd nooks among the mail-bags where they had settled, and put them on. Then we got down our coats, vests, pantaloons and heavy woolen shirts, from the arm-loops where they had been swinging all day, and clothed ourselves in them—for, there being no ladies either at the stations or in the coach, and the weather being hot, we had looked to our comfort by stripping to our underclothing, at nine o'clock in the morning. All things being now ready, we stowed the uneasy Dictionary where it would lie as quiet as possible, and placed the water-canteens and pistols where we could find them in the dark. Then we smoked a final pipe, and swapped a final yarn; after which, we put the pipes, tobacco and bag of coin in snug holes and caves among the mail-bags, and then fastened down the coach curtains all around, and made the place as "dark as the inside of a cow," as the conductor phrased it in his picturesque way. It was certainly as dark as any place could be—nothing was even dimly visible in it. And finally, we rolled ourselves up like silk-worms, each person in his own blanket, and sank peacefully to sleep.

Whenever the stage stopped to change horses, we would wake up, and try to recollect where we were—and succeed—and in a minute or two the stage would be off again, and we likewise. We began to get into country, now, threaded here and there with little streams. These had high, steep banks on each side, and every time we flew down one bank and scrambled up the other, our party inside got mixed somewhat. First we would all be down in a pile at the forward end of the stage, nearly in a sitting posture, and in a second we would shoot to the other end, and stand on our heads. And we would sprawl and kick, too, and ward off ends and corners of mail-bags that came lumbering over us and about us; and as the dust rose from the tumult, we would all sneeze in chorus, and the majority of us would grumble, and probably say some hasty thing, like: "Take your elbow out of my ribs!—can't you quit crowding?"

Every time we avalanched from one end of the stage to the other, the Unabridged Dictionary would come too; and every time it came it damaged somebody. One trip it "barked" the Secretary's elbow; the next trip it hurt me in the stomach, and the third it tilted Bemis's nose up till he could look down his nostrils—he said. The pistols and coin soon settled to the bottom, but the pipes, pipe-stems, tobacco and canteens clattered and floundered after the Dictionary every time it made an assault on us, and aided and abetted the book by spilling tobacco in our eyes, and water down our backs.

Still, all things considered, it was a very comfortable night. It wore gradually away, and when at last a cold gray light was visible through the puckers and chinks in the curtains, we yawned and stretched with satisfaction, shed our cocoons, and felt that we had slept as much as was necessary. By and by, as the sun rose up and warmed the world, we pulled off our clothes and got ready for breakfast. We were just pleasantly in time, for five minutes afterward the driver sent the weird music of his bugle winding over the grassy solitudes, and presently we detected a low hut or two in the distance. Then the rattling of the coach, the clatter of our six horses' hoofs, and the driver's crisp commands, awoke to a louder and stronger emphasis, and we went sweeping down on the station at our smartest speed. It was fascinating—that old overland stage-coaching.

We jumped out in undress uniform. The driver tossed his gathered reins out on the ground, gaped and stretched complacently, drew off his heavy buckskin gloves with great deliberation and insufferable dignity—taking not the slightest notice of a dozen solicitous inquiries after his health, and humbly facetious and flattering accostings, and obsequious tenders of service, from five or six hairy and half-civilized station-keepers and hostlers who were nimbly unhitching our steeds and bringing the fresh team out of the stables—for in the eyes of the stage-driver of that day, station-keepers and hostlers were a sort of good enough low creatures, useful in their place, and helping to make up a world, but not the kind of beings which a person of distinction could afford to concern himself with; while, on the contrary, in the eyes of the station-keeper and the hostler, the stage-driver was a hero—a great and shining dignitary, the world's favorite son, the envy of the people, the observed of the nations. When they spoke to him they received his insolent silence meekly, and as being the natural and proper conduct of so great a man; when he opened his lips they all hung on his words with admiration (he never honored a particular individual with a remark, but addressed it with a broad generality to the horses, the stables, the surrounding country and the human underlings); when he discharged a facetious insulting personality at a hostler, that hostler was happy for the day; when he uttered his one jest— old as the hills, coarse, profane, witless, and inflicted on the same audience, in the same language, every time his coach drove up there—the varlets roared, and slapped their thighs, and swore it was the best thing they'd ever heard in all their lives. And how they would fly around when he wanted a basin of water, a gourd of the same, or a light for his pipe!—but they would instantly insult a passenger if he so far forgot himself as to crave a favor at their hands. They could do that sort of insolence as well as the driver they copied it from—for, let it be borne in mind, the overland driver had but little less contempt for his passengers than he had for his hostlers.

The hostlers and station-keepers treated the really powerful *conductor* of the coach merely with the best of what was their idea of civility, but the *driver* was the only being they bowed down to and worshipped. How admiringly they would gaze up at him in his high seat as he gloved himself with lingering deliberation, while some happy hostler held the bunch of reins aloft, and waited patiently for him to take it! And how they would bombard him with glorifying ejaculations as he cracked his long whip and went careering away.

The station buildings were long, low huts, made of sun-dried, mud-colored bricks, laid up without mortar (*adobes,* the Spaniards call these bricks, and Americans shorten it to *'dobies*). The roofs, which had no slant to them worth speaking of, were thatched and then sodded or covered with a thick layer of earth, and from this sprung a pretty rank growth of weeds and grass. It was the first time we had ever seen a man's front yard on top of his house. The buildings consisted of barns, stable-room for twelve or fifteen horses, and a hut for an eating-room for passengers. This latter had bunks in it for the station-keeper and a hostler or two. You could rest your elbow on its eaves, and you had to bend in order to get in at the door. In place of a window there was a square hole about large enough for a man to crawl through, but this had no glass in it. There was no flooring, but the ground was packed hard. There was no stove, but the fire-place served all needful purposes. There were no shelves, no cupboards, no closets. In a corner stood an open sack of flour, and nestling against its base were a couple of black and venerable tin coffee-pots, a tin tea-pot, a little bag of salt, and a side of bacon.

By the door of the station-keeper's den, outside, was a tin wash-basin, on the ground. Near it was a pail of water and a piece of yellow bar soap, and from the eaves hung a hoary blue woolen shirt, significantly—but this latter was the station-keeper's private towel, and only two persons in all the party might venture to use it—the stage-driver and the conductor. The latter would not, from a sense of decency; the former would not, because he did not choose to encourage the advances of a station-keeper. We had towels—in the valise; they might as well have been in Sodom and Gomorrah. We (and the conductor) used our handkerchiefs, and the driver his pantaloons and sleeves. By the door, inside, was fastened a small old-fashioned looking-glass frame, with two little fragments of the original mirror lodged down in one corner of it. This arrangement afforded a pleasant double-barreled portrait of you when you looked into it, with one half of your head set up a couple of inches above the other half. From the glass frame hung the half of a comb by a string—but if I had to describe that patriarch or die, I believe I would order some sample coffins. It had come down from Esau and Samson, and had been accumulating hair ever since—along with certain impurities. In one corner of the room stood three or four rifles and muskets, together with horns and pouches of ammunition. The station-men wore pantaloons of coarse, country-woven stuff, and into the seat and the inside of the legs were sewed ample additions of buckskin, to do duty in place of leggings, when the man rode horseback—so the pants were half dull blue and half yellow, and unspeakably picturesque. The pants were stuffed into the tops of high boots, the heels whereof were armed with great Spanish spurs, whose little iron clogs and chains jingled with every step. The man wore a huge beard and mustachios, an old slouch hat, a blue woolen shirt, no suspenders, no vest, no coat—in a leathern sheath in his belt, a great long "navy" revolver (slung on right side, hammer to the front), and projecting from his boot a horn-handled bowie-knife. The furniture of the hut was neither gorgeous nor much in the way. The rocking-chairs and sofas were not present, and never had been, but they were represented by two three-legged stools, a pine-board bench four feet long, and two empty candle-boxes. The table was a greasy board on stilts, and the table-cloth and napkins had not come—and they were not looking for them, either. A battered tin platter, a knife and fork, and a tin pint cup, were at each man's place, and the driver had a queensware saucer that had seen better days. Of course this duke sat at the head of the table. There was one isolated piece of table furniture that bore about it a touching air of grandeur in misfortune. This was the caster. It was German silver, and crippled and rusty, but it was so preposterously out of place there that it was suggestive of a tattered exiled king among barbarians, and the majesty of its native position compelled respect even in its degradation. There was only one cruet left, and that was a stopperless, fly-specked, broken-necked thing, with two inches of vinegar in it, and a dozen preserved flies with their heels up and looking sorry they had invested there.

The station-keeper upended a disk of last week's bread, of the shape and size of an old-time cheese, and carved some slabs from it which were as good as Nicholson pavement,[3] and tenderer.

He sliced off a piece of bacon for each man, but only the experienced old hands made out to eat it, for it was condemned army bacon which the United States would not feed to its soldiers in the forts, and the stage company had bought it cheap for the sustenance of their passengers and employes. We may have found this condemned army bacon further out on the plains than the section I am locating it in, but we *found* it—there is no gainsaying that.

Then he poured for us a beverage which he called *"Slumgullion,"* and it is hard to think he was not inspired when he named it. It really pretended to be tea, but there was too much dish-rag, and sand, and old bacon-rind in it to deceive the intelligent traveler. He had no sugar and no milk—not even a spoon to stir the ingredients with.

We could not eat the bread or the meat, nor drink the "slumgullion." And when I looked at that melancholy vinegar-cruet, I thought of the anecdote (a very, very old one, even at that day) of the traveler who sat down to a table which had nothing on it but a mackerel and a pot of mustard. He asked the landlord if this was all. The landlord said:

"All! Why, thunder and lightning, I should think there was mackerel enough there for six."

"But I don't like mackerel."

"Oh—then help yourself to the mustard."

In other days I had considered it a good, a very good, anecdote, but there was a dismal plausibility about it, here, that took all the humor out of it.

Our breakfast was before us, but our teeth were idle.

I tasted and smelt, and said I would take coffee, I believed. The station-boss stopped dead still, and glared at me speechless. At last, when he came to, he turned away and said, as one who communes with himself upon a matter too vast to grasp:

"Coffee! Well, if that don't go clean ahead of me, I'm d——d!"

We could not eat, and there was no conversation among the hostlers and herdsmen —we all sat at the same board. At least there was no conversation further than a single hurried request, now and then, from one employe to another. It was always in the same form, and always gruffly friendly. Its western freshness and novelty startled me, at first, and interested me; but it presently grew monotonous, and lost its charm. It was:

"Pass the bread, you son of a skunk!" No, I forget—skunk was not the word; it seems to me it was still stronger than that; I know it was, in fact, but it is gone from

---

[3] Compound surface of wood blocks, gravel, and tar.

my memory, apparently. However, it is no matter—probably it was too strong for print, anyway. It is the landmark in my memory which tells me where I first encountered the vigorous new vernacular of the occidental plains and mountains.

We gave up the breakfast, and paid our dollar apiece and went back to our mail-bag bed in the coach, and found comfort in our pipes. Right here we suffered the first diminution of our princely state. We left our six fine horses and took six mules in their place. But they were wild Mexican fellows, and a man had to stand at the head of each of them and hold him fast while the driver gloved and got himself ready. And when at last he grasped the reins and gave the word, the men sprung suddenly away from the mules' heads and the coach shot from the station as if it had issued from a cannon. How the frantic animals did scamper! It was a fierce and furious gallop—and the gait never altered for a moment till we reeled off ten or twelve miles and swept up to the next collection of little station-huts and stables.

So we flew along all day. At 2 P.M. the belt of timber that fringes the North Platte and marks its windings through the vast level floor of the Plains came in sight. At 4 P.M. we crossed a branch of the river, and at 5 P.M. we crossed the Platte itself, and landed at Fort Kearney, *fifty-six hours out from St. Joe*—THREE HUNDRED MILES!

Now that was stage-coaching on the great overland, ten or twelve years ago, when perhaps not more than ten men in America, all told, expected to live to see a railroad follow that route to the Pacific. But the railroad is there, now, and it pictures a thousand odd comparisons and contrasts in my mind to read the following sketch, in the New York *Times,* of a recent trip over almost the very ground I have been describing. I can scarcely comprehend the new state of things:

"ACROSS THE CONTINENT.

"At 4.20 P.M., Sunday, we rolled out of the station at Omaha, and started westward on our long jaunt. A couple of hours out, dinner was announced—an "event" to those of us who had yet to experience what it is to eat in one of Pullman's hotels on wheels; so, stepping into the car next forward of our sleeping palace, we found ourselves in the dining-car. It was a revelation to us, that first dinner on Sunday. And though we continued to dine for four days, and had as many breakfasts and suppers, our whole party never ceased to admire the perfection of the arrangements, and the marvelous results achieved. Upon tables covered with snowy linen, and garnished with services of solid silver, Ethiop waiters, flitting about in spotless white, placed as by magic a repast at which Delmonico himself could have had no occasion to blush; and, indeed, in some respects it would be hard for that distinguished *chef* to match our *menu;* for, in addition to all that ordinarily makes up a first-chop dinner, had we not our antelope steak (the gormand who has not experienced this—bah! what does he know of the feast of fat things?) our delicious mountain-brook trout, and choice fruits and berries, and (sauce piquant and unpurchasable!) our sweet-scented, appetite-compelling air of the prairies? You may depend upon it, we all did justice to the good things, and as we washed them down with bumpers of sparkling Krug, whilst we sped along at the rate of thirty miles an hour, agreed it was the *fastest* living we had ever experienced. (We beat that, however, two days afterward when we made *twenty-seven miles in twenty-seven minutes,*

while our Champagne glasses filled to the brim spilled not a drop!) After dinner
we repaired to our drawing-room car, and, as it was Sabbath eve, intoned some
of the grand old hymns—"Praise God from whom," etc.; "Shining Shore,"
"Coronation," etc.—the voices of the men singers and of the women singers
blending sweetly in the evening air, while our train, with its great, glaring
Polyphemus eye, lighting up long vistas of prairie, rushed into the night and
the Wild. Then to bed in luxurious couches, where we slept the sleep of the
just and only awoke the next morning (Monday) at eight o'clock, to find
ourselves at the crossing of the North Platte, three hundred miles from
Omaha—*fifteen hours and forty minutes out.*" . . .

Chapter 7: [Bemis's Buffalo Hunt]

It did seem strange enough to see a town[4] again after what appeared to us such a long
acquaintance with deep, still, almost lifeless and houseless solitude! We tumbled out
into the busy street feeling like meteoric people crumbled off the corner of some other
world, and wakened up suddenly in this. For an hour we took as much interest in
Overland City as if we had never seen a town before. The reason we had an hour
to spare was because we had to change our stage (for a less sumptuous affair, called
a "mud-wagon") and transfer our freight of mails.

Presently we got under way again. We came to the shallow, yellow, muddy South
Platte, with its low banks and its scattering flat sand-bars and pigmy islands—a
melancholy stream straggling through the centre of the enormous flat plain, and only
saved from being impossible to find with the naked eye by its sentinel rank of
scattering trees standing on either bank. The Platte was "up," they said—which made
me wish I could see it when it was down, if it could look any sicker and sorrier. They
said it was a dangerous stream to cross, now, because its quicksands were liable to
swallow up horses, coach and passengers if an attempt was made to ford it. But the
mails had to go, and we made the attempt. Once or twice in midstream the wheels
sunk into the yielding sands so threateningly that we half believed we had dreaded
and avoided the sea all our lives to be shipwrecked in a "mud-wagon" in the middle
of a desert at last. But we dragged through and sped away toward the setting sun.

Next morning, just before dawn, when about five hundred and fifty miles from
St. Joseph, our mud-wagon broke down. We were to be delayed five or six hours,
and therefore we took horses, by invitation, and joined a party who were just starting
on a buffalo hunt. It was noble sport galloping over the plain in the dewy freshness
of the morning, but our part of the hunt ended in disaster and disgrace, for a wounded
buffalo bull chased the passenger Bemis nearly two miles, and then he forsook his horse
and took to a lone tree. He was very sullen about the matter for some twenty-four
hours, but at last he began to soften little by little, and finally he said:

"Well, it was not funny, and there was no sense in those gawks making themselves
so facetious over it. I tell you I was angry in earnest for awhile. I should have shot
that long gangly lubber they called Hank, if I could have done it without crippling
six or seven other people—but of course I couldn't, the old 'Allen's' so confounded
comprehensive. I wish those loafers had been up in the tree; they wouldn't have

[4] Julesburg, Colorado, here called Overland City.

wanted to laugh so. If I had had a horse worth a cent—but no, the minute he saw that buffalo bull wheel on him and give a bellow, he raised straight up in the air and stood on his heels. The saddle began to slip, and I took him round the neck and laid close to him, and began to pray. Then he came down and stood up on the other end awhile, and the bull actually stopped pawing sand and bellowing to contemplate the inhuman spectacle. Then the bull made a pass at him and uttered a bellow that sounded perfectly frightful, it was so close to me, and that seemed to literally prostrate my horse's reason, and make a raving distracted maniac of him, and I wish I may die if he didn't stand on his head for a quarter of a minute and shed tears. He was absolutely out of his mind—he was, as sure as truth itself, and he really didn't know what he was doing. Then the bull came charging at us, and my horse dropped down on all fours and took a fresh start—and then for the next ten minutes he would actually throw one hand-spring after another so fast that the bull began to get unsettled, too, and didn't know where to start in—and so he stood there sneezing, and shovelling dust over his back, and bellowing every now and then, and thinking he had got a fifteen-hundred dollar circus horse for breakfast, certain. Well, I was first out on his neck—the horse's, not the bull's—and then underneath, and next on his rump, and sometimes head up, and sometimes heels—but I tell you it seemed solemn and awful to be ripping and tearing and carrying on so in the presence of death, as you might say. Pretty soon the bull made a snatch for us and brought away some of my horse's tail (I suppose, but do not know, being pretty busy at the time), but *something* made him hungry for solitude and suggested to him to get up and hunt for it. And then you ought to have seen that spider-legged old skeleton go! and you ought to have seen the bull put out after him, too—head down, tongue out, tail up, bellowing like everything, and actually mowing down the weeds, and tearing up the earth, and boosting up the sand like a whirlwind! By George, it was a hot race! I and the saddle were back on the rump, and I had the bridle in my teeth and holding on to the pommel with both hands. First we left the dogs behind; then we passed a jackass rabbit; then we overtook a cayote, and were gaining on an antelope when the rotten girth let go and threw me about thirty yards off to the left, and as the saddle went down over the horse's rump he gave it a lift with his heels that sent it more than four hundred yards up in the air, I wish I may die in a minute if he didn't. I fell at the foot of the only solitary tree there was in nine counties adjacent (as any creature could see with the naked eye), and the next second I had hold of the bark with four sets of nails and my teeth, and the next second after that I was astraddle of the main limb and blaspheming my luck in a way that made my breath smell of brimstone. I *had* the bull, now, if he did not think of *one* thing. But that one thing I dreaded. I dreaded it very seriously. There was a possibility that the bull might not think of it, but there were greater chances that he would. I made up my mind what I would do in case he did. It was a little over forty feet to the ground from where I sat. I cautiously unwound the lariat from the pommel of my saddle—"

"Your *saddle?* Did you take your saddle up in the tree with you?"

"Take it up in the tree with me? Why, how you talk. Of course I didn't. No man could do that. It *fell* in the tree when it came down."

"Oh—exactly."

"Certainly. I unwound the lariat, and fastened one end of it to the limb. It was the very best green raw-hide, and capable of sustaining tons. I made a slip-noose in the other end, and then hung it down to see the length. It reached down twenty-two feet—half way to the ground. I then loaded every barrel of the Allen with a double charge. I felt satisfied. I said to myself, if he never thinks of that one thing that I dread, all right—but if he does, all right anyhow—I am fixed for him. But don't you know that the very thing a man dreads is the thing that always happens? Indeed it is so. I watched the bull, now, with anxiety—anxiety which no one can conceive of who has not been in such a situation and felt that at any moment death might come. Presently a thought came into the bull's eye. I knew it! said I—if my nerve fails now, I am lost. Sure enough, it was just as I had dreaded, he started in to climb the tree—"

"What, the bull?"

"Of course—who else?"

"But a bull can't climb a tree."

"He can't, can't he? Since you know so much about it, did you ever see a bull try?"

"No! I never dreamt of such a thing."

"Well, then, what is the use of your talking that way, then? Because you never saw a thing done, is that any reason why it can't be done?"

"Well, all right—go on. What did you do?"

"The bull started up, and got along well for about ten feet, then slipped and slid back. I breathed easier. He tried it again—got up a little higher—slipped again. But he came at it once more, and this time he was careful. He got gradually higher and higher, and my spirits went down more and more. Up he came—an inch at a time —with his eyes hot, and his tongue hanging out. Higher and higher—hitched his foot over the stump of a limb, and looked up, as much as to say, 'You are my meat, friend.' Up again—higher and higher, and getting more excited the closer he got. He was within ten feet of me! I took a long breath,—and then said I, 'It is now or never.' I had the coil of the lariat all ready; I paid it out slowly, till it hung right over his head; all of a sudden I let go of the slack, and the slip-noose fell fairly round his neck! Quicker than lightning I out with the Allen and let him have it in the face. It was an awful roar, and must have scared the bull out of his senses. When the smoke cleared away, there he was, dangling in the air, twenty foot from the ground, and going out of one convulsion into another faster than you could count! I didn't stop to count, anyhow—I shinned down the tree and shot for home."

"Bemis, is all that true, just as you have stated it?"

"I wish I may rot in my tracks and die the death of a dog if it isn't."

"Well, we can't refuse to believe it, and we don't. But if there were some proofs—"

"Proofs! Did I bring back my lariat?"

"No."

"Did I bring back my horse?"

"No."

"Did you ever see the bull again?"

"No."

"Well, then, what more do you want? I never saw anybody as particular as you are about a little thing like that."

I made up my mind that if this man was not a liar he only missed it by the skin of his teeth. This episode reminds me of an incident of my brief sojourn in Siam, years afterward. The European citizens of a town in the neighborhood of Bangkok had a prodigy among them by the name of Eckert, an Englishman—a person famous for the number, ingenuity and imposing magnitude of his lies. They were always repeating his most celebrated falsehoods, and always trying to "draw him out" before strangers; but they seldom succeeded. Twice he was invited to the house where I was visiting, but nothing could seduce him into a specimen lie. One day a planter named Bascom, an influential man, and a proud and sometimes irascible one, invited me to ride over with him and call on Eckert. As we jogged along, said he:

"Now, do you know where the fault lies? It lies in putting Eckert on his guard. The minute the boys go to pumping at Eckert he knows perfectly well what they are after, and of course he shuts up his shell. Anybody might know he would. But when we get there, we must play him finer than that. Let him shape the conversation to suit himself—let him drop it or change it whenever he wants to. Let him see that nobody is trying to draw him out. Just let him have his own way. He will soon forget himself and begin to grind out lies like a mill. Don't get impatient—just keep quiet, and let me play him. I will make him lie. It does seem to me that the boys must be blind to overlook such an obvious and simple trick as that."

Eckert received us heartily—a pleasant-spoken, gentle-mannered creature. We sat in the veranda an hour, sipping English ale, and talking about the king, and the sacred white elephant, the Sleeping Idol, and all manner of things; and I noticed that my comrade never led the conversation himself or shaped it, but simply followed Eckert's lead, and betrayed no solicitude and no anxiety about anything. The effect was shortly perceptible. Eckert began to grow communicative; he grew more and more at his ease, and more and more talkative and sociable. Another hour passed in the same way, and then all of a sudden Eckert said:

"Oh, by the way! I came near forgetting. I have got a thing here to astonish you. Such a thing as neither you nor any other man ever heard of—I've got a cat that will eat cocoanut! Common green cocoanut—and not only eat the meat, but drink the milk. It is so—I'll swear to it."

A quick glance from Bascom—a glance that I understood—then:

"Why, bless my soul, I never heard of such a thing. Man, it is impossible."

"I knew you would say it. I'll fetch the cat."

He went in the house. Bascom said:

"There—what did I tell you? Now, that is the way to handle Eckert. You see, I have petted him along patiently, and put his suspicions to sleep. I am glad we came. You tell the boys about it when you go back. Cat eat a cocoanut—oh, my! Now, that is just his way, exactly—he will tell the absurdest lie, and trust to luck to get out of it again. Cat eat a cocoanut—the innocent fool!"

Eckert approached with his cat, sure enough.

Bascom smiled. Said he:

"I'll hold the cat—you bring a cocoanut."

Eckert split one open, and chopped up some pieces. Bascom smuggled a wink to me, and proffered a slice of the fruit to puss. She snatched it, swallowed it ravenously, and asked for more!

We rode our two miles in silence, and wide apart. At least I was silent, though Bascom cuffed his horse and cursed him a good deal, notwithstanding the horse was behaving well enough. When I branched off homeward, Bascom said:

"Keep the horse till morning. And—you need not speak of this—foolishness to the boys."

from *Chapter 8: [The Pony Express]*

In a little while all interest was taken up in stretching our necks and watching for the "pony-rider"—the fleet messenger who sped across the continent from St. Joe to Sacramento, carrying letters nineteen hundred miles in eight days! Think of that for perishable horse and human flesh and blood to do! The pony-rider was usually a little bit of a man, brimful of spirit and endurance. No matter what time of the day or night his watch came on, and no matter whether it was winter or summer, raining, snowing, hailing, or sleeting, or whether his "beat" was a level straight road or a crazy trail over mountain crags and precipices, or whether it led through peaceful regions or regions that swarmed with hostile Indians, he must be always ready to leap into the saddle and be off like the wind! There was no idling-time for a pony-rider on duty. He rode fifty miles without stopping, by daylight, moonlight, starlight, or through the blackness of darkness—just as it happened. He rode a splendid horse that was born for a racer and fed and lodged like a gentleman; kept him at his utmost speed for ten miles, and then, as he came crashing up to the station where stood two men holding fast a fresh, impatient steed, the transfer of rider and mail-bag was made in the twinkling of an eye, and away flew the eager pair and were out of sight before the spectator could get hardly the ghost of a look. Both rider and horse went "flying light." The rider's dress was thin, and fitted close; he wore a "round-about," and a skull-cap, and tucked his pantaloons into his boot-tops like a race-rider. He carried no arms—he carried nothing that was not absolutely necessary, for even the postage on his literary freight was worth *five dollars a letter.* He got but little frivolous correspondence to carry—his bag had business letters in it, mostly. His horse was stripped of all unnecessary weight, too. He wore a little wafer of a racing-saddle, and no visible blanket. He wore light shoes, or none at all. The little flat mail-pockets strapped under the rider's thighs would each hold about the bulk of a child's primer. They held many and many an important business chapter and newspaper letter, but these were written on paper as airy and thin as gold-leaf, nearly, and thus bulk and weight were economized. The stage-coach traveled about a hundred to a hundred and twenty-five miles a day (twenty-four hours), the pony-rider about two hundred and fifty. There were about eighty pony-riders in the saddle all the time, night and day, stretching in a long, scattering procession from Missouri to California, forty flying eastward, and forty toward the west, and among them making four hundred gallant horses earn a stirring livelihood and see a deal of scenery every single day in the year.

We had had a consuming desire, from the beginning, to see a pony-rider, but somehow or other all that passed us and all that met us managed to streak by in the night, and so we heard only a whiz and a hail, and the swift phantom of the desert was gone before we could get our heads out of the windows. But now we were expecting one along every moment, and would see him in broad daylight. Presently the driver exclaims:

"HERE HE COMES!"

Every neck is stretched further, and every eye strained wider. Away across the endless dead level of the prairie a black speck appears against the sky, and it is plain that it moves. Well, I should think so! In a second or two it becomes a horse and

rider, rising and falling, rising and falling—sweeping toward us nearer and nearer—
growing more and more distinct, more and more sharply defined—nearer and still
nearer, and the flutter of the hoofs comes faintly to the ear—another instant a whoop
and a hurrah from our upper deck, a wave of the rider's hand, but no reply, and man
and horse burst past our excited faces, and go winging away like a belated fragment
of a storm!

So sudden is it all, and so like a flash of unreal fancy, that but for the flake of white
foam left quivering and perishing on a mail-sack after the vision had flashed by and
disappeared, we might have doubted whether we had seen any actual horse and man
at all, maybe. . . .

Chapter 21: [The "Washoe Zephyr"]

We were approaching the end of our long journey. It was the morning of the
twentieth day. At noon we would reach Carson City, the capital of Nevada Territory.
We were not glad, but sorry. It had been a fine pleasure trip; we had fed fat on
wonders every day; we were now well accustomed to stage life, and very fond of
it; so the idea of coming to a stand-still and settling down to a humdrum existence
in a village was not agreeable, but on the contrary depressing.

Visibly our new home was a desert, walled in by barren, snow-clad mountains.
There was not a tree in sight. There was no vegetation but the endless sage-brush and
greasewood. All nature was gray with it. We were plowing through great deeps of
powdery alkali dust that rose in thick clouds and floated across the plain like smoke
from a burning house. We were coated with it like millers; so were the coach, the
mules, the mail-bags, the driver—we and the sage-brush and the other scenery were
all one monotonous color. Long trains of freight wagons in the distance enveloped
in ascending masses of dust suggested pictures of prairies on fire. These teams and their
masters were the only life we saw. Otherwise we moved in the midst of solitude,
silence and desolation. Every twenty steps we passed the skeleton of some dead beast
of burthen, with its dust-coated skin stretched tightly over its empty ribs. Frequently
a solemn raven sat upon the skull or the hips and contemplated the passing coach with
meditative serenity.

By and by Carson City was pointed out to us. It nestled in the edge of a great
plain and was a sufficient number of miles away to look like an assemblage of mere
white spots in the shadow of a grim range of mountains overlooking it, whose
summits seemed lifted clear out of companionship and consciousness of earthly
things.

We arrived, disembarked, and the stage went on. It was a "wooden" town; its
population two thousand souls. The main street consisted of four or five blocks of
little white frame stores which were too high to sit down on, but not too high for
various other purposes; in fact, hardly high enough. They were packed close together,
side by side, as if room were scarce in that mighty plain. The sidewalk was of boards
that were more or less loose and inclined to rattle when walked upon. In the middle
of the town, opposite the stores, was the "plaza" which is native to all towns beyond
the Rocky Mountains—a large, unfenced, level vacancy, with a liberty pole in it, and
very useful as a place for public auctions, horse trades, and mass meetings, and likewise
for teamsters to camp in. Two other sides of the plaza were faced by stores, offices
and stables. The rest of Carson City was pretty scattering.

We were introduced to several citizens, at the stage-office and on the way up to the Governor's from the hotel—among others, to a Mr. Harris, who was on horseback; he began to say something, but interrupted himself with the remark:

"I'll have to get you to excuse me a minute; yonder is the witness that swore I helped to rob the California coach—a piece of impertinent intermeddling, sir, for I am not even acquainted with the man."

Then he rode over and began to rebuke the stranger with a six-shooter, and the stranger began to explain with another. When the pistols were emptied, the stranger resumed his work (mending a whiplash), and Mr. Harris rode by with a polite nod, homeward bound, with a bullet through one of his lungs, and several in his hips; and from them issued little rivulets of blood that coursed down the horse's sides and made the animal look quite picturesque. I never saw Harris shoot a man after that but it recalled to mind that first day in Carson.

This was all we saw that day, for it was two o'clock, now, and according to custom the daily "Washoe Zephyr" set in; a soaring dust-drift about the size of the United States set up edgewise came with it, and the capital of Nevada Territory disappeared from view. Still, there were sights to be seen which were not wholly uninteresting to new comers; for the vast dust cloud was thickly freckled with things strange to the upper air—things living and dead, that flitted hither and thither, going and coming, appearing and disappearing among the rolling billows of dust—hats, chickens and parasols sailing in the remote heavens; blankets, tin signs, sage-brush and shingles a shade lower; door-mats and buffalo robes lower still; shovels and coal scuttles on the next grade; glass doors, cats and little children on the next; disrupted lumber yards, light buggies and wheelbarrows on the next; and down only thirty or forty feet above ground was a scurrying storm of emigrating roofs and vacant lots.

It was something to see that much. I could have seen more, if I could have kept the dust out of my eyes.

But seriously a Washoe wind is by no means a trifling matter. It blows flimsy houses down, lifts shingle roofs occasionally, rolls up tin ones like sheet music, now and then blows a stage coach over and spills the passengers; and tradition says the reason there are so many bald people there, is, that the wind blows the hair off their heads while they are looking skyward after their hats. Carson streets seldom look inactive on Summer afternoons, because there are so many citizens skipping around their escaping hats, like chambermaids trying to head off a spider.

The "Washoe Zephyr" (Washoe is a pet nickname for Nevada) is a peculiarly Scriptural wind, in that no man knoweth "whence it cometh." That is to say, where it *originates*. It comes right over the mountains from the West, but when one crosses the ridge he does not find any of it on the other side! It probably is manufactured on the mountain-top for the occasion, and starts from there. It is a pretty regular wind, in the summer time. Its office hours are from two in the afternoon till two the next morning; and anybody venturing abroad during those twelve hours needs to allow for the wind or he will bring up a mile or two to leeward of the point he is aiming at. And yet the first complaint a Washoe visitor to San Francisco makes, is that the sea winds blow so, there! There is a good deal of human nature in that.

We found the state palace of the Governor of Nevada Territory to consist of a white frame one-story house with two small rooms in it and a stanchion supported shed in front—for grandeur—it compelled the respect of the citizen and inspired the Indians with awe. The newly arrived Chief and Associate Justices of the Territory, and other machinery of the government, were domiciled with less splendor. They were boarding around privately, and had their offices in their bedrooms.

The Secretary and I took quarters in the "ranch" of a worthy French lady by the name of Bridget O'Flannigan, a camp follower of his Excellency the Governor. She had known him in his prosperity as commander-in-chief of the Metropolitan Police of New York, and she would not desert him in his adversity as Governor of Nevada. Our room was on the lower floor, facing the plaza, and when we had got our bed, a small table, two chairs, the government fire-proof safe, and the Unabridged Dictionary into it, there was still room enough left for a visitor—may be two, but not without straining the walls. But the walls could stand it—at least the partitions could, for they consisted simply of one thickness of white "cotton domestic" stretched from corner to corner of the room. This was the rule in Carson—any other kind of partition was the rare exception. And if you stood in a dark room and your neighbors in the next had lights, the shadows on your canvas told queer secrets sometimes! Very often these partitions were made of old flour sacks basted together; and then the difference between the common herd and the aristocracy was, that the common herd had unornamented sacks, while the walls of the aristocrat were overpowering with rudimental fresco—*i.e.,* red and blue mill brands on the flour sacks. Occasionally, also, the better classes embellished their canvas by pasting pictures from *Harper's Weekly* on them. In many cases, too, the wealthy and the cultured rose to spittoons and other evidences of a sumptuous and luxurious taste.[5] We had a carpet and a genuine queen's-ware washbowl. Consequently we were hated without reserve by the other tenants of the O'Flannigan "ranch." When we added a painted oil-cloth window curtain, we simply took our lives into our own hands. To prevent bloodshed I removed up stairs and took up quarters with the untitled plebeians in one of the fourteen white pine cot-bedsteads that stood in two long ranks in the one sole room of which the second story consisted.

It was a jolly company, the fourteen. They were principally voluntary camp-followers of the Governor, who had joined his retinue by their own election at New York and San Francisco and came along, feeling that in the scuffle for little territorial crumbs and offices they could not make their condition more precarious than it was, and might reasonably expect to make it better. They were popularly known as the "Irish Brigade," though there were only four or five Irishmen among all the Governor's retainers. His good-natured Excellency was much annoyed at the gossip his henchmen created—especially when there arose a rumor that they were paid assassins of his, brought along to quietly reduce the democratic vote when desirable!

Mrs. O'Flannigan was boarding and lodging them at ten dollars a week apiece, and they were cheerfully giving their notes for it. They were perfectly satisfied, but Bridget presently found that notes that could not be discounted were but a feeble constitution for a Carson boarding-house. So she began to harry the Governor to find

---

[5] Twain's note: "Washoe people take a joke so hard that I must explain that the above description was only the rule; there were many honorable exceptions in Carson—plastered ceilings and houses that had considerable furniture in them."

employment for the "Brigade." Her importunities and theirs together drove him to a gentle desperation at last, and he finally summoned the Brigade to the presence. Then, said he:

"Gentlemen, I have planned a lucrative and useful service for you—a service which will provide you with recreation amid noble landscapes, and afford you never ceasing opportunities for enriching your minds by observation and study. I want you to survey a railroad from Carson City westward to a certain point! When the legislature meets I will have the necessary bill passed and the remuneration arranged."

"What, a railroad over the Sierra Nevada Mountains?"

"Well, then, survey it eastward to a certain point!"

He converted them into surveyors, chain-bearers and so on, and turned them loose in the desert. It was "recreation" with a vengeance! Recreation on foot, lugging chains through sand and sage-brush, under a sultry sun and among cattle bones, cayotes and tarantulas. "Romantic adventure" could go no further. They surveyed very slowly, very deliberately, very carefully. They returned every night during the first week, dusty, footsore, tired, and hungry, but very jolly. They brought in great store of prodigious hairy spiders—tarantulas—and imprisoned them in covered tumblers up stairs in the "ranch." After the first week, they had to camp on the field, for they were getting well eastward. They made a good many inquiries as to the location of that indefinite "certain point," but got no information. At last, to a peculiarly urgent inquiry of "How far eastward?" Governor Nye telegraphed back:

"To the Atlantic Ocean, blast you!—and then bridge it and go on!"

This brought back the dusty toilers, who sent in a report and ceased from their labors. The Governor was always comfortable about it; he said Mrs. O'Flannigan would hold him for the Brigade's board anyhow, and he intended to get what entertainment he could out of the boys; he said, with his old-time pleasant twinkle, that he meant to survey them into Utah and then telegraph Brigham to hang them for trespass!

The surveyors brought back more tarantulas with them, and so we had quite a menagerie arranged along the shelves of the room. Some of these spiders could straddle over a common saucer with their hairy, muscular legs, and when their feelings were hurt, or their dignity offended, they were the wickedest-looking desperadoes the animal world can furnish. If their glass prison-houses were touched ever so lightly they were up and spoiling for a fight in a minute. Starchy?—proud? Indeed, they would take up a straw and pick their teeth like a member of Congress. There was as usual a furious "zephyr" blowing the first night of the brigade's return, and about midnight the roof of an adjoining stable blew off, and a corner of it came crashing through the side of our ranch. There was a simultaneous awakening, and a tumultuous muster of the brigade in the dark, and a general tumbling and sprawling over each other in the narrow aisle between the bed-rows. In the midst of the turmoil, Bob H—— sprung up out of a sound sleep, and knocked down a shelf with his head. Instantly he shouted:

"Turn out, boys—the tarantulas is loose!"

No warning ever sounded so dreadful. Nobody tried, any longer, to leave the room, lest he might step on a tarantula. Every man groped for a trunk or a bed, and jumped on it. Then followed the strangest silence—a silence of grisly suspense it was, too—waiting, expectancy, fear. It was as dark as pitch, and one had to imagine the spectacle of those fourteen scant-clad men roosting gingerly on trunks and beds, for not a thing could be seen. Then came occasional little interruptions of the silence, and one could recognize a man and tell his locality by his voice, or locate any other sound a sufferer made by his gropings or changes of position. The occasional voices were not given to much speaking—you simply heard a gentle ejaculation of "Ow!" followed by a solid thump, and you knew the gentleman had felt a hairy blanket or something touch his bare skin and had skipped from a bed to the floor. Another silence. Presently you would hear a gasping voice say:

"Su-su-something's crawling up the back of my neck!"

Every now and then you could hear a little subdued scramble and a sorrowful "O Lord!" and then you knew that somebody was getting away from something he took for a tarantula, and not losing any time about it, either. Directly a voice in the corner rang out wild and clear:

"I've got him! I've got him!" [Pause, and probable change of circumstances.] "No, he's got me! Oh, ain't they *never* going to fetch a lantern!"

The lantern came at that moment, in the hands of Mrs. O'Flannigan, whose anxiety to know the amount of damage done by the assaulting roof had not prevented her waiting a judicious interval, after getting out of bed and lighting up, to see if the wind was done, now, up stairs, or had a larger contract.

The landscape presented when the lantern flashed into the room was picturesque, and might have been funny to some people, but was not to us. Although we were perched so strangely upon boxes, trunks and beds, and so strangely attired, too, we were too earnestly distressed and too genuinely miserable to see any fun about it, and there was not the semblance of a smile anywhere visible. I know I am not capable of suffering more than I did during those few minutes of suspense in the dark, surrounded by those creeping, bloody-minded tarantulas. I had skipped from bed to bed and from box to box in a cold agony, and every time I touched anything that was furzy I fancied I felt the fangs. I had rather go to war than live that episode over again. Nobody was hurt. The man who thought a tarantula had "got him" was mistaken—only a crack in a box had caught his finger. Not one of those escaped tarantulas was ever seen again. There were ten or twelve of them. We took candles and hunted the place high and low for them, but with no success. Did we go back to bed then? We did nothing of the kind. Money could not have persuaded us to do it. We sat up the rest of the night playing cribbage and keeping a sharp lookout for the enemy.

Chapter 22: [Lake Tahoe]

It was the end of August, and the skies were cloudless and the weather superb. In two or three weeks I had grown wonderfully fascinated with the curious new country, and concluded to put off my return to "the States" awhile. I had grown well accustomed to wearing a damaged slouch hat, blue woolen shirt, and pants crammed into boot-tops, and gloried in the absence of coat, vest and braces. I felt rowdyish and "bully," (as the historian Josephus phrases it, in his fine chapter upon the destruction of the Temple). It seemed to me that nothing could be so fine and so romantic. I had become an officer of the government, but that was for mere sublimity. The office was an unique sinecure. I had nothing to do and no salary. I was private Secretary to his majesty the Secretary and there was not yet writing enough for two of us. So Johnny K—— and I devoted our time to amusement. He was the young son of an Ohio nabob and was out there for recreation. He got it. We had heard a world of talk about the marvellous beauty of Lake Tahoe, and finally curiosity drove us thither to see it. Three or four members of the Brigade had been there and located some timber lands on its shores and stored up a quantity of provisions in their camp. We strapped a couple of blankets on our shoulders and took an axe apiece and started—for we intended to take up a wood ranch or so ourselves and become wealthy. We were on foot. The reader will find it advantageous to go horseback. We were told that the distance was eleven miles. We tramped a long time on level ground, and then toiled laboriously up a mountain about a thousand miles high and looked over. No lake there. We descended on the other side, crossed the valley and toiled up another mountain three or four thousand miles high, apparently, and looked over again. No lake yet. We sat down tired and perspiring, and hired a couple of Chinamen to curse those people who had beguiled us. Thus refreshed, we presently resumed the march with renewed vigor and determination. We plodded on, two or three hours longer, and at last the Lake burst upon us—a noble sheet of blue water lifted six thousand three hundred feet above the level of the sea, and walled in by a rim of snow-clad mountain peaks that towered aloft full three thousand feet higher still! It was a vast oval, and one would have to use up eighty or a hundred good miles in traveling around it. As it lay there with the shadows of the mountains brilliantly photographed upon its still surface I thought it must surely be the fairest picture the whole earth affords.

We found the small skiff belonging to the Brigade boys, and without loss of time set out across a deep bend of the lake toward the landmarks that signified the locality of the camp. I got Johnny to row—not because I mind exertion myself, but because it makes me sick to ride backwards when I am at work. But I steered. A three-mile pull brought us to the camp just as the night fell, and we stepped ashore very tired and wolfishly hungry. In a "cache" among the rocks we found the provisions and the cooking utensils, and then, all fatigued as I was, I sat down on a boulder and superintended while Johnny gathered wood and cooked supper. Many a man who had gone through what I had, would have wanted to rest.

It was a delicious supper—hot bread, fried bacon, and black coffee. It was a delicious solitude we were in, too. Three miles away was a saw-mill and some workmen, but there were not fifteen other human beings throughout the wide circumference of the lake. As the darkness closed down and the stars came out and spangled the great mirror with jewels, we smoked meditatively in the solemn hush and forgot our troubles and our pains. In due time we spread our blankets in the warm sand between two large boulders and soon fell asleep, careless of the procession of ants that passed in through rents in our clothing and explored our persons. Nothing could disturb the sleep that fettered us, for it had been fairly earned, and if our consciences had any sins on them they had to adjourn court for that night, any way. The wind rose just as we were losing consciousness, and we were lulled to sleep by the beating of the surf upon the shore.

It is always very cold on that lake shore in the night, but we had plenty of blankets and were warm enough. We never moved a muscle all night, but waked at early dawn in the original positions, and got up at once, thoroughly refreshed, free from soreness, and brim full of friskiness. There is no end of wholesome medicine in such an experience. That morning we could have whipped ten such people as we were the day before—sick ones at any rate. But the world is slow, and people will go to "water cures" and "movement cures" and to foreign lands for health. Three months of camp life on Lake Tahoe would restore an Egyptian mummy to his pristine vigor, and give him an appetite like an alligator. I do not mean the oldest and driest mummies, of course, but the fresher ones. The air up there in the clouds is very pure and fine, bracing and delicious. And why shouldn't it be?—it is the same the angels breathe. I think that hardly any amount of fatigue can be gathered together that a man cannot sleep off in one night on the sand by its side. Not under a roof, but under the sky; it seldom or never rains there in the summer time. I know a man who went there to die. But he made a failure of it. He was a skeleton when he came, and could barely stand. He had no appetite, and did nothing but read tracts and reflect on the future. Three months later he was sleeping out of doors regularly, eating all he could hold, three times a day, and chasing game over mountains three thousand feet high for recreation. And he was a skeleton no longer, but weighed part of a ton. This is no fancy sketch, but the truth. His disease was consumption. I confidently commend his experience to other skeletons.

I superintended again, and as soon as we had eaten breakfast we got in the boat and skirted along the lake shore about three miles and disembarked. We liked the appearance of the place, and so we claimed some three hundred acres of it and stuck our "notices" on a tree. It was yellow pine timber land—a dense forest of trees a hundred feet high and from one to five feet through at the butt. It was necessary to fence our property or we could not hold it. That is to say, it was necessary to cut down trees here and there and make them fall in such a way as to form a sort of enclosure (with pretty wide gaps in it). We cut down three trees apiece, and found it such heart-breaking work that we decided to "rest our case" on those; if they held the property, well and good; if they didn't, let the property spill out through the gaps and go; it was no use to work ourselves to death merely to save a few acres of land. Next day we came back to build a house—for a house was also necessary, in order to hold the property. We decided to build a substantial log-house and excite the envy of the Brigade boys; but by the time we had cut and trimmed the first log it seemed unnecessary to be so elaborate, and so we concluded to build it of saplings. However, two saplings, duly cut and trimmed, compelled recognition of the fact that a still modester architecture would satisfy the law, and so we concluded to build a "brush" house. We devoted the next day to this work, but we did so much "sitting around" and discussing, that by the middle of the afternoon we had achieved only a half-way sort of affair which one of us had to watch while the other cut brush, lest if both turned our backs we might not be able to find it again, it had such a strong family resemblance to the surrounding vegetation. But we were satisfied with it.

We were land owners now, duly seized and possessed, and within the protection of the law. Therefore we decided to take up our residence on our own domain and enjoy that large sense of independence which only such an experience can bring. Late the next afternoon, after a good long rest, we sailed away from the Brigade camp with all the provisions and cooking utensils we could carry off—borrow is the more accurate word—and just as the night was falling we beached the boat at our own landing.

Chapter 23: [A Bewildering Richness]

If there is any life that is happier than the life we led on our timber ranch for the next two or three weeks, it must be a sort of life which I have not read of in books or experienced in person. We did not see a human being but ourselves during the time, or hear any sounds but those that were made by the wind and the waves, the sighing of the pines, and now and then the far-off thunder of an avalanche. The forest about us was dense and cool, the sky above us was cloudless and brilliant with sunshine, the broad lake before us was glassy and clear, or rippled and breezy, or black and storm-tossed, according to Nature's mood; and its circling border of mountain domes, clothed with forests, scarred with land-slides, cloven by cañons and valleys, and helmeted with glittering snow, fitly framed and finished the noble picture. The view was always fascinating, bewitching, entrancing. The eye was never tired of gazing, night or day, in calm or storm; it suffered but one grief, and that was that it could not look always, but must close sometimes in sleep.

We slept in the sand close to the water's edge, between two protecting boulders, which took care of the stormy night-winds for us. We never took any paregoric to make us sleep. At the first break of dawn we were always up and running foot-races to tone down excess of physical vigor and exuberance of spirits. That is, Johnny was —but I held his hat. While smoking the pipe of peace after breakfast we watched the sentinel peaks put on the glory of the sun, and followed the conquering light as it swept down among the shadows, and set the captive crags and forests free. We watched the tinted pictures grow and brighten upon the water till every little detail of forest, precipice and pinnacle was wrought in and finished, and the miracle of the enchanter complete. Then to "business."

That is, drifting around in the boat. We were on the north shore. There, the rocks on the bottom are sometimes gray, sometimes white. This gives the marvelous transparency of the water a fuller advantage than it has elsewhere on the lake. We usually pushed out a hundred yards or so from shore, and then lay down on the thwarts, in the sun, and let the boat drift by the hour whither it would. We seldom talked. It interrupted the Sabbath stillness, and marred the dreams the luxurious rest and indolence brought. The shore all along was indented with deep, curved bays and coves, bordered by narrow sand-beaches; and where the sand ended, the steep mountain-sides rose right up aloft into space—rose up like a vast wall a little out of the perpendicular, and thickly wooded with tall pines.

So singularly clear was the water, that where it was only twenty or thirty feet deep the bottom was so perfectly distinct that the boat seemed floating in the air! Yes, where it was even *eighty* feet deep. Every little pebble was distinct, every speckled trout, every hand's-breadth of sand. Often, as we lay on our faces, a granite boulder, as large as a village church, would start out of the bottom apparently, and seem climbing up rapidly to the surface, till presently it threatened to touch our faces, and we could not resist the impulse to seize an oar and avert the danger. But the boat would float on, and the boulder descend again, and then we could see that when we had been exactly above it, it must still have been twenty or thirty feet below the surface. Down through the transparency of these great depths, the water was not *merely* transparent, but dazzlingly, brilliantly so. All objects seen through it had a bright, strong vividness, not only of outline, but of every minute detail, which they would not have had when seen simply through the same depth of atmosphere. So empty and airy did all spaces seem below us, and so strong was the sense of floating high aloft in mid-nothingness, that we called these boat-excursions "balloon-voyages."

We fished a good deal, but we did not average one fish a week. We could see trout by the thousand winging about in the emptiness under us, or sleeping in shoals on the bottom, but they would not bite—they could see the line too plainly, perhaps. We frequently selected the trout we wanted, and rested the bait patiently and persistently on the end of his nose at a depth of eighty feet, but he would only shake it off with an annoyed manner, and shift his position.

We bathed occasionally, but the water was rather chilly, for all it looked so sunny. Sometimes we rowed out to the "blue water," a mile or two from shore. It was as dead blue as indigo there, because of the immense depth. By official measurement the lake in its centre is one thousand five hundred and twenty-five feet deep!

Sometimes, on lazy afternoons, we lolled on the sand in camp, and smoked pipes and read some old well-worn novels. At night, by the camp-fire, we played euchre and seven-up to strengthen the mind—and played them with cards so greasy and defaced that only a whole summer's acquaintance with them could enable the student to tell the ace of clubs from the jack of diamonds.

We never slept in our "house." It never recurred to us, for one thing; and besides, it was built to hold the ground, and that was enough. We did not wish to strain it.

By and by our provisions began to run short, and we went back to the old camp and laid in a new supply. We were gone all day, and reached home again about night-fall, pretty tired and hungry. While Johnny was carrying the main bulk of the provisions up to our "house" for future use, I took the loaf of bread, some slices of bacon, and the coffee-pot, ashore, set them down by a tree, lit a fire, and went back to the boat to get the frying-pan. While I was at this, I heard a shout from Johnny, and looking up I saw that my fire was galloping all over the premises!

Johnny was on the other side of it. He had to run through the flames to get to the lake shore, and then we stood helpless and watched the devastation.

The ground was deeply carpeted with dry pine-needles, and the fire touched them off as if they were gunpowder. It was wonderful to see with what fierce speed the tall sheet of flame traveled! My coffee-pot was gone, and everything with it. In a minute and a half the fire seized upon a dense growth of dry manzanita chapparal six or eight feet high, and then the roaring and popping and crackling was something terrific. We were driven to the boat by the intense heat, and there we remained, spell-bound.

Within half an hour all before us was a tossing, blinding tempest of flame! It went surging up adjacent ridges—surmounted them and disappeared in the cañons beyond—burst into view upon higher and farther ridges, presently—shed a grander illumination abroad, and dove again—flamed out again, directly, higher and still higher up the mountain-side—threw out skirmishing parties of fire here and there, and sent them trailing their crimson spirals away among remote ramparts and ribs and gorges, till as far as the eye could reach the lofty mountain-fronts were webbed as it were with a tangled network of red lava streams. Away across the water the crags and domes were lit with a ruddy glare, and the firmament above was a reflected hell!

Every feature of the spectacle was repeated in the glowing mirror of the lake! Both pictures were sublime, both were beautiful; but that in the lake had a bewildering richness about it that enchanted the eye and held it with the stronger fascination.

We sat absorbed and motionless through four long hours. We never thought of supper, and never felt fatigue. But at eleven o'clock the conflagration had traveled beyond our range of vision, and then darkness stole down upon the landscape again.

Hunger asserted itself now, but there was nothing to eat. The provisions were all cooked, no doubt, but we did not go to see. We were homeless wanderers again, without any property. Our fence was gone, our house burned down; no insurance. Our pine forest was well scorched, the dead trees all burned up, and our broad acres of manzanita swept away. Our blankets were on our usual sand-bed, however, and so we lay down and went to sleep. The next morning we started back to the old camp, but while out a long way from shore, so great a storm came up that we dared not try to land. So I baled out the seas we shipped, and Johnny pulled heavily through the billows till we had reached a point three or four miles beyond the camp. The storm was increasing, and it became evident that it was better to take the hazard of beaching the boat than go down in a hundred fathoms of water; so we ran in, with tall white-caps following, and I sat down in the stern-sheets and pointed her head-on to the shore. The instant the bow struck, a wave came over the stern that washed crew and cargo ashore, and saved a deal of trouble. We shivered in the lee of a boulder all the rest of the day, and froze all the night through. In the morning the tempest had gone down, and we paddled down to the camp without any unnecessary delay. We were so starved that we ate up the rest of the Brigade's provisions, and then set out to Carson to tell them about it and ask their forgiveness. It was accorded, upon payment of damages.

We made many trips to the lake after that, and had many a hair-breadth escape and blood-curdling adventure which will never be recorded in any history.

Chapter 24: [A Genuine Mexican Plug]

I resolved to have a horse to ride. I had never seen such wild, free, magnificent horsemanship outside of a circus as these picturesquely-clad Mexicans, Californians and Mexicanized Americans displayed in Carson streets every day. How they rode! Leaning just gently forward out of the perpendicular, easy and nonchalant, with broad slouch-hat brim blown square up in front, and long *riata* swinging above the head, they swept through the town like the wind! The next minute they were only a sailing puff of dust on the far desert. If they trotted, they sat up gallantly and gracefully, and seemed part of the horse; did not go jiggering up and down after the silly Miss-Nancy fashion of the riding-schools. I had quickly learned to tell a horse from a cow, and was full of anxiety to learn more. I was resolved to buy a horse.

While the thought was rankling in my mind, the auctioneer came skurrying through the plaza on a black beast that had as many humps and corners on him as a dromedary, and was necessarily uncomely; but he was "going, going, at twenty-two—horse, saddle and bridle at twenty-two dollars, gentlemen!" and I could hardly resist.

A man whom I did not know (he turned out to be the auctioneer's brother) noticed the wistful look in my eye, and observed that that was a very remarkable horse to be going at such a price; and added that the saddle alone was worth the money. It was a Spanish saddle, with ponderous *tapidaros*,[6] and furnished with the ungainly

---

[6] Leather stirrup covers.

sole-leather covering with the unspellable name. I said I had half a notion to bid. Then this keen-eyed person appeared to me to be "taking my measure"; but I dismissed the suspicion when he spoke, for his manner was full of guileless candor and truthfulness. Said he:

"I know that horse—know him well. You are a stranger, I take it, and so you might think he was an American horse, maybe, but I assure you he is not. He is nothing of the kind; but—excuse my speaking in a low voice, other people being near—he is, without the shadow of a doubt, a Genuine Mexican Plug!"

I did not know what a Genuine Mexican Plug was, but there was something about this man's way of saying it, that made me swear inwardly that I would own a Genuine Mexican Plug, or die.

"Has he any other—er—advantages?" I inquired, suppressing what eagerness I could.

He hooked his forefinger in the pocket of my army-shirt, led me to one side, and breathed in my ear impressively these words:

"He can out-buck anything in America!"

"Going, going, going—at *twent—ty*-four dollars and a half, gen——"

"Twenty-seven!" I shouted, in a frenzy.

"And sold!" said the auctioneer, and passed over the Genuine Mexican Plug to me.

I could scarcely contain my exultation. I paid the money, and put the animal in a neighboring livery-stable to dine and rest himself.

In the afternoon I brought the creature into the plaza, and certain citizens held him by the head, and others by the tail, while I mounted him. As soon as they let go, he placed all his feet in a bunch together, lowered his back, and then suddenly arched it upward, and shot me straight into the air a matter of three or four feet! I came as straight down again, lit in the saddle, went instantly up again, came down almost on the high pommel, shot up again, and came down on the horse's neck—all in the space of three or four seconds. Then he rose and stood almost straight up on his hind feet, and I, clasping his lean neck desperately, slid back into the saddle, and held on. He came down, and immediately hoisted his heels into the air, delivering a vicious kick at the sky, and stood on his forefeet. And then down he came once more, and began the original exercise of shooting me straight up again. The third time I went up I heard a stranger say:

"Oh, *don't* he buck, though!"

While I was up, somebody struck the horse a sounding thwack with a leathern strap, and when I arrived again the Genuine Mexican Plug was not there. A Californian youth chased him up and caught him, and asked if he might have a ride. I granted him that luxury. He mounted the Genuine, got lifted into the air once, but sent his spurs home as he descended, and the horse darted away like a telegram. He soared over three fences like a bird, and disappeared down the road toward the Washoe Valley.

I sat down on a stone, with a sigh, and by a natural impulse one of my hands sought my forehead, and the other the base of my stomach. I believe I never appreciated, till then, the poverty of the human machinery—for I still needed a hand or two to place elsewhere. Pen cannot describe how I was jolted up. Imagination cannot conceive how disjointed I was—how internally, externally and universally I was unsettled, mixed up and ruptured. There was a sympathetic crowd around me, though.

One elderly-looking comforter said:

"Stranger, you've been taken in. Everybody in this camp knows that horse. Any child, any Injun, could have told you that he'd buck; he is the very worst devil to buck on the continent of America. You hear *me*. I'm Curry. *Old* Curry. Old *Abe* Curry. And moreover, he is a simon-pure, out-and-out, genuine d—d Mexican plug, and an uncommon mean one at that, too. Why, you turnip, if you had laid low and kept dark, there's chances to buy an *American* horse for mighty little more than you paid for that bloody old foreign relic."

I gave no sign; but I made up my mind that if the auctioneer's brother's funeral took place while I was in the Territory I would postpone all other recreations and attend it.

After a gallop of sixteen miles the Californian youth and the Genuine Mexican Plug came tearing into town again, shedding foam-lakes like the spume-spray that drives before a typhoon, and, with the final skip over a wheelbarrow and a Chinaman, cast anchor in front of the "ranch."

Such panting and blowing! Such spreading and contracting of the red equine nostrils, and glaring of the wild equine eye! But was the imperial beast subjugated? Indeed he was not. His lordship the Speaker of the House thought he was, and mounted him to go down to the Capitol; but the first dash the creature made was over a pile of telegraph poles half as high as a church; and his time to the Capitol —one mile and three quarters—remains unbeaten to this day. But then he took an advantage—he left out the mile, and only did the three quarters. That is to say, he made a straight cut across lots, preferring fences and ditches to a crooked road; and when the Speaker got to the Capitol he said he had been in the air so much he felt as if he had made the trip on a comet.

In the evening the Speaker came home afoot for exercise, and got the Genuine towed back behind a quartz wagon. The next day I loaned the animal to the Clerk of the House to go down to the Dana silver mine, six miles, and *he* walked back for exercise, and got the horse towed. Everybody I loaned him to always walked back; they never could get enough exercise any other way. Still, I continued to loan him to anybody who was willing to borrow him, my idea being to get him crippled, and throw him on the borrower's hands, or killed, and make the borrower pay for him. But somehow nothing ever happened to him. He took chances that no other horse ever took and survived, but he always came out safe. It was his daily habit to try experiments that had always before been considered impossible, but he always got through. Sometimes he miscalculated a little, and did not get his rider through intact, but *he* always got through himself. Of course I had tried to sell him; but that was a stretch of simplicity which met with little sympathy. The auctioneer stormed up and down the streets on him for four days, dispersing the populace, interrupting business, and destroying children, and never got a bid—at least never any but the eighteen-dollar one he hired a notoriously substanceless bummer to make. The people only smiled pleasantly, and restrained their desire to buy, if they had any. Then the auctioneer brought in his bill, and I withdrew the horse from the market. We tried to trade him off at private vendue next, offering him at a sacrifice for second-hand tombstones, old iron, temperance tracts—any kind of property. But holders were stiff, and we retired from the market again. I never tried to ride the horse any more. Walking was good enough exercise for a man like me, that had nothing the matter with him except ruptures, internal injuries, and such things. Finally I tried to give him away. But it was a failure. Parties said earthquakes were handy enough on the Pacific coast—they did not wish to own one. As a last resort I offered him to the Governor for the use of the "Brigade." His face lit up eagerly at first, but toned down again, and he said the thing would be too palpable.

Just then the livery stable man brought in his bill for six weeks' keeping—stall-room for the horse, fifteen dollars; hay for the horse, two hundred and fifty! The Genuine Mexican Plug had eaten a ton of the article, and the man said he would have eaten a hundred if he had let him.

I will remark here, in all seriousness, that the regular price of hay during that year and a part of the next was really two hundred and fifty dollars a ton. During a part of the previous year it had sold at five hundred a ton, in gold, and during the winter before that there was such scarcity of the article that in several instances small quantities had brought eight hundred dollars a ton in coin! The consequence might be guessed without my telling it: people turned their stock loose to starve, and before the spring arrived Carson and Eagle valleys were almost literally carpeted with their carcases! Any old settler there will verify these statements.

I managed to pay the livery bill, and that same day I gave the Genuine Mexican Plug to a passing Arkansas emigrant whom fortune delivered into my hand. If this ever meets his eye, he will doubtless remember the donation.

Now whoever has had the luck to ride a real Mexican plug will recognize the animal depicted in this chapter, and hardly consider him exaggerated—but the uninitiated will feel justified in regarding his portrait as a fancy sketch, perhaps.

Chapter 29: ["Bloated Millionaires"]

True knowledge of the nature of silver mining came fast enough. We went out "prospecting" with Mr. Ballou. We climbed the mountain sides, and clambered among sage-brush, rocks and snow till we were ready to drop with exhaustion, but found no silver—nor yet any gold. Day after day we did this. Now and then we came upon holes burrowed a few feet into the declivities and apparently abandoned; and now and then we found one or two listless men still burrowing. But there was no appearance of silver. These holes were the beginnings of tunnels, and the purpose was to drive them hundreds of feet into the mountain, and some day tap the hidden ledge where the silver was. Some day! It seemed far enough away, and very hopeless and dreary. Day after day we toiled, and climbed and searched, and we younger partners grew sicker and still sicker of the promiseless toil. At last we halted under a beetling rampart of rock which projected from the earth high upon the mountain. Mr. Ballou broke off some fragments with a hammer, and examined them long and attentively with a small eye-glass; threw them away and broke off more; said this rock was quartz, and quartz was the sort of rock that contained silver. *Contained* it! I had thought that at least it would be caked on the outside of it like a kind of veneering. He still broke off pieces and critically examined them, now and then wetting the piece with his tongue and applying the glass. At last he exclaimed:

"We've got it!"

We were full of anxiety in a moment. The rock was clean and white, where it was broken, and across it ran a ragged thread of blue. He said that that little thread had silver in it, mixed with base metals, such as lead and antimony, and other rubbish, and that there was a speck or two of gold visible. After a great deal of effort we managed to discern some little fine yellow specks, and judged that a couple of tons of them massed together might make a gold dollar, possibly. We were not jubilant, but Mr. Ballou said there were worse ledges in the world than that. He saved what he called the "richest" piece of the rock, in order to determine its value by the process called the "fire-assay." Then we named the mine "Monarch of the Mountains" (modesty of nomenclature is not a prominent feature in the mines), and Mr. Ballou wrote out and stuck up the following "notice," preserving a copy to be entered upon the books in the mining recorder's office in the town.

"NOTICE."

"We the undersigned claim three claims, of three hundred feet each (and one for discovery), on this silver-bearing quartz lead or lode, extend-north and south from this notice, with all its dips, spurs, and angles, variations and sinuosities, together with fifty feet of ground on either side for working the same."

We put our names to it and tried to feel that our fortunes were made. But when we talked the matter all over with Mr. Ballou, we felt depressed and dubious. He said that this surface quartz was not all there was of our mine; but that the wall or ledge of rock called the "Monarch of the Mountains," extended down hundreds and hundreds of feet into the earth—he illustrated by saying it was like a curb-stone, and maintained a nearly uniform thickness—say twenty feet—away down into the bowels of the earth, and was perfectly distinct from the casing rock on each side of it; and that it kept to itself, and maintained its distinctive character always, no matter how deep it extended into the earth or how far it stretched itself through and across the hills and valleys. He said it might be a mile deep and ten miles long, for all we knew; and that wherever we bored into it above ground or below, we would find gold and silver in it, but no gold or silver in the meaner rock it was cased between. And he said that down in the great depths of the ledge was its richness, and the deeper it went the richer it grew. Therefore, instead of working here on the surface, we must either bore down into the rock with a shaft till we came to where it was rich—say a hundred feet or so—or else we must go down into the valley and bore a long tunnel into the mountain side and tap the ledge far under the earth. To do either was plainly the labor of months; for we could blast and bore only a few feet a day—some five or six. But this was not all. He said that after we got the ore out it must be hauled in wagons to a distant silver-mill, ground up, and the silver extracted by a tedious and costly process. Our fortune seemed a century away!

But we went to work. We decided to sink a shaft. So, for a week we climbed the mountain, laden with picks, drills, gads, crowbars, shovels, cans of blasting powder and coils of fuse and strove with might and main. At first the rock was broken and loose and we dug it up with picks and threw it out with shovels, and the hole progressed very well. But the rock became more compact, presently, and gads and crowbars came into play. But shortly nothing could make an impression but blasting powder. That was the weariest work! One of us held the iron drill in its place and another would strike with an eight-pound sledge—it was like driving nails on a large scale. In the course of an hour or two the drill would reach a depth of two or three feet, making a hole a couple of inches in diameter. We would put in a charge of powder, insert half a yard of fuse, pour in sand and gravel and ram it down, then light the fuse and run. When the explosion came and the rocks and smoke shot into the air, we would go back and find about a bushel of that hard, rebellious quartz jolted out. Nothing more. One week of this satisfied me. I resigned. Clagget and Oliphant followed. Our shaft was only twelve feet deep. We decided that a tunnel was the thing we wanted.

So we went down the mountain side and worked a week; at the end of which time we had blasted a tunnel about deep enough to hide a hogshead in, and judged that about nine hundred feet more of it would reach the ledge. I resigned again, and the other boys only held out one day longer. We decided that a tunnel was not what we wanted. We wanted a ledge that was already "developed." There were none in the camp.

We dropped the "Monarch" for the time being.

Meantime the camp was filling up with people, and there was a constantly growing excitement about our Humboldt mines. We fell victims to the epidemic and strained every nerve to acquire more "feet." We prospected and took up new claims, put "notices" on them and gave them grandiloquent names. We traded some of our "feet" for "feet" in other people's claims. In a little while we owned largely in the "Gray Eagle," the "Columbiana," the "Branch Mint," the "Maria Jane," the "Universe," the "Root-Hog-or-Die," the "Samson and Delilah," the "Treasure Trove," the "Golconda," the "Sultana," the "Boomerang," the "Great Republic," the "Grand Mogul," and fifty other "mines" that had never been molested by a shovel or scratched with a pick. We had not less than thirty thousand "feet" apiece in the "richest mines on earth" as the frenzied cant phrased it—and were in debt to the butcher. We were stark mad with excitement—drunk with happiness—smothered under mountains of prospective wealth—arrogantly compassionate toward the plodding millions who knew not our marvellous canyon—but our credit was not good at the grocer's.

It was the strangest phase of life one can imagine. It was a beggars' revel. There was nothing doing in the district—no mining—no milling—no productive effort— no income—and not enough money in the entire camp to buy a corner lot in an eastern village, hardly; and yet a stranger would have supposed he was walking among bloated millionaires. Prospecting parties swarmed out of town with the first flush of dawn, and swarmed in again at nightfall laden with spoil—rocks. Nothing but rocks. Every man's pockets were full of them; the floor of his cabin was littered with them; they were disposed in labeled rows on his shelves.

Chapter 34: [The Great Landslide Case]

The mountains are very high and steep about Carson, Eagle and Washoe Valleys— very high and very steep, and so when the snow gets to melting off fast in the Spring and the warm surface-earth begins to moisten and soften, the disastrous land-slides commence. The reader cannot know what a land-slide is, unless he has lived in that country and seen the whole side of a mountain taken off some fine morning and deposited down in the valley, leaving a vast, treeless, unsightly scar upon the mountain's front to keep the circumstance fresh in his memory all the years that he may go on living within seventy miles of that place.

General Buncombe was shipped out to Nevada in the invoice of Territorial officers, to be United States Attorney. He considered himself a lawyer of parts, and he very much wanted an opportunity to manifest it—partly for the pure gratification of it and partly because his salary was Territorially meagre (which is a strong expression). Now the older citizens of a new territory look down upon the rest of the world with a calm, benevolent compassion, as long as it keeps out of the way—when it gets in the way they snub it. Sometimes this latter takes the shape of a practical joke.

One morning Dick Hyde rode furiously up to General Buncombe's door in Carson city and rushed into his presence without stopping to tie his horse. He seemed much excited. He told the General that he wanted him to conduct a suit for him and would pay him five hundred dollars if he achieved a victory. And then, with violent gestures and a world of profanity, he poured out his griefs. He said it was pretty well known that for some years he had been farming (or ranching as the more customary term is) in Washoe District, and making a successful thing of it, and furthermore it was known that his ranch was situated just in the edge of the valley, and that Tom Morgan owned a ranch immediately above it on the mountain side. And now the trouble was, that one of those hated and dreaded land-slides had come and slid Morgan's ranch, fences, cabins, cattle, barns and everything down on top of *his* ranch and exactly covered up every single vestige of his property, to a depth of about thirty-eight feet. Morgan was in possession and refused to vacate the premises—said was occupying own cabin and not interfering with anybody else's—and said the cabin was standing on the same dirt and same ranch it had always stood on, and he would like to see anybody make him vacate.

"And when I reminded him," said Hyde, weeping, "that it was on top of my ranch and that he was trespassing, he had the infernal meanness to ask me why didn't I *stay* on my ranch and hold possession when I see him a-coming! Why didn't I *stay* on it, the blathering lunatic—by George, when I heard that racket and looked up that hill it was just like the whole world was a-ripping and a-tearing down that mountain side—splinters, and cord-wood, thunder and lightning, hail and snow, odds and ends of hay stacks, and awful clouds of dust!—trees going end over end in the air, rocks as big as a house jumping 'bout a thousand feet high and busting into ten million pieces, cattle turned inside out and a-coming head on with their tails hanging out between their teeth!—and in the midst of all that wrack and destruction sot that cussed Morgan on his gate-post, a-wondering why I didn't *stay and hold possession!* Laws bless me, I just took one glimpse, General, and lit out'n the county in three jumps exactly.

"But what grinds me is that that Morgan hangs on there and won't move off'n that ranch—says it's his'n and he's going to keep it—likes it better'n he did when it was higher up the hill. Mad! Well, I've been so mad for two days I couldn't find my way to town—been wandering around in the brush in a starving condition—got anything here to drink, General? But I'm here *now,* and I'm a-going to law. You hear *me!*"

Never in all the world, perhaps, were a man's feelings so outraged as were the General's. He said he had never heard of such high-handed conduct in all his life as this Morgan's. And he said there was no use in going to law—Morgan had no shadow of right to remain where he was—nobody in the wide world would uphold him in it, and no lawyer would take his case and no judge listen to it. Hyde said that right there was where he was mistaken—everybody in town sustained Morgan; Hal Brayton, a very smart lawyer, had taken his case; the courts being in vacation, it was to be tried before a referee, and ex-Governor Roop had already been appointed to that office and would open his court in a large public hall near the hotel at two that afternoon.

The General was amazed. He said he had suspected before that the people of that Territory were fools, and now he knew it. But he said rest easy, rest easy and collect the witnesses, for the victory was just as certain as if the conflict were already over. Hyde wiped away his tears and left.

At two in the afternoon referee Roop's Court opened, and Roop appeared throned among his sheriffs, the witnesses, and spectators, and wearing upon his face a solemnity so awe-inspiring that some of his fellow-conspirators had misgivings that maybe he had not comprehended, after all, that this was merely a joke. An unearthly stillness prevailed, for at the slightest noise the judge uttered sternly the command:

"Order in the Court!"

And the sheriffs promptly echoed it. Presently the General elbowed his way through the crowd of spectators, with his arms full of law-books, and on his ears fell an order from the judge which was the first respectful recognition of his high official dignity that had ever saluted them, and it trickled pleasantly through his whole system:

"Way for the United States Attorney!"

The witnesses were called—legislators, high government officers, ranchmen, miners, Indians, Chinamen, negroes. Three fourths of them were called by the defendant Morgan, but no matter, their testimony invariably went in favor of the plaintiff Hyde. Each new witness only added new testimony to the absurdity of a man's claiming to own another man's property because his farm had slid down on top of it. Then the Morgan lawyers made their speeches, and seemed to make singularly weak ones—they did really nothing to help the Morgan cause. And now the General, with exultation in his face, got up and made an impassioned effort; he pounded the table, he banged the law-books, he shouted, and roared, and howled, he quoted from everything and everybody, poetry, sarcasm, statistics, history, pathos, bathos, blasphemy, and wound up with a grand war-whoop for free speech, freedom of the press, free schools, the Glorious Bird of America and the principles of eternal justice! (Applause.)

When the General sat down, he did it with the conviction that if there was anything in good strong testimony, a great speech and believing and admiring countenances all around, Mr. Morgan's case was killed. Ex-Governor Roop leant his head upon his hand for some minutes, thinking, and the still audience waited for his decision. Then he got up and stood erect, with bended head, and thought again. Then he walked the floor with long, deliberate strides, his chin in his hand, and still the audience waited. At last he returned to his throne, seated himself, and began, impressively:

"Gentlemen, I feel the great responsibility that rests upon me this day. This is no ordinary case. On the contrary it is plain that it is the most solemn and awful that ever man was called upon to decide. Gentlemen, I have listened attentively to the evidence, and have perceived that the weight of it, the overwhelming weight of it, is in favor of the plaintiff Hyde. I have listened also to the remarks of counsel, with high interest—and especially will I commend the masterly and irrefutable logic of the distinguished gentleman who represents the plaintiff. But gentlemen, let us beware how we allow mere human testimony, human ingenuity in argument and human ideas of equality, to influence us at a moment so solemn as this. Gentlemen, it ill becomes us, worms as we are, to meddle with the decrees of Heaven. It is plain to me that Heaven, in its inscrutable wisdom, has seen fit to move this defendant's ranch for a purpose. We are but creatures, and we must submit. If Heaven has chosen to favor the defendant Morgan in this marked and wonderful manner; and if Heaven, dissatisfied with the position of the Morgan ranch upon the mountain side, has chosen to remove it to a position more eligible and more advantageous for its owner, it ill becomes us, insects as we are, to question the legality of the act or inquire into the reasons that prompted it. No—Heaven created the ranches and it is Heaven's prerogative to rearrange them, to experiment with them, to shift them around at its pleasure. It is for us to submit, without repining. I warn you that this thing which has happened is a thing with which the sacrilegious hands and brains and tongues of men must not meddle. Gentlemen, it is the verdict of this court that the plaintiff, Richard Hyde, has been deprived of his ranch by the visitation of God! And from this decision there is no appeal."

Buncombe seized his cargo of law-books and plunged out of the court-room frantic with indignation. He pronounced Roop to be a miraculous fool, an inspired idiot. In all good faith he returned at night and remonstrated with Roop upon his extravagant decision, and implored him to walk the floor and think for half an hour, and see if he could not figure out some sort of modification of the verdict. Roop yielded at last and got up to walk. He walked two hours and a half, and at last his face lit up happily and he told Buncombe it had occurred to him that the ranch underneath the new Morgan ranch still belonged to Hyde, that his title to the ground was just as good as it had ever been, and therefore he was of opinion that Hyde had a right to dig it out from under there and—

The General never waited to hear the end of it. He was always an impatient and irascible man, that way. At the end of two months the fact that he had been played upon with a joke had managed to bore itself, like another Hoosac Tunnel,[7] through the solid adamant of his understanding.

Chapter 40: ["It's a Blind Lead"]

I now come to a curious episode—the most curious, I think, that had yet accented my slothful, valueless, heedless career. Out of a hillside toward the upper end of the town, projected a wall of reddish looking quartz-croppings, the exposed comb of a silver-bearing ledge that extended deep down into the earth, of course. It was owned by a company entitled the "Wide West." There was a shaft sixty or seventy feet deep on the under side of the croppings, and everybody was acquainted with the rock that came from it—and tolerably rich rock it was, too, but nothing extraordinary. I will remark here, that although to the inexperienced stranger all the quartz of a particular "district" looks about alike, an old resident of the camp can take a glance at a mixed pile of rock, separate the fragments and tell you which mine each came from, as easily as a confectioner can separate and classify the various kinds and qualities of candy in a mixed heap of the article.

[7] Railroad tunnel in northwestern Massachusetts under construction 1852–1873.

All at once the town was thrown into a state of extraordinary excitement. In mining parlance the Wide West had "struck it rich!" Everybody went to see the new developments, and for some days there was such a crowd of people about the Wide West shaft that a stranger would have supposed there was a mass meeting in session there. No other topic was discussed but the rich strike, and nobody thought or dreamed about anything else. Every man brought away a specimen, ground it up in a hand mortar, washed it out in his horn spoon, and glared speechless upon the marvelous result. It was not hard rock, but black, decomposed stuff which could be crumbled in the hand like a baked potato, and when spread out on a paper exhibited a thick sprinkling of gold and particles of "native" silver. Higbie brought a handful to the cabin, and when he had washed it out his amazement was beyond description. Wide West stock soared skywards. It was said that repeated offers had been made for it at a thousand dollars a foot, and promptly refused. We have all had the "blues" —the mere sky-blues—but mine were indigo, now—because I did not own in the Wide West. The world seemed hollow to me, and existence a grief. I lost my appetite, and ceased to take an interest in anything. Still I had to stay, and listen to other people's rejoicings, because I had no money to get out of the camp with.

The Wide West company put a stop to the carrying away of "specimens," and well they might, for every handful of the ore was worth a sum of some consequence. To show the exceeding value of the ore, I will remark that a sixteen-hundred-pounds parcel of it was sold, just as it lay, at the mouth of the shaft, at *one dollar a pound;* and the man who bought it "packed" it on mules a hundred and fifty or two hundred miles, over the mountains, to San Francisco, satisfied that it would yield at a rate that would richly compensate him for his trouble. The Wide West people also commanded their foreman to refuse any but their own operatives permission to enter the mine at any time or for any purpose. I kept up my "blue" meditations and Higbie kept up a deal of thinking, too, but of a different sort. He puzzled over the "rock," examined it with a glass, inspected it in different lights and from different points of view, and after each experiment delivered himself, in soliloquy, of one and the same unvarying opinion in the same unvarying formula:

"It is *not* Wide West rock!"

He said once or twice that he meant to have a look into the Wide West shaft if he got shot for it. I was wretched, and did not care whether he got a look into it or not. He failed that day, and tried again at night; failed again; got up at dawn and tried, and failed again. Then he lay in ambush in the sage brush hour after hour, waiting for the two or three hands to adjourn to the shade of a boulder for dinner; made a start once, but was premature—one of the men came back for something; tried it again, but when almost at the mouth of the shaft, another of the men rose up from behind the boulder as if to reconnoitre, and he dropped on the ground and lay quiet; presently he crawled on his hands and knees to the mouth of the shaft, gave a quick glance around, then seized the rope and slid down the shaft. He disappeared in the gloom of a "side drift" just as a head appeared in the mouth of the shaft and somebody shouted "Hello!"—which he did not answer. He was not disturbed any more. An hour later he entered the cabin, hot, red, and ready to burst with smothered excitement, and exclaimed in a stage whisper:

"I knew it! We are rich! IT'S A BLIND LEAD!"

I thought the very earth reeled under me. Doubt—conviction—doubt again—

exultation—hope, amazement, belief, unbelief—every emotion imaginable swept in wild procession through my heart and brain, and I could not speak a word. After a moment or two of this mental fury, I shook myself to rights, and said:

"Say it again!"

"It's a blind lead!"

"Cal., let's—let's burn the house—or kill somebody! Let's get out where there's room to hurrah! But what is the use? It is a hundred times too good to be true."

"It's a blind lead, for a million!—hanging wall—foot wall—clay casings—everything complete!" He swung his hat and gave three cheers, and I cast doubt to the winds and chimed in with a will. For I was worth a million dollars, and did not care "whether school kept or not!"

But perhaps I ought to explain. A "blind lead" is a lead or ledge that does not "crop out" above the surface. A miner does not know where to look for such leads, but they are often stumbled upon by accident in the course of driving a tunnel or sinking a shaft. Higbie knew the Wide West rock perfectly well, and the more he had examined the new developments the more he was satisfied that the ore could not have come from the Wide West vein. And so had it occurred to him alone, of all the camp, that there was a blind lead down in the shaft, and that even the Wide West people themselves did not suspect it. He was right. When he went down the shaft, he found that the blind lead held its independent way through the Wide West vein, cutting it diagonally, and that it was enclosed in its own well-defined casing-rocks and clay. Hence it was public property. Both leads being perfectly well defined, it was easy for any miner to see which one belonged to the Wide West and which did not.

We thought it well to have a strong friend, and therefore we brought the foreman of the Wide West to our cabin that night and revealed the great surprise to him. Higbie said:

"We are going to take possession of this blind lead, record it and establish ownership, and then forbid the Wide West company to take out any more of the rock. You cannot help your company in this matter—nobody can help them. I will go into the shaft with you and prove to your entire satisfaction that it is a blind lead. Now we propose to take you in with us, and claim the blind lead in our three names. What do you say?"

What could a man say who had an opportunity to simply stretch forth his hand and take possession of a fortune without risk of any kind and without wronging any one or attaching the least taint of dishonor to his name? He could only say, "Agreed."

The notice was put up that night, and duly spread upon the recorder's books before ten o'clock. We claimed two hundred feet each—six hundred feet in all—the smallest and compactest organization in the district, and the easiest to manage.

No one can be so thoughtless as to suppose that we slept, that night. Higbie and I went to bed at midnight, but it was only to lie broad awake and think, dream, scheme. The floorless, tumble-down cabin was a palace, the ragged gray blankets silk, the furniture rosewood and mahogany. Each new splendor that burst out of my visions of the future whirled me bodily over in bed or jerked me to a sitting posture just as if an electric battery had been applied to me. We shot fragments of conversation back and forth at each other. Once Higbie said:

"When are you going home—to the States?"

"To-morrow!"—with an evolution or two, ending with a sitting position. "Well—no—but next month, at furthest."

"We'll go in the same steamer."

"Agreed."

A pause.

"Steamer of the 10th?"

"Yes. No, the 1st."

"All right."

Another pause.

"Where are you going to live?" said Higbie.

"San Francisco."

"That's me!"

Pause.

"Too high—too much climbing"—from Higbie.

"What is?"

"I was thinking of Russian Hill—building a house up there."

"Too much climbing? Shan't you keep a carriage?"

"Of course. I forgot that."

Pause.

"Cal., what kind of a house are you going to build?"

"I was thinking about that. Three-story and an attic."

"But what *kind?*"

"Well, I don't hardly know. Brick, I suppose."

"Brick—bosh."

"Why? What is your idea?"

"Brown stone front—French plate glass—billiard-room off the dining-room—statuary and paintings—shrubbery and two-acre grass plat—greenhouse—iron dog on the front stoop—gray horses—landau, and a coachman with a bug on his hat!"

"By George!"

A long pause.

"Cal., when are you going to Europe?"

"Well—I hadn't thought of that. When are you?"

"In the Spring."

"Going to be gone all summer?"

"All summer! I shall remain there three years."

"No—but are you in earnest?"

"Indeed I am."

"I will go along too."

"Why of course you will."

"What part of Europe shall you go to?"

"All parts. France, England, Germany—Spain, Italy, Switzerland, Syria, Greece, Palestine, Arabia, Persia, Egypt—all over—everywhere."

"I'm agreed."

"All right."

"Won't it be a swell trip!"

"We'll spend forty or fifty thousand dollars trying to make it one, anyway."

Another long pause.

"Higbie, we owe the butcher six dollars, and he has been threatening to stop our—"

"Hang the butcher!"

"Amen."

And so it went on. By three o'clock we found it was no use, and so we got up and played cribbage and smoked pipes till sunrise. It was my week to cook. I always hated cooking—now, I abhorred it.

The news was all over town. The former excitement was great—this one was greater still. I walked the streets serene and happy. Higbie said the foreman had been offered two hundred thousand dollars for his third of the mine. I said I would like to see myself selling for any such price. My ideas were lofty. My figure was a million. Still, I honestly believe that if I had been offered it, it would have had no other effect than to make me hold off for more.

I found abundant enjoyment in being rich. A man offered me a three-hundred-dollar horse, and wanted to take my simple, unendorsed note for it. That brought the most realizing sense I had yet had that I was actually rich, beyond shadow of doubt. It was followed by numerous other evidences of a similar nature—among which I may mention the fact of the butcher leaving us a double supply of meat and saying nothing about money.

By the laws of the district, the "locators" or claimants of a ledge were obliged to do a fair and reasonable amount of work on their new property within ten days after the date of the location, or the property was forfeited, and anybody could go and seize it that chose. So we determined to go to work the next day. About the middle of the afternoon, as I was coming out of the post office, I met a Mr. Gardiner, who told me that Capt. John Nye was lying dangerously ill at his place (the "Nine-Mile Ranch"), and that he and his wife were not able to give him nearly as much care and attention as his case demanded. I said if he would wait for me a moment, I would go and help in the sick room. I ran to the cabin to tell Higbie. He was not there, but I left a note on the table for him, and a few minutes later I left town in Gardiner's wagon.

Chapter 41: ["We're Ruined—!"]

Captain Nye was very ill indeed, with spasmodic rheumatism. But the old gentleman was himself—which is to say, he was kind-hearted and agreeable when comfortable, but a singularly violent wild-cat when things did not go well. He would be smiling along pleasantly enough, when a sudden spasm of his disease would take him and he would go out of his smile into a perfect fury. He would groan and wail and howl with the anguish, and fill up the odd chinks with the most elaborate profanity that strong convictions and a fine fancy could contrive. With fair opportunity he could swear very well and handle his adjectives with considerable judgment; but when the spasm was on him it was painful to listen to him, he was so awkward. However, I had seen him nurse a sick man himself and put up patiently with the inconveniences of the situation, and consequently I was willing that he should have full license now that his own turn had come. He could not disturb me, with all his raving and ranting, for my mind had work on hand, and it labored on diligently, night and day, whether my hands were idle or employed. I was altering and amending the plans for my house, and thinking over the propriety of having the billiard-room in the attic, instead of on the same floor with the dining-room; also, I was trying to decide between green and blue for the upholstery of the drawing-room, for, although my preference was blue I feared it was a color that would be too easily damaged by dust and sunlight; likewise while I was content to put the coachman in a modest livery, I was uncertain about a footman—I needed one, and was even resolved to have one, but wished he could properly appear and perform his functions out of livery, for I somewhat dreaded so much show; and yet, inasmuch as my late grandfather had had a coachman and such things, but no liveries, I felt rather drawn to beat him;—or beat his ghost, at any rate; I was also systematizing the European trip, and managed to get it all laid out, as to route and length of time to be devoted to it—everything, with one exception— namely, whether to cross the desert from Cairo to Jerusalem per camel, or go by sea to Beirut, and thence down through the country per caravan. Meantime I was writing to the friends at home every day, instructing them concerning all my plans and intentions, and directing them to look up a handsome homestead for my mother and agree upon a price for it against my coming, and also directing them to sell my share of the Tennessee land and tender the proceeds to the widows' and orphans' fund of the typographical union of which I had long been a member in good standing. (This Tennessee land had been in the possession of the family many years, and promised to confer high fortune upon us some day; it still promises it, but in a less violent way.)

When I had been nursing the Captain nine days he was somewhat better, but very feeble. During the afternoon we lifted him into a chair and gave him an alcoholic vapor bath, and then set about putting him on the bed again. We had to be exceedingly careful, for the least jar produced pain. Gardiner had his shoulders and I his legs; in an unfortunate moment I stumbled and the patient fell heavily on the bed in an agony of torture. I never heard a man swear so in my life. He raved like a maniac, and tried to snatch a revolver from the table—but I got it. He ordered me out of the house, and swore a world of oaths that he would kill me wherever he caught me when he got on his feet again. It was simply a passing fury, and meant nothing. I knew he would forget it in an hour, and maybe be sorry for it, too; but it angered me a little, at the moment. So much so, indeed, that I determined to go back to Esmeralda. I thought he was able to get along alone, now, since he was on the war path. I took supper, and as soon as the moon rose, began my nine-mile journey, on foot. Even millionaires needed no horses, in those days, for a mere nine-mile jaunt without baggage.

As I "raised the hill" overlooking the town, it lacked fifteen minutes of twelve. I glanced at the hill over beyond the canyon, and in the bright moonlight saw what appeared to be about half the population of the village massed on and around the Wide West croppings. My heart gave an exulting bound, and I said to myself, "They have made a new strike to-night—and struck it richer than ever, no doubt." I started over there, but gave it up. I said the "strike" would keep, and I had climbed hills enough for one night. I went on down through the town, and as I was passing a little German bakery, a woman ran out and begged me to come in and help her. She said her husband had a fit. I went in, and judged she was right—he appeared to have a hundred of them, compressed into one. Two Germans were there, trying to hold him, and not making much of a success of it. I ran up the street half a block or so and routed out a sleeping doctor, brought him down half dressed, and we four wrestled with the maniac, and doctored, drenched and bled him, for more than an hour, and the poor German woman did the crying. He grew quiet, now, and the doctor and I withdrew and left him to his friends.

It was a little after one o'clock. As I entered the cabin door, tired but jolly, the dingy light of a tallow candle revealed Higbie, sitting by the pine table gazing stupidly at my note, which he held in his fingers, and looking pale, old, and haggard. I halted, and looked at him. He looked at me, stolidly. I said:

"Higbie, what—what is it?"

"We're ruined—we didn't do the work—THE BLIND LEAD'S RELOCATED!"

It was enough. I sat down sick, grieved—broken-hearted, indeed. A minute before, I was rich and brimful of vanity; I was a pauper now, and very meek. We sat still an hour, busy with thought, busy with vain and useless self-upbraidings, busy with "Why *didn't* I do this, and why *didn't* I do that," but neither spoke a word. Then we dropped into mutual explanations, and the mystery was cleared away. It came out that Higbie had depended on me, as I had on him, and as both of us had on the foreman. The folly of it! It was the first time that ever staid and steadfast Higbie had left an important matter to chance or failed to be true to his full share of a responsibility.

But he had never seen my note till this moment, and this moment was the first time he had been in the cabin since the day he had seen me last. He, also, had left a note for me, on that same fatal afternoon—had ridden up on horseback, and looked through the window, and being in a hurry and not seeing me, had tossed the note into the cabin through a broken pane. Here it was, on the floor, where it had remained undisturbed for nine days:

"Don't fail to do the work before the ten days expire. W. has passed through and given me notice. I am to join him at Mono Lake, and we shall go on from there to-night. He says he will find it this time, sure. CAL."

"W." meant Whiteman, of course. That thrice accursed "cement!"

That was the way of it. An old miner, like Higbie, could no more withstand the fascination of a mysterious mining excitement like this "cement" foolishness, than he could refrain from eating when he was famishing. Higbie had been dreaming about the marvelous cement for months; and now, against his better judgment, he had gone off and "taken the chances" on my keeping secure a mine worth a million undiscovered cement veins. They had not been followed this time. His riding out of town in broad daylight was such a commonplace thing to do that it had not attracted any attention. He said they prosecuted their search in the fastnesses of the mountains during nine days, without success; they could not find the cement. Then a ghastly fear came over him that something might have happened to prevent the doing of the necessary work to hold the blind lead (though indeed he thought such a thing hardly possible), and forthwith he started home with all speed. He would have reached Esmeralda in time, but his horse broke down and he had to walk a great part of the distance. And so it happened that as he came into Esmeralda by one road, I entered it by another. His was the superior energy, however, for he went straight to the Wide West, instead of turning aside as I had done—and he arrived there about five or ten minutes too late! The "notice" was already up, the "relocation" of our mine completed beyond recall, and the crowd rapidly dispersing. He learned some facts before he left the ground. The foreman had not been seen about the streets since the night we had located the mine—a telegram had called him to California on a matter of life and death, it was said. At any rate he had done no work and the watchful eyes of the community were taking note of the fact. At midnight of this woful tenth day, the ledge would be "relocatable," and by eleven o'clock the hill was black with men prepared to do the relocating. That was the crowd I had seen when I fancied a new "strike" had been made—idiot that I was. [We three had the same right to relocate the lead that other people had, provided we were quick enough.] As midnight was announced, fourteen men, duly armed and ready to back their proceedings, put up their "notice" and proclaimed their ownership of the blind lead, under the new name of the "Johnson." But A. D. Allen our partner (the foreman) put in a sudden appearance about that time, with a cocked revolver in his hand, and said his name must be added to the list, or he would "thin out the Johnson company some." He was a manly, splendid, determined fellow, and known to be as good as his word, and therefore a compromise was effected. They put in his name for a hundred feet, reserving to themselves the customary two hundred feet each. Such was the history of the night's events, as Higbie gathered from a friend on the way home.

Higbie and I cleared out on a new mining excitement the next morning, glad to get away from the scene of our sufferings, and after a month or two of hardship and disappointment, returned to Esmeralda once more. Then we learned that the Wide West and the Johnson companies had consolidated; that the stock, thus united, comprised five thousand feet, or shares; that the foreman, apprehending tiresome litigation, and considering such a huge concern unwieldy, had sold his hundred feet for ninety thousand dollars in gold and gone home to the States to enjoy it. If the stock was worth such a gallant figure, with five thousand shares in the corporation, it makes me dizzy to think what it would have been worth with only our original six hundred in it. It was the difference between six hundred men owning a house and five thousand owning it. We would have been millionaires if we had only worked with pick and spade one little day on our property and so secured our ownership!

It reads like a wild fancy sketch, but the evidence of many witnesses, and likewise that of the official records of Esmeralda District, is easily obtainable in proof that it is a true history. I can always have it to say that I was absolutely and unquestionably worth a million dollars, once, for ten days.

A year ago my esteemed and in every way estimable old millionaire partner, Higbie, wrote me from an obscure little mining camp in California that after nine or ten years of buffetings and hard striving, he was at last in a position where he could command twenty-five hundred dollars, and said he meant to go into the fruit business in a modest way. How such a thought would have insulted him the night we lay in our cabin planning European trips and brown stone houses on Russian Hill!

Chapter 47: [Buck Fanshaw's Funeral]

Somebody has said that in order to know a community, one must observe the style of its funerals and know what manner of men they bury with most ceremony. I cannot say which class we buried with most eclat in our "flush times," the distinguished public benefactor or the distinguished rough—possibly the two chief grades or grand divisions of society honored their illustrious dead about equally; and hence, no doubt the philosopher I have quoted from would have needed to see two representative funerals in Virginia before forming his estimate of the people.

There was a grand time over Buck Fanshaw when he died. He was a representative citizen. He had "killed his man"—not in his own quarrel, it is true, but in defence of a stranger unfairly beset by numbers. He had kept a sumptuous saloon. He had been the proprietor of a dashing helpmeet whom he could have discarded without the formality of a divorce. He had held a high position in the fire department and been a very Warwick in politics. When he died there was great lamentation throughout the town, but especially in the vast bottom-stratum of society.

On the inquest it was shown that Buck Fanshaw, in the delirium of a wasting typhoid fever, had taken arsenic, shot himself through the body, cut his throat, and jumped out of a four-story window and broken his neck—and after due deliberation, the jury, sad and tearful, but with intelligence unblinded by its sorrow, brought in a verdict of death "by the visitation of God." What could the world do without juries?

Prodigious preparations were made for the funeral. All the vehicles in town were hired, all the saloons put in mourning, all the municipal and fire-company flags hung at half-mast, and all the firemen ordered to muster in uniform and bring their machines duly draped in black. Now—let us remark in parenthesis—as all the peoples of the earth had representative adventurers in the Silverland, and as each adventurer had brought the slang of his nation or his locality with him, the combination made the slang of Nevada the richest and the most infinitely varied and copious that had ever existed anywhere in the world, perhaps, except in the mines of California in the "early days." Slang was the language of Nevada. It was hard to preach a sermon without it, and be understood. Such phrases as "You bet!" "Oh, no, I reckon not!" "No Irish need apply," and a hundred others, became so common as to fall from the lips of a speaker unconsciously—and very often when they did not touch the subject under discussion and consequently failed to mean anything.

After Buck Fanshaw's inquest, a meeting of the short-haired brotherhood[8] was held, for nothing can be done on the Pacific coast without a public meeting and an expression of sentiment. Regretful resolutions were passed and various committees appointed; among others, a committee of one was deputed to call on the minister, a fragile, gentle, spiritual new fledgling from an Eastern theological seminary, and as yet unacquainted with the ways of the mines. The committeeman, "Scotty" Briggs, made his visit; and in after days it was worth something to hear the minister tell about it. Scotty was a stalwart rough, whose customary suit, when on weighty official business, like committee work, was a fire helmet, flaming red flannel shirt, patent leather belt with spanner and revolver attached, coat hung over arm, and pants stuffed into boot tops. He formed something of a contrast to the pale theological student. It is fair to say of Scotty, however, in passing, that he had a warm heart, and a strong love for his friends, and never entered into a quarrel when he could reasonably keep out of it. Indeed, it was commonly said that whenever one of Scotty's fights was investigated, it always turned out that it had originally been no affair of his, but that out of native goodheartedness he had dropped in of his own accord to help the man who was getting the worst of it. He and Buck Fanshaw were bosom friends, for years, and had often taken adventurous "pot-luck" together. On one occasion, they had thrown off their coats and taken the weaker side in a fight among strangers, and after gaining a hard-earned victory, turned and found that the men they were helping had deserted early, and not only that, but had stolen their coats and made off with them!

[8] Firemen wore their hair short for safety reasons.

But to return to Scotty's visit to the minister. He was on a sorrowful mission, now, and his face was the picture of woe. Being admitted to the presence he sat down before the clergyman, placed his fire-hat on an unfinished manuscript sermon under the minister's nose, took from it a red silk handkerchief, wiped his brow and heaved a sight of dismal impressiveness, explanatory of his business. He choked, and even shed tears; but with an effort he mastered his voice and said in lugubrious tones:

"Are you the duck that runs the gospel-mill next door?"

"Am I the—pardon me, I believe I do not understand?"

With another sigh and a half-sob, Scotty rejoined:

"Why you see we are in a bit of trouble, and the boys thought maybe you would give us a lift, if we'd tackle you—that is, if I've got the rights of it and you are the head clerk of the doxology-works next door."

"I am the shepherd in charge of the flock whose fold is next door."

"The which?"

"The spiritual adviser of the little company of believers whose sanctuary adjoins these premises."

Scotty scratched his head, reflected a moment, and then said:

"You ruther hold over me, pard. I reckon I can't call that hand. Ante and pass the buck."

"How? I beg pardon. What did I understand you to say?"

"Well, you've ruther got the bulge on me. Or maybe we've both got the bulge, somehow. You don't smoke me and I don't smoke you. You see, one of the boys has passed in his checks and we want to give him a good send-off, and so the thing I'm on now is to roust out somebody to jerk a little chin-music for us and waltz him through handsome."

"My friend, I seem to grow more and more bewildered. Your observations are wholly incomprehensible to me. Cannot you simplify them in some way? At first I thought perhaps I understood you, but I grope now. Would it not expedite matters if you restricted yourself to categorical statements of fact unencumbered with obstructing accumulations of metaphor and allegory?"

Another pause, and more reflection. Then, said Scotty:

"I'll have to pass, I judge."

"How?"

"You've raised me out, pard."

"I still fail to catch your meaning."

"Why, that last lead of yourn is too many for me—that's the idea. I can't neither trump nor follow suit."

The clergyman sank back in his chair perplexed. Scotty leaned his head on his hand and gave himself up to thought. Presently his face came up, sorrowful but confident.

"I've got it now, so's you can savvy," he said. "What we want is a gospel-sharp. See?"

"A what?"

"Gospel-sharp. Parson."

"Oh! Why did you not say so before? I am a clergyman—a parson."

"Now you talk! You see my blind and straddle it like a man. Put it there!"—extending a brawny paw, which closed over the minister's small hand and gave it a shake indicative of fraternal sympathy and fervent gratification.

"Now we're all right, pard. Let's start fresh. Don't you mind my snuffling a little—becuz we're in a power of trouble. You see, one of the boys has gone up the flume—"

"Gone where?"

"Up the flume—throwed up the sponge, you understand."

"Thrown up the sponge?"

"Yes—kicked the bucket—"

"Ah—has departed to that mysterious country from whose bourne no traveler returns."

"Return! I reckon not. Why pard, he's *dead!*"

"Yes, I understand."

"Oh, you do? Well I thought maybe you might be getting tangled some more. Yes, you see he's dead again—"

"*Again?* Why, has he ever been dead before?"

"Dead before? No! Do you reckon a man has got as many lives as a cat? But you bet you he's awful dead now, poor old boy, and I wish I'd never seen this day. I don't want no better friend than Buck Fanshaw. I knowed him by the back; and when I know a man and like him, I freeze to him—you hear *me*. Take him all round, pard, there never was a bullier man in the mines. No man ever knowed Buck Fanshaw to go back on a friend. But it's all up, you know, it's all up. It ain't no use. They've scooped him."

"Scooped him?"

"Yes—death has. Well, well, well, we've got to give him up. Yes indeed. It's a kind of a hard world, after all, *ain't* it? But pard, he was a rustler! You ought to seen him get started once. He was a bully boy with a glass eye! Just spit in his face and give him room according to his strength, and it was just beautiful to see him peel and go in. He was the worst son of a thief that ever drawed breath. Pard, he was *on* it! He was on it bigger than an Injun!"

"On it? On what?"

"On the shoot. On the shoulder. On the fight, you understand. *He* didn't give a continental for *any* body. Beg your pardon, friend, for coming so near a cuss-word —but you see I'm on an awful strain, in this palaver, on account of having to cramp down and draw everything so mild. But we've got to give him up. There ain't any getting around that, I don't reckon. Now if we can get you to help plant him—"

"Preach the funeral discourse? Assist at the obsequies?"

"Obs'quies is good. Yes. That's it—that's our little game. We are going to get the thing up regardless, you know. He was always nifty himself, and so you bet you his funeral ain't going to be no slouch—solid silver door-plate on his coffin, six plumes on the hearse, and a nigger on the box in a biled shirt and a plug hat—how's that for high? And we'll take care of *you,* pard. We'll fix you all right. There'll be a kerridge for you; and whatever you want, you just 'scape out and we'll 'tend to it. We've got a shebang fixed up for you to stand behind, in No. 1's house, and don't you be afraid. Just go in and toot your horn, if you don't sell a clam. Put Buck through as bully as you can, pard, for anybody that knowed him will tell you that he was one of the whitest men that was ever in the mines. You can't draw it too strong. He never could stand it to see things going wrong. He's done more to make this town quiet and peaceable than any man in it. I've seen him lick four Greasers in eleven minutes, myself. If a thing wanted regulating, *he* warn't a man to go browsing around after somebody to do it, but he would prance in and regulate it himself. He warn't a Catholic. Scasely. He was down on 'em. His word was, 'No Irish need apply!' But it didn't make no difference about that when it came down to what a man's rights was—and so, when some roughs jumped the Catholic bone-yard and started in to stake out town-lots in it he *went* for 'em! And he *cleaned* 'em, too! I was there, pard, and I seen it myself."

"That was very well indeed—at least the impulse was—whether the act was strictly defensible or not. Had deceased any religious convictions? That is to say, did he feel a dependence upon, or acknowledge allegiance to a higher power?"

More reflection.

"I reckon you've stumped me again, pard. Could you say it over once more, and say it slow?"

"Well, to simplify it somewhat, was he, or rather had he ever been connected with any organization sequestered from secular concerns and devoted to self-sacrifice in the interests of morality?"

"All down but nine—set 'em up on the other alley, pard."

"What did I understand you to say?"

"Why, you're most too many for me, you know. When you get in with your left I hunt grass every time. Every time you draw, you fill; but I din't seem to have any luck. Lets have a new deal."

"How? Begin again?"

"That's it."

"Very well. Was he a good man, and—"

"There—I see that; don't put up another chip till I look at my hand. A good man, says you? Pard, it ain't no name for it. He was the best man that ever—pard, you would have doted on that man. He could lam any galoot of his inches in America. It was him that put down the riot last election before it got a start; and everybody said he was the only man that could have done it. He waltzed in with a spanner in one hand and a trumpet in the other, and sent fourteen men home on a shutter in less than three minutes. He had that riot all broke up and prevented nice before anybody ever got a chance to strike a blow. He was always for peace, and he would *have* peace—he could not stand disturbances. Pard, he was a great loss to this town. It would please the boys if you could chip in something like that and do him justice. Here once when the Micks got to throwing stones through the Methodis' Sunday school windows, Buck Fanshaw, all of his own notion, shut up his saloon and took a couple of six-shooters and mounted guard over the Sunday school. Says he, 'No Irish need apply!' And they didn't. He was the bulliest man in the mountains, pard! He could run faster, jump higher, hit harder, and hold more tangle-foot whisky without spilling it than any man in seventeen counties. Put that in, pard—it'll please the boys more than anything you could say. And you can say, pard, that he never shook his mother."

"Never shook his mother?"

"That's it—any of the boys will tell you so."

"Well, but why *should* he shake her?"

"That's what *I* say—but some people does."

"Not people of any repute?"

"Well, some that averages pretty so-so."

"In my opinion the man that would offer personal violence to his own mother, ought to—"

"Cheese it, pard; you've banked your ball clean outside the string. What I was a drivin' at, was, that he never *throwed off* on his mother—don't you see? No indeedy. He give her a house to live in, and town lots, and plenty of money; and he looked after her and took care of her all the time; and when she was down with the small-pox I'm d——d if he didn't set up nights and nuss her himself! *Beg* your pardon for saying it, but it hopped out too quick for yours truly. You've treated me like a gentleman, pard, and I ain't the man to hurt your feelings intentional. I think you're white. I think you're a square man, pard. I like you, and I'll lick any man that don't. I'll lick him till he can't tell himself from a last year's corpse! Put it *there!*" (Another fraternal handshake—and exit.)

The obsequies were all that "the boys" could desire. Such a marvel of funeral pomp had never been seen in Virginia. The plumed hearse, the dirge-breathing brass bands, the closed marts of business, the flags drooping at half mast, the long, plodding procession of uniformed secret societies, military battalions and fire companies, draped engines, carriages of officials, and citizens in vehicles and on foot, attracted multitudes of spectators to the sidewalks, roofs and windows; and for years afterward, the degree of grandeur attained by any civic display in Virginia was determined by comparison with Buck Fanshaw's funeral.

Scotty Briggs, as a pall-bearer and a mourner, occupied a prominent place at the funeral, and when the sermon was finished and the last sentence of the prayer for the dead man's soul ascended, he responded, in a low voice, but with feeling:

"AMEN. No Irish need apply."

As the bulk of the response was without apparent relevancy, it was probably nothing more than a humble tribute to the memory of the friend that was gone; for, as Scotty had once said, it was "his word."

Scotty Briggs, in after days, achieved the distinction of becoming the only convert to religion that was ever gathered from the Virginia roughs; and it transpired that the man who had it in him to espouse the quarrel of the weak out of inborn nobility of spirit was no mean timber whereof to construct a Christian. The making him one did not warp his generosity or diminish his courage; on the contrary it gave intelligent direction to the one and a broader field to the other. If his Sunday-school class progressed faster than the other classes, was it matter for wonder? I think not. He talked to his pioneer small-fry in a language they understood! It was my large privilege, a month before he died, to hear him tell the beautiful story of Joseph and his brethren to his class "without looking at the book." I leave it to the reader to fancy what it was like, as it fell, riddled with slang, from the lips of that grave, earnest teacher, and was listened to by his little learners with a consuming interest that showed that they were as unconscious as he was that any violence was being done to the sacred properties!

Chapter 53: [Grandfather's Old Ram]

Every now and then, in these days, the boys used to tell me I ought to get one Jim Blaine to tell me the stirring story of his grandfather's old ram—but they always added that I must not mention the matter unless Jim was drunk at the time—just comfortably and sociably drunk. They kept this up until my curiosity was on the rack to hear the story. I got to haunting Blaine; but it was of no use, the boys always found fault with his condition; he was often moderately but never satisfactorily drunk. I never watched a man's condition with such absorbing interest, such anxious solicitude; I never so pined to see a man uncompromisingly drunk before. At last, one evening I hurried to his cabin, for I learned that this time his situation was such that even the most fastidious could find no fault with it—he was tranquilly, serenely, symmetrically drunk—not a hiccup to mar his voice, not a cloud upon his brain thick enough to obscure his memory. As I entered, he was sitting upon an empty powder-keg, with a clay pipe in one hand and the other raised to command silence. His face was round, red, and very serious; his throat was bare and his hair tumbled; in general appearance and costume he was a stalwart miner of the period. On the pine table stood a candle, and its dim light revealed "the boys" sitting here and there on bunks, candle-boxes, powder-kegs, etc. They said:

"Sh——! Don't speak—he's going to commence."

The Story of the Old Ram

I found a seat at once, and Blaine said:

"I don't reckon them times will ever come again. There never was a more bullier old ram than what he was. Grandfather fetched him from Illinois—got him of a man by the name of Yates—Bill Yates—maybe you might have heard of him; his father was a deacon—Baptist—and he was a rustler, too; a man had to get up ruther early to get the start of old Thankful Yates; it was him that put the Greens up to jining teams with my grandfather when he moved west. Seth Green was prob'ly the pick of the flock; he married a Wilkerson—Sarah Wilkerson—a good cretur, she was— one of the likeliest heifers that was ever raised in old Stoddard, everybody said that knowed her. She could heft a bar'l of flour as easy as I can flirt a flapjack. And spin? Don't mention it! Independent? Humph! When Sile Hawkins come a browsing around her, she let him know that for all his tin he couldn't trot in harness alongside of *her.* You see, Sile Hawkins was—no, it warn't Sile Hawkins, after all—it was a galoot by the name of Filkins—I disremember his first name; but he *was* a stump— come into pra'r meeting drunk, one night, hooraying for Nixon, becuz he thought it was a primary; and old deacon Ferguson up and scooted him through the window and he lit on old Miss Jefferson's head, poor old filly. She was a good soul—had a glass eye and used to lend it to old Miss Wagner, that hadn't any, to receive company in; it warn't big enough, and when Miss Wagner warn't noticing, it would get twisted around in the socket, and look up, maybe, or out to one side, and every which way, while t' other one was looking as straight ahead as a spy-glass. Grown people didn't mind it, but it most always made the children cry, it was so sort of scary. She tried packing it in raw cotton, but it wouldn't work, somehow—the cotton would get loose and stick out and look so kind of awful that the children couldn't stand it no way. She was always dropping it out, and turning up her old dead-light on the company empty, and making them oncomfortable, becuz she never could tell when it hopped out, being blind on that side, you see. So somebody would have to hunch her and say, "Your game eye has fetched loose, Miss Wagner dear"—and then all of them would have to sit and wait till she jammed it in again—wrong side before, as a general thing, and green as a bird's egg, being a bashful cretur and easy sot back before company. But being wrong side before warn't much difference, anyway, becuz her own eye was sky-blue and the glass one was yaller on the front side, so whichever way she turned it it didn't match nohow. Old Miss Wagner was considerable on the borrow, she was. When she had a quilting, or Dorcas S'iety[9] at her house she gen'ally borrowed Miss Higgins's wooden leg to stump around on; it was considerable shorter than her other pin, but much *she* minded that. She said she couldn't abide crutches when she had company, becuz they were so slow; said when she had company and things had to be done, she wanted to get up and hump herself. She was as bald as a jug, and so she used to borrow Miss Jacops's wig—Miss Jacops was the coffin-peddler's wife—a ratty old buzzard, he was, that used to go roosting around where people was sick, waiting for 'em; and there that old rip would sit all day, in the shade, on a coffin that he judged would fit the can'idate; and if it was a slow customer and kind of uncertain, he'd fetch his rations and a blanket along and sleep in the coffin nights. He was anchored out that way, in frosty weather, for about three weeks, once, before old Robbins's place, waiting for him; and after that, for as much as two years, Jacops was not on speaking terms with the old man, on account of his disapp'inting him. He got one of his feet froze, and lost money, too, becuz old Robbins took a favorable turn and got well. The next time Robbins got sick, Jacops tried to make up with him, and varnished up the same old coffin and fetched it along; but old Robbins was too many for him; he had him in, and 'peared to be powerful weak; he bought the coffin for ten dollars and Jacops was to pay it back and twenty-five more besides if Robbins didn't like the coffin after he'd tried it. And then Robbins died, and at the funeral he bursted off the lid and riz up in his shroud and told the parson to let up on the performances, becuz he could *not* stand such a coffin as that. You see he had been in a trance once before, when he was young, and he took the chances on another, cal'lating that if he made the trip it was money in his pocket, and if he missed fire he couldn't lose a cent. And by George he sued Jacops for the rhino and got jedgment; and he set up the coffin in his back parlor and said he 'lowed to take his time, now. It was always an aggravation to Jacops, the way that miserable old thing acted. He moved back to Indiany pretty soon—went to Wellsville—Wellsville was the place the Hogadorns was from. Mighty fine family. Old Maryland stock. Old Squire Hogadorn could carry around more mixed licker, and cuss better than most any man I ever see. His second wife was the widder Billings—she that was Becky Martin; her dam was deacon Dunlap's first wife. Her oldest child, Maria, married a missionary and died in grace—et up by the savages. They et *him,* too, poor feller—biled him. It warn't the custom, so they say, but they explained to friends of his'n that went down there to bring away his things, that they'd tried missionaries every other way and never could get any good out of 'em—and so it annoyed all his relations to find out that that man's life was fooled away just out of a dern'd experiment, so to speak. But mind you, there ain't anything ever reely lost; everything that people can't understand and don't see the reason of does good if you only hold on and give it a fair shake; Prov'dence don't fire no blank ca'tridges, boys. That there missionary's substance, unbeknowns to himself, actu'ly converted every last one of them heathens that took a chance at the barbacue. Nothing ever fetched them but that.

---

[9] I.e., Dorcas Society, a church sewing circle.

Don't tell *me* it was an accident that he was biled. There ain't no such a thing as an accident. When my uncle Lem was leaning up agin a scaffolding once, sick, or drunk, or suthin, an Irishman with a hod full of bricks fell on him out of the third story and broke the old man's back in two places. People said it was an accident. Much accident there was about that. He didn't know what he was there for, but he was there for a good object. If he hadn't been there the Irishman would have been killed. Nobody can ever make me believe anything different from that. Uncle Lem's dog was there. Why didn't the Irishman fall on the dog? Becuz the dog would a seen him a coming and stood from under. That's the reason the dog warn't appinted. A dog can't be depended on to carry out a special providence. Mark my words it was a put-up thing. Accidents don't happen, boys. Uncle Lem's dog—I wish you could a seen that dog. He was a reglar shepherd—or ruther he was part bull and part shepherd—splendid animal; belonged to parson Hagar before Uncle Lem got him. Parson Hagar belonged to the Western Reserve Hagars; prime family; his mother was a Watson; one of his sisters married a Wheeler; they settled in Morgan county, and he got nipped by the machinery in a carpet factory and went through in less than a quarter of a minute; his widder bought the piece of carpet that had his remains wove in, and people come a hundred mile to 'tend the funeral. There was fourteen yards in the piece. She wouldn't let them roll him up, but planted him just so—full length. The church was middling small where they preached the funeral, and they had to let one end of the coffin stick out of the window. They didn't bury him—they planted one end, and let him stand up, same as a monument. And they nailed a sign on it and put—put on—put on it—sacred to—the m-e-m-o-r-y—of fourteen y-a-r-d-s—of three-ply—car—pet—containing all that was—m-o-r-t-a-l—of—of—W-i-l-l-i-a-m—W-h-e—"

Jim Blaine had been growing gradually drowsy and drowsier—his head nodded, once, twice, three times—dropped peacefully upon his breast, and he fell tranquilly asleep. The tears were running down the boys' cheeks—they were suffocating with suppressed laughter—and had been from the start, though I had never noticed it. I perceived that I was "sold." I learned then that Jim Blaine's peculiarity was that whenever he reached a certain stage of intoxication, no human power could keep him from setting out, with impressive unction, to tell about a wonderful adventure which he had once had with his grandfather's old ram—and the mention of the ram in the first sentence was as far as any man had ever heard him get, concerning it. He always maundered off, interminably, from one thing to another, till his whisky got the best of him and he fell asleep. What the thing was that happened to him and his grandfather's old ram is a dark mystery to this day, for nobody had ever yet found out.

Chapter 57: [That Rare and Blessed Spectacle, a Woman!]

It was in this Sacramento Valley, just referred to, that a deal of the most lucrative of the early gold mining was done, and you may still see, in places, its grassy slopes and levels torn and guttered and disfigured by the avaricious spoilers of fifteen and twenty years ago. You may see such disfigurements far and wide over California—and in some such places, where only meadows and forests are visible—not a living creature, not a house, no stick or stone or remnant of a ruin, and not a sound, not even a whisper to disturb the Sabbath stillness—you will find it hard to believe that there stood at one time a fiercely-flourishing little city, of two thousand or three thousand souls, with its newspaper, fire company, brass band, volunteer militia, bank, hotels, noisy Fourth of July processions and speeches, gambling hells crammed with tobacco smoke, profanity, and rough-bearded men of all nations and colors, with tables heaped with gold dust sufficient for the revenues of a German principality— streets crowded and rife with business—town lots worth four hundred dollars a front foot—labor, laughter, music, dancing, swearing, fighting, shooting, stabbing—a bloody inquest and a man for breakfast every morning—*everything* that delights and adorns existence—all the appointments and appurtenances of a thriving and prosper- ous and promising young city,—and *now* nothing is left of it all but a lifeless, homeless solitude. The men are gone, the houses have vanished, even the *name* of the place is forgotten. In no other land, in modern times, have towns so absolutely died and disappeared, as in the old mining regions of California.

It was a driving, vigorous, restless population in those days. It was a curious population. It was the *only* population of the kind that the world has ever seen gathered together, and it is not likely that the world will ever see its like again. For, observe, it was an assemblage of two hundred thousand *young* men—not simpering, dainty, kid-gloved weaklings, but stalwart, muscular, dauntless young braves, brimful of push and energy, and royally endowed with every attribute that goes to make up a peerless and magnificent manhood—the very pick and choice of the world's glorious ones. No women, no children, no gray and stooping veterans,—none but erect, bright-eyed, quick-moving, strong-handed young giants—the strangest population, the finest population, the most gallant host that ever trooped down the startled solitudes of an unpeopled land. And where are they now? Scattered to the ends of the earth—or prematurely aged and decrepit—or shot or stabbed in street affrays— or dead of disappointed hopes and broken hearts—all gone, or nearly all—victims devoted upon the altar of the golden calf—the noblest holocaust that ever wafted its sacrificial incense heavenward. It is pitiful to think upon.

It was a splendid population—for all the slow, sleepy, sluggish-brained sloths staid at home—you never find that sort of a people among pioneers—you cannot build pioneers out of that sort of material. It was that population that gave to California a name for getting up astounding enterprises and rushing them through with a magnificent dash and daring and a recklessness of cost or consequences, which she bears unto this day—and when she projects a new surprise, the grave world smiles as usual, and says "Well, that is California all over."

But they were rough in those times! They fairly reveled in gold, whisky, fights, and fandangoes, and were unspeakably happy. The honest miner raked from a hundred to a thousand dollars out of his claim a day, and what with the gambling dens and the other entertainments, he hadn't a cent the next morning, if he had any sort of luck. They cooked their own bacon and beans, sewed on their own buttons, washed their own shirts—blue woollen ones; and if a man wanted a fight on his hands without any annoying delay, all he had to do was to appear in public in a white shirt or a stove-pipe hat, and he would be accommodated. For those people hated aristocrats. They had a particular and malignant animosity toward what they called a "biled shirt."

It was a wild, free, disorderly, grotesque society! *Men*—only swarming hosts of stalwart *men*—nothing juvenile, nothing feminine, visible anywhere!

In those days miners would flock in crowds to catch a glimpse of that rare and blessed spectacle, a woman! Old inhabitants tell how, in a certain camp, the news went abroad early in the morning that a woman was come! They had seen a calico dress hanging out of a wagon down at the camping-ground—sign of emigrants from over the great plains. Everybody went down there, and a shout went up when an actual, bonafide dress was discovered fluttering in the wind! The male emigrant was visible. The miners said:

"Fetch her out!"

He said: "It is my wife, gentlemen—she is sick—we have been robbed of money, provisions, everything, by the Indians—we want to rest."

"Fetch her out! We've got to see her!"

"But, gentlemen, the poor thing, she—"

"FETCH HER OUT!"

He "fetched her out," and they swung their hats and sent up three rousing cheers and a tiger; and they crowded around and gazed at her, and touched her dress, and listened to her voice with the look of men who listened to a *memory* rather than a present reality—and then they collected twenty-five hundred dollars in gold and gave it to the man, and swung their hats again and gave three more cheers, and went home satisfied.

Once I dined in San Francisco with the family of a pioneer, and talked with his daughter, a young lady whose first experience in San Francisco was an adventure, though she herself did not remember it, as she was only two or three years old at the time. Her father said that, after landing from the ship, they were walking up the street, a servant leading the party with the little girl in her arms. And presently a huge miner, bearded, belted, spurred, and bristling with deadly weapons—just down from a long campaign in the mountains, evidently—barred the way, stopped the servant, and stood gazing, with a face all alive with gratification and astonishment. Then he said, reverently:

"Well, if it ain't a child!" And then he snatched a little leather sack out of his pocket and said to the servant:

"There's a hundred and fifty dollars in dust, there, and I'll give it to you to let me kiss the child!"

That anecdote is *true*.

But see how things change. Sitting at that dinner-table, listening to that anecdote, if I had offered double the money for the privilege of kissing the same child, I would have been refused. Seventeen added years have far more than doubled the price.

And while upon this subject I will remark that once in Star City, in the Humboldt Mountains, I took my place in a sort of long, post-office single file of miners, to patiently await my chance to peep through a crack in the cabin and get a sight of the splendid new sensation—a genuine, live Woman! And at the end of half of an hour my turn came, and I put my eye to the crack, and there she was, with one arm akimbo, and tossing flap-jacks in a frying-pan with the other. And she was one hundred and sixty-five years old, and hadn't a tooth in her head.

Chapter 61: [Dick Baker's Cat]

One of my comrades there[10]—another of those victims of eighteen years of unrequited toil and blighted hopes—was one of the gentlest spirits that ever bore its patient cross in a weary exile: grave and simple Dick Baker, pocket-miner of Dead-House Gulch. —He was forty-six, gray as a rat, earnest, thoughtful, slenderly educated, slouchily dressed and clay-soiled, but his heart was finer metal than any gold his shovel ever brought to light—than any, indeed, that ever was mined or minted.

Whenever he was out of luck and a little down-hearted, he would fall to mourning over the loss of a wonderful cat he used to own (for where women and children are not, men of kindly impulses take up with pets, for they must love something). And he always spoke of the strange sagacity of that cat with the air of a man who believed in his secret heart that there was something human about it—may be even supernatural.

I heard him talking about this animal once. He said:

"Gentlemen, I used to have a cat here, by the name of Tom Quartz, which you'd a took an interest in I reckon—most any body would. I had him here eight year— and he was the remarkablest cat I ever see. He was a large gray one of the Tom specie, an' he had more hard, natchral sense than any man in this camp—'n' a *power* of dignity —he wouldn't let the Gov'ner of Californy be familiar with him. He never ketched a rat in his life—'peared to be above it. He never cared for nothing but mining. He knowed more about mining, that cat did, than any man *I* ever, ever see. You couldn't tell *him* noth'n' 'bout placer diggin's—'n' as for pocket mining, why he was just born for it. He would dig out after me an' Jim when we went over the hills prospect'n', and he would trot along behind us for as much as five mile, if we went so fur. An' he had the best judgment, about mining ground—why you never see anything like it. When we went to work, he'd scatter a glance around, 'n' if he didn't think much of the indications, he would give a look as much as to say, 'Well, I'll have to get you to excuse *me*,' 'n' without another word he'd hyste his nose into the air 'n' shove for home. But if the ground suited him, he would lay low 'n' keep dark till the first pan was washed, 'n' then he would sidle up 'n' take a look, an' if there was about six or seven grains of gold *he* was satisfied—he didn't want no better prospect 'n' that—'n' then he would lay down on our coats and snore like a steamboat till we'd struck the pocket, an' then get up 'n' superintend. He was nearly lightnin' on superintending.

"Well, by an' by, up comes this yer quartz excitement. Every body was into it —every body was pick'n' 'n' blast'n' instead of shovelin' dirt on the hill side—every body was put'n' down a shaft instead of scrapin' the surface. Noth'n' would do Jim, but we must tackle the ledges, too, 'n' so we did. We commenced put'n' down a shaft, 'n' Tom Quartz he begin to wonder what in the Dickens it was all about. *He* hadn't ever seen any mining like that before, 'n' he was all upset, as you may say—he couldn't come to a right understanding of it no way—it was too many for *him*. He was down on it, too, you bet you—he was down on it powerful—'n' always appeared to consider it the cussedest foolishness out. But that cat, you know, was *always* agin new fangled arrangements—somehow he never could abide 'em. *You* know how it is with old habits. But by an' by Tom Quartz begin to git sort of reconciled a little, though he never *could* altogether understand that eternal sinkin' of a shaft an' never pannin' out any thing. At last he got to comin' down in the shaft, hisself, to try to cipher it out. An' when he'd git the blues, 'n' feel kind o' scruffy, 'n' aggravated 'n' disgusted —knowin' as he did, that the bills was runnin' up all the time an' we warn't makin' a cent—he would curl up on a gunny sack in the corner an' go to sleep. Well, one day when the shaft was down about eight foot, the rock got so hard that we had to put in a blast—the first blast'n' we'd ever done since Tom Quartz was born. An' then we lit the fuse 'n' clumb out 'n' got off 'bout fifty yards—'n' forgot 'n' left Tom Quartz sound asleep on the gunny sack. In 'bout a minute we seen a puff of smoke bust up out of the hole, 'n' then everything let go with an awful crash, 'n' about four million ton of rocks 'n' dirt 'n' smoke 'n' splinters shot up 'bout a mile an' a half into the air, an' by George, right in the dead centre of it was old Tom Quartz a goin' end over end, an' a snortin' an' a sneez'n', an' a clawin' an' a reachin' for things like all possessed. But it warn't no use, you know, it warn't no use. An' that was the last we see of *him* for about two minutes 'n' a half, an' then all of a sudden it begin to rain rocks and rubbage, an' directly he come down ker-whop about ten foot off f'm where we stood. Well, I reckon he was p'raps the orneriest lookin' beast you ever see. One ear was sot back on his neck, 'n' his tail was stove up, 'n' his eye-winkers were swinged off, 'n' he was all blacked up with powder an' smoke, an' all sloppy with mud 'n' slush f'm one end to the other. Well sir, it warn't no use to try to apologize—we couldn't say a word. He took a sort of a disgusted look at hisself, 'n' then he looked at us—an' it was just exactly the same as if he had said—'Gents, may be *you* think it's smart to take advantage of a cat that 'ain't had no experience of quartz minin', but *I* think *different*'—an' then he turned on his heel 'n' marched off home without ever saying another word.

"That was jest his style. An' may be you won't believe it, but after that you never see a cat so prejudiced agin quartz mining as what he was. An' by an' bye when he *did* get to goin' down in the shaft agin, you'd a been astonished at his sagacity. The minute we'd tetch off a blast 'n' the fuse'd begin to sizzle, he'd give a look as much as to say: "Well, I'll have to git you to excuse *me,*' an' it was surpris'n' the way he'd shin out of that hole 'n' go f'r a tree. Sagacity? It ain't no name for it. 'Twas *inspiration*!"

I said, "Well, Mr. Baker, his prejudice against quartz-mining *was* remarkable, considering how he came by it. Couldn't you ever cure him of it?"

"*Cure him!* No! When Tom Quartz was sot once, he was *always* sot—and you might a blowed him up as much as three million times 'n' you'd never a broken him of his cussed prejudice agin quartz mining."

The affection and the pride that lit up Baker's face when he delivered this tribute to the firmness of his humble friend of other days, will always be a vivid memory with me.

At the end of two months we had never "struck" a pocket. We had panned up and down the hillsides till they looked plowed like a field; we could have put in a crop of grain, then, but there would have been no way to get it to market. We got many good "prospects," but when the gold gave out in the pan and we dug down, hoping and longing, we found only emptiness—the pocket that should have been there was as barren as our own.—At last we shouldered our pans and shovels and struck out over the hills to try new localities. We prospected around Angel's Camp, in Calaveras county, during three weeks, but had no success. Then we wandered on foot among the mountains, sleeping under the trees at night, for the weather was mild, but still we remained as centless as the last rose of summer. That is a poor joke, but it is in pathetic harmony with the circumstances, since we were so poor ourselves. In accordance with the custom of the country, our door had always stood open and our board welcome to tramping miners—they drifted along nearly every day, dumped their paust shovels by the threshold and took "pot luck" with us—and now on our own tramp we never found cold hospitality.

Our wanderings were wide and in many directions; and now I could give the reader a vivid description of the Big Trees and the marvels of the Yo Semite—but what has this reader done to me that I should persecute him? I will deliver him into the hands of less conscientious tourists and take his blessing. Let me be charitable, though I fail in all virtues else.[11]

1872

---

from Old Times on the Mississippi

I: ["Cub" Wants to Be a Pilot]

When I was a boy, there was but one permanent ambition among my comrades in our village[1] on the west bank of the Mississippi River. That was, to be a steamboat-man. We had transient ambitions of other sorts, but they were only transient. When a circus came and went, it left us all burning to become clowns; the first negro minstrel show that came to our section left us all suffering to try that kind of life; now and then we had a hope that if we lived and were good, God would permit us to be pirates. These ambitions faded out, each in its turn; but the ambition to be a steamboatman always remained.

Once a day a cheap, gaudy packet arrived upward from St. Louis, and another downward from Keokuk. Before these events had transpired, the day was glorious with expectancy; after they had transpired, the day was a dead and empty thing. Not only the boys, but the whole village, felt this. After all these years I can picture that old time to myself now, just as it was then: the white town drowsing in the sunshine of a summer's morning; the streets empty, or pretty nearly so; one or two clerks sitting in front of the Water Street stores, with their splint-bottomed chairs tilted back against

---

[11] Twain's note: "Some of the phrases in the above are mining technicalities, purely, and may be a little obscure to the general reader. In *'placer diggings'* the gold is scattered all though the surface dirt; in *'pocket'* diggings it is concentrated in one litle spot; in *'quartz'* the gold is in a solid, continuous vein of rock, enclosed between distinct walls of some other kind of stone—and this is the most laborious and expensive of all the different kinds of mining. *'Prospecting'* is hunting for a *'placer'*; *'indications'* are signs of its presence; *'panning out'* refers to the washing process by which the grains of gold are separated from dirt; a *'prospect'* is what one finds in the first panful of dirt—and its value determines whether it is a good or a bad prospect, and whether it is worth while to tarry there or seek further."

[1] Hannibal, Missouri.

the wall, chins on breasts, hats slouched over their faces, asleep—with shingle-shavings enough around to show what broke them down; a sow and a litter of pigs loafing along the sidewalk, doing a good business in water-melon rinds and seeds; two or three lonely little freight piles scattered about the "levee;" a pile of "skids" on the slope of the stone-paved wharf, and the fragrant town drunkard asleep in the shadow of them; two or three wood flats at the head of the wharf, but nobody to listen to the peaceful lapping of the wavelets against them; the great Mississippi, the majestic, the magnificent Mississippi, rolling its mile-wide tide along, shining in the sun; the dense forest away on the other side; the "point" above the town, and the "point" below, bounding the river-glimpse and turning it into a sort of sea, and withal a very still and brilliant and lonely one. Presently a film of dark smoke appears above one of those remote "points;" instantly a negro drayman, famous for his quick eye and prodigious voice, lifts up the cry, "S-t-e-a-m-boat a-comin'!' " and the scene changes! The town drunkard stirs, the clerks wake up, a furious clatter of drays follows, every house and store pours out a human contribution, and all in a twinkling the dead town is alive and moving. Drays, carts, men, boys, all go hurrying from many quarters to a common centre, the wharf. Assembled there, the people fasten their eyes upon the coming boat as upon a wonder they are seeing for the first time. And the boat *is* rather a handsome sight, too. She is long and sharp and trim and pretty; she has two tall, fancy-topped chimneys, with a gilded device of some kind swung between them; a fanciful pilot-house, all glass and "gingerbread," perched on top of the "texas" deck behind them; the paddle-boxes are gorgeous with a picture or with gilded rays above the boat's name; the boiler deck, the hurricane deck, and the texas deck are fenced and orna-mented with clean white railings; there is a flag gallantly flying from the jack-staff; the furnace doors are open and the fires glaring bravely; the upper decks are black with passengers; the captain stands by the big bell, calm, imposing, the envy of all; great volumes of the blackest smoke are rolling and tumbling out of the chimneys —a husbanded grandeur created with a bit of pitch pine just before arriving at a town; the crew are grouped on the forecastle; the broad stage is run far out over the port bow, and an envied deck-hand stands picturesquely on the end of it with a coil of rope in his hand; the pent steam is screaming through the gauge-cocks; the captain lifts his hand, a bell rings, the wheels stop; then they turn back, churning the water to foam, and the steamer is at rest. Then such a scramble as there is to get aboard, and to get ashore, and to take in freight and to discharge freight, all at once and the same time; and such a yelling and cursing as the mates facilitate it all with! Ten minutes later the steamer is under way again, with no flag on the jack-staff and no black smoke issuing from the chimneys. After ten more minutes the town is dead again, and the town drunkard asleep by the skids once more.

My father was a justice of the peace, and I supposed he possessed the power of life and death over all men and could hang anybody that offended him. This was distinction enough for me as a general thing; but the desire to be a steamboatman kept intruding, nevertheless. I first wanted to be a cabin-boy, so that I could come out with a white apron on and shake a table-cloth over the side, where all my old comrades could see me; later I thought I would rather be the deck-hand who stood on the end of the stageplank with the coil of rope in his hand, because he was particularly conspicuous. But these were only daydreams—they were too heavenly to be contem-plated as real possibilities. By and by one of our boys went away. He was not heard of for a long time. At last he turned up as apprentice engineer or "striker" on a steamboat. This thing shook the bottom out of all my Sunday-school teachings. That boy had been notoriously worldly, and I just the reverse; yet he was exalted to this eminence, and I left in obscurity and misery. There was nothing generous about this fellow in his greatness. He would always manage to have a rusty bolt to scrub while his boat tarried at our town, and he would sit on the inside guard and scrub it, where we could all see him and envy him and loathe him. And whenever his boat was laid up he would come home and swell around the town in his blackest and greasiest clothes, so that nobody could help remembering that he was a steamboatman; and he used all sorts of steamboat technicalities in his talk, as if he were so used to them that he forgot common people could not understand them. He would speak of the "labboard" side of a horse in an easy, natural way that would make one wish he was dead. And he was always talking about "St. Looy" like an old citizen; he would refer casually to occasions when he "was coming down Fourth Street," or when he was "passing by the Planter's House," or when there was a fire and he took a turn on the brakes of "the old Big Missouri;" and then he would go on and lie about how many towns the size of ours were burned down there that day. Two or three of the boys had long been persons of consideration among us because they had been to St. Louis once and had a vague general knowledge of its wonders, but the day of their glory was over now. They lapsed into a humble silence, and learned to disappear when the ruthless "cub"-engineer approached. This fellow had money, too, and hair oil. Also an ignorant silver watch and a showy brass watch chain. He wore a leather belt and used no suspenders. If ever a youth was cordially admired and hated by his comrades, this one was. No girl could withstand his charms. He "cut out" every boy in the village. When his boat blew up at last, it diffused a tranquil contentment among us such as we had not known for months. But when he came home the next week, alive, renowned, and appeared in church all battered up and bandaged, a shining hero, stared at and wondered over by everybody, it seemed to us that the partiality of Providence for an undeserving reptile had reached a point where it was open to criticism.

This creature's career could produce but one result, and it speedily followed. Boy after boy managed to get on the river. The minister's son became an engineer. The doctor's and the postmaster's sons became "mud clerks;" the wholesale liquor dealer's son became a bar-keeper on a boat; four sons of the chief merchant, and two sons of the county judge, became pilots. Pilot was the grandest position of all. The pilot, even in those days of trivial wages, had a princely salary—from a hundred and fifty to two hundred and fifty dollars a month, and no board to pay. Two months of his wages would pay a preacher's salary for a year. Now some of us were left disconsolate. We could not get on the river—at least four parents would not let us.

So by and by I ran away. I said I never would come home again till I was a pilot and could come in glory. But somehow I could not manage it. I went meekly aboard a few of the boats that lay packed together like sardines at the long St. Louis wharf, and very humbly inquired for the pilots, but got only a cold shoulder and short words from mates and clerks. I had to make the best of this sort of treatment for the time being, but I had comforting daydreams of a future when I should be a great and honored pilot, with plenty of money, and could kill some of these mates and clerks and pay for them.

Months afterward the hope within me struggled to a reluctant death, and I found myself without an ambition. But I was ashamed to go home. I was in Cincinnati, and I set to work to map out a new career. I had been reading about the recent exploration of the river Amazon by an expedition sent out by our government. It was said that the expedition, owing to difficulties, had not thoroughly explored a part of the country lying about the head-waters, some four thousand miles from the mouth of the river. It was only about fifteen hundred miles from Cincinnati to New Orleans, where I could doubtless get a ship. I had thirty dollars left; I would go and complete the exploration of the Amazon. This was all the thought I gave to the subject. I never was great in matters of detail. I packed my valise, and took passage on an ancient tub called the Paul Jones, for New Orleans. For the sum of sixteen dollars I had the scarred and tarnished splendors of "her" main saloon principally to myself, for she was not a creature to attract the eye of wiser travelers.

When we presently got under way and went poking down the broad Ohio, I became a new being, and the subject of my own admiration. I was a traveler! A word never had tasted so good in my mouth before. I had an exultant sense of being bound for mysterious lands and distant climes which I never have felt in so uplifting a degree since. I was in such a glorified condition that all ignoble feelings departed out of me, and I was able to look down and pity the untraveled with a compassion that had hardly a trace of contempt in it. Still, when we stopped at villages and wood-yards, I could not help lolling carelessly upon the railings of the boiler deck to enjoy the envy of the country boys on the bank. If they did not seem to discover me, I presently sneezed to attract their attention, or moved to a position where they could not help seeing me. And as soon as I knew they saw me I gaped and stretched, and gave other signs of being mightily bored with traveling.

I kept my hat off all the time, and stayed where the wind and the sun could strike me, because I wanted to get the bronzed and weather-beaten look of an old traveler. Before the second day was half gone, I experienced a joy which filled me with the purest gratitude; for I saw that the skin had begun to blister and peel off my face and neck. I wished that the boys and girls at home could see me now.

We reached Louisville in time—at least the neighborhood of it. We stuck hard and fast on the rocks in the middle of the river and lay there four days. I was now beginning to feel a strong sense of being a part of the boat's family, a sort of infant son to the captain and younger brother to the officers. There is no estimating the pride I took in this grandeur, or the affection that began to swell and grow in me for those people. I could not know how the lordly steamboatman scorns that sort of presumption in a mere landsman. I particularly longed to acquire the least trifle of notice from the big stormy mate, and I was on the alert for an opportunity to do him a service to that end. It came at last. The riotous powwow of setting a spar was going on down on the forecastle, and I went down there and stood around in the way—or mostly skipping out of it—till the mate suddenly roared a general order for somebody to bring him a capstan bar. I sprang to his side and said: "Tell me where it is—I'll fetch it!"

If a rag-picker had offered to do a diplomatic service for the Emperor of Russia, the monarch could not have been more astounded than the mate was. He even stopped swearing. He stood and stared down at me. It took him ten seconds to scrape his disjointed remains together again. Then he said impressively: "Well, if this don't beat hell!" and turned to his work with the air of a man who had been confronted with a problem too abstruse for solution.

I crept away, and courted solitude for the rest of the day. I did not go to dinner; I stayed away from supper until everybody else had finished. I did not feel so much like a member of the boat's family now as before. However, my spirits returned, in installments, as we pursued our way down the river. I was sorry I hated the mate so, because it was not in (young) human nature not to admire him. He was huge and muscular, his face was bearded and whiskered all over; he had a red woman and a blue woman tattooed on his right arm,—one on each side of a blue anchor with a red rope to it; and in the matter of profanity he was perfect. When he was getting out cargo at a landing, I was always where I could see and hear. He felt all the sublimity of his great position, and made the world feel it, too. When he gave even the simplest order, he discharged it like a blast of lightning, and sent a long, reverberating peal of profanity thundering after it. I could not help contrasting the way in which the average landsman would give an order, with the mate's way of doing it. If the landsman should wish the gangplank moved a foot farther forward, he would probably say: "James, or William, one of you push that plank forward, please;" but put the mate in his place, and he would roar out: "Here, now, start that gang-plank for'ard! Lively, now! *What*'re you about! Snatch it! *snatch* it! There! there! Aft again! aft again! Don't you hear me? Dash it to dash! are you going to *sleep* over it! *'Vast* heaving. 'Vast heaving, I tell you! Going to heave it clear astern? WHERE're you going with that barrel! *for'ard* with it 'fore I make you swallow it, you dash-dash-dash-*dashed* split between a tired mud-turtle and a crippled hearse-horse!"

I wished I could talk like that.

When the soreness of my adventure with the mate had somewhat worn off, I began timidly to make up to the humblest official connected with the boat—the night watchman. He snubbed my advances at first, but I presently ventured to offer him a new chalk pipe, and that softened him. So he allowed me to sit with him by the big bell on the hurricane deck, and in time he melted into conversation. He could not well have helped it, I hung with such homage on his words and so plainly showed that I felt honored by his notice. He told me the names of dim capes and shadowy islands as we glided by them in the solemnity of the night, under the winking stars, and by and by got to talking about himself. He seemed oversentimental for a man whose salary was six dollars a week—or rather he might have seemed so to an older person than I. But I drank in his words hungrily, and with a faith that might have moved mountains if it had been applied judiciously. What was it to me that he was soiled and seedy and fragrant with gin? What was it to me that his grammar was bad, his construction worse, and his profanity so void of art that it was an element of weakness rather than strength in his conversation? He was a wronged man, a man who had seen trouble, and that was enough for me. As he mellowed into his plaintive history his tears dripped upon the lantern in his lap, and I cried, too, from sympathy. He said he was the son of an English nobleman—either an earl or an alderman, he could not remember which, but believed he was both; his father, the nobleman, loved him, but his mother hated him from the cradle; and so while he was still a little boy he was sent to "one of them old, ancient colleges"—he couldn't remember which; and by and by his father died and his mother seized the property and "shook" him, as he phrased it. After his mother shook him, members of the nobility with whom he was acquainted used their influence to get him the position of "loblolly-boy in a ship;" and from that point my watchman threw off all trammels of date and locality and branched out into a narrative that bristled all along with incredible adventures; a narrative that was so reeking with bloodshed and so crammed with hair-breadth escapes and the most engaging and unconscious personal villainies, that I sat speechless, enjoying, shuddering, wondering, worshiping.

It was a sore blight to find out afterwards that he was a low, vulgar, ignorant, sentimental, half-witted humbug, an untraveled native of the wilds of Illinois, who had absorbed wildcat literature and appropriated its marvels, until in time he had woven odds and ends of the mess into this yarn, and then gone on telling it to fledgelings like me, until he had come to believe it himself.

II: [A "Cub" Pilot's Experience; or, Learning the River]

What with lying on the rocks four days at Louisville, and some other delays, the poor old Paul Jones fooled away about two weeks in making the voyage from Cincinnati to New Orleans. This gave me a chance to get acquainted with one of the pilots, and he taught me how to steer the boat, and thus made the fascination of river life more potent than ever for me.

It also gave me a chance to get acquainted with a youth who had taken deck passage —more's the pity; for he easily borrowed six dollars of me on a promise to return to the boat and pay it back to me the day after we should arrive. But he probably died or forgot, for he never came. It was doubtless the former, since he had said his parents were wealthy, and he only traveled deck passage[2] because it was cooler.

I soon discovered two things. One was that a vessel would not be likely to sail for the mouth of the Amazon under ten or twelve years; and the other was that the nine or ten dollars still left in my pocket would not suffice for so imposing an exploration as I had planned, even if I could afford to wait for a ship. Therefore it followed that I must contrive a new career. The Paul Jones was now bound for St. Louis. I planned a siege against my pilot, and at the end of three hard days he surrendered. He agreed to teach me the Mississippi River from New Orleans to St. Louis for five hundred dollars, payable out of the first wages I should receive after graduating. I entered upon the small enterprise of "learning" twelve or thirteen hundred miles of the great Mississippi River with the easy confidence of my time of life. If I had really known what I was about to require of my faculties, I should not have had the courage to begin. I supposed that all a pilot had to do was to keep his boat in the river, and I did not consider that that could be much of a trick, since it was so wide.

The boat backed out from New Orleans at four in the afternoon, and it was "our watch" until eight. Mr. B——, my chief, "straightened her up," plowed her along past the sterns of the other boats that lay at the Levee, and then said, "Here, take her; shave those steamships as close as you'd peel an apple." I took the wheel, and my heart went down into my boots; for it seemed to me that we were about to scrape the side

[2] Steerage, the cheapest passage.

off every ship in the line, we were so close. I held my breath and began to claw the boat away from the danger; and I had my own opinion of the pilot who had known no better than to get us into such peril, but I was too wise to express it. In half a minute I had a wide margin of safety intervening between the Paul Jones and the ships; and within ten seconds more I was set aside in disgrace, and Mr. B—— was going into danger again and flaying me alive with abuse of my cowardice. I was stung, but I was obliged to admire the easy confidence with which my chief loafed from side to side of his wheel, and trimmed the ships so closely that disaster seemed ceaselessly imminent. When he had cooled a little he told me that the easy water was close ashore and the current outside, and therefore we must hug the bank, up-stream, to get the benefit of the former, and stay well out, downstream, to take advantage of the latter. In my own mind I resolved to be a down-stream pilot and leave the up-streaming to people dead to prudence.

Now and then Mr. B—— called my attention to certain things. Said he, "This is Six-Mile Point." I assented. It was pleasant enough information, but I could not see the bearing of it. I was not conscious that it was a matter of any interest to me. Another time he said, "This is Nine-Mile Point." Later he said, "This is Twelve-Mile Point." They were all about level with the water's edge; they all looked about alike to me; they were monotonously unpicturesque. I hoped Mr. B—— would change the subject. But no; he would crowd up around a point, hugging the shore with affection, and then say: "The slack water ends here, abreast this bunch of China-trees; now we cross over." So he crossed over. He gave me the wheel once or twice, but I had no luck. I either came near chipping off the edge of a sugar plantation, or else I yawed too far from shore, and so I dropped back into disgrace again and got abused.

The watch was ended at last, and we took supper and went to bed. At midnight the glare of a lantern shone in my eyes, and the night watchman said:—

"Come! turn out!"

And then he left. I could not understand this extraordinary procedure; so I presently gave up trying to, and dozed off to sleep. Pretty soon the watchman was back again, and this time he was gruff. I was annoyed. I said:—

"What do you want to come bothering around here in the middle of the night for? Now as like as not I'll not get to sleep again to-night."

The watchman said:—

"Well, if this an't good, I'm blest."

The "off-watch" was just turning in, and I heard some brutal laughter from them, and such remarks as "Hello, watchman! an't the new cub turned out yet? He's delicate, likely. Give him some sugar in a rag and send for the chambermaid to sing rock-a-by-baby to him."

About this time Mr. B—— appeared on the scene. Something like a minute later I was climbing the pilot-house steps with some of my clothes on and the rest in my arms. Mr. B—— was close behind, commenting. Here was something fresh—this thing of getting up in the middle of the night to go to work. It was a detail in piloting that had never occurred to me at all. I knew that boats ran all night, but somehow I had never happened to reflect that somebody had to get up out of a warm bed to run them. I began to fear that piloting was not quite so romantic as I had imagined it was; there was something very real and work-like about this new phase of it.

It was a rather dingy night, although a fair number of stars were out. The big mate was at the wheel, and he had the old tub pointed at a star and was holding her straight up the middle of the river. The shores on either hand were not much more than a mile apart, but they seemed wonderfully far away and ever so vague and indistinct. The mate said:—

"We've got to land at Jones's plantation, sir."

The vengeful spirit in me exulted. I said to myself, I wish you joy of your job, Mr. B——; you'll have a good time finding Mr. Jones's plantation such a night as this; and I hope you never *will* find it as long as you live.

Mr. B— said to the mate:—

"Upper end of the plantation, or the lower?"

"Upper."

"I can't do it. The stumps there are out of water at this stage. It's no great distance to the lower, and you'll have to get along with that."

"All right, sir. If Jones don't like it he'll have to lump it, I reckon."

And then the mate left. My exultation began to cool and my wonder to come up. Here was a man who not only proposed to find this plantation on such a night, but to find either end of it you preferred. I dreadfully wanted to ask a question, but I was carrying about as many short answers as my cargo-room would admit of, so I held my peace. All I desired to ask Mr. B—— was the simple question whether he was ass enough to really imagine he was going to find that plantation on a night when all plantations were exactly alike and all the same color. But I held in. I used to have fine inspirations of prudence in those days.

Mr. B—— made for the shore and soon was scraping it, just the same as if it had been daylight. And not only that, but singing—

"Father in heaven the day is declining," etc.

It seemed to me that I had put my life in the keeping of a peculiarly reckless outcast. Presently he turned on me and said:—

"What's the name of the first point above New Orleans?"

I was gratified to be able to answer promptly, and I did. I said I didn't know.

"Don't *know?*"

This manner jolted me. I was down at the foot again, in a moment. But I had to say just what I had said before.

"Well, you're a smart one," said Mr. B——. "What's the name of the *next* point?"

Once more I didn't know.

"Well this beats anything. Tell me the name of *any* point or place I told you."

I studied a while and decided that I couldn't.

"Look-a-here! What do you start out from, above Twelve-Mile Point, to cross over?"

"I—I—don't know."

"You—you—don't know?" mimicking my drawling manner of speech. "What *do* you know?"

"I—I—nothing, for certain."

"By the great Cæsar's ghost I believe you! You're the stupidest dunderhead I ever saw or ever heard of, so help me Moses! The idea of *you* being a pilot—*you!* Why, you don't know enough to pilot a cow down a lane."

Oh, but his wrath was up! He was a nervous man, and he shuffled from one side of his wheel to the other as if the floor was hot. He would boil a while to himself, and then overflow and scald me again.

"Look-a-here! What do you suppose I told you the names of those points for?"

I tremblingly considered a moment, and then the devil of temptation provoked me to say:—

"Well—to—to—be entertaining, I thought."

This was a red rag to the bull. He raged and stormed so (he was crossing the river at the time) that I judge it made him blind, because he ran over the steering-oar of a trading-scow. Of course the traders sent up a volley of red-hot profanity. Never was a man so grateful as Mr. B—— was: because he was brim full, and here were subjects who would *talk back.* He threw open a window, thrust his head out, and such an irruption followed as I never had heard before. The fainter and farther away the scowmen's curses drifted, the higher Mr. B—— lifted his voice and the weightier his adjectives grew. When he closed the window he was empty. You could have drawn a seine through his system and not caught curses enough to disturb your mother with. Presently he said to me in the gentlest way:—

"My boy, you must get a little memorandum-book, and every time I tell you a thing, put it down right away. There's only one way to be a pilot, and that is to get this entire river by heart. You have to know it just like A B C."

That was a dismal revelation to me; for my memory was never loaded with anything but blank cartridges. However, I did not feel discouraged long. I judged that it was best to make some allowances, for doubtless Mr. B—— was "stretching." Presently, he pulled a rope and struck a few strokes on the big bell. The stars were all gone, now, and the night was as black as ink. I could hear the wheels churn along the bank, but I was not entirely certain that I could see the shore. The voice of the invisible watchman called up from the hurricane deck:—

"What's this, sir?"

"Jones's plantation."

I said to myself, I wish I might venture to offer a small bet that it isn't. But I did not chirp. I only waited to see. Mr. B—— handled the engine bells, and in due time the boat's nose came to the land, a torch glowed from the forecastle, a man skipped ashore, a darky's voice on the bank said, "Gimme de carpet-bag, Mars' Jones," and the next moment we were standing up the river again, all serene. I reflected deeply a while, and then said,—but not aloud,—Well, the finding of that plantation was the luckiest accident that ever happened; but it couldn't happen again in a hundred years. And I fully believed it *was* an accident, too.

By the time we had gone seven or eight hundred miles up the river, I had learned to be a tolerably plucky upstream steersman, in daylight, and before we reached St. Louis I had made a trifle of progress in night-work, but only a trifle. I had a note-book that fairly bristled with the names of towns, "points," bars, islands, bends, reaches, etc.; but the information was to be found only in the note-book—none of it was in my head. It made my heart ache to think I had only got half of the river set down; for as our watch was four hours off and four hours on, day and night, there was a long four-hour gap in my book for every time I had slept since the voyage began.

My chief was presently hired to go on a big New Orleans boat, and I packed my satchel and went with him. She was a grand affair. When I stood in her pilot-house

I was so far above the water that I seemed perched on a mountain; and her decks stretched so far away, fore and aft, below me, that I wondered how I could ever have considered the little Paul Jones a large craft. There were other differences, too. The Paul Jones's pilot-house was a cheap, dingy, battered rattle-trap, cramped for room: but here was a sumptuous glass temple; room enough to have a dance in; showy red and gold window-curtains; an imposing sofa; leather cushions and a back to the high bench where visiting pilots sit, to spin yarns and "look at the river;" bright, fanciful "cuspadores" instead of a broad wooden box filled with sawdust; nice new oil-cloth on the floor; a hospitable big stove for winter; a wheel as high as my head, costly with inlaid work; a wire tiller-rope; bright brass knobs for the bells; and a tidy, white-aproned, black "texas-tender," to bring up tarts and ices and coffee during mid-watch, day and night. Now this was "something like;" and so I began to take heart once more to believe that piloting was a romantic sort of occupation after all. The moment we were under way I began to prowl about the great steamer and fill myself with joy. She was as clean and as dainty as a drawing-room; when I looked down her long, gilded saloon, it was like gazing through a splendid tunnel; she had an oil-picture, by some gifted sign-painter, on every state-room door; she glittered with no end of prism-fringed chandeliers; the clerk's office was elegant, the bar was marvelous, and the bar-keeper had been barbered and upholstered at incredible cost. The boiler deck (*i.e.,* the second story of the boat, so to speak) was as spacious as a church, it seemed to me; so with the forecastle; and there was no pitiful handful of deckhands, firemen, and roust-abouts down there, but a whole battalion of men. The fires were fiercely glaring from a long row of furnaces, and over them were eight huge boilers! This was unutterable pomp. The mighty engines—but enough of this. I had never felt so fine before. And when I found that the regiment of natty servants respectfully "sir'd" me, my satisfaction was complete.

When I returned to the pilot-house St. Louis was gone and I was lost. Here was a piece of river which was all down in my book, but I could make neither head nor tail of it: you understand, it was turned around. I had seen it, when coming up-stream, but I had never faced about to see how it looked when it was behind me. My heart broke again, for it was plain that I had got to learn this troublesome river *both ways.*

The pilot-house was full of pilots, going down to "look at the river." What is called the "upper river" (the two hundred miles between St. Louis and Cairo, where the Ohio comes in) was low; and the Mississippi changes its channel so constantly that the pilots used to always find it necessary to run down to Cairo to take a fresh look, when their boats were to lie in port a week, that is, when the water was at a low stage. A deal of this "looking at the river" was done by poor fellows who seldom had a berth, and whose only hope of getting one lay in their being always freshly posted and therefore ready to drop into the shoes of some reputable pilot, for a single trip, on account of such pilot's sudden illness, or some other necessity. And a good many of them constantly ran up and down inspecting the river, not because they ever really hoped to get a berth, but because (they being guests of the boat) it was cheaper to "look at the river" than stay ashore and pay board. In time these fellows grew dainty in their tastes, and only infested boats that had an established reputation for setting good tables. All visiting pilots were useful, for they were always ready and willing, winter or summer, night or day, to go out in the yawl and help buoy the channel or assist the boat's pilots in any way they could. They were likewise welcome because all pilots are tireless talkers, when gathered together, and as they talk only about the river they are always understood and are always interesting. Your true pilot cares nothing about anything on earth but the river, and his pride in his occupation surpasses the pride of kings.

We had a fine company of these river-inspectors along, this trip. There were eight or ten; and there was abundance of room for them in our great pilot-house. Two or three of them wore polished silk hats, elaborate shirtfronts, diamond breastpins, kid gloves, and patent-leather boots. They were choice in their English, and bore themselves with a dignity proper to men of solid means and prodigious reputation as pilots. The others were more or less loosely clad, and wore upon their heads tall felt cones that were suggestive of the days of the Commonwealth.

I was a cipher in this august company, and felt subdued, not to say torpid. I was not even of sufficient consequence to assist at the wheel when it was necessary to put the tiller hard down in a hurry; the guest that stood nearest did that when occasion required—and this was pretty much all the time, because of the crookedness of the channel and the scant water. I stood in a corner; and the talk I listened to took the hope all out of me. One visitor said to another:—

"Jim, how did you run Plum Point, coming up?"

"It was in the night, there, and I ran it the way one of the boys on the Diana told me; started out about fifty yards above the wood pile on the false point, and held on the cabin under Plum Point till I raised the reef—quarter less twain—then straightened up for the middle bar till I got well abreast the old one-limbed cotton-wood in the bend, then got my stern on the cotton-wood and head on the low place above the point, and came through a-booming—nine and a half."

"Pretty square crossing, an't it?"

"Yes, but the upper bar's working down fast."

Another pilot spoke up and said:—

"I had better water than that, and ran it lower down; started out from the false point—mark twain—raised the second reef abreast the big snag in the bend, and had quarter less twain."

There was no more trouble after that. Mr. B—— was a hero that night; and it was some little time, too, before his exploit ceased to be talked about by river men.

Fully to realize the marvelous precision required in laying the great steamer in her marks in that murky waste of water, one should know that not only must she pick her intricate way through snags and blind reefs, and then shave the head of the island so closely as to brush the overhanging foliage with her stern, but at one place she must pass almost within arm's reach of a sunken and invisible wreck that would snatch the hull timbers from under her if she should strike it, and destroy a quarter of a million dollars' worth of steamboat and cargo in five minutes, and maybe a hundred and fifty human lives into the bargain.

The last remark I heard that night was a compliment to Mr. B——, uttered in soliloquy and with unction by one of our guests. He said:—

"By the Shadow of Death, but he's a lightning pilot!"

1875

The Story of a Speech[*]

The Speech

This is an occasion peculiarly meet for the digging up of pleasant reminiscences concerning literary folk; therefore I will drop lightly into history myself. Standing here on the shore of the Atlantic and contemplating certain of its largest literary billows, I am reminded of a thing which happened to me thirteen years ago, when I had just succeeded in stirring up a little Nevadian literary puddle myself, whose spume-flakes were beginning to blow thinly Californiaward. I started an inspection tramp through the southern mines of California. I was callow and conceited, and I resolved to try the virtue of my *nom de guerre*.

I very soon had an opportunity. I knocked at a miner's lonely log cabin in the foot-hills of the Sierras just at nightfall. It was snowing at the time. A jaded, melancholy man of fifty, barefooted, opened the door to me. When he heard my *nom de guerre* he looked more dejected than before. He let me in—pretty reluctantly, I thought—and after the customary bacon and beans, black coffee, and hot whiskey, I took a pipe. This sorrowful man had not said three words up to this time. Now he spoke up and said, in the voice of one who is secretly suffering, "You're the fourth —I'm going to move." "The fourth what?" said I. "The fourth literary man that has been here in twenty-four hours—I'm going to move." "You don't tell me!" said I; "who were the others?" "Mr. Longfellow, Mr. Emerson, and Mr. Oliver Wendell Holmes—confound the lot!"

You can easily believe I was interested. I supplicated—three hot whiskies did the rest—and finally the melancholy miner began. Said he:

"They came here just at dark yesterday evening, and I let them in, of course. Said they were going to the Yosemite. They were a rough lot, but that's nothing; everybody looks rough that travels afoot. Mr. Emerson was a seedy little bit of a chap, redheaded. Mr. Holmes was as fat as a balloon; he weighed as much as three hundred, and had double chins all the way down to his stomach. Mr. Longfellow was built like a prize-fighter. His head was cropped and bristly, like as if he had a wig made of hair-brushes. His nose lay straight down his face, like a finger with the end joint tilted up. They had been drinking, I could see that. And what queer talk they used! Mr. Holmes inspected this cabin, then he took me by the buttonhole, and says he:

" 'Through the deep caves of thought
    I hear a voice that sings,
    Build thee more stately mansions,
    O my soul!'

"Says I, 'I can't afford it, Mr. Holmes, and moreover I don't want to.' Blamed if I liked it pretty well, either, coming from a stranger, that way. However, I started

---

[*] An address delivered in 1877, at a dinner given by the publishers of the *Atlantic Monthly*, followed by Twain's written assessment of it 29 years later.

to get out my bacon and beans, when Mr. Emerson came and looked on awhile, and then *he* takes me aside by the buttonhole and says:

> " 'Gives me agates for my meat;
>   Gives me cantharids to eat;
>   From air and ocean bring me foods,
>   From all zones and altitudes.'

"Says I, 'Mr. Emerson, if you'll excuse me, this ain't no hotel.' You see it sort of riled me—I warn't used to the ways of littery swells. But I went on a-sweating over my work and next comes Mr. Longfellow and buttonholes me, and interrupts me. Says he:

> " 'Honor be to Mudjekeewis!
>   You shall hear how Pau-Puk-Keewis—'

"But I broke in, and says I, 'Beg your pardon, Mr. Longfellow, if you'll be so kind as to hold your yawp for about five minutes and let me get this grub ready, you'll do me proud.' Well, sir, after they'd filled up I set out the jug. Mr. Holmes looks at it, and then he fires up all of sudden and yells:

> " 'Flash out a stream of blood-red wine!
>   For I would drink to other days.'

"By George, I was getting kind of worked up. I don't deny it, I was getting kind of worked up. I turns to Mr. Holmes, and says I, 'Looky here, my fat friend, I'm a-running this shanty, and if the court knows herself, you'll take whisky straight or you'll go dry.' Them's the very words I said to him. Now I don't want to sass such famous littery people, but you see they kind of forced me. There ain't nothing onreasonable 'bout me; I don't mind a passel of guests a-treadin' on my tail three or four times, but when it comes to *standing* on it it's different, 'and if the court knows herself,' I says, 'you'll take whisky straight or you'll go dry.' Well, between drinks they'd swell around the cabin and strike attitudes and spout; and pretty soon they got out a greasy old deck and went to playing euchre at ten cents a corner—on trust. I began to notice some pretty suspicious things. Mr. Emerson dealt, looked at his hand, shook his head, says:

> " 'I am the doubter and the doubt—'

and ca'mly bunched the hands and went to shuffling for a new layout. Says he:

> " 'They reckon ill who leave me out;
>   They know not well the subtle ways I keep
>   I pass and deal again!'

Hang'd if he didn't go ahead and do it, too! Oh, he was a cool one! Well, in about a minute things were running pretty tight, but all of a sudden I see by Mr. Emerson's eye he judged he had 'em. He had already corralled two tricks, and each of the others one. So now he kind of lifts a little in his chair and says:

" 'I tire of globes and aces!—
    Too long the game is played!'

—and down he fetched a right bower. Mr. Longfellow smiles as sweet as pie and says:

" 'Thanks thanks to thee, my worthy friend,
    For the lesson thou hast taught,'

—and blamed if he didn't down with *another* right bower! Emerson claps his hand on his bowie, Longfellow claps his on his revolver, and I went under a bunk. There was going to be trouble; but that monstrous Holmes rose up, wobbling his double chins, and says he, 'Order, gentlemen; the first man that draws, I'll lay down on him and smother him!' All quiet on the Potomac, you bet!

"They were pretty how-come-you-so by now, and they begun to blow. Emerson says, 'The nobbiest thing I ever wrote was "Barbara Frietchie." ' Says Longfellow, 'It don't begin with my "Biglow Papers." ' Says Holmes, 'My "Thanatopsis" lays over 'em both.' They mighty near ended in a fight. Then they wished they had some more company—and Mr. Emerson pointed to me and says:

" 'Is yonder squalid peasant all
    That this proud nursery could breed?'

He was a-whetting his bowie on his boot—so I let it pass. Well, sir, next they took it into their heads that they would like some music; so they made me stand up and sing "When Johnny Comes Marching Home" till I dropped—at thirteen minutes past four this morning. That's what I've been through, my friend. When I woke at seven, they were leaving, thank goodness, and Mr. Longfellow had my only boots on, and his'n under his arm. Says I, 'Hold on, there, Evangeline, what are you going to do with *them?*' He says, 'Going to make tracks with 'em; because:

" 'Lives of great men all remind us
    We can make our lives sublime;
    And, departing, leave behind us
    Footprints on the sands of time.'

As I said, Mr. Twain, you are the fourth in twenty-four hours—and I'm going to move; I ain't suited to a littery atmosphere."

I said to the miner, "Why, my dear sir, *these* were not the gracious singers to whom we and the world pay loving reverence and homage; these were impostors."

The miner investigated me with a calm eye for awhile; then said he, "Ah! impostors, were they? Are *you?*"

I did not pursue the subject, and since then I have not traveled on my *nom de guerre* enough to hurt. Such was the reminiscence I was moved to contribute, Mr. Chairman. In my enthusiasm I may have exaggerated the details a little, but you will easily forgive me that fault, since I believe it is the first time I have ever deflected from perpendicular fact on an occasion like this.

The Story

January 11, 1906.

Answer to a letter received this morning:

> DEAR MRS. H.,—I am forever your debtor for reminding me of that curious
> passage in my life. During the first year or two after it happened, I could not
> bear to think of it. My pain and shame were so intense, and my sense of having
> been an imbecile so settled, established and confirmed, that I drove the episode
> entirely from my mind—and so all these twenty-eight or twenty-nine years I
> have lived in the conviction that my performance of that time was coarse,
> vulgar, and destitute of humor. But your suggestion that you and your family
> found humor in it twenty-eight years ago moved me to look into the matter.
> So I commissioned a Boston typewriter[1] to delve among the Boston papers of
> that bygone time and send me a copy of it.
>   It came this morning, and if there is any vulgarity about it I am not to
> discover it. If it isn't innocently and ridiculously funny, I am no judge. I will
> see to it that you get a copy.

What I have said to Mrs. H. is true. I did suffer during a year or two from the
deep humiliations of the episode. But at last, in 1888, in Venice, my wife and I came
across Mr. and Mrs. A. P. C., of Concord, Massachusetts, and a friendship began then
of the sort which nothing but death terminates. The C.'s were very bright people and
in every way charming and companionable. We were together a month or two in
Venice and several months in Rome, afterward, and one day that lamented break of
mine was mentioned. And when I was on the point of lathering those people for
bringing it to my mind when I had gotten the memory of it almost squelched, I
perceived with joy that the C.'s were indignant about the way that my performance
had been received in Boston. They poured out their opinions most freely and frankly
about the frosty attitude of the people who were present at that performance, and
about the Boston newspapers for the position they had taken in regard to the matter.
That position was that I had been irreverent beyond belief, beyond imagination. Very
well; I had accepted that as a fact for a year or two, and had been thoroughly miserable
about it whenever I thought of it—which was not frequently, if I could help it.
Whenever I thought of it I wondered how I ever could have been inspired to do so
unholy a thing. Well, the C.'s comforted me, but they did not persuade me to continue
to think about the unhappy episode. I resisted that. I tried to get it out of my mind,
and let it die, and I succeeded. Until Mrs. H.'s letter came, it had been a good
twenty-five years since I had thought of that matter; and when she said that the thing
was funny I wondered if possibly she might be right. At any rate, my curiosity was
aroused, and I wrote to Boston and got the whole thing copied, as above set forth.
  I vaguely remembered some of the details of that gathering—dimly I can see a

---

[1] Typist.

you are going to get. But here is an innocent man. Bishop had never done you any harm, and see what you have done to him. He can never hold his head up again. The world can never look upon Bishop as being a live person. He is a corpse."

That is the history of that episode of twenty-eight years ago, which pretty nearly killed me with shame during that first year or two whenever it forced its way into my mind.

Now then, I take that speech up and examine it. As I said, it arrived this morning, from Boston. I have read it twice, and unless I am an idiot, it hasn't a single defect in it from the first word to the last. It is just as good as good can be. It is smart; it is saturated with humor. There isn't a suggestion of coarseness or vulgarity in it anywhere. What could have been the matter with that house? It is amazing, it is incredible, that they didn't shout with laughter, and those deities the loudest of them all. Could the fault have been with me? Did I lose courage when I saw those great men up there whom I was going to describe in such a strange fashion? If that happened, if I showed doubt, that can account for it, for you can't be successfully funny if you show that you are afraid of it. Well, I can't account for it, but if I had those beloved and revered old literary immortals back here now on the platform at Carnegie Hall I would take that same old speech, deliver it, word for word, and melt them till they'd run all over that stage. Oh, the fault must have been with *me,* it is not in the speech at all.

1923

---

from A Tramp Abroad

from **Chapter 2: Heidelberg**

[Language of Animals]

Animals talk to each other, of course. There can be no question about that; but I suppose there are very few people who can understand them. I never knew but one man who could. I knew he could, however, because he told me so himself. He was a middle-aged, simple-hearted miner who had lived in a lonely corner of California, among the woods and mountains, a good many years, and had studied the ways of his only neighbors, the beasts and the birds, until he believed he could accurately translate any remark which they made. This was Jim Baker. According to Jim Baker, some animals have only a limited education, and use only very simple words, and scarcely ever a comparison or a flowery figure; whereas, certain other animals have a large vocabulary, a fine command of language and a ready and fluent delivery; consequently these latter talk a great deal; they like it; they are conscious of their talent, and they enjoy "showing off." Baker said, that after long and careful observation, he had come to the conclusion that the blue-jays were the best talkers he had found among birds and beasts. Said he:—

"There's more *to* a blue-jay than any other creature. He has got more moods, and more different kinds of feelings than other creature; and mind you, whatever a blue-jay feels, he can put into language. And no mere commonplace language, either, but rattling, out-and-out book-talk—and bristling with metaphor, too—just bristling! And as for command of language—why *you* never see a blue-jay get stuck for a word. No man ever did. They just boil out of him! And another thing: I've noticed a good deal, and there's no bird, or cow, or anything that uses as good grammar as a blue-jay. You may say a cat uses good grammar. Well, a cat does—but you let a cat get excited, once; you let a cat get to pulling fur with another cat on a shed, nights, and you'll hear grammar that will give you the lockjaw. Ignorant people think it's the *noise* which fighting cats make that is so aggravating, but it ain't so; it's the sickening grammar they use. Now I've never heard a jay use bad grammar but very seldom; and when they do, they are as ashamed as a human; they shut right down and leave.

"You may call a jay a bird. Well, so he is, in a measure—because he's got feathers on him, and don't belong to no church, perhaps; but otherwise he is just as much a human as you be. And I'll tell you for why. A jay's gifts, and instincts, and feelings, and interests, cover the whole ground. A jay hasn't got any more principle than a Congressman. A jay will lie, a jay will steal, a jay will deceive, a jay will betray; and four times out of five, a jay will go back on his solemnest promise. The sacredness of an obligation is a thing which you can't cram into no blue-jay's head. Now on top of all this, there's another thing: a jay can out-swear any gentleman in the mines. You think a cat can swear. Well, a cat can; but you give a blue-jay a subject that calls for his reserve-powers, and where is your cat? Don't talk to *me*—I know too much about this thing. And there's yet another thing: in the one little particular of scolding—just good, clean, out-and-out scolding—a blue-jay can lay over anything, human or divine. Yes, sir, a jay is everything that a man is. A jay can cry, a jay can laugh, a jay can feel shame, a jay can reason and plan and discuss, a jay likes gossip and scandal, a jay has got a sense of humor, a jay knows when he is an ass just as well as you do—maybe better. If a jay ain't human, he better take in his sign, that's all. Now I'm going to tell you a perfectly true fact about some blue-jays." . . .

Chapter 3: Baker's Blue-Jay Yarn

"When I first begun to understand jay language correctly, there was a little incident happened here. Seven years ago, the last man in this region but me, moved away. There stands his house,—been empty ever since; a log house, with a plank roof—just one big room, and no more; no ceiling—nothing between the rafters and the floor. Well, one Sunday morning I was sitting out here in front of my cabin, with my cat, taking the sun, and looking at the blue hills, and listening to the leaves rustling so lonely in the trees, and thinking of the home away yonder in the States, that I hadn't heard from in thirteen years, when a blue jay lit on that house, with an acorn in his mouth, and says, 'Hello, I reckon I've struck something.' When he spoke, the acorn dropped out of his mouth and rolled down the roof, of course, but he didn't care; his mind was all on the thing he had struck. It was a knot-hole in the roof. He cocked his head to one side, shut one eye and put the other one to the hole, like a 'possum looking down a jug; then he glanced up with his bright eyes, gave a wink or two with his wings—which signifies gratification, you understand,—and says, 'It looks like a hole, it's located like a hole,—blamed if I don't believe it *is* a hole!'"

"Then he cocked his head down and took another look; he glances up perfectly joyful, this time; winks his wings and his tail both, and says, 'O, no, this ain't no fat thing, I reckon! If I ain't in luck!—why it's a perfectly elegant hole!' So he flew down and got that acorn, and fetched it up and dropped it in, and was just tilting his head back, with the heavenliest smile on his face, when all of a sudden he was paralyzed into a listening attitude and that smile faded gradually out of his countenance like a breath off'n a razor, and the queerest look of surprise took its place. Then he says, 'Why I didn't hear it fall!' He cocked his eye at the hole again, and took a long look; raised up and shook his head; stepped around to the other side of the hole and took another look from that side; shook his head again. He studied a while, then he just went into the *de* tails—walked round and round the hole and spied into it from every point of the compass. No use. Now he took a thinking attitude on the comb of the roof and scratched the back of his head with his right foot a minute, and finally says, 'Well, it's too many for *me,* that's certain; must be a mighty long hole; however, I ain't got no time to fool around here, I got to 'tend to business; I reckon it's all right —chance it, anyway.'

"So he flew off and fetched another acorn and dropped it in, and tried to flirt his eye to the hole quick enough to see what become of it, but he was too late. He held his eye there as much as a minute; then he raised up and sighed, and says, 'Confound it, I don't seem to understand this thing, no way; however, I'll tackle her again.' He fetched another acorn, and done his level best to see what become of it, but he couldn't. He says, 'Well, *I* never struck no such a hole as this, before; I'm of the opinion it's a totally new kind of a hole.' Then he begun to get mad. He held in for a spell, walking up and down the comb of the roof and shaking his head and muttering to himself; but his feelings got the upper hand of him, presently, and he broke loose and cussed himself black in the face. I never see a bird take on so about a little thing. When he got through he walks to the hole and looks in again for half a minute; then he says, 'Well, you're a long hole, and a deep hole, and a mighty singular hole altogether— but I've started in to fill you, and I'm d——d if I *don't* fill you, if it takes a hundred years!"

"And with that, away he went. You never see a bird work so since you was born. He laid into his work like a nigger, and the way he hove acorns into that hole for about two hours and a half was one of the most exciting and astonishing spectacles I ever struck. He never stopped to take a look any more—he just hove 'em in and went for more. Well at last he could hardly flop his wings, he was so tuckered out. He comes a-dropping down, once more, sweating like an ice-pitcher, drops his acorn in and says, '*Now* I guess I've got the bulge on you by this time!' So he bent down for a look. If you'll believe me, when his head came up again he was just pale with rage. He says, 'I've shoveled acorns enough in there to keep the family thirty years, and if I can see a sign of one of 'em I wish I may land in a museum with a belly full of sawdust in two minutes!'

"He just had strength enough to crawl up on to the comb and lean his back agin the chimbly, and then he collected his impressions and begun to free his mind. I see in a second that what I had mistook for profanity in the mines was only just the rudiments, as you may say.

"Another jay was going by, and heard him doing his devotions, and stops to inquire what was up. The sufferer told him the whole circumstance, and says, 'Now yonder's the hole, and if you don't believe me, go and look for yourself.' So this fellow went and looked, and comes back and says, 'How many did you say you put in there?' 'Not any less than two tons,' says the sufferer. The other jay went and looked again. He couldn't seem to make it out, so he raised a yell, and three more jays come. They all examined the hole, they all made the sufferer tell it over again, then they all discussed it, and got off as many leather-headed opinions about it as an average crowd of humans could have done.

"They called in more jays; then more and more, till pretty soon this whole region 'peared to have a blue flush about it. There must have been five thousand of them; and such another jawing and disputing and ripping and cussing, you never heard. Every jay in the whole lot put his eye to the hole and delivered a more chuckle-headed opinion about the mystery than the jay that went there before him. They examined the house all over, too. The door was standing half open, and at last one old jay happened to go and light on it and look in. Of course that knocked the mystery galley-west in a second. There lay the acorns, scattered all over the floor. He flopped his wings and raised a whoop. 'Come here!' he says, 'Come here, everybody; hang'd if this fool hasn't been trying to fill up a house with acorns!' They all came a-swooping down like a blue cloud, and as each fellow lit on the door and took a glance, the whole absurdity of the contract that that first jay had tackled hit him home and he fell over backwards suffocating with laughter, and the next jay took his place and done the same.

"Well, sir, they roosted around here on the house-top and the trees for an hour, and guffawed over that thing like human beings. It ain't any use to tell me a blue-jay hasn't got a sense of humor, because I know better. And memory, too. They brought jays here from all over the United States to look down that hole, every summer for three years. Other birds too. And they could all see the point, except an owl that come from Nova Scotia to visit the Yo Semite, and he took this thing in on his way back. He said he couldn't see anything funny in it. But then he was a good deal disappointed about Yo Semite, too."

1880

The Private History of a Campaign That Failed

You have heard from a great many people who did something in the war; is it not fair and right that you listen a little moment to one who started out to do something in it, but didn't? Thousands entered the war, got just a taste of it, and then stepped out again permanently. These, by their very numbers, are respectable, and are therefore entitled to a sort of voice—not a loud one, but a modest one; not a boastful one, but an apologetic one. They ought not to be allowed much space among better people —people who did something. I grant that; but they ought at least to be allowed to state why they didn't do anything, and also to explain the process by which they didn't do anything. Surely this kind of light must have a sort of value.

Out West there was a good deal of confusion in men's minds during the first months of the great trouble—a good deal of unsettledness, of leaning first this way, then that, then the other way. It was hard for us to get our bearings. I call to mind an instance of this. I was piloting on the Mississippi when the news came that South Carolina had gone out of the Union on the 20th of December, 1860. My pilot mate was a New-Yorker. He was strong for the Union; so was I. But he would not listen to me with any patience; my loyalty was smirched, to his eye, because my father had owned slaves. I said, in palliation of this dark fact, that I had heard my father say, some years before he died, that slavery was a great wrong, and that he would free the solitary negro he then owned if he could think it right to give away the property of the family when he was so straitened in means. My mate retorted that a mere impulse was nothing—anybody could pretend to a good impulse; and went on decrying my Unionism and libeling my ancestry. A month later the secession atmosphere had considerably thickened on the Lower Mississippi, and I became a rebel; so did he. We were together in New Orleans the 26th of January, when Louisiana went out of the Union. He did his full share of the rebel shouting, but was bitterly opposed to letting me do mine. He said that I came of bad stock—of a father who had been willing to set slaves free. In the following summer he was piloting a Federal gunboat and shouting for the Union again, and I was in the Confederate army. I held his note for some borrowed money. He was one of the most upright men I ever knew, but he repudiated that note without hesitation because I was a rebel and the son of a man who owned slaves.

In that summer—of 1861—the first wash of the wave of war broke upon the shores of Missouri. Our state was invaded by the Union forces. They took possession of St. Louis, Jefferson Barracks, and some other points. The Governor, Claib Jackson, issued his proclamation calling out fifty thousand militia to repel the invader.

I was visiting in the small town where my boyhood had been spent—Hannibal, Marion County. Several of us got together in a secret place by night and formed ourselves into a military company. One Tom Lyman, a young fellow of a good deal of spirit but of no military experience, was made captain; I was made second lieutenant. We had no first lieutenant; I do not know why; it was long ago. There were fifteen of us. By the advice of an innocent connected with the organization we called ourselves the Marion Rangers. I do not remember that any one found fault with the name. I did not; I thought it sounded quite well. The young fellow who proposed this title was perhaps a fair sample of the kind of stuff we were made of. He was young, ignorant, good-natured, well-meaning, trivial, full of romance, and given to reading chivalric novels and singing forlorn love-ditties. He had some pathetic little nickel-plated aristocratic instincts, and detested his name, which was Dunlap; detested it, partly because it was nearly as common in that region as Smith, but mainly because it had a plebeian sound to his ear. So he tried to ennoble it by writing it in this way: *d'Unlap.* That contented his eye, but left his ear unsatisfied, for people gave the new name the same old pronunciation—emphasis on the front end of it. He then did the bravest thing that can be imagined—a thing to make one shiver when one remembers how the world is given to resenting shams and affectations; he began to write his name so: *d'Un Lap.* And he waited patiently through the long storm of mud that was flung at this work of art, and he had his reward at last; for he lived to see that name accepted, and the emphasis put where he wanted it by people who had known him all his life, and to whom the tribe of Dunlaps had been as familiar as the rain and the sunshine for forty years. So sure of victory at last is the courage that can wait. He said he had found, by consulting some ancient French chronicles, that the name was rightly and originally written d'Un Lap; and said that if it were translated into English it would mean Peterson: *Lap,* Latin or Greek, he said, for stone or rock, same as the French *pierre,* that is to say, Peter: *d',* of or from; *un,* a or one; hence, d'Un Lap, of or from a stone or a Peter; that is to say, one who is the son of a stone, the son of a Peter —Peterson. Our militia company were not learned, and the explanation confused them; so they called him Peterson Dunlap. He proved useful to us in his way; he named our camps for us, and he generally struck a name that was "no slouch," as the boys said.

That is one sample of us. Another was Ed Stevens, son of the town jeweler— trim-built, handsome, graceful, neat as a cat; bright, educated, but given over entirely to fun. There was nothing serious in life to him. As far as he was concerned, this military expedition of ours was simply a holiday. I should say that about half of us looked upon it in the same way; not consciously, perhaps, but unconsciously. We did not think; we were not capable of it. As for myself, I was full of unreasoning joy to be done with turning out of bed at midnight and four in the morning for a while; grateful to have a change, new scenes, new occupations, a new interest. In my thoughts that was as far as I went; I did not go into the details; as a rule, one doesn't at twenty-four.

Another sample was Smith, the blacksmith's apprentice. This vast donkey had some pluck, of a slow and sluggish nature, but a soft heart; at one time he would knock a horse down for some impropriety, and at another he would get homesick and cry. However, he had one ultimate credit to his account which some of us hadn't; he stuck to the war, and was killed in battle at last.

Jo Bowers, another sample, was a huge, good-natured, flax-headed lubber; lazy, sentimental, full of harmless brag, a grumbler by nature; an experienced, industrious, ambitious, and often quite picturesque liar, and yet not a successful one, for he had had no intelligent training, but was allowed to come up just any way. This life was serious enough to him, and seldom satisfactory. But he was a good fellow, anyway, and the boys all liked him. He was made orderly sergeant; Stevens was made corporal.

These samples will answer—and they are quite fair ones. Well, this herd of cattle started for the war. What could you expect of them? They did as well as they knew how; but, really, what was justly to be expected of them? Nothing, I should say. That is what they did.

We waited for a dark night, for caution and secrecy were necessary; then, toward midnight, we stole in couples and from various directions to the Griffith place, beyond the town; from that point we set out together on foot. Hannibal lies at the extreme southeastern corner of Marion County, on the Mississippi River; our objective point was the hamlet of New London, ten miles away, in Ralls County.

The first hour was all fun, all idle nonsense and laughter. But that could not be kept up. The steady trudging came to be like work; the play had somehow oozed out of it; the stillness of the woods and the somberness of the night began to throw a depressing influence over the spirits of the boys, and presently the talking died out and each person shut himself up in his own thoughts. During the last half of the second hour nobody said a word.

Now we approached a log farm-house where, according to report, there was a guard of five Union soldiers. Lyman called a halt; and there, in the deep gloom of the overhanging branches, he began to whisper a plan of assault upon that house, which made the gloom more depressing than it was before. It was a crucial moment; we realized, with a cold suddenness, that here was no jest—we were standing face to face with actual war. We were equal to the occasion. In our response there was no hesitation, no indecision: we said that if Lyman wanted to meddle with those soldiers, he could go ahead and do it; but if he waited for us to follow him, he would wait a long time.

Lyman urged, pleaded, tried to shame us, but it had no effect. Our course was plain, our minds were made up: we would flank the farm-house—go out around. And that was what we did.

We struck into the woods and entered upon a rough time, stumbling over roots, getting tangled in vines, and torn by briers. At last we reached an open place in a safe region, and sat down, blown and hot, to cool off and nurse our scratches and bruises. Lyman was annoyed, but the rest of us were cheerful; we had flanked the farm-house, we had made our first military movement, and it was a success; we had nothing to fret about, we were feeling just the other way. Horse-play and laughing began again; the expedition was become a holiday frolic once more.

Then we had two more hours of dull trudging and ultimate silence and depression; then, about dawn, we straggled into New London, soiled, heel-blistered, fagged with our little march, and all of us except Stevens in a sour and raspy humor and privately down on the war. We stacked our shabby old shotguns in Colonel Ralls's barn, and then went in a body and breakfasted with that veteran of the Mexican War. Afterward he took us to a distant meadow, and there in the shade of a tree we listened to an old-fashioned speech from him, full of gun-powder and glory, full of that adjective-piling, mixed metaphor and windy declamation which were regarded as eloquence in that ancient time and that remote region; and then he swore us on the Bible to be faithful to the State of Missouri and drive all invaders from her soil, no matter whence they might come or under what flag they might march. This mixed us considerably, and we could not make out just what service we were embarked in; but Colonel Ralls, the practised politician and phrase-juggler, was not similarly in doubt; he knew quite clearly that he had invested us in the cause of the Southern Confederacy. He closed the solemnities by belting around me the sword which his neighbor, Colonel Brown, had worn at Buena Vista and Molino del Rey;[1] and he accompanied this act with another impressive blast.

Then we formed in line of battle and marched four miles to a shady and pleasant piece of woods on the border of the far-reaching expanses of a flowery prairie. It was an enchanting region for war—our kind of war.

We pierced the forest about half a mile, and took up a strong position, with some low, rocky, and wooded hills behind us, and a purling, limpid creek in front. Straightway half the command were in swimming and the other half fishing. The ass

[1] American victories (February and September 1847) in the Mexican War.

with the French name gave this position a romantic title, but it was too long, so the boys shortened and simplified it to Camp Ralls.

We occupied an old maple-sugar camp, whose half-rotted troughs were still propped against the trees. A long corn-crib served for sleeping-quarters for the battalion. On our left, half a mile away, were Mason's farm and house; and he was a friend to the cause. Shortly after noon the farmers began to arrive from several directions, with mules and horses for our use, and these they lent us for as long as the war might last, which they judged would be about three months. The animals were of all sizes, all colors, and all breeds. They were mainly young and frisky, and nobody in the command could stay on them long at a time; for we were town boys, and ignorant of horsemanship. The creature that fell to my share was a very small mule, and yet so quick and active that it could throw me without difficulty; and it did this whenever I got on it. Then it would bray—stretching its neck out, laying its ears back, and spreading its jaws till you could see down to its works. It was a disagreeable animal in every way. If I took it by the bridle and tried to lead it off the grounds, it would sit down and brace back, and no one could budge it. However, I was not entirely destitute of military resources, and I did presently manage to spoil this game; for I had seen many a steamboat aground in my time, and knew a trick or two which even a grounded mule would be obliged to respect. There was a well by the corn-crib; so I substituted thirty fathom of rope for the bridle, and fetched him home with the windlass.

I will anticipate here sufficiently to say that we did learn to ride, after some days' practice, but never well. We could not learn to like our animals; they were not choice ones, and most of them had annoying peculiarities of one kind or another. Stevens's horse would carry him, when he was not noticing, under the huge excrescences which form on the trunks of oak-trees, and wipe him out of the saddle; in this way Stevens got several bad hurts. Sergeant Bowers's horse was very large and tall, with slim, long legs, and looked like a railroad bridge. His size enabled him to reach all about, and as far as he wanted to, with his head; so he was always biting Bowers's legs. On the march, in the sun, Bowers slept a good deal; and as soon as the horse recognized that he was asleep he would reach around and bite him on the leg. His legs were black and blue with bites. This was the only thing that could ever make him swear, but this always did; whenever his horse bit him he always swore, and of course Stevens, who laughed at everything, laughed at this, and would even get into such convulsions over it as to lose his balance and fall off his horse; and then Bowers, already irritated by the pain of the horse-bite, would resent the laughter with hard language, and there would be a quarrel; so that horse made no end of trouble and bad blood in the command.

However, I will get back to where I was—our first afternoon in the sugar-camp. The sugar-troughs came very handy as horse-troughs, and we had plenty of corn to fill them with. I ordered Sergeant Bowers to feed my mule; but he said that if I reckoned he went to war to be a dry-nurse to a mule it wouldn't take me very long to find out my mistake. I believed that this was insubordination, but I was full of uncertainties about everything military, and so I let the thing pass, and went and ordered Smith, the blacksmith's apprentice, to feed the mule; but he merely gave me a large, cold, sarcastic grin, such as an ostensibly seven-year-old horse gives you when you lift his lip and find he is fourteen, and turned his back on me. I then went to the captain, and asked if it were not right and proper and military for me to have an orderly. He said it was, but as there was only one orderly in the corps, it was but right that he himself should have Bowers on his staff. Bowers said he wouldn't serve on anybody's staff; and if anybody thought he could make him, let him try it. So, of course, the thing had to be dropped; there was no other way.

Next, nobody would cook; it was considered a degradation; so we had no dinner. We lazied the rest of the pleasant afternoon away, some dozing under the trees, some smoking cob-pipes and talking sweethearts and war, some playing games. By late supper-time all hands were famished; and to meet the difficulty all hands turned to, on an equal footing, and gathered wood, built fires, and cooked the meal. Afterward everything was smooth for a while; then trouble broke out between the corporal and the sergeant, each claiming to rank the other. Nobody knew which was the higher office; so Lyman had to settle the matter by making the rank of both officers equal. The commander of an ignorant crew like that has many troubles and vexations which probably do not occur in the regular army at all. However, with the song-singing and yarn-spinning around the camp-fire, everything presently became serene again; and by and by we raked the corn down level in one end of the crib, and all went to bed on it, tying a horse to the door, so that he would neigh if any one tried to get in.[2]

We had some horsemanship drill every forenoon; then, afternoons, we rode off here and there in squads a few miles, and visited the farmers' girls, and had a youthful good time, and got an honest good dinner or supper, and then home again to camp, happy and content.

For a time life was idly delicious, it was perfect; there was nothing to mar it. Then came some farmers with an alarm one day. They said it was rumored that the enemy were advancing in our direction from over Hyde's prairie. The result was a sharp stir among us, and general consternation. It was a rude awakening from our pleasant trance. The rumor was but a rumor—nothing definite about it; so, in the confusion, we did not know which way to retreat. Lyman was for not retreating at all in these uncertain circumstances; but he found that if he tried to maintain that attitude he would fare badly, for the command were in no humor to put up with insubordination. So he yielded the point and called a council of war—to consist of himself and the three other officers; but the privates made such a fuss about being left out that we had to allow them to remain, for they were already present, and doing the most of the talking too. The question was, which way to retreat; but all were so flurried that nobody seemed to have even a guess to offer. Except Lyman. He explained in a few calm words that, inasmuch as the enemy were approaching from over Hyde's prairie, our course was simple: all we had to do was not to retreat *toward* him; any other direction would answer our needs perfectly. Everybody saw in a moment how true

[2] Twain's note: "It was always my impression that that was what the horse was there for, and I know that it was also the impression of at least one other of the command, for we talked about it at the time, and admired the military ingenuity of the device; but when I was out West, three years ago, I was told by Mr. A. G. Fuqua, a member of our company, that the horse was his; that the leaving him tied at the door was a matter of mere forgetfulness, and that to attribute it to intelligent invention was to give him quite too much credit. In support of his position he called my attention to the suggestive fact that the artifice was not employed again. I had not thought of that before."

this was, and how wise; so Lyman got a great many compliments. It was now decided that we should fall back on Mason's farm.

It was after dark by this time, and as we could not know how soon the enemy might arrive, it did not seem best to try to take the horses and things with us; so we only took the guns and ammunition, and started at once. The route was very rough and hilly and rocky, and presently the night grew very black and rain began to fall; so we had a troublesome time of it, struggling and stumbling along in the dark; and soon some person slipped and fell, and then the next person behind stumbled over him and fell, and so did the rest, one after the other; and then Bowers came, with the keg of powder in his arms, while the command were all mixed together, arms and legs, on the muddy slope; and so he fell, of course, with the keg, and this started the whole detachment down the hill in a body, and they landed in the brook at the bottom in a pile, and each that was undermost pulling the hair and scratching and biting those that were on top of him; and those that were being scratched and bitten scratching and biting the rest in their turn, and all saying they would die before they would ever go to war again if they ever got out of this brook this time, and the invader might rot for all they cared, and the country along with him—and all such talk as that, which was dismal to hear and take part in, in such smothered, low voices, and such a grisly dark place and so wet, and the enemy, maybe, coming any moment.

The keg of powder was lost, and the guns, too; so the growling and complaining continued straight along while the brigade pawed around the pasty hillside and slopped around in the brook hunting for these things; consequently we lost considerable time at this; and then we heard a sound, and held our breath and listened, and it seemed to be the enemy coming, though it could have been a cow, for it had a cough like a cow; but we did not wait, but left a couple of guns behind and struck out for Mason's again as briskly as we could scramble along in the dark. But we got lost presently among the rugged little ravines, and wasted a deal of time finding the way again, so it was after nine when we reached Mason's stile at last; and then before we could open our mouths to give the countersign several dogs came bounding over the fence, with great riot and noise, and each of them took a soldier by the slack of his trousers and began to back away with him. We could not shoot the dogs without endangering the persons they were attached to; so we had to look on helpless at what was perhaps the most mortifying spectacle of the Civil War. There was light enough, and to spare, for the Masons had now run out on the porch with candles in their hands. The old man and his son came and undid the dogs without difficulty, all but Bowers's; but they couldn't undo his dog, they didn't know his combination; he was of the bull kind, and seemed to be set with a Yale time-lock; but they got him loose at last with some scalding water, of which Bowers got his share and returned thanks. Peterson Dunlap afterward made up a fine name for this engagement, and also for the night march which preceded it, but both have long ago faded out of my memory.

We now went into the house, and they began to ask us a world of questions, whereby it presently came out that we did not know anything concerning who or what we were running from; so the old gentleman made himself very frank, and said we were a curious breed of soldiers, and guessed we could be depended on to end up the war in time, because no government could stand the expense of the shoe-leather we should cost it trying to follow us around. "Marion *Rangers!* good name, b'gosh!" said he. And wanted to know why we hadn't had a picket-guard at the place where the road entered the prairie, and why we hadn't sent out a scouting party to spy out the enemy and bring us an account of his strength, and so on, before jumping up and stampeding out of a strong position upon a mere vague rumor—and so on, and so forth, till he made us all feel shabbier than the dogs had done, not half so enthusiastically welcome. So we went to bed shamed and low-spirited; except Stevens. Soon Stevens began to devise a garment for Bowers which could be made to automatically display his battle-scars to the grateful, or conceal them from the envious, according to his occasions; but Bowers was in no humor for this, so there was a fight, and when it was over Stevens had some battle-scars of his own to think about.

Then we got a little sleep. But after all we had gone through, our activities were not over for the night; for about two o'clock in the morning we heard a shout of warning from down the lane, accompanied by a chorus from all the dogs, and in a moment everybody was up and flying around to find out what the alarm was about. The alarmist was a horseman who gave notice that a detachment of Union soldiers was on its way from Hannibal with orders to capture and hang any bands like ours which it could find, and said we had no time to lose. Farmer Mason was in a flurry this time himself. He hurried us out of the house with all haste, and sent one of his negroes with us to show us where to hide ourselves and our telltale guns among the ravines half a mile away. It was raining heavily.

We struck down the lane, then across some rocky pasture-land which offered good advantages for stumbling; consequently we were down in the mud most of the time, and every time a man went down he blackguarded the war, and the people that started it, and everybody connected with it, and gave himself the master dose of all for being so foolish as to go into it. At last we reached the wooded mouth of a ravine, and there we huddled ourselves under the streaming trees, and sent the negro back home. It was a dismal and heart-breaking time. We were like to be drowned with the rain, deafened with the howling wind and the booming thunder, and blinded by the lightning. It was, indeed, a wild night. The drenching we were getting was misery enough, but a deeper misery still was the reflection that the halter might end us before we were a day older. A death of this shameful sort had not occurred to us as being among the possibilities of war. It took the romance all out of the campaign, and turned our dreams of glory into a repulsive nightmare. As for doubting that so barbarous an order had been given, not one of us did that.

The long night wore itself out at last, and then the negro came to us with the news that the alarm had manifestly been a false one, and that breakfast would soon be ready. Straightway we were light-hearted again, and the world was bright, and life as full of hope and promise as ever—for we were young then. How long ago that was! Twenty-four years.

The mongrel child of philology named the night's refuge Camp Devastation, and no soul objected. The Masons gave us a Missouri country breakfast, in Missourian abundance, and we needed it: hot biscuits; hot "wheat bread," prettily criss-crossed in a lattice pattern on top; hot corn-pone; fried chicken; bacon, coffee, eggs, milk, buttermilk, etc.; and the world may be confidently challenged to furnish the equal of such a breakfast, as it is cooked in the South.

We stayed several days at Mason's; and after all these years the memory of the dullness, and stillness, and lifelessness of that slumberous farm-house still oppresses my spirit as with a sense of the presence of death and mourning. There was nothing to do, nothing to think about; there was no interest in life. The male part of the household were away in the fields all day, the women were busy and out of our sight; there was no sound but the plaintive wailing of a spinning-wheel, forever moaning out from some distant room—the most lonesome sound in nature, a sound steeped and sodden with homesickness and the emptiness of life. The family went to bed about dark every night, and as we were not invited to intrude any new customs we naturally followed theirs. Those nights were a hundred years long to youths accustomed to being up till twelve. We lay awake and miserable till that hour every time, and grew old and decrepit waiting through the still eternities for the clock-strikes. This was no place for town boys. So at last it was with something very like joy that we received news that the enemy were on our track again. With a new birth of the old warrior spirit we sprang to our places in line of battle and fell back on Camp Ralls.

Captain Lyman had taken a hint from Mason's talk, and he now gave orders that our camp should be guarded against surprise by the posting of pickets. I was ordered to place a picket at the forks of the road in Hyde's prairie. Night shut down black and threatening. I told Sergeant Bowers to go out to that place and stay till midnight; and, just as I was expecting, he said he wouldn't do it. I tried to get others to go, but all refused. Some excused themselves on account of the weather; but the rest were frank enough to say they wouldn't go in any kind of weather. This kind of thing sounds odd now, and impossible, but there was no surprise in it at the time. On the contrary, it seemed a perfectly natural thing to do. There were scores of little camps scattered over Missouri where the same thing was happening. These camps were composed of young men who had been born and reared to a sturdy independence, and who did not know what it meant to be ordered around by Tom, Dick, and Harry, whom they had known familiarly all their lives, in the village or on the farm. It is quite within the probabilities that this same thing was happening all over the South. James Redpath recognized the justice of this assumption, and furnished the following instance in support of it. During a short stay in East Tennessee he was in a citizen colonel's tent one day talking, when a big private appeared at the door, and, without salute or other circumlocution, said to the colonel:

"Say, Jim, I'm a-goin' home for a few days."

"What for?"

"Well, I hain't b'en there for a right smart while, and I'd like to see how things is comin' on."

"How long are you going to be gone?"

"'Bout two weeks."

"Well, don't be gone longer than that; and get back sooner if you can."

That was all, and the citizen officer resumed his conversation where the private had broken it off. This was in the first months of the war, of course. The camps in our part of Missouri were under Brigadier-General Thomas H. Harris. He was a townsman of ours, a first-rate fellow, and well liked; but we had all familiarly known him as the sole and modest-salaried operator in our telegraph-office, where he had to send about one despatch a week in ordinary times, and two when there was a rush of business; consequently, when he appeared in our midst one day, on the wing, and delivered a military command of some sort, in a large military fashion, nobody was surprised at the response which he got from the assembled soldiery:

"Oh, now, what'll you take to *don't*, Tom Harris?"

It was quite the natural thing. One might justly imagine that we were hopeless material for war. And so we seemed, in our ignorant state; but there were those among us who afterward learned the grim trade; learned to obey like machines; became valuable soldiers; fought all through the war, and came out at the end with excellent records. One of the very boys who refused to go out on picket duty that night, and called me an ass for thinking he would expose himself to danger in such a foolhardy way, had become distinguished for intrepidity before he was a year older.

I did secure my picket that night—not by authority, but by diplomacy. I got Bowers to go by agreeing to exchange ranks with him for the time being, and go along and stand the watch with him as his subordinate. We stayed out there a couple of dreary hours in the pitchy darkness and the rain, with nothing to modify the dreariness but Bowers's monotonous growlings at the war and the weather; then we began to nod, and presently found it next to impossible to stay in the saddle; so we gave up the tedious job, and went back to the camp without waiting for the relief guard. We rode into camp without interruption or objection from anybody, and the enemy could have done the same, for there were no sentries. Everybody was asleep; at midnight there was nobody to send out another picket, so none was sent. We never tried to establish a watch at night again, as far as I remember, but we generally kept a picket out in the daytime.

In that camp the whole command slept on the corn in the big corn-crib; and there was usually a general row before morning, for the place was full of rats, and they would scramble over the boys' bodies and faces, annoying and irritating everybody; and now and then they would bite some one's toe, and the person who owned the toe would start up and magnify his English and begin to throw corn in the dark. The ears were half as heavy as bricks, and when they struck they hurt. The persons struck would respond, and inside of five minutes every man would be locked in a death-grip with his neighbor. There was a grievous deal of blood shed in the corncrib, but this was all that was spilt while I was in the war. No, that is not quite true. But for one circumstance it would have been all. I will come to that now.

Our scares were frequent. Every few days rumors would come that the enemy were approaching. In these cases we always fell back on some other camp of ours; we never stayed where we were. But the rumors always turned out to be false; so at last even we began to grow indifferent to them. One night a negro was sent to our corn-crib with the same old warning: the enemy was hovering in our neighborhood. We all said let him hover. We resolved to stay still and be comfortable. It was a fine warlike resolution, and no doubt we all felt the stir of it in our veins—for a moment. We had been having a very jolly time, that was full of horse-play and schoolboy hilarity; but that cooled down now, and presently the fast-waning fire of forced jokes and forced laughs died out altogether, and the company became silent. Silent and nervous. And soon uneasy—worried—apprehensive. We had said we would stay, and we were committed. We could have been persuaded to go, but there was nobody brave enough to suggest it. An almost noiseless movement presently began in the dark by a general but unvoiced impulse. When the movement was completed each man knew that he was not the only person who had crept to the front wall and had his eye at a crack between the logs. No, we were all there; all there with our hearts in our throats, and staring out toward the sugar-troughs where the forest footpath came through. It was late, and there was a deep woodsy stillness everywhere. There was a veiled moonlight, which was only just strong enough to enable us to mark the general shape of objects. Presently a muffled sound caught our ears, and we recognized it as the hoof-beats of a horse or horses. And right away a figure appeared in the forest path; it could have been made of smoke, its mass had so little sharpness of outline. It was a man on horse-back, and it seemed to me that there were others behind him. I got hold of a gun in the dark, and pushed it through a crack between the logs, hardly knowing what I was doing, I was so dazed with fright. Somebody said "Fire!" I pulled the trigger. I seemed to see a hundred flashes and hear a hundred reports; then I saw the man fall down out of the saddle. My first feeling was of surprised gratification; my first impulse was an apprentice-sportsman's impulse to run and pick up his game. Somebody said, hardly audibly, "Good—we've got him!—wait for the rest." But the rest did not come. We waited—listened—still no more came. There was not a sound, not the whisper of a leaf; just perfect stillness; an uncanny kind of stillness, which was all the more uncanny on account of the damp, earthy, late-night smells now rising and pervading it. Then, wondering, we crept stealthily out, and approached the man. When we got to him the moon revealed him distinctly. He was lying on his back, with his arms abroad; his mouth was open and his chest heaving with long gasps, and his white shirt-front was all splashed with blood. The thought shot through me that I was a murderer; that I had killed a man—a man who had never done me any harm. That was the coldest sensation that ever went through my marrow. I was down by him in a moment, helplessly stroking his forehead; and I would have given anything then—my own life freely—to make him again what he had been five minutes before. And all the boys seemed to be feeling in the same way; they hung over him, full of pitying interest, and tried all they could to help him, and said all sorts of regretful things. They had forgotten all about the enemy; they thought only of this one forlorn unit of the foe. Once my imagination persuaded me that the dying man gave me a reproachful look out of his shadowy eyes, and it seemed to me that I could rather he had stabbed me than done that. He muttered and mumbled like a dreamer in his sleep about his wife and his child; and I thought with a new despair, "This thing that I have done does not end with him; it falls upon *them* too, and they never did me any harm, any more than he."

In a little while the man was dead. He was killed in war; killed in fair and legitimate war; killed in battle, as you may say; and yet he was as sincerely mourned by the opposing force as if he had been their brother. The boys stood there a half-hour sorrowing over him, and recalling the details of the tragedy, and wondering who he might be, and if he were a spy, and saying that if it were to do over again they would not hurt him unless he attacked them first. It soon came out that mine was not the only shot fired; there were five others—a division of the guilt which was a great relief to me, since it in some degree lightened and diminished the burden I was carrying. There were six shots fired at once; but I was not in my right mind at the time, and my heated imagination had magnified my one shot into a volley.

The man was not in uniform, and was not armed. He was a stranger in the country; that was all we ever found out about him. The thought of him got to preying upon me every night; I could not get rid of it. I could not drive it away, the taking of that unoffending life seemed such a wanton thing. And it seemed an epitome of war; that all war must be just that—the killing of strangers against whom you feel no personal animosity; strangers whom, in other circumstances, you would help if you found them in trouble, and who would help you if you needed it. My campaign was spoiled. It seemed to me that I was not rightly equipped for this awful business; that war was intended for men, and I for a child's nurse. I resolved to retire from this avocation of sham soldiership while I could save some remnant of my self-respect. These morbid thoughts clung to me against reason; for at bottom I did not believe I had touched that man. The law of probabilities decreed me guiltless of his blood; for in all my small experience with guns I had never hit anything I had tried to hit, and I knew I had done my best to hit him. Yet there was no solace in the thought. Against a diseased imagination demonstration goes for nothing.

The rest of my war experience was of a piece with what I have already told of it. We kept monotonously falling back upon one camp or another, and eating up the farmers and their families. They ought to have shot us; on the contrary, they were as hospitably kind and courteous to us as if we had deserved it. In one of these camps we found Ab Grimes, an Upper Mississippi pilot, who afterward became famous as a dare-devil rebel spy, whose career bristled with desperate adventures. The look and style of his comrades suggested that they had not come into the war to play, and their deeds made good the conjecture later. They were fine horsemen and good revolver shots; but their favorite arm was the lasso. Each had one at his pommel, and could snatch a man out of the saddle with it every time, on a full gallop, at any reasonable distance.

In another camp the chief was a fierce and profane old blacksmith of sixty, and he had furnished his twenty recruits with gigantic home-made bowie-knives, to be swung with two hands, like the *machetes* of the Isthmus. It was a grisly spectacle to see that earnest band practising their murderous cuts and slashes under the eye of that remorseless old fanatic.

The last camp which we fell back upon was in a hollow near the village of Florida, where I was born—in Monroe County. Here we were warned one day that a Union colonel was sweeping down on us with a whole regiment at his heel. This looked decidedly serious. Our boys went apart and consulted; then we went back and told the other companies present that the war was a disappointment to us, and we were going to disband. They were getting ready themselves to fall back on some place or other, and we were only waiting for General Tom Harris, who was expected to arrive at any moment; so they tried to persuade us to wait a little while, but the majority of us said no, we were accustomed to falling back, and didn't need any of Tom Harris's help; we could get along perfectly well without him—and save time, too. So about half of our fifteen, including myself, mounted and left on the instant; the others yielded to persuasion and stayed—stayed through the war.

An hour later we met General Harris on the road, with two or three people in his company—his staff, probably, but we could not tell; none of them were in uniform; uniforms had not come into vogue among us yet. Harris ordered us back; but we told him there was a Union colonel coming with a whole regiment in his wake, and it looked as if there was going to be a disturbance; so we had concluded to go home. He raged a little, but it was of no use; our minds were made up. We had done our share; had killed one man, exterminated one army, such as it was; let him go and kill the rest, and that would end the war. I did not see that brisk young general again until last year; then he was wearing white hair and whiskers.

In time I came to know that Union colonel whose coming frightened me out of the war and crippled the Southern cause to that extent—General Grant. I came within a few hours of seeing him when he was as unknown as I was myself; at a time when anybody could have said, "Grant?—Ulysses S. Grant? I do not remember hearing the name before." It seems difficult to realize that there was once a time when such a remark could be rationally made; but there was, and I was within a few miles of the place and the occasion, too, though proceeding in the other direction.

The thoughtful will not throw this war paper of mine lightly aside as being valueless. It has this value: it is a not unfair picture of what went on in many and many a militia camp in the first months of the rebellion, when the green recruits were without discipline, without the steadying and heartening influence of trained leaders; when all their circumstances were new and strange, and charged with exaggerated terrors, and before the invaluable experience of actual collision in the field had turned them from rabbits into soldiers. If this side of the picture of that early day has not before been put into history, then history has been to that degree incomplete, for it had and has its rightful place there. There was more Bull Run material scattered through the early camps of this country than exhibited itself at Bull Run. And yet it learned its trade presently, and helped to fight the great battles later. I could have become a soldier myself if I had waited. I had got part of it learned; I knew more about retreating than the man that invented retreating.

1885

Fenimore Cooper's Literary Offenses

> The Pathfinder *and* The Deerslayer *stand at the head of Cooper's novels as artistic creations. There are others of his works which contain parts as perfect as are to be found in these, and scenes even more thrilling. Not one can be compared with either of them as a finished whole.*
> *The defects in both of these tales are comparatively slight. They were pure works of art.*
>   Prof. Lounsbury

> *The five tales reveal an extraordinary fullness of invention. . . . One of the very greatest characters in fiction, Natty Bumppo. . . . The craft of the woodsman, the tricks of the trapper, all the delicate art of the forest, were familiar to Cooper from his youth up.*
>   Prof. Brander Matthews

> *Cooper is the greatest artist in the domain of romantic fiction yet produced by America.*
>   Wilkie Collins

It seems to me that it was far from right for the Professor of English Literature in Yale, the Professor of English Literature in Columbia, and Wilkie Collins to deliver opinions on Cooper's literature without having read some of it. It would have been much more decorous to keep silent and let persons talk who have read Cooper.

Cooper's art has some defects. In one place in *Deerslayer,* and in the restricted space of two-thirds of a page, Cooper has scored 114 offenses against literary art out of a possible 115. It breaks the record.

There are nineteen rules governing literary art in the domain of romantic fiction —some say twenty-two. In *Deerslayer* Cooper violated eighteen of them. These eighteen require:

1. That a tale shall accomplish something and arrive somewhere. But the *Deerslayer* tale accomplishes nothing and arrives in the air.

2. They require that the episodes of a tale shall be necessary parts of the tale, and shall help to develop it. But as the *Deerslayer* tale is not a tale, and accomplishes nothing and arrives nowhere, the episodes have no rightful place in the work, since there was nothing for them to develop.

3. They require that the personages in a tale shall be alive, except in the case of corpses, and that always the reader shall be able to tell the corpses from the others. But this detail has often been overlooked in the *Deerslayer* tale.

4. They require that the personages in a tale, both dead and alive, shall exhibit a sufficient excuse for being there. But this detail also has been overlooked in the *Deerslayer* tale.

5. They require that when the personages of a tale deal in conversation, the talk shall sound like human talk, and be talk such as human beings would be likely to talk in the given circumstances, and have a discoverable meaning, also a discoverable purpose, and a show of relevancy, and remain in the neighborhood of the subject in hand, and be interesting to the reader, and help out the tale, and stop when the people cannot think of anything more to say. But this requirement has been ignored from the beginning of the *Deerslayer* tale to the end of it.

6. They require that when the author describes the character of a personage in his tale, the conduct and conversation of that personage shall justify said description. But this law gets little or no attention in the *Deerslayer* tale, as Natty Bumppo's case will amply prove.

7. They require that when a personage talks like an illustrated, gilt-edged, tree-calf, hand-tooled, seven-dollar Friendship's Offering in the beginning of a paragraph, he shall not talk like a negro minstrel in the end of it. But this rule is flung down and danced upon in the *Deerslayer* tale.

8. They require that crass stupidities shall not be played upon the reader as "the craft of the woodsman, the delicate art of the forest," by either the author or the people in the tale. But this rule is persistently violated in the *Deerslayer* tale.

9. They require that the personages of a tale shall confine themselves to possibilities and let miracles alone; or, if they venture a miracle, the author must so plausibly set it forth as to make it look possible and reasonable. But these rules are not respected in the *Deerslayer* tale.

10. They require that the author shall make the reader feel a deep interest in the personages of his tale and in their fate; and that he shall make the reader love

the good people in the tale and hate the bad ones. But the reader of the *Deerslayer* tale dislikes the good people in it, is indifferent to the others, and wishes they would all get drowned together.

11. They require that the characters in a tale shall be so clearly defined that the reader can tell beforehand what each will do in a given emergency. But in the *Deerslayer* tale this rule is vacated.

In addition to these large rules there are some little ones. These require that the author shall

12. *Say* what he is proposing to say, not merely come near it.
13. Use the right word, not its second cousin.
14. Eschew surplusage.
15. Not omit necessary details.
16. Avoid slovenliness of form.
17. Use good grammar.
18. Employ a simple and straightforward style.

Even these seven are coldly and persistently violated in the *Deerslayer* tale.

Cooper's gift in the way of invention was not a rich endowment; but such as it was he liked to work it, he was pleased with the effects, and indeed he did some quite sweet things with it. In his little box of stage-properties he kept six or eight cunning devices, tricks, artifices for his savages and woodsmen to deceive and circumvent each other with, and he was never so happy as when he was working these innocent things and seeing them go. A favorite one was to make a moccasined person tread in the tracks of the moccasined enemy, and thus hide his own trail. Cooper wore out barrels and barrels of moccasins in working that trick. Another stage-property that he pulled out of his box pretty frequently was his broken twig. He prized his broken twig above all the rest of his effects, and worked it the hardest. It is a restful chapter in any book of his when somebody doesn't step on a dry twig and alarm all the reds and whites for two hundred yards around. Every time a Cooper person is in peril, and absolute silence is worth four dollars a minute, he is sure to step on a dry twig. There may be a hundred handier things to step on, but that wouldn't satisfy Cooper. Cooper requires him to turn out and find a dry twig; and if he can't do it, go and borrow one. In fact, the Leatherstocking Series ought to have been called the Broken Twig Series.

I am sorry there is not room to put in a few dozen instances of the delicate art of the forest, as practised by Natty Bumppo and some of the other Cooperian experts. Perhaps we may venture two or three samples. Cooper was a sailor—a naval officer; yet he gravely tells us how a vessel, driving toward a lee shore in a gale, is steered for a particular spot by her skipper because he knows of an *undertow* there which will hold her back against the gale and save her. For just pure woodcraft, or sailorcraft, or whatever it is, isn't that neat? For several years Cooper was daily in the society of artillery, and he ought to have noticed that when a cannon-ball strikes the ground it either buries itself or skips a hundred feet or so; skips again a hundred feet or so —and so on, till finally it gets tired and rolls. Now in one place he loses some "females"—as he always calls women—in the edge of a wood near a plain at night in a fog, on purpose to give Bumppo a chance to show off the delicate art of the forest before the reader. These mislaid people are hunting for a fort. They hear a cannon-blast, and a cannon-ball presently comes rolling into the wood and stops at their feet. To the females this suggests nothing. The case is very different with the admirable Bumppo. I wish I may never know peace again if he doesn't strike out promptly and *follow the track* of that cannon-ball across the plain through the dense fog and find the fort. Isn't it a daisy? If Cooper had any real knowledge of Nature's ways of doing things, he had a most delicate art in concealing the fact. For instance: one of his acute Indian experts, Chingachgook (pronounced Chicago, I think), has lost the trail of a person he is tracking through the forest. Apparently that trail is hopelessly lost. Neither you nor I could ever have guessed out the way to find it. It was very different with Chicago. Chicago was not stumped for long. He turned a running stream out of its course, and there, in the slush in its old bed, were that person's moccasin tracks. The current did not wash them away, as it would have done in all other like cases—no, even the eternal laws of Nature have to vacate when Cooper wants to put up a delicate job of woodcraft on the reader.

We must be a little wary when Brander Matthews tells us that Cooper's books "reveal an extraordinary fullness of invention." As a rule, I am quite willing to accept Brander Matthews's literary judgments and applaud his lucid and graceful phrasing of them; but that particular statement needs to be taken with a few tons of salt. Bless your heart, Cooper hadn't any more invention than a horse; and I don't mean a high-class horse, either; I mean a clothes-horse. It would be very difficult to find a really clever "situation" in Cooper's books, and still more difficult to find one of any kind which he has failed to render absurd by his handling of it. Look at the episodes of "the caves"; and at the celebrated scuffle between Maqua and those others on the table-land a few days later; and at Hurry Harry's queer water-transit from the castle to the ark; and at Deerslayer's half-hour with his first corpse; and at the quarrel between Hurry Harry and Deerslayer later; and at—but choose for yourself; you can't go amiss.

If Cooper had been an observer his inventive faculty would have worked better; not more interestingly, but more rationally, more plausibly. Cooper's proudest creations in the way of "situations" suffer noticeably from the absence of the observer's protecting gift. Cooper's eye was splendidly inaccurate. Cooper seldom saw anything correctly. He saw nearly all things as through a glass eye, darkly. Of course a man who cannot see the commonest little every-day matters accurately is working at a disadvantage when he is constructing a "situation." In the *Deerslayer* tale Cooper has a stream which is fifty feet wide where it flows out of a lake; it presently narrows to twenty as it meanders along for no given reason, and yet when a stream acts like that it ought to be required to explain itself. Fourteen pages later the width of the brook's outlet from the lake has suddenly shrunk thirty feet, and become "the narrowest part of the stream." This shrinkage is not accounted for. The stream has bends in it, a sure indication that it has alluvial banks and cuts them; yet these bends are only thirty and fifty feet long. If Cooper had been a nice and punctilious observer he would have noticed that the bends were oftener nine hundred feet long than short of it.

Cooper made the exit of that stream fifty feet wide, in the first place, for no particular reason; in the second place, he narrowed it to less than twenty to accommodate some Indians. He bends a "sapling" to the form of an arch over this narrow passage, and conceals six Indians in its foliage. They are "laying" for a settler's scow or ark which is coming up the stream on its way to the lake; it is being hauled against the stiff current by a rope whose stationary end is anchored in the lake; its rate of progress cannot be more than a mile an hour. Cooper describes the ark, but pretty obscurely. In the matter of dimensions "it was little more than a modern canal-boat." Let us guess, then, that it was about one hundred and forty feet long. It was of "greater breadth than common." Let us guess, then, that it was about sixteen feet wide. This leviathan had been prowling down bends which were but a third as long as itself, and scraping between banks where it had only two feet of space to spare on each side. We cannot too much admire this miracle. A low-roofed log dwelling occupies "two-thirds of the ark's length"—a dwelling ninety feet long and sixteen feet wide, let us say—a kind of vestibule train. The dwelling has two rooms—each forty-five feet long and sixteen feet wide, let us guess. One of them is the bedroom of the Hutter girls, Judith and Hetty; the other is the parlor in the daytime, at night it is papa's bedchamber. The ark is arriving at the stream's exit now, whose width has been reduced to less than twenty feet to accommodate the Indians—say to eighteen. There is a foot to spare on each side of the boat. Did the Indians notice that there was going to be a tight squeeze there? Did they notice that they could make money by climbing down out of that arched sapling and just stepping aboard when the ark scraped by? No, other Indians would have noticed these things, but Cooper's Indians never notice anything. Cooper thinks they are marvelous creatures for noticing, but he was almost always in error about his Indians. There was seldom a sane one among them.

The ark is one hundred and forty-feet long; the dwelling is ninety feet long. The idea of the Indians is to drop softly and secretly from the arched sapling to the dwelling as the ark creeps along under it at the rate of a mile an hour, and butcher the family. It will take the ark a minute and a half to pass under. It will take the ninety-foot dwelling a minute to pass under. Now, then, what did the six Indians do? It would take you thirty years to guess, and even then you would have to give it up, I believe. Therefore, I will tell you what the Indians did. Their chief, a person of quite extraordinary intellect for a Cooper Indian, warily watched the canal-boat as it squeezed along under him, and when he had got his calculations fined down to exactly the right shade, as he judged, he let go and dropped. And *missed the house!* That is actually what he did. He missed the house, and landed in the stern of the scow. It was not much of a fall, yet it knocked him silly. He lay there unconscious. If the house had been ninety-seven feet long he would have made the trip. The fault was Cooper's, not his. The error lay in the construction of the house. Cooper was no architect.

There still remained in the roost five Indians. The boat has passed under and is now out of their reach. Let me explain what the five did—you would not be able to reason it out for yourself. No. 1 jumped for the boat, but fell in the water astern of it. Then No. 2 jumped for the boat, but fell in the water still farther astern of it. Then No. 3 jumped for the boat, and fell a good way astern of it. Then No. 4 jumped for the boat, and fell in the water *away* astern. Then even No. 5 made a jump for the boat —for he was a Cooper Indian. In the matter of intellect, the difference between a Cooper Indian and the Indian that stands in front of the cigar-shop is not spacious. The scow episode is really a sublime burst of invention; but it does not thrill, because the inaccuracy of the details throws a sort of air of fictitiousness and general improbability over it. This comes of Cooper's inadequacy as an observer.

The reader will find some examples of Cooper's high talent for inaccurate observation in the account of the shooting-match in *The Pathfinder.*

A common wrought nail was driven lightly into the target, its head having been first touched with paint.

The color of the paint is not stated—an important omission, but Cooper deals freely in important omissions. No, after all, it was not an important omission; for this nail-head is *a hundred yards from* the marksmen, and could not be seen by them at that distance, no matter what its color might be. How far can the best eyes see a common house-fly? A hundred yards? It is quite impossible. Very well; eyes that cannot see a house-fly that is a hundred yards away cannot see an ordinary nail-head at that distance, for the size of the two objects is the same. It takes a keen eye to see a fly or a nail-head at fifty yards—one hundred and fifty feet. Can the reader do it?

The nail was lightly driven, its head painted, and game called. Then the Cooper miracles began. The bullet of the first marksman chipped an edge of the nail-head; the next man's bullet drove the nail a little way into the target—and removed all the paint. Haven't the miracles gone far enough now? Not to suit Cooper; for the purpose of this whole scheme is to show off his prodigy, Deerslayer-Hawkeye-Long-Rifle-Leatherstocking-Pathfinder-Bumppo before the ladies.

"Be all ready to clench it, boys!" cried out Pathfinder, stepping into his friend's tracks the instant they were vacant. "Never mind a new nail; I can see that, though the paint is gone, and what I can see I can hit at a hundred yards, though it were only a mosquito's eye. Be ready to clench!"

The rifle cracked, the bullet sped its way, and the head of the nail was buried in the wood, covered by the piece of flattened lead.

There, you see, is a man who could hunt flies with a rifle, and command a ducal salary in a Wild West show to-day if we had him back with us.

The recorded feat is certainly surprising just as it stands; but it is not surprising enough for Cooper. Cooper adds a touch. He has made Pathfinder do this miracle with another man's rifle; and not only that, but Pathfinder did not have even the advantage of loading it himself. He had everything against him, and yet he made that impossible shot; and not only made it, but did it with absolute confidence, saying, "Be ready to clench." Now a person like that would have undertaken that same feat with a brickbat, and with Cooper to help he would have achieved it, too.

Pathfinder showed off handsomely that day before the ladies. His very first feat was a thing which no Wild West show can touch. He was standing with the group of marksmen, observing—a hundred yards from the target, mind; one Jasper raised his rifle and drove the center of the bull's-eye. Then the Quartermaster fired. The target exhibited no result this time. There was a laugh. "It's a dead miss," said Major Lundie. Pathfinder waited an impressive moment or two; then said, in that calm, indifferent, know-it-all way of his, "No, Major, he has covered Jasper's bullet, as will be seen if any one will take the trouble to examine the target."

Wasn't it remarkable! How *could* he see that little pellet fly through the air and enter that distant bullet-hole? Yet that is what he did; for nothing is impossible to a Cooper person. Did any of those people have any deep-seated doubts about this thing? No; for that would imply sanity, and these were all Cooper people.

> The respect for Pathfinder's skill and for his quickness and accuracy of sight [the italics are mine] was so profound and general, that the instant he made this declaration the spectators began to distrust their own opinions, and a dozen rushed to the target in order to ascertain the fact. There, sure enough, it was found that the Quartermaster's bullet had gone through the hole made by Jasper's, and that, too, so accurately as to require a minute examination to be certain of the circumstance, which, however, was soon clearly established by discovering one bullet over the other in the stump against which the target was placed.

They made a "minute" examination; but never mind, how could they know that there were two bullets in that hole without digging the latest one out? For neither probe nor eyesight could prove the presence of any more than one bullet. Did they dig? No; as we shall see. It is the Pathfinder's turn now; he steps out before the ladies, takes aim, and fires.

But, alas! here is a disappointment; an incredible, an unimaginable disappointment —for the target's aspect is unchanged; there is nothing there but that same old bullet-hole!

> "If one dared to hint at such a thing," cried Major Duncan, "I should say that the Pathfinder has also missed the target!"

As nobody had missed it yet, the "also" was not necessary; but never mind about that, for the Pathfinder is going to speak.

> "No, no, Major," said he, confidently, "that *would* be a risky declaration. I didn't load the piece, and can't say what was in it; but if it was lead, you will find the bullet driving down those of the Quartermaster and Jasper, else is not my name Pathfinder."

A shout from the target announced the truth of this assertion.

Is the miracle sufficient as it stands? Not for Cooper. The Pathfinder speaks again, as he "now slowly advances toward the stage occupied by the females":

> "That's not all, boys, that's not all; if you find the target touched at all, I'll own to a miss. The Quartermaster cut the wood, but you'll find no wood cut by that last messenger."

The miracle is at last complete. He knew—doubtless *saw*—at the distance of a hundred yards—that his bullet had passed into the hole *without fraying the edges*. There were now three bullets in that one hole—three bullets embedded processionally in the body of the stump back of the target. Everybody knew this—somehow or other —and yet nobody had dug any of them out to make sure. Cooper is not a close observer, but he is interesting. He is certainly always that, no matter what happens. And he is more interesting when he is not noticing what he is about than when he is. This is a considerable merit.

The conversations in the Cooper books have a curious sound in our modern ears. To believe that such talk really ever came out of people's mouths would be to believe that there was a time when time was of no value to a person who thought he had something to say; when it was the custom to spread a two-minute remark out to ten; when a man's mouth was a rolling-mill, and busied itself all day long in turning four-foot pigs of thought into thirty-foot bars of conversational railroad iron by attenuation; when subjects were seldom faithfully stuck to, but the talk wandered all around and arrived nowhere; when conversations consisted mainly of irrelevancies, with here and there a relevancy, a relevancy with an embarrassed look, as not being able to explain how it got there.

Cooper was certainly not a master in the construction of dialogue. Inaccurate observation defeated him here as it defeated him in so many other enterprises of his. He even failed to notice that the man who talks corrupt English six days in the week must and will talk it on the seventh, and can't help himself. In the *Deerslayer* story he lets Deerslayer talk the showiest kind of book-talk sometimes, and at other times the basest of base dialects. For instance, when some one asks him if he has a sweetheart, and if so, where she abides, this is his majestic answer:

> "She's in the forest—hanging from the boughs of the trees, in a soft rain—in the dew on the open grass—the clouds that float about in the blue heavens— the birds that sing in the woods—the sweet springs where I slake my thirst— and in all the other glorious gifts that come from God's Providence!"

And he preceded that, a little before, with this:

> "It consarns me as all things that touches a fri'nd consarns a fri'nd."

And this is another of his remarks:

> "If I was Injin born, now, I might tell of this, or carry in the scalp and boast of the expl'ite afore the whole tribe; or if my inimy had only been a bear"— [and so on].

We cannot imagine such a thing as a veteran Scotch Commander-in-Chief comporting himself in the field like a windy melodramatic actor, but Cooper could. On one occasion Alice and Cora were being chased by the French through a fog in the neighborhood of their father's fort:

> *"Point de quartier aux coquins!"* cried an eager pursuer, who seemed to direct the operations of the enemy.

"Stand firm and be ready, my gallant 60ths!" suddenly exclaimed a voice above them; "wait to see the enemy; fire low, and sweep the glacis."

"Father! father!" exclaimed a piercing cry from out the mist; "it is I! Alice! thy own Elsie! spare, O! save your daughters!"

"Hold!" shouted the former speaker, in the awful tones of parental agony, the sound reaching even to the woods, and rolling back in solemn echo. "'Tis she! God has restored me my children! Throw open the sally-port; to the field, 60ths, to the field! pull not a trigger, lest ye kill my lambs! Drive off these dogs of France with your steel!"

Cooper's word-sense was singularly dull. When a person has a poor ear for music he will flat and sharp right along without knowing it. He keeps near the tune, but it is *not* the tune. When a person has a poor ear for words, the result is a literary flatting and sharping; you perceive what he is intending to say, but you also perceive that he doesn't say it. This is Cooper. He was not a word-musician. His ear was satisfied with the *approximate* word. I will furnish some circumstantial evidence in support of this charge. My instances are gathered from half a dozen pages of the tale called *Deerslayer.* He uses "verbal" for "oral"; "precision" for "facility"; "phenomena" for "marvels"; "necessary" for "predetermined"; "unsophisticated" for "primitive"; "preparation" for "expectancy"; "rebuked" for "subdued"; "dependent on" for "resulting from"; "fact" for "condition"; "fact" for "conjecture"; "precaution" for "caution"; "explain" for "determine"; "mortified" for "disappointed"; "meretricious" for "factitious"; "materially" for "considerably"; "decreasing" for "deepening"; "increasing" for "disappearing"; "embedded" for "inclosed"; "treacherous" for "hostile"; "stood" for "stooped"; "softened" for "replaced"; "rejoined" for "remarked"; "situation" for "condition"; "different" for "differing"; "insensible" for "unsentient"; "brevity" for "celerity"; "distrusted" for "suspicious"; "mental imbecility" for "imbecility"; "eyes" for "sight"; "counteracting" for "opposing"; "funeral obsequies" for "obsequies."

There have been daring people in the world who claimed that Cooper could write English, but they are all dead now—all dead but Lounsbury. I don't remember that Lounsbury makes the claim in so many words, still he makes it, for he says that *Deerslayer* is a "pure work of art." Pure, in that connection, means faultless—faultless in all details—and language is a detail. If Mr. Lounsbury had only compared Cooper's English with the English which he writes himself—but it is plain that he didn't; and so it is likely that he imagines until this day that Cooper's is as clean and compact as his own. Now I feel sure, deep down in my heart, that Cooper wrote about the poorest English that exists in our language, and that the English of *Deerslayer* is the very worst that even Cooper ever wrote.

I may be mistaken, but it does seem to me that *Deerslayer* is not a work of art in any sense; it does seem to me that it is destitute of every detail that goes to the making of a work of art; in truth, it seems to me that *Deerslayer* is just simply a literary *delirium tremens.*

A work of art? It has no invention; it has no order, system, sequence, or result; it has no life-likeness, no thrill, no stir, no seeming of reality; its characters are confusedly drawn, and by their acts and words they prove that they are not the sort of people the author claims that they are; its humor is pathetic; its pathos is funny;

its conversations are—oh! indescribable; its love-scenes odious; its English a crime against the language.

Counting these out, what is left is Art. I think we must all admit that.

1895

The War Prayer

It was a time of great and exalting excitement. The country was up in arms, the war was on, in every breast burned the holy fire of patriotism; the drums were beating, the bands playing, the toy pistols popping, the bunched firecrackers hissing and spluttering; on every hand and far down the receding and fading spread of roofs and balconies a fluttering wilderness of flags flashed in the sun; daily the young volunteers marched down the wide avenue gay and fine in their new uniforms, the proud fathers and mothers and sisters and sweethearts cheering them with voices choked with happy emotion as they swung by; nightly the packed mass meetings listened, panting, to patriot oratory which stirred the deepest deeps of their hearts, and which they interrupted at briefest intervals with cyclones of applause, the tears running down their cheeks the while; in the churches the pastors preached devotion to flag and country, and invoked the God of Battles, beseeching His aid in our good cause in outpouring of fervid eloquence which moved every listener. It was indeed a glad and gracious time, and the half dozen rash spirits that ventured to disapprove of the war and cast a doubt upon its righteousness straightway got such a stern and angry warning that for their personal safety's sake they quickly shrank out of sight and offended no more in that way.

Sunday morning came—next day the battalions would leave for the front; the church was filled; the volunteers were there, their young faces alight with martial dreams—visions of the stern advance, the gathering momentum, the rushing charge, the flashing sabers, the flight of the foe, the tumult, the enveloping smoke, the fierce pursuit, the surrender!—them home from the war, bronzed heroes, welcomed, adored, submerged in golden seas of glory! With the volunteers sat their dear ones, proud, happy, and envied by the neighbors and friends who had no sons and brothers to send forth to the field of honor, there to win for the flag, or, failing, die the noblest of noble deaths. The service proceeded; a war chapter from the Old Testament was read; the first prayer was said; it was followed by an organ burst that shook the building, and with one impulse the house rose, with glowing eyes and beating hearts, and poured out that tremendous invocation—

"God the all-terrible! Thou who ordainest,
Thunder thy clarion and lightning thy sword!"

Then came the "long" prayer. None could remember the like of it for passionate pleading and moving and beautiful language. The burden of its supplication was, that an ever-merciful and benignant Father of us all would watch over our noble young soldiers, and aid, comfort, and encourage them in their patriotic work; bless them, shield them in the day of battle and the hour of peril, bear them in His mighty hand, make them strong and confident, invincible in the bloody onset; help them to crush the foe, grant to them and to their flag and country imperishable honor and glory—

An aged stranger entered and moved with slow and noiseless step up the main aisle, his eyes fixed upon the minister, his long body clothed in a robe that reached to his feet, his head bare, his white hair descending in a frothy cataract to his shoulders, his seamy face unnaturally pale, pale even to ghastliness. With all eyes following him and wondering, he made his silent way; without pausing, he ascended to the preacher's side and stood there, waiting. With shut lids the preacher, unconscious of his presence, continued his moving prayer, and at last finished it with the words, uttered in fervent appeal, "Bless our arms, grant us the victory, O Lord our God, Father and Protector of our land and flag!"

The stranger touched his arm, motioned him to step aside—which the startled minister did—and took his place. During some moments he surveyed the spellbound audience with solemn eyes, in which burned an uncanny light; then in a deep voice he said:

"I come from the Throne—bearing a message from Almighty God!" The words smote the house with a shock; if the stranger perceived it he gave no attention. "He has heard the prayer of His servant your shepherd, and will grant it if such shall be your desire after I, His messenger, shall have explained to you its import—that is to say, its full import. For it is like unto many of the prayers of men, in that it asks for more than he who utters it is aware of—except he pause and think.

"God's servant and yours has prayed his prayer. Has he paused and taken thought? Is it one prayer? No, it is two—one uttered, the other not. Both have reached the ear of Him Who heareth all supplications, the spoken and the unspoken. Ponder this —keep it in mind. If you would beseech a blessing upon yourself, beware! lest without intent you invoke a curse upon a neighbor at the same time. If you pray for the blessing of rain upon your crop which needs it, by that act you are possibly praying for a curse upon some neighbor's crop which may not need rain and can be injured by it.

"You have heard your servant's prayer—the uttered part of it. I am commissioned of God to put into words the other part of it—that part which the pastor—and also you in your hearts—fervently prayed silently. And ignorantly and unthinkingly? God grant that it was so! You heard these words: 'Grant us the victory, O Lord our God!' That is sufficient. The *whole* of the uttered prayer is compact into those pregnant words. Elaborations were not necessary. When you have prayed for victory you have prayed for many unmentioned results which follow victory—*must* follow it, cannot help but follow it. Upon the listening spirit of God the Father fell also the unspoken part of the prayer. He commandeth me to put it into words. Listen!

"O Lord our Father, our young patriots, idols of our hearts, go forth to battle— be Thou near them! With them—in spirit—we also go forth from the sweet peace of our beloved firesides to smite the foe. O Lord our God, help us to tear their soldiers to bloody shreds with our shells; help us to cover their smiling fields with the pale forms of their patriot dead; help us to drown the thunder of the guns with the shrieks of their wounded, writhing in pain; help us to lay waste their humble homes with a hurricane of fire; help us to wring the hearts of their unoffending widows with unavailing grief; help us to turn them out roofless with their little children to wander unfriended the wastes of their desolated land in rags and hunger and thirst, sports of the sun flames of summer and the icy winds of winter, broken in spirit, worn with travail, imploring Thee for the refuge of the grave and denied it—for our sakes who adore Thee, Lord, blast their hopes, blight their lives, protract their bitter pilgrimage, make heavy their steps, water their way with their tears, stain the white snow with the blood of their wounded feet! We ask it, in the spirit of love, of Him Who is the Source of Love, and Who is the ever-faithful refuge and friend of all that are sore beset and seek His aid with humble and contrite hearts. Amen."

(After a pause.) "Ye have prayed it; if ye still desire it, speak! The messenger of the Most High waits."

It was believed afterward that the man was a lunatic, because there was no sense in what he said.

1923

Corn-Pone Opinions

Fifty years ago, when I was a boy of fifteen and helping to inhabit a Missourian village on the banks of the Mississippi, I had a friend whose society was very dear to me because I was forbidden by my mother to partake of it. He was a gay and impudent and satirical and delightful young black man—a slave—who daily preached sermons from the top of his master's woodpile, with me for sole audience. He imitated the pulpit style of the several clergymen of the village, and did it well, and with fine passion and energy. To me he was a wonder. I believed he was the greatest orator in the United States and would some day be heard from. But it did not happen; in the distribution of rewards he was overlooked. It is the way, in this world.

He interrupted his preaching, now and then, to saw a stick of wood; but the sawing was a pretense—he did it with his mouth; exactly imitating the sound the bucksaw makes in shrieking its way through the wood. But it served its purpose; it kept his master from coming out to see how the work was getting along. I listened to the sermons from the open window of a lumber room at the back of the house. One of his texts was this:

"You tell me whar a man gits his corn pone, en I'll tell you what his 'pinions is."

I can never forget it. It was deeply impressed upon me. By my mother. Not upon my memory, but elsewhere. She had slipped in upon me while I was absorbed and not watching. The black philosopher's idea was that a man is not independent, and cannot afford views which might interfere with his bread and butter. If he would prosper, he must train with the majority; in matters of large moment, like politics and religion, he must think and feel with the bulk of his neighbors, or suffer damage in his social standing and in his business prosperities. He must restrict himself to corn-pone opinions—at least on the surface. He must get his opinions from other people; he must reason out none for himself; he must have no first-hand views.

I think Jerry was right, in the main, but I think he did not go far enough.

1. It was his idea that a man conforms to the majority view of his locality by calculation and intention.

This happens, but I think it is not the rule.

2. It was his idea that there is such a thing as a first-hand opinion; an original opinion; an opinion which is coldly reasoned out in a man's head, by a searching analysis of the facts involved, with the heart unconsulted, and the jury room closed against outside influences. It may be that such an opinion has been born somewhere, at some time or other, but I suppose it got away before they could catch it and stuff it and put it in the museum.

I am persuaded that a coldly-thought-out and independent verdict upon a fashion in clothes, or manners, or literature, or politics, or religion, or any other matter that is projected into the field of our notice and interest, is a most rare thing—if it has indeed ever existed.

A new thing in costume appears—the flaring hoopskirt, for example—and the passers-by are shocked, and the irreverent laugh. Six months later everybody is reconciled; the fashion has established itself; it is admired, now, and no one laughs. Public opinion resented it before, public opinion accepts it now, and is happy in it. Why? Was the resentment reasoned out? Was the acceptance reasoned out? No. The instinct that moves to conformity did the work. It is our nature to conform; it is a force which not many can successfully resist. What is its seat? The inborn requirement of self-approval. We all have to bow to that; there are no exceptions. Even the woman who refuses from first to last to wear the hoopskirt comes under that law and is its slave; she could not wear the skirt and have her own approval; and that she *must* have, she cannot help herself. But as a rule our self-approval has its source in but one place and not elsewhere—the approval of other people. A person of vast consequences can introduce any kind of novelty in dress and the general world will presently adopt it —moved to do it, in the first place, by the natural instinct to passively yield to that vague something recognized as authority, and in the second place by the human instinct to train with the multitude and have its approval. An empress introduced the hoopskirt, and we know the result. A nobody introduced the bloomer, and we know the result. If Eve should come again, in her ripe renown, and reintroduce her quaint styles—well, we know what would happen. And we should be cruelly embarrassed, along at first.

The hoopskirt runs its course and disappears. Nobody reasons about it. One woman abandons the fashion; her neighbor notices this and follows her lead; this influences the next woman; and so on and so on, and presently the skirt has vanished out of the world, no one knows how nor why; nor cares, for that matter. It will come again, by and by; and in due course will go again.

Twenty-five years ago, in England, six or eight wine glasses stood grouped by each person's plate at a dinner party, and they were used, not left idle and empty; to-day there are but three or four in the group, and the average guest sparingly uses about two of them. We have not adopted this new fashion yet, but we shall do it presently. We shall not think it out; we shall merely conform, and let it go at that. We get our notions and habits and opinions from outside influences; we do not have to study them out.

Our table manners, and company manners, and street manners change from time to time, but the changes are not reasoned out; we merely notice and conform. We are creatures of outside influences; as a rule we do not think, we only imitate. We cannot invent standards that will stick; what we mistake for standards are only fashions, and perishable. We may continue to admire them, but we drop the use of them. We notice this in literature. Shakespeare is a standard, and fifty years ago we used to write tragedies which we couldn't tell from—from somebody else's; but we don't do it any more, now. Our prose standard, three quarters of a century ago, was ornate and diffuse; some authority or other changed it in the direction of compactness and simplicity, and conformity followed, without argument. The historical novel starts up suddenly, and sweeps the land. Everybody writes one, and the nation is glad. We had historical novels before; but nobody read them, and the rest of us conformed—without reasoning it out. We are conforming in the other way, now, because it is another case of everybody.

The outside influences are always pouring in upon us, and we are always obeying their orders and accepting their verdicts. The Smiths like the new play; the Joneses go to see it, and they copy the Smith verdict. Morals, religions, politics, get their following from surrounding influences and atmospheres, almost entirely; not from study, not from thinking. A man must and will have his own approval first of all, in each and every moment and circumstance of his life—even if he must repent of a self-approved act the moment after its commission, in order to get his self-approval *again:* but, speaking in general terms, a man's self-approval in the large concerns of life has its source in the approval of the peoples about him, and not in a searching personal examination of the matter. Mohammedans are Mohammedans because they are born and reared among that sect, not because they have thought it out and can furnish sound reasons for being Mohammedans; we know why Catholics are Catholics; why Presbyterians are Presbyterians; why Baptists are Baptists; why Mormons are Mormons; why thieves are thieves; why monarchists are monarchists; why Republicans are Republicans and Democrats, Democrats. We know it is a matter of association and sympathy, not reasoning and examination; that hardly a man in the world has an opinion upon morals, politics, or religion which he got otherwise than through his associations and sympathies. Broadly speaking, there are none but corn-pone opinions. And broadly speaking, corn-pone stands for self-approval. Self-approval is acquired mainly from the approval of other people. The result is conformity. Sometimes conformity has a sordid business interest—the bread-and-butter interest—but not in most cases, I think. I think that in the majority of cases it is unconscious and not calculated; that it is born of the human being's natural yearning to stand well with his fellows and have their inspiring approval and praise—a yearning which is commonly so strong and so insistent that it cannot be effectually resisted, and must have its way.

A political emergency brings out the corn-pone opinion in fine force in its two chief varieties—the pocketbook variety, which has its origin in self-interest, and the bigger variety, the sentimental variety—the one which can't bear to be outside the pale; can't bear to be in disfavor; can't endure the averted face and the cold shoulder; wants to stand well with his friends, wants to be smiled upon, wants to be welcome, wants to hear the precious words, *"He's* on the right track!" Uttered, perhaps by an ass, but still an ass of high degree, an ass whose approval is gold and diamonds to a smaller ass, and confers glory and honor and happiness, and membership in the herd. For these gauds many a man will dump his life-long principles into the street, and his conscience along with them. We have seen it happen. In some millions of instances.

Men think they think upon great political questions, and they do; but they think with their party, not independently; they read its literature, but not that of the other side; they arrive at convictions, but they are drawn from a partial view of the matter in hand and are of no particular value. They swarm with their party, they feel with their party, they are happy in their party's approval; and where the party leads they will follow, whether for right and honor, or through blood and dirt and a mush of mutilated morals.

In our late canvass half of the nation passionately believed that in silver lay salvation, the other half as passionately believed that that way lay destruction. Do you believe that a tenth part of the people, on either side, had any rational excuse for having an opinion about the matter at all? I studied that mighty question to the bottom —came out empty. Half of our people passionately believe in high tariff, the other half believe otherwise. Does this mean study and examination, or only feeling? The latter, I think. I have deeply studied that question, too—and didn't arrive. We all do no end of feeling, and we mistake it for thinking. And out of it we get an aggregation which we consider a boon. Its name is Public Opinion. It is held in reverence. It settles everything. Some think it the Voice of God.

1923

---

from Letter to Orion and Mollie Clemens

[October 19, 1865]

San F——— Oct. 19, 1865.

My Dear Bro & Sister:[1]

Orion there was *genius*—true, unmistakeable *genius*—in that sermon of yours. It was not the gilded base metal that passes for intellectual gold too generally in this world of ours. It is one of the few sermons that I have read with pleasure—I do not say profit, because I am beyond the reach of argument now. But seven or eight years ago that single sermon would have saved me. It even made me *think*—yea, & *regret*, for a while, as it was. (Don't preach from the above text next time.) Viewed as a *literary* production, that sermon was first-class.

And now let me preach *you* a sermon. I never had but two *powerful* ambitions in my life. One was to be a pilot, & the other a preacher of the gospel. I accomplished the one & failed in the other, *because* I could not supply myself with the necessary stock in trade—*i.e.* religion. I have given it up forever. I never had a "call" in that direction, anyhow, & my aspirations were the very ecstasy of presumption. But I *have* had a "call" to literature, of a low order—*i.e.* humorous. It is nothing to be proud of, but it is my strongest suit, & if I were to listen to that maxim of stern *duty* which says that to do right you *must* multiply the one or the two or the three talents which

---

[1] Mark Twain had accompanied his brother Orion to the Nevada Territory in 1861 (as told in *Roughing It,* Chapter 1). Mollie ("Sister") was Orion's wife.

the Almighty entrusts to your keeping, I would long ago have ceased to meddle with things for which I was by nature unfitted & turned my attention to seriously scribbling to excite the *laughter* of God's creatures. Poor, pitiful business! Though the Almighty did His part by me—for the talent is a mighty engine when supplied with the steam of *education*—which I have not got, & so its pistons & cylinders & shafts move feebly & for a holiday show & are useless for any good purpose.

But as I was saying, it is *human nature* to yearn to be what we were never intended for. It is singular, but it is so. I wanted to be a pilot or a preacher, & I was about as well calculated for either as is poor Emperor Norton[2] for Chief Justice of the United States. Now *you* aspire to be a *lawyer,* when the voice of God is thundering in your ears & you are willfully deaf & will not hear. *You* were *intended* for a preacher, & lo! you would be a scheming, groveling, mud-cat of a *lawyer.* A man *never is* willing to do what his Creator intended him to do. You are honest, pious, virtuous—what would you have more? *Go forth & preach.* When you preach from a pulpit, I will listen to you & not before. Until that time, I will read your sermons with sincere pleasure, but only as *literary gems.* That is my ultimatum. Ever since I got acquainted with you—which was in the autumn of 1861—I have thought many & many & *many* a time how you would tower head & shoulders above any of the small-fry preachers of my experience! I know what I am talking about. It is the nature of man to see as by the light of noonday the talents of his neighbor, (& to which that neighbor is blind as night,) & at the same time to be unaware of his own talents while he is gazing afar off at those of that neighbor, as aforesaid. *You* see in me a talent for humorous writing, & urge me to cultivate it. But I always regarded it as brotherly partiality on your part, & attached no value to it. It is only now, when editors of standard literary papers in the distant east give me high praise, & who do not know me & cannot of course be blinded by the glamour of partiality, that I really begin to believe there must be something in it.

But I'll toss up with you. Your letter has confirmed me. I *know*—I don't suppose —I *know* you would be great & useful as a minister of the gospel, & I am satisfied you will never be any better lawyer than a good many others. Now I don't know how you regard the ministry, but *I* would rather be a shining light in that department than the greatest lawyer that ever trod the earth. What is the pride of saving the widow's property or the homicide's trivial life, to snatching an immortal soul in mercy from the jaws of hell? Bah! The one is the feeble glitter of the fire-fly, & the other the regal glory of the sun.

But as I said, I will toss up with you. I will drop all trifling, & sighing after vain impossibilities, & strive for a fame—unworthy & evanescent though it must of necessity be—if you will record your promise to go hence to the States & preach the gospel when circumstances shall enable you to do so? I am in earnest. Shall it be so? . . .

Yr Bro Sam

P.S. You had better shove this in the stove—for if we strike a bargain I don't want any absurd "literary remains" & "unpublished letters of Mark Twain" published after I am planted. . . .

1961

---

[2] Celebrated street character in San Francisco and
self-proclaimed ruler of California and Mexico.

Letter to Will Bowen

[February 6, 1870]

Sunday Afternoon,
At Home, 472 Delaware Avenue,
Buffalo   Feb. 6, 1870

My First, & Oldest & Dearest Friend:[1]

My heart goes out to you just the same as ever. Your letter has stirred me to the
bottom. The fountains of my great deep are broken up & I have rained reminiscences for four & twenty hours. The old life has swept before me like a panorama;
the old days have trooped by in their old glory again; the old faces have looked out
of the mists of the past; old footsteps have sounded in my listening ears; old hands
have clasped mine, old voices have greeted me, & the songs I loved ages & ages ago
have come wailing down the centuries! Heavens what eternities have swung their
hoary cycles about us since those days were new!—Since we tore down Dick
Hardy's stable; since you had the measles & I went to your house purposely to catch
them; Since Henry Beebe kept that envied slaughter-house, & Joe Craig sold him
cats to kill in it; since old General Gaines used to say, "Whoop! Bow your neck &
spread!"; since Jimmy Finn was town drunkard & we stole his dinner while he slept
in the vat & fed it to the hogs in order to keep them still till we could mount them
& have a ride; since Clint Levering was drowned; since we taught that one-legged
nigger, Higgins, to offend Bill League's dignity by hailing him in public with his
exasperating "Hello, League!"—since we used to undress & play Robin Hood in
our shirt-tails, with lath swords, in the woods on Halliday's Hill on those long
summer days; since we used to go in swimming above the still-house branch—& at
mighty intervals wandered on vagrant fishing excursions clear up to "the Bay," &
wondered what was curtained away in the great world beyond that remote point;
since I jumped overboard from the ferry boat in the middle of the river that stormy
day to get my hat, & swam two or three miles after it (& *got* it,) while all the town
collected on the wharf & for an hour or so looked out across the angry waste of
"white-caps" toward where people said Sam. Clemens was last seen before he went
down; since we got up a rebellion against Miss Newcomb, under Ed. Stevens'
leadership, (to force her to let us all go over to Miss Torry's side of the schoolroom,) & gallantly "sassed" Laura Hawkins when she came out the third time to
call us in, & then afterward marched in in threatening & bloodthirsty array,—&
meekly yielded, & took each his little thrashing, & resumed his old seat entirely
"reconstructed"; since we used to indulge in that very peculiar performance on that
old bench outside the school-house to drive good old Bill Brown crazy while he
was eating his dinner; since we used to remain at school at noon & go hungry, in
order to persecute Bill Brown in all possible ways—poor old Bill, who *could* be
driven to such extremity of vindictiveness as to call us "You *infernal* fools!" &

---

[1] Will Bowen was a schoolmate of Mark Twain's in Hannibal, Missouri, and later a fellow pilot on the Mississippi. In this letter, written four days after his marriage to Olivia Langdon, Twain recalls many of the people and episodes in their shared experiences that were to figure in *Tom Sawyer* and *Huckleberry Finn*.

chase us round & round the school-house—& yet who never had the heart to hurt us when he caught us, & who always loved us & always took our part when the big boys wanted to thrash us; since we used to lay in wait for Bill Pitts at the pump & whale him; (I saw him two or three years ago, & was awful polite to his six feet two, & mentioned no reminiscences); since we used to be in Dave Garth's class in Sunday school & on week-days stole his leaf tobacco to run our miniature tobacco presses with; since Owsley shot Smar; since Ben Hawkins shot off his finger; since we accidentally burned up that poor fellow in the calaboose; since we used to shoot spool cannons, & cannons made of keys, while that envied & hated Henry Beebe drowned out our poor little popguns with his booming brazen little artillery on wheels; since Laura Hawkins was my sweetheart—

Hold: *That* rouses me out of my dream, & brings me violently back [unto this day & this generation. For behold I have at this moment the only sweetheart I ever *loved,* & bless her old heart she is lying asleep upstairs in a bed that I sleep in every night, & for four whole days she has been *Mrs. Samuel L. Clemens!*

I am thirty-four & she is twenty-four; I am young & very handsome (I make this statement with the fullest confidence, for I got it from her), & she is much the most beautiful girl I ever saw (I said that before she was anything to me, & so it is worthy of all belief) & she is the *best* girl, & the sweetest, & the gentlest, & the daintiest, & the most modest & unpretentious, & the wisest in all things she should be wise in & the most ignorant in all matters it would not grace her to know, & she is sensible & quick & loving & faithful, forgiving, full of charity—& her beautiful life is ordered by a religion that is all kindliness & unselfishness. Before the gentle majesty of her purity all evil things & evil ways & evil deeds stand abashed,—then surrender. Wherefore without effort, or struggle, or spoken exorcism, all the old vices & shameful habits that have possessed me these many many years, are falling away, one by one & departing into the darkness.

Bill, I know whereof I speak. I am too old & have moved about too much, & rubbed against too many people not to know human beings as well as we used to know "boils" from "breaks."

She is the very most perfect gem of womankind that ever I saw in my life—& I will stand by that remark till I die.

William, old boy, her father surprised us a little, the other night. We all arrived here in a night train (my little wife & I were going to board), & under pretense of taking us to the private boarding-house that had been selected for me while I was absent lecturing in New England, my new father-in-law & some old friends drove us in sleighs to the daintiest darlingest, loveliest little palace in America—& when I said "Oh, this won't do—people who can afford to live in this sort of style won't take boarders," that same blessed father-in-law] let out the secret that this was all *our* property—a present from himself. House & furniture cost $40,000 in cash, (including stable, horse & carriage), & is a most exquisite little palace (I saw no apartment in Europe so lovely as our drawing-room.)

Come along, you & Molly, just whenever you can, & pay us a visit, (giving us a little notice beforehand,) & if we don't make you comfortable nobody in the world can.

(And now my princess has come down for dinner (bless me, isn't it cosy, nobody but just us two, & three servants to wait on us & respectfully call us "Mr." and "Mrs. Clemens" instead of "Sam" & "Livy!") It took me many a year to work up to where

I can put on style, but now I'll do it.—My book gives me an income like a small lord, & my paper is a good profitable concern.

Dinner's ready. Good bye & God bless you, old friend, & keep your heart fresh & your memory green for the old days that will never come again.

Yrs always
Sam. Clemens.

1938

Letter to William Dean Howells

[July 21, 1885]

Elmira, July 21/85.

My Dear Howells—

You are really my only author; I am restricted to you; I wouldn't give a damn for the rest. I bored through Middlemarch[1] during the past week, with its labored & tedious analyses of feelings & motives, its paltry & tiresome people, its unexciting & uninteresting story, & its frequent blinding flashes of single-sentence poetry, philosophy, wit, & what-not, & nearly died from the over-work. I wouldn't read another of those books for a farm. I did try to read one other—Daniel Deronda.[2] I dragged through three chapters, losing flesh all the time, & then was honest enough to quit, & confess to myself that I haven't *any* romance-literature appetite, as far as I can see, except for your books.

But what I started to say, was, that I have just read Part II of Indian Summer,[3] & to my mind there isn't a waste-line in it, or one that could be improved. I read it yesterday, ending with that opinion; & read it again to-day, ending with the same opinion emphasized. I haven't read Part I yet, because that number must have reached Hartford after we left; but we are going to send down town for a copy, & when it comes I am to read both parts aloud to the family. It is a beautiful story, & makes a body laugh all the time, & cry inside, & feel so old & so forlorn; & gives him gracious glimpses of his lost youth that fill him with a measureless regret, & build up in him a cloudy sense of his having been a prince, once, in some enchanted far-off land, & of being in exile now, & desolate—& lord, no chance to ever get back there again! That is the thing that hurts. Well, you have done it with marvelous facility—& you make all the motives & feelings perfectly clear without analyzing the guts out of them, the way George Eliot does. I can't stand George Eliot, & Hawthorne & those people; I see what they are at, a hundred years before they get to it, & they just tire me to death. And as for the Bostonians,[4] I would rather be damned to John Bunyan's heaven than read that.   Yrs Ever

Mark.

1917

---

[1] Novel by George Eliot, published 1871–1872.
[2] Another novel by Eliot, published 1874–1876.
[3] Novel by Howells, serialized in *Harper's Monthly*.

[4] Novel by Henry James, serialized in the *Century Magazine*. Twain compares *The Bostonians* to John Bunyan's allegory *The Pilgrim's Progress* (1678).

William Dean Howells
1837–1920

William Dean Howells is best remembered for his ability to recognize how good other writers were, not for his own merits. Rather than stressing the implications of his first name ("he who asserts his own will"), we tend to focus on *Dean*, picturing Howells as the person high up in the administrative order who oversees and evaluates others. From his place in "The Editor's Study" and "The Easy Chair," titles given the influential monthly essays he wrote for *Harper's* magazine, Howells served as America's foremost critic and editor from 1886 into the early years of the twentieth century. But his reputation as the acknowledged spokesman for middle-class literary values, the cautiousness of his approach to matters of sexuality, and the canniness with which he orchestrated his own career are misleading. They make Howells seem older and grayer than in fact he was.

Howells started out as a brash young man with a background in a printer's shop and local newspapers. He came out of Ohio to storm the genteel Eastern literary redoubts in much the manner of heroes of the nineteenth-century *Bildungsroman* (a novel in which climbers from the provinces make their energetic way upward to social and professional acclaim in the major centers of power). Another example of the same type is Mark Twain, a man Howells helped to attain the level of success he himself already enjoyed.

Oddly enough, we think of Mark Twain as the eternal boy, even after his hair went snowy white. But Twain and Howells were almost exact contemporaries and shared several of the same early experiences: printing-shop apprenticeship, jobs with regional newspapers, and moves to the East in 1866 after sitting out the Civil War in other places (for Twain, the Nevada Territory, as secretary to the governor's secretary; for Howells, a consulship in Venice). But Howells's early days were, probably even more than Twain's, given over to the pugnacious attempt to get ahead. Twain seems the more energetic because he let his wildness show, while Howells carefully kept his under cover. Howells's main chance came through his role as critic and editor, positions that called for him to reject the personal flamboyance Twain found useful to his role as humorist and iconoclast. But Howells's temperament put his psychic energies to work in controlling, not releasing, the extremes of emotion that lay concealed beneath the smooth surface of the polite young man from Ohio.

One of eight children, Howells was born to a humble family in Martin's Ferry, Ohio, somewhat shakily supported by the father's work as an itinerant printer and newspaper editor. Though poor and peripatetic in their shifts around Ohio during the early years of Howells's childhood, the family was close. Howells was strongly affected by his father's championing of various reform movements and by his own avid reading in the literary classics. He set to work at once to turn himself into a capable journalist and writer of occasional poems and sketches. By the time he was twenty-one, he had begun to make his mark in Ohio as a writer and editor for important newspapers in and around Cincinnati and Columbus—the *Gazette* and the *Ohio State Journal*.

Howells's ambitions exceeded what Ohio had to offer, however. In 1860 he made two crucial moves: He wrote a campaign biography for Abraham Lincoln's presidential candidacy, and he made a trip to New England to meet such literary celebrities as Emerson, Holmes, Hawthorne, Lowell, and Thoreau. The Lincoln biography led to his appointment as American consul to Venice, and his visits with famous American writers gave him a glimpse into the nation's most prominent literary circle. The introductions he received to the Boston-Concord literary powers earned him early recognition for his talents and prepared the way, upon his return from Italy in 1865, for an assistant editorship at the country's most important journal, the *Atlantic Monthly,* where he was to become editor in chief in 1871. The *Atlantic* appointment was the start of what would be Howells's special fate: to be the arbiter of American letters and the judge of the careers of the next generation of writers.

From the time Howells settled in Boston, he began to pursue a second career as a novelist. The six novels he wrote while with the *Atlantic* not only helped him perfect his craft but also determined the kind of fiction he would urge on the American reading public, which heeded his judgments. Fiction had to be realistic, he maintained. It must give its attention to the details of the everyday lives of ordinary people. It must reject romanticized plots of passion and adventure to concentrate on stories of character and close observations of contemporary American life.

In 1881 Howells resigned his post with the *Atlantic* to free-lance. His first notable novel, *A Modern Instance,* appeared in 1882. *The Rise of Silas Lapham,* published in 1885, confirmed Howells's worth as a novelist. By 1886 he was back in an editor's chair, associated with *Harper's,* which had overtaken the *Atlantic* as the country's major literary arbiter. In 1889 he moved to New York, which had replaced Boston as the place where literary reputations were made or broken. Howells could work with the assurance that what he said for Realism and against the shoddily romantic would receive serious attention from a large, receptive, and international audience. Marked by the earnestness and commitment (as well as the humor and ironic touch) Howells brought to all his professional tasks, the essays and reviews he printed in the pages of *Harper's* helped make American literature what it became by 1900. The novels in the bookshops and lending libraries and in serial form in the popular magazines were no longer limited to the sentimental "weeper" or the historical costume romance.

This is not to suggest that the sentimental romance went out of style during Howells's day as the dean of American Realism; it flourished, but it did so in the face of the strong, new force in American writing that Howells made not only acceptable but respectable. White, middle-class readers could hardly think themselves *au courant* on the newest books if they were not familiar with the writings of such Americans as Hamlin Garland, Stephen Crane, and Frank Norris and with the names of such leading Continental writers as Tolstoy, Turgenev, Galdós, and Ibsen, as well as the Briton Thomas Hardy. Howells gave his editorial attention to American women writers—Sarah Orne Jewett, Mary E. Wilkins Freeman, Emily Dickinson, and Edith Wharton. He also encouraged new black writers like Paul Dunbar and Charles Chesnutt. Howells took it on himself, early and late, to declare the central importance of Mark Twain and

Henry James on the American cultural scene. Capable of appreciating their differing qualities as writers, Howells celebrated both the rowdiness of Twain's humor and the refined specialness of James's style. Part of Howells's talent was the ability to admire in others what he himself was unable to do. Certain literary leanings, differences in temperament, and deep-seated fears carried over from his childhood prevented Howells from speaking directly in his own fiction about the sex and violence that Stephen Crane and Frank Norris, for example, placed dead center in their works.

At the same time Howells helped several generations of Realists to get the notice they deserved, he continued to build up the bulk of his own writing. His most important essays and literary reminiscences trace the growth of the imaginative movement he himself helped to create: *Criticism and Fiction* (1891), *My Literary Passions* (1895), *Literary Friends and Acquaintances* (1900), and *My Mark Twain* (1910). Also noteworthy are his accounts of his youthful Ohio days, *A Boy's Town* (1890) and *My Year in a Log Cabin* (1893). In addition to *A Modern Instance* and *The Rise of Silas Lapham,* the foremost titles among his many novels are *Their Wedding Journey* (his first, 1878), *The Undiscovered Country* (1880), *Indian Summer* (1886), *A Hazard of New Fortunes* and *The Shadow of a Dream* (1890), *An Imperative Duty* (1892), *A Traveler from Altruria* (1894), *The Landlord at Lion's Head* (1897), *The Son of Royal Langbrith* (1904), and *The Leatherwood God* (1916). If all these titles were not enough, travel books, plays, and poems extended Howells's reach into other areas of writing.

Somehow there was time for other activities as well, both public and personal. On the political side, Howells took a number of courageous, well-publicized stands in the 1880s and 1890s: a forthright defense of the so-called Haymarket Anarchists in 1886, support of the founding of the NAACP, advocacy of socialism as the solution to the problem caused by the widening margin between the rich and the poor, encouragement of the suffragist movement, and criticism of the nation's imperialistic policies. On the private side, Howells, whose own psychological makeup had been vulnerable to jolts ever since young manhood, had to stave off further assaults to his mental stability, including breakdowns that came while he was at work on *A Modern Instance* in 1881 and 1882 and again in 1885 while completing *The Rise of Silas Lapham.*

The emotional history of Howells's wife and daughter Winifred was similar to that experienced by the Clemens household, as well as by the James and Adams families. It is a sad history—all too familiar to this period—of invalidism, nervous disorders, and early death. But Howells himself persevered, while trying to hold together the pieces of his family during Winny's illness in the 1880s, her death in 1889, and his wife's subsequent invalidism.

More and more honors were heaped upon his stocky body and graying head. Honorary degrees from Oxford, Princeton, Yale, and Columbia were bestowed on a man who had never had the chance back in Ohio to earn a regular grade-school education. By 1900 Howells commanded the literary scene. Over the next decade he was still deeply revered, but attention started to drift away from him toward the energetic young writers he had often been instrumental in getting started. By the 1920s Sinclar Lewis, H. L. Mencken, and other obstreperous young critics ridiculed Howells in a manner that was just as vigorous but less polite than the tone he had used as a young man to attack literary deadwood. By the 1930s the popularity of Melville and Poe was on the rise, while this honest Realist was shunted aside. Yet Howells's literary reputation began to regain attention in the 1940s as the concerns of the critics and historians turned once more toward the solid achievements of the post–Civil War generation.

Why is the praise that Howells gets sometimes begrudging? Certainly he introduced his readers to important "new" themes, something a literature requires if it is to keep pace with the events it tries to reflect. Among Howells's major themes are many that are still topical: the young American woman as a special type who sallies forth with somewhat reckless abandon to take on the world; the effects of divorce on couples in a society where admitting one's failures in marriage may be legally permissible but can be the cause of emotional devastation; the amorality of the business and professional classes, tenuously bound to the shaky morality of older values; the loss of religious certainties, with little of worth to replace them; the weakening position of "old families"; and the faltering relationships between parents and children. Howells portrays the shabby boredom of country life set against the more glamorous squalor and frenetic pace of city living; classes set against classes, both socially, in the drawing room, and economically, when strikers take to the street in protest; the shining veneer of manners that barely cover the fundamental crudity of people on the make. He is adept at the analysis of the female character and the discussion of the dream life that resists explanation by the most severe scientific scrutiny. Howells's main theme is the most modern theme of all: people at loose ends, displaced ethnically (with the "natives" drawing in their elbows in the presence of Irish, blacks, and other "aliens") and psychically (men and women going it alone in their professions or their marriages).

In addition to the new areas Howells opened up to the novelists of Realism, he took a clear position on several ethical issues. For Howells the acts of the artist are moral acts. To see realistically is to meet the world honestly, even though it means giving up faith in abstract absolutes. To see romantically is to deceive and to be deceived, thereby to live without moral validation. He wished to reject fatalism because he believed choice is necessary so that people can be responsible for what they do. He also scorned self-isolation, excessive subjectivism, and the sentimentality of people—especially women—given over to self-sacrifice and lives ground down by excessive attention to "duty."

Howells knew his American scene, and he was careful to single out what was most characteristically "American" about it. Howells believed that ordinariness was fine; optimism and small appetites were the national traits. Without self-contradiction, he wrote stories about the way common people react when placed at the extremes possible in ordinary lives—drug addiction, madness, alcoholism, suicide, emotional incest, repressed sexuality, violent death. Without denying his statement that American literature does best with the "smiling aspects" of life, he lived and worked on the edge of his own pessimism and doubts, as when, in the brief sketch "A Scene," he describes the holiday atmosphere surrounding the discovery of a young woman, pregnant but unmarried, who drowned herself. Howells did all these things, and handled these themes, because he was an ironist as well as a realist.

Irony is both Howells's greatest strength as an honest man and the source of the weakness that sapped his verve as a writer. We blame him most for not being exciting. But he would doubtless reply that he chose to keep himself and excitement apart. The love of novelty and the desire to set crazy things happening all at once, which attracts us to Mark Twain (because novelty and craziness pulled powerfully at Twain's imagination), were exactly what Howells tried to keep out of his life, his literature, and his pronouncements on the nature of Realism. Irony let him do this. It kept his fires banked, but it also held him to the truths of his life's intention: to re-create the American imagination in the image of his own self-limiting commitment to things exactly as they are.

Further Reading:

J. Woodress, *Howells and Italy*, 1952.
E. Carter, *Howells and the Age of Realism*, 1954.
E. Cady, *The Road to Realism: The Early Years, 1837–1885*, 1956.
E. Cady, *The Realist at War: The Mature Years, 1885–1920*, 1958.
O. Fryckstedt, *In Quest of America: A Study of Howells' Early Development as a Novelist*, 1958, 1971.
G. Bennett, *William Dean Howells: The Development of a Novelist*, 1959.
V. Brooks, *Howells: His Life and World*, 1959.
R. Hough, *The Quiet Rebel: William Dean Howells as Social Commentator*, 1959.
The War of the Critics over William Dean Howells, ed. E. Cady and D. Frazier, 1962.
R. Kirk and C. Kirk, *William Dean Howells*, 1962.
C. Kirk, *William Dean Howells and Art in His Time*, 1965.
G. Carrington, *The Immense Complex Drama: The World and Art of the Howells Novels*, 1966.

K. Vanderbilt, *The Achievement of William Dean Howells*, 1968.
E. Wagenknecht, *William Dean Howells: The Friendly Eye*, 1969.
K. Lynn, *William Dean Howells: An American Life*, 1971.
G. Bennett, *The Realism of William Dean Howells*, 1973.
William Dean Howells as Critic, ed. E. Cady, 1973.
E. Carter, *On the Trail of the Truth*, 1975.
Critics on William Dean Howells, ed. P. Eschholz, 1975.
G. C. Carrington, *Plots and Characters in the Fiction of William Dean Howells*, 1976.
W. Alexander, *William Dean Howells: The Realist as Humanist*, 1981.
K. E. Eble, *William Dean Howells*, 1982.
G. R. Uba, *Native Grains: Marriage and Family in the Fiction of William Dean Howells*, 1982.
E. S. Prioleau, *The Circle of Eros: Sexuality in the Work of William Dean Howells*, 1983.

Texts:

Suburban Sketches, 1884.
The Rise of Silas Lapham and *A Hazard of New Fortunes* from *A Selected Edition of William Dean Howells*, 41 vols. projected, ed. Cady et al., 1968–.
Criticism and Fiction, 1891.
Literary Friends and Acquaintances, 1900.
"Editha" from *Between the Dark and the*

Daylight, 1907.
See also M. Howells, *Life in Letters of William Dean Howells*, 2 vols., 1928, 1968.
William Dean Howells: Representative Selections, ed. C. Kirk and R. Kirk, 1950.
Mark Twain–Howells Letters: The Correspondence of Samuel L. Clemens and William Dean Howells, 1872–1910, ed. H. Smith and W. Gibson, 1960.

---

from Suburban Sketches

Scene: [The Drowned Girl]

On that loveliest autumn morning, the swollen tide had spread over all the russet levels, and gleamed in the sunlight a mile away. As the contributor moved onward down the street, luminous on either hand with crimsoning and yellowing maples, he was so filled with the tender serenity of the scene, as not to be troubled by the spectacle of small Irish houses standing miserably about on the flats ankle deep, as it were, in little pools of the tide, or to be aware at first, of a strange stir of people upon the streets: a fluttering to and fro and lively encounter and separation of groups of bareheaded women, a flying of children through the broken fences of the neighborhood, and across the vacant lots on which the insulted sign-boards forbade them to trespass; a sluggish movement of men through all, and a pause of different vehicles along the sidewalks. When a sense of these facts had penetrated his enjoyment, he asked a matron whose snowy arms, freshly taken from the wash-tub, were folded across a mighty chest, "What is the matter?"

"A girl drowned herself, sir-r-r, over there on the flats, last Saturday, and they're looking for her."

"It was the best thing she could do," said another matron grimly.

Upon this answer that literary soul fell at once to patching himself up a romantic story for the suicide, after the pitiful fashion of this fiction-ridden age, when we must relate everything we see to something we have read. He was the less to blame for it, because he could not help it; but certainly he is not to be praised for his associations with the tragic fact brought to his notice. Nothing could have been more trite or obvious, and he felt his intellectual poverty so keenly that he might almost have believed his discomfort a sympathy for the girl who had drowned herself last Saturday. But of course, this could not be, for he had but lately been thinking what a very tiresome figure to the imagination the Fallen Woman had become. As a fact of Christian civilization, she was a spectacle to wring one's heart, he owned; but he wished she were well out of the romances, and it really seemed a fatality that she should be the principal personage of this little scene. The preparation for it, whatever it was to be, was so deliberate, and the reality had so slight relation to the French roofs and modern improvements of the comfortable Charlesbridge[1] which he knew, that he could not consider himself other than as a spectator awaiting some entertainment, with a faint inclination to be critical.

In the mean time there passed through the motley crowd, not so much a cry as a sensation of "They've found her, they've found her!" and then the one terrible picturesque fact, "She was standing upright!"

Upon this there was wilder and wilder clamor among the people, dropping by degrees and almost dying away, before a flight of boys came down the street with the tidings, "They are bringing her—bringing her in a wagon."

The contributor knew that she whom they were bringing in the wagon, had had the poetry of love to her dismal and otherwise squalid death; but the history was of

---

[1] Area of Boston near the Charles River.

fancy, not of fact in his mind. Of course, he reflected, her lot must have been obscure and hard; the aspect of those concerned about her death implied that. But of her hopes and her fears, who could tell him anything? To be sure he could imagine the lovers, and how they first met, and where, and who he was that was doomed to work her shame and death; but here his fancy came upon something coarse and common: a man of her own race and grade, handsome after that manner of beauty which is so much more hateful than ugliness is; or, worse still, another kind of man whose deceit must have been subtler and wickeder; but whatever the person, a presence defiant of sympathy or even interest, and simply horrible. Then there were the details of the affair, in great degree common to all love affairs, and not varying so widely in any condition of life; for the passion which is so rich and infinite to those within its charm, is apt to seem a little tedious and monotonous in its character, and poor in resources to the cold looker-on.

Then, finally, there was the crazy purpose and its fulfillment: the headlong plunge from bank or bridge; the eddy, and the bubbles on the current that calmed itself above the suicide; the tide that rose and stretched itself abroad in the sunshine, carrying hither and thither the burden with which it knew not what to do; the arrest, as by some ghastly caprice of fate, of the dead girl, in that upright posture, in which she should meet the quest for her, as it were defiantly.

And now they were bringing her in a wagon.

Involuntarily all stood aside, and waited till the funeral car, which they saw, should come up toward them through the long vista of the maple-shaded street, a noiseless riot stirring the legs and arms of the boys into frantic demonstration, while the women remained quiet with arms folded or akimbo. Before and behind the wagon, driven slowly, went a guard of ragged urchins, while on the raised seat above sat two Americans, unperturbed by anything, and concerned merely with the business of the affair.

The vehicle was a grocer's cart which had perhaps been pressed into the service; and inevitably the contributor thought of Zenobia, and of Miles Coverdale's belief that if she could have foreboded all the *post-mortem* ugliness and grotesqueness of suicide, she never would have drowned herself.[2] This girl, too, had doubtless had her own ideas of the effect that her death was to make, her conviction that it was to wring one heart, at least, and to strike awe and pity to every other; and her woman's soul must have been shocked from death could she have known in what a ghastly comedy the body she put off was to play a part.

In the bottom of the cart lay something long and straight and terrible, covered with a red shawl that drooped over the end of the wagon; and on this thing were piled the baskets in which the grocers had delivered their orders for sugar and flour, and coffee and tea. As the cart jolted through their lines, the boys could no longer be restrained; they broke out with wild yells, and danced madly about it, while the red shawl hanging from the rigid feet nodded to their frantic mirth; and the sun dropped its light through the maples and shone bright upon the flooded flats.

1871

---

[2] The recollection is of *The Blithedale Romance* (1852) by Nathaniel Hawthorne, in which the woman Zenobia is found in an upright position in the river where she has drowned herself.

from # The Rise of Silas Lapham

I: [The Interview]

When Bartley Hubbard went to interview Silas Lapham for the "Solid Men of Boston" series, which he undertook to finish up in "The Events," after he replaced their original projector on that newspaper, Lapham received him in his private office by previous appointment.

"Walk right in!" he called out to the journalist, whom he caught sight of through the door of the counting-room.

He did not rise from the desk at which he was writing, but he gave Bartley his left hand for welcome, and he rolled his large head in the direction of a vacant chair. "Sit down! I'll be with you in just half a minute."

"Take your time," said Bartley, with the ease he instantly felt. "I'm in no hurry." He took a note-book from his pocket, laid it on his knee, and began to sharpen a pencil.

"There!" Lapham pounded with his great hairy fist on the envelope he had been addressing. "William!" he called out, and he handed the letter to a boy who came to get it. "I want that to go right away. Well, sir," he continued, wheeling round in his leather-cushioned swivel-chair, and facing Bartley, seated so near that their knees almost touched, "so you want my life, death, and Christian sufferings, do you, young man?"

"That's what I'm after," said Bartley. "Your money or your life."

"I guess you wouldn't want my life without the money," said Lapham, as if he were willing to prolong these moments of preparation.

"Take 'em both," Bartley suggested. "Don't want your money without your life, if you come to that. But you're just one million times more interesting to the public than if you hadn't a dollar; and you know that as well as I do, Mr. Lapham. There's no use beating about the bush."

"No," said Lapham, somewhat absently. He put out his huge foot and pushed the ground-glass door shut between his little den and the book-keepers, in their larger den outside.

"In personal appearance," wrote Bartley in the sketch for which he now studied his subject, while he waited patiently for him to continue, "Silas Lapham is a fine type of the successful American. He has a square, bold chin, only partially concealed by the short, reddish-gray beard, growing to the edges of his firmly closing lips. His nose is short and straight; his forehead good, but broad rather than high; his eyes blue, and with a light in them that is kindly or sharp according to his mood. He is of medium height, and fills an average arm-chair with a solid bulk, which, on the day of our interview, was unpretentiously clad in a business suit of blue serge. His head droops somewhat from a short neck, which does not trouble itself to rise far from a pair of massive shoulders."

"I don't know as I know just where you want me to begin," said Lapham.

"Might begin with your birth; that's where most of us begin," replied Bartley.

A gleam of humorous appreciation shot into Lapham's blue eyes.

"I didn't know whether you wanted me to go quite so far back as that," he said.

"But there's no disgrace in having been born, and I was born in the State of Vermont, pretty well up under the Canada line—so well up, in fact, that I came very near being an adoptive citizen; for I was bound to be an American of *some* sort, from the word Go! That was about—well, let me see!—pretty near sixty years ago: this is '75, and that was '20. Well, say I'm fifty-five years old; and I've *lived* 'em, too; not an hour of waste time about *me*, anywheres! I was born on a farm, and—"

"Worked in the fields summers and went to school winters: regulation thing?" Bartley cut in.

"Regulation thing," said Lapham, accepting this irreverent version of his history somewhat dryly.

"Parents poor, of course," suggested the journalist. "Any barefoot business? Early deprivations of any kind, that would encourage the youthful reader to go and do likewise? Orphan myself, you know," said Bartley, with a smile of cynical good comradery.

Lapham looked at him silently, and then said with quiet self-respect, "I guess if you see these things as a joke, my life won't inte*rest* you."

"Oh, yes, it will," returned Bartley, unabashed. "You'll see; it'll come out all right." And in fact it did so, in the interview which Bartley printed.

"Mr. Lapham," he wrote, "passed rapidly over the story of his early life, its poverty and its hardships, sweetened, however, by the recollections of a devoted mother, and a father who, if somewhat her inferior in education, was no less ambitious for the advancement of his children. They were quiet, unpretentious people, religious, after the fashion of that time, and of sterling morality, and they taught their children the simple virtues of the Old Testament and Poor Richard's Almanac."[1]

Bartley could not deny himself this gibe; but he trusted to Lapham's unliterary habit of mind for his security in making it, and most other people would consider it sincere reporter's rhetoric.

"You know," he explained to Lapham, "that we have to look at all these facts as material, and we get the habit of classifying them. Sometimes a leading question will draw out a whole line of facts that a man himself would never think of." He went on to put several queries, and it was from Lapham's answers that he generalized the history of his childhood. "Mr. Lapham, although he did not dwell on his boyish trials and struggles, spoke of them with deep feeling and an abiding sense of their reality." This was what he added in the interview, and by the time he had got Lapham past the period where risen Americans are all pathetically alike in their narrow circumstances, their sufferings, and their aspirations, he had beguiled him into forgetfulness of the check he had received, and had him talking again in perfect enjoyment of his autobiography.

"Yes, sir," said Lapham, in a strain which Bartley was careful not to interrupt again, "a man never sees all that his mother has been to him till it's too late to let her know that he sees it. Why, *my* mother—" he stopped. "It gives me a lump in the throat," he said apologetically, with an attempt at a laugh. Then he went on: "She was a little, frail thing, not bigger than a good-sized intermediate school-girl; but she did the whole work of a family of boys, and boarded the hired men besides. She cooked,

---

[1] *Poor Richard's Almanac*, published by Benjamin Franklin, was a compendium of commonsense advice about the virtues (and advantages) of hard work, thrift, and honesty.

swept, washed, ironed, made and mended from daylight till dark—and from dark till daylight, I was going to say; for I don't know how she got any time for sleep. But I suppose she did. She got time to go to church, and to teach us to read the Bible, and to misunderstand it in the old way. She was *good.* But it aint her on her knees in church that comes back to me so much like the sight of an angel, as her on her knees before me at night, washing my poor, dirty little feet, that I'd run bare in all day, and making me decent for bed. There were six of us boys; it seems to me we were all of a size; and she was just so careful with all of us. I can feel her hands on my feet yet!" Bartley looked at Lapham's No. 10 boots and softly whistled through his teeth. "We were patched all over; but we wa'n't ragged. *I* don't know how she got through it. She didn't seem to think it was anything; and I guess it was no more than my father expected of her. *He* worked like a horse in doors and out—up at daylight, feeding the stock, and groaning round all day with his rheumatism, but not stopping."

Bartley hid a yawn over his note-book, and probably, if he could have spoken his mind, he would have suggested to Lapham that he was not there for the purpose of interviewing his ancestry. But Bartley had learned to practice a patience with his victims which he did not always feel, and to feign an interest in their digressions till he could bring them up with a round turn.

"I tell you," said Lapham, jabbing the point of his penknife into the writing-pad on the desk before him, "when I hear women complaining nowadays that their lives are stunted and empty, I want to tell 'em about my *mother's* life. I could paint it out for 'em."

Bartley saw his opportunity at the word paint, and cut in. "And you say, Mr. Lapham, that you discovered this mineral paint on the old farm yourself?"

Lapham acquiesced in the return to business. "*I* didn't discover it," he said, scrupulously. "My father found it one day, in a hole made by a tree blowing down. There it was, laying loose in the pit, and sticking to the roots that had pulled up a big cake of dirt with 'em. *I* don't know what give him the idea that there was money in it, but he did think so from the start. I guess, if they'd had the word in those days, they'd considered him pretty much of a crank about it. He was trying as long as he lived to get that paint introduced; but he couldn't make it go. The country was so poor they couldn't paint their houses with anything; and father hadn't any facilities. It got to be a kind of joke with us; and I guess that paint-mine did as much as any one thing to make us boys clear out as soon as we got old enough. All my brothers went West and took up land; but I hung on to New England, and I hung on to the old farm, not because the paint-mine was on it, but because the old house was—and the graves. Well," said Lapham, as if unwilling to give himself too much credit, "there wouldn't been any market for it, anyway. You can go through that part of the State and buy more farms than you can shake a stick at for less money than it cost to build the barns on 'em. Of course, it's turned out a good thing. I keep the old house up in good shape, and we spend a month or so there every summer. M' wife kind of likes it, and the girls. Pretty place; sightly all round it. I've got a force of men at work there the whole time, and I've got a man and his wife in the house. Had a family meeting there last year; the whole connection from out West. There!" Lapham rose from his seat and took down a large warped, unframed photograph from the top of his desk, passing his hand over it, and then blowing vigorously upon it, to clear it of the dust. "There we are, *all* of us."

"I don't need to look twice at *you*," said Bartley, putting his finger on one of the heads.

"Well, that's Bill," said Lapham, with a gratified laugh. "He's about as brainy as any of us, I guess. He's one of their leading lawyers, out Dubuque way; been judge of the Common Pleas once or twice. That's his son—just graduated at Yale—alongside of my youngest girl. Good-looking chap, aint he?"

"*She's* a good-looking chap," said Bartley, with prompt irreverence. He hastened to add, at the frown which gathered between Lapham's eyes. "What a beautiful creature she is! What a lovely, refined, sensitive face! And she looks *good*, too."

"She *is* good," said the father, relenting.

"And, after all, that's about the best thing in a woman," said the potential reprobate. "If my wife wasn't good enough to keep both of us straight, I don't know what would become of me."

"My other daughter," said Lapham, indicating a girl with eyes that showed large, and a face of singular gravity. "Mis' Lapham," he continued, touching his wife's effigy with his little finger. "My brother Willard and his family—farm at Kankakee. Hazard Lapham and his wife—Baptist preacher in Kansas. Jim and his three girls—milling business at Minneapolis. Ben and his family—practicing medicine in Fort Wayne."

The figures were clustered in an irregular group in front of an old farm-house, whose original ugliness had been smartened up with a coat of Lapham's own paint and heightened with an incongruous piazza. The photographer had not been able to conceal the fact that they were all decent, honest-looking, sensible people, with a very fair share of beauty among the young girls; some of these were extremely pretty, in fact. He had put them into awkward and constrained attitudes, of course; and they all looked as if they had the instrument of torture which photographers call a head-rest under their occiputs. Here and there an elderly lady's face was a mere blur; and some of the younger children had twitched themselves into wavering shadows, and might have passed for spirit-photographs of their own little ghosts. It was the standard family-group photograph, in which most Americans have figured at some time or other; and Lapham exhibited a just satisfaction in it. "I presume," he mused aloud, as he put it back on top of his desk, "that we sha'n't soon get together again, all of us."

"And you say," suggested Bartley, "that you staid right along on the old place, when the rest cleared out West?"

"No-o-o-o," said Lapham, with a long, loud drawl; "I cleared out West too, first off. Went to Texas. Texas was all the cry in those days. But I got enough of the Lone Star in about three months, and I come back with the idea that Vermont was good enough for me."

"Fatted calf business?" queried Bartley, with his pencil poised above his note-book.

"I presume they were glad to see me," said Lapham, with dignity. "Mother," he added gently, "died that winter, and I staid on with father. I buried him in the spring; and then I came down to a little place called Lumberville, and picked up what jobs I could get. I worked round at the saw-mills, and I was ostler awhile at the hotel—I always *did* like a good horse. Well, I *wa'n't* exactly a college graduate, and I went to school odd times. I got to driving the stage after while, and by and by I *bought* the stage and run the business myself. Then I hired the tavern-stand, and—well, to make a long story short, then I got married. Yes," said Lapham, with pride, "I married the school-teacher. We did pretty well with the hotel, and my wife she was always at me to paint up. Well, I put it off, and *put* it off, as a man will, till one day I give in, and says I, 'Well, *let's* paint up. Why, Pert,'—m'wife's name's Persis,[2]—'I've got a whole paint-mine out on the farm. Let's go out and look at it.' So we drove out. I'd let the place for seventy-five dollars a year to a shif'less kind of a Kanuck[3] that had come down that way; and I'd hated to see the house with him in it; but we drove out one Saturday afternoon, and we brought back about a bushel of the stuff in the buggy-seat, and I tried it crude, and I tried it burnt; and I liked it. M'wife she liked it, too. There wa'n't any painter by trade in the village, and I mixed it myself. Well, sir, that tavern's got that coat of paint on it yet, and it haint ever had any other, and I don't know's it ever will. Well, you know, I felt as if it was a kind of a harumscarum experiment, all the while; and I presume I shouldn't have tried it, but I kind of liked to do it because father'd always set so much store by his paint-mine. And when I'd got the first coat on,"—Lapham called it *cut*,—"I presume I must have set as much as half an hour, looking at it and thinking how he would have enjoyed it. I've had my share of luck in this world, and I aint a-going to complain on my *own* account, but I've noticed that most things get along too late for most people. It made me feel bad, and it took all the pride out my success with the paint, thinking of father. Seemed to me I might 'a' taken more interest in it when he was by to see; but we've got to live and learn. Well, I called my wife out,—I'd tried it on the back of the house, you know,—and she left her dishes,—I can remember she came out with her sleeves rolled up and set down alongside of me on the trestle,—and says I, 'What do you think, Persis?' And says she, 'Well, you haint got a paint-mine, Silas Lapham; you've got a *gold*-mine.' She always was just so enthusiastic about things. Well, it was just after two or three boats had burnt up out West, and a lot of lives lost, and there was a great cry about non-inflammable paint, and I guess that was what was in her mind. 'Well, I guess it aint any gold-mine, Persis,' says I; 'but I guess it *is* a paint-mine. I'm going to have it analyzed, and if it turns out what I think it is, I'm going to work it. And if father hadn't had such a long name, I should call it the Nehemiah Lapham Mineral Paint. But, any rate, every barrel of it, and every keg, and every bottle, and every package, big or little, has got to have the initials and figures N. L. f. 1835, S. L. t. 1855, on it. Father found it in 1835, and I tried it in 1855.'"

"'S. T.—1860—X.' business," said Bartley.

"Yes," said Lapham, "but I hadn't heard of Plantation Bitters then, and I hadn't seen any of the fellow's labels. I set to work and I got a man down from Boston; and I carried him out to the farm, and he analyzed it—made a regular job of it. Well, sir, we built a kiln, and we kept a lot of that paint-ore red-hot for forty-eight hours; kept the Kanuck and his family up, firing. The presence of iron in the ore showed with the magnet from the start; and when he came to test it, he found out that it contained about seventy-five per cent. of the peroxide of iron."

Lapham pronounced the scientific phrases with a sort of reverent satisfaction, as if awed through his pride by a little lingering uncertainty as to what peroxide was. He accented it as if it were purr-ox-*eyed;* and Bartley had to get him to spell it.

"Well, and what then?" he asked, when he had made a note of the percentage.

[2] The verse from Romans 16:12 names Persis as the beloved who "labored much in the Lord"—suggestive of the moral qualities that such a woman would bring to her marriage.

[3] Derogatory term for a Canadian of French descent.

"What then?" echoed Lapham. "Well, then, the fellow set down and told me. 'You've got a paint here,' says he, 'that's going to drive every other mineral paint out of the market. Why,' says he, 'it'll drive 'em right into the Back Bay!'[4] Of course *I* didn't know what the Back Bay was then; but I begun to open my eyes; thought I'd had 'em open before, but I guess I hadn't. Says he, 'That paint has got hydraulic cement in it, and it can stand fire and water and acids'; he named over a lot of things. Says he, 'It'll mix easily with linseed oil, whether you want to use it boiled or raw; and it aint a-going to crack nor fade any; and it aint a-going to scale. When you've got your arrangements for burning it properly, you're going to have a paint that will stand like the everlasting hills, in every climate under the sun.' Then he went into a lot of particulars, and I begun to think he was drawing a long bow, and meant to make his bill accordingly. So I kept pretty cool; but the fellow's bill didn't amount to anything hardly—said I might pay him after I got going; young chap, and pretty easy; but every word he said was gospel. Well, I aint a-going to brag up my paint; I don't suppose you came here to hear me blow——"

"Oh, yes, I did," said Bartley. "That's what I want. Tell all there is to tell, and I can boil it down afterward. A man can't make a greater mistake with a reporter than to hold back anything out of modesty. It may be the very thing we want to know. What we want is the whole truth, and more; we've got so much modesty of our own that we can temper almost any statement."

Lapham looked as if he did not quite like this tone, and he resumed a little more quietly. "Oh, there isn't really very much more to say about the paint itself. But you can use it for almost anything where a paint is wanted, inside or out. It'll prevent decay, and it'll stop it, after it's begun, in tin or iron. You can paint the inside of a cistern or a bath-tub with it, and water wont hurt it; and you can paint a steam-boiler with it, and heat wont. You can cover a brick wall with it, or a railroad car, or the deck of a steam-boat, and you can't do a better thing for either."

"Never tried it on the human conscience, I suppose," suggested Bartley.

"No, sir," replied Lapham, gravely. "I guess you want to keep that as free from paint as you can, if you want much use of it. I never cared to try any of it on mine." Lapham suddenly lifted his bulk up out of his swivel-chair, and led the way out into the wareroom beyond the office partitions, where rows and ranks of casks, barrels, and kegs stretched dimly back to the rear of the building, and diffused an honest, clean, wholesome smell of oil and paint. They were labeled and branded as containing each so many pounds of Lapham's Mineral Paint, and each bore the mystic devices, *N. L. f. 1835—S. L. t. 1855.* "There!" said Lapham, kicking one of the largest casks with the toe of his boot, "that's about our biggest package; and here," he added, laying his hand affectionately on the head of a very small keg, as if it were the head of a child, which it resembled in size, "this is the smallest. We used to put the paint on the market dry, but now we grind every ounce of it in oil—very best quality of linseed oil—and warrant it. We find it gives more satisfaction. Now, come back to the office, and I'll show you our fancy brands."

It was very cool and pleasant in that dim wareroom, with the rafters showing

----

[4] Fashionable section of Boston and the location
of Beacon Street, where Lapham will build a
large new house.

overhead in a cloudy perspective, and darkening away into the perpetual twilight at the rear of the building; and Bartley had found an agreeable seat on the head of a half-barrel of the paint, which he was reluctant to leave. But he rose and followed the vigorous lead of Lapham back to the office, where the sun of a long summer afternoon was just beginning to glare in at the window. On shelves opposite Lapham's desk were tin cans of various sizes, arranged in tapering cylinders, and showing, in a pattern diminishing toward the top, the same label borne by the casks and barrels in the wareroom. Lapham merely waved his hand toward these; but when Bartley, after a comprehensive glance at them, gave his whole attention to a row of clean, smooth jars, where different tints of the paint showed through flawless glass, Lapham smiled and waited in pleased expectation.

"Hello!" said Bartley. "That's pretty!"

"Yes," assented Lapham, "it is rather nice. It's our latest thing, and we find it takes with customers first-rate. Look here!" he said, taking down one of the jars, and pointing to the first line of the label.

Bartley read, "THE PERSIS BRAND," and then he looked at Lapham and smiled.

"After *her*, of course," said Lapham. "Got it up and put the first of it on the market her last birthday. She was pleased."

"I should think she might have been," said Bartley, while he made a note of the appearance of the jars.

"I don't know about your mentioning it in your interview," said Lapham, dubiously.

"That's going into the interview, Mr. Lapham, if nothing else does. Got a wife myself, and I know just how you feel." It was in the dawn of Bartley's prosperity on the "Boston Events," before his troubles with Marcia had seriously begun.

"Is that so?" said Lapham, recognizing with a smile another of the vast majority of married Americans; a few underrate their wives, but the rest think them supernal in intelligence and capability. "Well," he added, "we must see about that. Where'd you say you lived?"

"We don't live; we board. Mrs. Nash, 13 Canary Place."

"Well, we've all got to commence that way," suggested Lapham, consolingly.

"Yes; but we've about got to the end of our string. I expect to be under a roof of my own on Clover street before long. I suppose," said Bartley, returning to business, "that you didn't let the grass grow under your feet much after you found out what was in your paint-mine?"

"No, sir," answered Lapham, withdrawing his eyes from a long stare at Bartley, in which he had been seeing himself a young man again, in the first days of his married life. "I went right back to Lumberville and sold out everything, and put all I could rake and scrape together into paint. And Mis' Lapham was with me every time. No hang back about *her*. I tell you she was a *woman*!"

Bartley laughed. "That's the sort most of us marry."

"No, we don't," said Lapham. "Most of us marry silly little girls grown up to *look* like women."

"Well, I guess that's about so," assented Bartley, as if upon second thought.

"If it hadn't been for her," resumed Lapham, "the paint wouldn't have come to anything. I used to tell her it wa'n't the seventy-five per cent. of purr-ox-eyed of iron in the *ore* that made that paint go; it was the seventy-five per cent. of purr-ox-eyed of iron in *her*."

"Good!" cried Bartley. "I'll tell Marcia that."

"In less'n six months there wa'n't a board-fence, nor a bridge-girder, nor a dead wall, nor a barn, nor a face of rock in that whole region that didn't have 'Lapham's Mineral Paint—Specimen' on it in the three colors we begun by making." Bartley had taken his seat on the window-sill, and Lapham, standing before him, now put up his huge foot close to Bartley's thigh; neither of them minded that.

"I've heard a good deal of talk about that S. T.—1860—X. man, and the stove-blacking man, and the kidney-cure man, because they advertised in that way; and I've read articles about it in the papers; but I don't see where the joke comes in, exactly. So long as the people that own the barns and fences don't object, I don't see what the public has got to do with it. And I never saw anything so very sacred about a big rock, along a river or in a pasture that it wouldn't do to put mineral paint on it in three colors. I wish some of the people that talk about the landscape, and *write* about it, had to bu'st one of them rocks *out* of the landscape with powder, or dig a hole to bury it in, as we used to have to do up on the farm; I guess they'd sing a little different tune about the profanation of scenery.[5] There aint any man enjoys a sightly bit of nature—a smooth piece of interval, with half a dozen good-sized wine-glass elms in it—more than *I* do. But I aint a-going to stand up for every big ugly rock I come across, as if we were all a set of dumn Druids.[6] I say the landscape was made for man, and not man for the landscape."

"Yes," said Bartley, carelessly; "it was made for the stove-polish man and the kidney-cure man."

"It was made for any man that knows how to use it," Lapham returned, insensible to Bartley's irony. "Let 'em go and live with nature in the *winter,* up there along the Canada line, and I guess they'll get enough of her for one while. Well—where was I?"

"Decorating the landscape," said Bartley.

"Yes, sir; I started right there at Lumberville, and it give the place a start, too. You wont find it on the map now; and you wont find it in the gazetteer. I give a pretty good lump of money to build a town-hall, about five years back, and the first meeting they held in it they voted to change the name,—Lumberville *wa'n't* a name,—and it's Lapham now."

"Isn't it somewhere up in that region that they get the old Brandon red?" asked Bartley.

"We're about ninety miles from Brandon. The Brandon's a good paint," said Lapham, conscientiously. "Like to show you round up at our place some odd time, if you get off."

"Thanks. I should like it first-rate. Works there?"

"Yes; Works there. Well, sir, just about the time I got started, the war broke out; and it knocked my paint higher than a kite. The thing dropped perfectly dead. I presume that if I'd had any sort of influence, I might have got it into government hands, for gun-carriages and army-wagons, and may be on board government vessels. But I hadn't, and we had to face the music. I was about broken-hearted, but m'wife

[5] As a late nineteenth-century industrialist, Lapham attacks the position taken by those who criticized the use of barn roofs, walls, rocks, and buildings for the display of large billboard advertising posters or painted signs.

[6] Probably an allusion to Stonehenge, the circle of stones considered sacred by the Druids, the priestly class of the Celts of ancient Britain.

she looked at it another way. 'I guess it's a providence,' says she. 'Silas, I guess you've got a country that's worth fighting for. Any rate, you better go out and give it a chance.' Well, sir, I went. I knew she meant business. It might kill her to have me go, but it would kill her sure if I staid. She was one of that kind. I went. Her last words was, 'I'll look after the paint, Si.' We hadn't but just one little girl then,— boy'd died,—and Mis' Lapham's mother was livin' with us; and I knew if times *did* anyways come up again, m'wife'd know just what to do. So I went. I got through; and you can call me Colonel, if you want to. Feel there!" Lapham took Bartley's thumb and forefinger and put them on a bunch in his leg, just above the knee. "Anything hard?"

"Ball?"[7]

Lapham nodded. "Gettysburg. That's my thermometer. If it wa'n't for that, I shouldn't know enough to come in when it rains."

Bartley laughed at a joke which betrayed some evidences of wear. "And when you came back, you took hold of the paint and rushed it?"

"I took hold of the paint and rushed it—all I could," said Lapham, with less satisfaction than he had hitherto shown in his autobiography. "But I found that I had got back to another world. The day of small things was past, and I don't suppose it will ever come again in this country. My wife was at me all the time to take a partner —somebody with capital; but I couldn't seem to bear the idea. That paint was like my own blood to me. To have anybody else concerned in it was like—well, I don't know what. I saw it was the thing to do; but I tried to fight it off, and I tried to joke it off. I used to say, 'Why didn't you take a partner yourself, Persis, while I was away?' And she'd say, 'Well, if you hadn't come back, I should, Si.' Always *did* like a joke about as well as any woman *I* ever saw. Well, I had to come to it. I took a partner." Lapham dropped the bold blue eyes with which he had been till now staring into Bartley's face, and the reporter knew that here was a place for asterisks in his interview, if interviews were faithful. "He had money enough," continued Lapham, with a suppressed sigh; "but he didn't know anything about paint. We hung on together for a year or two. And then we quit."

"And he had the experience," suggested Bartley, with companionable ease.

"I had some of the experience too," said Lapham, with a scowl; and Bartley divined, through the freemasonry[8] of all who have sore places in their memories, that this was a point which he must not touch again.

"And since that, I suppose, you've played it alone."

"I've played it alone."

"You must ship some of this paint of yours to foreign countries, Colonel?" suggested Bartley, putting on a professional air.

"We ship it to all parts of the world. It goes to South America, lots of it. It goes to Australia, and it goes to India, and it goes to China, and it goes to the Cape of Good Hope. It'll stand any climate. Of course, we don't export these fancy brands much. They're for home use. But we're introducing them elsewhere. Here." Lapham pulled open a drawer, and showed Bartley a lot of labels in different languages—

---

[7] Gunshot.

[8] In this context, mutual sympathy felt by those who have shared similar experiences.

Spanish, French, German, and Italian. "We expect to do a good business in all those countries. We've got our agencies in Cadiz now, and in Paris, and in Hamburg, and in Leghorn. It's a thing that's bound to make its way. Yes, sir. Wherever a man has got a ship, or a bridge, or a dock, or a house, or a car, or a fence, or a pig-pen, anywhere in God's universe, to paint, that's the paint for him, and he's bound to find it out sooner or later. You pass a ton of that paint dry through a blast-furnace, and you'll get a quarter of a ton of pig-iron. I believe in my paint. I believe it's a blessing to the world. When folks come in, and kind of smell round, and ask me what I mix it with, I always say, 'Well, in the first place, I mix it with *Faith,* and after that I grind it up with the best quality of boiled linseed oil that money will buy.'"

Lapham took out his watch and looked at it, and Bartley perceived that his audience was drawing to a close. "'F you ever want to run down and take a look at our Works, pass you over the road,"—he called it *rud,*—"and it sha'n't cost you a cent."

"Well, may be I shall, sometime," said Bartley. "Good afternoon, Colonel."

"Good afternoon. Or—hold on! My horse down there yet, William?" he called to the young man in the counting-room, who had taken his letter at the beginning of the interview. "Oh! All right!" he added, in response to something the young man said. "Can't I set you down somewhere, Mr. Hubbard? I've got my horse at the door, and I can drop you on my way home. I'm going to take Mis' Lapham to look at a house I'm driving piles for, down on the New Land."

"Don't care if I do," said Bartley.

Lapham put on a straw hat, gathered up some papers lying on his desk, pulled down its rolling cover, turned the key in it, and gave the papers to an extremely handsome young woman at one of the desks in the outer office. She was stylishly dressed, as Bartley saw, and her smooth, yellow hair was sculpturesquely waved over a low, white forehead. "Here," said Lapham, with the same prompt, gruff kindness that he had used in addressing the young man, "I want you should put these in shape, and give me a type-writer copy to-morrow."

"What an uncommonly pretty girl!" said Bartley, as they descended the rough stairway and found their way out to the street, past the dangling rope of a block and tackle wandering up into the cavernous darkness overhead.

"She does her work," said Lapham, shortly.

Bartley mounted to the left side of the open buggy standing at the curb-stone, and Lapham, gathering up the hitching-weight, slid it under the buggy-seat and mounted beside him.

"No chance to speed a horse here, of course," said Lapham, while the horse with a spirited gentleness picked her way, with a high, long action, over the pavement of the street. The streets were all narrow, and most of them crooked, in that quarter of the town; but at the end of one the spars of a vessel penciled themselves delicately against the cool blue of the afternoon sky. The air was full of a smell pleasantly compounded of oakum, of leather, and of oil. It was not the busy season, and they met only two or three trucks heavily straggling toward the wharf with their long string teams; but the cobble-stones of the pavement were worn with the dint of ponderous wheels, and discolored with iron-rust from them; here and there, in wandering streaks over its surface, was the gray stain of the salt water with which the street had been sprinkled.

After an interval of some minutes, which both men spent in looking round the dashboard from opposite sides to watch the stride of the horse, Bartley said, with a light sigh, "I had a colt once down in Maine that stepped just like that mare."

"Well!" said Lapham, sympathetically recognizing the bond that this fact created between them. "Well, now, I tell you what you do. You let me come for you 'most any afternoon, now, and take you out over the Milldam, and speed this mare a little. I'd like to show you what this mare can do. Yes, I would."

"All right," answered Bartley; "I'll let you know my first day off."

"Good," cried Lapham.

"Kentucky?" queried Bartley.

"No, sir. I don't ride behind anything but Vermont; never did. Touch of Morgan,[9] of course; but you can't have much Morgan in a horse if you want speed. Hambletonian mostly. Where'd you say you wanted to get out?"

"I guess you may put me down at the 'Events' office, just round the corner here. I've got to write up this interview while it's fresh."

"All right," said Lapham, impersonally assenting to Bartley's use of him as material.

He had not much to complain of in Bartley's treatment, unless it was the strain of extravagant compliment which it involved. But the flattery was mainly for the paint, whose virtues Lapham did not believe could be overstated, and himself and his history had been treated with as much respect as Bartley was capable of showing any one. He made a very picturesque thing of the discovery of the paint-mine. "Deep in the heart of the virgin forests of Vermont, far up toward the line of the Canadian snows, on a desolate mountain-side, where an autumnal storm had done its wild work, and the great trees, strewn hither and thither, bore witness to its violence, Nehemiah Lapham discovered, just forty years ago, the mineral which the alchemy of his son's enterprise and energy has transmuted into solid ingots of the most precious of metals. The colossal fortune of Colonel Silas Lapham lay at the bottom of a hole which an uprooted tree had dug for him, and which for many years remained a paint-mine of no more appreciable value than a soap-mine."

Here Bartley had not been able to forego another grin; but he compensated for it by the high reverence with which he spoke of Colonel Lapham's record during the war of the rebellion, and of the motives which impelled him to turn aside from an enterprise in which his whole heart was engaged and take part in the struggle. "The Colonel bears imbedded in the muscle of his right leg a little memento of the period in the shape of a minie-ball, which he jocularly referred to as his thermometer, and which relieves him from the necessity of reading 'The Probabilities' in his morning paper. This saves him just so much time; and for a man who, as he said, has not a moment of waste time on him anywhere, five minutes a day are something in the course of a year. Simple, clear, bold, and straightforward in mind and action, Colonel Silas Lapham, with a prompt comprehensiveness and a never-failing business sagacity, is, in the best sense of that much-abused term, one of nature's noblemen, to the last inch of his five eleven and a half. His life affords an example of single-minded application and unwavering perseverance which our young business men would do well to emulate. There is nothing showy or meretricious about the man. He believes in mineral paint, and he puts his heart and soul into it. He makes it a religion; though

[9] Breed of fine trotting horses. The Morgan, which came originally from Vermont, was eventually supplanted in popularity by the Hambletonian.

we would not imply that it *is* his religion. Colonel Lapham is a regular attendant at the Rev. Dr. Langworthy's church. He subscribes liberally to the Associated Charities, and no good object or worthy public enterprise fails to receive his support. He is not now actively in politics, and his paint is not partisan; but it is an open secret that he is, and always has been, a stanch Republican. Without violating the sanctities of private life, we cannot speak fully of various details which came out in the free and unembarrassed interview which Colonel Lapham accorded our representative. But we may say that the success of which he is justly proud he is also proud to attribute in great measure to the sympathy and energy of his wife—one of those women who, in whatever walk of life, seem born to honor the name of American Woman, and to redeem it from the national reproach of Daisy Millerism.[10] Of Colonel Lapham's family, we will simply add that it consists of two young lady daughters.

"The subject of this very inadequate sketch is building a house on the water side of Beacon street, after designs by one of our leading architectural firms, which, when complete, will be one of the finest ornaments of that exclusive avenue. It will, we believe, be ready for the occupancy of the family sometime in the spring."

When Bartley had finished his article, which he did with a good deal of inward derision, he went home to Marcia, still smiling over the thought of Lapham, whose burly simplicity had peculiarly amused him.

"He regularly turned himself inside out to me," he said, as he sat describing his interview to Marcia.

"Then I know you could make something nice out of it," said his wife; "and that will please Mr. Witherby."

"Oh, yes, I've done pretty well; but I couldn't let myself loose on him the way I wanted to. Confound the limitations of decency, anyway! I should like to have told just what Colonel Lapham thought of landscape advertising in Colonel Lapham's own words. I'll tell you one thing, Marsh: he had a girl there at one of the desks that you wouldn't let *me* have within gunshot of *my* office. Pretty? It aint any name for it!" Marcia's eyes began to blaze, and Bartley broke out into a laugh, in which he arrested himself at sight of a formidable parcel in the corner of the room.

"Hello! What's that?"

"Why, I don't know what it is," replied Marcia, tremulously. "A man brought it just before you came in, and I didn't like to open it."

"Think it was some kind of infernal machine?" asked Bartley, getting down on his knees to examine the package. "*Mrs.* B. Hubbard, heigh?" He cut the heavy hemp string with his penknife. "We must look into this thing. I should like to know who's sending packages to Mrs. Hubbard in my absence." He unfolded the wrappings of paper, growing softer and finer inward, and presently pulled out a handsome square glass jar, through which a crimson mass showed richly. "The Persis Brand!" he yelled. "I knew it!"

"Oh, what is it, Bartley?" quavered Marcia. Then, courageously drawing a little nearer: "Is it some kind of jam?" she implored.

---

[10] Reference to the controversy that arose over the character of the heroine of Henry James's novella *Daisy Miller* (1878). Some considered the story to be a criticism of the overly independent, perhaps immoral, young American woman; here Hubbard takes up this moralistic position.

"Jam? No!" roared Bartley. "It's *paint!* It's mineral paint—Lapham's paint!"

"Paint?" echoed Marcia, as she stood over him while he stripped their wrappings from the jars which showed the dark blue, dark green, light brown, dark brown, and black, with the dark crimson, forming the gamut of color of the Lapham paint. "Don't *tell* me it's paint that *I* can use, Bartley!"

"Well, I shouldn't advise you to use much of it—all at once," replied her husband. "But it's paint that you can use in moderation."

Marcia cast her arms round his neck and kissed him. "O Bartley, I think I'm the happiest girl in the world! I was just wondering what I should do. There are places in that Clover street house that need touching up so dreadfully. I shall be very careful. You needn't be afraid I shall overdo. But this just saves my life. Did you *buy* it, Bartley? You know we couldn't afford it, and you oughtn't to have done it! And what does the Persis Brand mean?"

"Buy it?" cried Bartley. "No! The old fool's sent it to you as a present. You'd better wait for the facts before you pitch into me for extravagance, Marcia. Persis is the name of his wife; and he named it after her because it's his finest brand. You'll see it in my interview. Put it on the market her last birthday for a surprise to her."

"What old fool?" faltered Marcia.

"Why, Lapham—the mineral paint man."

"Oh, what a good man!" sighed Marcia from the bottom of her soul. "Bartley! you *wont* make fun of him, as you do of some of those people? *Will* you?"

"Nothing that *he*'ll ever find out," said Bartley, getting up and brushing off the carpet-lint from his knees.

1885

---

from A Hazard of New Fortunes

from Part V: [The Strike]

from Chapter II

. . . The tide of his confused and aimless reverie had carried him far down-town, he thought;[1] but when he looked up from it to see where he was he found himself on Sixth Avenue, only a little below Thirty-ninth Street, very hot and blown; that idiotic fur overcoat was stifling. He could not possibly walk down to Eleventh; he did not want to walk even to the Elevated station at Thirty-fourth: he stopped at the corner to wait for a surface-car, and fell again into his bitter fancies. After a while he roused himself and looked up the track, but there was no car coming. He found himself beside a policeman, who was lazily swinging his club by its thong from his wrist.

---

[1] At this point in the narrative Angus Beaton, a somewhat feckless and ambitious young commercial artist, has made several false moves in his relations with the woman whose attention he has been courting. Disgruntled and out of sorts, he has been wandering aimlessly around Manhattan. This scene shows Beaton waiting for a streetcar, only to learn that the drivers have just gone out on strike.

"When do you suppose a car will be along?" he asked, rather in a general sarcasm of the absence of the cars than in any special belief that the policeman could tell him.

The policeman waited to discharge his tobacco-juice into the gutter. "In about a week," he said, nonchalantly.

"What's the matter?" asked Beaton, wondering what the joke could be.

"Strike," said the policeman. His interest in Beaton's ignorance seemed to overcome his contempt of it. "Knocked off everywhere this morning except Third Avenue and one or two cross-town lines." He spat again and kept his bulk at its incline over the gutter to glance at a group of men on the corner below. They were neatly dressed, and looked like something better than working-men, and they had a holiday air of being in their best clothes.

"Some of the strikers?" asked Beaton.

The policeman nodded.

"Any trouble yet?"

"There won't be any trouble till we begin to move the cars," said the policeman.

Beaton felt a sudden turn of his rage toward the men whose action would now force him to walk five blocks and mount the stairs of the Elevated station. "If you'd take out eight or ten of those fellows," he said, ferociously, "and set them up against a wall and shoot them, you'd save a great deal of bother."

"I guess we sha'n't have to shoot much," said the policeman, still swinging his locust. "Anyway, we sha'n't begin it. If it comes to a fight, though," he said, with a look at the men under the scooping rim of his helmet, "we can drive the whole six thousand of 'em into the East River without pullin' a trigger."

"Are there six thousand in it?"

"About."

"What do the infernal fools expect to live on?"

"The interest of their money, I suppose," said the officer, with a grin of satisfaction in his irony. "It's got to run its course. Then they'll come back with their heads tied up and their tails between their legs, and plead to be taken on again."

"If I was a manager of the roads," said Beaton, thinking of how much he was already inconvenienced by the strike, and obscurely connecting it as one of the series with the wrongs he had suffered at the hands of Mrs. Horn and Mrs. Mandel, "I would see them starve before I'd take them back—every one of them."

"Well," said the policeman, impartially, as a man might whom the companies allowed to ride free, but who had made friends with a good many drivers and conductors in the course of his free riding, "I guess that's what the roads would like to do if they could; but the men are too many for them, and there ain't enough other men to take their places."

"No matter," said Beaton, severely. "They can bring in men from other places."

"Oh, they'll do that fast enough," said the policeman.

A man came out of the saloon on the corner where the strikers were standing, noisy drunk, and they began, as they would have said, to have some fun with him. The policeman left Beaton, and sauntered slowly down toward the group as if in the natural course of an afternoon ramble. On the other side of the street Beaton could see another officer sauntering up from the block below. Looking up and down the avenue, so silent of its horse-car bells, he saw a policeman at every corner. It was rather impressive.

Chapter III

The strike made a good deal of talk in the office of *Every Other Week*—that is, it made Fulkerson[2] talk a good deal. He congratulated himself that he was not personally incommoded by it, like some of the fellows who lived up-town, and had not everything under one roof, as it were. He enjoyed the excitement of it, and he kept the office-boy running out to buy the extras which the newsmen came crying through the street almost every hour with a lamentable, unintelligible noise. He read not only the latest intelligence of the strike, but the editorial comments on it, which praised the firm attitude of both parties, and the admirable measures taken by the police to preserve order. Fulkerson enjoyed the interviews with the police captains and the leaders of the strike; he equally enjoyed the attempts of the reporters to interview the road managers, which were so graphically detailed, and with such a fine feeling for the right use of scare-heads as to have almost the value of direct expression from them, though it seemed that they had resolutely refused to speak. He said, at second-hand from the papers, that if the men behaved themselves and respected the rights of property, they would have public sympathy with them every time; but just as soon as they began to interfere with the roads' right to manage their own affairs in their own way, they must be put down with an iron hand; the phrase "iron hand" did Fulkerson almost as much good as if it had never been used before. News began to come of fighting between the police and the strikers when the roads tried to move their cars with men imported from Philadelphia, and then Fulkerson rejoiced at the splendid courage of the police. At the same time, he believed what the strikers said, and that the trouble was not made by them, but by gangs of roughs acting without their approval. In this juncture he was relieved by the arrival of the State Board of Arbitration, which took up its quarters, with a great many scare-heads, at one of the principal hotels, and invited the roads and the strikers to lay the matter in dispute before them; he said that now we should see the working of the greatest piece of social machinery in modern times. But it appeared to work only in the alacrity of the strikers to submit their grievance. The roads were as one road in declaring that there was nothing to arbitrate, and that they were merely asserting their right to manage their own affairs in their own way. One of the presidents was reported to have told a member of the Board, who personally summoned him, to get out and to go about his business. Then, to Fulkerson's extreme disappointment, the august tribunal, acting on behalf of the sovereign people in the interest of peace, declared itself powerless, and got out, and would, no doubt, have gone about its business if it had had any. Fulkerson did not know what to say, perhaps because the extras did not; but March[3] laughed at this result.

"It's a good deal like the military manœuvre of the King of France and his forty thousand men. I suppose somebody told him at the top of the hill that there was nothing to arbitrate, and to get out and go about his business, and that was the reason he marched down after he had marched up with all that ceremony. What amuses me is to find that in an affair of this kind the roads have rights and the strikers have rights, but the public has no rights at all. The roads and the strikers are allowed to fight out a private war in our midst—as thoroughly and precisely a private war as any we

---

[2] Fulkerson, the manager and entrepreneur of the newly formed biweekly magazine *Every Other Week*.

[3] Basil March, the editor of Fulkerson's journal and the main character in the novel.

despise the Middle Ages for having tolerated—as any street war in Florence or Verona—and to fight it out at our pains and expense, and we stand by like sheep and wait till they get tired. It's a funny attitude for a city of fifteen hundred thousand inhabitants."

"What would you do?" asked Fulkerson, a good deal daunted by this view of the case.

"Do? Nothing. Hasn't the State Board of Arbitration declared itself powerless? We have no hold upon the strikers; and we're so used to being snubbed and disobliged by common carriers that we have forgotten our hold on the roads and always allow them to manage their own affairs in their own way, quite as if we had nothing to do with them and they owed us no services in return for their privileges."

"That's a good deal so," said Fulkerson, disordering his hair. "Well, it's nuts for the colonel[4] nowadays. He says if he was boss of this town he would seize the roads on behalf of the people, and man 'em with policemen, and run 'em till the managers had come to terms with the strikers; and he'd do that every time there was a strike."

"Doesn't that rather savor of the paternalism he condemned in Lindau?"[5] asked March.

"I don't know. It savors of horse sense."

"You are pretty far gone, Fulkerson. I thought you were the most engaged man I ever saw; but I guess you're more father-in-lawed. And before you're married, too."

"Well, the colonel's a glorious old fellow, March. I wish he had the power to do that thing, just for the fun of looking on while he waltzed in. He's on the keen jump from morning till night, and he's up late and early to see the row. I'm afraid he'll get shot at some of the fights; he sees them all; *I* can't get any show at them: haven't seen a brickbat shied or a club swung yet. Have you?"

"No, I find I can philosophize the situation about as well from the papers, and that's what I really want to do, I suppose. Besides, I'm solemnly pledged by Mrs. March not to go near any sort of crowd, under penalty of having her bring the children and go with me. Her theory is that we must all die together; the children haven't been at school since the strike began. There's no precaution that Mrs. March hasn't used. She watches me whenever I go out, and sees that I start straight for this office."

Fulkerson laughed and said: "Well, it's probably the only thing that's saved your life. Have you seen anything of Beaton lately?"

"No. You don't mean to say *he's* killed!"

"Not if he knows it. But I don't know—What do you say, March? What's the reason you couldn't get us up a paper on the strike?"

"I knew it would fetch round to *Every Other Week,* somehow."

"No, but seriously. There'll be plenty of newspaper accounts. But you could treat it in the historical spirit—like something that happened several centuries ago; De Foe's *Plague of London* style.[6] Heigh? What made me think of it was Beaton. If I could get hold of him, you two could go round together and take down its æsthetic aspects.

---

[4] Colonel Woodburn, a transplanted Southerner, who continually voices outdated political and social values.

[5] Lindau is a German-born, aging, and crippled ex-veteran of the Union army, whose idealism in matters of social rights will lead him into the midst of the strike activities.

[6] *A Journal of the Plague Year* (1722) by Daniel Defoe (1660?–1731) is an early example of the coverage of a major catastrophe presented in a vividly journalistic style.

It's a big thing, March, this strike is. I tell you it's imposing to have a private war, as you say, fought out this way, in the heart of New York, and New York not minding it a bit. See? Might take that view of it. With your descriptions and Beaton's sketches—well, it would just be the greatest card! Come! What do you say?"

"Will you undertake to make it right with Mrs. March if I'm killed and she and the children are not killed with me?"

"Well, it would be difficult. I wonder how it would do to get Kendricks to do the literary part?"

"I've no doubt he'd jump at the chance. I've yet to see the form of literature that Kendricks wouldn't lay down his life for."

"Say!" March perceived that Fulkerson was about to vent another inspiration, and smiled patiently. "Look here! What's the reason we couldn't get one of the strikers to write it up for us?"

"Might have a symposium of strikers and presidents," March suggested.

"No; I'm in earnest. They say some of those fellows—especially the foreigners—are educated men. I know one fellow—a Bohemian[7]—that used to edit a Bohemian newspaper here. He could write it out in his kind of Dutch,[8] and we could get Lindau to translate it."

"I guess not," said March, dryly.

"Why not? He'd do it for the cause, wouldn't he? Suppose you put it up on him the next time you see him."

"I don't see Lindau any more," said March. He added, "I guess he's renounced me along with Mr. Dryfoos's money."

"Pshaw! You don't mean he hasn't been round since?"

"He came for a while, but he's left off coming now. I don't feel particularly gay about it," March said, with some resentment of Fulkerson's grin. "He's left me in debt to him for lessons to the children."

Fulkerson laughed out. "Well, he *is* the greatest old fool! Who'd 'a' thought he'd 'a' been in earnest with those 'brinciples' of his? But I suppose there have to be just such cranks; it takes all kinds to make a world."

"There has to be *one* such crank, it seems," March partially assented. "One's enough for me."

"I reckon this thing is nuts for Lindau, too," said Fulkerson. "Why, it must act like a schooner of beer on him all the while, to see 'gabidal' embarrassed like it is by this strike. It must make old Lindau feel like he was back behind those barricades at Berlin. Well, he's a splendid old fellow; pity he drinks, as I remarked once before."

When March left the office he did not go home so directly as he came, perhaps because Mrs. March's eye was not on him. He was very curious about some aspects of the strike, whose importance, as a great social convulsion, he felt people did not recognize; and, with his temperament in everything, he found its negative expressions as significant as its more violent phases. He had promised his wife solemnly that he would keep away from these, and he had a natural inclination to keep his promise; he had no wish to be that peaceful spectator who always gets shot when there is any firing on a mob. He interested himself in the apparent indifference of the mighty city,

---

[7] Originally, someone from the province in Czechoslovakia; later, someone with radical or highly liberal views.

[8] General term for the German language.

which kept on about its business as tranquilly as if the private war being fought out in its midst were a vague rumor of Indian troubles on the frontier; and he realized how there might once have been a street feud of forty years in Florence[9] without interfering materially with the industry and prosperity of the city. On Broadway there was a silence where a jangle and clatter of horse-car bells and hoofs had been, but it was not very noticeable; and on the avenues, roofed by the elevated roads, this silence of the surface tracks was not noticeable at all in the roar of the trains overhead. Some of the cross-town cars were beginning to run again, with a policeman on the rear of each; on the Third Avenue line, operated by non-union men, who had not struck, there were two policemen beside the driver of every car, and two beside the conductor, to protect them from the strikers. But there were no strikers in sight, and on Second Avenue they stood quietly about in groups on the corners. While March watched them at a safe distance, a car laden with policemen came down the track, but none of the strikers offered to molest it. In their simple Sunday best, March thought them very quiet, decent-looking people, and he could well believe that they had nothing to do with the riotous outbreaks in other parts of the city. He could hardly believe that there were any such outbreaks; he began more and more to think them mere newspaper exaggerations in the absence of any disturbance, or the disposition to it, that he could see. He walked on to the East River: Avenues A, B, and C presented the same quiet aspect as Second Avenue; groups of men stood on the corners, and now and then a police-laden car was brought unmolested down the tracks before them; they looked at it and talked together, and some laughed, but there was no trouble.

March got a cross-town car, and came back to the West Side. A policeman, looking very sleepy and tired, lounged on the platform.

"I suppose you'll be glad when this cruel war is over," March suggested, as he got in.

The officer gave him a surly glance and made him no answer.

His behavior, from a man born to the joking give and take of our life, impressed March. It gave him a fine sense of the ferocity which he had read of the French troops putting on toward the populace just before the *coup d'état;* he began to feel like the populace; but he struggled with himself and regained his character of philosophical observer. In this character he remained in the car and let it carry him by the corner where he ought to have got out and gone home, and let it keep on with him to one of the farthermost tracks westward, where so much of the fighting was reported to have taken place. But everything on the way was as quiet as on the East Side.

Suddenly the car stopped with so quick a turn of the brake that he was half thrown from his seat, and the policeman jumped down from the platform and ran forward.

from *Chapter IV*

... He[10] took the Elevated road. The strike seemed a very far-off thing, though the paper he bought to look up the stock-market was full of noisy typography about

[9] Reference to Florentine political feuds that continued for years during the Middle Ages.
[10] Jacob Dryfoos, a self-made businessman and financier, who has moved to New York City from his native Indiana.

yesterday's troubles on the surface lines. Among the millions in Wall Street there was some joking and some swearing, but not much thinking, about the six thousand men who had taken such chances in their attempt to better their condition. Dryfoos heard nothing of the strike in the lobby of the Stock Exchange, where he spent two or three hours watching a favorite stock of his go up and go down under the betting. By the time the Exchange closed it had risen eight points, and on this and some other investments he was five thousand dollars richer than he had been in the morning. But he had expected to be richer still, and he was by no means satisfied with his luck. All through the excitement of his winning and losing had played the dull, murderous rage he felt toward the child[11] who had defied him, and when the game was over and he started home his rage mounted into a sort of frenzy; he would teach her, he would break her. He walked a long way without thinking, and then waited for a car. None came, and he hailed a passing coupé.

"What has got all the cars?" he demanded of the driver, who jumped down from his box to open the door for him and get his direction.

"Been away?" asked the driver. "Hasn't been any car along for a week. Strike."

"Oh yes," said Dryfoos. He felt suddenly giddy, and he remained staring at the driver after he had taken his seat.

The man asked, "Where to?"

Dryfoos could not think of his street or number, and he said, with uncontrollable fury: "I told you once! Go up to West Eleventh, and drive along slow on the south side; I'll show you the place."

He could not remember the number of *Every Other Week* office, where he suddenly decided to stop before he went home. He wished to see Fulkerson, and ask him something about Beaton: whether he had been about lately, and whether he had dropped any hint of what had happened concerning Christine; Dryfoos believed that Fulkerson was in the fellow's confidence.

There was nobody but Conrad[12] in the counting-room, whither Dryfoos returned after glancing into Fulkerson's empty office. "Where's Fulkerson?" he asked, sitting down with his hat on.

"He went out a few moments ago," said Conrad, glancing at the clock. "I'm afraid he isn't coming back again to-day, if you wanted to see him."

Dryfoos twisted his head sidewise and upward to indicate March's room. "That other fellow out, too?"

"He went just before Mr. Fulkerson," answered Conrad.

"Do you generally knock off here in the middle of the afternoon?" asked the old man.

"No," said Conrad, as patiently as if his father had not been there a score of times and found the whole staff of *Every Other Week* at work between four and five. "Mr. March, you know, always takes a good deal of his work home with him, and I suppose Mr. Fulkerson went out so early because there isn't much doing to-day. Perhaps it's the strike that makes it dull."

"The strike—yes! It's a pretty piece of business to have everything thrown out because a parcel of lazy hounds want a chance to lay off and get drunk." Dryfoos

11 Christine Dryfoos, Jacob's headstrong daughter, who has just quarreled with her father over the fancy she has taken to Beaton.

12 Conrad Dryfoos, Jacob's idealistic son, whose social views run counter to his father's "public-be-damned" attitude.

seemed to think Conrad would make some answer to this, but the young man's mild face merely saddened, and he said nothing. "I've got a coupé out there now that I had to take because I couldn't get a car. If I had my way I'd have a lot of those vagabonds hung. They're waiting to get the city into a snarl, and then rob the houses—pack of dirty, worthless whelps. They ought to call out the militia, and fire into 'em. Clubbing is too good for them." Conrad was still silent, and his father sneered, "But I reckon *you* don't think so."

"I think the strike is useless," said Conrad.

"Oh, you *do,* do you? Comin' to your senses a little. Gettin' tired walkin' so much. I should like to know what your gentlemen over there on the East Side think about the strike, anyway."

The young fellow dropped his eyes. "I am not authorized to speak for them."

"Oh, indeed! And perhaps you're not authorized to speak for yourself?"

"Father, you know we don't agree about these things. I'd rather not talk—"

"But I'm goin' to *make* you talk this time!" cried Dryfoos, striking the arm of the chair he sat in with the side of his fist. A maddening thought of Christine came over him. "As long as you eat my bread, you have got to do as I say. I won't have my children telling me what I shall do and sha'n't do, or take on airs of being holier than me. Now, you just speak up! Do you think those loafers are right, or don't you? Come!"

Conrad apparently judged it best to speak. "I think they were very foolish to strike —at this time, when the Elevated roads can do the work."

"Oh, at this time, heigh! And I suppose they think over there on the East Side that it'd been wise to strike before we got the Elevated." Conrad again refused to answer, and his father roared, "What do you think?"

"I think a strike is always bad business. It's war; but sometime there don't seem any other way for the working-men to get justice. They say that sometimes strikes do raise the wages, after a while."

"Those lazy devils were paid enough already," shrieked the old man. "They got two dollars a day. How much do you think they ought to 'a' got? Twenty?"

Conrad hesitated, with a beseeching look at his father. But he decided to answer. "The men say that with partial work, and fines, and other things, they get sometimes a dollar, and sometimes ninety cents a day."

"They lie, and you *know* they lie," said his father, rising and coming toward him. "And what do you think the upshot of it all will be, after they've ruined business for another week, and made people hire hacks, and stolen the money of honest men? How is it going to end?"

"They will have to give in."

"Oh, give in, heigh! And what will you say *then,* I should like to know? How will you feel about it then? Speak!"

"I shall feel as I do now. I know you don't think that way, and I don't blame you —or anybody. But if I have got to say how I shall feel, why, I shall feel sorry they didn't succeed, for I believe they have a righteous cause, though they go the wrong way to help themselves."

His father came close to him, his eyes blazing, his teeth set. "Do you *dare* to say that to me?"

"Yes. I can't help it. I pity them; my whole heart is with those poor men."

"You impudent puppy!" shouted the old man. He lifted his hand and struck his son in the face. Conrad caught his hand with his own left, and, while the blood began to trickle from a wound that Christine's intaglio ring[13] had made in his temple, he looked at him with a kind of grieving wonder, and said, "Father!"

The old man wrenched his fist away and ran out of the house. He remembered his address now, and he gave it as he plunged into the coupé.[14] He trembled with his evil passion, and glared out of the windows at the passers as he drove home; he only saw Conrad's mild, grieving, wondering eyes, and the blood slowly trickling from the wound in his temple.

Conrad went to the neat-set bowl in Fulkerson's comfortable room and washed the blood away, and kept bathing the wound with the cold water till it stopped bleeding. The cut was not deep, and he thought he would not put anything on it. After a while he locked up the office and started out, he hardly knew where. But he walked on, in the direction he had taken, till he found himself in Union Square, on the pavement in front of Brentano's. It seemed to him that he heard some one calling gently to him, "Mr. Dryfoos!"

Chapter V

Conrad looked confusedly around, and the same voice said again, "Mr. Dryfoos!" and he saw that it was a lady speaking to him from a coupé beside the curbing, and then he saw that it was Miss Vance.[15]

She smiled when he gave signs of having discovered her, and came up to the door of her carriage. "I am so glad to meet you. I have been longing to talk to somebody; nobody seems to feel about it as I do. Oh, isn't it horrible? *Must* they fail? I saw cars running on all the lines as I came across; it made me sick at heart. *Must* those brave fellows give in? And everybody seems to hate them so—I can't bear it." Her face was estranged with excitement, and there were traces of tears on it. "You must think me almost crazy to stop you in the street this way; but when I caught sight of you I had to speak. I knew you would sympathize—I knew you would feel as I do. Oh, how can anybody help honoring those poor men for standing by one another as they do? They are risking all they have in the world for the sake of justice! Oh, they are true heroes! They are staking the bread of their wives and children on the dreadful chance they've taken! But no one seems to understand it. No one seems to see that they are willing to suffer more now that other poor men may suffer less hereafter. And those wretched creatures that are coming in to take their places—those traitors—"

"We can't blame them for wanting to earn a living, Miss Vance," said Conrad.

"No, no! I don't blame them. Who am I, to do such a thing? It's *we*—people like me, of my class—who make the poor betray one another. But this dreadful fighting —this hideous paper is full of it!" She held up an extra, crumpled with her nervous reading. "Can't something be done to stop it? Don't you think that if some one went among them, and tried to make them see how perfectly hopeless it was to resist the companies and drive off the new men, he might do some good? I have wanted to go

---

[13] During her quarrel with Dryfoos, Christine had flung at him the sharp-edged ring that Beaton had previously given her; Dryfoos had slipped it onto his own finger.

[14] Closed carriage.

[15] Margaret Vance, the woman Conrad Dryfoos idolizes and whose high-strung idealism provides Howells with yet another portrayal of the kinds of response the period's social ills were arousing.

and try; but I am a woman, and I mustn't! I shouldn't be afraid of the strikers, but I'm afraid of what people would say!" Conrad kept pressing his handkerchief to the cut in his temple, which he thought might be bleeding, and now she noticed this. "Are you hurt, Mr. Dryfoos? You look so pale."

"No, it's nothing—a little scratch I've got."

"Indeed, you look pale. Have you a carriage? How will you get home? Will you get in here with me and let me drive you?"

"No, no," said Conrad, smiling at her excitement. "I'm perfectly well—"

"And you don't think I'm foolish and wicked for stopping you here and talking in this way? But I know you feel as I do!"

"Yes, I feel as you do. You are right—right in every way—I mustn't keep you —Good-bye." He stepped back to bow, but she put her beautiful hand out of the window, and when he took it she wrung his hand hard.

"Thank you, thank you! You are good and you are just! But no one can do anything. It's useless!"

The type of irreproachable coachman on the box whose respectability had suffered through the strange behavior of his mistress in this interview drove quickly off at her signal, and Conrad stood a moment looking after the carriage. His heart was full of joy; it leaped; he thought it would burst. As he turned to walk away it seemed to him as if he mounted upon the air. The trust she had shown him, the praise she had given him, that crush of the hand: he hoped nothing, he formed no idea from it, but it all filled him with love that cast out the pain and shame he had been suffering. He believed that he could never be unhappy any more; the hardness that was in his mind toward his father went out of it; he saw how sorely he had tried him; he grieved that he had done it, but the means, the difference of his feeling about the cause of their quarrel, he was solemnly glad of that since she shared it. He was only sorry for his father. "Poor father!" he said under his breath as he went along. He explained to her about his father in his reverie, and she pitied his father, too.

He was walking over toward the West Side, aimlessly at first, and then at times with the longing to do something to save those mistaken men from themselves forming itself into a purpose. Was not that what she meant when she bewailed her woman's helplessness? She must have wished him to try if he, being a man, could not do something; or if she did not, still he would try, and if she heard of it she would recall what she had said and would be glad he had understood her so. Thinking of her pleasure in what he was going to do, he forgot almost what it was; but when he came to a street-car track he remembered it, and looked up and down to see if there were any turbulent gathering of men whom he might mingle with and help to keep from violence. He saw none anywhere; and then suddenly, as if at the same moment, for in his exalted mood all events had a dream-like simultaneity, he stood at the corner of an avenue, and in the middle of it, a little way off, was a street-car, and around the car a tumult of shouting, cursing, struggling men. The driver was lashing his horses forward, and a policeman was at their heads, with the conductor, pulling them; stones, clubs, brickbats hailed upon the car, the horses, the men trying to move them. The mob closed upon them in a body, and then a patrol-wagon whirled up from the other side, and a squad of policemen leaped out and began to club the rioters. Conrad could see how they struck them under the rims of their hats; the blows on their skulls sounded as if they had fallen on stone; the rioters ran in all directions.

One of the officers rushed up toward the corner where Conrad stood, and then he saw at his side a tall, old man, with a long, white beard, who was calling out at the policemen: "Ah, yes! Glup the strikerss—gif it to them! Why don't you co and glup the bresidents that insoalt your lawss, and gick your Boart of Arpidration out-of-toors? Glup the strikerss—they cot no friendts! They cot no money to pribe you, to dreat you!"

The officer lifted his club, and the old man threw his left arm up to shield his head. Conrad recognized Lindau, and now he saw the empty sleeve dangle in the air over the stump of his wrist. He heard a shot in that turmoil beside the car, and something seemed to strike him in the breast. He was going to say to the policeman: "Don't strike him! He's an old soldier! You see he has no hand!" but he could not speak, he could not move his tongue. The policeman stood there; he saw his face: it was not bad, not cruel; it was like the face of a statue, fixed, perdurable—a mere image of irresponsible and involuntary authority. Then Conrad fell forward, pierced through the heart by that shot fired from the car.

March heard the shot as he scrambled out of his car, and at the same moment he saw Lindau drop under the club of the policeman, who left him where he fell and joined the rest of the squad in pursuing the rioters. The fighting round the car in the avenue ceased; the driver whipped his horses into a gallop, and the place was left empty.

March would have liked to run; he thought how his wife had implored him to keep away from the rioting; but he could not have left Lindau lying there if he would. Something stronger than his will drew him to the spot, and there he saw Conrad dead beside the old man.

1890

---

from Criticism and Fiction

II: [Realism and the Common Man]

"As for those called critics," the author[1] says, "they have generally sought the rule of the arts in the wrong place; they have sought among poems, pictures, engravings, statues, and buildings; but art can never give the rules that make an art. This is, I believe, the reason why artists in general, and poets principally, have been confined in so narrow a circle; they have been rather imitators of one another than of nature. Critics follow them, and therefore can do little as guides. I can judge but poorly of anything while I measure it by no other standard than itself. The true standard of the arts is in every man's power; and an easy observation of the most common, sometimes of the meanest things, in nature will give the truest lights, where the greatest sagacity and industry that slights such observation must leave us in the dark, or, what is worse, amuse and mislead us by false lights."

[1] Edmund Burke (1729–1797), English statesman, in *Philosophical Inquiry into the Origins of Our Ideas on the Sublime and the Beautiful* (1756).

If this should happen to be true—and it certainly commends itself to acceptance—it might portend an immediate danger to the vested interests of criticism, only that it was written a hundred years ago; and we shall probably have the "sagacity and industry that slights the observation" of nature long enough yet to allow most critics the time to learn some more useful trade than criticism as they pursue it. Nevertheless, I am in hopes that the communistic era in taste foreshadowed by Burke is approaching, and that it will occur within the lives of men now overawed by the foolish old superstition that literature and art are anything but the expression of life, and are to be judged by any other test than that of their fidelity to it. The time is coming, I hope, when each new author, each new artist, will be considered, not in his proportion to any other author or artist, but in his relation to the human nature, known to us all, which it is his privilege, his high duty, to interpret. "The true standard of the artist is in every man's power" already, as Burke says; Michelangelo's "light of the piazza," the glance of the common eye, is and always was the best light on a statue;[2] Goethe's[3] "boys and blackbirds" have in all ages been the real connoisseurs of berries; but hitherto the mass of common men have been afraid to apply their own simplicity, naturalness, and honesty to the appreciation of the beautiful. They have always cast about for the instruction of some one who professed to know better, and who browbeat wholesome common-sense into the self-distrust that ends in sophistication. They have fallen generally to the worst of this bad species, and have been "amused"[4] and misled" (how pretty that quaint old use of amuse is!) "by the false lights" of critical vanity and self-righteousness. They have been taught to compare what they see and what they read, not with the things that they have observed and known, but with the things that some other artist or writer has done. Especially if they have themselves the artistic impulse in any direction they are taught to form themselves, not upon life, but upon the masters who became masters only by forming themselves upon life. The seeds of death are planted in them, and they can produce only the still-born, the academic. They are not told to take their work into the public square and see if it seems true to the chance passer, but to test it by the work of the very men who refused and decried any other test of their own work. The young writer who attempts to report the phrase and carriage of every-day life, who tries to tell just how he has heard men talk and seen them look, is made to feel guilty of something low and unworthy by the stupid people who would like to have him show how Shakespeare's men talked and looked, or Scott's, or Thackeray's, or Balzac's, or Hawthorne's, or Dickens's;[5] he is instructed to idealize his personages, that is, to take the life-likeness out of them, and put the book-likeness into them. He is approached in the spirit of the wretched pedantry into which learning, much or little, always decays when it withdraws itself and stands apart from experience in an attitude of imagined superiority, and which would say with the same confidence to the scientist: "I see that you are looking at a grasshopper there which you have found in the grass, and I suppose you intend to describe it. Now don't waste your time and sin against culture in that way. I've got a grasshopper here, which has been evolved at considera-

[2] Michelangelo's *David* (1504) may be meant as an example of a statue originally on public display in a Florentine *piazza*, or open square.
[3] Goethe: Johann Wolfgang von Goethe (1749–1832), German poet and dramatist.
[4] Beguiled, deceived.

[5] The novelists cited are Sir Walter Scott (1771–1832), William Makepeace Thackeray (1811–1863), Honoré de Balzac (1799–1850), Nathaniel Hawthorne (1804–1864), and Charles Dickens (1812–1870).

ble pains and expense out of the grasshopper in general; in fact, it's a type. It's made up of wire and cardboard, very prettily painted in a conventional tint, and it's perfectly indestructible. It isn't very much like a real grasshopper, but it's a great deal nicer, and it's served to represent the notion of a grasshopper ever since man emerged from barbarism. You may say that it's artificial. Well, it is artificial; but then it's ideal too; and what you want to do is cultivate the ideal. You'll find the books full of my kind of grasshopper, and scarcely a trace of yours in any of them. The thing that you are proposing to do is commonplace; but if you say that it isn't commonplace, for the very reason that it hasn't been done before, you'll have to admit that it's photographic."

As I said, I hope the time is coming when not only the artist, but the common, average man, who always "has the standard of the arts in his power," will have also the courage to apply it, and will reject the ideal grasshopper wherever he finds it, in science, in literature, in art, because it is not "simple, natural, and honest," because it is not like a real grasshopper. But I will own that I think the time is yet far off, and that the people who have been brought up on the ideal grasshopper, the heroic grasshopper, the impassioned grasshopper, the self-devoted, adventureful, good old romantic cardboard grasshopper, must die out before the simple, honest, and natural grasshopper can have a fair field. I am in no haste to compass the end of these good people, whom I find in the mean time very amusing. It is delightful to meet one of them, either in print or out of it—some sweet elderly lady or excellent gentleman whose youth was pastured on the literature of thirty or forty years ago—and to witness the confidence with which they preach their favorite authors as all the law and the prophets. They have commonly read little or nothing since, or, if they have, they have judged it by a standard taken from these authors, and never dreamed of judging it by nature; they are destitute of the documents in the case of the later writers; they suppose that Balzac was the beginning of realism, and that Zola[6] is its wicked end; they are quite ignorant, but they are ready to talk you down, if you differ from them, with an assumption of knowledge sufficient for any occasion. The horror, the resentment, with which they receive any question of their literary saints is genuine; you descend at once very far in the moral and social scale, and anything short of offensive personality is too good for you; it is expressed to you that you are one to be avoided, and put down even a little lower than you have naturally fallen.

These worthy persons are not to blame; it is part of their intellectual mission to represent the petrifaction of taste, and to preserve an image of a smaller and cruder and emptier world than we now live in, a world which was feeling its way towards the simple, the natural, the honest, but was a good deal "amused and misled" by lights now no longer mistakable for heavenly luminaries. They belong to a time, just passing away, when certain authors were considered authorities in certain kinds, when they must be accepted entire and not questioned in any particular. Now we are beginning to see and to say that no author is an authority except in those moments when he held his ear close to Nature's lips and caught her very accent. These moments are not continuous with any authors in the past, and they are rare with all. Therefore I am

---

[6] Émile Zola (1840–1902), the French novelist and critic, who championed the school of literary Naturalism.

not afraid to say now that the greatest classics are sometimes not at all great, and that we can profit by them only when we hold them, like our meanest contemporaries, to a strict accounting, and verify their work by the standard of the arts which we all have in our power, the simple, the natural, and the honest.

Those good people, those curious and interesting if somewhat musty back-numbers, must always have a hero, an idol of some sort, and it is droll to find Balzac, who suffered from their sort such bitter scorn and hate for his realism while he was alive, now become a fetich in his turn, to be shaken in the faces of those who will not blindly worship him. But it is no new thing in the history of literature: whatever is established is sacred with those who do not think. At the beginning of the century, when romance was making the same fight against effete classicism which realism is making to-day against effete romanticism, the Italian poet Monti[7] declared that "the romantic was the cold grave of the Beautiful," just as the realistic is now supposed to be. The romantic of that day and the real of this are in certain degree the same. Romanticism then sought, as realism seeks now, to widen the bounds of sympathy, to level every barrier against æsthetic freedom, to escape from the paralysis of tradition. It exhausted itself in this impulse; and it remained for realism to assert that fidelity to experience and probability of motive are essential conditions of a great imaginative literature. It is not a new theory, but it has never before universally characterized literary endeavor. When realism becomes false to itself, when it heaps up facts merely, and maps life instead of picturing it, realism will perish too. Every true realist instinctively knows this, and it is perhaps the reason why he is careful of every fact, and feels himself bound to express or to indicate its meaning at the risk of overmoralizing. In life he finds nothing insignificant; all tells for destiny and character; nothing that God has made is contemptible. He cannot look upon human life and declare this thing or that thing unworthy of notice, any more than the scientist can declare a fact of the material world beneath the dignity of his inquiry. He feels in every nerve the equality of things and the unity of men; his soul is exalted, not by vain shows and shadows and ideals, but by realities, in which alone the truth lives. In criticism it is his business to break the images of false gods and misshapen heroes, to take away the poor silly toys that many grown people would still like to play with. He cannot keep terms with Jack the Giant-killer or Puss in Boots, under any name or in any place, even when they appear as the convict Vautrec, or the Marquis de Montrivaut, or the Sworn Thirteen Noblemen.[8] He must say to himself that Balzac, when he imagined these monsters, was not Balzac, he was Dumas;[9] he was not realistic, he was romantic.

XXI: [The Nature of American Fiction]

It is no doubt such work as Mr. James's that an English essayist (Mr. E. Hughes)[10] has chiefly in mind, in a study of the differences of the English and American novel. He defines the English novel as working from within outwardly, and the American novel as working from without inwardly. The definition is very surprisingly accurate;

[7] Vincenzo Monti (1754–1828).
[8] Fictional characters depicted by Honoré de Balzac in *La Comédie Humaine,* the general title of the series of novels he wrote throughout his career.

[9] Alexandre Dumas the elder (1803–1870), French author of romantic novels, such as *The Three Musketeers* and *The Count of Monte Cristo.*
[10] The English critic Eilian Hughes, who wrote *Some Aspects of Humanity* in 1889.

and the critic's discovery of this fundamental difference is carried into particulars with a distinctness which is as unfailing as the courtesy he has in recognizing the present superiority of American work. He seems to think, however, that the English principle is the better, though why he should think so he does not make so clear. It appears a belated and rather voluntary effect of patriotism, disappointing in a philosopher of his degree; but it does not keep him from very explicit justice to the best characteristics of our fiction. "The American novelist is distinguished for the intellectual grip which he has of his characters. . . . He penetrates below the crust, and he recognizes no necessity of the crust to anticipate what is beneath. . . . He utterly discards heroics; he often even discards anything like a plot. . . . His story proper is often no more than a natural predicament. . . . It is no stage view we have of his characters, but one behind the scenes. . . . We are brought into contact with no strained virtues, illumined by strained light upon strained heights of situation. . . . Whenever he appeals to the emotions it would seem to be with an appeal to the intellect too. . . . because he weaves his story of the finer, less self-evident though common threads of human nature, seldom calling into play the grosser and more powerful strain. . . . Everywhere in his pages we come across acquaintances undisguised. . . . The characters in an American novel are never unapproachable to the reader. . . . The naturalness, with the every-day atmosphere which surrounds it, is one great charm of the American novel. . . . It is throughout examinative, discursory, even more—quizzical. Its characters are undergoing, at the hands of the author, calm, interested observation. . . . He is never caught identifying himself with them; he must preserve impartiality at all costs . . . but . . . the touch of nature is always felt, the feeling of kinship always follows. . . . The strength of the American novel is its optimistic faith. . . . If out of this persistent hopefulness it can evolve for men a new order of trustfulness, a tenet that between man and man there should be less suspicion, more confidence, since human nature sanctions it, its mission will have been more than an æsthetic, it will have been a moral one."

Not all of this will be found true of Mr. James, but all that relates to artistic methods and characteristics will, and the rest is true of American novels generally. For the most part in their range and tendency they are admirable. I will not say they are all good, or that any of them is wholly good; but I find in nearly every one of them a disposition to regard our life without the literary glasses so long thought desirable, and to see character, not as it is in other fiction, but as it abounds outside of all fiction. This disposition sometimes goes with poor enough performance, but in some of our novels it goes with performance that is excellent; and at any rate it is for the present more valuable than evenness of performance. It is what relates American fiction to the only living movement in imaginative literature, and distinguishes by a superior freshness and authenticity any group of American novels from a similarly accidental group of English novels, giving them the same good right to be as the like number of recent Russian novels, French novels, Spanish novels, Italian novels, Norwegian novels.

It is the difference of the American novelist's ideals from those of the English novelist that gives him his advantage, and seems to promise him the future. The love of the passionate and the heroic, as the Englishman has it, is such a crude and unwholesome thing, so deaf and blind to all the most delicate and important facts of art and life, so insensible to the subtle values in either that its presence or absence makes the whole difference, and enables one who is not obsessed by it to thank Heaven that he is not as that other man is.

There can be little question that many refinements of thought and spirit which every American is sensible of in the fiction of this continent, are necessarily lost upon our good kin beyond seas, whose thumb-fingered apprehension requires something gross and palpable for its assurance of reality. This is not their fault, and I am not sure that it is wholly their misfortune: they are made so as not to miss what they do not find, and they are simply content without those subtleties of life and character which it gives us so keen a pleasure to have noted in literature. If they perceive them at all it is as something vague and diaphanous, something that filmily wavers before their sense and teases them, much as the beings of an invisible world might mock one of our material frame by intimations of their presence. It is with reason, therefore, on the part of an Englishman, that Mr. Henley[11] complains of our fiction as a shadow-land, though we find more and more in it the faithful report of our life, its motives and emotions, and all the comparatively etherealized passions and ideals that influence it.

In fact, the American who chooses to enjoy his birthright to the full, lives in a world wholly different from the Englishman's, and speaks (too often through his nose) another language: he breathes a rarefied and nimble air full of shining possibilities and radiant promises which the fog-and-soot-clogged lungs of those less-favored islanders struggle in vain to fill themselves with. But he ought to be modest in his advantage, and patient with the coughing and sputtering of his cousin who complains of finding himself in an exhausted receiver[12] on plunging into one of our novels. To be quite just to the poor fellow, I have had some such experience as that myself in the atmosphere of some of our more attenuated romances.

Yet every now and then I read a book with perfect comfort and much exhilaration, whose scenes the average Englishman would gasp in. Nothing happens; that is, nobody murders or debauches anybody else; there is no arson or pillage of any sort; there is not a ghost, or a ravening beast, or a hair-breadth escape, or a shipwreck, or a monster of self-sacrifice, or a lady five thousand years old in the whole course of the story; "no promenade, no band of music, nossing!" as Mr. Du Maurier's Frenchman said of the meet for a fox-hunt.[13] Yet it is all alive with the keenest interest for those who enjoy the study of individual traits and general conditions as they make themselves known to American experience.

These conditions have been so favorable hitherto (though they are becoming always less so) that they easily account for the optimistic faith of our novel which Mr. Hughes notices. It used to be one of the disadvantages of the practice of romance in America, which Hawthorne more or less whimsically lamented, that there were so few shadows and inequalities in our broad level of prosperity; and it is one of the reflections suggested by Dostoïevsky's novel, The Crime and the Punishment,[14] that whoever struck a note so profoundly tragic in American fiction would do a false and mistaken thing—as false and as mistaken in its way as dealing in American fiction with

---

[11] William Ernest Henley (1849–1903), English critic and poet.
[12] A vacuum jar used in chemical experiments.
[13] From a sketch by the English writer and illustrator George Du Maurier (1834–1896),

included in his *Pictures of English Society* of 1884.
[14] Fédor Dostoyevski's novel *Crime and Punishment* was published in 1866.

certain nudities which the Latin peoples seem to find edifying. Whatever their deserts, very few American novelists have been led out to be shot, or finally exiled to the rigors of a winter at Duluth; and in a land where journeymen carpenters and plumbers strike for four dollars a day the sum of hunger and cold is comparatively small, and the wrong from class to class has been almost inappreciable, though all this is changing for the worse. Our novelists, therefore, concern themselves with the more smiling aspects of life, which are the more American, and seek the universal in the individual rather than the social interests. It is worth while, even at the risk of being called commonplace, to be true to our well-to-do actualities; the very passions themselves seem to be softened and modified by conditions which formerly at least could not be said to wrong any one, to cramp endeavor, or to cross lawful desire. Sin and suffering and shame there must always be in the world, I suppose, but I believe that in this new world of ours it is still mainly from one to another one, and oftener still from one to one's self. We have death too in America, and a great deal of disagreeable and painful disease, which the multiplicity of our patent medicines does not seem to cure; but this is tragedy that comes in the very nature of things, and is not peculiarly American, as the large, cheerful average of health and success and happy life is. It will not do to boast, but it is well to be true to the facts, and to see that, apart from these purely mortal troubles, the race here has enjoyed conditions in which most of the ills that have darkened its annals might be averted by honest work and unselfish behavior.

Fine artists we have among us, and right-minded as far as they go; and we must not forget this at evil moments when it seems as if all the women had taken to writing hysterical improprieties, and some of the men were trying to be at least as hysterical in despair of being as improper. If we kept to the complexion of a certain school— which sadly needs a school-master—we might very well be despondent; but, after all, that school is not representative of our conditions or our intentions. Other traits are much more characteristic of our life and our fiction. In most American novels, vivid and graphic as the best of them are, the people are segregated if not sequestered, and the scene is sparsely populated. The effect may be in instinctive response to the vacancy of our social life, and I shall not make haste to blame it. There are few places, few occasions among us, in which a novelist can get a large number of polite people together, or at least keep them together. Unless he carries a snap-camera his picture of them has no probability; they affect one like the figures perfunctorily associated in such deadly old engravings as that of "Washington Irving and his Friends." Perhaps it is for this reason that we excel in small pieces with three or four figures, or in studies of rustic communities, where there is propinquity if not society. Our grasp of more urbane life is feeble; most attempts to assemble it in our pictures are failures, possibly because it is too transitory, too intangible in its nature with us, to be truthfully represented as really existent.

I am not sure that the Americans have not brought the short story nearer perfection in the all-round sense than almost any other people, and for reasons very simple and near at hand. It might be argued from the national hurry and impatience that it was a literary form peculiarly adapted to the American temperament, but I suspect that its extraordinary development among us is owing much more to more tangible facts. The success of American magazines, which is nothing less than prodigious, is only commensurate with their excellence. Their sort of success is not only from the courage to decide what ought to please, but from the knowledge of what does please; and it is probable that, aside from the pictures, it is the short stories which please the readers of our best magazines. The serial novels they must have, of course; but rather more of course they must have short stories, and by operation of the law of supply and demand, the short stories, abundant in quantity and excellent in quality, are forthcoming because they are wanted. By another operation of the same law, which political economists have more recently taken account of, the demand follows the supply, and short stories are sought for because there is a proven ability to furnish them, and people read them willingly because they are usually very good. The art of writing them is now so disciplined and diffused with us that there is no lack either for the magazines or for the newspaper "syndicates" which deal in them almost to the exclusion of the serials. In other countries the feuilleton[15] of the journals is a novel continued from day to day, but with us the papers, whether daily or weekly, now more rarely print novels, whether they get them at first hand from the writers, as a great many do, or through the syndicates, which purvey a vast variety of literary wares, chiefly for the Sunday editions of the city journals. In the country papers the short story takes place of the chapters of a serial which used to be given.

1891

---

from Literary Friends and Acquaintance

from Part I: [My First Visit to New England]

XV: [Hawthorne]

Her[1] fellow-passenger was in far other excitement; he was to see Hawthorne, and in a manner to meet Priscilla and Zenobia, and Hester Prynne and little Pearl, and Miriam and Hilda, and Hollingsworth and Coverdale, and Chillingworth and Dimmesdale, and Donatello and Kenyon;[2] and he had no heart for any such poor little reality as that, who could not have been got into any story that one could respect, and must have been difficult even in a Heinesque[3] poem.

I wasted that whole evening and the next morning in fond delaying, and it was not until after the indifferent dinner I got at the tavern where I stopped, that I found courage to go and present Lowell's[4] letter to Hawthorne. I would almost have foregone meeting the weird genius only to have kept that letter, for it said certain infinitely precious things of me with such a sweetness, such a grace as Lowell alone could give his praise. Years afterwards, when Hawthorne was dead, I met Mrs. Hawthorne, and told her of the pang I had in parting with it, and she sent it me,

---

[15] The literary section of French newspapers.
[1] "Her" is an attractive young woman, a fellow passenger on the train Howells is taking, in 1860, out to Concord, Massachusetts; he is beginning a series of visits to the writers he considers his literary heroes.
[2] Characters from novels by Nathaniel

Hawthorne (1804–1864): *The Blithedale Romance* (1852), *The Scarlet Letter* (1850), and *The Marble Faun* (1860).
[3] In the manner of Heinrich Heine (1797–1856), German poet and essayist.
[4] James Russell Lowell (1819–1891), American poet, essayist, and diplomat.

doubly enriched by Hawthorne's keeping. But now if I were to see him at all I must give up my letter, and I carried it in my hand to the door of the cottage he called The Wayside. It was never otherwise than a very modest place, but the modesty was greater then than to-day, and there was already some preliminary carpentry at one end of the cottage, which I saw was to result in an addition to it. I recall pleasant fields across the road before it; behind rose a hill wooded with low pines, such as is made in *Septimius Felton*[5] the scene of the involuntary duel between Septimius and the young British officer. I have a sense of the woods coming quite down to the house, but if this was so I do not know what to do with a grassy slope which seems to have stretched part way up the hill. As I approached, I looked for the tower which the author was fabled to climb into at sight of the coming guest, and pull the ladder up after him; and I wondered whether he would fly before me in that sort, or imagine some easier means of escaping me.

The door was opened to my ring by a tall handsome boy whom I suppose to have been Mr. Julian Hawthorne;[6] and the next moment I found myself in the presence of the romancer, who entered from some room beyond. He advanced carrying his head with a heavy forward droop, and with a pace for which I decided that the word would be *pondering*. It was the pace of a bulky man of fifty, and his head was that beautiful head we all know from the many pictures of it. But Hawthorne's *look* was different from that of any picture of him that I have seen. It was sombre and brooding, as the look of such a poet should have been; it was the look of a man who had dealt faithfully and therefore sorrowfully with that problem of evil which forever attracted, forever evaded Hawthorne. It was by no means troubled; it was full of a dark repose. Others who knew him better and saw him oftener were familiar with other aspects, and I remember that one night at Longfellow's[7] table, when one of the guests happened to speak of the photograph of Hawthorne which hung in a corner of the room, Lowell said, after a glance at it, "Yes, it's good; but it hasn't his fine *accipitral*[8] look."

In the face that confronted me, however, there was nothing of keen alertness; but only a sort of quiet, patient intelligence, for which I seek the right word in vain. It was a very regular face, with beautiful eyes; the mustache, still entirely dark, was dense over the fine mouth. Hawthorne was dressed in black, and he had a certain effect which I remember, of seeming to have on a black cravat with no visible collar. He was such a man that if I had ignorantly met him anywhere I should have instantly felt him to be a personage.

I must have given him the letter myself, for I have no recollection of parting with it before, but I only remember his offering me his hand, and making me shyly and tentatively welcome. After a few moments of the demoralization which followed his hospitable attempts in me, he asked if I would not like to go up on his hill with him and sit there, where he smoked in the afternoon. He offered me a cigar, and when I said that I did not smoke, he lighted it for himself, and we climbed the hill together. At the top, where there was an outlook in the pines over the Concord meadows, we found a log, and he invited me to a place on it beside him, and at intervals of a minute or so he talked while he smoked. Heaven preserved me from the folly of trying to

[5] Unfinished story by Hawthorne about events during the Revolution.
[6] Hawthorne's only son, who became a writer of popular fiction. He was 14 at the time of Howells's visit.
[7] Henry Wadsworth Longfellow (1807–1882), the most famous of the New England poets of the time.
[8] As keen-sighted as a hawk.

tell him how much his books had been to me, and though we got on rapidly at no time, I think we got on better for this interposition. He asked me about Lowell, I dare say, for I told him of my joy in meeting him and Doctor Holmes,[9] and this seemed greatly to interest him. Perhaps because he was so lately from Europe, where our great men are always seen through the wrong end of the telescope, he appeared surprised at my devotion, and asked me whether I cared as much for meeting them as I should care for meeting the famous English authors. I professed that I cared much more, though whether this was true, I now have my doubts, and I think Hawthorne doubted it at the time. But he said nothing in comment, and went on to speak generally of Europe and America. He was curious about the West, which he seemed to fancy much more purely American, and said he would like to see some part of the country on which the shadow (or, if I must be precise, the damned shadow) of Europe had not fallen. I told him I thought the West must finally be characterized by the Germans, whom we had in great numbers, and, purely from my zeal for German poetry, I tried to allege some proofs of their present influence, though I could think of none outside of politics, which I thought they affected wholesomely. I knew Hawthorne was a Democrat, and I felt it well to touch politics lightly, but he had no more to say about the fateful election[10] then pending than Holmes or Lowell had.

With the abrupt transition of his talk throughout, he began somehow to speak of women, and said he had never seen a woman whom he thought quite beautiful. In the same way he spoke of the New England temperament, and suggested that the apparent coldness in it was also real, and that the suppression of emotion for generations would extinguish it at last. Then he questioned me as to my knowledge of Concord, and whether I had seen any of the notable people. I answered that I had met no one but himself, as yet, but I very much wished to see Emerson and Thoreau.[11] I did not think it needful to say that I wished to see Thoreau quite as much because he had suffered in the cause of John Brown[12] as because he had written the books which had taken me; and when he said that Thoreau prided himself on coming nearer the heart of a pine-tree than any other human being, I could say honestly enough that I would rather come near the heart of a man. This visibly pleased him, and I saw that it did not displease him, when he asked whether I was not going to see his next neighbor Mr. Alcott,[13] and I confessed that I had never heard of him. That surprised as well as pleased him; he remarked, with whatever intention, that there was nothing like recognition to make a man modest; and he entered into some account of the philosopher, whom I suppose I need not be much ashamed of not knowing then, since his influence was of the immediate sort that makes a man important to his townsmen while he is still strange to his countrymen.

Hawthorne descanted a little upon the landscape, and said certain of the pleasant

[9] Oliver Wendell Holmes (1809–1894), American writer and physician.

[10] In 1860 "the fateful election" was the presidential race, with a split ticket on the side of the Democrats (Stephen Douglas and John C. Breckinridge) and Abraham Lincoln as the Republican candidate.

[11] The next two men Howells had on his visiting list of Concord writers were Ralph Waldo Emerson (1803–1882) and Henry David Thoreau (1817–1862).

[12] Thoreau's lecture and essay on behalf of John Brown's militant antislavery activities (leading to Brown's capture at Harper's Ferry, Virginia, and his subsequent execution for the crime of attacking a federal arsenal) had been written and presented in October and November of 1859.

[13] Bronson Alcott (1799–1888), American educational reformer.

fields below us belonged to him; but he preferred his hill-top, and if he could have his way those arable fields should be grown up to pines too. He smoked fitfully, and slowly, and in the hour that we spent together, his whiffs were of the desultory and unfinal character of his words. When we went down, he asked me into his house again, and would have me stay to tea, for which we found the table laid. But there was a great deal of silence in it all, and at times, in spite of his shadowy kindness, I felt my spirits sink. After tea, he showed me a bookcase, where there were a few books toppling about on the half-filled shelves, and said, coldly, "This is my library." I knew that men were his books, and though I myself cared for books so much, I found it fit and fine that he should care so little, or seem to care so little. Some of his own romances were among the volumes on these shelves, and when I put my finger on the *Blithedale Romance* and said that I preferred that to the others, his face lighted up, and he said that he believed the Germans liked that best too.

Upon the whole we parted such good friends that when I offered to take leave he asked me how long I was to be in Concord, and not only bade me come to see him again, but said he would give me a card to Emerson, if I liked. I answered, of course, that I should like it beyond all things; and he wrote on the back of his card something which I found, when I got away, to be "I find this young man worthy." The quaintness, the little stiffness of it, if one pleases to call it so, was amusing to one who was not without his sense of humor, but the kindness filled me to the throat with joy. In fact, I entirely liked Hawthorne. He had been as cordial as so shy a man could show himself; and I perceived, with the repose that nothing else can give, the entire sincerity of his soul.

Nothing could have been further from the behavior of this very great man than any sort of posing, apparently, or a wish to affect me with a sense of his greatness. I saw that he was as much abashed by our encounter as I was; he was visibly shy to the point of discomfort, but in no ignoble sense was he conscious, and as nearly as he could with one so much his younger he made an absolute equality between us. My memory of him is without alloy one of the finest pleasures of my life. In my heart I paid him the same glad homage that I paid Lowell and Holmes, and he did nothing to make me think that I had overpaid him. This seems perhaps very little to say in his praise, but to my mind it is saying everything, for I have known but few great men, especially of those I met in early life, when I wished to lavish my admiration upon them, whom I have not the impression of having left in my debt. Then, a defect of the Puritan quality, which I have found in many New-Englanders, is that, wittingly or unwittingly, they propose themselves to you as an example, or if not quite this, that they surround themselves with a subtle ether of potential disapprobation, in which, at the first sign of unworthiness in you, they helplessly suffer you to gasp and perish; they have good hearts, and they would probably come to your succor out of humanity, if they knew how, but they do not know how. Hawthorne had nothing of this about him; he was no more tacitly than he was explicitly didactic. I thought him as thoroughly in keeping with his romances as Doctor Holmes had seemed with his essays and poems, and I met him as I had met the Autocrat[14] in the

---

[14] Title assumed by Oliver Wendell Holmes for the writing of his essays *The Autocrat of the Breakfast Table*, published in 1858.

supreme hour of his fame. He had just given the world the last of those incomparable works which it was to have finished from his hand; the *Marble Faun* had worthily followed, at a somewhat longer interval than usual, the *Blithedale Romance,* and the *House of Seven Gables,* [15] and the *Scarlet Letter,* and had perhaps carried his name higher than all the rest, and certainly farther. Everybody was reading it, and more or less bewailing its indefinite close, but yielding him that full honor and praise which a writer can hope for but once in his life. Nobody dreamed that thereafter only precious fragments, sketches more or less faltering, though all with the divine touch in them, were further to enrich a legacy which in its kind is the finest the race has received from any mind. As I have said, we are always finding new Hawthorne's, but the illusion soon wears away, and then we perceive that they were not Hawthornes at all; that he had some peculiar difference from them, which, by-and-by, we shall no doubt consent must be his difference from all men evermore.

I am painfully aware that I have not summoned before the reader the image of the man as it has always stood in my memory, and I feel a sort of shame for my failure. He was so altogether simple that it seems as if it would be easy to do so; but perhaps a spirit from the other world would be simple too, and yet would no more stand at parle, [16] or consent to be sketched, than Hawthorne. In fact, he was always more or less merging into the shadow, which was in a few years wholly to close over him; there was nothing uncanny in his presence, there was nothing even unwilling, but he had that apparitional quality of some great minds which kept Shakespeare largely unknown to those who thought themselves his intimates, and has at last left him a sort of doubt. There was nothing teasing or wilfully elusive in Hawthorne's impalpability, such as I afterwards felt in Thoreau; if he was not there to your touch, it was no fault of his; it was because your touch was dull, and wanted the use of contact with such natures. The hand passes through the veridical phantom [17] without a sense of its presence, but the phantom is none the less veridical for all that.

XVI: [Thoreau]

I kept the evening of the day I met Hawthorne wholly for the thoughts of him, or rather for that reverberation which continues in the young sensibilities after some important encounter. It must have been the next morning that I went to find Thoreau, and I am dimly aware of making one or two failures to find him, if I ever really found him at all.

He is an author who has fallen into that abeyance, awaiting all authors, great or small, at some time or another; but I think that with him, at least in regard to his most important book, it can be only transitory. I have not read the story of his hermitage beside Walden Pond since the year 1858, [18] but I have a fancy that if I should take it up now, I should think it a wiser and truer conception of the world than I thought it then. It is no solution of the problem; men are not going to answer the riddle of the painful earth by building themselves shanties and living upon beans and

---

[15] Another of Hawthorne's novels, published in 1851.
[16] Parley or discussion.

[17] A "truth-telling" phantom that appears simultaneously with the actual event it images.
[18] *Walden* was published in 1854.

watching ant-fights; but I do not believe Tolstoy[19] himself has more clearly shown the hollowness, the hopelessness, the unworthiness of the life of the world than Thoreau did in that book. If it were newly written it could not fail of a far vaster acceptance than it had then, when to those who thought and felt seriously it seemed that if slavery could only be controlled, all things else would come right of themselves with us. Slavery has not only been controlled, but it has been destroyed, and yet things have not begun to come right with us; but it was in the order of Providence that chattel slavery should cease before industrial slavery, and the infinitely crueler and stupider vanity and luxury bred of it, should be attacked. If there was then any prevision of the struggle now at hand, the seers averted their eyes, and strove only to cope with the less evil. Thoreau himself, who had so clear a vision of the falsity and folly of society as we still have it, threw himself into the tide that was already, in Kansas and Virginia,[20] reddened with war; he aided and abetted the John Brown raid, I do not recall how much or in what sort; and he had suffered in prison for his opinions and actions.[21] It was this inevitable heroism of his that, more than his literature even, made me wish to see him and revere him; and I do not believe that I should have found the veneration difficult, when at last I met him in his insufficient person, if he had otherwise been present to my glowing expectation. He came into the room a quaint, stump figure of a man, whose effect of long trunk and short limbs was heightened by his fashionless trousers being let down too low. He had a noble face, with tossed hair, a distraught eye, and a fine aquilinity of profile, which made me think at once of Don Quixote and of Cervantes;[22] but his nose failed to add that foot to his stature which Lamb[23] says a nose of that shape will always give a man. He tried to place me geographically after he had given me a chair not quite so far off as Ohio, though still across the whole room, for he sat against one wall, and I against the other; but apparently he failed to pull himself out of his revery by the effort, for he remained in a dreamy muse, which all my attempts to say something fit about John Brown and Walden Pond seemed only to deepen upon him. I have not the least doubt that I was needless and valueless about both, and that what I said could not well have prompted an important response; but I did my poor best, and I was terribly disappointed in the result. The truth is that in those days I was a helplessly concrete young person, and all forms of the abstract, the air-drawn, afflicted me like physical discomforts. I do not remember that Thoreau spoke of his books or of himself at all, and when he began to speak of John Brown, it was not the warm, palpable, loving, fearful old man of my conception, but a sort of John Brown type, a John Brown ideal, a John Brown principle, which we were somehow (with long pauses between the vague, orphic[24] phrases) to cherish, and to nourish ourselves upon.

It was not merely a defeat of my hopes, it was a rout, and I felt myself so scattered over the field of thought that I could hardly bring my forces together for retreat. I

---

[19] Count Leo Tolstoy (1828–1910), Russian novelist and social reformer.
[20] John Brown had carried out his militant antislavery efforts in the Kansas Territory in 1856 before launching his final raid on Harper's Ferry in 1859.
[21] Thoreau spent a night in the Concord jail for refusing to pay taxes to the state of Massachusetts because it was aiding the proslavery forces.
[22] Miguel de Cervantes (1547–1616), Spanish dramatist and novelist best known for the hero of his satiric narrative *Don Quixote*.
[23] Charles Lamb (1775–1834), English essayist and critic.
[24] Oracular, mystical.

must have made some effort, vain and foolish enough, to rematerialize my old demigod, but when I came away it was with the feeling that there was very little more left of John Brown than there was of me. His body was not mouldering in the grave, neither was his soul marching on;[25] his ideal, his type, his principle alone existed, and I did not know what to do with it. I am not blaming Thoreau; his words were addressed to a far other understanding than mine, and it was my misfortune if I could not profit by them. I think, or I venture to hope, that I could profit better by them now; but in this record I am trying honestly to report their effect with the sort of youth I was then.

XVII: [Emerson]

Such as I was, I rather wonder that I had the courage, after this experiment of Thoreau, to present the card Hawthorne had given me to Emerson. I must have gone to him at once, however, for I cannot make out any interval of time between my visit to the disciple and my visit to the master. I think it was Emerson himself who opened his door to me, for I have a vision of the fine old man standing tall on his threshold, with the card in his hand, and looking from it to me with a vague serenity,[26] while I waited a moment on the door-step below him. He must then have been about sixty, but I remember nothing of age in his aspect, though I have called him an old man. His hair, I am sure, was still entirely dark, and his face had a kind of marble youthfulness, chiselled to a delicate intelligence by the highest and noblest thinking that any man has done. There was a strange charm in Emerson's eyes, which I felt then and always, something like that I saw in Lincoln's, but shyer, but sweeter and less sad. His smile was the very sweetest I have ever beheld, and the contour of the mask and the line of the profile were in keeping with this incomparable sweetness of the mouth, at once grave and quaint, though quaint is not quite the word for it either, but subtly, not unkindly arch, which again is not the word.

It was his great fortune to have been mostly misunderstood, and to have reached the dense intelligence of his fellow-men after a whole lifetime of perfectly simple and lucid appeal, and his countenance expressed the patience and forbearance of a wise man content to bide his time. It would be hard to persuade people now that Emerson once represented to the popular mind all that was most hopelessly impossible, and that in a certain sort he was a national joke, the type of the incomprehensible, the byword of the poor paragrapher. He had perhaps disabused the community somewhat by presenting himself here and there as a lecturer, and talking face to face with men in terms which they could not refuse to find as clear as they were wise; he was more and more read, by certain persons, here and there; but we are still so far behind him in the reach of his far-thinking that it need not be matter of wonder that twenty years before his death he was the most misunderstood man in America. Yet in that twilight where he dwelt he loomed large upon the imagination; the minds that could not conceive him were still aware of his greatness. I myself had not read much of him,

---

[25] After John Brown's death in 1859, words in celebration of his cause were added to a popular marching tune. In 1861 Julia Ward Howe set other words to the same tune; the result was the "Battle Hymn of the Republic."

[26] By this date Emerson was beginning to show early signs of the senility that overtook him long before his death in 1882.

but I knew the essays he was printing in the *Atlantic,* [27] and I knew certain of his poems, though by no means many; yet I had this sense of him, that he was somehow, beyond and above my ken, a presence of force and beauty and wisdom, uncompanioned in our literature. He had lately stooped from his ethereal heights to take part in the battle of humanity, and I suppose that if the truth were told he was more to my young fervor because he had said that John Brown had made the gallows glorious like the cross, than because he had uttered all those truer and wiser things which will still a hundred years hence be leading the thought of the world.

I do not know in just what sort he made me welcome, but I am aware of sitting with him in his study or library, and of his presently speaking of Hawthorne, whom I probably celebrated as I best could, and whom he praised for his personal excellence, and for his fine qualities as a neighbor. "But his last book," he added, reflectively, "is a mere mush," and I perceived that this great man was no better equipped to judge an artistic fiction than the groundlings who were then crying out upon the indefinite close of the *Marble Faun.* Apparently he had read it, as they had, for the story, but it seems to me now, if it did not seem to me then, that as far as the problem of evil was involved, the book must leave it where it found it. That is forever insoluble, and it was rather with that than with his more or less shadowy people that the romancer was concerned. Emerson had, in fact, a defective sense as to specific pieces of literature; he praised extravagantly, and in the wrong place, especially among the new things, and he failed to see the worth of much that was fine and precious beside the line of his fancy.

He began to ask me about the West, and about some unknown man in Michigan, who had been sending him poems, and whom he seemed to think very promising, though he has not apparently kept his word to do great things. I did not find what Emerson had to say of my section very accurate or important, thought it was kindly enough, and just enough as to what the West ought to do in literature. He thought it a pity that a literary periodical which had lately been started in Cincinnati should be appealing to the East for contributions, instead of relying upon the writers nearer home; and he listened with what patience he could to my modest opinion that we had not the writers nearer home. I never was of those Westerners who believed that the West was kept out of literature by the jealousy of the East, and I tried to explain why we had not the men to write that magazine full in Ohio. He alleged the man in Michigan as one who alone could do much to fill it worthily, and again I had to say that I had never heard of him.

I felt rather guilty in my ignorance, and I had a notion that it did not commend me, but happily at this moment Mr. Emerson was called to dinner, and he asked me to come with him. After dinner we walked about in his "pleached garden" [28] a little, and then we came again into his library, where I meant to linger only till I could fitly get away. He questioned me about what I had seen of Concord, and whom besides Hawthorne I had met, and when I told him only Thoreau, he asked me if I knew the poems of Mr. William Henry Channing. [29] I have known them since, and felt their quality, which I have gladly owned a genuine and original poetry; but I answered

---

[27] The magazine *The Atlantic Monthly,* founded in 1857, was later headed by Howells, who became editor in 1871.

[28] Garden where shrubs and fruit trees have been bent and interlaced into an arbor.

[29] American poet (1810–1884).

then truly that I knew them only from Poe's criticisms:[30] cruel and spiteful things which I should be ashamed of enjoying as I once did.

"Whose criticisms?" asked Emerson.

"Poe's," I said again.

"Oh," he cried out, after a moment, as if he had returned from a far search for my meaning, *"you mean the jingle-man!"*

I do not know why this should have put me to such confusion, but if I had written the criticisms myself I do not think I could have been more abashed. Perhaps I felt an edge of reproof, of admonition, in a characterization of Poe which the world will hardly agree with; though I do not agree with the world about him, myself, in its admiration. At any rate, it made an end of me for the time, and I remained as if already absent, while Emerson questioned me as to what I had written in the *Atlantic Monthly*. He had evidently read none of my contributions, for he looked at them, in the bound volume of the magazine which he got down, with the effect of being wholly strange to them, and then gravely affixed my initials to each. He followed me to the door, still speaking of poetry, and as he took a kindly enough leave of me, he said one might very well give a pleasant hour to it now and then.

A pleasant hour to poetry! I was meaning to give all time and all eternity to poetry, and I should by no means have wished to find pleasure in it; I should have thought that a proof of inferior quality in the work; I should have preferred anxiety, anguish even, to pleasure. But if Emerson thought from the glance he gave my verses that I had better not lavish myself upon that kind of thing, unless there was a great deal more of me than I could have made apparent in our meeting, no doubt he was right. I was only too painfully aware of my shortcoming, but I felt that it was shorter-coming than it need have been. I had somehow not prospered in my visit to Emerson as I had with Hawthorne, and I came away wondering in what sort I had gone wrong. I was not a forth-putting youth, and I could not blame myself for anything in my approaches that merited withholding; indeed, I made no approaches; but as I must needs blame myself for something, I fell upon the fact that in my confused retreat from Emerson's presence I had failed in a certain slight point of ceremony, and I magnified this into an offence of capital importance. I went home to my hotel, and passed the afternoon in pure misery. I had moments of wild question when I debated whether it would be better to go back and own my error, or whether it would be better to write him a note, and try to set myself right in that way. But in the end I did neither, and I have since survived my mortal shame some forty years or more. But at the time it did not seem possible that I should live through the day with it, and I thought that I ought at least to go and confess it to Hawthorne, and let him disown the wretch who had so poorly repaid the kindness of his introduction by such misbehavior. I did indeed walk down by the Wayside, in the cool of the evening, and there I saw Hawthorne for the last time. He was sitting on one of the timbers beside his cottage, and smoking with an air of friendly calm. I had got on very well with him, and I longed to go in, and tell him how ill I had got on with Emerson; I believed that though he cast me off, he would understand me, and would perhaps see some hope for me in another world, though there could be none in this.

---

[30] Edgar Allan Poe (1809–1849), American writer of poetry, fiction, and literary criticism, had disdain for Channing and others who shared "transcendentalist" leanings.

But I had not the courage to speak of the affair to any one but Fields,[31] to whom I unpacked my heart when I got back to Boston, and he asked me about my adventures in Concord. By this time I could see it in a humorous light, and I did not much mind his lying back in his chair and laughing and laughing, till I thought he would roll out of it. He perfectly conceived the situation, and got an amusement from it that I could get only through sympathy with him. But I thought it a favorable moment to propose myself as the assistant editor of the *Atlantic Monthly,* which I had the belief I could very well become, with advantage to myself if not to the magazine. He seemed to think so too; he said that if the place had not just been filled, I should certainly have had it; and it was to his recollection of this prompt ambition of mine that I suppose I may have owed my succession to a like vacancy some four years later. He was charmingly kind; he entered with the sweetest interest into the story of my economic life, which had been full of changes and chances already. But when I said very seriously that now I was tired of these fortuities, and would like to be settled in something, he asked, with dancing eyes,

"Why, how old are you?"

"I am twenty-three," I answered, and then the laughing fit took him again.

"Well," he said, "you begin young, out there!"

In my heart I did not think that twenty-three was so very young, but perhaps it was; and if any one were to say that I had been portraying here a youth whose aims were certainly beyond his achievements, who was morbidly sensitive, and if not conceited was intolerably conscious, who had met with incredible kindness, and had suffered no more than was good for him, though he might not have merited his pain any more than his joy, I do not know that I should gainsay him, for I am not at all sure that I was not just that kind of youth when I paid my first visit to New England.

1900

Editha

The air was thick with the war[1] feeling, like the electricity of a storm which has not yet burst. Editha sat looking out into the hot spring afternoon, with her lips parted, and panting with the intensity of the question whether she could let him go. She had decided that she could not let him stay, when she saw him at the end of the still leafless avenue, making slowly up towards the house, with his head down and his figure relaxed. She ran impatiently out on the veranda, to the edge of the steps, and imperatively demanded greater haste of him with her will before she called aloud to him: "George!"

---

[31] James T. Fields, Boston publisher for many of the New England writers, editor of the *Atlantic,* and Howells's literary mentor.

[1] The Spanish-American War of 1898.

He had quickened his pace in mystical response to her mystical urgence, before he could have heard her; now he looked up and answered, "Well?"

"Oh, how united we are!" she exulted, and then she swooped down the steps to him. "What is it?" she cried.

"It's war," he said, and he pulled her up to him and kissed her.

She kissed him back intensely, but irrelevantly, as to their passion, and uttered from deep in her throat. "How glorious!"

"It's war," he repeated, without consenting to her sense of it; and she did not know just what to think at first. She never knew what to think of him; that made his mystery, his charm. All through their courtship, which was contemporaneous with the growth of the war feeling, she had been puzzled by his want of seriousness about it. He seemed to despise it even more than he abhorred it. She could have understood his abhorring any sort of bloodshed; that would have been a survival of his old life when he thought he would be a minister, and before he changed and took up the law. But making light of a cause so high and noble seemed to show a want of earnestness at the core of his being. Not but that she felt herself able to cope with a congenital defect of that sort, and make his love for her save him from himself. Now perhaps the miracle was already wrought in him. In the presence of the tremendous fact that he announced, all triviality seemed to have gone out of him; she began to feel that. He sank down on the top step, and wiped his forehead with his handkerchief, while she poured out upon him her question of the origin and authenticity of his news.

All the while, in her duplex emotioning, she was aware that now at the very beginning she must put a guard upon herself against urging him, by any word or act, to take the part that her whole soul willed him to take, for the completion of her ideal of him. He was very nearly perfect as he was, and he must be allowed to perfect himself. But he was peculiar, and he might very well be reasoned out of his peculiarity. Before her reasoning went her emotioning: her nature pulling upon his nature, her womanhood upon his manhood, without her knowing the means she was using to the end she was willing. She had always supposed that the man who won her would have done something to win her: she did not know what, but something. George Gearson had simply asked her for her love, on the way home from a concert, and she gave her love to him without, as it were, thinking. But now, it flashed upon her, if he could do something worthy to *have* won her—be a hero, *her* hero—it would be even better than if he had done it before asking her; it would be grander. Besides, she had believed in the war from the beginning.

"But don't you see, dearest," she said, "that it wouldn't have come to this if it hadn't been in the order of Providence? And I call any war glorious that is for the liberation of people who have been struggling for years against the cruelest oppression. Don't you think so, too?"

"I suppose so," he returned languidly. "But war! Is it glorious to break the peace of the world?"

"That ignoble peace! It was no peace at all, with that crime and shame at our very gates." She was conscious of parroting the current phrases of the newspapers, but it was no time to pick and choose her words. She must sacrifice anything to the high ideal she had for him, and after a good deal of rapid argument she ended with the climax: "But now it doesn't matter about the how or why. Since the war has come, all that is gone. There are no two sides any more. There is nothing now but our country."

He sat with his eyes closed and his head leant back against the veranda, and he remarked, with a vague smile, as if musing aloud, "Our country—right or wrong."[2]

"Yes, right or wrong!" she returned, fervidly. "I'll go and get you some lemonade." She rose rustling, and whisked away; when she came back with two tall glasses of clouded liquid on a tray, and the ice clucking in them, he still sat as she had left him, and she said, as if there had been no interruption: "But there is no question of wrong in this case. I call it a sacred war. A war for liberty and humanity, if ever there was one. And I know you will see it just as I do, yet."

He took half the lemonade at a gulp, and he answered as he set the glass down: "I know you always have the highest ideal. When I differ from you I ought to doubt myself."

A generous sob rose in Editha's throat for the humility of a man, so very nearly perfect, who was willing to put himself below her.

Besides, she felt, more subliminally, that he was never so near slipping through her fingers as when he took that meek way.

"You shall not say that! Only, for once I happen to be right." She seized his hand in her two hands, and poured her soul from her eyes into his. "Don't you think so?" she entreated him.

He released his hand and drank the rest of his lemonade, and she added, "Have mine too," but he shook his head in answering, "I've no business to think so, unless I act so, too."

Her heart stopped a beat before it pulsed on with leaps that she felt in her neck. She had noticed that strange thing in men: they seemed to feel bound to do what they believed, and not think a thing was finished when they said it, as girls did. She knew what was in his mind, but she pretended not, as she said, "Oh, I am not sure," and then faltered.

He went on as if to himself, without apparently heeding her: "There's only one way of proving one's faith in a thing like this."

She could not say that she understood, but she did understand.

He went on again. "If I believed—if I felt as you do about this war—Do you wish me to feel as you do?"

Now she was really not sure; so she said: "George, I don't know what you mean."

He seemed to muse away from her as before. "There is a sort of fascination in it. I suppose that at the bottom of his heart every man would like at times to have his courage tested, to see how he would act."

"How can you talk in that ghastly way?"

"It *is* rather morbid. Still, that's what it comes to, unless you're swept away by ambition or driven by conviction. I haven't the conviction or the ambition, and the other thing is what it comes to with me. I ought to have been a preacher, after all; then I couldn't have asked it of myself, as I must, now I'm a lawyer. And you believe

---

[2] During an engagement with the British fleet in 1816, this phrase was coined by Stephen Decatur, the American naval hero.

it's a holy war, Editha?" he suddenly addressed her. "Oh, I know you do! But you wish me to believe so, too?"

She hardly knew whether he was mocking or not, in the ironical way he always had with her plainer mind. But the only thing was to be outspoken with him.

"George, I wish you to believe whatever you think is true, at any and every cost. If I've tried to talk you into anything, I take it all back."

"Oh, I know that, Editha. I know how sincere you are, and how—I wish I had your undoubting spirit! I'll think it over; I'd like to believe as you do. But I don't, now; I don't, indeed. It isn't this war alone; though this seems peculiarly wanton and needless; but it's every war—so stupid; it makes me sick. Why shouldn't this thing have been settled reasonably?"

"Because," she said, very throatily again, "God meant it to be war."

"You think it was God? Yes, I suppose that is what people will say."

"Do you suppose it would have been war if God hadn't meant it?"

"I don't know. Sometimes it seems as if God had put this world into men's keeping to work it as they pleased."

"Now, George, that is blasphemy."

"Well, I won't blaspheme. I'll try to believe in your pocket Providence," he said, and then he rose to go.

"Why don't you stay to dinner?" Dinner at Balcom's Works was at one o'clock.

"I'll come back to supper, if you'll let me. Perhaps I shall bring you a convert."

"Well, you may come back, on that condition."

"All right. If I don't come, you'll understand."

He went away without kissing her, and she felt it a suspension of their engagement. It all interested her intensely; she was undergoing a tremendous experience, and she was being equal to it. While she stood looking after him, her mother came out through one of the long windows onto the veranda, with a catlike softness and vagueness.

"Why didn't he stay to dinner?"

"Because—because—war has been declared," Editha pronounced, without turning.

Her mother said, "Oh, my!" and then said nothing more until she had sat down in one of the large Shaker chairs[3] and rocked herself for some time. Then she closed whatever tacit passage of thought there had been in her mind with the spoken words: "Well, I hope *he* won't go."

"And *I* hope he *will*," the girl said, and confronted her mother with a stormy exaltation that would have frightened any creature less unimpressionable than a cat.

Her mother rocked herself again for an interval of cogitation. What she arrived at in speech was: "Well, I guess you've done a wicked thing, Editha Balcom."

The girl said, as she passed indoors through the same window her mother had come out by: "I haven't done anything—yet."

In her room, she put together all her letters and gifts from Gearson, down to the withered petals of the first flower he had offered, with that timidity of his veiled in

---

[3] Designed and manufactured by the Shakers, members of a religious community noted for the fine simplicity of their artifacts.

that irony of his. In the heart of the packet she enshrined her engagement ring which she had restored to the pretty box he had brought it her in. Then she sat down, if not calmly yet strongly, and wrote:

"GEORGE:—I understood when you left me. But I think we had better emphasize your meaning that if we cannot be one in everything we had better be one in nothing. So I am sending these things for your keeping till you have made up your mind.

"I shall always love you, and therefore I shall never marry any one else. But the man I marry must love his country first of all, and be able to say to me,

" 'I could not love thee, dear, so much,
Loved I not honor more.'[4]

"There is no honor above America with me. In this great hour there is no other honor.

"Your heart will make my words clear to you. I had never expected to say so much, but it has come upon me that I must say the utmost. EDITHA."

She thought she had worded her letter well, worded it in a way that could not be bettered; all had been implied and nothing expressed.

She had it ready to send with the packet she had tied with red, white, and blue ribbon, when it occurred to her that she was not just to him, that she was not giving him a fair chance. He had said he would go and think it over, and she was not waiting. She was pushing, threatening, compelling. That was not a woman's part. She must leave him free, free, free. She could not accept for her country or herself a forced sacrifice.

In writing her letter she had satisfied the impulse from which it sprang; she could well afford to wait till he had thought it over. She put the packet and the letter by, and rested serene in the consciousness of having done what was laid upon her by her love itself to do, and yet used patience, mercy, justice.

She had her reward. Gearson did not come to tea, but she had given him till morning, when, late at night there came up from the village the sound of a fife and drum, with a tumult of voices, in shouting, singing, and laughing. The noise drew nearer and nearer; it reached the street end of the avenue; there it silenced itself, and one voice, the voice she knew best, rose over the silence. It fell; the air was filled with cheers; the fife and drum struck up, with the shouting, singing, and laughing again, but now retreating; and a single figure came hurrying up the avenue.

She ran down to meet her lover and clung to him. He was very gay, and he put his arm round her with a boisterous laugh. "Well, you must call me Captain now; or Cap, if you prefer; that's what the boys call me. Yes, we've had a meeting at the town-hall, and everybody has volunteered; and they selected me for captain, and I'm going to the war, the big war, the glorious war, the holy war ordained by the pocket

[4] From the poem "To Lucasta, Going to the Wars," by Richard Lovelace (1618–1658).

Providence that blesses butchery. Come along; let's tell the whole family about it. Call them from their downy beds, father, mother, Aunt Hitty, and all the folks!"

But when they mounted the veranda steps he did not wait for a larger audience; he poured the story out upon Editha alone.

"There was a lot of speaking, and then some of the fools set up a shout for me. It was all going one way, and I thought it would be a good joke to sprinkle a little cold water on them. But you can't do that with a crowd that adores you. The first thing I knew I was sprinkling hell-fire on them. 'Cry havoc, and let slip the dogs of war.'[5] That was the style. Now that it had come to the fight, there were no two parties; there was one country, and the thing was to fight to a finish as quick as possible. I suggested volunteering then and there, and I wrote my name first of all on the roster. Then they elected me—that's all. I wish I had some ice-water."

She left him walking up and down the veranda, while she ran for the ice-pitcher and a goblet, and when she came back he was still walking up and down, shouting the story he had told her to her father and mother, who had come out more sketchily dressed than they commonly were by day. He drank goblet after goblet of the ice-water without noticing who was giving it, and kept on talking, and laughing through his talk wildly. "It's astonishing," he said, "how well the worse reason looks when you try to make it appear the better. Why, I believe I was the first convert to the war in that crowd to-night! I never thought I should like to kill a man; but now I shouldn't care; and the smokeless powder lets you see the man drop that you kill. It's all for the country! What a thing it is to have a country that *can't* be wrong, but if it is, is right, anyway!"

Editha had a great, vital thought, an inspiration. She set down the ice-pitcher on the veranda floor, and ran up-stairs and got the letter she had written him. When at last he noisily bade her father and mother, "Well, good-night. I forgot I woke you up; I sha'n't want any sleep myself," she followed him down the avenue to the gate. There, after the whirling words that seemed to fly away from her thoughts and refuse to serve them, she made a last effort to solemnize the moment that seemed so crazy, and pressed the letter she had written upon him.

"What's this?" he said. "Want me to mail it?"

"No, no. It's for you. I wrote it after you went this morning. Keep it—keep it —and read it sometime—" She thought, and then her inspiration came: "Read it if ever you doubt what you've done, or fear that I regret your having done it. Read it after you've started."

They strained each other in embraces that seemed as ineffective as their words, and he kissed her face with quick, hot breaths that were so unlike him, that made her feel as if she had lost her old lover and found a stranger in his place. The stranger said: "What a gorgeous flower you are, with your red hair, and your blue eyes that look black now, and your face with the color painted out by the white moonshine! Let me hold you under the chin, to see whether I love blood, you tiger-lily!" Then he laughed Gearson's laugh, and released her, scared and giddy. Within her wilfulness she had been frightened by a sense of subtler force in him, and mystically mastered as she had never been before.

[5] Shakespeare's *Julius Caesar*, Act III, Sc. i, l. 273.

She ran all the way back to the house, and mounted the steps panting. Her mother and father were talking of the great affair. Her mother said: "Wa'n't Mr. Gearson in rather of an excited state of mind? Didn't you think he acted curious?"

"Well, not for a man who'd just been elected captain and had set'em up for the whole of Company A," her father chuckled back.

"What in the world do you mean, Mr. Balcom? Oh! There's Editha!" She offered to follow the girl indoors.

"Don't come, mother!" Editha called, vanishing.

Mrs. Balcom remained to reproach her husband. "I don't see much of anything to laugh at."

"Well, it's catching. Caught it from Gearson. I guess it won't be much of a war, and I guess Gearson don't think so either. The other fellows will back down as soon as they see we mean it. I wouldn't lose any sleep over it. I'm going back to bed, myself."

Gearson came again next afternoon, looking pale and rather sick, but quite himself, even to his languid irony. "I guess I'd better tell you, Editha, that I consecrated myself to your god of battles last night by pouring too many libations to him down my own throat. But I'm all right now. One has to carry off the excitement, somehow."

"Promise me," she commanded, "that you'll never touch it again!"

"What! Not let the cannikin[6] clink? Not let the soldier drink? Well, I promise."

"You don't belong to yourself now; you don't even belong to *me*. You belong to your country, and you have a sacred charge to keep yourself strong and well for your country's sake. I have been thinking, thinking all night and all day long."

"You look as if you had been crying a little, too," he said, with his queer smile.

"That's all past. I've been thinking, and worshipping *you*. Don't you suppose I know all that you've been through, to come to this? I've followed you every step from your old theories and opinions."

"Well, you've had a long row to hoe."

"And I know you've done this from the highest motives—"

"Oh, there won't be much pettifogging to do till this cruel war is—"

"And you haven't simply done it for my sake. I couldn't respect you if you had."

"Well, then we'll say I haven't. A man that hasn't got his own respect intact wants the respect of all the other people he can corner. But we won't go into that. I'm in for the thing now, and we've got to face our future. My idea is that this isn't going to be a very protracted struggle; we shall just scare the enemy to death before it comes to a fight at all. But we must provide for contingencies, Editha. If anything happens to me—"

"Oh, George!" She clung to him, sobbing.

"I don't want you to feel foolishly bound to my memory. I should hate that, wherever I happened to be."

"I am yours, for time and eternity—time and eternity." She liked the words; they satisfied her famine for phrases.

---

[6] Cup. The reference is to the tradition of a soldier's right to drink before battle, as described in Shakespeare's *Othello,* Act II, Sc. iii, ll. 71–75.

"Well, say eternity; that's all right; but time's another thing; and I'm talking about time. But there is something! My mother! If anything happens—"

She winced, and he laughed, "You're not the bold soldier-girl of yesterday!" Then he sobered. "If anything happens, I want you to help my mother out. She won't like my doing this thing. She brought me up to think war a fool thing as well as a bad thing. My father was in the Civil War; all through it; lost his arm in it." She thrilled with the sense of the arm round her; what if that should be lost? He laughed as if divining her: "Oh, it doesn't run in the family, as far as I know!" Then he added, gravely: "He came home with misgivings about war, and they grew on him. I guess he and mother agreed between them that I was to be brought up in his final mind about it; but that was before my time. I only knew him from my mother's report of him and his opinions; I don't know whether they were hers first; but they were hers last. This will be a blow to her. I shall have to write and tell her—"

He stopped, and she asked: "Would you like me to write, too, George?"

"I don't believe that would do. No, I'll do the writing. She'll understand a little if I say that I thought the way to minimize it was to make war on the largest possible scale at once—that I felt I must have been helping on the war somehow if I hadn't helped keep it from coming, and I knew I hadn't; when it came, I had no right to stay out of it."

Whether his sophistries satisfied him or not, they satisfied her. She clung to his breast, and whispered, with closed eyes and quivering lips: "Yes, yes, yes!"

"But if anything should happen, you might go to her and see what you could do for her. You know? It's rather far off; she can't leave her chair—"

"Oh, I'll go, if it's the ends of the earth! But nothing will happen! Nothing *can*! I—"

She felt herself lifted with his rising, and Gearson was saying, with his arm still round her, to her father: "Well, we're off at once, Mr. Balcom. We're to be formally accepted at the capital, and then bunched up with the rest somehow, and sent into camp somewhere, and got to the front as soon as possible. We all want to be in the van, of course; we're the first company to report to the Governor. I came to tell Editha, but I hadn't got round to it."

She saw him again for a moment at the capital, in the station, just before the train started southward with his regiment. He looked well, in his uniform, and very soldierly, but somehow girlish, too, with his clean-shaven face and slim figure. The manly eyes and the strong voice satisfied her, and his preoccupation with some unexpected details of duty flattered her. Other girls were weeping and bemoaning themselves, but she felt a sort of noble distinction in the abstraction, the almost unconsciousness, with which they parted. Only at the last moment he said: "Don't forget my mother. It mayn't be such a walk-over as I supposed," and he laughed at the notion.

He waved his hand to her as the train moved off—she knew it among a score of hands that were waved to other girls from the platform of the car, for it held a letter which she knew was hers. Then he went inside the car to read it, doubtless, and she did not see him again. But she felt safe for him through the strength of what she called her love. What she called her God, always speaking the name in a deep voice and with the implication of a mutual understanding, would watch over him and keep him and bring him back to her. If with an empty sleeve, then he should have three arms instead of two, for both of hers should be his for life. She did not see, though, why she should always be thinking of the arm his father had lost.

There were not many letters from him, but they were such as she could have wished, and she put her whole strength into making hers such as she imagined he could have wished, glorifying and supporting him. She wrote to his mother glorifying him as their hero, but the brief answer she got was merely to the effect that Mrs. Gearson was not well enough to write herself, and thanking her for her letter by the hand of some one who called herself "Yrs truly, Mrs. W. J. Andrews."

Editha determined not to be hurt, but to write again quite as if the answer had been all she expected. Before it seemed as if she could have written, there came news of the first skirmish, and in the list of the killed, which was telegraphed as a trifling loss on our side, was Gearson's name. There was a frantic time of trying to make out that it might be, must be, some other Gearson; but the name and the company and the regiment and the State were too definitely given.

Then there was a lapse into depths out of which it seemed as if she never could rise again; then a lift into clouds far above all grief, black clouds, that blotted out the sun, but where she soared with him, with George—George! She had the fever that she expected of herself, but she did not die in it; she was not even delirious, and it did not last long. When she was well enough to leave her bed, her one thought was of George's mother, of his strangely worded wish that she should go to her and see what she could do for her. In the exaltation of the duty laid upon her—it buoyed her up instead of burdening her—she rapidly recovered.

Her father went with her on the long railroad journey from northern New York to western Iowa; he had business out at Davenport, and he said he could just as well go then as any other time; and he went with her to the little country town where George's mother lived in a little house on the edge of the illimitable cornfields, under trees pushed to a top of the rolling prairie. George's father had settled there after the Civil War, as so many other old soldiers had done; but they were Eastern people, and Editha fancied touches of the East in the June rose overhanging the front door, and the garden with early summer flowers stretching from the gate of the paling fence.

It was very low inside the house, and so dim, with the closed blinds, that they could scarcely see one another: Editha tall and black in her crapes which filled the air with smell of their dyes; her father standing decorously apart with his hat on his forearm, as at funerals; a woman rested in a deep arm-chair, and the woman who had let the strangers in stood behind the chair.

The seated woman turned her head round and up, and asked the woman behind her chair: "*Who* did you say?"

Editha, if she had done what she expected of herself, would have gone down on her knees at the feet of the seated figure and said, "I am George's Editha," for answer.

But instead of her own voice she heard that other woman's voice saying: "Well, I don't know as I *did* get the name just right. I guess I'll have to make a little more light in here," and she went and pushed two of the shutters ajar.

Then Editha's father said, in his public will-now-address-a few-remarks tone: "My name is Balcom, ma'am—Junius H. Balcom, of Balcom's Works, New York; my daughter—"

"Oh!" the seated woman broke in, with a powerful voice, the voice that always surprised Editha from Gearson's slender frame. "Let me see you. Stand round where the light can strike on your face," and Editha dumbly obeyed. "So, you're Editha Balcom," she sighed.

"Yes," Editha said, more like a culprit than a comforter.

"What did you come for?" Mrs. Gearson asked.

Editha's face quivered and her knees shook. "I came—because—because George—" She could go no further.

"Yes," the mother said, "he told me he had asked you to come if he got killed. You didn't expect that, I suppose, when you sent him."

"I would rather have died myself than done it!" Editha said, with more truth in her deep voice than she ordinarily found in it. "I tried to leave him free—"

"Yes, that letter of yours, that came back with his other things, left him free." Editha saw now where George's irony came from.

"It was not to be read before—unless—until—I told him so," she faltered.

"Of course, he wouldn't read a letter of yours, under the circumstances, till he thought you wanted him to. Been sick?" the woman abruptly demanded.

"Very sick," Editha said, with self-pity.

"Daughter's life," her father interposed, "was almost despaired of, at one time."

Mrs. Gearson gave him no heed. "I suppose you would have been glad to die, such a brave person as you! I don't believe *he* was glad to die. He was always a timid boy, that way; he was afraid of a good many things; but if he was afraid he did what he made up his mind to. I suppose he made up his mind to go, but I knew what it cost him by what it cost me when I heard of it. I had been through *one* war before. When you sent him you didn't expect he would get killed."

The voice seemed to compassionate Editha, and it was time. "No," she huskily murmured.

"No, girls don't; women don't when they give their men up to their country. They think they'll come marching back, somehow, just as gay as they went, or if it's an empty sleeve, or even an empty pantaloon, it's all the more glory, and they're so much the prouder of them, poor things!"

The tears began to run down Editha's face; she had not wept till then; but it was now such a relief to be understood that the tears came.

"No, you didn't expect him to get killed," Mrs. Gearson repeated, in a voice which was startlingly like George's again. "You just expected him to kill some one else, some of those foreigners, that weren't there because they had any say about it, but because they had to be there, poor wretches—conscripts, or whatever they call'em. You thought it would be all right for my George, *your* George, to kill the sons of those miserable mothers and the husbands of those girls that you would never see the faces of." The woman lifted her powerful voice in a psalmlike note. "I thank my God he didn't live to do it! I thank my God they killed him first, and that he ain't livin' with their blood on his hands!" She dropped her eyes, which she had raised with her voice, and glared at Editha. "What you got that black on for?" She lifted herself by her powerful arms so high that her helpless body seemed to hang limp its full length. "Take it off, take it off, before I tear it from your back!"

The lady who was passing the summer near Balcom's Works was sketching Editha's beauty, which lent itself wonderfully to the effects of a colorist. It had come to that confidence which is rather apt to grow between artist and sitter, and Editha had told her everything.

"To think of your having such tragedy in your life!" the lady said. She added: "I suppose there are people who feel that way about war. But when you consider the good this war has done—how much it has done for the country! I can't understand such people, for my part. And when you had come all the way out there to console her—got up out of a sick-bed! Well!"

"I think," Editha said, magnanimously, "she wasn't quite in her right mind; and so did papa."

"Yes," the lady said, looking at Editha's lips in nature and then at her lips in art, and giving an empirical touch to them in the picture. "But how dreadful of her! How perfectly—excuse me—how *vulgar!*"

A light broke upon Editha in the darkness which she felt had been without a gleam of brightness for weeks and months. The mystery that had bewildered her was solved by the word; and from that moment she rose from grovelling in shame and self-pity, and began to live again in the ideal.

1905

Henry Adams
1838–1918

To be born a member of the Adams family, one of the few dynastic powers to descend from the days of the American Revolution, portends a special fate. It was an honor and a burden keenly felt by Henry Brooks Adams, great-grandson of John Adams and grandson of John Quincy Adams, second and sixth presidents of the United States, and member of the family whose existence had helped make the United States into a nation with its own separate fate to fulfill. When the family gardener observed to the child Henry, "You'll be thinkin' you'll be President too!" the "causality of the remark made so strong an impression on [Adams's] mind that he never forgot it." But Henry Adams learned that such steady patterns of cause and effect were no guarantees in the helter-skelter society in which he grew up.

Henry Adams did not become president, or anything near. The centers of public power had been closed after the 1828 election, when Andrew Jackson blocked John Quincy Adams's attempt to gain a second term in office. The brash new values of Jacksonian democracy did not favor the eighteenth-century Federalist principles of America's premier family. Henry Adams had to create a career out of *not* being president, out of not being one of *those* Adamses. But since he could hardly escape the consequences of the evolutionary process he studied so closely, he spent a lifetime testing what it meant to be the descendent of the Adamses and of the mythic Adam (the progenitor of all human history). He also had to work out the personal significance of having been flung into one century at a time when it was speeding headlong toward the next. Henry Adams would not, therefore, make his way into the nation's history as a statesman or politician or an industrial leader. Writing served as the shaping power of his career as he became simultaneously the historian and the autobiographer of himself, of the Adams family, and of all the children of Adam.

Henry Adams was born and raised in Boston, summered at the Adamses' country residence in nearby Quincy, graduated from Harvard, studied some law in Germany, traveled around Europe, and acted as secretary to his father when Lincoln named Charles Francis Adams foreign minister to London during the Civil War years. After the war Adams, in his late twenties, knocked about for several years as a journalist writing on politics, economic matters, and historical events for the influential *Nation* and the *North American Review*. In 1870 Adams was cajoled into accepting a teaching post at Harvard. At the university he offered courses in medieval history to young men who would be unable to earn five dollars a day in the emerging commercial and industrial society with the information they got from his classes, however finely he honed their intellectual skills. He remained at Harvard until 1877 and developed an area of historical study where none had previously existed. (In the same way, his friend William James was just then teaching subjects at Harvard he had never taken as a student.)

The 1870s was a busy decade for Adams in other ways as well. He took on the editorship of the *North American Review* and used it as a forum to attack the political corruptions of the Gilded Age. In 1872 he married wealthy and clever Marion "Clover" Hooper of Boston. Adams had talent and energy to spare, together with enough of an independent income to assure him freedom to move from career to career or, as he would put it, from one kind of failed education to another.

Although Adams knew that he could never obtain political authority in the nation's capital, he decided he wanted to be where the power was. In 1877 he and Clover left New England and settled into the midst of "good" Washington, D.C., society. Here he could at least observe the nation's flaws and perhaps exert the influence of a sharp-eyed, caustic-tongued critic of the American scene.

Never an idler or quiescent observer, Adams launched himself into a full-time career as the historian of the Republic, especially of the period when the earlier Adamses had held center stage. His histories were actually extended biographies of the men who had, in addition to John Adams and John Quincy Adams, created a new country out of an old colony. Studies of Albert Gallatin (1879) and John Randolph (1882) joined with Adams's nine-volume *History of the United States of America During the Administrations of Thomas Jefferson and James Madison* (1889–1891) to give an overview of the period, one that is still considered essential to historical scholarship. He also published two anonymously written novels: *Democracy* (1880) and *Esther* (1884). Both novels make use of sensitive heroines to register the grievous flaws in American life that Adams and his wife found undermining confidence in the established beliefs—whether in government or in religion—that once gave Americans their sense of stability.

The growing loss of equilibrium on the public scene became almost unbearable for Adams when his wife committed suicide in 1885. Over and over he told his friends that he had died too, that what they saw in their midst was a dead man. The void caused by his wife's sudden death gave Adams a glimpse of "the supersensual chaos" that lay just below the surface of the elegant social world this husband and wife had shared. (Her suicide was an even greater shock than the one he had experienced as a young man when he stood at the bedside of his sister, dying terribly of lockjaw while the sun shone down upon the beauty of the world outside her window.) Marion's death also created a gap in the chronology Adams would give to his autobiography, *The Education of Henry Adams* (1918). When writing this, his most famous book, Adams deleted all mention of Marion or their marriage, omitting a twenty-year period in the chronology. But in actual life, the self-described "dead man" persevered.

Frenetic travel occupied Adams for several years after 1885. He and his friends zigzagged through Japan, Australia, the South Seas, Russia, the Middle East, as well as Europe, where he made almost annual trips. The habits of the student led him to continue his research into customs and artifacts of whatever cultures he came in contact with. *Historical Essays* about America was published in 1891, the same year as the final volume of *The History of the United States*. *Memoirs of Marau Taaroa*, about the Tahitian royal family, appeared in 1893.

As Adams's interests turned toward French history and culture, Paris and its environs became increasingly his home. The medievalist in him began to focus on the effects the Middle Ages had had on French civilization. Adams began to free himself from the weariness that had beset him since 1885 and to contemplate ways in which he might interpret his own era in terms of the past glories of Western culture. He hoped to be able to predict the future toward which he and his contemporaries were hurtling. He knew he could do nothing to control the social forces set loose by the new century. Perhaps he could learn how to interpret the laws that made it work. The cathedrals and religious monuments of northern France dedicated to the saints and the Virgin Mary attracted his imagination; so did the international expositions held in honor of the occult power of the dynamo, the most potent force of the new age of technology. *Mont-Saint-Michel and Chartres* (a "study of thirteenth-century unity") was completed and printed privately in 1904 and published in 1913. *The Education of Henry Adams* (a "study of twentieth-century multiplicity") was distributed to friends in 1907 but did not reach the hands of the general public until after Adams's death in 1918.

As Adams crisscrossed the ocean between the United States and the Continent during the final decade of his life, other writings concerned him. In 1901 Adams developed a theory of the future of human existence in "The Rule of Phase Applied to History." (With the increase in the quality of human consciousness, he noted, there was an alarming decline in the capacity of the mind to control the random forces of the universe.) While serving as the head of the American Historical Association, he gave an address that he later expanded into an essay, "A Letter to American Teachers of History" (1910), in which he argued that historical study must become more scientific and less impressionistic in its methods of research and interpretation. During an age increasingly scientific in temper and achievement, Adams thought history might become an anachronism through the acceleration of events marking the turn of the century. These two essays show Adams's continuing attempt to discover the kind of education that would permit him and his contemporaries to survive in a world of bewildering change.

In his sixties Adams turned to the study of X-rays, radiation, and thermodynamics. The new sciences were the essential education of the new age, an age neither his years at Harvard in the 1850s nor his subsequent experiences as a student of legal history, medieval philosophers, political skullduggery in London and Washington, nineteenth-century aesthetics, Darwinism, and the vagaries of the gold market had prepared him for.

Adams died the year the First World War came to its close. *The Education of Henry Adams* was published that year. It became an immediate best-seller and continues to hold its own as a masterpiece, though it has been more often praised than read. Among its fascinations are its power to foretell the course of future history: shaped by the ancient inertial weight of Russia in contention with China, by the nervous energy let loose by the New Woman, and by the explosive impersonality of the forces released by the new physics. The boy who had been born into the fourth decade of the nineteenth century with the assurance of meaning promised by his eighteenth-century mentality had lived long enough to face the fact that the twentieth century could not be mastered by any one of the forms of education available in the year 1900. The legacy Adams received from his distinguished Adams forebears had been insufficient. The value of the legacy that this childless man handed on to the sons of Adam could come only from the records he had kept of trying, failing, and trying once again—those unending processes by which the new Adam might yet make sense out of a welter of experiences.

The reasons for the somewhat begrudging attention paid to Adams's writing are not hard to find. His works are perceived to be arduous to read as literary texts. Their author is often difficult to stomach as a man because of his egotism and petty snobberies. Poe and Thoreau also wrote hard texts; as for liking their personalities, if one were making out a list of America's most lovable writers, the names of Poe and Thoreau would probably not appear either. But Adams suffers from special kinds of distaste that are brought to the reading of his big book. He wrote stories of failure that strike readers as not only depressing but arrogant. Adams has also been attacked for being too rich and privileged, somehow protected from life's trials. Even his ironic responses to social and cosmic ills make him seem more narrowly conservative than the interesting mix he claimed for himself—"Christian conservative anarchist." And there is no clear way around the often nasty bigotry by which he expressed his fear that the United States would be overrun by alien cultures and the unformed masses.

Still, Adams's merits continue to make a place for him as one of the most important writers of the late nineteenth century—perhaps even, as a steadily increasing number of readers insist, one of the major figures in American letters. Adams helped to redefine *education,* a word that Americans, from the Puritans through Franklin, Emerson, Melville, and Mark Twain, have thought crucial for the nation's survival. Adams also made himself into a masterly commentator on the nature of autobiography. His predecessors are not only Augustine, Rousseau, and Franklin (figures he specifically mentions) but also John Woolman, Frederick Douglass, and Henry David Thoreau—Americans all. In a secular age, he asked important questions about what it is we are to celebrate: the Lord, technology, or the self. He emphasized the importance of the mind at work creating facts as well as interpreting them. As a prose stylist he took earthbound words out into cosmic spaces; he grounded pure abstractions in the concrete world of political, social, and personal events. Reluctant as he was to leave the comforting tidiness of his old-fashioned boyhood in Quincy, he let himself be hurtled into the anxieties of the dynamo age.

Adams stood between Thoreau, who knew the questions and the answers—though he was unable to live according to them in the fullest sense—and the legion of twentieth-century worriers with uncertain questions and no answers. Adams shared with Gertrude Stein the brave ability to admit that he was not even certain which questions to ask or whether there were any. Snobbish, self-deprecating, a bit neurotic, and partially insulated by wealth, Adams took advantage of his privileged view to give us, in stunning literary style and with the discipline of historical scholarship, the state of affairs of the world as he found it. Subsequent generations of readers have undergone the shock of discovering that his world and the future he speculated about with such energy are essentially their world and their future. The "modern" perspective Adams brought to the writing of history reveals what a personal and universal story it is. History, as Adams writes it, is the same thing as autobiography: an unending education in what it means to experience the twentieth century and beyond.

Further Reading:

E. Samuels, *The Young Henry Adams*, 1948.
H. Jordy, *Henry Adams: Scientific Historian*, 1952, 1963.
J. C. Brunner, *Henry Adams: His Decline and Fall*, 1956.
H. H. Wasser, *The Scientific Thought of Henry Adams*, 1956.
J. Levenson, *The Mind and Art of Henry Adams*, 1957, 1968.
E. Samuels, *Henry Adams: The Middle Years*, 1958.
G. Hochfield, *Henry Adams: An Introduction and Interpretation*, 1962.
E. Samuels, *Henry Adams: The Major Phase*, 1964.
M. Lyon, *Symbol and Idea in Henry Adams*, 1969, 1970.
V. Wagner, *The Suspension of Henry Adams*, 1969.

J. Conder, *A Formula of His Own: Henry Adams' Literary Experiment*, 1970.
E. Scheyer, *The Circle of Henry Adams: Art and Artists*, 1970.
L. Auchincloss, *Henry Adams*, 1971.
J. Rowe, *Henry Adams and Henry James, The Emergence of the Modern Consciousness*, 1976.
E. Harbert, *The Force So Much Closer Home: Henry Adams and the Adams Family*, 1977.
D. R. Contosta, *Henry Adams and the American Experiment*, 1980.
W. Dusinberre, *Henry Adams: The Myth of Failure*, 1980.
Henry Adams/R. P. Blackmur, ed. V. Makowsky, 1980.
J. F. Byrnes, *The Virgin of Chartres*, 1981.
Critical Essays on Henry Adams, ed. E. N. Harbert, 1981.

Text:

The Education of Henry Adams, 1974.
See also *The Degradation of Democratic Dogma*, 1919, 1949.
Letters of Henry Adams, 2 vols., ed. W. Ford, 1930–1938.

Henry Adams and His Friends: A Collection of His Unpublished Letters, ed. H. Cater, 1947.
The Letters of Henry Adams, 3 vols., ed. J. Levenson, 1982.

from The Education of Henry Adams[*]

Preface

Jean Jacques Rousseau began his famous "Confessions" by a vehement appeal to the Deity: "I have shown myself as I was; contemptible and vile when I was so; good, generous, sublime when I was so; I have unveiled my interior such as Thou thyself hast seen it, Eternal Father! Collect about me the innumerable swarm of my fellows; let them hear my confessions; let them groan at my unworthiness; let them blush at my meannesses! Let each of them discover his heart in his turn at the foot of thy throne with the same sincerity; and then let any one of them tell thee if he dares: 'I was a better man!' "[1]

Jean Jacques was a very great educator in the manner of the eighteenth century, and has been commonly thought to have had more influence than any other teacher of his time; but his peculiar method of improving human nature has not been universally admired. Most educators of the nineteenth century have declined to show themselves before their scholars as objects more vile or contemptible than necessary, and even the humblest teacher hides, if possible, the faults with which nature has generously embellished us all, as it did Jean Jacques, thinking, as most religious minds are apt to do, that the Eternal Father himself may not feel unmixed pleasure at our thrusting under his eyes chiefly the least agreeable details of his creation.

As an unfortunate result the twentieth century finds few recent guides to avoid, or to follow. American literature offers scarcely one working model for high education. The student must go back, beyond Jean Jacques, to Benjamin Franklin,[2] to find a model even of self-teaching. Except in the abandoned sphere of the dead languages, no one has discussed what part of education has, in his personal experience, turned out to be useful, and what not. This volume attempts to discuss it.

As educator, Jean Jacques was in one respect, easily first; he erected a monument of warning against the Ego. Since his time, and largely thanks to him, the Ego has steadily tended to efface itself, and, for purposes of model, to become a manikin on which the toilet of education is to be draped in order to show the fit or misfit of the clothes. The object of study is the garment, not the figure. The tailor adapts the manikin as well as the clothes to his patron's wants. The tailor's object, in this volume, is to fit young men, in universities or elsewhere, to be men of the world, equipped for any emergency; and the garment offered to them is meant to show the faults of the patchwork fitted on their fathers.

At the utmost, the active-minded young man should ask of his teacher only mastery of his tools. The young man himself, the subject of education, is a certain form of energy; the object to be gained is economy of his force; the training is partly the

---

[*] Adams began work on *The Education* in 1903, completed it by 1905, and sent out the first copy of a private printing early in 1907; the Preface is dated February 16, 1907. The Massachusetts Historical Society brought out the first public edition in September 1918, after Adams's death in March of that year.

[1] Adams's own translation of sentences from *Confessions* by Jean Jacques Rousseau (1712–1778).

[2] The second model for the telling of one's life story cited by Adams is Benjamin Franklin's *Autobiography* (1818).

clearing away of obstacles, partly the direct application of effort. Once acquired, the tools and model may be thrown away.

The manikin, therefore, has the same value as any other geometrical figure of three or more dimensions, which is used for the study of relation. For that purpose it cannot be spared; it is the only measure of motion, of proportion, of human condition; it must have the air of reality; must be taken for real; must be treated as though it had life. Who knows? Possibly it had![3]

Chapter I: Quincy[4] (1838–1848)

Under the shadow of Boston State House, turning its back on the house of John Hancock,[5] the little passage called Hancock Avenue runs, or ran, from Beacon Street, skirting the State House grounds, to Mount Vernon Street, on the summit of Beacon Hill; and there, in the third house below Mount Vernon Place, February 16, 1838, a child was born, and christened later by his uncle, the minister of the First Church after the tenets of Boston Unitarianism, as Henry Brooks Adams.

Had he been born in Jerusalem under the shadow of the Temple and circumcised in the Synagogue by his uncle the high priest, under the name of Israel Cohen, he would scarcely have been more distinctly branded, and not much more heavily handicapped in the races of the coming century, in running for such stakes as the century was to offer; but, on the other hand, the ordinary traveller, who does not enter the field of racing, finds advantage in being, so to speak, ticketed through life, with the safeguards of an old, established traffic. Safeguards are often irksome, but sometimes convenient, and if one needs them at all, one is apt to need them badly. A hundred years earlier, such safeguards as his would have secured any young man's success; and although in 1838 their value was not very great compared with what they would have had in 1738, yet the mere accident of starting a twentieth-century career from a nest of associations so colonial—so troglodytic—as the First Church, the Boston State House, Beacon Hill, John Hancock and John Adams, Mount Vernon Street and Quincy, all crowding on ten pounds of unconscious babyhood, was so queer as to offer a subject of curious speculation to the baby long after he had witnessed the solution. What could become of such a child of the seventeenth and eighteenth centuries, when he should wake up to find himself required to play the game of the twentieth? Had he been consulted, would he have cared to play the game at all, holding such cards as he held, and suspecting that the game was to be one of which neither he nor anyone else back to the beginning of time knew the rules or the risks or the stakes? He was not consulted and was not responsible, but had he been taken into the confidence of his parents, he would certainly have told them to change nothing as far as concerned him. He would have been astounded by his own luck. Probably no child, born in the year, held better cards than he. Whether life was an honest game of chance, or whether the cards were marked and forced, he could not refuse to play his excellent hand. He could never make the usual plea of irresponsibil-

---

[3] A somewhat self-mocking paraphrase of a comment of Ralph Waldo Emerson (in his essay *Experience*) that we ought to treat men and women as though they were real.

[4] The family home of the Adamses near Boston.

[5] First signer of the Declaration of Independence and the first governor of Massachusetts.

ity. He accepted the situation as though he had been a party to it, and under the same circumstances would do it again, the more readily for knowing the exact values. To his life as a whole he was a consenting, contracting party and partner from the moment he was born to the moment he died. Only with that understanding—as a consciously assenting member in full partnership with the society of his age—had his education an interest to himself or to others.

As it happened, he never got to the point of playing the game at all; he lost himself in the study of it, watching the errors of the players; but this is the only interest in the story, which otherwise has no moral and little incident. A story of education— seventy years of it—the practical value remains to the end in doubt, like other values about which men have disputed since the birth of Cain and Abel; but the practical value of the universe has never been stated in dollars. Although everyone cannot be a Gargantua-Napoleon-Bismarck and walk off with the great bells of Notre Dame,[6] everyone must bear his own universe, and most persons are moderately interested in learning how their neighbors have managed to carry theirs.

This problem of education, started in 1838, went on for three years, while the baby grew, like other babies, unconsciously, as a vegetable, the outside world working as it never had worked before, to get his new universe ready for him. Often in old age he puzzled over the question whether, on the doctrine of chances, he was at liberty to accept himself or his world as an accident. No such accident had ever happened before in human experience. For him, alone, the old universe was thrown into the ash-heap and a new one created. He and his eighteenth-century, troglodytic Boston were suddenly cut apart—separated forever—in act if not in sentiment, by the opening of the Boston and Albany Railroad;[7] the appearance of the first Cunard steamers in the bay;[8] and the telegraphic messages which carried from Baltimore to Washington the news that Henry Clay and James K. Polk were nominated for the Presidency. This was in May, 1844; he was six years old; his new world was ready for use, and only fragments of the old met his eyes.

Of all this that was being done to complicate his education, he knew only the color of yellow. He first found himself sitting on a yellow kitchen floor in strong sunlight. He was three years old when he took this earliest step in education; a lesson of color. The second followed soon; a lesson of taste. On December 3, 1841, he developed scarlet fever. For several days he was as good as dead, reviving only under the careful nursing of his family. When he began to recover strength, about January 1, 1842, his hunger must have been stronger than any other pleasure or pain, for while in after life he retained not the faintest recollection of his illness, he remembered quite clearly his aunt entering the sick-room bearing in her hand a saucer with a baked apple.

The order of impressions retained by memory might naturally be that of color and taste, although one would rather suppose that the sense of pain would be first to educate. In fact, the third recollection of the child was that of discomfort. The moment he could be removed, he was bundled up in blankets and carried from the little house in Hancock Avenue to a larger one which his parents were to occupy for the rest of

---

[6] The feats of the giant Gargantua are taken from the *Life of Gargantua and Pantagruel* (1552) by François Rabelais (1494?–1553). Adams compares them to the achievements of other men of great historical force: Napoleon Bonaparte (1769–1821), who became emperor of France, and Otto von Bismarck (1815–1898), who controlled a united Germany as chancellor.
[7] In 1846.
[8] In 1840.

their lives in the neighboring Mount Vernon Street. The season was midwinter, January 10, 1842, and he never forgot his acute distress for want of air under his blankets, or the noises of moving furniture.

As a means of variation from a normal type, sickness in childhood ought to have a certain value not to be classed under any fitness or unfitness of natural selection,[9] and especially scarlet fever affected boys seriously, both physically and in character, though they might through life puzzle themselves to decide whether it had fitted or unfitted them for success; but this fever of Henry Adams took greater and greater importance in his eyes, from the point of view of education, the longer he lived. At first, the effect was physical. He fell behind his brothers two or three inches in height, and proportionally in bone and weight. His character and processes of mind seemed to share in this fining-down process of scale. He was not good in a fight, and his nerves were more delicate than boys' nerves ought to be. He exaggerated these weaknesses as he grew older. The habit of doubt; of distrusting his own judgment and of totally rejecting the judgment of the world; the tendency to regard every question as open; the hesitation to act except as a choice of evils; the shirking of responsibility; the love of line, form, quality; the horror of ennui; the passion for companionship and the antipathy to society—all these are well-known qualities of New England character in no way peculiar to individuals but in this instance they seemed to be stimulated by the fever, and Henry Adams could never make up his mind whether, on the whole, the change of character was morbid or healthy, good or bad for his purpose. His brothers were the type; he was the variation.

As far as the boy knew, the sickness did not affect him at all, and he grew up in excellent health, bodily and mental, taking life as it was given; accepting its local standards without a difficulty, and enjoying much of it as keenly as any other boy of his age. He seemed to himself quite normal, and his companions seemed always to think him so. Whatever was peculiar about him was education, not character, and came to him, directly and indirectly, as the result of that eighteenth-century inheritance which he took with his name.

The atmosphere of education in which he lived was colonial, revolutionary, almost Cromwellian,[10] as though he were steeped, from his greatest grandmother's birth, in the odor of political crime. Resistance to something was the law of New England nature; the boy looked out on the world with the instinct of resistance; for numberless generations his predecessors had viewed the world chiefly as a thing to be reformed, filled with evil forces to be abolished, and they saw no reason to suppose that they had wholly succeeded in the abolition; the duty was unchanged. That duty implied not only resistance to evil, but hatred of it. Boys naturally look on all force as an enemy, and generally find it so, but the New Englander, whether boy or man, in his long struggle with a stingy or hostile universe, had learned also to love the pleasure of hating; his joys were few.

Politics, as a practice, whatever its professions, had always been the systematic organization of hatreds, and Massachusetts politics had been as harsh as the cli-

---

[9] Here Adams makes the first of many references to the Darwinistic principles that had such an effect upon his generation.

[10] Oliver Cromwell (1599–1658), deposer of King Charles I in 1647 and later Lord Protector of England (1653–1658), was known in the colonies for his dictatorial rule.

mate. The chief charm of New England was harshness of contrasts and extremes of sensibility—a cold that froze the blood, and a heat that boiled it—so that the pleasure of hating—oneself if no better victim offered—was not its rarest amusement; but the charm was a true and natural child of the soil, not a cultivated weed of the ancients. The violence of the contrast was real and made the strongest motive of education. The double exterior nature gave life its relative values. Winter and summer, cold and heat, town and country, force and freedom, marked two modes of life and thought, balanced like lobes of the brain. Town was winter confinement, school, rule, discipline; straight, gloomy streets, piled with six feet of snow in the middle; frosts that made the snow sing under wheels or runners; thaws when the streets became dangerous to cross; society of uncles, aunts, and cousins who expected children to behave themselves, and who were not always gratified; above all else, winter represented the desire to escape and go free. Town was restraint, law, unity. Country, only seven miles away, was liberty, diversity, outlawry, the endless delight of mere sense impressions given by nature for nothing, and breathed by boys without knowing it.

Boys are wild animals, rich in the treasures of sense, but the New England boy had a wider range of emotions than boys of more equable climates. He felt his nature crudely, as it was meant. To the boy Henry Adams, summer was drunken. Among senses, smell was the strongest—smell of hot pine-woods and sweet-fern in the scorching summer noon; of new-mown hay; of ploughed earth; of box hedges; of peaches, lilacs, syringas; of stables, barns, cow-yards; of salt water and low tide on the marshes; nothing came amiss. Next to smell came taste, and the children knew the taste of everything they saw or touched, from pennyroyal and flagroot to the shell of pignut and the letters of a spelling-book—the taste of A-B, AB, suddenly revived on the boy's tongue sixty years afterwards. Light, line, and color as sensual pleasures, came later and were as crude as the rest. The New England light is glare, and the atmosphere harshens color. The boy was a full man before he ever knew what was meant by atmosphere; his idea of pleasure in light was the blaze of a New England sun. His idea of color was a peony, with the dew of early morning on its petals. The intense blue of the sea, as he saw it a mile or two away, from the Quincy hills; the cumuli in a June afternoon sky; the strong reds and greens and purples of colored prints and children's picture-books, as the American colors then ran; these were ideals. The opposites or antipathies, were the cold grays of November evenings, and the thick, muddy thaws of Boston winter. With such standards, the Bostonian could not but develop a double nature. Life was a double thing. After a January blizzard, the boy who could look with pleasure into the violent snow-glare of the cold white sunshine, with its intense light and shade, scarcely knew what was meant by tone. He could reach it only by education.

Winter and summer, then, were two hostile lives, and bred two separate natures. Winter was always the effort to live; summer was tropical license. Whether the children rolled in the grass, or waded in the brook, or swam in the salt ocean, or sailed in the bay, or fished for smelts in the creeks, or netted minnows in the salt-marshes, or took to the pine-woods and the granite quarries, or chased muskrats and hunted snapping-turtles in the swamps, or mushrooms or nuts on the autumn hills, summer and country were always sensual living, while winter was always compulsory learning. Summer was the multiplicity of nature; winter was school.

The bearing of the two seasons on the education of Henry Adams was no fancy;

it was the most decisive force he ever knew; it ran through life, and made the division between its perplexing, warring, irreconcilable problems, irreducible opposites, with growing emphasis to the last year of study. From earliest childhood the boy was accustomed to feel that, for him, life was double. Winter and summer, town and country, law and liberty, were hostile, and the man who pretended they were not, was in his eyes a schoolmaster—that is, a man employed to tell lies to little boys. Though Quincy was but two hours' walk from Beacon Hill,[11] it belonged in a different world. For two hundred years, every Adams, from father to son, had lived within sight of State Street,[12] and sometimes had lived in it, yet none had ever taken kindly to the town, or been taken kindly by it. The boy inherited his double nature. He knew as yet nothing about his great-grandfather, who had died a dozen years before his own birth: he took for granted that any great-grandfather of his must have always been good, and his enemies wicked; but he divined his great-grandfather's character from his own. Never for a moment did he connect the two ideas of Boston and John Adams; they were separate and antagonistic; the idea of John Adams went with Quincy. He knew his grandfather John Quincy Adams[13] only as an old man of seventy-five or eighty who was friendly and gentle with him, but except that he heard his grandfather always called "the President," and his grandmother "the Madam," he had no reason to suppose that his Adams grandfather differed in character from his Brooks grandfather[14] who was equally kind and benevolent. He liked the Adams side best, but for no other reason than that it reminded him of the country, the summer, and the absence of restraint. Yet he felt also that Quincy was in a way inferior to Boston, and that socially Boston looked down on Quincy. The reason was clear enough even to a five-year-old child. Quincy had no Boston style. Little enough style had either; a simpler manner of life and thought could hardly exist, short of cave-dwelling. The flint-and-steel with which his grandfather Adams used to light his own fires in the early morning was still on the mantelpiece of his study. The idea of a livery or even a dress for servants, or of an evening toilette, was next to blasphemy. Bathrooms, water-supplies, lighting, heating, and the whole array of domestic comforts, were unknown at Quincy. Boston had already a bathroom, a water-supply, a furnace, and gas. The superiority of Boston was evident, but a child liked it no better for that.

The magnificence of his grandfather Brooks's house in Pearl Street or South Street has long ago disappeared, but perhaps his country house at Medford may still remain to show what impressed the mind of a boy in 1845 with the idea of city splendor. The President's place at Quincy was the larger and older and far the more interesting of the two; but a boy felt at once its inferiority in fashion. It showed plainly enough its want of wealth. It smacked of colonial age, but not of Boston style or plush curtains. To the end of his life he never quite overcame the prejudice thus drawn in with his childish breath. He never could compel himself to care for nineteenth-century style. He was never able to adopt it, any more than his father or grandfather or

---

[11] Fashionable residential neighborhood of Boston's established families, and the center of Massachusetts political power.
[12] Where Boston's financial power was located.
[13] Sixth president of the United States, John Quincy Adams lived from 1767 to 1848. He

was the son of John Adams (1735–1826), second president and the founder of the Adams "dynasty."
[14] Peter Chardon Brooks (1767–1849), known as the wealthiest man in Boston.

great-grandfather had done. Not that he felt it as particularly hostile, for he reconciled himself to much that was worse; but because, for some remote reason, he was born an eighteenth-century child. The old house at Quincy was eighteenth century. What style it had was in its Queen Anne mahogany panels and its Louis Seize chairs and sofas.[15] The panels belonged to an old colonial Vassall who built the house; the furniture had been brought back from Paris in 1789 or 1801 or 1817, along with porcelain and books and much else of old diplomatic remnants; and neither of the two eighteenth-century styles—neither English Queen Anne nor French Louis Seize—was comfortable for a boy, or for anyone else. The dark mahogany had been painted white to suit daily life in winter gloom. Nothing seemed to favor, for a child's objects, the older forms. On the contrary, most boys, as well as grown-up people, preferred the new, with good reason, and the child felt himself distinctly at a disadvantage for the taste.

Nor had personal preference any share in his bias. The Brooks grandfather was as amiable and as sympathetic as the Adams grandfather. Both were born in 1767, and both died in 1848. Both were kind to children, and both belonged rather to the eighteenth than to the nineteenth centuries. The child knew no difference between them except that one was associated with winter and the other with summer; one with Boston, the other with Quincy. Even with Medford, the association was hardly easier. Once as a very young boy he was taken to pass a few days with his grandfather Brooks under charge of his aunt, but became so violently homesick that within twenty-four hours he was brought back in disgrace. Yet he could not remember ever being seriously homesick again.

The attachment to Quincy was not altogether sentimental or wholly sympathetic. Quincy was not a bed of thornless roses. Even there the curse of Cain[16] set its mark. There as elsewhere a cruel universe combined to crush a child. As though three or four vigorous brothers and sisters, with the best will, were not enough to crush any child, everyone else conspired towards an education which he hated. From cradle to grave this problem of running order through chaos, direction through space, discipline through freedom, unity through multiplicity, has always been, and must always be, the task of education, as it is the moral of religion, philosophy, science, art, politics, and economy; but a boy's will is his life, and he dies when it is broken, as the colt dies in harness, taking a new nature in becoming tame. Rarely has the boy felt kindly towards his tamers. Between him and his master has always been war. Henry Adams never knew a boy of his generation to like a master, and the task of remaining on friendly terms with one's own family, in such a relation, was never easy.

All the more singular it seemed afterwards to him that his first serious contact with the President should have been a struggle of will, in which the old man almost necessarily defeated the boy, but instead of leaving, as usual in such defeats, a lifelong sting, left rather an impression of as fair treatment as could be expected from a natural enemy. The boy met seldom with such restraint. He could not have been much more than six years old at the time—seven at the utmost—and his mother had taken him

[15] In the style prevalent during the reigns of Queen Anne of England (1707–1714) and of King Louis XVI of France (1774–1793).

[16] A curse was placed upon Cain for slaying his brother Abel, and he was sent to wander the earth (see Genesis 4:15–16). Reference to "Cain's curse" was thereafter applied to human existence in general.

to Quincy for a long stay with the President during the summer. What became of the rest of the family he quite forgot; but he distinctly remembered standing at the house door one summer morning in a passionate outburst of rebellion against going to school. Naturally his mother was the immediate victim of his rage; that is what mothers are for, and boys also; but in this case the boy had his mother at unfair disadvantage, for she was a guest, and had no means of enforcing obedience. Henry showed a certain tactical ability by refusing to start, and he met all efforts at compulsion by successful, though too vehement protest. He was in fair way to win, and was holding his own, with sufficient energy, at the bottom of the long staircase which led up to the door of the President's library, when the door opened, and the old man slowly came down. Putting on his hat, he took the boy's hand without a word, and walked with him, paralyzed by awe, up the road to the town. After the first moments of consternation at this interference in a domestic dispute, the boy reflected that an old gentleman close on eighty would never trouble himself to walk near a mile on a hot summer morning over a shadeless road to take a boy to school, and that it would be strange if a lad imbued with the passion of freedom could not find a corner to dodge around, somewhere before reaching the school door. Then and always, the boy insisted that this reasoning justified his apparent submission; but the old man did not stop, and the boy saw all his strategical points turned, one after another, until he found himself seated inside the school, and obviously the centre of curious if not malevolent criticism. Not till then did the President release his hand and depart.

The point was that this act, contrary to the inalienable rights of boys, and nullifying the social compact, ought to have made him dislike his grandfather for life. He could not recall that it had this effect even for a moment. With a certain maturity of mind, the child must have recognized that the President, though a tool of tyranny, had done his disreputable work with a certain intelligence. He had shown no temper, no irritation, no personal feeling, and had made no display of force. Above all, he had held his tongue. During their long walk he had said nothing; he had uttered no syllable of revolting cant about the duty of obedience and the wickedness of resistance to law; he had shown no concern in the matter; hardly even a consciousness of the boy's existence. Probably his mind at that moment was actually troubling itself little about his grandson's iniquities, and much about the iniquities of President Polk,[17] but the boy could scarcely at that age feel the whole satisfaction of thinking that President Polk was to be the vicarious victim of his own sins, and he gave his grandfather credit for intelligent silence. For this forbearance he felt instinctive respect. He admitted force as a form of right; he admitted even temper, under protest; but the seeds of a moral education would at that moment have fallen on the stoniest soil in Quincy, which is, as everyone knows, the stoniest glacial and tidal drift known in any Puritan land.

Neither party to this momentary disagreement can have felt rancor, for during these three or four summers the old President's relations with the boy were friendly and almost intimate. Whether his older brothers and sisters were still more favored he failed to remember, but he was himself admitted to a sort of familiarity which, when

[17] James K. Polk (1795–1849), who was considered by many in New England to be proslavery in his views.

in his turn he had reached old age, rather shocked him, for it must have sometimes tried the President's patience. He hung about the library; handled the books; deranged the papers; ransacked the drawers; searched the old purses and pocket-books for foreign coins; drew the sword-cane; snapped the travelling-pistols; upset everything in the corners, and penetrated the President's dressing-closet where a row of tumblers, inverted on the shelf, covered caterpillars which were supposed to become moths or butterflies, but never did. The Madam bore with fortitude the loss of the tumblers which her husband purloined for these hatcheries; but she made protest when he carried off her best cut-glass bowls to plant with acorns or peachstones that he might see the roots grow, but which, she said, he commonly forgot like the caterpillars.

At that time the President rode the hobby of tree-culture, and some fine old trees should still remain to witness it, unless they have been improved off the ground; but his was a restless mind, and although he took his hobbies seriously and would have been annoyed had his grandchild asked whether he was bored like an English duke, he probably cared more for the processes than for the results, so that his grandson was saddened by the sight and smell of peaches and pears, the best of their kind, which he brought up from the garden to rot on his shelves for seed. With the inherited virtues of his Puritan ancestors, the little boy Henry conscientiously brought up to him in his study the finest peaches he found in the garden, and ate only the less perfect. Naturally he ate more by way of compensation, but the act showed that he bore no grudge. As for his grandfather, it is even possible that he may have felt a certain self-reproach for his temporary rôle of schoolmaster—seeing that his own career did not offer proof of the worldly advantages of docile obedience—for there still exists somewhere a little volume of critically edited Nursery Rhymes with the boy's name in full written in the President's trembling hand on the fly-leaf. Of course there was also the Bible, given to each child at birth, with the proper inscription in the President's hand on the fly-leaf; while their grandfather Brooks supplied the silver mugs.

So many Bibles and silver mugs had to be supplied, that a new house, or cottage, was built to hold them. It was "on the hill," five minutes' walk above "the old house," with a far view eastward over Quincy Bay, and northward over Boston. Till his twelfth year, the child passed his summers there, and his pleasures of childhood mostly centered in it. Of education he had as yet little to complain. Country schools were not very serious. Nothing stuck to the mind except home impressions, and the sharpest were those of kindred children; but as influences that warped a mind, none compared with the mere effect of the back of the President's bald head, as he sat in his pew on Sundays, in line with that of President Quincy,[18] who, though some ten years younger, seemed to children about the same age. Before railways entered the New England town, every parish church showed half-a-dozen of these leading citizens, with gray hair, who sat on the main aisle in the best pews, and had sat there, or in some equivalent dignity, since the time of St. Augustine,[19] if not since the glacial epoch. It was unusual for boys to sit behind a President grandfather, and to read over his head the tablet

[18] Josiah Quincy (1772–1864), president of Harvard between 1829 and 1845, was actually only five years younger than John Quincy Adams.

[19] Bishop of the Latin Church in northern Africa, Augustine lived A.D. 354–430.

in memory of a President great-grandfather, who had "pledged his life, his fortune, and his sacred honor" to secure the independence of his country and so forth; but boys naturally supposed, without much reasoning, that other boys had the equivalent of President grandfathers, and that churches would always go on, with the bald-headed leading citizens on the main aisle, and Presidents or their equivalents on the walls. The Irish gardener once said to the child: "You'll be thinkin' you'll be President too!" The causality of the remark made so strong an impression on his mind that he never forgot it. He could not remember ever to have thought on the subject; to him, that there should be a doubt of his being President was a new idea. What had been would continue to be. He doubted neither about Presidents nor about Churches, and no one suggested at that time a doubt whether a system of society which had lasted since Adam would outlast one Adams more.

The Madam was a little more remote than the President, but more decorative. She stayed much in her own room with the Dutch tiles, looking out on her garden with the box walks, and seemed a fragile creature to a boy who sometimes brought her a note or a message, and took distinct pleasure in looking at her delicate face under what seemed to him very becoming caps. He liked her refined figure; her gentle voice and manner; her vague effect of not belonging there, but to Washington or to Europe, like her furniture, and writing-desk with little glass doors above and little eighteenth-century volumes in old binding, labelled "Peregrine Pickle" or "Tom Jones" or "Hannah More."[20] Try as she might, the Madam could never be Bostonian, and it was her cross in life, but to the boy it was her charm. Even at that age, he felt drawn to it. The Madam's life had been in truth far from Boston. She was born in London in 1775, daughter of Joshua Johnson, an American merchant, brother of Governor Thomas Johnson of Maryland; and Catherine Nuth, of an English family in London. Driven from England by the Revolutionary War, Joshua Johnson took his family to Nantes,[21] where they remained till the peace. The girl Louisa Catherine was nearly ten years old when brought back to London, and her sense of nationality must have been confused; but the influence of the Johnsons and the services of Joshua obtained for him from President Washington the appointment of Consul in London on the organization of the Government in 1790. In 1794 President Washington appointed John Quincy Adams Minister to The Hague.[22] He was twenty-seven years old when he returned to London, and found the Consul's house a very agreeable haunt. Louisa was then twenty.

At that time, and long afterwards, the Consul's house, far more than the Minister's, was the centre of contact for travelling Americans, either official or other. The Legation was a shifting point between 1785 and 1815; but the Consulate, far down in the City,[23] near the Tower, was convenient and inviting; so inviting that it proved fatal to young Adams. Louisa was charming, like a Romney portrait,[24] but among her many charms that of being a New England woman was not one. The defect was

---

[20] English novels by Tobias Smollett (1751) and Henry Fielding (1749), respectively. Hannah More (1745–1833) wrote on religious matters.
[21] City in France.
[22] Capital of the Netherlands.

[23] The financial center of London, near the Tower of London.
[24] That is, as lovely as the young women who appeared in the paintings by the English portraitist George Romney (1734–1802).

serious. Her future mother-in-law, Abigail,[25] a famous New England woman whose authority over her turbulent husband, the second President, was hardly so great as that which she exercised over her son, the sixth to be, was troubled by the fear that Louisa might not be made of stuff stern enough, or brought up on conditions severe enough, to suit a New England climate, or to make an efficient wife for her paragon son, and Abigail was right on that point, as on most others where sound judgment was involved; but sound judgment is sometimes a source of weakness rather than of force, and John Quincy already had reason to think that his mother held sound judgments on the subject of daughters-in-law which human nature, since the fall of Eve, made Adams helpless to realize. Being three thousand miles away from his mother, and equally far in love, he married Louisa in London, July 26, 1797, and took her to Berlin to be the head of the United States Legation. During three or four exciting years, the young bride lived in Berlin; whether she was happy or not, whether she was content or not, whether she was socially successful or not, her descendants did not surely know; but in any case she could by no chance have become educated there for a life in Quincy or Boston. In 1801 the overthrow of the Federalist Party[26] drove her and her husband to America, and she became at last a member of the Quincy household, but by that time her children needed all her attention, and she remained there with occasional winters in Boston and Washington, till 1809. Her husband was made Senator in 1803, and in 1809 was appointed Minister to Russia. She went with him to St. Petersburg, taking her baby, Charles Francis, born in 1807; but broken-hearted at having to leave her two older boys behind. The life at St. Petersburg was hardly gay for her; they were far too poor to shine in that extravagant society; but she survived it, though her little girl baby did not, and in the winter of 1814–15, alone with the boy of seven years old, crossed Europe from St. Petersburg to Paris, in her travelling-carriage, passing through the armies, and reaching Paris in the *Cent Jours*[27] after Napoleon's return from Elba. Her husband next went to England as Minister, and she was for two years at the Court of the Regent.[28] In 1817 her husband came home to be Secretary of State, and she lived for eight years in F Street, doing her work of entertainer for President Monroe's administration. Next she lived four miserable years in the White House. When that chapter was closed in 1829, she had earned the right to be tired and delicate, but she still had fifteen years to serve as wife of a Member of the House, after her husband went back to Congress in 1833. Then it was that the little Henry, her grandson, first remembered her, from 1843 to 1848, sitting in her panelled room, at breakfast, with her heavy silver teapot and sugar-bowl and cream-jug, which still exist somewhere as an heirloom of the modern safety-vault. By that time she was seventy years old or more, and thoroughly weary of being beaten about a stormy world. To the boy she seemed singularly peaceful, a vision of silver

[25] Abigail Smith Adams (1744–1818), known for her intelligence and advocacy of women's rights.

[26] Thomas Jefferson, a Republican, defeated John Adams, a Federalist, in his bid for reelection to the presidency in 1801.

[27] "The Hundred Days": the period between March and June 1815, when Napoleon, having

escaped from exile on the island of Elba, seized power in France and then met defeat at Waterloo.

[28] While his father George III was incapacitated by insanity, the prince of Wales ruled as regent between 1811 and 1820 before taking the throne as George IV.

gray, presiding over her old President and her Queen Anne mahogany; an exotic, like her Sèvres china; an object of deference to everyone, and of great affection to her son Charles; but hardly more Bostonian than she had been fifty years before, on her wedding-day, in the shadow of the Tower of London.

Such a figure was even less fitted than that of her old husband, the President, to impress on a boy's mind the standards of the coming century. She was Louis Seize, like the furniture. The boy knew nothing of her interior life, which had been, as the venerable Abigail, long since at peace, foresaw, one of severe stress and little pure satisfaction. He never dreamed that from her might come some of those doubts and self-questionings, those hesitations, those rebellions against law and discipline, which marked more than one of her descendants; but he might even then have felt some vague instinctive suspicion that he was to inherit from her the seeds of the primal sin, the fall from grace, the curse of Abel, that he was not of pure New England stock, but half exotic. As a child of Quincy he was not a true Bostonian, but even as a child of Quincy he inherited a quarter taint of Maryland blood. Charles Francis, half Marylander by birth, had hardly seen Boston till he was ten years old, when his parents left him there at school in 1817, and he never forgot the experience. He was to be nearly as old as his mother had been in 1845, before he quite accepted Boston, or Boston quite accepted him.

A boy who began his education in these surroundings, with physical strength inferior to that of his brothers, and with a certain delicacy of mind and bone, ought rightly to have felt at home in the eighteenth century and should, in proper self-respect, have rebelled against the standards of the nineteenth. The atmosphere of his first ten years must have been very like that of his grandfather at the same age, from 1767 till 1776, barring the battle of Bunker Hill, and even as late as 1846, the battle of Bunker Hill remained actual. The tone of Boston society was colonial. The true Bostonian always knelt in self-abasement before the majesty of English standards; far from concealing it as a weakness, he was proud of it as his strength. The eighteenth century ruled society long after 1850. Perhaps the boy began to shake it off rather earlier than most of his mates.

Indeed this prehistoric stage of education ended rather abruptly with his tenth year. One winter morning he was conscious of a certain confusion in the house in Mount Vernon Street, and gathered, from such words as he could catch, that the President, who happened to be then staying there, on his way to Washington, had fallen and hurt himself. Then he heard the word paralysis. After that day he came to associate the word with the figure of his grandfather, in a tall-backed, invalid armchair, on one side of the spare bedroom fireplace, and one of his old friends, Dr. Parkman or P. P. F. Degrand,[29] on the other side, both dozing.

The end of this first, or ancestral and Revolutionary, chapter came on February 21, 1848—and the month of February brought life and death as a family habit—when the eighteenth century, as an actual and living companion, vanished. If the scene on the floor of the House, when the old President fell,[30] struck the still simple-minded American public with a sensation unusually dramatic, its effect on a ten-year-old boy,

---

[29] The physician George Parkman (1790–1849) and the banker-politician Peter P. F. Degrand.
[30] John Quincy Adams died two days after he suffered a stroke while on the floor of the House of Representatives.

whose boy-life was fading away with the life of his grandfather, could not be slight. One had to pay for Revolutionary patriots; grandfathers and grandmothers; Presidents; diplomats; Queen Anne mahogany and Louis Seize chairs, as well as for Stuart[31] portraits. Such things warp young life. Americans commonly believed that they ruined it, and perhaps the practical common-sense of the American mind judged right. Many a boy might be ruined by much less than the emotions of the funeral service in the Quincy church, with its surroundings of national respect and family pride. By another dramatic chance it happened that the clergyman of the parish, Dr. Lunt, was an unusual pulpit orator, the ideal of a somewhat austere intellectual type, such as the school of Buckminster and Channing[32] inherited from the old Congregational clergy. His extraordinarily refined appearance, his dignity of manner, his deeply cadenced voice, his remarkable English and his fine appreciation, gave to the funeral service a character that left an overwhelming impression on the boy's mind. He was to see many great functions—funerals and festivals—in after-life, till his only thought was to see no more, but he never again witnessed anything nearly so impressive to him as the last services at Quincy over the body of one President and the ashes of another.

The effect of the Quincy service was deepened by the official ceremony which afterwards took place in Faneuil Hall,[33] when the boy was taken to hear his uncle, Edward Everett,[34] deliver a Eulogy. Like all Mr. Everett's orations, it was an admirable piece of oratory, such as only an admirable orator and scholar could create; too good for a ten-year-old boy to appreciate at its value; but already the boy knew that the dead President could not be in it, and had even learned why he would have been out of place there; for knowledge was beginning to come fast. The shadow of the War of 1812 still hung over State Street; the shadow of the Civil War to come had already begun to darken Faneuil Hall. No rhetoric could have reconciled Mr. Everett's audience to his subject. How could he say there, to an assemblage of Bostonians in the heart of mercantile Boston, that the only distinctive mark of all the Adamses, since old Sam Adams's father[35] a hundred and fifty years before, had been their inherited quarrel with State Street, which had again and again broken out into riot, bloodshed, personal feuds, foreign and civil war, wholesale banishments and confiscations, until the history of Florence was hardly more turbulent than that of Boston?[36] How could he whisper the word Hartford Convention[37] before the men who had made it? What would have been said had he suggested the chance of Secession and Civil War?

Thus already, at ten years old, the boy found himself standing face to face with a dilemma that might have puzzled an early Christian. What was he?—where was he going? Even then he felt that something was wrong, but he concluded that it must

---

[31] Gilbert Stuart (1755–1828), American portraitist, best known for his likenesses of George Washington.

[32] Unitarian clergymen Joseph Buckminster (1784–1812) and William Ellery Channing (1780–1842).

[33] Boston meeting hall.

[34] Everett (1794–1865) was at this time president of Harvard; he was also a Unitarian clergyman and a statesman renowned as a public speaker.

[35] Samuel Adams (1689–1748), colonial legislator and father of Sam Adams (1722–1803), had been

an active leader during the Revolutionary period.

[36] Adams compares the violent years of Florentine political struggles to the upheavals in Massachusetts politics, which pitted the idealistic, Unionist, antislavery Adamses against the mercantilist, sectionalist, proslavery factions of Boston.

[37] A meeting of men who wished to end the war against the British begun in 1812, even if it involved New England's leaving the Union.

be Boston. Quincy had always been right, for Quincy represented a moral principle —the principle of resistance to Boston. His Adams ancestors must have been right, since they were always hostile to State Street. If State Street was wrong, Quincy must be right! Turn the dilemma as he pleased, he still came back on the eighteenth century and the law of Resistance; of Truth; of Duty, and of Freedom. He was a ten-year-old priest and politician. He could under no circumstances have guessed what the next fifty years had in store, and no one could teach him; but sometimes, in his old age, he wondered—and could never decide—whether the most clear and certain knowledge would have helped him. Supposing he had seen a New York stock-list of 1900, and had studied the statistics of railways, telegraphs, coal, and steel—would he have quitted his eighteenth-century, his ancestral prejudices, his abstract ideals, his semi-clerical training, and the rest, in order to perform an expiatory pilgrimage to State Street, and ask for the fatted calf of his grandfather Brooks and a clerkship in the Suffolk Bank?[38]

Sixty years afterwards he was still unable to make up his mind. Each course had its advantages, but the material advantages, looking back, seemed to lie wholly in State Street.

Chapter XXV: The Dynamo and the Virgin (1900)

Until the Great Exposition of 1900[39] closed its doors in November, Adams haunted it, aching to absorb knowledge, and helpless to find it. He would have liked to know how much of it could have been grasped by the best-informed man in the world. While he was thus meditating chaos, Langley[40] came by, and showed it to him. At Langley's behest, the Exhibition dropped its superfluous rags and stripped itself to the skin, for Langley knew what to study, and why, and how; while Adams might as well have stood outside in the night, staring at the Milky Way. Yet Langley said nothing new, and taught nothing that one might not have learned from Lord Bacon,[41] three hundred years before; but though one should have known the "Advancement of Science" as well as one knew the "Comedy of Errors,"[42] the literary knowledge counted for nothing until some teacher should show how to apply it. Bacon took a vast deal of trouble in teaching King James I and his subjects, American or other, towards the year 1620, that true science was the development or economy of forces; yet an elderly American in 1900 knew neither the formula nor the forces; or even so much as to say to himself that his historical business in the Exposition concerned only the economies or developments of force since 1893, when he began the study at Chicago.

[38] Adams considers what would have been involved if he had denied his "Quincy" heritage to become like the Prodigal Son (Luke 15:11–32), returning to the wealth and power of Boston's State Street as represented by his maternal grandfather and by the Suffolk Bank.
[39] On display at the Paris Exposition of 1900 was an array of the most recent advances in the technology of electric motors, transformers, and dynamos.
[40] Samuel Langley (1834–1906), American scientist.
[41] Francis Bacon (1561–1628), English scientist.
[42] Play by William Shakespeare.

Nothing in education is so astonishing as the amount of ignorance it accumulates in the form of inert facts. Adams had looked at most of the accumulations of art in the storehouses called Art Museums; yet he did not know how to look at the art exhibits of 1900. He had studied Karl Marx and his doctrines of history[43] with profound attention, yet he could not apply them at Paris. Langley, with the ease of a great master of experiment, threw out of the field every exhibit that did not reveal a new application of force, and naturally threw out, to begin with, almost the whole art exhibit. Equally, he ignored almost the whole industrial exhibit. He led his pupil directly to the forces. His chief interest was in new motors to make his airship feasible, and he taught Adams the astonishing complexities of the new Daimler motor,[44] and of the automobile, which, since 1893, had become a nightmare at a hundred kilometres an hour, almost as destructive as the electric tram which was only ten years older; and threatening to become as terrible as the locomotive steam-engine itself, which was almost exactly Adams's own age.

Then he showed his scholar the great hall of dynamos,[45] and explained how little he knew about electricity or force of any kind, even of his own special sun, which spouted heat in inconceivable volume, but which, as far as he knew, might spout less or more, at any time, for all the certainty he felt in it. To him, the dynamo itself was but an ingenious channel for conveying somewhere the heat latent in a few tons of poor coal hidden in a dirty engine-house carefully kept out of sight; but to Adams the dynamo became a symbol of infinity. As he grew accustomed to the great gallery of machines, he began to feel the forty-foot dynamos as a moral force, much as the early Christians felt the Cross. The planet itself seemed less impressive, in its old-fashioned, deliberate, annual or daily revolution, than this huge wheel, revolving within arm's-length at some vertiginous speed, and barely murmuring—scarcely humming an audible warning to stand a hair's-breadth further for respect of power —while it would not wake the baby lying close against its frame. Before the end, one began to pray to it; inherited instinct taught the natural expression of man before silent and infinite force. Among the thousand symbols of ultimate energy, the dynamo was not so human as some, but it was the most expressive.

Yet the dynamo, next to the steam-engine, was the most familiar of exhibits. For Adams's objects its value lay chiefly in its occult mechanism. Between the dynamo in the gallery of machines and the engine-house outside, the break of continuity amounted to abysmal fracture for a historian's objects. No more relation could he discover between the steam and the electric current than between the Cross and the cathedral. The forces were interchangeable if not reversible, but he could see only an absolute *fiat* in electricity as in faith. Langley could not help him. Indeed, Langley seemed to be worried by the same trouble, for he constantly repeated that the new forces were anarchical, and especially that he was not responsible for the new rays,

[43] Marx's *Das Kapital* was published in 1867.
[44] Invented by the German Gottlieb Daimler (1834–1900), one of the primary developers of the internal combustion engine.
[45] The first electrical generator had been developed in 1831 by the British inventor Michael Faraday

(1791–1867). By Adams's time the dynamo had come to stand for the forces of industrial society that lacked the personal humanity Adams associated with the Virgin Mary as worshipped during the Middle Ages.

that were little short of parricidal in their wicked spirit towards science. His own rays, with which he had doubled the solar spectrum, were altogether harmless and beneficent; but Radium denied its God[46]— or, what was to Langley the same thing, denied the truths of his Science. The force was wholly new.

A historian who asked only to learn enough to be as futile as Langley or Kelvin,[47] made rapid progress under this teaching, and mixed himself up in the tangle of ideas until he achieved a sort of Paradise of ignorance vastly consoling to his fatigued senses. He wrapped himself in vibrations and rays which were new, and he would have hugged Marconi and Branly[48] had he met them, as he hugged the dynamo; while he lost his arithmetic in trying to figure out the equation between the discoveries and the economies of force. The economies, like the discoveries, were absolute, supersensual, occult; incapable of expression in horse-power. What mathematical equivalent could he suggest as the value of a Branly coherer? Frozen air, or the electric furnace, had some scale of measurement, no doubt, if somebody could invent a thermometer adequate to the purpose; but X-rays had played no part whatever in man's consciousness, and the atom itself had figured only as a fiction of thought. In these seven years man had translated himself into a new universe which had no common scale of measurement with the old. He had entered a supersensual world, in which he could measure nothing except by chance collisions of movements imperceptible to his senses, perhaps even imperceptible to his instruments, but perceptible to each other, and so to some known ray at the end of the scale. Langley seemed prepared for anything, even for an indeterminable number of universes interfused—physics stark mad in metaphysics.

Historians undertake to arrange sequences,—called stories, or histories—assuming in silence a relation of cause and effect. These assumptions, hidden in the depths of dusty libraries, have been astounding, but commonly unconscious and childlike; so much so, that if any captious critic were to drag them to light, historians would probably reply, with one voice, that they had never supposed themselves required to know what they were talking about. Adams, for one, had toiled in vain to find out what he meant. He had even published a dozen volumes of American history for no other purpose than to satisfy himself whether, by the severest process of stating, with the least possible comment, such facts as seemed sure, in such order as seemed rigorously consequent, he could fix for a familiar moment a necessary sequence of human movement. The result had satisfied him as little as at Harvard College. Where he saw sequence, other men saw something quite different, and no one saw the same unit of measure. He cared little about his experiments and less about his statesmen, who seemed to him quite as ignorant as himself and, as a rule, no more honest; but he insisted on a relation of sequence, and if he could not reach it by one method, he would try as many methods as science knew. Satisfied that the sequence of men led to nothing and that the sequence of their society could lead no further, while the mere sequence

---

[46] Radium's radiation, caused by atomic disintegration, went beyond any conception of cosmic force previously known, even that disclosed by Langley in 1881 in his measurements of solar radiation.

[47] William Thomson, Lord Kelvin (1824–1907), British scientist.

[48] Guglielmo Marconi (1874–1937) and Edouard Branly (1846–1940), Italian inventor of the radio telegraph and French inventor of the method for detecting radio waves, respectively.

of time was artificial, and the sequence of thought was chaos, he turned at last to the sequence of force; and thus it happened that, after ten years' pursuit, he found himself lying in the Gallery of Machines at the Great Exposition of 1900, with his historical neck broken by the sudden irruption of forces totally new.

Since no one else showed much concern, an elderly person without other cares had no need to betray alarm. The year 1900 was not the first to upset schoolmasters. Copernicus and Galileo[49] had broken many professional necks about 1600; Columbus had stood the world on its head towards 1500; but the nearest approach to the revolution of 1900 was that of 310, when Constantine[50] set up the Cross. The rays that Langley disowned, as well as those which he fathered, were occult, supersensual, irrational; they were a revelation of mysterious energy like that of the Cross; they were what, in terms of medieval science, were called immediate modes of the divine substance.

The historian was thus reduced to his last resources. Clearly if he was bound to reduce all these forces to a common value, this common value could have no measure but that of their attraction on his own mind. He must treat them as they had been felt; as convertible, reversible, interchangeable attractions on thought. He made up his mind to venture it; he would risk translating rays into faith. Such a reversible process would vastly amuse a chemist,[51] but the chemist could not deny that he, or some of his fellow physicists, could feel the force of both. When Adams was a boy in Boston, the best chemist in the place had probably never heard of Venus except by way of scandal,[52] or of the Virgin except as idolatry; neither had he heard of dynamos or automobiles or radium; yet his mind was ready to feel the force of all, though the rays were unborn and the women were dead.

Here opened another totally new education, which promised to be by far the most hazardous of all. The knife-edge along which he must crawl, like Sir Lancelot[53] in the twelfth century, divided two kingdoms of force which had nothing in common but attraction. They were as different as a magnet is from gravitation, supposing one knew what a magnet was, or gravitation, or love. The force of the Virgin was still felt at Lourdes,[54] and seemed to be as potent as X-rays; but in America neither Venus nor Virgin ever had value as force—at most as sentiment. No American had ever been truly afraid of either.

This problem in dynamics gravely perplexed an American historian. The Woman had once been supreme; in France she still seemed potent, not merely as a sentiment, but as a force. Why was she unknown in America? For evidently America was ashamed of her, and she was ashamed of herself, otherwise they would not have strewn fig-leaves so profusely all over her. When she was a true force, she was ignorant of fig-leaves,[55] but the monthly-magazine-made American female had not a feature that

---

[49] Copernicus (1473–1543) and Galileo (1564–1642) reformed existing conceptions concerning the motion of the earth around the sun.
[50] Christianity was made the official religion of the Roman Empire in A.D. 313 upon the proclamation of Emperor Constantine I.
[51] Druggist.
[52] By way of the treatment of venereal disease, associated with Venus, the love goddess.

[53] Reference to one of the chivalric tales concerning Sir Lancelot's heroic deeds.
[54] Shrine in France dedicated to the healing powers of the Virgin Mary.
[55] According to Genesis, Eve went naked in Eden until the Fall. She then covered her body with leaves from the fig tree because of her sense of shame. Adams refers to the prudery about the unclothed female form common to American magazines of the period.

would have been recognized by Adam. The trait was notorious, and often humorous, but anyone brought up among Puritans knew that sex was sin. In any previous age, sex was strength. Neither art nor beauty was needed. Everyone, even among Puritans, knew that neither Diana[56] of the Ephesians nor any of the Oriental goddesses was worshipped for her beauty. She was goddess because of her force; she was the animated dynamo; she was reproduction—the greatest and most mysterious of all energies; all she needed was to be fecund. Singularly enough, not one of Adams's many schools of education had ever drawn his attention to the opening lines of Lucretius, though they were perhaps the finest in all Latin literature, where the poet invoked Venus exactly as Dante invoked the Virgin:—

"Quae quoniam rerum naturam *sola* gubernas."[57]

The Venus of Epicurean philosophy survived in the Virgin of the Schools:[58]—

"Donna, sei tanto grande, e tanto vali,
   Che qual vuol grazia, e a te non ricorre,
   Sua disianza vuol volar senz' ali."[59]

All this was to American thought as though it had never existed. The true American knew something of the facts, but nothing of the feelings; he read the letter, but he never felt the law. Before this historical chasm, a mind like that of Adams felt itself helpless; he turned from the Virgin to the Dynamo as though he were a Branly coherer. On one side, at the Louvre and at Chartres, as he knew by the record of work actually done and still before his eyes, was the highest energy ever known to man, the creator of four-fifths of his noblest art, exercising vastly more attraction over the human mind than all the steam-engines and dynamos ever dreamed of; and yet this energy was unknown to the American mind. An American Virgin would never dare command; an American Venus would never dare exist.

The question, which to any plain American of the nineteenth century seemed as remote as it did to Adams, drew him almost violently to study, once it was posed; and on this point Langleys were as useless as though they were Herbert Spencers[60] or dynamos. The idea survived only as art. There one turned as naturally as though the artist were himself a woman. Adams began to ponder, asking himself whether he knew of any American artist who had ever insisted on the power of sex, as every classic had always done; but he could think only of Walt Whitman; Bret Harte, as far as the magazine would let him venture; and one or two painters, for the flesh-tones. All the rest had used sex for sentiment, never for force; to them, Eve was a tender flower, and Herodias[61] an unfeminine horror. American art, like the American language and

[56] Fertility goddess.
[57] From *De Rerum Natura* ("On the Nature of Things") by the Roman poet Lucretius (99?–55? B.C.): "Since thou alone dost govern the nature of things."
[58] That is, as described by the medieval scholastic philosophers.
[59] From Dante's *Divine Comedy* (*Paradiso* xxxiii,

13–15): "Lady [the Virgin], Thou art so great and so worthy, / That one who desires grace and does not seek after thee, / Would have his wish to soar without wings."
[60] Herbert Spencer (1820–1903): English advocate of social Darwinism.
[61] The wife of King Herod, who had John the Baptist slain.

American education, was as far as possible sexless. Society regarded this victory over sex as its greatest triumph, and the historian readily admitted it, since the moral issue, for the moment, did not concern one who was studying the relations of unmoral force. He cared nothing for the sex of the dynamo until he could measure its energy.

Vaguely seeking a clue, he wandered through the art exhibit, and, in his stroll, stopped almost every day before St. Gaudens's General Sherman,[62] which had been given the central post of honor. St. Gaudens himself was in Paris, putting on the work his usual interminable last touches, and listening to the usual contradictory suggestions of brother sculptors. Of all the American artists who gave to American art whatever life it breathed in the seventies, St. Gaudens was perhaps the most sympathetic, but certainly the most inarticulate. General Grant or Don Cameron[63] had scarcely less instinct of rhetoric than he. All the others—the Hunts, Richardson, John La Farge, Stanford White[64]—were exuberant; only St. Gaudens could never discuss or dilate on an emotion or suggest artistic arguments for giving to his work the forms that he felt. He never laid down the law or affected the despot, or became brutalized like Whistler[65] by the brutalities of his world. He required no incense; he was no egoist; his simplicity of thought was excessive; he could not imitate, or give any form but his own to the creations of his hand. No one felt more strongly than he the strength of other men, but the idea that they could affect him never stirred an image in his mind.

This summer his health was poor and his spirits were low. For such a temper, Adams was not the best companion, since his own gaiety was not *folle*;[66] but he risked going now and then to the studio on Mont Parnasse to draw him out for a stroll in the Bois de Boulogne,[67] or dinner as pleased his moods, and in return St. Gaudens sometimes let Adams go about in his company.

Once St. Gaudens took him down to Amiens, with a party of Frenchmen, to see the cathedral.[68] Not until they found themselves actually studying the sculpture of the western portal, did it dawn on Adams's mind that, for his purposes, St. Gaudens on that spot had more interest to him than the cathedral itself. Great men before great monuments express great truths, provided they are not taken too solemnly. Adams never tired of quoting the supreme phrase of his idol Gibbon, before the Gothic cathedrals: "I darted a contemptuous look on the stately monuments of superstition."[69] Even in the footnotes of his history, Gibbon had never inserted a bit of humor more human than this, and one would have paid largely for a photograph of the fat little historian, on the background of Notre Dame of Amiens, trying to persuade his readers —perhaps himself—that he was darting a contemptuous look on the stately monu-

[62] The statue of General William T. Sherman, Union general, was then on display in Paris; sculpted by Augustus Saint-Gaudens (1848–1907), it now stands at the edge of New York City's Central Park.

[63] James Donald Cameron (1833–1918), Pennsylvania senator and a man considered as inarticulate as President Grant, under whom he served as secretary of war.

[64] Well-known artists and architects of the period: William Morris Hunt (1824–1879); Richard Morris Hunt (1828–1895); Henry Richardson (1838–1886); John La Farge (1835–1910); Stanford White (1853–1906).

[65] James Abbott McNeil Whistler (1834–1903), who was apt to unloose vitriolic attacks against the artistic conventions of his day.

[66] French: "excessive" or "mad."

[67] Montparnasse was the Parisian artists' quarter; the Bois is a large park.

[68] The largest cathedral in France, dedicated to the Virgin Mary.

[69] English historian Edward Gibbon (1737–1794), author of *The Decline and Fall of the Roman Empire* (1776–1788), wrote this entry in his *French Journal* (February 21, 1763). Adams paraphrases here.

ment, for which he felt in fact the respect which every man of his vast study and active mind always feels before objects worthy of it; but besides the humor, one felt also the relation. Gibbon ignored the Virgin, because in 1789 religious monuments were out of fashion. In 1900 his remark sounded fresh and simple as the green fields to ears that had heard a hundred years of other remarks, mostly no more fresh and certainly less simple. Without malice, one might find it more instructive than a whole lecture of Ruskin. One sees what one brings, and at that moment Gibbon brought the French Revolution. Ruskin[70] brought reaction against the Revolution. St. Gaudens had passed beyond all. He liked the stately monuments much more than he liked Gibbon or Ruskin; he loved their dignity; their unity; their scale; their lines; their lights and shadows; their decorative sculpture; but he was even less conscious than they of the force that created it all—the Virgin, the Woman—by whose genius "the stately monuments of superstition" were built, through which she was expressed. He would have seen more meaning in Isis with the cow's horns, at Edfoo,[71] who expressed the same thought. The art remained, but the energy was lost even upon the artist.

Yet in mind and person St. Gaudens was a survival of the 1500's; he bore the stamp of the Renaissance, and should have carried an image of the Virgin round his neck, or stuck in his hat, like Louis XI.[72] In mere time he was a lost soul that had strayed by chance into the twentieth century, and forgotten where it came from. He writhed and cursed at his ignorance, much as Adams did at his own, but in the opposite sense. St. Gaudens was a child of Benvenuto Cellini,[73] smothered in an American cradle. Adams was a quintessence of Boston, devoured by curiosity to think like Benvenuto. St. Gaudens's art was starved from birth, and Adams's instinct was blighted from babyhood. Each had but half of a nature, and when they came together before the Virgin of Amiens they ought both to have felt in her the force that made them one; but it was not so. To Adams she became more than ever a channel of force; to St. Gaudens she remained as before a channel of taste.

For a symbol of power, St. Gaudens instinctively preferred the horse, as was plain in his horse and Victory of the Sherman monument. Doubtless Sherman also felt it so. The attitude was so American that, for at least forty years, Adams had never realized that any other could be in sound taste. How many years had he taken to admit a notion of what Michael Angelo and Rubens[74] were driving at? He could not say; but he knew that only since 1895 had he begun to feel the Virgin or Venus as force, and not everywhere even so. At Chartres—perhaps at Lourdes—possibly at Cnidos if one could still find there the divinely naked Aphrodite of Praxiteles[75]—but otherwise one must look for force to the goddesses of Indian mythology. The idea died out long ago in the German and English stock. St. Gaudens at Amiens was hardly less sensitive to the force of the female energy than Matthew Arnold at the Grande Chartreuse.[76] Neither of them felt goddesses as power—only as reflected emotion,

[70] John Ruskin (1819–1900), English writer on art and architecture.
[71] At Edfu on the Nile, Adams had seen such a statue of the fertility goddess Isis.
[72] King of France from 1423 to 1483.
[73] I.e., of the Italian Renaissance. The sculptor and writer Benvenuto Cellini lived from 1500 to 1571.
[74] Both the Italian artist and the Flemish painter emphasized the human form in their depiction of religious themes.
[75] Famous statue of Venus of the fourth century B.C. by the renowned Greek sculptor Praxiteles.
[76] The English poet (1822–1888) wrote "Stanzas from the Grande Chartreuse" (1855) in expression of his sense of the loss of the faith once held by the members of this medieval monastic community.

human expression, beauty, purity, taste, scarcely even as sympathy. They felt a railway train as power; yet they, and all other artists, constantly complained that the power embodied in a railway train could never be embodied in art. All the steam in the world could not, like the Virgin, build Chartres.

Yet in mechanics, whatever the mechanicians might think, both energies acted as interchangeable forces on man, and by action on man all known force may be measured. Indeed, few men of science measured force in any other way. After once admitting that a straight line was the shortest distance between two points, no serious mathematician cared to deny anything that suited his convenience, and rejected no symbol, unproved or unproveable, that helped him to accomplish work. The symbol was force, as a compass-needle or a triangle was force, as the mechanist might prove by losing it, and nothing could be gained by ignoring their value. Symbol or energy, the Virgin had acted as the greatest force the Western world ever felt, and had drawn man's activities to herself more strongly than any other power, natural or supernatural, had ever done; the historian's business was to follow the track of the energy; to find where it came from and where it went to; its complex source and shifting channels; its values, equivalents, conversions. It could scarcely be more complex than radium; it could hardly be deflected, diverted, polarized, absorbed more perplexingly than other radiant matter. Adams knew nothing about any of them, but as a mathematical problem of influence on human progress, though all were occult, all reacted on his mind, and he rather inclined to think the Virgin easiest to handle.

The pursuit turned out to be long and tortuous, leading at last into the vast forests of scholastic science. From Zeno to Descartes, hand in hand with Thomas Aquinas, Montaigne, and Pascal,[77] one stumbled as stupidly as though one were still a German student of 1860.[78] Only with the instinct of despair could one force one's self into this old thicket of ignorance after having been repulsed at a score of entrances more promising and more popular. Thus far, no path had led anywhere, unless perhaps to an exceedingly modest living. Forty-five years of study had proved to be quite futile for the pursuit of power; one controlled no more force in 1900 than in 1850, although the amount of force controlled by society had enormously increased. The secret of education still hid itself somewhere behind ignorance, and one fumbled over it as feebly as ever. In such labyrinths, the staff is a force almost more necessary than the legs; the pen becomes a sort of blind-man's dog, to keep him from falling into the gutters. The pen works for itself, and acts like a hand, modelling the plastic material over and over again to the form that suits it best. The form is never arbitrary, but is a sort of growth like crystallization, as any artist knows too well; for often the pencil or pen runs into side-paths and shapelessness, loses its relations, stops or is bogged. Then it has to return on its trail, and recover, if it can, its line of force. The result of a year's work depends more on what is struck out than on what is left in; on the sequence of the main lines of thought, than on their play or variety. Compelled once more to lean heavily on this support, Adams covered more thousands of pages with figures as formal as though they were algebra, laboriously striking out, altering, burning,

---

[77] Influential philosophers and mathematicians from the time of ancient Greece to the seventeenth century: Zeno of Elea (fifth century B.C.); René Descartes (1596–1650); St. Thomas Aquinas (1225?–1274); Michel de Montaigne (1533–1592); Blaise Pascal (1623–1662).

[78] Between 1858 and 1860 Adams studied in Germany.

experimenting, until the year had expired, the Exposition had long been closed, and winter drawing to its end, before he sailed from Cherbourg, on January 19, 1901, for home.

1905/1918

Ambrose Bierce
1842–1914

An account of Ambrose Bierce's life reads like one of the fantastic stories he wrote, down to the fact that there is no explanation provided for its ending. One day in 1912 he disappeared without a trace in Mexico. Rumors persist that he was killed there during the insurrection led by Pancho Villa's forces. Such a dramatic and mysterious conclusion would probably have pleased Bierce the storyteller; this ending to an existence marked by personal torment and family disasters would confirm the pessimism that earned him the nickname "Bitter Bierce."

The youngest of nine children of parents whose religious fanaticism turned him against both his family and their faith, Bierce was born in rural southeastern Ohio and raised on a farm in Indiana. Like Mark Twain, William Dean Howells, and Joel Chandler Harris (all born within ten years of one another), Bierce had early training as a printer's apprentice. As with so many other figures in American literature, he had little schooling. One year at the Kentucky Military Institute was his only attempt at formal education. He enlisted in the Union army as a drummer boy when the Civil War began, fought in several major battles, and rose in rank to lieutenant. At the war's end, he moved west, taking with him memories of the often brutal and always unhappy years of his childhood as well as the military horrors he had seen at first hand. By 1866 Bierce was settled into a journalist's life in San Francisco, where he worked alongside other young men (including Mark Twain, Bret Harte, and Joaquin Miller) who were making the newspaper world their entrance into the larger literary world. Then Bierce and his bride went to London to live for four years. There he learned new devices of satire and made his reputation for slash-and-cut journalism. As defined in *The Devil's Dictionary* of 1906, his views of marriage ("The state or condition of a community consisting of a master, a mistress, and two slaves, making in all, two"), religion ("A daughter of Hope and Fear, explaining to Ignorance the nature of the Unknowable"), and life ("A spiritual pickle preserving the body from decay") were bitingly sardonic, but his own experiences gave him sufficient cause for such reactions. Divorce, the suicide of friends, the murder of one son in a brawl, the death by alcoholism of another son, and the endless warfare carried out with relatives deepened his already pronounced cynicism into nihilism. But his savage way with words, his pungent black humor, and his apt critiques of topical follies and universal human stupidity won him immense popularity.

In 1876 Bierce returned to California, eventually to write for the *San Francisco*

Examiner, published by William Randolph Hearst, and to pour forth a variety of essays, reviews, political polemics, social commentaries, and works of fiction. Considered a major representative of post–Civil War literary realism, though he himself detested this mode, Bierce was also a master of the grotesque and the tale of the supernatural. In *Tales of Soldiers and Civilians* (1891) and *Can Such Things Be?* (1893), Bierce made clear with frightening vividness that he believed the ultimate reality lay in people's futile attempts to beat a cosmic system commanded by an impersonal fate.

When Bierce disappeared in 1912, the tradition he shared with many other writers did not vanish with him. Herman Melville had possessed "the darkness," and so did Bierce's contemporaries, Mark Twain and Stephen Crane—as would Ernest Hemingway, Nathanael West, and Thomas Pynchon in later generations. All were young men who confronted an unkind universe and made of it the stuff of a literary realism that seemed true in relation to its madness. The bad, mad, bitter man from San Francisco helped show American writers the way to hell.

Further Reading:
V. Starrett, *Ambrose Bierce,* 1920.
A. D. de Castro, *Portrait of Ambrose Bierce,* 1929.
C. Grattan, *Bitter Bierce: A Mystery of American Letters,* 1929.
C. McWilliams, *Ambrose Bierce: A Biography,* 1929, 1967.
W. Neale, *Life of Ambrose Bierce,* 1929.
F. D. Walker, *Ambrose Bierce, the Wickedest Man in San Francisco,* 1941.
P. Fatout, *Ambrose Bierce, the Devil's Lexicographer,* 1951.

P. Fatout, *Ambrose Bierce and the Black Hills,* 1956.
S. Woodruff, *The Short Stories of Ambrose Bierce: A Study in Polarity,* 1964.
R. O'Conner, *Ambrose Bierce: A Biography,* 1967.
M. Grenander, *Ambrose Bierce,* 1971.
From Fiction to Film: Ambrose Bierce's "An Occurrence at Owl Creek Bridge," ed. G. Barrett and T. Erskine, 1973.
C. N. Davidson, *Critical Essays on Ambrose Bierce,* 1982.

Text:
Tales of Soldiers and Civilians, 1892.
See also *Collected Works of Ambrose Bierce,* 12 vols., ed. W. Neale, 1909–1912.

The Letters of Ambrose Bierce, ed. B. Pope, 1922, 1967.

An Occurrence at Owl Creek Bridge

I

A man stood upon a railroad bridge in northern Alabama, looking down into the swift water twenty feet below. The man's hands were behind his back, the wrists bound with a cord. A rope loosely encircled his neck. It was attached to a stout cross-timber above his head, and the slack fell to the level of his knees. Some loose boards laid upon the sleepers[1] supporting the metals of the railway supplied a footing for him

---

[1] Railroad ties.

and his executioners—two private soldiers of the Federal army, directed by a sergeant, who in civil life may have been a deputy sheriff. At a short remove upon the same temporary platform was an officer in the uniform of his rank, armed. He was a captain. A sentinel at each end of the bridge stood with his rifle in the position known as "support," that is to say, vertical in front of the left shoulder, the hammer resting on the forearm thrown straight across the chest—a formal and unnatural position, enforcing an erect carriage of the body. It did not appear to be the duty of these two men to know what was occurring at the center of the bridge; they merely blockaded the two ends of the foot plank which traversed it.

Beyond one of the sentinels, nobody was in sight; the railroad ran straight away into a forest for a hundred yards, then, curving, was lost to view. Doubtless there was an outpost farther along. The other bank of the stream was open ground—a gentle acclivity crowned with a stockade of vertical tree trunks, loopholed for rifles, with a single embrasure through which protruded the muzzle of a brass cannon commanding the bridge. Midway of the slope between bridge and fort were the spectators— a single company of infantry in line, at "parade rest," the butts of the rifles on the ground, the barrels inclining slightly backward against the right shoulder, the hands crossed upon the stock. A lieutenant stood at the right of the line, the point of his sword upon the ground, his left hand resting upon his right. Excepting the group of four at the center of the bridge, not a man moved. The company faced the bridge, staring stonily, motionless. The sentinels, facing the banks of the stream, might have been statues to adorn the bridge. The captain stood with folded arms, silent, observing the work of his subordinates, but making no sign. Death is a dignitary who when he comes announced is to be received with formal manifestations of respect, even by those most familiar with him. In the code of military etiquette silence and fixity are forms of deference.

The man who was engaged in being hanged was apparently about thirty-five years of age. He was a civilian, if one might judge from his dress, which was that of a planter. His features were good—a straight nose, firm mouth, broad forehead, from which his long, dark hair was combed straight back, falling behind his ears to the collar of his well-fitting frock coat. He wore a mustache and pointed beard, but no whiskers: his eyes were large and dark gray, and had a kindly expression which one would hardly have expected in one whose neck was in the hemp. Evidently this was no vulgar assassin. The liberal military code makes provision for hanging many kinds of people, and gentlemen are not excluded.

The preparations being complete, the two private soldiers stepped aside and each drew away the plank upon which he had been standing. The sergeant turned to the captain, saluted, and placed himself immediately behind that officer, who in turn moved apart one pace. These movements left the condemned man and the sergeant standing on the two ends of the same plank, which spanned three of the crossties of the bridge. The end upon which the civilian stood almost, but not quite, reached a fourth. This plank had been held in place by the weight of the captain; it was now held by that of the sergeant. At a signal from the former, the latter would step aside, the plank would tilt, and the condemned man go down between two ties. The arrangement commended itself to his judgment as simple and effective. His face had not been covered nor his eyes bandaged. He looked a moment at his "unsteadfast footing," then let his gaze wander to the swirling water of the stream racing madly beneath his feet. A piece of dancing driftwood caught his attention and his eyes followed it down the current. How slowly it appeared to move! What a sluggish stream!

He closed his eyes in order to fix his last thoughts upon his wife and children. The water, touched to gold by the early sun, the brooding mists under the banks at some distance down the stream, the fort, the soldiers, the piece of drift—all had distracted him. And now he became conscious of a new disturbance. Striking through the thought of his dear ones was a sound which he could neither ignore nor understand, a sharp, distinct, metallic percussion like the stroke of a blacksmith's hammer upon the anvil; it had the same ringing quality. He wondered what it was, and whether immeasurably distant or near by—it seemed both. Its recurrence was regular, but as slow as the tolling of a death knell. He awaited each stroke with impatience and—he knew not why—apprehension. The intervals of silence grew progressively longer; the delays became maddening. With their greater infrequency the sounds increased in strength and sharpness. They hurt his ear like the thrust of a knife; he feared he would shriek. What he heard was the ticking of his watch.

He unclosed his eyes, and saw again the water below him. "If I could free my hands," he thought, "I might throw off the noose and spring into the stream. By diving I could evade the bullets, and, swimming vigorously, reach the bank, take to the woods, and get away home. My home, thank God, is as yet outside their lines; my wife and little ones are still beyond the invader's farthest advance."

As these thoughts, which have here to be set down in words, were flashed into the doomed man's brain rather than evolved from it, the captain nodded to the sergeant. The sergeant stepped aside.

II

Peyton Farquhar was a well-to-do planter of an old and highly respected Alabama family. Being a slave owner and like other slave owners a politician, he was naturally an original secessionist and ardently devoted to the Southern cause. Circumstances of an imperious nature, which it is unnecessary to relate here, had prevented him from taking service with the gallant army which had fought the disastrous campaigns ending with the fall of Corinth,[2] and he chafed under the inglorious restraint, longing for the release of his energies, the larger life of the soldier, the opportunity for distinction. That opportunity, he felt, would come, as it comes to all in war time. Meanwhile he did what he could. No service was too humble for him to perform in aid of the South, no adventure too perilous for him to undertake if consistent with the character of a civilian who was at heart a soldier, and who in good faith and without too much qualification assented to at least a part of the frankly villainous dictum that all is fair in love and war.

One evening while Farquhar and his wife were sitting on a rustic bench near the entrance to his grounds, a gray-clad soldier rode up to the gate and asked for a drink of water. Mrs. Farquhar was only too happy to serve him with her own white hands. While she was gone to fetch the water, her husband approached the dusty horseman and inquired eagerly for news from the front.

"The Yanks are repairing the railroads," said the man, "and are getting ready for

[2] The Union army seized Corinth, Mississippi, in the spring of 1862 during the Battle of Shiloh.

another advance. They have reached the Owl Creek bridge, put it in order, and built a stockade on the north bank. The commandant has issued an order, which is posted everywhere, declaring that any civilian caught interfering with the railroad, its bridges, tunnels, or trains will be summarily hanged. I saw the order."

"How far is it to the Owl Creek bridge?" Farquhar asked.

"About thirty miles."

"Is there no force on this side the creek?"

"Only a picket post half a mile out, on the railroad, and a single sentinel at this end of the bridge."

"Suppose a man—a civilian and student of hanging—should elude the picket post and perhaps get the better of the sentinel," said Farquhar, smiling, "what could he accomplish?"

The soldier reflected, "I was there a month ago," he replied. "I observed that the flood of last winter had lodged a great quantity of driftwood against the wooden pier at this end of the bridge. It is now dry and would burn like tow."

The lady had now brought the water, which the soldier drank. He thanked her ceremoniously, bowed to her husband, and rode away. An hour later, after nightfall, he repassed the plantation, going northward in the direction from which he had come. He was a Federal scout.

III

As Peyton Farquhar fell straight downward through the bridge he lost consciousness and was as one already dead. From this state he was awakened—ages later, it seemed to him—by the pain of a sharp pressure upon his throat, followed by a sense of suffocation. Keen, poignant agonies seemed to shoot from his neck downward through every fiber of his body and limbs. These pains appeared to flash along well-defined lines a ramification and to beat with an inconceivably rapid periodicity. They seemed like streams of pulsating fire heating him to an intolerable temperature. As to his head, he was conscious of nothing but a feeling of fullness—of congestion. These sensations were unaccompanied by thought. The intellectual part of his nature was already effaced: he had power only to feel, and feeling was torment. He was conscious of motion. Encompassed in a luminous cloud, of which he was now merely the fiery heart, without material substance, he swung through unthinkable arcs of oscillation, like a vast pendulum. Then all at once, with terrible suddenness, the light about him shot upward with the noise of a loud plash; a frightful roaring was in his ears, and all was cold and dark. The power of thought was restored; he knew that the rope had broken and he had fallen into the stream. There was no additional strangulation; the noose about his neck was already suffocating him and kept the water from his lungs. To die of hanging at the bottom of a river!—the idea seemed to him ludicrous. He opened his eyes in the darkness and saw above him a gleam of light, but how distant, how inaccessible! He was still sinking, for the light became fainter and fainter until it was a mere glimmer. Then it began to grow and brighten, and he knew that he was rising toward the surface—knew it with reluctance, for he was now very comfortable. "To be hanged and drowned," he thought, "that is not so bad; but I do not wish to be shot. No, I will not be shot, that is not fair."

He was not conscious of an effort, but a sharp pain in his wrist apprised him that he was trying to free his hands. He gave the struggle his attention, as an idler might observe the feat of a juggler, without interest in the outcome. What splendid effort! —what magnificent, what super-human strength! Ah, that was a fine endeavor! Bravo! The cord fell away; his arms parted and floated upward, the hands dimly seen on each side in the growing light. He watched them with a new interest as first one and then the other pounced upon the noose at his neck. They tore it away and thrust it fiercely aside, its undulations resembling those of a water snake. "Put it back, put it back!" He thought he shouted these words to his hands, for the undoing of the noose had been succeeded by the direst pang that he had yet experienced. His neck arched horribly; his brain was on fire; his heart, which had been fluttering faintly, gave a great leap, trying to force itself out at his mouth. His whole body was racked and wrenched with an insupportable anguish! But his disobedient hands gave no heed to the command. They beat the water vigorously with quick downward strokes, forcing him to the surface. He felt his head emerge; his eyes were blinded by the sunlight; his chest expanded convulsively, and with a supreme and crowning agony his lungs engulfed a great draught of air, which instantly he expelled in a shriek!

He was now in full possession of his physical senses. They were, indeed, preternaturally keen and alert. Something in the awful disturbance of his organic system had so exalted and refined them that they made record of things never before perceived. He felt the ripples upon his face and heard their separate sounds as they struck. He looked at the forest on the bank of the stream, saw the individual trees, the leaves and the veining of each leaf—saw the very insects upon them: the locusts, the brilliant-bodied flies, the gray spiders stretching their webs from twig to twig. He noted the prismatic colors in all the dewdrops upon a million blades of grass. The humming of the gnats that danced above the eddies of the stream, the beating of the dragonflies' wings, the strokes of the water spiders' legs, like oars which had lifted their boat—all these made audible music. A fish slid along beneath his eyes and he heard the rush of its body parting the water.

He had come to the surface facing down the stream; in a moment the visible world seemed to wheel slowly round, himself at the pivotal point, and he saw the bridge, the fort, the soldiers upon the bridge, the captain, the sergeant, the two privates, his executioners. They were in silhouette against the blue sky. They shouted and gesticulated, pointing at him. The captain had drawn his pistol, but did not fire; the others were unarmed. Their movements were grotesque and horrible, their forms gigantic.

Suddenly he heard a sharp report and something struck the water smartly within a few inches of his head, spattering his face with spray. He heard the second report, and saw one of the sentinels with his rifle at his shoulder, a light cloud of blue smoke rising from the muzzle. The man in the water saw the eye of the man on the bridge gazing into his own through the sights of the rifle. He observed that it was a gray eye and remembered having read that gray eyes were keenest, and that all famous marksmen had them. Nevertheless, this one had missed.

A counterswirl had caught Farquhar and turned him half round; he was again looking into the forest on the bank opposite the fort. The sound of a clear, high voice in a monotonous singsong now rang out behind him and came across the water with distinctness that pierced and subdued all other sounds, even the beating of the ripples in his ears. Although no soldier, he had frequented camps enough to know the dread significance of the deliberate, drawling, aspirated chant; the lieutenant on shore was taking part in the morning's work. How coldly and pitilessly—with what an even, calm intonation, presaging and enforcing tranquillity in the men—with what accurately measured intervals fell those cruel words:

"Attention, company! . . . Shoulder arms! . . . Ready! . . . Aim! . . . Fire!"

Farquhar dived—dived as deeply as he could. The water roared in his ears like the voice of Niagara, yet he heard the dulled thunder of the volley and, rising again toward the surface, met shining bits of metal, singularly flattened, oscillating slowly downward. Some of them touched him on the face and hands, then fell away, continuing their descent. One lodged between his collar and his neck; it was uncomfortably warm and he snatched it out.

As he rose to the surface, gasping for breath, he saw that he had been a long time under water; he was perceptibly farther downstream—nearer to safety. The soldiers had almost finished reloading; the metal ramrods flashed all at once in the sunshine as they were drawn from the barrels, turned in the air, and thrust into their sockets. The two sentinels fired again, independently and ineffectually.

The hunted man saw all this over his shoulder; he was now swimming vigorously with the current. His brain was energetic as his arms and legs; he thought with the rapidity of lightning.

"The officer," he reasoned, "will not make that martinet's error a second time. It is as easy to dodge a volley as a single shot. He has probably already given the command to fire at will. God help me, I cannot dodge them all!"

An appalling plash within two yards of him was followed by a loud, rushing sound, *diminuendo,*[3] which seemed to travel back through the air to the fort and died in an explosion which stirred the very river to its deeps! A rising sheet of water, which curved over him, fell down upon him, blinded him, strangled him! The cannon had taken a hand in the game. As he shook his head free from the commotion of the smitten water, he heard the deflected shot humming through the air ahead, and in an instant it was cracking and smashing the branches in the forest beyond.

"They will not do that again," he thought; "the next time they will use a charge of grape.[4] I must keep my eye upon the gun; the smoke will apprise me—the report arrives too late; it lags behind the missile. That is a good gun."

Suddenly he felt himself whirled round and round—spinning like a top. The water, the banks, the forests, the now distant bridge, fort, and men—all were commingled and blurred. Objects were represented by their colors only; circular horizontal streaks of color—that was all he saw. He had been caught in a vortex and was being whirled on with a velocity of advance and gyration which made him giddy and sick. In a few moments he was flung upon the gravel at the foot of the left bank of the stream —the southern bank—and behind a projecting point which concealed him from his enemies. The sudden arrest of his motion, the abrasion of one of his hands on the gravel, restored him, and he wept with delight. He dug his fingers into the sand, threw it over himself in handfuls, and audibly blessed it. It looked like gold, like diamonds, rubies, emeralds; he could think of nothing beautiful which it did not resemble. The trees upon the bank were giant garden plants; he noted a definite order in their

---

[3] Dying away in volume.
[4] Grapeshot; cannon charge made up of clusters of iron balls.

arrangement, inhaled the fragrance of their blooms. A strange, roseate light shone through the spaces among their trunks and the wind made in their branches the music of aeolian harps. He had no wish to perfect his escape—was content to remain in that enchanting spot until retaken.

A whiz and rattle of grapeshot among the branches high above his head roused him from his dream. The baffled cannoneer had fired him a random farewell. He sprang to his feet, rushed up the sloping bank, and plunged into the forest.

All that day he traveled, laying his course by the rounding sun. The forest seemed interminable; nowhere did he discover a break in it, not even a woodman's road. He had not known that he lived in so wild a region. There was something uncanny in the revelation.

By nightfall he was fatigued, footsore, famishing. The thought of his wife and children urged him on. At last he found a road which led him in what he knew to be the right direction. It was wide and straight as a city street, yet it seemed untraveled. No fields bordered it, no dwelling anywhere. Not so much as the barking of a dog suggested human habitation. The black bodies of the great trees formed a straight wall on both sides, terminating on the horizon in a point, like a diagram in a lesson in perspective. Overhead, as he looked up through this rift in the wood, shone great golden stars looking unfamiliar and grouped in strange constellations. He was sure they were arranged in some order which had a secret and malign significance. The wood on either side was full of singular noises, among which—once, twice, and again—he distinctly heard whispers in an unknown tongue.

His neck was in pain and lifting his hand to it he found it horribly swollen. He knew that it had a circle of black where the rope had bruised it. His eyes felt congested; he could no longer close them. His tongue was swollen with thirst; he relieved its fever by thrusting it forward from between his teeth into the cool air. How softly the turf had carpeted the untraveled avenue—he could no longer feel the roadway beneath his feet!

Doubtless, despite his suffering, he had fallen asleep while walking, for now he sees another scene—perhaps he has merely recovered from a delirium. He stands at the gate of his own home. All is as he left it, and all bright and beautiful in the morning sunshine. He must have traveled the entire night. As he pushes open the gate and passes up the wide white walk, he sees a flutter of female garments; his wife, looking fresh and cool and sweet, steps down from the veranda to meet him. At the bottom of the steps she stands waiting, with a smile of ineffable joy, an attitude of matchless grace and dignity. Ah, how beautiful she is! He springs forward with extended arms. As he is about to clasp her, he feels a stunning blow upon the back of the neck; a blinding white light blazes all about him with a sound like the shock of a cannon—then all is darkness and silence!

Peyton Farquhar was dead; his body, with a broken neck, swung gently from side to side beneath the timbers of the Owl Creek bridge.

1888–1891

William James
1842–1910

So new was the discipline of psychology to the American university, William James joked, that the first lectures he ever heard on the subject were the ones he gave at Harvard in the 1870s. In 1890 he drew together the basic assertions of the psychology he was developing into a two-volume work, *The Principles of Psychology.* This project remains a watershed between traditional and "modern" ways of defining the nature of human behavior.

In *The Principles of Psychology* and subsequent essays, James became the analyst of the modern consciousness. Where formerly the mind perceived the world as orderly and controllable, the mind itself was now likened to a jungle "where uncouth forms lurk in the shadows." The world and the perceiving mind were formed of the material of the "menagerie and the madhouse, the nursery, the prison, and the hospital," not of the sunlit terrace and the playground.

William James was a contemporary of Sigmund Freud and one of the sponsors of Freud's only appearance in this country when he lectured in 1909 at Clark University in Worcester, Massachusetts. Like the Viennese doctor, James explored the darker crevices of the psyche. The explanations he offered for what he found there were not sexual in the Freudian sense. James was a materialist in that he emphasized biological forces as the determinant of personal habits and collective social patterns. Yet James was a special kind of materialist: He was also a member of the James family, and none of *them* could let explanations for human behavior rest on flesh and bone alone.

A native New Yorker, William James was the first son of Henry James, Sr., and the elder brother (by fifteen months) of the novelist Henry James. Henry, Jr., characterized William as the one with a tremendous headstart; he pictured his energetic older brother as someone always just out of sight, several steps ahead in achieving the goals he chased with such confident energy. William had indeed begun his life on the run, but for the first thirty years he seemed to be running away from, as much as toward, the importance he later attained as psychologist, philosopher, teacher, writer, lecturer, and family man.

By eighteen William James was studying art, but he switched to science and then to medical studies at Harvard during the Civil War years. He sped off to the Amazon to join a scientific expedition organized by the famous Harvard zoologist Louis Agassiz, returned to Harvard and medical school in 1866, went to Europe in 1867 to immerse himself in the intellectual scene, and settled in at Harvard in 1869 to complete his M.D. degree. Several years of doubts and nervous ill health caught up with him in 1870. Like his father before him, and his sister Alice soon after, William experienced a serious nervous collapse. It threatened his ability to take on the daily task of dealing with overwhelming questions of existence in a universe whose purpose had become ambiguous and had gone beyond his ability to bear.

Although James had not given serious thought to taking up a career in philosophical studies, he had previously done extensive readings on various philosophers, among them France's Charles Renouvier. James emerged from his mental crisis with the conviction, supported by Renouvier, that whether one is free or not, one must believe in the freedom of choice that gives life meaning. In 1872 James began a long career as professor at Harvard (first in the physiological sciences, later in psychology and philosophy), lecturer, writer, and critic speaking out on such public issues as the territorial expansion of the United States into the Philippines (which he repudiated) and alternatives to armed conflict between nations.

William James is best known for his association with certain expressions he either originated or popularized: "pragmatism," "stream of consciousness," "the will to believe," "the sick soul," "the healthy-minded," "the Bitch-Goddess Success." He is also remembered for his forceful, expressive whiplash prose style, his friendship with other major intellectual figures of his generation (Charles Sanders Peirce, Josiah Royce, Henry Adams, George Santayana), and his thoroughly engaging personality. He spent much of his life refuting without seeming effort many of the principles by which his contemporaries liked to shape their comfortable lives. He did this so winningly and with such verve that he seemed to base his arguments on charm alone. Yet James remains both one of America's best writers and one of its most influential thinkers. In the midst of a society that wanted to hold to certain entrenched and unchanging laws of universal truth, James could say, "Damn the Absolute," smile disarmingly, argue persuasively, and capture the opposition.

But James is also easily misunderstood; the somewhat dubious meanings assigned by others to the term *pragmatism* indicate this. Just as *Darwinism* and *Freudianism* mean something other than "science according to Darwin" or "the position held by Freud," James's pragmatism is distinctly different from the corrupted readings given to the word when it is used without regard to its original meaning. For James (and for C. S. Peirce, the actual originator of the principles of philosophical pragmatism), the pragmatist held to a seriously moral set of values that, indeed, emphasize the importance of experience when summing up the success of human actions; but human actions also involve testing what "works" in the world against a thoughtful consideration of the collective good. Pragmatism, in the hands of James, was not the signal for ruthless self-aggrandizement and cynical manipulation of moral relativism; it was a guide to acts that succeed because they are *good* choices.

James did not just think, teach, and lecture. He also wrote, and to great effect. Among the best known and most influential of James's numerous publications are *The Will to Believe and Other Essays in Popular Philosophy* (1897), *Human Immortality* (1898), *Talks to Teachers on Psychology* (1899), and *The Varieties of Religious Experience* (1902). Ill health prevented him from continuing publication of his annual books between 1899 and 1901, but by 1901 he was back in force, delivering the Gifford Lectures on natural religion at the University of Edinburgh, giving lectures at the Lowell Institute in 1906 and at Columbia University in 1907. The latter two sets of addresses appeared as *Pragmatism: A New Name for Some Old Ways of Thinking* in 1907. The year before James died of heart failure in 1910, he published *The Meaning of Truth: A Sequel to "Pragmatism";* the essays in what he had come to call his philosophy of "radical empiricism" were published posthumously in 1911 and 1912.

William James left a multifold legacy: the realization of how close we all lie to failure; the belief in the power of intelligent will to overcome the demoralizing sense of defeat that an often cruel universe forces upon us; the wish to find sound and humane substitutes for war through the conversion of potentially destructive energies into a "moral equivalent" of the battlefield; a pluralism that embraced a diversity of definitions for every human experience; the refusal to think in narrow, bigoted terms.

James's dealings with his family (Henry and Alice in particular) reveal that he could both console them and annoy them with his stubborn shortsightedness. He was neither the best of men nor the greatest of American philosophers, but his vigorous presence left an indelible mark on the development of American ideas and ideals, both social and personal, at the turn of the century. And, as some have observed, William James ought to have written his brother Henry's novels —because of his direct writing style and his desire to cut straight to the core of consciousness. Yet American literature has both William and Henry—the philosopher and the novelist—to educate us in the complex fate of being human.

Further Reading:
C. Grattan, *The Three Jameses: A Family of Minds: Henry James, Sr., William James, Henry James,* 1922.
R. Perry, *The Thought and Character of William James,* 2 vols., 1935, 1948.
L. Morris, *William James: The Message of a Modern Mind,* 1950, 1969.
G. Allen, *William James: A Biography,* 1967.
B. Brennan, *William James,* 1968.
J. Roth, *Freedom and the Moral Life: The Ethics of William James,* 1969.
J. Wild, *The Radical Empiricism of William James,* 1969.
P. Dooley, *Pragmatism as Humanism: The Philosophy of William James,* 1974.
R. Hocks, *Henry James and Pragmatistic Thought: A Study in the Relationship Between the*

Philosophy of William James and the Literary Craft of Henry James, 1974.
C. Seigfried, *Chaos and Context: A Study in William James,* 1978.
H. Levinson, *The Religious Investigations of William James,* 1981.
R. Vanden Burgt, *The Religious Philosophy of William James,* 1981.
M. P. Ford, *William James's Philosophy: A New Perspective,* 1982.
E. Suckiel, *The Pragmatic Philosophy of William James,* 1982.
J. Barzun, *A Stroll with William James,* 1983.
D. Bjork, *The Compromised Scientist: William James in the Development of American Psychology,* 1983.

Text:
The Varieties of Religious Experience, 1916.
See also *The Writings of William James,* ed. J. McDermott, 1967, 1968.

The Letters of William James, 2 vols., ed. Henry James [his son], 1920.

from The Varieties of Religious Experience

from **The Sick Soul**

. . . Just as we saw that in healthy-mindedness there are shallower and profounder levels, happiness like that of the mere animal, and more regenerate sorts of happiness, so also are there different levels of the morbid mind, and the one is much more formidable than the other. There are people for whom evil means only a maladjustment with *things,* a wrong correspondence of one's life with the environment. Such evil as this is curable, in principle at least, upon the natural plane, for merely by modifying either the self or the things, or both at once, the two terms may be made to fit, and all go merry as a marriage bell again. But there are others for whom evil is no mere relation of the subject to particular outer things, but something more radical and general, a wrongness or vice in his essential nature, which no alteration of the environment, or any superficial rearrangement of the inner self, can cure, and which requires a supernatural remedy. On the whole, the Latin races have leaned more towards the former way of looking upon evil, as made up of ills and sins in the plural, removable in detail; while the Germanic races have tended rather to think of Sin in the singular, and with a capital S, as of something ineradicably ingrained in our natural subjectivity, and never to be removed by any superficial piecemeal operations. These comparisons of races are always open to exception, but undoubtedly the northern tone in religion has inclined to the more intimately pessimistic persuasion, and this way of feeling, being the more extreme, we shall find by far the more instructive for our study.

Recent psychology has found great use for the word 'threshold' as a symbolic designation for the point at which one state of mind passes into another. Thus we speak of the threshold of a man's consciousness in general, to indicate the amount of noise, pressure, or other outer stimulus which it takes to arouse his attention at all. One with a high threshold will doze through an amount of racket by which one with a low threshold would be immediately waked. Similarly, when one is sensitive to small differences in any order of sensation, we say he has a low 'difference-threshold'—his mind easily steps over it into the consciousness of the differences in question. And just so we might speak of a 'pain-threshold,' a 'fear-threshold,' a 'misery-threshold,' and find it quickly overpassed by the consciousness of some individuals, but lying too high in others to be often reached by their consciousness. The sanguine and healthy-minded live habitually on the sunny side of their misery-line, the depressed and melancholy live beyond it, in darkness and apprehension. There are men who seem to have started in life with a bottle or two of champagne inscribed to their credit; whilst others seem to have been born close to the pain-threshold, which the slightest irritants fatally send them over.

Does it not appear as if one who lived more habitually on one side of the pain-threshold might need a different sort of religion from one who habitually lived on the other? This question, of the relativity of different types of religion to different types of need, arises naturally at this point, and will become a serious problem ere we have done. But before we confront it in general terms, we must address ourselves to the unpleasant task of hearing what the sick souls, as we may call them in contrast to the healthy-minded, have to say of the secrets of their prison-house, their own peculiar form of consciousness. Let us then resolutely turn our backs on the once-born and their sky-blue optimistic gospel; let us not simply cry out, in spite of all appearances, "Hurrah for the Universe!—God's in his Heaven, all's right with the world." Let us see rather whether pity, pain, and fear, and the sentiment of human helplessness may not open a profounder view and put into our hands a more complicated key to the meaning of the situation.

To begin with, how *can* things so insecure as the successful experiences of this world afford a stable anchorage? A chain is no stronger than its weakest link, and life is after all a chain. In the healthiest and most prosperous existence, how many links of illness, danger, and disaster are always interposed? Unsuspectedly from the bottom of every fountain of pleasure, as the old poet said, something bitter rises up: a touch of nausea, a falling dead of the delight, a whiff of melancholy, things that sound a knell, for fugitive as they may be, they bring a feeling of coming from a deeper region and often have an appalling convincingness. The buzz of life ceases at their touch as a piano-string stops sounding when the damper falls upon it.

Of course the music can commence again;—and again and again,—at intervals. But with this the healthy-minded consciousness is left with an irremediable sense of precariousness. It is a bell with a crack; it draws its breath on sufferance and by an accident.

Even if we suppose a man so packed with healthy-mindedness as never to have experienced in his own person any of these sobering intervals, still, if he is a reflecting being, he must generalize and class his own lot with that of others; and, doing so, he must see that his escape is just a lucky chance and no essential difference. He might just as well have been born to an entirely different fortune. And then indeed the hollow security! What kind of a frame of things is it of which the best you can say is, "Thank God, it has let me off clear this time!" Is not its blessedness a fragile fiction? Is not your joy in it a very vulgar glee, not much unlike the snicker of any rogue at his success? If indeed it were all success, even on such terms as that! But take the happiest man, the one most envied by the world, and in nine cases out of ten his inmost consciousness is one of failure. Either his ideals in the line of his achievements are pitched far higher than the achievements themselves, or else he has secret ideals of which the world knows nothing, and in regard to which he inwardly knows himself to be found wanting.

When such a conquering optimist as Goethe[1] can express himself in this wise, how must it be with less successful men?

"I will say nothing," writes Goethe in 1824, "against the course of my existence. But at bottom it has been nothing but pain and burden, and I can affirm that during the whole of my 75 years, I have not had four weeks of genuine well-being. It is but the perpetual rolling of a rock that must be raised up again forever."

What single-handed man was ever on the whole as successful as Luther?[2] yet when he had grown old, he looked back on his life as if it were an absolute failure.

"I am utterly weary of life. I pray the Lord will come forthwith and carry me hence. Let him come, above all, with his last Judgment: I will stretch out my neck, the thunder will burst forth, and I shall be at rest."—And having a necklace of white agates in his hand at the time he added: "O God, grant that it may come without delay. I would readily eat up this necklace today, for the Judgment to come to-morrow."—The Electress Dowager, one day when Luther was dining with her, said to him: "Doctor, I wish you may live forty years to

---

[1] Johann Wolfgang Goethe (1749–1832), German poet, dramatist, and naturalist.

[2] Martin Luther (1483–1546), German theologian and leader of the Protestant Reformation.

come." "Madam," replied he, "rather than live forty years more, I would give up my chance of Paradise."

Failure then, failure! so the world stamps us at every turn. We strew it with our blunders, our misdeeds, our lost opportunities, with all the memorials of our inadequacy to our vocation. And with what a damning emphasis does it then blot us out! No easy fine, no mere apology or formal expiation, will satisfy the world's demands, but every pound of flesh exacted is soaked with all its blood. The subtlest forms of suffering known to man are connected with the poisonous humiliations incidental to these results.

And they are pivotal human experiences. A process so ubiquitous and everlasting is evidently an integral part of life. "There is indeed one element in human destiny," Robert Louis Stevenson[3] writes, "that not blindness itself can controvert. Whatever else we are intended to do, we are not intended to succeed; failure is the fate allotted."[4] And our nature being thus rooted in failure, is it any wonder that theologians should have held it to be essential, and thought that only through the personal experience of humiliation which it engenders the deeper sense of life's significance is reached?[5]

But this is only the first stage of the world-sickness. Make the human being's sensitiveness a little greater, carry him a little farther over the misery-threshold, and the good quality of the successful moments themselves when they occur is spoiled and vitiated. All natural goods perish. Riches take wings; fame is a breath; love is a cheat; youth and health and pleasure vanish. Can things whose end is always dust and disappointment be the real goods which our souls require? Back of everything is the great spectre of universal death, the all-encompassing blackness:[6]—

> "What profit hath a man of all his labour which he taketh under the Sun? I looked on all the works that my hands had wrought, and behold, all was vanity and vexation of spirit. For that which befalleth the sons of men befalleth beasts; as the one dieth, so dieth the other; all are of the dust, and all turn to dust again. . . . The dead know not anything, neither have they any more a reward; for the memory of them is forgotten. Also their love and their hatred and their envy is now perished; neither have they any more a portion for ever in anything that is done under the Sun. . . . Truly the light is sweet, and a pleasant thing it is for the eyes to behold the Sun: but if a man live many years and rejoice in them all, yet let him remember the days of darkness; for they shall be many."

[3] Scottish novelist, essayist, and poet (1850–1894).

[4] James's note: "He adds with characteristic healthy-mindedness: 'Our business is to continue to fail in good spirits.'"

[5] James's note: "The God of many men is little more than their court of appeal against the damnatory judgment passed on their failures by the opinion of this world. To our own consciousness there is usually a residuum of worth left over after our sins and errors have been told off—our capacity of acknowledging and regretting them is the germ of a better self *in posse* at least. But the world deals with us *in actu* and not *in posse:* and of this hidden germ, not to be guessed at from without, it never takes account. Then we turn to the All-knower, who knows our bad, but knows this good in us also, and who is just. We cast ourselves with our repentance on his mercy: only by an All-knower can we finally be judged. So the need of a God very definitely emerges from this sort of experience of life."

[6] James here quotes from various verses drawn from Ecclesiastes 1–3, 9, and 11.

In short, life and its negation are beaten up inextricably together. But if the life be good, the negation of it must be bad. Yet the two are equally essential facts of existence; and all natural happiness thus seems infected with a contradiction. The breath of the sepulchre surrounds it.

To a mind attentive to this state of things and rightly subject to the joy-destroying chill which such a contemplation engenders, the only relief that healthy-mindedness can give is by saying: 'Stuff and nonsense, get out into the open air!' or 'Cheer up, old fellow, you'll be all right erelong, if you will only drop your morbidness!' But in all seriousness, can such bald animal talk as that be treated as a rational answer? To ascribe religious value to mere happy-go-lucky contentment with one's brief chance at natural good is but the very consecration of forgetfulness and superficiality. Our troubles lie indeed too deep for *that* cure. The fact that we *can* die, that we *can* be ill at all, is what perplexes us; the fact that we now for a moment live and are well is irrelevant to that perplexity. We need a life not correlated with death, a health not liable to illness, a kind of good that will not perish, a good in fact that flies beyond the Goods of nature.

It all depends on how sensitive the soul may become to discords. "The trouble with me is that I believe too much in common happiness and goodness," said a friend of mine whose consciousness was of this sort, "and nothing can console me for their transiency. I am appalled and disconcerted at its being possible." And so with most of us: a little cooling down of animal excitability and instinct, a little loss of animal toughness, a little irritable weakness and descent of the pain-threshold, will bring the worm at the core of all our usual springs of delight into full view, and turn us into melancholy metaphysicians. The pride of life and glory of the world will shrivel. It is after all but the standing quarrel of hot youth and hoary eld.[7] Old age has the last word: the purely naturalistic look at life, however enthusiastically it may begin, is sure to end in sadness.

This sadness lies at the heart of every merely positivistic, agnostic, or naturalistic scheme of philosophy. Let sanguine healthy-mindedness do its best with its strange power of living in the moment and ignoring and forgetting, still the evil background is really there to be thought of, and the skull will grin in at the banquet. In the practical life of the individual, we know how his whole gloom or glee about any present fact depends on the remoter schemes and hopes with which it stands related. Its significance and framing give it the chief part of its value. Let it be known to lead nowhere, and however agreeable it may be in its immediacy, its glow and gilding vanish. The old man, sick with an insidious internal disease, may laugh and quaff his wine at first as well as ever, but he knows his fate now, for the doctors have revealed it; and the knowledge knocks the satisfaction out of all these functions. They are partners of death and the worm is their brother, and they turn to a mere flatness.

The lustre of the present hour is always borrowed from the background of possibilities it goes with. Let our common experiences be enveloped in an eternal moral order; let our suffering have an immortal significance; let Heaven smile upon the earth, and deities pay their visits; let faith and hope be the atmosphere which man breathes in;—and his days pass by with zest; they stir with prospects, they thrill with remoter values. Place round them on the contrary the curdling cold and gloom and

[7] Old age.

absence of all permanent meaning which for pure naturalism and the popular science evolutionism of our time are all that is visible ultimately, and the thrill stops short, or turns rather to an anxious trembling.

For naturalism, fed on recent cosmological speculations, mankind is in a position similar to that of a set of people living on a frozen lake, surrounded by cliffs over which there is no escape, yet knowing that little by little the ice is melting, and the inevitable day drawing near when the last film of it will disappear, and to be drowned ignominiously will be the human creature's portion. The merrier the skating, the warmer and more sparkling the sun by day, and the ruddier the bonfires at night, the more poignant the sadness with which one must take in the meaning of the total situation.

The early Greeks are continually held up to us in literary works as models of the healthy-minded joyousness which the religion of nature may engender. There was indeed much joyousness among the Greeks—Homer's flow of enthusiasm for most things that the sun shines upon is steady. But even in Homer the reflective passages are cheerless,[8] and the moment the Greeks grew systematically pensive and thought of ultimates, they became unmitigated pessimists.[9] The jealousy of the gods, the nemesis that follows too much happiness, the all-encompassing death, fate's dark opacity, the ultimate and unintelligible cruelty, were the fixed background of their imagination. The beautiful joyousness of their polytheism is only a poetic modern fiction. They knew no joys comparable in quality of preciousness to those which we shall erelong see that Brahmans, Buddhists,[10] Christians, Mohammedans, twice-born people whose religion is non-naturalistic, get from their several creeds of mysticism and renunciation.

Stoic[11] insensibility and Epicurean[12] resignation were the farthest advance which the Greek mind made in that direction. The Epicurean said: "Seek not to be happy, but rather to escape unhappiness; strong happiness is always linked with pain; therefore

---

[8] James's note: "E.g., Iliad, XVII. 446: 'Nothing then is more wretched anywhere than man of all that breathes and creeps upon this earth.'"

[9] James's note: "E.g., Theognis, 425–428: 'Best of all for all things upon earth is it not to be born nor to behold the splendors of the Sun; next best to traverse as soon as possible the gates of Hades.' See also the almost identical passage in Œdipus in Colonus, 1225.—The Anthology is full of pessimistic utterances: 'Naked came I upon the earth, naked I go below the ground—why then do I vainly toil when I see the end naked before me?'—'How did I come to be? Whence am I? Wherefore did I come? To pass away. How can I learn aught when naught I know? Being naught I came to life; once more shall I be what I was. Nothing and nothingness is the whole race of mortals.'—'For death we are all cherished and fattened like a herd of hogs that is wantonly butchered.'

"The difference between Greek pessimism and the oriental and modern variety is that the Greeks had not made the discovery that the pathetic mood may be idealized, and figure as a higher form of sensibility. Their spirit was still too essentially masculine for pessimism to be elaborated or lengthily dwelt on in their classic literature. They would have despised a life set wholly in a minor key, and summoned it to keep within the proper bounds of lachrymosity. The discovery that the enduring emphasis, so far as this world goes, may be laid on its pain and failure, was reserved for races more complex, and (so to speak) more feminine than the Hellenes had attained to being in the classic period. But all the same was the outlook of those Hellenes blackly pessimistic."

[10] Brahmans: priests of the highest caste of the Hindu faith; Buddhists: followers of Gautama Siddhartha (563?–483? B.C.), religious teacher of India.

[11] Stoics: followers of Zeno, Greek philosopher (c. 300 B.C.) who taught that we must calmly accept fate and live without passions;

[12] Epicureans: adherents of the teachings of Epicurus, Greek philosopher (342?–270 B.C.) who stressed the avoidance of pain.

hug the safe shore, and do not tempt the deeper raptures. Avoid disappointment by expecting little, and by aiming low; and above all do not fret." The Stoic said: "The only genuine good that life can yield a man is the free possession of his own soul; all other goods are lies." Each of these philosophies is in its degree a philosophy of despair in nature's boons. Trustful self-abandonment to the joys that freely offer has entirely departed from both Epicurean and Stoic; and what each proposes is a way of rescue from the resultant dust-and-ashes state of mind. The Epicurean still awaits results from economy of indulgence and damping of desire. The Stoic hopes for no results, and gives up natural good altogether. There is dignity in both these forms of resignation. They represent distinct stages in the sobering process which man's primitive intoxication with sense-happiness is sure to undergo. In the one the hot blood has grown cool, in the other it has become quite cold; and although I have spoken of them in the past tense, as if they were merely historic, yet Stoicism and Epicureanism will probably be to all time typical attitudes, marking a certain definite stage accomplished in the evolution of the world-sick soul.[13] They mark the conclusion of what we call the once-born period, and represent the highest flights of what twice-born religion would call the purely natural man—Epicureanism, which can only by great courtesy be called a religion, showing his refinement, and Stoicism exhibiting his moral will. They leave the world in the shape of an unreconciled contradiction, and seek no higher unity. Compared with the complex ecstasies which the supernaturally regenerated Christian may enjoy, or the oriental pantheist indulge in, their receipts for equanimity are expedients which seem almost crude in their simplicity.

Please observe, however, that I am not yet pretending finally to *judge* any of these attitudes. I am only describing their variety.

The securest way to the rapturous sorts of happiness of which the twice-born make report has as an historic matter of fact been through a more radical pessimism than anything that we have yet considered. We have seen how the lustre and enchantment may be rubbed off from the goods of nature. But there is a pitch of unhappiness so great that the goods of nature may be entirely forgotten, and all sentiment of their existence vanish from the mental field. For this extremity of pessimism to be reached, something more is needed than observation of life and reflection upon death. The individual must in his own person become the prey of a pathological melancholy. As the healthy-minded enthusiast succeeds in ignoring evil's very existence, so the subject of melancholy is forced in spite of himself to ignore that of all good whatever: for him it may no longer have the least reality. Such sensitiveness and susceptibility to mental pain is a rare occurrence where the nervous constitution is entirely normal; one seldom finds it in a healthy subject even where he is the victim of the most atrocious cruelties of outward fortune. So we note here the neurotic constitution, of which I said so much in my first lecture, making its active entrance on our scene, and

---

[13] James's note: "For instance, on the very day on which I write this page, the post brings me some aphorisms from a worldly-wise old friend in Heidelberg which may serve as a good contemporaneous expression of Epicureanism: 'By the word "happiness" every human being understands something different. It is a phantom pursued only by weaker minds. The wise man is satisfied with the more modest but much more definite term *contentment*. What education should chiefly aim at is to save us from a discontented life. Health is one favoring condition, but by no means an indispensable one, of contentment. Woman's heart and love are a shrewd device of Nature, a trap which she sets for the average man, to force him into working. But the wise man will always prefer work chosen by himself.' "

destined to play a part in much that follows. Since these experiences of melancholy are in the first instance absolutely private and individual, I can now help myself out with personal documents. Painful indeed they will be to listen to, and there is almost an indecency in handling them in public. Yet they lie right in the middle of our path; and if we are to touch the psychology of religion at all seriously, we must be willing to forget conventionalities, and dive below the smooth and lying official conversational surface.

One can distinguish many kinds of pathological depression. Sometimes it is mere passive joylessnesss and dreariness, discouragement, dejection, lack of taste and zest and spring. Professor Ribot[14] has proposed the name *anhedonia* to designate this condition.

"The state of *anhedonia*, if I may coin a new word to pair off with *analgesia*," he writes, "has been very little studied, but it exists. A young girl was smitten with a liver disease which for some time altered her constitution. She felt no longer any affection for her father and mother. She would have played with her doll, but it was impossible to find the least pleasure in the act. The same thing which formerly convulsed her with laughter entirely failed to interest her now. Esquirol observed the case of a very intelligent magistrate who was also a prey to hepatic disease. Every emotion appeared dead within him. He manifested neither perversion nor violence, but complete absence of emotional reaction. If he went to the theatre, which he did out of habit, he could find no pleasure there. The thought of his house, of his home, of his wife, and of his absent children moved him as little, he said, as a theorem of Euclid."

Prolonged seasickness will in most persons produce a temporary condition of anhedonia. Every good, terrestrial or celestial, is imagined only to be turned from with disgust. A temporary condition of this sort, connected with the religious evolution of a singularly lofty character, both intellectual and moral, is well described by the Catholic philosopher, Father Gratry, in his autobiographical recollections. In consequence of mental isolation and excessive study at the Polytechnic school, young Gratry fell into a state of nervous exhaustion with symptoms which he thus describes:—

"I had such a universal terror that I woke at night with a start, thinking that the Pantheon was tumbling on the Polytechnic school, or that the school was in flames, or that the Seine was pouring into the Catacombs, and that Paris was being swallowed up. And when these impressions were past, all day long without respite I suffered an incurable and intolerable desolation, verging on despair. I thought myself, in fact, rejected by God, lost, damned! I felt something like the suffering of hell. Before that I had never even thought of hell. My mind had never turned in that direction. Neither discourses nor reflections had impressed me in that way. I took no account of hell. Now, and all at once, I suffered in a measure what is suffered there.

"But what was perhaps still more dreadful is that every idea of heaven was

[14] Théodule Armand Ribot (1839–1916), author of *La Psychologie des Sentiments.* James adds the note "Psychologie des Sentiments, p. 54" to the extract immediately following.

taken away from me: I could no longer conceive of anything of the sort. Heaven did not seem to me worth going to. It was like a vacuum; a mythological elysium, an abode of shadows less real than the earth. I could conceive no joy, no pleasure in inhabiting it. Happiness, joy, light, affection, love—all these words were now devoid of sense. Without doubt I could still have talked of all these things, but I had become incapable of feeling anything in them, of understanding anything about them, of hoping anything from them, or of believing them to exist. There was my great and inconsolable grief! I neither perceived nor conceived any longer the existence of happiness or perfection. An abstract heaven over a naked rock. Such was my present abode for eternity."[15]

So much for melancholy in the sense of incapacity for joyous feeling. A much worse form of it is positive and active anguish, a sort of psychical neuralgia wholly unknown to healthy life. Such anguish may partake of various characters, having sometimes more the quality of loathing; sometimes that of irritation and exasperation; or again of self-mistrust and self-despair; or of suspicion, anxiety, trepidation, fear. The patient may rebel or submit; may accuse himself, or accuse outside powers; and he may or he may not be tormented by the theoretical mystery of why he should so have to suffer. Most cases are mixed cases, and we should not treat our classifications with too much respect. Moreover, it is only a relatively small proportion of cases that connect themselves with the religious sphere of experience at all. Exasperated cases, for instance, as a rule do not. I quote now literally from the first case of melancholy on which I lay my hand. It is a letter from a patient in a French asylum.

"I suffer too much in this hospital, both physically and morally. Besides the burnings and the sleeplessness (for I no longer sleep since I am shut up here, and the little rest I get is broken by bad dreams, and I am waked with a jump by nightmares, dreadful visions, lightning, thunder, and the rest), fear, atrocious fear, presses me down, holds me without respite, never lets me go. Where is the justice in it all! What have I done to deserve this excess of severity? Under what form will this fear crush me? What would I not owe to any one who would rid me of my life! Eat, drink, lie awake all night, suffer without interruption—such is the fine legacy I have received from my mother! What

---

[15] James's note: "A. GRATRY: Souvenirs de ma jeunesse, 1880, pp. 119–121, abridged. Some persons are affected with anhedonia permanently, or at any rate with a loss of the usual appetite for life. The annals of suicide supply such examples as the following:—

An uneducated domestic servant, aged nineteen, poisons herself, and leaves two letters expressing her motive for the act. To her parents she writes:—

'Life is sweet perhaps to some, but I prefer what is sweeter than life, and that is death. So good-by forever, my dear parents. It is nobody's fault, but a strong desire of my own which I have longed to fulfill for three or four years. I have always had a hope that some day I might have an opportunity of fulfilling it, and now it has come. . . . It is a wonder I have put this off so long, but I thought perhaps I should cheer up a bit and put all thought out of my head.' To her brother she writes: 'Good-by forever, my own dearest brother. By the time you get this I shall be gone forever. I know, dear love, there is no forgiveness for what I am going to do. . . . I am tired of living, so am willing to die. . . . Life may be sweet to some, but death to me is sweeter.' S. A. K. STRAHAN: Suicide and Insanity, 2d edition, London, 1894, p. 131."

I fail to understand is this abuse of power. There are limits to everything, there is a middle way. But God knows neither middle way nor limits. I say God, but why? All I have known so far has been the devil. After all, I am afraid of God as much as of the devil, so I drift along, thinking of nothing but suicide, but with neither courage nor means here to execute the act. As you read this, it will easily prove to you my insanity. The style and the ideas are incoherent enough —I can see that myself. But I cannot keep myself from being either crazy or an idiot; and, as things are, from whom should I ask pity? I am defenseless against the invisible enemy who is tightening his coils around me. I should be no better armed against him even if I saw him, or had seen him. Oh, if he would but kill me, devil take him! Death, death, once for all! But I stop. I have raved to you long enough. I say raved, for I can write no otherwise, having neither brain nor thoughts left. O God! what a misfortune to be born! Born like a mushroom, doubtless between an evening and a morning; and how true and right I was when in our philosophy-year in college I chewed the cud of bitterness with the pessimists. Yes, indeed, there is more pain in life than gladness—it is one long agony until the grave. Think how gay it makes me to remember that this horrible misery of mine, coupled with this unspeakable fear, may last fifty, one hundred, who knows how many more years!"[16]

This letter shows two things. First, you see how the entire consciousness of the poor man is so choked with the feeling of evil that the sense of there being any good in the world is lost for him altogether. His attention excludes it, cannot admit it: the sun has left his heaven. And secondly you see how the querulous temper of his misery keeps his mind from taking a religious direction. Querulousness of mind tends in fact rather towards irreligion; and it has played, so far as I know, no part whatever in the construction of religious systems.

Religious melancholy must be cast in a more melting mood. Tolstoy[17] has left us, in his book called My Confession, a wonderful account of the attack of melancholy which led him to his own religious conclusions. The latter in some respects are peculiar; but the melancholy presents two characters which make it a typical document for our present purpose. First it is a well-marked case of anhedonia, of passive loss of appetite for all life's values; and second, it shows how the altered and estranged aspect which the world assumed in consequence of this stimulated Tolstoy's intellect to a gnawing, carking questioning and effort for philosophic relief. I mean to quote Tolstoy at some length; but before doing so, I will make a general remark on each of these two points.

First on our spiritual judgments and the sense of value in general.

It is notorious that facts are compatible with opposite emotional comments, since the same fact will inspire entirely different feelings in different persons, and at different times in the same person; and there is no rationally deducible connection between any outer fact and the sentiments it may happen to provoke. These have their source in another sphere of existence altogether, in the animal and spiritual region of the

[16] James's note: "ROUBINOVITCH ET TOULOUSE: La Mélancolie, 1897, p. 170, abridged."

[17] Count Leo Tolstoy (1828–1910), Russian novelist and social reformer.

subject's being. Conceive yourself, if possible, suddenly stripped of all the emotion with which your world now inspires you, and try to imagine it *as it exists,* purely by itself, without your favorable or unfavorable, hopeful or apprehensive comment. It will be almost impossible for you to realize such a condition of negativity and deadness. No one portion of the universe would then have importance beyond another; and the whole collection of its things and series of its events would be without significance, character, expression, or perspective. Whatever of value, interest, or meaning our respective worlds may appear endued with are thus pure gifts of the spectator's mind. The passion of love is the most familiar and extreme example of this fact. If it comes, it comes; if it does not come, no process of reasoning can force it. Yet it transforms the value of the creature loved as utterly as the sunrise transforms Mont Blanc[18] from a corpse-like gray to a rosy enchantment; and it sets the whole world to a new tune for the lover and gives a new issue to his life. So with fear, with indignation, jealousy, ambition, worship. If they are there, life changes. And whether they shall be there or not depends almost always upon non-logical, often on organic conditions. And as the excited interest which these passions put into the world is our gift to the world, just so are the passions themselves *gifts,* —gifts to us, from sources sometimes low and sometimes high; but almost always non-logical and beyond our control. How can the moribund old man reason back to himself the romance, the mystery, the imminence of great things with which our old earth tingled for him in the days when he was young and well? Gifts, either of the flesh or of the spirit; and the spirit bloweth where it listeth; and the world's materials lend their surface passively to all the gifts alike, as the stage-setting receives indifferently whatever alternating colored lights may be shed upon it from the optical apparatus in the gallery.

Meanwhile the practically real world for each one of us, the effective world of the individual, is the compound world, the physical facts and emotional values in indistinguishable combination. Withdraw or pervert either factor of this complex resultant, and the kind of experience we call pathological ensues.

In Tolstoy's case the sense that life had any meaning whatever was for a time wholly withdrawn. The result was a transformation in the whole expression of reality. When we come to study the phenomenon of conversion or religious regeneration, we shall see that a not infrequent consequence of the change operated in the subject is a transfiguration of the face of nature in his eyes. A new heaven seems to shine upon new earth. In melancholiacs there is usually a similar change, only it is in the reverse direction. The world now looks remote, strange, sinister, uncanny. Its color is gone, its breath is cold, there is no speculation in the eyes it glares with. "It is as if I lived in another century," says one asylum patient. —"I see everything through a cloud," says another, "things are not as they were, and I am changed."—"I see," says a third, "I touch, but the things do not come near me, a thick veil alters the hue and look of everything."—"Persons move like shadows, and sounds seem to come from a distant world."—"There is no longer any past for me; people appear so strange; it is as if I could not see any reality, as if I were in a theatre; as if people were actors, and everything were scenery; I can no longer find myself; I walk, but why? Everything floats before my eyes, but leaves no impression."—"I weep false tears, I have

[18] The "White Mountain," highest peak in the Alps.

unreal hands: the things I see are not real things."—Such are expressions that naturally rise to the lips of melancholy subjects describing their changed state.[19]

Now there are some subjects whom all this leaves a prey to the profoundest astonishment. The strangeness is wrong. The unreality cannot be. A mystery is concealed, and a metaphysical solution must exist. If the natural world is so double-faced and unhomelike, what world, what thing is real? An urgent wondering and questioning is set up, a poring theoretic activity, and in the desperate effort to get into right relations with the matter, the sufferer is often led to what becomes for him a satisfying religious solution.

At about the age of fifty, Tolstoy relates that he began to have moments of perplexity, of what he calls arrest, as if he knew not 'how to live,' or what to do. It is obvious that these were moments in which the excitement and interest which our functions naturally bring had ceased. Life had been enchanting, it was now flat sober, more than sober, dead. Things were meaningless whose meaning had always been self-evident. The questions 'Why?' and 'What next?' began to beset him more and more frequently. At first it seemed as if such questions must be answerable, and as if he could easily find the answers if he would take the time; but as they ever became more urgent, he perceived that it was like those first discomforts of a sick man, to which he pays but little attention till they run into one continuous suffering, and then he realizes that what he took for a passing disorder means the most momentous thing in the world for him, means his death.

These questions 'Why?' 'Wherefore?' 'What for?' found no response.

"I felt," says Tolstoy, "that something had broken within me on which my life had always rested, that I had nothing left to hold on to, and that morally my life had stopped. An invincible force impelled me to get rid of my existence, in one way or another. It cannot be said exactly that I *wished* to kill myself, for the force which drew me away from life was fuller, more powerful, more general than any mere desire. It was a force like my old aspiration to live, only it impelled me in the opposite direction. It was an aspiration of my whole being to get out of life.

"Behold me then, a man happy and in good health hiding the rope in order not to hang myself to the rafters of the room where every night I went to sleep alone; behold me no longer going shooting, lest I should yield to the too easy temptation of putting an end to myself with my gun.

"I did not know what I wanted. I was afraid of life; I was driven to leave it; and in spite of that I still hoped something from it.

"All this took place at a time when so far as all my outer circumstances went, I ought to have been completely happy. I had a good wife who loved me and whom I loved; good children and a large property which was increasing with no pains taken on my part. I was more respected by my kinsfolk and acquaintance than I had ever been; I was loaded with praise by strangers; and without exaggeration I could believe my name already famous. Moreover I was neither

---

[19] James's note: "I cull these examples from the work of G. DUMAS: La Tristesse et la Joie, 1900."

insane nor ill. On the contrary, I possessed a physical and mental strength which I have rarely met in persons of my age. I could mow as well as the peasants, I could work with my brain eight hours uninterruptedly and feel no bad effects.

"And yet I could give no reasonable meaning to any actions of my life. And I was surprised that I had not understood this from the very beginning. My state of mind was as if some wicked and stupid jest was being played upon me by some one. One can live only so long as one is intoxicated, drunk with life; but when one grows sober one cannot fail to see that it is all a stupid cheat. What is truest about it is that there is nothing even funny or silly in it; it is cruel and stupid, purely and simply.

"The oriental fable of the traveler surprised in the desert by a wild beast is very old.

"Seeking to save himself from the fierce animal, the traveler jumps into a well with no water in it; but at the bottom of this well he sees a dragon waiting with open mouth to devour him. And the unhappy man, not daring to go out lest he should be the prey of the beast, not daring to jump to the bottom lest he should be devoured by the dragon, clings to the branches of a wild bush which grows out of one of the cracks of the well. His hands weaken, and he feels that he must soon give way to certain fate; but still he clings, and sees two mice, one white, the other black, evenly moving round the bush to which he hangs, and gnawing off its roots.

"The traveler sees this and knows that he must inevitably perish; but while thus hanging he looks about him and finds on the leaves of the bush some drops of honey. These he reaches with his tongue and licks them off with rapture.

"Thus I hang upon the boughs of life, knowing that the inevitable dragon of death is waiting ready to tear me, and I cannot comprehend why I am thus made a martyr. I try to suck the honey which formerly consoled me; but the honey pleases me no longer, and day and night the white mouse and the black mouse gnaw the branch to which I cling. I can see but one thing: the inevitable dragon and the mice—I cannot turn my gaze away from them.

"This is no fable, but the literal incontestable truth which every one may understand. What will be the outcome of what I do to-day? Of what I shall do to-morrow? What will be the outcome of all my life? Why should I live? Why should I do anything? Is there in life any purpose which the inevitable death which awaits me does not undo and destroy?

"These questions are the simplest in the world. From the stupid child to the wisest old man, they are in the soul of every human being. Without an answer to them, it is impossible, as I experienced, for life to go on.

" 'But perhaps,' I often said to myself, 'there may be something I have failed to notice or to comprehend. It is not possible that this condition of despair should be natural to mankind.' And I sought for an explanation in all the branches of knowledge acquired by men. I questioned painfully and protractedly and with no idle curiosity. I sought, not with indolence, but laboriously and obstinately for days and nights together. I sought like a man who is lost and seeks to save himself,—and I found nothing. I became convinced, moreover, that all those who before me had sought for an answer in the sciences have also found nothing. And not only this, but that they have recognized that the very thing which was leading me to despair—the meaningless absurdity of life—is the only incontestable knowledge accessible to man."

To prove this point, Tolstoy quotes the Buddha, Solomon, and Schopenhauer.[20] And he finds only four ways in which men of his own class and society are accustomed to meet the situation. Either mere animal blindness, sucking the honey without seeing the dragon or the mice,—"and from such a way," he says, "I can learn nothing, after what I now know;" or reflective epicureanism, snatching what it can while the day lasts,—which is only a more deliberate sort of stupefaction than the first; or manly suicide; or seeing the mice and dragon and yet weakly and plaintively clinging to the bush of life.

Suicide was naturally the consistent course dictated by the logical intellect.

"Yet," says Tolstoy, "whilst my intellect was working, something else in me was working too, and kept me from the dead—a consciousness of life, as I may call it, which was like a force that obliged my mind to fix itself in another direction and draw me out of my situation of despair. . . . During the whole course of this year, when I almost unceasingly kept asking myself how to end the business, whether by the rope or by the bullet, during all that time, alongside of all those movements of my ideas and observations, my heart kept languishing with another pining emotion. I can call this by no other name than that of a thirst for God. This craving for God had nothing to do with the movement of my ideas,—but it came from my heart. It was like a feeling of dread that made me seem like an orphan and isolated in the midst of all these things that were so foreign. And this feeling of dread was mitigated by the hope of finding the assistance of some one."[21]

Of the process, intellectual as well as emotional, which, starting from this idea of God, led to Tolstoy's recovery, I will say nothing in this lecture, reserving it for a later hour. The only thing that need interest us now is the phenomenon of his absolute disenchantment with ordinary life, and the fact that the whole range of habitual values may, to a man as powerful and full of faculty as he was, come to appear so ghastly a mockery.

When disillusionment has gone as far as this, there is seldom a *restitutio ad integrum*.[22] One has tasted of the fruit of the tree, and the happiness of Eden never comes again. The happiness that comes, when any does come,—and often enough it fails to return in an acute form, though its form is sometimes very acute,—is not the simple ignorance of ill, but something vastly more complex, including natural evil as one

---

[20] Arthur Schopenhauer (1788–1860), German philosopher who pitted the human renunciation of desire against the impersonal reality of the "will" of the universe.

[21] James's note: "My extracts are from the French translation by 'ZONIA.' In abridging I have taken the liberty of transposing one passage."

[22] Latin: "return to wholeness."

of its elements, but finding natural evil no such stumbling-block and terror because it now sees it swallowed up in supernatural good. The process is one of redemption, not of mere reversion to natural health, and the sufferer, when saved, is saved by what seems to him a second birth, a deeper kind of conscious being than he could enjoy before.

We find a somewhat different type of religious melancholy enshrined in literature in John Bunyan's autobiography.[23] Tolstoy's preoccupations were largely objective, for the purpose and meaning of life in general was what so troubled him; but poor Bunyan's troubles were over the condition of his own personal self. He was a typical case of the psychopathic temperament, sensitive of conscience to a diseased degree, beset by doubts, fears, and insistent ideas, and a victim of verbal automatisms, both motor and sensory. These were usually texts of Scripture which, sometimes damnatory and sometimes favorable, would come in a half-hallucinatory form as if they were voices, and fasten on his mind and buffet it between them like a shuttlecock. Added to this were a fearful melancholy self-contempt and despair.

"Nay, thought I, now I grow worse and worse; now I am farther from conversion than ever I was before. If now I should have burned at the stake, I could not believe that Christ had love for me; alas, I could neither hear him, nor see him, nor feel him, nor savor any of his things. Sometimes I would tell my condition to the people of God, which, when they heard, they would pity me, and would tell of the Promises. But they had as good have told me that I must reach the Sun with my finger as have bidden me receive or rely upon the Promise. [Yet] all this while as to the act of sinning, I never was more tender than now; I durst not take a pin or stick, though but so big as a straw, for my conscience now was sore, and would smart at every touch; I could not tell how to speak my words, for fear I should misplace them. Oh, how gingerly did I then go, in all I did or said! I found myself as on a miry bog that shook if I did but stir; and was as there left both by God and Christ, and the spirit, and all good things.

"But my original and inward pollution, that was my plague and my afflic-
tion. By reason of that, I was more loathsome in my own eyes than was a toad; and I thought I was so in God's eyes too. Sin and corruption, I said, would as naturally bubble out of my heart as water would bubble out of a fountain. I could have changed heart with anybody. I thought none but the Devil himself could equal me for inward wickedness and pollution of mind. Sure, thought I, I am forsaken of God; and thus I continued a long while, even for some years together.

"And now I was sorry that God had made me a man. The beasts, birds, fishes, etc., I blessed their condition, for they had not a sinful nature; they were not

[23] John Bunyan (1628–1688), English preacher and writer of Nonconformist religious works, is best known for *The Pilgrim's Progress* (1678). The quotation is from *Grace Abounding to the Chief of Sinners* (1666); James adds the note, "I have printed a number of detached passages continuously."

obnoxious to the wrath of God; they were not to go to hell-fire after death. I could therefore have rejoiced, had my condition been as any of theirs. Now I blessed the condition of the dog and toad, yea, gladly would I have been in the condition of the dog or horse, for I knew they had no soul to perish under the everlasting weight of Hell or Sin, as mine was like to do. Nay, and though I saw this, felt this, and was broken to pieces with it, yet that which added to my sorrow was, that I could not find with all my soul that I did desire deliverance. My heart was at times exceedingly hard. If I would have given a thousand pounds for a tear, I could not shed one; no, nor sometimes scarce desire to shed one.

"I was both a burthen and a terror to myself; nor did I ever so know, as now, what it was to be weary of my life, and yet afraid to die. How gladly would I have been anything but myself! Anything but a man! and in any condition but my own."

Poor patient Bunyan, like Tolstoy, saw the light again, but we must also postpone that part of his story to another hour. In a later lecture I will also give the end of the experience of Henry Alline, a devoted evangelist who worked in Nova Scotia a hundred years ago, and who thus vividly describes the high-water mark of the religious melancholy which formed its beginning. The type was not unlike Bunyan's.

"Everything I saw seemed to be a burden to me; the earth seemed accursed for my sake: all trees, plants, rocks, hills, and vales seemed to be dressed in mourning and groaning, under the weight of the curse, and everything around me seemed to be conspiring my ruin. My sins seemed to be laid open; so that I thought that every one I saw knew them, and sometimes I was almost ready to acknowledge many things, which I thought they knew: yea sometimes it seemed to me as if every one was pointing me out as the most guilty wretch upon earth. I had now so great a sense of the vanity and emptiness of all things here below, that I knew the whole world could not possibly make me happy, no, nor the whole system of creation. When I waked in the morning, the first thought would be, Oh, my wretched soul, what shall I do, where shall I go? And when I laid down, would say, I shall be perhaps in hell before morning. I would many times look on the beasts with envy, wishing with all my heart I was in their place, that I might have no soul to lose; and when I have seen birds flying over my head, have often thought within myself, Oh, that I could fly away from my danger and distress! Oh, how happy should I be, if I were in their place!"[24]

Envy of the placid beasts seems to be a very widespread affection in this type of sadness.

The worst kind of melancholy is that which takes the form of panic fear. Here is an excellent example, for permission to print which I have to thank the sufferer. The

[24] James's note: "The Life and Journal of the Rev, Mr. Henry Alline, Boston, 1806, pp. 25, 26. . . ."

original is in French, and though the subject was evidently in a bad nervous condition at the time of which he writes, his case has otherwise the merit of extreme simplicity. I translate freely.[25]

"Whilst in this state of philosophic pessimism and general depression of spirits about my prospects, I went one evening into a dressing-room in the twilight to procure some article that was there; when suddenly there fell upon me without any warning, just as if it came out of the darkness, a horrible fear of my own existence. Simultaneously there arose in my mind the image of an epileptic patient whom I had seen in the asylum, a black-haired youth with greenish skin, entirely idiotic, who used to sit all day on one of the benches, or rather shelves against the wall, with his knees drawn up against his chin, and the coarse gray undershirt, which was his only garment, drawn over them inclosing his entire figure. He sat there like a sort of sculptured Egyptian cat or Peruvian mummy, moving nothing but his black eyes and looking absolutely non-human. This image and my fear entered into a species of combination with each other. *That shape am I,* I felt, potentially. Nothing that I possess can defend me against that fate, if the hour for it should strike for me as it struck for him. There was such a horror of him, and such a perception of my own merely momentary discrepancy from him, that it was as if something hitherto solid within my breast gave way entirely, and I became a mass of quivering fear. After this the universe was changed for me altogether. I awoke morning after morning with a horrible dread at the pit of my stomach, and with a sense of the insecurity of life that I never knew before, and that I have never felt since.[26] It was like a revelation; and although the immediate feeling passed away, the experience has made me sympathetic with the morbid feelings of others ever since. It gradually faded, but for months I was unable to go out into the dark alone.

"In general I dreaded to be left alone. I remember wondering how other people could live, how I myself had ever lived, so unconscious of that pit of insecurity beneath the surface of life. My mother in particular, a very cheerful person, seemed to me a perfect paradox in her unconsciousness of danger, which you may well believe I was very careful not to disturb by revelations of my own state of mind. I have always thought that this experience of melancholia of mine had a religious bearing."

On asking this correspondent to explain more fully what he meant by these last words, the answer he wrote was this:—

[25] The following "quotation" is actually a personal account of the experience James had as a young man which led to a period of nervous collapse.

[26] James's note: "Compare Bunyan: 'There was I struck into a very great trembling insomuch that at some times I could, for days together, feel my very body, as well as my mind, to shake and totter under the sense of the dreadful judgment of God, that should fall on those that have sinned that most fearful and unpardonable sin. I felt also such clogging and heat at my stomach, by reason of this my terror, that I was, especially at some times, as if my breast-bone would have split asunder. . . . Thus did I wind, and twine, and shrink, under the burden that was upon me; which burden also did so oppress me that I could neither stand, nor go, nor lie, either at rest or quiet.' "

"I mean that the fear was so invasive and powerful that if I had not clung to scripture-texts like 'The eternal God is my refuge,' etc., 'Come unto me, all ye that labor and are heavy-laden,' etc., 'I am the resurrection and the life,' etc., I think I should have grown really insane."[27]

There is no need of more examples. The cases we have looked at are enough. One of them gives us the vanity of mortal things; another the sense of sin; and the remaining one describes the fear of the universe;—and in one or other of these three ways it always is that man's original optimism and self-satisfaction get leveled with the dust.

In none of these cases was there any intellectual insanity or delusion about matters of fact, but were we disposed to open the chapter of really insane melancholia, with its hallucinations and delusions, it would be a worse story still—desperation absolute and complete, the whole universe coagulating about the sufferer into a material of overwhelming horror, surrounding him without opening or end. Not the conception or intellectual perception of evil, but the grisly blood-freezing heart-palsying sensation of it close upon one, and no other conception or sensation able to live for a moment in its presence. How irrelevantly remote seem all our usual refined optimisms and intellectual and moral consolations in presence of a need of help like this! Here is the real core of the religious problem: Help! help! No prophet can claim to bring a final message unless he says things that will have a sound of reality in the ears of victims such as these. But the deliverance must come in as strong a form as the complaint, if it is to take effect; and that seems a reason why the coarser religions, revivalistic, orgiastic, with blood and miracles and supernatural operations, may possibly never be displaced. Some constitutions need them too much.

Arrived at this point, we can see how great an antagonism may naturally arise between the healthy-minded way of viewing life and the way that takes all this experience of evil as something essential. To this latter way, the morbid-minded way, as we might call it, healthy-mindedness pure and simple seems unspeakably blind and shallow. To the healthy-minded way, on the other hand, the way of the sick soul seems unmanly and diseased. With their grubbing in rat-holes instead of living in the light; with their manufacture of fears, and preoccupation with every unwholesome kind of misery, there is something almost obscene about these children of wrath and cravers of a second birth. If religious intolerance and hanging and burning could again become the order of the day, there is little doubt that, however it may have been in the past, the healthy-minded would at present show themselves the less indulgent party of the two.

In our own attitude, not yet abandoned, of impartial onlookers, what are we to say of this quarrel? It seems to me that we are bound to say that morbid-mindedness ranges over the wider scale of experience, and that its survey is the one that overlaps. The method of averting one's attention from evil, and living simply in the light of

[27] James's note in reference to a work by his father the elder Henry James, who also underwent a traumatic experience that resulted in psychological collapse: "For another case of fear equally sudden, see HENRY JAMES: Society the Redeemed Form of Man, Boston, 1879, pp. 43 ff."

good is splendid as long as it will work. It will work with many persons; it will work far more generally than most of us are ready to suppose; and within the sphere of its successful operation there is nothing to be said against it as a religious solution. But it breaks down impotently as soon as melancholy comes; and even though one be quite free from melancholy one's self, there is no doubt that healthy-mindedness is inadequate as a philosophical doctrine, because the evil facts which it refuses positively to account for are a genuine portion of reality; and they may after all be the best key to life's significance, and possibly the only openers of our eyes to the deepest levels of truth.

The normal process of life contains moments as bad as any of those which insane melancholy is filled with, moments in which radical evil gets its innings and takes its solid turn. The lunatic's visions of horror are all drawn from the material of daily fact. Our civilization is founded on the shambles, and every individual existence goes out in a lonely spasm of helpless agony. If you protest, my friend, wait til you arrive there yourself! To believe in the carnivorous reptiles of geologic times is hard for our imagination—they seem too much like mere museum specimens. Yet there is no tooth in any one of those museum-skulls that did not daily through long years of the foretime hold fast to the body struggling in despair of some fated living victim. Forms of horror just as dreadful to their victims, if on a smaller spatial scale, fill the world about us to-day. Here on our very hearths and in our garden the infernal cat plays with the panting mouse, or holds the hot bird fluttering in her jaws. Crocodiles and rattlesnakes and pythons are at this moment vessels of life as real as we are; their loathsome existence fills every minute of every day that drags its length along; and whenever they or other wild beasts clutch their living prey, the deadly horror which an agitated melancholiac feels is the literally right reaction on the situation.[28]

It may indeed be that no religious reconciliation with the absolute totality of things is possible. Some evils, indeed, are ministerial to higher forms of good; but it may be that there are forms of evil so extreme as to enter into no good system whatsoever, and that, in respect of such evil, dumb submission to neglect or notice is the only practical resource. This question must confront us on a later day. But provisionally, and as a mere matter of program and method, since the evil facts are as genuine parts of nature as the good ones, the philosophic presumption should be that they have some rational significance, and that systematic healthy-mindedness, failing as it does to

[28] James's note: "Example: 'It was about eleven o'clock at night . . . but I strolled on still with the people . . . Suddenly upon the left side of our road, a crackling was heard among the bushes; all of us were alarmed, and in an instant a tiger, rushing out of the jungle, pounced upon the one of the party that was foremost, and carried him off in the twinkling of an eye. The rush of the animal, and the crush of the poor victim's bones in his mouth, and his last cry of distress, "Ho hai!" involuntarily reëchoed by all of us, was over in three seconds; and then I know not what happened till I returned to my senses, when I found myself and companions lying down on the ground as if prepared to be devoured by our enemy, the sovereign of the forest. I find my pen incapable of describing the terror of that dreadful moment. Our limbs stiffened, our power of speech ceased, and our hearts beat violently, and only a whisper of the same "Ho hai!" was heard from us. In this state we crept on all fours for some distance back, and then ran for life with the speed of an Arab horse for about half an hour, and fortunately happened to come to a small village. . . . After this every one of us was attacked with fever, attended with shivering, in which deplorable state we remained till morning.'—Autobiography of Lutfullah, a Mohammedan Gentleman, Leipzig, 1857, p. 112."

accord to sorrow, pain, and death any positive and active attention whatever, is formally less complete than systems that try at least to include these elements in their scope.

The completest religions would therefore seem to be those in which the pessimistic elements are best developed. Buddhism, of course, and Christianity are the best known to us of these. They are essentially religions of deliverance: the man must die to an unreal life before he can be born in to the real life. In my next lecture, I will try to discuss some of the psychological conditions of this second birth. Fortunately from now onward we shall have to deal with more cheerful subjects than those which we have recently been dwelling on.

1902

Henry James
1843–1916

Literary historians of the United States and Great Britain both claim Henry James as their own. Modernist critics say he is of no country at all because he possessed an imagination that is "international" in scope. A few, like Mark Twain (who would not read one of James's novels on a bet), are indifferent as to who claims him.

It is natural that a man who has attracted so many different views of his worth has been given so many identifying labels. James is "the expatriate," the man who lived, observed, and wrote *between* cultures. Still, although he resided abroad for the bulk of his mature years and became a British citizen in the last year of his life, James is also recognized for his intensely "American" consciousness and for the slant that American quality gave to his international themes. James is also "the critic" or, in his own words, "the restless analyst." One of the first major American critical theorists, he possessed a penetrating social intelligence of the kind needed to aid Americans in better understanding their collective strengths and weaknesses. In the words of recent criticism, James is "the androgyne of the imagination." Neither exclusively male nor female in his sensibilities, he preferred to sort people out in terms of their behavior, not their gender. James is "the celibate priest," the writer who willingly sacrifices everything on what he called the altar of art. Finally, and most important, James is known as "the Master"—the influential force who helped bring an end to the nineteenth-century novel based on external plots and public events and initiated twentieth-century views of fiction as inner dramas of consciousness.

James denied himself the elements of personality that come to a man through marriage and through making his permanent home in his native country. Yet it is striking to realize that James began his life as one of the most American of children. Gertrude Stein once teasingly observed that Henry James had to suffer the ignominy of having no last name, only two first names—that is, having no real family identity. But James was born in 1843 into a securely upper-middle-class home in New York City's fashionable Washington Square neighborhood. He was very much the member of a pronounced family group, headed by the benign domination of the senior Henry James—philosopher, visionary, lecturer, and writer. The second son in a family of five precociously alert children (including William, the psychologist and philosopher, and Alice, the youngest of the lot), the younger Henry James remained somewhat to the side until his father's death in 1882. At that time, he shook himself loose from the first label he had had to wear—"Henry James, Junior," the name he used to sign the literary pieces he had presented to the public since his emergence as a professional writer in 1864.

Until his twenty-first year, Henry James was usually in tow as his father moved the family from New York to Newport, Rhode Island, and Cambridge, Massachusetts, and on to England, France, Germany, and Switzerland—always in quest of the perfect spiritual and intellectual education. In his late teens, James studied painting and then the law during a brief stint at Harvard. But it was "the life of the imagination" to which he would apply himself. Without the aid or liability of advanced schooling, James's intelligence was shaped into an acutely sensuous responsiveness by the theaters, art galleries, landscape vistas, and city scenes through which the senior James marched his troop of children. The young James responded most of all to the intricate give-and-take he saw played out in the midst of the intensely social nucleus of the James family.

James sensed very early in his career that the choreographed shifts of relationship between his fictional men and women that would form the basis of his mature literary art required settings steeped in generations of cultural and historical expressiveness. To his mind, the right people for his fictional needs were available anywhere he turned his watchful eye, but the proper background for his characters' activities was generally missing in his native country. For this reason, James left America in 1876 to take up residence abroad. Finally settling in England, he dedicated his life to the only thing that mattered: studying people having "scenes" and learning how to "make scenes" in his fiction.

James never broke loose altogether from his ties to the United States, nor did he dismiss his family or his American friends. His decision to become a British citizen in 1915 was the result of the shock caused by the First World War, when he came to view England as standing alone against the enemies of Western culture. But James remained an American of the kind that Henry Adams, Gertrude Stein, Henry David Thoreau, and even Edgar Allan Poe also represented: observers and critics who stood somewhat to the side of the American scene.

James had one of the longest and most sustained careers of any American writer, and he came to be considered one of the masters of fiction in Great Britain and the United States. In 1907 Scribner's publishing house began to put out the famous New York edition of his selected works in twenty-six volumes. James had not, however, leapt to fame overnight with the writing of a smashingly successful big book. With the exception of the relatively small popular success of *Daisy Miller* in 1879, that kind of fame always escaped him. Particularly at the very start of his career in the mid-1860s, James went through a long and often discouraging apprenticeship as a reviewer and writer of romantic tales, travel sketches, and what he later considered his "hideous" early attempts to write novels.

James's first notable appearance in print came in 1865 with a review of Walt Whitman's "Drum Taps," a collection of poems about the Civil War. (He did not care for it, but this early assessment of Whitman's poetry was revised sharply upward during his mature years.) His work as reviewer and writer of tales continued to appear in many of the more important journals of that period: the *North American Review,* the *Galaxy,* the *Nation,* and the newly formed *Atlantic Monthly.* James's first collection of stories was published in 1875, the same year that *Roderick Hudson* came out as an *Atlantic Monthly* serial; this was the novel he identified as the first serious expression of his powers as a writer of fiction. During that same decade, while on one of his frequent trips to the Continent, he met and conversed with Flaubert, Zola, Turgenev, and De Maupassant about literary matters. He also studied the works of his early favorites, Honoré de Balzac, the French chronicler of "the human comedy," and George Eliot, the English novelist. The late 1870s found James, settled in England and well into his chosen vocation, feeling increased confidence in his powers as a technician and storyteller. *The American* was published in 1877, quickly followed in 1878 by *The Europeans* and in 1879 by *Daisy Miller.* With *The Portrait of a Lady* in 1881, James completed his literary apprenticeship; he had fully arrived on the literary scene and was ready for the next stage of his developing career.

For the sake of convenience, students of James's career usually divide it into three periods. Analogous to the histories of the British monarchy, there is James I, James II, and James III (in the opinion of some of his detractors, James the Old Pretender). If *The Portrait of a Lady* stands out as the finest of James's early full-length novels (characteristic of the reign of James I), the middle period is highlighted by *The Bostonians, The Princess Casamassima* (both 1886), and *The Tragic Muse* (1889). None of these novels achieved the notoriety of *Daisy Miller.* James always longed for fame; at the same time, he trained his eye on the creation of a pure art. He wished to be free from compromises with the moral prudery of the public as well as the cheap sensationalism and easy sentimentality that brought big sales and wide publicity to lesser talents.

During the 1890s James turned to writing for the theater. There, he hoped, he would find the approval of the large theater-going public. But he encountered the same difficulties overcoming the theater audience's bent for superficiality as he had in capturing the attention of the readers of slickly presented fictions. This phase of his career was not the demoralizing failure it has sometimes been made to be. Yet clearly it was not a time of success. By 1895 James had returned to writing fiction, taking with him the skills of scenic presentation he had learned while trying his hand at drama. The loss in one area became a gain when he returned to writing novels and stories. Ten years of notable success followed as James wrote one after another intensely felt short tales, novellas, and long novels. Among his best known are "The Real Thing," "The Turn of the Screw," "The Beast in the Jungle," "The Aspern Papers," and "The Jolly Corner," as well as *The Spoils of Poynton* and *What Maisie Knew* in 1897 and *The Awkward Age* in 1899.

James's final period—the one that has made him one of the supreme masters of fiction in the minds of many and an overrated writer in the opinion of others— includes the three novels that were published in the years between 1902 and 1904: *The Wings of the Dove, The Ambassadors,* and *The Golden Bowl.* They were preceded and followed by the stylistic oddities of *The Sacred Fount* (1901), *The Sense of the Past,* and *The Ivory Tower,* the last two narratives remaining unfinished at the time of his death in 1916.

Any listing of James's major novels and novellas tends to overshadow two other areas of his productivity: the dozens of short stories he published throughout his fifty years as a writer and the great variety of nonfiction he wrote. In the latter grouping there are travel pieces, literary reviews, biographical descriptions, personal memoirs, and analyses of the social scene in the United States and abroad, including such memorable works as *The American Scene* (1907), *A Small Boy and Others* (1913), and *Notes of a Son and Brother* (1914). His reputation as a major influence on the art of the novel extends even further. The quantity and quality of his writings as a literary theorist must still be taken into account.

It was not that other American writers before Henry James paid no attention to the theory by which effective literary expression is formulated. Poe applied himself to this task. In varying degrees, Hawthorne and Whitman laid down principles of composition. And in James's own day, William Dean Howells was a constant commentator on the nature of literary composition. Hamlin Garland and Frank Norris also examined the matter of literary genres. But it was Henry James who over the years amassed a body of critical essays on both form and content that made him a major force in the definition of what prose fiction can do to create a sense of life on the page.

"The Art of Fiction" (1884), his notebooks, and the prefaces he supplied for each volume of the New York edition are but a few of the occasions he took to address, in public and in private, the long list of issues out of which modern literature has unfolded. James considered the essentially self-effacing role of the author who disappears inside the consciousnesses of his fictional characters or the generalized voice of the unseen narrator. He encouraged readers to give themselves willingly to a pleasureful encounter with complicated language and to delight in difficult syntax and ambiguities of verbal meaning. He experimented with the devices by which narrative time is compressed and expanded. He analyzed why emotion becomes intensified when the narrative is given over to one particularly alert fictional character whose singular point of view forms the story's drama. He refined the means for creating significant "scenes" out of barely perceptible incidents. Above all, James reiterated the importance of the literary techniques by which psychological complexities are revealed through the characters' responses to the environment that enfold them. Before James, writing good prose fiction had often been a happy accident; with James, writers and readers of literature alike became aware of fiction's conscious craft.

The same acute self-consciousness that Henry James lavished on his own and other writers' fiction provides the terms by which James himself can be assessed. Admired during his lifetime by a relatively small group of readers and fellow writers, James's loyal followers are matched by an equally intense group who find him infuriatingly or boringly difficult to read. The detail he gave to the nuances of individual consciousnesses within his stories seems liberating to many, stifling to some. Some see James responding to his characters with tender compassion for their frailties. To others he is a snob, a prude, an effete aesthete, and a social reactionary. The fact that many of the characters in his narratives are highly refined members of the leisured class, living and traveling far from American everyday doings, with all the Jamesian time in the world to linger with their exquisite consciousness, indicates for some that James was out of touch with his native land, his era, and real human life. Still others find in James's choice of subject and setting an inspired strategy for getting close to essential social and psychological concerns. These readers find their feelings mirrored by James's wide spectrum of human types—characters who discover they must (in the words of Lambert Strether, the hero of *The Ambassadors*) come to terms with what it means to live as though they were completely free, all the while remaining aware that they are gripped by binding limitations.

The value of James's influence on the art of fiction remains controversial. But all agree that, whether pernicious or inspiring, his influence has been immense and lasting. James remained convinced of his own greatness as a literary genius throughout his long devotion to his art. He would be pleased to know that his stamp is fixed on the face of fiction, altering the way we read about ourselves and others.

Further Reading:

F. Matthiessen, *Henry James: The Major Phase*, 1944.

The Question of Henry James, ed. F. Dupee, 1945.

J. Beach, *The Method of Henry James*, 1954.

Q. Anderson, *The American Henry James*, 1957.

L. Edel and D. Laurence, *A Bibliography of Henry James*, 1957.

F. Crews, *The Tragedy of Manners: Moral Drama in the Later Novels of Henry James*, 1957.

L. Levy, *Versions of Melodrama: A Study of the Fiction and Drama of Henry James, 1865–1897*, 1957.

C. Wegelin, *The Image of Europe in Henry James*, 1958.

R. Poirier, *The Comic Sense of Henry James: A Study of the Early Novels*, 1960.

O. Cargill, *The Novels of Henry James*, 1961, 1975.

J. Ward, *The Imagination of Disaster: Evil in the Fiction of Henry James*, 1961.

D. Krook, *The Ordeal of Consciousness in Henry James*, 1962.

W. Wright, *The Madness of Art: A Study of Henry James*, 1962.

Discussions of Henry James, ed. N. Lebowitz, 1962.

M. Geismar, *Henry James and the Jacobites*, 1963.

L. Holland, *The Expense of Vision: Essays on the Craft of Henry James*, 1964, 1982.

N. Lebowitz, *The Imagination of Loving*, 1965.

T. Tanner, *Henry James: Modern Comments*, 1968, 1970.

S. Sears, *The Negative Imagination: Form and Perspective in the Novels of Henry James*, 1969.

P. Buitenhuis, *The Grasping Imagination: The American Writing of Henry James*, 1970.

C. Samuel, *The Ambiguity of Henry James*, 1971.

M. Banta, *Henry James and the Occult*, 1972.

S. B. Chatman, *The Later Style of Henry James*, 1972.

Henry James's Major Novels: Essays in Criticism, ed. L. Powers, 1973.

R. A. Hocks, *Henry James and Pragmatistic Thought*, 1974.

L. Auchincloss, *Reading Henry James*, 1975.

G. H. Jones, *Henry James's Psychology of Experience*, 1975.

J. G. Moseley, *A Complex Inheritance: The Idea of Self-Transcendence in the Theology of Henry James, Sr., and the Novels of Henry James*, 1975.

T. Laitiner, *Aspects of Henry James's Style*, 1975.

W. R. Veeder, *Henry James: The Lesson of the Master: Popular Fiction and Personal Style in the Nineteenth Century*, 1975.

P. Brooks, *The Melodramatic Imagination: Balzac, Henry James, Melodrama, and the Mode of Excess*, 1976.

K. Graham, *Henry James: The Drama of Fulfillment*, 1976.

G. Leeming, *Who's Who in Henry James*, 1976.

M. MacKenzie, *Communities of Honor and Love in Henry James*, 1976.

J. Rowe, *Henry Adams and Henry James, The Emergence of a Modern Consciousness*, 1976.

R. Yeazell, *Language and Knowledge in the Late Novels of Henry James*, 1976.

C. Anderson, *Person, Place, and Thing in Henry James's Novels*, 1977.

S. Rimmon, *The Concept of Ambiguity: The Example of Henry James*, 1977.

S. Donadio, *Nietzsche, Henry James, and the Artist's Will*, 1978.

S. Perosa, *Henry James and the Experimental Novel*, 1978.
M. D. Springer, *A Rhetoric of Literary Character: Some Women of Henry James*, 1978.
E. Wagenknecht, *Eve and Henry James*, 1978.
N. Bradbury, *Henry James: The Later Novels*, 1979.
T. Tanner, *Henry James*, 1968.
T. Tanner, *Henry James*, 3 vols., 1979–1981.
P. Sicker, *Love and the Quest for Identity in the Fiction of Henry James*, 1980.
D. M. Fogel, *Henry James and the Structure of the Romantic Imagination*, 1981.
A. Habegger, *Gender, Fantasy, and Realism in American Literature*, 1982.
M. E. Jacobson, *Henry James and the Mass Market*, 1983.
E. Wagenknecht, *The Novels of Henry James*, 1983.
C. Kaston, *Imagination and Desire in the Novels of Henry James*, 1984.
M, Seltzer, *Henry James and the Art of Power*, 1984.
L. Edel, *Henry James: A Life*, 1985.

Texts:
Daisy Miller, "The Beast in the Jungle," "The Jolly Corner," preface to *The American*, and "The Turn of the Screw" from *The Novels and Tales of Henry James* (New York edition), 26 vols., 1907–1917.
Hawthorne, 1880.
The American Scene, 1968.
See also *The Art of the Novel: Critical Prefaces*, ed. R. Blackmur, 1943.
The Notebooks of Henry James, ed. F. Matthiessen and K. Murdock, 1947.
Plays of Henry James, ed. L. Edel, 1949.
Autobiography, ed. F. Dupee, 1956, 1983.
L. Edel and D. Laurence, *A Bibliography of Henry James*, 1957.
Henry James and H. G. Wells, ed. L. Edel and G. Ray, 1958.
Discovery of a Genius: William Dean Howells and Henry James, ed. A. Mordell, 1961.
Stories of the Supernatural, ed. L. Edel, 1949.
The Complete Tales of Henry James, 12 vols., ed. L. Edel, 1962–1965.
Letters of Henry James, 2 vols., ed. P. Lubbock, 1920.
The Letters of Henry James, 4 vols., ed. L. Edel, 1974–1984.

Daisy Miller

from Preface

It was in Rome during the autumn of 1877; a friend then living there but settled now in a South less weighted with appeals and memories happened to mention—which she might perfectly not have done—some simple and uninformed American lady of the previous winter, whose young daughter, a child of nature and of freedom, accompanying her from hotel to hotel, had "picked up" by the wayside, with the best conscience in the world, a good-looking Roman, of vague identity, astonished at his luck, yet (so far as might be, by the pair) all innocently, all serenely exhibited and introduced: this at least till the occurrence of some small social check, some interrupting incident, of no great gravity or dignity, and which I forget. I had never heard, save on this showing, of the amiable but not otherwise eminent ladies, who were n't in fact named, I think, and whose case had merely served to point a familiar moral; and it must have been just their want of salience that left a margin for the small pencil-mark inveterately signifying, in such connexions, "Dramatise, dramatise!" The result of my recognising a few months later the sense of my pencil-mark was the short chronicle of "Daisy Miller," which I indited in London the following spring and then addressed, with no conditions attached, as I remember, to the editor of a magazine that had its seat of publication at Philadelphia and had lately appeared to appreciate my contributions. That gentleman however (an historian of some repute) promptly returned me my missive, and with an absence of comment that struck me at the time as rather grim—as, given the circumstances, requiring indeed some explanation: till a friend to whom I appealed for light, giving him the thing to read, declared it could only have passed with the Philadelphian critic for "an outrage on American girlhood." This was verily a light, and of bewildering intensity; though I was presently to read into the matter a further helpful inference. To the fault of being outrageous this little composition added that of being essentially and pre-eminently a *nouvelle;*[1] a signal example in fact of that type, foredoomed at the best, in more cases than not, to editorial disfavour. If accordingly I was afterwards to be cradled, almost blissfully, in the conception that "Daisy" at least, among my productions, might approach "success," such success for example, on her eventual appearance, as the state of being promptly pirated in Boston—a sweet tribute I had n't yet received and was never again to know—the irony of things yet claimed its rights, I could n't but long continue to feel, in the circumstance that quite a special reprobation had waited on the first appearance in the world of the ultimately most prosperous child of my invention. So doubly discredited, at all events, this bantling met indulgence, with no great delay, in the eyes of my admirable friend the late Leslie Stephen and was published in two numbers of *The Cornhill Magazine* (1878).[2]

It qualified itself in that publication and afterwards as "a Study"; for reasons which I confess I fail to recapture unless they may have taken account simply of a certain flatness in my poor little heroine's literal denomination. Flatness indeed, one must have felt, was the very sum of her story; so that perhaps after all the attached epithet was meant but as a deprecation, addressed to the reader, of any great critical hope of stirring scenes. It provided for mere concentration, and on an object scant and superficially vulgar—from which, however, a sufficiently brooding tenderness might eventually extract a shy incongruous charm. I suppress at all events here the appended qualification—in view of the simple truth, which ought from the first to have been apparent to me, that my little exhibition is made to no degree whatever in critical but, quite inordinately and extravagantly, in poetical terms. It comes back to me that I was at a certain hour long afterwards to have reflected, in this connexion, on the characteristic free play of the whirligig of time. It was in Italy again—in Venice and in the prized society of an interesting friend, now dead, with whom I happened to wait, on the Grand Canal, at the animated water-steps of one of the hotels. The considerable little terrace there was so disposed as to make a salient stage for certain demonstrations on the part of two young girls, children *they,* if ever, of nature and of freedom, whose use of those resources, in the general public eye, and under our own as we sat in the gondola, drew from the lips of a second companion, sociably afloat with us, the remark that there before us, with no sign absent, were a couple of attesting Daisy Millers. Then it was that, in my charming hostess's prompt protest, the whirligig, as I have called it, at once betrayed itself. "How can you liken *those* creatures to a figure of which the only fault is touchingly to have transmuted so sorry a type and to have, by a poetic artifice, not only led our judgement of it astray, but made *any* judgement quite impossible?" With which this gentle lady and admirable

---

[1] Short prose narrative, one of James's favorite literary forms.

[2] British journal edited by Stephen, well-known writer and father of the writer Virginia Woolf.

critic turned on the author himself. "You *know* you quite falsified, by the turn you gave it, the thing you had begun with having in mind, the thing you had had, to satiety, the chance of 'observing': your pretty perversion of it, or your unprincipled mystification of our sense of it, does it really too much honour—in spite of which, none the less, as anything charming or touching always to that extent justifies itself, we after a fashion forgive and understand you. But why *waste* your romance? There are cases, too many, in which you 've done it again; in which, provoked by a spirit of observation at first no doubt sufficiently sincere, and with the measured and felt truth fairly twitching your sleeve, you have yielded to your incurable prejudice in favour of grace—to whatever it is in you that makes so inordinately for form and prettiness and pathos; not to say sometimes for misplaced drolling. Is it that you 've after all too much imagination? Those awful young women capering at the hotel-door, *they* are the real little Daisy Millers that were; whereas yours in the tale is such a one, more 's the pity, as—for pitch of the ingenuous, for quality of the artless—could n't possibly have been at all." My answer to all which bristled of course with more professions than I can or need report here; the chief of them inevitably to the effect that my supposedly typical little figure was of course pure poetry, and had never been anything else; since this is what helpful imagination, in however slight a dose, ever directly makes for. As for the original grossness of readers, I dare say I added, that was another matter—but one which at any rate had then quite ceased to signify. . . .

Daisy Miller

I

At the little town of Vevey, in Switzerland, there is a particularly comfortable hotel; there are indeed many hotels, since the entertainment of tourists is the business of the place, which, as many travellers will remember, is seated upon the edge of a remark-ably blue lake—a lake[3] that it behoves every tourist to visit. The shore of the lake presents an unbroken array of establishments of this order, of every category, from the "grand hotel" of the newest fashion, with a chalk-white front, a hundred balconies, and a dozen flags flying from its roof, to the small Swiss pension of an elder day, with its name inscribed in German-looking lettering upon a pink or yellow wall and an awkward summer-house in the angle of the garden. One of the hotels at Vevey, however, is famous, even classical, being distinguished from many of its upstart neighbours by an air both of luxury and of maturity. In this region, through the month of June, American travellers are extremely numerous; it may be said indeed that Vevey assumes at that time some of the characteristics of an American watering-place. There are sights and sounds that evoke a vision, an echo, of Newport and Saratoga.[4] There is a flitting hither and thither of "stylish" young girls, a rustling of muslin flounces, a rattle of dance-music in the morning hours, a sound of high-pitched voices at all times. You receive an impression of these things at the excellent inn of

---

[3] Lake Geneva.
[4] Fashionable resorts in Rhode Island and New York State, respectively.

the "Trois Couronnes,"[5] and are transported in fancy to the Ocean House or to Congress Hall.[6] But at the "Trois Couronnes," it must be added, there are other features much at variance with these suggestions: neat German waiters who look like secretaries of legation: Russian princesses sitting in the garden; little Polish boys walking about, held by the hand, with their governors; a view of the snowy crest of the Dent du Midi[7] and the picturesque towers of the Castle of Chillon.[8]

I hardly know whether it was the analogies or the differences that were uppermost in the mind of a young American, who, two or three years ago, sat in the garden of the "Trois Couronnes," looking about him rather idly at some of the graceful objects I have mentioned. It was a beautiful summer morning, and in whatever fashion the young American looked at things they must have seemed to him charming. He had come from Geneva the day before, by the little steamer, to see his aunt, who was staying at the hotel—Geneva having been for a long time his place of residence. But his aunt had a headache—his aunt had almost always a headache—and she was now shut up in her room smelling camphor, so that he was at liberty to wander about. He was some seven-and-twenty years of age; when his friends spoke of him they usually said that he was at Geneva "studying." When his enemies spoke of him they said—but after all he had no enemies: he was extremely amiable and generally liked. What I should say is simply that when certain persons spoke of him they conveyed that the reason of his spending so much time at Geneva was that he was extremely devoted to a lady who lived there—a foreign lady, a person older than himself. Very few Americans—truly I think none—had ever seen this lady, about whom there were some singular stories. But Winterbourne had an old attachment for the little capital of Calvinism;[9] he had been put to school there as a boy and had afterwards even gone, on trial—trial of the grey old "Academy"[10] on the steep and stony hillside—to college there; circumstances which had led to his forming a great many youthful friendships. Many of these he had kept, and they were a source of great satisfaction to him.

After knocking at his aunt's door and learning that she was indisposed he had taken a walk about the town and then he had come in to his breakfast. He had now finished that repast, but was enjoying a small cup of coffee which had been served him on a little table in the garden by one of the waiters who looked like *attachés*. At last he finished his coffee and lit a cigarette. Presently a small boy came walking along the path—an urchin of nine or ten. The child, who was diminutive for his years, had an aged expression of countenance, a pale complexion and sharp little features. He was dressed in knickerbockers and had red stockings that displayed his poor little spindle-shanks; he also wore a brilliant red cravat. He carried in his hand a long alpenstock, the sharp point of which he thrust into everything he approached—the flower-beds, the garden-benches, the trains of the ladies' dresses. In front of Winterbourne he paused, looking at him with a pair of bright and penetrating little eyes.

"Will you give me a lump of sugar?" he asked in a small sharp hard voice—a voice immature and yet somehow not young.

[5] French: "Three Crowns."
[6] Hotels at Newport and Saratoga, respectively.
[7] Peak of Mont Blanc in the Swiss Alps.
[8] Medieval castle situated on the lake and the setting for "The Prisoner of Chillon" (1816) by Lord Byron.
[9] Bastion of John Calvin's Protestant reform activities between 1541 and 1564.
[10] University of Geneva.

Winterbourne glanced at the light table near him, on which his coffee-service rested, and saw that several morsels of sugar remained. "Yes, you may take one," he answered; "but I don't think too much sugar good for little boys."

This little boy stepped forward and carefully selected three of the coveted fragments, two of which he buried in the pocket of his knickerbockers, depositing the other as promptly in another place. He poked his alpenstock, lance-fashion, into Winterbourne's bench and tried to crack the lump of sugar with his teeth.

"Oh blazes; it's har-r-d!" he exclaimed, divesting vowel and consonants, pertinently enough, of any taint of softness.

Winterbourne had immediately gathered that he might have the honour of claiming him as a countryman. "Take care you don't hurt your teeth," he said paternally.

"I have n't got any teeth to hurt. They've all come out. I've only got seven teeth. Mother counted them last night, and one came out right afterwards. She said she'd slap me if any more came out. I can't help it. It's this old Europe. It's the climate that makes them come out. In America they did n't come out. It's these hotels."

Winterbourne was much amused. "If you eat three lumps of sugar your mother will certainly slap you," he ventured.

"She's got to give me some candy then," rejoined his young interlocutor. "I can't get any candy here—any American candy. American candy's the best candy."

"And are American little boys the best little boys?" Winterbourne asked.

"I don't know. *I'm* an American boy," said the child.

"I see you're one of the best!" the young man laughed.

"Are you an American man?" pursued this vivacious infant. And then on his friend's affirmative reply, "American men are the best," he declared with assurance.

His companion thanked him for the compliment, and the child, who had now got astride of his alpenstock, stood looking about him while he attacked another lump of sugar. Winterbourne wondered if he himself had been like this in his infancy, for he had been brought to Europe at about the same age.

"Here comes my sister!" cried his young compatriot. "She's an American girl, you bet!"

Winterbourne looked along the path and saw a beautiful young lady advancing. "American girls are the best girls," he thereupon cheerfully remarked to his visitor.

"My sister ain't the best!" the child promptly returned. "She's always blowing at me."[11]

"I imagine that's your fault, not hers," said Winterbourne. The young lady meanwhile had drawn near. She was dressed in white muslin, with a hundred frills and flounces and knots of pale-coloured ribbon. Bareheaded, she balanced in her hand a large parasol with a deep border of embroidery; and she was strikingly, admirably pretty. "How pretty they are!" thought our friend, who straightened himself in his seat as if he were ready to rise.

The young lady paused in front of his bench, near the parapet of the garden, which overlooked the lake. The small boy had now converted his alpenstock into a vaulting-pole, by the aid of which he was springing about in the gravel and kicking it up not a little. "Why Randolph," she freely began, "What *are* you doing?"

"I'm going up the Alps!" cried Randolph. "This is the way!" And he gave another extravagant jump, scattering the pebbles about Winterbourne's ears.

---

[11] Slang for "criticizing me."

"That's the way they come down," said Winterbourne.

"He's an American man!" proclaimed Randolph in his harsh little voice.

The young lady gave no heed to this circumstance, but looked straight at her brother. "Well, I guess you'd better be quiet," she simply observed.

It seemed to Winterbourne that he had been in a manner presented. He got up and stepped slowly toward the charming creature, throwing away his cigarette. "This little boy and I have made acquaintance," he said with great civility. In Geneva, as he had been perfectly aware, a young man wasn't at liberty to speak to a young unmarried lady save under certain rarely-occurring conditions; but here at Vevey what conditions could be better than these?—a pretty American girl coming to stand in front of you in a garden with all the confidence in life. This pretty American girl, whatever that might prove, on hearing Winterbourne's observation simply glanced at him; she then turned her head and looked over the parapet, at the lake and the opposite mountains. He wondered whether he had gone too far, but decided that he must gallantly advance rather than retreat. While he was thinking of something else to say the young lady turned again to the little boy, whom she addressed quite as if they were alone together. "I should like to know where you got that pole."

"I bought it!" Randolph shouted.

"You don't mean to say you're going to take it to Italy!"

"Yes, I'm going to take it t' Italy!" the child rang out.

She glanced over the front of her dress and smoothed out a knot or two of ribbon. Then she gave her sweet eyes to the prospect again. "Well, I guess you'd better leave it somewhere," she dropped after a moment.

"Are you going to Italy?" Winterbourne now decided very respectfully to enquire.

She glanced at him with lovely remoteness. "Yes, sir," she then replied. And she said nothing more.

"And are you—a—thinking of the Simplon?"[12] he pursued with a slight drop of assurance.

"I don't know," she said. "I suppose it's some mountain. Randolph, what mountain are we thinking of?"

"Thinking of?"—the boy stared.

"Why going right over."

"Going to where?" he demanded.

"Why right down to Italy"—Winterbourne felt vague emulations.

"I don't know," said Randolph. "I don't want to go t' Italy. I want to go to America."

"Oh Italy's a beautiful place!" the young man laughed.

"Can you get candy there?" Randolph asked of all the echoes.

"I hope not," said his sister. "I guess you've had enough candy, and mother thinks so too."

"I haven't had any for ever so long—for a hundred weeks!" cried the boy, still jumping about.

The young lady inspected her flounces and smoothed her ribbons again; and Winterbourne presently risked an observation on the beauty of the view. He was ceasing to be in doubt, for he had begun to perceive that she was really not in the least embarrassed. She might be cold, she might be austere, she might even be prim;

---

[12] Alpine pass between Switzerland and Italy.

for that was apparently—he had already so generalised—what the most "distant" American girls did: they came and planted themselves straight in front of you to show how rigidly unapproachable they were. There had n't been the slightest flush in her fresh fairness however; so that she was clearly neither offended nor fluttered. Only she was composed—he had seen that before too—of charming little parts that didn't match and that made no *ensemble;*[13] and if she looked another way when he spoke to her, and seemed not particularly to hear him, this was simply her habit, her manner, the result of her having no idea whatever of "form" (with such a tell-tale appendage as Randolph where in the world would she have got it?) in any such connexion. As he talked a little more and pointed out some of the objects of interest in the view, with which she appeared wholly unacquainted, she gradually, none the less, gave him more of the benefit of her attention; and then he saw that act unqualified by the faintest shadow of reserve. It was n't however what would have been called a "bold" front that she presented, for her expression was as decently limpid as the very cleanest water. Her eyes were the very prettiest conceivable, and indeed Winterbourne had n't for a long time seen anything prettier than his fair countrywoman's various features— her complexion, her nose, her ears, her teeth. He took a great interest generally in that range of effects and was addicted to noting and, as it were, recording them; so that in regard to this young lady's face he made several observations. It was n't at all insipid, yet at the same time was n't pointedly—what point, on earth, could she ever make?—expressive; and though it offered such a collection of small finenesses and neatnesses he mentally accused it—very forgivingly—of a want of finish. He thought nothing more likely than that its wearer would have had her own experience of the action of her charms, as she would certainly have acquired a resulting confidence; but even should she depend on this for her main amusement her bright sweet superficial little visage gave out neither mockery nor irony. Before long it became clear that, however these things might be, she was much disposed to conversation. She remarked to Winterbourne that they were going to Rome for the winter—she and her mother and Randolph. She asked him if he was a "real American"; she would n't have taken him for one; he seemed more like a German—this flower was gathered as from a large field of comparison—especially when he spoke. Winterbourne, laughing, answered that he had met Germans who spoke like Americans, but not, so far as he remembered, any American with the resemblance she noted. Then he asked her if she might n't be more at ease should she occupy the bench he had just quitted. She answered that she liked hanging round, but she none the less resignedly, after a little, dropped to the bench. She told him she was from New York State—"if you know where that is"; but our friend really quickened this current by catching hold of her small slippery brother and making him stand a few minutes by his side.

"Tell me your honest name, my boy." So he artfully proceeded.

In response to which the child was indeed unvarnished truth. "Randolph C. Miller. And I'll tell you hers." With which he levelled his alpenstock at his sister.

"You had better wait till you're asked!" said this young lady quite at her leisure.

"I should like very much to know *your* name," Winterbourne made free to reply.

"Her name's Daisy Miller!" cried the urchin. "But that ain't her real name; that ain't her name on her cards."

---

[13] French: "harmonious whole."

"It's a pity you have n't got one of my cards!" Miss Miller quite as naturally remarked.

"Her real name's Annie P. Miller," the boy went on.

It seemed, all amazingly, to do her good. "Ask him *his* now"—and she indicated their friend.

But to this point Randolph seemed perfectly indifferent; he continued to supply information with regard to his own family. "My father's name is Ezra B. Miller. My father ain't in Europe—he's in a better place than Europe." Winterbourne for a moment supposed this the manner in which the child had been taught to intimate that Mr. Miller had been removed to the sphere of celestial rewards. But Randolph immediately added: "My father's in Schenectady. He's got a big business. My father's rich, you bet."

"Well!" ejaculated Miss Miller, lowering her parasol and looking at the embroidered border. Winterbourne presently released the child, who departed, dragging his alpenstock along the path. "He don't like Europe," said the girl as with an artless instinct for historic truth. "He wants to go back."

"To Schenectady, you mean?"

"Yes, he wants to go right home. He has n't got any boys here. There's one boy here, but he always goes round with a teacher. They won't let him play."

"And your brother has n't any teacher?" Winterbourne enquired.

It tapped, at a touch, the spring of confidence. "Mother thought of getting him one—to travel round with us. There was a lady told her of a very good teacher; an American lady—perhaps you know her—Mrs. Sanders. I think she came from Boston. She told her of this teacher, and we thought of getting him to travel round with us. But Randolph said he did n't want a teacher travelling round with us. He said he would n't have lessons when he was in the cars.[14] And we *are* in the cars about half the time. There was an English lady we met in the cars—I think her name was Miss Featherstone; perhaps you know her. She wanted to know why I did n't give Randolph lessons—give him 'instruction,' she called it. I guess he could give me more instruction than I could give him. He's very smart."

"Yes," said Winterbourne; "he seems very smart."

"Mother's going to get a teacher for him as soon as we get t' Italy. Can you get good teachers in Italy?"

"Very good, I should think," Winterbourne hastened to reply.

"Or else she's going to find some school. He ought to learn some more. He's only nine. He's going to college." And in this way Miss Miller continued to converse upon the affairs of her family and upon other topics. She sat there with her extremely pretty hands, ornamented with very brilliant rings, folded in her lap, and with her pretty eyes now resting upon those of Winterbourne, now wandering over the garden, the people who passed before her and the beautiful view. She addressed her new acquaintance as if she had known him a long time. He found it very pleasant. It was many years since he had heard a young girl talk so much. It might have been said of this wandering maiden who had come and sat down beside him upon a bench that she chattered. She was very quiet, she sat in a charming tranquil attitude; but her lips and her eyes were constantly moving. She had a soft slender agreeable voice, and her tone

---

[14] Railway cars.

was distinctly sociable. She gave Winterbourne a report of her movements and intentions, and those of her mother and brother, in Europe, and enumerated in particular the various hotels at which they had stopped. "That English lady in the cars," she said—"Miss Featherstone—asked me if we did n't all live in hotels in America. I told her I had never been in so many hotels in my life as since I came to Europe. I've never seen so many—it's nothing but hotels." But Miss Miller made this remark with no querulous accent; she appeared to be in the best humour with everything. She declared that the hotels were very good when once you got used to their ways and that Europe was perfectly entrancing. She was n't disappointed—not a bit. Perhaps it was because she had heard so much about it before. She had ever so many intimate friends who had been there ever so many times, and that way she had got thoroughly posted. And then she had had ever so many dresses and things from Paris. Whenever she put on a Paris dress she felt as if she were in Europe.

"It was a kind of a wishing-cap," Winterbourne smiled.

"Yes," said Miss Miller at once and without examining this analogy; "it always made me wish I was here. But I need n't have done that for dresses. I'm sure they send all the pretty ones to America; you see the most frightful things here. The only thing I don't like," she proceeded, "is the society. There ain't any society—or if there is I don't know where it keeps itself. Do you? I suppose there's some society somewhere, but I have n't seen anything of it. I'm very fond of society and I've always had plenty of it. I don't mean only in Schenectady, but in New York. I used to go to New York every winter. In New York I had lots of society. Last winter I had seventeen dinners given me, and three of them were by gentlemen," added Daisy Miller. "I've more friends in New York than in Schenectady—more gentlemen friends; and more young lady friends too," she resumed in a moment. She paused again for an instant; she was looking at Winterbourne with all her prettiness in her frank gay eyes and in her clear rather uniform smile. "I've always had," she said, "a great deal of gentlemen's society."

Poor Winterbourne was amused and perplexed—above all he was charmed. He had never yet heard a young girl express herself in just this fashion; never at least save in cases where to say such things was to have at the same time some rather complicated consciousness about them. And yet was he to accuse Miss Daisy Miller of an actual or a potential *arrière-pensée,* [15] as they said at Geneva? He felt he had lived at Geneva so long as to have got morally muddled; he had lost the right sense for the young American tone. Never indeed since he had grown old enough to appreciate things had he encountered a young compatriot of so "strong" a type as this. Certainly she was very charming, but how extraordinarily communicative and how tremendously easy! Was she simply a pretty girl from New York State—were they all like that, the pretty girls who had had a good deal of gentlemen's society? Or was she also a designing, an audacious, in short an expert young person? Yes, his instinct for such a question had ceased to serve him, and his reason could but mislead. Miss Daisy Miller looked extremely innocent. Some people had told him that after all American girls were exceedingly innocent, and others had told him that after all they were n't. He must on the whole take Miss Daisy Miller for a flirt—a pretty American flirt. He had never as yet had relations with representatives of that class. He had known here in Europe two or three women—persons older than Miss Daisy Miller and provided, for

[15] French: "ulterior motive."

respectability's sake, with husbands—who were great coquettes; dangerous terrible women with whom one's light commerce might indeed take a serious turn. But this charming apparition was n't a coquette in that sense; she was very unsophisticated; she was only a pretty American flirt. Winterbourne was almost grateful for having found the formula that applied to Miss Daisy Miller. He leaned back in his seat; he remarked to himself that she had the finest little nose he had ever seen; he wondered what were the regular conditions and limitations of one's intercourse with a pretty American flirt. It presently became apparent that he was on the way to learn.

"Have you been to that old castle?" the girl soon asked, pointing with her parasol to the far-shining walls of the Château de Chillon.

"Yes, formerly, more than once," said Winterbourne. "You too, I suppose, have seen it?"

"No, we have n't been there. I want to go there dreadfully. Of course I mean to go there. I would n't go away from here without having seen that old castle."

"It's a very pretty excursion," the young man returned, "and very easy to make. You can drive, you know, or you can go by the little steamer."

"You can go in the cars," said Miss Miller.

"Yes, you can go in the cars," Winterbourne assented.

"Our courier[16] says they take you right up to the castle," she continued. "We were going last week, but mother gave out. She suffers dreadfully from dyspepsia. She said she could n't any more go—!" But this sketch of Mrs. Miller's plea remained unfinished. "Randolph would n't go either; he says he don't think much of old castles. But I guess we'll go this week if we can get Randolph."

"Your brother is n't interested in ancient monuments?" Winterbourne indulgently asked.

He now drew her, as he guessed she would herself have said, every time. "Why no, he says he don't care much about old castles. He's only nine. He wants to stay at the hotel. Mother's afraid to leave him alone, and the courier won't stay with him; so we have n't been to many places. But it will be too bad if we don't go up there." And Miss Miller pointed again at the Château de Chillon.

"I should think it might be arranged," Winterbourne was thus emboldened to reply. "Could n't you get some one to stay—for the afternoon—with Randolph?"

Miss Miller looked at him a moment, and then with all serenity, "I wish *you'd* stay with him!" she said.

He pretended to consider it. "I'd much rather go to Chillon with you."

"With me?" she asked without a shadow of emotion.

She did n't rise blushing, as a young person at Geneva would have done; and yet, conscious that he had gone very far, he thought it possible she had drawn back. "And with your mother," he answered very respectfully.

But it seemed that both his audacity and his respect were lost on Miss Daisy Miller. "I guess mother would n't go—for *you,*" she smiled. "And she ain't much *bent* on going, anyway. She don't like to ride round in the afternoon." After which she familiarly proceeded: "But did you really mean what you said just now—that you'd like to go up there?"

"Most earnestly I meant it," Winterbourne declared.

[16] Person hired to aid travelers with hotel reservations and luggage.

"Then we may arrange it. If mother will stay with Randolph I guess Eugenio will."

"Eugenio?" the young man echoed.

"Eugenio's our courier. He does n't like to stay with Randolph—he's the most fastidious man I ever saw. But he's a splendid courier. I guess he'll stay at home with Randolph if mother does, and then we can go to the castle."

Winterbourne reflected for an instant as lucidly as possible: "we" could only mean Miss Miller and himself. This prospect seemed almost too good to believe; he felt as if he ought to kiss the young lady's hand. Possibly he would have done so,—and quite spoiled his chance; but at this moment another person—presumably Eugenio—appeared. A tall handsome man, with superb whiskers and wearing a velvet morning-coat and a voluminous watch-guard, approached the young lady, looking sharply at her companion. "Oh Eugenio!" she said with the friendliest accent.

Eugenio had eyed Winterbourne from head to foot; he now bowed gravely to Miss Miller. "I have the honour to inform Mademoiselle that luncheon's on table."

Mademoiselle slowly rose. "See here, Eugenio, I'm going to that old castle anyway."

"To the Château de Chillon, Mademoiselle?" the courier enquired. "Mademoiselle has made arrangements?" he added in a tone that struck Winterbourne as impertinent.

Eugenio's tone apparently threw, even to Miss Miller's own apprehension, a slightly ironical light on her position. She turned to Winterbourne with the slightest blush. "You won't back out?"

"I shall not be happy till we go!" he protested.

"And you're staying in this hotel?" she went on. "And you're really American?"

The courier still stood there with an effect of offence for the young man so far as the latter saw in it a tacit reflexion on Miss Miller's behaviour and an insinuation that she "picked up" acquaintances. "I shall have the honour of presenting to you a person who'll tell you all about me," he said, smiling, and referring to his aunt.

"Oh well, we'll go some day," she beautifully answered; with which she gave him a smile and turned away. She put up her parasol and walked back to the inn beside Eugenio. Winterbourne stood watching her, and as she moved away, drawing her muslin furbelows over the walk, he spoke to himself of her natural elegance.

II

He had, however, engaged to do more than proved feasible in promising to present his aunt, Mrs. Costello, to Miss Daisy Miller. As soon as that lady had got better of her headache he waited on her in her apartment and, after a show of the proper solicitude about her health, asked if she had noticed in the hotel an American family —a mamma, a daughter and an obstreperous little boy.

"An obstreperous little boy and a preposterous big courier?" said Mrs. Costello. "Oh yes, I've noticed them. Seen them, heard them and kept out of their way." Mrs. Costello was a widow of fortune, a person of much distinction and who frequently intimated that if she had n't been so dreadfully liable to sick-headaches she would probably have left a deeper impress on her time. She had a long pale face, a high nose and a great deal of very striking white hair, which she wore in large puffs and over the top of her head. She had two sons married in New York and another who was now in Europe. This young man was amusing himself at Homburg[17] and, though guided by his taste, was rarely observed to visit any particular city at the moment selected by his mother for her appearance there. Her nephew, who had come to Vevey expressly to see her, was therefore more attentive than, as she said, her very own. He had imbibed at Geneva the idea that one must be irreproachable in all such forms. Mrs. Costello had n't seen him for many years and was now greatly pleased with him, manifesting her approbation by initiating him into many of the secrets of that social sway which, as he could see she would like him to think, she exerted from her stronghold in Forty-Second Street. She admitted that she was very exclusive, but if he had been better acquainted with New York he would see that one had to be. And her picture of the minutely hierarchical constitution of the society of that city, which she presented to him in many different lights, was, to Winterbourne's imagination, almost oppressively striking.

He at once recognized from her tone that Miss Daisy Miller's place in the social scale was low. "I'm afraid you don't approve of them," he pursued in reference to his new friends.

"They're horribly common"—it was perfectly simple. "They're the sort of Americans that one does one's duty by just ignoring."

"Ah you just ignore them?"—the young man took it in.

"I can't *not,* my dear Frederick. I would n't if I had n't to, but I have to."

"The little girl's very pretty," he went on in a moment.

"Of course she's very pretty. But she's of the last crudity."

"I see what you mean of course," he allowed after another pause.

"She has that charming look they all have," his aunt resumed. "I can't think where they pick it up; and she dresses in perfection—no, you don't know how well she dresses. I can't think where they get their taste."

"But, my dear aunt, she's not, after all, a Comanche savage."

"She is a young lady," said Mrs. Costello, "who has an intimacy with her mamma's courier?"

"An 'intimacy' with him?" Ah there it was!

"There's no other name for such a relation. But the skinny little mother's just as bad! They treat the courier as a familiar friend—as a gentleman and a scholar. I should n't wonder if he dines with them. Very likely they've never seen a man with such good manners, such fine clothes, so *like* a gentleman—or a scholar. He probably corresponds to the young lady's idea of a count. He sits with them in the garden of an evening. I think he smokes in their faces."

Winterbourne listened with interest to these disclosures; they helped him to make up his mind about Miss Daisy. Evidently she was rather wild. "Well," he said, "I'm not a courier and I did n't smoke in her face, and yet she was very charming to me."

"You had better have mentioned at first," Mrs. Costello returned with dignity, "that you had made her valuable acquaintance."

"We simply met in the garden and talked a bit."

"By appointment—no? Ah that's still to come! Pray what did you say?"

"I said I should take the liberty of introducing her to my admirable aunt."

"Your admirable aunt's a thousand times obliged to you."

[17] German resort.

"It was to guarantee my respectability."

"And pray who's to guarantee hers?"

"Ah you're cruel!" said the young man. "She's a very innocent girl."

"You don't say that as if you believed it," Mrs. Costello returned.

"She's completely uneducated," Winterbourne acknowledged, "but she's wonderfully pretty, and in short she's very nice. To prove I believe it I'm going to take her to the Château de Chillon."

Mrs. Costello made a wondrous face. "You two are going off there together? I should say it proved just the contrary. How long had you known her, may I ask, when this interesting project was formed? You have n't been twenty-four hours in the house."

"I had known her half an hour!" Winterbourne smiled.

"Then she's just what I supposed."

"And what do you suppose?"

"Why that she's a horror."

Our youth was silent for some moments. "You really think then," he presently began, and with a desire for trustworthy information, "you really think that—" But he paused again while his aunt waited.

"Think what, sir?"

"That she's the sort of young lady who expects a man sooner or later to—well, we'll call it carry her off?"

"I have n't the least idea what such young ladies expect a man to do. But I really consider you had better not meddle with little American girls who are uneducated, as you mildly put it. You've lived too long out of the country. You'll be sure to make some great mistake. You're too innocent."

"My dear aunt, not so much as that comes to!" he protested with a laugh and a curl of his moustache.

"You're too guilty then!"

He continued all thoughtfully to finger the ornament in question. "You won't let the poor girl know you then?" he asked at last.

"Is it literally true that she's going to the Château de Chillon with you?"

"I've no doubt she fully intends it."

"Then, my dear Frederick," said Mrs. Costello, "I must decline the honour of her acquaintance. I'm an old woman, but I'm not too old—thank heaven—to be honestly shocked!"

"But don't they all do these things—the little American girls at home?" Winterbourne enquired.

Mrs. Costello stared a moment. "I should like to see my granddaughters do them!" she then grimly returned.

This seemed to throw some light on the matter, for Winterbourne remembered to have heard his pretty cousins in New York, the daughters of this lady's two daughters, called "tremendous flirts." If therefore Miss Daisy Miller exceeded the liberal licence allowed to these young women it was probable she did go even by the American allowance rather far. Winterbourne was impatient to see her again, and it vexed, it even a little humiliated him, that he should n't by instinct appreciate her justly.

Though so impatient to see her again he hardly knew what ground he should give for his aunt's refusal to become acquainted with her; but he discovered promptly enough that with Miss Daisy Miller there was no great need of walking on tiptoe. He found her that evening in the garden, wandering about in the warm starlight after the manner of an indolent sylph and swinging to and fro the largest fan he had ever beheld. It was ten o'clock. He had dined with his aunt, had been sitting with her since dinner, and had just taken leave of her till the morrow. His young friend frankly rejoiced to renew their intercourse; she pronounced it the stupidest evening she had ever passed.

"Have you been all alone?" he asked with no intention of an epigram and no effect of her perceiving one.

"I've been walking round with mother. But mother gets tired walking round," Miss Miller explained.

"Has she gone to bed?"

"No, she does n't like to go to bed. She does n't sleep scarcely any—not three hours. She says she does n't know how she lives. She's dreadfully nervous. I guess she sleeps more than she thinks. She's gone somewhere after Randolph; she wants to try to get him to go to bed. He does n't like to go to bed."

The soft impartiality of her *constatations,*[18] as Winterbourne would have termed them, was a thing by itself—exquisite little fatalist as they seemed to make her. "Let us hope she'll persuade him," he encouragingly said.

"Well, she'll talk to him all she can—but he does n't like her to talk to him": with which Miss Daisy opened and closed her fan. "She's going to try to get Eugenio to talk to him. But Randolph ain't afraid of Eugenio. Eugenio's a splendid courier, but he can't make much impression on Randolph! I don't believe he'll go to bed before eleven." Her detachment from any invidious judgement of this was, to her companion's sense, inimitable; and it appeared that Randolph's vigil was in fact triumphantly prolonged, for Winterbourne attended her in her stroll for some time without meeting her mother. "I've been looking round for that lady you want to introduce me to," she resumed—"I guess she's your aunt." Then on his admitting the fact and expressing some curiosity as to how she had learned it, she said she had heard all about Mrs. Costello from the chambermaid. She was very quiet and very *comme il faut;*[19] she wore white puffs; she spoke to no one and she never dined at the common table. Every two days she had a headache. "I think that's a lovely description, headache and all!" said Miss Daisy, chattering along in her thin gay voice. "I want to know her ever so much. I know just what *your* aunt would be; I know I'd like her. She'd be very exclusive. I like a lady to be exclusive; I'm dying to be exclusive myself. Well, I guess we *are* exclusive, mother and I. We don't speak to any one—or they don't speak to us. I suppose it's about the same thing. Anyway, I shall be ever so glad to meet your aunt."

Winterbourne was embarrassed—he could but trump up some evasion. "She'd be most happy, but I'm afraid those tiresome headaches are always to be reckoned with."

The girl looked at him through the fine dusk. "Well, I suppose she does n't have a headache every day."

He had to make the best of it. "She tells me she wonderfully does." He did n't know what else to say.

---

[18] French: "matter-of-fact conclusions."   [19] Attentive to the proprieties.

Miss Miller stopped and stood looking at him. Her prettiness was still visible in the darkness; she kept flapping to and fro her enormous fan. "She does n't want to know me!" she then lightly broke out. "Why don't you say so? You need n't be afraid. I'm not afraid!" And she quite crowed for the fun of it.

Winterbourne distinguished however a wee false note in this: he was touched, shocked, mortified by it. "My dear young lady, she knows no one. She goes through life immured. It's her wretched health."

The young girl walked on a few steps in the glee of the thing. "You need n't be afraid," she repeated. "Why should she want to know me?" Then she paused again; she was close to the parapet of the garden, and in front of her was the starlit lake. There was a vague sheen on its surface, and in the distance were dimly-seen mountain forms. Daisy Miller looked out at these great lights and shades and again proclaimed a gay indifference—"Gracious! she is exclusive!" Winterbourne wondered if she were seriously wounded and for a moment almost wished her sense of injury might be such as to make it becoming in him to reassure and comfort her. He had a pleasant sense that she would be all accessible to a respectful tenderness at that moment. He felt quite ready to sacrifice his aunt—conversationally; to acknowledge she was a proud rude woman and to make the point that they need n't mind her. But before he had time to commit himself to this questionable mixture of gallantry and impiety, the young lady, resuming her walk, gave an exclamation in quite another tone. "Well, here's mother! I guess she has n't got Randolph to go to bed." The figure of a lady appeared, at a distance, very indistinct in the darkness; it advanced with a slow and wavering step and then suddenly seemed to pause.

"Are you sure it's your mother? Can you make her out in this thick dusk?" Winterbourne asked.

"Well," the girl laughed, "I guess I know my own mother! And when she has got on my shawl too. She's always wearing my things."

The lady in question, ceasing now to approach, hovered vaguely about the spot at which she had checked her steps.

"I'm afraid your mother does n't see you," said Winterbourne. "Or perhaps," he added—thinking, with Miss Miller, the joke permissible—"perhaps she feels guilty about your shawl."

"Oh it's a fearful old thing!" his companion placidly answered. "I told her she could wear it if she did n't mind looking like a fright. She won't come here because she sees you."

"Ah then," said Winterbourne, "I had better leave you."

"Oh no—come on!" the girl insisted.

"I'm afraid your mother does n't approve of my walking with you."

She gave him, he thought, the oddest glance. "It is n't for me; it's for you—that is it's for her. Well, I don't know who it's for! But mother does n't like any of my gentlemen friends. She's right down timid. She always makes a fuss if I introduce a gentleman. But I do introduce them—almost always. If I did n't introduce my gentlemen friends to mother," Miss Miller added, in her small flat monotone, "I should n't think I was natural."

"Well, to introduce me," Winterbourne remarked, "you must know my name." And he proceeded to pronounce it.

"Oh my—I can't say all that!" cried his companion, much amused. But by this time they had come up to Mrs. Miller, who, as they drew near, walked to the parapet of the garden and leaned on it, looking intently at the lake and presenting her back to them. "Mother!" said the girl in a tone of decision—upon which the elder lady turned round. "Mr. Frederick Forsyth Winterbourne," said the latter's young friend, repeating his lesson of a moment before and introducing him very frankly and prettily. "Common" she might be, as Mrs. Costello had pronounced her; yet what provision was made by that epithet for her queer little native grace?

Her mother was a small spare light person, with a wandering eye, a scarce perceptible nose, and, as to make up for it, an unmistakeable forehead, decorated—but too far back, as Winterbourne mentally described it—with thin much-frizzled hair. Like her daughter Mrs. Miller was dressed with extreme elegance; she had enormous diamonds in her ears. So far as the young man could observe, she gave him no greeting —she certainly was n't looking at him. Daisy was near her, pulling her shawl straight. "What are you doing, poking round here?" this young lady enquired—yet by no means with the harshness of accent her choice of words might have implied.

"Well, I don't know"—and the new-comer turned to the lake again.

"I should n't think you'd want that shawl!" Daisy familiarly proceeded.

"Well—I do!" her mother answered with a sound that partook for Winterbourne of an odd strain between mirth and woe.

"Did you get Randolph to go to bed?" Daisy asked.

"No, I could n't induce him"—and Mrs. Miller seemed to confess to the same mild fatalism as her daughter. "He wants to talk to the waiter. He *likes* to talk to that waiter."

"I was just telling Mr. Winterbourne," the girl went on; and to the young man's ear her tone might have indicated that she had been uttering his name all her life.

"Oh yes!" he concurred—"I've the pleasure of knowing your son."

Randolph's mamma was silent; she kept her attention on the lake. But at last a sigh broke from her. "Well, I don't see how he lives!"

"Anyhow, it is n't so bad as it was at Dover,"[20] Daisy at least opined.

"And what occurred at Dover?" Winterbourne desired to know.

"He would n't go to bed at all. I guess he sat up all night—in the public parlour. He was n't in bed at twelve o'clock: it seemed as if he could n't budge."

"It was half-past twelve when *I* gave up," Mrs. Miller recorded with passionless accuracy.

It was of great interest to Winterbourne. "Does he sleep much during the day?"

"I guess he does n't sleep *very* much," Daisy rejoined.

"I wish he just *would!*" said her mother. "It seems as if he *must* make it up somehow."

"Well, I guess it's we that make it up. I think he's real tiresome," Daisy pursued.

After which, for some moments, there was silence. "Well, Daisy Miller," the elder lady then unexpectedly broke out, "I should n't think you'd want to talk against your own brother!"

"Well, he *is* tiresome, mother," said the girl, but with no sharpness of insistence.

"Well, he's only nine," Mrs. Miller lucidly urged.

"Well, he would n't go up to that castle, anyway," her daughter replied as for accommodation. "I'm going up there with Mr. Winterbourne."

To this announcement, very placidly made, Daisy's parent offered no response.

---

[20] Town on the English side of the Channel.

Winterbourne took for granted on this that she opposed such a course; but he said to himself at the same time that she was a simple easily-managed person and that a few deferential protestations would modify her attitude. "Yes," he therefore interposed, "your daughter has kindly allowed me the honour of being her guide."

Mrs. Miller's wandering eyes attached themselves with an appealing air to her other companion, who, however, strolled a few steps further, gently humming to herself. "I presume you'll go in the cars," she then quite colourlessly remarked.

"Yes, or in the boat," said Winterbourne.

"Well, of course I don't know," Mrs. Miller returned. "I've never been up to that castle."

"It is a pity you should n't go," he observed, beginning to feel reassured as to her opposition. And yet he was quite prepared to find that as a matter of course she meant to accompany her daughter.

It was on this view accordingly that light was projected for him. "We've been thinking ever so much about going, but it seems as if we could n't. Of course Daisy —she wants to go round everywhere. But there's a lady here—I don't know her name —she says she should n't think we'd want to go to see castles *here;* she should think we'd want to wait till we got t' Italy. It seems as if there would be so many there," continued Mrs. Miller with an air of increasing confidence. "Of course we only want to see the principal ones. We visited several in England," she presently added.

"Ah yes, in England there are beautiful castles," said Winterbourne. "But Chillon here is very well worth seeing."

"Well, if Daisy feels up to it—" said Mrs. Miller in a tone that seemed to break under the burden of such conceptions. "It seems as if there's nothing she won't undertake."

"Oh I'm pretty sure she'll enjoy it!" Winterbourne declared. And he desired more and more to make it a certainty that he was to have the privilege of a *tête-à-tête* [21] with the young lady who was still strolling along in front of them and softly vocalising. "You're not disposed, madam," he enquired, "to make the so interesting excursion yourself?"

So addressed Daisy's mother looked at him an instant with a certain scared obliquity and then walked forward in silence. Then, "I guess she had better go alone," she said simply.

It gave him occasion to note that this was a very different type of maternity from that of the vigilant matrons who massed themselves in the forefront of social intercourse in the dark old city at the other end of the lake. But his meditations were interrupted by hearing his name very distinctly pronounced by Mrs. Miller's unprotected daughter. "Mr. Winterbourne!" she piped from a considerable distance.

"Mademoiselle!" said the young man.

"Don't you want to take me out in a boat?"

"At present?" he asked.

"Why of course!" she gaily returned.

"Well, Annie Miller!" exclaimed her mother.

"I beg you, madam, to let her go," he hereupon eagerly pleaded; so instantly had he been struck with the romantic side of this chance to guide through the summer starlight a skiff freighted with a fresh and beautiful young girl.

[21] Intimate conversation.

"I should n't think she'd want to," said her mother. "I should think she'd rather go indoors."

"I'm sure Mr. Winterbourne wants to *take* me," Daisy declared. "He's so awfully devoted!"

"I'll row you over to Chillon under the stars."

"I don't believe it!" Daisy laughed.

"Well!" the elder lady again gasped, as in rebuke of this freedom.

"You haven't spoken to me for half an hour," her daughter went on.

"I've been having some very pleasant conversation with your mother," Winterbourne replied.

"Oh pshaw! I want you to take me out in a boat!" Daisy went on as if nothing else had been said. They had all stopped and she had turned round and was looking at her friend. Her face wore a charming smile, her pretty eyes gleamed in the darkness, she swung her great fan about. No, he felt, it was impossible to be prettier than that.

"There are half a dozen boats moored at that landing-place," and he pointed to a range of steps that descended from the garden to the lake. "If you'll do me the honour to accept my arm we'll go and select one of them."

She stood there smiling; she threw back her head; she laughed as for the drollery of this. "I like a gentleman to be formal!"

"I assure you it's a formal offer."

"I was bound I'd make you say something," Daisy agreeably mocked.

"You see it's not very difficult," said Winterbourne. "But I'm afraid you're chaffing me."

"I think not, sir," Mrs. Miller shyly pleaded.

"Do then let me give you a row," he persisted to Daisy.

"It's quite lovely, the way you say that!" she cried in reward.

"It will be still more lovely to do it."

"Yes, it would be lovely!" But she made no movement to accompany him; she only remained an elegant image of free light irony.

"I guess you'd better find out what time it is," her mother impartially contributed.

"It's eleven o'clock, Madam," said a voice with a foreign accent out of the neighbouring darkness; and Winterbourne, turning, recognised the florid personage he had already seen in attendance. He had apparently just approached.

"Oh Eugenio," said Daisy, "I'm going out with Mr. Winterbourne in a boat!"

Eugenio bowed. "At this hour of the night, Mademoiselle?"

"I'm going with Mr. Winterbourne," she repeated with her shining smile. "I'm going this very minute."

"Do tell her she can't, Eugenio," Mrs. Miller said to the courier.

"I think you had better not go out in a boat, Mademoiselle," the man declared.

Winterbourne wished to goodness this pretty girl were not on such familiar terms with her courier; but he said nothing, and she meanwhile added to his ground. "I suppose you don't think it's proper! My!" she wailed; "Eugenio does n't think anything's proper."

"I'm nevertheless quite at your service," Winterbourne hastened to remark.

"Does Mademoiselle propose to go alone?" Eugenio asked of Mrs. Miller.

"Oh no, with this gentleman!" cried Daisy's mamma for reassurance.

"I *meant* alone with the gentleman." The courier looked for a moment at Winterbourne—the latter seemed to make out in his face a vague presumptuous intelligence as at the expense of their companions—and then solemnly and with a bow, "As Mademoiselle pleases!" he said.

But Daisy broke off at this. "Oh I hoped you'd make a fuss! I don't care to go now."

"Ah but I myself shall make a fuss if you don't go," Winterbourne declared with spirit.

"That's all I want—a little fuss!" With which she began to laugh again.

"Mr. Randolph has retired for the night!" the courier hereupon importantly announced.

"Oh Daisy, now we can go then!" cried Mrs. Miller.

Her daughter turned away from their friend, all lighted with her odd perversity. "Good-night—I hope you're disappointed or disgusted or something!"

He looked at her gravely, taking her by the hand she offered. "I'm puzzled, if you want to know!" he answered.

"Well, I hope it won't keep you awake!" she said very smartly; and, under the escort of the privileged Eugenio, the two ladies passed toward the house.

Winterbourne's eyes followed them; he was indeed quite mystified. He lingered beside the lake a quarter of an hour, baffled by the question of the girl's sudden familiarities and caprices. But the only very definite conclusion he came to was that he should enjoy deucedly "going off" with her somewhere.

Two days later he went off with her to the Castle of Chillon. He waited for her in the large hall of the hotel, where the couriers, the servants, the foreign tourists were lounging about and staring. It was n't the place he would have chosen for a tryst, but she had placidly appointed it. She came tripping downstairs, buttoning her long gloves, squeezing her folded parasol against her pretty figure, dressed exactly in the way that consorted best, to his fancy, with their adventure. He was a man of imagination and, as our ancestors used to say, of sensibility;[22] as he took in her charming air and caught from the great staircase her impatient confiding step the note of some small sweet strain of romance, not intense but clear and sweet, seemed to sound for their start. He could have believed he was *really* going "off" with her. He led her out through all the idle people assembled—they all looked at her straight and hard: she had begun to chatter as soon as she joined him. His preference had been that they should be conveyed to Chillon in a carriage, but she expressed a lively wish to go in the little steamer—there would be such a lovely breeze upon the water and they should see such lots of people. The sail was n't long, but Winterbourne's companion found time for many characteristic remarks and other demonstrations, not a few of which were, from the extremity of their candour, slightly disconcerting. To the young man himself their small excursion showed so for delightfully irregular and incongruously intimate that, even allowing for her habitual sense of freedom, he had some expectation of seeing her appear to find in it the same savour. But it must be confessed that he was in this particular rather disappointed. Miss Miller was highly animated, she was in the brightest spirits; but she was clearly not at all in a nervous flutter— as she should have been to match *his* tension; she avoided neither his eyes nor those of any one else; she neither coloured from an awkward consciousness when she looked at him nor when she saw that people were looking at herself. People continued to

[22] Sensitive responses.

look at her a great deal, and Winterbourne could at least take pleasure in his pretty companion's distinguished air. He had been privately afraid she would talk loud, laugh overmuch, and even perhaps desire to move extravagantly about the boat. But he quite forgot his fears; he sat smiling with his eyes on her face while, without stirring from her place, she delivered herself of a great number of original reflexions. It was the most charming innocent prattle he had ever heard, for, by his own experience hitherto, when young persons were so ingenuous they were less articulate and when they were so confident were more sophisticated. If he had assented to the idea that she was "common," at any rate, *was* she proving so, after all, or was he simply getting used to her commonness? Her discourse was for the most part of what immediately and superficially surrounded them, but there were moments when it threw out a longer look or took a sudden straight plunge.

"What on *earth* are you solemn about?" she suddenly demanded, fixing her agreeable eyes on her friend's.

"Am I solemn?" he asked. "I had an idea I was grinning from ear to ear."

"You look as if you were taking me to a prayer-meeting or a funeral. If that's a grin your ears are very near together."

"Should you like me to dance a hornpipe on the deck?"

"Pray do, and I'll carry round your hat. It will pay the expenses of our journey."

"I never was better pleased in my life," Winterbourne returned.

She looked at him a moment, then let it renew her amusement. "I like to make you say those things. You're a queer mixture!"

In the castle, after they had landed, nothing could exceed the light independence of her humour. She tripped about the vaulted chambers, rustled her skirts in the corkscrew staircases, flirted back with a pretty little cry and a shudder from the edge of the oubliettes[23] and turned a singularly well-shaped ear to everything Winterbourne told her about the place. But he saw she cared little for mediæval history and that the grim ghosts of Chillon loomed but faintly before her. They had the good fortune to have been able to wander without other society than that of their guide; and Winterbourne arranged with this companion that they should n't be hurried—that they should linger and pause wherever they chose. He interpreted the bargain generously—Winterbourne on his side had been generous—and ended by leaving them quite to themselves. Miss Miller's observations were marked by no logical consistency; for anything she wanted to say she was sure to find a pretext. She found a great many, in the tortuous passages and rugged embrasures of the place, for asking her young man sudden questions about himself, his family, his previous history, his tastes, his habits, his designs, and for supplying information on corresponding points in her own situation. Of her own tastes, habits and designs the charming creature was prepared to give the most definite and indeed the most favourable account.

"Well, I hope you know enough!" she exclaimed after Winterbourne had sketched for her something of the story of the unhappy Bonnivard.[24] "I never saw a man that knew so much!" The history of Bonnivard had evidently, as they say, gone into one ear and out of the other. But this easy erudition struck her none the less as wonderful,

[23] Dungeon cells set below ground level with barred openings across the top.
[24] François de Bonnivard (1465?–1570), Swiss patriot held prisoner in a castle for seven years; hero of Byron's poem.

and she was soon quite sure she wished Winterbourne would travel with them and "go round" with them: they too in that case might learn something about something. "Don't you want to come and teach Randolph?" she asked; "I guess he'd improve with a gentleman teacher." Winterbourne was certain that nothing could possibly please him so much, but that he had unfortunately other occupations. "Other occupations? I don't believe a speck of it!" she protested. "What do you mean now? You're not in business." The young man allowed that he was not in business, but he had engagements which even within a day or two would necessitate his return to Geneva. "Oh bother!" she panted, "I don't believe it!" and she began to talk about something else. But a few moments later, when he was pointing out to her the interesting design of an antique fireplace, she broke our irrelevantly: "You don't mean to say you're going back to Geneva?"

"It is a melancholy fact that I shall have to report myself there to-morrow."

She met it with a vivacity that could only flatter him. "Well, Mr. Winterbourne, I think you're horrid!"

"Oh don't say such dreadful things!" he quite sincerely pleaded—"just at the last."

"The last?" the girl cried; "I call it the very first! I've half a mind to leave you here and go straight back to the hotel alone." And for the next ten minutes she did nothing but call him horrid. Poor Winterbourne was fairly bewildered; no young lady had as yet done him the honour to be so agitated by the mention of his personal plans. His companion, after this, ceased to pay any attention to the curiosities of Chillon or the beauties of the lake; she opened fire on the special charmer in Geneva whom she appeared to have instantly taken it for granted that he was hurrying back to see. How did Miss Daisy Miller know of that agent of his fate in Geneva? Winterbourne, who denied the existence of such a person, was quite unable to discover; and he was divided between amazement of the rapidity of her induction and amusement at the directness of her criticism. She struck him afresh, in all this, as an extraordinary mixture of innocence and crudity. "Does she never allow you more than three days at a time?" Miss Miller wished ironically to know. "Does n't she give you a vacation in summer? there's no one so hard-worked but they can get leave to go off somewhere at this season. I suppose if you stay another day she'll come right after you in the boat. Do wait over till Friday and I'll go down to the landing to see her arrive!" He began at last even to feel he had been wrong to be disappointed in the temper in which his young lady had embarked. If he had missed the personal accent, the personal accent was now making its appearance. It sounded very distinctly, toward the end, in her telling him she'd stop "teasing" him if he'd promise her solemnly to come down to Rome that winter.

"That's not a difficult promise to make," he hastened to acknowledge. "My aunt has taken an apartment in Rome from January and has already asked me to come and see her."

"I don't want you to come for your aunt," said Daisy; "I want you just to come for me." And this was the only allusion he was ever to hear her make again to his invidious kinswoman. He promised her that at any rate he would certainly come, and after this she forbore from teasing. Winterbourne took a carriage and they drove back to Vevey in the dusk; the girl at his side, her animation a little spent, was now quite distractingly passive.

In the evening he mentioned to Mrs. Costello that he had spent the afternoon at Chillon with Miss Daisy Miller.

"The Americans—of the courier?" asked this lady.

"Ah happily the courier stayed at home."

"She went with you all alone?"

"All alone."

Mrs. Costello sniffed a little at her smelling-bottle. "And that," she exclaimed, "is the little abomination you wanted me to know!"

III

Winterbourne, who had returned to Geneva the day after his excursion to Chillon, went to Rome toward the end of January. His aunt had been established there a considerable time and he had received from her a couple of characteristic letters. "Those people you were so devoted to last summer at Vevey have turned up here, courier and all," she wrote. "They seem to have made several acquaintances, but the courier continues to be the most *intime.* [25] The young lady, however, is also very intimate with various third-rate Italians, with whom she rackets about in a way that makes much talk. Bring me that pretty novel of Cherbuliez's—'Paule Méré' [26]—and don't come later than the 23d."

Our friend would in the natural course of events, on arriving in Rome, have presently ascertained Mrs. Miller's address at the American banker's and gone to pay his compliments to Miss Daisy. "After what happened at Vevey I certainly think I may call upon them," he said to Mrs. Costello.

"If after what happens—at Vevey and everywhere—you desire to keep up the acquaintance, you're very welcome. Of course you're not squeamish—a man may know every one. Men are welcome to the privilege!"

"Pray what is it then that 'happens'—here for instance?" Winterbourne asked.

"Well, the girl tears about alone with her unmistakeably low foreigners. As to what happens further you must apply elsewhere for information. She has picked up half a dozen of the regular Roman fortune-hunters of the inferior sort and she takes them about to such houses as she may put *her* nose into. When she comes to a party—such a party as she can come to—she brings with her a gentleman with a good deal of manner and a wonderful moustache."

"And where's the mother?"

"I have n't the least idea. They're very dreadful people."

Winterbourne thought them over in these new lights. "They're very ignorant—very innocent only, and utterly uncivilised. Depend on it they're not 'bad.'"

"They're hopelessly vulgar," said Mrs. Costello. "Whether or no being hopelessly vulgar is being 'bad' is a question for the metaphysicians. They're bad enough to blush for, at any rate; and for this short life that's quite enough."

The news that his little friend the child of nature of the Swiss lakeside was now surrounded by half a dozen wonderful moustaches checked Winterbourne's impulse to go straightway to see her. He had perhaps not definitely flattered himself that he had made an ineffaceable impression upon her heart, but he was annoyed at hearing of a state of affairs so little in harmony with an image that had lately flitted in and

---

[25] French: "intimate."

[26] Novel by Victor Cherbuliez (1829–1899), published in 1864.

out of his own meditations; the image of a very pretty girl looking out of an old Roman window and asking herself urgently when Mr. Winterbourne would arrive. If, however, he determined to wait a little before reminding this young lady of his claim to her faithful remembrance, he called with more promptitude on two or three other friends. One of these friends was an American lady who had spent several winters at Geneva, where she had placed her children at school. She was a very accomplished woman and she lived in Via Gregoriana.[27] Winterbourne found her in a little crimson drawing-room on a third floor; the room was filled with southern sunshine. He had n't been there ten minutes when the servant, appearing in the doorway, announced complacently "Madame Mila!" This announcement was presently followed by the entrance of little Randolph Miller, who stopped in the middle of the room and stood staring at Winterbourne. An instant later his pretty sister crossed the threshold; and then, after a considerable interval, the parent of the pair slowly advanced.

"I guess I know you!" Randolph broke ground without delay.

"I'm sure you know a great many things"—and his old friend clutched him all interestedly by the arm. "How's your education coming on?"

Daisy was engaged in some pretty babble with her hostess, but when she heard Winterbourne's voice she quickly turned her head with a "Well, I declare!" which he met smiling. "I told you I should come, you know."

"Well, I did n't believe it," she answered.

"I'm much obliged to you for that," laughed the young man.

"You might have come to see me then," Daisy went on as if they had parted the week before.

"I arrived only yesterday."

"I don't believe any such thing!" the girl declared afresh.

Winterbourne turned with a protesting smile to her mother, but this lady evaded his glance and, seating herself, fixed her eyes on her son. "We've got a bigger place than this," Randolph hereupon broke out. "It's all gold on the walls."

Mrs. Miller, more of a fatalist apparently than ever, turned uneasily in her chair. "I told you if I was to bring you you'd say something!" she stated as for the benefit of such of the company as might hear it.

"I told *you!*" Randolph retorted. "I tell *you,* sir!" he added jocosely, giving Winterbourne a thump on the knee. "It *is* bigger too!"

As Daisy's conversation with her hostess still occupied her Winterbourne judged it becoming to address a few words to her mother—such as "I hope you've been well since we parted at Vevey."

Mrs. Miller now certainly looked at him—at his chin. "Not very well, sir," she answered.

"She's got the dyspepsia," said Randolph. "I've got it too. Father's got it bad. But I've got it worst!"

This proclamation, instead of embarrassing Mrs. Miller, seemed to soothe her by reconstituting the environment to which she was most accustomed. "I suffer from the liver," she amiably whined to Winterbourne. "I think it's this climate; it's less bracing than Schenectady, especially in the winter season. I don't know whether you know

[27] Avenue in Rome.

we reside at Schenectady. I was saying to Daisy that I certainly had n't found any one like Dr. Davis and I did n't believe I *would*. Oh up in Schenectady, he stands first; they think everything of Dr. Davis. He has so much to do, and yet there was nothing he would n't do for *me*. He said he never saw anything like my dyspepsia, but he was bound to get at it. I'm sure there was nothing he would n't try, and I did n't care what he did to me if he only brought me relief. He was just going to try something new, and I just longed for it, when we came right off. Mr. Miller felt as if he wanted Daisy to see Europe for herself. But I could n't help writing the other day that I supposed it was all right for Daisy, but that I did n't know as I *could* get on much longer without Dr. Davis. At Schenectady he stands at the very top; and there's a great deal of sickness there too. It affects my sleep."

Winterbourne had a good deal of pathological gossip with Dr. Davis's patient, during which Daisy chattered unremittingly to her own companion. The young man asked Mrs. Miller how she was pleased with Rome. "Well, I say I'm disappointed," she confessed. "We had heard so much about it—I suppose we had heard too much. But we could n't help that. We had been led to expect something different."

Winterbourne, however, abounded in reassurance. "Ah wait a little, and you'll grow very fond of it."

"I hate it worse and worse every day!" cried Randolph.

"You're like the infant Hannibal,"[28] his friend laughed.

"No I ain't—like any infant!" Randolph declared at a venture.

"Well, that's so—and you never *were!*" his mother concurred. "But we've seen places," she resumed, "that I'd put a long way ahead of Rome." And in reply to Winterbourne's interrogation, "There's Zürich—up there in the mountains," she instanced; "I think Zürich's real lovely, and we had n't heard half so much about it."

"The best place we've seen's the *City of Richmond!*" said Randolph.

"He means the ship," Mrs. Miller explained. "We crossed in that ship. Randolph had a good time on the *City of Richmond*."

"It's the best place *I've* struck," the child repeated. "Only it was turned the wrong way."

"Well, we've got to turn the right way sometime," said Mrs. Miller with strained but weak optimism. Winterbourne expressed the hope that her daughter at least appreciated the so various interest of Rome, and she declared with some spirit that Daisy was quite carried away. "It's on account of the society—the society's splendid. She goes round everywhere; she has made a great number of acquaintances. Of course she goes round more than I do. I must say they've all been very sweet—they've taken her right in. And then she knows a great many gentlemen. Oh she thinks there's nothing like Rome. Of course it's a great deal pleasanter for a young lady if she knows plenty of gentlemen."

By this time Daisy had turned her attention again to Winterbourne, but in quite the same free form. "I've been telling Mrs. Walker how mean you were!"

"And what's the evidence you've offered?" he asked, a trifle disconcerted, for all his superior gallantry, by her inadequate measure of the zeal of an admirer who on his way down to Rome had stopped neither at Bologna nor at Florence, simply

[28] Carthaginian general (243–183? B.C.), who bore a hatred of Rome from childhood on.

because of a certain sweet appeal to his fond fancy, not to say to his finest curiosity. He remembered how a cynical compatriot had once told him that American women —the pretty ones, and this gave a largeness to the axiom—were at once the most exacting in the world and the least endowed with a sense of indebtedness.

"Why you were awfully mean up at Vevey," Daisy said. "You would n't do most anything. You would n't stay there when I asked you."

"Dearest young lady," cried Winterbourne, with generous passion, "have I come all the way to Rome only to be riddled by your silver shafts?"

"Just hear him say that!"—and she gave an affectionate twist to a bow on her hostess's dress. "Did you ever hear anything so quaint?"

"So 'quaint,' my dear?" echoed Mrs. Walker more critically—quite in the tone of a partisan of Winterbourne.

"Well, I don't know"—and the girl continued to finger her ribbons. "Mrs. Walker, I want to tell you something."

"Say, mother-r," broke in Randolph with his rough ends to his words, "I tell you you've got to go. Eugenio'll raise something!"

"I'm not afraid of Eugenio," said Daisy with a toss of her head. "Look here, Mrs. Walker," she went on, "you know I'm coming to your party."

"I'm delighted to hear it."

"I've got a lovely dress."

"I'm very sure of that."

"But I want to ask a favour—permission to bring a friend."

"I shall be happy to see any of your friends," said Mrs. Walker, who turned with a smile to Mrs. Miller.

"Oh they're not my friends," cried that lady, squirming in shy repudiation. "It seems as if they did n't take to *me*—I never spoke to one of them!"

"It's an intimate friend of mine, Mr. Giovanelli," Daisy pursued without a tremor in her young clearness or a shadow on her shining bloom.

Mrs. Walker had a pause and gave a rapid glance at Winterbourne. "I shall be glad to see Mr. Giovanelli," she then returned.

"He's just the finest kind of Italian," Daisy pursued with the prettiest serenity. "He's a great friend of mine and the handsomest man in the world—except Mr. Winterbourne! He knows plenty of Italians, but he wants to know some Americans. It seems as if he was crazy about Americans. He's tremendously bright. He's perfectly lovely!"

It was settled that this paragon should be brought to Mrs. Walker's party, and then Mrs. Miller prepared to take her leave. "I guess we'll go right back to the hotel," she remarked with a confessed failure of the larger imagination.

"You may go back to the hotel, mother," Daisy replied, "but I'm just going to walk round."

"She's going to go it with Mr. Giovanelli," Randolph unscrupulously commented.

"I'm going to go it on the Pincio,"[29] Daisy peaceably smiled, while the way that she "condoned" these things almost melted Winterbourne's heart.

"Alone, my dear—at this hour?" Mrs. Walker asked. The afternoon was drawing to a close—it was the hour for the throng of carriages and of contemplative pedestrians. "I don't consider it's safe, Daisy," her hostess firmly asserted.

[29] Roman hill with a panoramic vista.

"Neither do I then," Mrs. Miller thus borrowed confidence to add. "You'll catch the fever as sure as you live. Remember what Dr. Davis told you!"

"Give her some of that medicine before she starts in," Randolph suggested.

The company had risen to its feet; Daisy, still showing her pretty teeth, bent over and kissed her hostess. "Mrs. Walker, you're too perfect," she simply said. "I'm not going alone; I'm going to meet a friend."

"Your friend won't keep you from catching the fever even if it *is* his own second nature," Mrs. Miller observed.

"Is it Mr. Giovanelli that's the dangerous attraction?" Mrs. Walker asked without mercy.

Winterbourne was watching the challenged girl; at this question his attention quickened. She stood there smiling and smoothing her bonnet-ribbons; she glanced at Winterbourne. Then, while she glanced and smiled, she brought out all affirmatively and without a shade of hesitation: "Mr. Giovanelli—the beautiful Giovanelli."

"My dear young friend"—and, taking her hand, Mrs. Walker turned to pleading —"don't prowl off to the Pincio at this hour to meet a beautiful Italian."

"Well, he speaks first-rate English," Mrs. Miller incoherently mentioned.

"Gracious me," Daisy piped up, "I don't want to do anything that's going to affect my health—or my character either! There's an easy way to settle it." Her eyes continued to play over Winterbourne. "The Pincio's only a hundred yards off, and if Mr. Winterbourne were as polite as he pretends he'd offer to walk right in with me!"

Winterbourne's politeness hastened to proclaim itself, and the girl gave him gracious leave to accompany her. They passed downstairs before her mother, and at the door he saw Mrs. Miller's carriage drawn up, with the ornamental courier whose acquaintance he had made at Vevey seated within. "Goodbye, Eugenio," cried Daisy; "I'm going to take a walk!" The distance from Via Gregoriana to the beautiful garden at the other end of the Pincian Hill is in fact rapidly traversed. As the day was splendid, however, and the concourse of vehicles, walkers and loungers numerous, the young Americans found their progress much delayed. This fact was highly agreeable to Winterbourne, in spite of his consciousness of his singular situation. The slow-moving, idly-gazing Roman crowd bestowed much attention on the extremely pretty young woman of English race who passed through it, with some difficulty, on his arm; and he wondered what on earth had been in Daisy's mind when she proposed to exhibit herself unattended to its appreciation. His own mission, to her sense, was apparently to consign her to the hands of Mr. Giovanelli; but, at once annoyed and gratified, he resolved that he would do no such thing.

"Why have n't you been to see me?" she meanwhile asked. "You can't get out of that."

"I've had the honour of telling you that I've only just stepped out of the train."

"You must have stayed in the train a good while after it stopped!" she derisively cried. "I suppose you were asleep. You've had time to go to see Mrs. Walker."

"I knew Mrs. Walker—" Winterbourne began to explain.

"I know where you knew her. You knew her at Geneva. She told me so. Well, you knew me at Vevey. That's just as good. So you ought to have come." She asked him no other question than this; she began to prattle about her own affairs. "We've got splendid rooms at the hotel; Eugenio says they're the best rooms in Rome. We're going to stay all winter—if we don't die of the fever; and I guess we'll stay then! It's a great deal nicer than I thought; I thought it would be fearfully quiet—in fact I was sure it would be deadly pokey. I foresaw we should be going round all the time with one of those dreadful old men who explain about the pictures and things. But we only had about a week of that, and now I'm enjoying myself. I know ever so many people, and they're all so charming. The society's extremely select. There are all kinds—English and Germans and Italians. I think I like the English best. I like their style of conversation. But there are some lovely Americans. I never saw anything so hospitable. There's something or other every day. There's not much dancing—but I must say I never thought dancing was everything. I was always fond of conversation. I guess I'll have plenty at Mrs. Walker's—her rooms are so small." When they had passed the gate of the Pincian Gardens Miss Miller began to wonder where Mr. Giovanelli might be. "We had better go straight to that place in front, where you look at the view."

Winterbourne at this took a stand. "I certainly shan't help you to find him."

"Then I shall find him without you," Daisy said with spirit.

"You certainly won't leave me!" he protested.

She burst into her familiar little laugh. "Are you afraid you'll get lost—or run over? But there's Giovanelli leaning against that tree. He's staring at the women in the carriages: did you ever see anything so cool?"

Winterbourne descried hereupon at some distance a little figure that stood with folded arms and nursing its cane. It had a handsome face, a hat artfully poised, a glass in one eye and a nosegay in its buttonhole. Daisy's friend looked at it a moment and then said: "Do you mean to speak to that thing?"

"Do I mean to speak to him? Why you don't suppose I mean to communicate by signs!"

"Pray understand then," the young man returned, "that I intend to remain with you."

Daisy stopped and looked at him without a sign of troubled consciousness, with nothing in her face but her charming eyes, her charming teeth and her happy dimples. "Well, she's a cool one!" he thought.

"I don't like the way you say that," she declared. "It's too imperious."

"I beg your pardon if I say it wrong. The main point's to give you an idea of my meaning."

The girl looked at him more gravely, but with eyes that were prettier than ever. "I've never allowed a gentleman to dictate to me or to interfere with anything I do."

"I think that's just where your mistake has come in," he retorted. "You should sometimes listen to a gentleman—the right one."

At this she began to laugh again. "I do nothing but listen to gentlemen! Tell me if Mr. Giovanelli is the right one."

The gentleman with the nosegay in his bosom had now made out our two friends and was approaching Miss Miller with obsequious rapidity. He bowed to Winterbourne as well as to the latter's compatriot; he seemed to shine, in his coxcombical way, with the desire to please and the fact of his own intelligent joy, though Winterbourne thought him not a bad-looking fellow. But he nevertheless said to Daisy: "No, he's not the right one."

She had clearly a natural turn for free introductions: she mentioned with the easiest grace the name of each of her companions to the other. She strolled forward with one of them on either hand; Mr. Giovanelli, who spoke English very cleverly—Winterbourne afterwards learned that he had practised the idiom upon a great many American heiresses—addressed her a great deal of very polite nonsense. He had the best possible manners, and the young American, who said nothing, reflected on that depth of Italian subtlety, so strangely opposed to Anglo-Saxon simplicity, which enables people to show a smoother surface in proportion as they're more acutely displeased. Giovanelli of course had counted upon something more intimate—he had not bargained for a party of three; but he kept his temper in a manner that suggested far-stretching intentions. Winterbourne flattered himself he had taken his measure. "He's anything but a gentleman," said the young American; "he is n't even a very plausible imitation of one. He's a music-master or a penny-a-liner[30] or a third-rate artist. He's awfully on his good behaviour, but damn his fine eyes!" Mr. Giovanelli had indeed great advantages; but it was deeply disgusting to Daisy's other friend that something in her should n't have instinctively discriminated against such a type. Giovanelli chattered and jested and made himself agreeable according to his honest Roman lights. It was true that if he was an imitation the imitation was studied. "Nevertheless," Winterbourne said to himself, "a nice girl ought to know!" And then he came back to the dreadful question of whether this *was* in fact a nice girl. Would a nice girl—even allowing for her being a little American flirt—make a rendezvous with a presumbably low-lived foreigner? The rendezvous in this case indeed had been in broad daylight and in the most crowded corner of Rome; but was n't it possible to regard the choice of these very circumstances as a proof more of vulgarity than of anything else? Singular though it may seem, Winterbourne was vexed that the girl, in joining her *amoroso,*[31] should n't appear more impatient of his own company, and he was vexed precisely because of his inclination. It was impossible to regard her as a wholly unspotted flower—she lacked a certain indispensable fineness; and it would therefore much simplify the situation to be able to treat her as the subject of one of the visitations known to romancers as "lawless passions." That she should seem to wish to get rid of him would have helped him to think more lightly of her, just as to be able to think more lightly of her would have made her less perplexing. Daisy at any rate continued on this occasion to present herself as an inscrutable combination of audacity and innocence.

She had been walking some quarter of an hour, attended by her two cavaliers and responding in a tone of very childish gaiety, as it after all struck one of them, to the pretty speeches of the other, when a carriage that had detached itself from the revolving train drew up beside the path. At the same moment Winterbourne noticed that his friend Mrs. Walker—the lady whose house he had lately left—was seated in the vehicle and was beckoning to him. Leaving Miss Miller's side, he hastened to obey her summons—and all to find her flushed, excited, scandalised. "It's really too dreadful"—she earnestly appealed to him. "That crazy girl must n't do this sort of thing. She must n't walk here with you two men. Fifty people have remarked her."

Winterbourne—suddenly and rather oddly rubbed the wrong way by this—raised his grave eyebrows. "I think it's a pity to make too much fuss about it."

"It's a pity to let the girl ruin herself!"

---

[30] Low-paid hack writer.   [31] Italian: "lover"; "admirer."

"She's very innocent," he reasoned in his own troubled interest.

"She's very reckless," cried Mrs. Walker, "and goodness knows how far—left to itself—it may go. Did you ever," she proceeded to enquire, "see anything so blatantly imbecile as the mother? After you had all left me just now I couldn't sit still for thinking of it. It seemed too pitiful not even to attempt to save them. I ordered the carriage and put on my bonnet and came here as quickly as possible. Thank heaven I've found you!"

"What do you propose to do with us?" Winterbourne uncomfortably smiled.

"To ask her to get in, to drive her about here for half an hour—so that the world may see she's not running absolutely wild—and then take her safely home."

"I don't think it's a very happy thought," he said after reflexion, "but you're at liberty to try."

Mrs. Walker accordingly tried. The young man went in pursuit of their young lady who had simply nodded and smiled, from her distance, at her recent patroness in the carriage and then had gone her way with her own companion. On learning, in the event, that Mrs. Walker had followed her, she retraced her steps, however, with a perfect good grace and with Mr. Giovanelli at her side. She professed herself "enchanted" to have a chance to present this gentleman to her good friend, and immediately achieved the introduction; declaring with it, and as if it were of as little importance, that she had never in her life seen anything so lovely as that lady's carriage-rug.

"I'm glad you admire it," said her poor pursuer, smiling sweetly. "Will you get in and let me put it over you?"

"Oh no, thank you!"—Daisy knew her mind. "I'll admire it ever so much more as I see you driving round with it."

"Do get in and drive round *with* me," Mrs. Walker pleaded.

"That would be charming, but it's so fascinating just as I am!"—with which the girl radiantly took in the gentlemen on either side of her.

"It may be fascinating, dear child, but it's not the custom here," urged the lady of the victoria,[32] leaning forward in this vehicle with her hands devoutly clasped.

"Well, it ought to be then!" Daisy imperturbably laughed. "If I didn't walk I'd expire."

"You should walk with your mother, dear," cried Mrs. Walker with a loss of patience.

"With my mother dear?" the girl amusedly echoed. Winterbourne saw she scented interference. "My mother never walked ten steps in her life. And then, you know," she blandly added, "I'm more than five years old."

"You're old enough to be more reasonable. You're old enough, dear Miss Miller, to be talked about."

Daisy wondered to extravagance. "Talked about? What do you mean?"

"Come into my carriage and I'll tell you."

Daisy turned shining eyes again from one of the gentlemen beside her to the other. Mr. Giovanelli was bowing to and fro, rubbing down his gloves and laughing irresponsibly; Winterbourne thought the scene the most unpleasant possible. "I don't

[32] Horse-drawn carriage.

think I want to know what you mean," the girl presently said. "I don't think I should like it."

Winterbourne only wished Mrs. Walker would tuck up her carriage-rug and drive away; but this lady, as she afterwards told him, did n't feel she could "rest there." "Should you prefer being thought a very reckless girl?" she accordingly asked.

"Gracious me!" exclaimed Daisy. She looked again at Mr. Giovanelli, then she turned to her other companion. There was a small pink flush in her cheek; she was tremendously pretty. "Does Mr. Winterbourne think," she put to him with a wonderful bright intensity of appeal, "that—to save my reputation—I ought to get into the carriage?"

It really embarrassed him; for an instant he cast about—so strange was it to hear her speak that way of her "reputation." But he himself in fact had to speak in accordance with gallantry. The finest gallantry here was surely just to tell her the truth; and the truth, for our young man, as the few indications I have been able to give have made him known to the reader, was that his charming friend should listen to the voice of civilised society. He took in again her exquisite prettiness and then said the more distinctly: "I think you should get into the carriage."

Daisy gave the rein to her amusement. "I never heard anything so stiff! If this is improper, Mrs. Walker," she pursued, "then I'm *all* improper, and you had better give me right up. Good-bye; I hope you'll have a lovely ride!"—and with Mr. Giovanelli, who made a triumphantly obsequious salute, she turned away.

Mrs. Walker sat looking after her, and there were tears in Mrs. Walker's eyes. "Get in here, sir," she said to Winterbourne, indicating the place beside her. The young man answered that he felt bound to accompany Miss Miller; whereupon the lady of the victoria declared that if he refused her this favour she would never speak to him again. She was evidently wound up. He accordingly hastened to overtake Daisy and her more faithful ally, and, offering her his hand, told her that Mrs. Walker had made a stringent claim on his presence. He had expected her to answer with something rather free, something still more significant of the perversity from which the voice of society, through the lips of their distressed friend, had so earnestly endeavoured to dissuade her. But she only let her hand slip, as she scarce looked at him, through his slightly awkward grasp; while Mr. Giovanelli, to make it worse, bade him farewell with too emphatic a flourish of the hat.

Winterbourne was not in the best possible humour as he took his seat beside the author of his sacrifice. "That was not clever of you," he said candidly, as the vehicle mingled again with the throng of carriages.

"In such a case," his companion answered, "I don't want to be clever—I only want to be *true!*"

"Well, your truth has only offended the strange little creature—it has only put her off."

"It has happened very well"—Mrs. Walker accepted her work. "If she's so perfectly determined to compromise herself the sooner one knows it the better—one can act accordingly."

"I suspect she meant no great harm, you know," Winterbourne maturely opined.

"So I thought a month ago. But she has been going too far."

"What has she been doing?"

"Everything that's not done here. Flirting with any man she can pick up; sitting in corners with mysterious Italians; dancing all the evening with the same partners; receiving visits at eleven o'clock at night. Her mother melts away when the visitors come."

"But her brother," laughed Winterbourne, "sits up till two in the morning."

"He must be edified by what he sees. I'm told that at their hotel every one's talking about her and that a smile goes round among the servants when a gentleman comes and asks for Miss Miller."

"Ah we need n't mind the servants!" Winterbourne compassionately signified. "The poor girl's only fault," he presently added, "is her complete lack of education."

"She's naturally indelicate," Mrs. Walker, on her side, reasoned. "Take that example this morning. How long had you known her at Vevey?"

"A couple of days."

"Imagine then the taste of her making it a personal matter that you should have left the place!"

He agreed that taste was n't the strong point of the Millers—after which he was silent for some moments; but only at last to add: "I suspect, Mrs. Walker, that you and I have lived too long at Geneva!" And he further noted that he should be glad to learn with what particular design she had made him enter her carriage.

"I wanted to enjoin on you the importance of your ceasing your relations with Miss Miller; that of your not appearing to flirt with her; that of your giving her no further opportunity to expose herself; that of your in short letting her alone."

"I'm afraid I can't do anything quite so enlightened as *that*," he returned. "I like her awfully, you know."

"All the more reason you should n't help her to make a scandal."

"Well, there shall be nothing scandalous in my attentions to her," he was willing to promise.

"There certainly will be in the way she takes them. But I've said what I had on my conscience," Mrs. Walker pursued. "If you wish to rejoin the young lady I'll put you down. Here, by the way, you have a chance."

The carriage was engaged in that part of the Pincian drive which overhangs the wall of Rome and overlooks the beautiful Villa Borghese.[33] It is bordered by a large parapet, near which are several seats. One of these, at a distance, was occupied by a gentleman and a lady, toward whom Mrs. Walker gave a toss of her head. At the same moment these persons rose and walked to the parapet. Winterbourne had asked the coachman to stop; he now descended from the carriage. His companion looked at him a moment in silence and then, while he raised his hat, drove majestically away. He stood where he had alighted; he had turned his eyes toward Daisy and her cavalier. They evidently saw no one; they were too deeply occupied with each other. When they reached the low garden-wall they remained a little looking off at the great flat-topped pine-clusters of Villa Borghese; then the girl's attendant admirer seated himself familiarly on the broad ledge of the wall. The western sun in the opposite sky sent out a brilliant shaft through a couple of cloud-bars; whereupon the gallant Giovanelli took her parasol out of her hands and opened it. She came a little nearer

[33] Former summer palace of the Borghese family and now a museum, located in a public park.

and he held the parasol over her; then, still holding it, he let it so rest on her shoulder that both of their heads were hidden from Winterbourne. This young man stayed but a moment longer; then he began to walk. But he walked—not toward the couple united beneath the parasol, rather toward the residence of his aunt Mrs. Costello.

IV

He flattered himself on the following day that there was no smiling among the servants when he at least asked for Mrs. Miller at her hotel. This lady and her daughter, however, were not at home; and on the next day after, repeating his visit, Winterbourne again was met by a denial. Mrs. Walker's party took place on the evening of the third day, and in spite of the final reserves that had marked his last interview with that social critic our young man was among the guests. Mrs. Walker was one of those pilgrims from the younger world who, while in contact with the elder, make a point, in their own phrase, of studying European society; and she had on this occasion collected several specimens of diversely-born humanity to serve, as might be, for text-books. When Winterbourne arrived the little person he desired most to find was n't there; but in a few moments he saw Mrs. Miller come in alone, very shyly and ruefully. This lady's hair, above the dead waste of her temples, was more frizzled than ever. As she approached their hostess Winterbourne also drew near.

"You see I've come all alone," said Daisy's unsupported parent. "I'm so frightened I don't know what to do; it's the first time I've ever been to a party alone—especially in this country. I wanted to bring Randolph or Eugenio or some one, but Daisy just pushed me off by myself. I ain't used to going round alone."

"And does n't your daughter intend to favour us with her society?" Mrs. Walker impressively enquired.

"Well, Daisy's all dressed," Mrs. Miller testified with that accent of the dispassionate, if not of the philosophic, historian with which she always recorded the current incidents of her daughter's career. "She got dressed on purpose before dinner. But she has a friend of hers there; that gentleman—the handsomest of the Italians—that she wanted to bring. They've got going at the piano—it seems as if they could n't leave off. Mr. Giovanelli does sing splendidly. But I guess they'll come before very long," Mrs. Miller hopefully concluded.

"I'm sorry she should come—in that particular way," Mrs. Walker permitted herself to observe.

"Well, I told her there was no use in her getting dressed before dinner if she was going to wait three hours," returned Daisy's mamma. "I did n't see the use of her putting on such a dress as that to sit round with Mr. Giovanelli."

"This is most horrible!" said Mrs. Walker, turning away and addressing herself to Winterbourne. *"Elle s'affiche, la malheureuse."* [34] It's her revenge for my having ventured to remonstrate with her. When she comes I shan't speak to her."

Daisy came after eleven o'clock, but she was n't, on such an occasion, a young lady to wait to be spoken to. She rustled forward in radiant loveliness, smiling and

---

[34] French: "She's making a spectacle of herself, poor girl."

chattering, carrying a large bouquet and attended by Mr. Giovanelli. Every one stopped talking and turned and looked at her while she floated up to Mrs. Walker. "I'm afraid you thought I never was coming, so I sent mother off to tell you. I wanted to make Mr. Giovanelli practise some things before he came; you know he sings beautifully, and I want you to ask him to sing. This is Mr. Giovanelli; you know I introduced him to you; he's got the most lovely voice and he knows the most charming set of songs. I made him go over them this evening on purpose; we had the greatest time at the hotel." Of all this Daisy delivered herself with the sweetest brightest loudest confidence, looking now at her hostess and now at all the room, while she gave a series of little pats, round her very white shoulders, to the edges of her dress. "Is there any one I know?" she as undiscourageably asked.

"I think every one knows you!" said Mrs. Walker as with a grand intention; and she gave a very cursory greeting to Mr. Giovanelli. This gentleman bore himself gallantly; he smiled and bowed and showed his white teeth, he curled his moustaches and rolled his eyes and performed all the proper functions of a handsome Italian at an evening party. He sang, very prettily, half a dozen songs, though Mrs. Walker afterwards declared that she had been quite unable to find out who asked him. It was apparently not Daisy who had set him in motion—this young lady being seated a distance from the piano and though she had publicly, as it were, professed herself his musical patroness or guarantor, giving herself to gay and audible discourse while he warbled.

"It's a pity these rooms are so small; we can't dance," she remarked to Winterbourne as if she had seen him five minutes before.

"I'm not sorry we can't dance," he candidly returned. "I'm incapable of a step."

"Of course you're incapable of a step," the girl assented. "I should think your legs *would* be stiff cooped in there so much of the time in that victoria."

"Well, they were very restless three days ago," he amicably laughed; "all they really wanted was to dance attendance on you."

"Oh my other friend—my friend in need—stuck to me; he seems more at one with his limbs than you are—I'll say that for him. But did you ever hear anything so cool," Daisy demanded, "as Mrs. Walker's wanting me to get into her carriage and drop poor Mr. Giovanelli, and under the pretext that it was proper? People have different ideas! It would have been most unkind; he had been talking about that walk for ten days."

"He should n't have talked about it at all," Winterbourne decided to make answer on this: "he would never have proposed to a young lady of this country to walk about the streets of Rome with him."

"About the streets?" she cried with her pretty stare. "Where then would he have proposed to her to walk? The Pincio ain't the streets either, I guess; and I besides, thank goodness, am not a young lady of this country. The young ladies of this country have a dreadfully pokey time of it, by what I can discover; I don't see why I should change my habits for *such* stupids."

"I'm afraid your habits are those of a ruthless flirt," said Winterbourne with studied severity.

"Of course they are!"—and she hoped, evidently, by the manner of it, to take his breath away. "I'm a fearful frightful flirt! Did you ever hear of a nice girl that was n't? But I suppose you'll tell me now I'm not a nice girl."

He remained grave indeed under the shock of her cynical profession. "You're a very nice girl, but I wish you'd flirt with me, and me only."

"Ah thank you, thank you very much: you're the last man I should think of flirting with. As I've had the pleasure of informing you, you're too stiff."

"You say that too often," he resentfully remarked.

Daisy gave a delighted laugh. "If I could have the sweet hope of making you angry I'd say it again."

"Don't do that—when I'm angry I'm stiffer than ever. But if you won't flirt with me do cease at least to flirt with your friend at the piano. They don't," he declared as in full sympathy with "them," "understand that sort of thing here."

"I thought they understood nothing else!" Daisy cried with startling world-knowledge.

"Not in young unmarried women."

"It seems to me much more proper in young unmarried than in old married ones," she retorted.

"Well," said Winterbourne, "when you deal with natives you must go by the custom of the country. American flirting is a purely American silliness; it has—in its ineptitude of innocence—no place in *this* system. So when you show yourself in public with Mr. Giovanelli and without your mother—"

"Gracious, poor mother!"—and she made it beautifully unspeakable.

Winterbourne had a touched sense for this, but it did n't alter his attitude. "Though *you* may be flirting Mr. Giovanelli is n't—he means something else."

"He is n't preaching at any rate," she returned. "And if you want very much to know, we're neither of us flirting—not a little speck. We're too good friends for that. We're real intimate friends."

He was to continue to find her thus at moments inimitable. "Ah," he then judged, "if you're in love with each other it's another affair altogether!"

She had allowed him up to this point to speak so frankly that he had no thought of shocking her by the force of his logic; yet she now none the less immediately rose, blushing visibly and leaving him mentally to exclaim that the name of little American flirts was incoherence. "Mr. Giovanelli at least," she answered, sparing but a single small queer glance for it, a queerer small glance, he felt, than he had ever yet had from her—"Mr. Giovanelli never says to me such very disagreeable things."

It had an effect on him—he stood staring. The subject of their contention had finished singing; he left the piano, and his recognition of what—a little awkwardly —did n't take place in celebration of this might nevertheless have been an acclaimed operatic tenor's series of repeated ducks before the curtain. So he bowed himself over to Daisy. "Won't you come to the other room and have some tea?" he asked—offering Mrs. Walker's slightly thin refreshment as he might have done all the kingdoms of the earth.

Daisy at last turned on Winterbourne a more natural and calculable light. He was but the more muddled by it, however, since so inconsequent a smile made nothing clear—it seemed at the most to prove in her a sweetness and softness that reverted instinctively to the pardon of offences. "It has never occurred to Mr. Winterbourne to offer me any tea," she said with her finest little intention of torment and triumph.

"I've offered you excellent advice," the young man permitted himself to growl.

"I prefer weak tea!" cried Daisy, and she went off with the brilliant Giovanelli. She sat with him in the adjoining room, in the embrasure of the window, for the rest of the evening. There was an interesting performance at the piano, but neither of these conversers gave heed to it. When Daisy came to take leave of Mrs. Walker this lady conscientiously repaired the weakness of which she had been guilty at the moment of the girl's arrival—she turned her back straight on Miss Miller and left her to depart with what grace she might. Winterbourne happened to be near the door; he saw it all. Daisy turned very pale and looked at her mother, but Mrs. Miller was humbly unconscious of any rupture of any law or of any deviation from any custom. She appeared indeed to have felt an incongruous impulse to draw attention to her own striking conformity. "Good-night, Mrs. Walker," she said; "we've had a beautiful evening. You see if I let Daisy come to parties without me I don't want her to go away without me." Daisy turned away, looking with a small white prettiness, a blighted grace, at the circle near the door: Winterbourne saw that for the first moment she was too much shocked and puzzled even for indignation. He on his side was greatly touched.

"That was very cruel," he promptly remarked to Mrs. Walker.

But this lady's face was also as a stone. "She never enters my drawing-room again."

Since Winterbourne then, hereupon, was not to meet her in Mrs. Walker's drawing-room he went as often as possible to Mrs. Miller's hotel. The ladies were rarely at home, but when he found them the devoted Giovanelli was always present. Very often the glossy little Roman, serene in success, but not unduly presumptuous, occupied with Daisy alone the florid salon enjoyed by Eugenio's care, Mrs. Miller being apparently ever of the opinion that discretion is the better part of solicitude. Winterbourne noted, at first with surprise, that Daisy on these occasions was neither embarrassed nor annoyed by his own entrance; but he presently began to feel that she had no more surprises for him and that he really liked, after all, not making out what she was "up to." She showed no displeasure for the interruption of her tête-à-tête with Giovanelli; she could chatter as freshly and freely with two gentlemen as with one, and this easy flow had ever the same anomaly for her earlier friend that it was so free without availing itself of its freedom. Winterbourne reflected that if she was seriously interested in the Italian it was odd she should n't take more trouble to preserve the sanctity of their interviews, and he liked her the better for her innocent-looking indifference and her inexhaustible gaiety. He could hardly have said why, but she struck him as a young person not formed for a troublesome jealousy. Smile at such a betrayal though the reader may, it was a fact with regard to the women who had hitherto interested him that, given certain contingencies, Winterbourne could see himself afraid—literally afraid—of these ladies. It pleased him to believe that even were twenty other things different and Daisy should love him and he should know it and like it, he would still never be afraid of Daisy. It must be added that this conviction was not altogether flattering to her: it represented that she was nothing every way if not light.

But she was evidently very much interested in Giovanelli. She looked at him whenever he spoke; she was perpetually telling him to do this and to do that; she was constantly chaffing and abusing him. She appeared completely to have forgotten that her other friend had said anything to displease her at Mrs. Walker's entertainment. One Sunday afternoon, having gone to Saint Peter's with his aunt, Winterbourne became aware that the young woman held in horror by that lady was strolling about the great church under escort of her coxcomb of the Corso.[35] It amused him, after a debate, to point out the exemplary pair—even at the cost, as it proved, of Mrs. Costello's saying when she had taken them in through her eye-glass: "That's what makes you so pensive in these days, eh?"

"I had n't the least idea I was pensive," he pleaded.

"You're very much preoccupied; you're always thinking of something."

"And what is it," he asked, "that you accuse me of thinking of?"

"Of that young lady's, Miss Baker's, Miss Chandler's—what's her name?—Miss Miller's intrigue with that little barber's block."

"Do you call it an intrigue," he asked—"an affair that goes on with such peculiar publicity?"

"That's their folly," said Mrs. Costello, "it's not their merit."

"No," he insisted with a hint perhaps of the preoccupation to which his aunt had alluded—"I don't believe there's anything to be called an intrigue."

"Well"—and Mrs. Costello dropped her glass—"I've heard a dozen people speak of it: they say she's quite carried away by him."

"They're certainly as thick as thieves," our embarrassed young man allowed.

Mrs. Costello came back to them, however, after a little; and Winterbourne recognized in this a further illustration—than that supplied by his own condition—of the spell projected by the case. "He's certainly very handsome. One easily sees how it is. She thinks him the most elegant man in the world, the finest gentleman possible. She has never seen anything like him—he's better even than the courier. It was the courier probably who introduced him, and if he succeeds in marrying the young lady the courier will come in for a magnificent commission."

"I don't believe she thinks of marrying him," Winterbourne reasoned, "and I don't believe he hopes to marry her."

"You may be very sure she thinks of nothing at all. She romps on from day to day, from hour to hour, as they did in the Golden Age. I can imagine nothing more vulgar," said Mrs. Costello, whose figure of speech scarcely went on all fours. "And at the same time," she added, "depend upon it she may tell you any moment that she is 'engaged.'"

"I think that's more than Giovanelli really expects," said Winterbourne.

"And who is Giovanelli?"

"The shiny— but, to do him justice, not greasy—little Roman. I've asked questions about him and learned something. He's apparently a perfectly respectable little man. I believe he's in a small way a *cavaliere avvocato.*[36] But he does n't move in what are called the first circles. I think it really not absolutely impossible the courier introduced him. He's evidently immensely charmed with Miss Miller. If she thinks him the finest gentleman in the world, he, on his side, has never found himself in personal contact with such splendour, such opulence, such personal daintiness, as this young lady's. And then she must seem to him wonderfully pretty and interesting. Yes, he can't really hope to pull it off. That must appear to him too impossible a piece of luck. He has nothing but his handsome face to offer, and there's a substantial, a possibly explosive Mr. Miller in that mysterious land of dollars and six-shooters. Giovanelli's but too

[35] Roman street.   [36] Italian: "lawyer from the upper classes."

conscious that he has n't a title to offer. If he were only a count or a *marchese!*[37] What on earth can he make of the way they've taken him up?"

"He accounts for it by his handsome face and thinks Miss Miller a young lady *qui se passe ses fantaisies!*"[38]

"It's very true," Winterbourne pursued, "that Daisy and her mamma have n't yet risen to that stage of—what shall I call it—of culture, at which the idea of catching a count or a *marchese* begins. I believe them intellectually incapable of that conception."

"Ah but the *cavaliere avvocato* does n't believe them!" cried Mrs. Costello.

Of the observation excited by Daisy's "intrigue" Winterbourne gathered that day at Saint Peter's sufficient evidence. A dozen of the American colonists in Rome came to talk with his relative, who sat on a small portable stool at the base of one of the great pilasters. The vesper-service was going forward in splendid chants and organ-tones in the adjacent choir, and meanwhile, between Mrs. Costello and her friends, much was said about poor little Miss Miller's going really "too far." Winterbourne was not pleased with what he heard; but when, coming out upon the great steps of the church, he saw Daisy, who had emerged before him, get into an open cab with her accomplice and roll away through the cynical streets of Rome, the measure of her course struck him as simply there to take. He felt very sorry for her—not exactly that he believed she had completely lost her wits, but because it was painful to see so much that was pretty and undefended and natural sink so low in human estimation. He made an attempt after this to give a hint to Mrs. Miller. He met one day in the Corso a friend—a tourist like himself—who had just come out of the Doria Palace, where he had been walking through the beautiful gallery. His friend "went on" for some moments about the great portrait of Innocent X, by Velasquez,[39] suspended in one of the cabinets of the palace; and then said: "And in the same cabinet, by the way, I enjoyed sight of an image of a different kind; that little American who's so much more a work of nature than of art and whom you pointed out to me last week." In answer to Winterbourne's enquiries his friend narrated that the little American—prettier now than ever—was seated with a companion in the secluded nook in which the papal presence is enshrined.

"All alone?" the young man heard himself disingenuously ask.

"Alone with a little Italian who sports in his button-hole a stack of flowers. The girl's a charming beauty, but I thought I understood from you the other day that she's a young lady *du meilleur monde.*"[40]

"So she is!" said Winterbourne; and having assured himself that his informant had seen the interesting pair but ten minutes before, he jumped into a cab and went to call on Mrs. Miller. She was at home, but she apologised for receiving him in Daisy's absence.

"She's gone out somewhere with Mr. Giovanelli. She's always going round with Mr. Giovanelli."

"I've noticed they're intimate indeed," Winterbourne concurred.

[37] Marquis; one of noble rank.
[38] French: "who submits to her caprices."
[39] Diego Rodriguez de Silva y Velàsquez

(1599–1660), Spanish painter of the portrait of Pope Innocent X.
[40] French: "of the best society."

"Oh it seems as if they could n't live without each other!" said Mrs. Miller. "Well, he's a real gentleman anyhow. I guess I have the joke on Daisy—that she *must* be engaged!"

"And how does your daughter *take* the joke?"

"Oh she just says she ain't. But she might as *well* be!" this philosophic parent resumed. "She goes on as if she was. But I've made Mr. Giovanelli promise to tell me if Daisy don't. I'd want to write to Mr. Miller about it—would n't you?"

Winterbourne replied that he certainly should; and the state of mind of Daisy's mamma struck him as so unprecedented in the annals of parental vigilance that he recoiled before the attempt to educate at a single interview either her conscience or her wit.

After this Daisy was never at home and he ceased to meet her at the houses of their common acquaintance, because, as he perceived, these shrewd people had quite made up their minds as to the length she must have gone. They ceased to invite her, intimating that they wished to make, and make strongly, for the benefit of observant Europeans, the point that though Miss Daisy Miller was a pretty American girl all right, her behaviour was n't pretty at all—was in fact regarded by her compatriots as quite monstrous. Winterbourne wondered how she felt about all the cold shoulders that were turned upon her, and sometimes found himself suspecting with impatience that she simply did n't feel and did n't know. He set her down as hopelessly childish and shallow, as such mere giddiness and ignorance incarnate as was powerless either to heed or to suffer. Then at other moments he could n't doubt that she carried about in her elegant and irresponsible little organism a defiant, passionate, perfectly obser-vant consciousness of the impression she produced. He asked himself whether the defiance would come from the consciousness of innocence or from her being essen-tially a young person of the reckless class. Then it had to be admitted, he felt, that holding fast to a belief in her "innocence" was more and more but a matter of gallantry too fine-spun for use. As I have already had occasion to relate, he was reduced without pleasure to this chopping of logic and vexed at his poor fallibility, his want of instinctive certitude as to how far her extravagance was generic and national and how far it was crudely personal. Whatever it was he had helplessly missed her, and now it was too late. She was "carried away" by Mr. Giovanelli.

A few days after his brief interview with her mother he came across her at that supreme seat of flowering desolation known as the Palace of the Cæsars.[41] The early Roman spring had filled the air with bloom and perfume, and the rugged surface of the Palatine was muffled with tender verdure. Daisy moved at her ease over the great mounds of ruin that are embanked with mossy marble and paved with monumental inscriptions. It seemed to him he had never known Rome so lovely as just then. He looked off at the enchanting harmony of line and colour that remotely encircles the city—he inhaled the softly humid odours and felt the freshness of the year and the antiquity of the place reaffirm themselves in deep interfusion. It struck him also that Daisy had never showed to the eye for so utterly charming; but this had been his conviction on every occasion of their meeting. Giovanelli was of course at her side,

[41] Roman palace, now in ruins, on the Palatine Hill.

and Giovanelli too glowed as never before with something of the glory of his race.

"Well," she broke out upon the friend it would have been such mockery to designate as the latter's rival, "I should think you'd be quite lonesome!"

"Lonesome?" Winterbourne resignedly echoed.

"You're always going round by yourself. Can't you get any one to walk with you?"

"I'm not so fortunate," he answered, "as your gallant companion."

Giovanelli had from the first treated him with distinguished politeness; he listened with a deferential air to his remarks; he laughed punctiliously at his pleasantries; he attached such importance as he could find terms for to Miss Miller's cold compatriot. He carried himself in no degree like a jealous wooer; he had obviously a great deal of tact; he had no objection to any one's expecting a little humility of him. It even struck Winterbourne that he almost yearned at times for some private communication in the interest of his character for common sense; a chance to remark to him as another intelligent man that, bless him, *he* knew how extraordinary was their young lady and didn't flatter himself with confident—at least *too* confident and too delusive—hopes of matrimony and dollars. On this occasion he strolled away from his charming charge to pluck a sprig of almond-blossom which he carefully arranged in his button-hole.

"I know why you say that," Daisy meanwhile observed. "Because you think I go round too much with *him!*" And she nodded at her discreet attendant.

"Every one thinks so—if you care to know," was all Winterbourne found to reply.

"Of course I care to know!"—she made this point with much expression. "But I don't believe a word of it. They're only pretending to be shocked. They don't really care a straw what I do. Besides, I don't go round so much."

"I think you'll find they do care. They'll show it—disagreeably," he took on himself to state.

Daisy weighed the importance of that idea. "How—disagreeably?"

"Haven't you noticed anything?" he compassionately asked.

"I've noticed *you*. But I noticed you've no more 'give' than a ramrod the first time ever I saw you."

"You'll find at least that I've more 'give' than several others," he patiently smiled.

"How shall I find it?"

"By going to see the others."

"What will they do to me?"

"They'll show you the cold shoulder. Do you know what that means?"

Daisy was looking at him intently; she began to colour. "Do you mean as Mrs. Walker did the other night?"

"Exactly as Mrs. Walker did the other night."

She looked away at Giovanelli, still titivating with his almond-blossom. Then with her attention again on the important subject: "I should n't think you'd let people be so unkind!"

"How can I help it?"

"I should think you'd want to say something."

"I do want to say something"—and Winterbourne paused a moment. "I want to say that your mother tells me she believes you engaged."

"Well, I guess she does," said Daisy very simply.

The young man began to laugh. "And does Randolph believe it?"

"I guess Randolph does n't believe anything." This testimony to Randolph's scepticism excited Winterbourne to further mirth, and he noticed that Giovanelli was coming back to them. Daisy, observing it as well, addressed herself again to her countryman. "Since you've mentioned it," she said, "I *am* engaged." He looked at her hard—he had stopped laughing. "You don't believe it!" she added.

He asked himself, and it was for a moment like testing a heart-beat; after which, "Yes, I believe it!" he said.

"Oh no, you don't," she answered. "But *if* you possibly do," she still more perversely pursued—"well, I ain't!"

Miss Miller and her constant guide were on their way to the gate of the enclosure, so that Winterbourne, who had but lately entered, presently took leave of them. A week later on he went to dine at a beautiful villa on the Cælian Hill, and, on arriving, dismissed his hired vehicle. The evening was perfect, and he promised himself the satisfaction of walking home beneath the Arch of Constantine and past the vaguely-lighted monuments of the Forum.[42] Above was a moon half-developed, whose radiance was not brilliant but veiled in a thin cloud-curtain that seemed to diffuse and equalise it. When on his return from the villa at eleven o'clock he approached the dusky circle of the Colosseum the sense of the romantic in him easily suggested that the interior, in such an atmosphere, would well repay a glance. He turned aside and walked to one of the empty arches, near which, as he observed, an open carriage—one of the little Roman street-cabs—was stationed. Then he passed in among the cavernous shadows of the great structure and emerged upon the clear and silent arena. The place had never seemed to him more impressive. One half of the gigantic circus was in deep shade while the other slept in the luminous dusk. As he stood there he began to murmur Byron's famous lines out of "Manfred";[43] but before he had finished his quotation he remembered that if nocturnal meditation thereabouts was the fruit of a rich literary culture it was none the less deprecated by medical science. The air of other ages surrounded one; but the air of other ages, coldly analysed, was no better than a villainous miasma. Winterbourne sought, however, toward the middle of the arena, a further reach of vision, intending the next moment a hasty retreat. The great cross in the centre was almost obscured; only as he drew near did he make it out distinctly. He thus also distinguished two persons stationed on the low steps that formed its base. One of these was a woman seated; her companion hovered before her.

Presently the sound of the woman's voice came to him distinctly in the warm night-air. "Well, he looks at us as one of the old lions or tigers may have looked at the Christian martyrs!" These words were winged with their accent, so that they fluttered and settled about him in the darkness like vague white doves. It was Miss Daisy Miller who had released them for flight.

"Let us hope he's not very hungry"—the bland Giovanelli fell in with her humour. "He'll have to take *me* first; you'll serve for dessert."

Winterbourne felt himself pulled up with final horror now—and, it must be added, with final relief. It was as if a sudden clearance had taken place in the ambiguity of the poor girl's appearances and the whole riddle of her contradictions had grown easy

---

[42] Remnants of ancient constructions from the time of imperial Rome.

[43] Lord Byron's verse drama of 1817.

to read. She was a young lady about the *shades* of whose perversity a foolish puzzled gentleman need no longer trouble his head or his heart. That once questionable quantity *had* no shades—it was a mere black little blot. He stood there looking at her, looking at her companion too, and not reflecting that though he saw them vaguely he himself must have been more brightly presented. He felt angry at all his shiftings of view—he felt ashamed of all his tender little scruples and all his witless little mercies. He was about to advance again, and then again checked himself; not from the fear of doing her injustice, but from a sense of the danger of showing undue exhilaration for this disburdenment of cautious criticism. He turned away toward the entrance of the place; but as he did so he heard Daisy speak again.

"Why it was Mr. Winterbourne! He saw me and he cuts me dead!"

What a clever little reprobate she was, he was amply able to reflect at this, and how smartly she feigned, how promptly she sought to play off on him, a surprised and injured innocence! But nothing would induce him to cut her either "dead" or to within any measurable distance even of the famous "inch" of her life. He came forward again and went toward the great cross. Daisy had got up and Giovanelli lifted his hat. Winterbourne had now begun to think simply of the madness, on the ground of exposure and infection, of a frail young creature's lounging away such hours in a nest of malaria. What if she *were* the most plausible of little reprobates? That was no reason for her dying of the *perniciosa*. [44] "How long have you been 'fooling round' here?" he asked with conscious roughness.

Daisy, lovely in the sinister silver radiance, appraised him a moment, roughness and all. "Well, I guess all the evening." She answered with spirit and, he could see even then, with exaggeration. "I never saw anything so quaint."

"I'm afraid," he returned, "you'll not think a bad attack of Roman fever very quaint. This is the way people catch it. I wonder," he added to Giovanelli, "that you, a native Roman, should countenance such extraordinary rashness."

"Ah," said this seasoned subject, "for myself I have no fear."

"Neither have I—for you!" Winterbourne retorted in French. "I'm speaking for this young lady."

Giovanelli raised his well-shaped eyebrows and showed his shining teeth, but took his critic's rebuke with docility. "I assured Mademoiselle it was a grave indiscretion, but when was Mademoiselle ever prudent?"

"I never was sick, and I don't mean to be!" Mademoiselle declared. "I don't look like much, but I'm healthy! I was bound to see the Colosseum by moonlight—I wouldn't have wanted to go home without *that;* and we've had the most beautiful time, have n't we, Mr. Giovanelli? If there has been any danger Eugenio can give me some pills. Eugenio has got some splendid pills."

"*I* should advise you then," said Winterbourne, "to drive home as fast as possible and take one!"

Giovanelli smiled as for the striking happy thought. "What you say is very wise. I'll go and make sure the carriage is at hand." And he went forward rapidly.

Daisy followed with Winterbourne. He tried to deny himself the small fine anguish of looking at her, but his eyes themselves refused to spare him, and she seemed moreover not in the least embarrassed. He spoke no word; Daisy chattered over the

[44] Malaria, known locally as "the Roman fever."

beauty of the place: "Well, I *have* seen the Colosseum by moonlight—that's one thing I can rave about!" Then noticing her companion's silence she asked him why he was so stiff—it had always been her great word. He made no answer, but he felt his laugh an immense negation of stiffness. They passed under one of the dark archways; Giovanelli was in front with the carriage. Here Daisy stopped a moment, looking at her compatriot. "*Did* you believe I was engaged the other day?"

"It does n't matter now what I believed the other day!" he replied with infinite point.

It was a wonder how she did n't wince for it. "Well, what do you believe now?"

"I believe it makes very little difference whether you're engaged or not!"

He felt her lighted eyes fairly penetrate the thick gloom of the vaulted passage— as if to seek some access to him she had n't yet compassed. But Giovanelli, with a graceful inconsequence, was at present all for retreat. "Quick, quick; if we get in by midnight we're quite safe!"

Daisy took her seat in the carriage and the fortunate Italian placed himself beside her. "Don't forget Eugenio's pills!" said Winterbourne as he lifted his hat.

"I don't care," she unexpectedly cried out for this, "whether I have Roman fever or not!" On which the cab-driver cracked his whip and they rolled across the desultory patches of antique pavement.

Winterbourne—to do him justice, as it were—mentioned to no one that he had encountered Miss Miller at midnight in the Colosseum with a gentleman; in spite of which deep discretion, however, the fact of the scandalous adventure was known a couple of days later, with a dozen vivid details, to every member of the little American circle, and was commented accordingly. Winterbourne judged thus that the people about the hotel had been thoroughly empowered to testify, and that after Daisy's return there would have been an exchange of jokes between the porter and the cab-driver. But the young man became aware at the same moment of how thoroughly it had ceased to ruffle him that the little American flirt should be "talked about" by low-minded menials. These sources of current criticism a day or two later abounded still further: the little American flirt was alarmingly ill and the doctors now in possession of the scene. Winterbourne, when the rumour came to him, immediately went to the hotel for more news. He found that two or three charitable friends had preceded him and that they were being entertained in Mrs. Miller's salon by the all-efficient Randolph.

"It's going round at night that way, you bet—that's what has made her so sick. She's always going round at night. I should n't think she'd want to—it's so plaguey dark over here. You can't see anything over here without the moon's right up. In America they don't go round by the moon!" Mrs. Miller meanwhile wholly surrendered to her genius for unapparent uses; her salon knew her less than ever, and she was presumably now at least giving her daughter the advantage of her society. It was clear that Daisy was dangerously ill.

Winterbourne constantly attended for news from the sick-room, which reached him, however, but with worrying indirectness, though he once had speech, for a moment, of the poor girl's physician and once saw Mrs. Miller, who, sharply alarmed, struck him as thereby more happily inspired than he could have conceived and indeed as the most noiseless and light-handed of nurses. She invoked a good deal the remote shade of Dr. Davis, but Winterbourne paid her the compliment of taking her after all for less monstrous a goose. To this indulgence indeed something she further said perhaps even more insidiously disposed him. "Daisy spoke of you the other day quite pleasantly. Half the time she does n't know what she's saying, but that time I think she did. She gave me a message—she told me to tell you. She wanted you to know she never was engaged to that handsome Italian who was always round. I'm sure I'm very glad; Mr. Giovanelli has n't been near us since she was taken ill. I thought he was so much of a gentleman, but I don't call that very polite! A lady told me he was afraid I had n't approved of his being round with her so much evenings. Of course it ain't as if their evenings were as pleasant as ours—since *we* don't seem to feel that way about the poison. I guess I *don't* see the point now; but I suppose he knows I'm a lady and I'd scorn to raise a fuss. Anyway, she wants you to realise she ain't engaged. I don't know why she makes so much of it, but she said to me three times 'Mind you tell Mr. Winterbourne.' And then she told me to ask if you remembered the time you went up to that castle in Switzerland. But I said I would n't give any messages as *that*. Only if she ain't engaged I guess I'm glad to realise it too."

But, as Winterbourne had originally judged, the truth on this question had small actual relevance. A week after this the poor girl died; it had been indeed a terrible case of the *perniciosa*. A grave was found for her in the little Protestant cemetery, by an angle of the wall of imperial Rome, beneath the cypresses and the thick spring-flowers. Winterbourne stood there beside it with a number of other mourners; a number larger than the scandal excited by the young lady's career might have made probable. Near him stood Giovanelli, who came nearer still before Winterbourne turned away. Giovanelli, in decorous mourning, showed but a whiter face; his button-hole lacked its nosegay and he had visibly something urgent—and even to distress—to say, which he scarce knew how to "place." He decided at last to confide it with a pale convulsion to Winterbourne. "She was the most beautiful young lady I ever saw, and the most amiable." To which he added in a moment: "Also—naturally! —the most innocent."

Winterbourne sounded him with hard dry eyes, but presently repeated his words, "The most innocent?"

"The most innocent!"

It came somehow so much too late that our friend could only glare at its having come at all. "Why the devil," he asked, "did you take her to that fatal place?"

Giovanelli raised his neat shoulders and eyebrows to within suspicion of a shrug. "For myself I had no fear; and *she*—she did what she liked."

Winterbourne's eyes attached themselves to the ground. "She did what she liked!"

It determined on the part of poor Giovanelli a further pious, a further candid, confidence. "If she had lived I should have got nothing. She never would have married me."

It had been spoken as if to attest, in all sincerity, his disinterestedness, but Winterbourne scarce knew what welcome to give it. He said, however, with a grace inferior to his friend's: "I dare say not."

The latter was even by this not discouraged. "For a moment I hoped so. But no. I'm convinced."

Winterbourne took it in; he stood staring at the raw protuberance among the April daisies. When he turned round again his fellow mourner had stepped back.

He almost immediately left Rome, but the following summer he again met his aunt

Mrs. Costello at Vevey. Mrs. Costello extracted from the charming old hotel there a value that the Miller family had n't mastered the secret of. In the interval Winterbourne had often thought of the most interesting member of that trio—of her mystifying manners and her queer adventure. One day he spoke of her to his aunt —said it was on his conscience he had done her injustice.

"I'm sure I don't know"—that lady showed caution. "How did your injustice affect her?"

"She sent me a message before her death which I did n't understand at the time. But I've understood it since. She would have appreciated one's esteem."

"She took an odd way to gain it! But do you mean by what you say," Mrs. Costello asked, "that she would have reciprocated one's affection?"

As he made no answer to this she after a little looked round at him—he had n't been directly within sight; but the effect of that was n't to make her repeat her question. He spoke, however, after a while. "You were right in that remark that you made last summer. I was booked to make a mistake. I've lived too long in foreign parts." And this time she herself said nothing.

Nevertheless he soon went back to live at Geneva, whence there continue to come the most contradictory accounts of his motives of sojourn: a report that he's "studying" hard—an intimation that he's much interested in a very clever foreign lady.
1909

---

from Hawthorne

from **Chapter II: [American Negations and Additions]**

I know not at what age he began to keep a diary; the first entries in the American volumes are of the summer of 1835. There is a phrase in the preface to his novel of *Transformation*,[1] which must have lingered in the minds of many Americans who have tried to write novels, and to lay the scene of them in the Western world. "No author, without a trial, can conceive of the difficulty of writing a romance about a country where there is no shadow, no antiquity, no mystery, no picturesque and gloomy wrong, nor anything but a commonplace prosperity, in broad and simple daylight, as is happily the case with my dear native land." The perusal of Hawthorne's American Note-Books operates as a practical commentary upon this somewhat ominous text. It does so at least to my own mind; it would be too much, perhaps, to say that the effect would be the same for the usual English reader. An American reads between the lines—he completes the suggestions—he constructs a picture. I think I am not guilty of any gross injustice in saying that the picture he constructs from Hawthorne's American diaries, though by no means without charms of its own, is not, on the whole, an interesting one. It is characterised by an extraordinary blankness—a curious paleness of colour and paucity of detail. Hawthorne, as I have said, has a large and healthy

---

[1] Title given to Hawthorne's *The Marble Faun* (1860) in its English edition.

appetite for detail, and one is, therefore, the more struck with the lightness of the diet to which his observation was condemned. For myself, as I turn the pages of his journals, I seem to see the image of the crude and simple society in which he lived. I use these epithets, of course, not invidiously, but descriptively; if one desire to enter as closely as possible into Hawthorne's situation, one must endeavour to reproduce his circumstances. We are struck with the large number of elements that were absent from them, and the coldness, the thinness, the blankness, to repeat my epithet, present themselves so vividly that our foremost feeling is that of compassion for a romancer looking for subjects in such a field. It takes so many things, as Hawthorne must have felt later in life, when he made the acquaintance of the denser, richer, warmer European spectacle—it takes such an accumulation of history and custom, such a complexity of manners and types, to form a fund of suggestion for a novelist. If Hawthorne had been a young Englishman, or a young Frenchman of the same degree of genius, the same cast of mind, the same habits, his consciousness of the world around him would have been a very different affair; however obscure, however reserved, his own personal life, his sense of the life of his fellow-mortals would have been almost infinitely more various. The negative side of the spectacle on which Hawthorne looked out, in his contemplative saunterings and reveries, might, indeed, with a little ingenuity, be made almost ludicrous; one might enumerate the items of high civilization, as it exists in other countries, which are absent from the texture of American life, until it should become a wonder to know what was left. No State, in the European sense of the word, and indeed barely a specific national name. No sovereign, no court, no personal loyalty, no aristocracy, no church, no clergy, no army, no diplomatic service, no country gentlemen, no palaces, no castles, nor manors, nor old country-houses, nor parsonages, nor thatched cottages, nor ivied ruins; no cathedrals, nor abbeys, nor little Norman churches; no great Universities nor public schools— no Oxford, nor Eton, nor Harrow;[2] no literature, no novels, no museums, no pictures, no political society, no sporting class—no Epsom nor Ascot![3] Some such list as that might be drawn up of the absent things in American life—especially in the American life of forty years ago, the effect of which, upon an English or a French imagination, would probably, as a general thing, be appalling. The natural remark, in the almost lurid light of such an indictment, would be that if these things are left out, everything is left out. The American knows that a good deal remains; what it is that remains— that is his secret, his joke, as one may say. It would be cruel, in this terrible denudation, to deny him the consolation of his natural gift, that "American humour" of which of late years we have heard so much. . . .

from *Chapter V: [American Innocence]*

. . . Our hero was an American of the earlier and simpler type—the type of which it is doubtless premature to say that it has wholly passed away, but of which it may at least be said that the circumstances that produced it have been greatly modified. The generation to which he belonged, that generation which grew up with the century, witnessed during a period of fifty years the immense, uninterrupted material

---

[2] Eton and Harrow are upper-class English secondary boarding schools.

[3] English racecourses for thoroughbred racing.

development of the young Republic; and when one thinks of the scale on which it took place, of the prosperity that walked in its train and waited on its course, of the hopes it fostered and the blessings it conferred—of the broad morning sunshine, in a word, in which it all went forward—there seems to be little room for surprise that it should have implanted a kind of superstitious faith in the grandeur of the country, its duration, its immunity from the usual troubles of earthly empires. This faith was a simple and uncritical one, enlivened with an element of genial optimism, in the light of which it appeared that the great American state was not as other human institutions are, that a special Providence watched over it, that it would go on joyously forever, and that a country whose vast and blooming bosom offered a refuge to the strugglers and seekers of all the rest of the world, must come off easily, in the battle of the ages. From this conception of the American future the sense of its having problems to solve was blissfully absent; there were no difficulties in the programme, no looming complications, no rocks ahead. The indefinite multiplication of the population, and its enjoyment of the benefits of a common-school education and of unusual facilities for making an income—this was the form in which, on the whole, the future most vividly presented itself, and in which the greatness of the country was to be recognised of men. There was, indeed, a faint shadow in the picture—the shadow projected by the "peculiar institution" of the Southern States; but it was far from sufficient to darken the rosy vision of most good Americans, and, above all, of most good Democrats. Hawthorne alludes to it in a passage of his life of Pierce,[4] which I will quote, not only as a hint of the trouble that was in store for a cheerful race of men, but as an example of his own easy-going political attitude.

"It was while in the Lower House of Congress that Franklin Pierce took that stand on the Slavery question from which he has never since swerved by a hair's breadth. He fully recognised, by his votes and his voice, the rights pledged to the South by the Constitution. This, at the period when he declared himself, was an easy thing to do. But when it became more difficult, when the first imperceptible murmur of agitation had grown almost to a convulsion, his course was still the same. Nor did he ever shun the obloquy that sometimes threatened to pursue the Northern man who dared to love that great and sacred reality—his whole united country—better than the mistiness of a philanthropic theory."

This last invidious allusion is to the disposition, not infrequent at the North, but by no means general, to set a decisive limit to further legislation in favour of the cherished idiosyncrasy of the other half of the country. Hawthorne takes the license of a sympathetic biographer in speaking of his hero's having incurred obloquy by his conservative attitude on the question of Slavery. The only class in the American world that suffered in the smallest degree, at this time, from social persecution, was the little band of Northern Abolitionists, who were as unfashionable as they were indiscreet—which is saying much. Like most of his fellow-countrymen, Hawthorne had no idea that the respectable institution which he contemplated in impressive contrast to

[4] Biography of Franklin Pierce, classmate of Hawthorne at Bowdoin College, who was president of the United States 1853–1857.

humanitarian "mistiness," was presently to cost the nation four long years of bloodshed and misery, and a social revolution as complete as any the world has seen. When this event occurred, he was, therefore, proportionately horrified and depressed by it; it cut from beneath his feet the familiar ground which had long felt so firm, substituting a heaving and quaking medium in which his spirit found no rest. Such was the bewildered sensation of that earlier and simpler generation of which I have spoken; their illusions were rudely dispelled, and they saw the best of all possible republics given over to fratricidal carnage. This affair had no place in their scheme, and nothing was left for them but to hang their heads and close their eyes. The subsidence of that great convulsion has left a different tone from the tone it found, and one may say that the Civil War marks an era in the history of the American mind. It introduced into the national consciousness a certain sense of proportion and relation, of the world being a more complicated place than it had hitherto seemed, the future more treacherous, success more difficult. At the rate at which things are going, it is obvious that good Americans will be more numerous than ever; but the good American, in days to come, will be a more critical person than his complacent and confident grandfather. He has eaten of the tree of knowledge. He will not, I think, be a sceptic, and still less, of course, a cynic; but he will be, without discredit to his well-known capacity for action, an observer. He will remember that the ways of the Lord are inscrutable, and that this is a world in which everything happens; and eventualities, as the late Emperor of the French used to say, will not find him intellectually unprepared. The good American of which Hawthorne was so admirable a specimen was not critical, and it was perhaps for this reason that Franklin Pierce seemed to him a very proper President. . . .

1879

The Beast in the Jungle

I

What determined the speech that startled him in the course of their encounter scarcely matters, being probably but some words spoken by himself quite without intention —spoken as they lingered and slowly moved together after their renewal of acquaintance. He had been conveyed by friends an hour or two before to the house at which she was staying; the party of visitors at the other house, of whom he was one, and thanks to whom it was his theory, as always, that he was lost in the crowd, had been invited over to luncheon. There had been after luncheon much dispersal, all in the interest of the original motive, a view of Weatherend itself and the fine things, intrinsic features, pictures, heirlooms, treasures of all the arts, that made the place almost famous; and the great rooms were so numerous that guests could wander at their will, hang back from the principal group and in cases where they took such matters with the last seriousness give themselves up to mysterious appreciations and measurements. There were persons to be observed, singly or in couples, bending toward objects in out-of-the-way corners with their hands on their knees and their heads nodding quite as with the emphasis of an excited sense of smell. When they were two they either mingled their sounds of ecstasy or melted into silences of even deeper import, so that there were aspects of the occasion that gave it for Marcher much the air of the "look round," previous to a sale highly advertised, that excites or quenches, as may be, the dream of acquisition. The dream of acquisition at Weatherend would have had to be wild indeed, and John Marcher found himself, among such suggestions, disconcerted almost equally by the presence of those who knew too much and by that of those who knew nothing. The great rooms caused so much poetry and history to press upon him that he needed some straying apart to feel in a proper relation with them, though this impulse was not, as happened, like the gloating of some of his companions, to be compared to the movements of a dog sniffing a cupboard. It had an issue promptly enough in a direction that was not to have been calculated.

It led, briefly, in the course of the October afternoon, to his closer meeting with May Bartram, whose face, a reminder, yet not quite a remembrance, as they sat much separated at a very long table, had begun merely by troubling him rather pleasantly. It affected him as the sequel of something of which he had lost the beginning. He knew it, and for the time quite welcomed it, as a continuation, but did n't know what it continued, which was an interest or an amusement the greater as he was also somehow aware—yet without a direct sign from her—that the young woman herself had n't lost the thread. She had n't lost it, but she would n't give it back to him, he saw, without some putting forth of his hand for it; and he not only saw that, but saw several things more, things odd enough in the light of the fact that at the moment some accident of grouping brought them face to face he was still merely fumbling with the idea that any contact between them in the past would have had no importance. If it had had no importance he scarcely knew why his actual impression of her should so seem to have so much; the answer to which, however, was that in such a life as they all appeared to be leading for the moment one could but take things as they came. He was satisfied, without in the least being able to say why, that this young lady might roughly have ranked in the house as a poor relation; satisfied also that she was not there on a brief visit, but was more or less a part of the establishment—almost a working, a remunerated part. Did n't she enjoy at periods a protection that she paid for by helping, among other services, to show the place and explain it, deal with the tiresome people, answer questions about the dates of the building, the styles of the furniture, the authorship of the pictures, the favourite haunts of the ghost? It was n't that she looked as if you could have given her shillings—it was impossible to look less so. Yet when she finally drifted toward him, distinctly handsome, though ever so much older—older than when he had seen her before—it might have been as an effect of her guessing that he had, within the couple of hours, devoted more imagination to her than to all the others put together, and had thereby penetrated to a kind of truth that the others were too stupid for. She *was* there on harder terms than any one; she was there as a consequence of things suffered, one way and another, in the interval of years; and she remembered him very much as she was remembered—only a good deal better.

By the time they at last thus came to speech they were alone in one of the rooms —remarkable for a fine portrait over the chimney-place—out of which their friends had passed, and the charm of it was that even before they had spoken they had practically arranged with each other to stay behind for talk. The charm, happily, was in other things too—partly in there being scarce a spot at Weatherend without something to stay behind for. It was in the way the autumn day looked into the high windows as it waned; the way the red light, breaking at the close from under a low sombre sky, reached out in a long shaft and played over old wainscots, old tapestry, old gold, old colour. It was most of all perhaps in the way she came to him as if, since she had been turned on to deal with the simpler sort, he might, should he choose to keep the whole thing down, just take her mild attention for a part of her general business. As soon as he heard her voice, however, the gap was filled up and the missing link supplied; the slight irony he divined in her attitude lost its advantage. He almost jumped at it to get there before her. "I met you years and years ago in Rome. I remember all about it." She confessed to disappointment—she had been so sure he did n't; and to prove how well he did he began to pour forth the particular recollections that popped up as he called for them. Her face and her voice, all at his service now, worked the miracle—the impression operating like the torch of a lamplighter who touches into flame, one by one, a long row of gas-jets. Marcher flattered himself the illumination was brilliant, yet he was really still more pleased on her showing him, with amusement, that in his haste to make everything right he had got most things rather wrong. It had n't been at Rome—it had been at Naples; and it had n't been eight years before—it had been more nearly ten. She had n't been, either, with her uncle and aunt, but with her mother and her brother; in addition to which it was not with the Pembles *he* had been, but with the Boyers, coming down in their company from Rome—a point on which she insisted, a little to his confusion, and as to which she had her evidence in hand. The Boyers she had known, but did n't know the Pembles, though she had heard of them, and it was the people he was with who had made them acquainted. The incident of the thunderstorm that had raged round them with such violence as to drive them for refuge into an excavation—this incident had not occurred at the Palace of the Cæsars, but at Pompeii,[1] on an occasion when they had been present there at an important find.

He accepted her amendments, he enjoyed her corrections, though the moral of them was, she pointed out, that he *really* did n't remember the least thing about her; and he only felt it as a drawback that when all was made strictly historic there did n't appear much of anything left. They lingered together still, she neglecting her office —for from the moment he was so clever she had no proper right to him—and both neglecting the house, just waiting as to see if a memory or two more would n't again breathe on them. It had n't taken them many minutes, after all, to put down on the table, like the cards of a pack, those that constituted their respective hands; only what came out was that the pack was unfortunately not perfect—that the past, invoked, invited, encouraged, could give them, naturally, no more than it had. It had made them anciently meet—her at twenty, him at twenty-five; but nothing was so strange, they seemed to say to each other, as that, while so occupied, it had n't done a little more for them. They looked at each other as with the feeling of an occasion missed; the present would have been so much better if the other, in the far distance, in the

---

[1] I.e., not in Rome but at the ancient city near Naples.

foreign land, had n't been so stupidly meagre. There were n't apparently, all counted, more than a dozen little old things that had succeeded in coming to pass between them; trivialities of youth, simplicities of freshness, stupidities of ignorance, small possible germs, but too deeply buried—too deeply (did n't it seem?) to sprout after so many years. Marcher could only feel he ought to have rendered her some service—saved her from a capsized boat in the Bay or at least recovered her dressing-bag, filched from her cab in the streets of Naples by a lazzarone[2] with a stiletto. Or it would have been nice if he could have been taken with fever all alone at his hotel, and she could have come to look after him, to write to his people, to drive him out in convalescence. *Then* they would be in possession of the something or other that their actual show seemed to lack. It yet somehow presented itself, this show, as too good to be spoiled; so that they were reduced for a few minutes more to wondering a little helplessly why—since they seemed to know a certain number of the same people—their reunion had been so long averted. They did n't use that name for it but their delay from minute to minute to join the others was a kind of confession that they did n't quite want it to be a failure. Their attempted supposition of reasons for their not having met but showed how little they knew of each other. There came in fact a moment when Marcher felt a positive pang. It was vain to pretend she was an old friend, for all the communities were wanting, in spite of which it was as an old friend that he saw she would have suited him. He had new ones enough—was surrounded with them for instance on the stage of the other house; as a new one he probably would n't have so much as noticed her. He would have liked to invent something, get her to make-believe with him that some passage of a romantic or critical kind *had* originally occurred. He was really almost reaching out in imagination—as against time—for something that would do, and saying to himself that if it did n't come this sketch of a fresh start would show for quite awkwardly bungled. They would separate, and now for no second or no third chance. They would have tried and not succeeded. Then it was, just at the turn, as he afterwards made it out to himself, that, everything else failing, she herself decided to take up the case and, as it were, save the situation. He felt as soon as she spoke that she had been consciously keeping back what she said and hoping to get on without it; a scruple in her that immensely touched him when, by the end of three or four minutes more, he was able to measure it. What she brought out, at any rate, quite cleared the air and supplied the link—the link it was so odd he should frivolously have managed to lose.

"You know you told me something I've never forgotten and that again and again has made me think of you since; it was that tremendously hot day when we went to Sorrento,[3] across the bay, for the breeze. What I allude to was what you said to me, on the way back, as we sat under the awning of the boat enjoying the cool. Have you forgotten?"

He had forgotten and was even more surprised than ashamed. But the great thing was that he saw in this no vulgar reminder of any "sweet" speech. The vanity of women had long memories, but she was making no claim on him of a compliment or a mistake. With another woman, a totally different one, he might have feared the recall possibly even some imbecile "offer." So, in having to say that he had indeed

---

[2] Neapolitan beggar.   [3] On the Bay of Naples.

forgotten, he was conscious rather of a loss than of a gain; he already saw an interest in the matter of her mention. "I try to think—but I give it up. Yet I remember the Sorrento day."

"I'm not very sure you do," May Bartram after a moment said; "and I'm not very sure I ought to want you to. It's dreadful to bring a person back at any time to what he was ten years before. If you've lived away from it," she smiled, "so much the better."

"Ah if *you* have n't why should I?" he asked.

"Lived away, you mean, from what I myself was?"

"From what *I* was. I was of course an ass," Marcher went on; "but I would rather know from you just the sort of ass I was than——from the moment you have something in your mind—not know anything."

Still, however, she hesitated. "But if you've completely ceased to be that sort——?"

"Why I can then all the more bear to know. Besides, perhaps I have n't."

"Perhaps. Yet if you have n't," she added, "I should suppose you'd remember. Not indeed that *I* in the least connect with my impression the invidious name you use. If I had only thought you foolish," she explained, "the thing I speak of wouldn't so have remained with me. It was about yourself." She waited as if it might come to him; but as, only meeting her eyes in wonder, he gave no sign, she burnt her ships. "Has it ever happened?"

Then it was that, while he continued to stare, a light broke for him and the blood slowly came to his face, which began to burn with recognition. "Do you mean I told you——?" But he faltered, lest what came to him shouldn't be right, lest he should only give himself away.

"It was something about yourself that it was natural one should n't forget—that is if one remembered you at all. That's why I ask you," she smiled, "if the thing you then spoke of has ever come to pass?"

Oh then he saw, but he was lost in wonder and found himself embarrassed. This, he also saw, made her sorry for him, as if her allusion had been a mistake. It took him but a moment, however, to feel it had n't been, much as it had been a surprise. After the first little shock of it her knowledge on the contrary began, even if rather strangely, to taste sweet to him. She was the only other person in the world then who would have it, and she had had it all these years, while the fact of his having so breathed his secret had unaccountably faded from him. No wonder they could n't have met as if nothing had happened. "I judge," he finally said, "that I know what you mean. Only I had strangely enough lost any sense of having taken you so far into my confidence."

"Is it because you've taken so many others as well?"

"I've taken nobody. Not a creature since then."

"So that I'm the only person who knows?"

"The only person in the world."

"Well," she quickly replied, "I myself have never spoken. I've never, never repeated of you what you told me." She looked at him so that he perfectly believed her. Their eyes met over it in such a way that he was without a doubt. "And I never will."

She spoke with an earnestness that, as if almost excessive, put him at ease about her possible derision. Somehow the whole question was a new luxury to him—that is from the moment she was in possession. If she did n't take the sarcastic view she clearly took the sympathetic, and that was what he had had, in all the long time, from no one whomsoever. What he felt was that he could n't at present have begun to tell her, and yet could profit perhaps exquisitely by the accident of having done so of old. "Please don't then. We're just right as it is."

"Oh I am," she laughed, "if you are!" To which she added: "Then you do still feel in the same way?"

It was impossible he should n't take to himself that she was really interested, though it all kept coming as perfect surprise. He had thought of himself so long as abominably alone, and lo he was n't alone a bit. He had n't been, it appeared, for an hour—since those moments on the Sorrento boat. It was *she* who had been, he seemed to see as he looked at her—she who had been made so by the graceless fact of his lapse of fidelity. To tell her what he had told her—what had it been but to ask something of her? something that she had given, in her charity, without his having, by a remembrance, by a return of the spirit, failing another encounter, so much as thanked her. What he had asked of her had been simply at first not to laugh at him. She had beautifully not done so for ten years, and she was not doing so now. So he had endless gratitude to make up. Only for that he must see just how he had figured to her. "What, exactly, was the account I gave—?"

"Of the way you did feel? Well, it was very simple. You said you had had from your earliest time, as the deepest thing within you, the sense of being kept for something rare and strange, possibly prodigious and terrible, that was sooner or later to happen to you, that you had in your bones the foreboding and the conviction of, and that would perhaps overwhelm you."

"Do you call that very simple?" John Marcher asked.

She thought a moment. "It was perhaps because I seemed, as you spoke, to understand it."

"You do understand it?" he eagerly asked.

Again she kept her kind eyes on him. "You still have the belief?"

"Oh!" he exclaimed helplessly. There was too much to say.

"Whatever it's to be," she clearly made out, "it has n't yet come."

He shook his head in complete surrender now. "It has n't yet come. Only, you know, it is n't anything I'm to *do,* to achieve in the world, to be distinguished or admired for. I'm not such an ass as *that.* It would be much better, no doubt, if I were."

"It's to be something you're merely to suffer?"

"Well, say to wait for—to have to meet, to face, to see suddenly break out in my life; possibly destroying all further consciousness, possibly annihilating me; possibly, on the other hand, only altering everything, striking at the root of all my world and leaving me to the consequences, however they shape themselves."

She took this in, but the light in her eyes continued for him not to be that of mockery. "Is n't what you describe perhaps but the expectation—or at any rate the sense of danger, familiar to so many people—of falling in love?"

John Marcher wondered. "Did you ask me that before?"

"No—I was n't so free-and-easy then. But it's what strikes me now."

"Of course," he said after a moment, "it strikes you. Of course it strikes *me.* Of course what's in store for me may be no more than that. The only thing is," he went on, "that I think if it had been that I should by this time know."

"Do you mean because you've *been* in love?" And then as he but looked at her in silence: "You've been in love, and it has n't meant such a cataclysm, has n't proved the great affair?"

"Here I am, you see. It has n't been overwhelming."

"Then it has n't been love," said May Bartram.

"Well, I at least thought it was. I took it for that—I've taken it till now. It was agreeable, it was delightful, it was miserable," he explained. "But it was n't strange. It was n't what *my* affair 's to be."

"You want something all to yourself—something that nobody else knows or *has* known?"

"It is n't a question of what I 'want'—God knows I don't want anything. It's only a question of the apprehension that haunts me—that I live with day by day."

He said this so lucidly and consistently that he could see it further impose itself. If she had n't been interested before she'd have been interested now. "Is it a sense of coming violence?"

Evidently now too again he liked to talk of it. "I don't think of it as—when it does come—necessarily violent. I only think of it as natural and as of course above all unmistakable. I think of it simply as *the* thing. *The* thing will of itself appear natural."

"Then how will it appear strange?"

Marcher bethought himself. "It won't—to *me*."

"To whom then?"

"Well," he replied, smiling at last, "say to you."

"Oh then I'm to be present?"

"Why you *are* present—since you know."

"I see." She turned it over. "But I mean at the catastrophe."

At this, for a minute, their lightness gave way to their gravity; it was as if the long look they exchanged held them together. "It will only depend on yourself—if you'll watch with me."

"Are you afraid?" she asked.

"Don't leave me *now*," he went on.

"Are you afraid?" she repeated.

"Do you think me simply out of my mind?" he pursued instead of answering. "Do I merely strike you as a harmless lunatic?"

"No," said May Bartram. "I understand you. I believe you."

"You mean you feel how my obsession—poor old thing!—may correspond to some possible reality?"

"To some possible reality."

"Then you *will* watch with me?"

She hesitated, then for the third time put her question. "Are you afraid?"

"Did I tell you I was—at Naples?"

"No, you said nothing about it."

"Then I don't know. And I should *like* to know," said John Marcher. "You'll tell me yourself whether you think so. If you'll watch with me you'll see."

"Very good then." They had been moving by this time across the room, and at the door, before passing out, they paused as for the full wind-up of their understanding. "I'll watch with you," said May Bartram.

II

The fact that she "knew"—knew and yet neither chaffed him nor betrayed him—had in a short time begun to constitute between them a goodly bond, which became more marked when, within the year that followed their afternoon at Weatherend, the opportunities for meeting multiplied. The event that thus promoted these occasions was the death of the ancient lady her great-aunt, under whose wing, since losing her mother, she had to such an extent found shelter, and who, though but the widowed mother of the new successor to the property, had succeeded—thanks to a high tone and a high temper—in not forfeiting the supreme position at the great house. The deposition of this personage arrived but with her death, which, followed by many changes, made in particular a difference for the young woman in whom Marcher's expert attention had recognised from the first a dependent with a pride that might ache though it did n't bristle. Nothing for a long time had made him easier than the thought that the aching must have been much soothed by Miss Bartram's now finding herself able to set up a small home in London. She had acquired property, to an amount that made that luxury just possible, under her aunt's extremely complicated will, and when the whole matter began to be straightened out, which indeed took time, she let him know that the happy issue was at last in view. He had seen her again before that day, both because she had more than once accompanied the ancient lady to town and because he had paid another visit to the friends who so conveniently made of Weatherend one of the charms of their own hospitality. These friends had taken him back there; he had achieved there again with Miss Bartram some quiet detachment; and he had in London succeeded in persuading her to more than one brief absence from her aunt. They went together, on these latter occasions, to the National Gallery and the South Kensington Museum, where, among vivid reminders, they talked of Italy at large—not now attempting to recover, as at first, the taste of their youth and their ignorance. That recovery, the first day at Weatherend, had served its purpose well, had given them quite enough; so that they were, to Marcher's sense, no longer hovering about the headwaters of their stream, but had felt their boat pushed sharply off and down the current.

They were literally afloat together; for our gentleman this was marked, quite as marked as that the fortunate cause of it was just the buried treasure of her knowledge. He had with his own hands dug up this little hoard, brought to light—that is to within reach of the dim day constituted by their discretions and privacies—the object of value the hiding-place of which he had, after putting it into the ground himself, so strangely, so long forgotten. The rare luck of his having again just stumbled on the spot made him indifferent to any other question; he would doubtless have devoted more time to the odd accident of his lapse of memory if he had n't been moved to devote so much to the sweetness, the comfort, as he felt, for the future, that this accident itself had helped to keep fresh. It had never entered into his plan that any one should "know," and mainly for the reason that it was n't in him to tell any one. That would have been impossible, for nothing but the amusement of a cold world would have waited on it. Since, however, a mysterious fate had opened his mouth betimes, in spite of him, he would count that a compensation and profit by it to the utmost. That the right person *should* know tempered the asperity of his secret more even than his shyness had permitted him to imagine; and May Bartram was clearly right, because—well, because there she was. Her knowledge simply settled it; he would have been sure enough by this time had she been wrong. There was that in his situation, no doubt, that disposed him too much to see her as a mere confidant, taking all her light for him from the fact—the fact only—of her interest in his predicament; from her mercy, sympathy, seriousness, her consent not to regard him as the funniest of the funny. Aware, in fine, that her price for him was just in her giving him this constant sense of his being admirably spared, he was careful to remember that she had also a life of her own, with things that might happen to *her,* things that in friendship one should likewise take account of. Something fairly remarkable came to pass with him, for that matter, in this connexion—something represented by a certain passage of his consciousness, in the suddenest way, from one extreme to the other.

He had thought himself, so long as nobody knew, the most disinterested person in the world, carrying his concentrated burden, his perpetual suspense, ever so quietly, holding his tongue about it, giving others no glimpse of it nor of its effect upon his life, asking of them no allowance and only making on his side all those that were asked. He had n't disturbed people with the queerness of their having to know a haunted man, though he had had moments of rather special temptation on hearing them say they were forsooth "unsettled." If they were as unsettled as he was—he who had never been settled for an hour in his life—they would know what it meant. Yet it was n't, all the same, for him to make them, and he listened to them civilly enough. This was why he had such good—though possibly such rather colourless—manners; this was why, above all, he could regard himself, in a greedy world, as decently— as in fact perhaps even a little sublimely—unselfish. Our point is accordingly that he valued this character quite sufficiently to measure his present danger of letting it lapse, against which he promised himself to be much on his guard. He was quite ready, none the less, to be selfish just a little, since surely no more charming occasion for it had come to him. "Just a little," in a word, was just as much as Miss Bartram, taking one day with another, would let him. He never would be in the least coercive, and would keep well before him the lines on which consideration for her—the very highest— ought to proceed. He would thoroughly establish the heads under which her affairs, her requirements, her peculiarities—he went so far as to give them the latitude of that name—would come into their intercourse. All this naturally was a sign of how much he took the intercourse itself for granted. There was nothing more to be done about *that.* It simply existed; had sprung into being with her first penetrating question to him in the autumn light there at Weatherend. The real form it should have taken on the basis that stood out large was the form of their marrying. But the devil in this was that the very basis itself put marrying out of the question. His conviction, his apprehension, his obsession, in short, was n't a privilege he could invite a woman to share; and that consequence of it was precisely what was the matter with him. Something or other lay in wait for him, amid the twists and the turns of the months and the years, like a crouching beast in the jungle. It signified little whether the crouching beast were destined to slay him or to be slain. The definite point was the inevitable spring of the creature; and the definite lesson from that was that a man of feeling did n't cause himself to be accompanied by a lady on a tiger-hunt. Such was the image under which he had ended by figuring his life.

They had at first, none the less, in the scattered hours spent together, made no allusion to that view of it; which was a sign he was handsomely alert to give that he did n't expect, that he in fact did n't care, always to be talking about it. Such a feature in one's outlook was really like a hump on one's back. The difference it made every minute of the day existed quite independently of discussion. One discussed of course *like* a hunchback, for there was always, if nothing else, the hunchback face. That remained, and she was watching him; but people watched best, as a general thing, in silence, so that such would be predominantly the manner of their vigil. Yet he did n't want, at the same time, to be tense and solemn; tense and solemn was what he imagined he too much showed for with other people. The thing to be, with the one person who knew, was easy and natural—to make the reference rather than be seeming to avoid it, to avoid it rather than be seeming to make it, and to keep it, in any case, familiar, facetious even, rather than pedantic and portentous. Some such consideration as the latter was doubtless in his mind for instance when he wrote pleasantly to Miss Bartram that perhaps the great thing he had so long felt as in the lap of the gods was no more than this circumstance, which touched him so nearly, of her acquiring a house in London. It was the first allusion they had yet again made, needing any other hitherto so little; but when she replied, after having given him the news, that she was by no means satisfied with such a trifle as the climax to so special a suspense, she almost set him wondering if she had n't even a larger conception of singularity for him than he had for himself. He was at all events destined to become aware little by little, as time went by, that she was all the while looking at his life, judging it, measuring it, in the light of the thing she knew, which grew to be at last, with the consecration of the years, never mentioned between them save as "the real truth" about him. That had always been his own form of reference to it, but she adopted the form so quietly that, looking back at the end of a period, he knew there was no moment at which it was traceable that she had, as he might say, got inside his idea, or exchanged the attitude of beautifully indulging for that of still more beautifully believing him.

It was always open to him to accuse her of seeing him but as the most harmless of maniacs, and this, in the long run—since it covered so much ground—was his easiest description of their friendship. He had a screw loose for her, but she liked him in spite of it and was practically, against the rest of the world, his kind wise keeper, unremunerated but fairly amused and, in the absence of other near ties, not disreputably occupied. The rest of the world of course thought him queer, but she, she only, knew how, and above all why, queer; which was precisely what enabled her to dispose the concealing veil in the right folds. She took his gaiety from him—since it had to pass with them for gaiety—as she took everything else; but she certainly so far justified by her unerring touch his finer sense of the degree to which he had ended by convincing her. *She* at least never spoke of the secret of his life except as "the real truth about you," and she had in fact a wonderful way of making it seem, as such, the secret of her own life too. That was in fine how he so constantly felt her as allowing for him; he could n't on the whole call it anything else. He allowed for himself, but she, exactly, allowed still more; partly because, better placed for a sight of the matter, she traced his unhappy perversion through reaches of its course into which he could scarce follow it. He knew how he felt, but, besides knowing that, she knew how he *looked* as well; he knew each of the things of importance he was insidiously kept from doing, but she could add up the amount they made, understand how much, with a lighter weight on his spirit, he might have done, and thereby establish how, clever as he was, he fell short. Above all she was in the secret of the difference between the forms he went through—those of his little office under Government, those of caring for his modest patrimony, for his library, for his garden in the country, for the people in London whose invitations he accepted and repaid —and the detachment that reigned beneath them and that made of all behaviour, all that could in the least be called behaviour, a long act of dissimulation. What it had come to was that he wore a mask painted with the social simper, out of the eye-holes of which there looked eyes of an expression not in the least matching the other features. This the stupid world, even after years, had never more than half-discovered. It was only May Bartram who had, and she achieved, by an art indescribable, the feat of at once—or perhaps it was only alternately—meeting the eyes from in front and mingling her own vision, as from over his shoulder, with their peep through the apertures.

So while they grew older together she did watch with him, and so she let this association give shape and colour to her own existence. Beneath *her* forms as well detachment had learned to sit, and behaviour had become for her, in the social sense, a false account of herself. There was but one account of her that would have been true all the while and that she could give straight to nobody, least of all to John Marcher. Her whole attitude was a virtual statement, but the perception of that only seemed called to take its place for him as one of the many things necessarily crowded out of his consciousness. If she had moreover, like himself, to make sacrifices to their real truth, it was to be granted that her compensation might have affected her as more prompt and more natural. They had long periods, in this London time, during which, when they were together, a stranger might have listened to them without in the least pricking up his ears; on the other hand the real truth was equally liable at any moment to rise to the surface, and the auditor would have then wondered indeed what they were talking about. They had from an early hour made up their mind that society was, luckily, unintelligent, and the margin allowed them by this had fairly become one of their commonplaces. Yet there were still moments when the situation turned almost fresh—usually under the effect of some expression drawn from herself. Her expressions doubtless repeated themselves, but her intervals were generous. "What saves us, you know, is that we answer so completely to so usual an appearance: that of the man and woman whose friendship has become such a daily habit—or almost —as to be at last indispensable." That for instance was a remark she had frequently enough had occasion to make, though she had given it at different times different developments. What we are especially concerned with is the turn it happened to take from her one afternoon when he had come to see her in honour of her birthday. This anniversary had fallen on a Sunday, at a season of thick fog and general outward gloom; but he had brought her his customary offering, having known her now long enough to have established a hundred small traditions. It was one of his proofs to himself, the present he made her on her birthday, that he had n't sunk into real selfishness. It was mostly nothing more than a small trinket, but it was always fine of its kind, and he was regularly careful to pay for it more than he thought he could afford. "Our habit saves you at least, don't you see? because it makes you, after all, for the vulgar, indistinguishable from other men. What's the most inveterate mark of men in general? Why the capacity to spend endless time with dull women—to spend it I won't say without being bored, but without minding that they are, without being driven off at a tangent by it; which comes to the same thing. I'm your dull woman, a part of the daily bread for which you pray at church. That covers your tracks more than anything."

"And what covers yours?" asked Marcher, whom his dull woman could mostly to this extent amuse. "I see of course what you mean by your saving me, in this way and that, so far as other people are concerned—I've seen it all along. Only what is it that saves *you?* I often think, you know, of that."

She looked as if she sometimes thought of that too, but rather in a different way. "Where other people, you mean, are concerned?"

"Well, you're really so in with me, you know—as a sort of result of my being so in with yourself. I mean of my having such an immense regard for you, being so tremendously mindful of all you've done for me. I sometimes ask myself if it's quite fair. Fair I mean to have so involved and—since one may say it—interested you. I almost feel as if you had n't really had time to do anything else."

"Anything else but be interested?" she asked. "Ah what else does one ever want to be? If I've been 'watching' with you, as we long ago agreed I was to do, watching's always in itself an absorption."

"Oh certainly," John Marcher said, "if you had n't had your curiosity—! Only does n't it sometimes come to you as time goes on that your curiosity is n't being particularly repaid?"

May Bartram had a pause. "Do you ask that, by any chance, because you feel at all that yours is n't? I mean because you have to wait so long."

Oh he understood what she meant! "For the thing to happen that never does happen? For the beast to jump out? No, I'm just where I was about it. It is n't a matter as to which I can *choose,* I can decide for a change. It is n't one as to which there *can* be a change. It's in the lap of the gods. One's in the hands of one's law—there one is. As to the form the law will take, the way it will operate, that's its own affair."

"Yes," Miss Bartram replied; "of course one's fate's coming, of course it *has* come in its own form and its own way, all the while. Only, you know, the form and the way in your case were to have been—well, something so exceptional and, as one may say, so particularly *your* own."

Something in this made him look at her with suspicion. "You say 'were to *have* been,' as if in your heart you had begun to doubt."

"Oh!" she vaguely protested.

"As if you believed," he went on, "that nothing will now take place."

She shook her head slowly but rather inscrutably. "You're far from my thought."

He continued to look at her. "What then is the matter with you?"

"Well," she said after another wait, "the matter with me is simply that I'm more sure than ever my curiosity, as you call it, will be but too well repaid."

They were frankly grave now; he had got up from his seat, had turned once more about the little drawing-room to which, year after year, he brought his inevitable topic; in which he had, as he might have said, tasted their intimate community with every sauce, where every object was as familiar to him as the things of his own house and the very carpets were worn with his fitful walk very much as the desks in old counting-houses are worn by the elbows of generations of clerks. The generations of his nervous moods had been at work there, and the place was the written history of his whole middle life. Under the impression of what his friend had just said he knew himself, for some reason, more aware of these things; which made him, after a moment, stop again before her. "Is it possibly that you've grown afraid?"

"Afraid?" He thought, as she repeated the word, that his question had made her, a little, change colour; so that, lest he should have touched on a truth, he explained very kindly: "You remember that that was what you asked *me* long ago—that first day at Weatherend."

"Oh yes, and you told me you did n't know—that I was to see for myself. We've said little about it since, even in so long a time."

"Precisely," Marcher interposed—"quite as if it were too delicate a matter for us to make free with. Quite as if we might find, that I *am* afraid. For then," he said "we should n't, should we? quite know what to do."

She had for the time no answer to this question. "There have been days when I thought you were. Only, of course," she added, "there have been days when we have thought almost anything."

"Everything. Oh!" Marcher softly groaned as with a gasp, half-spent, at the face, more uncovered just then than it had been for a long while, of the imagination always with them. It had always had its incalculable moments of glaring out, quite as with the very eyes of the very Beast, and, used as he was to them, they could still draw from him the tribute of a sigh that rose from the depths of his being. All they had thought, first and last, rolled over him; the past seemed to have been reduced to mere barren speculation. This in fact was what the place had just struck him as so full of —the simplification of everything but the state of suspense. That remained only by seeming to hang in the void surrounding it. Even his original fear, if fear it had been, had lost itself in the desert. "I judge, however," he continued, "that you see I'm not afraid now."

"What I see, as I make it out, is that you've achieved something almost unprecedented in the way of getting used to danger. Living with it so long and so closely you've lost your sense of it; you know it's there, but you're indifferent, and you cease even, as of old, to have to whistle in the dark. Considering what the danger is," May Bartram wound up, "I'm bound to say I don't think your attitude could well be surpassed."

John Marcher faintly smiled. "It's heroic?"

"Certainly—call it that."

It was what he would have liked indeed to call it. "I *am* then a man of courage?"

"That's what you were to show me."

He still, however, wondered. "But does n't the man of courage know what he's afraid of—or *not* afraid of? I don't know *that,* you see. I don't focus it. I can't name it. I only know I'm exposed."

"Yes, but exposed—how shall I say?—so directly. So intimately. That's surely enough."

"Enough to make you feel then—as what we may call the end and the upshot of our watch—that I'm not afraid?"

"You're not afraid. But it is n't," she said, "the end of our watch. That is it is n't the end of yours. You've everything still to see."

"Then why have n't *you?*" he asked. He had had, all along, to-day, the sense of her keeping something back, and he still had it. As this was his first impression of that it quite made a date. The case was the more marked as she did n't at first answer; which in turn made him go on. "You know something I don't." Then his voice, for that of a man of courage, trembled a little. "You know what's to happen." Her silence, with the face she showed, was almost a confession—it made him sure. "You know, and you're afraid to tell me. It's so bad that you're afraid I'll find out."

All this might be true, for she did look as if, unexpectedly to her, he had crossed some mystic line that she had secretly drawn round her. Yet she might, after all, not have worried; and the real climax was that he himself, at all events, need n't. "You'll never find out."

III

It was all to have made, none the less, as I have said, a date; which came out in the fact that again and again, even after long intervals, other things that passed between them wore in relation to this hour but the character of recalls and results. Its immediate effect had been indeed rather to lighten insistence—almost to provoke a reaction; as if their topic had dropped by its own weight and as if moreover, for that matter, Marcher had been visited by one of his occasional warnings against egotism. He had kept up, he felt, and very decently on the whole, his consciousness of the importance of not being selfish, and it was true that he had never sinned in that direction without promptly enough trying to press the scales the other way. He often repaired his fault, the season permitting, by inviting his friend to accompany him to the opera; and it not infrequently thus happened that, to show he did n't wish her to have but one sort of food for her mind, he was the cause of her appearing there with him a dozen nights in the month. It even happened that, seeing her home at such times, he occasionally went in with her to finish, as he called it, the evening, and, the better to make his point, sat down to the frugal but always careful little supper that awaited his pleasure. His point was made, he thought, by his not eternally insisting with her on himself; made for instance, at such hours, when it befell that, her piano at hand and each of them familiar with it, they went over passages of the opera together. It chanced to be on one of these occasions, however, that he reminded her of her not having answered a certain question he had put to her during the talk that had taken place between them on her last birthday. "What is it that saves *you?*"—saved her, he meant, from that appearance of variation from the usual human type. If he had practically escaped remark, as she pretended, by doing, in the most important particular, what most men do—find the answer to life in patching up an alliance of a sort with a woman no better than himself—how had she escaped it, and how could the alliance, such as it was, since they must suppose it had been more or less noticed, have failed to make her rather positively talked about?

"I never said," May Bartram replied, "that it had n't made me a good deal talked about."

"Ah well then you're not 'saved.'"

"It has n't been a question for me. If you've had your woman I've had," she said, "my man."

"And you mean that makes you all right?"

Oh it was always as if there were so much to say! "I don't know why it should n't make me—humanly, which is what we're speaking of—as right as it makes you."

"I see," Marcher returned. " 'Humanly,' no doubt, as showing that you're living for something. Not, that is, just for me and my secret."

May Bartram smiled. "I don't pretend it exactly shows that I'm not living for you. It's my intimacy with you that's in question."

He laughed as he saw what she meant. "Yes, but since, as you say, I'm only, so far as people make out, ordinary, you're—are n't you?—no more than ordinary either. You help me to pass for a man like another. So if I *am,* as I understand you, you're not compromised. Is that it?"

She had another of her waits, but she spoke clearly enough. "That's it. It's all that concerns me—to help you to pass for a man like another."

He was careful to acknowledge the remark handsomely. "How kind, how beautiful, you are to me! How shall I ever repay you?"

She had her last grave pause, as if there might be a choice of ways. But she chose. "By going on as you are."

It was into this going on as he was that they relapsed, and really for so long a time that the day inevitably came for a further sounding of their depths. These depths, constantly bridged over by a structure firm enough in spite of its lightness and of its occasional oscillation in the somewhat vertiginous air, invited on occasion, in the interest of their nerves, a dropping of the plummet and a measurement of the abyss. A difference had been made moreover, once for all, by the fact that she had all the while not appeared to feel the need of rebutting his charge of an idea within her that she did n't dare to express—a charge uttered just before one of the fullest of their later discussions ended. It had come up for him then that she "knew" something and that what she knew was bad—too bad to tell him. When he had spoken of it as visibly so bad that she was afraid he might find it out, her reply had left the matter too equivocal to be let alone and yet, for Marcher's special sensibility, almost too formidable again to touch. He circled about it at a distance that alternately narrowed and widened and that still was n't much affected by the consciousness in him that there was nothing she could "know," after all, any better than he did. She had no source of knowledge he had n't equally—except of course that she might have finer nerves. That was what women had where they were interested; they made out things, where people were concerned, that the people often could n't have made out for themselves. Their nerves, their sensibility, their imagination, were conductors and revealers, and the beauty of May Bartram was in particular that she had given herself so to his case. He felt in these days what, oddly enough, he had never felt before, the growth of a dread of losing her by some catastrophe—some catastrophe that yet would n't at all be *the* catastrophe: partly because she had almost of a sudden begun to strike him as more useful to him than ever yet, and partly by reason of an appearance of uncertainty in her health, coincident and equally new. It was characteristic of the inner detachment he had hitherto so successfully cultivated and to which our whole account of him is a reference, it was characteristic that his complications, such as they were, had never yet seemed so as at this crisis to thicken about him, even to the point of making him ask himself if he were, by any chance, of a truth, within sight or sound, within touch or reach, within the immediate jurisdiction, of the thing that waited.

When the day came, as come it had to, that his friend confessed to him her fear of a deep disorder in her blood, he felt somehow the shadow of a change and the chill of a shock. He immediately began to imagine aggravations and disasters, and above all to think of her peril as the direct menace for himself of personal privation. This indeed gave him one of those partial recoveries of equanimity that were agreeable to him—it showed him that what was still first in his mind was the loss she herself might suffer. "What if she should have to die before knowing, before seeing—?" It would have been brutal, in the early stages of her trouble, to put that question to her; but it had immediately sounded for him to his own concern, and the possibility was what most made him sorry for her. If she did "know," moreover, in the sense of her having had some—what should he think?—mystical irresistible light, this would make the matter not better, but worse, inasmuch as her original adoption of his own curiosity had quite become the basis of her life. She had been living to see what would *be* to be seen, and it would quite lacerate her to have to give up before the accomplishment of the vision. These reflexions, as I say, quickened his generosity; yet, make them as he might, he saw himself, with the lapse of the period, more and more disconcerted. It lapsed for him with a strange steady sweep, and the oddest oddity was that it gave him, independently of the threat of much inconvenience, almost the only positive surprise his career, if career it could be called, had yet offered him. She kept the house as she had never done; he had to go to her to see her—she could meet him nowhere now, though there was scarce a corner of their loved old London in which she had n't in the past, at one time or another, done so; and he found her always seated by her fire in the deep old-fashioned chair she was less and less able to leave. He had been struck one day, after an absence exceeding his usual measure, with her suddenly looking much older to him than he had ever thought of her being; then he recognised that the suddenness was all on his side—he had just simply and suddenly noticed. She looked older because inevitably, after so many years, she *was* old, or almost; which was of course true in still greater measure of her companion. If she was old, or almost, John Marcher assuredly was, and yet it was her showing of the lesson, not his own, that brought the truth home to him. His surprises began here; when once they had begun they multiplied; they came rather with a rush: it was as if, in the oddest way in the world, they had all been kept back, sown in a thick cluster, for the late afternoon of life, the time at which for people in general the unexpected has died out.

One of them was that he should have caught himself—for he *had* so done—*really* wondering if the great accident would take form now as nothing more than his being condemned to see this charming woman, this admirable friend, pass away from him. He had never so unreservedly qualified her as while confronted in thought with such a possibility; in spite of which there was small doubt for him that as an answer to his long riddle the mere effacement of even so fine a feature of his situation would be an abject anticlimax. It would represent, as connected with his past attitude, a drop of dignity under the shadow of which his existence could only become the most grotesque of failures. He had been far from holding it a failure—long as he had waited for the appearance that was to make it a success. He had waited for quite another thing, not for such a thing as that. The breath of his good faith came short, however, as he recognised how long he had waited, or how long at least his companion had. That she, at all events, might be recorded as having waited in vain—this affected him sharply, and all the more because of his at first having done little more than amuse himself with the idea. It grew more grave as the gravity of her condition grew, and the state of mind it produced in him, which he himself ended by watching as if it had been some definite disfigurement of his outer person, may pass for another of his surprises. This conjoined itself still with another, the really stupefying consciousness of a question that he would have allowed to shape itself had he dared. What did everything mean—what, that is, did *she* mean, she and her vain waiting and her probable death and the soundless admonition of it all—unless that, at this time of day, it was simply, it was overwhelmingly too late? He had never at any stage of his queer consciousness admitted the whisper of such a correction; he had never till within these last few months been so false to his conviction as not to hold that what was to come to him had time, whether *he* struck himself as having it or not. That at last, at last, he certainly had n't it, to speak of, or had it but in the scantiest measure—such, soon enough, as things went with him, became the inference with which his old obsession had to reckon: and this it was not helped to do by the more and more confirmed appearance that the great vagueness casting the long shadow in which he had lived had, to attest itself, almost no margin left. Since it was in Time that he was to have met his fate, so it was in Time that his fate was to have acted; and as he waked up to the sense of no longer being young, which was exactly the sense of being stale, just as that, in turn, was the sense of being weak, he waked up to another matter beside. It all hung together; they were subject, he and the great vagueness, to an equal and indivisible law. When the possibilities themselves had accordingly turned stale, when the secret of the gods had grown faint, had perhaps even quite evaporated, that, and that only, was failure. It would n't have been failure to be bankrupt, dishonoured, pilloried, hanged; it was failure not to be anything. And so, in the dark valley into which his path had taken its unlooked-for twist, he wondered not a little as he groped. He did n't care what awful crash might overtake him, with what ignominy or what monstrosity he might yet be associated—since he was n't after all too utterly old to suffer—if it would only be decently proportionate to the posture he had kept, all his life, in the threatened presence of it. He had but one desire left—that he should n't have been "sold."

IV

Then it was that, one afternoon, while the spring of the year was young and new she met all in her own way his frankest betrayal of these alarms. He had gone in late to see her, but evening had n't settled and she was presented to him in that long fresh light of waning April days which affects us often with a sadness sharper than the greyest hours of autumn. The week had been warm, the spring was supposed to have begun early, and May Bartram sat, for the first time in the year, without a fire; a fact that, to Marcher's sense, gave the scene of which she formed part a smooth and ultimate look, an air of knowing, in its immaculate order and cold meaningless cheer, that it would never see a fire again. Her own aspect—he could scarce have said why—intensified this note. Almost as white as wax, with the marks and signs in her face as numerous and as fine as if they had been etched by a needle, with soft white draperies relieved by a faded green scarf on the delicate tone of which the years had further refined, she was the picture of a serene and exquisite but impenetrable sphinx, whose head, or indeed all whose person, might have been powdered with silver. She was a sphinx, yet with her white petals and green fronds she might have been a lily too—only an artificial lily, wonderfully imitated and constantly kept, without dust or stain, though not exempt from a slight droop and a complexity of faint creases, under some clear glass bell. The perfection of household care, of high polish and finish, always reigned in her rooms, but they now looked most as if everything had been wound up, tucked in, put away, so that she might sit with folded hands and with nothing more to do. She was "out of it," to Marcher's vision; her work was over; she communicated with him as across some gulf or from some island of rest that she had already reached, and it made him feel strangely abandoned. Was it—or rather was n't it—that if for so long she had been watching with him the answer to their question must have swum into her ken and taken on its name, so that her occupation was verily gone? He had as much as charged her with this in saying to her, many months before, that she even then knew something she was keeping from him. It was a point he had never since ventured to press, vaguely fearing as he did that it might become a difference, perhaps a disagreement, between them. He had in this later time turned nervous, which was what he in all the other years had never been; and the oddity was that his nervousness should have waited till he had begun to doubt, should have held off so long as he was sure. There was something, it seemed to him, that the wrong word would bring down on his head, something that would so at least ease off his tension. But he wanted not to speak the wrong word; that would make everything ugly. He wanted the knowledge he lacked to drop on him, if drop it could, by its own august weight. If she was to forsake him it was surely for her to take leave. This was why he did n't directly ask her again what she knew; but it was also why, approaching the matter from another side, he said to her in the course of his visit: "What do you regard as the very worst that at this time of day *can* happen to me?"

He had asked her that in the past often enough; they had, with the odd irregular rhythm of their intensities and avoidances, exchanged ideas about it and then had seen the ideas washed away by cool intervals, washed like figures traced in sea-sand. It had ever been the mark of their talk that the oldest allusions in it required but a little dismissal and reaction to come out again, sounding for the hour as new. She could thus at present meet his enquiry quite freshly and patiently. "Oh yes, I've repeatedly thought, only it always seemed to me of old that I could n't quite make up my mind. I thought of dreadful things, between which it was difficult to choose; and so must you have done."

"Rather! I feel now as if I had scarce done anything else. I appear to myself to have spent my life in thinking of nothing *but* dreadful things. A great many of them I've at different times named to you, but there were others I could n't name."

"They were too, too dreadful?"

"Too, too dreadful—some of them."

She looked at him a minute, and there came to him as he met it an inconsequent sense that her eyes, when one got their full clearness, were still as beautiful as they had been in youth, only beautiful with a strange cold light—a light that somehow was a part of the effect, if it was n't rather a part of the cause, of the pale hard sweetness of the season and the hour. "And yet," she said at last, "there are horrors we've mentioned."

It deepened the strangeness to see her, as such a figure in such a picture, talk of "horrors," but she was to do in a few minutes something stranger yet—though even of this he was to take the full measure but afterwards—and the note of it already trembled. It was, for the matter of that, one of the signs that her eyes were having again the high flicker of their prime. He had to admit, however, what she said. "Oh yes, there were times when we did go far." He caught himself in the act of speaking as if it all were over. Well, he wished it were; and the consummation depended for him clearly more and more on his friend.

But she had now a soft smile. "Oh far—!"

It was oddly ironic. "Do you mean you're prepared to go further?"

She was frail and ancient and charming as she continued to look at him, yet it was rather as if she had lost the thread. "Do you consider that we went far?"

"Why I thought it the point you were just making—that we *had* looked most things in the face."

"Including each other?" She still smiled. "But you're quite right. We've had together great imaginations, often great fears; but some of them have been unspoken."

"Then the worst—we have n't faced that. I *could* face it, I believe, if I knew what you think it. I feel," he explained, "as if I had lost my power to conceive such things." And he wondered if he looked as blank as he sounded. "It's spent."

"Then why do you assume," she asked, "that mine is n't?"

"Because you've given me signs to the contrary. It is n't a question for you of conceiving, imagining, comparing. It is n't a question now of choosing." At last he came out with it. "You know something I don't. You've shown me that before."

These last words had affected her, he made out in a moment, exceedingly, and she spoke with firmness. "I've shown you, my dear, nothing."

He shook his head. "You can't hide it."

"Oh, oh!" May Bartram sounded over what she could n't hide. It was almost a smothered groan.

"You admitted it months ago, when I spoke of it to you as of something you were afraid I should find out. Your answer was that I could n't, that I would n't, and I don't pretend I have. But you had something therefore in mind, and I now see how it must have been, how it still is, the possibility that, of all possibilities, has settled itself for you as the worst. This," he went on, "is why I appeal to you. I'm only afraid of ignorance to-day—I'm not afraid of knowledge." And then as for a while she said nothing: "What makes me sure is that I see in your face and feel here, in this air and amid these appearances, that you're out of it. You've done. You've had your experience. You leave me to my fate."

Well, she listened, motionless and white in her chair, as on a decision to be made, so that her manner was fairly an avowal, though still, with a small fine inner stiffness, an imperfect surrender. "It *would* be the worst," she finally let herself say. "I mean the thing I've never said."

It hushed him a moment. "More monstrous than all the monstrosities we've named?"

"More monstrous. Is n't that what you sufficiently express," she asked, "in calling it the worst?"

Marcher thought. "Assuredly—if you mean, as I do, something that includes all the loss and all the shame that are thinkable."

"It would if it *should* happen," said May Bartram. "What we're speaking of, remember, is only my idea."

"It's your belief," Marcher returned. "That's enough for me. I feel your beliefs are right. Therefore if, having this one, you give me no more light on it, you abandon me."

"No, no!" she repeated. "I'm with you—don't you see?—still." And as to make it more vivid to him she rose from her chair—a movement she seldom risked in these days—and showed herself, all draped and all soft, in her fairness and slimness. "I have n't forsaken you."

It was really, in its effort against weakness, a generous assurance, and had the success of the impulse not, happily, been great, it would have touched him to pain more than to pleasure. But the cold charm in her eyes had spread, as she hovered before him, to all the rest of her person, so that it was for the minute almost a recovery of youth. He could n't pity her for that; he could only take her as she showed—as capable even yet of helping him. It was as if, at the same time, her light might at any instant go out; wherefore he must make the most of it. There passed before him with intensity the three or four things he wanted most to know; but the question that came of itself to his lips really covered the others. "Then tell me if I shall consciously suffer."

She promptly shook her head. "Never!"

It confirmed the authority he imputed to her, and it produced on him an extraordinary effect. "Well, what's better than that? Do you call that the worst?"

"You think nothing is better?" she asked.

She seemed to mean something so special that he again sharply wondered, though still with the dawn of a prospect of relief. "Why not, if one does n't *know?*" After which, as their eyes, over his question, met in a silence, the dawn deepened and something to his purpose came prodigiously out of her very face. His own, as he took it in, suddenly flushed to the forehead, and he gasped with the force of a perception to which, on the instant, everything fitted. The sound of his gasp filled the air; then he became articulate. "I see—if I don't suffer!"

In her own look, however, was doubt. "You see what?"

"Why what you mean—what you've always meant."

She again shook her head. "What I mean is n't what I've always meant. It's different."

"It's something new?"

She hung back from it a little. "Something new. It's not what you think. I see what you think."

His divination drew breath then; only her correction might be wrong. "It is n't that I *am* a blockhead?" he asked between faintness and grimness. "It is n't that it's all a mistake?"

"A mistake?" she pityingly echoed. *That* possibility, for her, he saw, would be monstrous; and if she guaranteed him the immunity from pain it would accordingly not be what she had in mind. "Oh no," she declared; "it's nothing of that sort. You've been right."

Yet he could n't help asking himself if she were n't, thus pressed, speaking but to save him. It seemed to him he should be most in a hole if his history should prove all a platitude. "Are you telling me the truth, so that I shan't have been a bigger idiot than I can bear to know? I *have n't* lived with a vain imagination, in the most besotted illusion? I have n't waited but to see the door shut in my face?"

She shook her head again. "However the case stands *that* is n't the truth. Whatever the reality, it *is* a reality. The door is n't shut. The door's open," said May Bartram.

"Then something's to come?"

She waited once again, always with her cold sweet eyes on him. "It's never too late." She had, with her gliding step, diminished the distance between them, and she stood nearer to him, close to him, a minute, as if still charged with the unspoken. Her movement might have been for some finer emphasis of what she was at once hesitating and deciding to say. He had been standing by the chimney-piece, fireless and sparely adorned, a small perfect old French clock and two morsels of rosy Dresden constituting all its furniture; and her hand grasped the shelf while she kept him waiting, grasped it a little as for support and encouragement. She only kept him waiting, however; that is he only waited. It had become suddenly, from her movement and attitude, beautiful and vivid to him that she had something more to give him; her wasted face delicately shone with it—it glittered almost as with the white lustre of silver in her expression. She was right, incontestably, for what he saw in her face was the truth, and strangely, without consequence, while their talk of it as dreadful was still in the air, she appeared to present it as inordinately soft. This, prompting bewilderment, made him but gape the more gratefully for her revelation, so that they continued for some minutes silent, her face shining at him, her contact imponderably pressing, and his stare all kind but all expectant. The end, none the less, was that what he had expected failed to come to him. Something else took place instead, which seemed to consist at first in the mere closing of her eyes. She gave way at the same instant to a slow fine shudder, and though he remained staring—though he stared in fact but the harder—turned off and regained her chair. It was the end of what she had been intending, but it left him thinking only of that.

"Well, you don't say—?"

She had touched in her passage a bell near the chimney and had sunk back strangely pale. "I'm afraid I'm too ill."

"Too ill to tell me?" It sprang up sharp to him, and almost to his lips, the fear she might die without giving him light. He checked himself in time from so expressing his question, but she answered as if she had heard the words.

"Don't you know—now?"

"'Now'—?" She had spoken as if some difference had been made within the moment. But her maid, quickly obedient to her bell, was already with them. "I know nothing." And he was afterwards to say to himself that he must have spoken with odious impatience, such an impatience as to show that, supremely disconcerted, he washed his hands of the whole question.

"Oh!" said May Bartram.

"Are you in pain?" he asked as the woman went to her.

"No," said May Bartram.

Her maid, who had put an arm round her as if to take her to her room, fixed on him eyes that appealingly contradicted her; in spite of which, however, he showed once more his mystification. "What then has happened?"

She was once more, with her companion's help, on her feet, and, feeling withdrawal imposed on him, he had blankly found his hat and gloves and had reached the door. Yet he waited for her answer. "What *was* to," she said.

V

He came back the next day, but she was then unable to see him, and as it was literally the first time this had occurred in the long stretch of their acquaintance he turned away, defeated and sore, almost angry—or feeling at least that such a break in their custom was really the beginning of the end—and wandered alone with his thoughts, especially with the one he was least able to keep down. She was dying and he would lose her; she was dying and his life would end. He stopped in the Park, into which he had passed, and stared before him at his recurrent doubt. Away from her the doubt pressed again; in her presence he had believed her, but as he felt his forlornness he threw himself into the explanation that, nearest at hand, had most of a miserable warmth for him and least of a cold torment. She had deceived him to save him— to put him off with something in which he should be able to rest. What could the thing that was to happen to him be, after all, but just this thing that had begun to happen? Her dying, her death, his consequent solitude—*that* was what he had figured as the Beast in the Jungle, that was what had been in the lap of the gods. He had had her word for it as he left her—what else on earth could she have meant? It was n't a thing of a monstrous order; not a fate rare and distinguished; not a stroke of fortune that overwhelmed and immortalised; it had only the stamp of the common doom. But poor Marcher at this hour judged the common doom sufficient. It would serve his turn, and even as the consummation of infinite waiting he would bend his pride to accept it. He sat down on a bench in the twilight. He had n't been a fool. Something had *been,* as she had said, to come. Before he rose indeed it had quite struck him that the final fact really matched with the long avenue through which he had had to reach it. As sharing his suspense and as giving herself all, giving her life, to bring it to an end, she had come with him every step of the way. He had lived by her aid, and to leave her behind would be cruelly, damnably to miss her. What could be more overwhelming than that?

Well, he was to know within the week, for though she kept him a while at bay, left him restless and wretched during a series of days on each of which he asked about her only again to have to turn away, she ended his trial by receiving him where she had always received him. Yet she had been brought out at some hazard into the presence of so many of the things that were, consciously, vainly, half their past, and there was scant service left in the gentleness of her mere desire, all too visible, to check his obsession and wind up his long trouble. That was clearly what she wanted, the one thing more for her own peace while she could still put out her hand. He was so affected by her state that, once seated by her chair, he was moved to let everything go; it was she herself therefore who brought him back, took up again, before she dismissed him, her last word of the other time. She showed how she wished to leave their business in order. "I'm not sure you understood. You've nothing to wait for more. It *has* come."

Oh how he looked at her! "Really?"

"Really."

"The thing that, as you said, *was* to?"

"The thing that we began in our youth to watch for."

Face to face with her once more he believed her; it was a claim to which he had so abjectly little to oppose. "You mean that it has come as a positive definite occurrence, with a name and a date?"

"Positive. Definite. I don't know about the 'name,' but oh with a date!"

He found himself again too helplessly at sea. "But come in the night—come and passed me by?"

May Bartram had her strange faint smile. "Oh no, it has n't passed you by!"

"But if I have n't been aware of it and it has n't touched me—?"

"Ah your not being aware of it"—and she seemed to hesitate an instant to deal with this—"your not being aware of it is the strangeness *in* the strangeness. It's the wonder *of* the wonder." She spoke as with the softness almost of a sick child, yet now at last, at the end of all, with the perfect straightness of a sibyl. She visibly knew that she knew, and the effect on him was of something co-ordinate, in its high character, with the law that had ruled him. It was the true voice of the law; so on her lips would the law itself have sounded. "It *has* touched you," she went on. "It has done its office. It has made you all its own."

"So utterly without my knowing it?"

"So utterly without your knowing it." His hand, as he leaned to her, was on the arm of her chair, and, dimly smiling always now, she placed her own on it. "It's enough if *I* know it."

"Oh!" he confusedly breathed, as she herself of late so often had done.

"What I long ago said is true. You'll never know now, and I think you ought to be content. You've *had* it," said May Bartram.

"But had what?"

"Why what was to have marked you out. The proof of your law. It has acted. I'm too glad," she then bravely added, "to have been able to see what it's *not.*"

He continued to attach his eyes to her, and with the sense that it was all beyond him, and that *she* was too, he would still have sharply challenged her had n't he so felt it an abuse of her weakness to do more than take devoutly what she gave him, take it hushed as to a revelation. If he did speak, it was out of the foreknowledge of his loneliness to come. "If you're glad of what it's 'not' it might then have been worse?"

She turned her eyes away, she looked straight before her; with which after a moment: "Well, you know our fears."

He wondered. "It's something then we never feared?"

On this slowly she turned to him. "Did we ever dream, with all our dreams, that we should sit and talk of it thus?"

He tried for a little to make out that they had; but it was as if their dreams, numberless enough, were in solution in some thick cold mist through which thought lost itself. "It might have been that we could n't talk?"

"Well"—she did her best for him—"not from this side. This, you see," she said, "is the *other* side."

"I think," poor Marcher returned, "that all sides are the same to me." Then, however, as she gently shook her head in correction: "We might n't, as it were, have got across—?"

"To where we are—no. We're *here*"—she made her weak emphasis.

"And much good does it do us!" was her friend's frank comment.

"It does us the good it can. It does us the good that *it* is n't here. It's past. It's behind," said May Bartram. "Before—" but her voice dropped.

He had got up, not to tire her, but it was hard to combat his yearning. She after all told him nothing but that his light had failed—which he knew well enough without her. "Before—?" he blankly echoed.

"Before, you see, it was always to *come*. That kept it present."

"Oh I don't care what comes now! Besides," Marcher added, "it seems to me I liked it better present, as you say, than I can like it absent with *your* absence."

"Oh mine!"—and her pale hands made light of it.

"With the absence of everything." He had a dreadful sense of standing there before her for—so far as anything but this proved, this bottomless drop was concerned— the last time of their life. It rested on him with a weight he felt he could scarce bear, and this weight it apparently was that still pressed out what remained in him of speakable protest. "I believe you; but I can't begin to pretend I understand. *Nothing*, for me, is past; nothing *will* pass till I pass myself, which I pray my stars may be as soon as possible. Say, however," he added, "that I've eaten my cake, as you contend, to the last crumb—how can the thing I've never felt at all be the thing I was marked out to feel?"

She met him perhaps less directly, but she met him unperturbed. "You take your 'feelings' for granted. You were to suffer your fate. That was not necessarily to know it."

"How in the world—when what is such knowledge but suffering?"

She looked up at him a while in silence. "No—you don't understand."

"I suffer," said John Marcher.

"Don't, don't!"

"How can I help at least *that?*"

"Don't!" May Bartram repeated.

She spoke it in a tone so special, in spite of her weakness, that he stared an instant —stared as if some light, hitherto hidden, had shimmered across his vision. Darkness again closed over it, but the gleam had already become for him an idea. "Because I haven't the right—?"

"Don't *know*—when you need n't," she mercifully urged. "You need n't—for we should n't."

"Should n't?" If he could but know what she meant!

"No—it's too much."

"Too much?" he still asked but, with a mystification that was the next moment of a sudden to give way. Her words, if they meant something, affected him in this light—the light also of her wasted face—as meaning *all*, and the sense of what knowledge had been for herself came over him with a rush which broke through into a question. "Is it of that then you're dying?"

She but watched him, gravely at first, as to see, with this, where he was, and she might have seen something or feared something that moved her sympathy. "I would live for you still—if I could." Her eyes closed for a little, as if, withdrawn into herself, she were for a last time trying. "But I can't!" she said as she raised them again to take leave of him.

She could n't indeed, as but too promptly and sharply appeared, and he had no vision of her after this that was anything but darkness and doom. They had parted for ever in that strange talk; access to her chamber of pain, rigidly guarded, was almost wholly forbidden him; he was feeling now moreover, in the face of doctors, nurses, the two or three relatives attracted doubtless by the presumption of what she had to "leave," how few were the rights, as they were called in such cases, that he had to put forward, and how odd it might even seem that their intimacy should n't have given him more of them. The stupidest fourth cousin had more, even though she had been nothing in such a person's life. She had been a feature of features in *his,* for what else was it to have been so indispensable? Strange beyond saying were the ways of existence, baffling for him the anomaly of his lack, as he felt it to be, of producible claim. A woman might have been, as it were, everything to him, and it might yet present him in no connexion that any one seemed held to recognise. If this was the case in these closing weeks it was the case more sharply on the occasion of the last offices rendered, in the great grey London cemetery, to what had been mortal, to what had been precious, in his friend. The concourse at her grave was not numerous, but he saw himself treated as scarce more nearly concerned with it than if there had been a thousand others. He was in short from this moment face to face with the fact that he was to profit extraordinarily little by the interest May Bartram had taken in him. He could n't quite have said what he expected, but he had n't surely expected this approach to a double privation. Not only had her interest failed him, but he seemed to feel himself unattended—and for a reason he could n't seize—by the distinction, the dignity, the propriety, if nothing else, of the man markedly bereaved. It was as if in the view of society he had not *been* markedly bereaved, as if there still failed some sign or proof of it, and as if none the less his character could never be affirmed nor the deficiency ever made up. There were moments as the weeks went by when he would have liked, by some almost aggressive act, to take his stand on the intimacy of his loss, in order that it *might* be questioned and his retort, to the relief of his spirit, so recorded; but the moments of an irritation more helpless followed fast on these, the moments during which, turning things over with a good conscience but with a bare horizon, he found himself wondering if he ought n't to have begun, so to speak, further back.

He found himself wondering indeed at many things, and this last speculation had others to keep it company. What could he have done, after all, in her lifetime, without giving them both, as it were, away? He could n't have made known she was watching him, for that would have published the superstition of the Beast. This was what closed his mouth now—now that the Jungle had been threshed to vacancy and that the Beast had stolen away. It sounded too foolish and too flat; the difference for him in this particular, the extinction in his life of the element of suspense, was such as in fact to surprise him. He could scarce have said what the effect resembled; the abrupt cessation, the positive prohibition, of music perhaps, more than anything else, in some place all adjusted and all accustomed to sonority and to attention. If he could at any rate have conceived lifting the veil from his image at some moment of the past (what had he done, after all, if not lift it to *her?*) so to do this to-day, to talk to people at large of the Jungle cleared and confide to them that he now felt it as safe, would have been not only to see them listen as to a goodwife's tale, but really to hear himself tell one. What it presently came to in truth was that poor Marcher waded through his beaten grass, where no life stirred, where no breath sounded, where no evil eye seemed to gleam from a possible lair, very much as if vaguely looking for the Beast, and still more as if acutely missing it. He walked about in an existence that had grown strangely more spacious, and, stopping fitfully in places where the undergrowth of life struck him as closer, asked himself yearningly, wondered secretly and sorely, if it would have lurked here or there. It would have at all events *sprung;* what was at least complete was his belief in the truth itself of the assurance given him. The change from his old sense to his new was absolute and final: what was to happen *had* so absolutely and finally happened that he was as little able to know a fear for his future as to know a hope; so absent in short was any question of anything still to come. He was to live entirely with the other question, that of his unidentified past, that of his having to see his fortune impenetrably muffled and masked.

The torment of this vision became then his occupation; he could n't perhaps have consented to live but for the possibility of guessing. She had told him, his friend, not to guess; she had forbidden him, so far as he might, to know, and she had even in a sort denied the power in him to learn: which were so many things, precisely, to deprive him of rest. It was n't that he wanted, he argued for fairness, that anything past and done should repeat itself; it was only that he should n't, as an anticlimax, have been taken sleeping so sound as not to be able to win back by an effort of thought the lost stuff of consciousness. He declared to himself at moments that he would either win it back or have done with consciousness for ever; he made this idea his one motive in fine, made it so much his passion that none other, to compare with it, seemed ever to have touched him. The lost stuff of consciousness became thus for him as a strayed or stolen child to an unappeasable father; he hunted it up and down very much as if he were knocking at doors and enquiring of the police. This was the spirit in which, inevitably, he set himself to travel; he started on a journey that was to be as long as he could make it; it danced before him that, as the other side of the globe could n't possibly have less to say to him, it might, by a possibility of suggestion, have more. Before he quitted London, however, he made a pilgrimage to May Bartram's grave, took his way to it through the endless avenues of the grim suburban metropolis, sought it out in the wilderness of tombs, and, though he had come but for the renewal of the act of farewell, found himself, when he had at last stood by it, beguiled into long intensities. He stood for an hour, powerless to turn away and yet powerless to penetrate the darkness of death; fixing with his eyes her inscribed name and date, beating his forehead against the fact of the secret they kept, drawing his breath, while he waited, as if some sense would in pity of him rise from the stones. He kneeled on the stones, however, in vain; they kept what they concealed; and if the face of the tomb did become a face for him it was because her two names became a pair of eyes that did n't know him. He gave them a last long look, but no palest light broke.

VI

He stayed away, after this, for a year; he visited the depths of Asia, spending himself on scenes of romantic interest, of superlative sanctity; but what was present to him everywhere was that for a man who had known what *he* had known the world was vulgar and vain. The state of mind in which he had lived for so many years shone out to him, in reflexion, as a light that coloured and refined, a light beside which the glow of the East was garish cheap and thin. The terrible truth was that he had lost —with everything else—a distinction as well; the things he saw could n't help being common when he had become common to look at them. He was simply now one of them himself—he was in the dust, without a peg for the sense of difference; and there were hours when, before the temples of gods and the sepulchres of kings, his spirit turned for nobleness of association to the barely discriminated slab in the London suburb. That had become for him, and more intensely with time and distance, his one witness of a past glory. It was all that was left to him for proof or pride, yet the past glories of Pharaohs were nothing to him as he thought of it. Small wonder then that he came back to it on the morrow of his return. He was drawn there this time as irresistibly as the other, yet with a confidence, almost, that was doubtless the effect of the many months that had elapsed. He had lived, in spite of himself, into his change of feeling, and in wandering over the earth had wandered, as might be said, from the circumference to the centre of his desert. He had settled to his safety and accepted perforce his extinction; figuring to himself, with some colour, in the likeness of certain little old men he remembered to have seen, of whom, all meagre and wizened as they might look, it was related that they had in their time fought twenty duels or been loved by ten princesses. They indeed had been wondrous for others while he was but wondrous for himself; which, however, was exactly the cause of his haste to renew the wonder by getting back, as he might put it, into his own presence. That had quickened his steps and checked his delay. If his visit was prompt it was because he had been separated so long from the part of himself that alone he now valued.

It's accordingly not false to say that he reached his goal with a certain elation and stood there again with a certain assurance. The creature beneath the sod *knew* of his rare experience, so that, strangely now, the place had lost for him its mere blankness of expression. It met him in mildness—not, as before, in mockery; it wore for him the air of conscious greeting that we find, after absence, in things that have closely belonged to us and which seem to confess of themselves to the connexion. The plot of ground, the graven tablet, the tended flowers affected him so as belonging to him that he resembled for the hour a contented landlord reviewing a piece of property. Whatever had happened—well, had happened. He had not come back this time with the vanity of that question, his former worrying "What, *what?*" now practically so spent. Yet he would none the less never again so cut himself off from the spot; he would come back to it every month, for if he did nothing else by its aid he at least held up his head. It thus grew for him, in the oddest way, a positive resource; he carried out his idea of periodical returns, which took their place at last among the most inveterate of his habits. What it all amounted to, oddly enough, was that in his finally so simplified world this garden of death gave him the few square feet of earth on which he could still most live. It was as if, being nothing anywhere else for any one, nothing even for himself, he were just everything here, and if not for a crowd of witnesses or indeed for any witness but John Marcher, then by clear right of the register that he could scan like an open page. The open page was the tomb of his friend, and *there* were the facts of the past, there the truth of his life, there the backward reaches in which he could lose himself. He did this from time to time with such effect that he seemed to wander through the old years with his hand in the arm of a companion who was, in the most extraordinary manner, his other, his younger self; and to wander, which was more extraordinary yet, round and round a third presence —not wandering she, but stationary, still, whose eyes, turning with his revolution, never ceased to follow him, and whose seat was his point, so to speak, of orientation. Thus in short he settled to live—feeding all on the sense that he once *had* lived, and dependent on it not alone for a support but for an identity.

It sufficed him in its way for months and the year elapsed; it would doubtless even have carried him further but for an accident, superficially slight, which moved him, quite in another direction, with a force beyond any of his impressions of Egypt or of India. It was a thing of the merest chance—the turn, as he afterwards felt, of a hair, though he was indeed to live to believe that if light had n't come to him in this particular fashion it would still have come in another. He was to live to believe this, I say, though he was not to live, I may not less definitely mention, to do much else. We allow him at any rate the benefit of the conviction, struggling up for him at the end, that, whatever might have happened or not happened, he would have come round of himself to the light. The incident of an autumn day had put the match to the train laid from of old by his misery. With the light before him he knew that even of late his ache had only been smothered. It was strangely drugged, but it throbbed; at the touch it began to bleed. And the touch, in the event, was the face of a fellow mortal. This face, one grey afternoon when the leaves were thick in the alleys, looked into Marcher's own, at the cemetery, with an expression like the cut of a blade. He felt it, that is, so deep down that he winced at the steady thrust. The person who so mutely assaulted him was a figure he had noticed, on reaching his own goal, absorbed by a grave a short distance away, a grave apparently fresh, so that the emotion of the visitor would probably match it for frankness. This fact alone forbade further attention, though during the time he stayed he remained vaguely conscious of his neighbour, a middle-aged man apparently, in mourning, whose bowed back, among the clustered monuments and mortuary yews, was constantly presented. Marcher's theory that these were elements in contact with which he himself revived, had suffered, on this occasion, it may be granted, a marked, an excessive check. The autumn day was dire for him as none had recently been, and he rested with a heaviness he had not yet known on the low stone table that bore May Bartram's name. He rested without power to move, as if some spring in him, some spell vouchsafed, had suddenly been broken for ever. If he could have done that moment as he wanted he would simply have stretched himself on the slab that was ready to take him, treating it as a place prepared to receive his last sleep. What in all the wide world had he now to keep awake for? He stared before him with the question, and it was then that, as one of the cemetery walks passed near him, he caught the shock of the face.

His neighbour at the other grave had withdrawn, as he himself, with force enough in him, would have done by now, and was advancing along the path on his way to one of the gates. This brought him close, and his pace was slow, so that—and all the more as there was a kind of hunger in his look—the two men were for a minute directly confronted. Marcher knew him at once for one of the deeply stricken—a perception so sharp that nothing else in the picture comparatively lived, neither his dress, his age, nor his presumable character and class; nothing lived but the deep ravage of the features he showed. He *showed* them—that was the point; he was moved, as he passed, by some impulse that was either a signal for sympathy or, more possibly, a challenge to an opposed sorrow. He might already have been aware of our friend, might at some previous hour have noticed in him the smooth habit of the scene, with which the state of his own senses so scantly consorted, and might thereby have been stirred as by an overt discord. What Marcher was at all events conscious of was in the first place that the image of scarred passion presented to him was conscious too— of something that profaned the air; and in the second that, roused, startled, shocked, he was yet the next moment looking after it, as it went, with envy. The most extraordinary thing that had happened to him—though he had given that name to other matters as well—took place, after his immediate vague stare, as a consequence of this impression. The stranger passed, but the raw glare of his grief remained, making our friend wonder in pity what wrong, what wound it expressed, what injury not to be healed. What had the man *had,* to make him by the loss of it so bleed and yet live?

Something—and this reached him with a pang—that *he,* John Marcher, had n't; the proof of which was precisely John Marcher's arid end. No passion had ever touched him, for this was what passion meant; he had survived and maundered and pined, but where had been *his* deep ravage? The extraordinary thing we speak of was the sudden rush of the result of this question. The sight that had just met his eyes named to him, as in letters of quick flame, something he had utterly, insanely missed, and what he had missed made these things a train of fire, made them mark themselves in an anguish of inward throbs. He had seen *outside* of his life, not learned it within, the way a woman was mourned when she had been loved for herself: such was the force of his conviction of the meaning of the stranger's face, which still flared for him as a smoky torch. It had n't come to him, the knowledge, on the wings of experience; it had brushed him, jostled him, upset him, with the disrespect of chance, the insolence of accident. Now that the illumination had begun, however, it blazed to the zenith, and what he presently stood there gazing at was the sounded void of his life. He gazed, he drew breath, in pain; he turned in his dismay, and, turning, he had before him in sharper incision than ever the open page of his story. The name on the table smote him as the passage of his neighbour had done, and what it said to him, full in the face, was that *she* was what he had missed. This was the awful thought, the answer to all the past, the vision at the dread clearness of which he grew as cold as the stone beneath him. Everything fell together, confessed, explained, overwhelmed; leaving him most of all stupefied at the blindness he had cherished. The fate he had been marked for he had met with a vengeance—he had emptied the cup to the lees; he had been the man of his time, *the* man, to whom nothing on earth was to have happened. That was the rare stroke—that was his visitation. So he saw it, as we say, in pale horror, while the pieces fitted and fitted. So *she* had seen it while he did n't, and so she served at this hour to drive the truth home. It was the truth, vivid and monstrous, that all the while he had waited the wait was itself his portion. This the companion of his vigil had at a given moment made out, and she had then offered him the chance to baffle his doom. One's doom, however, was never baffled, and on the day she told him his own had come down she had seen him but stupidly stare at the escape she offered him.

The escape would have been to love her; then, *then* he would have lived. *She* had lived—who could say now with what passion?—since she had loved him for himself; whereas he had never thought of her (ah how it hugely glared at him!) but in the chill of his egotism and the light of her use. Her spoken words came back to him —the chain stretched and stretched. The Beast had lurked indeed, and the Beast, at its hour, had sprung; it had sprung in that twilight of the cold April when, pale, ill, wasted, but all beautiful, and perhaps even then recoverable, she had risen from her chair to stand before him and let him imaginably guess. It had sprung as he did n't guess; it had sprung as she hopelessly turned from him, and the mark, by the time he left her, had fallen where it *was* to fall. He had justified his fear and achieved his fate; he had failed, with the last exactitude, of all he was to fail of; and a moan now rose to his lips as he remembered she had prayed he might n't know. This horror of waking—*this* was knowledge, knowledge under the breath of which the very tears in his eyes seemed to freeze. Through them, none the less, he tried to fix it and hold it; he kept it there before him so that he might feel the pain. That at least, belated and bitter, had something of the taste of life. But the bitterness suddenly sickened him, and it was as if, horribly, he saw, in the truth, in the cruelty of his image, what had been appointed and done. He saw the Jungle of his life and saw the lurking Beast; then, while he looked, perceived it, as by a stir of the air, rise, huge and hideous, for the leap that was to settle him. His eyes darkened—it was close; and, instinctively turning, in his hallucination, to avoid it, he flung himself, face down, on the tomb.

1903

---

from Preface to *The American*

. . . If in "The American" I invoked the romantic association without malice prepense, yet with a production of the romantic effect that is for myself unmistakeable, the occasion is of the best perhaps for penetrating a little the obscurity of that principle. By what art or mystery, what craft of selection, omission or commission, does a given picture of life appear to us to surround its theme, its figures and images, with the air of romance while another picture close beside it may affect us as steeping the whole matter in the element of reality? . . .

(. . . The real represents to my perception the things we cannot possibly *not* know, sooner or later, in one way or another; it being but one of the accidents of our hampered state, and one of the incidents of their quantity and number, that particular instances have not yet come our way. The romantic stands, on the other hand, for the things that, with all the facilities in the world, all the wealth and all the courage and all the wit and all the adventure, we never *can* directly know; the things that can reach us only through the beautiful circuit and subterfuge of our thought and our desire.) There have been, I gather, many definitions of romance, as a matter indispensably of boats, or of caravans, or of tigers, or of "historical characters," or of ghosts, or of forgers, or of detectives, or of beautiful wicked women, or of pistols and knives, but they appear for the most part reducible to the idea of the facing of danger, the acceptance of great risks for the fascination, the very love, of their uncertainty, the joy of success if possible and of battle in any case. This would be a fine formula if it bore examination; but it strikes me as weak and inadequate, as by no means covering the true ground and yet as landing us in strange confusions.

The panting pursuit of danger is the pursuit of life itself, in which danger awaits us possibly at every step and faces us at every turn; so that the dream of an intenser experience easily becomes rather some vision of a sublime security like that enjoyed on the flowery plains of heaven, where we may conceive ourselves proceeding in ecstasy from one prodigious phase and form of it to another. And if it be insisted that the measure of the type is then in the *appreciation* of danger—the sign of our projection of the real being the smallness of its dangers, and that of our projection of the romantic the hugeness, the mark of the distinction being in short, as they say of collars and gloves and shoes, the size and "number" of the danger—this discrimination again surely fails, since it makes our difference not a difference of kind, which is what we want, but a difference only of degree, and subject by that condition to the indignity of a sliding scale and a shifting measure. There are immense and flagrant dangers that are but sordid and squalid ones, as we feel, tainting with their quality the very defiances they provoke; while there are common and covert ones, that "look like nothing" and that can be but inwardly and occultly dealt with, which involve the sharpest hazards to life and honour and the highest instant decisions and intrepidities of action. It is an arbitrary stamp that keeps these latter prosaic and makes the former heroic; and yet I should still less subscribe to a mere "subjective" division— I mean one that would place the difference wholly in the temper of the imperilled agent. It would be impossible to have a more romantic temper than Flaubert's Madame Bovary,[1] and yet nothing less resembles a romance than the record of her adventures. To classify it by that aspect—the definition of the spirit that happens to animate her —is like settling the question (as I have seen it witlessly settled) by the presence or absence of "costume." Where again then does costume begin or end?—save with the "run" of one or another sort of play? We must reserve vague labels for artless mixtures.

The only *general* attribute of projected romance that I can see, the only one that fits all its cases, is the fact of the kind of experience with which it deals—experience liberated, so to speak; experience disengaged, disembroiled, disencumbered, exempt from the conditions that we usually know to attach to it and, if we wish so to put the matter, drag upon it, and operating in a medium which relieves it, in a particular interest, of the inconvenience of a *related,* a measurable state, a state subject to all our vulgar communities. The greatest intensity may so be arrived at evidently—when the sacrifice of community, of the "related" sides of situations, has not been too rash. It must to this end not flagrantly betray itself; we must even be kept if possible, for our illusion, from suspecting any sacrifice at all. The balloon of experience is in fact of course tied to the earth, and under that necessity we swing, thanks to a rope of remarkable length, in the more or less commodious car of the imagination; but it is by the rope we know where we are, and from the moment that cable is cut we are at large and unrelated: we only swing apart from the globe—though remaining as exhilarated, naturally, as we like, especially when all goes well. The art of the romancer is, "for the fun of it," insidiously to cut the cable, to cut it without our detecting him. What I have recognised then in "The American," much to my surprise and after long years, is that the experience here represented is the disconnected and uncontrolled experience—uncontrolled by our general sense of "the way things happen"—which romance alone more or less successfully palms off on us. It is a case of Newman's[2] own intimate experience all, that being my subject, the thread of which, from beginning to end, is not once exchanged, however momentarily, for any other thread; and the experience of others concerning us, and concerning him, only so far as it touches him and as he recognises, feels or divines it. There is our general sense

---

[1] The heroine of the novel by the same name (1856), created by Gustave Flaubert (1821–1880), French novelist and literary acquaintance of James. Emma Bovary's temperament is as romantic as the narrative in which she figures is severely realistic.

[2] Newman: hero of *The American.*

of the way things happen—it abides with us indefeasibly, as readers of fiction, from the moment we demand that our fiction shall be intelligible; and there is our particular sense of the way they don't happen, which is liable to wake up unless reflexion and criticism, in us, have been skilfully and successfully drugged. There are drugs enough, clearly—it is all a question of applying them with tact; in which case the way things don't happen may be artfully made to pass for the way things do. . . .

1907

from The American Scene

from **Chapter II**

[The New York City Harbor]

. . . There is the beauty of light and air, the great scale of space, and, seen far away to the west, the open gates of the Hudson, majestic in their degree, even at a distance, and announcing still nobler things. But the real appeal, unmistakably, is in that note of vehemence in the local life of which I have spoken, for it is the appeal of a particular type of dauntless power.

The aspect the power wears then is indescribable; it is the power of the most extravagant of cities, rejoicing, as with the voice of the morning, in its might, its fortune, its unsurpassable conditions, and imparting to every object and element, to the motion and expression of every floating, hurrying, panting thing, to the throb of ferries and tugs, to the plash of waves and the play of winds and the glint of lights and the shrill of whistles and the quality and authority of breeze-borne cries—all, practically, a diffused, wasted clamour of *detonations*—something of its sharp free accent and, above all, of its sovereign sense of being "backed" and able to back. The universal *applied* passion struck me as shining unprecedentedly out of the composition; in the bigness and bravery and insolence, especially, of everything that rushed and shrieked; in the air as of a great intricate frenzied dance, half merry, half desperate, or at least half defiant, performed on the huge watery floor. This appearance of the bold lacing-together, across the waters, of the scattered members of the monstrous organism—lacing as by the ceaseless play of an enormous system of steam-shuttles or electric bobbins (I scarce know what to call them), commensurate in form with their infinite work—does perhaps more than anything else to give the pitch of the vision of energy. One has the sense that the monster grows and grows, flinging abroad its loose limbs even as some unmannered young giant at his "larks," and that the binding stitches must for ever fly further and faster and draw harder; the future complexity of the web, all under the sky and over the sea, becoming thus that of some colossal set of clockworks, some steel-souled machine-room of brandished arms and hammering fists and opening and closing jaws. The immeasurable bridges are but as the horizontal sheaths of pistons working at high pressure, day and night, and subject, one apprehends with perhaps inconsistent gloom, to certain, to fantastic, to merciless multiplication. In the light of this apprehension indeed the breezy brightness of the Bay puts on the semblance of the vast white page that awaits beyond any other perhaps the black overscoring of science.

Let me hasten to add that its present whiteness is precisely its charming note, the frankest of the signs you recognize and remember it by. That is the distinction I was just feeling my way to name as the main ground of its doing so well, for effect, without technical scenery. There are great imposing ports—Glasgow and Liverpool and London—that have already their page blackened almost beyond redemption from any such light of the picturesque as can hope to irradiate fog and grime, and there are others, Marseilles and Constantinople say, or, for all I know to the contrary, New Orleans, that contrive to abound before everything else in colour, and so to make a rich and instant and obvious show. But memory and the actual impression keep investing New York with the tone, predominantly, of summer dawns and winter frosts, of sea-foam, of bleached sails and stretched awnings, of blanched hulls, of scoured decks, of new ropes, of polished brasses, of streamers clear in the blue air; and it is by this harmony, doubtless, that the projection of the individual character of the place, of the candour of its avidity and the freshness of its audacity, is most conveyed. The "tall buildings," which have so promptly usurped a glory that affects you as rather surprised, as yet, at itself, the multitudinous sky-scrapers standing up to the view, from the water, like extravagant pins in a cushion already overplanted, and stuck in as in the dark, anywhere and anyhow, have at least the felicity of carrying out the fairness of tone, of taking the sun and the shade in the manner of towers of marble. They are not all of marble, I believe, by any means, even if some may be, but they are impudently new and still more impudently "novel"—this in common with so many other terrible things in America—and they are triumphant payers of dividends; all of which uncontested and unabashed pride, with flash of innumerable windows and flicker of subordinate gilt attributions, is like the flare, up and down their long, narrow faces, of the lamps of some general permanent "celebration.". . .

[Ellis Island]

In the Bay,[1] the rest of the morning, the dense raw fog that delayed the big boat, allowing sight but of the immediate ice-masses through which it thumped its way, was not less of the essence. Anything blander, as a medium, would have seemed a mockery of the facts of the terrible little Ellis Island,[2] the first harbour of refuge and stage of patience for the million or so of immigrants annually knocking at our official door. Before this door, which opens to them there only with a hundred forms and ceremonies, grindings and grumblings of the key, they stand appealing and waiting, marshalled, herded, divided, subdivided, sorted, sifted, searched, fumigated, for longer or shorter periods—the effect of all which prodigious process, an intendedly "scientific" feeding of the mill, is again to give the earnest observer a thousand more things to think of than he can pretend to retail. The impression of Ellis Island, in fine, would be—as I was to find throughout that so many of my impressions would be—a chapter by itself; and with a particular page for recognition of the degree in which the liberal

---

[1] New York Harbor.
[2] Ellis Island was opened in 1892 as the point of entry for the ever-increasing numbers of newly arrived immigrants.

hospitality of the eminent Commissioner of this wonderful service, to whom I had been introduced, helped to make the interest of the whole watched drama poignant and unforgettable. It is a drama that goes on, without a pause, day by day and year by year, this visible act of ingurgitation on the part of our body politic and social, and constituting really an appeal to amazement beyond that of any sword-swallowing or fire-swallowing of the circus. The wonder that one couldn't keep down was the thought that these two or three hours of one's own chance vision of the business were but as a tick or two of the mighty clock, the clock that never, never stops—least of all when it strikes, for a sign of so much winding-up, some louder hour of our national fate than usual. I think indeed that the simplest account of the action of Ellis Island on the spirit of any sensitive citizen who may have happened to "look in" is that he comes back from his visit not at all the same person that he went. He has eaten of the tree of knowledge, and the taste will be for ever in his mouth. He had thought he knew before, thought he had the sense of the degree in which it is his American fate to share the sanctity of his American consciousness, the intimacy of his American patriotism, with the inconceivable alien; but the truth had never come home to him with any such force. In the lurid light projected upon it by those courts of dismay it shakes him—or I like at least to imagine it shakes him—to the depths of his being; I like to think of him, I positively *have* to think of him, as going about ever afterwards with a new look, for those who can see it, in his face, the outward sign of the new chill in his heart. So is stamped, for detection, the questionably privileged person who has had an apparition, seen a ghost in his supposedly safe old house. Let not the unwary, therefore, visit Ellis Island.

The after-sense of that acute experience, however, I myself found, was by no means to be brushed away; I felt it grow and grow, on the contrary, wherever I turned: other impressions might come and go, but this affirmed claim of the alien, however immeasurably alien, to share in one's supreme relation was everywhere the fixed element, the reminder not to be dodged. One's supreme relation, as one had always put it, was one's relation to one's country—a conception made up so largely of one's countrymen and one's countrywomen. Thus it was as if, all the while, with such a fond tradition of what these products predominantly were, the idea of the country itself underwent something of that profane overhauling through which it appears to suffer the indignity of change. Is not our instinct in this matter, in general, essentially the safe one—that of keeping the idea simple and strong and continuous, so that it shall be perfectly sound? To touch it overmuch, to pull it about, is to put it in peril of weakening; yet on this free assault upon it, this readjustment of it in *their* monstrous, presumptuous interest, the aliens, in New York, seemed perpetually to insist. The combination there of their quantity and their quality—that loud primary stage of alienism which New York most offers to sight—operates, for the native, as their note of settled possession, something they have nobody to thank for; so that *un*settled possession is what we, on our side, seem reduced to—the implication of which, in its turn, is that, to recover confidence and regain lost ground, we, not they, must make the surrender and accept the orientation. We must go, in other words *more* than half-way to meet them; which is all the difference, for us, between possession and dispossession. This sense of dispossession, to be brief about it, haunted me so, I was to feel, in the New York streets and in the packed trajectiles to which one clingingly appeals from the streets, just as one tumbles back into the streets in appalled reaction from *them,* that the art of beguiling or duping it became an art to be cultivated—though the fond alternative vision was never long to be obscured, the imagination, exasperated to envy, of the ideal, in the order in question; of the luxury of some such close and sweet and *whole* national consciousness as that of the Switzer and the Scot. . . .

from **Chapter VII**

[The Rotary System]

. . . It is a consistent application of the rotary system[3]—the untried always awaiting its turn, and quite perceptibly stamping and snorting while it waits; all heedless as it is, poor innocent untried, of the certain hour of the impatiences before which it too will have to retreat. It is not indeed that the American laws, so operating, have not almost always their own queer interest; founded as they are, all together, on one of the strongest of the native impulses. We see this characteristic again and again at play, see it in especial wherever we see (which is more than frequently enough) a university or a college "started" or amplified.[4] This process almost always takes the form, primarily, of more lands and houses and halls and rooms, more swimming-baths and football-fields and gymnasia, a greater luxury of brick and mortar, a greater ingenuity, the most artful conceivable, of accommodation and installation. Such is the magic, such the presences, that tend, more than any other, to figure *as* the Institution, thereby perverting not a little, as need scarce be remarked, the finer collegiate idea: the theory being, doubtless, and again most characteristically, that with all the wrought stone and oak and painted glass, the immense provision, the multiplied marbles and tiles and cloisters and acres, "people will come," that is, individuals of value will, and in some manner work some miracle. In the early American time, doubtless, individuals of value had to wait too much for things; but that is now made up by the way things are waiting for individuals of value. . . .

from **Chapter XI**

[The American Woman]

. . . From the moment it is adequately borne in mind that the business-man, in the United States, may, with no matter what dim struggles, gropings, yearnings, never hope to be anything *but* a business-man, the size of the field he so abdicates is measured, as well as the fact of the other care to which his abdication hands it over. It lies there waiting, pleading from all its pores, to be occupied—the lonely waste, the boundless gaping void of "society"; which is but a rough name for all the *other* so numerous relations with the world he lives in that are imputable to the civilized being. Here it is then that the world he lives in accepts its doom and becomes, by his default, subject and plastic to his mate; his default having made, all around him, the unexampled

---

[3] I.e., the principle by which the old is constantly being replaced by the new for its own sake.

[4] James's observations were prompted by the new buildings erected on the campus of Harvard University during his twenty-year absence from Cambridge, Massachusetts.

opportunity of the woman—which she would have been an incredible fool not to pounce upon. It needs little contact with American life to perceive how she *has* pounced, and how, outside business, she has made it over in her image. She has been, up to now, on the vast residual tract, in peerless possession, and is occupied in developing and extending her wonderful conquest, which she appreciates to the last inch of its extent.

She has meanwhile probably her hours of amazement at the size of her windfall; she cannot quite live without wonder at the oddity of her so "sleeping" partner, the strange creature, by her side, with his values and his voids, but who is best known to her as having yielded what she would have clutched to the death. Yet these are mere mystic, inscrutable possibilities—dreams, for us, of her hushed, shrouded hours: the face she shows, on all the facts, is that of mere unwinking tribute to the matter of course. The effect of these high signs of assurance in her has been—and it is really her master-stroke—to represent the situation as perfectly normal. Her companion's attitude, totally destitute of high signs, does everything it can to further this feat; so that, as disposed together in the American picture, they testify, extraordinarily, to the *successful* rupture of a universal law, the sight is at first, for observation, most mystifying. Then the impunity of the whole thing gains upon us; the equilibrium strikes us, however strangely, as at least provisionally stable; we see that a society in many respects workable would seem to have been arrived at, and that we shall in any case have time to study it. The phenomenon may easily become, for a spectator, the sentence written largest in the American sky: when he is in search of the characteristic, what else so plays the part? The woman is two-thirds of the apparent life—which means that she is absolutely all of the social; and, as this is nowhere else the case, the occasion is unique for seeing what such a situation may make of her. The result elsewhere, in Europe generally, of conditions in which men have actively participated and to which, throughout, they personally contribute, she has only the old story to tell, and keeps telling it after her fashion. The woman produced by a women-made society alone has obviously quite a new story—to which it is not for a moment to be gainsaid that the world at large has, for the last thirty years in particular, found itself lending an attentive, at times even a charmed, ear. The extent and variety of this attention have been the specious measure of the personal success of the type in question, and are always referred to when its value happens to be challenged. "The American woman?—why, she has beguiled, she has conquered, the globe: look at her fortune everywhere and fail to accept her if you can."

She has been, accordingly, about the globe, beyond all doubt, a huge success of curiosity; she has at her best—and far beyond any consciousness and intention of her own, lively as these for the most part usually are—infinitely amused the nations. It has been found among them that, for more reasons than we can now go into, her manner of embodying and representing her sex has fairly made of her a new human convenience, not unlike fifty of the others, of a slightly different order, the ingenious mechanical appliances, stoves, refrigerators, sewing-machines, type-writers, cash-registers, that have done so much, in the household and the place of business, for the American name. By which I am of course far from meaning that the revelation has been of her utility as a domestic drudge; it has been much rather in the fact that the advantages attached to her being a woman at all have been so happily combined with the absence of the drawbacks, for persons intimately dealing with her, traditionally suggested by that condition. The corresponding advantages, in the light of almost any old order, have always seemed inevitably paid for by the drawbacks; but here, unmistakably, was a case in which—as at first appeared, certainly—they were to be enjoyed very nearly for nothing. What it came to, evidently, was that she had been grown in an air in which a hundred of the "European" complications and dangers didn't exist, and in which also she had had to take upon herself a certain training for freedom. It was not that she had had, in the vulgar sense, to "look out" for herself, inasmuch as it was of the very essence of her position not to be threatened or waylaid; but that she could develop her audacity on the basis of her security, just as she could develop her "powers" in a medium from which criticism was consistently absent. Thus she arrived, full-blown, on the general scene, the least criticized object, in proportion to her importance, that had ever adorned it. It would take long to say why her situation, under this retrospect, may affect the inner fibre of the critic himself as one of the most touching on record; he may merely note his perception that she was to have been after all but the sport of fate. For why need she originally, he wonders, have embraced so confidently, so gleefully, yet so unguardedly, the terms offered her to an end practically so perfidious? Why need she, unless in the interest of her eventual discipline, have turned away with so light a heart after watching the Man, the deep American man, retire into his tent and let down the flap? She had her "paper" from him, their agreement signed and sealed; but would she not, in some other air and under some other sky, have been visited by a saving instinct? . . .

[Washington, D.C.]

The "artistic" Federal city already announced spreads itself then before us, in plans elaborated even to the finer details, a city of palaces and monuments and gardens, symmetries and circles and far radiations, with the big Potomac for water-power and water-effect and the recurrent Maryland spring, so prompt and so full-handed, for a perpetual benediction. This imagery has, above all, the value, for the considering mind, that it presents itself as under the wide-spread wings of the general Government, which fairly make it figure to the rapt vision as the object caught up in eagle claws and lifted into fields of air that even the high brows of the municipal boss fail to sweep. The wide-spread wings affect us, in the prospect, as great fans that, by their mere tremor, will blow the work, at all steps and stages, clean and clear, disinfect it quite ideally of any germ of the job, and prepare thereby for the American voter, on the spot and in the pride of possession, quite a new kind of civic consciousness. The scheme looms largest, surely, as a demonstration of the possibilities of that service to him, and nothing about it will be more interesting than to measure—though this may take time —the nature and degree of his alleviation. Will the new pride I speak of sufficiently inflame him? Will the taste of the new consciousness, finding him so fresh to it, prove the right medicine? One can only regret that we must still rather indefinitely wait to see—and regret it all the more that there is always, in America, yet another lively source of interest involved in the execution of such designs, and closely involved just in proportion as the high intention, the formal majesty, of the thing seems assured. It comes back to what we constantly feel, throughout the country, to what the American scene everywhere depends on for half its appeal or its effect; to the fact that the social conditions, the material, pressing and pervasive, make the particular experiment or demonstration, whatever it may pretend to, practically a new and incalculable thing. This general Americanism is often the one tag of character attaching to the case after every other appears to have abandoned it. The thing is happening, or will have to happen, in the American way—that American way which is more different from all other native ways, taking country with country, than any of these latter are different from each other; and the question is of how, each time, the American way will see it through. . . .

from **Chapter XII**

[The Young Virginian]

The Richmond halls,[5] at any rate, appeared, through the chill of the season, scantly trodden, and I met in them no fellow-visitor but a young man of stalwart and ingenuous aspect who struck me so forcibly, after a little, as exhaling a natural piety that, as we happened at last to be rapt in contemplation of the same sad glass case, I took advantage of the occasion to ask him if he were a Southerner. His affirmative was almost eager, and he proved—for all the world like the hero of a famous novel —a gallant and nameless, as well as a very handsome, young Virginian. A farmer by occupation, he had come up on business from the interior to the capital, and, having a part of his morning on his hands, was spending it in this visitation—made, as I gathered, by no means for the first time, but which he still found absorbing. As a son of the new South he presented a lively interest of type—linguistically not least (since where doesn't the restless analyst grope for light?)—and his interest, the ground of my here recalling him, was promptly to arrive at a climax. He pointed out to me, amid an array of antique regimentals, certain objects identical with relics preserved in his own family and that had belonged to his father, who, enrolled at the earliest age, had fought to the end of the War. The old implements before us bore the number of the Virginia regiment in which this veteran had first seen service, and a question or two showed me how well my friend was acquainted with his parent's exploits. Enjoying, apparently—for he was intelligent and humorous and highly conversable —the opportunity to talk of such things (they being, as it were, so advantageously present there with a vague Northerner), he related, felicitously, some paternal adventure of which I have forgotten the particulars, but which comprised a desperate evasion of capture, or worse, by the lucky smashing of the skull of a Union soldier. I complimented him on his exact knowledge of these old, unhappy, far-off things, and it was his candid response that was charmingly suggestive. "Oh, I should be ready to do them all over again myself!" And then, smiling serenely, but as if it behoved even the least blatant of Northerners to understand: "That's the kind of Southerner *I* am!" I allowed that he was a capital kind of Southerner, and we afterwards walked together to the Public Library, where, on our finally parting, I could but thank him again for being so much the kind of Southerner I had wanted. He was a fine contemporary young American, incapable, so to speak, of hurting a Northern fly— *as* Northern; but whose consciousness would have been poor and unfurnished without this cool platonic passion. With what other pattern, personal views apart, *could* he

[5] The museum in Richmond, Virginia, dedicated to relics of the Confederacy.

have adorned its bare walls? So I wondered till it came to me that, though he wouldn't have hurt a Northern fly, there were things (ah, we had touched on some of these!) that, all fair, engaging, smiling, as he stood there, he would have done to a Southern negro. . . .

from **Chapter XIII**

[Florida and California]

. . . That was to come home to me presently in Florida—through the touched sense of the truth that Florida, ever so amiably, is weak. You may live there serenely, no doubt—as in a void furnished at the most with velvet air; you may in fact live there with an idea, if you are content that your idea shall consist of grapefruit and oranges. Oranges, grapefruit and velvet air constitute, in a manner, I admit, a feast; but press upon the board with any greater weight and it quite gives way—its three or four props treacherously forsake it. That is what I mean by the impression, in the great empty peninsula, of weakness; which I was to feel still clearer about on being able to compare it afterwards with the impression of California. California was to have —if I may decently be premature about it—her own treachery; but she was to wind one up much higher before she let one down. I was to find her, especially at the first flush, unlike sweet frustrated Florida, ever so amiably strong: which came from the art with which she makes the stoutnesses, as I have called them, of natural beauty stand you in temporary stead of the leannesses of everything else (everything that might be of an order equally interesting). This she is on a short acquaintance quite insolently able to do, thanks to her belonging so completely to the "handsome" side of the continent, of which she is the finest expression. The aspect of natural objects, up and down the Pacific coast, is as "aristocratic" as the comprehensive American condition permits anything to be: it indeed appears to the ingenious mind to represent an instinct on the part of Nature, a sort of shuddering, bristling need, to brace herself in advance against the assault of a society so much less marked with distinction than herself. If I was to conceive therefore under these later lights, that her spirit had put forth nowhere on the sub-tropical Atlantic shore anything to approach this conscious pride, so, doubtless, the Carolinian effect, even at its sweetest, was to strike me as related to it very much as a tinkle is related to a boom. . . .

from **Chapter XIV**

[The Railroads and the West]

. . . To what extent was hugeness, to what extent *could* it be, a ground for complacency of view, in any country not visited for the very love of wildness, for positive joy in barbarism?[6] Where was the charm of boundless immensity as overlooked from a car-window?—with the general pretension to charm, the general conquest of nature

---

[6] Traveling by train across the western states, James conjectures what the noise made by the Pullman cars is saying to him about the purposes to which the open spaces, laid claim to by the railroads, will be put in the future.

and space, affirmed, immediately round about you, by the general pretension of the Pullman, the great monotonous rumble of which seems forever to say to you: "See what I'm making of all this—see what I'm making, what I'm making!" I was to become later on still more intimately aware of the spirit of one's possible reply to that, but even then my consciousness served, and the eloquence of my exasperation seems, in its rude accents, to come back to me.

"I see what you are *not* making, oh, what you are ever so vividly not; and how can I help it if I am subject to that lucidity?—which appears never welcome to you, for its measure of truth, as it ought to be! How can I not be so subject, from the moment I don't just irreflectively gape? If I were one of the painted savages you have dispossessed, or even some tough reactionary trying to emulate him, what you are making would doubtless impress me more than what you are leaving unmade; for in that case it wouldn't be to *you* I should be looking in any degree for beauty or for charm. Beauty and charm would be for me in the solitude you have ravaged, and I should owe you my grudge for every disfigurement and every violence, for every wound with which you have caused the face of the land to bleed. No, since I accept your ravage, what strikes me is the long list of the arrears of your undone; and so constantly, right and left, that your pretended message of civilization is but a colossal recipe for the *creation* of arrears, and of such as can but remain forever out of hand. You touch the great lonely land—as one feels it still to be—only to plant upon it some ugliness about which, never dreaming of the grace of apology or contrition, you then proceed to brag with a cynicism all your own. You convert the large and noble sanities that I see around me, you convert them one after the other to crudities, to invalidities, hideous and unashamed; and you so leave them to add to the number of the myriad aspects you simply spoil, of the myriad unanswerable questions that you scatter about as some monstrous unnatural mother might leave a family of unfathered infants on doorsteps or in waiting-rooms. This is the meaning surely of the inveterate rule that you shall multiply the perpetrations you call 'places'—by the sign of some name as senseless, mostly, as themselves—to the sole end of multiplying to the eye, as one approaches, every possible source of displeasure. When nobody cares or notices or suffers, by all one makes out, when no displeasure, by what one can see, is ever felt or ever registered, why shouldn't you, you may indeed ask, be as much in your right as you need? But in that fact itself, that fact of the vast general unconsciousness and indifference, looms, for any restless analyst who may come along, the accumulation, on your hands, of the unretrieved and the irretrievable!"

1907

The Jolly Corner

I

"Every one asks me what I 'think' of everything," said Spencer Brydon; "and I make answer as I can—begging or dodging the question, putting them off with any nonsense. It would n't matter to any of them really," he went on, "for, even were it possible to meet in that stand-and-deliver way so silly a demand on so big a subject, my 'thoughts' would still be almost altogether about something that concerns only myself." He was talking to Miss Staverton, with whom for a couple of months now he had availed himself of every possible occasion to talk; this disposition and this resource, this comfort and support, as the situation in fact presented itself, having promptly enough taken the first place in the considerable array of rather unattenuated surprises attending his so strangely belated return to America. Everything was somehow a surprise; and that might be natural when one had so long and so consistently neglected everything, taken pains to give surprises so much margin for play. He had given them more than thirty years—thirty-three, to be exact; and they now seemed to him to have organised their performance quite on the scale of that licence. He had been twenty-three on leaving New York—he was fifty-six to-day: unless indeed he were to reckon as he had sometimes, since his repatriation, found himself feeling; in which case he would have lived longer than is often allotted to man. It would have taken a century, he repeatedly said to himself, and said also to Alice Staverton, it would have taken a longer absence and a more averted mind than those even of which he had been guilty, to pile up the differences, the newnesses, the queernesses, above all the bignesses, for the better or the worse, that at present assaulted his vision wherever he looked.

The great fact all the while however had been the incalculability; since he *had* supposed himself, from decade to decade, to be allowing, and in the most liberal and intelligent manner, for brilliancy of change. He actually saw that he had allowed for nothing; he missed what he would have been sure of finding, he found what he would never have imagined. Proportions and values were upside-down; the ugly things he had expected, the ugly things of his far-away youth, when he had too promptly waked up to a sense of the ugly—these uncanny phenomena placed him rather, as it happened, under the charm; whereas the "swagger" things, the modern, the monstrous, the famous things, those he had more particularly, like thousands of ingenuous enquirers every year, come over to see, were exactly his sources of dismay. They were as so many set traps for displeasure, above all for reaction, of which his restless tread was constantly pressing the spring. It was interesting, doubtless, the whole show, but it would have been too disconcerting had n't a certain finer truth saved the situation. He had distinctly not, in this steadier light, come over *all* for the monstrosities; he had come, not only in the last analysis but quite on the face of the act, under an impulse with which they had nothing to do. He had come—putting the thing pompously— to look at his "property," which he had thus for a third of a century not been within four thousand miles of; or, expressing it less sordidly, he had yielded to the humour of seeing again his house on the jolly corner, as he usually, and quite fondly, described it—the one in which he had first seen the light, in which various members of his family had lived and had died, in which the holidays of his overschooled boyhood had been passed and the few social flowers of his chilled adolescence gathered, and which, alienated then for so long a period, had, through the successive deaths of his two brothers and the termination of old arrangements, come wholly into his hands. He was the owner of another, not quite so "good"—the jolly corner having been, from far back, superlatively extended and consecrated; and the value of the pair represented his main capital, with an income consisting, in these later years, of their respective rents which (thanks precisely to their original excellent type) had never been depressingly low. He could live in "Europe," as he had been in the habit of living, on the product of these flourishing New York leases, and all the better since, that of the second structure, the mere number in its long row, having within a twelvemonth fallen in, renovation at a high advance had proved beautifully possible.

These were items of property indeed, but he had found himself since his arrival distinguishing more than ever between them. The house within the street, two bristling blocks westward, was already in course of reconstruction as a tall mass of flats; he had acceded, some time before, to overtures for this conversion—in which, now that it was going forward, it had been not the least of his astonishments to find himself able, on the spot, and though without a previous ounce of such experience, to participate with a certain intelligence, almost with a certain authority. He had lived his life with his back so turned to such concerns and his face addressed to those of so different an order that he scarce knew what to make of this lively stir, in a compartment of his mind never yet penetrated, of a capacity for business and a sense for construction. These virtues, so common all round him now, had been dormant in his own organism—where it might be said of them perhaps that they had slept the sleep of the just. At present, in the splendid autumn weather—the autumn at least was a pure boon in the terrible place—he loafed about his "work" undeterred, secretly agitated; not in the least "minding" that the whole proposition, as they said, was vulgar and sordid, and ready to climb ladders, to walk the plank, to handle materials and look wise about them, to ask questions, in fine, and challenge explanations and really "go into" figures.

It amused, it verily quite charmed him; and, by the same stroke, it amused, and even more, Alice Staverton, though perhaps charming her perceptibly less. She was n't however going to be better-off for it, as *he* was—and so astonishingly much: nothing was now likely, he knew, ever to make her better-off than she found herself, in the afternoon of life, as the delicately frugal possessor and tenant of the small house in Irving Place to which she had subtly managed to cling through her almost unbroken New York career. If he knew the way to it now better than to any other address among the dreadful multiplied numberings which seemed to him to reduce the whole place to some vast ledger-page, overgrown, fantastic, of ruled and criss-crossed lines and figures—if he had formed, for his consolation, that habit, it was really not a little because of the charm of his having encountered and recognised, in the vast wilderness of the wholesale, breaking through the mere gross generalisation of wealth and force and success, a small still scene where items and shades, all delicate things, kept the sharpness of the notes of a high voice perfectly trained, and where economy hung about like the scent of a garden. His old friend lived with one maid and herself dusted her relics and trimmed her lamps and polished her silver; she stood off, in the awful modern crush, when she could, but she sallied forth and did battle when the challenge was really to "spirit," the spirit she after all confessed to, proudly and a little shyly, as to that of the better time, that of *their* common, their quite far-away and antediluvian social period and order. She made use of the street-cars when need be, the terrible things that people scrambled for as the panic-stricken at sea scramble for the boats; she affronted, inscrutably, under stress, all the public concussions and ordeals; and yet, with that slim mystifying grace of her appearance, which defied you to say if she were a fair young woman who looked older through trouble, or a fine smooth older one who looked young through successful indifference; with her precious reference, above all, to memories and histories into which he could enter, she was as exquisite for him as some pale pressed flower (a rarity to begin with), and, failing other sweetnesses, she was a sufficient reward of his effort. They had communities of knowledge, "their" knowledge (this discriminating possessive was always on her lips) of presences of the other age, presences all overlaid, in his case, by the experience of a man and the freedom of a wanderer, overlaid by pleasure, by infidelity, by passages of life that were strange and dim to her, just by "Europe" in short, but still unobscured, still exposed and cherished, under that pious visitation of the spirit from which she had never been diverted.

She had come with him one day to see how his "apartment-house" was rising; he had helped her over gaps and explained to her plans, and while they were there had happened to have, before her, a brief but lively discussion with the man in charge, the representative of the building-firm that had undertaken his work. He had found himself quite "standing-up" to this personage over a failure on the latter's part to observe some detail of one of their noted conditions, and had so lucidly argued his case that, besides ever so prettily flushing, at the time, for sympathy in his triumph, she had afterwards said to him (though to a slightly greater effect of irony) that he had clearly for too many years neglected a real gift. If he had but stayed at home he would have anticipated the inventor of the sky-scraper. If he had but stayed at home he would have discovered his genius in time really to start some new variety of awful architectural hare and run it till it burrowed in a goldmine. He was to remember these words, while the weeks elapsed, for the small silver ring they had sounded over the queerest and deepest of his own lately most disguised and most muffled vibrations.

It had begun to be present to him after the first fortnight, it had broken out with the oddest abruptness, this particular wanton wonderment: it met him there—and this was the image under which he himself judged the matter, or at least, not a little, thrilled and flushed with it—very much as he might have been met by some strange figure, some unexpected occupant, at a turn of one of the dim passages of an empty house. The quaint analogy quite hauntingly remained with him, when he didn't indeed rather improve it by a still intenser form: that of his opening a door behind which he would have made sure of finding nothing, a door into a room shuttered and void, and yet so coming, with a great suppressed start, on some quite erect confronting presence, something planted in the middle of the place and facing him through the dusk. After that visit to the house in construction he walked with his companion to see the other and always so much the better one, which in the eastward direction formed one of the corners, the "jolly" one precisely, of the street now so generally dishonoured and disfigured in its westward reaches, and of the comparatively conservative Avenue.[1] The Avenue still had pretensions, as Miss Staverton said, to decency; the old people had mostly gone, the old names were unknown, and here and there an old association seemed to stray, all vaguely, like some very aged person, out too late, whom you might meet and feel the impulse to watch or follow, in kindness, for safe restoration to shelter.

They went in together, our friends; he admitted himself with his key, as he kept no one there, he explained, preferring, for his reasons, to leave the place empty, under a simple arrangement with a good woman living in the neighbourhood and who came

[1] Lower Fifth Avenue near Fourteenth Street, the New York City area where James grew up.

for a daily hour to open windows and dust and sweep. Spencer Brydon had his reasons and was growingly aware of them; they seemed to him better each time he was there, though he didn't name them all to his companion, any more than he told her as yet how often, how quite absurdly often, he himself came. He only let her see for the present, while they walked through the great blank rooms, that absolute vacancy reigned and that, from top to bottom, there was nothing but Mrs. Muldoon's broomstick, in a corner, to tempt the burglar. Mrs. Muldoon was then on the premises, and she loquaciously attended the visitors, preceding them from room to room and pushing back shutters and throwing up sashes—all to show them, as she remarked, how little there was to see. There was little indeed to see in the great gaunt shell where the main dispositions and the general apportionment of space, the style of an age of ampler allowances, had nevertheless for its master their honest pleading message, affecting him as some good old servant's, some lifelong retainer's appeal for a character, or even for a retiring-pension; yet it was also a remark of Mrs. Muldoon's that, glad as she was to oblige him by her noonday round, there was a request she greatly hoped he would never make of her. If he should wish her for any reason to come in after dark she would just tell him, if he "plased," that he must ask it of somebody else.

The fact that there was nothing to see did n't militate for the worthy woman against what one *might* see, and she put it frankly to Miss Staverton that no lady could be expected to like, could she? "craping up to thim top storeys in the ayvil hours." The gas and the electric light were off the house, and she fairly evoked a gruesome vision of her march through the great grey rooms—so many of them as there were too!—with her glimmering taper. Miss Staverton met her honest glare with a smile and the profession that she herself certainly would recoil from such an adventure. Spencer Brydon meanwhile held his peace—for the moment; the question of the "evil" hours in his old home had already become too grave for him. He had begun some time since to "crape," and he knew just why a packet of candles addressed to that pursuit had been stowed by his own hand, three weeks before, at the back of a drawer of the fine old sideboard that occupied, as a "fixture," the deep recess in the dining-room. Just now he laughed at his companions—quickly however changing the subject; for the reason that, in the first place, his laugh struck him even at that moment as starting the odd echo, the conscious human resonance (he scarce knew how to qualify it) that sounds made while he was there alone sent back to his ear or his fancy; and that, in the second, he imagined Alice Staverton for the instant on the point of asking him, with a divination, if he ever so prowled. There were divinations he was unprepared for, and he had at all events averted enquiry by the time Mrs. Muldoon had left them, passing on to other parts.

There was happily enough to say, on so consecrated a spot, that could be said freely and fairly; so that a whole train of declarations was precipitated by his friend's having herself broken out, after a yearning look round: "But I hope you don't mean they want you to pull *this* to pieces!" His answer came, promptly, with his re-awakened wrath: it was of course exactly what they wanted, and what they were "at" him for, daily, with the iteration of people who could n't for their life understand a man's liability to decent feelings. He had found the place, just as it stood and beyond what he could express, an interest and a joy. There were values other than the beastly rent-values, and in short, in short—! But it was thus Miss Staverton took him up.

"In short you're to make so good a thing of your sky-scraper that, living in luxury on *those* ill-gotten gains, you can afford for a while to be sentimental here!" Her smile had for him, with the words, the particular mild irony with which he found half her talk suffused; an irony without bitterness and that came, exactly, from her having so much imagination—not, like the cheap sarcasms with which one heard most people, about the world of "society," bid for the reputation of cleverness, from nobody's really having any. It was agreeable to him at this very moment to be sure that when he had answered, after a brief demur, "Well yes: so, precisely, you may put it!" her imagination would still do him justice. He explained that even if never a dollar were to come to him from the other house he would nevertheless cherish this one; and he dwelt, further, while they lingered and wandered, on the fact of the stupefaction he was already exciting, the positive mystification he felt himself create.

He spoke of the value of all he read into it, into the mere sight of the walls, mere shapes of the rooms, mere sound of the floors, mere feel, in his hand, of the old silver-plated knobs of the several mahogany doors, which suggested the pressure of the palms of the dead; the seventy years of the past in fine that these things represented, the annals of nearly three generations, counting his grandfather's, the one that had ended there, and the impalpable ashes of his long-extinct youth, afloat in the very air like microscopic motes. She listened to everything; she was a woman who answered intimately but who utterly did n't chatter. She scattered abroad therefore no cloud of words; she could assent, she could agree, above all she could encourage, without doing that. Only at the last she went a little further than he had done himself. "And then how do you know? You may still, after all, want to live here." It rather indeed pulled him up, for it was n't what he had been thinking, at least in her sense of the words. "You mean I may decide to stay on for the sake of it?"

"Well, *with* such a home—!" But, quite beautifully, she had too much tact to dot so monstrous an *i,* and it was precisely an illustration of the way she did n't rattle. How could any one—of any wit—insist on any one else's "wanting" to live in New York?

"Oh," he said, "I *might* have lived here (since I had my opportunity early in life); I might have put in here all these years. Then everything would have been different enough—and, I dare say, 'funny' enough. But that's another matter. And then the beauty of it—I mean of my perversity, of my refusal to agree to a 'deal'—is just in the total absence of a reason. Don't you see that if I had a reason about the matter at all it would *have* to be the other way, and would then be inevitably a reason of dollars? There are no reasons here *but* of dollars. Let us therefore have none whatever —not the ghost of one."

They were back in the hall then for departure, but from where they stood the vista was large, through an open door, into the great square main saloon, with its almost antique felicity of brave spaces between windows. Her eyes came back from that reach and met his own a moment. "Are you very sure the 'ghost' of one doesn't, much rather, serve—?"

He had a positive sense of turning pale. But it was as near as they were then to come. For he made answer, he believed, between a glare and a grin: "Oh ghosts— of course the place must swarm with them! I should be ashamed of it if it didn't. Poor Mrs. Muldoon's right, and it's why I haven't asked her to do more than look in."

Miss Staverton's gaze again lost itself, and things she did n't utter, it was clear, came and went in her mind. She might even for the minute, off there in the fine room, have imagined some element dimly gathering. Simplified like the death-mask of a handsome face, it perhaps produced for her just then an effect akin to the stir of an expression in the "set" commemorative plaster. Yet whatever her impression may have been she produced instead a vague platitude. "Well, if it were only furnished and lived in—!"

She appeared to imply that in case of its being still furnished he might have been a little less opposed to the idea of a return. But she passed straight into the vestibule, as if to leave her words behind her, and the next moment he had opened the house-door and was standing with her on the steps. He closed the door and, while he re-pocketed his key, looking up and down, they took in the comparatively harsh actuality of the Avenue, which reminded him of the assault of the outer light of the Desert on the traveller emerging from an Egyptian tomb. But he risked before they stepped into the street his gathered answer to her speech. "For me it *is* lived in. For me it *is* furnished." At which it was easy for her to sigh "Ah yes—!" all vaguely and discreetly; since his parents and his favourite sister, to say nothing of other kin, in numbers, had run their course and met their end there. That represented, within the walls, ineffaceable life.

It was a few days after this that, during an hour passed with her again, he had expressed his impatience of the too flattering curiosity—among the people he met— about his appreciation of New York. He had arrived at none at all that was socially producible, and as for that matter of his "thinking" (thinking the better or the worse of anything there) he was wholly taken up with one subject of thought. It was mere vain egoism, and it was moreover, if she liked, a morbid obsession. He found all things come back to the question of what he personally might have been, how he might have led his life and "turned out," if he had not so, at the outset, given it up. And confessing for the first time to the intensity within him of this absurd speculation—which but proved also, no doubt, the habit of too selfishly thinking—he affirmed the impotence there of any other source of interest, any other native appeal. "What would it have made of me, what would it have made of me? I keep for ever wondering, all idiotically; as if I could possibly know! I see what it has made of dozens of others, those I meet, and it positively aches within me, to the point of exasperation, that it would have made something of me as well. Only I can't make out *what,* and the worry of it, the small rage of curiosity never to be satisfied, brings back what I remember to have felt, once or twice, after judging best, for reasons, to burn some important letter unopened. I've been sorry, I've hated it—I've never known what was in the letter. You may of course say it's a trifle—!"

"I don't say it's a trifle," Miss Staverton gravely interrupted.

She was seated by her fire, and before her, on his feet and restless, he turned to and fro between this intensity of his idea and a fitful and unseeing inspection, through his single eye-glass, of the dear little old objects on her chimney-piece. Her interruption made him for an instant look at her harder. "I should n't care if you did!" he laughed, however; "and it's only a figure, at any rate, for the way I now feel. *Not* to have followed my perverse young course—and almost in the teeth of my father's curse, as I may say; not to have kept it up, so, 'over there,' from that day to this, without a doubt or a pang; not, above all, to have liked it, to have loved it, so much, loved it, no doubt, with such an abysmal conceit of my own preference: some variation from *that,* I say, must have produced some different effect for my life and for my 'form.' I should have stuck here—if it had been possible; and I was too young, at twenty-three, to judge, *pour deux sous,*[2] whether it *were* possible. If I had waited I might have seen it was, and then I might have been, by staying here, something nearer to one of these types who have been hammered so hard and made so keen by their conditions. It is n't that I admire them so much—the question of any charm in them, or of any charm, beyond that of the rank money-passion, exerted by their conditions *for* them, has nothing to do with the matter: it's only a question of what fantastic, yet perfectly possible, development of my own nature I may n't have missed. It comes over me that I had then a strange *alter ego* deep down somewhere within me, as the full-blown flower is in the small tight bud, and that I just took the course, I just transferred him to the climate, that blighted him for once and for ever."

"And you wonder about the flower," Miss Staverton said. "So do I, if you want to know; and so I've been wondering these several weeks. I believe in the flower," she continued, "I feel it would have been quite splendid, quite huge and monstrous."

"Monstrous above all!" her visitor echoed; "and I imagine, by the same stroke, quite hideous and offensive."

"You don't believe that," she returned; "if you did you would n't wonder. You'd know, and that would be enough for you. What you feel—and what I feel *for* you —is that you'd have had power."

"You'd have liked me that way?" he asked.

She barely hung fire. "How should I not have liked you?"

"I see. You'd have liked me, have preferred me, a billionaire!"

"How should I not have liked you?" she simply again asked.

He stood before her still—her question kept him motionless. He took it in, so much there was of it; and indeed his not otherwise meeting it testified to that. "I know at least what I am," he simply went on; "the other side of the medal's clear enough. I've not been edifying—I believe I'm thought in a hundred quarters to have been barely decent. I've followed strange paths and worshipped strange gods; it must have come to you again and again—in fact you've admitted to me as much—that I was leading, at any time these thirty years, a selfish frivolous scandalous life. And you see what it has made of me."

She just waited, smiling at him. "You see what it has made of *me.*"

"Oh you're a person whom nothing can have altered. You were born to be what you are, anywhere, anyway: you've the perfection nothing else could have blighted. And don't you see how, without my exile, I should n't have been waiting till now—?" But he pulled up for the strange pang.

"The great thing to see," she presently said, "seems to me to be that it has spoiled nothing. It has n't spoiled your being here at last. It has n't spoiled this. It has n't spoiled your speaking—" She also however faltered.

He wondered at everything her controlled emotion might mean. "Do you believe then—too dreadfully!—that I *am* as good as I might ever have been?"

"Oh no! Far from it!" With which she got up from her chair and was nearer to him. "But I don't care," she smiled.

[2] French: "for two cents" (that is, since inexperienced).

"You mean I'm good enough?"

She considered a little. "Will you believe it if I say so? I mean will you let that settle your question for you?" And then as if making out in his face that he drew back from this, that he had some idea which, however absurd, he could n't yet bargain away: "Oh you don't care either—but very differently: you don't care for anything but yourself."

Spencer Brydon recognised it—it was in fact what he had absolutely professed. Yet he importantly qualified. "*He* is n't myself. He's the just so totally other person. But I do want to see him," he added. "And I can. And I shall."

Their eyes met for a minute while he guessed from something in hers that she divined his strange sense. But neither of them otherwise expressed it, and her apparent understanding, with no protesting shock, no easy derision, touched him more deeply than anything yet, constituting for his stifled perversity, on the spot, an element that was like breatheable air. What she said however was unexpected. "Well, *I've* seen him."

"You—?"

"I've seen him in a dream."

"Oh a 'dream'—!" It let him down.

"But twice over," she continued. "I saw him as I see you now."

"You've dreamed the same dream—?"

"Twice over," she repeated. "The very same."

This did somehow a little speak to him, as it also gratified him. "You dream about me at that rate?"

"Ah about *him!*" she smiled.

His eyes again sounded her. "Then you know all about him." And as she said nothing more: "What's the wretch like?"

She hesitated, and it was as if he were pressing her so hard that, resisting for reasons of her own, she had to turn away. "I'll tell you some other time!"

II

It was after this that there was most of a virtue for him, most of a cultivated charm, most of a preposterous secret thrill, in the particular form of surrender to his obsession and of address to what he more and more believed to be his privilege. It was what in these weeks he was living for—since he really felt life to begin but after Mrs. Muldoon had retired from the scene and, visiting the ample house from attic to cellar, making sure he was alone, he knew himself in safe possession and, as he tacitly expressed it, let himself go. He sometimes came twice in the twenty-four hours; the moments he liked best were those of gathering dusk, of the short autumn twilight; this was the time of which, again and again, he found himself hoping most. Then he could, as seemed to him, most intimately wander and wait, linger and listen, feel his fine attention, never in his life before so fine, on the pulse of the great vague place: he preferred the lampless hour and only wished he might have prolonged each day the deep crepuscular spell. Later—rarely much before midnight, but then for a considerable vigil—he watched with his glimmering light; moving slowly, holding it high, playing it far, rejoicing above all, as much as he might, in open vistas, reaches of communication between rooms and by passages; the long straight chance or show, as he would have called it, for the revelation he pretended to invite. It was a practice he found he could perfectly "work" without exciting remark; no one was in the least the wiser for it; even Alice Staverton, who was moreover a well of discretion, did n't quite fully imagine.

He let himself in and let himself out with the assurance of calm proprietorship; and accident so far favoured him that, if a fat Avenue "officer" had happened on occasion to see him entering at eleven-thirty, he had never yet, to the best of his belief, been noticed as emerging at two. He walked there on the crisp November nights, arrived regularly at the evening's end; it was as easy to do this after dining out as to take his way to a club or to his hotel. When he left his club, if he had n't been dining out, it was ostensibly to go to his hotel; and when he left his hotel, if he had spent a part of the evening there, it was ostensibly to go to his club. Everything was easy in fine; everything conspired and promoted: there was truly even in the strain of his experience something that glossed over, something that salved and simplified, all the rest of consciousness. He circulated, talked, renewed, loosely and pleasantly, old relations—met indeed, so far as he could, new expectations and seemed to make out on the whole that in spite of the career, of such different contacts, which he had spoken of to Miss Staverton as ministering so little, for those who might have watched it, to edification, he was positively rather liked than not. He was a dim secondary social success—and all with people who had truly not an idea of him. It was all mere surface sound, this murmur of their welcome, this popping of their corks—just as his gestures of response were the extravagant shadows, emphatic in proportion as they meant little, of some game of *ombres chinoises*.[3] He projected himself all day, in thought, straight over the bristling line of hard unconscious heads and into the other, the real, the waiting life; the life that, as soon as he had heard behind him the click of his great house-door, began for him, on the jolly corner, as beguilingly as the slow opening bars of some rich music follows the tap of the conductor's wand.

He always caught the first effect of the steel point of his stick on the old marble of the hall pavement, large black-and-white squares that he remembered as the admiration of his childhood and that had then made in him, as he now saw, for the growth of an early conception of style. This effect was the dim reverberating tinkle as of some far-off bell hung who should say where?—in the depths of the house, of the past, of that mystical other world that might have flourished for him had he not, for weal or woe, abandoned it. On this impression he did ever the same thing; he put his stick noiselessly away in a corner—feeling the place once more in the likeness of some great glass bowl, all precious concave crystal, set delicately humming by the play of a moist finger round its edge. The concave crystal held, as it were, this mystical other world, and the indescribably fine murmur of its rim was the sigh there, the scarce audible pathetic wail to his strained ear, of all the old baffled forsworn possibilities. What he did therefore by this appeal of his hushed presence was to wake them into such measure of ghostly life as they might still enjoy. They were shy, all but unappeasably shy, but they were n't really sinister; at least they weren't as he had hitherto felt them—before they had taken the Form he so yearned to make them take, the Form he at moments saw himself in the light of fairly hunting on tiptoe, the points of his evening-shoes, from room to room and from storey to storey.

[3] French: "Chinese shadows," a show in which actors' shadows are projected upon a screen.

That was the essence of his vision—which was all rank folly, if one would, while he was out of the house and otherwise occupied, but which took on the last verisimilitude as soon as he was placed and posted. He knew what he meant and what he wanted; it was as clear as the figure on a cheque presented in demand for cash. His *alter ego* "walked"—that was the note of his image of him, while his image of his motive for his own odd pastime was the desire to waylay him and meet him. He roamed, slowly, warily, but all restlessly, he himself did—Mrs. Muldoon had been right, absolutely, with her figure of their "craping"; and the presence he watched for would roam restlessly too. But it would be as cautious and as shifty; the conviction of its probable, in fact its already quite sensible, quite audible evasion of pursuit grew for him from night to night, laying on him finally a rigour to which nothing in his life had been comparable. It had been the theory of many superficially-judging persons, he knew, that he was wasting that life in a surrender to sensations, but he had tasted of no pleasure so fine as his actual tension, had been introduced to no sport that demanded at once the patience and the nerve of this stalking of a creature more subtle, yet at bay perhaps more formidable, than any beast of the forest. The terms, the comparisons, the very practices of the chase positively came again into play; there were even moments when passages of his occasional experience as a sportsman, stirred memories, from his younger time, of moor and mountain and desert, revived for him—and to the increase of his keenness—by the tremendous force of analogy. He found himself at moments—once he had placed his single light on some mantel-shelf or in some recess—stepping back into shelter or shade, effacing himself behind a door or in an embrasure, as he had sought of old the vantage of rock and tree; he found himself holding his breath and living in the joy of the instant, the supreme suspense created by big game alone.

He was n't afraid (though putting himself the question as he believed gentlemen on Bengal tiger-shoots or in close quarters with the great bear of the Rockies had been known to confess to having put it); and this indeed—since here at least he might be frank!—because of the impression, so intimate and so strange, that he himself produced as yet a dread, produced certainly a strain, beyond the liveliest he was likely to feel. They fell for him into categories, they fairly became familiar, the signs, for his own perception, of the alarm his presence and his vigilance created; though leaving him always to remark, portentously, on his probably having formed a relation, his probably enjoying a consciousness, unique in the experience of man. People enough, first and last, had been in terror of apparitions, but who had ever before so turned the tables and become himself, in the apparitional world, an incalculable terror? He might have found this sublime had he quite dared to think of it; but he didn't too much insist, truly, on that side of his privilege. With habit and repetition he gained to an extraordinary degree the power to penetrate the dusk of distances and the darkness of corners, to resolve back into their innocence the treacheries of uncertain light, the evil-looking forms taken in the gloom by mere shadows, by accidents of the air, by shifting effects of perspective; putting down his dim luminary he could still wander on without it, pass into other rooms and, only knowing it was there behind him in case of need, see his way about, visually project for his purpose a comparative clearness. It made him feel, this acquired faculty, like some monstrous stealthy cat; he wondered if he would have glared at these moments with large shining yellow eyes, and what it might n't verily be, for the poor hard-pressed *alter ego,* to be confronted with such a type.

He liked however the open shutters; he opened everywhere those Mrs. Muldoon had closed, closing them as carefully afterwards, so that she should n't notice: he liked —oh this he did like, and above all in the upper rooms!—the sense of the hard silver of the autumn stars through the window-panes, and scarcely less the flare of the street-lamps below, the white electric lustre which it would have taken curtains to keep out. This was human actual social; this was of the world he had lived in, and he was more at his ease certainly for the countenance, coldly general and impersonal, that all the while and in spite of his detachment it seemed to give him. He had support of course mostly in the rooms at the wide front and the prolonged side; it failed him considerably in the central shades and the parts at the back. But if he sometimes, on his rounds, was glad of his optical reach, so none the less often the rear of the house affected him as the very jungle of his prey. The place was there more subdivided; a large "extension" in particular, where small rooms for servants had been multiplied, abounded in nooks and corners, in closets and passages, in the ramifications especially of an ample back staircase over which he leaned, many a time, to look far down— not deterred from his gravity even while aware that he might, for a spectator, have figured some solemn simpleton playing at hide-and-seek. Outside in fact he might himself make that ironic *rapprochement;*[4] but within the walls, and in spite of the clear windows, his consistency was proof against the cynical light of New York.

It had belonged to that idea of the exasperated consciousness of his victim to become a real test for him; since he had quite put it to himself from the first that, oh distinctly! he could "cultivate" his whole perception. He had felt it as above all open to cultivation—which indeed was but another name for his manner of spending his time. He was bringing it on, bringing it to perfection, by practice; in consequence of which it had grown so fine that he was now aware of impressions, attestations of his general postulate, that could n't have broken upon him at once. This was the case more specifically with a phenomenon at last quite frequent for him in the upper rooms, the recognition—absolutely unmistakeable, and by a turn dating from a particular hour, his resumption of his campaign after a diplomatic drop, a calculated absence of three nights—of his being definitely followed, tracked at a distance carefully taken and to the express end that he should the less confidently, less arrogantly, appear to himself merely to pursue. It worried, it finally quite broke him up, for it proved, of all the conceivable impressions, the one least suited to his book. He was kept in sight while remaining himself—as regards the essence of his position—sightless, and his only recourse then was in abrupt turns, rapid recoveries of ground. He wheeled about, retracing his steps, as if he might so catch in his face at least the stirred air of some other quick revolution. It was indeed true that his fully dislocalised thought of these manœuvres recalled to him Pantaloon, at the Christmas farce, buffeted and tricked from behind by ubiquitous Harlequin;[5] but it left intact the influence of the conditions themselves each time he was re-exposed to them, so that in fact this association, had he suffered it to become constant, would on a certain side have but ministered to his intenser gravity. He had made, as I have said, to create on the premises the baseless sense of a reprieve, his three absences; and the result of the third was to confirm the after-effect of the second.

<hr/>

[4] French: "restoration of harmonious relations."
[5] Pantaloon and Harlequin were characters in traditional pantomime comedies in which tricks are played upon aging fools.

On his return, that night—the night succeeding his last intermission—he stood in the hall and looked up the staircase with a certainty more intimate than any he had yet known. "He's *there,* at the top, and waiting—not, as in general, falling back for disappearance. He's holding his ground, and it's the first time—which is a proof, is n't it? that something has happened for him." So Brydon argued with his hand on the banister and his foot on the lowest stair; in which position he felt as never before the air chilled by his logic. He himself turned cold in it, for he seemed of a sudden to know what now was involved. "Harder pressed?—yes, he takes it in, with its thus making clear to him that I've come, as they say, 'to stay.' He finally does n't like and can't bear it, in the sense, I mean, that his wrath, his menaced interest, now balances with his dread. I've hunted him till he has 'turned': that, up there, is what has happened —he's the fanged or the antlered animal brought at last to bay." There came to him, as I say—but determined by an influence beyond my notation!—the acuteness of this certainty; under which however the next moment he had broken into a sweat that he would as little have consented to attribute to fear as he would have dared immediately to act upon it for enterprise. It marked none the less a prodigious thrill, a thrill that represented sudden dismay, no doubt, but also represented, and with the selfsame throb, the strangest, the most joyous, possibly the next minute almost the proudest, duplication of consciousness.

"He has been dodging, retreating, hiding, but now, worked up to anger, he'll fight!"—this intense impression made a single mouthful, as it were, of terror and applause. But what was wondrous was that the applause, for the felt fact, was so eager, since, if it was his other self he was running to earth, this ineffable identity was thus in the last resort not unworthy of him. It bristled there—somewhere near at hand, however unseen still—as the hunted thing, even as the trodden worm of the adage *must* at last bristle; and Brydon at this instant tasted probably of a sensation more complex than had ever before found itself consistent with sanity. It was as if it would have shamed him that a character so associated with his own should triumphantly succeed in just skulking, should to the end not risk the open; so that the drop of this danger was, on the spot, a great lift of the whole situation. Yet with another rare shift of the same subtlety he was already trying to measure by how much more he himself might now be in peril of fear; so rejoicing that he could, in another form, actively inspire that fear, and simultaneously quaking for the form in which he might passively know it.

The apprehension of knowing it must after a little have grown in him, and the strangest moment of his adventure perhaps, the most memorable or really most interesting, afterwards, of his crisis, was the lapse of certain instants of concentrated conscious *combat,* the sense of a need to hold on to something, even after the manner of a man slipping and slipping on some awful incline; the vivid impulse, above all, to move, to act, to charge, somehow and upon something—to show himself, in a word, that he was n't afraid. The state of "holding-on" was thus the state to which he was momentarily reduced; if there had been anything, in the great vacancy, to seize, he would presently have been aware of having clutched it as he might under a shock at home have clutched the nearest chair-back. He had been surprised at any rate— of this he *was* aware—into something unprecedented since his original appropriation of the place; he had closed his eyes, held them tight, for a long minute, as with that instinct of dismay and that terror of vision. When he opened them the room, the other contiguous rooms, extraordinarily, seemed lighter—so light, almost, that at first he took the change for day. He stood firm, however that might be, just where he had paused; his resistance had helped him—it was as if there were something he had tided over. He knew after a little what this was—it had been in the imminent danger of flight. He had stiffened his will against going; without this he would have made for the stairs, and it seemed to him that, still with his eyes closed, he would have descended them, would have known how, straight and swiftly, to the bottom.

Well, as he had held out, here he was—still at the top, among the more intricate upper rooms and with the gauntlet of the others, of all the rest of the house, still to run when it should be his time to go. He would go at his time—only at his time: did n't he go every night very much at the same hour? He took out his watch—there was light for that: it was scarcely a quarter past one, and he had never withdrawn so soon. He reached his lodgings for the most part at two—with his walk of a quarter of an hour. He would wait for the last quarter—he would n't stir till then; and he kept his watch there with his eyes on it, reflecting while he held it that this deliberate wait, a wait with an effort, which he recognised, would serve perfectly for the attestation he desired to make. It would prove his courage—unless indeed the latter might most be proved by his budging at last from his place. What he mainly felt now was that, since he had n't originally scuttled, he had his dignities—which had never in his life seemed so many—all to preserve and to carry aloft. This was before him in truth as a physical image, an image almost worthy of an age of greater romance. That remark indeed glimmered for him only to glow the next instant with a finer light; since what age of romance, after all, could have matched either the state of his mind or, "objectively," as they said, the wonder of his situation? The only difference would have been that, brandishing his dignities over his head as in a parchment scroll, he might then—that is in the heroic time—have proceeded downstairs with a drawn sword in his other grasp.

At present, really, the light he had set down on the mantel of the next room would have to figure his sword; which utensil, in the course of a minute, he had taken the requisite number of steps to possess himself of. The door between the rooms was open, and from the second another door opened to a third. These rooms, as he remembered, gave all three upon a common corridor as well, but there was a fourth, beyond them, without issue save through the preceding. To have moved, to have heard his step again, was appreciably a help; though even in recognising this he lingered once more a little by the chimney-piece on which his light had rested. When he next moved, just hesitating where to turn, he found himself considering a circumstance that, after his first and comparatively vague apprehension of it, produced in him the start that often attends some pang of recollection, the violent shock of having ceased happily to forget. He had come into sight of the door in which the brief chain of communication ended and which he now surveyed from the nearer threshold, the one not directly facing it. Placed at some distance to the left of this point, it would have admitted him to the last room of the four, the room without other approach or egress, had it not, to his intimate conviction, been closed *since* his former visitation, the matter probably of a quarter of an hour before. He stared with all his eyes at the wonder of the fact, arrested again where he stood and again holding his breath while he sounded its sense. Surely it had been *subsequently* closed—that is it had been on his previous passage indubitably open!

He took it full in the face that something had happened between—that he could n't not have noticed before (by which he meant on his original tour of all the rooms that evening) that such a barrier had exceptionally presented itself. He had indeed since that moment undergone an agitation so extraordinary that it might have muddled for him any earlier view; and he tried to convince himself that he might perhaps then have gone into the room and, inadvertently, automatically, on coming out, have drawn the door after him. The difficulty was that this exactly was what he never did; it was against his whole policy, as he might have said, the essence of which was to keep vistas clear. He had them from the first, as he was well aware, quite on the brain: the strange apparition, at the far end of one of them, of his baffled "prey" (which had become by so sharp an irony so little the term now to apply!) was the form of success his imagination had most cherished, projecting into it always a refinement of beauty. He had known fifty times the start of perception that had afterwards dropped; had fifty times gasped to himself "There!" under some fond brief hallucination. The house, as the case stood, admirably lent itself; he might wonder at the taste, the native architecture of the particular time, which could rejoice so in the multiplication of doors—the opposite extreme to the modern, the actual almost complete proscription of them; but it had fairly contributed to provoke this obsession of the presence encountered telescopically, as he might say, focussed and studied in diminishing perspective and as by a rest for the elbow.

It was with these considerations that his present attention was charged—they perfectly availed to make what he saw portentous. He *could n't,* by any lapse, have blocked that aperture; and if he had n't, if it was unthinkable, why what else was clear but that there had been another agent? Another agent?—he had been catching, as he felt, a moment back, the very breath of him; but when had he been so close as in this simple, this logical, this completely personal act? It was so logical, that is, that one might have *taken* it for personal; yet for what did Brydon take it, he asked himself, while, softly panting, he felt his eyes almost leave their sockets. Ah this time at last they *were,* the two, the opposed projections of him, in presence; and this time, as much as one would, the question of danger loomed. With it rose, as not before, the question of courage—for what he knew the blank face of the door to say to him was "Show us how much you have!" It stared, it glared back at him with that challenge; it put to him the two alternatives: should he just push it open or not? Oh to have this consciousness was to *think*—and to think, Brydon knew, as he stood there, was, with the lapsing moments, not to have acted! Not to have acted—that was the misery and the pang—was even still not to act; was in fact *all* to feel the thing in another, in a new and terrible way. How long did he pause and how long did he debate? There was presently nothing to measure it; for his vibration had already changed—as just by the effect of its intensity. Shut up there, at bay, defiant, and with the prodigy of the thing palpably proveably *done,* thus giving notice like some stark signboard— under that accession of accent the situation itself had turned; and Brydon at last remarkably made up his mind on what it had turned to.

It had turned altogether to a different admonition; to a supreme hint, for him, of the value of Discretion! This slowly dawned, no doubt—for it could take its time; so perfectly, on his threshold, had he been stayed, so little as yet had he either advanced or retreated. It was the strangest of all things that now when, by his taking ten steps and applying his hand to a latch, or even his shoulder and his knee, if necessary, to a panel, all the hunger of his prime need might have been met, his high curiosity crowned, his unrest assuaged—it was amazing, but it was also exquisite and rare, that insistence should have, at a touch, quite dropped from him. Discretion—he jumped at that; and yet not, verily, at such a pitch, because it saved his nerves or his skin, but because, much more valuably, it saved the situation. When I say he "jumped" at it I feel the consonance of this term with the fact that—at the end indeed of I know not how long—he did move again, he crossed straight to the door. He would n't touch it—it seemed now that he might *if* he would: he would only just wait there a little, to show, to prove, that he would n't. He had thus another station, close to the thin partition by which revelation was denied him; but with his eyes bent and his hands held off in a mere intensity of stillness. He listened as if there had been something to hear, but this attitude, while it lasted, was his own communication. "If you won't then—good: I spare you and I give up. You affect me as by the appeal positively for pity: you convince me that for reasons rigid and sublime—what do I know?—we both of us should have suffered. I respect them then, and, though moved and privileged as, I believe, it has never been given to man, I retire, I renounce—never, on my honour, to try again. So rest for ever—and let *me!*"

That, for Brydon was the deep sense of this last demonstration—solemn, measured, directed, as he felt it to be. He brought it to a close, he turned away; and now verily he knew how deeply he had been stirred. He retraced his steps, taking up his candle, burnt, he observed, well-nigh to the socket, and marking again, lighten it as he would, the distinctness of his footfall; after which, in a moment, he knew himself at the other side of the house. He did here what he had not yet done at these hours—he opened half a casement, one of those in the front, and let in the air of the night; a thing he would have taken at any time previous for a sharp rupture of his spell. His spell was broken now, and it did n't matter—broken by his concession and his surrender, which made it idle henceforth that he should ever come back. The empty street—its other life so marked even by the great lamplit vacancy—was within call, within touch; he stayed there as to be in it again, high above it though he was still perched; he watched as for some comforting common fact, some vulgar human note, the passage of a scavenger or a thief, some night-bird however base. He would have blessed that sign of life; he would have welcomed positively the slow approach of his friend the policeman, whom he had hitherto only sought to avoid, and was not sure that if the patrol had come into sight he might n't have felt the impulse to get into relation with it, to hail it, on some pretext, from his fourth floor.

The pretext that would n't have been too silly or too compromising, the explanation that would have saved his dignity and kept his name, in such a case, out of the papers, was not definite to him: he was so occupied with the thought of recording his Discretion—as an effect of the vow he had just uttered to his intimate adversary —that the importance of this loomed large and something had overtaken all ironically his sense of proportion. If there had been a ladder applied to the front of the house, even one of the vertiginous perpendiculars employed by painters and roofers and sometimes left standing overnight, he would have managed somehow, astride of the window-sill, to compass by outstretched leg and arm that mode of descent. If there had been some such uncanny thing as he had found in his room at hotels, a workable fire-escape in the form of notched cable or a canvas shoot, he would have availed himself of it as a proof—well, of his present delicacy. He nursed that sentiment, as the question stood, a little in vain, and even—at the end of he scarce knew, once more, how long—found it, as by the action on his mind of the failure of response of the outer world, sinking back to vague anguish. It seemed to him he had waited an age for some stir of the great grim hush; the life of the town was itself under a spell— so unnaturally, up and down the whole prospect of known and rather ugly objects, the blankness and the silence lasted. Had they ever, he asked himself, the hard-faced houses, which had begun to look livid in the dim dawn, had they ever spoken so little to any need of his spirit? Great builded voids, great crowded stillnesses put on, often, in the heart of cities, for the small hours, a sort of sinister mask, and it was of this large collective negation that Brydon presently became conscious—all the more that the break of day was, almost incredibly, now at hand, proving to him what a night he had made of it.

He looked again at his watch, saw what had become of his time-values (he had taken hours for minutes—not, as in other tense situations, minutes for hours) and the strange air of the streets was but the weak, the sullen flush of a dawn in which everything was still locked up. His choked appeal from his own open window had been the sole note of life, and he could but break off at last as for a worse despair. Yet while so deeply demoralised he was capable again of an impulse denoting—at least by his present measure—extraordinary resolution; of retracing his steps to the spot where he had turned cold with the extinction of his last pulse of doubt as to there being in the place another presence than his own. This required an effort strong enough to sicken him; but he had his reason, which overmastered for the moment everything else. There was the whole of the rest of the house to traverse, and how should he screw himself to that if the door he had seen closed were at present open? He could hold to the idea that the closing had practically been for him an act of mercy, a chance offered him to descend, depart, get off the ground and never again profane it. This conception held together, it worked; but what it meant for him depended now clearly on the amount of forbearance his recent action, or rather his recent inaction, had engendered. The image of the "presence," whatever it was, waiting there for him to go—this image had not yet been so concrete for his nerves as when he stopped short of the point at which certainty would have come to him. For, with all his resolution, or more exactly with all his dread, he did stop short—he hung back from really seeing. The risk was too great and his fear too definite: it took at this moment an awful specific form.

He knew—yes, as he had never known anything—that, *should* he see the door open, it would all too abjectly be the end of him. It would mean that the agent of his shame—for his shame was the deep abjection—was once more at large and in general possession; and what glared him thus in the face was the act that this would determine for him. It would send him straight about to the window he had left open, and by that window, be long ladder and dangling rope as absent as they would, he saw himself uncontrollably insanely fatally take his way to the street. The hideous chance of this he at least could avert; but he could only avert it by recoiling in time from assurance. He had the whole house to deal with, this fact was still there; only he now knew that uncertainty alone could start him. He stole back from where he had checked himself—merely to do so was suddenly like safety—and, making blindly for the greater staircase, left gaping rooms and sounding passages behind. Here was the top of the stairs, with a fine large dim descent and three spacious landings to mark off. His instinct was all for mildness, but his feet were harsh on the floors, and, strangely, when he had in a couple of minutes become aware of this, it counted somehow for help. He could n't have spoken, the tone of his voice would have scared him, and the common conceit or resource of "whistling in the dark" (whether literally or figuratively) have appeared basely vulgar; yet he liked none the less to hear himself go, and when he had reached his first landing—taking it all with no rush, but quite steadily—that stage of success drew from him a gasp of relief.

The house, withal, seemed immense, the scale of space again inordinate; the open rooms, to no one of which his eyes deflected, gloomed in their shuttered state like mouths of caverns; only the high skylight that formed the crown of the deep well created for him a medium in which he could advance, but which might have been, for queerness of colour, some watery under-world. He tried to think of something noble, as that his property was really grand, a splendid possession; but this nobleness took the form too of the clear delight with which he was finally to sacrifice it. They might come in now, the builders, the destroyers—they might come as soon as they would. At the end of two flights he had dropped to another zone, and from the middle of the third, with only one more left, he recognised the influence of the lower windows, of half-drawn blinds, of the occasional gleam of street-lamps, of the glazed spaces of the vestibule. This was the bottom of the sea, which showed an illumination of its own and which he even saw paved—when at a given moment he drew up to sink a long look over the banisters—with the marble squares of his childhood. By that time indubitably he felt, as he might have said in a commoner cause, better; it had allowed him to stop and draw breath, and the ease increased with the sight of the old black-and-white slabs. But what he most felt was that now surely, with the element of impunity pulling him as by hard firm hands, the case was settled for what he might have seen above had he dared that last look. The closed door, blessedly remote now, was still closed—and he had only in short to reach that of the house.

He came down further, he crossed the passage forming the access to the last flight; and if here again he stopped an instant it was almost for the sharpness of the thrill of assured escape. It made him shut his eyes—which opened again to the straight slope of the remainder of the stairs. Here was impunity still, but impunity almost excessive; inasmuch as the side-lights and the high fan-tracery of the entrance were glimmering straight into the hall; an appearance produced, he the next instant saw, by the fact that the vestibule gaped wide, that the hinged halves of the inner door had been thrown far back. Out of that again the *question* sprang at him, making his eyes, as he felt, half-start from his head, as they had done, at the top of the house, before the sign of the other door. If he had left that one open, had n't he left this one closed, and was n't he now in *most* immediate presence of some inconceivable occult activity? It was as sharp, the question, as a knife in his side, but the answer hung fire still and seemed to lose itself in the vague darkness to which the thin admitted dawn, glimmering archwise over the whole outer door, made a semicircular margin, a cold silvery nimbus that seemed to play a little as he looked—to shift and expand and contract.

It was as if there had been something within it, protected by indistinctness and corresponding in extent with the opaque surface behind, the painted panels of the last barrier to his escape, of which the key was in his pocket. The indistinctness mocked him even while he stared, affected him as somehow shrouding or challenging certitude, so that after faltering an instant on his step he let himself go with the sense that here *was* at last something to meet, to touch, to take, to know—something all unnatural and dreadful, but to advance upon which was the condition for him either of liberation or of supreme defeat. The penumbra, dense and dark, was the virtual screen of a figure which stood in it as still as some image erect in a niche or as some black-vizored sentinel guarding a treasure. Brydon was to know afterwards, was to recall and make out, the particular thing he had believed during the rest of his descent. He saw, in its great grey glimmering margin, the central vagueness diminish, and he felt it to be taking the very form toward which, for so many days, the passion of his curiosity had yearned. It gloomed, it loomed, it was something, it was somebody, the prodigy of a personal presence.

Rigid and conscious, spectral yet human, a man of his own substance and stature waited there to measure himself with his power to dismay. This only could it be—this only till he recognised, with his advance, that what made the face dim was the pair of raised hands that covered it and in which, so far from being offered in defiance, it was buried as for dark deprecation. So Brydon, before him, took him in; with every fact of him now, in the higher light, hard and acute—his planted stillness, his vivid truth, his grizzled bent head and white masking hands, his queer actuality of evening-dress, of dangling double eye-glass, of gleaming silk lappet and white linen, of pearl button and gold watch-guard and polished shoe. No portrait by a great modern master could have presented him with more intensity, thrust him out of his frame with more art, as if there had been "treatment," of the consummate sort, in his every shade and salience. The revulsion, for our friend, had become, before he knew it, immense—this drop, in the act of apprehension, to the sense of his adversary's inscrutable manœuvre. That meaning at least, while he gaped, it offered him; for he could but gape at his other self in this other anguish, gape as a proof that *he,* standing there for the achieved, the enjoyed, the triumphant life, could n't be faced in his triumph. Was n't the proof in the splendid covering hands, strong and completely spread?—so spread and so intentional that, in spite of a special verity that surpassed every other, the fact that one of these hands had lost two fingers, which were reduced to stumps, as if accidentally shot away, the face was effectually guarded and saved.

"Saved," though, *would* it be?—Brydon breathed his wonder till the very impunity of his attitude and the very insistence of his eyes produced, as he felt, a sudden stir which showed the next instant as a deeper portent, while the head raised itself, the betrayal of a braver purpose. The hands, as he looked, began to move, to open; then, as if deciding in a flash, dropped from the face and left it uncovered and presented. Horror, with the sight, had leaped into Brydon's throat, gasping there in a sound he could n't utter; for the bared identity was too hideous as *his,* and his glare was the passion of his protest. The face, *that* face, Spencer Brydon's?—he searched it still, but looking away from it in dismay and denial, falling straight from his height of sublimity. It was unknown, inconceivable, awful, disconnected from any possibility—! He had been "sold," he inwardly moaned, stalking such game as this: the presence before him was a presence, the horror within him a horror, but the waste of his nights had been only grotesque and the success of his adventure an irony. Such an identity fitted his at *no* point, made its alternative monstrous. A thousand times yes, as it came upon him nearer now—the face was the face of a stranger. It came upon him nearer now, quite as one of those expanding fantastic images projected by the magic lantern of childhood; for the stranger, whoever he might be, evil, odious, blatant, vulgar, had advanced as for aggression, and he knew himself give ground. Then harder pressed still, sick with the force of his shock, and falling back as under the hot breath and the roused passion of a life larger than his own, a rage of personality before which his own collapsed, he felt the whole vision turn to darkness and his very feet give way. His head went round; he was going; he had gone.

III

What had next brought him back, clearly—though after how long?—was Mrs. Muldoon's voice, coming to him from quite near, from so near that he seemed presently to see her as kneeling on the ground before him while he lay looking up at her; himself not wholly on the ground, but half-raised and upheld—conscious, yes, of tenderness of support and, more particularly, of a head pillowed in extraordinary softness and faintly refreshing fragrance. He considered, he wondered, his wit but half at his service; then another face intervened, bending more directly over him, and he finally knew that Alice Staverton had made her lap an ample and perfect cushion to him, and that she had to this end seated herself on the lowest degree of the staircase, the rest of his long person remaining stretched on his old black-and-white slabs. They were cold, these marble squares of his youth; but *he* somehow was not, in this rich return of consciousness—the most wonderful hour, little by little, that he had ever known, leaving him, as it did, so gratefully, so abysmally passive, and yet as with a treasure of intelligence waiting all round him for quiet appropriation; dissolved, he might call it, in the air of the place and producing the golden glow of a late autumn afternoon. He had come back, yes—come back from further away than any man but himself had ever travelled; but it was strange how with this sense what he had come back *to* seemed really the great thing, and as if his prodigious journey had been all for the sake of it. Slowly but surely his consciousness grew, his vision of his state thus completing itself: he had been miraculously *carried* back—lifted and carefully borne as from where he had been picked up, the uttermost end of an interminable grey passage. Even with this he was suffered to rest, and what had now brought him to knowledge was the break in the long mild motion.

It had brought him to knowledge, to knowledge—yes, this was the beauty of his state; which came to resemble more and more that of a man who has gone to sleep on some news of a great inheritance, and then, after dreaming it away, after profaning it with matters strange to it, has waked up again to serenity of certitude and has only to lie and watch it grow. This was the drift of his patience—that he had only to let it shine on him. He must moreover, with intermissions, still have been lifted and borne; since why and how else should he have known himself, later on, with the afternoon glow intenser, no longer at the foot of his stairs—situated as these now seemed at that dark other end of his tunnel—but on a deep window-bench of his high saloon, over which had been spread, couch-fashion, a mantle of soft stuff lined with grey fur that was familiar to his eyes and that one of his hands kept fondly feeling as for its pledge of truth. Mrs. Muldoon's face had gone, but the other, the second he had recognised, hung over him in a way that showed how he was still propped and pillowed. He took it all in, and the more he took it the more it seemed to suffice: he was as much at peace as if he had had food and drink. It was the two women who had found him, on Mrs. Muldoon's having plied, at her usual hour, her latch-key—and on her having above all arrived while Miss Staverton still lingered near the house. She had been turning away, all anxiety, from worrying the vain bell-handle—her calculation having been of the hour of the good woman's visit; but the latter, blessedly, had come up while she was still there, and they had entered together. He had then lain, beyond the vestibule, very much as he was lying now—quite, that is, as he appeared to have fallen, but all so wondrously without bruise or gash; only in a depth of stupor. What he most took in, however, at present, with the steadier clearance, was that Alice Staverton had for a long unspeakable moment not doubted he was dead.

"It must have been that I *was.*" He made it out as she held him. "Yes—I can only have died. You brought me literally to life. Only," he wondered, his eyes rising to her, "only, in the name of all the benedictions, how?"

It took her but an instant to bend her face and kiss him, and something in the manner of it, and in the way her hands clasped and locked his head while he felt the cool charity and virtue of her lips, something in all this beatitude somehow answered everything. "And now I keep you," she said.

"Oh keep me, keep me!" he pleaded while her face still hung over him: in response to which it dropped again and stayed close, clingingly close. It was the seal of their situation—of which he tasted the impress for a long blissful moment in silence. But he came back. "Yet how did you know—?"

"I was uneasy. You were to have come, you remember—and you had sent no word."

"Yes, I remember—I was to have gone to you at one to-day." It caught on to their "old" life and relation—which were so near and so far. "I was still out there in my strange darkness—where was it, what was it? I must have stayed there so long." He could but wonder at the depth and the duration of his swoon.

"Since last night?" she asked with a shade of fear for her possible indiscretion.

"Since this morning—it must have been: the cold dim dawn of to-day. Where have I been," he vaguely wailed, "where have I been?" He felt her hold him close, and it was as if this helped him now to make in all security his mild moan. "What a long dark day!"

All in her tenderness she had waited a moment. "In the cold dim dawn?" she quavered.

But he had already gone on piecing together the parts of the whole prodigy. "As I did n't turn up you came straight—?"

She barely cast about. "I went first to your hotel—where they told me of your absence. You had dined out last evening and had n't been back since. But they appeared to know you had been at your club."

"So you had the idea of *this*—?"

"Of what?" she asked in a moment.

"Well—of what has happened."

"I believed at least you'd have been here. I've known, all along," she said, "that you've been coming."

" 'Known' it—?"

"Well, I've believed it. I said nothing to you after that talk we had a month ago —but I felt sure. I knew you *would,*" she declared.

"That I'd persist, you mean?"

"That you'd see him."

"Ah but I did n't!" cried Brydon with his long wail. "There's somebody—an awful beast; whom I brought, too horribly, to bay. But it's not me."

At this she bent over him again, and her eyes were in his eyes. "No—it's not you." And it was as if, while her face hovered, he might have made out in it, had n't it been so near, some particular meaning blurred by a smile. "No, thank heaven," she repeated—"it's not you! Of course it was n't to have been."

"Ah but it *was,*" he gently insisted. And he stared before him now as he had been staring for so many weeks. "I was to have known myself."

"You could n't!" she returned consolingly. And then reverting, and as if to account further for what she had herself done, "But it was n't only *that,* that you had n't been at home," she went on. "I waited till the hour at which we had found Mrs. Muldoon that day of my going with you; and she arrived, as I've told you, while, failing to bring any one to the door, I lingered in my despair on the steps. After a little, if she had n't come, by such a mercy, I should have found means to hunt her up. But it was n't," said Alice Staverton, as if once more with her fine intention—"it was n't only that."

His eyes, as he lay, turned back to her. "What more then?"

She met it, the wonder she had stirred. "In the cold dim dawn, you say? Well, in the cold dim dawn of this morning I too saw you."

"Saw *me*—?"

"Saw *him,*" said Alice Staverton. "It must have been at the same moment."

He lay an instant taking it in—as if he wished to be quite reasonable. "At the same moment?"

"Yes—in my dream again, the same one I've named to you. He came back to me. Then I knew it for a sign. He had come to you."

At this Brydon raised himself; he had to see her better. She helped him when she understood his movement, and he sat up, steadying himself beside her there on the window-bench and with his right hand grasping her left. "*He* did n't come to me."

"You came to yourself," she beautifully smiled.

"Ah I've come to myself now—thanks to you, dearest. But this brute, with his awful face—this brute's a black stranger. He's none of *me,* even as I *might* have been," Brydon sturdily declared.

But she kept the clearness that was like the breath of infallibility. "Is n't the whole point that you'd have been different?"

He almost scowled for it. "As different as *that*—?"

Her look again was more beautiful to him than the things of this world. "Have n't you exactly wanted to know *how* different? So this morning," she said, "you appeared to me."

"Like *him?*"

"A black stranger!"

"Then how did you know it was I?"

"Because, as I told you weeks ago, my mind, my imagination, had worked so over what you might, what you might n't have been—to show you, you see, how I've thought of you. In the midst of that you came to me—that my wonder might be answered. So I knew," she went on; "and believed that, since the question held you too so fast, as you told me that day, you too would see for yourself. And when this morning I again saw I knew it would be because you had—and also then, from the first moment, because you somehow wanted me. *He* seemed to tell me of that. So why," she strangely smiled, "should n't I like him?"

It brought Spencer Brydon to his feet. "You 'like' that horror—?"

"I *could* have liked him. And to me," she said, "he was no horror. I had accepted him."

" 'Accepted'—?" Brydon oddly sounded.

"Before, for the interest of his difference—yes. And as *I* did n't disown him, as *I* knew him—which you at last, confronted with him in his difference, so cruelly did n't, my dear—well, he must have been, you see, less dreadful to me. And it may have pleased him that I pitied him."

She was beside him on her feet, but still holding his hand—still with her arm supporting him. But though it all brought for him thus a dim light, "You 'pitied' him?" he grudgingly, resentfully asked.

"He has been unhappy, he has been ravaged," she said.

"And have n't I been unhappy? Am not I—you've only to look at me!—ravaged?"

"Ah I don't say I like him *better,*" she granted after a thought. "But he's grim, he's worn—and things have happened to him. He does n't make shift, for sight, with your charming monocle."

"No"—it struck Brydon: "I could n't have sported mine 'downtown.' They'd have guyed me there."

"His great convex pince-nez—I saw it, I recognised the kind—is for his poor ruined sight. And his poor right hand—!"

"Ah!" Brydon winced—whether for his proved identity or for his lost fingers. Then, "He has a million a year," he lucidly added. "But he has n't you."

"And he is n't—no, he is n't—*you!*" she murmured as he drew her to his breast.

1908

The Turn of the Screw

The story had held us, round the fire, sufficiently breathless, but except the obvious remark that it was gruesome, as on Christmas Eve in an old house a strange tale should essentially be, I remember no comment uttered till somebody happened to note it as the only case he had met in which such a visitation had fallen on a child. The case, I may mention, was that of an apparition in just such an old house as had gathered us for the occasion—an appearance, of a dreadful kind, to a little boy sleeping in the room with his mother and waking her up in the terror of it; waking her not to dissipate his dread and soothe him to sleep again, but to encounter also herself, before she had succeeded in doing so, the same sight that had shocked him. It was this observation that drew from Douglas—not immediately, but later in the evening— a reply that had the interesting consequence to which I call attention. Some one else told a story not particularly effective, which I saw he was not following. This I took for a sign that he had himself something to produce and that we should only have to wait. We waited in fact till two nights later; but that same evening, before we scattered, he brought out what was in his mind.

"I quite agree—in regard to Griffin's ghost, or whatever it was—that its appearing first to the little boy, at so tender an age, adds a particular touch. But it's not the first occurrence of its charming kind that I know to have been concerned with a child. If the child gives the effect another turn of the screw, what do you say to *two* children—?"

"We say of course," somebody exclaimed, "that two children give two turns! Also that we want to hear about them."

I can see Douglas there before the fire, to which he had got up to present his back, looking down at this converser with his hands in his pockets. "Nobody but me, till now, has ever heard. It's quite too horrible." This was naturally declared by several voices to give the thing the utmost price, and our friend, with quiet art, prepared his triumph by turning his eyes over the rest of us and going on: "It's beyond everything. Nothing at all that I know touches it."

"For sheer terror?" I remember asking.

He seemed to say it was n't so simple as that; to be really at a loss how to qualify it. He passed his hand over his eyes, made a little wincing grimace. "For dreadful—dreadfulness!"

"Oh how delicious!" cried one of the women.

He took no notice of her; he looked at me, but as if, instead of me, he saw what he spoke of. "For general uncanny ugliness and horror and pain."

"Well then," I said, "just sit right down and begin."

He turned round to the fire, gave a kick to a log, watched it an instant. Then as he faced us again: "I can't begin. I shall have to send to town." There was a unanimous groan at this, and much reproach; after which, in his preoccupied way, he explained. "The story's written. It's in a locked drawer—it has not been out for years. I could write to my man and enclose the key; he could send down the packet as he finds it." It was to me in particular that he appeared to propound this—appeared almost to appeal for aid not to hesitate. He had broken a thickness of ice, the formation of many a winter; had had his reasons for a long silence. The others resented postponement, but it was just his scruples that charmed me. I adjured him to write by the first post and to agree with us for an early hearing; then I asked him if the experience in question had been his own. To this his answer was prompt. "Oh thank God, no!"

"And is the record yours? You took the thing down?"

"Nothing but the impression. I took that *here*"—he tapped his heart. "I've never lost it."

"Then your manuscript—?"

"Is in old faded ink and in the most beautiful hand." He hung fire[1] again. "A woman's. She has been dead these twenty years. She sent me the pages in question before she died." They were all listening now, and of course there was somebody to be arch, or at any rate to draw the inference. But if he put the inference by without

[1] Hesitated (descriptive of an explosive charge that does not go off immediately after being ignited).

a smile it was also without irritation. "She was a most charming person, but she was ten years older than I. She was my sister's governess," he quietly said. "She was the most agreeable woman I've ever known in her position; she'd have been worthy of any whatever. It was long ago, and this episode was long before. I was at Trinity,[2] and I found her at home on my coming down the second summer. I was much there that year—it was a beautiful one; and we had, in her off-hours, some strolls and talks in the garden—talks in which she struck me as awfully clever and nice. Oh yes; don't grin: I liked her extremely and am glad to this day to think she liked me too. If she had n't she would n't have told me. She had never told any one. It was n't simply that she said so, but that I knew she had n't. I was sure; I could see. You'll easily judge why when you hear."

"Because the thing had been such a scare?"

He continued to fix[3] me. "You'll easily judge," he repeated: "*you* will."

I fixed him too. "I see. She was in love."

He laughed for the first time. "You *are* acute. Yes, she was in love. That is she *had* been. That came out—she could n't tell her story without its coming out. I saw it, and she saw I saw it; but neither of us spoke of it. I remember the time and the place—the corner of the lawn, the shade of the great beeches and the long hot summer afternoon. It was n't a scene for a shudder; but oh—!" He quitted the fire and dropped back into his chair.

"You'll receive the packet Thursday morning?" I said.

"Probably not till the second post."

"Well then; after dinner—"

"You'll all meet me here?" He looked us round again. "Is n't anybody going?" It was almost the tone of hope.

"Everybody will stay!"

"*I* will—and *I* will!" cried the ladies whose departure had been fixed. Mrs. Griffin, however, expressed the need for a little more light. "Who was it she was in love with?"

"The story will tell," I took upon myself to reply.

"Oh I can't wait for the story!"

"The story *won't* tell," said Douglas; "not in any literal vulgar way."

"More's the pity then. That's the only way I ever understand."

"Won't *you* tell, Douglas?" somebody else enquired.

He sprang to his feet again. "Yes—to-morrow. Now I must go to bed. Good-night." And, quickly catching up a candlestick, he left us slightly bewildered. From our end of the great brown hall we heard his step on the stair; whereupon Mrs. Griffin spoke. "Well, if I don't know who she was in love with I know who *he* was."

"She was ten years older," said her husband.

"*Raison de plus*[4]—at that age! But it's rather nice, his long reticence."

"Forty years!" Griffin put in.

"With this outbreak at last."

"The outbreak," I returned, "will make a tremendous occasion of Thursday night"; and every one so agreed with me that in the light of it we lost all attention for

---

[2] One of the colleges of Oxford or Cambridge University in England.

[3] Stare at.

[4] French: "all the more reason."

everything else. The last story, however incomplete and like the mere opening of a serial, had been told; we handshook and "candlestuck," as somebody said, and went to bed.

I knew the next day that a letter containing the key had, by the first post, gone off to his London apartments; but in spite of—or perhaps just on account of—the eventual diffusion of this knowledge we quite let him alone till after dinner, till such an hour of the evening in fact as might best accord with the kind of emotion on which our hopes were fixed. Then he became as communicative as we could desire, and indeed gave us his best reason for being so. We had it from him again before the fire in the hall, as we had had our mild wonders of the previous night. It appeared that the narrative he had promised to read us really required for a proper intelligence a few words of prologue. Let me say here distinctly, to have done with it, that this narrative, from an exact transcript of my own made much later, is what I shall presently give. Poor Douglas, before his death—when it was in sight—committed to me the manuscript that reached him on the third of these days and that, on the same spot, with immense effect, he began to read to our hushed little circle on the night of the fourth. The departing ladies who had said they would stay did n't, of course, thank heaven, stay: they departed, in consequence of arrangements made, in a rage of curiosity, as they professed, produced by the touches with which he had already worked us up. But that only made his little final auditory more compact and select, kept it, round the hearth, subject to a common thrill.

The first of these touches conveyed that the written statement took up the tale at a point after it had, in a manner, begun. The fact to be in possession of was therefore that his old friend, the youngest of several daughters of a poor country parson,[5] had at the age of twenty, on taking service for the first time in the schoolroom, come up to London, in trepidation, to answer in person an advertisement that had already placed her in brief correspondence with the advertiser. This person proved, on her presenting herself for judgement at a house in Harley Street that impressed her as vast and imposing—this prospective patron proved a gentleman, a bachelor in the prime of life, such a figure as had never risen, save in a dream or an old novel, before a fluttered anxious girl out of a Hampshire vicarage.[6] One could easily fix his type; it never, happily, dies out. He was handsome and bold and pleasant, off-hand and gay and kind. He struck her, inevitably, as gallant and splendid, but what took her most of all and gave her the courage she afterwards showed was that he put the whole thing to her as a favour, an obligation he should gratefully incur. She figured him as rich, but as fearfully extravagant—saw him all in a glow of high fashion, of good looks, of expensive habits, of charming ways with women. He had for his town residence a big house filled with the spoils of travel and the trophies of the chase; but it was to his country home, an old family place in Essex, that he wished her immediately to proceed.

He had been left, by the death of his parents in India, guardian to a small nephew and a small niece, children of a younger, a military brother whom he had lost two years before. These children were, by the strangest of chances for a man in his position —a lone man without the right sort of experience or a grain of patience—very heavy on his hands. It had all been a great worry and, on his own part doubtless, a series of blunders, but he immensely pitied the poor chicks and had done all he could; had

---

[5] Clergyman of the Church of England.   [6] Residence of the vicar, or parson, of a parish.

in particular sent them down to his other house, the proper place for them being of course the country, and kept them there from the first with the best people he could find to look after them, parting even with his own servants to wait on them and going down himself, whenever he might, to see how they were doing. The awkward thing was that they had practically no other relations and that his own affairs took up all his time. He had put them in possession of Bly, which was healthy and secure, and had placed at the head of their little establishment—but belowstairs only—an excellent woman, Mrs. Grose, whom he was sure his visitor would like and who had formerly been maid to his mother. She was now housekeeper and was also acting for the time as superintendent to the little girl, of whom, without children of her own, she was by good luck extremely fond. There were plenty of people to help, but of course the young lady who should go down as governess would be in supreme authority. She would also have, in holidays, to look after the small boy, who had been for a term at school—young as he was to be sent, but what else could be done?— and who, as the holidays were about to begin, would be back from one day to the other. There had been for the two children at first a young lady whom they had had the misfortune to lose. She had done for them quite beautifully—she was a most respectable person—till her death, the great awkwardness of which had, precisely, left no alternative but the school for little Miles. Mrs. Grose, since then, in the way of manners and things, had done as she could for Flora; and there were, further, a cook, a housemaid, a dairywoman, an old pony, an old groom and an old gardener, all likewise thoroughly respectable.

So far had Douglas presented his picture when some one put a question. "And what did the former governess die of? Of so much respectability?"

Our friend's answer was prompt. "That will come out. I don't anticipate."

"Pardon me—I thought that was just what you *are* doing."

"In her successor's place," I suggested, "I should have wished to learn if the office brought with it—"

"Necessary danger to life?" Douglas completed my thought. "She did wish to learn, and she did learn. You shall hear to-morrow what she learnt. Meanwhile of course the prospect struck her as slightly grim. She was young, untried, nervous: it was a vision of serious duties and little company, of really great loneliness. She hesitated —took a couple of days to consult and consider. But the salary offered much exceeded her modest measure, and on a second interview she faced the music, she engaged." And Douglas, with this, made a pause that, for the benefit of the company, moved me to throw in—

"The moral of which was of course the seduction exercised by the splendid young man. She succumbed to it."

He got up and, as he had done the night before, went to the fire, gave a stir to a log with his foot, then stood a moment with his back to us. "She saw him only twice."

"Yes, but that's just the beauty of her passion."

A little to my surprise, on this, Douglas turned round to me. "It *was* the beauty of it. There were others," he went on, "who had n't succumbed. He told her frankly all his difficulty—that for several applicants the conditions had been prohibitive. They were somehow simply afraid. It sounded dull—it sounded strange; and all the more so because of his main condition."

"Which was—?"

"That she should never trouble him—but never, never: neither appeal nor complain nor write about anything; only meet all questions herself, receive all moneys from his solicitor;[7] take the whole thing over and let him alone. She promised to do this, and she mentioned to me that when, for a moment, disburdened, delighted, he held her hand, thanking her for the sacrifice, she already felt rewarded."

"But was that all her reward?" one of the ladies asked.

"She never saw him again."

"Oh!" said the lady; which, as our friend immediately again left us, was the only other word of importance contributed to the subject till, the next night, by the corner of the hearth, in the best chair, he opened the faded red cover of a thin old-fashioned gilt-edged album. The whole thing took indeed more nights than one, but on the first occasion the same lady put another question. "What's your title?"

"I have n't one."

"Oh *I* have!" I said. But Douglas, without heeding me, had begun to read with a fine clearness that was like a rendering to the ear of the beauty of his author's hand.

I

I remember the whole beginning as a succession of flights and drops, a little see-saw of the right throbs and the wrong. After rising, in town, to meet his appeal I had at all events a couple of very bad days—found all my doubts bristle again, felt indeed sure I had made a mistake. In this state of mind I spent the long hours of bumping swinging coach that carried me to the stopping-place at which I was to be met by a vehicle from the house. This convenience, I was told, had been ordered, and I found, toward the close of the June afternoon, a commodious fly[8] in waiting for me. Driving at that hour, on a lovely day, through a country the summer sweetness of which served as a friendly welcome, my fortitude revived and, as we turned into the avenue, took a flight that was probably but a proof of the point to which it had sunk. I suppose I had expected, or had dreaded, something so dreary that what greeted me was a good surprise. I remember as a thoroughly pleasant impression the broad clear front, its open windows and fresh curtains and the pair of maids looking out; I remember the lawn and the bright flowers and the crunch of my wheels on the gravel and the clustered tree-tops over which the rooks[9] circled and cawed in the golden sky. The scene had a greatness that made it a different affair from my own scant home, and there immediately appeared at the door, with a little girl in her hand, a civil person who dropped me as decent a curtsey as if I had been the mistress or a distinguished visitor. I had received in Harley Street a narrower notion of the place, and that, as I recalled it, made me think the proprietor still more of a gentleman, suggested that what I was to enjoy might be a matter beyond his promise.

I had no drop again till the next day, for I was carried triumphantly through the following hours by my introduction to the younger of my pupils. The little girl who accompanied Mrs. Grose affected me on the spot as a creature too charming not to make it a great fortune to have to do with her. She was the most beautiful child I

---

[7] Lawyer.
[8] Light, covered carriage.

[9] Birds similar to the American crow.

had ever seen, and I afterwards wondered why my employer had n't made more of a point to me of this. I slept little that night—I was too much excited; and this astonished me too, I recollect, remained with me, adding to my sense of the liberality with which I was treated. The large impressive room, one of the best in the house, the great state bed, as I almost felt it, the figured full draperies, the long glasses in which, for the first time, I could see myself from head to foot, all struck me—like the wonderful appeal of my small charge—as so many things thrown in. It was thrown in as well, from the first moment, that I should get on with Mrs. Grose in a relation over which, on my way, in the coach, I fear I had rather brooded. The one appearance indeed that in this early outlook might have made me shrink again was that of her being so inordinately glad to see me. I felt within half an hour that she was so glad —stout simple plain clean wholesome woman—as to be positively on her guard against showing it too much. I wondered even then a little why she should wish *not* to show it, and that, with reflexion, with suspicion, might of course have made me uneasy.

But it was a comfort that there could be no uneasiness in a connexion with anything so beatific as the radiant image of my little girl, the vision of whose angelic beauty had probably more than anything else to do with the restlessness that, before morning, made me several times rise and wander about my room to take in the whole picture and prospect; to watch from my open window the faint summer dawn, to look at such stretches of the rest of the house as I could catch, and to listen, while in the fading dusk the first birds began to twitter, for the possible recurrence of a sound or two, less natural and not without but within, that I had fancied I heard. There had been a moment when I believed I recognised, faint and far, the cry of a child; there had been another when I found myself just consciously starting as at the passage, before my door, of a light footstep. But these fancies were not marked enough not to be thrown off, and it is only in the light, or the gloom, I should rather say, of other and subsequent matters that they now come back to me. To watch, teach, "form" little Flora would too evidently be the making of a happy and useful life. It had been agreed between us downstairs that after this first occasion I should have her as a matter of course at night, her small white bed being already arranged, to that end, in my room. What I had undertaken was the whole care of her, and she had remained just this last time with Mrs. Grose only as an effect of our consideration for my inevitable strangeness and her natural timidity. In spite of this timidity—which the child herself, in the oddest way in the world, had been perfectly frank and brave about, allowing it, without a sign of uncomfortable consciousness, with the deep sweet serenity indeed of one of Raphael's holy infants,[10] to be discussed, to be imputed to her and to determine us—I felt quite sure she would presently like me. It was part of what I already liked Mrs. Grose herself for, the pleasure I could see her feel in my admiration and wonder as I sat at supper with four tall candles and with my pupil, in a high chair and a bib, brightly facing me between them over bread and milk. There were naturally things that in Flora's presence could pass between us only as prodigious and gratified looks, obscure and round-about allusions.

"And the little boy—does he look like her? Is he too so very remarkable?"

[10] The Italian High Renaissance painter was best known in the nineteenth century for his paintings of the Madonna and Child.

One would n't, it was already conveyed between us, too grossly flatter a child. "Oh Miss, *most* remarkable. If you think well of this one!"—and she stood there with a plate in her hand, beaming at our companion, who looked from one of us to the other with placid heavenly eyes that contained nothing to check us.

"Yes; if I do—?"

"You *will* be carried away by the little gentleman!"

"Well, that, I think, is what I came for—to be carried away. I'm afraid, however," I remember feeling the impulse to add, "I'm rather easily carried away. I was carried away in London!"

I can still see Mrs. Grose's broad face as she took this in. "In Harley Street?"

"In Harley Street."

"Well, Miss, you're not the first—and you won't be the last."

"Oh I've no pretensions," I could laugh, "to being the only one. My other pupil, at any rate, as I understand, comes back to-morrow?"

"Not to-morrow—Friday, Miss. He arrives, as you did, by the coach, under care of the guard, and is to be met by the same carriage."

I forthwith wanted to know if the proper as well as the pleasant and friendly thing would n't therefore be that on the arrival of the public conveyance I should await him with his little sister; a proposition to which Mrs. Grose assented so heartily that I somehow took her manner as a kind of comforting pledge—never falsified, thank heaven!—that we should on every question be quite at one. Oh she was glad I was there!

What I felt the next day was, I suppose, nothing that could be fairly called a reaction from the cheer of my arrival; it was probably at the most only a slight oppression produced by a fuller measure of the scale, as I walked round them, gazed up at them, took them in, of my new circumstances. They had, as it were, an extent and mass for which I had not been prepared and in the presence of which I found myself, freshly, a little scared not less than a little proud. Regular lessons, in this agitation, certainly suffered some wrong; I reflected that my first duty was, by the gentlest arts I could contrive, to win the child into the sense of knowing me. I spent the day with her out of doors; I arranged with her, to her great satisfaction, that it should be she, she only, who might show me the place. She showed it step by step and room by room and secret by secret, with droll delightful childish talk about it and with the result, in half an hour, of our becoming tremendous friends. Young as she was I was struck, throughout our little tour, with her confidence and courage, with the way, in empty chambers and dull corridors, on crooked staircases that made me pause and even on the summit of an old machicolated[11] square tower that made me dizzy, her morning music, her disposition to tell me so many more things than she asked, rang out and led me on. I have not seen Bly since the day I left it, and I dare say that to my present older and more informed eyes it would show a very reduced importance. But as my little conductress, with her hair of gold and her frock of blue, danced before me round corners and pattered down passages, I had the view of a castle of romance inhabited by a rosy sprite, such a place as would somehow,

[11] In medieval architecture, *machicolations* were projections built out from the battlements of a wall and pierced with holes, through which missiles or boiling liquids could be dropped on attackers.

for diversion of the young idea, take all colour out of story-books and fairy-tales. Was n't it just a story-book over which I had fallen a-doze and a-dream? No; it was a big ugly antique but convenient house, embodying a few features of a building still older, half-displaced and half-utilised, in which I had the fancy of our being almost as lost as a handful of passengers in a great drifting ship. Well, I was strangely at the helm!

II

This came home to me when, two days later, I drove over with Flora to meet, as Mrs. Grose said, the little gentleman; and all the more for an incident that, presenting itself the second evening, had deeply disconcerted me. The first day had been, on the whole, as I have expressed, reassuring; but I was to see it wind up to a change of note. The postbag that evening—it came late—contained a letter for me which, however, in the hand of my employer, I found to be composed but of a few words enclosing another, addressed to himself, with a seal still unbroken. "This, I recognise, is from the head-master, and the head-master's an awful bore. Read him, please; deal with him; but mind you don't report. Not a word. I'm off!" I broke the seal with a great effort —so great a one that I was a long time coming to it; took the unopened missive at last up to my room and only attacked it just before going to bed. I had better have let it wait till morning, for it gave me a second sleepless night. With no counsel to take, the next day, I was full of distress; and it finally got so the better of me that I determined to open myself at least to Mrs. Grose.

"What does it mean? The child's dismissed his school."

She gave me a look that I remarked at the moment; then, visibly, with a quick blankness, seemed to try to take it back. "But are n't they all—?"

"Sent home—yes. But only for the holidays. Miles may never go back at all."

Consciously, under my attention, she reddened. "They won't take him?"

"They absolutely decline."

At this she raised her eyes, which she had turned from me; I saw them fill with good tears. "What has he done?"

I cast about; then I judged best simply to hand her my document—which, however, had the effect of making her, without taking it, simply put her hands behind her. She shook her head sadly. "Such things are not for me, Miss."

My counsellor could n't read! I winced at my mistake, which I attenuated as I could, and opened the letter again to repeat it to her; then, faltering in the act and folding it up once more, I put it back in my pocket. "Is he really *bad?*"

The tears were still in her eyes. "Do the gentlemen say so?"

"They go into no particulars. They simply express their regret that it should be impossible to keep him. That can have but one meaning." Mrs. Grose listened with dumb emotion; she forbore to ask me what this meaning might be; so that, presently, to put the thing with some coherence and with the mere aid of her presence to my own mind, I went on: "That he's an injury to the others."

At this, with one of the quick turns of simple folk, she suddenly flamed up. "Master Miles!—*him* an injury?"

There was such a flood of good faith in it that, though I had not yet seen the child, my very fears made me jump to the absurdity of the idea. I found myself, to meet my friend the better, offering it, on the spot, sarcastically. "To his poor little innocent mates!"

"It's too dreadful," cried Mrs. Grose, "to say such cruel things! Why he's scarce ten years old."

"Yes, yes; it would be incredible."

She was evidently grateful for such a profession. "See him, Miss, first. *Then* believe it!" I felt forthwith a new impatience to see him; it was the beginning of a curiosity that, all the next hours, was to deepen almost to pain. Mrs. Grose was aware, I could judge, of what she had produced in me, and she followed it up with assurance. "You might as well believe it of the little lady. Bless her," she added the next moment— "*look* at her!"

I turned and saw that Flora, whom, ten minutes before, I had established in the schoolroom with a sheet of white paper, a pencil and a copy of nice "round O's," now presented herself to view at the open door. She expressed in her little way an extraordinary detachment from disagreeable duties, looking at me, however, with a great childish light that seemed to offer it as a mere result of the affection she had conceived for my person, which had rendered necessary that she should follow me. I needed nothing more than this to feel the full force of Mrs. Grose's comparison, and, catching my pupil in my arms, covered her with kisses in which there was a sob of atonement.

None the less, the rest of the day, I watched for further occasion to approach my colleague, especially as, toward evening, I began to fancy she rather sought to avoid me. I overtook her, I remember, on the staircase; we went down together and at the bottom I detained her, holding her there with a hand on her arm. "I take what you said to me at noon as a declaration that *you've* never known him to be bad."

She threw back her head; she had clearly by this time, and very honestly, adopted an attitude. "Oh never known him—I don't pretend *that!*"

I was upset again. "Then you *have* known him—?"

"Yes indeed, Miss, thank God!"

On reflexion I accepted this. "You mean that a boy who never is—?"

"Is no boy for *me!*"

I held her tighter. "You like them with the spirit to be naughty?" Then, keeping pace with her answer, "So do I!" I eagerly brought out. "But not to the degree to contaminate—"

"To contaminate?"—my big word left her at a loss.

I explained it. "To corrupt."

She stared, taking my meaning in; but it produced in her an odd laugh. "Are you afraid he'll corrupt *you?*" She put the question with such a fine bold humour that with a laugh, a little silly doubtless, to match her own, I gave way for the time to the apprehension of ridicule.

But the next day, as the hour for my drive approached, I cropped up in another place. "What was the lady who was here before?"

"The last governess? She was also young and pretty—almost as young and almost as pretty, Miss, even as you."

"Ah then I hope her youth and her beauty helped her!" I recollect throwing off. "He seems to like us young and pretty!"

"Oh he *did,*" Mrs. Grose assented: "it was the way he liked every one!" She had no sooner spoken indeed than she caught herself up. "I mean that's *his* way—the master's."

I was struck. "But of whom did you speak first?"

She looked blank, but she coloured. "Why of *him*."

"Of the master?"

"Of who else?"

There was so obviously no one else that the next moment I had lost my impression of her having accidentally said more than she meant; and I merely asked what I wanted to know. "Did *she* see anything in the boy—?"

"That was n't right? She never told me."

I had a scruple, but I overcame it. "Was she careful—particular?"

Mrs. Grose appeared to try to be conscientious. "About some things—yes."

"But not about all?"

Again she considered. "Well, Miss—she's gone. I won't tell tales."

"I quite understand your feeling," I hastened to reply; but I thought it after an instant not opposed to this concession to pursue: "Did she die here?"

"No—she went off."

I don't know what there was in this brevity of Mrs. Grose's that struck me as ambiguous. "Went off to die?" Mrs. Grose looked straight out of the window, but I felt that, hypothetically, I had a right to know what young persons engaged for Bly were expected to do. "She was taken ill, you mean, and went home?"

"She was not taken ill, so far as appeared, in this house. She left it, at the end of the year, to go home, as she said, for a short holiday, to which the time she had put in had certainly given her a right. We had then a young woman—a nursemaid who had stayed on and who was a good girl and clever; and *she* took the children altogether for the interval. But our young lady never came back, and at the very moment I was expecting her I heard from the master that she was dead."

I turned this over. "But of what?"

"He never told me! But please, Miss," said Mrs. Grose, "I must get to my work."

III

Her thus turning her back on me was fortunately not, for my just preoccupations, a snub that could check the growth of our mutual esteem. We met, after I had brought home little Miles, more intimately than ever on the ground of my stupefaction, my general emotion: so monstrous was I then ready to pronounce it that such a child as had now been revealed to me should be under an interdict. I was a little late on the scene of his arrival, and I felt, as he stood wistfully looking out for me before the door of the inn at which the coach had put him down, that I had seen him on the instant, without and within, in the great glow of freshness, the same positive fragrance of purity, in which I had from the first moment seen his little sister. He was incredibly beautiful, and Mrs. Grose had put her finger on it: everything but a sort of passion of tenderness for him was swept away by his presence. What I then and there took him to my heart for was something divine that I have never found to the same degree in any child—his indescribable little air of knowing nothing in the world but love. It would have been impossible to carry a bad name with a greater sweetness of innocence, and by the time I had got back to Bly with him I remained merely bewildered—so far, that is, as I was not outraged—by the sense of the horrible letter locked up in one of the drawers of my room. As soon as I could compass a private word with Mrs. Grose I declared to her that it was grotesque.

She promptly understood me. "You mean the cruel charge—?"

"It does n't live an instant. My dear woman, *look* at him!"

She smiled at my pretension to have discovered his charm. "I assure you, Miss, I do nothing else! What will you say then?" she immediately added.

"In answer to the letter?" I had made up my mind. "Nothing at all."

"And to his uncle?"

I was incisive. "Nothing at all."

"And to the boy himself?"

I was wonderful. "Nothing at all."

She gave with her apron a great wipe to her mouth. "Then I'll stand by you. We'll see it out."

"We'll see it out!" I ardently echoed, giving her my hand to make it a vow.

She held me there a moment, then whisked up her apron again with her detached hand. "Would you mind, Miss, if I used the freedom—"

"To kiss me? No!" I took the good creature in my arms and after we had embraced like sisters felt still more fortified and indignant.

This at all events was for the time: a time so full that as I recall the way it went it reminds me of all the art I now need to make it a little distinct. What I look back at with amazement is the situation I accepted. I had undertaken, with my companion, to see it out, and I was under a charm apparently that could smooth away the extent and the far and difficult connexions of such an effort. I was lifted aloft on a great wave of infatuation and pity. I found it simple, in my ignorance, my confusion and perhaps my conceit, to assume that I could deal with a boy whose education for the world was all on the point of beginning. I am unable even to remember at this day what proposal I framed for the end of his holidays and the resumption of his studies. Lessons with me indeed, that charming summer, we all had a theory that he was to have; but I now feel that for weeks the lessons must have been rather my own. I learnt something—at first certainly—that had not been one of the teachings of my small smothered life; learnt to be amused, and even amusing, and not to think for the morrow. It was the first time, in a manner, that I had known space and air and freedom, all the music of summer and all the mystery of nature. And then there was consideration—and consideration was sweet. Oh it was a trap—not designed but deep—to my imagination, to my delicacy, perhaps to my vanity; to whatever in me was most excitable. The best way to picture it all is to say that I was off my guard. They gave me so little trouble—they were of a gentleness so extraordinary. I used to speculate—but even this with a dim disconnectedness—as to how the rough future (for all futures are rough!) would handle them and might bruise them. They had the bloom of health and happiness; and yet, as if I had been in charge of a pair of little grandees, of princes of the blood, for whom everything, to be right, would have to be fenced about and ordered and arranged, the only form that in my fancy the after-years could take for them was that of a romantic, a really royal extension of the garden and the park. It may be of course above all that what suddenly broke into this gives the previous time a charm of stillness—that hush in which something gathers or crouches. The change was actually like the spring of a beast.

In the first weeks the days were long; they often, at their finest, gave me what I used to call my own hour, the hour when, for my pupils, tea-time and bed-time having come and gone, I had before my final retirement a small interval alone. Much as I liked my companions this hour was the thing in the day I liked most; and I liked it best of all when, as the light faded—or rather, I should say, the day lingered and the last calls of the last birds sounded, in a flushed sky, from the old trees—I could take a turn into the grounds and enjoy, almost with a sense of property that amused and flattered me, the beauty and dignity of the place. It was a pleasure at these moments to feel myself tranquil and justified; doubtless perhaps also to reflect that by my discretion, my quiet good sense and general high propriety, I was giving pleasure —if he ever thought of it!—to the person to whose pressure I had yielded. What I was doing was what he had earnestly hoped and directly asked of me, and that I *could,* after all, do it proved even a greater joy than I had expected. I dare say I fancied myself in short a remarkable young woman and took comfort in the faith that this would more publicly appear. Well, I needed to be remarkable to offer a front to the remarkable things that presently gave their first sign.

It was plump, one afternoon, in the middle of my very hour: the children were tucked away and I had come out for my stroll. One of the thoughts that, as I don't in the least shrink now from noting, used to be with me in these wanderings was that it would be as charming as a charming story suddenly to meet some one. Some one would appear there at the turn of a path and would stand before me and smile and approve. I did n't ask more than that—I only asked that he should *know;* and the only way to be sure he knew would be to see it, and the kind light of it, in his handsome face. That was exactly present to me—by which I mean the face was—when, on the first of these occasions, at the end of a long June day, I stopped short on emerging from one of the plantations and coming into view of the house. What arrested me on the spot—and with a shock much greater than any vision had allowed for—was the sense that my imagination had, in a flash, turned real. He did stand there!—but high up, beyond the lawn and at the very top of the tower to which, on that first morning, little Flora had conducted me. This tower was one of a pair—square incongruous crenellated[12] structures—that were distinguished, for some reason, though I could see little difference, as the new and the old. They flanked opposite ends of the house and were probably architectural absurdities, redeemed in a measure indeed by not being wholly disengaged nor of a height too pretentious, dating, in their gingerbread antiquity, from a romantic revival that was already a respectable past. I admired them, had fancies about them, for we could all profit in a degree, especially

---

[12] In medieval architecture, a *crenellation* was a notched battlement in a square, saw-tooth pattern.

when they loomed through the dusk, by the grandeur of their actual battlements; yet it was not at such an elevation that the figure I had so often invoked seemed most in place.

It produced in me, this figure, in the clear twilight, I remember, two distinct gasps of emotion, which were, sharply, the shock of my first and that of my second surprise. My second was a violent perception of the mistake of my first: the man who met my eyes was not the person I had precipitately supposed. There came to me thus a bewilderment of vision of which, after these years, there is no living view that I can hope to give. An unknown man in a lonely place is a permitted object of fear to a young woman privately bred; and the figure that faced me was—a few more seconds assured me—as little any one else I knew as it was the image that had been in my mind. I had not seen it in Harley Street—I had not seen it anywhere. The place moreover, in the strangest way in the world, had on the instant and by the very fact of its appearance become a solitude. To me at least, making my statement here with a deliberation with which I have never made it, the whole feeling of the moment returns. It was as if, while I took in, what I did take in, all the rest of the scene had been stricken with death. I can hear again, as I write, the intense hush in which the sounds of evening dropped. The rooks stopped cawing in the golden sky and the friendly hour lost for the unspeakable minute all its voice. But there was no other change in nature, unless indeed it were a change that I saw with a stranger sharpness. The gold was still in the sky, the clearness in the air, and the man who looked at me over the battlements was as definite as a picture in a frame. That's how I thought, with extraordinary quickness, of each person he might have been and that he was n't. We were confronted across our distance quite long enough for me to ask myself with intensity who then he was and to feel, as an effect of my inability to say, a wonder that in a few seconds more became intense.

The great question, or one of these, is afterwards, I know, with regard to certain matters, the question of how long they have lasted. Well, this matter of mine, think what you will of it, lasted while I caught at a dozen possibilities, none of which made a difference for the better, that I could see, in there having been in the house—and for how long, above all?—a person of whom I was in ignorance. It lasted while I just bridled a little with the sense of how my office seemed to require that there should be no such ignorance and no such person. It lasted while this visitant, at all events —and there was a touch of the strange freedom, as I remember, in the sign of familiarity of his wearing no hat—seemed to fix me, from his position, with just the question, just the scrutiny through the fading light, that his own presence provoked. We were too far apart to call to each other, but there was a moment at which, at shorter range, some challenge between us, breaking the hush, would have been the right result of our straight mutual stare. He was in one of the angles, the one away from the house, very erect, as it struck me, and with both hands on the ledge. So I saw him as I see the letters I form on this page; then, exactly, after a minute, as if to add to the spectacle, he slowly changed his place—passed, looking at me hard all the while, to the opposite corner of the platform. Yes, it was intense to me that during this transit he never took his eyes from me, and I can see at this moment the way his hand, as he went, moved from one of the crenellations to the next. He stopped at the other corner, but less long, and even as he turned away still markedly fixed me. He turned away; that was all I knew.

IV

It was not that I did n't wait, on this occasion, for more, since I was as deeply rooted as shaken. Was there a "secret" at Bly—a mystery of Udolpho[13] or an insane, an unmentionable relative kept in unsuspected confinement? I can't say how long I turned it over, or how long, in a confusion of curiosity and dread, I remained where I had had my collision; I only recall that when I re-entered the house darkness had quite closed in. Agitation, in the interval, certainly had held me and driven me, for I must, in circling about the place, have walked three miles; but I was to be later on so much more overwhelmed that this mere dawn of alarm was a comparatively human chill. The most singular part of it in fact—singular as the rest had been—was the part I became, in the hall, aware of in meeting Mrs. Grose. This picture comes back to me in the general train—the impression, as I received it on my return, of the wide white panelled space, bright in the lamplight and with its portraits and red carpet, and of the good surprised look of my friend, which immediately told me she had missed me. It came to me straightway, under her contact, that, with plain heartiness, mere relieved anxiety at my appearance, she knew nothing whatever that could bear upon the incident I had there ready for her. I had not suspected in advance that her comfortable face would pull me up, and I somehow measured the importance of what I had seen by my thus finding myself hesitate to mention it. Scarce anything in the whole history seems to me so odd as this fact that my real beginning of fear was one, as I may say, with the instinct of sparing my companion. On the spot, accordingly, in the pleasant hall and with her eyes on me, I, for a reason that I could n't then have phrased, achieved an inward revolution—offered a vague pretext for my lateness and, with the plea of the beauty of the night and of the heavy dew and wet feet, went as soon as possible to my room.

Here it was another affair; here, for many days after, it was a queer affair enough. There were hours, from day to day—or at least there were moments, snatched even from clear duties—when I had to shut myself up to think. It was n't so much yet that I was more nervous than I could bear to be as that I was remarkably afraid of becoming so; for the truth I had now to turn over was simply and clearly the truth that I could arrive at no account whatever of the visitor with whom I had been so inexplicably and yet, as it seemed to me, so intimately concerned. It took me little time to see that I might easily sound, without forms of enquiry and without exciting remark, any domestic complication. The shock I had suffered must have sharpened all my senses; I felt sure, at the end of three days and as the result of mere closer attention, that I had not been practised upon by the servants nor made the object of any "game." Of whatever it was that I knew nothing was known around me. There

---

[13] Reference to *The Mysteries of Udolpho*, an English Gothic novel by Ann Radcliffe (1764–1823), in which a young woman is carried off by her uncle to a castle filled with mysteries and ghostly manifestations that are later explained away as natural occurrences.

was but one sane inference: some one had taken a liberty rather monstrous. That was what, repeatedly, I dipped into my room and locked the door to say to myself. We had been, collectively, subject to an intrusion; some unscrupulous traveller, curious in old houses, had made his way in unobserved, enjoyed the prospect from the best point of view and then stolen out as he came. If he had given me such a bold hard stare, that was but a part of his indiscretion. The good thing, after all, was that we should surely see no more of him.

This was not so good a thing, I admit, as not to leave me to judge that what, essentially, made nothing else much signify was simply my charming work. My charming work was just my life with Miles and Flora, and through nothing could I so like it as through feeling that to throw myself into it was to throw myself out of my trouble. The attraction of my small charges was a constant joy, leading me to wonder afresh at the vanity of my original fears, the distaste I had begun by entertaining for the probable grey prose of my office. There was to be no grey prose, it appeared, and no long grind; so how could work not be charming that presented itself as daily beauty? It was all the romance of the nursery and the poetry of the school-room. I don't mean by this of course that we studied only fiction and verse; I mean that I can express no otherwise the sort of interest my companions inspired. How can I describe that except by saying that instead of growing deadly used to them—and it's a marvel for a governess: I call the sisterhood to witness!—I made constant fresh discoveries. There was one direction, assuredly, in which these discoveries stopped: deep obscurity continued to cover the region of the boy's conduct at school. It had been promptly given me, I have noted, to face that mystery without a pang. Perhaps even it would be nearer the truth to say that—without a word—he himself had cleared it up. He had made the whole charge absurd. My conclusion bloomed there with the real rose-flush of his innocence: he was only too fine and fair for the little horrid unclean school-world, and he had paid a price for it. I reflected acutely that the sense of such individual differences, such superiorities of quality, always, on the part of the majority—which could include even stupid sordid head-masters—turns infallibly to the vindictive.

Both the children had a gentleness—it was their only fault, and it never made Miles a muff[14]—that kept them (how shall I express it?) almost impersonal and certainly quite unpunishable. They were like those cherubs of the anecdote who had—morally at any rate—nothing to whack! I remember feeling with Miles in especial as if he had had, as it were, nothing to call even an infinitesimal history. We expect of a small child scant enough "antecedents," but there was in this beautiful little boy something extraordinarily sensitive, yet extraordinarily happy, that, more than in any creature of his age I have seen, struck me as beginning anew each day. He had never for a second suffered. I took this as a direct disproof of his having really been chastised. If he had been wicked he would have "caught" it, and I should have caught it by the rebound—I should have found the trace, should have felt the wound and the dishonour. I could reconstitute nothing at all, and he was therefore an angel. He never spoke of his school, never mentioned a comrade or a master; and I, for my part, was quite too much disgusted to allude to them. Of course I was under the spell, and the wonderful part is that, even at the time, I perfectly knew I was. But I gave myself

---

[14] British: a weak, ineffectual person.

up to it; it was an antidote to any pain, and I had more pains than one. I was in receipt in these days of disturbing letters from home, where things were not going well. But with this joy of my children what things in the world mattered? That was the question I used to put to my scrappy retirements. I was dazzled by their loveliness.

There was a Sunday—to get on—when it rained with such force and for so many hours that there could be no procession to church; in consequence of which, as the day declined, I had arranged with Mrs. Grose that, should the evening show improvement, we would attend together the late service. The rain happily stopped, and I prepared for our walk, which, through the park and by the good road to the village, would be a matter of twenty minutes. Coming downstairs to meet my colleague in the hall, I remembered a pair of gloves that had required three stitches and that had received them—with a publicity perhaps not edifying—while I sat with the children at their tea, served on Sundays, by exception, in that cold clean temple of mahogany and brass, the "grown-up" dining-room. The gloves had been dropped there, and I turned in to recover them. The day was grey enough, but the afternoon light still lingered, and it enabled me, on crossing the threshold, not only to recognise, on a chair near the wide window, then closed, the articles I wanted, but to become aware of a person on the other side of the window and looking straight in. One step into the room had sufficed; my vision was instantaneous; it was all there. The person looking straight in was the person who had already appeared to me. He appeared thus again with I won't say greater distinctness, for that was impossible, but with a nearness that represented a forward stride in our intercourse and made me, as I met him, catch my breath and turn cold. He was the same—he was the same, and seen, this time, as he had been seen before, from the waist up, the window, though the dining-room was on the ground floor, not going down to the terrace on which he stood. His face was close to the glass, yet the effect of this better view was, strangely, just to show me how intense the former had been. He remained but a few seconds—long enough to convince me he also saw and recognised; but it was as if I had been looking at him for years and had known him always. Something, however, happened this time that had not happened before; his stare into my face, through the glass and across the room, was as deep and hard as then, but it quitted me for a moment during which I could still watch it, see it fix successively several other things. On the spot there came to me the added shock of a certitude that it was not for me he had come. He had come for some one else.

The flash of this knowledge—for it was knowledge in the midst of dread—produced in me the most extraordinary effect, starting, as I stood there, a sudden vibration of duty and courage. I say courage because I was beyond all doubt already far gone. I bounded straight out of the door again, reached that of the house, got in an instant upon the drive and, passing along the terrace as fast as I could rush, turned a corner and came full in sight. But it was in sight of nothing now—my visitor had vanished. I stopped, almost dropped, with the real relief of this; but I took in the whole scene—I gave him time to reappear. I call it time, but how long was it? I can't speak to the purpose to-day of the duration of these things. That kind of measure must have left me: they could n't have lasted as they actually appeared to me to last. The terrace and the whole place, the lawn and the garden beyond it, all I could see of the park, were empty with a great emptiness. There were shrubberies and big trees, but I remember the clear assurance I felt that none of them concealed him. He was there or was not there: not there if I did n't see him. I got hold of this; then, instinctively, instead of returning as I had come, went to the window. It was confusedly present to me that I ought to place myself where he had stood. I did so; I applied my face to the pane and looked, as he had looked, into the room. As if, at this moment, to show me exactly what his range had been, Mrs. Grose, as I had done for himself just before, came in from the hall. With this I had the full image of a repetition of what had already occurred. She saw me as I had seen my own visitant; she pulled up short as I had done; I gave her something of the shock that I had received. She turned white, and this made me ask myself if I had blanched as much. She stared, in short, and retreated just on *my* lines, and I knew she had then passed out and come round to me and that I should presently meet her. I remained where I was, and while I waited I thought of more things than one. But there's only one I take space to mention. I wondered why *she* should be scared.

V

Oh she let me know as soon as, round the corner of the house, she loomed again into view. "What in the name of goodness is the matter—?" She was now flushed and out of breath.

I said nothing till she came quite near. "With me?" I must have made a wonderful face. "Do I show it?"

"You're as white as a sheet. You look awful."

I considered; I could meet on this, without scruple, any degree of innocence. My need to respect the bloom of Mrs. Grose's had dropped, without a rustle, from my shoulders, and if I wavered for the instant it was not with what I kept back. I put out my hand to her and she took it; I held her hard a little, liking to feel her close to me. There was a kind of support in the shy heave of her surprise. "You came for me for church, of course, but I can't go."

"Has anything happened?"

"Yes. You must know now. Did I look very queer?"

"Through this window? Dreadful!"

"Well," I said, "I've been frightened." Mrs. Grose's eyes expressed plainly that *she* had no wish to be, yet also that she knew too well her place not to be ready to share with me any marked inconvenience. Oh it was quite settled that she *must* share! "Just what you saw from the dining-room a minute ago was the effect of that. What *I* saw—just before—was much worse."

Her hand tightened. "What was it?"

"An extraordinary man. Looking in."

"What extraordinary man?"

"I have n't the least idea."

Mrs. Grose gazed round us in vain. "Then where is he gone?"

"I know still less."

"Have you seen him before?"

"Yes—once. On the old tower."

She could only look at me harder. "Do you mean he's a stranger?"

"Oh very much!"

"Yet you did n't tell me?"

"No—for reasons. But now that you've guessed—"

Mrs. Grose's round eyes encountered this charge. "Ah I have n't guessed!" she said very simply. "How can I if *you* don't imagine?"

"I don't in the very least."

"You've seen him nowhere but on the tower?"

"And on this spot just now."

Mrs. Grose looked round again. "What was he doing on the tower?"

"Only standing there and looking down at me."

She thought a minute. "Was he a gentleman?"

I found I had no need to think. "No." She gazed in deeper wonder. "No."

"Then nobody about the place? Nobody from the village?"

"Nobody—nobody. I did n't tell you, but I made sure."

She breathed a vague relief: this was, oddly, so much to the good. It only went indeed a little way. "But if he is n't a gentleman—"

"What *is* he? He's a horror."

"A horror?"

"He's—God help me if I know *what* he is!"

Mrs. Grose looked round once more; she fixed her eyes on the duskier distance and then, pulling herself together, turned to me with full inconsequence. "It's time we should be at church."

"Oh I'm not fit for church!"

"Won't it do you good?"

"It won't do *them*—!" I nodded at the house.

"The children?"

"I can't leave them now."

"You're afraid—?"

I spoke boldly. "I'm afraid of *him*."

Mrs. Grose's large face showed me, at this, for the first time, the far-away faint glimmer of a consciousness more acute: I somehow made out in it the delayed dawn of an idea I myself had not given her and that was as yet quite obscure to me. It comes back to me that I thought instantly of this as something I could get from her; and I felt it to be connected with the desire she presently showed to know more. "When was it—on the tower?"

"About the middle of the month. At this same hour."

"Almost at dark," said Mrs. Grose.

"Oh no, not nearly. I saw him as I see you."

"Then how did he get in?"

"And how did he get out?" I laughed. "I had no opportunity to ask him! This evening, you see," I pursued, "he has not been able to get in."

"He only peeps?"

"I hope it will be confined to that!" She had now let go my hand; she turned away a little. I waited an instant; then I brought out: "Go to church. Good-bye. I must watch."

Slowly she faced me again. "Do you fear for them?"

We met in another long look. "Don't *you?*" Instead of answering she came nearer to the window and, for a minute, applied her face to the glass. "You see how he could see," I meanwhile went on.

She did n't move. "How long was he here?"

"Till I came out. I came to meet him."

Mrs. Grose at last turned round, and there was still more in her face. "*I* could n't have come out."

"Neither could I!" I laughed again. "But I did come. I've my duty."

"So have I mine," she replied; after which she added: "What's he like?"

"I've been dying to tell you. But he's like nobody."

"Nobody?" she echoed.

"He has no hat." Then seeing in her face that she already, in this, with a deeper dismay, found a touch of picture, I quickly added stroke to stroke. "He has red hair, very red, close-curling, and a pale face, long in shape, with straight good features and little rather queer whiskers that are as red as his hair. His eyebrows are somehow darker; they look particularly arched and as if they might move a good deal. His eyes are sharp, strange—awfully; but I only know clearly that they're rather small and very fixed. His mouth's wide, and his lips are thin, and except for his little whiskers he's quite clean-shaven. He gives me a sort of sense of looking like an actor."

"An actor!" It was impossible to resemble one less, at least, than Mrs. Grose at that moment.

"I've never seen one, but so I suppose them. He's tall, active, erect," I continued, "but never—no, never!—a gentleman."

My companion's face had blanched as I went on; her round eyes started and her mild mouth gaped. "A gentleman?" she gasped, confounded, stupefied: "a gentleman *he?*"

"You know him then?"

She visibly tried to hold herself. "But he *is* handsome?"

I saw the way to help her. "Remarkably!"

"And dressed—?"

"In somebody's clothes. They're smart, but they're not his own."

She broke into a breathless affirmative groan. "They're the master's!"

I caught it up. "You *do* know him?"

She faltered but a second. "Quint!" she cried.

"Quint?"

"Peter Quint—his own man, his valet, when he was here!"

"When the master was?"

Gaping still, but meeting me, she pieced it all together. "He never wore his hat, but he did wear—well, there were waistcoats missed! They were both here—last year. Then the master went, and Quint was alone."

I followed, but halting a little. "Alone?"

"Alone with *us.*" Then as from a deeper depth, "In charge," she added.

"And what became of him?"

She hung fire so long that I was still more mystified. "He went too," she brought out at last.

"Went where?"

Her expression, at this, became extraordinary. "God knows where! He died."

"Died?" I almost shrieked.

She seemed fairly to square herself, plant herself more firmly to express the wonder of it. "Yes. Mr. Quint's dead."

VI

It took of course more than that particular passage to place us together in presence of what we had now to live with as we could, my dreadful liability to impressions of the order so vividly exemplified, and my companion's knowledge henceforth— a knowledge half consternation and half compassion—of that liability. There had been this evening, after the revelation that left me for an hour so prostrate—there had been for either of us no attendance on any service but a little service of tears and vows, of prayers and promises, a climax to the series of mutual challenges and pledges that had straightway ensued on our retreating together to the schoolroom and shutting ourselves up there to have everything out. The result of our having everything out was simply to reduce our situation to the last rigour of its elements. She herself had seen nothing, not the shadow of a shadow, and nobody in the house but the governess was in the governess's plight; yet she accepted without directly impugning my sanity the truth as I gave it to her, and ended by showing me on this ground an awestricken tenderness, a deference to my more than questionable privilege, of which the very breath has remained with me as that of the sweetest of human charities.

What was settled between us accordingly that night was that we thought we might bear things together; and I was not even sure that in spite of her exemption it was she who had the best of the burden. I knew at this hour, I think, as well as I knew later, what I was capable of meeting to shelter my pupils; but it took me some time to be wholly sure of what my honest comrade was prepared for to keep terms with so stiff an agreement. I was queer company enough—quite as queer as the company I received; but as I trace over what we went through I see how much common ground we must have found in the one idea that, by good fortune, *could* steady us. It was the idea, the second movement, that led me straight out, as I may say, of the inner chamber of my dread. I could take the air in the court, at least, and there Mrs. Grose could join me. Perfectly can I recall now the particular way strength came to me before we separated for the night. We had gone over and over every feature of what I had seen.

"He was looking for some one else, you say—some one who was not you?"

"He was looking for little Miles." A portentous clearness now possessed me. "*That's* whom he was looking for."

"But how do you know?"

"I know, I know, I know!" My exaltation grew. "And *you* know, my dear!"

She did n't deny this, but I required, I felt, not even so much telling as that. She took it up again in a moment. "What if *he* should see him?"

"Little Miles? That's what he wants!"

She looked immensely scared again. "The child?"

"Heaven forbid! The man. He wants to appear to *them*." That he might was an awful conception, and yet somehow I could keep it at bay; which moreover, as we lingered there, was what I succeeded in practically proving. I had an absolute certainty that I should see again what I had already seen, but something within me said that by offering myself bravely as the sole subject of such experience, by accepting, by inviting, by surmounting it all, I should serve as an expiatory victim and guard the tranquillity of the rest of the household. The children in especial I should thus fence about and absolutely save. I recall one of the last things I said that night to Mrs. Grose.

"It does strike me that my pupils have never mentioned—!"

She looked at me hard as I musingly pulled up. "His having been here and the time they were with him?"

"The time they were with him, and his name, his presence, his history, in any way. They've never alluded to it."

"Oh the little lady does n't remember. She never heard or knew."

"The circumstances of his death?" I thought with some intensity. "Perhaps not. But Miles would remember—Miles would know."

"Ah don't try him!" broke from Mrs. Grose.

I returned her the look she had given me. "Don't be afraid." I continued to think. "It *is* rather odd."

"That he has never spoken of him?"

"Never by the least reference. And you tell me they were 'great friends.'"

"Oh it was n't *him*!" Mrs. Grose with emphasis declared. "It was Quint's own fancy. To play with him, I mean—to spoil him." She paused a moment; then she added: "Quint was much too free."

This gave me, straight from my vision of his face—*such* a face!—a sudden sickness of disgust. "Too free with *my* boy?"

"Too free with every one!"

I forbore for the moment to analyse this description further than by the reflexion that a part of it applied to several of the members of the household, of the half-dozen maids and men who were still of our small colony. But there was everything, for our apprehension, in the lucky fact that no discomfortable legend, no perturbation of scullions,[15] had ever, within any one's memory, attached to the kind old place. It had neither bad name nor ill fame, and Mrs. Grose, most apparently, only desired to cling to me and to quake in silence. I even put her, the very last thing of all, to the test. It was when, at midnight, she had her hand on the schoolroom door to take leave. "I *have* it from you then—for it's of great importance—that he was definitely and admittedly bad?"

"Oh not admittedly. *I* knew it—but the master did n't."

"And you never told him?"

"Well, he did n't like tale-bearing—he hated complaints. He was terribly short with anything of that kind, and if people were all right to *him*—"

"He would n't be bothered with more?" This squared well enough with my impression of him: he was not a trouble-loving gentleman, nor so very particular perhaps about some of the company he himself kept. All the same, I pressed my informant. "I promise you *I* would have told!"

She felt my discrimination. "I dare say I was wrong. But really I was afraid."

"Afraid of what?"

"Of things that man could do. Quint was so clever—he was so deep."

I took this in still more than I probably showed. "You were n't afraid of anything else? Not of his effect—?"

[15] Kitchen workers.

"His effect?" she repeated with a face of anguish and waiting while I faltered.

"On innocent little precious lives. They were in your charge."

"No, they were n't in mine!" she roundly and distressfully returned. "The master believed in him and placed him here because he was supposed not to be quite in health and the country air so good for him. So he had everything to say. Yes"—she let me have it—"even about *them.*"

"Them—that creature?" I had to smother a kind of howl. "And you could bear it?"

"No. I could n't—and I can't now!" And the poor woman burst into tears.

A rigid control, from the next day, was, as I have said, to follow them; yet how often and how passionately, for a week, we came back together to the subject! Much as we had discussed it that Sunday night, I was, in the immediate later hours in especial —for it may be imagined whether I slept—still haunted with the shadow of something she had not told me. I myself had kept back nothing, but there was a word Mrs. Grose had kept back. I was sure moreover by morning that this was not from a failure of frankness, but because on every side there were fears. It seems to me indeed, in raking it all over, that by the time the morrow's sun was high I had restlessly read into the facts before us almost all the meaning they were to receive from subsequent and more cruel occurrences. What they gave me above all was just the sinister figure of the living man—the dead one would keep a while!—and of the months he had continuously passed at Bly, which, added up, made a formidable stretch. The limit of this evil time had arrived only when, on the dawn of a winter's morning, Peter Quint was found, by a labourer going to early work, stone dead on the road from the village: a catastrophe explained—superficially at least—by a visible wound to his head; such a wound as might have been produced (and as, on the final evidence, *had* been) by a fatal slip, in the dark and after leaving the public-house, on the steepish icy slope, a wrong path altogether, at the bottom of which he lay. The icy slope, the turn mistaken at night and in liquor, accounted for much—practically, in the end and after the inquest and boundless chatter, for everything; but there had been matters in his life, strange passages and perils, secret disorders, vices more than suspected, that would have accounted for a good deal more.

I scarce know how to put my story into words that shall be a credible picture of my state of mind; but I was in these days literally able to find a joy in the extraordinary flight of heroism the occasion demanded of me. I now saw that I had been asked for a service admirable and difficult; and there would be a greatness in letting it be seen —oh in the right quarter!—that I could succeed where many another girl might have failed. It was an immense help to me—I confess I rather applaud myself as I look back! —that I saw my response so strongly and so simply. I was there to protect and defend the little creatures in the world the most bereaved and the most loveable, the appeal of whose helplessness had suddenly become only too explicit, a deep constant ache of one's own engaged affection. We were cut off, really, together; we were united in our danger. They had nothing but me, and I—well, I had *them.* It was in short a magnificent chance. This chance presented itself to me in an image richly material. I was a screen—I was to stand before them. The more I saw the less they would. I began to watch them in a stifled suspense, a disguised tension, that might well, had it continued too long, have turned to something like madness. What saved me, as I now see, was that it turned to another matter altogether. It did n't last as suspense

—it was superseded by horrible proofs. Proofs, I say, yes—from the moment I really took hold.

This moment dated from an afternoon hour that I happened to spend in the grounds with the younger of my pupils alone. We had left Miles indoors, on the red cushion of a deep window-seat; he had wished to finish a book, and I had been glad to encourage a purpose so laudable in a young man whose only defect was a certain ingenuity of restlessness. His sister, on the contrary, had been alert to come out, and I strolled with her half an hour, seeking the shade, for the sun was still high and the day exceptionally warm. I was aware afresh with her, as we went, of how, like her brother, she contrived—it was the charming thing in both children—to let me alone without appearing to drop me and to accompany me without appearing to oppress. They were never importunate and yet never listless. My attention to them all really went to seeing them amuse themselves immensely without me: this was a spectacle they seemed actively to prepare and that employed me as an active admirer. I walked in a world of their invention—they had no occasion whatever to draw upon mine; so that my time was taken only with being for them some remarkable person or thing that the game of the moment required and that was merely, thanks to my superior, my exalted stamp, a happy and highly distinguished sinecure. I forget what I was on the present occasion; I only remember that I was something very important and very quiet and that Flora was playing very hard. We were on the edge of the lake, and, as we had lately begun geography, the lake was the Sea of Azof.[16]

Suddenly, amid these elements, I became aware that on the other side of the Sea of Azof we had an interested spectator. The way this knowledge gathered in me was the strangest thing in the world—the strangest, that is, except the very much stranger in which it quickly merged itself. I had sat down with a piece of work—for I was something or other that could sit—on the old stone bench which overlooked the pond; and in this position I began to take in with certitude and yet without direct vision the presence, a good way off, of a third person. The old trees, the thick shrubbery, made a great and pleasant shade, but it was all suffused with the brightness of the hot still hour. There was no ambiguity in anything; none whatever at least in the conviction I from one moment to another found myself forming as to what I should see straight before me and across the lake as a consequence of raising my eyes. They were attached at this juncture to the stitching in which I was engaged, and I can feel once more the spasm of my effort not to move them till I should so have steadied myself as to be able to make up my mind what to do. There was an alien object in view—a figure whose right of presence I instantly and passionately questioned. I recollect counting over perfectly the possibilities, reminding myself that nothing was more natural for instance than the appearance of one of the men about the place, or even of a messenger, a postman or a tradesman's boy, from the village. That reminder had as little effect on my practical certitude as I was conscious—still even without looking—of its having upon the character and attitude of our visitor. Nothing was more natural than that these things should be the other things they absolutely were not.

[16] Gulf of the Black Sea between Europe and Asia.

Of the positive identity of the apparition I would assure myself as soon as the small clock of my courage should have ticked out the right second; meanwhile, with an effort that was already sharp enough, I transferred my eyes straight to little Flora, who, at the moment, was about ten yards away. My heart had stood still for an instant with the wonder and terror of the question whether she too would see; and I held my breath while I waited for what a cry from her, what some sudden innocent sign either of interest or of alarm, would tell me. I waited, but nothing came; then in the first place —and there is something more dire in this, I feel, than in anything I have to relate —I was determined by a sense that within a minute all spontaneous sounds from her had dropped; and in the second by the circumstance that also within the minute she had, in her play, turned her back to the water. This was her attitude when I at last looked at her—looked with the confirmed conviction that we were still, together, under direct personal notice. She had picked up a small flat piece of wood which happened to have in it a little hole that had evidently suggested to her the idea of sticking in another fragment that might figure as a mast and make the thing a boat. This second morsel, as I watched her, she was very markedly and intently attempting to tighten in its place. My apprehension of what she was doing sustained me so that after some seconds I felt I was ready for more. Then I again shifted my eyes—I faced what I had to face.

VII

I got hold of Mrs. Grose as soon after this as I could; and I can give no intelligible account of how I fought out the interval. Yet I still hear myself cry as I fairly threw myself into her arms: "They *know*—it's too monstrous: they know, they know!"

"And what on earth—?" I felt her incredulity as she held me.

"Why all that *we* know—and heaven knows what more besides!" Then as she released me I made it out to her, made it out perhaps only now with full coherency even to myself. "Two hours ago, in the garden"—I could scarce articulate—"Flora *saw!*"

Mrs. Grose took it as she might have taken a blow in the stomach. "She has told you?" she panted.

"Not a word—that's the horror. She kept it to herself! The child of eight, *that* child!" Unutterable still for me was the stupefaction of it.

Mrs. Grose of course could only gape the wider. "Then how do you know?"

"I was there—I saw with my eyes: saw she was perfectly aware."

"Do you mean aware of *him?*"

"No—of *her.*" I was conscious as I spoke that I looked prodigious things, for I got the slow reflexion of them in my companion's face. "Another person—this time; but a figure of quite as unmistakeable horror and evil: a woman in black, pale and dreadful—with such an air also, and such a face!—on the other side of the lake. I was there with the child—quiet for the hour; and in the midst of it she came."

"Came how—from where?"

"From where they come from! She just appeared and stood there—but not so near."

"And without coming nearer?"

"Oh for the effect and the feeling she might have been as close as you!"

My friend, with an odd impulse, fell back a step. "Was she some one you've never seen?"

"Never. But some one the child has. Some one *you* have." Then to show how I had thought it all out: "My predecessor—the one who died."

"Miss Jessel?"

"Miss Jessel. You don't believe me?" I pressed.

She turned right and left in her distress. "How can you be sure?"

This drew from me, in the state of my nerves, a flash of impatience. "Then ask Flora—*she's* sure!" But I had no sooner spoken than I caught myself up. "No, for God's sake *don't!* She'll say she is n't—she'll lie!"

Mrs. Grose was not too bewildered instinctively to protest. "Ah how *can* you?"

"Because I'm clear. Flora does n't want me to know."

"It's only then to spare you."

"No, no—there are depths, depths! The more I go over it the more I see in it, and the more I see in it the more I fear. I don't know what I *don't* see, what I *don't* fear!"

Mrs. Grose tried to keep up with me. "You mean you're afraid of seeing her again?"

"Oh no; that's nothing—now!" Then I explained. "It's of *not* seeing her."

But my companion only looked wan. "I don't understand."

"Why, it's that the child may keep it up—and that the child assuredly *will*—without my knowing it."

At the image of this possibility Mrs. Grose for a moment collapsed, yet presently to pull herself together again as from the positive force of the sense of what, should we yield an inch, there would really be to give way to. "Dear, dear—we must keep our heads! And after all, if she does n't mind it—!" She even tried a grim joke. "Perhaps she likes it!"

"Like *such* things—a scrap of an infant!"

"Is n't it just a proof of her blest innocence?" my friend bravely enquired.

She brought me, for the instant, almost round. "Oh we must clutch at *that*—we must cling to it! If it is n't a proof of what you say, it's a proof of—God knows what! For the woman's a horror of horrors."

Mrs. Grose, at this, fixed her eyes a minute on the ground; then at last raising them, "Tell me how you know," she said.

"Then you admit it's what she was?" I cried.

"Tell me how you know," my friend simply repeated.

"Know? By seeing her! By the way she looked."

"At you, do you mean—so wickedly?"

"Dear me, no—I could have borne that. She gave me never a glance. She only fixed the child."

Mrs. Grose tried to see it. "Fixed her?"

"Ah with such awful eyes!"

She stared at mine as if they might really have resembled them. "Do you mean of dislike?"

"God help us, no. Of something much worse."

"Worse than dislike?"—this left her indeed at a loss.

"With a determination—indescribable. With a kind of fury of intention."

I made her turn pale. "Intention?"

"To get hold of her." Mrs. Grose—her eyes just lingering on mine—gave a shudder and walked to the window; and while she stood there looking out I completed my statement. "*That's* what Flora knows."

After a little she turned round. "The person was in black, you say?"

"In mourning—rather poor, almost shabby. But—yes—with extraordinary beauty." I now recognised to what I had at last, stroke by stroke, brought the victim of my confidence, for she quite visibly weighed this. "Oh handsome—very, very," I insisted; "wonderfully handsome. But infamous."

She slowly came back to me. "Miss Jessel—*was* infamous." She once more took my hand in both her own, holding it as tight as if to fortify me against the increase of alarm I might draw from this disclosure. "They were both infamous," she finally said.

So for a little we faced it once more together; and I found absolutely a degree of help in seeing it now so straight. "I appreciate," I said, "the great decency of your not having hitherto spoken; but the time has certainly come to give me the whole thing." She appeared to assent to this, but still only in silence; seeing which I went on: "I must have it now. Of what did she die? Come, there was something between them."

"There was everything."

"In spite of the difference—?"

"Oh of their rank, their condition"—she brought it woefully out. "*She* was a lady."

I turned it over; I again saw. "Yes—she was a lady."

"And he so dreadfully below," said Mrs. Grose.

I felt that I doubtless need n't press too hard, in such company, on the place of a servant in the scale; but there was nothing to prevent an acceptance of my companion's own measure of my predecessor's abasement. There was a way to deal with that, and I dealt; the more readily for my full vision—on the evidence—of our employer's late clever good-looking "own" man; impudent, assured, spoiled, depraved. "The fellow was a hound."

Mrs. Grose considered as if it were perhaps a little a case for a sense of shades. "I've never seen one like him. He did what he wished."

"With *her?*"

"With them all."

It was as if now in my friend's own eyes Miss Jessel had again appeared. I seemed at any rate for an instant to trace their evocation of her as distinctly as I had seen her by the pond; and I brought out with decision: "It must have been also what *she* wished!"

Mrs. Grose's face signified that it had been indeed, but she said at the same time: "Poor woman—she paid for it!"

"Then you do know what she died of?" I asked.

"No—I know nothing. I wanted not to know; I was glad enough I did n't; and I thanked heaven she was well out of this!"

"Yet you had then your idea—"

"Of her real reason for leaving? Oh yes—as to that. She could n't have stayed. Fancy it here—for a governess! And afterwards I imagined—and I still imagine. And what I imagine is dreadful."

"Not so dreadful as what I do," I replied; on which I must have shown her—as I was indeed but too conscious—a front of miserable defeat. It brought out again all her compassion for me, and at the renewed touch of her kindness my power to resist broke down. I burst, as I had the other time made her burst, into tears; she took me to her motherly breast, where my lamentation overflowed. "I don't do it!" I sobbed in despair; "I don't save or shield them! It's far worse than I dreamed. They're lost!"

VIII

What I had said to Mrs. Grose was true enough: there were in the matter I had put before her depths and possibilities that I lacked resolution to sound; so that when we met once more in the wonder of it we were of a common mind about the duty of resistance to extravagant fancies. We were to keep our heads if we should keep nothing else—difficult indeed as that might be in the face of all that, in our prodigious experience, seemed least to be questioned. Late that night, while the house slept, we had another talk in my room; when she went all the way with me as to its being beyond doubt that I had seen exactly what I had seen. I found that to keep her thoroughly in the grip of this I had only to ask her how, if I had "made it up," I came to be able to give, of each of the persons appearing to me, a picture disclosing, to the last detail, their special marks—a portrait on the exhibition of which she had instantly recognised and named them. She wished, of course—small blame to her!— to sink the whole subject; and I was quick to assure her that my own interest in it had now violently taken the form of a search for the way to escape from it. I closed with her cordially on the article of the likelihood that with recurrence—for recurrence we took for granted—I should get used to my danger; distinctly professing that my personal exposure had suddenly become the least of my discomforts. It was my new suspicion that was intolerable; and yet even to this complication the later hours of the day had brought a little ease.

On leaving her, after my first outbreak, I had of course returned to my pupils, associating the right remedy for my dismay with that sense of their charm which I had already recognised as a resource I could positively cultivate and which had never failed me yet. I had simply, in other words, plunged afresh into Flora's special society and there become aware—it was almost a luxury!—that she could put her little conscious hand straight upon the spot that ached. She had looked at me in sweet speculation and then had accused me to my face of having "cried." I had supposed the ugly signs of it brushed away; but I could literally—for the time at all events —rejoice, under this fathomless charity, that they had not entirely disappeared. To gaze into the depths of blue of the child's eyes and pronounce their loveliness a trick of premature cunning was to be guilty of a cynicism in preference to which I naturally preferred to abjure my judgement and, so far as might be, my agitation. I could n't abjure for merely wanting to, but I could repeat to Mrs. Grose—as I did there, over and over, in the small hours—that with our small friends' voices in the air, their pressure on one's heart and their fragrant faces against one's cheek, everything fell to the ground but their incapacity and their beauty. It was a pity that, somehow, to settle this once for all, I had equally to re-enumerate the signs of subtlety that, in the afternoon, by the lake, had made a miracle of my show of self-possession. It was a pity to be obliged to re-investigate the certitude of the moment itself and repeat how it had come to me as a revelation that the inconceivable communion I then surprised must have been for both parties a matter of habit. It was a pity I should have had to quaver out again the reasons for my not having, in my delusion, so much as questioned that the little girl saw our visitant even as I actually saw Mrs. Grose herself, and that she wanted, by just so much as she did thus see, to make me suppose she did n't, and at the same time, without showing anything, arrive at a guess as to whether I myself did! It was a pity I needed to recapitulate the portentous little activities by which she sought to divert my attention—the perceptible increase of movement, the greater intensity of play, the singing, the gabbling of nonsense and the invitation to romp.

Yet if I had not indulged, to prove there was nothing in it, in this review, I should have missed the two or three dim elements of comfort that still remained to me. I should n't for instance have been able to asseverate to my friend that I was certain —which was so much to the good—that *I* at least had not betrayed myself. I should n't have been prompted, by stress of need, by desperation of mind—I scarce know what to call it—to invoke such further aid to intelligence as might spring from pushing my colleague fairly to the wall. She had told me, bit by bit, under pressure, a great deal; but a small shifty spot on the wrong side of it all still sometimes brushed my brow like the wing of a bat; and I remember how on this occasion—for the sleeping house and the concentration alike of our danger and our watch seemed to help—I felt the importance of giving the last jerk to the curtain. "I don't believe anything so horrible," I recollect saying; "no, let us put it definitely, my dear, that I don't. But if I did, you know, there's a thing I should require now, just without sparing you the least bit more—oh not a scrap, come!—to get out of you. What was it you had in mind when, in our distress, before Miles came back, over the letter from his school, you said, under my insistence, that you did n't pretend for him he had n't literally *ever* been 'bad'? He has *not*, truly, 'ever,' in these weeks that I myself have lived with him and so closely watched him; he has been an imperturbable little prodigy of delightful loveable goodness. Therefore you might perfectly have made the claim for him if you had not, as it happened, seen an exception to take. What was your exception, and to what passage in your personal observation of him did you refer?"

It was a straight question enough, but levity was not our note, and in any case I had before the grey dawn admonished us to separate got my answer. What my friend had had in mind proved immensely to the purpose. It was neither more nor less than the particular fact that for a period of several months Quint and the boy had been perpetually together. It was indeed the very appropriate item of evidence of her having ventured to criticise the propriety, to hint at the incongruity, of so close an alliance, and even to go so far on the subject as a frank overture to Miss Jessel would take her. Miss Jessel had, with a very high manner about it, requested her to mind her business, and the good woman had on this directly approached little Miles. What she had said to him, since I pressed, was that *she* liked to see young gentlemen not forget their station.

I pressed again, of course, the closer for that. "You reminded him that Quint was only a base menial?"

"As you might say! And it was his answer, for one thing, that was bad."

"And for another thing?" I waited. "He repeated your words to Quint?"

"No, not that. It's just what he *would n't!*" she could still impress on me. "I was sure, at any rate," she added, "that he did n't. But he denied certain occasions."

"What occasions?"

"When they had been about together quite as if Quint were his tutor—and a very grand one—and Miss Jessel only for the little lady. When he had gone off with the fellow, I mean, and spent hours with him."

"He then prevaricated about it—he said he had n't?" Her assent was clear enough to cause me to add in a moment: "I see. He lied."

"Oh!" Mrs. Grose mumbled. This was a suggestion that it did n't matter; which indeed she backed up by a further remark. "You see, after all, Miss Jessel did n't mind. She did n't forbid him."

I considered. "Did he put that to you as a justification?"

At this she dropped again. "No, he never spoke of it."

"Never mentioned her in connexion with Quint?"

She saw, visibly flushing, where I was coming out. "Well, he did n't show anything. He denied," she repeated; "he denied."

Lord, how I pressed her now! "So that you could see he knew what was between the two wretches?"

"I don't know—I don't know!" the poor woman wailed.

"You do know, you dear thing," I replied; "only you have n't my dreadful boldness of mind, and you keep back, out of timidity and modesty and delicacy, even the impression that in the past, when you had, without my aid, to flounder about in silence, most of all made you miserable. But I shall get it out of you yet! There was something in the boy that suggested to you," I continued, "his covering and concealing their relation."

"Oh he could n't prevent—"

"Your learning the truth? I dare say! But, heavens," I fell, with vehemence, a-thinking, "what it shows that they must, to that extent, have succeeded in making of him!"

"Ah nothing that's not nice *now!*" Mrs. Grose lugubriously pleaded.

"I don't wonder you looked queer," I persisted, "when I mentioned to you the letter from his school!"

"I doubt if I looked as queer as you!" she retorted with homely force. "And if he was so bad then as that comes to, how is he such an angel now?"

"Yes indeed—and if he was a fiend at school! How, how, how? Well," I said in my torment, "you must put it to me again, though I shall not be able to tell you for some days. Only put it to me again!" I cried in a way that made my friend stare. "There are directions in which I must n't for the present let myself go." Meanwhile I returned to her first example—the one to which she had just previously referred —of the boy's happy capacity for an occasional slip. "If Quint—on your remonstrance at the time you speak of—was a base menial, one of the things Miles said to you, I find myself guessing, was that you were another." Again her admission was so adequate that I continued: "And you forgave him that?"

"Would n't *you?*"

"Oh yes!" And we exchanged there, in the stillness, a sound of the oddest amusement. Then I went on: "At all events, while he was with the man—"

"Miss Flora was with the woman. It suited them all!"

It suited me too, I felt, only too well; by which I mean that it suited exactly the particular deadly view I was in the very act of forbidding myself to entertain. But I so far succeeded in checking the expression of this view that I will throw, just here, no further light on it than may be offered by the mention of my final observation to Mrs. Grose. "His having lied and been impudent are, I confess, less engaging specimens than I had hoped to have from you of the outbreak in him of the little natural man. Still," I mused, "they must do, for they make me feel more than ever that I must watch."

It made me blush, the next minute, to see in my friend's face how much more unreservedly she had forgiven him than her anecdote struck me as pointing out to my own tenderness any way to do. This was marked when, at the schoolroom door, she quitted me. "Surely you don't accuse *him*—"

"Of carrying on an intercourse that he conceals from me? Ah remember that, until further evidence, I now accuse nobody." Then before shutting her out to go by another passage to her own place, "I must just wait," I wound up.

IX

I waited and waited, and the days took as they elapsed something from my consternation. A very few of them, in fact, passing, in constant sight of my pupils, without a fresh incident, sufficed to give to grievous fancies and even to odious memories a kind of brush of the sponge. I have spoken of the surrender to their extraordinary childish grace as a thing I could actively promote in myself, and it may be imagined if I neglected now to apply at this source for whatever balm it would yield. Stranger than I can express, certainly, was the effort to struggle against my new lights. It would doubtless have been a greater tension still, however, had it not been so frequently successful. I used to wonder how my little charges could help guessing that I thought strange things about them; and the circumstance that these things only made them more interesting was not by itself a direct aid to keeping them in the dark. I trembled lest they should see that they *were* so immensely more interesting. Putting things at the worst, at all events, as in meditation I so often did, any clouding of their innocence could only be—blameless and foredoomed as they were—a reason the more for taking risks. There were moments when I knew myself to catch them up by an irresistible impulse and press them to my heart. As soon as I had done so I used to wonder— "What will they think of that? Does n't it betray too much?" It would have been easy to get into a sad wild tangle about how much I might betray; but the real account, I feel, of the hours of peace I could still enjoy was that the immediate charm of my companions was a beguilement still effective even under the shadow of the possibility that it was studied. For if it occurred to me that I might occasionally excite suspicion by the little outbreaks of my sharper passion for them, so too I remember asking if I might n't see a queerness in the traceable increase of their own demonstrations.

They were at this period extravagantly and preternaturally fond of me; which, after all, I could reflect, was no more than a graceful response in children perpetually bowed down over and hugged. The homage of which they were so lavish succeeded in truth for my nerves quite as well as if I never appeared to myself, as I may say, literally to catch them at a purpose in it. They had never, I think, wanted to do so many things for their poor protectress; I mean—though they got their lessons better and better, which was naturally what would please her most—in the way of diverting, entertaining, surprising her; reading her passages, telling her stories, acting her charades, pouncing out at her, in disguises, as animals and historical characters, and above all astonishing her by the "pieces" they had secretly got by heart and could interminably recite. I should never get to the bottom—were I to let myself go even now—of the prodigious private commentary, all under still more private correction, with which I in these days overscored their full hours. They had shown me from the first a facility for everything, a general faculty which, taking a fresh start, achieved remarkable flights. They got their little tasks as if they loved them; they indulged, from the mere exuberance of the gift, in the most unimposed little miracles of memory. They not only popped out at me as tigers and as Romans, but as Shakespeareans, astronomers and navigators. This was so singularly the case that it had presumably much to do with the fact as to which, at the present day, I am at a loss for a different explanation: I allude to my unnatural composure on the subject of another school for Miles. What I remember is that I was content for the time not to open the question, and that contentment must have sprung from the sense of his perpetually striking show of cleverness. He was too clever for a bad governess, for a parson's daughter, to spoil; and the strangest if not the brightest thread in the pensive embroidery I just spoke of was the impression I might have got, if I had dared to work it out, that he was under some influence operating in his small intellectual life as a tremendous incitement.

If it was easy to reflect, however, that such a boy could postpone school, it was at least as marked that for such a boy to have been "kicked out" by a schoolmaster was a mystification without end. Let me add that in their company now—and I was careful almost never to be out of it—I could follow no scent very far. We lived in a cloud of music and affection and success and private theatricals. The musical sense in each of the children was of the quickest, but the elder in especial had a marvellous knack of catching and repeating. The schoolroom piano broke into all gruesome fancies; and when that failed there were confabulations in corners, with a sequel of one of them going out in the highest spirits in order to "come in" as something new. I had had brothers myself, and it was no revelation to me that little girls could be slavish idolaters of little boys. What surpassed everything was that there was a little boy in the world who could have for the inferior age, sex and intelligence so fine a consideration. They were extraordinarily at one, and to say that they never either quarrelled or complained is to make the note of praise coarse for their quality of sweetness. Sometimes perhaps indeed (when I dropped into coarseness) I came across traces of little understandings between them by which one of them should keep me occupied while the other slipped away. There is a naïf[17] side, I suppose, in all diplomacy; but if my pupils practised upon me it was surely with the minimum of grossness. It was all in the other quarter that, after a lull, the grossness broke out.

[17] Naive.

I find that I really hang back; but I must take my horrid plunge. In going on with the record of what was hideous at Bly I not only challenge the most liberal faith—for which I little care; but (and this is another matter) I renew what I myself suffered, I again push my dreadful way through it to the end. There came suddenly an hour after which, as I look back, the business seems to me to have been all pure suffering; but I have at least reached the heart of it, and the straightest road out is doubtless to advance. One evening—with nothing to lead up or prepare it—I felt the cold touch of the impression that had breathed on me the night of my arrival and which, much lighter then as I have mentioned, I should probably have made little of in memory had my subsequent sojourn been less agitated. I had not gone to bed; I sat reading by a couple of candles. There was a roomful of old books at Bly—last-century fiction some of it, which, to the extent of a distinctly deprecated renown, but never to so much as that of a stray specimen, had reached the sequestered home and appealed to the unavowed curiosity of my youth. I remember that the book I had in my hand was Fielding's "Amelia";[18] also that I was wholly awake. I recall further both a general conviction that it was horribly late and a particular objection to looking at my watch. I figure finally that the white curtain draping, in the fashion of those days, the head of Flora's little bed, shrouded, as I had assured myself long before, the perfection of childish rest. I recollect in short that though I was deeply interested in my author I found myself, at the turn of a page and with his spell all scattered, looking straight up from him and hard at the door of my room. There was a moment during which I listened, reminded of the faint sense I had had, the first night, of there being something undefinably astir in the house, and noted the soft breath of the open casement just move the half-drawn blind. Then, with all the marks of a deliberation that must have seemed magnificent had there been any one to admire it, I laid down my book, rose to my feet and, taking a candle, went straight out of the room and, from the passage, on which my light made little impression, noiselessly closed and locked the door.

I can say now neither what determined nor what guided me, but I went straight along the lobby, holding my candle high, till I came within sight of the tall window that presided over the great turn of the staircase. At this point I precipitately found myself aware of three things. They were practically simultaneous, yet they had flashes of succession. My candle, under a bold flourish, went out, and I perceived, by the uncovered window, that the yielding dusk of earliest morning rendered it unnecessary. Without it, the next instant, I knew that there was a figure on the stair. I speak of sequences, but I required no lapse of seconds to stiffen myself for a third encounter with Quint. The apparition had reached the landing halfway up and was therefore on the spot nearest the window, where, at sight of me, it stopped short and fixed me exactly as it had fixed me from the tower and from the garden. He knew me as well as I knew him; and so, in the cold faint twilight, with a glimmer in the high glass and another on the polish of the oak stair below, we faced each other in our common intensity. He was absolutely, on this occasion, a living detestable dangerous presence.

[18] Novel by Henry Fielding (1707–1754) in which the evils of society are portrayed through the trials and tribulations of a long-suffering, devoted wife who constantly forgives her weak, unfaithful husband. Amelia finally inherits a fortune, and the novel has a happy ending.

But that was not the wonder of wonders; I reserve this distinction for quite another circumstance: the circumstance that dread had unmistakeably quitted me and that there was nothing in me unable to meet and measure him.

I had plenty of anguish after that extraordinary moment, but I had, thank God, no terror. And he knew I had n't—I found myself at the end of an instant magnificently aware of this. I felt, in a fierce rigour of confidence, that if I stood my ground a minute I should cease—for the time at least—to have him to reckon with; and during the minute, accordingly, the thing was as human and hideous as a real interview: hideous just because it *was* human, as human as to have met alone, in the small hours, in a sleeping house, some enemy, some adventurer, some criminal. It was the dead silence of our long gaze at such close quarters that gave the whole horror, huge as it was, its only note of the unnatural. If I had met a murderer in such a place and at such an hour we still at least would have spoken. Something would have passed, in life, between us; if nothing had passed one of us would have moved. The moment was so prolonged that it would have taken but little more to make me doubt if even *I* were in life. I can't express what followed it save by saying that the silence itself —which was indeed in a manner an attestation of my strength—became the element into which I saw the figure disappear; in which I definitely saw it turn, as I might have seen the low wretch to which it had once belonged turn on receipt of an order, and pass, with my eyes on the villainous back that no hunch could have more disfigured, straight down the staircase and into the darkness in which the next bend was lost.

X

I remained a while at the top of the stair, but with the effect presently of understanding that when my visitor had gone, he had gone; then I returned to my room. The foremost thing I saw there by the light of the candle I had left burning was that Flora's little bed was empty; and on this I caught my breath with all the terror that, five minutes before, I had been able to resist. I dashed at the place in which I had left her lying and over which—for the small silk counterpane[19] and the sheets were disarranged —the white curtains had been deceivingly pulled forward; then my step, to my unutterable relief, produced an answering sound: I noticed an agitation of the window-blind, and the child, ducking down, emerged rosily from the other side of it. She stood there in so much of her candour and so little of her night-gown, with her pink bare feet and the golden glow of her curls. She looked intensely grave, and I had never had such a sense of losing an advantage acquired (the thrill of which had just been so prodigious) as on my consciousness that she addressed me with a reproach —"You naughty: where *have* you been?" Instead of challenging her own irregularity I found myself arraigned and explaining. She herself explained, for that matter, with the loveliest eagerest simplicity. She had known suddenly, as she lay there, that I was out of the room, and had jumped up to see what had become of me. I had dropped, with the joy of her reappearance, back into my chair—feeling then, and then only, a little faint; and she had pattered straight over to me, thrown herself upon my knee, given herself to be held with the flame of the candle full in the wonderful little face

---

[19] Bed covering.

that was still flushed with sleep. I remember closing my eyes an instant, yieldingly, consciously, as before the excess of something beautiful that shone out of the blue of her own. "You were looking for me out of the window?" I said. "You thought I might be walking in the grounds?"

"Well, you know, I thought some one was"—she never blanched as she smiled out that at me.

Oh how I looked at her now! "And did you see any one?"

"Ah *no!*" she returned almost (with the full privilege of childish inconsequence) resentfully, though with a long sweetness in her little drawl of the negative.

At that moment, in the state of my nerves, I absolutely believed she lied; and if I once more closed my eyes it was before the dazzle of the three or four possible ways in which I might take this up. One of these for a moment tempted me with such singular force that, to resist it, I must have gripped my little girl with a spasm that, wonderfully, she submitted to without a cry or a sign of fright. Why not break out at her on the spot and have it all over?—give it to her straight in her lovely little lighted face? "You see, you see, you *know* that you do and that you already quite suspect I believe it; therefore why not frankly confess it to me, so that we may at least live with it together and learn perhaps, in the strangeness of our fate, where we are and what it means?" This solicitation dropped, alas, as it came: if I could immediately have succumbed to it I might have spared myself—well, you'll see what. Instead of succumbing I sprang again to my feet, looked at her bed and took a helpless middle way. "Why did you pull the curtain over the place to make me think you were still there?"

Flora luminously considered; after which, with her little divine smile: "Because I don't like to frighten you!"

"But if I had, by your idea, gone out—?"

She absolutely declined to be puzzled; she turned her eyes to the flame of the candle as if the question were as irrelevant, or at any rate as impersonal, as Mrs. Marcet or nine-times-nine. "Oh but you know," she quite adequately answered, "that you might come back, you dear, and that you *have!*" And after a little, when she had got into bed, I had, a long time, by almost sitting on her for the retention of her hand, to show how I recognised the pertinence of my return.

You may imagine the general complexion, from that moment, of my nights. I repeatedly sat up till I did n't know when; I selected moments when my room-mate unmistakeably slept, and, stealing out, took noiseless turns in the passage. I even pushed as far as to where I had last met Quint. But I never met him there again, and I may as well say at once that I on no other occasion saw him in the house. I just missed, on the staircase, nevertheless, a different adventure. Looking down it from the top I once recognised the presence of a woman seated on one of the lower steps with her back presented to me, her body half-bowed and her head, in an attitude of woe, in her hands. I had been there but an instant, however, when she vanished without looking round at me. I knew, for all that, exactly what dreadful face she had to show; and I wondered whether, if instead of being above I had been below, I should have had the same nerve for going up that I had lately shown Quint. Well, there continued to be plenty of call for nerve. On the eleventh night after my latest encounter with that gentleman—they were all numbered now—I had an alarm that perilously skirted it and that indeed, from the particular quality of its unexpectedness, proved quite my sharpest shock. It was precisely the first night during this series that, weary with vigils, I had conceived I might again without laxity lay myself down at my old hour. I slept immediately and, as I afterwards knew, till about one o'clock; but when I woke it was to sit straight up, as completely roused as if a hand had shaken me. I had left a light burning, but it was now out, and I felt an instant certainty that Flora had extinguished it. This brought me to my feet and straight, in the darkness, to her bed, which I found she had left. A glance at the window enlightened me further, and the striking of a match completed the picture.

The child had again got up—this time blowing out the taper, and had again, for some purpose of observation or response, squeezed in behind the blind and was peering out into the night. That she now saw—as she had not, I had satisfied myself, the previous time—was proved to me by the fact that she was disturbed neither by my re-illumination nor by the haste I made to get into slippers and into a wrap. Hidden, protected, absorbed, she evidently rested on the sill—the casement opened forward —and gave herself up. There was a great still moon to help her, and this fact had counted in my quick decision. She was face to face with the apparition we had met at the lake, and could now communicate with it as she had not then been able to do. What I, on my side, had to care for was, without disturbing her, to reach, from the corridor, some other window turned to the same quarter. I got to the door without her hearing me; I got out of it, closed it and listened, from the other side, for some sound from her. While I stood in the passage I had my eyes on her brother's door, which was but ten steps off and which, indescribably, produced in me a renewal of the strange impulse that I lately spoke of as my temptation. What if I should go straight in and march to *his* window?—what if, by risking to his boyish bewilderment a revelation of my motive, I should throw across the rest of the mystery the long halter of my boldness?

This thought held me sufficiently to make me cross to his threshold and pause again. I preternaturally listened; I figured to myself what might portentously be; I wondered if his bed were also empty and he also secretly at watch. It was a deep soundless minute, at the end of which my impulse failed. He was quiet; he might be innocent; the risk was hideous; I turned away. There was a figure in the grounds—a figure prowling for a sight, the visitor with whom Flora was engaged; but it was n't the visitor most concerned with my boy. I hesitated afresh, but on other grounds and only a few seconds; then I had made my choice. There were empty rooms enough at Bly, and it was only a question of choosing the right one. The right one suddenly presented itself to me as the lower one—though high above the gardens—in the solid corner of the house that I have spoken of as the old tower. This was a large square chamber, arranged with some state as a bedroom, the extravagant size of which made it so inconvenient that it had not for years, though kept by Mrs. Grose in exemplary order, been occupied. I had often admired it and I knew my way about in it; I had only, after just faltering at the first chill gloom of its disuse, to pass across it and unbolt in all quietness one of the shutters. Achieving this transit I uncovered the glass without a sound and, applying my face to the pane, was able, the darkness without being much less than within, to see that I commanded the right direction. Then I saw something more. The moon made the night extraordinarily penetrable and showed me on the lawn a person, diminished by distance, who stood there motionless and as if fascinated, looking up to where I had appeared—looking, that is, not so much straight at me as at something that was apparently above me. There was clearly another person above me—there was a person on the tower; but the presence on the lawn was not in the least what I had conceived and had confidently hurried to meet. The presence on the lawn—I felt sick as I made it out—was poor little Miles himself.

XI

It was not till late next day that I spoke to Mrs. Grose; the rigour with which I kept my pupils in sight making it often difficult to meet her privately: the more as we each felt the importance of not provoking—on the part of the servants quite as much as on that of the children—any suspicion of a secret flurry or of a discussion of mysteries. I drew a great security in this particular from her mere smooth aspect. There was nothing in her fresh face to pass on to others the least of my horrible confidences. She believed me, I was sure, absolutely: if she had n't I don't know what would have become of me, for I could n't have borne the strain alone. But she was a magnificent monument to the blessing of a want of imagination, and if she could see in our little charges nothing but their beauty and amiability, their happiness and cleverness, she had no direct communication with the sources of my trouble. If they had been at all visibly blighted or battered she would doubtless have grown, on tracing it back, haggard enough to match them; as matters stood, however, I could feel her, when she surveyed them with her large white arms folded and the habit of serenity in all her look, thank the Lord's mercy that if they were ruined the pieces would still serve. Flights of fancy gave place, in her mind, to a steady fireside glow, and I had already begun to perceive how, with the development of the conviction that—as time went on without a public accident—our young things could, after all, look out for themselves, she addressed her greatest solicitude to the sad case presented by their deputy-guardian. That, for myself, was a sound simplification: I could engage that, to the world, my face should tell no tales, but it would have been, in the conditions, an immense added worry to find myself anxious about hers.

At the hour I now speak of she had joined me, under pressure, on the terrace, where, with the lapse of the season, the afternoon sun was now agreeable; and we sat there together while before us and at a distance, yet within call if we wished, the children strolled to and fro in one of their most manageable moods. They moved slowly, in unison, below us, over the lawn, the boy, as they went, reading aloud from a story-book and passing his arm round his sister to keep her quite in touch. Mrs. Grose watched them with positive placidity; then I caught the suppressed intellectual creak with which she conscientiously turned to take from me a view of the back of the tapestry. I had made her a receptacle of lurid things, but there was an odd recognition of my superiority—my accomplishments and my function—in her patience under my pain. She offered her mind to my disclosures as, had I wished to mix a witch's broth and proposed it with assurance, she would have held out a large clean saucepan. This had become thoroughly her attitude by the time that, in my recital of the events of the night, I reached the point of what Miles had said to me when, after seeing him, at such a monstrous hour, almost on the very spot where he happened now to be, I had gone down to bring him in; choosing then, at the window, with a concentrated need of not alarming the house, rather that method than any noisier process. I had left her meanwhile in little doubt of my small hope of representing with success even to her actual sympathy my sense of the real splendour of the little inspiration with which, after I had got him into the house, the boy met my final articulate challenge. As soon as I appeared in the moonlight on the terrace he had come to me as straight as possible; on which I had taken his hand without a word and led him, through the dark spaces, up the staircase where Quint had so hungrily hovered for him, along the lobby where I had listened and trembled, and so to his forsaken room.

Not a sound, on the way, had passed between us, and I had wondered—oh *how* I had wondered!—if he were groping about in his dreadful little mind for something plausible and not too grotesque. It would tax his invention certainly, and I felt, this time, over his real embarrassment, a curious thrill of triumph. It was a sharp trap for any game hitherto successful. He could play no longer at perfect propriety, nor could he pretend to it; so how the deuce would he get out of the scrape? There beat in me indeed, with the passionate throb of this question, an equal dumb appeal as to how the deuce *I* should. I was confronted at last, as never yet, with all the risk attached even now to sounding my own horrid note. I remember in fact that as we pushed into his little chamber, where the bed had not been slept in at all and the window, uncovered to the moonlight, made the place so clear that there was no need of striking a match—I remember how I suddenly dropped, sank upon the edge of the bed from the force of the idea that he must know how he really, as they say, "had" me. He could do what he liked, with all his cleverness to help him, so long as I should continue to defer to the old tradition of the criminality of those caretakers of the young who minister to superstitions and fears. He "had" me indeed, and in a cleft stick; for who would ever absolve me, who would consent that I should go unhung, if, by the faintest tremor of an overture, I were the first to introduce into our perfect intercourse an element so dire? No, no: it was useless to attempt to convey to Mrs. Grose, just as it is scarcely less so to attempt to suggest here, how, during our short stiff brush there in the dark, he fairly shook me with admiration. I was of course thoroughly kind and merciful; never, never yet had I placed on his small shoulders hands of such tenderness as those with which, while I rested against the bed, I held him there well under fire. I had no alternative but, in form at least, to put it to him.

"You must tell me now—and all the truth. What did you go out for? What were you doing there?"

I can still see his wonderful smile, the whites of his beautiful eyes and the uncovering of his clear teeth, shine to me in the dusk. "If I tell you why, will you understand?" My heart, at this, leaped into my mouth. *Would* he tell me why? I found no sound on my lips to press it, and I was aware of answering only with a vague repeated grimacing nod. He was gentleness itself, and while I wagged my head at him he stood there more than ever a little fairy prince. It was his brightness indeed that gave me a respite. Would it be so great if he were really going to tell me? "Well," he said at last, "just exactly in order that you should do this."

"Do what?"

"Think me—for a change—*bad!*" I shall never forget the sweetness and gaiety with which he brought out the word, nor how, on top of it, he bent forward and kissed me. It was practically the end of everything. I met his kiss and I had to make, while I folded him for a minute in my arms, the most stupendous effort not to cry. He had given exactly the account of himself that permitted least my going behind it, and it was only with the effect of confirming my acceptance of it that, as I presently glanced about the room, I could say—

"Then you did n't undress at all?"

He fairly glittered in the gloom. "Not at all. I sat up and read."

"And when did you go down?"

"At midnight. When I'm bad I *am* bad!"

"I see, I see—it's charming. But how could you be sure I should know it?"

"Oh I arranged that with Flora." His answers rang out with a readiness! "She was to get up and look out."

"Which is what she did do." It was I who fell into the trap!

"So she disturbed you, and, to see what she was looking at, you also looked—you saw."

"While you," I concurred, "caught your death in the night air!"

He literally bloomed so from this exploit that he could afford radiantly to assent. "How otherwise should I have been bad enough?" he asked. Then, after another embrace, the incident and our interview closed on my recognition of all the reserves of goodness that, for his joke, he had been able to draw upon.

XII

The particular impression I had received proved in the morning light, I repeat, not quite successfully presentable to Mrs. Grose, though I re-enforced it with the mention of still another remark that he had made before we separated. "It all lies in half a dozen words," I said to her, "words that really settle the matter. 'Think, you know, what I *might* do!' He threw that off to show me how good he is. He knows down to the ground what he 'might do.' That's what he gave them a taste of at school."

"Lord, you do change!" cried my friend.

"I don't change—I simply make it out. The four, depend upon it, perpetually meet. If on either of these last nights you had been with either child you'd clearly have understood. The more I've watched and waited the more I've felt that if there were nothing else to make it sure it would be made so by the systematic silence of each. *Never,* by a slip of the tongue, have they so much as alluded to either of their old friends, any more than Miles has alluded to his expulsion. Oh yes, we may sit here and look at them, and they may show off to us there to their fill; but even while they pretend to be lost in their fairy-tale they're steeped in their vision of the dead restored to them. He's not reading to her," I declared; "they're talking of *them*—they're talking horrors! I go on, I know, as if I were crazy; and it's a wonder I'm not. What I've seen would have made *you* so; but it has only made me more lucid, made me get hold of still other things."

My lucidity must have seemed awful, but the charming creatures who were victims of it, passing and repassing in their interlocked sweetness, gave my colleague something to hold on by; and I felt how tight she held as, without stirring in the breath of my passion, she covered them still with her eyes. "Of what other things have you got hold?"

"Why of the very things that have delighted, fascinated and yet, at bottom, as I now so strangely see, mystified and troubled me. Their more than earthly beauty, their absolutely unnatural goodness. It's a game," I went on; "it's a policy and a fraud!"

"On the part of little darlings—?"

"As yet mere lovely babies? Yes, mad as that seems!" The very act of bringing it out really helped me to trace it—follow it all up and piece it all together. "They have n't been good—they've only been absent. It has been easy to live with them because they're simply leading a life of their own. They're not mine—they're not ours. They're his and they're hers!"

"Quint's and that woman's?"

"Quint's and that woman's. They want to get to them."

Oh how, at this, poor Mrs. Grose appeared to study them! "But for what?"

"For the love of all the evil that, in those dreadful days, the pair put into them. And to ply them with that evil still, to keep up the work of demons, is what brings the others back."

"Laws!" said my friend under her breath. The exclamation was homely, but it revealed a real acceptance of my further proof of what, in the bad time—for there had been a worse even than this!—must have occurred. There could have been no such justification for me as the plain assent of her experience to whatever depth of depravity I found credible in our brace of scoundrels. It was in obvious submission of memory that she brought out after a moment: "They *were* rascals! But what can they now do?" she pursued.

"Do?" I echoed so loud that Miles and Flora, as they passed at their distance, paused an instant in their walk and looked at us. "Don't they do enough?" I demanded in a lower tone, while the children, having smiled and nodded and kissed hands to us, resumed their exhibition. We were held by it a minute; then I answered: "They can destroy them!" At this my companion did turn, but the appeal she launched was a silent one, the effect of which was to make me more explicit. "They don't know as yet quite how—but they're trying hard. They're seen only across, as it were, and beyond—in strange places and on high places, the top of towers, the roof of houses, the outside of windows, the further edge of pools; but there's a deep design, on either side, to shorten the distance and overcome the obstacle: so the success of the tempters is only a question of time. They've only to keep to their suggestions of danger."

"For the children to come?"

"And perish in the attempt!" Mrs. Grose slowly got up, and I scrupulously added: "Unless, of course, we can prevent!"

Standing there before me while I kept my seat she visibly turned things over. "Their uncle must do the preventing. He must take them away."

"And who's to make him?"

She had been scanning the distance, but she now dropped on me a foolish face. "You, Miss."

"By writing to him that his house is poisoned and his little nephew and niece mad?"

"But if they *are,* Miss?"

"And if I am myself, you mean? That's charming news to be sent him by a person enjoying his confidence and whose prime undertaking was to give him no worry."

Mrs. Grose considered, following the children again. "Yes, he do hate worry. That was the great reason—"

"Why those fiends took him in so long? No doubt, though his indifference must have been awful. As I'm not a fiend, at any rate, I should n't take him in."

My companion, after an instant and for all answer, sat down again and grasped my arm. "Make him at any rate come to you."

I stared. "To *me?*" I had a sudden fear of what she might do. " 'Him'?"

"He ought to *be* here—he ought to help."

I quickly rose and I think I must have shown her a queerer face than ever yet. "You see me asking him for a visit?" No, with her eyes on my face she evidently could n't. Instead of it even—as a woman reads another—she could see what I myself saw: his derision, his amusement, his contempt for the breakdown of my resignation at being left alone and for the fine machinery I had set in motion to attract his attention to my slighted charms. She did n't know—no one knew—how proud I had been to serve him and to stick to our terms; yet she none the less took the measure, I think, of the warning I now gave her. "If you should so lose your head as to appeal to him for me—"

She was really frightened. "Yes, Miss?"

"I would leave, on the spot, both him and you."

XIII

It was all very well to join them, but speaking to them proved quite as much as ever an effort beyond my strength—offered, in close quarters, difficulties as insurmountable as before. This situation continued a month, and with new aggravations and particular notes, the note above all, sharper and sharper, of the small ironic consciousness on the part of my pupils. It was not, I am as sure to-day as I was sure then, my mere infernal imagination: it was absolutely traceable that they were aware of my predicament and that this strange relation made, in a manner, for a long time, the air in which we moved. I don't mean that they had their tongues in their cheeks or did anything vulgar, for that was not one of their dangers: I do mean, on the other hand, that the element of the unnamed and untouched became, between us, greater than any other, and that so much avoidance could n't have been made successful without a great deal of tacit arrangement. It was as if, at moments, we were perpetually coming into sight of subjects before which we must stop short, turning suddenly out of alleys that we perceived to be blind, closing with a little bang that made us look at each other— for, like all bangs, it was something louder than we had intended—the doors we had indiscreetly opened. All roads lead to Rome, and there were times when it might have struck us that almost every branch of study or subject of conversation skirted forbidden ground. Forbidden ground was the question of the return of the dead in general and of whatever, in especial, might survive, for memory, of the friends little children had lost. There were days when I could have sworn that one of them had, with a small invisible nudge, said to the other: "She thinks she'll do it this time—but she *won't!*" To "do it" would have been to indulge for instance—and for once in a way —in some direct reference to the lady who had prepared them for my discipline. They had a delightful endless appetite for passages in my own history to which I had again and again treated them; they were in possession of everything that had ever happened to me, had had, with every circumstance, the story of my smallest adventures and of those of my brothers and sisters and of the cat and the dog at home, as well as many particulars of the whimsical bent of my father, of the furniture and arrangement of our house and of the conversation of the old women of our village. There were things enough, taking one with another, to chatter about, if one went very fast and knew by instinct when to go round. They pulled with an art of their own the strings of my invention and my memory; and nothing else perhaps, when I thought of such occasions afterwards, gave me so the suspicion of being watched from under cover. It was in any case over *my* life, *my* past and *my* friends alone that we could take anything like our ease; a state of affairs that led them sometimes without the least pertinence to break out into sociable reminders. I was invited—with no visible connexion—to repeat afresh Goody[20] Gosling's celebrated *mot*[21] or to confirm the details already supplied as to the cleverness of the vicarage pony.

It was partly at such junctures as these and partly at quite different ones that, with the turn my matters had now taken, my predicament, as I have called it, grew most sensible. The fact that the days passed for me without another encounter ought, it would have appeared, to have done something toward soothing my nerves. Since the light brush, that second night on the upper landing, of the presence of a woman at the foot of the stair, I had seen nothing, whether in or out of the house, that one had better not have seen. There was many a corner round which I expected to come upon Quint, and many a situation that, in a merely sinister way, would have favoured the appearance of Miss Jessel. The summer had turned, the summer had gone; the autumn had dropped upon Bly and had blown out half our lights. The place, with its grey sky and withered garlands, its bared spaces and scattered dead leaves, was like a theatre after the performance—all strewn with crumpled playbills. There were exactly states of the air, conditions of sound and of stillness, unspeakable impressions of the *kind* of ministering moment, that brought back to me, long enough to catch it, the feeling of the medium in which, that June evening out of doors, I had had my first sight of Quint, and in which too, at those other instants, I had, after seeing him through the window, looked for him in vain in the circle of shrubbery. I recognised the signs, the portents—I recognised the moment, the spot. But they remained unaccompanied and empty, and I continued unmolested; if unmolested one could call a young woman whose sensibility had, in the most extraordinary fashion, not declined but deepened. I had said in my talk with Mrs. Grose on that horrid scene of Flora's by the lake— and had perplexed her by so saying—that it would from that moment distress me much more to lose my power than to keep it. I had then expressed what was vividly in my mind: the truth that, whether the children really saw or not—since, that is, it was not yet definitely proved—I greatly preferred, as a safeguard, the fulness of my own exposure. I was ready to know the very worst that was to be known. What I had then had an ugly glimpse of was that my eyes might be sealed just while theirs were most opened. Well, my eyes *were* sealed, it appeared, at present—a consummation for which it seemed blasphemous not to thank God. There was, alas, a difficulty about that: I would have thanked him with all my soul had I not had in a proportionate measure this conviction of the secret of my pupils.

[20] More modern version of the archaic "Goodwife," a title applied to a married woman of low social position.

[21] French: "saying."

How can I retrace to-day the strange steps of my obsession? There were times of our being together when I would have been ready to swear that, literally, in my presence, but with my direct sense of it closed, they had visitors who were known and were welcome. Then it was that, had I not been deterred by the very chance that such an injury might prove greater than the injury to be averted, my exaltation would have broken out. "They're here, they're here, you little wretches," I would have cried, "and you can't deny it now!" The little wretches denied it with all the added volume of their sociability and their tenderness, just in the crystal depths of which—like the flash of a fish in a stream—the mockery of their advantage peeped up. The shock had in truth sunk into me still deeper than I knew on the night when, looking out either for Quint or for Miss Jessel under the stars, I had seen there the boy over whose rest I watched and who had immediately brought in with him—had straightway there turned on me—the lovely upward look with which, from the battlements above us, the hideous apparition of Quint had played. If it was a question of a scare my discovery on this occasion had scared me more than any other, and it was essentially in the scared state that I drew my actual conclusions. They harassed me so that sometimes, at odd moments, I shut myself up audibly to rehearse—it was at once a fantastic relief and a renewed despair—the manner in which I might come to the point. I approached it from one side and the other while, in my room, I flung myself about, but I always broke down in the monstrous utterance of names. As they died away on my lips I said to myself that I should indeed help them to represent something infamous if by pronouncing them I should violate as rare a little case of instinctive delicacy as any schoolroom probably had ever known. When I said to myself: "*They* have the manners to be silent, and you, trusted as you are, the baseness to speak!" I felt myself crimson and covered my face with my hands. After these secret scenes I chattered more than ever, going on volubly enough till one of our prodigious palpable hushes occurred—I can call them nothing else—the strange dizzy lift or swim (I try for terms!) into a stillness, a pause of all life, that had nothing to do with the more or less noise we at the moment might be engaged in making and that I could hear through any intensified mirth or quickened recitation or louder strum of the piano. Then it was that the others, the outsiders, were there. Though they were not angels they "passed," as the French say, causing me, while they stayed, to tremble with the fear of their addressing to their younger victims some yet more infernal message or more vivid image than they had thought good enough for myself.

What it was least possible to get rid of was the cruel idea that, whatever I had seen, Miles and Flora saw *more*— things terrible and unguessable and that sprang from dreadful passages of intercourse in the past. Such things naturally left on the surface, for the time, a chill that we vociferously denied we felt; and we had all three, with repetition, got into such splendid training that we went, each time, to mark the close of the incident, almost automatically through the very same movements. It was striking of the children at all events to kiss me inveterately with a wild irrelevance and never to fail—one or the other—of the precious question that had helped us through many a peril. "When do you think he *will* come? Don't you think we *ought* to write?"—there was nothing like that enquiry, we found by experience, for carrying off an awkwardness. "He" of course was their uncle in Harley Street; and we lived in much profusion of theory that he might at any moment arrive to mingle in our circle. It was impossible to have given less encouragement than he had administered to such a doctrine, but if we had not had the doctrine to fall back upon we should have deprived each other of some of our finest exhibitions. He never wrote to them —that may have been selfish, but it was a part of the flattery of his trust of myself; for the way in which a man pays his highest tribute to a woman is apt to be but by the more festal celebration of one of the sacred laws of his comfort. So I held that I carried out the spirit of the pledge given not to appeal to him when I let our young friends understand that their own letters were but charming literary exercises. They were too beautiful to be posted; I kept them myself; I have them all to this hour. This was a rule indeed which only added to the satiric effect of my being plied with the supposition that he might at any moment be among us. It was exactly as if our young friends knew how almost more awkward than anything else that might be for me. There appears to me moreover as I look back no note in all this more extraordinary than the mere fact that, in spite of my tension and of their triumph, I never lost patience with them. Adorable they must in truth have been, I now feel, since I did n't in these days hate them! Would exasperation, however, if relief had longer been postponed, finally have betrayed me? It little matters, for relief arrived. I call it relief though it was only the relief that a snap brings to a strain or the burst of a thunderstorm to a day of suffocation. It was at least change, and it came with a rush.

XIV

Walking to church a certain Sunday morning, I had little Miles at my side and his sister, in advance of us and at Mrs. Grose's, well in sight. It was a crisp clear day, the first of its order for some time; the night had brought a touch of frost and the autumn air, bright and sharp, made the church-bells almost gay. It was an odd accident of thought that I should have happened at such a moment to be particularly and very gratefully struck with the obedience of my little charges. Why did they never resent my inexorable, my perpetual society? Something or other had brought nearer home to me that I had all but pinned the boy to my shawl, and that in the way our companions were marshalled before me I might have appeared to provide against some danger of rebellion. I was like a gaoler[22] with an eye to possible surprises and escapes. But all this belonged—I mean their magnificent little surrender—just to the special array of the facts that were most abysmal. Turned out for Sunday by his uncle's tailor, who had had a free hand and a notion of pretty waistcoats and of his grand little air, Miles's whole title to independence, the rights of his sex and situation, were so stamped upon him that if he had suddenly struck for freedom I should have had nothing to say. I was by the strangest of chances wondering how I should meet him when the revolution unmistakeably occurred. I call it a revolution because I now see how, with the word he spoke, the curtain rose on the last act of my dreadful drama and the catastrophe was precipitated. "Look here, my dear, you know," he charmingly said, "when in the world, please, am I going back to school?"

Transcribed here the speech sounds harmless enough, particularly as uttered in the sweet, high, casual pipe with which, at all interlocutors, but above all at his eternal governess, he threw off intonations as if he were tossing roses. There was something in them that always made one "catch," and I caught at any rate now so effectually

[22] British: jailer.

that I stopped as short as if one of the trees of the park had fallen across the road. There was something new, on the spot, between us, and he was perfectly aware I recognised it, though to enable me to do so he had no need to look a whit less candid and charming than usual. I could feel in him how he already, from my at first finding nothing to reply, perceived the advantage he had gained. I was so slow to find anything that he had plenty of time, after a minute, to continue with his suggestive but inconclusive smile: "You know, my dear, that for a fellow to be with a lady *always*—!" His "my dear" was constantly on his lips for me, and nothing could have expressed more the exact shade of the sentiment with which I desired to inspire my pupils than its fond familiarity. It was so respectfully easy.

But oh how I felt that at present I must pick my own phrases! I remember that, to gain time, I tried to laugh, and I seemed to see in the beautiful face with which he watched me how ugly and queer I looked. "And always with the same lady?" I returned.

He neither blenched nor winked. The whole thing was virtually out between us. "Ah of course she's a jolly 'perfect' lady; but after all I'm a fellow, don't you see? who's—well, getting on."

I lingered there with him an instant ever so kindly. "Yes, you're getting on." Oh but I felt helpless!

I have kept to this day the heartbreaking little idea of how he seemed to know that and to play with it. "And you can't say I've not been awfully good, can you?"

I laid my hand on his shoulder, for though I felt how much better it would have been to walk on I was not yet quite able. "No, I can't say that, Miles."

"Except just that one night, you know—!"

"That one night?" I could n't look as straight as he.

"Why when I went down—went out of the house."

"Oh yes. But I forget what you did it for."

"You forget?"—he spoke with the sweet extravagance of childish reproach. "Why it was just to show you I could!"

"Oh yes—you could."

"And I can again."

I felt I might perhaps after all succeed in keeping my wits about me. "Certainly. But you won't."

"No, not *that* again. It was nothing."

"It was nothing," I said. "But we must go on."

He resumed our walk with me, passing his hand into my arm. "Then when *am* I going back?"

I wore, in turning it over, my most responsible air. "Were you very happy at school?"

He just considered. "Oh I'm happy enough anywhere!"

"Well then," I quavered, "if you're just as happy here—!"

"Ah but that is n't everything! Of course *you* know a lot—"

"But you hint that you know almost as much?" I risked as he paused.

"Not half I want to!" Miles honestly professed. "But it is n't so much that."

"What is it then?"

"Well—I want to see more life."

"I see; I see." We had arrived within sight of the church and of various persons, including several of the household of Bly, on their way to it and clustered about the door to see us go in. I quickened our step; I wanted to get there before the question between us opened up much further; I reflected hungrily that he would have for more than an hour to be silent; and I thought with envy of the comparative dusk of the pew and of the almost spiritual help of the hassock on which I might bend my knees. I seemed literally to be running a race with some confusion to which he was about to reduce me, but I felt he had got in first when, before we had even entered the churchyard, he threw out—

"I want my own sort!"

It literally made me bound forward. "There are n't many of your own sort, Miles!" I laughed. "Unless perhaps dear little Flora!"

"You really compare me to a baby girl?"

This found me singularly weak. "Don't you then *love* our sweet Flora?"

"If I did n't—and you too; if I did n't—!" he repeated as if retreating for a jump, yet leaving his thought so unfinished that, after we had come into the gate, another stop, which he imposed on me by the pressure of his arm, had become inevitable. Mrs. Grose and Flora had passed into the church, the other worshippers had followed and we were, for the minute, alone among the old thick graves. We had paused, on the path from the gate, by a low oblong table-like tomb.

"Yes, if you did n't—?"

He looked, while I waited, about at the graves. "Well, you know what!" But he did n't move, and he presently produced something that made me drop straight down on the stone slab as if suddenly to rest. "Does my uncle think what *you* think?"

I markedly rested. "How do you know what I think?"

"Ah well, of course I don't; for it strikes me you never tell me. But I mean does *he* know?"

"Know what, Miles?"

"Why the way I'm going on."

I recognised quickly enough that I could make, to this enquiry, no answer that would n't involve something of a sacrifice of my employer. Yet it struck me that we were all, at Bly, sufficiently sacrificed to make that venial. "I don't think your uncle much cares."

Miles, on this, stood looking at me. "Then don't you think he can be made to?"

"In what way?"

"Why by his coming down."

"But who'll get him to come down?"

"*I* will!" the boy said with extraordinary brightness and emphasis. He gave me another look charged with that expression and then marched off alone into church.

XV

The business was practically settled from the moment I never followed him. It was a pitiful surrender to agitation, but my being aware of this had somehow no power to restore me. I only sat there on my tomb and read into what our young friend had said to me the fulness of its meaning; by the time I had grasped the whole of which I had also embraced, for absence, the pretext that I was ashamed to offer my pupils and the rest of the congregation such an example of delay. What I said to myself above all was that Miles had got something out of me and that the gage of it for him would be just this awkward collapse. He had got out of me that there was something I was much afraid of, and that he should probably be able to make use of my fear to gain, for his own purpose, more freedom. My fear was of having to deal with the intolerable question of the grounds of his dismissal from school, since that was really but the question of the horrors gathered behind. That his uncle should arrive to treat with me of these things was a solution that, strictly speaking, I ought now to have desired to bring on; but I could so little face the ugliness and the pain of it that I simply procrastinated and lived from hand to mouth. The boy, to my deep discomposure, was immensely in the right, was in a position to say to me: "Either you clear up with my guardian the mystery of this interruption of my studies, or you cease to expect me to lead with you a life that's so unnatural for a boy." What was so unnatural for the particular boy I was concerned with was this sudden revelation of a consciousness and a plan.

That was what really overcame me, what prevented my going in. I walked round the church, hesitating, hovering; I reflected that I had already, with him, hurt myself beyond repair. Therefore I could patch up nothing and it was too extreme an effort to squeeze beside him into the pew: he would be so much more sure than ever to pass his arm into mine and make me sit there for an hour in close mute contact with his commentary on our talk. For the first minute since his arrival I wanted to get away from him. As I paused beneath the high east window and listened to the sounds of worship I was taken with an impulse that might master me, I felt, and completely, should I give it the least encouragement. I might easily put an end to my ordeal by getting away altogether. Here was my chance; there was no one to stop me; I could give the whole thing up—turn my back and bolt. It was only a question of hurrying again, for a few preparations, to the house which the attendance at church of so many of the servants would practically have left unoccupied. No one, in short, could blame me if I should just drive desperately off. What was it to get away if I should get away only till dinner? That would be in a couple of hours, at the end of which—I had the acute prevision—my little pupils would play at innocent wonder about my non-appearance in their train.

"What *did* you do, you naughty bad thing? Why in the world, to worry us so —and take our thoughts off too, don't you know?—did you desert us at the very door?" I couldn't meet such questions nor, as they asked them, their false little lovely eyes; yet it was all so exactly what I should have to meet that, as the prospect grew sharp to me, I at last let myself go.

I got, so far as the immediate moment was concerned, away; I came straight out of the churchyard and, thinking hard, retraced my steps through the park. It seemed to me that by the time I reached the house I had made up my mind to cynical flight. The Sunday stillness both of the approaches and of the interior, in which I met no one, fairly stirred me with a sense of opportunity. Were I to get off quickly this way I should get off without a scene, without a word. My quickness would have to be remarkable, however, and the question of a conveyance was the great one to settle. Tormented, in the hall, with difficulties and obstacles, I remember sinking down at the foot of the staircase—suddenly collapsing there on the lowest step and then, with a revulsion, recalling that it was exactly where, more than a month before, in the darkness of night and just so bowed with evil things, I had seen the spectre of the most horrible of women. At this I was able to straighten myself; I went the rest of the way up; I made, in my turmoil, for the schoolroom, where there were objects belonging to me that I should have to take. But I opened the door to find again, in a flash, my eyes unsealed. In the presence of what I saw I reeled straight back upon resistance.

Seated at my own table in the clear noonday light I saw a person whom, without my previous experience, I should have taken at the first blush for some house-maid who might have stayed at home to look after the place and who, availing herself of rare relief from observation and of the schoolroom table and my pens, ink and paper, had applied herself to the considerable effort of a letter to her sweetheart. There was an effort in the way that, while her arms rested on the table, her hands, with evident weariness, supported her head; but at the moment I took this in I had already become aware that, in spite of my entrance, her attitude strangely persisted. Then it was— with the very act of its announcing itself—that her identity flared up in a change of posture. She rose, not as if she had heard me, but with an indescribable grand melancholy of indifference and detachment, and, within a dozen feet of me, stood there as my vile predecessor. Dishonoured and tragic, she was all before me; but even as I fixed and, for memory, secured it, the awful image passed away. Dark as midnight in her black dress, her haggard beauty and her unutterable woe, she had looked at me long enough to appear to say that her right to sit at my table was as good as mine to sit at hers. While these instants lasted indeed I had the extraordinary chill of a feeling that it was I who was the intruder. It was as a wild protest against it that, actually addressing her—"You terrible miserable woman!"—I heard myself break into a sound that, by the open door, rang through the long passage and the empty house. She looked at me as if she heard me, but I had recovered myself and cleared the air. There was nothing in the room the next minute but the sunshine and the sense that I must stay.

XVI

I had so perfectly expected the return of the others to be marked by a demonstration that I was freshly upset at having to find them merely dumb and discreet about my desertion. Instead of gaily denouncing and caressing me they made no allusion to my having failed them, and I was left, for the time, on perceiving that she too said nothing, to study Mrs. Grose's odd face. I did this to such purpose that I made sure they had in some way bribed her to silence; a silence that, however, I would engage to break down on the first private opportunity. This opportunity came before tea: I secured five minutes with her in the housekeeper's room, where, in the twilight, amid a smell of lately-baked bread, but with the place all swept and garnished, I found her sitting in pained placidity before the fire. So I see her still, so I see her best: facing the flame from her straight chair in the dusky shining room, a large clean picture of the "put away"—of drawers closed and locked and rest without a remedy.

"Oh yes, they asked me to say nothing; and to please them—so long as they were there—of course I promised. But what had happened to you?"

"I only went with you for the walk," I said. "I had then to come back to meet a friend."

She showed her surprise. "A friend—*you?*"

"Oh yes, I've a couple!" I laughed. "But did the children give you a reason?"

"For not alluding to your leaving us? Yes; they said you'd like it better. *Do* you like it better?"

My face had made her rueful. "No, I like it worse!" But after an instant I added: "Did they say why I should like it better?"

"No; Master Miles only said 'We must do nothing but what she likes!'"

"I wish indeed he would! And what did Flora say?"

"Miss Flora was too sweet. She said 'Oh of course, of course!'—and I said the same."

I thought a moment. "You were too sweet too—I can hear you all. But none the less, between Miles and me, it's now all out."

"All out?" My companion stared. "But what, Miss?"

"Everything. It does n't matter. I've made up my mind. I came home, my dear," I went on, "for a talk with Miss Jessel."

I had by this time formed the habit of having Mrs. Grose literally well in hand in advance of my sounding that note; so that even now, as she bravely blinked under the signal of my word, I could keep her comparatively firm. "A talk! Do you mean she spoke?"

"It came to that. I found her, on my return, in the schoolroom."

"And what did she say?" I can hear the good woman still, and the candour of her stupefaction.

"That she suffers the torments—!"

It was this, of a truth, that made her, as she filled out my picture, gape. "Do you mean," she faltered "—of the lost?"

"Of the lost. Of the damned. And that's why, to share them—" I faltered myself with the horror of it.

But my companion, with less imagination, kept me up. "To share them—?"

"She wants Flora." Mrs. Grose might, as I gave it to her, fairly have fallen away from me had I not been prepared. I still held her there, to show I was. "As I've told you, however, it does n't matter."

"Because you've made up your mind? But to what?"

"To everything."

"And what do you call 'everything'?"

"Why to sending for their uncle."

"Oh Miss, in pity do," my friend broke out.

"Ah but I will, I *will!* I see it's the only way. What's 'out,' as I told you, with Miles is that if he thinks I'm afraid to—and has ideas of what he gains by that—he shall see he's mistaken. Yes, yes; his uncle shall have it here from me on the spot (and before the boy himself if necessary) that if I'm to be reproached with having done nothing again about more school—"

"Yes, Miss—" my companion pressed me.

"Well, there's that awful reason."

There were now clearly so many of these for my poor colleague that she was excusable for being vague. "But—a—which?"

"Why the letter from his old place."

"You'll show it to the master?"

"I ought to have done so on the instant."

"Oh no!" said Mrs. Grose with decision.

"I'll put it before him," I went on inexorably, "that I can't undertake to work the question on behalf of a child who has been expelled—"

"For we've never in the least known what!" Mrs. Grose declared.

"For wickedness. For what else—when he's so clever and beautiful and perfect? Is he stupid? Is he untidy? Is he infirm? Is he ill-natured? He's exquisite—so it can be only *that;* and that would open up the whole thing. After all," I said, "it's their uncle's fault. If he left here such people—!"

"He did n't really in the least know them. The fault's mine." She had turned quite pale.

"Well, you shan't suffer," I answered.

"The children shan't!" she emphatically returned.

I was silent a while; we looked at each other. "Then what am I to tell him?"

"You need n't tell him anything. *I'll* tell him."

I measured this. "Do you mean you'll write—?" Remembering she could n't, I caught myself up. "How do you communicate?"

"I tell the bailiff.[23] *He* writes."

"And should you like him to write our story?"

My question had a sarcastic force that I had not fully intended, and it made her after a moment inconsequently break down. The tears were again in her eyes. "Ah Miss, *you* write!"

"Well—to-night," I at last returned; and on this we separated.

XVII

I went so far, in the evening, as to make a beginning. The weather had changed back, a great wind was abroad, and beneath the lamp, in my room, with Flora at peace beside me, I sat for a long time before a blank sheet of paper and listened to the lash of the rain and the batter of the gusts. Finally I went out, taking a candle; I crossed the passage and listened a minute at Miles's door. What, under my endless obsession, I had been impelled to listen for was some betrayal of his not being at rest, and I presently caught one, but not in the form I had expected. His voice tinkled out. "I say, you there— come in." It was gaiety in the gloom!

I went in with my light and found him in bed, very wide awake but very much at his ease. "Well, what are *you* up to?" he asked with a grace of sociability in which it occurred to me that Mrs. Grose, had she been present, might have looked in vain for proof that anything was "out."

I stood over him with my candle. "How did you know I was there?"

"Why of course I heard you. Did you fancy you made no noise? You're like a troop of cavalry!" he beautifully laughed.

"Then you were n't asleep?"

"Not much! I lie awake and think."

I had put my candle, designedly, a short way off, and then, as he held out his

[23] Overseer of the estate.

friendly old hand to me, had sat down on the edge of his bed. "What is it," I asked, "that you think of?"

"What in the world, my dear, but *you*?"

"Ah the pride I take in your appreciation does n't insist on that! I had so far rather you slept."

"Well, I think also, you know, of this queer business of ours."

I marked the coolness of his firm little hand. "Of what queer business, Miles?"

"Why the way you bring me up. And all the rest!"

I fairly held my breath a minute, and even from my glimmering taper there was light enough to show how he smiled up at me from his pillow. "What do you mean by all the rest?"

"Oh you know, you know!"

I could say nothing for a minute, though I felt as I held his hand and our eyes continued to meet that my silence had all the air of admitting his charge and that nothing in the whole world of reality was perhaps at that moment so fabulous as our actual relation. "Certainly you shall go back to school," I said, "if it be that that troubles you. But not to the old place—we must find another, a better. How could I know it did trouble you, this question, when you never told me so, never spoke of it at all?" His clear listening face, framed in its smooth whiteness, made him for the minute as appealing as some wistful patient in a children's hospital; and I would have given, as the resemblance came to me, all I possessed on earth really to be the nurse or the sister of charity who might have helped to cure him. Well, even as it was I perhaps might help! "Do you know you've never said a word to me about your school—I mean the old one; never mentioned it in any way?"

He seemed to wonder; he smiled with the same loveliness. But he clearly gained time; he waited, he called for guidance. "Have n't I?" It was n't for *me* to help him —it was for the thing I had met!

Something in his tone and the expression of his face, as I got this from him, set my heart aching with such a pang as it had never yet known; so unutterably touching was it to see his little brain puzzled and his little resources taxed to play, under the spell laid on him, a part of innocence and consistency. "No, never—from the hour you came back. You've never mentioned to me one of your masters, one of your comrades, nor the least little thing that ever happened to you at school. Never, little Miles—no never—have you given me an inkling of anything that *may* have happened there. Therefore you can fancy how much I'm in the dark. Until you came out, that way, this morning, you had since the first hour I saw you scarce even made a reference to anything in your previous life. You seemed so perfectly to accept the present." It was extraordinary how my absolute conviction of his secret precocity—or whatever I might call the poison of an influence that I dared but half-phrase—made him, in spite of the faint breath of his inward trouble, appear as accessible as an older person, forced me to treat him as an intelligent equal. "I thought you wanted to go on as you are."

It struck me that at this he just faintly coloured. He gave, at any rate, like a convalescent slightly fatigued, a languid shake of his head. "I don't—I don't. I want to get away."

"You're tired of Bly?"

"Oh no, I like Bly."

"Well then—?"

"Oh *you* know what a boy wants!"

I felt I did n't know so well as Miles, and I took temporary refuge. "You want to go to your uncle?"

Again, at this, with his sweet ironic face, he made a movement on the pillow. "Ah you can't get off with that!"

I was silent a little, and it was I now, I think, who changed colour. "My dear, I don't want to get off!"

"You can't even if you do. You can't, you can't!"—he lay beautifully staring. "My uncle must come down and you must completely settle things."

"If we do," I returned with some spirit, "you may be sure it will be to take you quite away."

"Well, don't you understand that that's exactly what I'm working for? You'll have to *tell* him—about the way you've let it all drop: you'll have to tell him a tremendous lot!"

The exultation with which he uttered this helped me somehow for the instant to meet him rather more. "And how much will *you*, Miles, have to tell him? There are things he'll ask you!"

He turned it over. "Very likely. But what things?"

"The things you've never told me. To make up his mind what to do with you. He can't send you back—"

"I don't want to go back!" he broke in. "I want a new field."

He said it with admirable serenity, with positive unimpeachable gaiety; and doubtless it was that very note that most evoked for me the poignancy, the unnatural childish tragedy, of his probable reappearance at the end of three months with all this bravado and still more dishonour. It overwhelmed me now that I should never be able to bear that, and it made me let myself go. I threw myself upon him and in the tenderness of my pity I embraced him. "Dear little Miles, dear little Miles—!"

My face was close to his, and he let me kiss him, simply taking it with indulgent good humour. "Well, old lady?"

"Is there nothing—nothing at all that you want to tell me?"

He turned off a little, facing round toward the wall and holding up his hand to look at as one had seen sick children look. "I've told you—I told you this morning."

Oh I was sorry for him! "That you just want me not to worry you?"

He looked round at me now as if in recognition of my understanding him; then ever so gently, "To let me alone," he replied.

There was even a strange little dignity in it, something that made me release him, yet, when I had slowly risen, linger beside him. God knows *I* never wished to harass him, but I felt that merely, at this, to turn my back on him was to abandon or, to put it more truly, lose him. "I've just begun a letter to your uncle," I said.

"Well then, finish it!"

I waited a minute. "What happened before?"

He gazed up at me again. "Before what?"

"Before you came back. And before you went away."

For some time he was silent, but he continued to meet my eyes. "What happened?"

It made me, the sound of the words, in which it seemed to me I caught for the very first time a small faint quiver of consenting consciousness—it made me drop on my knees beside the bed and seize once more the chance of possessing him. "Dear little Miles, dear little Miles, if you *knew* how I want to help you! It's only that, it's nothing but that, and I'd rather die than give you a pain or do you a wrong—I'd rather die than hurt a hair of you. Dear little Miles"—oh I brought it out now even if I *should* go too far—"I just want you to help me to save you!" But I knew in a moment after this that I had gone too far. The answer to my appeal was instantaneous, but it came in the form of an extraordinary blast and chill, a gust of frozen air and a shake of the room as great as if, in the wild wind, the casement had crashed in. The boy gave a loud high shriek which, lost in the rest of the shock of sound, might have seemed, indistinctly, though I was so close to him, a note either of jubilation or of terror. I jumped to my feet again and was conscious of darkness. So for a moment we remained, while I stared about me and saw the drawn curtains unstirred and the window still tight. "Why the candle's out!" I then cried.

"It was I who blew it, dear!" said Miles.

XVIII

The next day, after lessons, Mrs. Grose found a moment to say to me quietly: "Have you written, Miss?"

"Yes—I've written." But I did n't add—for the hour—that my letter, sealed and directed, was still in my pocket. There would be time enough to send it before the messenger should go to the village. Meanwhile there had been on the part of my pupils no more brilliant, more exemplary morning. It was exactly as if they had both had at heart to gloss over any recent little friction. They performed the dizziest feats of arithmetic, soaring quite out of *my* feeble range, and perpetrated, in higher spirits than ever, geographical and historical jokes. It was conspicuous of course in Miles in particular that he appeared to wish to show how easily he could let me down. This child, to my memory, really lives in a setting of beauty and misery that no words can translate; there was a distinction all his own in every impulse he revealed; never was a small natural creature, to the uninformed eye all frankness and freedom, a more ingenious, a more extraordinary little gentleman. I had perpetually to guard against the wonder of contemplation into which my initiated view betrayed me; to check the irrelevant gaze and discouraged sigh in which I constantly both attacked and renounced the enigma of what such a little gentleman could have done that deserved a penalty. Say that, by the dark prodigy I knew, the imagination of all evil *had* been opened up to him: all the justice within me ached for the proof that it could ever have flowered into an act.

He had never at any rate been such a little gentleman as when, after our early dinner on this dreadful day, he came round to me and asked if I should n't like him for half an hour to play to me. David playing to Saul[24] could never have shown a finer sense of the occasion. It was literally a charming exhibition of tact, of magnanimity, and quite tantamount to his saying outright: "The true knights we love to read about never

[24] Reference to 1 Samuel 16:23: "And it came to pass, when the evil spirit from God was upon Saul, that David took an harp, and played with his hand: so Saul was refreshed, and was well, and the evil spirit departed from him." Saul was king of Israel; David succeeded him.

push an advantage too far. I know what you mean now: you mean that—to be let alone yourself and not followed up—you'll cease to worry and spy upon me, won't keep me so close to you, will let me go and come. Well, I 'come,' you see—but I don't go! There'll be plenty of time for that. I do really delight in your society and I only want to show you that I contended for a principle." It may be imagined whether I resisted this appeal or failed to accompany him again, hand in hand, to the schoolroom. He sat down at the old piano and played as he had never played; and if there are those who think he had better have been kicking a football I can only say that I wholly agree with them. For at the end of a time that under his influence I had quite ceased to measure I started up with a strange sense of having literally slept at my post. It was after luncheon, and by the schoolroom fire, and yet I had n't really in the least slept; I had only done something much worse—I had forgotten. Where all this time was Flora? When I put the question to Miles he played on a minute before answering, and then could only say: "Why, my dear, how do *I* know?"—breaking moreover into a happy laugh which immediately after, as if it were a vocal accompaniment, he prolonged into incoherent extravagant song.

I went straight to my room, but his sister was not there; then, before going downstairs, I looked into several others. As she was nowhere about she would surely be with Mrs. Grose, whom in the comfort of that theory I accordingly proceeded in quest of. I found her where I had found her the evening before, but she met my quick challenge with blank scared ignorance. She had only supposed that, after the repast, I had carried off both the children; as to which she was quite in her right, for it was the very first time I had allowed the little girl out of my sight without some special provision. Of course now indeed she might be with the maids, so that the immediate thing was to look for her without an air of alarm. This we promptly arranged between us; but when, ten minutes later and in pursuance of our arrangement, we met in the hall, it was only to report on either side that after guarded enquiries we had altogether failed to trace her. For a minute there, apart from observation, we exchanged mute alarms, and I could feel with what high interest my friend returned me all those I had from the first given her.

"She'll be above," she presently said—"in one of the rooms you have n't searched."

"No; she's at a distance." I had made up my mind. "She has gone out."

Mrs. Grose stared. "Without a hat?"

I naturally also looked volumes. "Is n't that woman always without one?"

"She's with *her*?"

"She's with *her*!" I declared. "We must find them."

My hand was on my friend's arm, but she failed for the moment, confronted with such an account of the matter, to respond to my pressure. She communed, on the contrary, where she stood, with her uneasiness. "And where's Master Miles?"

"Oh *he's* with Quint. They'll be in the schoolroom."

"Lord, Miss!" My view, I was myself aware—and therefore I suppose my tone —had never yet reached so calm an assurance.

"The trick's played," I went on; "they've successfully worked their plan. He found the most divine little way to keep me quiet while she went off."

" 'Divine'?" Mrs. Grose bewilderedly echoed.

"Infernal then!" I almost cheerfully rejoined. "He has provided for himself as well. But come!"

She had helplessly gloomed at the upper regions. "You leave him—?"

"So long with Quint? Yes—I don't mind that now."

She always ended at these moments by getting possession of my hand, and in this manner she could at present still stay me. But after gasping an instant at my sudden resignation, "Because of your letter?" she eagerly brought out.

I quickly, by way of answer, felt for my letter, drew it forth, held it up, and then, freeing myself, went and laid it on the great hall-table. "Luke will take it," I said as I came back. I reached the house-door and opened it; I was already on the steps.

My companion still demurred: the storm of the night and the early morning had dropped, but the afternoon was damp and grey. I came down to the drive while she stood in the doorway. "You go with nothing on?"

"What do I care when the child has nothing? I can't wait to dress," I cried, "and if you must do so I leave you. Try meanwhile yourself upstairs."

"With *them*?" Oh on this the poor woman promptly joined me!

XIX

We went straight to the lake, as it was called at Bly, and I dare say rightly called, though it may have been a sheet of water less remarkable than my untravelled eyes supposed it. My acquaintance with sheets of water was small, and the pool of Bly, at all events on the few occasions of my consenting, under the protection of my pupils, to affront its surface in the old flat-bottomed boat moored there for our use, had impressed me both with its extent and its agitation. The usual place of embarkation was half a mile from the house, but I had an intimate conviction that, wherever Flora might be, she was not near home. She had not given me the slip for any small adventure, and, since the day of the very great one that I had shared with her by the pond, I had been aware, in our walks, of the quarter to which she most inclined. This was why I had now given to Mrs. Grose's steps so marked a direction—a direction making her, when she perceived it, oppose a resistance that showed me she was freshly mystified. "You're going to the water, Miss?—you think she's *in*—?"

"She may be, though the depth is, I believe, nowhere very great. But what I judge most likely is that she's on the spot from which, the other day, we saw together what I told you."

"When she pretended not to see—?"

"With that astounding self-possession! I've always been sure she wanted to go back alone. And now her brother has managed it for her."

Mrs. Grose still stood where she had stopped. "You suppose they really *talk* of them?"

I could meet this with an assurance! "They say things that, if we heard them, would simply appal us."

"And if she *is* there—?"

"Yes?"

"Then Miss Jessel is?"

"Beyond a doubt. You shall see."

"Oh thank you!" my friend cried, planted so firm that, taking it in, I went straight on without her. By the time I reached the pool, however, she was close behind me, and I knew that, whatever, to her apprehension, might befall me, the exposure of sticking to me struck her as her least danger. She exhaled a moan of relief as we at last came in sight of the greater part of the water without a sight of the child. There was no trace of Flora on that nearer side of the bank where my observation of her had been most startling, and none on the opposite edge, where, save for a margin of some twenty yards, a thick copse[25] came down to the pond. This expanse, oblong in shape, was so narrow compared to its length that, with its ends out of view, it might have been taken for a scant river. We looked at the empty stretch, and then I felt the suggestion in my friend's eyes. I knew what she meant and I replied with a negative headshake.

"No, no; wait! She has taken the boat."

My companion stared at the vacant mooring-place and then again across the lake. "Then where is it?"

"Our not seeing it is the strongest of proofs. She has used it to go over, and then has managed to hide it."

"All alone—that child?"

"She's not alone, and at such times she's not a child: she's an old, old woman." I scanned all the visible shore while Mrs. Grose took again, into the queer element I offered her, one of her plunges of submission; then I pointed out that the boat might perfectly be in a small refuge formed by one of the recesses of the pool, an indentation masked, for the hither side, by a projection of the bank and by a clump of trees growing close to the water.

"But if the boat's there, where on earth's *she?*" my colleague anxiously asked.

"That's exactly what we must learn." And I started to walk further.

"By going all the way round?"

"Certainly, far as it is. It will take us but ten minutes, yet it's far enough to have made the child prefer not to walk. She went straight over."

"Laws!" cried my friend again: the chain of my logic was ever too strong for her. It dragged her at my heels even now, and when we had got halfway round—a devious tiresome process, on ground much broken and by a path choked with overgrowth —I paused to give her breath. I sustained her with a grateful arm, assuring her that she might hugely help me; and this started us afresh, so that in the course of but few minutes more we reached a point from which we found the boat to be where I had supposed it. It had been intentionally left as much as possible out of sight and was tied to one of the stakes of a fence that came, just there, down to the brink and that had been an assistance to disembarking. I recognised, as I looked at the pair of short thick oars, quite safely drawn up, the prodigious character of the feat for a little girl; but I had by this time lived too long among wonders and had panted to too many livelier measures. There was a gate in the fence, through which we passed, and that brought us after a trifling interval more into the open. Then "There she is!" we both exclaimed at once.

Flora, a short way off, stood before us on the grass and smiled as if her performance had now become complete. The next thing she did, however, was to stoop straight down and pluck—quite as if it were all she was there for—a big ugly spray of withered fern. I at once felt sure she had just come out of the copse. She waited for us, not herself taking a step, and I was conscious of the rare solemnity with which

[25] Grove of small trees.

we presently approached her. She smiled and smiled, and we met; but it was all done in a silence by this time flagrantly ominous. Mrs. Grose was the first to break the spell: she threw herself on her knees and, drawing the child to her breast, clasped in a long embrace the little tender yielding body. While this dumb convulsion lasted I could only watch it—which I did the more intently when I saw Flora's face peep at me over our companion's shoulder. It was serious now—the flicker had left it; but it strengthened the pang with which I at that moment envied Mrs. Grose the simplicity of *her* relation. Still, all this while, nothing more passed between us save that Flora had let her foolish fern again drop to the ground. What she and I had virtually said to each other was that pretexts were useless now. When Mrs. Grose finally got up she kept the child's hand, so that the two were still before me; and the singular reticence of our communion was even more marked in the frank look she addressed me. "I'll be hanged," it said, "if *I'll* speak!"

It was Flora who, gazing all over me in candid wonder, was the first. She was struck with our bareheaded aspect. "Why where are your things?"

"Where yours are, my dear!" I promptly returned.

She had already got back her gaiety and appeared to take this as an answer quite sufficient. "And where's Miles?" she went on.

There was something in the small valour of it that quite finished me: these three words from her were in a flash like the glitter of a drawn blade the jostle of the cup that my hand for weeks and weeks had held high and full to the brim and that now, even before speaking, I felt overflow in a deluge. "I'll tell you if you'll tell *me*—" I heard myself say, then heard the tremor in which it broke.

"Well, what?"

Mrs. Grose's suspense blazed at me, but it was too late now, and I brought the thing out handsomely. "Where, my pet, is Miss Jessel?"

XX

Just as in the churchyard with Miles, the whole thing was upon us. Much as I had made of the fact that this name had never once, between us, been sounded, the quick smitten glare with which the child's face now received it fairly likened my breach of the silence to the smash of a pane of glass. It added to the interposing cry, as if to stay the blow, that Mrs. Grose at the same instant uttered over my violence—the shriek of a creature scared, or rather wounded, which, in turn, within a few seconds, was completed by a gasp of my own. I seized my colleague's arm. "She's there, she's there!"

Miss Jessel stood before us on the opposite bank exactly as she had stood the other time, and I remember, strangely, as the first feeling now produced in me, my thrill of joy at having brought on a proof. She was there, so I was justified; she was there, so I was neither cruel nor mad. She was there for poor scared Mrs. Grose, but she was there most for Flora; and no moment of my monstrous time was perhaps so extraordinary as that in which I consciously threw out to her—with the sense that, pale and ravenous demon as she was, she would catch and understand it—an inarticulate message of gratitude. She rose erect on the spot my friend and I had lately quitted, and there wasn't in all the long reach of her desire an inch of her evil that fell short. This first vividness of vision and emotion were things of a few seconds, during which

Mrs. Grose's dazed blink across to where I pointed struck me as showing that she too at last saw, just as it carried my own eyes precipitately to the child. The revelation then of the manner in which Flora was affected startled me in truth far more than it would have done to find her also merely agitated, for direct dismay was of course not what I had expected. Prepared and on her guard as our pursuit had actually made her, she would repress every betrayal; and I was therefore at once shaken by my first glimpse of the particular one for which I had not allowed. To see her, without a convulsion of her small pink face, not even feign to glance in the direction of the prodigy I announced, but only, instead of that, turn at *me* an expression of hard still gravity, an expression absolutely new and unprecedented and that appeared to read and accuse and judge me—this was a stroke that somehow converted the little girl herself into a figure portentous. I gaped at her coolness even though my certitude of her thoroughly seeing was never greater than at that instant, and then, in the immediate need to defend myself, I called her passionately to witness. "She's there, you little unhappy thing—there, there, *there,* and you know it as well as you know me!" I had said shortly before to Mrs. Grose that she was not at these times a child, but an old, old woman, and my description of her could n't have been more strikingly confirmed than in the way in which, for all notice of this, she simply showed me, without an expressional concession or admission, a countenance of deeper and deeper, of indeed suddenly quite fixed reprobation. I was by this time—if I can put the whole thing at all together—more appalled at what I may properly call her manner than at anything else, though it was quite simultaneously that I became aware of having Mrs. Grose also, and very formidably, to reckon with. My elder companion, the next moment, at any rate, blotted out everything but her own flushed face and her loud shocked protest, a burst of high disapproval. "What a dreadful turn, to be sure, Miss! Where on earth do you see anything?"

I could only grasp her more quickly yet, for even while she spoke the hideous plain presence stood undimmed and undaunted. It had already lasted a minute, and it lasted while I continued, seizing my colleague, quite thrusting her at it and presenting her to it, to insist with my pointing hand. "You don't see her exactly as *we* see?—you mean to say you don't now—*now?* She's as big as a blazing fire! Only look, dearest woman, *look*—!" She looked, just as I did, and gave me, with her deep groan of negation, repulsion, compassion—the mixture with her pity of her relief at her exemption—a sense, touching to me even then, that she would have backed me up if she had been able. I might well have needed that, for with this hard blow of the proof that her eyes were hopelessly sealed I felt my own situation horribly crumble, I felt—I *saw*—my livid predecessor press, from her position, on my defeat, and I took the measure, more than all, of what I should have from this instant to deal with in the astounding little attitude of Flora. Into this attitude Mrs. Grose immediately and violently entered, breaking, even while there pierced through my sense of ruin a prodigious private triumph, into breathless reassurance.

"She is n't there, little lady, and nobody's there—and you never see nothing, my sweet! How can poor Miss Jessel—when poor Miss Jessel's dead and buried? *We* know, don't we, love?"—and she appealed, blundering in, to the child. "It's all a mere mistake and a worry and a joke—and we'll go home as fast as we can!"

Our companion, on this, had responded with a strange quick primness of propriety, and they were again, with Mrs. Grose on her feet, united, as it were, in shocked opposition to me. Flora continued to fix me with her small mask of disaffection, and even at that minute I prayed God to forgive me for seeming to see that, as she stood there holding tight to our friend's dress, her incomparable childish beauty had suddenly failed, had quite vanished. I've said it already—she was literally, she was hideously hard; she had turned common and almost ugly. "I don't know what you mean. I see nobody. I see nothing. I never *have*. I think you're cruel. I don't like you!" Then, after this deliverance, which might have been that of a vulgarly pert little girl in the street, she hugged Mrs. Grose more closely and buried in her skirts the dreadful little face. In this position she launched an almost furious wail. "Take me away, take me away—oh take me away from *her!*"

"From *me?*" I panted.

"From you—from you!" she cried.

Even Mrs. Grose looked across at me dismayed; while I had nothing to do but communicate again with the figure that, on the opposite bank, without a movement, as rigidly still as if catching, beyond the interval, our voices, was as vividly there for my disaster as it was not there for my service. The wretched child had spoken exactly as if she had got from some outside source each of her stabbing little words, and I could therefore, in the full despair of all I had to accept, but sadly shake my head at her. "If I had ever doubted all my doubt would at present have gone. I've been living with the miserable truth, and now it has only too much closed round me. Of course I've lost you: I've interfered, and you've seen, under *her* dictation"—with which I faced, over the pool again, our infernal witness—"the easy and perfect way to meet it. I've done my best, but I've lost you. Goodbye." For Mrs. Grose I had an imperative, an almost frantic "Go, go!" before which, in infinite distress, but mutely possessed of the little girl and clearly convinced, in spite of her blindness, that something awful had occurred and some collapse engulfed us, she retreated, by the way we had come, as fast as she could move.

Of what first happened when I was left alone I had no subsequent memory. I only knew that at the end of, I suppose, a quarter of an hour, an odorous dampness and roughness, chilling and piercing my trouble, had made me understand that I must have thrown myself, on my face, to the ground and given way to a wildness of grief. I must have lain there long and cried and wailed, for when I raised my head the day was almost done. I got up and looked a moment, through the twilight, at the grey pool and its blank haunted edge, and then I took, back to the house, my dreary and difficult course. When I reached the gate in the fence the boat, to my surprise, was gone, so that I had a fresh reflexion to make on Flora's extraordinary command of the situation. She passed that night, by the most tacit and, I should add, were not the word so grotesque a false note, the happiest of arrangements, with Mrs. Grose. I saw neither of them on my return, but on the other hand I saw, as by an ambiguous compensation, a great deal of Miles. I saw—I can use no other phrase—so much of him that it fairly measured more than it had ever measured. No evening I had passed at Bly was to have had the portentous quality of this one; in spite of which—and in spite also of the deeper depths of consternation that had opened beneath my feet —there was literally, in the ebbing actual, an extraordinarily sweet sadness. On reaching the house I had never so much as looked for the boy; I had simply gone straight to my room to change what I was wearing and to take in, at a glance, much material testimony to Flora's rupture. Her little belongings had all been removed.

When later, by the schoolroom fire, I was served with tea by the usual maid, I indulged, on the article of my other pupil, in no enquiry whatever. He had his freedom now—he might have it to the end! Well, he did have it; and it consisted —in part at least—of his coming in at about eight o'clock and sitting down with me in silence. On the removal of the tea-things I had blown out the candles and drawn my chair closer: I was conscious of a mortal coldness and felt as if I should never again be warm. So when he appeared I was sitting in the glow with my thoughts. He paused a moment by the door as if to look at me; then—as if to share them—came to the other side of the hearth and sank into a chair. We sat there in absolute stillness; yet he wanted, I felt, to be with me.

XXI

Before a new day, in my room, had fully broken, my eyes opened to Mrs. Grose, who had come to my bedside with worse news. Flora was so markedly feverish that an illness was perhaps at hand; she had passed a night of extreme unrest, a night agitated above all by fears that had for their subject not in the least her former but wholly her present governess. It was not against the possible re-entrance of Miss Jessel on the scene that she protested—it was conspicuously and passionately against mine. I was at once on my feet, and with an immense deal to ask; the more that my friend had discernibly now girded her loins to meet me afresh. This I felt as soon as I had put to her the question of her sense of the child's sincerity as against my own. "She persists in denying to you that she saw, or has ever seen, anything?"

My visitor's trouble truly was great. "Ah Miss, it is n't a matter on which I can push her! Yet it is n't either, I must say, as if I much needed to. It has made her, every inch of her, quite old."

"Oh I see her perfectly from here. She resents, for all the world like some high little personage, the imputation on her truthfulness and, as it were, her respectability. 'Miss Jessel indeed—*she*!' Ah she's 'respectable,' the chit! The impression she gave me there yesterday was, I assure you, the very strangest of all: it was quite beyond any of the others. I *did* put my foot in it! She'll never speak to me again."

Hideous and obscure as it all was, it held Mrs. Grose briefly silent; then she granted my point with a frankness which, I made sure, had more behind it. "I think indeed, Miss, she never will. She do have a grand manner about it!"

"And that manner"—I summed it up—"is practically what's the matter with her now."

Oh that manner, I could see in my visitor's face, and not a little else besides! "She asks me every three minutes if I think you're coming in."

"I see—I see." I too, on my side, had so much more than worked it out. "Has she said to you since yesterday—except to repudiate her familiarity with anything so dreadful—a single other word about Miss Jessel?"

"Not one, Miss. And of course, you know," my friend added, "I took it from her by the lake that just then and there at least there *was* nobody."

"Rather! And naturally you take it from her still."

"I don't contradict her. What else can I do?"

"Nothing in the world! You've the cleverest little person to deal with. They've made them—their two friends, I mean—still cleverer even than nature did; for it was wondrous material to play on! Flora has now her grievance, and she'll work it to the end."

"Yes, Miss; but to *what* end?"

"Why that of dealing with me to her uncle. She'll make me out to him the lowest creature—!"

I winced at the fair show of the scene in Mrs. Grose's face; she looked for a minute as if she sharply saw them together. "And him who thinks so well of you!"

"He has an odd way—it comes over me now," I laughed, "—of proving it! But that does n't matter. What Flora wants of course is to get rid of me."

My companion bravely concurred. "Never again to so much as look at you."

"So that what you've come to me now for," I asked, "is to speed me on my way?" Before she had time to reply, however, I had her in check. "I've a better idea—the result of my reflexions. My going *would* seem the right thing, and on Sunday I was terribly near it. Yet that won't do. It's *you* who must go. You must take Flora."

My visitor, at this, did speculate. "But where in the world—?"

"Away from here. Away from *them*. Away, even most of all, now, from me. Straight to her uncle."

"Only to tell on you—?"

"No, not 'only'! To leave me, in addition, with my remedy."

She was still vague. "And what *is* your remedy?"

"Your loyalty, to begin with. And then Miles's."

She looked at me hard. "Do you think he—?"

"Won't, if he has the chance, turn on me? Yes, I venture still to think it. At all events I want to try. Get off with his sister as soon as possible and leave me with him alone." I was amazed, myself, at the spirit I had still in reserve, and therefore perhaps a trifle the more disconcerted at the way in which, in spite of this fine example of it, she hesitated. "There's one thing, of course," I went on: "they must n't, before she goes, see each other for three seconds." Then it came over me that, in spite of Flora's presumable sequestration from the instant of her return from the pool, it might already be too late. "Do you mean," I anxiously asked, "that they *have* met?"

At this she quite flushed. "Ah, Miss, I'm not such a fool as that! If I've been obliged to leave her three or four times, it has been each time with one of the maids, and at present, though she's alone, she's locked in safe. And yet—and yet!" There were too many things.

"And yet what?"

"Well, are you so sure of the little gentleman?"

"I'm not sure of anything but *you*. But I have, since last evening, a new hope. I think he wants to give me an opening. I do believe that—poor little exquisite wretch! —he wants to speak. Last evening, in the firelight and the silence, he sat with me for two hours as if it were just coming."

Mrs. Grose looked hard through the window at the grey gathering day. "And did it come?"

"No, though I waited and waited I confess it did n't, and it was without a breach of the silence, or so much as a faint allusion to his sister's condition and absence, that we at last kissed for good-night. All the same," I continued, "I can't, if her uncle sees her, consent to his seeing her brother without my having given the boy—and most of all because things have got so bad—a little more time."

My friend appeared on this ground more reluctant than I could quite understand. "What do you mean by more time?"

"Well, a day or two—really to bring it out. He'll then be on *my* side—of which you see the importance. If nothing comes I shall only fail, and you at the worst have helped me by doing on your arrival in town whatever you may have found possible." So I put it before her, but she continued for a little so lost in other reasons that I came again to her aid. "Unless indeed," I wound up, "you really want *not* to go."

I could see it, in her face, at last clear itself: she put out her hand to me as a pledge. "I'll go—I'll go. I'll go this morning."

I wanted to be very just. "If you *should* wish still to wait I'd engage she should n't see me."

"No, no: it's the place itself. She must leave it." She held me a moment with heavy eyes, then brought out the rest. "Your idea's the right one. I myself, Miss—"

"Well?"

"I can't stay."

The look she gave me with it made me jump at possibilities. "You mean that, since yesterday, you *have* seen—?"

She shook her head with dignity. "I've *heard*—!"

"Heard?"

"From that child—horrors! There!" she sighed with tragic relief. "On my honour, Miss, she says things—!" But at this evocation she broke down; she dropped with a sudden cry upon my sofa and, as I had seen her do before, gave way to all the anguish of it.

It was quite in another manner that I for my part let myself go. "Oh thank God!"

She sprang up again at this, drying her eyes with a groan. "'Thank God'?"

"It so justifies me!"

"It does that, Miss!"

I could n't have desired more emphasis, but I just waited. "She's so horrible?"

I saw my colleague scarce knew how to put it. "Really shocking."

"And about me?"

"About you, Miss—since you must have it. It's beyond everything, for a young lady; and I can't think wherever she must have picked up—"

"The appalling language she applies to me? I can then!" I broke in with a laugh that was doubtless significant enough.

It only in truth left my friend still more grave. "Well, perhaps I ought to also—since I've heard some of it before! Yet I can't bear it," the poor woman went on while with the same movement she glanced, on my dressing-table, at the face of my watch. "But I must go back."

I kept her, however. "Ah if you can't bear it—!"

"How can I stop with her, you mean? Why just *for* that: to get her away. Far from this," she pursued, "far from *them*—"

"She may be different? she may be free?" I seized her almost with joy. "Then in spite of yesterday you *believe*—"

"In such doings?" Her simple description of them required, in the light of her expression, to be carried no further, and she gave me the whole thing as she had never done. "I believe."

Yes, it was a joy, and we were still shoulder to shoulder: if I might continue sure of that I should care but little what else happened. My support in the presence of disaster would be the same as it had been in my early need of confidence, and if my friend would answer for my honesty I would answer for all the rest. On the point of taking leave of her, none the less, I was to some extent embarrassed. "There's one thing of course—it occurs to me—to remember. My letter giving the alarm will have reached town before you."

I now felt still more how she had been beating about the bush and how weary at last it had made her. "Your letter won't have got there. Your letter never went."

"What then became of it?"

"Goodness knows! Master Miles—"

"Do you mean *he* took it?" I gasped.

She hung fire, but she overcame her reluctance. "I mean that I saw yesterday, when I came back with Miss Flora, that it was n't where you had put it. Later in the evening I had the chance to question Luke, and he declared that he had neither noticed nor touched it." We could only exchange, on this, one of our deeper mutual soundings, and it was Mrs. Grose who first brought up the plumb with an almost elate "You see!"

"Yes, I see that if Miles took it instead he probably will have read it and destroyed it."

"And don't you see anything else?"

I faced her a moment with a sad smile. "It strikes me that by this time your eyes are open even wider than mine."

They proved to be so indeed, but she could still almost blush to show it. "I make out now what he must have done at school." And she gave, in her simple sharpness, an almost droll disillusioned nod. "He stole!"

I turned it over—I tried to be more judicial. "Well—perhaps."

She looked as if she found me unexpectedly calm. "He stole *letters!*"

She could n't know my reasons for a calmness after all pretty shallow; so I showed them off as I might. "I hope then it was to more purpose than in this case! The note, at all events, that I put on the table yesterday," I pursued, "will have given him so scant an advantage—for it contained only the bare demand for an interview—that he's already much ashamed of having gone so far for so little, and that what he had on his mind last evening was precisely the need of confession." I seemed to myself for the instant to have mastered it, to see it all. "Leave us, leave us"—I was already, at the door, hurrying her off. "I'll get it out of him. He'll meet me. He'll confess. If he confesses he's saved. And if he's saved—"

"Then *you* are?" The dear woman kissed me on this, and I took her farewell. "I'll save you without him!" she cried as she went.

XXII

Yet it was when she had got off—and I missed her on the spot—that the great pinch really came. If I had counted on what it would give me to find myself alone with Miles I quickly recognised that it would give me at least a measure. No hour of my stay in fact was so assailed with apprehensions as that of my coming down to learn that the carriage containing Mrs. Grose and my younger pupil had already rolled out of the gates. Now I *was,* I said to myself, face to face with the elements, and for much of the rest of the day, while I fought my weakness, I could consider that I had been supremely rash. It was a tighter place still than I had yet turned round in; all the more that, for the first time, I could see in the aspect of others a confused reflexion of the crisis. What had happened naturally caused them all to stare; there was too little of the explained, throw out whatever we might, in the suddenness of my colleague's act. The maids and the men looked blank; the effect of which on my nerves was an aggravation until I saw the necessity of making it a positive aid. It was in short by just clutching the helm that I avoided total wreck; and I dare say that, to bear up at all, I became that morning very grand and very dry. I welcomed the consciousness that I was charged with much to do, and I caused it to be known as well that, left thus to myself, I was quite remarkably firm. I wandered with that manner, for the next hour or two, all over the place and looked, I have no doubt, as if I were ready for any onset. So, for the benefit of whom it might concern, I paraded with a sick heart.

The person it appeared least to concern proved to be, till dinner, little Miles himself. My perambulations had given me meanwhile no glimpse of him, but they had tended to make more public the change taking place in our relation as a consequence of his having at the piano, the day before, kept me, in Flora's interest, so beguiled and befooled. The stamp of publicity had of course been fully given by her confinement and departure, and the change itself was now ushered in by our non-observance of the regular custom of the schoolroom. He had already disappeared when, on my way down, I pushed open his door, and I learned below that he had breakfasted—in the presence of a couple of the maids—with Mrs. Grose and his sister. He had then gone out, as he said, for a stroll; than which nothing, I reflected, could better have expressed his frank view of the abrupt transformation of my office. What he would now permit this office to consist of was yet to be settled: there was at the least a queer relief— I mean for myself in especial—in the renouncement of one pretension. If so much had sprung to the surface I scarce put it too strongly in saying that what had perhaps sprung highest was the absurdity of our prolonging the fiction that I had anything more to teach him. It sufficiently stuck out that, by tacit little tricks in which even more than myself he carried out the care for my dignity, I had had to appeal to him to let me off straining to meet him on the ground of his true capacity. He had at any rate his freedom now; I was never to touch it again: as I had amply shown, moreover, when, on his joining me in the schoolroom the previous night, I uttered, in reference to the interval just concluded, neither challenge nor hint. I had too much, from this moment, my other ideas. Yet when he at last arrived the difficulty of applying them, the accumulations of my problem, were brought straight home to me by the beautiful little presence on which what had occurred had as yet, for the eye, dropped neither stain nor shadow.

To mark, for the house, the high state I cultivated I decreed that my meals with the boy should be served, as we called it, downstairs; so that I had been awaiting him in the ponderous pomp of the room outside the window of which I had had from Mrs. Grose, that first scared Sunday, my flash of something it would scarce have done to call light. Here at present I felt afresh—for I had felt it again and again—how my equilibrium depended on the success of my rigid will, the will to shut my eyes as tight as possible to the truth that what I had to deal with was, revoltingly, against nature. I could only get on at all by taking "nature" into my confidence and my account, by treating my monstrous ordeal as a push in a direction unusual, of course, and unpleasant, but demanding after all, for a fair front, only another turn of the screw of ordinary human virtue. No attempt, none the less, could well require more tact than just this attempt to supply, one's self, *all* the nature. How could I put even a little of that article into a suppression of reference to what had occurred? How on the other hand could I make a reference without a new plunge into the hideous obscure? Well, a sort of answer, after a time, had come to me, and it was so far confirmed as that I was met, incontestably, by the quickened vision of what was rare in my little companion. It was indeed as if he had found even now—as he had so often found at lessons—still some other delicate way to ease me off. Was n't there light in the fact which, as we shared our solitude, broke out with a specious glitter it had never yet quite worn?—the fact that (opportunity aiding, precious opportunity which had now come) it would be preposterous, with a child so endowed, to forego the help one might wrest from absolute intelligence? What had his intelligence been given him for but to save him? Might n't one, to reach his mind, risk the stretch of a stiff arm across his character? It was as if, when we were face to face in the dining-room, he had literally shown me the way. The roast mutton was on the table and I had dispensed with attendance. Miles, before he sat down, stood a moment with his hands in his pockets and looked at the joint, on which he seemed on the point of passing some humorous judgement. But what he presently produced was: "I say, my dear, is she really very awfully ill?"

"Little Flora? Not so bad but that she'll presently be better. London will set her up. Bly had ceased to agree with her. Come here and take your mutton."

He alertly obeyed me, carried the plate carefully to his seat and, when he was established, went on. "Did Bly disagree with her so terribly all at once?"

"Not so suddenly as you might think. One had seen it coming on."

"Then why did n't you get her off before?"

"Before what?"

"Before she became too ill to travel."

I found myself prompt. "She's *not* too ill to travel; she only might have become so if she had stayed. This was just the moment to seize. The journey will dissipate the influence"—oh I was grand!—"and carry it off."

"I see, I see"—Miles, for that matter, was grand too. He settled to his repast with the charming little "table manner" that, from the day of his arrival, had relieved me of all grossness of admonition. Whatever he had been expelled from school for, it was n't for ugly feeding. He was irreproachable, as always, today; but was unmistakeably more conscious. He was discernibly trying to take for granted more things than he found, without assistance, quite easy; and he dropped into peaceful silence while he felt his situation. Our meal was of the briefest—mine a vain pretence, and I had the things immediately removed. While this was done Miles stood again with his hands in his little pockets and his back to me—stood and looked out of the wide window through which, that other day, I had seen what pulled me up. We continued silent while the maid was with us—as silent, it whimsically occurred to me, as some young couple who, on their wedding-journey, at the inn, feel shy in the presence of the waiter. He turned round only when the waiter had left us. "Well—so we're alone!"

XXIII

"Oh more or less." I imagine my smile was pale. "Not absolutely. We should n't like that!" I went on.

"No—I suppose we should n't. Of course we've the others."

"We've the others—we've indeed the others," I concurred.

"Yet even though we have them," he returned, still with his hands in his pockets and planted there in front of me, "they don't much count, do they?"

I made the best of it, but I felt wan. "It depends on what you call 'much'!"

"Yes"—with all accommodation—"everything depends!" On this, however, he faced to the window again and presently reached it with his vague restless cogitating step. He remained there a while with his forehead against the glass, in contemplation of the stupid shrubs I knew and the dull things of November. I had always my hypocrisy of "work," behind which I now gained the sofa. Steadying myself with it there as I had repeatedly done at those moments of torment that I have described as the moments of my knowing the children to be given to something from which I was barred, I sufficiently obeyed my habit of being prepared for the worst. But an extraordinary impression dropped on me as I extracted a meaning from the boy's embarrassed back—none other than the impression that I was not barred now. This inference grew in a few minutes to sharp intensity and seemed bound up with the direct perception that it was positively *he* who was. The frames and squares of the great window were a kind of image, for him, of a kind of failure. I felt that I saw him, in any case, shut in or shut out. He was admirable but not comfortable: I took it in with a throb of hope. Was n't he looking through the haunted pane for something he could n't see?—and was n't it the first time in the whole business that he had known such a lapse? The first, the very first: I found it a splendid portent. It made him anxious, though he watched himself; he had been anxious all day and, even while in his usual sweet little manner he sat at table, had needed all his small strange genius to give it a gloss. When he at last turned round to meet me it was almost as if this genius had succumbed. "Well, I think I'm glad Bly agrees with *me*!"

"You'd certainly seem to have seen, these twenty-four hours, a good deal more of it than for some time before. I hope," I went on bravely, "that you've been enjoying yourself."

"Oh yes, I've been ever so far; all round about—miles and miles away. I've never been so free."

He had really a manner of his own, and I could only try to keep up with him. "Well, do you like it?"

He stood there smiling; then at last he put into two words—"Do *you?*"—more discrimination than I had ever heard two words contain. Before I had time to deal with that, however, he continued as if with the sense that this was an impertinence to be softened. "Nothing could be more charming than the way you take it, for of course if we're alone together now it's you that are alone most. But I hope," he threw in, "you don't particularly mind!"

"Having to do with you?" I asked. "My dear child, how can I help minding? Though I've renounced all claim to your company—you're so beyond me—I at least greatly enjoy it. What else should I stay on for?"

He looked at me more directly, and the expression of his face, graver now, struck me as the most beautiful I had ever found in it. "You stay on just for *that?*"

"Certainly. I stay on as your friend and from the tremendous interest I take in you till something can be done for you that may be more worth your while. That need n't surprise you." My voice trembled so that I felt it impossible to suppress the shake.

"Don't you remember how I told you, when I came and sat on your bed the night of the storm, that there was nothing in the world I would n't do for you?"

"Yes, yes!" He, on his side, more and more visibly nervous, had a tone to master; but he was so much more successful than I that, laughing out through his gravity, he could pretend we were pleasantly jesting. "Only that, I think, was to get me to do something for *you*!"

"It was partly to get you to do something," I conceded. "But, you know, you did n't do it."

"Oh yes," he said with the brightest superficial eagerness, "you wanted me to tell you something."

"That's it. Out, straight out. What you have on your mind, you know."

"Ah then is *that* what you've stayed over for?"

He spoke with a gaiety through which I could still catch the finest little quiver of resentful passion; but I can't begin to express the effect upon me of an implication of surrender even so faint. It was as if what I had yearned for had come at last only to astonish me. "Well, yes—I may as well make a clean breast of it. It was precisely for that."

He waited so long that I supposed it for the purpose of repudiating the assumption on which my action had been founded; but what he finally said was: "Do you mean now—here?"

"There could n't be a better place or time." He looked round him uneasily, and I had the rare—oh the queer!—impression of the very first symptom I had seen in him of the approach of immediate fear. It was as if he were suddenly afraid of me—which struck me indeed as perhaps the best thing to make him. Yet in the very pang of the effort I felt it vain to try sternness, and I heard myself the next instant so gentle as to be almost grotesque. "You want so to go out again?"

"Awfully!" He smiled at me heroically, and the touching little bravery of it was enhanced by his actually flushing with pain. He had picked up his hat, which he had brought in, and stood twirling it in a way that gave me, even as I was just nearly reaching port, a perverse horror of what I was doing. To do it in *any* way was an act of violence, for what did it consist of but the obtrusion of the idea of grossness and guilt on a small helpless creature who had been for me a revelation of the possibilities of beautiful intercourse? Was n't it base to create for a being so exquisite a mere alien awkwardness? I suppose I now read into our situation a clearness it could n't have had at the time, for I seem to see our poor eyes already lighted with some spark of a prevision of the anguish that was to come. So we circled about with terrors and scruples, fighters not daring to close. But it was for each other we feared! That kept us a little longer suspended and unbruised. "I'll tell you everything," Miles said—"I mean I'll tell you anything you like. You'll stay on with me, and we shall both be all right, and I *will* tell you—I *will*. But not now."

"Why not now?"

My insistence turned him from me and kept him once more at his window in a silence during which, between us, you might have heard a pin drop. Then he was before me again with the air of a person for whom, outside, some one who had frankly to be reckoned with was waiting. "I have to see Luke."

I had not yet reduced him to quite so vulgar a lie, and I felt proportionately ashamed. But, horrible as it was, his lies made up my truth. I achieved thoughtfully a few loops of my knitting. "Well then go to Luke, and I'll wait for what you promise. Only in return for that satisfy, before you leave me, one very much smaller request."

He looked as if he felt he had succeeded enough to be able still a little to bargain. "Very much smaller—?"

"Yes, a mere fraction of the whole. Tell me"—oh my work preoccupied me, and I was off-hand!—"if, yesterday afternoon, from the table in the hall, you took, you know, my letter."

XXIV

My grasp of how he received this suffered for a minute from something that I can describe only as a fierce split of my attention—a stroke that at first, as I sprang straight up, reduced me to the mere blind movement of getting hold of him, drawing him close and, while I just fell for support against the nearest piece of furniture, instinctively keeping him with his back to the window. The appearance was full upon us that I had already had to deal with here: Peter Quint had come into view like a sentinel before a prison. The next thing I saw was that, from outside, he had reached the window, and then I knew that, close to the glass and glaring in through it, he offered once more to the room his white face of damnation. It represents but grossly what took place within me at the sight to say that on the second my decision was made; yet I believe that no woman so overwhelmed ever in so short a time recovered her command of the *act*. It came to me in the very horror of the immediate presence that the act would be, seeing and facing what I saw and faced, to keep the boy himself unaware. The inspiration—I can call it by no other name—was that I felt how voluntarily, how transcendently, I *might*. It was like fighting with a demon for a human soul, and when I had fairly so appraised it I saw how the human soul—held out, in the tremor of my hands, at arms' length—had a perfect dew of sweat on a lovely childish forehead. The face that was close to mine was as white as the face against the glass, and out of it presently came a sound, not low nor weak, but as if from much further away, that I drank like a waft of fragrance.

"Yes—I took it."

At this, with a moan of joy, I enfolded, I drew him close; and while I held him to my breast, where I could feel in the sudden fever of his little body the tremendous pulse of his little heart, I kept my eyes on the thing at the window and saw it move and shift its posture. I have likened it to a sentinel, but its slow wheel, for a moment, was rather the prowl of a baffled beast. My present quickened courage, however, was such that, not too much to let it through, I had to shade, as it were, my flame. Meanwhile the glare of the face was again at the window, the scoundrel fixed as if to watch and wait. It was the very confidence that I might now defy him, as well as the positive certitude, by this time, of the child's unconsciousness, that made me go on. "What did you take it for?"

"To see what you said about me."

"You opened the letter?"

"I opened it."

My eyes were now, as I held him off a little again, on Miles's own face, in which the collapse of mockery showed me how complete was the ravage of uneasiness. What was prodigious was that at last, by my success, his sense was sealed and his communication stopped: he knew that he was in presence, but knew not of what, and knew still less that I also was and that I did know. And what did this strain of trouble matter when my eyes went back to the window only to see that the air was clear again and —by my personal triumph—the influence quenched? There was nothing there. I felt that the cause was mine and that I should surely get *all*. "And you found nothing!" —I let my elation out.

He gave the most mournful, thoughtful little headshake. "Nothing."

"Nothing, nothing!" I almost shouted in my joy.

"Nothing, nothing," he sadly repeated.

I kissed his forehead; it was drenched. "So what have you done with it?"

"I've burnt it."

"Burnt it?" It was now or never. "Is that what you did at school?"

Oh what this brought up! "At school?"

"Did you take letters?—or other things?"

"Other things?" He appeared now to be thinking of something far off and that reached him only through the pressure of his anxiety. Yet it did reach him. "Did I *steal*?"

I felt myself redden to the roots of my hair as well as wonder if it were more strange to put to a gentleman such a question or to see him take it with allowances that gave the very distance of his fall in the world. "Was it for that you might n't go back?"

The only thing he felt was rather a dreary little surprise. "Did you know I might n't go back?"

"I know everything."

He gave me at this the longest and strangest look. "Everything?"

"Everything. Therefore *did* you—?" But I could n't say it again.

Miles could, very simply. "No. I did n't steal."

My face must have shown him I believed him utterly; yet my hands—but it was for pure tenderness—shook him as if to ask him why, if it was all for nothing, he had condemned me to months of torment. "What then did you do?"

He looked in vague pain all round the top of the room and drew his breath, two or three times over, as if with difficulty. He might have been standing at the bottom of the sea and raising his eyes to some faint green twilight. "Well—I said things."

"Only that?"

"They thought it was enough!"

"To turn you out for?"

Never, truly, had a person "turned out" shown so little to explain it as this little person! He appeared to weigh my question, but in a manner quite detached and almost helpless. "Well, I suppose I ought n't."

"But to whom did you say them?"

He evidently tried to remember, but it dropped—he had lost it. "I don't know!"

He almost smiled at me in the desolation of his surrender, which was indeed practically, by this time, so complete that I ought to have left it there. But I was infatuated—I was blind with victory, though even then the very effect that was to have brought him so much nearer was already that of added separation. "Was it to every one?" I asked.

"No; it was only to—" But he gave a sick little headshake. "I don't remember their names."

"Were they then so many?"

"No—only a few. Those I liked."

Those he liked? I seemed to float not into clearness, but into a darker obscure, and within a minute there had come to me out of my very pity the appalling alarm of his being perhaps innocent. It was for the instant confounding and bottomless, for if he *were* what then on earth was I? Paralysed, while it lasted, by the mere brush of the question, I let him go a little, so that, with a deep-drawn sigh, he turned away from me again; which, as he faced toward the clear window, I suffered, feeling that I had nothing now there to keep him from. "And did they repeat what you said?" I went on after a moment.

He was soon at some distance from me, still breathing hard and again with the air, though now without anger for it, of being confined against his will. Once more, as he had done before, he looked up at the dim day as if, of what had hitherto sustained him, nothing was left but an unspeakable anxiety. "Oh yes," he nevertheless replied —"they must have repeated them. To those *they* liked," he added.

There was somehow less of it than I had expected; but I turned it over. "And these things came round—?"

"To the masters? Oh yes!" he answered very simply. "But I did n't know they'd tell."

"The masters? They did n't—they've never told. That's why I ask you."

He turned to me again his little beautiful fevered face. "Yes, it was too bad."

"Too bad?"

"What I suppose I sometimes said. To write home."

I can't name the exquisite pathos of the contradiction given to such a speech by such a speaker; I only know that the next instant I heard myself throw off with homely force: "Stuff and nonsense!" But the next after that I must have sounded stern enough. "What *were* these things?"

My sternness was all for his judge, his executioner; yet it made him avert himself again, and that movement made *me,* with a single bound and an irrepressible cry, spring straight upon him. For there again, against the glass, as if to blight his confession and stay his answer, was the hideous author of our woe—the white face of damnation. I felt a sick swim at the drop of my victory and all the return of my battle, so that the wildness of my veritable leap only served as a great betrayal. I saw him, from the midst of my act, meet it with a divination, and on the perception that even now he only guessed, and that the window was still to his own eyes free, I let the impulse flame up to convert the climax of his dismay into the very proof of his liberation. "No more, no more, no more!" I shrieked to my visitant as I tried to press him against me.

"Is she *here?*" Miles panted as he caught with his sealed eyes the direction of my words. Then as his strange "she" staggered me and, with a gasp, I echoed it, "Miss Jessel, Miss Jessel!" he with sudden fury gave me back.

I seized, stupefied, his supposition—some sequel to what we had done to Flora, but this made me only want to show him that it was better still than that. "It's not Miss Jessel! But it's at the window—straight before us. It's *there*—the coward horror, there for the last time!"

At this, after a second in which his head made the movement of a baffled dog's on a scent and then gave a frantic little shake for air and light, he was at me in a white rage, bewildered, glaring vainly over the place and missing wholly, though it now, to my sense, filled the room like the taste of poison, the wide overwhelming presence. "It's *he?*"

I was so determined to have all my proof that I flashed into ice to challenge him. "Whom do you mean by 'he'?"

"Peter Quint—you devil!" His face gave again, round the room, its convulsed supplication. *"Where?"*

They are in my ears still, his supreme surrender of the name and his tribute to my devotion. "What does he matter now, my own?—what will he *ever* matter? *I* have you," I launched at the beast, "but he has lost you for ever!" Then for the demonstration of my work, "There, *there!*" I said to Miles.

But he had already jerked straight round, stared, glared again, and seen but the quiet day. With the stroke of the loss I was so proud of he uttered the cry of a creature hurled over an abyss, and the grasp with which I recovered him might have been that of catching him in his fall. I caught him, yes, I held him—it may be imagined with what a passion; but at the end of a minute I began to feel what it truly was that I held. We were alone with the quiet day, and his little heart, dispossessed, had stopped.

1898

Alice James
1848–1892

It may be odd to give special recognition to a woman whose only accomplishment was that she died well. And for what purpose does one feature the relatively unknown member of a distinguished family of males? But Alice James is not a superfluous footnote to the lives of her older brothers. The diary she kept during the final two years of her invalidism recounts her drawn-out anticipation of "the grand mortuary moment" of death and what it meant to be a James who was *not* William, the famous philosopher-psychologist, or Henry, the famous novelist-critic. But she recorded other matters as well: in the main, "the resistance we bring to life," which promised the only true form of immortality that any of the Jameses, brothers and sister, could count on.

Alice James was the youngest of the five children of Henry James, Sr., and his wife Mary. Born in New York in 1848, she was preceded by William (1842), Henry, Jr. (1843), Garth Wilkinson (1845), and Robertson (1846). The senior James was a writer and lecturer on utopian schemes, a student of the writings of the mystic Emanuel Swedenborg, and an early socialist. The imprint he left on his brood of highly intelligent and sensitive children was simultaneously indulgent and demanding, liberating and restrictive. The mother's extreme self-effacement offered her daughter no lessons in independence. As the only girl, Alice James was reared in a demandingly masculine setting that seemed to make no room for her unique talents.

Alice James's girlhood and young womanhood sound like the lives of other well-brought-up young women of upper-middle-class families of the post–Civil War period, but with the addition of the darker edge of nervousness that worked against her ability to function with so-called normalcy. Her father and brothers also suffered from acute nervous disturbances at different periods in their lives, but they were able to come to better terms with their condition, perhaps because they, as males, had more chances to combat "the horrors." Active careers provided acceptable ways of expressing their ideas and their feelings. Hysteria and nervous collapse for Alice began in 1868, attacks that reappeared with increasing frequency. The family consulted a series of doctors, who prescribed the newest mind-cure treatments (electricity, motorpathy, and, later, hypnosis). To some degree Alice James's symptoms parallel those that marred the lives of Emily Dickinson, Elizabeth Barrett Browning, and the women who consulted that new Viennese doctor, Sigmund Freud. The causes of Alice's symptoms were too complex to be disentangled completely. The results stand out clearly.

In 1878, when Alice James deliberated killing herself, her father wisely gave his permission. This made it impossible for her to do so, since she would be responsible for such an act. The remainder of Alice James's life was given over, in the words of the critic Ruth Yeazell, to "a covert career in mortality," though she did not take to her bed as an invalid until 1884. In 1890 Alice James decided to keep a diary. She wished to write down her thoughts about her life from the perspective of her bedroom. This decision came after she went to live in England under the protective eyes of her brother Henry, by then a permanent British resident, and her friend Katharine Loring, who lived with her and cared for her until her death in 1892.

Alice James's existence seems strange and essentially tragic, but it was more than that. No public deeds or great poetry of the kind that Emily Dickinson wrote in her self-incarceration in the family house in Amherst were forthcoming. She dedicated her life instead to an analysis of consciousness. Her own consciousness was often fervid and intense—alternating between Whitmanesque exuberance ("I lay in a meadow until the unwrinkled serenity entered into my bones and made me one with the browsing kine, the still greenery, the drifting clouds, and the swooping birds") and a self-absorption about her ailments so great that, at times, she was transformed into a great headache. Still, she drew the world outside into her invalid's room. She asked questions, read newspapers and journals, made jokes. The Irish question about home rule, Henry's attempts to win acclaim in the popular theater, William's accomplishments as a celebrated thinker, and the lives of the London poor all found welcome room in her mind. They kept her alert, responsive, and amused until the day in 1892 when this sometimes difficult and snobbish, often unhappy, but always *interested* woman died, having achieved (as she wrote to William) "significance for myself."

Further Reading:
Alice James: Her Brothers, Her Journals, ed.
A. Burr, 1934.
The James Family, ed. F. Matthiessen, 1961.
J. Strouse, *Alice James: A Biography*, 1980.
The Death and Letters of Alice James, ed.
R. Yeazell, 1981.

Text:
The Diary of Alice James, ed. L. Edel, 1964.

from The Diary of Alice James

[May 31, 1889]

I think that if I get into the habit of writing a bit about what happens, or rather doesn't happen, I may lose a little of the sense of loneliness and desolation which abides with me. My circumstances allowing of nothing but the ejaculation of one-syllabled reflections, a written monologue by that most interesting being, *myself,* may have its yet to be discovered consolations. I shall at least have it all my own way and it may bring relief as an outlet to that geyser of emotions, sensations, speculations and reflections which ferments perpetually within my poor old carcass for its sins; so here goes, my first Journal!

[July 12, 1889]

H.[1] says, with his usual felicity, of Bob that he is an "extraordinary instance of a man's *nature* constituting his profession, his whole stock in trade." *His* journey to Damascus[2] casts a light upon the *naïfs*[3] mysteries of the Bible.—It's amusing to see how, even on my microscopic field, minute events are perpetually taking place illustrative of the broadest facts of human nature. Yesterday Nurse and I had a good laugh but I must allow that decidedly she "had" me. I was thinking of something that interested me very much and my mind was suddenly flooded by one of those luminous waves that sweep out of consciousness all but the living sense and overpower one with joy in the rich, throbbing complexity of life, when suddenly I looked up at Nurse, who was dressing me, and saw her primitive, rudimentary expression (so common here) as of no inherited quarrel with her destiny of putting petticoats over my head; the poverty and deadness of it contrasted to the tide of speculation that was coursing thro' my brain made me exclaim, "Oh! Nurse, don't you wish you were inside of *me!*"—her look of dismay and vehement disclaimer—"Inside of you, Miss, when you have just had a sick head-ache for five days!"—gave a greater blow to my vanity, than that much battered article has ever received. The headache had gone off in the night and I had clean forgotten it—when the little wretch confronted me with it, at this sublime moment when I was feeling within me the potency of a Bismarck,[4] and left me powerless before the immutable law that however great we may seem to our own consciousness no human being would exchange his for ours, and before the fact that *my* glorious rôle was to stand for *Sick headache* to mankind! What a grotesque I am

[1] Henry James (1843–1916), who was the second child of the family, next to William, born a year earlier. Robertson James (1846–1910), known as Bob, was the fourth child.
[2] I.e., a profound experience that radically changes one's life; in reference to the story of Saul (see Acts 9:1–22), who had been a

persecutor of the followers of Jesus until he underwent a spiritual conversion while on the road to Damascus and was thereafter known as Paul, leader and preacher of Christianity.
[3] French: "unaffected" or "artless."
[4] Otto von Bismarck (1815–1898), known as the Iron Chancellor and unifier of Germany.

to be sure! Lying in this room, with the resistance of a thistle-down, having illusory moments of throbbing with the pulse of the Race, the Mystery to be solved at the next breath and the fountain of all Happiness within me—the sense of vitality, in short, simply proportionate to the excess of weakness!—To sit by and watch these absurdities is amusing in its way and reminds me of how I used to *listen* to my "company manners" in the days when I had 'em, and how ridiculous they sounded.

Ah! Those strange people who have the courage to be unhappy! *Are* they unhappy, by-the-way?

[March 30, 1890]

March 30th

"How the poor live." Here is an instance taken from some evidence recently given in the Hebburn police-court:

> "Inspector Snowdon said that he went to Simpson's house No. 8 Williams-lane, Hebburn Quay, on the 15th ult. He had gone for two school-board fines which had not been paid. Simpson was getting some tea. All the children were present. Mrs. Simpson came out from the front room. She had a few rags on, hanging about her, but not sufficient to cover her nakedness. All the furniture in the house was two chairs, one without a back, and two iron beds, one of them in ruins, while there was a mattress black and glazed with filth. The children were in a filthy condition, hanging in rags and swarming with vermin. The house smelt dreadfully. There was no food in the house except a few potatoes. He afterwards went again to the house, but the door was fastened. He forced the door, and was led to believe that some person had been in the house, but looked all over the house without finding any one. On striking a match and looking up the chimney he found George there resting with his feet on one side and his back against the other side. There was no fire on. The boy said he often went there when any one was coming into the house. The girls told him that they slept in the bottom of a cupboard, and the mother on one of the shelves."
>
> Yet the father of this miserable family was a carpenter in Armstrong's, and his wages since the beginning of the year had averaged 25s. 7d. a week. Thanks to the "Children's Charter," he and his wife (who is stepmother to all the children except the youngest), are now undergoing two months' hard labour.
>
> (*P.M.G.,*[5] April 5th.)

In measuring such as the above Mrs. Lodge's story of the baby which was rescued from some den of misery is of inestimable value. The child was taken to a Home of some sort, laid in a spotless crib and all the comfortable layer of soil removed, when it began and roared all night and kept all the other children roaring for three days. The matron in despair sent off for the mother, who, on seeing it, immediately said: "Why, lay it on the floor"; which being done, the child went sound asleep all night.

[5] *Pall Mall Gazette,* a London newspaper.

But what could wring the hearts of pious old maids more than a baby lying on the floor of squalor?—baby meanwhile in bliss.

[June 18, 1890]

June 18th

It is very curious how, for the last year or two, I perpetually come across in my reading just what I have been thinking about, curious I mean, of course, because my reading is so haphazard. It reminds me of Wm.[6] in old days when his eyes were bad and I used to begin and tell him something which I thought of interest from whatever book I might be reading, when he would invariably say, "I glanced into the book yesterday and read that." I wonder what determines the *selection* of memory, why does one childish experience or impression stand out so luminous and solid against the, for the most part, vague and misty background? The things we remember have a *first-timeness* about them which suggests that that may be the reason of their survival. I must ask Wm. some day if there is any theory on the subject, or better, whether 'tis worth a theory. I remember so distinctly the first time I was conscious of a purely intellectual process. 'Twas the summer of '56 which we spent in Boulogne and the parents of Mlle. Marie Boningue our governess had a *campagne*[7] on the outskirts and invited us to spend the day, perhaps Marie's fête-day.[8] A large and shabby calèche came for us into which we were packed, save Wm.; all I can remember of the drive was a never-ending ribbon of dust stretching in front and the anguish greater even than usual of Wilky's and Bob's[9] heels grinding into my shins. Marie told us that her father had a scar upon his face caused by a bad scald in his youth and we must be sure and not look at him as he was very sensitive. How I remember the painful conflict between sympathy and the desire to look and the fear that my baseness should be discovered by the good man as he sat at the head of the table in charge of a big frosted-cake, sprinkled o'er with those pink and white worms in which lurk the caraway seed. How easy 'twould be to picture one's youth as a perpetual escape from that abhorred object!—I wonder if it is a blight upon children still?—But to arrive at the first flowering of me Intellect! We were turned into the garden to play, a sandy or rather dusty expanse with nothing in it, as I remember, but two or three scrubby apple-trees, from one of which hung a swing. As time went on Wilky and Bob disappeared, not to my grief, and the Boningues. Harry was sitting in the swing and I came up and stood near by as the sun began to slant over the desolate expanse, as the dready h[ou]rs, with that endlessness which they have for infancy, passed, when Harry suddenly exclaimed: "This might certainly be called pleasure under difficulties!" The stir of my whole being in response to the substance and exquisite, *original* form of this remark almost makes my heart beat now with the sisterly pride which was then awakened and it came to me in a flash, the higher nature of this appeal to the mind, as compared to the rudimentary solicitations which usually produced my childish explosions of laughter; and I can also feel distinctly the sense of self-satisfaction in that I could not only perceive, but

---

[6] William James (1842–1910), the eldest of the James children, who later became a professor of philosophy and psychology at Harvard.
[7] French: "little country house."

[8] Birthday or name day.
[9] Wilky: Garth Wilkinson James (1845–1883); Bob: Robertson James (1846–1910).

appreciate this subtlety, as if I had acquired a new sense, a sense whereby to measure intellectual things, wit as distinguished from giggling, for example.

[July 18, 1890]

July 18th

How well one has to be, to be ill! These confidences reveal to you, dear Inconnu,[10] so much mental debility that I don't want to rehearse herein my physical collapses in detail as well, altho' I am able to escape a general tone of lamentation. But this last prostration was rather excessive and comic in its combination, consisting of one of my usual attacks of rheumatic gout in that dissipated organ known in the family as "Alice's tum,"[11] in conjunction with an ulcerated tooth, and a very bad crick in my neck. By taking a very small dose of morphia, the first in three years, I was able to steady my nerves and *experience* the pain without distraction, for there is something very exhilarating in shivering whacks of crude pain which seem to lift you out of the present and its sophistications (great Men unable to have a tooth out without gas!) and ally you to long gone generations rent and torn with tooth-ache such as we can't dream of. I didn't succumb and send for my Primrose Knight, having no faith in anything but that time-honoured nostrum Patience, with its simple ingredients of refraining from muscular contractions and vocal exclamations lest you find yourself in a worse fix than you are already in!

[July 28, 1890]

July 28th

I lay in a meadow until the unwrinkled serenity entered into my bones and made me one with the browsing kine, the still greenery, the drifting clouds, and the swooping birds.

[October 26, 1890]

October 26th

William uses an excellent expression when he says in his paper on the "Hidden Self"[12] that the nervous victim "abandons" certain portions of his consciousness. It may be the word commonly used by his kind. It is just the right one at any rate, altho' I have never unfortunately been able to abandon my consciousness and get five minutes' rest. I have passed thro' an infinite succession of conscious abandonments and in looking back now I see how it began in my childhood, altho' I wasn't conscious of the necessity until '67 or '68 when I broke down first, acutely, and had violent turns of hysteria. As I lay prostrate after the storm with my mind luminous and active and susceptible of the clearest, strongest impressions, I saw so distinctly that it was a fight simply between my body and my will, a battle in which the former was to be triumphant to the end. Owing to some physical weakness, excess of nervous susceptibility, the

---

[10] Stranger.
[11] Stomach.
[12] The essay "The Hidden Self," which appeared

in *Scribner's,* March 1890, discusses the state of consciousness experienced in hysterics.

moral power *pauses,* as it were for a moment, and refuses to maintain muscular sanity, worn out with the strain of its constabulary functions. As I used to sit immovable reading in the library with waves of violent inclination suddenly invading my muscles taking some one of their myriad forms such as throwing myself out of the window, or knocking off the head of the benignant pater as he sat with his silver locks, writing at his table, it used to seem to me that the only difference between me and the insane was that I had not only all the horrors and suffering of insanity but the duties of doctor, nurse, and strait-jacket imposed upon me, too. Conceive of never being without the sense that if you let yourself go for a moment your mechanism will fall into pie and that at some given moment you must abandon it all, let the dykes break and the flood sweep in, acknowledging yourself abjectly impotent before the immutable laws. When all one's moral and natural stock in trade is a temperament forbidding the abandonment of an inch or the relaxation of a muscle, 'tis a never-ending fight. When the fancy took me of a morning at school to *study* my lessons by way of variety instead of shirking or wiggling thro' the most impossible sensations of upheaval, violent revolt in my head overtook me so that I had to "abandon" my brain, as it were. So it has always been, anything that sticks of itself is free to do so, but conscious and continuous cerebration is an impossible exercise and from just behind the eyes my head feels like a dense jungle into which no ray of light has ever penetrated. So, with the rest, you abandon the pit of your stomach, the palms of your hands, the soles of your feet, and refuse to keep them sane when you find in turn one moral impression after another producing despair in the one, terror in the other, anxiety in the third and so on until life becomes one long flight from remote suggestion and complicated eluding of the multifold traps set for your undoing.

[May 31, 1891]

May 31st

To him who waits, all things come! My aspirations may have been eccentric, but I cannot complain now, that they have not been brilliantly fulfilled. Ever since I have been ill, I have longed and longed for some palpable disease, no matter how conventionally dreadful a label it might have, but I was always driven back to stagger alone under the monstrous mass of subjective sensations, which that sympathetic being "the medical man" had no higher inspiration than to assure me I was personally responsible for, washing his hands of me with a graceful complacency under my very nose. Dr. Torry[13] was the only man who ever treated me like a rational being, who did not assume, because I was victim to many pains, that I was, of necessity, an arrested mental development too.

Notwithstanding all the happiness and comfort here, I have been going downhill at a steady trot; so they sent for Sir Andrew Clark four days ago, and the blessed being has endowed me not only with cardiac complications, but says that a lump that I have had in one of my breasts for three months, which has given me a great deal of pain, is a tumour, that nothing can be done for me but to alleviate pain, that it is only a question of time, etc. This with a delicate embroidery of "the most distressing case

[13] Dr. John Cooper Torry, like Sir Andrew Clark mentioned below, was a distinguished London physician consulted by Alice James.

of nervous hyperæsthesia" added to a spinal neurosis that has taken me off my legs for seven years; with attacks of rheumatic gout in my stomach for the last twenty, ought to satisfy the most inflated pathologic vanity. It is decidedly indecent to catalogue oneself in this way, but I put it down in a scientific spirit, to show that though I have no productive worth, I have a certain value as an indestructible quantity.

[June 1, 1891]

June 1st

To any one who has not been there, it will be hard to understand the enormous relief of Sir A.C.'s uncompromising verdict, lifting us out the formless vague and setting us within the very heart of the sustaining concrete. One would naturally not choose such an ugly and gruesome method of progression down the dark Valley of the Shadow of Death, and of course many of the moral sinews will snap by the way, but we shall gird up our loins and the blessed peace of the end will have no shadow cast upon it.

Having it to look forward to for a while seems to double the value of the event, for one becomes suddenly picturesque to oneself, and one's wavering little individuality stands out with a cameo effect and one has the tenderest indulgence for all the abortive little *stretchings out* which crowd in upon the memory. The grief is all for K. and H.,[14] who will *see* it all, whilst I shall only *feel* it, but they are taking it, of course, like archangels, and care for me with infinite tenderness and patience. Poor dear William with his exaggerated sympathy for suffering isn't to know anything about it until it is all over.[15]

[February 2, 1892]

February 2nd

This long slow dying is no doubt instructive, but it is disappointingly free from excitements: "naturalness" being carried to its supreme expression. One sloughs off the activities one by one, and never knows that they're gone, until one suddenly finds that the months have slipped away and the sofa will never more be laid upon, the morning paper read, or the loss of the new book regretted; one revolves with equal content within the narrowing circle until the vanishing point is reached, I suppose.

Vanity, however, maintains its undisputed sway, and I take satisfaction in feeling as much myself as ever, perhaps simply a more concentrated essence in this curtailment. If I could concern myself about the fate of my soul, it would give doubtless a savor of uncertainty to the fleeting moments, but I never felt so absolutely uninterested in the poor, shabby, old thing. The fact is, I have been dead so long and it has been simply such a grim shoving of the hours behind me as I faced a ceaseless possible horror, since that hideous summer of '78, when I went down to the deep sea, its dark waters closed over me and I knew neither hope nor peace; that now it's only the shrivelling of an empty pea pod that has to be completed.

---

[14] Katharine Loring, Alice's constant companion, and Henry James, her favorite brother.

[15] William James was told, however, of Alice's condition and visited her that autumn.

A little while ago we had rather an amusing episode with the kind and usually understanding Tuckey,[16] who was led away into assuring me that I should live a good bit still—I was terribly shocked and when he saw the havoc that he wrought, he reassuringly said: "but you'll be comfortable, too," at which I exclaimed: "Oh I don't care about that, but boo-hoo, it's so *inconvenient!*" and the poor man burst into a roar of laughter. I was glad afterwards that it happened, as I was taken quite by surprise, and was able to test the sincerity of my mortuary inclinations. I have always *thought* that I wanted to die, but I felt quite uncertain as to what my muscular demonstrations might be at the moment of transition, for I occasionally have a quiver as of an expected dentistical wrench when I fancy the actual moment. But my substance seemed equally outraged with my mind at Tuckey's dictum, so mayhap I shall be able to maintain a calm befitting so sublimated a spirit!—at any rate there is no humbuggy "strength of mind" about it, 'tis simply physical debility, 'twould be such a bore to be perturbed.

[March 4, 1892]

March 4th

I am being ground slowly on the grim grindstone of physical pain, and on two nights I had almost asked for K.'s lethal dose, but one steps hesitantly along such unaccustomed ways and endures from second to second; and I feel sure that it can't be possible but what the bewildered little hammer that keeps me going will very shortly see the decency of ending his distracted career; however this may be, physical pain however great ends in itself and falls away like dry husks from the mind, whilst moral discords and nervous horrors sear the soul. These last, Katharine has completely under the control of her rhythmic hand, so I go no longer in dread. Oh the wonderful moment when I felt myself floated for the first time into the deep sea of divine *cessation,* and saw all the dear old mysteries and miracles vanish into vapour! That first experience doesn't repeat itself, fortunately, for it might become a seduction.

Katharine can't help it, she's made that way, a simple embodiment of Health, as Baldwin called her, "the New England Professor of doing things."

Final Entry by Katharine P. Loring

All through Saturday the 5th and even in the night, Alice was making sentences. One of the last things she said to me was to make a correction in the sentence of March 4th "moral discords and nervous horrors."

This dictation of March 4th was rushing about in her brain all day, and although she was very weak and it tired her much to dictate, she could not get her head quiet until she had had it written: then she was relieved and I finished Miss Woolson's[17] story of "Dorothy" to her.

1889–1892/1934

K.P.L.

[16] Dr. Charles Lloyd Tuckey, the English physician who had suggested hypnosis as a possible aid for Alice's nervous symptoms. As her cancer pains increased, she found that this treatment helped soothe her.

[17] Constance Fenimore Woolson (1840–1894), American author and friend of Henry James.

George Washington Cable
1844–1925

George Washington Cable faced three sets of angry readers of his writings about Louisiana life and racial conditions in the post–Civil War South. The first were the Creoles among whom he had grown up. These descendants of early French and Spanish settlers in and around New Orleans came to feel that Cable had exposed their distinctive speech patterns and folkways to the derision of the "Yankees up North" who had taken to Cable's stories at their first appearance in the 1870s. Moreover, once Cable started to shift from writing fiction to lecturing and writing on such reform issues as the treatment of blacks in the Reconstruction era, other southerners turned against him as a renegade from their ideals. Still a third group was offended by Cable's narratives. Cable was an earnest, austerely pious man descended from both Virginian and New England stock, but his stories struck conventional magazine editors as unsavory; racial miscegenation and physical passion were considered unfit topics for audiences who preferred romantic love stories with "decent" endings. Despite these objections to his writings, Cable made his name in the literary world by the mid-1880s.

The way up had been a struggle for him from the start. At the age of fourteen Cable worked as a clerk in his native New Orleans to help support his family after the death of his father. Cable next served in the Confederate army during the Civil War and was twice wounded in action. After the war he made his living as a newspaperman, surveyor, and bookkeeper for a cotton broker. He wandered the back streets of New Orleans during his free time and began to accumulate materials about Creole life, which he first presented as sketches in one of the local newspapers. Cable gained national recognition when *Scribner's Monthly* published " 'Sieur George" in 1873. Throughout the 1870s Cable published many more tales of old New Orleans. Among them were "Belles Demoiselles Plantation," collected in *Old Creole Days* in 1879. His first and most important novel, *The Grandissimes,* published the next year, introduced Creole life to the reading public. *Madame Delphine* and *Dr. Sevier* followed in 1881 and 1884. All his novels and tales depict the romantic yet troubled lives and colorful, complex customs of the Creoles, who exist suspended between white and half-caste cultures. By this time Cable had achieved enough popular attention to be able to devote himself full-time to his writing, but he had also begun to rile many who objected to his pictures of social decadence, racial injustice, and moral murkiness. Cable took his family north to escape the hostility he faced daily in the South.

Settling in Northampton, Massachusetts, Cable devoted even more of his energies to social critiques, among them *The Silent South* (1885), *The Negro Question* (1892), and *John March, Southerner* (1894). Isolated from his origins and increasingly subservient to the demands for "niceness" imposed by editors and readers, Cable lived on well past the peak of his literary powers. Still, he left a legacy later extended by such major twentieth-century southern writers as William Faulkner, Thomas Wolfe, and Flannery O'Connor. These writers, as had

Cable, would present a complex mixture of melodrama and regional realism, ornate artificiality and stark verisimilitude that captures both the glamorous surface and violent underside of a southern culture where the relations between past and present, blacks and whites compound the fundamental issues of all American life.

Further Reading:

L. Bikle, *George W. Cable: His Life and Letters,* 1928.

G. Pugh, *George Washington Cable, a Biographical and Critical Study,* 1947.

K. Ekström, *George W. Cable: A Study of His Early Life and Works,* 1950.

C. P. Butcher, *George W. Cable as a Social Critic, 1887–1907,* 1956.

A. Turner, *George W. Cable: A Biography,* 1956.

P. Butcher, *George W. Cable: The Northampton Years,* 1959.

A. Turner, *Mark Twain and George Washington Cable,* 1960.

P. Butcher, *George W. Cable,* 1962.

L. D. Rubin, *George W. Cable,* 1969.

Critical Essays on George W. Cable, ed. A. Turner, 1980.

Text:

Old Creole Days, Part 1, 1879.

See also *Creoles and Cajuns: Stories of Old Louisiana,* ed. A. Turner, 1959.

A Southerner Looks at Negro Discrimination, ed. I. Manes, 1946.

Belles Demoiselles Plantation

The original grantee was Count ———, assume the name to be De Charleu; the old Creoles[1] never forgive a public mention. He was the French king's commissary. One day, called to France to explain the lucky accident of the commissariat having burned down with his account-books inside, he left his wife, a Choctaw Comptesse, behind.

Arrived at court, his excuses were accepted, and that tract granted him where afterwards stood Belles Demoiselles[2] Plantation. A man cannot remember every thing! In a fit of forgetfulness he married a French gentlewoman, rich and beautiful, and "brought her out."[3] However, "All's well that ends well;" a famine had been in the colony, and the Choctaw Comptesse had starved, leaving nought but a half-caste orphan family lurking on the edge of the settlement, bearing our French gentlewoman's own new name, and being mentioned in Monsieur's will.

And the new Comptesse—she tarried but a twelve-month, left Monsieur a lovely son, and departed, led out of this vain world by the swamp-fever.

From this son sprang the proud Creole family of De Charleu. It rose straight up, up, up, generation after generation, tall, branchless, slender, palm-like; and finally, in the time of which I am to tell, flowered with all the rare beauty of a century-plant, in Artemise, Innocente, Felicité, the twins Marie and Martha; Leontine and little

[1] Descendants of the original French and Spanish settlers of Louisiana and New Orleans.

[2] French: "Beautiful young ladies."

[3] Brought her across the Atlantic to America.

Septima; the seven beautiful daughters for whom their home had been fitly named
Belles Demoiselles.

The Count's grant had once been a long Pointe,[4] round which the Mississippi used
to whirl, and seethe, and foam, that it was horrid to behold. Big whirlpools would
open and wheel about in the savage eddies under the low bank, and close up again,
and others open, and spin, and disappear. Great circles of muddy surface would boil
up from hundreds of feet below, and gloss over, and seem to float away,—sink, come
back again under water, and with only a soft hiss surge up again, and again drift off,
and vanish. Every few minutes the loamy bank would tip down a great load of earth
upon its besieger, and fall back a foot,—sometimes a yard,—and the writhing river
would press after, until at last the Pointe was quite swallowed up, and the great river
glided by in a majestic curve, and asked no more; the bank stood fast, the "caving"
became a forgotten misfortune, and the diminished grant was a long, sweeping,
willowy bend, rustling with miles of sugar-cane.

Coming up the Mississippi in the sailing craft of those early days,[5] about the time
one first could descry the white spires of the old St. Louis Cathedral,[5] you would be
pretty sure to spy, just over to your right under the levee,[6] Belles Demoiselles
Mansion, with its broad veranda and red painted cypress roof, peering over the
embankment, like a bird in the nest, half hid by the avenue of willows which one
of the departed De Charleus,—he that married a Marot,—had planted on the levee's
crown.

The house stood unusually near the river, facing eastward, and standing four-
square, with an immense veranda about its sides, and a flight of steps in front spreading
broadly downward, as we open arms to a child. From the veranda nine miles of river
were seen; and in their compass, near at hand, the shady garden full of rare and
beautiful flowers; farther away broad fields of cane and rice, and the distant quarters
of the slaves, and on the horizon everywhere a dark belt of cypress forest.

The master was old Colonel De Charleu,—Jean Albert Henri Joseph De Charleu-
Marot, and "Colonel" by the grace of the first American governor.[7] Monsieur,—he
would not speak to any one who called him "Colonel,"—was a hoary-headed
patriarch. His step was firm, his form erect, his intellect strong and clear, his countenance classic, serene, dignified, commanding, his manners courtly, his voice musical,
—fascinating. He had had his vices,—all his life; but had borne them, as his race do,
with a serenity of conscience and a cleanness of mouth that left no outward blemish
on the surface of the gentleman. He had gambled in Royal Street,[8] drunk hard in
Orleans Street, run his adversary through in the duelling-ground at Slaughter-house
Point,[9] and danced and quarrelled at the St. Philippe-street-theatre quadroon balls.[10]
Even now, with all his courtesy and bounty, and a hospitality which seemed to be

---

[4] Pointed strip of land.
[5] Located in the heart of New Orleans.
[6] Riverside embankment raised to keep flood
waters from overflowing.
[7] Honorary title that would have been granted
after 1806, the year the United States took
control of the Louisiana Territory upon its
purchase from France.

[8] The gambling district of the city.
[9] The site of many duels during the early years
of the nineteenth century.
[10] Balls attended by upper-class white males and
beautiful young women who were one-quarter
black.

entertaining angels, he was bitter-proud and penurious, and deep down in his hard-finished heart loved nothing but himself, his name, and his motherless children. But these!—their ravishing beauty was all but excuse enough for the unbounded idolatry of their father. Against these seven goddesses he never rebelled. Had they even required him to defraud old De Carlos—

I can hardly say.

Old De Carlos was his extremely distant relative on the Choctaw side. With this single exception, the narrow thread-like line of descent from the Indian wife, diminished to a mere strand by injudicious alliances, and deaths in the gutters of old New Orleans, was extinct. The name, by Spanish contact, had become De Carlos; but this one surviving bearer of it was known to all, and known only, as Injin Charlie.

One thing I never knew a Creole to do. He will not utterly go back on the ties of blood, no matter what sort of knots those ties may be. For one reason, he is never ashamed of his or his father's sins; and for another,—he will tell you—he is "all heart!"

So the different heirs of the De Charleu estate had always strictly regarded the rights and interests of the De Carloses, especially their ownership of a block of dilapidated buildings in a part of the city, which had once been very poor property, but was beginning to be valuable. This block had much more than maintained the last De Carlos through a long and lazy lifetime, and, as his household consisted only of himself, and an aged and crippled negress, the inference was irresistible that he "had money." Old Charlie, though by *alias* an "Injin," was plainly a dark white man, about as old as Colonel De Charleu, sunk in the bliss of deep ignorance, shrewd, deaf, and, by repute at least, unmerciful.

The Colonel and he always conversed in English. This rare accomplishment, which the former had learned from his Scotch wife,—the latter from upriver traders,—they found an admirable medium of communication, answering, better than French could, a similar purpose to that of the stick which we fasten to the bit of one horse and breast-gear of another, whereby each keeps his distance. Once in a while, too, by way of jest, English found its way among the ladies of Belles Demoiselles, always signifying that their sire was about to have business with old Charlie.

Now a long-standing wish to buy out Charlie troubled the Colonel. He had no desire to oust him unfairly; he was proud of being always fair; yet he did long to engross the whole estate under one title. Out of his luxurious idleness he had conceived this desire, and thought little of so slight an obstacle as being already somewhat in debt to old Charlie for money borrowed, and for which Belles Demoiselles was, of course, good, ten times over. Lots, buildings, rents, all, might as well be his, he thought, to give, keep, or destroy. "Had he but the old man's heritage. Ah! he might bring that into existence which his *belles demoiselles* had been begging for, 'since many years;' a home,—and such a home,—in the gay city. Here he should tear down this row of cottages, and make his garden wall; there that long rope-walk[11] should give place to vine-covered arbors; the bakery yonder should make way for a costly conservatory; that wine warehouse should come down, and the mansion go up. It should be the finest in the State. Men should never pass it, but they should say—'the

[11] Building for the twisting of fibers into rope.

palace of the De Charleus; a family of grand descent, a people of elegance and bounty, a line as old as France, a fine old man, and seven daughters as beautiful as happy; whoever dare attempt to marry there must leave his own name behind him!'

"The house should be of stones fitly set, brought down in ships from the land of 'les Yankees,' and it should have an airy belvedere, with a gilded image tip-toeing and shining on its peak, and from it you should see, far across the gleaming folds of the river, the red roof of Belles Demoiselles, the country-seat. At the big stone gate there should be a porter's lodge, and it should be a privilege even to see the ground."

Truly they were a family fine enough, and fancy-free enough to have fine wishes, yet happy enough where they were, to have had no wish but to live there always.

To those, who, by whatever fortune, wandered into the garden of Belles Demoiselles some summer afternoon as the sky was reddening towards evening, it was lovely to see the family gathered out upon the tiled pavement at the foot of the broad front steps, gayly chatting and jesting, with that ripple of laughter that comes so pleasingly from a bevy of girls. The father would be found seated in their midst, the centre of attention and compliment, witness, arbiter, umpire, critic, by his beautiful children's unanimous appointment, but the single vassal, too, of seven absolute sovereigns.

Now they would draw their chairs near together in eager discussion of some new step in the dance, or the adjustment of some rich adornment. Now they would start about him with excited comments to see the eldest fix a bunch of violets in his button-hole. Now the twins would move down a walk after some unusual flower, and be greeted on their return with the high pitched notes of delighted feminine surprise.

As evening came on they would draw more quietly about their paternal centre. Often their chairs were forsaken, and they grouped themselves on the lower steps, one above another, and surrendered themselves to the tender influences of the approaching night. At such an hour the passer on the river, already attracted by the dark figures of the broad-roofed mansion, and its woody garden standing against the glowing sunset, would hear the voices of the hidden group rise from the spot in the soft harmonies of an evening song; swelling clearer and clearer as the thrill of music warmed them into feeling, and presently joined by the deeper tones of the father's voice; then, as the daylight passed quite away, all would be still, and he would know that the beautiful home had gathered its nestlings under its wings.

And yet, for mere vagary, it pleased them not to be pleased.

"Arti!" called one sister to another in the broad hall, one morning,—mock amazement in her distended eyes,—"something is goin' to took place!"

"*Comm-e-n-t?*"[12]—long-drawn perplexity.

"Papa is goin' to town!"

The news passed up stairs.

"Inno!"—one to another meeting in a doorway,—"something is goin' to took place!"

"*Qu'est-ce-que c'est!*"[13]—vain attempt at gruffness.

"Papa is goin' to town!"

The unusual tidings were true. It was afternoon of the same day that the Colonel tossed his horse's bridle to his groom, and stepped up to old Charlie, who was sitting

---

[12] French: "What?"   [13] French: "What is it?"

on his bench under a China-tree, his head as was his fashion, bound in a Madras handkerchief. The "old man" was plainly under the effect of spirits and smiled a deferential salutation without trusting himself to his feet.

"Eh, well Charlie!"—the Colonel raised his voice to suit his kinsman's deafness, —"how is those times with my friend Charlie?"

"Eh?" said Charlie, distractedly.

"Is that goin' well with my friend Charlie?"

"In de house,—call her,"—making a pretence of rising.

"Non, non! I don't want,"—the speaker paused to breathe—"ow is collection?"

"Oh!" said Charlie, "every day he make me more poorer!"

"What do you hask for it?" asked the planter indifferently, designating the house by a wave of his whip.

"Ask for w'at?" said Injin Charlie.

"De *house!* What you ask for it?"

"I don't believe," said Charlie.

"What you would *take* for it!" cried the planter.

"Wait for w'at?"

"What you would *take* for the whole block?"

"I don't want to sell him!"

"I'll give you *ten thousand dollah* for it."

"Ten t'ousand dollah for dis house? Oh, no, dat is no price. He is blame good old house,—dat old house." (Old Charlie and the Colonel never swore in presence of each other.) "Forty years dat old house didn't had to be paint! I easy can get fifty t'ousand dollah for dat old house."

"Fifty thousand picayunes; yes," said the Colonel.

"She's a good house. Can make plenty money," pursued the deaf man.

"That's what make you so rich, eh, Charlie?"

"Non, I don't make nothing. Too blame clever, me, dat's de troub'. She's a good house,—make money fast like a steamboat,—make a barrel full in a week! Me, I lose money all de days. Too blame clever."

"Charlie!"

"Eh?"

"Tell me what you'll take."

"Make? I don't make *nothing.* Too blame clever."

"What will you *take?*"

"Oh! I got enough already,—half drunk now."

"What will you take for the 'ouse?"

"You want to buy her?"

"I don't know,"—(shrug),—"may*be,*—if you sell it cheap."

"She's a bully old house."

There was a long silence. By and by old Charlie commenced—

"Old Injin Charlie is a low-down dog."

"C'est vrai, oui!"[14] retorted the Colonel in an undertone.

"He's got Injin blood in him."

The Colonel nodded assent.

---

[14] French: "Yes, that's so!"

"But he's got blame good blood, too, ain't it?"

The Colonel nodded impatiently.

"*Bien!*[15] Old Charlie's Injin blood says, 'sell de house, Charlie, you blame old fool!' *Mais,*[16] old Charlie's good blood says, 'Charlie! if you sell dat old house, Charlie, you low-down old dog, Charlie, what de Compte De Charleu make for you grace-gran'-muzzer, de dev' can eat you, Charlie, I don't care.'"

"But you'll sell it anyhow, won't you, old man?"

"No!" And the *no* rumbled off in muttered oaths like thunder out on the Gulf. The incensed old Colonel wheeled and started off.

"Curl!" (Colonel) said Charlie, standing up unsteadily.

The planter turned with an inquiring frown.

"I'll trade with you!" said Charlie.

The Colonel was tempted. "'Ow'l you trade?" he asked.

"My house for yours!"

The old Colonel turned pale with anger. He walked very quickly back, and came close up to his kinsman.

"Charlie!" he said.

"Injin Charlie,"—with a tipsy nod.

But by this time self-control was returning. "Sell Belles Demoiselles to you?" he said in a high key, and then laughed "Ho, ho, ho!" and rode away.

A cloud, but not a dark one, overshadowed the spirits of Belles Demoiselles' plantation. The old master, whose beaming presence had always made him a shining Saturn, spinning and sparkling within the bright circle of his daughters, fell into musing fits, started out of frowning reveries, walked often by himself, and heard business from his overseer fretfully.

No wonder. The daughters knew his closeness in trade, and attributed to it his failure to negotiate for the Old Charlie buildings,—so to call them. They began to depreciate Belles Demoiselles. If a north wind blew, it was too cold to ride. If a shower had fallen, it was too muddy to drive. In the morning the garden was wet. In the evening the grasshopper was a burden. *Ennui* was turned into capital; every headache was interpreted a premonition of ague; and when the native exuberance of a flock of ladies without a want or a care burst out in laughter in the father's face, they spread their French eyes, rolled up their little hands, and with rigid wrists and mock vehemence vowed and vowed again that they only laughed at their misery, and should pine to death unless they could move to the sweet city. "Oh! the theatre! Oh! Orleans Street! Oh! the masquerade! the Place d'Armes! the ball!" and they would call upon Heaven with French irreverence, and fall into each other's arms, and whirl down the hall singing a waltz, end with a grand collision and fall, and, their eyes streaming merriment, lay the blame on the slippery floor, that would some day be the death of the whole seven.

Three times more the fond father, thus goaded, managed, by accident,—business accident,—to see old Charlie and increase his offer; but in vain. He finally went to him formally.

"Eh?" said the deaf and distant relative. "For what you want him, eh? Why you don't stay where you halways be 'appy? Dis is a blame old rat-hole,—good for old Injin Charlie,—da's all. Why you don't stay where you be halways 'appy? Why you don't buy somewheres else?"

"That's none of your business," snapped the planter. Truth was, his reasons were unsatisfactory even to himself.

A sullen silence followed. Then Charlie spoke:

"Well, now, look here; I sell you old Charlie's house."

"*Bien!*[17] and the whole block," said the Colonel.

"Hold on," said Charlie. "I sell you de 'ouse and de block. Den I go and git drunk, and go to sleep; de dev' comes along and says, 'Charlie! old Charlie, you blame low-down old dog, wake up! What you doin' here? Where's de 'ouse what Monsieur le Compte give your grace-gran-muzzer? Don't you see dat fine gentyman, De Charleu, done gone and tore him down and make him over new, you blame old fool, Charlie, you low-down old Injin dog!' "

"I'll give you forty thousand dollars," said the Colonel.

"For de 'ouse?"

"For all."

The deaf man shook his head.

"Forty-five!" said the Colonel.

"What a lie? For what you tell me 'What a lie?' I don't tell you no lie."

"*Non, non!* I give you *forty-five!*" shouted the Colonel.

Charlie shook his head again.

"Fifty!"

He shook it again.

The figures rose and rose to—

"Seventy-five!"

The answer was an invitation to go away and let the owner alone, as he was, in certain specified respects, the vilest of living creatures, and no company for a fine gentyman.

The "fine gentyman" longed to blaspheme,—but before old Charlie!—in the name of pride, how could he? He mounted and started away.

"Tell you what I'll make wid you," said Charlie.

The other, guessing aright, turned back without dismounting, smiling.

"How much Belles Demoiselles hoes me now? asked the deaf one.

"One hundred and eighty thousand dollars," said the Colonel, firmly.

"Yass," said Charlie. "I don't want Belles Demoiselles."

The old Colonel's quiet laugh intimated it made no difference either way.

"But me," continued Charlie, "me,—I'm got le Compte De Charleu's blood in me, any'ow,—a litt' bit, any'ow, ain't it?"

The Colonel nodded that it was.

"*Bien!* If I go out of dis place and don't go to Belles Demoiselles, de peoples will say,—dey will say, 'Old Charlie he been all doze time tell a blame *lie!* He ain't no kin to his old grace-gran-muzzer, not a blame bit! He don't got nary drop of De Charleu blood to save his blame low-down old Injin soul!' No, sare! What I want wid money, den? No, sare! My place for yours!"

[17] French: "Good!"

He turned to go into the house, just too soon to see the Colonel make an ugly whisk at him with his riding-whip. Then the Colonel, too, moved off.

Two or three times over, as he ambled homeward, laughter broke through his annoyance, as he recalled old Charlie's family pride and the presumption of his offer. Yet each time he could but think better of—not the offer to swap, but the preposterous ancestral loyalty. It was so much better than he could have expected from his "low-down" relative, and not unlike his own whim withal—the proposition which went with it was forgiven.

This last defeat bore so harshly on the master of Belles Demoiselles, that the daughters, reading chagrin in his face, began to repent. They loved their father as daughters can, and when they saw their pretended dejection harassing him seriously they restrained their complaints, displayed more than ordinary tenderness, and heroically and ostentatiously concluded there was no place like Belles Demoiselles. But the new mood touched him more than the old, and only refined his discontent. Here was a man, rich without the care of riches, free from any real trouble, happiness as native to his house as perfume to his garden, deliberately, as it were with premeditated malice, taking joy by the shoulder and bidding her be gone to town, whither he might easily have followed, only that the very same ancestral nonsense that kept Injin Charlie from selling the old place for twice its value prevented him from choosing any other spot for a city home.

But by and by the charm of nature and the merry hearts around him prevailed; the fit of exalted sulks passed off, and after a while the year flared up at Christmas, flickered, and went out.

New Year came and passed; the beautiful garden of Belles Demoiselles put on its spring attire; the seven fair sisters moved from rose to rose; the cloud of discontent had warmed into invisible vapor in the rich sunlight of family affection, and on the common memory the only scar of last year's wound was old Charlie's sheer impertinence in crossing the caprice of the De Charleus. The cup of gladness seemed to fill with the filling of the river.

How high that river was! Its tremendous current rolled and tumbled and spun along, hustling the long funeral flotillas of drift,—and how near shore it came! Men were out day and night, watching the levee. On windy nights even the old Colonel took part, and grew light-hearted with occupation and excitement, as every minute the river threw a white arm over the levee's top, as though it would vault over. But all held fast, and, as the summer drifted in, the water sunk down into its banks and looked quite incapable of harm.

On a summer afternoon of uncommon mildness, old Colonel Jean Albert Henri Joseph De Charleu-Marot, being in a mood for revery, slipped the custody of his feminine rulers and sought the crown of the levee, where it was his wont to promenade. Presently he sat upon a stone bench,—a favorite seat. Before him lay his broad-spread fields; near by, his lordly mansion; and being still,—perhaps by female contact,—somewhat sentimental, he fell to musing on his past. It was hardly worthy to be proud of. All its morning was reddened with mad frolic, and far toward the meridian it was marred with elegant rioting. Pride had kept him well-nigh useless, and despised the honors won by valor; gaming had dimmed prosperity; death had taken his heavenly wife; voluptuous ease had mortgaged his lands; and yet his house still stood, his sweet-smelling fields were still fruitful, his name was fame enough; and yonder and yonder, among the trees and flowers, like angels walking in Eden, were the seven goddesses of his only worship.

Just then a slight sound behind him brought him to his feet. He cast his eyes anxiously to the outer edge of the little strip of bank between the levee's base and the river. There was nothing visible. He paused, with his ear toward the water, his face full of frightened expectation. Ha! There came a single plashing sound, like some great beast slipping into the river, and little waves in a wide semi-circle came out from under the bank and spread over the water!

"My God!"

He plunged down the levee and bounded through the low weeds to the edge of the bank. It was sheer, and the water about four feet below. He did not stand quite on the edge, but fell upon his knees a couple of yards away, wringing his hands, moaning and weeping, and staring through his watery eyes at a fine, long crevice just discernible under the matted grass, and curving outward on either hand toward the river.

"My God!" he sobbed aloud; "my God!" and even while he called, his God answered: the tough Bermuda grass stretched and snapped, the crevice slowly became a gape, and softly, gradually, with no sound but the closing of the water at last, a ton or more of earth settled into the boiling eddy and disappeared.

At the same instant a pulse of the breeze brought from the garden behind, the joyous, thoughtless laughter of the fair mistresses of Belles Demoiselles.

The old Colonel sprang up and clambered over the levee. Then forcing himself to a more composed movement, he hastened into the house and ordered his horse.

"Tell my children to make merry while I am gone," he left word. "I shall be back to-night," and the horse's hoofs clattered down a by-road leading to the city.

"Charlie," said the planter, riding up to a window, from which the old man's nightcap was thrust out, "what you say, Charlie,—my house for yours, eh, Charlie —what you say?"

"Ello!" said Charlie; "from where you come from dis time of to-night?"

"I come from the Exchange[18] in St. Louis Street." (A small fraction of the truth.)

"What you want?" said matter-of-fact Charlie.

"I come to trade."

The low-down relative drew the worsted[19] off his ears. "Oh! yass," he said with an uncertain air.

"Well, old man Charlie, what you say: my house for yours,—like you said,—eh, Charlie?"

"I dunno," said Charlie; "it's nearly mine now. Why you don't stay dare yourse'f?"

"*Because I don't want!*" said the Colonel savagely.

"Is dat reason enough for you? You better take me in de notion, old man, I tell you,—yes!"

Charlie never winced; but how his answer delighted the Colonel! Quoth Charlie: "I don't care—I take him!—*mais,* possession give right off."

"Not the whole plantation, Charlie; only"—

"I don't care," said Charlie; "we easy can fix dat. *Mais,* what for you don't want to keep him? I don't want him. You better keep him."

---

[18] A tavern.   [19] Nightcap of wool.

"Don't you try to make no fool of me, old man," cried the planter.

"Oh, no!" said the other. "Oh, no! but you make a fool of yourself, ain't it?" The dumbfounded Colonel stared; Charlie went on:

"Yass! Belles Demoiselles is more wort' dan tree block like dis one. I pass by dare since two weeks. Oh, pritty Belles Demoiselles! De cane was wave in de wind, de garden smell like a bouquet, de white-cap was jump up and down on de river; seven *belles demoiselles* was ridin' on horses. 'Pritty, pritty, pritty!' says old Charlie. Ah! *Monsieur le père,* 'ow 'appy, 'appy, 'appy!'"

"Yass!" he continued—the Colonel still staring—"le Compte De Charleu have two familie. One was low-down Choctaw, one was high up *noblesse.* He gave the low-down Choctaw dis old rat-hole; he give Belles Demoiselles to you gran-fozzer; and now you don't be *satisfait.* What I'll do wid Belles Demoiselles? She'll break me in two years, yass. And what you'll do wid old Charlie's house, eh? You'll tear her down and make you'se'f a blame old fool. I rather wouldn't trade!"

The planter caught a big breathful of anger, but Charlie went straight on:

"I rather wouldn't, *mais* I will do it for you;—just the same, like Monsieur le Compte would say, 'Charlie, you old fool, I want to shange houses wid you.'"

So long as the Colonel suspected irony he was angry, but as Charlie seemed, after all, to be certainly in earnest, he began to feel conscience-stricken. He was by no means a tender man, but his lately-discovered misfortune had unhinged him, and this strange, undeserved, disinterested family fealty on the part of Charlie touched his heart. And should he still try to lead him into the pitfall he had dug? He hesitated;—no, he would show him the place by broad daylight, and if he chose to overlook the "caving bank," it would be his own fault;—a trade's a trade.

"Come," said the planter, "come at my house to-night; to-morrow we look at the place before breakfast, and finish the trade."

"For what?" said Charlie.

"Oh, because I got to come in town in the morning."

"I don't want," said Charlie. "How I'm goin' to come dere?"

"I git you a horse at the liberty stable."

"Well—anyhow—I don't care—I'll go." And they went.

When they had ridden a long time, and were on the road darkened by hedges of Cherokee rose, the Colonel called behind him to the "low-down" scion:

"Keep the road, old man."

"Eh?"

"Keep the road."

"Oh, yes; all right; I keep my word; we don't goin' to play no tricks, eh?"

But the Colonel seemed not to hear. His ungenerous design was beginning to be hateful to him. Not only old Charlie's unprovoked goodness was prevailing; the eulogy on Belles Demoiselles had stirred the depths of an intense love for his beautiful home. True, if he held to it, the caving of the bank, at its present fearful speed, would let the house into the river within three months; but were it not better to lose it so, than sell his birthright? Again,—coming back to the first thought,—to betray his own blood! It was only Injin Charlie; but had not the De Charleu blood just spoken out in him? Unconsciously he groaned.

After a time they struck a path approaching the plantation in the rear, and a little after, passing from behind a clump of live-oaks, they came in sight of the villa. It looked so like a gem, shining through its dark grove, so like a great glow-worm in the dense foliage, so significant of luxury and gayety, that the poor master, from an overflowing heart, groaned again.

"What?" asked Charlie.

The Colonel only drew his rein, and, dismounting mechanically, contemplated the sight before him. The high, arched doors and windows were thrown wide to the summer air; from every opening the bright light of numerous candelabra darted out upon the sparkling foliage of magnolia and bay, and here and there in the spacious verandas a colored lantern swayed in the gentle breeze. A sound of revel fell on the ear, the music of harps; and across one window, brighter than the rest, flitted, once or twice, the shadows of dancers. But oh! the shadows flitting across the heart of the fair mansion's master!

"Old Charlie," said he, gazing fondly at his house. "You and me is both old, eh?"

"Yaas," said the stolid Charlie.

"And we has both been bad enough in our time, eh, Charlie?"

Charlie, surprised at the tender tone, repeated "Yaas."

"And you and me is mighty close?"

"Blame close, yaas."

"But you never know me to cheat, old man!"

"No,"—impassively.

"And do you think I would cheat you now?"

"I dunno," said Charlie. "I don't believe."

"Well, old man, old man,"—his voice began to quiver,—"I sha'n't cheat you now. My God!—old man, I tell you—you better not make the trade!"

"Because for what?" asked Charlie in plain anger; but both looked quickly toward the house! The Colonel tossed his hands wildly in the air, rushed forward a step or two, and giving one fearful scream of agony and fright, fell forward on his face in the path. Old Charlie stood transfixed with horror. Belles Demoiselles, the realm of maiden beauty, the home of merriment, the house of dancing, all in the tremor and glow of pleasure, suddenly sunk, with one short, wild wail of terror—sunk, sunk, down, down, down, into the merciless, unfathomable flood of the Mississippi.

Twelve long months were midnight to the mind of the childless father; when they were only half gone, he took his bed; and every day, and every night, old Charlie, the "low-down," the "fool," watched him tenderly, tended him lovingly, for the sake of his name, his misfortunes, and his broken heart. No woman's step crossed the floor of the sick-chamber, whose western dormer-windows overpeered the dingy architecture of old Charlie's block; Charlie and a skilled physician, the one all interest, the other all gentleness, hope, and patience—these only entered by the door; but by the window came in a sweet-scented evergreen vine, transplanted from the caving bank of Belles Demoiselles. It caught the rays of sunset in its flowery net and let them softly in upon the sick man's bed; gathered the glancing beams of the moon at midnight, and often wakened the sleeper to look, with his mindless eyes, upon their pretty silver fragments strewn upon the floor.

By and by there seemed—there was—a twinkling dawn of returning reason. Slowly, peacefully, with an increase unseen from day to day, the light of reason came into the eyes, and speech became coherent; but withal there came a failing of the wrecked body, and the doctor said that monsieur was both better and worse.

One evening, as Charlie sat by the vine-clad window with his fireless pipe in his hand, the old Colonel's eyes fell full upon his own, and rested there.

"Charl—," he said with an effort, and his delighted nurse hastened to the bedside and bowed his best ear. There was an unsuccessful effort or two, and then he whispered, smiling with sweet sadness,—

"We didn't trade."

The truth, in this case, was a secondary matter to Charlie; the main point was to give a pleasing answer. So he nodded his head decidedly, as who should say—"Oh yes, we did, it was a bonafide swap!" but when he saw the smile vanish, he tried the other expedient and shook his head with still more vigor, to signify that they had not so much as approached a bargain; and the smile returned.

Charlie wanted to see the vine recognized. He stepped backward to the window with a broad smile, shook the foliage, nodded and looked smart.

"I know," said the Colonel, with beaming eyes,"—many weeks."

The next day—

"Charl—"

The best ear went down.

"Send for a priest."

The priest came, and was alone with him a whole afternoon. When he left, the patient was very haggard and exhausted, but smiled and would not suffer the crucifix to be removed from his breast.

One more morning came. Just before dawn Charlie, lying on a pallet in the room, thought he was called, and came to the bedside.

"Old man," whispered the failing invalid, "is it caving yet?"

Charlie nodded.

"It won't pay you out."

"Oh, dat makes not'ing," said Charlie. Two big tears rolled down his brown face. "Dat makes not'in."

The Colonel whispered once more:

"*Mes belles demoiselles!* in paradise;—in the garden—I shall be with them at sunrise;" and so it was.

1879

Joel Chandler Harris
1848–1908

Well in advance of the twentieth-century development of folklore studies and cultural anthropology as academic disciplines, Joel Chandler Harris gathered the dialect tales he had heard in childhood told by black slaves. He placed them within a narrative context that made them available to a large white audience, sharpening the effects of their regional details and the age-old wisdom by which the enslaved outwit their masters. Because of Harris's accomplishments, American mainstream literature featured a memorable new character, Uncle Remus, as well as a new literary tradition.

Harris was like Mark Twain in this and other ways. Like Twain, Harris was slight of build, red-haired, and a printer's apprentice in boyhood. Like Twain, he grew up with stories he would introduce to Americans who had no direct contact with the rhythms of Negro speech. Harris's unique contribution was to reveal the skills by which unlettered slaves shaped miniature narratives of plantation life.

The way had been hard for Harris as a child in Georgia. His day-laborer father deserted his mother just before his birth. Helped by the local people of Putnam County, the mother and the child made do until young Harris went to work for a newspaper at fourteen. (Harris, Mark Twain, and George Washington Cable started to work at the same age; all three were largely self-taught.) Harris soon contributed humorous pieces to several Georgia papers, and he quickly gained a reputation in the newspaper world. In 1876 he joined the *Atlanta Constitution* in the city that became his permanent home. During this period Harris divided his time between editorial writing (urging southerners to "reconstruct" their habits and to rise above their past) and his dialect tales, which began to appear in print under the guise of Uncle Remus, the old slave.

His first collection of folk poems and proverbs was published in 1881 as *Uncle Remus: His Songs and His Sayings.* Further collections included *Nights with Uncle Remus* (1883), *Uncle Remus and His Friends* (1892), and *Uncle Remus and the Little Boy* (1905). As the titles suggest, relationships are important; they develop between the wide-eyed audience (likened to a little white boy from the main plantation household) and the narrator who acts as "best friend"—whiling away the hours with a seemingly endless supply of tales. The lasting impression of the Remus stories on readers of all ages and from many countries (there were translations into twenty-seven languages) stems from the force of their slave lore.

Genuine in its sources, "The Matter of Uncle Remus" goes back in time to African models, as well as to the animal fables of Aesop and Chaucer. Harris helped inspire other writers in the vernacular through his adroit use of narrative forms, his excellent ear for subtleties of dialect, and his ability to emphasize the universal nature of these classic standoffs between the weak and the powerful.

In addition to the Uncle Remus tales, Harris won recognition for his portrayals of the tragic dislocation felt by blacks in the postwar South, best seen in the stories in *Free Joe and Other Georgian Sketches* (1887). In whatever he did, Harris paid close attention to a body of folk legends that would reappear in different forms in the fiction of William Faulkner and Ralph Ellison.

Further Reading:
R. Wiggins, *The Life of Joel Chandler Harris from Obscurity in Boyhood to Fame in Early Manhood,* 1918.
A. Harlow, *Joel Chandler Harris (Uncle Remus): Plantation Storyteller,* 1941.
S. Brookes, *Joel Chandler Harris, Folklorist,* 1950.
P. Cousins, *Joel Chandler Harris: A Biography,* 1968.
R. B. Bickley, *Joel Chandler Harris,* 1978.
Critical Essays on Joel Chandler Harris, ed. R. B. Bickley, 1981.

Text:
Uncle Remus: His Songs and Sayings, 1899.
See also *The Complete Tales of Uncle Remus,* ed. R. Chase, 1955.
Joel Chandler Harris, Editor and Essayist: Miscellaneous Literary, Political, and Social Writings, ed. J. Harris, 1931.
The Life and Letters of Joel Chandler Harris, 1918, 1973.

from Uncle Remus

His Songs and Sayings

II: The Wonderful Tar-Baby Story

"Didn't the fox *never* catch the rabbit, Uncle Remus?" asked the little boy the next evening.

"He come mighty nigh it, honey, sho's you born—Brer Fox did. One day atter Brer Rabbit fool 'im wid dat calamus root, Brer Fox went ter wuk en got 'im some tar, en mix it wid some turkentime, en fix up a contrapshun wat he call a Tar-Baby, en he tuck dish yer Tar-Baby en he sot 'er in de big road, en den he lay off in de bushes fer to see wat de news wuz gwineter be. En he didn't hatter wait long, nudder, kaze bimeby here come Brer Rabbit pacin' down de road—lippity-clippity, clippity-lippity—dez ez sassy ez a jay-bird. Brer Fox, he lay low. Brer Rabbit come prancin' 'long twel he spy de Tar-Baby, en den he fotch up on his behime legs like he wuz 'stonished. De Tar-Baby, she sot dar, she did, en Brer Fox, he lay low.

" 'Mawnin'!' sez Brer Rabbit, sezee—'nice wedder dis mawnin',' sezee.

"Tar-Baby ain't sayin' nothin', en Brer Fox, he lay low.

" 'How duz yo' sym'tums seem ter segashuate?' sez Brer Rabbit, sezee.

"Brer Fox, he wink his eye slow, en lay low, en de Tar-Baby, she ain't sayin' nothin'.

" 'How you come on, den? Is you deaf?' sez Brer Rabbit, sezee. 'Kaze if you is, I kin holler louder,' sezee.

"Tar-Baby stay still, en Brer Fox, he lay low.

" 'Youer stuck up, dat's w'at you is,' says Brer Rabbit, sezee, 'en I'm gwineter kyore you, dat's w'at I'm a gwineter do,' sezee.

"Brer Fox, he sorter chuckle in his stummuck, he did, but Tar-Baby ain't sayin' nothin'.

" 'I'm gwineter larn you howter talk ter 'spectubble fokes ef hit's de las' ack,' sez Brer Rabbit, sezee. 'Ef you don't take off dat hat en tell me howdy, I'm gwineter bus' you wide open,' sezee.

"Tar-Baby stay still, en Brer Fox, he lay low.

"Brer Rabbit keep on axin' 'im, en de Tar-Baby, she keep on sayin' nothin', twel present'y Brer Rabbit draw back wid his fis', he did, en blip he tuck 'er side er de head. Right dar's whar he broke his merlasses jug. His fis' stuck, en he can't pull loose. De tar hilt 'im. But Tar-Baby, she stay still, en Brer Fox, he lay low.

" 'Ef you don't lemme loose, I'll knock you agin,' sez Brer Rabbit, sezee, en wid dat he fotch 'er a wipe wid de udder han', en dat stuck. Tar-Baby, she ain't sayin' nothin', en Brer Fox, he lay low.

" 'Tu'n me loose, fo' I kick de natal stuffin' outen you,' sez Brer Rabbit, sezee, but de Tar-Baby, she ain't sayin' nothin'. She des hilt on, en den Brer Rabbit lose de use er his feet in de same way. Brer Fox, he lay low. Den Brer Rabbit squall out dat ef de Tar-Baby don't tu'n 'im loose he butt 'er cranksided. En den he butted, en his head got stuck. Den Brer Fox, he sa'ntered fort', lookin' des ez innercent ez one er yo' mammy's mockin'-birds.

" 'Howdy, Brer Rabbit,' sez Brer Fox, sezee. 'You look sorter stuck up dis mawnin',' sezee, en den he rolled on de groun', en laughed en laughed twel he couldn't laugh no mo'. 'I speck you'll take dinner wid me dis time, Brer Rabbit. I done laid in some calamus root, en I ain't gwineter take no skuse,' sez Brer Fox, sezee."

Here Uncle Remus paused, and drew a two-pound yam out of the ashes.

"Did the fox eat the rabbit?" asked the little boy to whom the story had been told.

"Dat's all de fur de tale goes," replied the old man. "He mout, en den agin he moutent. Some say Jedge B'ar come 'long en loosed 'im—some say he didn't. I hear Miss Sally callin'. You better run 'long."

XVIII: Mr. Rabbit Finds His Match at Last

"Hit look like ter me dat I let on de udder night dat in dem days w'en de creeturs wuz santer'n 'roun' same like fokes, none un um wuz brash nuff fer ter ketch up wid Brer Rabbit," remarked Uncle Remus, reflectively.

"Yes," replied the little boy, "that's what you said."

"Well, den," continued the old man with unction, "dar's whar my 'membunce gin out, kaze Brer Rabbit did git kotched up wid, en hit cool 'im off like po'in' spring water on one er deze yer biggity fices."

"How was that, Uncle Remus?" asked the little boy.

"One day w'en Brer Rabbit wuz gwine lippity-clippitin' down de road, he meet up wid ole Brer Tarrypin,[1] en atter dey pass de time er day wid wunner nudder, Brer Rabbit, he 'low dat he wuz much 'blije ter Brer Tarrypin fer de han' he tuck in de rumpus dat day down at Miss Meadows's."

"When he dropped off of the water-shelf on the Fox's head," suggested the little boy.

"Dat's de same time, honey. Den Brer Tarrypin 'low dat Brer Fox run mighty fas' dat day, but dat ef he'd er bin atter 'im stidder Brer Rabbit, he'd er kotch 'im. Brer Rabbit say he could er kotch 'im hisse'f but he didn't keer 'bout leavin' de ladies. Dey keep on talkin', dey did, twel bimeby dey gotter 'sputin' 'bout w'ich wuz de swif'es'. Brer Rabbit, he say he kin outrun Brer Tarrypin, en Brer Tarrypin, he des vow dat he kin outrun Brer Rabbit. Up en down dey had it, twel fus news you know Brer Tarrypin say he got a fifty-dollar bill in de chink er de chimbly at home, en dat bill done tole 'im dat he could beat Brer Rabbit in a fa'r race. Den Brer Rabbit say he got a fifty-dollar bill w'at say dat he kin leave Brer Tarrypin so fur behime, dat he could sow barley ez he went 'long en hit 'ud be ripe nuff fer ter cut by de time Brer Tarrypin pass dat way.

"Enny how dey make de bet en put up de money, en ole Brer Tukky Buzzard, he wuz summonzd fer ter be de jedge, en de stakeholder; en 'twan't long 'fo' all de 'rangements wuz made. De race wuz a five-mile heat, en de groun' wuz medjud off, en at de een' er ev'ey mile a pos' wuz stuck up. Brer Rabbit wuz ter run down de

---

[1] Corruption of *terrapin,* one of a species of American tidewater turtles found near the Atlantic or Gulf coasts.

big road, en Brer Tarrypin, he say he'd gallup thoo de woods. Fokes tole 'im he could git long faster in de road, but ole Brer Tarrypin, he know w'at he doin'. Miss Meadows en de gals en mos' all de nabers got win' er de fun, en w'en de day wuz sot dey 'termin' fer ter be on han'. Brer Rabbit he train hisse'f ev'ey day, en he skip over de groun' des ez gayly ez a June cricket. Ole Brer Tarrypin, he lay low in de swamp. He had a wife en th'ee chilluns, ole Brer Tarrypin did, en dey wuz all de ve'y spit en image er de ole man. Ennybody w'at know one fum de udder gotter take a spy-glass, en den dey er li'ble fer ter git fooled.

"Dat's de way marters stan' twel de day er de race, en on dat day, ole Brer Tarrypin, en his ole 'oman, en his th'ee chilluns, dey got up 'fo' sun-up, en went ter de place. De ole 'oman, she tuck 'er stan' nigh de fus' mile-pos', she did, en de chilluns nigh de udders, up ter de las', en dar old Brer Tarrypin, he tuck his stan'. Bimeby, here come de fokes: Jedge Buzzard, he come, en Miss Meadows en de gals, dey come, en den yer come Brer Rabbit wid ribbins tied 'roun' his neck en streamin' fum his years. De fokes all went ter de udder een' er de track fer ter see how dey come out. W'en de time come Jedge Buzzard strut 'roun' en pull out his watch, en holler out:

" 'Gents, is you ready?'

"Brer Rabbit, he say 'yes,' en ole Miss Tarrypin holler 'go' fum de aidge er de woods. Brer Rabbit, he lit out on de race, en ole Miss Tarrypin, she put out for home. Jedge Buzzard, he riz en skimmed 'long fer ter see dat de race wuz runned fa'r. W'en Brer Rabbit got ter de fus' mile-pos' wunner de Tarrypin chilluns crawl out de woods, he did, en make fer de place. Brer Rabbit, he holler out:

" 'Whar is you, Brer Tarrypin?'

" 'Yer I come a bulgin',' sez de Tarrypin, sezee.

"Brer Rabbit so glad he's ahead dat he put out harder dan ever, en de Tarrypin, he make fer home. W'en he come ter de nex' pos', nudder Tarrypin crawl out er woods.

" 'Whar is you, Brer Tarrypin?' sez Brer Rabbit, sezee.

" 'Yer I come a bilin',' sez de Tarrypin, sezee.

"Brer Rabbit, he lit out, he did, en come ter nex' pos', en dar wuz de Tarrypin. Den he come ter nex', en dar wuz de Tarrypin. Den he had one mo' mile fer ter run, en he feel like he gittin' bellust. Bimeby, ole Brer Tarrypin look way off down de road en he see Jedge Buzzard sailin' 'long en he know hit's time fer 'im fer ter be up. So he scramble outen de woods, en roll 'cross de ditch, en shuffle thoo de crowd er folks en git ter de mile-pos' en crawl behime it. Bimeby, fus' news you know, yer come Brer Rabbit. He look 'roun' en he don't see Brer Tarrypin, en den he squall out:

" 'Gimme de money, Brer Buzzard! Gimme de money!'

"Den Miss Meadows en de gals, dey holler and laff fit ter kill deyse'f, en ole Brer Tarrypin, he raise up fum behime de pos' en sez, sezee:

" 'Ef you'll gimme time fer ter ketch my breff, gents en ladies, one en all, I speck I'll finger dat money myse'f,' sezee, en sho nuff, Brer Tarrypin tie de pu's 'roun' his neck en skaddle[2] off home."

---

[2] Harris's note: "It may be interesting to note here that in all probability the word 'skedaddle,' about which there was some controversy during the war, came from the Virginia negro's use of 'skaddle,' which is a corruption of 'scatter.' The matter, however, is hardly worth referring to."

"But, Uncle Remus," said the little boy, dolefully, "that was cheating."

"Co'se, honey. De creeturs 'gun ter cheat, en den fokes tuck it up, en hit keep on spreadin'. Hit mighty ketchin', en you mine yo' eye, honey, dat somebody don't cheat you 'fo' yo' ha'r git gray ez de ole nigger's."

1881

Sarah Orne Jewett
1849–1909

There is a direct line of influence from the inspiration taken by Sarah Orne Jewett from the regional stories of Harriet Beecher Stowe down to the impetus given by Jewett's writings to the young Mary Eleanor Wilkins Freeman and later to Willa Cather, who became one of Jewett's editors. With the exception of Cather, all these women were reared in New England. They gained almost immediate recognition for their talent to create literary annotations of a tight-knit way of life and a tradition of moral rigor that changed rapidly during their lifetimes. Of this group, Jewett's field of vision stands out for its attention to New England customs and local settings, made universal through its accounting of a people bound to family and community.

One of three daughters of a local practitioner and professor of medicine at Bowdoin College, Sarah Orne Jewett was born in South Berwick, Maine, a coastal town where her grandfather had been the leading sea captain and shipowner. In "The Custom House," preface to *The Scarlet Letter,* written in 1849–1850, Nathaniel Hawthorne could look back on the declining fortunes of once bustling Massachusetts port towns such as Salem. By the time of Jewett's adolescence in the 1860s, the shift from a maritime and entrepreneurial economic system to industrial America had already taken place. Spurred by her reading of Harriet Beecher Stowe's account of Maine coast life, *The Pearl of Orr's Island* (1862), and by the trips she made with her doctor-father on his buggy rounds to rural patients, Jewett decided in her teens to act as a literary amanuensis for the lives of the people of that region.

Jewett's earliest pieces, published under various pseudonyms, were written at the age of fourteen. These stories were often luridly overplotted in the manner of the popular fiction of the time, but she soon included local legends and observations of speech patterns and social mannerisms. Too sickly to receive a regular education, she read a great deal in the books of her father's library, with his constant encouragement. Most of all, she "read" the lives of people who were shaped both by the natural conditions of the villages, farms, and seaports of Maine and by the social complications introduced into a world that no longer seemed small enough to be manageable and pleasing.

By the age of twenty, Sarah Orne Jewett had had her story "Mr. Bruce" accepted by William Dean Howells for publication in the *Atlantic Monthly.* Her first collection of stories appeared as *Deephaven* (1877). In response to the praise she received for work that appeared in the country's best magazines (the *Atlantic,*

Harper's, and *Scribner's*), she published more than twenty volumes of stories over the years, culminating in 1896 with *The Country of the Pointed Firs,* her single best collection.

Even more than Mary E. Wilkins Freeman, who was markedly the reporter of present moments, Jewett became a recorder of times in the process of being lost forever—the "was" of her remembered childhood. She did not write rustic idylls about a perfect time and place, but in celebrating the modest pleasures and virtues of rural lives she proved how capable an unmarried woman from a sheltered background could be as the keeper of the literary annals of small-town New England. There was a large audience for such writing in her day. Later generations were reminded of a world they had never experienced personally; through Jewett, Americans came to believe they still possessed it as part of their national heritage.

Further Reading:
F. Matthiessen, *Sarah Orne Jewett,* 1960.
R. Cary, *Sarah Orne Jewett,* 1962.
M. Thorp, *Sarah Orne Jewett,* 1966.
Appreciation of Sarah Orne Jewett: 29 Interpretive Essays, ed. R. Cary, 1973.
J. Donovan, *Sarah Orne Jewett,* 1980.
P. Westbrook, *Acres of Flint: Sarah Orne Jewett and Her Contemporaries,* 1981.

Text:
Tales of New England, 1894.
See also *Deephaven and Other Stories,* ed. R. Cary, 1966.
The Uncollected Short Stories of Sarah Orne Jewett, ed. R. Cary, 1971.
Letters of Sarah Orne Jewett, ed. A. Fields, 1911.
Sarah Orne Jewett Letters, ed. R. Cary, 1956, 1967.

Miss Tempy's Watchers

The time of year was April; the place was a small farming town in New Hampshire, remote from any railroad. One by one the lights had been blown out in the scattered houses near Miss Tempy Dent's; but as her neighbors took a last look out-of-doors, their eyes turned with instinctive curiosity toward the old house, where a lamp burned steadily. They gave a little sigh. "Poor Miss Tempy!" said more than one bereft acquaintance; for the good woman lay dead in her north chamber, and the light was a watcher's light. The funeral was set for the next day, at one o'clock.

The watchers were two of the oldest friends, Mrs. Crowe and Sarah Ann Binson. They were sitting in the kitchen, because it seemed less awesome than the unused best room, and they beguiled the long hours by steady conversation. One would think that neither topics nor opinions would hold out, at that rate, all through the long spring night; but there was a certain degree of excitement just then, and the two women had risen to an unusual level of expressiveness and confidence. Each had already told the other more than one fact that she had determined to keep secret; they were again and again tempted into statements that either would have found impossible by daylight. Mrs. Crowe was knitting a blue yarn stocking for her husband; the foot was already so long that it seemed as if she must have forgotten to narrow it at the proper time. Mrs. Crowe knew exactly what she was about, however; she was of a much cooler disposition than Sister Binson, who made futile attempts at some sewing, only to drop her work into her lap whenever the talk was most engaging.

Their faces were interesting,—of the dry, shrewd, quick-witted New England type, with thin hair twisted neatly back out of the way. Mrs. Crowe could look vague and benignant, and Miss Binson was, to quote her neighbors, a little too sharp-set; but the world knew that she had need to be, with the load she must carry of supporting an inefficient widowed sister and six unpromising and unwilling nieces and nephews. The eldest boy was at last placed with a good man to learn the mason's trade. Sarah Ann Binson, for all her sharp, anxious aspect, never defended herself, when her sister whined and fretted. She was told every week of her life that the poor children never would have had to lift a finger if their father had lived, and yet she had kept her steadfast way with the little farm, and patiently taught the young people many useful things, for which, as everybody said, they would live to thank her. However pleasure-less her life appeared to outward view, it was brimful of pleasure to herself.

Mrs. Crowe, on the contrary, was well to do, her husband being a rich farmer and an easy-going man. She was a stingy woman, but for all that she looked kindly; and when she gave away anything, or lifted a finger to help anybody, it was thought a great piece of beneficence, and a compliment, indeed, which the recipient accepted with twice as much gratitude as double the gift that came from a poorer and more generous acquaintance. Everybody liked to be on good terms with Mrs. Crowe. Socially she stood much higher than Sarah Ann Binson. They were both old school-mates and friends of Temperance Dent, who had asked them, one day, not long before she died, if they would not come together and look after the house, and manage everything, when she was gone. She may have had some hope that they might become closer friends in this period of intimate partnership, and that the richer woman might better understand the burdens of the poorer. They had not kept the house the night before; they were too weary with the care of their old friend, whom they had not left until all was over.

There was a brook which ran down the hillside very near the house, and the sound of it was much louder than usual. When there was silence in the kitchen, the busy stream had a strange insistence in its wild voice, as if it tried to make the watchers understand something that related to the past.

"I declare, I can't begin to sorrow for Tempy yet. I am so glad to have her at rest," whispered Mrs. Crowe. "It is strange to set here without her, but I can't make it clear that she has gone. I feel as if she had got easy and dropped off to sleep, and I'm more scared about waking her up than knowing any other feeling."

"Yes," said Sarah Ann, "it's just like that, ain't it? But I tell you we are goin' to miss her worse than we expect. She's helped me through with many a trial, has Temperance. I ain't the only one who says the same, neither."

These words were spoken as if there were a third person listening; somebody beside Mrs. Crowe. The watchers could not rid their minds of the feeling that they were being watched themselves. The spring wind whistled in the window crack, now and then, and buffeted the little house in a gusty way that had a sort of companionable effect. Yet, on the whole, it was a very still night, and the watchers spoke in a half-whisper.

"She was the freest-handed woman that ever I knew," said Mrs. Crowe, decidedly. "According to her means, she gave away more than anybody. I used to tell her 't wa'n't right. I used really to be afraid that she went without too much, for we have a duty to ourselves."

Sister Binson looked up in a half-amused, unconscious way, and then recollected herself.

Mrs. Crowe met her look with a serious face. "It ain't so easy for me to give as it is for some," she said simply, but with an effort which was made possible only by the occasion. "I should like to say, while Tempy is laying here yet in her own house, that she has been a constant lesson to me. Folks are too kind, and shame me with thanks for what I do. I ain't such a generous woman as poor Tempy was, for all she had nothin' to do with, as one may say."

Sarah Binson was much moved at this confession, and was even pained and touched by the unexpected humility. "You have a good many calls on you"—she began, and then left her kind little compliment half finished.

"Yes, yes, but I've got means enough. My disposition's more of a cross to me as I grow older, and I made up my mind this morning that Tempy's example should be my pattern henceforth." She began to knit faster than ever.

" 'T ain't no use to get morbid: that's what Tempy used to say herself," said Sarah Ann, after a minute's silence. "Ain't it strange to say 'used to say'?" and her own voice choked a little. "She never did like to hear folks git goin' about themselves."

" 'T was only because they're apt to do it so as other folks will say 't was n't so, an' praise 'em up," humbly replied Mrs. Crowe, "and that ain't my object. There wa'n't a child but what Tempy set herself to work to see what she could do to please it. One time my brother's folks had been stopping here in the summer, from Massachusetts. The children was all little, and they broke up a sight of toys, and left 'em when they were going away. Tempy come right up after they rode by, to see if she could n't help me set the house to rights, and she caught me just as I was going to fling some of the clutter into the stove. I was kind of tired out, starting 'em off in season. 'Oh, give me them!' says she, real pleading; and she wropped 'em up and took 'em home with her when she went, and she mended 'em up and stuck 'em together, and made some young one or other happy with every blessed one. You'd thought I'd done her the biggest favor. 'No thanks to me. I should ha' burnt 'em, Tempy,' says I."

"Some of 'em came to our house, I know," said Miss Binson. "She'd take a lot o' trouble to please a child, 'stead o' shoving of it out o' the way, like the rest of us when we're drove."

"I can tell you the biggest thing she ever done, and I don't know's there's anybody left but me to tell it. I don't want it forgot," Sarah Binson went on, looking up at the clock to see how the night was going. "It was that pretty-looking Trevor girl, who taught the Corners school, and married so well afterwards, out in New York State. You remember her, I dare say?"

"Certain," said Mrs. Crowe, with an air of interest.

"She was a splendid scholar, folks said, and give the school a great start; but she'd overdone herself getting her education, and working to pay for it, and she all broke down one spring, and Tempy made her come and stop with her a while,—you remember that? Well, she had an uncle, her mother's brother, out in Chicago, who was well off and friendly, and used to write to Lizzie Trevor, and I dare say make her some presents; but he was a lively, driving man, and did n't take time to stop and think about his folks. He had n't seen her since she was a little girl. Poor Lizzie was so pale and weakly that she just got through the term o' school. She looked as if she was just going straight off in a decline. Tempy, she cosseted her up a while, and then, next thing folks knew, she was tellin' round how Miss Trevor had gone to see her uncle, and meant to visit Niagary Falls on the way, and stop over night. Now I happened to know, in ways I won't dwell on to explain, that the poor girl was in debt for her schoolin' when she come here, and her last quarter's pay had just squared it off at last, and left her without a cent ahead, hardly; but it had fretted her thinking of it, so she paid it all; those might have dunned her that she owed it to. An' I taxed Tempy about the girl's goin' off on such a journey till she owned up, rather 'n have Lizzie blamed, that she'd given her sixty dollars, same's if she was rolling in riches, and sent her off to have a good rest and vacation."

"Sixty dollars!" exclaimed Mrs. Crowe. "Tempy only had ninety dollars a year that came in to her; rest of her livin' she got by helpin' about, with what she raised off this little piece o' ground, sand one side an' clay the other. An' how often I've heard her tell, years ago, that she'd rather see Niagary than any other sight in the world!"

The women looked at each other in silence; the magnitude of the generous sacrifice was almost too great for their comprehension.

"She was just poor enough to do that!" declared Mrs. Crowe at last, in an abandonment of feeling. "Say what you may, I feel humbled to the dust," and her companion ventured to say nothing. She never had given away sixty dollars at once, but it was simply because she never had it to give. It came to her very lips to say in explanation, "Tempy was so situated;" but she checked herself in time, for she would not betray her own loyal guarding of a dependent household.

"Folks say a great deal of generosity, and this one's being public-sperited, and that one free-handed about giving," said Mrs. Crowe, who was a little nervous in the silence. "I suppose we can't tell the sorrow it would be to some folks not to give, same's 't would be to me not to save. I seem kind of made for that, as if 't was what I'd got to do. I should feel sights better about it if I could make it evident what I was savin' for. If I had a child, now, Sarah Ann," and her voice was a little husky, —"if I had a child, I should think I was heapin' of it up because he was the one trained by the Lord to scatter it again for good. But here's Mr. Crowe and me, we can't do anything with money, and both of us like to keep things same's they've always been. Now Priscilla Dance was talking away like a mill-clapper, week before last. She'd think I would go right off and get one o' them new-fashioned gilt-and-white papers for the best room, and some new furniture, an' a marble-top table. And I looked at her, all struck up. 'Why,' says I, 'Priscilla, that nice old velvet paper ain't hurt a mite. I should n't feel 't was my best room without it. Dan'el says 't is the first thing he can remember rubbin' his little baby fingers on to it, and how splendid he thought them red roses was.' I maintain," continued Mrs. Crowe stoutly, "that folks wastes sights o' good money doin' just such foolish things. Tearin' out the insides o' meetin'-houses, and fixin' the pews different; 't was good enough as 't was with mendin'; then times come, an' they want to put it all back same's 't was before."

This touched upon an exciting subject to active members of that parish. Miss Binson and Mrs. Crowe belonged to opposite parties, and had at one time come as near hard feelings as they could, and yet escape them. Each hastened to speak of other things and to show her untouched friendliness.

"I do agree with you," said Sister Binson, "that few of us know what use to make of money, beyond every-day necessities. You've seen more o' the world than I have, and know what's expected. When it comes to taste and judgment about such things, I ought to defer to others;" and with this modest avowal the critical moment passed when there might have been an improper discussion.

In the silence that followed, the fact of their presence in a house of death grew more clear than before. There was something disturbing in the noise of a mouse gnawing at the dry boards of a closet wall near by. Both the watchers looked up anxiously at the clock; it was almost the middle of the night and the whole world seemed to have left them alone with their solemn duty. Only the brook was awake.

"Perhaps we might give a look up-stairs now," whispered Mrs. Crowe, as if she hoped to hear some reason against their going just then to the chamber of death; but Sister Binson rose, with a serious and yet satisfied countenance, and lifted the small lamp from the table. She was much more used to watching than Mrs. Crowe, and much less affected by it. They opened the door into a small entry with a steep stairway; they climbed the creaking stairs, and entered the cold upper room on tiptoe. Mrs. Crowe's heart began to beat very fast as the lamp was put on a high bureau, and made long, fixed shadows about the walls. She went hesitatingly toward the solemn shape under its white drapery, and felt a sense of remonstrance as Sarah Ann gently, but in a business-like way, turned back the thin sheet.

"Seems to me she looks pleasanter and pleasanter," whispered Sarah Ann Binson impulsively, as they gazed at the white face with its wonderful smile. "To-morrow 't will all have faded out. I do believe they kind of wake up a day or two after they die, and it's then they go." She replaced the light covering, and they both turned quickly away; there was a chill in this upper room.

" 'T is a great thing for anybody to have got through, ain't it?" said Mrs. Crowe softly, as she began to go down the stairs on tiptoe. The warm air from the kitchen beneath met them with a sense of welcome and shelter.

"I don' know why it is, but I feel as near again to Tempy down here as I do up there," replied Sister Binson. "I feel as if the air was full of her, kind of. I can sense things, now and then, that she seems to say. Now I never was one to take up with no nonsense of sperits and such, but I declare I felt as if she told me just now to put some more wood into the stove."

Mrs. Crowe preserved a gloomy silence. She had suspected before this that her companion was of a weaker and more credulous disposition than herself. " 'T is a great thing to have got through," she repeated, ignoring definitely all that had last been said. "I suppose you know as well as I that Tempy was one that always feared death. Well, it's all put behind her now; she knows what 't is." Mrs. Crowe gave a little sigh, and Sister Binson's quick sympathies were stirred toward this other old friend, who also dreaded the great change.

"I'd never like to forgit almost those last words Tempy spoke plain to me," she said gently, like the comforter she truly was. "She looked up at me once or twice, that last afternoon after I come to set by her, and let Mis' Owen go home; and I says, 'Can I do anything to ease you, Tempy?' and the tears come into my eyes so I could n't see what kind of a nod she give me. 'No, Sarah Ann, you can't, dear,' says she; and then she got her breath again, and says she, looking at me real meanin', 'I'm only a-gettin' sleepier and sleepier; that's all there is,' says she, and smiled up at me kind of wishful, and shut her eyes. I knew well enough all she meant. She'd been lookin' out for a chance to tell me, and I don' know's she ever said much afterwards."

Mrs. Crowe was not knitting; she had been listening too eagerly. "Yes, 't will be a comfort to think of that sometimes," she said, in acknowledgment.

"I know that old Dr. Prince said once, in evenin' meetin', that he'd watched by many a dyin' bed, as we well knew, and enough o' his sick folks had been scared o' dyin' their whole lives through; but when they come to the last, he'd never seen one but was willin', and most were glad, to go. ' 'T is as natural as bein' born or livin' on,' he said. I don't know what had moved him to speak that night. You know he wa'n't in the habit of it, and 't was the monthly concert of prayer for foreign missions anyways," said Sarah Ann; "but 't was a great stay to the mind to listen to his words of experience."

"There never was a better man," responded Mrs. Crowe, in a really cheerful tone. She had recovered from her feeling of nervous dread, the kitchen was so comfortable with lamplight and firelight; and just then the old clock began to tell the hour of twelve with leisurely whirring strokes.

Sister Binson laid aside her work, and rose quickly and went to the cupboard. "We'd better take a little to eat," she explained. "The night will go fast after this. I want to know if you went and made some o' your nice cupcake, while you was home to-day?" she asked, in a pleased tone; and Mrs. Crowe acknowledged such a gratifying piece of thoughtfulness for this humble friend who denied herself all luxuries. Sarah Ann brewed a generous cup of tea, and the watchers drew their chairs up to the table presently, and quelled their hunger with good country appetites. Sister Binson put a spoon into a small, old-fashioned glass of preserved quince, and passed it to her friend. She was most familiar with the house, and played the part of hostess. "Spread some o' this on your bread and butter," she said to Mrs. Crowe. "Tempy wanted me to use some three or four times, but I never felt to. I know she'd like to have us comfortable now, and would urge us to make a good supper, poor dear."

"What excellent preserves she did make!" mourned Mrs. Crowe. "None of us has got her light hand at doin' things tasty. She made the most o' everything, too. Now, she only had that one old quince-tree down in the far corner of the piece, but she'd go out in the spring and tend to it, and look at it so pleasant, and kind of expect the old thorny thing into bloomin'."

"She was just the same with folks," said Sarah Ann. "And she'd never git more 'n a little apernful o' quinces, but she'd have every mite o' goodness out o' those, and set the glasses up onto her best-room closet shelf, *so* pleased. 'T wa'n't but a week ago to-morrow mornin' I fetched her a little taste o' jelly in a teaspoon; and she says 'Thank ye,' and took it, an' the minute she tasted it she looked up at me as worried as could be. 'Oh, I don't want to eat that,' says she. 'I always keep that in case o' sickness.' 'You're goin' to have the good o' one tumbler yourself,' says I. 'I'd just like to know who's sick now, if you ain't!' An' she couldn't help laughin', I spoke up so smart. Oh, dear me, how I shall miss talkin' over things with her! She always sensed things, and got just the p'int you meant."

"She did n't begin to age until two or three years ago, did she?" asked Mrs. Crowe. "I never saw anybody keep her looks as Tempy did. She looked young long after I begun to feel like an old woman. The doctor used to say 't was her young heart, and I don't know but what he was right. How she did do for other folks! There was one spell she was n't at home a day to a fortnight. She got most of her livin' so, and that made her own potatoes and things last her through. None o' the young folks could get married without her, and all the old ones was disappointed if she wa'n't round when they was down with sickness and had to go. An' cleanin', or tailorin' for boys, or rug-hookin',—there was nothin' but what she could do as handy as most. 'I do love to work,'—ain't you heard her say that twenty times a week?"

Sarah Ann Binson nodded, and began to clear away the empty plates. "We may want a taste o' somethin' more towards mornin'," she said. "There's plenty in the closet here; and in case some comes from a distance to the funeral, we'll have a little table spread after we get back to the house."

"Yes, I was busy all the mornin'. I've cooked up a sight o' things to bring over," said Mrs. Crowe. "I felt 't was the last I could do for her."

They drew their chairs near the stove again, and took up their work. Sister Binson's rocking-chair creaked as she rocked; the brook sounded louder than ever. It was more lonely when nobody spoke, and presently Mrs. Crowe returned to her thoughts of growing old.

"Yes, Tempy aged all of a sudden. I remember I asked her if she felt as well as common, one day, and she laughed at me good. There, when Mr. Crowe begun to look old, I couldn't help feeling as if somethin' ailed him, and like as not 't was somethin' he was goin' to git right over, and I dosed him for it stiddy, half of one summer."

"How many things we shall be wanting to ask Tempy!" exclaimed Sarah Ann Binson, after a long pause. "I can't make up my mind to doin' without her. I wish folks could come back just once, and tell us how 't is where they've gone. Seems then we could do without 'em better."

The brook hurried on, the wind blew about the house now and then; the house itself was a silent place, and the supper, the warm fire, and an absence of any new topics for conversation made the watchers drowsy. Sister Binson closed her eyes first, to rest them for a minute; and Mrs. Crowe glanced at her compassionately, with a new sympathy for the hard-worked little woman. She made up her mind to let Sarah Ann have a good rest, while she kept watch alone; but in a few minutes her own knitting was dropped, and she, too, fell asleep. Overhead, the pale shape of Tempy Dent, the outworn body of that generous, loving-hearted, simple soul, slept on also in its white raiment. Perhaps Tempy herself stood near, and saw her own life and its surroundings with new understanding. Perhaps she herself was the only watcher.

Later, by some hours, Sarah Ann Binson woke with a start. There was a pale light of dawn outside the small windows. Inside the kitchen, the lamp burned dim. Mrs. Crowe awoke, too.

"I think Tempy'd be the first to say 't was just as well we both had some rest," she said, not without a guilty feeling.

Her companion went to the outer door, and opened it wide. The fresh air was none too cold, and the brook's voice was not nearly so loud as it had been in the midnight darkness. She could see the shapes of the hills, and the great shadows that lay across the lower country. The east was fast growing bright.

" 'T will be a beautiful day for the funeral," she said, and turned again, with a sigh, to follow Mrs. Crowe up the stairs.

1888

Kate Chopin
1851–1904

To the age of nineteen, Katherine O'Flaherty experienced both the pleasures and the boring aimlessness that came to her as a belle caught up in the social swirl of St. Louis, a city flourishing in the aftermath of Civil War prosperity. Her father, an immigrant from Ireland, was a successful businessman; her mother was from an old Creole family that had settled in St. Louis. Her upbringing was Catholic, affluent, and "French" in its adherence to pious convent education, society balls, and French language and culture. Kate Chopin's later remarks about that period of giddy girlhood make clear that both nuns and debutantes lived lives of fantasy that excluded "real life." Real life is what Katherine O'Flaherty confronted in 1870 when she became Mrs. Oscar Chopin (pronounced in the French way, as in the name of the pianist Frédéric Chopin). She went to live in New Orleans, then, after business reversals, to a rural community near the cotton plantation owned by her husband's family. By 1884 she was back again in St. Louis, a widow with six children. Although she was not in financial want, Kate Chopin took up the literary career she had contemplated years earlier—the one she had been too busy raising her family to enter upon.

Kate Chopin set to work to learn how to write acceptable works of fiction. For her models of stories, sketches, and poetry she drew upon French writers— her contemporaries Émile Zola and Guy de Maupassant as well as the eighteenth-century literary and intellectual figure Madame de Staël. But what influenced her most was her experiences among the diverse cultures of Louisiana. Her fiction took as its home ground the lives of Creoles (descendants of the first French and Spanish settlers in the territory), Cajuns (progeny of the French immigrants who had been ignominiously expelled from Canada by the British conquerors in the eighteenth century), and the blacks and Indians of mixed blood who lived throughout Louisiana.

The history of Kate Chopin's reception by the reading public is a revealing one. The publication in 1894 of *Bayou Folk,* a collection of tales of rural life, earned her critical acceptance. *A Night in Acadie* (1897) confirmed her popularity as a teller of stories. Her readers were pleased by her attention to local customs and dialects. (They had taken in the same way to the tales of New England written by Mary Wilkins Freeman and Sarah Orne Jewett, which exerted a similar appeal with different material.) Newspapers and important national magazines, such as the newly formed *Vogue* and the well-established *Century,* featured her work. She had already written two novels of slight merit when *The Awakening* appeared in 1899. Almost immediately, her previously appreciative audience rose against her, not surprising when one realizes that the same middle-class readership had been unable to accept Stephen Crane's *Maggie, A Girl of the Streets* in 1893 and would reject Theodore Dreiser's *Sister Carrie* when it appeared in 1900.

Chopin had long been a loyal reader of Walt Whitman's *Leaves of Grass,* and the portrayal in *The Awakening* of Edna Pontellier's aroused sensuousness is indeed Whitmanesque. The young woman's increasing resentment of the constrictions imposed by married life and her flirtations with an attractive roué brought condemnation to the novel and its author; both were dropped from libraries and genteel society. Naturally upset by her fall from favor, Kate Chopin attempted little more writing before her death five years later.

The Awakening was rediscovered in the 1950s. What was once called bad behavior for a woman is now seen as good writing about a woman's turbulent feelings. During Chopin's lifetime, readers may have been drawn to her piquant tales of the exotic yet recognizably human types found in Creole and Cajun culture, but there was hardly approbation for her novel. Today appreciation comes easily to *The Awakening,* while her brief, almost anecdotal stories continue to surprise readers with their arresting portraits of passionate lives. In her accomplishments, Chopin demonstrated the characteristic American talent for writing fine short fiction heralded by Washington Irving, Edgar Allan Poe, and Nathaniel Hawthorne.

Further Reading:
D. Rankin, *Kate Chopin and Her Creole Stories,* 1932.
P. Seyersted, *Kate Chopin: A Critical Biography,* 1969, 1980.

Text:
The Complete Works of Kate Chopin, 2 vols., ed. P. Seyersted, 1969.

Désirée's Baby

As the day was pleasant, Madame Valmondé drove over to L'Abri to see Désirée and the baby.

It made her laugh to think of Désirée with a baby. Why, it seemed but yesterday that Désirée was little more than a baby herself; when Monsieur in riding through the gateway of Valmondé had found her lying asleep in the shadow of the big stone pillar.

The little one awoke in his arms and began to cry for "Dada." That was as much as she could do or say. Some people thought she might have strayed there of her own accord, for she was of the toddling age. The prevailing belief was that she had been purposely left by a party of Texans, whose canvas-covered wagon, late in the day, had crossed the ferry that Coton Maïs kept, just below the plantation. In time Madame Valmondé abandoned every speculation but the one that Désirée had been sent to her by a beneficent Providence to be the child of her affection, seeing that she was without child of the flesh. For the girl grew to be beautiful and gentle, affectionate and sincere, —the idol of Valmondé.

It was no wonder, when she stood one day against the stone pillar in whose shadow she had lain asleep, eighteen years before, that Armand Aubigny riding by and seeing her there, had fallen in love with her. That was the way all the Aubignys fell in love, as if struck by a pistol shot. The wonder was that he had not loved her before; for he had known her since his father brought him home from Paris, a boy of eight, after his mother died there. The passion that awoke in him that day, when he saw her at the gate, swept along like an avalanche, or like a prairie fire, or like anything that drives headlong over all obstacles.

Monsieur Valmondé grew practical and wanted things well considered: that is, the girl's obscure origin. Armand looked into her eyes and did not care. He was reminded that she was nameless. What did it matter about a name when he could give her one of the oldest and proudest in Louisiana? He ordered the *corbeille*[1] from Paris, and contained himself with what patience he could until it arrived; then they were married.

Madame Valmondé had not seen Désirée and the baby for four weeks. When she reached L'Abri she shuddered at the first sight of it, as she always did. It was a sad looking place, which for many years had not known the gentle presence of a mistress, old Monsieur Aubigny having married and buried his wife in France, and she having loved her own land too well ever to leave it. The roof came down steep and black like a cowl, reaching out beyond the wide galleries that encircled the yellow stuccoed house. Big, solemn oaks grew close to it, and their thick-leaved, far-reaching branches shadowed it like a pall. Young Aubigny's rule was a strict one, too, and under it his negroes had forgotten how to be gay, as they had been during the old master's easy-going and indulgent lifetime.

The young mother was recovering slowly, and lay full length, in her soft white muslins and laces, upon a couch. The baby was beside her, upon her arm, where he had fallen asleep, at her breast. The yellow nurse woman sat beside a window fanning herself.

Madame Valmondé bent her portly figure over Désirée and kissed her, holding her an instant tenderly in her arms. Then she turned to the child.

"This is not the baby!" she exclaimed, in startled tones. French was the language spoken at Valmondé in those days.

"I knew you would be astonished," laughed Désirée, "at the way he has grown. The little *cochon de lait!*[2] Look at his legs, mamma, and his hands and fingernails,—real fingernails. Zandrine had to cut them this morning. Is n't it true, Zandrine?"

The woman bowed her turbaned head majestically, "Mais si,[3] Madame."

"And the way he cries," went on Désirée, "is deafening. Armand heard him the other day as far away as La Blanche's cabin."

Madame Valmondé had never removed her eyes from the child. She lifted it and walked with it over to the window that was lightest. She scanned the baby narrowly, then looked as searchingly at Zandrine, whose face was turned to gaze across the fields.

"Yes, the child has grown, has changed," said Madame Valmondé, slowly, as she replaced it beside its mother. "What does Armand say?"

Désirée's face became suffused with a glow that was happiness itself.

"Oh, Armand is the proudest father in the parish, I believe, chiefly because it is a boy, to bear his name; though he says not,—that he would have loved a girl as well. But I know it is n't true. I know he says that to please me. And mamma," she added, drawing Madame Valmondé's head down to her, and speaking in a whisper,

---

[1] Wedding gifts from the groom to the bride.   [3] French: "But certainly."
[2] French: "Suckling pig."

"he has n't punished one of them—not one of them—since baby is born. Even Négrillon, who pretended to have burnt his leg that he might rest from work—he only laughed, and said Négrillon was a great scamp. Oh, mamma, I'm so happy; it frightens me."

What Désirée said was true. Marriage, and later the birth of his son had softened Armand Aubigny's imperious and exacting nature greatly. This was what made the gentle Désirée so happy, for she loved him desperately. When he frowned she trembled, but loved him. When he smiled, she asked no greater blessing of God. But Armand's dark, handsome face had not often been disfigured by frowns since the day he fell in love with her.

When the baby was about three months old, Désirée awoke one day to the conviction that there was something in the air menacing her peace. It was at first too subtle to grasp. It had only been a disquieting suggestion; an air of mystery among the blacks; unexpected visits from far-off neighbors who could hardly account for their coming. Then a strange, an awful change in her husband's manner, which she dared not ask him to explain. When he spoke to her, it was with averted eyes, from which the old love-light seemed to have gone out. He absented himself from home; and when there, avoided her presence and that of her child, without excuse. And the very spirit of Satan seemed suddenly to take hold of him in his dealings with the slaves. Désirée was miserable enough to die.

She sat in her room, one hot afternoon, in her *peignoir,* listlessly drawing through her fingers the strands of her long, silky brown hair that hung about her shoulders. The baby, half naked, lay asleep upon her own great mahogany bed, that was like a sumptuous throne, with its satin-lined half-canopy. One of La Blanche's little quadroon boys—half naked too—stood fanning the child slowly with a fan of peacock feathers. Désirée's eyes had been fixed absently and sadly upon the baby, while she was striving to penetrate the threatening mist that she felt closing about her. She looked from her child to the boy who stood beside him, and back again; over and over. "Ah!" It was a cry that she could not help; which she was not conscious of having uttered. The blood turned like ice in her veins, and a clammy moisture gathered upon her face.

She tried to speak to the little quadroon boy; but no sound would come, at first. When he heard his name uttered, he looked up, and his mistress was pointing to the door. He laid aside the great, soft fan, and obediently stole away, over the polished floor, on his bare tiptoes.

She stayed motionless, with gaze riveted upon her child, and her face the picture of fright.

Presently her husband entered the room, and without noticing her, went to a table and began to search among some papers which covered it.

"Armand," she called to him, in a voice which must have stabbed him, if he was human. But he did not notice. "Armand," she said again. Then she rose and tottered towards him. "Armand," she panted once more, clutching his arm, "look at our child. What does it mean? tell me."

He coldly but gently loosened her fingers from about his arm and thrust the hand away from him. "Tell me what it means!" she cried despairingly.

"It means," he answered lightly, "that the child is not white; it means that you are not white."

A quick conception of all that this accusation meant for her nerved her with unwonted courage to deny it. "It is a lie; it is not true, I am white! Look at my hair, it is brown; and my eyes are gray, Armand, you know they are gray. And my skin is fair," seizing his wrist. "Look at my hand; whiter than yours, Armand," she laughed hysterically.

"As white as La Blanche's," he returned cruelly; and went away leaving her alone with their child.

When she could hold a pen in her hand, she sent a despairing letter to Madame Valmondé.

"My mother, they tell me I am not white. Armand has told me I am not white. For God's sake tell them it is not true. You must know it is not true. I shall die. I must die. I cannot be so unhappy, and live."

The answer that came was as brief:

"My own Désirée: Come home to Valmondé; back to your mother who loves you. Come with your child."

When the letter reached Désirée she went with it to her husband's study, and laid it open upon the desk before which he sat. She was like a stone image: silent, white, motionless after she placed it there.

In silence he ran his cold eyes over the written words. He said nothing. "Shall I go, Armand?" she asked in tones sharp with agonized suspense.

"Yes, go."

"Do you want me to go?"

"Yes, I want you to go."

He thought Almighty God had dealt cruelly and unjustly with him; and felt, somehow, that he was paying Him back in kind when he stabbed thus into his wife's soul. Moreover he no longer loved her, because of the unconscious injury she had brought upon his home and his name.

She turned away like one stunned by a blow, and walked slowly towards the door, hoping he would call her back.

"Good-by, Armand," she moaned.

He did not answer her. That was his last blow at fate.

Désirée went in search of her child. Zandrine was pacing the sombre gallery with it. She took the little one from the nurse's arms with no word of explanation, and descending the steps, walked away, under the live-oak branches.

It was an October afternoon; the sun was just sinking. Out in the still fields the negroes were picking cotton.

Désirée had not changed the thin white garment nor the slippers which she wore. Her hair was uncovered and the sun's rays brought a golden gleam from its brown meshes. She did not take the broad, beaten road which led to the far-off plantation of Valmondé. She walked across a deserted field, where the stubble bruised her tender feet, so delicately shod, and tore her thin gown to shreds.

She disappeared among the reeds and willows that grew thick along the banks of the deep, sluggish bayou; and she did not come back again.

Some weeks later there was a curious scene enacted at L'Abri. In the centre of the smoothly swept back yard was a great bonfire. Armand Aubigny sat in the wide hallway that commanded a view of the spectacle; and it was he who dealt out to a half dozen negroes the material which kept this fire ablaze.

A graceful cradle of willow, with all its dainty furbishings, was laid upon the pyre, which had already been fed with the richness of a priceless *layette*. Then there were silk gowns, and velvet and satin ones added to these; laces, too, and embroideries; bonnets and gloves; for the *corbeille* had been of rare quality.

The last thing to go was a tiny bundle of letters; innocent little scribblings that Désirée had sent to him during the days of their espousal. There was the remnant of one back in the drawer from which he took them. But it was not Désirée's; it was part of an old letter from his mother to his father. He read it. She was thanking God for the blessing of her husband's love:—

"But, above all," she wrote, "night and day, I thank the good God for having so arranged our lives that our dear Armand will never know that his mother, who adores him, belongs to the race that is cursed with the brand of slavery."

1892

A Pair of Silk Stockings

Little Mrs. Sommers one day found herself the unexpected possessor of fifteen dollars. It seemed to her a very large amount of money, and the way in which it stuffed and bulged her worn old *porte-monnaie*[1] gave her a feeling of importance such as she had not enjoyed for years.

The question of investment was one that occupied her greatly. For a day or two she walked about apparently in a dreamy state, but really absorbed in speculation and calculation. She did not wish to act hastily, to do anything she might afterward regret. But it was during the still hours of the night when she lay awake revolving plans in her mind that she seemed to see her way clearly toward a proper and judicious use of the money.

A dollar or two should be added to the price usually paid for Janie's shoes, which would insure their lasting an appreciable time longer than they usually did. She would buy so and so many yards of percale for new shirt waists for the boys and Janie and Mag. She had intended to make the old ones do by skilful patching. Mag should have another gown. She had seen some beautiful patterns, veritable bargains in the shop windows. And still there would be left enough for new stockings—two pairs apiece —and what darning that would save for a while! She would get caps for the boys and sailor-hats for the girls. The vision of her little brood looking fresh and dainty and new for once in their lives excited her and made her restless and wakeful with anticipation.

The neighbors sometimes talked of certain "better days" that little Mrs. Sommers had known before she had ever thought of being Mrs. Sommers. She herself indulged

---

[1] French: "Pocketbook."

in no such morbid retrospection. She had no time—no second of time to devote to the past. The needs of the present absorbed her every faculty. A vision of the future like some dim, gaunt monster sometimes appalled her, but luckily to-morrow never comes.

Mrs. Sommers was one who knew the value of bargains; who could stand for hours making her way inch by inch toward the desired object that was selling below cost. She could elbow her way if need be; she had learned to clutch a piece of goods and hold it and stick to it with persistence and determination till her turn came to be served, no matter when it came.

But that day she was a little faint and tired. She had swallowed a light luncheon —no! when she came to think of it, between getting the children fed and the place righted, and preparing herself for the shopping bout, she had actually forgotten to eat any luncheon at all!

She sat herself upon a revolving stool before a counter that was comparatively deserted, trying to gather strength and courage to charge through an eager multitude that was besieging breast-works of shirting and figured lawn. An all-gone limp feeling had come over her and she rested her hand aimlessly upon the counter. She wore no gloves. By degrees she grew aware that her hand had encountered something very soothing, very pleasant to touch. She looked down to see that her hand lay upon a pile of silk stockings. A placard near by announced that they had been reduced in price from two dollars and fifty cents to one dollar and ninety-eight cents; and a young girl who stood behind the counter asked her if she wished to examine their line of silk hosiery. She smiled, just as if she had been asked to inspect a tiara of diamonds with the ultimate view of purchasing it. But she went on feeling the soft, sheeny luxurious things—with both hands now, holding them up to see them glisten, and to feel them glide serpent-like through her fingers.

Two hectic blotches came suddenly into her pale cheeks. She looked up at the girl.

"Do you think there are any eights-and-a-half among these?"

There were any number of eights-and-a-half. In fact, there were more of that size than any other. Here was a light-blue pair; there were some lavender, some all black and various shades of tan and gray. Mrs. Sommers selected a black pair and looked at them very long and closely. She pretended to be examining their texture, which the clerk assured her was excellent.

"A dollar and ninety-eight cents," she mused aloud. "Well, I'll take this pair." She handed the girl a five-dollar bill and waited for her change and for her parcel. What a very small parcel it was! It seemed lost in the depths of her shabby old shopping-bag.

Mrs. Sommers after that did not move in the direction of the bargain counter. She took the elevator, which carried her to an upper floor into the region of the ladies' waiting-rooms. Here, in a retired corner, she exchanged her cotton stockings for the new silk ones which she had just bought. She was not going through any acute mental process or reasoning with herself, nor was she striving to explain to her satisfaction the motive of her action. She was not thinking at all. She seemed for the time to be taking a rest from that laborious and fatiguing function and to have abandoned herself to some mechanical impulse that directed her actions and freed her of responsibility.

How good was the touch of the raw silk to her flesh! She felt like lying back in the cushioned chair and reveling for a while in the luxury of it. She did for a little while. Then she replaced her shoes, rolled the cotton stockings together and thrust them into her bag. After doing this she crossed straight over to the shoe department and took her seat to be fitted.

She was fastidious. The clerk could not make her out; he could not reconcile her shoes with her stockings, and she was not too easily pleased. She held back her skirts and turned her feet one way and her head another way as she glanced down at the polished, pointed-tipped boots. Her foot and ankle looked very pretty. She could not realize that they belonged to her and were a part of herself. She wanted an excellent and stylish fit, she told the young fellow who served her, and she did not mind the difference of a dollar or two more in the price so long as she got what she desired.

It was a long time since Mrs. Sommers had been fitted with gloves. On rare occasions when she had bought a pair they were always "bargains," so cheap that it would have been preposterous and unreasonable to have expected them to be fitted to the hand.

Now she rested her elbow on the cushion of the glove counter, and a pretty, pleasant young creature, delicate and deft of touch, drew a long-wristed "kid" over Mrs. Sommers' hand. She smoothed it down over the wrist and buttoned it neatly, and both lost themselves for a second or two in admiring contemplation of the little symmetrical gloved hand. But there were other places where money might be spent.

There were books and magazines piled up in the window of a stall a few paces down the street. Mrs. Sommers bought two high-priced magazines such as she had been accustomed to read in the days when she had been accustomed to other pleasant things. She carried them without wrapping. As well as she could she lifted her skirts at the crossings. Her stockings and boots and well fitting gloves had worked marvels in her bearing—had given her a feeling of assurance, a sense of belonging to the well-dressed multitude.

She was very hungry. Another time she would have stilled the cravings for food until reaching her own home, where she would have brewed herself a cup of tea and taken a snack of anything that was available. But the impulse that was guiding her would not suffer her to entertain any such thought.

There was a restaurant at the corner. She had never entered its doors; from the outside she had sometimes caught glimpses of spotless damask and shining crystal, and soft-stepping waiters serving people of fashion.

When she entered her appearance created no surprise, no consternation, as she had half feared it might. She seated herself at a small table alone, and an attentive waiter at once approached to take her order. She did not want a profusion; she craved a nice and tasty bite—a half dozen blue-points,[2] a plump chop with cress, a something sweet —a crème-frappée, for instance; a glass of Rhine wine, and after all a small cup of black coffee.

While waiting to be served she removed her gloves very leisurely and laid them beside her. Then she picked up a magazine and glanced through it, cutting the pages with a blunt edge of her knife. It was all very agreeable. The damask was even more spotless than it had seemed through the window, and the crystal more sparkling. There were quiet ladies and gentlemen, who did not notice her, lunching at the small tables like her own. A soft, pleasing strain of music could be heard, and a gentle breeze was blowing through the window. She tasted a bite, and she read a word or two, and she

[2] Small oysters.

sipped the amber wine and wiggled her toes in the silk stockings. The price of it made no difference. She counted the money out to the waiter and left an extra coin on his tray, whereupon he bowed before her as before a princess of royal blood.

There was still money in her purse, and her next temptation presented itself in the shape of a matinée poster.

It was a little later when she entered the theatre, the play had begun and the house seemed to her to be packed. But there were vacant seats here and there, and into one of them she was ushered, between brilliantly dressed women who had gone there to kill time and eat candy and display their gaudy attire. There were many others who were there solely for the play and acting. It is safe to say there was no one present who bore quite the attitude which Mrs. Sommers did to her surroundings. She gathered in the whole—stage and players and people in one wide impression, and absorbed it and enjoyed it. She laughed at the comedy and wept—she and the gaudy woman next to her wept over the tragedy. And they talked a little together over it. And the gaudy woman wiped her eyes and sniffled on a tiny square of filmy, perfumed lace and passed little Mrs. Sommers her box of candy.

The play was over, the music ceased, the crowd filed out. It was like a dream ended. People scattered in all directions. Mrs. Sommers went to the corner and waited for the cable car.

A man with keen eyes, who sat opposite to her, seemed to like the study of her small, pale face. It puzzled him to decipher what he saw there. In truth, he saw nothing —unless he were wizard enough to detect a poignant wish, a powerful longing that the cable car would never stop anywhere, but go on and on with her forever.

1897

The Storm

I

The leaves were so still that even Bibi thought it was going to rain. Bobinôt, who was accustomed to converse on terms of perfect equality with his little son, called the child's attention to certain sombre clouds that were rolling with sinister intention from the west, accompanied by a sullen, threatening roar. They were at Friedheimer's store and decided to remain there till the storm had passed. They sat within the door on two empty kegs. Bibi was four years old and looked very wise.

"Mama'll be 'fraid, yes," he suggested with blinking eyes.

"She'll shut the house. Maybe she got Sylvie helpin' her this evenin'," Bobinôt responded reassuringly.

"No; she ent got Sylvie. Sylvie was helpin' her yistiday," piped Bibi.

Bobinôt arose and going across to the counter purchased a can of shrimps, of which Calixta was very fond. Then he returned to his perch on the keg and sat stolidly holding the can of shrimps while the storm burst. It shook the wooden store and seemed to be ripping great furrows in the distant field. Bibi laid his little hand on his father's knee and was not afraid.

II

Calixta, at home, felt no uneasiness for their safety. She sat at a side window sewing furiously on a sewing machine. She was greatly occupied and did not notice the approaching storm. But she felt very warm and often stopped to mop her face on which the perspiration gathered in beads. She unfastened her white sacque[1] at the throat. It began to grow dark, and suddenly realizing the situation she got up hurriedly and went about closing windows and doors.

Out on the small front gallery she had hung Bobinôt's Sunday clothes to air and she hastened out to gather them before the rain fell. As she stepped outside, Alcée Laballière rode in at the gate. She had not seen him very often since her marriage, and never alone. She stood there with Bobinôt's coat in her hands, and the big rain drops began to fall. Alcée rode his horse under the shelter of a side projection where the chickens had huddled and there were plows and a harrow piled up in the corner.

"May I come and wait on your gallery till the storm is over, Calixta?" he asked.

"Come 'long in, M'sieur Alcée."

His voice and her own startled her as if from a trance, and she seized Bobinôt's vest. Alcée, mounting to the porch, grabbed the trousers and snatched Bibi's braided jacket that was about to be carried away by a sudden gust of wind. He expressed an intention to remain outside, but it was soon apparent that he might as well have been out in the open: the water beat in upon the boards in driving sheets, and he went inside, closing the door after him. It was even necessary to put something beneath the door to keep the water out.

"My! what a rain! It's good two years since it rain' like that," exclaimed Calixta as she rolled up a piece of bagging and Alcée helped her to thrust it beneath the crack.

She was a little fuller of figure than five years before when she married; but she had lost nothing of her vivacity. Her blue eyes still retained their melting quality; and her yellow hair, dishevelled by the wind and rain, kinked more stubbornly than ever about her ears and temples.

The rain beat upon the low, shingled roof with a force and clatter that threatened to break an entrance and deluge them there. They were in the dining room—the sitting room—the general utility room. Adjoining was her bed room, with Bibi's couch along side her own. The door stood open, and the room with its white, monumental bed, its closed shutters, looked dim and mysterious.

Alcée flung himself into a rocker and Calixta nervously began to gather up from the floor the lengths of a cotton sheet which she had been sewing.

"If this keeps up, *Dieu sait*[2] if the levees[3] goin' to stan' it!" she exclaimed.

"What have you got to do with the levees?"

"I got enough to do! An' there's Bobinôt with Bibi out in that storm—if he only didn' left Friedheimer's!"

"Let us hope, Calixta, that Bobinôt's got sense enough to come in out of a cyclone."

She went and stood at the window with a greatly disturbed look on her face. She

---

[1] Jacket.
[2] French: "God knows."
[3] Embankments built to keep the river from overflowing at flood times.

wiped the frame that was clouded with moisture. It was stiflingly hot. Alcée got up and joined her at the window, looking over her shoulder. The rain was coming down in sheets obscuring the view of far-off cabins and enveloping the distant wood in a gray mist. The playing of the lightning was incessant. A bolt struck a tall chinaberry tree at the edge of the field. It filled all visible space with a blinding glare and the crash seemed to invade the very boards they stood upon.

Calixta put her hands to her eyes, and with a cry, staggered backward. Alcée's arm encircled her, and for an instant he drew her close and spasmodically to him.

"*Bonté!*"[4] she cried, releasing herself from his encircling arm and retreating from the window, "the house'll go next! If I only knew w'ere Bibi was!" She would not compose herself; she would not be seated. Alcée clasped her shoulders and looked into her face. The contact of her warm, palpitating body when he had unthinkingly drawn her into his arms, had aroused all the old-time infatuation and desire for her flesh.

"Calixta," he said, "don't be frightened. Nothing can happen. The house is too low to be struck, with so many tall trees standing about. There! aren't you going to be quiet? say, aren't you?" He pushed her hair back from her face that was warm and steaming. Her lips were as red and moist as pomegranate seed. Her white neck and a glimpse of her full, firm bosom disturbed him powerfully. As she glanced up at him the fear in her liquid blue eyes had given place to a drowsy gleam that unconsciously betrayed a sensuous desire. He looked down into her eyes and there was nothing for him to do but to gather her lips in a kiss. It reminded him of Assumption.[5]

"Do you remember—in Assumption, Calixta?" he asked in a low voice broken by passion. Oh! she remembered; for in Assumption he had kissed her and kissed and kissed her; until his senses would well nigh fail, and to save her he would resort to a desperate flight. If she was not an immaculate dove in those days, she was still inviolate; a passionate creature whose very defenselessness had made her defense, against which his honor forbade him to prevail. Now—well, now—her lips seemed in a manner free to be tasted, as well as her round, white throat and her whiter breasts.

They did not heed the crashing torrents, and the roar of the elements made her laugh as she lay in his arms. She was a revelation in that dim, mysterious chamber; as white as the couch she lay upon. Her firm, elastic flesh that was knowing for the first time its birthright, was like a creamy lily that the sun invites to contribute its breath and perfume to the undying life of the world.

The generous abundance of her passion, without guile or trickery, was like a white flame which penetrated and found response in depths of his own sensuous nature that had never yet been reached.

When he touched her breasts they gave themselves up in quivering ecstasy, inviting his lips. Her mouth was a fountain of delight. And when he possessed her, they seemed to swoon together at the very borderland of life's mystery.

He stayed cushioned upon her, breathless, dazed, enervated, with his heart beating like a hammer upon her. With one hand she clasped his head, her lips lightly touching his forehead. The other hand stroked with a soothing rhythm his muscular shoulders.

The growl of the thunder was distant and passing away. The rain beat softly upon the shingles, inviting them to drowsiness and sleep. But they dared not yield.

---

[4] French: "Good gracious!"
[5] Festival of the Roman Catholic Church

honoring the ascent of the Virgin Mary into heaven.

The rain was over; and the sun was turning the glistening green world into a palace of gems. Calixta, on the gallery, watched Alcée ride away. He turned and smiled at her with a beaming face; and she lifted her pretty chin in the air and laughed aloud.

III

Bobinôt and Bibi, trudging home, stopped without at the cistern to make themselves presentable.

"My! Bibi, w'at will yo' mama say! You ought to be ashame'. You oughtn' put on those good pants. Look at 'em! An' that mud on yo' collar! How you got that mud on yo' collar, Bibi? I never saw such a boy!" Bibi was the picture of pathetic resignation. Bobinôt was the embodiment of serious solicitude as he strove to remove from his own person and his son's the signs of their tramp over heavy roads and through wet fields. He scraped the mud off Bibi's bare legs and feet with a stick and carefully removed all traces from his heavy brogans. Then, prepared for the worst—the meeting with an over-scrupulous housewife, they entered cautiously at the back door.

Calixta was preparing supper. She had set the table and was dripping coffee at the hearth. She sprang up as they came in.

"Oh, Bobinôt! You back! My! but I was uneasy. W'ere you been during the rain? An' Bibi? he ain't wet? he ain't hurt?" She had clasped Bibi and was kissing him effusively. Bobinôt's explanations and apologies which he had been composing all along the way, died on his lips as Calixta felt him to see if he were dry, and seemed to express nothing but satisfaction at their safe return.

"I brought you some shrimps, Calixta," offered Bobinôt, hauling the can from his ample side pocket and laying it on the table.

"Shrimps! Oh, Bobinôt! you too good fo' anything!" and she gave him a smacking kiss on the cheek that resounded. "*J'vous réponds,*[6] we'll have a feas' to night! umph-umph!"

Bobinôt and Bibi began to relax and enjoy themselves, and when the three seated themselves at table they laughed much and so loud that anyone might have heard them as far away as Laballière's.

IV

Alcée Laballière wrote to his wife, Clarisse, that night. It was a loving letter, full of tender solicitude. He told her not to hurry back, but if she and the babies liked it at Biloxi, to stay a month longer. He was getting on nicely; and though he missed them, he was willing to bear the separation a while longer—realizing that their health and pleasure were the first things to be considered.

V

As for Clarisse, she was charmed upon receiving her husband's letter. She and the babies were doing well. The society was agreeable; many of her old friends and

[6] French: "You bet!"

acquaintances were at the bay. And the first free breath since her marriage seemed to restore the pleasant liberty of her maiden days. Devoted as she was to her husband, their intimate conjugal life was something which she was more than willing to forego for a while.

So the storm passed and every one was happy.

1898

Mary E. Wilkins Freeman
1852–1930

Nathaniel Hawthorne called "the scribbling women" of his generation a menace to serious literature. The sentimentality and uncurbed fantasies commonly attributed by men to the popular fiction written by women in the pre–Civil War years may well have seemed to threaten a more accurate account of the innermost meanings of New England life. Current feminist criticism is reevaluating these charges through renewed interest in the novels many women then wrote to earn a living. More important, the situation altered significantly in the years following the Civil War. In fact, the work of women writers was one of the main origins of literary Realism. It is here that one finds portrayals of the bleak lives of the women of New England villages and farms—the ones who had gone a little crazy (as Robert Frost put it) when their men left them behind to set out for the cities or the Far West. The task of recording those women's fates frequently fell to the spinsters. On the surface these women might be thought to have been the most imaginatively bereft of the lot, but they had the time to think about their situation—and write about it with deadly accuracy.

Mary Eleanor Wilkins originally came from this band of unmarried women writers. She married Dr. Charles Freeman late, in 1902; it was initially a happy relationship that was progressively destroyed by his drunkenness and subsequent institutionalization in 1920. But during the long years before her marriage at forty-nine, Mary Wilkins established her reputation as a thoroughgoing regionalist and influential Realist.

Mary Wilkins grew up in frail health in Randolph, Massachusetts, south of Boston, and then in Brattleboro, Vermont. From the first, she had a love of reading that was a natural part of the imaginative lives of sensitive and isolated young girls of the Civil War period. Her formal education consisted of attendance at the Mount Holyoke Female Seminary for one year and the West Brattleboro Seminary for a second. But it was her devotion to the major literary figures of her century—Thackeray, Dickens, Poe, Hawthorne, Emerson, Thoreau, and Stowe—that stimulated her tastes. She supplemented her reading in fictional narrative and the essay by studying New England history, dialect, and folkways, adding to her love of received literary tradition the Realist's readiness to observe at first hand.

Her father's business failure in 1876 turned Mary Wilkins from writing occasional poems for children toward seriously considering a literary career. By the time she reached thirty, both her parents and her only sister were dead. Alone and impoverished, she had to make her way as a writer. In 1882 she won a literary contest with a prize of fifty dollars. By 1884 she established her name when *Harper's Bazar* (as it was then spelled) and other influential magazines provided a steady market for her stories. Readers both in this country and abroad gave her immediate approval. She eventually published thirty-nine volumes of stories, novels, and plays and received official recognition for her career in 1926 when the American Academy of Arts and Letters awarded her the William Dean Howells Medal for fiction. Still, her best work is bracketed by the years 1887 and 1892, during which time she brought out *A Humble Romance and Other Stories* (1887) and *A New England Nun and Other Stories* (1891).

Mary Wilkins Freeman emphasized the character of the people who inhabited the narrow valleys, small villages, and rocky farms of her native New England. Her stories attend less to the external details of place than to glimpses into the silent, inner lives of villagers and farmers who lived out what Thoreau (master observer of the same type fifty years earlier) called "lives of quiet desperation." To see her as a writer who moved far beyond the kind of writing Hawthorne deplored is to recognize the psychological authenticity she brought to her depiction of the mix of the human mind: the romantic's wistful desire for a brighter existence, the naturalist's acceptance of the impersonality of the universe, and the realist's awareness of the harsh facts of how people have to compromise their hopes if they are to continue to live together. As in "The Revolt of 'Mother,' " stubborn victories are won, on occasion, over circumstance, but the costs are high and the successes limited. The people about whom Mary Wilkins Freeman wrote are both very foolish and very brave. She gave them the respect of her writer's accurate gaze. As a consequence, both the tales and their teller command attention as important parts of American social and literary history that should not be overlooked.

Further Reading:
E. Foster, *Mary E. Wilkins Freeman*, 1956.
A. Hamblen, *The New England Art of Mary E. Wilkins Freeman*, 1966.
P. Westbrook, *Mary Wilkins Freeman*, 1967.

Text:
A New England Nun, 1891.
See also *The Best Stories of Mary Wilkins Freeman*, ed. H. Lanier, 1927.

The Revolt of "Mother"

"Father!"

"What is it?"

"What are them men diggin' over there in the field for?"

There was a sudden dropping and enlarging of the lower part of the old man's face, as if some heavy weight had settled therein; he shut his mouth tight, and went on harnessing the great bay mare. He hustled the collar on to her neck with a jerk.

"Father!"

The old man slapped the saddle upon the mare's back.

"Look here, father, I want to know what them men are diggin' over in the field for, an' I'm goin' to know."

"I wish you'd go into the house, mother, an' 'tend to your own affairs," the old man said then. He ran his words together, and his speech was almost as inarticulate as a growl.

But the woman understood; it was her most native tongue. "I ain't goin' into the house till you tell me what them men are doin' over there in the field," said she.

Then she stood waiting. She was a small woman, short and straight-waisted like a child in her brown cotton gown. Her forehead was mild and benevolent between the smooth curves of gray hair; there were meek downward lines about her nose and mouth; but her eyes, fixed upon the old man, looked as if the meekness had been the result of her own will, never of the will of another.

They were in the barn, standing before the wide open doors. The spring air, full of the smell of growing grass and unseen blossoms, came in their faces. The deep yard in front was littered with farm wagons and piles of wood; on the edges, close to the fence and the house, the grass was a vivid green, and there were some dandelions.

The old man glanced doggedly at his wife as he tightened the last buckles on the harness. She looked as immovable to him as one of the rocks in his pasture-land, bound to the earth with generations of blackberry vines. He slapped the reins over the horse, and started forth from the barn.

"*Father!*" said she.

The old man pulled up. "What is it?"

"I want to know what them men are diggin' over there in that field for."

"They're diggin' a cellar, I s'pose, if you've got to know."

"A cellar for what?"

"A barn."

"A barn? You ain't goin' to build a barn over there where we was goin' to have a house, father?"

The old man said not another word. He hurried the horse into the farm wagon, and clattered out of the yard, jouncing as sturdily on his seat as a boy.

The woman stood a moment looking after him, then she went out of the barn across a corner of the yard to the house. The house, standing at right angles with the great barn and a long reach of sheds and out-buildings, was infinitesimal compared with them. It was scarcely as commodious for people as the little boxes under the barn eaves were for doves.

A pretty girl's face, pink and delicate as a flower, was looking out of one of the house windows. She was watching three men who were digging over in the field which bounded the yard near the road line. She turned quietly when the woman entered.

"What are they digging for, mother?" said she. "Did he tell you?"

"They're diggin' for—a cellar for a new barn."

"Oh, mother, he ain't going to build another barn?"

"That's what he says."

A boy stood before the kitchen glass combing his hair. He combed slowly and painstakingly, arranging his brown hair in a smooth hillock over his forehead. He did not seem to pay any attention to the conversation.

"Sammy, did you know father was going to build a new barn?" asked the girl.

The boy combed assiduously.

"Sammy!"

He turned, and showed a face like his father's under his smooth crest of hair. "Yes, I s'pose I did," he said, reluctantly.

"How long have you known it?" asked his mother.

" 'Bout three months, I guess."

"Why didn't you tell of it?"

"Didn't think 'twould do no good."

"I don't see what father wants another barn for," said the girl, in her sweet, slow voice. She turned again to the window, and stared out at the digging men in the field. Her tender, sweet face was full of a gentle distress. Her forehead was as bald and innocent as a baby's, with the light hair strained back from it in a row of curl-papers. She was quite large, but her soft curves did not look as if they covered muscles.

Her mother looked sternly at the boy. "Is he goin' to buy more cows?" said she.

The boy did not reply; he was tying his shoes.

"Sammy, I want you to tell me if he's goin' to buy more cows."

"I s'pose he is."

"How many?"

"Four, I guess."

His mother said nothing more. She went into the pantry, and there was a clatter of dishes. The boy got his cap from a nail behind the door, took an old arithmetic from the shelf, and started for school. He was lightly built, but clumsy. He went out of the yard with a curious spring in the hips, that made his loose home-made jacket tilt up in the rear.

The girl went to the sink, and began to wash the dishes that were piled up there. Her mother came promptly out of the pantry, and shoved her aside. "You wipe 'em," said she; "I'll wash. There's a good many this mornin'."

The mother plunged her hands vigorously into the water, the girl wiped the plates slowly and dreamily. "Mother," said she, "don't you think it's too bad father's going to build that new barn, much as we need a decent house to live in?"

Her mother scrubbed a dish fiercely. "You ain't found out yet we're women-folks, Nanny Penn," said she. "You ain't seen enough of men-folks yet to. One of these days you'll find it out, an' then you'll know that we know only what men-folks think we do, so far as any use of it goes, an' how we'd ought to reckon men-folks in with Providence, an' not complain of what they do any more than we do of the weather."

"I don't care; I don't believe George is anything like that, anyhow," said Nanny. Her delicate face flushed pink, her lips pouted softly, as if she were going to cry.

"You wait an' see. I guess George Eastman ain't no better than other men. You hadn't ought to judge father, though. He can't help it, 'cause he don't look at things jest the way we do. An' we've been pretty comfortable here, after all. The roof don't leak—ain't never but once—that's one thing. Father's kept it shingled right up."

"I do wish we had a parlor."

"I guess it won't hurt George Eastman any to come to see you in a nice clean kitchen. I guess a good many girls don't have as good a place as this. Nobody's ever heard me complain."

"I ain't complained either, mother."

"Well, I don't think you'd better, a good father an' a good home as you've got. S'pose your father made you go out an' work for your livin'? Lots of girls have to that ain't no stronger an' better able to than you be."

Sarah Penn washed the frying-pan with a conclusive air. She scrubbed the outside of it as faithfully as the inside. She was a masterly keeper of her box of a house. Her one living-room never seemed to have in it any of the dust which the friction of life with inanimate matter produces. She swept, and there seemed to be no dirt to go before the broom; she cleaned, and one could see no difference. She was like an artist so perfect that he has apparently no art. To-day she got out a mixing bowl and a board, and rolled some pies, and there was no more flour upon her than upon her daughter who was doing finer work. Nanny was to be married in the fall, and she was sewing on some white cambric and embroidery. She sewed industriously while her mother cooked, her soft milk-white hands and wrists showed whiter than her delicate work.

"We must have the stove moved out in the shed before long," said Mrs. Penn. "Talk about not havin' things, it's been a real blessin' to be able to put a stove up in that shed in hot weather. Father did one good thing when he fixed that stove-pipe out there."

Sarah Penn's face as she rolled her pies had that expression of meek vigor which might have characterized one of the New Testament saints. She was making mince-pies. Her husband, Adoniram Penn, liked them better than any other kind. She baked twice a week. Adoniram often liked a piece of pie between meals. She hurried this morning. It had been later than usual when she began, and she wanted to have a pie baked for dinner. However deep a resentment she might be forced to hold against her husband, she would never fail in sedulous attention to his wants.

Nobility of character manifests itself at loop-holes when it is not provided with large doors. Sarah Penn's showed itself to-day in flaky dishes of pastry. So she made the pies faithfully, while across the table she could see, when she glanced up from her work, the sight that rankled in her patient and steadfast soul—the digging of the cellar of the new barn in the place where Adoniram forty years ago had promised her their new house should stand.

The pies were done for dinner. Adoniram and Sammy were home a few minutes after twelve o'clock. The dinner was eaten with serious haste. There was never much conversation at the table in the Penn family. Adoniram asked a blessing, and they ate promptly, then rose up and went about their work.

Sammy went back to school, taking soft sly lopes out of the yard like a rabbit. He wanted a game of marbles before school, and feared his father would give him some chores to do. Adoniram hastened to the door and called after him, but he was out of sight.

"I don't see what you let him go for, mother," said he. "I wanted him to help me unload that wood."

Adoniram went to work out in the yard unloading wood from the wagon. Sarah put away the dinner dishes, while Nanny took down her curl-papers and changed her dress. She was going down to the store to buy some more embroidery and thread.

When Nanny was gone, Mrs. Penn went to the door. "Father!" she called.

"Well, what is it!"

"I want to see you jest a minute, father."

"I can't leave this wood nohow. I've got to get it unloaded an' go for a load of gravel afore two o'clock. Sammy had ought to helped me. You hadn't ought to let him go to school so early."

"I want to see you jest a minute."

"I tell ye I can't, nohow, mother."

"Father, you come here." Sarah Penn stood in the door like a queen; she held her head as if it bore a crown; there was that patience which makes authority royal in her voice. Adoniram went.

Mrs. Penn led the way into the kitchen, and pointed to a chair. "Sit down, father," said she; "I've got somethin' I want to say to you."

He sat down heavily; his face was quite stolid, but he looked at her with restive eyes. "Well, what is it, mother?"

"I want to know what you're buildin' that new barn for, father?"

"I ain't got nothin' to say about it."

"It can't be you think you need another barn?"

"I tell ye I ain't got nothin' to say about it, mother; an' I ain't goin' to say nothin'."

"Be you goin' to buy more cows?"

Adoniram did not reply; he shut his mouth tight.

"I know you be, as well as I want to. Now, father, look here"—Sarah Penn had not sat down; she stood before her husband in the humble fashion of a Scripture woman[1]—"I'm goin' to talk real plain to you; I never have sence I married you, but I'm goin' to now. I ain't never complained, an' I ain't goin' to complain now, but I'm goin' to talk plain. You see this room here, father; you look at it well. You see there ain't no carpet on the floor, an' you see the paper is all dirty, an' droppin' off the walls. We ain't had no new paper on it for ten year, an' then I put it on myself, an' it didn't cost but ninepence a roll. You see this room, father; it's all the one I've had to work in an' eat in an' sit in sence we was married. There ain't another woman in the whole town whose husband ain't got half the means you have but what's got better. It's all the room Nanny's got to have her company in; an' there ain't one of her mates but what's got better, an' their fathers not so able as hers is. It's all the room she'll have to be married in. What would you have thought, father, if we had our weddin' in a room no better than this? I was married in my mother's parlor, with a carpet on the floor, an' stuffed furniture, an' a mahogany card-table. An' this is all the room my daughter will have to be married in. Look here, father!"

Sarah Penn went across the room as though it were a tragic stage. She flung open a door and disclosed a tiny bedroom, only large enough for a bed and bureau, with a path between. "There, father," said she—"there's all the room I've had to sleep in forty year. All my children were born there—the two that died, an' the two that's livin'. I was sick with a fever there."

She stepped to another door and opened it. It led into the small, ill-lighted pantry. "Here," said she, "is all the buttery I've got—every place I've got for my dishes, to set away my victuals in, an' to keep my milk-pans in. Father, I've been takin' care of the milk of six cows in this place, an' now you're goin' to build a new barn, an' keep more cows, an' give me more to do in it."

[1] Probably an allusion to the biblical figure Ruth,
a woman proverbially known for unswerving
loyalty to her husband.

She threw open another door. A narrow crooked flight of stairs wound upward from it. "There, father," said she, "I want you to look at the stairs that go up to them two unfinished chambers that are all the places our son an' daughter have had to sleep in all their lives. There ain't a prettier girl in town nor a more ladylike one than Nanny, an' that's the place she has to sleep in. It ain't so good as your horse's stall; it ain't so warm an' tight."

Sarah Penn went back and stood before her husband. "Now, father," said she, "I want to know if you think you're doin' right an' accordin' to what you profess. Here, when we was married, forty year ago, you promised me faithful that we should have a new house built in that lot over in the field before the year was out. You said you had money enough, an' you wouldn't ask me to live in no such place as this. It is forty year now, an' you've been makin' more money, an' I've been savin' of it for you ever since, an' you ain't built no house yet. You've built sheds an' cow-houses an' one new barn, an' now you're goin' to build another. Father, I want to know if you think it's right. You're lodgin' your dumb beasts better than you are your own flesh an' blood. I want to know if you think it's right."

"I ain't got nothin' to say."

"You can't say nothin' without ownin' it ain't right, father. An' there's another thing—I ain't complained; I've got along forty year, an' I s'pose I should forty more, if it wa'n't for that—if we don't have another house. Nanny she can't live with us after she's married. She'll have to go somewheres else to live away from us, an' it don't seem as if I could have it so, noways, father. She wa'n't ever strong. She's got considerable color, but there wa'n't never any backbone to her. I've always took the heft of everything off her, an' she ain't fit to keep house an' do everything herself. She'll be all worn out inside of a year. Think of her doin' all the washin' an' ironin' an' bakin' with them soft white hands an' arms, an' sweepin'! I can't have it so, noways, father."

Mrs. Penn's face was burning; her mild eyes gleamed. She had pleaded her little cause like a Webster;[2] she had ranged from severity to pathos; but her opponent employed that obstinate silence which makes eloquence futile with mocking echoes. Adoniram arose clumsily.

"Father, ain't you got nothin' to say?" said Mrs. Penn.

"I've got to go off after that load of gravel. I can't stan' here talkin' all day."

"Father, won't you think it over, an' have a house built there instead of a barn?"

"I ain't got nothin' to say."

Adoniram shuffled out. Mrs. Penn went into her bedroom. When she came out, her eyes were red. She had a roll of unbleached cotton cloth. She spread it out on the kitchen table, and began cutting out some shirts for her husband. The men over in the field had a team to help them this afternoon; she could hear their halloos. She had a scanty pattern for the shirts; she had to plan and piece the sleeves.

Nanny came home with her embroidery, and sat down with her needlework. She had taken down her curl-papers, and there was a soft roll of fair hair like an aureole over her forehead; her face was as delicately fine and clear as porcelain. Suddenly

[2] Reference to the statesman Daniel Webster (1782–1852), who was famous for his oratorical powers.

she looked up, and the tender red flamed all over her face and neck. "Mother," said she.

"What say?"

"I've been thinking—I don't see how we're goin' to have any—wedding in this room. I'd be ashamed to have his folks come if we didn't have anybody else."

"Mebbe we can have some new paper before then; I can put it on. I guess you won't have no call to be ashamed of your belongin's."

"We might have the wedding in the new barn," said Nanny, with gentle pettishness. "Why, mother, what makes you look so?"

Mrs. Penn had started, and was staring at her with a curious expression. She turned again to her work, and spread out a pattern carefully on the cloth. "Nothin'," said she.

Presently Adoniram clattered out of the yard in his two-wheeled dump cart, standing as proudly upright as a Roman charioteer. Mrs. Penn opened the door and stood there a minute looking out; the halloos of the men sounded louder.

It seemed to her all through the spring months that she heard nothing but the halloos and the noises of saws and hammers. The new barn grew fast. It was a fine edifice for this little village. Men came on pleasant Sundays, in their meeting suits and clean shirt bosoms, and stood around it admiringly. Mrs. Penn did not speak of it, and Adoniram did not mention it to her, although sometimes, upon a return from inspecting it, he bore himself with injured dignity.

"It's a strange thing how your mother feels about the new barn," he said, confidentially, to Sammy one day.

Sammy only grunted after an odd fashion for a boy; he had learned it from his father.

The barn was all completed ready for use by the third week in July. Adoniram had planned to move his stock in on Wednesday; on Tuesday he received a letter which changed his plans. He came in with it early in the morning. "Sammy's been to the post-office," said he, "an' I've got a letter from Hiram." Hiram was Mrs. Penn's brother, who lived in Vermont.

"Well," said Mrs. Penn, "what does he say about the folks?"

"I guess they're all right. He says he thinks if I come up country right off there's a chance to buy jest the kind of a horse I want." He stared reflectively out of the window at the new barn.

Mrs. Penn was making pies. She went on clapping the rolling-pin into the crust, although she was very pale, and her heart beat loudly.

"I dun' know but what I'd better go," said Adoniram. "I hate to go off jest now, right in the midst of hayin', but the ten-acre lot's cut, an' I guess Rufus an' the others can git along without me three or four days. I can't get a horse round here to suit me, nohow, an' I've got to have another for all that wood-haulin' in the fall. I told Hiram to watch out, an' if he got wind of a good horse to let me know. I guess I'd better go."

"I'll get out your clean shirt an' collar," said Mrs. Penn calmly.

She laid out Adoniram's Sunday suit and his clean clothes on the bed in the little bedroom. She got his shaving-water and razor ready. At last she buttoned on his collar and fastened his black cravat.

Adoniram never wore his collar and cravat except on extra occasions. He held his head high, with a rasped dignity. When he was all ready, with his coat and hat brushed, and a lunch of pie and cheese in a paper bag, he hesitated on the threshold of the door. He looked at his wife, and his manner was defiantly apologetic. "*If* them cows come to-day, Sammy can drive 'em into the new barn," said he; "an' when they bring the hay up, they can pitch it in there."

"Well," replied Mrs. Penn.

Adoniram set his shaven face ahead and started. When he had cleared the door-step, he turned and looked back with a kind of nervous solemnity. "I shall be back by Saturday if nothin' happens," said he.

"Do be careful, father," returned his wife.

She stood in the door with Nanny at her elbow and watched him out of sight. Her eyes had a strange, doubtful expression in them; her peaceful forehead was contracted. She went in, and about her baking again. Nanny sat sewing. Her wedding-day was drawing nearer, and she was getting pale and thin with her steady sewing. Her mother kept glancing at her.

"Have you got that pain in your side this mornin'?" she asked.

"A little."

Mrs. Penn's face, as she worked, changed, her perplexed forehead smoothed, her eyes were steady, her lips firmly set. She formed a maxim for herself, although incoherently with her unlettered thoughts. "Unsolicited opportunities are the guide-posts of the Lord to the new roads of life," she repeated in effect, and she made up her mind to her course of action.

"S'posin' I *had* wrote to Hiram," she muttered once, when she was in the pantry —"s'posin' I had wrote, an' asked him if he knew of any horse? But I didn't, an' father's goin' wa'n't none of my doin'. It looks like a providence." Her voice rang out quite loud at the last.

"What you talkin' about, mother?" called Nanny.

"Nothin'."

Mrs. Penn hurried her baking; at eleven o'clock it was all done. The load of hay from the west field came slowly down the cart track, and drew up at the new barn. Mrs. Penn ran out. "Stop!" she screamed—"stop!"

The men stopped and looked; Sammy upreared from the top of the load, and stared at his mother.

"Stop!" she cried out again. "Don't you put the hay in that barn; put it in the old one."

"Why, he said to put it in here," returned one of the hay-makers, wonderingly. He was a young man, a neighbor's son, whom Adoniram hired by the year to help on the farm.

"Don't you put the hay in the new barn; there's room enough in the old one, ain't there?" said Mrs. Penn.

"Room enough," returned the hired man, in his thick, rustic tones. "Didn't need the new barn, nohow, far as room's concerned. Well, I s'pose he changed his mind." He took hold of the horses' bridles.

Mrs. Penn went back to the house. Soon the kitchen windows were darkened, and a fragrance like warm honey came into the room.

Nanny laid down her work. "I thought father wanted them to put the hay into the new barn?" she said, wonderingly.

"It's all right," replied her mother.

Sammy slid down from the load of hay, and came in to see if dinner was ready.

"I ain't goin' to get a regular dinner to-day, as long as father's gone," said his mother. "I've let the fire go out. You can have some bread an' milk an' pie. I thought we could get along." She set out some bowls of milk, some bread, and a pie on the kitchen table. "You'd better eat your dinner now," said she. "You might jest as well get through with it. I want you to help me afterward."

Nanny and Sammy stared at each other. There was something strange in their mother's manner. Mrs. Penn did not eat anything herself. She went into the pantry, and they heard her moving dishes while they ate. Presently she came out with a pile of plates. She got the clothes-basket out of the shed, and packed them in it. Nanny and Sammy watched. She brought out cups and saucers, and put them in with the plates.

"What you goin' to do, mother?" inquired Nanny, in a timid voice. A sense of something unusual made her tremble, as if it were a ghost. Sammy rolled his eyes over his pie.

"You'll see what I'm goin' to do," replied Mrs. Penn. "If you're through, Nanny, I want you to go up-stairs an' pack up your things; an' I want you, Sammy, to help me take down the bed in the bedroom.'"

"Oh, mother, what for?" gasped Nanny.

"You'll see."

During the next few hours a feat was performed by this simple, pious New England mother which was equal in its way to Wolfe's storming of the Heights of Abraham.[3] It took no more genius and audacity of bravery for Wolfe to cheer his wondering soldiers up those steep precipices, under the sleeping eyes of the enemy, than for Sarah Penn, at the head of her children, to move all their little household goods into the new barn while her husband was away.

Nanny and Sammy followed their mother's instructions without a murmur; indeed, they were overawed. There is a certain uncanny and superhuman quality about all such purely original undertakings as their mother's was to them. Nanny went back and forth with her light loads, and Sammy tugged with sober energy.

At five o'clock in the afternoon the little house in which the Penns had lived for forty years had emptied itself into the new barn.

Every builder builds somewhat for unknown purposes, and is in a measure a prophet. The architect of Adoniram Penn's barn, while he designed it for the comfort of four-footed animals, had planned better than he knew for the comfort of humans. Sarah Penn saw at a glance its possibilities. Those great box-stalls, with quilts hung before them, would make better bedrooms than the one she had occupied for forty years, and there was a tight carriage-room. The harness-room, with its chimney and shelves, would make a kitchen of her dreams. The great middle space would make a parlor, by-and-by, fit for a palace. Up stairs there was as much room as down. With

[3] James Wolfe (1727–1759) was the British general who assaulted the French forces lodged on the cliffs near Quebec in the region known as the "Plains of Abraham"; the French were defeated, but Wolfe was killed during the battle that won Canada for Britain.

partitions and windows, what a house would there be! Sarah looked at the row of stanchions before the allotted space for cows, and reflected that she would have her front entry there.

At six o'clock the stove was up in the harness-room, the kettle was boiling, and the table set for tea. It looked almost as home-like as the abandoned house across the yard had ever done. The young hired man milked, and Sarah directed him calmly to bring the milk to the new barn. He came gaping, dropping little blots of foam from the brimming pails on the grass. Before the next morning he had spread the story of Adoniram Penn's wife moving into the new barn all over the little village. Men assembled in the store and talked it over, women with shawls over their heads scuttled into each other's houses before their work was done. Any deviation from the ordinary course of life in this quiet town was enough to stop all progress in it. Everybody paused to look at the staid, independent figure on the side track.[4] There was a difference of opinion with regard to her. Some held her to be insane; some, of a lawless and rebellious spirit.

Friday the minister went to see her. It was in the forenoon, and she was at the barn door shelling peas for dinner. She looked up and returned his salutation with dignity, then she went on with her work. She did not invite him in. The saintly expression of her face remained fixed, but there was an angry flush over it.

The minister stood awkwardly before her, and talked. She handled the peas as if they were bullets. At last she looked up, and her eyes showed the spirit that her meek front had covered for a lifetime.

"There ain't no use talkin', Mr. Hersey," said she. "I've thought it all over an' over, an' I believe I'm doin' what's right. I've made it the subject of prayer, an' it's betwixt me an' the Lord an' Adoniram. There ain't no call for nobody else to worry about it."

"Well, of course, if you have brought it to the Lord in prayer, and feel satisfied that you are doing right, Mrs. Penn," said the minister, helplessly. His thin gray-bearded face was pathetic. He was a sickly man; his youthful confidence had cooled; he had to scourge himself up to some of his pastoral duties as relentlessly as a Catholic ascetic, and then he was prostrated by the smart.

"I think it's right jest as much as I think it was right for our forefathers to come over from the old country 'cause they didn't have what belonged to 'em," said Mrs. Penn. She arose. The barn threshold might have been Plymouth Rock[5] from her bearing. "I don't doubt you mean well, Mr. Hersey," said she, "but there are things people hadn't ought to interfere with. I've been a member of the church for over forty year. I've got my own mind an' my own feet, an' I'm goin' to think my own thoughts an' go my own ways, an' nobody but the Lord is goin' to dictate to me unless I've a mind to have him. Won't you come in an' set down? How is Mis' Hersey?"

"She is well, I thank you," replied the minister. He added some more perplexed apologetic remarks; then he retreated.

He could expound the intricacies of every character study in the Scriptures, he was competent to grasp the Pilgrim Fathers and all historical innovators, but Sarah Penn was beyond him. He could deal with primal cases, but parallel ones worsted him. But,

---

[4] A spur line connected to the main railroad track.

[5] The spot associated with the landing of the Pilgrims on the Massachusetts coast in 1620.

after all, although it was aside from his province, he wondered more how Adoniram Penn would deal with his wife than how the Lord would. Everybody shared the wonder. When Adoniram's four new cows arrived, Sarah ordered three to be put in the old barn, the other in the house shed where the cooking-stove had stood. That added to the excitement. It was whispered that all four cows were domiciled in the house.

Towards sunset on Saturday, when Adoniram was expected home, there was a knot of men in the road near the new barn. The hired man had milked, but he still hung around the premises. Sarah Penn had supper all ready. There were brown-bread and baked beans and a custard pie; it was the supper that Adoniram loved on a Saturday night. She had on a clean calico, and she bore herself imperturbably. Nanny and Sammy kept close at her heels. Their eyes were large, and Nanny was full of nervous tremors. Still there was to them more pleasant excitement than anything else. An inborn confidence in their mother over their father asserted itself.

Sammy looked out of the harness-room window. "There he is," he announced, in an awed whisper. He and Nanny peeped around the casing. Mrs. Penn kept on about her work. The children watched Adoniram leave the new horse standing in the drive while he went to the house door. It was fastened. Then he went around to the shed. That door was seldom locked, even when the family was away. The thought how her father would be confronted by the cow flashed upon Nanny. There was a hysterical sob in her throat. Adoniram emerged from the shed and stood looking about in a dazed fashion. His lips moved; he was saying something, but they could not hear what it was. The hired man was peeping around a corner of the old barn, but nobody saw him.

Adoniram took the new horse by the bridle and led him across the yard to the new barn. Nanny and Sammy slunk close to their mother. The barn doors rolled back, and there stood Adoniram, with the long mild face of the great Canadian farm horse looking over his shoulder.

Nanny kept behind her mother, but Sammy stepped suddenly forward, and stood in front of her.

Adoniram stared at the group. "What on airth you all down here for?" said he. "What's the matter over to the house?"

"We've come here to live, father," said Sammy. His shrill voice quavered out bravely.

"What"—Adoniram sniffed—"what is it smells like cookin?" said he. He stepped forward and looked in the open door of the harness-room. Then he turned to his wife. His old bristling face was pale and frightened. "What on airth does this mean, mother?" he gasped.

"You come in here, father," said Sarah. She led the way into the harness-room and shut the door. "Now, father," said she, "you needn't be scared. I ain't crazy. There ain't nothin' to be upset over. But we've come here to live, an' we're goin' to live here. We've got jest as good a right here as new horses an' cows. The house wa'n't fit for us to live in any longer, an' I made up my mind I wa'n't goin' to stay there. I've done my duty by you forty year, an' I'm goin' to do it now; but I'm goin' to live here. You've got to put in some windows and partitions; an' you'll have to buy some furniture."

"Why, mother!" the old man gasped.

"You'd better take your coat off an' get washed—there's the wash-basin—an' then we'll have supper."

"Why, mother!"

Sammy went past the window, leading the new horse to the old barn. The old man saw him, and shook his head speechlessly. He tried to take off his coat, but his arms seemed to lack the power. His wife helped him. She poured some water into the tin basin, and put in a piece of soap. She got the comb and brush, and smoothed his thin gray hair after he had washed. Then she put the beans, hot bread, and tea on the table. Sammy came in, and the family drew up. Adoniram sat looking dazedly at his plate, and they waited.

"Ain't you goin' to ask a blessin', father?" said Sarah.

And the old man bent his head and mumbled.

All through the meal he stopped eating at intervals, and stared furtively at his wife; but he ate well. The home food tasted good to him, and his old frame was too sturdily healthy to be affected by his mind. But after supper he went out, and sat down on the step of the smaller door at the right of the barn, through which he had meant his Jerseys to pass in stately file, but which Sarah designed for her front house door, and he leaned his head on his hands.

After the supper dishes were cleared away and the milk-pans washed, Sarah went out to him. The twilight was deepening. There was a clear green glow in the sky. Before them stretched the smooth level of field; in the distance was a cluster of hay-stacks like the huts of a village; the air was very cool and calm and sweet. The landscape might have been an ideal one of peace.

Sarah bent over and touched her husband on one of his thin, sinewy shoulders. "Father!"

The old man's shoulders heaved: he was weeping.

"Why, don't do so, father," said Sarah.

"I'll—put up the—partitions, an'—everything you—want, mother."

Sarah put her apron up to her face; she was overcome by her own triumph.

Adoniram was like a fortress whose walls had no active resistance, and went down the instant the right besieging tools were used. "Why, mother," he said, hoarsely, "I hadn't no idee you was so set on't as all this comes to."

1891

Booker T. Washington
1856–1915

There has been a dramatic shift in Booker T. Washington's reputation since the turn of the century. His celebration as the almost mythic "Moses of his race" before World War I and his dismissal by black militants during the civil rights struggles of the 1960s as an Uncle Tom reveal the changing nature of black activism in America. Washington's contributions and his failings are being reassessed, but regardless of controversy about the man himself, his life and writings can hardly be dismissed. His autobiography alone confirms this. First published serially in the magazine *Outlook*, edited by the white liberal Lyman Abbott, Washington's *Up from Slavery* appeared in book form in 1901. Washington's life story caught the imagination of a large American audience. Whites in particular saw Washington as representing the "best" kind of black and the "right" kind of success. The period between the close of the Civil War and World War I has been called "the era of Booker T. Washington." In 1902, W. E. B. Du Bois, one of Washington's severest critics, could freely admit that Washington was "the one recognized spokesman of his ten million fellows and one of the most notable figures in a nation of seventy millions." What is currently in question is Washington's role in black history, not in whites' versions of that history.

Booker T. Washington was the son of an unidentified white slaveowner and a slave woman, born on an unknown date sometime in 1856 in Hale's Ford, Virginia. He did not even acquire a last name until he started school and took his stepfather's first name as his surname. After the end of the Civil War, he moved with his mother and stepfather to Malden, West Virginia, where he grew up poor. Consumed by the desire to get an education, he made the five-hundred-mile trek by foot and rail to Virginia's Hampton Institute, a school set up for the education of impoverished blacks. This incident forms one of the most vivid chapters in his tale of self-willed success. Out of his early experiences, Washington became a committed advocate of self-discipline and self-help (the very virtues that, in Benjamin Franklin's work ethic, could enable any poor boy to realize "the American dream").

Determined to succeed, Washington moved in 1881 to the Tuskegee Institute in Alabama, a manual arts school established after the Civil War to train blacks. He became the head of the institute, an effective fund-raiser, and promoter of its work in the Deep South, where lynchings and racial injustice were still common practice, despite the attempt of many whites to better the lot of the former slaves. In 1895 Washington earned national attention with his speech known as "The Atlanta Compromise." In this address he urged a moderate policy of reconciliation between aspiring blacks and nervous whites. Let blacks be given every means to improve their condition economically by learning useful trades, Washington urged, and they would be content to overlook the white community's failure to provide fundamental political rights. A practical man, Washington advocated a plan of compromise and trade-offs to secure his people the best chance to survive under difficult economic conditions. The assurance of jobs and living wages came first; social equality would come later. He knew the facts of power in a nation where animosity toward all minority groups was on the rise in the 1890s and where an essentially mercantile society responded to the appeal of money and management principles better than it did to suggestions that the moral fabric of the nation was being destroyed by inequality. Guest at a dinner given by President Theodore Roosevelt (not without riling many), recipient of an honorary degree from Harvard, praised by blacks and whites alike, Washington shrewdly did what he could to make blacks' lives more bearable.

When Washington is taken on his own terms, his autobiographical account of how clever, energetic boys go upward and onward in the face of practical contingencies has an undeniable impact on the imagination. He knew his times and used them well. He provided a model for black aspiration by his habit of seizing from history the essential social principles that led to material advancement while overlooking whatever might threaten that success.

Further Reading:

T. Boone, *The Philosophy of Booker T. Washington,* 1939.
B. Mathews, *Booker T. Washington, Educator and Interracial Interpreter,* 1948.
S. Spencer, *Booker T. Washington and the Negro's Place in American Life,* 1955.
Booker T. Washington and His Critics, Black Leadership in Crisis, ed. H. Hawkins, 1962.
A. Meier, *Negro Thought in America, 1880–1915: Racial Ideologies in the Age of Booker T. Washington,* 1963.

R. Brisbane, *The Black Vanguard,* 1970.
A. Bontemps, *Young Booker: Booker T. Washington's Early Days,* 1972.
L. Harlan, *Booker T. Washington: The Making of a Black Leader, 1856–1901,* 1972.
W. H. Delaney, *Learn by Doing: A Projected Educational Philosophy in the Thought of Booker T. Washington,* 1974.
L. Harlan, *Booker T. Washington: The Wizard of Tuskegee, 1901–1915,* 1983.

Text:
Up from Slavery, 1901.
See also *The Booker T. Washington Papers,* ed. L. Harlan, 11 vols., 1872–1981.

---

from Up from Slavery

Chapter III: The Struggle for an Education

One day, while at work in the coal-mine, I happened to overhear two miners talking about a great school for coloured people somewhere in Virginia. This was the first time that I had ever heard anything about any kind of school or college that was more pretentious than the little coloured school in our town.

In the darkness of the mine I noiselessly crept as close as I could to the two men who were talking. I heard one tell the other that not only was the school established for the members of my race, but that opportunities were provided by which poor but worthy students could work out all or a part of the cost of board, and at the same time be taught some trade or industry.

As they went on describing the school, it seemed to me that it must be the greatest place on earth, and not even Heaven presented more attractions for me at that time than did the Hampton Normal and Agricultural Institute in Virginia, about which these men were talking. I resolved at once to go to that school, although I had no idea where it was, or how many miles away, or how I was going to reach it; I remembered only that I was on fire constantly with one ambition, and that was to go to Hampton. This thought was with me day and night.

After hearing of the Hampton Institute, I continued to work for a few months longer in the coal-mine. While at work there, I heard of a vacant position in the household of General Lewis Ruffner, the owner of the salt-furnace and coal-mine. Mrs. Viola Ruffner, the wife of General Ruffner, was a "Yankee" woman from

Vermont. Mrs. Ruffner had a reputation all through the vicinity for being very strict with her servants, and especially with the boys who tried to serve her. Few of them had remained with her more than two or three weeks. They all left with the same excuse: she was too strict. I decided, however, that I would rather try Mrs. Ruffner's house than remain in the coal-mine, and so my mother applied to her for the vacant position. I was hired at a salary of $5 per month.

I had heard so much about Mrs. Ruffner's severity that I was almost afraid to see her, and trembled when I went into her presence. I had not lived with her many weeks, however, before I began to understand her. I soon began to learn that, first of all, she wanted everything kept clean about her, that she wanted things done promptly and systematically, and that at the bottom of everything she wanted absolute honesty and frankness. Nothing must be sloven or slipshod; every door, every fence, must be kept in repair.

I cannot now recall how long I lived with Mrs. Ruffner before going to Hampton, but I think it must have been a year and a half. At any rate, I here repeat what I have said more than once before, that the lessons that I learned in the home of Mrs. Ruffner were as valuable to me as any education I have ever gotten anywhere since. Even to this day I never see bits of paper scattered around a house or in the street that I do not want to pick them up at once. I never see a filthy yard that I do not want to clean it, a paling off of a fence that I do not want to put it on, an unpainted or unwhitewashed house that I do not want to paint or whitewash it, or a button off one's clothes, or a grease-spot on them or on a floor, that I do not want to call attention to it.

From fearing Mrs. Ruffner I soon learned to look upon her as one of my best friends. When she found that she could trust me she did so implicitly. During the one or two winters that I was with her she gave me an opportunity to go to school for an hour in the day during a portion of the winter months, but most of my studying was done at night, sometimes alone, sometimes under some one whom I could hire to teach me. Mrs. Ruffner always encouraged and sympathized with me in all my efforts to get an education. It was while living with her that I began to get together my first library. I secured a dry-goods box, knocked out one side of it, put some shelves in it, and began putting into it every kind of book that I could get my hands upon, and called it my "library."

Notwithstanding my success at Mrs. Ruffner's I did not give up the idea of going to the Hampton Institute. In the fall of 1872 I determined to make an effort to get there, although, as I have stated, I had no definite idea of the direction in which Hampton was, or of what it would cost to go there. I do not think that any one thoroughly sympathized with me in my ambition to go to Hampton unless it was my mother, and she was troubled with a grave fear that I was starting out on a "wild-goose chase." At any rate, I got only a half-hearted consent from her that I might start. The small amount of money that I had earned had been consumed by my stepfather and the remainder of the family, with the exception of a very few dollars, and so I had very little with which to buy clothes and pay my travelling expenses. My brother John helped me all that he could, but of course that was not a great deal, for his work was in the coal-mine, where he did not earn much, and most of what he did earn went in the direction of paying the household expenses.

Perhaps the thing that touched and pleased me most in connection with my starting for Hampton was the interest that many of the older coloured people took in the matter. They had spent the best days of their lives in slavery, and hardly expected to live to see the time when they would see a member of their race leave home to attend a boarding-school. Some of these older people would give me a nickel, others a quarter, or a handkerchief.

Finally the great day came, and I started for Hampton. I had only a small, cheap satchel that contained what few articles of clothing I could get. My mother at the time was rather weak and broken in health. I hardly expected to see her again, and thus our parting was all the more sad. She, however, was very brave through it all. At that time there were no through trains connecting that part of West Virginia with eastern Virginia. Trains ran only a portion of the way, and the remainder of the distance was travelled by stage-coaches.

The distance from Malden to Hampton is about five hundred miles. I had not been away from home many hours before it began to grow painfully evident that I did not have enough money to pay my fare to Hampton. One experience I shall long remember. I had been travelling over the mountains most of the afternoon in an old-fashioned stage-coach, when, late in the evening, the coach stopped for the night at a common, unpainted house called a hotel. All the other passengers except myself were whites. In my ignorance I supposed that the little hotel existed for the purpose of accommodating the passengers who travelled on the stage-coach. The difference that the colour of one's skin would make I had not thought anything about. After all the other passengers had been shown rooms and were getting ready for supper, I shyly presented myself before the man at the desk. It is true I had practically no money in my pocket with which to pay for bed or food, but I had hoped in some way to beg my way into the good graces of the landlord, for at that season in the mountains of Virginia the weather was cold, and I wanted to get indoors for the night. Without asking as to whether I had any money, the man at the desk firmly refused to even consider the matter of providing me with food or lodging. This was my first experience in finding out what the colour of my skin meant. In some way I managed to keep warm by walking about, and so got through the night. My whole soul was so bent upon reaching Hampton that I did not have time to cherish any bitterness toward the hotel-keeper.

By walking, begging rides both in wagons and in the cars, in some way, after a number of days, I reached the city of Richmond, Virginia, about eighty-two miles from Hampton. When I reached there, tired, hungry, and dirty, it was late in the night. I had never been in a large city, and this rather added to my misery. When I reached Richmond, I was completely out of money. I had not a single acquaintance in the place, and, being unused to city ways, I did not know where to go. I applied at several places for lodging, but they all wanted money, and that was what I did not have. Knowing nothing else better to do, I walked the streets. In doing this I passed by many foodstands where fried chicken and half-moon apple pies were piled high and made to present a most tempting appearance. At that time it seemed to me that I would have promised all that I expected to possess in the future to have gotten hold of one of those chicken legs or one of those pies. But I could not get either of these, nor anything else to eat.

I must have walked the streets till after midnight. At last I became so exhausted that I could walk no longer. I was tired, I was hungry, I was everything but discouraged. Just about the time when I reached extreme physical exhaustion, I came upon a portion of a street where the board sidewalk was considerably elevated. I waited for a few minutes, till I was sure that no passers-by could see me, and then crept under the sidewalk and lay for the night upon the ground, with my satchel of clothing for a pillow. Nearly all night I could hear the tramp of feet over my head. The next morning I found myself somewhat refreshed but I was extremely hungry, because it had been a long time since I had had sufficient food. As soon as it became light enough for me to see my surroundings I noticed that I was near a large ship, and that this ship seemed to be unloading a cargo of pig iron. I went at once to the vessel and asked the captain to permit me to help unload the vessel in order to get money for food. The captain, a white man, who seemed to be kind-hearted, consented. I worked long enough to earn money for my breakfast, and it seems to me, as I remember it now, to have been about the best breakfast that I have ever eaten.

My work pleased the captain so well that he told me if I desired I could continue working for a small amount per day. This I was very glad to do. I continued working on this vessel for a number of days. After buying food with the small wages I received there was not much left to add to the amount I must get to pay my way to Hampton. In order to economize in every way possible, so as to be sure to reach Hampton in a reasonable time, I continued to sleep under the same sidewalk that gave me shelter the first night I was in Richmond. Many years after that the coloured citizens of Richmond very kindly tendered me a reception at which there must have been two thousand people present. This reception was held not far from the spot where I slept the first night I spent in that city, and I must confess that my mind was more upon the sidewalk that first gave me shelter than upon the reception, agreeable and cordial as it was.

When I had saved what I considered enough money with which to reach Hampton, I thanked the captain of the vessel for his kindness, and started again. Without any unusual occurrence I reached Hampton, with a surplus of exactly fifty cents with which to begin my education. To me it had been a long, eventful journey; but the first sight of the large, three-story, brick school building seemed to have rewarded me for all that I had undergone in order to reach the place. If the people who gave the money to provide that building could appreciate the influence the sight of it had upon me, as well as upon thousands of other youths, they would feel all the more encouraged to make such gifts. It seemed to me to be the largest and most beautiful building I had ever seen. The sight of it seemed to give me new life. I felt that a new kind of existence had now begun—that life would now have a new meaning. I felt that I had reached the promised land, and I resolved to let no obstacle prevent me from putting forth the highest effort to fit myself to accomplish the most good in the world.

As soon as possible after reaching the grounds of the Hampton Institute, I presented myself before the head teacher for assignment to a class. Having been so long without proper food, a bath and change of clothing, I did not, of course, make a very favourable impression upon her, and I could see at once that there were doubts in her mind about the wisdom of admitting me as a student. I felt that I could hardly blame her if she got the idea that I was a worthless loafer or tramp. For some time she did not refuse to admit me, neither did she decide in my favour, and I continued to linger about her, and to impress her in all the ways I could with my worthiness. In the meantime I saw her admitting other students, and that added greatly to my discomfort, for I felt, deep down in my heart, that I could do as well as they, if I could only get a chance to show what was in me.

After some hours had passed, the head teacher said to me: "The adjoining recitation-room needs sweeping. Take the broom and sweep it."

It occurred to me at once that here was my chance. Never did I receive an order with more delight. I knew that I could sweep, for Mrs. Ruffner had thoroughly taught me how to do that when I lived with her.

I swept the recitation-room three times. Then I got a dusting-cloth and I dusted it four times. All the woodwork around the walls, every bench, table, and desk, I went over four times with my dusting-cloth. Besides, every piece of furniture had been moved and every closet and corner in the room had been thoroughly cleaned. I had the feeling that in a large measure my future depended upon the impression I made upon the teacher in the cleaning of that room. When I was through, I reported to the head teacher. She was a "Yankee" woman who knew just where to look for dirt. She went into the room and inspected the floor and closets; then she took her handkerchief and rubbed it on the woodwork about the walls, and over the table and benches. When she was unable to find one bit of dirt on the floor, or a particle of dust on any of the furniture, she quietly remarked, "I guess you will do to enter this institution."

I was one of the happiest souls on earth. The sweeping of that room was my college examination, and never did any youth pass an examination for entrance into Harvard or Yale that gave him more genuine satisfaction. I have passed several examinations since then, but I have always felt that this was the best one I ever passed.

I have spoken of my own experience in entering the Hampton Institute. Perhaps few, if any, had anything like the same experience that I had, but about that same period there were hundreds who found their way to Hampton and other institutions after experiencing something of the same difficulties that I went through. The young men and women were determined to secure an education at any cost.

The sweeping of the recitation-room in the manner that I did it seems to have paved the way for me to get through Hampton. Miss Mary F. Mackie, the head teacher, offered me a position as janitor. This, of course, I gladly accepted, because it was a place where I could work out nearly all the cost of my board. The work was hard and taxing, but I stuck to it. I had a large number of rooms to care for, and had to work late into the night, while at the same time I had to rise by four o'clock in the morning, in order to build the fires and have a little time in which to prepare my lessons. In all my career at Hampton, and ever since I have been out in the world, Miss Mary F. Mackie, the head teacher to whom I have referred, proved one of my strongest and most helpful friends. Her advice and encouragement were always helpful and strengthening to me in the darkest hour.

I have spoken of the impression that was made upon me by the buildings and general appearance of the Hampton Institute, but I have not spoken of that which made the greatest and most lasting impression upon me, and that was a great man—the noblest, rarest human being that it has ever been my privilege to meet. I refer to the late General Samuel C. Armstrong.

It has been my fortune to meet personally many of what are called great characters, both in Europe and America, but I do not hesitate to say that I never met any man who, in my estimation, was the equal of General Armstrong. Fresh from the degrading influences of the slave plantation and the coal-mines, it was a rare privilege for me to be permitted to come into direct contact with such a character as General Armstrong. I shall always remember that the first time I went into his presence he made the impression upon me of being a perfect man: I was made to feel that there was something about him that was superhuman. It was my privilege to know the General personally from the time I entered Hampton till he died, and the more I saw of him the greater he grew in my estimation. One might have removed from Hampton all the buildings, class-rooms, teachers, and industries, and given the men and women there the opportunity of coming into daily contact with General Armstrong, and that alone would have been a liberal education. The older I grow, the more I am convinced that there is no education which one can get from books and costly apparatus that is equal to that which can be gotten from contact with great men and women. Instead of studying books so constantly, how I wish that our schools and colleges might learn to study men and things!

General Armstrong spent two of the last six months of his life in my home at Tuskegee. At that time he was paralyzed to the extent that he had lost control of his body and voice in a very large degree. Notwithstanding his affliction, he worked almost constantly night and day for the cause to which he had given his life. I never saw a man who so completely lost sight of himself. I do not believe he ever had a selfish thought. He was just as happy in trying to assist some other institution in the South as he was when working for Hampton. Although he fought the Southern white man in the Civil War, I never heard him utter a bitter word against him afterward. On the other hand, he was constantly seeking to find ways by which he could be of service to the Southern whites.

It would be difficult to describe the hold that he had upon the students at Hampton, or the faith they had in him. In fact, he was worshipped by his students. It never occurred to me that General Armstrong could fail in anything that he undertook. There is almost no request that he could have made that would not have been complied with. When he was a guest at my home in Alabama, and was so badly paralyzed that he had to be wheeled about in an invalid's chair, I recall that one of the General's former students had occasion to push his chair up a long, steep hill that taxed his strength to the utmost. When the top of the hill was reached, the former pupil, with a glow of happiness on his face, exclaimed, "I am so glad that I have been permitted to do something that was real hard for the General before he dies!" While I was a student at Hampton, the dormitories became so crowded that it was impossible to find room for all who wanted to be admitted. In order to help remedy the difficulty the General conceived the plan of putting up tents to be used as rooms. As soon as it became known that General Armstrong would be pleased if some of the older students would live in the tents during the winter, nearly every student in school volunteered to go.

I was one of the volunteers. The winter that we spent in those tents was an intensely cold one, and we suffered severely—how much I am sure General Armstrong never knew, because we made no complaints. It was enough for us to know that we were pleasing General Armstrong, and that we were making it possible for an additional number of students to secure an education. More than once, during a cold night, when a stiff gale would be blowing, our tent was lifted bodily, and we would find ourselves in the open air. The General would usually pay a visit to the tents early in the morning, and his earnest, cheerful, encouraging voice would dispel any feeling of despondency.

I have spoken of my admiration for General Armstrong, and yet he was but a type of that Christlike body of men and women who went into the Negro schools at the close of the war by the hundreds to assist in lifting up my race. The history of the world fails to show a higher, purer, and more unselfish class of men and women than those who found their way into those Negro schools.

Life at Hampton was a constant revelation to me; was constantly taking me into a new world. The matter of having meals at regular hours, of eating on a tablecloth, using a napkin, the use of the bath-tub and of the tooth-brush, as well as the use of sheets upon the bed, were all new to me.

I sometimes feel that almost the most valuable lesson I got at the Hampton Institute was in the use and value of the bath. I learned there for the first time some of its value, not only in keeping the body healthy, but in inspiring self-respect and promoting virtue. In all my travels in the South and elsewhere since leaving Hampton I have always in some way sought my daily bath. To get it sometimes when I have been the guest of my own people in a single-roomed cabin has not always been easy to do, except by slipping away to some stream in the woods. I have always tried to teach my people that some provision for bathing should be a part of every house.

For some time, while a student at Hampton, I possessed but a single pair of socks, but when I had worn these till they became soiled, I would wash them at night and hang them by the fire to dry, so that I might wear them again the next morning.

The charge for my board at Hampton was ten dollars per month. I was expected to pay a part of this in cash and to work out the remainder. To meet this cash payment, as I have stated, I had just fifty cents when I reached the institution. Aside from a very few dollars that my brother John was able to send me once in a while, I had no money with which to pay my board. I was determined from the first to make my work as janitor so valuable that my services would be indispensable. This I succeeded in doing to such an extent that I was soon informed that I would be allowed the full cost of my board in return for my work. The cost of tuition was seventy dollars a year. This, of course, was wholly beyond my ability to provide. If I had been compelled to pay the seventy dollars for tuition, in addition to providing for my board, I would have been compelled to leave the Hampton school. General Armstrong, however, very kindly got Mr. S. Griffitts Morgan, of New Bedford, Mass., to defray the cost of my tuition during the whole time that I was at Hampton. After I finished the course at Hampton and had entered upon my lifework at Tuskegee, I had the pleasure of visiting Mr. Morgan several times.

After having been for a while at Hampton, I found myself in difficulty because I did not have books and clothing. Usually, however, I got around the trouble about books by borrowing from those who were more fortunate than myself. As to clothes, when I reached Hampton I had practically nothing. Everything that I possessed was in a small hand satchel. My anxiety about clothing was increased because of the fact that General Armstrong made a personal inspection of the young men in ranks, to see that their clothes were clean. Shoes had to be polished, there must be no buttons off the clothing, and no grease-spots. To wear one suit of clothes continually, while at work and in the schoolroom, and at the same time keep it clean, was rather a hard problem for me to solve. In some way I managed to get on till the teachers learned that I was in earnest and meant to succeed, and then some of them were kind enough to see that I was partly supplied with second-hand clothing that had been sent in barrels from the North. These barrels proved a blessing to hundreds of poor but deserving students. Without them I question whether I should ever have gotten through Hampton.

When I first went to Hampton I do not recall that I had ever slept in a bed that had two sheets on it. In those days there were not many buildings there, and room was very precious. There were seven other boys in the same room with me; most of them, however, students who had been there for some time. The sheets were quite a puzzle to me. The first night I slept under both of them, and the second night I slept on top of both of them; but by watching the other boys I learned my lesson in this, and have been trying to follow it ever since and to teach it to others.

I was among the youngest of the students who were in Hampton at that time. Most of the students were men and women—some as old as forty years of age. As I now recall the scene of my first year, I do not believe that one often has the opportunity of coming into contact with three or four hundred men and women who were so tremendously in earnest as these men and women were. Every hour was occupied in study or work. Nearly all had had enough actual contact with the world to teach them the need of education. Many of the older ones were, of course, too old to master the text-books very thoroughly, and it was often sad to watch their struggles; but they made up in earnestness much of what they lacked in books. Many of them were as poor as I was, and, besides having to wrestle with their books, they had to struggle with a poverty which prevented their having the necessities of life. Many of them had aged parents who were dependent upon them, and some of them were men who had wives whose support in some way they had to provide for.

The great and prevailing idea that seemed to take possession of every one was to prepare himself to lift up the people at his home. No one seemed to think of himself. And the officers and teachers, what a rare set of human beings they were! They worked for the students night and day, in season and out of season. They seemed happy only when they were helping the students in some manner. Whenever it is written—and I hope it will be—the part that the Yankee teachers played in the education of the Negroes immediately after the war will make one of the most thrilling parts of the history of this country. The time is not far distant when the whole South will appreciate this service in a way that it has not yet been able to do.

Chapter XIV: The Atlanta Exposition Address[1]

The Atlanta Exposition, at which I had been asked to make an address as a representative of the Negro race, as stated in the last chapter, was opened with a short address

[1] Delivered on September 18, 1895 before an audience of 2,000 at an exposition held in Atlanta, Georgia. This was the speech which brought Washington into national prominence. Because of the "compromise" he proposed for striking a balance between the aspirations of blacks and the fears of whites, he became a figure of controversy.

from Governor Bullock. After other interesting exercises, including an invocation from Bishop Nelson, of Georgia, a dedicatory ode by Albert Howell, Jr., and addresses by the President of the Exposition and Mrs. Joseph Thompson, the President of the Woman's Board, Governor Bullock introduced me with the words, "We have with us to-day a representative of Negro enterprise and Negro civilization."

When I arose to speak, there was considerable cheering, especially from the coloured people. As I remember it now, the thing that was uppermost in my mind was the desire to say something that would cement the friendship of the races and bring about hearty coöperation between them. So far as my outward surroundings were concerned, the only thing that I recall distinctly now is that when I got up, I saw thousands of eyes looking intently into my face. The following is the address which I delivered:—

MR. PRESIDENT AND GENTLEMEN OF THE BOARD OF DIRECTORS AND CITIZENS.

One-third of the population of the South is of the Negro race. No enterprise seeking the material, civil, or moral welfare of this section can disregard this element of our population and reach the highest success. I but convey to you, Mr. President and Directors, the sentiment of the masses of my race when I say that in no way have the value and manhood of the American Negro been more fittingly and generously recognized than by the managers of this magnificent Exposition at every stage of its progress. It is a recognition that will do more to cement the friendship of the two races than any occurrence since the dawn of our freedom.

Not only this, but the opportunity here afforded will awaken among us a new era of industrial progress. Ignorant and inexperienced, it is not strange that in the first years of our new life we began at the top instead of at the bottom; that a seat in Congress or the state legislature was more sought than real estate or industrial skill; that the political convention of stump speaking had more attractions than starting a dairy farm or truck garden.

A ship lost at sea for many days suddenly sighted a friendly vessel. From the mast of the unfortunate vessel was seen a signal, "Water, water; we die of thirst!" The answer from the friendly vessel at once came back, "Cast down your bucket where you are." A second time the signal, "Water, water; send us water!" ran up from the distressed vessel, and was answered, "Cast down your bucket where you are." And a third and fourth signal for water was answered, "Cast down your bucket where you are." The captain of the distressed vessel, at last heeding the injunction, cast down his bucket, and it came up full of fresh, sparkling water from the mouth of the Amazon River. To those of my race who depend on bettering their condition in a foreign land or who underestimate the importance of cultivating friendly relations with the Southern white man, who is their next-door neighbour, I would say: "Cast down your bucket where you are"—cast it down in making friends in every manly way of the people of all races by whom we are surrounded.

Cast it down in agriculture, mechanics, in commerce, in domestic service, and in the professions. And in this connection it is well to bear in mind that whatever other sins the South may be called to bear, when it comes to business, pure and simple, it is in the South that the Negro is given a man's chance in the commercial world, and in nothing is this Exposition more eloquent than in emphasizing this chance. Our greatest danger is that in the great leap from slavery to freedom we may overlook the fact that the masses of us are to live by the productions of our hands, and fail to keep in mind that we shall prosper in proportion as we learn to dignify and glorify common labour and put brains and skill into the common occupations of life; shall prosper in proportion as we learn to draw the line between the superficial and the substantial, the ornamental gewgaws of life and the useful. No race can prosper till it learns that there is as much dignity in tilling a field as in writing a poem. It is at the bottom of life we must begin, and not at the top. Nor should we permit our grievances to overshadow our opportunities.

To those of the white race who look to the incoming of those of foreign birth and strange tongue and habits for the prosperity of the South, were I permitted I would repeat what I say to my own race, "Cast down your bucket where you are." Cast it down among the eight millions of Negroes whose habits you know, whose fidelity and love you have tested in days when to have proved treacherous meant the ruin of your firesides. Cast down your bucket among these people who have, without strikes and labour wars, tilled your fields, cleared your forests, builded your railroads and cities, and brought forth treasures from the bowels of the earth, and helped make possible this magnificent representation of the progress of the South. Casting down your bucket among my people, helping and encouraging them as you are doing on these grounds, and to education of head, hand, and heart, you will find that they will buy your surplus land, make blossom the waste places in your fields, and run your factories. While doing this, you can be sure in the future, as in the past, that you and your families will be surrounded by the most patient, faithful, law-abiding, and unresentful people that the world has seen. As we have proved our loyalty to you in the past, in nursing your children, watching by the sick-bed of your mothers and fathers, and often following them with tear-dimmed eyes to their graves, so in the future, in our humble way, we shall stand by you with a devotion that no foreigner can approach, ready to lay down our lives, if need be, in defence of yours, interlacing our industrial, commercial, civil, and religious life with yours in a way that shall make the interests of both races one. In all things that are purely social we can be as separate as the fingers, yet one as the hand in all things essential to mutual progress.

There is no defence or security for any of us except in the highest intelligence and development of all. If anywhere there are efforts tending to curtail the fullest growth of the Negro, let these efforts be turned into stimulating, encouraging, and making him the most useful and intelligent citizen. Effort or means so invested will pay a thousand per cent interest. These efforts will be twice blessed—"blessing him that gives and him that takes."[2]

There is no escape through law of man or God from the inevitable:—

---

[2] Shakespeare's play *The Merchant of Venice,* Act IV, Sc. i, l. 1670.

The laws of changeless justice bind
    Oppressor with oppressed;
And close as sin and suffering joined
    We march to fate abreast.[3]

Nearly sixteen millions of hands will aid you in pulling the load upward, or they will pull against you the load downward. We shall constitute one-third and more of the ignorance and crime of the South, or one-third its intelligence and progress; we shall contribute one-third to the business and industrial prosperity of the South, or we shall prove a veritable body of death, stagnating, depressing, retarding every effort to advance the body politic.

Gentlemen of the Exposition, as we present to you our humble effort at an exhibition of our progress, you must not expect overmuch. Starting thirty years ago with ownership here and there in a few quilts and pumpkins and chickens (gathered from miscellaneous sources), remember the path that has led from these to the inventions and production of agricultural implements, buggies, steam-engines, newspapers, books, statuary, carving, paintings, the management of drug-stores and banks, has not been trodden without contact with thorns and thistles. While we take pride in what we exhibit as a result of our independent efforts, we do not for a moment forget that our part in this exhibition would fall far short of your expectations but for the constant help that has come to our educational life, not only from the Southern states, but especially from Northern philanthropists, who have made their gifts a constant stream of blessing and encouragement.

The wisest among my race understand that the agitation of questions of social equality is the extremest folly, and that progress in the enjoyment of all the privileges that will come to us must be the result of severe and constant struggle rather than of artificial forcing. No race that has anything to contribute to the markets of the world is long in any degree ostracized. It is important and right that all privileges of the law be ours, but it is vastly more important that we be prepared for the exercises of these privileges. The opportunity to earn a dollar in a factory just now is worth infinitely more than the opportunity to spend a dollar in an opera-house.

In conclusion, may I repeat that nothing in thirty years has given us more hope and encouragement, and drawn us so near to you of the white race, as this opportunity offered by the Exposition; and here bending, as it were, over the altar that represents the results of the struggles of your race and mine, both starting practically empty-handed three decades ago, I pledge that in your effort to work out the great and intricate problem which God has laid at the doors of the South, you shall have at all times the patient, sympathetic help of my race; only let this be constantly in mind, that, while

---

[3] "Song of the Negro Boatmen" by John
Greenleaf Whittier (1807–1892), New England
poet.

from representations in these buildings of the product of field, of forest, of mine, of factory, letters, and art, much good will come, yet far above and beyond material benefits will be that higher good, that, let us pray God, will come, in a blotting out of sectional differences and racial animosities and suspicions, in a determination to administer absolute justice, in a willing obedience among all classes to the mandates of law. This, this coupled with our material prosperity, will bring into our beloved South a new heaven and a new earth.

The first thing that I remember, after I had finished speaking, was that Governor Bullock rushed across the platform and took me by the hand, and that others did the same. I received so many and such hearty congratulations that I found it difficult to get out of the building. I did not appreciate to any degree, however, the impression which my address seemed to have made, until the next morning, when I went into the business part of the city. As soon as I was recognized, I was surprised to find myself pointed out and surrounded by a crowd of men who wished to shake hands with me. This was kept up on every street on to which I went, to an extent which embarrassed me so much that I went back to my boarding-place. The next morning I returned to Tuskegee. At the station in Atlanta, and at almost all of the stations at which the train stopped between that city and Tuskegee, I found a crowd of people anxious to shake hands with me.

The papers in all parts of the United States published the address in full, and for months afterward there were complimentary editorial references to it. Mr. Clark Howell, the editor of the Atlanta *Constitution,* telegraphed to a New York paper, among other words, the following, "I do not exaggerate when I say that Professor Booker T. Washington's address yesterday was one of the most notable speeches, both as to character and as to the warmth of its reception, ever delivered to a Southern audience. The address was a revelation. The whole speech is a platform upon which blacks and whites can stand with full justice to each other."

The Boston *Transcript* said editorially: "The speech of Booker T. Washington at the Atlanta Exposition, this week, seems to have dwarfed all the other proceedings and the Exposition itself. The sensation that it has caused in the press has never been equalled."

I very soon began receiving all kinds of propositions from lecture bureaus, and editors of magazines and papers, to take the lecture platform, and to write articles. One lecture bureau offered me fifty thousand dollars, or two hundred dollars a night and expenses, if I would place my services at its disposal for a given period. To all these communications I replied that my life-work was at Tuskegee; and that whenever I spoke it must be in the interests of the Tuskegee school and my race, and that I would enter into no arrangements that seemed to place a mere commercial value upon my services.

Some days after its delivery I sent a copy of my address to the President of the United States, the Hon. Grover Cleveland.[4] I received from him the following autograph reply:—

---

[4] At this time Grover Cleveland (1837–1908) was serving his second term as president (1893–1897); he had formerly served between 1885 and 1889.

GRAY GABLES, BUZZARD'S BAY, MASS.,
October 6, 1895.

BOOKER T. WASHINGTON, ESQ.:

MY DEAR SIR: I thank you for sending me a copy of your address delivered at the Atlanta Exposition.

I thank you with much enthusiasm for making the address. I have read it with intense interest, and I think the Exposition would be fully justified if it did not do more than furnish the opportunity for its delivery. Your words cannot fail to delight and encourage all who wish well for your race; and if our coloured fellow-citizens do not from your utterances gather new hope and form new determinations to gain every valuable advantage offered them by their citizenship, it will be strange indeed.

Yours very truly,

GROVER CLEVELAND.

Later I met Mr. Cleveland, for the first time, when, as President, he visited the Atlanta Exposition. At the request of myself and others he consented to spend an hour in the Negro Building, for the purpose of inspecting the Negro exhibit and of giving the coloured people in attendance an opportunity to shake hands with him. As soon as I met Mr. Cleveland I became impressed with his simplicity, greatness, and rugged honesty. I have met him many times since then, both at public functions and at his private residence in Princeton, and the more I see of him the more I admire him. When he visited the Negro Building in Atlanta he seemed to give himself up wholly, for that hour, to the coloured people. He seemed to be as careful to shake hands with some old coloured "auntie" clad partially in rags, and to take as much pleasure in doing so, as if he were greeting some millionnaire. Many of the coloured people took advantage of the occasion to get him to write his name in a book or on a slip of paper. He was as careful and patient in doing this as if he were putting his signature to some great state document.

Mr. Cleveland has not only shown his friendship for me in many personal ways, but has always consented to do anything I have asked of him for our school. This he has done, whether it was to make a personal donation or to use his influence in securing the donations of others. Judging from my personal acquaintance with Mr. Cleveland, I do not believe that he is conscious of possessing any colour prejudice. He is too great for that. In my contact with people I find that, as a rule, it is only the little, narrow people who live for themselves, who never read good books, who do not travel, who never open up their souls in a way to permit them to come into contact with other souls—with the great outside world. No man whose vision is bounded by colour can come into contact with what is highest and best in the world. In meeting men, in many places, I have found that the happiest people are those who do the most for others; the most miserable are those who do the least. I have also found that few things, if any, are capable of making one so blind and narrow as race prejudice. I often say to our students, in the course of my talks to them on Sunday evenings in the chapel, that the longer I live and the more experience I have of the world, the more I am convinced that, after all, the one thing that is most worth living for—and dying for, if need be—is the opportunity of making some one else more happy and more useful.

The coloured people and the coloured newspapers at first seemed to be greatly pleased with the character of my Atlanta address, as well as with its reception. But after the first burst of enthusiasm began to die away, and the coloured people began reading the speech in cold type, some of them seemed to feel that they had been hypnotized. They seemed to feel that I had been too liberal in my remarks toward the Southern whites, and that I had not spoken out strongly enough for what they termed the "rights" of the race. For a while there was a reaction, so far as a certain element of my own race was concerned, but later these reactionary ones seemed to have been won over to my way of believing and acting.

While speaking of changes in public sentiment, I recall that about ten years after the school at Tuskegee was established, I had an experience that I shall never forget. Dr. Lyman Abbott,[5] then the pastor of Plymouth Church, and also editor of the *Outlook* (then the *Christian Union*), asked me to write a letter for his paper giving my opinion of the exact condition, mental and moral, of the coloured ministers in the South, as based upon my observations. I wrote the letter, giving the exact facts as I conceived them to be. The picture painted was a rather black one—or, since I am black, shall I say "white"? It could not be otherwise with a race but a few years out of slavery, a race which had not had time or opportunity to produce a competent ministry.

What I said soon reached every Negro minister in the country, I think, and the letters of condemnation which I received from them were not few. I think that for a year after the publication of this article every association and every conference or religious body of any kind, of my race, that met, did not fail before adjourning to pass a resolution condemning me, or calling upon me to retract or modify what I had said. Many of these organizations went so far in their resolutions as to advise parents to cease sending their children to Tuskegee. One association even appointed a "missionary" whose duty it was to warn the people against sending their children to Tuskegee. This missionary had a son in the school, and I noticed that, whatever the "missionary" might have said or done with regard to others, he was careful not to take his son away from the institution. Many of the coloured papers, especially those that were the organs of religious bodies, joined in the general chorus of condemnation or demands for retraction.

During the whole time of the excitement, and through all the criticism, I did not utter a word of explanation or retraction. I knew that I was right, and that time and the sober second thought of the people would vindicate me. It was not long before the bishops and other church leaders began to make a careful investigation of the conditions of the ministry, and they found out that I was right. In fact, the oldest and most influential bishop in one branch of the Methodist Church said that my words were far too mild. Very soon public sentiment began making itself felt, in demanding a purifying of the ministry. While this is not yet complete by any means, I think I may say, without egotism, and I have been told by many of our most influential ministers, that my words had much to do with starting a demand for the placing of a higher type of men in the pulpit. I have had the satisfaction of having many who once condemned me thank me heartily for my frank words.

The change of the attitude of the Negro ministry, so far as regards myself, is so

---

[5] American clergyman, editor, author, and leader of "liberal" Protestantism (1835–1922).

complete that at the present time I have no warmer friends among any class than I have among the clergymen. The improvement in the character and life of the Negro ministers is one of the most gratifying evidences of the progress of the race. My experience with them, as well as other events in my life, convince me that the thing to do, when one feels sure that he has said or done the right thing, and is condemned, is to stand still and keep quiet. If he is right, time will show it.

In the midst of the discussion which was going on concerning my Atlanta speech, I received the letter which I give below, from Dr. Gilman, the President of Johns Hopkins University, who had been made chairman of the judges of award in connection with the Atlanta Exposition:—

JOHNS HOPKINS UNIVERSITY, BALTIMORE,
President's Office, September 30, 1895.

DEAR MR. WASHINGTON: Would it be agreeable to you to be one of the Judges of Award in the Department of Education at Atlanta? If so, I shall be glad to place your name upon the list. A line by telegraph will be welcomed.

Yours very truly,
D. C. GILMAN.

I think I was even more surprised to receive this invitation than I had been to receive the invitation to speak at the opening of the Exposition. It was to be a part of my duty, as one of the jurors, to pass not only upon the exhibits of the coloured schools, but also upon those of the white schools. I accepted the position, and spent a month in Atlanta in performance of the duties which it entailed. The board of jurors was a large one, consisting in all of sixty members. It was about equally divided between Southern white people and Northern white people. Among them were college presidents, leading scientists and men of letters, and specialists in many subjects. When the group of jurors to which I was assigned met for organization, Mr. Thomas Nelson Page,[6] who was one of the number, moved that I be made secretary of that division, and the motion was unanimously adopted. Nearly half of our division were Southern people. In performing my duties in the inspection of the exhibits of white schools I was in every case treated with respect, and at the close of our labours I parted from my associates with regret.

I am often asked to express myself more freely than I do upon the political condition and the political future of my race. These recollections of my experience in Atlanta give me the opportunity to do so briefly. My own belief is, although I have never before said so in so many words, that the time will come when the Negro in the South will be accorded all the political rights which his ability, character, and material possessions entitle him to. I think, though, that the opportunity to freely exercise such political rights will not come in any large degree through outside or artificial forcing, but will be accorded to the Negro by the Southern white people themselves, and that they will protect him in the exercise of those rights. Just as soon as the South gets over the old feeling that it is being forced by "foreigners," or "aliens," to do something which it does not want to do, I believe that the change in

---

[6] Southern writer of regional literature and diplomat (1853–1922).

the direction that I have indicated is going to begin. In fact, there are indications that it is already beginning in a slight degree.

Let me illustrate my meaning. Suppose that some months before the opening of the Atlanta Exposition there had been a general demand from the press and public platform outside the South that a Negro be given a place on the opening programme, and that a Negro be placed upon the board of jurors of award. Would any such recognition of the race have taken place? I do not think so. The Atlanta officials went as far as they did because they felt it to be a pleasure, as well as a duty, to reward what they considered merit in the Negro race. Say what we will, there is something in human nature which we cannot blot out, which makes one man, in the end, recognize and reward merit in another, regardless of colour or race.

I believe it is the duty of the Negro—as the greater part of the race is already doing —to deport himself modestly in regard to political claims, depending upon the slow but sure influences that proceed from the possession of property, intelligence, and high character for the full recognition of his political rights. I think that the according of the full exercise of political rights is going to be a matter of natural, slow growth, not an over-night, gourd-vine affair. I do not believe that the Negro should cease voting, for a man cannot learn the exercise of self-government by ceasing to vote any more than a boy can learn to swim by keeping out of the water, but I do believe that in his voting he should more and more be influenced by those of intelligence and character who are his next-door neighbours.

I know coloured men who, through the encouragement, help, and advice of Southern white people, have accumulated thousands of dollars' worth of property, but who, at the same time, would never think of going to those same persons for advice concerning the casting of their ballots. This, it seems to me, is unwise and unreasonable, and should cease. In saying this I do not mean that the Negro should truckle, or not vote from principle, for the instant he ceases to vote from principle he loses the confidence and respect of the Southern white man even.

I do not believe that any state should make a law that permits an ignorant and poverty-stricken white man to vote, and prevents a black man in the same condition from voting. Such a law is not only unjust, but it will react, as all unjust laws do, in time; for the effect of such a law is to encourage the Negro to secure education and property, and at the same time it encourages the white man to remain in ignorance and poverty. I believe that in time, through the operation of intelligence and friendly race relations, all cheating at the ballot box in the South will cease. It will become apparent that the white man who begins by cheating a Negro out of his ballot soon learns to cheat a white man out of his, and that the man who does this ends his career of dishonesty by the theft of property or by some equally serious crime. In my opinion, the time will come when the South will encourage all of its citizens to vote. It will see that it pays better, from every standpoint, to have healthy, vigorous life than to have that political stagnation which always results when one-half of the population has no share and no interest in the Government.

As a rule, I believe in universal, free suffrage, but I believe that in the South we are confronted with peculiar conditions that justify the protection of the ballot in many of the states, for a while at least, either by an educational test, a property test, or by both combined; but whatever tests are required, they should be made to apply with equal and exact justice to both races.

1900

Charles Waddell Chesnutt
1858–1932

"The everlasting problem"—as Charles Waddell Chesnutt characterized the consequences of the caste and color line in American society—formed the single theme of this black man's writings for the twenty years he devoted to stories, poems, novels, essays, speeches, and reviews about the troubled relationships between races in the post–Civil War years. Born in Cleveland three years before the start of the war, Chesnutt was the son of free blacks. His father had seen service in the Union army, then moved his family back to their hometown of Fayetteville, North Carolina, hoping that the government's Reconstruction policies would make the South a safe and sensible place in which to raise his children. Chesnutt experienced Carolina life between 1866 and 1883, directly absorbing the everyday facts of a light-skinned black in a region where the two races were uneasily coming to terms with each other under the conditions of the war's aftermath.

As a boy, Chesnutt studied French, German, and Greek and read widely in such classic writers as Shakespeare, Molière, Dickens, and Dumas, as well as Harriet Beecher Stowe and Albion Tourgée, whose pictures of black life were the best that white American culture could provide at that time. Before he was twenty, Chesnutt had taught in a series of segregated schools in North Carolina, but in 1883 he moved to the North, where he planned to make his mark, realizing he could not do so in the South. He spent six months in New York before returning to his birthplace. Cleveland remained his home until his death and the location of his varying successes as a lawyer, legal stenographer, and writer.

Chesnutt published sixteen short stories and a group of poems and essays between 1883 and 1887, the date when "The Goophered Grapevine"—appearing in the August 1887 issue of the *Atlantic Monthly*—brought him his first major attention. In 1899 two collections of his stories were published, *The Conjure Woman* and *The Wife of His Youth and Other Stories of the Color Line.* Three novels appeared over the next six years, *The House Behind the Cedars* in 1900, *The Marrow of Tradition* in 1901, and *The Colonial Dream* in 1905, after which Chesnutt virtually vanished from the national literary scene.

The public's varying responses to Chesnutt's literary activities can be traced to the changing nature of what he wrote and how he presented his material. His first stories had the same appeal that endeared the dialect folktales of Joel Chandler Harris to a large, white audience. (In fact, most of Chesnutt's readers assumed his white blood until he declared his racial identity to the world at large in 1899.) His own Uncle Remus figure, whom he called Uncle Julian, ironically manipulated the master-slave relationship far more than did Harris's figure, who with his cozy hearthside manner toward his master's little son has been viewed (perhaps unfairly) as an "Uncle Tom." But Chesnutt generally underplayed his mockery of the slavery system during the 1880s and 1890s. Although he recognized that other blacks had the right to express themselves with more anger, he himself was conservative by temperament and wrote best when he released his bitterness as irony.

In his novels of 1900 to 1905 Chesnutt spoke out with a candor that could not be mistaken and that in some areas could not be tolerated. Direct statements about the wrongs of American society marked Chesnutt's new method of attack. In this five-year period, he protested against the betrayal of the principles of equality by both whites and blacks. The devastating consequences when light-skinned blacks attempted to "pass" in a white world gave Chesnutt an effective theme by which he could dramatize the emotional scars caused by a color caste system. He gained genuine appreciation, but he realized that this respect took place within boundaries that society set around even its "best" blacks. Once he began to say what became too uncomfortable for easy listening, he had to be silenced. Although he completed six other novels, none was accepted for publication. His voice, in print at least, had been stilled.

Chesnutt continued to speak for racial justice in the Cleveland community, where he was held in esteem. In 1928, twenty-three years after the publication of his last novel, Chesnutt was given the NAACP Spingarn Medal for "pioneer work as a literary artist depicting the life and struggles of Americans of Negro descent, and for his long and useful career as scholar, worker, and freeman of one of America's greatest cities." Two generations after his death, Americans are once more heeding the narrative voices through which Chesnutt denounced the "barrier to the moral progress of the American people."

Further Reading:
H. Chesnutt, *Charles Waddell Chesnutt, Pioneer of the Color Line,* 1952.
J. Heermance, *Charles W. Chesnutt,* 1974.
F. Keller, *An American Crusade: The Life of Charles Waddell Chesnutt,* 1978.
S. Render, *Charles W. Chesnutt,* 1980.

Text:
The Wife of His Youth, 1899.
See also *The Short Fiction of Charles W. Chesnutt,* ed. S. Render, 1974, 1981.

The Sheriff's Children

Branson County, North Carolina, is in a sequestered district of one of the staidest and most conservative States of the Union. Society in Branson County is almost primitive in its simplicity. Most of the white people own the farms they till, and even before the war there were no very wealthy families to force their neighbors, by comparison, into the category of "poor whites."

To Branson County, as to most rural communities in the South, the war is the one historical event that overshadows all others. It is the era from which all local chronicles are dated,—births, deaths, marriages, storms, freshets. No description of the life of any Southern community would be perfect that failed to emphasize the all pervading influence of the great conflict.

Yet the fierce tide of war that had rushed through the cities and along the great highways of the country had comparatively speaking but slightly disturbed the sluggish current of life in this region, remote from railroads and navigable streams. To the north in Virginia, to the west in Tennessee, and all along the seaboard the war had raged; but the thunder of its cannon had not disturbed the echoes of Branson County, where the loudest sounds heard were the crack of some hunter's rifle, the baying of some deep-mouthed hound, or the yodel of some tuneful negro on his way through the pine forest. To the east, Sherman's army had passed on its march to the sea; but no straggling band of "bummers"[1] had penetrated the confines of Branson County. The war, it is true, had robbed the county of the flower of its young manhood; but the burden of taxation, the doubt and uncertainty of the conflict, and the sting of ultimate defeat, had been borne by the people with an apathy that robbed misfortune of half its sharpness.

The nearest approach to town life afforded by Branson County is found in the little village of Troy, the county seat, a hamlet with a population of four or five hundred.

Ten years make little difference in the appearance of these remote Southern towns. If a railroad is built through one of them, it infuses some enterprise; the social corpse is galvanized by the fresh blood of civilization that pulses along the farthest ramifications of our great system of commercial highways. At the period of which I write, no railroad had come to Troy. If a traveler, accustomed to the bustling life of cities, could have ridden through Troy on a summer day, he might easily have fancied himself in a deserted village. Around him he would have seen weather-beaten houses, innocent of paint, the shingled roofs in many instances covered with a rich growth of moss. Here and there he would have met a razor-backed hog lazily rooting his way along the principal thoroughfare; and more than once he would probably have had to disturb the slumbers of some yellow dog, dozing away the hours in the ardent sunshine, and reluctantly yielding up his place in the middle of the dusty road.

On Saturdays the village presented a somewhat livelier appearance, and the shade trees around the court house square and along Front Street served as hitching-posts for a goodly number of horses and mules and stunted oxen, belonging to the farmer-folk who had come in to trade at the two or three local stores.

A murder was a rare event in Branson County. Every well-informed citizen could tell the number of homicides committed in the county for fifty years back, and whether the slayer, in any given instance, had escaped, either by flight or acquittal, or had suffered the penalty of the law. So, when it became known in Troy early one Friday morning in summer, about ten years after the war, that old Captain Walker, who had served in Mexico under Scott, and had left an arm on the field of Gettysburg, had been foully murdered during the night, there was intense excitement in the village. Business was practically suspended, and the citizens gathered in little groups to discuss the murder, and speculate upon the identity of the murderer. It transpired from testimony at the coroner's inquest, held during the morning, that a strange mulatto had been seen going in the direction of Captain Walker's house the night before, and had been met going away from Troy early Friday morning, by a farmer on his way to town. Other circumstances seemed to connect the stranger with the crime. The sheriff organized a posse to search for him, and early in the evening, when most of

---

[1] Stray bands of Union army men who took the occasion of General Sherman's rapid sweep through the devastated areas of the Confederacy to loot and pillage.

the citizens of Troy were at supper, the suspected man was brought in and lodged in the county jail.

By the following morning the news of the capture had spread to the farthest limits of the county. A much larger number of people than usual came to town that Saturday,—bearded men in straw hats and blue homespun shirts, and butternut trousers[2] of great amplitude of material and vagueness of outline; women in homespun frocks and slat-bonnets, with faces as expressionless as the dreary sandhills which gave them a meagre sustenance.

The murder was almost the sole topic of conversation. A steady stream of curious observers visited the house of mourning, and gazed upon the rugged face of the old veteran, now stiff and cold in death; and more than one eye dropped a tear at the remembrance of the cheery smile, and the joke—sometimes superannuated, generally feeble, but always good-natured—with which the captain had been wont to greet his acquaintances. There was a growing sentiment of anger among these stern men, toward the murderer who had thus cut down their friend, and a strong feeling that ordinary justice was too slight a punishment for such a crime.

Toward noon there was an informal gathering of citizens in Dan Tyson's store.

"I hear it 'lowed that Square Kyahtah's too sick ter hol' co'te this evenin'," said one, "an' that the purlim'nary hearin' 'll haf ter go over 'tel nex' week."

A look of disappointment went round the crowd.

"Hit 's the durndes', meanes' murder ever committed in this caounty," said another, with moody emphasis.

"I s'pose the nigger 'lowed the Cap'n had some greenbacks," observed a third speaker.

"The Cap'n," said another, with an air of superior information, "has left two bairls of Confedrit money, which he 'spected 'ud be good some day er nuther."

This statement gave rise to a discussion of the speculative value of Confederate money; but in a little while the conversation returned to the murder.

"Hangin' air too good fer the murderer," said one; "he oughter be burnt, stidier bein' hung."

There was an impressive pause at this point, during which a jug of moonlight whiskey went the round of the crowd.

"Well," said a round-shouldered farmer, who, in spite of his peaceable expression and faded gray eye, was known to have been one of the most daring followers of a rebel guerrilla chieftain, "what air yer gwine ter do about it? Ef you fellers air gwine ter set down an' let a wuthless nigger kill the bes' white man in Branson, an' not say nuthin' ner do nuthin', I'll move outen the caounty."

This speech gave tone and direction to the rest of the conversation. Whether the fear of losing the round-shouldered farmer operated to bring about the result or not is immaterial to this narrative; but, at all events, the crowd decided to lynch the negro. They agreed that this was the least that could be done to avenge the death of their murdered friend, and that it was a becoming way in which to honor his memory. They had some vague notions of the majesty of the law and the rights of the citizen, but in the passion of the moment these sunk into oblivion; a white man had been killed by a negro.

---

[2] Trousers of homespun fabric dyed with, or the color of, the juice of butternuts.

"The Cap'n was an ole sodger," said one of his friends solemnly. "He'll sleep better when he knows that a co'te-martial has be'n hilt an' jestice done."

By agreement the lynchers were to meet at Tyson's store at five o'clock in the afternoon, and proceed thence to the jail, which was situated down the Lumberton Dirt Road (as the old turnpike antedating the plank-road was called), about half a mile south of the court-house. When the preliminaries of the lynching had been arranged, and a committee appointed to manage the affair, the crowd dispersed, some to go to their dinners, and some to secure recruits for the lynching party.

It was twenty minutes to five o'clock, when an excited negro, panting and perspiring, rushed up to the back door of Sheriff Campbell's dwelling, which stood at a little distance from the jail and somewhat farther than the latter building from the court-house. A turbaned colored woman came to the door in response to the negro's knock.

"Hoddy, Sis' Nance."

"Hoddy, Brer Sam."

"Is de shurff in," inquired the negro.

"Yas, Brer Sam, he's eatin' his dinner," was the answer.

"Will yer ax 'im ter step ter de do' a minute, Sis' Nance?"

The woman went into the dining-room, and a moment later the sheriff came to the door. He was a tall, muscular man, of a ruddier complexion than is usual among Southerners. A pair of keen, deep-set gray eyes looked out from under bushy eyebrows, and about his mouth was a masterful expression, which a full beard, once sandy in color, but now profusely sprinkled with gray, could not entirely conceal. The day was hot; the sheriff had discarded his coat and vest, and had his white shirt open at the throat.

"What do you want, Sam?" he inquired of the negro, who stood hat in hand, wiping the moisture from his face with a ragged shirt-sleeve.

"Shurff, dey gwine ter hang de pris'ner w'at's lock' up in de jail. Dey're comin' dis a-way now. I wuz layin' down on a sack er corn down at de sto', behine a pile er flour-bairls, w'en I hearn Doc' Cain en Kunnel Wright talkin' erbout it. I slip' outen de back do', en run here as fas' as I could. I hearn you say down ter de sto' once't dat you would n't let nobody take a pris'ner 'way fum you widout walkin' over yo' dead body, en I thought I'd let you know 'fo' dey come, so yer could pertec' de pris'ner."

The sheriff listened calmly, but his face grew firmer, and a determined gleam lit up his gray eyes. His frame grew more erect, and he unconsciously assumed the attitude of a soldier who momentarily expects to meet the enemy face to face.

"Much obliged, Sam," he answered. "I'll protect the prisoner. Who's coming?"

"I dunno who-all *is* comin'," replied the negro. "Dere's Mistah McSwayne, en Doc' Cain, en Maje' McDonal', en Kunnel Wright, en a heap er yuthers. I wuz so skeered I done furgot mo' d'n half un em. I spec' dey mus' be mos' here by dis time, so I'll git outen de way, fer I don' want nobody fer ter think I wuz mix' up in dis business." The negro glanced nervously down the road toward the town, and made a movement as if to go away.

"Won't you have some dinner first?" asked the sheriff.

The negro looked longingly in at the open door, and sniffed the appetizing odor of boiled pork and collards.

"I ain't got no time fer ter tarry, Shurff," he said, "but Sis' Nance mought gin me sump'n I could kyar in my han' en eat on de way."

A moment later Nancy brought him a huge sandwich of split corn-pone, with a thick slice of fat bacon inserted between the halves, and a couple of baked yams. The negro hastily replaced his ragged hat on his head, dropped the yams in the pocket of his capacious trousers, and, taking the sandwich in his hand, hurried across the road and disappeared in the woods beyond.

The sheriff reëntered the house, and put on his coat and hat. He then took down a double-barreled shotgun and loaded it with buckshot. Filling the chambers of a revolver with fresh cartridges, he slipped it into the pocket of the sack-coat which he wore.

A comely young woman in a calico dress watched these proceedings with anxious surprise.

"Where are you going, father?" she asked. She had not heard the conversation with the negro.

"I am goin' over to the jail," responded the sheriff. "There's a mob comin' this way to lynch the nigger we've got locked up. But they won't do it," he added with emphasis.

"Oh, father! don't go!" pleaded the girl, clinging to his arm; "they'll shoot you if you don't give him up."

"You never mind me, Polly," said her father reassuringly, as he gently unclasped her hands from his arm. "I'll take care of myself and the prisoner, too. There ain't a man in Branson County that would shoot me. Besides, I have faced fire too often to be scared away from my duty. You keep close in the house," he continued, "and if any one disturbs you just use the old horse-pistol in the top bureau drawer. It's a little old-fashioned, but it did good work a few years ago."

The young girl shuddered at this sanguinary allusion, but made no further objection to her father's departure.

The sheriff of Branson was a man far above the average of the community in wealth, education, and social position. His had been one of the few families in the county that before the war had owned large estates and numerous slaves. He had graduated at the State University at Chapel Hill, and had kept up some acquaintance with current literature and advanced thought. He had traveled some in his youth, and was looked up to in the county as an authority on all subjects connected with the outer world. At first an ardent supporter of the Union, he had opposed the secession movement in his native State as long as opposition availed to stem the tide of public opinion. Yielding at last to the force of circumstances, he had entered the Confederate service rather late in the war, and served with distinction through several campaigns, rising in time to the rank of colonel. After the war he had taken the oath of allegiance, and had been chosen by the people as the most available candidate for the office of sheriff, to which he had been elected without opposition. He had filled the office for several terms, and was universally popular with his constituents.

Colonel or Sheriff Campbell, as he was indifferently called, as the military or civil title happened to be most important in the opinion of the person addressing him, had a high sense of the responsibility attaching to his office. He had sworn to do his duty faithfully, and he knew what his duty was, as sheriff, perhaps more clearly than he had apprehended it in other passages of his life. It was, therefore, with no uncertainty in regard to his course that he prepared his weapons and went over to the jail. He had no fears for Polly's safety.

The sheriff had just locked the heavy front door of the jail behind him when a half dozen horsemen, followed by a crowd of men on foot, came round a bend in the road and drew near the jail. They halted in front of the picket fence that surrounded the building, while several of the committee of arrangements rode on a few rods farther to the sheriff's house. One of them dismounted and rapped on the door with his riding-whip.

"Is the sheriff at home?" he inquired.

"No, he has just gone out," replied Polly, who had come to the door.

"We want the jail keys," he continued.

"They are not here," said Polly. "The sheriff has them himself." Then she added, with assumed indifference, "He is at the jail now."

The man turned away, and Polly went into the front room, from which she peered anxiously between the slats of the green blinds of a window that looked toward the jail. Meanwhile the messenger returned to his companions and announced his discovery. It looked as though the sheriff had learned of their design and was preparing to resist it.

One of them stepped forward and rapped on the jail door.

"Well, what is it?" said the sheriff, from within.

"We want to talk to you, Sheriff," replied the spokesman.

There was a little wicket in the door; this the sheriff opened, and answered through it.

"All right, boys, talk away. You are all strangers to me, and I don't know what business you can have." The sheriff did not think it necessary to recognize anybody in particular on such an occasion; the question of identity sometimes comes up in the investigation of these extra-judicial executions.

"We're a committee of citizens and we want to get into the jail."

"What for? It ain't much trouble to get into jail. Most people want to keep out."

The mob was in no humor to appreciate a joke, and the sheriff's witticism fell dead upon an unresponsive audience.

"We want to have a talk with the nigger that killed Cap'n Walker."

"You can talk to that nigger in the court-house, when he's brought out for trial. Court will be in session here next week. I know what you fellows want, but you can't get my prisoner to-day. Do you want to take the bread out of a poor man's mouth? I get seventy-five cents a day for keeping this prisoner, and he's the only one in jail. I can't have my family suffer just to please you fellows."

One or two young men in the crowd laughed at the idea of Sheriff Campbell's suffering for want of seventy-five cents a day; but they were frowned into silence by those who stood near them.

"Ef yer don't let us in," cried a voice, "we 'll bu's' the do' open."

"Bust away," answered the sheriff, raising his voice so that all could hear. "But I give you fair warning. The first man that tries it will be filled with buckshot. I'm sheriff of this county; I know my duty, and I mean to do it."

"What's the use of kicking, Sheriff?" argued one of the leaders of the mob. "The nigger is sure to hang anyhow; he richly deserves it; and we've got to do something to teach the niggers their places, or white people won't be able to live in the county."

"There 's no use talking, boys," responded the sheriff. "I'm a white man outside, but in this jail I'm sheriff; and if this nigger's to be hung in this county, I propose to do the hanging. So you fellows might as well right-about-face, and march back to Troy. You've had a pleasant trip, and the exercise will be good for you. You know *me*. I've got powder and ball, and I've faced fire before now, with nothing between me and the enemy, and I don't mean to surrender this jail while I'm able to shoot." Having thus announced his determination, the sheriff closed and fastened the wicket, and looked around for the best position from which to defend the building.

The crowd drew off a little, and the leaders conversed together in low tones.

The Branson County jail was a small, two-story brick building, strongly constructed, with no attempt at architectural ornamentation. Each story was divided into two large cells by a passage running from front to rear. A grated iron door gave entrance from the passage to each of the four cells. The jail seldom had many prisoners in it, and the lower windows had been boarded up. When the sheriff had closed the wicket, he ascended the steep wooden stairs to the upper floor. There was no window at the front of the upper passage, and the most available position from which to watch the movements of the crowd below was the front window of the cell occupied by the solitary prisoner.

The sheriff unlocked the door and entered the cell. The prisoner was crouched in a corner, his yellow face, blanched with terror, looking ghastly in the semi-darkness of the room. A cold perspiration had gathered on his forehead, and his teeth were chattering with affright.

"For God's sake, Sheriff," he murmured hoarsely, "don't let 'em lynch me; I did n't kill the old man."

The sheriff glanced at the cowering wretch with a look of mingled contempt and loathing.

"Get up," he said sharply. "You will probably be hung sooner or later, but it shall not be to-day, if I can help it. I'll unlock your fetters, and if I can't hold the jail, you'll have to make the best fight you can. If I'm shot, I'll consider my responsibility at an end."

There were iron fetters on the prisoner's ankles, and handcuffs on his wrists. These the sheriff unlocked, and they fell clanking to the floor.

"Keep back from the window," said the sheriff. "They might shoot if they saw you."

The sheriff drew toward the window a pine bench which formed a part of the scanty furniture of the cell, and laid his revolver upon it. Then he took his gun in hand, and took his stand at the side of the window where he could with least exposure of himself watch the movements of the crowd below.

The lynchers had not anticipated any determined resistance. Of course they had looked for a formal protest, and perhaps a sufficient show of opposition to excuse the sheriff in the eye of any stickler for legal formalities. They had not however come prepared to fight a battle, and no one of them seemed willing to lead an attack upon the jail. The leaders of the party conferred together with a good deal of animated gesticulation, which was visible to the sheriff from his outlook, though the distance was too great for him to hear what was said. At length one of them broke away from the group, and rode back to the main body of the lynchers, who were restlessly awaiting orders.

"Well, boys," said the messenger, "we'll have to let it go for the present. The sheriff says he'll shoot, and he's got the drop on us this time. There ain't any of us that want to follow Cap'n Walker jest yet. Besides, the sheriff is a good fellow, and we don't want to hurt 'im. But," he added, as if to reassure the crowd, which began to show signs of disappointment, "the nigger might as well say his prayers, for he ain't got long to live."

There was a murmur of dissent from the mob, and several voices insisted that an attack be made on the jail. But pacific counsels finally prevailed, and the mob sullenly withdrew.

The sheriff stood at the window until they had disappeared around the bend in the road. He did not relax his watchfulness when the last one was out of sight. Their withdrawal might be a mere feint, to be followed by a further attempt. So closely, indeed, was his attention drawn to the outside, that he neither saw nor heard the prisoner creep stealthily across the floor, reach out his hand and secure the revolver which lay on the bench behind the sheriff, and creep as noiselessly back to his place in the corner of the room.

A moment after the last of the lynching party had disappeared there was a shot fired from the woods across the road; a bullet whistled by the window and buried itself in the wooden casing a few inches from where the sheriff was standing. Quick as thought, with the instinct born of a semi-guerrilla army experience, he raised his gun and fired twice at the point from which a faint puff of smoke showed the hostile bullet to have been sent. He stood a moment watching, and then rested his gun against the window, and reached behind him mechanically for the other weapon. It was not on the bench. As the sheriff realized this fact, he turned his head and looked into the muzzle of the revolver.

"Stay where you are, Sheriff," said the prisoner, his eyes glistening, his face almost ruddy with excitement.

The sheriff mentally cursed his own carelessness for allowing him to be caught in such a predicament. He had not expected anything of the kind. He had relied on the negro's cowardice and subordination in the presence of an armed white man as a matter of course. The sheriff was a brave man, but realized that the prisoner had him at an immense disadvantage. The two men stood thus for a moment, fighting a harmless duel with their eyes.

"Well, what do you mean to do?" asked the sheriff with apparent calmness.

"To get away, of course," said the prisoner, in a tone which caused the sheriff to look at him more closely, and with an involuntary feeling of apprehension; if the man was not mad, he was in a state of mind akin to madness, and quite as dangerous. The sheriff felt that he must speak the prisoner fair, and watch for a chance to turn the tables on him. The keen-eyed, desperate man before him was a different being altogether from the groveling wretch who had begged so piteously for life a few minutes before.

At length the sheriff spoke:—

"Is this your gratitude to me for saving your life at the risk of my own? If I had not done so, you would now be swinging from the limb of some neighboring tree."

"True," said the prisoner, "you saved my life, but for how long? When you came in, you said Court would sit next week. When the crowd went away they said I had not long to live. It is merely a choice of two ropes."

"While there's life there's hope," replied the sheriff. He uttered this commonplace mechanically, while his brain was busy in trying to think out some way of escape. "If you are innocent you can prove it."

The mulatto kept his eye upon the sheriff. "I did n't kill the old man," he replied;

"but I shall never be able to clear myself. I was at his house at nine o'clock. I stole from it the coat that was on my back when I was taken. I would be convicted, even with a fair trial, unless the real murderer were discovered beforehand."

The sheriff knew this only too well. While he was thinking what argument next to use, the prisoner continued:—

"Throw me the keys—no, unlock the door."

The sheriff stood a moment irresolute. The mulatto's eye glittered ominously. The sheriff crossed the room and unlocked the door leading into the passage.

"Now go down and unlock the outside door."

The heart of the sheriff leaped within him. Perhaps he might make a dash for liberty, and gain the outside. He descended the narrow stairs, the prisoner keeping close behind him.

The sheriff inserted the huge iron key into the lock. The rusty bolt yielded slowly. It still remained for him to pull the door open.

"Stop!" thundered the mulatto, who seemed to divine the sheriff's purpose. "Move a muscle, and I'll blow your brains out."

The sheriff obeyed; he realized that his chance had not yet come.

"Now keep on that side of the passage, and go back upstairs."

Keeping the sheriff under cover of the revolver, the mulatto followed him up the stairs. The sheriff expected the prisoner to lock him into the cell and make his own escape. He had about come to the conclusion that the best thing he could do under the circumstances was to submit quietly, and take his chances of recapturing the prisoner after the alarm had been given. The sheriff had faced death more than once upon the battlefield. A few minutes before, well armed, and with a brick wall between him and them he had dared a hundred men to fight; but he felt instinctively that the desperate man confronting him was not to be trifled with, and he was too prudent a man to risk his life against such heavy odds. He had Polly to look after, and there was a limit beyond which devotion to duty would be quixotic and even foolish.

"I want to get away," said the prisoner, "and I don't want to be captured; for if I am I know I will be hung on the spot. I am afraid," he added somewhat reflectively, "that in order to save myself I shall have to kill you."

"Good God!" exclaimed the sheriff in involuntary terror; "you would not kill the man to whom you owe your own life."

"You speak more truly than you know," replied the mulatto. "I indeed owe my life to you."

The sheriff started. He was capable of surprise, even in that moment of extreme peril. "Who are you?" he asked in amazement.

"Tom, Cicely's son," returned the other. He had closed the door and stood talking to the sheriff through the grated opening. "Don't you remember Cicely—Cicely whom you sold, with her child, to the speculator on his way to Alabama?"

The sheriff did remember. He had been sorry for it many a time since. It had been the old story of debts, mortgages, and bad crops. He had quarreled with the mother. The price offered for her and her child had been unusually large, and he had yielded to the combination of anger and pecuniary stress.

"Good God!" he gasped, "you would not murder your own father?"

"My father?" replied the mulatto. "It were well enough for me to claim the relationship, but it comes with poor grace from you to ask anything by reason of it. What father's duty have you ever performed for me? Did you give me your name, or even your protection? Other white men gave their colored sons freedom and money, and sent them to the free States. *You* sold *me* to the rice swamps."

"I at least gave you the life you cling to," murmured the sheriff.

"Life?" said the prisoner, with a sarcastic laugh. "What kind of a life? You gave me your own blood, your own features,—no man need look at us together twice to see that,—and you gave me a black mother. Poor wretch! She died under the lash, because she had enough womanhood to call her soul her own. You gave me a white man's spirit, and you made me a slave, and crushed it out."

"But you are free now," said the sheriff. He had not doubted, could not doubt, the mulatto's word. He knew whose passions coursed beneath that swarthy skin and burned in the black eyes opposite his own. He saw in this mulatto what he himself might have become had not the safeguards of parental restraint and public opinion been thrown around him.

"Free to do what?" replied the mulatto. "Free in name, but despised and scorned and set aside by the people to whose race I belong far more than to my mother's."

"There are schools," said the sheriff. "You have been to school." He had noticed that the mulatto spoke more eloquently and used better language than most Branson County people.

"I have been to school, and dreamed when I went that it would work some marvelous change in my condition. But what did I learn? I learned to feel that no degree of learning or wisdom will change the color of my skin and that I shall always wear what in my own country is a badge of degradation. When I think about it seriously I do not care particularly for such a life. It is the animal in me, not the man, that flees the gallows. I owe you nothing," he went on, "and expect nothing of you; and it would be no more than justice if I should avenge upon you my mother's wrongs and my own. But still I hate to shoot you; I have never yet taken human life—for I did *not* kill the old captain. Will you promise to give no alarm and make no attempt to capture me until morning, if I do not shoot?"

So absorbed were the two men in their colloquy and their own tumultuous thoughts that neither of them had heard the door below move upon its hinges. Neither of them had heard a light step come stealthily up the stairs, nor seen a slender form creep along the darkening passage toward the mulatto.

The sheriff hesitated. The struggle between his love of life and his sense of duty was a terrific one. It may seem strange that a man who could sell his own child into slavery should hesitate at such a moment, when his life was trembling in the balance. But the baleful influence of human slavery poisoned the very fountains of life, and created new standards of right. The sheriff was conscientious; his conscience had merely been warped by his environment. Let no one ask what his answer would have been; he was spared the necessity of a decision.

"Stop," said the mulatto, "you need not promise. I could not trust you if you did. It is your life for mine; there is but one safe way for me; you must die."

He raised his arm to fire, when there was a flash—a report from the passage behind him. His arm fell heavily at his side, and the pistol dropped at his feet.

The sheriff recovered first from his surprise, and throwing open the door secured the fallen weapon. Then seizing the prisoner he thrust him into the cell and locked the door upon him; after which he turned to Polly, who leaned half-fainting against the wall, her hands clasped over her heart.

"Oh, father, I was just in time!" she cried hysterically, and, wildly sobbing, threw herself into her father's arms.

"I watched until they all went away," she said. "I heard the shot from the woods and I saw you shoot. Then when you did not come out I feared something had happened, that perhaps you had been wounded. I got out the other pistol and ran over here. When I found the door open, I knew something was wrong, and when I heard voices I crept upstairs, and reached the top just in time to hear him say he would kill you. Oh, it was a narrow escape!"

When she had grown somewhat calmer, the sheriff left her standing there and went back into the cell. The prisoner's arm was bleeding from a flesh wound. His bravado had given place to a stony apathy. There was no sign in his face of fear or disappointment or feeling of any kind. The sheriff sent Polly to the house for cloth, and bound up the prisoner's wound with a rude skill acquired during his army life.

"I'll have a doctor come and dress the wound in the morning," he said to the prisoner. "It will do very well until then, if you will keep quiet. If the doctor asks you how the wound was caused, you can say that you were struck by the bullet fired from the woods. It would do you no good to have it known that you were shot while attempting to escape."

The prisoner uttered no word of thanks or apology, but sat in sullen silence. When the wounded arm had been bandaged, Polly and her father returned to the house.

The sheriff was in an unusually thoughtful mood that evening. He put salt in his coffee at supper, and poured vinegar over his pancakes. To many of Polly's questions he returned random answers. When he had gone to bed he lay awake for several hours.

In the silent watches of the night, when he was alone with God, there came into his mind a flood of unaccustomed thoughts. An hour or two before, standing face to face with death, he had experienced a sensation similar to that which drowning men are said to feel—a kind of clarifying of the moral faculty, in which the veil of the flesh, with its obscuring passions and prejudices, is pushed aside for a moment, and all the acts of one's life stand out, in the clear light of truth, in their correct proportions and relations,—a state of mind in which one sees himself as God may be supposed to see him. In the reaction following his rescue, this feeling had given place for a time to far different emotions. But now, in the silence of midnight, something of this clearness of spirit returned to the sheriff. He saw that he had owed some duty to this son of his,—that neither law nor custom could destroy a responsibility inherent in the nature of mankind. He could not thus, in the eyes of God at least, shake off the consequences of his sin. Had he never sinned, this wayward spirit would never have come back from the vanished past to haunt him. As these thoughts came, his anger against the mulatto died away, and in its place there sprang up a great pity. The hand of parental authority might have restrained the passions he had seen burning in the prisoner's eyes when the desperate man spoke the words which had seemed to doom his father to death. The sheriff felt that he might have saved this fiery spirit from the slough of slavery; that he might have sent him to the free North, and given him there, or in some other land, an opportunity to turn to usefulness and honorable pursuits the talents that had run to crime, perhaps to madness; he might, still less, have given this son of his the poor simulacrum of liberty which men of his caste could possess in a slave-holding community; or least of all, but still something, he might have kept the boy on the plantation, where the burdens of slavery would have fallen lightly upon him.

The sheriff recalled his own youth. He had inherited an honored name to keep untarnished; he had had a future to make; the picture of a fair young bride had beckoned him on to happiness. The poor wretch now stretched upon a pallet of straw between the brick walls of the jail had had none of these things,—no name, no father, no mother—in the true meaning of motherhood,—and until the past few years no possible future, and then one vague and shadowy in its outline, and dependent for form and substance upon the slow solution of a problem in which there were many unknown quantities.

From what he might have done to what he might yet do was an easy transition for the awakened conscience of the sheriff. It occurred to him, purely as a hypothesis, that he might permit his prisoner to escape; but his oath of office, his duty as sheriff, stood in the way of such a course, and the sheriff dismissed the idea from his mind. He could, however, investigate the circumstances of the murder, and move Heaven and earth to discover the real criminal, for he no longer doubted the prisoner's innocence; he could employ counsel for the accused, and perhaps influence public opinion in his favor. An acquittal once secured, some plan could be devised by which the sheriff might in some degree atone for his crime against this son of his—against society—against God.

When the sheriff had reached this conclusion he fell into an unquiet slumber, from which he awoke late the next morning.

He went over to the jail before breakfast and found the prisoner lying on his pallet, his face turned to the wall; he did not move when the sheriff rattled the door.

"Good-morning," said the latter, in a tone intended to waken the prisoner.

There was no response. The sheriff looked more keenly at the recumbent figure; there was an unnatural rigidity about its attitude.

He hastily unlocked the door and, entering the cell, bent over the prostrate form. There was no sound of breathing; he turned the body over—it was cold and stiff. The prisoner had torn the bandage from his wound and bled to death during the night. He had evidently been dead several hours.

1889

Charlotte Perkins Gilman
1860–1935

Charlotte Perkins Gilman is now studied primarily by social historians interested in her advocacy of women's rights, her often astute comments concerning the relation of female households to male economies, and her active career as a lecturer and writer on a large number of sociological themes. But she is largely ignored as a writer of specifically literary works; her fiction is combed to see what it reveals about social issues. However, one of her stories, "The Yellow Wallpaper," has been celebrated by two diverse groups: fans of horror tales and feminist critics. This ability to write a story with great personal intensity and to convert an unhappy bit of autobiography into a memorable fiction came once in Gilman's long career as a polemicist and social critic, but once was enough.

From her father's family, Charlotte Perkins inherited the approved attitudes toward female domesticity, but out of her mother's experience she formed more complex views toward family love, wifehood, and mothering.

Charlotte Anne Perkins, born in Hartford, Connecticut, was directly connected through her father to Lyman and Henry Ward Beecher, Catherine Beecher, and Harriet Beecher Stowe. The Beechers were famous for their ability to talk and to write about matters of religious piety and social reform and the need to affirm the values of middle-class America while correcting its ills. The various activities of the Beecher women can be interpreted as being against slavery in one form or another. At the same time—and this is the paradox that marked Gilman's own career—the Beechers upheld the supposedly enslaving institutions of hearth, home, and marriage.

However much a Beecher, Charlotte Perkins's father (himself an educated and influential writer) left his wife soon after the birth of his daughter. He remained aloof for the rest of his life from the ill fortune of his wife, who was left alone to support two children. Charlotte afterward attempted to gain her father's favor but was constantly thwarted. She had to experience the poverty and instability of a girlhood spent on the move as her mother wandered from place to place in search of a home she never found.

At twenty-four, after studying art and spending some time as an art teacher, Charlotte Perkins married Charles Stetson, an artist. When her only child was born the next year, 1885, she fell into a deep depression. At the urging of her husband she became a patient of S. Weir Mitchell, a famous Philadelphia physician who had evolved a cure for female nervous disorders in the 1870s. Mitchell's treatment consisted of total bed rest and the enforced isolation of the patient from all activities, physical and mental. Mitchell had some success with his procedures, and his emphasis on the need for the complete moral reliance of patient on physician paralleled the principles of Freudian analysis that were being introduced in Vienna. But these facts are overshadowed by the effect his treatment had on Charlotte Stetson; it was to drive her almost insane. She escaped this fate by fleeing both physician and husband for California, breaking free from these two men's well-intentioned domination over her mind and body. Not until 1892 was she able to take this bitter experience and convert it into her story "The Yellow Wallpaper," written with the purpose of exposing one of the ways by which women are reduced to the state of helpless children.

Charlotte Perkins accomplished a great deal besides writing one famous story. She developed several careers—first as a writer and then as a lecturer on issues of woman suffrage, socialism, and trade unionism. In 1900 she entered upon a successful marriage to George Gilman, her first cousin and another Beecher descendant. But marriage did not stay her hand as a critic of male society. Her best-known books (which the feminist movement has revived) are *Women and Economics* (1899), *The Home: Its Work and Influence* (1903), and *The Man-Made World, or Our Androcentric Culture* (1911). Her autobiography, *The Living of*

Charlotte Perkins Gilman, was published posthumously in 1935, the year she committed suicide in order to avoid the final torments of inoperable cancer.

Notwithstanding the questions of choice that arise from Gilman's final act, it is fortunate that, back in 1885, she was able, in spite of the terrible psychic experiences of that period, to will herself a different fate than that suffered by the woman in "The Yellow Wallpaper." She was able to end the mad repetition of defeat and despair that sent the nameless victim of that upstairs room crawling around and around the edges of the wallpaper. In contrast, Gilman was able to break out of that room and go on through a lifetime of considerable achievement.

Further Reading:
M. Hill, *Charlotte Perkins Gilman: The Making of a Radical Feminist, 1860–1896,* 1980.

Text:
The Charlotte Perkins Gilman Reader, ed. A. Lane, 1980.

The Yellow Wallpaper

It is very seldom that mere ordinary people like John and myself secure ancestral halls for the summer.

A colonial mansion, a hereditary estate, I would say a haunted house and reach the height of romantic felicity—but that would be asking too much of fate!

Still I will proudly declare that there is something queer about it.

Else, why should it be let so cheaply? And why have stood so long untenanted?

John laughs at me, of course, but one expects that.

John is practical in the extreme. He has no patience with faith, an intense horror of superstition, and he scoffs openly at any talk of things not to be felt and seen and put down in figures.

John is a physician, and *perhaps*— (I would not say it to a living soul, of course, but this is dead paper and a great relief to my mind)—*perhaps* that is one reason I do not get well faster.

You see, he does not believe I am sick! And what can one do?

If a physician of high standing, and one's own husband, assures friends and relatives that there is really nothing the matter with one but temporary nervous depression— a slight hysterical tendency—what is one to do?

My brother is also a physician, and also of high standing, and he says the same thing.

So I take phosphates or phosphites—whichever it is—and tonics, and air and exercise, and journeys, and am absolutely forbidden to "work" until I am well again.

Personally, I disagree with their ideas.

Personally, I believe that congenial work, with excitement and change, would do me good.

But what is one to do?

I did write for a while in spite of them; but it *does* exhaust me a good deal—having to be so sly about it, or else meet with heavy opposition.

I sometimes fancy that in my condition, if I had less opposition and more society and stimulus—but John says the very worst thing I can do is to think about my condition, and I confess it always makes me feel bad.

So I will let it alone and talk about the house.

The most beautiful place! It is quite alone, standing well back from the road, quite three miles from the village. It makes me think of English places that you read about, for there are hedges and walls and gates that lock, and lots of separate little houses for the gardeners and people.

There is a *delicious* garden! I never saw such a garden—large and shady, full of box-bordered paths, and lined with long grape-covered arbors with seats under them.

There were greenhouses, but they are all broken now.

There was some legal trouble, I believe, something about the heirs and co-heirs; anyhow, the place has been empty for years.

That spoils my ghostliness, I am afraid, but I don't care—there is something strange about the house—I can feel it.

I even said so to John one moonlight evening, but he said what I felt was a draught, and shut the window.

I get unreasonably angry with John sometimes. I'm sure I never used to be so sensitive. I think it is due to this nervous condition.

But John says if I feel so I shall neglect proper self-control; so I take pains to control myself—before him, at least, and that makes me very tired.

I don't like our room a bit. I wanted one downstairs that opened onto the piazza and had roses all over the window, and such pretty old-fashioned chintz hangings! But John would not hear of it.

He said there was only one window and not room for two beds, and no near room for him if he took another.

He is very careful and loving, and hardly lets me stir without special direction.

I have a schedule prescription for each hour in the day; he takes all care from me, and so I feel basely ungrateful not to value it more.

He said he came here solely on my account, that I was to have perfect rest and all the air I could get. "Your exercise depends on your strength, my dear," said he, "and your food somewhat on your appetite; but air you can absorb all the time." So we took the nursery at the top of the house.

It is a big, airy room, the whole floor nearly, with windows that look all ways, and air and sunshine galore. It was nursery first, and then playroom and gymnasium, I should judge, for the windows are barred for little children, and there are rings and things in the walls.

The paint and paper look as if a boys' school had used it. It is stripped off—the paper—in great patches all around the head of my bed, about as far as I can reach, and in a great place on the other side of the room low down. I never saw a worse paper in my life. One of those sprawling, flamboyant patterns committing every artistic sin.

It is dull enough to confuse the eye in following, pronounced enough constantly to irritate and provoke study, and when you follow the lame uncertain curves for a little distance they suddenly commit suicide—plunge off at outrageous angles, destroy themselves in unheard-of contradictions.

The color is repellent, almost revolting: a smouldering unclean yellow, strangely faded by the slow-turning sunlight. It is a dull yet lurid orange in some places, a sickly sulphur tint in others.

No wonder the children hated it! I should hate it myself if I had to live in this room long.

There comes John, and I must put this away—he hates to have me write a word.

We have been here two weeks, and I haven't felt like writing before, since that first day.

I am sitting by the window now, up in this atrocious nursery, and there is nothing to hinder my writing as much as I please, save lack of strength.

John is away all day, and even some nights when his cases are serious.

I am glad my case is not serious!

But these nervous troubles are dreadfully depressing.

John does not know how much I really suffer. He knows there is no reason to suffer, and that satisfies him.

Of course it is only nervousness. It does weigh on me so not to do my duty in any way!

I meant to be such a help to John, such a real rest and comfort, and here I am a comparative burden already!

Nobody would believe what an effort it is to do what little I am able—to dress and entertain, and order things.

It is fortunate Mary is so good with the baby. Such a dear baby!

And yet I *cannot* be with him, it makes me so nervous.

I suppose John never was nervous in his life. He laughs at me so about this wallpaper!

At first he meant to repaper the room, but afterward he said that I was letting it get the better of me, and that nothing was worse for a nervous patient than to give way to such fancies.

He said that after the wallpaper was changed it would be the heavy bedstead, and then the barred windows, and then that gate at the head of the stairs, and so on.

"You know the place is doing you good," he said, "and really, dear, I don't care to renovate the house just for a three months' rental."

"Then do let us go downstairs," I said. "There are such pretty rooms there."

Then he took me in his arms and called me a blessed little goose, and said he would go down cellar, if I wished, and have it whitewashed into the bargain.

But he is right enough about the beds and windows and things.

It is as airy and comfortable a room as anyone need wish, and, of course, I would not be so silly as to make him uncomfortable just for a whim.

I'm really getting quite fond of the big room, all but that horrid paper.

Out of one window I can see the garden—those mysterious deep-shaded arbors, the riotous old-fashioned flowers, and bushes and gnarly trees.

Out of another I get a lovely view of the bay and a little private wharf belonging to the estate. There is a beautiful shaded lane that runs down there from the house.

I always fancy I see people walking in these numerous paths and arbors, but John has cautioned me not to give way to fancy in the least. He says that with my imaginative power and habit of story-making, a nervous weakness like mine is sure to lead to all manner of excited fancies, and that I ought to use my will and good sense to check the tendency. So I try.

I think sometimes that if I were only well enough to write a little it would relieve the press of ideas and rest me.

But I find I get pretty tired when I try.

It is so discouraging not to have any advice and companionship about my work. When I get really well, John says we will ask Cousin Henry and Julia down for a long visit; but he says he would as soon put fireworks in my pillow-case as to let me have those stimulating people about now.

I wish I could get well faster.

But I must not think about that. This paper looks to me as if it *knew* what a vicious influence it had!

There is a recurrent spot where the pattern lolls like a broken neck and two bulbous eyes stare at you upside down.

I get positively angry with the impertinence of it and the ever-lastingness. Up and down and sideways they crawl, and those absurd unblinking eyes are everywhere. There is one place where two breadths didn't match, and the eyes go all up and down the line, one a little higher than the other.

I never saw so much expression in an inanimate thing before, and we all know how much expression they have! I used to lie awake as a child and get more entertainment and terror out of blank walls and plain furniture than most children could find in a toy-store.

I remember what a kindly wink the knobs of our big old bureau used to have, and there was one chair that always seemed like a strong friend.

I used to feel that if any of the other things looked too fierce I could always hop into that chair and be safe.

The furniture in this room is no worse than inharmonious, however, for we had to bring it all from downstairs. I suppose when this was used as a playroom they had to take the nursery things out, and no wonder! I never saw such ravages as the children have made here.

The wallpaper, as I said before, is torn off in spots, and it sticketh closer than a brother—they must have had perseverance as well as hatred.

Then the floor is scratched and gouged and splintered, the plaster itself is dug out here and there, and this great heavy bed, which is all we found in the room, looks as if it had been through the wars.

But I don't mind it a bit—only the paper.

There comes John's sister. Such a dear girl as she is, and so careful of me! I must not let her find me writing.

She is a perfect and enthusiastic housekeeper, and hopes for no better profession. I verily believe she thinks it is the writing which made me sick!

But I can write when she is out, and see her a long way off from these windows.

There is one that commands the road, a lovely shaded winding road, and one that just looks off over the country. A lovely country, too, full of great elms and velvet meadows.

This wallpaper has a kind of sub-pattern in a different shade, a particularly irritating one, for you can only see it in certain lights, and not clearly then.

But in the places where it isn't faded and where the sun is just so—I can see a strange, provoking, formless sort of figure that seems to skulk about behind that silly and conspicuous front design.

There's sister on the stairs!

Well, the Fourth of July is over! The people are all gone, and I am tired out. John thought it might do me good to see a little company, so we just had Mother and Nellie and the children down for a week.

Of course I didn't do a thing. Jennie sees to everything now.

But it tired me all the same.

John says if I don't pick up faster he shall send me to Weir Mitchell[1] in the fall.

But I don't want to go there at all. I had a friend who was in his hands once, and she says he is just like John and my brother, only more so!

Besides, it is such an undertaking to go so far.

I don't feel as if it was worthwhile to turn my hand over for anything, and I'm getting dreadfully fretful and querulous.

I cry at nothing, and cry most of the time.

Of course I don't when John is here, or anybody else, but when I am alone.

And I am alone a good deal just now. John is kept in town very often by serious cases, and Jennie is good and lets me alone when I want her to.

So I walk a little in the garden or down that lovely lane, sit on the porch under the roses, and lie down up here a good deal.

I'm getting really fond of the room in spite of the wallpaper. Perhaps *because* of the wallpaper.

It dwells in my mind so!

I lie here on this great immovable bed—it is nailed down, I believe—and follow that pattern about by the hour. It is as good as gymnastics, I assure you. I start, we'll say, at the bottom, down in the corner over there where it has not been touched, and I determine for the thousandth time that I *will* follow that pointless pattern to some sort of a conclusion.

I know a little of the principle of design, and I know this thing was not arranged on any laws of radiation, or alternation, or repetition, or symmetry, or anything else that I ever heard of.

It is repeated, of course, by the breadths, but not otherwise.

Looked at in one way, each breadth stands alone; the bloated curves and flourishes —a kind of "debased Romanesque"[2] with delirium tremens—go waddling up and down in isolated columns of fatuity.

But, on the other hand, they connect diagonally, and the sprawling outlines run off in great slanting waves of optic horror, like a lot of wallowing sea-weeds in full chase.

[1] American physician famous for his treatment of "neurotic females" by means of enforced bed rest and isolation. Herself a highly dissatisfied patient of Mitchell, Gilman intended this story as an attack against his methods.

[2] Style of architecture and decoration originating in the eleventh and twelfth centuries, here debased to ugliness.

The whole thing goes horizontally, too, at least it seems so, and I exhaust myself trying to distinguish the order of its going in that direction.

They have used a horizontal breadth for a frieze, and that adds wonderfully to the confusion.

There is one end of the room where it is almost intact, and there, when the crosslights fade and the low sun shines directly upon it, I can almost fancy radiation after all—the interminable grotesque seems to form around a common center and rush off in headlong plunges of equal distraction.

It makes me tired to follow it. I will take a nap, I guess.

I don't know why I should write this.

I don't want to.

I don't feel able.

And I know John would think it absurd. But I must say what I feel and think in some way—it is such a relief!

But the effort is getting to be greater than the relief.

Half the time now I am awfully lazy, and lie down ever so much. John says I mustn't lose my strength, and has me take cod liver oil and lots of tonics and things, to say nothing of ale and wine and rare meat.

Dear John! He loves me very dearly, and hates to have me sick. I tried to have a real earnest reasonable talk with him the other day, and tell him how I wish he would let me go and make a visit to Cousin Henry and Julia.

But he said I wasn't able to go, nor able to stand it after I got there; and I did not make out a very good case for myself, for I was crying before I had finished.

It is getting to be a great effort for me to think straight. Just this nervous weakness, I suppose.

And dear John gathered me up in his arms, and just carried me upstairs and laid me on the bed, and sat by me and read to me till it tired my head.

He said I was his darling and his comfort and all he had, and that I must take care of myself for his sake, and keep well.

He says no one but myself can help me out of it, that I must use my will and self-control and not let any silly fancies run away with me.

There's one comfort—the baby is well and happy, and does not have to occupy this nursery with the horrid wallpaper.

If we had not used it, that blessed child would have! What a fortunate escape! Why, I wouldn't have a child of mine, an impressionable little thing, live in such a room for worlds.

I never thought of it before, but it is lucky that John kept me here after all; I can stand it so much easier than a baby, you see.

Of course I never mention it to them any more—I am too wise—but I keep watch for it all the same.

There are things in that wallpaper that nobody knows about but me, or ever will.

Behind that outside pattern the dim shapes get clearer every day.

It is always the same shape, only very numerous.

And it is like a woman stooping down and creeping about behind that pattern. I don't like it a bit. I wonder—I begin to think—I wish John would take me away from here!

It is so hard to talk with John about my case, because he is so wise, and because he loves me so.

But I tried it last night.

It was moonlight. The moon shines in all around just as the sun does.

I hate to see it sometimes, it creeps so slowly, and always comes in by one window or another.

John was asleep and I hated to waken him, so I kept still and watched the moonlight on that undulating wallpaper till I felt creepy.

The faint figure behind seemed to shake the pattern, just as if she wanted to get out.

I got up softly and went to feel and see if the paper *did* move, and when I came back John was awake.

"What is it, little girl?" he said. "Don't go walking about like that—you'll get cold."

I thought it was a good time to talk, so I told him that I really was not gaining here, and that I wished he would take me away.

"Why, darling!" said he. "Our lease will be up in three weeks, and I can't see how to leave before.

"The repairs are not done at home, and I cannot possibly leave town just now. Of course, if you were in any danger, I could and would, but you really are better, dear, whether you can see it or not. I am a doctor, dear, and I know. You are gaining flesh and color, your appetite is better, I feel really much easier about you."

"I don't weigh a bit more," said I, "nor as much; and my appetite may be better in the evening when you are here but it is worse in the morning when you are away!"

"Bless her little heart!" said he with a big hug. "She shall be as sick as she pleases! But now let's improve the shining hours by going to sleep, and talk about it in the morning!"

"And you won't go away?" I asked gloomily.

"Why, how can I, dear? It is only three weeks more and then we will take a nice little trip of a few days while Jennie is getting the house ready. Really, dear, you are better!"

"Better in body perhaps—" I began, and stopped short, for he sat up straight and looked at me with such a stern, reproachful look that I could not say another word.

"My darling," said he, "I beg of you, for my sake and for our child's sake, as well as for your own, that you will never for one instant let that idea enter your mind! There is nothing so dangerous, so fascinating, to a temperament like yours. It is a false and foolish fancy. Can you not trust me as a physician when I tell you so?"

So of course I said no more on that score, and we went to sleep before long. He thought I was asleep first, but I wasn't, and lay there for hours trying to decide whether that front pattern and the back pattern really did move together or separately.

On a pattern like this, by daylight, there is a lack of sequence, a defiance of law, that is a constant irritant to a normal mind.

The color is hideous enough, and unreliable enough, and infuriating enough, but the pattern is torturing.

You think you have mastered it, but just as you get well under way in following, it turns a back-somersault and there you are. It slaps you in the face, knocks you down, and tramples upon you. It is like a bad dream.

The outside pattern is a florid arabesque, reminding one of a fungus. If you can imagine a toadstool in joints, an interminable string of toadstools, budding and sprouting in endless convolutions—why, that is something like it.

That is, sometimes!

There is one marked peculiarity about this paper, a thing nobody seems to notice but myself, and that is that it changes as the light changes.

When the sun shoots in through the east window—I always watch for that first long, straight ray—it changes so quickly that I never can quite believe it.

That is why I watch it always.

By moonlight—the moon shines in all night when there is a moon—I wouldn't know it was the same paper.

At night in any kind of light, in twilight, candlelight, lamplight, and worst of all by moonlight, it becomes bars! The outside pattern, I mean, and the woman behind it is as plain as can be.

I didn't realize for a long time what the thing was that showed behind, that dim sub-pattern, but now I am quite sure it is a woman.

By daylight she is subdued, quiet. I fancy it is the pattern that keeps her so still. It is so puzzling. It keeps me quiet by the hour.

I lie down ever so much now. John says it is good for me, and to sleep all I can.

Indeed he started the habit by making me lie down for an hour after each meal.

It is a very bad habit, I am convinced, for you see, I don't sleep.

And that cultivates deceit, for I don't tell them I'm awake—oh, no!

The fact is I am getting a little afraid of John.

He seems very queer sometimes, and even Jennie has an inexplicable look.

It strikes me occasionally, just as a scientific hypothesis, that perhaps it is the paper!

I have watched John when he did not know I was looking, and come into the room suddenly on the most innocent excuses, and I've caught him several times *looking at the paper!* And Jennie too. I caught Jennie with her hand on it once.

She didn't know I was in the room, and when I asked her in a quiet, a very quiet voice, with the most restrained manner possible, what she was doing with the paper, she turned around as if she had been caught stealing, and looked quite angry—asked me why I should frighten her so!

Then she said that the paper stained everything it touched, that she had found yellow smooches on all my clothes and John's and she wished we would be more careful!

Did not that sound innocent? But I know she was studying that pattern, and I am determined that nobody shall find it out but myself!

Life is very much more exciting now than it used to be. You see, I have something more to expect, to look forward to, to watch. I really do eat better, and am more quiet than I was.

John is so pleased to see me improve! He laughed a little the other day, and said I seemed to be flourishing in spite of my wallpaper.

I turned it off with a laugh. I had no intention of telling him it was *because* of the wallpaper—he would make fun of me. He might even want to take me away.

I don't want to leave now until I have found it out. There is a week more, and I think that will be enough.

I'm feeling so much better!

I don't sleep much at night, for it is so interesting to watch developments; but I sleep a good deal during the daytime.

In the daytime it is tiresome and perplexing.

There are always new shoots on the fungus, and new shades of yellow all over it. I cannot keep count of them, though I have tried conscientiously.

It is the strangest yellow, that wallpaper! It makes me think of all the yellow things I ever saw—not beautiful ones like buttercups, but old, foul, bad yellow things.

But there is something else about that paper—the smell! I noticed it the moment we came into the room but with so much air and sun it was not bad. Now we have had a week of fog and rain, and whether the windows are open or not, the smell is here.

It creeps all over the house.

I find it hovering in the dining-room, skulking in the parlor, hiding in the hall, lying in wait for me on the stairs.

It gets into my hair.

Even when I go to ride, if I turn my head suddenly and surprise it—there is that smell!

Such a peculiar odor, too! I have spent hours in trying to analyze it, to find what it smelled like.

It is not bad—at first—and very gentle, but quite the subtlest, most enduring odor I ever met.

In this damp weather it is awful. I wake up in the night and find it hanging over me.

It used to disturb me at first. I thought seriously of burning the house—to reach the smell.

But now I am used to it. The only thing I can think of that it is like is the *color* of the paper! A yellow smell.

There is a very funny mark on this wall, low down, near the mopboard. A streak that runs round the room. It goes behind every piece of furniture, except the bed, a long, straight, even *smooch,* as if it had been rubbed over and over.

I wonder how it was done and who did it, and what they did it for. Round and round and round—round and round and round—it makes me dizzy!

I really have discovered something at last.

Through watching so much at night, when it changes so, I have finally found out.

The front pattern *does* move—and no wonder! The woman behind shakes it!

Sometimes I think there are a great many women behind, and sometimes only one, and she crawls around fast, and her crawling shakes it all over.

Then in the very bright spots she keeps still, and in the very shady spots she just takes hold of the bars and shakes them hard.

And she is all the time trying to climb through. But nobody could climb through that pattern—it strangles so; I think that is why it has so many heads.

They get through, and then the pattern strangles them off and turns them upside down, and makes their eyes white!

If those heads were covered or taken off it would not be half so bad.

I think that woman gets out in the daytime!

And I'll tell you why—privately—I've seen her!

I can see her out of every one of my windows!

It is the same woman, I know, for she is always creeping, and most women do not creep by daylight.

I see her in that long shaded lane, creeping up and down. I see her in those dark grape arbors, creeping all around the garden.

I see her on that long road under the trees, creeping along, and when a carriage comes she hides under the blackberry vines.

I don't blame her a bit. It must be very humiliating to be caught creeping by daylight!

I always lock the door when I creep by daylight. I can't do it at night, for I know John would suspect something at once.

And John is so queer now that I don't want to irritate him. I wish he would take another room! Besides, I don't want anybody to get that woman out at night but myself.

I often wonder if I could see her out of all the windows at once.

But, turn as fast as I can, I can only see out of one at one time.

And though I always see her, she *may* be able to creep faster than I can turn! I have watched her sometimes away off in the open country, creeping as fast as a cloud shadow in a wind.

If only that top pattern could be gotten off from the under one! I mean to try it, little by little.

I have found out another funny thing, but I shan't tell it this time! It does not do to trust people too much.

There are only two more days to get this paper off, and I believe John is beginning to notice. I don't like the look in his eyes.

And I heard him ask Jennie a lot of professional questions about me. She had a very good report to give.

She said I slept a good deal in the daytime.

John knows I don't sleep very well at night, for all I'm so quiet!

He asked me all sorts of questions, too, and pretended to be very loving and kind.

As if I couldn't see through him!

Still, I don't wonder he acts so, sleeping under this paper for three months.

It only interests me, but I feel sure John and Jennie are affected by it.

. . . .

Hurrah! This is the last day, but it is enough. John is to stay in town over night, and won't be out until this evening.

Jennie wanted to sleep with me—the sly thing; but I told her I should undoubtedly rest better for a night all alone.

That was clever, for really I wasn't alone a bit! As soon as it was moonlight and that poor thing began to crawl and shake the pattern, I got up and ran to help her.

I pulled and she shook. I shook and she pulled, and before morning we had peeled off yards of that paper.

A strip about as high as my head and half around the room.

And then when the sun came and that awful pattern began to laugh at me, I declared I would finish it today!

We go away tomorrow, and they are moving all my furniture down again to leave things as they were before.

Jennie looked at the wall in amazement, but I told her merrily that I did it out of pure spite at the vicious thing.

She laughed and said she wouldn't mind doing it herself, but I must not get tired. How she betrayed herself that time!

But I am here, and no person touches this paper but Me—not *alive!*

She tried to get me out of the room—it was too patent! But I said it was so quiet and empty and clean now that I believed I would lie down again and sleep all I could, and not to wake me even for dinner—I would call when I woke.

So now she is gone, and the servants are gone, and the things are gone, and there is nothing left but that great bedstead nailed down, with the canvas mattress we found on it.

We shall sleep downstairs tonight, and take the boat home tomorrow.

I quite enjoy the room, now it is bare again.

How those children did tear about here!

This bedstead is fairly gnawed!

But I must get to work.

I have locked the door and thrown the key down into the front path.

I don't want to go out, and I don't want to have anybody come in, till John comes. I want to astonish him.

I've got a rope up here that even Jennie did not find. If that woman does get out, and tries to get away, I can tie her!

But I forgot I could not reach far without anything to stand on!

This bed will *not* move!

I tried to lift and push it until I was lame, and then I got so angry I bit off a little piece at one corner—but it hurt my teeth.

Then I peeled off all the paper I could reach standing on the floor. It sticks horribly and the pattern just enjoys it! All those strangled heads and bulbous eyes and waddling fungus growths just shriek with derision!

I am getting angry enough to do something desperate. To jump out of the window would be admirable exercise, but the bars are too strong even to try.

Besides I wouldn't do it. Of course not. I know well enough that a step like that is improper and might be misconstrued.

I don't like to *look* out of the windows even—there are so many of those creeping women, and they creep so fast.

I wonder if they all come out of that wallpaper as I did?

But I am securely fastened now by my well-hidden rope—you don't get *me* out in the road there!

I suppose I shall have to get back behind the pattern when it comes night, and that is hard!

It is so pleasant to be out in this great room and creep around as I please!

I don't want to go outside. I won't, even if Jennie asks me to.

For outside you have to creep on the ground, and everything is green instead of yellow.

But here I can creep smoothly on the floor, and my shoulder just fits in that long smooch around the wall, so I cannot lose my way.

Why, there's John at the door!

It is no use, young man, you can't open it!

How he does call and pound!

Now he's crying to Jennie for an axe.

It would be a shame to break down that beautiful door!

"John, dear!" said I in the gentlest voice. "The key is down by the front steps, under a plantain leaf!"

That silenced him for a few moments.

Then he said, very quietly indeed, "Open the door, my darling!"

"I can't," said I. "The key is down by the front door under a plantain leaf!" And then I said it again, several times, very gently and slowly, and said it so often that he had to go and see, and he got it of course, and came in. He stopped short by the door.

"What is the matter?" he cried. "For God's sake, what are you doing!"

I kept on creeping just the same, but I looked at him over my shoulder.

"I've got out at last," said I, "in spite of you and Jane. And I've pulled off most of the paper, so you can't put me back!"

Now why should that man have fainted? But he did, and right across my path by the wall, so that I had to creep over him every time!

1892

Hamlin Garland
1860–1940

At a time when art seemed to the American public to have separated itself from life, and literature from political and social action, Hamlin Garland fiercely insisted that such oppositions were neither necessary nor to be tolerated. The standards of both art and living were indissolubly linked, he decided, and this earnest young man from the Midwest desired to raise the level of both by means of a literary realism he called Veritism.

Garland was Wisconsin-born, the child of a farm family that had emigrated westward from Maine prior to the Civil War in hopes of finding better land and an easier livelihood. Wisconsin was succeeded by Iowa, then by the Dakota Territory, as failure followed failure. At twenty-four, Garland reversed the advice "Go west, young man" by heading toward Boston in 1884. There he was eventually taken up by William Dean Howells, another midwesterner transplanted to the East's fertile literary lands. Howells helped publicize Garland's fiction in reviews, but before the first collection of Garland's stories appeared in 1891 under the title *Main-Travelled Roads,* Garland had much to learn about the craft of writing and the sources he would need to draw on.

The years from 1884 to 1891 were a time of privation for Garland as he struggled to educate himself through hours of reading at the Boston Public Library. He finally managed to secure a teaching post at the Boston School of Oratory and to save enough money for two trips back to the family homestead in 1887 and 1889. These visits, shocking to this now visitor from "outside," convinced Garland of the story he had to tell: the spirit-wasting, body-crippling existences of hard-working men and women who had traveled in hope, either from Europe or the eastern states out to "the middle border" in pursuit of the Jeffersonian promise of decency and a piece of property. This dream promoted the heart-lifting democratic principles of a moral life and economic self-sufficiency. Garland was driven to set the record straight, a fact that tells a great deal about the fantasy life of the last decades of the nineteenth century. Garland knew that the dream of bucolic contentment on frontier farms had proved false, but many Americans back East had placed a romantic aura around scenes of rural life. This imaginative sleight of hand resulted once their own dream of finding happiness and the good life in the newly emerging cities was dashed.

If Garland tried to dispel the notion that a perfect past still remained out West, he also tried to sustain the possibility of a better world for the farmer in the future. He urged his readers to support the single-tax program of the social reformer Henry George and dramatized the position taken by the Populist Party in such novels as *Jason Edwards: An Average Man* and *A Spoil of Office,* both published in 1892. But Garland was better as the debunker of false dreams than as the supporter of new ones such as public ownership of the railroads and increased rights for farmers. For similar reasons, Garland appears sounder when he writes from a fierce honesty about tragic lives than when he concocts (as he often does) fantasies about brave, strong-willed, handsome young women who fall into the arms of brave, stalwart, handsome young men for whom they abdicate their wills.

Garland was at the peak of his literary strength when he turned in later years to writing memoirs rooted in direct knowledge of blighted rural regions, as in *A Son of the Middle Border* (1917) and *A Daughter of the Middle Border* (1921). These works, along with his essays on literary theory entitled *Crumbling Idols* (1894) and the stories he wrote in the 1890s, collected in 1910 as *Other Main-Travelled Roads,* assured Garland a place among the ardent literary Realists. What accounts then, for the somewhat embarrassing fact of the recurring strand of romantic idealization found in Garland's writings? It cannot simply be written off as the result of his growing older and more complacent or by saying he became a toady to the demands of a genteel audience. The mix we find in Garland of social reformer and novelist, realistic truth sayer and fantasist, is as much a part of the overall texture of his view of life as is a similar mix in Mark Twain's imagination. Garland is a Mark Twain without the humor and the genius. This subtracts something; it also leaves much to be admired.

Further Reading:
J. Holloway, *Hamlin Garland,* 1960, 1971.
D. Pizer, *Hamlin Garland's Early Work and Career,* 1960.
R. Gish, *Hamlin Garland: The Far West,* 1976.
J. McCullough, *Hamlin Garland,* 1978.
Critical Essays on Hamlin Garland, ed. J. Nagel, 1982.

Text:
"Under the Lion's Paw" from *Main-Travelled Roads,* 1891.
See also *Hamlin Garland's Diary,* ed. D. Pizer, 1968.

Under the Lion's Paw

I

It was the last of autumn and first day of winter coming together. All day long the ploughmen on their prairie farms had moved to and fro in their wide level fields through the falling snow, which melted as it fell, wetting them to the skin—all day, notwithstanding the frequent squalls of snow, the dripping, desolate clouds, and the muck of the furrows, black and tenacious as tar.

Under their dripping harness the horses swung to and fro silently, with that marvellous uncomplaining patience which marks the horse. All day the wild geese, honking wildly, as they sprawled sidewise down the wind, seemed to be fleeing from an enemy behind, and with neck outthrust and wings extended, sailed down the wind, soon lost to sight.

Yet the ploughman behind his plough, though the snow lay on his ragged great-coat, and the cold clinging mud rose on his heavy boots, fettering him like gyves, whistled in the very beard of the gale. As day passed, the snow, ceasing to melt, lay along the ploughed land, and lodged in the depth of the stubble, till on each slow round the last furrow stood out black and shining as jet between the ploughed land and the gray stubble.

When night began to fall, and the geese, flying low, began to alight invisibly in the near corn-field, Stephen Council was still at work "finishing a land." He rode on his sulky plough[1] when going with the wind, but walked when facing it. Sitting bent and cold but cheery under his slouch hat, he talked encouragingly to his four-in-hand.

"Come round there, boys!—Round agin! We got t' finish this land. Come in there, Dan! *Stiddy,* Kate,—stiddy! None o' y'r tantrums, Kittie. It's purty tuff, but got a be did. *Tchk! tchk!* Step along, Pete! Don't let Kate git y'r single-tree on the wheel. *Once* more!"

They seemed to know what he meant, and that this was the last round, for they worked with greater vigor than before.

"Once more, boys, an' then, sez I, oats an' a nice warm stall, an' sleep f'r all."

By the time the last furrow was turned on the land it was too dark to see the house, and the snow was changing to rain again. The tired and hungry man could see the light from the kitchen shining through the leafless hedge, and he lifted a great shout, "Supper f'r a half a dozen!"

It was nearly eight o'clock by the time he had finished his chores and started for supper. He was picking his way carefully through the mud, when the tall form of a man loomed up before him with a premonitory cough.

"Waddy ye want?" was the rather startled question of the farmer.

"Well, ye see," began the stranger, in a deprecating tone, "we'd like t' git in f'r the night. We've tried every house f'r the last two miles, but they hadn't any room f'r us. My wife's jest about sick, 'n' the children are cold and hungry—"

---

[1] Wheeled plow with a seat for the driver.

"Oh, y' want 'o stay all night, eh?"

"Yes, sir; it 'ud be a great accom——"

"Waal, I don't make it a practice t' turn anybuddy way hungry, not on sech nights as this. Drive right in. We ain't got much, but sech as it is——"

But the stranger had disappeared. And soon his steaming, weary team, with drooping heads and swinging single-trees, moved past the well to the block beside the path. Council stood at the side of the "schooner"[2] and helped the children out —two little half-sleeping children—and then a small woman with a babe in her arms.

"There ye go!" he shouted jovially, to the children. *"Now* we're all right! Run right along to the house there, an' tell Mam' Council you wants sumpthin' t' eat. Right this way, Mis'—keep right off t' the right there. I'll go an' git a lantern. Come," he said to the dazed and silent group at his side.

"Mother," he shouted, as he neared the fragrant and warmly lighted kitchen, "here are some wayfarers an' folks who need sumpthin' t' eat an' a place t' snooze." He ended by pushing them all in.

Mrs. Council, a large, jolly, rather coarse-looking woman, took the children in her arms. "Come right in, you little rabbits. 'Most asleep, hey? Now here's a drink o' milk f'r each o' ye. I'll have s'm tea in a minute. Take off y'r things and set up t' the fire."

While she set the children to drinking milk, Council got out his lantern and went out to the barn to help the stranger about his team, where his loud, hearty voice could be heard as it came and went between the haymow and the stalls.

The woman came to light as a small, timid, and discouraged-looking woman, but still pretty, in a thin and sorrowful way.

"Land sakes! An' you've travelled all the way from Clear Lake t'-day in this mud! Waal! waal! No wonder you're all tired out. Don't wait f'r the men, Mis' ——" She hesitated, waiting for the name.

"Haskins."

"Mis' Haskins, set right up to the table an' take a good swig o' tea whilst I make y' s'm toast. It's green tea, an' it's good. I tell Council as I git older I don't seem to enjoy Young Hyson n'r Gun-powder. I want the reel green tea, jest as it comes off 'n the vines. Seems t' have more heart in it, some way. Don't s'pose it has. Council says it's all in m' eye."

Going on in this easy way, she soon had the children filled with bread and milk and the woman thoroughly at home, eating some toast and sweet-melon pickles, and sipping the tea.

"See the little rats!" she laughed at the children. "They're full as they can stick now, and they want to go to bed. Now, don't git up, Mis' Haskins; set right where you are an' let me look after 'em. I know all about young ones, though I'm all alone now. Jane went an' married last fall. But, as I tell Council, it's lucky we keep our health. Set right there, Mis' Haskins; I won't have you stir a finger."

It was an unmeasured pleasure to sit there in the warm, homely kitchen, the jovial chatter of the housewife driving out and holding at bay the growl of the impotent, cheated wind.

[2] Covered wagon, sometimes referred to as a "prairie schooner."

The little woman's eyes filled with tears which fell down upon the sleeping baby in her arms. The world was not so desolate and cold and hopeless, after all.

"Now I hope Council won't stop out there and talk politics all night. He's the greatest man to talk politics an' read the *Tribune*—How old is it?"

She broke off and peered down at the face of the babe.

"Two months 'n' five days," said the mother, with a mother's exactness.

"Ye don't say! I want 'o know! The dear little pudzy-wudzy!" she went on, stirring it up in the neighborhood of the ribs with her fat forefinger.

"Pooty tough on 'oo to go gallivant'n' 'cross lots this way—"

"Yes, that's so; a man can't lift a mountain," said Council, entering the door. "Mother, this is Mr. Haskins, from Kansas. He's been eat up 'n' drove out by grasshoppers."

"Glad t' see yeh!—Pa, empty that wash-basin 'n' give him a chance t' wash."

Haskins was a tall man, with a thin, gloomy face. His hair was a reddish brown, like his coat, and seemed equally faded by the wind and sun, and his sallow face, though hard and set, was pathetic somehow. You would have felt that he had suffered much by the line of his mouth showing under his thin, yellow mustache.

"Hain't Ike got home yet, Sairy?"

"Hain't seen 'im."

"W-a-a-l, set right up, Mr. Haskins; wade right into what we've got; 'taint much, but we manage to live on it—she gits fat on it," laughed Council, pointing his thumb at his wife.

After supper, while the women put the children to bed, Haskins and Council talked on, seated near the huge cooking-stove, the steam rising from their wet clothing. In the Western fashion Council told as much of his own life as he drew from his guest. He asked but few questions, but by and by the story of Haskins' struggles and defeat came out. The story was a terrible one, but he told it quietly, seated with his elbows on his knees, gazing most of the time at the hearth.

"I didn't like the looks of the country, anyhow," Haskins said, partly rising and glancing at his wife. "I was ust t' northern Ingyannie, where we have lots o' timber 'n' lots o' rain, 'n' I didn't like the looks o' that dry prairie. What galled me the worst was goin' s' far away acrosst so much fine land layin' all through here vacant."

"And the 'hoppers eat ye four years, hand runnin', did they?"

"Eat! They wiped us out. They chawed everything that was green. They jest set around waitin' f'r us to die t' eat us, too. My God! I ust t' dream of 'em sittin' 'round on the bedpost, six feet long, workin' their jaws. They eet the fork-handles. They got worse 'n' worse till they jest rolled on one another, piled up like snow in winter. Well, it ain't no use. If I was t' talk all winter I couldn't tell nawthin'. But all the while I couldn't help thinkin' of all that land back here that nobuddy was usin' that I ought 'o had 'stead o' bein' out there in that cussed country."

"Waal, why didn't ye stop an' settle here?" asked Ike, who had come in and was eating his supper.

"Fer the simple reason that you fellers wantid ten 'r fifteen dollars an acre fer the bare land, and I hadn't no money fer that kind o' thing."

"Yes, I do my own work," Mrs. Council was heard to say in the pause which followed. "I'm a gettin' purty heavy t' be on m' laigs all day, but we can't afford t' hire, so I keep rackin' around somehow, like a foundered horse. S' lame—I tell Council he can't tell how lame I am, f'r I'm jest as lame in one laig as t' other." And the good soul laughed at the joke on herself as she took a handful of flour and dusted the biscuit-board to keep the dough from sticking.

"Well, I hain't *never* been very strong," said Mrs. Haskins. "Our folks was Canadians an' small-boned, and then since my last child I hain't got up again fairly. I don't like t' complain. Tim has about all he can bear now—but they was days this week when I jest wanted to lay right down an' die."

"Waal, now, I'll tell ye," said Council, from his side of the stove, silencing everybody with his good-natured roar, "I'd go down and *see* Butler, *anyway*, if I was you. I guess he'd let you have his place purty cheap; the farm's all run down. He's been anxious t' let t' somebuddy next year. It 'ud be a good chance fer you. Anyhow, you go to bed and sleep like a babe. I've got some ploughing t' do, anyhow, an' we'll see if somethin' can't be done about your case. Ike, you go out an' see if the horses is all right, an' I'll show the folks t' bed."

When the tired husband and wife were lying under the generous quilts of the spare bed, Haskins listened a moment to the wind in the eaves, and then said, with a slow and solemn tone,

"There are people in this world who are good enough t' be angels, an' only haff t' die to *be* angels."

II

Jim Butler was one of those men called in the West "land poor." Early in the history of Rock River he had come into the town and started in the grocery business in a small way, occupying a small building in a mean part of the town. At this period of his life he earned all he got, and was up early and late sorting beans, working over butter, and carting his goods to and from the station. But a change came over him at the end of the second year, when he sold a lot of land for four times what he paid for it. From that time forward he believed in land speculation as the surest way of getting rich. Every cent he could save or spare from his trade he put into land at forced sale, or mortgages on land, which were "just as good as the wheat," he was accustomed to say.

Farm after farm fell into his hands, until he was recognized as one of the leading landowners of the county. His mortgages were scattered all over Cedar County, and as they slowly but surely fell in he sought usually to retain the former owner as tenant.

He was not ready to foreclose; indeed, he had the name of being one of the "easiest" men in the town. He let the debtor off again and again, extending the time whenever possible.

"I don't want y'r land," he said. "All I'm after is the int'rest on my money—that's all. Now, if y' want 'o stay on the farm, why, I'll give y' a good chance. I can't have the land layin' vacant." And in many cases the owner remained as tenant.

In the meantime he had sold his store; he couldn't spend time in it; he was mainly occupied now with sitting around town on rainy days smoking and "gassin' with the boys," or in riding to and from his farms. In fishing-time he fished a good deal. Doc Grimes, Ben Ashley, and Cal Cheatham were his cronies on these fishing excursions or hunting trips in the time of chickens or partridges. In winter they went to Northern Wisconsin to shoot deer.

In spite of all these signs of easy life Butler persisted in saying he "hadn't enough money to pay taxes on his land," and was careful to convey the impression that he was poor in spite of his twenty farms. At one time he was said to be worth fifty thousand dollars, but land had been a little slow of sale of late, so that he was not worth so much.

A fine farm, known as the Higley place, had fallen into his hands in the usual way the previous year, and he had not been able to find a tenant for it. Poor Higley, after working himself nearly to death on it in the attempt to lift the mortgage, had gone off to Dakota, leaving the farm and his curse to Butler.

This was the farm which Council advised Haskins to apply for; and the next day Council hitched up his team and drove down to see Butler.

"You jest let *me* do the talkin'," he said. "We'll find him wearin' out his pants on some salt barrel somew'ers; and if he thought you *wanted* a place he'd sock it to you hot and heavy. You jest keep quiet; I'll fix 'im."

Butler was seated in Ben Ashley's store telling fish yarns when Council sauntered in casually.

"Hello, But; lyin' agin, hey?"

"Hello, Steve! How goes it?"

"Oh, so-so. Too dang much rain these days. I thought it was goin' t' freeze up f'r good last night. Tight squeak if I get m' ploughin' done. How's farmin' with *you* these days?"

"Bad. Ploughin' ain't half done."

"It 'ud be a religious idee f'r you t' go out an' take a hand y'rself."

"I don't haff to," said Butler, with a wink.

"Got anybody on the Higley place?"

"No. Know of anybody?"

"Waal, no; not eggsackly. I've got a relation back t' Michigan who's ben hot an' cold on the idee o' comin' West f'r some time. *Might* come if he could get a good lay-out. What do you talk on the farm?"

"Well, I d' know. I'll rent it on shares or I'll rent it money rent."

"Waal, how much money, say?"

"Well, say ten per cent, on the price—two-fifty."

"Wall, that ain't bad. Wait on 'im till 'e thrashes?"

Haskins listened eagerly to this important question, but Council was coolly eating a dried apple which he had speared out of a barrel with his knife. Butler studied him carefully.

"Well, knocks me out of twenty-five dollars interest."

"My relation'll need all he's got t' git his crops in," said Council, in the same, indifferent way.

"Well, all right; *say* wait," concluded Butler.

"All right; this is the man. Haskins, this is Mr. Butler—no relation to Ben—the hardest-working man in Cedar County."

On the way home Haskins said: "I ain't much better off. I'd like that farm; it's a good farm, but it's all run down, an' so 'm I. I could make a good farm of it if I had half a show. But I can't stock it n'r seed it."

"Waal, now, don't you worry," roared Council in his ear. "We'll pull y' through somehow till next harvest. He's agreed t' hire it ploughed, an' you can earn a hundred dollars ploughin' an' y' c'n git the seed o' me, an' pay me back when y' can."

Haskins was silent with emotion, but at last he said, "I ain't got nothin' t' live on."

"Now, don't you worry 'bout that. You jest make your headquarters at ol' Steve Council's. Mother'll take a pile o' comfort in havin' y'r wife an' children 'round. Y' see, Jane's married off lately, an' Ike's away a good 'eal, so we'll be darn glad t' have y' stop with us this winter. Nex' spring we'll see if y' can't git a start agin." And he chirruped to the team, which sprang forward with the rumbling, clattering wagon.

"Say, looky here, Council, you can't do this. I never saw—" shouted Haskins in his neighbor's ear.

Council moved about uneasily in his seat and stopped his stammering gratitude by saying: "Hold on, now; don't make such a fuss over a little thing. When I see a man down, an' things all on top of 'm, I jest like t' kick 'em off an' help 'm up. That's the kind of religion I got, an' it's about the *only* kind."

They rode the rest of the way home in silence. And when the red light of the lamp shone out into the darkness of the cold and windy night, and he thought of this refuge for his children and wife, Haskins could have put his arm around the neck of his burly companion and squeezed him like a lover. But he contented himself with saying, "Steve Council, you'll git y'r pay f'r this some day."

"Don't want any pay. My religion ain't run on such business principles."

The wind was growing colder, and the ground was covered with a white frost, as they turned into the gate of the Council farm, and the children came rushing out, shouting, "Papa's come!" They hardly looked like the same children who had sat at the table the night before. Their torpidity, under the influence of sunshine and Mother Council, had given way to a sort of spasmodic cheerfulness, as insects in winter revive when laid on the hearth.

III

Haskins worked like a fiend, and his wife, like the heroic woman that she was, bore also uncomplainingly the most terrible burdens. They rose early and toiled without intermission till the darkness fell on the plain, then tumbled into bed, every bone and muscle aching with fatigue, to rise with the sun next morning to the same round of the same ferocity of labor.

The eldest boy drove a team all through the spring, ploughing and seeding, milked the cows, and did chores innumerable, in most ways taking the place of a man.

An infinitely pathetic but common figure—this boy on the American farm, where there is no law against child labor. To see him in his coarse clothing, his huge boots, and his ragged cap, as he staggered with a pail of water from the well, or trudged in the cold and cheerless dawn out into the frosty field behind his team, gave the city-bred visitor a sharp pang of sympathetic pain. Yet Haskins loved his boy, and would have saved him from this if he could, but he could not.

By June the first year the result of such Herculean toil[3] began to show on the farm.

---

[3] After Hercules, whose heroic labors against great odds are described in classic myth.

The yard was cleaned up and sown to grass, the garden ploughed and planted, and the house mended.

Council had given them four of his cows.

"Take 'em an' run 'em on shares. I don't want 'o milk s' many. Ike's away s' much now, Sat'd'ys an' Sund'ys, I can't stand the bother anyhow."

Other men, seeing the confidence of Council in the newcomer, had sold him tools on time; and as he was really an able farmer, he soon had round him many evidences of his care and thrift. At the advice of Council he had taken the farm for three years, with the privilege of re-renting or buying at the end of the term.

"It's a good bargain, an' y' want 'o nail it," said Council. "If you have any kind ov a crop, you c'n pay y'r debts, an' keep seed an' bread."

The new hope which now sprang up in the hearts of Haskins and his wife grew almost as a pain by the time the wide field of wheat began to wave and rustle and swirl in the winds of July. Day after day he would snatch a few moments after supper to go and look at it.

"Have ye seen the wheat t'-day, Nettie?" he asked one night as he rose from supper.

"No, Tim, I ain't had time."

"Well, take time now. Le's go look at it."

She threw an old hat on her head—Tommy's hat—and looking almost pretty in her thin, sad way, went out with her husband to the hedge.

"Ain't it grand, Nettie? Just look at it."

It was grand. Level, russet here and there, heavy-headed, wide as a lake, and full of multitudinous whispers and gleams of wealth, it stretched away before the gazers like the fabled field of the cloth of gold.

"Oh, I think—I *hope* we'll have a good crop, Tim; and oh, how good the people have been to us!"

"Yes; I don't know where we'd be t'-day if it hadn't been f'r Council and his wife."

"They're the best people in the world," said the little woman, with a great sob of gratitude.

"We'll be in the field on Monday sure," said Haskins, gripping the rail on the fences as if already at the work of the harvest.

The harvest came, bounteous, glorious, but the winds came and blew it into tangles, and the rain matted it here and there close to the ground, increasing the work of gathering it threefold.

Oh, how they toiled in those glorious days! Clothing dripping with sweat, arms aching, filled with briars, fingers raw and bleeding, backs broken with the weight of heavy bundles, Haskins and his man toiled on. Tommy drove the harvester, while his father and a hired man bound on the machine. In this way they cut ten acres every day, and almost every night after supper, when the hand went to bed, Haskins returned to the field shocking the bound grain in the light of the moon. Many a night he worked till his anxious wife came out at ten o'clock to call him in to rest and lunch.

At the same time she cooked for the men, took care of the children, washed and ironed, milked the cows at night, made the butter, and sometimes fed the horses and watered them while her husband kept at the shocking.

No slave in the Roman galleys could have toiled so frightfully and lived, for this man thought himself a free man, and that he was working for his wife and babes.

When he sank into his bed with a deep groan of relief, too tired to change his grimy, dripping clothing, he felt that he was getting nearer and nearer to a home of his own, and pushing the wolf of want a little farther from his door.

There is no despair so deep as the despair of a homeless man or woman. To roam the roads of the country or the streets of the city, to feel there is no rood of ground on which the feet can rest, to halt weary and hungry outside lighted windows and hear laughter and song within,—these are the hungers and rebellions that drive men to crime and women to shame.

It was the memory of this homelessness, and the fear of its coming again, that spurred Timothy Haskins and Nettie, his wife, to such ferocious labor during that first year.

IV

"'M, yes; 'm, yes; first-rate," said Butler, as his eye took in the neat garden, the pig-pen, and the well-filled barnyard. "You're gitt'n' quite a stock around yeh. Done well, eh?"

Haskins was showing Butler around the place. He had not seen it for a year, having spent the year in Washington and Boston with Ashley, his brother-in-law, who had been elected to Congress.

"Yes, I've laid out a good deal of money durin' the last three years. I've paid out three hundred dollars f'r fencin'."

"Um—h'm! I see, I see," said Butler, while Haskins went on:

"The kitchen there cost two hundred; the barn ain't cost much in money, but I've put a lot o' time on it. I've dug a new well, and I—"

"Yes, yes, I see. You've done well. Stock worth a thousand dollars," said Butler, picking his teeth with a straw.

"About that," said Haskins, modestly. "We begin to feel's if we was gitt'n' a home f'r ourselves; but we've worked hard. I tell you we begin to feel it, Mr. Butler, and we're goin' t' begin to ease up purty soon. We've been kind o' plannin' a trip back t' her folks after the fall ploughin's done."

"*Eggs-actly!*" said Butler, who was evidently thinking of something else. "I suppose you've kind o' calc'lated on stayin' here three years more?"

"Well, yes. Fact is, I think I c'n buy the farm this fall, if you'll give me a reasonable show."

"Um—m! What do you call a reasonable show?"

"Well, say a quarter down and three years' time."

Butler looked at the huge stacks of wheat, which filled the yard, over which the chickens were fluttering and crawling, catching grasshoppers, and out of which the crickets were singing innumerably. He smiled in a peculiar way as he said, "Oh, I won't be hard on yeh. But what did you expect to pay f'r the place?"

"Why, about what you offered it for before, two thousand five hundred, or *possibly* three thousand dollars," he added quickly, as he saw the owner shake his head.

"This farm is worth five thousand and five hundred dollars," said Butler, in a careless and decided voice.

"*What!*" almost shrieked the astounded Haskins. "What's that? Five thousand? Why, that's double what you offered it for three years ago."

"Of course, and it's worth it. It was all run down then; now it's in good shape. You've laid out fifteen hundred dollars in improvements, according to your own story."

"But *you* had nothin' t' do about that. It's my work an' my money."

"You bet it was; but it's my land."

"But what's to pay me for all my—"

"Ain't you had the use of 'em?" replied Butler, smiling calmly into his face.

Haskins was like a man struck on the head with a sandbag; he couldn't think; he stammered as he tried to say: "But—I never'd git the use—You'd rob me! More'n that: you agreed—you promised that I could buy or rent at the end of three years at—"

"That's all right. But I didn't say I'd let you carry off the improvements, nor that I'd go on renting the farm at two-fifty. The land is doubled in value, it don't matter how; it don't enter into the question; an' now you can pay me five hundred dollars a year rent, or take it on your own terms at fifty-five hundred, or—git out."

He was turning away when Haskins, the sweat pouring from his face, fronted him, saying again:

"But *you've* done nothing to make it so. You hain't added a cent. I put it all there myself, expectin' to buy. I worked an' sweat to improve it. I was workin' for myself an' babes—"

"Well, why didn't you buy when I offered to sell? What y' kickin' about?"

"I'm kickin' about payin' you twice f'r my own things,—my own fences, my own kitchen, my own garden."

Butler laughed. "You're too green t' eat, young feller. *Your* improvements! The law will sing another tune."

"But I trusted your word."

"Never trust anybody, my friend. Besides, I didn't promise not to do this thing. Why, man, don't look at me like that. Don't take me for a thief. It's the law. The reg'lar thing. Everybody does it."

"I don't care if they do. It's stealin' jest the same. You take three thousand dollars of my money—the work o' my hands and my wife's." He broke down at this point. He was not a strong man mentally. He could face hardship, ceaseless toil, but he could not face the cold and sneering face of Butler.

"But I don't take it," said Butler, coolly. "All you've got to do is to go on jest as you've been a-doin', or give me a thousand dollars down, and a mortgage at ten per cent on the rest."

Haskins sat down blindly on a bundle of oats near by, and with staring eyes and drooping head went over the situation. He was under the lion's paw. He felt a horrible numbness in his heart and limbs. He was hid in a mist, and there was no path out.

Butler walked about, looking at the huge stacks of grain, and pulling now and again a few handfuls out, shelling the heads in his hands and blowing the chaff away. He hummed a little tune as he did so. He had an accommodating air of waiting.

Haskins was in the midst of the terrible toil of the last year. He was walking again in the rain and the mud behind his plough; he felt the dust and dirt of the threshing. The ferocious husking-time, with its cutting wind and biting, clinging snows, lay hard upon him. Then he thought of his wife, how she had cheerfully cooked and baked, without holiday and without rest.

"Well, what do you think of it?" inquired the cool, mocking, insinuating voice of Butler.

"I think you're a thief and a liar!" shouted Haskins, leaping up. "A black-hearted houn'!" Butler's smile maddened him; with a sudden leap he caught a fork in his hands, and whirled it in the air. "You'll never rob another man, damn ye!" he grated through his teeth, a look of pitiless ferocity in his accusing eyes.

Butler shrank and quivered, expecting the blow; stood, held hypnotized by the eyes of the man he had a moment before despised—a man transformed into an avenging demon. But in the deadly hush between the lift of the weapon and its fall there came a gush of faint, childish laughter and then across the range of his vision, far away and dim, he saw the sun-bright head of his baby girl, as, with the pretty, tottering run of a two-year-old, she moved across the grass of the dooryard. His hands relaxed: the fork fell to the ground; his head lowered.

"Make out y'r deed an' mor'gage, an' git off'n my land, an' don't ye never cross my line agin; if y' do, I'll kill ye."

Butler backed away from the man in wild haste, and climbing into his buggy with trembling limbs drove off down the road, leaving Haskins seated dumbly on the sunny pile of sheaves, his head sunk into his hands.

1889

Edith Wharton
1862–1937

There are many reasons why Mrs. Teddy Wharton (born Edith Newbold Jones) might not have become what she did, an important figure in American literature, a formidably acute recorder of social mores both here and abroad, and a sharp-minded organizer of both her own complex professional career and of relief agencies to aid refugees during the First World War. Edith Wharton was born into "old money"—that stratum of New York society that could take education, cultural refinement, and deference to class for granted. She never experienced the economic deprivations that drove, for example, Theodore Dreiser and Hamlin Garland on an upward scramble, nor did she know the uncertainties of the literary world that prompted William Dean Howells and Stephen Crane to run fast and far. As a woman of wealth and position, she could have remained throughout her lifetime essentially like many of the fictional characters in her stories and novels, characters who exist trivially in terms of glittering social events that mask their discontent and unsatisfied lives. This is not what happened, however. Slowly at first, but then with increasing momentum, Edith Wharton began to write about her life, not merely to acquiesce to its deadlier rhythms.

Edith Jones grew up in New York City, with interludes spent traveling abroad. Educated by a succession of governesses, she attained an early fluency in both foreign languages and the European outlook. This training was considered appropriate to a young woman in a patrician social circle that defined itself in terms of England and the Continent—not with any Whitmanesque democracy that lay somewhere vaguely west and north of Manhattan's chic avenues. She "came out" into society at eighteen according to the rigid rituals of her class— the class she later analyzed as rigorously as an anthropologist might the courtship habits of Fiji islanders. In the same year she also brought out some poems in the *Atlantic Monthly.* Printed anonymously, her poems signified little more than the fact that yet another young lady of good breeding believed she had something to say.

At twenty-three Edith Jones became the wife of Edward Wharton, a man of impeccable Boston ancestors. They settled into a childless, busy life. Edith Wharton threw her energies into being a society matron in New York, Newport, and Paris, and later at a large house she had built in the Massachusetts Berkshires. Marriage with Teddy (as this amiable but increasingly unstable man was known to his friends) lasted for twenty-eight generally unhappy years; it ended at last with a divorce in 1913 after his mental condition deteriorated into insanity. The decision to leave her husband pained Edith Wharton greatly. Their divorce was concluded in the courts after she proved him guilty of adultery. Everything in her nature that clung to tradition recoiled at this morally objectionable step, which she regarded as an act against "family."

She had made other, even more momentous choices than divorce prior to 1913. If the outward shows of Wharton's life continued to present her as a woman of leisure with the public style of a perennial hostess, she had long since begun to turn her private hours over to writing. Her first collection of short stories appeared in 1899 under the apt title *The Great Inclination;* it was a success that both amazed her and freed her to throw herself with even greater resolve into learning her craft. The novel *The Valley of Decision* followed in 1902, and another collection, *The Descent of Man,* in 1904. Her reputation was assured with *The House of Mirth* in 1905. From then on, Mrs. Teddy Wharton the society lady had a formidable competitor—Edith Wharton the acclaimed writer.

Wharton took up permanent residence in France in 1907. Personal and professional needs made her crave a more cosmopolitan setting than the United States could give her. Her writings poured forth, including three more collections of short stories, the last of which showed her skill at tales of the supernatural: *The Hermit and the Wild Woman and Other Stories* (1908), *Xingu and Other Stories* (1916), and *Tales of Men and Ghosts* (1910). The content of her work was by no means made up of the details of cosmopolitan society. The harshly bitter lives endured in the villages and farm areas of New England caught her attention and resulted in two powerful novels, *Ethan Frome* (1911) and *Summer* (1917). *The Custom of the Country* (1913) and *The Age of Innocence* (1920) returned Wharton to the city and to scenes of elegant society, her skill for satire still intact. Her targets continued to be both the "old society" and the "new society." The former was in the grip of outmoded values that gave idealistic young men and women little chance to survive under the new conditions. The latter was controlled by parvenues whose combative, often morally shabby actions undercut family, continuity, professional probity, and personal loyalties.

When World War I began, Wharton assumed the causes of France and Belgium as her own. She emerged from the war invigorated by the successes she had had organizing war relief programs for refugees as well as compiling several books of propaganda for the Allies.

By her midfifties Wharton had returned to her career as a literary figure. *The Age of Innocence* won her the Pulitzer Prize in 1920. *The Writing of Fiction* (1925) presented her views of her craft, and the autobiographical *A Backward Glance* (1934) revealed as much of her self as she chose. Kept out of her memoirs were mention of the difficult times she had spent as her mother's slighted child, the unhappiness of her marriage, and the brief but passionate affair she had had with an old friend, Morton Fullerton. Admitted were anecdotes of her friendships with Henry James, Sinclair Lewis, and Jean Cocteau.

Edith Wharton died in France, a member of a distinguished expatriate generation. The generation that came after—peopled by Hemingway, Stein, Dos Passos, and Fitzgerald—was also, in its own way, rebellious against convention and analytical about the mores of a newly evolving society. The life and writings of Edith Wharton might seem too special and too protected to this new throng in Paris, but she first explored some of the same literary territory settled by these later writers.

There are a number of points at which Edith Wharton's novels and stories align with those of her contemporaries. Living socially above the rank and file of Americans did not mean that Wharton existed beyond the absorptions and anxieties expressed by others. The extent to which human behavior is shaped by forces of environment and breeding is a major motif in Wharton's narratives, just as it was in those of Mark Twain, Frank Norris, and Theodore Dreiser. The manners that distinguish one group from another in a supposedly classless America called upon her powers as a social analyst, just as attention to manners absorbed Henry James and William Dean Howells in their fiction. Wharton paid the cost for sitting in judgment of her own country, just as did Henry James and Henry Adams. The annals of small-town life and the tragedies that come from the narrowing of individual aspirations are recorded in Wharton's *Ethan Frome* and *Summer,* as they were in the fiction of Sarah Orne Jewett and Mary Wilkins Freeman. A woman's experience of personal displacement and her longings to break free are presented as clearly in Wharton's stories as in those by Kate Chopin. The sharp-tongued critique of people who act like asses and rascals is as apparent in Wharton's satires as in Mark Twain's. In addition, both Wharton and Twain wrote, on occasion, reminiscences of the past that reveal their wistfulness over the loss of old values and simpler times.

Whatever the similarities between the well-bred lady from New York, Newport, and Paris and her literary contemporaries, Edith Wharton was her own woman. She frequently expressed her annoyance over being described as the too slavish pupil of Henry James. James was a friend and confidant, but she made it plain that she was not dependent on his example as a writer. Wharton's lucidity of style, her treatment of the inner life, and her eye and ear for cultural nuances are identifiably her own. She had served an arduous apprenticeship to her craft and to her life, and her strengths and weaknesses as a writer are to be credited to her alone. Now, with ever increasing interest, recent criticism is establishing Edith Wharton's place in American literary history. She is winning attention not only as a writer but also as a woman who wrote effectively about the toll taken on women in turn-of-the-century society and on the men who shared in their common fate.

Further Reading:

P. Lubbock, *Portrait of Edith Wharton*, 1947.
B. Nevius, *Edith Wharton: A Study of Her Fiction*, 1953.
M. Lyde, *Edith Wharton: Convention and Morality in the Work of a Novelist*, 1959.
Edith Wharton: A Collection of Critical Essays, ed. I. Home, 1962.
O. Coolidge, *Edith Wharton, 1862–1937*, 1964.
M. Bell, *Edith Wharton and Henry James: The Story of Their Friendship*, 1965.
G. Kellogg, *The Two Lives of Edith Wharton: The Woman and Her Work*, 1965.
L. Auchincloss, *Edith Wharton: A Woman in Her Time*, 1971.
R. W. B. Lewis, *Edith Wharton*, 1975.
G. Lindberg, *Edith Wharton and the Novel of Manners*, 1975.
M. McDowell, *Edith Wharton*, 1975.
M. B. McDowell, *Edith Wharton*, 1976.
R. H. Lawson, *Edith Wharton*, 1977.
C. Wolff, *A Feast of Words: The Triumph of Edith Wharton*, 1977.
E. Ammons, *Edith Wharton's Argument with America*, 1980.
C. Wershoven, *The Female Intruder in the Novels of Edith Wharton*, 1982.

Texts:

"The Other Two" from *The Collected Stories of Edith Wharton*, 2 vols., ed. R. W. B. Lewis, 1968.
Summer, 1917.
A Backward Glance, 1934.
See also *An Edith Wharton Treasury*, ed. A. Quinn, 1950.
Best Short Stories of Edith Wharton, ed. W. Andrews, 1958.
The Edith Wharton Reader, ed. L. Auchincloss, 1965.

The Other Two

I

Waythorn, on the drawing-room hearth, waited for his wife to come down to dinner.

It was their first night under his own roof, and he was surprised at his thrill of boyish agitation. He was not so old, to be sure—his glass gave him little more than the five-and-thirty years to which his wife confessed—but he had fancied himself already in the temperate zone; yet here he was listening for her step with a tender sense of all it symbolised, with some old trail of verse about the garlanded nuptial door-posts floating through his enjoyment of the pleasant room and the good dinner just beyond it.

They had been hastily recalled from their honeymoon by the illness of Lily Haskett, the child of Mrs. Waythorn's first marriage. The little girl, at Waythorn's desire, had been transferred to his house on the day of her mother's wedding, and the doctor, on their arrival, broke the news that she was ill with typhoid, but declared that all the symptoms were favourable. Lily could show twelve years of unblemished health, and the case promised to be a light one. The nurse spoke as reassuringly, and after a moment of alarm Mrs. Waythorn had adjusted herself to the situation. She was very fond of Lily—her affection for the child had perhaps been her decisive charm in Waythorn's eyes—but she had the perfectly balanced nerves which her little girl had inherited, and no woman ever wasted less tissue in unproductive worry. Waythorn was therefore quite prepared to see her come in presently, a little late because of a last look at Lily, but as serene and well-appointed as if good-night kiss had been laid on the brow of health. Her composure was restful to him; it acted as ballast to his somewhat unstable sensibilities. As he pictured her bending over the child's bed he thought how soothing her presence must be in illness: her very step would prognosticate recovery.

His own life had been a gray one, from temperament rather than circumstance, and he had been drawn to her by the unperturbed gaiety which kept her fresh and elastic at an age when most women's activities are growing either slack or febril. He knew what was said about her; for, popular as she was, there had always been a faint undercurrent of detraction. When she had appeared in New York, nine or ten years earlier, as the pretty Mrs. Haskett whom Gus Varick had unearthed somewhere—was it in Pittsburg or Utica?—society, while promptly accepting her, had reserved the right to cast a doubt on its own indiscrimination. Enquiry, however, established her undoubted connection with a socially reigning family, and explained her recent divorce as the natural result of a runaway match at seventeen; and as nothing was known of Mr. Haskett it was easy to believe the worst of him.

Alice Haskett's remarriage with Gus Varick was a passport to the set whose recognition she coveted, and for a few years the Varicks were the most popular couple in town. Unfortunately the alliance was brief and stormy, and this time the husband had his champions. Still, even Varick's stanchest supporters admitted that he was not meant for matrimony, and Mrs. Varick's grievances were of a nature to bear the inspection of the New York courts. A New York divorce is in itself a diploma of virtue, and in the semiwidowhood of this second separation Mrs. Varick took on an air of sanctity, and was allowed to confide her wrongs to some of the most scrupulous ears in town. But when it was known that she was to marry Waythorn there was a momentary reaction. Her best friends would have preferred to see her remain in the rôle of the injured wife, which was as becoming to her as crape to a rosy complexion. True, a decent time had elapsed, and it was not even suggested that Waythorn had supplanted his predecessor. People shook their heads over him, however, and one grudging friend, to whom he affirmed that he took the step with his eyes open, replied oracularly: "Yes—and with your ears shut."

Waythorn could afford to smile at these innuendoes. In the Wall Street phrase, he had "discounted" them. He knew that society has not yet adapted itself to the consequences of divorce, and that till the adaptation takes place every woman who uses the freedom the law accords her must be her own social justification. Waythorn had an amused confidence in his wife's ability to justify herself. His expectations were fulfilled, and before the wedding took place Alice Varick's group had rallied openly to her support. She took it all imperturbably: she had a way of surmounting obstacles without seeming to be aware of them, and Waythorn looked back with wonder at the trivialities over which he had worn his nerves thin. He had the sense of having found refuge in a richer, warmer nature than his own, and his satisfaction, at the moment, was humourously summed up in the thought that his wife, when she had done all she could for Lily, would not be ashamed to come down and enjoy a good dinner.

The anticipation of such enjoyment was not, however, the sentiment expressed by

Mrs. Waythorn's charming face when she presently joined him. Though she had put on her most engaging teagown she had neglected to assume the smile that went with it, and Waythorn thought he had never seen her look so nearly worried.

"What is it?" he asked. "Is anything wrong with Lily?"

"No; I've just been in and she's still sleeping." Mrs. Waythorn hesitated. "But something tiresome has happened."

He had taken her two hands, and now perceived that he was crushing a paper between them.

"This letter?"

"Yes—Mr. Haskett has written—I mean his lawyer has written."

Waythorn felt himself flush uncomfortably. He dropped his wife's hands.

"What about?"

"About seeing Lily. You know the courts—"

"Yes, yes," he interrupted nervously.

Nothing was known about Haskett in New York. He was vaguely supposed to have remained in the outer darkness from which his wife had been rescued, and Waythorn was one of the few who were aware that he had given up his business in Utica and followed her to New York in order to be near his little girl. In the days of his wooing, Waythorn had often met Lily on the doorstep, rosy and smiling, on her way "to see papa."

"I am so sorry," Mrs. Waythorn murmured.

He roused himself. "What does he want?"

"He wants to see her. You know she goes to him once a week."

"Well—he doesn't expect her to go to him now, does he?"

"No—he has heard of her illness; but he expects to come here."

"*Here?*"

Mrs. Waythorn reddened under his gaze. They looked away from each other.

"I'm afraid he has the right. . . . You'll see. . . ." She made a proffer of the letter.

Waythorn moved away with a gesture of refusal. He stood staring about the softly lighted room, which a moment before had seemed so full of bridal intimacy.

"I'm so sorry," she repeated. "If Lily could have been moved—"

"That's out of the question," he returned impatiently.

"I suppose so."

Her lip was beginning to tremble, and he felt himself a brute.

"He must come, of course," he said. "What is—his day?"

"I'm afraid—to-morrow."

"Very well. Send a note in the morning."

The butler entered to announce dinner.

Waythorn turned to his wife. "Come—you must be tired. It's beastly, but try to forget about it," he said, drawing her hand through his arm.

"You're so good, dear. I'll try," she whispered back.

Her face cleared at once, and as she looked at him across the flowers, between the rosy candle-shades, he saw her lips waver back into a smile.

"How pretty everything is!" she sighed luxuriously.

He turned to the butler. "The champagne at once, please. Mrs. Waythorn is tired."

In a moment or two their eyes met above the sparkling glasses. Her own were quite clear and untroubled: he saw that she had obeyed his injunction and forgotten.

II

Waythorn, the next morning, went down town earlier than usual. Haskett was not likely to come till the afternoon, but the instinct of flight drove him forth. He meant to stay away all day—he had thoughts of dining at his club. As his door closed behind him he reflected that before he opened it again it would have admitted another man who had as much right to enter it as himself, and the thought filled him with a physical repugnance.

He caught the "elevated"[1] at the employés' hour, and found himself crushed between two layers of pendulous humanity. At Eighth Street the man facing him wriggled out, and another took his place. Waythorn glanced up and saw that it was Gus Varick. The men were so close together that it was impossible to ignore the smile of recognition on Varick's handsome overblown face. And after all—why not? They had always been on good terms, and Varick had been divorced before Waythorn's attentions to his wife began. The two exchanged a word on the perennial grievance of the trains, and when a seat at their side was miraculously left empty the instinct of self-preservation made Waythorn slip into it after Varick.

The latter drew the stout man's breath of relief. "Lord—I was beginning to feel like a pressed flower." He leaned back, looking unconcernedly at Waythorn. "Sorry to hear that Sellers is knocked out again."

"Sellers?" echoed Waythorn, starting at his partner's name.

Varick looked surprised. "You didn't know he was laid up with the gout?"

"No. I've been away—I only got back last night," Waythorn felt himself reddening in anticipation of the other's smile.

"Ah—yes; to be sure. And Sellers's attack came on two days ago. I'm afraid he's pretty bad. Very awkward for me, as it happens, because he was just putting through a rather important thing for me."

"Ah?" Waythorn wondered vaguely since when Varick had been dealing in "important things." Hitherto he had dabbled only in the shallow pools of speculation, with which Waythorn's office did not usually concern itself.

It occurred to him that Varick might be talking at random, to relieve the strain of their propinquity. That strain was becoming momentarily more apparent to Waythorn, and when, at Cortlandt Street, he caught sight of an acquaintance and had a sudden vision of the picture he and Varick must present to an initiated eye, he jumped up with a muttered excuse.

"I hope you'll find Sellers better," said Varick civilly, and he stammered back: "If I can be of any use to you—" and let the departing crowd sweep him to the platform.

At his office he heard that Sellers was in fact ill with the gout, and would probably not be able to leave the house for some weeks.

"I'm sorry it should have happened so, Mr. Waythorn," the senior clerk said with affable significance. "Mr. Sellers was very much upset at the idea of giving you such a lot of extra work just now."

"Oh, that's no matter," said Waythorn hastily. He secretly welcomed the pressure of additional business, and was glad to think that, when the day's work was over, he would have to call at his partner's on the way home.

---

[1] Elevated railway.

He was late for luncheon, and turned in at the nearest restaurant instead of going to his club. The place was full, and the waiter hurried him to the back of the room to capture the only vacant table. In the cloud of cigar-smoke Waythorn did not at once distinguish his neighbours: but presently, looking about him, he saw Varick seated a few feet off. This time, luckily, they were too far apart for conversation, and Varick, who faced another way, had probably not even seen him; but there was an irony in their renewed nearness.

Varick was said to be fond of good living, and as Waythorn sat despatching his hurried luncheon he looked across half enviously at the other's leisurely degustation of his meal. When Waythorn first saw him he had been helping himself with critical deliberation to a bit of Camembert at the ideal point of liquefaction, and now, the cheese removed, he was just pouring his *café double* [2] from its little two-storied earthen pot. He poured slowly, his ruddy profile bent above the task, and one beringed white hand steadying the lid of the coffee-pot; then he stretched his other hand to the decanter of cognac at his elbow, filled a liqueur-glass, took a tentative sip, and poured the brandy into his coffee-cup.

Waythorn watched him in a kind of fascination. What was he thinking of—only of the flavour of the coffee and the liqueur? Had the morning's meeting left no more trace in his thoughts than on his face? Had his wife so completely passed out of his life that even this odd encounter with her present husband, within a week after her remarriage, was no more than an incident in his day? And as Waythorn mused, another idea struck him: had Haskett ever met Varick as Varick and he had just met? The recollection of Haskett perturbed him, and he rose and left the restaurant, taking a circuitous way out to escape the placid irony of Varick's nod.

It was after seven when Waythorn reached home. He thought the footman who opened the door looked at him oddly.

"How is Miss Lily?" he asked in haste.

"Doing very well, sir. A gentleman—"

"Tell Barlow to put off dinner for half an hour," Waythorn cut him off, hurrying upstairs.

He went straight to his room and dressed without seeing his wife. When he reached the drawing-room she was there, fresh and radiant. Lily's day had been good; the doctor was not coming back that evening.

At dinner Waythorn told her of Sellers's illness and of the resulting complications. She listened sympathetically, adjuring him not to let himself be overworked, and asking vague feminine questions about the routine of the office. Then she gave him the chronicle of Lily's day; quoted the nurse and doctor, and told him who had called to inquire. He had never seen her more serene and unruffled. It struck him, with a curious pang, that she was very happy in being with him, so happy that she found a childish pleasure in rehearsing the trivial incidents of her day.

After dinner they went to the library, and the servant put the coffee and liqueurs on a low table before her and left the room. She looked singularly soft and girlish in her rosy pale dress, against the dark leather of one of his bachelor armchairs. A day earlier the contrast would have charmed him.

He turned away now, choosing a cigar with affected deliberation.

[2] Strong coffee.

"Did Haskett come?" he asked, with his back to her.

"Oh, yes—he came."

"You didn't see him, of course?"

She hesitated a moment. "I let the nurse see him."

That was all. There was nothing more to ask. He swung round toward her, applying a match to his cigar. Well, the thing was over for a week, at any rate. He would try not to think of it. She looked up at him, a trifle rosier than usual, with a smile in her eyes.

"Ready for your coffee, dear?"

He leaned against the mantelpiece, watching her as she lifted the coffee-pot. The lamplight struck a gleam from her bracelets and tipped her soft hair with brightness. How light and slender she was, and how each gesture flowed into the next! She seemed a creature all compact of harmonies. As the thought of Haskett receded, Waythorn felt himself yielding again to the joy of possessorship. They were his, those white hands with their flitting motions, his the light haze of hair, the lips and eyes. . . .

She set down the coffee-pot, and reached for the decanter of cognac, measured off a liqueur-glass and poured it into his cup.

Waythorn uttered a sudden exclamation.

"What is the matter?" she said, startled.

"Nothing; only—I don't take cognac in my coffee."

"Oh, how stupid of me," she cried.

Their eyes met, and she blushed a sudden agonised red.

III

Ten days later, Mr. Sellers, still house-bound, asked Waythorn to call on his way down town.

The senior partner, with his swaddled foot propped up by the fire, greeted his associate with an air of embarrassment.

"I'm sorry, my dear fellow; I've got to ask you to do an awkward thing for me."

Waythorn waited, and the other went on, after a pause apparently given to the arrangement of his phrases: "The fact is, when I was knocked out I had just gone into a rather complicated piece of business for—Gus Varick."

"Well?" said Waythorn, with an attempt to put him at his ease.

"Well—it's this way: Varick came to me the day before my attack. He had evidently had an inside tip from somebody, and had made about a hundred thousand. He came to me for advice, and I suggested his going in with Vanderlyn."

"Oh, the deuce!" Waythorn exclaimed. He saw in a flash what had happened. The investment was an alluring one, but required negotiation. He listened quietly while Sellers put the case before him, and, the statement ended, he said: "You think I ought to see Varick?"

"I'm afraid I can't as yet. The doctor is obdurate. And this thing can't wait. I hate to ask you, but no one else in the office knows the ins and outs of it."

Waythorn stood silent. He did not care a farthing for the success of Varick's venture, but the honour of the office was to be considered, and he could hardly refuse to oblige his partner.

"Very well," he said, "I'll do it."

That afternoon, apprised by telephone, Varick called at the office. Waythorn, waiting in his private room, wondered what the others thought of it. The newspapers, at the time of Mrs. Waythorn's marriage, had acquainted their readers with every detail of her previous matrimonial ventures, and Waythorn could fancy the clerks smiling behind Varick's back as he was ushered in.

Varick bore himself admirably. He was easy without being undignified, and Waythorn was conscious of cutting a much less impressive figure. Varick had no experience of business, and the talk prolonged itself for nearly an hour while Waythorn set forth with scrupulous precision the details of the proposed transaction.

"I'm awfully obliged to you," Varick said as he rose. "The fact is I'm not used to having much money to look after, and I don't want to make an ass of myself—" He smiled, and Waythorn could not help noticing that there was something pleasant about his smile. "It feels uncommonly queer to have enough cash to pay one's bills. I'd have sold my soul for it a few years ago!"

Waythorn winced at the illusion. He had heard it rumoured that a lack of funds had been one of the determining causes of the Varick separation, but it did not occur to him that Varick's words were intentional. It seemed more likely that the desire to keep clear of embarrassing topics had fatally drawn him into one. Waythorn did not wish to be outdone in civility.

"We'll do the best we can for you," he said. "I think this is a good thing you're in."

"Oh, I'm sure it's immense. It's awfully good of you—" Varick broke off, embarrassed. "I suppose the thing's settled now—but if—"

"If anything happens before Sellers is about, I'll see you again," said Waythorn quietly. He was glad, in the end, to appear the more self-possessed of the two.

The course of Lily's illness ran smooth, and as the days passed Waythorn grew used to the idea of Haskett's weekly visit. The first time the day came round, he stayed out late, and questioned his wife as to the visit on his return. She replied at once that Haskett had merely seen the nurse downstairs, as the doctor did not wish any one in the child's sick-room till after the crisis.

The following week Waythorn was again conscious of the recurrence of the day, but had forgotten it by the time he came home to dinner. The crisis of the disease came a few days later, with a rapid decline of fever, and the little girl was pronounced out of danger. In the rejoicing which ensued the thought of Haskett passed out of Waythorn's mind, and one afternoon, letting himself into the house with a latch-key, he went straight to his library without noticing a shabby hat and umbrella in the hall.

In the library he found a small effaced-looking man with a thinnish gray beard sitting on the edge of a chair. The stranger might have been a piano-tuner, or one of those mysteriously efficient persons who are summoned in emergencies to adjust some detail of the domestic machinery. He blinked at Waythorn through a pair of gold-rimmed spectacles and said mildly: "Mr. Waythorn, I presume? I am Lily's father."

Waythorn flushed. "Oh—" he stammered uncomfortably. He broke off, disliking to appear rude. Inwardly he was trying to adjust the actual Haskett to the image of him projected by his wife's reminiscences. Waythorn had been allowed to infer that Alice's first husband was a brute.

"I am sorry to intrude," said Haskett, with his over-the-counter politeness.

"Don't mention it," returned Waythorn, collecting himself. "I suppose the nurse has been told?"

"I presume so. I can wait," said Haskett. He had a resigned way of speaking, as though life had worn down his natural powers of resistance.

Waythorn stood on the threshold, nervously pulling off his gloves.

"I'm sorry you've been detained. I will send for the nurse," he said; and as he opened the door he added with an effort: "I'm glad we can give you a good report of Lily." He winced as the *we* slipped out, but Haskett seemed not to notice it.

"Thank you, Mr. Waythorn. It's been an anxious time for me."

"Ah, well, that's past. Soon she'll be able to go to you." Waythorn nodded and passed out. In his own room he flung himself down with a groan. He hated the womanish sensibility which made him suffer so acutely from the grotesque chances of life. He had known when he married that his wife's former husbands were both living, and that amid the multiplied contacts of modern existence there were a thousand chances to one that he would run against one or the other, yet he found himself as much disturbed by his brief encounter with Haskett as though the law had not obligingly removed all difficulties in the way of their meeting.

Waythorn sprang up and began to pace the room nervously. He had not suffered half as much from his two meetings with Varick. It was Haskett's presence in his own house that made the situation so intolerable. He stood still, hearing steps in the passage.

"This way, please," he heard the nurse say. Haskett was being taken upstairs, then: not a corner of the house but was open to him. Waythorn dropped into another chair, staring vaguely ahead of him. On his dressing-table stood a photograph of Alice, taken when he had first known her. She was Alice Varick then—how fine and exquisite he had thought her! Those were Varick's pearls about her neck. At Waythorn's insistence they had been returned before her marriage. Had Haskett ever given her any trinkets—and what had become of them, Waythorn wondered? He realised suddenly that he knew very little of Haskett's past or present situation; but from the man's appearance and manner of speech he could reconstruct with curious precision the surroundings of Alice's first marriage. And it startled him to think that she had, in the background of her life, a phase of existence so different from anything with which he had connected her. Varick, whatever his faults, was a gentleman, in the conventional, traditional sense of the term: the sense which at that moment seemed, oddly enough, to have most meaning to Waythorn. He and Varick had the same social habits, spoke the same language, understood the same allusions. But this other man . . . it was grotesquely uppermost in Waythorn's mind that Haskett had worn a made-up tie attached with an elastic. Why should that ridiculous detail symbolise the whole man? Waythorn was exasperated by his own paltriness, but the fact of the tie expanded, forced itself on him, became as it were the key to Alice's past. He could see her, as Mrs. Haskett, sitting in a "front parlour" furnished in plush, with a pianola,[3] and a copy of "Ben Hur"[4] on the centre-table. He could see her going to the theatre with Haskett—or perhaps even to a "Church Sociable"—she in a "picture hat" and Haskett in a black frock-coat, a little creased, with the made-up tie on an elastic. On the way home they would stop and look at the illuminated shop-windows, lingering

---

[3] An automatic piano player.
[4] Best-selling novel (1880) by General Lew

Wallace (1827–1905). Like the pianola, suggestive of lower-middle-class tastes.

over the photographs of New York actresses. On Sunday afternoons Haskett would take her for a walk, pushing Lily ahead of them in a white enamelled perambulator, and Waythorn had a vision of the people they would stop and talk to. He could fancy how pretty Alice must have looked, in a dress adroitly constructed from the hints of a New York fashion-paper, and how she must have looked down on the other women, chafing at her life, and secretly feeling that she belonged in a bigger place.

For the moment his foremost thought was one of wonder at the way in which she had shed the phase of existence which her marriage with Haskett implied. It was as if her whole aspect, every gesture, every inflection, every allusion, were a studied negation of that period of her life. If she had denied being married to Haskett she could hardly have stood more convicted of duplicity than in this obliteration of the self which had been his wife.

Waythorn started up, checking himself in the analysis of her motives. What right had he to create a fantastic effigy of her and then pass judgment on it? She had spoken vaguely of her first marriage as unhappy, had hinted, with becoming reticence, that Haskett had wrought havoc among her young illusions. . . . It was a pity for Waythorn's peace of mind that Haskett's very inoffensiveness shed a new light on the nature of those illusions. A man would rather think that his wife has been brutalised by her first husband than that the process has been reversed.

IV

"Mr. Waythorn, I don't like that French governess of Lily's."

Haskett, subdued and apologetic, stood before Waythorn in the library, revolving his shabby hat in his hand.

Waythorn, surprised in his armchair over the evening paper, stared back perplexedly at his visitor.

"You'll excuse my asking to see you," Haskett continued. "But this is my last visit, and I thought if I could have a word with you it would be a better way than writing to Mrs. Waythorn's lawyer."

Waythorn rose uneasily. He did not like the French governess either; but that was irrelevant.

"I am not so sure of that," he returned stiffly; "but since you wish it I will give your message to—my wife." He always hesitated over the possessive pronoun in addressing Haskett.

The latter sighed. "I don't know as that will help much. She didn't like it when I spoke to her."

Waythorn turned red. "When did you see her?" he asked.

"Not since the first day I came to see Lily—right after she was taken sick. I remarked to her then that I didn't like the governess."

Waythorn made no answer. He remembered distinctly that, after that first visit, he had asked his wife if she had seen Haskett. She had lied to him then, but she had respected his wishes since; and the incident cast a curious light on her character. He was sure she would not have seen Haskett that first day if she had divined that Waythorn would object, and the fact that she did not divine it was almost as disagreeable to the latter as the discovery that she had lied to him.

"I don't like the woman," Haskett was repeating with mild persistency. "She ain't straight, Mr. Waythorn—she'll teach the child to be underhand. I've noticed a change in Lily—she's too anxious to please—and she don't always tell the truth. She used to be the straightest child, Mr. Waythorn—" He broke off, his voice a little thick. "Not but what I want her to have a stylish education," he ended.

Waythorn was touched. "I'm sorry, Mr. Haskett; but frankly, I don't quite see what I can do."

Haskett hesitated. Then he laid his hat on the table, and advanced to the hearth-rug, on which Waythorn was standing. There was nothing aggressive in his manner, but he had the solemnity of a timid man resolved on a decisive measure.

"There's just one thing you can do, Mr. Waythorn," he said. "You can remind Mrs. Waythorn that, by the decree of the courts, I am entitled to have a voice in Lily's bringing up." He paused, and went on more deprecatingly: "I'm not the kind to talk about enforcing my rights, Mr. Waythorn. I don't know as I think a man is entitled to rights he hasn't known how to hold on to; but this business of the child is different. I've never let go there—and I never mean to."

The scene left Waythorn deeply shaken. Shamefacedly, in indirect ways, he had been finding out about Haskett; and all that he had learned was favourable. The little man, in order to be near his daughter, had sold out his share in a profitable business in Utica, and accepted a modest clerkship in a New York manufacturing house. He boarded in a shabby street and had few acquaintances. His passion for Lily filled his life. Waythorn felt that this exploration of Haskett was like groping about with a dark-lantern in his wife's past; but he saw now that there were recesses his lantern had not explored. He had never enquired into the exact circumstances of his wife's first matrimonial rupture. On the surface all had been fair. It was she who had obtained the divorce, and the court had given her the child. But Waythorn knew how many ambiguities such a verdict might cover. The mere fact that Haskett retained a right over his daughter implied an unsuspected compromise. Waythorn was an idealist. He always refused to recognise unpleasant contingencies till he found himself confronted with them, and then he saw them followed by a special train of consequences. His next days were thus haunted, and he determined to try to lay the ghosts by conjuring them up in his wife's presence.

When he repeated Haskett's request a flame of anger passed over her face; but she subdued it instantly and spoke with a slight quiver of outraged motherhood.

"It is very ungentlemanly of him," she said.

The word grated on Waythorn. "That is neither here nor there. It's a bare question of rights."

She murmured: "It is not as if he could ever be a help to Lily—"

Waythorn flushed. This was even less to his taste. "The question is," he repeated, "what authority has he over her?"

She looked downward, twisting herself a little in her seat. "I am willing to see him —I thought you objected," she faltered.

In a flash he understood that she knew the extent of Haskett's claims. Perhaps it was not the first time she had resisted them.

"My objecting has nothing to do with it," he said coldly; "if Haskett has a right to be consulted you must consult him."

She burst into tears, and he saw that she expected him to regard her as a victim.

Haskett did not abuse his rights. Waythorn had felt miserably sure that he would not. But the governess was dismissed, and from time to time the little man demanded an interview with Alice. After the first outburst she accepted the situation with her usual adaptability. Haskett had once reminded Waythorn of the piano-tuner, and Mrs. Waythorn, after a month or two, appeared to class him with that domestic familiar. Waythorn could not but respect the father's tenacity. At first he had tried to cultivate the suspicion that Haskett might be "up to" something, that he had an object in securing a foothold in the house. But in his heart Waythorn was sure of Haskett's single-mindedness; he even guessed in the latter a mild contempt for such advantages as his relation with the Waythorns might offer. Haskett's sincerity of purpose made him invulnerable, and his successor had to accept him as a lien on the property.

Mr. Sellers was sent to Europe to recover from his gout, and Varick's affairs hung on Waythorn's hands. The negotiations were prolonged and complicated; they necessitated frequent conferences between the two men, and the interests of the firm forbade Waythorn's suggesting that his client should transfer his business to another office.

Varick appeared well in the transaction. In moments of relaxation his coarse streak appeared, and Waythorn dreaded his geniality; but in the office he was concise and clear-headed, with a flattering deference to Waythorn's judgment. Their business relations being so affably established, it would have been absurd for the two men to ignore each other in society. The first time they met in a drawing-room, Varick took up their intercourse in the same easy key, and his hostess's grateful glance obliged Waythorn to respond to it. After that they ran across each other frequently, and one evening at a ball Waythorn, wandering through the remoter rooms, came upon Varick seated beside his wife. She coloured a little, and faltered in what she was saying; but Varick nodded to Waythorn without rising, and the latter strolled on.

In the carriage, on the way home, he broke out nervously: "I didn't know you spoke to Varick."

Her voice trembled a little. "It's the first time—he happened to be standing near me; I didn't know what to do. It's so awkward, meeting everywhere—and he said you had been very kind about some business."

"That's different," said Waythorn.

She paused a moment. "I'll do just as you wish," she returned pliantly. "I thought it would be less awkward to speak to him when we meet."

Her pliancy was beginning to sicken him. Had she really no will of her own—no theory about her relation to these men? She had accepted Haskett—did she mean to accept Varick? It was "less awkward," as she had said, and her instinct was to evade difficulties or to circumvent them. With sudden vividness Waythorn saw how the instinct had developed. She was "as easy as an old shoe"—a shoe that too many feet had worn. Her elasticity was the result of tension in too many different directions. Alice Haskett—Alice Varick—Alice Waythorn—she had been each in turn, and had left hanging to each name a little of her privacy, a little of her personality, a little of the inmost self where the unknown god abides.

"Yes—it's better to speak to Varick," said Waythorn wearily.

V

The winter wore on, and society took advantage of the Waythorns' acceptance of Varick. Harassed hostesses were grateful to them for bridging over a social difficulty, and Mrs. Waythorn was held up as a miracle of good taste. Some experimental spirits could not resist the diversion of throwing Varick and his former wife together, and there were those who thought he found a zest in the propinquity. But Mrs. Waythorn's conduct remained irreproachable. She neither avoided Varick nor sought him out. Even Waythorn could not but admit that she had discovered the solution of the newest social problem.

He had married her without giving much thought to that problem. He had fancied that a woman can shed her past like a man. But now he saw that Alice was bound to hers both by the circumstances which forced her into continued relation with it, and by the traces it had left on her nature. With grim irony Waythorn compared himself to a member of a syndicate. He held so many shares in his wife's personality and his predecessors were his partners in the business. If there had been any element of passion in the transaction he would have felt less deteriorated by it. The fact that Alice took her change of husbands like a change of weather reduced the situation to mediocrity. He could have forgiven her for blunders, for excesses; for resisting Haskett, for yielding to Varick; for anything but her acquiescence and her tact. She reminded him of a juggler tossing knives; but the knives were blunt and he knew they would never cut her.

And then, gradually, habit formed a protecting surface for his sensibilities. If he paid for each day's comfort with the small change of his illusions, he grew daily to value the comfort more and set less store upon the coin. He had drifted into a dulling propinquity with Haskett and Varick and he took refuge in the cheap revenge of satirising the situation. He even began to reckon up the advantages which accrued from it, to ask himself if it were not better to own a third of a wife who knew how to make a man happy than a whole one who had lacked opportunity to acquire the art. For it *was* an art, and made up, like all others, of concessions, eliminations and embellishments; of lights judiciously thrown and shadows skilfully softened. His wife knew exactly how to manage the lights, and he knew exactly to what training she owed her skill. He even tried to trace the source of his obligations, to discriminate between the influences which had combined to produce his domestic happiness: he perceived that Haskett's commonness had made Alice worship good breeding, while Varick's liberal construction of the marriage bond had taught her to value the conjugal virtues; so that he was directly indebted to his predecessors for the devotion which made his life easy if not inspiring.

From this phase he passed into that of complete acceptance. He ceased to satirise himself because time dulled the irony of the situation and the joke lost its humour with its sting. Even the sight of Haskett's hat on the hall table had ceased to touch the springs of epigram. The hat was often seen there now, for it had been decided that it was better for Lily's father to visit her than for the little girl to go to his boarding-house. Waythorn, having acquiesced in this arrangement, had been surprised to find how little difference it made. Haskett was never obtrusive, and the few visitors who met him on the stairs were unaware of his identity. Waythorn did not know how often he saw Alice, but with himself Haskett was seldom in contact.

One afternoon, however, he learned on entering that Lily's father was waiting to see him. In the library he found Haskett occupying a chair in his usual provisional way. Waythorn always felt grateful to him for not leaning back.

"I hope you'll excuse me, Mr. Waythorn," he said rising. "I wanted to see Mrs. Waythorn about Lily, and your man asked me to wait here till she came in."

"Of course," said Waythorn, remembering that a sudden leak had that morning given over the drawing-room to the plumbers.

He opened his cigar-case and held it out to his visitor, and Haskett's acceptance seemed to mark a fresh stage in their intercourse. The spring evening was chilly, and Waythorn invited his guest to draw up his chair to the fire. He meant to find an excuse to leave Haskett in a moment; but he was tired and cold, and after all the little man no longer jarred on him.

The two were enclosed in the intimacy of their blended cigar-smoke when the door opened and Varick walked into the room. Waythorn rose abruptly. It was the first time that Varick had come to the house, and the surprise of seeing him, combined with the singular inopportuneness of his arrival, gave a new edge to Waythorn's blunted sensibilities. He stared at his visitor without speaking.

Varick seemed too preoccupied to notice his host's embarrassment.

"My dear fellow," he exclaimed in his most expansive tone, "I must apologise for tumbling in on you in this way, but I was too late to catch you down town, and so I thought—"

He stopped short, catching sight of Haskett, and his sanguine colour deepened to a flush which spread vividly under his scant blond hair. But in a moment he recovered himself and nodded slightly. Haskett returned the bow in silence, and Waythorn was still groping for speech when the footman came in carrying a tea-table.

The intrusion offered a welcome vent to Waythorn's nerves. "What the deuce are you bringing this here for?" he said sharply.

"I beg your pardon, sir, but the plumbers are still in the drawing-room, and Mrs. Waythorn said she would have tea in the library." The footman's perfectly respectful tone implied a reflection on Waythorn's reasonableness.

"Oh, very well," said the latter resignedly, and the footman proceeded to open the folding tea-table and set out its complicated appointments. While this interminable process continued the three men stood motionless, watching it with a fascinated stare, till Waythorn, to break the silence, said to Varick: "Won't you have a cigar?"

He held out the case he had just tendered to Haskett, and Varick helped himself with a smile. Waythorn looked about for a match, and finding none, proffered a light from his own cigar. Haskett, in the background, held his ground mildly, examining his cigar-tip now and then, and stepping forward at the right moment to knock its ashes into the fire.

The footman at last withdrew, and Varick immediately began: "If I could just say half a word to you about this business—"

"Certainly," stammered Waythorn; "in the dining-room—"

But as he placed his hand on the door it opened from without, and his wife appeared on the threshold.

She came in fresh and smiling, in her street dress and hat, shedding a fragrance from the boa[5] which she loosened in advancing.

_____

[5] Long scarf of fur or feathers worn around a woman's neck or shoulders.

"Shall we have tea in here, dear?" she began; and then she caught sight of Varick. Her smile deepened, veiling a slight tremor of surprise.

"Why, how do you do?" she said with a distinct note of pleasure.

As she shook hands with Varick she saw Haskett standing behind him. Her smile faded for a moment, but she recalled it quickly, with a scarcely perceptible side-glance at Waythorn.

"How do you do, Mr. Haskett?" she said, and shook hands with him a shade less cordially.

The three men stood awkwardly before her, till Varick, always the most self-possessed, dashed into an explanatory phrase.

"We—I had to see Waythorn a moment on business," he stammered, brick-red from chin to nape.

Haskett stepped forward with his air of mild obstinacy. "I am sorry to intrude; but you appointed five o'clock—" he directed his resigned glance to the timepiece on the mantel.

She swept aside their embarrassment with a charming gesture of hospitality.

"I'm so sorry—I'm always late; but the afternoon was so lovely." She stood drawing off her gloves, propitiatory and graceful, diffusing about her a sense of ease and familiarity in which the situation lost its grotesqueness. "But before talking business," she added brightly, "I'm sure every one wants a cup of tea."

She dropped into her low chair by the tea-table, and the two visitors, as if drawn by her smile, advanced to receive the cups she held out.

She glanced about for Waythorn, and he took the third cup with a laugh.

1904

Summer

I

A girl came out of lawyer Royall's house, at the end of the one street of North Dormer, and stood on the doorstep.

It was the beginning of a June afternoon. The springlike transparent sky shed a rain of silver sunshine on the roofs of the village, and on the pastures and larchwoods surrounding it. A little wind moved among the round white clouds on the shoulders of the hills, driving their shadows across the fields and down the grassy road that takes the name of street when it passes through North Dormer. The place lies high and in the open, and lacks the lavish shade of the more protected New England villages. The clump of weeping-willows about the duck pond, and the Norway spruces in front of the Hatchard gate, cast almost the only roadside shadow between lawyer Royall's house and the point where, at the other end of the village, the road rises above the church and skirts the black hemlock wall enclosing the cemetery.

The little June wind, frisking down the street, shook the doleful fringes of the Hatchard spruces, caught the straw hat of a young man just passing under them, and spun it clean across the road into the duck-pond.

As he ran to fish it out the girl on lawyer Royall's doorstep noticed that he was a stranger, that he wore city clothes, and that he was laughing with all his teeth, as the young and careless laugh at such mishaps.

Her heart contracted a little, and the shrinking that sometimes came over her when she saw people with holiday faces made her draw back into the house and pretend to look for the key that she knew she had already put into her pocket. A narrow greenish mirror with a gilt eagle over it hung on the passage wall, and she looked critically at her reflection, wished for the thousandth time that she had blue eyes like Annabel Balch, the girl who sometimes came from Springfield to spend a week with old Miss Hatchard, straightened the sunburnt hat over her small swarthy face, and turned out again into the sunshine.

"How I hate everything!" she murmured.

The young man had passed through the Hatchard gate, and she had the street to herself. North Dormer is at all times an empty place, and at three o'clock on a June afternoon its few able-bodied men are off in the fields or woods, and the women indoors, engaged in languid household drudgery.

The girl walked along, swinging her key on a finger, and looking about her with the heightened attention produced by the presence of a stranger in a familiar place. What, she wondered, did North Dormer look like to people from other parts of the world? She herself had lived there since the age of five, and had long supposed it to be a place of some importance. But about a year before, Mr. Miles, the new Episcopal clergyman at Hepburn, who drove over every other Sunday—when the roads were not ploughed up by hauling—to hold a service in the North Dormer church, had proposed, in a fit of missionary zeal, to take the young people down to Nettleton to hear an illustrated lecture on the Holy Land; and the dozen girls and boys who represented the future of North Dormer had been piled into a farm-waggon, driven over the hills to Hepburn, put into a way-train and carried to Nettleton. In the course of that incredible day Charity Royall had, for the first and only time, experienced railway-travel, looked into shops with plate-glass fronts, tasted cocoanut pie, sat in a theatre, and listened to a gentleman saying unintelligible things before pictures that she would have enjoyed looking at if his explanations had not prevented her from understanding them. This initiation had shown her that North Dormer was a small place, and developed in her a thirst for information that her position as custodian of the village library had previously failed to excite. For a month or two she dipped feverishly and disconnectedly into the dusty volumes of the Hatchard Memorial Library; then the impression of Nettleton began to fade, and she found it easier to take North Dormer as the norm of the universe than to go on reading.

The sight of the stranger once more revived memories of Nettleton, and North Dormer shrank to its real size. As she looked up and down it, from lawyer Royall's faded red house at one end to the white church at the other, she pitilessly took its measure. There it lay, a weather-beaten sunburnt village of the hills, abandoned of men, left apart by railway, trolley, telegraph, and all the forces that link life to life in modern communities. It had no shops, no theatres, no lectures, no "business block"; only a church that was opened every other Sunday if the state of the roads permitted, and a library for which no new books had been bought for twenty years, and where the old ones mouldered undisturbed on the damp shelves. Yet Charity Royall had always been told that she ought to consider it a privilege that her lot had been cast in North Dormer. She knew that, compared to the place she had come from, North

Dormer represented all the blessings of the most refined civilization. Everyone in the village had told her so ever since she had been brought there as a child. Even old Miss Hatchard had said to her, on a terrible occasion in her life: "My child, you must never cease to remember that it was Mr. Royall who brought you down from the Mountain."

She had been "brought down from the Mountain"; from the scarred cliff that lifted its sullen wall above the lesser slopes of Eagle Range, making a perpetual background of gloom to the lonely valley. The Mountain was a good fifteen miles away, but it rose so abruptly from the lower hills that it seemed almost to cast its shadow over North Dormer. And it was like a great magnet drawing the clouds and scattering them in storm across the valley. If ever, in the purest summer sky, there trailed a thread of vapour over North Dormer, it drifted to the Mountain as a ship drifts to a whirlpool, and was caught among the rocks, torn up and multiplied, to sweep back over the village in rain and darkness.

Charity was not very clear about the Mountain, but she knew it was a bad place, and a shame to have come from, and that, whatever befell her in North Dormer, she ought, as Miss Hatchard had once reminded her, to remember that she had been brought down from there, and hold her tongue and be thankful. She looked up at the Mountain, thinking of these things, and tried as usual to be thankful. But the sight of the young man turning in at Miss Hatchard's gate had brought back the vision of the glittering streets of Nettleton, and she felt ashamed of her old sun-hat, and sick of North Dormer, and jealously aware of Annabel Balch of Springfield, opening her blue eyes somewhere far off on glories greater than the glories of Nettleton.

"How I hate everything!" she said again.

Half way down the street she stopped at a weak-hinged gate. Passing through it, she walked down a brick path to a queer little brick temple with white wooden columns supporting a pediment on which was inscribed in tarnished gold letters: "The Honorius Hatchard Memorial Library, 1832."

Honorius Hatchard had been old Miss Hatchard's great-uncle; though she would undoubtedly have reversed the phrase, and put forward, as her only claim to distinction, the fact that she was his great-niece. For Honorius Hatchard, in the early years of the nineteenth century, had enjoyed a modest celebrity. As the marble tablet in the interior of the library informed its infrequent visitors, he had possessed marked literary gifts, written a series of papers called "The Recluse of Eagle Range," enjoyed the acquaintance of Washington Irving and Fitz-Greene Halleck,[1] and been cut off in his flower by a fever contracted in Italy. Such had been the sole link between North Dormer and literature, a link piously commemorated by the erection of the monument where Charity Royall, every Tuesday and Thursday afternoon, sat at her desk under a freckled steel engraving of the deceased author, and wondered if he felt any deader in his grave than she did in his library.

Entering her prison-house with a listless step she took off her hat, hung it on a plaster bust of Minerva, opened the shutters, leaned out to see if there were any eggs in the swallow's nest above one of the windows, and finally, seating herself behind

[1] Irving: American writer of tales, essays, and travel pieces (1783–1859); Halleck: American poet (1790–1867).

the desk, drew out a roll of cotton lace and a steel crochet hook. She was not an expert workwoman, and it had taken her many weeks to make the half-yard of narrow lace which she kept wound about the buckram back of a disintegrated copy of "The Lamplighter."[2] But there was no other way of getting any lace to trim her summer blouse, and since Ally Hawes, the poorest girl in the village, had shown herself in church with enviable transparencies about the shoulders, Charity's hook had travelled faster. She unrolled the lace, dug the hook into a loop, and bent to the task with furrowed brows.

Suddenly the door opened, and before she had raised her eyes she knew that the young man she had seen going in at the Hatchard gate had entered the library.

Without taking any notice of her he began to move slowly about the long vault-like room, his hands behind his back, his short-sighted eyes peering up and down the rows of rusty bindings. At length he reached the desk and stood before her.

"Have you a card-catalogue?" he asked in a pleasant abrupt voice; and the oddness of the question caused her to drop her work.

"A *what?*"

"Why, you know—" He broke off, and she became conscious that he was looking at her for the first time, having apparently, on his entrance, included her in his general short-sighted survey as part of the furniture of the library.

The fact that, in discovering her, he lost the thread of his remark, did not escape her attention, and she looked down and smiled. He smiled also.

"No, I don't suppose you *do* know," he corrected himself. "In fact, it would be almost a pity—"

She thought she detected a slight condescension in his tone, and asked sharply: "Why?"

"Because it's so much pleasanter, in a small library like this, to poke about by one's self—with the help of the librarian."

He added the last phrase so respectfully that she was mollified, and rejoined with a sigh: "I'm afraid I can't help you much."

"Why?" he questioned in his turn; and she replied that there weren't many books anyhow, and that she'd hardly read any of them. "The worms are getting at them," she added gloomily.

"Are they? That's a pity, for I see there are some good ones." He seemed to have lost interest in their conversation, and strolled away again, apparently forgetting her. His indifference nettled her, and she picked up her work, resolved not to offer him the least assistance. Apparently he did not need it, for he spent a long time with his back to her, lifting down, one after another, the tall cobwebby volumes from a distant shelf.

"Oh, I say!" he exclaimed; and looking up she saw that he had drawn out his handkerchief and was carefully wiping the edges of the book in his hand. The action struck her as an unwarranted criticism on her care of the books, and she said irritably: "It's not my fault if they're dirty."

He turned around and looked at her with reviving interest. "Ah—then you're not the librarian?"

[2] Popular novel, published in 1854, by Maria Susanna Cummins (1827–1866).

"Of course I am; but I can't dust all these books. Besides, nobody ever looks at them, now Miss Hatchard's too lame to come round."

"No, I suppose not." He laid down the book he had been wiping, and stood considering her in silence. She wondered if Miss Hatchard had sent him round to pry into the way the library was looked after, and the suspicion increased her resentment. "I saw you going into her house just now, didn't I?" she asked, with the New England avoidance of the proper name. She was determined to find out why he was poking about among her books.

"Miss Hatchard's house? Yes—she's my cousin and I'm staying there," the young man answered; adding, as if to disarm a visible distrust: "My name is Harney—Lucius Harney. She may have spoken of me."

"No, she hasn't," said Charity, wishing she could have said: "Yes, she has."

"Oh, well—" said Miss Hatchard's cousin with a laugh; and after another pause, during which it occurred to Charity that her answer had not been encouraging, he remarked: "You don't seem strong on architecture."

Her bewilderment was complete: the more she wished to appear to understand him the more unintelligible his remarks became. He reminded her of the gentleman who had "explained" the pictures at Nettleton, and the weight of her ignorance settled down on her again like a pall.

"I mean, I can't see that you have any books on the old houses about here. I suppose, for that matter, this part of the country hasn't been much explored. They all go on doing Plymouth and Salem. So stupid. My cousin's house, now, is remarkable. This place must have had a past—it must have been more of a place once." He stopped short, with the blush of a shy man who overhears himself, and fears he has been voluble. "I'm an architect, you see, and I'm hunting up old houses in these parts."

She stared. "Old houses? Everything's old in North Dormer, isn't it? The folks are, anyhow."

He laughed, and wandered away again.

"Haven't you any kind of a history of the place? I think there was one written about 1840: a book or pamphlet about its first settlement," he presently said from the farther end of the room.

She pressed her crochet hook against her lip and pondered. There was such a work, she knew: "North Dormer and the Early Townships of Eagle County." She had a special grudge against it because it was a limp weakly book that was always either falling off the shelf or slipping back and disappearing if one squeezed it in between sustaining volumes. She remembered, the last time she had picked it up, wondering how anyone could have taken the trouble to write a book about North Dormer and its neighbours: Dormer, Hamblin, Creston and Creston River. She knew them all, mere lost clusters of houses in the folds of the desolate ridges: Dormer, where North Dormer went for its apples; Creston River, where there used to be a papermill, and its grey walls stood decaying by the stream; and Hamblin, where the first snow always fell. Such were their titles to fame.

She got up and began to move about vaguely before the shelves. But she had no idea where she had last put the book, and something told her that it was going to play her its usual trick and remain invisible. It was not one of her lucky days.

"I guess it's somewhere," she said, to prove her zeal; but she spoke without conviction, and felt that her words conveyed none.

"Oh, well—" he said again. She knew he was going, and wished more than ever to find the book.

"It will be for next time," he added; and picking up the volume he had laid on the desk he handed it to her. "By the way, a little air and sun would do this good; it's rather valuable."

He gave her a nod and smile, and passed out.

II

The hours of the Hatchard Memorial librarian were from three to five; and Charity Royall's sense of duty usually kept her at her desk until nearly half-past four.

But she had never perceived that any practical advantage thereby accrued either to North Dormer or to herself; and she had no scruple in decreeing, when it suited her, that the library should close an hour earlier. A few minutes after Mr. Harney's departure she formed this decision, put away her lace, fastened the shutters, and turned the key in the door of the temple of knowledge.

The street upon which she emerged was still empty: and after glancing up and down it she began to walk toward her house. But instead of entering she passed on, turned into a field-path and mounted to a pasture on the hillside. She let down the bars of the gate, followed a trail along the crumbling wall of the pasture, and walked on till she reached a knoll where a clump of larches shook out their fresh tassels to the wind. There she lay down on the slope, tossed off her hat and hid her face in the grass.

She was blind and insensible to many things, and dimly knew it; but to all that was light and air, perfume and colour, every drop of blood in her responded. She loved the roughness of the dry mountain grass under her palms, the smell of the thyme into which she crushed her face, the fingering of the wind in her hair and through her cotton blouse, and the creak of the larches as they swayed to it.

She often climbed up the hill and lay there alone for the mere pleasure of feeling the wind and of rubbing her cheeks in the grass. Generally at such times she did not think of anything, but lay immersed in an inarticulate well-being. Today the sense of well-being was intensified by her joy at escaping from the library. She liked well enough to have a friend drop in and talk to her when she was on duty, but she hated to be bothered about books. How could she remember where they were, when they were so seldom asked for? Orma Fry occasionally took out a novel, and her brother Ben was fond of what he called "jography," and of books relating to trade and bookkeeping; but no one else asked for anything except, at intervals, "Uncle Tom's Cabin," or "Opening a Chestnut Burr," or Longfellow.[3] She had these under her hand, and could have found them in the dark; but unexpected demands came so rarely that they exasperated her like an injustice. . . .

She had liked the young man's looks, and his short-sighted eyes, and his odd way of speaking, that was abrupt yet soft, just as his hands were sunburnt and sinewy, yet with smooth nails like a woman's. His hair was sunburnt-looking too, or rather the

[3] Uncle Tom's Cabin: Harriet Beecher Stowe's best-selling antislavery novel, published in 1852; Opening a Chestnut Burr: popular novel by Edward Payson Roe, first published in 1874; Longfellow: Henry Wadsworth Longfellow (1807–1882), phenomenally popular New England poet of midcentury America.

colour of bracken after frost; his eyes grey, with the appealing look of the shortsighted, his smile shy yet confident, as if he knew lots of things she had never dreamed of, and yet wouldn't for the world have had her feel his superiority. But she did feel it, and liked the feeling; for it was new to her. Poor and ignorant as she was, and knew herself to be—humblest of the humble even in North Dormer, where to come from the Mountain was the worst disgrace—yet in her narrow world she had always ruled. It was partly, of course, owing to the fact that lawyer Royall was "the biggest man in North Dormer"; so much too big for it, in fact, that outsiders, who didn't know, always wondered how it held him. In spite of everything—and in spite even of Miss Hatchard—lawyer Royall ruled in North Dormer; and Charity ruled in lawyer Royall's house. She had never put it to herself in those terms; but she knew her power, knew what it was made of, and hated it. Confusedly, the young man in the library had made her feel for the first time what might be the sweetness of dependence.

She sat up, brushed the bits of grass from her hair, and looked down on the house where she held sway. It stood just below her, cheerless and untended, its faded red front divided from the road by a "yard" with a path bordered by gooseberry bushes, a stone well overgrown with traveller's joy, and a sickly Crimson Rambler tied to a fan-shaped support, which Mr. Royall had once brought up from Hepburn to please her. Behind the house a bit of uneven ground with clothes-lines strung across it stretched up to a dry wall, and beyond the wall a patch of corn and a few rows of potatoes strayed vaguely into the adjoining wilderness of rock and fern.

Charity could not recall her first sight of the house. She had been told that she was ill of a fever when she was brought down from the Mountain; and she could only remember waking one day in a cot at the foot of Mrs. Royall's bed, and opening her eyes on the cold neatness of the room that was afterward to be hers.

Mrs. Royall died seven or eight years later; and by that time Charity had taken the measure of most things about her. She knew that Mrs. Royall was sad and timid and weak; she knew that lawyer Royall was harsh and violent, and still weaker. She knew that she had been christened Charity (in the white church at the other end of the village) to commemorate Mr. Royall's disinterestedness in "bringing her down," and to keep alive in her a becoming sense of her dependence; she knew that Mr. Royall was her guardian, but that he had not legally adopted her, though everybody spoke of her as Charity Royall; and she knew why he had come back to live at North Dormer, instead of practising at Nettleton, where he had begun his legal career.

After Mrs. Royall's death there was some talk of sending her to a boarding-school. Miss Hatchard suggested it, and had a long conference with Mr. Royall, who, in pursuance of her plan, departed one day for Starkfield to visit the institution she recommended. He came back the next night with a black face; worse, Charity observed, than she had ever seen him; and by that time she had had some experience.

When she asked him how soon she was to start he answered shortly, "You ain't going," and shut himself up in the room he called his office; and the next day the lady who kept the school at Starkfield wrote that "under the circumstances" she was afraid she could not make room just then for another pupil.

Charity was disappointed; but she understood. It wasn't the temptations of Stark-field that had been Mr. Royall's undoing; it was the thought of losing her. He was a dreadfully "lonesome" man; she had made that out because she was so "lonesome" herself. He and she, face to face in that sad house, had sounded the depths of isolation;

and though she felt no particular affection for him, and not the slightest gratitude, she pitied him because she was conscious that he was superior to the people about him, and that she was the only being between him and solitude. Therefore, when Miss Hatchard sent for her a day or two later, to talk of a school at Nettleton, and to say that this time a friend of hers would "make the necessary arrangements," Charity cut her short with the announcement that she had decided not to leave North Dormer.

Miss Hatchard reasoned with her kindly, but to no purpose; she simply repeated: "I guess Mr. Royall's too lonesome."

Miss Hatchard blinked perplexedly behind her eye-glasses. Her long frail face was full of puzzled wrinkles, and she leant forward, resting her hands on the arms of her mahogany armchair, with the evident desire to say something that ought to be said.

"The feeling does you credit, my dear."

She looked about the pale walls of her sitting-room, seeking counsel of ancestral daguerreotypes and didactic samplers; but they seemed to make utterance more difficult.

"The fact is, it's not only—not only because of the advantages. There are other reasons. You're too young to understand—"

"Oh, no, I ain't," said Charity harshly; and Miss Hatchard blushed to the roots of her blonde cap. But she must have felt a vague relief at having her explanation cut short, for she concluded, again invoking the daguerreotypes: "Of course I shall always do what I can for you; and in case . . . in case . . . you know you can always come to me. . . ."

Lawyer Royall was waiting for Charity in the porch when she returned from this visit. He had shaved, and brushed his black coat, and looked a magnificent monument of a man; at such moments she really admired him.

"Well," he said, "is it settled?"

"Yes, it's settled. I ain't going."

"Not to the Nettleton school?"

"Not anywhere."

He cleared his throat and asked sternly: "Why?"

"I'd rather not," she said, swinging past him on her way to her room. It was the following week that he brought her up the Crimson Rambler and its fan from Hepburn. He had never given her anything before.

The next outstanding incident of her life had happened two years later, when she was seventeen. Lawyer Royall, who hated to go to Nettleton, had been called there in connection with a case. He still exercised his profession, though litigation languished in North Dormer and its outlying hamlets; and for once he had had an opportunity that he could not afford to refuse. He spent three days in Nettleton, won his case, and came back in high good-humour. It was a rare mood with him, and manifested itself on this occasion by his talking impressively at the supper-table of the "rousing welcome" his old friends had given him. He wound up confidentially: "I was a damn fool ever to leave Nettleton. It was Mrs. Royall that made me do it."

Charity immediately perceived that something bitter had happened to him, and that he was trying to talk down the recollection. She went up to bed early, leaving him seated in moody thought, his elbows propped on the worn oilcloth of the supper table. On the way up she had extracted from his overcoat pocket the key of the cupboard where the bottle of whiskey was kept.

She was awakened by a rattling at her door and jumped out of bed. She heard Mr. Royall's voice, low and peremptory, and opened the door, fearing an accident. No other thought had occurred to her; but when she saw him in the doorway, a ray from the autumn moon falling on his discomposed face, she understood.

For a moment they looked at each other in silence; then, as he put his foot across the threshold, she stretched out her arm and stopped him.

"You go right back from here," she said, in a shrill voice that startled her; "you ain't going to have that key tonight."

"Charity, let me in. I don't want the key. I'm a lonesome man," he began, in the deep voice that sometimes moved her.

Her heart gave a startled plunge, but she continued to hold him back contemptuously. "Well, I guess you made a mistake, then. This ain't your wife's room any longer."

She was not frightened, she simply felt a deep disgust; and perhaps he divined it or read it in her face, for after staring at her a moment he drew back and turned slowly away from the door. With her ear to her keyhole she heard him feel his way down the dark stairs, and toward the kitchen; and she listened for the crash of the cupboard panel. But instead she heard him, after an interval, unlock the door of the house, and his heavy steps came to her through the silence as he walked down the path. She crept to the window and saw his bent figure striding up the road in the moonlight. Then a belated sense of fear came to her with the consciousness of victory, and she slipped into bed, cold to the bone.

A day or two later poor Eudora Skeff, who for twenty years had been the custodian of the Hatchard library, died suddenly of pneumonia; and the day after the funeral Charity went to see Miss Hatchard, and asked to be appointed librarian. The request seemed to surprise Miss Hatchard: she evidently questioned the new candidate's qualifications.

"Why, I don't know, my dear. Aren't you rather too young?" she hesitated.

"I want to earn some money," Charity merely answered.

"Doesn't Mr. Royall give you all you require? No one is rich in North Dormer."

"I want to earn money enough to get away."

"To get away?" Miss Hatchard's puzzled wrinkles deepened, and there was a distressful pause. "You want to leave Mr. Royall?"

"Yes: or I want another woman in the house with me," said Charity resolutely.

Miss Hatchard clasped her nervous hands about the arms of her chair. Her eyes invoked the faded countenances on the wall, and after a faint cough of indecision she brought out: "The . . . the housework's too hard for you, I suppose?"

Charity's heart grew cold. She understood that Miss Hatchard had no help to give her and that she would have to fight her way out of her difficulty alone. A deeper sense of isolation overcame her; she felt incalculably old. "She's got to be talked to like a baby," she thought, with a feeling of compassion for Miss Hatchard's long immaturity. "Yes, that's it," she said aloud. "The housework's too hard for me: I've been coughing a good deal this fall."

She noted the immediate effect of this suggestion. Miss Hatchard paled at the memory of poor Eudora's taking-off, and promised to do what she could. But of course there were people she must consult: the clergyman, the selectmen of North Dormer, and a distant Hatchard relative at Springfield. "If you'd only gone to school!" she sighed. She followed Charity to the door, and there, in the security of the threshold, said with a glance of evasive appeal: "I know Mr. Royall is . . . trying at times; but his wife bore with him; and you must always remember, Charity, that it was Mr. Royall who brought you down from the Mountain."

Charity went home and opened the door of Mr. Royall's "office." He was sitting there by the stove reading Daniel Webster's[4] speeches. They had met at meals during the five days that had elapsed since he had come to her door, and she had walked at his side at Eudora's funeral; but they had not spoken a word to each other.

He glanced up in surprise as she entered, and she noticed that he was unshaved, and that he looked unusually old; but as she had always thought of him as an old man the change in his appearance did not move her. She told him she had been to see Miss Hatchard, and with what object. She saw that he was astonished; but he made no comment.

"I told her the housework was too hard for me, and I wanted to earn the money to pay for a hired girl. But I ain't going to pay for her: you've got to. I want to have some money of my own."

Mr. Royall's bushy black eyebrows were drawn together in a frown, and he sat drumming with ink-stained nails on the edge of his desk.

"What do you want to earn money for?" he asked.

"So's to get away when I want to."

"Why do you want to get away?"

Her contempt flashed out. "Do you suppose anybody'd stay at North Dormer if they could help it? You wouldn't, folks say!"

With lowered head he asked: "Where'd you go to?"

"Anywhere where I can earn my living. I'll try here first, and if I can't do it here I'll go somewhere else. I'll go up the Mountain if I have to." She paused on this threat, and saw that it had taken effect. "I want you should get Miss Hatchard and the selectmen to take me at the library: and I want a woman here in the house with me," she repeated.

Mr. Royall had grown exceedingly pale. When she ended he stood up ponderously, leaning against the desk; and for a second or two they looked at each other.

"See here," he said at length, as though utterance were difficult, "there's something I've been wanting to say to you; I'd ought to have said it before. I want you to marry me."

The girl still stared at him without moving. "I want you to marry me," he repeated, clearing his throat. "The minister'll be up here next Sunday and we can fix it up then. Or I'll drive you down to Hepburn to the Justice, and get it done there. I'll do whatever you say." His eyes fell under the merciless stare she continued to fix on him, and he shifted his weight uneasily from one foot to the other. As he stood there before her, unwieldy, shabby, disordered, the purple veins distorting the hands he pressed against the desk, and his long orator's jaw trembling with the effort of his avowal, he seemed like a hideous parody of the fatherly old man she had always known.

[4] Webster (1782–1852) was an American statesman noted for his powers as an orator.

"Marry you? Me?" she burst out with a scornful laugh. "Was that what you came to ask me the other night? What's come over you, I wonder? How long is it since you've looked at yourself in the glass?" She straightened herself, insolently conscious of her youth and strength. "I suppose you think it would be cheaper to marry me than to keep a hired girl. Everybody knows you're the closest man in Eagle County; but I guess you're not going to get your mending done for you that way twice."

Mr. Royall did not move while she spoke. His face was ash-coloured and his black eyebrows quivered as though the blaze of her scorn had blinded him. When she ceased he held up his hand.

"That'll do—that'll about do," he said. He turned to the door and took his hat from the hat-peg. On the threshold he paused. "People ain't been fair to me—from the first they ain't been fair to me," he said. Then he went out.

A few days later North Dormer learned with surprise that Charity had been appointed librarian of the Hatchard Memorial at a salary of eight dollars a month, and that old Verena Marsh, from the Creston Almshouse, was coming to live at lawyer Royall's and do the cooking.

III

It was not in the room known at the red house as Mr. Royall's "office" that he received his infrequent clients. Professional dignity and masculine independence made it necessary that he should have a real office, under a different roof; and his standing as the only lawyer of North Dormer required that the roof should be the same as that which sheltered the Town Hall and the post-office.

It was his habit to walk to this office twice a day, morning and afternoon. It was on the ground floor of the building, with a separate entrance, and a weathered name-plate on the door. Before going in he stepped in to the post-office for his mail —usually an empty ceremony—said a word or two to the town clerk, who sat across the passage in idle state, and then went over to the store on the opposite corner, where Carrick Fry, the storekeeper, always kept a chair for him, and where he was sure to find one or two selectmen leaning on the long counter, in an atmosphere of rope, leather, tar and coffee-beans. Mr. Royall, though monosyllabic at home, was not averse, in certain moods, to imparting his views to his fellow-townsmen; perhaps, also, he was unwilling that his rare clients should surprise him sitting, clerkless and unoccupied, in his dusty office. At any rate, his hours there were not much longer or more regular than Charity's at the library; the rest of the time he spent either at the store or in driving about the country on business connected with the insurance companies that he represented, or in sitting at home reading Bancroft's History of the United States[5] and the speeches of Daniel Webster.

Since the day when Charity had told him that she wished to succeed to Eudora Skeff's post their relations had undefinably but definitely changed. Lawyer Royall had kept his word. He had obtained the place for her at the cost of considerable manœuvering, as she guessed from the number of rival candidates, and from the

[5] George Bancroft (1800–1891) brought out and revised the volumes of his monumental history between 1834 and 1876.

acerbity with which two of them, Orma Fry and the eldest Targatt girl, treated her for nearly a year afterward. And he had engaged Verena Marsh to come up from Creston and do the cooking. Verena was a poor old widow, doddering and shiftless: Charity suspected that she came for her keep. Mr. Royall was too close a man to give a dollar a day to a smart girl when he could get a deaf pauper for nothing. But at any rate, Verena was there, in the attic just over Charity, and the fact that she was deaf did not greatly trouble the young girl.

Charity knew that what had happened on that hateful night would not happen again. She understood that, profoundly as she had despised Mr. Royall ever since, he despised himself still more profoundly. If she had asked for a woman in the house it was far less for her own defense than for his humiliation. She needed no one to defend her: his humbled pride was her surest protection. He had never spoken a word of excuse or extenuation; the incident was as if it had never been. Yet its consequences were latent in every word that he and she exchanged, in every glance they instinctively turned from each other. Nothing now would ever shake her rule in the red house.

On the night of her meeting with Miss Hatchard's cousin Charity lay in bed, her bare arms clasped under her rough head, and continued to think of him. She supposed that he meant to spend some time in North Dormer. He had said he was looking up the old houses in the neighbourhood; and though she was not very clear as to his purpose, or as to why anyone should look for old houses, when they lay in wait for one on every roadside, she understood that he needed the help of books, and resolved to hunt up the next day the volume she had failed to find, and any others that seemed related to the subject.

Never had her ignorance of life and literature so weighed on her as in reliving the short scene of her discomfiture. "It's no use trying to be anything in this place," she muttered to her pillow; and she shrivelled at the vision of vague metropolises, shining super-Nettletons, where girls in better clothes than Belle Balch's talked fluently of architecture to young men with hands like Lucius Harney's. Then she remembered his sudden pause when he had come close to the desk and had his first look at her. The sight had made him forget what he was going to say; she recalled the change in his face, and jumping up she ran over the bare boards to her washstand, found the matches, lit a candle, and lifted it to the square of looking-glass on the white-washed wall. Her small face, usually so darkly pale, glowed like a rose in the faint orb of light, and under her rumpled hair her eyes seemed deeper and larger than by day. Perhaps after all it was a mistake to wish they were blue. A clumsy band and button fastened her unbleached night-gown about the throat. She undid it, freed her thin shoulders, and saw herself a bride in low-necked satin, walking down an aisle with Lucius Harney. He would kiss her as they left the church. . . . She put down the candle and covered her face with her hands as if to imprison the kiss. At that moment she heard Mr. Royall's step as he came up the stairs to bed, and a fierce revulsion of feeling swept over her. Until then she had merely despised him; now deep hatred of him filled her heart. He became to her a horrible old man. . . .

The next day, when Mr. Royall came back to dinner, they faced each other in silence as usual. Verena's presence at the table was an excuse for their not talking, though her deafness would have permitted the freest interchange of confidences. But when the meal was over, and Mr. Royall rose from the table, he looked back at Charity, who had stayed to help the old woman clear away the dishes.

"I want to speak to you a minute," he said; and she followed him across the passage, wondering.

He seated himself in his black horse-hair arm-chair, and she leaned against the window, indifferently. She was impatient to be gone to the library, to hunt for the book on North Dormer.

"See here," he said, "why ain't you at the library the days you're supposed to be there?"

The question, breaking in on her mood of blissful abstraction, deprived her of speech, and she stared at him for a moment without answering.

"Who says I ain't?"

"There's been some complaints made, it appears. Miss Hatchard sent for me this morning—"

Charity's smouldering resentment broke into a blaze. "I know! Orma Fry, and that toad of a Targatt girl—and Ben Fry, like as not. He's going round with her. The low-down sneaks—I always knew they'd try to have me out! As if anybody ever came to the library, anyhow!"

"Somebody did yesterday, and you weren't there."

"Yesterday?" she laughed at her happy recollection. "At what time wasn't I there yesterday, I'd like to know?"

"Round about four o'clock."

Charity was silent. She had been so steeped in the dreamy remembrance of young Harney's visit that she had forgotten having deserted her post as soon as he had left the library.

"Who came at four o'clock?"

"Miss Hatchard did."

"Miss Hatchard? Why, she ain't ever been near the place since she's been lame. She couldn't get up the steps if she tried."

"She can be helped up, I guess. She was yesterday, anyhow, by the young fellow that's staying with her. He found you there, I understand, earlier in the afternoon; and he went back and told Miss Hatchard the books were in bad shape and needed attending to. She got excited, and had herself wheeled straight round; and when she got there the place was locked. So she sent for me, and told me about that, and about the other complaints. She claims you've neglected things, and that she's going to get a trained librarian."

Charity had not moved while he spoke. She stood with her head thrown back against the window-frame, her arms hanging against her sides, and her hands so tightly clenched that she felt, without knowing what hurt her, the sharp edge of her nails against her palms.

Of all Mr. Royall had said she had retained only the phrase: "He told Miss Hatchard the books were in bad shape." What did she care for the other charges against her? Malice or truth, she despised them as she despised her detractors. But that the stranger to whom she had felt herself so mysteriously drawn should have betrayed her! That at the very moment when she had fled up the hillside to think of him more deliciously he should have been hastening home to denounce her shortcomings! She remembered how, in the darkness of her room, she had covered her face to press his imagined kiss closer; and her heart raged against him for the liberty he had not taken.

"Well, I'll go," she said suddenly. "I'll go right off."

"Go where?" She heard the startled note in Mr. Royall's voice.

"Why, out of their old library: straight out, and never set foot in it again. They needn't think I'm going to wait round and let them say they've discharged me!"

"Charity—Charity Royall, you listen—" he began, getting heavily out of his chair; but she waved him aside, and walked out of the room.

Upstairs she took the library key from the place where she always hid it under her pincushion—who said she wasn't careful?—put on her hat, and swept down again and out into the street. If Mr. Royall heard her go he made no motion to detain her: his sudden rages probably made him understand the uselessness of reasoning with hers.

She reached the brick temple, unlocked the door and entered into the glacial twilight. "I'm glad I'll never have to sit in this old vault again when other folks are out in the sun!" she said aloud as the familiar chill took her. She looked with abhorrence at the long dingy rows of books, the sheep-nosed Minerva on her black pedestal, and the mild-faced young man in a high stock whose effigy pined above her desk. She meant to take out of the drawer her roll of lace and the library register, and go straight to Miss Hatchard to announce her resignation. But suddenly a great desolation overcame her, and she sat down and laid her face against the desk. Her heart was ravaged by life's cruellest discovery: the first creature who had come toward her out of the wilderness had brought her anguish instead of joy. She did not cry; tears came hard to her, and the storms of her heart spent themselves inwardly. But as she sat there in her dumb woe she felt her life to be too desolate, too ugly and intolerable.

"What have I ever done to it, that it should hurt me so?" she groaned, and pressed her fists against her lids, which were beginning to swell with weeping.

"I won't—I won't go there looking like a horror!" she muttered, springing up and pushing back her hair as if it stifled her. She opened the drawer, dragged out the register, and turned toward the door. As she did so it opened, and the young man from Miss Hatchard's came in whistling.

IV

He stopped and lifted his hat with a shy smile. "I beg your pardon," he said. "I thought there was no one here."

Charity stood before him, barring his way. "You can't come in. The library ain't open to the public Wednesdays."

"I know it's not; but my cousin gave me her key."

"Miss Hatchard's got no right to give her key to other folks, any more'n I have. I'm the librarian and I know the by-laws. This is my library."

The young man looked profoundly surprised.

"Why, I know it is; I'm so sorry if you mind my coming."

"I suppose you came to see what more you could say to set her against me? But you needn't trouble: it's my library today, but it won't be this time tomorrow. I'm on the way now to take her back the key and the register."

Young Harney's face grew grave, but without betraying the consciousness of guilt she had looked for.

"I don't understand," he said. "There must be some mistake. Why should I say things against you to Miss Hatchard—or to anyone?"

The apparent evasiveness of the reply caused Charity's indignation to overflow. "I don't know why you should. I could understand Orma Fry's doing it, because she's always wanted to get me out of here ever since the first day. I can't see why, when she's got her own home, and her father to work for her; nor Ida Targatt, neither, when she got a legacy from her step-brother on'y last year. But anyway we all live in the same place, and when it's a place like North Dormer it's enough to make people hate each other just to have to walk down the same street every day. But you don't live here, and you don't know anything about any of us, so what did you have to meddle for? Do you suppose the other girls'd have kept the books any better'n I did? Why, Orma Fry don't hardly know a book from a flat-iron! And what if I don't always sit round here doing nothing till it strikes five up at the church? Who cares if the library's open or shut? Do you suppose anybody ever comes here for books? What they'd like to come for is to meet the fellows they're going with—if I'd let 'em. But I wouldn't let Bill Sollas from over the hill hang round here waiting for the youngest Targatt girl, because I know him . . . that's all . . . even if I don't know about books all I ought to. . . ."

She stopped with a choking in her throat. Tremors of rage were running through her, and she steadied herself against the edge of the desk lest he should see her weakness.

What he saw seemed to affect him deeply, for he grew red under his sunburn, and stammered out, "But, Miss Royall, I assure you . . . I assure you . . ."

His distress inflamed her anger, and she regained her voice to fling back: "If I was you I'd have the nerve to stick to what I said!"

The taunt seemed to restore his presence of mind. "I hope I should if I knew; but I don't. Apparently something disagreeable has happened, for which you think I'm to blame. But I don't know what it is, because I've been up on Eagle Ridge ever since the early morning."

"I don't know where you've been this morning, but I know you were here in this library yesterday; and it was you that went home and told your cousin the books were in bad shape, and brought her round to see how I'd neglected them."

Young Harney looked sincerely concerned. "Was that what you were told? I don't wonder you're angry. The books *are* in bad shape, and as some are interesting it's a pity. I told Miss Hatchard they were suffering from dampness and lack of air; and I brought her here to show her how easily the place could be ventilated. I also told her you ought to have some one to help you do the dusting and airing. If you were given a wrong version of what I said I'm sorry; but I'm so fond of old books that I'd rather see them made into a bonfire than left to moulder away like these."

Charity felt her sobs rising and tried to stifle them in words. "I don't care what you say you told her. All I know is she thinks it's all my fault, and I'm going to lose my job, and I wanted it more'n anyone in the village, because I haven't got anybody belonging to me, the way other folks have. All I wanted was to put aside money enough to get away from here sometime. D'you suppose if it hadn't been for that I'd have kept on sitting day after day in this old vault?"

Of this appeal her hearer took up only the last question. "It *is* an old vault; but need it be? That's the point. And it's my putting the question to my cousin that seems to have been the cause of the trouble." His glance explored the melancholy penumbra of the long narrow room, resting on the blotched walls, the discoloured rows of books, and the stern rosewood desk surmounted by the portrait of the young Honorius. "Of course it's a bad job to do anything with a building jammed against a hill like this ridiculous mausoleum: you couldn't get a good draught through it without blowing a hole in the mountain. But it can be ventilated after a fashion, and the sun can be let in: I'll show you how if you like. . . ." The architect's passion for improvement had already made him lose sight of her grievance, and he lifted his stick instructively toward the cornice. But her silence seemed to tell him that she took no interest in the ventilation of the library, and turning back to her abruptly he held out both hands. "Look here—you don't mean what you said? You don't really think I'd do anything to hurt you?"

A new note in his voice disarmed her: no one had ever spoken to her in that tone.

"Oh, what *did* you do it for then?" she wailed. He had her hands in his, and she was feeling the smooth touch that she had imagined the day before on the hillside.

He pressed her hands lightly and let them go. "Why, to make things pleasanter for you here; and better for the books. I'm sorry if my cousin twisted around what I said. She's excitable, and she lives on trifles: I ought to have remembered that. Don't punish me by letting her think you take her seriously."

It was wonderful to hear him speak of Miss Hatchard as if she were a querulous baby: in spite of his shyness he had the air of power that the experience of cities probably gave. It was the fact of having lived in Nettleton that made lawyer Royall, in spite of his infirmities, the strongest man in North Dormer; and Charity was sure that this young man had lived in bigger places than Nettleton.

She felt that if she kept up her denunciatory tone he would secretly class her with Miss Hatchard; and the thought made her suddenly simple.

"It don't matter to Miss Hatchard how I take her. Mr. Royall says she's going to get a trained librarian; and I'd sooner resign than have the village say she sent me away."

"Naturally you would. But I'm sure she doesn't mean to send you away. At any rate, won't you give me the chance to find out first and let you know? It will be time enough to resign if I'm mistaken."

Her pride flamed into her cheeks at the suggestion of his intervening. "I don't want anybody should coax her to keep me if I don't suit."

He coloured too. "I give you my word I won't do that. Only wait till tomorrow, will you?" He looked straight into her eyes with his shy grey glance. "You can trust me, you know—you really can."

All the old frozen woes seemed to melt in her, and she murmured awkwardly, looking away from him: "Oh, I'll wait."

V

There had never been such a June in Eagle County. Usually it was a month of moods, with abrupt alternations of belated frost and midsummer heat; this year, day followed day in a sequence of temperate beauty. Every morning a breeze blew steadily from the hills. Toward noon it built up great canopies of white cloud that threw a cool shadow over fields and woods; then before sunset the clouds dissolved again, and the western light rained its unobstructed brightness on the valley.

On such an afternoon Charity Royall lay on a ridge above a sunlit hollow, her face pressed to the earth and the warm currents of the grass running through her. Directly in her line of vision a blackberry branch laid its frail white flowers and blue-green leaves against the sky. Just beyond, a tuft of sweet-fern uncurled between the beaded shoots of the grass, and a small yellow butterfly vibrated over them like a fleck of sunshine. This was all she saw; but she felt, above her and about her, the strong growth of the beeches clothing the ridge, the rounding of pale green cones on countless spruce-branches, the push of myriads of sweet-fern fronds in the cracks of the stony slope below the wood, and the crowding shoots of meadowsweet and yellow flags in the pasture beyond. All this bubbling of sap and slipping of sheaths and bursting of calyxes was carried to her on mingled currents of fragrance. Every leaf and bud and blade seemed to contribute its exhalation to the pervading sweetness in which the pungency of pine-sap prevailed over the spice of thyme and the subtle perfume of fern, and all were merged in a moist earth-smell that was like the breath of some huge sun-warmed animal.

Charity had lain there a long time, passive and sun-warmed as the slope on which she lay, when there came between her eyes and the dancing butterfly the sight of a man's foot in a large worn boot covered with red mud.

"Oh, don't!" she exclaimed, raising herself on her elbow and stretching out a warning hand.

"Don't what?" a hoarse voice asked above her head.

"Don't stamp on those bramble flowers, you dolt!" she retorted, springing to her knees. The foot paused and then descended clumsily on the frail branch, and raising her eyes she saw above her the bewildered face of a slouching man with a thin sunburnt beard, and white arms showing through his ragged shirt.

"Don't you ever *see* anything, Liff Hyatt?" she assailed him, as he stood before her with the look of a man who has stirred up a wasp's nest.

He grinned. "I seen you! That's what I come down for."

"Down from where?" she questioned, stooping to gather up the petals his foot had scattered.

He jerked his thumb toward the heights. "Been cutting down trees for Dan Targatt."

Charity sank back on her heels and looked at him musingly. She was not in the least afraid of poor Liff Hyatt, though he "came from the Mountain," and some of the girls ran when they saw him. Among the more reasonable he passed for a harmless creature, a sort of link between the mountain and civilized folk, who occasionally came down and did a little wood-cutting for a farmer when hands were short. Besides, she knew the Mountain people would never hurt her: Liff himself had told her so once when she was a little girl, and had met him one day at the edge of lawyer Royall's pasture. "They won't any of 'em touch you up there, f'ever you was to come up. . . . But I don't s'pose you will," he had added philosophically, looking at her new shoes, and at the red ribbon that Mrs. Royall had tied in her hair.

Charity had, in truth, never felt any desire to visit her birthplace. She did not care to have it known that she was of the Mountain, and was shy of being seen in talk with Liff Hyatt. But today she was not sorry to have him appear. A great many things had happened to her since the day when young Lucius Harney had entered the doors of the Hatchard Memorial, but none, perhaps, so unforeseen as the fact of her suddenly finding it a convenience to be on good terms with Liff Hyatt. She continued to look up curiously at his freckled weather-beaten face, with feverish hollows below the cheekbones and the pale yellow eyes of a harmless animal. "I wonder if he's related to me?" she thought, with a shiver of disdain.

"Is there any folks living in the brown house by the swamp, up under Porcupine?" she presently asked in an indifferent tone.

Liff Hyatt, for a while, considered her with surprise; then he scratched his head and shifted his weight from one tattered sole to the other.

"There's always the same folks in the brown house," he said with his vague grin.

"They're from up your way, ain't they?"

"Their name's the same as mine," he rejoined uncertainly.

Charity still held him with resolute eyes. "See here, I want to go there some day and take a gentleman with me that's boarding with us. He's up in these parts drawing pictures."

She did not offer to explain this statement. It was too far beyond Liff Hyatt's limitations for the attempt to be worth making. "He wants to see the brown house, and go all over it," she pursued.

Liff was still running his fingers perplexedly through his shock of straw-coloured hair. "Is it a fellow from the city?" he asked.

"Yes. He draws pictures of things. He's down there now drawing the Bonner house." She pointed to a chimney just visible over the dip of the pasture below the wood.

"The Bonner house?" Liff echoed incredulously.

"Yes. You won't understand—and it don't matter. All I say is: he's going to the Hyatts' in a day or two."

Liff looked more and more perplexed. "Bash is ugly sometimes in the afternoons."

"I know. But I guess he won't trouble me." She threw her head back, her eyes full on Hyatt's. "I'm coming too: you tell him."

"They won't none of them trouble you, the Hyatts won't. What d'you want to take a stranger with you, though?"

"I've told you, haven't I? You've got to tell Bash Hyatt."

He looked away at the blue mountains on the horizon; then his gaze dropped to the chimney-top below the pasture.

"He's down there now?"

"Yes."

He shifted his weight again, crossed his arms, and continued to survey the distant landscape. "Well, so long," he said at last, inconclusively; and turning away he shambled up the hillside. From the ledge above her, he paused to call down: "I wouldn't go there a Sunday"; then he clambered on till the trees closed in on him. Presently, from high overhead, Charity heard the ring of his axe.

She lay on the warm ridge, thinking of many things that the woodsman's appearance had stirred up in her. She knew nothing of her early life, and had never felt any curiosity about it: only a sullen reluctance to explore the corner of her memory where certain blurred images lingered. But all that had happened to her within the last few weeks had stirred her to the sleeping depths. She had become absorbingly interesting to herself, and everything that had to do with her past was illuminated by this sudden curiosity.

She hated more than ever the fact of coming from the Mountain; but it was no longer indifferent to her. Everything that in any way affected her was alive and vivid: even the hateful things had grown interesting because they were a part of herself.

"I wonder if Liff Hyatt knows who my mother was?" she mused; and it filled her with a tremor of surprise to think that some woman who was once young and slight, with quick motions of the blood like hers, had carried her in her breast, and watched her sleeping. She had always thought of her mother as so long dead as to be no more than a nameless pinch of earth; but now it occurred to her that the once-young woman might be alive, and wrinkled and elf-locked like the woman she had sometimes seen in the door of the brown house that Lucius Harney wanted to draw.

The thought brought her back to the central point in her mind, and she strayed away from the conjectures roused by Liff Hyatt's presence. Speculations concerning the past could not hold her long when the present was so rich, the future so rosy, and when Lucius Harney, a stone's throw away, was bending over his sketch-book, frowning, calculating, measuring, and then throwing his head back with the sudden smile that had shed its brightness over everything.

She scrambled to her feet, but as she did so she saw him coming up the pasture and dropped down on the grass to wait. When he was drawing and measuring one of "his houses," as she called them, she often strayed away by herself into the woods or up the hillside. It was partly from shyness that she did so: from a sense of inadequacy that came to her most painfully when her companion, absorbed in his job, forgot her ignorance and her inability to follow his least allusion, and plunged into a monologue on art and life. To avoid the awkwardness of listening with a blank face, and also to escape the surprised stare of the inhabitants of the houses before which he would abruptly pull up their horse and open his sketch-book, she slipped away to some spot from which, without being seen, she could watch him at work, or at least look down on the house he was drawing. She had not been displeased, at first, to have it known to North Dormer and the neighborhood that she was driving Miss Hatchard's cousin about the country in the buggy he had hired of lawyer Royall. She had always kept to herself, contemptuously aloof from village love-making, without exactly knowing whether her fierce pride was due to the sense of her tainted origin, or whether she was reserving herself for a more brilliant fate. Sometimes she envied the other girls their sentimental preoccupations, their long hours of inarticulate philandering with one of the few youths who still lingered in the village; but when she pictured herself curling her hair or putting a new ribbon on her hat for Ben Fry or one of the Sollas boys the fever dropped and she relapsed into indifference.

Now she knew the meaning of her disdains and reluctances. She had learned what she was worth when Lucius Harney, looking at her for the first time, had lost the thread of his speech, and leaned reddening on the edge of her desk. But another kind of shyness had been born in her: a terror of exposing to vulgar perils the sacred treasure of her happiness. She was not sorry to have the neighbors suspect her of "going with" a young man from the city; but she did not want it known to all the countryside how many hours of the long June days she spent with him. What she most feared was that the inevitable comments should reach Mr. Royall. Charity was instinctively aware that few things concerning her escaped the eyes of the silent man under whose roof she lived; and in spite of the latitude which North Dormer accorded to courting couples she had always felt that, on the day when she showed too open a preference, Mr. Royall might, as she phrased it, make her "pay for it." How, she did not know; and her fear was the greater because it was undefinable. If she had been accepting the attentions of one of the village youths she would have been less apprehensive: Mr. Royall could not prevent her marrying when she chose to. But everybody knew that "going with a city fellow" was a different and less straightforward affair: almost every village could show a victim of the perilous venture. And her dread of Mr. Royall's intervention gave a sharpened joy to the hours she spent with young Harney, and made her, at the same time, shy of being too generally seen with him.

As he approached she rose to her knees, stretching her arms above her head with the indolent gesture that was her way of expressing a profound well-being.

"I'm going to take you to that house up under Porcupine," she announced.

"What house? Oh, yes; that ramshackle place near the swamp, with the gipsy-looking people hanging about. It's curious that a house with traces of real architecture should have been built in such a place. But the people were a sulky-looking lot—do you suppose they'll let us in?"

"They'll do whatever I tell them," she said with assurance.

He threw himself down beside her. "Will they?" he rejoined with a smile. "Well, I should like to see what's left inside the house. And I should like to have a talk with the people. Who was it who was telling me the other day that they had come down from the Mountain?"

Charity shot a sideward look at him. It was the first time he had spoken of the Mountain except as a feature of the landscape. What else did he know about it, and about her relation to it? Her heart began to beat with the fierce impulse of resistance which she instinctively opposed to every imagined slight.

"The Mountain? I ain't afraid of the Mountain!"

Her tone of defiance seemed to escape him. He lay breast-down on the grass, breaking off sprigs of thyme and pressing them against his lips. Far off, above the folds of the nearer hills, the Mountain thrust itself up menacingly against a yellow sunset.

"I must go up there some day: I want to see it," he continued.

Her heart-beats slackened and she turned again to examine his profile. It was innocent of all unfriendly intention.

"What'd you want to go up the Mountain for?"

"Why, it must be rather a curious place. There's a queer colony up there, you know: sort of outlaws, a little independent kingdom. Of course you've heard them spoken of; but I'm told they have nothing to do with the people in the valleys—rather look down on them, in fact. I suppose they're rough customers; but they must have a good deal of character."

She did not quite know what he meant by having a good deal of character; but his tone was expressive of admiration, and deepened her dawning curiosity. It struck her now as strange that she knew so little about the Mountain. She had never asked, and no one had ever offered to enlighten her. North Dormer took the Mountain for granted, and implied its disparagement by an intonation rather than by explicit criticism.

"It's queer, you know," he continued, "that, just over there, on top of that hill, there should be a handful of people who don't give a damn for anybody."

The words thrilled her. They seemed the clue to her own revolts and defiances, and she longed to have him tell her more.

"I don't know much about them. Have they always been there?"

"Nobody seems to know exactly how long. Down at Creston they told me that the first colonists are supposed to have been men who worked on the railway that was built forty or fifty years ago between Springfield and Nettleton. Some of them took to drink, or got into trouble with the police, and went off—disappeared into the woods. A year or two later there was a report that they were living up on the Mountain. Then I suppose others joined them—and children were born. Now they say there are over a hundred people up there. They seem to be quite outside the jurisdiction of the valleys. No school, no church—and no sheriff ever goes up to see what they're about. But don't people ever talk of them at North Dormer?"

"I don't know. They say they're bad."

He laughed. "Do they? We'll go and see, shall we?"

She flushed at the suggestion, and turned her face to his. "You never heard, I suppose—I come from there. They brought me down when I was little."

"You?" He raised himself on his elbow, looking at her with sudden interest. "You're from the Mountain? How curious! I suppose that's why you're so different. . . ."

Her happy blood bathed her to the forehead. He was praising her—and praising her because she came from the Mountain!

"Am I . . . different?" she triumphed, with affected wonder.

"Oh, awfully!" He picked up her hand and laid a kiss on the sunburnt knuckles.

"Come," he said, "let's be off." He stood up and shook the grass from his loose grey clothes. "What a good day! Where are you going to take me tomorrow?"

VI

That evening after supper Charity sat alone in the kitchen and listened to Mr. Royall and young Harney talking in the porch.

She had remained indoors after the table had been cleared and old Verena had hobbled up to bed. The kitchen window was open, and Charity seated herself near it, her idle hands on her knee. The evening was cool and still. Beyond the black hills an amber west passed into pale green, and then to a deep blue in which a great star hung. The soft hoot of a little owl came through the dusk, and between its calls the men's voices rose and fell.

Mr. Royall's was full of a sonorous satisfaction. It was a long time since he had had anyone of Lucius Harney's quality to talk to: Charity divined that the young man symbolized all his ruined and unforgotten past. When Miss Hatchard had been called to Springfield by the illness of a widowed sister, and young Harney, by that time seriously embarked on his task of drawing and measuring all the old houses between

Nettleton and the New Hampshire border, had suggested the possibility of boarding at the red house in his cousin's absence, Charity had trembled lest Mr. Royall should refuse. There had been no question of lodging the young man: there was no room for him. But it appeared that he could still live at Miss Hatchard's if Mr. Royall would let him take his meals at the red house; and after a day's deliberation Mr. Royall consented.

Charity suspected him of being glad of the chance to make a little money. He had the reputation of being an avaricious man; but she was beginning to think he was probably poorer than people knew. His practice had become little more than a vague legend, revived only at lengthening intervals by a summons to Hepburn or Nettleton; and he appeared to depend for his living mainly on the scant produce of his farm, and on the commissions received from the few insurance agencies that he represented in the neighbourhood. At any rate, he had been prompt in accepting Harney's offer to hire the buggy at a dollar and a half a day; and his satisfaction with the bargain had manifested itself, unexpectedly enough, at the end of the first week, by his tossing a ten-dollar bill into Charity's lap as she sat one day retrimming her old hat.

"Here—go get yourself a Sunday bonnet that'll make all the other girls mad," he said, looking at her with a sheepish twinkle in his deep-set eyes; and she immediately guessed that the unwonted present—the only gift of money she had ever received from him—represented Harney's first payment.

But the young man's coming had brought Mr. Royall other than pecuniary benefit. It gave him, for the first time in years, a man's companionship. Charity had only a dim understanding of her guardian's needs; but she knew he felt himself above the people among whom he lived, and she saw that Lucius Harney thought him so. She was surprised to find how well he seemed to talk now that he had a listener who understood him; and she was equally struck by young Harney's friendly deference.

Their conversation was mostly about politics, and beyond her range; but tonight it had a peculiar interest for her, for they had begun to speak of the Mountain. She drew back a little, lest they should see she was in hearing.

"The Mountain? The Mountain?" she heard Mr. Royall say. "Why, the Mountain's a blot—that's what it is, sir, a blot. That scum up there ought to have been run in long ago—and would have, if the people down here hadn't been clean scared of them. The Mountain belongs to this township, and it's North Dormer's fault if there's a gang of thieves and outlaws living over there, in sight of us, defying the laws of their country. Why, there ain't a sheriff or a tax-collector or a coroner'd durst go up there. When they hear of trouble on the Mountain the selectmen look the other way, and pass an appropriation to beautify the town pump. The only man that ever goes up is the minister, and he goes because they send down and get him whenever there's any of them dies. They think a lot of Christian burial on the Mountain—but I never heard of their having the minister up to marry them. And they never trouble the Justice of the Peace either. They just herd together like the heathen."

He went on, explaining in somewhat technical language how the little colony of squatters had contrived to keep the law at bay, and Charity, with burning eagerness, awaited young Harney's comment; but the young man seemed more concerned to hear Mr. Royall's views than to express his own.

"I suppose you've never been up there yourself?" he presently asked.

"Yes, I have," said Mr. Royall with a contemptuous laugh. "The wiseacres down here told me I'd be done for before I got back; but nobody lifted a finger to hurt me. And I'd just had one of their gang sent up for seven years too."

"You went up after that?"

"Yes, sir: right after it. The fellow came down to Nettleton and ran amuck, the way they sometimes do. After they've done a wood-cutting job they come down and blow the money in; and this man ended up with manslaughter. I got him convicted, though they were scared of the Mountain even at Nettleton; and then a queer thing happened. The fellow sent for me to go and see him in gaol. I went, and this is what he says: 'The fool that defended me is a chicken-livered son of a ———— and all the rest of it,' he said. 'I've got a job to be done for me up on the Mountain, and you're the only man I seen in court that looks as if he'd do it.' He told me he had a child up there—or thought he had—a little girl; and he wanted her brought down and reared like a Christian. I was sorry for the fellow, so I went up and got the child." He paused, and Charity listened with a throbbing heart. "That's the only time I ever went up the Mountain," he concluded.

There was a moment's silence; then Harney spoke. "And the child—had she no mother?"

"Oh, yes: there was a mother. But she was glad enough to have her go. She'd have given her to anybody. They ain't half human up there. I guess the mother's dead by now, with the life she was leading. Anyhow, I've never heard of her from that day to this."

"My God, how ghastly," Harney murmured; and Charity, choking with humiliation, sprang to her feet and ran upstairs. She knew at last: knew that she was the child of a drunken convict and of a mother who wasn't "half human," and was glad to have her go; and she had heard this history of her origin related to the one being in whose eyes she longed to appear superior to the people about her! She had noticed that Mr. Royall had not named her, had even avoided any allusion that might identify her with the child he had brought down from the Mountain; and she knew it was out of regard for her that he had kept silent. But of what use was his discretion, since only that afternoon, misled by Harney's interest in the outlaw colony, she had boasted to him of coming from the Mountain? Now every word that had been spoken showed her how such an origin must widen the distance between them.

During his ten days' sojourn at North Dormer Lucius Harney had not spoken a word of love to her. He had intervened in her behalf with his cousin, and had convinced Miss Hatchard of her merits as a librarian; but that was a simple act of justice, since it was by his own fault that those merits had been questioned. He had asked her to drive him about the country when he hired lawyer Royall's buggy to go on his sketching expeditions; but that too was natural enough, since he was unfamiliar with the region. Lastly, when his cousin was called to Springfield, he had begged Mr. Royall to receive him as a boarder; but where else in North Dormer could he have boarded? Not with Carrick Fry, whose wife was paralysed, and whose large family crowded his table to over-flowing; not with the Targatts, who lived a mile up the road, nor with poor old Mrs. Hawes, who, since her eldest daughter had deserted her, barely had the strength to cook her own meals while Ally picked up her living as a seamstress. Mr. Royall's was the only house where the young man could have been offered a decent hospitality. There had been nothing, therefore, in the outward course of events to raise in Charity's breast the hopes with which it trembled.

But beneath the visible incidents resulting from Lucius Harney's arrival there ran an undercurrent as mysterious and potent as the influence that makes the forest break into leaf before the ice is off the pools.

The business on which Harney had come was authentic; Charity had seen the letter from a New York publisher commissioning him to make a study of the eighteenth century houses in the less familiar districts of New England. But incomprehensible as the whole affair was to her, and hard as she found it to understand why he paused enchanted before certain neglected and paintless houses, while others, refurbished and "improved" by the local builder, did not arrest a glance, she could not but suspect that Eagle County was less rich in architecture than he averred, and that the duration of his stay (which he had fixed at a month) was not unconnected with the look in his eyes when he had first paused before her in the library. Everything that had followed seemed to have grown out of that look: his way of speaking to her, his quickness in catching her meaning, his evident eagerness to prolong their excursions and to seize on every chance of being with her.

The signs of his liking were manifest enough; but it was hard to guess how much they meant, because his manner was so different from anything North Dormer had ever shown her. He was at once simpler and more deferential than any one she had known; and sometimes it was just when he was simplest that she most felt the distance between them. Education and opportunity had divided them by a width that no effort of hers could bridge, and even when his youth and his admiration brought him nearest, some chance word, some unconscious allusion, seemed to thrust her back across the gulf.

Never had it yawned so wide as when she fled up to her room carrying with her the echo of Mr. Royall's tale. Her first confused thought was the prayer that she might never see young Harney again. It was too bitter to picture him as the detached impartial listener to such a story. "I wish he'd go away: I wish he'd go tomorrow, and never come back!" she moaned to her pillow; and far into the night she lay there, in the disordered dress she had forgotten to take off, her whole soul a tossing misery on which her hopes and dreams spun about like drowning straws.

Of all this tumult only a vague heart-soreness was left when she opened her eyes the next morning. Her first thought was of the weather, for Harney had asked her to take him to the brown house under Porcupine, and then around by Hamblin; and as the trip was a long one they were to start at nine. The sun rose without a cloud, and earlier than usual she was in the kitchen, making cheese sandwiches, decanting buttermilk into a bottle, wrapping up slices of apple pie, and accusing Verena of having given away a basket she needed, which had always hung on a hook in the passage. When she came out into the porch, in her pink calico, which had run a little in the washing, but was still bright enough to set off her dark tints, she had such a triumphant sense of being a part of the sunlight and the morning that the last trace of her misery vanished. What did it matter where she came from, or whose child she was, when love was dancing in her veins, and down the road she saw young Harney coming toward her?

Mr. Royall was in the porch too. He had said nothing at breakfast, but when she came out in her pink dress, the basket in her hand, he looked at her with surprise. "Where you going to?" he asked.

"Why—Mr. Harney's starting earlier than usual today," she answered.

"Mr. Harney, Mr. Harney? Ain't Mr. Harney learned how to drive a horse yet?"

She made no answer, and he sat tilted back in his chair, drumming on the rail of the porch. It was the first time he had ever spoken of the young man in that tone, and Charity felt a faint chill of apprehension. After a moment he stood up and walked away toward the bit of ground behind the house, where the hired man was hoeing.

The air was cool and clear, with the autumnal sparkle that a north wind brings to the hills in early summer, and the night had been so still that the dew hung on everything, not as a lingering moisture, but in separate beads that glittered like diamonds on the ferns and grasses. It was a long drive to the foot of Porcupine: first across the valley, with blue hills bounding the open slopes; then down into the beech-woods, following the course of the Creston, a brown brook leaping over velvet ledges; then out again onto the farm-lands about Creston Lake, and gradually up the ridges of the Eagle Range. At last they reached the yoke of the hills, and before them opened another valley, green and wild, and beyond it more blue heights eddying away to the sky like the waves of a receding tide.

Harney tied the horse to a tree-stump, and they unpacked their basket under an aged walnut with a riven trunk out of which bumblebees darted. The sun had grown hot, and behind them was the noonday murmur of the forest. Summer insects danced on the air, and a flock of white butterflies fanned the mobile tips of the crimson fireweed. In the valley below not a house was visible; it seemed as if Charity Royall and young Harney were the only living beings in the great hollow of earth and sky.

Charity's spirits flagged and disquieting thoughts stole back on her. Young Harney had grown silent, and as he lay beside her, his arms under his head, his eyes on the network of leaves above him, she wondered if he were musing on what Mr. Royall had told him, and if it had really debased her in his thoughts. She wished he had not asked her to take him that day to the brown house; she did not want him to see the people she came from while the story of her birth was fresh in his mind. More than once she had been on the point of suggesting that they should follow the ridge and drive straight to Hamblin, where there was a little deserted house he wanted to see; but shyness and pride held her back. "He'd better know what kind of folks I belong to," she said to herself, with a somewhat forced defiance; for in reality it was shame that kept her silent.

Suddenly she lifted her hand and pointed to the sky. "There's a storm coming up."

He followed her glance and smiled. "Is it that scrap of cloud among the pines that frightens you?"

"It's over the Mountain; and a cloud over the Mountain always means trouble."

"Oh, I don't believe half the bad things you all say of the Mountain! But anyhow, we'll get down to the brown house before the rain comes."

He was not far wrong, for only a few isolated drops had fallen when they turned into the road under the shaggy flank of Porcupine, and came upon the brown house. It stood alone beside a swamp bordered with alder thickets and tall bulrushes. Not another dwelling was in sight, and it was hard to guess what motive could have actuated the early settler who had made his home in so unfriendly a spot.

Charity had picked up enough of her companion's erudition to understand what had attracted him to the house. She noticed the fan-shaped tracery of the broken light above the door, the flutings of the paintless pilasters at the corners, and the round window set in the gable; and she knew that, for reasons that still escaped her, these were things to be admired and recorded. Still, they had seen other houses far more "typical" (the word was Harney's); and as he threw the reins on the horse's neck he said with a slight shiver of repugnance: "We won't stay long."

Against the restless alders turning their white lining to the storm the house looked singularly desolate. The paint was almost gone from the clapboards, the window-panes were broken and patched with rags, and the garden was a poisonous tangle of nettles, burdocks and tall swamp-weeds over which big blue-bottles hummed.

At the sound of wheels a child with a tow-head and pale eyes like Liff Hyatt's peered over the fence and then slipped away behind an out-house. Harney jumped down and helped Charity out; and as he did so the rain broke on them. It came slantwise, on a furious gale, laying shrubs and young trees flat, tearing off their leaves like an autumn storm, turning the road into a river, and making hissing pools of every hollow. Thunder rolled incessantly through the roar of the rain, and a strange glitter of light ran along the ground under the increasing blackness.

"Lucky we're here after all," Harney laughed. He fastened the horse under a half-roofless shed, and wrapping Charity in his coat ran with her to the house. The boy had not reappeared, and as there was no response to their knocks Harney turned the door-handle and they went in.

There were three people in the kitchen to which the door admitted them. An old woman with a handkerchief over her head was sitting by the window. She held a sickly-looking kitten on her knees, and whenever it jumped down and tried to limp away she stooped and lifted it back without any change of her aged, unnoticing face. Another woman, the unkempt creature that Charity had once noticed in driving by, stood leaning against the window-frame and stared at them; and near the stove an unshaved man in a tattered shirt sat on a barrel asleep.

The place was bare and miserable and the air heavy with the smell of dirt and stale tobacco. Charity's heart sank. Old derided tales of the Mountain people came back to her, and the woman's stare was so disconcerting, and the face of the sleeping man so sodden and bestial, that her disgust was tinged with a vague dread. She was not afraid for herself; she knew the Hyatts would not be likely to trouble her; but she was not sure how they would treat a "city fellow."

Lucius Harney would certainly have laughed at her fears. He glanced about the room, uttered a general "How are you?" to which no one responded, and then asked the younger woman if they might take shelter till the storm was over.

She turned her eyes away from him and looked at Charity.

"You're the girl from Royall's, ain't you?"

The colour rose in Charity's face. "I'm Charity Royall," she said, as if asserting her right to the name in the very place where it might have been most open to question.

The woman did not seem to notice. "You kin stay," she merely said; then she turned away and stooped over a dish in which she was stirring something.

Harney and Charity sat down on a bench made of a board resting on two starch boxes. They faced a door hanging on a broken hinge, and through the crack they saw the eyes of the tow-headed boy and of a pale little girl with a scar across her cheek. Charity smiled, and signed to the children to come in; but as soon as they saw they were discovered they slipped away on bare feet. It occurred to her that they were afraid of rousing the sleeping man; and probably the woman shared their fear, for she moved about as noiselessly and avoided going near the stove.

The rain continued to beat against the house, and in one or two places it sent a stream through the patched panes and ran into pools on the floor. Every now and then the kitten mewed and struggled down, and the old woman stooped and caught it, holding it tight in her bony hands; and once or twice the man on the barrel half woke, changed his position and dozed again, his head falling forward on his hairy breast. As the minutes passed, and the rain still streamed against the windows, a loathing of the place and the people came over Charity. The sight of the weak-minded old woman, of the cowed children, and the ragged man sleeping off his liquor, made the setting of her own life seem a vision of peace and plenty. She thought of the kitchen at Mr. Royall's, with its scrubbed floor and dresser full of china, and the peculiar smell of yeast and coffee and soft-soap that she had always hated, but that now seemed the very symbol of household order. She saw Mr. Royall's room, with the high-backed horsehair chair, the faded rag carpet, the row of books on a shelf, the engraving of "The Surrender of Burgoyne"[6] over the stove, and the mat with a brown and white spaniel in a moss-green border. And then her mind travelled to Miss Hatchard's house, where all was freshness, purity and fragrance, and compared to which the red house had always seemed so poor and plain.

"This is where I belong—this is where I belong," she kept repeating to herself; but the words had no meaning for her. Every instinct and habit made her a stranger among these poor swamp-people living like vermin in their lair. With all her soul she wished she had not yielded to Harney's curiosity, and brought him there.

The rain had drenched her, and she began to shiver under the thin folds of her dress. The younger woman must have noticed it, for she went out of the room and came back with a broken teacup which she offered to Charity. It was half full of whiskey, and Charity shook her head; but Harney took the cup and put his lips to it. When he had set it down Charity saw him feel in his pocket and draw out a dollar; he hesitated a moment, and then put it back, and she guessed that he did not wish her to see him offering money to people she had spoken of as being her kin.

The sleeping man stirred, lifted his head and opened his eyes. They rested vacantly for a moment on Charity and Harney, and then closed again, and his head drooped; but a look of anxiety came into the woman's face. She glanced out of the window and then came up to Harney. "I guess you better go along now," she said. The young man understood and got to his feet. "Thank you," he said, holding out his hand. She seemed not to notice the gesture, and turned away as they opened the door.

The rain was still coming down, but they hardly noticed it: the pure air was like balm in their faces. The clouds were rising and breaking, and between their edges the light streamed down from remote blue hollows. Harney untied the horse, and they drove off through the diminishing rain, which was already beaded with sunlight.

---

[6] John Burgoyne (1722–1792), British general during the Revolution, was defeated at the Battle of Saratoga in October 1777.

For a while Charity was silent, and her companion did not speak. She looked timidly at his profile: it was graver than usual, as though he too were oppressed by what they had seen. Then she broke out abruptly: "Those people back there are the kind of folks I come from. They may be my relations, for all I know." She did not want him to think that she regretted having told him her story.

"Poor creatures," he rejoined. "I wonder why they came down to that fever-hole."

She laughed ironically. "To better themselves! It's worse up on the Mountain. Bash Hyatt married the daughter of the farmer that used to own the brown house. That was him by the stove, I suppose."

Harney seemed to find nothing to say and she went on: "I saw you take out a dollar to give to that poor woman. Why did you put it back?"

He reddened, and leaned forward to flick a swamp-fly from the horse's neck. "I wasn't sure—"

"Was it because you knew they were my folks, and thought I'd be ashamed to see you give them money?"

He turned to her with eyes full of reproach. "Oh, Charity—" It was the first time he had ever called her by her name. Her misery welled over.

"I ain't—I ain't ashamed. They're my people, and I ain't ashamed of them," she sobbed.

"My dear . . ." he murmured, putting his arm about her; and she leaned against him and wept out her pain.

It was too late to go around to Hamblin, and all the stars were out in a clear sky when they reached the North Dormer valley and drove up to the red house.

VII

Since her reinstatement in Miss Hatchard's favour Charity had not dared to curtail by a moment her hours of attendance at the library. She even made a point of arriving before the time, and showed a laudable indignation when the youngest Targatt girl, who had been engaged to help in the cleaning and rearranging of the books, came trailing in late and neglected her task to peer through the window at the Sollas boy. Nevertheless, "library days" seemed more than ever irksome to Charity after her vivid hours of liberty; and she would have found it hard to set a good example to her subordinate if Lucius Harney had not been commissioned, before Miss Hatchard's departure, to examine with the local carpenter the best means of ventilating the "Memorial."

He was careful to prosecute this inquiry on the days when the library was open to the public; and Charity was therefore sure of spending part of the afternoon in his company. The Targatt girl's presence, and the risk of being interrupted by some passer-by suddenly smitten with a thirst for letters, restricted their intercourse to the exchange of commonplaces; but there was a fascination to Charity in the contrast between these public civilities and their secret intimacy.

The day after their drive to the brown house was "library day," and she sat at her desk working at the revised catalogue, while the Targatt girl, one eye on the window, chanted out the titles of a pile of books. Charity's thoughts were far away, in the dismal house by the swamp, and under the twilight sky during the long drive home, when Lucius Harney had consoled her with endearing words. That day, for the first time since he had been boarding with them, he had failed to appear as usual at the midday meal. No message had come to explain his absence, and Mr. Royall who was more than usually taciturn, had betrayed no surprise, and made no comment. In itself this indifference was not particularly significant, for Mr. Royall, in common with most of his fellow-citizens, had a way of accepting events passively, as if he had long since come to the conclusion that no one who lived in North Dormer could hope to modify them. But to Charity, in the reaction from her mood of passionate exaltation, there was something disquieting in his silence. It was almost as if Lucius Harney had never had a part in their lives: Mr. Royall's imperturbable indifference seemed to relegate him to the domain of unreality.

As she sat at work, she tried to shake off her disappointment at Harney's non-appearing. Some trifling incident had probably kept him from joining them at midday; but she was sure he must be eager to see her again, and that he would not want to wait till they met at supper, between Mr. Royall and Verena. She was wondering what his first words would be, and trying to devise a way of getting rid of the Targatt girl before he came, when she heard steps outside, and he walked up the path with Mr. Miles.

The clergyman from Hepburn seldom came to North Dormer except when he drove over to officiate at the old white church which, by an unusual chance, happened to belong to the Episcopal communion. He was a brisk affable man, eager to make the most of the fact that a little nucleus of "church-people" had survived in the sectarian wilderness, and resolved to undermine the influence of the ginger-bread-coloured Baptist chapel at the other end of the village; but he was kept busy by parochial work at Hepburn, where there were paper-mills and saloons, and it was not often that he could spare time for North Dormer.

Charity, who went to the white church (like all the best people in North Dormer), admired Mr. Miles, and had even, during the memorable trip to Nettleton, imagined herself married to a man who had such a straight nose and such a beautiful way of speaking, and who lived in a brown-stone rectory covered with Virginia creeper. It had been a shock to discover the privilege was already enjoyed by a lady with crimped hair and a large baby; but the arrival of Lucius Harney had long since banished Mr. Miles from Charity's dreams, and as he walked up the path at Harney's side she saw him as he really was: a fat middle-aged man with a baldness showing under his clerical hat, and spectacles on his Grecian nose. She wondered what had called him to North Dormer on a weekday, and felt a little hurt that Harney should have brought him to the library.

It presently appeared that his presence there was due to Miss Hatchard. He had been spending a few days at Springfield, to fill a friend's pulpit, and had been consulted by Miss Hatchard as to young Harney's plan for ventilating the "Memorial." To lay hands on the Hatchard ark was a grave matter, and Miss Hatchard, always full of scruples, and of scruples about her scruples (it was Harney's phrase), wished to have Mr. Miles's opinion before deciding.

"I couldn't," Mr. Miles explained, "quite make out from your cousin what changes you wanted to make, and as the other trustees did not understand either I thought I had better drive over and take a look—though I'm sure," he added, turning his friendly spectacles on the young man, "that no one could be more competent—but of course this spot has its peculiar sanctity!"

"I hope a little fresh air won't desecrate it," Harney laughingly rejoined; and they walked to the other end of the library while he set forth his idea to the Rector.

Mr. Miles had greeted the two girls with his usual friendliness, but Charity saw that he was occupied with other things, and she presently became aware, by the scraps of conversation drifting over to her, that he was still under the charm of his visit to Springfield, which appeared to have been full of agreeable incidents.

"Ah, the Coopersons . . . yes, you know them, of course," she heard. "That's a fine old house! And Ned Cooperson has collected some really remarkable impressionist pictures. . . ." The names he cited were unknown to Charity. "Yes; yes; the Schaefer quartette played at Lyric Hall on Saturday evening; and on Monday I had the privilege of hearing them again at the Towers. Beautifully done . . . Bach and Beethoven . . . a lawn-party first . . . I saw Miss Balch several times, by the way . . . looking extremely handsome. . . ."

Charity dropped her pencil and forgot to listen to the Targatt girl's sing-song. Why had Mr. Miles suddenly brought up Annabel Balch's name?

"Oh, really?" she heard Harney rejoin; and, raising his stick, he pursued: "You see, my plan is to move these shelves away, and open a round window in this wall, on the axis of the one under the pediment."

"I suppose she'll be coming up here later to stay with Miss Hatchard?" Mr. Miles went on, following on his train of thought; then, spinning about and tilting his head back: "Yes, yes, I see—I understand: that will give a draught without materially altering the look of things. I can see no objection."

The discussion went on for some minutes, and gradually the two men moved back toward the desk. Mr. Miles stopped again and looked thoughtfully at Charity. "Aren't you a little pale, my dear? Not overworking? Mr. Harney tells me you and Mamie are giving the library a thorough overhauling." He was always careful to remember his parishioners' Christian names, and at the right moment he bent his benignant spectacles on the Targatt girl.

Then he turned to Charity. "Don't take things hard, my dear; don't take things hard. Come down and see Mrs. Miles and me some day at Hepburn," he said, pressing her hand and waving a farewell to Mamie Targatt. He went out of the library, and Harney followed him.

Charity thought she detected a look of constraint in Harney's eyes. She fancied he did not want to be alone with her; and with a sudden pang she wondered if he repented the tender things he had said to her the night before. His words had been more fraternal than lover-like; but she had lost their exact sense in the caressing warmth of his voice. He had made her feel that the fact of her being a waif from the Mountain was only another reason for holding her close and soothing her with consolatory murmurs; and when the drive was over, and she got out of the buggy, tired, cold, and aching with emotion, she stepped as if the ground were a sunlit wave and she the spray on its crest.

Why, then, had his manner suddenly changed, and why did he leave the library with Mr. Miles? Her restless imagination fastened on the name of Annabel Balch: from the moment it had been mentioned she fancied that Harney's expression had altered. Annabel Balch at a garden-party at Springfield, looking "extremely handsome" . . . perhaps Mr. Miles had seen her there at the very moment when Charity and Harney were sitting in the Hyatts' hovel, between a drunkard and a half-witted old woman! Charity did not know exactly what a garden-party was, but her glimpse of the flower-edged lawns of Nettleton helped her to visualize the scene, and envious recollections of the "old things" which Miss Balch avowedly "wore out" when she came to North Dormer made it only too easy to picture her in her splendour. Charity understood what associations the name must have called up, and felt the uselessness of struggling against the unseen influences in Harney's life.

When she came down from her room for supper he was not there; and while she waited in the porch she recalled the tone in which Mr. Royall had commented the day before on their early start. Mr. Royall sat at her side, his chair tilted back, his broad black boots with side-elastics resting against the lower bar of the railings. His rumpled grey hair stood up above his forehead like the crest of an angry bird, and the leather-brown of his veined cheeks was blotched with red. Charity knew that those red spots were the signs of a coming explosion.

Suddenly he said: "Where's supper? Has Verena Marsh slipped up again on her soda-biscuits?"

Charity threw a startled glance at him. "I presume she's waiting for Mr. Harney."

"Mr. Harney, is she? She'd better dish up, then. He ain't coming." He stood up, walked to the door, and called out, in the pitch necessary to penetrate the old woman's tympanum: "Get along with the supper, Verena."

Charity was trembling with apprehension. Something had happened—she was sure of it now—and Mr. Royall knew what it was. But not for the world would she have gratified him by showing her anxiety. She took her usual place, and he seated himself opposite, and poured out a strong cup of tea before passing her the tea-pot. Verena brought some scrambled eggs, and he piled his plate with them. "Ain't you going to take any?" he asked. Charity roused herself and began to eat.

The tone with which Mr. Royall had said "He's not coming" seemed to her full of an ominous satisfaction. She saw that he had suddenly begun to hate Lucius Harney, and guessed herself to be the cause of this change of feeling. But she had no means of finding out whether some act of hostility on his part had made the young man stay away, or whether he simply wished to avoid seeing her again after their drive back from the brown house. She ate her supper with a studied show of indifference, but she knew that Mr. Royall was watching her and that her agitation did not escape him.

After supper she went up to her room. She heard Mr. Royall cross the passage, and presently the sounds below her window showed that he had returned to the porch. She seated herself on her bed and began to struggle against the desire to go down and ask him what had happened. "I'd rather die than do it," she muttered to herself. With a word he could have relieved her uncertainty: but never would she gratify him by saying it.

She rose and leaned out of the window. The twilight had deepened into night, and she watched the frail curve of the young moon dropping to the edge of the hills. Through the darkness she saw one or two figures moving down the road; but the evening was too cold for loitering, and presently the strollers disappeared. Lamps were beginning to show here and there in the windows. A bar of light brought out the whiteness of a clump of lilies in the Hawes's yard: and farther down the street Carrick Fry's Rochester lamp cast its bold illumination on the rustic flower-tub in the middle of his grass-plot.

For a long time she continued to lean in the window. But a fever of unrest consumed her, and finally she went downstairs, took her hat from its hook, and swung out of the house. Mr. Royall sat in the porch, Verena beside him, her old hands crossed on her patched skirt. As Charity went down the steps Mr. Royall called after her: "Where you going?" She could easily have answered: "To Orma's," or "Down to the Targatts' "; and either answer might have been true, for she had no purpose. But she swept on in silence, determined not to recognize his right to question her.

At the gate she paused and looked up and down the road. The darkness drew her, and she thought of climbing the hill and plunging into the depths of the larch-wood above the pasture. Then she glanced irresolutely along the street, and as she did so a gleam appeared through the spruces at Miss Hatchard's gate. Lucius Harney was there, then—he had not gone down to Hepburn with Mr. Miles, as she had at first imagined. But where had he taken his evening meal, and what caused him to stay away from Mr. Royall's? The light was positive proof of his presence, for Miss Hatchard's servants were away on a holiday, and her farmer's wife came only in the mornings, to make the young man's bed and prepare his coffee. Beside that lamp he was doubtless sitting at this moment. To know the truth Charity had only to walk half the length of the village, and knock at the lighted window. She hesitated a minute or two longer, and then turned toward Miss Hatchard's.

She walked quickly, straining her eyes to detect anyone who might be coming along the street; and before reaching the Frys' she crossed over to avoid the light from their window. Whenever she was unhappy she felt herself at bay against a pitiless world, and a kind of animal secretiveness possessed her. But the street was empty and she passed unnoticed through the gate and up the path to the house. Its white front glimmered indistinctly through the trees, showing only one oblong of light on the lower floor. She had supposed that the lamp was in Miss Hatchard's sitting-room; but she now saw that it shone through a window at the farther corner of the house. She did not know the room to which this window belonged, and she paused under the trees, checked by a sense of strangeness. Then she moved on, treading softly on the short grass, and keeping so close to the house that whoever was in the room, even if roused by her approach, would not be able to see her.

The window opened on a narrow verandah with a trellised arch. She leaned close to the trellis, and parting the sprays of clematis that covered it looked into a corner of the room. She saw the foot of a mahogany bed, an engraving on the wall, a washstand on which a towel had been tossed, and one end of the green-covered table which held the lamp. Half of the lamp-shade projected into her field of vision, and just under it two smooth sunburnt hands, one holding a pencil and the other a ruler, were moving to and fro over a drawing-board.

Her heart jumped and then stood still. He was there, a few feet away; and while her soul was tossing on seas of woe he had been quietly sitting at his drawing-board. The sight of those two hands, moving with their usual skill and precision, woke her out of her dream. Her eyes were opened to the disproportion between what she had felt and the cause of her agitation; and she was turning away from the window when one hand abruptly pushed aside the drawing-board and the other flung down the pencil.

Charity had often noticed Harney's loving care of his drawings, and the neatness and method with which he carried on and concluded each task. The impatient sweeping aside of the drawing-board seemed to reveal a new mood. The gesture suggested sudden discouragement, or distaste for his work, and she wondered if he too were agitated by secret perplexities. Her impulse of flight was checked; she stepped up on the verandah and looked into the room.

Harney had put his elbows on the table and was resting his chin on his locked hands. He had taken off his coat and waistcoat, and unbuttoned the low collar of his flannel shirt; she saw the vigorous lines of his young throat, and the root of the muscles where they joined the chest. He sat staring straight ahead of him, a look of weariness and self-disgust on his face: it was almost as if he had been gazing at a distorted reflection of his own features. For a moment Charity looked at him with a kind of terror, as if he had been a stranger under familiar lineaments; then she glanced past him and saw on the floor an open portmanteau half full of clothes. She understood that he was preparing to leave, and that he had probably decided to go without seeing her. She saw that the decision, from whatever cause it was taken, had disturbed him deeply; and she immediately concluded that his change of plan was due to some surreptitious interference of Mr. Royall's. All her old resentments and rebellions flamed up, confusedly mingled with the yearning roused by Harney's nearness. Only a few hours earlier she had felt secure in his comprehending pity; now she was flung back on herself, doubly alone after that moment of communion.

Harney was still unaware of her presence. He sat without moving, moodily staring before him at the same spot in the wall-paper. He had not even had the energy to finish his packing, and his clothes and papers lay on the floor about the portmanteau. Presently he unlocked his clasped hands and stood up; and Charity, drawing back hastily, sank down on the step of the verandah. The night was so dark that there was not much chance of his seeing her unless he opened the window, and before that she would have time to slip away and be lost in the shadow of the trees. He stood for a minute or two looking around the room with the same expression of self-disgust, as if he hated himself and everything about him; then he sat down again at the table, drew a few more strokes, and threw his pencil aside. Finally he walked across the floor, kicking the portmanteau out of his way, and lay down on the bed, folding his arms under his head, and staring up morosely at the ceiling. Just so, Charity had seen him at her side, on the grass or the pine-needles, his eyes fixed on the sky, and pleasure flashing over his face like the flickers of sun the branches shed on it. But now the face was so changed that she hardly knew it; and grief at his grief gathered in her throat, rose to her eyes and ran over.

She continued to crouch on the steps, holding her breath and stiffening herself into complete immobility. One motion of her hand, one tap on the pane, and she could picture the sudden change in his face. In every pulse of her rigid body she was aware of the welcome his eyes and lips would give her; but something kept her from moving. It was not the fear of any sanction, human or heavenly; she had never in her life been afraid. It was simply that she had suddenly understood what would happen if she went in. It was the thing that *did* happen between young men and girls, and that North Dormer ignored in public and snickered over on the sly. It was what Miss Hatchard was still ignorant of, but every girl of Charity's class knew about before she left school. It was what had happened to Ally Hawes's sister Julia, and had ended in her going to Nettleton, and in people's never mentioning her name.

It did not, of course, always end so sensationally; nor, perhaps, on the whole, so untragically. Charity had always suspected that the shunned Julia's fate might have its compensations. There were other worse endings that the village knew of, mean, miserable, unconfessed; other lives that went on drearily, without visible change, in the same cramped setting of hypocrisy. But these were not the reasons that held her back. Since the day before, she had known exactly what she would feel if Harney should take her in his arms: the melting of palm into palm and mouth on mouth, and the long flame burning her from head to foot. But mixed with this feeling was another: the wondering pride in his liking for her, the startled softness that his sympathy had put into her heart. Sometimes, when her youth flushed up in her, she had imagined yielding like other girls to furtive caresses in the twilight; but she could not so cheapen herself to Harney. She did not know why he was going; but since he was going she felt she must do nothing to deface the image of her that he carried away. If he wanted her he must seek her: he must not be surprised into taking her as girls like Julia Hawes were taken. . . .

No sound came from the sleeping village, and in the deep darkness of the garden she heard now and then a secret rustle of branches, as though some night-bird brushed them. Once a footfall passed the gate, and she shrank back into her corner; but the steps died away and left a profounder quiet. Her eyes were still on Harney's tormented face: she felt she could not move till he moved. But she was beginning to grow numb from her constrained position, and at times her thoughts were so indistinct that she seemed to be held there only by a vague weight of weariness.

A long time passed in this strange vigil. Harney still lay on the bed, motionless and with fixed eyes, as though following his vision to its bitter end. At last he stirred and changed his attitude slightly, and Charity's heart began to tremble. But he only flung out his arms and sank back into his former position. With a deep sigh he tossed the hair from his forehead; then his whole body relaxed, his head turned sideways on the pillow, and she saw that he had fallen asleep. The sweet expression came back to his lips, and the haggardness faded from his face, leaving it as fresh as a boy's.

She rose and crept away.

VIII

She had lost the sense of time, and did not know how late it was till she came out into the street and saw that all the windows were dark between Miss Hatchard's and the Royall house.

As she passed from under the black pall of the Norway spruces she fancied she saw two figures in the shade about the duck-pond. She drew back and watched; but nothing moved, and she had stared so long into the lamp-lit room that the darkness confused her, and she thought she must have been mistaken.

She walked on, wondering whether Mr. Royall was still in the porch. In her exalted mood she did not greatly care whether he was waiting for her or not: she seemed to be floating high over life, on a great cloud of misery beneath which everyday realities had dwindled to mere specks in space. But the porch was empty, Mr. Royall's hat hung on its peg in the passage, and the kitchen lamp had been left to light her to bed. She took it and went up.

The morning hours of the next day dragged by without incident. Charity had imagined that, in some way or other, she would learn whether Harney had already left; but Verena's deafness prevented her being a source of news, and no one came to the house who could bring enlightenment.

Mr. Royall went out early, and did not return till Verena had set the table for the midday meal. When he came in he went straight to the kitchen and shouted to the old woman: "Ready for dinner—" then he turned into the dining-room, where Charity was already seated. Harney's plate was in its usual place, but Mr. Royall offered no explanation of his absence, and Charity asked none. The feverish exaltation of the night before had dropped, and she said to herself that he had gone away, indifferently, almost callously, and that now her life would lapse again into the narrow rut out of which he had lifted it. For a moment she was inclined to sneer at herself for not having used the arts that might have kept him.

She sat at table till the meal was over, lest Mr. Royall should remark on her leaving; but when he stood up she rose also, without waiting to help Verena. She had her foot on the stairs when he called to her to come back.

"I've got a headache. I'm going up to lie down."

"I want you should come in here first; I've got something to say to you."

She was sure from his tone that in a moment she would learn what every nerve in her ached to know; but as she turned back she made a last effort of indifference.

Mr. Royall stood in the middle of the office, his thick eyebrows beetling, his lower jaw trembling a little. At first she thought he had been drinking; then she saw that he was sober, but stirred by a deep and stern emotion totally unlike his usual transient angers. And suddenly she understood that, until then, she had never really noticed him or thought about him. Except on the occasion of his one offense he had been to her merely the person who is always there, the unquestioned central fact of life, as inevitable but as uninteresting as North Dormer itself, or any of the other conditions fate had laid on her. Even then she had regarded him only in relation to herself, and had never speculated as to his own feelings, beyond instinctively concluding that he would not trouble her again in the same way. But now she began to wonder what he was really like.

He had grasped the back of his chair with both hands, and stood looking hard at her. At length he said: "Charity, for once let's you and me talk together like friends."

Instantly she felt that something had happened, and that he held her in his hand.

"Where is Mr. Harney? Why hasn't he come back? Have you sent him away?" she broke out, without knowing what she was saying.

The change in Mr. Royall frightened her. All the blood seemed to leave his veins and against his swarthy pallor the deep lines in his face looked black.

"Didn't he have time to answer some of those questions last night? You was with him long enough!" he said.

Charity stood speechless. The taunt was so unrelated to what had been happening in her soul that she hardly understood it. But the instinct of self-defense awoke in her.

"Who says I was with him last night?"

"The whole place is saying it by now."

"Then it was you that put the lie into their mouths.—Oh, how I've always hated you!" she cried.

She had expected a retort in kind, and it startled her to hear her exclamation sounding on through silence.

"Yes, I know," Mr. Royall said slowly. "But that ain't going to help us much now."

"It helps me not to care a straw what lies you tell about me!"

"If they're lies, they're not my lies: my Bible oath on that, Charity. I didn't know where you were: I wasn't out of this house last night."

She made no answer and he went on: "Is it a lie that you were seen coming out of Miss Hatchard's nigh onto midnight?"

She straightened herself with a laugh, all her reckless insolence recovered. "I didn't look to see what time it was."

"You lost girl . . . you . . . you . . . Oh, my God, why did you tell me?" he broke out, dropping into his chair, his head bowed down like an old man's.

Charity's self-possession had returned with the sense of her danger. "Do you suppose I'd take the trouble to lie to *you?* Who are you, anyhow, to ask me where I go to when I go out at night?"

Mr. Royall lifted his head and looked at her. His face had grown quiet and almost gentle, as she remembered seeing it sometimes when she was a little girl, before Mrs. Royall died.

"Don't let's go on like this, Charity. It can't do any good to either of us. You were seen going into that fellow's house . . . you were seen coming out of it. . . . I've watched this thing coming, and I've tried to stop it. As God sees me, I have. . . ."

"Ah, it *was* you, then? I knew it was you that sent him away!"

He looked at her in surprise. "Didn't he tell you so? I thought he understood." He spoke slowly, with difficult pauses, "I didn't name you to him: I'd have cut my hand off sooner. I just told him I couldn't spare the horse any longer; and that the cooking was getting too heavy for Verena. I guess he's the kind that's heard the same thing before. Anyhow, he took it quietly enough. He said his job here was about done, anyhow; and there didn't another word pass between us. . . . If he told you otherwise he told you an untruth."

Charity listened in a cold trance of anger. It was nothing to her what the village said . . . but all this fingering of her dreams!

"I've told you he didn't tell me anything. I didn't speak with him last night."

"You didn't speak with him?"

"No. . . . It's not that I care what any of you say . . . but you may as well know. Things ain't between us the way you think . . . and the other people in this place. He was kind to me; he was my friend; and all of a sudden he stopped coming, and I knew it was you that done it—*you!*" All her unreconciled memory of the past flamed out at him. "So I went there last night to find out what you'd said to him: that's all."

Mr. Royall drew a heavy breath. "But then—if he wasn't there, what were you doing there all that time?—Charity, for pity's sake, tell me. I've got to know, to stop their talking."

This pathetic abdication of all authority over her did not move her: she could feel only the outrage of his interference.

"Can't you see that I don't care what anybody says? It's true I went there to see him; and he was in his room, and I stood outside for ever so long and watched him; but I dursn't go in for fear he'd think I'd come after him. . . ." She felt her voice breaking, and gathered it up in a last defiance. "As long as I live I'll never forgive you!" she cried.

Mr. Royall made no answer. He sat and pondered with sunken head, his veined hands clasped about the arms of his chair. Age seemed to have come down on him as winter comes on the hills after a storm. At length he looked up.

"Charity, you say you don't care; but you're the proudest girl I know, and the last to want people to talk against you. You know there's always eyes watching you: you're handsomer and smarter than the rest, and that's enough. But till lately you've never given them a chance. Now they've got it, and they're going to use it. I believe what you say, but they won't. . . . It was Mrs. Tom Fry seen you going in . . . and two or three of them watched for you to come out again. . . . You've been with the fellow all day long every day since he come here . . . and I'm a lawyer, and I know how hard slander dies." He paused, but she stood motionless, without giving him any sign of acquiescence or even of attention. "He's a pleasant fellow to talk to—I liked having him here myself. The young men up here ain't had his chances. But there's one thing as old as the hills and as plain as daylight: if he'd wanted you the right way he'd have said so."

Charity did not speak. It seemed to her that nothing could exceed the bitterness of hearing such words from such lips.

Mr. Royall rose from his seat. "See here, Charity Royall: I had a shameful thought once, and you've made me pay for it. Isn't that score pretty near wiped out? . . . There's a streak in me I ain't always master of; but I've always acted straight to you but that once. And you've known I would—you've trusted me. For all your sneers and your mockery you've always known I loved you the way a man loves a decent woman. I'm a good many years older than you, but I'm head and shoulders above this place and everybody in it, and you know that too. I slipped up once, but that's no reason for not starting again. If you'll come with me I'll do it. If you'll marry me we'll leave here and settle in some big town, where there's men, and business, and things doing. It's not too late for me to find an opening. . . . I can see it by the way folks treat me when I go down to Hepburn or Nettleton. . . ."

Charity made no movement. Nothing in his appeal reached her heart, and she thought only of words to wound and wither. But a growing lassitude restrained her. What did anything matter that he was saying? She saw the old life closing in on her, and hardly heeded his fanciful picture of renewal.

"Charity—Charity—say you'll do it," she heard him urge, all his lost years and wasted passion in his voice.

"Oh, what's the use of all this? When I leave here it won't be with you."

She moved toward the door as she spoke, and he stood up and placed himself between her and the threshold. He seemed suddenly tall and strong, as though the extremity of his humiliation had given him new vigour.

"That's all, is it? It's not much." He leaned against the door, so towering and powerful that he seemed to fill the narrow room. "Well, then—look here. . . . You're right: I've no claim on you—why should you look at a broken man like me? You want the other fellow . . . and I don't blame you. You picked out the best when you seen it . . . well, that was always my way." He fixed his stern eyes on her, and she had the sense that the struggle within him was at its highest. "Do you want him to marry you?" he asked.

They stood and looked at each other for a long moment, eye to eye, with the terrible equality of courage that sometimes made her feel as if she had his blood in her veins.

"Do you want him to—say? I'll have him here in an hour if you do. I ain't been in the law thirty years for nothing. He's hired Carrick Fry's team to take him to Hepburn, but he ain't going to start for another hour. And I can put things to him so he won't be long deciding. . . . He's soft: I could see that. I don't say you won't be sorry afterward—but, by God, I'll give you the chance to be, if you say so."

She heard him out in silence, too remote from all he was feeling and saying for any sally of scorn to relieve her. As she listened, there flitted through her mind the vision of Liff Hyatt's muddy boot coming down on the white bramble-flowers. The same thing had happened now; something transient and exquisite had flowered in her, and she had stood by and seen it trampled to earth. While the thought passed through her she was aware of Mr. Royall, still leaning against the door, but crestfallen, diminished, as though her silence were the answer he most dreaded.

"I don't want any chance you can give me: I'm glad he's going away," she said.

He kept his place a moment longer, his hand on the door-knob. "Charity!" he pleaded. She made no answer, and he turned the knob and went out. She heard him fumble with the latch of the front door, and saw him walk down the steps. He passed out of the gate, and his figure, stooping and heavy, receded slowly up the street.

For a while she remained where he had left her. She was still trembling with the humiliation of his last words, which rang so loud in her ears that it seemed as though they must echo through the village, proclaiming her a creature to lend herself to such vile suggestions. Her shame weighed on her like a physical oppression: the roof and walls seemed to be closing in on her, and she was seized by the impulse to get away, under the open sky, where there would be room to breathe. She went to the front door, and as she did so Lucius Harney opened it.

He looked graver and less confident than usual, and for a moment or two neither of them spoke. Then he held out his hand. "Are you going out?" he asked. "May I come in?"

Her heart was beating so violently that she was afraid to speak, and stood looking at him with tear-dilated eyes; then she became aware of what her silence must betray, and said quickly: "Yes: come in."

She led the way into the dining-room, and they sat down on opposite sides of the table, the cruet-stand and japanned bread-basket between them. Harney had laid his straw hat on the table, and as he sat there, in his easy-looking summer clothes, a brown tie knotted under his flannel collar, and his smooth brown hair brushed back from his forehead, she pictured him as she had seen him the night before, lying on his bed, with the tossed locks falling into his eyes, and his bare throat rising out of his unbuttoned shirt. He had never seemed so remote as at the moment when that vision flashed through her mind.

"I'm so sorry it's good-bye: I suppose you know I'm leaving," he began, abruptly and awkwardly; she guessed that he was wondering how much she knew of his reasons for going.

"I presume you found your work was over quicker than what you expected," she said.

"Well, yes—that is, no: there are plenty of things I should have liked to do. But my holiday's limited; and now that Mr. Royall needs the horse for himself it's rather difficult to find means of getting about."

"There ain't any too many teams for hire around here," she acquiesced; and there was another silence.

"These days here have been—awfully pleasant: I wanted to thank you for making them so," he continued, his colour rising.

She could not think of any reply, and he went on: "You've been wonderfully kind to me, and I wanted to tell you. . . . I wish I could think of you as happier, less lonely. . . . Things are sure to change for you by and by. . . ."

"Things don't change at North Dormer: people just get used to them."

The answer seemed to break up the order of his pre-arranged consolations, and he sat looking at her uncertainly. Then he said, with his sweet smile: "That's not true of you. It can't be."

The smile was like a knife-thrust through her heart: everything in her began to tremble and break loose. She felt her tears run over, and stood up.

"Well, good-bye," she said.

She was aware of his taking her hand, and of feeling that his touch was lifeless.

"Good-bye." He turned away, and stopped on the threshold. "You'll say good-bye for me to Verena?"

She heard the closing of the outer door and the sound of his quick tread along the path. The latch of the gate clicked after him.

The next morning when she arose in the cold dawn and opened her shutters she saw a freckled boy standing on the other side of the road and looking up at her. He was a boy from a farm three or four miles down the Creston road, and she wondered what he was doing there at that hour, and why he looked so hard at her window. When he saw her he crossed over and leaned against the gate unconcernedly. There was no one stirring in the house, and she threw a shawl over her night-gown and ran down and let herself out. By the time she reached the gate the boy was sauntering down the road, whistling carelessly; but she saw that a letter had been thrust between the slats and the crossbar of the gate. She took it out and hastened back to her room. The envelope bore her name, and inside was a leaf torn from a pocket-diary.

DEAR CHARITY:

I can't go away like this. I am staying for a few days at Creston River. Will you come down and meet me at Creston pool? I will wait for you till evening.

IX

Charity sat before the mirror trying on a hat which Ally Hawes, with much secrecy, had trimmed for her. It was of white straw, with a drooping brim and a cherry-coloured lining that made her face glow like the inside of the shell on the parlour mantelpiece.

She propped the square of looking-glass against Mr. Royall's black leather Bible, steadying it in front with a white stone on which a view of the Brooklyn Bridge was painted; and she sat before her reflection, bending the brim this way and that, while Ally Hawes's pale face looked over her shoulder like the ghost of wasted opportunities.

"I look awful, don't I?" she said at last with a happy sigh.

Ally smiled and took back the hat. "I'll stitch the roses on right here, so's you can put it away at once."

Charity laughed, and ran her fingers through her rough dark hair. She knew that Harney liked to see its reddish edges ruffled about her forehead and breaking into little rings at the nape. She sat down on her bed and watched Ally stoop over the hat with a careful frown.

"Don't you ever feel like going down to Nettleton for a day?" she asked.

Ally shook her head without looking up. "No, I always remember that awful time I went down with Julia—to that doctor's."

"Oh, Ally—"

"I can't help it. The house is on the corner of Wing Street and Lake Avenue. The trolley from the station goes right by it, and the day the minister took us down to see those pictures I recognized it right off, and couldn't seem to see anything else. There's a big black sign with gold letters all across the front—'Private Consultations.' She came near as anything to dying. . . ."

"Poor Julia!" Charity sighed from the height of her purity and her security. She had a friend whom she trusted and who respected her. She was going with him to spend the next day—the Fourth of July—at Nettleton. Whose business was it but hers, and what was the harm? The pity of it was that girls like Julia did not know how to choose, and to keep bad fellows at a distance. . . . Charity slipped down from the bed, and stretched out her hands.

"Is it sewed? Let me try it on again." She put the hat on and smiled at her image. The thought of Julia had vanished. . . .

The next morning she was up before dawn, and saw the yellow sunrise broaden behind the hills, and the silvery lustre preceding a hot day tremble across the sleeping fields.

Her plans had been made with great care. She had announced that she was going down to the Band of Hope picnic at Hepburn, and as no one else from North Dormer intended to venture so far it was not likely that her absence from the festivity would be reported. Besides, if it were she would not greatly care. She was determined to assert her independence, and if she stooped to fib about the Hepburn picnic it was chiefly from the secretive instinct that made her dread the profanation of her happiness. Whenever she was with Lucius Harney she would have liked some impenetrable mountain mist to hide her.

It was arranged that she should walk to a point of the Creston road where Harney was to pick her up and drive her across the hills to Hepburn in time for the nine-thirty train to Nettleton. Harney at first had been rather lukewarm about the trip. He declared himself ready to take her to Nettleton, but urged her not to go on the Fourth of July, on account of the crowds, the probable lateness of the trains, the difficulty of her getting back before night; but her evident disappointment caused him to give way, and even to affect a faint enthusiasm for the adventure. She understood why he was not more eager: he must have seen sights beside which even a Fourth of July at Nettleton would seem tame. But she had never seen anything; and a great longing possessed her to walk the streets of a big town on a holiday, clinging to his arm and jostled by idle crowds in their best clothes. The only cloud on the prospect was the fact that the shops would be closed; but she hoped he would take her back another day, when they were open.

She started out unnoticed in the early sunlight, slipping through the kitchen while Verena bent above the stove. To avoid attracting notice, she carried her new hat carefully wrapped up, and had thrown a long grey veil of Mrs. Royall's over the new white muslin dress which Ally's clever fingers had made for her. All of the ten dollars Mr. Royall had given her, and a part of her own savings as well, had been spent on renewing her wardrobe; and when Harney jumped out of the buggy to meet her she read her reward in his eyes.

The freckled boy who had brought her the note two weeks earlier was to wait with the buggy at Hepburn till their return. He perched at Charity's feet, his legs dangling between the wheels, and they could not say much because of his presence. But it did not greatly matter, for their past was now rich enough to have given them a private language; and with the long day stretching before them like the blue distance beyond the hills there was a delicate pleasure in postponement.

When Charity, in response to Harney's message, had gone to meet him at the Creston pool her heart had been so full of mortification and anger that his first words might easily have estranged her. But it happened that he had found the right word, which was one of simple friendship. His tone had instantly justified her, and put her guardian in the wrong. He had made no allusion to what had passed between Mr. Royall and himself, but had simply let it appear that he had left because means of conveyance were hard to find at North Dormer, and because Creston River was a more convenient centre. He told her that he had hired by the week the buggy of the freckled boy's father, who served as livery-stable keeper to one or two melancholy summer boarding-houses on Creston Lake, and had discovered, within driving distance, a number of houses worthy of his pencil; and he said that he could not, while he was in the neighbourhood, give up the pleasure of seeing her as often as possible.

When they took leave of each other she promised to continue to be his guide; and during the fortnight which followed they roamed the hills in happy comradeship. In most of the village friendships between youths and maidens lack of conversation was made up for by tentative fondling; but Harney, except when he had tried to comfort her in her trouble on their way back from the Hyatts', had never put his arm about her, or sought to betray her into any sudden caress. It seemed to be enough for him to breathe her nearness like a flower's; and since his pleasure at being with her, and his sense of her youth and her grace, perpetually shone in his eyes and softened the inflections of his voice, his reserve did not suggest coldness, but the deference due to a girl of his own class.

The buggy was drawn by an old trotter who whirled them along so briskly that the pace created a little breeze; but when they reached Hepburn the full heat of the airless morning descended on them. At the railway station the platform was packed with a sweltering throng, and they took refuge in the waiting-room, where there was another throng, already dejected by the heat and the long waiting for retarded trains.

Pale mothers were struggling with fretful babies, or trying to keep their older offspring from the fascination of the track; girls and their "fellows" were giggling and shoving, and passing about candy in sticky bags, and older men, collarless and perspiring, were shifting heavy children from one arm to the other, and keeping a haggard eye on the scattered members of their families.

At last the train rumbled in, and engulfed the waiting multitude. Harney swept Charity up on to the first car and they captured a bench for two, and sat in happy isolation while the train swayed and roared along through rich fields and languid tree-clumps. The haze of the morning had become a sort of clear tremor over everything, like the colourless vibration about a flame; and the opulent landscape seemed to droop under it. But to Charity the heat was a stimulant: it enveloped the whole world in the same glow that burned at her heart. Now and then a lurch of the train flung her against Harney, and through her thin muslin she felt the touch of his sleeve. She steadied herself, their eyes met, and the flaming breath of the day seemed to enclose them.

The train roared into the Nettleton station, the descending mob caught them on its tide, and they were swept out into a vague dusty square thronged with seedy "hacks" and long curtained omnibuses drawn by horses with tasselled fly-nets over their withers, who stood swinging their depressed heads drearily from side to side.

A mob of 'bus and hack drivers were shouting "To the Eagle House," "To the Washington House," "This way to the Lake," "Just starting for Greytop;" and through their yells came the popping of fire-crackers, the explosion of torpedoes, the banging of toy-guns, and the crash of a firemen's band trying to play the Merry Widow[7] while they were being packed into a waggonette streaming with bunting.

The ramshackle wooden hotels about the square were all hung with flags and paper lanterns, and as Harney and Charity turned into the main street, with its brick and granite business blocks crowding out the old low-storied shops, and its towering poles strung with innumerable wires that seemed to tremble and buzz in the heat, they saw the double line of flags and lanterns tapering away gaily to the park at the other end of the perspective. The noise and colour of this holiday version seemed to transform Nettleton into a metropolis. Charity could not believe that Springfield or even Boston had anything grander to show, and she wondered if, at this very moment, Annabel Balch, on the arm of as brilliant a young man, were threading her way through scenes as resplendent.

"Where shall we go first?" Harney asked; but as she turned her happy eyes on him he guessed the answer and said: "We'll take a look round, shall we?"

The street swarmed with their fellow-travellers, with other excursionists arriving from other directions, with Nettleton's own population, and with the mill-hands trooping in from the factories on the Creston. The shops were closed, but one would scarcely have noticed it, so numerous were the glass doors swinging open on saloons, on restaurants, on drug-stores gushing from every soda-water tap, on fruit and confectionery shops stacked with strawberry-cake, cocoanut drops, trays of glistening molasses candy, boxes of caramels and chewing-gum, baskets of sodden strawberries,

[7] Franz Lehar (1870–1948) composed the music for the operetta *The Merry Widow* in 1905; its most popular piece was the waltz, which even local bandsmen then attempted to play at public gatherings.

and dangling branches of bananas. Outside of some of the doors were trestles with banked-up oranges and apples, spotted pears and dusty raspberries; and the air reeked with the smell of fruit and stale coffee, beer and sarsaparilla and fried potatoes.

Even the shops that were closed offered, through wide expanses of plate-glass, hints of hidden riches. In some, waves of silk and ribbon broke over shores of imitation moss from which ravishing hats rose like tropical orchids. In others, the pink throats of gramophones opened their giant convolutions in a soundless chorus; or bicycles shining in neat ranks seemed to await the signal of an invisible starter; or tiers of fancy-goods in leatherette and paste and celluloid dangled their insidious graces; and, in one vast bay that seemed to project them into exciting contact with the public, wax ladies in daring dresses chatted elegantly, or, with gestures intimate yet blameless, pointed to their pink corsets and transparent hosiery.

Presently Harney found that his watch had stopped, and turned in at a small jeweller's shop which chanced to be still open. While the watch was being examined Charity leaned over the glass counter where, on a background of dark blue velvet, pins, rings and brooches glittered like the moon and stars. She had never seen jewellery so near by, and she longed to lift the glass lid and plunge her hand among the shining treasures. But already Harney's watch was repaired, and he laid his hand on her arm and drew her from her dream.

"Which do you like best?" he asked leaning over the counter at her side.

"I don't know. . . ." She pointed to a gold lily-of-the-valley with white flowers.

"Don't you think the blue pin's better?" he suggested, and immediately she saw that the lily of the valley was mere trumpery compared to the small round stone, blue as a mountain lake, with little sparks of light all round it. She coloured at her want of discrimination.

"It's so lovely I guess I was afraid to look at it," she said.

He laughed, and they went out of the shop; but a few steps away he exclaimed: "Oh, by Jove, I forgot something," and turned back and left her in the crowd. She stood staring down a row of pink gramophone throats till he rejoined her and slipped his arm through hers.

"You mustn't be afraid of looking at the blue pin any longer, because it belongs to you," he said; and she felt a little box being pressed into her hand. Her heart gave a leap of joy, but it reached her lips only in a shy stammer. She remembered other girls whom she had heard planning to extract presents from their fellows, and was seized with a sudden dread lest Harney should have imagined that she had leaned over the pretty things in the glass case in the hope of having one given to her. . . .

A little farther down the street they turned in at a glass doorway opening on a shining hall with a mahogany staircase, and brass cages in its corners, "We must have something to eat," Harney said; and the next moment Charity found herself in a dressing-room all looking-glass and lustrous surfaces, where a party of showy-looking girls were dabbing on powder and straightening immense plumed hats. When they had gone she took courage to bathe her hot face in one of the marble basins, and to straighten her own hat-brim, which the parasols of the crowd had indented. The dresses in the shops had so impressed her that she scarcely dared look at her reflection; but when she did so, the glow of her face under her cherry-coloured hat, and the curve of her young shoulders through the transparent muslin, restored her courage; and when she had taken the blue brooch from its box and pinned it on her bosom she walked toward the restaurant with her head high, as if she had always strolled through tessellated halls beside young men in flannels.

Her spirit sank a little at the sight of the slim-waisted waitresses in black, with bewitching mob-caps on their haughty heads, who were moving disdainfully between the tables. "Not f'r another hour," one of them dropped to Harney in passing; and he stood doubtfully glancing about him.

"Oh, well, we can't stay sweltering here," he decided; "let's try somewhere else—" and with a sense of relief Charity followed him from that scene of inhospitable splendour.

The "somewhere else" turned out—after more hot tramping, and several failures —to be, of all things, a little open-air place in a back street that called itself a French restaurant, and consisted in two or three rickety tables under a scarlet-runner, between a patch of zinnias and petunias and a big elm bending over from the next yard. Here they lunched on queerly flavoured things, while Harney, leaning back in a crippled rocking-chair, smoked cigarettes between the courses and poured into Charity's glass a pale yellow wine which he said was the very same one drank in just such jolly places in France.

Charity did not think the wine as good as sarsaparilla, but she sipped a mouthful for the pleasure of doing what he did, and of fancying herself alone with him in foreign countries. The illusion was increased by their being served by a deep-bosomed woman with smooth hair and a pleasant laugh, who talked to Harney in unintelligible words, and seemed amazed and overjoyed at his answering her in kind. At the other tables other people sat, mill-hands probably, homely but pleasant looking, who spoke the same shrill jargon, and looked at Harney and Charity with friendly eyes; and between the table-legs a poodle with bald patches and pink eyes nosed about for scraps, and sat up on his hind legs absurdly.

Harney showed no inclination to move, for hot as their corner was, it was at least shaded and quiet; and, from the main thoroughfares came the clanging of trolleys, the incessant popping of torpedoes, the jingle of street-organs, the bawling of mega-phone men and the loud murmur of increasing crowds. He leaned back, smoking his cigar, patting the dog, and stirring the coffee that steamed in their chipped cups. "It's the real thing, you know," he explained; and Charity hastily revised her previous conception of the beverage.

They had made no plans for the rest of the day, and when Harney asked her what she wanted to do next she was too bewildered by rich possibilities to find an answer. Finally she confessed that she longed to go to the Lake, where she had not been taken on her former visit, and when he answered, "Oh, there's time for that—it will be pleasanter later," she suggested seeing some pictures like the ones Mr. Miles had taken her to. She thought Harney looked a little disconcerted; but he passed his fine handkerchief over his warm brow, said gaily "Come along, then," and rose with a last pat for the pink-eyed dog.

Mr. Miles's pictures had been shown in an austere Y.M.C.A. hall, with white walls and an organ; but Harney led Charity to a glittering place—everything she saw seemed to glitter—where they passed, between immense pictures of yellow-haired beauties stabbing villains in evening dress, into a velvet-curtained auditorium packed with spectators to the last limit of compression. After that, for a while, everything was merged in her brain in swimming circles of heat and blinding alternations of light and darkness. All the world has to show seemed to pass before her in a chaos of palms and minarets, charging cavalry regiments, roaring lions, comic policemen and scowling murderers; and the crowd around her, the hundreds of hot sallow candy-munching faces, young, old, middle-aged, but all kindled with the same contagious excitement, became part of the spectacle, and danced on the screen with the rest.

Presently the thought of the cool trolley-run to the Lake grew irresistible, and they struggled out of the theatre. As they stood on the pavement, Harney pale with the heat, and even Charity a little confused by it, a young man drove by in an electric run-about with a calico band bearing the words: "Ten dollars to take you round the Lake." Before Charity knew what was happening, Harney had waved a hand, and they were climbing in. "Say, for twenny-five I'll run you out first to see the ball-game and back," the driver proposed with an insinuating grin; but Charity said quickly: "Oh, I'd rather go rowing on the Lake." The street was so thronged that progress was slow; but the glory of sitting in the little carriage while it wriggled its way between laden omnibuses and trolleys made the moments seem too short. "Next turn is Lake Avenue," the young man called out over his shoulder; and as they paused in the wake of a big omnibus groaning with Knights of Pythias[8] in cocked hats and swords, Charity looked up and saw on the corner a brick house with a conspicuous black and gold sign across its front. "Dr. Merkle; Private Consultations at all hours. Lady Attendants," she read; and suddenly she remembered Ally Hawes's words: "The house was at the corner of Wing Street and Lake Avenue . . . there's a big black sign across the front. . . ." Through all the heat and the rapture a shiver of cold ran over her.

X

The Lake at last—a sheet of shining metal brooded over by drooping trees. Charity and Harney had secured a boat and, getting away from the wharves and the refreshment-booths, they drifted idly along, hugging the shadow of the shore. Where the sun struck the water its shafts flamed back blindingly at the heat-veiled sky; and the least shade was black by contrast. The Lake was so smooth that the reflection of the trees on its edge seemed enamelled on a solid surface; but gradually, as the sun declined, the water grew transparent, and Charity, leaning over, plunged her fascinated gaze into depths so clear that she saw the inverted tree-tops interwoven with the green growths of the bottom.

They rounded a point at the farther end of the Lake, and entering an inlet pushed their bow against a protruding tree-trunk. A green veil of willows overhung them. Beyond the trees, wheat-fields sparkled in the sun; and all along the horizon the clear hills throbbed with light. Charity leaned back in the stern, and Harney unshipped the oars and lay in the bottom of the boat without speaking.

Ever since their meeting at the Creston pool he had been subject to these brooding silences, which were as different as possible from the pauses when they ceased to speak because words were needless. At such times his face wore the expression she had seen on it when she had looked in at him from the darkness, and again there came over her a sense of the mysterious distance between them; but usually his fits

---

[8] Secret fraternal order founded in 1864.

of abstraction were followed by bursts of gaiety that chased away the shadow before it chilled her.

She was still thinking of the ten dollars he had handed to the driver of the run-about. It had given them twenty minutes of pleasure, and it seemed unimaginable that anyone should be able to buy amusement at that rate. With ten dollars he might have bought her an engagement ring; she knew that Mrs. Tom Fry's, which came from Springfield, and had a diamond in it, had cost only eight seventy-five. But she did not know why the thought had occurred to her. Harney would never buy her an engagement ring: they were friends and comrades, but no more. He had been perfectly fair to her: he had never said a word to mislead her. She wondered what the girl was like whose hand was waiting for his ring. . . .

Boats were beginning to thicken on the Lake and the clang of incessantly arriving trolleys announced the return of the crowds from the ball-field. The shadows lengthened across the pearl-grey water and two white clouds near the sun were turning golden. On the opposite shore men were hammering hastily at a wooden scaffolding in a field. Charity asked what it was for.

"Why, the fireworks. I suppose there'll be a big show." Harney looked at her and a smile crept into his moody eyes. "Have you never seen any good fireworks?"

"Miss Hatchard always sends up lovely rockets on the Fourth," she answered doubtfully.

"Oh——" his contempt was unbounded. "I mean a big performance like this: illuminated boats, and all the rest."

She flushed at the picture. "Do they send them up from the Lake, too?"

"Rather. Didn't you notice that big raft we passed? It's wonderful to see the rockets completing their orbits down under one's feet." She said nothing, and he put the oars into the rowlocks. "If we stay we'd better go and pick up something to eat."

"But how can we get back afterward?" she ventured, feeling it would break her heart if she missed it.

He consulted a time-table, found a ten o'clock train and reassured her. "The moon rises so late that it will be dark by eight, and we'll have over an hour of it."

Twilight fell, and lights began to show along the shore. The trolleys roaring out from Nettleton became great luminous serpents coiling in and out among the trees. The wooden eating-houses at the Lake's edge danced with lanterns, and the dusk echoed with laughter and shouts and the clumsy splashing of oars.

Harney and Charity had found a table in the corner of a balcony built over the Lake, and were patiently awaiting an unattainable chowder. Close under them the water lapped the piles, agitated by the evolutions of a little white steamboat trellised with coloured globes which was to run passengers up and down the Lake. It was already black with them as it sheered off on its first trip.

Suddenly Charity heard a woman's laugh behind her. The sound was familiar, and she turned to look. A band of showily dressed girls and dapper young men wearing badges of secret societies, with new straw hats tilted far back on their square-clipped hair, had invaded the balcony and were loudly clamouring for a table. The girl in the lead was the one who had laughed. She wore a large hat with a long white feather, and from under its brim her painted eyes looked at Charity with amused recognition.

"Say! if this ain't like Old Home Week," she remarked to the girl at her elbow; and giggles and glances passed between them. Charity knew at once that the girl with the white feather was Julia Hawes. She had lost her freshness, and the paint under her eyes made her face seem thinner; but her lips had the same lovely curve, and the same cold mocking smile, as if there were some secret absurdity in the person she was looking at, and she had instantly detected it.

Charity flushed to the forehead and looked away. She felt herself humiliated by Julia's sneer, and vexed that the mockery of such a creature should affect her. She trembled lest Harney should notice that the noisy troop had recognized her; but they found no table free, and passed on tumultuously.

Presently there was a soft rush through the air and a shower of silver fell from the blue evening sky. In another direction, pale Roman candles shot up singly through the trees, and a fire-haired rocket swept the horizon like a portent. Between these intermittent flashes the velvet curtains of the darkness were descending, and in the intervals of eclipse the voices of the crowds seemed to sink to smothered murmurs.

Charity and Harney, dispossessed by newcomers, were at length obliged to give up their table and struggle through the throng about the boat-landings. For a while there seemed no escape from the tide of late arrivals; but finally Harney secured the last two places on the stand from which the more privileged were to see the fireworks. The seats were at the end of a row, one above the other. Charity had taken off her hat to have an uninterrupted view; and whenever she leaned back to follow the curve of some dishevelled rocket she could feel Harney's knees against her head.

After a while the scattered fireworks ceased. A longer interval of darkness followed, and then the whole night broke into flower. From every point of the horizon, gold and silver arches sprang up and crossed each other, sky-orchards broke into blossom, shed their flaming petals and hung their branches with golden fruit; and all the while the air was filled with a soft supernatural hum, as though great birds were building their nests in those invisible tree-tops.

Now and then there came a lull, and a wave of moonlight swept the Lake. In a flash it revealed hundreds of boats, steel-dark against lustrous ripples; then it withdrew as if with a furling of vast translucent wings. Charity's heart throbbed with delight. It was as if all the latent beauty of things had been unveiled to her. She could not imagine that the world held anything more wonderful; but near her she heard someone say, "You wait till you see the set piece," and instantly her hopes took a fresh flight. At last, just as it was beginning to seem as though the whole arch of the sky were one great lid pressed against her dazzled eyeballs, and striking out of them continuous jets of jewelled light, the velvet darkness settled down again, and a murmur of expectation ran through the crowd.

"Now—now!" the same voice said excitedly; and Charity, grasping the hat on her knee, crushed it tight in the effort to restrain her rapture.

For a moment the night seemed to grow more impenetrably black; then a great picture stood out against it like a constellation. It was surmounted by a golden scroll bearing the inscription, "Washington crossing the Delaware," and across a flood of motionless golden ripples the National Hero passed, erect, solemn and gigantic, standing with folded arms in the stern of a slowly moving golden boat.[9]

A long "Oh-h-h" burst from the spectators: the stand creaked and shook with their

---

[9] The fireworks display is based on the popular painting *Washington Crossing the Delaware* (1850) by the German-American artist Emanuel Leutze (1816–1868).

blissful trepidations. "Oh-h-h," Charity gasped: she had forgotten where she was, had at last forgotten even Harney's nearness. She seemed to have been caught up into the stars. . . .

The picture vanished and darkness came down. In the obscurity she felt her head clasped by two hands: her face was drawn backward, and Harney's lips were pressed on hers. With sudden vehemence he wound his arms about her, holding her head against his breast while she gave him back his kisses. An unknown Harney had revealed himself, a Harney who dominated her and yet over whom she felt herself possessed of a new mysterious power.

But the crowd was beginning to move, and he had to release her. "Come," he said in a confused voice. He scrambled over the side of the stand, and holding up his arm caught her as she sprang to the ground. He passed his arm about her waist, steadying her against the descending rush of people; and she clung to him, speechless, exultant, as if all the crowding and confusion about them were a mere vain stirring of the air.

"Come," he repeated, "we must try to make the trolley." He drew her along, and she followed, still in her dream. They walked as if they were one, so isolated in ecstasy that the people jostling them on every side seemed impalpable. But when they reached the terminus the illuminated trolley was already clanging on its way, its platforms black with passengers. The cars waiting behind it were as thickly packed; and the throng about the terminus was so dense that it seemed hopeless to struggle for a place.

"Last trip up the Lake," a megaphone bellowed from the wharf; and the lights of the little steamboat came dancing out of the darkness.

"No use waiting here; shall we run up the Lake?" Harney suggested.

They pushed their way back to the edge of the water just as the gang-plank was lowered from the white side of the boat. The electric light at the end of the wharf flashed full on the descending passengers, and among them Charity caught sight of Julia Hawes, her white feather askew, and the face under it flushed with coarse laughter. As she stepped from the gang-plank she stopped short, her dark-ringed eyes darting malice.

"Hullo, Charity Royall!" she called out; and then, looking back over her shoulder: "Didn't I tell you it was a family party? Here's grandpa's little darling come to take him home!"

A snigger ran through the group; and then, towering above them, and steadying himself by the hand-rail in a desperate effort at erectness, Mr. Royall stepped stiffly ashore. Like the young men of the party, he wore a secret society emblem in the buttonhole of his black frock-coat. His head was covered by a new Panama hat, and his narrow black tie, half undone, dangled down on his rumpled shirt-front. His face, a livid brown, with red blotches of anger and lips sunken in like an old man's, was a lamentable ruin in the searching glare.

He was just behind Julia Hawes, and had one hand on her arm; but as he left the gang-plank he freed himself, and moved a step or two away from his companions. He had seen Charity at once, and his glance passed slowly from her to Harney, whose arm was still about her. He stood staring at them, and trying to master the senile quiver of his lips; then he drew himself up with the tremulous majesty of drunkenness, and stretched out his arm.

"You whore—you damn—bare-headed whore, you!" he enunciated slowly.

There was a scream of tipsy laughter from the party, and Charity involuntarily put her hands to her head. She remembered that her hat had fallen from her lap when she jumped up to leave the stand; and suddenly she had a vision of herself, hatless, dishevelled, with a man's arm about her, confronting that drunken crew, headed by her guardian's pitiable figure. The picture filled her with shame. She had known since childhood about Mr. Royall's "habits": had seen him, as she went up to bed, sitting morosely in his office, a bottle at his elbow; or coming home, heavy and quarrelsome, from his business expeditions to Hepburn or Springfield; but the idea of his associating himself publicly with a band of disreputable girls and bar-room loafers was new and dreadful to her.

"Oh—" she said in a gasp of misery; and releasing herself from Harney's arm she went straight up to Mr. Royall.

"You come home with me—you come right home with me," she said in a low stern voice, as if she had not heard his apostrophe; and one of the girls called out: "Say, how many fellers does she want?"

There was another laugh, followed by a pause of curiosity, during which Mr. Royall continued to glare at Charity. At length his twitching lips parted. "I said, 'You—damn—whore!'" he repeated with precision, steadying himself on Julia's shoulder.

Laughs and jeers were beginning to spring up from the circle of people beyond their group; and a voice called out from the gangway: "Now, then, step lively there —all *aboard!*" The pressure of approaching and departing passengers forced the actors in the rapid scene apart, and pushed them back into the throng. Charity found herself clinging to Harney's arm and sobbing desperately. Mr. Royall had disappeared, and in the distance she heard the receding sound of Julia's laugh.

The boat, laden to the taffrail, was puffing away on her last trip.

XI

At two o'clock in the morning the freckled boy from Creston stopped his sleepy horse at the door of the red house, and Charity got out. Harney had taken leave of her at Creston River, charging the boy to drive her home. Her mind was still in a fog of misery, and she did not remember very clearly what had happened, or what they had said to each other, during the interminable interval since their departure from Nettleton; but the secretive instinct of the animal in pain was so strong in her that she had a sense of relief when Harney got out and she drove on alone.

The full moon hung over North Dormer, whitening the mist that filled the hollows between the hills and floated transparently above the fields. Charity stood a moment at the gate, looking out into the waning night. She watched the boy drive off, his horse's head wagging heavily to and fro; then she went around to the kitchen door and felt under the mat for the key. She found it, unlocked the door and went in. The kitchen was dark, but she discovered a box of matches, lit a candle and went upstairs. Mr. Royall's door, opposite hers, stood open on his unlit room; evidently he had not come back. She went into her room, bolted her door and began slowly to untie the ribbon about her waist, and to take off her dress. Under the bed she saw the paper bag in which she had hidden her new hat from inquisitive eyes. . . .

She lay for a long time sleepless on her bed, staring up at the moonlight on the low ceiling; dawn was in the sky when she fell asleep, and when she woke the sun was on her face.

She dressed and went down to the kitchen. Verena was there alone: she glanced at Charity tranquilly, with her old deaf-looking eyes. There was no sign of Mr. Royall about the house and the hours passed without his reappearing. Charity had gone up to her room, and sat there listlessly, her hands on her lap. Puffs of sultry air fanned her dimity window curtains and flies buzzed stiflingly against the bluish panes.

At one o'clock Verena hobbled up to see if she were not coming down to dinner; but she shook her head, and the old woman went away, saying: "I'll cover up, then."

The sun turned and left her room, and Charity seated herself in the window, gazing down the village street through the half-opened shutters. Not a thought was in her mind; it was just a dark whirlpool of crowding images; and she watched the people passing along the street, Dan Targatt's team hauling a load of pine-trunks down to Hepburn, the sexton's old white horse grazing on the bank across the way, as if she looked at these familiar sights from the other side of the grave.

She was roused from apathy by seeing Ally Hawes come out of the Frys' gate and walk slowly toward the red house with her uneven limping step. At the sight Charity recovered her severed contact with reality. She divined that Ally was coming to hear about her day: no one else was in the secret of the trip to Nettleton, and it had flattered Ally profoundly to be allowed to know of it.

At the thought of having to see her, of having to meet her eyes and answer or evade her questions, the whole horror of the previous night's adventure rushed back upon Charity. What had been a feverish nightmare became a cold and unescapable fact. Poor Ally, at that moment, represented North Dormer, with all its mean curiosities, its furtive malice, its sham unconsciousness of evil. Charity knew that, although all relations with Julia were supposed to be severed, the tender-hearted Ally still secretly communicated with her; and no doubt Julia would exult in the chance of retailing the scandal of the wharf. The story, exaggerated and distorted, was probably already on its way to North Dormer.

Ally's dragging pace had not carried her far from the Frys' gate when she was stopped by old Mrs. Sollas, who was a great talker, and spoke very slowly because she had never been able to get used to her new teeth from Hepburn. Still, even this respite would not last long; in another ten minutes Ally would be at the door, and Charity would hear her greeting Verena in the kitchen, and then calling up from the foot of the stairs.

Suddenly it became clear that flight, and instant flight, was the only thing conceivable. The longing to escape, to get away from familiar faces, from places where she was known, had always been strong in her in moments of distress. She had a childish belief in the miraculous power of strange scenes and new faces to transform her life and wipe out bitter memories. But such impulses were mere fleeting whims compared to the cold resolve which now possessed her. She felt she could not remain an hour longer under the roof of the man who had publicly dishonoured her, and face to face with the people who would presently be gloating over all the details of her humiliation.

Her passing pity for Mr. Royall had been swallowed up in loathing: everything in her recoiled from the disgraceful spectacle of the drunken old man apostrophizing her in the presence of a band of loafers and street-walkers. Suddenly, vividly, she relived again the horrible moment when he had tried to force himself into her room, and what she had before supposed to be a mad aberration now appeared to her as a vulgar incident in a debauched and degraded life.

While these thoughts were hurrying through her she had dragged out her old canvas school-bag, and was thrusting into it a few articles of clothing and the little packet of letters she had received from Harney. From under her pincushion she took the library key, and laid it in full view; then she felt at the back of a drawer for the blue brooch that Harney had given her. She would not have dared to wear it openly at North Dormer, but now she fastened it on her bosom as if it were a talisman to protect her in her flight. These preparations had taken but a few minutes, and when they were finished Ally Hawes was still at the Frys' corner talking to old Mrs. Sollas. . . .

She had said to herself, as she always said in moments of revolt: "I'll go to the Mountain—I'll go back to my own folks." She had never really meant it before; but now, as she considered her case, no other course seemed open. She had never learned any trade that would have given her independence in a strange place, and she knew no one in the big towns of the valley, where she might have hoped to find employment. Miss Hatchard was still away; but even had she been at North Dormer she was the last person to whom Charity would have turned, since one of the motives urging her to flight was the wish not to see Lucius Harney. Travelling back from Nettleton, in the crowded brightly-lit train, all exchange of confidence between them had been impossible; but during their drive from Hepburn to Creston River she had gathered from Harney's snatches of consolatory talk—again hampered by the freckled boy's presence—that he intended to see her the next day. At the moment she had found a vague comfort in the assurance; but in the desolate lucidity of the hours that followed she had come to see the impossibility of meeting him again. Her dream of comradeship was over; and the scene on the wharf—vile and disgraceful as it had been—had after all shed the light of truth on her minute of madness. It was as if her guardian's words had stripped her bare in the face of the grinning crowd and proclaimed to the world the secret admonitions of her conscience.

She did not think these things out clearly; she simply followed the blind propulsion of her wretchedness. She did not want, ever again, to see anyone she had known; above all, she did not want to see Harney. . . .

She climbed the hill-path behind the house and struck through the woods by a short-cut leading to the Creston road. A lead-coloured sky hung heavily over the fields, and in the forest the motionless air was stifling; but she pushed on, impatient to reach the road which was the shortest way to the Mountain.

To do so, she had to follow the Creston road for a mile or two, and go within half a mile of the village; and she walked quickly, fearing to meet Harney. But there was no sign of him, and she had almost reached the branch road when she saw the flanks of a large white tent projecting through the trees by the roadside. She supposed that it sheltered a travelling circus which had come there for the Fourth; but as she drew nearer she saw, over the folded-back flap, a large sign bearing the inscription, "Gospel Tent." The interior seemed to be empty; but a young man in a black alpaca coat, his lank hair parted over a round white face, stepped from under the flap and advanced toward her with a smile.

"Sister, your Saviour knows everything. Won't you come in and lay your guilt before Him?" he asked insinuatingly, putting his hand on her arm.

Charity started back and flushed. For a moment she thought the evangelist must have heard a report of the scene at Nettleton; then she saw the absurdity of the supposition.

"I on'y wish't I had any to lay!" she retorted, with one of her fierce flashes of self-derision; and the young man murmured, aghast: "Oh, Sister, don't speak blasphemy. . . ."

But she had jerked her arm out of his hold, and was running up the branch road, trembling with the fear of meeting a familiar face. Presently she was out of sight of the village, and climbing into the heart of the forest. She could not hope to do the fifteen miles to the Mountain that afternoon; but she knew of a place half-way to Hamblin where she could sleep, and where no one would think of looking for her. It was a little deserted house on a slope in one of the lonely rifts of the hills. She had seen it once, years before, when she had gone on a nutting expedition to the grove of walnuts below it. The party had taken refuge in the house from a sudden mountain storm, and she remembered that Ben Sollas, who liked frightening girls, had told them that it was said to be haunted.

She was growing faint and tired, for she had eaten nothing since morning, and was not used to walking so far. Her head felt light and she sat down for a moment by the roadside. As she sat there she heard the click of a bicycle-bell, and started up to plunge back into the forest; but before she could move the bicycle had swept around the curve of the road, and Harney, jumping off, was approaching her with outstretched arms.

"Charity! What on earth are you doing here?"

She stared as if he were a vision, so startled by the unexpectedness of his being there that no words came to her.

"Where were you going? Had you forgotten that I was coming?" he continued, trying to draw her to him; but she shrank from his embrace.

"I was going away—I don't want to see you—I want you should leave me alone," she broke out wildly.

He looked at her and his face grew grave, as though the shadow of a premonition brushed it.

"Going away—from me, Charity?"

"From everybody. I want you should leave me."

He stood glancing doubtfully up and down the lonely forest road that stretched away into sunflecked distances.

"Where were you going?"

"Home."

"Home—this way?"

She threw her head back defiantly. "To my home—up yonder: to the Mountain."

As she spoke she became aware of a change in his face. He was no longer listening to her, he was only looking at her, with the passionate absorbed expression she had seen in his eyes after they had kissed on the stand at Nettleton. He was the new Harney again, the Harney abruptly revealed in that embrace, who seemed so penetrated with the joy of her presence that he was utterly careless of what she was thinking or feeling.

He caught her hands with a laugh. "How do you suppose I found you?" he said gaily. He drew out the little packet of his letters and flourished them before her bewildered eyes.

"You dropped them, you imprudent young person—dropped them in the middle of the road, not far from here; and the young man who is running the Gospel tent picked them up just as I was riding by." He drew back, holding her at arm's length, and scrutinizing her troubled face with the minute searching gaze of his short-sighted eyes.

"Did you really think you could run away from me? You see you weren't meant to," he said; and before she could answer he had kissed her again, not vehemently, but tenderly, almost fraternally, as if he had guessed her confused pain, and wanted her to know he understood it. He wound his fingers through hers.

"Come—let's walk a little. I want to talk to you. There's so much to say."

He spoke with a boy's gaiety, carelessly and confidently, as if nothing had happened that could shame or embarrass them; and for a moment, in the sudden relief of her release from lonely pain, she felt herself yielding to his mood. But he had turned, and was drawing her back along the road by which she had come. She stiffened herself and stopped short.

"I won't go back," she said.

They looked at each other a moment in silence; then he answered gently: "Very well: let's go the other way, then."

She remained motionless, gazing silently at the ground, and he went on: "Isn't there a house up here somewhere—a little abandoned house—you meant to show me some day?" Still she made no answer, and he continued, in the same tone of tender reassurance: "Let us go there now and sit down and talk quietly." He took one of the hands that hung by her side and pressed his lips to the palm. "Do you suppose I'm going to let you send me away? Do you suppose I don't understand?"

The little old house—its wooden walls sun-bleached to a ghostly gray—stood in an orchard above the road. The garden palings had fallen, but the broken gate dangled between its posts, and the path to the house was marked by rose-bushes run wild and hanging their small pale blossoms above the crowding grasses. Slender pilasters and an intricate fan-light framed the opening where the door had hung; and the door itself lay rotting in the grass, with an old apple-tree fallen across it.

Inside, also, wind and weather had blanched everything to the same wan silvery tint: the house was as dry and pure as the interior of a long-empty shell. But it must have been exceptionally well built, for the little rooms had kept something of their human aspect: the wooden mantels with their neat classic ornaments were in place, and the corners of one ceiling retained a light film of plaster tracery.

Harney had found an old bench at the back door and dragged it into the house. Charity sat on it, leaning her head against the wall in a state of drowsy lassitude. He had guessed that she was hungry and thirsty, and had brought her some tablets of chocolate from his bicycle-bag, and filled his drinking-cup from a spring in the orchard; and now he sat at her feet, smoking a cigarette, and looking up at her without speaking. Outside, the afternoon shadows were lengthening across the grass, and through the empty window-frame that faced her she saw the Mountain thrusting its dark mass against a sultry sunset. It was time to go.

She stood up, and he sprang to his feet also, and passed his arm through hers with an air of authority. "Now, Charity, you're coming back with me."

She looked at him and shook her head. "I ain't ever going back. You don't know."

"What don't I know?" She was silent, and he continued: "What happened on the wharf was horrible—it's natural you should feel as you do. But it doesn't make any real difference: you can't be hurt by such things. You must try to forget. And you must try to understand that men . . . men sometimes . . ."

"I know about men. That's why."

He coloured a little at the retort, as though it had touched him in a way she did not suspect.

"Well, then . . . you must know one has to make allowances. . . . He'd been drinking. . . ."

"I know all that, too. I've seen him so before. But he wouldn't have dared speak to me that way if he hadn't . . ."

"Hadn't what? What do you mean?"

"Hadn't wanted me to be like those other girls. . . ." She lowered her voice and looked away from him. "So's 't he wouldn't have to go out. . . ."

Harney stared at her. For a moment he did not seem to seize her meaning; then his face grew dark. "The damned hound! The villainous low hound!" His wrath blazed up, crimsoning him to the temples. "I never dreamed—good God, it's too vile," he broke off, as if his thoughts recoiled from the discovery.

"I won't never go back there," she repeated doggedly.

"No—" he assented.

There was a long interval of silence, during which she imagined that he was searching her face for more light on what she had revealed to him; and a flush of shame swept over her.

"I know the way you must feel about me," she broke out, ". . . telling you such things. . . ."

But once more, as she spoke, she became aware that he was no longer listening. He came close and caught her to him as if he were snatching her from some imminent peril: his impetuous eyes were in hers, and she could feel the hard beat of his heart as he held her against it.

"Kiss me again—like last night," he said, pushing her hair back as if to draw her whole face up into his kiss.

XII

One afternoon toward the end of August a group of girls sat in a room at Miss Hatchard's in a gay confusion of flags, turkey-red, blue and white paper muslin, harvest sheaves and illuminated scrolls.

North Dormer was preparing for its Old Home Week. That form of sentimental decentralization was still in its early stages, and, precedents being few, and the desire to set an example contagious, the matter had become a subject of prolonged and passionate discussion under Miss Hatchard's roof. The incentive to the celebration had come rather from those who had left North Dormer than from those who had been obliged to stay there, and there was some difficulty in rousing the village to the proper state of enthusiasm. But Miss Hatchard's pale prim drawing-room was the centre of constant comings and goings from Hepburn, Nettleton, Springfield and even more distant cities; and whenever a visitor arrived he was led across the hall, and treated to a glimpse of the group of girls deep in their pretty preparations.

"All the old names . . . all the old names. . . ." Miss Hatchard would be heard, tapping across the hall on her crutches. "Targatt . . . Sollas . . . Fry: this is Miss Orma Fry sewing the stars on the drapery for the organ-loft. Don't move, girls . . . and this is Miss Ally Hawes, our cleverest needle-woman . . . and Miss Charity Royall making our garlands of evergreen. . . . I like the idea of its all being home-made, don't you? We haven't had to call in any foreign talent: my young cousin Lucius Harney, the architect—you know he's up here preparing a book on Colonial houses—he's taken the whole thing in hand so cleverly; but you must come and see his sketch for the stage we're going to put up in the Town Hall."

One of the first results of the Old Home Week agitation had, in fact, been the reappearance of Lucius Harney in the village street. He had been vaguely spoken of as being not far off, but for some weeks past no one had seen him at North Dormer, and there was a recent report of his having left Creston River, where he was said to have been staying, and gone away from the neighbourhood for good. Soon after Miss Hatchard's return, however, he came back to his old quarters in her house, and began to take a leading part in the planning of the festivities. He threw himself into the idea with extraordinary good-humour, and was so prodigal of sketches, and so inexhaustible in devices, that he gave immediate impetus to the rather languid movement, and infected the whole village with his enthusiasm.

"Lucius has such a feeling for the past that he has roused us all to a sense of our privileges," Miss Hatchard would say, lingering on the last word, which was a favourite one. And before leading her visitor back to the drawing-room she would repeat, for the hundredth time, that she supposed he thought it very bold of little North Dormer to start up and have a Home Week of its own, when so many bigger places hadn't thought of it yet; but that, after all, Associations counted more than the size of the population, didn't they? And of course North Dormer was so full of Associations . . . historic, literary (here a filial sigh for Honorius) and ecclesiastical . . . he knew about the old pewter communion service imported from England in 1769, she supposed? And it was so important, in a wealthy materialistic age, to set the example of reverting to the old ideals, the family and the homestead, and so on. This peroration usually carried her half-way back across the hall, leaving the girls to return to their interrupted activities.

The day on which Charity Royall was weaving hemlock garlands for the procession was the last before the celebration. When Miss Hatchard called upon the North Dormer maidenhood to collaborate in the festal preparations Charity had at first held aloof; but it had been made clear to her that her non-appearance might excite conjecture, and, reluctantly, she had joined the other workers. The girls, at first shy and embarrassed, and puzzled as to the exact nature of the projected commemoration, had soon become interested in the amusing details of their task, and excited by the notice they received. They would not for the world have missed their afternoons at Miss Hatchard's, and, while they cut out and sewed and draped and pasted, their tongues kept up such an accompaniment to the sewing-machine that Charity's silence sheltered itself unperceived under their chatter.

In spirit she was still almost unconscious of the pleasant stir about her. Since her return to the red house, on the evening of the day when Harney had overtaken her on her way to the Mountain, she had lived at North Dormer as if she were suspended in the void. She had come back there because Harney, after appearing to agree to the impossibility of her doing so, had ended by persuading her that any other course would be madness. She had nothing further to fear from Mr. Royall. Of this she had declared herself sure, though she had failed to add, in his exoneration, that he had twice offered to make her his wife. Her hatred of him made it impossible, at the moment, for her to say anything that might partly excuse him in Harney's eyes.

Harney, however, once satisfied of her security, had found plenty of reasons for urging her to return. The first, and the most unanswerable, was that she had nowhere else to go. But the one on which he laid the greatest stress was that flight would be equivalent to avowal. If—as was almost inevitable—rumours of the scandalous scene at Nettleton should reach North Dormer, how else would her disappearance be interpreted? Her guardian had publicly taken away her character, and she immediately vanished from his house. Seekers after motives could hardy fail to draw an unkind conclusion. But if she came back at once, and was seen leading her usual life, the incident was reduced to its true proportions, as the outbreak of a drunken old man furious at being surprised in disreputable company. People would say that Mr. Royall had insulted his ward to justify himself, and the sordid tale would fall into its place in the chronicle of his obscure debaucheries.

Charity saw the force of the argument; but if she acquiesced it was not so much because of that as because it was Harney's wish. Since that evening in the deserted house she could imagine no reason for doing or not doing anything except the fact that Harney wished or did not wish it. All her tossing contradictory impulses were merged in a fatalistic acceptance of his will. It was not that she felt in him any ascendency of character—there were moments already when she knew she was the stronger—but that all the rest of life had become a mere cloudy rim about the central glory of their passion. Whenever she stopped thinking about that for a moment she felt as she sometimes did after lying on the grass and staring up too long at the sky; her eyes were so full of light that everything about her was a blur.

Each time that Miss Hatchard, in the course of her periodical incursions into the work-room, dropped an allusion to her young cousin, the architect, the effect was the same on Charity. The hemlock garland she was wearing fell to her knees and she sat in a kind of trance. It was so manifestly absurd that Miss Hatchard should talk of Harney in that familiar possessive way, as if she had any claim on him, or knew anything about him. She, Charity Royall, was the only being on earth who really knew him, knew him from the soles of his feet to the rumpled crest of his hair, knew the shifting lights in his eyes, and the inflexions of his voice, and the things he liked and disliked, and everything there was to know about him, as minutely and yet unconsciously as a child knows the walls of the room it wakes up in every morning.

It was this fact, which nobody about her guessed, or would have understood, that made her life something apart and inviolable, as if nothing had any power to hurt or disturb her as long as her secret was safe.

The room in which the girls sat was the one which had been Harney's bedroom. He had been sent upstairs, to make room for the Home Week workers; but the furniture had not been moved, and as Charity sat there she had perpetually before her the vision she had looked in on from the midnight garden. The table at which Harney had sat was the one about which the girls were gathered; and her own seat was near the bed on which she had seen him lying. Sometimes, when the others were not looking, she bent over as if to pick up something, and laid her cheek for a moment against the pillow.

Toward sunset the girls disbanded. Their work was done, and the next morning at daylight the draperies and garlands were to be nailed up, and the illuminated scrolls put in place in the Town Hall. The first guests were to drive over from Hepburn in time for the midday banquet under a tent in Miss Hatchard's field; and after that the ceremonies were to begin. Miss Hatchard, pale with fatigue and excitement, thanked her young assistants, and stood in the porch, leaning on her crutches and waving a farewell as she watched them troop away down the street.

Charity had slipped off among the first; but at the gate she heard Ally Hawes calling after her, and reluctantly turned.

"Will you come over now and try on your dress?" Ally asked, looking at her with wistful admiration. "I want to be sure the sleeves don't ruck up the same as they did yesterday."

Charity gazed at her with dazzled eyes. "Oh, it's lovely," she said, and hastened away without listening to Ally's protest. She wanted her dress to be as pretty as the other girls'—wanted it, in fact, to outshine the rest, since she was to take part in the "exercises"—but she had no time just then to fix her mind on such matters. . . .

She sped up the street to the library, of which she had the key about her neck. From the passage at the back she dragged forth a bicycle, and guided it to the edge of the street. She looked about to see if any of the girls were approaching; but they had drifted away together toward the Town Hall, and she sprang into the saddle and turned toward the Creston road. There was an almost continual descent to Creston, and with her feet against the pedals she floated through the still evening air like one of the hawks she had often watched slanting downward on motionless wings. Twenty minutes from the time when she had left Miss Hatchard's door she was turning up the wood-road on which Harney had overtaken her on the day of her flight; and a few minutes afterward she had jumped from her bicycle at the gate of the deserted house.

In the gold-powdered sunset it looked more than ever like some frail shell dried and washed by many seasons; but at the back, whither Charity advanced, drawing her bicycle after her, there were signs of recent habitation. A rough door made of boards hung in the kitchen doorway, and pushing it open she entered a room furnished in primitive camping fashion. In the window was a table, also made of boards, with an earthenware jar holding a big bunch of wild asters. Two canvas chairs stood near by, and in one corner was a mattress with a Mexican blanket over it.

The room was empty, and leaning her bicycle against the house Charity clambered up the slope and sat down on a rock under an old apple-tree. The air was perfectly still, and from where she sat she would be able to hear the tinkle of a bicycle-bell a long way down the road. . . .

She was always glad when she got to the little house before Harney. She liked to have time to take in every detail of its secret sweetness—the shadows of the apple-trees swaying on the grass, the old walnuts rounding their domes below the road, the meadows sloping westward in the afternoon light—before his first kiss blotted it all out. Everything unrelated to the hours spent in that tranquil place was as faint as the remembrance of a dream. The only reality was the wondrous unfolding of her new self, the reaching out to the light of all her contracted tendrils. She had lived all her life among people whose sensibilities seemed to have withered for lack of use; and more wonderful, at first, than Harney's endearments were the words that were a part of them. She had always thought of love as something confused and furtive, and he made it as bright and open as the summer air.

On the morrow of the day when she had shown him the way to the deserted house he had packed up and left Creston River for Boston; but at the first station he had jumped off the train with a hand-bag and scrambled up into the hills. For two golden rainless August weeks he had camped in the house, getting eggs and milk from the solitary farm in the valley, where no one knew him, and doing his cooking over a spirit-lamp. He got up every day with the sun, took a plunge in a brown pool he knew of, and spent long hours lying in the scented hemlock-woods above the house, or wandering along the yoke of the Eagle Ridge, far above the misty blue valleys that swept away east and west between the endless hills. And in the afternoon Charity came to him.

With part of what was left of her savings she had hired a bicycle for a month, and every day after dinner, as soon as her guardian started to his office, she hurried to the library, got out her bicycle, and flew down the Creston road. She knew that Mr. Royall, like everyone else in North Dormer, was perfectly aware of her acquisition: possibly he, as well as the rest of the village, knew what use she made of it. She did not care: she felt him to be so powerless that if he had questioned her she would probably have told him the truth. But they had never spoken to each other since the night on the wharf at Nettleton. He had returned to North Dormer only on the third day after that encounter, arriving just as Charity and Verena were sitting down to supper. He had drawn up his chair, taken his napkin from the sideboard drawer, pulled it out of its ring, and seated himself as unconcernedly as if he had come in from his usual afternoon session at Carrick Fry's; and the long habit of the household made it seem almost natural that Charity should not so much as raise her eyes when he entered. She had simply let him understand that her silence was not accidental by leaving the table while he was still eating, and going up without a word to shut herself into her room. After that he formed the habit of talking loudly and genially to Verena whenever Charity was in the room; but otherwise there was no apparent change in their relations.

She did not think connectedly of these things while she sat waiting for Harney, but they remained in her mind as a sullen background against which her short hours with him flamed out like forest fires. Nothing else mattered, neither the good nor the bad, or what might have seemed so before she knew him. He had caught her up and carried her away into a new world, from which, at stated hours, the ghost of her came back to perform certain customary acts, but all so thinly and insubstantially that she sometimes wondered that the people she went about among could see her. . . .

Behind the swarthy Mountain the sun had gone down in waveless gold. From a pasture up the slope a tinkle of cow-bells sounded; a puff of smoke hung over the farm in the valley, trailed on the pure air and was gone. For a few minutes, in the clear light that is all shadow, fields and woods were outlined with an unreal precision; then the twilight blotted them out, and the little house turned gray and spectral under its wizened apple-branches.

Charity's heart contracted. The first fall of night after a day of radiance often gave her a sense of hidden menace: it was like looking out over the world as it would be when love had gone from it. She wondered if some day she would sit in that same place and watch in vain for her lover. . . .

His bicycle-bell sounded down the lane, and in a minute she was at the gate and his eyes were laughing in hers. They walked back through the long grass, and pushed open the door behind the house. The room at first seemed quite dark and they had to grope their way in hand in hand. Through the window-frame the sky looked light by contrast, and above the black mass of asters in the earthern jar one white star glimmered like a moth.

"There was such a lot to do at the last minute," Harney was explaining, "and I had to drive down to Creston to meet someone who has come to stay with my cousin for the show."

He had his arms about her, and his kisses were in her hair and on her lips. Under his touch things deep down in her struggled to the light and sprang up like flowers in sunshine. She twisted her fingers into his, and they sat down side by side on the improvised couch. She hardly heard his excuses for being late: in his absence a thousand doubts tormented her, but as soon as he appeared she ceased to wonder where he had come from, what had delayed him, who had kept him from her. It seemed as if the places he had been in, and the people he had been with, must cease to exist when he left them, just as her own life was suspended in his absence.

He continued, now, to talk to her volubly and gaily, deploring his lateness, grumbling at the demands on his time, and good-humouredly mimicking Miss Hatchard's benevolent agitation. "She hurried off Miles to ask Mr. Royall to speak at the Town Hall tomorrow: I didn't know till it was done." Charity was silent, and he added: "After all, perhaps it's just as well. No one else could have done it."

Charity made no answer: she did not care what part her guardian played in the morrow's ceremonies. Like all the other figures peopling her meagre world he had grown non-existent to her. She had even put off hating him.

"Tomorrow I shall only see you from far off," Harney continued. "But in the evening there'll be the dance in the Town Hall. Do you want me to promise not to dance with any other girl?"

Any other girl? Were there any others? She had forgotten even that peril, so enclosed did he and she seem in their secret world. Her heart gave a frightened jerk.

"Yes, promise."

He laughed and took her in his arms. "You goose—not even if they're hideous?"

He pushed the hair from her forehead, bending her face back, as his way was, and leaning over so that his head loomed black between her eyes and the paleness of the sky, in which the white star floated . . .

Side by side they sped back along the dark wood-road to the village. A late moon was rising, full orbed and fiery, turning the mountain ranges from fluid gray to a massive blackness, and making the upper sky so light that the stars looked as faint as their own reflections in water. At the edge of the wood, half a mile from North Dormer, Harney jumped from his bicycle, took Charity in his arms for a last kiss, and then waited while she went on alone.

They were later than usual, and instead of taking the bicycle to the library she propped it against the back of the wood-shed and entered the kitchen of the red house. Verena sat there alone; when Charity came in she looked at her with mild impenetrable eyes and then took a plate and a glass of milk from the shelf and set them silently on the table. Charity nodded her thanks, and sitting down fell hungrily upon her piece of pie and emptied the glass. Her face burned with her quick flight through the night, and her eyes were dazzled by the twinkle of the kitchen lamp. She felt like a night-bird suddenly caught and caged.

"He ain't come back since supper," Verena said. "He's down to the Hall."

Charity took no notice. Her soul was still winging through the forest. She washed her plate and tumbler, and then felt her way up the dark stairs. When she opened her door a wonder arrested her. Before going out she had closed her shutters against the afternoon heat, but they had swung partly open, and a bar of moonlight, crossing the room, rested on her bed and showed a dress of China silk laid out on it in virgin whiteness. Charity had spent more than she could afford on the dress, which was to surpass those of all the other girls; she had wanted to let North Dormer see that she was worthy of Harney's admiration. Above the dress, folded on the pillow, was the white veil which the young women who took part in the exercises were to wear under a wreath of asters; and beside the veil a pair of slim white satin shoes that Ally had produced from an old trunk in which she stored mysterious treasures.

Charity stood gazing at all the outspread whiteness. It recalled a vision that had come to her in the night after her first meeting with Harney. She no longer had such visions . . . warmer splendours had displaced them . . . but it was stupid of Ally to have paraded all those white things on her bed, exactly as Hattie Targatt's wedding dress from Springfield had been spread out for the neighbours to see when she married Tom Fry. . . .

Charity took up the satin shoes and looked at them curiously. By day, no doubt, they would appear a little worn, but in the moonlight they seemed carved of ivory. She sat down on the floor to try them on, and they fitted her perfectly, though when she stood up she lurched a little on the high heels. She looked down at her feet, which the graceful mould of the slippers had marvellously arched and narrowed. She had never seen such shoes before, even in the shop-windows at Nettleton . . . never, except . . . yes, once, she had noticed a pair of the same shape on Annabel Balch.

A blush of mortification swept over her. Ally sometimes sewed for Miss Balch when that brilliant being descended on North Dormer, and no doubt she picked up presents of cast-off clothing: the treasures in the mysterious trunk all came from the people she worked for. There could be no doubt that the white slippers were Annabel Balch's. . . .

As she stood there, staring down moodily at her feet, she heard the triple click-click-click of a bicycle-bell under her window. It was Harney's secret signal as he passed on his way home. She stumbled to the window on her high heels, flung open the shutters and leaned out. He waved to her and sped by, his black shadow dancing merrily ahead of him down the empty moonlit road; and she leaned there watching him till he vanished under the Hatchard spruces.

XIII

The Town Hall was crowded and exceedingly hot. As Charity marched into it, third in the white muslin file headed by Orma Fry, she was conscious mainly of the brilliant effect of the wreathed columns framing the green-carpeted stage toward which she was moving and of the unfamiliar faces turning from the front rows to watch the advance of the procession.

But it was all a bewildering blur of eyes and colours till she found herself standing at the back of the stage, her great bunch of asters and goldenrod held well in front of her, and answering the nervous glance of Lambert Sollas, the organist from Mr. Miles's church, who had come up from Nettleton to play the harmonium, and sat behind it, running his conductor's eye over the fluttered girls.

A moment later Mr. Miles, pink and twinkling, emerged from the background, as if buoyed up on his broad white gown, and briskly dominated the bowed heads in the front rows. He prayed energetically and briefly and then retired, and a fierce nod from Lambert Sollas warned the girls that they were to follow at once with "Home, Sweet Home." It was a joy to Charity to sing: it seemed as though, for the first time, her secret rapture might burst from her and flash its defiance at the world. All the glow in her blood, the breath of the summer earth, the rustle of the forest, the fresh call of birds at sunrise, and the brooding midday languors, seemed to pass into her untrained voice, lifted and led by the sustaining chorus.

And then suddenly the song was over, and after an uncertain pause, during which Miss Hatchard's pearl-grey gloves started a furtive signalling down the hall, Mr. Royall, emerging in turn, ascended the steps of the stage and appeared behind the flower-wreathed desk. He passed close to Charity, and she noticed that his gravely set face wore the look of majesty that used to awe and fascinate her childhood. His frock-coat had been carefully brushed and ironed, and the ends of his narrow black tie were so nearly even that the tying must have cost him a protracted struggle. His appearance struck her all the more because it was the first time she had looked him full in the face since the night at Nettleton, and nothing in his grave and impressive demeanour revealed a trace of the lamentable figure on the wharf.

He stood a moment behind the desk, resting his finger-tips against it, and bending slightly toward his audience; then he straightened himself and began.

At first she paid no heed to what he was saying: only fragments of sentences, sonorous quotations, allusions to illustrious men, including the obligatory tribute to Honorius Hatchard, drifted past her inattentive ears. She was trying to discover Harney among the notable people in the front row; but he was nowhere near Miss

Hatchard, who, crowned by a pearl-grey hat that matched her gloves, sat just below the desk, supported by Mrs. Miles and an important-looking unknown lady. Charity was near one end of the stage, and from where she sat the other end of the first row of seats was cut off by the screen of foliage masking the harmonium. The effort to see Harney around the corner of the screen, or through its interstices, made her unconscious of everything else; but the effort was unsuccessful, and gradually she found her attention arrested by her guardian's discourse.

She had never heard him speak in public before, but she was familiar with the rolling music of his voice when he read aloud, or held forth to the selectmen about the stove at Carrick Fry's. Today his inflections were richer and graver than she had ever known them: he spoke slowly, with pauses that seemed to invite his hearers to silent participation in his thought; and Charity perceived a light of response in their faces.

He was nearing the end of his address . . . "Most of you," he said, "most of you who have returned here today, to take contact with this little place for a brief hour, have come only on a pious pilgrimage, and will go back presently to busy cities and lives full of larger duties. But that is not the only way of coming back to North Dormer. Some of us, who went out from here in our youth . . . went out, like you, to busy cities and larger duties . . . have come back in another way—come back for good. I am one of those, as many of you know. . . ." He paused, and there was a sense of suspense in the listening hall. "My history is without interest, but it has its lesson: not so much for those of you who have already made your lives in other places, as for the young men who are perhaps planning even now to leave these quiet hills and go down into the struggle. Things they cannot foresee may send some of those young men back some day to the little township and the old homestead: they may come back for good. . . ." He looked about him, and repeated gravely : "For *good*. There's the point I want to make . . . North Dormer is a poor little place, almost lost in a mighty landscape: perhaps, by this time, it might have been a bigger place, and more in scale with the landscape, if those who had to come back had come with that feeling in their minds—that they wanted to come back for *good* . . . and not for bad . . . or just for indifference. . . .

"Gentlemen, let us look at things as they are. Some of us have come back to our native town because we'd failed to get on elsewhere. One way or other, things had gone wrong with us . . . what we'd dreamed of hadn't come true. But the fact that we had failed elsewhere is no reason why we should fail here. Our very experiments in larger places, even if they were unsuccessful, ought to have helped us to make North Dormer a larger place . . . and you young men who are preparing even now to follow the call of ambition, and turn your back on the old homes—well, let me say this to you, that if ever you do come back to them it's worth while to come back to them for their good. . . . And to do that, you must keep on loving them while you're away from them; and even if you come back against your will—and thinking it's all a bitter mistake of Fate or Providence—you must try to make the best of it, and to make the best of your old town; and after a while—well, ladies and gentlemen, I give you my recipe for what it's worth; after a while, I believe you'll be able to say, as I can say today: 'I'm glad I'm here.' Believe me, all of you, the best way to help the places we live in is to be glad we live there."

He stopped, and a murmur of emotion and surprise ran through the audience. It was not in the least what they had expected, but it moved them more than what they had expected would have moved them. "Hear, hear!" a voice cried out in the middle of the hall. An outburst of cheers caught up the cry, and as they subsided Charity heard Mr. Miles saying to someone near him: "That was a *man* talking—" He wiped his spectacles.

Mr. Royall had stepped back from the desk, and taken his seat in the row of chairs in front of the harmonium. A dapper white-haired gentleman—a distant Hatchard —succeeded him behind the goldenrod, and began to say beautiful things about the old oaken bucket, patient white-haired mothers, and where the boys used to go nutting . . . and Charity began again to search for Harney. . . .

Suddenly Mr. Royall pushed back his seat, and one of the maple branches in front of the harmonium collapsed with a crash. It uncovered the end of the first row and in one of the seats Charity saw Harney, and in the next a lady whose face was turned toward him, and almost hidden by the brim of her drooping hat. Charity did not need to see the face. She knew at a glance the slim figure, the fair hair heaped up under the hat-brim, the long pale wrinkled gloves with bracelets slipping over them. At the fall of the branch Miss Balch turned her head toward the stage, and in her pretty thin-lipped smile there lingered the reflection of something her neighbour had been whispering to her. . . .

Someone came forward to replace the fallen branch, and Miss Balch and Harney were once more hidden. But to Charity the vision of their two faces had blotted out everything. In a flash they had shown her the bare reality of her situation. Behind the frail screen of her lover's caresses was the whole inscrutable mystery of his life: his relations with other people—with other women—his opinions, his prejudices, his principles, the net of influences and interests and ambitions in which every man's life is entangled. Of all these she knew nothing, except what he had told her of his architectural aspirations. She had always dimly guessed him to be in touch with important people, involved in complicated relations—but she felt it all to be so far beyond her understanding that the whole subject hung like a luminous mist on the farthest verge of her thoughts. In the foreground, hiding all else, there was the glow of his presence, the light and shadow of his face, the way his short-sighted eyes, at her approach, widened and deepened as if to draw her down into them; and, above all, the flush of youth and tenderness in which his words enclosed her.

Now she saw him detached from her, drawn back into the unknown, and whisper-ing to another girl things that provoked the same smile of mischievous complicity he had so often called to her own lips. The feeling possessing her was not one of jealousy: she was too sure of his love. It was rather a terror of the unknown, of all the mysterious attractions that must even now be dragging him away from her, and of her own powerlessness to contend with them.

She had given him all she had—but what was it compared to the other gifts life held for him? She understood now the case of girls like herself to whom this kind of thing happened. They gave all they had, but their all was not enough: it could not buy more than a few moments. . . .

The heat had grown suffocating—she felt it descend on her in smothering waves, and the faces in the crowded hall began to dance like the pictures flashed on the screen at Nettleton. For an instant Mr. Royall's countenance detached itself from the general blur. He had resumed his place in front of the harmonium, and sat close to her, his eyes on her face; and his look seemed to pierce to the very centre of her confused sensations. . . . A feeling of physical sickness rushed over her—and then deadly apprehension. The light of the fiery hours in the little house swept back on her in a glare of fear. . . .

She forced herself to look away from her guardian, and became aware that the oratory of the Hatchard cousin had ceased, and that Mr. Miles was again flapping his wings. Fragments of his peroration floated through her bewildered brain. . . . "A rich harvest of hallowed memories. . . . A sanctified hour to which, in moments of trial, your thoughts will prayerfully return. . . . And now, O Lord, let us humbly and fervently give thanks for this blessed day of reunion, here in the old home to which we have come back from so far. Preserve it to us, O Lord, in times to come, in all its homely sweetness—in the kindliness and wisdom of its old people, in the courage and industry of its young men, in the piety and purity of this group of innocent girls—" He flapped a white wing in their direction, and at the same moment Lambert Sollas, with his fierce nod, struck the opening bars of "Auld Lang Syne." . . . Charity stared straight ahead of her and then, dropping her flowers, fell face downward at Mr. Royall's feet.

XIV

North Dormer's celebration naturally included the villages attached to its township, and the festivities were to radiate over the whole group, from Dormer and the two Crestons to Hamblin, the lonely hamlet on the north slope of the Mountain where the first snow always fell. On the third day there were speeches and ceremonies at Creston and Creston River; on the fourth the principal performers were to be driven in buck-boards to Dormer and Hamblin.

It was on the fourth day that Charity returned for the first time to the little house. She had not seen Harney alone since they had parted at the wood's edge the night before the celebrations began. In the interval she had passed through many moods, but for the moment the terror which had seized her in the Town Hall had faded to the edge of consciousness. She had fainted because the hall was stiflingly hot, and because the speakers had gone on and on. . . . Several other people had been affected by the heat, and had had to leave before the exercises were over. There had been thunder in the air all the afternoon, and everyone said afterward that something ought to have been done to ventilate the hall. . . .

At the dance that evening—where she had gone reluctantly, and only because she feared to stay away, she had sprung back into instant reassurance. As soon as she entered she had seen Harney waiting for her, and he had come up with kind gay eyes, and swept her off in a waltz. Her feet were full of music, and though her only training had been with the village youths she had no difficulty in tuning her steps to his. As they circled about the floor all her vain fears dropped from her, and she even forgot that she was probably dancing in Annabel Balch's slippers.

When the waltz was over Harney, with a last hand-clasp, left her to meet Miss Hatchard and Miss Balch, who were just entering. Charity had a moment of anguish as Miss Balch appeared; but it did not last. The triumphant fact of her own greater beauty, and of Harney's sense of it, swept her apprehensions aside. Miss Balch, in an unbecoming dress, looked sallow and pinched, and Charity fancied there was a worried expression in her pale-lashed eyes. She took a seat near Miss Hatchard and it was presently apparent that she did not mean to dance. Charity did not dance often either. Harney explained to her that Miss Hatchard had begged him to give each of the other girls a turn; but he went through the form of asking Charity's permission each time he led one out, and that gave her a sense of secret triumph even completer than when she was whirling about the room with him. . . .

She was thinking of all this as she waited for him in the deserted house. The late afternoon was sultry, and she had tossed aside her hat and stretched herself at full length on the Mexican blanket because it was cooler indoors than under the trees. She lay with her arms folded beneath her head, gazing out at the shaggy shoulder of the Mountain. The sky behind it was full of the splintered glories of the descending sun, and before long she expected to hear Harney's bicycle-bell in the lane. He had bicycled to Hamblin, instead of driving there with his cousin and her friends, so that he might be able to make his escape earlier and stop on the way back at the deserted house, which was on the road to Hamblin. They had smiled together at the joke of hearing the crowded buckboards roll by on the return, while they lay close in their hiding above the road. Such childish triumphs still gave her a sense of reckless security.

Nevertheless she had not wholly forgotten the vision of fear that had opened before her in the Town Hall. The sense of lastingness was gone from her and every moment with Harney would now be ringed with doubt.

The Mountain was turning purple against a fiery sunset from which it seemed to be divided by a knife-edge of quivering light; and above this wall of flame the whole sky was a pure pale green, like some cold mountain lake in shadow. Charity lay gazing up at it, and watching for the first white star. . . .

Her eyes were still fixed on the upper reaches of the sky when she became aware that a shadow had flitted across the glory-flooded room: it must have been Harney passing the window against the sunset. . . . She half raised herself, and then dropped back on her folded arms. The combs had slipped from her hair, and it trailed in a rough dark rope across her breast. She lay quite still, a sleepy smile on her lips, her indolent lids half shut. There was a fumbling at the padlock and she called out: "Have you slipped the chain?" The door opened, and Mr. Royall walked into the room.

She started up, sitting back against the cushions, and they looked at each other without speaking. Then Mr. Royall closed the door-latch and advanced a few steps.

Charity jumped to her feet. "What have you come for?" she stammered.

The last glare of the sunset was on her guardian's face, which looked ash-coloured in the yellow radiance.

"Because I knew you were here," he answered simply.

She had become conscious of the hair hanging loose across her breast, and it seemed as though she could not speak to him till she had set herself in order. She groped for her combs, and tried to fasten up the coil. Mr. Royall silently watched her.

"Charity," he said, "he'll be here in a minute. Let me talk to you first."

"You've got no right to talk to me. I can do what I please."

"Yes. What is it you mean to do?"

"I needn't answer that, or anything else."

He had glanced away, and stood looking curiously about the illuminated room.

Purple asters and red maple-leaves filled the jar on the table; on a shelf against the wall stood a lamp, the kettle, a little pile of cups and saucers. The canvas chairs were grouped about the table.

"So this is where you meet," he said.

His tone was quiet and controlled, and the fact disconcerted her. She had been ready to give him violence for violence, but this calm acceptance of things as they were left her without a weapon.

"See here, Charity—you're always telling me I've got no rights over you. There might be two ways of looking at that—but I ain't going to argue it. All I know is I raised you as good as I could, and meant fairly by you always—except once, for a bad half-hour. There's no justice in weighing that half-hour against the rest, and you know it. If you hadn't, you wouldn't have gone on living under my roof. Seems to me the fact of your doing that gives me some sort of a right; the right to try and keep you out of trouble. I'm not asking you to consider any other."

She listened in silence, and then gave a slight laugh. "Better wait till I'm in trouble," she said.

He paused a moment, as if weighing her words. "Is that all your answer?"

"Yes, that's all."

"Well—I'll wait."

He turned away slowly, but as he did so the thing she had been waiting for happened; the door opened again and Harney entered.

He stopped short with a face of astonishment, and then, quickly controlling himself, went up to Mr. Royall with a frank look.

"Have you come to see me, sir?" he said coolly, throwing his cap on the table with an air of proprietorship.

Mr. Royall again looked slowly about the room; then his eyes turned to the young man.

"Is this your house?" he inquired.

Harney laughed: "Well—as much as it's anybody's. I come here to sketch occasionally."

"And to receive Miss Royall's visits?"

"When she does me the honour—"

"Is this the home you propose to bring her to when you get married?"

There was an immense and oppressive silence. Charity, quivering with anger, started forward, and then stood silent, too humbled for speech. Harney's eyes had dropped under the old man's gaze; but he raised them presently, and looking steadily at Mr. Royall, said: "Miss Royall is not a child. Isn't it rather absurd to talk of her as if she were? I believe she considers herself free to come and go as she pleases, without any questions from anyone." He paused and added: "I'm ready to answer any she wishes to ask me."

Mr. Royall turned to her. "Ask him when he's going to marry you, then—" There was another silence, and he laughed in his turn—a broken laugh, with a scraping sound in it. "You darsn't!" he shouted out with sudden passion. He went close up to Charity, his right arm lifted, not in menace but in tragic exhortation.

"You darsn't, and you know it—and you know why!" He swung back again upon the young man. "And you know why you ain't asked her to marry you, and why you don't mean to. It's because you hadn't need to; nor any other man either. I'm the only one that was fool enough not to know that; and I guess nobody'll repeat my mistake—not in Eagle County, anyhow. They all know what she is, and what she came from. They all know her mother was a woman of the town from Nettleton, that followed one of those Mountain fellows up to his place and lived there with him like a heathen. I saw her there sixteen years ago, when I went to bring this child down. I went to save her from the kind of life her mother was leading—but I'd better have left her in the kennel she came from. . . ." He paused and stared darkly at the two young people, and out beyond them, at the menacing Mountain with its rim of fire; then he sat down beside the table on which they had so often spread their rustic supper, and covered his face with his hands. Harney leaned in the window, a frown on his face: he was twirling between his fingers a small package that dangled from a loop of string. . . . Charity heard Mr. Royall draw a hard breath or two, and his shoulders shook a little. Presently he stood up and walked across the room. He did not look again at the young people: they saw him feel his way to the door and fumble for the latch; and then he went out into the darkness.

After he had gone there was a long silence. Charity waited for Harney to speak; but he seemed at first not to find anything to say. At length he broke out irrelevantly: "I wonder how he found out?"

She made no answer and he tossed down the package he had been holding, and went up to her.

"I'm so sorry, dear . . . that this should have happened. . . ."

She threw her head back proudly. "I ain't ever been sorry—not a minute!"

"No."

She waited to be caught into his arms, but he turned away from her irresolutely. The last glow was gone from behind the Mountain. Everything in the room had turned grey and indistinct, and an autumnal dampness crept up from the hollow below the orchard, laying its cold touch on their flushed faces. Harney walked the length of the room, and then turned back and sat down at the table.

"Come," he said imperiously.

She sat down beside him, and he untied the string about the package and spread out a pile of sandwiches.

"I stole them from the love-feast at Hamblin," he said with a laugh, pushing them over to her. She laughed too, and took one, and began to eat.

"Didn't you make the tea?"

"No," she said. "I forgot—"

"Oh, well—it's too late to boil the water now." He said nothing more, and sitting opposite to each other they went on silently eating the sandwiches. Darkness had descended in the little room, and Harney's face was a dim blur to Charity. Suddenly he leaned across the table and laid his hand on hers.

"I shall have to go off for a while—a month or two, perhaps—to arrange some things; and then I'll come back . . . and we'll get married."

His voice seemed like a stranger's: nothing was left in it of the vibrations she knew. Her hand lay inertly under his, and she left it there, and raised her head, trying to answer him. But the words died in her throat. They sat motionless, in their attitude of confident endearment, as if some strange death had surprised them. At length Harney sprang to his feet with a slight shiver. "God! how damp—we couldn't have come here much longer." He went to the shelf, took down a tin candle-stick and lit the candle; then he propped an unhinged shutter against the empty window-frame and put the candle on the table. It threw up a queer shadow on his frowning forehead, and made the smile on his lips a grimace.

"But it's been good, though, hasn't it, Charity? . . . What's the matter—why do you stand there staring at me? Haven't the days here been good?" He went up to her and caught her to his breast. "And there'll be others—lots of others . . . jollier . . . even jollier . . . won't there, darling?"

He turned her head back, feeling for the curve of her throat below the ear, and kissing her there, and on the hair and eyes and lips. She clung to him desperately, and as he drew her to his knees on the couch she felt as if they were being sucked down together into some bottomless abyss.

XV

That night, as usual, they said good-bye at the wood's edge.

Harney was to leave the next morning early. He asked Charity to say nothing of their plans till his return, and, strangely even to herself, she was glad of the postponement. A leaden weight of shame hung on her, benumbing every other sensation, and she bade him good-bye with hardly a sign of emotion. His reiterated promises to return seemed almost wounding. She had no doubt that he intended to come back; her doubts were far deeper and less definable.

Since the fanciful vision of the future that had flitted through her imagination at their first meeting she had hardly ever thought of his marrying her. She had not had to put the thought from her mind; it had not been there. If ever she looked ahead she felt instinctively that the gulf between them was too deep, and that the bridge their passion had flung across it was as insubstantial as a rainbow. But she seldom looked ahead; each day was so rich that it absorbed her. . . . Now her first feeling was that everything would be different, and that she herself would be a different being to Harney. Instead of remaining separate and absolute, she would be compared with other people, and unknown things would be expected of her. She was too proud to be afraid, but the freedom of her spirit drooped. . . .

Harney had not fixed any date for his return; he had said he would have to look about first, and settle things. He had promised to write as soon as there was anything definite to say, and had left her his address, and asked her to write also. But the address frightened her. It was in New York, at a club with a long name in Fifth Avenue: it seemed to raise an insurmountable barrier between them. Once or twice, in the first days, she got out a sheet of paper, and sat looking at it, and trying to think what to say: but she had the feeling that her letter would never reach its destination. She had never written to anyone farther away than Hepburn.

Harney's first letter came after he had been gone about ten days. It was tender but grave, and bore no resemblance to the gay little notes he had sent her by the freckled boy from Creston River. He spoke positively of his intention of coming back, but named no date, and reminded Charity of their agreement that their plans should not be divulged till he had had time to "settle things." When that would be he could not yet foresee; but she could count on his returning as soon as the way was clear.

She read the letter with a strange sense of its coming from immeasurable distances and having lost most of its meaning on the way; and in reply she sent him a coloured post-card of Creston Falls, on which she wrote: "With love from Charity." She felt the pitiful inadequacy of this, and understood, with a sense of despair, that in her inability to express herself she must give him an impression of coldness and reluctance; but she could not help it. She could not forget that he had never spoken to her of marriage till Mr. Royall had forced the word from his lips; though she had not had the strength to shake off the spell that bound her to him she had lost all spontaneity of feeling, and seemed to herself to be passively awaiting a fate she could not avert.

She had not seen Mr. Royall on her return to the red house. The morning after her parting from Harney, when she came down from her room, Verena told her that her guardian had gone off to Worcester and Portland. It was the time of year when he usually reported to the insurance agencies he represented, and there was nothing unusual in his departure except its suddenness. She thought little about him, except to be glad he was not there. . . .

She kept to herself for the first days, while North Dormer was recovering from its brief plunge into publicity, and the subsiding agitation left her unnoticed. But the faithful Ally could not be long avoided. For the first few days after the close of the Old Home Week festivities Charity escaped her by roaming the hills all day when she was not at her post in the library; but after that a period of rain set in, and one pouring afternoon Ally, sure that she would find her friend indoors, came around to the red house with her sewing.

The two girls sat upstairs in Charity's room. Charity, her idle hands in her lap, was sunk in a kind of leaden dream, through which she was only half-conscious of Ally, who sat opposite her in a low rush-bottomed chair, her work pinned to her knee, and her thin lips pursed up as she bent above it.

"It was my idea running a ribbon through the gauging," she said proudly, drawing back to contemplate the blouse she was trimming. "It's for Miss Balch: she was awfully pleased." She paused and then added, with a queer tremor in her piping voice: "I darsn't have told her I got the idea from one I saw on Julia."

Charity raised her eyes listlessly. "Do you still see Julia sometimes?"

Ally reddened, as if the allusion had escaped her unintentionally. "Oh, it was a long time ago I seen her with those gaugings. . . ."

Silence fell again, and Ally presently continued: "Miss Balch left me a whole lot of things to do over this time."

"Why—has she gone?" Charity inquired with an inner start of apprehension.

"Didn't you know? She went off the morning after they had the celebration at Hamblin. I seen her drive by early with Mr. Harney."

There was another silence, measured by the steady tick of the rain against the window, and, at intervals, by the snipping sound of Ally's scissors.

Ally gave a meditative laugh. "Do you know what she told me before she went away? She told me she was going to send for me to come over to Springfield and make some things for her wedding."

Charity again lifted her heavy lids and stared at Ally's pale pointed face, which moved to and fro above her moving fingers.

"Is she going to get married?"

Ally let the blouse sink to her knee, and sat gazing at it. Her lips seemed suddenly dry, and she moistened them a little with her tongue.

"Why, I presume so . . . from what she said. . . . Didn't you know?"

"Why should I know?"

Ally did not answer. She bent above the blouse, and began picking out a basting thread with the point of the scissors.

"Why should I know?" Charity repeated harshly.

"I didn't know but what . . . folks here say she's engaged to Mr. Harney."

Charity stood up with a laugh, and stretched her arms lazily above her head.

"If all the people got married that folks say are going to you'd have your time full making wedding dresses," she said ironically.

"Why—don't you believe it?" Ally ventured.

"It wouldn't make it true if I did—nor prevent it if I didn't."

"That's so. . . . I only know I seen her crying the night of the party because her dress didn't set right. That was why she wouldn't dance any. . . ."

Charity stood absently gazing down at the lacy garment on Ally's knee. Abruptly she stooped and snatched it up.

"Well, I guess she won't dance in this either," she said with sudden violence; and grasping the blouse in her strong young hands she tore it in two and flung the tattered bits to the floor.

"Oh, Charity—" Ally cried, springing up. For a long interval the two girls faced each other across the ruined garment. Ally burst into tears.

"Oh, what'll I say to her? What'll I do? It was real lace!" she wailed between her piping sobs.

Charity glared at her unrelentingly. "You'd oughtn't to have brought it here," she said, breathing quickly. "I hate other people's clothes—it's just as if they were there themselves." The two stared at each other again over this avowal, till Charity brought out, in a gasp of anguish: "Oh, go—go—go—or I'll hate you too. . . ."

When Ally left her, she fell sobbing across her bed.

The long storm was followed by a north-west gale, and when it was over the hills took on their first umber tints, the sky grew more densely blue, and the big white clouds lay against the hills like snow-banks. The first crisp maple-leaves began to spin across Miss Hatchard's lawn, and the Virginia creeper on the Memorial splashed the white porch with scarlet. It was a golden triumphant September. Day by day the flame of the Virginia creeper spread to the hillsides in wider waves of carmine and crimson, the larches glowed like the thin yellow halo about a fire, the maples blazed and smouldered, and the black hemlocks turned to indigo against the incandescence of the forest.

The nights were cold, with a dry glitter of stars so high up that they seemed smaller and more vivid. Sometimes, as Charity lay sleepless on her bed through the long hours, she felt as though she were bound to those wheeling fires and swinging with them around the great black vault. At night she planned many things . . . it was then she wrote to Harney. But the letters were never put on paper, for she did not know how to express what she wanted to tell him. So she waited. Since her talk with Ally she had felt sure that Harney was engaged to Annabel Balch, and that the process of "settling things" would involve the breaking of this tie. Her first rage of jealousy over, she felt no fear on this score. She was still sure that Harney would come back, and she was equally sure that, for the moment at least, it was she whom he loved and not Miss Balch. Yet the girl, no less, remained a rival, since she represented all the things that Charity felt herself most incapable of understanding or achieving. Annabel Balch was, if not the girl Harney ought to marry, at least the kind of girl it would be natural for him to marry. Charity had never been able to picture herself as his wife; had never been able to arrest the vision and follow it out in its daily consequences; but she could perfectly imagine Annabel Balch in that relation to him.

The more she thought of these things the more the sense of fatality weighed on her: she felt the uselessness of struggling against the circumstances. She had never known how to adapt herself; she could only break and tear and destroy. The scene with Ally had left her stricken with shame at her own childish savagery. What would Harney have thought if he had witnessed it? But when she turned the incident over in her puzzled mind she could not imagine what a civilized person would have done in her place. She felt herself too unequally pitted against unknown forces. . . .

At length this feeling moved her to sudden action. She took a sheet of letter paper from Mr. Royall's office, and sitting by the kitchen lamp, one night after Verena had gone to bed, began her first letter to Harney. It was very short:

> I want you should marry Annabel Balch if you promised to. I think maybe you were afraid I'd feel too bad about it. I feel I'd rather you acted right.
>
> > Your loving
> > CHARITY.

She posted the letter early the next morning, and for a few days her heart felt strangely light. Then she began to wonder why she received no answer.

One day as she sat alone in the library pondering these things the walls of books began to spin around her, and the rosewood desk to rock under her elbows. The dizziness was followed by a wave of nausea like that she had felt on the day of the exercises in the Town Hall. But the Town Hall had been crowded and stiflingly hot, and the library was empty, and so chilly that she had kept on her jacket. Five minutes before she had felt perfectly well; and now it seemed as if she were going to die. The bit of lace at which she still languidly worked dropped from her fingers, and the steel crochet hook clattered to the floor. She pressed her temples hard between her damp hands, steadying herself against the desk while the wave of sickness swept over her. Little by little it subsided, and after a few minutes she stood up, shaken and terrified, groped for her hat, and stumbled out into the air. But the whole sunlit autumn world reeled and roared around her as she dragged herself along the interminable length of the road home.

As she approached the red house she saw a buggy standing at the door, and her heart gave a leap. But it was only Mr. Royall who got out, his travelling-bag in hand. He saw her coming, and waited in the porch. She was conscious that he was looking at her intently, as if there was something strange in her appearance, and she threw back her head with a desperate effort at ease. Their eyes met, and she said: "You back?" as if nothing had happened, and he answered: "Yes, I'm back," and walked in ahead of her, pushing open the door of his office. She climbed to her room, every step of the stairs holding her fast as if her feet were lined with glue.

Two days later, she descended from the train at Nettleton, and walked out of the station into the dusty square. The brief interval of cold weather was over, and the day was as soft, and almost as hot, as when she and Harney had emerged on the same scene on the Fourth of July. In the square the same broken-down hacks and carry-alls stood drawn up in a despondent line, and the lank horses with fly-nets over their withers swayed their heads drearily to and fro. She recognized the staring signs over the eating-houses and billiard saloons, and the long lines of wires on lofty poles tapering down the main street to the park at its other end. Taking the way the wires pointed, she went off hastily, with bent head, till she reached a wide transverse street with a brick building at the corner. She crossed this street and glanced furtively up at the front of the brick building; then she returned, and entered a door opening on a flight of steep brass-rimmed stairs. On the second landing she rang a bell, and a mulatto girl with a bushy head and a frilled apron let her into a hall where a stuffed fox on his hind legs proffered a brass card-tray to visitors. At the back of the hall was a glazed door marked: "Office." After waiting a few minutes in a handsomely furnished room, with plush sofas surmounted by large gold-framed photographs of showy young women, Charity was shown into the office. . . .

When she came out of the glazed door Dr. Merkle followed, and led her into another room, smaller, and still more crowded with plush and gold frames. Dr. Merkle was a plump woman with small bright eyes, an immense mass of black hair coming down low on her forehead, and unnaturally white and even teeth. She wore a rich black dress, with gold chains and charms hanging from her bosom. Her hands were large and smooth, and quick in all their movements; and she smelt of musk and carbolic acid.

She smiled on Charity with all her faultless teeth. "Sit down, my dear. Wouldn't you like a little drop of something to pick you up? . . . No. . . . Well, just lay back a minute then. . . . There's nothing to be done just yet; but in about a month, if you'll step round again . . . I could take you right into my own house for two or three days, and there wouldn't be a mite of trouble. Mercy me! The next time you'll know better'n to fret like this. . . ."

Charity gazed at her with widening eyes. This woman with the false hair, the false teeth, the false murderous smile—what was she offering her but immunity from some unthinkable crime? Charity, till then, had been conscious only of a vague self-disgust and a frightening physical distress; now, of a sudden, there came to her the grave surprise of motherhood. She had come to this dreadful place because she knew of no other way of making sure that she was not mistaken about her state; and the woman had taken her for a miserable creature like Julia. . . . The thought was so horrible that she sprang up, white and shaking, one of her great rushes of anger sweeping over her.

Dr. Merkle, still smiling, also rose. "Why do you run off in such a hurry? You can stretch out right here on my sofa. . . ." She paused, and her smile grew more motherly. "Afterwards—if there's been any talk at home, and you want to get away for a while . . . I have a lady friend in Boston who's looking for a companion . . . you're the very one to suit her, my dear. . . ."

Charity had reached the door. "I don't want to stay. I don't want to come back here," she stammered, her hand on the knob; but with a swift movement Dr. Merkle edged her from the threshold.

"Oh, very well. Five dollars, please."

Charity looked helplessly at the doctor's tight lips and rigid face. Her last savings had gone in repaying Ally for the cost of Miss Balch's ruined blouse, and she had had to borrow four dollars from her friend to pay for her railway ticket and cover the doctor's fee. It had never occurred to her that medical advice could cost more than two dollars.

"I didn't know . . . I haven't got that much . . ." she faltered, bursting into tears.

Dr. Merkle gave a short laugh which did not show her teeth, and inquired with concision if Charity supposed she ran the establishment for her own amusement? She leaned her firm shoulders against the door as she spoke, like a grim gaoler making terms with her captive.

"You say you'll come round and settle later? I've heard that pretty often too. Give me your address, and if you can't pay me I'll send the bill to your folks. . . . What? I can't understand what you say. . . . That don't suit you either? My, you're pretty particular for a girl that ain't got enough to settle her own bills. . . ." She paused, and fixed her eyes on the brooch with a blue stone that Charity had pinned to her blouse.

"Ain't you ashamed to talk that way to a lady that's got to earn her living, when you go about with jewellery like that on you? . . . It ain't in my line, and I do it only as a favour . . . but if you're a mind to leave that brooch as a pledge, I don't say no. . . . Yes, of course, you can get it back when you bring me my money. . . ."

On the way home, she felt an immense and unexpected quietude. It had been horrible to have to leave Harney's gift in the woman's hands, but even at that price the news she brought away had not been too dearly bought. She sat with half-closed eyes as the train rushed through the familiar landscape; and now the memories of her former journey, instead of flying before her like dead leaves, seemed to be ripening in her blood like sleeping grain. She would never again know what it was to feel herself alone. Everything seemed to have grown suddenly clear and simple. She no longer had any difficulty in picturing herself as Harney's wife now that she was the mother of his child; and compared to her sovereign right Annabel Balch's claim seemed no more than a girl's sentimental fancy.

That evening, at the gate of the red house, she found Ally waiting in the dusk. "I was down at the post-office just as they were closing up, and Will Targatt said there was a letter for you, so I brought it."

Ally held out the letter, looking at Charity with piercing sympathy. Since the scene of the torn blouse there had been a new and fearful admiration in the eyes she bent on her friend.

Charity snatched the letter with a laugh. "Oh, thank you—good-night," she called out over her shoulder as she ran up the path. If she had lingered a moment she knew she would have had Ally at her heels.

She hurried upstairs and felt her way into her dark room. Her hands trembled as she groped for the matches and lit her candle, and the flap of the envelope was so closely stuck that she had to find her scissors and slit it open. At length she read:

DEAR CHARITY:

I have your letter, and it touches me more than I can say. Won't you trust me, in return, to do my best? There are things it is hard to explain, much less to justify; but your generosity makes everything easier. All I can do now is to thank you from my soul for understanding. Your telling me that you wanted me to do right has helped me beyond expression. If ever there is a hope of realizing what we dreamed of you will see me back on the instant; and I haven't yet lost that hope.

She read the letter with a rush; then she went over and over it, each time more slowly and painstakingly. It was so beautifully expressed that she found it almost as difficult to understand as the gentleman's explanation of the Bible pictures at Nettleton; but gradually she became aware that the gist of its meaning lay in the last few words. "If ever there is a hope of realizing what we dreamed of . . ."

But then he wasn't even sure of that? She understood now that every word and every reticence was an avowal of Annabel Balch's prior claim. It was true that he was engaged to her, and that he had not yet found a way of breaking his engagement.

As she read the letter over Charity understood what it must have cost him to write it. He was not trying to evade an importunate claim; he was honestly and contritely struggling between opposing duties. She did not even reproach him in her thoughts for having concealed from her that he was not free: she could not see anything more reprehensible in his conduct than in her own. From the first she had needed him more than he had wanted her, and the power that had swept them together had been as far beyond resistance as a great gale loosening the leaves of the forest. . . . Only, there stood between them, fixed and upright in the general upheaval, the indestructible figure of Annabel Balch. . . .

Face to face with his admission of the fact, she sat staring at the letter. A cold tremor ran over her, and the hard sobs struggled up into her throat and shook her from head to foot. For a while she was caught and tossed on great waves of anguish that left her hardly conscious of anything but the blind struggle against their assaults. Then, little by little, she began to relive, with a dreadful poignancy, each separate stage of her poor romance. Foolish things she had said came back to her, gay answers Harney had made, his first kiss in the darkness between the fireworks, their choosing the blue brooch together, the way he had teased her about the letters she had dropped in her flight from the evangelist. All these memories, and a thousand others, hummed through her brain till his nearness grew so vivid that she felt his fingers in her hair, and his warm breath on her cheek as he bent her head back like a flower. These things were hers; they had passed into her blood, and become a part of her, they were building the child in her womb; it was impossible to tear asunder strands of life so interwoven.

The conviction gradually strengthened her, and she began to form in her mind the first words of the letter she meant to write to Harney. She wanted to write it at once, and with feverish hands she began to rummage in her drawer for a sheet of letter paper. But there was none left; she must go downstairs to get it. She had a superstitious feeling that the letter must be written on the instant, that setting down her secret in words would bring her reassurance and safety; and taking up her candle she went down to Mr. Royall's office.

At that hour she was not likely to find him there: he had probably had his supper and walked over to Carrick Fry's. She pushed open the door of the unlit room, and the light of her lifted candle fell on his figure, seated in the darkness in his high-backed chair. His arms lay along the arms of the chair, and his head was bent a little; but he lifted it quickly as Charity entered. She started back as their eyes met, remembering that her own were red with weeping, and that her face was livid with the fatigue and emotion of her journey. But it was too late to escape, and she stood and looked at him in silence.

He had risen from his chair, and came toward her with outstretched hands. The gesture was so unexpected that she let him take her hands in his, and they stood thus, without speaking, till Mr. Royall said gravely: "Charity—was you looking for me?"

She freed herself abruptly and fell back. "Me? No—" She set down the candle on his desk. "I wanted some letter-paper, that's all."

His face contracted, and the bushy brows jutted forward over his eyes. Without answering he opened the drawer of the desk, took out a sheet of paper and an envelope, and pushed them toward her. "Do you want a stamp too?" he asked.

She nodded, and he gave her the stamp. As he did so she felt that he was looking at her intently, and she knew that the candle light flickering up on her white face must be distorting her swollen features and exaggerating the dark rings about her eyes. She snatched up the paper, her reassurance dissolving under his pitiless gaze, in which she seemed to read the grim perception of her state, and the ironic recollection of the day when, in that very room, he had offered to compel Harney to marry her. His look seemed to say that he knew she had taken the paper to write to her lover, who had left her as he had warned her she would be left. She remembered the scorn with which she had turned from him that day, and knew, if he guessed the truth, what a list of old scores it must settle. She turned and fled upstairs; but when she got back to her room all the words that had been waiting had vanished. . . .

If she could have gone to Harney it would have been different; she would only have had to show herself to let his memories speak for her. But she had no money left, and there was no one from whom she could have borrowed enough for such a journey. There was nothing to do but to write, and await his reply. For a long time she sat bent above the blank page; but she found nothing to say that really expressed what she was feeling. . . .

Harney had written that she had made it easier for him, and she was glad it was so; she did not want to make things hard. She knew she had it in her power to do that; she held his fate in her hands. All she had to do was to tell him the truth; but that was the very fact that held her back. . . . Her five minutes face to face with Mr. Royall had stripped her of her last illusion, and brought her back to North Dormer's point of view. Distinctly and pitilessly there rose before her the fate of the girl who was married "to make things right." She had seen too many village love-stories end in that way. Poor Rose Cole's miserable marriage was of the number; and what good had come of it for her or for Halston Skeff? They had hated each other from the day the minister married them; and whenever old Mrs. Skeff had a fancy to humiliate her daughter-in-law she had only to say: "Who'd ever think the baby's only two? And for a seven months' child—ain't it a wonder what a size he is?" North Dormer had treasures of indulgence for brands in the burning, but only derision for those who succeeded in getting snatched from it; and Charity had always understood Julia Hawes's refusal to be snatched. . . .

Only—was there no alternative but Julia's? Her soul recoiled from the vision of the white-faced woman among the plush sofas and gilt frames. In the established order of things as she knew them she saw no place for her individual adventure. . . .

She sat in her chair without undressing till faint grey streaks began to divide the black slats of the shutters. Then she stood up and pushed them open, letting in the light. The coming of a new day brought a sharper consciousness of ineluctable reality, and with it a sense of the need of action. She looked at herself in the glass, and saw her face, white in the autumn dawn, with pinched cheeks and dark-ringed eyes, and all the marks of her state that she herself would never have noticed, but that Dr. Merkle's diagnosis had made plain to her. She could not hope that those signs would escape the watchful village; even before her figure lost its shape she knew her face would betray her.

Leaning from her window she looked out on the dark and empty scene; the ashen houses with shuttered windows, the grey road climbing the slope to the hemlock belt above the cemetery, and the heavy mass of the Mountain black against a rainy sky. To the east a space of light was broadening above the forest; but over that also the clouds hung. Slowly her gaze travelled across the fields to the rugged curve of the hills. She had looked out so often on that lifeless circle, and wondered if anything could ever happen to anyone who was enclosed in it. . . .

Almost without conscious thought her decision had been reached; as her eyes had followed the circle of the hills her mind had also travelled the old round. She supposed it was something in her blood that made the Mountain the only answer to her questioning, the inevitable escape from all that hemmed her in and beset her. At any rate it began to loom in her now as it loomed against the rainy dawn; and the longer she looked at it the more clearly she understood that now at last she was really going there.

XVI

The rain held off, and an hour later, when she started, wild gleams of sunlight were blowing across the fields.

After Harney's departure she had returned her bicycle to its owner at Creston, and she was not sure of being able to walk all the way to the Mountain. The deserted house was on the road; but the idea of spending the night there was unendurable, and she meant to try to push on to Hamblin, where she could sleep under a wood-shed if her strength should fail her. Her preparations had been made with quiet forethought. Before starting she had forced herself to swallow a glass of milk and eat a piece of bread; and she had put in her canvas satchel a little packet of the chocolate that Harney always carried in his bicycle bag. She wanted above all to keep up her strength, and reach her destination without attracting notice. . . .

Mile by mile she retraced the road over which she had so often flown to her lover. When she reached the turn where the wood-road branched off from the Creston highway she remembered the Gospel tent—long since folded up and transplanted—and her start of involuntary terror when the fat evangelist had said: "Your Saviour knows everything. Come and confess your guilt." There was no sense of guilt in her now, but only a desperate desire to defend her secret from irreverent eyes, and begin life again among people to whom the harsh code of the village was unknown. The impulse did not shape itself in thought: she only knew she must save her baby, and hide herself with it somewhere where no one would ever come to trouble them.

She walked on and on, growing more heavy-footed as the day advanced. It seemed a cruel chance that compelled her to retrace every step of the way to the deserted house; and when she came in sight of the orchard, and the silver-gray roof slanting crookedly through the laden branches, her strength failed her and she sat down by the roadside. She sat there a long time, trying to gather the courage to start again, and walk past the broken gate and the untrimmed rose-bushes strung with scarlet hips. A few drops of rain were falling, and she thought of the warm evenings when she and Harney had sat embraced in the shadowy room, and the noise of summer showers on the roof had rustled through their kisses. At length she understood that if she stayed any longer the rain might compel her to take shelter in the house overnight, and she got up and walked on, averting her eyes as she came abreast of the white gate and the tangled garden.

The hours wore on, and she walked more and more slowly, pausing now and then to rest, and to eat a little bread and an apple picked up from the roadside. Her body seemed to grow heavier with every yard of the way, and she wondered how she would be able to carry her child later, if already he laid such a burden on her. . . . A fresh wind had sprung up, scattering the rain and blowing down keenly from the mountain. Presently the clouds lowered again, and a few white darts struck her in the face: it was the first snow falling over Hamblin. The roofs of the lonely village were only half a mile ahead, and she was resolved to push beyond it, and try to reach the Mountain that night. She had no clear plan of action, except that, once in the settlement, she meant to look for Liff Hyatt, and get him to take her to her mother. She herself had been born as her own baby was going to be born and whatever her mother's subsequent life had been she could hardly help remembering the past, and receiving a daughter who was facing the trouble she had known.

Suddenly the deadly faintness came over her once more and she sat down on the bank and leaned her head against a tree-trunk. The long road and the cloudy landscape vanished from her eyes, and for a time she seemed to be circling about in some terrible wheeling darkness. Then that too faded.

She opened her eyes, and saw a buggy drawn up beside her, and a man who had jumped down from it and was gazing at her with a puzzled face. Slowly consciousness came back, and she saw that the man was Liff Hyatt.

She was dimly aware that he was asking her something, and she looked at him in silence, trying to find strength to speak. At length her voice stirred in her throat, and she said in a whisper: "I'm going up the Mountain."

"Up the Mountain?" he repeated, drawing aside a little; and as he moved she saw behind him, in the buggy, a heavily coated figure with a familiar pink face and gold spectacles on the bridge of a Grecian nose.

"Charity! What on earth are you doing here?" Mr. Miles exclaimed, throwing the reins on the horse's back and scrambling down from the buggy.

She lifted her heavy eyes to his. "I'm going to see my mother."

The two men glanced at each other, and for a moment neither of them spoke.

Then Mr. Miles said: "You look ill, my dear, and it's a long way. Do you think it's wise?"

Charity stood up. "I've got to go to her."

A vague mirthless grin contracted Liff Hyatt's face, and Mr. Miles again spoke uncertainly. "You know, then—you'd been told?"

She stared at him. "I don't know what you mean. I want to go to her."

Mr. Miles was examining her thoughtfully. She fancied she saw a change in his expression, and the blood rushed to her forehead. "I just want to go to her," she repeated.

He laid his hand on her arm. "My child, your mother is dying. Liff Hyatt came down to fetch me. . . . Get in and come with us."

He helped her up to the seat at his side, Liff Hyatt clambered in at the back, and they drove off toward Hamblin. At first Charity had hardly grasped what Mr. Miles was saying; the physical relief of finding herself seated in the buggy, and securely on her road to the Mountain, effaced the impression of his words. But as her head cleared she began to understand. She knew the Mountain had but the most infrequent intercourse with the valleys; she had often enough heard it said that no one ever went up there except the minister, when someone was dying. And now it was her mother who was dying . . . and she would find herself as much alone on the Mountain as anywhere else in the world. The sense of unescapable isolation was all she could feel for the moment; then she began to wonder at the strangeness of its being Mr. Miles who had undertaken to perform this grim errand. He did not seem in the least like the kind of man who would care to go up the Mountain. But here he was at her side, guiding the horse with a firm hand and bending on her the kindly gleam of his spectacles, as if there were nothing unusual in their being together in such circumstances.

For a while she found it impossible to speak, and he seemed to understand this, and made no attempt to question her. But presently she felt her tears rise and flow down over her drawn cheeks; and he must have seen them too, for he laid his hand on hers, and said in a low voice: "Won't you tell me what is troubling you?"

She shook her head, and he did not insist: but after a while he said, in the same low tone, so that they should not be overheard: "Charity, what do you know of your childhood, before you came down to North Dormer?"

She controlled herself, and answered: "Nothing only what I heard Mr. Royall say one day. He said he brought me down because my father went to prison."

"And you've never been up there since?"

"Never."

Mr. Miles was silent again, then he said: "I'm glad you're coming with me now. Perhaps we may find your mother alive, and she may know that you have come."

They had reached Hamblin, where the snow-flurry had left white patches in the rough grass on the roadside, and in the angles of the roofs facing north. It was a poor bleak village under the granite flank of the Mountain, and as soon as they left it they began to climb. The road was steep and full of ruts, and the horse settled down to a walk while they mounted and mounted, the world dropping away below them in great mottled stretches of forest and field, and stormy dark blue distances.

Charity had often had visions of this ascent of the Mountain but she had not known it would reveal so wide a country, and the sight of those strange lands reaching away on every side gave her a new sense of Harney's remoteness. She knew he must be miles and miles beyond the last range of hills that seemed to be the outmost verge of things, and she wondered how she had ever dreamed of going to New York to find him. . . .

As the road mounted the country grew bleaker, and they drove across fields of faded mountain grass bleached by long months beneath the snow. In the hollows a few white birches trembled, or a mountain ash lit its scarlet clusters; but only a scant growth of pines darkened the granite ledges. The wind was blowing fiercely across the open slopes; the horse faced it with bent head and straining flanks, and now and then the buggy swayed so that Charity had to clutch its side.

Mr. Miles had not spoken again; he seemed to understand that she wanted to be left alone. After a while the track they were following forked, and he pulled up the horse, as if uncertain of the way. Liff Hyatt craned his head around from the back, and shouted against the wind: "Left——" and they turned into a stunted pine-wood and began to drive down the other side of the Mountain.

A mile or two farther on they came out on a clearing where two or three low houses lay in stony fields, crouching among the rocks as if to brace themselves against the wind. They were hardly more than sheds, built of logs and rough boards, with tin stove-pipes sticking out of their roofs. The sun was setting, and dusk had already fallen on the lower world, but a yellow glare still lay on the lonely hillside and the crouching houses. The next moment it faded and left the landscape in dark autumn twilight.

"Over there," Liff called out, stretching his long arm over Mr. Miles's shoulder. The clergyman turned to the left, across a bit of bare ground overgrown with docks and nettles, and stopped before the most ruinous of the sheds. A stove-pipe reached its crooked arm out of one window, and the broken panes of the other were stuffed with rags and paper. In contrast to such a dwelling the brown house in the swamp might have stood for the home of plenty.

As the buggy drew up two or three mongrel dogs jumped out of the twilight with a great barking, and a young man slouched to the door and stood there staring. In the twilight Charity saw that his face had the same sodden look as Bash Hyatt's, the day she had seen him sleeping by the stove. He made no effort to silence the dogs, but leaned in the door, as if roused from a drunken lethargy, while Mr. Miles got out of the buggy.

"Is it here?" the clergyman asked Liff in a low voice; and Liff nodded.

Mr. Miles turned to Charity. "Just hold the horse a minute, my dear: I'll go in first," he said, putting the reins in her hands. She took them passively, and sat staring straight ahead of her at the darkening scene while Mr. Miles and Liff Hyatt went up to the house. They stood a few minutes talking with the man in the door, and then Mr. Miles came back. As he came close, Charity saw that his smooth pink face wore a frightened solemn look.

"Your mother is dead, Charity; you'd better come with me," he said.

She got down and followed him while Liff led the horse away. As she approached the door she said to herself: "This is where I was born . . . this is where I belong. . . ." She had said it to herself often enough as she looked across the sunlit valleys at the Mountain; but it had meant nothing then, and now it had become a reality. Mr. Miles took her gently by the arm, and they entered what appeared to be the only room in the house. It was so dark that she could just discern a group of a dozen people sitting or sprawling about a table made of boards laid across two barrels. They looked up listlessly as Mr. Miles and Charity came in, and a woman's thick voice said: "Here's the preacher." But no one moved.

Mr. Miles paused and looked about him; then he turned to the young man who had met them at the door.

"Is the body here?" he asked.

The young man, instead of answering, turned his head toward the group. "Where's the candle? I tole yer to bring a candle," he said with sudden harshness to a girl who was lolling against the table. She did not answer, but another man got up and took from some corner a candle stuck into a bottle.

"How'll I light it? The stove's out," the girl grumbled.

Mr. Miles fumbled under his heavy wrappings and drew out a match-box. He held a match to the candle, and in a moment or two a faint circle of light fell on the pale aguish heads that started out of the shadow like the heads of nocturnal animals.

"Mary's over there," someone said; and Mr. Miles, taking the bottle in his hand, passed behind the table. Charity followed him, and they stood before a mattress on the floor in a corner of the room. A woman lay on it, but she did not look like a dead woman; she seemed to have fallen across her squalid bed in a drunken sleep, and to have been left lying where she fell, in her ragged disordered clothes. One arm was flung above her head, one leg drawn up under a torn skirt that left the other bare to the knee: a swollen glistening leg with a ragged stocking rolled down about the ankle. The woman lay on her back, her eyes staring up unblinkingly at the candle that trembled in Mr. Miles's hand.

"She jus' dropped off," a woman said, over the shoulder of the others; and the young man added: "I jus' come in and found her."

An elderly man with lank hair and a feeble grin pushed between them. "It was like this: I says to her on'y the night before: if you don't take and quit, I says to her . . ."

Someone pulled him back and sent him reeling against a bench along the wall, where he dropped down muttering his unheeded narrative.

There was a silence; then the young woman who had been lolling against the table suddenly parted the group, and stood in front of Charity. She was healthier and robuster looking than the others, and her weather-beaten face had a certain sullen beauty.

"Who's the girl? Who brought her here?" she said, fixing her eyes mistrustfully on the young man who had rebuked her for not having a candle ready.

Mr. Miles spoke. "I brought her; she is Mary Hyatt's daughter."

"What? Her too?" the girl sneered; and the young man turned on her with an oath. "Shut your mouth, damn you, or get out of here," he said; then he relapsed into his former apathy, and dropped down on the bench, leaning his head against the wall.

Mr. Miles had set the candle on the floor and taken off his heavy coat. He turned to Charity. "Come and help me," he said.

He knelt down by the mattress, and pressed the lids over the dead woman's eyes. Charity, trembling and sick, knelt beside him, and tried to compose her mother's body. She drew the stocking over the dreadful glistening leg, and pulled the skirt down to the battered upturned boots. As she did so, she looked at her mother's face, thin yet swollen, with lips parted in a frozen gasp above the broken teeth. There was no sign in it of anything human: she lay there like a dead dog in a ditch. Charity's hands grew cold as they touched her.

Mr. Miles drew the woman's arms across her breast and laid his coat over her. Then he covered her face with his handkerchief, and placed the bottle with the candle in it at her head. Having done this he stood up.

"Is there no coffin?" he asked, turning to the group behind him.

There was a moment of bewildered silence; then the fierce girl spoke up. "You'd oughter brought it with you. Where'd we get one here, I'd like ter know?"

Mr. Miles, looking at the others, repeated: "Is it possible you have no coffin ready?"

"That's what I say: them that has it sleeps better," an old woman murmured. "But then she never had no bed. . . ."

"And the stove warn't hers," said the lank-haired man, on the defensive.

Mr. Miles turned away from them and moved a few steps apart. He had drawn a book from his pocket, and after a pause he opened it and began to read, holding the book at arm's length and low down, so that the pages caught the feeble light. Charity had remained on her knees by the mattress: now that her mother's face was covered it was easier to stay near her, and avoid the sight of the living faces which too horribly showed by what stages hers had lapsed into death.

"I am the Resurrection and the Life," Mr. Miles began; "he that believeth in me, though he were dead, yet shall he live. . . . Though after my skin worms destroy my body, yet in my flesh shall I see God. . . ."

In my flesh shall I see God! Charity thought of the gaping mouth and stony eyes under the handkerchief, and of the glistening leg over which she had drawn the stocking. . . .

"We brought nothing into this world and we shall take nothing out of it—"

There was a sudden muttering and a scuffle at the back of the group. "I brought the stove," said the elderly man with lank hair, pushing his way between the others. "I wen' down to Creston'n bought it . . . n' I got a right to take it outer here . . . n' I'll lick any feller says I ain't. . . ."

"Sit down, damn you!" shouted the tall youth who had been drowsing on the bench against the wall.

"For man walketh in a vain shadow, and disquieteth himself in vain; he heapeth up riches and cannot tell who shall gather them . . ."

"Well, it *are* his," a woman in the background interjected in a frightened whine.

The tall youth staggered to his feet. "If you don't hold your mouths I'll turn you all out o' here, the whole lot of you," he cried with many oaths. "G'wan, minister . . . don't let 'em faze you. . . ."

"Now is Christ risen from the dead and become the first-fruits of them that slept. . . . Behold, I show you a mystery. We shall not all sleep, but we shall all be changed, in a moment, in the twinkling of an eye, at the last trump. . . . For this corruptible must put on incorruption and this mortal must put on immortality. So when this corruption shall have put on incorruption, and when this mortal shall have put on immortality, then shall be brought to pass the saying that is written, Death is swallowed up in Victory. . . ."

One by one the mighty words fell on Charity's bowed head, soothing the horror, subduing the tumult, mastering her as they mastered the drink-dazed creatures at her back. Mr. Miles read to the last word, and then closed the book.

"Is the grave ready?" he asked.

Liff Hyatt, who had come in while he was reading, nodded a "Yes," and pushed forward to the side of the mattress. The young man on the bench, who seemed to assert some sort of right of kinship with the dead woman, got to his feet again, and the proprietor of the stove joined him. Between them they raised up the mattress; but their movements were unsteady, and the coat slipped to the floor, revealing the poor body in its helpless misery. Charity, picking up the coat, covered her mother once more. Liff had brought a lantern, and the old woman who had already spoken took it up, and opened the door to let the little procession pass out. The wind had dropped, and the night was very dark and bitterly cold. The old woman walked ahead, the lantern shaking in her hand and spreading out before her a pale patch of dead grass and coarse-leaved weeds enclosed in an immensity of blackness.

Mr. Miles took Charity by the arm, and side by side they walked behind the mattress. At length the old woman with the lantern stopped, and Charity saw the light fall on the stooping shoulders of the bearers and on a ridge of upheaved earth over which they were bending. Mr. Miles released her arm and approached the hollow on the other side of the ridge; and while the men stooped down, lowering the mattress into the grave, he began to speak again.

"Man that is born of woman hath but a short time to live and is full of misery. . . . He cometh up and is cut down . . . he fleeth as it were a shadow. . . . Yet, O Lord God most holy, O Lord most mighty, O holy and merciful Saviour, deliver us not into the bitter pains of eternal death. . . ."

"Easy there . . . is she down?" piped the claimant to the stove; and the young man called over his shoulder: "Lift the light there, can't you?"

There was a pause, during which the light floated uncertainly over the open grave. Someone bent over and pulled out Mr. Miles's coat—("No, no—leave the handkerchief," he interposed)—and then Liff Hyatt, coming forward with a spade, began to shovel in the earth.

"Forasmuch as it hath pleased Almighty God of His great mercy to take unto Himself the soul of our dear sister here departed, we therefore commit her body to the ground; earth to earth, ashes to ashes, dust to dust . . ." Liff's gaunt shoulders rose and bent in the lantern light as he dashed the clods of earth into the grave. "God— it's froze a'ready," he muttered, spitting into his palm and passing his ragged shirt-sleeve across his perspiring face.

"Through our Lord Jesus Christ, who shall change our vile body that it may be like unto His glorious body, according to the mighty working, whereby He is able to subdue all things unto Himself . . ." The last spadeful of earth fell on the vile body of Mary Hyatt, and Liff rested on his spade, his shoulder blades still heaving with the effort.

"Lord, have mercy upon us, Christ have mercy upon us, Lord have mercy upon us. . . ."

Mr. Miles took the lantern from the old woman's hand and swept its light across the circle of bleared faces. "Now kneel down, all of you," he commanded, in a voice of authority that Charity had never heard. She knelt down at the edge of the grave, and the others, stiffly and hesitatingly, got to their knees beside her. Mr. Miles knelt, too. "And now pray with me—you know this prayer," he said, and he began: "Our Father which art in Heaven . . ." One or two of the women falteringly took the words up, and when he ended, the lank-haired man flung himself on the neck of the tall youth. "It was this way," he said. "I tole her the night before, I says to her . . ." The reminiscence ended in a sob.

Mr. Miles had been getting into his coat again. He came up to Charity, who had remained passively kneeling by the rough mound of earth.

"My child, you must come. It's very late."

She lifted her eyes to his face: he seemed to speak out of another world.

"I ain't coming: I'm going to stay here."

"Here? Where? What do you mean?"

"These are my folks. I'm going to stay with them."

Mr. Miles lowered his voice. "But it's not possible—you don't know what you are doing. You can't stay among these people: you must come with me."

She shook her head and rose from her knees. The group about the grave had scattered in the darkness, but the old woman with the lantern stood waiting. Her mournful withered face was not unkind, and Charity went up to her.

"Have you got a place where I can lie down for the night?" she asked. Liff came up, leading the buggy out of the night. He looked from one to the other with his feeble smile. "She's my mother. She'll take you home," he said; and he added, raising his voice to speak to the old woman, "It's the girl from lawyer Royall's—Mary's girl . . . you remember. . . ."

The woman nodded and raised her sad old eyes to Charity's. When Mr. Miles and Liff clambered into the buggy she went ahead with the lantern to show them the track they were to follow; then she turned back, and in silence she and Charity walked away together through the night.

XVII

Charity lay on the floor on a mattress, as her dead mother's body had lain. The room in which she lay was cold and dark and low-ceilinged, and even poorer and barer than the scene of Mary Hyatt's earthly pilgrimage. On the other side of the fireless stove Liff Hyatt's mother slept on a blanket, with two children—her grandchildren, she said —rolled up against her like sleeping puppies. They had their thin clothes spread over them, having given the only other blanket to their guest.

Through the small square of glass in the opposite wall Charity saw a deep funnel of sky, so black, so remote, so palpitating with frosty stars that her very soul seemed to be sucked up into it. Up there somewhere, she supposed, the God whom Mr. Miles had invoked was waiting for Mary Hyatt to appear. What a long flight it was! And what would she have to say when she reached Him?

Charity's bewildered brain laboured with the attempt to picture her mother's past, and to relate it in any way to the designs of a just but merciful God; but it was impossible to imagine any link between them. She herself felt as remote from the poor creature she had seen lowered into her hastily dug grave as if the height of the heavens had divided them. She had seen poverty and misfortune in her life; but in a community where poor thrifty Mrs. Hawes and the industrious Ally represented the nearest approach to destitution there was nothing to suggest the savage misery of the Mountain farmers.

As she lay there, half-stunned by her tragic initiation, Charity vainly tried to think herself into the life about her. But she could not even make out what relationship these people bore to each other, or to her dead mother; they seemed to be herded together in a sort of passive promiscuity in which their common misery was the strongest link. She tried to picture to herself what her life would have been if she had grown up on the Mountain, running wild in rags, sleeping on the floor curled up against her mother, like the pale-faced children huddled against old Mrs. Hyatt, and turning into a fierce bewildered creature like the girl who had apostrophized her in such strange words. She was frightened by the secret affinity she had felt with this girl, and by the light it threw on her own beginnings. Then she remembered what Mr. Royall had said in telling her story to Lucius Harney: "Yes, there was a mother; but she was glad to have the child go. She'd have given her to anybody. . . ."

Well! after all, was her mother so much to blame? Charity, since that day, had always thought of her as destitute of all human feeling; now she seemed merely pitiful. What mother would not want to save her child from such a life? Charity thought of the future of her own child, and tears welled into her aching eyes, and ran down over her face. If she had been less exhausted, less burdened with his weight, she would have sprung up then and there and fled away. . . .

The grim hours of the night dragged themselves slowly by, and at last the sky paled and dawn threw a cold blue beam into the room. She lay in her corner staring at the dirty floor, the clothes-line hung with decaying rags, the old woman huddled against the cold stove, and the light gradually spreading across the wintry world, and bringing with it a new day in which she would have to live, to choose, to act, to make herself a place among these people—or to go back to the life she had left. A mortal lassitude weighed on her. There were moments when she felt that all she asked was to go on lying there unnoticed; then her mind revolted at the thought of becoming one of the miserable herd from which she sprang, and it seemed as though, to save her child from such a fate, she would find strength to travel any distance, and bear any burden life might put on her.

Vague thoughts of Nettleton flitted through her mind. She said to herself that she would find some quiet place where she could bear her child, and give it to decent people to keep; and then she would go out like Julia Hawes and earn its living and hers. She knew that girls of that kind sometimes made enough to have their children nicely cared for; and every other consideration disappeared in the vision of her baby, cleaned and combed and rosy, and hidden away somewhere where she could run in and kiss it, and bring it pretty things to wear. Anything, anything was better than to add another life to the nest of misery on the Mountain. . . .

The old woman and the children were still sleeping when Charity rose from her mattress. Her body was stiff with cold and fatigue, and she moved slowly lest her heavy steps should rouse them. She was faint with hunger, and had nothing left in her satchel; but on the table she saw the half of a stale loaf. No doubt it was to serve as the breakfast of old Mrs. Hyatt and the children; but Charity did not care; she had her own baby to think of. She broke off a piece of the bread and ate it greedily; then her glance fell on the thin faces of the sleeping children, and filled with compunction she rummaged in her satchel for something with which to pay for what she had taken. She found one of the pretty chemises that Ally had made for her, with a blue ribbon run through its edging. It was one of the dainty things on which she had squandered her savings, and as she looked at it the blood rushed to her forehead. She laid the chemise on the table, and stealing across the floor lifted the latch and went out. . . .

The morning was icy cold and a pale sun was just rising above the eastern shoulder of the Mountain. The houses scattered on the hillside lay cold and smokeless under the sun-flecked clouds, and not a human being was in sight. Charity paused on the threshold and tried to discover the road by which she had come the night before.

Across the field surrounding Mrs. Hyatt's shanty she saw the tumble-down house in which she supposed the funeral service had taken place. The trail ran across the ground between the two houses and disappeared in the pine-wood on the flank of the Mountain; and a little way to the right, under a wind-beaten thorn, a mound of fresh earth made a dark spot on the fawn-coloured stubble. Charity walked across the field to the mound. As she approached it she heard a bird's note in the still air, and looking up she saw a brown song-sparrow perched in an upper branch of the thorn above the grave. She stood a minute listening to his small solitary song; then she rejoined the trail and began to mount the hill to the pine-wood.

Thus far she had been impelled by the blind instinct of flight; but each step seemed to bring her nearer to the realities of which her feverish vigil had given only a shadowy image. Now that she walked again in a daylight world, on the way back to familiar things, her imagination moved more soberly. On one point she was still decided; she could not remain at North Dormer, and the sooner she got away from it the better. But everything beyond was darkness.

As she continued to climb the air grew keener, and when she passed from the shelter of the pines to the open grassy roof of the Mountain the cold wind of the night before sprang out on her. She bent her shoulders and struggled on against it for a while; but presently her breath failed, and she sat down under a ledge of rock overhung by shivering birches. From where she sat she saw the trail wandering across the bleached grass in the direction of Hamblin, and the granite wall of the Mountain falling away to infinite distances. On that side of the ridge the valleys still lay in wintry shadow; but in the plain beyond the sun was touching village roofs and steeples, and gilding the haze of smoke over far-off invisible towns.

Charity felt herself a mere speck in the lonely circle of the sky. The events of the last two days seemed to have divided her forever from her short dream of bliss. Even Harney's image had been blurred by that crushing experience: she thought of him as so remote from her that he seemed hardly more than a memory. In her fagged and fleeting mind only one sensation had the weight of reality; it was the bodily burden of her child. But for it she would have felt as rootless as the whiffs of thistledown the wind blew past her. Her child was like a load that held her down, and yet like a hand that pulled her to her feet. She said to herself that she must get up and struggle on. . . .

Her eyes turned back to the trail across the top of the Mountain, and in the distance she saw a buggy against the sky. She knew its antique outline, and the gaunt build of the old horse pressing forward with lowered head; and after a moment she recognized the heavy bulk of the man who held the reins. The buggy was following the trail and making straight for the pine-wood through which she had climbed; and she knew at once that the driver was in search of her. Her first impulse was to crouch down under the ledge till he had passed; but the instinct of concealment was overruled by the relief of feeling that someone was near her in the awful emptiness. She stood up and walked toward the buggy.

Mr. Royall saw her, and touched the horse with the whip. A minute or two later he was abreast of Charity; their eyes met, and without speaking he leaned over and helped her up into the buggy. She tried to speak, to stammer out some explanation, but no words came to her; and as he drew the cover over her knees he simply said: "The minister told me he'd left you up here, so I come up for you."

He turned the horse's head, and they began to jog back toward Hamblin. Charity sat speechless, staring straight ahead of her, and Mr. Royall occasionally uttered a word of encouragement to the horse: "Get along there, Dan. . . . I gave him a rest at Hamblin; but I brought him along pretty quick, and it's a stiff pull up here against the wind."

As he spoke it occurred to her for the first time that to reach the top of the Mountain so early he must have left North Dormer at the coldest hour of the night, and have travelled steadily but for the halt at Hamblin; and she felt a softness at her heart which no act of his had ever produced since he had brought her the Crimson Rambler because she had given up boarding-school to stay with him.

After an interval he began again: "It was a day just like this, only spitting snow, when I come up here for you the first time." Then, as if fearing that she might take his remark as a reminder of past benefits, he added quickly: "I dunno's you think it was such a good job, either."

"Yes, I do," she murmured, looking straight ahead of her.

"Well," he said, "I tried—"

He did not finish the sentence, and she could think of nothing more to say.

"Ho, there, Dan, step out," he muttered, jerking the bridle. "We ain't home yet. —You cold?" he asked abruptly.

She shook her head, but he drew the cover higher up and stooped to tuck it in about her ankles. She continued to look straight ahead. Tears of weariness and weakness were dimming her eyes and beginning to run over, but she dared not wipe them away lest he should observe the gesture.

They drove in silence, following the long loops of the descent upon Hamblin, and Mr. Royall did not speak again till they reached the outskirts of the village. Then he let the reins droop on the dashboard and drew out his watch.

"Charity," he said, "you look fair done up, and North Dormer's a goodish way off. I've figured out that we'd do better to stop here long enough for you to get a mouthful of breakfast and then drive down to Creston and take the train."

She roused herself from her apathetic musing. "The train—what train?"

Mr. Royall, without answering, let the horse jog on till they reached the door of the first house in the village. "This is old Mrs. Hobart's place," he said. "She'll give us something hot to drink."

Charity, half unconsciously, found herself getting out of the buggy and following him in at the open door. They entered a decent kitchen with a fire crackling in the stove. An old woman with a kindly face was setting out cups and saucers on the table. She looked up and nodded as they came in, and Mr. Royall advanced to the stove, clapping his numb hands together.

"Well, Mrs. Hobart, you got any breakfast for this young lady? You can see she's cold and hungry."

Mrs. Hobart smiled on Charity and took a tin coffee-pot from the fire. "My, you do look pretty mean," she said compassionately.

Charity reddened, and sat down at the table. A feeling of complete passiveness had once more come over her, and she was conscious only of the pleasant animal sensations of warmth and rest.

Mrs. Hobart put bread and milk on the table, and then went out of the house: Charity saw her leading the horse away to the barn across the yard. She did not come back, and Mr. Royall and Charity sat alone at the table with the smoking coffee between them. He poured out a cup for her, and put a piece of bread in the saucer, and she began to eat.

As the warmth of the coffee flowed through her veins her thoughts cleared and she began to feel like a living being again; but the return to life was so painful that the food choked in her throat and she sat staring down at the table in silent anguish.

After a while Mr. Royall pushed back his chair. "Now, then," he said, "if you're a mind to go along—" She did not move, and he continued: "We can pick up the noon train for Nettleton if you say so."

The words sent the blood rushing to her face, and she raised her startled eyes to his. He was standing on the other side of the table looking at her kindly and gravely; and suddenly she understood what he was going to say. She continued to sit motionless, a leaden weight upon her lips.

"You and me have spoke some hard things to each other in our time, Charity; and there's no good that I can see in any more talking now. But I'll never feel any way but one about you; and if you say so we'll drive down in time to catch that train, and go straight to the minister's house; and when you come back home you'll come as Mrs. Royall."

His voice had the grave persuasive accent that had moved his hearers at the Home Week festival; she had a sense of depths of mournful tolerance under that easy tone. Her whole body began to tremble with the dread of her own weakness.

"Oh, I can't—" she burst out desperately.

"Can't what?"

She herself did not know: she was not sure if she was rejecting what he offered, or already struggling against the temptation of taking what she no longer had a right to. She stood up, shaking and bewildered, and began to speak:

"I know I ain't been fair to you always; but I want to be now. . . . I want you to know . . . I want . . ." Her voice failed her and she stopped.

Mr. Royall leaned against the wall. He was paler than usual, but his face was composed and kindly, and her agitation did not appear to perturb him.

"What's all this about wanting?" he said as she paused. "Do you know what you really want? I'll tell you. You want to be took home and took care of. And I guess that's all there is to say."

"No . . . it's not all. . . ."

"Ain't it?" He looked at his watch. "Well, I'll tell you another thing. All *I* want is to know if you'll marry me. If there was anything else, I'd tell you so; but there ain't. Come to my age, a man knows the things that matter and the things that don't; that's about the only good turn life does us."

His tone was so strong and resolute that it was like a supporting arm about her. She felt her resistance melting, her strength slipping away from her as he spoke.

"Don't cry, Charity," he exclaimed in a shaken voice. She looked up, startled at his emotion, and their eyes met.

"See here," he said gently, "old Dan's come a long distance, and we've got to let him take it easy the rest of the way. . . ."

He picked up the cloak that had slipped to her chair and laid it about her shoulders. She followed him out of the house, and they walked across the yard to the shed, where the horse was tied. Mr. Royall unblanketed him and led him out into the road. Charity got into the buggy and he drew the cover about her and shook out the reins with a cluck. When they reached the end of the village he turned the horse's head toward Creston.

XVIII

They began to jog down the winding road to the valley at old Dan's languid pace. Charity felt herself sinking into deeper depths of weariness, and as they descended through the bare woods there were moments when she lost the exact sense of things, and seemed to be sitting beside her lover with the leafy arch of summer bending over them. But this illusion was faint and transitory. For the most part she had only a confused sensation of slipping down a smooth irresistible current; and she abandoned herself to the feeling as a refuge from the torment of thought.

Mr. Royall seldom spoke, but his silent presence gave her, for the first time, a sense of peace and security. She knew that where he was there would be warmth, rest, silence; and for the moment they were all she wanted. She shut her eyes, and even these things grew dim to her. . . .

In the train, during the short run from Creston to Nettleton, the warmth aroused her, and the consciousness of being under strange eyes gave her a momentary energy. She sat upright, facing Mr. Royall, and stared out of the window at the denuded country. Forty-eight hours earlier, when she had last traversed it, many of the trees still held their leaves; but the high wind of the last two nights had stripped them, and the lines of the landscape were as finely pencilled as in December. A few days of autumn cold had wiped out all trace of the rich fields and languid groves through which she had passed on the Fourth of July; and with the fading of the landscape those fervid hours had faded too. She could no longer believe that she was the being who had lived them; she was someone to whom something irreparable and overwhelming had happened, but the traces of the steps leading up to it had almost vanished.

When the train reached Nettleton and she walked out into the square at Mr. Royall's side the sense of unreality grew more overpowering. The physical strain of the night and day had left no room in her mind for new sensations and she followed Mr. Royall as passively as a tired child. As in a confused dream she presently found herself sitting with him in a pleasant room, at a table with a red and white table-cloth on which hot food and tea were placed. He filled her cup and plate and whenever she lifted her eyes from them she found his resting on her with the same steady tranquil gaze that had reassured and strengthened her when they had faced each other in old Mrs. Hobart's kitchen. As everything else in her consciousness grew more and more confused and immaterial, became more and more like the universal shimmer that dissolves the world to failing eyes, Mr. Royall's presence began to detach itself with rocky firmness from this elusive background. She had always thought of him—when she thought of him at all—as of someone hateful and obstructive, but whom she could outwit and dominate when she chose to make the effort. Only once, on the day of the Old Home Week celebration, while the stray fragments of his address drifted across her troubled mind, had she caught a glimpse of another being, a being so different from the dull-witted enemy with whom she had supposed herself to be living that even through the burning mist of her own dreams he had stood out with startling distinctness. For a moment, then, what he said—and something in his way of saying it—had made her see why he had always struck her as such a lonely man. But the mist of her dreams had hidden him again, and she had forgotten that fugitive impression.

It came back to her now, as they sat at the table, and gave her, through her own immeasurable desolation, a sudden sense of their nearness to each other. But all these feelings were only brief streaks of light in the grey blur of her physical weakness. Through it she was aware that Mr. Royall presently left her sitting by the table in the warm room, and came back after an interval with a carriage from the station— a closed "hack" with sun-burnt blue silk blinds—in which they drove together to a house covered with creepers and standing next to a church with a carpet of turf before it. They got out at this house, and the carriage waited while they walked up the path and entered a wainscoted hall and then a room full of books. In this room a clergyman whom Charity had never seen received them pleasantly, and asked them to be seated for a few minutes while witnesses were being summoned.

Charity sat down obediently, and Mr. Royall, his hands behind his back, paced slowly up and down the room. As he turned and faced Charity, she noticed that his lips were twitching a little; but the look in his eyes was grave and calm. Once he passed before her and said timidly: "Your hair's got kinder loose with the wind," and she lifted her hands and tried to smooth back the locks that had escaped from her braid. There was a looking-glass in a carved frame on the wall, but she was ashamed to look at herself in it, and she sat with her hands folded on her knee till the clergyman returned. Then they went out again, along a sort of arcaded passage, and into a low vaulted room with a cross on an altar, and rows of benches. The clergyman, who had left them at the door, presently reappeared before the altar in a surplice, and a lady who was probably his wife, and a man in a blue shirt who had been raking dead leaves on the lawn, came in and sat on one of the benches.

The clergyman opened a book and signed to Charity and Mr. Royall to approach. Mr. Royall advanced a few steps, and Charity followed him as she had followed him to the buggy when they went out of Mrs. Hobart's kitchen; she had the feeling that if she ceased to keep close to him, and do what he told her to do, the world would slip away from beneath her feet.

The clergyman began to read, and on her dazed mind there rose the memory of Mr. Miles, standing the night before in the desolate house of the Mountain, and reading out of the same book words that had the same dread sound of finality:

"I require and charge you both, as ye will answer at the dreadful day of judgment when the secrets of all hearts shall be disclosed, that if either of you know any impediment whereby ye may not be lawfully joined together . . ."

Charity raised her eyes and met Mr. Royall's. They were still looking at her kindly and steadily. "I will!" she heard him say a moment later, after another interval of words that she had failed to catch. She was so busy trying to understand the gestures the clergyman was signalling to her to make that she no longer heard what was being said. After another interval the lady on the bench stood up, and taking her hand put it in Mr. Royall's. It lay enclosed in his strong palm and she felt a ring that was too big for her being slipped onto her thin finger. She understood then that she was married. . . .

Late that afternoon Charity sat alone in a bedroom of the fashionable hotel where she and Harney had vainly sought a table on the Fourth of July. She had never before been in so handsomely furnished a room. The mirror above the dressing-table reflected the high head-board and fluted pillow-slips of the double bed, and a bedspread so spotlessly white that she had hesitated to lay her hat and jacket on it. The humming radiator diffused an atmosphere of drowsy warmth, and through a half-open door she saw the glitter of the nickel taps above twin marble basins.

For a while the long turmoil of the night and day had slipped away from her and she sat with closed eyes, surrendering herself to the spell of warmth and silence. But presently this merciful apathy was succeeded by the sudden acuteness of vision with which sick people sometimes wake out of a heavy sleep. As she opened her eyes they rested on the picture that hung above the bed. It was a large engraving with a dazzling white margin enclosed in a wide frame of bird's-eye maple with an inner scroll of gold. The engraving represented a young man in a boat on a lake overhung with trees. He was leaning over to gather water-lilies for the girl in a light dress who lay among the cushions in the stern. The scene was full of a drowsy midsummer radiance, and Charity averted her eyes from it and, rising from her chair, began to wander restlessly about the room.

It was on the fifth floor, and its broad window of plate glass looked over the roofs of the town. Beyond them stretched a wooded landscape in which the last fires of sunset were picking out a steely gleam. Charity gazed at the gleam with startled eyes. Even through the gathering twilight she recognized the contour of the soft hills encircling it, and the way the meadows sloped to its edge. It was Nettleton Lake that she was looking at.

She stood a long time in the window staring out at the fading water. The sight of it had roused her for the first time to a realization of what she had done. Even the feeling of the ring on her hand had not brought her this sharp sense of the irretrievable. For an instant the old impulse of flight swept through her; but it was only the lift of a broken wing. She heard the door open behind her, and Mr. Royall came in.

He had gone to the barber's to be shaved, and his shaggy grey hair had been trimmed and smoothed. He moved strongly and quickly, squaring his shoulders and carrying his head high, as if he did not want to pass unnoticed.

"What are you doing in the dark?" he called out in a cheerful voice. Charity made no answer. He went up to the window to draw down the blind, and putting his finger on the wall flooded the room with a blaze of light from the central chandelier. In this unfamiliar illumination husband and wife faced each other awkwardly for a moment; then Mr. Royall said: "We'll step down and have some supper, if you say so."

The thought of food filled her with repugnance; but not daring to confess it she smoothed her hair and followed him to the lift.

An hour later, coming out of the glare of the dining-room, she waited in the marble-panelled hall while Mr. Royall, before the brass lattice of one of the corner counters, selected a cigar and bought an evening paper. Men were lounging in rocking chairs under the blazing chandeliers, travellers coming and going, bells ringing, porters shuffling by with luggage. Over Mr. Royall's shoulder, as he leaned against the counter, a girl with her hair puffed high smirked and nodded at a dapper drummer who was getting his key at the desk across the hall.

Charity stood among these cross-currents of life as motionless and inert as if she had been one of the tables screwed to the marble floor. All her soul was gathered up into one sick sense of coming doom, and she watched Mr. Royall in fascinated terror while he pinched the cigars in successive boxes and unfolded his evening paper with a steady hand.

Presently he turned and joined her. "You go right along up to bed—I'm going to sit down here and have my smoke," he said. He spoke as easily and naturally as if they had been an old couple, long used to each other's ways, and her contracted heart gave a flutter of relief. She followed him to the lift, and he put her in and enjoined the buttoned and braided boy to show her to her room.

She groped her way in through the darkness, forgetting where the electric button was, and not knowing how to manipulate it. But a white autumn moon had risen, and the illuminated sky put a pale light in the room. By it she undressed, and after folding up the ruffled pillow-slips crept timidly under the spotless counterpane. She had never felt such smooth sheets or such light warm blankets; but the softness of the bed did not soothe her. She lay there trembling with a fear that ran through her veins like ice. "What have I done? Oh, what have I done?" she whispered, shuddering to her pillow; and pressing her face against it to shut out the pale landscape beyond the window she lay in the darkness straining her ears, and shaking at every footstep that approached. . . .

Suddenly she sat up and pressed her hands against her frightened heart. A faint sound had told her that someone was in the room; but she must have slept in the interval, for she had heard no one enter. The moon was setting beyond the opposite roofs, and in the darkness, outlined against the grey square of the window, she saw a figure seated in the rocking-chair. The figure did not move: it was sunk deep in the chair, with bowed head and folded arms, and she saw that it was Mr. Royall who sat there. He had not undressed, but had taken the blanket from the foot of the bed and laid it across his knees. Trembling and holding her breath she watched him, fearing that he had been roused by her movement; but he did not stir, and she concluded that he wished her to think he was asleep.

As she continued to watch him ineffable relief stole slowly over her, relaxing her strained nerves and exhausted body. He knew, then . . . he knew . . . it was because he knew that he had married her, and that he sat there in the darkness to show her she was safe with him. A stir of something deeper than she had ever felt in thinking of him flitted through her tired brain, and cautiously, noiselessly, she let her head sink on the pillow. . . .

When she woke the room was full of morning light, and her first glance showed her that she was alone in it. She got up and dressed, and as she was fastening her dress the door opened, and Mr. Royall came in. He looked old and tired in the bright daylight, but his face wore the same expression of grave friendliness that had reassured her on the Mountain. It was as if all the dark spirits had gone out of him.

They went downstairs to the dining-room for breakfast, and after breakfast he told her he had some insurance business to attend to. "I guess while I'm doing it you'd better step out and buy yourself whatever you need." He smiled, and added with an embarrassed laugh: "You know I always wanted you to beat all the other girls." He drew something from his pocket, and pushed it across the table to her; and she saw that he had given her two twenty-dollar bills. "If it ain't enough there's more where that come from—I want you to beat 'em all hollow," he repeated.

She flushed and tried to stammer out her thanks, but he had pushed back his chair and was leading the way out of the dining-room. In the hall he paused a minute to say that if it suited her they would take the three o'clock train back to North Dormer; then he took his hat and coat from the rack and went out.

A few minutes later Charity went out too. She had watched to see in what direction he was going, and she took the opposite way and walked quickly down that main street to the brick building on the corner of Lake Avenue. There she paused to look cautiously up and down the thoroughfare, and then climbed the brass-bound stairs to Dr. Merkle's door. The same bushy-headed mulatto girl admitted her, and after the same interval of waiting in the red plush parlor she was once more summoned to Dr. Merkle's office. The doctor received her without surprise, and led her into the inner plush sanctuary.

"I thought you'd be back, but you've come a mite too soon: I told you to be patient and not fret," she observed, after a pause of penetrating scrutiny.

Charity drew the money from her breast. "I've come to get my blue brooch," she said, flushing.

"Your brooch?" Dr. Merkle appeared not to remember. "My, yes—I get so many things of that kind. Well, my dear, you'll have to wait while I get it out of the safe. I don't leave valuables like that laying round like the noospaper."

She disappeared for a moment, and returned with a bit of twisted-up tissue paper from which she unwrapped the brooch.

Charity, as she looked at it, felt a stir of warmth at her heart. She held out an eager hand.

"Have you got the change?" she asked a little breathlessly, laying one of the twenty-dollar bills on the table.

"Change? What'd I want to have change for? I only see two twenties there," Dr. Merkle answered brightly.

Charity paused, disconcerted. "I thought . . . you said it was five dollars a visit. . . ."

"For *you,* as a favour—I did. But how about the responsibility—*and* the insurance? I don't s'pose you ever thought of that? This pin's worth a hundred dollars easy. If it had got lost or stole, where'd I been when you come to claim it?"

Charity remained silent, puzzled, and half-convinced by the argument, and Dr. Merkle promptly followed up her advantage. "I didn't ask you for your brooch, my dear. I'd a good deal ruther folks paid me my regular charge than have 'em put me to all this trouble."

She paused, and Charity, seized with a desperate longing to escape, rose to her feet and held out one of the bills.

"Will you take that?" she asked.

"No, I won't take that, my dear; but I'll take it with its mate, and hand you over a signed receipt if you don't trust me."

"Oh, but I can't—it's all I've got," Charity exclaimed.

Dr. Merkle looked up at her pleasantly from the plush sofa. "It seems you got married yesterday, up to the 'Piscopal church; I heard all about the wedding from the minister's chore-man. It would be a pity, wouldn't it, to let Mr. Royall know you had an account running here? I just put it to you as your own mother might."

Anger flamed up in Charity, and for an instant she thought of abandoning the brooch and letting Dr. Merkle do her worst. But how could she leave her only treasure with that evil woman? She wanted it for her baby: she meant it, in some mysterious way, to be a link between Harney's child and its unknown father. Trembling and hating herself while she did it, she laid Mr. Royall's money on the table, and catching up the brooch fled out of the room and the house. . . .

In the street she stood still, dazed by this last adventure. But the brooch lay in her bosom like a talisman, and she felt a secret lightness of heart. It gave her strength, after a moment, to walk on slowly in the direction of the post office, and go in through the swinging doors. At one of the windows she bought a sheet of letter-paper, an envelope and a stamp; then she sat down at a table and dipped the rusty post office pen in ink. She had come there possessed with a fear which had haunted her ever since she had felt Mr. Royall's ring on her finger; the fear that Harney might, after all, free himself and come back to her. It was a possibility which had never occurred to her during the dreadful hours after she had received his letter; only when the decisive step she had taken made longing turn to apprehension did such a contingency seem conceivable. She addressed the envelope, and on the sheet of paper she wrote:

I'm married to Mr. Royall. I'll always remember you.
                                        CHARITY.

The last words were not in the least what she had meant to write; they had flowed from her pen irresistibly. She had not had the strength to complete her sacrifice; but, after all, what did it matter? Now that there was no chance of ever seeing Harney again, why should she not tell him the truth?

When she had put the letter in the box she went out into the busy sunlit street and began to walk to the hotel. Behind the plate-glass windows of the department stores she noticed the tempting display of dresses and dress-materials that had fired her imagination on the day when she and Harney had looked in at them together. They reminded her of Mr. Royall's injunction to go out and buy all she needed. She looked down at her shabby dress, and wondered what she should say when he saw her coming back empty-handed. As she drew near the hotel she saw him waiting on the doorstep, and her heart began to beat with apprehension.

He nodded and waved his hand at her approach, and they walked through the hall and went upstairs to collect their possessions, so that Mr. Royall might give up the key of the room when they went down again for their midday dinner. In the bedroom, while she was thrusting back into the satchel the few things she had brought away with her, she suddenly felt that his eyes were on her and that he was going to speak. She stood still, her half-folded night-gown in her hand, while the blood rushed up to her drawn cheeks.

"Well, did you rig yourself out handsomely? I haven't seen any bundles round," he said jocosely.

"Oh, I'd rather let Ally Hawes make the few things I want," she answered.

"That so?" He looked at her thoughtfully for a moment and his eye-brows projected in a scowl. Then his face grew friendly again. "Well, I wanted you to go back looking stylisher than any of them; but I guess you're right. You're a good girl, Charity."

Their eyes met, and something rose in his that she had never seen there: a look that made her feel ashamed and yet secure.

"I guess you're good, too," she said, shyly and quickly. He smiled without answering, and they went out of the room together and dropped down to the hall in the glittering lift.

Late that evening, in the cold autumn moonlight, they drove up to the door of the red house.

1917

---

from A Backward Glance

from Chapter VIII: [Henry James Reads Brontë and Whitman]

He[1] knew I enjoyed our literary rough-and-tumbles, and no doubt for that reason scrupled the less to hit straight from the shoulder; but with others, though he tried to be more merciful, what he really thought was no less manifest. My own experience has taught me that nothing is more difficult than to talk indifferently or insincerely on the subject of one's craft. The writer, without much effort, can reel off polite humbug about pictures, the painter about books; but to fib about the art one practises is incredibly painful, and James's overscrupulous conscience, and passionate reverence for letters, while always inclining him to mercy, made deception doubly impossible.

I think it was James who first made me understand that genius is not an indivisible element, but one variously apportioned, so that the popular system of dividing humanity into geniuses and non-geniuses is a singularly inadequate way of estimating human complexity. In connection with this, I once brought him a phrase culled in a literary review. "Mr. ——— has *almost a streak* of genius." James, always an eager collector of verbal oddities, fell on the phrase with rapture, and earnest requests to every one to define the exact extent of "almost a streak" caused him amusement for months afterward. I mention this because so few people seem to have known in Henry James the ever-bubbling fountain of fun which was the delight of his intimates.

One of our joys, when the talk touched on any great example of prose or verse, was to get the book from the shelf, and ask one of the company to read the passage aloud. There were some admirable readers in the group, in whose gift I had long delighted; but I had never heard Henry James read aloud—or known that he enjoyed doing so—till one night some one alluded to Emily Brontë's poems, and I said I had

---

[1] Henry James (1843–1916), American author and a long-time friend and confidant of Wharton.

never read "Remembrance."[2] Immediately he took the volume from my hand, and, his eyes filling, and some far-away emotion deepening his rich and flexible voice, he began:

> Cold in the earth, and the deep snow piled above thee,
> Far, far removed, cold in the dreary grave,
> Have I forgot, my only Love, to love thee,
> Severed at last by Time's all-severing wave?

I had never before heard poetry read as he read it; and I never have since. He chanted it, and he was not afraid to chant it, as many good readers are, who, though they instinctively feel that the genius of the English poetical idiom requires it to be spoken *as poetry*, are yet afraid of yielding to their instinct because the present-day fashion is to chatter high verse as though it were colloquial prose. James, on the contrary, far from shirking the rhythmic emphasis, gave it full expression. His stammer ceased as by magic as soon as he began to read, and his ear, so sensitive to the convolutions of an intricate prose style, never allowed him to falter over the most complex prosody, but swept him forward on great rollers of sound till the full weight of his voice fell on the last cadence.

James's reading was a thing apart, an emanation of his inmost self, unaffected by fashion or elocutionary artifice. He read from his soul, and no one who never heard him read poetry knows what that soul was. Another day some one spoke of Whitman, and it was a joy to me to discover that James thought him, as I did, the greatest of American poets. "Leaves of Grass"[3] was put into his hands, and all that evening we sat rapt while he wandered from "The Song of Myself" to "When lilacs last in the door-yard bloomed" (when he read "Lovely and soothing Death" his voice filled the hushed room like an organ adagio), and thence let himself be lured on to the mysterious music of "Out of the Cradle," reading, or rather crooning it in a mood of subdued ecstasy till the fivefold invocation to Death tolled out like the knocks in the opening bars of the Fifth Symphony.[4]

James's admiration of Whitman, his immediate response to that mighty appeal, was a new proof of the way in which, above a certain level, the most divergent intelligences walk together like gods. We talked long that night of "Leaves of Grass," tossing back and forth to each other treasure after treasure; but finally James, in one of his sudden humorous drops from the heights, flung up his hands and cried out with the old stammer and twinkle: "Oh, yes, a great genius; undoubtedly a very great genius! Only one cannot help deploring his too-extensive acquaintance with the foreign languages."

1934

---

[2] Poem by Emily Brontë (1818–1848), British writer.
[3] "Leaves of Grass" by Walt Whitman (1819–1892) was first published in 1855 and

received many revisions over the years as further editions appeared.
[4] Symphony by Beethoven.

W. E. B. Du Bois
1868–1963

"The Niagara Movement" (the militant declaration of the need for blacks to demand equal rights) or "The Atlanta Compromise" (the placating request that whites allow blacks to remain quietly on the underside of American society in exchange for the promise of a moderate livelihood)—these are the two positions taken by the best-known and most articulate black leaders at the turn of the century, W. E. B. Du Bois and Booker T. Washington. Both men made a major difference in the directions taken in racial matters after the Civil War; but whereas Washington was once the figure favored by the majority of whites and blacks before World War I, today it is clearly Du Bois who enjoys the greatest approval.

Du Bois did not start out as an activist, nor did he have to struggle to survive, as did Washington, who had been born a slave. Du Bois had the good fortune to grow up under social conditions that allowed him time to reflect on the status of blacks in post–Civil War America and to develop the ideas that formed his later radicalism. Du Bois was born and raised in Great Barrington, Massachusetts, an amalgam, in his own words, of "a flood of Negro blood, a strain of French, a bit of Dutch, but thank God! no 'Anglo Saxon.' " His childhood was pleasant, if poor, marred only—but influentially—by the shock he had in grade school when he learned he was considered different from his fellow students because of his color.

Du Bois attended Fisk University in Nashville, Tennessee, and then went on to Harvard, where he graduated cum laude in 1890. While at Harvard, he attended classes conducted by the country's major philosophers, William James, George Santayana, and Josiah Royce. However reputable an institution Fisk was, it could not have provided Du Bois the association with prominent educators he gained at Harvard.

Du Bois remained at Harvard for two years of graduate school, then moved on to two more years of study on a fellowship at the University of Berlin. Thereafter, Du Bois interleaved his teaching position at Wilberforce University with the completion of a doctoral dissertation on the slave trade, published in the first volume of the *Harvard Historical Studies* series in 1896. Du Bois also taught at the University of Pennsylvania but moved in 1897 to Atlanta University, a black institution more receptive to his interest in Afro-American sociology.

During the late 1890s Du Bois was shaken out of his life as a scholar. In a time of violent racism, scarred by 3,500 lynchings between 1885 and 1910, Du Bois became increasingly active, both as a writer and as a political figure, working in concert with the most aggressive of the black leaders. American society appeared to offer blacks only two choices: follow the lead of Booker T. Washington, whose 1895 speech at the Atlanta Exposition counseled the acceptance of the status quo as the price for living in peace, though not with justice, or follow the lead of Du Bois, whose 1903 publication, *The Souls of Black Folk,* challenged Washington's position, advocated political radicalism, and provided an "autobiography" for blacks to counter Washington's own Horatio Alger–like myth of material success.

From 1910 into the 1930s, Du Bois edited *Crisis,* the journal of the National Association for the Advancement of Colored People, and crisis was the psychological condition he worked hard to instill in the minds of both blacks and whites. Having left Atlanta for New York in 1910, he saw that he could address large audiences on an ever broadening series of issues. His subsequent movement toward an "international" solution to the universal problem of race eventually led him into the Communist Party in 1961. He left the United States in 1963 for Ghana, where he applied for citizenship just before he died.

The nature of Du Bois's life's work is represented by certain expressions he reiterated in his writings and speeches: "the veil" (cast by whites, whose sense of revulsion toward "people of color" kept the latter safely "invisible"—the probable source for the title of Ralph Ellison's novel, *Invisible Man*), "the problem" (racism, the great issue the twentieth century has had to face), "the souls" (possessed by a people whose heritage of suffering must not be negated by bribes of semiskilled jobs and subsistence wages), and "crisis" (what the entire world society had to pass through before justice could be brought to everyone). Du Bois learned well the political fact that rhetoric and effective literary style can make the difference when major social changes hang in the balance. Du Bois's cosmopolitan education enabled him to respond in more complex ways to a complex social world than was possible for Booker T. Washington, whose focus remained on the needs of a rural southern past.

Further Reading:
F. Broderick, *W. E. B. Du Bois: A Negro Leader's Time of Crisis,* 1959.
E. Rudwick, *W. E. B. Du Bois: A Study in Minority Group Leadership,* 1968.
C. Contee, *W. E. B. Du Bois and African Naturalism, 1914–45,* 1970.
L. Lacy, *Cheer the Lonesome Traveler,* 1970.
E. Sterne, *His Was the Voice,* 1971.
W. E. B. Du Bois, ed. W. M. Tuttle, 1973.
A. Rampersad, *The Art and Imagination of W. E. B. Du Bois,* 1976.

Text:
The Thought and Writings of W. E. B. Du Bois, The Seventh Son, 2 vols., ed. J. Lester, 1971.
See also *The Autobiography of W. E. B. Du Bois: A Soliloquy on Viewing My Life from the Last Decade of Its First Century,* 1968.
The Selected Writings of W. E. B. Du Bois, ed. S. Wright, 1970.
W. E. B. Du Bois Speaks: Speeches and Addresses, ed. P. Foner, 1970.
W. E. B. Du Bois: A Reader, ed. M. Weinberg, 1970.
The Emerging Thought of W. E. B. Du Bois: Essays and Editorials from "The Crisis," ed. H. Moon, 1972.
The Correspondence of W. E. B. Du Bois, ed. H. Aptheker, 1973–1978.

---

from The Souls of Black Folk

Chapter III: Of Mr. Booker T. Washington and Others

From birth till death enslaved; in word, in deed, unmanned!

. . . .

Hereditary bondsmen! Know ye not
Who would be free themselves must strike the blow?[1]

Byron

Easily the most striking thing in the history of the American Negro since 1876[2] is the ascendancy of Mr. Booker T. Washington. It began at the time when war memories and ideals were rapidly passing; a day of astonishing commercial development was dawning; a sense of doubt and hesitation overtook the freedmen's sons,—then it was that his leading began. Mr. Washington came, with a single definite programme, at the psychological moment when the nation was a little ashamed of having bestowed so much sentiment on Negroes, and was concentrating its energies on Dollars. His programme of industrial education, conciliation of the South, and submission and silence as to civil and political rights, was not wholly original; the Free Negroes from 1830 up to war-time had striven to build industrial schools, and the American Missionary Association had from the first taught various trades; and Price[3] and others had sought a way of honorable alliance with the best of the Southerners. But Mr. Washington first indissolubly linked these things; he put enthusiasm, unlimited energy, and perfect faith into this programme, and changed it from a by-path into a veritable Way of Life. And the tale of the methods by which he did this is a fascinating study of human life.

It startled the nation to hear a Negro advocating such a programme after many decades of bitter complaint; it startled and won the applause of the South, it interested and won the admiration of the North; and after a confused murmur of protest, it silenced if it did not convert the Negroes themselves.

To gain the sympathy and coöperation of the various elements comprising the white South was Mr. Washington's first task; and this, at the time Tuskegee[4] was founded, seemed, for a black man, well-nigh impossible. And yet ten years later it was done in the word spoken at Atlanta: "In all things purely social we can be as separate as the five fingers, and yet one as the hand in all things essential to mutual progress." This "Atlanta Compromise"[5] is by all odds the most notable thing in Mr. Washington's career. The South interpreted it in different ways: the radicals received it as a complete surrender of the demand for civil and political equality; the conserva-

---

[1] From George Gordon, Lord Byron's *Childe Harold's Pilgrimage* (1812), Canto II.

[2] The year federal troops departed the South and the Reconstruction policy of support for black political power was ended.

[3] Thomas Frederick Price (1860–1919), Roman Catholic priest and editor, a founder of the American Missionary Association.

[4] Tuskegee Institute, Alabama, founded and built by Washington.

[5] In his 1895 speech, delivered at the Atlanta Exposition, Washington proposed that blacks be given vocational training in lieu of guaranteed civil rights; his intent was to promote racial stability by ensuring that blacks would receive the skills needed to obtain steady work.

tives, as a generously conceived working basis for mutual understanding. So both approved it, and to-day its author is certainly the most distinguished Southerner since Jefferson Davis,[6] and the one with the largest personal following.

Next to this achievement comes Mr. Washington's work in gaining place and consideration in the North. Others less shrewd and tactful had formerly essayed to sit on these two stools and had fallen between them; but as Mr. Washington knew the heart of the South from birth and training, so by singular insight he intuitively grasped the spirit of the age which was dominating the North. And so thoroughly did he learn the speech and thought of triumphant commercialism, and the ideals of material prosperity, that the picture of a lone black boy poring over a French grammar amid the weeds and dirt of a neglected home soon seemed to him the acme of absurdities. One wonders what Socrates and St. Francis of Assisi would say to this.[7]

And yet this very singleness of vision and thorough oneness with his age is a mark of the successful man. It is as though Nature must needs make men narrow in order to give them force. So Mr. Washington's cult has gained unquestioning followers, his work has wonderfully prospered, his friends are legion, and his enemies are confounded. To-day he stands as the one recognized spokesman of his ten million fellows, and one of the most notable figures in a nation of seventy millions. One hesitates, therefore, to criticise a life which, beginning with so little, has done so much. And yet the time is come when one may speak in all sincerity and utter courtesy of the mistakes and shortcomings of Mr. Washington's career, as well as of his triumphs, without being thought captious or envious, and without forgetting that it is easier to do ill than well in the world.

The criticism that has hitherto met Mr. Washington has not always been of this broad character. In the South especially has he had to walk warily to avoid the harshest judgments,—and naturally so, for he is dealing with the one subject of deepest sensitiveness to that section. Twice—once when at the Chicago celebration of the Spanish-American War he alluded to the color-prejudice that is "eating away the vitals of the South," and once when he dined with President Roosevelt[8]—has the resulting Southern criticism been violent enough to threaten seriously his popularity. In the North the feeling has several times forced itself into words, that Mr. Washington's counsels of submission overlooked certain elements of true manhood, and that his educational programme was unnecessarily narrow. Usually, however, such criticism has not found open expression, although, too, the spiritual sons of the Abolitionists have not been prepared to acknowledge that the schools founded before Tuskegee, by men of broad ideals and self-sacrificing spirit, were wholly failures or worthy of ridicule. While, then, criticism has not failed to follow Mr. Washington, yet the prevailing public opinion of the land has been but too willing to deliver the solution of a wearisome problem into his hands, and say, "If that is all you and your race ask, take it."

---

[6] An influential senator from Mississippi prior to the war, Davis became president of the Confederacy (1861–1865).

[7] Reference to the Greek philosopher and the founder of the Franciscan order, whose humble circumstances failed to detract from their wisdom.

[8] Theodore Roosevelt (1858–1919), when president of the United States (1901–1909), invited Washington to dinner, an incident that evoked severe criticism around the country.

Among his own people, however, Mr. Washington has encountered the strongest and most lasting opposition, amounting at times to bitterness, and even to-day continuing strong and insistent even though largely silenced in outward expression by the public opinion of the nation. Some of this opposition is, of course, mere envy; the disappointment of displaced demagogues and the spite of narrow minds. But aside from this, there is among educated and thoughtful colored men in all parts of the land a feeling of deep regret, sorrow, and apprehension at the wide currency and ascendancy which some of Mr. Washington's theories have gained. These same men admire his sincerity of purpose, and are willing to forgive much to honest endeavor which is doing something worth the doing. They coöperate with Mr. Washington as far as they conscientiously can; and, indeed, it is no ordinary tribute to this man's tact and power that, steering as he must between so many diverse interests and opinions, he so largely retains the respect of all.

But the hushing of the criticism of honest opponents is a dangerous thing. It leads some of the best of the critics to unfortunate silence and paralysis of effort, and others to burst into speech so passionately and intemperately as to lose listeners. Honest and earnest criticism from those whose interests are most nearly touched,—criticism of writers by readers, of government by those governed, of leaders by those led,—this is the soul of democracy and the safeguard of modern society. If the best of the American Negroes receive by outer pressure a leader whom they had not recognized before, manifestly there is here a certain palpable gain. Yet there is also irreparable loss,—a loss of that peculiarly valuable education which a group receives when by search and criticism it finds and commissions its own leaders. The way in which this is done is at once the most elementary and the nicest problem of social growth. History is but the record of such group-leadership; and yet how infinitely changeful is its type and character! And of all types and kinds, what can be more instructive than the leadership of a group within a group?—that curious double movement where real progress may be negative and actual advance be relative retrogression. All this is the social student's inspiration and despair.

Now in the past the American Negro has had instructive experience in the choosing of group leaders, founding thus a peculiar dynasty which in the light of present conditions is worth while studying. When sticks and stones and beasts form the sole environment of a people, their attitude is largely one of determined opposition to and conquest of natural forces. But when to earth and brute is added an environment of men and ideas, then the atttiude of the imprisoned group may take three main forms, —a feeling of revolt and revenge; an attempt to adjust all thought and action to the will of the greater group; or, finally, a determined effort at self-realization and self-development despite environing opinion. The influence of all of these attitudes at various times can be traced in the history of the American Negro, and in the evolution of his successive leaders.

Before 1750, while the fire of African freedom still burned in the veins of the slaves, there was in all leadership or attempted leadership but the one motive of revolt and revenge,—typified in the terrible Maroons, the Danish blacks, and Cato of Stono, and veiling all the Americas in fear of insurrection.[9] The liberalizing tendencies of the

[9] Reference to the slave insurrections in the West Indies and South Carolina during the seventeenth and eighteenth centuries, which caused consternation among slave owners.

latter half of the eighteenth century brought, along with kindlier relations between black and white, thoughts of ultimate adjustment and assimilation. Such aspiration was especially voiced in the earnest songs of Phyllis, in the martyrdom of Attucks, the fighting of Salem and Poor, the intellectual accomplishments of Banneker and Derham, and the political demands of the Cuffes.[10]

Stern financial and social stress after the war cooled much of the previous humanitarian ardor. The disappointment and impatience of the Negroes at the persistence of slavery and serfdom voiced itself in two movements. The slaves in the South, aroused undoubtedly by vague rumors of the Haytian revolt, made three fierce attempts at insurrection,—in 1800 under Gabriel in Virginia, in 1822 under Vesey in Carolina, and in 1831 again in Virginia under the terrible Nat Turner.[11] In the Free States, on the other hand, a new and curious attempt at self-development was made. In Philadelphia and New York color-prescription led to a withdrawal of Negro communicants from white churches and the formation of a peculiar socio-religious institution among the Negroes known as the African Church,—an organization still living and controlling in its various branches over a million of men.

Walker's wild appeal[12] against the trend of the times showed how the world was changing after the coming of the cotton-gin. By 1830 slavery seemed hopelessly fastened on the South, and the slaves thoroughly cowed into submission. The free Negroes of the North, inspired by the mulatto immigrants from the West Indies, began to change the basis of their demands; they recognized the slavery of slaves, but insisted that they themselves were freemen, and sought assimilation and amalgamation with the nation on the same terms with other men. Thus, Forten and Purvis of Philadelphia, Shad of Wilmington, Du Bois of New Haven, Barbadoes of Boston,[13] and others, strove singly and together as men, they said, not as slaves; as "people of color," not as "Negroes." The trend of the times, however, refused them recognition save in individual and exceptional cases, considered them as one with all the despised blacks, and they soon found themselves striving to keep even the rights they formerly had of voting and working and moving as freemen. Schemes of migration and colonization arose among them; but these they refused to entertain, and they eventually turned to the Abolition movement as a final refuge.

Here, led by Remond, Nell, Wells-Brown, and Douglass,[14] a new period of self-assertion and self-development dawned. To be sure, ultimate freedom and assimilation was the ideal before the leaders, but the assertion of the manhood rights of the

---

[10] Phyllis: Phillis Wheatley (ca. 1753–1784), a slave poet; Attucks: Crispus Attucks (ca. 1723–1770), slain leader of the "Boston Massacre" against the British troops; Salem and Poor: Peter Salem and Salem Poor, black soldiers during the American Revolution; Banneker: Benjamin Banneker (1731–1806), black astronomer and mathematician; Derham: James Derham (b. 1762), first acknowledged black physician; Cuffes: Paul Cuffe (1759–1817), black leader in the movement to resettle blacks in Africa.

[11] Gabriel Prosser, Denmark Vesey, and Nat Turner were slaves who led insurrections in

1800, 1822, and 1831, respectively; all were quelled and the leaders hanged.

[12] Antislavery pamphlet by the black leader David Walker (1785–1830).

[13] A roster of notable black political leaders in the prewar years: James Forten (1766–1842); Robert Purvis (1810–1898); Abraham Shadd; Alexander Du Bois (1803–1887), grandfather of W. E. B. Du Bois; and James G. Barbadoes.

[14] Remond: Charles Lenox Remond (1810–1873); Nell: William Cooper Nell (1816–1874); Wells-Brown: William Wells-Brown (1816?–1884); Douglass: Frederick Douglass (1817–1895).

Negro by himself was the main reliance, and John Brown's raid[15] was the extreme of its logic. After the war and emancipation, the great form of Frederick Douglass, the greatest of American Negro leaders, still led the host. Self-assertion, especially in political lines, was the main programme, and behind Douglass came Elliot, Bruce, and Langston, and the Reconstruction politicians, and, less conspicuous but of greater social significance Alexander Crummell and Bishop Daniel Payne.[16]

Then came the Revolution of 1876, the suppression of the Negro votes, the changing and shifting of ideals, and the seeking of new lights in the great night. Douglass, in his old age, still bravely stood for the ideals of his early manhood,— ultimate assimilation *through* self-assertion, and on no other terms. For a time Price arose as a new leader, destined, it seemed, not to give up, but to re-state the old ideals in a form less repugnant to the white South. But he passed away in his prime. Then came the new leader. Nearly all the former ones had become leaders by the silent suffrage of their fellows, had sought to lead their own people alone, and were usually, save Douglass, little known outside their race. But Booker T. Washington arose as essentially the leader not of one race but of two,—a compromiser between the South, the North, and the Negro. Naturally the Negroes resented, at first bitterly, signs of compromise which surrendered their civil and political rights, even though this was to be exchanged for larger chances of economic development. The rich and dominating North, however, was not only weary of the race problem, but was investing largely in Southern enterprises, and welcomed any method of peaceful coöperation. Thus, by national opinion, the Negroes began to recognize Mr. Washington's leadership; and the voice of criticism was hushed.

Mr. Washington represents in Negro thought the old attitude of adjustment and submission; but adjustment at such a peculiar time as to make his programme unique. This is an age of unusual economic development, and Mr. Washington's programme naturally takes an economic cast, becoming a gospel of Work and Money to such an extent as apparently almost completely to overshadow the higher aims of life. Moreover, this is an age when the more advanced races are coming in closer contact with the less developed races, and the race-feeling is therefore intensified; and Mr. Washington's programme practically accepts the alleged inferiority of the Negro races. Again, in our own land, the reaction from the sentiment of war time has given impetus to race-prejudice against Negroes, and Mr. Washington withdraws many of the high demands of Negroes as men and American citizens. In other periods of intensified prejudice all the Negro's tendency to self-assertion has been called forth; at this period a policy of submission is advocated. In the history of nearly all other races and peoples the doctrine preached at such crises has been that manly self-respect is worth more than lands and houses, and that a people who voluntarily surrender such respect, or cease striving for it, are not worth civilizing.

[15] The federal arsenal at Harper's Ferry, Virginia, was attacked by Brown and his followers on October 16, 1859, with the purpose of instigating a mass revolt of all slaves.

[16] Elliot: Robert Brown Elliot (1842–1884); Bruce: Blanche K. Bruce (1841–1898); Langston: John Mercer Langston (1829–1897); Crummell: Alexander Crummell (1819–1898); Payne: Daniel Alexander Payne (1811–1893), black congressman, senator, lawyer, clergyman, and educator, respectively, active after the end of the war.

In answer to this, it has been claimed that the Negro can survive only through submission. Mr. Washington distinctly asks that black people give up, at least for the present, three things,—

First, political power,

Second, insistence on civil rights,

Third, higher education of Negro youth,—

and concentrate all their energies on industrial education, the accumulation of wealth, and the conciliation of the South. This policy has been courageously and insistently advocated for over fifteen years, and has been triumphant for perhaps ten years. As a result of this tender of the palm-branch, what has been the return? In these years there have occurred:

1. The disfranchisement of the Negro.
2. The legal creation of a distinct status of civil inferiority for the Negro.
3. The steady withdrawal of aid from institutions for the higher training of the Negro.

These movements are not, to be sure, direct results of Mr. Washington's teachings; but his propaganda has, without a shadow of doubt, helped their speedier accomplishment. The question then comes: Is it possible, and probable, that nine millions of men can make effective progress in economic lines if they are deprived of political rights, made a servile caste, and allowed only the most meagre chance for developing their exceptional men? If history and reason give any distinct answer to these questions, it is an emphatic *No.* And Mr. Washington thus faces the triple paradox of his career:

1. He is striving nobly to make Negro artisans business men and property-owners; but it is utterly impossible, under modern competitive methods, for workingmen and property-owners to defend their rights and exist without the right of suffrage.
2. He insists on thrift and self-respect, but at the same time counsels a silent submission to civic inferiority such as is bound to sap the manhood of any race in the long run.
3. He advocates common-school[17] and industrial training, and depreciates institutions of higher learning; but neither the Negro common-schools, nor Tuskegee itself, could remain open a day were it not for teachers trained in Negro colleges, or trained by their graduates.

This triple paradox in Mr. Washington's position is the object of criticism by two classes of colored Americans. One class is spiritually descended from Toussaint the Savior,[18] through Gabriel, Vesey, and Turner, and they represent the attitude of revolt and revenge; they hate the white South blindly and distrust the white race generally, and so far as they agree on definite action, think that the Negro's only hope lies in emigration beyond the borders of the United States. And yet, by the irony of fate, nothing has more effectually made this programme seem hopeless than the recent course of the United States toward weaker and darker peoples in the West Indies,

---

[17] Public schools offering free instruction at the precollege level.

[18] Pierre Dominique Toussaint (1743–1803), later called Toussaint L'Ouverture, black leader of the slave revolt that resulted in Haitian independence.

Hawaii, and the Philippines—for where in the world may we go and be safe from lying and brute force?

The other class of Negroes who cannot agree with Mr. Washington has hitherto said little aloud. They deprecate the sight of scattered counsels, of internal disagreement; and especially they dislike making their just criticism of a useful and earnest man an excuse for a general discharge of venom from small-minded opponents. Nevertheless, the questions involved are so fundamental and serious that it is difficult to see how men like the Grimkes, Kelly Miller, J. W. E. Bowen,[19] and other representatives of this group, can much longer be silent. Such men feel in conscience bound to ask of this nation three things:

1. The right to vote.
2. Civic equality.
3. The education of youth according to ability.

They acknowledge Mr. Washington's invaluable service in counselling patience and courtesy in such demands; they do not ask that ignorant black men vote when ignorant whites are debarred, or that any reasonable restrictions in the suffrage should not be applied; they know that the low social level of the mass of the race is responsible for much discrimination against it, but they also know, and the nation knows, that relentless color-prejudice is more often a cause than a result of the Negro's degradation; they seek the abatement of this relic of barbarism, and not its systematic encouragement and pampering by all agencies of social power from the Associated Press to the Church of Christ. They advocate, with Mr. Washington, a broad system of Negro common schools supplemented by thorough industrial training; but they are surprised that a man of Mr. Washington's insight cannot see that no such educational system ever has rested or can rest on any other basis than that of the well-equipped college and university, and they insist that there is a demand for a few such institutions throughout the South to train the best of the Negro youth as teachers, professional men, and leaders.

This group of men honor Mr. Washington for his attitude of conciliation toward the white South; they accept the "Atlanta Compromise" in its broadest interpretation; they recognize, with him, many signs of promise, many men of high purpose and fair judgment, in this section; they know that no easy task has been laid upon a region already tottering under heavy burdens. But, nevertheless, they insist that the way to truth and right lies in straightforward honesty, not in indiscriminate flattery; in praising those of the South who do well and criticising uncompromisingly those who do ill; in taking advantage of the opportunities at hand and urging their fellows to do the same, but at the same time in remembering that only a firm adherence to their higher ideals and aspirations will ever keep those ideals within the realm of possibility. They do not expect that the free right to vote, to enjoy civic rights, and to be educated, will come in a moment; they do not expect to see the bias and prejudices of years

---

[19] Archibald Grimke (1849–1930) and Francis
Grimke (1850–1937); Kelly Miller (1863–1939);
J. W. E. Bowen (b. 1855).

disappear at the blast of a trumpet; but they are absolutely certain that the way for a people to gain their reasonable rights is not by voluntarily throwing them away and insisting that they do not want them; that the way for a people to gain respect is not by continually belittling and ridiculing themselves; that, on the contrary, Negroes must insist continually, in season and out of season, that voting is necessary to modern manhood, that color discrimination is barbarism, and that black boys need education as well as white boys.

In failing thus to state plainly and unequivocally the legitimate demands of their people, even at the cost of opposing an honored leader, the thinking classes of American Negroes would shirk a heavy responsibility,—a responsibility to themselves, a responsibility to the struggling masses, a responsibility to the darker races of men whose future depends so largely on this American experiment, but especially a responsibility to this nation,—this common Fatherland. It is wrong to aid and abet a national crime simply because it is unpopular not to do so. The growing spirit of kindliness and reconciliation between the North and South after the frightful difference of a generation ago ought to be a source of deep congratulation to all, and especially those whose mistreatment caused the war; but if that reconciliation is to be marked by the industrial slavery and civic death of those same black men, with permanent legislation into a position of inferiority, then those black men, if they are really men, are called upon by every consideration of patriotism and loyalty to oppose such a course by all civilized methods, even though such opposition involves disagreement with Mr. Booker T. Washington. We have no right to sit silently by while the inevitable seeds are sown for a harvest of disaster to our children, black and white.

First, it is the duty of black men to judge the South discriminatingly. The present generation of Southerners are not responsible for the past, and they should not be blindly hated or blamed for it. Furthermore, to no class is the indiscriminate endorsement of the recent course of the South toward Negroes more nauseating than to the best thought of the South. The South is not "solid"; it is a land in the ferment of social change, wherein forces of all kinds are fighting for supremacy; and to praise the ill the South is to-day perpetrating is just as wrong as to condemn the good. Discriminating and broad-minded criticism is what the South needs,—needs it for the sake of her own white sons and daughters, and for the insurance of robust, healthy mental and moral development.

To-day even the attitude of the Southern whites toward the blacks is not, as so many assume, in all cases the same; the ignorant Southerner hates the Negro, the workingmen fear his competition, the money-makers wish to use him as a laborer, some of the educated see a menace in his upward development, while others—usually the sons of the masters—wish to help him to rise. National opinion has enabled this last class to maintain the Negro common schools, and to protect the Negro partially in property, life, and limb. Through the pressure of the money-makers, the Negro is in danger of being reduced to semi-slavery, especially in the country districts; the workingmen, and those of the educated who fear the Negro, have united to disfranchise him, and some have urged his deportation; while the passions of the ignorant are easily aroused to lynch and abuse any black man. To praise this intricate whirl of thought and prejudice is nonsense; to inveigh indiscriminately against "the South" is unjust; but to use the same breath in praising Governor Aycock, exposing Senator Morgan, arguing with Mr. Thomas Nelson Page, and denouncing Senator Ben Tillman, is not only sane, but the imperative duty of thinking black men.[20]

It would be unjust to Mr. Washington not to acknowledge that in several instances he has opposed movements in the South which were unjust to the Negro; he sent memorials to the Louisiana and Alabama constitutional conventions, he has spoken against lynching, and in other ways has openly or silently set his influence against sinister schemes and unfortunate happenings. Notwithstanding this, it is equally true to assert that on the whole the distinct impression left by Mr. Washington's propaganda is, first, that the South is justified in its present attitude toward the Negro because of the Negro's degradation; secondly, that the prime cause of the Negro's failure to rise more quickly is his wrong education in the past; and, thirdly, that his future rise depends primarily on his own efforts. Each of these propositions is a dangerous half-truth. The supplementary truths must never be lost sight of: first, slavery and race-prejudice are potent if not sufficient causes of the Negro's position; second, industrial and common-school training were necessarily slow in planting because they had to await the black teachers trained by higher institutions,—it being extremely doubtful if any essentially different development was possible, and certainly a Tuskegee was unthinkable before 1880; and, third, while it is a great truth to say that the Negro must strive and strive mightily to help himself, it is equally true that unless his striving be not simply seconded, but rather aroused and encouraged by the initiative of the richer and wiser environing group, he cannot hope for great success.

In his failure to realize and impress this last point, Mr. Washington is especially to be criticised. His doctrine has tended to make the whites, North and South, shift the burden of the Negro problem to the Negro's shoulders and stand aside as critical and rather pessimistic spectators; when in fact the burden belongs to the nation, and the hands of none of us are clean if we bend not our energies to righting these great wrongs.

The South ought to be led, by candid and honest criticism, to assert her better self and do her full duty to the race she has cruelly wronged and is still wronging. The North—her co-partner in guilt—cannot salve her conscience by plastering it with gold. We cannot settle this problem by diplomacy and suaveness, by "policy" alone. If worse come to worst, can the moral fibre of this country survive the slow throttling and murder of nine millions of men?

The black men of America have a duty to perform, a duty stern and delicate,—a forward movement to oppose a part of the work of their greatest leader. So far as Mr. Washington preaches Thrift, Patience, and Industrial Training for the masses, we must hold up his hands and strive with him, rejoicing in his honors and glorying in the strength of this Joshua[21] called of God and of man to lead the headless host. But so far as Mr. Washington apologizes for injustice, North or South, does not rightly value the privilege and duty of voting, belittles the emasculating effects of caste distinctions, and opposes the higher training and ambition of our brighter minds,—

---

[20] Aycock, Morgan, Page, and Tillman were white leaders who took various positions regarding black suffrage in postwar affairs.

[21] Israelite leader who assumed the task of guiding the Jews in their flight from the Egyptians into the Promised Land after the death of Moses.

so far as he, the South, or the Nation, does this,—we must unceasingly and firmly oppose them. By every civilized and peaceful method we must strive for the rights which the world accords to men, clinging unwaveringly to those great words which the sons of the Fathers would fain forget: "We hold these truths to be self-evident: That all men are created equal; that they are endowed by their Creator with certain unalienable rights; that among these are life, liberty, and the pursuit of happiness."

Chapter VII: Of the Black Belt

I am black but comely, O ye daughters of Jerusalem,
As the tents of Kedar, as the curtains of Solomon.
Look not upon me, because I am black,
Because the sun hath looked upon me:
My mother's children were angry with me;
They made me the keeper of the vineyards;
But mine own vineyard have I not kept.
The Song of Solomon[22]

Out of the North the train thundered, and we woke to see the crimson soil of Georgia stretching away bare and monotonous right and left. Here and there lay straggling, unlovely villages, and lean men loafed leisurely at the depots; then again came the stretch of pines and clay. Yet we did not nod, nor weary of the scene; for this is historic ground. Right across our track, three hundred and sixty years ago, wandered the cavalcade of Hernando de Soto,[23] looking for gold and the Great Sea; and he and his foot-sore captives disappeared yonder in the grim forests to the west. Here sits Atlanta, the city of a hundred hills, with something Western, something Southern, and something quite its own, in its busy life. Just this side Atlanta is the land of the Cherokees and to the southwest, not far from where Sam Hose[24] was crucified, you may stand on a spot which is to-day the centre of the Negro problem,—the centre of those nine million men who are America's dark heritage from slavery and the slave-trade.

Not only is Georgia thus the geographical focus of our Negro population, but in many other respects, both now and yesterday, the Negro problems have seemed to be centered in this State. No other State in the Union can count a million Negroes among its citizens,—a population as large as the slave population of the whole Union in 1800; no other State fought so long and strenuously to gather this host of Africans. Oglethorpe[25] thought slavery against law and gospel; but the circumstances which gave Georgia its first inhabitants were not calculated to furnish citizens over-nice in their ideas about rum and slaves. Despite the prohibitions of the trustees, these Georgians, like some of their descendants, proceeded to take the law into their own hands; and so pliant were the judges, and so flagrant the smuggling, and so earnest were the prayers of Whitefield,[26] that by the middle of the eighteenth century all

[22] Song of Songs 1:5–6.
[23] Spanish explorer and discoverer of the Mississippi River (1500?–1542).
[24] Black accused of rape, tortured, and burned alive in Palmetto, Georgia, in 1899.

[25] James Edward Oglethorpe (1696–1785), English founder of the Georgia colony and antislavery crusader.
[26] George Whitefield (1711–1770), English Methodist preacher.

restrictions were swept away, and the slave-trade went merrily on for fifty years and more.

Down in Darien, where the Delegal riots took place some summers ago, there used to come a strong protest against slavery from the Scotch Highlanders; and the Moravians[27] of Ebenezer did not like the system. But not till the Haytian Terror of Toussaint was the trade in men even checked; while the national statute of 1808 did not suffice to stop it. How the Africans poured in!—fifty thousand between 1790 and 1810, and then, from Virginia and from smugglers, two thousand a year for many years more. So the thirty thousand Negroes of Georgia in 1790 were doubled in a decade,—were over a hundred thousand in 1810, had reached two hundred thousand in 1820, and half a million at the time of the war. Thus like a snake the black population writhed upward.

But we must hasten on our journey. This that we pass as we near Atlanta is the ancient land of the Cherokees,—that brave Indian nation which strove so long for its fatherland, until Fate and the United States Government drove them beyond the Mississippi. If you wish to ride with me you must come into the "Jim Crow Car."[28] There will be no objection,—already four other white men, and a little white girl with her nurse, are in there. Usually the races are mixed in there; but the white coach is all white. Of course this car is not so good as the other, but it is fairly clean and comfortable. The discomfort lies chiefly in the hearts of those four black men yonder —and in mine.

We rumble south in quite a business-like way. The bare red clay and pines of Northern Georgia begin to disappear, and in their place appears a rich rolling land, luxuriant, and here and there well tilled. This is the land of the Creek Indians; and a hard time the Georgians had to seize it. The towns grow more frequent and more interesting, and brand-new cotton mills rise on every side. Below Macon the world grows darker; for now we approach the Black Belt,—that strange land of shadows, at which even slaves paled in the past, and whence come now only faint and half-intelligible murmurs to the world beyond. The "Jim Crow Car" grows larger and a shade better; three rough field-hands and two or three white loafers accompany us, and the newsboy still spreads his wares at one end. The sun is setting, but we can see the great cotton country as we enter it,—the soil now dark and fertile, now thin and gray, with fruit-trees and dilapidated buildings,—all the way to Albany.

At Albany, in the heart of the Black Belt, we stop. Two hundred miles south of Atlanta, two hundred miles west of the Atlantic, and one hundred miles north of the Great Gulf lies Dougherty County, with ten thousand Negroes and two thousand whites. The Flint River winds down from Andersonville, and, turning suddenly at Albany, the county-seat, hurries on to join the Chattahoochee and the sea. Andrew Jackson knew the Flint well, and marched across it once to avenge the Indian Massacre at Fort Mims.[29] That was in 1814, not long before the battle of New Orleans;[30] and by the Creek treaty that followed this campaign, all Dougherty County, and much

[27] Protestant sect founded by John Huss around 1722.
[28] Jim Crow laws were tightened during the 1890s to enforce racial segregation in public places.
[29] Before Jackson (1767–1845) became the seventh president (serving from 1829 to 1837), he had

led troops against the Indians in the southern colonies.
[30] Jackson emerged as a national hero for his victory in this battle fought during the War of 1812.

other rich land, was ceded to Georgia. Still, settlers fought shy of this land, for the Indians were all about, and they were unpleasant neighbors in those days. The panic of 1837, which Jackson bequeathed to Van Buren,[31] turned the planters from the impoverished lands of Virginia, the Carolinas, and east Georgia, toward the West. The Indians were removed to Indian Territory, and settlers poured into these coveted lands to retrieve their broken fortunes. For a radius of a hundred miles about Albany, stretched a great fertile land, luxuriant with forests of pine, oak, ash, hickory, and poplar; hot with the sun and damp with the rich black swamp-land; and here the corner-stone of the Cotton Kingdom was laid.

Albany is to-day a wide-streeted, placid, Southern town, with a broad sweep of stores and saloons, and flanking rows of homes,—whites usually to the north, and blacks to the south. Six days in the week the town looks decidedly too small for itself, and takes frequent and prolonged naps. But on Saturday suddenly the whole county disgorges itself upon the place, and a perfect flood of black peasantry pours through the streets, fills the stores, blocks the sidewalks, chokes the thoroughfares, and takes full possession of the town. They are black, sturdy, uncouth country folk, good-natured and simple, talkative to a degree, and yet far more silent and brooding than the crowds of the Rhine-pfalz,[32] or Naples, or Cracow. They drink considerable quantities of whiskey, but do not get very drunk; they talk and laugh loudly at times, but seldom quarrel or fight. They walk up and down the streets, meet and gossip with friends, stare at the shop windows, buy coffee, cheap candy, and clothes, and at dusk drive home—happy? well no, not exactly happy, but much happier than as though they had not come.

Thus Albany is a real capital,—a typical Southern county town, the centre of the life of ten thousand souls; their point of contact with the outer world, their centre of news and gossip, their market for buying and selling, borrowing and lending, their fountain of justice and law. Once upon a time we knew country life so well and city life so little, that we illustrated city life as that of a closely crowded country district. Now the world has well-nigh forgotten what the country is, and we must imagine a little city of black people scattered far and wide over three hundred lonesome square miles of land, without train or trolley, in the midst of cotton and corn, and wide patches of sand and gloomy soil.

It gets pretty hot in Southern Georgia in July,—a sort of dull, determined heat that seems quite independent of the sun; so it took us some days to muster courage enough to leave the porch and venture out on the long country roads, that we might see this unknown world. Finally we started. It was about ten in the morning, bright with a faint breeze, and we jogged leisurely southward in the valley of the Flint. We passed the scattered box-like cabins of the brick-yard hands, and the long tenement-row facetiously called "The Ark," and were soon in the open country, and on the confines of the great plantations of other days. There is the "Joe Fields place"; a rough old fellow was he, and had killed many a "nigger" in his day. Twelve miles his plantation used to run,—a regular barony. It is nearly all gone now; only straggling bits belong to the family, and the rest has passed to Jews and Negroes. Even the bits

---

[31] Martin Van Buren (1782–1862), who succeeded Jackson as president, entered office during a time of national financial troubles.

[32] Territory in Germany; the Palatinate.

which are left are heavily mortgaged, and, like the rest of the land, tilled by tenants. Here is one of them now,—a tall brown man, a hard worker and a hard drinker, illiterate, but versed in farmlore, as his nodding crops declare. This distressingly new board house is his, and he has just moved out of yonder moss-grown cabin with its one square room.

From the curtains in Benton's house, down the road, a dark comely face is staring at the strangers; for passing carriages are not every-day occurrences here. Benton is an intelligent yellow man with a good-sized family, and manages a plantation blasted by the war and now the broken staff of the widow. He might be well-to-do, they say; but he carouses too much in Albany. And the half-desolate spirit of neglect born of the very soil seems to have settled on these acres. In times past there were cotton-gins and machinery here; but they have rotted away.

The whole land seems forlorn and forsaken. Here are the remnants of the vast plantations of the Sheldons, the Pellots, and the Rensons; but the souls of them are passed. The houses lie in half ruin, or have wholly disappeared; the fences have flown, and the families are wandering in the world. Strange vicissitudes have met these whilom masters. Yonder stretch the wide acres of Bildad Reasor; he died in war-time, but the upstart overseer hastened to wed the widow. Then he went, and his neighbors too, and now only the black tenant remains; but the shadow-hand of the master's grand-nephew or cousin or creditor stretches out of the gray distance to collect the rack-rent remorselessly, and so the land is uncared-for and poor. Only black tenants can stand such a system, and they only because they must. Ten miles we have ridden to-day and have seen no white face.

A resistless feeling of depression falls slowly upon us, despite the gaudy sunshine and the green cottonfields. This, then, is the Cotton Kingdom,—the shadow of a marvellous dream. And where is the King? Perhaps this is he,—the sweating plough-man, tilling his eighty acres with two lean mules, and fighting a hard battle with debt. So we sit musing, until, as we turn a corner on the sandy road, there comes a fairer scene suddenly in view,—a neat cottage snugly ensconced by the road, and near it a little store. A tall bronzed man rises from the porch as we hail him, and comes out to our carriage. He is six feet in height, with a sober face that smiles gravely. He walks too straight to be a tenant,—yes, he owns two hundred and forty acres. "The land is run down since the boom-days of eighteen hundred and fifty," he explains, and cotton is low. Three black tenants live on his place, and in his little store he keeps a small stock of tobacco, snuff, soap, and soda, for the neighborhood. Here is his gin-house with new machinery just installed. Three hundred bales of cotton went through it last year. Two children he has sent away to school. Yes, he says sadly, he is getting on, but cotton is down to four cents; I know how Debt sits staring at him.

Wherever the King may be, the parks and palaces of the Cotton Kingdom have not wholly disappeared. We plunge even now into great groves of oak and towering pine, with an undergrowth of myrtle and shrubbery. This was the "home-house" of the Thompsons,—slave-barons who drove their coach and four in the merry past. All is silence now, and ashes, and tangled weeds. The owner put his whole fortune into the rising cotton industry of the fifties, and with the falling prices of the eighties he packed up and stole away. Yonder is another grove, with unkempt lawn, great magnolias, and grass-grown paths. The Big House stands in half-ruin, its great front door staring blankly at the street, and the back part grotesquely restored for its black tenant. A shabby, well-built Negro he is, unlucky and irresolute. He digs hard to pay rent to the white girl who owns the remnant of the place. She married a policeman, and lives in Savannah.

Now and again we come to churches. Here is one now,—Shepherd's, they call it,—a great white-washed barn of a thing, perched on stilts of stone, and looking for all the world as though it were just resting here a moment and might be expected to waddle off down the road at almost any time. And yet it is the centre of a hundred cabin homes; and sometimes, of a Sunday, five hundred persons from far and near gather here and talk and eat and sing. There is a school-house near,—a very airy, empty shed; but even this is an improvement, for usually the school is held in the church. The churches vary from log-huts to those like Shepherd's, and the schools from nothing to this little house that sits demurely on the county line. It is a tiny plank-house, perhaps ten by twenty, and has within a double row of rough unplaned benches, resting mostly on legs, sometimes on boxes. Opposite the door is a square home-made desk. In one corner are the ruins of a stove, and in the other a dim blackboard. It is the cheerfulest schoolhouse I have seen in Dougherty, save in town. Back of the schoolhouse is a lodge-house two stories high and not quite finished. Societies meet there,—societies "to care for the sick and bury the dead"; and these societies grow and flourish.

We had come to the boundaries of Dougherty, and were about to turn west along the county-line, when all these sights were pointed out to us by a kindly old man, black, white-haired, and seventy. Forty-five years he had lived here, and now supports himself and his old wife by the help of the steer tethered yonder and the charity of his black neighbors. He shows us the farm of the Hills just across the county line in Baker,—a widow and two strapping sons, who raised ten bales (one need not add "cotton" down here) last year. There are fences and pigs and cows, and the soft-voiced, velvet-skinned young Memnon, who sauntered half-bashfully over to greet the strangers, is proud of his home. We turn now to the west along the county line. Great dismantled trunks of pines tower above the green cotton-fields, cracking their naked gnarled fingers toward the border of living forest beyond. There is little beauty in this region, only a sort of crude abandon that suggests power,—a naked grandeur, as it were. The houses are bare and straight; there are no hammocks or easy-chairs, and few flowers. So when, as here at Rawdon's, one sees a vine clinging to a little porch, and home-like windows peeping over the fences, one takes a long breath. I think I never before quite realized the place of the Fence in civilization. This is the Land of the Unfenced, where crouch on either hand scores of ugly one-room cabins, cheerless and dirty. Here lies the Negro problem in its naked dirt and penury. And here are no fences. But now and then the criss-cross rails or straight palings break into view, and then we know a touch of culture is near. Of course Harrison Gohagen, —a quiet yellow man, young, smooth-faced, and diligent,—of course he is lord of some hundred acres, and we expect to see a vision of well-kept rooms and fat beds and laughing children. For has he not fine fences? And those over yonder, why should they build fences on the rack-rented land? It will only increase their rent.

On we wind, through sand and pines and glimpses of old plantations, till there creeps into sight a cluster of buildings,—wood and brick, mills and houses, and scattered cabins. It seemed quite a village. As it came nearer and nearer, however, the aspect changed: the buildings were rotten, the bricks were falling out, the mills were silent, and the store was closed. Only in the cabins appeared now and then a bit of lazy life. I could imagine the place under some weird spell, and was half-minded to search out the princess. An old ragged black man, honest, simple, and improvident, told us the tale. The Wizard of the North—the Capitalist—had rushed down in the seventies to woo this coy dark soil. He bought a square mile or more, and for a time the field-hands sang, the gins groaned, and the mills buzzed. Then came a change. The agent's son embezzled the funds and ran off with them. Then the agent himself disappeared. Finally the new agent stole even the books, and the company in wrath closed its business and its houses, refused to sell, and let houses and furniture and machinery rust and rot. So the Waters-Loring plantation was stilled by the spell of dishonesty, and stands like some gaunt rebuke to a scarred land.

Somehow that plantation ended our day's journey; for I could not shake off the influence of that silent scene. Back toward town we glided, past the straight and thread-like pines, past a dark tree-dotted pond where the air was heavy with a dead sweet perfume. White slender-legged curlews flitted by us, and the garnet blooms of the cotton looked gay against the green and purple stalks. A peasant girl was hoeing in the field, white-turbaned and black-limbed. All this we saw, but the spell still lay upon us.

How curious a land is this,—how full of untold story, of tragedy and laughter, and the rich legacy of human life; shadowed with a tragic past, and big with future promise! This is the Black Belt of Georgia. Dougherty County is the west end of the Black Belt, and men once called it the Egypt of the Confederacy. It is full of historic interest. First there is the Swamp, to the west, where the Chickasawhatchee flows sullenly southward. The shadow of an old plantation lies at its edge, forlorn and dark. Then comes the pool; pendent gray moss and brackish waters appear, and forests filled with wildfowl. In one place the wood is on fire, smouldering in dull red anger; but nobody minds. Then the swamp grows beautiful; a raised road, built by chained Negro convicts, dips down into it, and forms a way walled and almost covered in living green. Spreading trees spring from a prodigal luxuriance of under-growth; great dark green shadows fade into the black background, until all is one mass of tangled semi-tropical foliage, marvellous in its weird savage splendor. Once we crossed a black silent stream, where the sad trees and writhing creepers, all glinting fiery yellow and green, seemed like some vast cathedral,—some green Milan[33] builded of wildwood. And as I crossed, I seemed to see again that fierce tragedy of seventy years ago. Osceola,[34] the Indian-Negro chieftain, had risen in the swamps of Florida, vowing vengeance. His war-cry reached the red Creeks of Dougherty, and their war-cry rang from the Chattahoochee to the sea. Men and women and children fled and fell before them as they swept into Dougherty. In yonder shadows a dark and hideously painted warrior glided stealthily on,—another and another, until three hundred had crept into the treacherous swamp. Then the false slime closing about them called the white men from the east. Waist-deep, they fought beneath the tall trees, until the war-cry was hushed and the Indians glided back into the west. Small wonder the wood is red.

Then came the black slaves. Day after day the clank of chained feet marching from

---

[33] The cathedral of Milan, Italy, is one of the largest church structures in Europe.

[34] Chief of the Seminoles (1804?–1838).

Virginia and Carolina to Georgia was heard in these rich swamp lands. Day after day the songs of the callous, the wail of the motherless, and the muttered curses of the wretched echoed from the Flint to the Chickasawhatchee, until by 1860 there had risen in West Dougherty perhaps the richest slave kingdom the modern world ever knew. A hundred and fifty barons commanded the labor of nearly six thousand negroes, held sway over farms with ninety thousand acres of tilled land, valued even in times of cheap soil at three millions of dollars. Twenty thousand bales of ginned cotton went yearly to England, New and Old; and men that came there bankrupt made money and grew rich. In a single decade the cotton output increased four-fold and the value of lands was tripled. It was the heyday of the *nouveau riche,* and a life of careless extravagance reigned among the masters. Four and six bob-tailed thoroughbreds rolled their coaches to town; open hospitality and gay entertainment were the rule. Parks and groves were laid out, rich with flower and vine, and in the midst stood the low wide-halled "big house," with its porch and columns and great fire-places.

And yet with all this there was something sordid, something forced,—a certain feverish unrest and recklessness; for was not all this show and tinsel built upon a groan? "This land was a little Hell," said a ragged, brown, and grave-faced man to me. We were seated near a roadside blacksmith-shop, and behind was the bare ruin of some master's home. "I've seen niggers drop dead in the furrow, but they were kicked aside, and the plough never stopped. And down in the guard-house, there's where the blood ran."

With such foundations a kingdom must in time sway and fall. The masters moved to Macon and Augusta, and left only the irresponsible overseers on the land. And the result is such ruin as this, the Lloyd "home-place":—great waving oaks, a spread of lawn, myrtles and chestnuts, all ragged and wild; a solitary gate-post standing where once was a castle entrance; an old rusty anvil lying amid rotting bellows and wood in the ruins of a blacksmith shop; a wide rambling old mansion, brown and dingy, filled now with the grandchildren of the slaves who once waited on its tables; while the family of the master has dwindled to two lone women, who live in Macon and feed hungrily off the remnants of an earldom. So we ride on, past phantom gates and falling homes,—past the once flourishing farms of the Smiths, the Gandys, and the Lagores,—and find all dilapidated and half ruined, even there where a solitary white woman, a relic of other days, sits alone in state among miles of Negroes and rides to town in her ancient coach each day.

This was indeed the Egypt of the Confederacy,—the rich granary whence potatoes and corn and cotton poured out to the famished and ragged Confederate troops as they battled for a cause lost long before 1861. Sheltered and secure, it became the place of refuge for families, wealth, and slaves. Yet even then the hard ruthless rape of the land began to tell. The red-clay sub-soil already had begun to peer above the loam. The harder the slaves were driven the more careless and fatal was their farming. Then came the revolution of war and Emancipation, the bewilderment of Reconstruction, —and now, what is the Egypt of the Confederacy, and what meaning has it for the nation's weal or woe?

It is a land of rapid contrasts and of curiously mingled hope and pain. Here sits a pretty blue-eyed quadroon hiding her bare feet; she was married only last week, and yonder in the field is her dark young husband, hoeing to support her, at thirty cents a day without board. Across the way is Gatesby, brown and tall, lord of two thousand acres shrewdly won and held. There is a store conducted by his black son, a blacksmith shop, and a ginnery. Five miles below here is a town owned and controlled by one white New Englander. He owns almost a Rhode Island county, with thousands of acres and hundreds of black laborers. Their cabins look better than most, and the farm, with machinery and fertilizers, is much more business-like than any in the county, although the manager drives hard bargains in wages. When now we turn and look five miles above, there on the edge of town are five houses of prostitutes,—two of blacks and three of whites; and in one of the houses of the whites a worthless black boy was harbored too openly two years ago; so he was hanged for rape. And here, too, is the high whitewashed fence of the "stockade," as the county prison is called; the white folks say it is ever full of black criminals,—the black folks say that only colored boys are sent to jail, and they not because they are guilty, but because the State needs criminals to eke out its income by their forced labor.

The Jew is the heir of the slave-baron in Dougherty; and as we ride westward, by wide stretching cornfields and stubby orchards of peach and pear, we see on all sides within the circle of dark forest a Land of Canaan.[35] Here and there are tales of projects for money-getting, born in the swift days of Reconstruction,[36]—"improvement" companies, wine companies, mills and factories; nearly all failed, and the Jew fell heir. It is a beautiful land, this Dougherty, west of the Flint. The forests are wonderful, the solemn pines have disappeared, and this is the "Oakey Woods," with its wealth of hickories, beeches, oaks, and palmettos. But a pall of debt hangs over the beautiful land; the merchants are in debt to the wholesalers, the planters are in debt to the merchants, the tenants owe the planters, and laborers bow and bend beneath the burden of it all. Here and there a man has raised his head above these murky waters. We passed one fenced stock-farm, with grass and grazing cattle, that looked very homelike after endless corn and cotton. Here and there are black freeholders: there is the gaunt dull-black Jackson, with his hundred acres. "I says, 'Look up! If you don't look up you can't get up,'" remarks Jackson, philosophically. And he's gotten up. Dark Carter's neat barns would do credit to New England. His master helped him to get a start, but when the black man died last fall the master's sons immediately laid claim to the estate. "And them white folks will get it, too," said my yellow gossip.[37]

I turn from these well-tended acres with a comfortable feeling that the Negro is rising. Even then, however, the fields, as we proceed, begin to redden and the trees disappear. Rows of old cabins appear filled with renters and laborers,—cheerless, bare, and dirty, for the most part, although here and there the very age and decay makes the scene picturesque. A young black fellow greets us. He is twenty-two, and just married. Until last year he had good luck renting; then cotton fell, and the sheriff seized and sold all he had. So he moved here, where the rent is higher, the land poorer, and the owner inflexible; he rents a forty-dollar mule for twenty dollars a year. Poor lad!—a slave at twenty-two. This plantation, owned now by a Russian Jew, was a part of the famous Bolton estate. After the war it was for many years worked by gangs of Negro convicts,—and black convicts then were even more plentiful than now; it

---

[35] The land God told Moses was promised to the Israelites upon their flight from bondage in Egypt; roughly equivalent to today's nation of Israel.

[36] The period between 1867 and 1877, during which the federal government initiated the process by which the Southern states were brought back into the Union; a time of great social, economic, and political change.

[37] Mulatto informant.

was a way of making Negroes work, and the question of guilt was a minor one. Hard tales of cruelty and mistreatment of the chained freemen are told, but the county authorities were deaf until the free-labor market was nearly ruined by wholesale migration. Then they took the convicts from the plantations, but not until one of the fairest regions of the "Oakey Woods" had been ruined and ravished into a red waste, out of which only a Yankee or his like could squeeze more blood from debt-cursed tenants.

No wonder that Luke Black, slow, dull, and discouraged, shuffles to our carriage and talks hopelessly. Why should he strive? Every year finds him deeper in debt. How strange that Georgia, the world-heralded refuge of poor debtors, should bind her own to sloth and misfortune as ruthlessly as ever England did! The poor land groans with its birth-pains, and brings forth scarcely a hundred pounds of cotton to the acre, where fifty years ago it yielded eight times as much. Of this meagre yield the tenant pays from a quarter to a third in rent, and most of the rest in interest on food and supplies bought on credit. Twenty years yonder sunken-cheeked, old black man has labored under that system, and now, turned day-laborer, is supporting his wife and boarding himself on his wages of a dollar and a half a week, received only part of the year.

The Bolton convict farm formerly included the neighboring plantation. Here it was that the convicts were lodged in the great log prison still standing. A dismal place it still remains, with rows of ugly huts filled with surly ignorant tenants. "What rent do you pay here?" I inquired. "I don't know,—what is it, Sam?" "All we make," answered Sam. It is a depressing place,—bare, unshaded, with no charm of past association, only a memory of forced human toil,—now, then, and before the war. They are not happy, these black men whom we meet throughout this region. There is little of the joyous abandon and playfulness which we are wont to associate with the plantation Negro. At best, the natural good-nature is edged with complaint or has changed into sullenness and gloom. And now and then it blazes forth in veiled but hot anger. I remember one big red-eyed black whom we met by the road-side. Forty-five years he had labored on this farm, beginning with nothing, and still having nothing. To be sure, he had given four children a common-school training, and perhaps if the new fence-law had not allowed unfenced crops in West Dougherty he might have raised a little stock and kept ahead. As it is, he is hopelessly in debt, disappointed, and embittered. He stopped us to inquire after the black boy in Albany, whom it was said a policeman had shot and killed for loud talking on the sidewalk. And then he said slowly: "Let a white man touch me, and he dies; I don't boast this, —I don't say it around loud, or before the children,—but I mean it. I've seen them whip my father and my old mother in them cotton-rows till the blood ran; by—" and we passed on.

Now Sears, whom we met next lolling under the chubby oak-trees, was of quite different fibre. Happy?—Well, yes; he laughed and flipped pebbles, and thought the world was as it was. He had worked here twelve years and has nothing but a mortgaged mule. Children? Yes, seven; but they hadn't been to school this year,— couldn't afford books and clothes, and couldn't spare their work. There go part of them to the fields now,—three big boys astride mules, and a strapping girl with bare brown legs. Careless ignorance and laziness here, fierce hate and vindictiveness there; —these are the extremes of the Negro problem which we met that day, and we scarce knew which we preferred.

Here and there we meet distinct characters quite out of the ordinary. One came out of a piece of newly cleared ground, making a wide detour to avoid the snakes. He was an old, hollow-cheeked man, with a drawn and characterful brown face. He had a sort of self-contained quaintness and rough humor impossible to describe; a certain cynical earnestness that puzzled one. "The niggers were jealous of me over on the other place," he said, "and so me and the old woman begged this piece of woods, and I cleared it up myself. Made nothing for two years, but I reckon I've got a crop now." The cotton looked tall and rich, and we praised it. He curtsied low, and then bowed almost to the ground, with an imperturbable gravity that seemed almost suspicious. Then he continued, "My mule died last week,"—a calamity in this land equal to a devastating fire in town,—"but a white man loaned me another." Then he added, eyeing us, "Oh, I gets along with white folks." We turned the conversation. "Bears? deer?" he answered, "well, I should say there were," and he let fly a string of brave oaths, as he told hunting-tales of the swamp. We left him standing still in the middle of the road looking after us, and yet apparently not noticing us.

The Whistle place, which includes his bit of land, was bought soon after the war by an English syndicate, the "Dixie Cotton and Corn Company." A marvellous deal of style their factor put on, with his servants and coach-and-six; so much so that the concern soon landed in inextricable bankruptcy. Nobody lives in the old house now, but a man comes each winter out of the North and collects his high rents. I know not which are the more touching,—such old empty houses, or the homes of the masters' sons. Sad and bitter tales lie hidden back of those white doors,—tales of poverty, of struggle, of disappointment. A revolution such as that of '63 is a terrible thing; they that rose rich in the morning often slept in paupers' beds. Beggars and vulgar speculators rose to rule over them, and their children went astray. See yonder sad-colored house, with its cabins and fences and glad crops! It is not glad within; last month the prodigal son of the struggling father wrote home from the city for money. Money! Where was it to come from? And so the son rose in the night and killed his baby, and killed his wife, and shot himself dead. And the world passed on.

I remember wheeling around a bend in the road beside a graceful bit of forest and a singing brook. A long low house faced us, with porch and flying pillars, great oaken door, and a broad lawn shining in the evening sun. But the window-panes were gone, the pillars were worm-eaten, and the moss-grown roof was falling in. Half curiously I peered through the unhinged door, and saw where, on the wall across the hall, was written in once gay letters a faded "Welcome."

Quite a contrast to the southwestern part of Dougherty County is the northwest. Soberly timbered in oak and pine, it has none of that half-tropical luxuriance of the southwest. Then, too, there are fewer signs of a romantic past, and more of systematic modern land-grabbing and money-getting. White people are more in evidence here, and farmer and hired labor replace to some extent the absentee landlord and rack-rented tenant. The crops have neither the luxuriance of the richer land nor the signs of neglect so often seen, and there were fences and meadows here and there. Most of this land was poor, and beneath the notice of the slave-baron, before the war. Since then his nephews and the poor whites and the Jews have seized it. The returns of the farmer are too small to allow much for wages, and yet he will not sell off small farms. There is the Negro Sanford; he has worked fourteen years as overseer on the Ladson place, and "paid out enough for fertilizers to have bought a farm," but the owner will not sell off a few acres.

Two children—a boy and a girl—are hoeing sturdily in the fields on the farm where Corliss works. He is smooth-faced and brown, and is fencing up his pigs. He used to run a successful cotton-gin, but the Cotton Seed Oil Trust has forced the price of ginning so low that he says it hardly pays him. He points out a stately old house over the way as the home of "Pa Willis." We eagerly ride over, for "Pa Willis" was the tall and powerful black Moses who led the Negroes for a generation, and led them well. He was a Baptist preacher, and when he died two thousand black people followed him to the grave; and now they preach his funeral sermon each year. His widow lives here,—a weazened, sharp-featured little woman, who curtsied quaintly as we greeted her. Further on lives Jack Delson, the most prosperous Negro farmer in the county. It is a joy to meet him—a great broad-shouldered, handsome black man, intelligent and jovial. Six hundred and fifty acres he owns, and has eleven black tenants. A neat and tidy home nestled in a flower-garden, and a little store stands beside it.

We pass the Munson place, where a plucky white widow is renting and struggling; and the eleven hundred acres of the Sennet plantation, with its Negro overseer. Then the character of the farms begins to change. Nearly all the lands belong to Russian Jews; the overseers are white, and the cabins are bare board-houses scattered here and there. The rents are high, and day-laborers and "contract" hands abound. It is a keen, hard struggle for living here, and few have time to talk. Tired with the long ride, we gladly drive into Gillonsville. It is a silent cluster of farm-houses standing on the cross-roads, with one of its stores closed and the other kept by a Negro preacher. They tell great tales of busy times at Gillonsville before all the railroads came to Albany; now it is chiefly a memory. Riding down the street, we stop at the preacher's and seat ourselves before the door. It was one of those scenes one cannot soon forget:— a wide, low, little house, whose motherly roof reached over and sheltered a snug little porch. There we sat, after the long hot drive, drinking cool water,—the talkative little store-keeper who is my daily companion; the silent old black woman patching pantaloons and saying never a word; the ragged picture of helpless misfortune who called in just to see the preacher; and finally the neat matronly preacher's wife, plump, yellow, and intelligent. "Own land?" said the wife; "well, only this house." Then she added quietly, "We did buy seven hundred acres up yonder, and paid for it; but they cheated us out of it. Sells was the owner." "Sells!" echoed the ragged misfortune, who was leaning against the balustrade and listening, "he's a regular cheat. I worked for him thirty-seven days this spring, and he paid me in cardboard checks which were to be cashed at the end of the month. But he never cashed them,—kept putting me off. Then the sheriff came and took my mule and corn and furniture—" "Furniture?" I asked; "but furniture is exempt from seizure by law." "Well, he took it just the same," said the hard-faced man.

1903

Edwin Arlington Robinson
1869–1935

The poets who preceded Edwin Arlington Robinson—Bryant, Whittier, Longfellow, and James Russell Lowell—have been grouped as "the fireside poets," and the name conveys their acceptability to the genteel tradition. Unlike these poets, Robinson had the lonely courage not to write conventionally pleasing verse. Instead he wrote lyrics stemming directly from his doomed sense of life. He was, in the existential bleakness of his vision, a forerunner of the disillusioned generation that created the modernist movement in art.

One of Robinson's brothers was an alcoholic, one a doctor addicted to drugs, and Robinson himself became an alcoholic. His father's business had failed, and it was only through local benefactors that Robinson managed to spend two years (like Robert Frost later) as a special student at Harvard. When he left Harvard, he returned home to Gardiner, Maine, where, trapped, unemployed, and in the force of his twenties, he wrote his most memorable poems. Robinson first anatomized his village (under the name "Tilbury Town") and its cast of local failures and eccentrics in the 1897 collection of poems *Children of the Night*. The most famous of his characters—the hopeless, backward-looking Miniver Cheevy and the immaculately dressed but suicidal Richard Cory—are perhaps self-caricatures and bear a special lyric force in their cruel self-satire. Nearing thirty, Robinson moved to New York, where he lived the rest of his life, although after 1911 he spent the summers in New Hampshire at the MacDowell Colony for artists. He never married.

In 1922 Robinson's *Collected Poems* was awarded the Pulitzer Prize. In his maturity, he was known chiefly for his long, Tennysonian poems on Arthurian themes, *Merlin* (1917), *Lancelot* (1920), and *Tristram* (1927), which have not aged well. He also wrote long psychological studies of character, among them *Cavender's House* (1929) and *Matthis at the Door* (1931). George Crabbe rather than Tennyson was Robinson's true English precursor. Crabbe's "hard, human pulse," his "plain excellence and stubborn skill," as Robinson called them, were Robinson's own aesthetic strengths. His brisk quatrains, the stern blank verse of his satires, his death-knell rhymes in "Eros Turannos"—"confusion, illusion, seclusion" or "striven, given, driven"—are marks of his care in composing.

Robinson's achievement in verse is now perceived, paradoxically, through the work of Robert Frost, who learned everything Robinson had to teach and brought it to rhythmic and lyric perfection. Without Robinson, we can scarcely imagine Frost's existence. Robinson's dark, sardonic nature appealed to Frost's grim side, and he also taught Frost how to be a regional poet. Robinson's revelation of the spoiled erotic life allowed Frost to draw aside curtains of privacy, and his insight into the tragic dramas enacted in rural life gave Frost one of his chief topics. When we look at Robinson now, we feel he must have been reading Frost; but the debt goes the other way.

Further Reading:
M. Van Doren, *Edwin Arlington Robinson,* 1927.
H. Hagedorn, *Edwin Arlington Robinson: A Biography,* 1938.
E. Kaplan, *Philosophy in the Poetry of Edwin Arlington Robinson,* 1940.
Y. Winters, *Edwin Arlington Robinson,* 1946.
E. Neff, *Edwin Arlington Robinson,* 1948.
E. Barnard, *Edwin Arlington Robinson: A Critical Study,* 1952.
E. S. Fussell, *Edwin Arlington Robinson: The Literary Background of a Traditional Poet,* 1954.
W. L. Anderson, *Edwin Arlington Robinson,*

1967.
W. R. Robinson, *Edwin Arlington Robinson: A Poetry of the Act,* 1967.
L. O. Coxe, *Edwin Arlington Robinson: The Life of Poetry,* 1968.
H. C. Franchere, *Edwin Arlington Robinson,* 1968.
Edwin Arlington Robinson: Centenary Essays, ed. E. Barnard, 1973.
R. Cary, *Early Reception of Edwin Arlington Robinson,* 1974.
N. C. Joyner, *Edwin Arlington Robinson,* 1978.

Text:
Collected Poems, 1940.
See also *Selected Poems of Edwin Arlington Robinson,* ed. M. D. Zabel, 1965, 1966.
Uncollected Poems and Prose of Edwin Arlington Robinson, ed. R. Cary, 1975.
Selected Letters of Edwin Arlington Robinson, ed. R. Torrence, 1940.

Richard Cory

Whenever Richard Cory went down town,
We people on the pavement looked at him:
He was a gentleman from sole to crown,
Clean favored, and imperially slim.

And he was always quietly arrayed,   5
And he was always human when he talked;
But still he fluttered pulses when he said,
"Good-morning," and he glittered when he walked.

And he was rich—yes, richer than a king—
And admirably schooled in every grace: 10
In fine, we thought that he was everything
To make us wish that we were in his place.

So on we worked, and waited for the light,
And went without the meat, and cursed the bread;
And Richard Cory, one calm summer night,   15
Went home and put a bullet through his head.

1896

George Crabbe[1]

Give him the darkest inch your shelf allows,
Hide him in lonely garrets, if you will,—
But his hard, human pulse is throbbing still
With the sure strength that fearless truth endows.
In spite of all fine science disavows,   5
Of his plain excellence and stubborn skill
There yet remains what fashion cannot kill,
Though years have thinned the laurel from his brows.

Whether or not we read him, we can feel
From time to time the vigor of his name   10
Against us like a finger for the shame
And emptiness of what our souls reveal
In books that are as altars where we kneel
To consecrate the flicker, not the flame.

1896

The Corridor

It may have been the pride in me for aught
I know, or just a patronizing whim;
But call it freak or fancy, or what not,
I cannot hide that hungry face of him.

I keep a scant half-dozen words he said,   5
And every now and then I lose his name;
He may be living or he may be dead,
But I must have him with me all the same.

I knew it, and I knew it all along,—
And felt it once or twice, or thought I did;   10
But only as a glad man feels a song
That sounds around a stranger's coffin lid.

---

[1] English poet (1754–1832) and author of *The Village* (1783), a bleak picture of rustic life.

I knew it, and he knew it, I believe,
But silence held us alien to the end;
And I have now no magic to retrieve   15
That year, to stop that hunger for a friend.
1902

But for the Grace of God

"There, but for the grace of God, goes . . ."

There is a question that I ask,
    And ask again:
What hunger was half-hidden by the mask
    That he wore then?

There was a word for me to say   5
    That I said not;
And in the past there was another day
    That I forgot:

A dreary, cold, unwholesome day,
    Racked overhead,—   10
As if the world were turning the wrong way,
    And the sun dead:

A day that comes back well enough
    Now he is gone.
What then? Has memory no other stuff   15
    To seize upon?

Wherever he may wander now
    In his despair,
Would he be more contented in the slough
    If all were there?   20

And yet he brought a kind of light
    Into the room;
And when he left, a tinge of something bright
    Survived the gloom.

Why will he not be where he is,   25
    And not with me?
The hours that are my life are mine, not his,—
    Or used to be.

What numerous imps invisible
  Has he at hand,   30
Far-flying and forlorn as what they tell
  At his command?

What hold of weirdness or of worth
  Can he possess,
That he may speak from anywhere on earth   35
  His loneliness?

Shall I be caught and held again
  In the old net?—
He brought a sorry sunbeam with him then,
  But it beams yet.   40

1910

Miniver Cheevy

Miniver Cheevy, child of scorn,
  Grew lean while he assailed the seasons;
He wept that he was ever born,
  And he had reasons.

Miniver loved the days of old   5
  When swords were bright and steeds were prancing;
The vision of a warrior bold
  Would set him dancing.

Miniver sighed for what was not,
  And dreamed, and rested from his labors;   10
He dreamed of Thebes[1] and Camelot,[2]
  And Priam's[3] neighbors.

Miniver mourned the ripe renown
  That made so many a name so fragrant;
He mourned Romance, now on the town,   15
  And Art, a vagrant.

---

[1] City in Greece made famous by Homer and the
Greek tragedians.
[2] Site of King Arthur's court.
[3] Priam was king of Troy. (The Trojan War is
described in Homer's *Iliad*.)

Miniver loved the Medici,[4]
  Albeit he had never seen one;
He would have sinned incessantly
  Could he have been one.   20

Miniver cursed the commonplace
  And eyed a khaki suit with loathing;
He missed the mediæval grace
  Of iron clothing.

Miniver scorned the gold he sought,   25
  But sore annoyed was he without it;
Miniver thought, and thought, and thought,
  And thought about it.

Miniver Cheevy, born too late,
  Scratched his head and kept on thinking;   30
Miniver coughed, and called it fate,
  And kept on drinking.

1910

For a Dead Lady

No more with overflowing light
Shall fill the eyes that now are faded,
Nor shall another's fringe with night
Their woman-hidden world as they did.
No more shall quiver down the days   5
The flowing wonder of her ways,
Whereof no language may requite
The shifting and the many-shaded.

The grace, divine, definitive,
Clings only as a faint forestalling;   10
The laugh that love could not forgive
Is hushed, and answers to no calling;
The forehead and the little ears
Have gone where Saturn keeps the years;
The breast where roses could not live   15
Has done with rising and with falling.

[4] One of the ruling families of the Italian
Renaissance.

The beauty, shattered by the laws
That have creation in their keeping,
No longer trembles at applause,
Or over children that are sleeping;   20
And we who delve in beauty's lore
Know all that we have known before
Of what inexorable cause
Makes Time so vicious in his reaping.
1910

Eros Turannos[1]

She fears him, and will always ask
   What fated her to choose him;
She meets in his engaging mask
   All reasons to refuse him;
But what she meets and what she fears   5
Are less than are the downward years,
Drawn slowly to the foamless weirs
   Of age, were she to lose him.

Between a blurred sagacity
   That once had power to sound him,   10
And Love, that will not let him be
   The Judas that she found him,
Her pride assuages her almost,
As if it were alone the cost.—
He sees that he will not be lost,   15
   And waits and looks around him.

A sense of ocean and old trees
   Envelops and allures him;
Tradition, touching all he sees,
   Beguiles and reassures him;   20
And all her doubts of what he says
Are dimmed with what she knows of days—
Till even prejudice delays
   And fades, and she secures him.

[1] Greek: "Love, the Ruler."

The falling leaf inaugurates   25
    The reign of her confusion;
The pounding wave reverberates
    The dirge of her illusion;
And home, where passion lived and died,
Becomes a place where she can hide,   30
While all the town and harbor side
    Vibrate with her seclusion.

We tell you, tapping on our brows,
    The story as it should be,—
As if the story of a house   35
    Were told, or ever could be;
We'll have no kindly veil between
Her visions and those we have seen,—
As if we guessed what hers have been,
    Or what they are or would be.   40

Meanwhile we do no harm; for they
    That with a god have striven,
Not hearing much of what we say,
    Take what the god has given;
Though like waves breaking it may be,   45
Or like a changed familiar tree,
Or like a stairway to the sea
    Where down the blind are driven.
1916

The Unforgiven

When he, who is the unforgiven,
    Beheld her first, he found her fair:
No promise ever dreamt in heaven
    Could then have lured him anywhere
    That would have been away from there;   5
And all his wits had lightly striven,
    Foiled with her voice, and eyes, and hair.

There's nothing in the saints and sages
    To meet the shafts her glances had,
Or such as hers have had for ages   10
    To blind a man till he be glad,

And humble him till he be mad.
The story would have many pages,
And would be neither good nor bad.

And, having followed, you would find him   15
Where properly the play begins;
But look for no red light behind him—
No fumes of many-colored sins,
Fanned high by screaming violins.
God knows what good it was to blind him,   20
Or whether man or woman wins.

And by the same eternal token,
Who knows just how it will all end?—
This drama of hard words unspoken,
This fireside farce, without a friend   25
Or enemy to comprehend
What augurs when two lives are broken,
And fear finds nothing left to mend.

He stares in vain for what awaits him,
And sees in Love a coin to toss;   30
He smiles, and her cold hush berates him
Beneath his hard half of the cross;
They wonder why it ever was;
And she, the unforgiving, hates him
More for her lack than for her loss.   35

He feeds with pride his indecision,
And shrinks from what will not occur,
Bequeathing with infirm derision
His ashes to the days that were,
Before she made him prisoner;   40
And labors to retrieve the vision
That he must once have had of her.

He waits, and there awaits an ending,
And he knows neither what nor when;
But no magicians are attending   45
To make him see as he saw then,
And he will never find again
The face that once had been the rending
Of all his purpose among men.

He blames her not, nor does he chide her,   50
And she has nothing new to say;
If he were Bluebeard he could hide her,

But that's not written in the play,
And there will be no change to-day;
Although, to the serene outsider,   55
There still would seem to be a way.
1916

The Mill

The miller's wife had waited long,
    The tea was cold, the fire was dead;
And there might yet be nothing wrong
    In how he went and what he said:
"There are no millers any more,"   5
    Was all that she had heard him say:
And he had lingered at the door
    So long that it seemed yesterday.

Sick with a fear that had no form
    She knew that she was there at last;   10
And in the mill there was a warm
    And mealy fragrance of the past.
What else there was would only seem
    To say again what he had meant;
And what was hanging from a beam   15
    Would not have heeded where she went.

And if she thought it followed her,
    She may have reasoned in the dark
That one way of the few there were
    Would hide her and would leave no mark: 20
Black water, smooth above the weir
    Like starry velvet in the night,
Though ruffled once, would soon appear
    The same as ever to the sight.
1920

The New Tenants

The day was here when it was his to know
How fared the barriers he had built between
His triumph and his enemies unseen,
For them to undermine and overthrow;
And it was his no longer to forego   5
The sight of them, insidious and serene,
Where they were delving always and had been
Left always to be vicious and to grow.

And there were the new tenants who had come,
By doors that were left open unawares,   10
Into his house, and were so much at home
There now that he would hardly have to guess,
By the slow guile of their vindictiveness,
What ultimate insolence would soon be theirs.

1920

from Not Always

II

There were long days when there was nothing said,
And there were longer nights where there was nought
But silence and recriminating thought
Between them like a field unharvested.
Antipathy was now their daily bread,   5
And pride the bitter drink they daily fought
To throw away. Release was all they sought
Of hope, colder than moonlight on the dead.

Wishing the other might at once be sure
And strong enough to shake the prison down,   10
Neither believed, although they strove together,
How long the stolid fabric would endure
That was a wall for them, and was to frown
And shine for them through many sorts of weather.

1925

New England

Here where the wind is always north-north-east
And children learn to walk on frozen toes,
Wonder begets an envy of all those
Who boil elsewhere with such a lyric yeast
Of love that you will hear them at a feast   5
Where demons would appeal for some repose,
Still clamoring where the chalice overflows
And crying wildest who have drunk the least.

Passion is here a soilure of the wits,
We're told, and Love a cross for them to bear;   10
Joy shivers in the corner where she knits
And Conscience always has the rocking-chair,
Cheerful as when she tortured into fits
The first cat that was ever killed by Care.
1925

Frank Norris
1870–1902

Frank Norris shuttled restlessly between coasts as a student at the University of
California at Berkeley and at Harvard. He studied art in Paris and London. He
acted as a newspaper correspondent in South Africa at the time of the Boer War
and in Cuba during the Spanish-American War. These journeys are matched by
the jumpy eagerness with which he set out to find the right materials and the
best literary devices to fulfill his intention to write "the Great American Novel."
But by age thirty-two he was dead of a ruptured appendix, and neither he nor
his readers had the chance to know how well he might have succeeded. He left
an array of novels, short stories, and critical essays that are as varied in method,
content, and quality as his short, hectic life.

The elements of Norris's work are uneven and diffuse: They include a long
poem set in the Middle Ages, *Yvernelle, A Tale of Feudal France* (1891), the
sea-adventure novel *Moran of the Lady Letty* (1898), and exposés of the greed that
corroded the men who ran the country's railroads and wheat farms—*The Octopus*
(1901) and *The Pit* (1902). Yet one theme appeared early in his writing and
continued to dominate his imagination. Since his student days and his reading of
Émile Zola, Norris cultivated the belief that the universe, society, and human
biology are profoundly deterministic. Whether Norris wrote in praise of the

romantic vision by which we color our dreams of happiness or whether he insisted on the brutal factors of heredity and environment upheld by the literary naturalists, he drove hard at "the red, living heart of things."

Norris was born in Chicago into a wealthy and cultivated family. The Norrises moved to San Francisco when he was fourteen. Soon afterward, he was encouraged by his father to take up painting and was sent off to spend a few years in Europe as an art student. But at twenty Norris shifted his attention to literature and relocated his studies to Berkeley. In 1894 he went to Harvard, where he stayed one year. The poem *Yvernelle* was published while he was a student, and two of his novels were largely written while at Cambridge (*McTeague,* published in 1899, and *Vandover and the Brute,* published posthumously in 1914).

After leaving Harvard, Norris worked as a journalist, acquiring an education in observation and dead-on-target language. He shared in the tradition of journalistic training embraced by a large number of young American writers— Mark Twain and William Dean Howells before him, Stephen Crane and Theodore Dreiser as his contemporaries, Sinclair Lewis and Ernest Hemingway in the next generation. Like Crane and Hemingway, Norris went into the field as a foreign war correspondent. But the wars he was most interested in covering were located in America: sociologically in the tensions between "the bosses" and "the people," psychologically within the embattled minds of humans drawn down toward the level of the bestial.

Norris desired to be completely honest about what people are capable of doing when transformed into killers by inner forces beyond their control. It is no surprise that *McTeague* proved a shocker when it appeared in 1899. The general public did not want to be reminded of what Norris was out to tell them—that the human heart is capable of great violence. But if Norris the writer had the reputation of morbidity and pessimism, there was also the Norris who concocted *Blix* and *A Man's Woman*—novels sentimental enough to appease the most tender-minded. Norris was back at his real strengths in *The Octopus* and *The Pit* in 1901 and 1902, the first two novels of a planned trilogy about corporate greed. Neither gained a wide audience. The book of essays *The Responsibilities of the Novelist,* appearing posthumously in 1903, shows that Norris sought popular approval, but not by catering to debased tastes that try to evade life's squalid meanings. Rather, he hoped to force his readers to meet the world head on. He tried to push them into thinking hard about the primitive impulses that lie outside the control of civilized patterns of "correct" behavior by their negation of human reasoning.

Norris died before he found the sure means by which he could suggest, with consistency from book to book, why we are victims of the universe. But when he succeeded, as in *McTeague,* readers are affected by the inevitability of disaster. Like the characters within the story, readers experience the power of fatality. The abrupt impact of Norris's language—with verbs that hurtle and nouns that stun— parallels the blind forces lodged at the core of the world. Placed under the spell of scenes in which primal impulses gain the upper hand over conventional codes of social behavior, we recognize that Norris's taste for the grotesque is exactly what a nightmare world requires.

Further Reading:
F. D. Walker, *Frank Norris*, 1932, 1963.
E. Marchand, *Frank Norris*, 1942.
W. French, *Frank Norris*, 1962.
D. Pizer, *The Novels of Frank Norris*, 1966.
W. Dillingham, *Frank Norris: Instinct and Art*,
1969.
C. Norris, *Frank Norris*, 1973.
A. Poncet, *Frank Norris, 1870–1902*, 1977.
D. Graham, *The Fiction of Frank Norris*, 1978.
Critical Essays on Frank Norris, ed. D. Graham,
1980.

Texts:
McTeague, 1899.
"A Plea for Romantic Fiction" from *The
Literary Criticism of Frank Norris*, ed. D. Pizer,
1962.
See also *The Complete Edition of Frank Norris*,
10 vols., 1928.
The Letters of Frank Norris, ed. F. Walker, 1956.

---

from McTeague
A Story of San Francisco

II: [The Dental Parlor][1]

After his breakfast the following Monday morning, McTeague looked over the appointments he had written down in the book-slate that hung against the screen. His writing was immense, very clumsy, and very round, with huge, full-bellied l's and h's. He saw that he had made appointment at one o'clock for Miss Baker, the retired dressmaker, a little old maid who had a tiny room a few doors down the hall. It adjoined that of Old Grannis.

Quite an affair had arisen from this circumstance. Miss Baker and Old Grannis were both over sixty, and yet it was current talk amongst the lodgers of the flat that the two were in love with each other. Singularly enough, they were not even acquaintances; never a word had passed between them. At intervals they met on the stairway; he on his way to his little dog hospital, she returning from a bit of marketing in the street. At such times they passed each other with averted eyes, pretending a certain preoccupation, suddenly seized with a great embarrassment, the timidity of a second childhood. He went on about his business, disturbed and thoughtful. She hurried up to her tiny room, her curious little false curls shaking with her agitation, the faintest suggestion of a flush coming and going in her withered cheeks. The emotion of one of these chance meetings remained with them during all the rest of the day.

Was it the first romance in the lives of each? Did Old Grannis ever remember a certain face amongst those that he had known when he was young Grannis—the face of some pale-haired girl, such as one sees in the old cathedral towns of England? Did Miss Baker still treasure up in a seldom opened drawer or box some faded daguerreotype, some strange old-fashioned likeness, with its curling hair and high stock? It was impossible to say.

Maria Macapa, the Mexican woman who took care of the lodgers' rooms, had been

---

[1] McTeague is a self-taught dentist with a modest practice leading a comfortable bachelor's existence in an apartment building in a lower-middle-class neighborhood of San Francisco at the turn of the century.

the first to call the flat's attention to the affair, spreading the news of it from room to room, from floor to floor. Of late she had made a great discovery; all the women folk of the flat were yet vibrant with it. Old Grannis came home from his work at four o'clock, and between that time and six Miss Baker would sit in her room, her hands idle in her lap, doing nothing, listening, waiting. Old Grannis did the same, drawing his armchair near to the wall, knowing that Miss Baker was upon the other side, conscious, perhaps that she was thinking of him; and there the two would sit through the hours of the afternoon, listening and waiting, they did not know exactly for what, but near to each other, separated only by the thin partition of their rooms. They had come to know each other's habits. Old Grannis knew that at quarter of five precisely Miss Baker made a cup of tea over the oil stove on the stand between the bureau and the window. Miss Baker felt instinctively the exact moment when Old Grannis took down his little binding apparatus from the second shelf of his clothes closet and began his favorite occupation of binding pamphlets—pamphlets that he never read, for all that.

In his "Parlors" McTeague began his week's work. He glanced in the glass saucer in which he kept his sponge-gold, and noticing that he had used up all his pellets, set about making some more. In examining Miss Baker's teeth at the preliminary sitting he had found a cavity in one of the incisors. Miss Baker had decided to have it filled with gold. McTeague remembered now that it was what is called a "proximate case," where there is not sufficient room to fill with large pieces of gold. He told himself that he should have to use "mats" in the filling. He made some dozen of these "mats" from his tape of non-cohesive gold, cutting it transversely into small pieces that could be inserted edgewise between the teeth and consolidated by packing. After he had made his "mats" he continued with the other kind of gold fillings, such as he would have occasion to use during the week; "blocks" to be used in large proximal cavities, made by folding the tape on itself a number of times and then shaping it with the soldering pliers; "cylinders" for commencing fillings, which he formed by rolling the tape around a needle called a "broach," cutting it afterwards into different lengths. He worked slowly, mechanically, turning the foil between his fingers with the manual dexterity that one sometimes sees in stupid persons. His head was quite empty of all thought, and he did not whistle over his work as another man might have done. The canary made up for his silence, trilling and chittering continually, splashing about in its morning bath, keeping up an incessant noise and movement that would have been maddening to any one but McTeague, who seemed to have no nerves at all.

After he had finished his fillings, he made a hook broach from a bit of piano wire to replace an old one that he had lost. It was time for his dinner then, and when he returned from the car conductors' coffee-joint, he found Miss Baker waiting for him.

The ancient little dressmaker was at all times willing to talk of Old Grannis to anybody that would listen, quite unconscious of the gossip of the flat. McTeague found her all a-flutter with excitement. Something extraordinary had happened. She had found out that the wall-paper in Old Grannis's room was the same as that in hers.

"It has led me to thinking, Doctor McTeague," she exclaimed, shaking her little false curls at him. "You know my room is so small, anyhow, and the wall-paper being the same—the pattern from my room continues right into his—I declare, I believe at one time that was all one room. Think of it, do you suppose it was? It almost amounts to our occupying the same room. I don't know—why, really—do you think

I should speak to the landlady about it? He bound pamphlets last night until half-past nine. They say that he's the younger son of a baronet; that there are reasons for his not coming to the title; his stepfather wronged him cruelly."

No one had ever said such a thing. It was preposterous to imagine any mystery connected with Old Grannis. Miss Baker had chosen to invent the little fiction, had created the title and the unjust stepfather from some dim memories of the novels of her girlhood.

She took her place in the operating chair. McTeague began the filling. There was a long silence. It was impossible for McTeague to work and talk at the same time.

He was just burnishing the last "mat" in Miss Baker's tooth, when the door of the "Parlors" opened, jangling the bell which he had hung over it, and which was absolutely unnecessary. McTeague turned, one foot on the pedal of his dental engine, the corundum disk whirling between his fingers.

It was Marcus Schouler who came in, ushering a young girl of about twenty.

"Hello, Mac," exclaimed Marcus; "busy? Brought my cousin round about that broken tooth."

McTeague nodded his head gravely.

"In a minute," he answered.

Marcus and his cousin Trina sat down in the rigid chairs underneath the steel engraving of the Court of Lorenzo de' Medici. They began talking in low tones. The girl looked about the room, noticing the stone pug dog, the rifle manufacturer's calendar, the canary in its little gilt prison, and the tumbled blankets on the unmade bed-lounge against the wall. Marcus began telling her about McTeague. "We're pals," he explained, just above a whisper. "Ah, Mac's all right, you bet. Say, Trina, he's the strongest duck you ever saw. What do you suppose? He can pull out your teeth with his fingers; yes, he can. What do you think of that? With his fingers, mind you; he can, for a fact. Get on to the size of him, anyhow. Ah, Mac's all right!"

Maria Macapa had come into the room while he had been speaking. She was making up McTeague's bed. Suddenly Marcus exclaimed under his breath: "Now we'll have some fun. It's the girl that takes care of the rooms. She's a greaser,[2] and she's queer in the head. She ain't regularly crazy, but *I* don't know, she's queer. Y'ought to hear her go on about a gold dinner service she says her folks used to own. Ask her what her name is and see what she'll say." Trina shrank back, a little frightened.

"No, you ask," she whispered.

"Ah, go on; what you 'fraid of?" urged Marcus. Trina shook her head energetically, shutting her lips together.

"Well, listen here," answered Marcus, nudging her; then raising his voice, he said:

"How do, Maria?" Maria nodded to him over her shoulder as she bent over the lounge.

"Workun hard nowadays, Maria?"

"Pretty hard."

"Didunt always have to work for your living, though, did you, when you ate offa gold dishes?" Maria didn't answer, except by putting her chin in the air and shutting her eyes, as though to say she knew a long story about that if she had a mind to talk.

---

[2] Derogatory term for a native of Latin America.

All Marcus's efforts to draw her out on the subject were unavailing. She only responded by movements of her head.

"Can't always start her going," Marcus told his cousin.

"What does she do, though, when you ask her about her name?"

"Oh, sure," said Marcus, who had forgotten. "Say, Maria, what's your name?"

"Huh?" asked Maria, straightening up, her hands on her hips.

"Tell us your name," repeated Marcus.

"Name is Maria—Miranda—Macapa." Then, after a pause, she added, as though she had but that moment thought of it, "Had a flying squirrel an' let him go."

Invariably Maria Macapa made this answer. It was not always she would talk about the famous service of gold plate, but a question as to her name never failed to elicit the same strange answer, delivered in a rapid undertone: "Name is Maria—Miranda —Macapa." Then, as if struck with an after thought, "Had a flying squirrel an' let him go."

Why Maria should associate the release of the mythical squirrel with her name could not be said. About Maria the flat knew absolutely nothing further than that she was Spanish-American. Miss Baker was the oldest lodger in the flat, and Maria was a fixture there as maid of all work when she had come. There was a legend to the effect that Maria's people had been at one time immensely wealthy in Central America.

Maria turned again to her work. Trina and Marcus watched her curiously. There was a silence. The corundum burr in McTeague's engine hummed in a prolonged monotone. The canary bird chittered occasionally. The room was warm, and the breathing of the five people in the narrow space made the air close and thick. At long intervals an acrid odor of ink floated up from the branch post-office immediately below.

Maria Macapa finished her work and started to leave. As she passed near Marcus and his cousin she stopped, and drew a bunch of blue tickets furtively from her pocket. "Buy a ticket in the lottery?" she inquired, looking at the girl. "Just a dollar."

"Go along with you, Maria," said Marcus, who had but thirty cents in his pocket. "Go along; it's against the law."

"Buy a ticket," urged Maria, thrusting the bundle toward Trina. "Try your luck. The butcher on the next block won twenty dollars the last drawing."

Very uneasy, Trina bought a ticket for the sake of being rid of her. Maria disappeared.

"Ain't she a queer bird?" muttered Marcus. He was much embarrassed and disturbed because he had not bought the ticket for Trina.

But there was a sudden movement. McTeague had just finished with Miss Baker.

"You should notice," the dressmaker said to the dentist, in a low voice, "he always leaves the door a little ajar in the afternoon." When she had gone out, Marcus Schouler brought Trina forward.

"Say, Mac, this is my cousin, Trina Sieppe." The two shook hands dumbly, McTeague slowly nodding his huge head with its great shock of yellow hair. Trina was very small and prettily made. Her face was round and rather pale; her eyes long and narrow and blue, like the half-open eyes of a little baby; her lips and the lobes of her tiny ears were pale, a little suggestive of anæmia; while across the bridge of her nose ran an adorable little line of freckles. But it was to her hair that one's attention was most attracted. Heaps and heaps of blue-black coils and braids, a royal crown of swarthy bands, a veritable sable tiara, heavy, abundant, odorous. All the vitality that should have given color to her face seemed to have been absorbed by this marvellous hair. It was the coiffure of a queen that shadowed the pale temples of this little bourgeoise. So heavy was it that it tipped her head backward, and the position thrust her chin out a little. It was a charming poise, innocent, confiding, almost infantile.

She was dressed all in black, very modest and plain. The effect of her pale face in all this contrasting black was almost monastic.

"Well," exclaimed Marcus suddenly, "I got to go. Must get back to work. Don't hurt her too much, Mac. S'long, Trina."

McTeague and Trina were left alone. He was embarrassed, troubled. These young girls disturbed and perplexed him. He did not like them, obstinately cherishing that intuitive suspicion of all things feminine—the perverse dislike of an overgrown boy. On the other hand, she was perfectly at her ease; doubtless the woman in her was not yet awakened; she was yet, as one might say, without sex. She was almost like a boy, frank, candid, unreserved.

She took her place in the operating chair and told him what was the matter, looking squarely into his face. She had fallen out of a swing the afternoon of the preceding day; one of her teeth had been knocked loose and the other altogether broken out.

McTeague listened to her with apparent stolidity, nodding his head from time to time as she spoke. The keenness of his dislike of her as a woman began to be blunted. He thought she was rather pretty, that he even liked her because she was so small, so prettily made, so good natured and straightforward.

"Let's have a look at your teeth," he said, picking up his mirror. "You better take your hat off." She leaned back in her chair and opened her mouth showing the rows of little round teeth, as white and even as the kernels on an ear of green corn, except where an ugly gap came at the side.

McTeague put the mirror into her mouth, touching one and another of her teeth with the handle of an excavator. By and by he straightened up, wiping the moisture from the mirror on his coat-sleeve.

"Well, Doctor," said the girl, anxiously, "it's a dreadful disfigurement, isn't it?" adding, "What can you do about it?"

"Well," answered McTeague, slowly, looking vaguely about on the floor of the room, "the roots of the broken tooth are still in the gum; they'll have to come out, and I guess I'll have to pull that other bicuspid. Let me look again. Yes," he went on in a moment, peering into her mouth with the mirror, "I guess that'll have to come out, too," The tooth was loose, discolored, and evidently dead. "It's a curious case," McTeague went on. "I don't know as I ever had a tooth like that before. It's what's called necrosis. It don't often happen. It'll have to come out sure."

Then a discussion was opened on the subject, Trina sitting up in the chair, holding her hat in her lap; McTeague leaning against the window frame, his hands in his pockets, his eyes wandering about on the floor. Trina did not want the other tooth removed; one hole like that was bad enough; but two—ah, no, it was not to be thought of.

But McTeague reasoned with her, tried in vain to make her understand that there was no vascular connection between the root and the gum. Trina was blindly persistent, with the persistency of a girl who has made up her mind.

McTeague began to like her better and better, and after a while commenced himself to feel that it would be a pity to disfigure such a pretty mouth. He became interested; perhaps he could do something, something in the way of a crown or bridge. "Let's look at that again," he said, picking up his mirror. He began to study the situation very carefully, really desiring to remedy the blemish.

It was the first bicuspid that was missing, and though part of the root of the second (the loose one) would remain after its extraction, he was sure it would not be strong enough to sustain a crown. All at once he grew obstinate, resolving, with all the strength of a crude and primitive man, to conquer the difficulty in spite of everything. He turned over in his mind the technicalities of the case. No, evidently the root was not strong enough to sustain a crown; besides that, it was placed a little irregularly in the arch. But, fortunately, there were cavities in the two teeth on either side of the gap—one in the first molar and one in the palatine surface of the cuspid; might he not drill a socket in the remaining root and sockets in the molar and cuspid, and, partly by bridging, partly by crowning, fill in the gap? He made up his mind to do it.

Why he should pledge himself to this hazardous case McTeague was puzzled to know. With most of his clients he would have contented himself with the extraction of the loose tooth and the roots of the broken one. Why should he risk his reputation in this case? He could not say why.

It was the most difficult operation he had ever performed. He bungled it considerably, but in the end he succeeded passably well. He extracted the loose tooth with his bayonet forceps and prepared the roots of the broken one as if for filling, fitting into them a flattened piece of platinum wire to serve as a dowel. But this was only the beginning; altogether it was a fortnight's work. Trina came nearly every other day, and passed two, and even three, hours in the chair.

By degrees McTeague's first awkwardness and suspicion vanished entirely. The two became good friends. McTeague even arrived at that point when he could work and talk to her at the same time—a thing that had never before been possible for him.

Never until then had McTeague become so well acquainted with a girl of Trina's age. The younger women of Polk Street—the shop girls, the young women of the soda fountains, the waitresses in the cheap restaurants—preferred another dentist, a young fellow just graduated from the college, a poser, a rider of bicycles, a man about town, who wore astonishing waistcoats and bet money on greyhound coursing. Trina was McTeague's first experience. With her the feminine element suddenly entered his little world. It was not only her that he saw and felt, it was the woman, the whole sex, an entire new humanity, strange and alluring, that he seemed to have discovered. How had he ignored it so long? It was dazzling, delicious, charming beyond all words. His narrow point of view was at once enlarged and confused, and all at once he saw that there was something else in life besides concertinas and steam beer. Everything had to be made over again. His whole rude idea of life had to be changed. The male virile desire in him tardily awakened, aroused itself, strong and brutal. It was resistless, untrained, a thing not to be held in leash an instant.

Little by little, by gradual, almost imperceptible degrees, the thought of Trina Sieppe occupied his mind from day to day, from hour to hour. He found himself thinking of her constantly; at every instant he saw her round, pale face; her narrow, milk-blue eyes; her little out-thrust chin; her heavy, huge tiara of black hair. At night he lay awake for hours under the thick blankets of the bed-lounge, staring upward into the darkness, tormented with the idea of her, exasperated at the delicate, subtle mesh in which he found himself entangled. During the forenoons, while he went about his work, he thought of her. As he made his plaster-of-paris moulds at the washstand in the corner behind the screen he turned over in his mind all that had happened, all that had been said at the previous sitting. Her little tooth that he had extracted he kept wrapped in a bit of newspaper in his vest pocket. Often he took it out and held it in the palm of his immense, horny hand, seized with some strange elephantine sentiment, wagging his head at it, heaving tremendous sighs. What a folly!

At two o'clock on Tuesdays, Thursdays, and Saturdays Trina arrived and took her place in the operating chair. While at his work McTeague was every minute obliged to bend closely over her; his hands touched her face, her cheeks, her adorable little chin; her lips pressed against his fingers. She breathed warmly on his forehead and on his eyelids, while the odor of her hair, a charming feminine perfume, sweet, heavy, enervating, came to his nostrils, so penetrating, so delicious, that his flesh pricked and tingled with it; a veritable sensation of faintness passed over this huge, callous fellow, with his enormous bones and corded muscles. He drew a short breath through his nose; his jaws suddenly gripped together vise-like.

But this was only at times—a strange, vexing spasm, that subsided almost immediately. For the most part, McTeague enjoyed the pleasure of these sittings with Trina with a certain strong calmness, blindly happy that she was there. This poor crude dentist of Polk Street, stupid, ignorant, vulgar, with his sham education and plebeian tastes, whose only relaxations were to eat, to drink steam beer,[3] and to play upon his concertina, was living through his first romance, his first idyl. It was delightful. The long hours he passed alone with Trina in the "Dental Parlors," silent, only for the scraping of the instruments and the purring of bud-burrs in the engine, in the foul atmosphere, overheated by the little stove and heavy with the smell of ether, creosote, and stale bedding, had all the charm of secret appointments and stolen meetings under the moon.

By degrees the operation progressed. One day, just after McTeague had put in the temporary gutta-percha fillings and nothing more could be done at that sitting, Trina asked him to examine the rest of her teeth. They were perfect, with one exception —a spot of white caries on the lateral surface of an incisor. McTeague filled it with gold, enlarging the cavity with hard-bits and hoe-excavators, and burring in afterward with half-cone burrs. The cavity was deep, and Trina began to wince and moan. To hurt Trina was a positive anguish for McTeague, yet an anguish which he was obliged to endure at every hour of the sitting. It was harrowing—he sweated under it—to be forced to torture her, of all women in the world; could anything be worse than that?

"Hurt?" he inquired, anxiously.

She answered by frowning, with a sharp intake of breath, putting her fingers over her closed lips and nodding her head. McTeague sprayed the tooth with glycerite of tannin, but without effect. Rather than hurt her he found himself forced to the use of anæsthesia, which he hated. He had a notion that the nitrous oxide gas was dangerous, so on this occasion, as on all others, used ether.

[3] Cheap form of beer.

He put the sponge a half dozen times to Trina's face, more nervous than he had ever been before, watching the symptoms closely. Her breathing became short and irregular; there was a slight twitching of the muscles. When her thumbs turned inward toward the palms, he took the sponge away. She passed off very quickly, and, with a long sigh, sank back into the chair.

McTeague straightened up, putting the sponge upon the rack behind him, his eyes fixed upon Trina's face. For some time he stood watching her as she lay there, unconscious and helpless, and very pretty. He was alone with her, and she was absolutely without defense.

Suddenly the animal in the man stirred and woke; the evil instincts that in him were so close to the surface leaped to life, shouting and clamoring.

It was a crisis—a crisis that had arisen all in an instant; a crisis for which he was totally unprepared. Blindly, and without knowing why, McTeague fought against it, moved by an unreasoned instinct of resistance. Within him, a certain second self, another better McTeague rose with the brute; both were strong, with the huge crude strength of the man himself. The two were at grapples. There in that cheap and shabby "Dental Parlor" a dreaded struggle began. It was the old battle, old as the world, wide as the world—the sudden panther leap of the animal, lips drawn, fangs aflash, hideous, monstrous, not to be resisted, and the simultaneous arousing of the other man, the better self that cries, "Down, down," without knowing why; that grips the monster; that fights to strangle it, to thrust it down and back.

Dizzied and bewildered with the shock, the like of which he had never known before, McTeague turned from Trina, gazing bewilderedly about the room. The struggle was bitter; his teeth ground themselves together with a little rasping sound; the blood sang in his ears; his face flushed scarlet; his hands twisted themselves together like the knotting of cables. The fury in him was the fury of a young bull in the heat of high summer. But for all that he shook his huge head from time to time, muttering: "No, by God! No, by God!"

Dimly he seemed to realize that should he yield now he would never be able to care for Trina again. She would never be the same to him, never so radiant, so sweet, so adorable; her charm for him would vanish in an instant. Across her forehead, her little pale forehead, under the shadow of her royal hair, he would surely see the smudge of a foul ordure, the footprint of the monster. It would be a sacrilege, an abomination. He recoiled from it, banding all his strength to the issue.

"No, by God! No, by God!"

He turned to his work, as if seeking a refuge in it. But as he drew near to her again, the charm of her innocence and helplessness came over him afresh. It was a final protest against his resolution. Suddenly he leaned over and kissed her, grossly, full on the mouth. The thing was done before he knew it. Terrified at his weakness at the very moment he believed himself strong, he threw himself once more into his work with desperate energy. By the time he was fastening the sheet of rubber upon the tooth, he had himself once more in hand. He was disturbed, still trembling, still vibrating with the throes of the crisis, but he was the master; the animal was downed, was cowed for this time, at least.

But for all that, the brute was there. Long dormant, it was now at last alive, awake. From now on he would feel its presence continually; would feel it tugging at its chain, watching its opportunity. Ah, the pity of it! Why could he not always love her purely, cleanly? What was this perverse, vicious thing that lived within him, knitted to his flesh?

Below the fine fabric of all that was good in him ran the foul stream of hereditary evil, like a sewer. The vices and sins of his father and of his father's father, to the third and fourth and five hundredth generation, tainted him. The evil of an entire race flowed in his veins. Why should it be? He did not desire it. Was he to blame?

But McTeague could not understand this thing. It had faced him, as sooner or later it faces every child of man; but its significance was not for him. To reason with it was beyond him. He could only oppose to it an instinctive stubborn resistance, blind, inert.

McTeague went on with his work. As he was rapping in the little blocks and cylinders with the mallet, Trina slowly came back to herself with a long sigh. She still felt a little confused, and lay quiet in the chair. There was a long silence, broken only by the uneven tapping of the hardwood mallet. By and by she said, "I never felt a thing," and then she smiled at him very prettily beneath the rubber dam. McTeague turned to her suddenly, his mallet in one hand, his pliers holding a pellet of sponge-gold in the other. All at once he said, with the unreasoned simplicity and directness of a child: "Listen here, Miss Trina, I like you better than any one else; what's the matter with us getting married?"

Trina sat up in the chair quickly, and then drew back from him, frightened and bewildered.

"Will you? Will you?" said McTeague. "Say, Miss Trina, will you?"

"What is it? What do you mean?" she cried, confusedly, her words muffled beneath the rubber.

"Will you?" repeated McTeague.

"No, no," she exclaimed, refusing without knowing why, suddenly seized with a fear of him, the intuitive feminine fear of the male. McTeague could only repeat the same thing over and over again. Trina, more and more frightened at his huge hands —the hands of the old-time car-boy—his immense square-cut head and his enormous brute strength, cried out: "No, no," behind the rubber dam, shaking her head violently, holding out her hands, and shrinking down before him in the operating chair. McTeague came nearer to her, repeating the same question. "No, no," she cried, terrified. Then, as she exclaimed, "Oh, I am sick," was suddenly taken with a fit of vomiting. It was the not unusual after effect of the ether, aided now by her excitement and nervousness. McTeague was checked. He poured some bromide of potassium into a graduated glass and held it to her lips.

"Here, swallow this," he said.

XXII: [Death Valley][4]

Within a month after his departure from San Francisco, Marcus had "gone in on a cattle ranch" in the Panamint Valley with an Englishman, an acquaintance of Mr.

[4] In this, the final chapter of the novel, McTeague is a fugitive from the law after his murder of Trina, who had become his wife, and his theft of a hoard of gold coins that she had kept hidden from him. Marcus has long since become McTeague's enemy, and in this episode the long story of revenge is played out in the alkali flats of Death Valley.

Sieppe's. His headquarters were at a place called Modoc, at the lower extremity of the valley, about fifty miles by trail to the south of Keeler.

His life was the life of a cowboy. He realized his former vision of himself, booted, sombreroed, and revolvered, passing his days in the saddle and the better part of his nights around the poker tables in Modoc's one saloon. To his intense satisfaction he even involved himself in a gun fight that arose over a disputed brand, with the result that two fingers of his left hand were shot away.

News from the outside world filtered slowly into the Panamint Valley, and the telegraph had never been built beyond Keeler. At intervals one of the local papers of Independence, the nearest large town, found its way into the cattle camps on the ranges, and occasionally one of the Sunday editions of a Sacramento journal, weeks old, was passed from hand to hand. Marcus ceased to hear from the Sieppes. As for San Francisco, it was as far from him as was London or Vienna.

One day, a fortnight after McTeague's flight from San Francisco, Marcus rode into Modoc, to find a group of men gathered about a notice affixed to the outside of the Wells-Fargo office. It was an offer of reward for the arrest and apprehension of a murderer. The crime had been committed in San Francisco, but the man wanted had been traced as far as the western portion of Inyo County, and was believed at that time to be in hiding in either the Pinto or Panamint hills, in the vicinity of Keeler.

Marcus reached Keeler on the afternoon of that same day. Half a mile from the town his pony fell and died from exhaustion. Marcus did not stop even to remove the saddle. He arrived in the barroom of the hotel in Keeler just after the posse had been made up. The sheriff, who had come down from Independence that morning, at first refused his offer of assistance. He had enough men already—too many, in fact. The country travelled through would be hard, and it would be difficult to find water for so many men and horses.

"But none of you fellers have ever seen um," vociferated Marcus, quivering with excitement and wrath. "I know um well. I could pick um out in a million. I can identify um, and you fellers can't. And I knew—I knew—good *God!* I knew that girl—his wife—in Frisco. She's a cousin of mine, she is—she was—I thought once of—This thing's a personal matter of mine—an' that money he got away with, that five thousand, belongs to me by rights. Oh, never mind, I'm going along. Do you hear?" he shouted, his fists raised, "I'm going along, I tell you. There ain't a man of you big enough to stop me. Let's see you try and stop me going. Let's see you once, any two of you." He filled the barroom with his clamor.

"Lord love you, come along, then," said the sheriff.

The posse rode out of Keeler that same night. The keeper of the general merchandise store, from whom Marcus had borrowed a second pony, had informed them that Cribbens and his partner, whose description tallied exactly with that given in the notice of reward, had outfitted at his place with a view to prospecting in the Panamint hills. The posse trailed them at once to their first camp at the head of the valley. It was an easy matter. It was only necessary to inquire of the cowboys and range riders of the valley if they had seen and noted the passage of two men, one of whom carried a bird cage.

Beyond this first camp the trail was lost, and a week was wasted in a bootless search around the mine at Gold Gulch, whither it seemed probable the partners had gone. Then a travelling peddler, who included Gold Gulch in his route, brought in the news of a wonderful strike of gold-bearing quartz some ten miles to the south on the western slope of the range. Two men from Keeler had made a strike, the peddler had said, and added the curious detail that one of the men had a canary bird in a cage with him.

The posse made Cribbens's camp three days after the unaccountable disappearance of his partner. Their man was gone, but the narrow hoof prints of a mule, mixed with those of huge hob-nailed boots, could be plainly followed in the sand. Here they picked up the trail and held to it steadily till the point was reached where, instead of tending southward it swerved abruptly to the east. The men could hardly believe their eyes.

"It ain't reason," exclaimed the sheriff. "What in thunder is he up to? This beats me. Cutting out into Death Valley at this time of year."

"He's heading for Gold Mountain over in the Armagosa, sure."

The men decided that this conjecture was true. It was the only inhabited locality in that direction. A discussion began as to the further movements of the posse.

"I don't figure on going into that alkali sink with no eight men and horses," declared the sheriff. "One man can't carry enough water to take him and his mount across, let alone *eight*. No, sir. Four couldn't do it. No, *three* couldn't. We've got to make a circuit round the valley and come up on the other side and head him off at Gold Mountain. That's what we got to do, and ride like hell to do it, too."

But Marcus protested with all the strength of his lungs against abandoning the trail now that they had found it. He argued that they were but a day and a half behind their man now. There was no possibility of their missing the trail—as distinct in the white alkali as in snow. They could make a dash into the valley, secure their man, and return long before their water failed them. He, for one, would not give up the pursuit, now that they were so close. In the haste of the departure from Keeler the sheriff had neglected to swear him in. He was under no orders. He would do as he pleased.

"Go on, then, you darn fool," answered the sheriff. "We'll cut on round the valley, for all that. It's a gamble he'll be at Gold Mountain before you're half way across. But if you catch him, here"—he tossed Marcus a pair of handcuffs—"put 'em on him and bring him back to Keeler."

Two days after he had left the posse, and when he was already far out in the desert, Marcus's horse gave out. In the fury of his impatience he had spurred mercilessly forward on the trail, and on the morning of the third day found that his horse was unable to move. The joints of his legs seemed locked rigidly. He would go his own length, stumbling and interfering, then collapse helplessly upon the ground with a pitiful groan. He was used up.

Marcus believed himself to be close upon McTeague now. The ashes at his last camp had still been smoldering. Marcus took what supplies of food and water he could carry, and hurried on. But McTeague was farther ahead than he had guessed, and by evening of his third day upon the desert Marcus, raging with thirst, had drunk his last mouthful of water and had flung away the empty canteen.

"If he ain't got water with um," he said to himself as he pushed on, "If he ain't got water with um, by damn! I'll be in a bad way. I will, for a fact."

At Marcus's shout McTeague looked up and around him. For the instant he saw no one. The white glare of alkali was still unbroken. Then his swiftly rolling eyes lighted upon a head and shoulder that protruded above the low crest of the break directly in front of him. A man was there, lying at full length upon the ground, covering him with a revolver. For a few seconds McTeague looked at the man stupidly, bewildered, confused, as yet without definite thought. Then he noticed that the man was singularly like Marcus Schouler. It *was* Marcus Schouler. How in the world did Marcus Schouler come to be in that desert? What did he mean by pointing a pistol at him that way? He'd best look out or the pistol would go off. Then his thoughts readjusted themselves with a swiftness born of a vivid sense of danger. Here was the enemy at last, the tracker he had felt upon his footsteps. Now at length he had "come on" and shown himself, after all those days of skulking. McTeague was glad of it. He'd show him now. They two would have it out right then and there. His rifle! He had thrown it away long since. He was helpless. Marcus had ordered him to put up his hands. If he did not, Marcus would kill him. He had the drop on him. McTeague stared, scowling fiercely at the levelled pistol. He did not move.

"Hands up!" shouted Marcus a second time. "I'll give you three to do it in. One, two—"

Instinctively McTeague put his hands above his head.

Marcus rose and came towards him over the break.

"Keep 'em up," he cried. "If you move 'em once I'll kill you, sure."

He came up to McTeague and searched him, going through his pockets; but McTeague had no revolver; not even a hunting knife.

"What did you do with that money, with that five thousand dollars?"

"It's on the mule," answered McTeague, sullenly.

Marcus grunted, and cast a glance at the mule, who was standing some distance away, snorting nervously, and from time to time flattening his long ears.

"Is that it there on the horn of the saddle, there in that canvas sack?" Marcus demanded.

"Yes, that's it."

A gleam of satisfaction came into Marcus's eyes, and under his breath he muttered: "Got it at last."

He was singularly puzzled to know what next to do. He had got McTeague. There he stood at length, with his big hands over his head, scowling at him sullenly. Marcus had caught his enemy, had run down the man for whom every officer in the State had been looking. What should he do with him now? He couldn't keep him standing there forever with his hands over his head.

"Got any water?" he demanded.

"There's a canteen of water on the mule."

Marcus moved toward the mule and made as if to reach the bridle-rein. The mule squealed, threw up his head, and galloped to a little distance, rolling his eyes and flattening his ears.

Marcus swore wrathfully.

"He acted that way once before," explained McTeague, his hands still in the air. "He ate some loco-weed back in the hills before I started."

For a moment Marcus hesitated. While he was catching the mule McTeague might get away. But where to, in heaven's name? A rat could not hide on the surface of that glistening alkali, and besides, all McTeague's store of provisions and his priceless supply of water were on the mule. Marcus ran after the mule, revolver in hand, shouting and cursing. But the mule would not be caught. He acted as if possessed, squealing, lashing out, and galloping in wide circles, his head high in the air.

"Come on," shouted Marcus, furious, turning back to McTeague. "Come on, help me catch him. We got to catch him. All the water we got is on the saddle."

McTeague came up.

"He's eatun some loco-weed," he repeated. "He went kinda crazy once before."

"If he should take it into his head to bolt and keep on running—"

Marcus did not finish. A sudden great fear seemed to widen around and inclose the two men. Once their water was gone, the end would not be long.

"We can catch him all right," said the dentist. "I caught him once before."

"Oh, I guess we can catch him," answered Marcus, reassuringly.

Already the sense of enmity between the two had weakened in the face of a common peril. Marcus let down the hammer of his revolver and slid it back into the holster.

The mule was trotting on ahead, snorting and throwing up great clouds of alkali dust. At every step the canvas sack jingled, and McTeague's bird cage, still wrapped in the flour-bags, bumped against the saddle-pads. By and by the mule stopped, blowing out his nostrils excitedly.

"He's clean crazy," fumed Marcus, panting and swearing.

"We ought to come up on him quiet," observed McTeague.

"I'll try and sneak up," said Marcus; "two of us would scare him again. You stay here."

Marcus went forward a step at a time. He was almost within arm's length of the bridle when the mule shied from him abruptly and galloped away.

Marcus danced with rage, shaking his fists, and swearing horribly. Some hundred yards away the mule paused and began blowing and snuffing in the alkali as though in search of feed. Then, for no reason, he shied again, and started off on a jog trot toward the east.

"We've *got* to follow him," exclaimed Marcus as McTeague came up. "There's no water within seventy miles of here."

Then began an interminable pursuit. Mile after mile, under the terrible heat of the desert sun, the two men followed the mule, racked with a thirst that grew fiercer every hour. A dozen times they could almost touch the canteen of water, and as often the distraught animal shied away and fled before them. At length Marcus cried:

"It's no use, we can't catch him, and we're killing ourselves with thirst. We got to take our chances." He drew his revolver from its holster, cocked it, and crept forward.

"Steady, now," said McTeague; "it won' do to shoot through the canteen."

Within twenty yards Marcus paused, made a rest of his left forearm and fired.

"You *got* him," cried McTeague. "No, he's up again. Shoot him again. He's going to bolt."

Marcus ran on, firing as he ran. The mule, one foreleg trailing, scrambled along, squealing and snorting. Marcus fired his last shot. The mule pitched forward upon his head, then, rolling sideways, fell upon the canteen, bursting it open and spilling its entire contents into the sand.

Marcus and McTeague ran up, and Marcus snatched the battered canteen from under the reeking, bloody hide. There was no water left. Marcus flung the canteen from him and stood up, facing McTeague. There was a pause.

"We're dead men," said Marcus.

McTeague looked from him out over the desert. Chaotic desolation stretched from them on either hand, flaming and glaring with the afternoon heat. There was the brazen sky and the leagues upon leagues of alkali, leper white. There was nothing more. They were in the heart of Death Valley.

"Not a drop of water," muttered McTeague; "not a drop of water."

"We can drink the mule's blood," said Marcus. "It's been done before. But—but—" he looked down at the quivering, gory body—"but I ain't thirsty enough for that yet."

"Where's the nearest water?"

"Well, it's about a hundred miles or more back of us in the Panamint hills," returned Marcus, doggedly. "We'd be crazy long before we reached it. I tell you, we're done for, by damn, we're *done* for. We ain't ever going to get outa here."

"Done for?" murmured the other, looking about stupidly. "Done for, that's the word. Done for? Yes, I guess we're done for."

"What are we going to do *now?*" exclaimed Marcus, sharply, after a while.

"Well, let's—let's be moving along—somewhere."

"*Where,* I'd like to know? What's the good of moving on?"

"What's the good of stopping here?"

There was a silence.

"Lord, it's hot," said the dentist, finally, wiping his forehead with the back of his hand. Marcus ground his teeth.

"Done for," he muttered; "done for."

"I never *was* so thirsty," continued McTeague. "I'm that dry I can hear my tongue rubbing against the roof of my mouth."

"Well, we can't stop here," said Marcus, finally; "we got to go somewhere. We'll try and get back, but it ain't no manner of use. Anything we want to take along with us from the mule? We can—"

Suddenly he paused. In an instant the eyes of the two doomed men had met as the same thought simultaneously rose in their minds. The canvas sack with its five thousand dollars was still tied to the horn of the saddle.

Marcus had emptied his revolver at the mule, and though he still wore his cartridge belt, he was for the moment as unarmed as McTeague.

"I guess," began McTeague coming forward a step, "I guess, even if we are done for, I'll take—some of my truck along."

"Hold on," exclaimed Marcus, with rising aggressiveness. "Let's talk about that. I ain't so sure about who that—who that money belongs to."

"Well, I *am,* you see," growled the dentist.

The old enmity between the two men, their ancient hate, was flaming up again.

"Don't try an' load that gun either," cried McTeague, fixing Marcus with his little eyes.

"Then don't lay your finger on that sack," shouted the other. "You're my prisoner, do you understand? You'll do as I say." Marcus had drawn the handcuffs from his pocket, and stood ready with his revolver held as a club. "You soldiered me out of that money once, and played me for a sucker, an' it's *my* turn now. Don't you lay your finger on that sack."

Marcus barred McTeague's way, white with passion. McTeague did not answer. His eyes drew to two fine, twinkling points, and his enormous hands knotted themselves into fists, hard as wooden mallets. He moved a step nearer to Marcus, then another.

Suddenly the men grappled, and in another instant were rolling and struggling upon the hot white ground. McTeague thrust Marcus backward until he tripped and fell over the body of the dead mule. The little bird cage broke from the saddle with the violence of their fall and rolled out upon the ground, the flour-bags slipping from it. McTeague tore the revolver from Marcus's grip and struck out with it blindly. Clouds of alkali dust, fine and pungent, enveloped the two fighting men, all but strangling them.

McTeague did not know how he killed his enemy, but all at once Marcus grew still beneath his blows. Then there was a sudden last return of energy. McTeague's right wrist was caught, something clicked upon it, then the struggling body fell limp and motionless with a long breath.

As McTeague rose to his feet, he felt a pull at his right wrist; something held it fast. Looking down, he saw that Marcus in that last struggle had found strength to handcuff their wrists together. Marcus was dead now; McTeague was locked to the body. All about him, vast, interminable, stretched the measureless leagues of Death Valley.

McTeague remained stupidly looking around him, now at the distant horizon, now at the ground, now at the half-dead canary chittering feebly in its little gilt prison.

1899

A Plea for Romantic Fiction

Let us at the start make a distinction. Observe that one speaks of romanticism and not sentimentalism. One claims that the latter is as distinct from the former as is that other form of art which is called Realism. Romance has been often put upon and overburdened by being forced to bear the onus of abuse that by right should fall to sentiment; but the two should be kept very distinct, for a very high and illustrious place will be claimed for romance, while sentiment will be handed down the scullery stairs.

Many people to-day are composing mere sentimentalism, and calling it and causing it to be called romance; so with those who are too busy to think much upon these subjects, but who none the less love honest literature, Romance, too, has fallen into disrepute. Consider now the cut-and-thrust stories. They are all labeled Romances, and it is very easy to get the impression that Romance must be an affair of cloaks and daggers, or moonlight and golden hair. But this is not so at all. The true Romance is a more serious business than this. It is not merely a conjurer's trick-box, full of flimsy quackeries, tinsel and claptraps, meant only to amuse, and relying upon deception to do even that. Is it not something better than this? Can we not see in it an instrument, keen, finely tempered, flawless—an instrument with which we may go straight through the clothes and tissues and wrappings of flesh down deep into the red, living heart of things?

Is all this too subtle, too merely speculative and intrinsic, too *precieuse*[1] and nice[2] and "literary"? Devoutly one hopes the contrary. So much is made of so-called Romanticism in present-day fiction that the subject seems worthy of discussion, and a protest against the misuse of a really noble and honest formula of literature appears to be timely—misuse, that is, in the sense of limited use. Let us suppose for the moment that a romance can be made out of a cut-and-thrust business. Good Heavens, are there no other things that are romantic, even in this—falsely, falsely, falsely called—humdrum world of to-day? Why should it be that so soon as the novelist addresses himself—seriously—to the consideration of contemporary life he must abandon Romance and take up that harsh, loveless, colourless, blunt tool called Realism?

Now, let us understand at once what is meant by Romance and what by Realism. Romance, I take it, is the kind of fiction that takes cognizance of variations from the type of normal life. Realism is the kind of fiction that confines itself to the type of normal life. According to this definition, then, Romance may even treat of the sordid, the unlovely—as for instance, the novels of M. Zola.[3] (Zola has been dubbed a Realist, but he is, on the contrary, the very head of the Romanticists.) Also, Realism, used as it sometimes is as a term of reproach, need not be in the remotest sense or degree offensive, but on the other hand respectable as a church and proper as a deacon—as, for instance, the novels of Mr. Howells.[4]

The reason why one claims so much for Romance, and quarrels so pointedly with Realism, is that Realism stultifies itself. It notes only the surface of things. For it, Beauty is not even skin deep, but only a geometrical plane, without dimensions and depth, a mere outside. Realism is very excellent so far as it goes, but it goes no further than the Realist himself can actually see, or actually hear. Realism is minute; it is the drama of a broken teacup, the tragedy of a walk down the block, the excitement of an afternoon call, the adventure of an invitation to dinner. It is the visit to my neighbour's house, a formal visit, from which I may draw no conclusions. I see my neighbour and his friends—very, oh, such very! probable people—and that is all. Realism bows upon the doormat and goes away and says to me, as we link arms on the sidewalk: "That is life." And I say it is not. It is not, as you would very well see if you took Romance with you to call upon your neighbour.

Lately you have been taking Romance a weary journey across the water—ages and the flood of years—and haling her into the fusby, musty, worm-eaten, moth-riddled, rust-corroded "Grandes Salles"[5] of the Middle Ages and the Renaissance, and she has found the drama of a bygone age for you there. But would you take her across the street to your neighbour's front parlour (with the bisque fisher-boy on the mantel and the photograph of Niagara Falls on glass hanging in the front window); would you introduce her there? Not you. Would you take a walk with her on Fifth Avenue, or Beacon Street, or Michigan Avenue?[6] No, indeed. Would you choose her for a

---

[1] Precious in the sense of being overly fastidious and affected.
[2] In the sense of being excessively refined.
[3] Émile Zola (1840–1902), French writer.
[4] William Dean Howells (1837–1920), American writer and editor, mentor of Norris.

[5] Great halls.
[6] Elegant thoroughfares in New York, Boston, and Chicago, respectively.

companion of a morning spent in Wall Street, or an afternoon in the Waldorf-Astoria?[7] You just guess you would not.

She would be out of place, you say—inappropriate. She might be awkward in my neighbour's front parlour, and knock over the little bisque fisher-boy. Well, she might. If she did, you might find underneath the base of the statuette, hidden away, tucked away—what? God knows. But something that would be a complete revelation of my neighbour's secretest life.

So you think Romance would stop in the front parlour and discuss medicated flannels and mineral waters[8] with the ladies? Not for more than five minutes. She would be off upstairs with you, prying, peeping, peering into the closets of the bedroom, into the nursery, into the sitting-room; yes, and into that little iron box screwed to the lower shelf of the closet in the library; and into those compartments and pigeon-holes of the *secretaire*[9] in the study. She would find a heartache (maybe) between the pillows of the mistress's bed, and a memory carefully secreted in the master's deed-box.[10] She would come upon a great hope amid the books and papers of the study-table of the young man's room, and—perhaps—who knows—an affair, or, great Heavens, an intrigue, in the scented ribbons and gloves and hairpins of the young lady's bureau. And she would pick here a little and there a little, making up a bag of hopes and fears and a package of joys and sorrows—great ones, mind you—and then come down to the front door, and, stepping out into the street, hand you the bags and package and say to you—"That is Life!"

Romance does very well in the castles of the Middle Ages and the Renaissance chateaux, and she has the *entrée* there and is very well received. That is all well and good. But let us protest against limiting her to such places and such times. You will find her, I grant you, in the chatelaine's chamber and the dungeon of the man-at-arms; but, if you choose to look for her, you will find her equally at home in the brownstone house on the corner and in the office-building downtown. And this very day, in this very hour, she is sitting among the rags and wretchedness, the dirt and despair of the tenements of the East Side of New York.

"What?" I hear you say, "look for Romance—the lady of the silken robes and golden crown, our beautiful, chaste maiden of soft voice and gentle eyes—look for her among the vicious ruffians, male and female, of Allen Street and Mulberry Bend?"[11] I tell you she is there, and to your shame be it said you will not know her in those surroundings. You, the aristocrats, who demand the fine linen and the purple in your fiction; you, the sensitive, the delicate, who will associate with your Romance only so long as she wears a silken gown. You will not follow her to the slums, for you believe that Romance should only amuse and entertain you, singing you sweet songs and touching the harp of silver strings with rosy-tipped fingers. If haply she should call to you from the squalour of a dive, or the awful degradation of a disorderly house, crying: "Look! listen! This, too, is life. These, too, are my children! Look at them, know them and, knowing, help!" Should she call thus you would stop your ears; you would avert your eyes and you would answer, "Come from there, Romance. Your

---

[7] Wall Street, the banking area located in lower Manhattan, and the Waldorf-Astoria, a recently opened hotel on Park Avenue, represented great wealth and fashion.

[8] Home remedies.

[9] French: "secretary," a kind of writing desk.

[10] Container for legal documents concerning property holdings.

[11] Squalid district near the Bowery, infamous as one of the most dangerous neighborhoods of New York City.

place is not there!" And you would make of her a harlequin, a tumbler, a sword-dancer, when, as a matter of fact, she should be by right divine a teacher sent from God.

She will not often wear the robe of silk, the gold crown, the jeweled shoon; will not always sweep the silver harp. An iron note is hers if so she choose, and coarse garments, and stained hands; and, meeting her thus, it is for you to know her as she passes—know her for the same young queen of the blue mantle and lilies. She can teach you if you will be humble to learn—teach you by showing. God help you if at last you take from Romance her mission of teaching; if you do not believe that she has a purpose—a nobler purpose and a mightier than mere amusement, mere entertainment. Let Realism do the entertaining with its meticulous presentation of teacups, rag carpets, wall-paper and haircloth sofas, stopping with these, going no deeper than it sees, choosing the ordinary, the untroubled, the commonplace.

But to Romance belongs the wide world for range, and the unplumbed depths of the human heart, and the mystery of sex, and the problems of life, and the black, unsearched penetralia of the soul of man. You, the indolent, must not always be amused. What matter the silken clothes, what matter the prince's houses? Romance, too, is a teacher, and if—throwing aside the purple—she wears the camel's-hair and feeds upon the locusts, it is to cry aloud unto the people, "Prepare ye the way of the Lord; make straight his path."[12]

1901

Stephen Crane
1871–1900

At nineteen Stephen Crane was best known for his skill as a baseball player. Any other distinctions while briefly a college student were negligible. Within ten years Crane was dead of tuberculosis, acclaimed as a journalist and as the author of *The Red Badge of Courage* (1894), the novel that alone assures his place in American fiction.

Between 1890 and 1900 Crane worked as a free-lance newspaper reporter observing life in New York's slums and as a correspondent reporting on often violent events taking place in Mexico, the American West, Cuba, and Greece. Because the role of the journalist and correspondent was made increasingly glamorous by the "romantic wars" of the 1890s, Crane became a celebrity. He lived in England in manorial splendor he could not afford with his common-law wife, the former madam of the Hotel de Dream in Jacksonville, Florida. He was the friend of writers of great importance, including Joseph Conrad, H. G. Wells, and Henry James. Throughout all this commotion—public and personal—Stephen

---

[12] Cry of John the Baptist (who wore camel's hair
and subsisted on locusts) as he announced the
coming of the Messiah (Matthew 3:3).

Crane feverishly wrote the ten volumes of material that make up his collected literary works.

The youngest of fourteen children, Crane was born in Newark, New Jersey, the son of a Methodist minister. The peripatetic nature of the father's ministry moved the Crane family from one small town to another in New Jersey and New York State. After Crane's abortive visits to the classrooms of Lafayette College in Pennsylvania and Syracuse University in New York, he turned full-time to the newspaper life. Crane had had some experience in the business, first as a boy working for his older brother's press bureau, then as the local correspondent of the *New York Tribune* while still a student at Syracuse University. Once he left college at the age of twenty, he had a living to earn and a good idea of how he was to do it.

Crane went to New York in 1891, held a post on the *New York Herald,* lost it, and turned to free-lance writing. He only infrequently sold filler stories to city papers that saw little merit in pieces reporting on what it feels like to live in the slums; exposés in the manner of the muckrakers were preferred. Crane lived hand to mouth, hanging about in the company of medical students and art students, with occasional stints back home in New Jersey. He knew from experience what being poor is like, and he brought to his studies of Bowery life a keenness of observation beyond that possible to the casually curious.

Maggie, a Girl of the Streets was completed in 1893 when Crane was twenty-one. Established publishers had no use for this portrayal of Irish immigrants hanging on to a Bowery existence. In contrast, Jacob Riis's *How the Other Half Lives* (1890) had quickly acquired a receptive readership for its straightforward account of the fetid places where the city's discards lived, perhaps because Riis's approach was patently that of the social reformer. Crane's fictional narrative of the short, dreary, dream-deluded life of Maggie, a young girl who goes "on the toif" as a streetwalker and ends drowned in the East River, was not so obviously uplifting. In an 1896 review of the republished version of *Maggie,* Frank Norris vividly described Crane's camera-eye techniques as "scores and scores of tiny flashlight photographs, instantaneous, caught as it were, on the run." But respectable readers in 1893 preferred the didacticism of the actual photographs Riis had used to dramatize his appeals for aid and reform of the poor to Crane's seemingly impersonal, amoral, sensational effects. *Maggie* came out under the pseudonym Johnston Smith and received little attention. But what attention it got mattered. Hamlin Garland and William Dean Howells recognized Crane's talent and became his mentors—Garland through his praise in *Crumbling Idols* (1894) and Howells in reviews placed in the *Philadelphia Press* (1893) and *Harper's Weekly* (1895).

Late in 1894 Crane's novel *The Red Badge of Courage* appeared as a syndicated feature in some 750 small newspapers across the country. Early the next year the *Philadelphia Press,* part of the chain that had printed *The Red Badge of Courage,* posted their hot young property on writing assignments out West. (From these experiences Crane would write "The Bride Comes to Yellow Sky" and "The Blue Hotel" in 1897.) In May 1895 his first collection of poems, *The Black Riders,* was published to unfavorable reviews. His experimentations in poetic form and the dark mood of his vision were too unconventional for popular acceptance. But in October 1895 *The Red Badge of Courage* was brought out by Appleton's, an important press, and Crane knew what it was like to be famous. Readers immediately took to the vivid tale of Civil War combat written by a young man born ten years after that war had been fought. Unlike *Maggie,* it created a stir among readers who were eager to read realistic accounts of Civil War battles but were uneasy with accounts of daily slum warfare. The serial publication of "Battles and Leaders of the Civil War" (published in four volumes in 1887 and 1888 by *Century* magazine) had roused public interest in the events of the war. Crane could count on excited attention from this moment on for anything he wrote or did.

For Crane, 1896 and 1897 were exceedingly productive years. *Maggie* was republished in 1896 by Appleton's under the eye of the writer-critic Frank Norris. The language of the original edition was cleaned up to meet current tastes in the printed word, and the novel received the approval it had failed to win in 1893. Also published in 1896 were *The Little Regiment,* a collection of Civil War stories, and *George's Mother,* the psychological account of the death-grip solicitude of a mother for her son. During the winter of 1896–1897 Crane was assigned to Cuba to cover the insurrection that led to the military confrontation in 1898 between Spain and the United States. He met and formed a permanent liaison with Cora Taylor of the Hotel de Dream. Early in 1897 he experienced the surprise of having the ship he was aboard sunk from under him as it headed for Cuba—an incident he immediately wrote up as a newspaper report and then developed into the short story "The Open Boat." In the midst of this activity, he published *The Third Violet,* a partly autobiographical novel about a young painter. By the summer of 1897, Crane was off to the Greco-Turkish war front, from whence he sent dispatches to American and British papers. By year's end he and Cora had gone to England to live.

Crane was once again in the Caribbean in 1898, reporting on the battles of the Spanish-American War for the famous Pulitzer paper, the *New York World.* By 1899 he had returned to England, already ill with tuberculosis and deep in debt. Over the next twelve months, Crane worked hard to earn the money he and Cora needed. He published *The Whilomville Stories* and *Wounds in the Rain;* prepared a second collection of poems, *War Is Kind;* completed the novel *Active Service;* wrote articles on major war battles published posthumously as *Great Battles of the World;* and pushed through the writing of twenty-five chapters of yet another novel, *The O'Ruddy.* Taken by Cora to a German sanatorium in the desperate hope that his illness could be arrested, Crane died on June 5, 1900.

That Crane was a literary prodigy is obvious. That he furnished American literature with a group of memorable tales and one novel-length masterwork is not at issue. The *kind* of writing Crane produced is what sparks controversy. Crane examined the inevitable conflict between self-made images that comfort and external facts that undercut romantic visions. But in his literary methods, was he primarily a realist, a naturalist, or an impressionist? Crane was a rebel against everything considered correct by the society he had left behind at twenty. The bohemian life he followed, the woman he lived with, and the material he wrote about all tell us this. But was he attempting to judge conventional society as a realist does, did he prefer to analyze its elements coolly in the manner of the naturalist, or was he most interested in imprinting impressionistic images for their own sake on his readers' minds?

The ironic tone that pervades Crane's narratives makes it difficult to determine his motives. Sometimes he appears hardly more than a very clever young man, and a rather cold one, who closes out the chance of getting at profound human feelings. At times Crane's compassion for those who yield to the stress of constant threats to their lives seems offset by a certain glibness. Those are the moments when he seems to be displaying what he knows (and his readers do not). At other times Crane appears to be trapped in unquestioned dreams of heroic male action. Consider for example, the problematic conclusion of *The Red Badge of Courage*. The young soldier Henry Fleming is now certain he knows the value of heroic action, but do the narrator's remarks in the closing sentences put the boy's certainty in doubt? Many of the endings Crane gives his stories are troublesome. They strike us as sophomoric exercises in facile cleverness—as with Mary Johnson's lament for her injured "goodness" in *Maggie,* the cash-register sign that flips up at the conclusion of "The Blue Hotel," Scratchy Wilson's double-take response to the news that the town marshal had gone and "got hisself married," and the final parade of small-town hypocrisies in "The Monster."

But Crane's imaginative force cannot be denied; nor can the way he finds apt images to encode human behavior. We detect in his writings the same discoveries made by William James's new psychology and by the theories of Charles Darwin and Herbert Spencer, which emphasize how susceptible we are to forces of inherited habits and environmental pressures. In one sense, *The Red Badge of Courage* is a determinist's primer about fears and falsehoods, but Crane manages to avoid trapping this story of a young soldier facing combat and his inner self in the doctrinaire. The novel is a very human tale, not a scientific treatise.

Crane lived quickly and wrote fast. His writing may have outrun his mind's ability or his heart's capacity to cut past the upper layers of that emotional cuticle where people under stress display their desires and terrors. But without question, Crane's reporter's eye is unfailingly accurate in its notations, just as his artist's touch is apparent in the images he has left permanently in his readers' memory.

Further Reading:

T. Beer, *Stephen Crane: A Study in American Letters,* 1923.
T. L. Raymond, *Stephen Crane,* 1923.
J. Berryman, *Stephen Crane,* 1950, 1962.
D. Hoffman, *The Poetry of Stephen Crane,* 1956, 1957.
C. Linson, *My Stephen Crane,* ed. E. Cady, 1958.
E. Cady, *Stephen Crane,* 1962, 1980.
E. Solomon, *Stephen Crane in England: A Portrait of the Artist,* 1964, 1965.
E. Solomon, *Stephen Crane: From Parody to Realism,* 1966.
Stephen Crane: A Collection of Critical Essays, ed. M. Bassan, 1967.
D. Gibson, *The Fiction of Stephen Crane,* 1968.

R. Stallman, *Stephen Crane: A Biography,* 1968.
Stephen Crane in the West and Mexico, ed. J. Katz, 1970.
R. M. Weatherford, *The Growth of Stephen Crane's Literary Reputation,* 1970.
M. La France, *A Reading of Stephen Crane,* 1971.
Stephen Crane in Transition: Centenary Essays, ed. J. Katz, 1972.
M. Holton, *Cylinder of Vision: The Fiction and Journalistic Writing of Stephen Crane,* 1972.
Stephen Crane's Career, ed. T. Gullason, 1973.
F. Bergon, *Stephen Crane's Artistry,* 1975.
J. Nagel, *Stephen Crane and Literary Impressionism,* 1980.
C. Wolford, *The Anger of Stephen Crane,* 1983.

Text:
The Works of Stephen Crane, 10 vols., ed.
F. Bowers, 1969–1976.
See also R. Stallman, *Stephen Crane: An
Omnibus,* 1952.
Stephen Crane: Letters, ed. R. Stallman and
L. Gilkes, 1960.
Stephen Crane: Uncollected Writings, ed.
O. Fryckstedt, 1963.

Completed Short Stories and Sketches, ed.
T. Gullason, 1963.
The Poems of Stephen Crane: A Critical Edition,
ed. J. Katz, 1966.
The Complete Novels, ed. T. Gullason, 1967.
*Stephen Crane: Sullivan County Tales and
Sketches,* ed. R. Stallman, 1968.

The Men in the Storm

At about three o'clock of the February afternoon, the blizzard began to swirl great clouds of snow along the streets, sweeping it down from the roofs and up from the pavements until the faces of pedestrians tingled and burned as from a thousand needle-prickings. Those on the walks huddled their necks closely in the collars of their coats and went along stooping like a race of aged people. The drivers of vehicles hurried their horses furiously on their way. They were made more cruel by the exposure of their positions, aloft on high seats. The street cars, bound up-town, went slowly, the horses slipping and straining in the spongy brown mass that lay between the rails. The drivers, muffled to the eyes, stood erect and facing the wind, models of grim philosophy. Overhead the trains rumbled and roared, and the dark structure of the elevated railroad, stretching over the avenue, dripped little streams and drops of water upon the mud and snow beneath it.

All the clatter of the street was softened by the masses that lay upon the cobbles until, even to one who looked from a window, it became important music, a melody of life made necessary to the ear by the dreariness of the pitiless beat and sweep of the storm. Occasionally one could see black figures of men busily shovelling the white drifts from the walks. The sounds from their labor created new recollections of rural experiences which every man manages to have in a measure. Later, the immense windows of the shops became aglow with light, throwing great beams of orange and yellow upon the pavement. They were infinitely cheerful, yet in a way they accented the force and discomfort of the storm, and gave a meaning to the pace of the people and the vehicles, scores of pedestrians and drivers, wretched with cold faces, necks and feet, speeding for scores of unknown doors and entrances, scattering to an infinite variety of shelters, to places which the imagination made warm with the familiar colors of home.

There was an absolute expression of hot dinners in the pace of the people. If one dared to speculate upon the destination of those who came trooping, he lost himself in a maze of social calculations; he might fling a handful of sand and attempt to follow the flight of each particular grain. But as to the suggestion of hot dinners, he was in firm lines of thought, for it was upon every hurrying face. It is a matter of tradition; it is from the tales of childhood. It comes forth with every storm.

However, in a certain part of a dark West-side street, there was a collection of men to whom these things were as if they were not. In this street was located a charitable house where for five cents the homeless of the city could get a bed at night and, in the morning, coffee and bread.

During the afternoon of the storm, the whirling snows acted as drivers, as men with whips, and at half-past three, the walk before the closed doors of the house was covered with wanderers of the street, waiting. For some distance on either side of the place they could be seen lurking in doorways and behind projecting parts of buildings, gathering in close bunches in an effort to get warm. A covered wagon drawn up near the curb sheltered a dozen of them. Under the stairs that led to the elevated railway station, there were six or eight, their hands stuffed deep in their pockets, their shoulders stooped, jiggling their feet. Others always could be seen coming, a strange procession, some slouching along with the characteristic hopeless gait of professional strays, some coming with hesitating steps wearing the air of men to whom this sort of thing was new.

It was an afternoon of incredible length. The snow, blowing in twisting clouds, sought out the men in their meagre hiding-places and skilfully beat in among them, drenching their persons with showers of fine, stinging flakes. They crowded together, muttering, and fumbling in their pockets to get their red, inflamed wrists covered by the cloth.

Newcomers usually halted at one of the groups and addressed a question, perhaps much as a matter of form, "Is it open yet?"

Those who had been waiting inclined to take the questioner seriously and become contemptuous. "No; do yeh think we'd be standin' here?"

The gathering swelled in numbers steadily and persistently. One could always see them coming, trudging slowly through the storm.

Finally, the little snow plains in the street began to assume a leaden hue from the shadows of evening. The buildings upreared gloomily save where various windows became brilliant figures of light that made shimmers and splashes of yellow on the snow. A street lamp on the curb struggled to illuminate, but it was reduced to impotent blindness by the swift gusts of sleet crusting its panes.

In this half-darkness, the men began to come from their shelter places and mass in front of the doors of charity. They were of all types, but the nationalities were mostly American, German and Irish. Many were strong, healthy, clear-skinned fellows with that stamp of countenance which is not frequently seen upon seekers after charity. There were men of undoubted patience, industry and temperance, who in time of ill-fortune, do not habitually turn to rail at the state of society, snarling at the arrogance of the rich and bemoaning the cowardice of the poor, but who at these times are apt to wear a sudden and singular meekness, as if they saw the world's progress marching from them and were trying to perceive where they had failed, what they had lacked, to be thus vanquished in the race. Then there were others of the shifting, Bowery[1] lodging-house element who were used to paying ten cents for a place to sleep, but who now came here because it was cheaper.

[1] Slum area of the lower East Side of New York City and location of cheap flophouses for vagrants.

But they were all mixed in one mass so thoroughly that one could not have discerned the different elements but for the fact that the laboring men, for the most part, remained silent and impassive in the blizzard, their eyes fixed on the windows of the house, statues of patience.

The sidewalk soon became completely blocked by the bodies of the men. They pressed close to one another like sheep in a winter's gale, keeping one another warm by the heat of their bodies. The snow came down upon this compressed group of men until, directly from above, it might have appeared like a heap of snow-covered merchandise, if it were not for the fact that the crowd swayed gently with a unanimous, rhythmical motion. It was wonderful to see how the snow lay upon the heads and shoulders of these men, in little ridges an inch thick perhaps in places, the flakes steadily adding drop and drop, precisely as they fall upon the unresisting grass of the fields. The feet of the men were all wet and cold and the wish to warm them accounted for the slow, gentle, rhythmical motion. Occasionally some man whose ears or nose tingled acutely from the cold winds would wriggle down until his head was protected by the shoulders of his companions.

There was a continuous murmuring discussion as to the probability of the doors being speedily opened. They persistently lifted their eyes toward the windows. One could hear little combats of opinion.

"There's a light in th' winder!"

"Naw; it's a reflection f'm across th' way."

"Well, didn't I see 'em lite it?"

"You did?"

"I did!"

"Well, then, that settles it!"

As the time approached when they expected to be allowed to enter, the men crowded to the doors in an unspeakable crush, jamming and wedging in a way that it seemed would crack bones. They surged heavily against the building in a powerful wave of pushing shoulders. Once a rumor flitted among all the tossing heads.

"They can't open th' doors! Th' fellers er smack up ag'in 'em."

Then a dull roar of rage came from the men on the outskirts; but all the time they strained and pushed until it appeared to be impossible for those that they cried out against to do anything but be crushed to pulp.

"Ah, git away f'm th' door!"

"Git outa that!"

"Throw 'em out!"

"Kill 'em!"

"Say, fellers, now, what th' 'ell? Give 'em a chanct t' open th' door!"

"Yeh damned pigs, give 'em a chanct t' open th' door!"

Men in the outskirts of the crowd occasionally yelled when a boot-heel of one of frantic trampling feet crushed on their freezing extremities.

"Git off me feet, yeh clumsy tarrier!"

"Say, don't stand on me feet! Walk on th' ground!"

A man near the doors suddenly shouted: "O-o-oh! Le' me out—le' me out!" And another, a man of infinite valor, once twisted his head so as to half face those who were pushing behind him. "Quit yer shovin', yeh—" and he delivered a volley of the most powerful and singular invective straight into the faces of the men behind him. It was as if he was hammering the noses of them with curses of triple brass. His face, red with rage, could be seen; upon it, an expression of sublime disregard of consequences. But nobody cared to reply to his imprecations; it was too cold. Many of them snickered and all continued to push.

In occasional pauses of the crowd's movement the men had opportunity to make jokes; usually grim things, and no doubt very uncouth. Nevertheless, they are notable —one does not expect to find the quality of humor in a heap of old clothes under a snowdrift.

The winds seemed to grow fiercer as time wore on. Some of the gusts of snow that came down on the close collection of heads cut like knives and needles, and the men huddled, and swore, not like dark assassins, but in a sort of an American fashion, grimly and desperately, it is true, but yet with a wondrous under-effect, indefinable and mystic, as if there was some kind of humor in this catastrophe, in this situation in a night of snow-laden winds.

Once, the window of the huge dry-goods shop across the street furnished material for a few moments of forgetfulness. In the brilliantly-lighted space appeared the figure of a man. He was rather stout and very well clothed. His whiskers were fashioned charmingly after those of the Prince of Wales.[2] He stood in an attitude of magnificent reflection. He slowly stroked his moustache with a certain grandeur of manner, and looked down at the snow-encrusted mob. From below, there was denoted a supreme complacence in him. It seemed that the sight operated inversely, and enabled him to more clearly regard his own environment, delightful relatively.

One of the mob chanced to turn his head and perceive the figure in the window. "Hello, lookit 'is whiskers," he said genially.

Many of the men turned then, and a shout went up. They called to him in all strange keys. They addressed him in every manner, from familiar and cordial greetings to carefully-worded advice concerning changes in his personal appearance. The man presently fled, and the mob chuckled ferociously like ogres who had just devoured something.

They turned then to serious business. Often they addressed the stolid front of the house.

"Oh, let us in fer Gawd's sake!"

"Let us in or we'll all drop dead!"

"Say, what's th' use o' keepin' all us poor Indians out in th' cold?"

And always some one was saying, "Keep off me feet."

The crushing of the crowd grew terrific toward the last. The men, in keen pain from the blasts, began almost to fight. With the pitiless whirl of snow upon them, the battle for shelter was going to the strong. It became known that the basement door at the foot of a little steep flight of stairs was the one to be opened, and they jostled

---

[2] Heir to the British throne, which he inherited upon the death of his mother Queen Victoria in 1901; known as a dandy.

and heaved in this direction like laboring fiends. One could hear them panting and groaning in their fierce exertion.

Usually some one in the front ranks was protesting to those in the rear: "O-o-ow! Oh, say, now, fellers, let up, will yeh? Do yeh wanta kill somebody?"

A policeman arrived and went into the midst of them, scolding and berating, occasionally threatening, but using no force but that of his hands and shoulders against these men who were only struggling to get in out of the storm. His decisive tones rang out sharply: "Stop that pushin' back there! Come, boys, don't push! Stop that! Here, you, quit yer shovin'! Cheese that!"

When the door below was opened, a thick stream of men forced a way down the stairs, which were of an extraordinary narrowness and seemed only wide enough for one at a time. Yet they somehow went down almost three abreast. It was a difficult and painful operation. The crowd was like a turbulent water forcing itself through one tiny outlet. The men in the rear, excited by the success of the others, made frantic exertions, for it seemed that this large band would more than fill the quarters and that many would be left upon the pavements. It would be disastrous to be of the last, and accordingly men with the snow biting their faces, writhed and twisted with their might. One expected that from the tremendous pressure, the narrow passage to the basement door would be so choked and clogged with human limbs and bodies that movement would be impossible. Once indeed the crowd was forced to stop, and a cry went along that a man had been injured at the foot of the stairs. But presently the slow movement began again, and the policeman fought at the top of the flight to ease the pressure on those who were going down.

A reddish light from a window fell upon the faces of the men when they, in turn, arrived at the last three steps and were about to enter. One could then note a change of expression that had come over their features. As they thus stood upon the threshold of their hopes, they looked suddenly content and complacent. The fire had passed from their eyes and the snarl had vanished from their lips: The very force of the crowd in the rear, which had previously vexed them, was regarded from another point of view, for it now made it inevitable that they should go through the little doors into the place that was cheery and warm with light.

The tossing crowd on the sidewalk grew smaller and smaller. The snow beat with merciless persistence upon the bowed heads of those who waited. The wind drove it up from the pavements in frantic forms of winding white, and it seethed in circles about the huddled forms, passing in, one by one, three by three, out of the storm.

1894

The Open Boat

A Tale Intended to Be After the Fact.
Being the Experience of Four Men
*from the Sunk Steamer Commodore**

I

None of them knew the color of the sky. Their eyes glanced level, and were fastened upon the waves that swept toward them. These waves were of the hue of slate, save for the tops, which were of foaming white, and all of the men knew the colors of the sea. The horizon narrowed and widened, and dipped and rose, and at all times its edge was jagged with waves that seemed thrust up in points like rocks.

Many a man ought to have a bath-tub larger than the boat which here rode upon the sea. These waves were most wrongfully and barbarously abrupt and tall, and each froth-top was a problem in small boat navigation.

The cook squatted in the bottom and looked with both eyes at the six inches of gunwale which separated him from the ocean. His sleeves were rolled over his fat forearms, and the two flaps of his unbuttoned vest dangled as he bent to bail out the boat. Often he said: "Gawd! That was a narrow clip." As he remarked it he invariably gazed eastward over the broken sea.

The oiler, steering with one of the two oars in the boat, sometimes raised himself suddenly to keep clear of water that swirled in over the stern. It was a thin little oar and it seemed often ready to snap.

The correspondent, pulling at the other oar, watched the waves and wondered why he was there.

The injured captain, lying in the bow, was at this time buried in that profound dejection and indifference which comes, temporarily at least, to even the bravest and most enduring when, willy nilly, the firm fails, the army loses, the ship goes down. The mind of the master of a vessel is rooted deep in the timbers of her, though he command for a day or a decade, and this captain had on him the stern impression of a scene in the grays of dawn of seven turned faces, and later a stump of a top-mast with a white ball on it that slashed to and fro at the waves, went low and lower, and down. Thereafter there was something strange in his voice. Although steady, it was deep with mourning, and of a quality beyond oration or tears.

"Keep' er a little more south, Billie," said he.

" 'A little more south,' sir," said the oiler in the stern.

A seat in this boat was not unlike a seat upon a bucking broncho, and, by the same token, a broncho is not much smaller. The craft pranced and reared, and plunged like

---

* Crane was on board the *Commodore* bound for Cuba to cover the revolution as a correspondent when the ship (carrying arms for the combatants) was sunk January 2, 1897, off the Florida coast. Together with four other men, Crane spent almost thirty hours in a dinghy before making a safe landing at Daytona. The New York *Press* ran Crane's account of his experiences on January 7. By June he had published his fictional version in *Scribner's Magazine* as "The Open Boat."

an animal. As each wave came, and she rose for it, she seemed like a horse making at a fence outrageously high. The manner of her scramble over these walls of water is a mystic thing, and, moreover, at the top of them were ordinarily these problems in white water, the foam racing down from the summit of each wave, requiring a new leap, and a leap from the air. Then, after scornfully bumping a crest, she would slide, and race, and splash down a long incline and arrive bobbing and nodding in front of the next menace.

A singular disadvantage of the sea lies in the fact that after successfully surmounting one wave you discover that there is another behind it just as important and just as nervously anxious to do something effective in the way of swamping boats. In a ten-foot dingey one can get an idea of the resources of the sea in the line of waves that is not probable to the average experience, which is never at sea in a dingey. As each salty wall of water approached, it shut all else from the view of the men in the boat, and it was the final outburst of the ocean, the last effort of the grim water. There was a terrible grace in the move of the waves, and they came in silence, save for the snarling of the crests.

In the wan light, the faces of the men must have been gray. Their eyes must have glinted in strange ways as they gazed steadily astern. Viewed from a balcony, the whole thing would doubtlessly have been weirdly picturesque. But the men in the boat had no time to see it, and if they had had leisure there were other things to occupy their minds. The sun swung steadily up the sky, and they knew it was broad day because the color of the sea changed from slate to emerald-green, streaked with amber lights, and the foam was like tumbling snow. The process of the breaking day was unknown to them. They were aware only of this effect upon the color of the waves that rolled toward them.

In disjointed sentences the cook and the correspondent argued as to the difference between a life-saving station and a house of refuge. The cook had said: "There's a house of refuge just north of the Mosquito Inlet Light, and as soon as they see us, they'll come off in their boat and pick us up."

"As soon as who see us?" said the correspondent.

"The crew," said the cook.

"Houses of refuge don't have crews," said the correspondent. "As I understand them, they are only places where clothes and grub are stored for the benefit of shipwrecked people. They don't carry crews."

"Oh, yes, they do," said the cook.

"No, they don't," said the correspondent.

"Well, we're not there yet, anyhow," said the oiler, in the stern.

"Well," said the cook, "perhaps it's not a house of refuge that I'm thinking of as being near Mosquito Inlet Light. Perhaps it's a life-saving station."

"We're not there yet," said the oiler, in the stern.

II

As the boat bounced from the top of each wave, the wind tore through the hair of the hatless men, and as the craft plopped her stern down again the spray slashed past them. The crest of each of these waves was a hill, from the top of which the men surveyed, for a moment, a broad tumultuous expanse, shining and wind-riven. It was probably splendid. It was probably glorious, this play of the free sea, wild with lights of emerald and white and amber.

"Bully good thing it's an on-shore wind," said the cook. "If not, where would we be? Wouldn't have a show."

"That's right," said the correspondent.

The busy oiler nodded his assent.

Then the captain, in the bow, chuckled in a way that expressed humor, contempt, tragedy, all in one. "Do you think we've got much of a show, now, boys?" said he.

Whereupon the three were silent, save for a trifle of hemming and hawing. To express any particular optimism at this time they felt to be childish and stupid, but they all doubtless possessed this sense of the situation in their mind. A young man thinks doggedly at such times. On the other hand, the ethics of their condition was decidedly against any open suggestion of hopelessness. So they were silent.

"Oh, well," said the captain, soothing his children, "we'll get ashore all right."

But there was that in his tone which made them think, so the oiler quoth: "Yes! If this wind holds!"

The cook was bailing. "Yes! If we don't catch hell in the surf."

Canton flannel gulls flew near and far. Sometimes they sat down on the sea, near patches of brown sea-weed that rolled over the waves with a movement like carpets on a line in a gale. The birds sat comfortably in groups, and they were envied by some in the dingey, for the wrath of the sea was no more to them than it was to a covey of prairie chickens a thousand miles inland. Often they came very close and stared at the men with black bead-like eyes. At these times they were uncanny and sinister in their unblinking scrutiny, and the men hooted angrily at them, telling them to be gone. One came, and evidently decided to alight on the top of the captain's head. The bird flew parallel to the boat and did not circle, but made short sidelong jumps in the air in chicken-fashion. His black eyes were wistfully fixed upon the captain's head. "Ugly brute," said the oiler to the bird. "You look as if you were made with a jack-knife." The cook and the correspondent swore darkly at the creature. The captain naturally wished to knock it away with the end of the heavy painter, but he did not dare do it, because anything resembling an emphatic gesture would have capsized this freighted boat, and so with his open hand, the captain gently and carefully waved the gull away. After it had been discouraged from the pursuit the captain breathed easier on account of his hair, and others breathed easier because the bird struck their minds at this time as being somehow grewsome and ominous.

In the meantime the oiler and the correspondent rowed. And also they rowed.

They sat together in the same seat, and each rowed an oar, then the oiler took both oars; then the correspondent took both oars; then the oiler; then the correspondent. They rowed and they rowed. The very ticklish part of the business was when the time came for the reclining one in the stern to take his turn at the oars. By the very last star of truth, it is easier to steal eggs from under a hen than it was to change seats in the dingey. First the man in the stern slid his hand along the thwart and moved with care, as if he were of Sèvres. Then the man in the rowing seat slid his hand along the other thwart. It was all done with the most extraordinary care. As the two sidled past each other, the whole party kept watchful eyes on the coming wave, and the captain cried: "Look out now! Steady there!"

The brown mats of sea-weed that appeared from time to time were like islands, bits of earth. They were travelling, apparently, neither one way nor the other. They were, to all intents, stationary. They informed the men in the boat that it was making progress slowly toward the land.

The captain, rearing cautiously in the bow, after the dingey soared on a great swell, said that he had seen the light-house at Mosquito Inlet. Presently the cook remarked that he had seen it. The correspondent was at the oars, then, and for some reason he too wished to look at the light-house, but his back was toward the far shore and the waves were important, and for some time he could not seize an opportunity to turn his head. But at last there came a wave more gentle than the others, and when at the crest of it he swiftly scoured the western horizon.

"See it?" said the captain.

"No," said the correspondent, slowly. "I didn't see anything."

"Look again," said the captain. He pointed. "It's exactly in that direction."

At the top of another wave, the correspondent did as he was bid, and this time his eyes chanced on a small still thing on the edge of the swaying horizon. It was precisely like the point of a pin. It took an anxious eye to find a light-house so tiny.

"Think we'll make it, Captain?"

"If this wind holds and the boat don't swamp, we can't do much else," said the captain.

The little boat, lifted by each towering sea, and splashed viciously by the crests, made progress that in the absence of sea-weed was not apparent to those in her. She seemed just a wee thing wallowing, miraculously, top-up, at the mercy of five oceans. Occasionally, a great spread of water, like white flame, swarmed into her.

"Bail her, cook," said the captain, serenely.

"All right, Captain," said the cheerful cook.

III

It would be difficult to describe the subtle brotherhood of men that was here established on the seas. No one said that it was so. No one mentioned it, but it dwelt in the boat, and each man felt it warm him. They were a captain, an oiler, a cook, and a correspondent, and they were friends, friends in a more curiously ironbound degree than may be common. The hurt captain, lying against the water-jar in the bow, spoke always in a low voice and calmly but he could never command a more ready and swiftly obedient crew than the motley three of the dingey. It was more than a mere recognition of what was best for the common safety. There was surely in it a quality that was personal and heartfelt. And after this devotion to the commander of the boat there was this comradeship that the correspondent, for instance, who had been taught to be cynical of men, knew even at the time was the best experience of his life. But no one said that it was so. No one mentioned it.

"I wish we had a sail," remarked the captain. "We might try my overcoat on the end of an oar and give you two boys a chance to rest." So the cook and the correspondent held the mast and spread wide the overcoat, the oiler steered, and the little boat made good way with her new rig. Sometimes the oiler had to scull sharply to keep a sea from breaking into the boat, but otherwise sailing was a success.

Meanwhile the light-house had been growing slowly larger. It had now almost assumed color, and appeared like a little gray shadow in the sky. The man at the oars could not be prevented from turning his head rather often to try for a glimpse of this little gray shadow.

At last, from the top of each wave the men in the tossing boat could see land. Even as the light-house was an upright shadow on the sky, this land seemed but a long black shadow on the sea. It certainly was thinner than paper. "We must be about opposite New Smyrna," said the cook, who had coasted this shore often in schooners. "Captain, by the way, I believe they abandoned that life-saving station there about a year ago."

"Did they?" said the captain.

The wind slowly died away. The cook and the correspondent were not now obliged to slave in order to hold high the oar. But the waves continued their old impetuous swooping at the dingey, and the little craft, no longer under way, struggled woundily over them. The oiler or the correspondent took the oars again.

Shipwrecks are *apropos* of nothing. If men could only train for them and have them occur when the men had reached pink condition, there would be less drowning at sea. Of the four in the dingey none had slept any time worth mentioning for two days and two nights previous to embarking in the dingey, and in the excitement of clambering about the deck of a foundering ship they had also forgotten to eat heartily.

For these reasons, and for others, neither the oiler nor the correspondent was fond of rowing at this time. The correspondent wondered ingenuously how in the name of all that was sane could there be people who thought it amusing to row a boat. It was not an amusement; it was a diabolical punishment, and even a genius of mental aberrations could never conclude that it was anything but a horror to the muscles and a crime against the back. He mentioned to the boat in general how the amusement of rowing struck him, and the weary-faced oiler smiled in full sympathy. Previously to the foundering, by the way, the oiler had worked double-watch in the engine-room of the ship.

"Take her easy, now, boys," said the captain. "Don't spend yourselves. If we have to run a surf you'll need all your strength, because we'll sure have to swim for it. Take your time."

Slowly the land arose from the sea. From a black line it became a line of black and a line of white—trees and sand. Finally, the captain said that he could make out a house on the shore. "That's the house of refuge, sure," said the cook. "They'll see us before long, and come out after us."

The distant light-house reared high. "The keeper ought to be able to make us out now, if he's looking through a glass," said the captain. "He'll notify the life-saving people."

"None of those other boats could have got ashore to give word of the wreck," said the oiler, in a low voice. "Else the life-boat would be out hunting us."

Slowly and beautifully the land loomed out of the sea. The wind came again. It had veered from the northeast to the southeast. Finally, a new sound struck the ears of the men in the boat. It was the low thunder of the surf on the shore. "We'll never be able to make the light-house now," said the captain. "Swing her head a little more north, Billie."

" 'A little more north,' sir," said the oiler.

Whereupon the little boat turned her nose once more down the wind, and all but the oarsman watched the shore grow. Under the influence of this expansion doubt and direful apprehension was leaving the minds of the men. The management of the boat was still most absorbing, but it could not prevent a quiet cheerfulness. In an hour, perhaps, they would be ashore.

Their back-bones had become thoroughly used to balancing in the boat and they now rode this wild colt of a dingey like circus men. The correspondent thought that he had been drenched to the skin, but happening to feel in the top pocket of his coat, he found therein eight cigars. Four of them were soaked with seawater; four were perfectly scatheless. After a search, somebody produced three dry matches, and thereupon the four waifs rode impudently in their little boat, and with an assurance of an impending rescue shining in their eyes, puffed at the big cigars and judged well and ill of all men. Everybody took a drink of water.

IV

"Cook," remarked the captain, "there don't seem to be any signs of life about your house of refuge."

"No," replied the cook. "Funny they don't see us!"

A broad stretch of lowly coast lay before the eyes of the men. It was dunes topped with dark vegetation. The roar of the surf was plain, and sometimes they could see the white lip of a wave as it spun up the beach. A tiny house was blocked out black upon the sky. Southward, the slim light-house lifted its little gray length.

Tide, wind, and waves were swinging the dingey northward. "Funny they don't see us," said the men.

The surf's roar was here dulled, but its tone was, nevertheless, thunderous and mighty. As the boat swam over the great rollers, the men sat listening to this roar. "We'll swamp sure," said everybody.

It is fair to say here that there was not a life-saving station within twenty miles in either direction, but the men did not know this fact and in consequence they made dark and opprobrious remarks concerning the eyesight of the nation's life-savers. Four scowling men sat in the dingey and surpassed records in the invention of epithets.

"Funny they don't see us."

The light-heartedness of a former time had completely faded. To their sharpened minds it was easy to conjure pictures of all kinds of incompetency and blindness and indeed, cowardice. There was the shore of the populous land, and it was bitter and bitter to them that from it came no sign.

"Well," said the captain, ultimately, "I suppose we'll have to make a try for ourselves. If we stay out here too long, we'll none of us have strength left to swim after the boat swamps."

And so the oiler, who was at the oars, turned the boat straight for the shore. There was a sudden tightening of muscles. There was some thinking.

"If we don't all get ashore—" said the captain. "If we don't all get ashore, I suppose you fellows know where to send news of my finish?"

They then briefly exchanged some addresses and admonitions. As for the reflections of the men, there was a great deal of rage in them. Perchance they might be formulated thus: "If I am going to be drowned—if I am going to be drowned—if I am going to be drowned, why, in the name of the seven mad gods who rule the sea, was I allowed to come thus far and contemplate sand and trees? Was I brought here merely to have my nose dragged away as I was about to nibble the sacred cheese of life? It is preposterous. If this old ninny-woman, Fate, cannot do better than this, she should be deprived of the management of men's fortunes. She is an old hen who knows not her intention. If she has decided to drown me, why did she not do it in the beginning and save me all this trouble. The whole affair is absurd. . . . But, no, she cannot mean to drown me. She dare not drown me. She cannot drown me. Not after all this work." Afterward the man might have had an impulse to shake his fist at the clouds. "Just you drown me, now, and then hear what I call you!"

The billows that came at this time were more formidable. They seemed always just about to break and roll over the little boat in a turmoil of foam. There was a preparatory and long growl in the speech of them. No mind unused to the sea would have concluded that the dingey could ascend these sheer heights in time, the shore was still afar, the oiler was a wily surfman. "Boys," he said, swiftly, "she won't live three minutes more and we're too far out to swim. Shall I take her to sea again, Captain?"

"Yes! Go ahead!" said the captain.

This oiler, by a series of quick miracles, and fast and steady oarsmanship, turned the boat in the middle of the surf and took her safely to sea again.

There was a considerable silence as the boat bumped over the furrowed sea to deeper water. Then somebody in gloom spoke. "Well, anyhow, they must have seen us from the shore by now."

The gulls went in slanting flight up the wind toward the gray desolate east. A squall, marked by dingy clouds, and clouds brick-red, like smoke from a burning building, appeared from the southeast.

"What do you think of those life-saving people? Ain't they peaches?"

"Funny they haven't seen us."

"Maybe they think we're out here for sport! Maybe they think we're fishin'. Maybe they think we're damned fools."

It was a long afternoon. A changed tide tried to force them southward, but wind and wave said northward. Far ahead, where coastline, sea, and sky formed their mighty angle, there were little dots which seemed to indicate a city on the shore.

"St. Augustine?"

The captain shook his head. "Too near Mosquito Inlet."

And the oiler rowed, and then the correspondent rowed. Then the oiler rowed. It was a weary business. The human back can become the seat of more aches and pains than are registered in books for the composite anatomy of a regiment. It is a limited area, but it can become the theatre of innumerable muscular conflicts, tangles, wrenches, knots, and other comforts.

"Did you ever like to row, Billie?" asked the correspondent.

"No," said the oiler. "Hang it."

When one exchanged the rowing-seat for a place in the bottom of the boat, he suffered a bodily depression that caused him to be careless of everything save an obligation to wiggle one finger. There was cold sea-water swashing to and fro in the boat, and he lay in it. His head, pillowed on a thwart, was within an inch of the swirl of a wave crest, and sometimes a particularly obstreperous sea came in-board and drenched him once more. But these matters did not annoy him. It is almost certain that if the boat had capsized he would have tumbled comfortably out upon the ocean as if he felt sure that it was a great soft mattress.

"Look! There's a man on the shore!"

"Where?"

"There! See 'im? See 'im?"

"Yes, sure! He's walking along."

"Now he's stopped. Look! He's facing us!"

"He's waving at us!"

"So he is! By thunder!"

"Ah, now, we're all right! Now we're all right! There'll be a boat out here for us in half an hour."

"He's going on. He's running. He's going up to that house there."

The remote beach seemed lower than the sea, and it required a searching glance to discern the little black figure. The captain saw a floating stick and they rowed to it. A bath-towel was by some weird chance in the boat, and, tying this on the stick, the captain waved it. The oarsman did not dare turn his head, so he was obliged to ask questions.

"What's he doing now?"

"He's standing still again. He's looking, I think. . . . There he goes again. Toward the house. . . . Now he's stopped again."

"Is he waving at us?"

"No, not now! he was, though."

"Look! There comes another man!"

"He's running."

"Look at him go, would you."

"Why, he's on a bicycle. Now he's met the other man. They're both waving at us. Look!"

"There comes something up the beach."

"What the devil is that thing?"

"Why, it looks like a boat."

"Why, certainly it's a boat."

"No, it's on wheels."

"Yes, so it is. Well, that must be the life-boat. They drag them along shore on a wagon."

"That's the life-boat, sure."

"No, by ———, it's—it's an omnibus."

"I tell you it's a life-boat."

"It is not! It's an omnibus. I can see it plain. See? One of those big hotel omnibuses."

"By thunder, you're right. It's an omnibus, sure as fate. What do you suppose they are doing with an omnibus? Maybe they are going around collecting the life-crew, hey?"

"That's it, likely. Look! There's a fellow waving a little black flag. He's standing on the steps of the omnibus. There come those other two fellows. Now they're all talking together. Look at the fellow with the flag. Maybe he ain't waving it!"

"That ain't a flag, is it? That's his coat. Why, certainly, that's his coat."

"So it is. It's his coat. He's taken it off and is waving it around his head. But would you look at him swing it!"

"Oh, say, there isn't any life-saving station there. That's just a winter resort hotel omnibus that has brought over some of the boarders to see us drown."

"What's that idiot with the coat mean? What's he signaling, anyhow?"

"It looks as if he were trying to tell us to go north. There must be a life-saving station up there."

"No! He thinks we're fishing. Just giving us a merry hand. See? Ah, there, Willie."

"Well, I wish I could make something out of those signals. What do you suppose he means?"

"He don't mean anything. He's just playing."

"Well, if he'd just signal us to try the surf again, or to go to sea and wait, or go north, or go south, or go to hell—there would be some reason in it. But look at him. He just stands there and keeps his coat revolving like a wheel. The ass!"

"There come more people."

"Now there's quite a mob. Look! Isn't that a boat?"

"Where? Oh, I see where you mean. No, that's no boat."

"That fellow is still waving his coat."

"He must think we like to see him do that, why don't he quit it. It don't mean anything."

"I don't know. I think he is trying to make us go north. It must be that there's a life-saving station there somewhere."

"Say, he ain't tired yet. Look at 'im wave."

"Wonder how long he can keep that up. He's been revolving his coat ever since he caught sight of us. He's an idiot. Why aren't they getting men to bring a boat out. A fishing boat—one of those big yawls—could come out here all right. Why don't he do something?"

"Oh, it's all right, now."

"They'll have a boat out here for us in less than no time, now that they've seen us."

A faint yellow tone came into the sky over the low land. The shadows on the sea slowly deepened. The wind bore coldness with it, and the men began to shiver.

"Holy smoke!" said one, allowing his voice to express his impious mood, "if we keep on monkeying out here! If we've got to flounder out here all night!"

"Oh, we'll never have to stay here all night! don't you worry. They've seen us now, and it won't be long before they'll come chasing out after us."

The shore grew dusky. The man waving a coat blended gradually into the gloom, and it swallowed in the same manner the omnibus and the group of people. The spray, when it dashed uproariously over the side, made the voyagers shrink and swear like men who were being branded.

"I'd like to catch the chump who waved the coat. I feel like soaking him one, just for luck."

"Why? What did he do?"

"Oh, nothing, but then he seemed so damned cheerful."

In the meantime the oiler rowed, and then the correspondent rowed, and then the oiler rowed. Gray-faced and bowed forward, they mechanically, turn by turn, plied the leaden oars. The form of the light-house had vanished from the southern horizon, but finally a pale star appeared, just lifting from the sea. The streaked saffron in the west passed before the all-merging darkness, and the sea to the east was black. The land had vanished, and was expressed only by the low and drear thunder of the surf.

"If I am going to be drowned—if I am going to be drowned—if I am going to be drowned, why, in the name of the seven mad gods who rule the sea, was I allowed to come thus far and contemplate sand and trees? Was I brought here merely to have my nose dragged away as I was about to nibble the sacred cheese of life?"

The patient captain, drooped over the water-jar, was sometimes obliged to speak to the oarsman.

"Keep her head up! Keep her head up!"

" 'Keep her head up,' sir." The voices were weary and low.

This was surely a quiet evening. All save the oarsman lay heavily and listlessly in the boat's bottom. As for him, his eyes were just capable of noting the tall black waves that swept forward in a most sinister silence, save for an occasional subdued growl of a crest.

The cook's head was on a thwart, and he looked without interest at the water under his nose. He was deep in other scenes. Finally he spoke. "Billie," he murmured, dreamfully, "what kind of pie do you like best?"

V

"Pie," said the oiler and the correspondent, agitatedly. "Don't talk about those things, blast you!"

"Well," said the cook, "I was just thinking about ham sandwiches, and——"

A night on the sea in an open boat is a long night. As darkness settled finally, the shine of the light, lifting from the sea in the south, changed to full gold. On the northern horizon a new light appeared, a small bluish gleam on the edge of the waters. These two lights were the furniture of the world. Otherwise there was nothing but waves.

Two men huddled in the stern, and distances were so magnificent in the dingey that the rower was enabled to keep his feet partly warmed by thrusting them under his companions. Their legs indeed extended far under the rowing-seat until they touched the feet of the captain forward. Sometimes, despite the efforts of the tired oarsman, a wave came piling into the boat, an icy wave of the night, and the chilling water soaked them anew. They would twist their bodies for a moment and groan, and sleep the dead sleep once more, while the water in the boat gurgled about them as the craft rocked.

The plan of the oiler and the correspondent was for one to row until he lost the ability, and then arouse the other from his sea-water couch in the bottom of the boat.

The oiler plied the oars until his head drooped forward, and the overpowering sleep blinded him. And he rowed yet afterward. Then he touched a man in the bottom of the boat, and called his name. "Will you spell me for a little while?" he said, meekly.

"Sure, Billie," said the correspondent, awakening and dragging himself to a sitting position. They exchanged places carefully, and the oiler, cuddling down in the sea-water at the cook's side, seemed to go to sleep instantly.

The particular violence of the sea had ceased. The waves came without snarling. The obligation of the man at the oars was to keep the boat headed so that the tilt of the rollers would not capsize her, and to preserve her from filling when the crests rushed past. The black waves were silent and hard to be seen in the darkness. Often one was almost upon the boat before the oarsman was aware.

In a low voice the correspondent addressed the captain. He was not sure that the captain was awake, although this iron man seemed to be always awake. "Captain, shall I keep her making for that light north, sir?"

The same steady voice answered him. "Yes. Keep it about two points off the port bow."

The cook had tied a life-belt around himself in order to get even the warmth which this clumsy cork contrivance could donate, and he seemed almost stove-like when a rower, whose teeth invariably chattered wildly as soon as he ceased his labor, dropped down to sleep.

The correspondent, as he rowed, looked down at the two men sleeping under foot. The cook's arm was around the oiler's shoulders, and, with their fragmentary clothing and haggard faces, they were the babes of the sea, a grotesque rendering of the old babes in the wood.

Later he must have grown stupid at his work, for suddenly there was a growling of water, and a crest came with a roar and a swash into the boat, and it was a wonder that it did not set the cook afloat in his life-belt. The cook continued to sleep, but the oiler sat up, blinking his eyes and shaking with the new cold.

"Oh, I'm awful sorry, Billie," said the correspondent, contritely.

"That's all right, old boy," said the oiler, and lay down again and was asleep.

Presently it seemed that even the captain dozed, and the correspondent thought that he was the one man afloat on all the oceans. The wind had a voice as it came over the waves, and it was sadder than the end.

There was a long, loud swishing astern of the boat, and a gleaming trail of phosphorescence, like blue flame, was furrowed on the black waters. It might have been made by a monstrous knife.

Then there came a stillness, while the correspondent breathed with the open mouth and looked at the sea.

Suddenly there was another swish and another long flash of bluish light, and this time it was alongside the boat, and might almost have been reached with an oar. The correspondent saw an enormous fin speed like a shadow through the water, hurling the crystalline spray and leaving the long glowing trail.

The correspondent looked over his shoulder at the captain. His face was hidden, and he seemed to be asleep. He looked at the babes of the sea. They certainly were asleep. So, being bereft of sympathy, he leaned a little way to one side and swore softly into the sea.

But the thing did not then leave the vicinity of the boat. Ahead or astern, on one side or the other, at intervals long or short, fled the long sparkling streak, and there was to be heard the whiroo of the dark fin. The speed and power of the thing was greatly to be admired. It cut the water like a gigantic and keen projectile.

The presence of this biding thing did not affect the man with the same horror that it would if he had been a picknicker. He simply looked at the sea dully and swore in an undertone.

Nevertheless, it is true that he did not wish to be alone with the thing. He wished one of his companions to awaken by chance and keep him company with it. But the captain hung motionless over the water-jar and the oiler and the cook in the bottom of the boat were plunged in slumber.

VI

"If I am going to be drowned—if I am going to be drowned—if I am going to be drowned, why, in the name of the seven mad gods who rule the sea, was I allowed to come thus far and contemplate sand and trees?"

During this dismal night, it may be remarked that a man would conclude that it was really the intention of the seven mad gods to drown him, despite the abominable injustice of it. For it was certainly an abominable injustice to drown a man who had worked so hard, so hard. The man felt it would be a crime most unnatural. Other people had drowned at sea since galleys swarmed with painted sails, but still—

When it occurs to a man that nature does not regard him as important, and that she feels she would not maim the universe by disposing of him, he at first wishes to throw bricks at the temple, and he hates deeply the fact that there are no bricks and no temples. Any visible expression of nature would surely be pelleted with his jeers.

Then, if there be no tangible thing to hoot he feels, perhaps, the desire to confront a personification and indulge in pleas, bowed to one knee, and with hands supplicant, saying: "Yes, but I love myself."

A high cold star on a winter's night is the word he feels that she says to him. Thereafter he knows the pathos of his situation.

The men in the dingey had not discussed these matters, but each had, no doubt, reflected upon them in silence and according to his mind. There was seldom any expression upon their faces save the general one of complete weariness. Speech was devoted to the business of the boat.

To chime the notes of his emotion, a verse mysteriously entered the correspondent's head. He had even forgotten that he had forgotten this verse, but it suddenly was in his mind.

> A soldier of the Legion lay dying in Algiers,
> There was lack of woman's nursing, there was dearth of woman's tears;
> But a comrade stood beside him, and he took that comrade's hand,
> And he said: "I never more shall see my own, my native land."[1]

In his childhood, the correspondent had been made acquainted with the fact that a soldier of the legion lay dying in Algiers, but he had never regarded it as important. Myriads of his school-fellows had informed him of the soldier's plight, but the dinning had naturally ended by making him perfectly indifferent. He had never considered it his affair that a soldier of the Legion lay dying in Algiers, nor had it appeared to him as a matter for sorrow. It was less to him than the breaking of a pencil's point.

Now, however, it quaintly came to him as a human, living thing. It was no longer merely a picture of a few throes in the breast of a poet, meanwhile drinking tea and warming his feet at the grate; it was an actuality—stern, mournful, and fine.

The correspondent plainly saw the soldier. He lay on the sand with his feet out straight and still. While his pale left hand was upon his chest in an attempt to thwart the going of his life, the blood came between his fingers. In the far Algerian distance,

---

[1] Crane's rendition of lines from a poem by
Caroline E. S. Norton, "Bingen on the Rhine"
(1883).

a city of low square forms was set against a sky that was faint with the last sunset hues. The correspondent, plying the oars and dreaming of the slow and slower movements of the lips of the soldier, was moved by a profound and perfectly impersonal comprehension. He was sorry for the soldier of the Legion who lay dying in Algiers.

The thing which had followed the boat and waited had evidently grown bored at the delay. There was no longer to be heard the slash of the cut-water, and there was no longer the flame of the long trail. The light in the north still glimmered, but it was apparently no nearer to the boat. Sometimes the boom of the surf rang in the correspondent's ears, and he turned the craft seaward then and rowed harder. Southward, some one had evidently built a watch-fire on the beach. It was too low and too far to be seen, but it made a shimmering, roseate reflection upon the bluff back of it, and this could be discerned from the boat. The wind came stronger, and sometimes a wave suddenly raged out like a mountain-cat and there was to be seen the sheen and sparkle of a broken crest.

The captain, in the bow, moved on his water-jar and sat erect. "Pretty long night," he observed to the correspondent. He looked at the shore. "Those life-saving people take their time."

"Did you see that shark playing around?"

"Yes, I saw him. He was a big fellow, all right."

"Wish I had known you were awake."

Later the correspondent spoke into the bottom of the boat. "Billie!" There was a slow and gradual disentanglement. "Billie, will you spell me?"

"Sure," said the oiler.

As soon as the correspondent touched the cold comfortable seawater in the bottom of the boat, and had huddled close to the cook's life-belt he was deep in sleep, despite the fact that his teeth played all the popular airs. This sleep was so good to him that it was but a moment before he heard a voice call his name in a tone that demonstrated the last stages of exhaustion. "Will you spell me?"

"Sure, Billie."

The light in the north had mysteriously vanished, but the correspondent took his course from the wide-awake captain.

Later in the night they took the boat farther out to sea, and the captain directed the cook to take one oar at the stern and keep the boat facing the seas. He was to call out if he should hear the thunder of the surf. This plan enabled the oiler and the correspondent to get respite together. "We'll give those boys a chance to get into shape again," said the captain. They curled down and, after a few preliminary chatterings and trembles, slept once more the dead sleep. Neither knew they had bequeathed to the cook the company of another shark, or perhaps the same shark.

As the boat carousel on the waves, spray occasionally bumped over the side and gave them a fresh soaking, but this had no power to break their repose. The ominous slash of the wind and the water affected them as it would have affected mummies.

"Boys," said the cook, with the notes of every reluctance in his voice, "she's drifted in pretty close. I guess one of you had better take her to sea again." The correspondent, aroused, heard the crash of the toppled crests.

As he was rowing, the captain gave him some whiskey and water, and this steadied the chills out of him. "If I ever get ashore and anybody shows me even a photograph of an oar——"

At last there was a short conversation.

"Billie. . . . Billie, will you spell me?"

"Sure," said the oiler.

VII

When the correspondent again opened his eyes, the sea and the sky were each of the gray hue of the dawning. Later, carmine and gold was painted upon the waters. The morning appeared finally, in its splendor, with a sky of pure blue, and the sunlight flamed on the tips of the waves.

On the distant dunes were set many little black cottages, and a tall white wind-mill reared above them. No man, nor dog, nor bicycle appeared on the beach. The cottages might have formed a deserted village.

The voyagers scanned the shore. A conference was held in the boat. "Well," said the captain, "if no help is coming, we might better try a run through the surf right away. If we stay out here much longer we will be too weak to do anything for ourselves at all." The others silently acquiesced in this reasoning. The boat was headed for the beach. The correspondent wondered if none ever ascended the tall wind-tower, and if then they never looked seaward. This tower was a giant, standing with its back to the plight of the ants. It represented in a degree, to the correspondent, the serenity of nature amid the struggles of the individual—nature in the wind, and nature in the vision of men. She did not seem cruel to him then, nor beneficent, nor treacherous, nor wise. But she was indifferent, flatly indifferent. It is, perhaps, plausible that a man in this situation, impressed with the unconcern of the universe, should see the innumerable flaws of his life and have them taste wickedly in his mind and wish for another chance. A distinction between right and wrong seems absurdly clear to him, then, in this new ignorance of the grave-edge, and he understands that if he were given another opportunity he would mend his conduct and his words, and be better and brighter during an introduction, or at a tea.

"Now, boys," said the captain, "she is going to swamp sure. All we can do is to work her in as far as possible, and then when she swamps, pile out and scramble for the beach. Keep cool now, and don't jump until she swamps sure."

The oiler took the oars. Over his shoulders he scanned the surf. "Captain," he said, "I think I'd better bring her about, and keep her head-on to the seas and back her in."

"All right, Billie," said the captain. "Back her in." The oiler swung the boat then and, seated in the stern, the cook and the correspondent were obliged to look over their shoulders to contemplate the lonely and indifferent shore.

The monstrous inshore rollers heaved the boat high until the men were again enabled to see the white sheets of water scudding up the slanted beach. "We won't get in very close," said the captain. Each time a man could wrest his attention from the rollers, he turned his glance toward the shore, and in the expression of the eyes during this contemplation there was a singular quality. The correspondent, observing the others, knew that they were not afraid, but the full meaning of their glances was shrouded.

As for himself, he was too tired to grapple fundamentally with the fact. He tried to coerce his mind into thinking of it, but the mind was dominated at this time by the muscles, and the muscles said they did not care. It merely occurred to him that if he should drown it would be a shame.

There were no hurried words, no pallor, no plain agitation. The men simply looked at the shore. "Now, remember to get well clear of the boat when you jump," said the captain.

Seaward the crest of a roller suddenly fell with a thunderous crash, and the long white comber came roaring down upon the boat.

"Steady now," said the captain. The men were silent. They turned their eyes from the shore to the comber and waited. The boat slid up the incline, leaped at the furious top, bounced over it, and swung down the long back of the wave. Some water had been shipped and the cook bailed it out.

But the next crest crashed also. The tumbling boiling flood of white water caught the boat and whirled it almost perpendicular. Water swarmed in from all sides. The correspondent had his hands on the gunwale at this time, and when the water entered at that place he swiftly withdrew his fingers, as if he objected to wetting them.

The little boat, drunken with this weight of water, reeled and snuggled deeper into the sea.

"Bail her out, cook! Bail her out," said the captain.

"All right, Captain," said the cook.

"Now, boys, the next one will do for us, sure," said the oiler. "Mind to jump clear of the boat."

The third wave moved forward, huge, furious, implacable. It fairly swallowed the dingey, and almost simultaneously the men tumbled into the sea. A piece of life-belt had lain in the bottom of the boat, and as the correspondent went overboard he held this to his chest with his left hand.

The January water was icy, and he reflected immediately that it was colder than he had expected to find it off the coast of Florida. This appeared to his dazed mind as a fact important enough to be noted at the time. The coldness of the water was sad; it was tragic. This fact was somehow so mixed and confused with his opinion of his own situation that it seemed almost a proper reason for tears. The water was cold.

When he came to the surface he was conscious of little but the noisy water. Afterward he saw his companions in the sea. The oiler was ahead in the race. He was swimming strongly and rapidly. Off to the correspondent's left, the cook's great white and corked back bulged out of the water, and in the rear the captain was hanging with his one good hand to the keel of the overturned dingey.

There is a certain immovable quality to a shore, and the correspondent wondered at it amid the confusion of the sea.

It seemed also very attractive, but the correspondent knew that it was a long journey, and he paddled leisurely. The piece of life-preserver lay under him, and sometimes he whirled down the incline of a wave as if he were on a hand-sled.

But finally he arrived at a place in the sea where travel was beset with difficulty. He did not pause swimming to inquire what manner of current had caught him, but there his progress ceased. The shore was set before him like a bit of scenery on a stage, and he looked at it and understood with his eyes each detail of it.

As the cook passed, much farther to the left, the captain was calling to him, "Turn over on your back, cook! Turn over on your back and use the oar."

"All right, sir." The cook turned on his back, and paddling with an oar, went ahead as if he were a canoe.

Presently the boat also passed to the left of the correspondent with the captain clinging with one hand to the keel. He would have appeared like a man raising himself to look over a board fence, if it were not for the extraordinary gymnastics of the boat. The correspondent marvelled that the captain could still hold it.

They passed on, nearer to shore—the oiler, the cook, the captain—and following them went the water-jar, bouncing gayly over the seas.

The correspondent remained in the grip of this strange new enemy—a current. The shore, with its white slope of sand and its green bluff, topped with little silent cottages, was spread like a picture before him. It was very near to him then, but he was impressed as one who in a gallery looks at a scene from Brittany or Holland.

He thought: "I am going to drown? Can it be possible? Can it be possible? Can it be possible?" Perhaps an individual must consider his own death to be the final phenomenon of nature.

But later a wave perhaps whirled him out of this small deadly current, for he found suddenly that he could again make progress toward the shore. Later still, he was aware that the captain, clinging with one hand to the keel of the dingey, had his face turned away from the shore and toward him, and was calling his name. "Come to the boat! Come to the boat!"

In his struggle to reach the captain and the boat, he reflected that when one gets properly wearied, drowning must really be a comfortable arrangement, a cessation of hostilities accompanied by a large degree of relief, and he was glad of it, for the main thing in his mind for some moments had been horror of the temporary agony. He did not wish to be hurt.

Presently he saw a man running along the shore. He was undressing with most remarkable speed. Coat, trousers, shirt, everything flew magically off him.

"Come to the boat," called the captain.

"All right, Captain." As the correspondent paddled, he saw the captain let himself down to bottom and leave the boat. Then the correspondent performed his one little marvel of the voyage. A large wave caught him and flung him with ease and supreme speed completely over the boat and far beyond it. It struck him even then as an event in gymnastics, and a true miracle of the sea. An overturned boat in the surf is not a plaything to a swimming man.

The correspondent arrived in water that reached only to his waist, but his condition did not enable him to stand for more than a moment. Each wave knocked him into a heap, and the under-tow pulled at him.

Then he saw the man who had been running and undressing, and undressing and running, come bounding into the water. He dragged ashore the cook, and then waded toward the captain, but the captain waved him away, and sent him to the correspondent. He was naked, naked as a tree in winter, but a halo was about his head, and he shone like a saint. He gave a strong pull, and a long drag, and a bully heave at the correspondent's hand. The correspondent, schooled in the minor formulae, said: "Thanks, old man." But suddenly the man cried: "What's that?" He pointed a swift finger. The correspondent said: "Go."

In the shallows, face downward, lay the oiler. His forehead touched sand that was periodically, between each wave, clear of the sea.

The correspondent did not know all that transpired afterward.

When he achieved safe ground he fell, striking the sand with each particular part of his body. It was as if he had dropped from a roof, but the thud was grateful to him.

It seems that instantly the beach was populated with men with blankets, clothes, and flasks, and women with coffee-pots and all the remedies sacred to their minds. The welcome of the land to the men from the sea was warm and generous, but a still and dripping shape was carried slowly up the beach, and the land's welcome for it could only be the different and sinister hospitality of the grave.

When it came night, the white waves paced to and fro in the moonlight, and the wind brought the sound of the great sea's voice to the men on shore, and they felt that they could then be interpreters.

1897

The Blue Hotel

I

The Palace Hotel at Fort Romper was painted a light blue, a shade that is on the legs of a kind of heron, causing the bird to declare its position against any background. The Palace Hotel, then, was always screaming and howling in a way that made the dazzling winter landscape of Nebraska seem only a gray swampish hush. It stood alone on the prairie, and when the snow was falling the town two hundred yards away was not visible. But when the traveler alighted at the railway station he was obliged to pass the Palace Hotel before he could come upon the company of low clap-board houses which composed Fort Romper, and it was not to be thought that any traveler could pass the Palace Hotel without looking at it. Pat Scully, the proprietor, had proved himself a master of strategy when he chose his paints. It is true that on clear days, when the great transcontinental expresses, long lines of swaying Pullmans, swept through Fort Romper, passengers were overcome at the sight, and the cult that knows the brown-reds and the subdivisions of the dark greens of the East expressed shame, pity, horror, in a laugh. But to the citizens of this prairie town, and to the people who would naturally stop there, Pat Scully had performed a feat. With this opulence and splendor, these creeds, classes, egotisms, that streamed through Romper on the rails day after day, they had no color in common.

As if the displayed delights of such a blue hotel were not sufficiently enticing, it was Scully's habit to go every morning and evening to meet the leisurely trains that stopped at Romper and work his seductions upon any man that he might see wavering, gripsack in hand.

One morning, when a snow-crusted engine dragged its long string of freight cars and its one passenger coach to the station, Scully performed the marvel of catching three men. One was a shaky and quick-eyed Swede, with a great shining cheap valise; one was a tall bronzed cowboy, who was on his way to a ranch near the Dakota line; one was a little silent man from the East, who didn't look it, and didn't announce it. Scully practically made them prisoners. He was so nimble and merry and kindly that each probably felt it would be the height of brutality to try to escape. They trudged off over the creaking board sidewalks in the wake of the eager little Irishman. He wore a heavy fur cap squeezed tightly down on his head. It caused his two red ears to stick out stiffly, as if they were made of tin.

At last, Scully, elaborately, with boisterous hospitality, conducted them through the portals of the blue hotel. The room which they entered was small. It seemed to be merely a proper temple for an enormous stove, which, in the center, was humming with god-like violence. At various points of its surface the iron had become luminous and glowed yellow from the heat. Beside the stove Scully's son Johnnie was playing High-Five with an old farmer who had whiskers both gray and sandy. They were quarreling. Frequently the old farmer turned his face toward a box of sawdust— colored brown from tobacco juice—that was behind the stove, and spat with an air of great impatience and irritation. With a loud flourish of words Scully destroyed the game of cards, and bustled his son upstairs with part of the baggage of the new guests. He himself conducted them to three basins of the coldest water in the world. The cowboy and the Easterner burnished themselves fiery red with this water, until it seemed to be some kind of a metal polish. The Swede, however, merely dipped his fingers gingerly and with trepidation. It was notable that throughout this series of small ceremonies the three travelers were made to feel that Scully was very benevolent. He was conferring great favors upon them. He handed the towel from one to the other with an air of philanthropic impulse.

Afterward they went to the first room, and, sitting about the stove, listened to Scully's officious clamor at his daughters, who were preparing the midday meal. They reflected in the silence of experienced men who tread carefully amid new people. Nevertheless, the old farmer, stationary, invincible in his chair near the warmest part of the stove, turned his face from the sawdust box frequently and addressed a glowing commonplace to the strangers. Usually he was answered in short but adequate sentences by either the cowboy or the Easterner. The Swede said nothing. He seemed to be occupied in making furtive estimates of each man in the room. One might have thought that he had the sense of silly suspicion which comes to guilt. He resembled a badly frightened man.

Later, at dinner, he spoke a little, addressing his conversation entirely to Scully. He volunteered that he had come from New York where for ten years he had worked as a tailor. These facts seemed to strike Scully as fascinating, and afterward he volunteered that he had lived at Romper for fourteen years. The Swede asked about the crops and the price of labor. He seemed barely to listen to Scully's extended replies. His eyes continued to rove from man to man.

Finally, with a laugh and a wink, he said that some of these Western communities were very dangerous; and after his statement he straightened his legs under the table, tilted his head and laughed again, loudly. It was plain that the demonstration had no meaning to the others. They looked at him wondering and in silence.

II

As the men trooped heavily back into the front room, the two little windows presented views of a turmoiling sea of snow. The huge arms of the wind were making attempts—mighty, circular, futile—to embrace the flakes as they sped. A gate-post like a still man with a blanched face stood aghast amid this profligate fury. In a hearty voice Scully announced the presence of a blizzard. The guests of the blue hotel, lighting their pipes, assented with grunts of lazy masculine contentment. No island of the sea could be exempt in the degree of this little room with its humming stove. Johnnie, son of Scully, in a tone which defined his opinion of his ability as a card-player, challenged the old farmer of both gray and sandy whiskers to a game of High-Five. The farmer agreed with a contemptuous and bitter scoff. They sat close to the stove, and squared their knees under a wide board. The cowboy and the Easterner watched the game with interest. The Swede remained near the window, aloof, but with a countenance that showed signs of an inexplicable excitement.

The play of Johnnie and the gray-beard was suddenly ended by another quarrel. The old man arose while casting a look of heated scorn at his adversary. He slowly buttoned his coat, and then stalked with fabulous dignity from the room. In the discreet silence of all other men the Swede laughed. His laughter rang somehow childish. Men by this time had begun to look at him askance, as if they wished to inquire what ailed him.

A new game was formed jocosely. The cowboy volunteered to become the partner of Johnnie, and they all then turned to ask the Swede to throw in his lot with the little Easterner. He asked some questions about the game, and learning that it wore many names, and that he had played it when it was under an alias, he accepted the invitation. He strode toward the men nervously, as if he expected to be assaulted. Finally, seated, he gazed from face to face and laughed shrilly. This laugh was so strange that the Easterner looked up quickly, the cowboy sat intent and with his mouth open, and Johnnie paused, holding the cards with still fingers.

Afterward there was a short silence. Then Johnnie said: "Well, let's get at it. Come on now!" They pulled their chairs forward until their knees were bunched under the board. They began to play, and their interest in the game caused the others to forget the manner of the Swede.

The cowboy was a board-whacker. Each time that he held superior cards he whanged them, one by one, with exceeding force, down upon the improvised table, and took the tricks with a glowing air of prowess and pride that sent thrills of indignation into the hearts of his opponents. A game with a board-whacker in it is sure to become intense. The countenances of the Easterner and the Swede were miserable whenever the cowboy thundered down his aces and kings, while Johnnie, his eye gleaming with joy, chuckled and chuckled.

Because of the absorbing play none considered the strange ways of the Swede. They paid strict heed to the game. Finally, during a lull caused by a new deal, the Swede suddenly addressed Johnnie: "I suppose there have been a good many men killed in this room." The jaws of the others dropped and they looked at him.

"What in hell are you talking about?" said Johnnie.

The Swede laughed again his blatant laugh, full of a kind of false courage and defiance. "Oh, you know what I mean all right," he answered.

"I'm a liar if I do!" Johnnie protested. The card was halted, and the men stared at the Swede. Johnnie evidently felt that as the son of the proprietor he should make a direct inquiry. "Now, what might you be drivin' at, mister?" he asked. The Swede winked at him. It was a wink full of cunning. His fingers shook on the edge of the board. "Oh, maybe you think I have been to nowheres. Maybe you think I'm a tenderfoot?"

"I don't know nothin' about you," answered Johnnie, "and I don't give a damn where you've been. All I got to say is that I don't know what you're driving at. There hain't never been nobody killed in this room."

The cowboy, who had been steadily gazing at the Swede, then spoke. "What's wrong with you, mister?"

Apparently it seemed to the Swede that he was formidably menaced. He shivered and turned white near the corners of his mouth. He sent an appealing glance in the direction of the little Easterner. During these moments he did not forget to wear his air of advanced pot-valor.[1] "They say they don't know what I mean," he remarked mockingly to the Easterner.

The latter answered after prolonged and cautious reflection. "I don't understand you," he said, impassively.

The Swede made a movement then which announced that he thought he had encountered treachery from the only quarter where he had expected sympathy if not help. "Oh, I see you are all against me. I see——"

The cowboy was in a state of deep stupefaction. "Say," he cried, as he tumbled the deck violently down upon the board. "Say, what are you gittin' at, hey?"

The Swede sprang up with the celerity of a man escaping from a snake on the floor. "I don't want to fight!" he shouted. "I don't want to fight!"

The cowboy stretched his long legs indolently and deliberately. His hands were in his pockets. He spat into the sawdust box. "Well, who the hell thought you did?" he inquired.

The Swede backed rapidly toward a corner of the room. His hands were out protectingly in front of his chest, but he was making an obvious struggle to control his fright. "Gentlemen," he quavered, "I suppose I am going to be killed before I can leave this house! I suppose I am going to be killed before I can leave this house!" In his eyes was the dying swan look. Through the windows could be seen the snow turning blue in the shadow of dusk. The wind tore at the house and some loose thing beat regularly against the clapboards like a spirit tapping.

A door opened, and Scully himself entered. He paused in surprise as he noted the tragic attitude of the Swede. Then he said: "What's the matter here?"

The Swede answered him swiftly and eagerly: "These men are going to kill me."

"Kill you!" ejaculated Scully. "Kill you! What are you talkin'?"

The Swede made the gesture of a martyr.

Scully wheeled sternly upon his son. "What is this, Johnnie?"

The lad had grown sullen. "Damned if I know," he answered. "I can't make no

---

[1] The bravado of drunkenness.

sense to it." He began to shuffle the cards, fluttering them together with an angry snap. "He says a good many men have been killed in this room, or something like that. And he says he's goin' to be killed here too. I don't know what ails him. He's crazy, I shouldn't wonder."

Scully then looked for explanation to the cowboy, but the cowboy simply shrugged his shoulders.

"Kill you?" said Scully again to the Swede. "Kill you? Man, you're off your nut."

"Oh, I know," burst out the Swede. "I know what will happen. Yes. I'm crazy —yes. Yes, of course, I'm crazy—yes. But I know one thing——" There was a sort of sweat of misery and terror upon his face. "I know I won't get out of here alive."

The cowboy drew a deep breath, as if his mind was passing into the last stages of dissolution. "Well, I'm dog-goned," he whispered to himself.

Scully wheeled suddenly and faced his son. "You've been troublin' this man!"

Johnnie's voice was loud with its burden of grievance. "Why, good Gawd, I ain't done nothin' to 'im."

The Swede broke in. "Gentlemen, do not disturb yourselves. I will leave this house. I will go 'way because——" He accused them dramatically with his glance. "Because I do not want to be killed."

Scully was furious with his son. "Will you tell me what is the matter, you young divil? What's the matter, anyhow? Speak out!"

"Blame it," cried Johnnie in despair, "don't I tell you I don't know. He—he says we want to kill him, and that's all I know. I can't tell what ails him."

The Swede continued to repeat: "Never mind, Mr. Scully, never mind. I will leave this house. I will go away, because I do not wish to be killed. Yes, of course, I am crazy—yes. But I know one thing! I will go away. I will leave this house. Never mind, Mr. Scully, never mind. I will go away."

"You will not go 'way," said Scully. "You will not go 'way until I hear the reason of this business. If anybody has troubled you I will take care of him. This is my house. You are under my roof, and I will not allow any peaceable man to be troubled here." He cast a terrible eye upon Johnnie, the cowboy, and the Easterner.

"Never mind, Mr. Scully, never mind. I will go 'way. I do not wish to be killed." The Swede moved toward the door, which opened upon the stairs. It was evidently his intention to go at once for his baggage.

"No, no," shouted Scully peremptorily; but the white-faced man slid by him and disappeared. "Now," said Scully severely, "what does this mane?" Johnnie and the cowboy cried together: "Why, we didn't do nothin' to im!"

Scully's eyes were cold. "No," he said, "you didn't?"

Johnnie swore a deep oath. "Why, this is the wildest loon I ever see. We didn't do nothin' at all. We were jest sittin' here playin' cards and he——"

The father suddenly spoke to the Easterner. "Mr. Blanc," he asked, "what has these boys been doin'?"

The Easterner reflected again. "I didn't see anything wrong at all," he said at last slowly.

Scully began to howl. "But what does it mane?" He stared ferociously at his son. "I have a mind to lather you for this, me boy."

Johnnie was frantic. "Well, what have I done?" he bawled at his father.

III

"I think you are tongue-tied," said Scully finally to his son, the cowboy and the Easterner, and at the end of this scornful sentence he left the room.

Upstairs the Swede was swiftly fastening the straps of his great valise. Once his back happened to be half-turned toward the door, and hearing a noise there, he wheeled and sprang up, uttering a loud cry. Scully's wrinkled visage showed grimly in the light of the small lamp he carried. This yellow effulgence, streaming upward, colored only his prominent features, and left his eyes, for instance, in mysterious shadow. He resembled a murderer.

"Man, man!" he exclaimed, "have you gone daffy?"

"Oh, no! Oh, no!" rejoined the other. "There are people in this world who know pretty nearly as much as you do—understand?"

For a moment they stood gazing at each other. Upon the Swede's deathly pale cheeks were two spots brightly crimson and sharply edged, as if they had been carefully painted. Scully placed the light on the table and sat himself on the edge of the bed. He spoke ruminatively. "By cracky, I never heard of such a thing in my life. It's a complete muddle. I can't for the soul of me think how you ever got this idea into your head." Presently he lifted his eyes and asked: "And did you sure think they were going to kill you?"

The Swede scanned the old man as if he wished to see into his mind. "I did," he said at last. He obviously suspected that this answer might precipitate an outbreak. As he pulled on a strap his whole arm shook, the elbow wavering like a bit of paper.

Scully banged his hand impressively on the foot-board of the bed. "Why, man, we're goin' to have a line of ilictric street-cars in this town next spring."

"'A line of electric street-cars,'" repeated the Swede stupidly.

"And," said Scully, "there's a new railroad goin' to be built down from Broken Arm to here. Not to mintion the four churches and the smashin' big brick school-house. Then there's the big factory, too. Why, in two years Romper'll be a met-tro-*pol*-is."

Having finished the preparation of his baggage, the Swede straightened himself. "Mr. Scully," he said with sudden hardihood, "how much do I owe you?"

"You don't owe me anythin'," said the old man angrily.

"Yes, I do," retorted the Swede. He took seventy-five cents from his pocket and tendered it to Scully; but the latter snapped his fingers in disdainful refusal. However, it happened that they both stood gazing in a strange fashion at three silver pieces on the Swede's open palm.

"I'll not take your money," said Scully at last. "Not after what's been goin' on here." Then a plan seemed to strike him. "Here," he cried, picking up his lamp and moving toward the door. "Here! Come with me a minute."

"No," said the Swede in overwhelming alarm.

"Yes," urged the old man. "Come on! I want you to come and see a picter—just across the hall—in my room."

The Swede must have concluded that his hour was come. His jaw dropped and his teeth showed like a dead man's. He ultimately followed Scully across the corridor, but he had the step of one hung in chains.

Scully flashed the light high on the wall of his own chamber. There was revealed a ridiculous photograph of a little girl. She was leaning against a balustrade of gorgeous decoration, and the formidable bang to her hair was prominent. The figure was as graceful as an upright sled-stake, and, withal, it was of the hue of lead. "There," said Scully tenderly. "That's the picter of my little girl that died. Her name was Carrie. She had the purtiest hair you ever saw! I was that fond of her, she—"

Turning then he saw that the Swede was not contemplating the picture at all, but, instead, was keeping keen watch on the gloom in the rear.

"Look, man!" shouted Scully heartily. "That's the picter of my little gal that died. Her name was Carrie. And then here's the picter of my oldest boy, Michael. He's a lawyer in Lincoln an' doin' well. I gave that boy a grand eddycation, and I'm glad for it now. He's fine boy. Look at 'im now. Ain't he bold as blazes, him there in Lincoln, an honored an' respicted gintleman. An honored an' respicted gintleman," concluded Scully with a flourish. And so saying, he smote the Swede jovially on the back.

The Swede faintly smiled.

"Now," said the old man, "there's only one more thing," He dropped suddenly to the floor and thrust his head beneath the bed. The Swede could hear his muffled voice. "I'd keep it under me piller if it wasn't for that boy Johnnie. Then there's the old woman—Where is it now? I never put it twice in the same place. Ah, now come out with you!"

Presently he backed clumsily from under the bed, dragging with him an old coat rolled into a bundle. "I've fetched him," he muttered. Kneeling on the floor he unrolled the coat and extracted from its heart a large yellow-brown whisky bottle.

His first maneuver was to hold the bottle up to the light. Reassured, apparently, that nobody had been tampering with it, he thrust it with a generous movement toward the Swede.

The weak-kneed Swede was about to eagerly clutch this element of strength, but he suddenly jerked his hand away and cast a look of horror upon Scully.

"Drink," said the old man affectionately. He had arisen to his feet, and now stood facing the Swede.

There was a silence. Then again Scully said: "Drink!"

The Swede laughed wildly. He grabbed the bottle, put it to his mouth, and as his lips curled absurdly around the opening and his throat worked, he kept his glance burning with hatred upon the old man's face.

IV

After the departure of Scully the three men, with the card-board still upon their knees, preserved for a long time an astounded silence. Then Johnnie said: "That's the dod-dangest Swede I ever see."

"He ain't no Swede," said the cowboy scornfully.

"Well, what is he then?" cried Johnnie. "What is he then?"

"It's my opinion," replied the cowboy deliberately, "he's some kind of a Dutchman." It was a venerable custom of the country to entitle as Swedes all light-haired men who spoke with a heavy tongue. In consequence the idea of the cowboy was not without its daring. "Yes, sir," he repeated. "It's my opinion this feller is some kind of a Dutchman."

"Well, he says he's a Swede, anyhow," muttered Johnnie sulkily. He turned to the Easterner: "What do you think, Mr. Blanc?"

"Oh, I don't know,'" replied the Easterner.

"Well, what do you think makes him act that way?" asked the cowboy.

"Why, he's frightened!" The Easterner knocked his pipe against a rim of the stove. "He's clear frightened out of his boots."

"What at?" cried Johnnie and cowboy together.

The Easterner reflected over his answer.

"What at?" cried the others again.

"Oh, I don't know, but it seems to me this man has been reading dime-novels, and he thinks he's right out in the middle of it—the shootin' and stabbin' and all."

"But," said the cowboy, deeply scandalized, "this ain't Wyoming, ner none of them places. This is Nebrasker."

"Yes," added Johnnie, "an' why don't he wait till he gits *out West?*"

The traveled Easterner laughed. "It isn't different there even—not in these days. But he thinks he's right in the middle of hell."

Johnnie and the cowboy mused long.

"It's awful funny," remarked Johnnie at last.

"Yes," said the cowboy. "This is a queer game. I hope we don't git snowed in, because then we'd have to stand this here man bein' around with us all the time. That wouldn't be no good."

"I wish pop would throw him out," said Johnnie.

Presently they heard a loud stamping on the stairs, accompanied by ringing jokes in the voice of old Scully, and laughter, evidently from the Swede. The men around the stove stared vacantly at each other. "Gosh," said the cowboy. The door flew open, and old Scully, flushed and anecdotal, came into the room. He was jabbering at the Swede, who followed him, laughing bravely. It was the entry of two roysterers from a banquet hall.

"Come now," said Scully sharply to the three seated men, "move up and give us a chance at the stove." The cowboy and the Easterner obediently sidled their chairs to make room for the newcomers. Johnnie, however, simply arranged himself in a more indolent attitude, and then remained motionless.

"Come! Git over, there," said Scully.

"Plenty of room on the other side of the stove," said Johnnie.

"Do you think we want to sit in the draught?" roared the father.

But the Swede here interposed with a grandeur of confidence. "No, no. Let the boy sit where he likes," he cried in a bullying voice to the father.

"All right! All right!" said Scully deferentially. The cowboy and the Easterner exchanged glances of wonder.

The five chairs were formed in a crescent about one side of the stove. The Swede began to talk; he talked arrogantly, profanely, angrily. Johnnie, the cowboy and the Easterner maintained a morose silence, while old Scully appeared to be receptive and eager, breaking in constantly with sympathetic ejaculations.

Finally the Swede announced that he was thirsty. He moved in his chair, and said that he would go for a drink of water.

"I'll git it for you," cried Scully at once.

"No," said the Swede contemptuously. "I'll get it for myself." He arose and stalked with the air of an owner off into the executive parts of the hotel.

As soon as the Swede was out of hearing Scully sprang to his feet and whispered intensely to the others. "Upstairs he thought I was tryin' to poison 'im."

"Say," said Johnnie, "this makes me sick. Why don't you throw 'im out in the snow?"

"Why, he's all right now," declared Scully. "It was only that he was from the East and he thought this was a tough place. That's all. He's all right now."

The cowboy looked with admiration upon the Easterner. "You were straight," he said. "You were on to that there Dutchman."

"Well," said Johnnie to his father, "he may be all right now, but I don't see it. Other time he was scared, and now he's too fresh."

Scully's speech was always a combination of Irish brogue and idiom, Western twang and idiom, and scraps of curiously formal diction taken from the storybooks and newspapers. He now hurled a strange mass of language at the head of his son. "What do I keep? What do I keep? What do I keep?" he demanded in a voice of thunder. He slapped his knee impressively, to indicate that he himself was going to make reply, and that all should heed. "I keep a hotel," he shouted. "A hotel, do you mind? A guest under my roof has sacred privileges. He is to be intimidated by none. Not one word shall he hear that would prijudice him in favor of goin' away. I'll not have it. There's no place in this here town where they can say they iver took in a guest of mine because he was afraid to stay here." He wheeled suddenly upon the cowboy and the Easterner. "Am I right?"

"Yes, Mr. Scully," said the cowboy, "I think you're right."

"Yes, Mr. Scully," said the Easterner, "I think you're right."

V

At six-o'clock supper, the Swede fizzed like a fire-wheel. He sometimes seemed on the point of bursting into riotous song, and in all his madness he was encouraged by old Scully. The Easterner was incased in reserve; the cowboy sat in wide-mouthed amazement, forgetting to eat, while Johnnie wrathily demolished great plates of food. The daughters of the house when they were obliged to replenish the biscuits approached as warily as Indians, and, having succeeded in their purposes, fled with ill-concealed trepidation. The Swede domineered the whole feast, and he gave it the appearance of a cruel bacchanal. He seemed to have grown suddenly taller; he gazed, brutally disdainful, into every face. His voice rang through the room. Once when he jabbed out harpoon-fashion with his fork to pinion a biscuit the weapon nearly impaled the hand of the Easterner which had been stretched quietly out for the same biscuit.

After supper, as the men filed toward the other room, the Swede smote Scully ruthlessly on the shoulder. "Well, old boy, that was a good square meal." Johnnie looked hopefully at his father; he knew that shoulder was tender from an old fall; and indeed it appeared for a moment as if Scully was going to flame out over the matter, but in the end he smiled a sickly smile and remained silent. The others understood from his manner that he was admitting his responsibility for the Swede's new viewpoint.

Johnnie, however, addressed his parent in an aside. "Why don't you license somebody to kick you downstairs?" Scully scowled darkly by way of reply.

When they were gathered about the stove, the Swede insisted on another game of High-Five. Scully gently deprecated the plan at first, but the Swede turned a wolfish glare upon him. The old man subsided, and the Swede canvassed the others. In his tone there was always a great threat. The cowboy and the Easterner both remarked indifferently that they would play. Scully said that he would presently have to go to meet the 6.58 train, and so the Swede turned menacingly upon Johnnie. For a moment their glances crossed like blades, and then Johnnie smiled and said, "Yes, I'll play."

They formed a square with the little board on their knees. The Easterner and the Swede were again partners. As the play went on, it was noticeable that the cowboy was not board-whacking as usual. Meanwhile, Scully, near the lamp, had put on his spectacles and, with an appearance curiously like an old priest, was reading a newspaper. In time he went out to meet the 6.58 train, and, despite his precautions, a gust of polar wind whirled into the room as he opened the door. Besides scattering the cards, it chilled the players to the marrow. The Swede cursed frightfully. When Scully returned, his entrance disturbed a cozy and friendly scene. The Swede again cursed. But presently they were once more intent, their heads bent forward and their hands moving swiftly. The Swede had adopted the fashion of board-whacking.

Scully took up his paper and for a long time remained immersed in matters which were extraordinarily remote from him. The lamp burned badly, and once he stopped to adjust the wick. The newspaper as he turned from page to page rustled with a slow and comfortable sound. Then suddenly he heard three terrible words: "You are cheatin'!"

Such scenes often prove that there can be little of dramatic import in environment. Any room can present a tragic front; any room can be comic. This little den was now hideous as a torture-chamber. The new faces of the men themselves had changed it upon the instant. The Swede held a huge fist in front of Johnnie's face, while the latter looked steadily over it into the blazing orbs of his accuser. The Easterner had grown pallid; the cowboy's jaw had dropped in that expression of bovine amazement which was one of his important mannerisms. After the three words, the first sound in the room was made by Scully's paper as it floated forgotten to his feet. His spectacles had also fallen from his nose, but by a clutch he had saved them in air. His hand, grasping the spectacles, now remained poised awkwardly and near his shoulder. He stared at the card-players.

Probably the silence was while a second elapsed. Then, if the floor had been suddenly twitched out from under the men they could not have moved quicker. The five had projected themselves headlong toward a common point. It happened that Johnnie in rising to hurl himself upon the Swede had stumbled slightly because of his curiously instinctive care for the cards and the board. The loss of the moment allowed time for the arrival of Scully, and also allowed the cowboy time to give the Swede a great push which sent him staggering back. The men found tongue together, and hoarse shouts of rage, appeal or fear burst from every throat. The cowboy pushed and jostled feverishly at the Swede, and the Easterner and Scully clung wildly to Johnnie; but, through the smoky air, above the swaying bodies of the peace-compellers, the eyes of the two warriors ever sought each other in glances of challenge that were at once hot and steely.

Of course the board had been overturned, and now the whole company of cards was scattered over the floor, where the boots of the men trampled the fat and painted kings and queens as they gazed with their silly eyes at the war that was waging above them.

Scully's voice was dominating the yells. "Stop now! Stop, I say! Stop, now—"

Johnnie, as he struggled to burst through the rank formed by Scully and the Easterner, was crying: "Well, he says I cheated! He says I cheated! I won't allow no man to say I cheated! If he says I cheated, he's a —————— ————!"

The cowboy was telling the Swede: "Quit, now! Quit, d'ye hear—"

The screams of the Swede never cease. "He did cheat! I saw him! I saw him—"

As for the Easterner, he was importuning in a voice that was not heeded. "Wait a moment, can't you? Oh, wait a moment. What's the good of a fight over a game of cards? Wait a moment—"

In this tumult no complete sentences were clear. "Cheat"—"Quit"—"He says"— These fragments pierced the uproar and rang out sharply. It was remarkable that whereas Scully undoubtedly made the most noise, he was the least heard of any of the riotous band.

Then suddenly there was a great cessation. It was as if each man had paused for breath, and although the room was still lighted with the anger of men, it could be seen that there was no danger of immediate conflict, and at once Johnnie, shouldering his way forward, almost succeeded in confronting the Swede. "What did you say I cheated for? What did you say I cheated for? I don't cheat and I won't let no man say I do!"

The Swede said: "I saw you! I saw you!"

"Well," cried Johnnie, "I'll fight any man what says I cheat!"

"No, you won't," said the cowboy. "Not here."

"Ah, be still, can't you?" said Scully, coming between them.

The quiet was sufficient to allow the Easterner's voice to be heard. He was repeating: "Oh, wait a moment, can't you? What's the good of a fight over a game of cards? Wait a moment."

Johnnie, his red face appearing above his father's shoulder, hailed the Swede again. "Did you say I cheated?"

The Swede showed his teeth. "Yes."

"Then," said Johnnie, "we must fight."

"Yes, fight," roared the Swede. He was like a demoniac. "Yes, fight! I'll show you what kind of a man I am! I'll show you who you want to fight! Maybe you think I can't fight! Maybe you think I can't! I'll show you, you skin, you card-sharp! Yes, you cheated! You cheated! You cheated!"

"Well, let's git at it, then, mister," said Johnnie coolly.

The cowboy's brow was beaded with sweat from his efforts in intercepting all sorts of raids. He turned in despair to Scully. "What are you goin' to do now?"

A change had come over the Celtic visage of the old man. He now seemed all eagerness; his eyes glowed.

"We'll let them fight," he answered stalwartly. "I can't put up with it any longer. I've stood this damned Swede till I'm sick. We'll let them fight."

VI

The men prepared to go out of doors. The Easterner was so nervous that he had great difficulty in getting his arms into the sleeves of his new leather-coat. As the cowboy drew his fur-cap down over his ears his hands trembled. In fact, Johnnie and old Scully were the only ones who displayed no agitation. These preliminaries were conducted without words.

Scully threw open the door. "Well, come on," he said. Instantly a terrific wind caused the flame of the lamp to struggle at its wick, while a puff of black smoke sprang from the chimney-top. The stove was in mid-current of the blast, and its voice swelled to equal the roar of the storm. Some of the scarred and bedabbled cards were caught up from the floor and dashed helplessly against the further wall. The men lowered their heads and plunged into the tempest as into a sea.

No snow was falling, but great whirls and clouds of flakes, swept up from the ground by the frantic winds, were streaming southward with the speed of bullets. The covered land was blue with the sheen of an unearthly satin, and there was no other hue save where at the low black railway station—which seemed incredibly distant —one light gleamed like a tiny jewel. As the men floundered into a thigh-deep drift, it was known that the Swede was bawling out something. Scully went to him, put a hand on his shoulder and projected an ear. "What's that you say?" he shouted.

"I say," bawled the Swede again, "I won't stand much show against this gang. I know you'll all pitch on me."

Scully smote him reproachfully on the arm. "Tut, man," he yelled. The wind tore the words from Scully's lips and scattered them far a-lee.

"You are all a gang of ———" boomed the Swede, but the storm also seized the remainder of this sentence.

Immediately turning their backs upon the wind, the men had swung around a corner to the sheltered side of the hotel. It was the function of the little house to preserve here, amid this great devastation of snow, an irregular V-shape of heavily-incrusted grass, which crackled beneath the feet. One could imagine the great drifts piled against the windward side. When the party reached the comparative peace of this spot it was found that the Swede was still bellowing.

"Oh, I know what kind of a thing this is! I know you'll all pitch on me. I can't lick you all!"

Scully turned upon him panther-fashion. "You'll not have to whip all of us. You'll have to whip my son Johnnie. An' the man what troubles you durin' that time will have me to dale with."

The arrangements were swiftly made. The two men faced each other, obedient to the harsh commands of Scully, whose face, in the subtly luminous gloom, could be seen set in the austere impersonal lines that are pictured on the countenances of the Roman veterans. The Easterner's teeth were chattering, and he was hopping up and down like a mechanical toy. The cowboy stood rock-like.

The contestants had not stripped off any clothing. Each was in his ordinary attire.

Their fists were up, and they eyed each other in a calm that had the elements of leonine cruelty in it.

During this pause, the Easterner's mind, like a film, took lasting impressions of three men—the iron-nerved master of the ceremony; the Swede, pale, motionless, terrible; and Johnnie, serene yet ferocious, brutish yet heroic. The entire prelude had in it a tragedy greater than the tragedy of action, and this aspect was accentuated by the long mellow cry of the blizzard, as it sped the tumbling and wailing flakes into the black abyss of the south.

"Now!" said Scully.

The two combatants leaped forward and crashed together like bullocks. There was heard the cushioned sound of blows, and of a curse squeezing out from between the tight teeth of one.

As for the spectators, the Easterner's pent-up breath exploded from him with a pop of relief, absolute relief from the tension of the preliminaries. The cowboy bounded into the air with a yowl. Scully was immovable as from supreme amazement and fear at the fury of the fight which he himself had permitted and arranged.

For a time the encounter in the darkness was such a perplexity of flying arms that it presented no more detail than would a swiftly-revolving wheel. Occasionally a face, as if illumined by a flash of light, would shine out, ghastly and marked with pink spots. A moment later, the men might have been known as shadows, if it were not for the involuntary utterance of oaths that came from them in whispers.

Suddenly a holocaust of warlike desire caught the cowboy, and he bolted forward with the speed of a broncho. "Go it, Johnnie; go it! Kill him! Kill him!"

Scully confronted him. "Kape back," he said; and by his glance the cowboy could tell that this man was Johnnie's father.

To the Easterner there was a monotony of unchangeable fighting that was an abomination. This confused mingling was eternal to his sense, which was concentrated in a longing for the end, the priceless end. Once the fighters lurched near him, and as he scrambled hastily backward, he heard them breathe like men on the rack.

"Kill him, Johnnie! Kill him! Kill him! Kill him!" The cowboy's face was contorted like one of those agony-masks in museums.

"Keep still," said Scully icily.

Then there was a sudden loud grunt, incomplete, cut-short, and Johnnie's body swung away from the Swede and fell with sickening heaviness to the grass. The cowboy was barely in time to prevent the mad Swede from flinging himself upon his prone adversary. "No, you don't," said the cowboy, interposing an arm. "Wait a second."

Scully was at his son's side. "Johnnie! Johnnie, me boy?" His voice had a quality of melancholy tenderness. "Johnnie? Can you go on with it?" He looked anxiously down into the bloody pulpy face of his son.

There was a moment of silence, and then Johnnie answered in his ordinary voice: "Yes, I—it—yes."

Assisted by his father he struggled to his feet. "Wait a bit now till you git your wind," said the old man.

A few paces away the cowboy was lecturing the Swede. "No, you don't! Wait a second!"

The Easterner was plucking at Scully's sleeve. "Oh, this is enough," he pleaded. "This is enough! Let it go as it stands. This is enough!"

"Bill," said Scully, "git out of the road." The cowboy stepped aside. "Now." The combatants were actuated by a new caution as they advanced toward collision. They glared at each other, and then the Swede aimed a lightning blow that carried with it his entire weight. Johnnie was evidently half-stupid from weakness, but he miraculously dodged, and his fist sent the over-balanced Swede sprawling.

The cowboy, Scully and the Easterner burst into a cheer that was like a chorus of triumphant soldiery, but before its conclusion the Swede had scuffled agilely to his feet and come in berserk abandon at his foe. There was another perplexity of flying arms, and Johnnie's body again swung away and fell, even as a bundle might fall from a roof. The Swede instantly staggered to a little wind-waved tree and leaned upon it, breathing like an engine, while his savage and flame-lit eyes roamed from face to face as the men bent over Johnnie. There was a splendor of isolation in his situation at this time which the Easterner felt once when, lifting his eyes from the man on the ground, he beheld that mysterious and lonely figure, waiting.

"Are you any good yet, Johnnie?" asked Scully in a broken voice.

The son gasped and opened his eyes languidly. After a moment he answered: "No —I ain't—any good—any—more." Then, from shame and bodily ill, he began to weep, the tears furrowing down through the blood-stains on his face. "He was too —too—too heavy for me."

Scully straightened and addressed the waiting figure. "Stranger," he said, evenly, "it's all up with our side." Then his voice changed into that vibrant huskiness which is commonly the tone of the most simple and deadly announcements. "Johnnie is whipped."

Without replying, the victor moved off on the route to the front door of the hotel.

The cowboy was formulating new and unspellable blasphemies. The Easterner was startled to find that they were out in a wind that seemed to come direct from the shadowed arctic floes. He heard again the wail of the snow as it was flung to its grave in the south. He knew now that all this time the cold had been sinking into him deeper and deeper, and he wondered that he had not perished. He felt indifferent to the condition of the vanquished man.

"Johnnie, can you walk?" asked Scully.

"Did I hurt—hurt him any?" asked the son.

"Can you walk, boy? Can you walk?"

Johnnie's voice was suddenly strong. There was a robust impatience in it. "I asked you whether I hurt him any!"

"Yes, yes, Johnnie," answered the cowboy consolingly; "he's hurt a good deal."

They raised him from the ground, and as soon as he was on his feet he went tottering off, rebuffing all attempts at assistance. When the party rounded the corner they were fairly blinded by the pelting of the snow. It burned their faces like fire. The cowboy carried Johnnie through the drift to the door. As they entered some cards again rose from the floor and beat against the wall.

The Easterner rushed to the stove. He was so profoundly chilled that he almost dared to embrace the glowing iron. The Swede was not in the room. Johnnie sank into a chair, and folding his arms on his knees, buried his face in them. Scully, warming one foot and then the other at a rim of the stove, muttered to himself with Celtic mournfulness. The cowboy had removed his fur-cap, and with a dazed and rueful air he was now running one hand through his tousled locks. From overhead they could hear the creaking of boards, as the Swede tramped here and there in his room.

The sad quiet was broken by the sudden flinging open of a door that led toward the kitchen. It was instantly followed by an inrush of women. They precipitated themselves upon Johnnie amid a chorus of lamentation. Before they carried their prey off to the kitchen, there to be bathed and harangued with that mixture of sympathy and abuse which is a feat of their sex, the mother straightened herself and fixed old Scully with an eye of stern reproach. "Shame be upon you, Patrick Scully!" she cried. "Your own son, too. Shame be upon you!"

"There, now! Be quiet, now!" said the old man weakly.

"Shame be upon you, Patrick Scully!" The girls, rallying to this slogan, sniffed disdainfully in the direction of these trembling accomplices, the cowboy and the Easterner. Presently they bore Johnnie away, and left the three men to dismal reflection.

VII

"I'd like to fight this here Dutchman myself," said the cowboy, breaking a long silence.

Scully wagged his head sadly. "No, that wouldn't do. It wouldn't be right. It wouldn't be right."

"Well, why wouldn't it?" argued the cowboy. "I don't see no harm in it."

"No," answered Scully with mournful heroism. "It wouldn't be right. It was Johnnie's fight, and now we mustn't whip the man just because he whipped Johnnie."

"Yes, that's true enough," said the cowboy: "but—he better not get fresh with me, because I couldn't stand no more of it."

"You'll not say a word to him," commanded Scully, and even then they heard the tread of the Swede on the stairs. His entrance was made theatric. He swept the door back with a bang and swaggered to the middle of the room. No one looked at him. 'Well," he cried, insolently, at Scully, "I s'pose you'll tell me now how much I owe you?"

The old man remained stolid. "You didn't owe me nothin'."

"Huh!" said the Swede, "huh! Don't owe 'im nothin'."

The cowboy addressed the Swede. "Stranger, I don't see how you come to be so gay around here."

Old Scully was instantly alert. "Stop!" he shouted, holding his hand forth, fingers upward. "Bill, you shut up!"

The cowboy spat carelessly into the sawdust box. "I didn't say a word, did I?" he asked.

"Mr. Scully," called the Swede, "how much do I owe you?" It was seen that he was attired for departure, and that he had his valise in his hand.

"You don't owe me nothin'," repeated Scully in his same imperturbable way.

"Huh!" said the Swede. "I guess you're right. I guess if it was any way at all, you'd owe me somethin'. That's what I guess." He turned to the cowboy. " 'Kill him! Kill him! Kill him!' " he mimicked, and then guffawed victoriously. " 'Kill him!' " He was convulsed with ironical humor.

But he might have been jeering the dead. The three men were immovable and silent, staring with glassy eyes at the stove.

The Swede opened the door and passed into the storm, giving one derisive glance backward at the still group.

As soon as the door was closed, Scully and the cowboy leaped to their feet and began to curse. They trampled to and fro, waving their arms and smashing into the air with their fists. "Oh, but that was a hard minute!" wailed Scully. "That was a hard minute! Him there leerin' and scoffin'! One bang at his nose was worth forty dollars to me that minute! How did you stand it, Bill?"

"How did I stand it?" cried the cowboy in a quivering voice. "How did I stand it? Oh!"

The old man burst into sudden brogue. "I'd loike to take that Swade," he wailed, "and hould 'im down on a shtone flure and bate 'im to a jelly wid a shtick!"

The cowboy groaned in sympathy. "I'd like to git him by the neck and ha-ammer him"—he brought his hand on a chair with a noise like a pistol-shot—"hammer that there Dutchman until he couldn't tell himself from a dead coyote!"

"I'd bate 'im until he—"

"I'd show *him* some things—"

And then together they raised a yearning fanatic cry. "Oh-o-oh! if we only could—"

"Yes!"

"Yes!"

"And then I'd—"

"O-o-oh!"

VIII

The Swede, tightly gripping his valise, tacked across the face of the storm as if he carried sails. He was following a line of little naked gasping trees, which he knew must mark the way of the road. His face, fresh from the pounding of Johnnie's fists, felt more pleasure than pain in the wind and the driving snow. A number of square shapes loomed upon him finally, and he knew them as the houses of the main body of the town. He found a street and made travel along it, leaning heavily upon the wind whenever, at a corner, a terrific blast caught him.

He might have been in a deserted village. We picture the world as thick with conquering and elated humanity, but here, with the bugles of the tempest pealing, it was hard to imagine a peopled earth. One viewed the existence of man then as a marvel, and conceded a glamour of wonder to these lice which were caused to cling to a whirling, fire-smote, ice-locked, disease-stricken, space-lost bulb. The conceit of man was explained by this storm to be the very engine of life. One was a coxcomb not to die in it. However, the Swede found a saloon.

In front of it an indomitable red light was burning, and the snow-flakes were made blood-color as they flew through the circumscribed territory of the lamp's shining. The Swede pushed open the door of the saloon and entered. A sanded expanse was before him, and at the end of it four men sat about a table drinking. Down one side of the room extended a radiant bar, and its guardian was leaning upon his elbows listening to the talk of the men at the table. The Swede dropped his valise upon the floor, and, smiling fraternally upon the barkeeper, said: "Gimme some whisky, will you?" The man placed a bottle, a whisky-glass, and a glass of ice-thick water upon the bar. The Swede poured himself an abnormal portion of whisky and drank it in three gulps. "Pretty bad night," remarked the bartender indifferently. He was making the pretension of blindness, which is usually a distinction of his class; but it could have been seen that he was furtively studying the half-erased blood-stains on the face of the Swede. "Bad night," he said again.

"Oh, it's good enough for me," replied the Swede, hardily, as he poured himself some more whisky. The barkeeper took his coin and maneuvered it through its reception by the highly-nickeled cash-machine. A bell rang; a card labeled "20 cts." had appeared.

"No," continued the Swede, "this isn't too bad weather. It's good enough for me."

"So?" murmured the barkeeper languidly.

The copious drams made the Swede's eyes swim, and he breathed a trifle heavier. "Yes, I like this weather. I like it. It suits me." It was apparently his design to impart a deep significance to these words.

"So?" murmured the bartender again. He turned to gaze dreamily at the scroll-like birds and bird-like scrolls which had been drawn with soap upon the mirrors back of the bar.

"Well, I guess I'll take another drink," said the Swede presently. "Have something?"

"No, thanks; I'm not drinkin'," answered the bartender. Afterward he asked: "How did you hurt your face?"

The Swede immediately began to boast loudly. "Why, in a fight. I thumped the soul out of a man down here at Scully's hotel."

The interest of the four men at the table was at last aroused.

"Who was it?" said one.

"Johnnie Scully," blustered the Swede. "Son of the man what runs it. He will be pretty near dead for some weeks, I can tell you. I made a nice thing of him, I did. He couldn't get up. They carried him in the house. Have a drink?"

Instantly the men in some subtle way incased themselves in reserve. "No, thanks," said one. The group was of curious formation. Two were prominent local business men; one was the district-attorney; and one was a professional gambler of the kind known as "square." But a scrutiny of the group would not have enabled an observer to pick the gambler from the men of more reputable pursuits. He was, in fact, a man so delicate in manner, when among people of fair class, and so judicious in his choice of victims, that in the strictly masculine part of the town's life he had come to be explicitly trusted and admired. People called him a thoroughbred. The fear and contempt with which his craft was regarded was undoubtedly the reason that his quiet dignity shone conspicuous above the quiet dignity of men who might be merely hatters, billiard-markers or grocery clerks. Beyond an occasional unwary traveler, who came by rail, this gambler was supposed to prey solely upon reckless and senile farmers, who, when flush with good crops, drove into town in all the pride and confidence of an absolutely invulnerable stupidity. Hearing at times in circuitous fashion of the despoilment of such a farmer, the important men of Romper invariably laughed in contempt of the victim, and if they thought of the wolf at all, it was with a kind of pride at the knowledge that he would never dare think of attacking their wisdom and courage. Besides, it was popular that this gambler had a real wife and two real children in a neat cottage in a suburb, where he led an exemplary home life, and when any one even suggested a discrepancy in his character, the crowd immediately vociferated descriptions of this virtuous family circle. Then men who led exemplary home lives, and men who did not lead exemplary home lives, all subsided in a bunch, remarking that there was nothing more to be said.

However, when a restriction was placed upon him—as, for instance, when a strong clique of members of the new Pollywog Club refused to permit him, even as a spectator, to appear in the rooms of the organization—the candor and gentleness with which he accepted the judgment disarmed many of his foes and made his friends more desperately partisan. He invariably distinguished between himself and a respectable Romper man so quickly and frankly that his manner actually appeared to be a continual broadcast compliment.

And one must not forget to declare the fundamental fact of his entire position in Romper. It is irrefutable that in all affairs outside of his business, in all matters that occur eternally and commonly between man and man, this thieving card-player was so generous, so just, so moral, that, in a contest, he could have put to flight the consciences of nine-tenths of the citizens of Romper.

And so it happened that he was seated in this saloon with the two prominent local merchants and the district-attorney.

The Swede continued to drink raw whisky, meanwhile babbling at the barkeeper and trying to induce him to indulge in potations. "Come on. Have a drink. Come on. What—no? Well a little one then. By gawd, I've whipped a man to-night, and I want to celebrate. I whipped him good, too. Gentlemen," the Swede cried to the men at the table, "have a drink?"

"Ssh!" said the barkeeper.

The group at the table, although furtively attentive, had been pretending to be deep in talk, but now a man lifted his eyes toward the Swede and said shortly: "Thanks. We don't want any more."

At this reply the Swede ruffled out his chest like a rooster. "Well," he exploded, "it seems I can't get anybody to drink with me in this town. Seems so, don't it? Well!"

"Ssh!" said the barkeeper.

"Say," snarled the Swede, "don't you try to shut me up. I won't have it. I'm a gentleman, and I want people to drink with me. And I want 'em to drink with me now. Now—do you understand?" He rapped the bar with his knuckles.

Years of experience had calloused the bartender. He merely grew sulky. "I hear you," he answered.

"Well," cried the Swede, "listen hard then. See those men over there? Well, they're going to drink with me, and don't you forget it. Now you watch."

"Hi!" yelled the barkeeper, "this won't do!"

"Why won't it?" demanded the Swede. He stalked over to the table, and by chance laid his hand upon the shoulder of the gambler. "How about this?" he asked, wrathfully. "I asked you to drink with me."

The gambler simply twisted his head and spoke over his shoulder. "My friend, I don't know you."

"Oh, hell!" answered the Swede, "come and have a drink."

"Now, my boy," advised the gambler kindly, "take your hand off my shoulder and go 'way and mind your own business." He was a little slim man, and it seemed strange to hear him use this tone of heroic patronage to the burly Swede. The other men at the table said nothing.

"What? You won't drink with me, you little dude! I'll make you then! I'll make you!" The Swede had grasped the gambler frenziedly at the throat, and was dragging him from his chair. The other men sprang up. The barkeeper dashed around the corner of his bar. There was a great tumult, and then was seen a long blade in the hand of the gambler. It shot forward, and a human body, this citadel of virtue, wisdom, power, was pierced as easily as if it had been a melon. The Swede fell with a cry of supreme astonishment.

The prominent merchants and the district-attorney must have at once tumbled out of the place backward. The bartender found himself hanging limply to the arm of a chair and gazing into the eyes of a murderer.

"Henry," said the latter, as he wiped his knife on one of the towels that hung beneath the bar-rail, "you tell 'em where to find me. I'll be home, waiting for 'em." Then he vanished. A moment afterward the barkeeper was in the street dinning through the storm for help, and, moreover, companionship.

The corpse of the Swede, alone in the saloon, had its eyes fixed upon a dreadful legend that dwelt a-top of the cash-machine. "This registers the amount of your purchase."

IX

Months later, the cowboy was frying pork over the stove of a little ranch near the Dakota line, when there was a quick thud of hoofs outside, and, presently, the Easterner entered with the letters and the papers.

"Well," said the Easterner at once, "the chap that killed the Swede had got three years. Wasn't much, was it?"

"He has? Three years?" The cowboy poised his pan of pork, while he ruminated upon the news. "Three years. That ain't much."

"No. It was a light sentence," replied the Easterner as he unbuckled his spurs. "Seems there was a good deal of sympathy for him in Romper."

"If the bartender had been any good," observed the cowboy thoughtfully, "he would have gone in and cracked that there Dutchman on the head with a bottle in the beginnin' of it and stopped all this here murderin'."

"Yes, a thousand things might have happened," said the Easterner tartly.

The cowboy returned his pan of pork to the fire, but his philosophy continued. "It's funny, ain't it? If he hadn't said Johnnie was cheatin' he'd be alive this minute. He was an awful fool. Game played for fun, too. Not for money. I believe he was crazy."

"I feel sorry for that gambler," said the Easterner.

"Oh, so do I," said the cowboy. "He don't deserve none of it for killin' who he did."

"The Swede might not have been killed if everything had been square."

"Might not have been killed?" exclaimed the cowboy. "Everythin' square? Why, when he said that Johnnie was cheatin' and acted like such a jackass? And then in the saloon he fairly walked up to git hurt?" With these arguments the cowboy brow-beat the Easterner and reduced him to rage.

"You're a fool!" cried the Easterner viciously. "You're a bigger jackass than the Swede by a million majority. Now let me tell you one thing. Let me tell you something. Listen! Johnnie *was* cheating!"

"'Johnnie,'" said the cowboy blankly. There was a minute of silence, and then he said robustly: "Why, no. The game was only for fun."

"Fun or not," said the Easterner, "Johnnie was cheating. I saw him. I know it. I saw him. And I refused to stand up and be a man. I let the Swede fight it out alone. And you—you were simply puffing around the place and wanting to fight. And then old Scully himself! We are all in it! This poor gambler isn't even a noun. He is kind of an adverb. Every sin is the result of a collaboration. We, five of us, have collaborated in the murder of this Swede. Usually there are from a dozen to forty women really involved in every murder, but in this case it seems to be only five men—you, I, Johnnie, old Scully, and that fool of an unfortunate gambler came merely as a culmination, the apex of a human movement, and gets all the punishment."

The cowboy, injured and rebellious, cried out blindly into this fog of mysterious theory: "Well, I didn't do anythin', did I?"

1898

The Bride Comes to Yellow Sky

I

The great Pullman was whirling onward with such dignity of motion that a glance from the window seemed simply to prove that the plains of Texas were pouring eastward. Vast flats of green grass, dull-hued spaces of mesquite and cactus, little groups of frame houses, woods of light and tender trees, all were sweeping into the east, sweeping over the horizon, a precipice.

A newly married pair had boarded this coach at San Antonio. The man's face was reddened from many days in the wind and sun, and a direct result of his new black clothes was that his brick-colored hands were constantly performing in a most conscious fashion. From time to time he looked down respectfully at his attire. He sat with a hand on each knee, like a man waiting in a barber's shop. The glances he devoted to other passengers were furtive and shy.

The bride was not pretty, nor was she very young. She wore a dress of blue cashmere, with small reservations of velvet here and there and with steel buttons abounding. She continually twisted her head to regard her puff sleeves, very stiff, straight, and high. They embarrassed her. It was quite apparent that she had cooked, and that she expected to cook, dutifully. The blushes caused by the careless scrutiny of some passengers as she had entered the car were strange to see upon this plain, under-class countenance, which was drawn in placid, almost emotionless lines.

They were evidently very happy. "Ever been in a parlor-car before?" he asked, smiling with delight.

"No," she answered. "I never was. It's fine, ain't it?"

"Great! And then after a while we'll go forward to the diner and get a big lay-out. Finest meal in the world. Charge a dollar."

"Oh, do they?" cried the bride. "Charge a dollar? Why, that's too much—for us —ain't it, Jack?"

"Not this trip, anyhow," he answered bravely. "We're going to go the whole thing."

Later, he explained to her about the trains. "You see, it's a thousand miles from one end of Texas to the other, and this train runs right across it and never stops but four times." He had the pride of an owner. He pointed out to her the dazzling fittings of the coach, and in truth her eyes opened wider as she contemplated the sea-green figured velvet, the shining brass, silver, and glass, the wood that gleamed as darkly brilliant as the surface of a pool of oil. At one end a bronze figure sturdily held a support for a separated chamber, and at convenient places on the ceiling were frescoes in olive and silver.

To the minds of the pair, their surroundings reflected the glory of their marriage that morning in San Antonio. This was the environment of their new estate, and the man's face in particular beamed with an elation that made him appear ridiculous to the negro porter. This individual at times surveyed them from afar with an amused and superior grin. On other occasions he bullied them with skill in ways that did not make it exactly plain to them that they were being bullied. He subtly used all the manners of the most unconquerable kind of snobbery. He oppressed them, but of this oppression they had small knowledge, and they speedily forgot that infrequently a number of travelers covered them with stares of derisive enjoyment. Historically there was supposed to be something infinitely humorous in their situation.

"We are due in Yellow Sky at 3.42," he said, looking tenderly into her eyes.

"Oh, are we?" she said, as if she had not been aware of it. To evince surprise at her husband's statement was part of her wifely amiability. She took from a pocket a little silver watch, and as she held it before her and stared at it with a frown of attention, the new husband's face shone.

"I bought it in San Anton' from a friend of mine," he told her gleefully.

"It's seventeen minutes past twelve," she said, looking up at him with a kind of shy and clumsy coquetry. A passenger, noting this play, grew excessively sardonic, and winked at himself in one of the numerous mirrors.

At last they went to the dining-car. Two rows of negro waiters in glowing white suits surveyed their entrance with the interest and also the equanimity of men who had been forewarned. The pair fell to the lot of a waiter who happened to feel pleasure in steering them through their meal. He viewed them with the manner of a fatherly pilot, his countenance radiant with benevolence. The patronage entwined with the ordinary deference was not plain to them. And yet as they returned to their coach they showed in their faces a sense of escape.

To the left, miles down a long purple slope, was a little ribbon of mist where moved the keening Rio Grande. The train was approaching it at an angle, and the apex was Yellow Sky. Presently it was apparent that as the distance from Yellow Sky grew shorter, the husband became commensurately restless. His brick-red hands were more insistent in their prominence. Occasionally he was even rather absent-minded and far-away when the bride leaned forward and addressed him.

As a matter of truth, Jack Potter was beginning to find the shadow of a deed weigh upon him like a leaden slab. He, the town marshal of Yellow Sky, a man known, liked, and feared in his corner, a prominent person, had gone to San Antonio to meet a girl he believed he loved, and there, after the usual prayers, had actually induced her to marry him, without consulting Yellow Sky for any part of the transaction. He was now bringing his bride before an innocent and unsuspecting community.

Of course, people in Yellow Sky married as it pleased them in accordance with a general custom; but such was Potter's thought of his duty to his friends, or of their idea of his duty, or of an unspoken form which does not control men in these matters, that he felt he was heinous. He had committed an extraordinary crime. Face to face with this girl in San Antonio, and spurred by his sharp impulse, he had gone headlong over all the social hedges. At San Antonio he was like a man hidden in the dark. A knife to sever any friendly duty, any form, was easy to his hand in that remote city. But the hour of Yellow Sky, the hour of daylight, was approaching.

He knew full well that his marriage was an important thing to his town. It could only be exceeded by the burning of the new hotel. His friends would not forgive him. Frequently he had reflected on the advisability of telling them by telegraph, but a new cowardice had been upon him. He feared to do it. And now the train was hurrying him toward a scene of amazement, glee, reproach. He glanced out of the window at the line of haze swinging slowly in toward the train.

Yellow Sky had a kind of brass band which played painfully to the delight of the populace. He laughed without heart as he thought of it. If the citizens could dream of his prospective arrival with his bride, they would parade the band at the station and escort them, amid cheers and laughing congratulations, to his adobe home.

He resolved that he would use all the devices of speed and plains-craft in making the journey from the station to his house. Once within that safe citadel, he could issue some sort of a vocal bulletin, and then not go among the citizens until they had time to wear off a little of their enthusiasm.

The bride looked anxiously at him. "What's worrying you, Jack?"

He laughed again. "I'm not worrying, girl. I'm only thinking of Yellow Sky."

She flushed in comprehension.

A sense of mutual guilt invaded their minds and developed a finer tenderness. They looked at each other with eyes softly aglow. But Potter often laughed the same nervous laugh. The flush upon the bride's face seemed quite permanent.

The traitor to the feelings of Yellow Sky narrowly watched the speeding landscape. "We're nearly there," he said.

Presently the porter came and announced the proximity of Potter's home. He held a brush in his hand and, with all his airy superiority gone, he brushed Potter's new clothes as the latter slowly turned this way and that way. Potter fumbled out a coin and gave it to the porter as he had seen others do. It was a heavy and muscle-bound business, as that of a man shoeing his first horse.

The porter took their bag, and as the train began to slow they moved forward to the hooded platform of the car. Presently the two engines and their long string of coaches rushed into the station of Yellow Sky.

"They have to take water here," said Potter, from a constricted throat and in mournful cadence as one announcing death. Before the train stopped his eye had swept the length of the platform, and he was glad and astonished to see there was none upon it but the station-agent, who, with a slightly hurried and anxious air, was walking toward the water-tanks. When the train had halted, the porter alighted first and placed in position a little temporary step.

"Come on, girl," said Potter hoarsely. As he helped her down they each laughed on a false note. He took the bag from the negro, and bade his wife cling to his arm. As they slunk rapidly away, his hang-dog glance perceived that they were unloading the two trunks, and also that the station-agent far ahead near the baggage-car had turned and was running toward him, making gestures. He laughed, and groaned as he laughed, when he noted the first effect of his marital bliss upon Yellow Sky. He gripped his wife's arm firmly to his side, and they fled. Behind them the porter stood chuckling fatuously.

II

The California Express on the Southern Railway was due at Yellow Sky in twenty-one minutes. There were six men at the bar of the Weary Gentleman saloon. One was a drummer[1] who talked a great deal and rapidly; three were Texans who did not care to talk at that time; and two were Mexican sheep-herders who did not talk as a general practice in the Weary Gentleman saloon. The bar-keeper's dog lay on the board-walk that crossed in front of the door. His head was on his paws, and he glanced drowsily here and there with the constant vigilance of a dog that is kicked on occasion. Across the sandy street were some vivid green grass plots, so wonderful in appearance amid the sands that burned near them in a blazing sun that they caused a doubt in the mind. They exactly resembled the grass mats used to represent lawns on the stage. At the cooler end of the railway station a man without a coat sat in a tilted chair and smoked his pipe. The fresh-cut bank of the Rio Grande circled near the town, and there could be seen beyond it a great plum-colored plain of mesquite.

Save for the busy drummer and his companions in the saloon, Yellow Sky was dozing. The new-comer leaned gracefully upon the bar, and recited many tales with the confidence of a bard who has come upon a new field.

"—and at the moment that the old man fell down stairs with the bureau in his arms, the old woman was coming up with two scuttles of coal, and, of course—"

The drummer's tale was interrupted by a young man who suddenly appeared in the open door. He cried: "Scratchy Wilson's drunk, and has turned loose with both hands." The two Mexicans at once set down their glasses and faded out of the rear entrance of the saloon.

The drummer, innocent and jocular, answered: "All right, old man. S'pose he has. Come in and have a drink, anyhow."

But the information had made such an obvious cleft in every skull in the room that the drummer was obliged to see its importance. All had become instantly morose. "Say," said he, mystified, "what is this?" His three companions made the introductory gesture of eloquent speech, but the young man at the door forestalled them.

"It means, my friend," he answered, as he came into the saloon, "that for the next two hours this town won't be a health resort."

The bar-keeper went to the door and locked and barred it. Reaching out of the

[1] Traveling salesman.

window, he pulled in heavy wooden shutters and barred them. Immediately a solemn, chapel-like gloom was upon the place. The drummer was looking from one to another.

"But say," he cried, "what is this, anyhow? You don't mean there is going to be a gun-fight?"

"Don't know whether there'll be a fight or not," answered one man grimly. "But there'll be some shootin'—some good shootin'."

The young man who had warned them waved his hand. "Oh, there'll be a fight fast enough, if anyone wants it. Anybody can get a fight out there in the street. There's a fight just waiting."

The drummer seemed to be swayed between the interest of a foreigner and a perception of personal danger.

"What did you say his name was?" he asked.

"Scratchy Wilson," they answered in chorus.

"And will he kill anybody? What are you going to do? Does this happen often? Does he rampage around like this once a week or so? Can he break in that door?"

"No, he can't break down that door," replied the bar-keeper. "He's tried it three times. But when he comes you'd better lay down on the floor, stranger. He's dead sure to shoot at it, and a bullet may come through."

Thereafter the drummer kept a strict eye upon the door. The time had not yet been called for him to hug the floor, but as a minor precaution he sidled near to the wall. "Will he kill anybody?" he said again.

The men laughed low and scornfully at the question.

"He's out to shoot, and he's out for trouble. Don't see any good in experimentin' with him."

"But what do you do in a case like this? What do you do?"

A man responded: "Why, he and Jack Potter—"

But, in chorus, the other men interrupted: "Jack Potter's in San Anton'."

"Well, who is he? What's he got to do with it?"

"Oh, he's the town marshal. He goes out and fights Scratchy when he gets on one of these tears."

"Wow," said the drummer, mopping his brow. "Nice job he's got."

The voices had toned away to mere whisperings. The drummer wished to ask further questions which were born of an increasing anxiety and bewilderment; but when he attempted them, the men merely looked at him in irritation and motioned him to remain silent. A tense waiting hush was upon them. In the deep shadows of the room their eyes shone as they listened for sounds from the street. One man made three gestures at the bar-keeper, and the latter, moving like a ghost, handed him a glass and a bottle. The man poured a full glass of whisky, and set down the bottle noiselessly. He gulped the whisky in a swallow, and turned again toward the door in immovable silence. The drummer saw that the bar-keeper, without a sound, had taken a Winchester from beneath the bar. Later he saw this individual beckoning to him, so he tiptoed across the room.

"You better come with me back of the bar."

"No, thanks," said the drummer, perspiring. "I'd rather be where I can make a break for the back door."

Whereupon the man of bottles made a kindly but peremptory gesture. The drummer obeyed it, and finding himself seated on a box with his head below the level of the bar, balm was laid upon his soul at sight of various zinc and copper fittings that bore a resemblance to armor-plate. The bar-keeper took a seat comfortably upon an adjacent box.

"You see," he whispered, "this here Scratchy Wilson is a wonder with a gun—a perfect wonder—and when he goes on the war trail, we hunt our holes—naturally. He's about the last one of the old gang that used to hang out along the river here. He's a terror when he's drunk. When he's sober he's all right—kind of simple—wouldn't hurt a fly—nicest fellow in town. But when he's drunk—whoo!"

There were periods of stillness. "I wish Jack Potter was back from San Anton'," said the bar-keeper. "He shot Wilson up once—in the leg—and he would sail in and pull out the kinks in this thing."

Presently they heard from a distance the sound of a shot, followed by three wild yowls. It instantly removed a bond from the men in the darkened saloon. There was a shuffling of feet. They looked at each other. "Here he comes," they said.

III

A man in a maroon-colored flannel shirt, which had been purchased for purposes of decoration and made, principally, by some Jewish women on the east side of New York, rounded a corner and walked into the middle of the main street of Yellow Sky. In either hand the man held a long, heavy blue-black revolver. Often he yelled, and these cries rang through a semblance of a deserted village, shrilly flying over the roofs in a volume that seemed to have no relation to the ordinary vocal strength of a man. It was as if the surrounding stillness formed the arch of a tomb over him. These cries of ferocious challenge rang against walls of silence. And his boots had red tops with gilded imprints, of the kind beloved in winter by little sledding boys on the hillsides of New England.

The man's face flamed in a rage begot of whisky. His eyes, rolling and yet keen for ambush, hunted the still door-ways and windows. He walked with the creeping movement of the midnight cat. As it occurred to him, he roared menacing information. The long revolvers in his hands were as easy as straws; they were moved with an electric swiftness. The little fingers of each hand played sometimes in a musician's way. Plain from the low collar of the shirt, the cords of his neck straightened and sank, straightened and sank, as passion moved him. The only sounds were his terrible invitations. The calm adobes preserved their demeanor at the passing of this small thing in the middle of the street.

There was no offer of fight; no offer of fight. The man called to the sky. There were no attractions. He bellowed and fumed and swayed his revolvers here and everywhere.

The dog of the bar-keeper of the Weary Gentleman saloon had not appreciated the advance of events. He yet lay dozing in front of his master's door. At sight of the dog, the man paused and raised his revolver humorously. At sight of the man, the dog sprang up and walked diagonally away, with a sullen head and growling. The man yelled, and the dog broke into a gallop. As it was about to enter an alley, there was a loud noise, a whistling, and something spat the ground directly before it. The dog screamed, and, wheeling in terror, galloped headlong in a new direction. Again there was a noise, a whistling, and sand was kicked viciously before it. Fear-stricken, the dog turned and flurried like an animal in a pen. The man stood laughing, his weapons at his hips.

Ultimately the man was attracted by the closed door of the Weary Gentleman saloon. He went to it, and hammering with a revolver, demanded drink.

The door remaining imperturbable, he picked a bit of paper from the walk and nailed it to the framework with a knife. He then turned his back contemptuously upon this popular resort, and walking to the opposite side of the street, and spinning there on his heel quickly and lithely, fired at the bit of paper. He missed it by a half inch. He swore at himself, and went away. Later, he comfortably fusilladed the windows of his most intimate friend. The man was playing with this town. It was a toy for him.

But still there was no offer of fight. The name of Jack Potter, his ancient antagonist, entered his mind, and he concluded that it would be a glad thing if he should go to Potter's house and by bombardment induce him to come out and fight. He moved in the direction of his desire, chanting Apache scalp-music.

When he arrived at it, Potter's house presented the same still, calm front as had the other adobes. Taking up a strategic position, the man howled a challenge. But this house regarded him as might a great stone god. It gave no sign. After a decent wait, the man howled further challenges, mingling with them wonderful epithets.

Presently there came the spectacle of a man churning himself into deepest rage over the immobility of a house. He fumed at it as the winter wind attacks a prairie cabin in the North. To the distance there should have gone the sound of a tumult like the fighting of two hundred Mexicans. As necessity bade him, he paused for breath or to reload his revolvers.

IV

Potter and his bride walked sheepishly and with speed. Sometimes they laughed together shamefacedly and low.

"Next corner, dear," he said finally.

They put forth the efforts of a pair walking bowed against a strong wind. Potter was about to raise a finger to point the first appearance of the new home when, as they circled the corner, they came face to face with a man in a maroon-colored shirt who was feverishly pushing cartridges into a large revolver. Upon the instant the man dropped this revolver to the ground, and, like lightning, whipped another from its holster. The second weapon was aimed at the bridegroom's chest.

There was a silence. Potter's mouth seemed to be merely a grave for his tongue. He exhibited an instinct to at once loosen his arm from the woman's grip, and he dropped the bag to the sand. As for the bride, her face had gone as yellow as old cloth. She was a slave to hideous rites gazing at the apparitional snake.

The two men faced each other at a distance of three paces. He of the revolver smiled with a new and quiet ferocity. "Tried to sneak up on me," he said. "Tried to sneak up on me!" His eyes grew more baleful. As Potter made a slight movement, the man thrust his revolver venomously forward. "No, don't you do it, Jack Potter. Don't you move a finger toward a gun just yet. Don't you move an eyelash. The time has come for me to settle with you, and I'm goin' to do it my own way and loaf along with no interferin'. So if you don't want a gun bent on you, just mind what I tell you."

Potter looked at his enemy. "I ain't got a gun on me, Scratchy," he said. "Honest, I ain't." He was stiffening and steadying, but yet somewhere at the back of his mind a vision of the Pullman floated, the sea-green figured velvet, the shining brass, silver, and glass, the wood that gleamed as darkly brilliant as the surface of a pool of oil —all the glory of the marriage, the environment of the new estate. "You know I fight when it comes to fighting, Scratchy Wilson, but I ain't got a gun on me. You'll have to do all the shootin' yourself."

His enemy's face went livid. He stepped forward and lashed his weapon to and fro before Potter's chest. "Don't you tell me you ain't got no gun on you, you whelp. Don't tell me no lie like that. There ain't a man in Texas ever seen you without no gun. Don't take me for no kid." He eyes blazed with light, and his throat worked like a pump.

"I ain't takin' you for no kid," answered Potter. His heels had not moved an inch backward. "I'm takin' you for a ———— fool. I tell you I ain't got a gun, and I ain't. If you're goin' to shoot me up, you better begin now. You'll never get a chance like this again."

So much enforced reasoning had told on Wilson's rage. He was calmer. "If you ain't got a gun, why ain't you got a gun?" he sneered. "Been to Sunday-school?"

"I ain't got a gun because I've just come from San Anton' with my wife. I'm married," said Potter. "And if I'd thought there was going to be any galoots like you prowling around when I brought my wife home, I'd had a gun, and don't you forget it."

"Married!" said Scratchy, not at all comprehending.

"Yes, married. I'm married," said Potter distinctly.

"Married?" said Scratchy. Seemingly for the first time he saw the drooping drowning woman at the other man's side. "No!" he said. He was like a creature allowed a glimpse of another world. He moved a pace backward, and his arm with the revolver dropped to his side. "Is this—is this the lady?" he asked.

"Yes, this is the lady," answered Potter.

There was another period of silence.

"Well," said Wilson at last, slowly, "I s'pose it's all off now."

"It's all off if you say so, Scratchy. You know I didn't make the trouble." Potter lifted his valise.

"Well, I 'low it's off, Jack," said Wilson. He was looking at the ground. "Married!" He was not a student of chivalry; it was merely that in the presence of this foreign condition he was a simple child of the earlier plains. He picked up his starboard revolver, and placing both weapons in their holsters, he went away. His feet made funnel-shaped tracks in the heavy sand.

1898

An Episode of War

The lieutenant's rubber blanket lay on the ground, and upon it he had poured the company's supply of coffee. Corporals and other representatives of the grimy and hot-throated men who lined the breastwork had come for each squad's portion.

The lieutenant was frowning and serious at this task of division. His lips pursed as he drew with his sword various crevices in the heap until brown squares of coffee, astoundingly equal in size, appeared on the blanket. He was on the verge of a great triumph in mathematics and the corporals were thronging forward, each to reap a little square, when suddenly the lieutenant cried out and looked quickly at a man near him as if he suspected it was a case of personal assault. The others cried out also when they saw blood upon the lieutenant's sleeve.

He had winced like a man stung, swayed dangerously, and then straightened. The sound of his hoarse breathing was plainly audible. He looked sadly, mystically, over the breastwork at the green face of a wood where now were many little puffs of white smoke. During this moment, the men about him gazed statue-like and silent, aston- ished and awed by this catastrophe which had happened when catastrophes were not expected—when they had leisure to observe it.

As the lieutenant stared at the wood, they too swung their heads so that for another moment all hands, still silent, contemplated the distant forest as if their minds were fixed upon the mystery of a bullet's journey.

The officer had, of course, been compelled to take his sword at once into his left hand. He did not hold it by the hilt. He gripped it at the middle of the blade, awkwardly. Turning his eyes from the hostile wood, he looked at the sword as he held it there, and seemed puzzled as to what to do with it, where to put it. In short this weapon had of a sudden become a strange thing to him. He looked at it in a kind of stupefaction, as if he had been miraculously endowed with a trident, a sceptre, or a spade.

Finally, he tried to sheath it. To sheath a sword held by the left hand, at the middle of the blade, in a scabbard hung at the left hip, is a feat worthy of a sawdust ring. This wounded officer engaged in a desperate struggle with the sword and the wobbling scabbard, and during the time of it, he breathed like a wrestler.

But at this instant the men, the spectators, awoke from their stone-like poses and crowded forward sympathetically. The orderly-sergeant took the sword and tenderly placed it in the scabbard. At the time, he leaned nervously backward, and did not allow even his finger to brush the body of the lieutenant. A wound gives strange dignity to him who bears it. Well men shy from this new and terrible majesty. It is as if the wounded man's hand is upon the curtain which hangs before the revelations of all existence, the meaning of ants, potentates, wars, cities, sunshine, snow, a feather dropped from a bird's wing, and the power of it sheds radiance upon a bloody form, and makes the other men understand sometimes that they are little. His comrades look at him with large eyes thoughtfully. Moreover, they fear vaguely that the weight of a finger upon him might send him headlong, precipitate the tragedy, hurl him at once into the dim grey unknown. And so the orderly-sergeant while sheathing the sword leaned nervously backward.

There were others who proffered assistance. One timidly presented his shoulder and asked the lieutenant if he cared to lean upon it, but the latter waved them away mournfully. He wore the look of one who knows he is the victim of a terrible disease and understands his helplessness. He again stared over the breast-work at the forest, and then turning went slowly rearward. He held his right wrist tenderly in his left hand, as if the wounded arm was made of very brittle glass.

And the men in silence stared at the wood, then at the departing lieutenant—then at the wood, then at the lieutenant.

As the wounded officer passed from the line of battle, he was enabled to see many things which as a participant in the fight were unknown to him. He saw a general on a black horse gazing over the lines of blue infantry at the green woods which veiled his problems. An aide galloped furiously, dragged his horse suddenly to a halt, saluted, and presented a paper. It was, for a wonder, precisely like an historical painting.

To the rear of the general and his staff, a group, composed of a bugler, two or three orderlies, and the bearer of the corps standard, all upon maniacal horses, were working like slaves to hold their ground, preserve their respectful interval, while the shells bloomed in the air about them, and caused their chargers to make furious quivering leaps.

A battery, a tumultuous and shining mass, was swirling toward the right. The wild thud of hoofs, the cries of the riders shouting blame and praise, menace and encouragement, and, last, the roar of the wheels, the slant of the glistening guns, brought the lieutenant to an intent pause. The battery swept in curves that stirred the heart; it made halts as dramatic as the crash of a wave on the rocks and when it fled onward, this aggregation of wheels, levers, motors, had a beautiful unity, as if it were a missile. The sound of it was a war-chorus that reached into the depths of man's emotion.

The lieutenant, still holding his arm as if it were of glass, stood watching this battery until all detail of it was lost, save the figures of the riders, which rose and fell and waved lashes over the black mass.

Later he turned his eyes toward the battle where the shooting sometimes crackled like bush-fires, sometimes sputtered with exasperating irregularity, and sometimes reverberated like the thunder. He saw the smoke rolling upward and saw crowds of men who ran and cheered, or stood and blazed away at the inscrutable distance.

He came upon some stragglers and they told him how to find the field hospital. They described its exact location. In fact these men, no longer having part in the battle, knew more of it than others. They told the performance of every corps, every division, the opinion of every general. The lieutenant, carrying his wounded arm rearward, looked upon them with wonder.

At the roadside a brigade was making coffee and buzzing with talk like a girls' boarding-school. Several officers came out to him and inquired concerning things of which he knew nothing. One, seeing his arm, began to scold. "Why, man, that's no way to do. You want to fix that thing." He appropriated the lieutenant and the lieutenant's wound. He cut the sleeve and laid bare the arm, every nerve of which softly fluttered under his touch. He bound his handkerchief over the wound, scolding away in the meantime. He tone allowed one to think that he was in the habit of being wounded every day. The lieutenant hung his head, feeling, in this presence, that he did not know how to be correctly wounded.

The low white tents of the hospital were grouped around an old school-house. There was here a singular commotion. In the foreground two ambulances interlocked wheels in the deep mud. The drivers were tossing the blame of it back and forth, gesticulating and berating, while from the ambulances, both crammed with wounded, there came an occasional groan. An interminable crowd of bandaged men were coming and going. Great numbers sat under the trees nursing heads or arms or legs. There was a dispute of some kind raging on the steps of the school-house. Sitting with his back against a tree a man with a face as grey as a new army blanket was serenely smoking a corn-cob pipe. The lieutenant wished to rush forward and inform him that he was dying.

A busy surgeon was passing near the lieutenant. "Good morning," he said with a friendly smile. Then he caught sight of the lieutenant's arm and his face at once changed. "Well, let's have a look at it." He seemed possessed suddenly of a great contempt for the lieutenant. This would evidently placed the latter on a very low social plane. The doctor cried out impatiently. What mutton-head had tied it up that way anyhow. The lieutenant answered: "Oh, a man."

When the wound was disclosed the doctor fingered it disdainfully. "Humph," he said. "You come along with me and I'll 'tend to you." His voice contained the same scorn as if he were saying: "You will have to go to jail."

The lieutenant had been very meek but now his face flushed, and he looked into the doctor's eyes. "I guess I won't have it amputated," he said.

"Nonsense, man! nonsense! nonsense!" cried the doctor. "Come along, now. I won't amputate it. Come along. Don't be a baby."

"Let go of me," said the lieutenant, holding back wrathfully. His glance fixed upon the door of the old school-house, as sinister to him as the portals of death.

And this is the story of how the lieutenant lost his arm. When he reached home his sisters, his mother, his wife, sobbed for a long time at the sight of the flat sleeve. "Oh, well," he said, standing shamefaced amid these tears, "I don't suppose it matters so much as all that."

1899

Theodore Dreiser
1871–1945

By the end of the nineteenth century, Indiana had become a major center of literary production, able to satisfy the needs of a large body of readers across the country. There had been General Lew Wallace's best-selling novel *Ben Hur*, about early Christians in Rome and Palestine, to provide the uplift of religious inspiration mixed with the romance of exotic times and places. There were the down-home humor and sentiment of James Whitcomb Riley's verses and the popular satires of George Ade and, later, Chic Sale. Best of all, there was Booth Tarkington, "the gentleman from Indiana," who provided middle-class parlors with the novels (such as *Seventeen*) and magazine pieces (the Penrod stories) that extolled the pleasures and pain of growing up as a boy in Indianapolis. Tarkington's Indiana (closely observed, with wit and good nature) was a nice place to be a boy and a dandy place to be a rich and famous author (especially one who could, as Tarkington did, also turn out such popular historical romances as *Monsieur Beaucaire* and astute comedies of manners like *The Magnificent Ambersons*). This Indiana, however, was not the one that Theodore Herman Albert Dreiser knew. He grew up poor and unhappy, the son of German immigrant parents, in Terre Haute, a rough river town down by the Ohio River.

Dreiser's imagination was midwestern through and through. It was not the Tarkington imagination, however. Dreiser was closer to the Hoosier author of an earlier generation, Edward Eggleston, who had portrayed the seamier, more violent sides of life when Indiana had been little more than a scattering of frontier settlements. Yet Dreiser's novels are most correctly associated with the Chicago school of Realism. Just as New York began to replace Boston as the primary center for work and culture by the 1880s, Indianapolis (locale for easygoing realism and genteel romancing) was displaced by Chicago in the 1890s and early 1900s. That boom city was both the literal place and the symbolic setting for lives and literature that dramatized the naturalistic principles that Dreiser's writings commandingly represent; for Dreiser, to live in Chicago was to experience the forces of environment and physical urges emphasized by his fiction.

Chicago was not the only place to stimulate Dreiser's imagination or to offer an arena for his struggles. Dreiser was a wanderer by nature; he characterized himself as a "cosmic waif." Like others of his generation, he felt buffeted by a willful and indifferent universe. He was always sympathetic toward his unhappy fictional characters because he felt himself to be as bereft as they. He took up lodgings in St. Louis, Pittsburgh, Cleveland, Chicago, and New York. He visited the Soviet Union for eleven weeks in 1927–1928. He acted as journalist, editor, and novelist—whatever his temporary stops called upon him to do. His brother Paul became a popular songwriter with the hit "On the Banks of the Wabash"— a nostalgic bit of "down-home" melody—but home was a place neither Theodore Dreiser nor his fictional characters ever had.

Dreiser had experienced almost too much family life when he was growing up. His family, especially his sisters with their wayward lives and illegitimate children, furnished him with ideas for the stories he would write. But it was not the life Booth Tarkington gave to his boys, Penrod or Sam. The bare, though hardly barren, facts of Dreiser's life are easy to review. He was the twelfth of thirteen children. His father (severe, a religious fanatic, and often out of work) and his mother (absorbed in her family, sympathetic, and illiterate) were unable to stave off the ruin and squalor that beset them. By the age of fifteen, Dreiser was on his own, living off small jobs he scared up around Terre Haute. A year at Indiana University followed in 1889 after a high school teacher who believed in him gave him money for further schooling. But Dreiser was eager to put as much distance between himself and his childhood as possible. As it had for other young men of the period, journalism offered a way out. From 1892 on, Dreiser gained experience on newspapers around the Midwest before heading for New

York. He supplemented his street knowledge as best he could with the contemporary literature that most appealed to him—the evolutionary theories of scientific and social determinism grounded on the work of Charles Darwin, Thomas Huxley, and Herbert Spencer.

The year 1900 saw the publication—and quick demise—of Dreiser's first novel, *Sister Carrie,* based in part on the elopement of one of his sisters and a story of the embezzlement of company funds that filled the newspapers at that time. *Sister Carrie* dropped from sight almost as soon as the publishers released it; they decided not to promote it because the publisher's wife found it shocking. Only recently has the full story of the tampering with Dreiser's novel come to light with the scholarly publication of the original manuscript. Dreiser had not only to suffer the evisceration of his original ideas but also to witness the disappearance from public view of the resulting bowdlerization.

Deeply disappointed by the failure of *Sister Carrie,* for which his royalties came to $68.40, Dreiser moved on to write a group of short stories. A nervous breakdown followed, debilitating him until 1904, the year he started to work for several magazines, including the Butterick publication *The Delineator.* In 1907 *Sister Carrie* was reissued and began both to receive the attention it deserved and to exert an influence on American literature's turn toward naturalism. *Jennie Gerhardt* was published in 1911; once again the plot came to Dreiser by way of a sister's experience as a rich man's mistress. In 1912 Dreiser brought out the first of three novels known as the Cowperwood trilogy: *The Financier,* followed by *The Titan* (1914) and *The Stoic* (posthumously published in 1947). A journalist by nature, Dreiser continued to base his fiction on contemporary figures whose stories were played out in the newspapers. (In the case of the Cowperwood novels, he modeled his hero on a well-known financial swashbuckler, Charles T. Yerkes.) By these means he dramatized the methods by which clever, ruthless entrepreneurs were taking control of the American system.

Autobiographical books followed: *The "Genius"* (1915) was a fictionalized version of Dreiser's early efforts as a writer; *A Book About Myself,* also known as *Newspaper Days* (1922), and *Dawn* (1931) were straightforward autobiographies. But it was the 1925 publication of *An American Tragedy,* based on an actual murder trial, that earned him the recognition he had been lumbering toward ever since his early days in Terre Haute.

Politics received most of Dreiser's attention in the last decades of his life. It is revealing that he simultaneously became a member of the Communist Party and a Quaker. He was a naive thinker and a somewhat confused social reformer, but to the end he tried to find a way out for individuals and social groups who wanted to escape the deadening grip of a mechanistic determinism that he both believed in and yearned to modify. Dreiser's example helps explain why American naturalism took a different approach to the universe from that upheld by Continental writers who worked from principles, based on their appraisal of human behavior, that attempted to be as clinically objective as any derived by laboratory observation of rats in a test cage.

Dreiser did his "homework" in the nineteenth-century evolutionary theory that had replaced Divine Providence with biology. He was a practicing journalist trained to report empirical facts. He was also a full-fledged participant in a literary movement that attempted to replace the self-delusions of romanticized fictions with honest, sobering accounts of how people react to real events. But Dreiser had to add hope to what he saw, however tragic the scene. This was how he expressed his own desires for happiness, material success, and sexual triumphs.

As Dreiser traveled around the United States—a country in the process of changing before his eyes—he wanted to be able to define the changes he witnessed as progress toward something better. He needed to associate the longings that frustrated his fictional characters and himself with the necessary birth pangs of a soul on its upward ascent. Dreiser once stopped in the middle of an outburst about the quiet farmlands of the Midwest, with their promise of stability and calm, and exclaimed, "But I have seen Pittsburgh!" That is, he had seen firsthand the hectic lives of people who worked silhouetted against the fires of the blast furnaces of the Pennsylvanian steel mills that gave the lie to an agricultural America. But if he contrasted the picture of Pittsburgh with the Ohio farmlands, he kept American ideals and rural idylls in his memory.

Carrie Meeber and George Hurstwood in *Sister Carrie* pass one another along the lines of ascent and descent that take the one to a celebrity's suite at the new Waldorf-Astoria and the other to suicide in a flophouse and a pauper's grave. In *An American Tragedy* Clyde Griffiths goes to his death for the murder of one young woman because of his longing for another, richer, more glamorous girl. His foolish dream of wealth is matched by the folly of his romantic desire for perfect love. Frank Cowperwood's life expresses his faith that he can take command of the machine that brings him financial success and sexual prowess. He rejects the notion that he can be broken by the mechanisms of a "hot" society and a "cold" universe. Money, sex, and power as the way (however abortive) to go "home" became major themes in twentieth-century literature, precisely because Dreiser made them important. His books and his life frequently demonstrate how freedom of choice and fulfillment of one's yearnings are often denied. But this did not stop him. He kept on writing as much about the power of desire as about the inevitability of defeat.

Further Reading:
D. Dudley, *Dreiser and the Land of the Free,* 1932, 1946.
R. Elias, *Theodore Dreiser, Apostle of Nature,* 1949, 1970.
H. Dreiser, *My Life with Dreiser,* 1951.
F. Matthiessen, *Theodore Dreiser,* 1951.
The Stature of Theodore Dreiser: A Critical Survey of the Man and His Work, ed. A. Kazin and C. Shapiro, 1955.
C. Shapiro, *Theodore Dreiser, Our Bitter Patriot,* 1962.
P. L. Gerber, *Theodore Dreiser,* 1964.
W. Swanberg, *Dreiser,* 1965.
M. Tjader, *Theodore Dreiser: A New Dimension,* 1965.
J. McAleer, *Theodore Dreiser: An Introduction and*

Interpretation, 1968.
R. Lehan, *Theodore Dreiser: His World and His Novels,* 1969.
E. Moers, *Two Dreisers,* 1969.
R. Warren, *Homage to Theodore Dreiser,* 1971.
Folcroft Library Editions, *Theodore Dreiser, America's Foremost Novelist,* 1973.
D. Pizer, *The Novels of Theodore Dreiser,* 1976.
P. L. Gerber, *Plots and Characters in the Fiction of Theodore Dreiser,* 1977.
Y. Hakutani, *Young Dreiser: A Critical Study,* 1980.
Critical Essays on Theodore Dreiser, ed. D. Pizer, 1981.
L. Hussman, *Dreiser and His Fiction,* 1983.

Text:
Sister Carrie, 1981.
See also *The Letters of Theodore Dreiser,* 3 vols., ed. R. Elias, 1959.

American Diaries, 1902–1926, ed. T. Riggio, 1982.

from Sister Carrie

Chapter III: [Looking for a Job]

Once across the river and into the wholesale district, she glanced about her for some likely door at which to apply.[1] As she contemplated the wide windows and imposing signs, she became conscious of being gazed upon and understood for what she was —a wage-seeker. She had never done this thing before and lacked courage. To avoid conspicuity and a certain indefinable shame she felt at being caught spying about for some place where she might apply for a position, she quickened her steps and assumed an air of indifference supposedly common to one upon an errand. In this way she passed many manufacturing and wholesale houses without once glancing in. At last, after several blocks of walking, she felt that this would not do, and began to look about again, though without relaxing her pace. A little way on she saw a great door which for some reason attracted her attention. It was ornamented by a small brass sign, and seemed to be the entrance to a vast hive of six or seven floors. "Perhaps," she thought, "they may want some one" and crossed over to enter, screwing up her courage to the sticking point as she went. When she came within a score of feet of the desired goal, she observed a young gentleman in a grey check suit, fumbling his watch-charm and looking out. That he had anything to do with the concern she could not tell, but because he happened to be looking in her direction, her weakening heart misgave her and she hurried by, too overcome with shame to enter in. After several blocks of walking, in which the uproar of the streets and the novelty of the situation had time to wear away the effect of this, her first defeat, she again looked about. Over the way stood a great six-story structure labeled "Storm and King," which she viewed with rising hope. It was a wholesale dry goods concern and employed women. She could see them moving about now and then upon the upper floors. This place she decided to enter, no matter what. She crossed over and walked directly toward the entrance. As she did so two men came out and paused in the door. A telegraph messenger in blue dashed past her and up the few steps which graced the entrance and disappeared. Several pedestrians out of the hurrying throng which filled the sidewalks passed about her as she paused, hesitating. She looked helplessly around and then, seeing herself observed, retreated. It was too difficult a task. She could not go past them.

So severe a defeat told sadly upon her nerves. She could scarcely understand her weakness and yet she could not think of gazing inquiringly about upon the surrounding scene. Her feet carried her mechanically forward, every foot of her progress being a satisfactory portion of a flight which she gladly made. Block after block passed by. Upon street lamps at the various corners she read names such as Madison, Monroe, La Salle, Clark, Dearborn, State; and still she went, her feet beginning to tire upon the broad stone flagging. She was pleased in part that the streets were bright and clean. The morning sun shining down with steadily increasing warmth made the shady side of the streets pleasantly cool. She looked at the blue sky overhead with more realization of its charm than had ever come to her before.

---

[1] Carrie Meeber, at 18, has arrived in Chicago from a small midwestern town in 1889 in the hope of finding a job and entering upon the exciting life of the big city.

Her cowardice began to trouble her in a way. She turned back along the street she had come, resolving to hunt up Storm and King and enter in. On the way she encountered a great wholesale shoe company, through the broad plate windows of which she saw an enclosed executive department, hidden by frosted glass. Without this enclosure, but just within the street entrance, sat a grey-haired gentleman at a small table, with a large open ledger of some kind before him. She walked by this institution several times hesitating, but finding herself unobserved she eventually gathered sufficient courage to falter past the screen door and stand humbly waiting.

"Well, young lady," observed the old gentleman looking at her somewhat kindly—"what is it you wish?"

"I am, that is, do you—I mean, do you need any help?" she stammered.

"Not just at present," he answered smiling. "Not just at present. Come in sometime next week. Occasionally we need some one."

She received the answer in silence and backed awkwardly out. The pleasant nature of her reception rather astonished her. She had expected that it would be more difficult, that something cold and harsh would be said—she knew not what. That she had not been put to shame and made to feel her unfortunate position seemed remarkable. She did not realize that it was just this which made her experience easy, but the result was the same. She felt greatly relieved.

Somewhat encouraged, she ventured into another large structure. It was a clothing company, and more people were in evidence—well-dressed men of forty and more, surrounded by brass railings and employed variously.

An office boy approached her.

"Who is it you wish to see?" he asked.

"I want to see the manager," she returned.

He ran away and spoke to one of a group of three men who were conferring together. One broke off and came towards her.

"Well?" he said, coldly. The greeting drove all courage from her at once.

"Do you need any help?" she stammered.

"No," he replied abruptly and turned upon his heel.

She went foolishly out, the office boy deferentially swinging the door for her, and gladly sank into the obscuring crowd. It was a severe set-back to her recently pleased mental state.

Now she walked quite aimlessly for a time, turning here and there, seeing one great company after another but finding no courage to prosecute her single inquiry. High noon came and with it hunger. She hunted out an unassuming restaurant and entered but was disturbed to find that the prices were exorbitant for the size of her purse. A bowl of soup was all that she could feel herself able to afford, and with this quickly eaten she went out again. It restored her strength somewhat and made her moderately bold to pursue the search.

In walking a few blocks to fix upon some probable place she again encountered the firm of Storm and King and this time managed to enter. Some gentlemen were conferring close at hand but took no notice of her. She was left standing, gazing nervously upon the floor, her confusion and mental distress momentarily increasing until at last she was ready to turn and hurry eagerly away. When the limit of her distress had been nearly reached she was beckoned to by a man at one of the many desks within the nearby railing.

"Who is it you wish to see?" he inquired.

"Why any one, if you please," she answered. "I am looking for something to do."

"Oh, you want to see Mr. McManus," he returned. "Sit down!" and he pointed to a chair against the neighboring wall. He went on leisurely writing until after a time a short stout gentleman came in from the street.

"Mr. McManus," called the man at the desk, "this young woman wants to see you."

The short gentleman turned about towards Carrie, and she arose and came forward.

"What can I do for you, Miss," he inquired surveying her curiously.

"I want to know if I can get a position," she inquired.

"As what?" he asked.

"Not as anything in particular," she faltered. "I—"

"Have you ever had any experience in the wholesale dry goods business?" he questioned.

"No sir," she replied.

"Are you a stenographer or typewriter?"[2]

"No sir."

"Well we haven't anything here," he said. "We employ only experienced help."

She began to step backward toward the door, when something about her plaintive face attracted him.

"Have you ever worked at anything before?" he inquired.

"No sir," she said.

"Well now, it's hardly possible that you would get anything to do in a wholesale house of this kind. Have you tried the department stores?"

She acknowledged that she had not.

"Well, if I were you," he said, looking at her rather genially, "I would try the department stores. They often need young women as clerks."

"Thank you," she said, her whole nature relieved by this spark of friendly interest.

"Yes," he said, as she moved toward the door, "you try the department stores," and off he went.

At that time the department store was in its earliest form of successful operation and there were not many. The first three in the United States, established about 1884, were in Chicago.[3] Carrie was familiar with the names of several through the advertisements in the "Daily News," and now proceeded to seek them. The words of Mr. McManus had somehow managed to restore her courage, which had fallen low, and she dared to hope that this new line would offer her something in the way of employment. Some time she spent in wandering up and down thinking to encounter the buildings by chance, so readily is the mind, bent upon prosecuting a hard but needful errand, eased by that self-deception which the semblance of search without the reality gives. At last she inquired of a police officer and was directed to proceed "two blocks up" where she would find The Fair. Following his advice she reached that institution and entered.

The nature of these vast retail combinations, should they ever permanently disappear, will form an interesting chapter in the commercial history of our nation. Such a flowering out of a modest trade principle the world had never witnessed up to that

---

[2] Typist.

[3] Reference to Marshall Field's, the Fair, and the Boston, stores that (although not literally the first in the country) brought commercial fame to Chicago during its time of growth after the 1871 fire.

time. They were along the line of the most effective retail organization, with hundreds of stores coordinated into one, and laid out upon the most imposing and economic basis. They were handsome, bustling, successful affairs, with a host of clerks and a swarm of patrons. Carrie passed along the busy aisles, much affected by the remarkable displays of trinkets, dress goods, shoes, stationery, jewelry. Each separate counter was a show place of dazzling interest and attraction. She could not help feeling the claim of each trinket and valuable upon her personally and yet she did not stop. There was nothing there which she could not have used—nothing which she did not long to own. The dainty slippers and stockings, the delicately frilled skirts and petticoats, the laces, ribbons, hair-combs, purses, all touched her with individual desire, and she felt keenly the fact that not any of these things were in the range of her purchase. She was a work-seeker, an outcast without employment, one whom the average employé could tell at a glance was poor and in need of a situation.

It must not be thought that anyone could have mistaken her for a nervous, sensitive, high-strung nature, cast unduly upon a cold, calculating and unpoetic world. Such certainly she was not. But women are peculiarly sensitive to the personal adornment or equipment of their person, even the dullest, and particularly is this true of the young. Your bright-eyed, rosy-cheeked maiden, over whom a poet might well rave for the flowerlike expression of her countenance and the lissome and dainty grace of her body, may reasonably be dead to every evidence of the artistic and poetic in the unrelated evidences of life, and yet not lack in material appreciation. Never, it might be said, does she fail in this. With her the bloom of a rose may pass unappreciated, but the bloom of a fold of silk, never. If nothing in the heavens, or the earth, or the waters, could elicit her fancy or delight her from its spiritual or artistic side, think not that the material would be lost. The glint of a buckle, the hue of a precious stone, the faintest tints of the watered silk, these she would devine and qualify as readily as your poet if not more so. The creak, the rustle, the glow—the least and best of the graven or spun—, these she would perceive and appreciate—if not because of some fashionable or hearsay quality, then on account of their true beauty, their innate fitness in any order of harmony, their place in the magical order and sequence of dress.

Not only did Carrie feel the drag of desire for all of this which was new and pleasing in apparel for women, but she noticed, too, with a touch at the heart, the fine ladies who elbowed and ignored her, brushing past in utter disregard of her presence, themselves eagerly enlisted in the materials which the store contained. Carrie was not familiar with the appearance of her more fortunate sisters of the city. Neither had she before known the nature and appearance of the shop girls, with whom she now compared poorly. They were pretty in the main, some even handsome, with a certain independence and toss of indifference which added, in the case of the more favored, a certain piquancy. Their clothes were neat, in many instances fine, and wherever she encountered the eye of one, it was only to recognize in it a keen analysis of her own position—her individual shortcomings of dress and that shadow of *manner* which she thought must hang about her and make clear to all who and what she was. A flame of envy lighted in her heart. She realized in a dim way how much the city held—wealth, fashion, ease—every adornment for women, and she longed for dress and beauty with a whole and fulsome heart.

On the second floor were the managerial offices, to which after some inquiry she was now directed. There she found other girls ahead of her, applicants like herself, but with more of that self-satisfied and independent air which experience of the city lends—girls who scrutinized her in a painful manner. After a wait of perhaps three-quarters of an hour she was called in turn.

"Now," said a sharp, quick-mannered Jew who was sitting at a roll-top desk near the window—"have you ever worked in any other store?"

"No sir," said Carrie.

"Oh, you haven't," he said, eyeing her keenly.

"No sir," she replied.

"Well, we prefer young women just now with some experience. I guess we can't use you."

Carrie stood waiting a moment, hardly certain whether the interview had terminated.

"Don't wait!" he exclaimed. "Remember we are very busy here."

Carrie began to move quickly to the door.

"Hold on," he said, calling her back. "Give me your name and address. We want girls occasionally."

When she had gotten safely out again into the street she could scarcely restrain tears. It was not so much the particular rebuff which she had just experienced, but the whole abashing trend of the day. She was tired and rather over-played upon in the nerves. She abandoned the thought of appealing to the other department stores and now wandered on, feeling a certain safety and relief in mingling with the crowd.

In her indifferent wandering she turned into Jackson Street, not far from the river, and was keeping her way along the south side of that imposing thoroughfare, when a piece of wrapping paper written on with marking ink and tacked upon a door attracted her attention. It read "Girls wanted—wrappers and stitchers." She hesitated for the moment, thinking surely to go in, but upon further consideration the added qualifications of "wrappers and stitchers" deterred her. She had no idea of what that meant. Most probably she would need to be experienced in it. She walked on a little way, mentally balancing as to whether or not to apply. Necessity triumphed however and she returned.

The entrance, which opened into a small hall, led to an elevator shaft, the elevator of which was up. It was a dingy affair, being used both as a freight and passenger entrance, and the woodwork was marked and splintered by the heavy boxes which were tumbled in and out, at intervals. A frowzy-headed German-American, about fourteen years of age, operated the elevator in his shirt sleeves and bare feet. His face was considerably marked with grease and dirt.

When the elevator stopped, the boy leisurely raised a protecting arm of wood and by grace of his superior privilege admitted her.

"Wear do you want to go?" he inquired.

"I want to see the manager," she replied.

"Wot manager?" he returned, surveying her caustically.

"Is there more than one?" she asked. "I thought it was all one firm."

"Naw," said the youth. "Der's six different people. Want to see Speigelheim?"

"I don't know," answered Carrie. She colored a little as she began to feel the necessity of explaining. "I want to see whoever put up that sign."

"Dot's Speigelheim," said the boy. "Fort floor." Therewith he proudly turned to his task of pulling the rope, and the elevator ascended.

The firm of Speigelheim and Co., makers of boys' caps, occupied one floor of fifty feet in width and some eighty feet in depth. It was a place rather dingily lighted, the darkest portions having incandescent lights, filled in part with machines and part with workbenches. At the latter labored quite a company of girls and some men. The former were drabby looking creatures, stained in face with oil and dust, clad in thin shapeless cotton dresses, and shod with more or less worn shoes. Many of them had their sleeves rolled up, revealing bare arms, and in some cases, owing to heat, their dresses were open at the neck. They were a fair type of nearly the lowest order of shop girls,—careless, rather slouchy, and more or less pale from confinement. They were not timid however, were rich in curiosity and strong in daring and slang.

Carrie looked about her, very much disturbed and quite sure that she did not want to work here. Aside from making her uncomfortable by sidelong glances, no one paid her the least attention. She waited until the whole department was aware of her presence. Then some word was sent round and a foreman in an apron and shirt sleeves, the latter rolled up to his shoulders, approached.

"Do you want to see me?" he asked.

"Do you need any help?" said Carrie, already learning directness of address.

"Do you know how to stitch caps?" he returned.

"No sir," she replied.

"Have you ever had any experience at this kind of work?" he inquired.

She owned that she hadn't.

"Well," said the foreman, scratching his ear meditatively, "we do need a stitcher. We like experienced help though. We've hardly got time to break people in." He paused and looked away out of the window. "We might, though, put you at finishing," he concluded reflectively.

"How much do you pay a week?" ventured Carrie, emboldened by a certain softness in the man's manner and his simplicity of address.

"Three and a half," he answered.

"Oh," she was about to exclaim, but checked herself, and allowed her thoughts to die without expression.

"We're not exactly in need of anybody," he went on vaguely, looking her over as one would a package. "You can come Monday morning though," he added, "and I'll put you to work."

"Thank you," said Carrie weakly.

"If you come, bring an apron," he added.

He walked away and left her standing by the elevator, never so much as inquiring her name.

While the appearance of the shop and the announcement of the price paid per week operated very much as a blow to Carrie's fancy, the fact that work of any kind, after so rude a round of experience, was offered her, was gratifying. She could not begin to believe that she would take the place, modest as her aspirations were. She had been used to better than that. Her mere experience and the free out-of-doors life of the country caused her nature to revolt at such confinement. Dirt had never been her share. Her sister's flat was clean. This place was grimy and low; the girls were careless and hardened. They must be bad-minded and -hearted, she imagined. Still a place had been offered her. Surely Chicago was not so bad if she could find one place in one day. She might find another and better later.

Her subsequent experiences were not of a reassuring nature, however. From all the more pleasing or imposing places she was turned away abruptly with the most chilling formality. In others where she applied, only the experienced were required. She met with painful rebuffs, the most trying of which had been in a cloak manufacturing house, where she had gone to the fourth floor to inquire.

"No, no," said the foreman, a rough, heavy-built individual who looked after a miserably lighted work shop, "we don't want anyone. Don't come here."

In another factory she was leered upon by a most sensual-faced individual who endeavored to turn the natural questions of the inquiry into a personal interview, asking all sorts of embarrassing questions and endeavoring to satisfy himself evidently that she was of loose enough morals to suit his purpose. In that case she had been relieved enough to get away and found the busy, indifferent streets to be again a soothing refuge.

With the wane of the afternoon went her hopes, her courage and her strength. She had been astonishingly persistent. So earnest an effort was well deserving of a better reward. On every hand, to her fatigued senses, the great business portion grew larger, harder, more stolid in its indifference. It seemed as if it was all closed to her, that the struggle was too fierce for her to hope to do anything at all. Men and women hurried by in long, shifting lines. She felt the flow of the tide of effort and interest, felt her own helplessness without quite realizing the wisp on the tide that she was. She cast about vainly for some possible place to apply but found no door which she had the courage to enter. It would be the same thing all over. The old humiliation of her pleas rewarded by curt denial. Sick at heart and in body, she turned to the west, the direction of Minnie's flat, which she had now fixed in mind, and began that wearisome, baffled retreat which the seeker for employment at nightfall too often makes. In passing through Fifth Avenue, south towards Van Buren Street, where she intended to take a car, she passed the door of a large wholesale shoe house, through the plate glass window of which she could see a middle-aged gentleman sitting at a small desk. One of those forlorn impulses which often grow out of a fixed sense of defeat, the last sprouting of a baffled and uprooted growth of ideas, seized upon her. She walked deliberately through the door and up to the gentleman who looked at her weary face with partially awakened interest.

"What is it?" he said.

"Can you give me something to do?" asked Carrie.

"Now I really don't know," he said kindly. "What kind of work is it you want —you're not a typewriter, are you?"

"Oh, no," answered Carrie.

"Well, we only employ book keepers and typewriters here. You might go round to the side and inquire upstairs. They did want some help upstairs a few days ago. Ask for Mr. Brown."

She hastened around to the side entrance and was taken up by the elevator to the fourth floor.

"Call Mr. Brown, Willie," said the elevator man to a boy near by.

Willie went off and presently returned with the information that Mr. Brown said she should sit down and that he would be around in a little while.

It was a portion of a stock room which gave no idea of the general character of the floor, and Carrie could form no opinion of the nature of the work.

"So you want something to do," said Mr. Brown, after he inquired concerning the nature of her errand. "Have you ever been employed in a shoe factory before?"

"No sir," said Carrie.

"What is your name?" he inquired, and being informed, "Well, I don't know as I have anything for you. Would you work for four and a half a week?"

Carrie was too worn by defeat not to feel that it was considerable. She had not expected that he would offer her less than six. She acquiesced, however, and he took her name and address.

"Well," he said finally—"you report here at eight o'clock Monday morning. I think I can find something for you to do."

He left her revived by the possibilities, sure that she had found something to do at last. Instantly the blood crept warmly over her body. Her nervous tension relaxed. She walked out into the busy street and discovered a new atmosphere. Behold, the throng was moving with a lightsome step. She noticed that men and women were smiling. Scraps of conversation and notes of laughter floated to her. The air was light. People were already pouring out of the buildings, their labor ended for the day. She noticed that they were pleased, and thoughts of her sister's home, and the meal that would be awaiting her, quickened her steps. She hurried on, tired perhaps, but no longer weary of foot. What would not Minnie say! Ah, the long winter in Chicago —the lights, the crowd, the amusement. This was a great, pleasing metropolis after all. Her new firm was a goodly institution. Its windows were of huge plate glass. She could probably do well there. Thoughts of Drouet[4] returned, of the things he had told her. She now felt that life was better. That it was livelier, sprightlier. She boarded a car in the best of spirits, feeling her blood still flowing pleasantly. She would live in Chicago, her mind kept saying to itself. She would have a better time than she ever had before—she would be happy.

Chapter V: [The Saloon]

Drouet did not call that evening. That worthy, after receiving the letter, had laid aside all thought of Carrie for the time being and was floating around having what he considered a gay time. On this particular evening he dined at Rector's, a restaurant of some local fame which occupied a basement at Clark and Monroe Streets. Thereafter he visited the resort of Hannah and Hogg's, which was in Adams Street opposite the somewhat imposing Federal Building. There he leaned over the splendid bar which it contained and swallowed a glass of plain whiskey and purchased a couple of cigars, one of which he lighted. This to him represented in part high life—a fair sample of what the whole must be.

Drouet was not a drinker, in the sense that that term is used to express excess. He was not a "monied" man. He only craved the best as his mind conceived it, and such doings seemed to him a part of the best. Rector's, with its polished marble walls and floor, its profusion of lights, its show of china and silverware, and above all its reputation as a resort for actors and professional men, seemed to him the proper place

[4] Charlie Drouet figures early in the novel as the traveling salesman who is Carrie's first seducer; he will be the one who introduces her to George Hurstwood, the manager of a fashionable Chicago saloon.

for a successful man to go. He loved fine clothes, good eating, and particularly the company and acquaintanceship of successful men. When dining it was a source of keen satisfaction to him to know that Joseph Jefferson was wont to come to this same place at some time or another, or that Henry E. Dixey, quite a well-known performer of the day, was there only a few tables off.[5] At Rector's he could always obtain this satisfaction, for there, particularly of an evening, one could encounter politicians, brokers, actors, some rich young "rounders" of the town, all eating and drinking amid a buzz of popular, commonplace conversation.

"That's so and so over there," was a common remark of these gentlemen among themselves, particularly among those who had not yet reached, but hoped to do so, the dazzling height which money to dine here, lavishly, represented.

"You don't say so," would be the reply.

"Why yes, didn't you know that? Why he's manager of the Grand Opera House."

When these things would fall upon Drouet's ears, he would straighten himself a little more stiffly and eat with solid comfort. If he had any vanity, this augmented it, and if he had any ambition, this stirred it. He would be able to flash a roll of greenbacks too someday. As it was, he could eat where *they* did.

His preference for Hannah and Hogg's Adams Street place was another yard off the same cloth. This was really a gorgeous saloon from a Chicago standpoint. Like Rector's it also was ornamented with a blaze of incandescent lights held in handsome chandeliers and set in graceful places. The floors were of brightly-colored tiles, the walls a composition of rich, dark-polished wood, which reflected the light, and colored stucco-work, which gave the place a very sumptuous appearance. The long bar was a blaze of lights, polished woodwork, colored and cut glassware and many fancy bottles. It was a truly swell saloon, with rich screens, fancy wines, and a line of bar goods unsurpassed in the country.

At Rector's, Drouet had met Mr. G. W. Hurstwood, manager of the Hannah and Hogg's Adams Street place, the latter having been pointed out as a very successful and well-known man about town. Hurstwood looked the part, for besides being slightly under forty, he had a good stout constitution, an active manner and a solid substantial air, which was composed in part of his fine clothes, his clean linen, his jewels, and, above all, his own sense of his importance. Drouet immediately conceived a notion of him as being someone worth knowing and was glad not only to meet him, but to visit the Adams Street bar thereafter whenever he wanted a drink or a cigar.

Hurstwood was an interesting character after his kind. He was shrewd and clever in many little things and capable of creating a good impression. His position, which was fairly important, was that of manager—a kind of stewardship which was imposing but lacked financial control. He had risen by perseverance and industry, through long years of service, from the position of barkeeper in a commonplace saloon to his present altitude. He had a little office in the place, set off in polished cherry and grillwork, where he kept in a roll-top desk the rather simple accounts of the place

[5] Jefferson; Dixey: two famous theater personalities of the time. Jefferson was best known for his portrayal of Rip Van Winkle in the dramatization of the Irving tale.

—supplies ordered and needed and so on. The chief executive and financial functions devolved upon the owners, Messrs. Hannah and Hogg, and upon a cashier, who looked after the money taken in.

For the most part he lounged about, dressed in excellent, tailored suits of imported goods, several rings upon his fingers, a fine blue diamond in his necktie, a striking vest of some new pattern and a watch chain of solid gold which held a charm of rich design and a watch of the latest make and engraving. He knew by name and could greet personally with a "Well, old fellow," hundreds of actors, merchants, politicians and the general run of successful characters about town, and it was a part of his success to do so. He had a finely graduated scale of informality and friendship, which improved from the "How do you do," addressed to the fifteen-dollar-a-week clerks and office attachés who by long frequenting of the place became aware of his position, to the "Why, old man, how are you," which he addressed to those noted or rich individuals who knew him and were inclined to be friendly. There was a class, however, too rich, too famous, or too successful, with whom he could not attempt any familiarity of address, and with these he was professionally tactful, assuming a grave and dignified attitude, paying them the deference which would win their good feeling without in the least compromising his own bearing and opinions. There were, in the last place, a few good followers, neither rich nor poor, famous nor yet remarkably successful, with whom he was friendly on the score of good fellowship. These were the kind of men whom he would converse with the longest and perhaps the most seriously. He loved to go out and have a good time once in a while,—to go to the races, the theatres, the sporting entertainments at some of the clubs and those more unmentionable resorts of vice—the gilded chambers of shame with which Chicago was then so liberally cursed. He kept a horse and neat trap, had his wife and two children who were well established in a neat house on the North Side, near Lincoln Park, and was altogether a very acceptable individual of our great American upper class—the first grade below the luxuriously rich.

Hurstwood liked Drouet. The latter's genial nature and dressy appearance pleased him. He knew that Drouet was only a traveling salesman, and not one of many years' standing at that, but the firm of Bartlett, Caryoe and Co. was a large and prosperous house, and Drouet stood well. Hurstwood knew Caryoe quite well, having drunk a glass now and then with him, in company with several others, when the conversation was general. Drouet had what was a help in his business, a moderate sense of humor, and could tell a good story when the occasion required. He could talk races with Hurstwood, tell interesting incidents concerning himself and his experiences with women, and report the state of trade in the cities which he visited, and so managed to make himself almost invariably agreeable. Tonight he was particularly so, since his report to the company had been favorably commented upon, his new samples had been satisfactorily selected and his trip marked out for the next six weeks.

"Why, hello, Charlie old man," said Hurstwood as Drouet came in that evening about eight o'clock. "How goes it?" The room was crowded.

Drouet shook hands, beaming good nature, and they strolled toward the bar.

"Oh, all right."

"I haven't seen you in six weeks. When did you get in?"

"Friday," said Drouet. "Had a fine trip."

"Glad of it," said Hurstwood, his black eyes lit with a warmth which half displaced the cold make-believe that usually dwelt in them. "What are you going to take?" he added, as the barkeeper, in snowy jacket and tie, leaned toward them from behind the bar.

"Old Hennessy," said Drouet.

"A little of the same for me," put in Hurstwood.

"How long are you in town this time?" inquired Hurstwood.

"Only until Wednesday. I'm going up to St. Paul."

"George Evans was in here Saturday and said he saw you in Milwaukee last week."

"Yes, I saw George," returned Drouet. "Great old boy, isn't he? We had quite a time there together."

The barkeeper was setting out the glasses and bottle before them, and they now poured out the draught as they talked, Drouet filling his to within a third of full as was considered proper and Hurstwood taking the barest suggestion of whiskey and modifying it with seltzer.

"What's become of Caryoe?" remarked Hurstwood. "I haven't seen him around here in two weeks."

"Laid up, they say," explained Drouet. "Say, he's a gouty old boy!"

"Made a lot of money in his time though, hasn't he?"

"Yes, wads of it," returned Drouet. "He won't live much longer. Barely comes down to the office now."

"Just one boy, hasn't he?" asked Hurstwood.

"Yes, and a swift-pacer," laughed Drouet.

"I guess he can't hurt the business very much though, with the other members all there."

"No, he can't injure that any, I guess."

Hurstwood was standing, his coat open, his thumbs in his pockets, the light on his jewels and rings relieving them with agreeable distinctness. He was the picture of fastidious comfort.

"Hello, George," said a voice, and Hurstwood turned around to put his hand in that of another worthy, resplendent in dress and figure, who had arrived from some other part of the country. They now conversed together in the same pointless phraseology, while Drouet drew out his purse to get a bill. The bartender saw his action however and signaled with his hands.

"It's on the manager," he said, smiling merrily. Hurstwood had them so trained that they knew.

"Let me introduce you to my friend here," Hurstwood said, coming up. He unloaded the newcomer on Drouet, who shook hands and immediately inquired if he would have something. Together they conversed, at first three-handed, with Hurstwood, then alone, while the latter went into his little office to talk with two fat, rosy-cheeked gentlemen who were there waiting to see him. Drouet could see that it was both a genial and interesting meeting for they talked with their heads together, then leaned back and laughed, then talked again and so on, while he exchanged commonplaces.

"What are you doing tonight?" said the newcomer after a time.

"Oh, I think I'll go over to the Grand in a little while," returned Drouet.

"What's there?"

"Hoyt's 'A Hole in the Ground.' "[6]

"Well, if I hadn't seen that several times, I'd join you," he remarked with that spirit of ready companionship which seems to be characteristic of the thoughtless.

Just then a third individual appeared who knew the second and took him away leaving Drouet to gaze, smoke and breathe with smiling satisfaction in the, to him, delightful atmosphere prevailing.

To one not inclined to drink, and gifted with a more serious turn of mind, such a bubbling, chattering, glittering chamber must ever seem an anomaly, a strange commentary on nature and life. Here come the moths in endless procession to bask in the light of the flame. Such conversation as one may hear would not warrant a commendation of the scene upon intellectual grounds. It seems plain that schemers would choose more sequestered quarters to arrange their plans, that politicians would not gather here in company to discuss anything save formalities where the sharp-eared may hear, and it would scarcely be justified on the score of thirst, for the majority of those who frequent these more gorgeous places have no craving for liquor. Nevertheless, the fact that here men gather, here chatter, here love to pass and rub elbows, must be explained upon some grounds. It must be that a strange bundle of passions and vague desires gives rise to such a curious social institution or it would not be.

Drouet, for one, was lured as much by his longing for pleasure as by his desire to shine among his betters. The many friends he met here dropped in because they craved, without perhaps consciously analyzing it, the company, the glow, the atmosphere, which they found. One might take it after all as an augur of the better social order, for the things which they satisfied here, though sensory, were not evil. No evil could come out of the contemplation of an expensively decorated chamber. The worst effect such a thing could have would be perhaps to stir up in the material-minded an ambition to arrange their lives upon a similarly splendid basis. In the last analysis, that would scarcely be called the fault of the decorations, but rather of the innate trend of the mind. That such a scene might stir the less expensively dressed to emulate the more expensively dressed could scarcely be laid at the door of anything save the false ambition of the minds of those so affected. Remove the element so thoroughly and solely complained of, liquor, and there would not be one to gainsay the qualities of beauty and enthusiasm which would remain. The pleased eye with which our modern restaurants of fashion are looked upon is proof positive of this assertion.

Yet here is the fact of the lighted chamber; the dressy, greedy company; the small, self-interested palaver; the disorganized, aimless, wandering mental action which it represents—the love of light and show and finery which, to one outside, under the serene light of the eternal stars, must seem a strange and shiny thing. Under the stars and sweeping night winds, what a lamp-flower it must bloom—a strange, glittering night-flower, odour-yielding, insect-drawing, insect-infested rose of pleasure.

"See that fellow coming in there?" said Hurstwood, returning and glancing at a gentleman just entering, arrayed in a high hat and Prince Albert coat, his fat cheeks puffed and red as with good eating.

"No, where?" said Drouet.

[6] Popular stage farce of the 1887 season, by Charles Hoyt.

"There," said Hurstwood, indicating the direction by a cast of his eye—"the man with the silk hat."

"Oh, yes," said Drouet, now affecting not to see. "Who is he?"

"That's Jules Wallace, the spiritualist."

Drouet followed him with his eyes, much interested.

"Doesn't look much like a man who sees spirits, does he?" said Drouet.

"Oh, I don't know," returned Hurstwood. "He's got the money, all right," and a little twinkle passed over his eyes.

"I don't go much on those things, do you?" asked Drouet.

"Well, you never can tell," said Hurstwood. "There may be something to it. I wouldn't bother about it myself though. By the way," he added, "are you going anywhere tonight?"

" 'A Hole in the Ground,' " said Drouet, mentioning the popular farce of the time.

"Well, you better be going. It's half after eight already," and he drew out his watch.

The crowd was already thinning out considerably—some bound for the theatres, some to their clubs, and some to that most fascinating of all the pleasures—for the type of man there represented at least—the ladies.

"Yes, I will," said Drouet.

"Come around after the show. I have something I want to show you," said Hurstwood.

"Sure," said Drouet, elated.

"You haven't anything on hand for the night, have you?" added Hurstwood.

"Not a thing!"

"Well, come round then."

"Is she a blonde?" said Drouet, laughing.

"Come around about twelve," said Hurstwood, ignoring the question.

"I struck a little peach coming in on the train Friday," remarked Drouet by way of parting. "By George, that's so. I must go and call on her before I go 'way."

"Oh, never mind her," Hurstwood remarked.

"Say, she was a little dandy, I tell you," went on Drouet confidentially, trying to impress his friend.

"Twelve o'clock," said Hurstwood.

"That's right," said Drouet, going out.

Thus was Carrie's name bandied about in the most frivolous and gay of places, and that also when the little toiler was bemoaning her narrow lot, which was almost inseparable from the early stages of this, her unfolding fate.

Chapter XLIV: [The Strike][7]

The barn at which Hurstwood applied was exceedingly short-handed, and was being operated practically by three men as directors. There were a lot of green hands around,

---

[7] The scene has shifted to New York City, where Hurstwood has fled with Carrie after taking a large amount of money from the safe of the Chicago saloon. Carrie has gone upon the stage as a chorus girl and is beginning to achieve some success, but Hurstwood's fortunes have declined so greatly that he is willing to take employment as a scab during a strike of the city's streetcar workers.

queer hungry-looking individuals, who looked as if want had driven them to desperate means. They tried to be lively and willing but there was an air of hang-dog diffidence about the place. Most all were awkward. All were silent, all poorly clothed.

Hurstwood presented the card given him.

"No experience, eh?" asked the man pleasantly enough.

"Not any," he replied.

"Well, I guess we'll have to teach you. Go out there in the yard and ask for Saunders. He'll show you."

Hurstwood went back through the barns and out into a large enclosed lot, where were a series of tracks and loops. A half-dozen cars were there, manned by instructors, each with a pupil at the lever. More pupils were waiting at one of the rear doors of the barn.

He took in the situation at once. Mr. Saunders need not be called for. All he had to do was stand here and wait his turn.

Presently one of the cars stopped near the barn end and a pupil got off.

"Next!" cried the teacher.

A shabby, thin-faced individual in a worn spring overcoat stepped away from Hurstwood's side and got on the platform. Then the teacher conferred with him quietly.

In silence Hurstwood viewed this scene and waited. His companions took his eye for awhile, though they did not interest him much more than the cars. They were an uncomfortable looking group, however. One or two were very thin and lean. Several were quite stout. Several others were rawboned and sallow, as if they had been beaten upon by all sorts of rough weather.

"Did you see by the paper they are going to call out the militia?" Hurstwood heard one of them remark.

"Oh, they'll do that," returned the other. "They always do."

"Think we're liable to have much trouble?" said another, whom Hurstwood did not see.

"Not very."

"That Scotchman that went out on the last car," put in a voice, "told me that they hit him in the ear with a cinder."

A small nervous laugh accompanied this.

"One of those fellows on the Fifth Avenue line must have had a hell of a time, according to the papers," drawled another. "They broke his car windows and pulled him off into the street 'fore the police could stop 'em."

"Yes, but there are more police around today," was added by another.

Hurstwood hearkened without much mental comment. These talkers seemed scared to him. Their gabbling was feverish—things said to quiet their own minds. He only looked out into the yard and waited.

Two of the men got around quite near him, but behind his back. They were rather social and he listened to what they said.

"Are you a railroad man?" said one.

"Me, no. I've always worked in a paper factory."

"I had a job in Newark, until last October," returned the other, with reciprocal feeling.

There were some words which passed, too low to hear. Then the conversation became strong again.

"I don't blame these fellers for strikin'," said one. "They got the right of it all right, but by God, I had to get something to do."

"Same here," said the other. "If I had my job in Newark, I wouldn't be over here takin' chances like these."

"It's hell these days, ain't it," said the man. "A poor man ain't nowhere. You could starve, by Jesus, right in the streets and there ain't most no one would help you."

"Right you are," said the other. "The job I had I lost 'cause they shut down. They run all summer and lay up a big stock, and then shut down."

Hurstwood paid some little attention to this. Somehow he felt a little superior to these two, a little better-off. To him they were ignorant and commonplace, poor sheep in a driver's hand.

"Poor devils," he thought, speaking out of the thoughts and feelings of a bygone period of success.

He was still listening to more of the same sort, which was his private opinion, when he was called.

"Next," said one of the instructors.

"You're next," said a neighbor, touching him.

He went out and climbed on the platform. The instructor took it for granted that no preliminaries were needed.

"You see this handle," he said, reaching up to an electric cut-off, which was fastened to the roof. "This throws the current off or on. If you want to reverse the car, you turn it over here. If you want to send it forward, you put it over here. If you want to cut off the power, you keep it in the middle."

Hurstwood smiled at the simple information.

"Now this handle here regulates your speed. To here," he said, pointing with his finger, "gives you about four miles an hour. This is eight. When it's full on, you make about fourteen miles an hour."

Hurstwood watched him calmly. He had seen motormen work before. He knew just about how they did it and was sure he could do as well, with a very little practise.

The instructor explained a few more details and then said:—

"Now we'll back her up."

Hurstwood stood placidly by, while the car rolled back into the yard.

"One thing you want to be careful about, and that is to start easy. Give one degree time to act before you add another. The one fault of most men is that they always want to throw her wide open. That's bad. It's dangerous too. Wears out the motor. You don't want to do that."

"I see," said Hurstwood.

He waited and waited, while the man talked on.

"Now you take it," he said finally.

The ex-manager laid hand to the lever and pushed gently, as he thought. It worked much easier than he imagined, however, with the result that the car jerked quickly forward, throwing him back almost against the door. He straightened up sheepishly, while the instructor stopped the car with the brake.

"You want to be careful about that," was all he said.

Hurstwood found, however, that handling a brake and regulating speed were not so instantly mastered as he had imagined. Once or twice he would have ploughed through the rear fence, if it had not been for the hand and word of his companion. The latter was rather patient with him, but he never smiled.

"You've got to get the knack of working both arms at once," he said. "It takes a little practise."

It came one o'clock while he was still on the car practising, and he began to feel hungry. The day set in snowing, and he was cold. He grew quite weary of running to and fro on the short track. He could see there was a knack to the thing which he had not quite mastered yet.

"Have you had your dinner yet?" asked the man, at last.

"No," he answered.

"Perhaps you'd better get it, then."

They ran the car to the end and both got off. Hurstwood went into the barn and sought a car step, pulling out his paper-wrapped lunch from his pocket. There was no water and the bread was dry, but he enjoyed it. There was no ceremony about dining. He swallowed and looked about, contemplating the dull, homely labor of the thing. It was disagreeable, miserably disagreeable, in all its phases. Not because he was bitter, but because it was hard. It would be hard to anyone, he thought.

After eating he stood about as before, waiting until his turn came. Among the men were those who impressed him as being against the strikers—grim, dull-looking individuals who maintained an unbroken silence. There was no index to the working of their minds. Hurstwood did not fancy these people. He was neutral himself, fairly well determined to work if he could, but willing to allow that the strikers had grievances. He would have preferred to see the others taking the situation in the same spirit.

When his turn came he perceived that he would not run a car this day. The intention was to give him an afternoon of practise, or such part of practise as he could get, along with others. A greater part of the time was spent in waiting about.

At last, evening came and with it hunger and a debate with himself as to how he should spend the night. It was half-past five. He must soon eat. If he tried to go home it would take him two hours and a half of cold walking and riding. Besides he had orders to report at seven the next morning, and going home would necessitate his rising at an unholy and disagreeable hour. More, he had only something like a dollar and fifteen cents of Carrie's money, with which he had intended to pay the week's coal bill, before the present idea struck him.

"They must have some place around here," he thought. "Where does that fellow from Newark stay?"

Finally he decided to ask. There was a young fellow standing near one of the doors in the cold, waiting a last turn. He was a mere boy in years—twenty-one about, but with a body which was lankly long, only because of privation. A little good living would have made this youth plump and swaggering.

"How do they arrange this, if a man hasn't got any money?" inquired Hurstwood discreetly.

The fellow turned a keen, watchful face on the inquirer.

"You mean eat?" he replied.

"Yes, and sleep. I can't go back to New York tonight."

"The foreman'll fix that if you ask him, I guess. He did me."

"That so?"

"Yes. I just told him I didn't have anything. Gee, I couldn't go home. I live way over in Hoboken."

Hurstwood only cleared his throat by way of acknowledgement.

"They've got a place upstairs here, I understand. I don't know what sort of a thing it is. Purty tough I guess. He gave me a meal ticket this noon. I know that wasn't much."

Hurstwood smiled grimly and the boy laughed.

"It ain't no fun, is it?" he inquired, wishing vainly for a cheery reply.

"Not much," answered Hurstwood.

"I'd tackle him now," volunteered the youth. "He may go 'way."

Hurstwood did so.

"Isn't there some place I can stay around here tonight?" he inquired. "If I have to go back to New York, I'm afraid I won't—"

"There's some cots upstairs," interrupted the man, "if you want one of them."

"That'll do," he assented.

He meant to ask for a meal ticket, but the seemingly proper moment never came and he decided to pay himself that night.

"I'll ask him in the morning."

He ate in a cheap restaurant in the vicinity and, being cold and lonely, went straight off to seek the loft in question. The company was not attempting to run cars after nightfall. It was so advised by the police.

The room seemed to have been a lounging place for night workers. There were some nine cots in the place, two or three wooden chairs, a soap box and a small round-bellied stove in which a fire was blazing. Early as he was, another man was there before him. The latter was sitting beside the stove, warming his hands.

Hurstwood approached and held out his own toward the fire. He was sick of the bareness and privation of all things connected with this venture already, but was steeling himself to hold out. He fancied he could for awhile.

"Cold isn't it?" said the early guest.

"Rather."

A long silence.

"Not much of a place to sleep in is it?" said the man.

"Better than nothing," replied Hurstwood.

Another silence.

"I believe I'll turn in," said the man.

Rising, he went to one of the cots and stretched himself, removing only his shoes and pulling the one blanket and dirty old comforter over him in a sort of bundle. The sight disgusted Hurstwood, but he did not dwell on it, choosing to gaze into the stove and think of something else. Presently he decided to retire and picked a cot, also removing his shoes.

While he was doing so, the youth who had advised him to come here entered and, seeing Hurstwood, tried to be genial.

"Better'n nothin'," he observed, looking around.

Hurstwood did not take this to himself. He thought it to be an expression of individual satisfaction and so did not answer. The youth imagined he was out of sorts and set to whistling softly. Seeing another man asleep, he quit that and lapsed into silence.

Hurstwood made the best of a bad lot by keeping on his clothes, and pushing away the covering, which was dirty, from his head; but at last he dozed in sheer weariness. The covering became more and more comfortable; its character was forgotten and he slept.

In the morning he was aroused out of a pleasant dream by several men stirring about in a cold, cheerless room. He had been back in Chicago in fancy, in his own comfortable home. Jessica had been arranging to go somewhere and he had been talking with her about it. She was so clear in his mind, that he was startled now by the contrast of this room. He raised his head, and the cold bitter reality jarred him into wakefulness.

"Guess I'd better get up," he said.

There was no water on this floor. He fastened on his shoes in the cold and stood up, shaking himself in his stiffness. His clothes felt disagreeable, his hair bad.

"Hell," he muttered, as he put on his hat.

Downstairs things were stirring again.

He found a hydrant with a trough which had once been used for horses, but there was no towel here and his handkerchief was soiled from yesterday. He contented himself with wetting his eyes with the ice-cold water. Then he sought the foreman, who was already on the ground.

"Had your breakfast yet?" inquired that worthy.

"No," said Hurstwood.

"Better get it then. Your car won't be ready for a little while."

Hurstwood hesitated.

"Could you let me have a meal-ticket?" he asked with an effort.

"Here you are," said the man, handing him one.

He breakfasted as poorly as the night before on some fried steak and bad coffee. Then he went back.

"Here," said the foreman, motioning to him when he came in. "You take this car out in a few minutes."

Hurstwood climbed upon the platform in the gloomy barn and waited for a signal. He was nervous, and yet the thing was a relief. Anything was better than the barn.

On this, the fourth day of the strike, the situation had taken a turn for the worse. The strikers, following the counsel of their leaders and the newspapers, had struggled peaceably enough. There had been no great violence done. Cars had been stopped, it is true, and the men argued with. Some crews had been won over and led away; some windows broken, some jeering and yelling done; but in no more than five or six instances had men been seriously injured. These by crowds whose acts the leaders disclaimed.

Idleness, however, and the sight of the company, backed by the police, triumphing, angered the men. They saw that each day more cars were going on, each day more declarations were being made by the company officials that the effective opposition of the strikers was broken. This angered the men and put desperate thoughts in their minds. Peaceful methods meant, they saw, that the companies would soon run all their cars, and those who had complained would be forgotten. There was nothing so helpful to the companies as peaceful methods.

All at once they blazed forth, and for a week there was storm and stress. Cars were assailed, men attacked, policemen struggled with, tracks torn up and shots fired, until at last street fights and mob movements became frequent, and the city was invested with militia.

Hurstwood knew nothing of the change of temper.

"Run your car out," called the foreman, waving a vigorous hand at him. A green conductor jumped up behind and rang the bell twice as a signal to start. Hurstwood turned the lever, and ran the car out through the door into the street in front of the barn. Here two brawny policemen got up beside him on the platform—one on either hand.

At the sound of a gong near the barn door, two bells were given by the conductor and Hurstwood opened his lever.

The two policemen looked about them calmly.

" 'Tis cold, all right, this morning," said the one on the left, who possessed a rich brogue.

"I had enough of it yesterday," said the other. "I wouldn't want a steady job of this."

"Nor I."

Neither paid the slightest attention to Hurstwood, who stood facing the cold wind, which was chilling him completely, and thinking of his orders.

"Keep a steady gait," the foreman had said. "Don't stop for anyone who doesn't look like a real passenger. Whatever you do, don't stop for a crowd."

The two officers kept silent for a few moments.

"The last man must have gone through all right," said the officer on the left. "I don't see his car anywhere."

"Who's on there?" asked the second officer, referring of course to its complement of policemen.

"Schaeffer and Ryan."

There was another silence in which the car ran smoothly along. There were not so many houses along this part of the way. Hurstwood did not see many people either. The situation was not wholly disagreeable to him. If he wasn't so cold, he thought, he would do real well.

He was brought out of this feeling by the sudden appearance of a curve ahead, which he had not expected. He shut off the current and did an energetic turn at the brakes, but not in time sufficient to avoid an unnaturally quick turn. It shook him up quite a bit and made him feel like making some apologetic remarks, but he refrained.

"You want to look out for them things," said the officer on the left, condescendingly.

"That's right," agreed Hurstwood, shame-facedly.

"There's lots of them on this line," said the officer on the right.

Around the corner, a more populated way appeared. One or two pedestrians were in view ahead. A boy coming out of a gate, with a tin milk bucket, gave Hurstwood his first objectionable greeting.

"Scab!" he yelled. "Scab!"

Hurstwood heard it but tried to make no comment, even to himself. He knew he would get that and much more of the same sort probably.

At a corner farther up a man stood by the track and signaled the car to stop.

"Never mind him," said one of the officers. "He's up to some game."

Hurstwood obeyed. At the corner he saw the wisdom of it. No sooner did the man perceive the intention to ignore him, than he shook his fist.

"Ah! you bloody coward!" he yelled.

Some half-dozen men, standing on the corner, flung taunts and jeers after the speeding car.

Hurstwood winced the least bit. The real thing was slightly worse than the thoughts of it had been.

Now came in sight, three or four blocks farther on, a heap of something on the track.

"They've been at work here, all right," said one of the policemen.

"We'll have an argument maybe," said the other.

Hurstwood ran the car close and stopped. He had not done so wholly, however, before a crowd was gathered about. It was composed of ex-motormen and conductors in part, with a sprinkling of friends and sympathizers.

"Come off the car, pardner," said one of the men in a voice meant to be conciliatory. "You don't want to take the bread out of another man's mouth, do you?"

Hurstwood held to his brake and lever, pale and very uncertain what to do.

"Stand back!" yelled one of the officers, leaning over the platform railing. "Clear out of this now. Give the man a chance to do his work."

"Listen, pardner," said the leader, ignoring the policeman and addressing Hurstwood. "We're all working men, like yourself. If you were a regular motorman and had been treated as we've been, you wouldn't want anyone to come in and take your place, would you? You wouldn't want anyone to do you out of your chance to get your rights, would you?"

"Shut her off! Shut her off!" urged the other of the policemen roughly. "Get out of this now," and he jumped the railing and landed before the crowd, and began shoving. Instantly the other officer was down beside him.

"Stand back now!" they yelled. "Get out of this. What the hell do you mean— out now!"

It was like a small swarm of bees.

"Don't shove me," said one of the strikers determinedly. "I'm not doing anything."

"Get out of this!" cried the officer, swinging his club. "I'll give ye a bat on the sconce! Back now!"

"What the hell!" cried another of the strikers, pushing the other way, adding at the same time some lusty oaths.

Crack came an officer's club on his forehead. He blinked his eyes blindly a few times, wobbled on his legs, threw up his hands and staggered back. In return a swift fist landed on the officer's neck.

Infuriated by this, the latter plunged left and right, laying about madly with his club. He was ably assisted by his brother of the blue, who poured ponderous oaths upon the troubled waters. No severe damage was done, owing to the agility of the strikers in keeping out of reach. They stood about the side walk now and jeered.

"Where is the conductor?" yelled one of the officers, getting his eye on that individual, who had come nervously forward to stand by Hurstwood. The latter had stood gazing upon the scene with more astonishment than fear.

"Why the hell don't you come down here and get these stones off the track?" inquired the officer. "What you standing there for? Do you want to stay here all day? Get down."

Hurstwood breathed heavily in excitement and jumped down with the nervous conductor, as if he had been called.

"Hurry up now," said the other policeman.

Cold as it was, these officers were hot and mad. Hurstwood worked with the conductor, lifting stone after stone and warming himself by the work.

"Ah, you scab you!" yelled the crowd. "You coward! Steal a man's job, will you? Rob the poor, will you—you thief! We'll get you yet, now. Wait!"

Not all of this was delivered by one man. It came from here and there, incorporated with much more of the same sort and curses.

"Work, you blackguards!" yelled a voice. "Do the dirty work! You're the suckers that keep the poor people down—you bastards!"

"May God starve ye yet!" yelled an old Irishwoman, who now threw open a nearby window and stuck out her head.

"Yes and you!" she added, catching the eye of one of the policemen. "You bloody, murtherin thafe! Crack my son over the head, will you, you hard-hearted murtherin divil! Ah, ye—"

But the officer turned a deaf ear.

"Go to the devil, you old hag," he half-muttered as he stared round upon the scattered company.

Now the stones were off and Hurstwood took his place again amid a continued chorus of epithets. Both officers got up beside him, and the conductor rang the bell, when, bang! bang! through window and door came rocks and stones. One narrowly grazed Hurstwood's head. Another shattered the window behind.

"Throw open your lever," yelled one of the officers, grabbing at the handle himself.

Hurstwood complied and the car shot away, followed by a rattle of stones and a rain of curses.

"That ——— ——— hit me in the neck," said one of the officers. "I gave him a good crack for it though."

"I think I must have left spots on some of them," said the other.

"I know that big guy that called me a ——— ———," said the first. "I'll get him yet for that."

"I thought we were in for it sure, once there," said the second.

Thus they talked. Hurstwood, warm and excited, gazed steadily ahead. It was an astonishing experience for him. He had read of these things but the reality seemed something altogether new. He was no coward in spirit. The fact that he had suffered this much now rather operated to arouse a stolid determination to stick it out. He did not recur in thought to New York or the flat. This one trip seemed a consuming thing.

They now ran into the business heart of Brooklyn uninterrupted, though not without reminders of the fact that they might expect more. People gazed at the broken windows of the car and at Hurstwood in his plain clothes. Voices called "scab" now and then, as well as other epithets, but no crowd attacked the car. At the down-town end of the line, one of the officers went to call up his station and report the trouble.

"There's a gang out there," he said, "laying for us yet. Better send some one over there and clean them out."

The car ran back more quietly, hooted, watched, flung at, but not attacked. Hurstwood breathed freely when he saw the barns.

"Well," he observed to himself, "I came out of that all right."

The car was turned in and he was allowed to loaf awhile, but at last he was again called. This time a new team of officers were aboard. Slightly more confident, he sped the car along the commonplace streets and felt somewhat less fearful. On one side, however, he suffered intensely. The day was raw, with a sprinkling of snow, and a gusty wind, which was made all the more intolerable by the speed of the car. His clothing was not intended for this sort of work. He shivered, stamped his feet and beat his arms as he had seen other conductors do in the past, but said nothing. The novelty and danger of the situation modified, in a way, his disgust and distress at being compelled to be here, but not enough to prevent him from feeling grim and sour. This was a dog's life, he thought. It was a tough thing to have to come to.

The one thought that strengthened him was the insult offered by Carrie. He was not down so low as to take all that, he thought. He could do something—this even —for awhile. It would get better. He would save a little.

A boy threw a clod of mud while he was thus reflecting and hit him upon the arm. It hurt sharply and angered him more than he had been any time since morning.

"The little cur," he muttered.

"Hurt you?" asked one of the policemen.

"No," he answered.

At one of the corners where the car slowed up because of a turn, an ex-motorman, standing on the sidewalk, called to him.

"Won't you come out, pardner, and be a man? Remember we're fighting for a decent day's wages, that's all. We've got families to support." The man seemed most peaceably inclined.

Hurstwood pretended not to see him. He kept his eyes straight on before and opened the lever wide. The voice had something appealing in it.

All morning this went on and long into the afternoon. He made three trips which were not any more difficult than the last described. The dinner he had was no stay for such work, and the cold was telling on him. Numb as he seemed to become to it, nevertheless it seemed to get worse. At each end of the line he stopped to thaw out, but he could have groaned at the anguish of it. One of the barn-men, out of pity, loaned him a heavy cap and a pair of sheepskin gloves, and for once he was extremely thankful. These were things he needed much.

On the second trip of the afternoon he ran into a crowd about half-way along the line, which blocked the car's progress with an old telegraph pole.

"Get that thing off the track!" shouted the two policemen.

"Yah, yah, yah!" yelled the crowd. "Get it off yourself!"

The two policemen got down and Hurstwood started to follow.

"You stay there," one called. "Some one will run away with your car."

Amid the babel of voices, Hurstwood heard one close beside him.

"Come down, partner, and be a man. Don't fight the poor. Leave that to the corporations."

He saw the same individual who had called to him from the corner. Now as before he pretended not to hear.

"Come down," the man repeated gently. "You don't want to fight poor men. Don't fight at all." It was a most philosophic and jesuitical motorman.

A third policeman joined the other two from somewhere, and someone ran to telephone for more officers. Hurstwood gazed about, determined but fearful.

A man grabbed him by the coat.

"Come off of that!" he exclaimed, jerking at him and trying to pull him over the railing.

"Let go!" said Hurstwood savagely.

"I'll show you—you scab!" cried a young Irishman, jumping up on the coupler and aiming a blow at Hurstwood. The latter ducked and caught it on the shoulder instead of the jaw.

"Away from here!" shouted an officer, hastening to the rescue and adding, of course, the usual oaths.

Hurstwood recovered himself, pale and trembling in the hands. It was becoming serious with him now. People were looking up and jeering at him. One girl was making faces.

"Ah, ya! ya!" she cried. It was the hissing, jeering mob of Christ's time.

He had begun to waver in his resolution when a patrol wagon rolled up and more officers dismounted. Now the track was quickly cleared and the release effected.

"Let her go now, quick," said the officer, and again he was off.

Another trial of the afternoon came when, delayed by a crowd, the officer commanded him to open up and plough his way through them.

"Run over 'em," he said, hoarsely.

Hurstwood complied and scattered a small throng, amid jeers.

The end came with a real mob which met the car on its return trip a mile or two from the barns. It was an exceedingly poor-looking neighborhood. He wanted to run fast through it but again the track was blocked. He saw men carrying something out to it when he was yet a half-dozen blocks away.

"There they are again!" exclaimed one policeman.

"I'll give them something this time," said the second officer, whose patience was becoming worn. Hurstwood suffered a qualm of body as the car rolled up to this.

As before the crowd began hooting, but now, rather than come near, they threw things. One or two windows were smashed and Hurstwood dodged a stone.

Both policemen ran out towards the crowd, but the latter replied by running toward the car. A woman, a mere girl in appearance, was among these, bearing a rough stick. She was exceedingly wrathful and struck at Hurstwood, who dodged. Thereupon her companions, duly encouraged, jumped on the car and pulled Hurstwood over. He had hardly time to speak or shout before he fell.

"Let go of me," he said, falling on his side.

"Ah, you sucker," he heard some one say. There were kicks and blows rained on him. He seemed to be suffocating. Then two men seemed to be dragging him off and he wrestled for freedom.

"Let up," said a voice. "You're all right. Stand up."

He was let loose, and sort of recovered himself. Now he recognized the two officers. He felt as if he would faint from exhaustion. Something was wet on his chin. He put up his hand and felt—then looked. It was red.

"They cut me," he said, foolishly, fishing for his handkerchief.

"Now, now," said one of the officers. "It's only a scratch."

His senses became clearer now and he looked around. He was standing in a little store where they left him for the moment. Outside, he could see, as he stood wiping his chin, the car and the excited crowd. A patrol wagon was there and another.

He walked over, and looked out. It was an ambulance, backing in.

He saw some energetic charging by the police and arrests being made.

"Come on now, if you want to take your car in," said an officer, opening the door and looking in.

He walked out, feeling rather uncertain of himself. He was very cold and frightened.

"Where's the conductor?" he asked.

"Oh, he's not here now," said the policeman.

Hurstwood went towards the car and stepped nervously on. As he did so, there was a pistol shot. Something stung his shoulder.

"Who fired that!" he heard an officer exclaim. "By God, who did that!" Both left him, running towards a certain building. He paused a moment and then got down.

"By God," he said vaguely—"this is too much for me."

He walked nervously to the corner and hurried down a side street.

"Wheh!" he said, drawing in his breath.

A half-block away, a small girl gazed at him.

"You better sneak," she called after him.

He walked homeward in a blinding snow storm, reaching the ferry by dusk. The cabins were filled with a few comfortable souls who studied him curiously. His head was still in such a whirl that he felt confused. All the wonder of the twinkling lights of the river in a white storm passed for nothing. He trudged doggedly on until he reached the flat. There he entered and found the room warm. Carrie was gone. A couple of evening papers were lying on the table where she left them. He lit the gas and sat down. Then he got up and stripped to examine his shoulder. It was a mere scratch. He washed his hands and face, still in a brown study, apparently, and combed his hair. Then he looked for something to eat, and finally, his hunger gone, sat down in his comfortable rocking chair. It was a wonderful relief.

He put his hand to his chin, forgetting for the moment the papers.

"Well," he said after a time, his nature recovering itself. "That's a pretty tough game over there."

Then he turned and saw the papers. With a half a sigh, he picked up the "World."[8]

"Strike Spreading in Brooklyn," he read. "Rioting Breaks Out in All Parts of the City."

He adjusted his paper very comfortably and continued. It was the one thing he read with absorbing interest.

[8] The New York *World,* the popular newspaper published by Joseph Pulitzer.

Chapter L: [The Two New Yorks][9]

In the city at that time there were a number of charities, similar in nature to the Captain's, which Hurstwood patronized in a similarly unfortunate way. One was a convent missionhouse of the Sisters of Mercy in 15th Street—a row of red brick family dwellings before the door of which hung a plain wooden contribution box, on which was painted the statement that every noon a meal was given free to all those who might apply and ask for aid. This simple announcement was modest in the extreme, covering as it did a charity so broad. Institutions and charities are so large and so numerous in New York that such things as this are not often noticed by the more comfortably situated. But to one whose mind is upon the matter, they grow exceedingly under inspection. Unless one were looking up this matter in particular, he could have stood at Sixth Avenue and 15th Street for days around the noon hour and never have noticed that out of the vast crowd that surged along that busy thoroughfare there turned out, every few seconds, some weatherbeaten, heavy-footed specimen of humanity, gaunt in countenance and dilapidated in the matter of clothes. The fact is none the less true, however, and the colder the day the more apparent it became. Space and a lack of culinary room in the mission house compelled an arrangement which permitted of only twenty-five or thirty eating at one time, so that a line had to be formed outside and an orderly entrance effected. This caused a daily spectacle which, however, had become so common by repetition during a number of years that now nothing was thought of it. The men waited patiently like cattle in the coldest weather, often for several hours, before they could be admitted. No questions were asked and no service rendered. They ate and went away again, some of them returning regularly day after day the winter through.

A big, motherly woman invariably stood guard at the door during the entire operation and counted in the admissible number. The men moved up in solemn order. There was no haste and no eagerness displayed. It was almost a dumb procession. In the bitterest weather this line was to be found here. Under an icy wind there was a prodigious slapping of hands and a dancing of feet. Fingers and the features of the face looked as if severely nipped by the cold. A study of these men in broad light proved them to be nearly all of a type. They belonged to the class that sits on the park benches during the endurable days and sleeps upon them during the summer nights. They frequent the Bowery and those down-at-the-heels East Side streets where poor clothes and shrunken features are not singled out as curious. They are the men who are in the lodging house sitting rooms during bleak and bitter weather and who swarm about the cheaper shelters which only open at six in a number of the lower East Side streets. Miserable food, ill-timed and greedily eaten, had played havoc with bone and muscle. They were all pale, flabby, sunken-eyed, hollow-chested, with eyes that glinted and shone, and lips that were a sickly red by contrast. Their hair was but half attended to, their ears anæmic in hue, and their shoes broken in leather and run down at heel and toe. They were of the class which simply floats and drifts, every wave of people washing up one as breakers do driftwood upon a stormy shore.

For nearly a quarter of a century in another section of the city, Fleischmann, the caterer, had given a loaf of bread to anyone who would come for it to the rear door

---

[9] Hurstwood and Carrie have separated. She has attained stardom on the musical comedy stage; he has become a vagrant and beggar on the New York streets.

of his restaurant at the corner of Broadway and 9th Street, at midnight. Every night, during twenty years, about three hundred men had formed in line and at the appointed time marched past the doorway, picked their loaf from a great box, placed just outside, and vanished again into the night. From the beginning to the present time there had been little change in the character or number of these men. There were two or three figures that had grown familiar to those who had seen this little procession pass year after year. Two of them had missed scarcely a night in fifteen years. There were about forty more-or-less regular callers. The remainder of the line was formed of strangers. In times of panic and unusual hardships, there were seldom more than three hundred. In times of prosperity, when little is heard of the unemployed, there were seldom less. The same number winter and summer, in storm or calm, in good times and bad, held this melancholy midnight rendezvous at Fleischmann's bread box.

At both of these two charities, during the severe winter which was now on, Hurstwood was a frequent visitor. On one occasion it was peculiarly cold, and, finding no comfort in begging about the streets, he waited until noon before seeking this free offering to the poor. Already at eleven o'clock of this morning, several such as he had shambled forward out of Sixth Avenue, their thin clothes flapping and fluttering in the wind. They leaned against the iron railing which protects the walls of the 9th Regiment Armory, which fronts upon that section of 15th Street, having come early in order to be first in. Having an hour to wait, they at first lingered at a respectful distance, but others coming up, they moved closer in order to forfend against being forestalled in the matter of precedence. To this collection Hurtstood came up from the west out of Seventh Avenue and stopped close to the door, nearer than all the others. Those who had been waiting before him, but farther away, now drew near and by a certain stolidity of demeanor, no words being spoken, indicated that they were first. Seeing the opposition to his action he looked sullenly along the line and then moved out, taking his place at the foot. When order had been restored, the animal feeling of opposition relaxed.

"Must be pretty near noon," ventured one.

"It is," said another. "I've been waitin' nearly an hour."

"Gee but it's cold."

They peered eagerly at the door where all must enter. A groceryman drove up and carried in several baskets of edibles. This started some words upon grocerymen and the cost of food in general.

"I see meat's gone up," said one.

"If there wuz war it would help this country a lot."

The line was growing rapidly. Already there were fifty or more, and those at the head by their demeanor evidently congratulated themselves upon not having so long to wait as those at the foot. There was much jerking of heads and looking down the line.

"It don't matter much how near you get to the front so long as you're in the first twenty-five," commented one of the first twenty-five. "You all go in together."

"Hmph!" ejaculated Hurstwood, who had been so sturdily displaced.

"This here Single Tax is the thing,"[10] said another. "There ain't gone to be no order till it comes."

<hr>

[10] During the 1880s and 1890s, the Single Tax movement, intended to provide equitable taxation that would close the gap between the rich and the poor, was led by Henry George.

For the most part there was silence, gaunt men shuffling, glancing and beating their arms.

At last the door opened and the motherly sister looked out. She only looked an order. Slowly the line moved up and one by one passed in until thirty were counted. Then she interposed a stout arm and the line halted with six men on the steps. Of these the ex-manager was one. Waiting thus, some talked, some ejaculated concerning the misery of it, some brooded, as did Hurstwood. At last he was admitted and, having eaten, came away, almost angered because of his pains in getting it.

At eleven o'clock of another evening perhaps two weeks later, he was at the midnight offering of a loaf, waiting patiently. It had been an unfortunate day with him, but now he took his fate with a touch of philosophy. If he could secure no supper, or was hungry late in the evening, here was a place where he could come. A few minutes before twelve a great box of bread was pushed out and exactly on the hour a portly, round-faced German took position by it, calling "Ready." The whole line at once moved forward, each taking his load in turn and going his separate way. On this occasion the ex-manager ate his as he went, plodding the dark streets in silence to his bed.

By January he had about concluded that the game was up with him. Life had always seemed a precious thing, but now constant want and a weakened vitality had made the charms of earth rather dull and inconspicuous. Several times, when fortune pressed most harshly, he thought he would end his troubles, but with a change of weather, or the arrival of a quarter or a dime, his mood would change and he would wait. Each day he would find some old paper lying about and look into it to see if there was any trace of Carrie, but all summer and fall he had looked in vain. Then he noticed that his eyes were beginning to hurt him, and rapidly this ailment increased until in the dark chambers of the lodgings he frequented he did not attempt to read. Bad and irregular eating was sapping every function of his body. The one recourse left him was to doze, when a place offered and he could get the money to occupy it.

He was beginning to find, in his wretched clothing and meagre state of body, that people took him for a chronic type of bum and beggar. Police hustled him along, restaurant and lodging-house keepers turned him out promptly the moment he had his due, pedestrians waved him off. He found it more and more difficult to get anything from anybody.

At last he admitted to himself that the game was up. It was after a long series of appeals to pedestrians in which he had been refused and refused, everyone hastening from contact.

"Give me a little something, will you mister?" he said to the last one. "For God's sake do. I'm starving."

"Ah, get out," said the man, who happened to be a common type himself, holdholding a small official position under Tammany.[11] "You no good. I'll give you nawthin."

Hurstwood put his hands, red from cold, down in his pockets. Tears came into his eyes.

---

[11] The powerful political machine run by the Democratic party in New York City.

"That's right," he said, "I'm no good now. I was all right. I had money. I'm going to quit this," and with death in his heart he started down toward the Bowery.[12] People had turned on the gas before and died. Why shouldn't he? He remembered a lodging house where there were little closed rooms with gas jets in them, almost pre-arranged, he thought, for this which he wanted to do, which rented for fifteen cents. Then he remembered that he had no fifteen cents.

On the way he met a comfortable-looking gentleman coming clean-shaven out of a fine barber shop.

"Would you mind giving me a little something?" he asked this man boldly.

The gentleman looked him over and fished for a dime. Nothing but quarters were in his pocket.

"Here," he said, handing him one to be rid of him. "Be off now."

Hurstwood moved on, wondering. The sight of the large, bright coin pleased him a little. He remembered that he was hungry and that he could get a bed for ten cents. With this, the idea of death passed for the time being out of his mind. It was only when he could get nothing but insults that death seemed worth while.

One day in the middle of the winter, the sharpest spell of the season set in. It broke gray and cold on the first day and on the second snowed. Poor luck pursuing him, he had secured but ten cents by nightfall, and this he had spent for food. At evening he found himself at the Boulevard and 67th Street, where he finally turned his face Bowery-ward. Especially fatigued because of the wandering propensity which had seized him in the morning, he now half dragged his wet feet, slopping the soles upon the sidewalk. An old, thin coat was turned up about his red ears—his cracked derby hat was pulled down until it turned the same hearing organs outward. His hands were in his pockets.

"I'll just go down Broadway," he said to himself.

When he reached 42nd Street, the fire signs were already blazing bright. Crowds were hastening to dine. Through bright windows at every corner might be seen gay companies in luxuriant restaurants. There were coaches, and crowded cable cars.

In his weary and hungry state he should never have come here. The contrast was too sharp. Even he was recalled keenly to better things.

"What's the use," he thought. "It's all up with me. I'll quit this."

People turned to look after him, so uncouth was his shambling figure. Several officers followed him with their eyes to see that he did not beg of anybody.

Once he paused in an aimless, incoherent sort of way and looked through the windows of an imposing restaurant, before which blazed a fire sign and through the large plate windows of which could be seen the red and gold decorations, the palms, the white napery and shiny glassware, and above all, the comfortable crowd. Weak as his mind had become, his hunger was sharp enough to show the importance of this. He stopped stock still, his frayed pants soaking in the slush, and peered foolishly in.

"Eat," he mumbled. "That's right, eat. Nobody else wants any."

Then his voice dropped even lower and his mind half lost the fancy it had.

---

[12] The district on the lower East Side of the city known for its flophouses, cheap saloons, and poverty, in contrast to the affluence and glamor of Carrie's Broadway, lined with fashionable hotels, restaurants, and theaters.

"It's mighty cold," he said. "Awful cold."

At Broadway and 39th Street was blazing, in incandescent fire, Carrie's name. "Carrie Madenda," it read, "and the Casino Company." All the wet, snowy sidewalk was bright with this radiated fire. It was so bright that it attracted Hurstwood's gaze. He looked up, and then at a large gilt-framed poster-board on which was a fine lithograph of Carrie, life-size.

Hurstwood gazed at it a moment, snuffling and hunching one shoulder as if something were scratching him. He was so run-down, however, that his mind was not exactly clear.

"That's you," he said at last, addressing her. "Wasn't good enough for you, was I? Huh."

He lingered, trying to think logically. This was no longer possible with him.

"She's got it," he said, incoherently, thinking of money. "Let her give me some."

He started around to the side door. Then he forgot what he was going for and paused, pushing his hands deeper to warm the wrists. Suddenly it returned. The stage door! That was it.

He approached that entrance and went in.

"Well," said the attendant, staring at him. Seeing him pause he went over and shoved him. "Get out of here," he said.

"I want to see Miss Madenda," he said.

"You do, eh!" the other said, almost tickled at the spectacle. "Get out of here," and he shoved him again.

Hurstwood had no strength to resist.

"I want to see Miss Madenda," he tried to explain, even as he was being hustled away. "I'm all right. I—"

The man gave him a last push and closed the door. As he did so Hurstwood slipped and fell in the snow. It hurt him and some old vague sense of shame returned. He began to cry and swear foolishly.

"God damned dog!" he said. "Damned old cur," wiping the slush from his worthless coat. "I—I hired such people as you once."

Now a fierce feeling against Carrie welled up—just one fierce, angry thought before the whole thing slipped out of his mind.

"She owes me something to eat," he said. "She owes it to me."

Hopelessly he turned back into Broadway again and slopped onward, and away, begging, crying, losing track of his thoughts, one after another, as a mind decayed and disjointed is wont to do.

It was a truly wintry evening a few days later when his one distinguished mental decision was reached. Already at four o'clock the sombre hue of night was thickening the air. A heavy snow was falling—a fine, picking, whipping snow, borne forward by a swift wind in long, thin lines. The streets were bedded with it, six inches of cold, soft carpet, churned to a dirty brown by the crush of teams and the feet of men. Along Broadway, men picked their way in ulsters and umbrellas. Along the Bowery, men slouched through it with collars up and hats pulled over their ears. In the former thoroughfare, business men and travellers were making for comfortable hotels. In the latter, crowds on cold errands shifted past dingy stores, in the deep recesses of which lights were already gleaming. There were early lights in the cable cars, whose usual clatter was reduced by the mantle about the wheels. The whole city was muffled by its fast-thickening mantle.

In her comfortable chambers at the Waldorf,[13] Carrie was reading, at this time, "Père Goriot,"[14] which Ames had recommended to her. It was so strong, and Ames's mere commendation had so aroused her interest, that she caught nearly the full sympathetic significance of it. For the first time it was being borne in upon her how silly and worthless had been her earlier reading, as a whole. Becoming wearied, however, she yawned and came to the window, looking out upon the old unending procession of carriages rolling up Fifth Avenue.

"Isn't it bad," she observed to Lola.

"Terrible," said that little lady, joining her. "I hope it snows enough to go sleigh riding."

"Oh, dear," said Carrie, with whom the sufferings of father Goriot were still keen. "That's all you think of. Aren't you sorry for the people who haven't got anything tonight?"

"Of course I am," said Lola, "but what can I do? I haven't got anything."

Carrie smiled.

"You wouldn't care if you had," she returned.

"I would too," said Lola. "But people never gave me anything when I was hard up."

"Isn't it just awful," said Carrie, studying the winter's storm.

"Look at that man over there," laughed Lola, who had caught sight of someone falling down. "How sheepish men look when they fall, don't they?"

"We'll have to take a coach[15] tonight," answered Carrie absently.

In the lobby of the Imperial,[16] Mr. Charles Drouet was just arriving, shaking the snow from a very handsome ulster. Bad weather had driven him home early and stirred his desires for those pleasures which shut out the snow and gloom of life. A good dinner, the company of a young woman, and an evening at the theatre were the chief things for him.

"Why hello, Harry," he said, addressing a lounger in one of the comfortable lobby chairs—"how are you?"

"Oh, about six and six," said the other.

"Rotten weather, isn't it."

"Well, I should say," said the other. "I've been just sitting here, thinking where I'd go tonight."

"Come along with me," said Drouet. "I can introduce you to something dead swell."

[13] The Waldorf-Astoria, which opened on Fifth Avenue at Thirty-third Street in 1893, quickly became known as one of the most luxurious hotels of the city.
[14] *Le Père Goriot,* a novel by Honoré de Balzac, was published in 1834; it relates the sad story of the lives of unfortunates in Paris.

[15] Covered carriage.
[16] The Imperial Hotel, at Thirty-second Street and Broadway, was a popular hotel frequented by businessmen.

"Who is it?" said the other.

"Oh, a couple of girls over here in 40th Street. We could have a dandy time. I was just looking for you."

"Supposing we get 'em and take 'em out to dinner."

"Sure," said Drouet. "Wait'll I go upstairs and change my clothes."

"Well, I'll be in the barber shop," said the other. "I want to get a shave."

"All right," said Drouet, creaking off in his good shoes toward the elevator. The old butterfly was as light on the wing as ever.

On an incoming vestibuled Pullman, speeding at forty miles an hour through the snow of the evening, were three others, all related.[17]

"First call for dinner in the dining car," a Pullman servant was announcing, as he hastened through the aisle in snow-white apron and jacket.

"I don't believe I want to play any more," said the youngest, a black-haired beauty (turned supercilious by fortune) as she pushed a euchre hand away from her.

"Shall we go in to dinner?" inquired her husband, who was all that fine raiment can make.

"Oh, not yet," she answered. "I don't want to play any more, though."

"Jessica," said her mother, who was also a study in what good clothing can do for age, "push that pin down in your tie—it's coming up."

Jessica obeyed, incidentally touching at her lovely hair, and looking at a little jewel-faced watch. Her husband studied her, for beauty, even cold, is fascinating from one point of view.

"Well, we won't have much more of this weather," he said. "It only takes two weeks to get to Rome."

Mrs. Hurstwood nestled comfortably in her corner and smiled. It was so nice to be mother-in-law of a rich young man—one whose financial state had borne her personal inspection.

"Do you suppose the boat will sail promptly," asked Jessica, "if it keeps up like this?"

"Oh, yes," answered her husband. "This won't make any difference."

Passing down the aisle came a very fair-haired banker's son, also of Chicago, who had long eyed this supercilious beauty. Even now he did not hesitate to glance at her, and she was conscious of it. With a specially conjured show of indifference she turned her pretty face wholly away. It was not wifely modesty at all. By so much was her pride satisfied.

The last of this small and once partially united company, however, was elsewhere, having reached a distinguished decision. Before a dirty four-story building in a side street quite near the Bowery, whose one-time coat of buff had been changed by soot and rain, he mingled with a significant crowd of men—a crowd which had been and was still gathering by degrees. It began with the approach of two or three who hung about the closed wooden doors and beat their feet to keep them warm. They had on faded derby hats with dents in them. Their misfit coats were heavy with melted snow

---

[17] Hurstwood's estranged wife, daughter, and the daughter's new husband, who are traveling together by railway from Chicago to New York City at the start of a pleasure trip to Europe.

and turned up at the collars. Their trousers were mere bags, frayed at the bottoms and wobbling over big, soppy shoes, torn at the sides and worn almost to shreds. They made no effort to go in but shifted ruefully about, digging their hands deep in their pockets and leering at the crowd and the increasing lamps. With the minutes increased the numbers. There were old men with grizzled beards and sunken eyes, men who were comparatively young but shrunken by diseases, men who were middle-aged. None was fat. There was a face in the thick of the collection which was as white as drained veal. There was another red as brick. Some came with thin, rounded shoulders; others with wooden legs; still others with frames so lean that clothes only flapped about them. There were great ears, swollen noses, thick lips, and above all, red, bloodshot eyes. Not a normal, healthy face in the whole mass; not a straight figure; not a straightforward, steady glance.

In the drive of the wind and sleet they pushed in on one another. There were wrists, unprotected by coat or pocket, which were red with cold. There were ears, half-covered by every conceivable semblance of a hat, which still looked stiff and bitten. In the snow they shifted, now one foot, now another, almost rocking in unison.

With the growth of the crowd about the door came a murmur. It was not conversation but a running comment directed at anyone in general. It contained oaths and slang phrases.

"By damn, I wisht they'd hurry up."

"Jesus."

"Look at the copper watchin'."

"Maybe it ain't winter, nuther."

"I wisht I was in Sing Sing."[18]

Now a sharper lash of wind cut down and they huddled closer. It was an edging, shifting, pushing throng. There was no anger, no pleading, no threatening words. It was all sullen endurance, unlightened by either wit or good fellowship.

A carriage went jingling by with some reclining figure in it. One of the members nearest the door saw it.

"Look at the bloke, ridin'."

"He ain't so cold!"

"Eh! Eh! Eh!" yelled another, the carriage having long since passed out of hearing.

Little by little the night crept on. Along the walk a crowd turned out on its way home. Men and shop girls went by with quick steps. The cross-town cars began to be crowded. The gas lamps were blazing and every window bloomed ruddy with steady flames. Still the crowd hung about the door, unwavering.

"Ain't they ever goin' to open up?" queried a hoarse voice suggestively.

This seemed to renew general interest in the closed door, and many gazed in that direction. They looked at it as dumb brutes look, as dogs paw and whine and study the knob. They shifted and blinked and muttered, now a curse, now a comment. Still they waited and still the snow whirled and cut them with biting flakes. On the old hats and peaked shoulders it was piling. It gathered in little heaps and curves and no one brushed it off. In the centre of the crowd the warmth and steam melted it, and

[18] New York State prison, located up the Hudson
River from Manhattan.

water trickled off hat-rims and down noses, which the owners could not reach to scratch. On the outer rim the piles remained unmelted. Those who could not get in the centre lowered their heads to the weather and bent their forms.

A light appeared through the transom overhead. It sent a thrill of possibility through the watchers. There was a murmur of recognition. At last the bars grated inside and the crowd pricked up its ears. Footsteps shuffled within and it murmured again. Some one called: "Slow up there now," and then the door opened. It was push and jam for a minute, with grim, beast silence to prove its quality, and then it melted inward, like logs floating, and disappeared. There were wet hats and wet shoulders, a cold, shrunken, disgruntled mass pouring in between bleak walls. It was just six o'clock and there was supper in every hurrying pedestrian's face. And yet no supper was provided here—nothing but beds. Of these, Hurstwood was claiming one.

He laid down his fifteen cents and crept off with weary steps to his allotted room. It was a dingy affair, wooden, dusty, hard. A small gas jet furnished sufficient light for so rueful a corner.

"Hm," he said, clearing his throat and locking the door.

Now he began leisurely to take off his clothes, but stopped first with his coat and tucked it along the crack under the door. His vest he arranged in the same place. His old wet, cracked hat he laid softly upon the table. Then he pulled off his shoes and lay down.

It seemed as if he thought awhile for now he arose and turned the gas out, standing calmly in the blackness, hidden from view. After a few moments in which he reviewed nothing, but merely hesitated, he turned the gas on again, but applying no match. Even then he stood there, hidden wholly in that blindness which is night, while the uprising fumes filled the room. When the odor reached his nostrils he quit his attitude and fumbled for the bed.

"What's the use," he said wearily, as he stretched himself to rest.

1900

Willa Cather
1873–1947

The old settlements of Virginia and the new lands of Nebraska formed the bedding ground for Willa Cather's talents; so did the layers of memory she found elsewhere across the North American continent, from New Mexico to Canada. Cather was born on the family farm in the hills of Virginia; she lived there until she was nine, when she moved with her parents to Nebraska. After several farming ventures there proved unsuccessful, the Cathers decided to live in the small town of Red Cloud. A young community, Red Cloud nevertheless offered the usual mix of frontier activities. It was flavored by the customs of newcomers from Scandinavia, Germany, and Central Europe as well as by "eastern cultivation" based on classical languages, music, and literature.

Willa Cather was graduated from the University of Nebraska in 1895, then returned East to Pittsburgh. She supported herself first as a journalist and later as a high school teacher. By 1900 she was placing stories and poems in such well-known, large-circulation magazines as *McClure's* and *Cosmopolitan. April Twilight,* a collection of poems, appeared in 1903; it was followed in 1905 by *The Troll Garden,* a grouping of short stories. On the move again, she arrived in New York in 1906 and worked as managing editor of *McClure's* until 1912, the publication date of her first novel, *Alexander's Bridge.* She decided to support herself solely by writing fiction. The appreciation commanded by her earliest work continued and grew, and her decision to be a full-time professional writer proved to be a wise one.

Until 1912 Willa Cather had only hovered around her childhood experiences in Nebraska as possible material for her writings. The next five years saw a burst of literary activity stimulated by those memories, three novels that make clear her affinity for recording dreams of an ordered life whose every moment had significance. They show her mind stimulated by the ahistorical, semimythic landscapes of Nebraska and Arizona. *O Pioneers!* (1913), *Song of the Lark* (1915), and *My Ántonia* (1918) reveal the aspirations of young men and women on the frontier who try to trick defeat and betrayal with their hopes and unflinching will.

Youth and the Bright Medusa, a collection of stories, emerged in 1920. In 1922, the year her war novel, *One of Ours,* was published, Cather's writing career and personal life faltered when the woman she loved got married. She regained her psychic strength, however, and over the next five years wrote three more novels: *A Lost Lady* (1923), *The Professor's House* (1925), and *Death Comes for the Archbishop* (1927). *Shadows on the Rock* followed in 1931, as did other books of less note. Throughout the 1920s and early 1930s she received a number of awards, confirming her place as an important literary voice.

The twin roles of religious faith and memory are strong forces in Willa Cather's fiction. The human need for illusion, dreams, and a vision of a world that lies beyond the material frame permeates her accounts of characters whose lives are made greater, though not necessarily happier, by their insistence on linking their present desires with the aspirations experienced by previous generations. Repeatedly, she portrays the psychological patterns of those who make pilgrimages of the spirit into virginal territories, either geographical or spiritual. Her confirmation as a Protestant Episcopalian in 1922 made her especially responsive to the traditions of Roman Catholicism that had led priests into the frontier areas of New Mexico and French Canada. Priests and pioneers shared the same tradition of heart's longings that are central to much of her fiction.

Cather specifically rejected the realism she associated with a journalist's itemization of facts. She worked more closely with the modernist writers of her generation, who approached their subjects by means of suggestion and the power of descriptive language. But however oblique her treatment, Cather's analysis of why we dream of something better and of how those dreams result in courage and not in defeat makes her narratives of hopeful immigrants and sensitive carriers of culture seem accurate deep down at the bone of truth.

Further Reading:
A. Porterfield, *Willa Cather*, 1928.
R. Rapin, *Willa Cather*, 1930.
M. Bennett, *The World of Willa Cather*, 1951, 1961.
D. Daiches, *Willa Cather: A Critical Introduction*, 1951, 1962.
E. Brown and L. Edel, *Willa Cather: A Critical Biography*, 1953.
E. Lewis, *Willa Cather Living*, 1953.
E. Sergeant, *Willa Cather: A Memoir*, 1953, 1963.
N. W. Smith, *Willa Cather's Art of Fiction*, 1954.
J. Randall, *The Landscape and the Looking Glass: Willa Cather's Search for Value*, 1960, 1973.
E. A. Bloom, *Willa Cather's Gift of Sympathy*, 1962, 1965.
Dorothy Van Ghent, *Willa Cather*, 1964.

Willa Cather and Her Critics, ed. J. Schroeter, 1967.
R. Giannone, *Music in Willa Cather's Fiction*, 1968.
B. Bonham, *Willa Cather*, 1970.
J. Woodress, *Willa Cather: Her Life and Art*, 1970.
D. T. McFarland, *Willa Cather*, 1972.
P. L. Yongue, *The Immense Design*, 1972.
P. Gerber, *Willa Cather*, 1975.
D. McFarland, *Willa Cather's Imagination*, 1975.
M. Pers, *Willa Cather's Children*, 1975.
D. Stouck, *Willa Cather's Imagination*, 1975.
M. Brown, *Only One Point of the Compass: Willa Cather in the Northeast*, 1980.
K. Bryne, *Chrysalis: Willa Cather in Pittsburgh, 1896–1906*, 1980.

Texts:
"The Sculptor's Funeral" from *Willa Cather's Collected Short Fiction*, ed. V. Faulkner, 1970.
"Neighbour Rosicky" from *Obscure Destinies*, 1930.
See also *The Novels and Stories of Willa Cather*, 13 vols., 1934–1941.

The Kingdom of Art: Willa Cather's First Principles and Critical Statements, 1893–1896, ed. B. Slote, 1966.
The World and the Parish: Willa Cather's Articles and Reviews, 1893–1902, ed. W. Curtin, 1970.

The Sculptor's Funeral

A group of the townspeople stood on the station siding of a little Kansas town, awaiting the coming of the night train, which was already twenty minutes overdue. The snow had fallen thick over everything; in the pale starlight the line of bluffs across the wide, white meadows south of the town made soft, smoke-coloured curves against the clear sky. The men on the siding stood first on one foot and then on the other, their hands thrust deep into their trousers pockets, their overcoats open, their shoulders screwed up with the cold; and they glanced from time to time toward the southeast, where the railroad track wound along the river shore. They conversed in low tones and moved about restlessly, seeming uncertain as to what was expected of them. There was but one of the company who looked as though he knew exactly why he was there; and he kept conspicuously apart; walking to the far end of the platform, returning to the station door, then pacing up the track again, his chin sunk in the high collar of his overcoat, his burly shoulders drooping forward, his gait heavy and dogged. Presently he was approached by a tall, spare, grizzled man clad in a faded Grand Army suit,[1] who shuffled out from the group and advanced with a certain deference, craning

---

[1] Uniform of members of the Grand Army of the Republic, an association of veterans of the Civil War who had fought on the Union side.

his neck forward until his back made the angle of a jack-knife three-quarters open.

"I reckon she's a-goin' to be pretty late agin to-night, Jim," he remarked in a squeaky falsetto. "S'pose it's the snow?"

"I don't know," responded the other man with a shade of annoyance, speaking from out an astonishing cataract of red beard that grew fiercely and thickly in all directions.

The spare man shifted the quill toothpick he was chewing to the other side of his mouth. "It ain't likely that anybody from the East will come with the corpse, I s'pose," he went on reflectively.

"I don't know," responded the other, more curtly than before.

"It's too bad he didn't belong to some lodge or other. I like an order funeral myself. They seem more appropriate for people of some repytation," the spare man continued, with an ingratiating concession in his shrill voice, as he carefully placed his toothpick in his vest pocket. He always carried the flag at the G.A.R. funerals in the town.

The heavy man turned on his heel, without replying, and walked up the siding. The spare man shuffled back to the uneasy group. "Jim's ez full ez a tick, ez ushel," he commented commiseratingly.

Just then a distant whistle sounded, and there was a shuffling of feet on the platform. A number of lanky boys of all ages appeared as suddenly and slimily as eels wakened by the crack of thunder; some came from the waiting-room, where they had been warming themselves by the red stove, or half asleep on the slat benches; others uncoiled themselves from baggage trucks or slid out of express wagons. Two clambered down from the driver's seat of a hearse that stood backed up against the siding. They straightened their stooping shoulders and lifted their heads, and a flash of momentary animation kindled their dull eyes at that cold, vibrant scream, the world-wide call for men. It stirred them like the note of a trumpet; just as it had often stirred the man who was coming home to-night, in his boyhood.

The night express shot, red as a rocket, from out the eastward marsh lands and wound along the river shore under the long lines of shivering poplars that sentinelled the meadows, the escaping steam hanging in grey masses against the pale sky and blotting out the Milky Way. In a moment the red glare from the headlight streamed up the snow-covered track before the siding and glittered on the wet, black rails. The burly man with the dishevelled red beard walked swiftly up the platform toward the approaching train, uncovering his head as he went. The group of men behind him hesitated, glanced questioningly at one another, and awkwardly followed his example. The train stopped, and the crowd shuffled up to the express car just as the door was thrown open, the spare man in the G.A.R. suit thrusting his head forward with curiosity. The express messenger appeared in the doorway, accompanied by a young man in a long ulster and travelling cap.

"Are Mr. Merrick's friends here?" inquired the young man.

The group on the platform swayed and shuffled uneasily. Philip Phelps, the banker, responded with dignity: "We have come to take charge of the body. Mr. Merrick's father is very feeble and can't be about."

"Send the agent out here," growled the express messenger, "and tell the operator to lend a hand."

The coffin was got out of its rough box and down on the snowy platform. The townspeople drew back enough to make room for it and then formed a close semicircle about it, looking curiously at the palm leaf which lay across the black cover.

No one said anything. The baggage man stood by his truck, waiting to get at the trunks. The engine panted heavily, and the fireman dodged in and out among the wheels with his yellow torch and long oil-can, snapping the spindle boxes. The young Bostonian, one of the dead sculptor's pupils who had come with the body, looked about him helplessly. He turned to the banker, the only one of that black, uneasy, stoop-shouldered group who seemed enough of an individual to be addressed.

"None of Mr. Merrick's brothers are here?" he asked uncertainly.

The man with the red beard for the first time stepped up and joined the group. "No, they have not come yet; the family is scattered. The body will be taken directly to the house." He stooped and took hold of one of the handles of the coffin.

"Take the long hill road up, Thompson, it will be easier on the horses," called the liveryman as the undertaker snapped the door of the hearse and prepared to mount to the driver's seat.

Laird, the red-bearded lawyer, turned again to the stranger: "We didn't know whether there would be any one with him or not," he explained. "It's a long walk, so you'd better go up in the hack." He pointed to a single battered conveyance, but the young man replied stiffly: "Thank you, but I think I will go up with the hearse. If you don't object," turning to the undertaker, "I'll ride with you."

They clambered up over the wheels and drove off in the starlight up the long, white hill toward the town. The lamps in the still village were shining from under the low, snow-burdened roofs; and beyond, on every side, the plains reached out into emptiness, peaceful and wide as the soft sky itself, and wrapped in a tangible, white silence.

When the hearse backed up to a wooden sidewalk before a naked, weather-beaten frame house, the same composite, ill-defined group that had stood upon the station siding was huddled about the gate. The front yard was an icy swamp, and a couple of warped planks, extending from the sidewalk to the door, made a sort of rickety footbridge. The gate hung on one hinge, and was opened wide with difficulty. Steavens, the young stranger, noticed that something black was tied to the knob of the front door.

The grating sound made by the casket, as it was drawn from the hearse, was answered by a scream from the house; the front door was wrenched open, and a tall, corpulent woman rushed out bareheaded into the snow and flung herself upon the coffin, shrieking: "My boy, my boy! And this is how you've come home to me!"

As Steavens turned away and closed his eyes with a shudder of unutterable repulsion, another woman, also tall, but flat and angular, dressed entirely in black, darted out of the house and caught Mrs. Merrick by the shoulders, crying sharply: "Come, come, mother; you musn't go on like this!" Her tone changed to one of obsequious solemnity as she turned to the banker: "The parlour is ready, Mr. Phelps."

The bearers carried the coffin along the narrow boards, while the undertaker ran ahead with the coffin-rests. They bore it into a large, unheated room that smelled of dampness and disuse and furniture polish, and set it down under a hanging lamp ornamented with jingling glass prisms and before a "Rogers group" of John Alden and Priscilla,[2] wreathed with smilax. Henry Steavens stared about him with the

---

[2] Small plaster statuary group depicting the hero and heroine of Longfellow's poem "The Courtship of Miles Standish," manufactured by John Rogers (1829–1904). "Rogers groups" were a popular, sentimental form of art that the sculptor Merrick would have disdained.

sickening conviction that there had been some horrible mistake, and that he had somehow arrived at the wrong destination. He looked painfully about over the clover-green Brussels,[3] the fat plush upholstery; among the handpainted china plaques and panels, and vases, for some mark of identification, for something that might once conceivably have belonged to Harvey Merrick. It was not until he recognized his friend in the crayon portrait of a little boy in kilts and curls hanging above the piano, that he felt willing to let any of these people approach the coffin.

"Take the lid off, Mr. Thompson; let me see my boy's face," wailed the elder woman between her sobs. This time Steavens looked fearfully, almost beseechingly into her face, red and swollen under its masses of strong, black, shiny hair. He flushed, dropped his eyes, and then, almost incredulously, looked again. There was a kind of power about her face—a kind of brutal handsomeness, even, but it was scarred and furrowed by violence, and so coloured and coarsened by fiercer passions that grief seemed never to have laid a gentle finger there. The long nose was distended and knobbed at the end, and there were deep lines on either side of it; her heavy, black brows almost met across her forehead, her teeth were large and square, and set far apart —teeth that could tear. She filled the room; the men were obliterated, seemed tossed about like twigs in an angry water, and even Steavens felt himself being drawn into the whirlpool.

The daughter—the tall, raw-boned woman in crêpe, with a mourning comb in her hair which curiously lengthened her long face—sat stiffly upon the sofa, her hands, conspicuous for their large knuckles, folded in her lap, her mouth and eyes drawn down, solemnly awaiting the opening of the coffin. Near the door stood a mulatto woman, evidently a servant in the house, with a timid bearing and an emaciated face pitifully sad and gentle. She was weeping silently, the corner of her calico apron lifted to her eyes, occasionally suppressing a long, quivering sob. Steavens walked over and stood beside her.

Feeble steps were heard on the stairs, and an old man, tall and frail, odorous of pipe smoke, with shaggy, unkept grey hair and a dingy beard, tobacco stained about the mouth, entered uncertainly. He went slowly up to the coffin and stood rolling a blue cotton handkerchief between his hands, seeming so pained and embarrassed by his wife's orgy of grief that he had no consciousness of anything else.

"There, there, Annie, dear, don't take on so," he quavered timidly, putting out a shaking hand and awkwardly patting her elbow. She turned with a cry, and sank upon his shoulder with such violence that he tottered a little. He did not even glance toward the coffin, but continued to look at her with a dull, frightened, appealing expression, as a spaniel looks at the whip. His sunken cheeks slowly reddened and burned with miserable shame. When his wife rushed from the room, her daughter strode after her with set lips. The servant stole up to the coffin, bent over it for a moment, and then slipped away to the kitchen, leaving Steavens, the lawyer and the father to themselves. The old man stood trembling and looking down at his dead son's face. The sculptor's splendid head seemed even more noble in its rigid stillness than in life. The dark hair had crept down upon the wide forehead; the face seemed strangely long, but in it there was not that beautiful and chaste repose which we expect to find in the faces of the

---

[3] Cheap carpeting of the type made in Brussels, Belgium.

dead. The brows were so drawn that there were two deep lines above the beaked nose, and the chin was thrust forward defiantly. It was as though the strain of life had been so sharp and bitter that death could not at once wholly relax the tension and smooth the countenance into perfect peace—as though he were still guarding something precious and holy, which might even yet be wrested from him.

The old man's lips were working under his stained beard. He turned to the lawyer with timid deference: "Phelps and the rest are comin' back to set up with Harve, ain't they?" he asked. "Thank 'ee, Jim, thank 'ee." He brushed the hair back gently from his son's forehead. "He was a good boy, Jim; always a good boy. He was ez gentle ez a child and the kindest of 'em all—only we didn't none of us ever onderstand him." The tears trickled slowly down his beard and dropped upon the sculptor's coat.

"Martin, Martin. Oh, Martin! come here," his wife wailed from the top of the stairs. The old man started timorously: "Yes, Annie, I'm coming." He turned away, hesitated, stood for a moment in miserable indecision; then reached back and patted the dead man's hair softly, and stumbled from the room.

"Poor old man, I didn't think he had any tears left. Seems as if his eyes would have gone dry long ago. At his age nothing cuts very deep," remarked the lawyer.

Something in his tone made Steavens glance up. While the mother had been in the room, the young man had scarcely seen anyone else; but now, from the moment he first glanced into Jim Laird's florid face and blood-shot eyes, he knew that he had found what he had been heartsick at not finding before—the feeling, the understanding, that must exist in some one, even here.

The man was red as his beard, with features swollen and blurred by dissipation, and a hot, blazing blue eye. His face was strained—that of a man who is controlling himself with difficulty—and he kept plucking at his beard with a sort of fierce resentment. Steavens, sitting by the window, watched him turn down the glaring lamp, still its jangling pendants with an angry gesture, and then stand with his hands locked behind him, staring down into the master's face. He could not help wondering what link there could have been between the porcelain vessel and so sooty a lump of potter's clay.

From the kitchen an uproar was sounding; when the dining-room door opened, the import of it was clear. The mother was abusing the maid for having forgotten to make the dressing for the chicken salad which had been prepared for the watchers. Steavens had never heard anything in the least like it; it was injured, emotional, dramatic abuse, unique and masterly in its excruciating cruelty, as violent and unrestrained as had been her grief of twenty minutes before. With a shudder of disgust the lawyer went into the dining-room and closed the door into the kitchen.

"Poor Roxy's getting it now," he remarked when he came back. "The Merricks took her out of the poor-house years ago; and if her loyalty would let her, I guess the poor old thing could tell tales that would curdle your blood. She's the mulatto woman who was standing in here a while ago, with her apron to her eyes. The old woman is a fury; there never was anybody like her for demonstrative piety and ingenious cruelty. She made Harvey's life a hell for him when he lived at home; he was so sick ashamed of it. I never could see how he kept himself so sweet."

"He was wonderful," said Steavens slowly, "wonderful; but until to-night I have never known how wonderful."

"That is the true and eternal wonder of it, anyway; that it can come even from such a dung heap as this," the lawyer cried, with a sweeping gesture which seemed to indicate much more than the four walls within which they stood.

"I think I'll see whether I can get a little air. The room is so close I am beginning to feel rather faint," murmured Steavens, struggling with one of the windows. The sash was stuck, however, and would not yield, so he sat down dejectedly and began pulling at his collar. The lawyer came over, loosened the sash with one blow of his red fist and sent the window up a few inches. Steavens thanked him, but the nausea which had been gradually climbing into his throat for the last half hour left him with but one desire—a desperate feeling that he must get away from this place with what was left of Harvey Merrick. Oh, he comprehended well enough now the quiet bitterness of the smile that he had seen so often on his master's lips!

He remembered that once, when Merrick returned from a visit home, he brought with him a singularly feeling and suggestive bas-relief of a thin, faded old woman, sitting and sewing something pinned to her knee; while a full-lipped, full-blooded little urchin, his trousers held up by a single gallus, stood beside her, impatiently twitching her gown to call her attention to a butterfly he had caught. Steavens, impressed by the tender and delicate modelling of the thin, tired face, had asked him if it were his mother. He remembered the dull flush that had burned up in the sculptor's face.

The lawyer was sitting in a rocking-chair beside the coffin, his head thrown back and his eyes closed. Steavens looked at him earnestly, puzzled at the line of the chin, and wondering why a man should conceal a feature of such distinction under that disfiguring shock of beard. Suddenly, as though he felt the young sculptor's keen glance, he opened his eyes.

"Was he always a good deal of an oyster?" he asked abruptly. "He was terribly shy as a boy."

"Yes, he was an oyster, since you put it so," rejoined Steavens. "Although he could be very fond of people, he always gave one the impression of being detached. He disliked violent emotion; he was reflective, and rather distrustful of himself—except, of course, as regarded his work. He was sure-footed enough there. He distrusted men pretty thoroughly and women even more, yet somehow without believing ill of them. He was determined, indeed, to believe the best, but he seemed afraid to investigate."

"A burnt dog dreads the fire," said the lawyer grimly, and closed his eyes.

Steavens went on and on, reconstructing that whole miserable boyhood. All this raw, biting ugliness had been the portion of the man whose tastes were refined beyond the limits of the reasonable—whose mind was an exhaustless gallery of beautiful impressions, and so sensitive that the mere shadow of a poplar leaf flickering against a sunny wall would be etched and held there forever. Surely, if ever a man had the magic word in his finger tips, it was Merrick. Whatever he touched, he revealed its holiest secret; liberated it from enchantment and restored it to its pristine loveliness, like the Arabian prince who fought the enchantress spell for spell. Upon whatever he had come in contact with, he had left a beautiful record of the experience—a sort of ethereal signature; a scent, a sound, a colour that was his own.

Steavens understood now the real tragedy of his master's life; neither love nor wine, as many had conjectured; but a blow which had fallen earlier and cut deeper than these could have done—a shame not his, and yet so unescapably his, to hide in his heart from his very boyhood. And without—the frontier warfare; the yearning of a boy, cast ashore upon a desert of newness and ugliness and sordidness, for all that is chastened and old, and noble with traditions.

At eleven o'clock the tall, flat woman in black crêpe entered and announced that the watchers were arriving, and asked them "to step into the dining-room." As Steavens rose, the lawyer said dryly: "You go on—it'll be a good experience for you, doubtless; as for me, I'm not equal to that crowd to-night; I've had twenty years of them."

As Steavens closed the door after him he glanced back at the lawyer, sitting by the coffin in the dim light, with his chin resting on his hand.

The same misty group that had stood before the door of the express car shuffled into the dining-room. In the light of the kerosene lamp they separated and became individuals. The minister, a pale, feeble-looking man with white hair and blond chin-whiskers, took his seat beside a small side table and placed his Bible upon it. The Grand Army man sat down behind the stove and tilted his chair back comfortably against the wall, fishing his quill toothpick from his waistcoat pocket. The two bankers, Phelps and Elder, sat off in a corner behind the dinner-table where they could finish their discussion of the new usury law and its effect on chattel security loans. The real estate agent, an old man with a smiling, hypocritical face, soon joined them. The coal and lumber dealer and the cattle shipper sat on opposite sides of the hard coal-burner, their feet on the nickel-work. Steavens took a book from his pocket and began to read. The talk around him ranged through various topics of local interest while the house was quieting down. When it was clear that the members of the family were in bed, the Grand Army man hitched his shoulders and, untangling his long legs, caught his heels on the rounds of his chair.

"S'pose there'll be a will, Phelps?" he queried in his weak falsetto.

The banker laughed disagreeably and began trimming his nails with a pearl-handled pocket-knife.

"There'll scarcely be any need for one, will there?" he queried in his turn.

The restless Grand Army man shifted his position again, getting his knees still nearer his chin. "Why, the ole man says Harve's done right well lately," he chirped.

The other banker spoke up. "I reckon he means by that Harve ain't asked him to mortgage any more farms lately, so as he could go on with his education."

"Seems like my mind don't reach back to a time when Harve wasn't bein' edycated," tittered the Grand Army man.

There was a general chuckle. The minister took out his handkerchief and blew his nose sonorously. Banker Phelps closed his knife with a snap. "It's too bad the old man's sons didn't turn out better," he remarked with reflective authority. "They never hung together. He spent money enough on Harve to stock a dozen cattle-farms and he might as well have poured it into Sand Creek. If Harve had stayed at home and helped nurse what little they had, and gone into stock on the old man's bottom farm, they might all have been well fixed. But the old man had to trust everything to tenants and was cheated right and left."

"Harve never could have handled stock none," interposed the cattleman. "He hadn't it in him to be sharp. Do you remember when he bought Sander's mules for eight-year-olds, when everybody in town knew that Sander's father-in-law give 'em to his wife for a wedding present eighteen years before, an' they was full-grown mules then."

Everyone chuckled, and the Grand Army man rubbed his knees with a spasm of childish delight.

"Harve never was much account for anything practical, and he shore was never fond of work," began the coal and lumber dealer. "I mind the last time he was home; the day he left, when the old man was out to the barn helpin' his hand hitch up to take Harve to the train, and Cal Moots was patchin' up the fence, Harve, he come out on the step and sings out, in his lady-like voice: 'Cal Moots, Cal Moots! please come cord my trunk.'"

"That's Harve for you," approved the Grand Army man gleefully. "I kin hear him howlin' yet when he was a big feller in long pants and his mother used to whale him with a rawhide in the barn for lettin' the cows git foundered in the cornfield when he was drivin' 'em home from pasture. He killed a cow of mine that-a-way onct— a pure Jersey and the best milker I had, an' the ole man had to put up for her. Harve, he was watchin' the sun set acrost the marshes when the anamile got away; he argued that sunset was oncommon fine."

"Where the old man made his mistake was in sending the boy East to school," said Phelps, stroking his goatee and speaking in a deliberate, judicial tone. "There was where he got his head full of trapesing to Paris and all such folly. What Harve needed, of all people, was a course in some first-class Kansas City business college."

The letters were swimming before Steavens's eyes. Was it possible that these men did not understand, that the palm on the coffin meant nothing to them? The very name of their town would have remained forever buried in the postal guide had it not been now and again mentioned in the world in connection with Harvey Merrick's. He remembered what his master had said to him on the day of his death, after the congestion of both lungs had shut off any probability of recovery, and the sculptor had asked his pupil to send his body home. "It's not a pleasant place to be lying while the world is moving and doing and bettering," he had said with a feeble smile, "but it rather seems as though we ought to go back to the place we came from in the end. The townspeople will come in for a look at me; and after they have had their say I shan't have much to fear from the judgment of God. The wings of the Victory, in there"—with a weak gesture toward his studio—"will not shelter me."

The cattleman took up the comment. "Forty's young for a Merrick to cash in; they usually hang on pretty well. Probably he helped it along with whisky."

"His mother's people were not long lived, and Harvey never had a robust constitution," said the minister mildly. He would have liked to say more. He had been the boy's Sunday-school teacher, and had been fond of him; but he felt that he was not in a position to speak. His own sons had turned out badly, and it was not a year since one of them had made his last trip home in the express car, shot in a gambling-house in the Black Hills.

"Nevertheless, there is no disputin' that Harve frequently looked upon the wine when it was red, also variegated, and it shore made an oncommon fool of him," moralized the cattleman.

Just then the door leading into the parlour rattled loudly, and everyone started involuntarily, looking relieved when only Jim Laird came out. His red face was convulsed with anger, and the Grand Army man ducked his head when he saw the spark in his blue, blood-shot eye. They were all afraid of Jim; he was a drunkard, but he could twist the law to suit his client's needs as no other man in all western

Kansas could do; and there were many who tried. The lawyer closed the door gently behind him, leaned back against it and folded his arms, cocking his head a little to one side. When he assumed this attitude in the court-room, ears were always pricked up, as it usually foretold a flood of withering sarcasm.

"I've been with you gentlemen before," he began in a dry, even tone, "when you've sat by the coffins of boys born and raised in this town; and, if I remember rightly, you were never any too well satisfied when you checked them up. What's the matter, anyhow? Why is it that reputable young men are as scarce as millionaires in Sand City? It might almost seem to a stranger that there was some way something the matter with your progressive town. Why did Ruben Sayer, the brightest young lawyer you ever turned out, after he had come home from the university as straight as a die, take to drinking and forge a check and shoot himself? Why did Bill Merrit's son die of the shakes in a saloon in Omaha? Why was Mr. Thomas's son, here, shot in a gambling-house? Why did young Adams burn his mill to beat the insurance companies and go to the pen?"

The lawyer paused and unfolded his arms, laying one clenched fist quietly on the table. "I'll tell you why. Because you drummed nothing but money and knavery into their ears from the time they wore knickerbockers; because you carped away at them as you've been carping here to-night, holding our friends Phelps and Elder up to them for their models, as our grandfathers held up George Washington and John Adams. But the boys, worse luck, were young, and raw at the business you put them to; and how could they match coppers with such artists as Phelps and Elder? You wanted them to be successful rascals; they were only unsuccessful ones—that's all the difference. There was only one boy ever raised in this borderland between ruffianism and civilization, who didn't come to grief, and you hated Harvey Merrick more for winning out than you hated all the other boys who got under the wheels. Lord, Lord, how you did hate him! Phelps, here, is fond of saying that he could buy and sell us all out any time he's a mind to; but he knew Harve wouldn't have given a tinker's damn for his bank and all his cattle-farms put together; and a lack of appreciation, that way, goes hard with Phelps.

"Old Nimrod, here, thinks Harve drank too much; and this from such as Nimrod and me!

"Brother Elder says Harve was too free with the old man's money—fell short in filial consideration, maybe. Well, we can all remember the very tone in which brother Elder swore his own father was a liar, in the county court; and we all know that the old man came out of that partnership with his son as bare as a sheared lamb. But maybe I'm getting personal, and I'd better be driving ahead at what I want to say."

The lawyer paused a moment, squared his heavy shoulders, and went on: "Harvey Merrick and I went to school together, back East. We were dead in earnest, and we wanted you all to be proud of us some day. We meant to be great men. Even I, and I haven't lost my sense of humour, gentlemen, I meant to be a great man. I came back here to practise, and I found you didn't in the least want me to be a great man. You wanted me to be a shrewd lawyer—oh, yes! Our veteran here wanted me to get him an increase of pension, because he had dyspepsia; Phelps wanted a new county survey that would put the widow Wilson's little bottom farm inside his south line; Elder wanted to lend money at 5 per cent a month, and get it collected; old Stark here wanted to wheedle old women up in Vermont into investing their annuities in real estate mortgages that are not worth the paper they are written on. Oh, you needed me hard enough, and you'll go on needing me; and that's why I'm not afraid to plug the truth home to you this once.

"Well, I came back here and became the damned shyster you wanted me to be. You pretend to have some sort of respect for me; and yet you'll stand up and throw mud at Harvey Merrick, whose soul you couldn't dirty and whose hands you couldn't tie. Oh, you're a discriminating lot of Christians! There have been times when the sight of Harvey's name in some Eastern paper has made me hang my head like a whipped dog; and, again, times when I liked to think of him off there in the world, away from all this hog-wallow, doing his great work and climbing the big, clean up-grade he'd set for himself.

"And we? Now that we've fought and lied and sweated and stolen, and hated as only the disappointed strugglers in a bitter, dead little Western town know how to do, what have we got to show for it? Harvey Merrick wouldn't have given one sunset over your marshes for all you've got put together, and you know it. It's not for me to say why, in the inscrutable wisdom of God, a genius should ever have been called from this place of hatred and bitter waters; but I want this Boston man to know that the drivel he's been hearing here to-night is the only tribute any truly great man could ever have from such a lot of sick, side-tracked, burnt-dog, land-poor sharks as the here-present financiers of Sand City—upon which town may God have mercy!"

The lawyer thrust out his hand to Steavens as he passed him, caught up his overcoat in the hall, and had left the house before the Grand Army man had had time to lift his ducked head and crane his long neck about at his fellows.

Next day Jim Laird was drunk and unable to attend the funeral services. Steavens called twice at his office, but was compelled to start East without seeing him. He had a presentiment that he would hear from him again, and left his address on the lawyer's table; but if Laird found it, he never acknowledged it. The thing in him that Harvey Merrick had loved must have gone underground with Harvey Merrick's coffin; for it never spoke again, and Jim got the cold he died of driving across the Colorado mountains to defend one of Phelps's sons who had got into trouble out there by cutting government timber.

1905

Neighbour Rosicky

I

When Doctor Burleigh told neighbour Rosicky he had a bad heart, Rosicky protested.

"So? No, I guess my heart was always pretty good. I got a little asthma, maybe. Just a awful short breath when I was pitchin' hay last summer, dat's all."

"Well now, Rosicky, if you know more about it than I do, what did you come to me for? It's your heart that makes you short of breath, I tell you. You're sixty-five years old, and you've always worked hard, and your heart's tired. You've got to be careful from now on, and you can't do heavy work any more. You've got five boys at home to do it for you."

The old farmer looked up at the Doctor with a gleam of amusement in his queer triangular-shaped eyes. His eyes were large and lively, but the lids were caught up in the middle in a curious way, so that they formed a triangle. He did not look like a sick man. His brown face was creased but not wrinkled, he had a ruddy colour in his smooth-shaven cheeks and in his lips, under his long brown moustache. His hair was thin and ragged around his ears, but very little grey. His forehead, naturally high and crossed by deep parallel lines, now ran all the way up to his pointed crown. Rosicky's face had the habit of looking interested,—suggested a contented disposition and a reflective quality that was gay rather than grave. This gave him a certain detachment, the easy manner of an onlooker and observer.

"Well, I guess you ain't got no pills fur a bad heart, Doctor Ed. I guess the only thing is fur me to git me a new one."

Doctor Burleigh swung round in his desk-chair and frowned at the old farmer. "I think if I were you I'd take a little care of the old one, Rosicky."

Rosicky shrugged. "Maybe I don't know how. I expect you mean fur me not to drink my coffee no more."

"I wouldn't, in your place. But you'll do as you choose about that. I've never yet been able to separate a Bohemian[1] from his coffee or his pipe. I've quit trying. But the sure thing is you've got to cut out farm work. You can feed the stock and do chores about the barn, but you can't do anything in the fields that makes you short of breath."

"How about shelling corn?"

"Of course not!"

Rosicky considered with puckered brows.

"I can't make my heart go no longer'n it wants to, can I, Doctor Ed?"

"I think it's good for five or six years yet, maybe more, if you'll take the strain off it. Sit around the house and help Mary. If I had a good wife like yours, I'd want to stay around the house."

His patient chuckled. "It ain't no place fur a man. I don't like no old man hanging round the kitchen too much. An' my wife, she's a awful hard worker her own self."

"That's it; you can help her a little. My Lord, Rosicky, you are one of the few men I know who has a family he can get some comfort out of; happy dispositions, never quarrel among themselves, and they treat you right. I want to see you live a few years and enjoy them."

"Oh, they're good kids, all right," Rosicky assented.

The Doctor wrote him a prescription and asked him how his oldest son, Rudolph, who had married in the spring, was getting on. Rudolph had struck out for himself, on rented land. "And how's Polly? I was afraid Mary mightn't like an American daughter-in-law, but it seems to be working out all right."

"Yes, she's a fine girl. Dat widder woman bring her daughters up very nice. Polly got lots of spunk, an' she got some style, too. Da's nice, for young folks to have some

---

[1] Native of Bohemia, a province of Czechoslovakia.

style." Rosicky inclined his head gallantly. His voice and his twinkly smile were an affectionate compliment to his daughter-in-law.

"It looks like a storm, and you'd better be getting home before it comes. In town in the car?" Doctor Burleigh rose.

"No, I'm in de wagon. When you got five boys, you ain't got much chance to ride round in de Ford. I ain't much for cars, noway."

"Well, it's a good road out to your place; but I don't want you bumping around in a wagon much. And never again on a hay-rake, remember!"

Rosicky placed the Doctor's fee delicately behind the desk-telephone, looking the other way, as if this were an absent-minded gesture. He put on his plush cap and his corduroy jacket with a sheepskin collar, and went out.

The Doctor picked up his stethoscope and frowned at it as if he were seriously annoyed with the instrument. He wished it had been telling tales about some other man's heart, some old man who didn't look the Doctor in the eye so knowingly, or hold out such a warm brown hand when he said good-bye. Doctor Burleigh had been a poor boy in the country before he went away to medical school; he had known Rosicky almost ever since he could remember, and he had a deep affection for Mrs. Rosicky.

Only last winter he had had such a good breakfast at Rosicky's, and that when he needed it. He had been out all night on a long, hard confinement case[2] at Tom Marshall's,—a big rich farm where there was plenty of stock and plenty of feed and a great deal of expensive farm machinery of the newest model, and no comfort whatever. The woman had too many children and too much work, and she was no manager. When the baby was born at last, and handed over to the assisting neighbour woman, and the mother was properly attended to, Burleigh refused any breakfast in that slovenly house, and drove his buggy—the snow was too deep for a car—eight miles to Anton Rosicky's place. He didn't know another farm-house where a man could get such a warm welcome, and such good strong coffee with rich cream. No wonder the old chap didn't want to give up his coffee!

He had driven in just when the boys had come back from the barn and were washing up for breakfast. The long table, covered with a bright oilcloth, was set out with dishes waiting for them, and the warm kitchen was full of the smell of coffee and hot biscuit and sausage. Five big handsome boys, running from twenty to twelve, all with what Burleigh called natural good manners,—they hadn't a bit of the painful self-consciousness he himself had to struggle with when he was a lad. One ran to put his horse away, another helped him off with his fur coat and hung it up, and Josephine, the youngest child and the only daughter, quickly set another place under her mother's direction.

With Mary, to feed creatures was the natural expression of affection,—her chickens, the calves, her big hungry boys. It was a rare pleasure to feed a young man whom she seldom saw and of whom she was as proud as if he belonged to her. Some country housekeepers would have stopped to spread a white cloth over the oilcloth, to change the thick cups and plates for their best china, and the wooden-handled knives for plated ones. But not Mary.

[2] I.e., the delivery of a baby.

"You must take us as you find us, Doctor Ed. I'd be glad to put out my good things for you if you was expected, but I'm glad to get you any way at all."

He knew she was glad,—she threw back her head and spoke out as if she were announcing him to the whole prairie. Rosicky hadn't said anything at all; he merely smiled his twinkling smile, put some more coal on the fire, and went into his own room to pour the Doctor a little drink in a medicine glass. When they were all seated, he watched his wife's face from his end of the table and spoke to her in Czech. Then, with the instinct of politeness which seldom failed him, he turned to the Doctor and said slyly; "I was just tellin' her not to ask you no questions about Mrs. Marshall till you eat some breakfast. My wife, she's terrible fur to ask questions."

The boys laughed, and so did Mary. She watched the Doctor devour her biscuit and sausage, too much excited to eat anything herself. She drank her coffee and sat taking in everything about her visitor. She had known him when he was a poor country boy, and was boastfully proud of his success, always saying: "What do people go to Omaha for, to see a doctor, when we got the best one in the State right here?" If Mary liked people at all, she felt physical pleasure in the sight of them, personal exultation in any good fortune that came to them. Burleigh didn't know many women like that, but he knew she was like that.

When his hunger was satisfied, he did, of course, have to tell them about Mrs. Marshall, and he noticed what a friendly interest the boys took in the matter.

Rudolph, the oldest one (he was still living at home then), said: "The last time I was over there, she was lifting them big heavy milk-cans, and I knew she oughtn't to be doing it."

"Yes, Rudolph told me about that when he come home, and I said it wasn't right," Mary put in warmly. "It was all right for me to do them things up to the last, for I was terrible strong, but that woman's weakly. And do you think she'll be able to nurse it, Ed?" She sometimes forgot to give him the title she was so proud of. "And to think of your being up all night and then not able to get a decent breakfast! I don't know what's the matter with such people."

"Why, Mother," said one of the boys, "if Doctor Ed had got breakfast there, we wouldn't have him here. So you ought to be glad."

"He knows I'm glad to have him, John, any time. But I'm sorry for that poor woman, how bad she'll feel the Doctor had to go away in the cold without his breakfast."

"I wish I'd been in practice when these were getting born." The doctor looked down the row of close-clipped heads. "I missed some good breakfasts by not being."

The boys began to laugh at their mother because she flushed so red, but she stood her ground and threw up her head. "I don't care, you wouldn't have got away from this house without breakfast. No doctor ever did. I'd have had something ready fixed that Anton could warm up for you."

The boys laughed harder than ever, and exclaimed at her: "I'll bet you would!" "She would, that!"

"Father, did you get breakfast for the doctor when we were born?"

"Yes, and he used to bring me my breakfast, too, mighty nice. I was always awful hungry!" Mary admitted with a guilty laugh.

While the boys were getting the Doctor's horse, he went to the window to examine the house plants. "What do you do to your geraniums to keep them blooming all winter, Mary? I never pass this house that from the road I don't see your windows full of flowers."

She snapped off a dark red one, and a ruffled new green leaf, and put them in his buttonhole. "There, that looks better. You look too solemn for a young man, Ed. Why don't you git married? I'm worried about you. Settin' at breakfast, I looked at you real hard, and I seen you've got some grey hairs already."

"Oh, yes! They're coming. Maybe they'd come faster if I married."

"Don't talk so. You'll ruin your health eating at the hotel. I could send your wife a nice loaf of nut bread, if you only had one. I don't like to see a young man getting grey. I'll tell you something, Ed; you make some strong black tea and keep it handy in a bowl, and every morning just brush it into your hair, an' it'll keep the grey from showin' much. That's the way I do!"

Sometimes the Doctor heard the gossipers in the drug-store wondering why Rosicky didn't get on faster. He was industrious, and so were his boys, but they were rather free and easy, weren't pushers, and they didn't always show good judgment. They were comfortable, they were out of debt, but they didn't get much ahead. Maybe, Doctor Burleigh reflected, people as generous and warm-hearted and affectionate as the Rosickys never got ahead much; maybe you couldn't enjoy your life and put it into the bank, too.

II

When Rosicky left Doctor Burleigh's office he went into the farm-implement store to light his pipe and put on his glasses and read over the list Mary had given him. Then he went into the general merchandise place next door and stood about until the pretty girl with the plucked eyebrows, who always waited on him, was free. Those eyebrows, two thin India-ink strokes, amused him, because he remembered how they used to be. Rosicky always prolonged his shopping by a little joking; the girl knew the old fellow admired her, and she liked to chaff with him.

"Seems to me about every other week you buy ticking, Mr. Rosicky, and always the best quality," she remarked as she measured off the heavy bolt with red stripes.

"You see, my wife is always makin' goose-fedder pillows, an' de thin stuff don't hold in dem little down-fedders."

"You must have lots of pillows at your house."

"Sure. She makes quilts of dem, too. We sleeps easy. Now she's makin' a fedder quilt for my son's wife. You know Polly, that married my Rudolph. How much my bill, Miss Pearl?"

"Eight eighty-five."

"Chust make it nine, and put in some candy fur de women."

"As usual. I never did see a man buy so much candy for his wife. First thing you know, she'll be getting too fat."

"I'd like dat. I ain't much fur all dem slim women like what de style is now."

"That's one for me, I suppose, Mr. Bohunk!" Pearl sniffed and elevated her India-ink strokes.

When Rosicky went out to his wagon, it was beginning to snow,—the first snow of the season, and he was glad to see it. He rattled out of town and along the highway through a wonderfully rich stretch of country, the finest farms in the county. He admired this High Prairie, as it was called, and always liked to drive through it. His own place lay in a rougher territory, where there was some clay in the soil and it was not so productive. When he bought his land, he hadn't the money to buy on High Prairie; so he told his boys, when they grumbled, that if their land hadn't some clay in it, they wouldn't own it at all. All the same, he enjoyed looking at these fine farms, as he enjoyed looking at a prize bull.

After he had gone eight miles, he came to the graveyard, which lay just at the edge of his own hay-land. There he stopped his horses and sat still on his wagon seat, looking about at the snowfall. Over yonder on the hill he could see his own house, crouching low, with the clump of orchard behind and the windmill before, and all down the gentle hill-slope the rows of pale gold cornstalks stood out against the white field. The snow was falling over the cornfield and the pasture and the hay-land, steadily, with very little wind,—a nice dry snow. The graveyard had only a light wire fence about it and was all overgrown with long red grass. The fine snow, settling into this red grass and upon the few little evergreens and the headstones, looked very pretty.

It was a nice graveyard, Rosicky reflected, sort of snug and homelike, not cramped or mournful,—a big sweep all round it. A man could lie down in the long grass and see the complete arch of the sky over him, hear the wagons go by; in summer the mowing-machine rattled right up to the wire fence. And it was so near home. Over there across the cornstalks his own roof and windmill looked so good to him that he promised himself to mind the Doctor and take care of himself. He was awful fond of his place, he admitted. He wasn't anxious to leave it. And it was a comfort to think that he would never have to go farther than the edge of his own hayfield. The snow, falling over his barnyard and the graveyard, seemed to draw things together like. And they were all old neighbours in the graveyard, most of them friends; there was nothing to feel awkward or embarrassed about. Embarrassment was the most disagreeable feeling Rosicky knew. He didn't often have it,—only with certain people whom he didn't understand at all.

Well, it was a nice snowstorm; a fine sight to see the snow falling so quietly and graciously over so much open country. On his cap and shoulders, on the horses' backs and manes, light, delicate, mysterious it fell; and with it a dry cool fragrance was released into the air. It meant rest for vegetation and men and beasts, for the ground itself; a season of long nights for sleep, leisurely breakfasts, peace by the fire. This and much more went through Rosicky's mind, but he merely told himself that winter was coming, clucked to his horses, and drove on.

When he reached home, John, the youngest boy, ran out to put away his team for him, and he met Mary coming up from the outside cellar with her apron full of carrots. They went into the house together. On the table, covered with oilcloth figured with clusters of blue grapes, a place was set, and he smelled hot coffee-cake of some kind. Anton never lunched in town; he thought that extravagant, and anyhow he didn't like the food. So Mary always had something ready for him when he got home.

After he was settled in his chair, stirring his coffee in a big cup, Mary took out of the oven a pan of *kolache* stuffed with apricots, examined them anxiously to see whether they had got too dry, put them beside his plate, and then sat down opposite him.

Rosicky asked her in Czech if she wasn't going to have any coffee.

She replied in English, as being somehow the right language for transacting business: "Now what did Doctor Ed say, Anton? You tell me just what."

"He said I was to tell you some compliments, but I forgot 'em." Rosicky's eyes twinkled.

"About you, I mean. What did he say about your asthma?"

"He says I ain't got no asthma." Rosicky took one of the little rolls in his broad brown fingers. The thickened nail of his right thumb told the story of his past.

"Well, what is the matter? And don't try to put me off."

"He don't say nothing much, only I'm a little older, and my heart ain't so good like it used to be."

Mary started and brushed her hair back from her temples with both hands as if she were a little out of her mind. From the way she glared, she might have been in a rage with him.

"He says there's something the matter with your heart? Doctor Ed says so?"

"Now don't yell at me like I was a hog in de garden, Mary. You know I always did like to hear a woman talk soft. He didn't say anything de matter wid my heart, only it ain't so young like it used to be, an' he tell me not to pitch hay or run de corn-sheller."

Mary wanted to jump up, but she sat still. She admired the way he never under any circumstances raised his voice or spoke roughly. He was city-bred, and she was country-bred; she often said she wanted her boys to have their papa's nice ways.

"You never have no pain there, do you? It's your breathing and your stomach that's been wrong. I wouldn't believe nobody but Doctor Ed about it. I guess I'll go see him myself. Didn't he give you no advice?"

"Chust to take it easy like, an' stay round de house dis winter. I guess you got some carpenter work for me to do. I kin make some new shelves for you, and I want dis long time to build a closet in de boys' room and make dem two little fellers keep dere clo'es hung up."

Rosicky drank his coffee from time to time, while he considered. His moustache was of the soft long variety and came down over his mouth like the teeth of a buggy-rake over a bundle of hay. Each time he put down his cup, he ran his blue handkerchief over his lips. When he took a drink of water, he managed very neatly with the back of his hand.

Mary sat watching him intently, trying to find any change in his face. It is hard to see anyone who has become like your own body to you. Yes, his hair had got thin, and his high forehead had deep lines running from left to right. But his neck, always clean shaved except in the busiest seasons, was not loose or baggy. It was burned a dark reddish brown, and there were deep creases in it, but it looked firm and full of blood. His cheeks had a good colour. On either side of his mouth there was a half-moon down the length of his cheek, not wrinkles, but two lines that had come there from his habitual expression. He was shorter and broader than when she married him; his back had grown broad and curved, a good deal like the shell of an old turtle, and his arms and legs were short.

He was fifteen years older than Mary, but she had hardly ever thought about it before. He was her man, and the kind of man she liked. She was rough, and he was gentle,—city-bred, as she always said. They had been shipmates on a rough voyage and had stood by each other in trying times. Life had gone well with them because, at bottom, they had the same ideas about life. They agreed, without discussion, as to what was most important and what was secondary. They didn't often exchange opinions, even in Czech,—it was as if they had thought the same thought together. A good deal had to be sacrificed and thrown overboard in a hard life like theirs, and they had never disagreed as to the things that could go. It had been a hard life, and a soft life, too. There wasn't anything brutal in the short, broad-backed man with the three-cornered eyes and the forehead that went on to the top of his skull. He was a city man, a gentle man, and though he had married a rough farm girl, he had never touched her without gentleness.

They had been at one accord not to hurry through life, not to be always skimping and saving. They saw their neighbours buy more land and feed more stock than they did, without discontent. Once when the creamery agent came to the Rosickys to persuade them to sell him their cream, he told them how much money the Fasslers, their nearest neighbours, had made on their cream last year.

"Yes," said Mary, "and look at them Fassler children! Pale, pinched little things, they look like skimmed milk. I'd rather put some colour into my children's faces than put money into the bank."

The agent shrugged and turned to Anton.

"I guess we'll do like she says," said Rosicky.

III

Mary very soon got into town to see Doctor Ed, and then she had a talk with her boys and set a guard over Rosicky. Even John, the youngest, had his father on his mind. If Rosicky went to throw hay down from the loft, one of the boys ran up the ladder and took the fork from him. He sometimes complained that though he was getting to be an old man, he wasn't an old woman yet.

That winter he stayed in the house in the afternoons and carpentered, or sat in the chair between the window full of plants and the wooden bench where the two pails of drinking-water stood. This spot was called "Father's corner," though it was not a corner at all. He had a shelf there, where he kept his Bohemian papers and his pipes and tobacco, and his shears and needles and thread and tailor's thimble. Having been a tailor in his youth, he couldn't bear to see a woman patching at his clothes, or at the boys'. He liked tailoring, and always patched all the overalls and jackets and work shirts. Occasionally he made over a pair of pants one of the older boys had outgrown, for the little fellow.

While he sewed, he let his mind run back over his life. He had a good deal to remember, really; life in three countries. The only part of his youth he didn't like to remember was the two years he had spent in London, in Cheapside, working for a German tailor who was wretchedly poor. Those days, when he was nearly always hungry, when his clothes were dropping off him for dirt, and the sound of a strange language kept him in continual bewilderment, had left a sore spot in his mind that wouldn't bear touching.

He was twenty when he landed at Castle Garden[3] in New York, and he had a protector who got him work in a tailor shop in Vesey Street, down near the Washington Market. He looked upon that part of his life as very happy. He became a good workman, he was industrious, and his wages were increased from time to time. He minded his own business and envied nobody's good fortune. He went to night school and learned to read English. He often did overtime work and was well paid for it, but somehow he never saved anything. He couldn't refuse a loan to a friend, and he was self-indulgent. He liked a good dinner, and a little went for beer, a little for tobacco; a good deal went to the girls. He often stood through an opera on Saturday nights; he could get standing-room for a dollar. Those were the great days of opera in New York, and it gave a fellow something to think about for the rest of the week. Rosicky had a quick ear, and a childish love of all the stage splendour; the scenery, the costumes, the ballet. He usually went with a chum, and after the performance they had beer and maybe some oysters somewhere. It was a fine life; for the first five years or so it satisfied him completely. He was never hungry or cold or dirty, and everything amused him: a fire, a dog fight, a parade, a storm, a ferry ride. He thought New York the finest, richest, friendliest city in the world.

Moreover, he had what he called a happy home life. Very near the tailor shop was a small furniture-factory, where an old Austrian, Loeffler, employed a few skilled men and made unusual furniture, most of it to order, for the rich German housewives up-town. The top floor of Loeffler's five-storey factory was a loft, where he kept his choice lumber and stored the odd pieces of furniture left on his hands. One of the young workmen he employed was a Czech, and he and Rosicky became fast friends. They persuaded Loeffler to let them have a sleeping-room in one corner of the loft. They bought good beds and bedding and had their pick of the furniture kept up there. The loft was low-pitched, but light and airy, full of windows, and good-smelling by reason of the fine lumber put up there to season. Old Loeffler used to go down to the docks and buy wood from South America and the East from the sea captains. The young men were as foolish about their house as a bridal pair. Zichec, the young cabinet-maker, devised every sort of convenience, and Rosicky kept their clothes in order. At night and on Sundays, when the quiver of machinery underneath was still, it was the quietest place in the world, and on summer nights all the sea winds blew in. Zichec often practised on his flute in the evening. They were both fond of music and went to the opera together. Rosicky thought he wanted to live like that for ever.

But as the years passed, all alike, he began to get a little restless. When spring came round, he would begin to feel fretted, and he got to drinking. He was likely to drink too much of a Saturday night. On Sunday he was languid and heavy, getting over his spree. On Monday he plunged into work again. So he never had time to figure out what ailed him, though he knew something did. When the grass turned green in Park Place, and the lilac hedge at the back of Trinity churchyard put out its blossoms,[4] he was tormented by a longing to run away. That was why he drank too much; to get a temporary illusion of freedom and wide horizons.

Rosicky, the old Rosicky, could remember as if it were yesterday the day when the young Rosicky found out what was the matter with him. It was on a Fourth of

[3] Entry point for immigrants, replaced in 1892 by   [4] In the area at the southern end of Manhattan.
Ellis Island.

July afternoon, and he was sitting in Park Place in the sun. The lower part of New York was empty. Wall Street, Liberty Street, Broadway, all empty. So much stone and asphalt with nothing going on, so many empty windows. The emptiness was intense, like the stillness in a great factory when the machinery stops and the belts and bands cease running. It was too great a change, it took all the strength out of one. Those blank buildings, without the stream of life pouring through them, were like empty jails. It struck young Rosicky that this was the trouble with big cities; they built you in from the earth itself, cemented you away from any contact with the ground. You lived in an unnatural world, like the fish in an aquarium, who were probably much more comfortable than they ever were in the sea.

On that very day he began to think seriously about the articles he had read in the Bohemian papers, describing prosperous Czech farming communities in the West. He believed he would like to go out there as a farm hand; it was hardly possible that he could ever have land of his own. His people had always been workmen; his father and grandfather had worked in shops. His mother's parents had lived in the country, but they rented their farm and had a hard time to get along. Nobody in his family had ever owned any land,—that belonged to a different station of life altogether. Anton's mother died when he was little, and he was sent into the country to her parents. He stayed with them until he was twelve, and formed those ties with the earth and the farm animals and growing things which are never made at all unless they are made early. After his grandfather died, he went back to live with his father and stepmother, but she was very hard on him, and his father helped him to get passage to London.

After that Fourth of July day in Park Place, the desire to return to the country never left him. To work on another man's farm would be all he asked; to see the sun rise and set and to plant things and watch them grow. He was a very simple man. He was like a tree that has not many roots, but one tap-root that goes down deep. He subscribed for a Bohemian paper printed in Chicago, then for one printed in Omaha. His mind got farther and farther west. He began to save a little money to buy his liberty. When he was thirty-five, there was a great meeting in New York of Bohemian athletic societies, and Rosicky left the tailor shop and went home with the Omaha delegates to try his fortune in another part of the world.

IV

Perhaps the fact that his own youth was well over before he began to have a family was one reason why Rosicky was so fond of his boys. He had almost a grandfather's indulgence for them. He had never had to worry about any of them—except, just now, a little about Rudolph.

On Saturday night the boys always piled into the Ford, took little Josephine, and went to town to the moving-picture show. One Saturday morning they were talking at the breakfast table about starting early that evening, so that they would have an hour or so to see the Christmas things in the stores before the show began. Rosicky looked down the table.

"I hope you boys ain't disappointed, but I want you to let me have de car tonight. Maybe some of you can go in with de neighbours."

Their faces fell. They worked hard all week, and they were still like children. A new jackknife or a box of candy pleased the older ones as much as the little fellow.

"If you and Mother are going to town," Frank said, "maybe you could take a couple of us along with you, anyway."

"No, I want to take de car down to Rudolph's, and let him an' Polly go in to de show. She don't git into town enough, an' I'm afraid she's gettin' lonesome, an' he can't afford no car yet."

That settled it. The boys were a good deal dashed. Their father took another piece of apple-cake and went on: "Maybe next Saturday night de two little fellers can go along wid dem."

"Oh, is Rudolph going to have the car every Saturday night?"

Rosicky did not reply at once; then he began to speak seriously: "Listen, boys; Polly ain't lookin' so good. I don't like to see nobody lookin' sad. It comes hard fur a town girl to be a farmer's wife. I don't want no trouble to start in Rudolph's family. When it starts, it ain't so easy to stop. An American girl don't git used to our ways all at once. I like to tell Polly she and Rudolph can have the car every Saturday night till after New Year's, if it's all right with you boys."

"Sure it's all right, Papa," Mary cut in. "And it's good you thought about that. Town girls is used to more than country girls. I lay awake nights, scared she'll make Rudolph discontented with the farm."

The boys put as good a face on it as they could. They surely looked forward to their Saturday nights in town. That evening Rosicky drove the car the half-mile down to Rudolph's new, bare little house.

Polly was in a short-sleeved gingham dress, clearing away the supper dishes. She was a trim, slim little thing, with blue eyes and shingled yellow hair, and her eyebrows were reduced to a mere brush-stroke, like Miss Pearl's.

"Good evening, Mr. Rosicky. Rudolph's at the barn, I guess." She never called him father, or Mary mother. She was sensitive about having married a foreigner. She never in the world would have done it if Rudolph hadn't been such a handsome, persuasive fellow and such a gallant lover. He had graduated in her class in the high school in town, and their friendship began in the ninth grade.

Rosicky went in, though he wasn't exactly asked. "My boys ain't goin' to town tonight, an' I brought de car over fur you two to go in to de picture show."

Polly, carrying dishes to the sink, looked over her shoulder at him. "Thank you. But I'm late with my work tonight, and pretty tired. Maybe Rudolph would like to go in with you."

"Oh, I don't go to de shows! I'm too old-fashioned. You won't feel so tired after you ride in de air a ways. It's a nice clear night, an' it ain't cold. You go an' fix yourself up, Polly, an' I'll wash de dishes an' leave everything nice fur you."

Polly blushed and tossed her bob. "I couldn't let you do that, Mr. Rosicky. I wouldn't think of it."

Rosicky said nothing. He found a bib apron on a nail behind the kitchen door. He slipped it over his head and then took Polly by her two elbows and pushed her gently toward the door of her own room. "I washed up de kitchen many times for my wife, when de babies was sick or somethin'. You go an' make yourself look nice. I like you to look prettier'n any of dem town girls when you go in. De young folks must have some fun, an' I'm goin' to look out fur you, Polly."

That kind, reassuring grip on her elbows, the old man's funny bright eyes, made

Polly want to drop her head on his shoulder for a second. She restrained herself, but she lingered in his grasp at the door of her room, murmuring tearfully: "You always lived in the city when you were young, didn't you? Don't you ever get lonesome out here?"

As she turned round to him, her hand fell naturally into his, and he stood holding it and smiling into her face with his peculiar, knowing, indulgent smile without a shadow of reproach in it. "Dem big cities is all right fur de rich, but dey is terrible hard fur de poor."

"I don't know. Sometimes I think I'd like to take a chance. You lived in New York, didn't you?"

"An' London. Da's bigger still. I learned my trade dere. Here's Rudolph comin', you better hurry."

"Will you tell me about London some time?"

"Maybe. Only I ain't no talker, Polly. Run an' dress yourself up."

The bedroom door closed behind her, and Rudolph came in from the outside, looking anxious. He had seen the car and was sorry any of his family should come just then. Supper hadn't been a very pleasant occasion. Halting in the doorway, he saw his father in a kitchen apron, carrying dishes to the sink. He flushed crimson and something flashed in his eye. Rosicky held up a warning finger.

"I brought de car over fur you an' Polly to go to de picture show, an' I made her let me finish here so you won't be late. You go put on a clean shirt, quick!"

"But don't the boys want the car, Father?"

"Not tonight dey don't." Rosicky fumbled under his apron and found his pants pocket. He took out a silver dollar and said in a hurried whisper: "You go an' buy dat girl some ice cream an' candy tonight, like you was courtin'. She's awful good friends wid me."

Rudolph was very short of cash, but he took the money as if it hurt him. There had been a crop failure all over the county. He had more than once been sorry he'd married this year.

In a few minutes the young people came out, looking clean and a little stiff. Rosicky hurried them off, and then he took his own time with the dishes. He scoured the pots and pans and put away the milk and swept the kitchen. He put some coal in the stove and shut off the draughts, so the place would be warm for them when they got home late at night. Then he sat down and had a pipe and listened to the clock tick.

Generally speaking, marrying an American girl was certainly a risk. A Czech should marry a Czech. It was lucky that Polly was the daughter of a poor widow woman; Rudolph was proud, and if she had a prosperous family to throw up at him, they could never make it go. Polly was one of four sisters, and they all worked; one was book-keeper in the bank, one taught music, and Polly and her younger sister had been clerks, like Miss Pearl. All four of them were musical, had pretty voices, and sang in the Methodist choir, which the eldest sister directed.

Polly missed the sociability of a store position. She missed the choir, and the company of her sisters. She didn't dislike housework, but she disliked so much of it. Rosicky was a little anxious about this pair. He was afraid Polly would grow so discontented that Rudy would quit the farm and take a factory job in Omaha. He had worked for a winter up there, two years ago, to get money to marry on. He had done very well, and they would always take him back at the stockyards. But to Rosicky that meant the end of everything for his son. To be a landless man was to be a wage-earner, a slave, all your life; to have nothing, to be nothing.

Rosicky thought he would come over and do a little carpentering for Polly after the New Year. He guessed she needed jollying. Rudolph was a serious sort of chap, serious in love and serious about his work.

Rosicky shook out his pipe and walked home across the fields. Ahead of him the lamplight shone from his kitchen windows. Suppose he were still in a tailor shop on Vesey Street, with a bunch of pale, narrow-chested sons working on machines, all coming home tired and sullen to eat supper in a kitchen that was a parlour also; with another crowded, angry family quarrelling just across the dumb-waiter shaft, and squeaking pulleys at the windows where dirty washings hung on dirty lines above a court full of old brooms and mops and ash-cans. . . .

He stopped by the windmill to look up at the frosty winter stars and draw a long breath before he went inside. That kitchen with the shining windows was dear to him; but the sleeping fields and bright stars and the noble darkness were dearer still.

V

On the day before Christmas the weather set in very cold; no snow, but a bitter, biting wind that whistled and sang over the flat land and lashed one's face like fine wires. There was baking going on in the Rosicky kitchen all day, and Rosicky sat inside, making over a coat that Albert had outgrown into an overcoat for John. Mary had a big red geranium in bloom for Christmas, and a row of Jerusalem cherry trees, full of berries. It was the first year she had ever grown these; Doctor Ed brought her the seeds from Omaha when he went to some medical convention. They reminded Rosicky of plants he had seen in England; and all afternoon, as he stitched, he sat thinking about those two years in London, which his mind usually shrank from even after all this while.

He was a lad of eighteen when he dropped down into London, with no money and no connexions except the address of a cousin who was supposed to be working at a confectioner's. When he went to the pastry shop, however, he found that the cousin had gone to America. Anton tramped the streets for several days, sleeping in doorways and on the Embankment,[5] until he was in utter despair. He knew no English, and the sound of the strange language all about him confused him. By chance he met a poor German tailor who had learned his trade in Vienna, and could speak a little Czech. This tailor, Lifschnitz, kept a repair shop in a Cheapside basement, underneath a cobbler. He didn't much need an apprentice, but he was sorry for the boy and took him in for no wages but his keep and what he could pick up. The pickings were supposed to be coppers given you when you took work home to a customer. But most of the customers called for their clothes themselves, and the coppers that came Anton's way were very few. He had, however, a place to sleep. The tailor's family lived upstairs in three rooms; a kitchen, a bedroom, where Lifschnitz and his wife and five children slept, and a living-room. Two corners of this

[5] The region of London alongside the Thames River.

living-room were curtained off for lodgers; in one Rosicky slept on an old horsehair sofa, with a feather quilt to wrap himself in. The other corner was rented to a wretched, dirty boy, who was studying the violin. He actually practised there. Rosicky was dirty, too. There was no way to be anything else. Mrs. Lifschnitz got the water she cooked and washed with from a pump in a brick court, four flights down. There were bugs in the place, and multitudes of fleas, though the poor woman did the best she could. Rosicky knew she often went empty to give another potato or a spoonful of dripping to the two hungry, sad-eyed boys who lodged with her. He used to think he would never get out of there, never get a clean shirt to his back again. What would he do, he wondered, when his clothes actually dropped to pieces and the worn cloth wouldn't hold patches any longer?

It was still early when the old farmer put aside his sewing and his recollections. The sky had been a dark grey all day, with not a gleam of sun, and the light failed at four o'clock. He went to shave and change his shirt while the turkey was roasting. Rudolph and Polly were coming over for supper.

After supper they sat round in the kitchen, and the younger boys were saying how sorry they were it hadn't snowed. Everybody was sorry. They wanted a deep snow that would lie long and keep the wheat warm, and leave the ground soaked when it melted.

"Yes, sir!" Rudolph broke out fiercely; "if we have another dry year like last year, there's going to be hard times in this country."

Rosicky filled his pipe. "You boys don't know what hard times is. You don't owe nobody, you got plenty to eat an' keep warm, an' plenty water to keep clean. When you got them, you can't have it very hard."

Rudolph frowned, opened and shut his big right hand, and dropped it clenched upon his knee. "I've got to have a good deal more than that, Father, or I'll quit this farming gamble. I can always make good wages railroading, or at the packing house, and be sure of my money."

"Maybe so," his father answered dryly.

Mary, who had just come in from the pantry and was wiping her hands on the roller towel, thought Rudy and his father were getting too serious. She brought her darning-basket and sat down in the middle of the group.

"I ain't much afraid of hard times, Rudy," she said heartily. "We've had a plenty, but we've always come through. Your father wouldn't never take nothing very hard, not even hard times. I got a mind to tell you a story on him. Maybe you boys can't hardly remember the year we had that terrible hot wind, that burned everything up on the Fourth of July? All the corn an' the gardens. An' that was in the days when we didn't have alfalfa yet,—I guess it wasn't invented.

"Well, that very day your father was out cultivatin' corn, and I was here in the kitchen makin' plum preserves. We had bushels of plums that year. I noticed it was terrible hot, but it's always hot in the kitchen when you're preservin', an' I was too busy with my plums to mind. Anton come in from the field about three o'clock, an' I asked him what was the matter.

" 'Nothin',' he says, 'but it's pretty hot, an' I think I won't work no more today.' He stood round for a few minutes, an' then he says: 'Ain't you near through? I want you should git up a nice supper for us tonight. It's Fourth of July.'

"I told him to git along, that I was right in the middle of preservin', but the plums would taste good on hot biscuit. 'I'm goin' to have fried chicken, too,' he says, and he went off an' killed a couple. You three oldest boys was little fellers, playin' round outside, real hot an' sweaty, an' your father took you to the horse tank down by the windmill an' took off your clothes an' put you in. Them two box-elder trees was little then, but they made shade over the tank. Then he took off all his own clothes, an' got in with you. While he was playin' in the water with you, the Methodist preacher drove into our place to say how all the neighbours was goin' to meet at the school-house that night, to pray for rain. He drove right to the windmill, of course, and there was your father and you three with no clothes on. I was in the kitchen door, an' I had to laugh, for the preacher acted like he ain't never seen a naked man before. He surely was embarrassed, an' your father couldn't git to his clothes; they was all hangin' up on the windmill to let the sweat dry out of 'em. So he laid in the tank where he was, an' put one of you boys on top of him to cover him up a little, an' talked to the preacher.

"When you got through playin' in the water, he put clean clothes on you and a clean shirt on himself, an' by that time I'd begun to get supper. He says: 'It's too hot in here to eat comfortable. Let's have a picnic in the orchard. We'll eat our supper behind the mulberry hedge, under them linden trees.'

"So he carried our supper down, an' a bottle of my wild-grape wine, an' everything tasted good, I can tell you. The wind got cooler as the sun was goin' down, and it turned out pleasant, only I noticed how the leaves was curled up on the linden trees. That made me think, an' I asked your father if that hot wind all day hadn't been terrible hard on the gardens an' the corn.

" 'Corn,' he says, 'there ain't no corn.'

" 'What you talkin' about?' I said. 'Ain't we got forty acres?'

" 'We ain't got an ear,' he says, 'nor nobody else ain't got none. All the corn in this country was cooked by three o'clock today, like you'd roasted it in an oven.'

" 'You mean you won't get no crop at all?' I asked him. I couldn't believe it, after he'd worked so hard.

" 'No crop this year,' he says. 'That's why we're havin' a picnic. We might as well enjoy what we got.'

"An' that's how your father behaved, when all the neighbours was so discouraged they couldn't look you in the face. An' we enjoyed ourselves that year, poor as we was, an' our neighbours wasn't a bit better off for bein' miserable. Some of 'em grieved till they got poor digestions and couldn't relish what they did have."

The younger boys said they thought their father had the best of it. But Rudolph was thinking that, all the same, the neighbours had managed to get ahead more, in the fifteen years since that time. There must be something wrong about his father's way of doing things. He wished he knew what was going on in the back of Polly's mind. He knew she liked his father, but he knew, too, that she was afraid of something. When his mother sent over coffee-cake or prune tarts or a loaf of fresh bread, Polly seemed to regard them with a certain suspicion. When she observed to him that his brothers had nice manners, her tone implied that it was remarkable they should have. With his mother she was stiff and on her guard. Mary's hearty frankness and gusts of good humour irritated her. Polly was afraid of being unusual or conspicuous in any way, of being "ordinary," as she said!

When Mary had finished her story, Rosicky laid aside his pipe.

"You boys like me to tell you about some of dem hard times I been through in London?" Warmly encouraged, he sat rubbing his forehead along the deep creases. It was bothersome to tell a long story in English (he nearly always talked to the boys in Czech), but he wanted Polly to hear this one.

"Well, you know about dat tailor shop I worked in in London? I had one Christmas dere I ain't never forgot. Times was awful bad before Christmas; de boss ain't got much work, an' have it awful hard to pay his rent. It ain't so much fun, bein' poor in a big city like London, I'll say! All de windows is full of good t'ings to eat, an' all de pushcarts in de streets is full, an' you smell 'em all de time, an' you ain't got no money,—not a damn bit. I didn't mind de cold so much, though I didn't have no overcoat, chust a short jacket I'd outgrowed so it wouldn't meet on me, an' my hands was chapped raw. But I always had a good appetite, like you all know, an' de sight of dem pork pies in de windows was awful fur me!

"Day before Christmas was terrible foggy dat year, an' dat fog gits into your bones and makes you all damp like. Mrs. Lifschnitz didn't give us nothin' but a little bread an' drippin' for supper, because she was savin' to try for to give us a good dinner on Christmas Day. After supper de boss say I can go an' enjoy myself, so I went into de streets to listen to de Christmas singers. Dey sing old songs an' make very nice music, an' I run round after dem a good ways, till I got awful hungry. I t'ink maybe if I go home, I can sleep till morning an' forgit my belly.

"I went into my corner real quiet, and roll up in my fedder quilt. But I ain't got my head down, till I smell somet'ing good. Seem like it git stronger an' stronger, an' I can't git to sleep noway. I can't understand dat smell. Dere was a gas light in a hall across de court, dat always shine in at my window a little. I got up an' look round. I got a little wooden box in my corner fur a stool, 'cause I ain't got no chair. I picks up dat box, and under it dere is a roast goose on a platter! I can't believe my eyes. I carry it to de window where de light comes in, an' touch it and smell it to find out, an' den I taste it to be sure. I say, I will eat chust one little bite of dat goose, so I can go to sleep, and tomorrow I won't eat none at all. But I tell you, boys, when I stop, one half of dat goose was gone!"

The narrator bowed his head, and the boys shouted. But little Josephine slipped behind his chair and kissed him on the neck beneath his ear.

"Poor little Papa, I don't want him to be hungry!"

"Da's long ago, child. I ain't never been hungry since I had your mudder to cook fur me."

"Go on and tell us the rest, please," said Polly.

"Well, when I come to realize what I done, of course, I felt terrible. I felt better in de stomach, but very bad in de heart. I set on my bed wid dat platter on my knees, an' it all come to me; how hard dat poor woman save to buy dat goose, and how she get some neighbour to cook it dat got more fire, an' how she put it in my corner to keep it away from dem hungry children. Dey was a old carpet hung up to shut my corner off, an' de children wasn't allowed to go in dere. An' I know she put it in my corner because she trust me more'n she did de violin boy. I can't stand it to face her after I spoil de Christmas. So I put on my shoes and go out into de city. I tell myself I better throw myself in de river; but I guess I ain't dat kind of a boy.

"It was after twelve o'clock, an' terrible cold, an' I start out to walk about London all night. I walk along de river awhile, but dey was lots of drunks all along; men, and women too. I chust move along to keep away from de police. I git onto de Strand, an' den over to New Oxford Street,[6] where dere was a big German restaurant on de ground floor, wid big windows all fixed up fine, an' I could see de people havin' parties inside. While I was lookin' in, two men and two ladies come out, laughin' and talkin' and feelin' happy about all dey been eatin' an' drinkin', and dey was speakin' Czech,—not like de Austrians, but like de home folks talk it.

"I guess I went crazy, an' I done what I ain't never done before nor since. I went right up to dem gay people an' begun to beg dem: 'Fellow-countrymen, for God's sake give me money enough to buy a goose!'

"Dey laugh, of course, but de ladies speak awful kind to me, an' dey take me back into de restaurant and give me hot coffee and cakes, an' make me tell all about how I happened to come to London, an' what I was doin' dere. Dey take my name and where I work down on paper, an' both of dem ladies give me ten shillings.

"De big market at Covent Garden ain't very far away, an' by dat time it was open. I go dere an' buy a big goose an' some pork pies, an' potatoes and onions, an' cakes an' oranges fur de children,—all I could carry! When I git home, everybody is still asleep. I pile all I bought on de kitchen table, an' go in an' lay down on my bed, an' I ain't waken up till I hear dat woman scream when she come out into her kitchen. My goodness, but she was surprise! She laugh an' cry at de same time, an' hug me and waken all de children. She ain't stop fur no breakfast; she git de Christmas dinner ready dat morning, and we all sit down an' eat all we can hold. I ain't never seen dat violin boy have all he can hold before.

"Two three days after dat, de two men come to hunt me up, an' dey ask my boss, and he give me a good report an' tell dem I was a steady boy all right. One of dem Bohemians was very smart an' run a Bohemian newspaper in New York, an' de odder was a rich man, in de importing business, an' dey been travelling togedder. Dey told me how t'ings was easier in New York, an' offered to pay my passage when dey was goin' home soon on a boat. My boss say to me: 'You go. You ain't got no chance here, an' I like to see you git ahead, fur you always been a good boy to my woman, and fur dat fine Christmas dinner you give us all.' An' da's how I got to New York."

That night when Rudolph and Polly, arm in arm, were running home across the fields with the bitter wind at their backs, his heart leaped for joy when she said she thought they might have his family come over for supper on New Year's Eve. "Let's get up a nice supper, and not let your mother help at all; make her be company for once."

"That would be lovely of you, Polly," he said humbly. He was a very simple, modest boy, and he, too, felt vaguely that Polly and her sisters were more experienced and worldly than his people.

VI

The winter turned out badly for farmers. It was bitterly cold, and after the first light snows before Christmas there was no snow at all,—and no rain. March was as bitter

---

[6] Fashionable area of London with shops, theaters, and restaurants.

as February. On those days when the wind fairly punished the country, Rosicky sat by his window. In the fall he and the boys had put in a big wheat planting, and now the seed had frozen in the ground. All that land would have to be ploughed up and planted over again, planted in corn. It had happened before, but he was younger then, and he never worried about what had to be. He was sure of himself and of Mary; he knew they could bear what they had to bear, that they would always pull through somehow. But he was not so sure about the young ones, and he felt troubled because Rudolph and Polly were having such a hard start.

Sitting beside his flowering window while the panes rattled and the wind blew in under the door, Rosicky gave himself to reflection as he had not done since those Sundays in the loft of the furniture-factory in New York, long ago. Then he was trying to find what he wanted in life for himself; now he was trying to find what he wanted for his boys, and why it was he so hungered to feel sure they would be here, working this very land, after he was gone.

They would have to work hard on the farm, and probably they would never do much more than make a living. But if he could think of them as staying here on the land, he wouldn't have to fear any great unkindness for them. Hardships, certainly; it was a hardship to have the wheat freeze in the ground when seed was so high; and to have to sell your stock because you had no feed. But there would be other years when everything came along right, and you caught up. And what you had was your own. You didn't have to choose between bosses and strikers, and go wrong either way. You didn't have to do with dishonest and cruel people. They were the only things in his experience he had found terrifying and horrible; the look in the eyes of a dishonest and crafty man, of a scheming and rapacious woman.

In the country, if you had a mean neighbour, you could keep off his land and make him keep off yours. But in the city, all the foulness and misery and brutality of your neighbours was part of your life. The worst things he had come upon in his journey through the world were human,—depraved and poisonous specimens of man. To this day he could recall certain terrible faces in the London streets. There were mean people everywhere, to be sure, even in their own country town here. But they weren't tempered, hardened, sharpened, like the treacherous people in cities who live by grinding or cheating or poisoning their fellow-men. He had helped to bury two of his fellow-workmen in the tailoring trade, and he was distrustful of the organized industries that see one out of the world in big cities. Here, if you were sick, you had Doctor Ed to look after you; and if you died, fat Mr. Haycock, the kindest man in the world, buried you.

It seemed to Rosicky that for good, honest boys like his, the worst they could do on the farm was better than the best they would be likely to do in the city. If he'd had a mean boy, now, one who was crooked and sharp and tried to put anything over on his brothers, then town would be the place for him. But he had no such boy. As for Rudolph, the discontented one, he would give the shirt off his back to anyone who touched his heart. What Rosicky really hoped for his boys was that they could get through the world without ever knowing much about the cruelty of human beings. "Their mother and me ain't prepared them for that," he sometimes said to himself.

These thoughts brought him back to a grateful consideration of his own case. What an escape he had had, to be sure! He, too, in his time, had had to take money for repair work from the hand of a hungry child who let it go so wistfully; because it was money due his boss. And now, in all these years, he had never had to take a cent from anyone in bitter need,—never had to look at the face of a woman become like a wolf's from struggle and famine. When he thought of these things, Rosicky would put on his cap and jacket and slip down to the barn and give his work-horses a little extra oats, letting them eat it out of his hand in their slobbery fashion. It was his way of expressing what he felt, and made him chuckle with pleasure.

The spring came warm, with blue skies,—but dry, dry as a bone. The boys began ploughing up the wheat-fields to plant them over in corn. Rosicky would stand at the fence corner and watch them, and the earth was so dry it blew up in clouds of brown dust that hid the horses and the sulky plough and the driver. It was a bad outlook.

The big alfalfa-field that lay between the home place and Rudolph's came up green, but Rosicky was worried because during that open windy winter a great many Russian thistle plants had blown in there and lodged. He kept asking the boys to rake them out; he was afraid their seed would root and "take the alfalfa." Rudolph said that was nonsense. The boys were working so hard planting corn, their father felt he couldn't insist about the thistles, but he set great store by that big alfalfa field. It was a feed you could depend on,—and there was some deeper reason, vague, but strong. The peculiar green of that clover woke early memories in old Rosicky, went back to something in his childhood in the old world. When he was a little boy, he had played in fields of that strong blue-green colour.

One morning, when Rudolph had gone to town in the car, leaving a work-team idle in his barn, Rosicky went over to his son's place, put the horses to the buggy-rake, and set about quietly raking up those thistles. He behaved with guilty caution, and rather enjoyed stealing a march on Doctor Ed, who was just then taking his first vacation in seven years of practice and was attending a clinic in Chicago. Rosicky got the thistles raked up, but did not stop to burn them. That would take some time, and his breath was pretty short, so he thought he had better get the horses back to the barn.

He got them into the barn and to their stalls, but the pain had come on so sharp in his chest that he didn't try to take the harness off. He started for the house, bending lower with every step. The cramp in his chest was shutting him up like a jack-knife. When he reached the windmill, he swayed and caught at the ladder. He saw Polly coming down the hill, running with the swiftness of a slim greyhound. In a flash she had her shoulder under his armpit.

"Lean on me, Father, hard! Don't be afraid. We can get to the house all right."

Somehow they did, though Rosicky became blind with pain; he could keep on his legs, but he couldn't steer his course. The next thing he was conscious of was lying on Polly's bed, and Polly bending over him wringing out bath towels in hot water and putting them on his chest. She stopped only to throw coal into the stove, and she kept the tea-kettle and the black pot going. She put these hot applications on him for nearly an hour, she told him afterwards, and all that time he was drawn up stiff and blue, with the sweat pouring off him.

As the pain gradually loosed its grip, the stiffness went out of his jaws, the black circles round his eyes disappeared, and a little of his natural colour came back. When his daughter-in-law buttoned his shirt over his chest at last, he sighed.

"Da's fine, de way I feel now, Polly. It was a awful bad spell, an' I was so sorry it all come on you like it did."

Polly was flushed and excited. "Is the pain really gone? Can I leave you long enough to telephone over to your place?"

Rosicky's eyelids fluttered. "Don't telephone, Polly. It ain't no use to scare my wife. It's nice and quiet here, an' if I ain't too much trouble to you, just let me lay still till I feel like myself. I ain't got no pain now. It's nice here."

Polly bent over him and wiped the moisture from his face. "Oh, I'm so glad it's over!" she broke out impulsively. "It just broke my heart to see you suffer so, Father."

Rosicky motioned her to sit down on the chair where the tea-kettle had been, and looked up at her with that lively affectionate gleam in his eyes. "You was awful good to me, I won't never forgit dat. I hate it to be sick on you like dis. Down at de barn I say to myself, dat young girl ain't had much experience in sickness, I don't want to scare her, an' maybe she's got a baby comin' or somet'ing."

Polly took his hand. He was looking at her so intently and affectionately and confidingly; his eyes seemed to caress her face, to regard it with pleasure. She frowned with her funny streaks of eyebrows, and then smiled back at him.

"I guess maybe there is something of that kind going to happen. But I haven't told anyone yet, not my mother or Rudolph. You'll be the first to know."

His hand pressed hers. She noticed that it was warm again. The twinkle in his yellow-brown eyes seemed to come nearer.

"I like mighty well to see dat little child, Polly," was all he said. Then he closed his eyes and lay half-smiling. But Polly sat still, thinking hard. She had a sudden feeling that nobody in the world, not her mother, not Rudolph, or anyone, really loved her as much as old Rosicky did. It perplexed her. She sat frowning and trying to puzzle it out. It was as if Rosicky had a special gift for loving people, something that was like an ear for music or an eye for colour. It was quiet, unobtrusive; it was merely there. You saw it in his eyes,—perhaps that was why they were merry. You felt it in his hands, too. After he dropped off to sleep, she sat holding his warm, broad, flexible brown hand. She had never seen another in the least like it. She wondered if it wasn't a kind of gypsy hand, it was so alive and quick and light in its communications,—very strange in a farmer. Nearly all the farmers she knew had huge lumps of fists, like mauls,[7] or they were knotty and bony and uncomfortable-looking, with stiff fingers. But Rosicky's was like quicksilver, flexible, muscular, about the colour of a pale cigar, with deep, deep creases across the palm. It wasn't nervous, it wasn't a stupid lump; it was a warm brown human hand, with some cleverness in it, a great deal of generosity, and something else which Polly could only call "gypsy-like,"—something nimble and lively and sure, in the way that animals are.

Polly remembered that hour long afterwards; it had been like an awakening to her. It seemed to her that she had never learned so much about life from anything as from old Rosicky's hand. It brought her to herself; it communicated some direct and untranslatable message.

When she heard Rudolph coming in the car, she ran out to meet him.

[7] Heavy mallets.

"Oh, Rudy, your father's been awful sick! He raked up those thistles he's been worrying about, and afterwards he could hardly get to the house. He suffered so I was afraid he was going to die."

Rudolph jumped to the ground. "Where is he now?"

"On the bed. He's asleep. I was terribly scared, because, you know, I'm so fond of your father." She slipped her arm through his and they went into the house. That afternoon they took Rosicky home and put him to bed, though he protested that he was quite well again.

The next morning he got up and dressed and sat down to breakfast with his family. He told Mary that his coffee tasted better than usual to him, and he warned the boys not to bear any tales to Doctor Ed when he got home. After breakfast he sat down by his window to do some patching and asked Mary to thread several needles for him before she went to feed her chickens,—her eyes were better than his, and her hands steadier. He lit his pipe and took up John's overalls. Mary had been watching him anxiously all morning, and as she went out of the door with her bucket of scraps, she saw that he was smiling. He was thinking, indeed, about Polly, and how he might never have known what a tender heart she had if he hadn't got sick over there. Girls nowadays didn't wear their heart on their sleeve. But now he knew Polly would make a fine woman after the foolishness wore off. Either a woman had that sweetness at her heart or she hadn't. You couldn't always tell by the look of them; but if they had that, everything came out right in the end.

After he had taken a few stitches, the cramp began in his chest, like yesterday. He put his pipe cautiously down on the window-sill and bent over to ease the pull. No use,—he had better try to get to his bed if he could. He rose and groped his way across the familiar floor, which was rising and falling like the deck of a ship. At the door he fell. When Mary came in, she found him lying there, and the moment she touched him she knew that he was gone.

Doctor Ed was away when Rosicky died, and for the first few weeks after he got home he was hard driven. Every day he said to himself that he must get out to see that family that had lost their father. One soft, warm moonlight night in early summer he started for the farm. His mind was on other things, and not until his road ran by the graveyard did he realize that Rosicky wasn't over there on the hill where the red lamplight shone, but here, in the moonlight. He stopped his car, shut off the engine, and sat there for a while.

A sudden hush had fallen on his soul. Everything here seemed strangely moving and significant, though signifying what, he did not know. Close by the wire fence stood Rosicky's mowing-machine, where one of the boys had been cutting hay that afternoon; his own work-horses had been going up and down there. The new-cut hay perfumed all the night air. The moonlight silvered the long, billowy grass that grew over the graves and hid the fence; the few little evergreens stood out black in it, like shadows in a pool. The sky was very blue and soft, the stars rather faint because the moon was full.

For the first time it struck Doctor Ed that this was really a beautiful graveyard. He thought of city cemeteries; acres of shrubbery and heavy stone, so arranged and lonely and unlike anything in the living world. Cities of the dead, indeed; cities of the forgotten, of the "put away." But this was open and free, this little square of long grass which the wind for ever stirred. Nothing but the sky overhead, and the many-coloured fields running on until they met that sky. The horses worked here in summer; the neighbours passed on their way to town; and over yonder, in the cornfield, Rosicky's own cattle would be eating fodder as winter came on. Nothing could be more undeathlike than this place; nothing could be more right for a man who had helped to do the work of great cities and had always longed for the open country and had got to it at last. Rosicky's life seemed to him complete and beautiful.

1928/1930

Jack London
1876–1916

One of the most popular and most highly paid writers of his time, Jack London was born in San Francisco on January 12, 1876, the illegitimate son of William Henry Chaney, an itinerant astrologer, and Flora Wellman, a spiritualist. He took the name of his stepfather, John London, an unsuccessful rancher who moved the family to Oakland in 1886. As London records in his autobiography, *John Barleycorn* (1913), he quit Oakland High School at fourteen and began a life of odd jobs, heavy drinking, and daring adventures: He earned money as an oyster pirate in San Francisco Bay, worked long hours in a cannery, frequented the Oakland libraries and saloons, and sailed as an able-bodied seaman to Japan. In 1894 he tramped halfway across the country with Kelley's Industrial Army, a California group of unemployed who staged a protest march on Washington. This experience not only led to his long embrace of socialism but also impelled him, especially after being arrested for vagrancy in Buffalo, New York, to begin what he called his "frantic pursuit of knowledge." In 1896 he enrolled as a special student at the University of California at Berkeley, but after a semester he decided he would rather spend the winter prospecting for gold in the Klondike. He found no gold; instead he returned with experiences and material he would mine for a lifetime as a writer. His first collection of short stories, *The Son of the Wolf*, appeared in 1900.

Three years later he published a best-selling novel, *The Call of the Wild,* in which he attempted to enter into the consciousness of an animal: "There is an ecstasy that marks the summit of life and beyond which life cannot rise. . . . This ecstasy comes when one is most alive, and it comes as a complete forgetfulness that one is alive." London believed that such elemental and ecstatic forms of consciousness could also be attained by people, though mainly in moments of violent struggle with forces larger than themselves.

Though the drama of extremely reduced states of consciousness, as depicted in such famous London stories as "To Build a Fire," informs much of his writing, there is another side to London's work, one more dependent on Marxist economics than Darwinian biology. A year before *Call of the Wild* appeared, London spent six weeks disguised as an out-of-work American sailor roaming the slums of London's East End while he gathered material for the one book he claimed to love the most, *People of the Abyss* (1903). An indictment of capitalism and the class system, the book revealed an intellectual conflict in the writer that would become increasingly strained in his later work. London never satisfactorily reconciled his intense desire for social justice with his equally intense belief in the survival of the powerful. If his Marxism was tainted by an almost ferocious faith in individualism and racial superiority ("I am first of all a white man and only then a socialist"), his Darwinism was diluted by his affection for the underdog and his collectivist sympathies. Throughout his career, he alternated between the rugged individualism of Theodore Roosevelt and the quest for solidarity of Eugene Debs.

The main difficulty with London's personal philosophy, however, was not his inability to reconcile Darwin and Marx but his inability to extend his thoughts past their crudest formulations. He once wrote in a letter:

> I assert, with Hobbes, that it is impossible to separate thought from matter that thinks.
> I assert, with Bacon, that all human understanding arises from the world of sensations.
> I assert, with Locke, that all human ideas are due to the functions of the senses.
> I assert, with Kant, the mechanical origin of the universe, and that creation is a natural and historical process.
> I assert, with Laplace, that there is no need of the hypothesis of a Creator.

This manifesto typifies the blunt style of London's thinking. He tended to see ideas in much the same way that he saw nature—as elemental forces to be reckoned with. Yet, like Rudyard Kipling, whom he greatly admired, London was a natural storyteller. In its narrative energy and mythic power, London's best writing transcends whatever philosophical slogans he set out to portray.

During the height of his popularity as a novelist, London continued to lead a strenuous and adventurous life. After completing one of his most successful novels, *The Sea Wolf,* in 1904, he went to Japan and Korea to cover the Russo-Japanese War for the Hearst papers. In 1905 he ran unsuccessfully for the second time as the Socialist candidate for mayor of Oakland. He published another successful novel, *White Fang,* in 1906 and wrote one of his most highly respected books, the semiautobiographical novel *Martin Eden,* in 1908 and 1909 while sailing his homemade yacht to the South Pacific. When the Mexican Revolution broke out in 1914, he rushed to Veracruz as a correspondent for *Collier's.* In 1915, exhausted and in failing health, he traveled to Hawaii, where during the day he produced hack work to keep up his dwindling fortune (he had made over a million dollars from his writing) and at night read Freud and Jung. Back in California, suffering from acute uremia, he injected a larger dose of painkilling morphine than he had been accustomed to and died early in the morning of November 22, 1916.

Further Reading:
P. Foner, *Jack London, American Rebel*, 1947.
E. Labor, *Jack London*, 1974.
J. McClintock, *White Logic: Jack London's Short Stories*, 1975.
A. Sinclair, *Jack: A Biography of Jack London*, 1977.
C. Watson, *The Novels of Jack London: A Reappraisal*, 1982.

Text:
Lost Face, 1910.

To Build a Fire*

Day had broken cold and gray, exceedingly cold and gray, when the man turned aside from the main Yukon trail and climbed the high earth-bank, where a dim and little-travelled trail led eastward through the fat spruce timberland. It was a steep bank, and he paused for breath at the top, excusing the act to himself by looking at his watch. It was nine o'clock. There was no sun nor hint of sun, though there was not a cloud in the sky. It was a clear day, and yet there seemed an intangible pall over the face of things, a subtle gloom that made the day dark, and that was due to the absence of sun. This fact did not worry the man. He was used to the lack of sun. It had been days since he had seen the sun, and he knew that a few more days must pass before that cheerful orb, due south, would just peep above the sky line and dip immediately from view.

The man flung a look back along the way he had come. The Yukon lay a mile wide and hidden under three feet of ice. On top of this ice were as many feet of snow. It was all pure white, rolling in gentle undulations where the ice jams of the freeze-up had formed. North and south, as far as his eye could see, it was unbroken white, save for a dark hairline that curved and twisted from around the spruce-covered island to the south, and that curved and twisted away into the north, where it disappeared behind another spruce-covered island. This dark hairline was the trail—the main trail —that led south five hundred miles to the Chilcoot Pass, Dyea, and salt water; and that led north seventy miles to Dawson, and still on to the north a thousand miles to Nulato, and finally to St. Michael, on Bering Sea, a thousand miles and half a thousand more.

But all this—the mysterious, far-reaching hairline trail, the absence of sun from the sky, the tremendous cold, and the strangeness and weirdness of it all—made no impression on the man. It was not because he was long used to it. He was a newcomer in the land, a *chechaquo*, and this was his first winter. The trouble with him was that he was without imagination. He was quick and alert in the things of life, but only in the things, and not in the significances. Fifty degrees below zero meant eighty-odd degrees of frost. Such fact impressed him as being cold and uncomfortable, and that

---

* An earlier version of this story first appeared in *Youth's Companion* in May 1902.

was all. It did not lead him to meditate upon his frailty as a creature of temperature, and upon man's frailty in general, able only to live within certain narrow limits of heat and cold; and from there on it did not lead him to the conjectural field of immortality and man's place in the universe. Fifty degrees below zero stood for a bite of frost that hurt and that must be guarded against by the use of mittens, ear flaps, warm moccasins, and thick socks. Fifty degrees below zero was to him just precisely fifty degrees below zero. That there should be anything more to it than that was a thought that never entered his head.

As he turned to go on, he spat speculatively. There was a sharp, explosive crackle that startled him. He spat again. And again, in the air, before it could fall to the snow, the spittle crackled. He knew that at fifty below spittle crackled on the snow, but this spittle had crackled in the air. Undoubtedly it was colder than fifty below—how much colder he did not know. But the temperature did not matter. He was bound for the old claim on the left fork of Henderson Creek, where the boys were already. They had come over across the divide from the Indian Creek country, while he had come the roundabout way to take a look at the possibilities of getting out logs in the spring from the islands in the Yukon. He would be in to camp by six o'clock; a bit after dark, it was true, but the boys would be there, a fire would be going, and a hot supper would be ready. As for lunch, he pressed his hand against the protruding bundle under his jacket. It was also under his shirt, wrapped up in a handkerchief and lying against the naked skin. It was the only way to keep the biscuits from freezing. He smiled agreeably to himself as he thought of those biscuits, each cut open and sopped in bacon grease, and each enclosing a generous slice of fried bacon.

He plunged in among the big spruce trees. The trail was faint. A foot of snow had fallen since the last sled had passed over, and he was glad he was without a sled, travelling light. In fact, he carried nothing but the lunch wrapped in the handkerchief. He was surprised, however, at the cold. It certainly was cold, he concluded, as he rubbed his numb nose and cheekbones with his mittened hand. He was a warm-whiskered man, but the hair on his face did not protect the high cheekbones and the eager nose that thrust itself aggressively into the frosty air.

At the man's heels trotted a dog, a big native husky, the proper wolf dog, gray-coated and without any visible or temperamental difference from its brother, the wild wolf. The animal was depressed by the tremendous cold. It knew that it was no time for travelling. Its instinct told it a truer tale than was told to the man by the man's judgment. In reality, it was not merely colder than fifty below zero; it was colder than sixty below, than seventy below. It was seventy-five below zero. Since the freezing point is thirty-two above zero, it meant that one hundred and seven degrees of frost obtained. The dog did not know anything about thermometers. Possibly in its brain there was no sharp consciousness of a condition of very cold such as was in the man's brain. But the brute had its instinct. It experienced a vague but menacing apprehension that subdued it and made it slink along at the man's heels, and that made it question eagerly every unwonted movement of the man as if expecting him to go into camp or to seek shelter somewhere and build a fire. The dog had learned fire, and it wanted fire, or else to burrow under the snow and cuddle its warmth away from the air.

The frozen moisture of its breathing had settled on its fur in a fine powder of frost, and especially were its jowls, muzzle, and eyelashes whitened by its crystalled breath.

The man's red beard and mustache were likewise frosted, but more solidly, the deposit taking the form of ice and increasing with every warm, moist breath he exhaled. Also, the man was chewing tobacco, and the muzzle of ice held his lips so rigidly that he was unable to clear his chin when he expelled the juice. The result was that a crystal beard of the color and solidity of amber was increasing its length on his chin. If he fell down it would shatter itself, like glass, into brittle fragments. But he did not mind the appendage. It was the penalty all tobacco chewers paid in that country, and he had been out before in two cold snaps. They had not been so cold as this, he knew, but by the spirit thermometer at Sixty Mile he knew they had been registered at fifty below and at fifty-five.

He held on through the level stretch of woods for several miles, crossed a wide flat of nigger heads, and dropped down a bank to the frozen bed of a small stream. This was Henderson Creek, and he knew he was ten miles from the forks. He looked at his watch. It was ten o'clock. He was making four miles an hour, and he calculated that he would arrive at the forks at half-past twelve. He decided to celebrate that event by eating his lunch there.

The dog dropped in again at his heels, with a tail drooping discouragement, as the man swung along the creek bed. The furrow of the old sled trail was plainly visible, but a dozen inches of snow covered the marks of the last runners. In a month no man had come up or down that silent creek. The man held steadily on. He was not much given to thinking, and just then particularly he had nothing to think about save that he would eat lunch at the forks and that at six o'clock he would be in camp with the boys. There was nobody to talk to; and, had there been, speech would have been impossible because of the ice muzzle on his mouth. So he continued monotonously to chew tobacco and to increase the length of his amber beard.

Once in a while the thought reiterated itself that it was very cold and that he had never experienced such cold. As he walked along he rubbed his cheekbones and nose with the back of his mittened hand. He did this automatically, now and again changing hands. But, rub as he would, the instant he stopped his cheekbones went numb, and the following instant the end of his nose went numb. He was sure to frost his cheeks; he knew that, and experienced a pang of regret that he had not devised a nose strap of the sort Bud wore in cold snaps. Such a strap passed across the cheeks, as well, and saved them. But it didn't matter much, after all. What were frosted cheeks? A bit painful, that was all; they were never serious.

Empty as the man's mind was of thoughts, he was keenly observant, and he noticed the changes in the creek, the curves and bends and timber jams, and always he sharply noted where he placed his feet. Once, coming around a bend, he shied abruptly, like a startled horse, curved away from the place where he had been walking, and retreated several paces back along the trail. The creek he knew was frozen clear to the bottom —no creek could contain water in that arctic winter—but he knew also that there were springs that bubbled out from the hillsides and ran along under the snow and on top the ice of the creek. He knew that the coldest snaps never froze these springs, and he knew likewise their danger. They were traps. They hid pools of water under the snow that might be three inches deep, or three feet. Sometimes a skin of ice half an inch thick covered them, and in turn was covered by the snow. Sometimes there were alternate layers of water and ice skin, so that when one broke through he kept on breaking through for a while, sometimes wetting himself to the waist.

That was why he had shied in such panic. He had felt the give under his feet and heard the crackle of a snow-hidden ice skin. And to get his feet wet in such a temperature meant trouble and danger. At the very least it meant delay, for he would be forced to stop and build a fire, and under its protection to bare his feet while he dried his socks and moccasins. He stood and studied the creek bed and its banks, and decided that the flow of water came from the right. He reflected awhile, rubbing his nose and cheeks, then skirted to the left, stepping gingerly and testing the footing for each step. Once clear of the danger, he took a fresh chew of tobacco and swung along at his four-mile gait.

In the course of the next two hours he came upon several similar traps. Usually the snow above the hidden pools had a sunken, candied appearance that advertised the danger. Once again, however, he had a close call; and once, suspecting danger, he compelled the dog to go on in front. The dog did not want to go. It hung back until the man shoved it forward, and then it went quickly across the white, unbroken surface. Suddenly it broke through, floundered to one side, and got away to firmer footing. It had wet its forefeet and legs, and almost immediately the water that clung to it turned to ice. It made quick efforts to lick the ice off its legs, then dropped down in the snow and began to bite out the ice that had formed between the toes. This was matter of instinct. To permit the ice to remain would mean sore feet. It did not know this. It merely obeyed the mysterious prompting that arose from the deep crypts of its being. But the man knew, having achieved a judgment on the subject, and he removed the mitten from his right hand and helped tear out the ice particles. He did not expose his fingers more than a minute, and was astonished at the swift numbness that smote them. It certainly was cold. He pulled on the mitten hastily, and beat the hand savagely across his chest.

At twelve o'clock the day was at its brightest. Yet the sun was too far south on its winter journey to clear the horizon. The bulge of the earth intervened between it and Henderson Creek, where the man walked under a clear sky at noon and cast no shadow. At half-past twelve, to the minute, he arrived at the forks of the creek. He was pleased at the speed he had made. If he kept it up, he would certainly be with the boys by six. He unbuttoned his jacket and shirt and drew forth his lunch. The action consumed no more than a quarter of a minute, yet in that brief moment the numbness laid hold of the exposed fingers. He did not put the mitten on, but, instead, struck the fingers a dozen sharp smashes against his leg. Then he sat down on a snow-covered log to eat. The sting that followed upon the striking of his fingers against his leg ceased so quickly that he was startled. He had had no chance to take a bit of biscuit. He struck the fingers repeatedly and returned them to the mitten, baring the other hand for the purpose of eating. He tried to take a mouthful, but the ice muzzle prevented. He had forgotten to build a fire and thaw out. He chuckled at his foolishness, and as he chuckled he noted the numbness creeping into the exposed fingers. Also, he noted that the stinging which had first come to his toes when he sat down was already passing away. He wondered whether the toes were warm or numb. He moved them inside the moccasins and decided that they were numb.

He pulled the mitten on hurriedly and stood up. He was a bit frightened. He stamped up and down until the stinging returned into the feet. It certainly was cold, was his thought. That man from Sulphur Creek had spoken the truth when telling how cold it sometimes got in the country. And he had laughed at him at the time!

That showed one must not be too sure of things. There was no mistake about it, it was cold. He strode up and down, stamping his feet and threshing his arms, until reassured by the returning warmth. Then he got out matches and proceeded to make a fire. From the undergrowth, where high water of the previous spring had lodged a supply of seasoned twigs, he got his firewood. Working carefully from a small beginning, he soon had a roaring fire, over which he thawed the ice from his face and in the protection of which he ate his biscuits. For the moment the cold of space was outwitted. The dog took satisfaction in the fire, stretching out close enough for warmth and far enough away to escape being singed.

When the man had finished, he filled his pipe and took his comfortable time over a smoke. Then he pulled on his mittens, settled the ear flaps of his cap firmly about his ears, and took the creek trail up the left fork. The dog was disappointed and yearned back toward the fire. This man did not know cold. Possibly all the generations of his ancestry had been ignorant of cold, of real cold, of cold one hundred and seven degrees below freezing point. But the dog knew; all its ancestry knew, and it had inherited the knowledge. And it knew that it was not good to walk abroad in such fearful cold. It was the time to lie snug in a hole in the snow and wait for a curtain of cloud to be drawn across the face of outer space whence this cold came. On the other hand, there was no keen intimacy between the dog and the man. The one was the toil slave of the other, and the only caresses it had ever received were the caresses of the whip lash and of harsh and menacing throat sounds that threatened the whip lash. So the dog made no effort to communicate its apprehension to the man. It was not concerned in the welfare of the man; it was for its own sake that it yearned back toward the fire. But the man whistled, and spoke to it with the sound of whip lashes, and the dog swung in at the man's heels and followed after.

The man took a chew of tobacco and proceeded to start a new amber beard. Also, his moist breath quickly powdered with white his mustache, eyebrows, and lashes. There did not seem to be so many springs on the left fork of the Henderson, and for half an hour the man saw no signs of any. And then it happened. At a place where there were no signs, where the soft, unbroken snow seemed to advertise solidity beneath, the man broke through. It was not deep. He wet himself halfway to the knees before he floundered out to the firm crust.

He was angry, and cursed his luck aloud. He had hoped to get into camp with the boys at six o'clock, and this would delay him an hour, for he would have to build a fire and dry out his footgear. This was imperative at that low temperature—he knew that much; and he turned aside to the bank, which he climbed. On top, tangled in the underbrush about the trunks of several small spruce trees, was a highwater deposit of dry firewood—sticks and twigs, principally, but also larger portions of seasoned branches and fine, dry, last year's grasses. He threw down several large pieces on top of the snow. This served for a foundation and prevented the young flame from drowning itself in the snow it otherwise would melt. The flame he got by touching a match to a small shred of birch bark that he took from his pocket. This burned even more readily than paper. Placing it on the foundation, he fed the young flame with wisps of dry grass and with the tiniest dry twigs.

He worked slowly and carefully, keenly aware of his danger. Gradually, as the flame grew stronger, he increased the size of the twigs with which he fed it. He squatted in the snow, pulling the twigs out from their entanglement in the brush and feeding directly to the flame. He knew there must be no failure. When it is seventy-five below zero, a man must not fail in his first attempt to build a fire—that is, if his feet are wet. If his feet are dry, and he fails, he can run along the trail for half a mile and restore his circulation. But the circulation of wet and freezing feet cannot be restored by running when it is seventy-five below. No matter how fast he runs, the wet feet will freeze the harder. All this the man knew. The old-timer on Sulphur Creek had told him about it the previous fall, and now he was appreciating the advice. Already all sensation had gone out of his feet. To build the fire he had been forced to remove his mittens, and the fingers had quickly gone numb. His pace of four miles an hour had kept his heart pumping blood to the surface of his body and to all the extremities. But the instant he stopped, the action of the pump eased down. The cold of space smote the unprotected tip of the planet, and he, being on that unprotected tip, received the full force of the blow. The blood of his body recoiled before it. The blood was alive, like the dog, and like the dog it wanted to hide away and cover itself up from the fearful cold. So long as he walked four miles an hour, he pumped that blood, willy-nilly, to the surface; but now it ebbed away and sank down into the recesses of his body. The extremities were the first to feel its absence. His wet feet froze the faster, and his exposed fingers numbed the faster, though they had not yet begun to freeze. Nose and cheeks were already freezing, while the skin of all his body chilled as it lost its blood.

But he was safe. Toes and nose and cheeks would be only touched by the frost, for the fire was beginning to burn with strength. He was feeding it with twigs the size of his finger. In another minute he would be able to feed it with branches the size of his wrist, and then he could remove his wet footgear, and, while it dried, he could keep his naked feet warm by the fire, rubbing them at first, of course, with snow. The fire was a success. He was safe. He remembered the advice of the old-timer on Sulphur Creek, and smiled. The old-timer had been very serious in laying down the law that no man must travel alone in the Klondike after fifty below. Well, here he was; he had had the accident; he was alone; and he had saved himself. Those old-timers were rather womanish, some of them, he thought. All a man had to do was to keep his head, and he was all right. Any man who was a man could travel alone. But it was surprising, the rapidity with which his cheeks and nose were freezing. And he had not thought his fingers could go lifeless in so short a time. Lifeless they were, for he could scarcely make them move together to grip a twig, and they seemed remote from his body and from him. When he touched a twig, he had to look and see whether or not he had hold of it. The wires were pretty well down between him and his finger ends.

All of which counted for little. There was the fire, snapping and crackling and promising life with every dancing flame. He started to untie his moccasins. They were coated with ice; the thick German socks were like sheaths of iron halfway to the knees; and the moccasin strings were like rods of steel all twisted and knotted as by some conflagration. For a moment he tugged with his numb fingers, then, realizing the folly of it, he drew his sheath knife.

But before he could cut the strings, it happened. It was his own fault or, rather, his mistake. He should not have built the fire under the spruce tree. He should have built it in the open. But it had been easier to pull the twigs from the brush and drop them directly on the fire. Now the tree under which he had done this carried a weight of snow on its boughs. No wind had blown for weeks, and each bough was fully freighted. Each time he had pulled a twig he had communicated a slight agitation to the tree—an imperceptible agitation, so far as he was concerned, but an agitation sufficient to bring about the disaster. High up in the tree one bough capsized its load of snow. This fell on the boughs beneath, capsizing them. This process continued, spreading out and involving the whole tree. It grew like an avalanche, and it descended without warning upon the man and the fire, and the fire was blotted out! Where it had burned was a mantle of fresh and disordered snow.

The man was shocked. It was as though he had just heard his own sentence of death. For a moment he sat and stared at the spot where the fire had been. Then he grew very calm. Perhaps the old-timer on Sulphur Creek was right. If he had only had a trail mate he would have been in no danger now. The trail mate could have built the fire. Well, it was up to him to build the fire over again, and this second time there must be no failure. Even if he succeeded, he would most likely lose some toes. His feet must be badly frozen by now, and there would be some time before the second fire was ready.

Such were his thoughts, but he did not sit and think them. He was busy all the time they were passing through his mind. He made a new foundation for a fire, this time in the open, where no treacherous tree could blot it out. Next he gathered dry grasses and tiny twigs from the highwater flotsam. He could not bring his fingers together to pull them out, but he was able to gather them by the handful. In this way he got many rotten twigs and bits of green moss that were undesirable, but it was the best he could do. He worked methodically, even collecting an armful of the larger branches to be used later when the fire gathered strength. And all the while the dog sat and watched him, a certain yearning wistfulness in its eyes, for it looked upon him as the fire provider, and the fire was slow in coming.

When all was ready, the man reached in his pocket for a second piece of birch bark. He knew the bark was there, and, though he could not feel it with his fingers, he could hear its crisp rustling as he fumbled for it. Try as he would, he could not clutch hold of it. And all the time, in his consciousness, was the knowledge that each instant his feet were freezing. This thought tended to put him in a panic, but he fought against it and kept calm. He pulled on his mittens with his teeth, and threshed his arms back and forth, beating his hands with all his might against his sides. He did this sitting down, and he stood up to do it; and all the while the dog sat in the snow, its wolf brush of a tail curled around warmly over its forefeet, its sharp wolf ears pricked forward intently as it watched the man. And the man, as he beat and threshed with his arms and hands, felt a great surge of envy as he regarded the creature that was warm and secure in its natural covering.

After a time he was aware of the first faraway signals of sensation in his beaten fingers. The faint tingling grew stronger till it evolved into a stinging ache that was excruciating, but which the man hailed with satisfaction. He stripped the mitten from his right hand and fetched forth the birch bark. The exposed fingers were quickly going numb again. Next he brought out his bunch of sulphur matches. But the tremendous cold had already driven the life out of his fingers. In his effort to separate one match from the others, the whole bunch fell in the snow. He tried to pick it out of the snow, but failed. The dead fingers could neither touch nor clutch. He was very careful. He drove the thought of his freezing feet, and nose, and cheeks, out of his mind, devoting his whole soul to the matches. He watched, using the sense of vision in place of that of touch, and when he saw his fingers on each side the bunch, he closed them—that is, he willed to close them, for the wires were down, and the fingers did not obey. He pulled the mitten on the right hand, and beat it fiercely against his knee. Then, with both mittened hands, he scooped the bunch of matches, along with much snow, into his lap. Yet he was no better off.

After some manipulation he managed to get the bunch between the heels of his mittened hands. In this fashion he carried it to his mouth. The ice crackled and snapped when by a violent effort he opened his mouth. He drew the lower jaw in, curled the upper lip out of the way, and scraped the bunch with his upper teeth in order to separate a match. He succeeded in getting one, which he dropped on his lap. He was no better off. He could not pick it up. Then he devised a way. He picked it up in his teeth and scratched it on his leg. Twenty times he scratched before he succeeded in lighting it. As it flamed he held it with his teeth to the birch bark. But the burning brimstone went up his nostrils and into his lungs, causing him to cough spasmodically. The match fell into the snow and went out.

The old-timer on Sulphur Creek was right, he thought in the moment of controlled despair that ensued: after fifty below, a man should travel with a partner. He beat his hands, but failed in exciting any sensation. Suddenly he bared both hands, removing the mittens with his teeth. He caught the whole bunch between the heels of his hands. His arm muscles not being frozen enabled him to press the hand heels tightly against the matches. Then he scratched the bunch along his leg. It flared into flame, seventy sulphur matches at once! There was no wind to blow them out. He kept his head to one side to escape the strangling fumes, and held the blazing bunch to the birch bark. As he so held it, he became aware of sensation in his hand. His flesh was burning. He could smell it. Deep down below the surface he could feel it. The sensation developed into pain that grew acute. And still he endured it, holding the flame of the matches clumsily to the bark that would not light readily because his own burning hands were in the way, absorbing most of the flame.

At last, when he could endure no more, he jerked his hands apart. The blazing matches fell sizzling into the snow, but the birch bark was alight. He began laying dry grasses and the tiniest twigs on the flame. He could not pick and choose, for he had to lift the fuel between the heels of his hands. Small pieces of rotten wood and green moss clung to the twigs, and he bit them off as well as he could with his teeth. He cherished the flame carefully and awkwardly. It meant life, and it must not perish. The withdrawal of blood from the surface of his body now made him begin to shiver, and he grew more awkward. A large piece of green moss fell squarely on the little fire. He tried to poke it out with his fingers, but his shivering frame made him poke too far, and he disrupted the nucleus of the little fire, the burning grasses and tiny twigs separating and scattering. He tried to poke them together again, but in spite of the tenseness of the effort, his shivering got away with him, and the twigs were hopelessly scattered. Each twig gushed a puff of smoke and went out. The fire provider had failed. As he looked apathetically about him, his eyes chanced on the dog, sitting across the ruins of the fire from him, in the snow, making restless, hunching movements, slightly lifting one forefoot and then the other, shifting its weight back and forth on them with wistful eagerness.

The sight of the dog put a wild idea into his head. He remembered the tale of the man, caught in a blizzard, who killed a steer and crawled inside the carcass, and so was saved. He would kill the dog and bury his hands in the warm body until the numbness went out of them. Then he could build another fire. He spoke to the dog, calling it to him; but in his voice was a strange note of fear that frightened the animal, who had never known the man to speak in such way before. Something was the matter, and its suspicious nature sensed danger—it knew not what danger, but somewhere, somehow, in its brain arose an apprehension of the man. It flattened its ears down at the sound of the man's voice, and its restless, hunching movements and the liftings and shiftings of its forefeet became more pronounced; but it would not come to the man. He got on his hands and knees and crawled toward the dog. This unusual posture again excited suspicion, and the animal sidled mincingly away.

The man sat up in the snow for a moment and struggled for calmness. Then he pulled on his mittens, by means of his teeth, and got upon his feet. He glanced down at first in order to assure himself that he was really standing up, for the absence of sensation in his feet left him unrelated to the earth. His erect position in itself started to drive the webs of suspicion from the dog's mind; and when he spoke peremptorily, with the sound of whip lashes in his voice, the dog rendered its customary allegiance and came to him. As it came within reaching distance, the man lost his control. His arms flashed out to the dog, and he experienced genuine surprise when he discovered that his hands could not clutch, that there was neither bend nor feeling in the fingers. He had forgotten for the moment that they were frozen and that they were freezing more and more. All this happened quickly, and before the animal could get away, he encircled its body with his arms. He sat down in the snow, and in this fashion held the dog, while it snarled and whined and struggled.

But it was all he could do, hold its body encircled in his arms and sit there. He realized that he could not kill the dog. There was no way to do it. With his helpless hands he could neither draw nor hold his sheath knife nor throttle the animal. He released it, and it plunged wildly away, with tail between its legs, and still snarling. It halted forty feet away and surveyed him curiously, with ears sharply pricked forward.

The man looked down at his hands in order to locate them, and found them hanging on the ends of his arms. It struck him as curious that one should have to use his eyes in order to find out where his hands were. He began threshing his arms back and forth, beating the mittened hands against his sides. He did this for five minutes, violently, and his heart pumped enough blood up to the surface to put a stop to his shivering. But no sensation was aroused in the hands. He had an impression that they hung like weights on the ends of his arms, but when he tried to run the impression down, he could not find it.

A certain fear of death, dull and oppressive, came to him. This fear quickly became poignant as he realized that it was no longer a mere matter of freezing his fingers and toes, or of losing his hands and feet, but that it was a matter of life and death with the chances against him. This threw him into a panic, and he turned and ran up the creek bed along the old, dim trail. The dog joined in behind and kept up with him. He ran blindly, without intention, in fear such as he had never known in his life. Slowly, as he plowed and floundered through the snow, he began to see things again —the banks of the creek, the old timber jams, the leafless aspens, and the sky. The running made him feel better. He did not shiver. Maybe, if he ran on, his feet would thaw out; and, anyway, if he ran far enough, he would reach camp and the boys. Without doubt he would lose some fingers and toes and some of his face; but the boys would take care of him, and save the rest of him when he got there. And at the same time there was another thought in his mind that said he would never get to the camp and the boys; that it was too many miles away, that the freezing had too great a start on him, and that he would soon be stiff and dead. This thought he kept in the background and refused to consider. Sometimes it pushed itself forward and demanded to be heard, but he thrust it back and strove to think of other things.

It struck him as curious that he could run at all on feet so frozen that he could not feel them when they struck the earth and took the weight of his body. He seemed to himself to skim along above the surface, and to have no connection with the earth. Somewhere he had once seen a winged Mercury, and he wondered if Mercury felt as he felt when skimming over the earth.

His theory of running until he reached camp and the boys had one flaw in it: he lacked the endurance. Several times he stumbled, and finally he tottered, crumpled up, and fell. When he tried to rise, he failed. He must sit and rest, he decided, and next time he would merely walk and keep on going. As he sat and regained his breath, he noted that he was feeling quite warm and comfortable. He was not shivering, and it even seemed that a warm glow had come to his chest and trunk. And yet, when he touched his nose or cheeks, there was no sensation. Running would not thaw them out. Nor would it thaw out his hands and feet. Then the thought came to him that the frozen portions of his body must be extending. He tried to keep this thought down, to forget it, to think of something else; he was aware of the panicky feeling that it caused, and he was afraid of the panic. But the thought asserted itself, and persisted, until it produced a vision of his body totally frozen. This was too much, and he made another wild run along the trail. Once he slowed down to a walk, but the thought of the freezing extending itself made him run again.

And all the time the dog ran with him, at his heels. When he fell down a second time, it curled its tail over its forefeet and sat in front of him, facing him, curiously eager and intent. The warmth and security of the animal angered him, and he cursed it till it flattened down its ears appeasingly. This time the shivering came more quickly upon the man. He was losing in his battle with the frost. It was creeping into his body from all sides. The thought of it drove him on, but he ran no more than a hundred feet, when he staggered and pitched headlong. It was his last panic. When he had recovered his breath and control, he sat up and entertained in his mind the conception of meeting death with dignity. However, the conception did not come to him in such terms. His idea of it was that he had been making a fool of himself, running around like a chicken with its head cut off—such was the simile that occurred to him. Well, he was bound to freeze anyway, and he might as well take it decently. With this new-found peace of mind came the first glimmerings of drowsiness. A good idea, he thought, to sleep off to death. It was like taking an anesthetic. Freezing was not so bad as people thought. There were lots worse ways to die.

He pictured the boys finding his body next day. Suddenly he found himself with them, coming along the trail and looking for himself. And, still with them, he came around a turn in the trail and found himself lying in the snow. He did not belong with himself any more, for even then he was out of himself, standing with the boys and looking at himself in the snow. It certainly was cold, was his thought. When he got back to the States he could tell the folks what real cold was. He drifted on from this to a vision of the old-timer on Sulphur Creek. He could see him quite clearly, warm and comfortable, and smoking a pipe.

"You were right, old hoss; you were right," the man mumbled to the old-timer of Sulphur Creek.

Then the man drowsed off into what seemed to him the most comfortable and satisfying sleep he had ever known. The dog sat facing him and waiting. The brief day drew to a close in a long, slow twilight. There were no signs of a fire to be made, and, besides, never in the dog's experience had it known a man to sit like that in the snow and make no fire. As the twilight drew on, its eager yearning for the fire mastered it, and with a great lifting and shifting of forefeet, it whined softly, then flattened its ears down in anticipation of being chidden by the man. But the man remained silent. Later the dog whined loudly. And still later it crept close to the man and caught the scent of death. This made the animal bristle and back away. A little longer it delayed, howling under the stars that leaped and danced and shone brightly in the cold sky. Then it turned and trotted up the trail in the direction of the camp it knew, where were the other food providers and fire providers.

1908

Upton Sinclair
1878–1968

There is no use pretending that Upton Sinclair was a literary man. He is to be appreciated for what his novel *The Jungle* clearly represents: one of the most effective polemical tracts ever produced by the reform movements at the turn of the twentieth century. *The Jungle* is a notable example of muckraking, the journalistic attack against corrupt practices that had become an important literary subgenre during the years just prior to World War I. Using the devices of melodrama and newspaper writing, the muckrakers set out to expose the misdemeanors and felonies of the corporations and industry, the political machines and social institutions that were controlling the lives of essentially helpless people. Sensational plots in the form of screaming headlines were the means the reformers took to gain their ends. *The Jungle* was privately printed in 1906 after five publishers turned it down. Sinclair's friend Jack London announced its intent. "What *Uncle Tom's Cabin* did for the black slaves," London declared, "*The Jungle* has a large chance to do for the white slaves of today."

The Jungle became a best-seller once it was picked up by an established publishing house and translated into seventeen languages. But it was not a success for the reason that the reading public was shocked on behalf of the proletarian workers in whose cause it was written. Set in the Chicago stockyards, the novel, with its brutally effective scenes of the slaughter of diseased cattle and hogs, did not arouse the indignation of readers over the conditions under which the stockyard men had to work. "I realized with bitterness," Sinclair wrote later, "that I had been made a 'celebrity,' not because the public cared anything about the workers, but simply because the public did not want to eat tubercular beef." The outcry stirred up by Sinclair's novel eventually led to the passage of the Pure Food Bill in 1907, signed into law by President Theodore Roosevelt. The book had won a battle, though not the one Sinclair had had in mind. Sinclair's miscalculation about his readers' responses reflects what the critic Alfred Kazin has observed: that Sinclair possessed an old-fashioned idealism and quaint personal romanticism that was already vanishing from American writing by the early 1900s.

Upton Sinclair was born in Baltimore, a child of the failed branch of an influential and aristocratic family. He grew up poor in New York City, made his way through the City College of New York and Columbia University, then went to work in the 1890s to earn a meager living as the hack writer of adventure stories for boys' magazines. Between 1901 and 1906 he also wrote five novels, which earned him a total of one thousand dollars. At the age of twenty he had become a confirmed Socialist and an unorthodox Marxist. With the money that came to him from the success of *The Jungle,* he sponsored a utopian experiment in New Jersey. When the dormitory, Helicon Hall, burned down, he lost everything.

In the years following, most of the gains Sinclair made from his publishing successes went into failed reform schemes; but he struggled on, living at the edge, writing with cheerful, humorless, boyish enthusiasm about a variety of social issues. Syphilis, education, hygiene, and religion were among the topics that captured his attention as the books poured forth. In 1942 Sinclair was the most widely read of all American authors. No less than 772 translations of his books had been published in forty-seven languages in thirty-nine countries, ranging from the Soviet-bloc nations to Japan and China. *The Metropolis* and *The Moneychanger* (both 1908), *King Coal* (1917), *Oil!* (1927), and *The Flivver-King: A Story of Ford-America* (1937) vividly headline the areas of American commercial life Sinclair made it his business to expose. But in the 1930s and 1940s, Sinclair turned from deflating the myths created by others to concocting some of his own. His Lanny Budd series told the fictional adventures of a man who is portrayed as the friend and adviser of Franklin Delano Roosevelt and other men in authority throughout the world. A maker of history, not merely an observer, Sinclair's new hero was the final working out of his creator's earnest, exuberant literary fantasies of justice and power. *The Jungle,* however, is the novel for which Sinclair will rightly be remembered. In both subject and method, it struck the consciousness of the American public with the force of one of the sledges used to fell cattle in the Chicago stockyards.

Further Reading:
F. Dell, *Upton Sinclair: A Study in Social Protest,* 1927.
J. Duram, *Upton Sinclair's Realistic Romanticism,* 1970.
Critics on Upton Sinclair, ed. A. Blinderman, 1975.
L. Harris, *Upton Sinclair, American Rebel,* 1975.
W. A. Bloodworth, *Upton Sinclair,* 1977.

Text:
The Jungle, 1906.
See also *Autobiography,* 1902.
The Cry for Justice: An Anthology of the Literature of Social Protest by Upton Sinclair, introduction by Jack London, 1915.
Candid Reminiscences: My First Thirty Years, 1932.
Upton Sinclair Anthology, ed. I. Evans, 1934.

from The Jungle

Chapter III: [The Slaughterhouse]

In his capacity as delicatessen vender, Jokubas Szedvilas had many acquaintances. Among these was one of the special policemen employed by Durham, whose duty it frequently was to pick out men for employment. Jokubas had never tried it, but he expressed a certainty that he could get some of his friends a job through this man. It was agreed, after consultation, that he should make the effort with old Antanas and with Jonas. Jurgis was confident of his ability to get work for himself, unassisted by any one.

As we have said before, he was not mistaken in this. He had gone to Brown's and stood there not more than half an hour before one of the bosses noticed his form towering above the rest, and signalled to him. The colloquy which followed was brief and to the point:—

"Speak English?"

"No; Lit-uanian." (Jurgis had studied this word carefully.)

"Job?"

"Je." (A nod.)

"Worked here before?"

"No 'stand."

(Signals and gesticulations on the part of the boss. Vigorous shakes of the head by Jurgis.)

"Shovel guts?"

"No 'stand." (More shakes of the head.)

"Zarnos. Pagaiksztis. Szluota!" (Imitative motions.)

"Je."

"See door. Durys?" (Pointing.)

"Je."

"To-morrow, seven o'clock. Understand? Rytoj! Prieszpietys! Septyni!"

"Dekui, tamistai!" (Thank you, sir.) And that was all. Jurgis turned away, and then in a sudden rush the full realization of his triumph swept over him, and he gave a yell and a jump, and started off on a run. He had a job! He had a job! And he went all the way home as if upon wings, and burst into the house like a cyclone, to the rage of the numerous lodgers who had just turned in for their daily sleep.

Meantime Jokubas had been to see his friend the policeman, and received encouragement, so it was a happy party. There being no more to be done that day, the shop was left under the care of Lucija, and her husband sallied forth to show his friends the sights of Packingtown. Jokubas did this with the air of a country gentleman escorting a party of visitors over his estate; he was an old-time resident, and all these wonders had grown up under his eyes, and he had a personal pride in them. The packers might own the land, but he claimed the landscape, and there was no one to say nay to this.

They passed down the busy street that led to the yards. It was still early morning, and everything was at its high tide of activity. A steady stream of employees was pouring through the gate—employees of the higher sort, at this hour, clerks and stenographers and such. For the women there were waiting big two-horse wagons, which set off at a gallop as fast as they were filled. In the distance there was heard again the lowing of the cattle, a sound as of a far-off ocean calling. They followed it, this time, as eager as children in sight of a circus menagerie—which, indeed, the scene a good deal resembled. They crossed the railroad tracks, and then on each side of the street were the pens full of cattle; they would have stopped to look, but Jokubas hurried them on, to where there was a stairway and a raised gallery, from which everything could be seen. Here they stood, staring, breathless with wonder.

There is over a square mile of space in the yards, and more than half of it is occupied by cattle-pens; north and south as far as the eye can reach there stretches a sea of pens. And they were all filled—so many cattle no one had ever dreamed existed in the world. Red cattle, black, white, and yellow cattle; old cattle and young cattle; great bellowing bulls and little calves not an hour born; meek-eyed milch cows and fierce, long-horned Texas steers. The sound of them here was as of all the barnyards of the universe; and as for counting them—it would have taken all day simply to count the pens. Here and there ran long alleys, blocked at intervals by gates; and Jokubas told them that the number of these gates was twenty-five thousand. Jokubas had recently been reading a newspaper article which was full of statistics such as that, and he was very proud as he repeated them and made his guests cry out with wonder. Jurgis too had a little of this sense of pride. Had he not just gotten a job, and become a sharer in all this activity, a cog in this marvellous machine?

Here and there about the alleys galloped men upon horseback, booted, and carrying long whips; they were very busy, calling to each other, and to those who were driving the cattle. They were drovers and stock-raisers, who had come from far states, and brokers and commission-merchants, and buyers for all the big packing-houses. Here and there they would stop to inspect a bunch of cattle, and there would be a parley, brief and businesslike. The buyer would nod or drop his whip, and that would mean a bargain; and he would note it in his little book, along with hundreds of others he had made that morning. Then Jokubas pointed out the place where the cattle were driven to be weighed, upon a great scale that would weigh a hundred thousand pounds at once and record it automatically. It was near to the east entrance that they stood, and all along this east side of the yards ran the railroad tracks, into which the cars were run, loaded with cattle. All night long this had been going on, and now the pens were full; by to-night they would all be empty, and the same thing would be done again.

"And what will become of all these creatures?" cried Teta Elzbieta.

"By to-night," Jokubas answered, "they will all be killed and cut up; and over there on the other side of the packing-houses are more railroad tracks, where the cars come to take them away."

There were two hundred and fifty miles of track within the yards, their guide went on to tell them. They brought about ten thousand head of cattle every day, and as many hogs, and half as many sheep—which meant some eight or ten million live creatures turned into food every year. One stood and watched, and little by little caught the drift of the tide, as it set in the direction of the packing-houses. There were groups of cattle being driven to the chutes, which were roadways about fifteen feet wide, raised high above the pens. In these chutes the stream of animals was continuous;

it was quite uncanny to watch them, pressing on to their fate, all unsuspicious—a very river of death. Our friends were not poetical, and the sight suggested to them no metaphors of human destiny; they thought only of the wonderful efficiency of it all. The chutes into which the hogs went climbed high up—to the very top of the distant buildings; and Jokubas explained that the hogs went up by the power of their own legs, and then their weight carried them back through all the processes necessary to make them into pork.

"They don't waste anything here," said the guide, and then he laughed and added a witticism, which he was pleased that his unsophisticated friends should take to be his own: "They use everything about the hog except the squeal." In front of Brown's General Office building there grows a tiny plot of grass, and this, you may learn, is the only bit of green thing in Packingtown; likewise this jest about the hog and his squeal, the stock in trade of all the guides, is the one gleam of humor that you will find there.

After they had seen enough of the pens, the party went up the street, to the mass of buildings which occupy the centre of the yards. These buildings, made of brick and stained with innumerable layers of Packingtown smoke, were painted all over with advertising signs, from which the visitor realized suddenly that he had come to the home of many of the torments of his life. It was here that they made those products with the wonders of which they pestered him so—by placards that defaced the landscape when he travelled, and by staring advertisements in the newspapers and magazines—by silly little jingles that he could not get out of his mind, and gaudy pictures that lurked for him around every street corner. Here was where they made Brown's Imperial Hams and Bacon, Brown's Dressed Beef, Brown's Excelsior Sausages! Here was the headquarters of Durham's Pure Leaf Lard, of Durham's Breakfast Bacon, Durham's Canned Beef, Potted Ham, Devilled Chicken, Peerless Fertilizer!

Entering one of the Durham buildings, they found a number of other visitors waiting; and before long there came a guide, to escort them through the place. They make a great feature of showing strangers through the packing-plants, for it is a good advertisement. But *ponas* Jokubas whispered maliciously that the visitors did not see any more than the packers wanted them to.

They climbed a long series of stairways outside of the building, to the top of its five or six stories. Here were the chute, with its river of hogs, all patiently toiling upward; there was a place for them to rest to cool off, and then through another passageway they went into a room from which there is no returning for hogs.

It was a long, narrow room, with a gallery along it for visitors. At the head there was a great iron wheel, about twenty feet in circumference, with rings here and there along its edge. Upon both sides of this wheel there was a narrow space, into which came the hogs at the end of their journey; in the midst of them stood a great burly negro, bare-armed and bare-chested. He was resting for the moment, for the wheel had stopped while men were cleaning up. In a minute or two, however, it began slowly to revolve, and then the men upon each side of it sprang to work. They had chains which they fastened about the leg of the nearest hog, and the other end of the chain they hooked into one of the rings upon the wheel. So, as the wheel turned, a hog was suddenly jerked off his feet and borne aloft.

At the same instant the ear was assailed by a most terrifying shriek; the visitors started in alarm, the women turned pale and shrank back. The shriek was followed by another, louder and yet more agonizing—for once started upon that journey, the hog never came back; at the top of the wheel he was shunted off upon a trolley, and went sailing down the room. And meantime another was swung up, and then another, and another, until there was a double line of them, each dangling by a foot and kicking in frenzy—and squealing. The uproar was appalling, perilous to the ear-drums; one feared there was too much sound for the room to hold—that the walls must give way or the ceiling crack. There were high squeals and low squeals, grunts, and wails of agony; there would come a momentary lull, and then a fresh outburst, louder than ever, surging up to a deafening climax. It was too much for some of the visitors—the men would look at each other, laughing nervously, and the women would stand with hands clenched, and the blood rushing to their faces, and the tears starting in their eyes.

Meantime, heedless of all these things, the men upon the floor were going about their work. Neither squeals of hogs nor tears of visitors made any difference to them; one by one they hooked up the hogs, and one by one with a swift stroke they slit their throats. There was a long line of hogs, with squeals and life-blood ebbing away together; until at last each started again, and vanished with a splash into a huge vat of boiling water.

It was all so very businesslike that one watched it fascinated. It was pork-making by machinery, pork-making by applied mathematics. And yet somehow the most matter-of-fact person could not help thinking of the hogs; they were so innocent, they came so very trustingly; and they were so very human in their protests—and so perfectly within their rights! They had done nothing to deserve it; and it was adding insult to injury, as the thing was done here, swinging them up in this cold-blooded, impersonal way, without a pretence at apology, without the homage of a tear. Now and then a visitor wept, to be sure; but this slaughtering-machine ran on, visitors or no visitors. It was like some horrible crime committed in a dungeon, all unseen and unheeded, buried out of sight and of memory.

One could not stand and watch very long without becoming philosophical, without beginning to deal in symbols and similes, and to hear the hog-squeal of the universe. Was it permitted to believe that there was nowhere upon the earth, or above the earth, a heaven for hogs, where they were requited for all this suffering? Each one of these hogs was a separate creature. Some were white hogs, some were black; some were brown, some were spotted; some were old, some were young; some were long and lean, some were monstrous. And each of them had an individuality of his own, a will of his own, a hope and a heart's desire; each was full of self-confidence, of self-importance, and a sense of dignity. And trusting and strong in faith he had gone about his business, the while a black shadow hung over him and a horrid Fate waited in his pathway. Now suddenly it had swooped upon him, and had seized him by the leg. Relentless, remorseless, it was; all his protests, his screams, were nothing to it—it did its cruel will with him, as if his wishes, his feelings, had simply no existence at all; it cut his throat and watched him gasp out his life. And now was one to believe that there was nowhere a god of hogs, to whom this hog-personality was precious, to whom these hog-squeals and agonies had a meaning? Who would take this hog into his arms and comfort him, reward him for his work well done, and show him the meaning of his sacrifice? Perhaps some glimpse of all this was in the thoughts of our humble-minded Jurgis, as he turned to go on with the rest of the party, and muttered: "Dieve—but I'm glad I'm not a hog!"

The carcass hog was scooped out of the vat by machinery, and then it fell to the second floor, passing on the way through a wonderful machine with numerous scrapers, which adjusted themselves to the size and shape of the animal, and sent it out at the other end with nearly all of its bristles removed. It was then again strung up by machinery, and sent upon another trolley ride; this time passing between two lines of men, who sat upon a raised platform, each doing a certain single thing to the carcass as it came to him. One scraped the outside of a leg; another scraped the inside of the same leg. One with a swift stroke cut the throat; another with two swift strokes severed the head, which fell to the floor and vanished through a hole. Another made a slit down the body; a second opened the body wider; a third with a saw cut the breast-bone; a fourth loosened the entrails; a fifth pulled them out—and they also slid through a hole in the floor. There were men to scrape each side and men to scrape the back; there were men to clean the carcass inside, to trim it and wash it. Looking down this room, one saw, creeping slowly, a line of dangling hogs a hundred yards in length; and for every yard there was a man, working as if a demon were after him. At the end of this hog's progress every inch of the carcass had been gone over several times; and then it was rolled into the chilling-room, where it stayed for twenty-four hours, and where a stranger might lose himself in a forest of freezing hogs.

Before the carcass was admitted here, however, it had to pass a government inspector, who sat in the doorway and felt of the glands in the neck for tuberculosis. This government inspector did not have the manner of a man who was worked to death; he was apparently not haunted by a fear that the hog might get by him before he had finished his testing. If you were a sociable person, he was quite willing to enter into conversation with you, and to explain to you the deadly nature of the ptomaines which are found in tubercular pork; and while he was talking with you you could hardly be so ungrateful as to notice that a dozen carcasses were passing him untouched. This inspector wore a blue uniform, with brass buttons, and he gave an atmosphere of authority to the scene, and, as it were, put the stamp of official approval upon the things which were done in Durham's.

Jurgis went down the line with the rest of the visitors, staring open-mouthed, lost in wonder. He had dressed hogs himself in the forest of Lithuania; but he had never expected to live to see one hog dressed by several hundred men. It was like a wonderful poem to him, and he took it all in guilelessly—even to the conspicuous signs demanding immaculate cleanliness of the employees. Jurgis was vexed when the cynical Jokubas translated these signs with sarcastic comments, offering to take them to the secret-rooms where the spoiled meats went to be doctored.

The party descended to the next floor, where the various waste materials were treated. Here came the entrails, to be scraped and washed clean for sausage-casings; men and women worked here in the midst of a sickening stench, which caused the visitors to hasten by, gasping. To another room came all the scraps to be "tanked," which meant boiling and pumping off the grease to make soap and lard; below they took out the refuse, and this, too, was a region in which the visitors did not linger. In still other places men were engaged in cutting up the carcasses that had been through the chilling-rooms. First there were the "splitters," the most expert workmen in the plant, who earned as high as fifty cents an hour, and did not a thing all day except chop hogs down the middle. Then there were "cleaver men," great giants with muscles of iron; each had two men to attend him—to slide the half carcass in front of him on the table, and hold it while he chopped it, and then turn each piece so that he might chop it once more. His cleaver had a blade about two feet long, and he never made but one cut; he made it so neatly, too, that his implement did not smite through and dull itself—there was just enough force for a perfect cut, and no more. So through various yawning holes there slipped to the floor below—to one room hams, to another forequarters, to another sides of pork. One might go down to this floor and see the pickling-rooms, where the hams were put into vats, and the great smoke-rooms, with their air-tight iron doors. In other rooms they prepared salt-pork—there were whole cellars full of it, built up in great towers to the ceiling. In yet other rooms they were putting up meat in boxes and barrels, and wrapping hams and bacon in oiled paper, sealing and labelling and sewing them. From the doors of these rooms went men with loaded trucks, to the platform where freight-cars were waiting to be filled; and one went out there and realized with a start that he had come at last to the ground floor of this enormous building.

Then the party went across the street to where they did the killing of beef—where every hour they turned four or five hundred cattle into meat. Unlike the place they had left, all this work was done on one floor; and instead of there being one line of carcasses which moved to the workmen, there were fifteen or twenty lines, and the men moved from one to another of these. This made a scene of intense activity, a picture of human power wonderful to watch. It was all in one great room, like a circus amphitheatre, with a gallery for visitors running over the centre.

Along one side of the room ran a narrow gallery, a few feet from the floor; into which gallery the cattle were driven by men with goads which gave them electric shocks. Once crowded in here, the creatures were prisoned, each in a separate pen, by gates that shut, leaving them no room to turn around; and while they stood bellowing and plunging, over the top of the pen there leaned one of the "knockers," armed with a sledge-hammer, and watching for a chance to deal a blow. The room echoed with the thuds in quick succession, and the stamping and kicking of the steers. The instant the animal had fallen, the "knocker" passed on to another; while a second man raised a lever, and the side of the pen was raised, and the animal, still kicking and struggling, slid out to the "killing-bed." Here a man put shackles about one leg, and pressed another lever, and the body was jerked up into the air. There were fifteen or twenty such pens, and it was a matter of only a couple of minutes to knock fifteen or twenty cattle and roll them out. Then once more the gates were opened, and another lot rushed in; and so out of each pen there rolled a steady stream of carcasses, which the men upon the killing-beds had to get out of the way.

The manner in which they did this was something to be seen and never forgotten. They worked with furious intensity, literally upon the run—at a pace with which there is nothing to be compared except a football game. It was all highly specialized labor, each man having his task to do; generally this would consist of only two or three specific cuts, and he would pass down the line of fifteen or twenty carcasses, making these cuts upon each. First there came the "butcher," to bleed them; this meant one swift stroke, so swift that you could not see it—only the flash of the knife; and before you could realize it, the man had darted on to the next line, and a stream of bright red was pouring out upon the floor. This floor was half an inch deep with blood, in spite of the best efforts of men who kept shovelling it through holes; it must have made the floor slippery, but no one could have guessed this by watching the men at work.

The carcass hung for a few minutes to bleed; there was no time lost, however, for there were several hanging in each line, and one was always ready. It was let down to the ground, and there came the "headsman," whose task it was to sever the head, with two or three swift strokes. Then came the "floorsman," to make the first cut in the skin; and then another to finish ripping the skin down the centre; and then half a dozen more in swift succession, to finish the skinning. After they were through, the carcass was again swung up; and while a man with a stick examined the skin, to make sure that it had not been cut, and another rolled it up and tumbled it through one of the inevitable holes in the floor, the beef proceeded on its journey. There were men to cut it, and men to split it, and men to gut it and scrape it clean inside. There were some with hose which threw jets of boiling water upon it, and others who removed the feet and added the final touches. In the end, as with the hogs, the finished beef was run into the chilling-room, to hang its appointed time.

The visitors were taken there and shown them, all neatly hung in rows, labelled conspicuously with the tags of the government inspectors—and some, which had been killed by a special process, marked with the sign of the "kosher" rabbi, certifying that it was fit for sale to the orthodox. And then the visitors were taken to the other parts of the building, to see what became of each particle of the waste material that had vanished through the floor; and to the pickling-rooms, and the salting-rooms, the canning-rooms, and the packing-rooms, where choice meat was prepared for shipping in refrigerator-cars, destined to be eaten in all the four corners of civilization. Afterward they went outside, wandering about among the mazes of buildings in which was done the work auxiliary to this great industry. There was scarcely a thing needed in the business that Durham and Company did not make for themselves. There was a great steam-power plant and an electricity plant. There was a barrel factory, and a boiler-repair shop. There was a building to which the grease was piped, and made into soap and lard; and then there was a factory for making lard cans, and another for making soap boxes. There was a building in which the bristles were cleaned and dried, for the making of hair cushions and such things; there was a building where the skins were dried and tanned, there was another where heads and feet were made into glue, and another where bones were made into fertilizer. No tiniest particle of organic matter was wasted in Durham's. Out of the horns of the cattle they made combs, buttons, hair-pins, and imitation ivory; out of the shin bones and other big bones they cut knife and tooth-brush handles, and mouthpieces for pipes; out of the hoofs they cut hair-pins and buttons, before they made the rest into glue. From such things as feet, knuckles, hide clippings, and sinews came such strange and unlikely products as gelatin, isinglass, and phosphorus, bone-black, shoe-blacking, and bone-oil. They had curled-hair works for the cattle tails, and a "wool-pullery" for the sheep skins; they made pepsin from the stomachs of the pigs, and albumen from the blood, and violin strings from the ill-smelling entrails. When there was nothing else to be done with a thing, they first put it into a tank and got out of it all the tallow and grease, and then they made it into fertilizer. All these industries were gathered into buildings near by, connected by galleries and railroads with the main establishment;

and it was estimated that they had handled nearly a quarter of a billion of animals since the founding of the plant by the elder Durham a generation and more ago. If you counted with it the other big plants—and they were now really all one—it was, so Jokubas informed them, the greatest aggregation of labor and capital ever gathered in one place. It employed thirty thousand men; it supported directly two hundred and fifty thousand people in its neighborhood, and indirectly it supported half a million. It sent its products to every country in the civilized world, and it furnished the food for not less than thirty million people!

To all of these things our friends would listen open-mouthed—it seemed to them impossible of belief that anything so stupendous could have been devised by mortal man. That was why to Jurgis it seemed almost profanity to speak about the place as did Jokubas, sceptically; it was a thing as tremendous as the universe—the laws and ways of its working no more than the universe to be questioned or understood. All that a mere man could do, it seemed to Jurgis, was to take a thing like this as he found it, and do as he was told; to be given a place in it and a share in its wonderful activities was a blessing to be grateful for, as one was grateful for the sunshine and the rain. Jurgis was even glad that he had not seen the place before meeting with his triumph, for he felt that the size of it would have overwhelmed him. But now he had been admitted—he was a part of it all! He had the feeling that this whole huge establishment had taken him under its protection, and had become responsible for his welfare. So guileless was he, and ignorant of the nature of business, that he did not even realize that he had become an employee of Brown's, and that Brown and Durham were supposed by all the world to be deadly rivals—were even required to be deadly rivals by the law of the land, and ordered to try to ruin each other under penalty of fine and imprisonment!

1906

The Literature of Modernism: Prose 1912–1940

 American writers of the early twentieth century were born into a society that was still young and a culture that was still raw. In 1890, the year in which Gertrude Stein turned sixteen and Sherwood Anderson turned fourteen, the great Sioux chief Sitting Bull died. Throughout the 1890s, the decade in which William Faulkner, F. Scott Fitzgerald, and Ernest Hemingway were born, the United States remained on the circumference of civilization. It had no palaces or castles, Henry James once noted, no cathedrals or abbeys or ivied ruins. Even its thriving cities were less elegant than those of Europe. Americans took pride in the achievement of their painters (from Benjamin West in the late eighteenth century to James McNeill Whistler in the late nineteenth) and their writers (from Edgar Allan Poe through Nathaniel Hawthorne to Mark Twain and Henry James), but they knew that their life remained comparatively crude, their art and literature comparatively thin.

To balance their sense of cultural inferiority, Americans held tightly to a sense of social and moral superiority. Many Americans respected—and some envied—Europe for its rich culture. But they scorned Europe's accumulated strata of gentility—piled, Henry James wrote, "upwards into vague regions of privilege"—and they condemned its wickedness and weariness. Even parents who sent their children to tour Europe or study there sought first to inoculate

Grant Wood,
Stone City, Iowa,
oil on canvas, 1930.
Joslyn Art Museum,
Omaha, Nebraska.

Archibald J. Motley, Jr.,
Chicken Shack,
oil on canvas, 1936.
National Archives,
Washington, D.C.

"This Vast Shaggy Continent"

The church-going classes . . . form the backbone of philanthropic social interest, of social reform through political action, of pacifism, of popular education. They embody and express the spirit of kindly goodwill towards classes which are at an economic disadvantage and towards other nations, especially when the latter show any disposition towards a republican form of government. The Middle West, the prairie country, has been the centre of active social philanthropy and political progressivism because it is the chief home of this folk.

John Dewey, "The American Intellectual Frontier" (1922)

Into this vast shaggy continent of ours poured the first feeble tide of European settlement. European men, institutions, and ideas were lodged in the American wilderness, and this great American West took them to her bosom, taught them a new way of looking upon the destiny of the common man, trained them in adaptation to the conditions of the New World, to the creation of new institutions to meet new needs; and ever as society on her eastern border grew to resemble the Old World in its social forms and its industry, ever, as it began to lose faith in the ideal of democracy, she opened new provinces, and dowered new democracies in her most distant domains with her material treasures and with the ennobling influence that the fierce love of freedom, the strength that came from hewing out a home, making a school and a church, and creating a higher future for his family, furnished to the pioneer.

Frederick Jackson Turner, *The Frontier in American History* (1920)

them against Europe's decadence. However crude and raw American culture might be, its "triumphant democracy" (to borrow the title of Andrew Carnegie's celebration of America) was a model of some things and proof of others: a model of political freedom, economic opportunity, and moral rectitude and proof that to remain young and vigorous a society must remain open and democratic. In a famous address delivered in Chicago at the American Historical Association in 1893, Frederick Jackson Turner announced that American democracy drew its force not from its European heritage but from its frontier experience. Twenty years later, on June 17, 1914, Turner reiterated his celebrated announcement: "American democracy was born of no theorist's dream; it was not carried in the *Susan Constant* to Virginia, nor in the *Mayflower* to Plymouth. It came stark and strong and full of life out of the American forest, and it gained new strength each time it touched a new frontier."

To live on the edge of civilization was, then, from an American point of view, to be blessed as well as deprived. Writing in the mid-nineteenth century, Henry David Thoreau captured America's characteristic ambivalence in an epigraph: "I love the wild not less than the good." Americans sometimes attributed their energy and good hope—twin tokens of superiority—to their close ties to nature, their proximity to the frontier, or their love of the wild, sometimes to what Henry James called the overriding "importance of the individual in the American world," and sometimes to the continuing presence of divine favor. But since they regarded these things as interrelated and interdependent, they also saw youth and simplicity rather than age and sophistication as the bedrock of America's strength. American culture might be raw, but American society was vital, its future assured: "The old nations of the earth creep at a snail's pace," Andrew Carnegie wrote in 1886; "the Republic thunders past with the rush of the express." As they spread across the continent, furthermore, and then later began the long trek from the soil of their farms to the sidewalks of their cities, they carried their convictions with them. The ambivalence that New Englanders learned early to feel toward Europe, mixing a sense of cultural inferiority with a sense of social and moral superiority, westerners came to feel toward easterners and rural folk toward city dwellers.

"The East Was Haunted for Me"

When I came back from the East last autumn I felt that I wanted the world to be in uniform and at a sort of moral attention forever. . . .

Even when the East excited me most, even when I was most keenly aware of its superiority to the bored, sprawling, swollen towns beyond the Ohio, with their interminable inquisitions which spared only the children and the very old —even then it had always for me a quality of distortion. West Egg, especially, still figures in my more fantastic dreams. I see it as a night scene by El Greco: a hundred houses, at once conventional and grotesque, crouching under a sullen, overhanging sky and a lustreless moon. In the foreground four solemn men in dress suits are walking along the sidewalk with a stretcher on which lies a drunken woman in a white evening dress. Her hand, which dangles over the side, sparkles cold with jewels. Gravely the men turn in at a house—the wrong house. But no one knows the woman's name, and no one cares.

After Gatsby's death the East was haunted for me like that, distorted beyond my eyes' power of correction. So when the blue smoke of brittle leaves was in the air and the wind blew the wet laundry stiff on the line I decided to come back home.

F. Scott Fitzgerald, *The Great Gatsby* (1925)

The Transformation of American Culture

By the early twentieth century, the waves of immigration that had diversified American society were also diversifying its literature. In 1908, Israel Zangwill's play *The Melting-Pot* became a major hit in New York. Although some writers of the early twentieth century, including H. L. Mencken and Edmund Wilson, came from established communities along the eastern seaboard, many came from out-of-the-way places and diverse backgrounds. Abraham Cahan (1860–1951), Gertrude Stein (1874–1946), Nathanael West (1903–1940), and Henry Roth (b. 1906) became the first major Jewish writers of American literature. Writers were more likely to be poor, more likely to be female, and more likely to be black. They came from the South: William Faulkner and Richard Wright from Mississippi, Thomas Wolfe from North Carolina, Zora Neale Hurston from Florida. They came from California, like John Steinbeck, or even from remote frontier communities like Indian Creek, Texas, the birthplace of Katherine Anne Porter. Above all they came from the Midwest: a few from its cities, John Dos Passos from Chicago and F. Scott Fitzgerald from St. Paul, and scores from its smaller communities. Sherwood Anderson was born in Camden, Ohio; Sinclair

---

I Pray Thee Ask No Questions. This Is That Golden Land.

The small white steamer, *Peter Stuyvesant,* that delivered the immigrants from the stench and throb of the steerage to the stench and the throb of New York tenements, rolled slightly on the water beside the stone quay in the lee of the weathered barracks and new brick buildings of Ellis Island. Her skipper was waiting for the last of the officials, laborers and guards to embark upon her before he cast off and started for Manhattan. . . .

It was May of the year 1907, the year that was destined to bring the greatest number of immigrants to the shores of the United States. All that day, as on all the days since spring began, her decks had been thronged by hundreds upon hundreds of foreigners, natives from almost every land in the world, the jowled close-cropped Teuton, the full-bearded Russian, the scraggly-whiskered Jew, and among them Slovack peasants with docile faces, smooth-cheeked and swarthy Armenians, pimply Greeks, Danes with wrinkled eyelids. All day her decks had been colorful, a matrix of the vivid costumes of other lands, the speckled green-and-yellow aprons, the flowered kerchief, embroidered homespun, the silver-braided sheepskin vest, the gaudy scarfs, yellow boots, fur caps, caftans, dull gabardines. All day the guttural, the high-pitched voices, the astonished cries, the gasps of wonder, reiterations of gladness had risen from her decks in a motley billow of sound. But now her decks were empty, quiet, spreading out under the sunlight almost as if the warm boards were relaxing from the strain and the pressure of the myriads of feet.

Henry Roth, prologue to *Call It Sleep* (1934)

Lewis, in Sauk Center, Minnesota; Ernest Hemingway, in Oak Park, Illinois; and Langston Hughes, in Joplin, Missouri. "The Middle West," Ford Madox Ford wrote from Paris, "was seething with literary impulse."

Together these writers transformed the cultural landscape of America and enlarged its cultural role. In the same years in which the United States was emerging as a world power, its writers were becoming a major force in the development of literary modernism. In addition to producing remarkable literature, writers like T. S. Eliot, Gertrude Stein, and Ernest Hemingway began playing prominent roles in the cultural affairs of London and Paris. At the same time, however, they reclaimed native literary traditions and transformed colloquial American English into a medium for serious fiction. "All modern American literature," Ernest Hemingway asserted, evoking America's colloquial tradition, "comes from one book by Mark Twain called *Huckleberry Finn.*" H. L. Mencken's celebration of American English, *The American Language* (1919), with its four revisions and two supplements, still stands as his masterpiece.

The reassessment of American literature that began with W. C. Brownell's *American Prose Masters* (1909) and John Macy's *The Spirit of American Literature* (1913) continued through Van Wyck Brooks's *America's Coming of Age* (1915) and Waldo Frank's *Our America* (1919) to produce two works of lasting value— D. H. Lawrence's *Studies in Classic American Literature* (1922) and Lewis Mumford's *The Golden Day* (1926). Through this broad reassessment, Emily Dickinson was discovered, Herman Melville was rediscovered, and writers from James Fenimore Cooper to Mark Twain and Henry James were reinterpreted. Simultaneously, Stein and Anderson inaugurated a remarkable flowering of American fiction that culminated in the work of Faulkner, Fitzgerald, Hemingway, and scores of other writers. Theirs was, as the distinguished French critic Claude-Edmonde Magny called it, *L'Age du roman américain* ("The Age of the American Novel").

The Age of the American Novel

These youngsters are attempting a first-hand examination of the national scene, and making an effort to represent it in terms that are wholly American. They are the pioneers of a literature that, whatever its defects in the abstract, will at least be a faithful reflection of the national life. . . . In England the novel subsides into formulae, the drama is submerged in artificialities, and even poetry, despite occasional revolts, moves toward scholarliness and emptiness. But in America, since the war, all three show the artless and superabundant energy of little children. They lack, only too often, manner and urbanity; it is no wonder they are often shocking to pedants. But there is the breath of life in them, and that life is nearer its beginning than its end.

H. L. Mencken, *Prejudices: Fourth Series* (1924)

The Great War and a Literature of Disenchantment

"In its essence literature is concerned with the self," Lionel Trilling has written, "and the particular concern of the literature of the last two centuries has been with the self in its standing quarrel with culture." For writers born in the 1890s, the grounds of that quarrel were shifting. Like Walt Whitman and William Dean Howells, Faulkner, Fitzgerald, and Hemingway saw life in America as a test case of life in the modern world; America remained for them, to borrow one of Howells's titles, *A Modern Instance* (1882). But for them even more than for their predecessors, the world they had inherited seemed, as James T. Farrell put it in one of his titles, *A World I Never Made* (1936). In their most characteristic moments, American writers appear both fascinated with the details of American life and ambivalent toward the values that inform it. Some of their protagonists bear the scars of old injuries and wounds; others suffer from a profound sense of disappointment that culture does so little to nourish their lives or enlarge their happiness. Virtually all of them appear ill equipped to cope both with the alluring, threatening worlds that they inhabit and with the sharp, contradictory needs that they harbor. Some are conscious of themselves primarily as people to whom things happen, as creatures shaped by social forces. Their sense of themselves is one we associate with literary Realism; they feel the force of history impinging upon them from moment to moment. Others are conscious of themselves primarily as creatures acting out of control, as creatures driven by overwhelming needs and desires. Their sense of themselves is one we associate with literary Naturalism; they feel the irresistible force of nature welling up within them from moment to moment. In both cases, however, the notion of the individual as a special force capable of fashioning or making its self and remaking its world—a notion that arose in the Renaissance and later acquired an American flavor in Benjamin Franklin's *Autobiography*—becomes deeply imperiled. Protagonists of modern fiction characteristically move back and forth between moments in which their lives are a series of set tasks and mundane repetitions and moments in which their lives become dramas of momentous decisions to which no prior experience speaks. If on one side culture fails them because it imposes rigid schedules or tedious tasks, on the other it fails them because it provides neither rules nor principles nor even useful analogies by which they can hope to give direction and purpose to their lives. When human existence consists "merely in the unique and the present," Thomas Mann once noted, people do "not know how to conduct" themselves. In modern literature, protagonists sometimes flee, sometimes withdraw, and sometimes improvise, but they rarely act with confidence in themselves or in their worlds.

The ambivalence that defines modern American literature stemmed in part from disillusionment triggered by the First World War. "That's what you all are. . . . You are a lost generation," Gertrude Stein said to Ernest Hemingway, describing those who had survived the war. To present-day readers, the literary outcry that followed World War I may well seem excessive. People had died, Ezra Pound wrote, "For an old bitch gone in the teeth, / For a botched civilization." But such words reflect more than a sense of disappointment with the untidiness of history. The Great War exacted a terrible toll. America's own substantial losses (48,000 killed, 2,900 missing, 56,000 dead from disease) pale beside those of Germany (1.8 million killed), Russia (1.7 million), France (1.4 million), Austria-Hungary (1.2 million), and Britain (947,000). Virtually the whole of Europe emerged from the war not only decimated but depleted, exhausted, and debt-ridden, still racked with inflation and political unrest. But as heinous deeds led to reprisals yet more heinous, the war had also taken on the aspect of a terrible betrayal. "All the horrors of all the ages were brought together," Winston Churchill declared, "and not only armies but whole populations were thrust into the midst of them. . . . Neither peoples nor rulers drew the line at any deed which they thought could help them to win. . . ."

A century earlier, a series of great intellectual explorers and rebels—Sir Charles Lyell, Charles Darwin, Karl Marx, Friedrich Nietzsche, and Sigmund Freud—had mounted an assault against orthodox religious faith that continued from the nineteenth century into the twentieth. Biblical criticism, historical scholarship, science, and social thought had weakened many apparently secure truths and beliefs, and with them several familiar sources of consolation and restraint. "The stupendous failure of Christianity tortured history," Henry Adams asserts in his *Education*. In exchange for religious faith, the nineteenth century offered faith in progress as assuring both continued scientific development and continued extension of rational control over the affairs of humankind—and thus promoting both prosperity and peace. Against such a backdrop, the staggering casualties and the unspeakable atrocities of the Great War made the promise of

---

"All the Horrors of All the Ages Were Brought Together"

Germany, having let Hell loose, kept well in the van of terror; but she was followed step by step by the desperate and ultimately avenging nations she had assailed. Every outrage against humanity or international law was repaid by reprisals—often of a greater scale and of longer duration. No truce or parley mitigated the strife of the armies. The wounded died between the lines: the dead mouldered into the soil. Merchant ships and neutral ships and hospital ships were sunk on the seas and all on board left to their fate, or killed as they swam. Every effort was made to starve whole nations into submission without regard to age or sex. Cities and monuments were smashed by artillery. Bombs from the air were cast down indiscriminately. Poison gas in many forms stifled or seared the soldiers. Liquid fire was projected upon their bodies. Men fell from the air in flames, or were smothered often slowly in the dark recesses of the sea. The fighting strength of armies was limited only by the manhood of their countries. Europe and large parts of Asia and Africa became one vast battlefield on which after years of struggle not armies but nations broke and ran. When all was over, Torture and Cannibalism were the only two expedients that the civilized, scientific, Christian States had been able to deny themselves: and they were of doubtful utility.

Winston Churchill (ca. 1920)

the nineteenth century seem nothing so much as a fool's paradise. "The plunge of civilization into this abyss of blood and horror," Henry James wrote, "so gives away the whole long age during which we have supposed the world to be, with whatever abatement, gradually bettering, that to have to take it all now for what the treacherous years were really making for and *meaning* is too tragic for any words."

The United States entered the war reluctantly, it entered late, and it remained uncertain of its own motives. "The world must be made safe for democracy," proclaimed Woodrow Wilson. "We are going into war upon the command of gold," countered Senator George Norris of Nebraska. Still, on April 4, 1917, the Senate voted 82 to 6 for war, and two days later, on a bleak Good Friday morning, the House followed suit, 373 to 50. Given the severe losses already suffered from England across Europe to Russia, the United States shifted the balance of power substantially. Despite its late entry, it played a major role in determining both the outcome of the war and the terms of peace. By the war's end, the United States had become a world power. Many of its citizens, including several of its writers—some as soldiers, others as ambulance drivers— had seen the war's slaughter firsthand. In the years following the war, Hemingway, who had been seriously wounded, created several almost wholly disillusioned characters: "I was always embarrassed," Frederic Henry remarks in *A Farewell to Arms* (1929), "by the words sacred, glorious, and sacrifice and the expression in vain. We had heard them . . . and had read them . . . , and I had seen nothing sacred, and the things that were glorious had no glory and the sacrifices were like the stockyards at Chicago if nothing was done with the meat except to bury it. There were many words that you could not stand to hear and finally only the names of places had dignity."

People wholly emptied of beliefs have, of course, always been rare, and they remained rare even when "the great century" became "the treacherous years." But with the war behind them, people began to see more clearly that the same intellectual explorers and rebels who had undermined traditional beliefs had also unmasked hidden realities that challenged some of the nineteenth century's most cherished assumptions—such as faith in progress, faith in human uniqueness, and faith in rationality as the shaping force of the human psyche and human society. Henry Adams's nightmare vision, of the human mind struggling "like a frightened bird to escape the chaos which caged it" and of human life terribly diminished, spoke with special force to writers of the early twentieth century as they searched for ground on which they could stand.

Politics in general and reform in particular, allied as they were with the faith that had crumbled, became almost as unfashionable among writers and intellectuals as orthodox religious belief. The populism of the 1890s, which had culminated in William Jennings Bryan's presidential campaign of 1896, was followed in the early twentieth century by the even stronger progressive movement. Yet, despite the presence of politically engaged writers like H. L. Mencken, John Dos Passos, Jean Toomer, Edmund Wilson, and Sinclair Lewis, the progressives' surge of reform suffered major reversals after 1914. By the

---

"Looking Blankly into the Void of Death"

Every fabulist has told how the human mind has always struggled like a frightened bird to escape the chaos which caged it; how—appearing suddenly and inexplicably out of some unknown and unimaginable void; passing half its known life in the mental chaos of sleep; victim even when awake, to its own ill-adjustment, to disease, to age, to external suggestion, to nature's compulsion; doubting its sensations, and, in the last resort, trusting only to instruments and averages—after sixty or seventy years of growing astonishment, the mind wakes to find itself looking blankly into the void of death. That it should profess itself pleased by this performance was all that the highest rules of good breeding could ask; but that it should actually be satisfied would prove that it existed only as idiocy.

Henry Adams, *The Education of Henry Adams* (1918)

---

mid-1920s, it was in near eclipse: The Jazz Age, Fitzgerald announced, "had no interest in politics at all." Like religious belief, the appeal of social reform would not mount much of a comeback among "highbrows" until the 1930s and the heyday of New Deal politics.

In the meantime, writers turned hither and yon. The Jazz Age, Fitzgerald also asserted, "was an age of miracles, it was an age of art, it was an age of excess, and it was an age of satire." The noted drama critic George Jean Nathan adopted a deliberately cynical and hedonistic posture. "The great problems of the world—social, political, economic, and theological—do not concern me in the slightest . . . ," he proclaimed. "What concerns me alone is myself, and the interests of a few close friends. For all I care the rest of the world may go to hell at today's sunset." Mencken, another iconoclast, relied on wit and satire. Others, like James G. Huneker, turned to aestheticism, as though to make a religion of art by balancing its form and beauty against the clumsy force and mess of life. "Highbrows," the journalist and novelist Ben Hecht complained, talked about art as if it were their dead grandmother. John Keats's "Ode on a Grecian Urn," William Faulkner said, with deliberate irreverence, is worth any number of old ladies. But the era's aestheticism represented more than flight. In its concern for craftsmanship and in its stress on conscious experimentation in style and form, even in its desire to isolate literature from the social and moral problems of the time, aestheticism represented a need to find in art a way of saying no to a world that seemed at once fragmented and diminished. "In an age of disbelief, or, what is the same thing, in a time that is largely humanistic, in one sense or another, it is for the poet to supply the satisfactions of belief," Wallace Stevens wrote, "in his measure and in his style."

"The Firm Foundation of Unyielding Despair"

Such, in outline, but even more purposeless, more void of meaning, is the world which Science presents for our belief. Amid such a world, if anywhere, our ideals henceforth must find a home. That Man is the product of causes which had no prevision of the end they were achieving; that his origin, his growth, his hopes and fears, his loves and his beliefs, are but the outcome of accidental collocations of atoms; that no fire, no heroism, no intensity of thought and feeling, can preserve an individual life beyond the grave; that all the labors of the ages, all the devotion, all the inspiration, all the noonday brightness of human genius, are destined to extinction in the vast death of the solar system, and that the whole temple of Man's achievement must inevitably be buried beneath the debris of a universe in ruins—all these things, if not quite beyond dispute, are yet so nearly certain, that no philosophy which rejects them can hope to stand. Only within the scaffolding of these truths, only on the firm foundation of unyielding despair, can the soul's habitation henceforth be safely built.

Bertrand Russell, "A Free Man's Worship" (1918)

Big Business and the Transformation of American Society

Another source of disillusionment, more varied than the Great War and more immediate to writers who had not seen the war firsthand, was the rapid transformation of American society that had commenced in America in the mid-nineteenth century, accelerated with the Civil War, and then accelerated again with World War I. Americans were accustomed, almost by birthright, to encounters with historical change and cultural dislocation. Their story was, at least in part, the story of a shifting frontier that had first drawn people from England and Europe to America and then across the continent to the Pacific. Many Americans were still on the road, moving on, seemingly confident of their ability to cope with motion and change. To writers born in the 1890s, however, the world's disarray seemed almost total. "We are unsettled to the very roots of our being," Walter Lippmann wrote in 1914. "There isn't a human relation, whether of parent and child, husband and wife, worker and employer, that doesn't move in a strange situation." "The civilized world has disposed of supernaturalism," Mencken reported, "and is engaged in a destructive criticism of the old faith's residuum—morality."

As early as the seventeenth century, Americans had begun to associate respectability with success and success with money—and both with what Hawthorne, in a sketch titled "The Sister Years," calls the "moral influence of wealth." But after the Civil War, America's general belief in progress became a specific belief in the beneficence of material progress—a belief shared by businessmen, politicians, social thinkers, and ministers alike. Even dissenters like Thorstein Veblen (1857–1929) found it easier to attack the distribution of wealth than to question the adequacy of material progress as an end or the feasibility of continuous economic growth as a means. By the turn of the century, changes were coming from every side. A new form of capitalism, organized and corporate, had replaced the dispersed, entrepreneurial capitalism of the early nineteenth century. A more centralized democracy that gave a greater role to people of wealth had replaced the loose confederation of the nation's beginning. Soon the nation's industry, like its government, was moving concertedly to serve the interests of business, assuming that business could satisfy as well as serve the needs of the people. The trust-busting and social reform of the late nineteenth and early twentieth centuries notwithstanding, the primary commitment of the nation—as articulated in its ideology and supported by its economy, its government, and its technology—was to making itself a model of economic growth.

Although major portions of the United States remained rural and agricultural well into the twentieth century, and though the South remained poor as well, a new pattern—urban, industrial, commercial, affluent, and secular—had been established for American life. Powerful first in the East, it spread rapidly across the upper Midwest and eventually prevailed even in the South. In the brief span between the close of the Civil War in 1865 and the outbreak of World War I in 1914, the nation saw the traditional authority of both the church and the family seriously erode; it saw its cities commence a period of rapid, unabated growth; and it saw its most successful businesses begin to produce and market on a national scale—first in cities, the easier targets, and then, as railroads, canals, and telegraphs extended their networks, in villages. Stimulated by a wartime economy, growth in productivity exploded after World War I. With national income soaring from $59.4 billion in 1920 to $87.2 billion in 1928, the United States achieved the highest standard of living the world had ever known. By 1929 it accounted for 34.4 percent of total world production, compared with 39.6 by Great Britain, France, Germany, Russia, and Japan combined.

The nation's new affluence ushered in a new mode of conspicuous consumption. Cosmetics and cigarettes, refrigerators and porcelain bathtubs, along with scores of new gadgets, fascinated the nation as they fascinated Sinclair Lewis's George Babbitt. The number of telephones installed in the nation rose from under 1.4 million in 1900 to over 20.2 million in 1930; the number of automobiles produced soared from 4,000 in 1900 to 4.8 million in 1929. In the autumn of 1920, Americans heard their first public radio broadcast; in 1929, they spent $852 million purchasing radios. Movies, boxing, and baseball became big businesses, making idols of Rudolph Valentino and Greta Garbo, heroes of Jack Dempsey and Babe Ruth. Clothing styles changed with each new season. Where the boundaries of what was permissible in language, manners, and behavior were not abolished, they were extended, and a "revolution in morals" was under way.

The Role of Artists in an Era of Wild Oscillations

Writers and artists participated in much of the remaking of America and dominated some of it. The ships that carried them to Europe almost invariably featured black jazz bands, as did many of the Parisian clubs they frequented. In

1919 and again in 1921, the "Original Dixieland Jazz Band" played in England; by 1925, black jazz performers had played in major cities from London and Paris to Berlin and Moscow. Soon the music of jazz and swing bands was altering not only the play of writers like Fitzgerald but the rhythm of their prose. In their campaign against priggishness and censorship, Randolph Bourne, Van Wyck Brooks, and H. L. Mencken made *Puritan* an epithet for people who fear pleasure and love power and *Puritanism* a scapegoat for most known forms of blindness, greed, and repression. Although the era created competing diversions—the radio, big-time sports, and the movies, for example—its technology, its expanding

---

The Writer and the Movie

Around quitting time, Tod Hackett heard a great din on the road outside his office. The groan of leather mingled with the jangle of iron and over all beat the tatoo of a thousand hooves. He hurried to the window.

An army of cavalry and foot was passing. It moved like a mob; its lines broken, as though fleeing from some terrible defeat. The dolmans of the hussars, the heavy shakos of the guards, Hanoverian light horse, with their flat leather caps and flowing red plumes, were all jumbled together in bobbing disorder. Behind the cavalry came the infantry, a wild sea of waving sabretaches, sloped muskets, crossed shoulder belts and swinging cartridge boxes. Tod recognized the scarlet infantry of England with their white shoulder pads, the black infantry of the Duke of Brunswick, the French grenadiers with their enormous white gaiters, the Scotch with bare knees under plaid skirts.

While he watched, a little fat man, wearing a cork sun-helmet, polo shirt and knickers, darted around the corner of the building in pursuit of the army.

"Stage Nine—you bastards—Stage Nine!" he screamed through a small megaphone.

The cavalry put spur to their horses and the infantry broke into a dogtrot. The little man in the cork hat ran after them, shaking his fist and cursing.

Tod watched until they had disappeared behind half a Mississippi steamboat, then put away his pencils and drawing board, and left the office. On the sidewalk outside the studio he stood for a moment trying to decide whether to walk home or take a streetcar. He had been in Hollywood less than three months and still found it a very exciting place, but he was lazy and didn't like to walk. He decided to take the streetcar as far as Vine Street and walk the rest of the way.

A talent scout for National Films had brought Tod to the Coast after seeing some of his drawings in an exhibit of undergraduate work at the Yale School of Fine Arts. He had been hired by telegram.

Nathanael West, *The Day of the Locust* (1939)

communications network, and its growing advertising industry encouraged the development of new magazines and new publishing firms (Alfred A. Knopf in 1915; Boni & Liveright in 1917; Harcourt, Brace in 1919; Viking in 1925). With publishers courting writers and magazines competing for stories, writers were able to make more money and reach a larger audience than ever before. The 1920s were the age of the Book of the Month Club and the Literary Guild. Although book prices were low, royalties were high, and magazines paid large fees for stories. Many writers shared in the nation's new affluence. Near the end of his career, Jack London made more than $75,000 per year. F. Scott Fitzgerald's first novel, *This Side of Paradise* (1920), sold more than 40,000 copies in its first year, launching Fitzgerald on a career in which he made unheard-of sums of money. After 1927, when *The Jazz Singer* transformed the use of sound in motion pictures, Hollywood began using lucrative contracts to draw hundreds of writers, including Fitzgerald and Faulkner, Dashiell Hammett and Nathanael West, to California.

Still, writers found much to offend and little to sustain them in the sharp contrasts and wild oscillations triggered by the nation's headlong rush to make money. Women had emerged from the Great War hoping for a new beginning. In 1920, after nearly a century of agitation, they won suffrage with adoption of the Nineteenth Amendment. But what followed was neither the reconstitution of American society that they had prophesied nor the disintegration of it that their enemies had predicted. The right of women to vote had little discernible impact on the nation's politics and almost none on its economy. In Dorothy Canfield Fisher's *The Home-Maker* (1924), a wife who has failed as a mother trades places with her husband, who has failed as a businessman, and both find happiness. But in fact the force of the women's movement began to dissipate rapidly after the war, leaving women who had believed in its promise disillusioned. Several older writers—Edith Wharton (1862–1937), Ellen Glasgow (1874–1945), Gertrude Stein (1874–1946), and Willa Cather (1876–1947)—survived the 1920s, and several younger ones—Katherine Anne Porter (1890–1980), Josephine Herbst (1897–1969), and Zora Neale Hurston (ca. 1901–1960)—emerged during them. But for the most part they encountered what the heroines of Fitzgerald and Hemingway novels and stories encounter—more suspicion and fear than affirmation and support. Both the literature and the life of the era reflect familiar anxieties with renewed intensity: among women, fear of being isolated or punished; among men, fear of being displaced or devoured.

At the same time, racism not only survived but flourished. On one side, it manifested itself in appeals to racial pride, particularly among so-called Aryans; on the other, it manifested itself in appeals to racial fear, particularly of "the darker types," including immigrants from southern and eastern Europe as well as black Americans. In books like *The Passing of the Great Race* (1916) and *The Rising Tide of Color* (1920), men bearing resonant names—Madison Grant and Lothrop Stoddard—not only celebrated Aryans as stalwart builders and champions of culture but also condemned people of color as fertile, dark, devious, and dangerous.

" 'The Rise of the Colored Empires' "

"Civilization's going to pieces," broke out Tom violently. "I've gotten to be a terrible pessimist about things. Have you read 'The Rise of the Colored Empires' by this man Goddard?"

"Why, no," I answered, rather surprised by his tone.

"Well, it's a fine book, and everybody ought to read it. The idea is if we don't look out the white race will be—will be utterly submerged. It's all scientific stuff; it's been proved."

"Tom's getting very profound," said Daisy, with an expression of unthoughtful sadness. "He reads deep books with long words in them. What was that word we—"

"Well, these books are all scientific," insisted Tom, glancing at her impatiently. "This fellow has worked out the whole thing. It's up to us, who are the dominant race, to watch out or these other races will have control of things."

"We've got to beat them down," whispered Daisy, winking ferociously toward the fervent sun.

"You ought to live in California—" began Miss Baker, but Tom interrupted her by shifting heavily in his chair.

"This idea is that we're Nordics. I am, and you are, and you are, and—" After an infinitesimal hesitation he included Daisy with a slight nod, and she winked at me again. "—And we've produced all the things that go to make civilization—oh, science and art, and all that. Do you see?"

F. Scott Fitzgerald, *The Great Gatsby* (1925)

On a markedly different front, Aimee Semple McPherson and Billy Sunday sought to counter the assault on religious faith by directing large evangelical enterprises designed to recruit new converts. Other citizens opposed "the revolution in morals" by attempting to legislate morality, particularly where alcohol was concerned. In 1919, when the Eighteenth Amendment established Prohibition, the tension between "highbrows" and evangelical Protestants began to intensify. Ironically, however, Prohibition tended not only to encourage lawlessness and to finance organized crime but also to associate drinking with sophistication—with consequences that are still being felt. Washington, D.C., had three hundred licensed saloons before Prohibition and seven hundred speakeasies, supplied by four thousand bootleggers, during it. Boston had more than four thousand speakeasies; Detroit, more than twenty thousand.

The era also witnessed wholesale violations of civil liberties. Both the Red Scare in 1919 and the Palmer Raids in 1920 fanned hostility toward "aliens" and "anarchists" and "Communists." The long, divisive trial of Nicola Sacco and Bartolomeo Vanzetti (1920–1927) and their execution served further to polarize the nation, as did the National Origins Act of 1924, which halted immigration from the Orient and restricted immigration from southern and eastern Europe. Encouraged by such actions, private citizens began organizing their own vigilante persecutions of political, religious, and racial minorities. In 1920, concerned citizens countered such actions by creating the American Civil Liberties Union. But the dominant mood of the nation was more clearly expressed by the Ku Klux Klan—bands of white-hooded men who rode through the night to terrorize people for not being born white and Protestant. Between 1920 and 1925, membership in the Klan rose from roughly five thousand to five million.

Given such stark contrasts, the juxtaposition of the cronyism and corruption of Warren Harding's administration (1920–1923) with the stern asceticism of Calvin Coolidge's (1923–1929) did nothing so much as reinforce the fear that America's only shared commitment was to establishing "a businessman's government." Above all, it was the materialism of the era that writers repudiated. "Feeling like aliens in the commercial world," Malcolm Cowley wrote, scores of writers, from Gertrude Stein to Ernest Hemingway to Richard Wright, sailed for Europe "as soon as they had money enough to pay for their steamer tickets." Even those like F. Scott Fitzgerald, who participated in the nation's high jinks and shared in its prosperity, felt uncomfortable in a land so totally preoccupied with business. Suddenly America seemed not merely gross and vulgar but so single-minded and so heedless in its pursuit of material progress as to doom each "new generation . . . more than the last," Fitzgerald wrote, "to the fear of poverty and the worship of success." A favorite story among writers of the period recalled the day a thirty-six-year-old man named Sherwood Anderson walked out of the office of his paint factory in Elyria, Ohio, to search for meaning in art. "I hardly know what I can teach," Anderson wrote his brother Karl, "except anti-success."

Both the inadequacy of mere success and the hostility of American society to art, or more generally to mind and spirit, coalesce in the story told of Anderson. In fact, however, Anderson's dramatic turn from business to art was triggered more by a nervous breakdown than by a startling conversion, his being one of the fortunate crises of his time. Years later, looking back, remembering especially Fitzgerald's crack-up, Edmund Wilson remarked that his own generation's journey had not been so gay "as we expected when we first started out. . . . We, too, have had our casualties." At times, a sense of hollowness seemed to touch almost everything, from the nation's dream of colossal wealth and meretricious beauty to the revolt of its highbrows and the rebellion of its youth.

Big Ideas for Big Business

What is the finest game? Business. The soundest science? Business. The truest art? Business. The fullest education? Business. The fairest opportunity? Business. The cleanest philanthropy? Business. The sanest religion? Business.

Edward Earl Purington (1921)

The Great Crash and a Revival of Reform

When the Great Crash came, bringing what Fitzgerald later termed "history's most expensive orgy" to a halt, it struck with an abruptness that remains difficult to comprehend. On December 4, 1928, in his last address to Congress, President Coolidge assured the nation that it had never "met with a more pleasing prospect." "The country can regard the present with satisfaction," he concluded, "and anticipate the future with optimism." Over the next several months, the speculative binges of the 1920s culminated in what came to be called the Great Bull Market. In 1923, the volume of sales on the New York Stock Exchange had topped 236 million shares; in 1928, the volume reached over 1.1 billion shares. As thousands rushed to borrow money and buy stock, millions rushed to read newspapers and listen to radios, making the market a spectator sport as well as business at its biggest. Between 1925 and 1928, General Motors stock climbed from 99 to 212. During three weeks in March 1929, Radio Corporation of America stock shot from 94 1/2 to 178. In the summer of 1929, industrials gained 110 points, or nearly 25 percent. Suddenly the nation's dream of overwhelming prosperity actually seemed to lie within reach. Then, in the fall of 1929, less than a year after President Coolidge's speech, the market broke: Radio Corporation of America lost 32 points in a matter of days; industrials lost 228 points between early September and early November, a decline of 50 percent. Having reached 452 in September 1929, industrials sank to 58 in 1932, at the bottom of the Great Depression. During the same period, Montgomery Ward fell from a high of 138 to a low of 4, General Motors from 212 to 8. With confidence collapsing and

---

"The *Debacle* of Idealism"

For . . . many men and women the new day so sonorously heralded by the optimists and propagandists of war-time had turned into night before it ever arrived, and in the uncertain blackness they did not know which way to turn. They could revolt against stupidity and mediocrity, they could derive a meager pleasure from regarding themselves with pity as members of a lost generation, but they could not find peace.

Frederick Lewis Allen, *Only Yesterday* (1931)

What most distinguishes the generation who have approached maturity since the *debacle* of idealism at the end of the war is not their rebellion against the religion and the moral code of their parents, but their disillusionment with their own rebellion. It is common for young men and women to rebel, but that they should rebel sadly and without faith in their rebellion, and that they should distrust the new freedom no less than the old certainties—that is something of a novelty.

Walter Lippmann, *A Preface to Morals* (1929)

reserves disappearing, income began to fall, banks to fail, and unemployment to rise. Soon it seemed that almost everyone was poor and that no one knew what to do—President Herbert Hoover even less than the governors and the mayors.

Bread lines and soup kitchens; "Hoovervilles," as the shantytowns that dotted the country were called; families leaving foreclosed homes in search of some place to make a new start; millions of men and hundreds of thousands of young boys riding the rails, seeking in motion a sense of release even more final than the one other people found watching movies, listening to radio programs, or dancing to the sound of the big bands—these became the trademarks of the 1930s. To those already skeptical, as many writers were, the magnitude of the Great Depression did nothing so much as confirm that something had gone drastically wrong with the nation's way of life.

"The Literary Delirium"

There has come a sort of break in the literary movement that was beginning to feel its first strength in the years 1912–1916. . . . For us [then], a variety of elements seemed to contribute to produce an atmosphere that was liberating and stimulating. The American writer . . . seemed at last to be getting all the breaks. . . . The young man or young woman was scarcely out of college when his first novel was seized on by a publisher who exploited instead of censoring whatever in it was improper or disturbing, and he soon found himself a figure of glamour in the world between the Algonquin and Greenwich Village, at a kind of fancy-dress party of frantic self-advertisement. . . .

In any case, at the end of the twenties, a kind of demoralization set in. . . . There was suddenly very little money around, and the literary delirium seemed clearing. The sexual taboos of the age before had been dismissed both from books and from life, and there was no need to be feverish about them; liquor was legal again, and the stock market lay gasping its last. The new "classes" of intellectuals—it was a feature of the post-boom period that they tended to think of themselves as "intellectuals" rather than as "writers"—were in general sober and poor, and they applied the analysis of Marxism to the scene of wreckage they faced. This at least offered a discipline for the mind, gave a coherent picture of history and promised not only employment but the triumph of the constructive intellect. But then, within the decade that followed, the young journalists and novelists and poets who had tried to base their dreams on bedrock, had the spectacle, not of the advent of "the first truly human culture," the ideal of Lenin and Trotsky, but of the rapid domination of Europe by the state socialism of Hitler and Stalin, with its strangling of political discussion and its contemptuous extermination of art; and they no longer knew what to think.

Edmund Wilson, "Thoughts on Being Bibliographed" (1943)

Given the haunting quality of the 1920s, the suddenness of the Crash inevitably provoked feelings of nostalgia and bafflement. Yet there was also, as Malcolm Cowley remarked, "a sense of relief" on coming out of the 1920s, "as on coming out of a room too full of talk and people into the sunlight of the winter streets." Soon writers began looking back on the 1920s, as Josephine Herbst later noted, less as a unified period of miracles and art than as "crumbs and pieces" that contradicted each other—as an era of "flux and change" in which "artistic movements" interacted with "political crises," and even as an era in which such seemingly abandoned ideas as "social service, justice, and religious reaction" had found "special spokesmen."

By appealing to America's idealism rather than to its established preoccupation with big business, Franklin Delano Roosevelt became the first president since Woodrow Wilson to capture the attention of writers. With the New Deal, reform politics became once again respectable. The Federal Writers' Project alone provided support for hundreds of writers. Concern for stylistic and formal experimentation in literature continued, but the 1930s also inspired a sense of urgency that literature make contact with the critical social and cultural problems of the time. Young writers wanted to prove, Alfred Kazin asserted, that they could move "the streets, the stockyards, the hiring halls into literature" and so make their "radical strength . . . carry on the experimental impulse of modern literature."

The 1930s became the heyday of documentary literature in America. In books like Ruth McKenny's *Industrial Valley,* George Leighton's *Five Cities,* Erskine Caldwell and Margaret Bourke-White's *You Have Seen Their Faces,* and the WPA's record of case histories, *These Are Our Lives,* writers sought to record the deprivation, poverty, and suffering of the poor. At the same time, an intensified fascination with the idea of culture began giving phrases like the "American dream" and the "American way of life" fresh authority in the nation's search for values. During the 1920s Sigmund Freud had taught writers, including some who had never read his writings, a new vocabulary. Beyond that, he had taught writers to regard all experience, even telltale slips of tongue and pen, as symptomatic, thus inaugurating an age of suspicion and skepticism as well as

---

"Something Has Got to Change in America"

There's a song that says, "the time ain't long." That song is right. Something has got to change in America—and change soon. We must help that change to come. . . .

We want a new and better America, where there won't be any poor, where there won't be any more Jim Crow, where there won't be any lynchings, where there won't be any munition makers, where we won't need philanthropy, nor charity, nor the New Deal, nor Home Relief.

We want an America that will be ours, a world that will be ours—we Negro workers and white workers! Black writers and white! We'll make that world.

Langston Hughes, "To Negro Writers" (1935)

critical analysis. During the 1930s, as the Depression deepened and crisis followed crisis, the influence of Karl Marx spread rapidly—particularly his critique of capitalism as interpreted by Max Eastman, Waldo Frank, and John Reed. What Freud did to human utterances—namely, insist that they should never be taken simply on their own terms but must instead be viewed skeptically—Marx did for human institutions. Soon a new form of suspicion and skepticism, as well as a new form of critical analysis, was gaining currency. Americans began wondering whether their economic system ("free enterprise capitalism") might not be at odds with their political system ("egalitarian democracy"). "Thousands were convinced and hundreds of thousands were half-persuaded that no simple operation would save us," Cowley wrote; "there had to be the complete renovation of society that Karl Marx had prophesied in 1848. Unemployment would be ended, war and fascism would vanish from the earth, but only after the revolution."

Although some writers influenced by Marx permitted their work to become propagandistic and ephemeral, others, as different as John Dos Passos, Nathanael West, and Richard Wright, did not. They wrote of the poor, often of the very poor, from the farms of the South and the ghettos of the North. Whereas writers like Theodore Dreiser had written of poor people who actually hope to escape poverty and share in power and prosperity, writers of the 1930s frequently wrote of people whose hardship, privation, and misery are intensified by hopelessness. A sense of violent protest accordingly runs through the fiction of the 1930s. If the stronger writers of the period avoided slogans—"the toiling masses," for example —it was, as Josephine Herbst asserted, in part because slogans seemed to provide no answers to "terrible questions," in part because slogans seemed to throttle struggling impulses, and in part because fiction's proper subject still seemed to them to be the individual human spirit "with its own peculiar past." But in the 1930s, more than in any other period in our history, those individual spirits tend to be marginal human beings. They are rootless poets and fierce, defiant gangsters; they are vagabonds and sharecroppers; they are people of mixed or uncertain racial identity or ambiguous sexuality; they are those Edward Dahlberg called *Bottom Dogs* (1930), Jack Conroy, *The Disinherited* (1933), Tess Slesinger, *The Unpossessed* (1934).

Despair and Compliance

One policeman sat in the rear with me while the other one drove. We were traveling very fast and the siren was blowing. It was the same kind of a siren they had used at the marathon dance when they wanted to wake us up.

"Why did you kill her?" the policeman in the rear seat asked.

"She asked me to," I said.

"You hear that, Ben?"

"Ain't he an obliging bastard?" Ben said, over his shoulder.

"Is that the only reason you got?" the policeman in the rear seat asked.

"They shoot horses, don't they?" I said.

Horace McCoy, *They Shoot Horses, Don't They?* (1935)

Shortly after the elevation of Hitler to power in 1933, the threat of war began to spread across Europe. With Hitler's staggering persecution of Jews, thousands of writers, scholars, painters, musicians, scientists, and philosophers—people like Thomas Mann, Hannah Arendt, Vladimir Nabokov, and Albert Einstein—sought refuge in the United States. Yet despite this dramatic new immigration, the United States remained throughout the 1930s preoccupied with its own internal problems and committed to neutrality. Reforms designed to offset the consequences of the Great Depression and stimulate recovery from it dominated the nation's domestic policy, just as isolationism dominated its foreign policy. Despite Roosevelt's reforms, however, recovery from the rapid economic decline and soaring unemployment of the Great Depression was painfully slow. Full economic recovery would not come until after the nation shifted its attention and abandoned its policy of neutrality by entering World War II—an event that would accelerate the United States' rise as a world power and change its literature once again.

Alienation and Experimentation

American writers of the early twentieth century began in alienation and repudiation, moods that were intensified by the Great War and transformed by the Great Depression. The sense that the world had somehow broken in two haunted them. Feeling cut off from the past, they turned to it, in search of some usable heritage. Allusions and echoes of earlier writers fill their stories. "In a city," Ezra Pound once remarked, "visual impressions succeed each other, overlap, overcross, they are 'cinematographic.'" In villages, he continued, people possess a sense of sequence and a sense of shared knowledge; because they know who did what before, during, and after the cataclysmic changes in their history, their life "is narrative." Convinced that individual experience had become disjointed and communal experience chaotic, writers of the early twentieth century struggled with the wild shifts and swings of their era, as with bits and pieces, trying to make art of them. Dos Passos shaped his fiction out of fragments taken from movies, newsreels, newspapers, and popular songs; Faulkner shaped his out of "the rag-tag and bob-ends of old tales and talking." In different ways, both sought to confront the radically discontinuous and fragmentary aspects of their world. As though to remind us that discontinuity threatens narrative as well as history, art as well as life, writers made the story sequence, a form of discontinuous narrative, one of the representative fictional forms of their era—a form highlighted in Stein's *Three Lives,* Anderson's *Winesburg, Ohio,* Hemingway's *In Our Time,* and Faulkner's *Go Down, Moses.*

At the same time, writers struggled to combine the variety and resilience of idiomatic American English with the resonance and allusional density of more traditional literary language. In some moments, they reflect a deep fascination with American life; in others, they disclose a disenchantment so profound as to approximate what the great French poet Baudelaire called the "sublime literature" of despair, in which degradation and hopelessness persuade the reader to "long for

---

"The Noises of America"

The tall, impossibly tall, incomparably tall, city shoulderingly upward into hard
sunlight leaned a little through the octaves of its parallel edges, leaningly strode
upward into firm hard snowy sunlight; the noises of America nearingly
throbbed with smokes and hurrying dots which are men and which are women
and which are things new and curious and hard and strange and vibrant and
immense, lifting with a great undulous stride firmly into immortal sunlight.

E. E. Cummings, *The Enormous Room* (1922)

Three gulls wheel above the broken boxes, orangerinds, spoiled cabbage heads
that heave between the splintered plank walls, the green waves spume under the
round bow as the ferry, skidding on the tide, crashes, gulps the broken water,
slides, settles slowly into the slip. Handwinches whirl with jingle of chains.
Gates fold upwards, feet step out across the crack, men and women press
through the manuresmelling wooden tunnel of the ferryhouse, crushed and
jostling like apples fed down a chute into a press.

John Dos Passos, *Manhattan Transfer* (1925)

---

goodness as a remedy." Some of the voices Dos Passos created are so public as to
seem familiar, while some of those Faulkner created are so private as to seem
strange, bizarre, even deranged. If, however, one part of the achievement of
Faulkner, Stein, Hemingway, Dos Passos, and Wright was to reform and extend
the language of American literature, another part was to reshape the tastes and
skills of the readers of that literature. Implicit in their works is the task of
teaching us the skills required to read them. By extending the range of our
literature, they hoped also to expand its audience.

One manifestation of the alienation that writers of the early twentieth century
felt was their need to create places more their own. "I would say," Faulkner once
remarked, "that in our culture there is really no place for the artist." In New
Orleans, Memphis, Chicago, New York, London, and Paris, writers gravitated
toward enclaves where money mattered less, literature and art more. In addition,
however, several of these enclaves were identified with specific regions (Chicago
with the Midwest; Memphis and New Orleans with the South) or with racial
minorities (Harlem) and so provided a counterbalance not only to materialism
and its consequences but also to the strong centralizing forces that had begun to
dominate American society. Although the Northeast had declined as a source of
literary art, it retained its power as literary arbiter of the nation, primarily
through the great publishing houses of New York. As a result, the writing of the
Northeast continued to be regarded as "American" literature, the writing of the
Midwest and especially the writing of the South as "regional" literature, and the
writing of black Americans as "minority" literature.

"Paris Was Always Worth It"

There is never any ending to Paris and the memory of each person who has
lived in it differs from that of any other. We always returned to it no matter
who we were or how it was changed or with what difficulties, or ease, it could
be reached. Paris was always worth it and you received return for whatever you
brought to it. But this is how Paris was in the early days when we were very
poor and very happy.

Ernest Hemingway, *A Moveable Feast* (1964)

On a different front, the rise of national magazines and even more of the
movies and radio was rapidly nationalizing American popular culture. In the year
1922, a total of 40 million people attended the movies; in 1930, an average of
100 million bought tickets each week. By 1928, when radio sales soared to $852
million, radio programs were reaching millions of homes each day. Writers
needed places in which they could enter the world of art and find support for
what they were doing; but they also needed some means of holding fast to the
particular subcultures they knew, whether those subcultures were to be defined
regionally, racially, or sexually. Many of the nation's stronger writers moved
from regional centers to New York, London, or Paris—as was the case with
Wright. A few moved back home, as was the case with Faulkner, but many
found in regional enclaves precisely what they needed—a second country, slightly
more romantic and considerably more supportive than any place they had known,
where they could still maintain contact with the folkways and voices that fed
their art, a way station poised between the worlds they actually knew and those
they were trying to create.

In and outside their enclaves, they established "little magazines"—*Poetry* and
The Little Review in Chicago; *The Criterion* and *Blast* in London; *Transition* and
Transatlantic Review in Paris; *Broom* in Rome; *The Seven Arts* and *The Dial* in
New York; *The Fugitive* in Nashville; *The Double Dealer* in New Orleans.
Writers published stories in popular magazines, of course, as well as in little
magazines—in *The Saturday Evening Post* as well as *The Double Dealer*—and they
published many works that are now ignored as well as some that are still read.
But the little magazines served an important double purpose. First, by publishing
works of minor writers, they added depth and resonance to the literary life of
early twentieth-century America. Second, by publishing some of the more
experimental works of writers who later became famous, they provided a market
for works that played a major role in revolutionizing the taste and reading skills
of the nation's most avid readers, including emerging writers.

Like Whitman, writers of the twentieth century have celebrated the magic of
the commonplace. And like Whitman's, their disaffection with American life has

coexisted with fascination. The disaffection and alienation that mark American fiction of the early twentieth century run deep, in part because our writers have felt so acutely the failure of American life to meet the needs of mind and spirit that no material possession can ever satisfy. Like T. S. Eliot, our writers have tended to be suspicious of the dream of creating social systems so perfect that no one would need to be good, and like Herman Melville, they have tended to feel greater solidarity with the poor, the forgotten, and the defeated than with the rich and the victorious. They have confronted more honestly and courageously than most of us the incongruities and anxieties that shape our lives. One thing they had inherited from the nineteenth century, besides a suspect faith in the sufficiency of material progress itself, was the promise of more freedom: a willingness to blur or even dissolve all limitations, all restrictions, all taboos, in art as well as in life. Yet even as they enjoyed the rewards of material progress and advocated freedom, our writers have remained convinced that freedom suffices only when people truly know what they want, and then only when what they want corresponds to their deepest needs and so matches their capacity for wonder.

Recently, in another connection, I spoke of the modern self as characterized by its intense and adverse imagination of the culture in which it had its being, and by certain powers of indignant perception which, turned upon the subconscious portions of culture, have made it accessible to conscious thought. Freud's view of culture is marked by this *adverse* awareness, by this indignant perception. He does indeed see the self as formed by its culture. But he also sees the self as set against the culture, struggling against it, having been from the first reluctant to enter it. . . .

In its essence literature is concerned with the self; and the particular concern of the literature of the last two centuries has been with the self in its standing quarrel with culture. We cannot mention the name of any great writer of the modern period whose work has not in some way, and usually in a passionate and explicit way, insisted on this quarrel, who has not expressed the bitterness of his discontent with civilization, who has not said that the self made greater legitimate demands than any culture could hope to satisfy. This intense conviction of the existence of the self apart from culture is, as culture well knows, its noblest and most generous achievement. At the present moment it must be thought of as a liberating idea without which our developing ideal of community is bound to defeat itself. We can speak no greater praise of Freud than to say that he placed this idea at the very center of his thought.

Lionel Trilling, *Freud and the Crisis of Our Culture* (1955)

American writers of the early twentieth century were heirs, then, less of the dominant culture of the nineteenth century than of its great intellectual rebels. Much of the daring, even the headiness, of the assaults that Darwin, Marx, Nietzsche, and Freud had led against apparently secure truths and beliefs found new expression in the extraordinary boldness and the sheer presumption of writers as different as Stein, Dos Passos, and Faulkner as they set out to invent literature anew. When these writers looked to the past, seeking ancestors and a heritage, they often turned to forgotten, out-of-the-way figures. In fact, however, their cavalier dismissal of their most immediate heritage, that of Victorian thinking and writing, was often overstated: Many of them remained closet loyalists where the nineteenth century was concerned. In a similar vein, one may say that their brashness outstripped their assurance; even Stein, Faulkner, and Wright, as brash as any, lived on close terms with most known forms of doubt, including self-doubt. Yet their gifts survived. An almost fierce determination to deal with the past on no terms except their own not only marked them as rebels but also shaped their art. Modern American fiction is often pessimistic and violent, even brutal and despairing. But it is also infused with great boldness of spirit, as we see especially in the remarkable formal experiments that give it a special place in one of the great outpourings of innovative expression in the history of Western literature.

Further Reading:
F. L. Allen, *Only Yesterday*, 1931.
M. Cowley, *After the Genteel Tradition: American Writing, 1910–1930*, 1937.
A. Kazin, *On Native Grounds: An Interpretation of Modern American Prose Literature*, 1942.
L. Trilling, *The Liberal Imagination*, 1950.
M. Cowley, *Exile's Return: A Narrative of Ideas, 1934*, 1951.
E. Goldman, *Rendezvous with Destiny*, 1952.
E. Wilson, *The Shores of Light: A Literary Chronicle of the Twenties and Thirties*, 1952.
F. J. Hoffman, *The Twenties: American Writing in the Postwar Decade*, 1955.
R. Hofstadter, *The Age of Reform: From Bryan to FDR*, 1955.
L. Trilling, *The Opposing Self*, 1955.
L. Trilling, *Freud and the Crisis of Our Culture*, 1956.
S. P. Hays, *The Response to Industrialism: 1885–1914*, 1957.
W. Leuchtenburg, *The Perils of Prosperity: 1914–1932*, 1958.
W. Morris, *The Territory Ahead*, 1958.

D. Aaron, *Writers on the Left*, 1961
W. Berthoff, *The Ferment of Realism: American Literature 1884–1919*, 1965.
R. Bridgman, *The Colloquial Style in America*, 1966.
N. L. Huggins, *Harlem Renaissance*, 1971.
H. Kenner, *The Pound Era*, 1971.
R. Miller, *Black American Literature: 1760 to the Present*, 1971.
H. Kenner, *A Homemade World*, 1975.
M. Cowley, *And I Worked at the Writer's Trade: American Writing, Chapters of Literary History, 1918–1978*, 1978.
W. Morris, *Earthly Delights, Unearthly Adornments: American Writers as Image Makers*, 1978.
R. Stepto, *From Behind the Veil: A Study of Afro-American Narrative*, 1979.
J. Lears, *No Place of Grace: Antimodernism and the Transformation of American Culture, 1880–1920*, 1981.
P. Johnson, *Modern Times: The World from the Twenties to the Eighties*, 1983.

Gertrude Stein
1874–1946

Gertrude Stein was one of the most resolute champions in American letters for the worth of ordinary things. Live in the middle, she admonished. Yet Stein is generally thought of in terms of the experimental in writing and the unconventional in living. The first Jewish writer to have a large impact on American literature, she became the friend and patron of leaders of the avant-garde in the halcyon days before World War I. She collected juicy anecdotes as well as paintings; she entertained famous people, and she sponsored and even tutored young writers. She dispersed clever aphorisms ("You are all a lost generation"), unforgettable lines ("A rose is a rose is a rose is a rose"), and sharp admonitions ("Look facts in the face look facts in the face look facts in the face"). Having instructed others to live in the middle, she lived nearer the edge —by living as she chose and saying what she thought. She was the longtime lover of Alice B. Toklas, who became famous in her own right for her hashish fudge. Stein was frequently sharp-tongued. She studied with the experimental psychologist and philosopher William James (who praised her) and tutored Ernest Hemingway (who reluctantly gave credit where it was due).

Such items as these make good gossip. In some discussions of Paris and the surge of modernism, the mere mention of Gertrude Stein's name has been used to counteract excessive seriousness. As witty as Stein was in conversation, however, and as much amusement as she provides readers in her delightful, games-playing *Tender Buttons* or *The Autobiography of Alice B. Toklas,* her enduring importance to modern literature lies elsewhere. It lies, aptly enough, exactly where she said it should: with the middle way of familiar values and concerns. Her writings constitute a celebration and a critique of the importance of work, of the uses of self-deception, and of the importance of paying constant attention to both material things and the weight of words. Throughout her work, she resolutely places both abstract thought and complex reasoning at the service of forcefulness rather than of mere clarity.

In her own times, and in her own way, Gertrude Stein, the daughter of a talented, well-situated family one generation removed from Germany, was the intellectual child of Ralph Waldo Emerson. Both Emerson and Stein endeavored to match up linguistic signs, natural sounds, and psychic meanings. Stein also carried forward the interests of her Harvard psychology professor, William James; like him, she was fascinated with the effects of habit, memory, and the unfoldings of consciousness. In addition, she was the imaginative compatriot of William Carlos Williams, Ezra Pound, T. S. Eliot, and Sherwood Anderson. Determined to make things new, Stein broke most rules governing punctuation and syntax and many governing diction. The playfulness of her mind manifested itself in many ways, particularly in its ability to make us pay close attention to even the simplest words. Using familiar words, many of them monosyllabic, she confronted us with fundamental distinctions, such as that between being and remembering and between consciousness and self-consciousness. "At any moment

when you are you you are you without the memory of yourself," she wrote in
What Are Masterpieces (1940), "because if you remember yourself while you are
you you are not for the purposes of creating you."

Gertrude Stein was born in Allegheny, Pennsylvania, a town now part of
Pittsburgh, the youngest of seven children. Despite the security and privilege in
which she lived, Stein never took her existence for granted. Both she and her
brother Leo knew that their parents had "allowed" them to be born only because
two older siblings had died. "Gertrude doesn't like to be frightened," she wrote,
and she didn't; yet she persisted in testing herself at almost every turn from early
in her life to its end.

The year after her birth in 1874, the Stein family went abroad, remaining
there until 1879. Gertrude Stein thus had the advantage of an early exposure to
European languages, but she stubbornly insisted that her only true language was
English. In 1880 the Steins moved to Oakland, California, where Stein spent her
youth. (Of Oakland she would later say, "There is no there there.") She was
close neither to her parents nor to any of her siblings other than Leo. By 1892,
both her parents were dead. Financially independent, she was free to move out
into the world. In 1893 she entered Radcliffe College, which a year later
affiliated with Harvard University, where she encountered the new philosophy of
Josiah Royce and George Santayana and the new psychology of William James,
under whose direction she worked on laboratory experiments in 1894. She
graduated magna cum laude, then spent two years at Johns Hopkins University as
a medical student before abandoning her plans for a career as a physiological
psychologist. In 1902 she moved to London, where she immersed herself in
studying the English language at the British Museum, preparing to be a writer.

Precisely why Stein decided to give up her medical studies remains unclear.
She may have decided to put distance between herself and an unmanageable love
affair with two women, a situation she describes in a novel *OED, or Things as
They Are* (written 1903, published 1950). Or perhaps she wished to remain near
Leo. She had already followed him from California to Harvard and from
Harvard to Johns Hopkins. Now Leo had decided to explore the possibilities of
French culture. In 1903, after one year in London, Stein moved into an
apartment with Leo on the Left Bank in Paris, at 27 rue de Fleurus, near the
center of Europe's literary and artistic circles, where she would live for many
years.

In Paris, both Gertrude and Leo Stein found a perfect "second country." They
soon turned their attention to modern painters. They promoted the art of
Cézanne, Renoir, Gauguin, Manet, and Toulouse-Lautrec, as well as two even
newer painters, Matisse and Picasso—all of whose works they began collecting
before the artists became so famous as to be prohibitively expensive. Soon the
Steins' apartment became a famous meeting place for painters and writers, making
Gertrude a celebrated international hostess who ruled, as Katherine Anne Porter
once reported disparagingly, "in such masterly freedom as only a few early
medieval queens had equalled." But Gertrude Stein did more than collect art and
entertain. She also wrote, experimenting with words as the painters she knew
experimented with forms, shapes, and colors.

In 1905 Gertrude Stein completed her first book, *Three Lives*. It consists of three stories—"The Good Anna," "Melanctha," and "The Gentle Lena." These stories have been praised both for their stylistic innovations and for the poignant ways in which they explore the lives of three very different Baltimore women. In 1908 Stein completed *The Making of Americans*. In this unconventional "novel," she sets out to tell "everybody's history" by drawing heavily on the history of her family, at the same time minimizing the importance of action and avoiding dialogue. Neither *Three Lives* nor *The Making of Americans* was published commercially at the time it was written. Stein's first book was published in 1909 at her own expense; the second appeared in print in 1925, after Stein had established a name for herself with other writings.

Alice B. Toklas moved into the Steins' rue de Fleurus apartment in 1909, and she became Gertrude Stein's lifelong companion, amanuensis, lover, and joint hostess in charge of looking after the spouses of the geniuses who came to call. Later, when Leo decided to move, the Steins' valuable collection of paintings was divided; and Gertrude and Alice were left to get on with Gertrude's career.

Gertrude Stein's writing expanded in the years before World War I, and her fame seemed assured with *Tender Buttons* (1914), a series of paragraphs, some playful and witty, others brief prose poems, that focus on different subjects. Her experiments with language and literary forms coincided with and mirrored the increasing attention being given by painters to abstractions, collages, visual puns, and "in" jokes. Stein's juggling of words rejected conventional expectations of syntax, chronology, and definable meanings. As Hemingway commented in a 1948 letter, "She could never fail; nor strike out; nor be knocked out of the box because she made the rules and played under her own rules." Her portraits of people and objects were often whimsical in the extreme—seemingly thrown together at random.

But Gertrude Stein was also a theorist whose pronouncements about time, punctuation, and narration were taken seriously by other writers. In recognition of the crucial role she had come to play in the emergence of a distinctively modern literature, she was invited to present her theories as a series of lectures at Oxford and Cambridge in 1926. In 1934 and 1935 she made a triumphant tour of the United States. Both her British and American lectures, dealing with visual space as well as language and literature, were published under the titles *Composition as Explanation* (1926), *Narration* (1935), and *Geographical History of America* (1936). In them we follow Stein's pursuit of "the excitingness of pure being" and of the desire to put intensity back in language. Despite her travels, however, she continued to think of Paris as her adopted home, the vantage point from which she could best describe and interpret her native land as well as theorize about language and literature.

Stein's most famous works are autobiographical—*Everybody's Autobiography* (1937) and especially *The Autobiography of Alice B. Toklas* (1933). Both are filled with her barbed opinions about people, food, parties, writing, and the arts; both bear witness to her wide influence; and both provoked sharp rejoinders from her acquaintances and rivals. Never again would her strong-willed peers sit in silent awe of the woman Hemingway described as looking like a Roman emperor, adding that one might not prefer women to look like that. Literary critics and cultural historians joined Stein's "students" (Hemingway, Anderson, and others) in openly expressing their ambivalent feelings toward her. In 1935 a group of Parisian writers and artists published *Testimony Against Gertrude Stein,* primarily in response to *The Autobiography of Alice B. Toklas.* Yet Stein's reputation has continued to grow, especially among those who had nothing personally at stake in the issue of just how important she was.

Stein collaborated with Virgil Thompson on two operas, *Four Saints in Three Acts* (1934) and *The Mother of Us All* (1945–1946), a celebration of Susan B. Anthony. *Wars I Have Seen* (1945) provides a witty yet poignant assessment of the wars that had punctuated Stein's life. *Brewsie and Willie* (1946) offers a lively account of the popularity she enjoyed with the American soldiers who sought her out as a bona fide tourist attraction once France (where she continued to live during World War II) was liberated from German occupation in 1945. To the end of her life, however, even as she cultivated her reputation as a woman who lived an unconventional life amid people and events that stood traditional culture on its head, she remained a hardworking woman devoted to living in the middle. In 1946, following a sharp decline in her health, she entered the American hospital in Paris, where she underwent surgery that failed. On July 27, shortly before she died, she summoned the energy to say, "What is the answer?" and, hearing no reply, to murmur, "In that case, what is the question?"

Gertrude Stein sometimes acted like a comfortable anarchist. She was in fact an uneasy searcher after order who resolutely insisted on being honest about the kinds of stability the modern world could provide. She made use of all the continuities she could find—even those in "the language of dishes and daylight." But her world is a world of gerunds (her favorite verbal form, since gerunds insist on a life of continuous action), a world of consciousness where nothing stands still and where the most solid of realities is one's essential "bottom nature" caught in a flash of words and depicted verbally in "the continuous present." "Let no one think that anything has come to stay," she wrote. She held strong opinions about everything, yet she knew them for what they were—temporarily improvised certainties. After conducting a seminar at the University of Chicago in 1934, she attributed her popularity not to her sharp opinions but to this: "You see why they talk to me is that I am like them I do not know the answer. . . . I do not even know whether there is a question let alone having answers for a question."

Convinced that the twentieth century differed radically from the nineteenth, Stein sought to foster a radical shift in sensibility. Her end was immediacy of presentation in a continuous present. She wanted to give each moment its own successive emphasis, its difference, its place; her art celebrates the "thing seen at the moment it is seen." Time and again her art forces us to examine or reexamine not only relations between words and things but also relations between the composition of language and the process of consciousness: "I had in hundreds of ways related words, then sentences then paragraphs to the thing at which I was looking."

Further Reading:
W. Rogers, *When This You See, Remember Me:
Gertrude Stein in Person,* 1948, 1971, 1973.
D. Sutherland, *Gertrude Stein: A Biography of
Her Work,* 1951, 1971.
E. Sprigge, *Gertrude Stein: Her Life and Work,*
1957.
R. Reid, *Art by Subtraction: A Dissenting
Opinion of Gertrude Stein,* 1958.
J. M. Brinnin, *The Third Rose: Gertrude Stein
and Her World,* 1959.
F. Hoffman, *Gertrude Stein,* 1961.
A. Stewart, *Gertrude Stein and the Present,* 1967.
N. Weinstein, *Gertrude Stein and the Literature of
the Modern Consciousness,* 1970.
R. Bridgman, *Gertrude Stein in Pieces,* 1971.
A. Burnett, *Gertrude Stein,* 1972.

H. Greenfield, *Gertrude Stein: A Biography,* 1973.
Staying Alone: Letters of Alice B. Toklas, ed.
E. Burns, 1974.
J. Mellows, *Charmed Circles: Gertrude Stein and
Company,* 1974.
Gertrude Stein: A Companion Portrait, ed.
L. Simon, 1974.
C. Copeland, *Language & Time & Gertrude
Stein,* 1975.
M. Hoffman, *Gertrude Stein,* 1976.
W. Steiner, *Exact Resemblance to Exact
Resemblance: The Literary Portraiture of Gertrude
Stein,* 1978.
S. Neuman, *Gertrude Stein: Autobiography and the
Problem of Narration,* 1979.

Texts:
Wars I Have Seen, 1945.
The Autobiography of Alice B. Toklas, 1960.
Three Lives, 1945.
"The Work" and "Miguel (Collusion). Giumpe.
Candle." in *Bee Time Vine and Other Pieces,*
1953.
See also *Selected Writings of Gertrude Stein,* ed.
C. Van Vechten, 1946, 1962.
*Two: Gertrude Stein and Her Brother, and Other
Early Portraits, 1908–1912,* ed. J. Flannery, 1951,

1969.
*Stanzas in Meditation, and Other Poems,
1929–1933,* ed. D. Sutherland, 1956.
Writings and Lectures, 1911–1945, ed. P.
Meyerowitz, 1967.
Selected Operas and Plays of Gertrude Stein, ed.
J. M. Brinnin, 1970.
The Yale Gertrude Stein: Selections, ed.
R. Kostelanetz, 1980.

from Wars I Have Seen

I do not know whether to put in the things I do not remember as well as the things
I do remember. To begin with I was born, that I do not remember but I was told
about it quite often, I was not born during the night but about eight o'clock in the
morning and my father whenever I had anything the matter with me always reproached me by telling me that I had been born a perfect baby. I do not know whether
the four living and the two dead older children had not been born equally perfect
babies at any rate my father never reproached them with it when there was anything
the matter with them. Anyway though I could not remember it from the beginning
there was no doubt that I was the youngest of the children and as such naturally I
had privileges the privilege of petting the privilege of being the youngest one. If
that does happen it is not lost all the rest of one's life, there you are you are privileged, nobody can do anything but take care of you, that is the way I was and that
is the way I still am, and any one who is like that necessarily liked it. I did and
do. . . .

Born that way there is no reason why I should have seen so many wars. I have seen three. The Spanish-American war, the first world war and now the second world war.

There were of course a number of others that did not particularly concern me. The Boer war I remembered that one, the Japanese-Chinese war, and the Russian-Japanese war I remember that one very well too. Each one of these wars I remember for another reason. I suppose it is not so remarkable that I should have seen so many wars having seen a good many countries when I was a baby and having a feeling about countries which I suppose sooner or later since wars are make you be one of those that see them. . . .

In time of war you know much more what children feel than in time of peace, not that children feel more but you have to know more about what they feel. In time of peace what children feel concerns the lives of the children as children but in time of war there is a mingling there is not children's lives and grown up lives there is just lives and so quite naturally you have to know what children feel. And so it being now war and I seeing just incidentally but nevertheless inevitably seeing and knowing of the feeling of children of any age I do not now have to remember about my feeling but just feel the feeling of having been a certain age. And so there was life in California from about six to sixteen, and as each thing happened it did happen. So many things happened but really in remembering not more than one or two a year certainly not one every month certainly not one every week certainly not one every day. Well say two or three a year. Quite enough too to remember because the rest of the time was just the rest of the time.

During these years there was no war and if there was it was not any war of mine. But of course there was history, and there were novels historical novels and so there was in a way war all the time. Why not when there is always war and sometimes a nice war and sometimes an interesting war. And children do not take war seriously as war. War is soldiers and soldiers have not to be war but they have to be soldiers. Which is a nice thing. I remember that the only war that was not soldiers to me but war was the civil war. The other wars were soldiers emotion and something to see. They said things that sounded like soldiers not like war, but the civil war, not the other wars in America, not the revolutionary war or Indian wars they were soldiers not war. . . .

And so to go back to historical wars. I naturally liked history and Shakespeare's plays and historical novels and there was always war. Of course ancient history was full of wars and the Decline and Fall of the Roman Empire[1] was full of war but these did not any of them interest me as wars. English wars interested me, some French wars and the American civil war. And I was right because the American civil war was the prototype of all the wars the two big wars that I have completely lived. Also the American civil war.

Naturally my mother being Baltimore there was the South, and naturally there was the north. My father I never took on in war although he was north.

Of course there were Indian wars naturally there was no cinema then but if there

---

[1] English historian Edward Gibbon (1737–1794) wrote *The Decline and Fall,* a history of the Roman Empire published in six volumes between 1776 and 1788.

had been, Indian wars would have been like that, although one could know people who had been in them and could see them the real Indians on the stage and there was Fenimore Cooper they were not real wars, not as real as some English wars in history and certainly not as real as the American civil war. A very real war.

But naturally all my childhood was not taken up with enjoying past wars, although as an omnivorous reader naturally there was a great deal of war. There was one very funny thing about wars as a child sees it, although there are so many killed there being so many dead is not very real at all, my feeling about that was quite a separate thing and had nothing to do with wars. And that is natural enough. However near a war is it is always not very near. Even when it is here. It is very funny that but it is true. Perhaps if one were a boy it would be different but I do not think so. I think even when men are in a war actually in a war it is not very near, it is here but it is not very near. That is the way it seems to me from all I can hear and from all I can see. But the civil war was quite near. As near as a war can be. But as I say my childhood actual childhood had nothing to do with wars. As it really happened there were no wars just then none at all. There were just at the end of my adolescence but never before. From babyhood to the Boer war there was no war. No war at all.

So I had my childhood and my adolescence without outside of me there being any war.

What is there inside in one that makes one know all about war. You ask questions now why in Russia do not the Germans surrender when they are surrounded. And there is no answer except that perhaps they are afraid to. Perhaps. What is there inside one that makes one know all about war.

Death starts history and fears. And that begins very soon and dies out little by little or not at all or all.

A farmer on a hill said of the Germans, do not say that it had to do with their leaders, they are a people whose fate it is to always choose a man whom they force to lead them in a direction in which they do not want to go.

This same person on this same hill was saying, it was after a thunderstorm and we were talking about it together. Yes he said it is like them to call it a thunder and lightning war. Thunder and lightning a storm of thunder and lightning can cause a fair amount of damage and frightens you enormously but leaves nothing else behind it, no after-effect at all.

And so from the time I was little all through my adolescence although I read and read about wars, if you like history and historical novels you have to and historical plays, but there was no really outside war at least none that I noticed or that anybody around me noticed. . . .

It is funny about wars, they ought to be different but they are not.

In a way that is what makes it nice about France. In one war they upset the Germans by resisting unalterably steadily and patiently and valiantly for four years, in the next war they upset them just as much by not resisting at all and going under completely in six weeks. Well that is what makes them changeable enough to create styles. . . .

It was when I was between twelve and seventeen that I went through the dark and dreadful days of adolescence, in which predominated the fear of death, not so much of death as of dissolution, and naturally is war like that. It is and it is not. One really can say that in war-time there is death death and death but is there dissolution. I wonder. May that not be one of the reasons among so many others why wars go on, and why particularly adolescents need it.

It was a very long time between twelve and seventeen, between Shakespeare and the Boer war which was the first war I knew to be a war, a real war where a country that was a natural country was at war.

And in between there was religion, which too had to do with adolescence and with war.

There is no love interest in these modern wars. I am speaking of the world wars but particularly of the 1939 war, there is no love interest, very little religion and no love interest. Religious people in these world wars are religious but otherwise they are like everybody in what they do and lovers the same way they may be in love but otherwise they are like everybody which was not at all as war was to me from babyhood to 1900, not at all.

From babyhood to fourteen which is the beginning of adolescence, life is mostly taken up with slowly knowing that stars are worlds, that words are ways and that force is strength and that wiles are ways as words are, in other words that one is one and that the others can come to be with that one. That is what is most occupying from babyhood to fourteen, and during that time there are things like having apples given one to take home one for you and the other four for the other four and slowly one by one they are eaten until there is none, and there is the reason for eating the last one because since the other ones are eaten then of course there is no sense in keeping the last one, because then the story has to be told and why should it since after all all your life you can have it as remorse that it has been done. War is like that, it goes on like that it keeps going on like that and soon nobody has anything to eat that is nobody who does not take what does not belong to them and later although there is remorse the very last one has been eaten if not there has to be an explanation and if there is an explanation that does not help remorse nor does it help any one, remorse does not and not eating it does not, and so as I was then so am I now, and war, was not then but the feeling was just the same and eating was just the same in so many ways. A fish bone can even be a worry anything that can happen or has happened or has not happened can be a worry and that is what war is, and so what is the difference between life and war. There is none.

So then between babyhood and fourteen there are all these things, and romantic war with them, not to believe in but to dream.

Between babyhood and fourteen there was frequent change of scene. Modern wars all wars are like that, they go places, where they never heard of in many cases, and between babyhood and fourteen there had been so many changes of scene. And different ways of traveling about, and that also is like war. Just now all the young men of France have to go, they do not know where, some of them run away and when they run away they do not know where and a great many of them are taken away they do not know where and this is all as it was between babyhood and fourteen. Europe and America and railroad and water and stage coach and walking and horse back and in every there was no astonishment and that is the way war is.

I remember being very worried in reading, if anybody in the book died and did not have children because then nobody in that family could be living yet, and if they were not living yet how could they hear what was happening. This always bothered me from that time on until just now and now well now it does seem that the future is not important any more, the world has become so shrunken and it will never be different and so it does not mean much and there is no love interest, it is mostly parents who suffer, perhaps it was like that between babyhood and fourteen.

Dear Life life is strife Claribel used to say, but she did say dear life and in any way it is and she did say life is strife but is it.

It was all that between babyhood and fourteen, and it was the nineteenth century between babyhood and fourteen and the nineteenth century dies hard all centuries do that is why the last war to kill it is so long, it is still being killed now in 1942, the nineteenth century just as the eighteenth century took from the revolution to 1840 to kill, so the nineteenth century is taking from 1914 to 1943 to kill. It is hard to kill a century almost impossible, as was the old joke about mothers-in-law, and centuries get to be like that they get to be wearing like a mother-in-law. So as I was saying from babyhood to fourteen and of course longer much longer it was the nineteenth century and the wars civil domestic and foreign were nineteenth century wars, naturally enough.

Saint George and the Dragon, Siegfried and the dragon, anybody and the dragon, the dragon is always the century any century that anybody is trying to kill, and the worst of it all is that the one that says he is trying to kill the century that has to be killed is the last piece of the century that has to be killed and often the most long-lived, such as a Napoleon a Hitler or a Julius Cæsar the century has to be killed and they are the embodiment the most persistent end of it they are to live while really in its being killed they have to go, only nobody does tell them so, nobody and so they never do know, never do know.

However when I was a baby and then on to fourteen, the nineteenth century was full on.

In the nineteenth century, there was reading, there was evolution, there was war and antiwar which was the same thing, and there was eating. Even now I always resent when in a book they say they sat down to a hearty meal and they do not tell just what it was they ate. In the nineteenth century they often did. And in these days 1943 when eating well actually it is like prohibition one is so certain that one is never going to eat again that one is not greedy but one does eat everything well in these days you would imagine that you would not take pleasure in what the characters in a novel ate when they did eat, but one does enormously, well anyway the nineteenth century, liked to cry liked to try liked to eat liked to pursue evolution and liked war, war and peace peace and war and no more.

When I was then I liked revolutions I liked to eat I liked to eat I liked to cry not in real life but in books in real life there was nothing much to cry about but in books oh dear me, it was wonderful there was so much to cry about and then there was evolution. Evolution was all over my childhood, walks abroad with an evolutionist and the world was full of evolution, biological and botanical evolution, with music as a background for emotion and books as a reality, and a great deal of fresh air as a necessity, and a great deal of eating as an excitement and as an orgy, and now well just then there was no war no actual war anywhere.

In the nineteenth century there was nothing more exciting than climbing a high hill or a mountain and seeing the rain driving across a wide plain or valley with the sun following.

There was nothing more interesting in the nineteenth century than little by little realising the detail of natural selection in insects flowers and birds and butterflies and comparing things and animals and noticing protective coloring nothing more interesting, and this made the nineteenth century what it is, the white man's burden, the gradual domination of the globe as piece by piece it became known and became all of a piece, and the hope of Esperanto or a universal language. Now they can do the radio in so many languages that nobody any longer dreams of a single language, and there should not any longer be dreams of conquest because the globe is all one, anybody can hear everything and everybody can hear the same thing, so what is the use of conquering, and so the nineteenth century now in '43 is slowly coming to an end. . . .

Fifteen to twenty-four, yes there was a war there, the Boer war.

Fifteen the time does not pass slowly but a great deal of time there is nothing to do except stand around, in games and in the evening and in the day, stand around, not even get up and sit down but just stand around. And now, just now, everybody has to grow something to eat or run around to find something to eat now in 1943 so it is not like fifteen, but more like twenty-two, at twenty-two, everybody is very busy just to be you.

And that was the time there was the Boer war and it was a shock and a surprise to know that armies could surrender, not many killed and they could surrender and the war not be over. That was the new thing the Boer war told us, the English could surrender even when there was a smaller percent of them dead than there should have been according to statistics before they did surrender but they did not lose the war. And that was a new thing. When they had surrendered like that in our revolutionary war then the war was over, they lost it but in the Boer war when they did like that the war was not over and they had not lost it and that was a new thing. That went very well with my being twenty-two or something very well indeed.

But at fifteen there was no war when I was fifteen no war at all.

Between fifteen and twenty-two it is not natural that some one surrounded by enemies who would not speak to him ate the only piece of chocolate and they were men not boys and they all wanted it. Naturally enough in 1943. When you are fifteen it is rather wonderful that any one can do such a thing, have enemies who will not speak to him and eat the chocolate cake the only piece and all the enemies who would not speak to him wanting it. It is a funny thing about enemies. It does take such a long time to believe in them believe that they are enemies, and then after all nobody really does seem to believe in them believe that they are enemies. It is about when one is fifteen that one first begins to hear about enemies not in books of course books are full of enemies, but in life. What are enemies and what is war, and are there enemies in war or are they not. From fifteen on one can begin to wonder about such a thing, along with eternity and clouds and beauty and faith. Enemies are not important whether they are real or not, I can remember when I was sixteen seeing a play then modern in which a woman or was it a girl had so many enemies among the other women or girls and could I believe it, no I could not. But he who in 1943 ate the chocolate cake he always believed that he had enemies and that enemies were real even when one was fifteen. But about war well he was not so sure that enemies are enemies during a war. And perhaps they are and perhaps they are not.

Our two servants, they are sisters, we are just in this house a nice big modern house alone against a mountain with a lovely park all full of bushes and big trees, and firs, and the two sisters one a good cook and the other a very perfect chamber maid, they know all about enemies, in war and in peace. Now in 1943 they have forgotten about peace, perhaps there is no such thing but they know all about enemies in war real enemies and enemies that are enemies. It sounds like the same thing but it is not.

There are so many enemies in Shakespeare.

Between fifteen and twenty-four there is so much time in which you do nothing but stand around and wait for it to happen. Now in 1942 in April 1942 there is no longer any standing around waiting for something to happen that is among those who are not fighting of course those who are fighting are like that, they are standing around waiting to do something but everybody else is now as is normal in adult life they are busy not necessarily with everything but they know from day to day that they will do something to-morrow. From fifteen to twenty-three or four nobody does know really know that they will do something to-morrow.

Between the ages of fifteen and twenty-three nobody ever can get back in time.

And now in 1943 at any age nobody can get back in time. And for the same reason, there is so much to do, there is nothing to do, there is no way for anybody to leave home and everybody is on the road and everybody talks to everybody and beside sometimes you know them all of which makes it impossible for anybody to get home in time. In time for what. Well just to get home in time or to get back in time and that is the way it usually is between fifteen and twenty-three. Nobody can get back in time.

War and enemies.

As I was saying there are so many enemies in Shakespeare. . . .

It is funny and when you are fifteen you begin to know that enemies are not what they seem, and then by twenty-four you know enemies are enemies and in between well and then later and now it is not certain that enemies are what they seem.

At fifteen man and animals fruit trees and flowers beginning not to be things to pick but to feel. In the year '43, milk was more and more difficult to have. There was no milk not even skimmed milk and so everybody who could had a goat. We had a goat. When I was fifteen I did not care for goats I like a wall and I had read about fruit trees growing on the sunny side of a wall and I always said when I was fifteen that when I was older and could have it I would have a wall and have fruit trees growing on the sunny side of a wall. I remember the first time I ever saw fruit trees arranged to grow on a wall. It was just after the Spanish American war and we were in Paris for the exposition and McKinley had just been shot and I saw fruit trees trained to grow on the sunny side of walls and it reminded me of when I was fifteen and I wanted to grow fruit trees on sunny sides of the wall and my brother said that he would keep a goat on the wall to eat the fruit trees. And now it is 1943 and there is no milk and we keep a goat and I walk the goat and I like the goat, goats are very willful and I have found out why we like flowers. Because goats pick flowers to eat, and children pick flowers because animals pick flowers to eat and children pick flowers like that.

At fifteen flowers commence to have other meanings, beauty is beauty and flowers are flowers and flowers are no longer flowers as the goat picks them.

Beauty is its own excuse for being, that begins at fifteen that and that enemies are not what they seem, that all belongs at fifteen. At fifteen overbearing that is the need to be the one that has to dominate the other one by not studying, by studying, by fighting, by not fighting, by war, red war, white war, green war and black war. Black war is fighting, red war is war, white war is exciting and green war is disappointing. And at fifteen war has begun, and every one knows that with the sun or without the sun war has begun. . . .

And so the Boer war was disagreeable but not really serious not even for the Boers, like all defeated people they got the best of it, it is better to be defeated and win than win and be defeated. Now here in 1943 it seems so strange to see the enemy weakening just slowly weakening, quickly weakening, not being defeated or anything but just weakening, the French do better, they get defeated but they do not weaken, while the Germans do not get defeated they weaken, and when they weaken enough to go out like a lamp with no oil, or with no wire, out, it does not die it just weakens to nothing. Until they weaken everybody says about them but they are still strong, and then they weaken. There you are, that is to say here we are 1943.

After the Spanish-American war there was the Boer war, and that was no longer fifteen that was older, I was in the medical school then the first year and I went out to San Francisco to see my brother Mike who had just been married.

The Spanish-American war was the first to me modern war. Modern is like realism, modern is always modern to some one as realism is always real to some one, not to some one but to a great many at one time. Modern, how nicely it is modern now then and when.

What was modern then was seeing all the middle western men, young men, boys too many, going out to San Francisco, and catching everything and then going off in boats to the Philippines. I was just reading Shakespeare's Henry the Fifth and I found it astonishing how easily they talked of transporting ten thousand, fifteen thousand even twenty thousand soldiers across the water from England to France. How when they had such comparatively little tonnage, did they get so many of them across, how did they, well anyway so they say they did. Call it modern if you like but soldiers any quantity of them at any time can be carried across the ocean, any quantity of them at any time and now here in June 1943, we are waiting for them, waiting for them, to bring us shoes and stockings and dental floss, here in the country we have plenty to eat although we would like more cake and sugar and butter but still here in the country having a goat and chickens we do have plenty to eat and fish, we do have plenty to eat. But one does get so tired of seeing everybody planting and growing vegetables you think how nice it will be to have those happy days come back when vegetables grew not in the ground but in tins. A vegetable garden in the beginning looks so promising and then after all little by little it grows nothing but vegetables, nothing, nothing but vegetables.

Well anyway the Spanish-American war was modern but it was completely nineteenth century, there was nothing but the question of sea power and whose sea power was it, we all read a book that told us it, but then we had known it anyway, because of Nelson, and now we were doing it again, and it was very exciting, we were all finding out about the difficulty of having to have two fleets a Pacific one and an Atlantic one, and we were all getting to feel that we were to be, well there it was still nineteenth century completely nineteenth century and we were not thinking about a twentieth century, and we were so excited that we were not realising that the nineteenth century was beginning to be over, not the least bit in the world. I was young then but I can still see those young men in San Francisco, those middle-western young men of twenty and twenty-one, with their undeveloped necks, their rather doughy faces, I see why they call them dough-boys,[2] they are like that between twenty and twenty-one, they go to sleep anywhere sitting or standing, their heads and their mouths and their eyes can go to sleep anywhere, and open or not open, that is what it is to be twenty or twenty-one, and now here and now, it is just the same, the young of twenty-one, the young Frenchmen of twenty-one are all being deported to Germany, two came to see me to say good-bye to ask how I could encourage them and all I could say was try to study them and learn their language and get to know their literature, think of yourselves as a tourist and not as a prisoner, and they were worried and nervous and they said will the Americans like it if we think of them like that, sure I said all the Americans want is to make you free, and they said yes we know that. It makes me feel very very much like that, I used to say to any Frenchman or Frenchwoman who complained of anything, I said but every time I go out in the village of Bilignin there I see all your young men whatever is happening they are still there and that is everything that they are not gone. But now they are gone and going. Some of them betake themselves to the mountains others are conspiring, the son of our dentist a boy of eighteen has just been taken because he was helping and will he be shot or not. Oh dear. We all cry. But there is nothing to do but wait for us to come nothing to do. And they look so, I saw a train full of them, everybody was handing them up wine and bread, although nobody has much of it for themselves or to give them, and there they were with the gendarmes,[3] going away. And they were awake then and pretty soon they will be tired out and go to sleep any way that it is possible to be sleeping, in a chair or standing or in any way.

It is funny but my memory of those middle-western boys going out to the Philippines was that they were just like these French boys twenty and twenty-one going off to Germany, as deported and held away from every one. Dear me.

So that was realism. Anything is realism but that certainly was realism. . . .

So the Spanish-American war and seeing all those middle-western men in San Francisco, made me realise what realism is.

Just to-night June 1943 I was out walking in the twilight in the mountain village of Culoz where I live now and my dog Basket was running around and a young man in working clothes said he is a nice dog but I have been whistling to him and he wont come. Oh I said you have to do more than whistle, you have to talk English and he said my father could and I could too once but I now have forgotten. And I said but how is that not that you have forgotten but that your father talked English, that he said is very simple he is an American, ah I said yes, he came to France in the last war as a soldier he married a Frenchwoman, he got a good job at Chaumont and he stayed,

[2] United States Army infantry soldiers. The expression was coined during the Mexican War of the mid-nineteenth century and was in common usage through World War I.

[3] Literally, "men of arms"; French policemen.

and in '38 we intended to go away but my mother fell ill and we did not leave. And she, I said, oh she is dead, and he, oh he is in a concentration camp when America came into the war they came and took him, and you, we are four brothers and a sister, and the oldest is an actor in the Comedie Française and the second is a plumber and the third is head butcher in a camp of youth and here I am working for farmers and my name is Robert Nelson White and I looked as if I was not sure that all he said was so and he said here are my papers, they do not spell white right, but my name there is Robert White, I left out the Nelson all right. And it all made me feel a little funny anything these days these strange days can make you feel a little funny so I shook hands with him and we went up Basket and I up the hill and he Robert Nelson White went on down, down the hill.

Now all that made me feel all the more how different was that Spanish-American war. I asked Robert Nelson White if his father was a Frenchman by blood, if his grandfather or grandmother either one was French but no he said he was always American his people never had been anything but American and his little sister of fourteen was at school and he and his brother had crossed the lines at night to come into the free zone and here he was.

In the Spanish-American war romance was simple and realistic like the young Californians who went to the war and General King wrote novels about it and in one he said and I threw the bridle of my horse to my orderly Ned Hanford, and it was Ned Hanford and when he read these simple words, he had a thrill he always had a thrill. That was the way it was then in the Spanish-American war. It was then that they began to think about realism. The Red Badge of Courage by Crane, and any simple description of war as done by the Russians, later on a naval battle in the next war, the Russo-Japanese war, which described it just as it was not as it felt or looked. But anyway there they were they middle-western boys in San Francisco, and there was Chinatown and there was the French quarter, and there were the Lurline baths and there was everything that they never had seen before. It is always that way in war, always.

And now in June 1943, it is trying, there are so many sad things happening, so many in prison, so many going away, our dentist's son and he was only eighteen and he should have been taking his entrance university examinations and he with others in a camion took shoes and clothes and weapons to give to the young men who had taken themselves to the mountains, to avoid being sent away and what has happened to him and to them. I have just met a very charming woman courageous and lives in an old castle and has five children and the youngest one is twenty-one and he has gone, she has never lost any money but life is always dearer and she and her children have worked very hard to keep their castle sheared their own sheep, and everything, and now she said, of course she would not mind Christian's going away, that is to say not to mind if it were not the times are so uncertain and so troubling, and he is very sweet and he is big and tall and very winning and since he was born there have never been three months without their seeing him, never and now, well I said he hopes to come back for the vintage and she had clear eyes very wide open and she said yes.

And all that makes one think more and more of the strangeness and the unreality of those middle-western boys who were naturally called dough-boys, being in San

Francisco, and then going to the Philippines, when they got to the Philippines and back again I never saw them so I do not really know what happened to them, by that time we were all interested in realism in literature, and that kind of went on until 1938, when it was all over, there was an end of the nineteenth century and realism was the last thing the nineteenth century did completely. Anybody can understand that there is no point in being realistic about here and now, no use at all not any, and so it is not the nineteenth but the twentieth century, there is no realism now, life is not real it is not earnest, it is strange which is an entirely different matter. . . .

Realism.

After all there has to be realism realism in romance and in novels and the reason why is this. Novels have to resemble something and in order that they do there must be realism. Of course all writers had had realism, writers and readers always have a realism, after all living is in a way always real, that is to say what one hears and sees, even what one feels is in a way always real, but the realism of the present seems new because the realism of the past is no longer real.

And so just at the time of the Spanish-American war, there commenced the difference between Kipling's realism, which was romanticism, but real enough, and the French and Russian realism, which was so real that it was real enough. Was it real as anybody could know realism, or was it not. Just at the time of the Spanish-American war and later the Russo-Japanese war this question of realism was becoming the vital question for Americans who having a land with a clear light manufacturing light and resistant steel, their life needed a clean and resistant realism but at the same time they needed to move around and you cannot keep moving around without feeling romantic. The nineteenth century was then in its full strength and everybody knew it, and everybody knew that when a thing is like that you have to begin to try to forget it, and they all began to they all began to begin to forget it. . . .

This is my scientific history. Not Saint Odile, but this, that I am about to tell.

August 1943. Here we can see every night when the moon is bright and even when it is not, we cannot see them but we hear them, they hum and then from time to time they drop a light and they give us all a very great deal of delight. And why. Because they are going to drop bombs on the Italians. Anybody can like an Italian but just the same we can have a great deal of pleasure in hearing all these airplanes hum and see them drop lights on their way to bomb Italians. Why we all say do they not give in. Not so exciting perhaps but more useful, useful that is if you want to go on living in a country that has not been overwhelmed by destruction. Last night just before the airplanes came there was a complete eclipse of the moon, the shadow of the earth fell on the moon, none too soon and then slowly it passed away, it was very nice, but none of the newspapers and none of the radios mentioned it. Eclipses are an amusement for peace time and yet all the same said my neighbor, she is a country-woman, it makes one think of all those worlds turning around and around. Yes I said it is more terrifying even than war. Yes she said. And it was twelve o'clock at night and the moon was shining bright again and we went to bed and a little after we heard the airplanes humming and we saw the lights dropping and then we shut out the moon-light and then we were sleeping. All this is an introduction to the nineteenth century feeling about science.

To believe in progress and in science you had to know what science was and what progress might be. Having been born in the nineteenth century it was natural enough to know what science was. Darwin[4] was still alive and Huxley[5] and Agassiz[6] and after all they all made the difference of before and after. And now in 1943 none of it means more than it did. Not so much more as not more. Not more at all.

And I began with evolution. Most pleasant and exciting and decisive. It justified peace and justified war. It also justified life and it also justified death and it also justified life. Evolution did all that. And now. Evolution is no longer interesting. It is historical now and no longer actual. Not even pleasant or exciting, not at all. To those of us who were interested in science then it had to do tremendously with the history of the world, the history of all animals, the history of death and life, and all that had to do with the round world. Evolution was as exciting as the discovery of America, by Columbus quite as exciting, and quite as much an opening up and a limiting, quite as much. By that I mean that discovering America, by reasoning and then finding, opened up a new world and at the same time closed the circle, there was no longer any beyond. Evolution did the same thing, it opened up the history of all animals vegetables and minerals, and man, and at the same time it made them all confined, confined within a circle, no excitement of creation any more. It is funny all this and this was my childhood and youth and beginning of existence. War oh yes war but logical and incessant war, and peace oh yes, peace because if war is completely understood then peace was the ideal. It was just like that.

Stars are not really more than just what they look like. If they are then are they really realer than war. It is just that that makes the twentieth century, know what science teaches and whether it is or whether it is not what science teaches, since war is really and therefore it is what it is, that is everybody gets to meet anybody friends and enemies we have then now enemies in the house and in the barn, and it does not make any difference about the stars and it does not make any difference about war, only really it does make a difference about war seeing the trains pass with the enemy on them yes it does, but the stars whether they are what they look like or what science teaches, does it make any difference and anybody can answer that it does not.

I did live in the nineteenth century and the difference was that then the answer was that it did make a difference, that the stars were what science teaches and now in August 1943 it does not.

Naturally if you were born in the nineteenth century when evolution first began to be known, and everything was being understood, really understood everybody knew that if everything was really being and going to be understood, and if everything was understood then there would be progress and if there was going to be progress there would not be any wars, and if there were not any wars then everything could be and would be understood, and even if death and life were not understood and eternity and beginning was not understood well that is to say if they were not understood more than science understood them better after all except in the unhappi-

---

[4] Charles Darwin (1809–1882), English scientist who formulated what is commonly known today as the "theory of evolution," which he explained in *The Origin of the Species* (1859).

[5] Thomas Henry Huxley (1825–1895), also an Englishman and one of three scientists whose approval Darwin sought before publishing *The Origin of the Species;* Huxley was one of Darwin's chief supporters in the controversy surrounding this work.

[6] Louis Agassiz (1807–1873), Swiss-born naturalist, educator, and author, was an influential opponent of Darwin's theory of evolution.

ness of adolescence better not think about that. That was what the nineteenth century knew to be true, and they wanted it to be like that. To be sure there were a great many wars, but on the other hand there was a great deal of civilising going on so much so that by the time the twentieth century began almost any one could read and write, and now in the twentieth century anybody can listen to the radio, in any language and everybody is civilised enough to do that, but wars are more than ever and now everybody knows that although everybody is civilised there is no progress and everybody knows even though anybody flies higher and higher they cannot explain eternity any more than before, and everybody can persecute anybody just as much if not more than ever, it is rather ridiculous so much science, so much civilisation that is so much reading and writing and listening to the radio, and they persecute anybody, and put books on the index, that and ban them publicly just like that. It is funny. . . .

1945

from The Autobiography of Alice B. Toklas

from **6: The War**

Americans living in Europe before the war never really believed that there was going to be war. Gertrude Stein always tells about the little janitor's boy who, playing in the court, would regularly every couple of years assure her that papa was going to the war. Once some cousins of hers were living in Paris, they had a country girl as a servant. It was the time of the russian-japanese war and they were all talking about the latest news. Terrified she dropped the platter and cried, and are the germans at the gates.

William Cook's father was an Iowan who at seventy years of age was making his first trip in Europe in the summer of nineteen fourteen. When the war was upon them he refused to believe it and explained that he could understand a family fighting among themselves, in short a civil war, but not a serious war with one's neighbours.

Gertrude Stein in 1913 and 1914 had been very interested reading the newspapers. She rarely read french newspapers, she never read anything in french, and she always read the Herald. That winter she added the Daily Mail. She liked to read about the suffragettes and she liked to read about Lord Roberts' campaign for compulsory military service in England. Lord Roberts had been a favourite hero of hers early in her life. His Forty-One Years In India was a book she often read and she had seen Lord Roberts when she and her brother, then taking a college vacation, had seen Edward the Seventh's coronation procession. She read the Daily Mail, although, as she said, she was not interested in Ireland.

We went to England July fifth and went according to programme to see John Lane at his house Sunday afternoon.

There were a number of people there and they were talking of many things but some of them were talking about war. One of them, some one told me he was an editorial writer on one of the big London dailies, was bemoaning the fact that he would not be able to eat figs in August in Provence as was his habit. Why not, asked some one. Because of the war, he answered. Some one else, Walpole or his brother I think it was, said that there was no hope of beating Germany as she had such an excellent system, all her railroad trucks were numbered in connection with locomotives and switches. But, said the eater of figs, that is all very well as long as the trucks remain in Germany on their own lines and switches, but in an aggressive war they will leave the frontiers of Germany and then, well I promise you then there will be a great deal of numbered confusion.

This is all I remember definitely of that Sunday afternoon in July.

As we were leaving, John Lane said to Gertrude Stein that he was going out of town for a week and he made a rendezvous with her in his office for the end of July, to sign the contract for Three Lives. I think, he said, in the present state of affairs I would rather begin with that than with something more entirely new. I have confidence in that book. Mrs. Lane is very enthusiastic and so are the readers.

Having now ten days on our hands we decided to accept the invitation of Mrs. Mirlees, Hope's mother, and spend a few days in Cambridge. We went there and thoroughly enjoyed ourselves.

It was a most comfortable house to visit. Gertrude Stein liked it, she could stay in her room or in the garden as much as she liked without hearing too much conversation. The food was excellent, scotch food, delicious and fresh, and it was very amusing meeting all the University of Cambridge dignitaries. We were taken into all the gardens and invited into many of the homes. It was lovely weather, quantities of roses, morris-dancing by all the students and girls and generally delightful. We were invited to lunch at Newnham, Miss Jane Harrison, who had been Hope Mirlees' pet enthusiasm, was much interested in meeting Gertrude Stein. We sat up on the dais with the faculty and it was very awe inspiring. The conversation was not however particularly amusing. Miss Harrison and Gertrude Stein did not particularly interest each other.

We had been hearing a good deal about Doctor and Mrs. Whitehead.[1] They no longer lived in Cambridge. The year before Doctor Whitehead had left Cambridge to go to London University. They were to be in Cambridge shortly and they were to dine at the Mirlees'. They did and I met my third genius.

It was a pleasant dinner. I sat next to Housman, the Cambridge poet, and we talked about fishes and David Starr Jordan but all the time I was more interested in watching Doctor Whitehead. Later we went into the garden and he came and sat next to me and we talked about the sky in Cambridge.

Gertrude Stein and Doctor Whitehead and Mrs. Whitehead all became interested in each other. Mrs. Whitehead asked us to dine at her house in London and then to spend a week end, the last week end in July with them in their country home in Lockridge, near Salisbury Plain. We accepted with pleasure.

[1] Alfred North Whitehead (1861–1947), English philosopher and mathematician, was co-author, with Bertrand Russell, of *Principia Mathematica,* author of *Science in the Modern World* (1925), and proponent of the technique of "extensive abstraction" (the derivation of concepts from conscious perception).

We went back to London and had a lovely time. We were ordering some comfortable chairs and a comfortable couch covered with chintz to replace some of the italian furniture that Gertrude Stein's brother had taken with him. This took a great deal of time. We had to measure ourselves into the chairs and into the couch and to choose chintz that would go with the pictures, all of which we successfully achieved. These chairs and this couch, and they are comfortable, in spite of war came to the door one day in January, nineteen fifteen at the rue de Fleurus and were greeted by us with the greatest delight. One needed such comforting and such comfort in those days. We dined with the Whiteheads and liked them more than ever and they liked us more than ever and were kind enough to say so.

Gertrude Stein kept her appointment with John Lane at the Bodley Head. They had a very long conversation, this time so long that I quite exhausted all the shop windows of that region for quite a distance, but finally Gertrude Stein came out with a contract. It was a gratifying climax.

Then we took the train to Lockridge to spend the week end with the Whiteheads. We had a week-end trunk, we were very proud of our week-end trunk, we had used it on our first visit and now we were actively using it again. As one of my friends said to me later, they asked you to spend the week end and you stayed six weeks. We did.

There was quite a house party when we arrived, some Cambridge people, some young men, the younger son of the Whiteheads, Eric, then fifteen years old but very tall and flower-like and the daughter Jessie just back from Newnham. There could not have been much serious thought of war because they were all talking of Jessie Whitehead's coming trip to Finland. Jessie always made friends with foreigners from strange places, she had a passion for geography and a passion for the glory of the British Empire. She had a friend, a finn, who had asked her to spend the summer with her people in Finland and had promised Jessie a possible uprising against Russia. Mrs. Whitehead was hesitating but had practically consented. There was an older son North who was away at the time.

Then suddenly, as I remember, there were the conferences to prevent the war, Lord Grey and the russian minister of foreign affairs. And then before anything further could happen the ultimatum to France. Gertrude Stein and I were completely miserable as was Evelyn Whitehead, who had french blood and who had been raised in France and had strong french sympathies. Then came the days of the invasion of Belgium and I can still hear Doctor Whitehead's gentle voice reading the papers out loud and then all of them talking about the destruction of Louvain and how they must help the brave little belgians. Gertrude Stein desperately unhappy said to me, where is Louvain. Don't you know, I said. No, she said, nor do I care, but where is it.

Our week end was over and we told Mrs. Whitehead that we must leave. But you cannot get back to Paris now, she said. No, we answered, but we can stay in London. Oh no, she said, you must stay with us until you can get back to Paris. She was very sweet and we were very unhappy and we liked them and they liked us and we agreed to stay. And then to our infinite relief England came into the war. . . .

Evelyn Whitehead was very busy planning war work and helping every one and I as far as possible helped her. Gertrude Stein and Doctor Whitehead walked endlessly around the country. They talked of philosophy and history, it was during these days that Gertrude Stein realised how completely it was Doctor Whitehead and not Russell who had had the ideas for their great book.[2] Doctor Whitehead, the gentlest and most simply generous of human beings never claimed anything for himself and enormously admired anyone who was brilliant, and Russell undoubtedly was brilliant.

Gertrude Stein used to come back and tell me about these walks and the country still the same as in the days of Chaucer, with the green paths of the early britons that could still be seen in long stretches, and the triple rainbows of that strange summer. They used, Doctor Whitehead and Gertrude Stein, to have long conversations with game-keepers and mole-catchers. The mole-catcher had said, but sir, England has never been in a war but that she has been victorious. Doctor Whitehead turned to Gertrude Stein with a gentle smile. I think we may say so, he said. The game-keeper, when Doctor Whitehead seemed discouraged said to him, but Doctor Whitehead, England is the predominant nation, is she not. I hope she is, yes I hope she is, replied Doctor Whitehead gently.

The germans were getting nearer and nearer Paris. One day Doctor Whitehead said to Gertrude Stein, they were just going through a rough little wood and he was helping her, have you any copies of your writings or are they all in Paris. They are all in Paris, she said. I did not like to ask, said Doctor Whitehead, but I have been worrying.

The germans were getting nearer and nearer Paris and the last day Gertrude Stein could not leave her room, she sat and mourned. She loved Paris, she thought neither of manuscripts nor of pictures, she thought only of Paris and she was desolate. I came up to her room, I called out, it is alright Paris is saved, the germans are in retreat. She turned away and said, don't tell me these things. But it's true, I said, it is true. And then we wept together. . . .

I remember the leaving London very little, I cannot even remember whether it was day-light or not but it must have been because when we were on the channel boat it was day-light. The boat was crowded. There were quantities of belgian soldiers and officers escaped from Antwerp, all with tired eyes. It was our first experience of the tired but watchful eyes of soldiers. We finally were able to arrange a seat for Mrs. Whitehead who had been ill and soon we were in France. Mrs. Whitehead's papers were so overpowering that there were no delays and soon we were in the train and about ten o'clock at night we were in Paris. We took a taxi and drove through Paris, beautiful and unviolated, to the rue de Fleurus. We were once more at home. . . .

from 7: After the War

1919–1932

We were, in these days as I look back at them, constantly seeing people.

It is a confused memory those first years after the war and very difficult to think back and remember what happened before or after something else. Picasso once said,

---

[2] *Principia Mathematica* (1910–1913), a rigorous development of pure mathematics through formal logic.

I have already told, when Gertrude Stein and he were discussing dates, you forget that when we were young an awful lot happened in a year. During the years just after the war as I look in order to refresh my memory over the bibliography of Gertrude Stein's work, I am astonished when I realise how many things happened in a year. Perhaps we were not so young then but there were a great many young in the world and perhaps that comes to the same thing.

The old crowd had disappeared. Matisse was now permanently in Nice and in any case although Gertrude Stein and he were perfectly good friends when they met, they practically never met. This was the time when Gertrude Stein and Picasso were not seeing each other. They always talked with the tenderest friendship about each other to any one who had known them both but they did not see each other. Guillaume Apollinaire was dead. Braque and his wife we saw from time to time, he and Picasso by this time were fairly bitterly on the outs. I remember one evening Man Ray brought a photograph that he had made of Picasso to the house and Braque happened to be there. The photograph was being passed around and when it came to Braque he looked at it and said, I ought to know who that gentleman is, je dois connaître ce monsieur. It was a period this and a very considerable time afterward that Gertrude Stein celebrated under the title, Of Having for a Long Time Not Continued to be Friends. . . .

We began to meet new people all the time.

Some one told us, I have forgotten who, that an american woman had started a lending library of english books in our quarter. We had in those days of economy given up Mudie's, but there was the American Library which supplied us a little, but Gertrude Stein wanted more. We investigated and we found Sylvia Beach.[3] Sylvia Beach was very enthusiastic about Gertrude Stein and they became friends. She was Sylvia Beach's first annual subscriber and Sylvia Beach was proportionately proud and grateful. Her little place was in a little street near the Ecole de Médecine. It was not then much frequented by americans. There was the author of Beebie the Beebeist and there was the niece of Marcel Schwob and there were a few stray irish poets. We saw a good deal of Sylvia those days, she used to come to the house and also go out into the country with us in the old car. We met Adrienne Monnier and she brought Valéry Larbaud to the house and they were all very interested in Three Lives and Valéry Larbaud, so we understood, meditated translating it. It was at this time that Tristan Tzara first appeared in Paris. Adrienne Monnier was much excited by his advent. Picabia had found him in Switzerland during the war and they had together created dadaism, and out of dadaism, with a great deal of struggle and quarrelling came surréalisme.

Tzara came to the house, I imagine Picabia brought him but I am not quite certain. I have always found it very difficult to understand the stories of his violence and his wickedness, at least I found it difficult then because Tzara when he came to the house sat beside me at the tea table and talked to me like a pleasant and not very exciting cousin.

[3] American bookseller and publisher (1887–1962). An expatriate in Paris, she ran the famous Shakespeare & Co. bookstore, located at 12 rue de l'Odéon, and encouraged new, young writers of all nationalities. Beach was the first publisher of James Joyce's *Ulysses* (1922), which was banned in the United States for over ten years. Her autobiography *Shakespeare and Company*, was published in 1959.

Adrienne Monnier wanted Sylvia to move to the rue de l'Odéon and Sylvia hesitated but finally she did so and as a matter of fact we did not see her very often afterward. They gave a party just after Sylvia moved in and we went and there Gertrude Stein first discovered that she had a young Oxford following. There were several young Oxford men there and they were awfully pleased to meet her and they asked her to give them some manuscripts and they published them that year nineteen twenty, in the Oxford Magazine.

Sylvia Beach from time to time brought groups of people to the house, groups of young writers and some older women with them. It was at that time that Ezra Pound came, no that was brought about in another way. She later ceased coming to the house but she sent word that Sherwood Anderson had come to Paris and wanted to see Gertrude Stein and might he come. Gertrude Stein sent back word that she would be very pleased and he came with his wife and Rosenfeld, the musical critic.

For some reason or other I was not present on this occasion, some domestic complication in all probability, at any rate when I did come home Gertrude Stein was moved and pleased as she has very rarely been. Gertrude Stein was in those days a little bitter, all her unpublished manuscripts, and no hope of publication or serious recognition. Sherwood Anderson came and quite simply and directly as is his way told her what he thought of her work and what it had meant to him in his development. He told it to her then and what was even rarer he told it in print immediately after. Gertrude Stein and Sherwood Anderson have always been the best of friends but I do not believe even he realises how much his visit meant to her. It was he who thereupon wrote the introduction to Geography and Plays. . . .

As I have said there was Broom.[4]

Before the war we had known a young fellow, not known him much but a little; Elmer Harden, who was in Paris studying music. During the war we heard that Elmer Harden had joined the french army and had been badly wounded. It was rather an amazing story. Elmer Harden had been nursing french wounded in the american hospital and one of his patients, a captain with an arm fairly disabled, was going back to the front. Elmer Harden could not content himself any longer nursing. He said to Captain Peter, I am going with you. But it is impossible, said Captain Peter. But I am, said Elmer stubbornly. So they took a taxi and they went to the war office and to a dentist and I don't know where else, but by the end of the week Captain Peter had rejoined and Elmer Harden was in his regiment as a soldier. He fought well and was wounded. After the war we met him again and then we met often. He and the lovely flowers he used to send us were a great comfort in those days just after the peace. He and I always say that he and I will be the last people of our generation to remember the war. I am afraid we both of us have already forgotten it a little. Only the other day though Elmer announced that he had had a great triumph, he had made Captain Peter and Captain Peter is a breton admit that it was a nice war. Up to this time when he had said to Captain Peter, it was a nice war, Captain Peter had

---

[4] *Broom* was published from November 1921 to January 1924 and was originally edited by Harold A. Loeb and Alfred Kreymborg. The latter has been called the patron saint of the little-magazine movement, of which *Broom* is one of the best-known and more lavish examples. The term "little magazine" is usually applied specifically to small, short-lived, avant-garde publications that encourage innovation and experimentation as opposed to orthodoxy and tradition. *Broom* takes its name from the proverb "A new broom sweeps clean."

not answered, but this time when Elmer said, it was a nice war, Captain Peter said, yes Elmer, it was a nice war.

Kate Buss came from the same town as Elmer, from Medford, Mass. She was in Paris and she came to see us. I do not think Elmer introduced her but she did come to see us. She was much interested in the writings of Gertrude Stein and owned everything that up to that time could be bought. She brought Kreymborg to see us. Kreymborg had come to Paris with Harold Loeb to start Broom. Kreymborg and his wife came to the house frequently. He wanted very much to run The Long Gay Book, the thing Gertrude Stein had written just after The Making of Americans, as a serial. Of course Harold Loeb would not consent to that. Kreymborg used to read out the sentences from this book with great gusto. He and Gertrude Stein had a bond of union beside their mutual liking because the Grafton Press that had printed Three Lives had printed his first book and about the same time.

Kate Buss brought lots of people to the house. She brought Djuna Barnes and Mina Loy and they had wanted to bring James Joyce but they didn't. We were glad to see Mina whom we had known in Florence as Mina Haweis. Mina brought Glenway Wescott on his first trip to Europe. Glenway impressed us greatly by his english accent. Hemingway explained. He said, when you matriculate at the University of Chicago you write down just what accent you will have and they give it to you when you graduate. You can have a sixteenth century or modern, whatever you like. Glenway left behind him a silk cigarette case with his initials, we kept it until he came back again and then gave it to him.

Mina also brought Robert McAlmon. McAlmon was very nice in those days, very mature and very good-looking. It was much later that he published The Making of Americans in the Contact press and that everybody quarrelled. But that is Paris, except that as a matter of fact Gertrude Stein and he never became friends again.

Kate Buss brought Ernest Walsh, he was very young then and very feverish and she was very worried about him. We met him later with Hemingway and then in Belley, but we never knew him very well.

We met Ezra Pound at Grace Lounsbery's house, he came home to dinner with us and he stayed and he talked about japanese prints among other things. Gertrude Stein liked him but did not find him amusing. She said he was a village explainer, excellent if you were a village, but if you were not, not. Ezra also talked about T. S. Eliot. It was the first time any one had talked about T.S. at the house. Pretty soon everybody talked about T.S. Kitty Buss talked about him and much later Hemingway talked about him as the Major. Considerably later Lady Rothermere talked about him and invited Gertrude Stein to come and meet him. They were founding the Criterion.[5] We had met Lady Rothermere through Muriel Draper whom we had seen again for the first time after many years. Gertrude Stein was not particularly anxious to go to Lady Rothermere's and meet T. S. Eliot, but we all insisted she should, and she gave a doubtful yes. I had no evening dress to wear for this occasion and started to make one. The bell rang and in walked Lady Rothermere and T.S.

[5] Another of the so-called little magazines, published in London in 1922 and edited for a time by the poet T. S. Eliot.

Eliot and Gertrude Stein had a solemn conversation, mostly about split infinitives and other grammatical solecisms and why Gertrude Stein used them. Finally Lady Rothermere and Eliot rose to go and Eliot said that if he printed anything of Gertrude Stein's in the Criterion it would have to be her very latest thing. They left and Gertrude Stein said, don't bother to finish your dress, now we don't have to go, and she began to write a portrait of T. S. Eliot and called it the fifteenth of November, that being this day and so there could be no doubt but that it was her latest thing. It was all about wool is wool and silk is silk or wool is woollen and silk is silken. She sent it to T. S. Eliot and he accepted it but naturally he did not print it.

Then began a long correspondence, not between Gertrude Stein and T. S. Eliot, but between T. S. Eliot's secretary and myself. We each addressed the other as Sir, I signing myself A. B. Toklas and she signing initials. It was only considerably afterwards that I found out that his secretary was not a young man. I don't know whether she ever found out that I was not.

In spite of all this correspondence nothing happened and Gertrude Stein mischievously told the story to all the english people coming to the house and at that moment there were a great many english coming in and out. At any rate finally there was a note, it was now early spring, from the Criterion asking would Miss Stein mind if her contribution appeared in the October number. She replied that nothing could be more suitable than the fifteenth of November on the fifteenth of October.

Once more a long silence and then this time came proof of the article. We were surprised but returned the proof promptly. Apparently a young man had sent it without authority because very shortly came an apologetic letter saying that there had been a mistake, the article was not to be printed just yet. This was also told to the passing english with the result that after all it was printed. Thereafter it was reprinted in the Georgian Stories. Gertrude Stein was delighted when later she was told that Eliot had said in Cambridge that the work of Gertrude Stein was very fine but not for us.

But to come back to Ezra. Ezra did come back and he came back with the editor of The Dial.[6] This time it was worse than japanese prints, it was much more violent. In his surprise at the violence Ezra fell out of Gertrude Stein's favourite little armchair, the one I have since tapestried with Picasso designs, and Gertrude Stein was furious. Finally Ezra and the editor of The Dial left, nobody too well pleased. Gertrude Stein did not want to see Ezra again. Ezra did not quite see why. He met Gertrude Stein one day near the Luxembourg gardens and said, but I do want to come to see you. I am so sorry, answered Gertrude Stein, but Miss Toklas has a bad tooth and beside we are busy picking wild flowers. All of which was literally true, like all of Gertrude Stein's literature, but it upset Ezra, and we never saw him again. . . .

The first thing that happened when we were back in Paris was Hemingway with a letter of introduction from Sherwood Anderson.

I remember very well the impression I had of Hemingway that first afternoon. He

[6] Published, with numerous changes in editorial policy, from 1880 to 1929. In 1916 *The Dial* was moved from Chicago to New York and began publishing the work of new writers. In 1919 it began to publish the works of internationally known authors. This, the most famous of the so-called little magazines, is the third of four with this name to have appeared in America since 1840.

was an extraordinarily good-looking young man, twenty-three years old. It was not long after that that everybody was twenty-six. It became the period of being twenty-six. During the next two or three years all the young men were twenty-six years old. It was the right age apparently for that time and place. There were one or two under twenty, for example George Lynes but they did not count as Gertrude Stein carefully explained to them. If they were young men they were twenty-six. Later on, much later on they were twenty-one and twenty-two.

So Hemingway was twenty-three, rather foreign looking, with passionately interested, rather than interesting eyes. He sat in front of Gertrude Stein and listened and looked.

They talked then, and more and more, a great deal together. He asked her to come and spend an evening in their apartment and look at his work. Hemingway had then and has always a very good instinct for finding apartments in strange but pleasing localities and good femmes de ménage and good food. This his first apartment was just off the place du Tertre. We spent the evening there and he and Gertrude Stein went over all the writing he had done up to that time. He had begun the novel that it was inevitable he would begin and there were the little poems afterwards printed by McAlmon in the Contract Edition. Gertrude Stein rather liked the poems, they were direct, Kiplingesque, but the novel she found wanting. There is a great deal of description in this, she said, and not particularly good description. Begin over again and concentrate, she said.

Hemingway was at this time Paris correspondent for a canadian newspaper. He was obliged there to express what he called the canadian viewpoint.

He and Gertrude Stein used to walk together and talk together a great deal. One day she said to him, look here, you say you and your wife have a little money between you. Is it enough to live on if you live quietly. Yes, he said. Well, she said, then do it. If you keep on doing newspaper work you will never see things, you will only see words and that will not do, that is of course if you intend to be a writer. Hemingway said he undoubtedly intended to be a writer. . . .

In those early days Hemingway liked all his contemporaries except Cummings. He accused Cummings of having copied everything, not from anybody but from somebody. Gertrude Stein who had been much impressed by The Enormous Room said that Cummings did not copy, he was the natural heir of the New England tradition with its aridity and its sterility, but also with its individuality. They disagreed about this. They also disagreed about Sherwood Anderson. Gertrude Stein contended that Sherwood Anderson had a genius for using a sentence to convey a direct emotion, this was in the great american tradition, and that really except Sherwood there was no one in America who could write a clear and passionate sentence. Hemingway did not believe this, he did not like Sherwood's taste. Taste has nothing to do with sentences, contended Gertrude Stein. She also added that Fitzgerald was the only one of the younger writers who wrote naturally in sentences.

Gertrude Stein and Fitzgerald are very peculiar in their relation to each other. Gertrude Stein had been very much impressed by This Side of Paradise. She read it when it came out and before she knew any of the young american writers. She said of it that it was this book that really created for the public the new generation. She has never changed her opinion about this. She thinks this equally true of *The Great Gatsby*. She thinks Fitzgerald will be read when many of his well known contemporaries are forgotten. Fitzgerald always says that he thinks Gertrude Stein says these things just to annoy him by making him think that she means them, and he adds in his favourite way, and her doing it is the cruellest thing I ever heard. They always however have a very good time when they meet. And the last time they met they had a good time with themselves and Hemingway.

Then there was McAlmon. McAlmon had one quality that appealed to Gertrude Stein, abundance, he could go on writing, but she complained that it was dull.

There was also Glenway Wescott but Glenway Wescott at no time interested Gertrude Stein. He has a certain syrup but it does not pour.

So then Hemingway's career was begun. For a little while we saw less of him and then he began to come again. He used to recount to Gertrude Stein the conversations that he afterwards used in The Sun Also Rises and they talked endlessly about the character of Harold Loeb. At this time Hemingway was preparing his volume of short stories to submit to publishers in America. One evening after we had not seen him for a while he turned up with Shipman. Shipman was an amusing boy who was to inherit a few thousand dollars when he came of age. He was not of age. He was to buy the Transatlantic Review[7] when he came of age, so Hemingway said. He was to support a surrealist review when he came of age, André Masson said. He was to buy a house in the country when he came of age, Josette Gris said. As a matter of fact when he came of age nobody who had known him then seemed to know what he did do with his inheritance. Hemingway brought him with him to the house to talk about buying the Transatlantic and incidentally he brought the manuscript he intended sending to America. He handed it to Gertrude Stein. He had added to his stories a little story of meditations and in these he said that The Enormous Room was the greatest book he had ever read. It was then that Gertrude Stein said, Hemingway, remarks are not literature. . . .

For some time now many people, and publishers, have been asking Gertrude Stein to write her autobiography and she had always replied, not possibly.

She began to tease me and say that I should write my autobiography. Just think, she would say, what a lot of money you would make. She then began to invent titles for my autobiography. My Life With The Great, Wives of Geniuses I Have Sat With, My Twenty-five Years With Gertrude Stein.

Then she began to get serious and say, but really seriously you ought to write your autobiography. Finally I promised that if during the summer I could find time I would write my autobiography.

When Ford Madox Ford was editing the Transatlantic Review he once said to Gertrude Stein, I am a pretty good writer and a pretty good editor and a pretty good business man but I find it very difficult to be all three at once.

I am a pretty good housekeeper and a pretty good gardener and a pretty good needlewoman and a pretty good secretary and a pretty good editor and a pretty good vet for dogs and I have to do them all at once and I found it difficult to add being a pretty good author.

[7] Another of the well-known little magazines, published in Paris from 1924 to 1925 and edited by the novelist Ford Madox Ford. Its assistant editor was Ernest Hemingway, whose work it often published.

About six weeks ago Gertrude Stein said, it does not look to me as if you were ever going to write that autobiography. You know what I am going to do. I am going to write it for you. I am going to write it as simply as Defoe did the autobiography of Robinson Crusoe. And she has and this is it.

1933

---

from Three Lives

The Gentle Lena

Lena was patient, gentle, sweet and German. She had been a servant for four years and had liked it very well.

Lena had been brought from Germany to Bridgepoint by a cousin and had been in the same place there for four years.

This place Lena had found very good. There was a pleasant, unexacting mistress and her children, and they all liked Lena very well.

There was a cook there who scolded Lena a great deal but Lena's German patience held no suffering and the good incessant woman really only scolded so for Lena's good.

Lena's German voice when she knocked and called the family in the morning was as awakening, as soothing, and as appealing, as a delicate soft breeze in midday, summer. She stood in the hallway every morning a long time in her unexpectant and unsuffering German patience calling to the young ones to get up. She would call and wait a long time and then call again, always even, gentle, patient, while the young ones fell back often into that precious, tense, last bit of sleeping that gives a strength of joyous vigour in the young, over them that have come to the readiness of middle age, in their awakening.

Lena had good hard work all morning and on the pleasant sunny afternoons she was sent out into the park to sit and watch the little two year old girl baby of the family.

The other girls, all them that make the pleasant lazy crowd, that watch the children in the sunny afternoons out in the park, all liked the simple, gentle, German Lena very well. They all, too, liked very well to tease her, for it was so easy to make her mixed and troubled, and all helpless, for she could never learn to know just what the other quicker girls meant by the queer things they said.

The two or three of these girls, the ones that Lena always sat with, always worked together to confuse her. Still it was pleasant, all this life for Lena.

The little girl fell down sometimes and cried, and then Lena had to soothe her. When the little girl would drop her hat, Lena had to pick it up and hold it. When the little girl was bad and threw away her playthings, Lena told her she could not have them and took them from her to hold until the little girl should need them.

It was all a peaceful life for Lena, almost as peaceful as a pleasant leisure. The other girls, of course, did tease her, but then that only made a gentle stir within her.

Lena was a brown and pleasant creature, brown as blonde races often have them brown, brown, not with the yellow or the red or the chocolate brown of sun burned countries, but brown with the clear colour laid flat on the light toned skin beneath, the plain, spare brown that makes it right to have been made with hazel eyes, and not too abundant straight, brown hair, hair that only later deepens itself into brown from the straw yellow of a German childhood.

Lena had the flat chest, straight back and forward falling shoulders of the patient and enduring working woman, though her body was now still in its milder girlhood and work had not yet made these lines too clear.

The rarer feeling that there was with Lena, showed in all the even quiet of her body movements, but in all it was the strongest in the patient, old-world ignorance, and earth made pureness of her brown, flat, soft featured face. Lena had eyebrows that were a wondrous thickness. They were black, and spread, and very cool, with their dark colour and their beauty, and beneath them were her hazel eyes, simple and human, with the earth patience of the working gentle, German woman.

Yes it was all a peaceful life for Lena. The other girls, of course, did tease her, but then that only made a gentle stir within her.

"What you got on your finger Lena," Mary, one of the girls she always sat with, one day asked her. Mary was good natured, quick, intelligent and Irish.

Lena had just picked up the fancy paper made accordion that the little girl had dropped beside her, and was making it squeak sadly as she pulled it with her brown, strong, awkward finger.

"Why, what is it, Mary, paint?" said Lena, putting her finger to her mouth to taste the dirt spot.

"That's awful poison Lena, don't you know?" said Mary, "that green paint that you just tasted."

Lena had sucked a good deal of the green paint from her finger. She stopped and looked hard at the finger. She did not know just how much Mary meant by what she said.

"Ain't it poison, Nellie, that green paint, that Lena sucked just now," said Mary. "Sure it is Lena, it's real poison, I ain't foolin' this time anyhow."

Lena was a little troubled. She looked hard at her finger where the paint was, and she wondered if she had really sucked it.

It was still a little wet on the edges and she rubbed it off a long time on the inside of her dress, and in between she wondered and looked at the finger and thought, was it really poison that she had just tasted.

"Ain't it too bad, Nellie, Lena should have sucked that," Mary said.

Nellie smiled and did not answer. Nellie was dark and thin, and looked Italian. She had a big mass of black hair that she wore high up on her head, and that made her face look very fine.

Nellie always smiled and did not say much, and then she would look at Lena to perplex her.

And so they all three sat with their little charges in the pleasant sunshine a long time. And Lena would often look at her finger and wonder if it was really poison that she had just tasted and then she would rub her finger on her dress a little harder.

Mary laughed at her and teased her and Nellie smiled a little and looked queerly at her.

Then it came time, for it was growing cooler, for them to drag together the little ones, who had begun to wander, and to take each one back to its own mother. And Lena never knew for certain whether it was really poison, that green stuff that she had tasted.

During these four years of service, Lena always spent her Sundays out at the house of her aunt, who had brought her four years before to Bridgepoint.

This aunt, who had brought Lena, four years before, to Bridgepoint, was a hard, ambitious, well meaning, German woman. Her husband was a grocer in the town, and they were very well to do. Mrs. Haydon, Lena's aunt, had two daughters who were just beginning as young ladies, and she had a little boy who was not honest and who was very hard to manage.

Mrs. Haydon was a short, stout, hard built, German woman. She always hit the ground very firmly and compactly as she walked. Mrs. Haydon was all a compact and well hardened mass, even to her face, reddish and darkened from its early blonde, with its hearty, shiny, cheeks, and doubled chin well covered over with the uproll from her short, square neck.

The two daughters, who were fourteen and fifteen, looked like unkneaded, unformed mounds of flesh beside her.

The elder girl, Mathilda, was blonde, and slow, and simple, and quite fat. The younger, Bertha, who was almost as tall as her sister, was dark, and quicker, and she was heavy, too, but not really fat.

These two girls the mother had brought up very firmly. They were well taught for their position. They were always both well dressed, in the same kinds of hats and dresses, as is becoming in two German sisters. The mother liked to have them dressed in red. Their best clothes were red dresses made of good heavy cloth, and strongly trimmed with braid of a glistening black. They had stiff, red felt hats, trimmed with black velvet ribbon, and a bird. The mother dressed matronly, in a bonnet and in black, always sat between her two big daughters, firm, directing, and repressed.

The only weak spot in this good German woman's conduct was the way she spoiled her boy, who was not honest and who was very hard to manage.

The father of this family was a decent, quiet, heavy, and uninterfering German man. He tried to cure the boy of his bad ways, and make him honest, but the mother could not make herself let the father manage, and so the boy was brought up very badly.

Mrs. Haydon's girls were now only just beginning as young ladies, and so to get her niece, Lena, married, was just then the most important thing that Mrs. Haydon had to do.

Mrs. Haydon had four years before gone to Germany to see her parents, and had taken the girls with her. This visit had been for Mrs. Haydon most successful, though her children had not liked it very well.

Mrs. Haydon was a good and generous woman, and she patronized her parents grandly, and all the cousins who came from all about to see her. Mrs. Haydon's people were of the middling class of farmers. They were not peasants, and they lived in a town of some pretension, but it all seemed very poor and smelly to Mrs. Haydon's American born daughters.

Mrs. Haydon liked it all. It was familiar, and then here she was so wealthy and important. She listened and decided, and advised all of her relations how to do things better. She arranged their present and their future for them, and showed them how in the past they had been wrong in all their methods.

Mrs. Haydon's only trouble was with her two daughters, whom she could not make behave well to her parents. The two girls were very nasty to all their numerous relations. Their mother could hardly make them kiss their grandparents, and every day the girls would get a scolding. But then Mrs. Haydon was so very busy that she did not have time to really manage her stubborn daughters.

These hard working, earth-rough German cousins were to these American born children, ugly and dirty, and as far below them as were Italian or negro workmen, and they could not see how their mother could ever bear to touch them, and then all the women dressed so funny, and were worked all rough and different.

The two girls stuck up their noses at them all, and always talked in English to each other about how they hated all these people and how they wished their mother would not do so. The girls could talk some German, but they never chose to use it.

It was her eldest brother's family that most interested Mrs. Haydon. Here there were eight children, and out of the eight, five of them were girls.

Mrs. Haydon thought it would be a fine thing to take one of these girls back with her to Bridgepoint and get her well started. Everybody liked that she should do so, and they were all willing that it should be Lena.

Lena was the second girl in her large family. She was at this time just seventeen years old. Lena was not an important daughter in the family. She was always sort of dreamy and not there. She worked hard and went very regularly at it, but even good work never seemed to bring her near.

Lena's age just suited Mrs. Haydon's purpose. Lena could first go out to service, and learn how to do things, and then, when she was a little older, Mrs. Haydon could get her a good husband. And then Lena was so still and docile, she would never want to do things her own way. And then, too, Mrs. Haydon, with all her hardness had wisdom, and she could feel the rarer strain there was in Lena.

Lena was willing to go with Mrs. Haydon. Lena did not like her German life very well. It was not the hard work but the roughness that disturbed her. The people were not gentle, and the men when they were glad were very boisterous, and would lay hold of her and roughly tease her. They were good people enough around her, but it was all harsh and dreary for her.

Lena did not really know that she did not like it. She did not know that she was always dreamy and not there. She did not think whether it would be different for her away off there in Bridgepoint. Mrs. Haydon took her and got her different kinds of dresses, and then took her with them to the steamer. Lena did not really know what it was that had happened to her.

Mrs. Haydon, and her daughters, and Lena travelled second class on the steamer. Mrs. Haydon's daughters hated that their mother should take Lena. They hated to have a cousin, who was to them, little better than a nigger, and then everybody on the steamer there would see her. Mrs. Haydon's daughters said things like this to their mother, but she never stopped to hear them, and the girls did not dare to make their meaning very clear. And so they could only go on hating Lena hard, together. They could not stop her from going back with them to Bridgepoint.

Lena was very sick on the voyage. She thought, surely before it was over that she would die. She was so sick she could not even wish that she had not started. She could not eat, she could not moan, she was just blank and scared, and sure that every minute she would die. She could not hold herself in, nor help herself in her trouble. She just stayed where she had been put, pale, and scared, and weak, and sick, and sure that she was going to die.

Mathilda and Bertha Haydon had no trouble from having Lena for a cousin on the voyage, until the last day that they were on the ship, and by that time they had made their friends and could explain.

Mrs. Haydon went down every day to Lena, gave her things to make her better, held her head when it was needful, and generally was good and did her duty by her.

Poor Lena had no power to be strong in such trouble. She did not know how to yield to her sickness nor endure. She lost all her little sense of being in her suffering. She was so scared, and then at her best, Lena, who was patient, sweet and quiet, had not self-control, nor any active courage.

Poor Lena was so scared and weak, and every minute she was sure that she would die.

After Lena was on land again a little while, she forgot all her bad suffering. Mrs. Haydon got her the good place, with the pleasant unexacting mistress, and her children, and Lena began to learn some English and soon was very happy and content.

All her Sundays out Lena spent at Mrs. Haydon's house. Lena would have liked much better to spend her Sundays with the girls she always sat with, and who often asked her, and who teased her and made a gentle stir within her, but it never came to Lena's unexpectant and unsuffering German nature to do something different from what was expected of her, just because she would like it that way better. Mrs. Haydon had said that Lena was to come to her house every other Sunday, and so Lena always went there.

Mrs. Haydon was the only one of her family who took any interest in Lena. Mr. Haydon did not think much of her. She was his wife's cousin and he was good to her, but she was for him stupid, and a little simple, and very dull, and sure some day to need help and to be in trouble. All young poor relations, who were brought from Germany to Bridgepoint were sure, before long, to need help and to be in trouble.

The little Haydon boy was always very nasty to her. He was a hard child for anyone to manage, and his mother spoiled him very badly. Mrs. Haydon's daughters as they grew older did not learn to like Lena any better. Lena never knew that she did not like them either. She did not know that she was only happy with the other quicker girls, she always sat with in the park, and who laughed at her and always teased her.

Mathilda Haydon, the simple, fat, blonde, older daughter felt very badly that she had to say that this was her cousin Lena, this Lena who was little better for her than a nigger. Mathilda was an overgrown, slow, flabby, blonde, stupid, fat girl, just beginning as a woman; thick in her speech and dull and simple in her mind, and very jealous of all her family and of other girls, and proud that she could have good dresses and new hats and learn music, and hating very badly to have a cousin who was a common servant. And then Mathilda remembered very strongly that dirty nasty place that Lena came from and that Mathilda had so turned up her nose at, and where she had been made so angry because her mother scolded her and liked all those rough cow-smelly people.

Then, too, Mathilda would get very mad when her mother had Lena at their parties, and when she talked about how good Lena was, to certain German mothers in whose sons, perhaps, Mrs. Haydon might find Lena a good husband. All this would make the dull, blonde, fat Mathilda very angry. Sometimes she would get so angry that she would, in her thick, slow way, and with jealous anger blazing in her light blue eyes, tell her mother that she did not see how she could like that nasty Lena; and then her mother would scold Mathilda, and tell her that she knew her cousin Lena was poor and Mathilda must be good to poor people.

Mathilda Haydon did not like relations to be poor. She told all her girl friends what she thought of Lena, and so the girls would never talk to Lena at Mrs. Haydon's parties. But Lena in her unsuffering and unexpectant patience never really knew that she was slighted. When Mathilda was with her girls in the street or in the park and would see Lena, she always turned up her nose and barely nodded to her, and then she would tell her friends how funny her mother was to take care of people like that Lena, and how, back in Germany, all Lena's people lived just like pigs.

The younger daughter, the dark, large, but not fat, Bertha Haydon, who was very quick in her mind, and in her ways, and who was the favourite with her father, did not like Lena, either. She did not like her because for her Lena was a fool and so stupid, and she would let those Irish and Italian girls laugh at her and tease her, and everybody always made fun of Lena, and Lena never got mad, or even had sense enough to know that they were all making an awful fool of her.

Bertha Haydon hated people to be fools. Her father, too, thought Lena was a fool, and so neither the father nor the daughter ever paid any attention to Lena, although she came to their house every other Sunday.

Lena did not know how all the Haydons felt. She came to her aunt's house all her Sunday afternoons that she had out, because Mrs. Haydon had told her she must do so. In the same way Lena always saved all of her wages. She never thought of any way to spend it. The German cook, the good woman who always scolded Lena, helped her to put it in the bank each month, as soon as she got it. Sometimes before it got into the bank to be taken care of, somebody would ask Lena for it. The little Haydon boy sometimes asked and would get it, and sometimes some of the girls, the ones Lena always sat with, needed some more money; but the German cook, who always scolded Lena, saw to it that this did not happen very often. When it did happen she would scold Lena very sharply, and for the next few months she would not let Lena touch her wages, but put it in the bank for her on the same day that Lena got it.

So Lena always saved her wages, for she never thought to spend them, and she always went to her aunt's house for her Sundays because she did not know that she could do anything different.

Mrs. Haydon felt more and more every year that she had done right to bring Lena back with her, for it was all coming out just as she had expected. Lena was good and never wanted her own way, she was learning English, and saving all her wages, and soon Mrs. Haydon would get her a good husband.

All these four years Mrs. Haydon was busy looking around among all the German people that she knew for the right man to be Lena's husband, and now at last she was quite decided.

The man Mrs. Haydon wanted for Lena was a young German-American tailor, who worked with his father. He was good and all the family were very saving, and

Mrs. Haydon was sure that this would be just right for Lena, and then too, this young tailor always did whatever his father and his mother wanted.

This old German tailor and his wife, the father and the mother of Herman Kreder, who was to marry Lena Mainz, were very thrifty, careful people. Herman was the only child they had left with them, and he always did everything they wanted. Herman was now twenty-eight years old, but he had never stopped being scolded and directed by his father and his mother. And now they wanted to see him married.

Herman Kreder did not care much to get married. He was a gentle soul and a little fearful. He had a sullen temper, too. He was obedient to his father and his mother. He always did his work well. He often went out on Saturday nights and on Sundays, with other men. He liked it with them but he never became really joyous. He liked to be with men and he hated to have women with them. He was obedient to his mother, but he did not care much to get married.

Mrs. Haydon and the elder Kreders had often talked the marriage over. They all three liked it very well. Lena would do anything that Mrs. Haydon wanted, and Herman was always obedient in everything to his father and his mother. Both Lena and Herman were saving and good workers and neither of them ever wanted their own way.

The elder Kreders, everybody knew, had saved up all their money, and they were hard, good German people, and Mrs. Haydon was sure that with these people Lena would never be in any trouble. Mr. Haydon would not say anything about it. He knew old Kreder had a lot of money and owned some good houses, and he did not care what his wife did with that simple, stupid Lena, so long as she would be sure never to need help or to be in trouble.

Lena did not care much to get married. She liked her life very well where she was working. She did not think much about Herman Kreder. She thought he was a good man and she always found him very quiet. Neither of them ever spoke much to the other. Lena did not care much just then about getting married.

Mrs. Haydon spoke to Lena about it very often. Lena never answered anything at all. Mrs. Haydon thought, perhaps Lena did not like Herman Kreder. Mrs. Haydon could not believe that any girl not even Lena, really had no feeling about getting married.

Mrs. Haydon spoke to Lena very often about Herman. Mrs. Haydon sometimes got very angry with Lena. She was afraid that Lena, for once, was going to be stubborn, now when it was all fixed right for her to be married.

"Why you stand there so stupid, why don't you answer, Lena," said Mrs. Haydon one Sunday, at the end of a long talking that she was giving Lena about Herman Kreder, and about Lena's getting married to him.

"Yes ma'am," said Lena, and then Mrs. Haydon was furious with this stupid Lena. "Why don't you answer with some sense, Lena, when I ask you if you don't like Herman Kreder. You stand there so stupid and don't answer just like you ain't heard a word what I been saying to you. I never see anybody like you, Lena. If you going to burst out at all, why don't you burst out sudden instead of standing there so silly and don't answer. And here I am so good to you, and find you a good husband so you can have a place to live in all your own. Answer me, Lena, don't you like Herman Kreder? He is a fine young fellow, almost too good for you, Lena, when you stand there so stupid and don't make no answer. There ain't many poor girls that get the chance you got now to get married."

"Why, I do anything you say, Aunt Mathilda. Yes, I like him. He don't say much to me, but I guess he is a good man, and I do anything you say for me to do."

"Well then Lena, why you stand there so silly all the time and not answer when I asked you."

"I didn't hear you say you wanted I should say anything to you. I didn't know you wanted me to say nothing. I do whatever you tell me it's right for me to do. I marry Herman Kreder, if you want me."

And so for Lena Mainz the match was made.

Old Mrs. Kreder did not discuss the matter with her Herman. She never thought that she needed to talk such things over with him. She just told him about getting married to Lena Mainz who was a good worker and very saving and never wanted her own way, and Herman made his usual little grunt in answer to her.

Mrs. Kreder and Mrs. Haydon fixed the day and made all the arrangements for the wedding and invited everybody who ought to be there to see them married.

In three months Lena Mainz and Herman Kreder were to be married.

Mrs. Haydon attended to Lena's getting all the things that she needed. Lena had to help a good deal with the sewing. Lena did not sew very well. Mrs. Haydon scolded because Lena did not do it better, but then she was very good to Lena, and she hired a girl to come and help her. Lena still stayed on with her pleasant mistress, but she spent all her evenings and her Sundays with her aunt and all the sewing.

Mrs. Haydon got Lena some nice dresses. Lena liked that very well. Lena liked having new hats even better, and Mrs. Haydon had some made for her by a real milliner who made them very pretty.

Lena was nervous these days, but she did not think much about getting married. She did not know really what it was, that, which was always coming nearer.

Lena liked the place where she was with the pleasant mistress and the good cook, who always scolded, and she liked the girls she always sat with. She did not ask if she would like being married any better. She always did whatever her aunt said and expected, but she was always nervous when she saw the Kreders with their Herman. She was excited and she liked her new hats, and everybody teased her and every day her marrying was coming nearer, and yet she did not really know what it was, this that was about to happen to her.

Herman Kreder knew more what it meant to be married and he did not like it very well. He did not like to see girls and he did not want to have to have one always near him. Herman always did everything that his father and his mother wanted and now they wanted that he should be married.

Herman had a sullen temper; he was gentle and he never said much. He liked to go out with other men, but he never wanted that there should be any women with them. The men all teased him about getting married. Herman did not mind the teasing but he did not like very well the getting married and having a girl always with him.

Three days before the wedding day, Herman went away to the country to be gone over Sunday. He and Lena were to be married Tuesday afternoon. When the day came Herman had not been seen or heard from.

The older Kreder couple had not worried much about it. Herman always did everything they wanted and he would surely come back in time to get married. But when Monday night came, and there was no Herman, they went to Mrs. Haydon to tell her what had happened.

Mrs. Haydon got very much excited. It was hard enough to work so as to get everything all ready, and then to have that silly Herman go off that way, so no one could tell what was going to happen. Here was Lena and everything all ready, and now they would have to make the wedding later so that they would know that Herman would be sure to be there.

Mrs. Haydon was very much excited, and then she could not say much to the old Kreder couple. She did not want to make them angry, for she wanted very badly now that Lena should be married to their Herman.

At last it was decided that the wedding should be put off a week longer. Old Mr. Kreder would go to New York to find Herman, for it was very likely that Herman had gone there to his married sister.

Mrs. Haydon sent word around, about waiting until a week from that Tuesday, to everybody that had been invited, and then Tuesday morning she sent for Lena to come down to see her.

Mrs. Haydon was very angry with poor Lena when she saw her. She scolded her hard because she was so foolish, and now Herman had gone off and nobody could tell where he had gone to, and all because Lena always was so dumb and silly. And Mrs. Haydon was just like a mother to her, and Lena always stood there so stupid and did not answer what anybody asked her, and Herman was so silly too, and now his father had to go and find him. Mrs. Haydon did not think that any old people should be good to their children. Their children always were so thankless, and never paid any attention, and older people were always doing things for their good. Did Lena think it gave Mrs. Haydon any pleasure, to work so hard to make Lena happy, and get her a good husband, and then Lena was so thankless and never did anything that anybody wanted. It was a lesson to poor Mrs. Haydon not to do things any more for anybody. Let everybody take care of themselves and never come to her with any troubles; she knew better now than to meddle to make other people happy. It just made trouble for her and her husband did not like it. He always said she was too good, and nobody ever thanked her for it, and there Lena was always standing stupid and not answering anything anybody wanted. Lena could always talk enough to those silly girls she liked so much, and always sat with, but who never did anything for her except to take away her money, and here was her aunt who tried so hard and was so good to her and treated her just like one of her own children and Lena stood there, and never made any answer and never tried to please her aunt, or to do anything that her aunt wanted. "No, it ain't no use your standin' there and cryin', now, Lena. It's too late now to care about that Herman. You should have cared some before, and then you wouldn't have to stand and cry now, and be a disappointment to me, and then I get scolded by my husband for taking care of everybody, and nobody ever thankful. I am glad you got the sense to feel sorry now, Lena, anyway, and I try to do what I can to help you out in your trouble, only you don't deserve to have anybody take any trouble for you. But perhaps you know better next time. You go home now and take care you don't spoil your clothes and that new hat, you had no business to be wearin' that this morning, but you ain't got no sense at all, Lena. I never in my life see anybody be so stupid."

Mrs. Haydon stopped and poor Lena stood there in her hat, all trimmed with pretty flowers, and the tears coming out of her eyes, and Lena did not know what it was that she had done, only she was not going to be married and it was a disgrace for a girl to be left by a man on the very day she was to be married.

Lena went home all alone, and cried in the street car.

Poor Lena cried very hard all alone in the street car. She almost spoiled her new hat with her hitting it against the window in her crying. Then she remembered that she must not do so.

The conductor was a kind man and he was very sorry when he saw her crying. "Don't feel so bad, you get another feller, you are such a nice girl," he said to make her cheerful. "But Aunt Mathilda said now, I never get married," poor Lena sobbed out for her answer. "Why you really got trouble like that," said the conductor, "I just said that now to josh you. I didn't ever think you really was left by a feller. He must be a stupid feller. But don't you worry, he wasn't much good if he could go away and leave you, lookin' to be such a nice girl. You just tell all your trouble to me, and I help you." The car was empty and the conductor sat down beside her to put his arm around her, and to be comfort to her. Lena suddenly remembered where she was, and if she did things like that her aunt would scold her. She moved away from the man into the corner. He laughed, "Don't be scared," he said, "I wasn't going to hurt you. But you just keep up your spirit. You are a real nice girl, and you'll be sure to get a real good husband. Don't you let nobody fool you. You're all right and I don't want to scare you."

The conductor went back to his platform to help a passenger get on the car. All the time Lena stayed in the street car, he would come in every little while and reassure her, about her not to feel so bad about a man who hadn't no more sense than to go away and leave her. She'd be sure yet to get a good man, she needn't be so worried he frequently assured her.

He chatted with the other passenger who had just come in, a very well dressed old man, and then with another who came in later, a good sort of a working man, and then another who came in, a nice lady, and he told them all about Lena's having trouble, and it was too bad there were men who treated a poor girl so badly. And everybody in the car was sorry for poor Lena and the workman tried to cheer her, and the old man looked sharply at her, and said she looked like a good girl, but she ought to be more careful and not to be so careless, and things like that would not happen to her, and the nice lady went and sat beside her and Lena liked it, though she shrank away from being near her.

So Lena was feeling a little better when she got off the car, and the conductor helped her, and he called out to her, "You be sure you keep up a good heart now. He wasn't no good that feller and you were lucky for to lose him. You'll get a real man yet, one that will be better for you. Don't you be worried, you're a real nice girl as I ever see in such trouble," and the conductor shook his head and went back into his car to talk it over with the other passengers he had there.

The German cook, who always scolded Lena, was very angry when she heard the story. She never did think Mrs. Haydon would do so much for Lena, though she was always talking so grand about what she could do for everybody. The good German cook always had been a little distrustful of her. People who always thought they were so much never did really do things right for anybody. Not that Mrs. Haydon wasn't a good woman. Mrs. Haydon was a real, good, German woman, and she did really mean to do well by her niece Lena. The cook knew that very well, and she had always said so, and she always had liked and respected Mrs. Haydon, who always acted very proper to her, and Lena was so backward, when there was a man to talk to, Mrs. Haydon did have hard work when she tried to marry Lena. Mrs. Haydon was a good woman, only she did talk sometimes too grand. Perhaps this trouble would make her see it wasn't always so easy to do, to make everybody do everything just like she wanted. The cook was very sorry now for Mrs. Haydon. All this must be such a disappointment, and such a worry to her, and she really had always been very good to Lena. But Lena had better go and put on her other clothes and stop with all that crying. That wouldn't do nothing now to help her, and if Lena would be a good girl, and just be real patient, her aunt would make it all come out right yet for her. "I just tell Mrs. Aldrich, Lena, you stay here yet a little longer. You know she is always so good to you, Lena, and I know she let you and I tell her all about that stupid Herman Kreder. I got no patience, Lena, with anybody who can be so stupid. You just stop now with your crying, Lena, and take off them good clothes and put them away so you don't spoil them when you need them, and you can help me with the dishes and everything will come off better for you. You see if I ain't right by what I tell you. You just stop crying now Lena quick, or else I scold you."

Lena still choked a little and was very miserable inside her but she did everything just as the cook told her.

The girls Lena always sat with were very sorry to see her look so sad with her trouble. Mary the Irish girl sometimes got very angry with her. Mary was always very hot when she talked of Lena's aunt Mathilda, who thought she was so grand, and had such stupid, stuck up daughters. Mary wouldn't be a fat fool like that ugly tempered Mathilda Haydon, not for anything anybody could ever give her. How Lena could keep on going there so much when they all always acted as if she was just dirt to them, Mary never could see. But Lena never had any sense of how she should make people stand round for her, and that was always all the trouble with her. And poor Lena, she was so stupid to be sorry for losing that gawky fool who didn't ever know what he wanted and just said "ja" to his mamma and his papa, like a baby, and was scared to look at a girl straight, and then sneaked away the last day like as if somebody was going to do something to him. Disgrace, Lena talking about disgrace! It was a disgrace for a girl to be seen with the likes of him, let alone to be married to him. But that poor Lena, she never did know how to show herself off for what she was really. Disgrace to have him go away and leave her. Mary would just like to get a chance to show him. If Lena wasn't worth fifteen like Herman Kreder, Mary would just eat her own head all up. It was a good riddance Lena had of that Herman Kreder and his stingy, dirty parents, and if Lena didn't stop crying about it,—Mary would just naturally despise her.

Poor Lena, she knew very well how Mary meant it all, this she was always saying to her. But Lena was very miserable inside her. She felt the disgrace it was for a decent German girl that a man should go away and leave her. Lena knew very well that her aunt was right when she said the way Herman had acted to her was a disgrace to everyone that knew her. Mary and Nellie and the other girls she always sat with were always very good to Lena but that did not make her trouble any better. It was a disgrace the way Lena had been left, to any decent family, and that could never be made any different to her.

And so the slow days wore on, and Lena never saw her Aunt Mathilda. At last on Sunday she got word by a boy to go and see her Aunt Mathilda. Lena's heart beat quick for she was very nervous now with all this that had happened to her. She went just as quickly as she could to see her Aunt Mathilda.

Mrs. Haydon quick, as soon as she saw Lena, began to scold her for keeping her aunt waiting so long for her, and for not coming in all the week to see her, to see if her aunt should need her, and so her aunt had to send a boy to tell her. But it was easy, even for Lena, to see that her aunt was not really angry with her. It wasn't Lena's fault, went on Mrs. Haydon, that everything was going to happen all right for her. Mrs. Haydon was very tired taking all this trouble for her, and when Lena couldn't even take trouble to come and see her aunt, to see if she needed anything to tell her. But Mrs. Haydon really never minded things like that when she could do things for anybody. She was tired now, all the trouble she had been taking to make things right for Lena, but perhaps now Lena heard it she would learn a little to be thankful to her. "You get all ready to be married Tuesday, Lena, you hear me," said Mrs. Haydon to her. "You come here Tuesday morning and I have everything all ready for you. You wear your new dress I got you, and your hat with all them flowers on it, and you be very careful coming you don't get your things all dirty, you so careless all the time, Lena, and not thinking, and you act sometimes you never got no head at all on you. You go home now, and you tell your Mrs. Aldrich that you leave her Tuesday. Don't you go forgetting now, Lena, anything I ever told you what you should do to be careful. You be a good girl, now Lena. You get married Tuesday to Herman Kreder." And that was all Lena ever knew of what had happened all this week to Herman Kreder. Lena forgot there was anything to know about it. She was really to be married Tuesday, and her Aunt Mathilda said she was a good girl, and now there was no disgrace left upon her.

Lena now fell back into the way she always had of being always dreamy and not there, the way she always had been, except for the few days she was so excited, because she had been left by a man the very day she was to have been married. Lena was a little nervous all these last days, but she did not think much about what it meant for her to be married.

Herman Kreder was not so content about it. He was quiet and was sullen and he knew he could not help it. He knew now he just had to let himself get married. It was not that Herman did not like Lena Mainz. She was as good as any other girl could be for him. She was a little better perhaps than other girls he saw, she was so very quiet, but Herman did not like to always have to have a girl around him. Herman had always done everything that his mother and his father wanted. His father had found him in New York, where Herman had gone to be with his married sister.

Herman's father when he had found him coaxed Herman a long time and went on whole days with his complaining to him, always troubled but gentle and quite patient with him, and always he was worrying to Herman about what was the right way his boy Herman should always do, always whatever it was his mother ever wanted from him, and always Herman never made him any answer.

Old Mr. Kreder kept on saying to him, he did not see how Herman could think now, it could be any different. When you make a bargain you just got to stick right to it, that was the only way old Mr. Kreder could ever see it, and saying you would get married to a girl and she got everything all ready, that was a bargain just like one you make in business and Herman he had made it, and now Herman he would just have to do it, old Mr. Kreder didn't see there was any other way a good boy like his Herman had, to do it. And then too that Lena Mainz was such a nice girl and Herman hadn't ought to really give his father so much trouble and make him pay out all that money, to come all the way to New York just to find him, and they both lose all that time from their working, when all Herman had to do was just to stand up, for an hour, and then he would be all right married, and it would be all over for him, and then everything at home would never be any different to him.

And his father went on; there was his poor mother saying always how her Herman always did everything before she ever wanted, and now just because he got notions in him, and wanted to show people how he could be stubborn, he was making all this trouble for her, and making them pay all that money just to run around and find him. "You got no idea Herman, how bad mama is feeling about the way you been acting Herman," said old Mr. Kreder to him. "She says she never can understand how you can be so thankless Herman. It hurts her very much you been so stubborn, and she find you such a nice girl for you, like Lena Mainz who is always just so quiet and always saves up all her wages, and she never wanting her own way at all like some girls are always all the time to have it, and your mama trying so hard, just so you could be comfortable Herman to be married, and then you act so stubborn Herman. You like all young people Herman, you think only about yourself, and what you are just wanting, and your mama she is thinking only what is good for you to have, for you in the future. Do you think your mama wants to have a girl around to be a bother, for herself, Herman. It's just for you Herman she is always thinking, and she talks always about how happy she will be, when she sees her Herman married to a nice girl, and then when she fixed it all up so good for you, so it never would be any bother to you, just the way she wanted you should like it, and you say yes all right, I do it, and then you go away like this and act stubborn, and make all this trouble everybody to take for you, and we spend money, and I got to travel all round to find you. You come home now with me Herman and get married, and I tell your mama she better not say anything to you about how much it cost me to come all the way to look for you—Hey Herman," said his father coaxing, "hey, you come home now and get married. All you got to do Herman is just to stand up for an hour Herman and then you don't never to have any more bother to it—Hey Herman!— you come home with me to-morrow and get married. Hey Herman."

Herman's married sister liked her brother Herman, and she had always tried to help him, when there was anything she knew he wanted. She liked it that he was so good and always did everything that their father and their mother wanted, but still she wished it could be that he could have more his own way, if there was anything he ever wanted.

But now she thought Herman with his girl was very funny. She wanted that Herman should be married. She thought it would do him lots of good to get married. She laughed at Herman when she heard the story. Until his father came to find him, she did not know why it was Herman had come just then to New York to see her. When she heard the story she laughed a good deal at her brother Herman and teased him a good deal about his running away, because he didn't want to have a girl to be all the time around him.

Herman's married sister liked her brother Herman, and she did not want him not to like to be with women. He was good, her brother Herman, and it would surely do him good to get married. It would make him stand up for himself stronger. Herman's sister always laughed at him and always she would try to reassure him. "Such a nice man as my brother Herman acting like as if he was afraid of women. Why the girls all like a man like you Herman, if you didn't always run away when you saw them. It do you good really Herman to get married, and then you got somebody you can boss around when you want to. It do you good Herman to get married, you see if you don't like it, when you really done it. You go along home now with papa, Herman and get married to that Lena. You don't know how nice you like it Herman when you try once how you can do it. You just don't be afraid of nothing, Herman. You good enough for any girl to marry, Herman. Any girl be glad to have a man like you to be always with them Herman. You just go along home with papa and try it what I say, Herman. Oh you so funny Herman, when you sit there, and then run away and leave your girl behind you. I know she is crying like anything Herman for to lose you. Don't be bad to her Herman. You go along home with papa now and get married Herman. I'd be awful ashamed Herman, to really have a brother didn't have spirit enough to get married, when a girl is just dying for to have him. You always like me to be with you Herman. I don't see why you say you don't want a girl to be all the time around you. You always been good to me Herman, and I know you always be good to that Lena, and you soon feel just like as if she had always been there with you. Don't act like as if you wasn't a nice strong man, Herman. Really I laugh at you Herman, but you know I like awful well to see you real happy. You go home and get married to that Lena, Herman. She is a real pretty girl and real nice and good and quiet and she make my brother Herman very happy. You just stop your fussing now with Herman, papa. He go with you to-morrow papa, and you see he like it so much to be married, he make everybody laugh just to see him be so happy. Really truly, that's the way it will be with you Herman. You just listen to me what I tell you Herman." And so his sister laughed at him and reassured him, and his father kept on telling what the mother always said about her Herman, and he coaxed him and Herman never said anything in answer, and his sister packed his things up and was very cheerful with him, and she kissed him, and then she laughed and then she kissed him, and his father went and bought the tickets for the train, and at last late on Sunday he brought Herman back to Bridgepoint with him.

It was always very hard to keep Mrs. Kreder from saying what she thought, to her Herman, but her daughter had written her a letter, so as to warn her not to say anything about what he had been doing, to him, and her husband came in with Herman and said, "Here we are come home mama, Herman and me, and we are very tired it was so crowded coming," and then he whispered to her. "You be good to Herman, mama, he didn't mean to make us so much trouble," and so old Mrs. Kreder, held in what she felt was so strong in her to say to her Herman. She just said very stiffly to him, "I'm glad to see you come home to-day, Herman." Then she went to arrange it all with Mrs. Haydon.

Herman was now again just like he always had been, sullen and very good, and very quiet, and always ready to do whatever his mother and his father wanted. Tuesday morning came, Herman got his new clothes on and went with his father and his mother to stand up for an hour and get married. Lena was there in her new dress, and her hat with all the pretty flowers, and she was very nervous for now she knew she was really very soon to be married. Mrs. Haydon had everything all ready.

Everybody was there just as they should be and very soon Herman Kreder and Lena Mainz were married.

When everything was really over, they went back to the Kreder house together. They were all now to live together, Lena and Herman and the old father and the old mother, in the house where Mr. Kreder had worked so many years as a tailor, with his son Herman always there to help him.

Irish Mary had often said to Lena she never did see how Lena could ever want to have anything to do with Herman Kreder and his dirty stingy parents. The old Kreders were to an Irish nature, a stingy, dirty couple. They had not the free-hearted, thoughtless, fighting, mud bespattered, ragged, peat-smoked cabin dirt that Irish Mary knew and could forgive and love. Theirs was the German dirt of saving, of being dowdy and loose and foul in your clothes so as to save them and yourself in washing, having your hair greasy to save it in the soap and drying, having your clothes dirty, not in freedom, but because so it was cheaper, keeping the house close and smelly, because so it cost less to get it heated, living so poorly not only so as to save money but so they should never even know themselves that they had it, working all the time not only because from their nature they just had to and because it made them money but also that they never could be put in any way to make them spend their money.

This was the place Lena now had for her home and to her it was very different than it could be for an Irish Mary. She too was German and was thrifty, though she was always so dreamy and not there. Lena was always careful with things and she always saved her money, for that was the only way she knew how to do it. She never had taken care of her own money and she never had thought how to use it.

Lena Mainz had been, before she was Mrs. Herman Kreder, always clean and decent in her clothes and in her person, but it was not because she ever thought about it or really needed so to have it, it was the way her people did in the German country where she came from, and her Aunt Mathilda and the good German cook who always scolded, had kept her on and made her, with their scoldings, always more careful to keep clean and to wash real often. But there was no deep need in all this for Lena and so, though Lena did not like the old Kreders, though she really did not know that, she did not think about their being stingy dirty people.

Herman Kreder was cleaner than the old people, just because it was his nature to keep cleaner, but he was used to his mother and his father, and he never thought that they should keep things cleaner. And Herman too always saved all his money, except for that little beer he drank when he went out with other men of an evening the way he always liked to do it, and he never thought of any other way to spend it. His father had always kept all the money for them and he always was doing business with it. And then too Herman really had no money, for he always had worked for his father, and his father had never thought to pay him.

And so they began all four to live in the Kreder house together, and Lena began soon with it to look careless and a little dirty, and to be more lifeless with it, and nobody ever noticed much what Lena wanted, and she never really knew herself what she needed.

The only real trouble that came to Lena with their living all four there together, was the way old Mrs. Kreder scolded. Lena had always been used to being scolded, but this scolding of old Mrs. Kreder was very different from the way she ever before had had to endure it.

Herman, now he was married to her, really liked Lena very well. He did not care very much about her but she never was a bother to him being there around him, only when his mother worried and was nasty to them because Lena was so careless, and did not know how to save things right for them with their eating, and all the other ways with money, that the old woman had to save it.

Herman Kreder had always done everything his mother and his father wanted but he did not really love his parents very deeply. With Herman it was always only that he hated to have any struggle. It was all always all right with him when he could just go along and do the same thing over every day with his working, and not to hear things, and not to have people make him listen to their anger. And now his marriage, and he just knew it would, was making trouble for him. It made him hear more what his mother was always saying, with her scolding. He had to really hear it now because Lena was there, and she was so scared and dull always when she heard it. Herman knew very well with his mother, it was all right if one ate very little and worked hard all day and did not hear her when she scolded, the way Herman always had done before they were so foolish about his getting married and having a girl there to be all the time around him, and now he had to help her so the girl could learn too, not to hear it when his mother scolded and not to look so scared, and not to eat much, and always to be sure to save it.

Herman really did not know very well what he could do to help Lena to understand it. He could never answer his mother back to help Lena, that never would make things any better for her, and he never could feel in himself any way to comfort Lena, to make her strong not to hear his mother, in all the awful ways she always scolded. It just worried Herman to have it like that all the time around him. Herman did not know much about how a man could make a struggle with a mother, to do much to keep her quiet, and indeed Herman never knew much how to make a struggle against anyone who really wanted to have anything very badly. Herman all his life never wanted anything so badly, that he would really make a struggle against any one to get it. Herman all his life only wanted to live regular and quiet, and not talk much and to do the same way every day like every other with his working. And now his mother had made him get married to this Lena and now with his mother making all that scolding, he had all this trouble and this worry always on him.

Mrs. Haydon did not see Lena now very often. She had not lost her interest in her niece Lena, but Lena could not come much to her house to see her, it would not be right, now Lena was a married woman. And then too Mrs. Haydon had her hands full just then with her two daughters, for she was getting them ready to find them good husbands, and then too her own husband now worried her very often about her always spoiling that boy of hers, so he would be sure to turn out no good and be a disgrace to a German family, and all because his mother always spoiled him. All these things were very worrying now to Mrs. Haydon, but still she wanted to be good to Lena, though she could not see her very often. She only saw her when Mrs. Haydon went to call on Mrs. Kreder or when Mrs. Kreder came to see Mrs. Haydon, and that never could be very often. Then too these days Mrs. Haydon could not scold Lena, Mrs. Kreder was always there with her, and it would not be right to scold Lena when Mrs. Kreder was there, who had now the real right to do it. And so her aunt always said nice things now to Lena, and though Mrs. Haydon sometimes was a little worried when she saw Lena looking sad and not careful, she did not have time just then to really worry much about it.

Lena now never any more saw the girls she always used to sit with. She had no way now to see them and it was not in Lena's nature to search out ways to see them, nor did she now ever think much of the days when she had been used to see them. They never any of them had come to the Kreder house to see her. Not even Irish Mary had ever thought to come to see her. Lena had been soon forgotten by them. They had soon passed away from Lena and now Lena never thought any more that she had ever known them.

The only one of her old friends who tried to know what Lena liked and what she needed, and who always made Lena come to see her, was the good German cook who had always scolded. She now scolded Lena hard for letting herself go so, and going out when she was looking so untidy. "I know you going to have a baby Lena, but that's no way for you to be looking. I am ashamed most to see you come and sit here in my kitchen, looking so sloppy and like you never used to Lena. I never see anybody like you Lena. Herman is very good to you, you always say so, and he don't treat you bad ever though you don't deserve to have anybody good to you, you so careless all the time, Lena, letting yourself go like you never had anybody tell you what was the right way you should know how to be looking. No, Lena, I don't see no reason you should let yourself go so and look so untidy Lena, so I am ashamed to see you sit there looking so ugly, Lena. No Lena that ain't no way ever I see a woman make things come out better, letting herself go so every way and crying all the time like as if you had real trouble. I never wanted to see you marry Herman Kreder, Lena, I knew what you got to stand with that old woman always, and that old man, he is so stingy too and he don't say things out but he ain't any better in his heart than his wife with her bad ways, I know that Lena, I know they don't hardly give you enough to eat, Lena, I am real sorry for you Lena, you know that Lena, but that ain't anyway to be going round so untidy Lena, even if you have got all that trouble. You never see me do like that Lena, though sometimes I got a headache so I can't see to stand to be working hardly, and nothing comes right with all my cooking, but I always see Lena, I look decent. That's the only way a German girl can make things come out right Lena. You hear me what I am saying to you, Lena. Now you eat something nice Lena, I got it all ready for you, and you wash up and be careful Lena and the baby will come all right to you, and then I make your Aunt Mathilda see that you live in a house soon all alone with Herman and your baby, and then everything go better for you. You hear me what I say to you Lena. Now don't let me ever see you come looking like this any more Lena, and you just stop with that always crying. You ain't got no reason to be sitting there now with all that crying, I never see anybody have trouble it did them any good to do the way you are doing, Lena. You hear me Lena. You go home now and you be good the way I tell you Lena, and I see what I can do. I make your Aunt Mathilda make old Mrs. Kreder let you be till you get your baby all right. Now don't you be scared and so silly Lena. I don't like to see you act so Lena when really you got a nice man and so many things really any girl should be grateful to be having. Now you go home Lena to-day and you do the way I say, to you, and I see what I can do to help you."

"Yes Mrs. Aldrich" said the good German woman to her mistress later, "Yes Mrs. Aldrich that's the way it is with them girls when they want so to get married. They don't know when they got it good Mrs. Aldrich. They never know what it is they're really wanting when they got it, Mrs. Aldrich. There's that poor Lena, she just been here crying and looking so careless so I scold her, but that was no good that marrying for that poor Lena, Mrs. Aldrich. She do look so pale and sad now Mrs. Aldrich, it just break my heart to see her. She was a good girl was Lena, Mrs. Aldrich, and I never had no trouble with her like I got with so many young girls nowadays Mrs. Aldrich, and I never see any girl any better to work right than our Lena, and now she got to stand it all the time with that old woman Mrs. Kreder. My! Mrs. Aldrich, she is a bad old woman to her. I never see Mrs. Aldrich how old people can be so bad to young girls and not have no kind of patience with them. If Lena could only live with her Herman, he ain't so bad the way men are, Mrs. Aldrich, but he is just the way always his mother wants him, he ain't got no spirit in him, and so I don't really see no help for that poor Lena. I know her aunt, Mrs. Haydon, meant it all right for her Mrs. Aldrich, but poor Lena, it would be better for her if her Herman had stayed there in New York that time he went away to leave her. I don't like it the way Lena is looking now, Mrs. Aldrich. She looks like as if she don't have no life left in her hardly, Mrs. Aldrich, she just drags around and looks so dirty and after all the pains I always took to teach her and to keep her nice in her ways and looking. It don't do no good to them, for them girls to get married Mrs. Aldrich, they are much better when they only know it, to stay in a good place when they got it, and keep on regular with their working. I don't like it the way Lena looks now Mrs. Aldrich. I wish I knew some way to help that poor Lena, Mrs. Aldrich, but she is a bad old woman, that old Mrs. Kreder, Herman's mother. I speak to Mrs. Haydon real soon, Mrs. Aldrich, I see what we can do now to help that poor Lena."

These were really bad days for poor Lena. Herman always was real good to her and now he even sometimes tried to stop his mother from scolding Lena. "She ain't well now mama, you let her be now you hear me. You tell me what it is you want she should be doing, I tell her. I see she does it right just the way you want it mama. You let be, I say now mama, with that always scolding Lena. You let be, I say now, you wait till she is feeling better." Herman was getting really strong to struggle, for he could see that Lena with that baby working hard inside her, really could not stand it any longer with his mother and the awful ways she always scolded.

It was a new feeling Herman now had inside him that made him feel he was strong to make a struggle. It was new for Herman Kreder really to be wanting something, but Herman wanted strongly now to be a father, and he wanted badly that his baby should be a boy and healthy. Herman never had cared really very much about his father and his mother, though always, all his life, he had done everything just as they wanted, and he had never really cared much about his wife, Lena, though he always had been very good to her, and had always tried to keep his mother off her, with the awful way she always scolded, but to be really a father of a little baby, that feeling took hold of Herman very deeply. He was almost ready, so as to save his baby from all trouble, to really make a strong struggle with his mother and with his father, too, if he would not help him to control his mother.

Sometimes Herman even went to Mrs. Haydon to talk all this trouble over. They decided then together, it was better to wait there all four together for the baby, and Herman could make Mrs. Kreder stop a little with her scolding, and then when Lena was a little stronger, Herman should have his own house for her, next door to his father, so he could always be there to help him in his working, but so they could eat and sleep in a house where the old woman could not control them and they could not hear her awful scolding.

And so things went on, the same way, a little longer. Poor Lena was not feeling any joy to have a baby. She was scared the way she had been when she was so sick on the water. She was scared now every time when anything would hurt her. She was scared and still and lifeless, and sure that every minute she would die. Lena had no power to be strong in this kind of trouble, she could only sit still and be scared, and dull, and lifeless, and sure that every minute she would die.

Before very long, Lena had her baby. He was a good, healthy little boy, the baby. Herman cared very much to have the baby. When Lena was a little stronger he took a house next door to the old couple, so he and his own family could eat and sleep and do the way they wanted. This did not seem to make much change now for Lena. She was just the same as when she was waiting with her baby. She just dragged around and was careless with her clothes and all lifeless, and she acted always and lived on just as if she had no feeling. She always did everything regular with the work, the way she always had had to do it, but she never got back any spirit in her. Herman was always good and kind, and always helped her with her working. He did everything he knew to help her. He always did all the active new things in the house and for the baby. Lena did what she had to do the way she always had been taught it. She always just kept going now with her working, and she was always careless, and dirty, and a little dazed, and lifeless. Lena never got any better in herself of this way of being that she had had ever since she had been married.

Mrs. Haydon never saw any more of her niece, Lena. Mrs. Haydon had now so much trouble with her own house, and her daughters getting married, and her boy, who was growing up, and who always was getting so much worse to manage. She knew she had done right by Lena. Herman Kreder was a good man, she would be glad to get one so good, sometimes, for her own daughters, and now they had a home to live in together, separate from the old people, who had made their trouble for them. Mrs. Haydon felt she had done very well by her niece Lena, and she never thought now she needed any more to go and see her. Lena would do very well now without her aunt to trouble herself any more about her.

The good German cook who had always scolded, still tried to do her duty like a mother to poor Lena. It was very hard now to do right by Lena. Lena never seemed to hear now what anyone was saying to her. Herman was always doing everything he could to help her. Herman always, when he was home, took good care of the baby. Herman loved to take care of his baby. Lena never thought to take him out or to do anything she didn't have to.

The good cook sometimes made Lena come to see her. Lena would come with her baby and sit there in the kitchen, and watch the good woman cooking, and listen to her sometimes a little, the way she used to, while the good German woman scolded her for going around looking so careless when now she had no trouble, and sitting there so dull, and always being just so thankless. Sometimes Lena would wake up a little and get back into her face her old, gentle, patient, and unsuffering sweetness, but mostly Lena did not seem to hear much when the good German woman scolded. Lena always liked it when Mrs. Aldrich her good mistress spoke to her kindly, and then Lena would seem to go back and feel herself to be like she was when she had been in service. But mostly Lena just lived along and was careless in her clothes, and dull, and lifeless.

By and by Lena had two more little babies. Lena was not so much scared now when she had the babies. She did not seem to notice very much when they hurt her, and she never seemed to feel very much now about anything that happened to her.

They were very nice babies, all these three that Lena had, and Herman took good care of them always. Herman never really cared much about his wife, Lena. The only things Herman ever really cared for were his babies. Herman always was very good to his children. He always had a gentle, tender way when he held them. He learned to be very handy with them. He spent all the time he was not working, with them. By and by he began to work all day in his own home so that he could have his children always in the same room with him.

Lena always was more and more lifeless and Herman now mostly never thought about her. He more and more took all the care of their three children. He saw to their eating right and their washing, and he dressed them every morning, and he taught them the right way to do things, and he put them to their sleeping, and he was now always every minute with them. Then there was to come to them, a fourth baby. Lena went to the hospital near by to have the baby. Lena seemed to be going to have much trouble with it. When the baby was come out at last, it was like its mother lifeless. While it was coming, Lena had grown very pale and sicker. When it was all over Lena had died, too, and nobody knew just how it had happened to her.

The good German cook who had always scolded Lena, and had always to the last day tried to help her, was the only one who ever missed her. She remembered how nice Lena had looked all the time she was in service with her, and how her voice had been so gentle and sweet-sounding, and how she always was a good girl, and how she never had to have any trouble with her, the way she always had with all the other girls who had been taken into the house to help her. The good cook sometimes spoke so of Lena when she had time to have a talk with Mrs. Aldrich, and this was all the remembering there now ever was of Lena.

Herman Kreder now always lived very happy, very gentle, very quiet, very well content alone with his three children. He never had a woman any more to be all the time around him. He always did all his own work in his house, when he was through every day with the work he was always doing for his father. Herman always was alone, and he always worked alone, until his little ones were big enough to help him. Herman Kreder was very well content now and he always lived very regular and peaceful, and with every day just like the next one, always alone now with his three good, gentle children.

1909

The Work

Not fierce and tender but sweet.
This is our impression of the soldiers.
We call our machine Aunt Pauline.
Fasten it fat, that is us, we say Aunt Pauline.
When we left Paris we had rain.
Not snow now nor that in between.
We did have snow then.

Now we are bold.

We are accustomed to it.

All the weights are measures.

By this we mean we know how much oil we use for the machine.

Splendid.

We say are they plateful.

Girls are.

By this we mean that it is reasonable to be well fed and they are in France. It is astonishing how well everything works.

Women.

Treasures in song.

I mean that we feel that way.

Really we do not sing and as yet we have no phonograph.

The soldiers would like it.

I see a mountain wheeler.

This was when we were frightened and there was no reason as the wheels were good.

I see a capstan.

This meant that we knew the direction.

I see a straight, I see a rattle, all things are breathing.

This means that I had learnt to go down hill.

Then we came to warmer climbs.

Can you say see me.

Hurrah for America.

Here we met a Captain and take him part way.

A day's sun.

Is this Miss.

Yes indeed our mat.

We meant by this that we were always meeting people and that it was pleasant.

We can thank you.

We thank you.

Soldiers of course spoke to us.

Come together.

Come to me there now.

They read on our van American Committee in aid of French wounded.

All of it is bit.

Bitter.

This is the way they say we do help.

In the meaning of bright.

Bright not light.

This comforts them when they speak to me. I often discuss America with them and what we hope to do. They listen well and say we hope so too. We all do.

Light to me.

Then say the essence.

Here I must confess I am introducing my own troubles. There is always a certain amount of trouble in getting essence but everybody is so kind.

Not a nightingale.

We hope to hear one soon.

Wild animals are not fierce neither are sponges.

This means that the french fight well and make no suggestions. They like to talk about life. They say it is for you to decide what you will bring them. They can criticise but you know how to ask them to tell you what they meant. They are so reasonable.

Can you see her dressed or him.

In this way we cough.

This makes me sad. I hate to hear of them that they are not going to be well. We need them. Not to fight only but to live. You can imagine how I feel.

What can a mayor do.

All the mayors have been most kind.

In this new school in this new school they are ladies and now you mention gifts and lists.

This refers to long conversations and after all they are devoted and all devotion begins with one another. They feel they must answer for all. In this way we know whom to ask. We cannot say we can be pleased but we are very careful in our distribution. That is as it should be.

Can you believe.

Then then.

All the leaves.

This means that as we went South there were leaves.

All the hotels.

Of course there were hotels and many of them were most sympathetic. I remember one where the landlady told us of her son. She had another one. He was then the one the one the only one and he would not be the one to do what was offered him. To remain. Not that he would do more than he did. No indeed. And a boy was an officer. Not one of her children. Were they fighting. They would never remain different in living. Let us hope they are not dying. I cannot tell you what it means to be fighting.

Cooks cook.

We are so happy.

In the land.

You mean a lady.

Nobody speaks of that work.

They do love rabbits.

Can we have imagination.

They ask have we a stocking.

This is apropos of the colonials. We see a great many. They fight so bravely and as they have many of them no people they are so grateful we like them so much. And they have such pleasant ways of speaking to each other. We get to talk to them.

We have to.

It is not a joke.

A war is not a joke.

Did he die there because he was mortal and we leave Rivesaltes. Be nice to me.

This is apropos of the birthplace of Marechal Joffre. We visited it and we have sent postal cards of it. The committee will be pleased.

It is not a bother to be a soldier.
I think kindly of that bother.
Can you say lapse.
Then think about it.
Indeed it is yet.
We are so pleased.
With the flag.
With the flag of sets.
Sets of color.
Do you like flags.
Blue flags smell sweetly.
Blue flags in a whirl.

We did this we had ribbon of the American flag and we cut it up and we gave each soldier one with a pin and they pinned it on and we were pleased and we received a charming letter from a telephonist at the front who heard from a friend in Perpignan that we were giving this bit of ribbon and he asked for some and we sent them and we hope that they are all living.

The wind blows.
And the automobile goes.
Can you guess boards.
Wood.

Naturally we think about wind because this country of Rousillon is the windiest corner in France. Also it is a great wine country.

Can you guess hoop.
Barrels.
Can you guess girls.
Servants.
The women of the country still wear the caps of the country.
Can you guess messages.
Indeed.
Then there are meats to buy.
This is apropos of the small Benevol hospitals who try to supply the best food.
We like asparagus so.
This is an interview.
Soldiers like a fuss.
Give them their way.
This is meant to be read they like a fuss made over them, and they do.
Yes indeed we will.
We are not mighty.
Nor merry.
We are happy.
Very.
In the morning.
We believe in the morning.
Do we.

This means that I have always had the habit of late rising but for hospital visiting I have to rise early.

Please be an interview.
This is when we do not think we would know what to say.
Please be an interview with dogs.
Please comfort me.
Please plan a game.
Please then and places.
This is apropos of the fact that I always ask where they come from and then I am ashamed to say I don't know all the Departments but I am learning them.
In the meantime.
In the meantime we are useful.
That is what I mean to say.
In the meantime can you have beds. This means that knowing the number of beds you begin to know the hospital.
Kindly call a brother.
What is a cure.
I speak french.
What one means.
I can call it in time.
By the way where are fish.
They all love fishing.
In that case are there any wonders.
Many wonders are women.
I could almost say that that was apropos of my cranking my machine.
And men too.
We smile.
In the way sentences.
He does not feel as we do.
But he did have the coat.
He blushed a little.
This is sometimes when they can't quite help themselves and they want to help us.
We do not understand the weather. That astonishes me.
Camellias in Perpignan.
Camellias finish when roses begin.
Thank you in smiles.
In this way we go on. So far we have had no troubles yet and yet we do need material.
It is astonishing that those who have fought so hard and so well should pick yellow irises and fish in a stream.
And then a pansy.
I did not ask for it.
It smells.
A sweet smell.
With acacia.
Call it locusts.
Call it me.
I finish by saying that the french soldier is the person we should all help.

1917/1953

Miguel (Collusion). Guimpe. Candle.

Collection of eggs white, white as know excellent.

Are the holds extra skinned.

A bland is curtain grease with a fine tart. A field might a field might. Blame cross extermination. Please porouses. Please porouses contumely. A glass plate. A glass white is a shadow in the bun. A shadow in the begun oar box. Or not pleasing. Or not white. In read old lozenges. Instead. In that bread. In that bred and a lower a real old heard, a real cold curry able to be at it with a crush in without, with out all ox holds at neither best.

A clinging fancy, clinging lightly in astrakhan and silver and a sweet tooth surely swelling. A sigh in distributed add in dresses and a little lounge a clean piece of murder girder to seem high long. And yet coloratura in the beef.

Nicely.

Cold in, cold in, why not a servant wedding. Why not peak pillow with a peck. So creek.

Out on pledges and a intwine, out occasional. Out in occasion to be sold gracious goodness, it in, it in seen.

Bay win. Bay cake.

Be cake saddle and mud or a can be so much. More mew. More clever stroked beside the lead of liver cake in shake. In shake.

Miguel, migall in all to lend a stand to lend it bender to lend an upright circle an upright circle beam, beam in loads, why are knees feet.

A lamb a white long loan and an ostrich and a tin bin a real cold cake with season and a little blind oak, a coon is sooner.

Cup up, Cube in, Cube in a sand curl.

Cheese and a dirty weight.

My dear sir. The left place which shows a signer, the left place which shows a signer and please please be a mercy, pertain to more clothes than older and a little twinkle almost a shouter and a study, almost that blind.

Could not a bee line a coat with guimpes and tin peas and a cold ice. The rest of the funnel is nice and strong and relieved all went.

Cooled queue, glass, a guile which is toes in cuts more angels. Let us say, let us say girls, let us say furls, let us select haughty bowls and a little towels and leaves wild stolen leaves and sleeves, combined sleeves. A little tun is likely to mean a standing step. The rest is deep. Cold, mingle.

Just let me say that there is a little tall thing to catch, just listen to it and say more spanish, more spanish finish, more finish that just manage and a little thing a little thing means a light steady, not so steady as flowers and any way there are twenty counting, not likely that there should.

A second better.

A wilderness causes stirrups, a cool pet is native.

Chimera.

Woods long, to let a branch of cases and please, see the tea and cold. A best chance is with the tool and long bedrooms are divided really divided uttering the tune. Best low, best quite too painful with little cut tigers where there are transoms. The less best flower is white with roses and a team a whole team is scarce it runs on the hill. Who would know that donkey, who would cherish houses and little paints and clear white beans with more pressings. Just the same the gold is blue. A chance bow with a piece of strewn heel so that anyway there is a dam factory. The like white is steak. So long meal.

Guimpe.

Consider the kind call, make it show, make it beady make it please the name of called pieces.

If a change comes to pay darlings, if it seizes the plain chill of the told price and a little ladder is brightly, a little light has no seam no solid bounce.

Then the purse then the tiled rubber roof is collision and really what is fur, fur is summer.

A little date pretty a little date pretty with a log, a little date pretty with a horse and cow and cheese real cheese that repeats the call the call of the untamed harbor and legs and everything.

Please pay that, please pay a kind of succeeding peaches and little curls.

Will wild rubbers single out paces, will they ease cold hares and little sturgeons will they rarely be soluble.

A beet in the foundry is likely to be sat forward, it is naturally suggested that long tall pinches are pleasant.

I am clad in sweet syrup and odors.

A way to build collars with little cs and heights, the way to build collars with a two old boat, a way to build cellars with coins and shadows and real old bouts.

Too soon a vacation, two pieces and another, a ran old cut with a juice with juice, could bursts shower, could a clean boat move politely. Egg off egg off the leader, egg and a persuasion. Little told, little too collared with a sodden beam. Is it final is it so bellowing, is it not that three names are singular only two are audacious the third is contrasting that is to say they are three together. Black, black sill, black still will frill, frill calm, frill in a bother in a bother together, the noise is boiled.

Miguel, Miguel is not boweled by a little water founting away behind a table center. Not there harry no night nice in peep, nuts and sound shades put in the place of upright and tunes piano tunes.

A Mother.

Cool with the spring of a dark respectable lantern question.

Calling.

Calling in that exercises walking so that if there is a night there is long excuse with a shade of a piece of labor, much labor if tables are waiting so that they need washing and window cleaning.

A little pull perplexed shows a result in.

Continue so that when a regular base ball is put there is no choice in blots and anyway there is no hesitation in not biting. The least best is naughty. Cold bowls mean somewhere.

Why should waking be old. A little waiter naturally peeps and lets a bag sigh and meddles with rocks. A little wedding shows intelligence and calm and slices and all the reason why bites are black. Leave kindly saloon leave kindly saloon in white slices and little onions. A church is colored. It shows papers. Papers are so many.

Really big special willows.

Pack waist in dog. A case short, laugh lump of wood pieces lessly.

Two between cold and hot entirely turned to change silence to a lung which makes rash seals.

The right of a case and the back of a deal a deal square short with lazy thorns. The best ungainly little rasp which makes tall not twins twins are a bloom two four and this makes a lawn biter with lapse of little angles which means nails hand nails and length.

A class a class is beaten, it has necklaces and spy glasses and measures and slats and little ferns and bugs and nice paws and a pine a pine rabbit and even a bell a long bell.

Certainly a clamor means a steak a steak to push. And really a little language means a dog a dog to sober. Naturally pans are sweet and neighborly and almost a blind a really blind call, a sweet long tall towel which hums hums by the day. A little of seize a clam a billow a rack a lantern settler and a pall a pell mell shoulder.

Petunia Wilmington.

Such is sucking when there is a pack of sound which is goats which is lamb last lambling. Loaf. A hole is in seen and likely is to pudding when color is to buds. Buds when in seen solid, no coats, no black necessaries. A real kind is dew real cue act one.

A bed, suppose hair pleats in easy canisters so that in again have check to a blossom. My house. A land to call water.

A little please to pay, a time to choose figs and baled asses and nearly all the cooks and little pieces and more oil puddings. There is no use.

A blame to little gutter and ruin all ruin to a choice mind a mind chosen to burnish little asters and big golds entirely and leave plates leaves plates with sugar and extra almost extra.

A single ruin a return a lively dog a lively dog to sit, to place collections in little blouse in cold and so called arch change. Really it is no use. The best day is complete with hoes. All hoes and all places.

A cow shapes leaves and salt and flesh behind. More ice more catching of the pills that sigh. The rest is meat and cold grapes and a sad a sole sad chase.

Leave little tones to blink with a constitution.

Sad board. Negligible undertaking. Leading mattresses. Celebrate. Collect class. Be so.

The best pealing, necessitate more oiled opera glasses which show such nice, such near bolts and shoes.

Paul paul.

Unheld bore bore what water wine eye glass and summer rain. Gnats little flies and coffee not cups. Not nearly good enough to exchange for places. I exchange more next day than before.

Leave little wheels so that the whole case is this. Beg more and say that chick chicken is rested. The best way is not to say anything, press it in a flavor and put it in to answer. Really that is an occupation not like the lazy lily.

Please bite, please bite this.

Please bite.

Please bite please bite this.

An awful chance to be a cook's cake.

Little teas are bitten able and the knives are best away. Little miser is in hale brothers to mean a mother and eight children with four twins. Four twins are two. No check. Lest the noise fogs a supple ended plight. Cigarettes are mud. Least is said. Show a correction. More please bananas.

More fat what, bail it, putter white, beady in the fly, hit chat, left more, gale glass no so syrup, joist, joist with, no pretty little seat to fizzle with the summer so.

No next collapse with confusion in a in a taste with lungs taste not taste and little pleasing and oh cans oh cans see. Least is the party vogue and necessary and instant craning with a loud perpendicular neglected coat more.

1913/1953

Sherwood Anderson
1876–1941

Sherwood Anderson was born on September 13, 1876, in Camden, Ohio, a small town near the Kentucky border. During the first eighteen years of his life, his family moved from one Ohio town to the next, as his father, a harness maker and inveterate storyteller whom Anderson described as a "colorful no account," shifted from job to job. Anderson's formal education was brief and spotty. As a boy he worked at many jobs—as a newsboy, a housepainter, a stableboy, a farmhand, and a laborer in a bicycle factory. At fourteen, when his mother died, he dropped out of school altogether. When he was eighteen, his family settled in Clyde, Ohio, the town that he would later imaginatively transform into Winesburg, Ohio, the fictional setting that ensured his literary reputation. In 1896, however, after only two years in Clyde, Anderson moved to Chicago, where he worked as a warehouse laborer. In 1898 he enlisted in the army during the Spanish-American War and served briefly in Cuba. Back from the army, he drifted into business, first as an advertising copywriter in Chicago and later as the manager of two paint firms in Ohio. By 1904, when he married the first of his four wives, he was living the life of a successful businessman.

At the same time, Anderson was secretly writing fiction and building toward a crisis. Everything came to a head on November 27, 1912, when suddenly, in the middle of dictating a letter, he walked out of his office in Elyria, Ohio, and disappeared for several days. He turned up in Cleveland disturbed, disheveled, and disoriented. He later dramatized this apparently confused gesture as an artistic repudiation of the business world. It also became an integral part of his literary achievement. The critic Clifton Fadiman remarked of Anderson that "the dramatization of this moment is his major contribution to the interpretation of American life. . . . He is obsessed with the experience of sudden self-discovery."

Having recovered from his nervous collapse, Anderson moved again to Chicago, hoping this time to combine a career writing advertising copy with a career writing fiction. But he was now moving steadily toward art. He was reading receptively the work of Sigmund Freud, D. H. Lawrence, and Gertrude Stein. He was also receiving encouragement from some of the leading figures of the Chicago "Renaissance," including Theodore Dreiser, Ben Hecht, Floyd Dell, and Carl Sandburg. Soon he began publishing verse and short fiction in *The Little Review, Poetry, The Masses,* and *The Seven Arts.* In 1916 he published his first novel, *Windy McPherson's Son,* an autobiographical story based on memories of his father and his own recent disillusionment with the world of business. A second novel, *Marching Men* (1917), dealt with a militant brotherhood of industrial workers. In 1918 Anderson published a volume of poems in the Carl Sandburg manner, *Mid-American Chants.*

In the late fall of 1915 Anderson began writing the 23 tales that would compose the only one of his books still regarded as a major achievement, *Winesburg, Ohio* (1919). By the middle of the next year he had finished most of "The Tales and the Persons" that make up his "Book of the Grotesque." Thematically, Anderson's Winesburg tales (the name of the fictional town suggests a combination of the dreamy and the mundane) anticipate the wasteland image explored by T. S. Eliot, Ernest Hemingway, F. Scott Fitzgerald, and Nathanael West. The truncation of life that his characters experience becomes a kind of living death. Their senses seem anesthetized, their sensibilities numbed, their spirits shrunken. Though the feeling of small-town paralysis derived directly from Anderson's experiences, *Winesburg, Ohio* was structurally indebted to such collections as Ivan Turgenev's *A Sportsman's Sketches* (1852), James Joyce's *Dubliners* (1914), and particularly Edgar Lee Masters's *Spoon River Anthology* (1915). Anderson acknowledged the influence of Gertrude Stein's *Three Lives* (1909)—"She is making new, strange and to my ears sweet combinations of words"—in the development of his repetitive, colloquial prose style. So deliberately did Anderson resist fancy writing ("I have had a great fear of phrase-making") that his prose might be said to approach a poetry of inarticulation. Nearly all of his characters struggle at self-expression and, as stories like "Hands" and "Mother" clearly reveal, live in a conversational world of unfocused feelings and awkward silences.

Winesburg, Ohio has had an enormous influence on the development of the American short story. Its sequential pattern anticipates such collections as Jean Toomer's *Cane,* Ernest Hemingway's *In Our Time,* William Faulkner's *Go Down, Moses,* and more recently, John Barth's *Lost in the Funhouse.* Its preoccupation with American eccentrics and "grotesques" foreshadowed the characterizations of such later short-story writers as Flannery O'Connor and Carson McCullers. And its spare poetry of ordinary American speech anticipates the recent working-class tales of Raymond Carver and Bobbie Ann Mason. Anderson also demonstrated in his stories and critical essays an aesthetic resistance to the literary slickness of contrived plots: No Americans, he wrote, "lived, felt, or talked as the average American novel makes them live, feel, or talk and as for the plot short stories of the magazines—those bastard children of de Maupassant, Poe, and O. Henry—it was certain that there were no plot stories ever lived in any life."

As much as any writer of his time, Anderson combined the fate of being a flawed writer ("For all my egotism," he remarked late in his life, "I know I am but a minor figure") and a major force ("He was the father of my generation of

American writers and the tradition of American writing which our successors will carry on," remarked William Faulkner). None of Anderson's subsequent books had the literary impact of *Winesburg, Ohio,* though collections of short stories such as *The Triumph of the Egg* (1921), *Horses and Men* (1923), and *Death in the Woods and Other Stories* (1933) contain a number of excellent tales. Anderson continued to write novels, the most successful of which is *Poor White* (1920), the story of an aspiring midwestern inventor who realizes that his industrial genius is destroying the environment. His later novels include *Many Marriages* (1923), *Dark Laughter* (1925), *Beyond Desire* (1932), and *Kit Brandon* (1936). Anderson also published several collections of essays on American industrial and rural conditions, *Perhaps Women* (1931), *Puzzled America* (1935), and *Home Town* (1940), and a collection of literary profiles, *No Swank* (1934).

In the summer of 1922, a year after he had traveled to Europe and met Gertrude Stein, Anderson was finally able to give up copywriting. In 1924 he moved with his third wife to Marion, Virginia, where he edited two local newspapers, one Democratic and the other Republican. He collected his editorials in *Hello, Towns* (1929). In 1941, while on a State Department goodwill tour of South America, he died of peritonitis caused by his accidentally having swallowed a fragment of a toothpick at a cocktail party.

One explanation of the discrepancy between Anderson's achievement and his influence has to do with his origins. Many critics and readers were easterners who nevertheless believed, as Van Wyck Brooks put it, "that the heart of America lay in the West" and that "Sherwood was the essence of his West." A second explanation lies in the overriding importance of the theme and scene that Anderson sought to explore: the loneliness of the modern world as manifested in the social, cultural, and spiritual impoverishment of small-town America. The isolation that haunts Anderson's characters is religious as well as social; felt as a form of orphanhood, a kind of ultimate separation, it leads them almost inevitably to flight that is undertaken as a kind of return. The struggle his characters wage, they wage in the name of reestablishing ties with a community, a family, or a self that they have somehow lost. A third explanation lies in Anderson's capacity for deliberate self-dramatization. Like Walt Whitman, Anderson viewed himself as a composite of us all; he was the American as writer. In the tales he told about himself, in his three volumes of autobiographical writing, *A Story-Teller's Story* (1924), *Tar: A Midwest Childhood* (1926), and the posthumous *Sherwood Anderson's Memoirs* (1942), and in his letters, he insisted on mixing his life and art, on making himself into a fictional character for his time as well as for himself. In this, too, his motives were mixed: They were social and even didactic as well as personal and artistic. Anderson wanted to teach us, among other things, the value of dropping out and breaking away. "I hardly know what I can teach except anti-success," he wrote his brother Karl in 1931. Most of all, Anderson wanted to teach us that the purpose of art, like the purpose of love, is self-transcendence. "I think the whole glory of writing lies in the fact that it forces us out of ourselves and into the lives of others," he said later in his life. "In the end the real writer becomes a lover."

Further Reading:
I. Howe, *Sherwood Anderson*, 1951.
R. Burbank, *Sherwood Anderson*, 1964.
B. Weber, *Sherwood Anderson*, 1964.
The Achievement of Sherwood Anderson: Essays in Criticism, ed. R. L. White, 1966.

Texts:
"The Book of the Grotesque" and "Hands"
from *Winesburg, Ohio*, 1919.
"Mother" and "Departure" from the edition of 1958.
"The Egg" from *The Triumph of the Egg*, 1921.

---

from Winesburg, Ohio

The Book of the Grotesque

The writer, an old man with a white mustache, had some difficulty in getting into bed. The windows of the house in which he lived were high and he wanted to look at the trees when he awoke in the morning. A carpenter came to fix the bed so that it would be on a level with the window.

Quite a fuss was made about the matter. The carpenter, who had been a soldier in the Civil War, came into the writer's room and sat down to talk of building a platform for the purpose of raising the bed. The writer had cigars lying about and the carpenter smoked.

For a time the two men talked of the raising of the bed and then they talked of other things. The soldier got on the subject of the war. The writer, in fact, led him to that subject. The carpenter had once been a prisoner in Andersonville prison and had lost a brother. The brother had died of starvation, and whenever the carpenter got upon that subject he cried. He, like the old writer, had a white mustache, and when he cried he puckered up his lips and the mustache bobbed up and down. The weeping old man with the cigar in his mouth was ludicrous. The plan the writer had for the raising of his bed was forgotten and later the carpenter did it in his own way and the writer, who was past sixty, had to help himself with a chair when he went to bed at night.

In his bed the writer rolled over on his side and lay quite still. For years he had been beset with notions concerning his heart. He was a hard smoker and his heart fluttered. The idea had got into his mind that he would some time die unexpectedly and always when he got into bed he thought of that. It did not alarm him. The effect in fact was quite a special thing and not easily explained. It made him more alive, there in bed, than at any other time. Perfectly still he lay and his body was old and not of much use any more, but something inside him was altogether young. He was like a pregnant woman, only that the thing inside him was not a baby but a youth. No, it wasn't a youth, it was a woman, young, and wearing a coat of mail like a knight. It is absurd, you see, to try to tell what was inside the old writer as he lay on his high bed and listened to the fluttering of his heart. The thing to get at is what the writer, or the young thing within the writer, was thinking about.

The old writer, like all of the people in the world, had got, during his long life, a great many notions in his head. He had once been quite handsome and a number of women had been in love with him. And then, of course, he had known people, many people, known them in a peculiarly intimate way that was different from the way in which you and I know people. At least that is what the writer thought and the thought pleased him. Why quarrel with an old man concerning his thoughts?

In the bed the writer had a dream that was not a dream. As he grew somewhat sleepy but was still conscious, figures began to appear before his eyes. He imagined the young indescribable thing within himself was driving a long procession of figures before his eyes.

You see the interest in all this lies in the figures that went before the eyes of the writer. They were all grotesques. All of the men and women the writer had ever known had become grotesques.

The grotesques were not all horrible. Some were amusing, some almost beautiful, and one, a woman all drawn out of shape, hurt the old man by her grotesqueness. When she passed he made a noise like a small dog whimpering. Had you come into the room you might have supposed the old man had unpleasant dreams or perhaps indigestion.

For an hour the procession of grotesques passed before the eyes of the old man, and then, although it was a painful thing to do, he crept out of bed and began to write. Some one of the grotesques had made a deep impression on his mind and he wanted to describe it.

At his desk the writer worked for an hour. In the end he wrote a book which he called "The Book of the Grotesque." It was never published, but I saw it once and it made an indelible impression on my mind. The book had one central thought that is very strange and has always remained with me. By remembering it I have been able to understand many people and things that I was never able to understand before. The thought was involved but a simple statement of it would be something like this:

That in the beginning when the world was young there were a great many thoughts but no such thing as a truth. Man made the truths himself and each truth was a composite of a great many vague thoughts. All about in the world were the truths and they were all beautiful.

The old man had listed hundreds of the truths in his book. I will not try to tell you of all of them. There was the truth of virginity and the truth of passion, the truth of wealth and of poverty, of thrift and of profligacy, of carelessness and abandon. Hundreds and hundreds were the truths and they were all beautiful.

And then the people came along. Each as he appeared snatched up one of the truths and some who were quite strong snatched up a dozen of them.

It was the truths that made the people grotesques. The old man had quite an elaborate theory concerning the matter. It was his notion that the moment one of the people took one of the truths to himself, called it his truth, and tried to live his life by it, he became a grotesque and the truth he embraced became a falsehood.

You can see for yourself how the old man, who had spent all of his life writing and was filled with words, would write hundreds of pages concerning this matter. The subject would become so big in his mind that he himself would be in danger of becoming a grotesque. He didn't, I suppose, for the same reason that he never published the book. It was the young thing inside him that saved the old man.

Concerning the old carpenter who fixed the bed for the writer, I only mentioned him because he, like many of what are called very common people, became the nearest thing to what is understandable and lovable of all the grotesques in the writer's book.

Hands

Upon the half decayed veranda of a small frame house that stood near the edge of a ravine near the town of Winesburg, Ohio, a fat little old man walked nervously up and down. Across a long field that had been seeded for clover but that had produced only a dense crop of yellow mustard weeds, he could see the public highway along which went a wagon filled with berry pickers returning from the fields. The berry pickers, youths and maidens, laughed and shouted boisterously. A boy clad in a blue shirt leaped from the wagon and attempted to drag after him one of the maidens, who screamed and protested shrilly. The feet of the boy in the road kicked up a cloud of dust that floated across the face of the departing sun. Over the long field came a thin girlish voice. "Oh, you Wing Biddlebaum, comb your hair, it's falling into your eyes," commanded the voice to the man, who was bald and whose nervous little hands fiddled about the bare white forehead as though arranging a mass of tangled locks.

Wing Biddlebaum, forever frightened and beset by a ghostly band of doubts, did not think of himself as in any way a part of the life of the town where he had lived for twenty years. Among all the people of Winesburg but one had come close to him. With George Willard, son of Tom Willard, the proprietor of the New Willard House, he had formed something like a friendship. George Willard was the reporter on the *Winesburg Eagle* and sometimes in the evenings he walked out along the highway to Wing Biddlebaum's house. Now as the old man walked up and down on the veranda, his hands moving nervously about, he was hoping that George Willard would come and spend the evening with him. After the wagon containing the berry pickers had passed, he went across the field through the tall mustard weeds and climbing a rail fence peered anxiously along the road to the town. For a moment he stood thus, rubbing his hands together and looking up and down the road, and then, fear overcoming him, ran back to walk again upon the porch on his own house.

In the presence of George Willard, Wing Biddlebaum, who for twenty years had been the town mystery, lost something of his timidity, and his shadowy personality, submerged in a sea of doubts, came forth to look at the world. With the young reporter at his side, he ventured in the light of day into Main Street or strode up and down on the rickety front porch of his own house, talking excitedly. The voice that had been low and trembling became shrill and loud. The bent figure straightened. With a kind of wriggle, like a fish returned to the brook by the fisherman, Biddlebaum the silent began to talk, striving to put into words the ideas that had been accumulated by his mind during long years of silence.

Wing Biddlebaum talked much with his hands. The slender expressive fingers, forever active, forever striving to conceal themselves in his pockets or behind his back, came forth and became the piston rods of his machinery of expression.

The story of Wing Biddlebaum is a story of hands. Their restless activity, like unto the beating of the wings of an imprisoned bird, had given him his name. Some obscure poet of the town had thought of it. The hands alarmed their owner. He wanted to keep them hidden away and looked with amazement at the quiet inexpressive hands of other men who worked beside him in the fields, or passed, driving sleepy teams on country roads.

When he talked to George Willard, Wing Biddlebaum closed his fists and beat with them upon a table or on the walls of his house. The action made him more comfortable. If the desire to talk came to him when the two were walking in the fields, he sought out a stump or the top board of a fence and with his hands pounding busily talked with renewed ease.

The story of Wing Biddlebaum's hands is worth a book in itself. Sympathetically set forth it would tap many strange, beautiful qualities in obscure men. It is a job for a poet. In Winesburg the hands had attracted attention merely because of their activity. With them Wing Biddlebaum had picked as high as a hundred and forty quarts of strawberries in a day. They became his distinguishing feature, the source of his fame. Also they made more grotesque an already grotesque and elusive individuality. Winesburg was proud of the hands of Wing Biddlebaum in the same spirit in which it was proud of Banker White's new stone house and Wesley Moyer's bay stallion, Tony Tip, that had won the two-fifteen trot at the fall races in Cleveland.

As for George Willard, he had many times wanted to ask about the hands. At times an almost overwhelming curiosity had taken hold of him. He felt that there must be a reason for their strange activity and their inclination to keep hidden away and only a growing respect for Wing Biddlebaum kept him from blurting out the questions that were often in his mind.

Once he had been on the point of asking. The two were walking in the fields on a summer afternoon and had stopped to sit upon a grassy bank. All afternoon Wing Biddlebaum had talked as one inspired. By a fence he had stopped and beating like a giant woodpecker upon the top board had shouted at George Willard, condemning his tendency to be too much influenced by the people about him. "You are destroying yourself," he cried. "You have the inclination to be alone and to dream and you are afraid of dreams. You want to be like others in town here. You hear them talk and you try to imitate them."

On the grassy bank Wing Biddlebaum had tried again to drive his point home. His voice became soft and reminiscent, and with a sigh of contentment he launched into a long rambling talk, speaking as one lost in a dream.

Out of the dream Wing Biddlebaum made a picture for George Willard. In the picture men lived again in a kind of pastoral golden age. Across a green open country came clean-limbed young men, some afoot, some mounted upon horses. In crowds the young men came to gather about the feet of an old man who sat beneath a tree in a tiny garden and who talked to them.

Wing Biddlebaum became wholly inspired. For once he forgot the hands. Slowly they stole forth and lay upon George Willard's shoulders. Something new and bold came into the voice that talked. "You must try to forget all you have learned," said the old man. "You must begin to dream. From this time on you must shut your ears to the roaring of the voices."

Pausing in his speech, Wing Biddlebaum looked long and earnestly at George Willard. His eyes glowed. Again he raised the hands to caress the boy and then a look of horror swept over his face.

With a convulsive movement of his body, Wing Biddlebaum sprang to his feet and thrust his hands deep into his trousers pockets. Tears came to his eyes. "I must be getting along home. I can talk no more with you," he said nervously.

Without looking back, the old man had hurried down the hillside and across a meadow, leaving George Willard perplexed and frightened upon the grassy slope. With a shiver of dread the boy arose and went along the road toward town. "I'll not ask him about his hands," he thought, touched by the memory of the terror he had seen in the man's eyes. "There's something wrong, but I don't want to know what it is. His hands have something to do with his fear of me and of everyone."

And George Willard was right. Let us look briefly into the story of the hands. Perhaps our talking of them will arouse the poet who will tell the hidden wonder story of the influence for which the hands were but fluttering pennants of promise.

In his youth Wing Biddlebaum had been a school teacher in a town in Pennsylvania. He was not then known as Wing Biddlebaum, but went by the less euphonic name of Adolph Myers. As Adolph Myers he was much loved by the boys of his school.

Adolph Myers was meant by nature to be a teacher of youth. He was one of those rare, little-understood men who rule by a power so gentle that it passes as a lovable weakness. In their feeling for the boys under their charge such men are not unlike the finer sort of women in their love of men.

And yet that is but crudely stated. It needs the poet there. With the boys of his school, Adolph Myers had walked in the evening or had sat talking until dusk upon the schoolhouse steps lost in a kind of dream. Here and there went his hands, caressing the shoulders of the boys, playing about the tousled heads. As he talked his voice became soft and musical. There was a caress in that also. In a way the voice and the hands, the stroking of the shoulders and the touching of the hair were a part of the schoolmaster's effort to carry a dream into the young minds. By the caress that was in his fingers he expressed himself. He was one of those men in whom the force that creates life is diffused, not centralized. Under the caress of his hands doubt and disbelief went out of the minds of the boys and they began also to dream.

And then the tragedy. A half-witted boy of the school became enamored of the young master. In his bed at night he imagined unspeakable things and in the morning went forth to tell his dreams as facts. Strange, hideous accusations fell from his loose-hung lips. Through the Pennsylvania town went a shiver. Hidden, shadowy doubts that had been in men's minds concerning Adolph Myers were galvanized into beliefs.

The tragedy did not linger. Trembling lads were jerked out of bed and questioned. "He put his arms about me," said one. "His fingers were always playing in my hair," said another.

One afternoon a man of the town, Henry Bradford, who kept a saloon, came to the schoolhouse door. Calling Adolph Myers into the school yard he began to beat him with his fists. As his hard knuckles beat down into the frightened face of the schoolmaster, his wrath became more and more terrible. Screaming with dismay, the children ran here and there like disturbed insects. "I'll teach you to put your hands on my boy, you beast," roared the saloon keeper, who, tired of beating the master, had begun to kick him about the yard.

Adolph Myers was driven from the Pennsylvania town in the night. With lanterns in their hands a dozen men came to the door of the house where he lived alone and commanded that he dress and come forth. It was raining and one of the men had a rope in his hands. They had intended to hang the schoolmaster, but something in his figure, so small, white, and pitiful, touched their hearts and they let him escape. As he ran away into the darkness they repented of their weakness and ran after him, swearing and throwing sticks and great balls of soft mud at the figure that screamed and ran faster and faster into the darkness.

For twenty years Adolph Myers had lived alone in Winesburg. He was but forty but looked sixty-five. The name of Biddlebaum he got from a box of goods seen at a freight station as he hurried through an eastern Ohio town. He had an aunt in Winesburg, a black-toothed old woman who raised chickens, and with her he lived until she died. He had been ill for a year after the experience in Pennsylvania, and after his recovery worked as a day laborer in the fields, going timidly about and striving to conceal his hands. Although he did not understand what had happened he felt that the hands must be to blame. Again and again the fathers of the boys had talked of the hands. "Keep your hands to yourself," the saloon keeper had roared, dancing with fury in the schoolhouse yard.

Upon the veranda of his house by the ravine, Wing Biddlebaum continued to walk up and down until the sun had disappeared and the road beyond the field was lost in the grey shadows. Going into his house he cut slices of bread and spread honey upon them. When the rumble of the evening train that took away the express cars loaded with the day's harvest of berries had passed and restored the silence of the summer night, he went again to walk upon the veranda. In the darkness he could not see the hands and they became quiet. Although he still hungered for the presence of the boy, who was the medium through which he expressed his love of man, the hunger became again a part of his loneliness and his waiting. Lighting a lamp, Wing Bid-dlebaum washed the few dishes soiled by his simple meal and, setting up a folding cot by the screen door that led to the porch, prepared to undress for the night. A few stray white bread crumbs lay on the cleanly washed floor by the table; putting the lamp upon a low stool he began to pick up the crumbs, carrying them to his mouth one by one with unbelievable rapidity. In the dense blotch of light beneath the table, the kneeling figure looked like a priest engaged in some service of his church. The nervous expressive fingers, flashing in and out of the light, might well have been mistaken for the fingers of the devotee going swiftly through decade after decade of his rosary.

Mother

Elizabeth Willard, the mother of George Willard, was tall and gaunt and her face was marked with smallpox scars. Although she was but forty-five, some obscure disease had taken the fire out of her figure. Listlessly she went about the disorderly old hotel looking at the faded wall-paper and the ragged carpets and, when she was able to be about, doing the work of a chambermaid among beds soiled by the slumbers of fat traveling men. Her husband, Tom Willard, a slender, graceful man with square shoulders, a quick military step, and a black mustache trained to turn sharply up at the ends, tried to put the wife out of his mind. The presence of the tall ghostly figure, moving slowly through the halls, he took as a reproach to himself. When he thought of her he grew angry and swore. The hotel was unprofitable and forever on the edge of failure and he wished himself out of it. He thought of the old house and the woman who lived there with him as things defeated and done for. The hotel in which he had begun life so hopefully was now a mere ghost of what a hotel should be. As he went spruce and business-like through the streets of Winesburg, he sometimes stopped and turned quickly about as though fearing that the spirit of the hotel and of the woman would follow him even into the streets. "Damn such a life, damn it!" he sputtered aimlessly.

Tom Willard had a passion for village politics and for years had been the leading Democrat in a strongly Republican community. Some day, he told himself, the tide of things political will turn in my favor and the years of ineffectual service count big in the bestowal of rewards. He dreamed of going to Congress and even of becoming governor. Once when a younger member of the party arose at a political conference and began to boast of his faithful service, Tom Willard grew white with fury. "Shut up, you," he roared, glaring about. "What do you know of service? What are you but a boy? Look at what I've done here! I was a Democrat here in Winesburg when it was a crime to be a Democrat. In the old days they fairly hunted us with guns."

Between Elizabeth and her one son George there was a deep unexpressed bond of sympathy, based on a girlhood dream that had long ago died. In the son's presence she was timid and reserved, but sometimes while he hurried about town intent upon his duties as a reporter, she went into his room and closing the door knelt by a little desk, made of a kitchen table, that sat near a window. In the room by the desk she went through a ceremony that was half a prayer, half a demand, addressed to the skies. In the boyish figure she yearned to see something half forgotten that had once been a part of herself re-created. The prayer concerned that. "Even though I die, I will in some way keep defeat from you," she cried, and so deep was her determination that her whole body shook. Her eyes glowed and she clenched her fists. "If I am dead and see him becoming a meaningless drab figure like myself, I will come back," she declared. "I ask God now to give me that privilege. I demand it. I will pay for it. God may beat me with his fists. I will take any blow that may befall if but this my boy be allowed to express something for us both." Pausing uncertainly, the woman stared about the boy's room. "And do not let him become smart and successful either," she added vaguely.

The communion between George Willard and his mother was outwardly a formal thing without meaning. When she was ill and sat by the window in her room he sometimes went in the evening to make her a visit. They sat by a window that looked over the roof of a small frame building into Main Street. By turning their heads they could see through another window, along an alleyway that ran behind the Main Street stores and into the back door of Abner Groff's bakery. Sometimes as they sat thus a picture of village life presented itself to them. At the back door of his shop appeared Abner Groff with a stick or an empty milk bottle in his hand. For a long time there was a feud between the baker and a grey cat that belonged to Sylvester West, the druggist. The boy and his mother saw the cat creep into the door of the bakery and presently emerge followed by the baker, who swore and waved his arms about. The baker's eyes were small and red and his black hair and beard were filled with flour dust. Sometimes he was so angry that, although the cat had disappeared, he hurled sticks, bits of broken glass, and even some of the tools of his trade about. Once he broke a window at the back of Sinning's Hardware Store. In the alley the grey cat crouched behind barrels filled with torn paper and broken bottles above which flew a black swarm of flies. Once when she was alone, and after watching a prolonged and ineffectual outburst on the part of the baker, Elizabeth Willard put her head down on her long white hands and wept. After that she did not look along the alleyway any more, but tried to forget the contest between the bearded man and the cat. It seemed like a rehearsal of her own life, terrible in its vividness.

In the evening when the son sat in the room with his mother, the silence made them both feel awkward. Darkness came on and the evening train came in at the station. In the street below feet tramped up and down upon a board sidewalk. In the station yard, after the evening train had gone, there was a heavy silence. Perhaps Skinner Leason, the express agent, moved a truck the length of the station platform. Over on Main Street sounded a man's voice, laughing. The door of the express office banged. George Willard arose and crossing the room fumbled for the doorknob. Sometimes he knocked against a chair, making it scrape along the floor. By the window sat the sick woman, perfectly still, listless. Her long hands, white and bloodless, could be seen drooping over the ends of the arms of the chair. "I think you had better be out among the boys. You are too much indoors," she said, striving to relieve the embarrassment of the departure. "I thought I would take a walk," replied George Willard, who felt awkward and confused.

One evening in July, when the transient guests who made the New Willard House their temporary home had become scarce, and the hallways, lighted only by kerosene lamps turned low, were plunged in gloom, Elizabeth Willard had an adventure. She had been ill in bed for several days and her son had not come to visit her. She was alarmed. The feeble blaze of life that remained in her body was blown into a flame by her anxiety and she crept out of bed, dressed and hurried along the hallway toward her son's room, shaking with exaggerated fears. As she went along she steadied herself with her hand, slipped along the papered walls of the hall and breathed with difficulty. The air whistled through her teeth. As she hurried forward she thought how foolish she was. "He is concerned with boyish affairs," she told herself. "Perhaps he has now begun to walk about in the evening with girls."

Elizabeth Willard had a dread of being seen by guests in the hotel that had once belonged to her father and the ownership of which still stood recorded in her name in the county courthouse. The hotel was continually losing patronage because of its shabbiness and she thought of herself as also shabby. Her own room was in an obscure corner and when she felt able to work she voluntarily worked among the beds, preferring the labor that could be done when the guests were abroad seeking trade among the merchants of Winesburg.

By the door of her son's room the mother knelt upon the floor and listened for some sound from within. When she heard the boy moving about and talking in low tones a smile came to her lips. George Willard had a habit of talking aloud to himself and to hear him doing so had always given his mother a peculiar pleasure. The habit in him, she felt, strengthened the secret bond that existed between them. A thousand times she had whispered to herself of the matter. "He is groping about, trying to find himself," she thought. "He is not a dull clod, all words and smartness. Within him there is a secret something that is striving to grow. It is the thing I let be killed in myself."

In the darkness in the hallway by the door the sick woman arose and started again toward her own room. She was afraid that the door would open and the boy come upon her. When she had reached a safe distance and was about to turn a corner into a second hallway she stopped and bracing herself with her hands waited, thinking to shake off a trembling fit of weakness that had come upon her. The presence of the boy in the room had made her happy. In her bed, during the long hours alone, the little fears that had visited her had become giants. Now they were all gone. "When I get back to my room I shall sleep," she murmured gratefully.

But Elizabeth Willard was not to return to her bed and to sleep. As she stood trembling in the darkness the door of her son's room opened and the boy's father, Tom Willard, stepped out. In the light that streamed out at the door he stood with the knob in his hand and talked. What he said infuriated the woman.

Tom Willard was ambitious for his son. He had always thought of himself as a successful man, although nothing he had ever done had turned out successfully. However, when he was out of sight of the New Willard House and had no fear of coming upon his wife, he swaggered and began to dramatize himself as one of the chief men of the town. He wanted his son to succeed. He it was who had secured for the boy the position on the *Winesburg Eagle*. Now, with a ring of earnestness in his voice, he was advising concerning some course of conduct. "I tell you what, George, you've got to wake up," he said sharply. "Will Henderson has spoken to me three times concerning the matter. He says you go along for hours not hearing when you are spoken to and acting like a gawky girl. What ails you?" Tom Willard laughed good-naturedly. "Well, I guess you'll get over it," he said. "I told Will that. You're not a fool and you're not a woman. You're Tom Willard's son and you'll wake up. I'm not afraid. What you say clears things up. If being a newspaper man had put the notion of becoming a writer into your mind that's all right. Only I guess you'll have to wake up to do that too, eh?"

Tom Willard went briskly along the hallway and down a flight of stairs to the office. The woman in the darkness could hear him laughing and talking with a guest who was striving to wear away a dull evening by dozing in a chair by the office door. She returned to the door of her son's room. The weakness had passed from her body as by a miracle and she stepped boldly along. A thousand ideas raced through her head. When she heard the scraping of a chair and the sound of a pen scratching upon paper, she again turned and went back along the hallway to her own room.

A definite determination had come into the mind of the defeated wife of the Winesburg hotel keeper. The determination was the result of long years of quiet and rather ineffectual thinking. "Now," she told herself, "I will act. There is something threatening my boy and I will ward it off." The fact that the conversation between Tom Willard and his son had been rather quiet and natural, as though an understanding existed between them, maddened her. Although for years she had hated her husband, her hatred had always before been a quite impersonal thing. He had been merely a part of something else that she hated. Now, and by the few words at the door, he had become the thing personified. In the darkness of her own room she clenched her fists and glared about. Going to a cloth bag that hung on a nail by the wall she took out a long pair of sewing scissors and held them in her hand like a dagger. "I will stab him," she said aloud. "He has chosen to be the voice of evil and I will kill him. When I have killed him something will snap within myself and I will die also. It will be a release for all of us."

In her girlhood and before her marriage with Tom Willard, Elizabeth had borne a somewhat shaky reputation in Winesburg. For years she had been what is called "stage-struck" and had paraded through the streets with traveling men guests at her father's hotel, wearing loud clothes and urging them to tell her of life in the cities out of which they had come. Once she startled the town by putting on men's clothes and riding a bicycle down Main Street.

In her own mind the tall dark girl had been in those days much confused. A great restlessness was in her and it expressed itself in two ways. First there was an uneasy desire for change, for some big definite movement to her life. It was this feeling that had turned her mind to the stage. She dreamed of joining some company and wandering over the world, seeing always new faces and giving something out of herself to all people. Sometimes at night she was quite beside herself with the thought, but when she tried to talk of the matter to the members of the theatrical companies that came to Winesburg and stopped at her father's hotel, she got nowhere. They did not seem to know what she meant, or if she did get something of her passion expressed, they only laughed. "It's not like that," they said. "It's as dull and uninteresting as this here. Nothing comes of it."

With the traveling men when she walked about with them, and later with Tom Willard, it was quite different. Always they seemed to understand and sympathize with her. On the side streets of the village, in the darkness under the trees, they took hold of her hand and she thought that something unexpressed in herself came forth and became a part of an unexpressed something in them.

And then there was the second expression of her restlessness. When that came she felt for a time released and happy. She did not blame the men who walked with her and later she did not blame Tom Willard. It was always the same, beginning with kisses and ending, after strange wild emotions, with peace and then sobbing repentance. When she sobbed she put her hand upon the face of the man and had always the same thought. Even though he were large and bearded she thought he had become suddenly a little boy. She wondered why he did not sob also.

In her room, tucked away in a corner of the old Willard House, Elizabeth Willard lighted a lamp and put it on a dressing table that stood by the door. A thought had come into her mind and she went to a closet and brought out a small square box and set it on the table. The box contained material for make-up and had been left with other things by a theatrical company that had once been stranded in Winesburg. Elizabeth Willard had decided that she would be beautiful. Her hair was still black and there was a great mass of it braided and coiled about her head. The scene that was to take place in the office below began to grow in her mind. No ghostly worn-out figure should confront Tom Willard, but something quite unexpected and startling. Tall and with dusky cheeks and hair that fell in a mass from her shoulders, a figure should come striding down the stairway before the startled loungers in the hotel office. The figure would be silent—it would be swift and terrible. As a tigress whose cub had been threatened would she appear, coming out of the shadows, stealing noiselessly along and holding the long wicked scissors in her hand.

With a little broken sob in her throat, Elizabeth Willard blew out the light that stood upon the table and stood weak and trembling in the darkness. The strength that had been as a miracle in her body left and she half reeled across the floor, clutching at the back of the chair in which she had spent so many long days staring out over the tin roofs into the main street of Winesburg. In the hallway there was the sound of footsteps and George Willard came in at the door. Sitting in a chair beside his mother he began to talk. "I'm going to get out of here," he said. "I don't know where I shall go or what I shall do but I am going away."

The woman in the chair waited and trembled. An impulse came to her. "I suppose you had better wake up," she said. "You think that? You will go to the city and make money, eh? It will be better for you, you think, to be a business man, to be brisk and smart and alive?" She waited and trembled.

The son shook his head. "I suppose I can't make you understand, but oh, I wish I could," he said earnestly. "I can't even talk to father about it. I don't try. There isn't any use. I don't know what I shall do. I just want to go away and look at people and think."

Silence fell upon the room where the boy and woman sat together. Again, as on the other evenings, they were embarrassed. After a time the boy tried again to talk. "I suppose it won't be for a year or two but I've been thinking about it," he said, rising and going toward the door. "Something father said makes it sure that I shall have to go away." He fumbled with the door knob. In the room the silence became unbearable to the woman. She wanted to cry out with joy because of the words that had come from the lips of her son, but the expression of joy had become impossible to her. "I think you had better go out among the boys. You are too much indoors," she said. "I thought I would go for a little walk," replied the son stepping awkwardly out of the room and closing the door.

Departure

Young George Willard got out of bed at four in the morning. It was April and the young tree leaves were just coming out of their buds. The trees along the residence streets in Winesburg are maple and the seeds are winged. When the wind blows they whirl crazily about, filling the air and making a carpet underfoot.

George came downstairs into the hotel office carrying a brown leather bag. His trunk was packed for departure. Since two o'clock he had been awake thinking of the journey he was about to take and wondering what he would find at the end of his journey. The boy who slept in the hotel office lay on a cot by the door. His mouth was open and he snored lustily. George crept past the cot and went out into the silent deserted main street. The east was pink with the dawn and long streaks of light climbed into the sky where a few stars still shone.

Beyond the last house on Trunion Pike in Winesburg there is a great stretch of open fields. The fields are owned by farmers who live in town and drive homeward at evening along Trunion Pike in light creaking wagons. In the fields are planted berries and small fruits. In the late afternoon in the hot summers when the road and the fields are covered with dust, a smoky haze lies over the great flat basin of land. To look across it is like looking out across the sea. In the spring when the land is green the effect is somewhat different. The land becomes a wide green billiard table on which tiny human insects toil up and down.

All through his boyhood and young manhood George Willard had been in the habit of walking on Trunion Pike. He had been in the midst of the great open place on winter nights when it was covered with snow and only the moon looked down at him; he had been there in the fall when bleak winds blew and on summer evenings when the air vibrated with the song of insects. On the April morning he wanted to go there again, to walk again in the silence. He did walk to where the road dipped down by a little stream two miles from town and then turned and walked silently back again. When he got to Main Street clerks were sweeping the sidewalks before the stores. "Hey, you George. How does it feel to be going away?" they asked.

The westbound train leaves Winesburg at seven forty-five in the morning. Tom Little is conductor. His train runs from Cleveland to where it connects with a great trunk line railroad with terminals in Chicago and New York. Tom has what in railroad circles is called an "easy run." Every evening he returns to his family. In the fall and spring he spends his Sundays fishing in Lake Erie. He has a round red face and small blue eyes. He knows the people in the towns along his railroad better than a city man knows the people who live in his apartment building.

George came down the little incline from the New Willard House at seven o'clock. Tom Willard carried his bag. The son had become taller than the father.

On the station platform everyone shook the young man's hand. More than a dozen people waited about. Then they talked of their own affairs. Even Will Henderson, who was lazy and often slept until nine, had got out of bed. George was embarrassed. Gertrude Wilmot, a tall thin woman of fifty who worked in the Winesburg post office, came along the station platform. She had never before paid any attention to George. Now she stopped and put out her hand. In two words she voiced what everyone felt. "Good luck," she said sharply and then turning went on her way.

When the train came into the station George felt relieved. He scampered hurriedly aboard. Helen White came running along Main Street hoping to have a parting word with him, but he had found a seat and did not see her. When the train started Tom Little punched his ticket, grinned and, although he knew George well and knew on what adventure he was just setting out, made no comment. Tom had seen a thousand George Willards go out of their towns to the city. It was a commonplace enough incident with him. In the smoking car there was a man who had just invited Tom to go on a fishing trip to Sandusky Bay. He wanted to accept the invitation and talk over details.

George glanced up and down the car to be sure no one was looking, then took out his pocketbook and counted his money. His mind was occupied with a desire not to appear green. Almost the last words his father had said to him concerned the matter of his behavior when he got to the city. "Be a sharp one," Tom Willard had said. "Keep your eyes on your money. Be awake. That's the ticket. Don't let anyone think you're a greenhorn."

After George counted his money he looked out of the window and was surprised to see that the train was still in Winesburg.

The young man, going out of his town to meet the adventure of life, began to think but he did not think of anything very big or dramatic. Things like his mother's death, his departure from Winesburg, the uncertainty of his future life in the city, the serious and larger aspects of his life did not come into his mind.

He thought of little things—Turk Smollet wheeling boards through the main street of his town in the morning, a tall woman, beautifully gowned, who had once stayed overnight at his father's hotel, Butch Wheeler the lamp lighter of Winesburg hurrying through the streets on a summer evening and holding a torch in his hand, Helen White standing by a window in the Winesburg post office and putting a stamp on an envelope.

The young man's mind was carried away by his growing passion for dreams. One looking at him would not have thought him particularly sharp. With the recollection of little things occupying his mind he closed his eyes and leaned back in the car seat. He stayed that way for a long time and when he aroused himself and again looked out of the car window the town of Winesburg had disappeared and his life there had become but a background on which to paint the dreams of his manhood.

1919

The Egg[*]

My father was, I am sure, intended by nature to be a cheerful, kindly man. Until he was thirty-four years old he worked as a farm-hand for a man named Thomas Butterworth whose place lay near the town of Bidwell, Ohio. He had then a horse of his own and on Saturday evenings drove into town to spend a few hours in social intercourse with other farm-hands. In town he drank several glasses of beer and stood about in Ben Head's saloon—crowded on Saturday evenings with visiting farm-hands. Songs were sung and glasses thumped on the bar. At ten o'clock father drove home along a lonely country road, made his horse comfortable for the night and himself went to bed, quite happy in his position in life. He had at that time no notion of trying to rise in the world.

It was in the spring of his thirty-fifth year that father married my mother, then a country school-teacher, and in the following spring I came wriggling and crying into the world. Something happened to the two people. They became ambitious. The American passion for getting up in the world took possession of them.

It may have been that mother was responsible. Being a school-teacher she had no doubt read books and magazines. She had, I presume, read of how Garfield, Lincoln, and other Americans rose from poverty to fame and greatness and as I lay beside her —in the days of her lying-in—she may have dreamed that I would some day rule men and cities. At any rate she induced father to give up his place as a farm-hand, sell his horse and embark on an independent enterprise of his own. She was a tall silent woman with a long nose and troubled grey eyes. For herself she wanted nothing. For father and myself she was incurably ambitious.

The first venture into which the two people went turned out badly. They rented ten acres of poor stony land on Griggs's Road, eight miles from Bidwell, and launched into chicken raising. I grew into boyhood on the place and got my first impressions of life there. From the beginning they were impressions of disaster and if, in my turn, I am a gloomy man inclined to see the darker side of life, I attribute it to the fact

---

[*] First published in 1920 in *The Dial* as "The Triumph of the Egg."

that what should have been for me the happy joyous days of childhood were spent on a chicken farm.

One unversed in such matters can have no notion of the many and tragic things that can happen to a chicken. It is born out of an egg, lives for a few weeks as a tiny fluffy thing such as you will see pictured on Easter cards, then becomes hideously naked, eats quantities of corn and meal bought by the sweat of your father's brow, gets diseases called pip, cholera, and other names, stands looking with stupid eyes at the sun, becomes sick and dies. A few hens and now and then a rooster, intended to serve God's mysterious ends, struggle through to maturity. The hens lay eggs out of which come other chickens and the dreadful cycle is thus made complete. It is all unbelievably complex. Most philosophers must have been raised on chicken farms. One hopes for so much from a chicken and is so dreadfully disillusioned. Small chickens, just setting out on the journey of life, look so bright and alert and they are in fact so dreadfully stupid. They are so much like people they mix one up in one's judgments of life. If disease does not kill them they wait until your expectations are thoroughly aroused and then walk under the wheels of a wagon—to go squashed and dead back to their maker. Vermin infest their youth, and fortunes must be spent for curative powders. In later life I have seen how a literature has been built up on the subject of fortunes to be made out of the raising of chickens. It is intended to be read by the gods who have just eaten of the tree of the knowledge of good and evil. It is a hopeful literature and declares that much may be done by simple ambitious people who own a few hens. Do not be led astray by it. It was not written for you. Go hunt for gold on the frozen hills of Alaska, put your faith in the honesty of a politician, believe if you will that the world is daily growing better and that good will triumph over evil, but do not read and believe the literature that is written concerning the hen. It was not written for you.

I, however, digress. My tale does not primarily concern itself with the hen. If correctly told it will center on the egg. For ten years my father and mother struggled to make our chicken farm pay and then they gave up that struggle and began another. They moved into the town of Bidwell, Ohio and embarked in the restaurant business. After ten years of worry with incubators that did not hatch, and with tiny—and in their own way lovely—balls of fluff that passed on into semi-naked pullethood and from that into dead henhood, we threw all aside and packing our belongings on a wagon drove down Griggs's Road toward Bidwell, a tiny caravan of hope looking for a new place from which to start on our upward journey through life.

We must have been a sad looking lot, not, I fancy, unlike refugees fleeing from a battlefield. Mother and I walked in the road. The wagon that contained our goods had been borrowed for the day from Mr. Albert Griggs, a neighbor. Out of its sides stuck the legs of cheap chairs and at the back of the pile of beds, tables, and boxes filled with kitchen utensils was a crate of live chickens, and on top of that the baby carriage in which I had been wheeled about in my infancy. Why we stuck to the baby carriage I don't know. It was unlikely other children would be born and the wheels were broken. People who have few possessions cling tightly to those they have. That is one of the facts that make life so discouraging.

Father rode on top of the wagon. He was then a bald-headed man of forty-five, a little fat and from long association with mother and the chickens he had become habitually silent and discouraged. All during our ten years on the chicken farm he had worked as a laborer on neighboring farms and most of the money he had earned had been spent for remedies to cure chicken diseases, on Wilmer's White Wonder Cholera Cure or Professor Bidlow's Egg Producer or some other preparations that mother found advertised in the poultry papers. There were two little patches of hair on father's head just above his ears. I remember that as a child I used to sit looking at him when he had gone to sleep in a chair before the stove on Sunday afternoons in the winter. I had at that time already begun to read books and have notions of my own and the bald path that led over the top of his head was, I fancied, something like a broad road, such a road as Caesar might have made on which to lead his legions out of Rome and into the wonders of an unknown world. The tufts of hair that grew above father's ears were, I thought, like forests. I fell into a half-sleeping, half-waking state and dreamed I was a tiny thing going along the road into a far beautiful place where there were no chicken farms and where life was a happy eggless affair.

One might write a book concerning our flight from the chicken farm into town. Mother and I walked the entire eight miles—she to be sure that nothing fell from the wagon and I to see the wonders of the world. On the seat of the wagon beside father was his greatest treasure. I will tell you of that.

On a chicken farm where hundreds and even thousands of chickens come out of eggs surprising things sometimes happen. Grotesques are born out of eggs as out of people. The accident does not often occur—perhaps once in a thousand births. A chicken is, you see, born that has four legs, two pairs of wings, two heads or what not. The things do not live. They go quickly back to the hand of their maker that has for a moment trembled. The fact that the poor little things could not live was one of the tragedies of life to father. He had some sort of notion that if he could but bring into henhood or roosterhood a five-legged hen or a two-headed rooster his fortune would be made. He dreamed of taking the wonder about to county fairs and of growing rich by exhibiting it to other farm-hands.

At any rate he saved all the little monstrous things that had been born on our chicken farm. They were preserved in alcohol and put each in its own glass bottle. These he had carefully put into a box and on our journey into town it was carried on the wagon seat beside him. He drove the horses with one hand and with the other clung to the box. When we got to our destination the box was taken down at once and the bottles removed. All during our days as keepers of a restaurant in the town of Bidwell, Ohio, the grotesques in their little glass bottles sat on a shelf back of the counter. Mother sometimes protested but father was a rock on the subject of his treasure. The grotesques were, he declared, valuable. People, he said, liked to look at strange and wonderful things.

Did I say that we embarked in the restaurant business in the town of Bidwell, Ohio? I exaggerated a little. The town itself lay at the foot of a low hill and on the shore of a small river. The railroad did not run through the town and the station was a mile away to the north at a place called Pickleville. There had been a cider mill and pickle factory at the station, but before the time of our coming they had both gone out of business. In the morning and in the evening busses came down to the station along a road called Turner's Pike from the hotel on the main street of Bidwell. Our going to the out of the way place to embark in the restaurant business was mother's idea. She talked of it for a year and then one day went off and rented an empty store building opposite the railroad station. It was her idea that the restaurant would be profitable. Travelling men, she said, would be always waiting around to take trains out of town and town people would come to the station to await incoming trains. They would come to the restaurant to buy pieces of pie and drink coffee. Now that I am older I know that she had another motive in going. She was ambitious for me. She wanted me to rise in the world, to get into a town school and become a man of the towns.

At Pickleville father and mother worked hard as they always had done. At first there was the necessity of putting our place into shape to be a restaurant. That took a month. Father built a shelf on which he put tins of vegetables. He painted a sign on which he put his name in large red letters. Below his name was the sharp command —"EAT HERE"—that was so seldom obeyed. A show case was bought and filled with cigars and tobacco. Mother scrubbed the floor and the walls of the room. I went to school in the town and was glad to be away from the farm and from the presence of the discouraged, sad-looking chickens. Still I was not very joyous. In the evening I walked home from school along Turner's Pike and remembered the children I had seen playing in the town school yard. A troop of little girls had gone hopping about and singing. I tried that. Down along the frozen road I went hopping solemnly on one leg. "Hippity Hop To The Barber Shop," I sang shrilly. Then I stopped and looked doubtfully about. I was afraid of being seen in my gay mood. It must have seemed to me that I was doing a thing that should not be done by one who, like myself, had been raised on a chicken farm where death was a daily visitor.

Mother decided that our restaurant should remain open at night. At ten in the evening a passenger train went north past our door followed by a local freight. The freight crew had switching to do in Pickleville and when the work was done they came to our restaurant for hot coffee and food. Sometimes one of them ordered a fried egg. In the morning at four they returned north-bound and again visited us. A little trade began to grow up. Mother slept at night and during the day tended the restaurant and fed our boarders while father slept. He slept in the same bed mother had occupied during the night and I went off to the town of Bidwell and to school. During the long nights, while mother and I slept, father cooked meats that were to go into sandwiches for the lunch baskets of our boarders. Then an idea in regard to getting up in the world came into his head. The American spirit took hold of him. He also became ambitious.

In the long nights when there was little to do father had time to think. That was his undoing. He decided that he had in the past been an unsuccessful man because he had not been cheerful enough and that in the future he would adopt a cheerful outlook on life. In the early morning he came upstairs and got into bed with mother. She woke and the two talked. From my bed in the corner I listened.

It was father's idea that both he and mother should try to entertain the people who came to eat at our restaurant. I cannot now remember his words, but he gave the impression of one about to become in some obscure way a kind of public entertainer. When people, particularly young people from the town of Bidwell, came into our place, as on very rare occasions they did, bright entertaining conversation was to be made. From father's words I gathered that something of the jolly inn-keeper effect was to be sought. Mother must have been doubtful from the first, but she said nothing discouraging. It was father's notion that a passion for the company of himself and mother would spring up in the breasts of the younger people of the town of Bidwell. In the evening bright happy groups would come singing down Turner's Pike. They would troop shouting with joy and laughter into our place. There would be song and festivity. I do not mean to give the impression that father spoke so elaborately of the matter. He was as I have said an uncommunicative man. "They want some place to go. I tell you they want some place to go," he said over and over. That was as far as he got. My own imagination has filled in the blanks.

For two or three weeks this notion of father's invaded our house. We did not talk much, but in our daily lives tried earnestly to make smiles take the place of glum looks. Mother smiled at the boarders and I, catching the infection, smiled at our cat. Father became a little feverish in his anxiety to please. There was no doubt, lurking somewhere in him, a touch of the spirit of the showman. He did not waste much of his ammunition on the railroad men he served at night but seemed to be waiting for a young man or woman from Bidwell to come in to show what he could do. On the counter in the restaurant there was a wire basket kept always filled with eggs, and it must have been before his eyes when the idea of being entertaining was born in his brain. There was something pre-natal about the way eggs kept themselves connected with the development of his idea. At any rate an egg ruined his new impulse in life. Late one night I was awakened by a roar of anger coming from father's throat. Both mother and I sat upright in our beds. With trembling hands she lighted a lamp that stood on a table by her head. Downstairs the front door of our restaurant went shut with a bang and in a few minutes father tramped up the stairs. He held an egg in his hand and his hand trembled as though he were having a chill. There was a half insane light in his eyes. As he stood glaring at us I was sure he intended throwing the egg at either mother or me. Then he laid it gently on the table beside the lamp and dropped on his knees beside mother's bed. He began to cry like a boy and I, carried away by his grief, cried with him. The two of us filled the little upstairs room with our wailing voices. It is ridiculous, but of the picture we made I can remember only the fact that mother's hand continually stroked the bald path that ran across the top of his head. I have forgotten what mother said to him and how she induced him to tell her of what had happened downstairs. His explanation also has gone out of my mind. I remember only my own grief and fright and the shiny path over father's head glowing in the lamp light as he knelt by the bed.

As to what happened downstairs. For some unexplainable reason I know the story as well as though I had been a witness to my father's discomfiture. One in time gets to know many unexplainable things. On that evening young Joe Kane, son of a merchant of Bidwell, came to Pickleville to meet his father, who was expected on the ten o'clock evening train from the South. The train was three hours late and Joe came into our place to loaf about and to wait for its arrival. The local freight train came in and the freight crew were fed. Joe was left alone in the restaurant with father.

From the moment he came into our place the Bidwell young man must have been puzzled by my father's actions. It was his notion that father was angry at him for hanging around. He noticed that the restaurant keeper was apparently disturbed by his presence and he thought of going out. However, it began to rain and he did not fancy the long walk to town and back. He bought a five-cent cigar and ordered a cup of coffee. He had a newspaper in his pocket and took it out and began to read. "I'm waiting for the evening train. It's late," he said apologetically.

For a long time father, whom Joe Kane had never seen before, remained silently gazing at his visitor. He was no doubt suffering from an attack of stage fright. As so often happens in life he had thought so much and so often of the situation that now confronted him that he was somewhat nervous in its presence.

For one thing, he did not know what to do with his hands. He thrust one of them nervously over the counter and shook hands with Joe Kane. "How-de-do," he said. Joe Kane put his newspaper down and stared at him. Father's eye lighted on the basket of eggs that sat on the counter and he began to talk. "Well," he began hesitatingly, "well, you have heard of Christopher Columbus, eh?" He seemed to be angry. "That Christopher Columbus was a cheat," he declared emphatically. "He talked of making an egg stand on its end. He talked, he did, and then he went and broke the end of the egg."

My father seemed to his visitor to be beside himself at the duplicity of Christopher Columbus. He muttered and swore. He declared it was wrong to teach children that Christopher Columbus was a great man when, after all, he cheated at the critical moment. He had declared he would make an egg stand on end and then when his bluff had been called he had done a trick. Still grumbling at Columbus, father took an egg from the basket on the counter and began to walk up and down. He rolled the egg between the palms of his hands. He smiled genially. He began to mumble words regarding the effect to be produced on an egg by the electricity that comes out of the human body. He declared that without breaking its shell and by virtue of rolling it back and forth in his hands he could stand the egg on its end. He explained that the warmth of his hands and the gentle rolling movement he gave the egg created a new centre of gravity, and Joe Kane was mildly interested. "I have handled thousands of eggs," father said. "No one knows more about eggs than I do."

He stood the egg on the counter and it fell on its side. He tried the trick again and again, each time rolling the egg between the palms of his hands and saying the words regarding the wonders of electricity and the laws of gravity. When after a half hour's effort he did succeed in making the egg stand for a moment he looked up to find that his visitor was no longer watching. By the time he had succeeded in calling Joe Kane's attention to the success of his effort the egg had again rolled over and lay on its side.

Afire with the showman's passion and at the same time a good deal disconcerted by the failure of his first effort, father now took the bottles containing the poultry monstrosities down from their place on the shelf and began to show them to his visitor. "How would you like to have seven legs and two heads like this fellow?" he asked, exhibiting the most remarkable of his treasures. A cheerful smile played over his face. He reached over the counter and tried to slap Joe Kane on the shoulder as he had seen men do in Ben Head's saloon when he was a young farm-hand and drove to town on Saturday evenings. His visitor was made a little ill by the sight of the body of the terribly deformed bird floating in the alcohol in the bottle and got up to go. Coming from behind the counter father took hold of the young man's arm and led him back to his seat. He grew a little angry and for a moment had to turn his face away and force himself to smile. Then he put the bottles back on the shelf. In an outburst of generosity he fairly compelled Joe Kane to have a fresh cup of coffee and another cigar at his expense. Then he took a pan and filling it with vinegar, taken from a jug that sat beneath the counter, he declared himself about to do a new trick. "I will heat this egg in this pan of vinegar," he said. "Then I will put it through the neck of a bottle without breaking the shell. When the egg is inside the bottle it will resume its normal shape and the shell will become hard again. Then I will give the bottle with the egg in it to you. You can take it about with you wherever you go. People will want to know how you got the egg in the bottle. Don't tell them. Keep them guessing. That is the way to have fun with this trick."

Father grinned and winked at his visitor. Joe Kane decided that the man who confronted him was mildly insane but harmless. He drank the cup of coffee that had been given him and began to read his paper again. When the egg had been heated in vinegar father carried it on a spoon to the counter and going into a back room got an empty bottle. He was angry because his visitor did not watch him as he began to do his trick, but nevertheless went cheerfully to work. For a long time he struggled, trying to get the egg to go through the neck of the bottle. He put the pan of vinegar back on the stove, intending to reheat the egg, then picked it up and burned his fingers. After a second bath in the hot vinegar the shell of the egg had been softened a little but not enough for his purpose. He worked and worked and a spirit of desperate determination took possession of him. When he thought that at last the trick was about to be consummated the delayed train came in at the station and Joe Kane started to go nonchalantly out at the door. Father made a last desperate effort to conquer the egg and make it do the thing that would establish his reputation as one who knew how to entertain guests who came into his restaurant. He worried the egg. He attempted to be somewhat rough with it. He swore and the sweat stood out on his forehead. The egg broke under his hand. When the contents spurted over his clothes, Joe Kane, who had stopped at the door, turned and laughed.

A roar of anger rose from my father's throat. He danced and shouted a string of inarticulate words. Grabbing another egg from the basket on the counter, he threw it, just missing the head of the young man as he dodged through the door and escaped.

Father came upstairs to mother and me with an egg in his hand. I do not know what he intended to do. I imagine he had some idea of destroying it, of destroying all eggs, and that he intended to let mother and me see him begin. When, however, he got into the presence of mother something happened to him. He laid the egg gently on the table and dropped on his knees by the bed as I have already explained. He later decided to close the restaurant for the night and to come upstairs and get into bed. When he did so he blew out the light and after much muttered conversation both he and mother went to sleep. I suppose I went to sleep also, but my sleep was troubled. I awoke at dawn and for a long time looked at the egg that lay on the table. I wondered why eggs had to be and why from the egg came the hen who again laid the egg. The question got into my blood. It has stayed there, I imagine, because I am the son of my father. At any rate, the problem remains unsolved in my mind. And that, I conclude, is but another evidence of the complete and final triumph of the egg—at least as far as my family is concerned.

1920

H. L. Mencken
1880–1956

At the age of nine, armed with his first library card, H. L. Mencken began, as he reports in his autobiography, "to inhabit a world that was two-thirds letterpress and one-third trees, fields, streets, and people. I acquired round shoulders, spindly shanks, and a despondent view of humanity. I read everything that I could find in English. . . . To this day [at age sixty] I am still what might be called a reader, and have a high regard for authors." Long before he wrote these words, H. L. Mencken had become an astute reader and critic of American life as well as a prolific and controversial writer.

A journalist, magazine editor, essayist, humorist, and philologist, Mencken wrote on virtually every important issue in the first half of twentieth-century America. His list of books, articles, reviews, poems, newspaper reports, and columns runs well over three hundred pages. Intellectually, Mencken was drawn to everything, and everything he wrote was marked by a distinctive imaginative intelligence: impertinent and acerbic, but also always clearheaded and often quite humorous. As a cultural and political commentator, Mencken had few peers. His uncompromising criticism of what he saw as the nation's declining standards of literary taste as well as what he called the "unwarranted pretensions" of government officials and public institutions found grateful audiences among several generations of disgruntled Americans.

Henry Louis Mencken was born in Baltimore to prosperous German-American parents on September 12, 1880, and he lived in Baltimore nearly all his life. He had ten years of formal education before beginning his career in journalism as a reporter for the *Baltimore Herald* in 1899. Within four years he had risen to city editor. In 1906 he moved to the *Baltimore Sun* as editor-in-chief and began a lifelong association with the *Sun* papers. His early newspaper style recalled the sardonic frontier journalism of Mark Twain and Ambrose Bierce, and he used writing for much the same purposes—to expose pretension, quackery, and ignorance wherever he found it. Mencken's most celebrated reports focus on the national political conventions and the Scopes "monkey trial" in Tennessee during the summer of 1925.

While practicing his trade as a journalist, Mencken also began a long and distinguished career as a magazine editor. From 1914 to 1923 he helped edit the influential *Smart Set,* which he used as a forum to attack "Victorian" standards in art and morality, an action that first gained him notoriety as a literary critic. He promoted, for example, the naturalism of Theodore Dreiser and the satire of Sinclair Lewis at the expense of "the genteel tradition" represented by Henry James and William Dean Howells. His controversial literary criticism is collected in *A Book of Prefaces* (1917), which also contains his acerbic defense of his own amorality and his belief in freedom of expression. In 1924 he became editor of *The American Mercury,* another iconoclastic magazine, where he published the works of Carl Sandburg, Vachel Lindsay, and Lewis Mumford. Eventually, however, as the Great Depression deepened, Mencken's conservatism and scorn for

Franklin Roosevelt's New Deal cost the magazine many readers, and in 1933 he resigned as editor.

By the mid-1930s Mencken had written more than a dozen books. His most ambitious work was *The American Language* (1919), a brilliant historical analysis of the origins and growth of the second of two major "streams of English." Through the rest of his life, he continued to correct, enlarge, and rewrite *The American Language,* gradually adding several supplementary volumes to the original project. But the book that earned him the largest readership was *In Defense of Women* (1928), in which he defended the proposition that "the average American woman, despite her deficiencies, is greatly superior to the average American man."

In his six volumes of *Prejudices,* published between 1919 and 1928, Mencken turned his comic invective toward American politics, religion, and the foibles of the general public—the "booboisie," as he called them. His was a raucous comic personality, full of exaggeration, raillery, and bile for those he disliked and compassion, generosity, and loyalty for those he admired. Although he sometimes strikes readers as being against everything, he usually finds a way of doing justice to his principles as well as his prejudices.

In 1930 Mencken married Sara Haardt, a writer and English professor, who died in 1935 from tuberculosis. Thereafter Mencken lived with his brother August in the Baltimore home where they had been born. During a temporary respite from journalism in World War II, Mencken completed three volumes of an autobiography: *Happy Days, 1880–1892* (1940), *Newspaper Days, 1899–1906* (1941), and *Heathen Days, 1890–1936* (1943). A week after filing a scathing report on the 1948 Republican convention, Mencken suffered a stroke, which terminated his career. He died in 1956.

As a writer, Mencken always sought to be entertaining. He never forgot his readers. In fact, he cultivated an audience that he encouraged to regard itself as the "truly civilized minority." Ridicule was one of his chief weapons, humor another. He once described his humor as "a capacity to discover hidden and surprising relations between apparently disparate things, and to invent novel and arresting turns of speech." But his larger talent derived from the clarity with which he knew his own mind and the witty precision with which he expressed it, a point he made in the final lines of his last book, appropriately titled *Minority Report* (1956): "The imbeciles who have printed acres of comments on my books have seldom noticed the chief character of my style. It is that I write with almost scientific precision—that my meaning is never obscure." Yet if Mencken used his pen with the precision of a brain surgeon, he also relied on the emotive power of language. Rarely did he unfold a colorless rational argument. He mastered the art of public discourse and worked the language for all it was worth.

Near the end of his career, Mencken offered the following assessment of his own work:

> Those who explore these pages will find them marked with a certain ribaldry, even when they discuss topics commonly regarded as grave. I do not apologize for this, for life in the Republic has always seemed to me far more comic than serious. We live in a land of absolute quackeries, and if we do not learn how

to laugh we succumb to the melancholy disease which afflicts the race with viewers-with-alarm. I have had too good a time of it in this world to go down that chute.

A singular presence in twentieth-century American literature, Mencken recognized that "the life of every man who dissents from prevailing ideas is bound to be more or less lonely." He left no literary heirs.

Further Reading:
C. Bode, *Mencken*, 1969.
D. C. Stenerson, *H. L. Mencken: Iconoclast from Baltimore*, 1971.
C. A. Fecher, *Mencken: A Study of His Thought*, 1978.
On Mencken, ed. J. Dorsey, 1980.

Texts:
The American Language: A Preliminary Inquiry into the Development of English in the United States, 1919.
All other selections from *A Mencken Chrestomathy*, 1949.
See also *Letters of H. L. Mencken*, ed. G. J. Forgue, 1961.
The American Scene: A Reader, 1965.
The Young Mencken: The Best of His Work, ed. C. Bode, 1973.
The New Mencken Letters, ed. C. Bode, 1976.
A Choice of Days, 1980.

from The American Language

from **Euphemisms**

The American, probably more than any other man, is prone to be apologetic about the trade he follows. He seldom believes that it is quite worthy of his virtues and talents; almost always he thinks that he would have adorned something far gaudier. Unfortunately, it is not always possible for him to escape, or even for him to dream plausibly of escaping, so he soothes himself by assuring himself that he belongs to a superior section of his craft, and very often he invents a sonorous name to set himself off from the herd. Here we glimpse the origin of a multitude of characteristic American euphemisms, *e.g.*, *mortician* for *undertaker*, *realtor* for *real-estate agent*, *electragist* for *electrical contractor*, *aisle manager* for *floor-walker*, *beautician* for *hairdresser*, *exterminating engineer* for *rat-catcher*, and so on. *Realtor* was devised by a high-toned real-estate agent of Minneapolis, Charles N. Chadbourn by name. He thus describes its genesis:

> It was in November, 1915, on my way to a meeting of the Minneapolis Real Estate Board, that I was annoyed by the strident peddling of a scandal sheet: "All About the Robbery of a Poor Widow by a Real Estate Man." The "real estate man" thus exposed turned out to be an obscure hombre with desk-room in a back office in a rookery, but the incident set me to thinking. "Every member of our board," I thought, "is besmirched by this scandal article. Anyone, however unworthy or disreputable, may call himself a real estate man. Why do

not the members of our board deserve a distinctive title? Each member is vouched for by the board, subscribes to its Code of Ethics, and must behave himself or get out." So the idea incubated for three or four weeks, and was then sprung on the local brethren.[1]

As to the etymology of the term, Mr. Chadbourn says:

Real estate originally meant a royal grant. It is so connected with land in the public mind that *realtor* is easily understood, even at a first hearing. The suffix *-or* means a doer, one who performs an act, as in *grantor, executor, sponsor, administrator.*

The Minneapolis brethren were so pleased with their new name that Mr. Chadbourn was moved to dedicate it to the whole profession. In March, 1916, he went to the convention of the National Association of Real Estate Boards at New Orleans, and made a formal offer of it. It was accepted gratefully, and is now defined by the association as follows:

A person engaged in the real estate business who is an active member of a member board of the National Association of Real Estate Boards, and as such, an affiliated member of the National Association, who is subject to its rules and regulations, who observes its standards of conduct, and is entitled to its benefits.[2]

In 1920 the Minneapolis Real Estate Board and the National Association of Real Estate Boards applied to Judge Joseph W. Molyneaux of Minneapolis for an injunction restraining the Northwestern Telephone Exchange Company from using *realtor* to designate some of its hirelings, and on September 10 the learned judge duly granted this relief. Since then the National Association has obtained similar injunctions in Virginia, Utah and other States. Its general counsel is heard from every time *realtor* is taken in vain, and when, in 1922, Sinclair Lewis applied it to George F. Babbitt,[3] there was an uproar. But when Mr. Chadbourn was appealed to he decided that Babbitt was "fairly well described," for he was "a prominent member of the local board and of the State association," and one could scarcely look for anything better in "a book written in the ironic vein of the author of 'Main Street.'"[4] Mr. Chadbourn believes that *realtor* should be capitalized, "like *Methodist* or *American,*"[5] but so far it has not been generally done. In June, 1925, at a meeting of the National Association of Real Estate Boards in Detroit, the past presidents of the body presented him with

[1] Mencken's note: "Private communication, Sept. 28, 1935."
[2] Mencken's note: *"Realtor: Its Meaning and Use;* Chicago (National Association of Real Estate Boards), 1925."
[3] Sinclair Lewis (1885–1951) in 1921 published *Babbitt,* a novel that satirically portrays a real estate dealer as a standardized product of modern American civilization.

[4] Mencken's note: "Letter to W. A. Frisbie, editor of the *Minneapolis Daily News.* This was in 1922. The letter was subscribed 'Yours realtorially.' A copy was sent to Mr. Lewis, who preserves it in his archives."
[5] Mencken's note: "Private communication, Sept. 4, 1935."

a gold watch as a token of their gratitude for his contribution to the uplift of their profession. On May 30, 1934, the following letter from Nathan William MacChesney, general counsel of the National Association, appeared in the *New Republic:*

> [*Realtor*] is not a word, but a trade right, coined and protected by law by the National Association of Real Estate Boards, and the term is a part of the trade-mark as registered in some forty-four States and Canada. Something over $200,000 has been spent in its protection by the National Association of Real Estate Boards in attempting to confine its use to those real estate men who are members of the National Association of Real Estate Boards, subject to its code for ethics and to its discipline for violation. It has been a factor in making the standards of the business generally during the past twenty years, and the exclusive right of the National Association of Real Estate Boards has been sustained in a series of court decisions, a large number of injunctions having been issued, restraining its improper use.

In 1924 the *Realtors' Bulletin* of Baltimore reported that certain enemies of realtric science were trying to show that *realtor* was derived from the English word *real* and the Spanish word *toro,* a bull, and to argue that it thus meant *real bull.* But this obscenity apparently did not go far; probably a hint from the alert general counsel was enough to stop it. During the same year I was informed by Herbert U. Nelson, executive secretary of the National Association, that "the real-estate men of London, through the Institute of Estate Agents and Auctioneers, after studying our experience in this respect, are planning to coin the word *estator* and to protect it by legal steps." This plan, I believe, came to fruition, but *estator* never caught on, and I can't find it in the Supplement to the Oxford Dictionary. *Realtor,* however, is there—and the first illustrative quotation is from "Babbitt"! In March, 1927, J. Foster Hagan, of Ballston, Va., reported to *American Speech* that he had encountered *realtress* on the window of a real-estate office there, but this charming derivative seems to have died a-bornin'. In 1925 or thereabout certain ambitious insurance solicitors, inflamed by *realtor,* began to call themselves *insurors,* but it, too, failed to make any progress.

Electragist, like *realtor,* seems to be the monopoly of the lofty technicians who affect it: "it is copyrighted by the Association of Electragists International, whose members alone may use it."[6] But *mortician* is in the public domain. It was proposed by a writer in the *Embalmers' Monthly* for February, 1895, but the undertakers, who were then *funeral-directors,* did not rise to it until some years later. On September 16, 1916, some of the more eminent of them met at Columbus, O., to form a national association, on the lines of the American College of Surgeons, the American Association of University Professors, and the Society of the Cincinnati, and a year later they decided upon National Selected *Morticians* as its designation.[7] To this day the association remains so exclusive that, of the 24,000 undertakers in the United States, only 200

---

[6] Mencken's note: "*Electragist,* by Corneil Ridderhof. *American Speech,* Aug., 1927, p. 477. It means, according to Mr. Ridderhof, 'a combined electrical dealer and contractor.'"

[7] Mencken's note: "I am indebted here to Mr. W. M. Krieger, executive secretary of the organization, the headquarters of which are in Chicago."

belong to it. But any one of the remaining 23,800 is free to call himself a *mortician,* and to use all the other lovely words that the advance of human taxidermy has brought in. *Mortician,* of course, was suggested by *physician,* for undertakers naturally admire and like to pal with the resurrection men, and there was a time when some of them called themselves *embalming surgeons.* A *mortician* never handles a *corpse;* he *prepares a body* or *patient.* This business is carried on in a *preparation-room* or *operating-room,* and when it is achieved the patient is put into a *casket*[8] and stored in the *reposing-room* or *slumber-room* of a *funeral-home.* On the day of the funeral he is moved to the *chapel* therein for the last exorcism, and then hauled to the cemetery in a *funeral-car* or *casket-coach.*[9] The old-time shroud is now a *négligé* or *slumber-shirt* or *slumber-robe,* the mortician's work-truck is an *ambulance,* and the cemetery is fast becoming a *memorial-park.* In the West cemeteries are being supplanted by public mausoleums, which sometimes go under the names of *cloisters, burial-abbeys,* etc.[10] To be laid away in one runs into money. The vehicle that morticians use for their expectant hauling of the ill is no longer an *ambulance,* but an *invalid-coach. Mortician* has been a favorite butt of the national wits, but they seem to have made no impression on it. In January, 1932, it was barred from the columns of the Chicago *Tribune.* "This decree goes forth," announced the *Tribune,* "not for lack of sympathy with the ambition of undertakers to be well regarded, but because of it. If they haven't the sense to save themselves from their own lexicographers, we shall not be guilty of abetting them in their folly."[11] But *mortician* not only continues to flourish; it also begets progeny, *e.g., beautician, cosmetician, radiotrician* and *bootician.*[12] The barbers, so far, have not devised a name for themselves in *-ician,* but they may be trusted to do so anon. In my youth they were *tonsorial artists,* but in recent years some of them have been calling themselves *chirotonsors.*[13] Practically all American press-agents are now *public relations counsel, contact-managers* or *publicists,* all tree-trimmers are *tree-surgeons,* all milk-wagon and bakery-wagon drivers have become *salesmen,* nearly all janitors are *superintendents,* many gardeners have become *landscape-architects* (in England even the whales of the profession are simple *landscape-gardeners*), cobblers are beginning to call themselves *shoe-rebuilders,*[14] and the corn-doctors, after a generation as *chiropodists,* have burst forth as *podiatrists.* The American fondness for such sonorous appellations

---

[8] Mencken's note: " 'Casket' seems to have come in during the Civil War period. In 1863 Nathaniel Hawthorne denounced it in *Our Old Home* as 'a vile modern phrase, which compels a person . . . to shrink . . . from the idea of being buried at all.' At the start it had a rival in case. The latter was used in the Richmond *Examiner's* report of the funeral of Gen. J. E. B. Stuart, May 13, 1864. But the *Examiner,* in the same report, used 'corpse' and 'hearse.' "

[9] Mencken's note: *"Mortuary Nomenclature, Hygeia,* Nov., 1925, p. 651."

[10] Mencken's note: *"The Mortician,* by Elmer Davis, *American Mercury,* May, 1927."

[11] Mencken's note: *"Editor and Publisher,* Jan. 30, 1932."

[12] Mencken's note: "I proposed the use of 'bootician' to designate a high-toned big-city bootlegger in the *American Mercury,* April,

1925, p. 450. The term met a crying need, and had considerable success. In March, 1927, the San Jose *Mercury-Herald* said: 'Our bootleggers are now calling themselves "booticians." It seems that bootlegger has some trace of odium about it, while "bootician" has none.' (Reprinted in the Baltimore *Evening Sun,* April 4, 1927). On July 23, 1931, according to the Associated Press, a man arrested in Chicago, on being asked his profession answered proudly that he was a 'bootician.' "

[13] Mencken's note: "In 1924 representatives of 1000 of them met in Chicago, and voted for 'chirotonsor.' See the *Commonweal,* Nov. 26, 1924, p. 58."

[14] Mencken's note: "There is a *Shoe Rebuilders'* Association in Baltimore. See the Baltimore *Evening Sun,* Oct. 17, 1935."

arrested the interest of W. L. George, the English novelist, when he visited the United States in 1920. He said:

Business titles are given in America more readily than in England. I know one *president* whose staff consists of two typists. Many firms have four *vice-presidents.* In the magazines you seldom find merely an *editor;* the others need their share of honor, so they are *associate* (not *assistant*) *editors.* A dentist is called a *doctor.* I wandered into a university, knowing nobody, and casually asked for the *dean.* I was asked, "Which *dean?*" In that building there were enough deans to stock all the English cathedrals. The master of a secret society is *royal supreme knight commander.* Perhaps I reached the extreme at a theatre in Boston, when I wanted something, I forgot what, and was told that I must apply to the *chief of the ushers.* He was a mild little man, who had something to do with people getting into their seats, rather a come-down from the pomp and circumstance of his title. Growing interested, I examined my programme, with the following result: It is not a large theatre, but it has a *press-representative,* a *treasurer* (box-office clerk), an *assistant treasurer* (box-office junior clerk), an *advertising-agent,* our old friend the *chief of the ushers,* a *stage-manager,* a *head-electrician,* a *master of properties* (in England called *props*), a *leader of the orchestra* (pity this—why not *president?*), and a *matron* (occupation unknown).[15]

George might have unearthed some even stranger magnificoes in other playhouses. I once knew an ancient bill-sticker, attached to a Baltimore theatre, who boasted the sonorous title of *chief lithographer.* Today, in all probability, he would be called a *lithographic-engineer.* For a number of years the *Engineering News-Record,* the organ of the legitimate engineers, used to devote a column every week to just such uninvited invaders of the craft, and some of the species it unearthed were so fantastic that it was constrained to reproduce their business cards photographically in order to convince its readers that it was not spoofing. One of its favorite exhibits was a bedding manufacturer who first became a *mattress-engineer* and then promoted himself to the lofty dignity of *sleep-engineer.* No doubt he would have called himself a *morphician* if he had thought of it. Another exhilarating specimen was a tractor-driver who advertised for a job as a *caterpillar-engineer.* A third was a beautician who burst out as an *appearance-engineer.* In an Atlanta department-store the *News-Record* found an *engineer of good taste*—a young woman employed to advise newly-married couples patronizing the furniture department, and elsewhere it unearthed *display-engineers* who had been lowly window-dressers until some visionary among them made the great leap, *demolition-engineers* who were once content to be house-wreckers, and *sanitary-engineers* who had an earlier incarnation as garbage-men. . . .

Euphemisms for things are almost as common in the United States as euphemisms for avocations. Dozens of forlorn little fresh-water colleges are called *universities,* and almost all *pawn-shops* are *loan-offices.* When *movie-cathedral* came in a few scoffers snickered, but by the generality of fans it was received gravely. *City,* in England, used to be confined to the seats of bishops, and even today it is applied only to considerable places, but in the United States it is commonly assumed by any town with paved

[15] Mencken's note: *"Hail, Columbia!;* New York, 1921, pp. 92-3."

streets, and in the statistical publications of the Federal government it is applied to all places of 8000 or more population. The American use of *store* for *shop,* like that of *help* for *servant,* is probably the product of an early effort at magnification. Before Prohibition saloons used to be *sample-rooms, buffets, exchanges, cafés* and *restaurants;* now they are *taverns, cocktail-rooms, taprooms, American-bars, stubes* and what not. Not long ago the *Furnished-Room Guide* undertook to substitute *hotelette* for *rooming-house,*[16] and in 1928 President E. L. Robins of the National *Fertilizer* Association proposed that the name of that organization be changed to the National Association of *Plant Food* Manufacturers or the American *Plant Food* Association.[17] In Pasadena the public garbage-wagons bear the legend: *Table-Waste Disposal Department.* The word *studio* is heavily overworked; there are *billiard-studios, tonsorial-studios, candy-studios,* and even *shoe-studios.*[18] Nor is this reaching out for sweet and disarming words confined to the lowly. Some time ago, in the *Survey,* the trade journal of the American uplifters, Dr. Thomas Dawes Eliot, associate professor of sociology in Northwestern University, printed a solemn argument in favor of abandoning all such harsh terms as *reformatory, house of refuge, reform school* and *jail.* "Each time a new phrase is developed," he said, "it seems to bring with it, or at least to be accompanied by, some measure of permanent gain, in standards or in viewpoint, even though much of the old may continue to masquerade as the new. The series, *alms, philanthropy, relief, rehabilitation, case work, family welfare,* shows such a progression from cruder to more refined levels of charity." Among the substitutions proposed by the learned professor were *habit-disease* for *vice, psycho-neurosis* for *sin, failure to compensate* for *disease, treatment* for *punishment, delinquent* for *criminal, unmarried mother* for *illegitimate mother, out of wedlock* for *bastard, behavior problem* for *prostitute, colony* for *penitentiary, school* for *reformatory, psychopathic hospital* for *insane asylum,* and *house of detention* for *jail.*[19] Many of these terms (or others like them) have been actually adopted. Practically all American insane asylums are now simple *hospitals,* many reformatories and houses of correction have been converted into *homes* or *schools,* all almshouses are now *infirmaries, county-farms* or *county-homes,* and most of the more advanced American penologists now speak of criminals as *psychopathic personalities.* By a law of New York it is provided that "in any local law, ordinance or resolution, or in any public or judicial proceeding, or in any process, notice, order, decree, judgment, record or other public document or paper, the term *bastard* or *illegitimate child* shall not be used, but the term *child born out of wedlock* shall be used in substitution therefor, and with the same force and effect."[20] Meanwhile, such harsh terms as *second-hand* and *ready-made* disappear from the American vocabulary. For the former the automobile dealers, who are ardent euphemists, have substituted *reconditioned, rebuilt, repossessed* and *used,* and for the latter department-stores offer *ready-tailored, ready-to-wear* and *ready-to-put-on.* For *shop-worn* two of the current euphemisms are *store-used* and *slightly-second.* . . .

1919

[16] Mencken's note: "See the *New Yorker,* Jan. 9, 1935, p. 74. The *New Yorker* expressed a waggish preference for 'furnished-roomateria.' "
[17] Mencken's note: "United Press report, Nov. 13, 1925."
[18] Mencken's note: "See *Studio,* by John T. Krumpelmann, *American Speech,* Dec., 1926, p. 158."

[19] Mencken's note: "*A Limbo for Cruel Words, Survey,* June 15, 1922."
[20] Mencken's note: "Laws of 1925, Ch. 515, in force April 9, 1925. I have to thank Mr. Sylvan Baruch of the New York Bar for calling my attention to this statute."

American Culture

The capital defect in the culture of These States is the lack of a civilized aristocracy, secure in its position, animated by an intelligent curiosity, skeptical of all facile generalizations, superior to the sentimentality of the mob, and delighting in the battle of ideas for its own sake. The word I use, despite the qualifying adjective, has got itself meanings, of course, that I by no means intend to convey. Any mention of an aristocracy, to a public fed upon democratic fustian, is bound to bring up images of stockbrokers' wives lolling obscenely in opera boxes, or of haughty Englishmen slaughtering whole generations of grouse in an inordinate and incomprehensible manner, or of bogus counts coming over to work their magic upon the daughters of breakfast-food and bathtub kings. This misconception belongs to the general American tradition. Its depth and extent are constantly revealed by the naïve assumption that the so-called fashionable folk of the large cities—chiefly wealthy industrials in the interior-decorator and country-club stage of culture—constitute an aristocracy, and by the scarcely less remarkable assumption that the peerage of England is identical with the gentry—that is, that such men as Lord Northcliffe, Lord Riddel and even Lord Reading were English gentlemen.[1]

Here, as always, the worshiper is the father of the gods, and no less when they are evil than when they are benign. The inferior man must find himself superiors, that he may marvel at his political equality with them, and in the absence of recognizable superiors *de facto* he creates superiors *de jure*.[2] The sublime principle of one man, one vote must be translated into terms of dollars, diamonds, fashionable intelligence; the equality of all men before the law must have clear and dramatic proofs. Sometimes, perhaps, the thing goes further and is more subtle. The inferior man needs an aristocracy to demonstrate, not only his mere equality, but also his actual superiority. The society columns in the newspapers may have some such origin. They may visualize once more the accomplished journalist's understanding of the mob mind that he plays upon so skillfully, as upon some immense and cacophonous organ, always going *fortissimo*.[3] What the inferior man and his wife see in the sinister revels of those brummagem first families, I suspect, is often a massive witness to their own higher rectitude—in brief, to their firmer grasp upon the immutable axioms of Christian virtue, the one sound boast of the nether nine-tenths of humanity in every land under the cross.

But this bugaboo aristocracy is actually bogus, and the evidence of its bogusness lies in the fact that it is insecure. One gets into it only onerously, but out of it very easily. Entrance is effected by dint of a long and bitter struggle, and the chief incidents of that struggle are almost intolerable humiliations. The aspirant must school and steel himself to sniffs and sneers; he must see the door slammed upon him a hundred times

---

[1] Lord Northcliffe: Alfred Charles William Harmsworth, British publisher of "At the War" (1916); Lord Riddel: George Allardice, British press representative at peace conferences (1919–1922); Lord Reading: Rufus Daniel Isaacs, high commissioner and special ambassador to the United States (1918).

[2] *De facto* (Latin): "In fact" or "actually"; *de jure* (Latin): "by right" or "by law."

[3] Musical term (Italian) for "very loud."

before ever it is thrown open to him. To get in at all he must show a talent for abasement—and abasement makes him timorous. Worse, that timorousness is not cured when he succeeds at last. On the contrary, it is made even more tremulous, for what he faces within the gates is a scheme of things made up almost wholly of harsh and often unintelligible taboos, and the penalty for violating even the least of them is swift and disastrous. He must exhibit exactly the right social habits, appetites and prejudices, public and private. He must harbor exactly the right enthusiasms and indignations. He must have a hearty taste for exactly the right sports and games. His attitude toward the fine arts must be properly tolerant and yet not a shade too eager. He must read and like exactly the right books, pamphlets and public journals. He must put up at the right hotels when he travels. His wife must patronize the right milliners. He himself must stick to the right haberdashery. He must live in the right neighborhood. He must even embrace the right doctrines of religion. It would ruin him, for all society column purposes, to move to Union Hill, N. J., or to drink coffee from his saucer, or to marry a chambermaid with a gold tooth, or to join the Seventh Day Adventists. Within the boundaries of his curious order he is worse fettered than a monk in a cell. Its obscure conception of propriety, its nebulous notion that this or that is honorable, hampers him in every direction, and very narrowly. What he resigns when he enters, even when he makes his first deprecating knock at the door, is every right to attack the ideas that happen to prevail within. Such as they are, he must accept them without question. And as they shift and change he must shift and change with them, silently and quickly.

Obviously, that order cannot constitute a genuine aristocracy, in any rational sense. A genuine aristocracy is grounded upon very much different principles. Its first and most salient character is its interior security, and the chief visible evidence of that security is the freedom that goes with it—not only freedom in act, the divine right of the aristocrat to do what he damn well pleases, so long as he does not violate the primary guarantees and obligations of his class, but also and more importantly freedom in thought, the liberty to try and err, the right to be his own man. It is the instinct of a true aristocracy, not to punish eccentricity by expulsion, but to throw a mantle of protection about it—to safeguard it from the suspicions and resentments of the lower orders. Those lower orders are inert, timid, inhospitable to ideas, hostile to changes, faithful to a few maudlin superstitions. All progress goes on on the higher levels. It is there that salient personalities, made secure by artificial immunities, may oscillate most widely from the normal track. It is within that entrenched fold, out of reach of the immemorial certainties of the mob, that extraordinary men of the lower orders may find their city of refuge, and breathe a clear air. This, indeed, is at once the hall-mark and the justification of a genuine aristocracy—that it is beyond responsibility to the general masses of men, and hence superior to both their degraded longings and their no less degraded aversions. It is nothing if it is not autonomous, curious, venturesome, courageous, and everything if it is. It is the custodian of the qualities that make for change and experiment; it is the class that organizes danger to the service of the race; it pays for its high prerogatives by standing in the forefront of the fray.

No such aristocracy, it must be plain, is now on view in the United States. The makings of one were visible in the Virginia of the Eighteenth Century, but with Jefferson and Washington the promise died. In New England, it seems to me, there was never anything of the sort, either in being or in nascency: there was only a theocracy that degenerated very quickly into a plutocracy on the one hand and a caste of sterile pedants on the other—the passion for God splitting into a lust for dollars and a weakness for mere words. Despite the common notion to the contrary—a notion generated by confusing literacy with intelligence—the New England of the great days never showed any genuine enthusiasm for ideas. It began its history as a slaughter-house of ideas, and it is today not easily distinguishable from a cold-storage plant. Its celebrated adventures in mysticism, once apparently so bold and significant, are now seen to have been little more than an elaborate hocus-pocus—respectable Unitarians shocking the peasantry and scaring the horned cattle in the fields by masquerading in the robes of Rosicrucians. The notions that it embraced in those austere and far-off days were stale, and when it had finished with them they were dead. So in politics. Since the Civil War it has produced fewer political ideas, as political ideas run in the Republic, than any average county in Kansas or Nebraska. Appomattox seemed to be a victory for New England idealism. It was actually a victory for the New England plutocracy, and that plutocracy has dominated thought about the Housatonic ever since. The sect of professional idealists has so far dwindled that it has ceased to be of any importance, even as an opposition. When the plutocracy is challenged now, it is challenged by the proletariat.

Well, what is on view in New England is on view in all other parts of the nation, sometimes with ameliorations, but usually with the colors merely exaggerated. What one beholds, sweeping the eye over the land, is a culture that, like the national literature, is in three layers—the plutocracy on top, a vast mass of undifferentiated human blanks bossed by demagogues at the bottom, and a forlorn *intelligentsia* gasping out a precarious life between. I need not set out at any length, I hope, the intellectual deficiencies of the plutocracy—its utter failure to show anything even remotely resembling the makings of an aristocracy. It is badly educated, it is stupid, it is full of low-caste superstitions and indignations, it is without decent traditions or informing vision; above all, it is extraordinarily lacking in the most elemental independence and courage. Out of this class comes the grotesque fashionable society of our big towns, already described. It shows all the stigmata of inferiority—moral certainty, cruelty, suspicion of ideas, fear. Never does it function more revealingly than in the recurrent *pogroms* against radicalism, *i.e.,* against humorless persons who, like Andrew Jackson, take the platitudes of democracy seriously. And what is the theory at the bottom of all these proceedings? So far as it can be reduced to comprehensible terms it is much less a theory than a fear—a shivering, idiotic, discreditable fear of a mere banshee—an overpowering, paralyzing dread that some extra-eloquent Red, permitted to emit his balderdash unwhipped, may eventually convert a couple of courageous men, and that the courageous men, filled with indignation against the plutocracy, may take to the highroad, burn down a nail-factory or two, and slit the throat of some virtuous profiteer.

Obviously, it is out of reason to look for any hospitality to ideas in a class so extravagantly fearful of even the most palpably absurd of them. Its philosophy is firmly grounded upon the thesis that the existing order must stand forever free from attack, and not only from attack, but also from mere academic criticism, and its ethics are as firmly grounded upon the thesis that every attempt at any such criticism is a proof of moral turpitude. Within its own ranks, protected by what may be regarded as the privilege of the order, there is nothing to take the place of this criticism. In other countries the plutocracy has often produced men of reflective and analytical habit, eager to rationalize its instincts and to bring it into some sort of relationship to the main streams of human thought. The case of David Ricardo at once comes to mind, and there have been many others: John Bright, Richard Cobden, George Grote. But in the United States no such phenomenon has been visible. Nor has the plutocracy ever fostered an inquiring spirit among its intellectual valets and footmen, which is to say, among the gentlemen who compose headlines and leading articles for its newspapers. What chiefly distinguishes the daily press of the United States from the press of all other countries pretending to culture is not its lack of truthfulness or even its lack of dignity and honor, for these deficiencies are common to newspapers everywhere, but its incurable fear of ideas, its constant effort to evade the discussion of fundamentals by translating all issues into a few elemental fears, its incessant reduction of all reflection to mere emotion. It is, in the true sense, never well-informed. It is seldom intelligent, save in the arts of the mob-master. It is never courageously honest. Held harshly to a rigid correctness of opinion, it sinks rapidly into formalism and feebleness. Its yellow section is perhaps its best section, for there the only vestige of the old free journalist survives. In the more respectable papers one finds only a timid and petulant animosity to all questioning of the existing order, however urbane and sincere—a pervasive and ill-concealed dread that the mob now heated up against the orthodox hobgoblins may suddenly begin to unearth hobgoblins of its own, and so run amok.

    For it is upon the emotions of the mob, of course, that the whole comedy is played. Theoretically, the mob is the repository of all political wisdom and virtue; actually, it is the ultimate source of all political power. Even the plutocracy cannot make war upon it openly, or forget the least of its weaknesses. The business of keeping it in order must be done discreetly, warily, with delicate technique. In the main that business consists in keeping alive its deep-seated fears—of strange faces, of unfamiliar ideas, of unhackneyed gestures, of untested liberties and responsibilities. The one permanent emotion of the inferior man, as of all the simpler mammals, is fear—fear of the unknown, the complex, the inexplicable. What he wants beyond everything else is security. His instincts incline him toward a society so organized that it will protect him at all hazards, and not only against perils to his hide but also against assaults upon his mind—against the need to grapple with unaccustomed problems, to weigh ideas, to think things out for himself, to scrutinize the platitudes upon which his everyday thinking is based.

1920

Imperial Purple

Most of the rewards of the Presidency, in these days, have come to be very trashy. The President continues, of course, to be an eminent man, but only in the sense that Jack Dempsey, Lindbergh, Babe Ruth and Henry Ford have been eminent men. He sees little of the really intelligent and amusing people of the country: most of them, in fact, make it a sort of point of honor to avoid him. His time is put in mainly with shabby politicians and other such designing fellows—in brief, with rogues and ig-noramuses. When he takes a little holiday his customary companions are vermin that no fastidious man would consort with. Dr. Harding, forced to entertain them, resorted to poteen as an analgesic; Dr. Coolidge loaded them aboard the *Mayflower,* and then fled to his cabin, took off his vest and shirt, and went to sleep; Dr. Hoover hauled them to the Rapidan at 60 miles an hour, and back at 80 or 90.[1]

The honors that are heaped upon a President are seldom of a kind to impress and content a civilized man. People send him turkeys, opossums, pieces of wood from the *Constitution,*[2] goldfish, carved peach kernels, models of the State capitols of Wyoming and Arkansas, and pressed flowers from the Holy Land. Once a year some hunter in Montana or Idaho sends him 20 pounds of bearsteak, usually collect. It arrives in a high state, and has to be fed to the White House dog. He receives 20 or 30 chain-prayer letters every day, and fair copies of 40 or 50 sets of verse. Colored clergymen send him illustrated Bibles, madstones and boxes of lucky powders, usually accompanied by applications for appointment as collector of customs at New Orleans, Mobile or Wilmington, N. C., or as Register of the Treasury. His public rewards come in the form of LL.D.'s[3] from colleges eager for the publicity—and on the same day others precisely like it are given to a champion lawn-tennis player, a banker known to be without heirs of his body, and a general in the Army. No one ever thinks to give him any other academic honor; he is never made a Litt.D., a D.D., an S.T.D., a D.D.S., or a J.U.D.,[4] but always an LL.D. Dr. Hoover, to date, has 30 or 40 such degrees. He apparently knows as little about law as a court catchpoll, but he is more solidly *legum doctor* than Blackstone or Pufendorf.[5]

The health of a President is watched very carefully, not only by the Vice-President but also by medical men detailed for the purpose by the Army or Navy. These medical men have high-sounding titles, and perform the duties of their office in full uniform, with swords on one side and stethoscopes on the other. The diet of their imperial patient is rigidly scrutinized. If he eats a few peanuts they make a pother; if he goes in for some steamed hard crabs at night, washed down by what passes in Washington for malt liquor, they complain to the newspapers. Every morning they look at his tongue, take his pulse and temperature, determine his blood pressure, and examine his eye-grounds and his knee-jerks. The instant he shows the slightest sign of being upset they clap him into bed, post Marines to guard him, put him on a regimen fit for a Trappist,[6] and issue bulletins to the newspapers.

When a President goes traveling he never goes alone, but always with a huge staff

---

[1] Warren G. Harding, twenty-ninth president (1921–1923), drank poteen, an illicitly distilled whiskey of Ireland; Calvin Coolidge, thirtieth president (1923–1929), enjoyed the privileges of the president's yacht, the *Mayflower;* Herbert Hoover, thirty-first president (1929–1933), escaped to his "summer White House," located at Rapidan, Virginia.

[2] U.S. frigate known as "Old Ironsides," built in 1797 and permanently berthed in Boston.

[3] LL.D.: Doctor of Laws (*Legum Doctor*).

[4] Litt.D.: Doctor of Letters (*Litterarum Doctor*);

D.D.: Doctor of Divinity (*Divinitatis Doctor*); S.T.D.: Doctor of Sacred Theology (*Sacrae Theologiae Doctor*); D.D.S.: Doctor of Dental Surgery; J.U.D.: Doctor of Both Laws (i.e., canon and civil) (*Juris Utriusque Doctor*).

[5] Blackstone: Sir William Blackstone (1723–1780), English jurist and law commentator; Pufendorf: Samuel Pufendorf (1632–1694), German jurist and theologian.

[6] Monk of the Trappist order, in which perpetual silence and strict discipline are enforced.

of secretaries, Secret Service agents, doctors, nurses, and newspaper reporters. Even so stingy a fellow as Dr. Coolidge had to hire two whole Pullman cars to carry his entourage. The cost, to be sure, is borne by the taxpayers, but the President has to put up with the company. As he rolls along thousands of boys rush out to put pennies on the track, and now and then one of them loses a finger or a toe, and the train has to be backed up to comfort his mother, who, it usually turns out, cannot speak English. When the train arrives anywhere all the town bores and scoundrels gather to greet the Chief Magistrate, and that night he has to eat a bad dinner, and to listen to three hours of bad speeches.

The President has less privacy than any other American. Thousands of persons have the right of access to him, beginning with the British Ambassador and running down to the secretary of the Republican county committee of Ziebach county, South Dakota. Among them are the 96 members of the United States Senate, perhaps the windiest and most tedious group of men in Christendom. If a Senator were denied admission to the White House the whole Senate would rise in indignation. And if the minister from Albania were kicked out even the French and British Ambassadors would join in protesting. Many of these gentlemen drop in, not because they have anything to say, but simply to prove to their employers or customers that they can do it. How long they stay is only partly determined by the President himself. Dr. Coolidge used to get rid of them by falling asleep in their faces, but that device is impossible to Presidents with a more active interest in the visible world. It would not do to have them heaved out by the Secret Service men or by the White House police, or to insult and affront them otherwise, for many of them have wicked tongues. On two occasions within historic times Presidents who were irritable with such bores were reported in Washington to be patronizing the jug, and it took a lot of fine work to put down the scandal.

All day long the right hon. lord of us all sits listening solemnly to bores and quacks. Anon a secretary rushes in with the news that some eminent movie actor or football coach has died, and the President must seize a pen and write a telegram of condolence to the widow. Once a year he is repaid by receiving a cable on his birthday from King George.[7] Such things are cherished by Presidents, and they leave them, *post mortem,*[8] to the Library of Congress. Anon there comes a day of public ceremonial, and a chance to make a speech. Alas, it must be made at the annual banquet of some organization that is discovered, at the last minute, to be made up mainly of gentlemen under indictment, or at the tomb of some statesman who escaped impeachment by a hair. Twenty million voters with IQ's below 60 have their ears glued to the radio; it takes four days' hard work to concoct a speech without a sensible word in it. Next day a dam must be opened somewhere. Four Senators get drunk and try to neck a lady politician built like an overloaded tramp steamer. The Presidential automobile runs over a dog. It rains.

1931

---

[7] George V (George Frederick Ernest Albert) (1865–1936), king of England (1910–1936).   [8] Latin: "after death."

Sinclair Lewis
1885–1951

Satirists give us new vocabularies for showing how ideals degenerate into follies. Sinclair Lewis performed that service for the 1920s. The titles of his two major novels, *Main Street* and *Babbitt,* came quickly to summarize for his generation the mediocrity and narrowness of small-town life—its corruption of the American dream through an infatuation with boosterism and a worship of material wealth, as well as its betrayal of individualism through an intolerant fear of behavior that departed from accepted norms. As much as any writer of his time, Lewis extended into direct encounter with the culture of the 1920s the view of stultifying small-town life that we associate with Sarah Orne Jewett and Sherwood Anderson.

Sinclair Lewis was born in 1885 in Sauk Centre, Minnesota, into a prominent, prosperous family. A tall, ungainly, lonely boy, he became a tall, ungainly, lonely man. In both playground games and social gatherings, around children and adults, he felt awkward and ill at ease. Nearly friendless, variously pitied and teased, he soon discovered that hiking and reading could provide means of getting away from the people and scenes that oppressed him. He took long, solitary rambles through the countryside, and he began reading about other worlds. He was particularly drawn to nineteenth-century poets, especially Alfred Lord Tennyson and Charles Swinburne, and to medieval culture. Yet Lewis was also fortunate to be born in a small town in the heartland of the United States near the turn of the century, just when the nation's literary center had begun to shift from the East to the Midwest and South and just before it began to shift from small towns to cities. By the time Lewis came to write *Main Street,* he had his fictional community of Gopher Prairie already at hand.

At age seventeen Lewis left the Midwest to attend Yale. Again friendless and alone, he continued to feel the need to get away. He read widely, particularly about medieval culture, and he began writing, signing his name "H. Sinclayre Lewys." He also began planning long excursions—two that took him to Europe by cattle boat and one that took him across Mexico in a series of long hikes. Near the beginning of his senior year, he left Yale to join Upton Sinclair's experimental commune, Helicon Hall, located outside Englewood Cliffs, New Jersey. From there he went to New York and then to Panama before returning to Yale, from which he graduated in 1908.

After graduation, Lewis lived in Iowa, California, Washington, and New York, working as a reporter for various newspapers and selling story plots for $5 each. For a short time he lived in a bohemian colony in Carmel, California, where he met Jack London. But it was not until he turned back to the Midwest, to the scenes he had encountered earliest and knew best, that fiction began to work for him. To augment his own memories and observations, he conducted research almost as an amateur sociologist might. His notebooks consist of long lists of names, turns of speech, descriptions of people and places, maps, statistics, and the like. During the next decade Lewis wrote five novels and many stories.

In *Main Street* (1920) and *Babbitt* (1922), later in *Arrowsmith* (1925), *Elmer Gantry* (1927), "The Man Who Knew Coolidge" (1928), and *Dodsworth* (1929), he launched a decade-long attack against both the greediness of American business and the stifling effect of American provincialism. In 1930, having emerged from obscurity to acclaim, he became the first American writer to win the Nobel Prize for literature.

Lewis's major literary themes reach back through Edgar Lee Masters's *Spoon River Anthology* to the "Whilomville" stories of Stephen Crane and the novels of William Dean Howells. In Mark Twain's "The Man That Corrupted Hadleyburg," the Dawson's Landing setting of *Puddn'head Wilson,* and the river town described in *Huckleberry Finn,* we can locate the literary origins of similarly satiric views of village life. But it was Lewis's novels, even more than Mencken's essays on American "boobery," that lifted these themes to prominence immediately after World War I. In *Main Street,* Lewis presents a character who embodies some of the best and combats some of the worst qualities of "middletown" America. In *Babbitt,* he presents a character who embodies some of the worst forms of boosterism, materialism, and intolerance yet retains deeper needs and desires that he struggles to express.

If Sinclair Lewis set out to deflate myths—by satirizing evangelical preachers on the make, shrewd yet limited businessmen, hypocritical doctors and teachers, and racial bigots—he also tried to create myths of his own. This tendency is most evident in *Arrowsmith,* in which an idealistic young doctor devoted to research is pitted against people who want to exploit his contributions for profit. Satire lends itself to good/bad, either/or conflicts, and Lewis liked to pit knights of idealism against dragons of cynical materialism.

As a result, the fiction that won Lewis acclaim and helped change American literature also brought him vilification. To some readers, his works offered revelations of the unfulfilled dreams and the rising discontent of people who find little sense of shared happiness in the organizations they join, fleeting pleasure in the gadgets they buy, and limited fulfillment in the values they boost; to others, his works represented unfair depictions or even bitter denunciations of the American way of life. Both *Main Street* and *Babbitt* draw heavily on the qualities that most clearly marked Lewis's dominant frame of mind during his youth and apprenticeship: his uneasy estrangement and his restless longings. In addition, however, these novels depend heavily on his capacity for close attention to the local and the immediate. The clothes and manners, the mores and gadgets, the foibles and hypocrisies, the emptiness and aspirations of "middletown" America form the center of his best fiction. Inseparable from his capacity for close observation is the characteristic ambivalence he acquired early and cultivated throughout his life—of estrangement and kinship, judgment and affection. In his crude yet telling art, close familiarity and a detached, even bitter perspective mingle with youthful yearning. As a result, his fiction combines satire, realism, and romance in shifting and sometimes strained combinations.

Lewis continued to write until his death in 1951. But the Nobel Prize in 1930 came near the end of his short life as a writer of significant work. In some respects, he was as much a journalist of the muckraking tradition of the generation that immediately preceded him (producing, for example, Upton

Sinclair's *The Jungle*) as he was a novelist. Like the muckrakers, he was skilled at satirizing his victims. His portrayals of Babbitt and Dodsworth, however, allowed Lewis to show compassion for his small-town go-getters; he recognized the basic pathos of their mistaken devotion to the idols of the marketplace—which William James called "the bitch-goddess success." When Lewis set out directly to celebrate idealistic young devotees of freedom or simply to debunk village philistines and corporate crooks, his work lost its edge. It possessed staying power only when his need to flail his misguided fools was balanced by his sense of compassion for them. In *Arrowsmith* and *Elmer Gantry,* and above all in *Main Street* and *Babbitt,* he exposes the sometimes pathetic and sometimes terrible inadequacies of the commonplace. In the process, he finds words for America's hidden fears and hopes.

Further Reading:

C. Van Doren, *Sinclair Lewis,* 1933.
P. Miller, "The Incorruptible Sinclair Lewis," *Atlantic,* April 1951.
From Main Street to Stockholm, 1919–1930, ed. H. Smith, 1952.
M. Schorer, *Sinclair Lewis: An American Life,* 1961.
S. Grebstein, *Sinclair Lewis,* 1962.
Sinclair Lewis: A Collection of Critical Essays, ed.

M. Schorer, 1962.
D. Dooley, *The Art of Sinclair Lewis,* 1967.
R. O'Connor, *Sinclair Lewis,* 1971.
S. Sherman, *The Significance of Sinclair Lewis,* 1922, 1971.
J. Lundquist, *Sinclair Lewis,* 1973.
M. Light, *The Quixotic Vision of Sinclair Lewis,* 1975.

Texts:

Babbitt, 1922, 1950.
Main Street, 1920, 1948.
See also *Selected Short Stories of Sinclair Lewis,*

1935.
The Man from Main Street: A Sinclair Lewis Reader, ed. H. Maule and M. Cane, 1953.

from Babbitt

Chapter III: [George F. Babbitt and the Fairy Girl]

I

To George F. Babbitt, as to most prosperous citizens of Zenith, his motor car was poetry and tragedy, love and heroism. The office was his pirate ship but the car his perilous excursion ashore.

Among the tremendous crises of each day none was more dramatic than starting the engine. It was slow on cold mornings; there was the long, anxious whirr of the starter; and sometimes he had to drip ether into the cocks of the cylinders, which was so very interesting that at lunch he would chronicle it drop by drop, and orally calculate how much each drop had cost him.

This morning he was darkly prepared to find something wrong, and he felt belittled when the mixture exploded sweet and strong, and the car didn't even brush the door-jamb, gouged and splintery with many bruisings by fenders, as he backed out of the garage. He was confused. He shouted "Morning!" to Sam Doppelbrau with more cordiality than he had intended.

Babbitt's green and white Dutch Colonial house was one of three in that block on Chatham Road. To the left of it was the residence of Mr. Samuel Doppelbrau, secretary of an excellent firm of bathroom-fixture jobbers. His was a comfortable house with no architectural manners whatever; a large wooden box with a squat tower, a broad porch, and glossy paint yellow as a yolk. Babbitt disapproved of Mr. and Mrs. Doppelbrau as "Bohemian." From their house came midnight music and obscene laughter; there were neighborhood rumors of bootlegged whisky and fast motor rides. They furnished Babbitt with many happy evenings of discussion, during which he announced firmly, "I'm not strait-laced, and I don't mind seeing a fellow throw in a drink once in a while, but when it comes to deliberately trying to get away with a lot of hell-raising all the while like the Doppelbraus do, it's too rich for my blood!"

On the other side of Babbitt lived Howard Littlefield, Ph.D., in a strictly modern house whereof the lower part was dark red tapestry brick, with a leaded oriel, the upper part of pale stucco like spattered clay, and the roof red-tiled. Littlefield was the Great Scholar of the neighborhood; the authority on everything in the world except babies, cooking, and motors. He was a Bachelor of Arts of Blodgett College, and a Doctor of Philosophy in economics of Yale. He was the employment-manager and publicity-counsel of the Zenith Street Traction Company. He could, on ten hours' notice, appear before the board of aldermen or the state legislature and prove, absolutely, with figures all in rows and with precedents from Poland and New Zealand, that the street-car company loved the Public and yearned over its employees; that all its stock was owned by Widows and Orphans; and that whatever it desired to do would benefit property-owners by increasing rental values, and help the poor by lowering rents. All his acquaintances turned to Littlefield when they desired to know the date of the battle of Saragossa, the definition of the word "sabotage," the future of the German mark, the translation of *"hinc illæ lachrimæ,"*[1] or the number of products of coal tar. He awed Babbitt by confessing that he often sat up till midnight reading the figures and footnotes in Government reports, or skimming (with amusement at the author's mistakes) the latest volumes of chemistry, archeology, and ichthyology.

But Littlefield's great value was as a spiritual example. Despite his strange learnings he was as strict a Presbyterian and as firm a Republican as George F. Babbitt. He confirmed the business men in the faith. Where they knew only by passionate instinct that their system of industry and manners was perfect, Dr. Howard Littlefield proved it to them, out of history, economics, and the confessions of reformed radicals.

Babbitt had a good deal of honest pride in being the neighbor of such a savant, and in Ted's intimacy with Eunice Littlefield. At sixteen Eunice was interested in no statistics save those regarding the ages and salaries of motion-picture stars, but—as Babbitt definitively put it—"she was her father's daughter."

The difference between a light man like Sam Doppelbrau and a really fine character

---

[1] Latin: "hence these tears"; from *Andria* by Terence (ca. 195–159 B.C.).

like Littlefield was revealed in their appearances. Doppelbrau was disturbingly young for a man of forty-eight. He wore his derby on the back of his head, and his red face was wrinkled with meaningless laughter. But Littlefield was old for a man of forty-two. He was tall, broad, thick; his gold-rimmed spectacles were engulfed in the folds of his long face; his hair was a tossed mass of greasy blackness; he puffed and rumbled as he talked; his Phi Beta Kappa key shone against a spotty black vest; he smelled of old pipes; he was altogether funereal and archidiaconal; and to real-estate brokerage and the jobbing of bathroom-fixtures he added an aroma of sanctity.

This morning he was in front of his house, inspecting the grass parking between the curb and the broad cement sidewalk. Babbitt stopped his car and leaned out to shout "Mornin'!" Littlefield lumbered over and stood with one foot up on the running-board.

"Fine morning," said Babbitt, lighting—illegally early—his second cigar of the day.

"Yes, it's a mighty fine morning," said Littlefield.

"Spring coming along fast now."

"Yes, it's real spring now, all right," said Littlefield.

"Still cold nights, though. Had to have a couple blankets, on the sleeping-porch last night."

"Yes, it wasn't any too warm last night," said Littlefield.

"But I don't anticipate we'll have any more real cold weather now."

"No, but still, there was snow at Tiflis, Montana, yesterday," said the Scholar, "and you remember the blizzard they had out West three days ago—thirty inches of snow at Greeley, Colorado—and two years ago we had a snow-squall right here in Zenith on the twenty-fifth of April."

"Is that a fact! Say, old man, what do you think about the Republican candidate? Who'll they nominate for president? Don't you think it's about time we had a real business administration?"

"In my opinion, what the country needs, first and foremost, is a good, sound, business-like conduct of its affairs. What we need is—a business administration!" said Littlefield.

"I'm glad to hear you say that! I certainly am glad to hear you say that! I didn't know how you'd feel about it, with all your associations with colleges and so on, and I'm glad you feel that way. What the country needs—just at this present juncture —is neither a college president nor a lot of monkeying with foreign affairs, but a good —sound—economical—business—administration, that will give us a chance to have something like a decent turnover."

"Yes. It isn't generally realized that even in China the schoolmen are giving way to more practical men, and of course you can see what that implies."

"Is that a fact! Well, well!" breathed Babbitt, feeling much calmer, and much happier about the way things were going in the world. "Well, it's been nice to stop and parleyvoo a second. Guess I'll have to get down to the office now and sting a few clients. Well, so long, old man. See you tonight. So long."

II

They had labored, these solid citizens. Twenty years before, the hill on which Floral Heights was spread, with its bright roofs and immaculate turf and amazing comfort, had been a wilderness of rank second-growth elms and oaks and maples. Along the precise streets were still a few wooded vacant lots, and the fragment of an old orchard. It was brilliant to-day; the apple boughs were lit with fresh leaves like torches of green fire. The first white of cherry blossoms flickered down a gully, and robins clamored.

Babbitt sniffed the earth, chuckled at the hysteric robins as he would have chuckled at kittens or at a comic movie. He was, to the eye, the perfect office-going executive —a well-fed man in a correct brown soft hat and frameless spectacles, smoking a large cigar, driving a good motor along a semi-suburban parkway. But in him was some genius of authentic love for his neighborhood, his city, his clan. The winter was over; the time was come for the building, the visible growth, which to him was glory. He lost his dawn depression; he was ruddily cheerful when he stopped on Smith Street to leave the brown trousers, and to have the gasoline-tank filled.

The familiarity of the rite fortified him: the sight of the tall red iron gasoline-pump, the hollow-tile and terra-cotta garage, the window full of the most agreeable accessories—shiny casings, spark-plugs with immaculate porcelain jackets, tire-chains of gold and silver. He was flattered by the friendliness with which Sylvester Moon, dirtiest and most skilled of motor mechanics, came out to serve him. "Mornin', Mr. Babbitt!" said Moon, and Babbitt felt himself a person of importance, one whose name even busy garagemen remembered—not one of these cheap-sports flying around in flivvers. He admired the ingenuity of the automatic dial, clicking off gallon by gallon; admired the smartness of the sign: "A fill in time saves getting stuck—gas to-day 31 cents"; admired the rhythmic gurgle of the gasoline as it flowed into the tank, and the mechanical regularity with which Moon turned the handle.

"How much we takin' to-day?" asked Moon, in a manner which combined the independence of the great specialist, the friendliness of a familiar gossip, and respect for a man of weight in the community, like George F. Babbitt.

"Fill 'er up."

"Who you rootin' for for Republican candidate, Mr. Babbitt?"

"It's too early to make any predictions yet. After all, there's still a good month and two weeks—no, three weeks—must be almost three weeks—well, there's more than six weeks in all before the Republican convention, and I feel a fellow ought to keep an open mind and give all the candidates a show—look 'em all over and size 'em up, and then decide carefully."

"That's a fact, Mr. Babbitt."

"But I'll tell you—and my stand on this is just the same as it was four years ago, and eight years ago, and it'll be my stand four years from now—yes, and eight years from now! What I tell everybody, and it can't be too generally understood, is that what we need first, last, and all the time is a good, sound business administration!"

"By golly, that's right!"

"How do those front tires look to you?"

"Fine! Fine! Wouldn't be much work for garages if everybody looked after their car the way you do."

"Well, I do try and have some sense about it." Babbitt paid his bill, said adequately, "Oh, keep the change," and drove off in an ecstasy of honest self-appreciation. It was with the manner of a Good Samaritan that he shouted at a respectable-looking man who was waiting for a trolley car, "Have a lift?" As the man climbed in Babbitt condescended, "Going clear down-town? Whenever I see a fellow waiting for a trolley, I always make it a practice to give him a lift—unless, of course, he looks like a bum."

"Wish there were more folks that were so generous with their machines," dutifully said the victim of benevolence.

"Oh, no, 'tain't a question of generosity, hardly. Fact, I always feel—I was saying to my son just the other night—it's a fellow's duty to share the good things of this world with his neighbors, and it gets my goat when a fellow gets stuck on himself and goes around tooting his horn merely because he's charitable."

The victim seemed unable to find the right answer. Babbitt boomed on:

"Pretty punk service the Company giving us on these car-lines. Nonsense to only run the Portland Road cars once every seven minutes. Fellow gets mighty cold on a winter morning, waiting on a street corner with the wind nipping at his ankles."

"That's right. The Street Car Company don't care a damn what kind of a deal they give us. Something ought to happen to 'em."

Babbitt was alarmed. "But still, of course it won't do to just keep knocking the Traction Company and not realize the difficulties they're operating under, like these cranks that want municipal ownership. The way these workmen hold up the Company for high wages is simply a crime, and of course the burden falls on you and me that have to pay a seven-cent fare! Fact, there's remarkable service on all their lines—considering."

"Well—" uneasily.

"Darn fine morning," Babbitt explained. "Spring coming along fast."

"Yes, it's real spring now."

The victim had no originality, no wit, and Babbitt fell into a great silence and devoted himself to the game of beating trolley cars to the corner: a spurt, a tail-chase, nervous speeding between the huge yellow side of the trolley and the jagged row of parked motors, shooting past just as the trolley stopped—a rare game and valiant.

And all the while he was conscious of the loveliness of Zenith. For weeks together he noticed nothing but clients and the vexing To Rent signs of rival brokers. To-day, in mysterious malaise, he raged or rejoiced with equal nervous swiftness, and to-day the light of spring was so winsome that he lifted his head and saw.

He admired each district along his familiar route to the office: The bungalows and shrubs and winding irregular drive-ways of Floral Heights. The one-story shops on Smith Street, a glare of plate-glass and new yellow brick; groceries and laundries and drug-stores to supply the more immediate needs of East Side housewives. The market gardens in Dutch Hollow, their shanties patched with corrugated iron and stolen doors. Billboards with crimson goddesses nine feet tall advertising cinema films, pipe tobacco, and talcum powder. The old "mansions" along Ninth Street, S.E., like aged dandies in filthy linen; wooden castles turned into boarding-houses, with muddy walks and rusty hedges, jostled by fast-intruding garages, cheap apartment-houses, and fruit-stands conducted by bland, sleek Athenians. Across the belt of railroad-tracks, factories with high-perched water-tanks and tall stacks—factories producing condensed milk, paper boxes, lighting-fixtures, motor cars. Then the business center, the thickening darting traffic, the crammed trolleys unloading, and high doorways of marble and polished granite.

It was big—and Babbitt respected bigness in anything; in mountains, jewels, muscles, wealth, or words. He was, for a spring-enchanted moment, the lyric and almost unselfish lover of Zenith. He thought of the outlying factory suburbs; of the

Chaloosa River with its strangely eroded banks; of the orchard-dappled Tonawanda Hills to the North, and all the fat dairy land and big barns and comfortable herds. As he dropped his passenger he cried, "Gosh, I feel pretty good this morning!"

III

Epochal as starting the car was the drama of parking it before he entered his office. As he turned from Oberlin Avenue round the corner into Third Street, N.E., he peered ahead for a space in the line of parked cars. He angrily just missed a space as a rival driver slid into it. Ahead, another car was leaving the curb, and Babbitt slowed up, holding out his hand to the cars pressing on him from behind, agitatedly motioning an old woman to go ahead, avoiding a truck which bore down on him from one side. With front wheels nicking the wrought-steel bumper of the car in front, he stopped, feverishly cramped his steering-wheel, slid back into the vacant space and, with eighteen inches of room, manœuvered to bring the car level with the curb. It was a virile adventure masterfully executed. With satisfaction he locked a thief-proof steel wedge on the front wheel, and crossed the street to his real-estate office on the ground floor of the Reeves Building.

The Reeves Building was as fireproof as a rock and as efficient as a typewriter; fourteen stories of yellow pressed brick, with clean, upright, unornamented lines. It was filled with the offices of lawyers, doctors, agents for machinery, for emery wheels, for wire fencing, for mining-stock. Their gold signs shone on the windows. The entrance was too modern to be flamboyant with pillars; it was quiet, shrewd, neat. Along the Third Street side were a Western Union Telegraph Office, the Blue Delft Candy Shop, Shotwell's Stationery Shop, and the Babbitt-Thompson Realty Company.

Babbitt could have entered his office from the street, as customers did, but it made him feel an insider to go through the corridor of the building and enter by the back door. Thus he was greeted by the villagers.

The little unknown people who inhabited the Reeves Building corridors—elevator-runners, starter, engineers, superintendent, and the doubtful-looking lame man who conducted the news and cigar stand—were in no way city-dwellers. They were rustics, living in a constricted valley, interested only in one another and in The Building. Their Main Street was the entrance hall, with its stone floor, severe marble ceiling, and the inner windows of the shops. The liveliest place on the street was the Reeves Building Barber Shop, but this was also Babbitt's one embarrassment. Himself, he patronized the glittering Pompeian Barber Shop in the Hotel Thornleigh, and every time he passed the Reeves shop—ten times a day, a hundred times—he felt untrue to his own village.

Now, as one of the squirearchy, greeted with honorable salutations by the villagers, he marched into his office, and peace and dignity were upon him, and the morning's dissonances all unheard.

They were heard again, immediately.

Stanley Graff, the outside salesman, was talking on the telephone with tragic lack of that firm manner which disciplines clients: "Say, uh, I think I got just the house that would suit you—the Percival House, in Linton. . . . Oh, you've seen it. Well, how'd it strike you? . . . Huh? . . . Oh," irresolutely, "oh, I see."

As Babbitt marched into his private room, a coop with semi-partition of oak and frosted glass, at the back of the office, he reflected how hard it was to find employees who had his own faith that he was going to make sales.

There were nine members of the staff, besides Babbitt and his partner and father-in-law, Henry Thompson, who rarely came to the office. The nine were Stanley Graff, the outside salesman—a youngish man given to cigarettes and the playing of pool; old Mat Penniman, general utility man, collector of rents and salesman of insurance —broken, silent, gray; a mystery, reputed to have been a "crack" real-estate man with a firm of his own in haughty Brooklyn; Chester Kirby Laylock, resident salesman out at the Glen Oriole acreage development—an enthusiastic person with a silky mustache and much family; Miss Theresa McGoun, the swift and rather pretty stenographer; Miss Wilberta Bannigan, the thick, slow, laborious accountant and file-clerk; and four freelance part-time commission salesmen.

As he looked from his own cage into the main room Babbitt mourned, "McGoun's a good stenog., smart's a whip, but Stan Graff and all those bums——" The zest of the spring morning was smothered in the stale office air.

Normally he admired the office, with a pleased surprise that he should have created this sure lovely thing; normally he was stimulated by the clean newness of it and the air of bustle; but to-day it seemed flat—the tiled floor, like a bathroom, the ocher-colored metal ceiling, the faded maps on the hard plaster walls, the chairs of varnished pale oak, the desks and filing-cabinets of steel painted in olive drab. It was a vault, a steel chapel where loafing and laughter were raw sin.

He hadn't even any satisfaction in the new water-cooler! And it was the very best of water-coolers, up-to-date, scientific, and right-thinking. It had cost a great deal of money (in itself a virtue). It possessed a non-conducting fiber ice-container, a porcelain water-jar (guaranteed hygienic), a dripless non-clogging sanitary faucet, and machine-painted decorations in two tones of gold. He looked down the relentless stretch of tiled floor at the water-cooler, and assured himself that no tenant of the Reeves Building had a more expensive one, but he could not recapture the feeling of social superiority it had given him. He astoundingly grunted, "I'd like to beat it off to the woods right now. And loaf all day. And go to Gunch's again to-night, and play poker, and cuss as much as I feel like, and drink a hundred and nine-thousand bottles of beer."

He sighed; he read through his mail; he shouted "Msgoun," which meant "Miss McGoun"; and began to dictate.

This was his own version of his first letter:

"Omar Gribble, send it to his office, Miss McGoun, yours of twentieth to hand and in reply would say look here, Gribble, I'm awfully afraid if we go on shilly-shallying like this we'll just naturally lose the Allen sale, I had Allen up on carpet day before yesterday and got right down to cases and think I can assure you—uh, uh, no, change that: all my experience indicates he is all right, means to do business, looked into his financial record which is fine—that sentence seems to be a little balled up, Miss McGoun; make a couple sentences out of it if you have to, period, new paragraph.

"He is perfectly willing to pro rate the special assessment and strikes me, am dead sure there will be no difficulty in getting him to pay for title insurance, so now for heaven's sake let's get busy—no, make that: so now let's go to it and get down— no, that's enough—you can tie those sentences up a little better when you type 'em, Miss McGoun—your sincerely, etcetera."

This is the version of his letter which he received, typed, from Miss McGoun that afternoon:

BABBITT-THOMPSON REALTY CO.
Homes for Folks
Reeves Bldg., Oberlin Avenue & 3rd St., N.E.
Zenith

Omar Gribble, Esq.,
576 North American Building,
Zenith.

Dear Mr. Gribble:
      Your letter of the twentieth to hand. I must say I'm awfully afraid that if we go on shilly-shallying like this we'll just naturally lose the Allen sale. I had Allen up on the carpet day before yesterday, and got right down to cases. All my experience indicates that he means to do business. I have also looked into his financial record, which is fine.

He is perfectly willing to pro rate the special assessment and there will be no difficulty in getting him to pay for title insurance.
   So let's go!
                 Yours sincerely,

As he read and signed it, in his correct flowing business-college hand, Babbitt reflected, "Now that's a good, strong letter, and clear's a bell. Now what the— I never told McGoun to make a third paragraph there! Wish she'd quit trying to improve on my dictation! But what I can't understand is: why can't Stan Graff or Chet Laylock write a letter like that? With punch! With a kick!"

The most important thing he dictated that morning was the fortnightly form-letter, to be mimeographed and sent out to a thousand "prospects." It was diligently imitative of the best literary models of the day; of heart-to-heart-talk advertisements, "sales-pulling" letters, discourses on the "development of Will-power," and hand-shaking house-organs, as richly poured forth by the new school of Poets of Business. He had painfully written out a first draft, and he intoned it now like a poet delicate and distrait:

SAY, OLD MAN!
      I just want to know can I do you a whaleuva favor? Honest! No kidding! I know you're interested in getting a house, not merely a place where you hang up the old bonnet but a love-nest for the wife and kiddies—and maybe for the flivver out beyant (be sure and spell that b-e-y-a-n-t, Miss McGoun) the spud garden. Say, did you ever stop to think that we're here to save you trouble? That's how we make a living—folks don't pay us for our lovely beauty! Now take a look:
      Sit right down at the handsome carved mahogany escritoire and shoot us in a line telling us just what you want, and if we can find it we'll come hopping down your lane with the good tidings, and if we can't, we won't bother you.

To save your time, just fill out the blank enclosed. On request will also send blank regarding store properties in Floral Heights, Silver Grove, Linton, Bellevue, and all East Side residential districts.

Yours for service,

P.S.—Just a hint of some plums we can pick for you—some genuine bargains that came in to-day:

SILVER GROVE.—Cute four-room California bungalow, a.m.i., garage, dandy shade tree, swell neighborhood, handy car line. $3700, $780 down and balance liberal, Babbitt-Thompson terms, cheaper than rent.

DORCHESTER.—A corker! Artistic two-family house, all oak trim, parquet floors, lovely gas log, big porches, colonial, HEATED ALL-WEATHER GARAGE, a bargain at $11,250.

Dictation over, with its need of sitting and thinking instead of bustling around and making a noise and really doing something, Babbitt sat creakily back in his revolving desk-chair and beamed on Miss McGoun. He was conscious of her as a girl, of black bobbed hair against demure cheeks. A longing which was indistinguishable from loneliness enfeebled him. While she waited, tapping a long, precise pencil-point on the desk-tablet, he half identified her with the fairy girl of his dreams. He imagined their eyes meeting with terrifying recognition; imagined touching her lips with frightened reverence and— She was chirping, "Any more, Mist' Babbitt?" He grunted, "That winds it up, I guess," and turned heavily away.

For all his wandering thoughts, they had never been more intimate than this. He often reflected, "Nev' forget how old Jake Offutt said a wise bird never goes love-making in his own office or his own home. Start trouble. Sure. But—"

In twenty-three years of married life he had peered uneasily at every graceful ankle, every soft shoulder; in thought he had treasured them; but not once had he hazarded respectability by adventuring. Now, as he calculated the cost of repapering the Styles house, he was restless again, discontented about nothing and everything, ashamed of his discontentment, and lonely for the fairy girl.

1922

---

from Main Street

from Chapter III: [Gopher Prairie]

II

To each of the passengers his seat was his temporary home, and most of the passengers were slatternly housekeepers. But one seat looked clean and deceptively cool. In it were an obviously prosperous man and a black-haired, fine-skinned girl whose pumps rested on an immaculate horsehide bag.

They were Dr. Will Kennicott and his bride, Carol.

They had been married at the end of a year of conversational courtship, and they were on their way to Gopher Prairie after a wedding journey in the Colorado mountains.

The hordes of the way-train were not altogether new to Carol. She had seen them on trips from St. Paul to Chicago. But now that they had become her own people, to bathe and encourage and adorn, she had an acute and uncomfortable interest in them. They distressed her. They were so stolid. She had always maintained that there is no American peasantry, and she sought now to defend her faith by seeing imagination and enterprise in the young Swedish farmers, and in a traveling man working over his order-blanks. But the older people, Yankees as well as Norwegians, Germans, Finns, Canucks, had settled into submission to poverty. They were peasants, she groaned.

"Isn't there any way of waking them up? What would happen if they understood scientific agriculture?" she begged of Kennicott, her hand groping for his.

It had been a transforming honeymoon. She had been frightened to discover how tumultuous a feeling could be roused in her. Will had been lordly—stalwart, jolly, impressively competent in making camp, tender and understanding through the hours when they had lain side by side in a tent pitched among pines high up on a lonely mountain spur.

His hand swallowed hers as he started from thoughts of the practise to which he was returning. "These people? Wake 'em up? What for? They're happy."

"But they're so provincial. No, that isn't what I mean. They're—oh, so sunk in the mud."

"Look here, Carrie. You want to get over your city idea that because a man's pants aren't pressed, he's a fool. These farmers are mighty keen and up-and-coming."

"I know! That's what hurts. Life seems so hard for them—these lonely farms and this gritty train."

"Oh, they don't mind it. Besides, things are changing. The auto, the telephone, rural free delivery; they're bringing the farmers in closer touch with the town. Takes time, you know, to change a wilderness like this was fifty years ago. But already, why, they can hop into the Ford or the Overland and get in to the movies on Saturday evening quicker than you could get down to 'em by trolley in St. Paul."

"But if it's these towns we've been passing that the farmers run to for relief from their bleakness— Can't you understand? Just *look* at them!"

Kennicott was amazed. Ever since childhood he had seen these towns from trains on this same line. He grumbled, "Why, what's the matter with 'em? Good hustling burgs. It would astonish you to know how much wheat and rye and corn and potatoes they ship in a year."

"But they're so ugly."

"I'll admit they aren't comfy like Gopher Prairie. But give 'em time."

"What's the use of giving them time unless some one has desire and training enough to plan them? Hundreds of factories trying to make attractive motor cars, but these towns—left to chance. No! That can't be true. It must have taken genius to make them so scrawny!"

"Oh, they're not so bad," was all he answered. He pretended that his hand was the cat and hers the mouse. For the first time she tolerated him rather than encouraged him. She was staring out at Schoenstrom, a hamlet of perhaps a hundred and fifty inhabitants, at which the train was stopping.

A bearded German and his pucker-mouthed wife tugged their enormous imitation-leather satchel from under a seat and waddled out. The station agent hoisted a dead calf aboard the baggage-car. There were no other visible activities in Schoenstrom. In the quiet of the halt, Carol could hear a horse kicking his stall, a carpenter shingling a roof.

The business-center of Schoenstrom took up one side of one block, facing the railroad. It was a row of one-story shops covered with galvanized iron, or with clapboards painted red and bilious yellow. The buildings were as ill-assorted, as temporary-looking, as a mining-camp street in the motion-pictures. The railroad station was a one-room frame box, a mirey cattle-pen on one side and a crimson wheat-elevator on the other. The elevator, with its cupola on the ridge of a shingled roof, resembled a broad-shouldered man with a small, vicious, pointed head. The only habitable structures to be seen were the florid red-brick Catholic church and rectory at the end of Main Street.

Carol picked at Kennicott's sleeve. "You wouldn't call this a not-so-bad town, would you?"

"These Dutch burgs *are* kind of slow. Still, at that— See that fellow coming out of the general store there, getting into the big car? I met him once. He owns about half the town, besides the store. Rauskukle, his name is. He owns a lot of mortgages, and he gambles in farm-lands. Good nut on him, that fellow. Why, they say he's worth three or four hundred thousand dollars! Got a dandy great big yellow brick house with tiled walks and a garden and everything, other end of town—can't see it from here—I've gone past it when I've driven through here. Yes sir!"

"Then, if he has all that, there's no excuse whatever for this place! If his three hundred thousand went back into the town, where it belongs, they could burn up these shacks, and build a dream-village, a jewel! Why do the farmers and the town-people let the Baron keep it?"

"I must say I don't quite get you sometimes, Carrie. Let him? They can't help themselves! He's a dumm old Dutchman, and probably the priest can twist him around his finger, but when it comes to picking good farming land, he's a regular wiz!"

"I see. He's their symbol of beauty. The town erects him, instead of erecting buildings."

"Honestly, don't know what you're driving at. You're kind of played out, after this long trip. You'll feel better when you get home and have a good bath, and put on the blue negligée. That's some vampire costume, you witch!"

He squeezed her arm, looked at her knowingly.

They moved on from the desert stillness of the Schoenstrom station. The train creaked, banged, swayed. The air was nauseatingly thick. Kennicott turned her face from the window, rested her head on his shoulder. She was coaxed from her unhappy mood. But she came out of it unwillingly, and when Kennicott was satisfied that he had corrected all her worries and had opened a magazine of saffron detective stories, she sat upright.

Here—she meditated—is the newest empire of the world; the Northern Middle-west; a land of dairy herds and exquisite lakes, of new automobiles and tar-paper shanties and silos like red towers, of clumsy speech and a hope that is boundless. An empire which feeds a quarter of the world—yet its work is merely begun. They are pioneers, these sweaty wayfarers, for all their telephones and bank-accounts and automatic pianos and co-operative leagues. And for all its fat richness, theirs is a pioneer land. What is its future? she wondered. A future of cities and factory smut where now are loping empty fields? Homes universal and secure? Or placid châteaux ringed with sullen huts? Youth free to find knowledge and laughter? Willingness to sift the sanctified lies? Or creamy-skinned fat women, smeared with grease and chalk, gorgeous in the skins of beasts and the bloody feathers of slain birds, playing bridge with puffy pink-nailed jeweled fingers, women who after much expenditure of labor and bad temper still grotesquely resemble their own flatulent lap-dogs? The ancient stale inequalities, or something different in history, unlike the tedious maturity of other empires? What future and what hope?

Carol's head ached with the riddle.

She saw the prairie, flat in giant patches or rolling in long hummocks. The width and bigness of it, which had expanded her spirit an hour ago, began to frighten her. It spread out so; it went on so uncontrollably; she could never know it. Kennicott was closeted in his detective story. With the loneliness which comes most depressingly in the midst of many people she tried to forget problems, to look at the prairie objectively.

The grass beside the railroad had been burnt over; it was a smudge prickly with charred stalks of weeds. Beyond the undeviating barbed-wire fences were clumps of golden rod. Only this thin hedge shut them off from the plains—shorn wheat-lands of autumn, a hundred acres to a field, prickly and gray near-by but in the blurred distance like tawny velvet stretched over dipping hillocks. The long rows of wheat-shocks marched like soldiers in worn yellow tabards. The newly plowed fields were black banners fallen on the distant slope. It was a martial immensity, vigorous, a little harsh, unsoftened by kindly gardens.

The expanse was relieved by clumps of oaks with patches of short wild grass; and every mile or two was a chain of cobalt slews, with the flicker of blackbirds' wings across them.

All this working land was turned into exuberance by the light. The sunshine was dizzy on open stubble; shadows from immense cumulus clouds were forever sliding across low mounds; and the sky was wider and loftier and more resolutely blue than the sky of cities . . . she declared.

"It's a glorious country; a land to be big in," she crooned.

Then Kennicott startled her by chuckling, "D' you realize the town after the next is Gopher Prairie? Home!"

III

That one word—home—it terrified her. Had she really bound herself to live, inescapably, in this town called Gopher Prairie? And this thick man beside her, who dared to define her future, he was a stranger! She turned in her seat, stared at him. Who was he? Why was he sitting with her? He wasn't of her kind! His neck was heavy; his speech was heavy; he was twelve or thirteen years older than she; and about him was none of the magic of shared adventures and eagerness. She could not believe that she had ever slept in his arms. That was one of the dreams which you had but did not officially admit.

She told herself how good he was, how dependable and understanding. She touched his ear, smoothed the plane of his solid jaw, and, turning away again, concentrated upon liking his town. It wouldn't be like these barren settlements. It couldn't be! Why, it had three thousand population. That was a great many people. There would be six hundred houses or more. And— The lakes near it would be so lovely. She'd seen them in the photographs. They had looked charming . . . hadn't they?

As the train left Wahkeenyan she began nervously to watch for the lakes—the entrance to all her future life. But when she discovered them, to the left of the track, her only impression of them was that they resembled the photographs.

A mile from Gopher Prairie the track mounts a curving low ridge, and she could see the town as a whole. With a passionate jerk she pushed up the window, looked out, the arched fingers of her left hand trembling on the sill, her right hand at her breast.

And she saw that Gopher Prairie was merely an enlargement of all the hamlets which they had been passing. Only to the eyes of a Kennicott was it exceptional. The huddled low wooden houses broke the plains scarcely more than would a hazel thicket. The fields swept up to it, past it. It was unprotected and unprotecting; there was no dignity in it nor any hope of greatness. Only the tall red grain-elevator and a few tinny church-steeples rose from the mass. It was a frontier camp. It was not a place to live in, not possibly, not conceivably.

The people—they'd be as drab as their houses, as flat as their fields. She couldn't stay here. She would have to wrench loose from this man, and flee.

She peeped at him. She was at once helpless before his mature fixity, and touched by his excitement as he sent his magazine skittering along the aisle, stooped for their bags, came up with flushed face, and gloated, "Here we are!"

She smiled loyally, and looked away. The train was entering town. The houses on the outskirts were dusky old red mansions with wooden frills, or gaunt frame shelters like grocery boxes, or new bungalows with concrete foundations imitating stone.

Now the train was passing the elevator, the grim storage-tanks for oil, a creamery, a lumber-yard, a stock-yard muddy and trampled and stinking. Now they were stopping at a squat red frame station, the platform crowded with unshaven farmers and with loafers—unadventurous people with dead eyes. She was here. She could not go on. It was the end—the end of the world. She sat with closed eyes, longing to push past Kennicott, hide somewhere in the train, flee on toward the Pacific.

Something large arose in her soul and commanded, "Stop it! Stop being a whining baby!" She stood up quickly; she said, "Isn't it wonderful to be here at last!"

He trusted her so. She would make herself like the place. And she was going to do tremendous things—

She followed Kennicott and the bobbing ends of the two bags which he carried. They were held back by the slow line of disembarking passengers. She reminded herself that she was actually at the dramatic moment of the bride's home-coming. She ought to feel exalted. She felt nothing at all except irritation at their slow progress toward the door.

Kennicott stooped to peer through the windows. He shyly exulted:

"Look! Look! There's a bunch come down to welcome us! Sam Clark and the missus and Dave Dyer and Jack Elder, and, yes sir, Harry Haydock and Juanita, and a whole crowd! I guess they see us now. Yuh, yuh sure, they see us! See 'em waving!"

She obediently bent her head to look out at them. She had hold of herself. She was ready to love them. But she was embarrassed by the heartiness of the cheering group. From the vestibule she waved to them, but she clung a second to the sleeve of the brakeman who helped her down before she had the courage to dive into the cataract of hand-shaking people, people whom she could not tell apart. She had the impression that all the men had coarse voices, large damp hands, tooth-brush mustaches, bald spots, and Masonic watch-charms.

She knew that they were welcoming her. Their hands, their smiles, their shouts, their affectionate eyes overcame her. She stammered, "Thank you, oh, thank you!"

One of the men was clamoring at Kennicott, "I brought my machine down to take you home, doc."

"Fine business, Sam!" cried Kennicott; and, to Carol, "Let's jump in. That big Paige over there. Some boat, too, believe me! Sam can show speed to any of these Marmons from Minneapolis!"

Only when she was in the motor car did she distinguish the three people who were to accompany them. The owner, now at the wheel, was the essence of decent self-satisfaction; a baldish, largish, level-eyed man, rugged of neck but sleek and round of face—face like the back of a spoon bowl. He was chuckling at her, "Have you got us all straight yet?"

"Course she has! Trust Carrie to get things straight and get 'em darn quick! I bet she could tell you every date in history!" boasted her husband.

But the man looked at her reassuringly and with a certainty that he was a person whom she could trust she confessed, "As a matter of fact I haven't got anybody straight."

"Course you haven't, child. Well, I'm Sam Clark, dealer in hardware, sporting goods, cream separators, and almost any kind of heavy junk you can think of. You can call me Sam—anyway, I'm going to call you Carrie, seein' 's you've been and gone and married this poor fish of a bum medic that we keep round here." Carol smiled lavishly, and wished that she called people by their given names more easily. "The fat cranky lady back there beside you, who is pretending that she can't hear me giving her away, is Mrs. Sam'l Clark; and this hungry-looking squirt up here beside me is Dave Dyer, who keeps his drug store running by not filling your hubby's prescriptions right—fact you might say he's the guy that put the 'shun' in 'prescription.' So! Well, leave us take the bonny bride home. Say, doc, I'll sell you the Candersen place for three thousand plunks. Better be thinking about building a new home for Carrie. Prettiest *Frau* in G. P., if you asks me!"

Contentedly Sam Clark drove off, in the heavy traffic of three Fords and the Minniemashie House Free 'Bus.

"I shall like Mr. Clark . . . I *can't* call him 'Sam'! They're all so friendly." She glanced at the houses; tried not to see what she saw; gave way in: "Why do these stories lie so? They always make the bride's home-coming a bower of roses. Complete trust in noble spouse. Lies about marriage. I'm *not* changed. And this town—O my God! I can't go through with it. This junk-heap!"

Her husband bent over her. "You look like you were in a brown study. Scared? I don't expect you to think Gopher Prairie is a paradise, after St. Paul. I don't expect you to be crazy about it, at first. But you'll come to like it so much—life's so free here and best people on earth."

She whispered to him (while Mrs. Clark considerately turned away), "I love you for understanding. I'm just—I'm beastly over-sensitive. Too many books. It's my lack of shoulder-muscles and sense. Give me time, dear."

"You bet! All the time you want!"

She laid the back of his hand against her cheek, snuggled near him. She was ready for her new home.

Kennicott had told her that, with his widowed mother as housekeeper, he had occupied an old house, "but nice and roomy, and well-heated, best furnace I could find on the market." His mother had left Carol her love, and gone back to Lac-qui-Meurt.

It would be wonderful, she exulted, not to have to live in Other People's Houses, but to make her own shrine. She held his hand tightly and stared ahead as the car swung round a corner and stopped in the street before a prosaic frame house in a small parched lawn. . . .

from **Chapter IV: [A Walk down Main Street]**

I

"The Clarks have invited some folks to their house to meet us, tonight," said Kennicott, as he unpacked his suit-case.

"Oh, that is nice of them!"

"You bet. I told you you'd like 'em. Squarest people on earth. Uh, Carrie—Would you mind if I sneaked down to the office for an hour, just to see how things are?"

"Why, no. Of course not. I know you're keen to get back to work."

"Sure you don't mind?"

"Not a bit. Out of my way. Let me unpack."

But the advocate of freedom in marriage was as much disappointed as a drooping bride at the alacrity with which he took that freedom and escaped to the world of men's affairs. She gazed about their bedroom, and its full dismalness crawled over her: the awkward knuckly L-shape of it; the black walnut bed with apples and spotty pears carved on the headboard; the imitation maple bureau, with pink-daubed scent-bottles and a petticoated pin-cushion on a marble slab uncomfortably like a gravestone; the plain pine washstand and the garlanded water-pitcher and bowl. The scent was of horsehair and plush and Florida Water.

"How could people ever live with things like this?" she shuddered. She saw the furniture as a circle of elderly judges, condemning her to death by smothering. The tottering brocade chair squeaked, "Choke her—choke her—smother her." The old linen smelled of the tomb. She was alone in this house, this strange still house, among the shadows of dead thoughts and haunting repressions. "I hate it! I hate it!" she panted. "Why did I ever—"

She remembered that Kennicott's mother had brought these family relics from the old home in Lac-qui-Meurt. "Stop it! They're perfectly comfortable things. They're —comfortable. Besides— Oh, they're horrible! We'll change them, right away."

Then, "But of course he *has* to see how things are at the office—"

She made a pretense of busying herself with unpacking. The chintz-lined, silver-fitted bag which had seemed so desirable a luxury in St. Paul was an extravagant vanity here. The daring black chemise of frail chiffon and lace was a hussy at which the deep-bosomed bed stiffened in disgust, and she hurled it into a bureau drawer, hid it beneath a sensible linen blouse.

She gave up unpacking. She went to the window, with a purely literary thought of village charm—hollyhocks and lanes and apple-cheeked cottages. What she saw was the side of the Seventh-Day Adventist Church—a plain clapboard wall of a sour liver color; the ash-pile back of the church; an unpainted stable; and an alley in which a Ford delivery-wagon had been stranded. This was the terraced garden below her boudoir; this was to be her scenery for—

"I mustn't! I mustn't! I'm nervous this afternoon. Am I sick? . . . Good Lord, I hope it isn't that! Not now! How people lie! How these stories lie! They say the bride is always so blushing and proud and happy when she finds that out, but—I'd hate it! I'd be scared to death! Some day but— Please, dear nebulous Lord, not now! Bearded sniffy old men sitting and demanding that we bear children. If *they* had to bear them—! I wish they did have to! Not now! Not till I've got hold of this job of liking the ash-pile out there! . . . I must shut up. I'm mildly insane. I'm going out for a walk. I'll see the town by myself. My first view of the empire I'm going to conquer!"

She fled from the house.

She stared with seriousness at every concrete crossing, every hitching-post, every rake for leaves; and to each house she devoted all her speculation. What would they come to mean? How would they look six months from now? In which of them would she be dining? Which of these people whom she passed, now mere arrangements of hair and clothes, would turn into intimates, loved or dreaded, different from all the other people in the world? . . .

II

When Carol had walked for thirty-two minutes she had completely covered the town, east and west, north and south; and she stood at the corner of Main Street and Washington Avenue and despaired.

Main Street with its two-story brick shops, its story-and-a-half wooden residences, its muddy expanse from concrete walk to walk, its huddle of Fords and lumber-wagons, was too small to absorb her. The broad, straight, unenticing gashes of the streets let in the grasping prairie on every side. She realized the vastness and the emptiness of the land. The skeleton iron windmill on the farm a few blocks away, at the north end of Main Street, was like the ribs of a dead cow. She thought of the coming of the Northern winter, when the unprotected houses would crouch together in terror of storms galloping out of that wild waste. They were so small and weak, the little brown houses. They were shelters for sparrows, not homes for warm laughing people.

She told herself that down the street the leaves were a splendor. The maples were orange; the oaks a solid tint of raspberry. And the lawns had been nursed with love. But the thought would not hold. At best the trees resembled a thinned woodlot. There was no park to rest the eyes. And since not Gopher Prairie but Wakamin was the county-seat, there was no court-house with its grounds.

She glanced through the fly-specked windows of the most pretentious building in sight, the one place which welcomed strangers and determined their opinion of the charm and luxury of Gopher Prairie—the Minniemashie House. It was a tall lean shabby structure, three stories of yellow-streaked wood, the corners covered with sanded pine slabs purporting to symbolize stone. In the hotel office she could see a stretch of bare unclean floor, a line of rickety chairs with brass cuspidors between, a writing-desk with advertisements in mother-of-pearl letters upon the glass-covered back. The dining-room beyond was a jungle of stained table-cloths and catsup bottles.

She looked no more at the Minniemashie House.

A man in cuffless shirt-sleeves with pink arm-garters, wearing a linen collar but no tie, yawned his way from Dyer's Drug Store across to the hotel. He leaned against the wall, scratched a while, sighed, and in a bored way gossiped with a man tilted back in a chair. A lumber-wagon, its long green box filled with large spools of barbed-wire fencing, creaked down the block. A Ford, in reverse, sounded as though it were shaking to pieces, then recovered and rattled away. In the Greek candy-store was the whine of a peanut-roaster, and the oily smell of nuts.

There was no other sound nor sign of life.

She wanted to run, fleeing from the encroaching prairie, demanding the security of a great city. Her dreams of creating a beautiful town were ludicrous. Oozing out from every drab wall, she felt a forbidding spirit which she could never conquer.

She trailed down the street on one side, back on the other, glancing into the cross streets. It was a private Seeing Main Street tour. She was within ten minutes beholding not only the heart of a place called Gopher Prairie, but ten thousand towns from Albany to San Diego:

Dyer's Drug Store, a corner building of regular and unreal blocks of artificial stone. Inside the store, a greasy marble soda-fountain with an electric lamp of red and green and curdled-yellow mosaic shade. Pawed-over heaps of tooth-brushes and combs and packages of shaving-soap. Shelves of soap-cartons, teething-rings, garden-seeds, and patent medicines in yellow packages—nostrums for consumption, for "women's diseases"—notorious mixtures of opium and alcohol, in the very shop to which her husband sent patients for the filling of prescriptions.

From a second-story window the sign "W. P. Kennicott, Phys. & Surgeon," gilt on black sand.

A small wooden motion-picture theater called "The Rosebud Movie Palace." Lithographs announcing a film called "Fatty in Love."

Howland & Gould's Grocery. In the display window, black, overripe bananas and lettuce on which a cat was sleeping. Shelves lined with red crêpe paper which was now faded and torn and concentrically spotted. Flat against the wall of the second story the signs of lodges—the Knights of Pythias, the Maccabees, the Woodmen, the Masons.

Dahl & Oleson's Meat Market—a reek of blood.

A jewelry shop with tinny-looking wrist-watches for women. In front of it, at the curb, a huge wooden clock which did not go.

A fly-buzzing saloon with a brilliant gold and enamel whisky sign across the front. Other saloons down the block. From them a stink of stale beer, and thick voices bellowing pidgin German or trolling out dirty songs—vice gone feeble and unenterprising and dull—the delicacy of a mining-camp minus its vigor. In front of the saloons, farmwives sitting on the seats of wagons, waiting for their husbands to become drunk and ready to start home.

A tobacco shop called "The Smoke House," filled with young men shaking dice for cigarettes. Racks of magazines, and pictures of coy fat prostitutes in striped bathing-suits.

A clothing store with a display of "ox-blood-shade Oxfords with bull-dog toes." Suits which looked worn and glossless while they were still new, flabbily draped on dummies like corpses with painted cheeks.

The Bon Ton Store—Haydock & Simons'—the largest shop in town. The first-story front of clear glass, the plates cleverly bound at the edges with brass. The second story of pleasant tapestry brick. One window of excellent clothes for men, interspersed with collars of floral piqué which showed mauve daisies on a saffron ground. Newness and an obvious notion of neatness and service. Haydock & Simons. Haydock. She had met a Haydock at the station; Harry Haydock; an active person of thirty-five. He seemed great to her, now, and very like a saint. His shop was clean!

Axel Egge's General Store, frequented by Scandinavian farmers. In the shallow dark window-space heaps of sleazy sateens, badly woven galateas, canvas shoes designed for women with bulging ankles, steel and red glass buttons upon cards with broken edges, a cottony blanket, a granite-ware frying-pan reposing on a sun-faded crêpe blouse.

Sam Clark's Hardware Store. An air of frankly metallic enterprise. Guns and churns and barrels of nails and beautiful shiny butcher knives.

Chester Dashaway's House Furnishing Emporium. A vista of heavy oak rockers with leather seats, asleep in a dismal row.

Billy's Lunch. Thick handleless cups on the wet oilcloth-covered counter. An odor of onions and the smoke of hot lard. In the doorway a young man audibly sucking a toothpick.

The warehouse of the buyer of cream and potatoes. The sour smell of a dairy.

The Ford Garage and the Buick Garage, competent one-story brick and cement buildings opposite each other. Old and new cars on grease-blackened concrete floors. Tire advertisements. The roaring of a tested motor; a racket which beat at the nerves. Surly young men in khaki union-overalls. The most energetic and vital places in town.

A large warehouse for agricultural implements. An impressive barricade of green and gold wheels, of shafts and sulky seats, belonging to machinery of which Carol knew nothing—potato-planters, manure-spreaders, silage-cutters, disk-harrows, breaking-plows.

A feed store, its windows opaque with the dust of bran, a patent medicine advertisement painted on its roof.

Ye Art Shoppe, Prop. Mrs. Mary Ellen Wilks, Christian Science Library open daily free. A touching fumble at beauty. A one-room shanty of boards recently covered with rough stucco. A show-window delicately rich in error: vases starting out to imitate tree-trunks but running off into blobs of gilt—an aluminum ash-tray labeled "Greetings from Gopher Prairie"—a Christian Science magazine—a stamped sofa-cushion portraying a large ribbon tied to a small poppy, the correct skeins of embroidery-silk lying on the pillow. Inside the shop, a glimpse of bad carbon prints of bad and famous pictures, shelves of phonograph records and camera films, wooden toys, and in the midst an anxious small woman sitting in a padded rocking chair.

A barber shop and pool room. A man in shirt sleeves, presumably Del Snafflin the proprietor, shaving a man who had a large Adam's apple.

Nat Hicks's Tailor Shop, on a side street off Main. A one-story building. A fashion-plate showing human pitchforks in garments which looked as hard as steel plate.

On another side street a raw red-brick Catholic Church with a varnished yellow door.

The post-office—merely a partition of glass and brass shutting off the rear of a mildewed room which must once have been a shop. A tilted writing-shelf against a wall rubbed black and scattered with official notices and army recruiting-posters.

The damp, yellow-brick schoolbuilding in its cindery grounds.

The State Bank, stucco masking wood.

The Farmers' National Bank. An Ionic temple of marble. Pure, exquisite, solitary. A brass plate with "Ezra Stowbody, Pres't."

A score of similar shops and establishments.

Behind them and mixed with them, the houses, meek cottages or large, comfortable, soundly uninteresting symbols of prosperity.

In all the town not one building save the Ionic bank which gave pleasure to Carol's eyes; not a dozen buildings which suggested that, in the fifty years of Gopher Prairie's existence, the citizens had realized that it was either desirable or possible to make this, their common home, amusing or attractive.

It was not only the unsparing unapologetic ugliness and the rigid straightness which overwhelmed her. It was the planlessness, the flimsy temporariness of the buildings, their faded unpleasant colors. The street was cluttered with electric-light poles, telephone poles, gasoline pumps for motor cars, boxes of goods. Each man had built with the most valiant disregard of all the others. Between a large new "block" of two-story brick shops on one side, and the fire-brick Overland garage on the other side, was a one-story cottage turned into a millinery shop. The white temple of the Farmers' Bank was elbowed back by a grocery of glaring yellow brick. One store-building had a patchy galvanized iron cornice; the building beside it was crowned with battlements and pyramids of brick capped with blocks of red sandstone.

She escaped from Main Street, fled home.

She wouldn't have cared, she insisted, if the people had been comely. She had noted a young man loafing before a shop, one unwashed hand holding the cord of an awning; a middle-aged man who had a way of staring at women as though he had been married too long and too prosaically; an old farmer, solid, wholesome, but not clean—his face like a potato fresh from the earth. None of them had shaved for three days.

"If they can't build shrines, out here on the prairie, surely there's nothing to prevent their buying safety-razors!" she raged.

She fought herself: "I must be wrong. People do live here. It *can't* be as ugly as —as I know it is! I must be wrong. But I can't do it. I can't go through with it."

She came home too seriously worried for hysteria; and when she found Kennicott waiting for her, and exulting, "Have a walk? Well, like the town? Great lawns and trees, eh?" she was able to say, with a self-protective maturity new to her, "It's very interesting."

1920

Eugene O'Neill
1888–1953

Nobel Prize–winning playwright Eugene Gladstone O'Neill was born in a
Broadway hotel room, in the center of New York's theater district, and grew up
in the world of the American theater. "You might say I started as a trouper," he
once reported. "I knew only actors and the stage. My mother nursed me in the
wings and in dressing rooms." His father, James O'Neill, was an extremely
successful, Irish-born actor who played the lead in over 6,000 performances of
The Count of Monte Cristo, a melodrama based on Alexandre Dumas's famous
novel. By his late teens O'Neill had begun to despise the popular Victorian
theater that his father represented. Later he would set out to create a new
dramatic style and idiom—to completely transform the American stage.

O'Neill was educated in Catholic boarding schools and private academies. His
only regular home in childhood was in New London, Connecticut, where his
family lived during the summer, and where he grew to love both the sea and the
gritty waterfront life of sailors and saloons. He entered Princeton in 1906, but
collegiate life soon clashed with his hard-drinking, rebellious behavior, and he
was suspended in his first year. He spent several years "just drifting" and in 1909
was secretly married against the wishes of both his and his wife's parents. A few
months later he embarked on the experiences as a seaman that would provide him
with much of the material for his later plays. He sailed to Honduras to prospect
for gold and spent two years before the mast, sailing to Buenos Aires, England,
and South Africa.

On his return, divorced and the father of a two-year-old son, O'Neill hung
around disreputable New York waterfront backrooms, several of which became
settings for later plays; passed a few months on tour with his father's company;
and found a position as a reporter for a New London newspaper, where he
contributed local news items and light verse. Toward the end of 1912, however,
he was hospitalized for six months with tuberculosis. The event proved to be a
turning point in his life. While recovering in a Connecticut sanitorium, he
started to read drama seriously—especially Strindberg, Ibsen, and the Greek tragic
poets—and decided to become a playwright. In the summer of 1914 he applied
to George Pierce Baker's famous drama workshop at Harvard ("because I want to
be an artist or nothing") to study for one year as a special student, and that same
year he published his first book, *Thirst, and Other One-Act Plays.*

After a semester at Harvard, O'Neill moved to Greenwich Village, where he
became a leading member of two avant-garde groups, the Provincetown Players
and the Greenwich Village Theatre, both of which helped to lay the foundation
for the modern "little theater" movement. On July 28, 1916, O'Neill's first play,
Bound East for Cardiff, was produced at the Wharf Theatre in Provincetown,
Massachusetts. Written in 1914 and included as a writing sample with his
Harvard application, this one-act play showed O'Neill's gift for evoking a
powerful atmosphere and his keen ear for the vernacular. These two elements,

voice and atmosphere, became prominent features of every O'Neill stage production.

In 1918 O'Neill remarried and, despite severe bouts of alcoholism, began working on longer plays. His first full-length play, *Beyond the Horizon,* was produced in New York in 1920 and won a Pulitzer Prize. In the same year the Provincetown Playhouse staged *The Emperor Jones.* An experimental drama that blends fantasy and reality against an incessant beat of drums, it established O'Neill as America's most promising playwright. A year later that promise seemed fulfilled when he won his second Pulitzer Prize for *Anna Christie.* To O'Neill, however, *Anna Christie* seemed a backward-looking work, full of "Broadway tricks," rather than a new theatrical form designed to get beneath conventional dramatic surfaces—"behind life," as he put it.

Following *Anna Christie,* O'Neill began a period of restless experimentation and colossal productivity. The early 1920s brought the deaths in close succession of his father, mother, and brother and were marred by his own continued drinking problems and a deteriorating marriage. Yet twenty of his plays were produced on New York stages. These included a series of experimental plays: *The Hairy Ape* (1922), *All God's Chillun Got Wings* (1924), *Desire Under the Elms* (1924), *The Great God Brown* (1926), and the nine-act *Strange Interlude* (1928), which won him a third Pulitzer Prize. With *Strange Interlude* O'Neill achieved a new dramatic language, one that stressed breakdowns in communication, with private voices submerged beneath social voices. A stage direction from the play offers an indication of the "interior dialogue" that O'Neill was striving for: "They stare straight ahead and remain motionless. They speak, ostensibly one to the other, but showing by their tone it is a thinking aloud to oneself, and neither appears to hear what the other has said." In 1929 O'Neill, recovered from his alcoholism, divorced his second wife and married the actress Carlotta Monterey in France, where they were to live for several years. Two years later, The Theatre Guild produced one of O'Neill's most ambitious plays, *Mourning Becomes Electra,* a trilogy that focuses on the passions of an old New England family at the conclusion of the Civil War.

O'Neill's later drama turned increasingly to personal memories. *Ah, Wilderness!* (1933), which featured George M. Cohan, is a domestic comedy—O'Neill called it a "comedy of recollection"—about a rebellious adolescent growing up, like O'Neill himself, in a turn-of-the-century Connecticut family. In *The Iceman Cometh* (1946), O'Neill delved back into his New York waterfront days. Set in a backroom world of drunk and hopeless individuals, the four and one-half hour drama climaxes in an astonishing soliloquy, perhaps the longest in American drama. The last of O'Neill's plays to be produced on Broadway during his lifetime, *The Iceman Cometh* achieved greater success during its revival in the 1950s than in its first production, and it is now among his most widely acclaimed works.

In 1932 O'Neill and his wife moved to Sea Island, Georgia. Four years later he was awarded the Nobel Prize. As his health continued to decline, he moved, first to California, where he lived in relative seclusion, and then to New York. During this period he wrote several plays, all of which were produced in Sweden after his death in 1953. Of these, the most impressive is another four and one-half hour play, *Long Day's Journey into Night,* for which O'Neill received posthumously his fourth Pulitzer Prize. An intense, autobiographical drama concerning a writer's miserly father, drug-addicted mother, and alcoholic brother, *Long Day's Journey into Night* is probably O'Neill's finest work. After seeing a London production of the play, T. S. Eliot called it "one of the most moving plays I have ever seen." The critic Brendan Gill considered it "the finest play written in English in my lifetime." The play opened in New York in 1956 and has been successfully revived twice on Broadway, most recently in 1986.

Three other plays received posthumous premieres: *A Touch of the Poet, Hughie,* and *More Stately Mansions.* Of these, the most successful is *Hughie,* written in 1940 but not performed in America until 1964. Echoing many of O'Neill's themes, this fifty-minute play returns to the spare, almost claustrophobic settings of his first sea plays. A drama of voice and atmosphere rather than of plot, it shows O'Neill's remarkable sensitivity to sound and to the poetry of urban slang. O'Neill once wrote that critics had generally missed the best part of his work: "But where I feel myself most neglected is just where I set most store by myself —as a bit of a poet, who has labored with the spoken word to evolve original rhythms of beauty where beauty apparently isn't." A one-act masterpiece, *Hughie* captures the essence of O'Neill's dramatic lyricism.

Further Reading:
B. H. Clark, *Eugene O'Neill: The Man and His Plays,* 1947.
E. Engel, *The Haunted Heroes of Eugene O'Neill,* 1953.
D. Alexander, *The Tempering of Eugene O'Neill,* 1962.
A. and B. Gelb, *O'Neill,* 1962, 1973.
J. Raleigh, *The Plays of Eugene O'Neill,* 1965.

L. Schaeffer, *O'Neill, Son and Playwright,* 1968.
T. Bogard, *Contour in Time: The Plays of Eugene O'Neill,* 1972.
L. Chabrowe, *Ritual and Pathos: The Theater of O'Neill,* 1976.
Eugene O'Neill: A Collection of Criticism, ed. E. Griffin, 1976.

Text:
Hughie, 1959.

Hughie

Characters

"Erie" Smith, a teller of tales

A Night Clerk

Scene: The desk and a section of lobby of a small hotel on a West Side street in midtown New York. It is between 3 and 4 A.M. of a day in the summer of 1928. It is one of those hotels, built in the decade 1900–10

on the side streets of the Great White Way[1] sector,
which began as respectable second class but soon were
forced to deteriorate in order to survive. Following the
First World War and Prohibition, it had given up all
pretense of respectability, and now is anything a paying
guest wants it to be, a third class dump, catering to the
catch-as-catch-can trade. But still it does not prosper. It
has not shared in the Great Hollow Boom of the
twenties. The Everlasting Opulence of the New
Economic Law has overlooked it. It manages to keep
running by cutting the overhead for service, repairs, and
cleanliness to a minimum.

The desk faces left along a section of seedy lobby
with shabby chairs. The street entrance is off-stage, left.
Behind the desk are a telephone switchboard and the
operator's stool. At right, the usual numbered tiers of
mailboxes, and above them a clock.

The NIGHT CLERK sits on the stool, facing front, his
back to the switchboard. There is nothing to do. He is
not thinking. He is not sleepy. He simply droops and
stares acquiescently at nothing. It would be discouraging
to glance at the clock. He knows there are several
hours to go before his shift is over. Anyway, he does
not need to look at clocks. He has been a night clerk
in New York hotels so long he can tell time by sounds
in the street.

He is in his early forties. Tall, thin, with a
scrawny neck and jutting Adam's apple. His face is
long and narrow, greasy with perspiration, sallow,
studded with pimples from ingrowing hairs. His nose is
large and without character. So is his mouth. So are
his ears. So is his thinning brown hair, powdered with
dandruff. Behind horn-rimmed spectacles, his blank
brown eyes contain no discernible expression. One
would say they had even forgotten how it feels to be
bored. He wears an ill-fitting blue serge suit, white
shirt and collar, a blue tie. The suit is old and shines
at the elbows as if it had been waxed and polished.

Footsteps echo in the deserted lobby as someone
comes in from the street. The Night Clerk rises
wearily. His eyes remain empty but his gum-
my lips part automatically in a welcoming
The-Patron-Is-Always-Right grimace, intended as a
smile. His big uneven teeth are in bad condition.

ERIE SMITH enters and approaches the desk. He is
about the same age as the Clerk and has the same

---

[1] The theatrical section of Broadway.

pasty, perspiry, night-life complexion. There the resemblance ends. Erie is around medium height but appears shorter because he is stout and his fat legs are too short for his body. So are his fat arms. His big head squats on a neck which seems part of his beefy shoulders. His face is round, his snub nose flattened at the tip. His blue eyes have drooping lids and puffy pouches under them. His sandy hair is falling out and the top of his head is bald. He walks to the desk with a breezy, familiar air, his gait a bit waddling because of his short legs. He carries a Panama hat and mops his face with a red and blue silk handkerchief. He wears a light grey suit cut in the extreme, tight-waisted, Broadway mode, the coat open to reveal an old and faded but expensive silk shirt in a shade of blue that sets teeth on edge, and a gay red and blue foulard tie, its knot stained by perspiration. His trousers are held up by a braided brown leather belt with a brass buckle. His shoes are tan and white, his socks white silk.

In manner, he is consciously a Broadway sport and a Wise Guy—the type of small fry gambler and horse player, living hand to mouth on the fringe of the rackets. Infesting corners, doorways, cheap restaurants, the bars of minor speakeasies, he and his kind imagine they are in the Real Know, cynical oracles of the One True Grapevine.

Erie usually speaks in a low, guarded tone, his droop-lidded eyes suspiciously wary of nonexistent eavesdroppers. His face is set in the prescribed pattern of gambler's dead pan. His small, pursy mouth is always crooked in the cynical leer of one who possesses superior, inside information, and his shifty once-over glances never miss the price tags he detects on everything and everybody. Yet there is something phoney about his characterization of himself, some sentimental softness behind it which doesn't belong in the hard-boiled picture.

Erie avoids looking at the Night Clerk, as if he resented him.

Erie: *Peremptorily.* Key.

Then as the Night Clerk gropes with his memory— grudgingly.

Forgot you ain't seen me before. Erie Smith's the name. I'm an old timer in this fleabag. 492.

Night Clerk: In a tone of one who is wearily relieved when he does not have to remember anything—he plucks out the key. 492. Yes, sir.

Erie: Taking the key, gives the Clerk the once-over. He appears not unfavorably impressed but his tone still holds resentment. How long you been on the job? Four, five days, huh? I been off on a drunk. Come to now, though. Tapering off. Well, I'm glad they fired that young squirt they took on when Hughie got sick. One of them fresh wise punks. Couldn't tell him nothing. Pleased to meet you, Pal. Hope you stick around.

> *He shoves out his hand. The Night Clerk takes it obediently.*

Night Clerk: With a compliant, uninterested smile. Glad to know you, Mr. Smith.

Erie: What's your name?

Night Clerk: As if he had half forgotten because what did it matter, anyway? Hughes. Charlie Hughes.

Erie: Starts. Huh? Hughes? Say, is that on the level?

Night Clerk: Charlie Hughes.

Erie: Well, I be damned! What the hell d'you know about that!

> *Warming toward the Clerk.*

Say, now I notice, you don't look like Hughie, but you remind me of him somehow. You ain't by any chance related?

Night Clerk: You mean to the Hughes who had this job so long and died recently? No, sir. No relation.

Erie: Gloomily. No, that's right. Hughie told me he didn't have no relations left —except his wife and kids, of course.

> *He pauses—more gloomily.*

Yeah. The poor guy croaked last week. His funeral was what started me off on a bat.

> *Then boastfully, as if defending himself against gloom.*

Some drunk! I don't go on one often. It's bum dope in my book. A guy gets careless and gabs about things he knows and when he comes to he's liable to find there's guys who'd feel easier if he wasn't around no more. That's the trouble with knowing things. Take my tip, Pal. Don't never know nothin'. Be a sap and stay healthy.

> *His manner has become secretive, with sinister*
> *undertones. But the Night Clerk doesn't notice this.*
> *Long experience with guests who stop at his desk in*
> *the small hours to talk about themselves has given him*

> *a foolproof technique of self-defense. He appears to
> listen with agreeable submissiveness and be impressed,
> but his mind is blank and he doesn't hear unless a
> direct question is put to him, and sometimes not even
> then. Erie thinks he is impressed.*

But hell, I always keep my noggin working, booze or no booze. I'm no sucker.
What was I sayin'? Oh, some drunk. I sure hit the high spots. You shoulda seen
the doll I made night before last. And did she take me to the cleaners! I'm a
sucker for blondes.

> *He pauses—giving the Night Clerk a cynical,
> contemptuous glance.*

You're married, ain't you?
Night Clerk: Long ago he gave up caring whether questions were personal or not. Yes,
sir.
Erie: Yeah, I'd'a laid ten to one on it. You got that old look. Like Hughie had.
Maybe that's the resemblance.

> *He chuckles contemptuously.*

Kids, too, I bet?
Night Clerk: Yes, sir. Three.
Erie: You're worse off than Hughie was. He only had two. Three, huh? Well,
that's what comes of being careless!

> *He laughs. The Night Clerk smiles at a guest. He had
> been a little offended when a guest first made that crack
> —must have been ten years ago—yes, Eddie, the
> oldest, is eleven now—or is it twelve? Erie goes on
> with good-natured tolerance.*

Well, I suppose marriage ain't such a bum racket, if you're made for it. Hughie
didn't seem to mind it much, although if you want my low-down, his wife is a
bum—in spades! Oh, I don't mean cheatin'. With her puss and figure, she'd
never make no one except she raided a blind asylum.

> *The Night Clerk feels that he has been standing a
> long time and his feet are beginning to ache and he
> wishes 492 would stop talking and go to bed so he can
> sit down again and listen to the noises in the street and
> think about nothing. Erie gives him an amused,
> condescending glance.*

How old are you? Wait! Let me guess. You look fifty or over but I'll lay ten to
one you're forty-three or maybe forty-four.
Night Clerk: I'm forty-three.

> *He adds vaguely.*

Or maybe it is forty-four.

Erie: Elated. I win, huh? I sure can call the turn on ages, Buddy. You ought to see the dolls get sored up when I work it on them! You're like Hughie. He looked like he'd never see fifty again and he was only forty-three. Me, I'm forty-five. Never think it, would you? Most of the dames don't think I've hit forty yet.

> *The Night Clerk shifts his position so he can lean more on the desk. Maybe those shoes he sees advertised for fallen arches— But they cost eight dollars, so that's out— Get a pair when he goes to heaven. Erie is sizing him up with another cynical, friendly glance.*

I make another bet about you. Born and raised in the sticks, wasn't you?

Night Clerk: Faintly aroused and defensive. I come originally from Saginaw, Michigan, but I've lived here in the Big Town so long I consider myself a New Yorker now.

> *This is a long speech for him and he wonders sadly why he took the trouble to make it.*

Erie: I don't deserve no medal for picking that one. Nearly every guy I know on the Big Stem[2]—and I know most of 'em—hails from the sticks. Take me. You'd never guess it but I was dragged up in Erie, P-a. Ain't that a knockout! Erie, P-a! That's how I got my moniker. No one calls me nothing but Erie. You better call me Erie, too, Pal, or I won't know when you're talkin' to me.

Night Clerk: All right, Erie.

Erie: Atta Boy.

> *He chuckles.*

Here's another knockout. Smith is my real name. A Broadway guy like me named Smith and it's my real name! Ain't that a knockout!

> *He explains carefully so there will be no misunderstanding.*

I don't remember nothing much about Erie, P-a, you understand—or want to. Some punk burg! After grammar school, my Old Man put me to work in his store, dealing out groceries. Some punk job! I stuck it till I was eighteen before I took a run-out powder.

---

[2] I.e., the larger of the two peninsulas forming Michigan.

The Night Clerk seems turned into a drooping
waxwork, draped along the desk. This is what he used
to dread before he perfected his technique of not
listening: The Guest's Story of His Life. He fixes his
mind on his aching feet. Erie chuckles.

Speaking of marriage, that was the big reason I ducked. A doll nearly had me
hooked for the old shotgun ceremony. Closest I ever come to being played for a
sucker. This doll in Erie—Daisy's her name—was one of them dumb wide-open
dolls. All the guys give her a play. Then one day she wakes up and finds she's
going to have a kid. I never figured she meant to frame me in particular. Way I
always figured, she didn't have no idea who, so she holds a lottery all by herself.
Put about a thousand guys' names in a hat—all she could remember—and drew
one out and I was it. Then she told her Ma, and her Ma told her Pa, and her Pa
come round looking for me. But I was no fall guy even in them days. I took it
on the lam. For Saratoga, to look the bangtails[3] over. I'd started to be a horse
player in Erie, though I'd never seen a track. I been one ever since.

With a touch of bravado.

And I ain't done so bad, Pal. I've made some killings in my time the gang still
gab about. I've been in the big bucks. More'n once, and I will be again. I've had
tough breaks too, but what the hell, I always get by. When the horses won't run
for me, there's draw or stud. When they're bad, there's a crap game. And when
they're all bad, there's always bucks to pick up for little errands I ain't talkin'
about, which they give a guy who can keep his clam shut. Oh, I get along,
Buddy. I get along fine.

He waits for approving assent from the Night Clerk,
but the latter is not hearing so intently he misses his
cue until the expectant silence crashes his ears.

Night Clerk: Hastily, gambling on "yes." Yes, Sir.
Erie: Bitingly. Sorry if I'm keeping you up, Sport.

With an aggrieved air.

Hughie was a wide-awake guy. He was always waiting for me to roll in. He'd
say, "Hello, Erie, how'd the bangtails treat you?" Or, "How's luck?" Or, "Did
you make the old bones behave?" Then I'd tell him how I'd done. He'd ask,
"What's new along the Big Stem?" and I'd tell him the latest off the grapevine.

He grins with affectionate condescension.

---

[3] Racehorses.

It used to hand me a laugh to hear old Hughie crackin' like a sport. In all the years I knew him, he never bet a buck on nothin'.

Excusingly.

But it ain't his fault. He'd have took a chance, but how could he with his wife keepin' cases on every nickel of his salary? I showed him lots of ways he could cross her up, but he was too scared.

He chuckles.

The biggest knockout was when he'd kid me about dames. He'd crack, "What? No blonde to-night, Erie? You must be slippin'." Jeez, you never see a guy more bashful with a doll around than Hughie was. I used to introduce him to the tramps I'd drag home with me. I'd wise them up to kid him along and pretend they'd fell for him. In two minutes, they'd have him hanging on the ropes. His face'd be red and he'd look like he wanted to crawl under the desk and hide. Some of them dolls was raw babies. They'd make him pretty raw propositions. He'd stutter like he was paralyzed. But he ate it up, just the same. He was tickled pink. I used to hope maybe I could nerve him up to do a little cheatin'. I'd offer to fix it for him with one of my dolls. Hell, I got plenty, I wouldn't have minded. I'd tell him, "Just let that wife of yours know you're cheatin', and she'll have some respect for you." But he was too scared.

He pauses—boastfully.

Some queens I've brought here in my time, Brother—frails from the Follies, or the Scandals, or the Frolics,[4] that'd knock your eye out! And I still can make 'em. You watch. I ain't slippin'.

> *He looks at the Night Clerk expecting reassurance, but the Clerk's mind has slipped away to the clanging bounce of garbage cans in the outer night. He is thinking: "A job I'd like. I'd bang those cans louder than they do! I'd wake up the whole damned city!" Erie mutters disgustedly to himself.*

Jesus, what a dummy!

> *He makes a move in the direction of the elevator, off right front—gloomily.*

Might as well hit the hay, I guess.

---

[4] Follies; Scandals; Frolics: stage revues.

Night Clerk: Comes to—with the nearest approach to feeling he has shown in many a long night—approvingly. Good night, Mr. Smith. I hope you have a good rest.

> *But Erie stops, glancing around the deserted lobby with forlorn distaste, jiggling the room key in his hand.*

Erie: What a crummy dump! What did I come back for? I shoulda stayed on a drunk. You'd never guess it, Buddy, but when I first come here this was a classy hotel—and clean, can you believe it?

> *He scowls.*

I've been campin' here, off and on, fifteen years, but I've got a good notion to move out. It ain't the same place since Hughie was took to the hospital.

> *Gloomily.*

Hell with going to bed! I'll just lie there worrying—

> *He turns back to the desk. The Clerk's face would express despair, but the last time he was able to feel despair was back around World War days when the cost of living got so high and he was out of a job for three months. Erie leans on the desk—in a dejected, confidential tone.*

Believe me, Brother, I never been a guy to worry, but this time I'm on a spot where I got to, if I ain't a sap.

Night Clerk: In the vague tone of a corpse which admits it once overheard a favorable rumor about life. That's too bad, Mr. Smith. But they say most of the things we worry about never happen.

> *His mind escapes to the street again to play bouncing cans with the garbage men.*

Erie: Grimly. This thing happens, Pal. I ain't won a bet at nothin' since Hughie was took to the hospital. I'm jinxed. And that ain't all— But to hell with it! You're right, at that. Something always turns up for me. I was born lucky. I ain't worried. Just moaning low. Hell, who don't when they're getting over a drunk? You know how it is. The Brooklyn Boys march over the bridge with bloodhounds to hunt you down. And I'm still carrying the torch for Hughie. His checking out was a real K.O. for me. Damn if I know why. Lots of guys I've been pals with, in a way, croaked from booze or something, or got rubbed out, but I always took it as part of the game. Hell, we all gotta croak.

Here today, gone tomorrow, so what's the good of beefin'? When a guy's dead, he's dead. He don't give a damn, so why should anybody else?

> *But this fatalistic philosophy is no comfort and Erie sighs.*

I miss Hughie, I guess. I guess I'd got to like him a lot.

> *Again he explains carefully so there will be no misunderstanding.*

Not that I was ever real pals with him, you understand. He didn't run in my class. He didn't know none of the answers. He was just a sucker.

> *He sighs again.*

But I sure am sorry he's gone. You missed a lot not knowing Hughie, Pal. He sure was one grand little guy.

> *He stares at the lobby floor. The Night Clerk regards him with vacant, bulging eyes full of a vague envy for the blind. The garbage men have gone their predestined way. Time is that much older. The Clerk's mind remains in the street to greet the noise of a far-off El train. Its approach is pleasantly like a memory of hope; then it roars and rocks and rattles past the nearby corner, and the noise pleasantly deafens memory; then it recedes and dies, and there is something melancholy about that. But there is hope. Only so many El trains pass in one night, and each one passing leaves one less to pass, so the night recedes, too, until at last it must die and join all the other long nights in Nirvana,[5] the Big Night of Nights. And that's life. "What I always tell Jess when she nags me to worry about something: 'That's life, isn't it? What can you do about it?'" Erie sighs again—then turns to the Clerk, his foolishly wary, wise-guy eyes defenseless, his poker face as self-betraying as a hurt dog's—appealingly.*

Say, you do remind me of Hughie somehow, Pal. You got the same look on your map.

> *But the Clerk's mind is far away attending the obsequies of night, and it takes it some time to get back. Erie is hurt—contemptuously.*

[5] Paradise.

But I guess it's only that old night clerk look! There's one of 'em born every
minute!
Night Clerk: His mind arrives just in time to catch this last—with a bright grimace.
   Yes, Mr. Smith. That's what Barnum[6] said, and it's certainly true, isn't it?
Erie: Grateful even for this sign of companionship, growls. Nix on the Mr. Smith
   stuff, Charlie. There's ten of *them* born every minute. Call me Erie, like I told
   you.
Night Clerk: Automatically, as his mind tiptoes into the night again. All right, Erie.
Erie: Encouraged, leans on the desk, clacking his room key like a castanet. Yeah.
   Hughie was one grand little guy. All the same, like I said, he wasn't the kind
   of guy you'd ever figger a guy like me would take to. Because he was a
   sucker, see—the kind of sap you'd take to the cleaners a million times and
   he'd never wise up he was took. Why, night after night, just for a gag, I'd
   get him to shoot crap with me here on the desk. With *my* dice. And he'd
   never ask to give 'em the once-over. Can you beat that!

He chuckles—then earnestly.

Not that I'd ever ring in no phoneys on a pal. I'm no heel.

He chuckles again.

And anyway, I didn't need none to take Hughie because he never even made me
knock 'em against nothing. Just a roll on the desk here. Boy, if they'd ever let
me throw 'em that way in a real game, I'd be worth ten million dollars.

He laughs.

You'da thought Hughie woulda got wise something was out of order when, no
matter how much he'd win on a run of luck like suckers have sometimes, I'd
always take him to the cleaners in the end. But he never suspicioned nothing. All
he'd say was "Gosh, Erie, no wonder you took up gambling. You sure were
born lucky."

He chuckles.

Can you beat that?

He hastens to explain earnestly.

Of course, like I said, it was only a gag. We'd play with real jack,[7] just to make
it look real, but it was all my jack. He never had no jack. His wife dealt him
four bits a day for spending money. So I'd stake him at the start to half of what
I got—in chicken feed, I mean. We'd pretend a cent was a buck, and a nickel
was a fin and so on. Some big game! He got a big kick out of it. He'd get all

---

[6] P. T. Barnum (1810–1891), the American   [7] Money.
showman, was supposed to have coined the
phrase "There's a sucker born every minute."

het up.[8] It give me a kick, too—especially when he'd say, "Gosh, Erie, I don't wonder you never worry about money, with your luck."

He laughs.

That guy would believe anything! Of course, I'd stall him off when he'd want to shoot nights when I didn't have a goddamned nickel.

He chuckles.

What laughs he used to hand me! He'd always call horses "the bangtails," like he'd known 'em all his life—and he'd never seen a race horse, not till I kidnaped him one day and took him down to Belmont. What a kick he got out of that! I got scared he'd pass out with excitement. And he wasn't doing no betting either. All he had was four bits. It was just the track, and the crowd, and the horses got him. Mostly the horses.

With a surprised, reflective air.

Y'know, it's funny how a dumb, simple guy like Hughie will all of a sudden get something right. He says, "They're the most beautiful things in the world, I think." And he wins! I tell you, Pal, I'd rather sleep in the same stall with old Man o' War[9] than make the whole damn Follies. What do you think?
Night Clerk: His mind darts back from a cruising taxi and blinks bewilderedly in the light: "Say yes." Yes, I agree with you, Mr.—I mean, Erie.
Erie: With good-natured contempt. Yeah? I bet you never seen one, except back at the old Fair Grounds in the sticks. I don't mean them kind of turtles. I mean a real horse.

The Clerk wonders what horses have to do with anything—or for that matter, what anything has to do with anything—then gives it up. Erie takes up his tale.

And what d'you think happened the next night? Damned if Hughie didn't dig two bucks out of his pants and try to slip 'em to me. "Let this ride on the nose of whatever horse you're betting on tomorrow," he told me. I got sore. "Nix," I told him, "if you're going to start playin' sucker and bettin' on horse races, you don't get no assist from me."

He grins wryly.

Was that a laugh! Me advising a sucker not to bet when I've spent a lot of my life tellin' saps a story to make 'em bet! I said, "Where'd you grab this dough?

---

[8] Excited ("heated up").
[9] The champion racehorse that won the Belmont Stakes in 1920.

Outa the Little Woman's purse, huh? What tale you going to give her when you lose it? She'll start breaking up the furniture with you!" "No," he says, "she'll just cry." "That's worse," I said, "no guy can beat that racket. I had a doll cry on me once in a restaurant full of people till I had to promise her a diamond engagement ring to sober her up." Well, anyway, Hughie sneaked the two bucks back in the Little Woman's purse when he went home that morning, and that was the end of that.

Cynically.

Boy Scouts got nothin' on me, Pal, when it comes to good deeds. That was one I done. It's too bad I can't remember no others.

> *He is well wound up now and goes on without
> noticing that the Night Clerk's mind has left the
> premises in his sole custody.*

Y'know I had Hughie sized up for a sap the first time I see him. I'd just rolled in from Tia Juana. I'd made a big killing down there and I was lousy with jack. Came all the way in a drawing room, and I wasn't lonely in it neither. There was a blonde movie doll on the train—and I was lucky in them days. Used to follow the horses South every winter. I don't no more. Sick of traveling. And I ain't as lucky as I was—

Hastily.

Anyway, this time I'm talkin' about, soon as I hit this lobby I see there's a new night clerk, and while I'm signing up for the bridal suite I make a bet with myself he's never been nothin' but a night clerk. And I win. At first, he wouldn't open up. Not that he was cagey about gabbin' too much. But like he couldn't think of nothin' about himself worth saying. But after he'd seen me roll in here the last one every night, and I'd stop to kid him along and tell him the tale of what I'd win that day, he got friendly and talked. He'd come from a hick burg upstate. Graduated from high school, and had a shot at different jobs in the old home town but couldn't make the grade until he was took on as night clerk in the hotel there. Then he made good. But he wasn't satisfied. Didn't like being only a night clerk where everybody knew him. He'd read somewhere—in the Suckers' Almanac, I guess—that all a guy had to do was come to the Big Town and Old Man Success would be waitin' at the Grand Central[10] to give him the key to the city. What a gag that is! Even I believed that once, and no one could ever call me a sap. Well, anyway, he made the break and come here and the only job he could get was night clerk. Then he fell in love—or kidded himself he was—and got married. Met her on a subway train. It stopped sudden and she was jerked into him, and he put his arms around her, and they started talking, and the poor boob never stood a chance. She was a sales girl in some punk

---

[10] Grand Central Station, in midtown New York.

department store, and she was sick of standing on her dogs all day, and all the way home to Brooklyn, too. So, the way I figger it, knowing Hughie and dames, she proposed and said "yes" for him, and married him, and after that, of course, he never dared stop being a night clerk, even if he could.

He pauses.

Maybe you think I ain't giving her a square shake. Well, maybe I ain't. She never give me one. She put me down as a bad influence, and let her chips ride. And maybe Hughie couldn't have done no better. Dolls didn't call him no riot. Hughie and her seemed happy enough the time he had me out to dinner in their flat. Well, not happy. Maybe contented. No, that's boosting it, too. Resigned comes nearer, as if each was givin' the other a break by thinking, "Well, what more could I expect?"

Abruptly he addresses the Night Clerk with contemptuous good nature.

How d'you and your Little Woman hit it off, Brother?
Night Clerk: *His mind has been counting the footfalls of the cop on the beat as they recede, sauntering longingly toward the dawn's release. "If he'd only shoot it out with a gunman some night! Nothing exciting has happened in any night I've ever lived through!" He stammers gropingly among the echoes of Erie's last words.* Oh—you mean *my* wife? Why, we get along all right, I guess.
Erie: *Disgustedly.* Better lay off them headache pills, Pal. First thing you know, some guy is going to call you a dope.

But the Night Clerk cannot take this seriously. It is years since he cared what anyone called him. So many guests have called him so many things. The Little Woman has, too. And, of course, he has, himself. But that's all past. Is daybreak coming now? No, too early yet. He can tell by the sound of that surface car. It is still lost in the night. Flat wheeled and tired. Distant the carbarn,[11] and far away the sleep. Erie, having soothed resentment with his wisecrack, goes on with a friendly grin.

Well, keep hoping, Pal. Hughie was as big a dope as you until I give him some interest in life.

Slipping back into narrative.

That time he took me home to dinner. Was that a knockout! It took him a hell of a while to get up nerve to ask me. "Sure, Hughie," I told him, "I'll be tickled

---

[11] Bus or railway terminal.

to death." I was thinking, I'd rather be shot. For one thing, he lived in Brooklyn, and I'd sooner take a trip to China. Another thing, I'm a guy that likes to eat what I order and not what somebody deals me. And he had kids and a wife, and the family racket is out of my line. But Hughie looked so tickled I couldn't welsh on him. And it didn't work out so bad. Of course, what he called home was only a dump of a cheap flat. Still, it wasn't so bad for a change. His wife had done a lot of stuff to doll it up. Nothin' with no class, you understand. Just cheap stuff to make it comfortable. And his kids wasn't the gorillas I'd expected, neither. No throwin' spitballs in my soup or them kind of gags. They was quiet like Hughie. I kinda liked 'em. After dinner I started tellin' 'em a story about a race horse a guy I know owned once. I thought it was up to me to put out something, and kids like animal stories, and this one was true, at that. This old turtle never wins a race, but he was as foxy as ten guys, a natural born crook, the goddamnedest thief, he'd steal anything in reach that wasn't nailed down— Well, I didn't get far. Hughie's wife butt in and stopped me cold. Told the kids it was bedtime and hustled 'em off like I was giving 'em measles. It got my goat, kinda. I coulda liked her—a little—if she'd give me a chance. Not that she was nothin' Ziegfeld[12] would want to glorify. When you call her plain, you give her all the breaks.

Resentfully.

Well, to hell with it. She had me tagged for a bum, and seein' me made her sure she was right. You can bet she told Hughie never invite me again, and he never did. He tried to apologize, but I shut him up quick. He says, "Irma was brought up strict. She can't help being narrow-minded about gamblers." I said, "What's it to me? I don't want to hear your dame troubles. I got plenty of my own. Remember that doll I brung home night before last? She gives me an argument I promised her ten bucks. I told her, 'Listen, Baby, I got an impediment in my speech. Maybe it sounded like ten, but it was two, and that's all you get. Hell, I don't want to buy your soul! What would I do with it?' Now she's peddling the news along Broadway I'm a rat and a chiseler, and of course all the rats and chiselers believe her. Before she's through, I won't have a friend left."

He pauses—confidentially.

I switched the subject on Hughie, see, on purpose. He never did beef to me about his wife again.

He gives a forced chuckle.

Believe me, Pal, I can stop guys that start telling me their family troubles!
Night Clerk: His mind has hopped an ambulance clanging down Sixth, and is asking without curiosity: "Will he die, Doctor, or isn't he lucky?" "I'm afraid not, but he'll

---

[12] Florenz Ziegfeld (1869–1932), producer of the Follies.

have to be absolutely quiet for months and months." "With a pretty nurse taking care of him?" "Probably not pretty." "Well, anyway, I claim he's lucky. And now I must get back to the hotel. 492 won't go to bed and insists on telling me jokes. It must have been a joke because he's chuckling." *He laughs with a heartiness which has forgotten that heart is more than a word used in "Have a heart," an old slang expression.* Ha— Ha! That's a good one, Erie. That's the best I've heard in a long time!

Erie: *For a moment is so hurt and depressed he hasn't the spirit to make a sarcastic crack. He stares at the floor, twirling his room key—to himself.* Jesus, this sure is a dead dump. About as homey as the Morgue.

He glances up at the clock.

Gettin' late. Better beat it up to my cell and grab some shut eye.

He makes a move to detach himself from the desk but fails and remains wearily glued to it. His eyes prowl the lobby and finally come to rest on the Clerk's glistening, sallow face. He summons up strength for a withering crack.

Why didn't you tell me you was deef, Buddy? I know guys is sensitive about them little afflictions, but I'll keep it confidential.

But the Clerk's mind has rushed out to follow the siren wail of a fire engine. "A fireman's life must be exciting." *His mind rides the engine, and asks a fireman with disinterested eagerness:* "Where's the fire? Is it a real good one this time? Has it a good start? Will it be big enough, do you think?" *Erie examines his face—bitingly.*

Take my tip, Pal, and don't never try to buy from a dope peddler. He'll tell you you had enough already.

The Clerk's mind continues its dialogue with the fireman: "I mean, big enough to burn down the whole damn city?" "Sorry, Brother, but there's no chance. There's too much stone and steel. There'd always be something left." "Yes, I guess you're right. There's too much stone and steel. I wasn't really hoping, anyway. It really doesn't matter to me." *Erie gives him up and again attempts to pry himself from the desk, twirling his key frantically as if it were a fetish which might set him free.*

Well, me for the hay.

> *But he can't dislodge himself—dully.*

Christ, it's lonely. I wish Hughie was here. By God, if he was, I'd tell him a tale that'd make his eyes pop! The bigger the story the harder he'd fall. He was that kind of sap. He thought gambling was romantic. I guess he saw me like a sort of dream guy, the sort of guy he'd like to be if he could take a chance. I guess he lived a sort of double life listening to me gabbin' about hittin' the high spots. Come to figger it, I'll bet he even cheated on his wife that way, using me and my dolls.

> *He chuckles.*

No wonder he liked me, huh? And the bigger I made myself the more he lapped it up. I went easy on him at first. I didn't lie—not any more'n a guy naturally does when he gabs about the bets he wins and the dolls he's made. But I soon see he was cryin' for more, and when a sucker cries for more, you're a dope if you don't let him have it. Every tramp I made got to be a Follies' doll. Hughie liked 'em to be Follies' dolls. Or in the Scandals or Frolics. He wanted me to be the Sheik of Araby, or something that any blonde 'd go round-heeled about. Well, I give him plenty of that. And I give him plenty of gambling tales. I explained my campin' in this dump was because I don't want to waste jack on nothin' but gambling. It was like dope to me, I told him. I couldn't quit. He lapped that up. He liked to kid himself I'm mixed up in the racket. He thought gangsters was romantic. So I fed him some baloney about highjacking I'd done once. I told him I knew all the Big Shots. Well, so I do, most of 'em, to say hello, and sometimes they hello back. Who wouldn't know 'em that hangs around Broadway and the joints? I run errands for 'em sometimes, because there's dough in it, but I'm cagey about gettin' in where it ain't healthy. Hughie wanted to think me and Legs Diamond[13] was old pals. So I give him that too. I give him anything he cried for.

> *Earnestly.*

Don't get the wrong idea, Pal. What I fed Hughie wasn't all lies. The tales about gambling wasn't. They was stories of big games and killings that really happened since I've been hangin' round. Only I wasn't in on 'em like I made out—except one or two from way back when I had a run of big luck and was in the bucks for a while until I was took to the cleaners.

> *He stops to pay tribute of a sigh to the memory of brave days that were and that never were—then meditatively.*

---

[13] John Henry Diamond (1896–1931), gangster of the prohibition era.

Yeah, Hughie lapped up my stories like they was duck soup,[14] or a beakful of heroin. I sure took him around with me in tales and showed him one hell of a time.

> *He chuckles—then seriously.*

And, d'you know, it done me good, too, in a way. Sure. I'd get to seein' myself like he seen me. Some nights I'd come back here without a buck, feeling lower than a snake's belly, and first thing you know I'd be lousy with jack, bettin' a grand a race. Oh, I was wise I was kiddin' myself. I ain't a sap. But what the hell, Hughie loved it, and it didn't cost nobody nothin', and if every guy along Broadway who kids himself was to drop dead there wouldn't be nobody left. Ain't it the truth, Charlie?

> *He again stares at the Night Clerk appealingly, forgetting past rebuffs. The Clerk's face is taut with vacancy. His mind has been trying to fasten itself to some noise in the night, but a rare and threatening pause of silence has fallen on the city, and here he is, chained behind a hotel desk forever, awake when everyone else in the world is asleep, except Room 492, and he won't go to bed, he's still talking, and there is no escape.*

Night Clerk: *His glassy eyes stare through Erie's face. He stammers deferentially.*
  Truth? I'm afraid I didn't get— What's the truth?
Erie: *Hopelessly.* Nothing, Pal. Not a thing.

> *His eyes fall to the floor. For a while he is too defeated even to twirl his room key. The Clerk's mind still cannot make a getaway because the city remains silent, and the night vaguely reminds him of death, and he is vaguely frightened, and now that he remembers, his feet are giving him hell, but that's no excuse not to act as if the Guest is always right: "I should have paid 492 more attention. After all, he is company. He is awake and alive. I should use him to help me live through the night. What's he been talking about? I must have caught some of it without meaning to." The Night Clerk's forehead puckers perspiringly as he tries to remember. Erie begins talking again but this time it is obviously aloud to himself, without hope of a listener.*

I could tell by Hughie's face before he went to the hospital, he was through. I've seen the same look on guys' faces when they knew they was on the spot, just

---

[14] Something easy to take.

before guys caught up with them. I went to see him twice in the hospital. The first time, his wife was there and give me a dirty look, but he cooked up a smile and said, "Hello, Erie, how're the bangtails treating you?" I see he wants a big story to cheer him, but his wife butts in and says he's weak and he mustn't get excited. I felt like crackin', "Well, the Docs in this dump got the right dope. Just leave you with him and he'll never get excited." The second time I went, they wouldn't let me see him. That was near the end. I went to his funeral, too. There wasn't nobody but a coupla his wife's relations. I had to feel sorry for her. She looked like she ought to be parked in a coffin, too. The kids was bawlin'. There wasn't no flowers but a coupla lousy wreaths. It woulda been a punk showing for poor old Hughie, if it hadn't been for my flower piece.

He swells with pride.

That was some display, Pal. It'd knock your eye out! Set me back a hundred bucks, and no kiddin'! A big horseshoe of red roses! I knew Hughie'd want a horseshoe because that made it look like he'd been a horse player. And around the top printed in forget-me-nots was "Good-by, Old Pal." Hughie liked to kid himself he was my pal.

He adds sadly.

And so he was, at that—even if he was a sucker.

> *He pauses, his false poker face as nakedly forlorn as an organ grinder's monkey's. Outside, the spell of abnormal quiet presses suffocatingly upon the street, enters the deserted, dirty lobby. The Night Clerk's mind cowers away from it. He cringes behind the desk, his feet aching like hell. There is only one possible escape. If his mind could only fasten onto something 492 has said. "What's he been talking about? A clerk should always be attentive. You even are duty bound to laugh at a guest's smutty jokes, no matter how often you've heard them. That's the policy of the hotel. 492 has been gassing[15] for hours. What's he been telling me? I must be slipping. Always before this I've been able to hear without bothering to listen, but now when I need company— Ah! I've got it! Gambling! He said a lot about gambling. That's something I've always wanted to know more about, too. Maybe he's a professional gambler. Like Arnold Rothstein."[16]*

Night Clerk: Blurts out with an uncanny, almost lifelike eagerness. I beg your pardon, Mr.—Erie- -but did I understand you to say you are a gambler by profession? Do you, by any chance, know the Big Shot, Arnold Rothstein?

---

[15] Talking emptily.
[16] Rothstein (1882–1928), New York area gambler known for high stakes, was murdered in his hotel room, supposedly for reneging on a bet.

But this time it is Erie who doesn't hear him. And the Clerk's mind is now suddenly impervious to the threat of Night and Silence as it pursues an ideal of fame and glory within itself called Arnold Rothstein.

Erie: *With mournful longing.* Christ, I wish Hughie was alive and kickin'. I'd tell him I win ten grand from the bookies, and ten grand at stud, and ten grand in a crap game! I'd tell him I bought one of those Mercedes sport roadsters with nickel pipes sticking out of the hood! I'd tell him I lay three babes from the Follies—two blondes and one brunette!

The Night Clerk dreams, a rapt hero worship transfiguring his pimply face: "Arnold Rothstein! He must be some guy! I read a story about him. He'll gamble for any limit on anything, and always wins. The story said he wouldn't bother playing in a poker game unless the smallest bet you could make—one white chip!—was a hundred dollars. Christ, that's going some! I'd like to have the dough to get in a game with him once! The last pot everyone would drop out but him and me. I'd say, 'Okay, Arnold, the sky's the limit,' and I'd raise him five grand, and he'd call, and I'd have a royal flush to his four aces. Then I'd say, 'Okay, Arnold, I'm a good sport, I'll give you a break. I'll cut you double or nothing. Just one cut. I want quick action for my dough.' And I'd cut the ace of spades and win again." Beatific vision swoons on the empty pools of the Night Clerk's eyes. He resembles a holy saint, recently elected to Paradise. Erie breaks the silence—bitterly resigned.

But Hughie's better off, at that, being dead. He's got all the luck. He needn't do no worryin' now. He's out of the racket. I mean, the whole goddamned racket. I mean life.

Night Clerk: *Kicked out of his dream—with detached, pleasant acquiescence.* Yes, it is a goddamned racket when you stop to think, isn't it, 492? But we might as well make the best of it, because— Well, you can't burn it all down, can you? There's too much steel and stone. There'd always be something left to start it going again.

Erie: *Scowls bewilderedly.* Say, what is this? What the hell you talkin' about?

Night Clerk: *At a loss—in much confusion.* Why, to be frank, I really don't— Just something that came into my head.

Erie: *Bitingly, but showing he is comforted at having made some sort of contact.* Get it out of your head quick, Charlie, or some guys in uniform will walk in here with a butterfly net and catch you.

He changes the subject—earnestly.

Listen, Pal, maybe you guess I was kiddin' about that flower piece for Hughie costing a hundred bucks? Well, I ain't! I didn't give a damn what it cost. It was up to me to give Hughie a big-time send-off, because I knew nobody else would.

Night Clerk: Oh, I'm not doubting your word, Erie. You won the money gambling, I suppose— I mean, I beg your pardon if I'm mistaken, but you are a gambler, aren't you?

Erie: *Preoccupied.* Yeah, sure, when I got scratch[17] to put up. What of it? But I don't win that hundred bucks. I don't win a bet since Hughie was took to the hospital. I had to get down on my knees and beg every guy I know for a sawbuck here and a sawbuck there until I raised it.

Night Clerk: *His mind concentrated on the Big Ideal—insistently.* Do you by any chance know—Arnold Rothstein?

Erie: *His train of thought interrupted—irritably.* Arnold? What's he got to do with it? He wouldn't loan a guy like me a nickel to save my grandmother from streetwalking.

Night Clerk: *With humble awe.* Then you do know him!

Erie: Sure I know the bastard. Who don't on Broadway? And he knows me— when he wants to. He uses me to run errands when there ain't no one else handy. But he ain't my trouble, Pal. My trouble is, some of these guys I put the bite on is dead wrong G's,[18] and they expect to be paid back next Tuesday, or else I'm outa luck and have to take it on the lam, or I'll get beat up and maybe sent to a hospital.

> *He suddenly rouses himself and there is something pathetically but genuinely gallant about him.*

But what the hell. I was wise I was takin' a chance. I've always took a chance, and if I lose I pay, and no welshing! It sure was worth it to give Hughie the big send-off.

> *He pauses. The Night Clerk hasn't paid any attention except to his own dream. A question is trembling on his parted lips, but before he can get it out Erie goes on gloomily.*

But even that ain't my big worry, Charlie. My big worry is the run of bad luck I've had since Hughie got took to the hospital. Not a win. That ain't natural. I've always been a lucky guy—lucky enough to get by and pay up, I mean. I wouldn't never worry about owing guys, like I owe them guys. I'd always know I'd make a win that'd fix it. But now I got a lousy hunch when I lost Hughie I lost my luck—I mean, I've lost the old confidence. He used to give me confidence.

> *He turns away from the desk.*

---

[17] Betting money. A sawbuck (below) is a ten-dollar bill.

[18] I.e., some are owed several thousand dollars.

No use gabbin' here all night. You can't do me no good.

He starts toward the elevator.

Night Clerk: *Pleadingly.* Just a minute, Erie, if you don't mind.

With awe.

So you're an old friend of Arnold Rothstein! Would you mind telling me if it's really true when Arnold Rothstein plays poker, one white chip is—a hundred dollars?

Erie: *Dully exasperated.* Say, for Christ's sake, what's it to you— ?

He stops abruptly, staring probingly at the Clerk. There is a pause. Suddenly his face lights up with a saving revelation. He grins warmly and saunters confidently back to the desk.

Say, Charlie, why didn't you put me wise before, you was interested in gambling? Hell, I got you all wrong, Pal. I been tellin' myself, this guy ain't like old Hughie. He ain't got no sportin' blood. He's just a dope.

Generously.

Now I see you're a right guy. Shake.

He shoves out his hand which the Clerk clasps with a limp pleasure. Erie goes on with gathering warmth and self-assurance.

That's the stuff. You and me'll get along. I'll give you all the breaks, like I give Hughie.

Night Clerk: *Gratefully.* Thank you, Erie.

Then insistently.

Is it true when Arnold Rothstein plays poker, one white chip—

Erie: *With magnificent carelessness.* Sets you back a hundred bucks? Sure. Why not? Arnold's in the bucks, ain't he? And when you're in the bucks, a C note[19] is chicken feed. I ought to know, Pal. I was in the bucks when Arnold was a piker.[20] Why, one time down in New Orleans I lit a cigar with a C note, just for a gag, y'understand. I was with a bunch of high class dolls and I wanted to see their eyes pop out—and believe me, they sure popped! After that, I coulda made 'em one at a time or all together! Hell, I once win twenty grand on a single race. That's action! A good crap game is action, too. Hell, I've been in games where there was a hundred grand in real folding money lying around the floor. That's travelin'!

---

[19] One-hundred-dollar bill.   [20] Small-time gambler.

> *He darts a quick glance at the Clerk's face and begins to hedge warily. But he needn't. The Clerk sees him now as the Gambler in 492, the Friend of Arnold Rothstein—and nothing is incredible. Erie goes on.*

Of course, I wouldn't kid you. I'm not in the bucks now—not right this moment. You know how it is, Charlie. Down today and up tomorrow. I got some dough ridin' on the nose of a turtle in the 4th at Saratoga. I hear a story he'll be so full of hop, if the joc can keep him from jumpin' over the grandstand, he'll win by a mile. So if I roll in here with a blonde that'll knock your eyes out, don't be surprised.

> *He winks and chuckles.*

Night Clerk: *Ingratiatingly pally, smiling.* Oh, you can't surprise me that way. I've been a night clerk in New York all my life, almost.

> *He tries out a wink himself.*

I'll forget the house rules, Erie.

Erie: *Dryly.* Yeah. The manager wouldn't like you to remember something he ain't heard of yet.

> *Then slyly feeling his way.*

How about shootin' a little crap, Charlie? I mean just in fun, like I used to with Hughie. I know you can't afford takin' no chances. I'll stake you, see? I got a coupla bucks. We gotta use real jack or it don't look real. It's all my jack, get it? You can't lose. I just want to show you how I'll take you to the cleaners. It'll give me confidence.

> *He has taken two one-dollar bills and some change from his pocket. He pushes most of it across to the Clerk.*

Here y'are.

> *He produces a pair of dice—carelessly.*

Want to give these dice the once-over before we start?

Night Clerk: *Earnestly.* What do you think I am? I know I can trust you.

Erie: *Smiles.* You remind me a lot of Hughie, Pal. He always trusted me. Well, don't blame me if I'm lucky.

> *He clicks the dice in his hand—thoughtfully.*

Y'know, it's time I quit carryin' the torch for Hughie. Hell, what's the use? It don't do him no good. He's gone. Like we all gotta go. Him yesterday, me or you tomorrow, and who cares, and what's the difference? It's all in the racket, huh?

> *His soul is purged of grief, his confidence restored.*

I shoot two bits.

Night Clerk: Manfully, with an excited dead-pan expression he hopes resembles Arnold Rothstein's. I fade you.[21]

Erie: Throws the dice. Four's my point.

> *Gathers them up swiftly and throws them again.*

Four it is.

> *He takes the money.*

Easy when you got my luck—and know how. Huh, Charlie?

> *He chuckles, giving the Night Clerk the slyly amused,
> contemptuous, affectionate wink with which a Wise
> Guy regales a Sucker.*

CURTAIN

1941/1958;1959

Katherine Anne Porter
1890–1980

Katherine Anne Porter was born Callie Porter on May 15, 1890, in a simple L-shaped log cabin in Indian Creek, Texas, a small frontier community. She received, as she put it, a "fragmentary, but strangely useless and ornamental education" in various convent schools. Looking back, she saw herself as having been taught not at "schools at all but by five writers: Henry James, James Joyce, W. B. Yeats, T. S. Eliot, and Ezra Pound." Throughout her life, she spread misrepresentations, concoctions, and fabrications about her family and childhood, evoking a grand family plantation and distinguished ancestry that bore little resemblance to the actualities of the hard, uprooted life she experienced but considerable resemblance to elements of the stories she wrote.

During her long life, Porter lived in towns all over Texas and in cities throughout the United States—Denver, Chicago, New Orleans, New York, and

---

[21] Accept your bet. (The first roll of the dice here
becomes the point, or goal, of successive rolls.)

Washington, to name a few—where she worked on newspapers and later held teaching positions. She also lived in Mexico, where she was politically active, as well as Belgium, Switzerland, France, and Germany. Approaching forty, she reported "that she had had four husbands and thirty-seven lovers." Over the last half of her life, there were two more husbands and many more lovers, including several after she reached the age of seventy. "Love," she said, is "purely a creation of the human imagination": it is the "most important example of how the imagination continually outruns the creature it inhabits." In addition to men, Porter collected furs, jewels, fine silver and china, antique furniture, gossip, and fables.

Porter's need to glamorize and enhance the facts of her life emerged early and lasted as long as she lived. Her finest fiction, however, which clearly sprang in part from needs like those expressed in her fabrications, was largely concentrated in the middle years of her life, especially the decade of the 1930s. "I went to Europe in 1931 an unknown," she later remarked, "and returned to find myself a celebrity." This success was based on two collections of stories and short novels, *Flowering Judas* (published in 1930 and augmented in 1935) and *Noon Wine* (1937). Her critical reputation was enhanced by *Pale Horse, Pale Rider: Three Short Novels* (1938) and *The Leaning Tower and Other Stories* (1944). In his review of *The Leaning Tower,* Edmund Wilson admitted that Porter was "baffling" to him and struggled to formulate the "elusive" quality that made her "absolutely a first-rate artist":

> These stories are not illustrations of anything that is reducible to a moral law or a political or social analysis or even a principle of human behavior. What they show us are human relations in their constantly shifting phases and in the moments of which their existence is made. There is no place for general reflections; you are to live through the experience as the characters do.

Like Sherwood Anderson, Porter believed that the short story did not require a "plot." The writer, she said, "needed *first* a *theme,* and then a point of view, a certain knowledge of human nature and strong feeling about it, and style—that is to say, his own special way of telling a thing that makes it precisely his own and no one else's." As Eudora Welty pointed out in a review of *The Collected Stories of Katherine Anne Porter* (1965), she cared nothing for conventionally dramatic construction: "The suspense—so acute and so real—in Katherine Anne Porter's work never did depend for its life on disclosure of the happenings of the narrative . . . but in the writing of the story, which becomes one single long sustained moment for the reader."

Even in Porter's finest work we observe a tension between a desire to confront and disclose the significance of her experience and a countervailing desire to disguise and conceal that significance. The conflict between these impulses sometimes results in a rarefied, ethereal prose, as though Porter were reaching for the timeless and the universal before making sufficient contact with the local and the immediate. Both her aestheticism and her evasiveness, her reluctance to confront fully the significances lurking in her own experience of the world she knew best, occasionally limit her achievement. In works such as "Old Mortality," however, she masters the tension between her sense of herself as a stylist seeking timelessness and universality and her sense of herself as a storyteller drawing upon perceptions and memories of local scenes and human actions.

Porter's only novel, *Ship of Fools,* which she wrote laboriously over a thirty-year period, appeared in 1962 and attracted considerable attention, in part because it had been so long awaited. The novel, an account of a voyage from Veracruz, Mexico, to Bremerhaven, Germany, in 1931, during the Nazi regime, explores the wreckage of modern civilization by focusing on the often vicious private histories and behavior of the ship's passengers. The vision of the book is a bleak one and apparently derives from Porter's longstanding belief that art offered the only hope, however small and fragile, in a darkening world. In 1940 she wrote in an introduction to a new edition of *Flowering Judas:* "All the conscious and recollected years of my life have been lived to this day under the heavy threat of world catastrophe, and most of the energies of my mind and spirit have been spent in the effort to grasp the meaning of those threats, to trace them to their sources and to understand the logic of this majestic and terrible failure of the life of man in the Western world." In 1952 Porter published *The Days Before: Collected Essays and Occasional Writings,* a volume that was expanded in 1970; the essays range from an interpretation of nuclear fear to a profile of Jacqueline Kennedy. Katherine Anne Porter died on September 18, 1980, in the Carriage Hill Nursing Center in Silver Spring, Maryland.

Further Reading:
H. J. Mooney, *The Fiction and Criticism of Katherine Anne Porter,* 1962.
R. B. West, Jr., *Katherine Anne Porter,* 1963.
E. Welty, "The Eye of the Story," *Yale Review,* December 1965.
J. Givner, *Katherine Anne Porter: A Life,* 1982.

Text:
Pale Horse, Pale Rider, 1939.

Old Mortality

Part I: 1885–1902

She was a spirited-looking young woman, with dark curly hair cropped and parted on the side, a short oval face with straight eyebrows, and a large curved mouth. A round white collar rose from the neck of her tightly buttoned black basque, and round white cuffs set off lazy hands with dimples in them, lying at ease in the folds of her flounced skirt which gathered around to a bustle. She sat thus, forever in the pose of being photographed, a motionless image in her dark walnut frame with silver oak leaves in the corners, her smiling gray eyes following one about the room. It was a reckless indifferent smile, rather disturbing to her nieces Maria and Miranda. Quite often they wondered why every older person who looked at the picture said, "How lovely"; and why everyone who had known her thought her so beautiful and charming.

There was a kind of faded merriment in the background, with its vase of flowers and draped velvet curtains, the kind of vase and the kind of curtains no one would have any more. The clothes were not even romantic looking, but merely most terribly out of fashion, and the whole affair was associated, in the minds of the little girls, with dead things: the smell of Grandmother's medicated cigarettes and her furniture that smelled of beeswax, and her old-fashioned perfume, Orange Flower. The woman in the picture had been Aunt Amy, but she was only a ghost in a frame, and a sad, pretty story from old times. She had been beautiful, much loved, unhappy, and she had died young.

Maria and Miranda, aged twelve and eight years, knew they were young, though they felt they had lived a long time. They had lived not only their own years; but their memories, it seemed to them, began years before they were born, in the lives of the grown-ups around them, old people above forty, most of them, who had a way of insisting that they too had been young once. It was hard to believe.

Their father was Aunt Amy's brother Harry. She had been his favorite sister. He sometimes glanced at the photograph and said, "It's not very good. Her hair and her smile were her chief beauties, and they aren't shown at all. She was much slimmer than that, too. There were never any fat women in the family, thank God."

When they heard their father say things like that, Maria and Miranda simply wondered, without criticism, what he meant. Their grandmother was thin as a match; the pictures of their mother, long since dead, proved her to have been a candle-wick, almost. Dashing young ladies, who turned out to be, to Miranda's astonishment, merely more of Grandmother's grandchildren, like herself, came visiting from school for the holidays, boasting of their eighteen-inch waists. But how did their father account for great-aunt Eliza, who quite squeezed herself through doors, and who, when seated, was one solid pyramidal monument from floor to neck? What about great-aunt Keziah, in Kentucky? Her husband, great-uncle John Jacob, had refused to allow her to ride his good horses after she had achieved two hundred and twenty pounds. "No," said great-uncle John Jacob, "my sentiments of chivalry are not dead in my bosom; but neither is my common sense, to say nothing of charity to our faithful dumb friends. And the greatest of these is charity." It was suggested to great-uncle John Jacob that charity should forbid him to wound great-aunt Keziah's female vanity by such a comment on her figure. "Female vanity will recover," said great-uncle John Jacob, callously, "but what about my horses' backs? And if she had the proper female vanity in the first place, she would never have got into such shape." Well, great-aunt Keziah was famous for her heft, and wasn't she in the family? But something seemed to happen to their father's memory when he thought of the girls he had known in the family of his youth, and he declared steadfastly they had all been, in every generation without exception, as slim as reeds and graceful as sylphs.

This loyalty of their father's in the face of evidence contrary to his ideal had its springs in family feeling, and a love of legend that he shared with the others. They loved to tell stories, romantic and poetic, or comic with a romantic humor; they did not gild the outward circumstance, it was the feeling that mattered. Their hearts and imaginations were captivated by their past, a past in which worldly considerations had played a very minor role. Their stories were almost always love stories against a bright blank heavenly blue sky.

Photographs, portraits by inept painters who meant earnestly to flatter, and the festival garments folded away in dried herbs and camphor were disappointing when the little girls tried to fit them to the living beings created in their minds by the breathing words of their elders. Grandmother, twice a year compelled in her blood by the change of seasons, would sit nearly all of one day beside old trunks and boxes in the lumber room, unfolding layers of garments and small keepsakes; she spread them out on sheets on the floor around her, crying over certain things, nearly always the same things, looking again at pictures in velvet cases, unwrapping locks of hair and dried flowers, crying gently and easily as if tears were the only pleasure she had left.

If Maria and Miranda were very quiet, and touched nothing until it was offered, they might sit by her at these times, or come and go. There was a tacit understanding that her grief was strictly her own, and must not be noticed or mentioned. The little girls examined the objects, one by one, and did not find them, in themselves, impressive. Such dowdy little wreaths and necklaces, some of them made of pearly shells; such moth-eaten bunches of pink ostrich feathers for the hair; such clumsy big breast pins and bracelets of gold and colored enamel; such silly-looking combs, standing up on tall teeth capped with seed pearls and French paste. Miranda, without knowing why, felt melancholy. It seemed such a pity that these faded things, these yellowed long gloves and misshapen satin slippers, these broad ribbons cracking where they were folded, should have been all those vanished girls had to decorate themselves with. And where were they now, those girls, and the boys in the odd-looking collars? The young men seemed even more unreal than the girls, with their high-buttoned coats, their puffy neckties, their waxed mustaches, their waving thick hair combed carefully over their foreheads. Who could have taken them seriously, looking like that?

No, Maria and Miranda found it impossible to sympathize with those young persons, sitting rather stiffly before the camera, hopelessly out of fashion, but they were drawn and held by the mysterious love of the living, who remembered and cherished these dead. The visible remains were nothing; they were dust, perishable as the flesh; the features stamped on paper and metal were nothing, but their living memory enchanted the little girls. They listened, all ears and eager minds, picking here and there among the floating ends of narrative, patching together as well as they could fragments of tales that were like bits of poetry or music, indeed were associated with the poetry they had heard or read, with music, with the theater.

"Tell me again how Aunt Amy went away when she was married." "She ran into the gray cold and stepped into the carriage and turned and smiled with her face as pale as death, and called out 'Good-by, good-by,' and refused her cloak, and said, 'Give me a glass of wine.' And none of us saw her alive again." "Why wouldn't she wear her cloak, Cousin Cora?" "Because she was not in love, my dear." Ruin hath taught me thus to ruminate, that time will come and take my love away.[1] "Was she really beautiful, Uncle Bill?" "As an angel, my child." There were golden-haired angels with long blue pleated skirts dancing around the throne of the Blessed Virgin. None of them resembled Aunt Amy in the least, nor the type of beauty they had been brought up to admire. There were points of beauty by which one was judged severely. First, a beauty must be tall; whatever color the eyes, the hair must be dark, the darker the better; the skin must be pale and smooth. Lightness and swiftness of movement were

[1] From Shakespeare's Sonnet 64 ("When I have seen by time's fell hand defaced"), ll. 11–12.

important points. A beauty must be a good dancer, superb on horseback, with a serene manner, an amiable gaiety tempered with dignity at all hours. Beautiful teeth and hands, of course, and over and above all this, some mysterious crown of enchantment that attracted and held the heart. It was all very exciting and discouraging.

Miranda persisted through her childhood in believing, in spite of her smallness, thinness, her little snubby nose saddled with freckles, her speckled gray eyes and habitual tantrums, that by some miracle she would grow into a tall, cream-colored brunette, like cousin Isabel; she decided always to wear a trailing white satin gown. Maria, born sensible, had no such illusions. "We are going to take after Mamma's family," she said. "It's no use, we are. We'll never be beautiful, we'll always have freckles. And *you*," she told Miranda, "haven't even a good disposition."

Miranda admitted both truth and justice in this unkindness, but still secretly believed that she would one day suddenly receive beauty, as by inheritance, riches laid suddenly in her hands through no deserts of her own. She believed for quite a while that she would one day be like Aunt Amy, not as she appeared in the photograph, but as she was remembered by those who had seen her.

When Cousin Isabel came out in her tight black riding habit, surrounded by young men, and mounted gracefully, drawing her horse up and around so that he pranced learnedly on one spot while the other riders sprang to their saddles in the same sedate flurry, Miranda's heart would close with such a keen dart of admiration, envy, vicarious pride it was almost painful; but there would always be an elder present to lay a cooling hand upon her emotions. "She rides almost as well as Amy, doesn't she? But Amy had the pure Spanish style, she could bring out paces in a horse no one else knew he had." Young namesake Amy, on her way to a dance, would swish through the hall in ruffled white taffeta, glimmering like a moth in the lamplight, carrying her elbows pointed backward stiffly as wings, sliding along as if she were on rollers, in the fashionable walk of her day. She was considered the best dancer at any party, and Maria, sniffing the wave of perfume that followed Amy, would clasp her hands and say, "Oh, I can't *wait* to be grown up." But the elders would agree that the first Amy had been lighter, more smooth and delicate in her waltzing; young Amy would never equal her. Cousin Molly Parrington, far past her youth, indeed she belonged to the generation before Aunt Amy, was a noted charmer. Men who had known her all her life still gathered about her; now that she was happily widowed for the second time there was no doubt that she would yet marry again. But Amy, said the elders, had the same high spirits and wit without boldness, and you really could not say that Molly had ever been discreet. She dyed her hair, and made jokes about it. She had a way of collecting the men around her in a corner, where she told them stories. She was an unnatural mother to her ugly daughter Eva, an old maid past forty while her mother was still the belle of the ball. "Born when I was fifteen, you remember," Molly would say shamelessly, looking an old beau straight in the eye, both of them remembering that he had been best man at her first wedding when she was past twenty-one. "Everyone said I was like a little girl with her doll."

Eva, shy and chinless, straining her upper lip over two enormous teeth, would sit in corners watching her mother. She looked hungry, her eyes were strained and tired. She wore her mother's old clothes, made over, and taught Latin in a Female Seminary. She believed in votes for women, and had traveled about, making speeches. When her mother was not present, Eva bloomed out a little, danced prettily, smiled, showing all her teeth, and was like a dry little plant set out in a gentle rain. Molly was merry about her ugly duckling. "It's lucky for me my daughter is an old maid. She's not so apt," said Molly naughtily, "to make a grandmother of me." Eva would blush as if she had been slapped.

Eva was a blot, no doubt about it, but the little girls felt she belonged to their everyday world of dull lessons to be learned, stiff shoes to be limbered up, scratchy flannels to be endured in cold weather, measles and disappointed expectations. Their Aunt Amy belonged to the world of poetry. The romance of Uncle Gabriel's long, unrewarded love for her, her early death, was such a story as one found in old books: unworldly books, but true, such as the Vita Nuova, the Sonnets of Shakespeare and the Wedding Song of Spenser;[2] and poems by Edgar Allan Poe. "Her tantalized spirit now blandly reposes, Forgetting or never regretting its roses. . . ." Their father read that to them, and said, "He was our greatest poet," and they knew that "our" meant he was Southern. Aunt Amy was real as the pictures in the old Holbein and Dürer[3] books were real. The little girls lay flat on their stomachs and peered into a world of wonder, turning the shabby leaves that fell apart easily, not surprised at the sight of the Mother of God sitting on a hollow log nursing her Child; not doubting either Death or the Devil riding at the stirrups of the grim knight; not questioning the propriety of the stiffly dressed ladies of Sir Thomas More's[4] household, seated in dignity on the floor, or seeming to be. They missed all the dog and pony shows, and lantern-slide entertainments, but their father took them to see "Hamlet," and "The Taming of the Shrew," and "Richard the Third," and a long sad play with Mary, Queen of Scots, in it. Miranda thought the magnificent lady in black velvet was truly the Queen of Scots, and was pained to learn that the real Queen had died long ago, and not at all on the night she, Miranda, had been present.

The little girls loved the theater, that world of personages taller than human beings, who swept upon the scene and invested it with their presences, their more than human voices, their gestures of gods and goddesses ruling a universe. But there was always a voice recalling other and greater occasions. Grandmother in her youth had heard Jenny Lind, and thought that Nellie Melba[5] was much overrated. Father had seen Bernhardt, and Madame Modjeska[6] was no sort of rival. When Paderewski[7] played for the first time in their city, cousins came from all over the state and went from the grandmother's house to hear him. The little girls were left out of this great occasion. They shared the excitement of the going away, and shared the beautiful moment of return, when cousins stood about in groups, with coffee cups and glasses in their hands, talking in low voices, awed and happy. The little girls, struck with

[2] *La Vita Nuova* (*The New Life*): a long poem by Dante Alighieri (1265–1321), celebrating his intensely spiritual love for Beatrice. Wedding Song: The "Epithalamion" (1595), poem by Edmund Spenser (1552?–1599), possibly to celebrate his own marriage in 1594.

[3] Hans Holbein (1497–1543) and Albrecht Dürer (1471–1528), German painters.

[4] Sir Thomas More (1478–1535), English statesman and scholar, martyred for his refusal to acknowledge Henry VIII's repudiation of the authority of the Pope.

[5] Jenny Lind (1820–1887): Swedish coloratura soprano, known as the Swedish nightingale; Nellie Melba: stage name of Helen Porter Armstrong (1861–1931), Australian coloratura soprano.

[6] Sarah Bernhardt (1844–1923), popular French actress; Helena Modjeska (1840–1909), Polish-American actress.

[7] Ignace Paderewski (1860–1941), Polish pianist, composer, and statesman.

the sense of a great event, hung about in their nightgowns and listened, until someone noticed and hustled them away from the sweet nimbus of all that glory. One old gentleman, however, had heard Rubinstein[8] frequently. He could not but feel that Rubinstein had reached the final height of musical interpretation, and, for him, Paderewski had been something of an anticlimax. The little girls heard him muttering on, holding up one hand, patting the air as if he were calling for silence. The others looked at him, and listened, without any disturbance of their grave tender mood. They had never heard Rubinstein; they had, one hour since, heard Paderewski, and why should anyone need to recall the past? Miranda, dragged away, half understanding the old gentleman, hated him. She felt that she too had heard Paderewski.

There was then a life beyond a life in this world, as well as in the next; such episodes confirmed for the little girls the nobility of human feeling, the divinity of man's vision of the unseen, the importance of life and death, the depths of the human heart, the romantic value of tragedy. Cousin Eva, on a certain visit, trying to interest them in the study of Latin, told them the story of John Wilkes Booth, who, handsomely garbed in a long black cloak, had leaped to the stage after assassinating President Lincoln. "Sic semper tyrannis,"[9] he had shouted superbly, in spite of his broken leg. The little girls never doubted that it had happened in just that way, and the moral seemed to be that one should always have Latin, or at least a good classical poetry quotation, to depend upon in great or desperate moments. Cousin Eva reminded them that no one, not even a good Southerner, could possibly approve of John Wilkes Booth's deed. It was murder, after all. They were to remember that. But Miranda, used to tragedy in books and in family legends—two great-uncles had committed suicide and a remote ancestress had gone mad for love—decided that, without the murder, there would have been no point to dressing up and leaping to the stage shouting in Latin. So how could she disapprove of the deed? It was a fine story. She knew a distantly related old gentleman who had been devoted to the art of Booth, had seen him in a great many plays, but not, alas, at his greatest moment. Miranda regretted this; it would have been so pleasant to have the assassination of Lincoln in the family.

Uncle Gabriel, who had loved Aunt Amy so desperately, still lived somewhere, though Miranda and Maria had never seen him. He had gone away, far away, after her death. He still owned racehorses, and ran them at famous tracks all over the country, and Miranda believed there could not possibly be a more brilliant career. He had married again, quite soon, and had written to Grandmother, asking her to accept his new wife as a daughter in place of Amy. Grandmother had written coldly, accepting, inviting them for a visit, but Uncle Gabriel had somehow never brought his bride home. Harry had visited them in New Orleans, and reported that the second wife was a very good-looking well-bred blonde girl who would undoubtedly be a good wife for Gabriel. Still, Uncle Gabriel's heart was broken. Faithfully once a year he wrote a letter to someone of the family, sending money for a wreath for Amy's grave. He had written a poem for her gravestone, and had come home, leaving his second wife in Atlanta, to see that it was carved properly. He could never account

[8] Anton Rubinstein (1829–1894), Russian pianist, who toured in the U.S. as well as Europe.   [9] Latin: "Thus ever tyranny."

for having written this poem; he had certainly never tried to write a single rhyme since leaving school. Yet one day when he had been thinking about Amy, the verse occurred to him, out of the air. Maria and Miranda had seen it, printed in gold on a mourning card. Uncle Gabriel had sent a great number of them to be handed around among the family.

> "She lives again who suffered life,
> Then suffered death, and now set free
> A singing angel, she forgets
> The griefs of old mortality."

"Did she really sing?" Maria asked her father.

"Now what has that to do with it?" he asked. "It's a poem."

"I think it's very pretty," said Miranda, impressed. Uncle Gabriel was second cousin to her father and Aunt Amy. It brought poetry very near.

"Not so bad for tombstone poetry," said their father, "but it should be better."

Uncle Gabriel had waited five years to marry Aunt Amy. She had been ill, her chest was weak; she was engaged twice to other young men and broke her engagements for no reason; and she laughed at the advice of older and kinder-hearted persons who thought it very capricious of her not to return the devotion of such a handsome and romantic young man as Gabriel, her second cousin, too; it was not as if she would be marrying a stranger. Her coldness was said to have driven Gabriel to a wild life and even to drinking. His grandfather was wealthy and Gabriel was his favorite; they had quarreled over the racehorses, and Gabriel had shouted, "By God, I must have *something.*" As if he had not everything already: youth, health, good looks, the prospect of riches, and a devoted family circle. His grandfather pointed out to him that he was little better than an ingrate, and showed signs of being a wastrel as well. Gabriel said, "You had racehorses, and made a good thing of them." "I never depended upon them for a livelihood, sir," said his grandfather.

Gabriel wrote letters about this and many other things to Amy from Saratoga and from Kentucky and from New Orleans, sending her presents, and flowers packed in ice, and telegrams. The presents were amusing, such as a huge cage full of small green lovebirds; or, as an ornament for her hair, a full-petaled enameled rose with paste dewdrops, with an enameled butterfly in brilliant colors suspended quivering on a gold wire about it; but the telegrams always frightened her mother, and the flowers, after a journey by train and then by stage into the country, were much the worse for wear. He would send roses when the rose garden at home was in full bloom. Amy could not help smiling over it, though her mother insisted it was touching and sweet of Gabriel. It must prove to Amy that she was always in his thoughts.

"That's no place for me," said Amy, but she had a way of speaking, a tone of voice, which made it impossible to discover what she meant by what she said. It was possible always that she might be serious. And she would not answer questions.

"Amy's wedding dress," said the grandmother, unfurling an immense cloak of dove-colored cut velvet, spreading beside it a silvery-gray watered-silk frock, and a small gray velvet toque with a dark red breast of feathers. Cousin Isabel, the beauty, sat with her. They talked to each other, and Miranda could listen if she chose.

"She would not wear white, nor a veil," said Grandmother. "I couldn't oppose her, for I had said my daughters should each have exactly the wedding dress they wanted. But Amy surprised me. 'Now what would I look like in white satin?' she asked. It's true she was pale, but she would have been angelic in it, and all of us told her so. 'I shall wear mourning if I like,' she said, 'it is *my* funeral, you know.' I reminded her that Lou and your mother had worn white with veils and it would please me to have my daughters all alike in that. Amy said, 'Lou and Isabel are not like me,' but I could not persuade her to explain what she meant. One day when she was ill she said, 'Mammy, I'm not long for this world,' but not as if she meant it. I told her, 'You might live as long as anyone, if only you will be sensible.' 'That's the whole trouble,' said Amy. 'I feel sorry for Gabriel,' she told me. 'He doesn't know what he's asking for.'

"I tried to tell her once more," said the grandmother, "that marriage and children would cure her of everything. 'All women of our family are delicate when they are young,' I said. 'Why, when I was your age no one expected me to live a year. It was called greensickness,[10] and everybody knew there was only one cure.' 'If I live for a hundred years and turn green as grass,' said Amy, 'I still shan't want to marry Gabriel.' So I told her very seriously that if she truly felt that way she must never do it, and Gabriel must be told once for all, and sent away. He would get over it. 'I have told him, and I have sent him away,' said Amy. 'He just doesn't listen.' We both laughed at that, and I told her young girls found a hundred ways to deny they wished to be married, and a thousand more to test their power over men, but that she had more than enough of that, and now it was time for her to be entirely sincere and make her decision. As for me," said the grandmother, "I wished with all heart to marry your grandfather, and if he had not asked me, I should have asked him most certainly. Amy insisted that she could not imagine wanting to marry anybody. She would be, she said, a nice old maid like Eva Parrington. For even then it was pretty plain that Eva was an old maid, born. Harry said, 'Oh, Eva—Eva has no chin, that's her trouble. If you had no chin, Amy, you'd be in the same fix as Eva, no doubt.' Your Uncle Bill would say, 'When women haven't anything else, they'll take a vote for consolation. A pretty thin bed-fellow,' said your Uncle Bill. 'What I really need is a good dancing partner to guide me through life,' said Amy, 'that's the match I'm looking for.' It was no good trying to talk to her."

Her brothers remembered her tenderly as a sensible girl. After listening to their comments on her character and ways, Maria decided that they considered her sensible because she asked their advice about her appearance when she was going out to dance. If they found fault in any way, she would change her dress or her hair until they were pleased, and say, "You are an angel not to let your poor sister go out looking like a freak." But she would not listen to her father, nor to Gabriel. If Gabriel praised the frock she was wearing, she was apt to disappear and come back in another. He loved her long black hair, and once, lifting it up from her pillow when she was ill, said, "I love your hair, Amy, the most beautiful hair in the world." When he returned on his next visit, he found her with her hair cropped and curled close to her head.

[10] Chlorosis, an iron-deficiency anemia chiefly affecting girls at puberty and characterized by greenish skin color.

He was horrified, as if she had willfully mutilated herself. She would not let it grow again, not even to please her brothers. The photograph hanging on the wall was one she had made at that time to send to Gabriel, who sent it back without a word. This pleased her, and she framed the photograph. There was a thin inky scrawl low in one corner, "To dear brother Harry, who likes my hair cut."

This was a mischievous reference to a very grave scandal. The little girls used to look at their father, and wonder what would have happened if he had really hit the young man he shot at. The young man was believed to have kissed Aunt Amy, when she was not in the least engaged to him. Uncle Gabriel was supposed to have had a duel with the young man, but Father had got there first. He was a pleasant, everyday sort of father, who held his daughters on his knee if they were prettily dressed and well behaved, and pushed them away if they had not freshly combed hair and nicely scrubbed fingernails. "Go away, you're disgusting," he would say, in a matter-of-fact voice. He noticed if their stocking seams were crooked. He caused them to brush their teeth with a revolting mixture of prepared chalk, powdered charcoal and salt. When they behaved stupidly he could not endure the sight of them. They understood dimly that all this was for their own future good; and when they were snively with colds, he prescribed delicious hot toddy for them, and saw that it was given them. He was always hoping they might not grow up to be so silly as they seemed to him at any given moment, and he had a disconcerting way of inquiring, "How do you *know?*" when they forgot and made dogmatic statements in his presence. It always came out embarrassingly that they did not know at all, but were repeating something they had heard. This made conversation with him difficult, for he laid traps and they fell into them, but it became important to them that their father should not believe them to be fools. Well, this very father had gone to Mexico once and stayed there for nearly a year, because he had shot at a man with whom Aunt Amy had flirted at a dance. It had been very wrong of him, because he should have challenged the man to a duel, as Uncle Gabriel had done. Instead, he just took a shot at him, and this was the lowest sort of manners. It had caused great disturbance in the whole community and had almost broken up the affair between Aunt Amy and Uncle Gabriel for good. Uncle Gabriel insisted that the young man had kissed Aunt Amy, and Aunt Amy insisted that the young man had merely paid her a compliment on her hair.

During the Mardi Gras holidays there was to be a big gay fancy-dress ball. Harry was going as a bull-fighter because his sweetheart, Mariana, had a new black lace mantilla and high comb from Mexico. Maria and Miranda had seen a photograph of their mother in this dress, her lovely face without a trace of coquetry looking gravely out from under a tremendous fall of lace from the peak of the comb, a rose tucked firmly over her ear. Amy copied her costume from a small Dresden-china shepherdess which stood on the mantel piece in the parlor; a careful copy with ribboned hat, gilded crook, very low-laced bodice, short basket skirts, green slippers and all. She wore it with a black half-mask, but it was no disguise. "You would have known it was Amy at any distance," said Father. Gabriel, six feet three in height as he was, had got himself up to match, and a spectacle he provided in pale blue satin knee breeches and a blond curled wig with a hair ribbon. "He felt a fool, and he looked like one," said Uncle Bill, "and he behaved like one before the evening was over."

Everything went beautifully until the party gathered downstairs to leave for the ball. Amy's father—he must have been born a grandfather, thought Miranda—gave one glance at his daughter, her white ankles shining, bosom deeply exposed, two round spots of paint on her cheeks, and fell into a frenzy of outraged propriety. "It's disgraceful," he pronounced, loudly. "No daughter of mine is going to show herself in such a rig-out. It's bawdy," he thundered. "Bawdy!"

Amy had taken off her mask to smile at him. "Why, Papa," she said very sweetly, "what's wrong with it? Look on the mantelpiece. She's been there all along, and you were never shocked before."

"There's all the difference in the world," said her father, "all the difference, young lady, and you know it. You go upstairs this minute and pin up that waist in front and let down those skirts to a decent length before you leave this house. *And wash your face!*"

"I see nothing wrong with it," said Amy's mother, firmly, "and you shouldn't use such language before innocent young girls." She and Amy sat down with several females of the household to help, and they made short work of the business. In ten minutes Amy returned, face clean, bodice filled in with lace, shepherdess skirt modestly sweeping the carpet behind her.

When Amy appeared from the dressing room for her first dance with Gabriel, the lace was gone from her bodice, her skirts were tucked up more daringly than before, and the spots on her cheeks were like pomegranates. "Now Gabriel, tell me truly, wouldn't it have been a pity to spoil my costume?" Gabriel, delighted that she had asked his opinion, declared it was perfect. They agreed with kindly tolerance that old people were often tiresome, but one need not upset them by open disobedience: their youth was gone, what had they to live for?

Harry, dancing with Mariana who swung a heavy train around her expertly at every turn of the waltz, began to be uneasy about his sister Amy. She was entirely too popular. He saw young men make beelines across the floor, eyes fixed on those white silk ankles. Some of the young men he did not know at all, others he knew too well and could not approve of for his sister Amy. Gabriel, unhappy in his lyric satin and wig, stood about holding his ribboned crook as though it had sprouted thorns. He hardly danced at all with Amy, he did not enjoy dancing with anyone else, and he was having a thoroughly wretched time of it.

There appeared late, alone, got up as Jean Lafitte, a young Creole gentleman who had, two years before, been for a time engaged to Amy. He came straight to her, with the manner of a happy lover, and said, clearly enough for everyone near by to hear him, "I only came because I knew you were to be here. I only want to dance with you and I shall go again." Amy, with a face of delight, cried out, "Raymond!" as if to a lover. She had danced with him four times, and had then disappeared from the floor on his arm.

Harry and Mariana, in conventional disguise of romance, irreproachably betrothed, safe in their happiness, were waltzing slowly to their favorite song, the melancholy farewell of the Moorish King on leaving Granada. They sang in whispers to each other, in their uncertain Spanish, a song of love and parting and that sword's point of grief that makes the heart tender towards all other lost and disinherited creatures: Oh, mansion of love, my earthly paradise . . . that I shall see no more . . . whither flies the poor swallow, weary and homeless, seeking for shelter where no shelter is? I too am far from home without the power to fly. . . . Come to my heart, sweet bird, beloved pilgrim, build your nest near my bed, let me listen to your song, and weep for my lost land of joy. . . .

Into this bliss broke Gabriel. He had thrown away his shepherd's crook and he was carrying his wig. He wanted to speak to Harry at once, and before Mariana knew what was happening she was sitting beside her mother and the two excited young men were gone. Waiting, disturbed and displeased, she smiled at Amy who waltzed past with a young man in Devil costume, including ill-fitting scarlet cloven hoofs. Almost at once, Harry and Gabriel came back, with serious faces, and Harry darted on the dance floor, returning with Amy. The girls and the chaperones were asked to come at once, they must be taken home. It was all mysterious and sudden, and Harry said to Mariana, "I will tell you what is happening, but not now—"

The grandmother remembered of this disgraceful affair only that Gabriel brought Amy home alone and that Harry came in somewhat later. The other members of the party straggled in at various hours, and the story came out piecemeal. Amy was silent and, her mother discovered later, burning with fever. "I saw at once that something was very wrong. 'What has happened, Amy?' 'Oh, Harry goes about shooting at people at a party,' she said, sitting down as if she were exhausted. 'It was on your account, Amy,' said Gabriel. 'Oh, no, it was not,' said Amy. 'Don't believe him, Mammy.' So I said, 'Now enough of this. Tell me what happened, Amy. And Amy said, 'Mammy, this is it. Raymond came in, and you know I like Raymond, and he is a good dancer. So we danced together, too much, maybe. We went on the gallery for a breath of air, and stood there. He said, "How well your hair looks. I like this new shingled style." ' She glanced at Gabriel. 'And then another young man came out and said, "I've been looking everywhere. This is our dance, isn't it?" And I went in to dance. And now it seems that Gabriel went out at once and challenged Raymond to a duel about something or other, but Harry doesn't wait for that. Raymond had already gone out to have his horse brought, I suppose one doesn't duel in fancy dress,' she said, looking at Gabriel, who fairly shriveled in his blue satin shepherd's costume, 'and Harry simply went out and shot at him. I don't think that was fair,' said Amy."

Her mother agreed that indeed it was not fair; it was not even decent, and she could not imagine what her son Harry thought he was doing. "It isn't much of a way to defend your sister's honor," she said to him afterward. "I didn't want Gabriel to go fighting duels," said Harry. "That wouldn't have helped much, either."

Gabriel had stood before Amy, leaning over, asking once more the question he had apparently been asking her all the way home. "Did he kiss you, Amy?"

Amy took off her shepherdess hat and pushed her hair back. "Maybe he did," she answered, "and maybe I wished him to."

"Amy, you must not say such things," said her mother. "Answer Gabriel's question."

"He hasn't the right to ask it," said Amy, but without anger.

"Do you love him, Amy?" asked Gabriel, the sweat standing out on his forehead.

"It doesn't matter," answered Amy, leaning back in her chair.

"Oh, it does matter; it matters terribly," said Gabriel. "You must answer me now." He took both of her hands and tried to hold them. She drew her hands away firmly and steadily so that he had to let go.

"Let her alone, Gabriel," said Amy's mother. "You'd better go now. We are all tired. Let's talk about it tomorrow."

She helped Amy to undress, noticing the changed bodice and the shortened skirt. "You shouldn't have done that, Amy. That was not wise of you. It was better the other way."

Amy said, "Mammy, I'm sick of this world. I don't like anything in it. It's so *dull,*" she said, and for a moment she looked as if she might weep. She had never been tearful, even as a child, and her mother was alarmed. It was then she discovered that Amy had fever.

"Gabriel is dull, Mother—he sulks," she said. "I could see him sulking every time I passed. It spoils things," she said. "Oh, I want to go to sleep."

Her mother sat looking at her and wondering how it had happened she had brought such a beautiful child into the world. "Her face," said her mother, "was angelic in sleep."

Some time during that fevered night, the projected duel between Gabriel and Raymond was halted by the offices of friends on both sides. There remained the open question of Harry's impulsive shot, which was not so easily settled. Raymond seemed vindictive about that, it was possible he might choose to make trouble. Harry, taking the advice of Gabriel, his brothers and friends, decided that the best way to avoid further scandal was for him to disappear for a while. This being decided upon, the young men returned about daybreak, saddled Harry's best horse and helped him pack a few things; accompanied by Gabriel and Bill, Harry set out for the border, feeling rather gay and adventurous.

Amy, being wakened by the stirring in the house, found out the plan. Five minutes after they were gone, she came down in her riding dress, had her own horse saddled, and struck out after them. She rode almost every morning; before her parents had time to be uneasy over her prolonged absence, they found her note.

What had threatened to be a tragedy became a rowdy lark. Amy rode to the border, kissed her brother Harry good-by, and rode back again with Bill and Gabriel. It was a three days' journey, and when they arrived Amy had to be lifted from the saddle. She was really ill by now, but in the gayest of humors. Her mother and father had been prepared to be severe with her, but, at sight of her, their feelings changed. They turned on Bill and Gabriel. "Why did you let her do this?" they asked.

"You know we could not stop her," said Gabriel helplessly, "and she did enjoy herself so much!"

Amy laughed. "Mammy, it was splendid, the most delightful trip I ever had. And if I am to be the heroine of this novel, why shouldn't I make the most of it?" The scandal, Maria and Miranda gathered, had been pretty terrible. Amy simply took to bed and stayed there, and Harry had skipped out blithely to wait until the little affair blew over. The rest of the family had to receive visitors, write letters, go to church, return calls, and bear the whole brunt, as they expressed it. They sat in the twilight of scandal in their little world, holding themselves very rigidly, in a shared tension as if all their nerves began at a common center. This center had received a blow, and family nerves shuddered, even into the farthest reaches of Kentucky. From whence in due time great-great-aunt Sally Rhea addressed a letter to *Mifs Amy Rhea.* In deep brown ink like dried blood, in a spidery hand adept at archaic symbols and abbreviations, great-great-aunt Sally informed Amy that she was fairly convinced that this calamity was only the forerunner of a series shortly to be visited by the Almighty God upon a race already condemned through its own wickedness, a warning that man's time was short, and that they must all prepare for the end of the world. For herself, she had long expected it, she was entirely resigned to the prospect of meeting her Maker; and Amy, no less than her wicked brother Harry, must likewise place herself in God's hands and prepare for the worst. *"Oh, my dear unfortunate young relative,"* twittered great-great-aunt Sally, *"we must in our Extremty join hands and appr before ye Dread Throne of Jdgmnt a United Fmly, if One is Mssg from ye Flock, what will Jesus say?"*

Great-great-aunt Sally's religious career had become comic legend. She had forsaken her Catholic rearing for a young man whose family were Cumberland Presbyterians. Unable to accept their opinions, however, she was converted to the Hard-Shell Baptists, a sect as loathsome to her husband's family as the Catholic could possibly be. She had spent a life of vicious self-indulgent martyrdom to her faith; as Harry commented: "Religion put claws on Aunt Sally and gave her a post to whet them on." She had out-argued, out-fought, and out-lived her entire generation, but she did not miss them. She bedeviled the second generation without ceasing, and was beginning hungrily on the third.

Amy, reading this letter, broke into her gay full laugh that always caused everyone around her to laugh too, even before they knew why, and her small green lovebirds in their cage turned and eyed her solemnly. "Imagine drawing a pew in heaven beside Aunt Sally," she said. "What a prospect."

"Don't laugh too soon," said her father. "Heaven was made to order for Aunt Sally. She'll be on her own territory there."

"For my sins," said Amy, "I must go to heaven with Aunt Sally."

During the uncomfortable time of Harry's absence, Amy went on refusing to marry Gabriel. Her mother could hear their voices going on in their endless colloquy, during many long days. One afternoon Gabriel came out, looking very sober and discouraged. He stood looking down at Amy's mother as she sat sewing, and said, "I think it is all over, I believe now that Amy will never have me." The grandmother always said afterward, "Never have I pitied anyone as I did poor Gabriel at that moment. But I told him, very firmly, 'Let her alone, then, she is ill.'" So Gabriel left, and Amy had no word from him for more than a month.

The day after Gabriel was gone, Amy rose looking extremely well, went hunting with her brothers Bill and Stephen, bought a velvet wrap, had her hair shingled and curled again, and wrote long letters to Harry, who was having a most enjoyable exile in Mexico City.

After dancing all night three times in one week, she woke one morning in a hemorrhage. She seemed frightened and asked for the doctor, promising to do whatever he advised. She was quiet for a few days, reading. She asked for Gabriel. No one knew where he was. "You should write him a letter; his mother will send it on." "Oh, no," she said. "I miss him coming in with his sour face. Letters are no good."

Gabriel did come in, only a few days later, with a very sour face and unpleasant news. His grandfather had died, after a day's illness. On his death bed, in the name of God, being of a sound and disposing mind, he had cut off his favorite grandchild Gabriel with one dollar. "In the name of God, Amy," said Gabriel, "the old devil has ruined me in one sentence."

It was the conduct of his immediate family in the matter that had embittered him, he said. They could hardly conceal their satisfaction. They had known and envied Gabriel's quite just, well-founded expectations. Not one of them offered to make any private settlement. No one even thought of repairing this last-minute act of senile vengeance. Privately they blessed their luck. "I have been cut off with a dollar," said

Gabriel, "and they are all glad of it. I think they feel somehow that this justifies every criticism they ever made against me. They were right about me all along. I am a worthless poor relation," said Gabriel. "My God, I wish you could see them."

Amy said, "I wonder how you will ever support a wife, now."

Gabriel said, "Oh, it isn't so bad as that. If you would, Amy—"

Amy said, "Gabriel, if we get married now there'll be just time to be in New Orleans for Mardi Gras. If we wait until after Lent, it may be too late."

"Why, Amy," said Gabriel, "how could it ever be too late?"

"You might change your mind," said Amy. "You know how fickle you are."

There were two letters in the grandmother's many packets of letters that Maria and Miranda read after they were grown. One of them was from Amy. It was dated ten days after her marriage.

"Dear Mammy, New Orleans hasn't changed as much as I have since we saw each other last. I am now a staid old married woman, and Gabriel is very devoted and kind. Footlights won a race for us yesterday, she was the favorite, and it was wonderful. I go to the races every day, and our horses are doing splendidly; I had my choice of Erin Go Bragh[11] or Miss Lucy, and I chose Miss Lucy. She is mine now, she runs like a streak. Gabriel says I made a mistake, Erin Go Bragh will stay better. I think Miss Lucy will stay my time.

"We are having a lovely visit. I'm going to put on a domino and take to the streets with Gabriel sometime during Mardi Gras. I'm tired of watching the show from a balcony. Gabriel says it isn't safe. He says he'll take me if I insist, but I doubt it. Mammy, he's very nice. Don't worry about me. I have a beautiful black-and-rose-colored velvet gown for the Proteus Ball. Madame, my new mother-in-law, wanted to know if it wasn't a little dashing. I told her I hoped so or I had been cheated. It is fitted perfectly smooth in the bodice, very low in the shoulders—Papa would not approve—and the skirt is looped with wide silver ribbons between the waist and knees in front, and then it surges around and is looped enormously in the back, with a train just one yard long. I now have an eighteen-inch waist, thanks to Madame Duré. I expect to be so dashing that my mother-in-law will have an attack. She has them quite often. Gabriel sends love. Please take good care of Graylie and Fiddler. I want to ride them again when I come home. We're going to Saratoga, I don't know just when. Give everybody my dear dear love. It rains all the time here, of course. . . .

"P.S. Mammy, as soon as I get a minute to myself, I'm going to be terribly homesick. Good-by, my darling Mammy."

The other was from Amy's nurse, dated six weeks after Amy's marriage.

"I cut off the lock of hair because I was sure you would like to have it. And I do not want you to think I was careless, leaving her medicine where she could get it, the doctor has written and explained. It would not have done her any harm except that her heart was weak. She did not know how much she was taking, often she said

---

[11] Gaelic: "Ireland forever."

to me, one more of those little capsules wouldn't do any harm, and so I told her to be careful and not take anything except what I gave her. She begged me for them sometimes but I would not give her more than the doctor said. I slept during the night because she did not seem to be so sick as all that and the doctor did not order me to sit up with her. Please accept my regrets for your great loss and please do not think that anybody was careless with your dear daughter. She suffered a great deal and now she is at rest. She could not get well but she might have lived longer. Yours respectfully. . . ."

The letters and all the strange keepsakes were packed away and forgotten for a great many years. They seemed to have no place in the world.

Part II: 1904

During vacation on their grandmother's farm, Maria and Miranda, who read as naturally and constantly as ponies crop grass, and with much the same kind of pleasure, had by some happy chance laid hold of some forbidden reading matter, brought in and left there with missionary intent, no doubt, by some Protestant cousin. It fell into the right hands if enjoyment had been its end. The reading matter was printed in poor type on spongy paper, and was ornamented with smudgy illustrations all the more exciting to the little girls because they could not make head or tail of them. The stories were about beautiful but unlucky maidens, who for mysterious reasons had been trapped by nuns and priests in dire collusion; they were then "immured" in convents, where they were forced to take the veil—an appalling rite during which the victims shrieked dreadfully—and condemned forever after to most uncomfortable and disorderly existences. They seemed to divide their time between lying chained in dark cells and assisting other nuns to bury throttled infants under stones in moldering rat-infested dungeons.

Immured! It was the word Maria and Miranda had been needing all along to describe their condition at the Convent of the Child Jesus, in New Orleans, where they spent the long winters trying to avoid an education. There were no dungeons at the Child Jesus, and this was only one of numerous marked differences between convent life as Maria and Miranda knew it and the thrilling paper-backed version. It was no good at all trying to fit the stories to life, and they did not even try. They had long since learned to draw the lines between life, which was real and earnest, and the grave was not its goal; poetry, which was true but not real; and stories, or forbidden reading matter, in which things happened as nowhere else, with the most sublime irrelevance and unlikelihood, and one need not turn a hair, because there was not a word of truth in them.

It was true the little girls were hedged and confined, but in a large garden with trees and a grotto; they were locked at night into a long cold dormitory, with all the windows open, and a sister sleeping at either end. Their beds were curtained with muslin, and small night-lamps were so arranged that the sisters could see through the curtains, but the children could not see the sisters. Miranda wondered if they ever slept, or did they sit there all night quietly watching the sleepers through the muslin? She tried to work up a little sinister thrill about this, but she found it impossible to care much what either of the sisters did. They were very dull good-natured women who managed to make the whole dormitory seem dull. All days and all things in the Convent of the Child Jesus were dull, in fact, and Maria and Miranda lived for Saturdays.

No one had even hinted that they should become nuns. On the contrary Miranda felt that the discouraging attitude of Sister Claude and Sister Austin and Sister Ursula towards her expressed ambition to be a nun barely veiled a deeply critical knowledge of her spiritual deficiencies. Still Maria and Miranda had got a fine new word out of their summer reading, and they referred to themselves as "immured." It gave a romantic glint to what was otherwise a very dull life for them, except for blessed Saturday afternoons during the racing season.

If the nuns were able to assure the family that the deportment and scholastic achievements of Maria and Miranda were at least passable, some cousin or other always showed up smiling, in holiday mood, to take them to the races, where they were given a dollar each to bet on any horse they chose. There were black Saturdays now and then, when Maria and Miranda sat ready, hats in hand, curly hair plastered down and slicked behind their ears, their stiffly pleated navy-blue skirts spread out around them, waiting with their hearts going down slowly into their high-topped laced-up black shoes. They never put on their hats until the last minute, for somehow it would have been too horrible to have their hats on, when, after all, Cousin Henry and Cousin Isabel, or Uncle George and Aunt Polly, were not coming to take them to the races. When no one appeared, and Saturday came and went a sickening waste, they were then given to understand that it was a punishment for bad marks during the week. They never knew until it was too late to avoid the disappointment. It was very wearing.

One Saturday they were sent down to wait in the visitors' parlor, and there was their father. He had come all the way from Texas to see them. They leaped at sight of him, and then stopped short, suspiciously. Was he going to take them to the races? If so, they were happy to see him.

"Hello," said father, kissing their cheeks. "Have you been good girls? Your Uncle Gabriel is running a mare at the Crescent City today, so we'll all go and bet on her. Would you like that?"

Maria put on her hat without a word, but Miranda stood and addressed her father sternly. She had suffered many doubts about this day. "*Why* didn't you send word yesterday? I could have been looking forward all this time."

"We didn't know," said father, in his easiest paternal manner, "that you were going to deserve it. Remember Saturday before last?"

Miranda hung her head and put on her hat, with the round elastic under the chin. She remembered too well. She had, in midweek, given way to despair over her arithmetic and had fallen flat on her face on the classroom floor, refusing to rise until she was carried out. The rest of the week had been a series of novel deprivations, and Saturday a day of mourning; secret mourning, for if one mourned too noisily, it simply meant another bad mark against deportment.

"Never mind," said father, as if it were the smallest possible matter, "today you're going. Come along now. We've barely time."

These expeditions were all joy, every time, from the moment they stepped into a closed one-horse cab, a treat in itself with its dark, thick upholstery, soaked with strange perfumes and tobacco smoke, until the thrilling moment when they walked into a restaurant under big lights and were given dinner with things to eat they never had at home, much less at the convent. They felt worldly and grown up, each with her glass of water colored pink with claret.

The great crowd was always exciting as if they had never seen it before, with the beautiful, incredibly dressed ladies, all plumes and flowers and paint, and the elegant gentlemen with yellow gloves. The bands played in turn with thundering drums and brasses, and now and then a wild beautiful horse would career around the track with a tiny, monkey-shaped boy on his back, limbering up for his race.

Miranda had a secret personal interest in all this which she knew better than to confide to anyone, even Maria. Least of all to Maria. In ten minutes the whole family would have known. She had lately decided to be a jockey when she grew up. Her father had said one day that she was going to be a little thing all her life, she would never be tall; and this meant, of course, that she would never be a beauty like Aunt Amy, or Cousin Isabel. Her hope of being a beauty died hard, until the notion of being a jockey came suddenly and filled all her thoughts. Quietly, blissfully, at night before she slept, and too often in the daytime when she should have been studying, she planned her career as jockey. It was dim in detail, but brilliant at the right distance. It seemed too silly to be worried about arithmetic at all, when what she needed for her future was to ride better—much better. "You ought to be ashamed of yourself," said father, after watching her gallop full tilt down the lane at the farm, on Trixie, the mustang mare. "I can see the sun, moon and stars between you and the saddle every jump." Spanish style meant that one sat close to the saddle, and did all kinds of things with the knees and reins. Jockeys bounced lightly, their knees almost level with the horse's back, rising and falling like a rubber ball. Miranda felt she could do that easily. Yes, she would be a jockey, like Tod Sloan, winning every other race at least. Meantime, while she was training, she would keep it a secret, and one day she would ride out, bouncing lightly, with the other jockeys, and win a great race, and surprise everybody, her family most of all.

On that particular Saturday, her idol, the great Tod Sloan, was riding, and he won two races. Miranda longed to bet her dollar on Tod Sloan, but father said, "Not now, honey. Today you must bet on Uncle Gabriel's horse. Save your dollar for the fourth race, and put it on Miss Lucy. You've got a hundred to one shot. Think if she wins."

Miranda knew well enough that a hundred to one shot was no bet at all. She sulked, the crumpled dollar in her hand grew damp and warm. She could have won three dollars already on Tod Sloan. Maria said virtuously, "It wouldn't be nice not to bet on Uncle Gabriel. That way, we keep the money in the family." Miranda put out her under lip at her sister. Maria was too prissy for words. She wrinkled her nose back at Miranda.

They had just turned their dollar over to the bookmaker for the fourth race when a vast bulging man with a red face and immense tan ragged mustaches fading into gray hailed them from a lower level of the grandstand, over the heads of the crowd, "Hey, there, Harry?" Father said, "Bless my soul, there's Gabriel." He motioned to the man, who came pushing his way heavily up the shallow steps. Maria and Miranda stared, first at him, then at each other. "Can that be our Uncle Gabriel?" their eyes asked. "Is that Aunt Amy's handsome romantic beau? Is that the man who wrote the poem about our Aunt Amy?" Oh, what did grown-up people *mean* when they talked, anyway?

He was a shabby fat man with bloodshot blue eyes, sad beaten eyes, and a big melancholy laugh, like a groan. He towered over them shouting to their father, "Well, for God's sake, Harry, it's been a coon's age. You ought to come out and look 'em over. You look just like yourself, Harry, how are you?"

The band struck up "Over the River" and Uncle Gabriel shouted louder. "Come on, let's get out of this. What are you doing up here with the pikers?"[12]

"Can't," shouted Father. "Brought my little girls. Here they are."

Uncle Gabriel's bleared eyes beamed blindly upon them. "Fine looking set, Harry," he bellowed, "pretty as pictures, how old are they?"

"Ten and fourteen now," said Father; "awkward ages. Nest of vipers," he boasted, "perfect batch of serpent's teeth. Can't do a thing with 'em." He fluffed up Miranda's hair, pretending to tousle it.

"Pretty as pictures," bawled Uncle Gabriel, "but rolled into one they don't come up to Amy, do they?"

"No, they don't," admitted their father at the top of his voice, "but they're only half-baked." *Over the river, over the river,* moaned the band, *my sweetheart's waiting for me.*

"I've got to get back now," yelled Uncle Gabriel. The little girls felt quite deaf and confused. "Got the God-damnedest jockey in the world, Harry, just my luck. Ought to tie him on. Fell off Fiddler yesterday, just plain fell off on his tail— Remember Amy's mare, Miss Lucy? Well, this is her namesake, Miss Lucy IV. None of 'em ever came up to the first one, though. Stay right where you are, I'll be back."

Maria spoke up boldly. "Uncle Gabriel, tell Miss Lucy we're betting on her." Uncle Gabriel bent down and it looked as if there were tears in his swollen eyes. "God bless your sweet heart," he bellowed, "I'll tell her." He plunged down through the crowd again, his fat back bowed slightly in his loose clothes, his thick neck rolling over his collar.

Miranda and Maria, disheartened by the odds, by their first sight of their romantic Uncle Gabriel, whose language was so coarse, sat listlessly without watching, their chances missed, their dollars gone, their hearts sore. They didn't even move until their father leaned over and hauled them up. "Watch your horse," he said, in a quick warning voice, "watch Miss Lucy come home."

They stood up, scrambled to their feet on the bench, every vein in them suddenly beating so violently they could hardly focus their eyes, and saw a thin little mahogany-colored streak flash by the judges' stand, only a neck ahead, but their Miss Lucy, oh, their darling, their lovely—oh, Miss Lucy, their Uncle Gabriel's Miss Lucy, had won, had won. They leaped up and down screaming and clapping their hands, their hats falling back on their shoulders, their hair flying wild. *Whoa, you heifer,* squalled the band with snorting brasses, and the crowd broke into a long roar like the falling of the walls of Jericho.

The little girls sat down, feeling quite dizzy, while their father tried to pull their hats straight, and taking out his handkerchief held it to Miranda's face, saying very gently, "Here, blow your nose," and he dried her eyes while he was about it. He stood up then and shook them out of their daze. He was smiling with deep laughing wrinkles

---

[12] Misers or persons unwilling to take risks; hence, small bettors.

around his eyes, and spoke to them as if they were grown young ladies he was squiring around.

"Let's go out and pay our respects to Miss Lucy," he said. "She's the star of the day."

The horses were coming in, looking as if their hides had been drenched and rubbed with soap, their ribs heaving, their nostrils flaring and closing. The jockeys sat bowed and relaxed, their faces calm, moving a little at the waist with the movement of their horses. Miranda noted this for future use; that was the way you came in from a race, easy and quiet, whether you had won or lost. Miss Lucy came last, and a little handful of winners applauded her and cheered the jockey. He smiled and lifted his whip, his eyes and shriveled brown face perfectly serene. Miss Lucy was bleeding at the nose, two thick red rivulets were stiffening her tender mouth and chin, the round velvet chin that Miranda thought the nicest kind of chin in the world. Her eyes were wild and her knees were trembling, and she snored when she drew her breath.

Miranda stood staring. That was winning, too. Her heart clinched tight; that was winning, for Miss Lucy. So instantly and completely did her heart reject that victory, she did not know when it happened, but she hated it, and was ashamed that she had screamed and shed tears for joy when Miss Lucy, with her bloodied nose and bursting heart had gone past the judges' stand a neck ahead. She felt empty and sick and held to her father's hand so hard that he shook her off a little impatiently and said, "What is the matter with you? Don't be so fidgety."

Uncle Gabriel was standing there waiting, and he was completely drunk. He watched the mare go in, then leaned against the fence with its white-washed posts and sobbed openly. "She's got the nosebleed, Harry," he said. "Had it since yesterday. We thought we had her all fixed up. But she did it, all right. She's got a heart like a lion. I'm going to breed her, Harry. Her heart's worth a million dollars, by itself, God bless her." Tears ran over his brick-colored face and into his straggling mustaches. "If anything happens to her now I'll blow my brains out. She's my last hope. She saved my life. I've had a run," he said, groaning into a large handkerchief and mopping his face all over, "I've had a run of luck that would break a brass billy goat. God, Harry, let's go somewhere and have a drink."

"I must get the children back to school first, Gabriel," said their father, taking each by a hand.

"No, no, don't go yet," said Uncle Gabriel desperately. "Wait here a minute, I want to see the vet and take a look at Miss Lucy, and I'll be right back. Don't go, Harry, for God's sake. I want to talk to you a few minutes."

Maria and Miranda, watching Uncle Gabriel's lumbering, unsteady back, were thinking that this was the first time they had ever seen a man that they knew to be drunk. They had seen pictures and read descriptions, and had heard descriptions, so they recognized the symptoms at once. Miranda felt it was an important moment in a great many ways.

"Uncle Gabriel's a drunkard, isn't he?" she asked her father, rather proudly.

"Hush, don't say such things," said father, with a heavy frown, "or I'll never bring you here again." He looked worried and unhappy, and, above all, undecided. The little girls stood stiff with resentment against such obvious injustice. They loosed their hands from his and moved away coldly, standing together in silence. Their father did not notice, watching the place where Uncle Gabriel had disappeared. In a few minutes he came back, still wiping his face, as if there were cobwebs on it, carrying his big black hat. He waved at them from a short distance, calling out in a cheerful way, "She's going to be all right, Harry. It's stopped now. Lord, this will be good news for Miss Honey. Come on, Harry, let's all go home and tell Miss Honey. She deserves some good news."

Father said, "I'd better take the children back to school first, then we'll go."

"No, no," said Uncle Gabriel, fondly. "I want her to see the girls. She'll be tickled pink to see them, Harry. Bring 'em along."

"Is it another race horse we're going to see?" whispered Miranda in her sister's ear.

"Don't be silly," said Maria. "It's Uncle Gabriel's second wife."

"Let's find a cab, Harry," said Uncle Gabriel, "and take your little girls out to cheer up Miss Honey. Both of 'em rolled into one look a lot like Amy, I swear they do. I want Miss Honey to see them. She's always liked our family, Harry, though of course she's not what you'd call an expansive kind of woman."

Maria and Miranda sat facing the driver, and Uncle Gabriel squeezed himself in facing them beside their father. The air became at once bitter and sour with his breathing. He looked sad and poor. His necktie was on crooked and his shirt was rumpled. Father said, "You're going to see Uncle Gabriel's second wife, children," exactly as if they had not heard everything; and to Gabriel, "How *is* your wife nowadays? It must be twenty years since I saw her last."

"She's pretty gloomy, and that's a fact," said Uncle Gabriel. "She's been pretty gloomy for years now, and nothing seems to shake her out of it. She never did care for horses, Harry, if you remember; she hasn't been near the track three times since we were married. When I think how Amy wouldn't have missed a race for anything . . . She's very different from Amy, Harry, a very different kind of woman. As fine a woman as ever lived in her own way, but she hates change and moving around, and she just lives in the boy."

"Where is Gabe now?" asked father.

"Finishing college," said Uncle Gabriel; "a smart boy, but awfully like his mother. Awfully like," he said, in a melancholy way. "She hates being away from him. Just wants to sit down in the same town and wait for him to get through with his education. Well, I'm sorry it can't be done if that's what she wants, but God Almighty —And this last run of luck has about got her down. I hope you'll be able to cheer her up a little, Harry, she needs it."

The little girls sat watching the streets grow duller and dingier and narrower, and at last the shabbier and shabbier white people gave way to dressed-up Negroes, and then to shabby Negroes, and after a long way the cab stopped before a desolate-looking little hotel in Elysian Fields. Their father helped Maria and Miranda out, told the cabman to wait, and they followed Uncle Gabriel through a dirty damp-smelling patio, down a long gas-lighted hall full of a terrible smell, Miranda couldn't decide what it was made of but it had a bitter taste even, and up a long staircase with a ragged carpet. Uncle Gabriel pushed open a door without warning, saying, "Come in, here we are."

A tall pale-faced woman with faded straw-colored hair and pink-rimmed eyelids rose suddenly from a squeaking rocking chair. She wore a stiff blue-and-white-striped shirtwaist and a stiff black skirt of some hard shiny material. Her large knuckled hands rose to her round, neat pompadour at sight of her visitors.

"Honey," said Uncle Gabriel, with large false heartiness, "you'll never guess who's come to see you." He gave her a clumsy hug. Her face did not change and her eyes rested steadily on the three strangers. "Amy's brother Harry, Honey, you remember, don't you?"

"Of course," said Miss Honey, putting out her hand straight as a paddle, "of course I remember you, Harry." She did not smile.

"And Amy's two little nieces," went on Uncle Gabriel, bringing them forward. They put out their hands limply, and Miss Honey gave each one a slight flip and dropped it. "And we've got good news for you," went on Uncle Gabriel, trying to bolster up the painful situation. "Miss Lucy stepped out and showed 'em today, Honey. We're rich again, old girl, cheer up."

Miss Honey turned her long, despairing face towards her visitors. "Sit down," she said with a heavy sigh, seating herself and motioning towards various rickety chairs. There was a big lumpy bed, with a grayish-white counterpane on it, a marble-topped washstand, grayish coarse lace curtains on strings at the two small windows, a small closed fireplace with a hole in it for a stovepipe, and two trunks, standing at odds as if somebody were just moving in, or just moving out. Everything was dingy and soiled and neat and bare; not a pin out of place.

"We'll move to the St. Charles tomorrow," said Uncle Gabriel, as much to Harry as to his wife. "Get your best dresses together, Honey, the long dry spell is over."

Miss Honey's nostrils pinched together and she rocked slightly, with her arms folded. "I've lived in the St. Charles before, and I've lived here before," she said, in a tight deliberate voice, "and this time I'll just stay where I am, thank you. I prefer it to moving back here in three months. I'm settled now, I feel at home here," she told him, glancing at Harry, her pale eyes kindling with blue fire, a stiff white line around her mouth.

The little girls sat trying not to stare, miserably ill at ease. Their grandmother had pronounced Harry's children to be the most unteachable she had ever seen in her long experience with the young; but they had learned by indirection one thing well—nice people did not carry on quarrels before outsiders. Family quarrels were sacred, to be waged privately in fierce hissing whispers, low choked mutters and growls. If they did yell and stamp, it must be behind closed doors and windows. Uncle Gabriel's second wife was hopping mad and she looked ready to fly out at Uncle Gabriel any second, with him sitting there like a hound when someone shakes a whip at him.

"She loathes and despises everybody in this room," thought Miranda, coolly, "and she's afraid we won't know it. She needn't worry, we knew it when we came in." With all her heart she wanted to go, but her father, though his face was a study, made no move. He seemed to be trying to think of something pleasant to say. Maria, feeling guilty, though she couldn't think why, was calculating rapidly, "Why, she's only Uncle Gabriel's second wife, and Uncle Gabriel was only married before to Aunt Amy, why, she's no kin at all, and I'm glad of it." Sitting back easily, she let her hands fall open in her lap; they would be going in a few minutes, undoubtedly, and they need never come back.

Then father said, "We mustn't be keeping you, we just dropped in for a few minutes. We wanted to see how you are."

Miss Honey said nothing, but she made a little gesture with her hands, from the wrist, as if to say, "Well, you see how I am, and now what next?"

"I must take these young ones back to school," said father, and Uncle Gabriel said stupidly, "Look, Honey, don't you think they resemble Amy a little? Especially around the eyes, especially Maria, don't you think, Harry?"

Their father glanced at them in turn. "I really couldn't say," he decided, and the little girls saw he was more monstrously embarrassed than ever. He turned to Miss Honey, "I hadn't seen Gabriel for so many years," he said, "we thought of getting out for a talk about old times together. You know how it is."

"Yes, I know," said Miss Honey, rocking a little, and all that she knew gleamed forth in a pallid, unquenchable hatred and bitterness that seemed enough to bring her long body straight up out of the chair in a fury, "I know," and she sat staring at the floor. Her mouth shook and straightened. There was a terrible silence, which was broken when the little girls saw their father rise. They got up, too, and it was all they could do to keep from making a dash for the door.

"I must get the young ones back," said their father. "They've had enough excitement for one day. They each won a hundred dollars on Miss Lucy. It was a good race," he said, in complete wretchedness, as if he simply could not extricate himself from the situation. "Wasn't it, Gabriel?"

"It was a grand race," said Gabriel, brokenly, "a grand race."

Miss Honey stood up and moved a step towards the door. "Do you take them to the races, actually?" she asked, and her lids flickered towards them as if they were loathsome insects, Maria felt.

"If I feel they deserve a little treat, yes," said their father, in an easy tone but with wrinkled brow.

"I had rather, much rather," said Miss Honey clearly, "see my son dead at my feet than hanging around a race track."

The next few moments were rather a blank, but at last they were out of it, going down the stairs, across the patio, with Uncle Gabriel seeing them back into the cab. His face was sagging, the features had fallen as if the flesh had slipped from the bones, and his eyelids were puffed and blue. "Good-by, Harry," he said soberly. "How long you expect to be here?"

"Starting back tomorrow," said Harry. "Just dropped in on a little business and to see how the girls were getting along."

"Well," said Uncle Gabriel, "I may be dropping into your part of the country one of these days. Good-by, children," he said, taking their hands one after the other in his big warm paws. "They're nice children, Harry. I'm glad you won on Miss Lucy," he said to the little girls, tenderly. "Don't spend your money foolishly, now. Well, so long, Harry." As the cab jolted away he stood there fat and sagging, holding up his arm and wagging his hand at them.

"Goodness," said Maria, in her most grown-up manner, taking her hat off and hanging it over her knee, "I'm glad that's over."

"What I want to know is," said Miranda, "*is* Uncle Gabriel a real drunkard?"

"Oh, hush," said their father, sharply, "I've got the heartburn."

There was a respectful pause, as before a public monument. When their father had the heartburn it was time to lay low. The cab rumbled on, back to clean gay streets, with the lights coming on in the early February darkness, past shimmering shop windows, smooth pavements, on and on, past beautiful old houses set in deep gardens, on, on back to the dark walls with the heavy-topped trees hanging over them. Miranda sat thinking so hard she forgot and spoke out in her thoughtless way: "I've decided I'm not going to be a jockey, after all." She could as usual have bitten her tongue, but as usual it was too late.

Father cheered up and twinkled at her knowingly, as if that didn't surprise him in the least. "Well, well," said he, "so you aren't going to be a jockey! That's very sensible of you. I think she ought to be a lion-tamer, don't you, Maria? That's a nice, womanly profession."

Miranda, seeing Maria from the height of her fourteen years suddenly joining with their father to laugh at her, made an instant decision and laughed with them at herself. That was better. Everybody laughed and it was such a relief.

"Where's my hundred dollars?" asked Maria, anxiously.

"It's going in the bank," said their father, "and yours too," he told Miranda. "That is your nest-egg."

"Just so they don't buy my stockings with it," said Miranda, who had long resented the use of her Christmas money by their grandmother. "I've got enough stockings to last me a year."

"I'd like to buy a racehorse," said Maria, "but I know it's not enough." The limitations of wealth oppressed her. "*What* could you buy with a hundred dollars?" she asked fretfully.

"Nothing, nothing at all," said their father, "a hundred dollars is just something you put in the bank."

Maria and Miranda lost interest. They had won a hundred dollars on a horse race once. It was already in the far past. They began to chatter about something else.

The lay sister opened the door on a long cord, from behind the grille; Maria and Miranda walked in silently to their familiar world of shining bare floors and insipid wholesome food and cold-water washing and regular prayers; their world of poverty, chastity and obedience, of early to bed and early to rise, of sharp little rules and tittle-tattle. Resignation was in their childish faces as they held them up to be kissed.

"Be good girls," said their father, in the strange serious, rather helpless way he always had when he told them good-by. "Write to your daddy, now, nice long letters," he said, holding their arms firmly for a moment before letting go for good. Then he disappeared, and the sister swung the door closed after him.

Maria and Miranda went upstairs to the dormitory to wash their faces and hands and slick down their hair again before supper.

Miranda was hungry. "We didn't have a thing to eat, after all," she grumbled. "Not even a chocolate nut bar. I think that's mean. We didn't even get a quarter to spend," she said.

"Not a living bite," said Maria. "Not a nickel." She poured out cold water into the bowl and rolled up her sleeves.

Another girl about her own age came in and went to a washbowl near another bed. "Where have you been?" she asked. "Did you have a good time?"

"We went to the races, with our father," said Maria, soaping her hands.

"Our uncle's horse won," said Miranda.

"My goodness," said the other girl, vaguely, "that must have been grand."

Maria looked at Miranda, who was rolling up her own sleeves. She tried to feel martyred, but it wouldn't go. "Immured for another week," she said, her eyes sparkling over the edge of her towel.

Part III: 1912

Miranda followed the porter down the stuffy aisle of the sleeping-car, where the berths were nearly all made down and the dusty green curtains buttoned, to a seat at the further end. "Now yo' berth's ready any time, Miss," said the porter.

"But I want to sit up a while," said Miranda. A very thin old lady raised choleric black eyes and fixed upon her a regard of unmixed disapproval. She had two immense front teeth and a receding chin, but she did not lack character. She had piled her luggage around her like a barricade, and she glared at the porter when he picked some of it up to make room for his new passenger. Miranda sat, saying mechanically, "May I?"

"You may, indeed," said the old lady, for she seemed old in spite of a certain brisk, rustling energy. Her taffeta petticoats creaked like hinges every time she stirred. With ferocious sarcasm, after a half second's pause, she added, "You may be so good as to get off my hat!"

Miranda rose instantly in horror, and handed to the old lady a wilted contrivance of black horsehair braid and shattered white poppies. "I'm dreadfully sorry," she stammered, for she had been brought up to treat ferocious old ladies respectfully, and this one seemed capable of spanking her, then and there. "I didn't dream it was your hat."

"And whose hat did you dream it might be?" inquired the old lady, baring her teeth and twirling the hat on a forefinger to restore it.

"I didn't think it was a hat at all," said Miranda with a touch of hysteria.

"Oh, you didn't think it was a hat? Where on earth are your eyes, child?" and she proved the nature and function of the object by placing it on her head at a somewhat tipsy angle, though still it did not much resemble a hat. "Now can you see what it is?"

"Yes, oh, yes," said Miranda, with a meekness she hoped was disarming. She ventured to sit again after a careful inspection of the narrow space she was to occupy.

"Well, well," said the old lady, "let's have the porter remove some of these encumbrances," and she stabbed the bell with a lean sharp forefinger. There followed a flurry of rearrangements, during which they both stood in the aisle, the old lady giving a series of impossible directions to the Negro which he bore philosophically while he disposed of the luggage exactly as he had meant to do. Seated again, the old lady asked in a kindly, authoritative tone, "And what might your name be, child?"

At Miranda's answer, she blinked somewhat, unfolded her spectacles, straddled them across her high nose competently, and took a good long look at the face beside her.

"If I'd had my spectacles on," she said, in an astonishingly changed voice, "I might have known. I'm Cousin Eva Parrington," she said, "Cousin Molly Parrington's daughter, remember? I knew you when you were a little girl. You were a lively little girl," she added as if to console her, "and very opinionated. The last thing I heard about you, you were planning to be a tight-rope walker. You were going to play the violin and walk the tight rope at the same time."

"I must have seen it at the vaudeville show," said Miranda. "I couldn't have invented it. Now I'd like to be an air pilot!"

"I used to go to dances with your father," said Cousin Eva, busy with her own thoughts, "and to big holiday parties at your grandmother's house, long before you were born. Oh, indeed, yes, a long time before."

Miranda remembered several things at once. Aunt Amy had threatened to be an old maid like Eva. Oh, Eva, the trouble with her is she has no chin. Eva has given up, and is teaching Latin in a Female Seminary. Eva's gone out for votes for women, God help her. The nice thing about an ugly daughter is, she's not apt to make me a grandmother. . . . "They didn't do you much good, those parties, dear Cousin Eva," thought Miranda.

"They didn't do me much good, those parties," said Cousin Eva aloud as if she were a mind-reader, and Miranda's head swam for a moment with fear that she had herself spoken aloud. "Or at least, they didn't serve their purpose, for I never got married; but I enjoyed them, just the same. I had a good time at those parties, even if I wasn't a belle. And so you are Harry's child, and here I was quarreling with you. You do remember me, don't you?"

"Yes," said Miranda, and thinking that even if Cousin Eva had been really an old maid ten years before, still she couldn't be much past fifty now, and she looked so withered and tired, so famished and sunken in the cheeks, so *old,* somehow. Across the abyss separating Cousin Eva from her own youth, Miranda looked with painful premonition. "Oh, must I ever be like that?" She said aloud, "Yes, you used to read Latin to me, and tell me not to bother about the sense, to get the sound in my mind, and it would come easier later."

"Ah, so I did," said Cousin Eva, delighted. "So I did. You don't happen to remember that I once had a beautiful sapphire velvet dress with a train on it?"

"No, I don't remember that dress," said Miranda.

"It was an old dress of my mother's made over and cut down to fit," said Eva, "and it wasn't in the least becoming to me, but it was the only really good dress I ever had, and I remember it as if it were yesterday. Blue was never my color." She sighed with a humorous bitterness. The humor seemed momentary, but the bitterness was a constant state of mind.

Miranda, trying to offer the sympathy of fellow suffering, said, "I know. I've had Maria's dresses made over for me, and they were never right. It was dreadful."

"Well," said Cousin Eva, in the tone of one who did not wish to share her unique disappointments. "How is your father? I always liked him. He was one of the finest-looking young men I ever saw. Vain, too, like all his family. He wouldn't ride any but the best horses he could buy, and I used to say he made them prance and then watched his own shadow. I used to tell this on him at dinner parties, and he hated me for it. I feel pretty certain he hated me." An overtone of complacency in Cousin Eva's voice explained better than words that she had her own method of commanding attention and arousing emotion. "How *is* your father, I asked you, my dear?"

"I haven't seen him for nearly a year," answered Miranda, quickly, before Cousin Eva could get ahead again. "I'm going home now to Uncle Gabriel's funeral; you know, Uncle Gabriel died in Lexington and they have brought him back to be buried beside Aunt Amy."

"So that's how we meet," said Cousin Eva. "Yes, Gabriel drank himself to death at last. I'm going to the funeral, too. I haven't been home since I went to Mother's funeral, it must be, let's see, yes, it will be nine years next July. I'm going to Gabriel's funeral, though. I wouldn't miss that. Poor fellow, what a life he had. Pretty soon, they'll all be gone."

Miranda said, "We're left, Cousin Eva," meaning those of her own generation, the young, and Cousin Eva said, "Pshaw, you'll live forever, and you won't bother to come to our funerals." She didn't seem to think this was a misfortune, but flung the remark from her like a woman accustomed to saying what she thought.

Miranda sat thinking, "Still, I suppose it would be pleasant if I could say something to make her believe that she and all of them would be lamented, but—but—" With a smile which she hoped would be her denial of Cousin Eva's cynicism about the younger generation, she said, "You were right about the Latin, Cousin Eva, your reading did help when I began with it. I still study," she said. "Latin, too."

"And why shouldn't you?" asked Cousin Eva, sharply, adding at once mildly, "I'm glad you are going to use your mind a little, child. Don't let yourself rust away. Your mind outwears all sorts of things you may set your heart upon; you can enjoy it when all other things are taken away." Miranda was chilled by her melancholy. Cousin Eva went on: "In our part of the country, in my time, we were so provincial—a woman didn't dare to think or act for herself. The whole world was a little that way," she said, "but we were the worst, I believe. I suppose you must know how I fought for votes for women when it almost made a pariah of me—I was turned out of my chair at the Seminary, but I'm glad I did it and I would do it again. You young things don't realize. You'll live in a better world because we worked for it."

Miranda knew something of Cousin Eva's career. She said sincerely, "I think it was brave of you, and I'm glad you did it, too. I loved your courage."

"It wasn't just showing off, mind you," said Cousin Eva, rejecting praise, fretfully. "Any fool can be brave. We were working for something we knew was right, and it turned out that we needed a lot of courage for it. That was all. I didn't expect to go to jail, but I went three times, and I'd go three times three more if it were necessary. We aren't voting yet," she said, "but we will be."

Miranda did not venture any answer, but she felt convinced that indeed women would be voting soon if nothing fatal happened to Cousin Eva. There was something in her manner which said such things could be left safely to her. Miranda was dimly fired for the cause herself; it seemed heroic and worth suffering for, but discouraging, too, to those who came after: Cousin Eva so plainly had swept the field clear of opportunity.

They were silent for a few minutes, while Cousin Eva rummaged in her handbag, bringing up odds and ends: peppermint drops, eye drops, a packet of needles, three handkerchiefs, a little bottle of violet perfume, a book of addresses, two buttons, one black, one white, and, finally, a packet of headache powders.

"Bring me a glass of water, will you, my dear?" she asked Miranda. She poured the headache powder on her tongue, swallowed the water, and put two peppermints in her mouth.

"So now they're going to bury Gabriel near Amy," she said after a while, as if her eased headache had started her on a new train of thought. "Miss Honey would like that, poor dear, if she could know. After listening to stories about Amy for twenty-five years, she must lie alone in her grave in Lexington while Gabriel sneaks off to Texas to make his bed with Amy again. It was a kind of life-long infidelity, Miranda, and now an eternal infidelity on top of that. He ought to be ashamed of himself."

"It was Aunt Amy he loved," said Miranda, wondering what Miss Honey could have been like before her long troubles with Uncle Gabriel. "First, anyway."

"Oh, that Amy," said Cousin Eva, her eyes glittering. "Your Aunt Amy was a devil and a mischief-maker, but I loved her dearly. I used to stand up for Amy when her reputation wasn't worth that." Her fingers snapped like castanets. "She used to say to me, in that gay soft way she had, 'Now, Eva, don't go talking votes for women when the lads ask you to dance. Don't recite Latin poems to 'em,' she would say, 'they got sick of that in school. Dance and say nothing, Eva,' she would say, her eyes perfectly devilish, 'and hold your chin up, Eva.' My chin was my weak point, you see. 'You'll never catch a husband if you don't look out,' she would say. Then she would laugh and fly away, and where did she fly to?" demanded Cousin Eva, her sharp eyes pinning Miranda down to the bitter facts of the case, "To scandal and to death, nowhere else."

"She was joking, Cousin Eva," said Miranda, innocently, "and everybody loved her."

"Not everybody, by a long shot," said Cousin Eva in triumph. "She had enemies. If she knew, she pretended she didn't. If she cared, she never said. You couldn't make her quarrel. She was sweet as a honeycomb to everybody. *Everybody,*" she added, "that was the trouble. She went through life like a spoiled darling, doing as she pleased and letting other people suffer for it, and pick up the pieces after her. I never believed for one moment," said Cousin Eva, putting her mouth close to Miranda's ear and breathing peppermint hotly into it, "that Amy was an impure woman. Never! But let me tell you, there were plenty who did believe it. There were plenty to pity poor Gabriel for being so completely blinded by her. A great many persons were not surprised when they heard that Gabriel was perfectly miserable all the time, on their honeymoon, in New Orleans. Jealousy. And why not? But I used to say to such persons that, no matter what the appearances were, I had faith in Amy's virtue. Wild, I said, indiscreet, I said, heartless, I said, but *virtuous,* I feel certain. But you could hardly blame anyone for being mystified. The way she rose up suddenly from death's door to marry Gabriel Breaux, after refusing him and treating him like a dog for years, looked odd, to say the least. To say the very least," she added, after a moment, "odd is a mild word for it. And there was something very mysterious about her death, only six weeks after marriage."

Miranda roused herself. She felt she knew this part of the story and could set Cousin Eva right about one thing. "She died of a hemorrhage from the lungs," said Miranda. "She had been ill for five years, don't you remember?"

Cousin Eva was ready for that. "Ha, that was the story, indeed. The official account, you might say. Oh, yes, I heard that often enough. But did you ever hear about that fellow Raymond somebody-or-other from Calcasieu Parish, almost a stranger, who persuaded Amy to elope with him from a dance one night, and she just ran out into the darkness without even stopping for her cloak, and your poor dear nice father Harry—you weren't even thought of then—had to run him down to earth and shoot him?"

Miranda leaned back from the advancing flood of speech. "Cousin Eva, my father shot *at* him, don't you remember? He didn't hit him. . . ."

"Well, that's a pity."

". . . and they had only gone out for a breath of air between dances. It was Uncle Gabriel's jealousy. And my father shot at the man because he thought that was better than letting Uncle Gabriel fight a duel about Aunt Amy. There was *nothing* in the whole affair except Uncle Gabriel's jealousy."

"You poor baby," said Cousin Eva, and pity gave a light like daggers to her eyes, "you dear innocent, you—do you believe that? How old are you, anyway?"

"Just past eighteen," said Miranda.

"If you don't understand what I tell you," said Cousin Eva portentously, "you will later. Knowledge can't hurt you. You mustn't live in a romantic haze about life. You'll understand when you're married, at any rate."

"I'm married now, Cousin Eva," said Miranda, feeling for almost the first time that it might be an advantage, "nearly a year. I eloped from school." It seemed very unreal even as she said it, and seemed to have nothing at all to do with the future; still, it was important, it must be declared, it was a situation in life which people seemed to be most exacting about, and the only feeling she could rouse in herself about it was an immense weariness as if it were an illness that she might one day hope to recover from.

"Shameful, shameful," cried Cousin Eva, genuinely repelled. "If you had been my child I should have brought you home and spanked you."

Miranda laughed out. Cousin Eva seemed to believe things could be arranged like that. She was so solemn and fierce, so comic and baffled.

"And you must know I should have just gone straight out again, through the nearest window," she taunted her. "If I went the first time, why not the second?"

"Yes, I suppose so," said Cousin Eva. "I hope you married rich."

"Not so very," said Miranda. "Enough." As if anyone could have stopped to think of such a thing!

Cousin Eva adjusted her spectacles and sized up Miranda's dress, her luggage, examined her engagement ring and wedding ring, with her nostrils fairly quivering as if she might smell out wealth on her.

"Well, that's better than nothing," said Cousin Eva. "I thank God every day of my life that I have a small income. It's a Rock of Ages.[13] What would have become of me if I hadn't a cent of my own? Well, you'll be able now to do something for your family."

Miranda remembered what she had always heard about the Parringtons. They were money-hungry, they loved money and nothing else, and when they had got some they kept it. Blood was thinner than water between the Parringtons where money was concerned.

"We're pretty poor," said Miranda, stubbornly allying herself with her father's family instead of her husband's, "but a rich marriage is no way out," she said, with the snobbishness of poverty. She was thinking, "You don't know my branch of the family, dear Cousin Eva, if you think it is."

"Your branch of the family," said Cousin Eva, with that terrifying habit she had of lifting phrases out of one's mind, "has no more practical sense than so many children. Everything for love," she said, with a face of positive nausea, "that was it. Gabriel would have been rich if his grandfather had not disinherited him, but would Amy be sensible and marry him and make him settle down so the old man would have been pleased with him? No. And what could Gabriel do without money? I wish

[13] An allusion to the epithet for the Almighty in the hymn "Rock of Ages, Cleft for Me."

you could have seen the life he led Miss Honey, one day buying her Paris gowns and the next day pawning her earrings. It just depended on how the horses ran, and they ran worse and worse, and Gabriel drank more and more."

Miranda did not say, "I saw a little of it." She was trying to imagine Miss Honey in a Paris gown. She said, "But Uncle Gabriel was so mad about Aunt Amy, there was no question of her not marrying him at last, money or no money."

Cousin Eva strained her lips tightly over her teeth, let them fly again and leaned over, gripping Miranda's arm. "What I ask myself, what I ask myself over and over again," she whispered, "is, what connection did this man Raymond from Calcasieu have with Amy's sudden marriage to Gabriel, and *what* did Amy do to make away with herself so soon afterward? For mark my words, child, Amy wasn't so ill as all that. She'd been flying around for years after the doctors said her lungs were weak. Amy did away with herself to escape some disgrace, some exposure that she faced."

The beady black eyes glinted; Cousin Eva's face was quite frightening, so near and so intent. Miranda wanted to say, "Stop. Let her rest. What harm did she ever do you?" but she was timid and unnerved, and deep in her was a horrid fascination with the terrors and the darkness Cousin Eva had conjured up. What was the end of this story?

"She was a bad, wild girl, but I was fond of her to the last," said Cousin Eva. "She got into trouble somehow, and she couldn't get out again, and I have every reason to believe she killed herself with the drug they gave her to keep her quiet after a hemorrhage. If she didn't, what happened, what happened?"

"I don't know," said Miranda. "How should I know? She was very beautiful," she said, as if this explained everything. "Everybody said she was very beautiful."

"Not everybody," said Cousin Eva, firmly, shaking her head. "I for one never thought so. They made entirely too much fuss over her. She was good-looking enough, but why did they think she was beautiful? I cannot understand it. She was too thin when she was young, and later I always thought she was too fat, and again in her last year she was altogether too thin. She always got herself up to be looked at, and so people looked, of course. She rode too hard, and she danced too freely, and she talked too much, and you'd have to be blind, deaf and dumb not to notice her. I don't mean she was loud or vulgar, she wasn't, but she was *too free,*" said Cousin Eva. She stopped for breath and put a peppermint in her mouth. Miranda could see Cousin Eva on the platform, making her speeches, stopping to take a peppermint. But why did she hate Aunt Amy so, when Aunt Amy was dead and she alive? Wasn't being alive enough?

"And her illness wasn't romantic either," said Cousin Eva, "though to hear them tell it she faded like a lily. Well, she coughed blood, if that's romantic. If they had made her take proper care of herself, if she had been nursed sensibly, she might have been alive today. But no, nothing of the kind. She lay wrapped in beautiful shawls on a sofa with flowers around her, eating as she liked or not eating, getting up after a hemorrhage and going out to ride or dance, sleeping with the windows closed; with crowds coming in and out laughing and talking at all hours, and Amy sitting up so her hair wouldn't get out of curl. And why wouldn't that sort of thing kill a well person in time? I have almost died twice in my life," said Cousin Eva, "and both times I was sent to a hospital where I belonged and left there until I came out. And I came out," she said, her voice deepening to a bugle note, "and I went to work again."

"Beauty goes, character stays," said the small voice of axiomatic morality in Miranda's ear. It was a dreary prospect; why was a strong character so deforming? Miranda felt she truly wanted to be strong, but how could she face it, seeing what it did to one?

"She had a lovely complexion," said Cousin Eva, "perfectly transparent with a flush on each cheekbone. But it was tuberculosis, and is disease beautiful? And she brought it on herself by drinking lemon and salt to stop her periods when she wanted to go to dances. There was a superstition among young girls about that. They fancied that young men could tell what ailed them by touching their hands, or even by looking at them. As if it mattered? But they were terribly self-conscious and they had immense respect for man's worldly wisdom in those days. My own notion is that a man couldn't—but anyway, the whole thing was stupid."

"I should have thought they'd have stayed at home if they couldn't manage better than that," said Miranda, feeling very knowledgeable and modern.

"They didn't dare. Those parties and dances were their market, a girl couldn't afford to miss out, there were always rivals waiting to cut the ground from under her. The rivalry—" said Cousin Eva, and her head lifted, she arched like a cavalry horse getting a whiff of the battlefield—"you can't imagine what the rivalry was like. The way those girls treated each other—nothing was too mean, nothing too false—"

Cousin Eva wrung her hands. "It was just sex," she said in despair; "their minds dwelt on nothing else. They didn't call it that, it was all smothered under pretty names, but that's all it was, sex." She looked out of the window into the darkness, her sunken cheek near Miranda flushed deeply. She turned back. "I took to the soap box and the platform when I was called upon," she said proudly, "and I went to jail when it was necessary, and my condition didn't make any difference. I was booed and jeered and shoved around just as if I had been in perfect health. But it was part of our philosophy not to let our physical handicaps make any difference to our work. You know what I mean," she said, as if until now it was all mystery. "Well, Amy carried herself with more spirit than the others, and she didn't seem to be making any sort of fight, but she was simply sex-ridden, like the rest. She behaved as if she hadn't a rival on earth, and she pretended not to know what marriage was about, but I know better. None of them had, and they didn't want to have, anything else to think about, and they didn't really know anything about that, so they simply festered inside—they festered—"

Miranda found herself deliberately watching a long procession of living corpses, festering women stepping gaily towards the charnel house, their corruption concealed under laces and flowers, their dead faces lifted smiling, and thought quite coldly, "Of course it was not like that. This is no more true than what I was told before, it's every bit as romantic," and she realized that she was tired of her intense Cousin Eva, she wanted to go to sleep, she wanted to be at home, she wished it were tomorrow and she could see her father and her sister, who were so alive and solid; who would mention her freckles and ask her if she wanted something to eat.

"My mother was not like that," she said, childishly. "My mother was a perfectly natural woman who liked to cook. I have seen some of her sewing," she said. "I have read her diary."

"Your mother was a saint," said Cousin Eva, automatically.

Miranda sat silent, outraged. "My mother was nothing of the sort," she wanted to fling in Cousin Eva's big front teeth. But Cousin Eva had been gathering bitterness until more speech came of it.

" 'Hold your chin up, Eva,' Amy used to tell me," she began, doubling up both her fists and shaking them a little. "All my life the whole family bedeviled me about my chin. My entire girlhood was spoiled by it. Can you imagine," she asked, with a ferocity that seemed much too deep for this one cause, "people who call themselves civilized spoiling life for a young girl because she had one unlucky feature? Of course, you understand perfectly it was all in the very best humor, everybody was very amusing about it, no harm meant—oh, no, no harm at all. That is the hellish thing about it. It is that I can't forgive," she cried out, and she twisted her hands together as if they were rags. "Ah, the family," she said, releasing her breath and sitting back quietly, "the whole hideous institution should be wiped from the face of the earth. It is the root of all human wrongs," she ended, and relaxed, and her face became calm. She was trembling. Miranda reached out and took Cousin Eva's hand and held it. The hand fluttered and lay still, and Cousin Eva said, "You've not the faintest idea what some of us went through, but I wanted you to hear the other side of the story. And I'm keeping you up when you need your beauty sleep," she said grimly, stirring herself with an immense rustle of petticoats.

Miranda pulled herself together, feeling limp, and stood up. Cousin Eva put out her hand again, and drew Miranda down to her. "Good night, you dear child," she said, "to think you're grown up." Miranda hesitated, then quite suddenly kissed her Cousin Eva on the cheek. The black eyes shown brightly through water for an instant, and Cousin Eva said with a warm note in her sharp clear orator's voice, "Tomorrow we'll be at home again. I'm looking forward to it, aren't you? Good night."

Miranda fell asleep while she was getting off her clothes. Instantly it was morning again. She was still trying to close her suitcase when the train pulled into the small station, and there on the platform she saw her father, looking tired and anxious, his hat pulled over his eyes. She rapped on the window to catch his attention, then ran out and threw herself upon him. He said, "Well, here's my big girl," as if she were still seven, but his hands on her arms held her off, the tone was forced. There was no welcome for her, and there had not been since she had run away. She could not persuade herself to remember how it would be; between one home-coming and the next her mind refused to accept its own knowledge. Her father looked over her head and said, without surprise, "Why, hello, Eva, I'm glad somebody sent you a telegram." Miranda, rebuffed again, let her arms fall away again, with the same painful dull jerk of the heart.

"No one in my family," said Eva, her face framed in the thin black veil she reserved, evidently, for family funerals, "ever sent me a telegram in my life. I had the news from young Keziah who had it from young Gabriel. I suppose Gabe is here?"

"Everybody seems to be here," said Father. "The house is getting full."

"I'll go to the hotel if you like," said Cousin Eva.

"Damnation, no," said Father. "I didn't mean that. You'll come with us where you belong."

Skid, the handy man, grabbed the suitcases and started down the rocky village street. "We've got the car," said Father. He took Miranda by the hand, then dropped it again, and reached for Cousin Eva's elbow.

"I'm perfectly able, thank you," said Cousin Eva, shying away.

"If you're so independent now," said Father, "God help us when you get that vote."

Cousin Eva pushed back her veil. She was smiling merrily. She liked Harry, she always had liked him, he could tease as much as he liked. She slipped her arm through his. "So it's all over with poor Gabriel, isn't it?"

"Oh, yes," said Father, "it's all over, all right. They're pegging out pretty regularly now. It will be our turn next, Eva?"

"I don't know, and I don't care," said Eva, recklessly. "It's good to be back now and then, Harry, even if it is only for funerals. I feel sinfully cheerful."

"Oh, Gabriel wouldn't mind, he'd like seeing you cheerful. Gabriel was the cheerfulest cuss I ever saw, when we were young. Life for Gabriel," said Father, "was just one perpetual picnic."

"Poor fellow," said Cousin Eva.

"Poor old Gabriel," said Father, heavily.

Miranda walked along beside her father, feeling homeless, but not sorry for it. He had not forgiven her, she knew that. When would he? She could not guess, but she felt it would come of itself, without words and without acknowledgment on either side, for by the time it arrived neither of them would need to remember what had caused their division, nor why it had seemed so important. Surely old people cannot hold their grudges forever because the young want to live, too, she thought, in her arrogance, her pride. I will make my own mistakes, not yours; I cannot depend upon you beyond a certain point, why depend at all? There was something more beyond, but this was a first step to take, and she took it, walking in silence beside her elders who were no longer Cousin Eva and Father, since they had forgotten her presence, but had become Eva and Harry, who knew each other well, who were comfortable with each other, being contemporaries on equal terms, who occupied by right their place in this world, at the time of life to which they had arrived by paths familiar to them both. They need not play their roles of daughter, of son, to aged persons who did not understand them; nor of father and elderly female cousin to young persons whom they did not understand. They were precisely themselves; their eyes cleared, their voices relaxed into perfect naturalness, they need not weigh their words or calculate the effect of their manner. "It is I who have no place," thought Miranda. "Where are my own people and my own time?" She resented, slowly and deeply and in profound silence, the presence of these aliens who lectured and admonished her, who loved her with bitterness and denied her the right to look at the world with her own eyes, who demanded that she accept their version of life and yet could not tell her the truth, not in the smallest thing. "I hate them both," her most inner and secret mind said plainly, *"I will be free of them, I shall not even remember them."*

She sat in the front seat with Skid, the Negro boy. "Come back with us, Miranda," said Cousin Eva, with the sharp little note of elderly command, "there is plenty of room."

"No, thank you," said Miranda, in a firm cold voice. "I'm quite comfortable. Don't disturb yourself."

Neither of them noticed her voice or her manner. They sat back and went on talking steadily in their friendly family voices, talking about their dead, their living, their affairs, their prospects, their common memories, interrupting each other, catching each other up on small points of dispute, laughing with a gaiety and freshness Miranda had not known they were capable of, going over old stories and finding new points of interest in them.

Miranda could not hear the stories above the noisy motor, but she felt she knew them well, or stories like them. She knew too many stories like them, she wanted something new of her own. The language was familiar to them, but not to her, not any more. The house, her father had said, was full. It would be full of cousins, many of them strangers. Would there be any young cousins there, to whom she could talk about things they both knew? She felt a vague distaste for seeing cousins. There were too many of them and her blood rebelled against the ties of blood. She was sick to death of cousins. She did not want any more ties with this house, she was going to leave it, and she was not going back to her husband's family either. She would have no more bonds that smothered her in love and hatred. She knew now why she had run away to marriage, and she knew that she was going to run away from marriage, and she was not going to stay in any place, with anyone, that threatened to forbid her making her own discoveries, that said "No" to her. She hoped no one had taken her old room, she would like to sleep there once more, she would say good-by there where she had loved sleeping once, sleeping and waking and waiting to be grown, to begin to live. Oh, what is life, she asked herself in desperate seriousness, in those childish unanswerable words, and what shall I do with it? It is something of my own, she thought in a fury of jealous possessiveness, what shall I make of it? She did not know that she asked herself this because all her earliest training had argued that life was a substance, a material to be used, it took shape and direction and meaning only as the possessor guided and worked it; living was a progress of continuous and varied acts of the will directed towards a definite end. She had been assured that there were good and evil ends, one must make a choice. But what was good, and what was evil? I hate love, she thought, as if this were the answer, I hate loving and being loved, I hate it. And her disturbed and seething mind received a shock of comfort from this sudden collapse of an old painful structure of distorted images and misconceptions. "You don't know anything about it," said Miranda to herself, with extraordinary clearness as if she were an elder admonishing some younger misguided creature. "You have to find out about it." But nothing in her prompted her to decide, "I will now do this, I will be that, I will go yonder, I will take a certain road to a certain end." There are questions to be asked first, she thought, but who will answer them? No one, or there will be too many answers, none of them right. What is the truth, she asked herself as intently as if the question had never been asked, the truth, even about the smallest, the least important of all the things I must find out? and where shall I begin to look for it? Her mind closed stubbornly against remembering, not the past but the legend of the past, other people's memory of the past, at which she had spent her life peering in wonder like a child at a magic-lantern show. Ah, but there is my own life to come yet, she thought, my own life now and beyond. I don't want any promises, I won't have false hopes, I won't be romantic about myself. I can't live in their world any longer, she told herself, listening to the voices back of her. Let them tell their stories to each other. Let them go on explaining how things happened. I don't care. At least I can know the truth about what happens to me, she assured herself silently, making a promise to herself, in her hopefulness, her ignorance.

1938

Jean Toomer
1894–1967

For a time, the poet and novelist Jean Toomer was regarded as the most talented writer of the "Harlem Renaissance," a literary movement of black writers who had congregated in New York City in the early 1920s and had transformed Harlem into the intellectual and cultural center of black America. The group included an impressive number of painters, photographers, and musicians, as well as such writers as Langston Hughes, Countee Cullen, Zora Neale Hurston, and Claude McKay. In its magazines and anthologies, the movement promoted the creative work of the "New Negro," of whom Jean Toomer was thought to be one of the outstanding examples in literature. He was so highly regarded not only because he wrote truthfully and sensitively about black life but because he did so, as one member of the movement put it, "without the surrender or compromise of the artist's vision."

Jean Toomer was born in Washington, D.C., in 1894. His father was Nathan Toomer, a black planter, and his mother was the daughter of P. B. S. Pinchback, a Reconstruction governor of Louisiana whose own racial background was apparently mixed. Toomer's early years were severely complicated by his father's desertion in 1895, when Toomer was only one year old; they were perhaps even more severely complicated by what Toomer later termed his "racial composition and position." From early on, his life took him back and forth between what he later described as the "white" world and the "black" in a land where life itself was viewed "as if it were divided into white and black." "In my body were many bloods, some dark blood, all blended . . . ," he wrote. "I was . . . either a new type of man or the very oldest." He once claimed seven blood strains ("French, Dutch, Welsh, Negro, German, Jewish, and Indian"). Yet at other times Toomer doubted "whether there is any colored blood in me or not." Both of his marriages were to white women—the first to a promising writer who was a descendant of the Puritan poet Anne Bradstreet.

Toomer lived for several years in New Rochelle, New York, then moved back to Washington, where he finished high school. He then enrolled at the University of Wisconsin but abandoned his studies there after a year and wandered about—all the while working at odd jobs, studying, and writing—to Chicago, New York, Massachusetts, Wisconsin again, and New Jersey. Returning to Washington, he began to write more concertedly. In 1921 he moved to Sparta, Georgia, near his father's original home, and took a job briefly as a teacher at the Georgia Normal and Industrial Institute. It was there that he conceived and began *Cane* (1923), the book that established him as an important literary figure.

During the early 1920s Toomer contributed regularly to such leading black journals as *The Crisis* and *Opportunity* and to such experimental magazines as *Broom, The Little Review,* and *The Double Dealer.* The experimental nature of his work, and particularly his interest in combining dramatic and narrative sketches, drew praise from a wide range of writers, including Sherwood Anderson, Allen Tate, and Hart Crane. Shortly after publishing *Cane,* Toomer became intrigued by the Russian spiritual teacher George Gurdjieff, who believed that through proper discipline and meditation an individual could achieve cosmic consciousness. Toomer traveled to France in the summer of 1926 to study at the Gurdjieff Institute and returned to Harlem prepared to set up classes in the philosophy of "Unitism." Looking back, Langston Hughes described this period in Toomer's life with a blend of humor and sorrow. People in Harlem, Hughes wrote in *The Big Sea* (1940), "had to work all day to make a living" and so turned out to be reluctant converts:

> Their advance toward cosmic consciousness was slow and their hope of achieving awareness distant indeed. . . . So Jean Toomer shortly left his Harlem group and went downtown to drop the seeds of Gurdjieff in less dark and poverty-stricken fields. . . . From downtown New York, Toomer carried Gurdjieff to Chicago's Gold Coast—and the Negroes lost one of the most talented of all their writers—the author of the beautiful book of prose and verse, *Cane*.

Though Toomer disappeared from the literary scene, he continued to write poetry, plays, essays, and fiction, much of it going unpublished. Works such as *Essentials* (1931) and *Portage Potential* (1932) reflect his mounting interests in different forms of mystical philosophy (he became deeply involved in Quaker pietism) and poetry, while the long poem *Blue Meridian* (1936) reflects his continuing effort artistically to resolve the problems generated by racial tensions in America. But Toomer's literary reputation still rests primarily on the book conceived during the four months he lived near his father's home in Georgia.

In *Cane*, Toomer draws heavily on the folk songs, the folktales, and the syncopated rhythms of the language of the black people he encountered in Georgia. By mixing poems with both dramatic and prose sketches, he not only created one of the distinctive literary experiments of the 1920s but also fashioned a work of lasting historical and artistic significance. Historically, *Cane* played a major role in the efforts of black writers to enlarge the cultural life of black people in America. Artistically, it celebrates the power of exotic and primitive impulses to triumph over the tyranny of culture. What holds these two different aspects of Toomer's achievement together is his celebration of a freedom that is physical and psychic as well as aesthetic.

Further Reading:

H. M. Gloster, *Negro Voices in American Fiction*, 1948.
A. Bontemps, "The Negro Renaissance: Jean Toomer and the Harlem Writers of the 1920's" in *Anger and Beyond: The Negro Writer in the*
United States, ed. H. Hill, 1966.
D. T. Turner, *In a Minor Chord: Three Afro-American Writers and Their Search for Identity*, 1971.
N. Y. McKay, *Jean Toomer, Artist*, 1984.

Text:
Cane, 1923.

from Cane

Blood-Burning Moon

1

Up from the skeleton stone walls, up from the rotting floor boards and the solid hand-hewn beams of oak of the pre-war cotton factory, dusk came. Up from the dusk the full moon came. Glowing like a fired pine-knot, it illumined the great door and soft showered the Negro shanties aligned along the single street of factory town. The full moon in the great door was an omen. Negro women improvised songs against its spell.

Louisa sang as she came over the crest of the hill from the white folks' kitchen. Her skin was the color of oak leaves on young trees in fall. Her breasts, firm and up-pointed like ripe acorns. And her singing had the low murmur of winds in fig trees. Bob Stone, younger son of the people she worked for, loved her. By the way the world reckons things, he had won her. By measure of that warm glow which came into her mind at thought of him, he had won her. Tom Burwell, whom the whole town called Big Boy, also loved her. But working in the fields all day, and far away from her, gave him no chance to show it. Though often enough of evenings he had tried to. Somehow, he never got along. Strong as he was with hands upon the ax or plow, he found it difficult to hold her. Or so he thought. But the fact was that he held her to factory town more firmly than he thought for. His black balanced, and pulled against, the white of Stone, when she thought of them. And her mind was vaguely upon them as she came over the crest of the hill, coming from the white folks' kitchen. As she sang softly at the evil face of the full moon.

A strange stir was in her. Indolently, she tried to fix upon Bob or Tom as the cause of it. To meet Bob in the canebrake, as she was going to do an hour or so later, was nothing new. And Tom's proposal which she felt on its way to her could be indefinitely put off. Separately, there was no unusual significance to either one. But for some reason, they jumbled when her eyes gazed vacantly at the rising moon. And from the jumble came the stir that was strangely within her. Her lips trembled. The slow rhythm of her song grew agitant and restless. Rusty black and tan spotted hounds, lying in the dark corners of porches or prowling around back yards, put their noses in the air and caught its tremor. They began plaintively to yelp and howl. Chickens woke up and cackled. Intermittently, all over the countryside dogs barked and roosters crowed as if heralding a weird dawn or some ungodly awakening. The women sang lustily. Their songs were cotton-wads to stop their ears. Louisa came down into factory town and sank wearily upon the step before her home. The moon was rising towards a thick cloud-bank which soon would hide it.

Red nigger moon. Sinner!
Blood-burning moon. Sinner!
Come out that fact'ry door.

2

Up from the deep dusk of a cleared spot on the edge of the forest a mellow glow arose and spread fan-wise into the low-hanging heavens. And all around the air was heavy with the scent of boiling cane. A large pile of cane-stalks lay like ribboned shadows upon the ground. A mule, harnessed to a pole, trudged lazily round and round the pivot of the grinder. Beneath a swaying oil lamp, a Negro alternately whipped out at the mule, and fed cane-stalks to the grinder. A fat boy waddled pails of fresh ground juice between the grinder and the boiling stove. Steam came from the copper boiling pan. The scent of cane came from the copper pan and drenched the forest and the hill that sloped to factory town, beneath its fragrance. It drenched the men in circle seated around the stove. Some of them chewed at the white pulp of stalks, but there was no need for them to, if all they wanted was to taste the cane. One tasted it in factory town. And from factory town one could see the soft haze thrown by the glowing stove upon the low-hanging heavens.

Old David Georgia stirred the thickening syrup with a long ladle, and ever so often drew it off. Old David Georgia tended his stove and told tales about the white folks, about moonshining and cotton picking, and about sweet nigger gals, to the men who sat there about his stove to listen to him. Tom Burwell chewed cane-stalk and laughed with the others till someone mentioned Louisa. Till some one said something about Louisa and Bob Stone, about the silk stockings she must have gotten from him. Blood ran up Tom's neck hotter than the glow that flooded from the stove. He sprang up. Glared at the men and said, "She's my gal." Will Manning laughed. Tom strode over to him. Yanked him up and knocked him to the ground. Several of Manning's friends got up to fight for him. Tom whipped out a long knife and would have cut them to shreds if they hadnt ducked into the woods. Tom had had enough. He nodded to Old David Georgia and swung down the path to factory town. Just then, the dogs started barking and the roosters began to crow. Tom felt funny. Away from the fight, away from the stove, chill got to him. He shivered. He shuddered when he saw the full moon rising towards the cloud-bank. He who didnt give a godam for the fears of old women. He forced his mind to fasten on Louisa. Bob Stone. Better not be. He turned into the street and saw Louisa sitting before her home. He went towards her, ambling, touched the brim of a marvelously shaped, spotted, felt hat, said he wanted to say something to her, and then found that he didnt know what he had to say, or if he did, that he couldnt say it. He shoved his big fists in his overalls, grinned, and started to move off.

"Youall want me, Tom?"

"Thats what us wants, sho, Louisa."

"Well, here I am—"

"An here I is, but that aint ahelpin none, all th same."

"You wanted to say something? . . ."

"I did that, sho. But words is like th spots on dice: no matter how y fumbles em, there's times when they jes wont come. I dunno why. Seems like th love I feels fo yo done stole m tongue. I got it now. Whee! Louisa, honey, I oughtnt tell y, I feel I oughtnt cause yo is young an goes t church an I has had other gals, but Louisa I sho do love y. Lil gal, Ise watched y from them first days when youall sat right here befo yo door befo th well an sang sometimes in a way that like t broke m heart. Ise carried y with me into th fields, day after day, an after that, an I sho can plow when yo is there, an I can pick cotton. Yassur! Come near beatin Barlo yesterday. I sho did. Yassur! An next year if ole Stone'll trust me, I'll have a farm. My own. My bales will buy yo what y gets from white folks now. Silk stockings an purple dresses—course I dont believe what some folks been whisperin as t how y gets them things now. White folks always did do for niggers what they likes. An they jes cant help alikin yo, Louisa. Bob Stone likes y. Course he does. But not th way folks is awhisperin. Does he, hon?"

"I dont know what you mean, Tom."

"Course y dont. Ise already cut two niggers. Had t hon, t tell em so. Niggers always tryin t make somethin out a nothin. An then besides, white folks aint up t them tricks so much nowadays. Godam better not be. Leastawise not with yo. Cause I wouldnt stand f it. Nassur."

"What would you do, Tom?"

"Cut him jes like I cut a nigger."

"No, Tom—"

"I said I would an there aint no mo to it. But that aint th talk f now. Sing, honey Louisa, an while I'm listenin t y I'll be makin love."

Tom took her hand in his. Against the tough thickness of his own, hers felt soft and small. His huge body slipped down to the step beside her. The full moon sank upward into the deep purple of the cloud-bank. An old woman brought a lighted lamp and hung it on the common well whose bulky shadow squatted in the middle of the road, opposite Tom and Louisa. The old woman lifted the well-lid, took hold the chain, and began drawing up the heavy bucket. As she did so, she sang. Figures shifted, restlesslike, between lamp and window in the front rooms of the shanties. Shadows of the figures fought each other on the gray dust of the road. Figures raised the windows and joined the old woman in song. Louisa and Tom, the whole street, singing:

> Red nigger moon. Sinner!
> Blood-burning moon. Sinner!
> Come out that fact'ry door.

3

Bob Stone sauntered from his veranda out into the gloom of fir trees and magnolias. The clear white of his skin paled, and the flush of his cheeks turned purple. As if to balance this outer change, his mind became consciously a white man's. He passed the house with its huge open hearth which, in the days of slavery, was the plantation cookery. He saw Louisa bent over that hearth. He went in as a master should and took her. Direct, honest, bold. None of this sneaking that he had to go through now. The contrast was repulsive to him. His family had lost ground. Hell no, his family still owned the niggers, practically. Damned if they did, or he wouldnt have to duck around so. What would they think if they knew? His mother? His sister? He shouldnt mention them, shouldnt think of them in this connection. There in the dusk he blushed at doing so. Fellows about town were all right, but how about his friends up North? He could see them incredible, repulsed. They didnt know. The thought first made him laugh. Then, with their eyes still upon him, he began to feel embarrassed. He felt the need of explaining things to them. Explain hell. They wouldnt understand, and moreover, who ever heard of a Southerner getting on his knees to any Yankee, or anyone. No sir. He was going to see Louisa to-night, and love her. She was lovely —in her way. Nigger way. What way was that? Damned if he knew. Must know. He'd known her long enough to know. Was there something about niggers that you couldnt know? Listening to them at church didnt tell you anything. Looking at them didnt tell you anything. Talking to them didnt tell you anything—unless it was gossip, unless they wanted to talk. Of course, about farming, and licker, and craps —but those werent nigger. Nigger was something more. How much more? Something to be afraid of, more? Hell no. Who ever heard of being afraid of a nigger? Tom Burwell. Cartwell had told him that Tom went with Louisa after she reached home. No sir. No nigger had ever been with his girl. He'd like to see one try. Some position for him to be in. Him, Bob Stone, of the old Stone family, in a scrap with a nigger over a nigger girl. In the good old days . . . Ha! Those were the days. His family had lost ground. Not so much, though. Enough for him to have to cut through old Lemon's canefield by way of the woods, that he might meet her. She was worth it. Beautiful nigger gal. Why nigger? Why not, just gal? No, it was because she was nigger that he went to her. Sweet . . . The scent of boiling cane came to him. Then he saw the rich glow of the stove. He heard the voices of the men circled around it. He was about to skirt the clearing when he heard his own name mentioned. He stopped. Quivering. Leaning against a tree, he listened.

"Bad nigger. Yassur, he sho is one bad nigger when he gets started."

"Tom Burwell's been on th gang three times fo cuttin men."

"What y think he's agwine t do t Bob Stone?"

"Dunno yet. He aint found out. When he does—Baby!"

"Aint no tellin."

"Young Stone aint no quitter an I ken tell y that. Blood of th old uns in his veins."

"Thats right. He'll scrap, sho."

"Be gettin too hot f niggers round this away."

"Shut up, nigger. Y dont know what y talkin bout."

Bob Stone's ears burned as though he had been holding them over the stove. Sizzling heat welled up within him. His feet felt as if they rested on red-hot coals. They stung him to quick movement. He circled the fringe of the glowing. Not a twig cracked beneath his feet. He reached the path that led to factory town. Plunged furiously down it. Halfway along, a blindness within him veered him aside. He crashed into the bordering canebrake. Cane leaves cut his face and lips. He tasted blood. He threw himself down and dug his fingers in the ground. The earth was cool. Cane-roots took the fever from his hands. After a long while, or so it seemed to him, the thought came to him that it must be time to see Louisa. He got to his feet and walked calmly to their meeting place. No Louisa. Tom Burwell had her. Veins in his forehead bulged and distended. Saliva moistened the dried blood on his lips. He bit down on his lips. He tasted blood. Not his own blood; Tom Burwell's blood. Bob drove through the cane and out again upon the road. A hound swung down the path before him towards factory town. Bob couldnt see it. The dog loped aside to let him pass. Bob's blind rushing made him stumble over it. He fell with a thud that dazed him. The hound yelped. Answering yelps came from all over the countryside. Chickens cackled. Roosters crowed, heralding the bloodshot eyes of southern awakening. Singers in the town were silenced. They shut their windows down. Palpitant between the rooster crows, a chill hush settled upon the huddled forms of Tom and Louisa. A figure rushed from the shadow and stood before them. Tom popped to his feet.

"Whats y want?"

"I'm Bob Stone."

"Yassur—an I'm Tom Burwell. Whats y want?"

Bob lunged at him. Tom side-stepped, caught him by the shoulder, and flung him to the ground. Straddled him.

"Let me up."

"Yassur—but watch yo doins, Bob Stone."

A few dark figures, drawn by the sound of scuffle, stood about them. Bob sprang to his feet.

"Fight like a man, Tom Burwell, an I'll lick y."

Again he lunged. Tom side-stepped and flung him to the ground. Straddled him.

"Get off me, you godam nigger you."

"Yo sho has started somethin now. Get up."

Tom yanked him up and began hammering at him. Each blow sounded as if it smashed into a precious, irreplaceable soft something. Beneath them, Bob staggered back. He reached in his pocket and whipped out a knife.

"Thats my game, sho."

Blue flash, a steel blade slashed across Bob Stone's throat. He had a sweetish sick feeling. Blood began to flow. Then he felt a sharp twitch of pain. He let his knife drop. He slapped one hand against his neck. He pressed the other on top of his head as if to hold it down. He groaned. He turned, and staggered towards the crest of the hill in the direction of white town. Negroes who had seen the fight slunk into their homes and blew the lamps out. Louisa, dazed, hysterical, refused to go indoors. She slipped, crumbled, her body loosely propped against the woodwork of the well. Tom Burwell leaned against it. He seemed rooted there.

Bob reached Broad Street. White men rushed up to him. He collapsed in their arms.

"Tom Burwell. . . ."

White men like ants upon a forage rushed about. Except for the taut hum of their moving, all was silent. Shotguns, revolvers, rope, kerosene, torches. Two high-powered cars with glaring search-lights. They came together. The taut hum rose to a low roar. Then nothing could be heard but the flop of their feet in the thick dust of the road. The moving body of their silence preceded them over the crest of the hill into factory town. It flattened the Negroes beneath it. It rolled to the wall of the factory, where it stopped. Tom knew that they were coming. He couldnt move. And then he saw the search-lights of the two cars glaring down on him. A quick shock went through him. He stiffened. He started to run. A yell went up from the mob. Tom wheeled about and faced them. They poured down on him. They swarmed. A large man with dead-white face and flabby cheeks came to him and almost jabbed a gun-barrel through his guts.

"Hands behind y, nigger."

Tom's wrists were bound. The big man shoved him to the well. Burn him over it, and when the woodwork caved in, his body would drop to the bottom. Two deaths for a godam nigger. Louisa was driven back. The mob pushed in. Its pressure, its momentum was too great. Drag him to the factory. Wood and stakes already there. Tom moved in the direction indicated. But they had to drag him. They reached the great door. Too many to get in there. The mob divided and flowed around the walls to either side. The big man shoved him through the door. The mob pressed in from the sides. Taut humming. No words. A stake was sunk into the ground. Rotting floor boards piled around it. Kerosene poured on the rotting floor boards. Tom bound to the stake. His breast was bare. Nails scratches let little lines of blood trickle down and mat into the hair. His face, his eyes were set and stony. Except for irregular breathing, one would have thought him already dead. Torches were flung onto the pile. A great flare muffled in black smoke shot upward. The mob yelled. The mob was silent. Now Tom could be seen within the flames. Only his head, erect, lean, like a blackened stone. Stench of burning flesh soaked the air. Tom's eyes popped. His head settled downward. The mob yelled. Its yell echoed against the skeleton stone walls and sounded like a hundred yells. Like a hundred mobs yelling. Its yell thudded against the thick front wall and fell back. Ghost of a yell slipped through the flames and out the great door of the factory. It fluttered like a dying thing down the single street of factory town. Louisa, upon the step before her home, did not hear it, but her eyes opened slowly. They saw the full moon glowing in the great door. The full moon, an evil thing, an omen, soft showering the homes of folks she knew. Where were they, these people? She'd sing, and perhaps they'd come out and join her. Perhaps Tom Burwell would come. At any rate, the full moon in the great door was an omen which she must sing to:

Red nigger moon. Sinner!
Blood-burning moon. Sinner!
Come out that fact'ry door.

1923

John Dos Passos
1896–1970

John Roderigo Dos Passos was born on January 14, 1896, in a hotel in Chicago, Illinois, the illegitimate son of Lucy Addison Sprigg Madison, who was forty-eight when her son was born, and John Randolph Dos Passos, a wealthy attorney of Portuguese descent, who had written a book on the superiority of Anglo-Saxon political traditions. After years of living discreetly apart, Dos Passos's parents were finally married in 1910, though it was not until Dos Passos finished his college education that he was formally acknowledged by his father. Raised by his mother with his father's generous financial support, Dos Passos lived a comfortable early life. He later referred to these years as a "hotel childhood." He toured Europe extensively, and he experienced early, steady exposure to good music, art, and books as well as to fine clothes, fine food, and fine schools. Having first attended private schools in England and Connecticut, he went on to Harvard College, where he graduated with honors in 1916.

By the time he entered Harvard, Dos Passos had already substantially defined the two interests that would shape his life—literary aestheticism and reform politics. "It was characteristic of the Jazz Age," F. Scott Fitzgerald remarked, "that it had no interest in politics at all." In contrast to many of his contemporaries, however, Dos Passos was directly influenced by the leaders of the reform movements of the prewar years. At Harvard he studied Thorstein Veblen's penetrating analyses of capitalistic society as well as Walter Pater's aesthetic theories, and he read Theodore Dreiser as well as Gustave Flaubert. It was characteristic of him that his contributions to the *Harvard Advocate* included a review of the radical John Reed's *Insurgent Mexico* as well as reviews of the experimental poetry of Ezra Pound and T. S. Eliot.

After graduation, Dos Passos followed his father's advice and left for Spain to study architecture, but in 1917, upon his father's death and America's entry into the First World War, he followed his own inclinations and joined the Norton-Harjes volunteer ambulance service in France. He later served with the Red Cross ambulance service in Italy, then with the United States Army Medical Corps. He also spent some time in Paris, where during one offensive he volunteered to help with the wounded: "It was my job," he recalled, "to carry off buckets full of amputated arms and hands and legs from an operating room." These war experiences led to his first two novels, *One Man's Initiation, 1917* (1920) and the critically well-received *Three Soldiers* (1921), both of which focus on the disillusioning impact of the Great War on sensitive young American soldiers.

With the war behind him, Dos Passos resumed the mixed career he had envisaged earlier, as a free-lance journalist, an aspiring artist, and a political activist. By 1920 he was publishing widely in *The Liberator, The Freeman, Dial,* and *The Nation.* He also published a volume of poems, *A Pushcart at the Curb* (1922), and two modernist plays, *The Garbage Man* (1926) and *Airways, Inc.* (1928). In 1926 he joined the executive board of *New Masses,* an avowedly Communist journal that he helped found. In 1927 he was jailed in Boston for picketing the statehouse in support of Sacco and Vanzetti. And in 1928, following a tour of the USSR, he agreed to serve as "contributing editor" to the *Daily Worker.* Though he never joined the Communist party—in 1930 he called himself only "a middle-class liberal"—he found himself, as the Great Depression deepened, increasingly entangled in labor disputes and related controversies, yet also more and more disenchanted by the strong-arm tactics of communism. In 1931 Dos Passos, along with Theodore Dreiser, was indicted for criminal syndicalism for aiding the striking miners in Harlan County, Kentucky. He served as treasurer of the National Committee for Defense of Political Prisoners in 1932, and in 1940 as treasurer of the Joint Campaign for Political Refugees.

Throughout this period—in fact, throughout his life—Dos Passos traveled extensively. Travel played a large part in his creative imagination, both as a direct stimulus for several travel books and as a metaphor for the rootlessness of modern technological society. Like his friend Ernest Hemingway, Dos Passos was for a time enamored of Spain, and he immersed himself in Spanish culture and politics. In 1922 he published a collection of essays on Spain, *Rosinante to the Road Again,* in which he examined Spanish civilization and at the same time explored his own Iberian background. Later his passionate disagreement with

Hemingway over the Spanish civil war—Dos Passos was disgusted by the way the Communists used the war to their own advantage—led to an irreparable breach in what had been a close, mutually supportive friendship. Toward the end of his life, Dos Passos continued to use his ethnic roots as a motive for travel and writing: He published *Brazil on the Move* in 1963 and *The Portugal Story* in 1969.

Dos Passos's fiction, like his politics, reflects his desire to confront imaginatively the large-scale transformation of American society from a predominantly rural, agricultural, traditional society into an increasingly urban, industrial, commercial, secular, and disoriented one. In *Manhattan Transfer* (1925), the impact of the First World War is placed against the larger backdrop of an emerging urban, technological civilization. In this, his first major novel, Dos Passos began to develop the tone that became characteristic of his work, a tone in which protest and despair mingle with some residual, irrepressible hope. But he also began experimenting with style and structure in ways that continued to mark his art. Sinclair Lewis said of *Manhattan Transfer* that its composition was based on the "technique of the movie, in its flashes, its cut-backs, its speed." In narrative shifts and jumps (with an absence of transitions reminiscent of Ezra Pound's *Cantos,* T. S. Eliot's *The Waste Land,* and Hart Crane's *The Bridge*), Dos Passos also began finding techniques that would convey the stark contrasts and abrupt changes of urban life. In subways and skyscrapers he began finding images of a society whose great energies and skills, lacking purpose, are surrendered to mere motion and empty innovation.

In his masterpiece, *U.S.A.* (1937), a trilogy comprising three separately published novels—*The 42nd Parallel* (1930), *1919* (1932), and *The Big Money* (1936)—Dos Passos created a story that extends chronologically from the prewar years to 1936 and reaches geographically from New York to California, from Chicago to Mexico, and beyond America to Europe. His panoramic canvas includes isolated farms and airplane factories, picket lines and ghetto streets, union offices and corporate headquarters. Matching his canvas, his cast of characters includes farmhands and factory laborers, hoboes and vagabonds, advertising executives and Hollywood actresses, entrepreneurs and financiers. Yet despite the vast sweep of his story and the shifts that characterize it, Dos Passos establishes the central conflict of his story as a conflict between "two nations"—a small group of rich and powerful people who successfully manipulate the social and economic forces that shape history and a large group of poor and sometimes hopeless people who are used by those forces only to be abandoned or destroyed.

In addition to telling the individual stories of eleven major characters in *U.S.A.,* Dos Passos employs three supplemental devices that broaden the scope of his work. In the first of these, called "Newsreel," he presents materials that create a public framework for the incidents and themes of his narrative. "Newsreel" includes headlines and snippets of articles from newspapers ("Wall Street Stunned"); lines from slogans, mottoes, and popular songs (from a ballad about Casey Jones or a union protest song); and bits and pieces from public reports and political oratory. In the second supplemental device, called "Camera Eye," he presents bits and pieces expressive of private and subjective feelings that are sometimes lyrical, sometimes elegiac, sometimes satiric, sometimes angry, and sometimes threatening (" 'all right we are two nations' "). In the third supplemental device, Dos Passos brings twenty-seven carefully crafted biographical sketches of prominent public figures (movie stars like Rudolph Valentino, politicians like Woodrow Wilson, inventors like Thomas Edison, financiers like J. P. Morgan, social critics like Thorstein Veblen, labor leaders like Eugene Debs) into his narrative. Like the stories of his own fictional characters, the stories of these actual personages focus on different modes of failure and success and on the social and economic forces that shape success and failure alike. They thus serve to extend Dos Passos's chronicle of the transformation of the United States in the first third of this century.

In *U.S.A.,* more than in any other of his novels, Dos Passos blends literary aestheticism and reformist politics by combining innovative language and technique with a detailed survey of contemporary history and politics. A less stylistically conscious reformer, Upton Sinclair, found the books deplorably difficult to read. A less politically conscious stylist, Ernest Hemingway, thought Dos Passos might be sacrificing his fictional characters to propaganda: "Keep them people, people, people, and don't let them get to be symbols. Remember the race is older than the economic system." The French philosopher and writer Jean Paul Sartre, however, regarded *U.S.A.* as a supreme literary and political achievement and called Dos Passos the greatest novelist of the twentieth century.

The idea of calling his trilogy *U.S.A.* came to Dos Passos at about the same time that he broke with Hemingway and returned to the United States planning to write the "truth" about the Communist activities in Spain. In 1937 Dos Passos wrote an article, "Farewell to Europe," and began an intensive program of reading in American history that not only culminated in such books as *The Living Thoughts of Tom Paine* (1940), *The Ground We Stand On* (1941), *The Head and Heart of Thomas Jefferson* (1954), and a narrative history, *The Men Who Made the Nation* (1957), but also reinforced an increasingly patriotic and conservative stance. Although he remained aware of the many imperfections of the United States, Dos Passos also became convinced that in a corrupt world the United States remained the best hope for individual liberty and human progress. As early as 1937 he had described "the one hope for the future of the type of western civilization which furnishes the frame of our lives" as "the system of popular government based on individual liberty." In 1939 his disillusionment with the Spanish civil war found fictional form in *The Adventures of a Young Man,* which became the first volume in a second trilogy, *District of Columbia* (1952). The second volume of the trilogy, *Number One* (1943), is a novelistic exposé of political corruption loosely based on the career of Huey Long; the third, *The Grand Design* (1949), is a satire on New Deal bureaucracy. In *Mid-Century* (1961), Dos Passos attempted to revive the style and methods of *U.S.A.* in a fictional attack on the power of financiers and labor unions.

Largely because of the success of *U.S.A.,* Dos Passos tends to be identified as a writer of the 1930s. Yet he wrote passionately and productively from the 1920s through the Cold War era of the 1950s and the counterculture of the 1960s. In *Mid-Century* he laments what he considers the loss of heroic ideals among "kids who'd been soaked in wartime prosperity . . . raised on the gibblegabble of the radio between the family car and the corner drugstore and the Five and Ten." Staunchly anti-Communist, he supported President Nixon's 1970 invasion of

Cambodia ("the first rational military step taken in the whole war"). In June 1970 he wrote his daughter cantankerously about the impact that the documentary movie *Woodstock* had on his conception of the young: "To me it was endlessly depressing. . . . If Nixon fails [in Cambodia] it is just this generation that is raising such cain that will have to bear the brunt of the results. I'll be in my grave re-entering the carbon cycle." Three months later, on September 27, 1970, he died of a heart attack in Baltimore, Maryland.

Further Reading:
J. H. Wrenn, *John Dos Passos*, 1961.
R. G. Davis, *John Dos Passos*, 1962.
Studies in U.S.A., ed. D. Sanders, 1972.
M. Landesberg, *Dos Passos' Path to U.S.A.: A Political Biography, 1912–1936*, 1972.
Ludington, T. *John Dos Passos: Twentieth Century Odyssey*, 1980.

Text:
U.S.A., 1974.
See also *The Fourteenth Chronicle: Letters and Diaries of John Dos Passos*, ed. T. Ludington, 1973.

from # U.S.A.*

from ## The Big Money

Newsreel XLV

'Twarn't for powder and for storebought hair
De man I love would not gone nowhere

if one should seek a simple explanation of his career, it would doubtless be found in that extraordinary decision to forsake the ease of a clerkship for the wearying labor of a section hand. The youth who so early in life had so much of judgment and willpower could not fail to rise above the general run of men. He became the intimate of bankers

St. Louis woman wid her diamon' rings
Pulls dat man aroun' by her apron strings

Tired of walking, riding a bicycle or riding in streetcars, he is likely to buy a Ford.

DAYLIGHT HOLDUP SCATTERS CROWD

Just as soon as his wife discovers that every Ford is like every other Ford and that nearly everyone has one, she is likely to influence him to step into the next social group, of which the Dodge is the most conspicuous example.

---

* The trilogy *U.S.A.*, containing the three novels *The 42nd Parallel, 1919,* and *The Big Money,* was first published in 1938. These novels had been published separately in 1930, 1932, and 1936, respectively.

DESPERATE REVOLVER BATTLE FOLLOWS

The next step comes when daughter comes back from college and the family moves into a new home. Father wants economy. Mother craves opportunity for her children, daughter desires social prestige and son wants travel, speed, get-up-and-go.

MAN SLAIN NEAR HOTEL MAJESTIC BY THREE FOOTPADS

I hate to see de evenin sun go down
Hate to see de evenin sun go down
'Cause my baby he done lef' dis town

such exploits may indicate a dangerous degree of bravado but they display the qualities that made a boy of highschool age the acknowledged leader of a gang that has been a thorn in the side of the State of

The American Plan

Frederick Winslow Taylor (they called him Speedy Taylor in the shop) was born in Germantown, Pennsylvania, the year of Buchanan's election. His father was a lawyer, his mother came from a family of New Bedford whalers; she was a great reader of Emerson, belonged to the Unitarian Church and the Browning Society. She was a fervent abolitionist and believed in democratic manners; she was a housekeeper of the old school, kept everybody busy from dawn till dark. She laid down the rules of conduct:

selfrespect, selfreliance, selfcontrol
and a cold long head for figures.

But she wanted her children to appreciate the finer things, so she took them abroad for three years on the Continent, showed them cathedrals, grand opera, Roman pediments, the old masters under their brown varnish in their great frames of tarnished gilt.

Later Fred Taylor was impatient of these wasted years, stamped out of the room when people talked about the finer things; he was a testy youngster, fond of practical jokes, and a great hand at rigging up contraptions and devices.

At Exeter he was head of his class and captain of the ballteam, the first man to pitch overhand. (When umpires complained that overhand pitching wasn't in the rules of the game, he answered that it got results.)

As a boy he had nightmares; going to bed was horrible for him; he thought they came from sleeping on his back. He made himself a leather harness with wooden pegs that stuck into his flesh when he turned over. When he was grown he slept in a chair or in bed in a sitting position propped up with pillows. All his life he suffered from sleeplessness.

He was a crackerjack tennisplayer. In 1881, with his friend Clark, he won the National Doubles Championship. (He used a spoonshaped racket of his own design.)

At school he broke down from overwork, his eyes went back on him. The doctor suggested manual labor. So instead of going to Harvard he went into the machineshop of a small pumpmanufacturing concern, owned by a friend of the family's, to learn the trade of patternmaker and machinist. He learned to handle a lathe and to dress and cuss like a workingman.

Fred Taylor never smoked tobacco or drank liquor or used tea or coffee; he couldn't understand why his fellowmechanics wanted to go on sprees and get drunk and raise cain Saturday nights. He lived at home; when he wasn't reading technical books he'd play parts in amateur theatricals or step up to the piano in the evening and sing a good tenor in *A Warrior Bold* or *A Spanish Cavalier.*

He served his first year's apprenticeship in the machineshop without pay; the next two years he made a dollar and a half a week, the last year two dollars.

Pennsylvania was getting rich off iron and coal. When he was twentytwo, Fred Taylor went to work at the Midvale Iron Works. At first he had to take a clerical job, but he hated that and went to work with a shovel. At last he got them to put him on a lathe. He was a good machinist, he worked ten hours a day and in the evenings followed an engineering course at Stevens. In six years he rose from machinist's helper to keeper of toolcribs to gangboss to foreman to mastermechanic in charge of repairs to chief draftsman and director of research to chief engineer of the Midvale Plant.

The early years he was a machinist with the other machinists in the shop, cussed and joked and worked with the rest of them, soldiered on the job when they did. Mustn't give the boss more than his money's worth. But when he got to be foreman, he was on the management's side of the fence, *gathering in on the part of those on the management's side all the great mass of traditional knowledge which in the past has been in the heads of the workmen and in the physical skill and knack of the workman.* He couldn't stand to see an idle lathe or an idle man.

Production went to his head and thrilled his sleepless nerves like liquor or women on a Saturday night. He never loafed and he'd be damned if anybody else would. Production was an itch under his skin.

He lost his friends in the shop; they called him niggerdriver. He was a stockily built man with a temper and a short tongue.

I was a young man in years, but I give you my word I was a great deal older than I am now, what with the worry, meanness, and contemptibleness of the whole damn thing. It's a horrid life for any man to live, not being able to look any workman in the face without seeing hostility there, and a feeling that every man around you is your virtual enemy.

That was the beginning of the Taylor System of Scientific Management.

He was impatient of explanations, he didn't care whose hide he took off in enforcing the laws he believed inherent in the industrial process.

When starting an experiment in any field, question everything, question the very foundations upon which the art rests, question the simplest, the most selfevident, the most universally accepted facts; prove everything,

except the dominant Quaker Yankee (the New Bedford skippers were the greatest niggerdrivers on the whaling seas) rules of conduct. He boasted he'd never ask a workman to do anything he couldn't do.

He devised an improved steamhammer; he standardized tools and equipment, he filled the shop with college students with stopwatches and diagrams, tabulating, standardizing. *There's the right way of doing a thing and the wrong way of doing it; the right way means increased production, lower costs, higher wages, bigger profits:* the American plan.

He broke up the foreman's job into separate functions, speedbosses, gangbosses, timestudy men, order-of-work men

The skilled mechanics were too stubborn for him; what he wanted was a plain handyman who'd do what he was told. If he was a firstclass man and did firstclass work, Taylor was willing to let him have firstclass pay; that's where he began to get into trouble with the owners.

At thirtyfour he married and left Midvale and took a flyer for the big money in connection with a pulpmill started in Maine by some admirals and political friends of Grover Cleveland's;

the panic of '93 made hash of that enterprise,

so Taylor invented for himself the job of Consulting Engineer in Management and began to build up a fortune by careful investments.

The first paper he read before the American Society of Mechanical Engineers was anything but a success; they said he was crazy. *I have found,* he wrote in 1909, *that any improvement is not only opposed but aggressively and bitterly opposed by the majority of men.*

He was called in by Bethlehem Steel. It was in Bethlehem he made his famous experiments with handling pigiron; he taught a Dutchman named Schmidt to handle fortyseven tons instead of twelve and a half tons of pigiron a day and got Schmidt to admit he was as good as ever at the end of the day.

He was a crank about shovels, every job had to have a shovel of the right weight and size for that job alone; every job had to have a man of the right weight and size for that job alone; but when he began to pay his men in proportion to the increased efficiency of their work,

the owners, who were a lot of greedy smalleyed Dutchmen, began to raise Hail Columbia; when Schwab bought Bethlehem Steel in 1901

Fred Taylor

inventor of efficiency

who had doubled the production of the stampingmill by speeding up the main lines of shafting from ninetysix to twohundred and twentyfive revolutions a minute

was unceremoniously fired.

After that Fred Taylor always said he couldn't afford to work for money.

He took to playing golf (using golfclubs of his own design), doping out methods for transplanting huge boxtrees into the garden of his home.

At Boxly in Germantown he kept open house for engineers, factorymanagers, industrialists;

he wrote papers,

lectured in colleges,

appeared before a congressional committee,

everywhere preached the virtues of scientific management and the Barth slide rule, the cutting-down of waste and idleness, the substitution for skilled mechanics of the plain handyman (like Schmidt the pigiron handler) who'd move as he was told and work by the piece:

production;

more steel rails more bicycles more spools of thread more armorplate for battleships more bedpans more barbedwire more needles more lightningrods more ballbearings more dollarbills;

(the old Quaker families of Germantown were growing rich, the Pennsylvania millionaires were breeding billionaires out of iron and coal)

production would make every firstclass American rich who was willing to work at piecework and not drink or raise cain or think or stand mooning at his lathe.

Thrifty Schmidt the pigiron handler can invest his money and get to be an owner like Schwab and the rest of the greedy smalleyed Dutchmen and cultivate a taste for Bach and have hundredyearold boxtrees in his garden at Bethlehem or Germantown or Chestnut Hill,

and lay down the rules of conduct;

the American plan

But Fred Taylor never saw the working of the American plan;

in 1915 he went to the hospital in Philadelphia suffering from a breakdown.

Pneumonia developed; the nightnurse heard him winding his watch;

on the morning of his fiftyninth birthday, when the nurse went into his room to look at him at fourthirty,

he was dead with his watch in his hand.

The Camera Eye (46)

walk the streets and walk the streets inquiring of Coca-Cola signs Lucky Strike ads pricetags in storewindows scraps of overheard conversations stray tatters of newsprint yesterday's headlines sticking out of ashcans

for a set of figures a formula of action an address you don't quite know you've forgotten the number the street may be in Brooklyn a train leaving for somewhere a steamboat whistle stabbing your ears a job chalked up in front of an agency

to do to make there are more lives than walking desperate the streets hurry underdog do make

a speech urging action in the crowded hall after handclapping the pats and smiles of others on the platform the scrape of chairs the expectant hush the few coughs during the first stuttering attempt to talk straight tough going the snatch for a slogan they are listening and then the easy climb slogan by slogan to applause (if somebody in your head didn't say liar to you and on Union Square

that time you leant from a soapbox over faces avid young opinionated old the middleaged numb with overwork eyes bleared with newspaperreading trying to tell them the straight dope make them laugh tell them what they want to hear wave a flag whispers the internal agitator crazy to succeed)

you suddenly falter ashamed flush red break out in sweat why not tell these men stamping in the wind that we stand on a quicksand?

that doubt is the whetstone of understanding is too hard hurts instead of urging

picket John D. Rockefeller the bastard if the cops knock your blocks off it's all for the advancement of the human race while I go home after a drink and a hot meal and read (with some difficulty in the Loeb Library trot) the epigrams of Martial and ponder the course of history and what leverage might pry the owners loose from power and bring back (I too Walt Whitman) our storybook democracy

and all the time in my pocket that letter from that collegeboy asking me to explain why being right which he admits   the radicals are in their private lives such shits

lie abed underdog (peeling the onion of doubt) with the book unread in your hand and swing on the seesaw maybe after all maybe topdog   make

money   you understand what he meant the old party with the white beard beside the crystal inkpot at the cleared varnished desk in the walnut office in whose voice boomed all the clergymen of childhood and shrilled the hosannahs of the offkey female choirs. All you say is very true but there's such a thing as sales   And I have daughters   I'm sure you too will end by thinking differently   make

money in New York (lipstick kissed off the lips of a girl fashionablydressed fragrant at five o'clock in a taxicab careening down Park Avenue when at the end of each crosstown street the west is flaming with gold and white smoke billows from the smokestacks of steamboats leaving port and the sky is lined with greenbacks

the riveters are quiet the trucks of the producers are shoved off onto the marginal avenues

winnings sing from every streetcorner

crackle in the ignitions of the cars swish smooth in ballbearings sparkle in the lights going on in the showwindows croak in the klaxons tootle in the horns of imported millionaire shining towncars

dollars are silky in her hair soft in her dress sprout in the elaborately contrived rosepetals that you kiss become pungent and crunchy in the speakeasy dinner sting shrill in the drinks

make loud the girlandmusic show set off the laughing jag in the cabaret swing in the shufflingshuffling orchestra click sharp in the hatcheck girl's goodnight)

if not why not?   walking the streets rolling on your bed eyes sting from peeling the speculative onion of doubt if somebody in your head   topdog?   underdog? didn't (and on Union Square) say liar to you

Newsreel XLVII

boy seeking future offered opportunity . . . good positions for bright . . . CHANCE FOR ADVANCEMENT . . . boy to learn . . . errand boy . . . office boy

YOUNG MAN WANTED

Oh tell me how long
I'll have to wait

OPPORTUNITY

in bank that chooses its officers from the ranks, for wideawake ambitious book-keeper . . . architectural draftsman with experience on factory and industrial buildings in brick, timber, and reinforced concrete . . . bronzefitter . . . letterer . . . patternmaker . . . carriage painter . . . firstclass striper and finisher . . . young man for hosiery, underwear, and notion house . . . assistant in order department . . . firstclass penman accurate at figures . . . energetic hardworker for setting dies in powerpresses for metal parts

canvasser . . . flavor chemist . . . freightelevator man . . . housesalesman . . . insuranceman . . . insuranceman . . . invoice clerk . . . jeweler . . . laborer . . . machinist . . . millingmachine man . . . shipping clerk . . . shipping clerk . . . shipping clerk . . . shoe salesman . . . signwriter . . . solicitor for retail fishmarket . . . teacher . . . timekeeper . . . tool and diemaker, tracer, toolroom foreman, translator, typist . . . windowtrimmer . . . wrapper

OPPORTUNITY FOR

Do I get it now
Or must I hesitate

young man not afraid of hard work
young man for office
young man for stockroom
young man as stenographer
young man to travel
young man to learn

OPPORTUNITY

Oh tell me how long

to superintend municipal light, water, and ice plant in beautiful growing, healthful town in Florida's highlands . . . to take charge of underwear department in large wholesale mailhouse . . . to assist in railroad investigation . . . to take charge of about twenty men on tools, dies, gigs, and gauges . . . as bookkeeper in stockroom . . . for light porter work . . . civil engineer . . . machinery and die appraiser . . . building estimator . . . electrical and powerplant engineer

Newsreel LXVI

HOLMES DENIES STAY

A better world's in birth

Tiny wasps imported from Korea in battle to death with Asiatic beetle

BOY CARRIED MILE DOWN SEWER; SHOT OUT
ALIVE

CHICAGO BARS MEETINGS

For justice thunders condemnation

WASHINGTON KEEPS EYE ON RADICALS

Arise rejected of the earth

PARIS BRUSSELS MOSCOW GENEVA ADD THEIR
VOICES

It is the final conflict
Let each stand in his place

GEOLOGIST LOST IN CAVE SIX DAYS

The International Party

SACCO AND VANZETTI MUST DIE

Shall be the human race.

Much I thought of you when I was lying in the death house—the singing, the kind tender voices of the children from the playground where there was all the life and the joy of liberty —just one step from the wall that contains the buried agony of three buried souls. It would remind me so often of you and your sister and I wish I could see you every moment, but I feel better that you will not come to the death house so that you could not see the horrible picture of three living in agony waiting to be electrocuted.

The Camera Eye (50)

they have clubbed us off the streets   they are stronger   they are rich   they hire and fire the politicians the newspapereditors the old judges the small men with reputations the collegepresidents the wardheelers (listen businessmen collegepresidents judges America will not forget her betrayers) they hire the men with guns the uniforms the policecars the patrolwagons

all right you have won   you will kill the brave men our friends tonight

there is nothing left to do   we are beaten   we the beaten crowd together in these old dingy schoolrooms on Salem Street   shuffle up and down the gritty creaking stairs sit hunched with bowed heads on benches and hear the old words of the haters of oppression   made new in sweat and agony tonight

our work is over   the scribbled phrases   the nights typing releases the smell of the printshop the sharp reek of newprinted leaflets the rush for Western Union stringing words into wires the search for stinging words to make you feel who are your oppressors America

America our nation has been beaten by strangers who have turned our language inside out who have taken the clean words our fathers spoke and made them slimy and foul

their hired men sit on the judge's bench they sit back with their feet on the tables under the dome of the State House they are ignorant of our beliefs they have the dollars the guns the armed forces the powerplants they have built the electricchair and hired the executioner to throw the switch all right we are two nations

America our nation has been beaten by strangers who have bought the laws and fenced off the meadows and cut down the woods for pulp and turned our pleasant cities into slums and sweated the wealth out of our people and when they want to they hire the executioner to throw the switch

but do they know that the old words of the immigrants are being renewed in blood and agony tonight do they know that the old American speech of the haters of oppression is new tonight in the mouth of an old woman from Pittsburgh of a husky boilermaker from Frisco who hopped freights clear from the Coast to come here in the mouth of a Back Bay socialworker in the mouth of an Italian printer of a hobo from Arkansas   the language of the beaten nation is not forgotten in our ears tonight

the men in the deathhouse made the old words new before they died

If it had not been for these things, I might have lived out my life talking at streetcorners to scorning men. I might have died unknown, unmarked, a failure. This is our career and our triumph. Never in our full life can we hope to do such work for tolerance, for justice, for man's understanding of man as now we do by an accident.

now their work is over   the immigrants haters of oppression lie quiet in black suits in the little undertaking parlor in the North End   the city is quiet   the men of the conquering nation are not to be seen on the streets

they have won why are they scared to be seen on the streets?   on the streets you see only the downcast faces of the beaten   the streets belong to the beaten nation all the way to the cemetery where the bodies of the immigrants are to be burned   we line the curbs in the drizzling rain we crowd the wet sidewalks elbow to elbow silent pale looking with scared eyes at the coffins

we stand defeated America

Newsreel LXVIII

WALL STREET STUNNED

This is not Thirtyeight but it's old Ninetyseven
You must put her in Center on time

MARKET SURE TO RECOVER FROM SLUMP

DECLINE IN CONTRACTS

POLICE TURN MACHINE GUNS ON COLORADO
MINE STRIKERS KILL 5 WOUND 40

sympathizers appeared on the scene just as thousands of office workers were pouring out of the buildings at the lunch hour. As they raised their placard high and started an indefinite march from one side to the other, they were jeered and hooted not only by the office workers but also by workmen on a building under construction

NEW METHODS OF SELLING SEEN

RESCUE CREWS TRY TO UPEND ILL-FATED CRAFT
WHILE WAITING FOR PONTOONS

He looked 'round an' said to his black greasy fireman
Jus' shovel in a little more coal
And when we cross that White Oak Mountain
You can watch your Ninety-seven roll

I find your column interesting and need advice. I have saved four thousand
dollars which I want to invest for a better income. Do you think I might buy
stocks?

POLICE KILLER FLICKS CIGARETTE AS HE GOES
TREMBLING TO DOOM

PLAY AGENCIES IN RING OF SLAVE GIRL MARTS

MAKER OF LOVE DISBARRED AS LAWYER

Oh the right wing clothesmakers
And the Socialist fakers
They make by the workers . . .
Double cross

They preach Social-ism
But practice Fasc-ism
To keep capitalism
By the boss

MOSCOW CONGRESS OUSTS OPPOSITION

It's a mighty rough road from Lynchburg to Danville
An' a line on a three mile grade
It was on that grade he lost his average
An' you see what a jump he made

MILL THUGS IN MURDER RAID

here is the most dangerous example of how at the decisive moment the bourgeois
ideology liquidates class solidarity and turns a friend of the workingclass of yesterday
into a most miserable propagandist for imperialism today

RED PICKETS FINED FOR PROTESTS HERE

We leave our home in the morning
We kiss our children goodbye

OFFICIALS STILL HOPE FOR RESCUE OF MEN

He was goin' downgrade makin' ninety miles an hour
When his whistle broke into a scream
He was found in the wreck with his hand on the throttle
An' was scalded to death with the steam

RADICALS FIGHT WITH CHAIRS AT UNITY MEETING

PATROLMEN PROTECT REDS

U.S. CHAMBER OF COMMERCE URGES CONFIDENCE

REAL VALUES UNHARMED

While we slave for the bosses
Our children scream an' cry
But when we draw our money
Our grocery bills to pay

PRESIDENT SEES PROSPERITY NEAR

Not a cent to spend for clothing
Not a cent to lay away

STEAMROLLER IN ACTION AGAINST MILITANTS

MINERS BATTLE SCABS

But we cannot buy for our children
Our wages are too low
Now listen to me you workers
Both you women and men
Let us win for them the victory
I'm sure it ain't no sin

CARILLON PEALS IN SINGING TOWER

the President declared it was impossible to view the increased advantages for the many without smiling at those who a short time ago expressed so much fear lest our country might come under the control of a few individuals of great wealth.

HAPPY CROWDS THRONG CEREMONY

on a tiny island nestling like a green jewel in the lake that mirrors the singing tower, the President today participated in the dedication of a bird sanctuary and its pealing carillon, fulfilling the dream of an immigrant boy

The Camera Eye (51)

at the head of the valley in the dark of the hills on the broken floor of a lurchedover cabin a man halfsits halflies propped up by an old woman two wrinkled girls that might be young   chunks of coal flare in the hearth flicker in his face white and sagging as dough   blacken the cavedin mouth the taut throat the belly swelled enormous with the wound he got working on the minetipple

the barefoot girl brings him a tincup of water   the woman wipes sweat off his streaming face with a dirty denim sleeve   the firelight flares in his eyes stretched big with fever in the women's scared eyes and in the blanched faces of the foreigners

without help in the valley hemmed by dark strikesilent hills the man will die (my father died we know what it is like to see a man die) the women will lay him out on the rickety cot the miners will bury him

in the jail it's light too hot the steamheat hisses we talk through the greenpainted iron bars to a tall white mustachioed old man some smiling miners in shirtsleeves a boy   faces white from mining have already the tallowy look of jailfaces

foreigners what can we say to the dead?   foreigners what can we say to the jailed?

the representative of the political party talks fast through the bars join up with us and no other union we'll send you tobacco candy solidarity our lawyers will write briefs speakers will shout your names at meetings they'll carry your names on cardboards on picketlines   the men in jail shrug their shoulders smile thinly our eyes look in their eyes through the bars   what can I say?

(in another continent I have seen the faces looking out through the barred basement windows behind the ragged sentry's boots I have seen before day the straggling footsore prisoners herded through the streets limping between bayonets   heard the volley

I have seen the dead lying out in those distant deeper valleys) what can we say to the jailed?

in the law's office we stand against the wall the law is a big man with eyes angry in a big pumpkinface   who sits and stares at us meddling foreigners through the door the deputies crane with their guns   they stand guard at the mines   they blockade the miners' soupkitchens   they've cut off the road up the valley   the hiredmen with guns stand ready to shoot (they have made us foreigners in the land where we were born they are the conquering army that has filtered into the country unnoticed they have taken the hilltops by stealth they levy toll they stand at the minehead   they stand at the polls   they stand by when the bailiffs carry the furniture of the family evicted from the city tenement out on the sidewalk they are there when the bankers foreclose on a farm they are ambushed and ready to shoot down the strikers marching behind the flag up the switchback road to the mine   those that the guns spare they jail)

the law stares across the desk out of angry eyes his face reddens in splotches like a gobbler's neck with the strut of the power of submachineguns sawedoffshotguns teargas and vomitinggas the power that can feed you or leave you to starve sits easy at his desk his back is covered he feels strong behind him he feels the prosecutingattorney the judge an owner himself the political boss the minesuperintendent the board of directors   the president of the utility the manipulator of the holdingcompany

he lifts his hand towards the telephone

the deputies crowd in the door

we have only words against

Power Superpower

In eighteen-eighty when Thomas Edison's agent was hooking up the first telephone in London, he put an ad in the paper for a secretary and stenographer. The eager young cockney with sprouting muttonchop whiskers who answered it

had recently lost his job as officeboy. In his spare time he had been learning shorthand and bookkeeping and taking dictation from the editor of the English *Vanity Fair* at night and jotting down the speeches in Parliament for the papers. He came of temperance smallshopkeeper stock; already he was butting his bullethead against the harsh structure of caste that doomed boys of his class to a life of alpaca jackets, penmanship, subordination. To get a job with an American firm was to put a foot on the rung of a ladder that led up into the blue.

He did his best to make himself indispensable; they let him operate the switchboard for the first halfhour when the telephone service was opened. Edison noticed his weekly reports on the electrical situation in England

and sent for him to be his personal secretary.

Samuel Insull landed in America on a raw March day in eightyone. Immediately he was taken out to Menlo Park, shown about the little group of laboratories, saw the strings of electriclightbulbs shining at intervals across the snowy lots, all lit from the world's first central electric station. Edison put him right to work and he wasn't through till midnight. Next morning at six he was on the job; Edison had no use for any nonsense about hours or vacations. Insull worked from that time on until he was seventy without a break; no nonsense about hours or vacations. Electric power turned the ladder into an elevator.

Young Insull made himself indispensable to Edison and took more and more charge of Edison's business deals. He was tireless, ruthless, reliable as the tides, Edison used to say, and fiercely determined to rise.

In ninetytwo he induced Edison to send him to Chicago and put him in as president of the Chicago Edison Company. Now he was on his own. *My engineering,* he said once in a speech, when he was sufficiently czar of Chicago to allow himself the luxury of plain speaking, *has been largely concerned with engineering all I could out of the dollar.*

He was a stiffly arrogant redfaced man with a closecropped mustache; he lived on Lake Shore Drive and was at the office at 7:10 every morning. It took him fifteen years to merge the five electrical companies into the Commonwealth Edison Company. *Very early I discovered that the first essential, as in other public utility business, was that it should be operated as a monopoly.*

When his power was firm in electricity he captured gas, spread out into the surrounding townships in northern Illinois. When politicians got in his way, he bought them, when laborleaders got in his way he bought them. Incredibly his power grew. He was scornful of bankers, lawyers were his hired men. He put his own lawyer in as corporation counsel and through him ran Chicago. When he found to his amazement that there were men (even a couple of young lawyers, Richberg and Ickes) in Chicago that he couldn't buy, he decided he'd better put on a show for the public;

Big Bill Thompson, the Builder:

punch King George in the nose,

the hunt for the treeclimbing fish,

the Chicago Opera.

It was too easy; the public had money, there was one of them born every minute, with the founding of Middlewest Utilities in nineteen twelve Insull began to use the public's money to spread his empire. His companies began to have open stockholders' meetings, to ballyhoo service, the small investor could sit there all day hearing the bigwigs talk. It's fun to be fooled. Companyunions hypnotized his employees; everybody had to buy stock in his companies, employees had to go out and sell stock, officeboys, linemen, trolleyconductors. Even Owen D. Young was afraid of him. *My experience is that the greatest aid in the efficiency of labor is a long line of men waiting at the gate.*

War shut up the progressives (no more nonsense about trustbusting, controlling monopoly, the public good) and raised Samuel Insull to the peak.

He was head of the Illinois State Council of Defense. *Now,* he said delightedly, *I can do anything I like.* With it came the perpetual spotlight, the purple taste of empire. If anybody didn't like what Samuel Insull did he was a traitor. Chicago damn well kept its mouth shut.

The Insull companies spread and merged put competitors out of business until Samuel Insull and his stooge brother Martin controlled through the leverage of holdingcompanies and directorates and blocks of minority stock

light and power, coalmines and tractioncompanies

in Illinois, Michigan, the Dakotas, Nebraska, Arkansas, Oklahoma, Missouri, Maine, Kansas, Wisconsin, Virginia, Ohio, North Carolina, Indiana, New York, New Jersey, Texas, in Canada, in Louisiana, in Georgia, in Florida and Alabama.

(It has been figured out that one dollar in Middle West Utilities controlled seventeen hundred and fifty dollars invested by the public in the subsidiary companies that actually did the work of producing electricity. With the delicate lever of a voting trust controlling the stock of the two top holdingcompanies he controlled a twelfth of the power output of America.)

Samuel Insull began to think he owned all that the way a man owns the roll of bills in his back pocket.

Always he'd been scornful of bankers. He owned quite a few in Chicago. But the New York bankers were laying for him; they felt he was a bounder, whispered that this financial structure was unsound. Fingers itched to grasp the lever that so delicately moved this enormous power over lives,

superpower, Insull liked to call it.

A certain Cyrus S. Eaton of Cleveland, an exBaptistminister, was the David that brought down this Goliath. Whether it was so or not he made Insull believe that Wall Street was behind him.

He started buying stock in the three Chicago utilities. Insull in a panic for fear he'd lose his control went into the market to buy against him. Finally the Reverend Eaton let himself be bought out, shaking down the old man for a profit of twenty million dollars.

The stockmarket crash.

Paper values were slipping. Insull's companies were intertwined in a tangle that no bookkeeper has ever been able to unravel.

The gas hissed out of the torn balloon. Insull threw away his imperial pride and went on his knees to the bankers.

The bankers had him where they wanted him. To save the face of the tottering czar he was made a receiver of his own concerns. But the old man couldn't get out of his head the illusion that the money was all his. When it was discovered that he was using the stockholders' funds to pay off his brothers' brokerage accounts it was too thick even for a federal judge. Insull was forced to resign.

He held directorates in eightyfive companies, he was chairman of sixtyfive, president of eleven: it took him three hours to sign his resignations.

As a reward for his services to monopoly his companies chipped in on a pension of eighteen thousand a year. But the public was shouting for criminal prosecution. When the handouts stopped newspapers and politicians turned on him. Revolt against the moneymanipulators was in the air. Samuel Insull got the wind up and ran off to Canada with his wife.

Extradition proceedings. He fled to Paris. When the authorities began to close in on him there he slipped away to Italy, took a plane to Tirana, another to Saloniki and then the train to Athens. There the old fox went to earth. Money talked as sweetly in Athens as it had in Chicago in the old days.

The American ambassador tried to extradite him. Insull hired a chorus of Hellenic lawyers and politicos and sat drinking coffee in the lobby of the Grande Bretagne, while they proceeded to tie up the ambassador in a snarl of chicanery as complicated as the bookkeeping of his holdingcompanies. The successors of Demosthenes were delighted. The ancestral itch in many a Hellenic palm was temporarily assuaged. Samuel Insull settled down cozily in Athens, was stirred by the sight of the Parthenon, watched the goats feeding on the Pentelic slopes, visited the Areopagus, admired marble fragments ascribed to Phidias, talked with the local bankers about reorganizing the public utilities of Greece, was said to be promoting Macedonian lignite. He was the toast of the Athenians; Madame Kouryoumdjouglou, the vivacious wife of a Bagdad datemerchant, devoted herself to his comfort. When the first effort at extradition failed, the old gentleman declared in the courtroom, as he struggled out from the embraces of his four lawyers: *Greece is a small but great country.*

The idyll was interrupted when the Roosevelt Administration began to put the heat on the Greek Foreign Office. Government lawyers in Chicago were accumulating truckloads of evidence and chalking up more and more drastic indictments.

Finally after many a postponement (he had hired physicians as well as lawyers, they cried to high heaven that it would kill him to leave the genial climate of the Attic plain),

he was ordered to leave Greece as an undesirable alien, to the great indignation of Balkan society and of Madame Kouryoumdjouglou.

He hired the *Maiotis* a small and grubby Greek freighter and panicked the foreignnews services by slipping off for an unknown destination.

It was rumored that the new Odysseus was bound for Aden, for the islands of the

South Seas, that he'd been invited to Persia. After a few days he turned up rather seasick in the Bosporus on his way, it was said, to Rumania where Madame Kouryoumdjouglou had advised him to put himself under the protection of her friend la Lupescu.

At the request of the American ambassador the Turks were delighted to drag him off the Greek freighter and place him in a not at all comfortable jail. Again money had been mysteriously wafted from England, the healing balm began to flow, lawyers were hired, interpreters expostulated, doctors made diagnoses;

but Angora was boss

and Insull was shipped off to Smyrna to be turned over to the assistant federal districtattorney who had come all that way to arrest him.

The Turks wouldn't even let Madame Kouryoumdjouglou, on her way back from making arrangements in Bucharest, go ashore to speak to him. In a scuffle with the officials on the steamboat the poor lady was pushed overboard

and with difficulty fished out of the Bosporus.

Once he was cornered the old man let himself tamely be taken home on the *Exilona*, started writing his memoirs, made himself agreeable to his fellow passengers, was taken off at Sandy Hook and rushed to Chicago to be arraigned.

In Chicago the government spitefully kept him a couple of nights in jail; men he'd never known, so the newspapers said, stepped forward to go on his twohundredand-fiftythousanddollar bail. He was moved to a hospital that he himself had endowed. Solidarity. The leading businessmen in Chicago were photographed visiting him there. Henry Ford paid a call.

The trial was very beautiful. The prosecution got bogged in finance technicalities. The judge was not unfriendly. The Insulls stole the show.

They were folks, they smiled at reporters, they posed for photographers, they went down to the courtroom by bus. Investors might have been ruined but so, they allowed it to be known, were the Insulls; the captain had gone down with the ship.

Old Samuel Insull rambled amiably on the stand, told his lifestory: from officeboy to powermagnate, his struggle to make good, his love for his home and the kiddies. He didn't deny he'd made mistakes; who hadn't, but they were honest errors. Samuel Insull wept. Brother Martin wept. The lawyers wept. With voices choked with emotion headliners of Chicago business told from the witnessstand how much Insull had done for business in Chicago. There wasn't a dry eye in the jury.

Finally driven to the wall by the prosecutingattorney Samuel Insull blurted out that yes, he had made an error of some ten million dollars in accounting but that it had been an honest error.

Verdict: Not Guilty.

Smiling through their tears the happy Insulls went to their towncar amid the cheers of the crowd. Thousands of ruined investors, at least so the newspapers said, who had lost their life savings sat crying over the home editions at the thought of how Mr. Insull had suffered. The bankers were happy, the bankers had moved in on the properties.

In an odor of sanctity the deposed monarch of superpower, the officeboy who made good, enjoys his declining years spending the pension of twentyone thousand a year that the directors of his old companies dutifully restored to him. *After fifty years of work,* he said, *my job is gone.*

1936

F. Scott Fitzgerald
1896–1940

Francis Scott Key Fitzgerald belonged, as Edmund Wilson once noted, as much to "the middle west of large cities and country clubs" as Sinclair Lewis belonged to "the middle west of the prairies and little towns." Born in St. Paul, Minnesota, on September 24, 1896, Fitzgerald was descended on his father's side from a socially prominent family of once-prosperous landowners and legislators, including the author of "The Star-Spangled Banner," and on his mother's from a family of newly prosperous and still thriving Irish immigrants. The former, he later noted, possessed "that series of reticences and obligations that go under the poor old shattered word 'breeding,'" while the latter "had the money." From this divided heritage, Fitzgerald acquired not only a deep ambivalence toward both status and money but also a sense of entanglement in America's history. "I look out at it," he once said of that history, "and I think it is the most beautiful history in the world. It is the history of me and my people. . . . It is the history of all aspiration—not just the American dream but the human dream." Yet Fitzgerald's hold on his heritage, as on almost everything, remained precarious. "That was always my experience," he observed near the end of his life, "a poor boy in a rich town; a poor boy in a rich boy's school; a poor boy in a rich man's club."

From St. Paul, Fitzgerald went on to Princeton and New York and Paris and Hollywood. No major writer of his time lived so extravagant a version of success, and none experienced a more devastating version of failure. He was at once a striking embodiment and a scathing critic of his age, primarily because he possessed, as his friend John Peale Bishop remarked, "the rare faculty of being able to experience romantic and ingenuous emotions and a half hour later regard them with satiric detachment." Many of Fitzgerald's emotions, like those of his age, derived from the almost religious awe that he felt toward the idealization of great wealth and the romanticization of sexual love, by both of which he felt simultaneously attracted and repulsed, enchanted and offended. At the same time, however, his fiction discloses a preoccupation with and a sensitivity to social class that is unusual in American fiction. In both his writing and his life, Fitzgerald continually demonstrated the tensions of a divided consciousness. Toward the end of his life, in a series of remarkably personal and vulnerable essays about his "crack-up," he said that "the test of a first-rate intelligence is the ability to hold two opposed ideas in the mind at the same time, and still retain the ability to function."

At a Catholic prep school in New Jersey and then at Princeton, where poor examination scores barely qualified him in 1913 for admission "with conditions," Fitzgerald sacrificed academic achievement to social success. He very early equated literature with celebrity and success, claiming in "The Crack-up" (1936) that "it seemed a romantic business to be a successful literary man—you were not ever going to be famous as a movie star but what note you had was probably longer-lived—you were never going to have the power of a man of strong political or religious convictions but you were certainly more independent." At Princeton, Fitzgerald compiled a dismal scholastic record—he was in academic trouble every semester—yet managed to distinguish himself socially and intellectually through his writing. He wrote clever plots and lyrics for Triangle Club shows (in one he played a glamorous show girl, and a photograph of him in costume appeared in the *New York Times*), along with short stories, poems, and plays for literary and humor magazines.

In 1917 Fitzgerald conveniently eased himself out of Princeton, where he had fallen a year behind because of poor grades, by accepting a commission in the U.S. Infantry. That winter, at Fort Leavenworth, Kansas (where his platoon captain was Dwight David Eisenhower), Fitzgerald began a novel, *The Romantic Egoist,* which, after several drafts and rejections, was eventually salvaged as *This Side of Paradise* (1920). Fitzgerald worked desperately at the novel—keeping at it while in the army, including a tour in Montgomery, Alabama (he never got overseas), and then after the army while working briefly in New York and while living at his parents' house in St. Paul—because he optimistically equated its publication with both literary and romantic success. While stationed in Montgomery, Fitzgerald had fallen in love with a recent high school graduate, a beautiful, high-spirited, talented, precariously balanced debutante named Zelda Sayre. "If I stopped working to finish the novel," Fitzgerald later wrote, "I lost the girl." With the publication of *This Side of Paradise,* an autobiographical novel set in Princeton, Fitzgerald not only won Zelda's hand but also made himself a cultural hero to the "flappers and philosophers" of the era he named "the Jazz Age." A whole generation of college students listened to Fitzgerald as one might listen to an oracle.

The novel proved to be an immediate sensation; it sold over 40,000 copies in its first year and made Fitzgerald an overnight celebrity. It also immensely improved his income: "Counting the bag, I found that in 1919 I had made $800 by writing, that in 1920 I had made $18,000 [from] stories, picture rights, and book. My story price had gone from $30 to $1,000." Fitzgerald had been publishing his short stories since the spring of 1919, first in H. L. Mencken's *The Smart Set* and later in the mass-circulation *Saturday Evening Post,* where he published story after story for the next seventeen years. Though Fitzgerald remains one of the finest American short-story writers, he often expressed contempt for the form—"I don't enjoy it & just do it for the money"—and considered the novel as the best expression of his art. Nevertheless, Fitzgerald would publish in his lifetime four significant collections of stories: *Flappers and Philosophers* (1920), *Tales of the Jazz Age* (1922), *All the Sad Young Men* (1926) (which featured "The Rich Boy" as the lead story), and *Taps at Reveille* (1935). Several collections of stories were also published posthumously. Edmund Wilson, who met Fitzgerald at Princeton and who became one his closest friends, had warned Fitzgerald after reading *This Side of Paradise* that he was in danger of becoming a "very popular trashy novelist." In selling scores of stories to popular magazines over the years, Fitzgerald, it is apparent, did not always heed Wilson's warning.

After their marriage in April 1920, Fitzgerald and Zelda set out on a life together that was glamorous, extravagant, emotionally stormy, and usually good publicity. Through the 1920s and into the 1930s they dressed fashionably, stayed in expensive hotels, swam in public fountains, and danced on restaurant tables. They partied for nights at a time, drank excessively, and enjoyed being evicted from public places, all the while spending money even more rapidly than Fitzgerald could earn it. A second novel, *The Beautiful and Damned,* a story of moral and sexual dissolution partly stimulated by the fast style of the Fitzgeralds' marriage, appeared in 1922 and received many disappointing reviews. Between 1922 and 1924 Fitzgerald lived in Great Neck, Long Island, where he became friends with Ring Lardner and where he tried his hand at an unsuccessful play, *The Vegetable* (1923). In 1924 the Fitzgeralds sailed for an extended European trip, during which Fitzgerald met Gertrude Stein and Ezra Pound and began a tense, competitive friendship with Ernest Hemingway. In 1925 Fitzgerald published his finest novel, *The Great Gatsby,* which has continued to exercise a remarkable hold on both the popular and the academic imagination. Three movies have been based on it, and scores of critical articles have been written about it. The novel is about the mysterious, fabulously wealthy Jay Gatsby, who throws lavish parties at his Long Island estate and who tries to relive a previous idyllic romance. For all his vulgarity, Gatsby possesses "some heightened sensitivity to the promises of life . . . an extraordinary gift for hope, a romantic readiness." The enormous popularity of the book derives in part from its focus on two of Fitzgerald's favorite themes, love and money, while its enormous critical success derives from Fitzgerald's ability to imbue a popular subject with cultural myth and literary seriousness.

Fitzgerald returned to the United States in December 1926 and spent a few months scriptwriting in Hollywood. The Fitzgeralds then settled outside of Wilmington, Delaware, where they tried to piece their lives together. Zelda felt unproductive and frustrated; Fitzgerald's drinking had reached dangerous proportions. In the summer of 1928 they returned to Paris, where Zelda, always a talented dancer and desperately searching for an independent identity, tried too late to find a creative outlet in ballet. Two years later, while on another trip to Europe, Zelda suffered the first of a series of mental breakdowns that forced her to spend most of the last seventeen years of her life in sanatoriums. By 1931, when the Fitzgeralds returned to America, the Great Depression was deepening and Fitzgerald was experiencing an abrupt reversal of fortune. Guilt-ridden and depressed by Zelda's collapse, humbled by his own rising self-doubts, he began drinking more and writing less.

In 1932 Zelda Fitzgerald published a novel, *Save Me the Waltz,* which she had written while she was receiving treatment at the Johns Hopkins clinic. Two years later Fitzgerald published *Tender Is the Night,* the story of an alcoholic American psychiatrist who falls in love with and disastrously marries one of his wealthy patients. (The book's title comes from "Ode to a Nightingale," one of several Keats poems that had long exerted a powerful influence on Fitzgerald's fiction.) But nothing could revitalize Fitzgerald's financial situation. The royalties on works that had earned hundreds of thousands of dollars in the 1920s brought him a total of $50 in 1932 and 1933. Sorely in debt, Fitzgerald returned to Hollywood in 1937 on a lucrative contract as a scriptwriter. But his effort to translate his genius for narrative fiction into screenplays also failed. Although he worked on numerous scripts, he managed to receive only one screen credit over the next two years. His drinking binges continued to get him in trouble with the studios, and he gradually drifted into free-lance jobs. In 1940, at the age of forty-four, he died in Hollywood of a heart attack at the home of the journalist Sheilah Graham. His new novel—Fitzgerald liked to think of it as "a Western" —about a self-made Hollywood producer, *The Last Tycoon,* remained unfinished. Over the next eight years, Zelda continued to struggle with bouts of severe depression. In 1947, she was burned to death in a North Carolina hospital fire.

"I am not a great man," Fitzgerald said to his daughter, near the end of his life, "but sometimes I think the impersonal and objective quality of my talent and the sacrifices of it, in pieces, to preserve its essential value has some sort of epic grandeur." At the time of his death, Fitzgerald's reputation, like his income, had fallen very low. In the years since, however, readers have discovered, in *The Great Gatsby, Tender Is the Night,* and a handful of stories, including "The Rich Boy," works of permanent value. At its best, the lyricism of his prose arises from and is interlaced with dramatic situations that disclose something of the emptiness and something of the hope of our world. The critic Lionel Trilling regarded Fitzgerald as "perhaps the last notable writer to affirm the Romantic fantasy, descended from the Renaissance, of personal ambition or heroism, of life committed to, or thrown away for, some ideal of self."

Further Reading:
K. Eble, *F. Scott Fitzgerald,* 1963.
W. Goldhurst, *F. Scott Fitzgerald and His Contemporaries,* 1963.
A. Mizener, *The Far Side of Paradise,* rev. ed., 1965.
J. F. Callahan, *The Illusions of a Nation: Myth and History in the Novels of F. Scott Fitzgerald,* 1972.
M. J. Bruccoli, *Some Sort of Epic Grandeur: The Life of F. Scott Fitzgerald,* 1981.

Texts:
"The Rich Boy" from *Babylon Revisited and Other Stories,* 1950.
The Crack-up, 1945.

The Rich Boy

[I]

Begin with an individual, and before you know it you find that you have created a type; begin with a type, and you find that you have created—nothing. That is because we are all queer fish, queerer behind our faces and voices than we want any one to know or than we know ourselves. When I hear a man proclaiming himself an "average, honest, open fellow," I feel pretty sure that he has some definite and perhaps terrible abnormality which he has agreed to conceal—and his protestation of being average and honest and open is his way of reminding himself of his misprision.

There are no types, no plurals. There is a rich boy, and this is his and not his brothers' story. All my life I have lived among his brothers but this one has been my friend. Besides, if I wrote about his brothers I should have to begin by attacking all the lies that the poor have told about the rich and the rich have told about themselves —such a wild structure they have erected that when we pick up a book about the rich, some instinct prepares us for unreality. Even the intelligent and impassioned reporters of life have made the country of the rich as unreal as fairy-land.

Let me tell you about the very rich. They are different from you and me. They possess and enjoy early, and it does something to them, makes them soft where we are hard, and cynical where we are trustful, in a way that, unless you were born rich, it is very difficult to understand. They think, deep in their hearts, that they are better than we are because we had to discover the compensations and refuges of life for ourselves. Even when they enter deep into our world or sink below us, they still think that they are better than we are. They are different. The only way I can describe young Anson Hunter is to approach him as if he were a foreigner and cling stubbornly to my point of view. If I accept his for a moment I am lost—I have nothing to show but a preposterous movie.

II

Anson was the eldest of six children who would some day divide a fortune of fifteen million dollars, and he reached the age of reason—is it seven?—at the beginning of the century when daring young women were already gliding along Fifth Avenue in electric "mobiles." In those days he and his brother had an English governess who spoke the language very clearly and crisply and well, so that the two boys grew to speak as she did—their words and sentences were all crisp and clear and not run together as ours are. They didn't talk exactly like English children but acquired an accent that is peculiar to fashionable people in the city of New York.

In the summer the six children were moved from the house on 71st Street to a big estate in northern Connecticut. It was not a fashionable locality—Anson's father wanted to delay as long as possible his children's knowledge of that side of life. He was a man somewhat superior to his class, which composed New York society, and to his period, which was the snobbish and formalized vulgarity of the Gilded Age, and he wanted his sons to learn habits of concentration and have sound constitutions and grow up into right-living and successful men. He and his wife kept an eye on them as well as they were able until the two older boys went away to school, but in huge establishments this is difficult—it was much simpler in the series of small and medium-sized houses in which my own youth was spent—I was never far out of the reach of my mother's voice, of the sense of her presence, her approval or disapproval.

Anson's first sense of his superiority came to him when he realized the half-grudging American deference that was paid to him in the Connecticut village. The parents of the boys he played with always inquired after his father and mother, and were vaguely excited when their own children were asked to the Hunters' house. He accepted this as the natural state of things, and a sort of impatience with all groups of which he was not the centre—in money, in position, in authority—remained with him for the rest of his life. He disdained to struggle with other boys for precedence —he expected it to be given him freely, and when it wasn't he withdrew into his family. His family was sufficient, for in the East money is still a somewhat feudal thing, a clan-forming thing. In the snobbish West, money separates families to form "sets."

At eighteen, when he went to New Haven, Anson was tall and thick-set, with a clear complexion and a healthy color from the ordered life he had led in school. His hair was yellow and grew in a funny way on his head, his nose was beaked—these two things kept him from being handsome—but he had a confident charm and a certain brusque style, and the upper-class men who passed him on the street knew without being told that he was a rich boy and had gone to one of the best schools. Nevertheless, his very superiority kept him from being a success in college—the independence was mistaken for egotism, and the refusal to accept Yale standards with the proper awe seemed to belittle all those who had. So, long before he graduated, he began to shift the centre of his life to New York.

He was at home in New York—there was his own house with "the kind of servants you can't get any more"—and his own family, of which, because of his good humor and a certain ability to make things go, he was rapidly becoming the centre, and the débutante parties, and the correct manly world of the men's clubs, and the occasional wild spree with the gallant girls[1] whom New Haven only knew from the fifth row. His aspirations were conventional enough—they included even the irreproachable shadow he would some day marry, but they differed from the aspirations of the majority of young men in that there was no mist over them, none of that quality which is variously known as "idealism" or "illusion." Anson accepted without reservation the world of high finance and high extravagance, of divorce and dissipation, of snobbery and of privilege. Most of our lives end as a compromise—it was as a compromise that his life began.

He and I first met in the late summer of 1917 when he was just out of Yale, and, like the rest of us, was swept up into the systematized hysteria of the war. In the blue-green uniform of the naval aviation he came down to Pensacola, where the hotel orchestras played "I'm sorry, dear," and we young officers danced with the girls. Every one liked him, and though he ran with the drinkers and wasn't an especially good pilot, even the instructors treated him with a certain respect. He was always having long talks with them in his confident, logical voice—talks which ended by his getting himself, or, more frequently, another officer, out of some impending trouble. He was convivial, bawdy, robustly avid for pleasure, and we were all surprised when he fell in love with a conservative and rather proper girl.

Her name was Paula Legendre, a dark, serious beauty from somewhere in California. Her family kept a winter residence just outside of town, and in spite of her primness she was enormously popular; there is a large class of men whose egotism can't endure humor in a woman. But Anson wasn't that sort, and I couldn't understand the attraction of her "sincerity"—that was the thing to say about her—for his keen and somewhat sardonic mind.

Nevertheless, they fell in love—and on her terms. He no longer joined the twilight gathering at the De Soto bar, and whenever they were seen together they were engaged in a long, serious dialogue, which must have gone on several weeks. Long afterward he told me that it was not about anything in particular but was composed on both sides of immature and even meaningless statements—the emotional content that gradually came to fill it grew up not out of the words but out of its enormous seriousness. It was a sort of hypnosis. Often it was interrupted, giving way to that

---

[1] I.e., chorus girls or performers in burlesque theaters.

emasculated humor we call fun; when they were alone it was resumed again, solemn, low-keyed, and pitched so as to give each other a sense of unity in feeling and thought. They came to resent any interruptions of it, to be unresponsive to facetiousness about life, even to the mild cynicism of their contemporaries. They were only happy when the dialogue was going on, and its seriousness bathed them like the amber glow of an open fire. Toward the end there came an interruption they did not resent—it began to be interrupted by passion.

Oddly enough, Anson was as engrossed in the dialogue as she was and as profoundly affected by it, yet at the same time aware that on his side much was insincere, and on hers much was merely simple. At first, too, he despised her emotional simplicity as well, but with his love her nature deepened and blossomed, and he could despise it no longer. He felt that if he could enter into Paula's warm safe life he would be happy. The long preparation of the dialogue removed any constraint—he taught her some of what he had learned from more adventurous women, and she responded with a rapt holy intensity. One evening after a dance they agreed to marry, and he wrote a long letter about her to his mother. The next day Paula told him that she was rich, that she had a personal fortune of nearly a million dollars.

III

It was exactly as if they could say "Neither of us has anything: we shall be poor together"—just as delightful that they should be rich instead. It gave them the same communion of adventure. Yet when Anson got leave in April, and Paula and her mother accompanied him North, she was impressed with the standing of his family in New York and with the scale on which they lived. Alone with Anson for the first time in the rooms where he had played as a boy, she was filled with a comfortable emotion, as though she were pre-eminently safe and taken care of. The pictures of Anson in a skull cap at his first school, of Anson on horseback with the sweetheart of a mysterious forgotten summer, of Anson in a gay group of ushers and bridesmaids at a wedding, made her jealous of his life apart from her in the past, and so completely did his authoritative person seem to sum up and typify these possessions of his that she was inspired with the idea of being married immediately and returning to Pensacola as his wife.

But an immediate marriage wasn't discussed—even the engagement was to be secret until after the war. When she realized that only two days of his leave remained, her dissatisfaction crystallized in the intention of making him as unwilling to wait as she was. They were driving to the country for dinner, and she determined to force the issue that night.

Now a cousin of Paula's was staying with them at the Ritz, a severe, bitter girl who loved Paula but was somewhat jealous of her impressive engagement, and as Paula was late in dressing, the cousin, who wasn't going to the party, received Anson in the parlor of the suite.

Anson had met friends at five o'clock and drunk freely and indiscreetly with them for an hour. He left the Yale Club at a proper time, and his mother's chauffeur drove him to the Ritz, but his usual capacity was not in evidence, and the impact of the steam-heated sitting-room made him suddenly dizzy. He knew it, and he was both amused and sorry.

Paula's cousin was twenty-five, but she was exceptionally naïve, and at first failed to realize what was up. She had never met Anson before, and she was surprised when he mumbled strange information and nearly fell off his chair, but until Paula appeared it didn't occur to her that what she had taken for the odor of a dry-cleaned uniform was really whiskey. But Paula understood as soon as she appeared; her only thought was to get Anson away before her mother saw him, and at the look in her eyes the cousin understood too.

When Paula and Anson descended to the limousine they found two men inside, both asleep; they were the men with whom he had been drinking at the Yale Club, and they were also going to the party. He had entirely forgotten their presence in the car. On the way to Hempstead they awoke and sang. Some of the songs were rough, and though Paula tried to reconcile herself to the fact that Anson had few verbal inhibitions, her lips tightened with shame and distaste.

Back at the hotel the cousin, confused and agitated, considered the incident, and then walked into Mrs. Legendre's bedroom, saying: "Isn't he funny?"

"Who is funny?"

"Why—Mr. Hunter. He seemed so funny."

Mrs. Legendre looked at her sharply.

"How is he funny?"

"Why, he said he was French. I didn't know he was French."

"That's absurd. You must have misunderstood." She smiled: "It was a joke."

The cousin shook her head stubbornly.

"No. He said he was brought up in France. He said he couldn't speak any English, and that's why he couldn't talk to me. And he couldn't!"

Mrs. Legendre looked away with impatience just as the cousin added thoughtfully, "Perhaps it was because he was so drunk," and walked out of the room.

This curious report was true. Anson, finding his voice thick and uncontrollable, had taken the unusual refuge of announcing that he spoke no English. Years afterwards he used to tell that part of the story, and he invariably communicated the uproarious laughter which the memory aroused in him.

Five times in the next hour Mrs. Legendre tried to get Hempstead on the phone. When she succeeded, there was a ten-minute delay before she heard Paula's voice on the wire.

"Cousin Jo told me Anson was intoxicated."

"Oh, no. . . ."

"Oh, yes. Cousin Jo says he was intoxicated. He told her he was French, and fell off his chair and behaved as if he was very intoxicated. I don't want you to come home with him."

"Mother, he's all right! Please don't worry about—"

"But I do worry. I think it's dreadful. I want you to promise me not to come home with him."

"I'll take care of it, mother. . . ."

"I don't want you to come home with him."

"All right, mother. Good-by."

"Be sure now, Paula. Ask some one to bring you."

Deliberately Paula took the receiver from her ear and hung it up. Her face was flushed with helpless annoyance. Anson was stretched out asleep in a bedroom up-stairs, while the dinner-party below was proceeding lamely toward conclusion.

The hour's drive had sobered him somewhat—his arrival was merely hilarious—and Paula hoped that the evening was not spoiled, after all, but two imprudent cocktails before dinner completed the disaster. He talked boisterously and somewhat offensively to the party at large for fifteen minutes, and then slid silently under the table; like a man in an old print—but, unlike an old print, it was rather horrible without being at all quaint. None of the young girls present remarked upon the incident—it seemed to merit only silence. His uncle and two other men carried him up-stairs, and it was just after this that Paula was called to the phone.

An hour later Anson awoke in a fog of nervous agony, through which he perceived after a moment the figure of his uncle Robert standing by the door.

". . . I said are you better?"

"What?"

"Do you feel better, old man?"

"Terrible," said Anson.

"I'm going to try you on another bromo-seltzer. If you can hold it down, it'll do you good to sleep."

With an effort Anson slid his legs from the bed and stood up.

"I'm all right," he said dully.

"Take it easy."

"I thin' if you gave me a glassbrandy I could go down-stairs."

"Oh, no—"

"Yes, that's the only thin'. I'm all right now. . . . I suppose I'm in Dutch dow' there."

"They know you're a little under the weather," said his uncle deprecatingly. "But don't worry about it. Schuyler didn't even get here. He passed away in the locker-room over at the Links."

Indifferent to any opinion, except Paula's, Anson was nevertheless determined to save the débris of the evening, but when after a cold bath he made his appearance most of the party had already left. Paula got up immediately to go home.

In the limousine the old serious dialogue began. She had known that he drank, she admitted, but she had never expected anything like this—it seemed to her that perhaps they were not suited to each other, after all. Their ideas about life were too different, and so forth. When she finished speaking, Anson spoke in turn, very soberly. Then Paula said she'd have to think it over; she wouldn't decide to-night; she was not angry but she was terribly sorry. Nor would she let him come into the hotel with her, but just before she got out of the car she leaned and kissed him unhappily on the cheek.

The next afternoon Anson had a long talk with Mrs. Legendre while Paula sat listening in silence. It was agreed that Paula was to brood over the incident for a proper period and then, if mother and daughter thought it best, they would follow Anson to Pensacola. On his part he apologized with sincerity and dignity—that was all; with every card in her hand Mrs. Legendre was unable to establish any advantage over him. He made no promises, showed no humility, only delivered a few serious comments on life which brought him off with rather a moral superiority at the end. When they came South three weeks later, neither Anson in his satisfaction nor Paula in her relief at the reunion realized that the psychological moment had passed forever.

IV

He dominated and attracted her, and at the same time filled her with anxiety. Confused by his mixture of solidity and self-indulgence, of sentiment and cynicism—incongruities which her gentle mind was unable to resolve—Paula grew to think of him as two alternating personalities. When she saw him alone, or at a formal party, or with his casual inferiors, she felt a tremendous pride in his strong, attractive presence, the paternal, understanding stature of his mind. In other company she became uneasy when what had been a fine imperviousness to mere gentility showed its other face. The other face was gross, humorous, reckless of everything but pleasure. It startled her mind temporarily away from him, even led her into a short covert experiment with an old beau, but it was no use—after four months of Anson's enveloping vitality there was an anæmic pallor in all other men.

In July he was ordered abroad, and their tenderness and desire reached a crescendo. Paula considered a last-minute marriage—decided against it only because there were always cocktails on his breath now, but the parting itself made her physically ill with grief. After his departure she wrote him long letters of regret for the days of love they had missed by waiting. In August Anson's plane slipped down into the North Sea. He was pulled onto a destroyer after a night in the water and sent to hospital with pneumonia; the armistice was signed before he was finally sent home.

Then, with every opportunity given back to them, with no material obstacle to overcome, the secret weavings of their temperaments came between them, drying up their kisses and their tears, making their voices less loud to one another, muffling the intimate chatter of their hearts until the old communication was only possible by letters, from far away. One afternoon a society reporter waited for two hours in the Hunters' house for a confirmation of their engagement. Anson denied it; nevertheless an early issue carried the report as a leading paragraph—they were "constantly seen together at Southhampton, Hot Springs, and Tuxedo Park." But the serious dialogue had turned a corner into a long-sustained quarrel, and the affair was almost played out. Anson got drunk flagrantly and missed an engagement with her, whereupon Paula made certain behavioristic demands. His despair was helpless before his pride and his knowledge of himself: the engagement was definitely broken.

"Dearest," said their letters now, "Dearest, Dearest, when I wake up in the middle of the night and realize that after all it was not to be, I feel that I want to die. I can't go on living any more. Perhaps when we meet this summer we may talk things over and decide differently—we were so excited and sad that day, and I don't feel that I can live all my life without you. You speak of other people. Don't you know there are no other people for me, but only you. . . ."

But as Paula drifted here and there around the East she would sometimes mention her gaieties to make him wonder. Anson was too acute to wonder. When he saw a man's name in her letters he felt more sure of her and a little disdainful—he was always superior to such things. But he still hoped that they would some day marry.

Meanwhile he plunged vigorously into all the movement and glitter of postbellum New York, entering a brokerage house, joining half a dozen clubs, dancing late, and moving in three worlds—his own world, the world of young Yale graduates, and that section of the half-world which rests one end on Broadway. But there was always a thorough and infractible eight hours devoted to his work in Wall Street, where the combination of his influential family connection, his sharp intelligence, and his abundance of sheer physical energy brought him almost immediately forward. He had one of those invaluable minds with partitions in it; sometimes he appeared at his office refreshed by less than an hour's sleep, but such occurrences were rare. So early as 1920 his income in salary and commissions exceeded twelve thousand dollars.

As the Yale tradition slipped into the past he became more and more of a popular figure among his classmates in New York, more popular than he had ever been in college. He lived in a great house, and had the means of introducing young men into other great houses. Moreover, his life already seemed secure, while theirs, for the most part, had arrived again at precarious beginnings. They commenced to turn to him for amusement and escape, and Anson responded readily, taking pleasure in helping people and arranging their affairs.

There were no men in Paula's letters now, but a note of tenderness ran through them that had not been there before. From several sources he heard that she had "a heavy beau," Lowell Thayer, a Bostonian of wealth and position, and though he was sure she still loved him, it made him uneasy to think that he might lose her, after all. Save for one unsatisfactory day she had not been in New York for almost five months, and as the rumors multiplied he became increasingly anxious to see her. In February he took his vacation and went down to Florida.

Palm Beach sprawled plump and opulent between the sparkling sapphire of Lake Worth, flawed here and there by house-boats at anchor, and the great turquoise bar of the Atlantic Ocean. The huge bulks of the Breakers and the Royal Poinciana rose as twin paunches from the bright level of the sand, and around them clustered the Dancing Glade, Bradley's House of Chance, and a dozen modistes and milliners with goods at triple prices from New York. Upon the trellised veranda of the Breakers two hundred women stepped right, stepped left, wheeled, and slid in that then celebrated calisthenic known as the double-shuffle, while in half-time to the music two thousand bracelets clicked up and down on two hundred arms.

At the Everglades Club after dark Paula and Lowell Thayer and Anson and a casual fourth played bridge with hot cards. It seemed to Anson that her kind, serious face was wan and tired—she had been around now for four, five, years. He had known her for three.

"Two spades."

"Cigarette? . . . Oh, I beg your pardon. By me."

"By."

"I'll double three spades."

There were a dozen tables of bridge in the room, which was filling up with smoke. Anson's eyes met Paula's, held them persistently even when Thayer's glance fell between them. . . .

"What was bid?" he asked abstractedly.

"Rose of Washington Square"

sang the young people in the corners:

"I'm withering there
    In basement air—"

The smoke banked like fog, and the opening of a door filled the room with blown swirls of ectoplasm. Little Bright Eyes streaked past the tables seeking Mr. Conan Doyle among the Englishmen who were posing as Englishmen about the lobby.

"You could cut it with a knife."

". . . cut it with a knife."

". . . . a knife."

At the end of the rubber Paula suddenly got up and spoke to Anson in a tense, low voice. With scarcely a glance at Lowell Thayer, they walked out the door and descended a long flight of stone steps—in a moment they were walking hand in hand along the moonlit beach.

"Darling, darling. . . ." They embraced recklessly, passionately, in a shadow. . . . Then Paula drew back her face to let his lips say what she wanted to hear—she could feel the words forming as they kissed again. . . . Again she broke away, listening, but as he pulled her close once more she realized that he had said nothing—only *"Darling! Darling!"* in that deep, sad whisper that always made her cry. Humbly, obediently, her emotions yielded to him and the tears streamed down her face, but her heart kept on crying: "Ask me—oh, Anson, dearest, ask me!"

"Paula. . . . *Paula!*"

The words wrung her heart like hands, and Anson, feeling her tremble, knew that emotion was enough. He need say no more, commit their destinies to no practical enigma. Why should he, when he might hold her so, biding his own time, for another year—forever? He was considering them both, her more than himself. For a moment, when she said suddenly that she must go back to her hotel, he hesitated, thinking, first, "This is the moment, after all," and then: "No, let it wait—she is mine. . . ."

He had forgotten that Paula too was worn away inside with the strain of three years. Her mood passed forever in the night.

He went back to New York next morning filled with a certain restless dissatisfaction. Late in April, without warning, he received a telegram from Bar Harbor in which Paula told him that she was engaged to Lowell Thayer, and that they would be married immediately in Boston. What he never really believed could happen had happened at last.

Anson filled himself with whiskey that morning, and going to the office, carried on his work without a break—rather with a fear of what would happen if he stopped. In the evening he went out as usual, saying nothing of what had occurred; he was cordial, humorous, unabstracted. But one thing he could not help—for three days, in any place, in any company, he would suddenly bend his head into his hands and cry like a child.

V

In 1922 when Anson went abroad with the junior partner to investigate some London loans, the journey intimated that he was to be taken into the firm. He was twenty-seven now, a little heavy without being definitely stout, and with a manner older than his years. Old people and young people liked him and trusted him, and mothers felt safe when their daughters were in his charge, for he had a way, when he came into a room, of putting himself on a footing with the oldest and most conservative people there. "You and I," he seemed to say, "we're solid. We understand."

He had an instinctive and rather charitable knowledge of the weaknesses of men and women, and, like a priest, it made him the more concerned for the maintenance of outward forms. It was typical of him that every Sunday morning he taught in a fashionable Episcopal Sunday-school—even though a cold shower and a quick change into a cutaway coat were all that separated him from the wild night before.

After his father's death he was the practical head of his family, and, in effect, guided the destinies of the younger children. Through a complication his authority did not extend to his father's estate, which was administrated by his Uncle Robert, who was the horsey member of the family, a good-natured, hard-drinking member of that set which centres about Wheatley Hills.

Uncle Robert and his wife, Edna, had been great friends of Anson's youth, and the former was disappointed when his nephew's superiority failed to take a horsey form. He backed him for a city club which was the most difficult in America to enter —one could only join if one's family had "helped to build up New York" (or, in other words, were rich before 1880)—and when Anson, after his election, neglected it for the Yale Club, Uncle Robert gave him a little talk on the subject. But when on top of that Anson declined to enter Robert Hunter's own conservative and somewhat neglected brokerage house, his manner grew cooler. Like a primary teacher who has taught all he knew, he slipped out of Anson's life.

There were so many friends in Anson's life—scarcely one for whom he had not done some unusual kindness and scarcely one whom he did not occasionally embarrass by his bursts of rough conversation or his habit of getting drunk whenever and however he liked. It annoyed him when any one else blundered in that regard—about his own lapses he was always humorous. Odd things happened to him and he told them with infectious laughter.

I was working in New York that spring, and I used to lunch with him at the Yale Club, which my university was sharing until the completion of our own. I had read of Paula's marriage, and one afternoon, when I asked him about her, something moved him to tell me the story. After that he frequently invited me to family dinners at his house and behaved as though there was a special relation between us, as though with his confidence a little of that consuming memory had passed into me.

I found that despite the trusting mothers, his attitude toward girls was not indiscriminately protective. It was up to the girl—if she showed an inclination toward looseness, she must take care of herself, even with him.

"Life," he would explain sometimes, "has made a cynic of me."

By life he meant Paula. Sometimes, especially when he was drinking, it became a little twisted in his mind, and he thought that she had callously thrown him over.

This "cynicism," or rather his realization that naturally fast girls were not worth sparing, led to his affair with Dolly Karger. It wasn't his only affair in those years, but it came nearest to touching him deeply, and it had a profound effect upon his attitude toward life.

Dolly was the daughter of a notorious "publicist" who had married into society. She herself grew up into the Junior League, came out at the Plaza, and went to the Assembly; and only a few old families like the Hunters could question whether or not she "belonged," for her picture was often in the papers, and she had more enviable attention than many girls who undoubtedly did. She was dark-haired, with carmine lips and a high, lovely color, which she concealed under pinkish-gray powder all through the first year out, because high color was unfashionable—Victorian-pale was the thing to be. She wore black, severe suits and stood with her hands in her pockets leaning a little forward, with a humorous restraint on her face. She danced exquisitely —better than anything she liked to dance—better than anything except making love. Since she was ten she had always been in love, and, usually, with some boy who didn't respond to her. Those who did—and there were many—bored her after a brief encounter, but for her failures she reserved the warmest spot in her heart. When she met them she would always try once more—sometimes she succeeded, more often she failed.

It never occurred to this gypsy of the unattainable that there was a certain resemblance in those who refused to love her—they shared a hard intuition that saw through to her weakness, not a weakness of emotion but a weakness of rudder. Anson perceived this when he first met her, less than a month after Paula's marriage. He was drinking rather heavily, and he pretended for a week that he was falling in love with her. Then he dropped abruptly and forgot—immediately he took up the commanding position in her heart.

Like so many girls of that day Dolly was slackly and indiscreetly wild. The unconventionality of a slightly older generation had been simply one facet of a post-war movement to discredit obsolete manners—Dolly's was both older and shabbier, and she saw in Anson the two extremes which the emotionally shiftless woman seeks, an abandon to indulgence alternating with a protective strength. In his character she felt both the sybarite and the solid rock, and these two satisfied every need of her nature.

She felt that it was going to be difficult, but she mistook the reason—she thought that Anson and his family expected a more spectacular marriage, but she guessed immediately that her advantage lay in his tendency to drink.

They met at the large débutante dances, but as her infatuation increased they managed to be more and more together. Like most mothers, Mrs. Karger believed that Anson was exceptionally reliable, so she allowed Dolly to go with him to distant country clubs and suburban houses without inquiring closely into their activities or questioning her explanations when they came in late. At first these explanations might have been accurate, but Dolly's worldly ideas of capturing Anson were soon engulfed in the rising sweep of her emotion. Kisses in the back of taxis and motor-cars were no longer enough; they did a curious thing:

They dropped out of their world for a while and made another world just beneath it where Anson's tippling and Dolly's irregular hours would be less noticed and commented on. It was composed, this world, of varying elements—several of Anson's Yale friends and their wives, two or three young brokers and bond salesmen and a handful of unattached men, fresh from college, with money and a propensity to dissipation. What this world lacked in spaciousness and scale it made up for by allowing them a liberty that it scarcely permitted itself. Moreover, it centred around them and permitted Dolly the pleasure of a faint condescension—a pleasure which Anson, whose whole life was a condescension from the certitudes of his childhood, was unable to share.

He was not in love with her, and in the long feverish winter of their affair he frequently told her so. In the spring he was weary—he wanted to renew his life at some other source—moreover, he saw that either he must break with her now or accept the responsibility of a definite seduction. Her family's encouraging attitude precipitated his decision—one evening when Mr. Karger knocked discreetly at the library door to announce that he had left a bottle of old brandy in the dining-room, Anson felt that life was hemming him in. That night he wrote her a short letter in which he told her that he was going on his vacation, and that in view of all the circumstances they had better meet no more.

It was June. His family had closed up the house and gone to the country, so he was living temporarily at the Yale Club. I had heard about his affair with Dolly as it developed—accounts salted with humor, for he despised unstable women, and granted them no place in the social edifice in which he believed—and when he told me that night that he was definitely breaking with her I was glad. I had seen Dolly here and there, and each time with a feeling of pity at the hopelessness of her struggle, and of shame at knowing so much about her that I had no right to know. She was what is known as "a pretty little thing," but there was a certain recklessness which rather fascinated me. Her dedication to the goddess of waste would have been less obvious had she been less spirited—she would most certainly throw herself away, but I was glad when I heard that the sacrifice would not be consummated in my sight.

Anson was going to leave the letter of farewell at her house next morning. It was one of the few houses left open in the Fifth Avenue district, and he knew that the Kargers, acting upon erroneous information from Dolly, had foregone a trip abroad to give their daughter her chance. As he stepped out the door of the Yale Club into Madison Avenue the postman passed him, and he followed back inside. The first letter that caught his eye was in Dolly's hand.

He knew what it would be—a lonely and tragic monologue, full of the reproaches he knew, the invoked memories, the "I wonder if's"—all the immemorial intimacies that he had communicated to Paula Legendre in what seemed another age. Thumbing over some bills, he brought it on top again and opened it. To his surprise it was a short, somewhat formal note, which said that Dolly would be unable to go to the country with him for the week-end, because Perry Hull from Chicago had unexpectedly come to town. It added that Anson had brought this on himself: "—if I felt that you loved me as I love you I would go with you at any time, any place, but Perry is *so* nice, and he so much wants me to marry him—"

Anson smiled contemptuously—he had had experience with such decoy epistles. Moreover, he knew how Dolly had labored over this plan, probably sent for the faithful Perry and calculated the time of his arrival—even labored over the note so that it would make him jealous without driving him away. Like most compromises, it had neither force nor vitality but only a timorous despair.

Suddenly he was angry. He sat down in the lobby and read it again. Then he went to the phone, called Dolly and told her in his clear, compelling voice that he had received her note and would call for her at five o'clock as they had previously planned. Scarcely waiting for the pretended uncertainty of her "Perhaps I can see you for an hour," he hung up the receiver and went down to his office. On the way he tore his own letter into bits and dropped it in the street.

He was not jealous—she meant nothing to him—but at her pathetic ruse everything stubborn and self-indulgent in him came to the surface. It was a presumption from a mental inferior and it could not be overlooked. If she wanted to know to whom she belonged she would see.

He was on the door-step at quarter past five. Dolly was dressed for the street, and he listened in silence to the paragraph of "I can only see you for an hour," which she had begun on the phone.

"Put on your hat, Dolly," he said, "we'll take a walk."

They strolled up Madison Avenue and over to Fifth while Anson's shirt dampened upon his portly body in the deep heat. He talked little, scolding her, making no love to her, but before they had walked six blocks she was his again, apologizing for the note, offering not to see Perry at all as an atonement, offering anything. She thought that he had come because he was beginning to love her.

"I'm hot," he said when they reached 71st Street. "This is a winter suit. If I stop by the house and change, would you mind waiting for me down-stairs? I'll only be a minute."

She was happy; the intimacy of his being hot, of any physical fact about him, thrilled her. When they came to the iron-grated door and Anson took out his key she experienced a sort of delight.

Down-stairs it was dark, and after he ascended in the lift Dolly raised a curtain and looked out through opaque lace at the houses over the way. She heard the lift machinery stop, and with the notion of teasing him pressed the button that brought it down. Then on what was more than an impulse she got into it and sent it up to what she guessed was his floor.

"Anson," she called, laughing a little.

"Just a minute," he answered from his bedroom . . . then after a brief delay: "Now you can come in."

He had changed and was buttoning his vest.

"This is my room," he said lightly. "How do you like it?"

She caught sight of Paula's picture on the wall and stared at it in fascination, just as Paula had stared at the pictures of Anson's childish sweethearts five years before. She knew something about Paula—sometimes she tortured herself with fragments of the story.

Suddenly she came close to Anson, raising her arms. They embraced. Outside the area window a soft artificial twilight already hovered, though the sun was still bright on a back roof across the way. In half an hour the room would be quite dark. The uncalculated opportunity overwhelmed them, made them both breathless, and they clung more closely. It was imminent, inevitable. Still holding one another, they raised their heads—their eyes fell together upon Paula's picture, staring down at them from the wall.

Suddenly Anson dropped his arms, and sitting down at his desk tried the drawer with a bunch of keys.

"Like a drink?" he asked in a gruff voice.

"No, Anson."

He poured himself half a tumbler of whiskey, swallowed it, and then opened the door into the hall.

"Come on," he said.

Dolly hesitated.

"Anson—I'm going to the country with you tonight, after all. You understand that, don't you?"

"Of course," he answered brusquely.

In Dolly's car they rode on to Long Island, closer in their emotions than they had ever been before. They knew what would happen—not with Paula's face to remind them that something was lacking, but when they were alone in the still, hot Long Island night they did not care.

The estate in Port Washington where they were to spend the weekend belonged to a cousin of Anson's who had married a Montana copper operator. An interminable drive began at the lodge and twisted under imported poplar saplings toward a huge, pink Spanish house. Anson had often visited there before.

After dinner they danced at the Linx Club. About midnight Anson assured himself that his cousins would not leave before two—then he explained that Dolly was tired; he would take her home and return to the dance later. Trembling a little with excitement, they got into a borrowed car together and drove to Port Washington. As they reached the lodge he stopped and spoke to the night-watchman.

"When are you making a round, Carl?"

"Right away."

"Then you'll be here till everybody's in?"

"Yes, sir."

"All right. Listen: if any automobile, no matter whose it is, turns in at this gate, I want you to phone the house immediately." He put a five-dollar bill into Carl's hand. "Is that clear?"

"Yes, Mr. Anson." Being of the Old World, he neither winked nor smiled. Yet Dolly sat with her face turned slightly away.

Anson had a key. Once inside he poured a drink for both of them—Dolly left hers untouched—then he ascertained definitely the location of the phone, and found that it was within easy hearing distance of their rooms, both of which were on the first floor.

Five minutes later he knocked at the door of Dolly's room.

"Anson?" He went in, closing the door behind him. She was in bed, leaning up anxiously with elbows on the pillow; sitting beside her he took her in his arms.

"Anson, darling."

He didn't answer.

"Anson. . . . . Anson! I love you. . . . . Say you love me. Say it now—can't you say it now? Even if you don't mean it?"

He did not listen. Over her head he perceived that the picture of Paula was hanging here upon this wall.

He got up and went close to it. The frame gleamed faintly with thrice-reflected moonlight—within was a blurred shadow of a face that he saw he did not know. Almost sobbing, he turned around and stared with abomination at the little figure on the bed.

"This is all foolishness," he said thickly. "I don't know what I was thinking about. I don't love you and you'd better wait for somebody that loves you. I don't love you a bit, can't you understand?"

His voice broke, and he went hurriedly out. Back in the salon he was pouring himself a drink with uneasy fingers, when the front door opened suddenly, and his cousin came in.

"Why, Anson, I hear Dolly's sick," she began solicitously. "I hear she's sick. . . . ."

"It was nothing," he interrupted, raising his voice so that it would carry into Dolly's room. "She was a little tired. She went to bed."

For a long time afterward Anson believed that a protective God sometimes interfered in human affairs. But Dolly Karger, lying awake and staring at the ceiling, never again believed in anything at all.

VI

When Dolly married during the following autumn, Anson was in London on business. Like Paula's marriage, it was sudden, but it affected him in a different way. At first he felt that it was funny, and had an inclination to laugh when he thought of it. Later it depressed him—it made him feel old.

There was something repetitive about it—why, Paula and Dolly had belonged to different generations. He had a foretaste of the sensation of a man of forty who hears that the daughter of an old flame has married. He wired congratulations and, as was not the case with Paula, they were sincere—he had never really hoped that Paula would be happy.

When he returned to New York, he was made a partner in the firm, and, as his responsibilities increased, he had less time on his hands. The refusal of a life-insurance company to issue him a policy made such an impression on him that he stopped drinking for a year, and claimed that he felt better physically, though I think he missed the convivial recounting of those Celliniesque adventures[2] which, in his early twenties, had played such a part in his life. But he never abandoned the Yale Club. He was a figure there, a personality, and the tendency of his class, who were now seven years out of college, to drift away to more sober haunts was checked by his presence.

His day was never too full nor his mind too weary to give any sort of aid to any one who asked it. What had been done at first through pride and superiority had become a habit and a passion. And there was always something—a younger brother in trouble at New Haven, a quarrel to be patched up between a friend and his wife, a position to be found for this man, an investment for that. But his specialty was the solving of problems for young married people. Young married people fascinated him and their apartments were almost sacred to him—he knew the story of their love-affair, advised them where to live and how, and remembered their babies' names. Toward young wives his attitude was circumspect: he never abused the trust which their husbands—strangely enough in view of his unconcealed irregularities—invariably reposed in him.

He came to take a vicarious pleasure in happy marriages, and to be inspired to an almost equally pleasant melancholy by those that went astray. Not a season passed that he did not witness the collapse of an affair that perhaps he himself had fathered. When Paula was divorced and almost immediately remarried to another Bostonian, he talked about her to me all one afternoon. He would never love any one as he had loved Paula, but he insisted that he no longer cared.

[2] I.e., love affairs like those of Benvenuto Cellini (1500–1571), Italian sculptor and legendary lover.

"I'll never marry," he came to say; "I've seen too much of it, and I know a happy marriage is a very rare thing. Besides, I'm too old."

But he did believe in marriage. Like all men who spring from a happy and successful marriage, he believed in it passionately—nothing he had seen would change his belief, his cynicism dissolved upon it like air. But he did really believe he was too old. At twenty-eight he began to accept with equanimity the prospect of marrying without romantic love; he resolutely chose a New York girl of his own class, pretty, intelligent, congenial, above reproach—and set about falling in love with her. The things he had said to Paula with sincerity, to other girls with grace, he could no longer say at all without smiling, or with the force necessary to convince.

"When I'm forty," he told his friends, "I'll be ripe. I'll fall for some chorus girl like the rest."

Nevertheless, he persisted in his attempt. His mother wanted to see him married, and he could now well afford it—he had a seat on the Stock Exchange, and his earned income came to twenty-five thousand a year. The idea was agreeable: when his friends —he spent most of his time with the set he and Dolly had evolved—closed themselves in behind domestic doors at night, he no longer rejoiced in his freedom. He even wondered if he should have married Dolly. Not even Paula had loved him more, and he was learning the rarity, in a single life, of encountering true emotion.

Just as this mood began to creep over him a disquieting story reached his ear. His Aunt Edna, a woman just this side of forty, was carrying on an open intrigue with a dissolute, hard-drinking young man named Cary Sloane. Every one knew of it except Anson's Uncle Robert, who for fifteen years had talked long in clubs and taken his wife for granted.

Anson heard the story again and again with increasing annoyance. Something of his old feeling for his uncle came back to him, a feeling that was more than personal, a reversion toward that family solidarity on which he had based his pride. His intuition singled out the essential point of the affair, which was that his uncle shouldn't be hurt. It was his first experiment in unsolicited meddling, but with his knowledge of Edna's character he felt that he could handle the matter better than a district judge or his uncle.

His uncle was in Hot Springs. Anson traced down the sources of the scandal so that there should be no possibility of mistake and then he called Edna and asked her to lunch with him at the Plaza next day. Something in his tone must have frightened her, for she was reluctant, but he insisted, putting off the date until she had no excuse for refusing.

She met him at the appointed time in the Plaza lobby, a lovely, faded, gray-eyed blonde in a coat of Russian sable. Five great rings, cold with diamonds and emeralds, sparkled on her slender hands. It occurred to Anson that it was his father's intelligence and not his uncle's that had earned the fur and the stones, the rich brilliance that buoyed up her passing beauty.

Though Edna scented his hostility, she was unprepared for the directness of his approach.

"Edna, I'm astonished at the way you've been acting," he said in a strong, frank voice. "At first I couldn't believe it."

"Believe what?" she demanded sharply.

"You needn't pretend with me, Edna. I'm talking about Cary Sloane. Aside from any other consideration, I didn't think you could treat Uncle Robert—"

"Now look here, Anson—" she began angrily, but his peremptory voice broke through hers:

"—and your children in such a way. You've been married eighteen years, and you're old enough to know better."

"You can't talk to me like that! You—"

"Yes, I can. Uncle Robert has always been my best friend." He was tremendously moved. He felt a real distress about his uncle, about his three young cousins.

Edna stood up, leaving her crab-flake cocktail untasted.

"This is the silliest thing—"

"Very well, if you won't listen to me I'll go to Uncle Robert and tell him the whole story—he's bound to hear it sooner or later. And afterward I'll go to old Moses Sloane."

Edna faltered back into her chair.

"Don't talk so loud," she begged him. Her eyes blurred with tears. "You have no idea how your voice carries. You might have chosen a less public place to make all these crazy accusations."

He didn't answer.

"Oh, you never liked me, I know," she went on. "You're just taking advantage of some silly gossip to try and break up the only interesting friendship I've ever had. What did I ever do to make you hate me so?"

Still Anson waited. There would be the appeal to his chivalry, then to his pity, finally to his superior sophistication—when he had shouldered his way through all these there would be the admissions, and he could come to grips with her. By being silent, by being impervious, by returning constantly to his main weapon, which was his own true emotion, he bullied her into frantic despair as the luncheon hour slipped away. At two o'clock she took out a mirror and a handkerchief, shined away the marks of her tears and powdered the slight hollows where they had lain. She had agreed to meet him at her own house at five.

When he arrived she was stretched on a *chaise-longue* which was covered with cretonne for the summer, and the tears he had called up at luncheon seemed still to be standing in her eyes. Then he was aware of Cary Sloane's dark anxious presence upon the cold hearth.

"What's this idea of yours?" broke out Sloane immediately. "I understand you invited Edna to lunch and then threatened her on the basis of some cheap scandal."

Anson sat down.

"I have no reason to think it's only scandal."

"I hear you're going to take it to Robert Hunter, and to my father."

Anson nodded.

"Either you break it off—or I will," he said.

"What God damned business is it of yours, Hunter?"

"Don't lose your temper, Cary," said Edna nervously. "It's only a question of showing him how absurd—"

"For one thing, it's my name that's being handed around," interrupted Anson. "That's all that concerns you, Cary."

"Edna isn't a member of your family."

"She most certainly is!" His anger mounted. "Why—she owes this house and the rings on her fingers to my father's brains. When Uncle Robert married her she didn't have a penny."

They all looked at the rings as if they had a significant bearing on the situation. Edna made a gesture to take them from her hand.

"I guess they're not the only rings in the world," said Sloane.

"Oh, this is absurd," cried Edna. "Anson, will you listen to me? I've found out how the silly story started. It was a maid I discharged who went right to the Chilicheffs—all these Russians pump things out of their servants and then put a false meaning on them." She brought down her fist angrily on the table: "And after Robert lent them the limousine for a whole month when we were South last winter—"

"Do you see?" demanded Sloane eagerly. "This maid got hold of the wrong end of the thing. She knew that Edna and I were friends, and she carried it to the Chilicheffs. In Russia they assume that if a man and a woman—"

He enlarged the theme to a disquisition upon social relations in the Caucasus.

"If that's the case it better be explained to Uncle Robert," said Anson dryly, "so that when the rumors do reach him he'll know they're not true."

Adopting the method he had followed with Edna at luncheon he let them explain it all away. He knew that they were guilty and that presently they would cross the line from explanation into justification and convict themselves more definitely than he could ever do. By seven they had taken the desperate step of telling him the truth —Robert Hunter's neglect, Edna's empty life, the casual dalliance that had flamed up into passion—but like so many true stories it had the misfortune of being old, and its enfeebled body beat helplessly against the armor of Anson's will. The threat to go to Sloane's father sealed their helplessness, for the latter, a retired cotton broker out of Alabama, was a notorious fundamentalist who controlled his son by a rigid allowance and the promise that at his next vagary the allowance would stop forever.

They dined at a small French restaurant, and the discussion continued—at one time Sloane resorted to physical threats, a little later they were both imploring him to give them time. But Anson was obdurate. He saw that Edna was breaking up, and that her spirit must not be refreshed by any renewal of their passion.

At two o'clock in a small night-club on 53d Street, Edna's nerves suddenly collapsed, and she cried to go home. Sloane had been drinking heavily all evening, and he was faintly maudlin, leaning on the table and weeping a little with his face in his hands. Quickly Anson gave them his terms. Sloane was to leave town for six months, and he must be gone within forty-eight hours. When he returned there was to be no resumption of the affair, but at the end of a year Edna might, if she wished, tell Robert Hunter that she wanted a divorce and go about it in the usual way.

He paused, gaining confidence from their faces for his final word.

"Or there's another thing you can do," he said slowly, "if Edna wants to leave her children, there's nothing I can do to prevent your running off together."

"I want to go home!" cried Edna again. "Oh, haven't you done enough to us for one day?"

Outside it was dark, save for a blurred glow from Sixth Avenue down the street. In that light those two who had been lovers looked for the last time into each other's tragic faces, realizing that between them there was not enough youth and strength to avert their eternal parting. Sloane walked suddenly off down the street and Anson tapped a dozing taxi-driver on the arm.

It was almost four; there was a patient flow of cleaning water along the ghostly pavement of Fifth Avenue, and the shadows of two night women flitted over the dark façade of St. Thomas's church. Then the desolate shrubbery of Central Park where Anson had often played as a child, and the mounting numbers, significant as names, of the marching streets. This was his city, he thought, where his name had flourished through five generations. No change could alter the permanence of its place here, for change itself was the essential substratum by which he and those of his name identified themselves with the spirit of New York. Resourcefulness and a powerful will—for his threats in weaker hands would have been less than nothing—had beaten the gathering dust from his uncle's name, from the name of his family, from even this shivering figure that sat beside him in the car.

Cary Sloane's body was found next morning on the lower shelf of a pillar of Queensboro Bridge. In the darkness and in his excitement he had thought that it was the water flowing black beneath him, but in less than a second it made no possible difference—unless he had planned to think one last thought of Edna, and call out her name as he struggled feebly in the water.

VII

Anson never blamed himself for his part in this affair—the situation which brought it about had not been of his making. But the just suffer with the unjust, and he found that his oldest and somehow his most precious friendship was over. He never knew what distorted story Edna told, but he was welcome in his uncle's house no longer.

Just before Christmas Mrs. Hunter retired to a select Episcopal heaven, and Anson became the responsible head of his family. An unmarried aunt who had lived with them for years ran the house, and attempted with helpless inefficiency to chaperone the younger girls. All the children were less self-reliant than Anson, more conventional both in their virtues and in their shortcomings. Mrs. Hunter's death had postponed the début of one daughter and the wedding of another. Also it had taken something deeply material from all of them, for with her passing the quiet, expensive superiority of the Hunters came to an end.

For one thing, the estate, considerably diminished by two inheritance taxes and soon to be divided among six children, was not a notable fortune any more. Anson saw a tendency in his youngest sisters to speak rather respectfully of families that hadn't "existed" twenty years ago. His own feeling of precedence was not echoed in them—sometimes they were conventionally snobbish, that was all. For another thing, this was the last summer they would spend on the Connecticut estate; the clamor against it was too loud: "Who wants to waste the best months of the year shut up in that dead old town?" Reluctantly he yielded—the house would go into the market in the fall, and next summer they would rent a smaller place in Westchester County. It was a step down from the expensive simplicity of his father's idea, and, while he sympathized with the revolt, it also annoyed him; during his mother's lifetime he had gone up there at least every other week-end—even in the gayest summers.

Yet he himself was part of this change, and his strong instinct for life had turned him in his twenties from the hollow obsequies of that abortive leisure class. He did not see this clearly—he still felt that there was a norm, a standard of society. But there was no norm, it was doubtful if there ever had been a true norm in New York. The few who still paid and fought to enter a particular set succeeded only to find that as a society it scarcely functioned—or, what was more alarming, that the Bohemia from which they fled sat above them at table.

At twenty-nine Anson's chief concern was his own growing loneliness. He was sure now that he would never marry. The number of weddings at which he had officiated as best man or usher was past all counting—there was a drawer at home that bulged with the official neckties of this or that wedding-party, neckties standing for romances that had not endured a year, for couples who had passed completely from his life. Scarf-pins, gold pencils, cuff-buttons, presents from a generation of grooms had passed through his jewel-box and been lost—and with every ceremony he was less and less able to imagine himself in the groom's place. Under his hearty good-will toward all those marriages there was despair about his own.

And as he neared thirty he became not a little depressed at the inroads that marriage, especially lately, had made upon his friendships. Groups of people had a disconcerting tendency to dissolve and disappear. The men from his own college—and it was upon them he had expended the most time and affection—were the most elusive of all. Most of them were drawn deep into domesticity, two were dead, one lived abroad, one was in Hollywood writing continuities for pictures that Anson went faithfully to see.

Most of them, however, were permanent commuters with an intricate family life centring around some suburban country club, and it was from these that he felt his estrangement most keenly.

In the early days of their married life they had all needed him; he gave them advice about their slim finances, he exorcised their doubts about the advisability of bringing a baby into two rooms and a bath, especially he stood for the great world outside. But now their financial troubles were in the past and the fearfully expected child had evolved into an absorbing family. They were always glad to see old Anson, but they dressed up for him and tried to impress him with their present importance, and kept their troubles to themselves. They needed him no longer.

A few weeks before his thirtieth birthday the last of his early and intimate friends was married. Anson acted in his usual rôle of best man, gave his usual silver tea-service, and went down to the usual *Homeric*[3] to say good-by. It was a hot Friday afternoon in May, and as he walked from the pier he realized that Saturday closing had begun and he was free until Monday morning.

"Go where?" he asked himself.

The Yale Club, of course; bridge until dinner, then four or five raw cocktails in somebody's room and a pleasant confused evening. He regretted that this afternoon's groom wouldn't be along—they had always been able to cram so much into such nights: they knew how to attach women and how to get rid of them, how much consideration any girl deserved from their intelligent hedonism. A party was an adjusted thing—you took certain girls to certain places and spent just so much on their amusement; you drank a little, not much more than you ought to drink, and at a

[3] An ocean liner; a cruise was a popular
honeymoon trip.

certain time in the morning you stood up and said you were going home. You avoided college boys, sponges, future engagements, fights, sentiment, and indiscretions. That was the way it was done. All the rest was dissipation.

In the morning you were never violently sorry—you made no resolutions, but if you had overdone it and your heart was slightly out of order, you went on the wagon for a few days without saying anything about it, and waited until an accumulation of nervous boredom projected you into another party.

The lobby of the Yale Club was unpopulated. In the bar three very young alumni looked up at him, momentarily and without curiosity.

"Hello, there, Oscar," he said to the bartender. "Mr. Cahill been around this afternoon?"

"Mr. Cahill's gone to New Haven."

"Oh . . . that so?"

"Gone to the ball game. Lot of men gone up."

Anson looked once again into the lobby, considered for a moment, and then walked out and over to Fifth Avenue. From the broad window of one of his clubs—one that he had scarcely visited in five years—a gray man with watery eyes stared down at him. Anson looked quickly away—that figure sitting in vacant resignation, in supercilious solitude, depressed him. He stopped and, retracing his steps, started over 47th Street toward Teak Warden's apartment. Teak and his wife had once been his most familiar friends—it was a household where he and Dolly Karger had been used to go in the days of their affair. But Teak had taken to drink, and his wife had remarked publicly that Anson was a bad influence on him. The remark reached Anson in an exaggerated form—when it was finally cleared up, the delicate spell of intimacy was broken, never to be renewed.

"Is Mr. Warden at home?" he inquired.

"They've gone to the country."

The fact unexpectedly cut at him. They were gone to the country and he hadn't known. Two years before he would have known the date, the hour, come up at the last moment for a final drink, and planned his first visit to them. Now they had gone without a word.

Anson looked at his watch and considered a week-end with his family, but the only train was a local that would jolt through the aggressive heat for three hours. And to-morrow in the country, and Sunday—he was in no mood for porch-bridge with polite undergraduates, and dancing after dinner at a rural roadhouse, a diminutive of gaiety which his father had estimated too well.

"Oh, no," he said to himself. . . . "No."

He was a dignified, impressive young man, rather stout now, but otherwise unmarked by dissipation. He could have been cast for a pillar of something—at times you were sure it was not society, at others nothing else—for the law, for the church. He stood for a few minutes motionless on the sidewalk in front of a 47th Street apartment-house; for almost the first time in his life he had nothing whatever to do.

Then he began to walk briskly up Fifth Avenue, as if he had just been reminded of an important engagement there. The necessity of dissimulation is one of the few characteristics that we share with dogs, and I think of Anson on that day as some well-bred specimen who had been disappointed at a familiar back door. He was going to see Nick, once a fashionable bartender in demand at all private dances, and now employed in cooling non-alcoholic champagne among the labyrinthine cellars of the Plaza Hotel.

"Nick," he said, "what's happened to everything?"

"Dead," Nick said.

"Make me a whiskey sour." Anson handed a pint bottle over the counter. "Nick, the girls are different; I had a little girl in Brooklyn and she got married last week without letting me know."

"That a fact? Ha-ha-ha," responded Nick diplomatically. "Slipped it over on you."

"Absolutely," said Anson. "And I was out with her the night before."

"Ha-ha-ha," said Nick, "ha-ha-ha!"

"Do you remember the wedding, Nick, in Hot Springs where I had the waiters and the musicians singing 'God save the King'?"

"Now where was that, Mr. Hunter?" Nick concentrated doubtfully. "Seems to me that was—"

"Next time they were back for more, and I began to wonder how much I'd paid them," continued Anson.

"—seems to me that was at Mr. Trenholm's wedding."

"Don't know him," said Anson decisively. He was offended that a strange name should intrude upon his reminiscences; Nick perceived this.

"Na—aw—" he admitted, "I ought to know that. It was one of *your* crowd— Brakins . . . Baker—"

"Bicker Baker," said Anson responsively. "They put me in a hearse after it was over and covered me up with flowers and drove me away."

"Ha-ha-ha," said Nick. "Ha-ha-ha."

Nick's simulation of the old family servant paled presently and Anson went up-stairs to the lobby. He looked around—his eyes met the glance of an unfamiliar clerk at the desk, then fell upon a flower from the morning's marriage hesitating in the mouth of a brass cuspidor. He went out and walked slowly toward the blood-red sun over Columbus Circle. Suddenly he turned around and, retracing his steps to the Plaza, immured himself in a telephone-booth.

Later he said that he tried to get me three times that afternoon, that he tried every one who might be in New York—men and girls he had not seen for years, an artist's model of his college days whose faded number was still in his address book—Central told him that even the exchange existed no longer. At length his quest roved into the country, and he held brief disappointing conversations with emphatic butlers and maids. So-and-so was out, riding, swimming, playing golf, sailed to Europe last week. Who shall I say phoned?

It was intolerable that he should pass the evening alone—the private reckonings which one plans for a moment of leisure lose every charm when the solitude is enforced. There were always women of a sort, but the ones he knew had temporarily vanished, and to pass a New York evening in the hired company of a stranger never occurred to him—he would have considered that that was something shameful and secret, the diversion of a travelling salesman in a strange town.

Anson paid the telephone bill—the girl tried unsuccessfully to joke with him about its size—and for the second time that afternoon started to leave the Plaza and go he knew not where. Near the revolving door the figure of a woman, obviously with child, stood sideways to the light—a sheer beige cape fluttered at her shoulders when the door turned and, each time, she looked impatiently toward it as if she were weary of waiting. At the first sight of her a strong nervous thrill of familiarity went over him, but not until he was within five feet of her did he realize that it was Paula.

"Why, Anson Hunter!"

His heart turned over.

"Why, Paula—"

"Why, this is wonderful. I can't believe it, *Anson!*"

She took both his hands, and he saw in the freedom of the gesture that the memory of him had lost poignancy to her. But not to him—he felt that old mood that she evoked in him stealing over his brain, that gentleness with which he had always met her optimism as if afraid to mar its surface.

"We're at Rye for the summer. Pete had to come East on business—you know of course I'm Mrs. Peter Hagerty now—so we brought the children and took a house. You've got to come out and see us."

"Can I?" he asked directly. "When?"

"When you like. Here's Pete." The revolving door functioned, giving up a fine tall man of thirty with a tanned face and a trim mustache. His immaculate fitness made a sharp contrast with Anson's increasing bulk, which was obvious under the faintly tight cut-away coat.

"You oughtn't to be standing," said Hagerty to his wife. "Let's sit down here." He indicated lobby chairs, but Paula hesitated.

"I've got to go right home," she said. "Anson, why don't you—why don't you come out and have dinner with us to-night? We're just getting settled, but if you can stand that—"

Hagerty confirmed the invitation cordially.

"Come out for the night."

Their car waited in front of the hotel, and Paula with a tired gesture sank back against silk cushions in the corner.

"There's so much I want to talk to you about," she said, "it seems hopeless."

"I want to hear about you."

"Well"—she smiled at Hagerty—"that would take a long time too. I have three children—by my first marriage. The oldest is five, then four, then three." She smiled again. "I didn't waste much time having them, did I?"

"Boys?"

"A boy and two girls. Then—oh, a lot of things happened, and I got a divorce in Paris a year ago and married Pete. That's all—except that I'm awfully happy."

In Rye they drove up to a large house near the Beach Club, from which there issued presently three dark, slim children who broke from an English governess and approached them with an esoteric cry. Abstractedly and with difficulty Paula took each one into her arms, a caress which they accepted stiffly, as they had evidently been told not to bump into Mummy. Even against their fresh faces Paula's skin showed scarcely any weariness—for all her physical languor she seemed younger than when he had last seen her at Palm Beach seven years ago.

At dinner she was preoccupied, and afterward, during the homage to the radio, she lay with closed eyes on the sofa, until Anson wondered if his presence at this time were not an intrusion. But at nine o'clock, when Hagerty rose and said pleasantly that he was going to leave them by themselves for a while, she began to talk slowly about herself and the past.

"My first baby," she said—"the one we call Darling, the biggest little girl—I wanted to die when I knew I was going to have her, because Lowell was like a stranger to me. It didn't seem as though she could be my own. I wrote you a letter and tore it up. Oh, you were *so* bad to me, Anson."

It was the dialogue again, rising and falling. Anson felt a sudden quickening of memory.

"Weren't you engaged once?" she asked—"a girl named Dolly something?"

"I wasn't ever engaged. I tried to be engaged, but I never loved anybody but you, Paula."

"Oh," she said. Then after a moment: "This baby is the first one I ever really wanted. You see, I'm in love now—at last."

He didn't answer, shocked at the treachery of her remembrance. She must have seen that the "at last" bruised him, for she continued:

"I was infatuated with you, Anson—you could make me do anything you liked. But we wouldn't have been happy. I'm not smart enough for you. I don't like things to be complicated like you do." She paused. "You'll never settle down," she said.

The phrase struck at him from behind—it was an accusation that of all accusations he had never merited.

"I could settle down if women were different," he said. "If I didn't understand so much about them, if women didn't spoil you for other women, if they had only a little pride. If I could go to sleep for a while and wake up into a home that was really mine—why, that's what I'm made for, Paula, that's what women have seen in me and liked in me. It's only that I can't get through the preliminaries any more."

Hagerty came in a little before eleven; after a whiskey Paula stood up and announced that she was going to bed. She went over and stood by her husband.

"Where did you go, dearest?" she demanded.

"I had a drink with Ed Saunders."

"I was worried. I thought maybe you'd run away."

She rested her head against his coat.

"He's sweet, isn't he, Anson?" she demanded.

"Absolutely," said Anson, laughing.

She raised her face to her husband.

"Well, I'm ready," she said. She turned to Anson: "Do you want to see our family gymnastic stunt?"

"Yes," he said in an interested voice.

"All right. Here we go!"

Hagerty picked her up easily in his arms.

"This is called the family acrobatic stunt," said Paula. "He carries me up-stairs. Isn't it sweet of him?"

"Yes," said Anson.

Hagerty bent his head slightly until his face touched Paula's.

"And I love him," she said. "I've just been telling you, haven't I, Anson?"

"Yes," he said.

"He's the dearest thing that ever lived in this world; aren't you, darling? . . . Well, good night. Here we go. Isn't he strong?"

"Yes," Anson said.

"You'll find a pair of Pete's pajamas laid out for you. Sweet dreams—see you at breakfast."

"Yes," Anson said.

VIII

The older members of the firm insisted that Anson should go abroad for the summer. He had scarcely had a vacation in seven years, they said. He was stale and needed a change. Anson resisted.

"If I go," he declared, "I won't come back any more."

"That's absurd, old man. You'll be back in three months with all this depression gone. Fit as ever."

"No." He shook his head stubbornly. "If I stop, I won't go back to work. If I stop, that means I've given up—I'm through."

"We'll take a chance on that. Stay six months if you like—we're not afraid you'll leave us. Why, you'd be miserable if you didn't work."

They arranged his passage for him. They liked Anson—every one liked Anson—and the change that had been coming over him cast a sort of pall over the office. The enthusiasm that had invariably signalled up business, the consideration toward his equals and his inferiors, the lift of his vital presence—within the past four months his intense nervousness had melted down these qualities into the fussy pessimism of a man of forty. On every transaction in which he was involved he acted as a drag and a strain.

"If I go I'll never come back," he said.

Three days before he sailed Paula Legendre Hagerty died in childbirth. I was with him a great deal then, for we were crossing together, but for the first time in our friendship he told me not a word of how he felt, nor did I see the slightest sign of emotion. His chief preoccupation was with the fact that he was thirty years old—he would turn the conversation to the point where he could remind you of it and then fall silent, as if he assumed that the statement would start a chain of thought sufficient to itself. Like his partners, I was amazed at the change in him, and I was glad when the *Paris* moved off into the wet space between the worlds, leaving his principality behind.

"How about a drink?" he suggested.

We walked into the bar with that defiant feeling that characterizes the day of departure and ordered four Martinis. After one cocktail a change came over him—he suddenly reached across and slapped my knee with the first joviality I had seen him exhibit for months.

"Did you see that girl in the red tam?" he demanded, "the one with the high color who had the two police dogs down to bid her good-by."

"She's pretty," I agreed.

"I looked her up in the purser's office and found out that she's alone. I'm going down to see the steward in a few minutes. We'll have dinner with her to-night."

After a while he left me, and within an hour he was walking up and down the deck with her, talking to her in his strong, clear voice. Her red tam was a bright spot of color against the steel-green sea, and from time to time she looked up with a flashing bob of her head, and smiled with amusement and interest, and anticipation. At dinner we had champagne, and were very joyous—afterward Anson ran the pool with infectious gusto, and several people who had seen me with him asked me his name. He and the girl were talking and laughing together on a lounge in the bar when I went to bed.

I saw less of him on the trip than I had hoped. He wanted to arrange a foursome, but there was no one available, so I saw him only at meals. Sometimes, though, he would have a cocktail in the bar, and he told me about the girl in the red tam, and his adventures with her, making them all bizarre and amusing, as he had a way of doing, and I was glad that he was himself again, or at least the self that I knew, and with which I felt at home. I don't think he was ever happy unless some one was in love with him, responding to him like filings to a magnet, helping him to explain himself, promising him something. What it was I do not know. Perhaps they promised that there would always be women in the world who would spend their brightest, freshest, rarest hours to nurse and protect that superiority he cherished in his heart.

1926

---

from The Crack-up

[I]

February, 1936

Of course all life is a process of breaking down, but the blows that do the dramatic side of the work—the big sudden blows that come, or seem to come, from outside—the ones you remember and blame things on and, in moments of weakness, tell your friends about, don't show their effect all at once. There is another sort of blow that comes from within—that you don't feel until it's too late to do anything about it, until you realize with finality that in some regard you will never be as good a man again. The first sort of breakage seems to happen quick—the second kind happens almost without your knowing it but is realized suddenly indeed.

Before I go on with this short history, let me make a general observation—the test of a first-rate intelligence is the ability to hold two opposed ideas in the mind at the same time, and still retain the ability to function. One should, for example, be able to see that things are hopeless and yet be determined to make them otherwise. This philosophy fitted on to my early adult life, when I saw the improbable, the implausible, often the "impossible," come true. Life was something you dominated if you were any good. Life yielded easily to intelligence and effort, or to what proportion could be mustered of both. It seemed a romantic business to be a successful literary man—you were not ever going to be as famous as a movie star but what note you had was probably longer-lived—you were never going to have the power of a man of strong political or religious convictions but you were certainly more independent. Of course within the practice of your trade you were forever unsatisfied—but I, for one, would not have chosen any other.

As the twenties passed, with my own twenties marching a little ahead of them, my two juvenile regrets—at not being big enough (or good enough) to play football in college, and at not getting overseas during the war—resolved themselves into childish waking dreams of imaginary heroism that were good enough to go to sleep on in restless nights. The big problems of life seemed to solve themselves, and if the business of fixing them was difficult, it made one too tired to think of more general problems.

Life, ten years ago, was largely a personal matter. I must hold in balance the sense of the futility of effort and the sense of the necessity to struggle; the conviction of the inevitability of failure and still the determination to "succeed"—and, more than these, the contradiction between the dead hand of the past and the high intentions of the future. If I could do this through the common ills—domestic, professional and personal—then the ego would continue as an arrow shot from nothingness to nothingness with such force that only gravity would bring it to earth at last.

For seventeen years, with a year of deliberate loafing and resting out in the center —things went on like that, with a new chore only a nice prospect for the next day. I was living hard, too, but: "Up to forty-nine it'll be all right," I said. "I can count on that. For a man who's lived as I have, that's all you could ask."

—And then, ten years this side of forty-nine, I suddenly realized that I had prematurely cracked.

II

Now a man can crack in many ways—can crack in the head—in which case the power of decision is taken from you by others! or in the body, when one can but submit to the white hospital world; or in the nerves. William Seabrook[1] in an unsympathetic book tells, with some pride and a movie ending, of how he became a public charge. What led to his alcoholism or was bound up with it, was a collapse of his nervous system. Though the present writer was not so entangled—having at the time not tasted so much as a glass of beer for six months—it was his nervous reflexes that were giving way—too much anger and too many tears.

Moreover, to go back to my thesis that life has a varying offensive, the realization of having cracked was not simultaneous with a blow, but with a reprieve.

Not long before, I had sat in the office of a great doctor and listened to a grave sentence. With what, in retrospect, seems some equanimity, I had gone on about my affairs in the city where I was then living, not caring much, not thinking how much had been left undone, or what would become of this and that responsibility, like people do in books; I was well insured and anyhow I had been only a mediocre caretaker of most of the things left in my hands, even of my talent.

But I had a strong sudden instinct that I must be alone. I didn't want to see any people at all. I had seen so many people all my life—I was an average mixer, but more than average in a tendency to identify myself, my ideas, my destiny, with those of all classes that I came in contact with. I was always saving or being saved—in a single morning I would go through the emotions ascribable to Wellington at Water-

---

[1] William Buehler Seabrook (1886–1945), American adventurer and travel writer. An alcoholic, he was confined to a mental hospital for seven months in 1933. *Asylum* (1935) is his account of his commitment and experiences there.

loo. I lived in a world of inscrutable hostiles and inalienable friends and supporters.

But now I wanted to be absolutely alone and so arranged a certain insulation from ordinary cares.

It was not an unhappy time. I went away and there were fewer people. I found I was good-and-tired. I could lie around and was glad to, sleeping or dozing sometimes twenty hours a day and in the intervals trying resolutely not to think—instead I made lists—made lists and tore them up, hundreds of lists: of cavalry leaders and football players and cities, and popular tunes and pitchers, and happy times, and hobbies and houses lived in and how many suits since I left the army and how many pairs of shoes (I didn't count the suit I bought in Sorrento that shrunk, nor the pumps and dress shirt and collar that I carried around for years and never wore, because the pumps got damp and grainy and the shirt and collar got yellow and starch-rotted). And lists of women I'd liked, and of the times I had let myself be snubbed by people who had not been my betters in character or ability.

—And then suddenly, surprisingly, I got better.

—And cracked like an old plate as soon as I heard the news.

That is the real end of this story. What was to be done about it will have to rest in what used to be called the "womb of time." Suffice it to say that after about an hour of solitary pillow-hugging, I began to realize that for two years my life had been a drawing on resources that I did not possess, that I had been mortgaging myself physically and spiritually up to the hilt. What was the small gift of life given back in comparison to that?—when there had once been a pride of direction and a confidence in enduring independence.

I realized that in those two years, in order to preserve something—an inner hush maybe, maybe not—I had weaned myself from all the things I used to love—that every act of life from the morning tooth-brush to the friend at dinner had become an effort. I saw that for a long time I had not liked people and things, but only followed the rickety old pretense of liking. I saw that even my love for those closest to me was become only an attempt to love, that my casual relations—with an editor, a tobacco seller, the child of a friend, were only what I remembered I *should* do, from other days. All in the same month I became bitter about such things as the sound of the radio, the advertisements in the magazines, the screech of tracks, the dead silence of the country—contemptuous at human softness, immediately (if secretively) quarrelsome toward hardness—hating the night when I couldn't sleep and hating the day because it went toward night. I slept on the heart side now because I knew that the sooner I could tire that out, even a little, the sooner would come that blessed hour of nightmare which, like a catharsis, would enable me to better meet the new day.

There were certain spots, certain faces I could look at. Like most Middle Westerners, I have never had any but the vaguest race prejudices—I always had a secret yen for the lovely Scandinavian blondes who sat on porches in St. Paul but hadn't emerged enough economically to be part of what was then society. They were too nice to be "chickens" and too quickly off the farmlands to seize a place in the sun, but I remember going round blocks to catch a single glimpse of shining hair—the bright shock of a girl I'd never known. This is urban, unpopular talk. It strays afield from the fact that in these latter days I couldn't stand the sight of Celts, English, Politicians,

Strangers, Virginians, Negroes (light or dark), Hunting People, or retail clerks, and middlemen in general, all writers (I avoided writers very carefully because they can perpetuate trouble as no one else can)—and all the classes as classes and most of them as members of their class . . .

Trying to cling to something, I liked doctors and girl children up to the age of about thirteen and well-brought-up boy children from about eight years old on. I could have peace and happiness with these few categories of people. I forgot to add that I liked old men—men over seventy, sometimes over sixty if their faces looked seasoned. I liked Katharine Hepburn's face on the screen, no matter what was said about her pretentiousness, and Miriam Hopkins' face, and old friends if I only saw them once a year and could remember their ghosts.

All rather inhuman and undernourished, isn't it? Well, that, children, is the true sign of cracking up.

It is not a pretty picture. Inevitably it was carted here and there within its frame and exposed to various critics. One of them can only be described as a person whose life makes other people's lives seem like death—even this time when she was cast in the usually unappealing role of Job's comforter. In spite of the fact that this story is over, let me append our conversation as a sort of postscript:

"Instead of being so sorry for yourself, listen—" she said. (She always says "Listen," because she thinks while she talks—*really* thinks.) So she said: "Listen. Suppose this wasn't a crack in you—suppose it was a crack in the Grand Canyon."

"The crack's in me," I said heroically.

"Listen! The world only exists in your eyes—your conception of it. You can make it as big or as small as you want to. And you're trying to be a little puny individual. By God, if I ever cracked, I'd try to make the world crack with me. Listen! The world only exists through your apprehension of it, and so it's much better to say that it's not you that's cracked—it's the Grand Canyon."

"Baby et up all her Spinoza?"

"I don't know anything about Spinoza. I know—" She spoke, then, of old woes of her own, that seemed, in the telling, to have been more dolorous than mine, and how she had met them, over-ridden them, beaten them.

I felt a certain reaction to what she said, but I am a slow-thinking man, and it occurred to me simultaneously that of all natural forces, vitality is the incommunicable one. In days when juice came into one as an article without duty, one tried to distribute it—but always without success; to further mix metaphors, vitality never "takes." You have it or you haven't it, like health or brown eyes or honor or a baritone voice. I might have asked some of it from her, neatly wrapped and ready for home cooking and digestion, but I could never have got it—not if I'd waited around for a thousand hours with the tin cup of self-pity. I could walk from her door, holding myself very carefully like cracked crockery, and go away into the world of bitterness, where I was making a home with such materials as are found there—and quote to myself after I left her door:

"*Ye are the salt of the earth. But if the salt hath lost its savour, wherewith shall it be salted?*"

Matthew 5-13.

1936

William Faulkner
1897–1962

Eudora Welty said that to be a writer in Mississippi after Faulkner was like living next door to a mountain. Brilliant and erratic (even after he won the Nobel Prize in 1949, he was still capable of producing work his editors hesitated to publish), Faulkner is today generally regarded as the greatest twentieth-century American writer of fiction, and his work is routinely ranked with the literary achievements of Hawthorne, Melville, Twain, and James. Although Faulkner's novels and tales have been frequently described as difficult and obscure, his explanation of them was simple: He wrote, he said in his Nobel Prize acceptance speech, of "the problems of the human heart in conflict with itself which alone can make good writing because only that is worth writing about, worth the agony and the sweat."

Born on September 25, 1897, in New Albany, Mississippi, Faulkner soon moved with his family to Oxford, Mississippi, where he lived most of his life. He grew up with legends about his ancestors, most notably his great-grandfather, William Clark Falkner, a lawyer and a Civil War colonel prominent in the region for his colorful exploits, his political influence and wealth, his keen sense of honor, and his popular romantic novel, *The White Rose of Memphis* (1881). "When I was a little boy," Faulkner said, "there'd be sometimes twenty or thirty people in the house, mostly relatives, . . . some maybe coming for overnight and staying on for months, swapping stories about the family and about the past, while I sat in a corner and listened. That's where I got my books." The Falkner family had made its money in railroad and banking enterprises during the post–Civil War era, but after the family railroad was sold in 1902, Faulkner's father ran a livery stable, then a hardware store, and eventually became business manager of the University of Mississippi.

A good student in his early years, Faulkner soon became restive in school and was often truant. Though he liked to read, draw, and write poetry, he attended classes during his last two years of high school mainly to play football. In 1915 he dropped out of school for good, planning to work in his grandfather's bank. For two years he frequented the University of Mississippi campus, writing poems and submitting his drawings to student publications. Distressed when his childhood sweetheart decided to marry another man, Faulkner tried to enlist in the U.S. Army, only to be told that he was too small (he was five feet five and a half inches tall). In the spring of 1918 he moved to New Haven, Connecticut, to be close to an Oxford friend, Phil Stone, who was attending Yale Law School and who had already begun to encourage and promote Faulkner's literary talents. Later that year Faulkner changed the spelling of his name from Falkner to Faulkner and enlisted with the Royal Air Force in Canada. After spending several months in Toronto, he returned to Oxford dressed in an officer's uniform and armed with dramatic tales of his adventures in the skies over France.

As a veteran, Faulkner was allowed in the fall of 1919 to enroll as a special student at the University of Mississippi, where he studied French and wrote for

University periodicals. He had a poem accepted by *The New Republic,* and his first published short story, an aviation tale, appeared in the college newspaper. But Faulkner soon found college little more to his liking than high school had been, and after a year and a half he again dropped out. He continued to read, write, and sketch while working for brief intervals as a salesman in a New York City bookstore and as a carpenter, a house painter, and a university postmaster in Oxford, earning for himself a reputation as a ne'er-do-well. "Count No Count," the people of Oxford called him.

During his early years as a writer, Faulkner thought of himself as a poet (he would later describe himself as a "failed poet"). His reading continued to range widely, from French and English poetry of the nineteenth and early twentieth centuries to Cervantes and Shakespeare, Fielding and Dickens, Hawthorne and Melville, Balzac, Conrad, and Joyce. But most of his early writing is poetry, much of it written in the pastoral mode and all of it full not only of echoes but of borrowed words and borrowed sentiments, taken especially from the Romantics, particularly John Keats; from the Victorians, particularly Alfred Lord Tennyson; from the aesthetes and decadents of the late nineteenth and early twentieth centuries, particularly Algernon Charles Swinburne and A. E. Housman; and from his own contemporaries, particularly T. S. Eliot. In 1924, with the energetic help of his friend Phil Stone, who acted from time to time as critic, editor, agent, and publicist, Faulkner published his first book, a slim volume of poetry called—in echo of Hawthorne—*The Marble Faun.* Stone also wrote the book's preface, promoting Faulkner as a promising local celebrity, "a man steeped in the soil of his native land, a Southerner by every instinct, and, more than that, a Mississippian."

The first major turning point in Faulkner's career came in the fall of 1924, when he visited New Orleans and met Sherwood Anderson, whose writing he admired; at the time, Faulkner thought Conrad's *Heart of Darkness* and Anderson's "I'm a Fool" the two best stories he had ever read. The following year, he spent several months with Anderson, discussing books, spinning yarns, and drinking, while he contributed to the new literary magazine, *The Double Dealer,* and wrote sketches of New Orleans for the *Times-Picayune* (these were collected in 1968 as *New Orleans Sketches*). With Anderson's encouragement, Faulkner was turning increasingly to prose. While in New Orleans he finished *Soldiers' Pay* (1926), a novel about the homecoming of a badly scarred and dying air force veteran. In the summer of 1925 Faulkner traveled to Europe, visiting Italy, Switzerland, France, and England. Upon his return, he alternated between Oxford and New Orleans.

In 1937 Faulkner brought out his second novel, *Mosquitoes,* a story about a sophisticated New Orleans literary crowd on a yachting expedition that is written in the "conversational" mode Aldous Huxley had made fashionable in the 1920s. It is, however, in the work that followed *Mosquitoes,* the work set in his mythical Mississippi county, Yoknapatawpha, that Faulkner established the special themes—having to do with the complexities of sexual, familial, social, and racial identities and the force and burden of the past—that would eventually make him famous. In writing a book originally called *Flags in the Dust* but published as *Sartoris* (1929), Faulkner made the discovery that marked the second turning point in his career: "I discovered that my own little postage stamp of native soil was worth writing about and that I would never live long enough to exhaust it, and that by sublimating the actual into the apocryphal I might have complete liberty to use whatever talent I might have to its absolute top. I opened up a gold mine of other people, so I created a cosmos of my own." In *Sartoris,* a novel about the history of several generations of a distinguished Mississippi family, modeled in part on his own family, Faulkner introduced many of the characters and themes he would work with in his fiction throughout his career.

In the best of the Yoknapatawpha fiction, Faulkner created works unequaled in America in this century. Of his twenty novels, fifteen are set in Yoknapatawpha County, a location based on Lafayette County in northern Mississippi. *The Sound and the Fury* (1929), one of the great twentieth-century novels, treats the economic and emotional deterioration of the Compson family in four magnificent chapters, each one dramatizing a different consciousness with a different conception of time and language. The famous opening chapter, for example, is narrated by Benjy Compson, a thirty-three-year-old idiot, as his mind alternates between sense impressions and memories. No less innovative in its narrative method is Faulkner's next novel, *As I Lay Dying* (1930), which he wrote while working the night shift in a University of Mississippi boiler room. The novel, told from the multiple perspectives of fifteen "interior monologues," moves between horror and comedy as it recounts the adventures of a poor white family's efforts to fulfill the mother's wish to have her body decently buried in her hometown. Plot summary can give no sense of Faulkner's stylistic achievement in these books and those that were to follow. Trying to capture the effect on the reader of Faulkner's narrative technique, Jean-Paul Sartre wrote:

> Faulkner's vision of the world can be compared to that of a man sitting in a convertible looking backward. At every moment shadows emerge on his right, and on his left flickering and quavering points of light, which become trees, men, and cars only when they are seen in perspective. The past here gains a surrealistic quality; its outline is hard, clear, and immutable. The indefinable and elusive present is helpless before it; it is full of holes through which past things, fixed, motionless, and silent, invade it.

In 1929 Faulkner finally succeeded in marrying his childhood sweetheart, not long after she had divorced her first husband and moved back to Oxford with her two children. The following year he bought and restored an antebellum mansion; he was also beginning to sell his fiction to national magazines. In 1931 he published *Sanctuary,* the tale of a collegiate "flapper," Temple Drake, who gets involved with criminals, drugs, and prostitution. Following *Sanctuary,* the first of his novels to enjoy any commercial success, Faulkner immediately wrote several of his finest novels. In 1932 he published *Light in August,* a story of sexual passion, racism, and religious fanaticism that traces the parallel destinies of two wandering orphans—a pregnant country girl, Lena Grove, who is searching for her fleeing lover, and a presumed murderer, Joe Christmas, who is eventually shot and castrated. In *Absalom, Absalom!* (1936), Faulkner explored the intricate family history of a poor white man, Thomas Sutpen, whose dream of founding a dynasty in Mississippi ends in the tragic ruin of almost everyone involved. In 1938 Faulkner collected seven stories concerning the Sartoris family in *The Unvanquished.* He also published two non-Yoknapatawpha books during this period: *Pylon* (1935), a novel that grew out of Faulkner's flying lessons in 1933 and that traces the adventures of barnstorming airplane pilots, and *Wild Palms* (1939), a novel with two stories arranged in alternating chapters—one the tale of two doomed lovers and the other the story of a convict caught in a flood.

In 1940 Faulkner completed *The Hamlet,* the story of a grasping and rising family of poor whites, the Snopeses, who are described as "just Snopes, like colonies of rats or termites." Faulkner later added two more episodic novels about the Snopes family, *The Town* (1957) and *The Mansion* (1959), the three books usually being referred to as the Snopes trilogy. In 1942 Faulkner completed *Go Down, Moses,* which explores the history of the racially mixed McCaslin family. Faulkner frequently incorporated stories into his novels. "Spotted Horses," for example, evolved into a section of *The Hamlet.* Many stories, furthermore, deal with characters who also appear in the novels. The Compsons of "That Evening Sun," for example, are the central characters in *The Sound and the Fury.*

Because of his complex narrative methods and his morally oriented subject matter, Faulkner did not greatly interest sociologically minded critics during the Depression years; by the mid-1940s, of all his books, only *Sanctuary* remained in print. During the late 1940s and the early 1950s, however, a reappraisal of Faulkner's achievement began, spurred in part by the publication in 1948 of *Intruder in the Dust,* a "detective" story about an elderly black man who refuses to "act like a nigger" and whose surprising innocence in a murder case leaves him a "tyrant over the whole county's white conscience." In 1950, shortly after the appearance of his *Collected Stories,* Faulkner learned that he had won the Nobel Prize for literature. In the early 1950s he made several trips to Europe and lectured frequently on college campuses. In 1954 he published *The Fable,* a dense allegory that takes place during the false armistice of 1918. The novel won both the National Book Award and the Pulitzer Prize. A month before his death from a heart attack in 1962, Faulkner published his last novel, *The Reivers,* a nostalgic and comic story based on events remembered from his childhood.

Although Faulkner's finest fiction deals with one imaginary county in Mississippi, it explores the whole of human experience, a fact recognized when Faulkner received the Nobel Prize. No American writer of his time has exerted wider influence. His fiction has been translated into many languages, and it has exercised a deep, varied influence on writers not only in Europe, especially France, but throughout South America and even Japan, where he traveled on a State Department trip in 1955. In his work readers have discovered a feeling for the American South—and for the South's history—that bespeaks a concern for human beings both in the modern world and in some larger, more inclusive realm as well. In addition, readers have recognized that Faulkner's work is strikingly innovative in structure, form, and style. In its rhetorical extravagance and its dry understatement, in its rich allusions and intricate design, readers have found themselves amply challenged and amply rewarded. "The study of Faulkner," said Robert Penn Warren, "is the most challenging single task in contemporary American literature for criticism to undertake. Here is a novelist who, in mass of work, in scope of material, in range of effect, in reportorial accuracy and symbolic subtlety, in philosophical weight can be put beside the masters of our own past literature."

Shortly before Faulkner died on July 6, 1962, he wrote in a letter to a friend that he had finally gotten "some perspective on all that I have done. I mean, the work apart from me, the work which I did, apart from what I am. . . . And now I realise for the first time what an amazing gift I had. . . . I don't know where it came from." Though Faulkner sometimes feared that words bore too little relation to life, his fiction demonstrates the power of words—their power to serve, as one of his characters puts it, as a "meager and fragile thread . . . by which the little surface corners and edges of men's secret and solitary lives may be joined for an instant now and then," and their power, as another of his characters puts it, when brought "into a happy conjunction" to "produce something that lives."

Further Reading:
C. Brooks, *William Faulkner: The Yoknapatawpha Country*, 1963.
J. Blotner, *Faulkner: A Biography*, 1974.
C. Brooks, *William Faulkner: Toward Yoknapatawpha and Beyond*, 1978.
D. Kartiganer, *The Fragile Thread: The Meaning of Form in Faulkner's Novels*, 1979.
D. Minter, *William Faulkner: His Life and Work*, 1980.
Faulkner: New Perspectives, ed. R. H. Brodhead, 1983.

Texts:
"Spotted Horses" from *Uncollected Stories of William Faulkner*, 1979.
"That Evening Sun" from *Collected Stories of William Faulkner*, 1950.
Nobel Prize Address from *The Faulkner Reader*, 1954.

Spotted Horses

I

Yes, sir. Flem Snopes has filled that whole country full of spotted horses. You can hear folks running them all day and all night, whooping and hollering, and the horses running back and forth across them little wooden bridges ever now and then kind of like thunder. Here I was this morning pretty near half way to town, with the team ambling along and me setting in the buckboard about half asleep, when all of a sudden something come swurging up outen the bushes and jumped the road clean, without touching hoof to it. It flew right over my team, big as a billboard and flying through the air like a hawk. It taken me thirty minutes to stop my team and untangle the harness and the buckboard and hitch them up again.

That Flem Snopes. I be dog if he ain't a case, now. One morning about ten years ago, the boys was just getting settled down on Varner's porch for a little talk and tobacco, when here come Flem out from behind the counter, with his coat off and his hair all parted, like he might have been clerking for Varner for ten years already. Folks all knowed him; it was a big family of them about five miles down the bottom. That year, at least. Share-cropping. They never stayed on any place over a year. Then they would move on to another place, with the chap or maybe the twins of that year's litter. It was a regular nest of them. But Flem. The rest of them stayed tenant farmers, moving ever year, but here come Flem one day, walking out from behind Jody Varner's counter like he owned it. And he wasn't there but a year or two before folks knowed that, if him and Jody was both still in that store in ten years more, it would be Jody clerking for Flem Snopes. Why, that fellow could make a nickel where it wasn't but four cents to begin with. He skun me in two trades, myself, and the fellow that can do that, I just hope he'll get rich before I do; that's all.

All right. So here Flem was, clerking at Varner's, making a nickel here and there and not telling nobody about it. No, sir. Folks never knowed when Flem got the better of somebody lessen the fellow he beat told it. He'd just set there in the store-chair, chewing his tobacco and keeping his own business to hisself, until about a week later we'd find out it was somebody else's business he was keeping to hisself—provided the fellow he trimmed was mad enough to tell it. That's Flem.

We give him ten years to own ever thing Jody Varner had. But he never waited no ten years. I reckon you-all know that gal of Uncle Billy Varner's, the youngest one; Eula. Jody's sister. Ever Sunday ever yellow-wheeled buggy and curried riding horse in that country would be hitched to Bill Varner's fence, and the young bucks setting on the porch, swarming around Eula like bees around a honey pot. One of these here kind of big, soft-looking gals that could giggle richer than plowed new-ground. Wouldn't none of them leave before the others, and so they would set there on the porch until time to go home, with some of them with nine and ten miles to ride and then get up tomorrow and go back to the field. So they would all leave together and they would ride in a clump down to the creek ford and hitch them curried horses and yellow-wheeled buggies and get out and fight one another. Then they would get in the buggies again and go on home.

Well, one day about a year ago, one of them yellow-wheeled buggies and one of them curried saddle-horses quit this country. We heard they was heading for Texas. The next day Uncle Billy and Eula and Flem come in to town in Uncle Bill's surrey, and when they come back, Flem and Eula was married. And on the next day we heard that two more of them yellow-wheeled buggies had left the country. They mought have gone to Texas, too. It's a big place.

Anyway, about a month after the wedding, Flem and Eula went to Texas, too. They was gone pretty near a year. Then one day last month, Eula come back, with a baby. We figgured up, and we decided that it was as well-growed a three-months-old baby as we ever see. It can already pull up on a chair. I reckon Texas makes big men quick, being a big place. Anyway, if it keeps on like it started, it'll be chewing tobacco and voting time it's eight years old.

And so last Friday here come Flem himself. He was on a wagon with another fellow. The other fellow had one of these two-gallon hats and a ivory-handled pistol and a box of gingersnaps sticking out of his hind pocket, and tied to the tail-gate of the wagon was about two dozen of them Texas ponies, hitched to one another with barbed wire. They was colored like parrots and they was quiet as doves, and ere a one of them would kill you quick as a rattlesnake. Nere a one of them had two eyes the same color, and nere a one of them had ever see a bridle, I reckon; and when that Texas man got down offen the wagon and walked up to them to show how gentle they was, one of them cut his vest clean offen him, same as with a razor.

Flem had done already disappeared; he had went on to see his wife, I reckon, and to see if that ere baby had done gone on to the field to help Uncle Billy plow maybe. It was the Texas man that taken the horses on to Mrs. Littlejohn's lot. He had a little trouble at first, when they come to the gate, because they hadn't never see a fence before, and when he finally got them in and taken a pair of wire cutters and unhitched them and got them into the barn and poured some shell corn into the trough, they durn nigh tore down the barn. I reckon they thought that shell corn was bugs, maybe. So he left them in the lot and he announced that the auction would begin at sunup to-morrow.

That night we was setting on Mrs. Littlejohn's porch. You-all mind the moon was nigh full that night, and we could watch them spotted varmints swirling along the fence and back and forth across the lot same as minnows in a pond. And then now and then they would all kind of huddle up against the barn and rest themselves by biting and kicking one another. We would hear a squeal, and then a set of hoofs would go Bam! against the barn, like a pistol. It sounded just like a fellow with a pistol, in a nest of cattymounts, taking his time.

II

It wasn't ere a man knowed yet if Flem owned them things or not. They just knowed one thing: that they wasn't never going to know for sho if Flem did or not, or if maybe he didn't just get on that wagon at the edge of town, for the ride or not. Even Eck Snopes didn't know, Flem's own cousin. But wasn't nobody surprised at that. We knowed that Flem would skin Eck quick as he would ere a one of us.

They was there by sunup next morning, some of them come twelve and sixteen miles, with seed-money tied up in tobacco sacks in their overalls, standing along the fence, when the Texas man come out of Mrs. Littlejohn's after breakfast and clumb onto the gate post with that ere white pistol butt sticking outen his hind pocket. He taken a new box of gingersnaps outen his pocket and bit the end offen it like a cigar and spit out the paper, and said the auction was open. And still they was coming up in wagons and a horse- and mule-back and hitching the teams across the road and coming to the fence. Flem wasn't nowhere in sight.

But he couldn't get them started. He begun to work on Eck, because Eck holp him last night to get them into the barn and feed them that shell corn. Eck got out just in time. He come outen that barn like a chip on the crest of a busted dam of water, and clumb into the wagon just in time.

He was working on Eck when Henry Armstid come up in his wagon. Eck was saying he was skeered to bid on one of them, because he might get it, and the Texas man says, "Them ponies? Them little horses?" He clumb down offen the gate post and went toward the horses. They broke and run, and him following them, kind of chirping to them, with his hand out like he was fixing to catch a fly, until he got three or four of them cornered. Then he jumped into them, and then we couldn't see nothing for a while because of the dust. It was a big cloud of it, and them blare-eyed, spotted things swoaring outen it twenty foot to a jump, in forty directions without counting up. Then the dust settled and there they was, that Texas man and the horse. He had its head twisted clean around like a owl's head. Its legs was braced and it was trembling like a new bride and groaning like a saw mill, and him holding its head wrung clean around on its neck so it was snuffing sky. "Look it over," he says, with his heels dug too and that white pistol sticking outen his pocket and his neck swole up like a spreading adder's until you could just tell what he was saying, cussing the horse and talking to us all at once: "Look him over, the fiddleheaded son of fourteen fathers. Try him, buy him; you will get the best—" Then it was all dust again, and we couldn't see nothing but spotted hide and mane, and that ere Texas man's boot-heels like a couple of walnuts on two strings, and after a while that two-gallon hat come sailing out like a fat old hen crossing a fence.

When the dust settled again, he was just getting outen the far fence corner, brushing himself off. He come and got his hat and brushed it off and come and clumb onto the gate post again. He was breathing hard. He taken the gingersnap box outen his pocket and et one, breathing hard. The hammer-head horse was still running round and round the lot like a merry-go-round at a fair. That was when Henry Armstid come shoving up to the gate in them patched overalls and one of them dangle-armed shirts of hisn. Hadn't nobody noticed him until then. We was all watching the Texas man and the horses. Even Mrs. Littlejohn; she had done come out and built a fire under the wash-pot in her back yard, and she would stand at the fence a while and then go back into the house and come out again with a arm full of wash and stand at the fence again. Well, here come Henry shoving up, and then we see Mrs. Armstid right behind him, in that ere faded wrapper and sunbonnet and them tennis shoes. "Git on back to that wagon," Henry says.

"Henry," she says.

"Here, boys," the Texas man says; "make room for missus to git up and see. Come on, Henry," he says; "here's your chance to buy that saddle-horse missus has been wanting. What about ten dollars, Henry?"

"Henry," Mrs. Armstid says. She put her hand on Henry's arm. Henry knocked her hand down.

"Git on back to that wagon, like I told you," he says.

Mrs. Armstid never moved. She stood behind Henry, with her hands rolled into her dress, not looking at nothing. "He hain't no more despair than to buy one of them things," she says. "And us not five dollars ahead of the pore house, he hain't no more despair." It was the truth, too. They ain't never made more than a bare living offen that place of theirs, and them with four chaps and the very clothes they wears she earns by weaving by the firelight at night while Henry's asleep.

"Shut your mouth and git on back to that wagon," Henry says. "Do you want I taken a wagon stake to you here in the big road?"

Well, that Texas man taken one look at her. Then he begun on Eck again, like Henry wasn't even there. But Eck was skeered. "I can git me a snapping turtle or a water moccasin for nothing. I ain't going to buy none."

So the Texas man said he would give Eck a horse. "To start the auction, and because you holp me last night. If you'll start the bidding on the next horse," he says, "I'll give you that fiddle-head horse."

I wish you could have seen them, standing there with their seed-money in their pockets, watching that Texas man give Eck Snopes a live horse, all fixed to call him a fool if he taken it or not. Finally Eck says he'll take it. "Only I just starts the bidding," he says. "I don't have to buy the next one lessen I ain't overtopped." The Texas man said all right, and Eck bid a dollar on the next one, with Henry Armstid standing there with his mouth already open, watching Eck and the Texas man like a mad-dog or something. "A dollar," Eck says.

The Texas man looked at Eck. His mouth was already open too, like he had started to say something and what he was going to say had up and died on him. "A dollar?" he says. "One dollar? You mean, *one* dollar, Eck?"

"Durn it," Eck says; "two dollars, then."

Well, sir, I wish you could a seen that Texas man. He taken out that gingersnap box and held it up and looked into it, careful, like it might have been a diamond ring in it, or a spider. Then he threwed it away and wiped his face with a bandanna. "Well," he says. "Well. Two dollars. Two dollars. Is your pulse all right, Eck?" he says. "Do you have ager-sweats at night, maybe?" he says. "Well," he says, "I got to take it. But are you boys going to stand there and see Eck get two horses at a dollar a head?"

That done it. I be dog if he wasn't nigh as smart as Flem Snopes. He hadn't no more than got the words outen his mouth before here was Henry Armstid, waving his hand. "Three dollars," Henry says. Mrs. Armstid tried to hold him again. He knocked her hand off, shoving up to the gate post.

"Mister," Mrs. Armstid says, "we got chaps in the house and not corn to feed the stock. We got five dollars I earned my chaps a-weaving after dark, and him snoring in the bed. And he hain't no more despair."

"Henry bids three dollars," the Texas man says. "Raise him a dollar, Eck, and the horse is yours."

"Henry," Mrs. Armstid says.

"Raise him, Eck," the Texas man says.

"Four dollars," Eck says.

"Five dollars," Henry says, shaking his fist. He shoved up right under the gate post. Mrs. Armstid was looking at the Texas man too.

"Mister," she says, "if you take that five dollars I earned my chaps a-weaving for one of them things, it'll be a curse onto you and yourn during all the time of man."

But it wasn't no stopping Henry. He had shoved up, waving his fist at the Texas man. He opened it; the money was in nickels and quarters, and one dollar bill that looked like a cow's cud. "Five dollars," he says. "And the man that raises it'll have to beat my head off, or I'll beat hisn."

"All right," the Texas man says. "Five dollars is bid. But don't you shake your hand at me."

III

It taken till nigh sundown before the last one was sold. He got them hotted up once and the bidding got up to seven dollars and a quarter, but most of them went around three or four dollars, him setting on the gate post and picking the horses out one at a time by mouth-word, and Mrs. Littlejohn pumping up and down at the tub and stopping and coming to the fence for a while and going back to the tub again. She had done got done too, and the wash was hung on the line in the back yard, and we could smell supper cooking. Finally they was all sold; he swapped the last two and the wagon for a buckboard.

We was all kind of tired, but Henry Armstid looked more like a mad-dog than ever. When he bought, Mrs. Armstid had went back to the wagon, setting in it behind them two rabbit-sized, bone-pore mules, and the wagon itself looking like it would fall all to pieces soon as the mules moved. Henry hadn't even waited to pull it outen the road; it was still in the middle of the road and her setting in it, not looking at nothing, ever since this morning.

Henry was right up against the gate. He went up to the Texas man. "I bought a horse and I paid cash," Henry says. "And yet you expect me to stand around here until they are all sold before I can get my horse. I'm going to take my horse outen that lot."

The Texas man looked at Henry. He talked like he might have been asking for a cup of coffee at the table. "Take your horse," he says.

Then Henry quit looking at the Texas man. He begun to swallow, holding onto the gate. "Ain't you going to help me?" he says.

"It ain't my horse," the Texas man says.

Henry never looked at the Texas man again, he never looked at nobody. "Who'll help me catch my horse?" he says. Never nobody said nothing. "Bring the plowline," Henry says. Mrs. Armstid got outen the wagon and brought the plowline. The Texas man got down offen the post. The woman made to pass him, carrying the rope.

"Don't you go in there, missus," the Texas man says.

Henry opened the gate. He didn't look back. "Come on here," he says.

"Don't you go in there, missus," the Texas man says.

Mrs. Armstid wasn't looking at nobody, neither, with her hands across her middle, holding the rope. "I reckon I better," she says. Her and Henry went into the lot. The horses broke and run. Henry and Mrs. Armstid followed.

"Get him into the corner," Henry says. They got Henry's horse cornered finally, and Henry taken the rope, but Mrs. Armstid let the horse get out. They hemmed it up again, but Mrs. Armstid let it get out again, and Henry turned and hit her with the rope. "Why didn't you head him back?" Henry says. He hit her again. "Why didn't you?" It was about that time I looked around and see Flem Snopes standing there.

It was the Texas man that done something. He moved fast for a big man. He caught the rope before Henry could hit the third time, and Henry whirled and made like he would jump at the Texas man. But he never jumped. The Texas man went and taken Henry's arm and led him outen the lot. Mrs. Armstid come behind them and the Texas man taken some money outen his pocket and he give it into Mrs. Armstid's hand. "Get him into the wagon and take him on home," the Texas man says, like he might have been telling them he enjoyed his supper.

Then here come Flem. "What's that for, Buck?" Flem says.

"Thinks he bought one of them ponies," the Texas man says. "Get him on away, missus."

But Henry wouldn't go. "Give him back that money," he says. "I bought that horse and I aim to have him if I have to shoot him."

And there was Flem, standing there with his hands in his pockets, chewing, like he had just happened to be passing.

"You take your money and I take my horse," Henry says. "Give it back to him," he says to Mrs. Armstid.

"You don't own no horse of mine," the Texas man says. "Get him on home, missus."

Then Henry seen Flem. "You got something to do with these horses," he says. "I bought one. Here's the money for it." He taken the bill outen Mrs. Armstid's hand. He offered it to Flem. "I bought one. Ask him. Here. Here's the money," he says, giving the bill to Flem.

When Flem taken the money, the Texas man dropped the rope he had snatched outen Henry's hand. He had done sent Eck Snopes's boy up to the store for another box of gingersnaps, and he taken the box outen his pocket and looked into it. It was empty and he dropped it on the ground. "Mr. Snopes will have your money for you to-morrow," he says to Mrs. Armstid. "You can get it from him to-morrow. He don't own no horse. You get him into the wagon and get him on home." Mrs. Armstid went back to the wagon and got in. "Where's that ere buckboard I bought?" the Texas man says. It was after sundown then. And then Mrs. Littlejohn come out on the porch and rung the supper bell.

IV

I come on in and et supper. Mrs. Littlejohn would bring in a pan of bread or something, then she would go out to the porch a minute and come back and tell us. The Texas man had hitched his team to the buckboard he had swapped them last two horses for, and him and Flem had gone, and then she told that the rest of them that never had ropes had went back to the store with I. O. Snopes to get some ropes, and wasn't nobody at the gate but Henry Armstid, and Mrs. Armstid setting in the wagon in the road, and Eck Snopes and that boy of hisn. "I don't care how many of them fool men gets killed by them things," Mrs. Littlejohn says, "but I ain't going to let Eck Snopes take that boy into that lot again." So she went down to the gate, but she come back without the boy or Eck neither.

"It ain't no need to worry about that boy," I says. "He's charmed." He was right behind Eck last night when Eck went to help feed them. The whole drove of them jumped clean over that boy's head and never touched him. It was Eck that touched him. Eck snatched him into the wagon and taken a rope and frailed the tar outen him.

So I had done et and went to my room and was undressing, long as I had a long trip to make next day; I was trying to sell a machine to Mrs. Bundren up past Whiteleaf; when Henry Armstid opened that gate and went in by hisself. They couldn't make him wait for the balance of them to get back with their ropes. Eck Snopes said he tried to make Henry wait, but Henry wouldn't do it. Eck said Henry walked right up to them and that when they broke, they run clean over Henry like a hay-mow breaking down. Eck said he snatched that boy of hisn out of the way just in time and that them things went through that gate like a creek flood and into the wagons and teams hitched side the road, busting wagon tongues and snapping harness like it was fishing-line, with Mrs. Armstid still setting in their wagon in the middle of it like something carved outen wood. Then they scattered, wild horses and tame mules with pieces of harness and single trees dangling offen them, both ways up and down the road.

"There goes ourn, paw!" Eck says his boy said. "There it goes, into Mrs. Little-john's house." Eck says it run right up the steps and into the house like a boarder late for supper. I reckon so. Anyway, I was in my room, in my underclothes, with one sock on and one sock in my hand, leaning out the window when the commotion busted out, when I heard something run into the melodeon in the hall; it sounded like a railroad engine. Then the door to my room come sailing in like when you throw a tin bucket top into the wind and I looked over my shoulder and see something that looked like a fourteen-foot pinwheel a-blaring its eyes at me. It had to blare them fast, because I was already done jumped out the window.

I reckon it was anxious, too. I reckon it hadn't never seen barbed wire or shell corn before, but I know it hadn't never seen underclothes before, or maybe it was a sewing-machine agent it hadn't never seen. Anyway, it swirled and turned to run back up the hall and outen the house, when it met Eck Snopes and that boy just coming in, carrying a rope. It swirled again and run down the hall and out the back door just in time to meet Mrs. Littlejohn. She had just gathered up the clothes she had washed, and she was coming onto the back porch with a armful of washing in one hand and a scrubbing-board in the other, when the horse skidded up to her, trying to stop and swirl again. It never taken Mrs. Littlejohn no time a-tall.

"Git outen here, you son," she says. She hit it across the face with the scrubbing-board; that ere scrubbing-board split as neat as ere a axe could have done it, and when the horse swirled to run back up the hall, she hit it again with what was left of the scrubbing-board, not on the head this time. "And stay out," she says.

Eck and that boy was half-way down the hall by this time. I reckon that horse looked like a pinwheel to Eck too. "Git to hell outen here, Ad!" Eck says. Only there wasn't time. Eck dropped flat on his face, but the boy never moved. The boy was about a yard tall maybe, in overhalls just like Eck's; that horse swoared over his head without touching a hair. I saw that, because I was just coming back up the front steps, still carrying that ere sock and still in my underclothes, when the horse come onto the porch again. It taken one look at me and swirled again and run to the end of the porch and jumped the banisters and the lot fence like a hen-hawk and lit in the lot running and went out the gate again and jumped eight or ten upside-down wagons and went on down the road. It was a full moon then. Mrs. Armstid was still setting in the wagon like she had done been carved outen wood and left there and forgot.

That horse. It ain't never missed a lick. It was going about forty miles a hour when it come to the bridge over the creek. It would have had a clear road, but it so happened that Vernon Tull was already using the bridge when it got there. He was coming back from town; he hadn't heard about the auction; him and his wife and three daughters and Mrs. Tull's aunt, all setting in chairs in the wagon bed, and all asleep, including the mules. They waked up when the horse hit the bridge one time, but Tull said the first he knew was when the mules tried to turn the wagon around in the middle of the bridge and he seen that spotted varmint run right twixt the mules and run up the wagon tongue like a squirrel. He said he just had time to hit it across the face with his whip-stock, because about that time the mules turned the wagon around on that ere one-way bridge and that horse clumb across one of the mules and jumped down onto the bridge again and went on, with Vernon standing up in the wagon and kicking at it.

Tull said the mules turned in the harness and clumb back into the wagon too, with Tull trying to beat them out again, with the reins wrapped around his wrist. After that he says all he seen was overturned chairs and womenfolks' legs and white drawers shining in the moonlight, and his mules and that spotted horse going on up the road like a ghost.

The mules jerked Tull outen the wagon and drug him a spell on the bridge before the reins broke. They thought at first that he was dead, and while they was kneeling around him, picking the bridge splinters outen him, here come Eck and that boy, still carrying the rope. They was running and breathing a little hard. "Where'd he go?" Eck says.

V

I went back and got my pants and shirt and shoes on just in time to go and help get Henry Armstid outen the trash in the lot. I be dog if he didn't look like he was dead, with his head hanging back and his teeth showing in the moonlight, and a little rim of white under his eyelids. We could still hear them horses, here and there; hadn't none of them got more than four-five miles away yet, not knowing the country, I reckon. So we could hear them and folks yelling now and then: "Whooey. Head him!"

We toted Henry into Mrs. Littlejohn's. She was in the hall; she hadn't put down the armful of clothes. She taken one look at us, and she laid down the busted scrubbing-board and taken up the lamp and opened a empty door. "Bring him in here," she says.

We toted him in and laid him on the bed. Mrs. Littlejohn set the lamp on the dresser, still carrying the clothes. "I'll declare, you men," she says. Our shadows was way up the wall, tiptoeing too; we could hear ourselves breathing. "Better get his wife," Mrs. Littlejohn says. She went out, carrying the clothes.

"I reckon we had," Quick says. "Go get her, somebody."

"Whyn't you go?" Winterbottom says.

"Let Ernest git her," Durley says. "He lives neighbors with them."

Ernest went to fetch her. I be dog if Henry didn't look like he was dead. Mrs. Littlejohn come back, with a kettle and some towels. She went to work on Henry, and then Mrs. Armstid and Ernest come in. Mrs. Armstid come to the foot of the bed and stood there, with her hands rolled into her apron, watching what Mrs. Littlejohn was doing, I reckon.

"You men git outen the way," Mrs. Littlejohn says. "Git outside," she says. "See if you can't find something else to play with that will kill some more of you."

"Is he dead?" Winterbottom says.

"It ain't your fault if he ain't," Mrs. Littlejohn says. "Go tell Will Varner to come up here. I reckon a man ain't so different from a mule, come long come short. Except maybe a mule's got more sense."

We went to get Uncle Billy. It was a full moon. We could hear them, now and then, four mile away: "Whooey. Head him." The country was full of them, one on ever wooden bridge in the land, running across it like thunder: "Whooey. There he goes. Head him."

We hadn't got far before Henry begun to scream. I reckon Mrs. Littlejohn's water had brung him to; anyway, he wasn't dead. We went on to Uncle Billy's. The house was dark. We called to him, and after a while the window opened and Uncle Billy put his head out, peart as a peckerwood, listening. "Are they still trying to catch them durn rabbits?" he says.

He come down, with his britches on over his night-shirt and his suspenders dangling, carrying his horse-doctoring grip. "Yes, sir," he says, cocking his head like a woodpecker; "they're still a-trying."

We could hear Henry before we reached Mrs. Littlejohn's. He was going Ah-Ah-Ah. We stopped in the yard. Uncle Billy went on in. We could hear Henry. We stood in the yard, hearing them on the bridges, this-a-way and that: "Whooey. Whooey."

"Eck Snopes ought to caught hisn," Ernest says.

"Looks like he ought," Winterbottom said.

Henry was going Ah-Ah-Ah steady in the house; then he begun to scream. "Uncle Billy's started," Quick says. We looked into the hall. We could see the light where the door was. Then Mrs. Littlejohn come out.

"Will needs some help," she says. "You, Ernest. You'll do." Ernest went into the house.

"Hear them?" Quick said. "That one was on Four Mile bridge." We could hear them; it sounded like thunder a long way off; it didn't last long:

"Whooey."

We could hear Henry: "Ah-Ah-Ah-Ah-Ah."

"They are both started now," Winterbottom says. "Ernest too."

That was early in the night. Which was a good thing, because it taken a long night for folks to chase them things right and for Henry to lay there and holler, being as Uncle Billy never had none of this here chloryfoam to set Henry's leg with. So it was considerate in Flem to get them started early. And what do you reckon Flem's com-ment was?

That's right. Nothing. Because he wasn't there. Hadn't nobody see him since that Texas man left.

VI

That was Saturday night. I reckon Mrs. Armstid got home about daylight, to see about the chaps. I don't know where they thought her and Henry was. But lucky the oldest one was a gal, about twelve, big enough to take care of the little ones. Which she did for the next two days. Mrs. Armstid would nurse Henry all night and work in the kitchen for hern and Henry's keep, and in the afternoon she would drive home (it was about four miles) to see to the chaps. She would cook up a pot of victuals and leave it on the stove, and the gal would bar the house and keep the little ones quiet. I would hear Mrs. Littlejohn and Mrs. Armstid talking in the kitchen. "How are the chaps making out?" Mrs. Littlejohn says.

"All right," Mrs. Armstid says.

"Don't they git skeered at night?" Mrs. Littlejohn says.

"Ina May bars the door when I leave," Mrs. Armstid says. "She's got the axe in bed with her. I reckon she can make out."

I reckon they did. And I reckon Mrs. Armstid was waiting for Flem to come back to town; hadn't nobody seen him until this morning; to get her money the Texas man said Flem was keeping for her. Sho. I reckon she was.

Anyway, I heard Mrs. Armstid and Mrs. Littlejohn talking in the kitchen this morning while I was eating breakfast. Mrs. Littlejohn had just told Mrs. Armstid that Flem was in town. "You can ask him for that five dollars," Mrs. Littlejohn says.

"You reckon he'll give it to me?" Mrs. Armstid says.

Mrs. Littlejohn was washing dishes, washing them like a man, like they was made out of iron. "No," she says. "But asking him won't do no hurt. It might shame him. I don't reckon it will, but it might."

"If he wouldn't give it back, it ain't no use to ask," Mrs. Armstid says.

"Suit yourself," Mrs. Littlejohn says. "It's your money."

I could hear the dishes.

"Do you reckon he might give it back to me?" Mrs. Armstid says. "That Texas man said he would. He said I could get it from Mr. Snopes later."

"Then go and ask him for it," Mrs. Littlejohn says.

I could hear the dishes.

"He won't give it back to me," Mrs. Armstid says.

"All right," Mrs. Littlejohn says. "Don't ask him for it, then."

I could hear the dishes; Mrs. Armstid was helping. "You don't reckon he would, do you?" she says. Mrs. Littlejohn never said nothing. It sounded like she was throwing the dishes at one another. "Maybe I better go and talk to Henry about it," Mrs. Armstid says.

"I would," Mrs. Littlejohn says. I be dog if it didn't sound like she had two plates in her hands, beating them together. "Then Henry can buy another five-dollar horse with it. Maybe he'll buy one next time that will out and out kill him. If I thought that, I'd give you back the money, myself."

"I reckon I better talk to him first," Mrs. Armstid said. Then it sounded like Mrs. Littlejohn taken up all the dishes and throwed them at the cook-stove, and I come away.

That was this morning. I had been up to Bundren's and back, and I thought that things would have kind of settled down. So after breakfast, I went up to the store. And there was Flem, setting in the store-chair and whittling, like he might not have ever moved since he come to clerk for Jody Varner. I. O. was leaning in the door, in his shirt sleeves and with his hair parted too, same as Flem was before he turned the clerking job over to I. O. It's a funny thing about them Snopes: they all looks alike, yet there ain't ere a two of them that claims brothers. They're always just cousins, like Flem and Eck and Flem and I. O. Eck was there too, squatting against the wall, him and that boy, eating cheese and crackers outen a sack; they told me that Eck hadn't been home a-tall. And that Lon Quick hadn't got back to town, even. He followed his horse clean down to Samson's Bridge, with a wagon and a camp outfit. Eck finally caught one of hisn. It run into a blind lane at Freeman's and Eck and the boy taken and tied their rope across the end of the lane, about three foot high. The horse come to the end of the lane and whirled and run back without ever stopping. Eck says it never seen the rope a-tall. He says it looked just like one of these here Christmas pinwheels. "Didn't it try to run again?" I says.

"No," Eck says, eating a bite of cheese offen his knife blade. "Just kicked some."

"Kicked some?" I says.

"It broke its neck," Eck says.

Well, they was squatting there, about six of them, talking, talking at Flem; never nobody knowed yet if Flem had ere a interest in them horses or not. So finally I come right out and asked him. "Flem's done skun all of us so much," I says, "that we're proud of him. Come on, Flem," I says, "how much did you and that Texas man make offen them horses? You can tell us. Ain't nobody here but Eck that bought one of them; the others ain't got back to town yet, and Eck's your own cousin; he'll be proud to hear, too. How much did you-all make?"

They was all whittling, not looking at Flem, making like they was studying. But you could a heard a pin drop. And I. O. He had been rubbing his back up and down on the door, but he stopped now, watching Flem like a pointing dog. Flem finished cutting the sliver offen his stick. He spit across the porch, into the road. " 'Twarn't none of my horses," he says.

I. O. cackled, like a hen, slapping his legs with both hands. "You boys might just as well quit trying to get ahead of Flem," he said.

Well, about that time I see Mrs. Armstid come outen Mrs. Littlejohn's gate, coming up the road. I never said nothing. I says, "Well, if a man can't take care of himself in a trade, he can't blame the man that trims him."

Flem never said nothing, trimming at the stick. He hadn't seen Mrs. Armstid. "Yes, sir," I says. "A fellow like Henry Armstid ain't got nobody but hisself to blame."

"Course he ain't," I. O. says. He ain't seen her, neither. "Henry Armstid's a born fool. Always is been. If Flem hadn't a got his money, somebody else would."

We looked at Flem. He never moved. Mrs. Armstid come on up the road.

"That's right," I says. "But, come to think of it, Henry never bought no horse." We looked at Flem; you could a heard a match drop. "That Texas man told her to get that five dollars back from Flem next day. I reckon Flem's done already taken that money to Mrs. Littlejohn's and give it to Mrs. Armstid."

We watched Flem. I. O. quit rubbing his back against the door again. After a while Flem raised his head and spit across the porch, into the dust. I. O. cackled, just like a hen. "Ain't he a beating fellow, now?" I. O. says.

Mrs. Armstid was getting closer, so I kept on talking, watching to see if Flem would look up and see her. But he never looked up. I went on talking about Tull, about how he was going to sue Flem, and Flem setting there, whittling his stick, not saying nothing else after he said they wasn't none of his horses.

Then I. O. happened to look around. He seen Mrs. Armstid. "Pssssst!" he says. Flem looked up. "Here she comes!" I. O. says. "Go out the back. I'll tell her you done went in to town to-day."

But Flem never moved. He just set there, whittling, and we watched Mrs. Armstid come up onto the porch, in that ere faded sunbonnet and wrapper and them tennis shoes that made a kind of hissing noise on the porch. She come onto the porch and stopped, her hands rolled into her dress in front, not looking at nothing.

"He said Saturday," she says, "that he wouldn't sell Henry no horse. He said I could get the money from you."

Flem looked up. The knife never stopped. It went on trimming off a sliver same as if he was watching it. "He taken that money off with him when he left," Flem says.

Mrs. Armstid never looked at nothing. We never looked at her, neither, except that boy of Eck's. He had a half-et cracker in his hand, watching her, chewing.

"He said Henry hadn't bought no horse," Mrs. Armstid says. "He said for me to get the money from you today."

"I reckon he forgot about it," Flem said. "He taken that money off with him Saturday." He whittled again. I. O. kept on rubbing his back, slow. He licked his lips. After a while the woman looked up the road, where it went on up the hill, toward the graveyard. She looked up that way for a while, with that boy of Eck's watching her and I. O. rubbing his back slow against the door. Then she turned back toward the steps.

"I reckon it's time to get dinner started," she says.

"How's Henry this morning, Mrs. Armstid?" Winterbottom says.

She looked at Winterbottom; she almost stopped. "He's resting, I thank you kindly," she says.

Flem got up, outen the chair, putting his knife away. He spit across the porch. "Wait a minute, Mrs. Armstid," he says. She stopped again. She didn't look at him. Flem went on into the store, with I. O. done quit rubbing his back now, with his head craned after Flem, and Mrs. Armstid standing there with her hands rolled into her dress, not looking at nothing. A wagon come up the road and passed; it was Freeman, on the way to town. Then Flem come out again, with I. O. still watching him. Flem had one of these little striped sacks of Jody Varner's candy; I bet he still owes Jody that nickel, too. He put the sack into Mrs. Armstid's hand, like he would have put it into a hollow stump. He spit again across the porch. "A little sweetening for the chaps," he says.

"You're right kind," Mrs. Armstid says. She held the sack of candy in her hand, not looking at nothing. Eck's boy was watching the sack, the half-et cracker in his hand; he wasn't chewing now. He watched Mrs. Armstid roll the sack into her apron. "I reckon I better get on back and help with dinner," she says. She turned and went back across the porch. Flem set down in the chair again and opened his knife. He spit across the porch again, past Mrs. Armstid where she hadn't went down the steps yet. Then she went on, in that ere sunbonnet and wrapper all the same color, back down the road toward Mrs. Littlejohn's. You couldn't see her dress move, like a natural woman walking. She looked like a old snag still standing up and moving along on a high water. We watched her turn in at Mrs. Littlejohn's and go outen sight. Flem was whittling. I. O. begun to rub his back on the door. Then he begun to cackle, just like a durn hen.

"You boys might just as well quit trying," I. O. says. "You can't git ahead of Flem. You can't touch him. Ain't he a sight, now?"

I be dog if he ain't. If I had brung a herd of wild cattymounts into town and sold them to my neighbors and kinfolks, they would have lynched me. Yes, sir.

1931

That Evening Sun[1]

I

Monday is no different from any other weekday in Jefferson now. The streets are paved now, and the telephone and electric companies are cutting down more and more of the shade trees—the water oaks, the maples and locusts and elms—to make room for iron poles bearing clusters of bloated and ghostly and bloodless grapes, and we

---

[1] Probably an echo of "I hate to see that evening sun go down," from the 1914 song "St. Louis Blues," by W. C. Handy.

have a city laundry which makes the rounds on Monday morning, gathering the bundles of clothes into bright-colored, specially-made motor cars: the soiled wearing of a whole week now flees apparitionlike behind alert and irritable electric horns, with a long diminishing noise of rubber and asphalt like tearing silk, and even the Negro women who still take in white people's washing after the old custom, fetch and deliver it in automobiles.

But fifteen years ago, on Monday morning the quiet, dusty, shady streets would be full of Negro women with, balanced on their steady, turbaned heads, bundles of clothes tied up in sheets, almost as large as cotton bales, carried so without touch of hand between the kitchen door of the white house and the blackened washpot beside a cabin door in Negro Hollow.

Nancy would set her bundle on the top of her head, then upon the bundle in turn she would set the black straw sailor hat which she wore winter and summer. She was tall, with a high, sad face sunken a little where her teeth were missing. Sometimes we would go a part of the way down the lane and across the pasture with her, to watch the balanced bundle and the hat that never bobbed nor wavered, even when she walked down into the ditch and up the other side and stooped through the fence. She would go down on her hands and knees and crawl through the gap, her head rigid, uptilted, the bundle steady as a rock or a balloon, and rise to her feet again and go on.

Sometimes the husbands of the washing women would fetch and deliver the clothes, but Jesus never did that for Nancy, even before father told him to stay away from our house, even when Dilsey was sick and Nancy would come to cook for us.

And then about half the time we'd have to go down the lane to Nancy's cabin and tell her to come on and cook breakfast. We would stop at the ditch, because father told us to not have anything to do with Jesus—he was a short black man, with a razor scar down his face—and we would throw rocks at Nancy's house until she came to the door, leaning her head around it without any clothes on.

"What yawl mean, chunking my house?" Nancy said. "What you little devils mean?"

"Father says for you to come on and get breakfast," Caddy said. "Father says it's over a half an hour now, and you've got to come this minute."

"I aint studying no breakfast," Nancy said. "I going to get my sleep out."

"I bet you're drunk," Jason said. "Father says you're drunk. Are you drunk, Nancy?"

"Who says I is?" Nancy said. "I got to get my sleep out. I aint studying no breakfast."

So after a while we quit chunking the cabin and went back home. When she finally came, it was too late for me to go to school. So we thought it was whisky until that day they arrested her again and they were taking her to jail and they passed Mr Stovall. He was the cashier in the bank and a deacon in the Baptist church, and Nancy began to say:

"When you going to pay me, white man? When you going to pay me, white man? It's been three times now since you paid me a cent—" Mr Stovall knocked her down, but she kept on saying, "When you going to pay me, white man? It's been three times now since—" until Mr Stovall kicked her in the mouth with his heel and the marshal caught Mr Stovall back, and Nancy lying in the street, laughing. She turned her head and spat out some blood and teeth and said, "It's been three times now since he paid me a cent."

That was how she lost her teeth, and all that day they told about Nancy and Mr Stovall, and all that night the ones that passed the jail could hear Nancy singing and yelling. They could see her hands holding to the window bars, and a lot of them stopped along the fence, listening to her and to the jailer trying to make her stop. She didn't shut up until almost daylight, when the jailer began to hear a bumping and scraping upstairs and he went up there and found Nancy hanging from the window bar. He said that it was cocaine and not whisky, because no nigger would try to commit suicide unless he was full of cocaine, because a nigger full of cocaine wasn't a nigger any longer.

The jailer cut her down and revived her; then he beat her, whipped her. She had hung herself with her dress. She had fixed it all right, but when they arrested her she didn't have on anything except a dress and so she didn't have anything to tie her hands with and she couldn't make her hands let go of the window ledge. So the jailer heard the noise and ran up there and found Nancy hanging from the window, stark naked, her belly already swelling out a little, like a little balloon.

When Dilsey was sick in her cabin and Nancy was cooking for us, we could see her apron swelling out; that was before father told Jesus to stay away from the house. Jesus was in the kitchen, sitting behind the stove, with his razor scar on his black face like a piece of dirty string. He said it was a watermelon that Nancy had under her dress.

"It never come off of your vine, though," Nancy said.

"Off of what vine?" Caddy said.

"I can cut down the vine it did come off of," Jesus said.

"What makes you want to talk like that before these chillen?" Nancy said. "Whyn't you go on to work? You done et. You want Mr Jason to catch you hanging around his kitchen, talking that way before these chillen?"

"Talking what way?" Caddy said. "What vine?"

"I cant hang around white man's kitchen," Jesus said. "But white man can hang around mine. White man can come in my house, but I cant stop him. When white man want to come in my house, I aint got no house. I cant stop him, but he cant kick me outen it. He cant do that."

Dilsey was still sick in her cabin. Father told Jesus to stay off our place. Dilsey was still sick. It was a long time. We were in the library after supper.

"Isn't Nancy through in the kitchen yet?" mother said. "It seems to me that she has had plenty of time to have finished the dishes."

"Let Quentin go and see," father said. "Go and see if Nancy is through, Quentin. Tell her she can go on home."

I went to the kitchen. Nancy was through. The dishes were put away and the fire was out. Nancy was sitting in a chair, close to the cold stove. She looked at me.

"Mother wants to know if you are through," I said.

"Yes," Nancy said. She looked at me. "I done finished." She looked at me.

"What is it?" I said. "What is it?"

"I aint nothing but a nigger," Nancy said. "It aint none of my fault."

She looked at me, sitting in the chair before the cold stove, the sailor hat on her head. I went back to the library. It was the cold stove and all, when you think of a kitchen being warm and busy and cheerful. And with a cold stove and the dishes all put away, and nobody wanting to eat at that hour.

"Is she through?" mother said.

"Yessum," I said.

"What is she doing?" mother said.

"She's not doing anything. She's through."

"I'll go and see," father said.

"Maybe she's waiting for Jesus to come and take her home," Caddy said.

"Jesus is gone," I said. Nancy told us how one morning she woke up and Jesus was gone.

"He quit me," Nancy said. "Done gone to Memphis, I reckon. Dodging them city *po*-lice for a while, I reckon."

"And a good riddance," father said. "I hope he stays there."

"Nancy's scaired of the dark," Jason said.

"So are you," Caddy said.

"I'm not," Jason said.

"Scairy cat," Caddy said.

"I'm not," Jason said.

"You, Candace!" mother said. Father came back.

"I am going to walk down the lane with Nancy," he said. "She says that Jesus is back."

"Has she seen him?" mother said.

"No. Some Negro sent her word that he was back in town. I wont be long."

"You'll leave me alone, to take Nancy home?" mother said. "Is her safety more precious to you than mine?"

"I wont be long," father said.

"You'll leave these children unprotected, with that Negro about?"

"I'm going too," Caddy said. "Let me go, Father."

"What would he do with them, if he were unfortunate enough to have them?" father said.

"I want to go, too," Jason said.

"Jason!" mother said. She was speaking to father. You could tell that by the way she said the name. Like she believed that all day father had been trying to think of doing the thing she wouldn't like the most, and that she knew all the time that after a while he would think of it. I stayed quiet, because father and I both knew that mother would want him to make me stay with her if she just thought of it in time. So father didn't look at me. I was the oldest. I was nine and Caddy was seven and Jason was five.

"Nonsense," father said. "We wont be long."

Nancy had her hat on. We came to the lane. "Jesus always been good to me," Nancy said. "Whenever he had two dollars, one of them was mine." We walked in the lane. "If I can just get through the lane," Nancy said, "I be all right then."

The lane was always dark. "This is where Jason got scared on Hallowe'en," Caddy said.

"I didn't," Jason said.

"Cant Aunt Rachel do anything with him?" father said. Aunt Rachel was old. She lived in a cabin beyond Nancy's, by herself. She had white hair and she smoked a pipe in the door, all day long; she didn't work any more. They said she was Jesus' mother. Sometimes she said she was and sometimes she said she wasn't any kin to Jesus.

"Yes, you did," Caddy said. "You were scairder than Frony. You were scairder than T.P. even. Scairder than niggers."

"Cant nobody do nothing with him," Nancy said. "He say I done woke up the devil in him and aint but one thing going to lay it down again."

"Well, he's gone now," father said. "There's nothing for you to be afraid of now. And if you'd just let white men alone."

"Let what white men alone?" Caddy said. "How let them alone?"

"He aint gone nowhere," Nancy said. "I can feel him. I can feel him now, in this lane. He hearing us talk, every word, hid somewhere, waiting. I aint seen him, and I aint going to see him again but once more, with that razor in his mouth. That razor on that string down his back, inside his shirt. And then I aint going to be even surprised."

"I wasn't scaired," Jason said.

"If you'd behave yourself, you'd have kept out of this," father said. "But it's all right now. He's probably in St. Louis now. Probably got another wife by now and forgot all about you."

"If he has, I better not find out about it," Nancy said. "I'd stand there right over them, and every time he wropped her, I'd cut that arm off. I'd cut his head off and I'd slit her belly and I'd shove—"

"Hush," father said.

"Slit whose belly, Nancy?" Caddy said.

"I wasn't scaired," Jason said. "I'd walk right down this lane by myself."

"Yah," Caddy said. "You wouldn't dare to put your foot down in it if we were not here too."

II

Dilsey was still sick, so we took Nancy home every night until mother said, "How much longer is this going on? I to be left alone in this big house while you take home a frightened Negro?"

We fixed a pallet in the kitchen for Nancy. One night we waked up, hearing the sound. It was not singing and it was not crying, coming up the dark stairs. There was a light in mother's room and we heard father going down the hall, down the back stairs, and Caddy and I went into the hall. The floor was cold. Our toes curled away from it while we listened to the sound. It was like singing and it wasn't like singing, like the sounds that Negroes make.

Then it stopped and we heard father going down the back stairs, and we went to the head of the stairs. Then the sound began again, in the stairway, not loud, and we could see Nancy's eyes halfway up the stairs, against the wall. They looked like cat's eyes do, like a big cat against the wall, watching us. When we came down the steps to where she was, she quit making the sound again, and we stood there until father came back up from the kitchen, with his pistol in his hand. He went back down with Nancy and they came back with Nancy's pallet.

We spread the pallet in our room. After the light in mother's room went off, we could see Nancy's eyes again. "Nancy," Caddy whispered, "are you asleep, Nancy?"

Nancy whispered something. It was oh or no, I dont know which. Like nobody had made it, like it came from nowhere and went nowhere, until it was like Nancy was not there at all; that I had looked so hard at her eyes on the stairs that they had got printed on my eyeballs, like the sun does when you have closed your eyes and there is no sun. "Jesus," Nancy whispered. "Jesus."

"Was it Jesus?" Caddy said. "Did he try to come into the kitchen?"

"Jesus," Nancy said. Like this: Jeeeeeeeeeeeeeeeesus, until the sound went out, like a match or a candle does.

"It's the other Jesus she means," I said.

"Can you see us, Nancy?" Caddy whispered. "Can you see our eyes too?"

"I aint nothing but a nigger," Nancy said. "God knows. God knows."

"What did you see down there in the kitchen?" Caddy whispered. "What tried to get in?"

"God knows," Nancy said. We could see her eyes. "God knows."

Dilsey got well. She cooked dinner. "You'd better stay in bed a day or two longer," father said.

"What for?" Dilsey said. "If I had been a day later, this place would be to rack and ruin. Get on out of here now, and let me get my kitchen straight again."

Dilsey cooked supper too. And that night, just before dark, Nancy came into the kitchen.

"How do you know he's back?" Dilsey said. "You aint seen him."

"Jesus is a nigger," Jason said.

"I can feel him," Nancy said. "I can feel him laying yonder in the ditch."

"Tonight?" Dilsey said. "Is he there tonight?"

"Dilsey's a nigger too," Jason said.

"You try to eat something," Dilsey said.

"I dont want nothing," Nancy said.

"I aint a nigger," Jason said.

"Drink some coffee," Dilsey said. She poured a cup of coffee for Nancy. "Do you know he's out there tonight? How come you know it's tonight?"

"I know," Nancy said. "He's there, waiting. I know. I done lived with him too long. I know what he is fixing to do fore he know it himself."

"Drink some coffee," Dilsey said. Nancy held the cup to her mouth and blew into the cup. Her mouth pursed out like a spreading adder's, like a rubber mouth, like she had blown all the color out of her lips with blowing the coffee.

"I aint a nigger," Jason said. "Are you a nigger, Nancy?"

"I hellborn, child," Nancy said. "I wont be nothing soon. I going back where I come from soon."

III

She began to drink the coffee. While she was drinking, holding the cup in both hands, she began to make the sound again. She made the sound into the cup and the coffee sploshed out onto her hands and her dress. Her eyes looked at us and she sat there, her elbows on her knees, holding the cup in both hands, looking at us across the wet cup, making the sound. "Look at Nancy," Jason said. "Nancy cant cook for us now. Dilsey's got well now."

"You hush up," Dilsey said. Nancy held the cup in both hands, looking at us, making the sound, like there were two of them: one looking at us and the other making the sound. "Whyn't you let Mr Jason telefoam the marshal?" Dilsey said. Nancy stopped then, holding the cup in her long brown hands. She tried to drink some coffee again, but it sploshed out of the cup, onto her hands and her dress, and she put the cup down. Jason watched her.

"I cant swallow it," Nancy said. "I swallows but it wont go down me."

"You go down to the cabin," Dilsey said. "Frony will fix you a pallet and I'll be there soon."

"Wont no nigger stop him," Nancy said.

"I aint a nigger," Jason said. "Am I, Dilsey?"

"I reckon not," Dilsey said. She looked at Nancy. "I dont reckon so. What you going to do, then?"

Nancy looked at us. Her eyes went fast, like she was afraid there wasn't time to look, without hardly moving at all. She looked at us, at all three of us at one time. "You member that night I stayed in yawls' room?" she said. She told about how we waked up early the next morning, and played. We had to play quiet, on her pallet, until father woke up and it was time to get breakfast. "Go and ask your maw to let me stay here tonight," Nancy said. "I wont need no pallet. We can play some more."

Caddy asked mother. Jason went too. "I cant have Negroes sleeping in the bed-rooms," mother said. Jason cried. He cried until mother said he couldn't have any dessert for three days if he didn't stop. Then Jason said he would stop if Dilsey would make a chocolate cake. Father was there.

"Why dont you do something about it?" mother said. "What do we have officers for?"

"Why is Nancy afraid of Jesus?" Caddy said. "Are you afraid of father, mother?"

"What could the officers do?" father said. "If Nancy hasn't seen him, how could the officers find him?"

"Then why is she afraid?" mother said.

"She says he is there. She says she knows he is there tonight."

"Yet we pay taxes," mother said. "I must wait here alone in this big house while you take a Negro woman home."

"You know that I am not lying outside with a razor," father said.

"I'll stop if Dilsey will make a chocolate cake," Jason said. Mother told us to go out and father said he didn't know if Jason would get a chocolate cake or not, but he knew what Jason was going to get in about a minute. We went back to the kitchen and told Nancy.

"Father said for you to go home and lock the door, and you'll be all right," Caddy said. "All right from what, Nancy? Is Jesus mad at you?" Nancy was holding the coffee cup in her hands again, her elbows on her knees and her hands holding the cup between her knees. She was looking into the cup. "What have you done that made Jesus mad?" Caddy said. Nancy let the cup go. It didn't break on the floor, but the coffee spilled out, and Nancy sat there with her hands still making the shape of the cup. She began to make the sound again, not loud. Not singing and not unsinging. We watched her.

"Here," Dilsey said. "You quit that, now. You get aholt of yourself. You wait here. I going to get Versh to walk home with you." Dilsey went out.

We looked at Nancy. Her shoulders kept shaking, but she quit making the sound. We watched her. "What's Jesus going to do to you?" Caddy said. "He went away."

Nancy looked at us. "We had fun that night I stayed in yawls' room, didn't we?"

"I didn't," Jason said. "I didn't have any fun."

"You were asleep in mother's room," Caddy said. "You were not there."

"Let's go down to my house and have some more fun," Nancy said.

"Mother wont let us," I said. "It's too late now."

"Dont bother her," Nancy said. "We can tell her in the morning. She wont mind."

"She wouldn't let us," I said.

"Dont ask her now," Nancy said. "Dont bother her now."

"She didn't say we couldn't go," Caddy said.

"We didn't ask," I said.

"If you go, I'll tell," Jason said.

"We'll have fun," Nancy said. "They won't mind, just to my house. I been working for yawl a long time. They won't mind."

"I'm not afraid to go," Caddy said. "Jason is the one that's afraid. He'll tell."

"I'm not," Jason said.

"Yes, you are," Caddy said. "You'll tell."

"I won't tell," Jason said. "I'm not afraid."

"Jason ain't afraid to go with me," Nancy said. "Is you, Jason?"

"Jason is going to tell," Caddy said. The lane was dark. We passed the pasture gate. "I bet if something was to jump out from behind that gate, Jason would holler."

"I wouldn't," Jason said. We walked down the lane. Nancy was talking loud.

"What are you talking so loud for, Nancy?" Caddy said.

"Who; me?" Nancy said. "Listen at Quentin and Caddy and Jason saying I'm talking loud."

"You talk like there was five of us here," Caddy said. "You talk like father was here too."

"Who; me talking loud, Mr Jason?" Nancy said.

"Nancy called Jason 'Mister,'" Caddy said.

"Listen how Caddy and Quentin and Jason talk," Nancy said.

"We're not talking loud," Caddy said. "You're the one that's talking like father—"

"Hush," Nancy said; "hush, Mr Jason."

"Nancy called Jason 'Mister' aguh—"

"Hush," Nancy said. She was talking loud when we crossed the ditch and stooped through the fence where she used to stoop through with the clothes on her head. Then we came to her house. We were going fast then. She opened the door. The smell of the house was like the lamp and the smell of Nancy was like the wick, like they were waiting for one another to begin to smell. She lit the lamp and closed the door and put the bar up. Then she quit talking loud, looking at us.

"What're we going to do?" Caddy said.

"What do yawl want to do?" Nancy said.

"You said we would have some fun," Caddy said.

There was something about Nancy's house; something you could smell besides Nancy and the house. Jason smelled it, even. "I don't want to stay here," he said. "I want to go home."

"Go home, then," Caddy said.

"I don't want to go by myself," Jason said.

"We're going to have some fun," Nancy said.

"How?" Caddy said.

Nancy stood by the door. She was looking at us, only it was like she had emptied her eyes, like she had quit using them. "What do you want to do?" she said.

"Tell us a story," Caddy said. "Can you tell a story?"

"Yes," Nancy said.

"Tell it," Caddy said. We looked at Nancy. "You don't know any stories."

"Yes," Nancy said. "Yes, I do."

She came and sat in a chair before the hearth. There was a little fire there. Nancy built it up, when it was already hot inside. She built a good blaze. She told a story. She talked like her eyes looked, like her eyes watching us and her voice talking to us did not belong to her. Like she was living somewhere else, waiting somewhere else. She was outside the cabin. Her voice was inside and the shape of her, the Nancy that could stoop under a barbed wire fence with a bundle of clothes balanced on her head as though without weight, like a balloon, was there. But that was all. "And so this here queen come walking up to the ditch, where that bad man was hiding. She was walking up to the ditch, and she say, 'If I can just get past this here ditch,' was what she say . . ."

"What ditch?" Caddy said. "A ditch like that one out there? Why did a queen want to go into a ditch?"

"To get to her house," Nancy said. She looked at us. "She had to cross the ditch to get into her house quick and bar the door."

"Why did she want to go home and bar the door?" Caddy said.

IV

Nancy looked at us. She quit talking. She looked at us. Jason's legs stuck straight out of his pants where he sat on Nancy's lap. "I don't think that's a good story," he said. "I want to go home."

"Maybe we had better," Caddy said. She got up from the floor. "I bet they are looking for us right now." She went toward the door.

"No," Nancy said. "Don't open it." She got up quick and passed Caddy. She didn't touch the door, the wooden bar.

"Why not?" Caddy said.

"Come back to the lamp," Nancy said. "We'll have fun. You don't have to go."

"We ought to go," Caddy said. "Unless we have a lot of fun." She and Nancy came back to the fire, the lamp.

"I want to go home," Jason said. "I'm going to tell."

"I know another story," Nancy said. She stood close to the lamp. She looked at Caddy, like when your eyes look up at a stick balanced on your nose. She had to look down to see Caddy, but her eyes looked like that, like when you are balancing a stick.

"I won't listen to it," Jason said. "I'll bang on the floor."

"It's a good one," Nancy said. "It's better than the other one."

"What's it about?" Caddy said. Nancy was standing by the lamp. Her hand was on the lamp, against the light, long and brown.

"Your hand is on that hot globe," Caddy said. "Don't it feel hot to your hand?"

Nancy looked at her hand on the lamp chimney. She took her hand away, slow. She stood there, looking at Caddy, wringing her long hand as though it were tied to her wrist with a string.

"Let's do something else," Caddy said.

"I want to go home," Jason said.

"I got some popcorn," Nancy said. She looked at Caddy and then at Jason and then at me and then at Caddy again. "I got some popcorn."

"I don't like popcorn," Jason said. "I'd rather have candy."

Nancy looked at Jason. "You can hold the popper." She was still wringing her hand; it was long and limp and brown.

"All right," Jason said. "I'll stay a while if I can do that. Caddy can't hold it. I'll want to go home again if Caddy holds the popper."

Nancy built up the fire. "Look at Nancy putting her hands in the fire," Caddy said. "What's the matter with you, Nancy?"

"I got popcorn," Nancy said. "I got some." She took the popper from under the bed. It was broken. Jason began to cry.

"Now we can't have any popcorn," he said.

"We ought to go home, anyway," Caddy said. "Come on, Quentin."

"Wait," Nancy said; "wait. I can fix it. Don't you want to help me fix it?"

"I don't think I want any," Caddy said. "It's too late now."

"You help me, Jason," Nancy said. "Don't you want to help me?"

"No," Jason said. "I want to go home."

"Hush," Nancy said; "hush. Watch. Watch me. I can fix it so Jason can hold it and pop the corn." She got a piece of wire and fixed the popper.

"It won't hold good," Caddy said.

"Yes, it will," Nancy said. "Yawl watch. Yawl help me shell some corn."

The popcorn was under the bed too. We shelled it into the popper and Nancy helped Jason hold the popper over the fire.

"It's not popping," Jason said. "I want to go home."

"You wait," Nancy said. "It'll begin to pop. We'll have fun then." She was sitting close to the fire. The lamp was turned up so high it was beginning to smoke.

"Why don't you turn it down some?" I said.

"It's all right," Nancy said. "I'll clean it. Yawl wait. The popcorn will start in a minute."

"I don't believe it's going to start," Caddy said. "We ought to start home, anyway. They'll be worried."

"No," Nancy said. "It's going to pop. Dilsey will tell um yawl with me. I been working for yawl long time. They won't mind if yawl at my house. You wait, now. It'll start popping any minute now."

Then Jason got some smoke in his eyes and he began to cry. He dropped the popper into the fire. Nancy got a wet rag and wiped Jason's face, but he didn't stop crying.

"Hush," she said. "Hush." But he didn't hush. Caddy took the popper out of the fire.

"It's burned up," she said. "You'll have to get some more popcorn, Nancy."

"Did you put all of it in?" Nancy said.

"Yes," Caddy said. Nancy looked at Caddy. Then she took the popper and opened it and poured the cinders into her apron and began to sort the grains, her hands long and brown, and we watching her.

"Haven't you got any more?" Caddy said.

"Yes," Nancy said; "yes. Look. This here ain't burnt. All we need to do is—"

"I want to go home," Jason said. "I'm going to tell."

"Hush," Caddy said. We all listened. Nancy's head was already turned toward the barred door, her eyes filled with red lamplight. "Somebody is coming," Caddy said.

Then Nancy began to make that sound again, not loud, sitting there above the fire, her long hands dangling between her knees; all of a sudden water began to come out on her face in big drops, running down her face, carrying in each one a little turning ball of firelight like a spark until it dropped off her chin. "She's not crying," I said.

"I ain't crying," Nancy said. Her eyes were closed. "I ain't crying. Who is it?"

"I don't know," Caddy said. She went to the door and looked out. "We've got to go now," she said. "Here comes father."

"I'm going to tell," Jason said. "Yawl made me come."

The water still ran down Nancy's face. She turned in her chair. "Listen. Tell him. Tell him we going to have fun. Tell him I take good care of yawl until in the morning. Tell him to let me come home with yawl and sleep on the floor. Tell him I won't need no pallet. We'll have fun. You member last time how we had so much fun?"

"I didn't have fun," Jason said. "You hurt me. You put smoke in my eyes. I'm going to tell."

V

Father came in. He looked at us. Nancy did not get up.

"Tell him," she said.

"Caddy made us come down here," Jason said. "I didn't want to."

Father came to the fire. Nancy looked up at him. "Can't you go to Aunt Rachel's and stay?" he said. Nancy looked up at father, her hands between her knees. "He's not here," father said. "I would have seen him. There's not a soul in sight."

"He in the ditch," Nancy said. "He waiting in the ditch yonder."

"Nonsense," father said. He looked at Nancy. "Do you know he's there?"

"I got the sign," Nancy said.

"What sign?"

"I got it. It was on the table when I come in. It was a hog-bone, with blood meat still on it, laying by the lamp. He's out there. When yawl walk out that door, I gone."

"Gone where, Nancy?" Caddy said.

"I'm not a tattletale," Jason said.

"Nonsense," father said.

"He out there," Nancy said. "He looking through that window this minute, waiting for yawl to go. Then I gone."

"Nonsense," father said. "Lock up your house and we'll take you on to Aunt Rachel's."

"'Twont do no good," Nancy said. She didn't look at father now, but he looked down at her, at her long, limp, moving hands. "Putting it off wont do no good."

"Then what do you want to do?" father said.

"I don't know," Nancy said. "I can't do nothing. Just put it off. And that don't do no good. I reckon it belong to me. I reckon what I going to get ain't no more than mine."

"Get what?" Caddy said. "What's yours?"

"Nothing," father said. "You all must get to bed."

"Caddy made me come," Jason said.

"Go on to Aunt Rachel's," father said.

"It won't do no good," Nancy said. She sat before the fire, her elbows on her knees, her long hands between her knees. "When even your own kitchen wouldn't do no good. When even if I was sleeping on the floor in the room with your chillen, and the next morning there I am, and blood—"

"Hush," father said. "Lock the door and put out the lamp and go to bed."

"I scared of the dark," Nancy said. "I scared for it to happen in the dark."

"You mean you're going to sit right here with the lamp lighted?" father said. Then Nancy began to make the sound again, sitting before the fire, her long hands between her knees. "Ah, damnation," father said. "Come along, chillen. It's past bedtime."

"When yawl go home, I gone," Nancy said. She talked quieter now, and her face looked quiet, like her hands. "Anyway, I got my coffin money saved up with Mr. Lovelady." Mr. Lovelady was a short, dirty man who collected the Negro insurance, coming around to the cabins or the kitchens every Saturday morning, to collect fifteen cents. He and his wife lived at the hotel. One morning his wife committed suicide. They had a child, a little girl. He and the child went away. After a week or two he came back alone. We would see him going along the lanes and the back streets on Saturday mornings.

"Nonsense," father said. "You'll be the first thing I'll see in the kitchen tomorrow morning."

"You'll see what you'll see, I reckon," Nancy said. "But it will take the Lord to say what that will be."

VI

We left her sitting before the fire.

"Come and put the bar up," father said. But she didn't move. She didn't look at us again, sitting quietly there between the lamp and the fire. From some distance down the lane we could look back and see her through the open door.

"What, Father?" Caddy said. "What's going to happen?"

"Nothing," father said. Jason was on father's back, so Jason was the tallest of all of us. We went down into the ditch. I looked at it, quiet. I couldn't see much where the moonlight and the shadows tangled.

"If Jesus is hid here, he can see us, can't he?" Caddy said.

"He's not there," father said. "He went away a long time ago."

"You made me come," Jason said, high; against the sky it looked like father had two heads, a little one and a big one. "I didn't want to."

We went up out of the ditch. We could still see Nancy's house and the open door, but we couldn't see Nancy now, sitting before the fire with the door open, because she was tired. "I just done got tired," she said. "I just a nigger. It ain't no fault of mine."

But we could hear her, because she began just after we came up out of the ditch, the sound that was not singing and not unsinging. "Who will do our washing now, Father?" I said.

"I'm not a nigger," Jason said, high and close above father's head.

"You're worse," Caddy said, "you are a tattletale. If something was to jump out, you'd be scairder than a nigger."

"I wouldn't," Jason said.
"You'd cry," Caddy said.
"Caddy," father said.
"I wouldn't!" Jason said.
"Scairy cat," Caddy said.
"Candace!" father said.

1931

Nobel Prize Address

[Stockholm, December 10, 1950]

I feel that this award was not made to me as a man, but to my work—a life's work in the agony and sweat of the human spirit, not for glory and least of all for profit, but to create out of the materials of the human spirit something which did not exist before. So this award is only mine in trust. It will not be difficult to find a dedication for the money part of it commensurate with the purpose and significance of its origin. But I would like to do the same with the acclaim too, by using this moment as a pinnacle from which I might be listened to by the young men and women already dedicated to the same anguish and travail, among whom is already that one who will some day stand here where I am standing.

Our tragedy today is a general and universal physical fear so long sustained by now that we can even bear it. There are no longer problems of the spirit. There is only the question: When will I be blown up? Because of this, the young man or woman writing today has forgotten the problems of the human heart in conflict with itself which alone can make good writing because only that is worth writing about, worth the agony and the sweat.

He must learn them again. He must teach himself that the basest of all things is to be afraid; and, teaching himself that, forget it forever, leaving no room in his workshop for anything but the old verities and truths of the heart, the old universal truths lacking which any story is ephemeral and doomed—love and honor and pity and pride and compassion and sacrifice. Until he does so, he labors under a curse. He writes not of love but of lust, of defeats in which nobody loses anything of value, of victories without hope and, worst of all, without pity or compassion. His griefs grieve on no universal bones, leaving no scars. He writes not of the heart but of the glands.

Until he relearns these things, he will write as though he stood among and watched the end of man. I decline to accept the end of man. It is easy enough to say that man is immortal simply because he will endure: that when the last ding-dong of doom has clanged and faded from the last worthless rock hanging tideless in the last red and dying evening, that even then there will still be one more sound: that of his puny inexhaustible voice, still talking. I refuse to accept this. I believe that man will not merely endure: he will prevail. He is immortal, not because he alone among creatures has an inexhaustible voice, but because he has a soul, a spirit capable of compassion and sacrifice and endurance. The poet's, the writer's, duty is to write about these things. It is his privilege to help man endure by lifting his heart, by reminding him of the courage and honor and hope and pride and compassion and pity and sacrifice which have been the glory of his past. The poet's voice need not merely be the record of man, it can be one of the props, the pillars to help him endure and prevail.

1950/1950

Ernest Hemingway
1899–1961

No other major American writer has ever equaled the popular success and worldwide reputation of Ernest Hemingway. During his lifetime he attained the status of an international celebrity; his activities were reported by gossip columnists along with the disport of the movie stars and the athletes he became friends with. His prose style became one of the most recognizable literary "trademarks" of all time and is still widely imitated and parodied.

Hemingway was born on July 21, 1899, in Oak Park, Illinois, a suburb just west of Chicago. His father was a prosperous physician; his mother, a devoted member of the Congregational church who, having tried to pursue a career as an opera singer, taught music. In high school Hemingway participated in several organized sports, including football and boxing. He played the cello in the school orchestra (his mother hoped he would become a cellist) and wrote for the school's newspaper and literary magazine. But the most intense of his early experiences, if we may judge by the memories he carried with him, centered on the hunting and fishing he did with his father near the family cottage on the upper peninsula of northern Michigan. There, under his father's tutelage, he learned things he never forgot—the ritual of the hunt and the code of the hunter, lessons that stressed the primacy of elemental physical confrontations and the importance of physical prowess, physical endurance, and physical courage. His father, who committed suicide in 1928, gave Hemingway his first fishing rod at age two and his first gun at age ten: "I am so pleased and proud you have grown to be such a fine big manly fellow," he wrote his son in 1915.

In 1917, having finished high school, Hemingway decided to forgo college. Setting out on his own, he found work as a cub reporter on the Kansas City *Star,* where he began cultivating the restrained yet vigorous prose style that later, when he shaped it into literature under the influence of Sherwood Anderson, Ezra Pound, and Gertrude Stein, would make him famous. Though he enjoyed newspaper work, he soon left it for Europe, drawn by the first of several wars in which he would serve. Rejected by the army because of an eye defect, he volunteered for the Red Cross ambulance corps. In 1918, after a brief stay in France, he entered active duty in Italy, where he was severely wounded by the explosion of a mortar shell. Throughout his life he wore a platinum kneecap and bore numerous shrapnel scars. Yet the experience proved exhilarating as well as traumatic. "Wounds don't matter," he wrote his family jauntily in a letter from a Milan hospital that was published in the Oak Park newspaper; "I wouldn't mind being wounded again so much because I know just what it is like . . . and it does give you an awfully satisfactory feeling to be wounded." Wounds— physical and psychic—would play a significant role not only in Hemingway's writing but also in his life. Remarkably accident-prone, he was repeatedly injured —in car crashes, plane crashes, shooting mishaps, freak accidents, and fires. Nearly everywhere he went—Italy, Spain, France, England, Africa, Montana, Idaho, the Florida Keys, Cuba—something happened, making his scarred body a personal geography of wounds.

After the war Hemingway returned home, decorated by the Italians for conspicuous valor. For the next two years he tried to resume the life he had left behind. He hunted and fished with friends in northern Michigan and began writing for the Toronto *Star*. But he could not adjust to the United States and Canada and itched to return to Europe. He would always be attacked by critics for not concentrating on the "American scene" ("Difference with us guys," he wrote Faulkner, "is I always lived out of country"), and most of his writing is set in other countries. In 1921 he married the first of his four wives and left the United States to join the growing band of self-exiled artists and writers who were gathering in Paris.

Paris attracted Americans such as Hemingway not only because it was the exciting center of a modernist revolution in art and literature but also because of its more liberal moral climate, the availability of liquor (Prohibition had gone into effect in the United States in 1919), and the highly favorable exchange rate. Back in the spring of 1921 Hemingway had met Sherwood Anderson, and it was through Anderson's courteous letters of introduction that the younger midwestern writer met Gertrude Stein and Ezra Pound. Later, Hemingway would get to know John Dos Passos, James Joyce (whose *Ulysses* he considered a "most goddamn wonderful book"), and F. Scott Fitzgerald. Though all of these writers in one way or another helped Hemingway launch his literary career, he ended up quarreling—at times nastily—with nearly everyone who had helped him.

"That's what you are, that's what you all are," Gertrude Stein said to Hemingway, speaking of those who had survived the war. "You are a lost generation." And it was in part a sense of loss, disillusionment, and disenchantment that Hemingway shared with the other expatriates in Paris. The Great War, like the grand words used to justify it, seemed to him a terrible betrayal. He was beginning to discover in violence and the consequences of violence one of his major themes and in war and its aftermath one of his favorite settings. The violence of the modern world, ritualized in hunting, fishing, and bullfighting (in which he saw a combination of "valor and art"), began to preoccupy his imagination. At the same time, he continued to write articles as the European correspondent of the Toronto *Star:* He interviewed Mussolini, covered the Greco-Turkish War, and wrote about crime. In 1923 he published his first book, *Three Stories and Ten Poems,* and returned to Toronto, where he resumed newspaper work and where his first child was born.

A year later Hemingway was back in Paris, trying to support a family on his meager income from journalism and publishing short stories in small literary journals. One of his early stories, "My Old Man," was selected for an anthology of the best stories of 1923, though the editor of the volume consistently misspelled Hemingway's name. Gradually, however, Hemingway was building a reputation as a meticulous craftsman. His stories, he warned a publisher, "are written so tight and so hard that the alteration of a word can throw an entire story out of key." In 1925 he published *In Our Time,* a story sequence that included several stories set in the Michigan of his boyhood. A year earlier he had published a slightly different collection in Paris under the lowercase title *in our time.* The main sequence of stories, which concludes with "Big Two-Hearted River, Parts I and II," is introduced and interspersed with a series of brief and elliptically related interchapters that begins with the violence of the Turkish War and concludes with the violence of bullfighting and political execution.

Although, as its title indicates, Hemingway clearly intended *In Our Time* to have the immediacy and impact of journalism, its style is far from the representational realism of modern reporting. In a 1958 interview, Hemingway expressed his literary concern in a way that shows how his art both depends on and radically departs from conventional "realism": "From things that have happened and from things as they exist and from all the things that you know and all those that you cannot know, you make something through your invention that is not a representation but a whole new thing truer than any thing true and alive." The two parts of "Big Two-Hearted River" are firmly grounded in Hemingway's firsthand knowledge of fishing the Fox River north of Seney, Michigan, yet, as he said to Gertrude Stein, in writing the story he was "trying to do the country like Cézanne," a reference to Cézanne's now famous landscape paintings of the Provence countryside, which became the creative force behind cubism.

By 1926 Hemingway had grown increasingly annoyed at critical references to his artistic indebtedness to Sherwood Anderson. As a response, he published an insensitive and even vicious parody of Anderson called *The Torrents of Spring,* a book that is widely regarded as one of his weakest efforts. Yet in the same year he published *The Sun Also Rises,* which brought him international fame and is still widely regarded as the best of his novels. *The Sun Also Rises* centers on a group of heavy-drinking, tough-talking, and hard-living expatriates and is narrated by an American reporter in Paris. For many readers, *The Sun Also Rises* perfectly captured the postwar mood of the "lost generation"; to emphasize the point, Hemingway used Gertrude Stein's phrase as an epigraph to the book. A second collection of stories, *Men Without Women,* followed in 1927, and two years later his second serious novel, *A Farewell to Arms,* the story of an American ambulance officer in Italy who is seriously wounded and falls in love with a British nurse. After discovering that she is pregnant, he deserts the service and escapes with her to Switzerland, where for a few idyllic months in the mountains they find a "separate peace" that is disastrously shattered when both mother and infant die in childbirth.

In 1930, at the suggestion of John Dos Passos, Hemingway bought a house in Key West, Florida. By this time he was married for a second time, was sporting a full beard, weighed a burly 208 pounds, and was already referring to himself as "Papa." It was a persona he would use for the rest of his life. In Key West, Hemingway developed a lifelong passion for sailing and deep-sea fishing. "A sportsman," James Joyce had called him, "and ready to live the life he writes about. He would never have written it if his body had not allowed him to live it." In his writing and behavior, Hemingway consistently promoted a conventionally "masculine" way of life; for a biographical sketch, he once listed his hobbies as "ski-ing, fishing, shooting, and drinking." Yet even during his life, his insistently male performances, though good for publicity, were the subject of critical ridicule. Edmund Wilson had been among the first to praise Hemingway's early stories. In the Key West Hemingway, however, "the Hemingway of the handsome photographs with the sportsman's tan and the outdoor grin, with the ominous resemblance to Clark Gable, who poses with giant marlin which he has just hauled in," Wilson saw an "arrogant, belligerent and boastful" man who was "certainly the worst-invented character to be found in the author's work."

For all his public posturing, however, Hemingway continued to write. In 1932 he published a now classic book about bullfighting, *Death in the Afternoon,* which contains much of what can be called the author's "philosophy of life"—his fascination with danger and death and his unswerving commitment to honor, valor, and a quality of style he called "grace under pressure." Another excellent collection of short stories, *Winner Take Nothing,* appeared in 1933, and in 1935 Hemingway used the experiences gathered on African safaris to write *The Green Hills of Africa,* a book that blends literary commentary and travel description with a metaphysics of big-game hunting. Out of his African experience also came two of his finest stories, "The Snows of Kilimanjaro" and "The Short Happy Life of Francis Macomber."

Throughout the 1930s Hemingway was criticized by leftist critics for ignoring progressive causes and retreating into a hedonistic sporting life. Hemingway was always suspicious of politically motivated fiction: "There is no left and right in writing," he claimed; "there is only good and bad writing." Yet in his next book, *To Have and Have Not* (1937), his only novel that uses an American setting, Hemingway created the hard-bitten, pragmatic hero Harry Morgan, a Florida fishing boat captain who fights a separate war against the Depression by smuggling rum from Cuba to Key West. Morgan's often-quoted dying words— "One man alone ain't got no bloody f——ing chance"—appealed to "socially aware" readers who were perhaps too eager to see in the book a statement of Hemingway's social conscience. In 1936 Hemingway went to Spain with Dos Passos to work on an anti-Fascist documentary film, *The Spanish Earth.* His journalistic coverage of the civil war in Spain provided him with the material for a play called *The Fifth Column* (1938) and a novel called *For Whom the Bell Tolls* (1940), an enormously popular story about an American academic, Robert Jordan, who teams up with a small group of peasant guerrillas and heroically sacrifices his life in what proves to be a losing cause.

In 1940, married for the third time, Hemingway moved to an estate in Cuba, where he fished for marlin, drank excessively, raised fighting cocks, and played lavish host to actors and actresses, matadors, fighters, politicos, and an assortment of international celebrities. When the United States entered the Second World War, Hemingway volunteered his prized fishing vessel for antisubmarine duty. In 1944, as a war correspondent, he participated in the Normandy invasion and eventually took such an "active" role with the U.S. Army's 4th Infantry Division in France and Germany that he was awarded the Bronze Star. After the war, he married again and spent time in Venice, the city that served as the setting for one of his most poorly received novels, the idyllic romance, *Across the River and into the Trees* (1950). He returned to Cuba and started working on a long "sea novel" that he had much difficulty with and that eventually was published posthumously as *Islands in the Stream* (1970). In 1952, however, Hemingway selected one long self-contained section of that novel and published it as *The Old Man and the Sea* —a parable-like tale of an old Cuban fisherman who catches a giant marlin but is unable to keep the sharks from mutilating it before he can get it safely to shore. This novella became Hemingway's biggest-selling book, won him the Pulitzer Prize, and led directly to his being awarded the Nobel Prize in 1954.

During the final years of his life, Hemingway made several trips to Spain and engaged in another African safari, during which he barely survived back-to-back plane crashes. But his health was giving out. As political tension mounted in Cuba, he left his estate and moved to Ketchum, Idaho, where he underwent both medical and psychiatric treatment. In 1960 he used some notes and reportage that had survived from the 1920s as the basis for a collection of reminiscences, *A Moveable Feast*, which appeared posthumously in 1964. In 1961 he found himself unable to write one sentence for a volume to be presented to President John F. Kennedy: "It just won't come any more," he said. "How simple the writing of literature would be," he had written in his Nobel Prize acceptance speech, "if it were only necessary to write in another way what has been well written."

A sense of loss and the threat of violence had informed almost everything Hemingway wrote. In a deceptively simple, spare, disciplined prose (he said of *In Our Time*, "There is no writing in it that anybody with a high-school education cannot read"), he labored to find ways of restoring the force of words that had lost their edge. His heroes bear scars that are psychological as well as physical, and they carry with them memories of violence as well as premonitions of death. Facing a disordered, hypocritical world, they seek to discover some code by which to live, some style for comporting themselves in reality. Their cause, that of finding some way gracefully to endure the pain and accept the futility of life without cant or illusion, is based on the assumption that learning how to live life can sometimes help us to understand it. On July 2, 1961, in Ketchum, Idaho, Hemingway chose, as his father had before him, to end his own life violently. He pressed a double-barreled shotgun to his forehead and pulled both triggers.

Further Reading:
Ernest Hemingway: The Man and His Work, ed. J. K. M. McCaffrey, 1950.
P. Young, *Ernest Hemingway,* rev. ed., 1966.
C. Baker, *Ernest Hemingway: A Life Story,* 1969.
G. H. Hemingway, *Papa,* 1976.
A. Burgess, *Ernest Hemingway and His World,* 1978.

Texts:
"Big Two-Hearted River" from *In Our Time,* 1925.
"A Man of the World" and "Get a Seeing-Eyed Dog" from *Atlantic Monthly,* 1957.

Big Two-Hearted River

Part I

The train went on up the track out of sight, around one of the hills of burnt timber. Nick sat down on the bundle of canvas and bedding the baggage man had pitched out of the door of the baggage car. There was no town, nothing but the rails and the burned-over country. The thirteen saloons that had lined the one street of Seney had not left a trace. The foundations of the Mansion House hotel stuck up above the ground. The stone was chipped and split by the fire. It was all that was left of the town of Seney. Even the surface had been burned off the ground.

Nick looked at the burned-over stretch of hillside, where he had expected to find the scattered houses of the town and then walked down the railroad track to the bridge over the river. The river was there. It swirled against the log spiles of the bridge. Nick looked down into the clear, brown water, colored from the pebbly bottom, and watched the trout keeping themselves steady in the current with wavering fins. As he watched them they changed their positions by quick angles, only to hold steady in the fast water again. Nick watched them a long time.

He watched them holding themselves with their noses into the current, many trout in deep, fast moving water, slightly distorted as he watched far down through the glassy convex surface of the pool, its surface pushing and swelling smooth against the resistance of the log-driven piles of the bridge. At the bottom of the pool were the big trout. Nick did not see them at first. Then he saw them at the bottom of the pool, big trout looking to hold themselves on the gravel bottom in a varying mist of gravel and sand, raised in spurts by the current.

Nick looked down into the pool from the bridge. It was a hot day. A kingfisher flew up the stream. It was a long time since Nick had looked into a stream and seen trout. They were very satisfactory. As the shadow of the kingfisher moved up the stream, a big trout shot upstream in a long angle, only his shadow marking the angle, then lost his shadow as he came through the surface of the water, caught the sun, and then, as he went back into the stream under the surface, his shadow seemed to float down the stream with the current, unresisting, to his post under the bridge where he tightened facing up into the current.

Nick's heart tightened as the trout moved. He felt all the old feeling.

He turned and looked down the stream. It stretched away, pebbly-bottomed with shallows and big boulders and a deep pool as it curved away around the foot of a bluff.

Nick walked back up the ties to where his pack lay in the cinders beside the railway track. He was happy. He adjusted the pack harness around the bundle, pulling straps tight, slung the pack on his back, got his arms through the shoulder straps and took some of the pull off his shoulders by leaning his forehead against the wide band of the tump-line. Still, it was too heavy. It was much too heavy. He had his leather rod-case in his hand and leaning forward to keep the weight of the pack high on his shoulders he walked along the road that paralleled the railway track, leaving the burned town behind in the heat, and then turned off around a hill with a high, fire-scarred hill on either side onto a road that went back into the country. He walked along the road feeling the ache from the pull of the heavy pack. The road climbed steadily. It was hard work walking up-hill. His muscles ached and the day was hot, but Nick felt happy. He felt he had left everything behind, the need for thinking, the need to write, other needs. It was all back of him.

From the time he had gotten down off the train and the baggage man had thrown his pack out of the open car door things had been different. Seney was burned, the country was burned over and changed, but it did not matter. It could not all be burned. He knew that. He hiked along the road, sweating in the sun, climbing to cross the range of hills that separated the railway from the pine plains.

The road ran on, dipping occasionally, but always climbing. Nick went on up. Finally the road after going parallel to the burnt hillside reached the top. Nick leaned back against a stump and slipped out of the pack harness. Ahead of him, as far as he could see, was the pine plain. The burned country stopped off at the left with the range of hills. On ahead islands of dark pine trees rose out of the plain. Far off to the left was the line of the river. Nick followed it with his eye and caught glints of the water in the sun.

There was nothing but the pine plain ahead of him, until the far blue hills that marked the Lake Superior height of land. He could hardly see them, faint and far away in the heat-light over the plain. If he looked too steadily they were gone. But if he only half-looked they were there, the far off hills of the height of land.

Nick sat down against the charred stump and smoked a cigarette. His pack balanced on the top of the stump, harness holding ready, a hollow molded in it from his back. Nick sat smoking, looking out over the country. He did not need to get his map out. He knew where he was from the position of the river.

As he smoked, his legs stretched out in front of him, he noticed a grasshopper walk along the ground and up onto his woolen sock. The grasshopper was black. As he had walked along the road, climbing, he had started many grasshoppers from the dust. They were all black. They were not the big grasshoppers with yellow and black or red and black wings whirring out from their black wing sheathing as they fly up. These were just ordinary hoppers, but all a sooty black in color. Nick had wondered about them as he walked, without really thinking about them. Now, as he watched the black hopper that was nibbling at the wool of his sock with its fourway lip, he realized that they had all turned black from living in the burned-over land. He realized that the fire must have come the year before, but the grasshoppers were all black now. He wondered how long they would stay that way.

Carefully he reached his hand down and took hold of the hopper by the wings. He turned him up, all his legs walking in the air, and looked at his jointed belly. Yes, it was black too, iridescent where the back and head were dusty.

"Go on, hopper," Nick said, speaking out loud for the first time, "Fly away somewhere."

He tossed the grasshopper up into the air and watched him sail away to a charcoal stump across the road.

Nick stood up. He leaned his back against the weight of his pack where it rested upright on the stump and got his arms through the shoulder straps. He stood with the pack on his back on the brow of the hill looking out across the country, toward the distant river and then struck down the hillside away from the road. Underfoot the ground was good walking. Two hundred yards down the hillside the fire line stopped. Then it was sweet fern, growing ankle high, to walk through, and clumps of jack pines; a long undulating country with frequent rises and descents, sandy underfoot and the country alive again.

Nick kept his direction by the sun. He knew where he wanted to strike the river and he kept on through the pine plain, mounting small rises to see other rises ahead of him and sometimes from the top of a rise a great solid island of pines off to his right or his left. He broke off some sprigs of the heathery sweet fern, and put them under his pack straps. The chafing crushed it and he smelled it as he walked.

He was tired and very hot, walking across the uneven, shadeless pine plain. At any time he knew he could strike the river by turning off to his left. It could not be more than a mile away. But he kept on toward the north to hit the river as far upstream as he could go in one day's walking.

For some time as he walked Nick had been in sight of one of the big islands of pine standing out above the rolling high ground he was crossing. He dipped down and then as he came slowly up to the crest of the ridge he turned and made toward the pine trees.

There was no underbrush in the island of pine trees. The trunks of the trees went straight up or slanted toward each other. The trunks were straight and brown without branches. The branches were high above. Some interlocked to make a solid shadow on the brown forest floor. Around the grove of trees was a bare space. It was brown and soft underfoot as Nick walked on it. This was the over-lapping of the pine needle floor, extending out beyond the width of the high branches. The trees had grown tall and the branches moved high, leaving in the sun this bare space they had once covered with shadow. Sharp at the edge of this extension of the forest floor commenced the sweet fern.

Nick slipped off his pack and lay down in the shade. He lay on his back and looked up into the pine trees. His neck and back and the small of his back rested as he stretched. The earth felt good against his back. He looked up at the sky, through the branches, and then shut his eyes. He opened them and looked up again. There was a wind high up in the branches. He shut his eyes again and went to sleep.

Nick woke stiff and cramped. The sun was nearly down. His pack was heavy and the straps painful as he lifted it on. He leaned over with the pack on and picked up the leather rod-case and started out from the pine trees across the sweet fern swale, toward the river. He knew it could not be more than a mile.

He came down a hillside covered with stumps into a meadow. At the edge of the meadow flowed the river. Nick was glad to get to the river. He walked upstream through the meadow. His trousers were soaked with the dew as he walked. After the hot day, the dew had come quickly and heavily. The river made no sound. It was too fast and smooth. At the edge of the meadow, before he mounted to a piece of high ground to make camp, Nick looked down the river at the trout rising. They were rising to insects come from the swamp on the other side of the stream when the sun went down. The trout jumped out of water to take them. While Nick walked through the little stretch of meadow alongside the stream, trout had jumped high out of water. Now as he looked down the river, the insects must be settling on the surface, for the trout were feeding steadily all down the stream. As far down the long stretch as he could see, the trout were rising, making circles all down the surface of the water, as though it were starting to rain.

The ground rose, wooded and sandy, to overlook the meadow, the stretch of river and the swamp. Nick dropped his pack and rod-case and looked for a level piece of ground. He was very hungry and he wanted to make his camp before he cooked. Between two jack pines, the ground was quite level. He took the ax out of the pack and chopped out two projecting roots. That leveled a piece of ground large enough to sleep on. He smoothed out the sandy soil with his hand and pulled all the sweet fern bushes by their roots. His hands smelled good from the sweet fern. He smoothed the uprooted earth. He did not want anything making lumps under the blankets. When he had the ground smooth, he spread his three blankets. One he folded double, next to the ground. The other two he spread on top.

With the ax he slit off a bright slab of pine from one of the stumps and split it into pegs for the tent. He wanted them long and solid to hold in the ground. With the tent unpacked and spread on the ground, the pack, leaning against a jackpine, looked much smaller. Nick tied the rope that served the tent for a ridge-pole to the trunk of one of the pine trees and pulled the tent up off the ground with the other end of the rope and tied it to the other pine. The tent hung on the rope like a canvas blanket on a clothes line. Nick poked a pole he had cut up under the back peak of the canvas and then made it a tent by pegging out the sides. He pegged the sides out taut and drove the pegs deep, hitting them down into the ground with the flat of the ax until the rope loops were buried and the canvas was drum tight.

Across the open mouth of the tent Nick fixed cheese cloth to keep out mosquitoes. He crawled inside under the mosquito bar with various things from the pack to put at the head of the bed under the slant of the canvas. Inside the tent the light came through the brown canvas. It smelled pleasantly of canvas. Already there was something mysterious and homelike. Nick was happy as he crawled inside the tent. He had not been unhappy all day. This was different though. Now things were done. There had been this to do. Now it was done. It had been a hard trip. He was very tired. That was done. He had made his camp. He was settled. Nothing could touch him. It was a good place to camp. He was there, in the good place. He was in his home where he had made it. Now he was hungry.

He came out, crawling under the cheese cloth. It was quite dark outside. It was lighter in the tent.

Nick went over to the pack and found, with his fingers, a long nail in a paper sack of nails, in the bottom of the pack. He drove it into the pine tree, holding it close and hitting it gently with the flat of the ax. He hung the pack up on the nail. All his supplies were in the pack. They were off the ground and sheltered now.

Nick was hungry. He did not believe he had ever been hungrier. He opened and emptied a can of pork and beans and a can of spaghetti into the frying pan.

"I've got a right to eat this kind of stuff, if I'm willing to carry it," Nick said. His voice sounded strange in the darkening woods. He did not speak again.

He started a fire with some chunks of pine he got with the ax from a stump. Over the fire he stuck a wire grill, pushing the four legs down into the ground with his boot. Nick put the frying pan on the grill over the flames. He was hungrier. The beans and spaghetti warmed. Nick stirred them and mixed them together. They began to bubble, making little bubbles that rose with difficulty to the surface. There was a good smell. Nick got out a bottle of tomato catchup and cut four slices of bread. The little bubbles were coming faster now. Nick sat down beside the fire and lifted the frying pan off. He poured about half the contents out into the tin plate. It spread slowly on the plate. Nick knew it was too hot. He poured on some tomato catchup. He knew the beans and spaghetti were still too hot. He looked at the fire, then at the tent, he was not going to spoil it all by burning his tongue. For years he had never enjoyed fried bananas because he had never been able to wait for them to cool. His tongue was very sensitive. He was very hungry. Across the river in the swamp, in the almost dark, he saw a mist rising. He looked at the tent once more. All right. He took a full spoonful from the plate.

"Chrise," Nick said, "Geezus Chrise," he said happily.

He ate the whole plateful before he remembered the bread. Nick finished the second plateful with the bread, mopping the plate shiny. He had not eaten since a cup of coffee and a ham sandwich in the station restaurant at St. Ignace. It had been a very fine experience. He had been that hungry before, but had not been able to satisfy it. He could have made camp hours before if he had wanted to. There were plenty of good places to camp on the river. But this was good.

Nick tucked two big chips of pine under the grill. The fire flared up. He had forgotten to get water for the coffee. Out of the pack he got a folding canvas bucket and walked down the hill, across the edge of the meadow, to the stream. The other bank was in the white mist. The grass was wet and cold as he knelt on the bank and dipped the canvas bucket into the stream. It bellied and pulled hard in the current. The water was ice cold. Nick rinsed the bucket and carried it full up to the camp. Up away from the stream it was not so cold.

Nick drove another big nail and hung up the bucket full of water. He dipped the coffee pot half full, put some more chips under the grill onto the fire and put the pot on. He could not remember which way he made coffee. He could remember an argument about it with Hopkins, but not which side he had taken. He decided to bring it to a boil. He remembered now that was Hopkins's way. He had once argued about everything with Hopkins. While he waited for the coffee to boil, he opened a small can of apricots. He liked to open cans. He emptied the can of apricots out into a tin cup. While he watched the coffee on the fire, he drank the juice syrup of the apricots, carefully at first to keep from spilling, then meditatively, sucking the apricots down. They were better than fresh apricots.

The coffee boiled as he watched. The lid came up and coffee and grounds ran down the side of the pot. Nick took it off the grill. It was a triumph for Hopkins. He put sugar in the empty apricot cup and poured some of the coffee out to cool. It was too hot to pour and he used his hat to hold the handle of the coffee pot. He would not let it steep in the pot at all. Not the first cup. It should be straight Hopkins all the way. Hop deserved that. He was a very serious coffee maker. He was the most serious man Nick had ever known. Not heavy, serious. That was a long time ago. Hopkins spoke without moving his lips. He had played polo. He made millions of dollars in Texas. He had borrowed carfare to go to Chicago, when the wire came that his first big well had come in. He could have wired for money. That would have been too slow. They called Hop's girl the Blonde Venus. Hop did not mind because she was not his real girl. Hopkins said very confidently that none of them would make fun of his real girl. He was right. Hopkins went away when the telegram came. That was on the Black River. It took eight days for the telegram to reach him. Hopkins gave away his .22 caliber Colt automatic pistol to Nick. He gave his camera to Bill. It was to remember him always by. They were all going fishing again next summer. The Hop Head was rich. He would get a yacht and they would all cruise along the north shore of Lake Superior. He was excited but serious. They said good-bye and all felt bad. It broke up the trip. They never saw Hopkins again. That was a long time ago on the Black River.

Nick drank the coffee, the coffee, according to Hopkins. The coffee was bitter. Nick laughed. It made a good ending to the story. His mind was starting to work. He knew he could choke it because he was tired enough. He spilled the coffee out of the pot and shook the grounds loose into the fire. He lit a cigarette and went inside the tent. He took off his shoes and trousers, sitting on the blankets, rolled the shoes up inside the trousers for a pillow and got in between the blankets.

Out through the front of the tent he watched the glow of the fire, when the night wind blew on it. It was a quiet night. The swamp was perfectly quiet. Nick stretched under the blanket comfortably. A mosquito hummed close to his ear. Nick sat up and lit a match. The mosquito was on the canvas, over his head. Nick moved the match quickly up to it. The mosquito made a satisfactory hiss in the flame. The match went out. Nick lay down again under the blankets. He turned on his side and shut his eyes. He was sleepy. He felt sleep coming. He curled up under the blanket and went to sleep.

Part II

In the morning the sun was up and the tent was starting to get hot. Nick crawled out under the mosquito netting stretched across the mouth of the tent, to look at the morning. The grass was wet on his hands as he came out. He held his trousers and his shoes in his hands. The sun was just up over the hill. There was the meadow, the river and the swamp. There were birch trees in the green of the swamp on the other side of the river.

The river was clear and smoothly fast in the early morning. Down about two hundred yards were three logs all the way across the stream. They made the water smooth and deep above them. As Nick watched, a mink crossed the river on the logs and went into the swamp. Nick was excited. He was excited by the early morning and the river. He was really too hurried to eat breakfast, but he knew he must. He built a little fire and put on the coffee pot. While the water was heating in the pot he took an empty bottle and went down over the edge of the high ground to the meadow. The meadow was wet with dew and Nick wanted to catch grasshoppers for bait before the sun dried the grass. He found plenty of good grasshoppers. They were at the base of the grass stems. Sometimes they clung to a grass stem. They were cold and wet with the dew, and could not jump until the sun warmed them. Nick picked them up, taking only the medium sized brown ones, and put them into the bottle. He turned over a log and just under the shelter of the edge were several hundred hoppers. It was a grasshopper lodging house. Nick put about fifty of the medium browns into the bottle. While he was picking up the hoppers the others warmed in the sun and commenced to hop away. They flew when they hopped. At first they made one flight and stayed stiff when they landed, as though they were dead.

Nick knew that by the time he was through with breakfast they would be as lively as ever. Without dew in the grass it would take him all day to catch a bottle full of good grasshoppers and he would have to crush many of them, slamming at them with his hat. He washed his hands at the stream. He was excited to be near it. Then he walked up to the tent. The hoppers were already jumping stiffly in the grass. In the bottle, warmed by the sun, they were jumping in a mass. Nick put in a pine stick as a cork. It plugged the mouth of the bottle enough, so the hoppers could not get out and left plenty of air passage.

He had rolled the log back and knew he could get grasshoppers there every morning.

Nick laid the bottle full of jumping grasshoppers against a pine trunk. Rapidly he mixed some buckwheat flour with water and stirred it smooth, one cup of flour, one cup of water. He put a handful of coffee in the pot and dipped a lump of grease out of a can and slid it sputtering across the hot skillet. On the smoking skillet he poured smoothly the buckwheat batter. It spread like lava, the grease spitting sharply. Around the edges the buckwheat cake began to firm, then brown, then crisp. The surface was bubbling slowly to porousness. Nick pushed under the browned under surface with a fresh pine chip. He shook the skillet sideways and the cake was loose on the surface. I won't try and flop it, he thought. He slid the chip of clean wood all the way under the cake, and flopped it over onto its face. It sputtered in the pan.

When it was cooked Nick regreased the skillet. He used all the batter. It made another big flapjack and one smaller one.

Nick ate a big flapjack and a smaller one, covered with apple butter. He put apple butter on the third cake, folded it over twice, wrapped it in oiled paper and put it in his shirt pocket. He put the apple butter jar back in the pack and cut bread for two sandwiches.

In the pack he found a big onion. He sliced it in two and peeled the silky outer skin. Then he cut one half into slices and made onion sandwiches. He wrapped them in oiled paper and buttoned them in the other pocket of his khaki shirt. He turned the skillet upside down on the grill, drank the coffee, sweetened and yellow brown with the condensed milk in it, and tidied up the camp. It was a nice little camp.

Nick took his fly rod out of the leather rod-case, jointed it, and shoved the rod-case back into the tent. He put on the reel and threaded the line through the guides. He had to hold it from hand to hand, as he threaded it, or it would slip back through its own weight. It was a heavy, double tapered fly line. Nick had paid eight dollars for it a long time ago. It was made heavy to lift back in the air and come forward flat and heavy and straight to make it possible to cast a fly which has no weight. Nick opened the aluminum leader box. The leaders were coiled between the damp flannel pads. Nick had wet the pads at the water cooler on the train up to St. Ignace. In the damp pads the gut leaders had softened and Nick unrolled one and tied it by a loop at the end to the heavy fly line. He fastened a hook on the end of the leader. It was a small hook; very thin and springy.

Nick took it from his hook book, sitting with the rod across his lap. He tested the knot and the spring of the rod by pulling the line taut. It was a good feeling. He was careful not to let the hook bite into his finger.

He started down to the stream, holding his rod, the bottle of grasshoppers hung from his neck by a thong tied in half hitches around the neck of the bottle. His landing net hung by a hook from his belt. Over his shoulder was a long flour sack tied at each corner into an ear. The cord went over his shoulder. The sack flapped against his legs.

Nick felt awkward and professionally happy with all his equipment hanging from him. The grasshopper bottle swung against his chest. In his shirt the breast pockets bulged against him with the lunch and his fly book.

He stepped into the stream. It was a shock. His trousers clung tight to his legs. His shoes felt the gravel. The water was a rising cold shock.

Rushing, the current sucked against his legs. Where he stepped in, the water was over his knees. He waded with the current. The gravel slid under his shoes. He looked down at the swirl of water below each leg and tipped up the bottle to get a grasshopper.

The first grasshopper gave a jump in the neck of the bottle and went out into the water. He was sucked under in the whirl by Nick's right leg and came to the surface a little way down stream. He floated rapidly, kicking. In a quick circle, breaking the smooth surface of the water, he disappeared. A trout had taken him.

Another hopper poked his head out of the bottle. His antennæ wavered. He was getting his front legs out of the bottle to jump, Nick took him by the head and held him while he threaded the slim hook under his chin, down through his thorax and into the last segments of his abdomen. The grasshopper took hold of the hook with his front feet, spitting tobacco juice on it. Nick dropped him into the water.

Holding the rod in his right hand he let out line against the pull of the grasshopper in the current. He stripped off line from the reel with his left hand and let it run free. He could see the hopper in the little waves of the current. It went out of sight.

There was a tug on the line. Nick pulled against the taut line. It was his first strike. Holding the now living rod across the current he brought in the line with his left hand. The rod bent in jerks, the trout pumping against the current. Nick knew it was a small one. He lifted the rod straight up in the air. It bowed with the pull.

He saw the trout in the water jerking with his head and body against the shifting tangent of the line in the stream.

Nick took the line in his left hand and pulled the trout, thumping tiredly against the current, to the surface. His back was mottled the clear, water-over-gravel color, his side flashing in the sun. The rod under his right arm, Nick stooped, dipping his right hand into the current. He held the trout, never still, with his moist right hand, while he unhooked the barb from his mouth, then dropped him back into the stream.

He hung unsteadily in the current, then settled to the bottom beside a stone. Nick reached down his hand to touch him, his arm to the elbow under water. The trout was steady in the moving stream, resting on the gravel, beside a stone. As Nick's fingers touched him, touched his smooth, cool, underwater feeling he was gone, gone in a shadow across the bottom of the stream.

He's all right, Nick thought. He was only tired.

He had wet his hand before he touched the trout, so he would not disturb the delicate mucus that covered him. If a trout was touched with a dry hand, a white fungus attacked the unprotected spot. Years before when he had fished crowded streams, with fly fishermen ahead of him and behind him, Nick had again and again come on dead trout, furry with white fungus, drifted against a rock, or floating belly up in some pool. Nick did not like to fish with other men on the river. Unless they were of your party, they spoiled it.

He wallowed down the stream, above his knees in the current, through the fifty yards of shallow water above the pile of logs that crossed the stream. He did not rebait his hook and held it in his hand as he waded. He was certain he could catch small trout in the shallows, but he did not want them. There would be no big trout in the shallows this time of day.

Now the water deepened up his thighs sharply and coldly. Ahead was the smooth dammed-back flood of water above the logs. The water was smooth and dark; on the left, the lower edge of the meadow; on the right the swamp.

Nick leaned back against the current and took a hopper from the bottle. He threaded the hopper on the hook and spat on him for good luck. Then he pulled several yards of line from the reel and tossed the hopper out ahead onto the fast, dark water. It floated down towards the logs, then the weight of the line pulled the bait under the surface. Nick held the rod in his right hand, letting the line run out through his fingers.

There was a long tug. Nick struck and the rod came alive and dangerous, bent double, the line tightening, coming out of water, tightening, all in a heavy, dangerous, steady pull. Nick felt the moment when the leader would break if the strain increased and let the line go.

The reel ratcheted into a mechanical shriek as the line went out in a rush. Too fast. Nick could not check it, the line rushing out, the reel note rising as the line ran out.

With the core of the reel showing, his heart feeling stopped with the excitement, leaning back against the current that mounted icily his thighs, Nick thumbed the reel hard with his left hand. It was awkward getting his thumb inside the fly reel frame.

As he put on pressure the line tightened into sudden hardness and beyond the logs a huge trout went high out of water. As he jumped, Nick lowered the tip of the rod. But he felt, as he dropped the tip to ease the strain, the moment when the strain was too great; the hardness too tight. Of course, the leader had broken. There was no mistaking the feeling when all spring left the line and it became dry and hard. Then it went slack.

His mouth dry, his heart down, Nick reeled in. He had never seen so big a trout. There was a heaviness, a power not to be held, and then the bulk of him, as he jumped. He looked as broad as a salmon.

Nick's hand was shaky. He reeled in slowly. The thrill had been too much. He felt vaguely, a little sick, as though it would be better to sit down.

The leader had broken where the hook was tied to it. Nick took it in his hand. He thought of the trout somewhere on the bottom, holding himself steady over the gravel, far down below the light, under the logs, with the hook in his jaw. Nick knew the trout's teeth would cut through the snell of the hook. The hook would imbed itself in his jaw. He'd bet the trout was angry. Anything that size would be angry. That was a trout. He had been solidly hooked. Solid as a rock. He felt like a rock, too, before he started off. By God, he was a big one. By God, he was the biggest one I ever heard of.

Nick climbed out onto the meadow and stood, water running down his trousers and out of his shoes, his shoes squlchy. He went over and sat on the logs. He did not want to rush his sensations any.

He wriggled his toes in the water, in his shoes, and got out a cigarette from his breast pocket. He lit it and tossed the match into the fast water below the logs. A tiny trout rose at the match, as it swung around in the fast current. Nick laughed. He would finish the cigarette.

He sat on the logs, smoking, drying in the sun, the sun warm on his back, the river shallow ahead entering the woods, curving into the woods, shallows, light glittering, big water-smooth rocks, cedars along the bank and white birches, the logs warm in the sun smooth to sit on, without bark, gray to the touch; slowly the feeling of disappointment left him. It went away slowly, the feeling of disappointment that came sharply after the thrill that made his shoulders ache. It was all right now. His rod lying out on the logs, Nick tied a new hook on the leader, pulling the gut tight until it grimped into itself in a hard knot.

He baited up, then picked up the rod and walked to the far end of the logs to get into the water, where it was not too deep. Under and beyond the logs was a deep pool. Nick walked around the shallow shelf near the swamp shore until he came out on the shallow bed of the stream.

On the left, where the meadow ended and the woods began, a great elm tree was uprooted. Gone over in a storm, it lay back into the woods, its roots clotted with dirt, grass growing in them, rising a solid bank beside the stream. The river cut to the edge of the uprooted tree. From where Nick stood he could see deep channels, like ruts, cut in the shallow bed of the stream by the flow of the current. Pebbly where he stood and pebbly and full of boulders beyond; where it curved near the tree roots, the bed of the stream was marly and between the ruts of deep water green weed fronds swung in the current.

Nick swung the rod back over his shoulder and forward, and the line, curving forward, laid the grasshopper down on one of the deep channels in the weeds. A trout struck and Nick hooked him.

Holding the rod far out toward the uprooted tree and sloshing backward in the current, Nick worked the trout, plunging, the rod bending alive, out of the danger of the weeds into the open river. Holding the rod, pumping alive against the current, Nick brought the trout in. He rushed, but always came, the spring of the rod yielding to the rushes, sometimes jerking under water, but always bringing him in. Nick eased downstream with the rushes. The rod above his head he led the trout over the net, then lifted.

The trout hung heavy in the net, mottled trout back and silver sides in the meshes. Nick unhooked him; heavy sides, good to hold, big undershot jaw, and slipped him, heaving and big sliding, into the long sack that hung from his shoulders in the water.

Nick spread the mouth of the sack against the current and it filled, heavy with water. He held it up, the bottom in the stream, and the water poured out through the sides. Inside at the bottom was the big trout, alive in the water.

Nick moved downstream. The sack out ahead of him, sunk, heavy in the water, pulling from his shoulders.

It was getting hot, the sun hot on the back of his neck.

Nick had one good trout. He did not care about getting many trout. Now the stream was shallow and wide. There were trees along both banks. The trees of the left bank made short shadows on the current in the forenoon sun. Nick knew there were trout in each shadow. In the afternoon, after the sun had crossed toward the hills, the trout would be in the cool shadows on the other side of the stream.

The very biggest ones would lie up close to the bank. You could always pick them up there on the Black. When the sun was down they all moved out into the current. Just when the sun made the water blinding in the glare before it went down, you were liable to strike a big trout anywhere in the current. It was almost impossible to fish then, the surface of the water was blinding as a mirror in the sun. Of course, you could fish upstream, but in a stream like the Black, or this, you had to wallow against the current and in a deep place, the water piled up on you. It was no fun to fish upstream with this much current.

Nick moved along through the shallow stretch watching the banks for deep holes. A beech tree grew close beside the river, so that the branches hung down into the water. The stream went back in under the leaves. There were always trout in a place like that.

Nick did not care about fishing that hole. He was sure he would get hooked in the branches.

It looked deep though. He dropped the grasshopper so the current took it under water, back in under the overhanging branch. The line pulled hard and Nick struck. The trout threshed heavily, half out of water in the leaves and branches. The line was caught. Nick pulled hard and the trout was off. He reeled in and holding the hook in his hand, walked down the stream.

Ahead, close to the left bank, was a big log. Nick saw it was hollow; pointing up river the current entered it smoothly, only a little ripple spread each side of the log. The water was deepening. The top of the hollow log was gray and dry. It was partly in the shadow.

Nick took the cork out of the grasshopper bottle and a hopper clung to it. He picked him off, hooked him and tossed him out. He held the rod far out so that the hopper on the water moved into the current flowing into the hollow log. Nick lowered the rod and the hopper floated in. There was a heavy strike. Nick swung the rod against the pull. It felt as though he were hooked into the log itself, except for the live feeling.

He tried to force the fish out into the current. It came, heavily.

The line went slack and Nick thought the trout was gone. Then he saw him, very near, in the current, shaking his head, trying to get the hook out. His mouth was clamped shut. He was fighting the hook in the clear flowing current.

Looping in the line with his left hand, Nick swung the rod to make the line taut and tried to lead the trout toward the net but he was gone, out of sight, the line pumping. Nick fought him against the current, letting him thump in the water against the spring of the rod. He shifted the rod to his left hand, worked the trout upstream, holding his weight, fighting on the rod, and then let him down into the net. He lifted him clear of the water, a heavy half circle in the net, the net dripping, unhooked him and slid him into the sack.

He spread the mouth of the sack and looked down in at the two big trout alive in the water.

Through the deepening water, Nick waded over to the hollow log. He took the sack off, over his head, the trout flopping as it came out of water, and hung it so the trout were deep in the water. Then he pulled himself up on the log and sat, the water from his trousers and boots running down into the stream. He laid his rod down, moved along to the shady end of the log and took the sandwiches out of his pocket. He dipped the sandwiches in the cold water. The current carried away the crumbs. He ate the sandwiches and dipped his hat full of water to drink, the water running out through his hat just ahead of his drinking.

It was cool in the shade, sitting on the log. He took a cigarette out and struck a match to light it. The match sunk into the gray wood, making a tiny furrow. Nick leaned over the side of the log, found a hard place and lit the match. He sat smoking and watching the river.

Ahead the river narrowed and went into a swamp. The river became smooth and deep and the swamp looked solid with cedar trees, their trunks close together, their branches solid. It would not be possible to walk through a swamp like that. The branches grew so low. You would have to keep almost level with the ground to move at all. You could not crash through the branches. That must be why the animals that lived in swamps were built the way they were, Nick thought.

He wished he had brought something to read. He felt like reading. He did not feel like going on into the swamp. He looked down the river. A big cedar slanted all the way across the stream. Beyond that the river went into the swamp.

Nick did not want to go in there now. He felt a reaction against deep wading with the water deepening up under his armpits, to hook big trout in places impossible to land them. In the swamp the banks were bare, the big cedars came together overhead, the sun did not come through, except in patches; in the fast deep water, in the half light, the fishing would be tragic. In the swamp fishing was a tragic adventure. Nick did not want it. He did not want to go down the stream any further today.

He took out his knife, opened it and stuck it in the log. Then he pulled up the sack, reached into it and brought out one of the trout. Holding him near the tail, hard to hold, alive, in his hand, he whacked him against the log. The trout quivered, rigid. Nick laid him on the log in the shade and broke the neck of the other fish the same way. He laid them side by side on the log. They were fine trout.

Nick cleaned them, slitting them from the vent to the tip of the jaw. All the insides and the gills and tongue came out in one piece. They were both males; long gray-white strips of milt, smooth and clean. All the insides clean and compact, coming out all together. Nick tossed the offal ashore for the minks to find.

He washed the trout in the stream. When he held them back up in the water they looked like live fish. Their color was not gone yet. He washed his hands and dried them on the log. Then he laid the trout on the sack spread out on the log, rolled them up in it, tied the bundle and put it in the landing net. His knife was still standing, blade stuck in the log. He cleaned it on the wood and put it in his pocket.

Nick stood up on the log, holding his rod, the landing net hanging heavy, then stepped into the water and splashed ashore. He climbed the bank and cut up into the woods, toward the high ground. He was going back to camp. He looked back. The river just showed through the trees. There were plenty of days coming when he could fish the swamp.

1925

A Man of the World

The blind man knew the sounds of all the different machines in the saloon. I don't know how long it took him to learn the sounds of the machines but it must have taken him quite a time because he only worked one saloon at a time. He worked two towns though and he would start out of The Flats along after it was good and dark on his way up to Jessup. He'd stop by the side of the road when he heard a car coming and their lights would pick him up and either they would stop and give him a ride or they wouldn't and would go on by on the icy road. It would depend on how they were loaded and whether there were women in the car because the blind man smelled plenty strong and especially in winter. But someone would always stop for him because he was a blind man.

Everybody knew him and they called him Blindy which is a good name for a blind man in that part of the country, and the name of the saloon that he threw his trade to was The Pilot. Right next to it was another saloon, also with gambling and a dining room, that was called The Index. Both of these were the names of mountains and they were both good saloons with old-days bars and the gambling was about the same in one as in the other except you are better in The Pilot probably, although you got a better sizzling steak at The Index. Then The Index was open all night long and got the early morning trade and from daylight until ten o'clock in the morning the drinks were on the house. They were the only saloons in Jessup and they did not have to do that kind of thing. But that was the way they were.

Blindy probably preferred The Pilot because the machines were right along the left-hand wall as you came in and faced the bar. This gave him better control over them than he would have had at The Index where they were scattered on account it was a bigger place with more room. On this night it was really cold outside and he came in with icicles on his mustache and small pus icicles out of both eyes and he didn't look really very good. Even his smell was froze but that wasn't for very long and he started to put out almost as soon as the door was shut. It was always hard for me to look at him but I was looking at him carefully because I knew he always rode and I didn't see how he would be frozen up so bad. Finally I asked him.

"Where you walk from, Blindy?"

"Willie Sawyer put me out of his car down below the railway bridge. There weren't no more cars come and I walked in."

"What did he put you afoot for?" somebody asked.

"Said I smelled too bad."

Someone had pulled the handle on a machine and Blindy started listening to the whirr. It came up nothing. "Any dudes playing?" he asked me.

"Can't you hear?"

"Not yet."

"No dudes, Blindy, and it's a Wednesday."

"I know what night it is. Don't start telling me what night it is."

Blindy went down the line of machines feeling in all of them to see if anything had been left in the cups by mistake. Naturally there wasn't anything, but that was the first part of his pitch. He came back to the bar where we were and Al Chaney asked him to have a drink.

"No," Blindy said. "I got to be careful on those roads."

"What you mean those roads?" somebody asked him. "You only go on one road. Between here and The Flats."

"I been on lots of roads," Blindy said. "And any time I may have to take off and go on more."

Somebody hit on a machine but it wasn't any heavy hit. Blindy moved on it just the same. It was a quarter machine and the young fellow who was playing it gave him a quarter sort of reluctantly. Blindy felt it before he put it in his pocket.

"Thank you," he said. "You'll never miss it."

The young fellow said, "Nice to know that," and put a quarter back in the machine and pulled down again.

He hit again but this time pretty good and he scooped in the quarters and gave a quarter to Blindy.

"Thanks," Blindy said. "You're doing fine."

"Tonight's my night," the young fellow who was playing said.

"Your night is my night," Blindy said and the young fellow went on playing but he wasn't doing any good any more and Blindy was so strong standing by him and he looked so awful and finally the fellow quit playing and came over to the bar. Blindy had run him out but he had no way of noticing it because the fellow didn't say anything, so Blindy just checked the machines again with his hand and stood there waiting for someone else to come in and make a play.

There wasn't any play at the wheel nor at the crap table and at the poker game there were just gamblers sitting there and cutting each other up. It was a quiet evening on a week night in town and there wasn't any excitement. The place was not making a nickel except at the bar. But at the bar it was pleasant and the place had been nice until Blindy had come in. Now everybody was figuring they might as well go next door to The Index or else cut out and go home.

"What will yours be, Tom?" Frank the bartender asked me. "This is on the house."

"I was figuring on shoving."

"Have one first then."

"The same with ditch," I said. Frank asked the young fellow, who was wearing heavy Oregon Cities and a black hat and was shaved clean and had a snow-burned face, what he would drink and the young fellow took the same. The whisky was Old Forester.

I nodded to him and raised my drink and we both sipped at the drinks. Blindy was down at the far end of the machines. I think he figured maybe no one would come in if they saw him at the door. Not that he was self-conscious.

"How did that man lose his sight?" the young fellow asked me.

"I wouldn't know," I told him.

"In a fight," Frank told him.

"Him fight?" the stranger said. He shook his head.

"Yeah," Frank said. "He got that high voice out of the same fight. Tell him, Tom."

"I never heard of it."

"No. You wouldn't of," Frank said. "Of course not. You wasn't here, I suppose. Mister, it was a night about as cold as tonight. Maybe colder. It was a quick fight too. I didn't see the start of it. Then they come fighting out of the door of The Index. Blackie, him that's Blindy now, and this other boy Willie Sawyer, and they were slugging and kneeing and gouging and biting and I see one of Blackie's eyes hanging down on his cheek. They were fighting on the ice of the road with the snow all banked up and the light from this door and The Index door, and Hollis Sands was right behind Willie Sawyer who was gouging for the eye and Hollis kept hollering, 'Bite it off! Bite it off just like it was a grape!' Blackie was biting onto Willie Sawyer's face and he had a good holt and it gave way with a jerk and then he had another good holt and they were down on the ice now and Willie Sawyer was gouging him to make him let go and then Blackie gave a yell like you've never heard. Worse than when they cut a boar."

Blindy had come up opposite us and we smelled him and turned around.

" 'Bite it off just like it was a grape,' " he said in his high-pitched voice and looked at us, moving his head up and down. "That was the left eye. He got the other one without no advice. Then he stomped me when I couldn't see. That was the bad part." He patted himself.

"I could fight good then," he said. "But he got the eye before I knew even what was happening. He got it with a lucky gouge. Well," Blindy said without any rancor, "that put a stop to my fighting days."

"Give Blackie a drink," I said to Frank.

"Blindy's the name, Tom. I earned that name. You seen me earn it. That's the same fellow who put me adrift down the road tonight. Fellow bit the eye. We ain't never made friends."

"What did you do to him?" the stranger asked.

"Oh you'll see him around," Blindy said. "You'll recognize him any time you see him. I'll let it come as a surprise."

"You don't want to see him," I told the stranger.

"You know that's one of the reasons I'd like to see sometimes," Blindy said. "I'd like to just have one good look at him."

"You know what he looks like," Frank told him. "You went up and put your hands on his face once."

"Did it again tonight too," Blindy said happily. "That's why he put me out of the car. He ain't got no sense of humor at all. I told him on a cold night like this he'd ought to bundle up so the whole inside of his face wouldn't catch cold. He didn't even think that was funny. You know that Willie Sawyer he'll never be a man of the world."

"Blackie, you have one on the house," Frank said. "I can't drive you home because I only live just down the road. But you can sleep in the back of the place."

"That's mighty good of you, Frank. Only just don't call me Blackie. I'm not Blackie any more. Blindy's my name."

"Have a drink, Blindy."

"Yes, sir," Blindy said. His hand reached out and found the glass and he raised it accurately to the three of us.

"That Willie Sawyer," he said. "Probably alone home by himself. That Willie Sawyer he don't know how to have any fun at all."

1957

Get a Seeing-Eyed Dog

"And what did we do then?" he asked her. She told him.

"That part is very strange. I can't remember that at all."

"Can you remember the safari leaving?"

"I should. But I don't. I remember the women going down the trail to the beach for the water with the pots on their heads and I remember the flock of geese the toto[1] drove back and forth to the water. I remember how slowly they all went and they were always going down or coming up. There was a very big tide too and the flats were yellow and the channel ran by the far island. The wind blew all the time and there were no flies and no mosquitoes. There was a roof and a cement floor and the poles that held the roof up, and the wind blew through all the time. It was cool all day and lovely and cool at night."

"Do you remember when the big dhow[2] came in and careened on the low tide?"

"Yes, I remember her and the crew coming ashore in her boats and coming up the path from the beach, and the geese were afraid of them and so were the women."

"That was the day we caught so many fish but had to come in because it was so rough."

"I remember that."

"You're remembering well today," she said. "Don't do it too much."

"I'm sorry you didn't get to fly to Zanzibar," he said. "That upper beach from where we were was a fine place to land. You could have landed and taken off from there quite easily."

"We can always go to Zanzibar. Don't try to remember too much today. Would you like me to read to you? There's always something in the old *New Yorkers* that we missed."

"No, please don't read," he said. "Just talk. Talk about the good days."

"Do you want to hear about what it's like outside?"

"It's raining," he said. "I know that."

"It's raining a big rain," she told him. "There won't be any tourists out with this weather. The wind is very wild and we can go down and sit by the fire."

"We could anyway. I don't care about them any more. I like to hear them talk."

"Some of them are awful," she said. "But some of them are quite nice. I think it's really the nicest ones that go out to Torcello."

"That's quite true," he said. "I hadn't thought of that. There's really nothing for them to see unless they are a little bit nice."

"Can I make you a drink?" she asked. "You know how worthless a nurse I am. I wasn't trained for it and I haven't any talent. But I can make drinks."

"Let's have a drink."

"What do you want?"

"Anything," he said.

---

[1] Bantu: "child."   [2] Arab low-masted sailing vessel.

"I'll make a surprise. I'll make it downstairs."

He heard the door open and close and her feet on the stairs and he thought, I must get her to go on a trip. I must figure out some way to do it. I have to think up something practical. I've got this now for the rest of my life and I must figure out ways not to destroy her life and ruin her with it. She has been so good and she was not built to be good. I mean this sort of good. I mean good every day and dull good.

He heard her coming up the stairs and noticed the difference in her tread when she was carrying two glasses and when she had walked down bare-handed. He heard the rain on the windowpane and he smelled the beech logs burning in the fireplace. As she came into the room he put his hand out for the drink a little too soon. But then he felt it tall and cold and closed his hand on it and felt her touch the glass with her own.

"It's our old drink for out here," she said. "Campari and Gordon's with ice."

"I'm certainly glad you're not a girl who would say 'on the rocks.'"

"No," she said. "I wouldn't ever say that. We've *been* on the rocks."

"On our own two feet when the chips were down and for keeps," he remembered. "Do you remember when we barred those phrases?"

"That was in the time of my lion. Wasn't he a wonderful lion? I can't wait till we see him."

"I can't either," he said.

"I'm sorry."

"Do you remember when we barred that phrase?"

"I nearly said it again."

"You know," he told her, "we're awfully lucky to have come here. I remember it so well that it is palpable. That's a new word and we'll bar it soon. But it really is wonderful. When I hear the rain I can see it on the stones and on the canal and on the lagoon, and I know the way the trees bend in every wind and how the church and the tower are in every sort of light. We couldn't have come to a better place for me. It's really perfect. We've got the good radio and a fine tape recorder and I'm going to write better than I ever could. If you take your time with the tape recorder you can get the words right. I can work slow and I can see the words when I say them. If they're wrong I hear them wrong and I can do them over and work on them until I get them right. Honey, in lots of ways we couldn't have it better."

"Oh Philip—"

"Shit," he said. "The dark is just the dark. This isn't like the real dark. I can see very well inside and now my head is better all the time and I can remember and I can make up well. You wait and see. Didn't I remember better today?"

"You remember better all the time. And you're getting strong."

"I am strong," he said. "Now if you—"

"If me what?"

"If you'd go away for a while and get a rest and a change from this."

"Don't you want me?"

"Of course I want you, darling."

"Then why do we have to talk about me going away? I know I'm not good at looking after you but I can do things other people can't do and we do love each other. You love me and you know it and we know things nobody else knows."

"We do wonderful things in the dark," he said.

"And we did wonderful things in the daytime too."

"You know I rather like the dark. In some ways it is an improvement."

"Don't lie too much," she said. "You don't have to be so bloody noble."

"Listen to it rain," he said. "How is the tide now?"

"It's way out and the wind has driven the water even further out. You could almost walk to Burano."

"All except one place," he said. "Are there many birds?"

"Mostly gulls and terns. They are down on the flats and when they get up the wind catches them."

"Aren't there any shore birds?"

"There are a few working on the part of the flats that only comes out when we have this wind and this tide."

"Do you think it will ever be spring?"

"I don't know," she said. "It certainly doesn't act like it."

"Have you drunk all your drink?"

"Just about. Why don't you drink yours?"

"I was saving it."

"Drink it up," she said. "Wasn't it awful when you couldn't drink at all?"

"No, you see," he said. "What I was thinking about when you went downstairs was that you could go to Paris and then to London and you'd see people and could have some fun and then you'd come back and it would have to be spring by then and you could tell me all about everything."

"No," she said.

"I think it would be intelligent to do," he said. "You know this is a long sort of stupid business and we have to learn to pace ourselves. And I don't want to wear you out. You know—"

"I wish you wouldn't say 'you know' so much."

"You see? That's one of the things. I could learn to talk in a non-irritating way. You might be mad about me when you came back."

"What would you do nights?"

"Nights are easy."

"I'll bet they are. I suppose you've learned how to sleep too."

"I'm going to," he told her and drank half the drink. "That's part of The Plan. You know this is how it works. If you go away and have some fun then I have a good conscience. Then for the first time in my life with a good conscience I sleep automatically. I take a pillow which represents my good conscience and I put my arms around it and off I go to sleep. If I wake up by any odd chance I just think beautiful happy dirty thoughts. Or I make wonderful fine good resolutions. Or I remember things. You know I want you to have fun—"

"Please don't say 'you know.'"

"I'll concentrate on not saying it. It's barred but I forget and let the bars down. Any way I don't want you just to be a seeing-eyed dog."

"I'm not and you know it. Anyway it's seeing-eye not seeing-eyed."

"I knew that," he told her. "Come and sit here, would you mind very much?"

She came and sat by him on the bed and they both heard the rain hard against the pane of the window and he tried not to feel her head and her lovely face the way a blind man feels and there was no other way that he could touch her face except that way. He held her close and kissed the top of her head. I will have to try it another day, he thought. I must not be so stupid about it. She feels so lovely and I love her so much and have done her so much damage and I must learn to take good care of her in every way I can. If I think of her and of her only, everything will be all right.

"I won't say 'you know' all the time any more," he told her. "We can start with that."

She shook her head and he could feel her tremble.

"You say it all you want," she said and kissed him.

"Please don't cry, my blessed," he said.

"I don't want you to sleep with any lousy pillow," she said.

"I won't. Not *any* lousy pillow."

Stop it, he said to himself. Stop it right now.

"Look, *tu,*"[3] he said. "We'll go down now and have lunch in our old fine place by the fire and I'll tell you what a wonderful kitten you are and what lucky kittens we are."

"We really are."

"We'll work everything out fine."

"I just don't want to be sent away."

"Nobody is ever going to send you away."

But walking down the stairs feeling each stair carefully and holding to the banister he thought, I must get her away and get her away as soon as I can without hurting her. Because I am not doing too well at this. That I can promise you. But what else can you do? Nothing, he thought. There's nothing you can do. But maybe, as you go along, you will get good at it.

1957

Thomas Wolfe
1900–1938

Thomas Wolfe was born in Asheville, North Carolina, on October 3, 1900, the youngest of eight children. His mother, Julia Westall, was a sociable woman who liked to have other people as well as her family around her. She was also a strong-willed person whose penchant for discipline and restraint served both a practical and an ambitious streak. She felt little tolerance for carelessness and none for drinking liquor—sentiments that clashed with the habits of her husband, William Oliver Wolfe. Called W. O., Wolfe's father was a tall, angular stonecutter who liked to tell stories in a booming, oratorical voice that his son remembered as being unexpectedly tender. Impulsive and extravagant in virtually everything he did, W. O. was especially careless in the way he spent money and the way he drank whiskey; his binges could last days, sometimes weeks. Wolfe adopted many of his father's traits, admiring his eccentricities and especially his

[3] French: "you."

expressiveness: "He dramatized his emotions to a greater extent," he wrote, "than anyone I had ever known."

By the time Wolfe was six years old, his mother had turned her family's rambling home into a boardinghouse, as part of a larger effort to make money, and his parents had turned their lives into a battleground. Looking back, Wolfe saw the childhood that furnished so much of the material of his fiction as having included many invaluable experiences, but he also saw it as dominated by a fatal misalliance, the principals of which were parents and the victims their children. "I think I learned about being alone when I was a child about eight years old," he wrote one of his sisters in 1933, "and I think that I have known about it ever since."

From Asheville, Wolfe—an ungainly six and a half feet tall, studious, sensitive, and unathletic, hungering for experiences and learning—went to Chapel Hill, where he studied literature and philosophy at the University of North Carolina. He edited the college newspaper and literary magazine and after graduation in 1920 continued his studies at Harvard, where he was accepted in George Pierce Baker's famous drama course (the "47 Workshop"). Wolfe had written several plays in college, and while at Harvard it seemed for a time that he might become a successful playwright. One of his graduate school plays, *Welcome to Our City,* like all of his drama at the time based on a southern theme, was produced at Harvard and came close to being accepted on Broadway. Needing money desperately, Wolfe left Harvard with an M.A. in 1924 and took a job teaching freshman English at New York University ("Details and the teaching of mechanics—the rules of grammar—torture me"). The following year Wolfe traveled to Europe and from a foreign perspective began writing stories that ambitiously took America as their theme. "I will know this country," he had written his mother in 1923, ". . . as I know the palm of my hand, and I will put it on paper, and make it true and beautiful."

Wolfe spent the next three years alternately teaching English and touring Europe while working on a massive novel, called *O Lost,* that he completed in 1928. In 1929, after extensive editorial revision ("We have cut out great hunks of the original book") the novel was published as *Look Homeward, Angel.* Subtitled *A Story of the Buried Life,* the novel portrays the bitter conflicts and strong affections of the Gants, a large southern family, as seen by Eugene Gant, an emotionally tormented adolescent and future writer who "escapes" from his family and the confines of his small town by going north to Harvard. A huge success, *Look Homeward, Angel* enabled Wolfe to resign his teaching position and devote himself to writing. In 1930 he won a Guggenheim fellowship and traveled to Europe to gather material for his next books. The foreign perspective once again left him with a vivid image of America: "During that summer in Paris [1930]," he wrote, "I think I felt this great homesickness more than ever before, and I really believe that from this emotion, this constant and almost intolerable effort of memory and desire, the material and structure of the books I now began to write were derived."

"I do not think the history of the Gant family is over," Wolfe wrote his mother in 1930, and when he returned to the United States the following year he worked on a continuation of his first novel. *Of Time and the River* (1935) describes Eugene Gant's career at Harvard, his friendships and travels. During this period Wolfe also produced a collection of short stories, *From Death to Morning* (1935), and a self-analytical statement of his literary intentions, *The Story of a Novel* (1936), in which he identified his creative ambition with the "enormous space and energy of American life." In 1935 Wolfe once again sailed for Europe, and his experiences of Nazi Germany were published in a short novel, *I Have a Thing to Tell You* (1937). In 1938 Wolfe made a long tour of the Pacific Northwest, leaving with his publisher the manuscript of a long, unruly novel, *The Web and the Rock,* in which Wolfe claimed to be replacing Eugene Gant with a less egocentric character, George Weber, whose own significance as a writer lay "in his personal identity to the life of every man." In September 1938, just short of his thirty-eighth birthday, Wolfe died in Baltimore, Maryland, following repeated bouts with pneumonia, when tuberculosis bacteria resulted in a cerebral infection. Wolfe's publisher severely edited *The Web and the Rock,* which appeared in 1939, and reconstructed out of a mass of deleted, extraneous, and previously published material, another novel, *You Can't Go Home Again* (1940), which continued the story of George Weber. Now a successful novelist, Weber returns to the small town where he grew up and finds it devastatingly changed. In 1941 a collection of Wolfe's stories and miscellaneous writings was published as *The Hills Beyond.* It contained "The Lost Boy," a story based on the death of his brother, first published in 1937.

Like Walt Whitman's poetry, Thomas Wolfe's fiction draws heavily on his ability to identify and exploit correlations between his sense of his own life and his sense of America. The story of his protagonists is characteristically a story of the search for a lost father, a lost home, a lost sense of certitude and order. "The deepest search in life. . . ," he said, "was man's search to find a father, not merely the father of his flesh, not merely the lost father of his youth, but the image of a strength and wisdom external to his need and superior to his hunger, to which the belief and power of his own life could be united." It was this story—one of the oldest, most personal, and most profoundly religious of our stories—that Wolfe saw as informing the story of America. What he termed in one of his letters "the whole intolerable memory of America, its violence, savagery, immensity, beauty, ugliness, and glory," he presented in his fiction as America's search for a meaningful destiny, for a strength and wisdom of its own.

Wolfe drew on his own experience and his own personality as directly and persistently as any other significant novelist of his time. There are clear risks and limitations in such a strategy, even for so shaggy a giant as Wolfe and for so prodigious a talent as he possessed: He is almost always criticized—even by his admirers—for his inflated descriptions, florid writing, lack of narrative detachment, and emotional excesses. But there were many times when his strategy led to powerful, creative achievement, as it did in *Look Homeward, Angel* and, on a smaller scale, "The Lost Boy."

Further Reading:
H. J. Muller, *Thomas Wolfe,* 1947.
H. Holman, *Thomas Wolfe,* 1960.
E. Nowell, *Thomas Wolfe,* 1960.

Text:
The Hills Beyond, 1941.

The Lost Boy

I

Light came and went and came again, the booming strokes of three o'clock beat out across the town in thronging bronze from the courthouse bell, light winds of April blew the fountain out in rainbow sheets, until the plume returned and pulsed, as Grover turned into the Square. He was a child, dark-eyed and grave, birthmarked upon his neck—a berry of warm brown—and with a gentle face, too quiet and too listening for his years. The scuffed boy's shoes, the thick-ribbed stockings gartered at the knees, the short knee pants cut straight with three small useless buttons at the side, the sailor blouse, the old cap battered out of shape, perched sideways up on top of the raven head, the old soiled canvas bag slung from the shoulder, empty now, but waiting for the crisp sheets of the afternoon—these friendly, shabby garments, shaped by Grover, uttered him. He turned and passed along the north side of the Square and in that moment saw the union of Forever and of Now.

Light came and went and came again, the great plume of the fountain pulsed and winds of April sheeted it across the Square in a rainbow gossamer of spray. The fire department horses drummed on the floors with wooden stomp, most casually, and with dry whiskings of their clean, coarse tails. The street cars ground into the Square from every portion of the compass and halted briefly like wound toys in their familiar quarter-hourly formula. A dray, hauled by a boneyard nag, rattled across the cobbles on the other side before his father's shop. The courthouse bell boomed out its solemn warning of immediate three, and everything was just the same as it had always been.

He saw that haggis of vexed shapes with quiet eyes—that hodgepodge of ill-sorted architectures that made up the Square, and he did not feel lost. For "Here," thought Grover, "here is the Square as it has always been—and papa's shop, the fire department and the City Hall, the fountain pulsing with its plume, the street cars coming in and halting at the quarter hour, the hardware store on the corner there, the row of old brick buildings on this side of the street, the people passing and the light that comes and changes and that always will come back again, and everything that comes and goes and changes in the Square, and yet will be the same again. And here," the boy thought, "is Grover with his paper bag. Here is old Grover, almost twelve years old. Here is the month of April, 1904. Here is the courthouse bell and three o'clock. Here is Grover on the Square that never changes. Here is Grover, caught upon this point of time."

It seemed to him that the Square, itself the accidental masonry of many years, the chance agglomeration of time and of disrupted strivings, was the center of the universe. It was for him, in his soul's picture, the earth's pivot, the granite core of changelessness, the eternal place where all things came and passed, and yet abode forever and would never change.

He passed the old shack on the corner—the wooden fire-trap where S. Goldberg ran his wiener stand. Then he passed the Singer place next door, with its gleaming display of new machines. He saw them and admired them, but he felt no joy. They brought back to him the busy hum of housework and of women sewing, the intricacy of stitch and weave, the mystery of style and pattern, the memory of women bending over flashing needles, the pedaled tread, the busy whir. It was women's work: it filled him with unknown associations of dullness and of vague depression. And always, also, with a moment's twinge of horror, for his dark eye would always travel toward that needle stitching up and down so fast the eye could never follow it. And then he would remember how his mother once had told him she had driven the needle through her finger, and always, when he passed this place, he would remember it and for a moment crane his neck and turn his head away.

He passed on then, but had to stop again next door before the music store. He always had to stop by places that had shining perfect things in them. He loved hardware stores and windows full of accurate geometric tools. He loved windows full of hammers, saws, and planing boards. He liked windows full of strong new rakes and hoes, with unworn handles, of white perfect wood, stamped hard and vivid with the maker's seal. He loved to see such things as these in the windows of hardware stores. And he would fairly gloat upon them and think that someday he would own a set himself.

Also, he always stopped before the music and piano store. It was a splendid store. And in the window was a small white dog upon his haunches, with head cocked gravely to one side, a small white dog that never moved, that never barked, that listened attentively at the flaring funnel of a horn to hear "His Master's Voice"—a horn forever silent, and a voice that never spoke. And within were many rich and shining shapes of great pianos, an air of splendor and of wealth.

And now, indeed, he *was* caught, held suspended. A waft of air, warm, chocolate-laden, filled his nostrils. He tried to pass the white front of the little eight-foot shop; he paused, struggling with conscience; he could not go on. It was the little candy shop run by old Crocker and his wife. And Grover could not pass.

"Old stingy Crockers!" he thought scornfully. "I'll not go there any more. But—" as the maddening fragrance of rich cooking chocolate touched him once again—"I'll just look in the window and see what they've got." He paused a moment, looking with his dark and quiet eyes into the window of the little candy shop. The window, spotlessly clean, was filled with trays of fresh-made candy. His eyes rested on a tray of chocolate drops. Unconsciously he licked his lips. Put one of them upon your tongue and it just melted there, like honeydew. And then the trays full of rich homemade fudge. He gazed longingly at the deep body of the chocolate fudge, reflectively at maple walnut, more critically, yet with longing, at the mints, the nougatines, and all the other dainties.

"Old stingy Crockers!" Grover muttered once again, and turned to go. "I wouldn't go in *there* again."

And yet he did not go away. "Old stingy Crockers" they might be; still, they did make the best candy in town, the best, in fact, that he had ever tasted.

He looked through the window back into the little shop and saw Mrs. Crocker there. A customer had gone in and had made a purchase, and as Grover looked he saw Mrs. Crocker, with her little wrenny face, her pinched features, lean over and peer primly at the scales. She had a piece of fudge in her clean, bony, little fingers, and as Grover looked, she broke it, primly, in her little bony hands. She dropped a morsel down into the scales. They weighted down alarmingly, and her thin lips tightened. She snatched the piece of fudge out of the scales and broke it carefully once again. This time the scales wavered, went down very slowly, and came back again. Mrs. Crocker carefully put the reclaimed piece of fudge back in the tray, dumped the remainder in a paper bag, folded it and gave it to the customer, counted the money carefully and doled it out into the till, the pennies in one place, the nickels in another.

Grover stood there, looking scornfully. "Old stingy Crocker—afraid that she might give a crumb away!"

He grunted scornfully and again he turned to go. But now Mr. Crocker came out from the little partitioned place where they made all their candy, bearing a tray of fresh-made fudge in his skinny hands. Old Man Crocker rocked along the counter to the front and put it down. He really rocked along. He was a cripple. And like his wife, he was a wrenny, wizened little creature, with bony hands, thin lips, a pinched and meager face. One leg was inches shorter than the other, and on this leg there was an enormous thick-soled boot, with a kind of wooden, rocker-like arrangement, six inches high at least, to make up for the deficiency. On this wooden cradle Mr. Crocker rocked along, with a prim and apprehensive little smile, as if he were afraid he was going to lose something.

"Old stingy Crocker!" muttered Grover. "Humph! He wouldn't give you anything!"

And yet—he did not go away. He hung there curiously, peering through the window, with his dark and gentle face now focused and intent, alert and curious, flattening his nose against the glass. Unconsciously he scratched the thick-ribbed fabric of one stockinged leg with the scuffed and worn toe of his old shoe. The fresh, warm odor of the new-made fudge was delicious. It was a little maddening. Half consciously he began to fumble in one trouser pocket, and pulled out his purse, a shabby worn old black one with a twisted clasp. He opened it and prowled about inside.

What he found was not inspring—a nickel and two pennies and—he had forgotten them—the stamps. He took the stamps out and unfolded them. There were five twos, eight ones, all that remained of the dollar-sixty-cents' worth which Reed, the pharmacist, had given him for running errands a week or two before.

"Old Crocker," Grover thought, and looked somberly at the grotesque little form as it rocked back into the shop again, around the counter, and up the other side. "Well—" again he looked indefinitely at the stamps in his hand—"he's had all the rest of them. He might as well take these."

So, soothing conscience with this sop of scorn, he went into the shop and stood looking at the trays in the glass case and finally decided. Pointing with a slightly grimy finger at the fresh-made tray of chocolate fudge, he said, "I'll take fifteen cents' worth of this, Mr. Crocker." He paused a moment, fighting with embarrassment, then he lifted his dark face and said quietly, "And please, I'll have to give you stamps again."

Mr. Crocker made no answer. He did not look at Grover. He pressed his lips together primly. He went rocking away and got the candy scoop, came back, slid open the door of the glass case, put fudge into the scoop, and, rocking to the scales, began to weigh the candy out. Grover watched him as he peered and squinted, he watched him purse and press his lips together, he saw him take a piece of fudge and break it in two parts. And then old Crocker broke two parts in two again. He weighed, he squinted, and he hovered, until it seemed to Grover that by calling *Mrs.* Crocker stingy he had been guilty of a rank injustice. But finally, to his vast relief, the job was over, the scales hung there, quivering apprehensively, upon the very hair-line of nervous balance, as if even the scales were afraid that one more move from Old Man Crocker and they would be undone.

Mr. Crocker took the candy then and dumped it in a paper bag and, rocking back along the counter toward the boy, he dryly said: "Where are the stamps?" Grover gave them to him. Mr. Crocker relinquished his clawlike hold upon the bag and set it down upon the counter. Grover took the bag and dropped it in his canvas sack, and then remembered. "Mr. Crocker—" again he felt the old embarrassment that was almost like strong pain— "I gave you too much," Grover said. "There were eighteen cents in stamps. You—you can just give me three ones back."

Mr. Crocker did not answer. He was busy with his bony little hands, unfolding the stamps and flattening them out on top of the glass counter. When he had done so, he peered at them sharply for a moment, thrusting his scrawny neck forward and running his eye up and down, like a bookkeeper who totes up rows of figures.

When he had finished, he said tartly: "I don't like this kind of business. If you want candy, you should have the money for it. I'm not a post office. The next time you come in here and want anything, you'll have to pay me money for it."

Hot anger rose in Grover's throat. His olive face suffused with angry color. His tarry eyes got black and bright. He was on the verge of saying: "Then why did you take my other stamps? Why do you tell me now, when you have taken all the stamps I had, that you don't want them?"

But he was a boy, a boy of eleven years, a quiet, gentle, gravely thoughtful boy, and he had been taught how to respect his elders. So he just stood there looking with his tar-black eyes. Old Man Crocker, pursing at the mouth a little, without meeting Grover's gaze, took the stamps up in his thin, parched fingers and, turning, rocked away with them down to the till.

He took the twos and folded them and laid them in one rounded scallop, then took the ones and folded them and put them in the one next to it. Then he closed the till and started to rock off, down toward the other end. Grover, his face now quiet and grave, kept looking at him, but Mr. Crocker did not look at Grover. Instead he began to take some stamped cardboard shapes and fold them into boxes.

In a moment Grover said, "Mr. Crocker, will you give me the three ones, please?"

Mr. Crocker did not answer. He kept folding boxes, and he compressed his thin lips quickly as he did so. But Mrs. Crocker, back turned to her spouse, also folding boxes with her birdlike hands, muttered tartly: "Hm! *I'd* give him nothing!"

Mr. Crocker looked up, looked at Grover, said, "What are you waiting for?"

"Will you give me the three ones, please?" Grover said.

"I'll give you nothing," Mr. Crocker said.

He left his work and came rocking forward along the counter. "Now you get out of here! Don't you come in here with any more of those stamps," said Mr. Crocker.

"I should like to know where he gets them—that's what *I* should like to know," said Mrs. Crocker.

She did not look up as she said these words. She inclined her head a little to the side, in Mr. Crocker's direction, and continued to fold the boxes with her bony fingers.

"You get out of here!" said Mr. Crocker. "And don't you come back here with any stamps. . . . Where did you get those stamps?" he said.

"That's just what *I've* been thinking," Mrs. Crocker said. "*I've* been thinking all along."

"You've been coming in here for the last two weeks with those stamps," said Mr. Crocker. "I don't like the look of it. Where did you get those stamps?" he said.

"That's what *I've* been thinking," said Mrs. Crocker, for a second time.

Grover had got white underneath his olive skin. His eyes had lost their luster. They looked like dull, stunned balls of tar. "From Mr. Reed," he said. "I got the stamps from Mr. Reed." Then he burst out desperately: "Mr. Crocker—Mr. Reed will tell you how I got the stamps. I did some work for Mr. Reed, he gave me those stamps two weeks ago."

"Mr. Reed," said Mrs. Crocker acidly. She did not turn her head. "I call it mighty funny."

"Mr. Crocker," Grover said, "if you'll just let me have three ones—"

"You get out of here!" cried Mr. Crocker, and he began rocking forward toward Grover. "Now don't you come in here again, boy! There's something funny about this whole business! I don't like the look of it," said Mr. Crocker. "If you can't pay as other people do, then I don't want your trade."

"Mr. Crocker," Grover said again, and underneath the olive skin his face was gray, "if you'll just let me have those three—"

"You get out of here!" Mr. Crocker cried, rocking down toward the counter's end. "If you don't get out, boy—"

"*I'd* call a policeman, that's what I'd do," Mrs. Crocker said.

Mr. Crocker rocked around the lower end of the counter. He came rocking up to Grover. "You get out," he said.

He took the boy and pushed him with his bony little hands, and Grover was sick and gray down to the hollow pit of his stomach.

"You've got to give me those three ones," he said.

"You get out of here!" shrilled Mr. Crocker. He seized the screen door, pulled it open, and pushed Grover out. "Don't you come back in here," he said, pausing for a moment, and working thinly at the lips. He turned and rocked back in the shop again. The screen door slammed behind him. Grover stood there on the pavement. And light came and went and came again into the Square.

The boy stood there, and a wagon rattled past. There were some people passing by, but Grover did not notice them. He stood there blindly, in the watches of the sun, feeling this was Time, this was the center of the universe, the granite core of changelessness, and feeling, this is Grover, this the Square, this is Now.

But something had gone out of day. He felt the overwhelming, soul-sickening guilt that all the children, all the good men of the earth, have felt since Time began. And even anger had died down, had been drowned out, in this swelling tide of guilt, and "This is the Square"—thought Grover as before—"This is Now. There is my father's shop. And all of it is as it has always been—save I."

And the Square reeled drunkenly around him, light went in blind gray motes before his eyes, the fountain sheeted out to rainbow iridescence and returned to its proud, pulsing plume again. But all the brightness had gone out of day, and "Here is the Square, and here is permanence, and here is Time—and all of it the same as it has always been, save I."

The scuffed boots of the lost boy moved and stumbled blindly. The numb feet crossed the pavement—reached the cobbled street, reached the plotted central square —the grass plots, and the flower beds, so soon to be packed with red geraniums.

"I want to be alone," thought Grover, "where I cannot go near him. . . . Oh God, I hope he never hears, that no one ever tells him—"

The plume blew out, the iridescent sheet of spray blew over him. He passed through, found the other side and crossed the street, and— "Oh God, if papa ever hears!" thought Grover, as his numb feet started up the steps into his father's shop.

He found and felt the steps—the width and thickness of old lumber twenty feet in length. He saw it all—the iron columns on his father's porch, painted with the dull anomalous black-green that all such columns in this land and weather come to; two angels, fly-specked, and the waiting stones. Beyond and all around, in the stonecutter's shop, cold shapes of white and marble, rounded stone, the languid angel with strong marble hands of love.

He went on down the aisle, the white shapes stood around him. He went on to the back of the workroom. This he knew—the little cast-iron stove in left-hand corner, caked, brown, heat-blistered, and the elbow of the long stack running out across the shop; the high and dirty window looking down across the Market Square toward Niggertown; the rude old shelves, plank-boarded, thick, the wood not smooth but pulpy, like the strong hair of an animal; upon the shelves the chisels of all sizes and a layer of stone dust; an emery wheel with pump tread; and a door that let out on the alleyway, yet the alleyway twelve feet below. Here in the room, two trestles of this coarse spiked wood upon which rested gravestones, and at one, his father at work.

The boy looked, saw the name was Creasman: saw the carved analysis of John, the symmetry of the s, the fine sentiment that was being polished off beneath the name and date: "John Creasman, November 7, 1903."

Gant looked up. He was a man of fifty-three, gaunt-visaged, mustache cropped, immensely long and tall and gaunt. He wore good dark clothes—heavy, massive— save he had no coat. He worked in shirt-sleeves with his vest on, a strong watch chain stretching across his vest, wing collar and black tie, Adam's apple, bony forehead, bony nose, light eyes, gray-green, undeep and cold, and, somehow, lonely-looking, a striped apron going up around his shoulders, and starched cuffs. And in one hand a tremendous rounded wooden mallet like a butcher's bole; and in his other hand, a strong cold chisel.

"How are you, son?"

He did not look up as he spoke. He spoke quietly, absently. He worked upon the chisel and the wooden mallet, as a jeweler might work on a watch, except that in the man and in the wooden mallet there was power too.

"What is it, son?" he said.

He moved around the table from the head, started up on "J" once again.

"Papa, I never stole the stamps," said Grover.

Gant put down the mallet, laid the chisel down. He came around the trestle.

"What?" he said.

As Grover winked his tar-black eyes, they brightened, the hot tears shot out. "I never stole the stamps," he said.

"Hey? What is this?" his father said. "What stamps?"

"That Mr. Reed gave me, when the other boy was sick and I worked there for three days. . . . And Old Man Crocker," Grover said, "he took all the stamps. And

I told him Mr. Reed had given them to me. And now he owes me three ones—and Old Man Crocker says he don't believe that they were mine. He says—he says—that I must have taken them somewhere," Grover blurted out.

"The stamps that Reed gave you—hey?" the stonecutter said. "The stamps you had—" He wet his thumb upon his lips, threw back his head and slowly swung his gaze around the ceiling then turned and strode quickly from his workshop out into the storeroom.

Almost at once he came back again, and as he passed the old gray painted-board partition of his office he cleared his throat and wet his thumb and said, "Now, I tell you—"

Then he turned and strode up toward the front again and cleared his throat and said, "I tell you now—" He wheeled about and started back, and as he came along the aisle between the marshaled rows of gravestones he said beneath his breath, "By God, now—"

He took Grover by the hand and they went out flying. Down the aisle they went by all the gravestones, past the fly-specked angels waiting there, and down the wooden steps and across the Square. The fountain pulsed, the plume blew out in sheeted iridescence, and it swept across them; an old gray horse, with a peaceful look about his torn lips, swucked up the cool mountain water from the trough as Grover and his father went across the Square, but they did not notice it.

They crossed swiftly to the other side in a direct line to the candy shop. Gant was still dressed in his long striped apron, and he was still holding Grover by the hand. He opened the screen door and stepped inside.

"Give him the stamps," Gant said.

Mr. Crocker came rocking forward behind the counter, with the prim and careful look that now was somewhat like a smile. "It was just—" he said.

"Give him the stamps," Gant said, and threw some coins down on the counter.

Mr. Crocker rocked away and got the stamps. He came rocking back. "I just didn't know—" he said.

The stonecutter took the stamps and gave them to the boy. And Mr. Crocker took the coins.

"It was just that—" Mr. Crocker began again, and smiled.

Gant cleared his throat: "You never were a father," he said. "You never knew the feelings of a father, or understood the feelings of a child; and that is why you acted as you did. But a judgment is upon you. God has cursed you. He has afflicted you. He has made you lame and childless as you are—and lame and childless, miserable as you are, you will go to your grave and be forgotten!"

And Crocker's wife kept kneading her bony little hands and said, imploringly, "Oh, no—oh don't say that, please don't say that."

The stonecutter, the breath still hoarse in him, left the store, still holding the boy tightly by the hand. Light came again into the day.

"Well, son," he said, and laid his hand on the boy's back. "Well, son," he said, "now don't you mind."

They walked across the Square, the sheeted spray of iridescent light swept out on them, the horse swizzled at the water-trough, and "Well, son," the stonecutter said.

And the old horse sloped down, ringing with his hoofs upon the cobblestones.

"Well, son," said the stonecutter once again, "be a good boy."

And he trod his own steps then with his great stride and went back again into his shop.

The lost boy stood upon the Square, hard by the porch of his father's shop.

"This is Time," thought Grover. "Here is the Square, here is my father's shop, and here am I."

And light came and went and came again—but now not quite the same as it had done before. The boy saw the pattern of familiar shapes and knew that they were just the same as they had always been. But something had gone out of day, and something had come in again. Out of the vision of those quiet eyes some brightness had gone, and into their vision had come some deeper color. He could not say, he did not know through what transforming shadows life had passed within that quarter hour. He only knew that something had been lost—something forever gained.

Just then a buggy curved out through the Square, and fastened to the rear end was a poster, and it said "St. Louis" and "Excursion" and "The Fair."[1]

II: The Mother

As we went down through Indiana—you were too young, child, to remember it—but I always think of all of you the way you looked that morning, when we went down through Indiana, going to the Fair. All of the apple trees were coming out, and it was April; it was the beginning of spring in southern Indiana and everything was getting green. Of course we don't have farms at home like those in Indiana. The childern had never seen such farms as those, and I reckon, kidlike, they had to take it in.

So all of them kept running up and down the aisle—well, no, except for you and Grover. *You* were too young, Eugene. You were just three, I kept you with me. As for Grover—well, I'm going to tell you about that.

But the rest of them kept running up and down the aisle and from one window to another. They kept calling out and hollering to each other every time they saw something new. They kept trying to look out on all sides, in every way at once, as if they wished they had eyes at the back of their heads. It was the first time any of them had ever been in Indiana, and I reckon that it all seemed strange and new.

And so it seemed they couldn't get enough. It seemed they never could be still. They kept running up and down and back and forth, hollering and shouting to each other, until—"I'll vow! You childern! I never saw the beat of you!" I said. "The way that you keep running up and down and back and forth and never can be quiet for a minute beats all I ever saw," I said.

You see, they were excited about going to St. Louis, and so curious over everything they saw. They couldn't help it, and they wanted to see everything. But—"I'll vow!" I said. "If you childern don't sit down and rest you'll be worn to a frazzle before we ever get to see St. Louis and the Fair!"

Except for Grover! He—no, sir! not him. Now, boy, I want to tell you—I've raised the lot of you—and if I do say so, there wasn't a numbskull in the lot. But *Grover!* Well, you've all grown up now, all of you have gone away, and none of

[1] The World's Fair, held in St. Louis in 1904.

you are childern any more. . . . And of course, I hope that, as the fellow says, you have reached the dignity of man's estate. I suppose you have the judgment of grown men. . . . But *Grover! Grover* had it even then!

Oh, even as a child, you know—at a time when I was almost afraid to trust the rest of you out of my sight—I could depend on Grover. He could go anywhere, I could send him anywhere, and I'd always know he'd get back safe, and do exactly what I told him to!

Why, I didn't even have to tell him. You could send that child to market and tell him what you wanted, and he'd come home with *twice* as much as you could get yourself for the same money!

Now you know, I've always been considered a good trader. But *Grover!*—why, it got so finally that I wouldn't even tell him. Your papa said to me: "You'd be better off if you'd just tell him what you want and leave the rest to him. For," your papa says, "damned if I don't believe he's a better trader than you are. He gets more for the money than anyone I ever saw."

Well, I had to admit it, you know. I had to own up then. Grover, even as a child, was a far better trader than I was. . . . Why, yes, they told it on him all over town, you know. They said all of the market men, all of the farmers, knew him. They'd begin to laugh when they saw him coming—they'd say: "Look out! Here's Grover! Here's one trader you're not going to fool!"

And they were right! *That* child! I'd say, "Grover, suppose you run uptown and see if they've got anything good to *eat* today"—and I'd just wink at him, you know, but he'd know what I meant. I wouldn't let on that I *wanted* anything exactly, but I'd say, "Now it just occurs to me that some good fresh stuff may be coming in from the country, so suppose you take this dollar and just see what you can do with it."

Well, sir, that was all that was needed. The minute you told that child that you depended on his judgment, he'd have gone to the ends of the earth for you—and, let me tell you something, he wouldn't *miss,* either!

His eyes would get as black as coals—oh! the way that child would look at you, the intelligence and sense in his expression. He'd say: "Yes, *ma'am!* Now don't you worry, mama. You leave it all to me—and I'll do *good*!" said Grover.

And he'd be off like a streak of lightning and—oh Lord! As your father said to me, "I've been living in this town for almost thirty years," he said—"I've seen it grow up from a crossroads village, and I thought I knew everything there was to know about it—but that child—" your papa says—"he knows places that I never heard of!" . . . Oh, he'd go right down there to that place below your papa's shop where the draymen and the country people used to park their wagons—or he'd go down there to those old lots on Concord Street where the farmers used to keep their wagons. And, child that he was, he'd go right in among them, sir—*Grover* would!—go right in and barter with them like a grown man!

And he'd come home with things he'd bought that would make your eyes stick out. . . . Here he comes one time with another boy, dragging a great bushel basket full of ripe termaters between them. "Why, Grover!" I says. "How on earth are we ever going to use them? Why they'll go bad on us before we're half way through with them." "Well, mama," he says, "I know—" oh, just as solemn as a judge—"but they were the last the man had," he says, "and he wanted to go home, and so I got them for ten cents," he says. "They were so cheap," said Grover, "I thought it was a shame to let 'em go, and I figgered that what we couldn't eat—why," says Grover, "you could *put up*!" Well, the way he said it—so earnest and so serious—I had to laugh. "But I'll vow!" I said. "If you don't beat all!" . . . But that was *Grover*!— the way he was in *those* days! As everyone said, boy that he was, he had the sense and judgment of a grown man. . . . Child, child, I've seen you all grow up, and all of you were bright enough. There were no half-wits in *my* family. But for all-round intelligence, judgment, and general ability, Grover surpassed the whole crowd. I've never seen his equal, and everyone who knew him as a child will say the same.

So that's what I tell them now when they ask me about all of you. I have to tell the truth. I always said that *you* were smart enough, Eugene—but when they come around and brag to me about you, and about how you have got on and have a kind of name—I don't let on, you know. I just sit there and let them talk. I don't brag on you—if *they* want to brag on you, that's *their* business. I never bragged on one of my own childern in my life. When father raised us up, we were all brought up to believe that it was not good breeding to brag about your kin. "If the others want to do it," father said, "well, let *them* do it. Don't ever let on by a word or sign that you know what they are talking about. Just let *them* do the talking, and say nothing."

So when they come around and tell me all about the things *you've* done—I don't let on to them, I never say a word. Why yes!—why, here, you know—oh, along about a month or so ago, this feller comes—a well-dressed man, you know—he looked intelligent, a good substantial sort of person. He said he came from New Jersey, or somewhere up in that part of the country, and he began to ask me all sorts of questions—what you were like when you were a boy, and all such stuff as that.

I just pretended to study it all over and then I said, "Well, yes"—real serious-like, you know—"well, yes—I reckon I ought to know a little something about him. Eugene was my child, just the same as all the others were. I brought him up just the way I brought up all the others. And," I says—oh, just as solemn as you please— "he wasn't a *bad* sort of a boy. Why," I says, "up to the time that he was twelve years old he was just about the same as any other boy—a good, average, normal sort of fellow."

"Oh," he says. "But didn't you notice something? Wasn't there something kind of strange?" he says—"something different from what you noticed in the other children?"

I didn't let on, you know—I just took it all in and looked as solemn as an owl—I just pretended to study it all over, just as serious as you please.

"Why no," I says, real slow-like, after I'd studied it all over. "As I remember it, he was a good, ordinary, normal sort of boy, just like all the others."

"Yes," he says—oh, all excited-like, you know—"But didn't you notice how brilliant he was? Eugene must have been more brilliant than the rest!"

"Well, now," I says, and pretended to study that all over too. "Now let me see. . . . Yes," I says—I just looked him in the eye, as solemn as you please—"he did pretty well. . . . Well, yes," I says, "I guess he was a fairly bright sort of a boy. I never had no complaints to make of him on that score. He was bright enough," I says. "The only trouble with him was that he was lazy."

"Lazy!" he says—oh, you should have seen the look upon his face, you know— he jumped like someone had stuck a pin in him. "Lazy!" he says. "Why, you don't mean to tell me—"

"Yes," I says—oh, I never cracked a smile—"I was telling him the same thing myself the last time that I saw him. I told him it was a mighty lucky thing for him that he had the gift of gab. Of course, he went off to college and read a lot of books, and I reckon that's where he got this flow of language they say he has. But as I said to him the last time that I saw him: 'Now look a-here,' I said. 'If you can earn your living doing a light, easy class of work like this you do,' I says, 'you're mighty lucky, because none of the rest of your people,' I says, 'had any such luck as that. They had to work hard for a living.'"

Oh, I told him, you know. I came right out with it. I made no bones about it. And I tell you what—I wish you could have seen his face. It was a study.

"Well," he says, at last, "you've got to admit this, haven't you—he was the brightest boy you had, now wasn't he?"

I just looked at him a moment. I had to tell the truth. I couldn't fool him any longer. "No," I says. "He was a good, bright boy—I got no complaint to make about him on that score—but the brightest boy I had, the one that surpassed all the rest of them in sense, and understanding, and in judgment—the best boy I had—the smartest boy I ever saw—was—well, it wasn't Eugene," I said. "It was another one."

He looked at me a moment, then he said, "Which boy was that?"

Well, I just looked at him, and smiled. I shook my head, you know. I wouldn't tell him. "I never brag about my own," I said. "You'll have to find out for yourself."

But—I'll have to tell *you*—and you know yourself, I brought the whole crowd up, I knew you all. And you can take my word for it—the best one of the lot was —*Grover!*

And when I think of Grover as he was along about that time, I always see him sitting there, so grave and earnest-like, with his nose pressed to the window, as we went down through Indiana in the morning, to the Fair.

All through that morning we were going down along beside the Wabash River —the Wabash River flows through Indiana, it is the river that they wrote the song about—so all that morning we were going down along the river. And I sat with all you childern gathered about me as we went down through Indiana, going to St. Louis, to the Fair.

And Grover sat there, so still and earnest-like, looking out the window, and he didn't move. He sat there like a man. He was just eleven and a half years old, but he had more sense, more judgment, and more understanding than any child I ever saw.

So here he sat beside this gentleman and looked out the window. I never knew the man—I never asked his name—but I tell you what! He was certainly a fine-looking, well-dressed, good, substantial sort of man, and I could see that he had taken a great liking to Grover. And Grover sat there looking out, and then turned to this gentleman, as grave and earnest as a grown-up man, and says, "What kind of crops grow here, sir?" Well, this gentleman threw his head back and just hah-hahed. "Well, I'll see if I can tell you," says this gentleman, and then, you know, he talked to him, they talked together, and Grover took it all in, as solemn as you please, and asked this gentleman every sort of question—what the trees were, what was growing there, how big the farms were—all sorts of questions, which this gentleman would answer, until I said: "Why, I'll vow, Grover! You shouldn't ask so many questions. You'll bother the very life out of this gentleman."

The gentleman threw his head back and laughed right out. "Now you leave that boy alone. He's all right," he said. "He doesn't bother me a bit, and if I know the answers to his questions I will answer him. And if I don't know, why, then, I'll tell him so. But he's *all right*," he said, and put his arm round Grover's shoulders. "You leave him alone. He doesn't bother me a bit."

And I can still remember how he looked that morning, with his black eyes, his black hair, and with the birthmark on his neck—so grave, so serious, so earnest-like —as he sat by the train window and watched the apple trees, the farms, the barns, the houses, and the orchards, taking it all in, I reckon, because it was strange and new to him.

It was so long ago, but when I think of it, it all comes back, as if it happened yesterday. Now all of you have either died or grown up and gone away, and nothing is the same as it was then. But all of you were there with me that morning and I guess I should remember how the others looked, but somehow I don't. Yet I can still see Grover just the way he was, the way he looked that morning when we went down through Indiana, by the river, to the Fair.

III: The Sister

Can you remember, Eugene, how Grover used to look? I mean the birthmark, the black eyes, the olive skin. The birthmark always showed because of those open sailor blouses kids used to wear. But I guess you must have been too young when Grover died. . . . I was looking at that old photograph the other day. You know the one I mean—that picture showing mama and papa and all of us children before the house on Woodson Street. *You* weren't there, Eugene. *You* didn't get in. *You* hadn't arrived when that was taken. . . . You remember how mad you used to get when we'd tell you that you were only a dishrag hanging out in Heaven when something happened?

You were the baby. That's what you get for being the baby. You don't get in the picture, do you? . . . I was looking at that old picture just the other day. There we were. And, my God, what is it all about? I mean, when you see the way we were —Daisy and Ben and Grover, Steve and all of us—and then how everyone either dies or grows up and goes away—and then—look at us now! Do you ever get to feeling funny? You know what I mean—do you ever get to feeling *queer*—when you try to figure these things out? You've been to college and you ought to know the answer—and I wish you'd tell me if you know.

My Lord, when I think sometimes of the way I used to be—the dreams I used to have. Playing the piano, practicing seven hours a day, thinking that some day I would be a great pianist. Taking singing lessons from Aunt Nell because I felt that some day I was going to have a great career in opera. . . . Can you beat it now? Can you imagine it? *Me!* In grand opera! . . . Now I want to ask you. I'd like to know.

My Lord! When I go uptown and walk down the street and see all these funny-looking little boys and girls hanging around the drug store—do you suppose any of them have ambitions the way we did? Do you suppose any of these funny-looking little girls are thinking about a big career in opera? . . . Didn't you ever see that picture of us? I was looking at it just the other day. It was made before the old house down on Woodson Street, with papa standing there in his swallow-tail, and mama there beside him—and Grover, and Ben, and Steve, and Daisy, and myself, with our feet upon our bicycles. Luke, poor kid, was only four or five. *He* didn't have a bicycle like us. But there he was. And there were all of us together.

Well, there I was, and my poor old skinny legs and long white dress, and two pigtails hanging down my back. And all the funny-looking clothes we wore, with the doo-lolley business on them. . . . But I guess you can't remember. You weren't born.

But, well, we were a right nice-looking set of people, if I do say so. And there was "86" the way it used to be, with the front porch, the grape vines, and the flower beds before the house—and "Miss Eliza" standing there by papa, with a watch charm pinned upon her waist. . . . I shouldn't laugh, but "Miss Eliza"—well, mama was a pretty woman then. Do you know what I mean? "Miss Eliza" was a right good-looking woman, and papa in his swallow-tail was a good-looking man. Do you remember how he used to get dressed up on Sunday? And how grand we thought he was? And how he let me take his money out and count it? And how rich we all thought he was? And how wonderful that dinkey little shop on the Square looked to us? . . . Can you beat it, now? Why we thought that papa was the biggest man in town and—oh, you can't tell me! You can't tell me! He had his faults, but papa was a wonderful man. You know he was!

And there was Steve and Ben and Grover, Daisy, Luke, and me lined up there before the house with one foot on our bicycles. And I got to thinking back about it all. It all came back.

Do you remember anything about St. Louis? You were only three or four years old then, but you must remember something. . . . Do you remember how you used to bawl when I would scrub you? How you'd bawl for Grover? Poor kid, you used to yell for Grover every time I'd get you in the tub. . . . He was a sweet kid and he was crazy about you—he almost brought you up.

That year Grover was working at the Inside Inn out on the Fair Grounds. Do you remember the old Inside Inn? That big old wooden thing inside the Fair? And how I used to take you there to wait for Grover when he got through working? And old fat Billy Pelham at the newsstand—how he always used to give you a stick of chewing gum?

They were all crazy about Grover. Everybody liked him. . . . And how proud Grover was of you! Don't you remember how he used to show you off? How he used to take you around and make you talk to Billy Pelham? And Mr. Curtis at the desk? And how Grover would try to make you talk and get you to say "Grover"? And you couldn't say it—you couldn't pronounce the "r." You'd say "Gova." Have you forgotten that? You shouldn't forget *that,* because—you were a *cute* kid, then —Ho-ho-ho-ho-ho—I don't know where it's gone to, but you were a big hit in those days. . . . I tell you, boy, you were Somebody back in those days.

And I was thinking of it all the other day when I was looking at that photograph. How we used to go and meet Grover there, and how he'd take us to the Midway. Do you remember the Midway? The Snake-Eater and the Living Skeleton, the Fat Woman and the Chute-the-chute, the Scenic Railway and the Ferris Wheel? How you bawled the night we took you up on the Ferris Wheel? You yelled your head off—I tried to laugh it off, but I tell you, I was scared myself. Back in those days, that was Something. And how Grover laughed at us and told us there was no danger. . . . My lord! poor little Grover. He wasn't quite twelve years old at the time, but he seemed so grown up to us. I was two years older, but I thought he knew it all.

It was always that way with him. Looking back now, it sometimes seems that it was Grover who brought us up. He was always looking after us, telling us what to do, bringing us something—some ice cream or some candy, something he had bought out of the poor little money he'd gotten at the Inn.

Then I got to thinking of the afternoon we sneaked away from home. Mama had gone out somewhere. And Grover and I got on the street car and went downtown. And my Lord, we thought that we were going Somewhere. In those days, that was what we called a *trip*. A ride in the street car was something to write home about in those days. . . . I hear that it's all built up around there now.

So we got on the car and rode the whole way down into the business section of St. Louis. We got out on Washington Street and walked up and down. And I tell you, boy, we thought that that was Something. Grover took me into a drug store and set me up to soda water. Then we came out and walked around some more, down to the Union Station and clear over to the river. And both of us half scared to death at what we'd done and wondering what mama would say if she found out.

We stayed down there till it was getting dark, and we passed by a lunchroom —an old one-armed joint with one-armed chairs and people sitting on stools and eating at the counter. We read all the signs to see what they had to eat and how much it cost, and I guess nothing on the menu was more than fifteen cents, but it couldn't have looked grander to us if it had been Delmonico's. So we stood there with our noses pressed against the window, looking in. Two skinny little kids, both of us scared half to death, getting the thrill of a lifetime out of it. You know what I mean? And smelling everything with all our might and thinking how good it all smelled. . . . Then Grover turned to me and whispered: "Come on, Helen. Let's go in. It says fifteen cents for pork and beans. And I've got the money," Grover said. "I've got sixty cents."

I was so scared I couldn't speak. I'd never been in a place like that before. But I kept thinking, "Oh Lord, if mama should find out!" I felt as if we were committing some big crime. . . . Don't you know how it is when you're a kid? It was the thrill of a lifetime. . . . I couldn't resist. So we both went in and sat down on those high stools before the counter and ordered pork and beans and a cup of coffee. I suppose we were too frightened at what we'd done really to enjoy anything. We just gobbled it all up in a hurry, and gulped our coffee down. And I don't know whether it was the excitement—I guess the poor kid was already sick when we came in there and didn't know it. But I turned and looked at him, and he was white as death. . . . And when I asked him what was the matter, he wouldn't tell me. He was too proud. He said he was all right, but I could see that he was sick as a dog. . . . So he paid the bill. It came to forty cents—I'll never forget *that* as long as I live. . . . And sure enough, we no more than got out the door—he hardly had time to reach the curb—before it all came up.

And the poor kid was so scared and so ashamed. And what scared him so was not that he had gotten sick, but that he had spent all that money and it had come to nothing. And mama would find out. . . . Poor kid, he just stood there looking at me and he whispered: "Oh Helen, don't tell mama. She'll be mad if she finds out." Then we hurried home, and he was still white as a sheet when we got there.

Mama was waiting for us. She looked at us—you know how "Miss Eliza" looks at you when she thinks you've been doing something that you shouldn't. Mama said, "Why, where on earth have you two children been?" I guess she was all set to lay us out. Then she took one look at Grover's face. That was enough for her. She said, "Why, child, what in the world!" She was white as a sheet herself. . . . And all that Grover said was—"Mama, I feel sick."

He was sick as a dog. He fell over on the bed, and we undressed him and mama put her hand upon his forehead and came out in the hall—she was so white you could have made a black mark on her face with chalk—and whispered to me, "Go get the doctor quick, he's burning up."

And I went chasing up the street, my pigtails flying, to Dr. Packer's house. I brought him back with me. When he came out of Grover's room he told mama what to do but I don't know if she even heard him.

Her face was white as a sheet. She looked at me and looked right through me. She never saw me. And oh, my Lord, I'll never forget the way she looked, the way my heart stopped and came up in my throat. I was only a skinny little kid of fourteen. But she looked as if she was dying right before my eyes. And I knew that if anything happened to him, she'd never get over it if she lived to be a hundred.

Poor old mama. You know, he always was her eyeballs—you know that, don't you?—not the rest of us!—no, sir! I know what I'm talking about. It always has been Grover—she always thought more of him than she did of any of the others. And— poor kid!—he was a sweet kid. I can still see him lying there, and remember how sick he was, and how scared I was! I don't know why I was so scared. All we'd done had been to sneak away from home and go into a lunchroom—but I felt guilty about the whole thing, as if it was my fault.

It all came back to me the other day when I was looking at that picture, and I thought, my God, we were two kids together, and I was only two years older than Grover was, and now I'm forty-six. . . . Can you believe it? Can you figure it out —the way we grow up and change and go away? . . . And my Lord, Grover seemed so grown-up to me. He was such a quiet kid—I guess that's why he seemed older than the rest of us.

I wonder what Grover would say now if he could see that picture. All my hopes and dreams and big ambitions have come to nothing, and it's all so long ago, as if it happened in another world. Then it comes back, as if it happened yesterday. . . . Sometimes I lie awake at night and think of all the people who have come and gone, and how everything is different from the way we thought that it would be. Then I go out on the street next day and see the faces of the people that I pass. . . . Don't they look strange to you? Don't you see something funny in people's eyes, as if all of them were puzzled about something? As if they were wondering what had happened to them since they were kids? Wondering what it is that they have lost? . . . Now am I crazy, or do you know what I mean? You've been to college, Gene, and I want you to tell me if you know the answer. Now do they look that way to you? I never noticed that look in people's eyes when I was a kid—did you?

My God, I wish I knew the answer to these things. I'd like to find out what is wrong—what has changed since then—and if we have the same queer look in our eyes, too. Does it happen to us all, to everyone? . . . Grover and Ben, Steve, Daisy, Luke, and me—all standing there before that house on Woodson Street in Altamont —there we are, and you see the way we were—and how it all gets lost. What is it, anyway, that people lose?

How is it that nothing turns out the way we thought it would be? It all gets lost until it seems that it has never happened—that it is something we dreamed somewhere. . . . You see what I mean? . . . It seems that it must be something we heard somewhere—that it happened to someone else. And then it all comes back again.

And suddenly you remember just how it was, and see again those two funny, frightened, skinny little kids with their noses pressed against the dirty window of that lunchroom thirty years ago. You remember the way it felt, the way it smelled, even the strange smell in the old pantry in that house we lived in then. And the steps before the house, the way the rooms looked. And those two little boys in sailor suits who used to ride up and down before the house on tricycles. . . . And the birthmark on Grover's neck. . . . The Inside Inn. . . . St. Louis, and the Fair.

It all comes back as if it happened yesterday. And then it goes away again, and seems farther off and stranger than if it happened in a dream.

IV: The Brother

"*This* is King's Highway," the man said.

And then Eugene looked and saw that it was just a street. There were some big new buildings, a large hotel, some restaurants and "bar-grill" places of the modern kind, the livid monotone of neon lights, the ceaseless traffic of motor cars—all this was new, but it was just a street. And he knew that it had always been just a street, and nothing more—but somehow—well, he stood there looking at it, wondering what else he had expected to find.

The man kept looking at him with inquiry in his eyes, and Eugene asked him if the Fair had not been out this way.

"Sure, the Fair was out beyond here," the man said. "Out where the park is now. But this street you're looking for—don't you remember the name of it or nothing?" the man said.

Eugene said he thought the name of the street was Edgemont, but that he wasn't sure. Anyhow it was something like that. And he said the house was on the corner of that street and of another street.

Then the man said: "What was that other street?"

Eugene said he did not know, but that King's Highway was a block or so away, and that an interurban line ran past about half a block from where he once had lived.

"What line was this?" the man said, and stared at him.

"The interurban line," Eugene said.

Then the man stared at him again, and finally, "I don't know no interurban line," he said.

Eugene said it was a line that ran behind some houses, and that there were board fences there and grass beside the tracks. But somehow he could not say that it was summer in those days and that you could smell the ties, a wooden, tarry smell, and feel a kind of absence in the afternoon after the car had gone. He only said the interurban line was back behind somewhere between the backyards of some houses and some old board fences, and that King's Highway was a block or two away.

He did not say that King's Highway had not been a street in those days but a kind of road that wound from magic out of some dim and haunted land, and that along the way it had got mixed in with Tom the Piper's son, with hot cross buns, with all the light that came and went, and with coming down through Indiana in the morning, and the smell of engine smoke, the Union Station, and most of all with voices lost and far and long ago that said "King's Highway."

He did not say these things about King's Highway because he looked about him and he saw what King's Highway was. All he could say was that the street was near King's Highway, and was on the corner, and that the interurban trolley line was close to there. He said it was a stone house, and that there were stone steps before it, and a strip of grass. He said he thought the house had had a turret at one corner, he could not be sure.

The man looked at him again, and said, "This is King's Highway, but I never heard of any street like that."

Eugene left him then, and went on till he found the place. And so at last he turned into the street, finding the place where the two corners met, the huddled block, the turret, and the steps, and paused a moment, looking back, as if the street were Time.

For a moment he stood there, waiting—for a word, and for a door to open, for the child to come. He waited, but no words were spoken; no one came.

Yet all of it was just as it had always been, except that the steps were lower, the porch less high, the strip of grass less wide, than he had thought. All the rest of it was as he had known it would be. A graystone front, three-storied, with a slant slate roof, the side red brick and windowed, still with the old arched entrance in the center for the doctor's use.

There was a tree in front, and a lamp post; and behind and to the side, more trees than he had known there would be. And all the slatey turret gables, all the slatey window gables, going into points, and the two arched windows, in strong stone, in the front room.

It was all so strong, so solid, and so ugly—and all so enduring and so good, the way he had remembered it, except he did not smell the tar, the hot and caulky dryness of the old cracked ties, the boards of backyard fences and the coarse and sultry grass, and absence in the afternoon when the street car had gone, and the twins, sharp-visaged in their sailor suits, pumping with furious shrillness on tricycles up and down before the house, and the feel of the hot afternoon, and the sense that everyone was absent at the Fair.

Except for this, it all was just the same; except for this and for King's Highway, which was now a street; except for this, and for the child that did not come.

It was a hot day. Darkness had come. The heat rose up and hung and sweltered like a sodden blanket in St. Louis. It was wet heat, and one knew that there would be no relief or coolness in the night. And when one tried to think of the time when the heat would go away, one said: "It cannot last. It's bound to go away," as we always say it in America. But one did not believe it when he said it. The heat soaked down and men sweltered in it; the faces of the people were pale and greasy with the heat. And in their faces was a patient wretchedness, and one felt the kind of desolation that one feels at the end of a hot day in a great city in America—when one's home is far away, across the continent, and he thinks of all that distance, all that heat, and feels, "Oh God! but it's a big country!"

And he feels nothing but absence, absence, and the desolation of America, the loneliness and sadness of the high, hot skies, and evening coming on across the Middle West, across the sweltering and heat-sunken land, across all the lonely little towns, the farms, the fields, the oven swelter of Ohio, Kansas, Iowa, and Indiana at the close of day, and voices, casual in the heat, voices at the little stations, quiet, casual, somehow faded into that enormous vacancy and weariness of heat, of space, and of the immense, the sorrowful, the most high and awful skies.

Then he hears the engine and the wheel again, the wailing whistle and the bell, the sound of shifting in the sweltering yard, and walks the street, and walks the street, beneath the clusters of hard lights, and by the people with sagged faces, and is drowned in desolation and in no belief.

He feels the way one feels when one comes back, and knows that he should not have come, and when he sees that, after all, King's Highway is—a street; and St. Louis —the enchanted name—a big, hot, common town upon the river, sweltering in wet, dreary heat, and not quite South, and nothing else enough to make it better.

It had not been like this before. He could remember how it would get hot, and how good the heat was, and how he would lie out in the backyard on an airing mattress, and how the mattress would get hot and dry and smell like a hot mattress full of sun, and how the sun would make him want to sleep, and how, sometimes, he would go down into the basement to feel coolness, and how the cellar smelled as cellars always smell—a cool, stale smell, the smell of cobwebs and of grimy bottles. And he could remember, when you opened the door upstairs, the smell of the cellar would come up to you—cool, musty, stale and dank and dark—and how the thought of the dark cellar always filled him with a kind of numb excitement, a kind of visceral expectancy.

He could remember how it got hot in the afternoons, and how he would feel a sense of absence and vague sadness in the afternoons, when everyone had gone away. The house would seem so lonely, and sometimes he would sit inside, on the second step of the hall stairs, and listen to the sound of silence and of absence in the afternoon. He could smell the oil upon the floor and on the stairs, and see the sliding doors with their brown varnish and the beady chains across the door, and thrust his hands among the beady chains, and gather them together in his arms, and let them clash, and swish with light beady swishings all around him. He could feel darkness, absence, varnished darkness, and stained light within the house, through the stained glass of the window on the stairs, through the small stained glasses by the door, stained light and absence, silence and the smell of floor oil and vague sadness in the house on a hot mid-afternoon. And all these things themselves would have a kind of life: would seem to wait attentively, to be most living and most still.

He would sit there and listen. He could hear the girl next door practice her piano lessons in the afternoon, and hear the street car coming by between the backyard fences, half a block away, and smell the dry and sultry smell of backyard fences, the smell of coarse hot grasses by the car tracks in the afternoon, the smell of tar, of dry caulked ties, the smell of bright worn flanges, and feel the loneliness of backyards in the afternoon and the sense of absence when the car was gone.

Then he would long for evening and return, the slant of light, and feet along the street, the sharp-faced twins in sailor suits upon their tricycles, the smell of supper and the sound of voices in the house again, and Grover coming from the Fair.

That is how it was when he came into the street, and found the place where the two corners met, and turned at last to see if Time was there. He passed the house: some lights were burning, the door was open, and a woman sat upon the porch. And presently he turned, came back, and stopped before the house again. The corner light fell blank upon the house. He stood looking at it, and put his foot upon the step.

Then he said to the woman who was sitting on the porch: "This house—excuse me—but could you tell me, please, who lives here in this house?"

He knew his words were strange and hollow, and he had not said what he wished to say. She stared at him a moment, puzzled.

Then she said: "I live here. Who are you looking for?"

He said, "Why, I am looking for—"

And then he stopped, because he knew he could not tell her what it was that he was looking for.

"There used to be a house—" he said.

The woman was now staring at him hard.

He said, "I think I used to live here."

She said nothing.

In a moment he continued, "I used to live here in this house," he said, "when I was a little boy."

She was silent, looking at him, then she said: "Oh. Are you sure this was the house? Do you remember the address?"

"I have forgotten the address," he said, "but it was Edgemont Street, and it was on the corner. And I know this is the house."

"This isn't Edgemont Street," the woman said. "The name is Bates."

"Well, then, they changed the name of the street," he said, "but this is the same house. It hasn't changed."

She was silent a moment, then she nodded: "Yes. They did change the name of the street. I remember when I was a child they called it something else," she said. "But that was a long time ago. When was it that you lived here?"

"In 1904."

Again she was silent, looking at him. Then presently: "Oh. That was the year of the Fair. You were here then?"

"Yes." He now spoke rapidly, with more confidence. "My mother had the house, and we were here for seven months. And the house belonged to Dr. Packer," he went on. "We rented it from him."

"Yes," the woman said, and nodded, "this was Dr. Packer's house. He's dead now, he's been dead for many years. But this was the Packer house, all right."

"That entrance on the side," he said, "where the steps go up, that was for Dr. Packer's patients. That was the entrance to his office."

"Oh," the woman said, "I didn't know that. I've often wondered what it was. I didn't know what it was for."

"And this big room in front here," he continued, "that was the office. And there were sliding doors, and next to it, a kind of alcove for his patients—"

"Yes, the alcove is still there, only all of it has been made into one room now—and I never knew just what the alcove was for."

"And there were sliding doors on this side, too, that opened on the hall—and a stairway going up upon this side. And halfway up the stairway, at the landing, a little window of colored glass—and across the sliding doors here in the hall, a kind of curtain made of strings of beads."

She nodded, smiling. "Yes, it's just the same—we still have the sliding doors and the stained glass window on the stairs. There's no bead curtain any more," she said, "but I remember when people had them. I know what you mean."

"When we were here," he said, "we used the doctor's office for a parlor—except later on—the last month or two—and then we used it for—a bedroom."

"It is a bedroom now," she said. "I run the house—I rent rooms—all of the rooms upstairs are rented—but I have two brothers and they sleep in this front room."

Both of them were silent for a moment, then Eugene said, "My brother stayed there too."

"In the front room?" the woman said.

He answered, "Yes."

She paused, then said: "Won't you come in? I don't believe it's changed much. Would you like to see?"

He thanked her and said he would, and he went up the steps. She opened the screen door to let him in.

Inside it was just the same—the stairs, the hallway, the sliding doors, the window of stained glass upon the stairs. And all of it was just the same, except for absence, the stained light of absence in the afternoon, and the child who once had sat there, waiting on the stairs.

It was all the same except that as a child he had sat there feeling things were *Somewhere*—and now he *knew*. He had sat there feeling that a vast and sultry river was somewhere—and now he knew! He had sat there wondering what King's Highway was, where it began, and where it ended—now he knew! He had sat there haunted by the magic word "downtown"—now he knew!—and by the street car, after it had gone—and by all things that came and went and came again, like the cloud shadows passing in a wood, that never could be captured.

And he felt that if he could only sit there on the stairs once more, in solitude and absence in the afternoon, he would be able to get it back again. Then would he be able to remember all that he had seen and been—the brief sum of himself, the universe of his four years, with all the light of Time upon it—that universe which was so short to measure, and yet so far, so endless, to remember. Then would he be able to see his own small face again, pooled in the dark mirror of the hall, and peer once more into the grave eyes of the child that he had been, and discover there in his quiet three-years' self the lone integrity of "I," knowing: "Here is the House, and here House listening; here is Absence, Absence in the afternoon; and here in this House, this Absence, is my core, my kernel—here am I!"

But as he thought it, he knew that even if he could sit here alone and get it back again, it would be gone as soon as seized, just as it had been then—first coming like the vast and drowsy rumors of the distant and enchanted Fair, then fading like cloud shadows on a hill, going like faces in a dream—coming, going, coming, possessed and held but never captured, like lost voices in the mountains long ago—and like the dark eyes and quiet face of the dark, lost boy, his brother, who, in the mysterious rhythms of his life and work, used to come into this house, then go, and then return again.

The woman took Eugene back into the house and through the hall. He told her of the pantry, told her where it was and pointed to the place, but now it was no longer there. And he told her of the backyard, and of the old board fence around the yard. But the old board fence was gone. And he told her of the carriage house, and told her it was painted red. But now there was a small garage. And the backyard was still there, but smaller than he thought, and now there was a tree.

"I did not know there was a tree," he said. "I do not remember any tree."

"Perhaps it was not there," she said. "A tree could grow in thirty years." And then they came back through the house again and paused at the sliding doors.

"And could I see this room?" he said.

She slid the doors back. They slid open smoothly, with a rolling heaviness, as they used to do. And then he saw the room again. It was the same. There was a window at the side, the two arched windows at the front, the alcove and the sliding doors, the fireplace with the tiles of mottled green, the mantel of dark mission wood, the mantel posts, a dresser and a bed, just where the dresser and the bed had been so long ago.

"Is this the room?" the woman said. "It hasn't changed?"

He told her that it was the same.

"And your brother slept here where my brothers sleep?"

"This is his room," he said.

They were silent. He turned to go, and said, "Well, thank you. I appreciate your showing me."

She said that she was glad and that it was no trouble. "And when you see your family, you can tell them that you saw the house," she said. "My name is Mrs. Bell. You can tell your mother that a Mrs. Bell has the house now. And when you see your brother, you can tell him that you saw the room he slept in, and that you found it just the same."

He told her then that his brother was dead.

The woman was silent for a moment. Then she looked at him and said: "He died here, didn't he? In this room?"

He told her that it was so.

"Well, then," she said, "I knew it. I don't know how. But when you told me he was here, I knew it."

He said nothing. In a moment the woman said, "What did he die of?"

"Typhoid."

She looked shocked and troubled, and said involuntarily, "My two brothers—"

"That was a long time ago," he said. "I don't think you need to worry now."

"Oh, I wasn't thinking about that," she said. "It was just hearing that a little boy—your brother—was—was in this room that my two brothers sleep in now—"

"Well, maybe I shouldn't have told you then. But he was a good boy—and if you'd known him you wouldn't mind."

She said nothing, and he added quickly: "Besides, he didn't stay here long. This wasn't really his room—but the night he came back with my sister he was so sick—they didn't move him."

"Oh," the woman said, "I see." And then: "Are you going to tell your mother you were here?"

"I don't think so."

"I—I wonder how she feels about this room."

"I don't know. She never speaks of it."

"Oh. . . . How old was he?"

"He was twelve."

"You must have been pretty young yourself."

"I was not quite four."

"And—you just wanted to see the room, didn't you? That's why you came back."

"Yes."

"Well—" indefinitely—"I guess you've seen it now."

"Yes, thank you."

"I guess you don't remember much about him, do you? I shouldn't think you would."

"No, not much."

The years dropped off like fallen leaves: the face came back again—the soft dark oval, the dark eyes, the soft brown berry on the neck, the raven hair, all bending down, approaching—the whole appearing to him ghost-wise, intent and instant.

"Now say it—*Grover!*"

"Gova."

"No—not Gova—*Grover!* . . . Say it!"

"Gova."

"Ah-h—you didn't say it. You said Gova. *Grover*—now say it!"

"Gova."

"Look, I tell you what I'll do if you say it right. Would you like to go down to King's Highway? Would you like Grover to set you up? All right, then. If you say Grover and say it right, I'll take you to King's Highway and set you up to ice cream. Now say it right—*Grover!*"

"Gova."

"Ah-h, you-u. You're the craziest little old boy I ever did see. Can't you even say Grover?"

"Gova."

"Ah-h, you-u. Old Tongue-Tie, that's what you are. . . . Well, come on, then, I'll set you up anyway."

It all came back, and faded, and was lost again. Eugene turned to go, and thanked the woman and said good-bye.

"Well, then, good-bye," the woman said, and they shook hands. "I'm glad if I could show you. I'm glad if—" She did not finish, and at length she said: "Well, then, that was a long time ago. You'll find everything changed now, I guess. It's all built up around here now—and way out beyond here, out beyond where the Fair Grounds used to be. I guess you'll find it changed."

They had nothing more to say. They just stood there for a moment on the steps, and then shook hands once more.

"Well, good-bye."

And again he was in the street, and found the place where the corners met, and for the last time turned to see where Time had gone.

And he knew that he would never come again, and that lost magic would not come again. Lost now was all of it—the street, the heat, King's Highway, and Tom the Piper's son, all mixed in with the vast and drowsy murmur of the Fair, and with the sense of absence in the afternoon, and the house that waited, and the child that dreamed. And out of the enchanted wood, that thicket of man's memory, Eugene knew that the dark eye and the quiet face of his friend and brother—poor child, life's stranger, and life's exile, lost like all of us, a cipher in blind mazes, long ago—the lost boy was gone forever, and would not return.

1937

Zora Neale Hurston
ca. 1901–1960

Zora Neale Hurston was born—the date is uncertain—in Eatonville, Florida, a town she described as "the first [incorporated] Negro community" and "the first attempt at organized self-government on the part of Negroes in America." After her mother's death in 1904, her father, a tenant farmer and preacher, placed her in a school in Jacksonville. At fourteen, when want of money forced her father to remove her from school, she joined a traveling Gilbert and Sullivan troupe as a maid, hoping to save money so that she could return to school. Near the end of her life, Hurston entered another period of wandering: She worked again as a maid, then as a librarian, as a part-time teacher, and as a reporter. On January 28, 1960, she died in the County Welfare Home in Fort Pierce, Florida. Between her troubled beginnings and her lonely end, however, during the 1920s, the 1930s, and into the 1940s, Hurston lived a remarkably full and varied life, one she autobiographically recorded in what may be her finest book, *Dust Tracks on the Road* (1942).

In 1923 Hurston entered Howard University, where she began to write. In 1926 she won a scholarship to Barnard College, where she was the first black woman to be admitted and where she continued to write. She also began to cultivate an interest in anthropology. By the time she graduated in 1928, she had attracted the attention of Columbia University's distinguished anthropologist Franz Boas, with whom she worked off and on for more than ten years. From 1928 to 1931 she collected folklore throughout the South and in 1935 published *Mules & Men,* anthropological stories of voodoo among southern blacks. In 1937 and 1938, sponsored by two successive Guggenheim fellowships, she did field research in Jamaica, Haiti, and Bermuda, investigations that led to another book of anthropology, *Tell My Horse* (1938). Later still, she collected folklore in

Florida for the Works Progress Administration. "Voodooism" and "black magic" became abiding interests, as did the oral folk literature of the black South and the Caribbean. "She was always getting scholarships and things from wealthy white people," Langston Hughes recalled, "some of whom simply paid her just to sit around and represent the Negro race for them. . . . She was full of side-splitting anecdotes, humorous tales, and tragicomic stories, remembered out of her life in the South as a daughter of a travelling minister of God."

In part because she was a flamboyant, charismatic woman, and especially because she was a remarkably gifted writer, Hurston played a major role in the Harlem Renaissance during the late 1920s and the early 1930s. No writer of the period did more than she to show the glamour, the excitement, and the promise that enabled American cities to draw hundreds of thousands of black people to them. And none did more than she to expose the loneliness, emptiness, and brutality that people often found once they had reached their destinations. Her deeper subject, however, one embedded in the move of people from the farms and villages to the cities, lay in the strength and wisdom that people found in the folkways, the music, and the stories they carried with them. Many of these themes were explored in a series of novels: *Jonah's Gourd Vine* (1934), a narrative based on the lives of Hurston's parents; *Their Eyes Were Watching God* (1937), a love story set in Eatonville and the surrounding farm community; *Moses, Man of the Mountain* (1939), a re-creation and reinterpretation of the Old Testament Hebrews in the form of Negro folktales; and *Seraph on the Suwanee* (1948), the tale of a love affair between a white man and a black woman.

Hurston's point of view was so distinctly and powerfully her own that she seldom pleased anyone entirely and sometimes pleased no one at all. Since her writing often went counter to the more recent literature of black protest, making her seem politically unrealistic, Hurston's reputation suffered in the 1950s a severe decline that continued in the years following her lonely death. During the last several years, however, her achievement has received new recognition, based, as Alice Walker has noted, on the sense that she was "before her time" in presenting "black people as complete, complex, *undiminished* human beings, a sense that is lacking in so much black writing and literature."

Further Reading:
L. Hughes, *The Big Sea*, 1940.
A. Rayson, "The Novels of Zora Neale Hurston," *Studies in Black Literature*, Winter 1974.
A. Walker, "In Search of Zora Neale Hurston," *Ms. Magazine*, March 1975.
R. E. Hemenway, *Zora Neale Hurston: A Literary Biography*, 1977.

Texts:
"The Gilded Six-bits" from *The Best Short Stories by Negro Writers*, ed. Langston Hughes, 1967.
"Their Eyes Were Watching God" from *I Love Myself When I Am Laughing . . . and Then Again When I Am Looking Mean and Impressive*, ed. A. Walker, 1979.

The Gilded Six-bits[1]

It was a Negro yard around a Negro house in a Negro settlement that looked to the payroll of the G. and G. Fertilizer works for its support.

But there was something happy about the place. The front yard was parted in the middle by a sidewalk from gate to doorstep, a sidewalk edged on either side by quart bottles driven neck down into the ground on a slant. A mess of homey flowers planted without a plan but blooming cheerily from their helter-skelter places. The fence and house were whitewashed. The porch and steps scrubbed white.

The front door stood open to the sunshine so that the floor of the front room could finish drying after its weekly scouring. It was Saturday. Everything clean from the front gate to the privy house. Yard raked so that the strokes of the rake would make a pattern. Fresh newspaper cut in fancy edge on the kitchen shelves.

Missie May was bathing herself in the galvanized washtub in the bedroom. Her dark-brown skin glistened under the soapsuds that skittered down from her washrag. Her stiff young breasts thrust forward aggressively, like broad-based cones with the tips lacquered in black.

She heard men's voices in the distance and glanced at the dollar clock on the dresser.

"Humph! Ah'm way behind time t'day! Joe gointer be heah 'fore Ah git mah clothes on if Ah don't make haste."

She grabbed the clean meal sack at hand and dried herself hurriedly and began to dress. But before she could tie her slippers, there came the ring of singing metal on wood. Nine times.

Missie May grinned with delight. She had not seen the big tall man come stealing in the gate and creep up the walk grinning happily at the joyful mischief he was about to commit. But she knew that it was her husband throwing silver dollars in the door for her to pick up and pile beside her plate at dinner. It was this way every Saturday afternoon. The nine dollars hurled into the open door, he scurried to a hiding place behind the Cape jasmine bush and waited.

Missie May promptly appeared at the door in mock alarm.

"Who dat chunkin' money in mah do'way?" she demanded. No answer from the yard. She leaped off the porch and began to search the shrubbery. She peeped under the porch and hung over the gate to look up and down the road. While she did this, the man behind the jasmine darted to the chinaberry tree. She spied him and gave chase.

"Nobody ain't gointer be chunkin' money at me and Ah not do 'em nothin'," she shouted in mock anger. He ran around the house with Missie May at his heels. She overtook him at the kitchen door. He ran inside but could not close it after him before she crowded in and locked with him in a rough-and-tumble. For several minutes the two were a furious mass of male and female energy. Shouting, laughing, twisting, turning, tussling, tickling each other in the ribs; Missie May clutching onto Joe and Joe trying, but not too hard, to get away.

[1] Seventy-five cents.

"Missie May, take yo' hand out mah pocket!" Joe shouted out between laughs.

"Ah ain't, Joe, not lessen you gwine gimme whateve' it is good you got in yo' pocket. Turn it go, Joe, do Ah'll tear yo' clothes."

"Go on tear 'em. You de one dat pushes de needles round heah. Move yo' hand, Missie May."

"Lemme git dat paper sack out yo' pocket. Ah bet it's candy kisses."

"Tain't. Move yo' hand. Woman ain't got no business in a man's clothes nohow. Go way."

Missie May gouged way down and gave an upward jerk and triumphed.

"Unhhunh! Ah got it! It 'tis so candy kisses. Ah knowed you had somethin' for me in yo' clothes. Now Ah got to see whut's in every pocket you got."

Joe smiled indulgently and let his wife go through all of his pockets and take out the things that he had hidden there for her to find. She bore off the chewing gum, the cake of sweet soap, the pocket handkerchief as if she had wrested them from him, as if they had not been bought for the sake of this friendly battle.

"Whew! dat play-fight done got me all warmed up!" Joe exclaimed. "Got me some water in de kittle?"

"Yo' water is on de fire and yo' clean things is cross de bed. Hurry up and wash yo'self and git changed so we kin eat. Ah'm hongry." As Missie said this, she bore the steaming kettle into the bedroom.

"You ain't hongry, sugar," Joe contradicted her. "Youse jes' a little empty. Ah'm de one whut's hongry. Ah could eat up camp meetin', back off 'ssociation, and drink Jurdan dry. Have it on de table when Ah git out de tub."

"Don't you mess wid mah business, man. You git in yo' clothes. Ah'm a real wife, not no dress and breath. Ah might not look lak one, but if you burn me, you won't git a thing but wife ashes."

Joe splashed in the bedroom and Missie May fanned around in the kitchen. A fresh red-and-white checked cloth on the table. Big pitcher of buttermilk beaded with pale drops of butter from the churn. Hot fried mullet, crackling bread, ham hock atop a mound of string beans and new potatoes, and perched on the windowsill a pone of spicy potato pudding.

Very little talk during the meal but that little consisted of banter that pretended to deny affection but in reality flaunted it. Like when Missie May reached for a second helping of the tater pone. Joe snatched it out of her reach.

After Missie May had made two or three unsuccessful grabs at the pan, she begged, "Aw, Joe, gimme some mo' dat tater pone."

"Nope, sweetenin' is for us menfolks. Y'all pritty lil frail eels don't need nothin' lak dis. You too sweet already."

"Please, Joe."

"Naw, naw. Ah don't want you to git no sweeter than whut you is already. We goin' down de road a lil piece t'night so you go put on yo' Sunday-go-to-meetin' things."

Missie May looked at her husband to see if he was playing some prank. "Sho nuff, Joe?"

"Yeah. We goin' to de ice cream parlor."

"Where de ice cream parlor at, Joe?"

"A new man done come heah from Chicago and he done got a place and took and opened it up for a ice cream parlor, and bein' as it's real swell, Ah wants you to be one de first ladies to walk in dere and have some set down."

"Do Jesus, Ah ain't knowed nothin' bout it. Who de man done it?"

"Mister Otis D. Slemmons, of spots and places—Memphis, Chicago, Jacksonville, Philadelphia and so on."

"Dat heavyset man wid his mouth full of gold teeths?"

"Yeah. Where did you see 'im at?"

"Ah went down to de sto' tuh git a box of lye and Ah seen 'im standin' on de corner talkin' to some of de mens, and Ah come on back and went to scrubbin' de floor, and he passed and tipped his hat whilst Ah was scourin' de steps. Ah thought Ah never seen *him* befo'."

Joe smiled pleasantly. "Yeah, he's up-to-date. He got de finest clothes Ah ever seen on a colored man's back."

"Aw, he don't look no better in his clothes than you do in yourn. He got a puzzlegut[2] on 'im and he so chuckleheaded[3] he got a pone behind his neck."

Joe looked down at his own abdomen and said wistfully: "Wisht Ah had a build on me lak he got. He ain't puzzlegutted, honey. He jes' got a corperation. Dat make 'm look lak a rich white man. All rich mens is got some belly on 'em."

"Ah seen de pitchers of Henry Ford and he's a spare-built man and Rockefeller look lak he ain't got but one gut. But Ford and Rockefeller and dis Slemmons and all de rest kin be as many-gutted as dey please, Ah's satisfied wid you jes' lak you is, baby. God took pattern after a pine tree and built you noble. Youse a pritty man, and if Ah knowed any way to make you mo' pritty still Ah'd take and do it."

Joe reached over gently and toyed with Missie May's ear. "You jes' say dat cause you love me, but Ah know Ah can't hold no light to Otis D. Slemmons. Ah ain't never been nowhere and Ah ain't got nothin' but you."

Missie May got on his lap and kissed him and he kissed back in kind. Then he went on. "All de womens is crazy 'bout 'im everywhere he go."

"How you know dat, Joe?"

"He tole us so hisself."

"Dat don't make it so. His mouf is cut crossways, ain't it? Well, he kin lie jes' lak anybody else."

"Good Lawd, Missie! You womens sho is hard to sense into things. He's got a five-dollar gold piece for a stickpin and he got a ten-dollar gold piece on his watch chain and his mouf is jes' crammed full of gold teeths. Sho wisht it wuz mine. And whut make it so cool, he got money 'cumulated. And womens give it all to 'im."

"Ah don't see whut de womens see on 'im. Ah wouldn't give 'im a wink if de sheriff wuz after 'im."

"Well, he tole us how de white womens in Chicago give 'im all dat gold money. So he don't 'low nobody to touch it at all. Not even put day finger on it. Dey tole 'im not to. You kin make 'miration at it, but don't tetch it."

"Whyn't he stay up dere where dey so crazy 'bout 'im?"

"Ah reckon dey done made 'im vast-rich and he wants to travel some. He says dey wouldn't leave 'im hit a lick of work. He got mo' lady people crazy 'bout him than he kin shake a stick at."

---

[2] Potbelly.   [3] Stupid.

"Joe, Ah hates to see you so dumb. Dat stray nigger jes' tell y'all anything and y'all b'lieve it."

"Go 'head on now, honey, and put on yo' clothes. He talkin' 'bout his pritty womens—Ah want 'im to see *mine*."

Missie May went off to dress and Joe spent the time trying to make his stomach punch out like Slemmons's middle. He tried the rolling swagger of the stranger, but found that his tall bone-and-muscle stride fitted ill with it. He just had time to drop back into his seat before Missie May came in dressed to go.

On the way home that night Joe was exultant. "Didn't Ah say ole Otis was swell? Can't he talk Chicago talk? Wuzn't dat funny whut he said when great big fat ole Ida Armstrong come in? He asted me, 'Who is dat broad wid de forte shake?' Dat's a new word. Us always thought forty was a set of figgers but he showed us where it means a whole heap of things. Sometimes he don't say forty, he jes' say thirty-eight and two and dat mean de same thing. Know whut he tole me when Ah wuz payin' for our ice cream? He say, Ah have to hand it to you, Joe. Dat wife of yours is jes' thirty-eight and two. Yessuh, she's forte! Ain't he killin'?"

"He'll do in case of a rush. But he sho is got uh heap uh gold on 'im. Dat's de first time Ah ever seed gold money. It lookted good on him sho nuff, but it'd look a whole heap better on you."

"Who, me? Missie May, youse crazy! Where would a po' man lak me git gold money from?"

Missie May was silent for a minute, then she said, "Us might find some goin' long de road some time. Us could."

"Who would be losin' gold money round heah? We ain't even seen none dese white folks wearin' no gold money on dey watch chain. You must be figgerin' Mister Packard or Mister Cadillac goin' pass through heah."

"You don't know whut been lost 'round heah. Maybe somebody way back in memorial times lost they gold money and went on off and it ain't never been found. And then if we wuz to find it, you could wear some 'thout havin' no gang of womens lak dat Slemmons say he got."

Joe laughed and hugged her. "Don't be so wishful 'bout me. Ah'm satisfied de way Ah is. So long as Ah be yo' husband. Ah don't keer 'bout nothin' else. Ah'd ruther all de other womens in de world to be dead than for you to have de toothache. Less we go to bed and git our night rest."

It was Saturday night once more before Joe could parade his wife in Slemmons's ice cream parlor again. He worked the night shift and Saturday was his only night off. Every other evening around six o'clock he left home, and dying dawn saw him hustling home around the lake, where the challenging sun flung a flaming sword from east to west across the trembling water.

That was the best part of life—going home to Missie May. Their whitewashed house, the mock battle on Saturday, the dinner and ice cream parlor afterwards, church on Sunday nights when Missie outdressed any woman in town—all, everything, was right.

One night around eleven the acid ran out at the G. and G. The foreman knocked off the crew and let the steam die down. As Joe rounded the lake on his way home, a lean moon rode the lake in a silver boat. If anybody had asked Joe about the moon on the lake, he would have said he hadn't paid it any attention. But he saw it with his feelings. It made him yearn painfully for Missie. Creation obsessed him. He thought about children. They had been married more than a year now. They had money put away. They ought to be making little feet for shoes. A little boy child would be about right.

He saw a dim light in the bedroom and decided to come in through the kitchen door. He could wash the fertilizer dust off himself before presenting himself to Missie May. It would be nice for her not to know that he was there until he slipped into his place in bed and hugged her back. She always liked that.

He eased the kitchen door open slowly and silently, but when he went to set his dinner bucket on the table he bumped it into a pile of dishes, and something crashed to the floor. He heard his wife gasp in fright and hurried to reassure her. "Iss me, honey. Don't git skeered."

There was a quick, large movement in the bedroom. A rustle, a thud, and a stealthy silence. The light went out.

What? Robbers? Murderers? Some varmint attacking his helpless wife, perhaps. He struck a match, threw himself on guard and stepped over the doorsill into the bedroom.

The great belt on the wheel of Time slipped and eternity stood still. By the match light he could see the man's legs fighting with his breeches in his frantic desire to get them on. He had both chance and time to kill the intruder in his helpless condition —half in and half out of his pants—but he was too weak to take action. The shapeless enemies of humanity that live in the hours of Time had waylaid Joe. He was assaulted in his weakness. Like Samson awakening after his haircut. So he just opened his mouth and laughed.

The match went out and he struck another and lit the lamp. A howling wind raced across his heart, but underneath its fury he heard his wife sobbing and Slemmons pleading for his life. Offering to buy it with all that he had. "Please, suh, don't kill me. Sixty-two dollars at de sto'. Gold money."

Joe just stood. Slemmons looked at the window, but it was screened. Joe stood out like a rough-backed mountain between him and the door. Barring him from escape, from sunrise, from life.

He considered a surprise attack upon the big clown that stood there laughing like a chessy cat. But before his fist could travel an inch, Joe's own rushed out to crush him like a battering ram. Then Joe stood over him.

"Git into yo' damn rags, Slemmons, and dat quick."

Slemmons scrambled to his feet and into his vest and coat. As he grabbed his hat, Joe's fury overrode his intentions and he grabbed at Slemmons with his left hand and struck at him with his right. The right landed. The left grazed the front of his vest. Slemmons was knocked a somersault into the kitchen and fled through the open door. Joe found himself alone with Missie May, with the golden watch charm clutched in his left fist. A short bit of broken chain dangled between his fingers.

Missie May was sobbing. Wails of weeping without words. Joe stood, and after a while he found out that he had something in his hand. And then he stood and felt without thinking and without seeing with his natural eyes. Missie May kept on crying and Joe kept on feeling so much, and not knowing what to do with all his feelings, he put Slemmons's watch charm in his pants pocket and took a good laugh and went to bed.

"Missie May, whut you cryin' for?"

"Cause Ah love you so hard and Ah know you don't love *me* no mo'."

Joe sank his face into the pillow for a spell, then he said huskily, "You don't know de feelings of dat yet, Missie May."

"Oh Joe, honey, he said he wuz gointer give me dat gold money and he jes' kept on after me—"

Joe was very still and silent for a long time. Then he said, "Well, don't cry no mo', Missie May. Ah got yo' gold piece for you."

The hours went past on their rusty ankles. Joe still and quiet on one bed rail and Missie May wrung dry of sobs on the other. Finally the sun's tide crept upon the shore of night and drowned all its hours. Missie May with her face stiff and streaked towards the window saw the dawn come into her yard. It was day. Nothing more. Joe wouldn't be coming home as usual. No need to fling open the front door and sweep off the porch, making it nice for Joe. Never no more breakfast to cook; no more washing and starching of Joe's jumper-jackets and pants. No more nothing. So why get up?

With this strange man in her bed, she felt embarrassed to get up and dress. She decided to wait till he had dressed and gone. Then she would get up, dress quickly and be gone forever beyond reach of Joe's looks and laughs. But he never moved. Red light turned to yellow, then white.

From beyond the no-man's land between them came a voice. A strange voice that yesterday had been Joe's.

"Missie May, ain't you gonna fix me no breakfus'?"

She sprang out of bed. "Yeah, Joe. Ah didn't reckon you wuz hongry."

No need to die today. Joe needed her for a few more minutes anyhow.

Soon there was a roaring fire in the cookstove. Water bucket full and two chickens killed. Joe loved fried chicken and rice. She didn't deserve a thing and good Joe was letting her cook him some breakfast. She rushed hot biscuits to the table as Joe took his seat.

He ate with his eyes in his plate. No laughter, no banter.

"Missie May, you ain't eatin' yo' breakfus'."

"Ah don't choose none, Ah thank yuh."

His coffee cup was empty. She sprang to refill it. When she turned from the stove and bent to set the cup beside Joe's plate, she saw the yellow coin on the table between them.

She slumped into her seat and wept into her arms.

Presently Joe said calmly, "Missie May, you cry too much. Don't look back lak Lot's wife and turn to salt."

The sun, the hero of every day, the impersonal old man that beams as brightly on death as on birth, came up every morning and raced across the blue dome and dipped into the sea of fire every morning. Water ran downhill and birds nested.

Missie knew why she didn't leave Joe. She couldn't. She loved him too much, but she could not understand why Joe didn't leave her. He was polite, even kind at times, but aloof.

There were no more Saturday romps. No ringing silver dollars to stack beside her plate. No pockets to rifle. In fact, the yellow coin in his trousers was like a monster hiding in the cave of his pockets to destroy her.

She often wondered if he still had it, but nothing could have induced her to ask nor yet to explore his pockets to see for herself. Its shadow was in the house whether or no.

One night Joe came home around midnight and complained of pains in the back. He asked Missie to rub him down with liniment. It had been three months since Missie had touched his body and it all seemed strange. But she rubbed him. Grateful for the chance. Before morning youth triumphed and Missie exulted. But the next day, as she joyfully made up their bed, beneath her pillow she found the piece of money with the bit of chain attached.

Alone to herself, she looked at the thing with loathing, but look she must. She took it into her hands with trembling and saw first thing that it was no gold piece. It was a gilded half dollar. Then she knew why Slemmons had forbidden anyone to touch his gold. He trusted village eyes at a distance not to recognize his stickpin as a gilded quarter, and his watch charm as a four-bit piece.

She was glad at first that Joe had left it there. Perhaps he was through with her punishment. They were man and wife again. Then another thought came clawing at her. He had come home to buy from her as if she were any woman in the longhouse. Fifty cents for her love. As if to say that he could pay as well as Slemmons. She slid the coin into his Sunday pants pocket and dressed herself and left his house.

Halfway between her house and the quarters she met her husband's mother, and after a short talk she turned and went back home. Never would she admit defeat to that woman who prayed for it nightly. If she had not the substance of marriage she had the outside show. Joe must leave *her*. She let him see she didn't want his old gold four-bits, too.

She saw no more of the coin for some time though she knew that Joe could not help finding it in his pocket. But his health kept poor, and he came home at least every ten days to be rubbed.

The sun swept around the horizon, trailing its robes of weeks and days. One morning as Joe came in from work, he found Missie May chopping wood. Without a word he took the ax and chopped a huge pile before he stopped.

"You ain't got no business choppin' wood, and you know it."

"How come? Ah been choppin' it for de last longest."

"Ah ain't blind. You makin' feet for shoes."

"Won't you be glad to have a lil baby chile, Joe?"

"You know dat 'thout astin' me."

"Iss gointer be a boy chile and de very spit of you."

"You reckon, Missie May?"

"Who else could it look lak?"

Joe said nothing, but he thrust his hand deep into his pocket and fingered something there.

It was almost six months later Missie May took to bed and Joe went and got his mother to come wait on the house.

Missie May was delivered of a fine boy. Her travail was over when Joe came in from work one morning. His mother and the old women were drinking great bowls of coffee around the fire in the kitchen.

The minute Joe came into the room his mother called him aside.

"How did Missie May make out?" he asked quickly.

"Who, dat gal? She strong as a ox. She gointer have plenty mo'. We done fixed her wid de sugar and lard to sweeten her for de nex' one."

Joe stood silent awhile.

"You ain't ask 'bout de baby, Joe. You oughter be mighty proud cause he sho is de spittin' image of yuh, son. Dat's yourn all right, if you never git another one, dat un is yourn. And you know Ah'm mighty proud too, son, cause Ah never thought well of you marryin' Missie May cause her ma used tuh fan her foot round right smart and Ah been mighty skeered dat Missie May wuz gointer git misput on her road."

Joe said nothing. He fooled around the house till late in the day, then, just before he went to work, he went and stood at the foot of the bed and asked his wife how she felt. He did this every day during the week.

On Saturday he went to Orlando to make his market. It had been a long time since he had done that.

Meat and lard, meal and flour, soap and starch. Cans of corn and tomatoes. All the staples. He fooled around town for a while and bought bananas and apples. Way after while he went around to the candy store.

"Hello, Joe," the clerk greeted him. "Ain't seen you in a long time."

"Nope, Ah ain't been heah. Been round in spots and places."

"Want some of them molasses kisses you always buy?"

"Yessuh." He threw the gilded half dollar on the counter. "Will dat spend?"

"What is it, Joe? Well, I'll be doggone! A gold-plated four-bit piece. Where'd you git it, Joe?"

"Offen a stray nigger dat come through Eatonville. He had it on his watch chain for a charm—goin' round making out iss gold money. Ha ha! He had a quarter on his tiepin and it wuz all golded up too. Tryin' to fool people. Makin' out he so rich and everything. Ha! Ha! Tryin' to tole off folkses wives from home."

"How did you git it, Joe? Did he fool you, too?"

"Who, me? Naw suh! He ain't fooled me none. Know whut Ah done? He come round me wid his smart talk. Ah hauled off and knocked 'im down and took his old four-bits away from 'im. Gointer buy my wife some good ole lasses kisses wid it. Gimme fifty cents worth of dem candy kisses."

"Fifty cents buys a mighty lot of candy kisses, Joe. Why don't you split it up and take some chocolate bars, too? They eat good, too."

"Yessuh, dey do, but Ah wants all dat in kisses. Ah got a lil boy chile home now. Tain't a week old yet, but he kin suck a sugar tit and maybe eat one them kisses hisself."

Joe got his candy and left the store. The clerk turned to the next customer. "Wisht I could be like these darkies. Laughin' all the time. Nothin' worries 'em."

Back in Eatonville, Joe reached his own front door. There was the ring of singing metal on wood. Fifteen times. Missie May couldn't run to the door, but she crept there as quickly as she could.

"Joe Banks, Ah hear you chunkin' money in mah do'way. You wait till Ah got mah strength back and Ah'm gointer fix you for dat."

1933

from Their Eyes Were Watching God

There are years that ask questions and years that answer. Janie had had no chance to know things, so she had to ask. Did marriage end the cosmic loneliness of the unmated? Did marriage compel love like the sun the day?

In the few days to live before she went to Logan Killicks and his often-mentioned sixty acres, Janie asked inside of herself and out. She was back and forth to the pear tree continuously wondering and thinking. Finally out of Nanny's talk and her own conjectures she made a sort of comfort for herself. Yes, she would love Logan after they were married. She could see no way for it to come about, but Nanny and the old folks had said it so it must be so. Husbands and wives always loved each other, and that was what marriage meant. It was just so. Janie felt glad of the thought for then it wouldn't seem so destructive and mouldy. She wouldn't be lonely anymore.

Janie and Logan got married in Nanny's parlor of a Saturday evening with three cakes and big platters of fried rabbit and chicken. Everything to eat in abundance. Nanny and Mrs. Washburn had seen to that. But nobody put anything on the seat of Logan's wagon to make it ride glorious on the way to his house. It was a lonesome place like a stump in the middle of the woods where nobody had ever been. The house was absent of flavor, too. But anyhow Janie went on inside to wait for love to begin. The new moon had been up and down three times before she got worried in mind. Then she went to see Nanny in Mrs. Washburn's kitchen on the day for beaten biscuits.

Nanny beamed all out with gladness and made her come up to the bread board so she could kiss her.

"Lawd a'mussy, honey. Ah sho is glad tuh see mah chile! G'wan inside and let Mis' Washburn know youse heah. Umph! Umph! Umph! How is dat husband uh your?"

Janie didn't go into where Mrs. Washburn was. She didn't say anything to match up with Nanny's gladness either. She just fell on a chair with her hips and sat there. Between the biscuits and her beaming pride Nanny didn't notice for a minute. But after a while she found the conversation getting lonesome so she looked up at Janie.

"Whut's de matter, sugar? You ain't none too spry dis mornin'."

"Oh, nothin' much, Ah reckon. Ah come to get a lil information from you."

The old woman looked amazed, then gave a big clatter of laughter. "Don't tell me you done got knocked up already, less see—dis Saturday it's two month and two weeks."

"No'm, Ah don't think so anyhow." Janie blushed a little.

"You ain't got nothin' to be shamed of, honey, youse uh married 'oman. You got yo' lawful husband same as Mis' Washburn or anybody else!"

"Ah'm all right day way. Ah *know* 'tain't nothin' dere."

"You and Logan been fussin'? Lawd, Ah know dat grass-gut, liver-lipted nigger ain't done took and beat mah baby already! Ah'll take a stick and salivate 'im!"

"No'm, he ain't even talked 'bout hittin' me. He says he never mean to lay de weight uh his hand on me in malice. He chops all de wood he think Ah wants and den he totes it inside de kitchin for me. Keeps both water buckets full."

"Humph! don't 'spect all dat tuh keep up. He ain't kissin' yo' mouf when he carry on over yuh lak dat. He's kissin' yo' foot and 'taint in uh man tuh kiss foot long. Mouf kissin' is on uh equal and dat's natural but when dey got to bow down tuh love, dey soon straightens up."

"Yes'm."

"Well, if he do all dat whut you come in heah wid uh face long as mah arm for?"

"'Cause you told me Ah mus gointer love him, and, and Ah don't. Maybe if somebody was to tell me how, Ah could do it."

"You come heah wid yo' mouf full uh foolishness on uh busy day. Heah you got uh prop tuh lean on all yo' bawn days, and big protection, and everybody got tuh tip dey hat tuh you and call you Mis' Killicks and you come worryin' me 'bout love."

"But Nanny, Ah wants to want him sometimes. Ah don't want him to do all de wantin'."

"If you don't want him, you sho oughta. Heah you is wid de onliest organ in town, amongst colored folks, in yo' parlor. Got a house bought and paid for and sixty acres uh land right on de big road and. . . . Lawd have mussy! Dat's de very prong all us black women gits hung on. Dis love! Dat's just whut's got us uh pullin' and uh haulin' and sweatin' and doin' from can't see in de mornin' till can't see at night. Dat's how come de ole folks say dat bein' uh fool don't kill nobody. It jus' makes you sweat. Ah betcha you wants some dressed up dude dat got to look at de sole of his shoe everytime he cross de street tuh see whether he got enough leather dere tuh make it across. You can buy and sell such as dem wid what you got. In fact you can buy 'em and give 'em away."

"Ah ain't studyin' 'bout none of 'em. At de same time Ah ain't takin' dat ole land tuh heart neither. Ah could throw ten acres of it over de fence every day and never look back to see where it fell. Ah feel de same way 'bout Mr. Killicks too. Some folks never was meant to be loved and he's one of 'em."

"How come?"

"'Cause Ah hates de way his head is so long one way and so flat on de sides and dat pone uh fat back uh his neck."

"He never made his own head. You talk so silly."

"Ah don't keer who made it. Ah don't like de job. His belly is too big too, now, and his toe-nails look lak mule foots. And 'tain't nothin' in de way of him washin' his feet every evenin' before he comes tuh bed. 'Taint nothin' tuh hinder him 'cause Ah places de water for him. Ah'd ruther be shot wid tacks than tuh turn over in de bed and stir up de air whilst he is in dere. He don't even never mention nothin' pretty."

She began to cry.

"Ah wants things sweet wid mah marriage lak when you sit under a pear tree and think. Ah . . ."

"'Tain't no use in you cryin', Janie. Grandma done been long uh few roads herself. But folks is meant to cry 'bout somethin' or other. Better leave things de way dey is. Youse young yet. No tellin' whut mout happen befo' you die. Wait awhile, baby. Yo' mind will change."

Nanny sent Janie along with a stern mien, but she dwindled all the rest of the day as she worked. And when she gained the privacy of her own little shack she stayed on her knees so long she forgot she was there herself. There is a basin in the mind where words float around on thought and thought on sound and sight. Then there is a depth of thought untouched by words, and deeper still a gulf of formless feelings untouched by thought. Nanny entered this infinity of conscious pain again on her old knees. Towards morning she muttered, "Lawd, you know mah heart. Ah done de best Ah could do. De rest is left to you." She scuffled up from her knees and fell heavily across the bed. A month later she was dead.

So Janie waited a bloom time, and a green time and an orange time. But when the pollen again gilded the sun and sifted down on the world she began to stand around the gate and expect things. What things? She didn't know exactly. Her breath was gusty and short. She knew things that nobody had ever told her. For instance, the words of the trees and the wind. She often spoke to falling seeds and said, "Ah hope you fall on soft ground," because she had heard seeds saying that to each other as they passed. She knew the world was a stallion rolling in the blue pasture of ether. She knew that God tore down the old world every evening and built a new one by sun-up. It was wonderful to see it take form with the sun and emerge from the gray dust of its making. The familiar people and things had failed her so she hung over the gate and looked up the road towards way off. She knew now that marriage did not make love. Janie's first dream was dead, so she became a woman. . . .

After that night Jody moved his things and slept in a room downstairs. He didn't really hate Janie, but he wanted her to think so. He had crawled off to lick his wounds. They didn't talk too much around the store either. Anybody that didn't know would have thought that things had blown over, it looked so quiet and peaceful around. But the stillness was the sleep of swords. So new thoughts had to be thought and new words said. She didn't want to live like that. Why must Joe be so mad with her for making him look small when he did it to her all the time? Had been doing it for years. Well, if she must eat out of a long-handled spoon, she must. Jody might get over his mad spell any time at all and begin to act like somebody towards her.

Then too she noticed how baggy Joe was getting all over. Like bags hanging from an ironing board. A little sack hung from the corners of his eyes and rested on his cheek-bones; a loose-filled bag of feathers hung from his ears and rested on his neck beneath his chin. A sack of flabby something hung from his loins and rested on his thighs when he sat down. But even these things were running down like candle grease as time moved on.

He made new alliances too. People he never bothered with one way or another now seemed to have his ear. He had always been scornful of root-doctors and all their kind, but now she saw a faker from over around Altamonte Springs, hanging around the place almost daily. Always talking in low tones when she came near, or hushed altogether. She didn't know that he was driven by a desperate hope to appear the oldtime body in her sight. She was sorry about the root-doctor because she feared that Joe was depending on the scoundrel to make him well when what he needed was a doctor, and a good one. She was worried about his not eating his meals, till she found out he was having old lady Davis to cook for him. She knew that she was a much better cook than the old woman, and cleaner about the kitchen. So she bought a beef-bone and made him some soup.

"Naw, thank you," he told her shortly. "Ah'm havin' uh hard enough time tuh try and git well as it is."

She was stunned at first and hurt afterwards. So she went straight to her bosom friend, Pheoby Watson, and told her about it.

"Ah'd ruther be dead than for Jody tuh think Ah'd hurt him," she sobbed to Pheoby. "It ain't always been too pleasant, 'cause you know how Joe worships de works of his own hands, but God in heben knows Ah wouldn't do one thing tuh hurt nobody. It's too underhand and mean."

"Janie, Ah thought maybe de thing would die down and you never would know nothin' 'bout it, but it's been singin' round here ever since de big fuss in de store dat Joe was 'fixed' and you wuz the one dat did it."

"Pheoby, for de longest time, Ah been feelin' dat somethin' set for still-bait, but dis is—is—oh Pheoby! What *kin* I do?"

"You can't do nothin' but make out you don't know it. It's too late fuh y'all tuh be splittin' up and gittin' divorce. Just g'wan back home and set down on yo' royal diasticutis and say nothin'. Nobody don't b'lieve it nohow."

"Tuh think Ah been wid Jody twenty yeahs and Ah just now got tuh bear de name uh poisonin' him! It's 'bout to kill me, Pheoby. Sorrow dogged by sorrow is in mah heart."

"Dat's lie dat trashy nigger dat calls hisself uh two-headed doctor brought tuh 'im in order tuh git in wid Jody. He seen he wuz sick—everybody been knowin' dat for de last longest, and den Ah reckon he hear y'all wuz kind of at variance, so dat wuz his chance. Last summer dat multiplied cock-roach wuz round heah tryin' tuh sell gophers!"

"Phoeby, Ah don't even b'lieve Jody b'lieve dat lie. He ain't never took no stock in de mess. He just make out he b'lieve it tuh hurt me. Ah'm stone dead from standin' still and tryin' tuh smile."

She cried often in the weeks that followed. Joe got too weak to look after things and took to his bed. But he relentlessly refused to admit her to his sickroom. People came and went in the house. This one and that one came into her house with covered plates of broth and other sick-room dishes without taking the least notice of her as Joe's wife. People who had never known what it was to enter the gate of the Mayor's yard unless it were to do some menial job now paraded in and out as his confidants. They came to the store and ostentatiously looked over whatever she was doing and went back to report to him at the house. Said things like "Mr. Starks need *somebody* tuh sorta look out for 'im till he kin git on his feet again and look for hisself."

But Jody was never to get on his feet again. Janie had Sam Watson to bring her the news from the sick room, and when he told her how things were, she had him bring a doctor from Orlando without giving Joe a chance to refuse, and without saying she sent for him.

"Just a matter of time," the doctor told her. "When a man's kidneys stop working altogether, there is no way for him to live. He needed medical attention two years ago. Too late now."

So Janie began to think of Death. Death, that strange being with the huge square toes who lived way in the West. The great one who lived in the straight house like a platform without sides to it, and without a roof. What need has Death for a cover, and what winds can blow against him? He stands in his high house that overlooks the world. Stands watchful and motionless all day with his sword drawn back, waiting for the messenger to bid him come. Been standing there before there was a where or a when or a then. She was liable to find a feather from his wings lying in her yard any day now. She was sad and afraid too. Poor Jody! He ought not to have to wrassle in there by himself. She sent Sam in to suggest a visit, but Jody said No. These medical doctors wuz all right with the Godly sick, but they didn't know a thing about a case like his. He'd be all right just as soon as the two-headed man found what had been buried against him. He wasn't going to die at all. That was what he thought. But Sam told her different, so she knew. And then if he hadn't, the next morning she was bound to know, for people began to gather in the big yard under the palm and chinaberry trees. People who would not have dared to foot the place before crept in and did not come to the house. Just squatted under the trees and waited. Rumor, that wingless bird, had shadowed over the town.

She got up that morning with the firm determination to go in there and have a good talk with Jody. But she sat a long time with the walls creeping in on her. Four walls squeezing her breath out. Fear lest he depart while she sat trembling upstairs nerved her and she was inside the room before she caught her breath. She didn't make the cheerful, casual start that she had thought out. Something stood like an oxen's foot on her tongue, and then too, Jody, no Joe, gave her a ferocious look. A look with all the unthinkable coldness of outer space. She must talk to a man who was ten immensities away.

He was lying on his side facing the door like he was expecting somebody or something. A sort of changing look on his face. Weak-looking but sharp-pointed about the eyes. Through the thin counterpane she could see what was left of his belly huddled before him on the bed like some helpless thing seeking shelter.

The half-washed bedclothes hurt her pride for Jody. He had always been so clean.

"Whut you doin' in heah, Janie?"

"Come tuh see 'bout you and how you wuz makin' out."

He gave a deep-growling sound like a hog dying down in the swamp and trying to drive off disturbance. "Ah come in heah tuh git shet uh you but look lak 'tain't doin' me no good. G'wan out. Ah needs tuh rest."

"Naw, Jody, Ah come in heah tuh talk widja and Ah'm gointuh do it too. It's for both of our sakes Ah'm talkin'."

He gave another ground grumble and eased over on his back.

"Jody, maybe Ah ain't been sich uh good wife tuh you, but Jody—"

"Dat's 'cause you ain't got de right feelin' for nobody. You oughter have some sympathy 'bout yo'self. You ain't no hog."

"But, Jody, Ah meant tuh be awful nice."

"Much as Ah done fuh yuh. Holdin' me up tuh scorn. No sympathy!"

"Naw, Jody, it wasn't because Ah didn't have no sympathy. Ah had uh lavish uh dat. Ah just didn't never git no chance tuh use none of it. You wouldn't let me."

"Dat's right, blame everything on me. Ah wouldn't let you show no feelin'! When, Janie, dat's all Ah ever wanted or desired. Now you come blamin' me!"

"'Tain't dat, Jody. Ah ain't here tuh blame nobody. Ah'm just tryin' tuh make you know what kind a person Ah is befo' it's too late."

"Too late?" he whispered.

His eyes buckled in a vacant-mouthed terror and she saw the awful surprise in his face and answered it.

"Yeah, Jody, don't keer whut dat multiplied cock-roach told yuh tuh git yo' money, you got tuh die, and yuh can't live."

A deep sob came out of Jody's weak frame. It was like beating a bass drum in a hen-house. Then it rose high like pulling in a trombone.

"Janie! Janie! don't tell me Ah got tuh die, and Ah ain't used tuh thinkin' 'bout it."

"'Tain't really no need of you dying, Jody, if you had of—de doctor—but it don't do no good bringin' dat up now. Dat's just whut Ah wants tuh say, Jody. You wouldn't listen. You done lived wid me for twenty years and you don't half know me atall. And you could have but you was so busy worshippin' de works of yo' own hands, and cuffin' folks around in their minds till you didn't see uh whole heap uh things yuh could have."

"Leave heah, Janie. Don't come heah—"

"Ah knowed you wasn't gointuh lissen tuh me. You changes everything but nothin' don't change you—not even death. But Ah ain't goin' outa here and Ah ain't gointuh hush. Naw, you gointuh listen tuh me one time befo' you die. Have yo' way all yo' life, trample and mash down and then die ruther than tuh let yo'self heah 'bout it. Listen, Jody, you ain't de Jody Ah run off down de road wid. You'se whut's left after he died. Ah run off tuh keep house wid you in uh wonderful way. But you wasn't satisfied wid me de way Ah was. Naw! Mah own mind had tuh be squeezed and crowded out tuh make room for yours in me."

"Shut up! Ah wish thunder and lightnin' would kill yuh!"

"Ah know it. And now you got tuh die tuh find out dat you got tuh pacify somebody besides yo'self if you wants any love and any sympathy in dis world. You ain't tried tuh pacify *nobody* but yo'self. Too busy listening tuh yo' own big voice."

"All dis tearin' down talk!" Jody whispered with sweat globules forming all over his face and arms. "Git outa heah!"

"All dis bowin' down, all dis obedience under yo' voice—dat ain't whut Ah rushed off down de road tuh find out about you."

A sound of strife in Jody's throat, but his eyes stared unwillingly into a corner of the room so Janie knew the futile fight was not with her. The icy sword of the square-toed one had cut off his breath and left his hands in a pose of agonizing protest. Janie gave them peace on his breast, then she studied his dead face for a long time.

"Dis sittin' in de rulin' chair is been hard on Jody," she muttered out loud. She was full of pity for the first time in years. Jody had been hard on her and others but life had mishandled him too. Poor Joe! Maybe if she had known some other way to try, she might have made his fate different. But what the other way could be, she had no idea. She thought back and forth about what had happened in the making of a voice out of a man. Then thought about herself. Years ago, she had told her girl self to wait for her in the looking glass. It had been a long time since she had remembered. Perhaps she'd better look. She went over to the dresser and looked hard at her skin and features. The young girl was gone, but a handsome woman had taken her place. She tore off the kerchief from her head and let down her plentiful hair. The weight, the length, the glory was there. She took careful stock of herself, then combed her hair and tied it back up again. Then she starched and ironed her face, forming it into just what people wanted to see, and opened up the window and cried, "Come heah people! Jody is dead. Mah husband is gone from me."

Joe's funeral was the finest thing Orange County had ever seen with Negro eyes. The motor hearse, the Cadillac and Buick carriages; Dr. Henderson there in his Lincoln; the hosts from far and wide. Then again the gold and red and purple, the gloat and glamor of the secret orders, each with its insinuations of power and glory undreamed of by the uninitiated. People on farm horses and mules; babies riding astride of brothers' and sisters' backs. The Elks band ranked at the church door and playing "Safe in the Arms of Jesus" with such a dominant drum rhythm that it could be stepped off smartly by the long line as it filed inside. The Little Emperor of the cross-roads was leaving Orange County as he had come—with the out-stretched hand of power.

Janie starched and ironed her face and came set in the funeral behind her veil. It was like a wall of stone and steel. The funeral was going on outside. All things concerning death and burial were said and done. Finish. End. Nevermore. Darkness. Deep hole. Dissolution. Eternity. Weeping and wailing outside. Inside the expensive black folds were resurrection and life. She did not reach outside for anything, nor did the things of death reach inside to disturb her calm. She sent her face to Joe's funeral, and herself went rollicking with the springtime across the world. After a while the people finished their celebration and Janie went on home.

Before she slept that night she burnt up every one of her head rags and went about the house the next morning with her hair in one thick braid swinging well before her waist. That was the only change people saw in her. She kept the store in the same way except of evenings she sat on the porch and listened and sent Hezekiah in to wait on late customers. She saw no reason to rush at changing things around. She would have the rest of her life to do as she pleased.

1937

Langston Hughes
1902–1967

The most influential black writer in the history of American literature, Langston Hughes was at the center of the Harlem Renaissance of the 1920s and was one of its most productive figures. Besides editing numerous anthologies of black writing, Hughes published ten volumes of poetry, nine books of fiction, nine plays, two autobiographies, several biographies and histories, and an impressive amount of humor and journalism. Practically a cultural institution in himself, by the mid-1930s he had become the first black American writer to establish a truly international reputation. Hughes was also the first American black to carve out for himself a wholly independent literary career.

James Langston Hughes was born in Joplin, Missouri, on February 1, 1902. His racial ancestry was complex: black, Jewish, Scottish, English, and Cherokee. His grandmother had been married to one of the men killed in John Brown's attack on Harpers Ferry. Hughes's parents separated when he was still quite young (Hughes's father, a lawyer and engineer, moved to Mexico to escape American racism), and Hughes was brought up by his mother and grandmother in Kansas and later in Cleveland, Ohio, where he graduated from high school. Hughes then spent a year in Mexico with his father, who offered to finance his education at Columbia, provided he study engineering. Quarrels with his father drove Hughes nearly to the brink of suicide, but he nevertheless entered Columbia in 1921. Dissatisfied with his studies, restless, and determined to be a writer, Hughes left college the following year and in 1923 joined the merchant marines. He worked as a cook's helper, traveling to Africa, Italy, and France, where he spent a year working as a dishwasher in a Paris nightclub. Hughes returned to the United States in 1925; while working as a busboy in a Washington, D.C., hotel, he met the then prominent poet Vachel Lindsay, who immediately publicized the "bus-boy poet" in local papers and thus helped launch Hughes's literary career.

A precocious writer, Hughes began composing poetry in early adolescence. In high school he read Carl Sandburg and Edgar Lee Masters and wrote for the literary magazine. One of his best-known poems, "The Negro Speaks of Rivers," was written while he was still in high school and was published (as were several other of his poems) in *The Crisis,* the magazine of the National Association for the Advancement of Colored People (NAACP). Eleven of Hughes's poems were selected for *The New Negro* (1925), Alain Locke's influential anthology representing the best work of the Harlem Renaissance. In 1926 Hughes returned to college, enrolling at Lincoln University in Pennsylvania, from which he graduated in 1929. During this period he published two books of poetry, *The Weary Blues* (1926) and *Fine Clothes to the Jew* (1927), and wrote a novel about everyday black life, *Not Without Laughter* (1930), which won an award and convinced him that he could make a living—however precarious—by writing.

After graduation Hughes received a monthly sum from an affluent white woman and so was able to live in suburban New Jersey and write. Soon, however, sensing that he was disappointing his patroness (who wanted him "to be more African than Harlem—primitive in the simple, intuitive and noble sense of the word"), he set out on his own. After a tour of Cuba and Haiti, he began supporting himself by conducting an extensive reading tour that took him throughout the South, the Southwest, and California. In 1932 he was invited to participate in a movie about American race relations to be filmed in the Soviet Union; the film was never made, but it permitted Hughes to travel throughout Russia, China, and Japan. Hughes's childhood years and the account of his many travels are the subjects of his two autobiographical books, *The Big Sea* (1940) and *I Wonder as I Wander* (1956).

While in Russia, Hughes discovered the stories of D. H. Lawrence and began writing short fiction: "If D. H. Lawrence," he thought, "can write such psychologically powerful accounts of folks in England, that send shivers up and down my spine, maybe I could write stories like his about folks in America." The results of Hughes's efforts were contained in two collections of stories, *The Ways of White Folks* (1934) and *Laughing to Keep from Crying* (1952), stories mostly written while Hughes lived at the artists' colony in Carmel, California. In 1935 his play *Mulatto* (written in 1930), which he called "a problem play on race relations," was successfully produced on Broadway, and in 1937 Hughes traveled to Spain, where he covered the civil war for the Baltimore *Afro-American* and met many writers, including Ernest Hemingway. Throughout his career, Hughes continued to write plays, the most famous of which is *Tambourines to Glory* (1963), based on his 1959 novel of that name. A remarkably versatile writer, Hughes also tried his hand at librettos, film scripts, songs, children's books, and translations. He never, however, lost touch with poetry: In 1951 he published one of his most famous books, *Montage of a Dream Deferred,* which he followed with *Ask Your Mama: Twelve Moods for Jazz* (1961) and *The Panther and the Lash: Poems of Our Times* (1967).

Aside from his own considerable body of published work, Hughes left several indelible marks on American cultural life. He collaborated on projects with Zora Neale Hurston and Arna Bontemps; he organized and led poetry-reading tours for black writers; he fostered the reading of poetry to musical accompaniment; he promoted the work of a host of other writers as well as several musicians; and he founded the Harlem Suitcase Theater in New York (1938), the New Negro Theater in Los Angeles (1939), and the Skyloft Players in Chicago (1942). In his own work he used elements taken from black songs and folktales as well as the rhythms of blues and jazz. In many of his poems he employs the metrical forms of the blues and the improvisational techniques of the jam session. His was an effort to capture the cunning and the richness of the idiomatic black English he had heard both in the rural South and in the urban North. Through it he sought to convey the resilience and strength of the dispossessed as they struggled to develop popular art forms that would combat the debilitating monotony, weariness, fear, and pain of their lives.

In 1943 Hughes began a long series of character vignettes for the *Chicago Defender* that now ranks among his most important work. At the center of the series is a humorous, street-wise Harlem workingman, Jesse B. Simple, whose musings and opinions on contemporary affairs—war, racism, feminism, cities, poverty, sports, and so on—are communicated to an educated black narrator. Hughes claimed that the origins of Simple were probably to be found in his reading of *Don Quixote,* though he also claimed that he modeled Simple after a factory worker he had interviewed in 1942 in a Harlem café. Hughes asked the man what he made at the plant:

> "Cranks," he answered.
> "What kind of cranks?"
> "Oh, man, I don't know what kind of cranks."
> "Well," asked Hughes, "do they crank cars, trucks, buses, planes, or what?"
> "I don't know what them cranks cranks," he said.
> At which his girl friend, a little annoyed, put in, "You've been working there long enough. By now you ought to know what them cranks crank."
> "Aw woman," he said, "you know white folks don't tell colored folks what cranks cranks."

The first collection of sketches, *Simple Speaks His Mind,* appeared in 1950; it was followed by *Simple Takes a Wife* (1952), *Simple Stakes a Claim* (1957), *The Best of Simple* (1961), and *Simple's Uncle Sam* (1965). Langston Hughes died on May 22, 1967.

Further Reading:
J. Emmanuel, *Langston Hughes*, 1967.
M. Meltzer, *Langston Hughes: A Biography*, 1968.
T. B. O'Daniel, *Langston Hughes, Black Genius: A Critical Evaluation*, 1972.
F. Berry, *Langston Hughes: Before and Beyond Harlem*, 1983.

Texts:
"Feet Live Their Own Life" from *The Best of Simple*, 1961.
"Thank You M'am" from *Something in Common*, 1963.

Feet Live Their Own Life

"If you want to know about my life," said Simple as he blew the foam from the top of the newly filled glass the bartender put before him, "don't look at my face, don't look at my hands. Look at my feet and see if you can tell how long I been standing on them."

"I cannot see your feet through your shoes," I said.

"You do not need to see through my shoes," said Simple. "Can't you tell by the shoes I wear—not pointed, not rockingchair, not French-toed, not nothing but big, long, broad, and flat—that I been standing on these feet a long time and carrying some heavy burdens? They ain't flat from standing at no bar, neither, because I always sets at a bar. Can't you tell that? You know I do not hang out in a bar unless it has stools, don't you?"

"That I have observed," I said, "but I did not connect it with your past life."

"Everything I do is connected up with my past life," said Simple. "From Virginia to Joyce, from my wife to Zarita, from my mother's milk to this glass of beer, everything is connected up."

"I trust you will connect up with that dollar I just loaned you when you get paid," I said. "And who is Virginia? You never told me about her."

"Virginia is where I was borned," said Simple. "I *would* be borned in a state named after a woman. From that day on, women never give me no peace."

"You, I fear, are boasting. If the women were running after you as much as you run after them, you would not be able to sit here on this bar stool in peace. I don't see any women coming to call you out to go home, as some of these fellows' wives do around here."

"Joyce better not come in no bar looking for me," said Simple. "That is why me and my wife busted up—one reason. I do not like to be called out of no bar by a female. It's a man's perogative to just set and drink sometimes."

"How do you connect that prerogative with your past?" I asked.

"When I was a wee small child," said Simple, "I had no place to set and think in, being as how I was raised up with three brothers, two sisters, seven cousins, one married aunt, a common-law uncle, and the minister's grandchild—and the house only had four rooms. I never had no place just to set and think. Neither to set and drink—not even much my milk before some hongry child snatched it out of my hand. I were not the youngest, neither a girl, nor the cutest. I don't know why, but I don't think nobody liked me much. Which is why I was afraid to like anybody for a long time myself. When I did like somebody, I was full-grown and then I picked out the wrong woman because I had no practice in liking anybody before that. We did not get along."

"Is that when you took to drink?"

"Drink took to me," said Simple. "Whiskey just naturally likes me but beer likes me better. By the time I got married I had got to the point where a cold bottle was almost as good as a warm bed, especially when the bottle could not talk and the bed-warmer could. I do not like a woman to talk to me too much—I mean about me. Which is why I like Joyce. Joyce most in generally talks about herself."

"I am still looking at your feet," I said, "and I swear they do not reveal your life to me. Your feet are no open book."

"You have eyes but you see not," said Simple. "These feet have stood on every rock from the Rock of Ages to 135th and Lenox. These feet have supported everything from a cotton bale to a hongry woman. These feet have walked ten thousand miles working for white folks and another ten thousand keeping up with colored. These feet have stood at altars, crap tables, free lunches, bars, graves, kitchen doors, betting windows, hospital clinics, WPA desks, social security railings, and in all kinds of lines from soup lines to the draft. If I just had four feet, I could have stood in more places longer. As it is, I done wore out seven hundred pairs of shoes, eighty-nine tennis shoes, twelve summer sandals, also six loafers. The socks that these feet have bought could build a knitting mill. The corns I've cut away would dull a German razor. The bunions I forgot would make you ache from now till Judgment Day. If anybody was to write the history of my life, they should start with my feet."

"Your feet are not all that extraordinary," I said. "Besides, everything you are saying is general. Tell me specifically some one thing your feet have done that makes them different from any other feet in the world, just one."

"Do you see that window in that white man's store across the street?" asked Simple. "Well, this right foot of mine broke out that window in the Harlem riots right smack in the middle. Didn't no other foot in the world break that window but mine. And this left foot carried me off running as soon as my right foot came down. Nobody else's feet saved me from the cops that night but these *two* feet right here. Don't tell me these feet ain't had a life of their own."

"For shame," I said, "going around kicking out windows. Why?"

"Why?" said Simple. "You have to ask my great-great-grandpa why. He must of been simple—else why did he let them capture him in Africa and sell him for a slave to breed my great-grandpa in slavery to breed my grandpa in slavery to breed my pa to breed me to look at that window and say, 'It ain't mine! Bam-mmm-mm-m!' and kick it out?"

"This bar glass is not yours either," I said. "Why don't you smash it?"

"It's got my beer in it," said Simple.

Just then Zarita came in wearing her Thursday-night rabbit-skin coat. She didn't stop at the bar, being dressed up, but went straight back to a booth. Simple's hand went up, his beer went down, and the glass back to its wet spot on the bar.

"Excuse me a minute," he said, sliding off the stool.

Just to give him pause, the dozens, that old verbal game of maligning a friend's female relatives, came to mind. "Wait," I said. "You have told me about what to ask your great-great-grandpa. But I want to know what to ask your great-great-grandma."

"I don't play the dozens that far back," said Simple, following Zarita into the smoky juke-box blue of the back room.

1950

Thank You, M'am

She was a large woman with a large purse that had everything in it but a hammer and nails. It had a long strap, and she carried it slung across her shoulder. It was about eleven o'clock at night, dark, and she was walking alone, when a boy ran up behind her and tried to snatch her purse. The strap broke with the sudden single tug the boy gave it from behind. But the boy's weight and the weight of the purse combined caused him to loose his balance. Instead of taking off full blast as he had hoped, the boy fell on his back on the sidewalk and his legs flew up. The large woman simply turned around and kicked him right square in his blue-jeaned sitter. Then she reached down, picked the boy up by his shirt front, and shook him until his teeth rattled.

After that the woman said, "Pick up my pocketbook, boy, and give it here."

She still held him tightly. But she bent down enough to permit him to stoop and pick up her purse. Then she said, "Now ain't you ashamed of yourself?"

Firmly gripped by his shirt front, the boy said, "Yes'm."

The woman said, "What did you want to do it for?"

The boy said, "I didn't aim to."

She said, "You a lie!"

By that time two or three people passed, stopped, turned to look, and some stood watching.

"If I turn you loose, will you run?" asked the woman.

"Yes'm," said the boy.

"Then I won't turn you loose," said the woman. She did not release him.

"Lady, I'm sorry," whispered the boy.

"Um-hum! Your face is dirty. I got a great mind to wash your face for you. Ain't you got nobody home to tell you to wash your face?"

"No'm," said the boy.

"Then it will get washed this evening," said the large woman, starting up the street, dragging the frightened boy behind her.

He looked as if he were fourteen or fifteen, frail and willow-wild, in tennis shoes and blue jeans.

The woman said, "You ought to be my son. I would teach you right from wrong. Least I can do right now is to wash your face. Are you hungry?"

"No'm," said the being-dragged boy. "I just want you to turn me loose."

"Was I bothering *you* when I turned that corner?" asked the woman.

"No'm."

"But you put yourself in contact with *me,*" said the woman. "If you think that that contact is not going to last awhile, you got another thought coming. When I get through with you, sir, you are going to remember Mrs. Luella Bates Washington Jones."

Sweat popped out on the boy's face and he began to struggle. Mrs. Jones stopped, jerked him around in front of her, put a half nelson about his neck, and continued to drag him up the street. When she got to her door, she dragged the boy inside, down a hall, and into a large kitchenette-furnished room at the rear of the house. She switched on the light and left the door open. The boy could hear other roomers laughing and talking in the large house. Some of their doors were open, too, so he knew he and the woman were not alone. The woman still had him by the neck in the middle of her room.

She said, "What is your name?"

"Roger," answered the boy.

"Then, Roger, you go to that sink and wash your face," said the woman, whereupon she turned him loose—at last. Roger looked at the door—looked at the woman—looked at the door—*and went to the sink.*

"Let the water run until it gets warm," she said. "Here's a clean towel."

"You gonna take me to jail?" asked the boy, bending over the sink.

"Not with that face, I would not take you nowhere," said the woman. "Here I am trying to get home to cook me a bite to eat, and you snatch my pocketbook! Maybe you ain't been to your supper either, late as it be. Have you?"

"There's nobody home at my house," said the boy.

"Then we'll eat," said the woman. "I believe you're hungry—or been hungry—to try to snatch my pocketbook!"

"I want a pair of blue suede shoes," said the boy.

"Well, you didn't have to snatch *my* pocketbook to get some suede shoes," said Mrs. Luella Bates Washington Jones. "You could of asked me."

"M'am?"

The water dripping from his face, the boy looked at her. There was a long pause. A very long pause. After he had dried his face and not knowing what else to do, dried it again, the boy turned around, wondering what next. The door was open. He could make a dash for it down the hall. He could run, run, run, *run!*

The woman was sitting on the day bed. After a while she said, "I were young once and I wanted things I could not get."

There was another long pause. The boy's mouth opened. Then he frowned, not knowing he frowned.

The woman said, "Um-hum! You thought I was going to say *but,* didn't you? You thought I was going to say, *but I didn't snatch people's pocketbooks.* Well, I wasn't going to say that." Pause. Silence. "I have done things, too, which I would not tell you, son—neither tell God, if He didn't already know. Everybody's got something in common. So you set down while I fix us something to eat. You might run that comb through your hair so you will look presentable."

In another corner of the room behind a screen was a gas plate and an icebox. Mrs. Jones got up and went behind the screen. The woman did not watch the boy to see if he was going to run now, nor did she watch her purse, which she left behind her on the day bed. But the boy took care to sit on the far side of the room, away from the purse, where he thought she could easily see him out of the corner of her eye if she wanted to. He did not trust the woman *not* to trust him. And he did not want to be mistrusted now.

"Do you need somebody to go to the store," asked the boy, "maybe to get some milk or something?"

"Don't believe I do," said the woman, "unless you just want sweet milk yourself. I was going to make cocoa out of this canned milk I got here."

"That will be fine," said the boy.

She heated some lima beans and ham she had in the icebox, made the cocoa, and set the table. The woman did not ask the boy anything about where he lived, or his folks, or anything else that would embarrass him. Instead, as they ate, she told him about her job in a hotel beauty shop that stayed open late, what the work was like, and how all kinds of women came in and out, blondes, redheads, and Spanish. Then she cut him a half of her ten-cent cake.

"Eat some more, son," she said.

When they were finished eating, she got up and said, "Now here, take this ten dollars and buy yourself some blue suede shoes. And next time, do not make the mistake of latching onto *my* pocketbook *nor nobody else's*—because shoes got by devilish ways will burn your feet. I got to get my rest now. But from here on in, son, I hope you will behave yourself."

She led him down the hall to the front door and opened it. "Good night! Behave yourself, boy!" she said, looking out into the street as he went down the steps.

The boy wanted to say something other than, "Thank you, m'am," to Mrs. Luella Bates Washington Jones, but although his lips moved, he couldn't even say that as he turned at the foot of the barren stoop and looked up at the large woman in the door. Then she shut the door.

1958

John Steinbeck
1902–1968

John Steinbeck was born on February 27, 1902, in Salinas, California, in the heart of Monterey County and the Salinas Valley, whose scenery and people left indelible marks on much of his finest fiction. His father was county treasurer and his mother a schoolteacher. In high school, Steinbeck participated in basketball and track, wrote for the school paper, and was elected president of the senior class. In 1919 he entered Stanford University, where he attended classes off and on for several years without taking a degree. During this period he also worked sporadically at odd jobs—as a hand on farms and ranches, a laborer on a road gang, a seaman on a cattle boat, a bricklayer, a surveyor, and a reporter. His single-minded ambition, however, from the age of seventeen, was to become a writer. For ten years he consistently wrote stories and novels—which publishers consistently rejected. But Steinbeck managed to stick through this period, even though he had very little money, apparently because his need to write was deeper than his need to be published. "If my characters are sad or happy," he said in 1931, "I reflect their emotions. I have no personal nor definitive emotions of my own. Indeed, when there is no writing in progress, I feel like an uninhabited body. I think I am only truly miserable at such times."

In 1926 Steinbeck left California, determined to establish himself as a writer and convinced that New York was the place to do it. Soon he was back in California, working again at odd jobs and writing persistently. His first novel, *Cup of Gold,* a fictionalized account of the pirate Henry Morgan, was published in 1929. But neither it nor Steinbeck's next two books—*The Pastures of Heaven* (1932), a collection of short stories about a California farming community, and *To a God Unknown* (1933), a novel about a California farmer's pagan fertility cult—attracted much attention.

In 1930, however, Steinbeck met a marine biologist and naturalist, Edward F. Ricketts, who exerted an enormous influence over his thinking and writing. Ricketts introduced Steinbeck to theories of organisms that today would probably be regarded as sociobiology. Steinbeck responded with an intellectual enthusiasm that was at once deep and decisive; he realized not only that he had found his "theme" but that he had been heading toward similar notions in his writing for some time ("I have written this theme over and over and did not know what I was writing"). The main idea was that the essential biological difference between individuals and groups was *qualitative* rather than quantitative. As Steinbeck put it, "When acting as a group, men do not partake of their ordinary natures at all. The group can change its nature. . . . The greatest group unit, that is the whole race, has qualities which the individual lacks entirely." Armed with such biological ideas as well as with his innate storytelling power, Steinbeck became, for a brief time, one of the most prominent writers in America.

Between 1935 and 1941 Steinbeck published his finest work: *Tortilla Flat* (1935), a novel that deals with the *paisanos* of the Salinas Valley in a manner deliberately reminiscent of Malory's tales of King Arthur and the Knights of the Round Table; *In Dubious Battle* (1936), the story of a strike by migrant fruit pickers; *Of Mice and Men* (1937), a folk parable of itinerent farmhands who dream of a piece of land they can call their own; *The Long Valley* (1938), a collection of short fiction that contains many of Steinbeck's most famous tales, such as "The Red Pony," "The Snake," "The Chrysanthemums," and "The Leader of the People"; *The Grapes of Wrath* (1939), the Pulitzer Prize–winning odyssey of a family of dispossessed sharecroppers who migrate from the Oklahoma dust bowl to the "promised land" of California; and *The Sea of Cortez*

(1941), the record of a biological expedition to collect specimens along the California peninsula that Steinbeck wrote in collaboration with Edward Ricketts.

All of Steinbeck's major works, and especially the stories of *The Long Valley,* are populated by characters who—like those of his fellow-Californian predecessor Jack London—display severely reduced states of consciousness. Steinbeck is fond of portraying simpletons, idiots, illiterates, and animals. In fact, animal imagery and animal behavior, as Edmund Wilson pointed out, pervade Steinbeck's books, from the Pirate in *Tortilla Flat,* who lives with his dogs in a kennel, to the famous description of a turtle crossing a highway in *The Grapes of Wrath,* a progress that prefigures the human journey. Even Steinbeck's "group" consciousness finds its equivalent in animal behavior. The westward migration in "The Leader of the People" is described as "a whole bunch of people made into one big crawling beast. . . . Every man wanted something for himself, but the big beast that was all of them wanted only westering."

During the Second World War, Steinbeck worked as a war correspondent and in 1942 wrote a popular tale about Norway's resistance to the Nazis, *The Moon Is Down* (1942), which like many of his later books seemed to be originally conceived as a play and was quickly turned into a highly successful Broadway production. Steinbeck's ability to write stories that were almost scenarios was perhaps first apparent in *Of Mice and Men,* and it led not only to numerous film adaptations of his works but to many screenwriting assignments. In 1944 Steinbeck published *Cannery Row,* a "down-and-out" tale of the Monterey docks based on the work of Edward Ricketts; it was followed by the story of a microcosmic group of stranded travelers, *The Wayward Bus* (1947), then by another symbolic examination of society, *The Pearl* (1948), a parable of a poor Mexican fisherman whose sudden wealth brings only misery to his community. In 1952 Steinbeck brought out a family saga patterned after the biblical tale of Cain and Abel, *East of Eden.* (While he wrote it, he simultaneously kept a journal documenting his writing process; this was published posthumously in 1969 as *Journal of a Novel: The East of Eden Letters.*) His two last novels were *The Short Reign of Pippin IV* (1957), a slight comedy about a contemporary French king, and *The Winter of Our Discontent* (1961), a story of moral and political corruption that he described as "part Kafka and part Booth Tarkington." In 1962, the year he was awarded the Nobel Prize for literature, Steinbeck published *Travels with Charlie in Search of America,* the record of an automobile tour of forty states.

Steinbeck's greatest subject, the story of lowly, dispossessed people, of their indignant fear and their inherent dignity, had a poignancy during the Great Depression that it has since lost for some readers. Yet it is not a subject we can afford to lose. In *The Pastures of Heaven,* Steinbeck pictures an old man, looking down into a valley, wishing that he "could go down there and . . . think over all" the events of his life; "maybe," he concludes, "I could make something out of them, something all in one piece that had a meaning, instead of all these trailing ends." Some such motive, the desire to become a cohesive imagination and an articulate voice for the broken dreams and lives of common people, lies at the heart of the work for which Steinbeck is now best remembered.

Further Reading:
P. Lisca, *The Wide World of John Steinbeck*,
1958.
W. French, *John Steinbeck*, 1961.
J. Fontenrose, *John Steinbeck: An Introduction and
Interpretation*, 1963.
T. Kiernan, *The Intricate Music: A Biography of
John Steinbeck*, 1979.
J. J. Benson, *The True Adventures of John
Steinbeck, Writer: A Biography*, 1984.

Text:
The Long Valley, 1938.

The Leader of the People[*]

On Saturday afternoon Billy Buck, the ranch-hand, raked together the last of the old
year's haystack and pitched small forkfuls over the wire fence to a few mildly
interested cattle. High in the air small clouds like puffs of cannon smoke were driven
eastward by the March wind. The wind could be heard whishing in the brush on the
ridge crests, but no breath of it penetrated down into the ranch-cup.

The little boy, Jody, emerged from the house eating a thick piece of buttered bread.
He saw Billy working on the last of the haystack. Jody tramped down scuffing his
shoes in a way he had been told was destructive to good shoe-leather. A flock of white
pigeons flew out of the black cypress tree as Jody passed, and circled the tree and landed
again. A half-grown tortoise-shell cat leaped from the bunkhouse porch, galloped on
stiff legs across the road, whirled and galloped back again. Jody picked up a stone to
help the game along, but he was too late, for the cat was under the porch before the
stone could be discharged. He threw the stone into the cypress tree and started the
white pigeons on another whirling flight.

Arriving at the used-up haystack, the boy leaned against the barbed wire fence.
"Will that be all of it, do you think?" he asked.

The middle-aged ranch-hand stopped his careful raking and stuck his fork into the
ground. He took off his black hat and smoothed down his hair. "Nothing left of it
that isn't soggy from ground moisture," he said. He replaced his hat and rubbed his
dry leathery hands together.

"Ought to be plenty mice," Jody suggested.

"Lousy with them," said Billy. "Just crawling with mice."

"Well, maybe, when you get all through, I could call the dogs and hunt the mice."

"Sure, I guess you could," said Billy Buck. He lifted a forkful of the damp
ground-hay and threw it into the air. Instantly three mice leaped out and burrowed
frantically under the hay again.

Jody sighed with satisfaction. Those plump, sleek, arrogant mice were doomed. For

---

[*] Originally Part IV of *The Red Pony*, published
in 1937, "The Leader of the People" was
published for the first time as a separate
collected work in *The Long Valley* (1938).

eight months they had lived and multiplied in the haystack. They had been immune from cats, from traps, from poison and from Jody. They had grown smug in their security, overbearing and fat. Now the time of disaster had come; they would not survive another day.

Billy looked up at the top of the hills that surrounded the ranch. "Maybe you better ask your father before you do it," he suggested.

"Well, where is he? I'll ask him now."

"He rode up to the ridge ranch after dinner. He'll be back pretty soon."

Jody slumped against the fence post. "I don't think he'd care."

As Billy went back to his work he said ominously, "You'd better ask him anyway. You know how he is."

Jody did know. His father, Carl Tiflin, insisted upon giving permission for any-thing that was done on the ranch, whether it was important or not. Jody sagged farther against the post until he was sitting on the ground. He looked up at the little puffs of wind-driven cloud. "Is it like to rain, Billy?"

"It might. The wind's good for it, but not strong enough."

"Well, I hope it don't rain until after I kill those damn mice." He looked over his shoulder to see whether Billy had noticed the mature profanity. Billy worked on without comment.

Jody turned back and looked at the side-hill where the road from the outside world came down. The hill was washed with lean March sunshine. Silver thistles, blue lupins and a few poppies bloomed among the sage bushes. Halfway up the hill Jody could see Doubletree Mutt, the black dog, digging in a squirrel hole. He paddled for a while and then paused to kick bursts of dirt out between his hind legs, and he dug with an earnestness which belied the knowledge he must have had that no dog had ever caught a squirrel by digging in a hole.

Suddenly, while Jody watched, the black dog stiffened, and backed out of the hole and looked up the hill toward the cleft in the ridge where the road came through. Jody looked up too. For a moment Carl Tiflin on horseback stood out against the pale sky and then he moved down the road toward the house. He carried something white in his hand.

The boy started to his feet. "He's got a letter," Jody cried. He trotted away toward the ranch house, for the letter would probably be read aloud and he wanted to be there. He reached the house before his father did, and ran in. He heard Carl dismount from his creaking saddle and slap the horse on the side to send it to the barn where Billy would unsaddle it and turn it out.

Jody ran into the kitchen. "We got a letter!" he cried.

His mother looked up from a pan of beans. "Who has?"

"Father has. I saw it in his hand."

Carl strode into the kitchen then, and Jody's mother asked, "Who's the letter from, Carl?"

He frowned quickly. "How did you know there was a letter?"

She nodded her head in the boy's direction. "Big-Britches Jody told me."

Jody was embarrassed.

His father looked down at him contemptuously. "He *is* getting to be a Big-

Britches," Carl said. "He's minding everybody's business but his own. Got his big nose into everything."

Mrs. Tiflin relented a little. "Well, he hasn't enough to keep him busy. Who's the letter from?"

Carl still frowned on Jody. "I'll keep him busy if he isn't careful." He held out a sealed letter. "I guess it's from your father."

Mrs. Tiflin took a hairpin from her head and slit open the flap. Her lips pursed judiciously. Jody saw her eyes snap back and forth over the lines. "He says," she translated, "he says he's going to drive out Saturday to stay for a little while. Why, this is Saturday. The letter must have been delayed." She looked at the postmark. "This was mailed day before yesterday. It should have been here yesterday." She looked up questioningly at her husband, and then her face darkened angrily. "Now what have you got that look on you for? He doesn't come often."

Carl turned his eyes away from her anger. He could be stern with her most of the time, but when occasionally her temper arose, he could not combat it.

"What's the matter with you?" she demanded again.

In his explanation there was a tone of apology Jody himself might have used. "It's just that he talks," Carl said lamely. "Just talks."

"Well, what of it? You talk yourself."

"Sure I do. But your father only talks about one thing."

"Indians!" Jody broke in excitedly. "Indians and crossing the plains!"

Carl turned fiercely on him. "You get out, Mr. Big-Britches! Go on, now! Get out!"

Jody went miserably out the back door and closed the screen with elaborate quietness. Under the kitchen window his shamed, downcast eyes fell upon a curiously shaped stone, a stone of such fascination that he squatted down and picked it up and turned it over in his hands.

The voices came clearly to him through the open kitchen window. "Jody's damn well right," he heard his father say. "Just Indians and crossing the plains. I've heard that story about how the horses got driven off about a thousand times. He just goes on and on, and he never changes a word in the things he tells."

When Mrs. Tiflin answered her tone was so changed that Jody, outside the window, looked up from his study of the stone. Her voice had become soft and explanatory. Jody knew how her face would have changed to match the tone. She said quietly, "Look at it this way, Carl. That was the big thing in my father's life. He led a wagon train clear across the plains to the coast, and when it was finished, his life was done. It was a big thing to do, but it didn't last long enough. Look!" she continued, "it's as though he was born to do that, and after he finished it, there wasn't anything more for him to do but think about it and talk about it. If there'd been any farther west to go, he'd have gone. He's told me so himself. But at last there was the ocean. He lives right by the ocean where he had to stop."

She had caught Carl, caught him and entangled him in her soft tone. "I've seen him," he agreed quietly. "He goes down and stares off west over the ocean." His voice sharpened a little. "And then he goes up to the Horseshoe Club in Pacific Grove, and he tells people how the Indians drove off the horses."

She tried to catch him again. "Well, it's everything to him. You might be patient with him and pretend to listen."

Carl turned impatiently away. "Well, if it gets too bad, I can always go down to the bunkhouse and sit with Billy," he said irritably. He walked through the house and slammed the front door after him.

Jody ran to his chores. He dumped the grain to the chickens without chasing any of them. He gathered the eggs from the nests. He trotted into the house with the wood and interlaced it so carefully in the wood-box that two armloads seemed to fill it to overflowing.

His mother had finished the beans by now. She stirred up the fire and brushed off the stove-top with a turkey wing. Jody peered cautiously at her to see whether any rancor toward him remained. "Is he coming today?" Jody asked.

"That's what his letter said."

"Maybe I better walk up the road to meet him."

Mrs. Tiflin clanged the stove-lid shut. "That would be nice," she said. "He'd probably like to be met."

"I guess I'll just do it then."

Outside, Jody whistled shrilly to the dogs. "Come on up the hill," he commanded. The two dogs waved their tails and ran ahead. Along the roadside the sage had tender new tips. Jody tore off some pieces and rubbed them on his hands until the air was filled with the sharp wild smell. With a rush the dogs leaped from the road and yapped into the brush after a rabbit. That was the last Jody saw of them, for when they failed to catch the rabbit, they went back home.

Jody plodded on up the hill toward the ridge top. When he reached the little cleft where the road came through, the afternoon wind struck him and blew up his hair and ruffled his shirt. He looked down on the little hills and ridges below and then out at the huge green Salinas Valley. He could see the white town of Salinas far out in the flat and the flash of its windows under the waning sun. Directly below him, in an oak tree, a crow congress had convened. The tree was black with crows all cawing at once.

Then Jody's eyes followed the wagon road down from the ridge where he stood, and lost it behind a hill, and picked it up again on the other side. On that distant stretch he saw a cart slowly pulled by a bay horse. It disappeared behind the hill. Jody sat down on the ground and watched the place where the cart would reappear again. The wind sang on the hilltops and the puff-ball clouds hurried eastward.

Then the cart came into sight and stopped. A man dressed in black dismounted from the seat and walked to the horse's head. Although it was so far away, Jody knew he had unhooked the check-rein, for the horse's head dropped forward. The horse moved on, and the man walked slowly up the hill beside it. Jody gave a glad cry and ran down the road toward them. The squirrels bumped along off the road, and a road-runner flirted its tail and raced over the edge of the hill and sailed out like a glider.

Jody tried to leap into the middle of his shadow at every step. A stone rolled under his foot and he went down. Around a little bend he raced, and there, a short distance ahead, were his grandfather and the cart. The boy dropped from his unseemly running and approached at a dignified walk.

The horse plodded stumble-footedly up the hill and the old man walked beside it. In the lowering sun their giant shadows flickered darkly behind them. The grandfather was dressed in a black broadcloth suit and he wore kid congress gaiters[1] and a black tie on a short, hard collar. He carried his black slouch hat in his hand. His white beard was cropped close and his white eyebrows overhung his eyes like moustaches. The blue eyes were sternly merry. About the whole face and figure there was a granite dignity, so that every motion seemed an impossible thing. Once at rest, it seemed the old man would be stone, would never move again. His steps were slow and certain. Once made, no step could ever be retraced; once headed in a direction, the path would never bend nor the pace increase nor slow.

When Jody appeared around the bend, Grandfather waved his hat slowly in welcome, and he called, "Why, Jody! Come down to meet me, have you?"

Jody sidled near and turned and matched his step to the old man's step and stiffened his body and dragged his heels a little. "Yes, sir," he said. "We got your letter only today."

"Should have been here yesterday," said Grandfather. "It certainly should. How are all the folks?"

"They're fine, sir." He hesitated and then suggested shyly, "Would you like to come on a mouse hunt tomorrow, sir?"

"Mouse hunt, Jody?" Grandfather chuckled. "Have the people of this generation come down to hunting mice? They aren't very strong, the new people, but I hardly thought mice would be game for them."

"No, sir. It's just play. The haystack's gone. I'm going to drive out the mice to the dogs. And you can watch, or even beat the hay a little."

The stern, merry eyes turned down on him. "I see. You don't eat them, then. You haven't come to that yet."

Jody explained, "The dogs eat them, sir. It wouldn't be much like hunting Indians, I guess."

"No, not much—but then later, when the troops were hunting Indians and shooting children and burning teepees, it wasn't much different from your mouse hunt."

They topped the rise and started down into the ranch cup, and they lost the sun from their shoulders. "You've grown," Grandfather said. "Nearly an inch, I should say."

"More," Jody boasted. "Where they mark me on the door, I'm up more than an inch since Thanksgiving even."

Grandfather's rich throaty voice said, "Maybe you're getting too much water and turning to pith and stalk. Wait until you head out, and then we'll see."

Jody looked quickly into the old man's face to see whether his feelings should be hurt, but there was no will to injure, no punishing nor putting-in-your-place light in the keen blue eyes. "We might kill a pig," Jody suggested.

"Oh, no! I couldn't let you do that. You're just humoring me. It isn't the time and you know it."

"You know Riley, the big boar, sir?"

"Yes. I remember Riley well."

[1] Ankle-high shoes with elastic in the sides (also called "congress boots").

"Well, Riley ate a hole into that same haystack, and it fell down on him and smothered him."

"Pigs do that when they can," said Grandfather.

"Riley was a nice pig, for a boar, sir. I rode him sometimes, and he didn't mind."

A door slammed at the house below them, and they saw Jody's mother standing on the porch waving her apron in welcome. And they saw Carl Tiflin walking up from the barn to be at the house for the arrival.

The sun had disappeared from the hills by now. The blue smoke from the house chimney hung in flat layers in the purpling ranch-cup. The puff-ball clouds, dropped by the falling wind, hung listlessly in the sky.

Billy Buck came out of the bunkhouse and flung a wash basin of soapy water on the ground. He had been shaving in mid-week, for Billy held Grandfather in reverence, and Grandfather said that Billy was one of the few men of the new generation who had not gone soft. Although Billy was in middle age, Grandfather considered him a boy. Now Billy was hurrying toward the house too.

When Jody and Grandfather arrived, the three were waiting for them in front of the yard gate.

Carl said, "Hello, sir. We've been looking for you."

Mrs. Tiflin kissed Grandfather on the side of his beard, and stood still while his big hand patted her shoulder. Billy shook hands solemnly, grinning under his straw moustache. "I'll put up your horse," said Billy, and he led the rig away.

Grandfather watched him go, and then, turning back to the group, he said as he had said a hundred times before, "There's a good boy. I knew his father, old Mule-tail Buck. I never knew why they called him Mule-tail except he packed mules."

Mrs. Tiflin turned and led the way into the house. "How long are you going to stay, Father? Your letter didn't say."

"Well, I don't know. I thought I'd stay about two weeks. But I never stay as long as I think I'm going to."

In a short while they were sitting at the white oilcloth table eating their supper. The lamp with the tin reflector hung over the table. Outside the dining-room windows the big moths battered softly against the glass.

Grandfather cut his steak into tiny pieces and chewed slowly. "I'm hungry," he said. "Driving out here got my appetite up. It's like when we were crossing. We all got so hungry every night we could hardly wait to let the meat get done. I could eat about five pounds of buffalo meat every night."

"It's moving around does it," said Billy. "My father was a government packer. I helped him when I was a kid. Just the two of us could about clean up a deer's ham."

"I knew your father, Billy," said Grandfather. "A fine man he was. They called him Mule-tail Buck. I don't know why except he packed mules."

"That was it," Billy agreed. "He packed mules."

Grandfather put down his knife and fork and looked around the table. "I remember one time we ran out of meat—" His voice dropped to a curious low sing-song, dropped into a tonal groove the story had worn for itself. "There was no buffalo, no antelope; not even rabbits. The hunters couldn't even shoot a coyote. That was the time for the leader to be on the watch. I was the leader, and I kept my eyes open. Know why? Well, just the minute the people began to get hungry they'd start slaughtering the team oxen. Do you believe that? I've heard of parties that just ate up their draft cattle. Started from the middle and worked toward the ends. Finally they'd eat the lead pair, and then the wheelers. The leader of a party had to keep them from doing that."

In some manner a big moth got into the room and circled the hanging kerosene lamp. Billy got up and tried to clap it between his hands. Carl struck with a cupped palm and caught the moth and broke it. He walked to the window and dropped it out.

"As I was saying," Grandfather began again, but Carl interrupted him. "You'd better eat some more meat. All the rest of us are ready for our pudding."

Jody saw a flash of anger in his mother's eyes. Grandfather picked up his knife and fork. "I'm pretty hungry, all right," he said. "I'll tell you about that later."

When supper was over, when the family and Billy Buck sat in front of the fireplace in the other room, Jody anxiously watched Grandfather. He saw the signs he knew. The bearded head leaned forward; the eyes lost their sternness and looked wonderingly into the fire; the big lean fingers laced themselves on the black knees. "I wonder," he began, "I just wonder whether I ever told you how those thieving Piutes drove off thirty-five of our horses."

"I think you did," Carl interrupted. "Wasn't it just before you went up into the Tahoe country?"

Grandfather turned quickly toward his son-in-law. "That's right. I guess I must have told you that story."

"Lots of times," Carl said cruelly, and he avoided his wife's eyes. But he felt the angry eyes on him, and he said, "'Course I'd like to hear it again."

Grandfather looked back at the fire. His fingers unlaced and laced again. Jody knew how he felt, how his insides were collapsed and empty. Hadn't Jody been called a Big-Britches that very afternoon? He arose to heroism and opened himself to the term Big-Britches again. "Tell about Indians," he said softly.

Grandfather's eyes grew stern again. "Boys always want to hear about Indians. It was a job for men, but boys want to hear about it. Well, let's see. Did I ever tell you how I wanted each wagon to carry a long iron plate?"

Everyone but Jody remained silent. Jody said, "No. You didn't."

"Well, when the Indians attacked, we always put the wagons in a circle and fought from between the wheels. I thought that if every wagon carried a long plate with rifle holes, the men could stand the plates on the outside of the wheels when the wagons were in the circle and they would be protected. It would save lives and that would make up for the extra weight of the iron. But of course the party wouldn't do it. No party had done it before and they couldn't see why they should go to the expense. They lived to regret it, too."

Jody looked at his mother, and knew from her expression that she was not listening at all. Carl picked at a callus on his thumb and Billy Buck watched a spider crawling up the wall.

Grandfather's tone dropped into its narrative groove again. Jody knew in advance exactly what words would fall. The story droned on, speeded up for the attack, grew sad over the wounds, struck a dirge at the burials on the great plains. Jody sat quietly watching Grandfather. The stern blue eyes were detached. He looked as though he were not very interested in the story himself.

When it was finished, when the pause had been politely respected as the frontier of the story, Billy Buck stood up and stretched and hitched his trousers. "I guess I'll turn in," he said. Then he faced Grandfather. "I've got an old powder horn and a cap and ball pistol down to the bunkhouse. Did I ever show them to you?"

Grandfather nodded slowly. "Yes, I think you did, Billy. Reminds me of a pistol I had when I was leading the people across." Billy stood politely until the little story was done, and then he said, "Good night," and went out of the house.

Carl Tiflin tried to turn the conversation then. "How's the country between here and Monterey? I've heard it's pretty dry."

"It is dry," said Grandfather. "There's not a drop of water in the Laguna Seca. But it's a long pull from '87. The whole country was powder then, and in '61 I believe all the coyotes starved to death. We had fifteen inches of rain this year."

"Yes, but it all came too early. We could do with some now." Carl's eye fell on Jody. "Hadn't you better be getting to bed?"

Jody stood up obediently. "Can I kill the mice in the old haystack, sir?"

"Mice? Oh! Sure, kill them all off. Billy said there isn't any good hay left."

Jody exchanged a secret and satisfying look with Grandfather. "I'll kill every one tomorrow," he promised.

Jody lay in his bed and thought of the impossible world of Indians and buffaloes, a world that had ceased to be forever. He wished he could have been living in the heroic time, but he knew he was not of heroic timber. No one living now, save possibly Billy Buck, was worthy to do the things that had been done. A race of giants had lived then, fearless men, men of a staunchness unknown in this day. Jody thought of the wide plains and of the wagons moving across like centipedes. He thought of Grandfather on a huge white horse, marshaling the people. Across his mind marched the great phantoms, and they marched off the earth and they were gone.

He came back to the ranch for a moment, then. He heard the dull rushing sound that space and silence make. He heard one of the dogs, out in the doghouse, scratching a flea and bumping his elbow against the floor with every stroke. Then the wind arose again and the black cypress groaned and Jody went to sleep.

He was up half an hour before the triangle sounded for breakfast. His mother was rattling the stove to make the flames roar when Jody went through the kitchen. "You're up early," she said. "Where are you going?"

"Out to get a good stick. We're going to kill the mice today."

"Who is 'we'?"

"Why, Grandfather and I."

"So you've got him in it. You always like to have someone in with you in case there's blame to share."

"I'll be right back," said Jody. "I just want to have a good stick ready for after breakfast."

He closed the screen door after him and went out into the cool blue morning. The birds were noisy in the dawn and the ranch cats came down from the hill like blunt snakes. They had been hunting gophers in the dark, and although the four cats were full of gopher meat, they sat in a semi-circle at the back door and mewed piteously for milk. Doubletree Mutt and Smasher moved sniffing along the edge of the brush, performing the duty with rigid ceremony, but when Jody whistled, their heads jerked up and their tails waved. They plunged down to him, wriggling their skins and yawning. Jody patted their heads seriously, and moved on to the weathered scrap pile. He selected an old broom handle and a short piece of inch-square scrap wood. From his pocket he took a shoelace and tied the ends of the sticks loosely together to make a flail. He whistled his new weapon through the air and struck the ground experimentally, while the dogs leaped aside and whined with apprehension.

Jody turned and started down past the house toward the old haystack ground to look over the field of slaughter, but Billy Buck, sitting patiently on the back steps, called to him, "You better come back. It's only a couple of minutes till breakfast."

Jody changed his course and moved toward the house. He leaned his flail against the steps. "That's to drive the mice out," he said. "I'll bet they're fat. I'll bet they don't know what's going to happen to them today."

"No, nor you either," Billy remarked philosophically, "nor me, nor anyone."

Jody was staggered by this thought. He knew it was true. His imagination twitched away from the mouse hunt. Then his mother came out on the back porch and struck the triangle, and all thoughts fell in a heap.

Grandfather hadn't appeared at the table when they sat down. Billy nodded at his empty chair. "He's all right? He isn't sick?"

"He takes a long time to dress," said Mrs. Tiflin. "He combs his whiskers and rubs up his shoes and brushes his clothes."

Carl scattered sugar on his mush. "A man that's led a wagon train across the plains has got to be pretty careful how he dresses."

Mrs. Tiflin turned on him. "Don't do that, Carl! Please don't!" There was more of threat than of request in her tone. And the threat irritated Carl.

"Well, how many times do I have to listen to the story of the iron plates, and the thirty-five horses? That time's done. Why can't he forget it, now it's done?" He grew angrier while he talked, and his voice rose. "Why does he have to tell them over and over? He came across the plains. All right! Now it's finished. Nobody wants to hear about it over and over."

The door into the kitchen closed softly. The four at the table sat frozen. Carl laid his mush spoon on the table and touched his chin with his fingers.

Then the kitchen door opened and Grandfather walked in. His mouth smiled tightly and his eyes were squinted. "Good morning," he said, and he sat down and looked at his mush dish.

Carl could not leave it there. "Did—did you hear what I said?"

Grandfather jerked a little nod.

"I don't know what got into me, sir. I didn't mean it. I was just being funny."

Jody glanced in shame at his mother, and he saw that she was looking at Carl, and that she wasn't breathing. It was an awful thing that he was doing. He was tearing himself to pieces to talk like that. It was a terrible thing to him to retract a word, but to retract it in shame was infinitely worse.

Grandfather looked sidewise. "I'm trying to get right side up," he said gently. "I'm not being mad. I don't mind what you said, but it might be true, and I would mind that."

"It isn't true," said Carl. "I'm not feeling well this morning. I'm sorry I said it."

"Don't be sorry, Carl. An old man doesn't see things sometimes. Maybe you're right. The crossing is finished. Maybe it should be forgotten, now it's done."

Carl got up from the table. "I've had enough to eat. I'm going to work. Take your time, Billy!" He walked quickly out of the dining-room. Billy gulped the rest of his food and followed soon after. But Jody could not leave his chair.

"Won't you tell any more stories?" Jody asked.

"Why, sure I'll tell them, but only when—I'm sure people want to hear them."

"I like to hear them, sir."

"Oh! Of course you do, but you're a little boy. It was a job for men, but only little boys like to hear about it."

Jody got up from his place. "I'll wait outside for you, sir. I've got a good stick for those mice."

He waited by the gate until the old man came out on the porch. "Let's go down and kill the mice now," Jody called.

"I think I'll just sit in the sun, Jody. You go kill the mice."

"You can use my stick if you like."

"No, I'll just sit here a while."

Jody turned disconsolately away, and walked down toward the old haystack. He tried to whip up his enthusiasm with thoughts of the fat juicy mice. He beat the ground with his flail. The dogs coaxed and whined about him, but he could not go. Back at the house he could see Grandfather sitting on the porch, looking small and thin and black.

Jody gave up and went to sit on the steps at the old man's feet.

"Back already? Did you kill the mice?"

"No, sir. I'll kill them some other day."

The morning flies buzzed close to the ground and the ants dashed about in front of the steps. The heavy smell of sage slipped down the hill. The porch boards grew warm in the sunshine.

Jody hardly knew when Grandfather started to talk. "I shouldn't stay here, feeling the way I do." He examined his strong old hands. "I feel as though the crossing wasn't worth doing." His eyes moved up the side-hill and stopped on a motionless hawk perched on a dead limb. "I tell those old stories, but they're not what I want to tell. I only know how I want people to feel when I tell them.

"It wasn't Indians that were important, nor adventures, nor even getting out here. It was a whole bunch of people made into one big crawling beast. And I was the head. It was westering and westering. Every man wanted something for himself, but the big beast that was all of them wanted only westering. I was the leader, but if I hadn't been there, someone else would have been the head. The thing had to have a head.

"Under the little bushes the shadows were black at white noonday. When we saw the mountains at last, we cried—all of us. But it wasn't getting here that mattered, it was movement and westering.

"We carried life out here and set it down the way those ants carry eggs. And I was the leader. The westering was as big as God, and the slow steps that made the movement piled up and piled up until the continent was crossed.

"Then we came down to the sea, and it was done." He stopped and wiped his eyes until the rims were red. "That's what I should be telling instead of stories."

When Jody spoke, Grandfather started and looked down at him. "Maybe I could lead the people some day," Jody said.

The old man smiled. "There's no place to go. There's the ocean to stop you. There's a line of old men along the shore hating the ocean because it stopped them."

"In boats I might, sir."

"No place to go, Jody. Every place is taken. But that's not the worst—no, not the worst. Westering has died out of the people. Westering isn't a hunger any more.

It's all done. Your father is right. It is finished." He laced his fingers on his knee and looked at them.

Jody felt very sad. "If you'd like a glass of lemonade I could make it for you."

Grandfather was about to refuse, and then he saw Jody's face. "That would be nice," he said. "Yes, it would be nice to drink a lemonade."

Jody ran into the kitchen where his mother was wiping the last of the breakfast dishes. "Can I have a lemon to make a lemonade for Grandfather?"

His mother mimicked—"And another lemon to make a lemonade for you."

"No, ma'am. I don't want one."

"Jody! You're sick!" Then she stopped suddenly. "Take a lemon out of the cooler," she said softly. "Here, I'll reach the squeezer down to you."

1938

Nathanael West
1903–1940

As a teenager, Nathan Weinstein went to a summer camp in the Adirondack Mountains called Camp Paradox—an appropriate start to the strange, brief life of the writer who changed his name to Nathanael West, wrote four vividly grotesque short novels in eight years, and died with his bride of six months in a car crash at the age of thirty-seven. West was born in New York City, the first child of prosperous Lithuanian Jewish immigrants. But his parents' hope that he would prove to be a success in school and then in business soon was dashed. An indifferent student, West spent most of his boyhood and youth playing baseball and reading unassigned books. Tolstoy, Dostoevski, Flaubert, and Henry James were far more important to him than school assignments. In 1921, having left high school without a diploma, he forged the documents he needed to gain admittance to Tufts University, only to withdraw within two months because of poor grades. Still restless, he gained admission to Brown University by passing himself off as another student, also named Nathan Weinstein, who possessed the proper credentials for admission and had already matriculated.

While at Brown, West appropriated the clothes of a dandy and the manner of a gentile in a somewhat frantic attempt to disown his own Jewishness. Intellectually and imaginatively, he experimented with different strains of the aesthete, the decadent, and the mystic. He reveled in readings from medieval Catholicism, the French Symbolists, Friedrich Nietzsche, and James Joyce and in the bizarre stories of J. K. Huysmans and Arthur Machen, as well as in the latest experiments in literary form. Discovering that his double had already conveniently passed the subjects he most disliked, such as science and mathematics, he began to concentrate on English and other more congenial subjects. Two and one-half years later, in 1924, he graduated.

Degree in hand, West persuaded his father to postpone the time when he, as the only son, would be expected to join the family's business as a building contractor. He spent the next two years in Paris, reading and trying to write, then returned to New York, where he again begged off working for his father, this time to clerk first in one small hotel and then another. Over the next several years he continued to write and began to cadge free rooms for such indigent writer-friends as Dashiell Hammett, Erskine Caldwell, and James T. Farrell.

By ruining his family's business, the stock market crash of 1929 saved West from ever having to return to the fold. In 1931 he published his first novel, *The Dream Life of Balso Snell,* under his new name, Nathanael West. Although *Balso Snell* went virtually unnoticed, West's second novel, *Miss Lonelyhearts* (written at the slow speed of a hundred words a day), attracted considerable attention when it first appeared in 1933. Then, just as the demand for copies was increasing, West's publisher went bankrupt, with only eight hundred copies sold.

Between 1932 and 1934 West did a stint editing little magazines, including work with the poet William Carlos Williams on *Contact.* In 1934 he published a novel, *A Cool Million,* which vanished from sight almost as soon as it had appeared. Disheartened, West moved to Hollywood to try his luck at screenwriting, which he took to with surprising ease. Disillusioned by California, West returned to New York, only to decide that the East was a dead end. In 1935 he went back to Hollywood, trying once again to follow the advice of Horace Greeley's nineteenth-century motto—"Go west, young man"—which West insisted had been both the inspiration for the name he had created for himself in 1931 and the catalyst for his first trip to California in 1934.

Back in Hollywood, West soon began making a great deal of money. He had time not only for writing but also for hunting, which he loved, and radical politics, which he needed. A speedy scriptwriter, he spent his spare time hunting, joining in Communist rallies, and completing *The Day of the Locust.* Published in 1939, *The Day of the Locust* received good reviews but had poor sales because, according to his publisher, women did not take to the story. Happiness came to him in 1940 with marriage in April to Eileen McKenney, the subject of Ruth McKenney's *My Sister Eileen* (1938), as well as with a better job at Columbia Pictures and the sale of the movie rights to *A Cool Million.* In December he and his wife were killed in an automobile accident near El Centro, California, on their return from a hunting trip in Mexico. His body was returned to the East at his family's request and laid to rest in a Jewish cemetery.

During the years following his death, Nathanael West gradually acquired a large underground reputation. It was not until 1957, however, with the publication of his collected novels, that he began to receive public acclaim. His talent for parody, brilliant nastiness, grotesquerie, and unsympathetically rendered characters is immense. At the time of his death, West was planning to move on to serious political novels as well as "simple, warm, and kindly books." But his enormous conscience did not lend itself to earnest expression, which in his hands too easily became maudlin. He cared about the people he portrayed, but preaching about their failings was not his way of showing his concern. His satires are fast and funny rather than somber and uplifting. His vision of horror and betrayal, apocalypse and self-delusion sometimes combines the brevity of Poe and the mordancy of Melville, but it always retains the disillusionment of the bright and strangely earnest young man who had read a great deal of Dostoevski and Nietzsche while conning his way through college.

In West's strange art, bizarre fantasies, sexual confusion, social alienation, and tortured sensibilities mingle and collide. The masks his characters don and the roles they play, like the role of Miss Lonelyhearts, come somehow to dominate and even tyrannize them. In his art, society tends rather to manipulate and use human beings, even to mock and taunt them, than to support, serve, and sustain them. At times the world of Miss Lonelyhearts seems almost like a cartoon. It is a stark world, a world of grotesque, misshapen characters, of strange, contorted images, of apocalyptic signs. Yet despite the stark contrasts that define it, it is not a simple world. Miss Lonelyhearts, West's fool of pity, is only in part a victim of his world and its confusions; he is also a victim of himself.

Further Reading:
J. Light, *Nathanael West: An Interpretive Study*, 1961.
S. Hyman, *Nathanael West*, 1962.
R. Reid, *Nathanael West*, 1962.
V. Comerchero, *Nathanael West, The Ironic Prophet*, 1964.
R. Reid, *The Fiction of Nathanael West: No Redeemer, No Promised Land*, 1967.
J. Martin, *Nathanael West: The Art of His Life*, 1970.
Nathanel West: A Collection of Critical Essays, ed. J. Martin, 1971.
N. Scott, *Nathanael West: A Critical Essay*, 1971.
I. Malin, *Nathanael West's Novels*, 1972.
Nathanael West: The Cheaters and the Cheated: A Collection of Critical Essays, ed. D. Madden, 1973.
K. Widmer, *Nathanael West*, 1982.

Text:
The Complete Works of Nathanael West, 1957, 1960, 1970.
See also *The Collected Works of Nathanael West,* 1975.

---

from Miss Lonelyhearts

Miss Lonelyhearts, Help Me, Help Me

The Miss Lonelyhearts of The New York *Post-Dispatch* (Are-you-in-trouble?—Do-you-need-advice?—Write-to-Miss-Lonelyhearts-and-she-will-help-you) sat at his desk and stared at a piece of white cardboard. On it a prayer had been printed by Shrike, the feature editor.

"Soul of Miss L, glorify me.
Body of Miss L, nourish me
Blood of Miss L, intoxicate me.
Tears of Miss L, wash me.
Oh good Miss L, excuse my plea,
And hide me in your heart,
And defend me from mine enemies.
Help me, Miss L, help me, help me.
In sæcula sæculorum.[1] Amen."

Although the deadline was less than a quarter of an hour away, he was still working on his leader. He had gone as far as: "Life *is* worth while, for it is full of dreams

---

[1] Latin: "world without end."

and peace, gentleness and ecstasy, and faith that burns like a clear white flame on a grim dark altar." But he found it impossible to continue. The letters were no longer funny. He could not go on finding the same joke funny thirty times a day for months on end. And on most days he received more than thirty letters, all of them alike, stamped from the dough of suffering with a heart-shaped cookie knife.

On his desk were piled those he had received this morning. He started through them again, searching for some clue to a sincere answer.

Dear Miss Lonelyhearts—

I am in such pain I don't know what to do sometimes I think I will kill myself my kidneys hurt so much. My husband thinks no woman can be a good catholic and not have children irregardless of the pain. I was married honorable from our church but I never knew what married life meant as I never was told about man and wife. My grandmother never told me and she was the only mother I had but made a big mistake by not telling me as it dont pay to be inocent and is only a big disapointment. I have 7 children in 12 yrs and ever since the last 2 I have been so sick. I was operatored on twice and my husband promised no more children on the doctors advice as he said I might die but when I got back from the hospital he broke his promise and now I am going to have a baby and I dont think I can stand it my kidneys hurt so much. I am so sick and scared because I cant have an abortion on account of being a catholic and my husband so religious. I cry all the time it hurts so much and I dont know what to do.

Yours respectfully,
Sick-of-it-all

Miss Lonelyhearts threw the letter into an open drawer and lit a cigarette.

Dear Miss Lonelyhearts—

I am sixteen years old now and I dont know what to do and would appreciate it if you could tell me what to do. When I was a little girl it was not so bad because I got used to the kids on the block makeing fun of me, but now I would like to have boy friends like the other girls and go out on Saturday nites, but no boy will take me because I was born without a nose—although I am a good dancer and have a nice shape and my father buys me pretty clothes.

I sit and look at myself all day and cry. I have a big hole in the middle of my face that scares people even myself so I cant blame the boys for not wanting to take me out. My mother loves me, but she crys terrible when she looks at me.

What did I do to deserve such a terrible bad fate? Even if I did do some bad things I didnt do any before I was a year old and I was born this way. I asked Papa and he says he doesnt know, but that maybe I did something in the other world before I was born or that maybe I was being punished for his sins. I dont believe that because he is a very nice man. Ought I commit suicide?

Sincerely yours,
Desperate

The cigarette was imperfect and refused to draw. Miss Lonelyhearts took it out of his mouth and stared at it furiously. He fought himself quiet, then lit another one.

Dear Miss Lonelyhearts—

I am writing to you for my little sister Gracie because something awfull hapened to her and I am afraid to tell mother about it. I am 15 years old and Gracie is 13 and we live in Brooklyn. Gracie is deaf and dumb and biger than me but not very smart on account of being deaf and dumb. She plays on the roof of our house and dont go to school except to deaf and dumb school twice a week on tuesdays and thursdays. Mother makes her play on the roof because we dont want her to get run over as she aint very smart. Last week a man came on the roof and did something dirty to her. She told me about it and I dont know what to do as I am afraid to tell mother on account of her being liable to beat Gracie up. I am afraid that Gracie is going to have a baby and I listened to her stomack last night for a long time to see if I could hear the baby but I couldn't. If I tell mother she will beat Gracie up awfull because I am the only one who loves her and last time when she tore her dress they loked her in the closet for 2 days and if the boys on the blok hear about it they will say dirty things like they did on Peewee Conors sister the time she got caught in the lots. So please what would you do if the same hapened in your family.

Yours truly,
Harold S.

He stopped reading. Christ was the answer, but, if he did not want to get sick, he had to stay away from the Christ business. Besides, Christ was Shrike's particular joke. "Soul of Miss L, glorify me. Body of Miss L, save me. Blood of . . ." He turned to his typewriter.

Although his cheap clothes had too much style, he still looked like the son of a Baptist minister. A beard would become him, would accent his Old-Testament look. But even without a beard no one could fail to recognize the New England puritan. His forehead was high and narrow. His nose was long and fleshless. His bony chin was shaped and cleft like a hoof. On seeing him for the first time, Shrike had smiled and said, "The Susan Chesters, the Beatrice Fairfaxes and the Miss Lonelyhearts are the priests of twentieth-century America."

A copy boy came up to tell him that Shrike wanted to know if the stuff was ready. He bent over the typewriter and began pounding its keys.

But before he had written a dozen words, Shrike leaned over his shoulder. "The same old stuff," Shrike said. "Why don't you give them something new and hopeful? Tell them about art. Here, I'll dictate:

"Art Is a Way Out.

"Do not let life overwhelm you. When the old paths are choked with the débris of failure, look for newer and fresher paths. Art is just such a path. Art is distilled from suffering. As Mr. Polnikoff exclaimed through his fine Russian beard, when, at the age of eighty-six, he gave up his business to learn Chinese, 'We are, as yet, only at the beginning. . . .'

"Art Is One of Life's Richest Offerings.

"For those who have not the talent to create, there is appreciation. For those . . .

"Go on from there."

Miss Lonelyhearts and the Cripple

Miss Lonelyhearts dodged Betty because she made him feel ridiculous. He was still trying to cling to his humility, and the farther he got below self-laughter, the easier it was for him to practice it. When Betty telephoned, he refused to answer and after he had twice failed to call her back, she left him alone.

One day, about a week after he had returned from the country, Goldsmith asked him out for a drink. When he accepted, he made himself so humble that Goldsmith was frightened and almost suggested a doctor.

They found Shrike in Delehanty's and joined him at the bar. Goldsmith tried to whisper something to him about Miss Lonelyhearts' condition, but he was drunk and refused to listen. He caught only part of what Goldsmith was trying to say.

"I must differ with you, my good Goldsmith," Shrike said. "Don't call sick those who have faith. They are the well. It is you who are sick."

Goldsmith did not reply and Shrike turned to Miss Lonelyhearts. "Come, tell us, brother, how it was that you first came to believe. Was it music in a church, or the death of a loved one, or mayhap, some wise old priest?"

The familiar jokes no longer had any effect on Miss Lonelyhearts. He smiled at Shrike as the saints are supposed to have smiled at those about to martyr them.

"Ah, but how stupid of me," Shrike continued. "It was the letters, of course. Did I myself not say that the Miss Lonelyhearts are the priests of twentieth-century America?"

Goldsmith laughed, and Shrike, in order to keep him laughing, used an old trick; he appeared to be offended. "Goldsmith, you are the nasty product of this unbelieving age. You cannot believe, you can only laugh. You take everything with a bag of salt and forget that salt is the enemy of fire as well as of ice. Be warned, the salt you use is not Attic salt, it is coarse butcher's salt. It doesn't preserve; it kills."

The bartender who was standing close by, broke in to address Miss Lonelyhearts. "Pardon me, sir, but there's a gent here named Doyle who wants to meet you. He says you know his wife."

Before Miss Lonelyhearts could reply, he beckoned to someone standing at the other end of the bar. The signal was answered by a little cripple, who immediately started in their direction. He used a cane and dragged one of his feet behind him in a box-shaped shoe with a four-inch sole. As he hobbled along, he made many waste motions, like those of a partially destroyed insect.

The bartender introduced the cripple as Mr. Peter Doyle. Doyle was very excited and shook hands twice all around, then with a wave that was meant to be sporting, called for a round of drinks.

Before lifting his glass, Shrike carefully inspected the cripple. When he had finished, he winked at Miss Lonelyhearts and said, "Here's to humanity." He patted Doyle on the back. "Mankind, mankind . . ." he sighed, wagging his head sadly. "What is man that . . ."

The bartender broke in again on behalf of his friend and tried to change the conversation to familiar ground. "Mr. Doyle inspects meters for the gas company."

"And an excellent job it must be," Shrike said. "He should be able to give us the benefit of a different viewpoint. We newspapermen are limited in many ways and I like to hear both sides of a case."

Doyle had been staring at Miss Lonelyhearts as though searching for something, but he now turned to Shrike and tried to be agreeable. "You know what people say, Mr. Shrike?"

"No, my good man, what is it that people say?"

"Everybody's got a frigidaire nowadays, and they say that we meter inspectors take the place of the iceman in the stories." He tried, rather diffidently, to leer.

"What!" Shrike roared at him. "I can see, sir, that you are not the man for us. You can know nothing about humanity; you are humanity. I leave you to Miss Lonelyhearts." He called to Goldsmith and stalked away.

The cripple was confused and angry. "Your friend is a nut," he said. Miss Lonelyhearts was still smiling, but the character of his smile had changed. It had become full of sympathy and a little sad.

The new smile was for Doyle and he knew it. He smiled back gratefully.

"Oh, I forgot," Doyle said, "the wife asked me, if I bumped into you, to ask you to our house to eat. That's why I made Jake introduce us."

Miss Lonelyhearts was busy with his smile and accepted without thinking of the evening he had spent with Mrs. Doyle. The cripple felt honored and shook hands for a third time. It was evidently his only social gesture.

After a few more drinks, when Doyle said that he was tired, Miss Lonelyhearts suggested that they go into the back room. They found a table and sat opposite each other.

The cripple had a very strange face. His eyes failed to balance; his mouth was not under his nose; his forehead was square and bony; and his round chin was like a forehead in miniature. He looked like one of those composite photographs used by screen magazines in guessing contests.

They sat staring at each other until the strain of wordless communication began to excite them both. Doyle made vague, needless adjustments to his clothing. Miss Lonelyhearts found it very difficult to keep his smile steady.

When the cripple finally labored into speech, Miss Lonelyhearts was unable to understand him. He listened hard for a few minutes and realized that Doyle was making no attempt to be understood. He was giving birth to groups of words that lived inside of him as things, a jumble of the retorts he had meant to make when insulted and the private curses against fate that experience had taught him to swallow.

Like a priest, Miss Lonelyhearts turned his face slightly away. He watched the play of the cripple's hands. At first they conveyed nothing but excitement, then gradually they became pictorial. They lagged behind to illustrate a matter with which he was already finished, or ran ahead to illustrate something he had not yet begun to talk about. As he grew more articulate, his hands stopped trying to aid his speech and began to dart in and out of his clothing. One of them suddenly emerged from a pocket of his coat, dragging some sheets of letter paper. He forced these on Miss Lonelyhearts.

Dear Miss Lonelyhearts—

I am kind of ashamed to write you because a man like me dont take stock in things like that but my wife told me you were a man and not some dopey woman so I thought I would write to you after reading your answer to Disillusioned. I am a cripple 41 yrs of age which I have been all my life and I have never let myself get blue until lately when I have been feeling lousy all the time on account of not getting anywhere and asking myself what is it all for. You have a education so I figured may be you no. What I want to no is why I go around pulling my leg up and down stairs reading meters for the gas company for a stinking $22.50 per while the bosses ride around in swell cars living off the fat of the land. Dont think I am a greasy red. I read where they shoot cripples in Russia because they cant work but

I can work better than any park bum and support a wife and child to. But thats not what I am writing you about. What I want to no is what is it all for my pulling my god damed leg along the streets and down in stinking cellars with it all the time hurting fit to burst so that near quitting time I am crazy with pain and when I get home all I hear is money money which aint no home for a man like me. What I want to no is what in hell is the use day after day with a foot like mine when you have to go around pulling and scrambling for a lousy three squares with a toothache in it that comes from useing the foot so much. The doctor told me I ought to rest it for six months but who will pay me when I am resting it. But that aint what I mean either because you might tell me to change my job and where could I get another one I am lucky to have one at all. It aint the job that I am complaining about but what I want to no is what is the whole stinking business for.

Please write me an answer not in the paper because my wife reads your stuff and I dont want her to no I wrote to you because I always said the papers is crap but I figured maybe you no something about it because you have read a lot of books and I never even finished high.

Yours truly,
Peter Doyle

While Miss Lonelyhearts was puzzling out the crabbed writing, Doyle's damp hand accidentally touched his under the table. He jerked away, but then drove his hand back and forced it to clasp the cripple's. After finishing the letter, he did not let go, but pressed it firmly with all the love he could manage. At first the cripple covered his embarrassment by disguising the meaning of the clasp with a handshake, but he soon gave in to it and they sat silently, hand in hand.

Miss Lonelyhearts Has a Religious Experience

After a long night and morning, towards noon, Miss Lonelyhearts welcomed the arrival of fever. It promised heat and mentally unmotivated violence. The promise was soon fulfilled; the rock became a furnace.

He fastened his eyes on the Christ that hung on the wall opposite his bed. As he stared at it, it became a bright fly, spinning with quick grace on a background of blood velvet sprinkled with tiny nerve stars.

Everything else in the room was dead—chairs, table, pencils, clothes, books. He thought of this black world of things as a fish. And he was right, for it suddenly rose to the bright bait on the wall. It rose with a splash of music and he saw its shining silver belly.

Christ is life and light.

"Christ! Christ!" This shout echoed through the innermost cells of his body.

He moved his head to a cooler spot on the pillow and the vein in his forehead became less swollen. He felt clean and fresh. His heart was a rose and in his skull another rose bloomed.

The room was full of grace. A sweet, clean grace, not washed clean, but clean as the innersides of the inner petals of a newly forced rosebud.

Delight was also in the room. It was like a gentle wind, and his nerves rippled under it like small blue flowers in a pasture.

He was conscious of two rhythms that were slowly becoming one. When they became one, his identification with God was complete. His heart was the one heart, the heart of God. And his brain was likewise God's.

God said, "Will you accept it, now?"

And he replied, "I accept, I accept."

He immediately began to plan a new life and his future conduct as Miss Lonelyhearts. He submitted drafts of his column to God and God approved them. God approved his every thought.

Suddenly the door bell rang. He climbed out of bed and went into the hall to see who was coming. It was Doyle, the cripple, and he was slowly working his way up the stairs.

God had sent him so that Miss Lonelyhearts could perform a miracle and be certain of his conversion. It was a sign. He would embrace the cripple and the cripple would be made whole again, even as he, a spiritual cripple, had been made whole.

He rushed down the stairs to meet Doyle with his arms spread for the miracle.

Doyle was carrying something wrapped in a newspaper. When he saw Miss Lonelyhearts, he put his hand inside the package and stopped. He shouted some kind of a warning, but Miss Lonelyhearts continued his charge. He did not understand the cripple's shout and heard it as a cry for help from Desperate, Harold S., Catholic-mother, Broken-hearted, Broad-shoulders, Sick-of-it-all, Disillusioned-with-tubercular-husband. He was running to succor them with love.

The cripple turned to escape, but he was too slow and Miss Lonelyhearts caught him.

While they were struggling, Betty came in through the street door. She called to them to stop and started up the stairs. The cripple saw her cutting off his escape and tried to get rid of the package. He pulled his hand out. The gun inside the package exploded and Miss Lonelyhearts fell, dragging the cripple with him. They both rolled part of the way down the stairs.

1933

Richard Wright
1908–1960

Richard Wright was born into an impoverished black sharecropper family on a cotton plantation near Natchez, Mississippi, on September 4, 1908. His father deserted the family when Wright was five years old, and when he was ten his mother suffered the first of a series of strokes that left her partially paralyzed. As a child Wright was shuttled about among various relatives and spent some time in an orphanage. A good student, he graduated from Smith-Robinson High School in Jackson, Mississippi, in 1925 and moved to Memphis, where he took menial jobs and began writing. Two years later he moved to Chicago, then in 1937 to New York City. In 1947 he moved to Paris, where he lived as an expatriate until his fatal heart attack on November 28, 1960.

Although each of the places Wright lived marked his life, none marked it more deeply than Mississippi, which inspired the characteristic tone of anguish and anger that we find in all his best work. The deprivation that Wright felt in the Deep South was partly physical—he was often hungry, and he was always poor. But it was also psychological, intellectual, and spiritual. Both his mother and his maternal grandmother, who helped raise him, were rigidly moralistic and believed in harsh corporal punishment. In the society around him, the threat of far worse forms of violence was constant. In the schools he attended, education was not only limited but restrictive. In Memphis he once tried to get books from the library by forging a note from a white borrower: *"Dear Madam:"* he later wrote in "The Library Card," *"Will you please let this nigger boy . . . have some books by H. L. Mencken?"* The deception reflects not only the iconoclastic role Mencken later came to play for Wright but also the sense Wright had of having been deliberately denied access to the books he most needed. An avid reader, Wright often turned to books for the emotional fulfillment he could not find in life: "It had been only through books," he wrote, ". . . that I had managed to keep myself alive."

After his move to Chicago, Wright worked as a porter, a dishwasher, a salesman for a disreputable burial insurance agency, and as a postal worker. With the onset of the Depression, he was forced to go on relief and work as a street sweeper before gravitating toward the Federal Negro Theater and the Federal Writer's Project, both of which were sponsored by the WPA. Wright also became active in radical politics; he began writing poetry for leftist journals, and in 1933 he joined the Chicago John Reed Club shortly before officially becoming a member of the Communist party. In 1935 Wright began to contribute articles and reviews to the intellectual and politically radical journal, *The New Masses.*

With his move to New York City in 1937, Wright became Harlem editor of the Communist newspaper *The Daily Worker* and soon began writing the books that made him famous. That year he finished his first novel, *Lawd Today,* an experimental work (not published until 1963) about twenty-four hours in the life of a middle-class Chicago black that Wright self-consciously modeled after James Joyce's *Ulysses* and John Dos Passos's *U.S.A.* A year later Wright published his first book, *Uncle Tom's Children: Four Novellas,* a collection of stories that viscerally concern racial prejudice, black resistance, and violence in the Deep South. Wright said of one of the stories, "Long Black Song," that he was influenced by both Gertrude Stein and Ernest Hemingway as he tried to find a way to handle serious social issues in a simple, naturalistic style. In 1940, while on a Guggenheim fellowship, Wright published *Native Son,* the grim, nightmarish tale of a young black man who accidentally murders the liberal daughter of his white employer. As Theodore Dreiser had done with *An American Tragedy* (1925), Wright based his story on an actual murder case; like Dreiser's, Wright's intentions were more literary than documentary. He wanted, he wrote, to put the case of the Negro squarely into American literary tradition:

> We do have in the Negro the embodiment of a past, tragic enough to appease the spiritual hunger of even a [Henry] James and we have in the oppression of the Negro a shadow athwart our national life dense and heavy enough to satisfy even the gloomy broodings of a Hawthorne. And if Poe were alive, he would not have to invent horror; horror would invent him.

An enormous publishing success, *Native Son* was the first book written by an American black to be selected for the Book of the Month Club.

In 1941 Wright wrote the text for *Twelve Million Black Voices,* a book that combined words and pictures to express the "folk history of the Negro in the United States." The following year, while giving a talk at Fisk University on growing up black in America, Wright decided to compose his autobiography:

> It was not half-way through my speech that it crashed upon me that I was saying things that whites had forbidden Negroes to say. . . . Later, I learned that I had accidentally blundered into the secret, black, hidden core of race relations in the United States. That core is this: nobody is ever expected to speak honestly about this problem.

The result of his autobiographical efforts was another best-selling book, *Black Boy* (1945), which contained the story of his life up until his move to Chicago. Deleted at the time were several chapters dealing with his life in Chicago and his increasing disenchantment with the Communist party; this material was eventually published posthumously as *American Hunger* (1977). Wright had left the Communist party in 1944, following a bitter struggle in which the party accused him of harboring anti-Stalinist sentiments and resisting party discipline.

In the spring of 1946 Wright and his family visited France for several months on the invitation of Gertrude Stein. The Wrights returned to Paris in 1947, where they settled permanently and where Wright, by now a vehement anti-Communist, met Jean-Paul Sartre and immersed himself in existentialist philosophy. Wright's work had long concerned itself with such issues as freedom, alienation, dread, and identity through violence ("When a man kills, it's for something. . . . I didn't know I was really alive in this world until I felt things hard enough to kill for 'em," says the hero of *Native Son*), but in his later work, such as *The Outsider* (1953), *Savage Holiday* (1954), and *The Long Dream* (1958), philosophy became a more explicit and less effective part of his fiction. These novels focus on heroes who, finding themselves cut off from the world around them as well as from the past, determine to make virtues of isolation and rootlessness. Throughout the 1950s Wright also traveled extensively in an attempt to understand the origins and legacy of black slavery: *Black Power: A Report of Reactions in a Land of Pathos* (1954) is an account of a trip to the Gold Coast (Ghana); *The Color Curtain* (1956) reports on his coverage of a conference in Indonesia; and *Pagan Spain* (1957) is an attempt to find answers to the history of slavery in the paradoxes of Spanish culture. In 1957 Wright also brought out a collection of his European lectures on politics, racism, and black literature. A collection of short stories, *Eight Men,* was published posthumously in 1961.

Wright's early work, which is also his most powerful, focuses on the large demographic shift of black people from the rural South toward the urban North. In these works his heroes struggle against accepting both the "place" of powerlessness and the "role" of subservience and silence that their society has assigned them. Since this struggle often leads Wright's heroes into defiance that society regards as criminal—and sometimes leads them directly into criminality— they characteristically find themselves threatened by social rejection as well as terrible punishment. Both of these threats, one psychological, the other physical, haunt Wright's characters as they attempt to force people who occupy positions of power and prestige to see, hear, and acknowledge them. It was a struggle Wright, too, continually endured: "I had elected," he wrote in *American Hunger,* "in my fevered search for honorable adjustment to the American scene, not to submit and in doing so I had embraced the daily horror of anxiety, of tension, of eternal disquiet."

Further Reading:
J. Baldwin, "Everybody's Protest Novel" in *Notes of a Native Son,* 1955.
I. Howe, "Black Boys and Native Sons" in *A World More Attractive,* 1963.
R. Ellison, "Richard Wright's Blues" in *Shadow and Act,* 1964.
C. Webb, *Richard Wright: A Biography,* 1968.
D. McCall, *The Example of Richard Wright,* 1969.

Texts:
Black Boy, 1945.
"Long Black Song" from *Uncle Tom's Children,* 1940.

from Black Boy

Chapter Thirteen: [The Library Card]

One morning I arrived early at work and went into the bank lobby where the Negro porter was mopping. I stood at a counter and picked up the Memphis *Commercial Appeal* and began my free reading of the press. I came finally to the editorial page and saw an article dealing with one H. L. Mencken. I knew by hearsay that he was the editor of the *American Mercury,* but aside from that I knew nothing about him. The article was a furious denunciation of Mencken, concluding with one, hot, short sentence: Mencken is a fool.

I wondered what on earth this Mencken had done to call down upon him the scorn of the South. The only people I had ever heard denounced in the South were Negroes, and this man was not a Negro. Then what ideas did Mencken hold that made a newspaper like the *Commercial Appeal* castigate him publicly? Undoubtedly he must be advocating ideas that the South did not like. Were there, then, people other than Negroes who criticized the South? I knew that during the Civil War the South had hated northern whites, but I had not encountered such hate during my life. Knowing no more of Mencken than I did at that moment, I felt a vague sympathy for him. Had not the South, which had assigned me the role of a non-man, cast at him its hardest words?

Now, how could I find out about this Mencken? There was a huge library near the riverfront, but I knew that Negroes were not allowed to patronize its shelves any more than they were the parks and playgrounds of the city. I had gone into the library several times to get books for the white men on the job. Which of them would now help me to get books? And how could I read them without causing concern to the white men with whom I worked? I had so far been successful in hiding my thoughts and feelings from them, but I knew that I would create hostility if I went about this business of reading in a clumsy way.

I weighed the personalities of the men on the job. There was Don, a Jew; but I distrusted him. His position was not much better than mine and I knew that he was uneasy and insecure; he had always treated me in an offhand, bantering way that barely concealed his contempt. I was afraid to ask him to help me to get books; his frantic desire to demonstrate a racial solidarity with the whites against Negroes might make him betray me.

Then how about the boss? No, he was a Baptist and I had the suspicion that he would not be quite able to comprehend why a black boy would want to read Mencken. There were other white men on the job whose attitudes showed clearly that they were Kluxers or sympathizers, and they were out of the question.

There remained only one man whose attitude did not fit into an anti-Negro category, for I had heard the white men refer to him as a "Pope lover." He was an Irish Catholic and was hated by the white Southerners. I knew that he read books, because I had got him volumes from the library several times. Since he, too, was an object of hatred, I felt that he might refuse me but would hardly betray me. I hesitated, weighing and balancing the imponderable realities.

One morning I paused before the Catholic fellow's desk.

"I want to ask you a favor," I whispered to him.

"What is it?"

"I want to read. I can't get books from the library. I wonder if you'd let me use your card?"

He looked at me suspiciously.

"My card is full most of the time," he said.

"I see," I said and waited, posing my question silently.

"You're not trying to get me into trouble, are you, boy?" he asked, staring at me.

"Oh, no, sir."

"What book do you want?"

"A book by H. L. Mencken."

"Which one?"

"I don't know. Has he written more than one?"

"He has written several."

"I didn't know that."

"What makes you want to read Mencken?"

"Oh, I just saw his name in the newspaper," I said.

"It's good of you to want to read," he said. "But you ought to read the right things."

I said nothing. Would he want to supervise my reading?

"Let me think," he said. "I'll figure out something."

I turned from him and he called me back. He stared at me quizzically.

"Richard, don't mention this to the other white men," he said.

"I understand," I said. "I won't say a word."

A few days later he called me to him.

"I've got a card in my wife's name," he said. "Here's mine."

"Thank you, sir."

"Do you think you can manage it?"

"I'll manage fine," I said.

"If they suspect you, you'll get in trouble," he said.

"I'll write the same kind of notes to the library that you wrote when you sent me for books," I told him. "I'll sign your name."

He laughed.

"Go ahead. Let me see what you get," he said.

That afternoon I addressed myself to forging a note. Now, what were the names of books written by H. L. Mencken? I did not know any of them. I finally wrote what I thought would be a foolproof note: *Dear Madam: Will you please let this nigger boy*—I used the word "nigger" to make the librarian feel that I could not possibly be the author of the note—*have some books by H. L. Mencken?* I forged the white man's name.

I entered the library as I had always done when on errands for whites, but I felt that I would somehow slip up and betray myself. I doffed my hat, stood a respectful distance from the desk, looked as unbookish as possible, and waited for the white patrons to be taken care of. When the desk was clear of people, I still waited. The white librarian looked at me.

"What do you want, boy?"

As though I did not possess the power of speech, I stepped forward and simply handed her the forged note, not parting my lips.

"What books by Mencken does he want?" she asked.

"I don't know, ma'am," I said, avoiding her eyes.

"Who gave you this card?"

"Mr. Falk," I said.

"Where is he?"

"He's at work, at the M—— Optical Company," I said. "I've been in here for him before."

"I remember," the woman said. "But he never wrote notes like this."

Oh, God, she's suspicious. Perhaps she would not let me have the books? If she had turned her back at that moment, I would have ducked out the door and never gone back. Then I thought of a bold idea.

"You can call him up, ma'am," I said, my heart pounding.

"You're not using these books, are you?" she asked pointedly.

"Oh, no, ma'am. I can't read."

"I don't know what he wants by Mencken," she said under her breath.

I knew now that I had won; she was thinking of other things and the race question had gone out of her mind. She went to the shelves. Once or twice she looked over her shoulder at me, as though she was still doubtful. Finally she came forward with two books in her hand.

"I'm sending him two books," she said. "But tell Mr. Falk to come in next time, or send me the names of the books he wants. I don't know what he wants to read."

I said nothing. She stamped the card and handed me the books. Not daring to glance at them, I went out of the library, fearing that the woman would call me back for further questioning. A block away from the library I opened one of the books and read a title: *A Book of Prefaces*. I was nearing my nineteenth birthday and I did not know how to pronounce the word "preface." I thumbed the pages and saw strange words and strange names. I shook my head, disappointed. I looked at the other book;

it was called *Prejudices*. I knew what that word meant; I had heard it all my life. And right off I was on guard against Mencken's books. Why would a man want to call a book *Prejudices?* The word was so stained with all my memories of racial hate that I could not conceive of anybody using it for a title. Perhaps I had made a mistake about Mencken? A man who had prejudices must be wrong.

When I showed the books to Mr. Falk, he looked at me and frowned.

"That librarian might telephone you," I warned him.

"That's all right," he said. "But when you're through reading those books, I want you to tell me what you get out of them."

That night in my rented room, while letting the hot water run over my can of pork and beans in the sink, I opened *A Book of Prefaces* and began to read. I was jarred and shocked by the style, the clear, clean, sweeping sentences. Why did he write like that? And how did one write like that? I pictured the man as a raging demon, slashing with his pen, consumed with hate, denouncing everything American, extolling everything European or German, laughing at the weaknesses of people, mocking God, authority. What was this? I stood up, trying to realize what reality lay behind the meaning of the words . . . Yes, this man was fighting, fighting with words. He was using words as a weapon, using them as one would use a club. Could words be weapons? Well, yes, for here they were. Then, maybe, perhaps, I could use them as a weapon? No. It frightened me. I read on and what amazed me was not what he said, but how on earth anybody had the courage to say it.

Occasionally I glanced up to reassure myself that I was alone in the room. Who were these men about whom Mencken was talking so passionately? Who was Anatole France? Joseph Conrad? Sinclair Lewis, Sherwood Anderson, Dostoevski, George Moore, Gustave Flaubert, Maupassant, Tolstoy, Frank Harris, Mark Twain, Thomas Hardy, Arnold Bennett, Stephen Crane, Zola, Norris, Gorky, Bergson, Ibsen, Balzac, Bernard Shaw, Dumas, Poe, Thomas Mann, O. Henry, Dreiser, H. G. Wells, Gogol, T. S. Eliot, Gide, Baudelaire, Edgar Lee Masters, Stendhal, Turgenev, Huneker, Nietzsche, and scores of others? Were these men real? Did they exist or had they existed? And how did one pronounce their names?

I ran across many words whose meanings I did not know, and I either looked them up in a dictionary or, before I had a chance to do that, encountered the word in a context that made its meaning clear. But what strange world was this? I concluded the book with the conviction that I had somehow overlooked something terribly important in life. I had once tried to write, had once reveled in feeling, had let my crude imagination roam, but the impulse to dream had been slowly beaten out of me by experience. Now it surged up again and I hungered for books, new ways of looking and seeing. It was not a matter of believing or disbelieving what I read, but of feeling something new, of being affected by something that made the look of the world different.

As dawn broke I ate my pork and beans, feeling dopey, sleepy. I went to work, but the mood of the book would not die; it lingered, coloring everything I saw, heard, did. I now felt that I knew what the white men were feeling. Merely because I had read a book that had spoken of how they lived and thought, I identified myself with that book. I felt vaguely guilty. Would I, filled with bookish notions, act in a manner that would make the whites dislike me?

I forged more notes and my trips to the library became frequent. Reading grew into a passion. My first serious novel was Sinclair Lewis's *Main Street*. It made me see my boss, Mr. Gerald, and identify him as an American type. I would smile when I saw him lugging his golf bags into the office. I had always felt a vast distance separating me from the boss, and now I felt closer to him, though still distant. I felt now that I knew him, that I could feel the very limits of his narrow life. And this had happened because I had read a novel about a mythical man called George F. Babbitt.

The plots and stories in the novels did not interest me so much as the point of view revealed. I gave myself over to each novel without reserve, without trying to criticize it; it was enough for me to see and feel something different. And for me, everything was something different. Reading was like a drug, a dope. The novels created moods in which I lived for days. But I could not conquer my sense of guilt, my feeling that the white men around me knew that I was changing, that I had begun to regard them differently.

Whenever I brought a book to the job, I wrapped it in newspaper—a habit that was to persist for years in other cities and under other circumstances. But some of the white men pried into my packages when I was absent and they questioned me.

"Boy, what are you reading those books for?"

"Oh, I don't know, sir."

"That's deep stuff you're reading, boy."

"I'm just killing time, sir."

"You'll addle your brains if you don't watch out."

I read Dreiser's *Jennie Gerhardt* and *Sister Carrie* and they revived in me a vivid sense of my mother's suffering; I was overwhelmed. I grew silent, wondering about the life around me. It would have been impossible for me to have told anyone what I derived from these novels, for it was nothing less than a sense of life itself. All my life had shaped me for the realism, the naturalism of the modern novel, and I could not read enough of them.

Steeped in new moods and ideas, I bought a ream of paper and tried to write; but nothing would come, or what did come was flat beyond telling. I discovered that more than desire and feeling were necessary to write and I dropped the idea. Yet I still wondered how it was possible to know people sufficiently to write about them? Could I ever learn about life and people? To me, with my vast ignorance, my Jim Crow station in life, it seemed a task impossible of achievement. I now knew what being a Negro meant. I could endure the hunger. I had learned to live with hate. But to feel that there were feelings denied me, that the very breath of life itself was beyond my reach, that more than anything else hurt, wounded me. I had a new hunger.

In buoying me up, reading also cast me down, made me see what was possible, what I had missed. My tension returned, new, terrible, bitter, surging, almost too great to be contained. I no longer *felt* that the world about me was hostile, killing; I *knew* it. A million times I asked myself what I could do to save myself, and there were no answers. I seemed forever condemned, ringed by walls.

I did not discuss my reading with Mr. Falk, who had lent me his library card; it would have meant talking about myself and that would have been too painful. I smiled each day, fighting desperately to maintain my old behavior, to keep my disposition seemingly sunny. But some of the white men discerned that I had begun to brood.

"Wake up there, boy!" Mr. Olin said one day.

"Sir!" I answered for the lack of a better word.

"You act like you've stolen something," he said.

I laughed in the way I knew he expected me to laugh, but I resolved to be more conscious of myself, to watch my every act, to guard and hide the new knowledge that was dawning within me.

If I went north, would it be possible for me to build a new life then? But how could a man build a life upon vague, unformed yearnings? I wanted to write and I did not even know the English language. I bought English grammars and found them dull. I felt that I was getting a better sense of the language from novels than from grammars. I read hard, discarding a writer as soon as I felt that I had grasped his point of view. At night the printed page stood before my eyes in sleep.

Mrs. Moss, my landlady, asked me one Sunday morning:

"Son, what is this you keep on reading?"

"Oh, nothing. Just novels."

"What you get out of 'em?"

"I'm just killing time," I said.

"I hope you know your own mind," she said in a tone which implied that she doubted if I had a mind.

I knew of no Negroes who read the books I liked and I wondered if any Negroes ever thought of them. I knew that there were Negro doctors, lawyers, newspapermen, but I never saw any of them. When I read a Negro newspaper I never caught the faintest echo of my preoccupation in its pages. I felt trapped and occasionally, for a few days, I would stop reading. But a vague hunger would come over me for books, books that opened up new avenues of feeling and seeing, and again I would forge another note to the white librarian. Again I would read and wonder as only the naïve and unlettered can read and wonder, feeling that I carried a secret, criminal burden about with me each day.

That winter my mother and brother came and we set up housekeeping, buying furniture on the installment plan, being cheated and yet knowing no way to avoid it. I began to eat warm food and to my surprise found that regular meals enabled me to read faster. I may have lived through many illnesses and survived them, never suspecting that I was ill. My brother obtained a job and we began to save toward the trip north, plotting our time, setting tentative dates for departure. I told none of the white men on the job that I was planning to go north; I knew that the moment they felt I was thinking of the North they would change toward me. It would have made them feel that I did not like the life I was living, and because my life was completely conditioned by what they said or did, it would have been tantamount to challenging them.

I could calculate my chances for life in the South as a Negro fairly clearly now.

I could fight the southern whites by organizing with other Negroes, as my grandfather had done. But I knew that I could never win that way; there were many whites and there were but few blacks. They were strong and we were weak. Outright black rebellion could never win. If I fought openly I would die and I did not want to die. News of lynchings were frequent.

I could submit and live the life of a genial slave, but that was impossible. All of my life had shaped me to live by my own feelings and thoughts. I could make up to Bess and marry her and inherit the house. But that, too, would be the life of a slave; if I did that, I would crush to death something within me, and I would hate myself as much as I knew the whites already hated those who had submitted. Neither could I ever willingly present myself to be kicked, as Shorty had done. I would rather have died than do that.

I could drain off my restlessness by fighting with Shorty and Harrison. I had seen many Negroes solve the problem of being black by transferring their hatred of themselves to others with a black skin and fighting them. I would have to be cold to do that, and I was not cold and I could never be.

I could, of course, forget what I had read, thrust the whites out of my mind, forget them; and find release from anxiety and longing in sex and alcohol. But the memory of how my father had conducted himself made that course repugnant. If I did not want others to violate my life, how could I voluntarily violate it myself?

I had no hope whatever of being a professional man. Not only had I been so conditioned that I did not desire it, but the fulfillment of such an ambition was beyond my capabilities. Well-to-do Negroes lived in a world that was almost as alien to me as the world inhabited by whites.

What, then, was there? I held my life in my mind, in my consciousness each day, feeling at times that I would stumble and drop it, spill it forever. My reading had created a vast sense of distance between me and the world in which I lived and tried to make a living, and that sense of distance was increasing each day. My days and nights were one long, quiet, continuously contained dream of terror, tension, and anxiety. I wondered how long I could bear it.

1937

Long Black Song

I

Go t sleep, baby
Papas gone t town
Go t sleep, baby
The suns goin down
Go t sleep, baby
Yo candys in the sack
Go t sleep, baby
Papas comin back . . .

Over and over she crooned, and at each lull of her voice she rocked the wooden cradle with a bare black foot. But the baby squalled louder, its wail drowning out the song. She stopped and stood over the cradle, wondering what was bothering it, if its stomach hurt. She felt the diaper; it was dry. She lifted it up and patted its back. Still it cried, longer and louder. She put it back into the cradle and dangled a string of red beads before its eyes. The little black fingers clawed them away. She bent over, frowning, murmuring: "Whuts the mattah, chile? Yuh wan some watah?" She held a dripping gourd to the black lips, but the baby turned its head and kicked its legs. She stood a moment, perplexed. Whuts wrong wid that chile? She ain never carried on like this this tima day. She picked it up and went to the open door. "See the sun, baby?" she asked, pointing to a big ball of red dying between the branches of trees. The baby pulled back and strained its round black arms and legs against her stomach and shoulders. She knew it was tired; she could tell by the halting way it opened its mouth to draw in air. She sat on a wooden stool, unbuttoned the front of her dress, brought the baby closer and offered it a black teat.

"Don baby wan suppah?" It pulled away and went limp, crying softly, piteously, as though it would never stop. Then it pushed its fingers against her breasts and wailed. Lawd, chile, what yuh wan? Yo ma cant hep yuh less she knows whut yuh wan. Tears gushed; four white teeth flashed in red gums; the little chest heaved up and down and round black fingers stretched floorward. Lawd, chile, whuts wrong wid yuh? She stooped slowly, allowing her body to be guided by the downward tug. As soon as the little fingers touched the floor the wail quieted into a broken sniffle. She turned the baby loose and watched it crawl toward a corner. She followed and saw the little fingers reach for the tail-end of an old eight-day clock. "Yuh wan tha ol clock?" She dragged the clock into the center of the floor. The baby crawled after it, calling, "Ahh!" Then it raised its hands and beat on the top of the clock Bink! Bink! Bink! "Naw, yuhll hurt yo hans!" She held the baby and looked around. It cried and struggled. "Wait, baby!" She fetched a small stick from the top of a rickety dresser. "Here," she said, closing the little fingers about it. "Beat wid this, see?" She heard each blow landing squarely on top of the clock. Bang! Bang! Bang! And with each bang the baby smiled and said, "Ahh!" Mabbe thall keep yuh quiet erwhile. Mabbe Ah kin git some res now. She stood in the doorway. Lawd, tha chiles a pain! She mus be teethin. Er something . . .

She wiped sweat from her forehead with the bottom of her dress and looked out over the green fields rolling up the hillsides. She sighed, fighting a feeling of loneliness. Lawd, its sho hard t pass the days wid Silas gone. Been mos a week now since he took the wagon outta here. Hope ain nothin wrong. He must be buyin a heapa stuff there in Colwatah t be stayin all this time. Yes; maybe Silas would remember and bring that five-yard piece of red calico she wanted. Oh, Lawd! Ah *hope* he don fergit it!

She saw green fields wrapped in the thickening gloam. It was as if they had left the earth, those fields, and were floating slowly skyward. The afterglow lingered, red, dying, somehow tenderly sad. And far away, in front of her, earth and sky met in a soft swoon of shadow. A cricket chirped, sharp and lonely; and it seemed she could hear it chirping long after it had stopped. Silas oughta c mon soon. Ahm tireda staying here by mahsef.

Loneliness ached in her. She swallowed, hearing Bang! Bang! Bang! Tom been gone t war mos a year now. N tha ol wars over n we ain heard nothing yit. Lawd, don let Tom be dead! She frowned into the gloam and wondered about that awful war so far away. They said it was over now. Yeah, Gawd had t stop em fo they killed everybody. She felt that merely to go so far away from home was a kind of death in itself. Just to go that far away was to be killed. Nothing good could come from men going miles across the sea to fight. N how come they wanna kill each other? How come they wanna make blood? Killing was not what men ought to do. Shucks! she thought.

She sighed, thinking of Tom, hearing Bang! Bang! Bang! She saw Tom, saw his big black smiling face; her eyes went dreamily blank, drinking in the red afterglow. Yes, God; it could have been Tom instead of Silas who was having her now. Yes; it could have been Tom she was loving. She smiled and asked herself, Lawd, Ah wondah how would it been wid Tom? Against the plush sky she saw a white bright day and a green cornfield and she saw Tom walking in his overalls and she was with Tom and he had his arm about her waist. She remembered how weak she had felt feeling his fingers sinking into the flesh of her hips. Her knees had trembled and she had had a hard time trying to stand up and not just sink right there to the ground. Yes; that was what Tom had wanted her to do. But she had held Tom up and he had held her up; they had held each other up to keep from slipping to the ground there in the green cornfield. Lawd! Her breath went and she passed her tongue over her lips. But that was not as exciting as that winter evening when the grey skies were sleeping and she and Tom were coming home from church down dark Lover's Lane. She felt the tips of her teats tingling and touching the front of her dress as she remembered how he had crushed her against him and hurt her. She had closed her eyes and was smelling the acrid scent of dry October leaves and had gone weak in his arms and had felt she could not breathe any more and had torn away and run, run home. And the sweet ache which had frightened her then was stealing back to her loins now with the silence and the cricket calls and the red afterglow and Bang! Bang! Bang! Lawd, Ah wondah how would it been wid Tom?

She stepped out on the porch and leaned against the wall of the house. Sky sang a red song. Fields whispered a green prayer. And song and prayer were dying in silence and shadow. Never in all her life had she been so much alone as she was now. Days were never so long as these days; and nights were never so empty as these nights. She jerked her head impatiently, hearing Bang! Bang! Bang! Shucks! she thought. When Tom had gone something had ebbed so slowly that at first she had not noticed it. Now she felt all of it as though the feeling had no bottom. She tried to think just how it had happened. Yes; there had been all her life the long hope of white bright days and the deep desire of dark black nights and then Tom had gone. Bang! Bang! Bang! There had been laughter and eating and singing and the long gladness of green cornfields in summer. There had been cooking and sewing and sweeping and the deep dream of sleeping grey skies in winter. Always it had been like that and she had been happy. But no more. The happiness of those days and nights, of those green cornfields and grey skies had started to go from her when Tom had gone to war. His leaving had left an empty black hole in her heart, a black hole that Silas had come in and filled. But not quite. Silas had not quite filled that hole. No; days and nights were not as they were before.

She lifted her chin, listening. She had heard something, a dull throb like she had heard that day Silas had called her outdoors to look at the airplane. Her eyes swept the sky. But there was no plane. Mabbe its behin the house? She stepped into the yard and looked upward through paling light. There were only a few big wet stars trembling in the east. Then she heard the throb again. She turned, looking up and

down the road. The throb grew louder, droning; and she heard Bang! Bang! Bang!
There! A car! Wondah whuts a car doin coming out here? A black car was winding
over a dusty road, coming toward her. Mabbe some white mans bringing Silas home
wida loada goods? But, Lawd, Ah *hope* its no trouble! The car stopped in front of
the house and a white man got out. Wondah whut he wans? She looked at the car,
but could not see Silas. The white man was young; he wore a straw hat and had no
coat. He walked toward her with a huge black package under his arm.

"Well, howre yuh today, Aunty?"

"Ahm well. How yuh?"

"Oh, so-so. Its sure hot today, hunh?"

She brushed her hand across her forehead and sighed.

"Yeah; it is kinda warm."

"You busy?"

"Naw, Ah ain doin nothin."

"Ive got something to show you. Can I sit here, on your porch?"

"Ah reckon so. But, Mistah, Ah ain got no money."

"Haven't you sold your cotton yet?"

"Silas gone t town wid it now."

"Whens he coming back?"

"Ah don know. Ahm waitin fer im."

She saw the white man take out a handkerchief and mop his face. Bang! Bang!
Bang! He turned his head and looked through the open doorway, into the front room.

"Whats all that going on in there?"

She laughed.

"Aw, thas jus Ruth."

"Whats she doing?"

"She beatin tha ol clock."

"Beating a *clock?*"

She laughed again.

"She wouldnt go t sleep so Ah give her tha ol clock t play wid."

The white man got up and went to the front door; he stood a moment looking
at the black baby hammering on the clock. Bang! Bang! Bang!

"But why let her tear your clock up?"

"It ain no good."

"You could have it fixed."

"We ain got no money t be fixin' no clocks."

"Haven't you got a clock?"

"Naw."

"But how do you keep time?"

"We git erlong widout time."

"But how do you know when to get up in the morning?"

"We jus git up, thas all."

"But how do you know what time it is when you get up?"

"We git up wid the sun."

"And at night, how do you tell when its night?"

"It gits dark when the sun goes down."

"Haven't you ever had a clock?"

She laughed and turned her face toward the silent fields. "Mistah, we don need no clock."

"Well, this beats everything! I don't see how in the world anybody can live without time."

"We just don need no time, Mistah."

The white man laughed and shook his head; she laughed and looked at him. The white man was funny. Jus like lil boy. Astin how do Ah know when t git up in the mawnin! She laughed again and mused on the baby, hearing Bang! Bang! Bang! She could hear the white man breathing at her side; she felt his eyes on her face. She looked at him; she saw he was looking at her breasts. Hes jus lika lil boy. Acks like he cant understand *nothin!*

"But you need a clock," the white man insisted. "Thats what Im out here for. Im selling clocks and graphophones. The clocks are made right into the graphophones, a nice sort of combination, hunh? You can have music and time all at once. Ill show you . . ."

"Mistah, we don need no clock!"

"You dont have to buy it. It wont cost you anything just to look."

He unpacked the big black box. She saw the strands of his auburn hair glinting in the afterglow. His back bulged against his white shirt as he stooped. He pulled out a square brown graphophone. She bent forward, looking. Lawd, but its pretty! She saw the face of a clock under the horn of the graphophone. The gilt on the corners sparkled. The color in the wood glowed softly. It reminded her of the light she saw sometimes in the baby's eyes. Slowly she slid a finger over a beveled edge; she wanted to take the box into her arms and kiss it.

"Its eight o'clock," he said.

"Yeah?"

"It only costs fifty dollars. And you dont have to pay for it all at once. Just five dollars down and five dollars a month."

She smiled. The white man was just like a little boy. Jus like a chile. She saw him grinding the handle of the box.

There was a sharp, scratching noise; then she moved nervously, her body caught in the ringing coils of music.

When the trumpet of the Lord shall sound . . .

She rose on circling waves of white bright days and dark black nights.

. . . and time shall be no more . . .

Higher and higher she mounted.

And the morning breaks . . .

Earth fell far behind, forgotten.

. . . eternal, bright and fair . . .

Echo after echo sounded.

When the saved of the earth shall gather . . .

Her blood surged like the long gladness of summer.

. . . over the other shore . . .

Her blood ebbed like the deep dream of sleep in winter.

And when the roll is called up yonder . . .

She gave up, holding her breath.

I'll be there . . .

A lump filled her throat. She leaned her back against a post, trembling, feeling the rise and fall of days and nights, of summer and winter; surging, ebbing, leaping about her, beyond her, far out over the fields to where earth and sky lay folded in darkness. She wanted to lie down and sleep, or else leap up and shout. When the music stopped she felt herself coming back, being let down slowly. She sighed. It was dark now. She looked into the doorway. The baby was sleeping on the floor. Ah gotta git up n put tha chile t bed, she thought.

"Wasnt that pretty?"

"It wuz pretty, awright."

"When do you think your husbands coming back?"

"Ah don know, Mistah."

She went into the room and put the baby into the cradle. She stood again in the doorway and looked at the shadowy box that had lifted her up and carried her away. Crickets called. The dark sky had swallowed up the earth, and more stars were hanging, clustered, burning. She heard the white man sigh. His face was lost in shadow. She saw him rub his palms over his forehead. Hes just lika lil boy.

"Id like to see your husband tonight," he said. "Ive got to be in Lilydale at six o'clock in the morning and I wont be back through here soon. I got to pick up my buddy over there and we're heading North."

She smiled into the darkness. He was just like a little boy. A little boy selling clocks.

"Yuh sell them things alla time?" she asked.

"Just for the summer," he said. "I go to school in winter. If I can make enough money out of this Ill go to Chicago to school this fall . . ."

"Whut yuh gonna be?"

"*Be?* What do you mean?"

"Whut yuh goin to school fer?"

"Im studying science."

"Whuts tha?"

"Oh, er . . ." He looked at her. "Its about why things are as they are."

"Why things is as they *is?*"

"Well, its something like that."

"How come yuh wanna study tha?"

"Oh, you wouldnt understand."

She sighed.

"Naw, Ah guess Ah wouldnt."

"Well, I reckon Ill be getting along," said the white man. "Can I have a drink of water?"

"Sho. But we ain got nothin but well-watah, n yuhll have t come n git."

"Thats all right."

She slid off the porch and walked over the ground with bare feet. She heard the shoes of the white man behind her, falling to the earth in soft whispers. It was dark now. She led him to the well, groped her way, caught the bucket and let it down with a rope; she heard a splash and the bucket grew heavy. She drew it up, pulling against its weight, throwing one hand over the other, feeling the cool wet of the rope on her palms.

"Ah don git watah outa here much," she said, a little out of breath. "Silas gits the watah mos of the time. This buckets too heavy fer me."

"Oh, wait! Ill help!"

His shoulder touched hers. In the darkness she felt his warm hands fumbling for the rope.

"Where is it?"

"Here."

She extended the rope through the darkness. His fingers touched her breasts.

"Oh!"

She said it in spite of herself. He would think she was thinking about that. And he was a white man. She was sorry she had said that.

"Wheres the gourd?" he asked. "Gee, its dark!"

She stepped back and tried to see him.

"Here."

"I cant see!" he said, laughing.

Again she felt his fingers on the tips of her breasts. She backed away, saying nothing this time. She thrust the gourd out from her. Warm fingers met her cold hands. He had the gourd. She heard him drink; it was the faint, soft music of water going down a dry throat, the music of water in a silent night. He sighed and drank again.

"I was thirsty," he said. "I hadnt had any water since noon."

She knew he was standing in front of her; she could not see him, but she felt him. She heard the gourd rest against the wall of the well. She turned, then felt his hands full on her breasts. She struggled back.

"Naw, Mistah!"

"Im not going to hurt you!"

White arms were about her, tightly. She was still. But hes a *white* man. A *white* man. She felt his breath coming hot on her neck and where his hands held her breasts the flesh seemed to knot. She was rigid, poised; she swayed backward, then forward. She caught his shoulders and pushed.

"Naw, naw . . . Mistah, Ah cant do that!"

She jerked away. He caught her hand.

"Please . . ."

"Lemme go!"

She tried to pull her hand out of his and felt his fingers tighten. She pulled harder, and for a moment they were balanced, one against the other. Then he was at her side again, his arms about her.

"I wont hurt you! I wont hurt you . . ."

She leaned backward and tried to dodge his face. Her breasts were full against him; she gasped, feeling the full length of his body. She held her head far to one side; she knew he was seeking her mouth. His hands were on her breasts again. A wave of warm blood swept into her stomach and loins. She felt his lips touching her throat and where he kissed it burned.

"Naw, naw . . ."

Her eyes were full of the wet stars and they blurred, silver and blue. Her knees were loose and she heard her own breathing; she was trying to keep from falling. But hes a *white* man! A *white* man! Naw! Naw! And still she would not let him have her lips; she kept her face away. Her breasts hurt where they were crushed against him and each time she caught her breath she held it and while she held it it seemed that if she would let it go it would kill her. Her knees were pressed hard against his and she clutched the upper parts of his arms, trying to hold on. Her loins ached. She felt her body sliding.

"Gawd . . ."

He helped her up. She could not see the stars now; her eyes were full of the feeling that surged over her body each time she caught her breath. He held her close, breathing into her ear; she straightened, rigidly, feeling that she had to straighten or die. And then her lips felt his and she held her breath and dreaded ever to breathe again for fear of the feeling that would sweep down over her limbs. She held tightly, hearing a mountain tide of blood beating against her throat and temples. Then she gripped him, tore her face away, emptied her lungs in one long despairing gasp and went limp. She felt his hand; she was still, taut, feeling his hand, then his fingers. The muscles in her legs flexed and she bit her lips and pushed her toes deep into the wet dust by the side of the well and tried to wait and tried to wait until she could wait no longer. She whirled away from him and a streak of silver and blue swept across her blood. The wet ground cooled her palms and knee-caps. She stumbled up and ran, blindly, her toes flicking warm, dry dust. Her numbed fingers grabbed at a rusty nail in the post at the porch and she pushed ahead of hands that held her breasts. Her fingers found the door-facing; she moved into the darkened room, her hands before her. She touched the cradle and turned till her knees hit the bed. She went over, face down, her fingers trembling in the crumpled folds of his shirt. She moved and moved again and again, trying to keep ahead of the warm flood of blood that sought to catch her. A liquid metal covered her and she rode on the curve of white bright days and dark black nights and the surge of the long gladness of summer and the ebb of the deep dream of sleep in winter till a high red wave of hotness drowned her in a deluge of silver and blue and boiled her blood and blistered her flesh *bangbangbang* . . .

II

"Yuh bettah go," she said.

She felt him standing by the side of the bed, in the dark. She heard him clear his throat. His belt-buckle tinkled.

"Im leaving that clock and graphophone," he said.

She said nothing. In her mind she saw the box glowing softly, like the light in the baby's eyes. She stretched out her legs and relaxed.

"You can have it for forty instead of fifty. Ill be by early in the morning to see if your husbands in."

She said nothing. She felt the hot skin of her body growing steadily cooler.

"Do you think hell pay ten on it? Hell only owe thirty then."

She pushed her toes deep into the quilt, feeling a night wind blowing through the door. Her palms rested lightly on top of her breasts.

"Do you think hell pay ten on it?"

"Hunh?"

"Hell pay ten, wont he?"

"Ah don know," she whispered.

She heard his shoe hit against a wall; footsteps echoed on the wooden porch. She started nervously when she heard the roar of his car; she followed the throb of the motor till she heard it when she could hear it no more, followed it till she heard it roaring faintly in her ears in the dark and silent room. Her hands moved on her breasts and she was conscious of herself, all over; she felt the weight of her body resting heavily on shucks. She felt the presence of fields lying out there covered with night. She turned over slowly and lay on her stomach, her hands tucked under her. From somewhere came a creaking noise. She sat upright, feeling fear. The wind sighed. Crickets called. She lay down again, hearing shucks rustle. Her eyes looked straight up in the darkness and her blood sogged. She had lain a long time, full of a vast peace, when a far away tinkle made her feel the bed again. The tinkle came through the night; she listened, knowing that soon she would hear the rattle of Silas' wagon. Even then she tried to fight off the sound of Silas' coming, even then she wanted to feel the peace of night filling her again; but the tinkle grew louder and she heard the jangle of a wagon and the quick trot of horses. Thas Silas! She gave up and waited. She heard horses neighing. Out of the window bare feet whispered in the dust, then crossed the porch, echoing in soft booms. She closed her eyes and saw Silas come into the room in his dirty overalls as she had seen him come in a thousand times before.

"Yuh sleep, Sarah?"

She did not answer. Feet walked across the floor and a match scratched. She opened her eyes and saw Silas standing over her with a lighted lamp. His hat was pushed far back on his head and he was laughing.

"Ah reckon yuh thought Ah waznt never comin back, hunh? Cant yuh wake up? See, Ah got that red cloth yuh wanted . . ." He laughed again and threw the red cloth on the mantel.

"Yuh hongry?" she asked.

"Naw, Ah kin make out till mawnin." Shucks rustled as he sat on the edge of the bed. "Ah got two hundred n fifty fer mah cotton."

"Two hundred n fifty?"

"Nothin different! N guess whut Ah done?"

"Whut?"

"Ah bought ten mo acres o lan. Got em from ol man Burgess. Paid im a hundred n fifty dollahs down. Ahll pay the rest next year ef things go erlong awright. Ahma have t git a man t hep me nex spring . . ."

"Yuh mean hire somebody?"

"Sho, hire somebody! Whut yuh think? Ain tha the way the white folks do? Ef yuhs gonna git anywheres yuhs gotta do just like they do." He paused. "Whut yuh been doin since Ah been gone?"

"Nothin. Cookin, cleanin, n . . ."

"How Ruth?"

"She awright." She lifted her head. "Silas, yuh git any lettahs?"

"Naw. But Ah heard Tom wuz in town."

"In *town?*"

She sat straight up.

"Yeah, thas whut the folks wuz sayin at the sto."

"Back from the war?"

"Ah ast erroun t see ef Ah could fin im. But Ah couldnt."

"Lawd, Ah wish hed c mon home."

"Them white folks shos glad the wars over. But things wuz kinda bad there in town. Everywhere Ah looked wuznt nothin but black n white soljers. N them white folks beat up a black soljer yestiddy. He was jus in from France. Wuz still wearin his soljers suit. They claimed he sassed a white woman . . ."

"Who wuz he?"

"Ah don know. Never saw im befo."

"Yuh see An Peel?"

"Naw."

"Silas!" she said reprovingly.

"Aw, Sarah, Ah jus couldnt git out there."

"Whut else yuh bring sides the cloth?"

"Ah got yuh some high-top shoes." He turned and looked at her in the dim light of the lamp. "Woman, ain yuh glad Ah bought yuh some shoes n cloth?" He laughed and lifted his feet to the bed. "Lawd, Sarah, yuhs sho sleepy, ain yuh?"

"Bettah put tha lamp out, Silas . . ."

"Aw . . ." He swung out of the bed and stood still for a moment. She watched him, then turned her face to the wall.

"Whuts that by the windah?" he asked.

She saw him bending over and touching the graphophone with his fingers.

"Thasa graphophone."

"Where yuh git it from?"

"A man lef it here."

"When he bring it?"

"Today."

"But how come he t leave it?"

"He says hell be out here in the mawnin to see ef yuh wans t buy it."

He was on his knees, feeling the wood and looking at the gilt on the edges of the box. He stood up and looked at her.

"Yuh ain never said yuh wanted one of these things."

She said nothing.

"Where wuz the man from?"

"Ah don know."

"He white?"

"Yeah."

He put the lamp back on the mantel. As he lifted the globe to blow out the flame, his hand paused.

"Whos hats this?"

She raised herself and looked. A straw hat lay bottom upwards on the edge of the mantel. Silas picked it up and looked back to the bed, to Sarah.

"Ah guess its the white mans. He must a lef it . . ."

"Whut he doin *in our room?*"

"He wuz talkin t me bout that graphophone."

She watched him go to the window and stoop again to the box. He picked it up, fumbled with the price-tag and took the box to the light.

"Whut this thing cos?"

"Forty dollahs."

"But its marked fifty here."

"Oh, Ah means he said fifty . . ."

He took a step toward the bed.

"Yuh lyin t me!"

"Silas!"

He heaved the box out of the front door; there was a smashing, tinkling noise as it bounded off the front porch and hit the ground. "Whut in hell yuh lie t me fer?"

"Yuh broke the box!"

"Ahma break yo Gawddam neck ef yuh don stop lyin t me!"

"Silas, Ah ain lied t yuh!"

"Shut up, Gawddammit! Yuh did!"

He was standing by the bed with the lamp trembling in his hand. She stood on the other side, between the bed and the wall.

"How come yuh tell me that thing cos *forty* dollahs when it cos *fifty?*"

"Thas whut he tol me."

"How come he take *ten* dollars off fer yuh?"

"He ain took nothin off fer me, Silas!"

"Yuh lyin t me! N yuh lied t me bout Tom, too!"

She stood with her back to the wall, her lips parted, looking at him silently, steadily. Their eyes held for a moment. Silas looked down, as though he were about to believe her. Then he stiffened.

"Whos this?" he asked, picking up a short, yellow pencil from the crumpled quilt. She said nothing. He started toward her.

"Yuh wan me t take mah raw-hide whip n make yuh talk?"

"Naw, naw, Silas! Yuh wrong! He wuz figgerin wid tha pencil!"

He was silent a moment, his eyes searching her face.

"Gawddam yo black soul t hell, don yuh try lyin t me! Ef yuh start layin wid white men Ahll hosswhip yuh t a incha yo life. Shos theres a Gawd in Heaven Ah will! From sunup t sundown Ah works mah guts out t pay them white trash bastards whut Ah owe em, n then Ah comes n fins they been in mah house! Ah cant go into their houses, n yuh know Gawddam well Ah cant! They don have no mercy on no black folks; wes jus like dirt under their feet! Fer ten years Ah slaves lika dog t git mah farm free, givin ever penny Ah kin t em, n then Ah comes n fins they been in mah house . . ." He was speechless with outrage. "If yuh wans t eat at mah table yuhs gonna keep them white trash bastards out, yuh hear? Tha white ape kin come n git tha damn box n Ah ain gonna pay im a cent! He had no bisness leavin it here, n yuh had no bisness lettin im! Ahma tell tha sonofabitch something when he comes out here in the mawnin, so hep me Gawd! Now git back in tha bed!"

She slipped beneath the quilt and lay still, her face turned to the wall. Her heart thumped slowly and heavily. She heard him walk across the floor in his bare feet. She heard the bottom of the lamp as it rested on the mantel. She stiffened when the room darkened. Feet whispered across the floor again. The shucks rustled from Silas' weight as he sat on the edge of the bed. She was still, breathing softly. Silas was mumbling. She felt sorry for him. In the darkness it seemed that she could see the hurt look on his black face. The crow of a rooster came from far away, came so faintly that it seemed she had not heard it. The bed sank and the shucks cried out in dry whispers; she knew Silas had stretched out. She heard him sigh. Then she jumped because he jumped. She could feel the tenseness of his body; she knew he was sitting bolt upright. She felt his hands fumbling jerkily under the quilt. Then the bed heaved amid a wild shout of shucks and Silas' feet hit the floor with a loud boom. She snatched herself to her elbows, straining her eyes in the dark, wondering what was wrong now. Silas was moving about, cursing under his breath.

"Don wake Ruth up!" she whispered.

"Ef yuh say one mo word t me Ahma slap yuh inter a black spasm!"

She grabbed her dress, got up and stood by the bed, the tips of her fingers touching the wall behind her. A match flared in yellow flame; Silas' face was caught in a circle of light. He was looking downward, staring intently at a white wad of cloth balled in his hand. His black cheeks were hard, set; his lips were tightly pursed. She looked closer; she saw that the white cloth was a man's handkerchief. Silas' fingers loosened; she heard the handkerchief hit the floor softly, damply. The match went out.

"Yuh little bitch!"

Her knees gave. Fear oozed from her throat to her stomach. She moved in the dark toward the door, struggling with the dress, jamming it over her head. She heard the thick skin of Silas' feet swish across the wooden planks.

"Ah got mah raw-hide whip n Ahm takin yuh t the barn!"

She ran on tiptoe to the porch and paused, thinking of the baby. She shrank as something whined through the air. A red streak of pain cut across the small of her back and burned its way into her body, deeply.

"Silas!" she screamed.

She grabbed for the post and fell in dust. She screamed again and crawled out of reach.

"Git t the barn, Gawddammit!"

She scrambled up and ran through the dark, hearing the baby cry. Behind her leather thongs hummed and feet whispered swiftly over the dusty ground.

"C mere, yuh bitch! C mere, Ah say!"

She ran to the road and stopped. She wanted to go back and get the baby, but she dared not. Not as long as Silas had that whip. She stiffened, feeling that he was near.

"Yuh jus as well c mon back n git yo beatin!"

She ran again, slowing now and then to listen. If she only knew where he was she would slip back into the house and get the baby and walk all the way to Aunt Peel's.

"Yuh ain comin back in mah house till Ah beat yuh!"

She was sorry for the anger she knew he had out there in the field. She had a bewildering impulse to go to him and ask him not to be angry; she wanted to tell him that there was nothing to be angry about; that what she had done did not matter; that she was sorry; that after all she was his wife and still loved him. But there was no way she could do that now; if she went to him he would whip her as she had seen him whip a horse.

"Sarah! Sarah!"

His voice came from far away. Ahm goin git Ruth. Back through dust she sped, going on her toes, holding her breath.

"Saaaarah!"

From far off his voice floated over the fields. She ran into the house and caught the baby in her arms. Again she sped through dust on her toes. She did not stop till she was so far away that his voice sounded like a faint echo falling from the sky. She looked up; the stars were paling a little. Mus be gittin near mawnin. She walked now, letting her feet sink softly into the cool dust. The baby was sleeping; she could feel the little chest swelling against her arm. She looked up again; the sky was solid black. Its gittin near mawnin. Ahma take Ruth t An Peels. N mabbe Ahll fin Tom . . . But she could not walk all that distance in the dark. Not now. Her legs were tired. For a moment a memory of surge and ebb rose in her blood; she felt her legs straining, upward. She sighed. Yes, she would go to the sloping hillside back of the garden and wait until morning. Then she would slip away. She stopped, listened. She heard a faint, rattling noise. She imagined Silas' kicking or throwing the smashed graphophone. Hes mad! Hes sho mad! Aw, Lawd! . . . She stopped stock still, squeezing the baby till it whimpered. What would happen when that white man came out in the morning? She had forgotten him. She would have to head him off and tell him. Yeah, cause Silas jus mad ernuff t kill! Lawd, hes mad ernuff t kill!

III

She circled the house widely, climbing a slope, groping her way, holding the baby high in her arms. After awhile she stopped and wondered where on the slope she was. She remembered there was an elm tree near the edge; if she could find it she would know. She groped farther, feeling with her feet. Ahm gittin los! And she did not want to fall with the baby. Ahma stop here, she thought. When morning came she would see the car of the white man from this hill and she would run down the road and tell him to go back; and then there would be no killing. Dimly she saw in her mind a picture of men killing and being killed. White men killed the black and black men killed the white. White men killed the black men because they could, and the black men killed the white men to keep from being killed. And killing was blood. Lawd, Ah wish Tom wuz here. She shuddered, sat on the ground and watched the sky for signs of morning. Mabbe Ah oughta walk on down the road? Naw . . . Her legs were tired. Again she felt her body straining. Then she saw Silas holding the white man's handkerchief. She heard it hit the floor, softly, damply. She was sorry for what she had done. Silas was as good to her as any black man could be to a black woman. Most of the black women worked in the fields as croppers. But Silas had given her her own home, and that was more than many others had done for their women. Yes, she knew how Silas felt. Always he had said he was as good as any white man. He had worked hard and saved his money and bought a farm so he could grow his own crops like white men. Silas hates white folks! Lawd, he sho hates em!

The baby whimpered. She unbuttoned her dress and nursed her in the dark. She looked toward the east. There! A tinge of grey hovered. It wont be long now. She could see ghostly outlines of trees. Soon she would see the elm, and by the elm she would sit till it was light enough to see the road.

The baby slept. Far off a rooster crowed. Sky deepened. She rose and walked slowly down a narrow, curving path and came to the elm tree. Standing on the edge of a slope, she saw a dark smudge in a sea of shifting shadows. That was her home. Wondah how come Silas didnt light the lamp? She shifted the baby from her right hip to her left, sighed, struggled against sleep. She sat on the ground again, caught the baby close and leaned against the trunk of a tree. Her eye-lids drooped and it seemed that a hard, cold hand caught hold of her right leg or was it her left leg—she did not know which —and began to drag her over a rough litter of shucks and when she strained to see who it was that was pulling her no one was in sight but far ahead was darkness and it seemed that out of the darkness some force came and pulled her like a magnet and she went sliding along over a rough bed of screeching shucks and it seemed that a wild fear made her want to scream but when she opened her mouth to scream she could not scream and she felt she was coming to a wide black hole and again she made ready to scream and then it was too late for she was already over the wide black hole falling falling falling . . .

She awakened with a start and blinked her eyes in the sunshine. She found she was clutching the baby so hard that it had begun to cry. She got to her feet, trembling from fright of the dream, remembering Silas and the white man and Silas' running her out of the house and the white man's coming. Silas was standing in the front yard; she caught her breath. Yes, she had to go and head that white man off! Naw! She could not do that, not with Silas standing there with that whip in his hand. If she tried to climb any of those slopes he would see her surely. And Silas would never forgive her for something like that. If it were anybody but a white man it would be different.

Then, while standing there on the edge of the slope looking wonderingly at Silas striking the whip against his overall-leg—and then, while standing there looking— she froze. There came from the hills a distant throb. Lawd! The baby whimpered. She loosened her arms. The throb grew louder, droning. Hes comin fas! She wanted to run to Silas and beg him not to bother the white man. But he had that whip in his hand. She should not have done what she had done last night. This was all her fault. Lawd, ef anything happens t im its mah blame . . . Her eyes watched a black car speed over the crest of a hill. She should have been out there on the road instead of sleeping here by the tree. But it was too late now. Silas was standing in the yard; she saw him turn with a nervous jerk and sit on the edge of the porch. He was holding the whip stiffly. The car came to a stop. A door swung open. A white man got out. Thas im! She saw another white man in the front seat of the car. N thats his buddy . . . The white man who had gotten out walked over the ground, going to Silas. They faced each other, the white man standing up and Silas sitting down; like two toy men they faced each other. She saw Silas point the whip to the smashed graphophone. The white man looked down and took a quick step backward. The white man's shoulders were bent and he shook his head from left to right. Then Silas got up and they faced each other again; like two dolls, a white doll and a black doll, they faced each other in the valley below. The white man pointed his finger into Silas' face. Then Silas' right arm went up; the whip flashed. The white man turned, bending, flinging his hands to shield his head. Silas' arm rose and fell, rose and fell. She saw the white man crawling in dust, trying to get out of reach. She screamed when she saw the other white man get out of the car and run to Silas. Then all three were on the ground, rolling in dust, grappling for the whip. She clutched the baby and ran. Lawd! Then she stopped, her mouth hanging open. Silas had broken loose and was running toward the house. She knew he was going for his gun.

"Silas!"

Running, she stumbled and fell. The baby rolled in the dust and bawled. She grabbed it up and ran again. The white men were scrambling for their car. She reached level ground, running. Hell be killed! Then again she stopped. Silas was on the front porch, aiming a rifle. One of the white men was climbing into the car. The other was standing, waving his arms, shouting at Silas. She tried to scream, but choked; and she could not scream till she heard a shot ring out.

"Silas!"

One of the white men was on the ground. The other was in the car. Silas was aiming again. The car started, running in a cloud of dust. She fell to her knees and hugged the baby close. She heard another shot, but the car was roaring over the top of the southern hill. Fear was gone now. Down the slope she ran. Silas was standing on the porch, holding his gun and looking at the fleeing car. Then she saw him go to the white man lying in dust and stoop over him. He caught one of the man's legs and dragged the body into the middle of the road. Then he turned and came slowly back to the house. She ran, holding the baby, and fell at his feet.

"Silas!"

IV

"Git up, Sarah!"

His voice was hard and cold. She lifted her eyes and saw blurred black feet. She wiped tears away with dusty fingers and pulled up. Something took speech from her and she stood with bowed shoulders. Silas was standing still, mute; the look on his face condemned her. It was as though he had gone far off and had stayed a long time and had come back changed even while she was standing there in the sunshine before him. She wanted to say something, to give herself. She cried.

"Git the chile up, Sarah!"

She lifted the baby and stood waiting for him to speak, to tell her something to change all this. But he said nothing. He walked toward the house. She followed. As she attempted to go in, he blocked the way. She jumped to one side as he threw the red cloth outdoors to the ground. The new shoes came next. Then Silas heaved the baby's cradle. It hit the porch and a rocker splintered; the cradle swayed for a second, then fell to the ground, lifting a cloud of brown dust against the sun. All of her clothes and the baby's clothes were thrown out.

"Silas!"

She cried, seeing blurred objects sailing through the air and hearing them hit softly in the dust.

"Git you things n go!"

"Silas!"

"Ain no use yuh sayin *nothin* now!"

"But theyll kill yuh!"

"There ain nothin Ah kin do. N there ain nothin yuh kin do. Yuh done done too
Gawddam much awready. Git yo things n go!"

"Theyll kill yuh, Silas!"

He pushed her off the porch.

"GIT YO THINGS N GO T AN PEELS!"

"Les *both* go, Silas!"

"Ahm stayin here till they come back!"

She grabbed his arm and he slapped her hand away. She dropped to the edge of
the porch and sat looking at the ground.

"Go way," she said quietly. "Go way fo they comes. Ah didnt mean no harm . . ."

"Go way fer whut?"

"Theyll *kill* yuh . . ."

"It don make no difference." He looked out over the sunfilled fields. "Fer ten years
Ah slaved mah life out t git mah farm free . . ." His voice broke off. His lips moved
as though a thousand words were spilling silently out of his mouth, as though he did
not have breath enough to give them sound. He looked to the sky, and then back
to the dust. "Now, its all gone. *Gone . . .* Ef Ah run erway, Ah ain got nothin. Ef
Ah stay n fight, Ah ain got nothin. It dont make no difference which way Ah go.
Gawd! Gawd, Ah wish all them white folks wuz dead! *Dead,* Ah tell yuh! Ah wish
Gawd would kill em *all!*"

She watched him run a few steps and stop. His throat swelled. He lifted his hands
to his face; his fingers trembled. Then he bent to the ground and cried. She touched
his shoulders.

"Silas!"

He stood up. She saw he was staring at the white man's body lying in the dust
in the middle of the road. She watched him walk over to it. He began to talk to no
one in particular; he simply stood over the dead white man and talked out of his life,
out of a deep and final sense that now it was all over and nothing could make any
difference.

"The white folks ain never gimme a chance! They ain never give no black man
a chance! There ain nothin in yo whole life yuh kin keep from em! They take yo
lan! They take yo freedom! They take yo women! N then they take yo life!" He
turned to her, screaming. "N then Ah gits stabbed in the back by mah own blood!
When mah eyes is on the white folks to keep em from killin me, mah own blood
trips me up!" He knelt in the dust again and sobbed; after a bit he looked to the sky,
his face wet with tears. "Ahm gonna be hard like they is! So hep me, Gawd, Ah'm
gonna be *hard!* When they come fer me Ahm gonna *be here!* N when they git me
outta here theys gonna *know Ahm gone! Ef Gawd lets me live Ahm gonna make em
feel* it!" He stopped and tried to get his breath. "But, Lawd, Ah don wanna be this
way! I don mean nothin! Yuh die ef yuh fight! Yuh die ef yuh don fight! Either
way yuh die n it don mean nothin . . ."

He was lying flat on the ground, the side of his face deep in dust. Sarah stood
nursing the baby with eyes black and stony. Silas pulled up slowly and stood again
on the porch.

"Git on t An Peels, Sarah!"

A dull roar came from the south. They both turned. A long streak of brown dust was weaving down the hillside.

"Silas!"

"Go on cross the fiels, Sarah!"

"We kin *both* go! Git the hosses!"

He pushed her off the porch, grabbed her hand, and led her to the rear of the house, past the well, to where a path led up a slope to the elm tree.

"Silas!"

"Yuh git on fo they ketch yuh too!"

Blind from tears, she went across the swaying fields, stumbling over blurred grass. It ain no use! She knew it was now too late to make him change his mind. The calves of her legs knotted. Suddenly her throat tightened, aching. She stopped, closed her eyes and tried to stem a flood of sorrow that drenched her. Yes, killing of white men by black men and killing of black men by white men went on in spite of the hope of white bright days and the desire of dark black nights and the long gladness of green cornfields in summer and the deep dream of sleepy grey skies in winter. And when killing started it went on, like a river flowing. Oh, she felt sorry for Silas! Silas. . . . He was following that long river of blood. Lawd, how come he wans t stay there like tha? And he did not want to die; she knew he hated dying by the way he talked of it. Yet he followed the old river of blood, knowing that it meant nothing. He followed it, cursing and whimpering. But he followed it. She stared before her at the dry, dusty grass. Somehow, men, black men and white men, land and houses, green cornfields and grey skies, gladness and dreams, were all a part of that which made life good. Yes, somehow, they were linked, like the spokes in a spinning wheel. She felt they were. She knew they were. She felt it when she breathed and knew it when she looked. But she could not say how; she could not put her finger on it and when she thought hard about it it became all mixed up, like milk spilling suddenly. Or else it knotted in her throat and chest in a hard, aching lump, like the one she felt now. She touched her face to the baby's face and cried again.

There was a loud blare of auto horns. The growing roar made her turn round. Silas was standing, seemingly unafraid, leaning against a post of the porch. The long line of cars came speeding in clouds of dust. Silas moved toward the door and went in. Sarah ran down the slope a piece, coming again to the elm tree. Her breath was slow and hard. The cars stopped in front of the house. There was a steady drone of motors and drifting clouds of dust. For a moment she could not see what was happening. Then on all sides white men with pistols and rifles swarmed over the fields. She dropped to her knees, unable to take her eyes away, unable, it seemed, to breathe. A shot rang out. A white man fell, rolling over, face downward.

"Hes gotta gun!"

"Git back!"

"Lay down!"

The white men ran back and crouched behind cars. Three more shots came from the house. She looked, her head and eyes aching. She rested the baby in her lap and shut her eyes. Her knees sank into the dust. More shots came, but it was no use looking now. She knew it all by heart. She could feel it happening even before it happened. There were men killing and being killed. Then she jerked up, being compelled to look.

"Burn the bastard out!"

"Set the sonofabitch on fire!"

"Cook the coon!"

"Smoke im out!"

She saw two white men on all fours creeping past the well. One carried a gun and the other a red tin can. When they reached the back steps the one with the tin can crept under the house and crept out again. Then both rose and ran. Shots. One fell. A yell went up. A yellow tongue of fire licked out from under the back steps.

"Burn the nigger!"

"C mon out, nigger, n git yos!"

She watched from the hill-slope; the back steps blazed. The white men fired a steady stream of bullets. Black smoke spiraled upward in the sunshine. Shots came from the house. The white men crouched out of sight, behind their cars.

"Make up your mind, nigger!"

"C mon out er burn, yuh black bastard!"

"Yuh think yuhre white now, nigger?"

The shack blazed, flanked on all sides by whirling smoke filled with flying sparks. She heard the distant hiss of flames. White men were crawling on their stomachs. Now and then they stopped, aimed, and fired into the bulging smoke. She looked with a tense numbness; she looked, waiting for Silas to scream, or run out. But the house crackled and blazed, spouting yellow plumes to the blue sky. The white men shot again, sending a hail of bullets into the furious pillars of smoke. And still she could not see Silas running out, or hear his voice calling. Then she jumped, standing. There was a loud crash; the roof caved in. A black chimney loomed amid crumbling wood. Flames roared and black smoke billowed, hiding the house. The white men stood up, no longer afraid. Again she waited for Silas, waited to see him fight his way out, waited to hear his call. Then she breathed a long, slow breath, emptying her lungs. She knew now. Silas had killed as many as he could and stayed on to burn, had stayed without a murmur. She filled her lungs with a quick gasp as the walls fell in; the house was hidden by eager plumes of red. She turned and ran with the baby in her arms, ran blindly across the fields, crying, "Naw, Gawd!"

1938

Walker Evans,
Brooklyn Bridge,
photograph, ca. 1928.
The J. Paul Getty Museum.

Georgia O'Keeffe,
Brooklyn Bridge,
oil on masonite, 1948.
The Brooklyn Museum.
Bequest of Mary Childs Draper.

The Literature of Modernism: Poetry 1912–1940

 The generation of poets that came to adulthood in the early years of the twentieth century had been brought up to believe that American culture was far inferior to European culture. Black poets, like Langston Hughes and Countee Cullen, bore the double burden of having been told that their race had no culture and that the only way to be literary was to imitate a white tradition. The great accomplishment of American poetry of the modernist period was to equal English poetry—not by the work of a single genius like Whitman or Dickinson but rather by the productions of a long line of poets changing the face of the art. The new American poets defiantly claimed equal status with the parent literature and explored to the full the native resources of the American language. A number of black poets, for instance, encouraged by the example of Langston Hughes, began to write in the black vernacular, taking as their rhythmic base not the English pentameter but the syncopation of jazz, the first black art form to be incorporated into American life.

Hughes's vignettes of Harlem life participated in the large democratization of poetry sponsored by his contemporaries. Dissatisfied with the historically aristocratic role of poetry in Europe, some modern American poets—Robert Frost, E. E. Cummings, William Carlos Williams—began writing poetry for a mass audience, a poetry in which that audience could find reflected its own environment and concerns. "My nonliterary listeners," said Langston

Hughes in *I Wonder as I Wander* (1956), "would be ready [at this point in the reading] to think in terms of their own problems":

> Then I read poems about women domestics, workers on the Florida roads, poor
> black students wanting to shatter the darkness of ignorance and prejudice, and
> one about the sharecroppers of Mississippi. . . . Many of my verses were
> documentary, journalistic, and topical.

While Hughes was documenting Harlem and Mississippi, Cummings was sketching, in slang, the flappers of the jazz age, Williams was writing proletarian portraits, and Frost was describing, in terms the common reader could understand, the bleak isolation, hostility, and seclusion of rural New England. But American readers, on the whole, were not prepared for the new poets, even these most accessible ones; all of the American modernists found themselves writing in a raw culture not yet ready for them.

American Culture and the International Style

In the early part of the century, when the poets were exploring Europe and European avant-garde writing, America was firmly isolationist. Even America's late participation in World War I only confirmed in most Americans a sense that the country's strength lay in its turning its back on European quarrels. After all, most Americans had repudiated Europe (for political, religious, or economic reasons) in deciding to emigrate to America, and many immigrant families Americanized themselves, linguistically and culturally, as fast as possible.

World War I, decimating Europe, had left America relatively untouched. After Woodrow Wilson's death, America returned to its isolationist mood during the "normalcy" of the twenties under Warren Harding, Calvin Coolidge, and Herbert Hoover. The business boom of the twenties collapsed in the crash of the stock market in October 1929, an event that plunged America into a depression that turned American attention even more drastically toward its own concerns. Despite the efforts of Franklin Delano Roosevelt after 1932, the depression was finally ended only by the increase in manufacturing caused by America's entrance into World War II in 1941. Until the end of that war, America remained a provincial nation, wary of all things European.

The writers of this era responded variously to American isolationism and provinciality. Many writers left America for London or Paris—among them T. S. Eliot, Ezra Pound, Cummings, and Frost (though of these only Eliot and Pound became permanent expatriates). The first books of poetry by Pound, Frost, and Marianne Moore were all published abroad, where public taste was more accustomed to avant-garde art. Pound wrote, in disgust, that "the age demanded an image / Of its accelerated grimace, / . . . a mould in plaster, / Made with no loss of time, / . . . [not] alabaster / Or the 'sculpture' of rhyme" ("Hugh Selwyn Mauberley"). American taste preferred genteel Anglophilia or robust American good sense to the sort of experimentation being carried on by its new poets.

Credo

If a certain thing was said once for all in Atlantis or Arcadia, in 450 before Christ or in 1290 after, it is not for us moderns to go saying it over, or to go obscuring the memory of the dead by saying the same thing with less skill and less conviction.

My pawing over the ancients and semi-ancients has been one struggle to find out what has been done, once for all, better than it can ever be done again, and to find out what remains for us to do, and plenty does remain, for if we still feel the same emotions as those which launched the thousand ships, it is quite certain that we come on these feelings differently, through different nuances, by different intellectual gradations. Each age has its own abounding gifts yet only some ages transmute them into matter of duration. No good poetry is ever written in a manner twenty years old, for to write in such a manner shows conclusively that the writer thinks from books, convention and *cliché*, and not from life.

Ezra Pound (1911)

That experimentation, as observed with the advantage of hindsight, directed itself chiefly against the prescribed English models. The "international style" that American modernist work exhibits (in common with modern French and Italian poetry) distinguishes it sharply from nineteenth-century American poetry. Though some nineteenth-century poets, notably Longfellow, had borrowed from European literature, their borrowings were domesticated into a "fireside" style and on the whole did not exhibit linguistic experimentation. But now Eliot, who had studied comparative literature at Harvard, began to imitate topics and tones that he had found in French poets—the urban *ennui* of Charles Baudelaire, the satire of the bourgeoisie of Jules Laforgue. Pound, who had studied comparative literature at the University of Pennsylvania, looked for his inspiration to a European period before the English Renaissance, imitating the *dolce stil nuovo* ("sweet new style") of fourteenth-century Italian poets such as Guido Cavalcanti. This hybridizing of the English poetic heritage with French and Italian models produced the poems that appeared in Pound's *A Lume Spento* (1908) and Eliot's *Prufrock and Other Observations* (1917). Eliot's European poems adopted a weary irony foreign to American literature, and Pound's poems took on archaic language and medieval postures. Later, Eliot, who had studied Sanskrit and Buddhism, would turn to the religious poetry of the Indian Upanishads as a lyric source, and Pound would incorporate Chinese, Anglo-Saxon, and Latin models into his *Cantos*. It must quickly be added that, for all this display of foreign influence, both Pound and Eliot wrote solidly in the British tradition. Pound's masters were Robert Browning, for the dramatic monologue, and Dante Gabriel Rossetti, who wrote poems derived from medieval Italian models, especially Dante, Petrarch, and Cavalcanti. Eliot's masters were Matthew Arnold, Browning, Tennyson (whose musicality he imitated), and the post-Shakespearean Jacobean dramatists (whom Eliot admired for their macabre theatricality of style).

Tradition and the Individual Talent

No poet, no artist of any art, has his complete meaning alone. His significance, his appreciation is the appreciation of his relation to the dead poets and artists. You cannot value him alone; you must set him, for contrast and comparison, among the dead. I mean this as a principle of æsthetic, not merely historical, criticism. The necessity that he shall conform, that he shall cohere, is not one-sided; what happens when a new work of art is created is something that happens simultaneously to all the works of art which preceded it. The existing monuments form an ideal order among themselves, which is modified by the introduction of the new (the really new) work of art among them. The existing order is complete before the new work arrives; for order to persist after the supervention of novelty, the *whole* existing order must be, if ever so slightly, altered; and so the relations, proportions, values of each work of art toward the whole are readjusted; and this is conformity between the old and the new. Whoever has approved this idea of order, of the form of European, of English literature, will not find it preposterous that the past should be altered by the present as much as the present is directed by the past. And the poet who is aware of this will be aware of great difficulties and responsibilities.

T. S. Eliot (1919)

Eliot and Pound were not the only poets to borrow from foreign sources. E. E. Cummings learned his typographical play from the French modernist poets Guillaume Apollinaire and Stéphane Mallarmé, and he adopted an aesthetic based on the manifestos issued by the French Surrealists and Dadaists, poets who detached literature from referential meaning and linked it to experimental play. (The Surrealist manifestos were imitated by Pound, who, in his short-lived journal *Blast* in 1914 and 1915 issued irascible proclamations of his own, influenced by the Italian Futurist writers, who wanted a poetry geared to a technological world.)

In quieter ways, Frost, Wallace Stevens, and Moore were also influenced by international models. Frost wrote a rural poetry influenced not only by the English tradition from Wordsworth to Hardy but also by Latin eclogues and georgic poetry. He rightly suspected that he might find a more cordial reception in England for such poetry than in America, and his friendship with the English poet Edward Thomas (who reviewed Frost's work enthusiastically) gave him the support he sought. Although Frost returned to America after three years in England, it is symptomatic of the condition of American culture that it was in London that he and Pound should meet. Pound, finding in Frost an indigenous American voice of the sort he had been calling for, sponsored Frost's first American publication.

Stevens, though he never in his long life traveled abroad, was a devoted reader of French poetry and collector of French painting. "French and English," he wrote, "constitute a single language," and he composed his inventive lines as though they did: "The gaiety of language is our seigneur." For all the depth of his roots in Wordsworth and Keats, Stevens, like Eliot, found his way as a young poet at Harvard only by imitating the new harmonies—abrupt, nonchalant, oblique—of the French symbolists. And Marianne Moore, though she went abroad only once, served for four years (1925–1929) as the editor of *The Dial,* the New York magazine that, more than any other, brought the news of avant-garde art (including painting, sculpture, and music) to the American audience. Her expert knowledge of French was probably instrumental in her form of rebellion against English prosody when she decided to count syllables in her verse, as the French do, in lieu of feet.

Almost all the modernist American poets lived their creative years in cities. The American hinterland offered no base for poetry. Eliot left St. Louis for Cambridge and, eventually, London; Pound's family went from Idaho to Philadelphia, and Pound left the United States for Venice, Paris, London, and eventually various cities in Italy; Frost's family moved back east from San Francisco, and Frost remained always within easy reach of Boston. In the United States, only New York (and to a lesser extent Boston and Cambridge) contained enough artists for company, support, and journal publishing.

New York became the center toward which most poets converged. Moore's family made their way from St. Louis to Carlisle, Pennsylvania, to New York; E. E. Cummings left Cambridge for New York; William Carlos Williams, though he practiced medicine in New Jersey, joined, as did Stevens, the New York group clustered around *The Dial* and *Others* (a journal of experimental writing); Hart Crane left Ohio for Manhattan; and the writers of the Harlem Renaissance, though they may have been born in the South, found in New York the personal and intellectual stimulus necessary for a black literary movement.

But New York was not the only city to produce poetry. There was a "Chicago school" of poets that included Edgar Lee Masters and Carl Sandburg; and the magazine *Poetry,* founded and edited by Harriet Monroe, was published in Chicago. There was also a "southern school" of poetry clustered around John Crowe Ransom, a school that would produce Allen Tate, Robert Penn Warren, and even Robert Lowell. Still, New York was where the modernist movement in poetry, supported from abroad by its expatriate wing, was created and sustained. The poets were sustained, too, by artistic events in New York, notably the famous Armory show of 1913, which introduced modernist French painting to the American audience and radically changed American conceptions of art. Even though American poetry in the first part of the century was, for the most part, confined to one city on one coast, it was no longer narrowly parochial in content or in form.

American Themes in the New Poetry

Though the international aesthetic of modernism is the one that gave American poetry a wider perspective on the world, there were American poets who embraced a different, and no less powerful, aesthetic. William Carlos Williams

American Scenes

Mr. Frost is an honest writer, writing from himself, from his own knowledge and emotion; not simply picking up the manner which magazines are accepting at the moment, and applying it to topics in vogue. He is quite consciously and definitely putting New England rural life into verse. He is not using themes that anybody could have cribbed out of Ovid.

There are only two passions in art; there are only love and hate—with endless modifications. Frost has been honestly fond of the New England people, I dare say with spells of irritation. He has given their life honestly and seriously. He has never turned aside to make fun of it. He has taken their tragedy as tragedy, their stubbornness as stubbornness. I know more of farm life than I did before I had read his poems. That means I know more of 'Life.'

Ezra Pound, reviewing *North of Boston* (1914)

and Hart Crane opposed Eliot's and Pound's search for foreign materials for poetry. Williams, whose father was English and mother Puerto Rican, experienced the shakiness of being a first-generation child in America. His early Anglophile poetry imitated Keats, but he soon became defiantly American. Though Williams was powerfully influenced by the concepts of modernist art (he knew the French painters Francis Picabia and Marcel Duchamp), he embodied those concepts in poems treating American scenes, poems expressed in a resolutely colloquial language. Crane, believing that Eliot had taken a fatally wrong turn in using continental materials in *The Waste Land,* set himself, as had Williams in *Paterson,* the task of writing an American epic, which he called *The Bridge.* As *Paterson* uses documentary materials concerning the history and ongoing life of an ordinary American city, so *The Bridge* confronts modern American technology (the Brooklyn Bridge), the American past (Pocahontas and Rip Van Winkle), and the American present (hoboes riding the rails during the Depression).

Both Crane and Williams, though themselves from the middle class, felt social and political sympathy for the poor. This sympathy may have arisen in Williams through his practice of medicine among New Jersey's immigrants and in Crane through his sexual companionship with working-class men. The "Europeanizing" modernists, on the other hand, were conservative in their social and political alignments: Eliot declared himself an Anglo-Catholic royalist, Pound eventually came to sympathize with Fascism, and Frost and Stevens became increasingly Republican. The southern writers, though Democrats, preached an agrarianism that was profoundly conservative in its preference for the southern agricultural past over the northern technological present.

The division in American literary life between left and right wings has been the cause of bitter quarrels and literary scandals, the most famous centering on Ezra Pound, who in 1948 was awarded the Library of Congress Bollingen Prize for poetry while under indictment for treason for his World War II Italian radio broadcasts supporting Mussolini. Pound's literary supporters—of all political persuasions—argued that the poetry could be separated from the politics, since Pound had been declared of unsound mind and was incarcerated in St. Elizabeth's mental hospital; political antagonists replied that Pound's alliance with Fascism and his declared anti-Semitism should have precluded any award for his poetry. The controversy revealed the persistent American tendency to judge a poet's work by his life and to demand an ethical standard for literature to the exclusion of an aesthetic one.

American poets of the twentieth century did not, in short, enter a sympathetic culture. American suspicion of poetry originated long before the modernist period, however. In a frontier society, it has been argued, the fine arts have no practical value. It is also true that the dissenting founders of the northeastern colonies adopted a moral and instrumental, rather than aesthetic, view of literature. But the deepening of the estrangement between the common reader and the poet came about partly because of the gap in learning between the modernist poets and a reading public that knew no foreign cultures, ancient or modern, and partly because of the obliquity and nondiscursive form of the new poetry.

Longfellow, for instance, had been careful to explain his sources and allusions and to present his foreign material to his audience in an accommodated form. But *The Waste Land* and Pound's *Cantos* scattered bits of the literary and historical past over the page and expected the reader to perform as archaeologist, piecing together the fragments of a ruined culture. Even in *Paterson* and *The Bridge,* development was neither linear nor logical. These works, American in theme, were nonetheless radically modernist in form. *Paterson* mixed prose with poetry, history with lyricism, personal letters with dramatic vignettes; *The Bridge* mixed myth with history, narrative with rhapsody, stanzaic forms with free verse. Moore's patchwork of quotations, united by a quirky intellectual associationism, was no easier for the common reader to appreciate. The public embraced Frost and Cummings because they seemed accessible, brief, and explicit. Yet the public simplified both poets, seeking the sage more than the skeptic in Frost and preferring the sentimental to the satiric Cummings, reducing the one to a benign pastoral poet and the other to a poet of easy eroticism.

Yet the modernist poets, whatever their early estranged relation with the immediate public, were not indifferent to the common life of their generation. Like everyone else of the period, they were affected by World War I and the Depression and reacted variously to these events. Because Eliot and Pound saw the war from the European side, they felt a shock similar to that experienced by European poets, and the total work of each can be seen as a long meditation on the dissolution of the cultural past. Both used anthropological and archaeological methods to explore the myths that have sustained the West. Pound's reaction to

"What Is the Poet's Function?"

Certainly it is not to lead people out of the confusion in which they find themselves. Nor is it, I think, to comfort them while they follow their leaders to and fro. I think that his function is to make his imagination theirs and that he fulfills himself only as he sees his imagination become the light in the minds of others. His role, in short, is to help people live their lives.

Wallace Stevens, from The Necessary Angel (1951)

Ethics are no more a part of poetry than they are of painting.

The aesthetic order includes all other orders but is not limited to them.

Poetry is a purging of the world's poverty and change and evil and death. It is a present perfecting, a satisfaction in the irremediable poverty of life.

We never arrive intellectually. But emotionally we arrive constantly (as in poetry, happiness, high mountains, vistas).

Wallace Stevens, from Adagia

World War I was to attack capitalism itself and to urge a return to an economic system that did not permit "usury," the making of money by lending money. Williams, Crane, and Hughes, on the other hand, dealt more immediately with domestic events. Williams wrote about the 1920 trial of Sacco and Vanzetti (two Italian anarchist immigrants who were executed, perhaps wrongly, for murder), but he also treated the urban poverty and squalor that he saw among his patients. Crane wrote about the gains and losses of a technological society, criticizing the quantification of life but admiring the mastery of technological power; Hughes commemorated the wrongful trial, in 1931, of the Scottsboro "boys," nine blacks accused of the rape of two white women. The skepticism about the American dream generated by the Depression reached even such a politically inactive poet as Stevens. He was stung by the criticism (voiced in the Marxist journal *The Masses* by the critic Stanley Burnshaw) that his poetry averted its gaze from those suffering in the Depression. As a result, Stevens embarked on *Owl's Clover*, a long poem treating the social function of art and raising questions of the permanence and relevance of European art to the future.

All of the modernist poets, by their interest in the social fabric and its intellectual base, enlarged the range of topics considered appropriate to poetry. In the Pre-Raphaelite and Georgian poets of turn-of-the-century England, poetry had become almost purely "lyric," attenuated, inward-looking. Eliot made the revolutionary move of including, in *The Waste Land,* a sordid lower-class pub discussion of abortion and also a meaningless copulation between a bored typist and her "young man carbuncular." In another surprising move, Frost retold, in an American locale and with American characters, what the English poet Thomas Gray had called "the short and simple annals of the poor," including those who were backward, criminal, or mad. Pound, although he never abandoned entirely his Pre-Raphaelite lyric beginnings, thrust up against lyric passages inconsequential and trivial details of ordinary experience. Williams sketched the urban underclass, while Crane brought into his poetry all sorts of diverse social realities—Charlie Chaplin, advertising, Indian dances, black oppression, urban suicide. Cummings introduced comic obscenity and political satire; Hughes and Toomer began to make visible in poetry the life of blacks, northern and southern. And Wallace Stevens, though he was rarely a poet of historical events, introduced into modern poetry topics of philosophical and cognitive subtlety.

A New American Literary Language

But modernist poetry did not stake its claim chiefly by being innovative in thematic ways. Rather, like all interesting poetry, it distinguished itself, in W. H. Auden's words, by "new styles of architecture, a change of heart." The new style manifested itself in many ways. Some poetry could be distinctively American in language, as in Frost's "sentence sounds" and Hughes's black vernacular, or it could rewrite in American idiom (as in Frost and Robinson) traditional genres like the Wordsworthian pastoral narrative. Frost learned from Longfellow and Whittier and Bryant that rural New England was worthy poetic territory, but he learned even more, stylistically, from the Latin poets, especially Horace and Lucretius. His domestication, in American poetry, of the language of Roman stoicism is a brilliant native achievement. Prosody too is a distinguishing feature of modernist poetry: Both Eliot and Pound, but in different ways, brought free verse into prominence. Eliot's extreme musicality, visible throughout all his work, culminated in his calling his last poems "quartets" after the example of Beethoven; Pound, on the other hand, amassed Imagist phrases into a fragmentary line that broke off after each breath.

   Modernist poetry is distinguished by structure, too, from the traditional poetry of earlier centuries; it is a poetry of fragments. Many of the modernist poets wrote long poems, but they constructed them on a principle different from the apparent unity that governs the sustained epics of Milton and Wordsworth. *The Waste Land,* the *Cantos, Paterson,* and *The Bridge* are all discontinuous epics, coming at their topics from a variety of perspectives. They borrow from art the metonymic technique of collage, in which one thing after another is glued onto a surface, and they borrow from film the technique of montage, in which one frame is contrasted with the next. They also change disconcertingly from "high" to "low" language instead of keeping a constant level of diction. The *ars poetica* of Wallace Stevens, a long poem called *Notes Toward a Supreme Fiction,* is similarly unpredictable in diction and form; it is sometimes serious, sometimes farcical, sometimes philosophical, sometimes anecdotal.

"A Machine Made of Words"

A poem is a small (or large) machine made of words. When I say there's nothing sentimental about a poem I mean that there can be no part, as in any other machine, that is redundant.

Prose may carry a load of ill-defined matter like a ship. But poetry is the machine which drives it, pruned to a perfect economy. As in all machines its movement is intrinsic, undulant, a physical more than a literary character. In a poem this movement is distinguished in each case by the character of the speech from which it arises. . . .

There is no poetry of distinction without formal invention, for it is in the intimate form that works of art achieve their exact meaning, in which they most resemble the machine, to give language its highest dignity, its illumination in the environment to which it is native.

William Carlos Williams (1944)

All poetry is experimental poetry.

Wallace Stevens, from *Adagia*

By the end of the modernist period, there was no longer a single American literary language—elevated, discursive, logical, genteel, expository. Instead, literary language had been shattered into a thousand bright reflecting parts, and the literary artists turned the kaleidoscope of poetry to make successive new patterns of the shining fragments. Not only language, but topics and conventions had been reworked. All the poetic genres—elegy, epic, love poetry, the sonnet—had been given new American embodiments. The Muse, as Whitman had predicted in "Song of the Exposition," had come as an "illustrious émigré" to these shores.

The view of America that we can gather from modernist testimony is full of contradictory elements. Except for Frost and Crane, the modernist poets are sharply critical of their country, either explicitly or implicitly—and even Frost and Crane see much that they deplore, such as the deprivation and misery present among both the rural and the urban poor. Pound, in a fervor driven by mounting eccentricity rising to madness, attempted to persuade America away from its entanglements with munition makers and back to what he believed to be its political first principles. Eliot satirized Boston provinciality, and Cummings mocked "the Cambridge ladies that live in furnished souls." Cullen and Hughes uttered bitter indictments of the oppressive racism of the American majority. Stevens wondered how a country with more wilderness than settled land, and only a brief history of cultural production, could ever generate a native aesthetic.

"I Am Concerned with the Future of America"

I am concerned with the Future of America, but not because I think that America has any so-called par value as a state or as a group of people. . . . It is only because I feel persuaded that here are destined to be discovered certain as yet undefined spiritual quantities, perhaps a new hierarchy of faith not to be developed so completely elsewhere. And in this process I like to feel myself as a potential factor; certainly I must speak in its terms and what discoveries I may make are situated in its experience.

Hart Crane, "General Aims and Theories" (1937)

And yet, for all this criticism, a certain piety toward America distills itself from this poetry. Eliot displays piety toward Gloucester and the New England past; Frost takes pride in the stubbornness of the New England conscience; Crane makes a radiant claim for a single American tradition reaching from Indian dances to the suspension bridge; Williams expresses a humorous and tolerant love of life in a small American city; Moore asserts that superiority, which "has never been confined to one locality," can exist in America as well as in the older cultures of Europe or China; Cummings finds ebullient amusement in watching the American character, appealing in spite of its foolishness; and Hughes makes appreciative notations of the resilience of his Harlem neighbors even in hard times. It is the ambivalence of American poetry about American social reality that renders it believable.

If we look to the philosophical base of modernity, we can see that the modernist poets—except for the later Eliot—create either a world without a God or a world in which a corrosive skepticism attaches itself to belief. Their secular sense of the world revises the subject matter, attitude, and style of poetry. Wallace Stevens wrote:

To see the gods dispelled in mid-air and dissolve like clouds is one of the great human experiences. . . . It was their annihilation, not ours, and yet it left us feeling that in a measure, we, too, had been annihilated.

In varying degrees, this is the story of one whole generation of poets. They look to an Emersonian natural transcendence but find that it fails to sustain them. They can settle on no doctrinal or communal form of belief. Each of them—again, the later Eliot excepted—constructs a world of which the individual is, necessarily, the center and in which human mortality defines a final horizon of expectation. Even when these poets are believers—as Moore was—the aesthetic of the poetry is founded on social, not supernatural, meaning.

"The Figure a Poem Makes"

The figure a poem makes. It begins in delight and ends in wisdom. The figure is the same as for love. No one can really hold that the ecstasy should be static and stand still in one place. It begins in delight, it inclines to the impulse, it assumes direction with the first line laid down, it runs a course of lucky events, and ends in a clarification of life—not necessarily a great clarification, such as sects and cults are founded on, but in a momentary stay against confusion. It has denouement. It has an outcome that though unforeseen was predestined from the first image of the original mood—and indeed from the very mood. It is but a trick poem and no poem at all if the best of it was thought of first and saved for the last. It finds its own name as it goes and discovers the best waiting for it in some final phrase at once wise and sad—the happy-sad blend of the drinking song.

Robert Frost (1939)

Faced with the absence of a prescriptive religious or social order, many of these poets eventually find an exhilarating sense of personal freedom. An exploration of this freedom, coupled with a parallel exploration of linguistic possibility, becomes for these poets the chief avenue to creative work. They become historians of modernist culture, examining the possible representations—both individual and communal—of our century. As they cleanse language and culture of old and worn-out meanings and introduce to poetry what is American in thought, sensibility, perception, observation, and diction, they become exemplary of the modern endeavors of consciousness itself.

Further Reading:
S. Brown, *Negro Poetry and Drama,* 1937.
H. Gregory and M. Zaturenska, *A History of American Poetry, 1900–1940,* 1946.
L. Bogan, *Achievement in American Poetry 1900–1950,* 1951.
R. H. Pearce, *The Continuity of American Poetry,* 1961.
M. Cowley, *After the Genteel Tradition: American Writers 1910–1930,* rev. ed. 1964.
J. H. Miller, *Poets of Reality,* 1965.
R. Bridgman, *The Colloquial Style in America,* 1966.
E. Margolies, *Native Sons: A Critical Study of Twentieth-Century Negro Authors,* 1968.
H. H. Waggoner, *American Poets: From the Puritans to the Present Day,* 1968.
J. Mazzaro, *Modern American Poetry,* 1970.

N. I. Huggins, *Harlem Renaissance,* 1971.
H. Kenner, *The Pound Era,* 1971.
A. Gelpi, *The Tenth Muse: The Psyche of the American Poet,* 1975.
D. Perkins, *History of Modern Poetry,* 1976.
E. S. Watts, *The Poetry of American Women from 1632 to 1945,* 1977.
M. L. Rosenthal, *Sailing into the Unknown: Yeats, Pound, and Eliot,* 1978.
M. Borroff, *Language and the Poet: Verbal Artistry in Frost, Stevens, and Moore,* 1979.
H. Vendler, *Part of Nature, Part of Us: Modern American Poets,* 1980.
M. Perloff, *The Poetics of Indeterminacy: Rimbaud to Cage,* 1981.
D. E. Stanford, *Revolution and Convention in Modern Poetry,* 1983.

Robert Frost
1875–1963

Robert Frost is the best known of our modern American poets: His poems find their way into high school textbooks and into popular memory far more quickly than do the poems of his contemporaries. In part, Frost's popularity may be due to the apparent simplicity of his subject matter, but it is surely more profoundly due to his uncanny feeling for what he called "sentence sounds," the sounds and syntactic patterns into which the American language naturally falls. Frost's lines are remembered without effort: "The land was ours before we were the land's"; "But I have promises to keep"; "Nothing gold can stay"; "Earth's the right place for love"; "Good fences make good neighbors." Frost's immense talent as a reader of his own work made him something of a national institution; the gravel-voiced old man with a shock of white hair who was seen on television reading "The Gift Outright" at John F. Kennedy's inauguration in 1961 was already a figure known to most viewers. But they also knew his work; he was probably the one living poet whose poetry had touched them in school.

Frost's gift for an intimate lyricism was learned in part from Whitman; "You come too" (from "The Pasture") was an invitation that Whitman had often extended to his readers. Whitman's patriotism, too, finds a kindred echo in Frost's faith in the continuity of American principle, evident in a poem like "Immigrants," where every immigrant ship is said to have the *Mayflower* as its convoy. And Emerson, the ancestor of both Whitman and Frost, stands behind Frost's resolute transcendental confidence that we can stay—anchor—our minds on something like a star.

And yet these American ancestors do not fully account for Frost. Since Lionel Trilling first emphasized the darker side of Frost's imagination, critics have increasingly seen how many-sided Frost is. Biographers have drawn links between the events of Frost's own life—a Gothic chronicle of disasters—and the poetry. Frost's father, a transplanted easterner, died in San Francisco when Frost was eleven. (Frost's mother returned to New Hampshire, and Frost took the region for his own.) But it was not only the early death of his father that convinced Frost of the evil in existence. His own first child died in infancy; his only son committed suicide; one daughter died after childbirth, and another was mentally ill; his embittered wife refused on her deathbed to admit him to her room. The "rage" that Frost saw in the natural order ("Once by the Pacific") had for him its counterpart in the social order, where any "flower" could be subverted; the poem "The Subverted Flower" suggests a fundamental incompatibility between male sexual desire and female fear and disgust. In many of his grimmer poems (like "Design") Frost comes close to Thomas Hardy in suspecting that the universe may be governed by a malevolent God or, worse, not governed at all— by anyone.

Like many American writers, Frost had to expatriate himself to find his first success. Before he went to England in 1912 at the age of thirty-eight, he had been writing poetry for a long time. He had been class poet at his graduation in

1892 from high school in Lawrence, Massachusetts, where his future wife, Elinor White, was co-valedictorian with him. Frost went on to Dartmouth but dropped out after only one term. He continued to write while working at odd jobs— bobbin boy at a cotton mill, cobbler, schoolteacher, journalist. In 1897 he came to Harvard for two years as a special student, where he carried on the study of Latin that he had begun in high school. At Harvard he attended the philosophy lectures of George Santayana and read William James; their skepticism and pragmatism influenced the philosophical temper of his poetry. In 1899 his grandfather bought a farm for him in Derry, New Hampshire; but though Frost lived there and worked the farm for ten years, he was no nearer to publishing a book. After three more years of teaching at Pinkerton Academy in Derry, Frost left for England, where he published his first volume, *A Boy's Will* (1913). The title comes from Longfellow: "A boy's will is the wind's will, / And the thoughts of youth are long, long thoughts." In choosing this title, Frost made explicit his own derivation from and competition with Longfellow, New England's regional poet, and in fact Longfellow's "Schooner Hesperus" and "Hiawatha" have now been displaced in our literary history by Frost's regional poetry of New Hampshire.

In England, Frost met Ezra Pound, who helped publish Frost's second book, *North of Boston* (1914), a volume containing several of Frost's most stunning poems, including "Mending Wall," "Home Burial," and "After Apple-Picking." His reputation made, Frost returned to the United States to take a teaching position at Amherst College in 1917, through he taught there only intermittently. His many other teaching stints and his poetry readings, together with his royalties, supported Frost for the rest of his life. He was far more popular, and more successful financially, than the majority of his contemporaries.

Frost's poems tend to fall, formally speaking, into two groups: the long blank-verse poems like "Home Burial," often embodying some form of New England rural suffering, and the short, exquisite, rhymed lyrics, including philosophical sonnets like "Design." The narratives, which reopen a vein already worked by Edwin Arlington Robinson, represent the strains of life lived under pinched, emotionally thwarting conditions. They are a powerful corrective to the European pastoral tradition that represents nature as bountiful and gracious and man's life in nature as healing and joyful. They are also a corrective to the optimistic Emersonian view of nature as an authentic teacher. After reading the harsh accusations in "Home Burial," no reader can continue to think nature or domesticity merciful. The troglodytic farmer in "Mending Wall" is more a savage than a noble savage.

Frost's songlike lyrics ("Reluctance" or "Stopping by Woods on a Snowy Evening") stem directly from the most musical of English poems (Shakespeare's songs, Keats's odes, Shelley's choruses); his more philosophical lyrics are given their sternness by Horace and Lucretius. Frost's long reading in the Latin poets is visible not merely in his use of hendecasyllabics (eleven-syllable lines) in "For Once, Then, Something," but more powerfully in his pre-Christian view of nature. In repudiating the Christian tradition of a sacramental nature in favor of a nature enigmatic ("The Most of It"), elusive ("For Once, Then, Something"), or unreadable ("Time Out"), Frost adds to his nature poetry a metaphysical element of philosophic commentary. But his deftness of touch ("If design govern in a thing so small") retains his poetry within a colloquial tradition, just as his reliance on rhyme (he objected to free verse, saying it was like playing tennis without a net) retains his poetry within the tradition of the European lyric.

Frost represents a powerful antithesis to the modernist poetic represented by Pound and Eliot. As they face Europe, he faces America; as they assume and display learning, he is only obliquely allusive; as they write free verse, he writes in meter; as they lament a fragmented culture, he records a culture that can still muster a living, if forgotten, tradition. No one has better incorporated American speed into verse; Frost was delighted when he wrote, as a final line to "The Pauper Witch of Grafton," "I might have, but it doesn't seem as if"—a line that, in its vernacular lilt, could never have closed a British poem. In his grimly comic, sometimes even mischievous poetry, Frost preserved a vein of American humor that we are more likely to associate with prose like Twain's. And in his essays on poetry—aphoristic, pithy, and profound—Frost is one of the best theorists of a skeptical, questioning modern poetry that settles for no easy answers.

Further Reading:
L. R. Thompson, *Fire and Ice: The Art and Thought of Robert Frost,* 1942.
S. Cox, *A Swinger of Birches,* 1957.
R. L. Cook, *The Dimensions of Robert Frost,* 1959.
J. F. Lynan, *The Pastoral Art of Robert Frost,* 1960.
R. Squires, *The Major Themes of Robert Frost,* 1963.
R. Brower, *The Poetry of Robert Frost,* 1963.
P. L. Gerber, *Robert Frost,* 1966.
L. R. Thompson, *Robert Frost: The Early Years,* 1966.
L. R. Thompson, *Robert Frost: The Years of Triumph,* 1970.

F. Lentricchia, *Robert Frost: Modern Poetics and the Landscape of Self,* 1975.
L. R. Thompson and R. H. Winnick, *Robert Frost: The Later Years,* 1976.
F. Lentricchia and M. C. Lentricchia, *Robert Frost: A Bibliography,* 1976.
R. Poirier, *Robert Frost: The Work of Knowing,* 1977.
L. Wagner, *Robert Frost: The Critical Reception,* 1977.
J. C. Kemp, *Robert Frost and New England,* 1979.
L. R. Thompson, *Robert Frost,* 1981.
Critical Essays on Robert Frost, ed. P. L. Gerber, 1982.

Text:
The Poetry of Robert Frost, ed. E. C. Lathem, 1969 (punctuation corrected from *The Selected Poems of Robert Frost,* 1963).
See also *Selected Letters of Robert Frost,* ed. L. R.

Thompson, 1964.
Selected Prose of Robert Frost, ed. H. Cox and E. C. Lathem, 1966.

Mowing

There was never a sound beside the wood but one,
And that was my long scythe whispering to the ground.
What was it it whispered? I knew not well myself;
Perhaps it was something about the heat of the sun,

Something, perhaps, about the lack of sound—
And that was why it whispered and did not speak.
It was no dream of the gift of idle hours,
Or easy gold at the hand of fay or elf:
Anything more than the truth would have seemed too weak
To the earnest love that laid the swale[1] in rows,
Not without feeble-pointed spikes of flowers
(Pale orchises), and scared a bright green snake.
The fact is the sweetest dream that labor knows.
My long scythe whispered and left the hay to make.

1913

October

O hushed October morning mild,
Thy leaves have ripened to the fall;
Tomorrow's wind, if it be wild,
Should waste them all.
The crows above the forest call;
Tomorrow they may form and go.
O hushed October morning mild,
Begin the hours of this day slow.
Make the day seem to us less brief.
Hearts not averse to being beguiled,
Beguile us in the way you know.
Release one leaf at break of day;
At noon release another leaf;
One from our trees, one far away.
Retard the sun with gentle mist;
Enchant the land with amethyst.
Slow, slow!
For the grapes' sake, if they were all,
Whose leaves already are burnt with frost,
Whose clustered fruit must else be lost—
For the grapes' sake along the wall.

1913

---

[1] Low-lying meadow.

Reluctance

Out through the fields and the woods
    And over the walls I have wended;
I have climbed the hills of view
    And looked at the world, and descended;
I have come by the highway home,   5
    And lo, it is ended.

The leaves are all dead on the ground,
    Save those that the oak is keeping
To ravel them one by one
    And let them go scraping and creeping   10
Out over the crusted snow,
    When others are sleeping.

And the dead leaves lie huddled and still,
    No longer blown hither and thither;
The last lone aster is gone;   15
    The flowers of the witch hazel wither;
The heart is still aching to seek,
    But the feet question "Whither?"

Ah, when to the heart of man
    Was it ever less than a treason   20
To go with the drift of things,
    To yield with a grace to reason,
And bow and accept the end
    Of a love or a season?

1913

Mending Wall

Something there is that doesn't love a wall,[1]
That sends the frozen-ground-swell under it
And spills the upper boulders in the sun,
And makes gaps even two can pass abreast.

---

[1] It is frost (a pun on Frost himself) that is
inimical to walls.

The work of hunters is another thing: 5
I have come after them and made repair
Where they have left not one stone on a stone,
But they would have the rabbit out of hiding,
To please the yelping dogs. The gaps I mean,
No one has seen them made or heard them made,   10
But at spring mending-time we find them there.
I let my neighbor know beyond the hill;
And on a day we meet to walk the line
And set the wall between us once again.
We keep the wall between us as we go.   15
To each the boulders that have fallen to each.
And some are loaves and some so nearly balls
We have to use a spell to make them balance:
"Stay where you are until our backs are turned!"
We wear our fingers rough with handling them.   20
Oh, just another kind of outdoor game,
One on a side. It comes to little more:
There where it is we do not need the wall:
He is all pine and I am apple orchard.
My apple trees will never get across   25
And eat the cones under his pines, I tell him.
He only says, "Good fences make good neighbors."
Spring is the mischief in me, and I wonder
If I could put a notion in his head:
"*Why* do they make good neighbors? Isn't it   30
Where there are cows? But here there are no cows.
Before I built a wall I'd ask to know
What I was walling in or walling out,
And to whom I was like to give offense.
Something there is that doesn't love a wall,   35
That wants it down." I could say "Elves" to him,
But it's not elves exactly, and I'd rather
He said it for himself. I see him there,
Bringing a stone grasped firmly by the top
In each hand, like an old-stone savage armed.   40
He moves in darkness as it seems to me,
Not of woods only and the shade of trees.
He will not go behind his father's saying,
And he likes having thought of it so well
He says again, "Good fences make good neighbors."   45
1914

Home Burial

He saw her from the bottom of the stairs
Before she saw him. She was starting down,
Looking back over her shoulder at some fear.
She took a doubtful step and then undid it
To raise herself and look again. He spoke   5
Advancing toward her: "What is it you see
From up there always—for I want to know."
She turned and sank upon her skirts at that,
And her face changed from terrified to dull.
He said to gain time: "What is it you see,"   10
Mounting until she cowered under him.
"I will find out now—you must tell me, dear."
She, in her place, refused him any help,
With the least stiffening of her neck and silence.
She let him look, sure that he wouldn't see,   15
Blind creature; and awhile he didn't see.
But at last he murmured, "Oh," and again, "Oh."

"What is it—what?" she said.

                       "Just that I see."

"You don't," she challenged. "Tell me what it is."

"The wonder is I didn't see at once.   20
I never noticed it from here before.
I must be wonted to it—that's the reason.
The little graveyard where my people are!
So small the window frames the whole of it.
Not so much larger than a bedroom, is it?   25
There are three stones of slate and one of marble,
Broad-shouldered little slabs there in the sunlight
On the sidehill. We haven't to mind *those*.
But I understand: it is not the stones,
But the child's mound——"

                   "Don't, don't, don't, don't," she cried.   30

She withdrew, shrinking from beneath his arm
That rested on the banister, and slid downstairs;
And turned on him with such a daunting look,
He said twice over before he knew himself:
"Can't a man speak of his own child he's lost?"   35

"Not you! Oh, where's my hat? Oh, I don't need it!
I must get out of here. I must get air.
I don't know rightly whether any man can."

"Amy! Don't go to someone else this time.
Listen to me. I won't come down the stairs." 40
He sat and fixed his chin between his fists.
"There's something I should like to ask you, dear."

"You don't know how to ask it."

                              "Help me, then."

Her fingers moved the latch for all reply.

"My words are nearly always an offense. 45
I don't know how to speak of anything
So as to please you. But I might be taught
I should suppose. I can't say I see how.
A man must partly give up being a man
With womenfolk. We could have some arrangement 50
By which I'd bind myself to keep hands off
Anything special you're a-mind to name.
Though I don't like such things 'twixt those that love.
Two that don't love can't live together without them.
But two that do can't live together with them." 55
She moved the latch a little. "Don't—don't go.
Don't carry it to someone else this time.
Tell me about it if it's something human.
Let me into your grief. I'm not so much
Unlike other folks as your standing there 60
Apart would make me out. Give me my chance.
I do think, though, you overdo it a little.
What was it brought you up to think it the thing
To take your mother-loss of a first child
So inconsolably—in the face of love. 65
You'd think his memory might be satisfied——"

"There you go sneering now!"

                    "I'm not, I'm not!
You make me angry. I'll come down to you.
God, what a woman! And it's come to this,
A man can't speak of his own child that's dead." 70

"You can't because you don't know how to speak.
If you had any feelings, you that dug

With your own hand—how could you?—his little grave;
I saw you from that very window there,
Making the gravel leap and leap in air,   75
Leap up, like that, like that, and land so lightly
And roll back down the mound beside the hole.
I thought, Who is that man? I didn't know you.
And I crept down the stairs and up the stairs
To look again, and still your spade kept lifting.   80
Then you came in. I heard your rumbling voice
Out in the kitchen, and I don't know why,
But I went near to see with my own eyes.
You could sit there with the stains on your shoes
Of the fresh earth from your own baby's grave   85
And talk about your everyday concerns.
You had stood the spade up against the wall
Outside there in the entry, for I saw it."

"I shall laugh the worst laugh I ever laughed.
I'm cursed. God, if I don't believe I'm cursed."   90

"I can repeat the very words you were saying.
'Three foggy mornings and one rainy day
Will rot the best birch fence a man can build.'
Think of it, talk like that at such a time!
What had how long it takes a birch to rot   95
To do with what was in the darkened parlor.
You *couldn't* care! The nearest friends can go
With anyone to death, comes so far short
They might as well not try to go at all.
No, from the time when one is sick to death,   100
One is alone, and he dies more alone.
Friends make pretense of following to the grave,
But before one is in it, their minds are turned
And making the best of their way back to life
And living people, and things they understand.   105
But the world's evil. I won't have grief so
If I can change it. Oh, I won't, I won't!"

"There, you have said it all and you feel better.
You won't go now. You're crying. Close the door.
The heart's gone out of it: why keep it up.   110
Amy! There's someone coming down the road!"

"You—oh, you think the talk is all. I must go—
Somewhere out of this house. How can I make you——"

"If—you—do!" She was opening the door wider.
"Where do you mean to go? First tell me that.   115
I'll follow and bring you back by force. I *will!*—"
1914

After Apple-Picking

My long two-pointed ladder's sticking through a
    tree
Toward heaven still,
And there's a barrel that I didn't fill
Beside it, and there may be two or three
Apples I didn't pick upon some bough.   5
But I am done with apple-picking now.
Essence of winter sleep is on the night,
The scent of apples: I am drowsing off.
I cannot rub the strangeness from my sight
I got from looking through a pane of glass   10
I skimmed this morning from the drinking trough
And held against the world of hoary grass.
It melted, and I let it fall and break.
But I was well
Upon my way to sleep before it fell,   15
And I could tell
What form my dreaming was about to take.
Magnified apples appear and disappear,
Stem end and blossom end,
And every fleck of russet showing clear.   20
My instep arch not only keeps the ache,
It keeps the pressure of a ladder-round.
I feel the ladder sway as the boughs bend.
And I keep hearing from the cellar bin
The rumbling sound   25
Of load on load of apples coming in.
For I have had too much
Of apple-picking: I am overtired
Of the great harvest I myself desired.
There were ten thousand thousand fruit to touch,   30
Cherish in hand, lift down, and not let fall.
For all
That struck the earth,
No matter if not bruised or spiked with stubble,

Went surely to the cider-apple heap   35
As of no worth.
One can see what will trouble
This sleep of mine, whatever sleep it is.
Were he not gone,
The woodchuck could say whether it's like his   40
Long sleep, as I describe its coming on,
Or just some human sleep.

1914

The Road Not Taken

Two roads diverged in a yellow wood,
And sorry I could not travel both
And be one traveler, long I stood
And looked down one as far as I could
To where it bent in the undergrowth;   5

Then took the other, as just as fair,
And having perhaps the better claim,
Because it was grassy and wanted wear;
Though as for that the passing there
Had worn them really about the same,   10

And both that morning equally lay
In leaves no step had trodden black.
Oh, I kept the first for another day!
Yet knowing how way leads on to way,
I doubted if I should ever come back.   15

I shall be telling this with a sigh
Somewhere ages and ages hence:
Two roads diverged in a wood, and I—
I took the one less traveled by,
And that has made all the difference.   20

1916

The Oven Bird

There is a singer everyone has heard,
Loud, a mid-summer and a mid-wood bird,
Who makes the solid tree trunks sound again.
He says that leaves are old and that for flowers
Mid-summer is to spring as one to ten.   5
He says the early petal-fall is past
When pear and cherry bloom went down in
    showers
On sunny days a moment overcast;
And comes that other fall we name the fall.[1]
He says the highway dust is over all.   10
The bird would cease and be as other birds
But that he knows in singing not to sing.
The question that he frames in all but words
Is what to make of a diminished thing.
1916

Birches

When I see birches bend to left and right
Across the lines of straighter darker trees,
I like to think some boy's been swinging them.
But swinging doesn't bend them down to stay
As ice storms do. Often you must have seen them   5
Loaded with ice a sunny winter morning
After a rain. They click upon themselves
As the breeze rises, and turn many-colored
As the stir cracks and crazes their enamel.
Soon the sun's warmth makes them shed crystal shells   10
Shattering and avalanching on the snow crust—
Such heaps of broken glass to sweep away
You'd think the inner dome of heaven had fallen.
They are dragged to the withered bracken[1] by the load,
And they seem not to break; though once they are bowed   15
So low for long, they never right themselves:

---

[1] The English call the season "autumn."   [1] Fern.

You may see their trunks arching in the woods
Years afterwards, trailing their leaves on the ground
Like girls on hands and knees that throw their hair
Before them over their heads to dry in the sun.   20
But I was going to say when Truth broke in
With all her matter of fact about the ice storm
I should prefer to have some boy bend them
As he went out and in to fetch the cows—
Some boy too far from town to learn baseball,   25
Whose only play was what he found himself,
Summer or winter, and could play alone.
One by one he subdued his father's trees
By riding them down over and over again
Until he took the stiffness out of them,   30
And not one but hung limp, not one was left
For him to conquer. He learned all there was
To learn about not launching out too soon
And so not carrying the tree away
Clear to the ground. He always kept his poise   35
To the top branches, climbing carefully
With the same pains you use to fill a cup
Up to the brim, and even above the brim.
Then he flung outward, feet first, with a swish,
Kicking his way down through the air to the ground.   40
So was I once myself a swinger of birches.
And so I dream of going back to be.
It's when I'm weary of considerations,
And life is too much like a pathless wood
Where your face burns and tickles with the cobwebs   45
Broken across it, and one eye is weeping
From a twig's having lashed across it open.
I'd like to get away from earth awhile
And then come back to it and begin over.
May no fate willfully misunderstand me   50
And half grant what I wish and snatch me away
Not to return. Earth's the right place for love:
I don't know where it's likely to go better.
I'd like to go by climbing a birch tree,
And climb black branches up a snow-white trunk   55
Toward heaven, till the tree could bear no more,
But dipped its top and set me down again.
That would be good both going and coming back.
One could do worse than be a swinger of birches.
1916

Fire and Ice

Some say the world will end in fire,
Some say in ice.
From what I've tasted of desire
I hold with those who favor fire.
But if it had to perish twice,   5
I think I know enough of hate
To say that for destruction ice
Is also great
And would suffice.

1923

Nothing Gold Can Stay

Nature's first green is gold,
Her hardest hue to hold.
Her early leaf's a flower;
But only so an hour.
Then leaf subsides to leaf.   5
So Eden sank to grief,
So dawn goes down to day.
Nothing gold can stay.

1923

Stopping by Woods on a Snowy Evening

Whose woods these are I think I know.
His house is in the village, though;
He will not see me stopping here
To watch his woods fill up with snow.

My little horse must think it queer   5
To stop without a farmhouse near
Between the woods and frozen lake
The darkest evening of the year.

He gives his harness bells a shake
To ask if there is some mistake.   10
The only other sound's the sweep
Of easy wind and downy flake.

The woods are lovely, dark and deep,
But I have promises to keep,
And miles to go before I sleep,   15
And miles to go before I sleep.

1923

For Once, Then, Something*

Others taunt me with having knelt at well-curbs
Always wrong to the light, so never seeing
Deeper down in the well than where the water
Gives me back in a shining surface picture
Me myself in the summer heaven godlike   5
Looking out of a wreath of fern and cloud puffs.
Once, when trying with chin against a well-curb,
I discerned, as I thought, beyond the picture,
Through the picture, a something white, uncertain,
Something more of the depths—and then I lost it.   10
Water came to rebuke the too clear water.
One drop fell from a fern, and lo, a ripple
Shook whatever it was lay there at bottom,
Blurred it, blotted it out. What was that whiteness?
Truth? A pebble of quartz? For once, then, something.¹   15
1923

---

* The poem is written in hendecasyllabics, a Latin form of 11 syllables per line.
¹ Cf. Diogenes (412?–323 B.C.), Greek Cynic philosopher: "Truth lies at the bottom of a well."

To Earthward

Love at the lips was touch
As sweet as I could bear;
And once that seemed too much;
I lived on air

That crossed me from sweet things,   5
The flow of—was it musk
From hidden grapevine springs
Down hill at dusk?

I had the swirl and ache
From sprays of honeysuckle   10
That when they're gathered shake
Dew on the knuckle.

I craved strong sweets, but those
Seemed strong when I was young;
The petal of the rose   15
It was that stung.

Now no joy but lacks salt
That is not dashed with pain
And weariness and fault;
I crave the stain   20

Of tears, the aftermark
Of almost too much love,
The sweet of bitter bark
And burning clove.

When stiff and sore and scarred   25
I take away my hand
From leaning on it hard
In grass and sand,

The hurt is not enough:
I long for weight and strength   30
To feel the earth as rough
To all my length.

1923

The Need of Being Versed
in Country Things

The house had gone to bring again
To the midnight sky a sunset glow.
Now the chimney was all of the house that stood,
Like a pistil after the petals go.

The barn opposed across the way,   5
That would have joined the house in flame
Had it been the will of the wind, was left
To bear forsaken the place's name.

No more it opened with all one end
For teams that came by the stony road   10
To drum on the floor with scurrying hoofs
And brush the mow with the summer load.

The birds that came to it through the air
At broken windows flew out and in,
Their murmur more like the sigh we sigh   15
From too much dwelling on what has been.

Yet for them the lilac renewed its leaf,
And the aged elm, though touched with fire;
And the dry pump flung up an awkward arm;
And the fence post carried a strand of wire.   20

For them there was really nothing sad.
But though they rejoiced in the nest they kept,
One had to be versed in country things
Not to believe the phoebes wept.

1923

Once by the Pacific

The shattered water made a misty din.
Great waves looked over others coming in,
And thought of doing something to the shore
That water never did to land before.
The clouds were low and hairy in the skies,   5
Like locks blown forward in the gleam of eyes.
You could not tell, and yet it looked as if
The shore was lucky in being backed by cliff,
The cliff in being backed by continent;
It looked as if a night of dark intent   10
Was coming, and not only a night, an age.
Someone had better be prepared for rage.
There would be more than ocean-water broken
Before God's last *Put out the Light* was spoken.[1]

1928

Immigrants

No ship of all that under sail or steam
Have gathered people to us more and more
But Pilgrim-manned the *Mayflower* in a dream
Has been her anxious convoy in to shore.

1928

Desert Places

Snow falling and night falling fast, oh, fast
In a field I looked into going past,
And the ground almost covered smooth in snow,
But a few weeds and stubble showing last.

---

[1] God's first words in Genesis are, "Let there be Light."

The woods around it have it—it is theirs.   5
All animals are smothered in their lairs.
I am too absent-spirited to count;
The loneliness includes me unawares.

And lonely as it is, that loneliness
Will be more lonely ere it will be less—   10
A blanker whiteness of benighted[1] snow
With no expression, nothing to express.

They cannot scare me with their empty spaces
Between stars—on stars where no human race is.
I have it in me so much nearer home   15
To scare myself with my own desert places.

1936

Design[1]

I found a dimpled spider, fat and white,
On a white heal-all,[2] holding up a moth
Like a white piece of rigid satin cloth—
Assorted characters of death and blight
Mixed ready to begin the morning right,   5
Like the ingredients of a witches' broth—
A snow-drop spider, a flower like a froth,[3]
And dead wings carried like a paper kite.

What had that flower to do with being white,
The wayside blue and innocent heal-all?   10
What brought the kindred spider to that height,
Then steered the white moth thither in the night?
What but design of darkness to appall?—
If design govern in a thing so small.

1936

---

[1] Ignorant; overtaken by spiritual and physical
darkness.
[1] The argument from design (order in nature)
was often urged as a proof for the existence of
God.
[2] A flower, normally blue.

[3] In the octave (first eight lines), Frost
complicates his task by using the only four
common words ending with the sound *ŏth;* he
also continues the octave rhyme sound *īte* in the
sestet (last six lines).

Provide, Provide

The witch that came (the withered hag)
To wash the steps with pail and rag
Was once the beauty Abishag,[1]

The picture pride of Hollywood.
Too many fall from great and good   5
For you to doubt the likelihood.

Die early and avoid the fate.
Or if predestined to die late,
Make up your mind to die in state.

Make the whole stock exchange your own!   10
If need be occupy a throne,
Where nobody can call *you* crone.

Some have relied on what they knew,
Others on being simply true.
What worked for them might work for you.   15

No memory of having starred
Atones for later disregard,
Or keeps the end from being hard.

Better to go down dignified
With boughten friendship at your side   20
Than none at all. Provide, provide!

1936

The Most of It

He thought he kept the universe alone;
For all the voice in answer he could wake
Was but the mocking echo of his own
From some tree-hidden cliff across the lake.

[1] Young girl brought in as a sexual partner for
King David in his old age (see 1 Kings 1:2–4).

Some morning from the boulder-broken beach   5
He would cry out on life, that what it wants
Is not its own love back in copy speech,
But counter-love, original response.
And nothing ever came of what he cried
Unless it was the embodiment that crashed   10
In the cliff's talus¹ on the other side,
And then in the far-distant water splashed,
But after a time allowed for it to swim,
Instead of proving human when it neared
And someone else additional to him,   15
As a great buck it powerfully appeared,
Pushing the crumpled water up ahead,
And landed pouring like a waterfall,
And stumbled through the rocks with horny tread,
And forced the underbrush—and that was all.   20

1942

The Gift Outright

The land was ours before we were the land's.
She was our land more than a hundred years
Before we were her people. She was ours
In Massachusetts, in Virginia,
But we were England's, still colonials,   5
Possessing what we still were unpossessed by,
Possessed by what we now no more possessed.
Something we were withholding made us weak
Until we found out that it was ourselves
We were withholding from our land of living,   10
And forthwith found salvation in surrender.
Such as we were we gave ourselves outright
(The deed of gift was many deeds of war)
To the land vaguely realizing westward,
But still unstoried, artless, unenhanced,   15
Such as she was, such as she would become.

1942

¹ Slope.

Time Out

It took that pause to make him realize
The mountain he was climbing had the slant
As of a book held up before his eyes
(And was a text albeit done in plant).
Dwarf cornel, gold-thread, and maianthemum, 5
He followingly fingered as he read,
The flowers fading on the seed to come;
But the thing was the slope it gave his head:
The same for reading as it was for thought,
So different from the hard and level stare 10
Of enemies defied and battles fought.
It was the obstinately gentle air
That may be clamored at by cause and sect,
But it will have its moment to reflect.

1942

Carl Sandburg
1878–1967

With his fellow Chicago poet Edgar Lee Masters, Carl Sandburg was one of the
early rebels of the modern period, reacting against the genteel tradition in the
name of Walt Whitman and America. Writing in free verse and about such
unpoetic subjects as the vigorous, even violent poor of Chicago, the "Hog
Butcher for the World," he sought to be a poet of the people in the Whitman
tradition. Sandburg was strongly populist in his political sympathies; he celebrated
grass-roots American characters and circumstances, often in poems that drew
clearly on Whitman for their verse technique. "Chicago," for example, teems
with people and attempts to recreate, in a modern and stridently vitalist way, the
energy of Whitman's chants. His main concern as a poet was the vivid
presentation of unrefined reality, and poems like "Fog" resemble the work of the
Imagists in their brevity, their juxtaposition of images to catch objective reality,
and their clean, simple language. Sandburg characteristically wrote other kinds of
poems as well—most notably poems of social protest, such as "Graceland," and
emotional, reflective poems, such as "Cool Tombs" and "Grass."

Carl Sandburg was born in 1878 to a family of Swedish immigrants in Illinois,
where his father was employed in the railroad yards. Raised in poverty, Sandburg
was forced to quit school at the age of thirteen to earn money at a variety of
odd jobs—milkman, porter, dishwasher. After the Spanish-American war, in
which he volunteered for the army and was sent to Puerto Rico, he enrolled in

Lombard College, supporting himself while there by working for the local fire department; he left abruptly in 1902 without graduating. He again found work of various sorts, including a stint as salesman of stereoscopic photographs. He even spent some time riding the rails with hoboes and served a short jail term in Pittsburgh. His experiences helped reinforce his strong populist convictions, and in 1907 and 1908 he worked for the Social Democratic party as journalist and organizer. Meanwhile he was trying to settle down, and in 1908 he married the sister of the photographer Edward Steichen.

In 1914 Harriet Monroe published a group of his poems, entitled "Chicago Poems," in *Poetry;* two years later a book with the same title appeared. It marked the start of Sandburg's fame, which by the end of his life was considerable. *Cornhuskers* appeared in 1918, followed by *Smoke and Steel* (1920), *Slabs of the Sunburnt West* (1922), and *The People, Yes* (1936). His six-volume biography of Abraham Lincoln (1940) earned him the Pulitzer Prize for history. Other prose writings include children's stories (beginning with *Rootabaga Stories,* 1922), historical commentary (*Storm over the Land,* 1942, and *Home Front Memos,* 1943), and a novel (*Remembrance Rock,* 1950). The poet who toured the country, reading and singing folksongs while accompanying himself on guitar, interspersing his performances with homespun philosophizing, became a celebrated public figure. He was asked to be a candidate for the presidency in 1940, and his birthplace was made a museum that same year; his 75th birthday was declared Carl Sandburg Day by the governor of Illinois. Sandburg received the Presidential Medal of Freedom in 1964.

He was not admired, on the whole, by his fellow poets. Ezra Pound once suggested that the University of Pennsylvania set up a fellowship for creative ability; he had Sandburg in mind as a possible recipient, for he feared Sandburg would remain imperfect for lack of culture. William Carlos Williams also criticized Sandburg's artlessness, but Frost's observation, after their first meeting, was the most acid:

> We've been having a dose of Carl Sandburg. He's another person I find it hard to do justice to. He was possibly [three] hours in town and he spent one of those washing his white hair and toughening his expression for his public performance. His mandolin pleased some people, his poetry a very few, and his infantile talk none. His affectations have almost buried him out of sight. He is probably the most artificial and studied ruffian the world has had.

Often as artless in life as he appeared to be in his writing, Sandburg had walked away from that meeting feeling that a friendship had begun. "Met Frost," he wrote, "about the strongest, loneliest, friendliest personality among the poets today; I'm going to write him once a year; and feel the love of him every day."

In a tradition in which the poet as primitive occupies a central, if complicated, place, Sandburg might have become an important figure. But, from Whitman on, to be "one of the roughs," to be artless in American literature, has been a creation of highly self-conscious art. By those standards Sandburg was lacking. Where others sought to create the illusion of unsophisticated spontaneity, Sandburg *was* artistically unsophisticated; almost paradoxically, he therefore seemed, at least to an observer like Frost, affected. Behind Pound's and Williams's apparently casual Imagist poems lay an almost obsessive concern with craft and, in Pound's case in particular, considerable acquaintance with the literary past that he sought to make new. Behind Whitman's chants of America lay far more than the desire to present American figures in all their vitality. The Americans Whitman wrote of, including himself in his own complicated self-portrayal, were part of a comprehensive vision of divine, natural, social, and psychological reality, and Whitman's language ranged from the demotic to the sublime in his attempt to give flesh to this vision. Against that achievement, Sandburg's work as a whole seems notable primarily for its part in the modernist revolution in literature. It is best appreciated for the real power of some of the individual poems, where Sandburg achieved a memorable freshness and vigor of expression.

Further Reading:

B. Weirick, *From Whitman to Sandburg*, 1924.
K. Detzer, *Carl Sandburg*, 1941.
H. Durnell, *The America of Carl Sandburg*, 1945.
R. Crowder, *Carl Sandburg*, 1964.

J. Haas, *Carl Sandburg*, 1967.
N. Callahan, *Carl Sandburg, Lincoln of Our Literature*, 1969.
G. W. Allen, *Carl Sandburg*, 1972.

Text:
Complete Poems, 1950.

Chicago

    Hog Butcher for the World,
    Tool Maker, Stacker of Wheat,
    Player with Railroads and the Nation's Freight Handler;
    Stormy, husky, brawling,
    City of the Big Shoulders: 5

They tell me you are wicked and I believe them, for I have seen your painted
    women under the gas lamps luring the farm boys.
And they tell me you are crooked and I answer: Yes, it is true I have seen the
    gunman kill and go free to kill again.
And they tell me you are brutal and my reply is: On the faces of women and
    children I have seen the marks of wanton hunger.
And having answered so I turn once more to those who sneer at this my city,
    and I give them back the sneer and say to them:
Come and show me another city with lifted head singing so proud to be alive
    and coarse and strong and cunning.   10
Flinging magnetic curses amid the toil of piling job on job, here is a tall bold
    slugger set vivid against the little soft cities;
Fierce as a dog with tongue lapping for action, cunning as a savage pitted
    against the wilderness,

Bareheaded,
Shoveling,
Wrecking,   15
Planning,
Building, breaking, rebuilding,
Under the smoke, dust all over his mouth, laughing with white teeth,
Under the terrible burden of destiny laughing as a young man laughs,
Laughing even as an ignorant fighter laughs who has never lost a battle,   20
Bragging and laughing that under his wrist is the pulse, and under his ribs the
    heart of the people,
             Laughing!
Laughing the stormy, husky, brawling laughter of Youth, half-naked, sweating,
    proud to be Hog Butcher, Tool Maker, Stacker of Wheat, Player with
    Railroads and Freight Handler to the Nation.

1914

Graceland

Tomb of a millionaire,
A multi-millionaire, ladies and gentlemen,
Place of the dead where they spend every year
The usury of twenty-five thousand dollars
    For upkeep and flowers   5
To keep fresh the memory of the dead.
The merchant prince gone to dust
Commanded in his written will
Over the signed name of his last testament
Twenty-five thousand dollars be set aside   10
For roses, lilacs, hydrangeas, tulips,
For perfume and color, sweetness of remembrance
Around his last long home.

(A hundred cash girls want nickels to go to the movies tonight.
In the back stalls of a hundred saloons, women are at tables   15
Drinking with men or waiting for men jingling loose silver dollars in their
    pockets.
In a hundred furnished rooms is a girl who sells silk or dress goods or leather
    stuff for six dollars a week wages
And when she pulls on her stockings in the morning she is reckless about God
    and the newspapers and the police, the talk of her home town or the name
    people call her.)

1916

Fog

The fog comes
on little cat feet.

It sits looking
over harbor and city
on silent haunches   5
and then moves on.

1916

Portrait of a Motorcar

It's a lean car . . . a long-legged dog of a car . . . a gray-ghost eagle car.
The feet of it eat the dirt of a road . . . the wings of it eat the hills.
Danny the driver dreams of it when he sees women in red skirts and red sox in
   his sleep.
It is in Danny's life and runs in the blood of him . . . a lean gray-ghost car.

1918

Cool Tombs

When Abraham Lincoln was shoveled into the tombs, he forgot the copperheads[1]
   and the assassin . . . in the dust, in the cool tombs.

And Ulysses Grant lost all thought of con men and Wall Street, cash and
   collateral turned ashes . . . in the dust, in the cool tombs.

Pocahontas' body, lovely as a poplar, sweet as a red haw[2] in November or a
   pawpaw[3] in May, did she wonder? does she remember? . . . in the dust, in
   the cool tombs?

[1] Copperhead: species of poisonous snake, but
here a derogatory epithet for Northerners who
sided with the Confederacy during the Civil
War.

[2] Hawthorn berry.
[3] Fruit of the pawpaw tree, much like papaya.

Take any streetful of people buying clothes and groceries, cheering a hero or
    throwing confetti and blowing tin horns . . . tell me if the lovers are losers
    . . . tell me if any get more than the lovers . . . in the dust . . . in the cool
    tombs.

1918

Grass

Pile the bodies high at Austerlitz¹ and Waterloo.
Shovel them under and let me work—
                    I am the grass; I cover all.

And pile them high at Gettysburg
And pile them high at Ypres and Verdun.   5
Shovel them under and let me work.
Two years, ten years, and passengers ask the conductor:
                    What place is this?
                    Where are we now?

                    I am the grass.   10
                    Let me work.

1918

Wallace Stevens
1879–1955

Wallace Stevens's extraordinary first book, *Harmonium* (1923), is one of those
books, like T. S. Eliot's *Prufrock and Other Observations* and Marianne Moore's
Observations, by which we have come to define American modernism. Each of
these collections struck a clear new note in formal terms; each was in some way
self-displaying. Stevens's book was not a success; even in 1931, when it was
reprinted in an expanded form, it had only a *succès d'estime.* It was full of odd
poems with odd names, like "Thirteen Ways of Looking at a Blackbird" and
"Metaphors of a Magnifico." These strange-looking poems did not at all resemble
the other poems in the volume, which were recognizably in a traditional vein,

---

¹ The places named in the poem were the scenes
of major battles during the Napoleonic Wars,
the Civil War, and World War I, respectively.

with reminiscences of Wordsworth, Keats, Browning, and Tennyson. Even the seemingly conventional poems, however, had strange titles like "Le Monocle de Mon Oncle" and "The Comedian as the Letter C." The book did contain one conventionally named poem in a conventional style—"Sunday Morning." But this poem, soon to become very famous, was unconventional in theme; it was a bold declaration of the death of God. In the poem a sensuous aestheticism and agnosticism became substitutes for religious observance.

At least one of those who read the second edition of *Harmonium* when it appeared in the depths of the Great Depression found it shocking that the poet was not addressing the social ills of the day. Stanley Burnshaw's criticism of *Harmonium* in *The New Masses* stung Stevens into his attempts, in *Owl's Clover* (1936) and *Parts of a World* (1942), to treat social issues, including the war in Ethiopia and World War II. But these poems achieved no real stylistic success, and Stevens remained, for the rest of his career, preeminently a poet of the inner life. Nonetheless, Stevens never lost his concern with the social function of poetry, that "postcard from a volcano" addressed to future generations.

Stevens's nature was both religious and romantic; yet the two beliefs he had wholeheartedly entered into, religion and romantic love, both turned out, in his eyes, to be delusory. By these striking evidences of the mind's capacity to delude itself he was led to meditate on the ways that the mind contructs objects and worlds responsive to desire, then sees them shatter and dissolve. The inadequacy of the world to our desire, coupled with our apparently incorrigible pursuit of belief and desire, gave Stevens the great paradox on which he was to brood all his life, the incommensurability of desire and its object. For him, the imagination was what desired; "reality" was what the imagination constructed as a response to desire. "Reality" therefore changes always, as desire is frustrated and a new fictive construct must be shaped yet once again. In this way, new political states are constructed after the collapse of old ones, new art forms are invented when the old become withered, and a new religion replaces the stale religion of the past. Stevens's skepticism about these successive reconstructions of reality comes from his taking the long historical view of the psyche's inner life.

At the same time, though Stevens held seriously to the absolute power of the imagination in the construction of the self and culture, he could treat his theme with gaiety, mockery, and brio. Many of the short poems in *Harmonium* are what we would now call "conceptual art"—the originality of the idea behind them, rather than the linguistic execution, gives them their poetic energy. "Anecdote of the Jar" is such a poem, in its witty reversal of Keats's "Ode on a Grecian Urn." The British poet may have an illustrated marble urn in the British Museum, but the American poet has only a bare gray stoneware jar in the Tennessee wilderness. And whereas the British poet can write in opulent stanzas derived from Shakespeare and the sonnet, the American poet cannot find any diction or stanza form that he is comfortable in. In this respect, Stevens's laconic wit is often turned against himself as the clumsy American trying to utter "heavenly labials in a world of gutturals." In the many volumes following *Harmonium,* Stevens's seriousness of subject and gaiety of treatment continue to create a style peculiar to him, in which he deepens his exploration of the inner life of desire.

During his life as a poet, Stevens carried on a parallel life as a lawyer and insurance executive. He was the son of a Reading, Pennsylvania, lawyer who sent all three of his sons to law school. After three years at Harvard, where he wrote poetry and was president of the literary magazine, Stevens left without taking a degree; his father would not pay for a final year, as only three years of college were required for admission at some law schools. Since the Harvard Law School required four years of college, Stevens could not be admitted there; instead, he entered New York Law School, but after graduation he was relatively unsuccessful in his first professional jobs. At this time in New York, Stevens associated with other young poets, especially his Harvard classmate Alfred Kreymborg, who edited a journal called *Others*. In the *Others* group Stevens met William Carlos Williams and Marianne Moore, a lifelong friend. But as Stevens's professional duties increased, he drifted away from literary society; his move to Hartford, Connecticut, in 1916 removed him from the New York scene. He eventually became a very successful insurance lawyer; at his death he was a vice-president of the Hartford Accident and Indemnity Company.

From 1916 to his death in 1955, Stevens lived in Hartford, and although he made many business trips in America, he never went to Europe. His chief literary life, aside from poetry, took place through correspondence with friends and students of his poetry. His marriage to Elsie Kachel seems to have been unhappy. They had one child, born in 1924, named by Stevens, because her birth came near Christmas, Holly Bright.

By the end of his life, Stevens was recognized as a major poet. His *Collected Poems* (1955) won the National Book Award and a Pulitzer Prize. Although Stevens's daughter has published, in *The Palm at the End of the Mind* (1971), a group of his poems arranged in chronological order, the *Collected Poems* remains the way to know Stevens, to read the poems as he himself arranged them in successive volumes. To Stevens, his *Collected Poems,* when he saw them bound, seemed like the whole world in reduced form, like the terrestrial globe used in geography classes. The volume was "the planet on the table," and he, as poet, was like Shakespeare's airy spirit Ariel: "Ariel was glad he had written his poems."

In 1951 Stevens published a remarkable collection of essays, *The Necessary Angel.* Here, and in essays published after his death in *Opus Posthumous* (1957), he displays the outlines of his theory of poetry. Stevens saw poetry as an "accuracy with respect to the structure of reality"; it was formed by the pressure of the mind against the outside pressure of reality. Imagination was for him a "third planet," comparable in power to the sun and moon, allowing us to see the world in a personal way, different with each mood. Poetry is "the gaiety of language," "a holiday in reality"; but it is also a voice, speaking in "ghostlier demarcations, keener sounds," "of ourselves and of our origins." Stevens's most concise view of the poet's role in society appears in the poem "Academic Discourse at Havana," where he says of the poet:

As part of nature he is part of us.
His rarities are ours: may they be fit
And reconcile us to our selves in those
True reconcilings, dark, pacific words,
And the adroiter harmonies of their fall.

Stevens showed American poetry a new way of being American—not by regionalism (though he wrote memorable poems about Connecticut), not by patriotism, not through use of the common vernacular, but by an adaptation of English literature to the American language. In his long poems he invented a new pentameter, freer in its metric than the English model, returning to Whitman's largeness of motion. And in his skeptical, ironic, and whimsical humor he lightens into modern American speculativeness the seriousness of English discursive verse.

Further Reading:

F. Kermode, *Wallace Stevens*, 1961.
J. G. Benziger, *Images of Eternity*, 1962.
The Achievement of Wallace Stevens, ed. A. Brown and R. Haller, 1962.
D. Fuchs, *The Comic Spirit of Wallace Stevens*, 1962.
G. Cambon, *The Inclusive Flame*, 1963.
J. J. Enck, *Wallace Stevens: Images and Judgments*, 1964.
H. Wells, *Introduction to Wallace Stevens*, 1964.
J. N. Riddell, *The Clairvoyant Eye*, 1965.
E. P. Nasser, *Wallace Stevens: An Anatomy of Figuration*, 1965.
F. Doggett, *Stevens' Poetry of Thought*, 1966.
H. J. Stern, *Wallace Stevens: Art of Uncertainty*, 1966.
R. Buttel, *Wallace Stevens: The Making of "Harmonium,"* 1967.
R. Sukenick, *Wallace Stevens: Musing the Obscure*, 1967.
J. Baird, *The Dome and the Rock: Structure in the Poetry of Wallace Stevens*, 1968.
W. Burney, *Wallace Stevens*, 1968.

H. Vendler, *On Extended Wings: Wallace Stevens' Longer Poems*, 1969.
R. Blessing, *Wallace Stevens's "Whole Harmonium,"* 1970.
S. F. Morse, *Wallace Stevens: Poetry as Life*, 1970.
M. Benamou, *Wallace Stevens and the Symbolist Imagination*, 1972.
W. A. Litz, *Introspective Voyage: The Poetic Development of Wallace Stevens*, 1972.
L. Beckett, *Wallace Stevens*, 1977.
H. Bloom, *Wallace Stevens: The Poems of Our Climate*, 1977.
H. Stevens, *Souvenirs and Prophecies: The Young Wallace Stevens*, 1977.
S. B. Weston, *Wallace Stevens: An Introduction*, 1977.
F. Doggett, *Wallace Stevens: The Making of a Poem*, 1980.
Wallace Stevens: A Celebration, ed. F. Doggett and R. Buttel, 1980.
H. Vendler, *Wallace Stevens: Words Chosen out of Desire*, 1985.

Text:
The Palm at the End of the Mind, ed. H. Stevens, 1971.

Sunday Morning

I

Complacencies of the peignoir, and late
Coffee and oranges in a sunny chair,[1]
And the green freedom of a cockatoo
Upon a rug mingle to dissipate
The holy hush of ancient sacrifice.[2]   5
She dreams a little, and she feels the dark
Encroachment of that old catastrophe,
As a calm darkens among water-lights.
The pungent oranges and bright, green wings
Seem things in some procession of the dead,   10
Winding across wide water, without sound.
The day is like wide water, without sound,
Stilled for the passing of her dreaming feet
Over the seas, to silent Palestine,
Dominion of the blood and sepulchre.[3]   15

II

Why should she give her bounty to the dead?
What is divinity if it can come
Only in silent shadows and in dreams?
Shall she not find in comforts of the sun,
In pungent fruit and bright, green wings, or else   20
In any balm or beauty of the earth,
Things to be cherished like the thought of heaven?
Divinity must live within herself:
Passions of rain, or moods in falling snow;
Grievings in loneliness, or unsubdued   25
Elations when the forest blooms; gusty
Emotions on wet roads on autumn nights;
All pleasures and all pains, remembering
The bough of summer and the winter branch.
These are the measures destined for her soul.   30

III

Jove[4] in the clouds had his inhuman birth.
No mother suckled him, no sweet land gave

---

[1] The agnostic lady does not attend a Sunday
church service; instead, she remains in her
peignoir and breakfasts.

[2] The death of Jesus.
[3] The passion and entombment of Jesus.
[4] In mythology, the king of the gods.

Large-mannered motions to his mythy mind.
He moved among us, as a muttering king,
Magnificent, would move among his hinds,   35
Until our blood, commingling, virginal,[5]
With heaven, brought such requital to desire
The very hinds[6] discerned it, in a star.
Shall our blood fail? Or shall it come to be
The blood of paradise? And shall the earth   40
Seem all of paradise that we shall know?
The sky will be much friendlier then than now,
A part of labor and a part of pain,
And next in glory to enduring love,
Not this dividing and indifferent blue.   45

IV

She says, "I am content when wakened birds,
Before they fly, test the reality
Of misty fields, by their sweet questionings;
But when the birds are gone, and their warm fields
Return no more, where, then, is paradise?"   50
There is not any haunt of prophecy,
Nor any old chimera[7] of the grave,
Neither the golden underground,[8] nor isle
Melodious,[9] where spirits gat them home,
Nor visionary south, nor cloudy palm[10]   55
Remote on heaven's hill, that has endured
As April's green endures; or will endure
Like her remembrance of awakened birds,
Or her desire for June and evening, tipped
By the consummation of the swallow's wings.   60

V

She says, "But in contentment I still feel
The need of some imperishable bliss."
Death is the mother of beauty; hence from her,
Alone, shall come fulfilment to our dreams
And our desires. Although she strews the leaves   65
Of sure obliteration on our paths,
The path sick sorrow took, the many paths

---

[5] Like the Virgin Mary, impregnated by the
Holy Spirit.
[6] The shepherds who saw the Christmas star.
[7] Ghost, illusion.
[8] The Elysian fields, in mythology the heaven of
heroes.

[9] Avalon, where King Arthur was taken after
death.
[10] The palm was the reward given to Christian
martyrs in heaven.

Where triumph rang its brassy phrase, or love
Whispered a little out of tenderness,
She makes the willow shiver in the sun   70
For maidens who were wont to sit and gaze
Upon the grass, relinquished to their feet.
She causes boys to pile new plums and pears
On disregarded plate.[11] The maidens taste
And stray impassioned in the littering leaves.   75

VI

Is there no change of death in paradise?
Does ripe fruit never fall? Or do the boughs
Hang always heavy in that perfect sky,
Unchanging, yet so like our perishing earth,
With rivers like our own that seek for seas   80
They never find, the same receding shores
That never touch with inarticulate pang?
Why set the pear upon those river-banks
Or spice the shores with odors of the plum?
Alas, that they should wear our colors there,   85
The silken weavings of our afternoons,
And pick the strings of our insipid lutes!
Death is the mother of beauty, mystical,
Within whose burning bosom we devise
Our earthly mothers waiting, sleeplessly.   90

VII

Supple and turbulent, a ring of men
Shall chant in orgy on a summer morn
Their boisterous devotion to the sun,
Not as a god, but as a god might be,
Naked among them, like a savage source.   95
Their chant shall be a chant of paradise,
Out of their blood, returning to the sky;
And in their chant shall enter, voice by voice,
The windy lake wherein their lord delights,
The trees, like serafin,[12] and echoing hills,   100
That choir among themselves long afterward.
They shall know well the heavenly fellowship
Of men that perish and of summer morn.
And whence they came and whither they shall go
The dew upon their feet shall manifest.   105

[11] Silver dishes.   [12] Seraphim; angels.

VIII

She hears, upon that water without sound,
A voice that cries, "The tomb in Palestine[13]
Is not the porch of spirits lingering.
It is the grave of Jesus, where he lay."
We live in an old chaos of the sun,   110
Or old dependency of day and night,
Or island solitude, unsponsored, free,
Of that wide water, inescapable.
Deer walk upon our mountains, and the quail
Whistle about us their spontaneous cries;   115
Sweet berries ripen in the wilderness;
And, in the isolation of the sky,
At evening, casual flocks of pigeons make
Ambiguous undulations as they sink,
Downward to darkness, on extended wings.   120

1923

Thirteen Ways of Looking at a Blackbird

I

Among twenty snowy mountains,
The only moving thing
Was the eye of the blackbird.

II

I was of three minds,
Like a tree   5
In which there are three blackbirds.

III

The blackbird whirled in the autumn winds.
It was a small part of the pantomime.

---

[13] When Jesus' friends went to the sepulcher, they found that the door-stone had been rolled away and the tomb was empty. An angel sat on the stone and said, "He is not here, for he is risen" (Matthew 28:2–6; Mark 16:4–6). (In Luke 24:1–6 and in John 20:11–12, there are two angels at the tomb.)

IV

A man and a woman
Are one.   10
A man and a woman and a blackbird
Are one.

V

I do not know which to prefer,
The beauty of inflections
Or the beauty of innuendoes,   15
The blackbird whistling
Or just after.

VI

Icicles filled the long window
With barbaric glass.
The shadow of the blackbird   20
Crossed it, to and fro.
The mood
Traced in the shadow
An indecipherable cause.

VII

O thin men of Haddam,[1]   25
Why do you imagine golden birds?
Do you not see how the blackbird
Walks around the feet
Of the women about you?

VIII

I know noble accents
And lucid, inescapable rhythms;   30
But I know, too,
That the blackbird is involved
In what I know.

IX

When the blackbird flew out of sight,   35
It marked the edge
Of one of many circles.

[1] Town in Connecticut.

X

At the sight of blackbirds
Flying in a green light,
Even the bawds of euphony[2]   40
Would cry out sharply.

XI

He rode over Connecticut
In a glass coach.
Once a fear pierced him,
In that he mistook   45
The shadow of his equipage
For blackbirds.

XII

The river is moving.
The blackbird must be flying.

XIII

It was evening all afternoon.   50
It was snowing
And it was going to snow.
The blackbird sat
In the cedar-limbs.

1923

Anecdote of the Jar

I placed a jar in Tennessee,
And round it was, upon a hill.
It made the slovenly wilderness
Surround that hill.

The wilderness rose up to it,   5
And sprawled around, no longer wild.
The jar was round upon the ground
And tall and of a port in air.

---

[2] Those touting harmony as the highest aesthetic
virtue.

It took dominion everywhere.
The jar was gray and bare.   10
It did not give of bird or bush,
Like nothing else in Tennessee.

1923

The Paltry Nude Starts on a Spring Voyage

But not on a shell,[1] she starts,
Archaic, for the sea.
But on the first-found weed
She scuds[2] the glitters,
Noiselessly, like one more wave.   5

She too is discontent
And would have purple stuff upon her arms,
Tired of the salty harbors,
Eager for the brine and bellowing
Of the high interiors of the sea.   10

The wind speeds her,
Blowing upon her hands
And watery back.
She touches the clouds, where she goes
In the circle of her traverse of the sea.   15

Yet this is meagre play
In the scurry[3] and water-shine,
As her heels foam—
Not as when the goldener nude
Of a later day   20

Will go, like the centre of sea-green pomp,
In an intenser calm,
Scullion[4] of fate,
Across the spick torrent, ceaselessly,
Upon her irretrievable way.   25

1923

---

[1] In classical myth the spring goddess, Venus, was
born of sea-foam and appears in paintings (as in
Botticelli's *Birth of Venus*) nude, borne on a
seashell, and with drapery of royal purple.
[2] Runs swiftly, as if driven forward.

[3] An invented word.
[4] Here, the "new broom" that "sweeps clean";
literally, a kitchen servant whose chief task is
cleaning dishes.

The Snow Man

One must have a mind of winter
To regard the frost and the boughs
Of the pine-trees crusted with snow;

And have been cold a long time
To behold the junipers shagged with ice,   5
The spruces rough in the distant glitter

Of the January sun; and not to think
Of any misery in the sound of the wind,
In the sound of a few leaves,

Which is the sound of the land   10
Full of the same wind
That is blowing in the same bare place

For the listener, who listens in the snow,
And, nothing himself, beholds
Nothing that is not there and the nothing that is.   15

1923

The Emperor of Ice-Cream

Call the roller of big cigars,
The muscular one,[1] and bid him whip
In kitchen cups concupiscent curds.
Let the wenches dawdle in such dress
As they are used to wear, and let the boys   5
Bring flowers in last month's newspapers.
Let be be finale of seem.
The only emperor is the emperor of ice-cream.

[1] It required muscles to operate the large machines that rolled tobacco leaves flat in cigar factories. The poem may be a Key West poem; at Cuban wakes in Key West, Florida, ice cream was often served.

Take from the dresser of deal,[2]
Lacking the three glass knobs, that sheet   10
On which she embroidered fantails[3] once
And spread it so as to cover her face.
If her horny feet protrude, they come
To show how cold she is, and dumb.
Let the lamp affix its beam.   15
The only emperor is the emperor of ice-cream.

1923

The Idea of Order at Key West

She sang beyond the genius of the sea.
The water never formed to mind or voice,
Like a body wholly body, fluttering
Its empty sleeves; and yet its mimic motion
Made constant cry, caused constantly a cry,   5
That was not ours although we understood,
Inhuman, of the veritable ocean.

The sea was not a mask. No more was she.
The song and water were not medleyed sound
Even if what she sang was what she heard,
Since what she sang was uttered word by word.   10
It may be that in all her phrases stirred
The grinding water and the gasping wind;
But it was she and not the sea we heard.

For she was the maker of the song she sang.
The ever-hooded, tragic-gestured sea   15
Was merely a place by which she walked to sing.
Whose spirit is this? we said, because we knew
It was the spirit that we sought and knew
That we should ask this often as she sang.   20

If it was only the dark voice of the sea
That rose, or even colored by many waves;
If it was only the outer voice of sky

---

[2] Pine (the cheapest wood).
[3] Embroidery pattern resembling the tails of
fantail pigeons.

And cloud, of the sunken coral water-walled,
However clear, it would have been deep air,   25
The heaving speech of air, a summer sound
Repeated in a summer without end
And sound alone. But it was more than that,
More even than her voice, and ours, among
The meaningless plungings of water and the wind,   30
Theatrical distances, bronze shadows heaped
On high horizons, mountainous atmospheres
Of sky and sea.
                    It was her voice that made
The sky acutest at its vanishing.   35
She measured to the hour its solitude.
She was the single artificer of the world
In which she sang. And when she sang, the sea,
Whatever self it had, became the self
That was her song, for she was the maker. Then we,   40
As we beheld her striding there alone,
Knew that there never was a world for her
Except the one she sang and, singing, made.

Ramon Fernandez,[1] tell me, if you know,
Why, when the singing ended and we turned   45
Toward the town, tell why the glassy lights,
The lights in the fishing boats at anchor there,
As the night descended, tilting in the air,
Mastered the night and portioned out the sea,
Fixing emblazoned zones and fiery poles,[2]   50
Arranging, deepening, enchanting night.

Oh! Blessed rage for order, pale Ramon,
The maker's rage to order words of the sea,
Words of the fragrant portals, dimly-starred,
And of ourselves and of our origins,   55
In ghostlier demarcations, keener sounds.
1936

---

[1] Stevens said that he invented this name.
[2] The zones and poles are like those geographers
invent to demarcate the terrestrial globe.

A Postcard from the Volcano[*]

Children picking up our bones
Will never know that these were once
As quick as foxes on the hill;

And that in autumn, when the grapes
Made sharp air sharper by their smell   5
These had a being, breathing frost;

And least will guess that with our bones
We left much more, left what still is
The look of things, left what we felt

At what we saw. The spring clouds blow   10
Above the shuttered mansion-house,
Beyond our gate and the windy sky

Cries out a literate despair.
We knew for long the mansion's look
And what we said of it became   15

A part of what it is . . . Children,
Still weaving budded aureoles,
Will speak our speech and never know,

Will say of the mansion that it seems
As if he that lived there left behind   20
A spirit storming in blank walls,

A dirty house in a gutted world,
A tatter of shadows peaked to white,
Smeared with the gold of the opulent sun.

1936

[*] The poem is written as a message from an inhabitant of a town covered over by lava after a volcanic eruption long ago. The dead man lived in a "mansion-house" still visible.

Arrival at the Waldorf[1]

Home from Guatemala, back at the Waldorf.
This arrival in the wild country of the soul,
All approaches gone, being completely there,

Where the wild poem is a substitute
For the woman one loves or ought to love,   5
One wild rhapsody a fake for another.

You touch the hotel the way you touch moonlight
Or sunlight and you hum and the orchestra
Hums and you say "The world in a verse,

A generation sealed, men remoter than mountains,   10
Women invisible in music and motion and color,"
After that alien, point-blank, green and actual Guatemala.

1942

No Possum, No Sop, No Taters[1]

He is not here, the old sun,
As absent as if we were asleep.

The field is frozen. The leaves are dry.
Bad is final in this light.

In this bleak air the broken stalks   5
Have arms without hands. They have trunks

Without legs or, for that, without heads.
They have heads in which a captive cry

Is merely the moving of a tongue.
Snow sparkles like eyesight falling to earth,   10

[1] Famous and expensive hotel in New York City.
[1] Rustic American for "No meat (opossum), no
bread to dip in gravy, no potatoes."

Like seeing fallen brightly away.
The leaves hop, scraping on the ground.

It is deep January. The sky is hard.
The stalks are firmly rooted in ice.

It is in this solitude, a syllable,   15
Out of these gawky flitterings,

Intones its single emptiness,
The savagest hollow of winter-sound.

It is here, in this bad, that we reach
The last purity of the knowledge of good.   20

The crow looks rusty as he rises up.
Bright is the malice in his eye . . .

One joins him there for company.
But at a distance, in another tree.

1947

The Auroras of Autumn[1]

I

This is where the serpent[2] lives, the bodiless.
His head is air. Beneath his tip at night
Eyes open and fix on us in every sky.

Or is this another wriggling out of the egg,
Another image at the end of the cave,   5
Another bodiless for the body's slough?

This is where the serpent lives. This is his nest,
These fields, these hills, these tinted distances,
And the pines above and along and beside the sea.

[1] I.e., the aurora borealis, or northern lights.
[2] The snake, because he repeatedly sheds his skin,
is a symbol of change over time.

This is form gulping after formlessness,   10
Skin flashing to wished-for disappearances
And the serpent body flashing without the skin.

This is the height emerging and its base . . .
These lights may finally attain a pole[3]
In the midmost midnight and find the serpent there,   15

In another nest, the master of the maze
Of body and air and forms and images,
Relentlessly in possession of happiness.

This is his poison: that we should disbelieve
Even that. His meditations in the ferns,   20
When he moved so slightly to make sure of sun,

Made us no less as sure.[4] We saw in his head,
Black beaded on the rock, the flecked animal,
The moving grass, the Indian in his glade.

II

Farewell to an idea . . . A cabin[5] stands,   25
Deserted, on a beach. It is white,
As by a custom or according to

An ancestral theme or as a consequence
Of an infinite course. The flowers against the wall
Are white, a little dried, a kind of mark   30

Reminding, trying to remind, of a white
That was different, something else, last year
Or before, not the white of an aging afternoon,

Whether fresher or duller, whether of winter cloud
Or of winter sky, from horizon to horizon.   35
The wind is blowing the sand across the floor.

Here, being visible is being white,
Is being of the solid of white, the accomplishment
Of an extremist in an exercise . . .

---

[3] The North Pole.
[4] I.e., sure that a serpent lurked in the grass.
[5] In an earlier poem, "The Comedian as the Letter C," Stevens's protagonist, Crispin, had settled down in a cabin with a wife and four daughters.

The season changes. A cold wind chills the beach.   40
The long lines of it grow longer, emptier,
A darkness gathers though it does not fall

And the whiteness grows less vivid on the wall.
The man who is walking turns blankly on the sand.
He observes how the north is always enlarging the change,   45

With its frigid brilliances, its blue-red sweeps
And gusts of great enkindlings, its polar green,
The color of ice and fire and solitude.

III

Farewell to an idea . . . The mother's face,
The purpose of the poem, fills the room.   50
They are together, here, and it is warm,

With none of the prescience of oncoming dreams.
It is evening. The house is evening, half dissolved.
Only the half they can never possess remains,

Still-starred. It is the mother they possess,   55
Who gives transparence to their present peace.
She makes that gentler that can gentle be.

And yet she too is dissolved, she is destroyed.
She gives transparence. But she has grown old.
The necklace is a carving not a kiss.   60

The soft hands are a motion not a touch.
The house will crumble and the books will burn.
They are at ease in a shelter of the mind

And the house is of the mind and they and time,
Together, all together. Boreal night   65
Will look like frost as it approaches them

And to the mother as she falls asleep
And as they say good-night, good-night. Upstairs
The windows will be lighted, not the rooms.

A wind will spread its windy grandeurs round   70
And knock like a rifle-butt against the door.
The wind will command them with invincible sound.

IV

Farewell to an idea . . . The cancellings,
The negations are never final: The father sits
In space, wherever he sits, of bleak regard,   75

As one that is strong in the bushes[6] of his eyes.
He says no to no and yes to yes. He says yes
To no; and in saying yes he says farewell.

He measures the velocities of change.
He leaps from heaven to heaven more rapidly   80
Than bad angels leap from heaven to hell in flames.

But now he sits in quiet and green-a-day.[7]
He assumes the great speeds of space and flutters them
From cloud to cloudless, cloudless to keen clear

In flights of eye and ear, the highest eye   85
And the lowest ear, the deep ear that discerns,
At evening, things that attend it until it hears

The supernatural preludes of its own,
At the moment when the angelic eye defines
Its actors approaching, in company, in their masks.   90

Master O master seated by the fire
And yet in space and motionless and yet
Of motion the ever-brightening origin,

Profound, and yet the king and yet the crown,
Look at this present throne. What company,   95
In masks, can choir it with the naked wind?

V

The mother invites humanity to her house
And table. The father fetches tellers of tales
And musicians who mute much, muse much, on the tales.

The father fetches negresses to dance,   100
Among the children, like curious ripenesses
Of pattern in the dance's ripening.

---

[6] I.e., bushy eyebrows.   [7] Pastoral rusticity.

For these the musicians make insidious tones,
Clawing the sing-song of their instruments.
The children laugh and jangle a tinny time.   105

The father fetches pageants out of air,
Scenes of the theatre, vistas and blocks of woods
And curtains like a naive pretence of sleep.

Among these the musicians strike the instinctive poem.
The father fetches his unherded herds,   110
Of barbarous tongue, slavered and panting halves

Of breath, obedient to his trumpet's touch.
This then is Chatillon[8] or as you please.
We stand in the tumult of a festival.

What festival? This loud, disordered mooch?   115
These hospitaliers?[9] These brute-like guests?
These musicians dubbing at a tragedy,

A-dub, a-dub, which is made up of this:
That there are no lines to speak? There is no play.
Or, the persons act one merely by being here.   120

VI

It[10] is a theatre floating through the clouds,
Itself a cloud, although of misted rock
And mountains running like water, wave on wave,

Through waves of light. It is of cloud transformed
To cloud transformed again, idly, the way   125
A season changes color to no end,

Except the lavishing of itself in change,
As light changes yellow into gold and gold
To its opal elements and fire's delight,

Splashed wide-wise because it likes magnificence   130
And the solemn pleasures of magnificent space.
The cloud drifts idly through half-thought-of forms.

[8] Of uncertain meaning.   [10] I.e., the aurora borealis.
[9] Unruly military monks.

The theatre is filled with flying birds,
Wild wedges, as of a volcano's smoke, palm-eyed[11]
And vanishing, a web in a corridor   135

Or massive portico. A capitol,
It may be, is emerging or has just
Collapsed. The denouement has to be postponed . . .

This is nothing until in a single man contained,
Nothing until this named thing nameless is   140
And is destroyed. He opens the door of his house

On flames. The scholar of one candle sees
An Arctic effulgence flaring on the frame
Of everything he is. And he feels afraid.

VII

Is there an imagination that sits enthroned   145
As grim as it is benevolent, the just
And the unjust, which in the midst of summer stops

To imagine winter? When the leaves are dead,
Does it take its place in the north and enfold itself,
Goat-leaper,[12] crystalled and luminous, sitting   150

In highest night? And do these heavens adorn
And proclaim it, the white creator of black, jetted
By extinguishings, even of planets as may be,

Even of earth, even of sight, in snow,
Except as needed by way of majesty,   155
In the sky, as crown and diamond cabala?[13]

It leaps through us, through all our heavens leaps,
Extinguishing our planets, one by one,
Leaving, of where we were and looked, of where

We knew each other and of each other thought,   160
A shivering residue, chilled and foregone,
Except for that crown and mystical cabala.

---

[11] I.e., tropical. (The birds are those that gaze on   [13] Esoteric doctrine.
palms.)
[12] The Goat, Capricorn, is the winter sign of the
Zodiac.

But it dare not leap by chance in its own dark.
It must change from destiny to slight caprice.
And thus its jetted tragedy, its stele[14]   165

And shape and mournful making move to find
What must unmake it and, at last, what can,
Say, a flippant communication under the moon.

VIII

There may be always a time of innocence.
There is never a place. Or if there is no time,   170
If it is not a thing of time, nor of place,

Existing in the idea of it, alone,
In the sense against calamity, it is not
Less real. For the oldest and coldest philosopher,

There is or may be a time of innocence   175
As pure principle. Its nature is its end,
That it should be, and yet not be, a thing

That pinches the pity of the pitiful man,
Like a book at evening beautiful but untrue,
Like a book on rising beautiful and true.   180

It is like a thing of ether that exists
Almost as predicate. But it exists,
It exists, it is visible, it is, it is.

So, then, these lights are not a spell of light,
A saying out of a cloud, but innocence.   185
An innocence of the earth and no false sign

Or symbol of malice. That we partake thereof,
Lie down like children in this holiness,
As if, awake, we lay in the quiet of sleep,

As if the innocent mother sang in the dark   190
Of the room and on an accordion, half-heard,
Created the time and place in which we breathed . . .

[14] Carved commemorative stone.

IX

And of each other thought—in the idiom
Of the work, in the idiom of an innocent earth,
Not of the enigma of the guilty dream.   195

We were as Danes in Denmark[15] all day long
And knew each other well, hale-hearted landsmen,
For whom the outlandish was another day

Of the week, queerer than Sunday. We thought alike
And that made brothers of us in a home   200
In which we fed on being brothers, fed

And fattened as on a decorous honeycomb.
This drama that we live—We lay sticky with sleep.
This sense of the activity of fate—

The rendezvous, when she[16] came alone,   205
By her coming became a freedom of the two,
An isolation which only the two could share.

Shall we be found hanging in the trees next spring?
Of what disaster is this the imminence:
Bare limbs, bare trees and a wind as sharp as salt?   210

The stars are putting on their glittering belts.
They throw around their shoulders cloaks that flash
Like a great shadow's last embellishment.

It[17] may come tomorrow in the simplest word,
Almost as part of innocence, almost,   215
Almost as the tenderest and the truest part.

X

An unhappy people in a happy world—
Read, rabbi,[18] the phases of this difference.
An unhappy people in an unhappy world—

Here are too many mirrors for misery.   220
A happy people in an unhappy world—
It cannot be. There's nothing there to roll

[15] I.e., at home on the earth.
[16] The beloved.
[17] The disaster (literally, the misfortune caused by
the disfavor of the stars), death.

[18] The scholar or teacher, reading to a
congregation.

On the expressive tongue, the finding fang.
A happy people in a happy world—
Buffo! A ball, an opera, a bar.   225

Turn back to where we were when we began:
An unhappy people in a happy world.
Now, solemnize the secretive syllables.

Read to the congregation, for today
And for tomorrow, this extremity,   230
This contrivance of the spectre of the spheres,[19]

Contriving balance to contrive a whole,
The vital, the never-failing genius,
Fulfilling his meditations, great and small.

In these unhappy he meditates a whole,   235
The full of fortune and the full of fate,
As if he lived all lives, that he might know,

In hall harridan, not hushful paradise,
To a haggling of wind and weather, by these lights
Like a blaze of summer straw, in winter's nick.   240

1950

Angel Surrounded by Paysans[*]

One of the countrymen:

                                        There is
    A welcome at the door to which no one comes?
The angel:
    I am the angel of reality,   5
    Seen for a moment standing in the door.

    I have neither ashen wing nor wear of ore[1]
    And live without a tepid aureole,

---

[19] The creator of the world.

[*] In his *Letters* (New York: Knopf, 1966), Stevens says that the poem was written about a still life representing a Venetian glass bowl (the "angel") standing on a table amid other glass and pottery vessels (the "peasants"). "The point of the poem," Stevens writes, "is that there must be in the world about us things that solace us quite as fully as any heavenly visitation could."

[1] Gold.

Or stars that follow me, not to attend,
But, of my being and its knowing, part.   10

I am one of you and being one of you
Is being and knowing what I am and know.

Yet I am the necessary angel of earth,
Since, in my sight, you see the earth again,

Cleared of its stiff and stubborn, man-locked set,   15
And, in my hearing, you hear its tragic drone

Rise liquidly in liquid lingerings,
Like watery words awash; like meanings said

By repetitions of half-meanings. Am I not,
Myself, only half of a figure of a sort,   20

A figure half seen, or seen for a moment, a man
Of the mind, an apparition apparelled in

Apparels of such lightest look that a turn
Of my shoulder and quickly, too quickly, I am gone?

1950

Final Soliloquy of the Interior Paramour*

Light the first light of evening, as in a room
In which we rest and, for small reason, think
The world imagined is the ultimate good.

This is, therefore, the intensest rendezvous.
It is in that thought that we collect ourselves,   5
Out of all the indifferences, into one thing:

Within a single thing, a single shawl
Wrapped tightly round us, since we are poor, a warmth,
A light, a power, the miraculous influence.

---

* The poem is spoken by the "interior
paramour," or muse, to the poet.

Here, now, we forget each other and ourselves.   10
We feel the obscurity of an order, a whole,
A knowledge, that which arranged the rendezvous,

Within its vital boundary, in the mind.
We say God and the imagination are one . . .
How high that highest candle lights the dark.   15

Out of this same light, out of the central mind,
We make a dwelling in the evening air,
In which being there together is enough.
1953

The Plain Sense of Things

After the leaves have fallen, we return
To a plain sense of things. It is as if
We had come to an end of the imagination,
Inanimate in an inert savoir.[1]

It is difficult even to choose the adjective   5
For this blank cold, this sadness without cause.
The great structure has become a minor house.
No turban walks across the lessened floors.

The greenhouse never so badly needed paint.
The chimney is fifty years old and slants to one side.   10
A fantastic effort has failed, a repetition
In a repetitiousness of men and flies.

Yet the absence of the imagination had
Itself to be imagined. The great pond,
The plain sense of it, without reflections, leaves,   15
Mud, water like dirty glass, expressing silence

Of a sort, silence of a rat come out to see,
The great pond and its waste of the lilies, all this
Had to be imagined as an inevitable knowledge,
Required, as a necessity requires.   20
1954

[1] French: "knowledge."

The Planet on the Table[1]

Ariel[2] was glad he had written his poems.
They were of a remembered time
Or of something seen that he liked.

Other makings of the sun
Were waste and welter   5
And the ripe shrub writhed.

His self and the sun were one
And his poems, although makings of his self,
Were no less makings of the sun.

It was not important that they survive.   10
What mattered was that they should bear
Some lineament or character,

Some affluence, if only half-perceived,
In the poverty of their words,
Of the planet of which they were part.   15

1954

The River of Rivers in Connecticut[1]

There is a great river this side of Stygia,[2]
Before one comes to the first black cataracts
And trees that lack the intelligence of trees.

In that river, far this side of Stygia,
The mere flowing of the water is a gayety,   5
Flashing and flashing in the sun. On its banks,

[1] The "planet" is a terrestrial globe, representing
the world in miniature. Stevens uses this as an
image for his *Collected Poems* (1954).
[2] The tree spirit in Shakespeare's play *The
Tempest*. The character Ariel sings several songs
in the course of the play. Here, Ariel
symbolizes the poet.
[1] *Connecticut* is an Indian word meaning "land of

many rivers." The Connecticut River is the
largest in the state, where Stevens lived. The
phrase "River of Rivers" is formed in imitation
of such Biblical phrases as "King of Kings" and
"Holy of Holies."
[2] The land of the dead, named from the River
Styx, which the shades of the dead must cross
in the boatman Charon's ferry.

No shadow walks. The river is fateful,
Like the last one. But there is no ferryman.
He could not bend against its propelling force.

It is not to be seen beneath the appearances   10
That tell of it. The steeple at Farmington
Stands glistening and Haddam[3] shines and sways.

It is the third commonness with light and air,
A curriculum,[4] a vigor, a local abstraction . . .
Call it, once more, a river, an unnamed flowing,   15

Space-filled, reflecting the seasons, the folk-lore
Of each of the senses; call it, again and again,
The river that flows nowhere, like a sea.
1954

Not Ideas About the Thing
but the Thing Itself[1]

At the earliest ending of winter,
In March, a scrawny cry from outside
Seemed like a sound in his mind.

He knew that he heard it,
A bird's cry, at daylight or before,   5
In the early March wind.

The sun was rising at six,
No longer a battered panache[2] above snow . . . .
It would have been outside.

It was not from the vast ventriloquism   10
Of sleep's faded papier-mâché . . .[3]
The sun was coming from outside.

---

[3] Farmington and Haddam are towns in Connecticut.
[4] Body of knowledge; the word has the same root as *current*.
[1] The *Ding-an-sich* (German) or "thing as it is in itself," was thought by Kantian philosophers to be beyond the reach of our perceptions, which could attain only to phenomena. Stevens put this poem last in his *Collected Poems* (1954).
[2] Tuft of feathers on a helmet.
[3] Material of paper and paste used to make ephemeral masks, statues, etc.

That scrawny cry—It was
A chorister whose c preceded the choir.[4]
It was part of the colossal sun,   15

Surrounded by its choral rings,
Still far away. It was like
A new knowledge of reality.

1954

The Course of a Particular

Today the leaves cry, hanging on branches swept by wind,
Yet the nothingness of winter becomes a little less.
It is still full of icy shades and shapen snow.

The leaves cry . . . One holds off and merely hears the cry.
It is a busy cry, concerning someone else.   5
And though one says that one is part of everything,

There is a conflict, there is a resistance involved;
And being part is an exertion that declines:
One feels the life of that which gives life as it is.

The leaves cry. It is not a cry of divine attention,   10
Nor the smoke-drift of puffed-out heroes, nor human cry.
It is the cry of leaves that do not transcend themselves,

In the absence of fantasia, without meaning more
Than they are in the final finding of the ear, in the thing
Itself, until, at last, the cry concerns no one at all.   15

1957

---

[4] The chorister sounds the note C on a pitch pipe
to give the choir its starting key.

Of Mere Being

The palm at the end of the mind,
Beyond the last thought, rises
In the bronze decor,

A gold-feathered bird
Sings in the palm, without human meaning,   5
Without human feeling, a foreign song.

You know then that it is not the reason
That makes us happy or unhappy.
The bird sings. Its feathers shine.

The palm stands on the edge of space.   10
The wind moves slowly in the branches.
The bird's fire-fangled feathers dangle down.
1957

William Carlos Williams
1883–1963

William Carlos Williams was long viewed as the homespun poet for the
technological age. A New Jersey physician, he was mistaken for a hobbyist-poet
jotting verses at odd moments between patients. Only with the 1946 publication
of Book One of his modern industrial-age American epic, *Paterson,* did readers
begin to appreciate Williams's achievement as a major twentieth-century
American writer. Thereafter, students, young poets, and critics looked closely and
with increasing admiration at his formally innovative books of poetry, fiction,
drama, and criticism. Dr. Williams had been writing in relative obscurity since
before 1920. At last, at midcentury, his readers caught up with the poet and
began to realize that Williams deserved the recognition and honor already
accorded to the select group of twentieth-century American poets that included
T. S. Eliot, Robert Frost, and Wallace Stevens.

His *Autobiography* (1951) presents young Billy Williams as an all-American
boy playing baseball and pranks, but in several ways his youth was not typically
American. Williams was born in 1883 in Rutherford, a northern New Jersey
town across the Meadowlands from New York City. He was the elder son of
William George and Raquel Helene Hoheb Williams. His father, an Englishman
earning his living as a traveling salesman in the Caribbean and in Latin America,
had met Helene, of Basque and Jewish origins, in Puerto Rico. After their

marriage he settled with her in Rutherford, where neither had friends or family. "Imagine," Williams later wrote of the town in the 1880s, "no sewers, no water supply, no gas even, not even a trolley car. The sidewalks were of wood." Williams's father was periodically away on business, while his mother, knowing little English, was somewhat reclusive in the town. More difficult still, there was mental disorder in the family. His father's brother, Uncle Godwin, who lived with them, terrified young Billy with his erratic behavior. Helene herself was subject periodically to seizures combined with changes of voice, which embarrassed and doubtless frightened the child.

Yet Williams's parents were a cultured couple. As a young woman, his mother had studied art in the *beaux arts* tradition in Paris, and throughout her life she conveyed her love of all things European, especially art, which Williams later considered studying. His father passed along his literary interests to the boy by reading aloud from the Afro-American poet Paul Lawrence Dunbar, from Gilbert and Sullivan, and from a collection of English Romantic and Victorian poets, including Keats. The household was bilingual in English and Spanish, and in boyhood the Williams sons, including Billy's younger brother Edgar, took music lessons and tasted life abroad, including a year of school in Switzerland and several months in Paris. This family background has proved significant to Williams's readers, who continue to discover important strains of European artistic influence in writing that is self-professedly American.

Ambitious for his sons' education, George Williams sent them, at considerable financial sacrifice, to Horace Mann High School in New York City, a two-hour daily commute each way. With the family's blessing, Edgar, evidently the academically superior student, prepared to study architecture, while William was readied for a career in dentistry. At the turn of the century, college work was not required for admission to some American medical schools, and Williams entered the School of Medicine at the University of Pennsylvania in Philadelphia following his graduation from high school. In retrospect, it was a happy choice. Within the year he had transferred from dentistry into medicine. Meanwhile, in a moment crucial for his life as a writer, he met the aspiring artist Charles Demuth, the young poet H. D. (Hilda Doolittle), and a graduate student, Ezra Pound, who became his lifelong friend and critic.

Through medical school and his interning years in New York (1902–1909), Williams, an earnest and dutiful young man, remained a Sunday painter and sustained his literary ambitions. Unknown to him then, his medical education, emphasizing rapid diagnosis and note-taking on cases, would later become an integral part of his poetic practice. In those early years, however, Williams still wrote well-meant clichés ("the only way to be truly happy is to make others happy") that echoed the Christian liberalism of his Rutherford culture. His first book, *Poems* (1909), self-published, was ambitious but sentimental and derivative —"bad Keats" he later called it. At that point poetry was his haven, a respite from the daily experience of blood and childbirth, roach-infested laboratories and disease.

At twenty-six, while a medical intern, Williams began the courtship of Charlotte Herman, the daughter of a prosperous German-American printer in Rutherford whose family became the subject of Williams's Stecher trilogy of novels (*White Mule*, 1937; *In the Money*, 1940; *The Build-Up*, 1952). When she refused him, Williams immediately proposed to her quieter, plainer, younger sister Florence. Williams and "Flossie" became informally engaged in 1909, just before he left for a year of postgraduate medical study in Leipzig, Germany. He also visited Pound in London and saw his brother Ed, who was studying architecture at the American Academy in Rome. After touring in Spain, Williams returned to America to begin medical practice in his hometown. He married Flossie in December 1912, and within two years had a mortgage, the first of two infant sons, and a practice that included evening office hours and house calls. Nonetheless, he determined to continue his literary life.

Manhattan, Rutherford, and their surroundings thereafter became Williams's main compass points. The Rutherford area provided abundant material for his writing, while an hour's drive away in a Model-T Ford, a wide circle of cosmopolitan artists and writers in New York kept him abreast of the contemporary movement in the arts known as modernism. In 1913, the year in which Pound arranged for the publication of Williams's second book of poems, *The Tempers*, Williams probably learned of the latest European work of artists like Matisse, Cézanne, and Braque, whose works were displayed at the New York Armory. By the midteens, Williams had affiliated with the Others group of artists and writers and had met Marianne Moore, Wallace Stevens, and Marcel Duchamp, who were revolutionizing the arts through their efforts to break down and restructure space and time.

But the cultural influences on Williams were broad-based. One was the efficiency movement of the 1910s, which was meant to encourage more productive labor and which taught Americans to think in ever finer, more precise subdivisions of time and motion. Even as Williams criticized this glorification of speed, he was writing prodigiously and sustaining a busy, multifaceted life.

Williams's break with traditional forms and subject matter came with *Al Que Quiere!* ("To Him Who Wants It!"), a book of iconoclastic lyrics, and with *Kora in Hell: Improvisations* (1920). *Kora* was an experimental montage of passages written "automatically" to tap subconscious funds of poetic energy; portions of unpremeditated writing were coupled with Williams's commentary on them. *Kora* appeared in the same issues of *The Little Review* that carried James Joyce's *Ulysses,* a work that was to influence Williams profoundly, as it did numerous other American writers. (Williams met Joyce in 1924, while on sabbatical in Europe with Flossie.)

The 1920s were an especially prolific period for Williams. Continuously experimenting in form, he spoke in the voice that is unmistakably his. Often angry and irreverent in tone, it was defiant of all conventions—formal, political, and religious. A self-consciously American poet, he was angered by—and jealous of—T. S. Eliot, whose insistence on the British tradition Williams thought retrograde. During those years, various small presses published many of Williams's most lasting works, including *Spring and All* (1923), which combined prose and poetry, *The Great American Novel* (1923), and *In the American Grain* (1925), a personal revision of American history and culture. Williams always remained innovative. He believed the repetition of familiar forms to be a kind of living death for a poet.

During the Great Depression, Williams published a collection of short stories aptly entitled *The Knife of the Times* (1932) and saw two major collections of poems through the press. From the wartime 1940s, as successive books of his long poem *Paterson* appeared and his reputation grew, Williams began to suffer health problems. Through heart attacks and strokes he continued, with the tireless help of Flossie, to read, write, travel, and lecture. Two major works, *The Desert Music* (1954) and *Pictures from Brueghel* (1962) came from the efforts of those years, as he struggled toward a flexible verse form he called the variable foot.

By now Williams was earning prestigious prizes for his poetry. Still he resolutely encouraged the younger poets who wrote him letters and appeared on his Rutherford doorstep. He never forgot how hard it was to make his way or how difficult his isolation had often been. He remarked in 1950, "I think the artist, generally speaking, feels lonely. Perhaps his recourse to art, in any form, comes from his essential loneliness. He is usually in rebellion against the world."

Further Reading:

J. H. Miller, *Poets of Reality*, 1965.
J. Guimond, *The Art of William Carlos Williams*, 1968.
S. Paul, *The Music of Survival*, 1968.
B. Dijkstra, *The Hieroglyphics of a New Speech*, 1969.
J. Breslin, *William Carlos Williams*, 1970.
J. Conarroe, *William Carlos Williams'*

"*Paterson*," 1970.
B. Sankey, *A Companion to William Carlos Williams' "Paterson,"* 1971.
D. Tashjian, *William Carlos Williams and the American Scene, 1920–1940*, 1978.
P. Mariani, *William Carlos Williams*, 1981.
William Carlos Williams: Man and Poet, ed. C. Terrell, 1983.

Texts:

The Collected Earlier Poems of William Carlos Williams, 1966.

The Collected Later Poems of William Carlos Williams, 1967.

The Young Housewife

At ten A.M. the young housewife
moves about in negligee behind
the wooden walls of her husband's house.
I pass solitary in my car.

Then again she comes to the curb   5
to call the ice-man, fish-man, and stands
shy, uncorseted, tucking in
stray ends of hair, and I compare her
to a fallen leaf.

The noiseless wheels of my car   10
rush with a crackling sound over
dried leaves as I bow and pass smiling.

1917

El Hombre[1]

It's a strange courage
you give me ancient star:

Shine alone in the sunrise
toward which you lend no part!
1917

Danse Russe[1]

If when my wife is sleeping
and the baby and Kathleen
are sleeping
and the sun is a flame-white disc
in silken mists   5
above shining trees,—
if I in my north room
dance naked, grotesquely
before my mirror
waving my shirt round my head   10
and singing softly to myself:
"I am lonely, lonely.
I was born to be lonely,
I am best so!"
If I admire my arms, my face,   15
my shoulders, flanks, buttocks
against the yellow drawn shades,—
Who shall say I am not
the happy genius of my household?[2]
1917

---

[1] Spanish: "the man" or "the brave man."
[1] French: "Russian dance."

[2] The *genius loci* (Latin) is the tutelary deity of a place.

Love Song

I lie here thinking of you:—

the stain of love
is upon the world!
Yellow, yellow, yellow
it eats into the leaves,   5
smears with saffron
the horned branches that lean
heavily
against a smooth purple sky!
There is no light   10
only a honey-thick stain
that drips from leaf to leaf
and limb to limb
spoiling the colors
of the whole world—   15

you far off there under
the wine-red selvage[1] of the west!

1917

Queen Anne's Lace[1]

Her body is not so white as
anemone petals nor so smooth—nor
so remote a thing. It is a field
of the wild carrot taking
the field by force; the grass   5
does not raise above it.
Here is no question of whiteness,
white as can be, with a purple mole
at the center of each flower.
Each flower is a hand's span   10
of her whiteness. Wherever

[1] Finished edge of fabric.
[1] The wild carrot; its flower is composed of multiple white blossoms, giving a lacelike appearance.

his hand has lain there is
a tiny purple blemish. Each part
is a blossom under his touch
to which the fibres of her being   15
stem one by one, each to its end,
until the whole field is a
white desire, empty, a single stem,
a cluster, flower by flower,
a pious wish to whiteness gone over—   20
or nothing.

1921

Paterson[1]

Before the grass is out the people are out
and bare twigs still whip the wind—
when there is nothing, in the pause between
snow and grass in the parks and at the street ends
—Say it, no ideas but in things—   5
nothing but the blank faces of the houses
and cylindrical trees
bent, forked by preconception and accident
split, furrowed, creased, mottled, stained
secret—into the body of the light—   10
These are the ideas, savage and tender
somewhat of the music, et cetera
of Paterson, that great philosopher—

From above, higher than the spires, higher
even than the office towers, from oozy fields   15
abandoned to grey beds of dead grass
black sumac, withered weed stalks
mud and thickets cluttered with dead leaves—
the river comes pouring in above the city
and crashes from the edge of the gorge   20
in a recoil of spray and rainbow mists—
—Say it, no ideas but in things—
and factories crystallized from its force,
like ice from spray upon the chimney rocks

[1] The New Jersey city is anthropomorphized here
and in Williams's epic narrative.

Say it! No ideas but in things. Mr.   25
Paterson has gone away
to rest and write. Inside the bus one sees
his thoughts sitting and standing. His thoughts
alight and scatter—

Who are these people (how complex   30
this mathematic) among whom I see myself
in the regularly ordered plateglass of
his thoughts, glimmering before shoes and bicycles—?
They walk incommunicado, the
equation is beyond solution, yet   35
its sense is clear—that they may live
his thought is listed in the Telephone
Directory—
      and there's young Alex Shorn
whose dad the boot-black bought a house   40
and painted it inside
with seascapes of a pale green monochrome[2]—
the infant Dionysus springing from
Apollo's arm—the floors oakgrained in
Balkan fashion—Hermes' nose, the body   45
of a gourmand, the lips of Cupid, the eyes
the black eyes of Venus' sister—

But who! who are these people? It is
his flesh making the traffic, cranking the car
buying the meat—   50
Defeated in achieving the solution they
fall back among cheap pictures, furniture
filled silk, cardboard shoes, bad dentistry
windows that will not open, poisonous gin
scurvy, toothache—   55

But never, in despair and anxiety
forget to drive wit in, in till it
discover that his thoughts are decorous and simple
and never forget that though his thoughts are decorous
and simple, the despair and anxiety   60
the grace and detail of
a dynamo—

Divine thought! Jacob fell backwards off the press
and broke his spine. What pathos, what mercy

---

[2] The bootblack's paintings are of mythological subjects; his house borrows its floor pattern from Europe. In the incongruity of these transplanted fashions Williams questions the suitability of European themes for American art and architecture.

of nurses (who keep birthday books)   65
and doctors who can't speak proper english—
is here correctly on a spotless bed
painless to the Nth power—the two legs
perfect without movement or sensation

Twice a month Paterson receives letters   70
from the Pope, his works are translated
into French, the clerks in the post office
ungum the rare stamps from his packages
and steal them for their children's albums
So in his high decorum he is wise   75

What wind and sun of children stamping the snow
stamping the snow and screaming drunkenly
The actual, florid detail of cheap carpet
amazingly upon the floor and paid for
as no portrait ever was—Canary singing   80
and geraniums in tin cans spreading their leaves
reflecting red upon the frost—
They are the divisions and imbalances
of his whole concept, made small by pity
and desire, they are—no ideas beside the facts—   85
1921

Spring and All

By the road to the contagious hospital
under the surge of the blue
mottled clouds driven from the
northeast—a cold wind. Beyond, the
waste of broad, muddy fields   5
brown with dried weeds, standing and fallen

patches of standing water
the scattering of tall trees

All along the road the reddish
purplish, forked, upstanding, twiggy   10
stuff of bushes and small trees
with dead, brown leaves under them
leafless vines—

Lifeless in appearance, sluggish
dazed spring approaches—   15

They enter the new world naked,
cold, uncertain of all
save that they enter. All about them
the cold, familiar wind—

Now the grass, tomorrow   20
the stiff curl of wildcarrot leaf
One by one objects are defined—
It quickens: clarity, outline of leaf

But now the stark dignity of
entrance—Still, the profound change   25
has come upon them: rooted they
grip down and begin to awaken
1923

The Rose

The rose is obsolete
but each petal ends in
an edge, the double facet
cementing the grooved
columns of air—The edge   5
cuts without cutting
meets—nothing—renews
itself in metal or porcelain—

whither? It ends—

But if it ends   10
the start is begun
so that to engage roses
becomes a geometry—

Sharper, neater, more cutting
figured in majolica[1]—   15
the broken plate
glazed with a rose

[1] A type of ornamental glazed pottery.

Somewhere the sense
makes copper roses
steel roses—   20

The rose carried weight of love
but love is at an end—of roses
It is at the edge of the
petal that love waits

Crisp, worked to defeat   25
laboredness—fragile
plucked, moist, half-raised
cold, precise, touching

What

The place between the petal's   30
edge and the

From the petal's edge a line starts
that being of steel
infinitely fine, infinitely
rigid penetrates   35
the Milky Way
without contact—lifting
from it—neither hanging
nor pushing—

The fragility of the flower   40
unbruised
penetrates space
1923

To Elsie

The pure products of America[1]
go crazy—
mountain folk from Kentucky

or the ribbed north end of
Jersey   5
with its isolate lakes and

[1] The "pure products of America" are those living in such isolated pockets that they have been produced by generations of inbreeding, with consequent multiplication of genetic defects.

valleys, its deaf-mutes, thieves
old names
and promiscuity between

devil-may-care men who have taken   10
to railroading
out of sheer lust of adventure—

and young slatterns, bathed
in filth
from Monday to Saturday   15

to be tricked out that night
with gauds²
from imaginations which have no

peasant traditions to give them
character   20
but flutter and flaunt

sheer rags—succumbing without
emotion
save numbed terror

under some hedge of choke-cherry   25
or viburnum—
which they cannot express—

Unless it be that marriage
perhaps
with a dash of Indian blood   30

will throw up a girl so desolate
so hemmed round
with disease or murder

that she'll be rescued by an
agent—   35
reared by the state and

sent out at fifteen to work in
some hard pressed
house in the suburbs—

some doctor's family, some Elsie—   40
voluptuous water
expressing with broken

² Jewelry (archaic).

brain the truth about us—
her great
ungainly hips and flopping breasts   45

addressed to cheap
jewelry
and rich young men with fine eyes

as if the earth under our feet
were   50
an excrement of some sky

and we degraded prisoners
destined
to hunger until we eat filth

while the imagination strains   55
after deer
going by fields of goldenrod in

the stifling heat of September
Somehow
it seems to destroy us   60

It is only in isolate flecks that
something
is given off

No one
to witness   65
and adjust, no one to drive the car
1923

The Red Wheelbarrow

so much depends
upon

a red wheel
barrow

glazed with rain   5
water

beside the white
chickens
1923

The Sea-Elephant[1]

Trundled from
the strangeness of the sea—
a kind of
heaven—

Ladies and Gentlemen!   5
the greatest
sea-monster ever exhibited
alive

the gigantic
sea-elephant! O wallow   10
of flesh where
are

there fish enough for
that
appetite stupidity   15
cannot lessen?

Sick
of April's smallness
the little
leaves—   20

Flesh has lief of you
enormous sea—
Speak!
Blouaugh! (feed

[1] Largest of the fin-footed mammals. (The male's weight averages 5,000 pounds.) It can produce a deep roar from its snout; it feeds on small fish, shellfish, and squid. Although clumsy on land, it is swift and graceful in the ocean. The poem is set at a sideshow, where a barker is exhibiting a sea elephant in captivity.

me) my
flesh is riven—
fish after fish into his maw
unswallowing   25

to let them glide down
gulching back
half spittle half   30
brine

the
troubled eyes—torn
from the sea.
(In   35

a practical voice) They
ought
to put it back where
it came from.   40

Gape.
Strange head—
told by old sailors—
rising

bearded   45
to the surface—and
the only
sense out of them

is that woman's
Yes   50
it's wonderful but they
ought to

put it
back into the sea where
it came from.   55
Blouaugh!

Swing—ride
walk
on wires—toss balls
stoop and   60

contort yourselves—
But I

am love. I am
from the sea—

Blouaugh!   65
there is no crime save
the too-heavy
body

the sea
held playfully—comes   70
to the surface
the water

boiling
about the head the cows[2]
scattering   75
fish dripping from

the bounty
of. . . . and spring
they say
Spring is icummen in[3]—   80

1934

The Botticellian Trees[1]

The alphabet of
the trees

is fading in the
song of the leaves

the crossing   5
bars of the thin

---

[2] Female sea elephants.
[3] Adaptation of medieval lyric, "Sumer Is Icumen In."

[1] In the painting *La Primavera (Spring)* by the Italian Sandro Botticelli (1444–1510) the trees are coming into leaf.

          letters that spelled
          winter

          and the cold
          have been illumined   10

          with
          pointed green

          by the rain and sun—
          The strict simple

          principles of   15
          straight branches

          are being modified
          by pinched-out

          ifs of color, devout
          conditions   20

          the smiles of love—
          . . . . . .

          until the stript
          sentences

          move as a woman's
          limbs under cloth   25

          and praise from secrecy
          quick with desire

          love's ascendancy
          in summer—

          In summer the song   30
          sings itself

          above the muffled words—
          1932

This Is Just to Say

I have eaten
the plums
that were in
the icebox

and which   5
you were probably
saving
for breakfast

Forgive me
they were delicious   10
so sweet
and so cold
1934

Flowers by the Sea

When over the flowery, sharp pasture's
edge, unseen, the salt ocean

lifts its form—chicory and daisies
tied, released, seem hardly flowers alone

but color and the movement—or the shape   5
perhaps—of restlessness, whereas

the sea is circled and sways
peacefully upon its plantlike stem
1935

To a Poor Old Woman

munching a plum on
the street a paper bag
of them in her hand

They taste good to her
They taste good   5
to her. They taste
good to her

You can see it by
the way she gives herself
to the one half   10
sucked out in her hand

Comforted
a solace of ripe plums
seeming to fill the air
They taste good to her   15
1935

The Yachts

contend in a sea which the land partly encloses
shielding them from the too-heavy blows
of an ungoverned ocean which when it chooses

tortures the biggest hulls, the best man knows
to pit against its beatings, and sinks them pitilessly.   5
Mothlike in mists, scintillant in the minute

brilliance of cloudless days, with broad bellying sails
they glide to the wind tossing green water
from their sharp prows while over them the crew crawls

ant-like, solicitously grooming them, releasing,   10
making fast as they turn, lean far over and having
caught the wind again, side by side, head for the mark.

In a well guarded arena of open water surrounded by
lesser and greater craft which, sycophant, lumbering
and flittering follow them, they appear youthful, rare   15

as the light of a happy eye, live with the grace
of all that in the mind is fleckless, free and
naturally to be desired. Now the sea which holds them

is moody, lapping their glossy sides, as if feeling
for some slightest flaw but fails completely.   20
Today no race. Then the wind comes again. The yachts

move, jockeying for a start, the signal is set and they
are off. Now the waves strike at them but they are too
well made, they slip through, though they take in canvas.

Arms with hands grasping seek to clutch at the prows.   25
Bodies thrown recklessly in the way are cut aside.
It is a sea of faces about them in agony, in despair

until the horror of the race dawns staggering the mind,
the whole sea become an entanglement of watery bodies
lost to the world bearing what they cannot hold. Broken,   30

beaten, desolate, reaching from the dead to be taken up
they cry out, failing, failing! their cries rising
in waves still as the skillful yachts pass over.

1935

The Poor

It's the anarchy of poverty
delights me, the old
yellow wooden house indented
among the new brick tenements

Or a cast-iron balcony   5
with panels showing oak branches
in full leaf. It fits
the dress of the children

reflecting every stage and
custom of necessity——
Chimneys, roofs, fences of
wood and metal in an unfenced   10

age and enclosing next to
nothing at all: the old man
in a sweater and soft black
hat who sweeps the sidewalk——   15

his own ten feet of it
in a wind that fitfully
turning his corner has
overwhelmed the entire city   20

1938

These

are the desolate, dark weeks
when nature in its barrenness
equals the stupidity of man.

The year plunges into night
and the heart plunges
lower than night   5

to an empty, windswept place
without sun, stars or moon
but a peculiar light as of thought

that spins a dark fire——   10
whirling upon itself until,
in the cold, it kindles

to make a man aware of nothing
that he knows, not loneliness
itself——Not a ghost but   15

would be embraced——emptiness,
despair——(They
whine and whistle) among

the flashes and booms of war;
houses of whose rooms   20
the cold is greater than can be thought,

the people gone that we loved,
the beds lying empty, the couches
damp, the chairs unused—

Hide it away somewhere   25
out of the mind, let it get roots
and grow, unrelated to jealous

ears and eyes—for itself.
In this mine they come to dig—all.
Is this the counterfoil to sweetest   30

music? The source of poetry that
seeing the clock stopped, says,
The clock has stopped

that ticked yesterday so well?
and hears the sound of lakewater   35
splashing—that is now stone.
1938

Paterson: The Falls

What common language to unravel?
The falls, combed into straight lines
from that rafter of a rock's
lip. Strike in! the middle of

some trenchant phrase, some   5
well packed clause. Then . . .
This is my plan. 4 sections: First,
the archaic persons of the drama.

An eternity of bird and bush,
resolved. An unraveling: 10
the confused streams aligned, side
by side, speaking! Sound

married to strength, a strength
of falling—from a height! The wild

voice of the shirt-sleeved   15
Evangelist[1] rivaling, Hear

me! I am the Resurrection
and the Life! echoing
among the bass and pickerel, slim
eels from Barbados, Sargasso   20

Sea,[2] working up the coast to that
bounty, ponds and wild streams—
Third, the old town: Alexander Hamilton
working up from St. Croix,[3]

from that sea! and a deeper, whence   25
he came! stopped cold
by that unmoving roar, fastened
there: the rocks silent

but the water, married to the stone,
voluble, though frozen; the water   30
even when and though frozen
still whispers and moans—

And in the brittle air
a factory bell clangs, at dawn, and
snow whines under their feet. Fourth,   35
the modern town, a

disembodied roar! the cataract and
its clamor broken apart—and from
all learning, the empty
ear struck from within, roaring . . .   40
1944

Burning the Christmas Greens

Their time past, pulled down
cracked and flung to the fire
—go up in a roar

All recognition lost, burnt clean
clean in the flame, the green   5

dispersed, a living red,
flame red, red as blood wakes
on the ash—

and ebbs to a steady burning
the rekindled bed become   10
a landscape of flame

At the winter's midnight
we went to the trees, the coarse
holly, the balsam and
the hemlock for their green   15

At the thick of the dark
the moment of the cold's
deepest plunge we brought branches
cut from the green trees

to fill our need, and over   20
doorways, about paper Christmas
bells covered with tinfoil
and fastened by red ribbons

we stuck the green prongs
in the windows hung   25
woven wreaths and above pictures
the living green. On the

mantle we built a green forest
and among those hemlock
sprays put a herd of small   30
white deer as if they

were walking there. All this!
and it seemed gentle and good
to us. Their time past,
relief! The room bare. We   35

stuffed the dead grate
with them upon the half burnt out
log's smoldering eye, opening
red and closing under them

and we stood there looking down.   40
Green is a solace
a promise of peace, a fort
against the cold (though we

did not say so) a challenge
above the snow's   45
hard shell. Green (we might
have said) that, where

small birds hide and dodge
and lift their plaintive
rallying cries, blocks for them   50
and knocks down

the unseeing bullets of
the storm. Green spruce boughs
pulled down by a weight of
snow—Transformed!   55

Violence leaped and appeared.
Recreant!¹ roared to life
as the flame rose through and
our eyes recoiled from it.

In the jagged flames green   60
to red, instant and alive. Green!
those sure abutments . . . Gone!
lost to mind

and quick in the contracting
tunnel of the grate   65
appeared a world! Black
mountains, black and red—as

yet uncolored—and ash white,
an infant landscape of shimmering
ash and flame and we, in   70
that instant, lost,

breathless to be witnesses,
as if we stood
ourselves refreshed among
the shining fauna of that fire.   75
1944

---

¹ Pun on *recreant* (betraying one's allegiance) and
re-creant (re-creating).

Impromptu: The Suckers*

Take it out in vile whiskey, take it out
in lifting your skirts to show your silken
crotches; it is this that is intended.
You are it. Your pleas will always be denied.
You too will always go up with the two guys,   5
scapegoats to save the Republic and
especially the State of Massachusetts. The
Governor says so and you ain't supposed
to ask for details—

Your case has been reviewed by high-minded   10
and unprejudiced observers (like hell
they were!) the president of a great
university, the president of a noteworthy
technical school and a judge too old to sit
on the bench, men already rewarded for   15
their services to pedagogy and the enforcement
of arbitrary statutes. In other words
pimps to tradition—

Why in hell didn't they choose some other
kind of "unprejudiced adviser" for their   20
death council? instead of sticking to that
autocratic strain of Boston backwash, except
that the council was far from unprejudiced
but the product of a rejected, discredited
class long since outgrown except for use in   25
courts and school, and that they
wanted it so—

Why didn't they choose at least one decent
Jew or some fair-minded Negro or anybody
but such a triumvirate of inversion, the   30
New England aristocracy, bent on working off
a grudge against you, Americans, you
are the suckers, you are the ones who will

---

* This satiric "improvisation," addressed to recent immigrants, centers on the Sacco-Vanzetti case. In 1920, in Massachusetts, a paymaster and his guard were shot and killed by two men who escaped with over $15,000. Nicola Sacco and Bartolomeo Vanzetti, Italian anarchists, were found guilty of the crime in 1921 and sentenced to death. They were executed in the electric chair in 1927, after prolonged judicial review by a committee appointed by the governor of Massachusetts. However, their guilt is still a matter of dispute.

be going up on the eleventh to get the current
shot into you, for the glory of the state   35
and the perpetuation of abstract justice—

And all this in the face of the facts: that
the man who swore, and deceived the jury
wilfully by so doing, that the bullets found
in the bodies of the deceased could be   40
identified as having been fired from the pistol
of one of the accused—later
acknowledged that he could not so identify
them; that the jurors now seven years after
the crime do not remember the details and   45
have wanted to forget them; that the
prosecution has never succeeded in
apprehending the accomplices nor in connecting
the prisoners with any of the loot stolen—

The case is perfect against you, all the   50
documents say so—in spite of the fact that
it is reasonably certain that you were not
at the scene of the crime, shown, quite as
convincingly as the accusing facts in the
court evidence, by better reasoning to have   55
been committed by someone else with whom
the loot can be connected and among whom the
accomplices can be found—

It's no use, you are Americans, just the dregs.
It's all you deserve. You've got the cash,   60
what the hell do you care? You've got
nothing to lose. You are inheritors of a great
tradition. My country right or wrong!
You do what you're told to do. You don't
answer back the way Tommy Jeff did or Ben   65
Frank or Georgie Washing. I'll say you
don't. You're civilized. You let your
betters tell you where you get off. Go
ahead—

But after all, the thing that swung heaviest   70
against you was that you were scared when
they copped you. Explain that you
nature's nobleman! For you know that every
American is innocent and at peace in his
own heart. He hasn't a damned thing to be   75
afraid of. He knows the government is for

him. Why, when a cop steps up and grabs
you at night you just laugh and think it's
a hell of a good joke—

This is what was intended from the first.   80
So take it out in your rotten whisky and
silk underwear. That's what you get out of
it. But put it down in your memory that this
is the kind of stuff that they can't get away
with. It is there and it's loaded. No one   85
can understand what makes the present age
what it is. They are mystified by certain
insistences.

1941

The Last Words of My English Grandmother

1920

There were some dirty plates
and a glass of milk
beside her on a small table
near the rank, disheveled bed—

Wrinkled and nearly blind   5
she lay and snored
rousing with anger in her tones
to cry for food,

Gimme something to eat—
They're starving me—   10
I'm all right I won't go
to the hospital. No, no, no

Give me something to eat
Let me take you
to the hospital, I said   15
and after you are well

you can do as you please.
She smiled, Yes

you do what you please first
then I can do what I please—   20

Oh, oh, oh! she cried
as the ambulance men lifted
her to the stretcher—
Is this what you call

making me comfortable?   25
By now her mind was clear—
Oh you think you're smart
you young people,

she said, but I'll tell you
you don't know anything.   30
Then we started.
On the way

we passed a long row
of elms. She looked at them
awhile out of   35
the ambulance window and said,

What are all those
fuzzy-looking things out there?
Trees? Well, I'm tired
of them and rolled her head away.   40
1949

The Three Graces[1]

We have the picture of you in mind,
when you were young, posturing
(for a photographer) in scarves
(if you could have done it) but now,
for none of you is immortal, ninety-   5
three, the three, ninety and three,
Mary, Ellen and Emily, what

[1] Conventionally depicted as three maidens with
arms enlaced, a common subject in classical and
Renaissance art.

beauty is it clings still about you?
Undying? Magical? For there is still
no answer, why we live or why   10
you will not live longer than I
or that there should be an answer why
any should live and whatever other
should die. Yet you live
and all that can be said is that   15
you live, time cannot alter it—
and as I write this Mary has died.

1950

The Descent

The descent beckons
      as the ascent beckoned.
            Memory is a kind
of accomplishment,
      a sort of renewal   5
           even
an initiation, since the spaces it opens are new places
      inhabited by hordes
           heretofore unrealized,
of new kinds—   10
      since their movements
           are toward new objectives
(even though formerly they were abandoned).

No defeat is made up entirely of defeat—since
the world it opens is always a place   15
      formerly
           unsuspected. A
world lost,
      a world unsuspected,
           beckons to new places   20
and no whiteness (lost) is so white as the memory
of whiteness   .

With evening, love wakens
      though its shadows
           which are alive by reason   25

of the sun shining—
      grow sleepy now and drop away
          from desire   .
Love without shadows stirs now
        beginning to awaken
             as night   30
advances.

The descent
      made up of despairs
         and without accomplishment   35
realizes a new awakening:
        which is a reversal
of despair.
      For what we cannot accomplish, what
is denied to love,
                                     40
      what we have lost in the anticipation—
        a descent follows,
endless and indestructible   .

1954

A Negro Woman

      carrying a bunch of marigolds
          wrapped
               in an old newspaper:
She carries them upright,
         bareheaded,   5
             the bulk
of her thighs
         causing her to waddle
            as she walks
looking into   10
        the store window which she passes
             on her way.
What is she
      but an ambassador
            from another world   15
a world of pretty marigolds
        of two shades
            which she announces

not knowing what she does
        other   20
            than walk the streets
holding the flowers upright
      as a torch[1]
          so early in the morning.

1955

Poem

The rose fades
and is renewed again
by its seed, naturally
but where

save in the poem   5
shall it go
to suffer no diminution
of its splendor

1962

The Rewaking

Sooner or later
we must come to the end
of striving

to re-establish
the image the image of   5
the rose

but not yet
you say extending the
time indefinitely

---

[1] The torch is one of the symbols of Demeter,
the Greek goddess of the harvest and fertility.

10

by
your love until a whole
spring

rekindle
the violet to the very
lady's-slipper

15

and so by
your love the very sun
itself is revived
1962

Ezra Pound
1885–1972

Ezra Pound set himself the goal of knowing by the age of thirty "more about poetry than any man living." Accomplished and influential as a poet and—perhaps more notably—as critic, translator, and literary entrepreneur, he pursued his many-sided literary career with ambition and intensity. There can be "no doubt," a reviewer remarked, "as to his vitality and his determination to burst his way into Parnassus." He remains one of the writers most responsible for the modernist revolution in English poetry and prose.

Pound was born in Hailey, Idaho, and raised in Philadelphia in middle-class circumstances. At Hamilton College and the University of Pennsylvania, he specialized in medieval and Renaissance literature in Spanish, Italian, French, and Latin, including a "special study" of Martial, Catullus, and Tacitus. By the time he received his M.A. in 1906, he had "spatted with nearly everybody" and decided against continuing toward the Ph.D. A short period teaching at Wabash College ("the last or at least sixth circle of desolation") only confirmed him in his often heated contempt of American college professors. Dismissed abruptly after a scandal about keeping a woman overnight in his room, Pound traveled to Venice. There he began his lifelong struggle to live for and, wherever possible, on his writing.

In Venice, he had his first book, *A Lume Spento* (1908), published, but at his own expense. He tried working as a gondolier (he was not strong enough) and, briefly, as a publicist for a friend ("the greatest livin' she pianist") before moving in 1908 to London, "the place for poetry." He immediately began to transform English literature—without, however, sacrificing his pleasure in ostentatiously playing the raw and vital American. He frequently cultivated, in speech and writing, a parodic version of the American language; he also was an occasional self-appointed expert on native manners, as when, at lunch with the novelists D. H. Lawrence and Ford Madox Ford, he demonstrated, in a suitably barbaric fashion, how an American ate an apple.

In London, Pound entered a milieu of poets dedicated to writing what, he determined, had already been written in language that was already worn. He responded with poetry that was at once conservative and revolutionary. His famous rallying cry—"make it new!"—meant not a break with the past, but remaining faithful to the spirit of the past while attempting to modernize it, to rediscover its vigor through the creation of new forms. This was something that, Pound vehemently believed, most did not do, because of the sterile academism of most scholarship and the formulaic rhetoric of conventional literary styles. Pound was thus a maverick iconoclast who denounced both the academic scholarship and conventional verse of his day; he was, at the same time, however eccentrically, a passionately learned, even bookish writer. These apparently contradictory tendencies account for much of the energy in an early poem like "Sestina: Altaforte," which is in the difficult sestina form, on a historical subject, and in the tradition of the dramatic monologue associated with Robert Browning. Despite all this indebtedness to literary tradition and history, Pound sought to project himself into the speaker so completely that he became him, and to make thereby a poem that was not archaizing but vitally alive—so alive that when Pound read the poem at a poets' dinner at the Tour Eiffel restaurant, the management put a screen around his table.

Pound's success in infusing the books he touched and the history he recounted with immediacy and passion was so great that some have seen in his intense immersion in experience a sort of mysticism. The English writer and artist Wyndham Lewis observed that Pound "has really walked with Sophocles beside the Aegean; he has *seen* the Florence of Cavalcanti." When Pound continually exhorted himself and others that "every literaryism, every book word, fritters away a scrap of the reader's patience, a scrap of his sense of your sincerity," he did so with an evangelist's intensity. Literature was for him an intensification of life, and he treated his own lapses into "literaryisms"—his poems that echoed the dead letter of an old language rather than the living spirit of the past—with as much severity as he did those of others. After Ford Madox Ford looked through the copy of Pound's third book of poetry, *Canzoni* (1911), he rolled on the floor of his room in mock horror at the book's artificial language. That roll, Pound wrote, "saved me at least two years, perhaps more."

Pound's engagement with the past throughout his career encompassed a wide variety of literary traditions and historical eras, from classical Greece and Rome to medieval Europe, ancient China, and eighteenth-century America. The result was frequently poetry studded with covert references, difficult to the point of inaccessibility. Yet part of the reason for this difficulty was Pound's increasing exploration of an essentially simple poetic technique. At the beginning of his career he called it the technique of the "luminous detail"; later it became the "ideogrammatic method." In his early work it meant to evoke by means of a few, spare words, used without narrative context, moments of transcendent beauty. Later, employed with greater compression and allusiveness, the same technique could evoke the "intelligence of a period."

The first uses of the technique were purely literary. The luminous detail was essential to the Imagist movement in poetry, of which Pound was the originator and, for a little while, the leader. Under the banner of Imagism, he advocated poetry that eschewed all rhetoric and "emotional slither," that would be, objectively and concretely, an image—which Pound defined as "that which presents an intellectual and emotional 'complex' in an instant of time." The Imagist poem showed with as much immediacy as possible a luminous moment; it sought to owe little or nothing, therefore, to narrative or expository structures. When, shortly after defining the Imagist poem, Pound discovered Ernest Fenellosa's essay on the Chinese written character, he was able to extend the implications of the Imagist aesthetic considerably. In that essay, Fenellosa argued that Chinese characters were pictographs and that Chinese poetry was a succession of these "concrete pictures." Poetry of this sort could, Pound felt, in its presentation of a succession of luminous moments, approach the grammarless immediacy of perception, an ontological ideal that remained crucial to his poetry throughout his career. In 1914 Pound joined Wyndham Lewis in founding the Vorticism movement, which stood in essence for an aggressive version of these ideas.

The short Imagist poem "In a Station of the Metro" is representative, in compressed form, of Pound's technique. Pound presents concretely a moment of perception. The language is economical, free of "emotional slither." And, thanks to the unexplained juxtaposition of the two lines—a juxtaposition that avoids the use of logical and narrative connectives—the poem approaches, Pound would maintain, the grammarless immediacy of nature. Reality, the poem implies, is a construction of such relationships, and poetic perception is a succession of moments in which those relationships become luminously manifest.

By the end of the decade, Pound was the author of a number of books of poetry, of which *Personae* (1909), *Ripostes* (1912), and *Lustra* (1915) are the most important. The best poems from the latter two were later added to an expanded version of *Personae*. Pound also distinguished himself during this time as one of the century's outstanding, though sometimes controversial, translators of poetry. The most famous of his translations are those from the Chinese, done from the notes of Fenellosa and collected under the title *Cathay* (1915), and from the Latin poet Propertius, published as *Homage to Sextus Propertius* (1917).

With the appearance in 1920 of *Hugh Selwyn Mauberley: Life and Contacts* and the first sections of the poem that was to occupy him for the rest of his life, *The Cantos,* it was clear that Pound had decisively expanded on and complicated his poetic technique. With his friends T. S. Eliot and James Joyce, he shared the ambition to exploit and to overcome the often depressing, often comic disparity between ancient and modern cultures by writing an epic for the modern world. Increasingly concerned with the relationships of art and society, Pound began working in longer, more complex forms. *Hugh Selwyn Mauberley* was a sequence of short, crisp cameos; it was, Pound wrote, "a study in form, an attempt to condense the James novel." *The Cantos,* by contrast, were not condensations but a finally unending, encyclopedic long poem in open form, one that could include, however chaotically, all that was on Pound's mind, from personal anecdotes to literary allusions of an enormous variety and range. Both these works extended the technique of the luminous detail. It became, in the *Mauberley* poems, more decisively a historiographical technique, as details, allusions, and fragments of quotations were inserted in the separate sections of the poem as means of evoking the whole flavor of the society and era from which they came. Once again, narrative structure, though hard to avoid, was suppressed wherever possible. In

The Cantos this technique of often cryptic, fragmented, and highly allusive references was vastly extended, and narrative and expository structure was more daringly put aside. The result is a poem of greater flexibility and difficulty, if one that finally lacks the coherence of an overall design.

While Pound was attempting to establish his own career as a poet, he was passionately interested in the careers of other writers. Indeed, his own work was often overshadowed by that of the writers he admired and worked on behalf of. Pound was as passionately generous as he was egoistic. He attempted to aid, practically and artistically, an astonishing number of the century's most important writers. A short list would include Lawrence, Joyce, Eliot, Lewis, William Butler Yeats, William Carlos Williams, Robert Frost, and Ernest Hemingway. He served as corresponding editor in Europe for Harriet Monroe's Chicago-based *Poetry,* the literary magazine most responsible for exporting the modernist revolution to America, and as editor or contributing editor for numerous other magazines. He once made unauthorized changes in some poems that Yeats had entrusted to him for submission to *Poetry;* once Yeats got over his shock, he sought Pound's help in modernizing his style. Pound acted as an editor for Eliot's *Waste Land,* cutting a number of lines and passages from it. Pound also tried to help Eliot at one point by setting up a fund to enable his friend to stop working in a bank and to devote himself to writing poetry full-time. On numerous occasions, Pound helped writers financially from his own pocket. He encouraged other writers even when their achievements made him jealous (*The Waste Land* evoked from Pound the response "Complimenti, you bitch. I am wracked by the seven jealousies") or when he detested them, as he did Lawrence.

Between 1915 and 1920, as Pound worked on the *Mauberley* poems and the beginning of *The Cantos,* he became a committed social critic and theorist. The *Mauberley* poems show vividly how Pound's bitter reaction to World War I, which convinced him of the bankruptcy of Western history, helped launch him on his ultimately disastrous career as social analyst and critic. "There died a myriad, / And of the best, among them, / For an old bitch gone in the teeth / For a botched civilization," he wrote in Section V; among the best who were killed, he was doubtless thinking of his friend the sculptor Henri Gaudier-Brzeska, who died at the front in 1915. But the crucial point in Pound's transformation into a passionately engaged social critic came with his discovery of the economic theories of Major C. H. Douglas. Pound felt he had discovered in them the answer to many of the evils of the current system. In particular, he saw in Douglas's theories of social credit the basis for a monetary system that would change the disenfranchised position of the artist in the modern commercial world. Governments would grant citizens social credit for work done. They would consider, in doing so, the inherent and social value of the work that went into making something; the laws of the marketplace, the laws of cost, supply, and demand would be set aside. Pound threw himself as passionately into the fray as social critic as he had as literary critic. "Usurers"—a category which for Pound consisted of capitalists, Jews, and bankers—acted against the common good. As a prose work like *Jefferson and Mussolini* (1935) illustrates, he made them the targets of repeated virulent attacks.

Pound left England for France in 1921. Dissatisfied there, he moved in 1924 to Rapallo, Italy, where he stayed until the end of World War II. He became more and more obsessed with his missionary role as social critic, turning his enormous vigor in that direction in letters, essays, and poems. He met Mussolini in 1933 and was greatly impressed; Mussolini had found Pound's *A Draft of XXX Cantos* "entertaining," and Pound saw in Mussolini someone who had outdone the aesthetes in their own field. Feeling that Fascist Italy was a nation that was likely to adopt his economic theories, Pound supported it more and more vigorously. The most notorious form of that support was his broadcasting a regular program on Rome Radio in which he discussed both aesthetic and political matters and propagandized for Fascism even after America had entered the war. In 1939 he wrote, "Usury is the cancer of the world, and only the surgeon's knife of Fascism can cut it out of the life of the nations." His support of Fascism included an equally strenuous anti-Semitism.

At the end of the war Pound was imprisoned in an American camp for prisoners of war at Pisa. He was first put in a cage that had been reinforced with heavy steel, where he was exposed to the weather. After three weeks, he became so thin and weak that he was transferred to a tent in the medical compound. There, on the dispensary typewriter, he wrote (along with letters for other prisoners) what many regard as his best poems, *The Pisan Cantos*. At the end of six months he was taken to America to stand trial for treason. Declared legally insane, he was transferred to St. Elizabeth's mental hospital in Washington, D.C., where he was incarcerated for thirteen years. At last, after receiving the Bollingen Prize for poetry and after work on his behalf by a number of writers, including Frost, Hemingway, Archibald MacLeish, and the ever-faithful Eliot, he was released to return to Italy. He died in 1972, last of the great leaders of the modernist movement.

Though he spent his formative years as an artist in England and lived abroad most of his life, and though he uttered, on more than one occasion, the sentiment that "residence in America is most revolting to think of," Pound remains a distinctively American author. Like Walt Whitman, the poet he likened to a "pig-headed father" in "Pact," Pound was pig-headed, exhibitionistic, and egoistic, yet equally generous in both his attachments and his commitment to the renewal of poetry in his age. He wrote poetry that was as indecorous as it was sublime, in the way that Whitman's verse had echoed for Emerson both the Bhagavad-Gita and the *New York Herald*. And Pound spent the bulk of his poetic career working on a long poem in the Whitmanesque tradition. *The Cantos* has been variously assessed, by Pound and others, as a success or a failure in its accomplishment; it is, at least in ambition, based on an epic model and frequently messianic in impulse. Confused and confusing, it is often capricious in its use of juxtaposition without structural connection, the technique that Pound came to label in later years the ideogrammatic method. In its confusion, however, *The Cantos* too, like Walt Whitman's "Song of Myself," contains multitudes—of ideas, insights, characters, and events—from the wide-ranging play of Pound's sometimes nobly impassioned, sometimes violently satiric personality. Though the theater of the poems is not the American scene and circumstance but world history, it was here that Pound came closest to living up to the egotism of his early comment about Whitman: "I honor him for he prophesized me." Pound's place as critic, aesthetician, and central figure in the tradition of American poetry is still disputed. But though his work is variously assessed, none would deny

Pound's importance to the modernist movement: as literary entrepreneur, generous publicist for the work of others, and literary journalist.

Further Reading:

C. Norman, *Ezra Pound*, 1960.
L. Dembo, *The Confucian Odes of Ezra Pound*, 1963.
G. Dekker, *The Cantos of Ezra Pound*, 1963.
N. de Nagy, *Ezra Pound's Poetics and Literary Tradition*, 1966.
K. L. Goodwin, *The Influence of Ezra Pound*, 1966.
J. Cornell, *The Trial of Ezra Pound*, 1966.
N. Stock, *Reading the Cantos*, 1967.
T. H. Jackson, *The Early Poetry of Ezra Pound*, 1968.
W. Yip, *Ezra Pound's Cathay*, 1969.
New Approaches to Ezra Pound, ed. E. Hesse, 1969.
N. Stock, *The Life of Ezra Pound*, 1970.
M. de Rachewiltz, *Discretions*. 1971.
C. Brooke-Rose, *A ZBC of Ezra Pound*, 1971.
H. Kenner, *The Pound Era*, 1972.
D. Davie, *Ezra Pound*, 1976.

R. Bush, *The Genesis of Pound's Cantos*, 1976.
J. Wilhelm, *The Later Cantos of Ezra Pound*, 1977.
M. Alexander, *The Poetic Achievement of Ezra Pound*, 1979.
M. S. Bernstein, *The Tale of the Tribe: Ezra Pound and Modern Verse Epic*, 1980.
W. Flory, *Ezra Pound and the Cantos*, 1980.
G. Kearn, *Guide to Ezra Pound's Selected Cantos*, 1980.
C. Terrell, *A Companion to the Cantos of Ezra Pound*, 1980.
P. Ackroyd, *Ezra Pound and His World*, 1981.
I. F. A. Bell, *Critic as Scientist: The Modernist Poetics of Ezra Pound*, 1981.
C. Froula, *A Guide to Ezra Pound's Selected Poems*, 1982.
E. Fuller Torrey, *The Roots of Treason: Ezra Pound and the Secret of St. Elizabeth's*, 1983.

Texts:

Personae, 1949.
The Cantos of Ezra Pound, 1970.
See also *The Letters of Ezra Pound, 1907–1941*, ed. D. D. Paige, 1950.
Pound/Joyce: Letters and Essays, ed. F. Read, 1967.

Sestina: Altaforte

LOQUITUR: En *Bertrans de Born.*[1]
   Dante Alighieri put this man in hell for that he was a stirrer up of strife.[2]
   Eccovi![2]
   Judge ye!
   Have I dug him up again?
   The scene is at his castle, Altaforte. "Papiols" is his jongleur.[3]
   "The Leopard," the device[4] *of Richard Cœur de Lion.*

I

Damn it all! all this our South stinks peace.
You whoreson dog, Papiols, come! Let's to music!
I have no life save when the swords clash.

---

[1] "Lord Bertrans de Born speaks." Bertrans de Born, Provençal poet (1140–1209), appears in Dante's *Inferno*, 28, as the promoter of strife between two brothers, Henry Plantagenet and King Richard I of England (1157–1199), called Richard Cœur de Lion (the Lionhearted).

[2] "Behold!"
[3] *Altaforte*, in Italian, means "high and strong"; jongleur: minstrel.
[4] Heraldic emblem.

But ah! when I see the standards gold, vair,[5] purple,
  opposing
And the broad fields beneath them turn crimson,   5
Then howl I my heart nigh mad with rejoicing.

II

In hot summer have I great rejoicing
When the tempests kill the earth's foul peace,
And the lightnings from black heav'n flash crimson,
And the fierce thunders roar me their music   10
And the winds shriek through the clouds mad,
  opposing,
And through all the riven skies God's swords clash.

III

Hell grant soon we hear again the swords clash!
And the shrill neighs of destriers[6] in battle rejoicing,
Spiked breast to spiked breast opposing!   15
Better one hour's stour[7] than a year's peace
With fat boards, bawds, wine and frail music!
Bah! there's no wine like the blood's crimson!

IV

And I love to see the sun rise blood-crimson.
And I watch his spears through the dark clash   20
And it fills all my heart with rejoicing
And pries wide my mouth with fast music
When I see him so scorn and defy peace,
His lone might 'gainst all darkness opposing.

V

The man who fears war and squats opposing   25
My words for stour, hath no blood of crimson
But is fit only to rot in womanish peace
Far from where worth's won and the swords clash
For the death of such sluts I go rejoicing;
Yea, I fill all the air with my music.   30

VI

Papiols, Papiols, to the music!
There's no sound like to swords swords opposing,

---

[5] Alternating argent (silver) and azure bell-shapes
on a standard, resembling those on a heraldic
emblem.   [6] Battle horses.
   [7] Combat.

No cry like the battle's rejoicing
When our elbows and swords drip the crimson
And our charges 'gainst "The Leopard's" rush clash.   35
May God damn for ever all who cry "Peace!"

VII

And let the music of the swords make them
    crimson!
Hell grant soon we hear again the swords clash!
Hell blot black for alway the thought "Peace"!
1909

The River-Merchant's Wife: A Letter*

While my hair was still cut straight across my forehead
I played about the front gate, pulling flowers.
You came by on bamboo stilts, playing horse,
You walked about my seat, playing with blue plums.
And we went on living in the village of Chokan: 5
Two small people, without dislike or suspicion.

At fourteen I married My Lord you.
I never laughed, being bashful.
Lowering my head, I looked at the wall.
Called to, a thousand times, I never looked back.   10

At fifteen I stopped scowling,
I desired my dust to be mingled with yours
Forever and forever and forever.
Why should I climb the look out?

At sixteen you departed,   15
You went into far Ku-to-yen, by the river of swirling eddies,
And you have been gone five months.
The monkeys make sorrowful noise overhead.

---

* Adapted from the Chinese of Li Po (700?–762).
Ernest Fenollosa (1853–1908), an American
orientalist and collector, made the translation
from which Pound worked.

You dragged your feet when you went out.
By the gate now, the moss is grown, the different mosses,   20
Too deep to clear them away!
The leaves fall early this autumn, in wind.
The paired butterflies are already yellow with August
Over the grass in the West garden;
They hurt me. I grow older.   25
If you are coming down through the narrows of the river Kiang,
Please let me know beforehand,
And I will come out to meet you
            As far as Cho-fu-Sa.
1915

The Garden

En robe de parade.[1]
Samain

Like a skein of loose silk blown against a wall
She walks by the railing of a path in Kensington Gardens,
And she is dying piece-meal
            of a sort of emotional anæmia.

And round about there is a rabble   5
Of the filthy, sturdy, unkillable infants of the very poor.
They shall inherit the earth.

In her is the end of breeding.
Her boredom is exquisite and excessive.
She would like some one to speak to her,   10
And is almost afraid that I
            will commit that indiscretion.
1916

---

[1] French: "dressed for going out."

Salutation

O generation of the thoroughly smug
   and thoroughly uncomfortable,
I have seen fishermen picknicking in the sun,
I have seen them with untidy families,
I have seen their smiles full of teeth   5
   and heard ungainly laughter.
And I am happier than you are,
And they were happier than I am;
And the fish swim in the lake
   and do not even own clothing.   10

1916

A Pact

I make a pact with you, Walt Whitman—
I have detested you long enough.
I come to you as a grown child
Who has had a pig-headed father;
I am old enough now to make friends.   5
It was you that broke the new wood,
Now is a time for carving.
We have one sap and one root—
Let there be commerce between us.

1916

In a Station of the Metro[1]

The apparition of these faces in the crowd;
Petals on a wet, black bough.

1916

---

[1] The Paris subway.

from Hugh Selwyn Mauberley
(Life and Contacts)

"*Vocat æstus in umbram*"[1]
NEMESIANUS, *Ec. IV*

I: E. P. Ode pour l'Election de Son Sepulchre[2]

For three years, out of key with his time,
He strove to resuscitate the dead art
Of poetry; to maintain "the sublime"
In the old sense. Wrong from the start—

No, hardly, but seeing he had been born   5
In a half savage country, out of date;
Bent resolutely on wringing lilies from the acorn;
Capaneus;[3] trout for factitious bait;

᾽Ίδμεν γάρ τοι πάνθ᾽, ὂσ᾽ ἐνὶ Τροίη[4]
Caught in the unstopped ear;   10
Giving the rocks small lee-way
The chopped seas held him, therefore, that year.

His true Penelope was Flaubert,[5]
He fished by obstinate isles;
Observed the elegance of Circe's[6] hair   15
Rather than the mottoes on sun-dials.

Unaffected by "the march of events,"
He passed from men's memory in *l'an trentiesme*
De son eage;[7] the case presents
No adjunct to the Muses' diadem.   20

II

The age demanded an image
Of its accelerated grimace,

---

[1] Latin: "Heat summons us into the shade." From the fourth *Eclogue* of Nemesianus, Roman poet (fl. A.D. 283).

[2] Adaptation of the title of an ode by the French Renaissance poet Pierre de Ronsard (1524–1585), *On the Selection of His Tomb.*

[3] One of the Seven against Thebes, struck by lightning for his rebellion.

[4] From the song the Sirens sang (*Odyssey* 12.189): "For we know all the toils [endured] in wide Troy." Odysseus stopped his comrades' ears with wax so they would not be seduced by the song.

[5] Penelope: Odysseus' faithful wife; Flaubert: Gustave Flaubert (1821–1880), French novelist who cultivated "the right word," *le mot juste.*

[6] Circe: Enchantress with whom Odysseus remained for a year.

[7] "His thirtieth year." Adapted from *The Testament* of François Villon, French Renaissance poet.

Something for the modern stage,
Not, at any rate, an Attic grace;

Not, not certainly, the obscure reveries   5
Of the inward gaze;
Better mendacities
Than the classics in paraphrase!

The "age demanded" chiefly a mould in plaster,
Made with no loss of time,   10
A prose kinema,[8] not, not assuredly, alabaster
Or the "sculpture" of rhyme.

III

The tea-rose tea-grown, etc.
Supplants the mousseline of Cos,[9]
The pianola "replaces"
Sappho's barbitos.[10]

Christ follows Dionysus,[11]   5
Phallic and ambrosial
Made way for macerations;[12]
Caliban casts out Ariel.[13]

All things are a flowing,
Sage Heracleitus[14] says;   10
But a tawdry cheapness
Shall outlast our days.

Even the Christian beauty
Defects—after Samothrace;[15]
We see τὸ καλόν[16]   15
Decreed in the market place.

Faun's flesh is not to us,
Nor the saint's vision.
We have the press for wafer;
Franchise for circumcision.   20

---

[8] Greek for "motion"; also the root of *cinema*, motion pictures.
[9] Mousseline of Cos: light fabric woven in the Aegean island of Cos.
[10] Lyrelike instrument used by Sappho, Greek woman poet who lived during the sixth century B.C.
[11] Greek god of wine and sexual frenzy.
[12] Mortification of the flesh.
[13] Caliban; Ariel: in Shakespeare's *Tempest,* the earth-bound and airy figures, respectively.
[14] Greek philosopher who taught that all things are in flux.
[15] Aegean island where the statute *The Winged Victory* was found.
[16] Greek: "the beautiful."

All men, in law, are equals.
Free of Pisistratus,[17]
We choose a knave or an eunuch
To rule over us.

O bright Apollo,   25
τίν' ἄνδρα, τίν' ἤρωα, τίνα θεόν,[18]
What god, man, or hero
Shall I place a tin wreath upon!

IV

These fought in any case,
and some believing,
                  pro domo,[19] in any case . . .

Some quick to arm,
some for adventure,   5
some from fear of weakness,
some from fear of censure,
some for love of slaughter, in imagination,
learning later . . .
some in fear, learning love of slaughter;   10

Died some, pro patria,
                  non "dulce" non
                  "et decor" . . .[20]
walked eye-deep in hell
believing in old men's lies, then unbelieving
came home, home to a lie,   15
home to many deceits,
home to old lies and new infamy;
usury age-old and age-thick
and liars in public places.

Daring as never before, wastage as never before.   20
Young blood and high blood,
fair cheeks, and fine bodies;

fortitude as never before

frankness as never before,
disillusions as never told in the old days,   25

---

[17] Athenian tyrant.
[18] "What god, what hero, what man shall we loudly praise?" From Pindar's *Olympian Odes*, II, 2.

[19] Latin: "for the home."
[20] "For the homeland, not sweetly, not gloriously." Adapted from Horace: "Dulce et decorum est pro patria mori" (*Odes*, III, ii, 13).

> hysterias, trench confessions,
> laughter out of dead bellies.

V

> There died a myriad,
> And of the best, among them,
> For an old bitch gone in the teeth,
> For a botched civilization,
>
> Charm, smiling at the good mouth,   5
> Quick eyes gone under earth's lid,
>
> For two gross of broken statues,
> For a few thousand battered books.

1920

---

from The Cantos

I

And then went down to the ship,[1]
Set keel to breakers, forth on the godly sea, and
We set up mast and sail on that swart ship,
Bore sheep aboard her, and our bodies also
Heavy with weeping, and winds from sternward   5
Bore us out onward with bellying canvas,
Circe's[2] this craft, the trim-coifed goddess.
Then sat we amidships, wind jamming the tiller,
Thus with stretched sail, we went over sea till day's end.
Sun to his slumber, shadows o'er all the ocean,   10
Came we then to the bounds of deepest water,
To the Kimmerian lands,[3] and peopled cities
Covered with close-webbed mist, unpierced ever
With glitter of sun-rays
Nor with stars stretched, nor looking back from heaven   15
Swartest night stretched over wretched men there.
The ocean flowing backward, came we then to the place
Aforesaid by Circe.
Here did they rites, Perimedes and Eurylochus,[4]

---

[1] Adapted from Book XI of Homer's *Odyssey*, retelling Odysseus' sacrifice, summoning up the spirits of the dead in Hades.
[2] In myth, Circe was the enchantress who turned men to beasts; she sent Odysseus into the underworld to seek Tiresias, who would give him directions for returning home to Ithaca.
[3] Lands of darkness at the edge of the earth; the entrance to Hades.
[4] Two of Odysseus' companions.

And drawing sword from my hip   20
I dug the ell-square pitkin;⁵
Poured we libations unto each the dead,
First mead and then sweet wine, water mixed with white flour.
Then prayed I many a prayer to the sickly death's-heads;
As set in Ithaca, sterile bulls of the best   25
For sacrifice, heaping the pyre with goods,
A sheep to Tiresias only, black and a bell-sheep.
Dark blood flowed in the fosse,
Souls out of Erebus,⁶ cadaverous dead, of brides
Of youths and of the old who had borne much;   30
Souls stained with recent tears, girls tender,
Men many, mauled with bronze lance heads,
Battle spoil, bearing yet dreory⁷ arms,
These many crowded about me; with shouting,
Pallor upon me, cried to my men for more beasts;   35
Slaughtered the herds, sheep slain of bronze;
Poured ointment, cried to the gods,
To Pluto the strong, and praised Proserpine;⁸
Unsheathed the narrow sword,
I sat to keep off the impetuous impotent dead,   40
Till I should hear Tiresias.
But first Elpenor⁹ came, our friend Elpenor,
Unburied, cast on the wide earth,
Limbs that we left in the house of Circe,
Unwept, unwrapped in sepulchre, since toils urged other.   45
Pitiful spirit. And I cried in hurried speech:
"Elpenor, how art thou come to this dark coast?
"Cam'st thou afoot, outstripping seamen?"
            And he in heavy speech:
"Ill fate and abundant wine. I slept in Circe's ingle.¹⁰   50
"Going down the long ladder unguarded,
"I fell against the buttress,
"Shattered the nape-nerve, the soul sought Avernus.¹¹
"But thou, O King, I bid remember me, unwept, unburied,
"Heap up mine arms, be tomb by sea-bord, and inscribed: 55
"A man of no fortune, and with a name to come.
"And set my oar up, that I swung mid fellows."

And Anticlea¹² came, whom I beat off, and then Tiresias Theban,
Holding his golden wand, knew me, and spoke first:
"A second time?¹³ why? man of ill star,   60

---

⁵ Small pit.
⁶ Hades.
⁷ Old English: "bloody."
⁸ Pluto; Proserpine: king and queen of Hades.
⁹ Companion of Ulysses who died in a fall from
  Circe's roof and was left unburied.

¹⁰ Corner (i.e., house).
¹¹ Lake thought to be the entrance of Hades.
¹² Odysseus' mother; he may not speak to her
  until Tiresias speaks, having drunk the blood of
  the libation.
¹³ They had met once in life.

"Facing the sunless dead and this joyless region?
"Stand from the fosse, leave me my bloody bever[14]
"For soothsay."

        And I stepped back,
And he strong with the blood, said then: "Odysseus   65
"Shalt return through spiteful Neptune,[15] over dark seas,
"Lose all companions." And then Anticlea came.
Lie quiet Divus. I mean, that is Andreas Divus,
In officina Wecheli, 1538, out of Homer.[16]
And he sailed, by Sirens and thence outward and away   70
And unto Circe.

        Venerandam,[17]
In the Cretan's phrase, with the golden crown, Aphrodite,[18]
Cypri munimenta sortita est,[19] mirthful, orichalchi,[20] with golden
Girdles and breast bands, thou with dark eyelids   75
Bearing the golden bough of Argicida.[21] So that:

1925

from **XVI**[22]

And they looked at it, and I can still hear the old admiral,
"Was it? it was
       Lord Byron
Dead drunk, with the face of an a y n. . . . . . .
He pulled it out long, like that: 5
      the face of a y n . . . . gel."

And because that son of a bitch,
      Franz Josef of Austria. . . . . .[23]
And because that son of a bitch Napoléon Barbiche . . .[24]
They put Aldington[25] on Hill 70, in a trench   10
      dug through corpses

[14] Libation (from French *boire*: "to drink").
[15] Neptune, god of the sea, would delay by a storm Odysseus' return to Ithaca.
[16] Pound used the Latin translation of the *Odyssey* produced in the workshop ("officina") of Wechel in Paris by Andreas Divus.
[17] "Worthy of veneration." Phrase used of Aphrodite in the second Homeric Hymn, translated into Latin verse in the fifteenth century by the Cretan Georgius Dartona.
[18] Goddess of sexual love and beauty.
[19] Latin: "She won by lot from the fortresses of Cyprus."
[20] "Of copper," a phrase referring to the gifts given to Aphrodite, recounted in the second Homeric Hymn.

[21] *Argicida* means "killer of Argus." This is a refernce to the god Hermes, whose caduceus, or magic wand, is here associated with the golden bough offered by Odysseus to Proserpina.
[22] This canto is spoken by Victor Platt, an older poet.
[23] Emperor of Austria (d. 1916) whose policies helped to bring about World War I. The remainder of the canto concerns the war and Pound's friends who fought in it, some of whom died.
[24] French emperor (the "Bearded One"), whose policies helped cause the war.
[25] Pound's friend the poet Richard Aldington, who, with his wife H.D., began the Imagist movement.

With a lot of kids of sixteen,
Howling and crying for their mamas,
And he sent a chit back to his major:
             I can hold out for ten minutes
With my sergeant and a machine-gun.   15
                And they rebuked him for levity.
And Henri Gaudier[26] went to it,
         and they killed him,
And killed a good deal of sculpture,
And ole T.E.H.[27] he went to it,   20
With a lot of books from the library,
London Library, and a shell buried 'em in a dug-out,
And the Library expressed its annoyance.
              And a bullet hit him on the elbow   25
. . .gone through the fellow in front of him,
And he read Kant in the Hospital, in Wimbledon,[28]
           in the original,
And the hospital staff didn't like it.

And Wyndham Lewis[29] went to it,   30
With a heavy bit of artillery,
         and the airmen came by with a mitrailleuse,
And cleaned out most of his company,
         and a shell lit on his tin hut,
While he was out in the privvy,   35
         and he was all there was left of that outfit.

Windeler[30] went to it,
         and he was out in the Ægæan,
And down in the hold of his ship
         pumping gas into a sausage,   40
And the boatswain looked over the rail,
         down into amidships, and he said:
         Gees! look a' the Kept'n,
The Kept'n's a-gettin' 'er up.

And Ole Captain Baker[31] went to it,   45
         with his legs full of rheumatics,
So much so he couldn't run,
         so he was six months in hospital,
Observing the mentality of the patients.

[26] Pound's friend the sculptor Henri
Gaudier-Brzeska, who was killed in the war.
[27] T. E. Hulme, the poet, also killed in the war.
[28] The hospital staff did not like Hulme's reading
the German philosopher's works.

[29] Novelist, painter, and friend of Pound's. Lewis
died in 1957.
[30] Unidentified friend of Pound's.
[31] Unidentified friend of Pound's.

And Fletcher[32] was 19 when he went to it,   50
And his major went mad in the control pit,
      about midnight, and started throwing the 'phone about
And he had to keep him quiet
            till about six in the morning,
And direct that bunch of artillery.   55

And Ernie Hemingway went to it,
            too much in a hurry,
And they buried him for four days.

Et ma foi, vous savez,[33]
            tous les nerveux. Non,   60
Y a une limite; les bêtes, les bêtes ne sont
Pas faites pour ça, c'est peu de chose un cheval.
Les hommes de 34 ans à quatre pattes
            qui criaient "maman." Mais les costauds,
La fin, là à Verdun, n'y avait que ces gros bonshommes   65
            Et y voyaient extrêmement clair.
. . . .

1925

from **XLV**

With *Usura*[34]

With usura hath no man a house of good stone
each block cut smooth and well fitting
that design might cover their face,
with usura   5
hath no man a painted paradise on his church wall
harpes et luz[35]
or where virgin receiveth message
and halo projects from incision,
with usura   10
seeth no man Gonzaga[36] his heirs and his concubines
no picture is made to endure nor to live with
but it is made to sell and sell quickly

---

[32] John Gould Fletcher, young American poet and a friend of Pound's.
[33] The passage beginning here and ending at l. 66 enumerates the horrors of the war in what appears to be the reminiscence of a French soldier: "And really, you know, / so many were 'nervous.' No, / There's a limit; animals, even animals aren't / Made for that, [but] a horse doesn't matter much. / There were thirty-four-year-old men on all fours / calling

'Mama!' But only the big tough guys, / At the end, at [the battle of] Verdun, were left, / And they knew the whole score."
[34] Latin: "usury," exorbitant interest paid for money borrowed; more generally, avarice of all sorts.
[35] French: "harps and lutes," from Jacques Villon's prayer for his mother.
[36] Luigi Gonzaga (1267–1360), ruler of Mantua.

with usura, sin against nature,
is thy bread ever more of stale rags   15
is thy bread dry as paper,
with no mountain wheat, no strong flour
with usura the line grows thick
with usura is no clear demarcation
and no man can find site for his dwelling.   20
Stonecutter is kept from his stone
weaver is kept from his loom
WITH USURA
wool comes not to market
sheep bringeth no gain with usura   25
Usura is a murrain,[37] usura
blunteth the needle in the maid's hand
and stoppeth the spinner's cunning. Pietro Lombardo[38]
came not by usura
Duccio[39] came not by usura   30
nor Pier della Francesca;[40] Zuan Bellin'[41] not by usura
nor was 'La Calunnia'[42] painted.
Came not by usura Angelico;[43] came not Ambrogio Praedis,[44]
Came no church of cut stone signed: *Adamo me fecit.*[45]
Not by usura St Trophime[46]   35
Not by usura Saint Hilaire,[47]
Usura rusteth the chisel
It rusteth the craft and the craftsman
It gnaweth the thread in the loom
None learneth to weave gold in her pattern;   40
Azure hath a canker by usura; cramoisi[48] is unbroidered
Emerald findeth no Memling[49]
Usura slayeth the child in the womb
It stayeth the young man's courting
It hath brought palsey to bed, lyeth   45
between the young bride and her bridegroom
                     CONTRA NATURAM[50]
They have brought whores for Eleusis[51]
Corpses are set to banquet
at behest of usura.   50
1937

---

[37] Disease.
[38] Italian sculptor (1435–1515).
[39] Sienese painter (1260?–1318?).
[40] Florentine painter (1420?–1492).
[41] Giovanni Bellini (1430?–1516), Venetian painter.
[42] Italian: "Calumny," painting by Sandro Botticelli (1445?–1510).
[43] Fra Angelico (1387?–1455), Florentine painter.
[44] Ambrogio de Predis (1455?–1506), Italian painter.
[45] Latin: "Adam made me," the inscription by the architect on the Church of San Zeno Maggiore in Verona.
[46] Church in Arles, France.
[47] Church in Poitiers, France.
[48] Crimson cloth.
[49] Hans Memling (1430?–1495), Flemish painter.
[50] Latin: "against nature."
[51] Shrine of Demeter, the mother goddess.

from LXXXI

Has he tempered the viol's wood
To enforce   both the grave   and the acute?
Has he curved us the bowl of the lute?
             Lawes and Jenkyns guard thy rest
             Dolmetsch ever be thy guest[52]   5
Hast 'ou fashioned so airy a mood
   To draw up leaf from the root?
Hast 'ou found   a cloud   so light
   As seemed neither mist nor shade?[53]

             Then resolve me, tell me aright   10
             If Waller sang or Dowland played.[54]

          Your eyen two wol sleye me sodenly
          I may the beauté of hem nat susteyne[55]

And for 180 years almost nothing.

Ed ascoltando al leggier mormorio[56]
   there came new subtlety of eyes into my tent,   15
whether of spirit or hypostasis,
   but what the blindfold hides
or at carneval
             nor any pair showed anger   20
   Saw but the eyes and stance between the eyes,
colour, diastasis,[57]
   careless or unaware it had not the
   whole tent's room
nor was place for the full 'Ειδώς[58]   25
interpass, penetrate
   casting but shade beyond the other lights
      sky's clear
      night's sea
      green of the mountain pool   30
      shone from the unmasked eyes in half-mask's space.

---

[52] Henry Lawes (1596–1662) and John Jenkyns (1592–1678) were seventeenth-century English composers. Arnold Dolmetsch (1858–1940) was the resuscitator of early music played on authentic instruments.

[53] An imitation of Ben Jonson's lyric "Her Triumph," ll. 23–27: "Ha'you marked but the fall o'the snow / Before the soil hath smutched it? / Ha'you felt the wool o'the beaver, / Or swansdown ever? / Or have smelt o'the bud o'the briar. . . ."

[54] Edmund Waller (1606–1687), English poet, and John Dowland (1563–1626), English composer and lutanist.

[55] From Geoffrey Chaucer's poem "Merciles Beaute."

[56] Italian: "And listening to the light murmur."

[57] Separation, as opposed to "hypostasis" (l. 17), meaning both human and divine.

[58] Greek: "knowing" or "vision."

What thou lovest well remains,
      the rest is dross
What thou lov'st well shall not be reft from thee
What thou lov'st well is thy true heritage
Whose world, or mine or theirs   35
     or is it of none?
First came the seen, then thus the palpable
  Elysium,[59] though it were in the halls of hell,
What thou lovest well is thy true heritage   40
What thou lov'st well shall not be reft from thee

The ant's a centaur in his dragon world.
Pull down thy vanity, it is not man
Made courage, or made order, or made grace,
  Pull down thy vanity, I say pull down.   45
Learn of the green world what can be thy place
In scaled invention or true artistry,
Pull down thy vanity,
     Paquin[60] pull down!
The green casque[61] has outdone your elegance.   50

"Master thyself, then others shall thee beare"[62]
  Pull down thy vanity
Thou art a beaten dog beneath the hail,
A swollen magpie in a fitful sun,
Half black half white   55
Nor knowst'ou wing from tail
Pull down thy vanity
    How mean thy hates
Fostered in falsity,
    Pull down thy vanity,   60
Rathe[63] to destroy, niggard[64] in charity,
Pull down thy vanity,
   I say pull down.

But to have done instead of not doing
    this is not vanity   65
To have, with decency, knocked
That a Blunt[65] should open[66]
   To have gathered from the air a live tradition
or from a fine old eye the unconquered flame

[59] Paradise.
[60] Parisian designer.
[61] Helmet (i.e., of the insects).
[62] Paraphrase of line 13 of Chaucer's poem
 "Truth" or "Balade of Bon Conseyl."
[63] Quick.

[64] Stingy.
[65] Wilfred Blunt (1840–1922), English poet
 admired by Pound as an elder statesman of art
 and politics.
[66] See Matthew 7:7: "Knock, and it shall be
 opened unto you."

This is not vanity.
      Here error is all in the not done,
all in the diffidence that faltered . . .

1948

              from **CXV**

The scientists are in terror
      and the European mind stops
Wyndham Lewis[67] chose blindness
      rather than have his mind stop.
Night under wind mid garofani,[68]   5
      the petals are almost still
Mozart, Linnaeus, Sulmona,[69]
When one's friends hate each other
      how can there be peace in the world?
Their asperities diverted me in my green time.   10
A blown husk that is finished
      but the light sings eternal
a pale flare over marshes
         where the salt hay whispers to tide's change
Time, space,   15
      neither life nor death is the answer.
And of man seeking good,
      doing evil.
In meiner Heimat[70]
      where the dead walked   20
         and the living were made of cardboard.

1969

Robinson Jeffers
1887–1962

Robinson Jeffers was a poet of long forms who remained a poetic conservative,
choosing traditional narrative over the innovative open form of Walt Whitman's
"Song of Myself." Yet, as much as Whitman, Jeffers worked to articulate with
evangelical intensity a vision of America and the cosmos, a vision that was at
once religious, historical, psychological, and scientific in its points of reference.
He differed from Whitman in depicting his primitive American characters against

[67] See note 29.
[68] Italian: "carnations."
[69] Linnaeus: Swedish taxonomist Carolus Linnaeus

(1707–1778); Sulmona: town in central Italy,
respectively.
[70] German: "in my native land."

the background of classical tragedy rather than the epic tradition; he once professed to be pleased by a description of himself as "striding morosely over the hills with a copy of Aeschylus in one hand and a shilling shocker in the other."

Jeffers was born in 1887 to a prosperous family in Pittsburgh, Pennsylvania. His father, a Presbyterian preacher and theologian who taught at Western Theological Seminary, could afford to send his son to study in Switzerland and Germany. After graduation in 1905 from Occidental College (his family having moved west to Long Beach, California, in 1903), the young Jeffers began work on an M.A. at the University of Southern California, studied in Zurich in 1906, and returned to U.S.C. as a medical student in 1907.

At U.S.C. Jeffers met Una Call Kuster, who was then married to a prominent Los Angeles lawyer. It was the first of what he later called the two "accidents that changed and directed my life." As their relationship deepened and grew to trouble them both, Jeffers broke away to study forestry in Washington State; but within an hour of his return to California in 1911, he saw Una in the street, and their relationship recommenced. In a last attempt to save the marriage, her husband persuaded her to spend a year abroad; it did not succeed. In 1913 Una divorced Kuster and married Jeffers. Years later, Jeffers touchingly acknowledged his personal debt to Una with a characteristically self-deprecating tribute: "My nature is cold and undiscriminating; she excited and focused it, gave it eyes and nerves and sympathies. She never saw any of my poems until they were typed, yet by her presence and conversation she has coauthored every one of them." Una also served, as Jeffers wrote in 1953, in many practical ways as a mediator between him and the world, something that his extreme shyness made necessary.

In 1914, aided by a modest inheritance, Jeffers settled in Carmel, California. Happening upon that region was the second of the two accidents that directed his life. There, Jeffers wrote, he "could see people living—amid magnificent unspoiled scenery—essentially as they did in the Idylls, or the Sagas, or in Homer's Ithaca." The region was to furnish much of both the settings and the spirit of his major poetry. In 1919 he started work on Tor House and Hawk Tower, the stone buildings that became his lifelong home. As Jeffers "helped the mason shift and place the wave and wind-worn granite," Una wrote, he became "aware of strengths in himself unknown before." In a poem published in 1951, "The Old Stonemason," Jeffers linked working with stone with some of the major preoccupations of his poetry, the strength that allows one to struggle out of the "tidewash" of human passions and illusions, and the ability to face the "enormous inhuman beauty of things." In 1924 Jeffers's first major work, *Tamar and Other Poems,* was privately published; it was reissued with the narrative "Roan Stallion" in 1925. The success of these poems marked the beginning of his public career as a poet and his emerging identity as a sort of cult figure. From the nature of his poetry, which was often sensational, tragic, and philosophical (he also, though less frequently, philosophized in prose), it was not difficult to picture him as a solitary, brooding, prophetic figure who, from his rugged house overlooking the Pacific, wrote of the suicidal passions of a self-deluded mankind.

By now the pattern of the rest of his reclusive, outwardly uneventful life was set. With Una to manage his limited contact with the public world, he could stay in the seclusion he so required, a seclusion that had less to do with the misanthropy many readers have found in his works than it did with Jeffers's shyness and extreme self-protectiveness. When he did have contact with others, he showed himself consistently to be a conscientious and considerate man. Though a stoical detachment from the passions of mankind was an important theme and a heroic posture in much of his poetry, Jeffers's personal need for solitude had humbler and tenderer roots. As Una remarked, "Many people work best, I think, when they are stimulated by outside influences and clashing with other minds, but not my husband, who gets quite *numb* when he cannot pursue his own quiet and solitary way." So shy of contact was he that once, when Una was away, he hid in the bedroom with their dog to avoid two strangers who had knocked at the door. The great tragedy of his life was Una's death in 1950. The "passage of time does not make it more endurable," he wrote a year later, in refusing an invitation to give a reading in Chicago. He died after years of illness in 1962.

Jeffers's work consists primarily of two kinds of poems. Long tragic narratives like *Tamar* and "Roan Stallion" and, later, *The Women at Point Sur, Cawdor, Thurso's Landing,* and *Give Your Heart to the Hawks* are complemented by short meditative lyrics, typically set on the dramatic Pacific coastline. In all his poems, Jeffers saw himself as an exponent of what he called "inhumanism," a philosophy so austere and forbidding that it has, along with the sensationalistic plots of his longer works, limited Jeffers's appeal. His view of the world, molded as it was by the disillusionment that followed World War I, was as prophetically stern as his domestic life was quiet and devoted. He believed that "man is a part of nature, but a nearly infinitesimal part; the human race will cease after a while and leave no trace, but the great splendors of nature will go on." Most fear to face this truth, Jeffers believed; as a result, the life of the bulk of humankind is characterized by "immoderate racial introversion," with "ninety-odd percent of people's activities turned in on other people instead of outward on the world." Human social and historical concerns, he believed, are blind and vain. They isolate humankind as a species from awareness of the far greater, inhuman beauty of the cosmos it inhabits. Jeffers occasionally took comfort in the thought of the extinction of the human race, when nature will have purified itself of man. More frequently, he condemned his fellows for their many forms of self-degradation. Jeffers interpreted such differing phenomena as urbanization and world war as signs of the self-destructive self-preoccupation of the species, and he could sound quite strident, even foolish in his condemnations. He once described the life of the masses with disgust as "this horrible entwining of people libidinously listening to *crooners,* etc." His work frequently uses the theme of incest to express symbolically how the species causes its own suffering by turning away from the grandeur of nonhuman nature to focus its energies and passions on itself.

Against this collective degradation, lonely individuals of a higher sort could stand out in bold relief insofar as they sought the triumph of an extreme and painful self-transcendence. In such moments, moments that usually came in the midst of a great tragedy that burned away the all-too-human in them, a few of Jeffers's heroes were capable of looking directly on inhuman reality in all its terrible beauty. For Jeffers, this was the equivalent of looking directly at God. In these moments his characters found in themselves an austere, stony stoicism. Jeffers once wrote a characteristically stern version of the biblical commandments: One must love God with all one's heart and soul and one's neighbor as oneself—"as much as that, but as *little* as that."

Further Reading:

L. Powell, *Robinson Jeffers, The Man and His Work*, 1934, 1940.
R. Gilbert, *Shine, Perishing Republic: Robinson Jeffers and the Tragic Sense in Modern Poetry*, 1936.
R. Squires, *The Loyalties of Robinson Jeffers*, 1956, 1963.
M. C. Monjian, *Robinson Jeffers, a Study in Inhumanism*, 1958.
M. Bennett, *The Stone Mason of Tor House: The Life and Work of Robinson Jeffers*, 1966.

Brother Antonius (W. Everson), *Robinson Jeffers: Fragments of an Older Fury*, 1968.
A. B. Coffin, *Robinson Jeffers: Poet of Inhumanism*, 1970.
R. Brophy, *Robinson Jeffers: Myth, Ritual, and Symbol in the Narrative Poems*, 1973.
J. Shebl, *In This Wild Water*, 1976.
W. Nolte, *Rock and Hawk: Robinson Jeffers and the Romantic Agony*, 1978.
R. Zaller, *The Cliffs of Solitude: A Reading of Robinson Jeffers*, 1983.

Texts:

"Boats in a Fog" and "Apology for Bad Dreams" from *The Selected Poetry of Robinson Jeffers*, 1959.
"The Torch-Bearers' Race" from *Robinson*

Jeffers: Selected Poems, 1965.
See also *The Selected Letters of Robinson Jeffers, 1897–1962*, ed. A. Ridgeway, 1968.

Boats in a Fog

Sports and gallantries, the stage, the arts, the antics of dancers,
The exuberant voices of music,
Have charm for children but lack nobility; it is bitter earnestness
That makes beauty; the mind
Knows, grown adult.
        A sudden fog-drift muffled the ocean,   5
A throbbing of engines moved in it,
At length, a stone's throw out, between the rocks and the vapor,
One by one moved shadows
Out of the mystery, shadows, fishing-boats, trailing each other
Following the cliff for guidance,   10
Holding a difficult path between the peril of the sea-fog
And the foam on the shore granite.
One by one, trailing their leader, six crept by me,
Out of the vapor and into it,
The throb of their engines subdued by the fog, patient and cautious,   15
Coasting all round the peninsula
Back to the buoys in Monterey[1] harbor. A flight of pelicans
Is nothing lovelier to look at;

---

[1] California coastal town just to the north of Carmel, the site of Jeffers's Tor House.

The flight of the planets is nothing nobler; all the arts lose virtue
Against the essential reality   20
Of creatures going about their business among the equally
Earnest elements of nature.

1925

Apology for Bad Dreams

I

In the purple light, heavy with redwood, the slopes drop seaward,
Headlong convexities of forest, drawn in together to the steep ravine. Below,
    on the sea-cliff,
A lonely clearing; a little field of corn by the streamside, a roof under spared
    trees. Then the ocean
Like a great stone someone has cut to a sharp edge and polished to shining.
    Beyond it, the fountain
And furnace of incredible light flowing up from the sunk sun. In the little
    clearing a woman   5
Is punishing a horse; she had tied the halter to a sapling at the edge of the
    wood, but when the great whip
Clung to the flanks, the creature kicked so hard she feared he would snap the
    halter; she called from the house
The young man her son; who fetched a chain tie-rope, they working together
Noosed the small rusty links round the horse's tongue
And tied him by the swollen tongue to the tree.   10
Seen from this height they are shrunk to insect size.
Out of all human relation. You cannot distinguish
The blood dripping from where the chain is fastened,
The beast shuddering; but the thrust neck and the legs
Far apart. You can see the whip fall on the flanks . . .   15
The gesture of the arm. You cannot see the face of the woman.[1]
The enormous light beats up out of the west across the cloud-bars of the
    trade-wind. The ocean
Darkens, the high clouds brighten, the hills darken together. Unbridled and
    unbelievable beauty
Covers the evening world . . . not covers, grows apparent out of it, as Venus
    down there grows out

---

[1] In a letter, Jeffers provides a source for this scene: "The woman who tied up the horse to the tree to lash, with the chain around its tongue—*she* was real and she did just that. *And* this isnt [*sic*] in the poem[:] we heard later she was killed by one of her horses falling on her as they were crossing a stream. Pinioned her in the water!"

From the lit sky. What said the prophet? "I create good: and I create evil: I am
    the Lord."[2]   20

II

This coast crying out for tragedy like all beautiful places,
(The quiet ones ask for quieter suffering: but here the granite cliff the gaunt
    cypresses crown
Demands what victim? The dykes of red lava and black what Titan? The hills
    like pointed flames
Beyond Soberanes,[3] the terrible peaks of the bare hills under the sun, what
    immolation?)
This coast crying out for tragedy like all beautiful places: and like the
    passionate spirit of humanity   25
Pain for its bread: God's, many victims', the painful deaths, the horrible
    transfigurations: I said in my heart,
"Better invent than suffer: imagine victims
Lest your own flesh be chosen the agonist, or you
Martyr some creature in the beauty of the place." And I said,
"Burn sacrifices once a year to magic   30
Horror away from the house, this little house here
You have built over the ocean with your own hands
Beside the standing boulders: for what are we,
The beast that walks upright, with speaking lips
And little hair, to think we should always be fed,   35
Sheltered, intact, and self-controlled? We sooner more liable
Than the other animals. Pain and terror, the insanities of desire; not accidents
    but essential,
And crowd up from the core:" I imagined victims for those wolves, I made
    them phantoms to follow,
They have hunted the phantoms and missed the house. It is not good to forget
    over what gulfs the spirit
Of the beauty of humanity, the petal of a lost flower blown seaward by the
    night-wind, floats to its quietness.   40

III

Boulders blunted like an old bear's teeth break up from the headland; below
    them
All the soil is thick with shells, the tide-rock feasts of a dead people.
Here the granite flanks are scarred with ancient fire, the ghosts of the tribe
Crouch in the nights beside the ghost of a fire, they try to remember the
    sunlight,

---

[2] For Jeffers, God is not bound by the human
categories of good and evil; God includes all
phenomena.

[3] Point on the California coast.

Light has died out of their skies. These have paid something for the future 45
Luck of the country, while we living keep old griefs in memory: though God's
Envy is not a likely fountain of ruin, to forget evils calls down
Sudden reminders from the cloud: remembered deaths be our redeemers;
Imagined victims our salvation: white as the half moon at midnight
Someone flamelike passed me, saying, "I am Tamar Cauldwell,[4] I have my
    desire," 50
Then the voice of the sea returned, when she had gone by, the stars to their
    towers.
. . . Beautiful country burn again. Point Pinos down to the Sur Rivers
Burn as before with bitter wonders, land and ocean and the Carmel water.

IV

He brays[5] humanity in a mortar[6] to bring the savor
From the bruised root: a man having bad dreams, who invents victims, is only
    the ape of that God. 55
He washes it out with tears and many waters, calcines it with fire in the red
    crucible,
Deforms it, makes it horrible to itself: the spirit flies out and stands naked, he
    sees the spirit,
He takes it in the naked ecstasy; it breaks in his hand, the atom is broken, the
    power that massed it
Cries to the power that moves the stars, "I have come home to myself, behold
    me.
I bruised myself in the flint mortar and burnt me 60
In the red shell, I tortured myself, I flew forth,
Stood naked of myself and broke me in fragments,
And here am I moving the stars that are me."
I have seen these ways of God:[7] I know of no reason
For fire and change and torture and the old returnings. 65
He being sufficient might be still. I think they admit no reason; they are the
    ways of my love.
Unmeasured power, incredible passion, enormous craft: no thought apparent but
    burns darkly

---

[4] Heroine of Jeffers's early narrative poem *Tamar.* Her "desire" ultimately leads to a sensationalistic *liebestod* (love-death), in which she and her "three lovers" (a group that includes her brother and father) are burned to death.
[5] Crushes or grinds.
[6] Vessel for pulverizing and pounding.
[7] Jeffers's comment about his poem "At the Birth of an Age" is relevant here: "All the prevalent religions think of God as blessed or happy, or at least at peace; even the pantheist mystic finds peace in God. Therefore this conception of God as pain is hardly admitted by the reader's mind. . . . It is a conception that runs through my verses. . . . If God is all, he must be suffering, since an unreckoned part of the universe is always suffering. But his suffering must be self-inflicted, for he is all; there is no one outside himself to inflict it.—I suppose the idea carries psychological as well as cosmic or religious implications. Man as well as God must suffer in order to discover; and it is often voluntary—self-inflicted suffering."

Smothered with its own smoke in the human brain-vault: no thought outside: a
    certain measure in phenomena:
The fountains of the boiling stars, the flowers on the foreland, the
    ever-returning roses of dawn.

1925

The Torch-Bearers' Race

Here is the world's end. When our fathers forded the first river in Asia we
    crossed the world's end;
And when the North Sea throbbed under their keels, the world's end;
And when the Atlantic surge rolled English oak in the sea-trough; always there
    was farther to go,
A new world piecing out the old one: but ours, our new world?[1]
Dark and enormous rolls the surf; down on the mystical tide-line under the
    cliffs at moonset   5
Dead tribes move, remembering the scent of their hills, the lost hunters
Our fathers hunted; they driven westward died the sun's death, they dread the
    depth and hang at the land's hem,
And are unavenged; frail ghosts, and ghostlike in their lives too,
Having only a simple hunger for all our complication of desires. Dark and
    enormous
Rolls the surf of the far storms of the heart of the ocean;   10
The old granite breaks into white torches the heavy-shouldered children of the
    wind . . . our ancient wanderings
West from the world's birth what sea-bound breaking shall flame up torchlike?
I am building a thick stone pillar upon this shore, the very turn of the world,
    the long migration's
End; the sun goes on but we have come up to an end.[2]
We have climbed at length to a height, to an end, this end: shall we go down
    again to Mother Asia?[3]   15
Some of us will go down, some will abide, but we sought
More than to return to a mother. This huge, inhuman, remote, unruled, this
    ocean will show us

---

[1] The poem's opening lines contain Jeffers's
capsule summary of the development of human
civilization. Beginning in Asia, then moving
westward, the bearers of civilization crossed
into Europe, England, and then across the
Atlantic surge into America. With each step, it
seemed that mankind had crossed "the world's
end."

[2] America's westward migration was frequently

taken in American literature to be an emblem
of the closing of the circle of mankind's
development. Civilization began in the Orient
and moved westward as it grew. Jeffers thus
stands at the end of world historical
development; he also stands at the beginning of
something greater than merely human history.

[3] Asia was the cradle of human civilization.

The inhuman road, the unruled attempt, the remote lodestar.
The torch-bearers' race: it is run in a dusk; when the emptied racer drops unseen
    at the end of his course
A fresh hand snatches the hilt of the light, the torch flies onward   20
Though the man die. Not a runner knows where the light was lighted, not a
    runner knows where it carries fire to,
Hand kisses hand in the dark, the torch passes, the man
Falls, and the torch passes. It gleamed across Euphrates mud, shone on Nile
    shore, it lightened
The little homely Ionian water and the sweet Ægean.[4]
O perfect breathing of the runners, those narrow courses, names like the stars'
    names, Sappho, Alcæus,   25
And Æschylus[5] a name like the first eagle's; but the torch westering
The seas widened, the earth's bloom hardened, the stone rose Rome seeding the
    earth, but the torch northering
Lightened the Atlantic . . . O flame, O beauty and shower of beauty,
There is yet one ocean and then no more, God whom you shine to walks there
    naked, on the final Pacific,
Not in a man's form.
                  The torch answered: Have I kindled a morning?   30
For again, this old world's end is the gate of a world fire new, of your wild
    future, wild as a hawk's[6] dream,
Ways hung on nothing, like stars, feet shaking earth off; that long way
Was a labor in a dream, will you wake now? The eaglets rustle in the aerie, the
    red eyes of dawn stabbing up through the nest-side,
You have walked in a dream, consumed with your fathers and your mothers,
    you have loved
Inside the four walls of humanity, passions turned inward, incestuous desires and
    a fighting against ghosts, but the clarions   35
Of light have called morning.
               What, not to be tangled any more in the blinding
Rays of reflected desire, the man with the woman, the woman with the child,
    the daughter with the father, but freed
Of the web self-woven, the burning and the blistering strands running inward?
Those rays to be lightened awide, to shine up the star-path, subduing the world
    outward? Oh chicks in the high nest be fledged now,
Having found out flight in the air to make wing to the height, fierce eye-flames 40
Of the eaglets be strengthened, to drink of the fountain of the beauty of the
    sun of the stars, and to gaze in his face, not a father's,
And motherless and terrible and here.

[4] The Euphrates: river in Mesopotamia, site of the Babylonian Empire; the Nile: river in Egypt, home of the empire of the Pharoahs; the Ionian water: sea between Greece and Italy; the Aegean: sea between Greece and Asia Minor, location of classical Greek civilization.
[5] Sappho: Greek poet of the sixth century B.C.;

Alcaeus: Greek lyric poet of the sixth century B.C.; Aeschylus: Greek tragic dramatist of the fifth century B.C.
[6] Hawks and eagles were frequently used by Jeffers as symbols for the higher, self-transcendent individual.

But I at the gate, I falling

On the gate-sill add this: When the ancient wisdom is folded like a
    wine-stained cloth and laid up in darkness.
And the old symbols forgotten, in the glory of that your hawk's dream
Remember that the life of mankind is like the life of a man, a flutter from
    darkness to darkness
Across the bright hair of a fire, so much of the ancient
Knowledge will not be annulled. What unimaginable opponent to end you?
    There is one fountain
Of power, yours and that last opponent's, and of long peace.

45

1925

Marianne Moore
1887–1972

Marianne Moore, by the end of her long life, was treated somewhat as a lovable
mascot to be patronized by those who thought her eccentricities (the black
tricorn hat or her love of the Brooklyn Dodgers) charming. This latter image
obscured the real person, the clever and scornful writer who came on the literary
scene praised by T. S. Eliot, in 1921. Moore's clear and avant-garde intelligence
made *The Dial,* under her editorship (1925–1929), the magazine anyone interested
in new art and writing in the 1920s had to read. In her poetry, she was a precise
artist for whom a few words sketched an ethical problem, an exotic animal, or a
landscape.

Moore was born within a year of Emily Dickinson's death; it was not, in fact,
until Moore was in her twenties that Dickinson's art was understood and her
rank as a major poet established. Moore looked to Dickinson as a model, but
looked even more to various English sources, especially George Herbert, John
Bunyan, and other religious writers. She had been brought up in strict
Presbyterianism, and the strong ethical bent that this training produced in her
remained in lifelong tension (at first productive, later destructive) with her
appreciation of the multiplicity and aesthetic diversity of life's natural and human
products. She gazed at lizards and medieval tapestries with equal interest; she
relished the lore of bestiaries and newspaper quotations, advertising copy and
guidebooks, fashion reporting and the Bible. But her moral side urged the
strictness of principles, the plainness of axioms, and the geometry of the righteous
life. Her relish she called "gusto," her love of the plain style she called
"sincerity," and in the antiphony between "gusto" and "sincerity" her poetry
takes form.

The form it takes is both strict and free. Moore would write out a stanza
until the phrases all fell right and the lines were satisfactory. Then she would
create other stanzas on the model of the first, counting the syllables in each line
of the original stanza and replicating that number in subsequent stanzas. She
insisted that she wrote by stanzas, not in syllabic lines. By fixing a relatively

inflexible number of syllables in each line, she established the rule of control that a poet needs for ingenious invention to be pressed into service. Though many of her poems are written in free verse, the elegant and quirky motion of her syllabic poems (including "The Fish" and "Poetry") made her famous.

Moore's father went insane before she was born; she never knew him. For the first seven years of her life she lived with her mother and her elder brother in the house of her maternal grandparents in St. Louis. Her mother took a teaching job and moved the family to Carlisle, Pennsylvania; there they continued the intense closeness reflected in their subsequent lives. Moore lived with her mother all her life and remained closely attached to her brother. Moore graduated from Bryn Mawr College; her grades were not good enough for her to major in English—an ironic fate—so she majored in biology, beginning that training of the eye that, together with the act of the commenting mind, gave her second book its punning title, *Observations* (1924).

In fact, that book contained mostly poems reprinted from her first book, *Poems* (1921), published (without her knowledge or permission) by two of her friends, American writers living in London, Winifred Bryher and Hilda Dolittle. Moore's poems had already appeared in such American avant-garde journals as *Poetry* and *Others*. She was moving in a circle that included Alfred Kreymborg (the editor of *Others*), Wallace Stevens, William Carlos Williams, and various painters and sculptors. She was thought beautiful by many who knew her, but marriage (which it takes "all one's criminal ingenuity to avoid") was something she turned away from, though her long poem "Marriage" shows she had considered both its seductions and its rewards. Her mother's bitter experience may have deterred her, or, like Emily Dickinson, she may have reserved her attention for her work.

"One detects creative power," wrote Moore, "by its capacity to conquer one's detachment." To read Moore's best pages is to find one's detachment conquered as one is drawn into an odd, unpredictable, satiric, learned mind, offering "neatness of finish! neatness of finish!" side by side with the sprawling grandeur of "an octopus of ice"—as Moore called the many-armed glacier covering Mt. Rainier. A great deal of Moore's creative power was spent, as in "An Octopus," thinking about America, both critically and approvingly. Her symbol for America is Mt. Rainier itself—enormous, half threat, half invitation, hospitable to all sorts of enterprising and hardy mountain fauna but at the same time the site of terrible geographic, climatic, and aesthetic extremes. Moore was tart when she looked at American failings: Against the American disposition to listen to "snake-charming controversialists" she argued that "it is one thing to change one's mind, / another to eradicate it." Against those who saw in New York only a commercial center she argued "it is not the plunder, / but 'accessibility to experience.'" Against Anglophiles she argued that excellence "has never been confined to one locality." She hated the "half limping and half-ladyfied" rhetoric of diplomats; she scoffed at those who complacently announced that woman was "circumscribed by a / heritage of blindness and native / incompetence." Generally, the prejudiced, in Moore's poetry, condemn themselves; their words, quoted back at them and embedded in Moore's surgical cleanness of style, resound in foolishness. Moore's habit of quoting, however, extended far beyond the satirical quoting of the words of fools; she collected with the temperament of a magpie all sorts of things to quote. The Rosenbach Foundation Museum in Philadelphia preserves her living room; its drawers are full of the accumulation of a lifetime— conversation notebooks in which she recorded sayings (especially of her mother and brother) and files of clippings. Her poems are mosaics, or collages; many pieces are arranged until they fit together. The impossible ideal hovering under the surface is that of an assemblage so perfect that it would need no authorially supplied connective tissue.

The aesthetic pleasures to be found in Moore are those of exquisite appositeness, lightness of touch combined with depth of feeling, ingenuity and surprise, and conversational urbanity and wit. In her later years her morality ("this is mortality, / this is eternity") and her whimsy ("O to be a dragon") disturbed the delicate balance maintained in the best of her poetry, but *Observations* remains, like T. S. Eliot's *Prufrock and Other Observations* and Wallace Stevens's *Harmonium,* one of the treasures of American modernist writing.

Further Reading:
F. Engel, *Marianne Moore,* 1964.
J. Garrigue, *Marianne Moore,* 1965.
A. K. Weatherhead, *The Edge of the Image: Marianne Moore, William Carlos Williams, and Some Other Poets,* 1967.
G. W. Nitchie, *Marianne Moore: An Introduction to the Poetry,* 1969.
Marianne Moore: A Collection of Critical Essays, ed. C. Tomlinson, 1969.
D. Hall, *Marianne Moore: The Cage and the Animal,* 1970.
C. S. Abbot, *Marianne Moore: A Reference Guide,* 1980.
B. Costello, *Marianne Moore: Imaginary Possessions,* 1981.

Texts:
"Poetry" and "Melancthon" from *Collected Poems,* 1951.
All other selections from *The Complete Poems of Marianne Moore,* 1981.
See also *A Marianne Moore Reader,* 1961.

Poetry[*]

I, too, dislike it: there are things that are important beyond all this fiddle.
  Reading it, however, with a perfect contempt for it, one discovers in
    it after all, a place for the genuine.
      Hands that can grasp, eyes
        that can dilate, hair that can rise
          if it must, these things are important not because a   5

---

[*] This poem was revised several times and in the end (1967) reduced to its first two sentences. The version here is from *Collected Poems* (1951).

high-sounding interpretation can be put upon them but because they are
  useful. When they become so derivative as to become unintelligible,
  the same thing may be said for all of us, that we
    do not admire what
    we cannot understand: the bat
      holding on upside down or in quest of something to

eat, elephants pushing, a wild horse taking a roll, a tireless wolf under
  a tree, the immovable critic twitching his skin like a horse that feels a flea,
    the base-
  ball fan, the statistician—
    nor is it valid
      to discriminate against 'business documents and

school-books';' all these phenomena are important. One must make a
    distinction
  however: when dragged into prominence by half poets, the result is not
    poetry,
  nor till the poets among us can be
    'literalists of
      the imagination'²—above
        insolence and triviality and can present

for inspection, 'imaginary gardens with real toads in them', shall we have
  it. In the meantime, if you demand on the one hand,
    the raw material of poetry in
      all its rawness³ and
        that which is on the other hand
          genuine, you are interested in poetry.

1921

---

¹ Moore's note: "*Diary of Tolstoy* (Dutton), p. 84.
'Where the boundary between prose and poetry
lies, I shall never be able to understand. The
question is raised in manuals of style, yet the
answer to it lies beyond me. Poetry is verse;
prose is not verse. Or else poetry is everything
with the exception of business documents and
school books.'"
² Moore's note: "*Yeats: Ideas of Good and Evil* (A.
H. Bullen), p. 182. 'The limitation of his view
was from the very intensity of his vision; he
was a too literal realist of imagination, as others
are of nature; and because he believed that the
figures seen by the mind's eye, when exalted by
inspiration, were "eternal existences," symbols
of divine essences, he hated every grace of style
that might obscure their lineaments.' "
³ Moore saved a clipping from *The Spectator*
(London) for May 10, 1913, in which a
contributor, called "C," asked why the Greek
Anthology still charms us, says: "All [of its
poems] appeal to emotions which endure for all
time, and which, it has been aptly said, are the
true raw material of poetry."

The Fish

wade
through black jade.[1]
   Of the crow-blue mussel-shells, one keeps
   adjusting the ash-heaps;[2]
      opening and shutting itself like   5

an
injured fan.
   The barnacles which encrust the side
   of the wave, cannot hide
      there for the submerged shafts of the   10

sun,
split like spun
   glass, move themselves with spotlight swiftness
   into the crevices—
      in and out, illuminating   15

the
turquoise sea
   of bodies. The water drives a wedge
   of iron through the iron edge
      of the cliff; whereupon the stars,[3]   20

pink
rice-grains, ink-
   bespattered jelly-fish, crabs like green
   lilies, and submarine
      toadstools, slide each on the other.   25

All
external
   marks of abuse are present on this
   defiant edifice—
      all the physical features of   30

---

[1] The ocean waters.   [3] Starfish.
[2] I.e., the heaps of mussels look like lumps of
burnt coal.

ac-
cident—lack
   of cornice, dynamite grooves, burns, and
   hatchet strokes, these things stand
      out on it; the chasm-side is   35

dead.
Repeated
   evidence has proved that it can live
   on what can not revive
      its youth. The sea grows old in it.   40

1924

In the Days of Prismatic Color[1]

not in the days of Adam and Eve, but when Adam
   was alone;[2] when there was no smoke and color was
fine, not with the refinement
   of early civilization art, but because
of its originality; with nothing to modify it but the   5

mist that went up, obliqueness was a variation
   of the perpendicular, plain to see and
to account for: it is no
   longer that; nor did the blue-red-yellow band
of incandescence that was color keep its stripe: it also is one of   10

those things into which much that is peculiar can be
   read; complexity is not a crime, but carry
it to the point of murkiness
   and nothing is plain. Complexity,
moreover, that has been committed to darkness, instead of   15

granting itself to be the pestilence that it is, moves all a-
   bout as if to bewilder us with the dismal
fallacy that insistence
   is the measure of achievement and that all
truth must be dark. Principally throat, sophistication is as it al-   20

[1] Light split into all the colors of the spectrum
by being passed through a prism.   [2] I.e., before the creation of Eve.

ways has been—at the antipodes from the initial great truths. "Part of it was crawling, part of it
was about to crawl, the rest
   was torpid in its lair."[3] In the short-legged, fit-
ful advance, the gurgling and all the minutiae—we have the classic   25

multitude of feet. To what purpose! Truth is no Apollo
   Belvedere,[4] no formal thing. The wave may go over it if it likes.
Know that it will be there when it says,
   "I shall be there when the wave has gone by."[5]

1924

England

with its baby rivers and little towns, each with its abbey or its cathedral,
with voices—one voice perhaps, echoing through the transept[1]—the
criterion of suitability and convenience: and Italy
with its equal shores—contriving an epicureanism[2]
from which the grossness has been extracted: 5

and Greece with its goat and its gourds,
the nest of modified illusions: and France,
the "chrysalis of the nocturnal butterfly,"[3]
in whose products mystery of construction
diverts one from what was originally one's object—   10
substance at the core: and the East[4] with its snails, its emotional

shorthand[5] and jade cockroaches, its rock crystal and its imperturbability,
all of museum quality: and America where there
is the little old ramshackle victoria[6] in the south,

---

[3] Moore's note: " 'Part of it was crawling,' etc. Nestor, *Greek Anthology* (Loeb Classical Library) Vol. III, p. 129." Moore borrows the metaphor of the reptile emerging from its lair from Nestor.

[4] The statue of Apollo, a Roman copy of a Greek original, was long considered the epitome of ancient art and beauty.

[5] The quotation is borrowed from a remark made by Moore's brother John in conversation: "I'm stubborn—I feel sometimes as if the wave can go over me if it likes and I'll be there when it's gone by." The remark is recorded in Moore's *Conversation Notebook.*

[1] The part of a cruciform (cross-shaped) church perpendicular to the nave (long center aisle).

[2] Refined pleasure of the senses.

[3] The fashion designer Erté designed evening gowns described in these words. Moore's note simply gives the quotation followed by "Erté."

[4] I.e., China.

[5] Ideograms.

[6] Type of carriage.

where cigars are smoked on the street in the north;   15
where there are no proof-readers, no silkworms, no digressions;

the wild man's land; grassless, linksless,[7] languageless country in which letters are
    written
not in Spanish, not in Greek, not in Latin, not in shorthand,
but in plain American which cats and dogs can read!
The letter *a* in psalm and calm when   20
pronounced with the sound of *a* in candle, is very noticeable, but

why should continents of misapprehension
have to be accounted for by the fact?
Does it follow that because there are poisonous toadstools
which resemble mushrooms, both are dangerous?   25
Of mettlesomeness which may be mistaken for appetite,
of heat which may appear to be haste,
no conclusions may be drawn.

To have misapprehended the matter is to have confessed that one has not looked
    far enough.
The sublimated wisdom of China, Egyptian discernment,   30
the cataclysmic torrent of emotion
compressed in the verbs of the Hebrew language,
the books of the man who is able to say,
"I envy nobody but him, and him only,
who catches more fish than I do"[8]—   35
the flower and fruit of all that noted superiority—
if not stumbled upon in America,
must one imagine that it is not there?
It has never been confined to one locality.

1921

When I Buy Pictures

or what is closer to the truth,
when I look at that of which I may regard myself as the imaginary possessor,
I fix upon what would give me pleasure in my average moments:
the satire upon curiosity in which no more is discernible
than the intensity of the mood;   5

---

[7] I.e., lacking golf courses.
[8] From *The Compleat Angler* by Izaak Walton
(1593–1683), as Moore's note remarks.

or quite the opposite—the old thing, the medieval decorated hat-box,
in which there are hounds with waists diminishing like the waist of the
    hour-glass,
and deer and birds and seated people;
it may be no more than a square of parquetry; the literal biography perhaps,
in letters standing well apart upon a parchment-like expanse;   10
an artichoke in six varieties of blue; the snipe-legged hieroglyphic in three
    parts;[1]
the silver fence protecting Adam's grave,[2] or Michael taking Adam by the wrist.
Too stern an intellectual emphasis upon this quality or that detracts from one's
    enjoyment.
It must not wish to disarm anything; nor may the approved triumph easily be
    honored—
that which is great because something else is small.   15
It comes to this: of whatever sort it is,
it must be "lit with piercing glances into the life of things";[3]
it must acknowledge the spiritual forces which have made it.

1921

A Grave

Man looking into the sea,
taking the view from those who have as much right to it as you have to it
    yourself,
it is human nature to stand in the middle of a thing,
but you cannot stand in the middle of this;
the sea has nothing to give but a well excavated grave.   5
The firs stand in a procession, each with an emerald turkey-foot at the top,
reserved as their contours, saying nothing;
repression, however, is not the most obvious characteristic of the sea;
the sea is a collector, quick to return a rapacious look.
There are others besides you who have worn that look—   10
whose expression is no longer a protest; the fish no longer investigate them
for their bones have not lasted:
men lower nets, unconscious of the fact that they are desecrating a grave,
and row quickly away—the blades of the oars
moving together like the feet of water-spiders as if there were no such thing as
    death.   15

---

[1] These are instances of various forms of illustration and calligraphy.
[2] Moore's note: " 'A silver fence was erected by Constantine to enclose the grave of Adam.'

Literary Digest, January 5, 1918; descriptive paragraph with photograph."
[3] Moore's note: "A. R. Gordon, *The Poets of the Old Testament* (Hodder and Stoughton, 1919)."

The wrinkles progress among themselves in a phalanx—beautiful under
    networks of foam,
and fade breathlessly while the sea rustles in and out of the seaweed;
the birds swim through the air at top speed, emitting cat-calls as heretofore—
the tortoise-shell scourges about the feet of the cliffs, in motion beneath them;
and the ocean, under the pulsation of lighthouses and noise of bell-buoys,   20
advances as usual, looking as if it were not that ocean in which dropped things
    are bound to sink—
in which if they turn and twist, it is neither with volition nor consciousness.

1924

New York

the savage's romance,
accreted where we need the space for commerce—
the center of the wholesale fur trade,[1]
starred with tepees of ermine and peopled with foxes,
the long guard-hairs waving two inches beyond the body of the pelt;   5
the ground dotted with deer-skins—white with white spots,
"as satin needlework in a single color may carry a varied pattern,"[2]
and wilting eagle's-down compacted by the wind;
and picardels[3] of beaver-skin; white ones alert with snow.
It is a far cry from the "queen full of jewels"   10
and the beau with the muff,
from the gilt coach shaped like a perfume-bottle,
to the conjunction of the Monongahela and the Allegheny,[4]
and the scholastic philosophy of the wilderness.[5]
It is not the dime-novel exterior,   15
Niagara Falls, the calico horses and the war-canoe;
it is not that "if the fur is not finer than such as one sees others wear,

[1] Moore's note: "In 1921 New York succeeded St. Louis as the center of the wholesale fur trade."

[2] Moore's note quotes a description of a white fawn with white spots, of which these words are used.

[3] Renaissance collars made of pieces of material sewn together.

[4] The two rivers meet at Pittsburgh, Pennsylvania.

[5] Moore copied into her 1916–1921 *Reading Notebook* a statement from Henry Osborn Taylor's *The Medieval Mind* about the difficult scholastic philosophy of Duns Scotus (ca. 1266–1308): "If you enter his lists you are lost. The right way to attack him is to stand outside and laugh." Although Moore lived in the city, she took an ironic view of its commerce.

one would rather be without it"[6]—
that estimated in raw meat and berries, we could feed the universe;
it is not the atmosphere of ingenuity,   20
the otter, the beaver, the puma skins
without shooting-irons or dogs;
it is not the plunder,
but "accessibility to experience."[7]

1924

No Swan So Fine[*]

"No water so still as the
        dead fountains of Versailles."[1] No swan,
with swart blind look askance
and gondoliering legs, so fine
        as the chintz china one with fawn-   5
brown eyes and toothed gold
collar on to show whose bird it was.

Lodged in the Louis Fifteenth
        candelabrum-tree of cockscomb-
tinted buttons, dahlias,   10
sea-urchins, and everlastings,
        it perches on the branching foam
of polished sculptured
flowers—at ease and tall. The king is dead.

1935

---

[6] Moore attributes this remark, slightly altered, to
Isabella, duchess of Gonzaga, quoted in Frank
Alvah Parson's *The Psychology of Dress* (1920).
[7] Moore's note: "Henry James."
[*] According to Moore, the poem concerns a pair
of Louis XV (1723–1774) candelabra
ornamented with Dresden china flowers and
swans, a piece of art still "alive" though the
king in whose reign it was made is long dead.
[1] The king's palace at Versailles, near Paris, has
elaborate fountains. Moore's note: "'There is no
water so still as the dead fountains of
Versailles.' Percy Phillip, *New York Times
Magazine*, May 10, 1931."

The Monkey Puzzle[1]

A kind of monkey or pine-lemur
not of interest to the monkey,
in a kind of Flaubert's Carthage,[2] it defies one—
this "Paduan cat with lizard," this "tiger in a bamboo thicket."
"An interwoven somewhat," it will not come out.   5
Ignore the Foo dog and it is forthwith more than a dog,
its tail superimposed upon itself in a complacent half spiral,
this pine-tree—this pine-tiger, is a tiger, not a dog.
It knows that if a nomad may have dignity,
Gibraltar has had more—   10
that "it is better to be lonely than unhappy."
A conifer contrived in imitation of the glyptic work of jade and hard-stone
    cutters,
a true curio in this bypath of curio-collecting,
it is worth its weight in gold, but no one takes it
from these woods in which society's not knowing is colossal,   15
the lion's ferocious chrysanthemum head seeming kind by comparison.
This porcupine-quilled, complicated starkness—
this is beauty—"a certain proportion in the skeleton which gives the best
    results."[3]
One is at a loss, however, to know why it should be here,
in this morose part of the earth—   20
to account for its origin at all;
but we prove, we do not explain our birth.

1935

---

[1] The tree, popularly called the monkey-puzzle tree, belongs to the species *Araucaria imbricata* and is also known as the Chile pine. Its large branches curl in on themselves.

[2] Moore quoted in an interview the injunction of the French novelist Gustave Flaubert (1821–1880): "Describe a tree so no other tree could be mistaken for it," an act she accomplishes in this poem. Flaubert, in his novel *Salammbô* (1863), describes in exact detail the ancient city of Carthage; thus "Flaubert's Carthage" refers to a meticulously descriptive system.

[3] Moore's note for this quotation, the only one in the poem for which she cites a source, is: "Lafcadio Hearn, *Talks to Writers* (Dodd, Mead)." Moore often put into quotation marks remarks by others, which she had noted in her "conversation notebooks." The quoted fragments in this poem may be remarks of this kind made perhaps by her mother, with whom she lived. Lafcadio Hearn (1850–1904) was a naturalized American citizen, born in Greece, famous for his travel books.

Nevertheless

you've seen a strawberry
    that's had a struggle;[1] yet
    was, where the fragments met,

a hedgehog or a star-
    fish for the multitude   5
    of seeds. What better food

than apple-seeds—the fruit
    within the fruit—locked in
    like counter-curved twin

hazel-nuts? Frost that kills   10
    the little rubber-plant-
    leaves of *kok-saghyz*[2]-stalks can't

harm the roots; they still grow
    in frozen ground. Once where
    there was a prickly-pear-   15

leaf clinging to barbed wire,
    a root shot down to grow
    in earth two feet below;

as carrots form mandrakes
    or a ram's-horn root some-   20
    times. Victory won't come

to me unless I go
    to it; a grape-tendril
    ties a knot in knots till

knotted thirty times,—so   25
    the bound twig that's under-
    gone and over-gone, can't stir.

[1] The contemporary novelist Marguerite Young
recalled Moore's coming across a deformed
strawberry and remarking, "There's a strawberry
that had a struggle."

[2] Russian: "dandelion."

The weak overcomes its
    menace, the strong over-
    comes itself. What is there   30

like fortitude! What sap
    went through that little thread
    to make the cherry red!

1944

His Shield

The pin-swin or spine-swine
    (the edgehog miscalled hedgehog) with all his edges out,
  echidna[1] and echinoderm[2] in distressed-
pin-cushion thorn-fur coats, the spiny pig or porcupine,
    the rhino with horned snout—   5
  everything is battle-dressed.

Pig-fur won't do, I'll wrap
    myself in salamander-skin like Presbyter John.[3]
  A lizard in the midst of flames, a firebrand
that is life, asbestos-eyed asbestos-eared, with tattooed nap   10
    and permanent pig on
  the instep; he can withstand

fire and won't drown. In his
    unconquerable country of unpompous gusto,
  gold was so common none considered it; greed   15
and flattery were unknown. Though rubies large as tennis-
    balls conjoined in streams so
  that the mountain seemed to bleed,

the inextinguishable
    salamander styled himself but presbyter. His shield   20
  was his humility. In Carpasian
linen coat, flanked by his household lion-cubs and sable
    retinue, he revealed
  a formula safer than

[1] Nocturnal egg-laying mammal with a spiny
back, native to Australia.
[2] Sea urchin.
[3] Prester John, whose kingdom is described in the
following lines, was a legendary Christian priest
and monarch of a wealthy empire in Asia or
Africa. This legend first appeared in the twelfth
century and persisted long afterward.

an armorer's: the power of relinquishing   25
    what one would keep; that is freedom. Become dinosaur-
  skulled, quilled or salamander-wooled, more ironshod
and javelin-dressed than a hedgehog battalion of steel, but be
    dull. Don't be envied or
  armed with a measuring-rod.   30

1951

Melancthon[*]

Openly, yes,
with the naturalness
  of the hippopotamus or the alligator
    when it climbs out on the bank to experience the

sun, I do these   5
things which I do, which please
  no one but myself. Now I breathe and now I am submerged; the blemishes stand up and shout when the object

in view was a
renaissance; shall I say   10
  the contrary? The sediment of the river which
  encrusts my joints, makes me very grey but I am used

to it, it may
remain there; do away
  with it and I am myself done away with, for the   15
  patina of circumstance can but enrich what was

there to begin
with. This elephant-skin
  which I inhabit, fibred over like the shell of
  the cocoanut, this piece of black glass through which no light 20

can filter—cut
into checkers by rut

---

[*] This poem was dropped from the 1967 *Complete
Poems*. The version printed here is from the
1951 *Collected Poems*. First published in 1915, it
was originally entitled "Black Earth," of which
"Melancthon" is the Greek equivalent. The
poem is spoken by a black elephant, whose
wrinkled skin resembles black earth.

upon rut of unpreventable experience—
it is a manual for the peanut-tongued and the

hairy-toed. Black   25
but beautiful,[1] my back
    is full of the history of power. Of power? What
    is powerful and what is not? My soul shall never

be cut into
by a wooden spear; through-   30
    out childhood to the present time, the unity of
    life and death has been expressed by the circumference

described by my
trunk; nevertheless I
    perceive feats of strength to be inexplicable after   35
    all; and I am on my guard; external poise, it

has its centre
well nurtured—we know
    where—in pride; but spiritual poise, it has its centre where?
    My ears are sensitized to more than the sound of   40

the wind. I see
and I hear, unlike the
    wandlike body of which one hears so much,[2] which was made
    to see and not to see; to hear and not to hear;

that tree-trunk without   45
roots, accustomed to shout
    its own thoughts to itself like a shell, maintained intact
    by who knows what strange pressure of the atmosphere; that

spiritual
brother to the coral-   50
    plant, absorbed into which, the equable sapphire light
    becomes a nebulous green. The I of each is to

the I of each
a kind of fretful speech
    which sets a limit on itself; the elephant is   55
    black earth preceded by a tendril? Compared with those

[1] Song of Solomon 1:5: "I am black, but comely. . . ."   [2] The elephant's view of man, further described in lines 46–60.

phenomena
which vacillate like a
   translucence of the atmosphere, the elephant is
   that on which darts cannot strike decisively the first   60

time, a substance
needful as an instance
   of the indestructibility of matter; it
   has looked at electricity and at the earth-

quake and is still   65
here; the name means thick. Will
   depth be depth, thick skin be thick, to one who can see no
   beautiful element of unreason under it?

1951

T. S. Eliot
1888–1965

T. S. Eliot's *The Waste Land*, like Walt Whitman's "Song of Myself," changed the course of American literary history. Eliot's long poem, published in 1922, consolidated the despair felt throughtout Europe after World War I and thus spoke for the collapse of a whole culture. Its fragments of civilization seemed like the rubbish heap of history. But it was the exquisite musicality of the poem, its instantly memorable lines, that made it haunt the literary imagination.

The poet of *The Waste Land* was an expatriate American living in London. At the time he wrote the poem he had been driven, by fears of a permanent breakdown, to psychiatric treatment in Lausanne. There, in the midst of polyglot Switzerland, in the center of Europe, he looked inward to his own nervous collapse and outward to the fragmentation of Europe. But behind the European voices and landscapes of this famous poem lay an American story. In fact, Eliot had originally begun his poem with a scene in Boston's Scollay Square (the home of brothels and burlesque shows). In deleting his original opening scene and affixing instead an opening unmistakably European, Eliot turned his back on the New World and placed himself resolutely in the Old.

Eliot's family had come to the United States from England, and the pull back to family origins in East Coker, Somersetshire, is given its due in the second poem of his later sequence, *Four Quartets*. Eliot's own branch of the family had moved from Gloucester, Massachusetts, to St. Louis, where Eliot's grandfather founded Washington University in 1853. Eliot's father made money manufacturing bricks from Mississippi clay; it was Eliot's mother (author of a long verse-drama on Savonarola, which her son paid to have published) who sponsored the literary education of the poet. Eliot was a brilliantly successful student at Harvard (1906–1910 as an undergraduate studying literature, 1911–1914 as a graduate student in Sanskrit and philosophy). Though he completed a Ph.D.

dissertation on the work of the skeptical idealist philosopher F. H. Bradley, Eliot never took the degree. He was studying at Oxford when World War I broke out; by the time it ended, when he could have returned to America to defend the dissertation, he had married and had chosen poetry over the academic life.

The marriage was unhappy from the beginning. Eliot's wife, Vivien Haigh-Wood, was constantly ill with an assortment of maladies, in part psychosomatic but nonetheless agonizing. Eliot's father, disapproving of the marriage, changed his will and died leaving Eliot only the income, not the capital, from his share of the estate. It was after his father's death, the punishment of the will, and a London visit by his mother and sister that Eliot experienced the breakdown preceding the composition of *The Waste Land*.

With the recovery of his health, a change of job from banking to publishing (at Faber & Faber), and the publication of *The Waste Land* in *The Criterion* (a journal that he edited), Eliot's life found renewed stability. In 1932 he obtained a legal separation from his wife, whose condition had considerably worsened and who eventually died in a mental hospital in 1947. After World War II, Eliot lived for over ten years in London with John Hayward, a bibliophile, editor, and reviewer who was confined to a wheelchair by muscular dystrophy. In 1957, at age sixty-eight, Eliot married Valerie Fletcher, for many years his secretary at Faber.

Eliot's sensibility sometimes seems, to use Ezra Pound's term, a "vortex" into which the whole of modern culture was absorbed. Even as an undergraduate, Eliot adopted the irony and *ennui* of the French poets Charles Baudelaire and Jules Laforgue, whom he had discovered through Arthur Symons's influential book, *The Symbolist Movement in Literature*. In "The Love Song of J. Alfred Prufrock" the French influence is brilliantly crossed with a Tennysonian music and a Browningesque dramatic monologue. Eliot's surrealism, combining the etherized patient, the catlike fog, the butt-ends of days, and the impaled Prufrock wriggling on the wall, was something altogether new in American poetry, far from the inert Imagism of Amy Lowell and equally far from the pieties of the nineteenth-century "fireside poets."

Prufrock and Other Observations (1917) is, like Wallace Stevens's *Harmonium* (1923) and Marianne Moore's *Observations* (1924), one of the landmarks of American modernism. It was followed rapidly by *Gerontion* (1919), *Poems* (1920), and *Poems 1909–1925*, which contained *The Waste Land*. These books remain Eliot's chief poetic achievement. In them we see Eliot's most striking lyric invention, a play of voices deployed almost as instruments in an orchestra, as he drew into lyric the vocal theatricality he had found in Elizabethan and Jacobean drama. Eliot's original title for *The Waste Land* had been "He do the police in different voices," a quotation from Dickens's *Our Mutual Friend*, describing a character who would read aloud newspaper accounts of police-blotter business, giving all the characters different dramatic voicings. Escaping from "personality" (the lyric self of the conventional lyric speaker), Eliot found freedom in multiplying his poetic voices, both in *The Waste Land* and in his later plays.

At the same time, Eliot was becoming the most brilliant literary critic in English since Coleridge. As assistant editor of *The Egoist* from 1917 to 1919 and editor of *The Criterion* for seventeen years (1922–1939), he wrote the essays collected in *The Sacred Wood* (1920), *Homage to Dryden* (1924), and *For Lancelot*

Andrewes (1928). Eliot's essays took up polemical positions in the service of his own theory of poetry, projecting his own "dissociation of sensibility" back into the post-metaphysical poets, defending the macabre extremes of tension in the Jacobeans, and (after his conversion to Anglicanism in 1927) arguing for the glories of Anglican literature (Lancelot Andrewes, George Herbert). Eliot's most influential essay, "Tradition and the Individual Talent," published in *The Sacred Wood,* repudiates both the avant-garde conviction that modern poetry should break utterly from the past and the Wordsworthian definition of poetry as "emotion recollected in tranquillity." It argues that the modern poet cannot succeed without a profound incorporation of the literature of the past. It argues as well that the poet is a medium, serving as a catalyst for new combinations of language, and that the poet must therefore escape from individual personality and emotion in composing poetry. In turning away from biographical and historical information and toward language and style in his essays on individual poets (Milton, Herbert), Eliot gave a new direction to the practice of literary criticism. The so-called New Criticism, advocated in England by I. A. Richards and in the United States by such followers of Eliot as Allen Tate and John Crowe Ransom, brought a new sophistication, after the manner of Eliot, to the analysis of poetry.

Eliot's valuing of complexity, irony, and paradox, his powerful sense of the unity of a literary work, and his conviction that the work provided an "objective correlative" for the state of mind of its creator pervaded his critical writing in the 1920s. In later essays Eliot's political views became increasingly conservative until, in 1934, in a book he later retracted, *After Strange Gods* (based on lectures given at the University of Virginia), he argued against the desirability of "any large number of free-thinking Jews" in any Christian society. Eliot, who remained in many ways a Victorian intellectual preoccupied with the dissolution of social consensus and Christian belief, was pained by the increasing democratization of society and the increasing secularism of education. Both of these, he thought, entailed the loss of the fabric of common culture he believed indispensable to literature and government alike.

Though Eliot was acquainted with the avant-garde English writers of Bloomsbury, he could not greet with any joy their enthusiasm for change, reflected in Virginia Woolf's statement that in 1910 the world had changed, had become modern. His own balance was too precarious to welcome any external disruptions. Eliot may have displayed a failure of nerve in being unable to embrace social change, but that change found no more sensitive seismographer than its horrified poet-witness.

Eliot's major work after *The Waste Land* was the sequence now known as *Four Quartets* ("Burnt Norton," "East Coker," "The Dry Salvages," and "Little Gidding"). The first was written in 1935, the others during World War II; they were published together in the United States in 1943. They should be read, in part, as war poems, as well as poems having a relation, as Eliot said, to "the four seasons and the four elements." In wartime, Eliot's confidence in the value of writing was momentarily shaken: "It is hard . . . to feel confident that morning after morning spent fiddling with words and rhythms is justified activity—especially as there is never any certainty that the whole thing won't have to be scrapped."

Yet Eliot's career as a writer continued, not only in the autobiographical and historical accounts of temporal mutability in the *Quartets* but also in a series of plays. He had earlier composed *Sweeney Agonistes* (1926–1927), a brilliant adaptation of vaudeville rhythms; *Murder in the Cathedral* (1935), a dramatization of the temptation of Thomas à Becket; and *The Family Reunion* (1939), a play about marital guilt. After the *Quartets*, Eliot wrote more plays—*The Cocktail Party* (1949), which introduced a psychiatrist into a drama of Christian expiation of guilt; *The Confidential Clerk* (1953); and *The Elder Statesman* (1959). Only the first of these succeeded on the stage.

In 1948 Eliot was awarded the Nobel Prize for literature. His reputation fluctuated even during his lifetime, and it will require the publication of manuscripts, letters, and other such documents before a full history of his significance and influence can be written. He is indubitably the greatest writer of modern free verse in America and the greatest of our literary critics, a man whose taste set the taste of his era. Eliot's conviction that he was witnessing the death of culture, conveyed most powerfully in his myths of historical decline, gripped his first auditors. More skeptical readers may believe his later ironic statement that *The Waste Land* represented merely "a personal grudge," a catastrophe of the inner life rather than of the life of civilization. Those readers will see it as one of the great lyrics of a crisis in consciousness, an American long poem to be ranked with Milton's "Lycidas" and Wordsworth's "Ode: On the Intimations of Immortality" as a comprehensive account of the human predicament.

Further Reading:

F. R. Leavis, *New Bearings in English Poetry*, 1932.
F. O. Matthiessen, *The Achievement of T. S. Eliot*, 1935, 1947.
T. S. Eliot: A Selected Critique, ed. L. Unger, 1948.
E. Drew, *T. S. Eliot: The Design of His Poetry*, 1949.
H. Gardner, *The Art of T. S. Eliot*, 1949.
D. E. S. Maxwell, *The Poetry of T. S. Eliot*, 1952.
G. Williamson, *A Reader's Guide to T. S. Eliot*, 1953.
G. Smith, *T. S. Eliot's Poetry and Plays*, 1956.
H. Kenner, *The Invisible Poet: T. S. Eliot*, 1959.
D. E. Jones, *The Plays of T. S. Eliot*, 1960.
K. Smidt, *Poetry and Belief in the Work of T. S. Eliot*, 1961.
A. G. George, *T. S. Eliot: His Mind and Art*, 1962.
P. R. Headings, *T. S. Eliot*, 1964.
H. Howarth, *Notes of Some Figures Behind T. S. Eliot*, 1964.
L. Unger, *T. S. Eliot: Monuments and Patterns*, 1966.
H. Blamires, *Word Unheard: A Guide Through Eliot's Four Quartets*, 1969.
A. Austin, *T. S. Eliot: The Literary and Social Criticism*, 1971.
B. Bergonzi, *T. S. Eliot*, 1971.
G. Patterson, *T. S. Eliot: Poems in the Making*, 1971.
R. Sencourt, *T. S. Eliot: A Memoir*, 1971.
R. Kirk, *Eliot and His Age*, 1972.
R. Kojecky, *T. S. Eliot's Social Criticism*, 1972.
J. D. Margolis, *T. S. Eliot's Intellectual Development*, 1972.
B. Rajan, *The Overwhelming Question: A Study of the Poetry of T. S. Eliot*, 1976.
S. Spender, *T. S. Eliot*, 1976.
D. Traversi, *T. S. Eliot: The Longer Poems*, 1976.
H. Gardner, *The Composition of the "Four Quartets,"* 1977.
L. Gordon, *Eliot's Early Years*, 1977.
J. E. Miller, *T. S. Eliot's Personal Waste Land*, 1977.
The Literary Criticism of T. S. Eliot: New Essays, ed. D. Newton-DeMolina, 1977.
N. Frye, *T. S. Eliot*, 1981.
C. Behr, *T. S. Eliot: A Chronology of His Life and Works*, 1982.
E. K. Hay, *T. S. Eliot's Negative Way*, 1982.
R. Bush, *T. S. Eliot: A Study in Character and Style*, 1983.

Texts:

"Death of St. Narcissus" from *Poems Written in Early Youth*, 1967.

Remaining selections from *Complete Poems and Plays*, 1962.

The Death of Saint Narcissus[1]

Come under the shadow of this gray rock—
Come in under the shadow of this gray rock,
And I will show you something different from either
Your shadow sprawling over the sand at daybreak, or
Your shadow leaping behind the fire against the red rock: 5
I will show you his bloody cloth and limbs
And the gray shadow on his lips.

He walked once between the sea and the high cliffs
When the wind made him aware of his limbs smoothly passing each other
And of his arms crossed over his breast.   10
When he walked over the meadows
He was stifled and soothed by his own rhythm.
By the river
His eyes were aware of the pointed corners of his eyes
And his hands aware of the pointed tips of his fingers.   15

Struck down by such knowledge
He could not live men's ways, but became a dancer before God.
If he walked in city streets
He seemed to tread on faces, convulsive thighs and knees.
So he came out under the rock.   20

First he was sure that he had been a tree,[2]
Twisting its branches among each other.
And tangling its roots among each other.

Then he knew that he had been a fish
With slippery white belly held tight in his own fingers,   25
Writhing in his own clutch, his ancient beauty
Caught fast in the pink tips of his new beauty.

Then he had been a young girl
Caught in the woods by a drunken old man
Knowing at the end the taste of his own whiteness,   30
The horror of his own smoothness,
And he felt drunken and old.

[1] The title represents a conflation of the mythological Narcissus—who fell in love with his own image in a pool and is consequently the symbol of autoeroticism—and Saint Sebastian, a Christian who was martyred by being shot through with arrows. The death of Saint Sebastian was a favorite subject in the Renaissance for painters wishing to depict the male nude.
[2] The doctrine of the transmigration of the soul here shows the soul rising in the evolutionary scale as it passes from one body to another.

So he became a dancer to God.
Because his flesh was in love with the burning arrows
He danced on the hot sand   35
Until the arrows came.
As he embraced them his white skin surrendered itself to the redness of
      blood, and satisfied him.
Now he is green, dry and stained
With the shadow in his mouth.

1967

The Love Song of J. Alfred Prufrock

S'io credesse che mia risposta fosse
A persona che mai tornasse al mondo,
Questa fiamma staria senza piu scosse.
Ma perciocche giammai di questo fondo
Non torno vivo alcun, s'i'odo il vero,
Senza tema d'infamia it rispondo.[1]

Let us go then, you and I,
When the evening is spread out against the sky
Like a patient etherised upon a table;
Let us go, through certain half-deserted streets,
The muttering retreats   5
Of restless nights in one-night cheap hotels
And sawdust restaurants with oyster-shells:
Streets that follow like a tedious argument
Of insidious intent
To lead you to an overwhelming question. . .   10
Oh, do not ask, "What is it?"
Let us go and make our visit.

In the room the women come and go
Talking of Michelangelo.

The yellow fog that rubs its back upon the window-panes,   15
The yellow smoke that rubs its muzzle on the window-panes,
Licked its tongue into the corners of the evening,

[1] From Dante's *Inferno*, XXVII, 61–66. Guido da Montefeltro speaks, after Dante questions him: "If I thought that my reply were to be to someone who would ever return to the world, this flame would be still, without further motion. But since no one has ever returned alive from this depth, if what I hear is true, I answer you without fear of shame." In the poem, Prufrock speaks, similarly, an inner truth to an unnamed "you."

Lingered upon the pools that stand in drains,
Let fall upon its back the soot that falls from chimneys,
Slipped by the terrace, made a sudden leap,   20
And seeing that it was a soft October night,
Curled once about the house, and fell asleep.

    And indeed there will be time
For the yellow smoke that slides along the street,
Rubbing its back upon the window-panes;   25
There will be time, there will be time
To prepare a face to meet the faces that you meet;
There will be time to murder and create,
And time for all the works and days² of hands
That lift and drop a question on your plate;   30
Time for you and time for me,
And time yet for a hundred indecisions,
And for a hundred visions and revisions,
Before the taking of a toast and tea.

    In the room the women come and go   35
Talking of Michelangelo.

    And indeed there will be time
To wonder, "Do I dare?" and, "Do I dare?"
Time to turn back and descend the stair,
With a bald spot in the middle of my hair—   40
(They will say: "How his hair is growing thin!")
My morning coat, my collar mounting firmly to the chin,
My necktie rich and modest, but asserted by a simple pin—
(They will say: "But how his arms and legs are thin!")
Do I dare   45
Disturb the universe?
In a minute there is time
For decisions and revisions which a minute will reverse.

    For I have known them all already, known them all—
Have known the evenings, mornings, afternoons,   50
I have measured out my life with coffee spoons;
I know the voices dying with a dying fall
Beneath the music from a farther room.
    So how should I presume?

    And I have known the eyes already, known them all— 55
The eyes that fix you in a formulated phrase,
And when I am formulated, sprawling on a pin,

---

² The Greek poet Hesiod (eighth century B.C.)
wrote *Works and Days,* a georgic poem.

When I am pinned and wriggling on the wall,
Then how should I begin
To spit out all the butt-ends of my days and ways?   60
    And how should I presume?

    And I have known the arms already, known them all—
Arms that are braceleted and white and bare
(But in the lamplight, downed with light brown hair!)
Is it perfume from a dress   65
That makes me so digress?
Arms that lie along a table, or wrap about a shawl.
    And should I then presume?
    And how should I begin?

    . . . . .

    Shall I say, I have gone at dusk through narrow streets   70
And watched the smoke that rises from the pipes
Of lonely men in shirt-sleeves, leaning out of windows? . . .

    I should have been a pair of ragged claws
Scuttling across the floors of silent seas.

    . . . . .

    And the afternoon, the evening, sleeps so peacefully!   75
Smoothed by long fingers,
Asleep . . . tired . . . or it malingers,
Stretched on the floor, here beside you and me.
Should I, after tea and cakes and ices,
Have the strength to force the moment to its crisis?   80
But though I have wept and fasted, wept and prayed,
Though I have seen my head (grown slightly bald) brought in upon a platter,[3]
I am no prophet—and here's no great matter;
I have seen the moment of my greatness flicker,
And I have seen the eternal Footman hold my coat, and snicker, 85
And in short, I was afraid.

    And would it have been worth it, after all,
After the cups, the marmalade, the tea,
Among the porcelain, among some talk of you and me,
Would it have been worth while,   90
To have bitten off the matter with a smile,
To have squeezed the universe into a ball
To roll it toward some overwhelming question,
To say: "I am Lazarus, come from the dead,[4]
Come back to tell you all, I shall tell you all"—   95

---

[3] The head of John the Baptist was delivered on a platter to Salome (Matthew 14:1–11).

[4] Lazarus was raised from the dead by Jesus (John 11:1–44).

If one, settling a pillow by her head,
   Should say: "That is not what I meant at all.
   That is not it, at all."

   And would it have been worth it, after all,
Would it have been worth while,   100
After the sunsets and the dooryards and the sprinkled streets,
After the novels, after the teacups, after the skirts that trail along the floor—
And this, and so much more?—
It is impossible to say just what I mean!
But as if a magic lantern threw the nerves in patterns on a screen: 105
Would it have been worth while
If one, settling a pillow or throwing off a shawl,
And turning toward the window, should say:
   "That is not it at all,
   That is not what I meant, at all."   110
   . . . . .

No! I am not Prince Hamlet,[5] nor was meant to be;
Am an attendant lord, one that will do
To swell a progress,[6] start a scene or two,
Advise the prince; no doubt, an easy tool,
Deferential, glad to be of use,   115
Politic, cautious, and meticulous;
Full of high sentence,[7] but a bit obtuse;
At times, indeed, almost ridiculous—
Almost, at times, the Fool.

   I grow old . . . I grow old . . .   120
I shall wear the bottoms of my trousers rolled.

   Shall I part my hair behind? Do I dare to eat a peach?
I shall wear white flannel trousers, and walk upon the beach.
I have heard the mermaids singing, each to each.

I do not think that they will sing to me.   125

I have seen them riding seaward on the waves
Combing the white hair of the waves blown back
When the wind blows the water white and black.

We have lingered in the chambers of the sea
By sea-girls wreathed with seaweed red and brown   130
Till human voices wake us, and we drown.
1917

---

[5] I.e., Prufrock will be, not like Hamlet the hero,   [6] Royal procession.
but rather like Polonius, a fussy court advisor.   [7] Sententiousness.

La Figlia Che Piange[1]

O quam te memorem virgo . . .[2]

Stand on the highest pavement of the stair—
Lean on a garden urn—
Weave, weave the sunlight in your hair—
Clasp your flowers to you with a pained surprise—
Fling them to the ground and turn   5
With a fugitive resentment in your eyes:
But weave, weave the sunlight in your hair.

So I would have had him leave,
So I would have had her stand and grieve,
So he would have left   10
As the soul leaves the body torn and bruised,
As the mind deserts the body it has used.
I should find
Some way incomparably light and deft,
Some way we both should understand,   15
Simple and faithless as a smile and shake of the hand.

She turned away, but with the autumn weather
Compelled my imagination many days,
Many days and many hours:
Her hair over her arms and her arms full of flowers.
And I wonder how they should have been together!   20
I should have lost a gesture and a pose.
Sometimes these cogitations still amaze
The troubled midnight and the noon's repose.

1917

Whispers of Immortality

Webster[1] was much possessed by death
And saw the skull beneath the skin;
And breastless creatures under ground
Leaned backward with a lipless grin.

---

[1] Italian: "The Weeping Girl."
[2] From Virgil's *Aeneid*, I, 327: "By what name shall I call thee, O maiden?" This is Aeneas' salutation to the huntress who is in fact his mother, Venus.

[1] John Webster, English dramatist (1580?–1634) and author of the play *The Duchess of Malfi* (ca. 1614).

Daffodil bulbs instead of balls   5
Stared from the sockets of the eyes!
He knew that thought clings round dead limbs
Tightening its lusts and luxuries.

Donne, I suppose, was such another
Who found no substitute for sense,   10
To seize and clutch and penetrate;
Expert beyond experience,

He knew the anguish of the marrow
The ague of the skeleton;
No contact possible to flesh   15
Allayed the fever of the bone.

. . . . .

Grishkin is nice: her Russian eye
Is underlined for emphasis;
Uncorseted, her friendly bust
Gives promise of pneumatic bliss.   20

The couched Brazilian jaguar
Compels the scampering marmoset
With subtle effluence of cat;
Grishkin has a maisonette;[2]

The sleek Brazilian jaguar   25
Does not in its arboreal gloom
Distil so rank a feline smell
As Grishkin in a drawing-room.

And even the Abstract Entities
Circumambulate her charm;   30
But our lot crawls between dry ribs
To keep our metaphysics warm.
1920

----

[2] Apartment with two stories.

Sweeney Among the Nightingales

ὤμοι, πέπληγμαι καιρίαν πληγὴν ἔσω.[1]

Apeneck Sweeney[2] spreads his knees
Letting his arms hang down to laugh,
The zebra stripes along his jaw
Swelling to maculate[3] giraffe.

The circles of the stormy moon   5
Slide westward toward the River Plate,[4]
Death and the Raven drift above
And Sweeney guards the hornèd gate.[5]

Gloomy Orion and the Dog[6]
Are veiled; and hushed the shrunken seas;   10
The person in the Spanish cape
Tries to sit on Sweeney's knees

Slips and pulls the table cloth
Overturns a coffee-cup,
Reorganized upon the floor   15
She yawns and draws a stocking up;

The silent man in mocha brown
Sprawls at the window-sill and gapes;
The waiter brings in oranges
Bananas figs and hothouse grapes;   20

The silent vertebrate in brown
Contracts and concentrates, withdraws;
Rachel *née* Rabinovitch
Tears at the grapes with murderous paws;

She and the lady in the cape   25
Are suspect, thought to be in league;
Therefore the man with heavy eyes
Declines the gambit, shows fatigue,

[1] "Alas, I am struck a mortal blow within,"
Agamemnon's cry as he is murdered by his wife
and her lover (Aeschylus, *Agamemnon*, l. 1343).
[2] Sweeney, with his apelike neck and gorillalike
arms, is Eliot's figure for brutish man.
[3] Spotted.

[4] In Argentina.
[5] In Hades, the gate through which true dreams
pass.
[6] The constellation Orion and the Dog Star,
Sirius.

Leaves the room and reappears
Outside the window, leaning in,   30
Branches of wistaria
Circumscribe a golden grin;

The host with someone indistinct
Converses at the door apart,
The nightingales are singing near   35
The Convent of the Sacred Heart,

And sang within the bloody wood
When Agamemnon cried aloud,
And let their liquid siftings fall
To stain the stiff dishonoured shroud.   40

1920

The Waste Land

The Waste Land was printed first in 1922 in The Criterion and The Dial; when it
was expanded to book form later that year, Eliot added notes. "In the early
poems," said Eliot at seventy-six in a Paris Review interview, "it was a question
of . . . having more to say than one knew how to say. . . . In The Waste Land, I
wasn't even bothering whether I understood what I was saying." In his thirties
Eliot was perhaps writing under the compulsions of extreme marital unhappiness
and self-disgust, yet his agile and retentive mind was not quite so unconscious as
he later suggested.

The Waste Land is based on a few well-known literary and aesthetic sources,
most of them myths manipulated so that they yield unhappy endings (the death
of the vegetation god; the death of the father; shipwreck; the devastation of the
land when its king, symbolically wounded in the thigh, is impotent). Eliot also
found for his poem myths that already had unhappy endings: the destruction of
Valhalla through human greed, dramatized by Wagner in The Ring of the
Nibelung; the death of the cities that symbolize civilization (Jerusalem, Athens,
Alexandria, Rome, London); and the death of cultures, like that of Renaissance
England personified in Queen Elizabeth. These myths are for Eliot macrocosmic
cultural versions of the death of personal love between man and wife and the
death of generosity and freedom in the heart. The Waste Land sees history—both
universal history and personal history—as unredeemable on its own terms.

Sexual malaise lies at the heart of The Waste Land. The neurasthenic
upper-class couple driven mad by each other's presence are paired, in "A Game of
Chess," with a squalid lower-class couple whose marriage is foundering because
of bad teeth, abortion, and sexual infidelity. Girls at Margate are seduced and

abandoned, just as Philomela was raped and tortured long ago; Tristan sees only a blank sea instead of Isolde; Ophelia goes mad after Hamlet's desertion. Sexual squalor appears in the joyless affair of the typist and the "young man carbuncular," in Sweeney's vulgar conjunction with Mrs. Porter, and in the unsavory offer of a homosexual weekend by Mr. Eugenides. Women become surreal seducers surrounded by bats with baby faces. Salome, enraged by John the Baptist's persistence in speaking of Jesus from the cistern in which he is imprisoned, takes revenge for his rejection of her by ordering his execution.

The central figure in the poem, one who has "foresuffered all," is Tiresias, the prophet who had experienced sexuality as both man and woman. The androgynous voice of this "old man with wrinkled female breasts" mediates this poem, so full of loathing for the sexual principle.

The poem is also an elegy. It begins with the ritual of the burial of the dead, and at its nerve center we see the immemorial topic of elegy, the death of the beautiful young man, "Phlebas, who was once handsome and tall as you." (Eliot had dedicated *Prufrock and Other Observations* to the memory of Jean Verdenal, a young doctor he had known in Paris, who had drowned during World War I.) The elegiac subject is also multiple—the "so many" undone by death, the drowned Phoenician Sailor, the Hanged Man, the corpse planted in the garden, "the king my brother's wreck," and "the king my father's death before him."

Against the twin horrors of sexuality and death, Eliot sets certain luminous fragments of value—the young steersman's love song to his Irish love, Spenser's refrain in his betrothal song, Ophelia's poignant "goodnight" spoken in madness, the Rhinemaidens' ecstatic water song, the repentance of St. Augustine, the Buddha's fire sermon. He asserts also the consolatory powers of literature; he has shored fragments of literature as his only bulwark against his ruins. Seen in this way, the poem is an assemblage of what Matthew Arnold called "touchstones," those lines of literature that move us deeply and against which we test other lines for greatness. In these closing "touchstones," the poem reminds itself of the chant of salvation (sung by boy sopranos in Wagner's *Parsifal*), when the grail knight cures the impotent king and restores the land to fertility. It invokes a Dantesque purgation in the refining fire and recalls a sonnet in which the disinherited speaker ("El Desdichado") says that he is the inconsolable widower whose beloved has died, whose tower is ruined. It invokes ideas of madness and vengeance in its allusion to *The Spanish Tragedy*. In finding lines of poetry appropriate to his own disinherited and mad state, to his dead father's cruelty and his own sexual failure, Eliot condensed his wide and polyglot reading to "touchstones," ending with one line of sexual longing ("The swallow has its mate; when shall I be as the swallow?") and one line of ethical and religious Buddhist resignation ("Give. Sympathize. Control. Peace. Peace. Peace.").

This collage of literary fragments, this archaeological heap of literary ruins, is the mirror of Eliot's acute inspection of his own spiritual and literary predicament. How could he forge a new literature out of the ruins of European culture? The refusal here to end with a Christian solution marks only one resting place of Eliot's long mental and aesthetic journey. It is, however, deservedly, the most famous pause in his career. In spite of its initial difficulty, *The Waste Land* has rapidly become domesticated in our literature, its combination of the ferociously colloquial and a stylized exaltation of diction setting a new level of literary daring.

The manuscript of *The Waste Land* was edited by Ezra Pound into its present form, gaining him Eliot's grateful dedication as "the better craftsman." But it should not be forgotten that Eliot could have edited it himself—as he did previous and subsequent poems—and that its glories are his invention. Its music is so pervasive that long stretches resound in the mind long after the pages are closed. At a time of suicidal grief—the epigraph, after all, says "I want to die"— Eliot raised himself, in this one poem, to a fury of self-analysis and cultural polemic that remains unsurpassed in modern literature.

The Waste Land[*]

> "*Nam Sibyllam quidem Cumis ego ipse oculis meis vidi in ampulla pendere, et cum illi pueri dicerent:* Σίβυλλα τί θέλεις; *respondebat illa:* ἀποθανεῖν θέλω."[1]

For Ezra Pound
il miglior fabbro.[2]

I. The Burial of the Dead[3]

April is the cruellest month, breeding
Lilacs out of the dead land, mixing
Memory and desire, stirring
Dull roots with spring rain.
Winter kept us warm, covering   5
Earth in forgetful snow, feeding
A little life with dried tubers.
Summer surprised us, coming over the Starnbergersee[4]
With a shower of rain; we stopped in the colonnade,
And went on in sunlight, into the Hofgarten,[5]   10
And drank coffee, and talked for an hour.
Bin gar keine Russin, stamm' aus Litauen, echt deutsch.[6]
And when we were children, staying at the archduke's,
My cousin's, he took me out on a sled,

---

[*] Eliot's notes are printed after the text of the poem. His notes are referred to in parentheses in the footnotes that follow by an *E* followed by the section number of the poem in Roman numerals and the line number in Arabic, e.g., (E.,II,32).
[1] "For I myself saw with my own eyes the Cumaean Sibyl hanging in a bottle, and when the boys said to her, 'Sibyl, what do you want?,' she would reply, 'I want to die'" (Petronius, *Satyricon,* XLVIII). The Sibyl, in requesting longevity from Apollo, had forgotten to ask for perpetual youth and had therefore shriveled with age.

[2] "The better craftsman" (Dante, *Purgatorio,* XXVI, 117). Eliot's tribute to Pound, whose editorial help can be seen in the facsimile *Waste Land* (1971), which transcribes the original manuscript of the poem.
[3] Title of the funeral service in the Anglican *Book of Common Prayer.*
[4] Lake near Munich.
[5] Park in Munich.
[6] German: "I'm not Russian at all, I come from Lithuania, pure German."

And I was frightened. He said, Marie,
Marie, hold on tight. And down we went.
In the mountains, there you feel free.
I read, much of the night, and go south in the winter. 15

What are the roots that clutch, what branches grow
Out of this stony rubbish? Son of man,[7] 20
You cannot say, or guess, for you know only
A heap of broken images, where the sun beats,
And the dead tree gives no shelter, the cricket no relief,[8]
And the dry stone no sound of water. Only
There is shadow under this red rock, 25
(Come in under the shadow of this red rock),[9]
And I will show you something different from either
Your shadow at morning striding behind you
Or your shadow at evening rising to meet you;
I will show you fear in a handful of dust.[10] 30
        Frisch weht der Wind
        Der Heimat zu
        Mein Irisch Kind,
        Wo weilest du?[11]
"You gave me hyacinths first a year ago; 35
"They called me the hyacinth girl."
—Yet when we came back, late, from the Hyacinth garden,
Your arms full, and your hair wet, I could not
Speak, and my eyes failed, I was neither
Living nor dead, and I knew nothing, 40
Looking into the heart of light, the silence.
Oed' und leer das Meer.[12]

    Madame Sosostris, famous clairvoyante,
Had a bad cold, nevertheless
Is known to be the wisest woman in Europe, 45
With a wicked pack of cards.[13] Here, said she,
Is your card, the drowned Phoenician Sailor,
(Those are pearls that were his eyes.[14] Look!)
Here is Belladonna, the Lady of the Rocks,
The lady of situations. 50

---

[7] God's address to the prophet Ezekiel (E.,I,20).

[8] "The grasshopper shall be a burden" in old age, when "desire shall fail," says the Preacher in Ecclesiastes (E.,I,23).

[9] Cf. Isaiah 32:1–2, where the coming of the Messiah will be "as the shadow of a great rock in a weary land."

[10] "Dust thou art, and unto dust thou shalt return," as in the funeral service.

[11] From Richard Wagner's opera *Tristan und Isolde*

(E.,I,34), the young steersman's lyric song: "The wind blows fresh / To the homeland / My Irish girl, / Where are you waiting?"

[12] "Empty and barren the sea" (E.,I, 42), Tristan's lament as he lies dying, thinking that he will die before Isolde arrives.

[13] Tarot cards, used to tell fortunes (E.,I,46).

[14] From Shakespeare's *The Tempest* (Act I, Sc. ii, l. 398); said of a drowned father.

Here is the man with three staves, and here the Wheel,
And here is the one-eyed merchant, and this card,
Which is blank, is something he carries on his back,
Which I am forbidden to see. I do not find
The Hanged Man. Fear death by water.   55
I see crowds of people, walking round in a ring.
Thank you. If you see dear Mrs. Equitone,
Tell her I bring the horoscope myself:
One must be so careful these days.

    Unreal City,   60
Under the brown fog of a winter dawn,
A crowd flowed over London Bridge, so many,
I had not thought death had undone so many.[15]
Sighs, short and infrequent, were exhaled,
And each man fixed his eyes before his feet.   65
Flowed up the hill and down King William Street,
To where Saint Mary Woolnoth[16] kept the hours
With a dead sound on the final stroke of nine.
There I saw one I knew, and stopped him, crying: "Stetson!
"You who were with me in the ships at Mylae![17]   70
"That corpse you planted last year in your garden,
"Has it begun to sprout? Will it bloom this year?
"Or has the sudden frost disturbed its bed?
"Oh keep the Dog far hence, that's friend to men,
"Or with his nails he'll dig it up again![18]   75
"You! hypocrite lecteur!—mon semblable,—mon frère!"[19]

II. A Game of Chess[20]

The Chair she sat in, like a burnished throne,
Glowed on the marble,[21] where the glass
Held up by standards wrought with fruited vines
From which a golden Cupidon[22] peeped out   80
(Another hid his eyes behind his wing)
Doubled the flames of sevenbranched candelabra
Reflecting light upon the table as
The glitter of her jewels rose to meet it,

[15] Quoted from Dante's *Inferno* (E.,I,63).
[16] London church.
[17] Naval battle (260 B.C.) in which the Romans defeated the Carthaginians.
[18] An echo from the play *The White Devil* (1612) by John Webster. The original reads: "But keep the wolf far thence, that's foe to men, / For with his nails he'll dig them up again" (Act V, Sc. iv, ll. 97–98).
[19] Quote from Baudelaire's poem "Au

Lecteur"("To the Reader"): "Hypocrite reader! —my double,—my brother!" (E.,I,76).
[20] Title of a play by Thomas Middleton (1627) about a marriage of convenience.
[21] Echo of a passage in Shakespeare's *Antony and Cleopatra* (Act II, Sc. ii, ll. 196–197), referring to Cleopatra's barge: "The barge she sat in, like a burnish'd throne, / Burn'd on the water."
[22] Statue of Cupid, god of love in Roman mythology.

From satin cases poured in rich profusion; 85
In vials of ivory and coloured glass
Unstoppered, lurked her strange synthetic perfumes,
Unguent, powdered, or liquid—troubled, confused
And drowned the sense in odours; stirred by the air
That freshened from the window, these ascended 90
In fattening the prolonged candle-flames,
Flung their smoke into the laquearia,[23]
Stirring the pattern on the coffered ceiling.
Huge sea-wood fed with copper
Burned green and orange, framed by the coloured stone, 95
In which sad light a carvèd dolphin swam.
Above the antique mantel was displayed
As though a window gave upon the sylvan scene[24]
The change of Philomel,[25] by the barbarous king
So rudely forced; yet there the nightingale 100
Filled all the desert with inviolable voice
And still she cried, and still the world pursues,
"Jug Jug"[26] to dirty ears.
And other withered stumps of time
Were told upon the walls; staring forms 105
Leaned out, leaning, hushing the room enclosed.
Footsteps shuffled on the stair.
Under the firelight, under the brush, her hair
Spread out in fiery points
Glowed into words, then would be savagely still. 110

    "My nerves are bad to-night. Yes, bad. Stay with me.
"Speak to me. Why do you never speak. Speak.
  "What are you thinking of? What thinking? What?
"I never know what you are thinking. Think."

    I think we are in rats' alley 115
Where the dead men lost their bones.

    "What is that noise?"
               The wind under the door.
"What is that noise now? What is the wind doing?"
            Nothing again nothing. 120
                       "Do
"You know nothing? Do you see nothing? Do you remember
"Nothing?"

---

[23] Paneled ceiling as described in a passage in
Virgil's *Aeneid* telling of Dido's welcome of
Aeneas to Carthage. When Aeneas left her,
Dido committed suicide (E.,II,92).

[24] Allusion to the Garden of Eden in John
Milton's *Paradise Lost* (IV, 140).

[25] Ovid, in the *Metamorphoses*, retells the story of
the rape of Philomel by her brother-in-law
Tereus; he cut out her tongue, but the gods, in
compensation, turned her into a nightingale.

[26] Conventional Elizabethan rendering of the
nightingale's song.

      I remember
Those are pearls that were his eyes.
"Are you alive, or not? Is there nothing in your head?"   125
                                                 But

O O O O that Shakespeherian Rag—
It's so elegant
So intelligent[27]   130
"What shall I do now? What shall I do?"
"I shall rush out as I am, and walk the street
"With my hair down, so. What shall we do to-morrow?
"What shall we ever do?"
                          The hot water at ten.   135
And if it rains, a closed car at four.
And we shall play a game of chess,
Pressing lidless eyes and waiting for a knock upon the door.

      When Lil's husband got demobbed,[28] I said—
I didn't mince my words, I said to her myself,   140
HURRY UP PLEASE ITS TIME[29]
Now Albert's coming back, make yourself a bit smart.
He'll want to know what you done with that money he gave you
To get yourself some teeth. He did, I was there.
You have them all out, Lil, and get a nice set,   145
He said, I swear, I can't bear to look at you.
And no more can't I, I said, and think of poor Albert,
He's been in the army four years, he wants a good time,
And if you don't give it him, there's others will, I said.
Oh is there, she said. Something o' that, I said.   150
Then I'll know who to thank, she said, and give me a straight look.
HURRY UP PLEASE ITS TIME
If you don't like it you can get on with it, I said.
Others can pick and choose if you can't.
But if Albert makes off, it won't be for lack of telling.   155
You ought to be ashamed, I said, to look so antique.
(And her only thirty-one.)
I can't help it, she said, pulling a long face,
It's them pills I took, to bring it off,[30] she said.
(She's had five already, and nearly died of young George.)   160
The chemist[31] said it would be all right, but I've never been the same.
You are a proper fool, I said.
Well, if Albert won't leave you alone, there it is, I said,
What you get married for if you don't want children?
HURRY UP PLEASE ITS TIME   165

[27] Lines adapted from a popular song, "That Shakesperian Rag."

[28] Demobilized from the army (slang).

[29] English pubkeeper's announcement of closing time.

[30] I.e., to cause an abortion.

[31] In England: "pharmacist."

Well, that Sunday Albert was home, they had a hot gammon,[32]
And they asked me in to dinner, to get the beauty of it hot—
HURRY UP PLEASE ITS TIME
HURRY UP PLEASE ITS TIME
Goonight Bill. Goodnight Lou. Goonight May. Goonight.   170
Ta ta. Goonight. Goonight.
Good night, ladies, good night, sweet ladies, good night, good night.[33]

III. The Fire Sermon[34]

The river's tent is broken: the last fingers of leaf
Clutch and sink into the wet bank. The wind
Crosses the brown land, unheard. The nymphs are departed.   175
Sweet Thames, run softly, till I end my song.[35]
The river bears no empty bottles, sandwich papers,
Silk handkerchiefs, cardboard boxes, cigarette ends
Or other testimony of summer nights. The nymphs are departed.
And their friends, the loitering heirs of city directors;[36]   180
Departed, have left no addresses.
By the waters of Leman I sat down and wept . . .[37]
Sweet Thames, run softly till I end my song,
Sweet Thames, run softly, for I speak not loud or long.
But at my back in a cold blast I hear[38]   185
The rattle of the bones, and chuckle spread from ear to ear.
A rat crept softly through the vegetation
Dragging its slimy belly on the bank
While I was fishing in the dull canal
On a winter evening round behind the gashouse   190
Musing upon the king my brother's wreck
And on the king my father's death before him.[39]
White bodies naked on the low damp ground
And bones cast in a little low dry garret,
Rattled by the rat's foot only, year to year.   195
But at my back from time to time I hear
The sound of horns and motors, which shall bring

---

[32] Bacon.

[33] From Ophelia's mad speech, after Hamlet has repudiated her (Shakespeare's *Hamlet*, Act IV, Sc. ii, ll. 72–74).

[34] Title of a sermon by the Buddha, denouncing the fires of passion, hatred, and infatuation with which the senses burn (E.,III,308).

[35] From Edmund Spenser's "Prothalamion," a nuptial eulogy describing a wedding party on the river Thames, including nymphs and swans.

[36] The "city" is London's financial district.

[37] Echo of Psalm 137, lamenting the Jews' exile from Jerusalem: "By the rivers of Babylon, there we sat down, yea, we wept, when we remembered Zion." Eliot substitutes "Leman," the French name for Lake Geneva. (Eliot was hospitalized in Lausanne, Switzerland, while writing *The Waste Land*.)

[38] Adapted from "To His Coy Mistress" by Andrew Marvell (1621–1678): "But at my back I always hear / Time's wingèd chariot hurrying near."

[39] Adapted from Shakespeare's *Tempest* (Act I, Sc. ii, ll. 389–391), as Ferdinand laments his father's presumed death: "Sitting on a bank, / Weeping against the king my father's wreck, / This music crept by me upon the waters."

Sweeney to Mrs. Porter in the spring.[40]
O the moon shone bright on Mrs. Porter
And on her daughter
They wash their feet in soda water   200
Et O ces voix d'enfants, chantant dans la coupole![41]

    Twit twit twit
Jug jug jug jug jug jug
So rudely forc'd.
Tereu[42]   205

    Unreal City
Under the brown fog of a winter noon
Mr. Eugenides, the Smyrna[43] merchant
Unshaven, with a pocket full of currants
C.i.f. London:[44] documents at sight,   210
Asked me in demotic[45] French
To luncheon at the Cannon Street Hotel[46]
Followed by a weekend at the Metropole.

    At the violet hour, when the eyes and back   215
Turn upward from the desk, when the human engine waits
Like a taxi throbbing waiting,
I Tiresias, though blind, throbbing between two lives,[47]
Old man with wrinkled female breasts, can see
At the violet hour, the evening hour that strives   220
Homeward, and brings the sailor home from sea,[48]
The typist home at teatime, clears her breakfast, lights
Her stove, and lays out food in tins.
Out of the window perilously spread
Her drying combinations[49] touched by the sun's last rays,   225
On the divan are piled (at night her bed)
Stockings, slippers, camisoles, and stays.[50]

---

[40] Sweeney, as in Eliot's other poems, represents
vulgar humanity. Mrs. Porter and her daughter
appear in a bawdy song from World War I.
The allusion (E.,III,197) is to a poem by John
Day (1574–1640?) that mentions Actaeon's
violation of the goddess Diana's privacy as he
spied on her as she was bathing, an offense that
was punished by death.

[41] French: "And O those treble voices, singing in
the dome!" This is the closing line of the
sonnet "Parsifal" by Paul Verlaine (1844–1896).
In Wagner's opera *Parsifal*, the voices of boy
sopranos are heard up high, from the wings, in
the final affirmation of Parsifal's salvation once
he has defeated the seductress Kundry, thereby
preserving his sexual purity.

[42] A reprise of the nightingale's song and the story
of Philomel and Tereus.

[43] Turkish port.

[44] "Carriage and insurance free" to London.

[45] Vulgar.

[46] Presumably, a homosexual assignation in a
luxury hotel in Brighton.

[47] Tiresias, a blind prophet, had been transformed
into a woman for seven years; when asked by
the gods who had greater pleasure in sex, men
or women, he answered that it was women
(E.,III,218).

[48] The allusion is to Sappho's poem (CXLIX) on
the evening star, which brings all things home
that the morning had dispersed.

[49] Underwear.

[50] Corsets.

I Tiresias, old man with wrinkled dugs[51]
Perceived the scene, and foretold the rest—
I too awaited the expected guest.   230
He, the young man carbuncular,[52] arrives,
A small house agent's clerk, with one bold stare,
One of the low on whom assurance sits
As a silk hat on a Bradford millionaire.[53]
The time is now propitious, as he guesses,   235
The meal is ended, she is bored and tired,
Endeavours to engage her in caresses
Which still are unreproved, if undesired.
Flushed and decided, he assaults at once;
Exploring hands encounter no defence;   240
His vanity requires no response,
And makes a welcome of indifference.
(And I Tiresias have foresuffered all
Enacted on this same divan or bed;
I who have sat by Thebes below the wall   245
And walked among the lowest of the dead.)[54]
Bestows one final patronising kiss,
And gropes his way, finding the stairs unlit . . .

   She turns and looks a moment in the glass,
Hardly aware of her departed lover;   250
Her brain allows one half-formed thought to pass:
"Well now that's done: and I'm glad it's over."
When lovely woman stoops to folly and
Paces about her room again, alone,
She smoothes her hair with automatic hand,   255
And puts a record on the gramophone.[55]

   "This music crept by me upon the waters"
And along the Strand,[56] up Queen Victoria Street.
O City city, I can sometimes hear
Beside a public bar in Lower Thames Street,   260
The pleasant whining of a mandoline
And a clatter and a chatter from within
Where fishmen lounge at noon: where the walls
Of Magnus Martyr[57] hold
Inexplicable splendour of Ionian white and gold.   265

[51] Breasts.
[52] I.e., suffering from acne.
[53] A *nouveau riche* industrialist from Bradford, Yorkshire.
[54] Tiresias lived in Thebes, and in the afterlife in Hades.
[55] Echo of *The Vicar of Wakefield* by Oliver Goldsmith (1728–1774), in which Olivia recalls her seduction: "When lovely woman stoops to folly, / And finds too late that men betray, / What charm can soothe her melancholy? / What art can wash her guilt away?"
[56] London street.
[57] London church built by the famous architect Sir Christopher Wren (1632–1723) (E.,III,264).

The river sweats
Oil and tar
The barges drift
With the turning tide
Red sails   270
Wide
To leeward, swing on the heavy spar.
The barges wash
Drifting logs
Down Greenwich reach[58]   275
Past the Isle of Dogs.[59]
              Weialala leia
              Wallala leialala[60]

     Elizabeth and Leicester[61]
Beating oars   280
The stern was formed
A gilded shell
Red and gold
The brisk swell
Rippled both shores   285
Southwest wind
Carried down stream
The peal of bells
White towers
              Weialala leia   290
              Wallala leialala

"Trams[62] and dusty trees.
Highbury bore me. Richmond and Kew
Undid me.[63] By Richmond I raised my knees
Supine on the floor of a narrow canoe."   295

   "My feet are at Moorgate,[64] and my heart
Under my feet. After the event
He wept. He promised 'a new start.'
I made no comment. What should I resent?"

---

[58] Along the Thames River at Greenwich.
[59] Peninsula in the Thames opposite Greenwich
where Queen Elizabeth I was born.
[60] From the song of the Rhinemaidens in
Wagner's *Ring* cycle. These are the river
nymphs who open the tetralogy and who
repossess their Rhinegold at the end.
[61] Queen Elizabeth I and Robert Dudley, earl of
Leicester. The account of their boat ride on the

Thames (E.,III,279) is drawn from an incident,
retold by the Spanish ambassador, in which
Elizabeth and Leicester joked about their
marrying. Of course no marriage took place.
[62] Streetcars.
[63] Highbury, Richmond, and Kew are areas near
London. The passage rephrases Dante's "Siena
bore me; Maremma undid me" (E.,III,64).
[64] Slum in East London.

"On Margate Sands.[65]   300
I can connect
Nothing with nothing.
The broken fingernails of dirty hands.
My people humble people who expect
Nothing."   305
                    la la

To Carthage then I came[66]

        Burning burning burning burning[67]
O Lord Thou pluckest me out[68]
O Lord Thou pluckest   310

burning

IV. Death by Water[69]

Phlebas the Phoenician, a fortnight dead,
Forgot the cry of gulls, and the deep sea swell
And the profit and loss.
                        A current under sea   315
Picked his bones in whispers. As he rose and fell
He passed the stages of his age and youth
Entering the whirlpool.
                        Gentile or Jew
O you who turn the wheel and look to windward,   320
Consider Phlebas, who was once handsome and tall as you.

V. What the Thunder Said[70]

After the torchlight red on sweaty faces
After the frosty silence in the gardens
After the agony in stony places
The shouting and the crying   325
Prison and palace and reverberation
Of thunder of spring over distant mountains
He who was living is now dead[71]
We who were living are now dying
With a little patience   330

[65] Resort on the Thames estuary.
[66] From the *Confessions* of St. Augustine; in
Carthage, Augustine continued his life of sexual
sin (E.,III,309).
[67] From the Buddha's Fire Sermon.
[68] St. Augustine (*Confessions*) thanks God for
having plucked him out of the life of sin.
[69] Eliot had dedicated his first volume of verse to
the memory of his French friend Jean Verdenal,
who had drowned. (See Madame Sosostris's
warning [I, 55].)
[70] The thunder is the voice of God in the Indian
Upanishads (E.,V,402).
[71] The opening of this section recalls Jesus' agony
in the Garden of Gethsemane, his betrayal by
Judas, his judging by Pontius Pilate in the
palace, and his death.

Here is no water but only rock
Rock and no water and the sandy road
The road winding above among the mountains
Which are mountains of rock without water
If there were water we should stop and drink   335
Amongst the rock one cannot stop or think
Sweat is dry and feet are in the sand
If there were only water amongst the rock
Dead mountain mouth of carious[72] teeth that cannot spit
Here one can neither stand nor lie nor sit   340
There is not even silence in the mountains
But dry sterile thunder without rain
There is not even solitude in the mountains
But red sullen faces sneer and snarl
From doors of mudcracked houses   345
                    If there were water

     And no rock
     If there were rock
     And also water
     And water   350
     A spring
     A pool among the rock
     If there were the sound of water only
     Not the cicada
     And dry grass singing   355
     But sound of water over a rock
     Where the hermit-thrush sings in the pine trees
     Drip drop drip drop drop drop drop
     But there is no water

     Who is the third who walks always beside you?[73]   360
When I count, there are only you and I together
But when I look ahead up the white road
There is always another one walking beside you
Gliding wrapt in a brown mantle, hooded
I do not know whether a man or a woman   365
—But who is that on the other side of you?

     What is that sound high in the air
Murmur of maternal lamentation
Who are those hooded hordes swarming
Over endless plains, stumbling in cracked earth   370
Ringed by the flat horizon only
What is the city over the mountains

---

[72] Decayed.
[73] Eliot suggests here the hallucinations of
Antarctic explorers; he also recalls (E.,V, introductory note) Christ's accompanying, unrecognized, two disciples to Emmaus after his resurrection.

Cracks and reforms and bursts in the violet air
Falling towers
Jerusalem Athens Alexandria   375
Vienna London
Unreal

    A woman drew her long black hair out tight
And fiddled whisper music on those strings
And bats with baby faces in the violet light   380
Whistled, and beat their wings
And crawled head downward down a blackened wall
And upside down in air were towers
Tolling reminiscent bells, that kept the hours
And voices singing out of empty cisterns and exhausted wells.   385

    In this decayed hole among the mountains
In the faint moonlight, the grass is singing
Over the tumbled graves, about the chapel
There is the empty chapel,[74] only the wind's home.
It has no windows, and the door swings,   390
Dry bones can harm no one.
Only a cock stood on the rooftree
Co co rico co co rico
In a flash of lightning. Then a damp gust
Bringing rain   395

    Ganga[75] was sunken, and the limp leaves
Waited for rain, while the black clouds
Gathered far distant, over Himavant.[76]
The jungle crouched, humped in silence.
Then spoke the thunder   400
DA
Datta:[77] what have we given?
My friend, blood shaking my heart
The awful daring of a moment's surrender
Which an age of prudence can never retract   405
By this, and this only, we have existed
Which is not to be found in our obituaries
Or in memories draped by the beneficent spider
Or under seals broken by the lean solicitor
In our empty rooms   410
DA

[74] In Arthurian legend, the Chapel Perilous, where the Grail knights prayed before they set out to find the Holy Grail.
[75] The Ganges, India's sacred river.
[76] The Himalayas.
[77] Sanskrit for "give," the first word of the thunder in the Upanishads.

Dayadhvam:[78] I have heard the key
Turn in the door once and turn once only
We think of the key, each in his prison
Thinking of the key, each confirms a prison   415
Only at nightfall, aethereal rumours
Revive for a moment a broken Coriolanus[79]
DA
Damyata:[80] The boat responded
Gaily, to the hand expert with sail and oar   420
The sea was calm, your heart would have responded
Gaily, when invited, beating obedient
To controlling hands

                       I sat upon the shore
Fishing,[81] with the arid plain behind me   425
Shall I at least set my lands in order?[82]
London Bridge is falling down falling down falling down
Poi s'ascose nel foco che gli affina[83]
Quando fiam uti chelidon[84]—O swallow swallow
Le Prince d'Aquitaine à la tour abolie[85]   430
These fragments I have shored against my ruins
Why then Ile fit you. Hieronymo's mad againe.[86]
Datta. Dayadhvam. Damyata.
           Shantih shantih shantih[87]

1922

Notes on "The Waste Land"[88]

Not only the title, but the plan and a good deal of the incidental symbolism of the
poem were suggested by Miss Jessie L. Weston's book on the Grail legend: *From*

[78] Sanskrit: "sympathize."
[79] Shakespeare's tragic hero who betrayed his own country and then betrayed the opposite camp.
[80] Sanskrit: "Control yourselves."
[81] Eliot's note refers to the Fisher King of the Grail legend (E.,V,425).
[82] Allusion to God's command in Isaiah 38:1: "Set thine house in order: for thou shalt die, and not live."
[83] In the *Purgatorio* (*Purgatory*) of Dante's *Divine Comedy,* the Provençal poet Arnaut Daniel implores Dante's regard: "Then he hid himself in the fire that refines them."
[84] "When will I be like the swallow" (and have a mate and be able to sing again)? From the late Latin poem *Pervigilium Veneris* (*The Vigil of Venus*), a love complaint (E.,V,429).
[85] French: "The prince of Aquitaine of the ruined tower." From the sonnet "El Desdichado" ("The Disinherited Son") by Gérard de Nerval

(1808–1855). The passage reads: "I am the man of shadows, the widower, unconsoled, / The prince of Aquitaine of the ruined tower, / My only star is dead, and my starry lute / Bears the black sun of melancholia."
[86] Lines from Elizabethan playwright Thomas Kyd's revenge play *The Spanish Tragedy.* "I'll suit your wish," says the bereaved father Hieronymo, agreeing to write a play by means of which, even though mad, he revenges himself for the murder of his son and then kills himself.
[87] Sanskrit: the formal ending of an Upanishad; equivalent, says Eliot, to "the peace which passeth understanding" (E.,v.,434).
[88] In its original appearance in journals in both England and America, *The Waste Land* had no notes. When it appeared as a separate publication, Eliot was asked to fill out the pages and added the notes.

Ritual to Romance (Cambridge). Indeed, so deeply am I indebted, Miss Weston's book will elucidate the difficulties of the poem much better than my notes can do; and I recommend it (apart from the great interest of the book itself) to any who think such elucidation of the poem worth the trouble. To another work of anthropology I am indebted in general, one which has influenced our generation profoundly; I mean *The Golden Bough*;[89] I have used especially the two volumes *Adonis, Attis, Osiris*.[90] Anyone who is acquainted with these works will immediately recognise in the poem certain references to vegetation ceremonies.

I. The Burial of the Dead

Line 20. Cf. Ezekiel II, i.

    23. Cf. Ecclesiastes XII, v.

    31. V. Tristan und Isolde, I, verses 5–8.

    42. Id. III, verse 24.

    46. I am not familiar with the exact constitution of the Tarot pack of cards, from which I have obviously departed to suit my own convenience. The Hanged Man, a member of the traditional pack, fits my purpose in two ways: because he is associated in my mind with the Hanged God of Frazer, and because I associate him with the hooded figure in the passage of the disciples to Emmaus in Part V. The Phoenician Sailor and the Merchant appear later; also the "crowds of people," and Death by Water is executed in Part IV. The Man with Three Staves (an authentic member of the Tarot pack) I associate, quite arbitrarily, with the Fisher King himself.

    60. Cf. Baudelaire:

      "Fourmillante cité, cité pleine de rêves,

      "Où le spectre en plein jour raccroche le passant."[91]

    63. Cf. Inferno III, 55–57:

                "si lunga tratta

      di gente, ch'io non avrei mai creduto

      che morte tanta n'avesse disfatta."[92]

    64. Cf. Inferno IV, 25–27:

      "Quivi, secondo che per ascoltare,

      "non avea pianto, ma' che di sospiri,

      "che l'aura eterna facevan tremare."[93]

    68. A phenomenon which I have often noticed.

    74. Cf. the Dirge in Webster's *White Devil*.

    76. V. Baudelaire, Preface to *Fleurs du Mal*.

---

[89] Sir James Frazer's compendium of myths and religions (1890).

[90] Vegetation gods who die and are reborn.

[91] From "Les Sept Vieillards" ("The Seven Old Men") of Charles Baudelaire (1821–1867): "Swarming city, city of dreams, / Where in broad daylight a ghost accosts the passerby."

[92] Dante: "such a long train / of people, that I would never have believed / that death had undone so many."

[93] Dante: "Here, as far as hearing could ascertain, / was no complaint, except for sighs, / that made the eternal air tremble."

II. A Game of Chess

77. Cf. *Antony and Cleopatra*, II, ii, l. 190.

92. Laquearia. V. *Aeneid*, I, 726:
    dependent lychni laquearibus aureis incensi / et noctem flammis funalia vincunt.[94]

98. Sylvan scene. V. Milton, *Paradise Lost*, IV, 140.

99. V. Ovid, *Metamorphoses*, VI, Philomela.

100. Cf. Part III, l. 204.

115. Cf. Part III, l. 195.

118. Cf. Webster: "Is the wind in that door still?"[95]

126. Cf. Part I, l. 37, 48.

138. Cf. the game of chess in Middleton's *Women beware Women*.[96]

III. The Fire Sermon

176. V. Spenser, *Prothalamion*.

192. Cf. *The Tempest*, I, ii.

196. Cf. Marvell, *To His Coy Mistress*.

197. Cf. Day, *Parliament of Bees*:
    "When of the sudden, listening, you shall hear,
    "A noise of horns and hunting, which shall bring
    "Actaeon to Diana in the spring,
    "Where all shall see her naked skin . . ."

199. I do not know the origin of the ballad from which these lines are taken: it was reported to me from Sydney, Australia.

202. V. Verlaine, *Parsifal*.

210. The currants were quoted at a price "carriage and insurance free to London"; and the Bill of Lading etc. were to be handed to the buyer upon payment of the sight draft.

218. Tiresias, although a mere spectator and not indeed a "character," is yet the most important personage in the poem, uniting all the rest. Just as the one-eyed merchant, seller of currants, melts into the Phoenician Sailor, and the latter is not wholly distinct from Ferdinand Prince of Naples,[97] so all the women are one woman, and the two sexes meet in Tiresias. What Tiresias *sees*, in fact, is the substance of the poem. The whole passage from Ovid is of great anthropological interest:
    . . . Cum Iunone iocos et 'maior vestra profecto est
    Quam, quae contingit maribus,' dixisse, 'voluptas.'
    Illa negat; placuit quae sit sententia docti
    Quaerere Tiresiae: venus huic erat utraque nota.

[94] "Lighted lamps hang from the gold-paneled ceiling, and flaming torches vanquish the night."
[95] In John Webster's play *The Devil's Law-Case* (1623) this is said of a dying man, meaning "Is there still breath coming from his mouth?"
[96] In this play by Thomas Middleton (1657), a guardian plays a game of chess while her ward is seduced.
[97] In Shakespeare's *The Tempest*.

Nam duo magnorum viridi coeuntia silva
Corpora serpentum baculi violaverat ictu
Deque viro factus, mirabile, femina septem
Egerat autumnos; octavo rursus eosdem
Vidit et 'est vestrae si tanta potentia plagae,'
Dixit 'ut auctoris sortem in contraria mutet,
Nunc quoque vos feriam!' percussis anguibus isdem
Forma prior rediit genetivaque venit imago.
Arbiter hic igitur sumptus de lite iocosa
Dicta Iovis firmat; gravius Saturnia iusto
Nec pro materia fertur doluisse suique
Iudicis aeterna damnavit lumina nocte,
At pater omnipotens (neque enim licet inrita cuiquam
Facta dei fecisse deo) pro lumine adempto
Scire futura dedit poenamque levavit honore.[98]

221. This may not appear as exact as Sappho's lines, but I had in mind the "longshore" or "dory" fisherman, who returns at nightfall.

253. V. Goldsmith, the song in *The Vicar of Wakefield*.

257. V. *The Tempest*, as above.

264. The interior of St. Magnus Martyr is to my mind one of the finest among Wren's interiors. See *The Proposed Demolition of Nineteen City Churches*: (P. S. King & Son, Ltd.).

266. The Song of the (three) Thames-daughters begins here. From line 292 to 306 inclusive they speak in turn. V. *Götterdämmerung*, III, i: the Rhine-daughters.

279. V. Froude, *Elizabeth*, Vol. I, ch. iv, letter of De Quadra to Philip of Spain:

"In the afternoon we were in a barge, watching the games on the river. (The queen) was alone with Lord Robert and myself on the poop, when they began to talk nonsense, and went so far that Lord Robert at last said, as I was on the spot there was no reason why they should not be married if the queen pleased."

293. Cf. *Purgatorio*, V, 133:

"Ricorditi di me, che son la Pia;
"Siena mi fe', disfecemi Maremma."[99]

307. V. St. Augustine's *Confessions*: "to Carthage then I came, where a cauldron of unholy loves sang all about mine ears."

---

[98] The passage Eliot quotes is from Ovid's *Metamorphoses* II, 421–43: "Jove said jestingly to Juno: 'You wives have greater pleasure in love than husbands.' She denied it. It pleased them to ask the opinion of the learned Tiresias, who knew both sorts of love. For once, with a blow of his staff, he had separated two copulating snakes in the forest, and was miraculously changed instantly from a man into a woman, remaining so for seven years. In the eighth year he saw the same snakes again and said, 'If striking you is so powerful that it changes the sex of the one dealing the blow, then I will now strike you again.' As soon as he struck them, his former shape and masculine form were restored. As arbiter of the jesting quarrel, he supported Jove's opinion. Juno, disturbed by the decision, decreed that he should be condemned to eternal blindness. But the omnipotent god (since no god can undo what has been done by another god) gave him the power to know the future, with this honor redeeming his loss of sight."

[99] La Pia, born in Siena, was murdered by her husband in his castle at Maremma: "Remember me, who am La Pia; / Siena made me, Maremma undid me."

308. The complete text of the Buddha's Fire Sermon (which corresponds in importance to the Sermon on the Mount) from which these words are taken, will be found translated in the late Henry Clarke Warren's *Buddhism in Translation* (Harvard Oriental Series). Mr. Warren was one of the great pioneers of Buddhist studies in the Occident.

309. From St. Augustine's *Confessions* again. The collocation of these two representatives of eastern and western asceticism, as the culmination of this part of the poem, is not an accident.

V. What the Thunder Said

In the first part of Part V three themes are employed: the journey to Emmaus, the approach to the Chapel Perilous (see Miss Weston's book) and the present decay of Eastern Europe.

357. This is *Turdus aonalaschkae pallasii,* the hermit-thrush which I have heard in Quebec Province. Chapman says (*Handbook of Birds of Eastern North America*) "it is most at home in secluded woodland and thickety retreats. . . . Its notes are not remarkable for variety or volume, but in purity and sweetness of tone and exquisite modulation they are unequalled." Its "water-dripping song" is justly celebrated.

360. The following lines were stimulated by the account of one of the Antarctic expeditions (I forget which, but I think one of Shackleton's): it was related that the party of explorers, at the extremity of their strength, had the constant delusion that there was *one more member* than could actually be counted.

367–77. Cf. Hermann Hesse, *Blick ins Chaos:* "Schon ist halb Europa, schon ist zumindest der halbe Osten Europas auf dem Wege zum Chaos, fährt betrunken im heiligem Wahn am Abgrund entlang und singt dazu, singt betrunken und hymnisch wie Dmitri Karamasoff sang. Ueber diese Lieder lacht der Bürger beleidigt, der Heilige und Seher hört sie mit Tränen."[100]

402. "Datta, dayadhvam, damyata" (Give, sympathise, control). The fable of the meaning of the Thunder is found in the *Brihadaranyaka—Upanishad,* 5, 1. A translation is found in Deussen's *Sechzig Upanishads des Veda,* p. 489.

408. Cf. Webster, *The White Devil,* V, vi:

> ". . . they'll remarry
> Ere the worm pierce your winding-sheet, ere the spider
> Make a thin curtain for your epitaphs."

412. Cf. *Inferno,* XXXIII, 46:

> "ed io senti chiavar l'uscio di sotto
> all'orribile torre."[101]

Also F. H. Bradley, *Appearance and Reality,* p. 346. "My external sensations are no less private to myself than are my thoughts or my feelings. In either case my experience falls within my own circle, a circle closed on

---

[100] "Already half of Europe, already at least half of Eastern Europe, is on the way to chaos, traveling drunken in a sort of holy ecstasy, headlong toward the abyss, singing the while, singing drunken hymns, as Dmitri Karamazov sang. The offended bourgeois laughs at these songs; the saint and the seer hear them with tears."

[101] Ugolino was imprisoned with his children, and they starved to death: "And I heard the key turn below in the door / of the horrible tower."

the outside; and, with all its elements alike, every sphere is opaque to the others which surround it. . . . In brief, regarded as an existence which appears in a soul, the whole world for each is peculiar and private to that soul."

425. V. Weston: *From Ritual to Romance;* chapter on the Fisher King.

428. V. *Purgatorio,* XXVI, 148.

> " 'Ara vos prec per aquella valor
> 'que vos guida al som de l'escalina,
> 'sovegna vos a temps de ma dolor.'
> Poi s'ascose nel foco che gli affina."[102]

429. V. *Pervigilium Veneris.* Cf. Philomela in Parts II and III.

430. V. Gérard de Nerval, Sonnet *El Desdichado.*

432. V. Kyd's *Spanish Tragedy.*

434. Shantih. Repeated as here, a formal ending to an Upanishad. "The peace which passeth understanding" is our equivalent to this word.

1922

---

from Four Quartets

Burnt Norton[*]

> τοῦ λόγου δ'ἐόντος ξυνοῦ ζώουσιν οἱ πολλοί
> ὡς ἰδίαν ἔχοντες φρόνησιν.
> *I. p. 77. Fr. 2.*
>
> ὁδὸς ἄνω κάτω μία καὶ ωὐτή.
> *I. p. 89. Fr. 60.*
> Diels: Die Fragmente der Vorsokratiker (*Herakleitos*).[1]

I

Time present and time past
Are both perhaps present in time future,
And time future contained in time past.
If all time is eternally present
All time is unredeemable.   5
What might have been is an abstraction
Remaining a perpetual possibility
Only in a world of speculation.

---

[102] The speaker is the troubadour poet Arnaut Daniel: " 'I pray you now, by the goodness / that guides you to the top of the staircase, / remember my suffering in due time.' / Then he hid himself in the fire that refines them."

[*] The poem is the first of Eliot's "Four Quartets," the other three being "East Coker," "The Dry Salvages," and "Little Gidding." Burnt Norton was a country house in Gloucestershire, visited by Eliot in 1934.

[1] Both epigraphs, quoted from Diels's *Fragments of the Presocratics,* are from the Greek philosopher Heraclitus (sixth century B.C.), who believed the whole world to be constantly in flux: "Although the Word, the Logos, is universal, most people live as though they had their own special rules." "The way up and the way down are one and the same."

What might have been and what has been
Point to one end, which is always present.
Footfalls echo in the memory
Down the passage which we did not take
Towards the door we never opened
Into the rose-garden. My words echo
Thus, in your mind.
                   But to what purpose
Disturbing the dust on a bowl of rose-leaves
I do not know.
              Other echoes
Inhabit the garden. Shall we follow?
Quick, said the bird, find them, find them,
Round the corner. Through the first gate,
Into our first world, shall we follow
The deception of the thrush? Into our first world.
There they were, dignified, invisible,
Moving without pressure, over the dead leaves,
In the autumn heat, through the vibrant air,
And the bird called, in response to
The unheard music hidden in the shrubbery,
And the unseen eyebeam crossed, for the roses
Had the look of flowers that are looked at.
There they were as our guests, accepted and accepting.
So we moved, and they, in a formal pattern,
Along the empty alley, into the box circle,
To look down into the drained pool.
Dry the pool, dry concrete, brown edged,
And the pool was filled with water out of sunlight,
And the lotos rose, quietly, quietly,
The surface glittered out of heart of light,
And they were behind us, reflected in the pool.
Then a cloud passed, and the pool was empty.
Go, said the bird, for the leaves were full of children,
Hidden excitedly, containing laughter.
Go, go, go, said the bird: human kind
Cannot bear very much reality.
Time past and time future
What might have been and what has been
Point to one end, which is always present.

II

Garlic and sapphires in the mud
Clot the bedded axle-tree.[2]

---

[2] The axle on which the world turns.

The trilling wire in the blood
Sings below inveterate scars
And reconciles forgotten wars.
The dance along the artery
The circulation of the lymph
Are figured in the drift of stars
Ascend to summer in the tree
We move above the moving tree
In light upon the figured leaf
And hear upon the sodden floor
Below, the boarhound and the boar
Pursue their pattern as before
But reconciled among the stars.

At the still point of the turning world. Neither flesh nor fleshless;
Neither from nor towards; at the still point, there the dance is,
But neither arrest nor movement. And do not call it fixity,
Where past and future are gathered. Neither movement from nor towards,
Neither ascent nor decline. Except for the point, the still point,
There would be no dance, and there is only the dance.
I can only say, *there* we have been: but I cannot say where.
And I cannot say, how long, for that is to place it in time.

The inner freedom from the practical desire,
The release from action and suffering, release from the inner
And the outer compulsion, yet surrounded
By a grace of sense, a white light still and moving,
Erhebung,[3] without motion, concentration
Without elimination, both a new world
And the old made explicit, understood
In the completion of its partial ecstasy,
The resolution of its partial horror.
Yet the enchainment of past and future
Woven in the weakness of the changing body,
Protects mankind from heaven and damnation
Which flesh cannot endure.
                    Time past and time future
Allow but a little consciousness.
To be conscious is not to be in time
But only in time can the moment in the rose-garden,
The moment in the arbour where the rain beat,
The moment in the draughty church at smokefall
Be remembered; involved with past and future.
Only through time time is conquered.

[3] German: "exaltation."

III

Here is a place of disaffection
Time before and time after
In a dim light: neither daylight
Investing form with lucid stillness
Turning shadow into transient beauty
With slow rotation suggesting permanence   95
Nor darkness to purify the soul
Emptying the sensual with deprivation
Cleansing affection from the temporal.
Neither plenitude nor vacancy. Only a flicker
Over the strained time-ridden faces   100
Distracted from distraction by distraction
Filled with fancies and empty of meaning
Tumid apathy with no concentration
Men and bits of paper, whirled by the cold wind
That blows before and after time,   105
Wind in and out of unwholesome lungs
Time before and time after.
Eructation[4] of unhealthy souls
Into the faded air, the torpid
Driven on the wind that sweeps the gloomy hills of London,   110
Hampstead and Clerkenwell, Campden and Putney,
Highgate, Primrose and Ludgate. Not here
Not here the darkness, in this twittering world.

   Descend lower, descend only
Into the world of perpetual solitude,   115
World not world, but that which is not world,
Internal darkness, deprivation
And destitution of all property,
Desiccation of the world of sense,
Evacuation of the world of fancy,   120
Inoperancy of the world of spirit;
This is the one way, and the other
Is the same, not in movement
But abstention from movement; while the world moves
In appetency, on its metalled ways   125
Of time past and time future.

IV

Time and the bell have buried the day,
The black cloud carries the sun away.

---
[4] Belching.

Will the sunflower turn to us, will the clematis
Stray down, bend to us; tendril and spray 130
Clutch and cling?
Chill
Fingers of yew be curled
Down on us? After the kingfisher's wing
Has answered light to light, and is silent, the light is still 135
At the still point of the turning world.

V

Words move, music moves
Only in time; but that which is only living
Can only die. Words, after speech, reach
Into the silence. Only by the form, the pattern, 140
Can words or music reach
The stillness, as a Chinese jar still
Moves perpetually in its stillness.
Not the stillness of the violin, while the note lasts,
Not that only, but the co-existence, 145
Or say that the end precedes the beginning,
And the end and the beginning were always there
Before the beginning and after the end.
And all is always now. Words strain,
Crack and sometimes break, under the burden, 150
Under the tension, slip, slide, perish,
Decay with imprecision, will not stay in place,
Will not stay still. Shrieking voices
Scolding, mocking, or merely chattering,
Always assail them. The Word in the desert 155
Is most attacked by voices of temptation,[5]
The crying shadow in the funeral dance,
The loud lament of the disconsolate chimera.

The detail of the pattern is movement,
As in the figure of the ten stairs.[6] 160
Desire itself is movement
Not in itself desirable;
Love is itself unmoving,
Only the cause and end of movement,
Timeless, and undesiring 165
Except in the aspect of time

[5] Reference to Satan's temptation of Jesus in the desert (Luke 4:1–12).
[6] The stairway to perfection, a Christian concept derived from the ladder on which Jacob saw angels ascending to and descending from heaven. St. John of the Cross said that the soul ascends to God by way of "the Ten Degrees of the Mystical Ladder of Divine Love."

Caught in the form of limitation
Between un-being and being.
Sudden in a shaft of sunlight
Even while the dust moves   170
There rises the hidden laughter
Of children in the foliage
Quick now, here, now, always—
Ridiculous the waste sad time
Stretching before and after.   175
1936

John Crowe Ransom
1888–1974

John Crowe Ransom, the best southern poet of his generation, combined faultless
irony with a faultless civility and tenderness, achieving a tone quite unlike that
of any other poet, a tone as far as possible from the dryly angular metaphysical
poetry of another southern poet and critic, Allen Tate. Ransom was a poet of
line rather than of color. Though he, like Tate, was influenced as an adult reader
by the English seventeenth-century poets, he also received the literary past
indirectly through the southern culture into which he was born.

The son of a Methodist minister in Tennessee, Ransom studied Latin and
Greek at Vanderbilt before going on to Oxford as a Rhodes scholar. After
military service between 1917 and 1919, he returned to teach at Vanderbilt for
almost twenty years. In 1937 he left Vanderbilt for Kenyon College in Ohio,
where he founded *The Kenyon Review* in 1939. Ransom wrote most of his poetry
between 1914 and 1927, roughly between the ages of twenty-five and forty.
Poems About God (1919), *Chills and Fever* (1924), and *Two Gentlemen in Bonds*
(1926) made his reputation as a poet, though in his *Selected Poems* (1945) he did
not include any work from his first volume. Revised editions of the *Selected
Poems* (1963, 1969) were awarded the Bollingen Prize and the National Book
Award. In his later life, Ransom was known chiefly as the writer of the book
The New Criticism (1941), which gave its name to a literary school. In that book,
Ransom discussed the critical work of four eminent contemporary writers—
I. A. Richards, T. S. Eliot, Yvor Winters, and William Empson—and suggested,
in closing, that what was wanted for the modern age was "an ontological critic,"
one who would see the literary work as a part of "the world's body," a being
rich in its own right, not one to be appropriated to abstract ideological ends. In
his own writing about poetry, Ransom emphasized the "texture" of the literary
artifact, its highly wrought fabric of language.

While Ransom was at Vanderbilt, he and a group that included Allen Tate
and Robert Penn Warren became known as the Fugitives, after the name of their
journal, a little magazine that ran for only nineteen issues over three years. The
conservative political philosophy of the Fugitives, based on a wish to preserve the

religious and economic status quo of the old South, consorted oddly with their avant-garde taste in poetry and critical theory.

Ransom, their chief theorist, knew from his own experience the work of making a poem, the delicate interrelations of its parts, the weaving of its motivations, its figures, and its rhetorical drama. As a poet, he objected to teachers' filling up time in class by discussing, for example, the Puritan revolution or Puritan theology in preference to, or to the exclusion of, any discussion of Milton's aesthetic work in making his epic poem. In arguing for pedagogical attention to the complexity of poetic texture and to the aesthetic achievement of the poem, Ransom wished to correct the philological, philosophical, and historical emphasis in American literary study. It was logical that such a corrective should come from the South, always the region in which belles lettres were best understood, while the Northeast had been formed in the theologically serious mode of Puritan reading.

Ransom's own poetry has all the delight in texture, all the irony and subtlety that one would expect from the mind that argued that attention should be paid to such matters. Though Ransom wrote in formal rhyming stanzas, his metric was accentual, based on the number of beats per line rather than on isometric feet. His tone is always at once light and grave, classical in its reserve but gracious in its tenderness. Ransom writes often about the conflict between body and spirit, about death, and about aspirations that end in defeat. He reflected on the nature of poetry in the New World: In a poem about Philomela, the grieving nightingale who stands symbolically for poetry, he asks despairingly about her status in America:

> How could her delicate dirge run democratic,
> Delivered in a cloudless boundless public place
> To an inordinate race?

Ransom brought to American literature qualities we associate with classical poetry—urbanity, shapeliness, and equilibrium. In perceiving the distinct separateness of the civilization and literature of the South, Ransom helped preserve and continue our oldest American belletristic tradition. And by turning American academic minds to the ontological uniqueness of art, Ransom profoundly influenced the aesthetic development of a generation.

Further Reading:

J. L. Stewart, *John Crowe Ransom*, 1962.
K. F. Knight, *The Poetry of John Crowe Ransom*, 1964.
R. Buffington, *The Equilibrist: A Study of John Crowe Ransom's Poems 1916–1963*, 1967.
John Crowe Ransom: Critical Essays and a Bibliography, ed. N. H. Young, 1968.
T. H. Parsons, *John Crowe Ransom*, 1969.

J. E. Magner, Jr., *John Crowe Ransom: Critical Principles and Preoccupations*, 1971.
T. D. Young, ed., *John Crowe Ransom*, 1971.
J. L. Stewart, *John Crowe Ransom*, 1972.
M. Williams, *The Poetry of John Crowe Ransom*, 1972.
T. H. Young, *Gentleman in a Dustcoat: A Biography of John Crowe Ransom*, 1977.

Text:
Selected Poems, 1978.

Piazza Piece

—I am a gentleman in a dustcoat trying
To make you hear. Your ears are soft and small
And listen to an old man not at all,
They want the young men's whispering and sighing.
But see the roses on your trellis dying   5
And hear the spectral singing of the moon;
For I must have my lovely lady soon,
I am a gentleman in a dustcoat trying.

—I am a lady young in beauty waiting
Until my truelove comes, and then we kiss.   10
But what grey man among the vines is this
Whose words are dry and faint as in a dream?
Back from my trellis, Sir, before I scream!
I am a lady young in beauty waiting.

1927

Vision by Sweetwater

Go and ask Robin to bring the girls over
To Sweetwater, said my Aunt; and that was why
It was like a dream of ladies sweeping by
The willows, clouds, deep meadowgrass, and river.

Robin's sisters and my Aunt's lily daughter   5
Laughed and talked, and tinkled light as wrens
If there were a little colony all hens
To go walking by the steep turn of Sweetwater.

Let them alone, dear Aunt, just for one minute
Till I go fishing in the dark of my mind: 10
Where have I seen before, against the wind,
These bright virgins, robed and bare of bonnet,

Flowing with music of their strange quick tongue
And adventuring with delicate paces by the stream,—
Myself a child, old suddenly at the scream   15
From one of the white throats which it hid among?

1927

Parting, Without a Sequel

She has finished and sealed the letter
At last, which he so richly has deserved,
With characters venomous and hatefully curved,
And nothing could be better.

But even as she gave it   5
Saying to the blue-capped functioner of doom,
"Into his hands," she hoped the leering groom
Might somewhere lose and leave it.

Then all the blood
Forsook the face. She was too pale for tears,   10
Observing the ruin of her younger years.
She went and stood

Under her father's vaunting oak
Who kept his peace in wind and sun, and glistened
Stoical in the rain; to whom she listened   15
If he spoke.

And now the agitation of the rain
Rasped his sere leaves, and he talked low and
     gentle
Reproaching the wan daughter by the lintel;
Ceasing and beginning again.   20

Away went the messenger's bicycle,
His serpent's track went up the hill forever,
And all the time she stood there hot as fever
And cold as any icicle.

1927

Dead Boy

The little cousin is dead, by foul subtraction,
A green bough from Virginia's aged tree,
And none of the county kin like the transaction,
Nor some of the world of outer dark, like me.

A boy not beautiful, nor good, nor clever,   5
A black cloud full of storms too hot for keeping,
A sword beneath his mother's heart—yet never
Woman bewept her babe as this is weeping.

A pig with a pasty face, so I had said,
Squealing for cookies, kinned by poor pretense   10
With a noble house. But the little man quite dead,
I see the forbears' antique lineaments.

The elder men have strode by the box of death
To the wide flag porch, and muttering low send round
The bruit¹ of the day. O friendly waste of breath!   15
Their hearts are hurt with a deep dynastic wound.

He was pale and little, the foolish neighbors say;
The first-fruits, saith the Preacher, the Lord hath taken;
But this was the old tree's late branch wrenched away,
Grieving the sapless limbs, the shorn and shaken.   20
1927

The Equilibrists

Full of her long white arms and milky skin
He had a thousand times remembered sin.
Alone in the press of people traveled he,
Minding her jacinth, and myrrh, and ivory.

Mouth he remembered: the quaint orifice   5
From which came heat that flamed upon the kiss,
Till cold words came down spiral from the head,
Grey doves from the officious tower illsped.

Body: it was a white field ready for love,
On her body's field, with the gaunt tower above,   10
The lilies grew, beseeching him to take,
If he would pluck and wear them, bruise and break.

Eyes talking: Never mind the cruel words,
Embrace my flowers, but not embrace the swords.

¹ Rumor.

But what they said, the doves came straightway flying   15
And unsaid: Honor, Honor, they came crying.

Importunate her doves. Too pure, too wise,
Clambering on his shoulder, saying, Arise,
Leave me now, and never let us meet,
Eternal distance now command thy feet.   20

Predicament indeed, which thus discovers
Honor among thieves, Honor between lovers.
O such a little word is Honor, they feel!
But the grey word is between them cold as steel.

At length I saw these lovers fully were come   25
Into their torture of equilibrium;
Dreadfully had forsworn each other, and yet
They were bound each to each, and they did not forget.

And rigid as two painful stars, and twirled
About the clustered night their prison world,   30
They burned with fierce love always to come near,
But Honor beat them back and kept them clear.

Ah, the strict lovers, they are ruined now!
I cried in anger. But with puddled brow
Devising for those gibbeted and brave   35
Came I descanting: Man, what would you have?

For spin your period out, and draw your breath,
A kinder sæculum¹ begins with Death.
Would you ascend to Heaven and bodiless dwell?
Or take your bodies honorless to Hell?   40

In Heaven you have heard no marriage is,
No white flesh tinder to your lecheries,
Your male and female tissue sweetly shaped
Sublimed away, and furious blood escaped.

Great lovers lie in Hell, the stubborn ones   45
Infatuate of the flesh upon the bones;
Stuprate,² they rend each other when they kiss,
The pieces kiss again, no end to this.

But still I watched them spinning, orbited nice.
Their flames were not more radiant than their ice.   50

---

¹ World.   ² Violated.

I dug in the quiet earth and wrought the tomb
And made these lines to memorize their doom:—

> #### EPITAPH
>
> *Equilibrists lie here; stranger, tread light;*
> *Close, but untouching in each other's sight;*
> *Mouldered the lips and ashy the tall skull.*
> *Let them lie perilous and beautiful.*

55

1927

E. E. Cummings
1894–1962

Cummings belongs to the part of the modernist movement that wanted to experiment with the visual appearance of the printed page. Both Guillaume Apollinaire and Stéphane Mallarmé in France had scattered typography over the page, and Cummings adopted their inventions (which would later engender "concrete poetry") to his own purposes. Numbers and letters fall like confetti down his pages, giving his *Collected Poems* the look of a volume printed by a tipsy typesetter. Cummings's typographical experiments arose in part from his visual gifts. He was a painter all his life, and his sophisticated and humorous paintings and drawings are still regularly shown in museums. But his experiments arose perhaps even more from his wish to upset the predictability of the printed page and the expectations of conventional readers.

Cummings was born in Cambridge, Massachusetts, the child of cultured parents. His father was a Congregational minister and professor at Harvard, but it was chiefly his mother, to whom Cummings was devoted all his life, who encouraged her son's writing. It seems likely that a good deal of Cummings's wish to shock stemmed originally from his repudiation of his father's way of life. For all Cummings's protestations of filial piety in "my father moved through dooms of love," he was irritated by his father's unremitting seriousness, so alien to his own volatile temperament; the role of *enfant terrible* was one Cummings never tired of playing.

Cummings's father taught English and social ethics at Harvard, and Cummings himself graduated from Harvard in 1915 and took an M.A. in literature there the following year. At Harvard, through knowledgeable friends like Scofield Thayer and Witter Bynner, Cummings discovered new art and music. At his Harvard graduation, having won the privilege of delivering one of the commencement "parts" (or speeches), Cummings praised cubist painting and Stravinsky's music. He knew such tastes were opposed by the majority of his teachers and fellow students. In his writing he continually pitted the values of what he scornfully called "mostpeople" against the bohemian tastes of the artist.

Cummings went off to France in 1917 as a volunteer ambulance driver for the Red Cross. Through his own unconventional behavior, he was suspected of being a spy and was detained, with his friend Slater Brown, for three months in a French internment camp. His father wrote letters to friends in Washington pleading for intervention on his son's behalf; through the influence of President Woodrow Wilson, Cummings was freed. He described his imprisonment in *The Enormous Room* (1922), the book that first brought him fame.

Cummings lived in France from 1921 to 1923, where he was exposed to a bohemian culture that he imitated when he finally settled, in 1924, in New York's Greenwich Village, where he spent the rest of his life writing and painting. His mother helped to support him until she died. Cummings married three times and had a daughter by his first wife, who concealed Cummings's paternity from the child because she had remarried and wished the child to believe that her second husband was the father. Cummings acknowledged his daughter when she was in her twenties, and they became affectionately attached to each other.

Cummings's first poems were published in *The Dial* in 1920. In his lifetime, his most frequently anthologized poems were those in which he was most sentimental. But his greatest gift was as a satirist. He could take the measure of literary falsity, patriotic cant, or intellectual humbug with a scathing phrase; he scorned conventional verbal and political pieties and conventional standards of behavior. He preached a neo-paganism of untroubled sexual pleasure, childlike egotism, and irrepressible impudence; a myth of spontaneity animated his aesthetic. Of course, the ingenuity visible in his poems about the grasshopper and the falling leaf demonstrates how unspontaneous such compositions actually are. An acrobat of words, Cummings scorned discursive logic and political strategy. If this world did not suit, "there's a hell / of a good universe next door; let's go." He establishes only two poles of thought, ignorance and belief; there is, to him, something suspect about the middle ground of learning, on the one hand, and skepticism, on the other.

In American literary history, Cummings ranks as a memorable documentary writer because of *The Enormous Room* and *Eimi* (1933), his account of travels in Russia after the rise of Stalin (whom he hated). Both books are vivid in rapidly noted sensory detail and irrepressibly energetic in style. Cummings's early poetry remains a body of inventive and ebullient work, raising provocative aesthetic questions. Is something that cannot be read aloud a poem? If so, what do we mean by the word *poem*? Can a poem incorporate slang, obscenity, advertising jargon, dialect? Is all language material for poetry? Must the line be the unit of the poem? Does the eye have as much right to the poem as the ear? Is the sonnet dead or can it be resuscitated? Can satiric lyrics be written in puritanical America? These questions are still relevant.

Cummings's wish to believe that all people are at heart alike in love and that all desires are simple ones led him into a conventional sentimentalizing of the erotic life. But his capacity for play in language and for vivid satire of America and its institutions ensures him a permanent place in American literature.

Further Reading:
C. Norman, *The Magic Maker, E. E. Cummings,* 1958.
N. Friedman, *E. E. Cummings: The Art of His Poetry,* 1960.
N. Friedman, *E. E. Cummings: The Growth of a Writer,* 1964.
B. A. Marks, *E. E. Cummings,* 1964.
R. E. Wegner, *The Poetry and Prose of E. E. Cummings,* 1965.
E. Triem, *E. E. Cummings,* 1969.
B. K. Dumas, *A Remembrance of Miracles,*

1974.
G. Lane, *I Am: A Study of E. E. Cummings' Poems,* 1976.
P. Lauter, *E. E. Cummings,* 1976.
R. Kidder, *E. E. Cummings: An Introduction to the Poetry,* 1979.
R. S. Kennedy, *Dreams in the Mirror: A Biography of E. E. Cummings,* 1980.
A Concordance to the Poems of E. E. Cummings, ed. K. McBride, 1982.

Text:
Complete Poems, 1972.
See also *Selected Letters of E. E. Cummings,* ed.

F. W. Dupee and G. Stade, 1969.

[in Just-]

in Just-
spring   when the world is mud-
luscious the little
lame balloonman

whistles   far   and wee   5

and eddieandbill come
running from marbles and
piracies and it's
spring

when the world is puddle-wonderful   10

the queer
old balloonman whistles
far   and   wee
and bettyandisbel come dancing

from hop-scotch and jump-rope and   15

```
          it's
          spring
          and
              the

                    goat-footed[1]                                   20

          balloonMan        whistles
          far
          and
          wee
          1923
```

[the Cambridge ladies who live in furnished souls]

the Cambridge ladies who live in furnished souls
are unbeautiful and have comfortable minds
(also, with the church's protestant blessings
daughters, unscented shapeless spirited)
they believe in Christ and Longfellow,[1] both dead,   5
are invariably interested in so many things—
at the present writing one still finds
delighted fingers knitting for the is it Poles?
perhaps. While permanent faces coyly bandy
scandal of Mrs. N and Professor D   10
. . . . the Cambridge ladies do not care, above
Cambridge if sometimes in its box of
sky lavender and cornerless, the
moon rattles like a fragment of angry candy
          1923

[1] Characteristic of Pan, ancient Greek god of woods and shepherds.

[1] Henry Wadsworth Longfellow (1807–1882), Cambridge poet and Harvard professor.

[mr youse needn't be so spry]

mr youse needn't be so spry
concernin questions arty

each has his tastes but as for i
i likes a certain party

gimme the he-man's solid bliss   5
for youse ideas i'll match youse

a pretty girl who naked is
is worth a million statues
1926

[she being Brand]

she being Brand

-new; and you
know consequently a
little stiff i was
careful of her and(having   5

thoroughly oiled the universal
joint tested my gas felt of
her radiator made sure her springs were O.

K.)i went right to it flooded-the-carburetor cranked her

up,slipped the   10
clutch(and then somehow got into reverse she
kicked what
the hell)next
minute i was back in neutral tried and

again slo-wly; bare,ly nudg.   ing(my   15

lev-er Right-
oh and her gears being in
A I shape passed
from low through
second-in-to-high like   20
greasedlightning)just as we turned the corner of Divinity

avenue[1] i touched the accelerator and give

her the juice,good

                        (it
was the first ride and believe i we was   25
happy to see how nice she acted right up to
the last minute coming back down by the Public
Gardens[2] i slammed on
the

internalexpanding   30
&
externalcontracting
brakes Bothatonce and
brought allofher tremB
-ling   35
to a: dead.

stand-
;Still)
1926

["next to of course god america i]

"next to of course god america i
love you land of the pilgrims' and so forth oh
say can you see by the dawn's early my
country 'tis of centuries come and go
and are no more what of it we should worry   5
in every language even deafanddumb

---

[1] Street in Cambridge, Massachusetts, where the
Harvard Divinity School is located.
    [2] Properly, the Public Garden, a park in Boston.

thy sons acclaim your glorious name by gorry
by jingo by gee by gosh by gum
why talk of beauty what could be more beaut-
iful than these heroic happy dead   10
who rushed like lions to the roaring slaughter
they did not stop to think they died instead
then shall the voice of liberty be mute?"

He spoke. And drank rapidly a glass of water
1926

[my sweet old etcetera]

my sweet old etcetera
aunt lucy during the recent

war could and what
is more did tell you just
what everybody was fighting   5

for,
my sister

isabel created hundreds
(and
hundreds) of socks not to   10
mention shirts fleaproof earwarmers

etcetera wristers etcetera, my
mother hoped that

i would die etcetera
bravely of course my father used   15
to become hoarse talking about how it was
a privilege and if only he
could meanwhile my

self etcetera lay quietly
in the deep mud et   20

cetera
(dreaming,

et
    cetera, of
Your smile   25
eyes knees and of your Etcetera)
1926

[i sing of Olaf glad and big]

i sing of Olaf glad and big
whose warmest heart recoiled at war:
a conscientious object—or

his wellbelovéd colonel(trig
westpointer most succinctly bred)   5
took erring Olaf soon in hand;
but—though an host of overjoyed
noncoms(first knocking on the head
him)do through icy waters roll
that helplessness which others stroke   10
with brushes recently employed
anent this muddy toiletbowl,
while kindred intellects evoke
allegiance per blunt instruments—
Olaf(being to all intents   15
a corpse and wanting any rag
upon what God unto him gave)
responds, without getting annoyed
"I will not kiss your fucking flag"

straightway the silver bird looked grave   20
(departing hurriedly to shave)

but—though all kinds of officers
(a yearning nation's blueeyed pride)
their passive prey did kick and curse
until for wear their clarion   25
voices and boots were much the worse,
and egged the firstclassprivates on
his rectum wickedly to tease
by means of skilfully applied
bayonets roasted hot with heat—   30

Olaf(upon what were once knees)
does almost ceaselessly repeat
"there is some shit I will not eat"

our president, being of which
assertions duly notified   35
threw the yellowsonofabitch
into a dungeon, where he died

Christ(of His mercy infinite)
i pray to see; and Olaf, too

preponderatingly because   40
unless statistics lie he was
more brave than me:more blond than you.
1931

[r-p-o-p-h-e-s-s-a-g-r]

                 r-p-o-p-h-e-s-s-a-g-r
        who
a)s w(e loo)k
upnowgath
        PPEGORHRASS   5
                  eringint(o-
aThe):l
   eA
      !p:
S   a   10
      (r
rIvInG   gRrEaPsPhOs)
                    to
rea(be)rran(com)gi(e)ngly
,grasshopper;   15
1935

[may i feel said he]

may i feel said he
(i'll squeal said she
just once said he)
it's fun said she

(may i touch said he   5
how much said she
a lot said he)
why not said she

(let's go said he
not too far said she   10
what's too far said he
where you are said she)

may i stay said he
(which way said she
like this said he   15
if you kiss said she

may i move said he
is it love said she)
if you're willing said he
(but you're killing said she   20

but it's life said he
but your wife said she
now said he)
ow said she

(tiptop said he   25
don't stop said she
oh no said he)
go slow said she

(cccome?said he   30
ummm said she)
you're divine!said he
(you are Mine said she)
1935

[this little bride & groom are]

this little bride & groom are
standing)in a kind
of crown he dressed
in black candy she

veiled with candy white   5
carrying a bouquet of
pretend flowers this
candy crown with this candy

little bride & little
groom in it kind of stands on   10
a thin ring which stands on a much
less thin very much more

big & kinder of ring & which
kinder of stands on a
much more than very much   15
biggest & thickest & kindest

of ring & all one two three rings
are cake & everything is protected by-
cellophane against anything(because
nothing really exists   20

1938

[anyone lived in a pretty how town]

anyone lived in a pretty how town
(with up so floating many bells down)
spring summer autumn winter
he sang his didn't he danced his did.

Women and men(both little and small)   5
cared for anyone not at all
they sowed their isn't they reaped their same
sun moon stars rain

children guessed(but only a few
and down they forgot as up they grew   10
autumn winter spring summer)
that noone loved him more by more

when by now and tree by leaf
she laughed his joy she cried his grief
bird by snow and stir by still   15
anyone's any was all to her

someones married their everyones
laughed their cryings and did their dance
(sleep wake hope and then)they
said their nevers they slept their dream   20

stars rain sun moon
(and only the snow can begin to explain
how children are apt to forget to remember
with up so floating many bells down)

one day anyone died i guess   25
(and noone stooped to kiss his face)
busy folk buried them side by side
little by little and was by was

all by all and deep by deep   30
and more by more they dream their sleep
noone and anyone earth by april
wish by spirit and if by yes.

Women and men(both dong and ding)
summer autumn winter spring   35
reaped their sowing and went their came
sun moon stars rain
1940

[1(a]

```
1(a

le
af
fa

ll                                                        5

s)
one
l

iness
```

1958

Hart Crane
1899–1932

In his short life, Hart Crane left a small legacy of highly worked and powerfully
thought-through poems in which the legacy of the modernist French poets
Rimbaud and Mallarmé first entered our literature. Like Rimbaud in his "Bateau
Ivre," Crane wrote a poetry of headlong momentum, his precipitous current
flowing, like the Mississippi, toward a revelatory ocean. Like Mallarmé, Crane
pressed syntax to its utmost compression, and by transferred epithets and
periphrases he made up a heady texture rich with music and light. Crane's poems
name Emily Dickinson, Herman Melville, and Walt Whitman as his predecessors,
but Robert Lowell was right in calling Crane "the Shelley of our age"; Crane
had learned from Shelley the ecstatic hope and incandescent love that opposed
themselves to skepticism and irony, which they both nonetheless knew well.

Nothing in Crane's life or background explains his meteoric poetic genius. He
was born in Cleveland, Ohio, of unhappily married parents, who were divorced
when he was seventeen. Crane's businessman father, a candy manufacturer, hoped
that his son would enter his business. Crane's predatory mother, from whom he
had eventually to cut himself off, bound her son ever more tightly to her.
Crane's schooling was interrupted by his mother's insisting he accompany her on
trips; lacking enough credits at the end of high school to enter college, Crane
took jobs in advertising, first in Cleveland and then New York. The jobs bored
him, but as he moved, he found friends. In New York these included Sherwood
Anderson, Allen Tate, and Gorham Munson, editor of *The Pagan,* where in 1916

Crane had published a poem. In Cleveland again, from 1919 to 1921, while working for his father, Crane made the acquaintance of other artists, who recognized him as one of their own.

Crane returned to New York, where he published his first collection, *White Buildings,* in 1926 and began work on *The Bridge* (he had already completed *Voyages,* his love sequence for Emil Opffer, a sailor with whom he shared an apartment with a view of the Brooklyn Bridge). Grants from the philanthropist Otto Kahn, as well as money from his family and friends, enabled Crane to live without steady work. But already Crane's drinking and his search for homosexual liaisons in dock bars were proving dangerous.

Crane's uncontrollable alcoholism proved so destructive that it led him to his early suicide. Toward the end of his life there was a chaotic period in Mexico, where he attempted to forsake his lifelong homosexuality by beginning an affair with Peggy Cowley (previously married to the critic Malcolm Cowley). In Mexico, Crane was imprisoned for disturbing the peace. In 1932 he set sail for New York but jumped into the Gulf of Mexico, the last impulsive act of an impulsive life.

Although the surface of Crane's poetry is difficult, behind his opaque texture lie careful reasons for his choice of words, as his patient letters to his friends show and as close reading will confirm. He had epic ambitions (fulfilled only partly by his sequence *The Bridge*), and many of his poems attempt epic scope within a lyric compass as they retell a decisive journey or voyage. They do this with a profound commitment to modernity.

The modern poet must, Crane thought, "absorb the machine." In opposing himself to Eliot's more conservative Europeanizing of American poetry, Crane looked resolutely not eastward to Europe but westward to America's frontiers. In *The Bridge,* Crane connects the bridge, the technological symbol of the machine age, to the dance of Pocahontas, to Whitman's mapping of the American continent, to the hoboes riding the freight trains, and to New Yorkers in the subway. Each portion of the sequence has its own form, ranging from first-person monologue to third-person description to second-person colloquy; the sequence employs both rhyme and free verse. In recognizing the Indian dance as the primal American aesthetic and religious form, and, later, in wanting to write an epic called *The Conquistadors,* Crane demonstrated his conviction that the present is constructed upon the past. America, he thought, must retain historical memory, not the memory of Europe so much as the memory of what has occurred on American soil. And unlike Pound and Frost, he turned not only to the New England past but to Spanish sources. *The Bridge* included not only political events (Columbus's voyage) but also aesthetic ones, from *Rip Van Winkle* to the works of Poe.

In 1930, after the publication of *The Bridge* (to mixed reviews), Crane received a Guggenheim fellowship and traveled to Mexico, but it became increasingly difficult for him to write. In the brief peaceful period with Peggy Cowley, he completed his last lyric, "The Broken Tower." In it what Crane called "the logic of metaphor" appears fully coherent, and the poem becomes an example of the sort of verse that would assemble itself into one great organized "single new word, never before spoken." At their best, Crane's assimilative powers produce a poetry that is at once rapidly cumulative and disintegrating, in which atmospheres dissolve as fast as they are created. This instability of essence in Crane affronted conservative critics, among them Yvor Winters, who argued that Crane's suicide was the logical result of his Emersonian and Whitmanesque individualism.

Crane's ambition was halted by his rapidly worsening alcoholism. But he left, besides the uneven *Bridge,* many exquisite smaller pieces (from the tender "Chaplinesque" to the symphonic *Voyages*) by which he will be remembered, and in his essays and letters he bequeathed a strict body of working aesthetic theory. Its chief tenet is the forsaking of a discursive or expository appearance to the poem. The logic of the poem must be impeccable, but it is not the explanatory or instructional logic of versified prose. Instead, the logic of the poem is associational, governed by the succession of feelings acted out by the words of the poem. Crane often uses transferred epithets—for example, "adagios of islands" —to combine two ideas—here, moving slowly (as in a musical adagio) and an ocean voyage through islands. Such writing conveys much information in a small compass, and subsequent poets (especially Robert Lowell in his sonnets and Allen Ginsberg in his telegraphic descriptions) have learned to write in Crane's rapid notation. In turning poetry away from the instructional and toward the associational, Crane taught other poets how to render brilliant impressions, in language duplicating the dazzling multiplicity of human sensations and thoughts.

Further Reading:

B. Weber, *Hart Crane: A Biographical and Critical Study,* 1948, 1970.

V. Quinn, *Hart Crane,* 1963.

R. W. B. Lewis, *The Poetry of Hart Crane,* 1969.

J. E. Unterecker, *Voyager: A Life of Hart Crane,* 1969.

S. Paul, *Hart's Bridge,* 1972.

M. D. Uroff, *Hart Crane: The Patterns of His Poetry,* 1974.

P. Horton, *Hart Crane,* 1976.

R. Sugg, *Hart Crane's* The Bridge, 1976.

H. Nilsen, *Hart Crane's Divided Vision: An Analysis of* The Bridge, 1980.

D. R. Clark, *Critical Essays on Hart Crane,* 1982.

A. Trachtenberg, *Hart Crane: A Collection of Critical Essays,* 1982.

J. Schwartz, *Hart Crane: A Reference Guide,* 1983.

Text:

The Complete Poems and Selected Letters and Prose of Hart Crane, ed. B. Weber, 1966.

See also *The Letters of Hart Crane, 1916–1932,* ed. B. Weber, 1952, 1965.

Black Tambourine

The interests of a black man in a cellar
Mark tardy judgment on the world's closed door.
Gnats toss in the shadow of a bottle,
And a roach spans a crevice in the floor.

AEsop, driven to pondering, found   5
Heaven with the tortoise and the hare;
Fox brush and sow ear top his grave
And mingling incantations on the air.

The black man, forlorn in the cellar,
Wanders in some mid-kingdom, dark, that lies,   10
Between his tambourine, stuck on the wall,
And, in Africa, a carcass quick with flies.

1926

Chaplinesque[1]

We make our meek adjustments,
Contented with such random consolations
As the wind deposits
In slithered and too ample pockets.

For we can still love the world, who find   5
A famished kitten on the step, and know
Recesses for it from the fury of the street,
Or warm torn elbow coverts.

We will sidestep, and to the final smirk
Dally the doom of that inevitable thumb   10
That slowly chafes its puckered index toward us,
Facing the dull squint with what innocence
And what surprise!

And yet these fine collapses are not lies
More than the pirouettes of any pliant cane;   15
Our obsequies are, in a way, no enterprise.
We can evade you, and all else but the heart:
What blame to us if the heart live on.

The game enforces smirks; but we have seen
The moon in lonely alleys make   20
A grail of laughter of an empty ash can,
And through all sound of gaiety and quest
Have heard a kitten in the wilderness.

1926

---

[1] In the manner of Charles Chaplin.

Repose of Rivers

The willows carried a slow sound,
A sarabande the wind mowed on the mead.
I could never remember
That seething, steady leveling of the marshes
Till age had brought me to the sea.   5

Flags, weeds. And remembrance of steep alcoves
Where cypresses shared the noon's
Tyranny; they drew me into hades almost.
And mammoth turtles climbing sulphur dreams
Yielded, while sun-silt rippled them   10
Asunder . . .

How much I would have bartered! the black gorge
And all the singular nestings in the hills
Where beavers learn stitch and tooth.
The pond I entered once and quickly fled—   15
I remember now its singing willow rim.

And finally, in that memory all things nurse;
After the city that I finally passed
With scalding unguents spread and smoking darts
The monsoon cut across the delta   20
At gulf gates . . . There, beyond the dykes

I heard wind flaking sapphire, like this summer,
And willows could not hold more steady sound.
1926

Passage

Where the cedar leaf divides the sky
I heard the sea.
In sapphire arenas of the hills
I was promised an improved infancy.

Sulking, sanctioning the sun,   5
My memory I left in a ravine,—

Casual louse that tissues the buckwheat,
Aprons rocks, congregates pears
In moonlit bushels
And wakens alleys with a hidden cough.   10

Dangerously the summer burned
(I had joined the entrainments of the wind).
The shadows of boulders lengthened my back:
In the bronze gongs of my cheeks
The rain dried without odour.   15

"It is not long, it is not long;
See where the red and black
Vine-stanchioned valleys—": but the wind
Died speaking through the ages that you know
And hug, chimney-sooted heart of man!   20

So was I turned about and back, much as your smoke
Compiles a too well-known biography.

The evening was a spear in the ravine
That throve through very oak. And had I walked
The dozen particular decimals of time?   25
Touching an opening laurel, I found
A thief beneath, my stolen book in hand.

"Why are you back here—smiling an iron coffin?"
"To argue with the laurel," I replied:
"Am justified in transience, fleeing   30
Under the constant wonder of your eyes—."

He closed the book. And from the Ptolemies
Sand troughed us in a glittering abyss.
A serpent swam a vertex to the sun
—On unpaced beaches leaned its tongue and drummed.   35
What fountains did I hear? what icy speeches?
Memory, committed to the page, had broke.
1926

At Melville's Tomb*

Often beneath the wave, wide from this ledge
The dice of drowned men's bones he saw bequeath
An embassy. Their numbers as he watched,
Beat on the dusty shore and were obscured.

And wrecks passed without sound of bells,   5
The calyx[1] of death's bounty giving back
A scattered chapter, livid hieroglyph,
The portent wound in corridors of shells.

Then in the circuit calm of one vast coil,
Its lashings charmed and malice reconciled,   10
Frosted eyes there were that lifted altars;
And silent answers crept across the stars.

Compass, quadrant and sextant[2] contrive
No farther tides . . . High in the azure steeps
Monody[3] shall not wake the mariner.   15
This fabulous shadow only the sea keeps.

1926

Voyages

I

Above the fresh ruffles of the surf
Bright striped urchins flay each other with sand.
They have contrived a conquest for shell shucks,
And their fingers crumble fragments of baked weed
Gaily digging and scattering.   5

And in answer to their treble interjections
The sun beats lightning on the waves,

---

* Written in memory of Herman Melville
(1819–1891), author of *Moby-Dick* (1851). The
poem imitates the French convention of the
poem at the tomb of the artist-predecessor.

[1] Used metaphorically of the vortex made in the
ocean by a sinking ship.
[2] Instruments used in navigation.
[3] Ode sung by one voice.

The waves fold thunder on the sand;
And could they hear me I would tell them:

O brilliant kids, frisk with your dog,   10
Fondle your shells and sticks, bleached
By time and the elements; but there is a line
You must not cross nor ever trust beyond it
Spry cordage[1] of your bodies to caresses
Too lichen-faithful from too wide a breast.   15
The bottom of the sea is cruel.

II

—And yet this great wink of eternity,
Of rimless floods, unfettered leewardings,
Samite[2] sheeted and processioned where
Her undinal[3] vast belly moonward bends,   20
Laughing the wrapt inflections of our love;

Take this Sea, whose diapason[4] knells
On scrolls of silver snowy sentences,
The sceptred terror of whose sessions rends
As her demeanors motion well or ill,   25
All but the pieties of lovers' hands.

And onward, as bells off San Salvador
Salute the crocus lustres of the stars,
In these poinsettia meadows of her tides,—
Adagios[5] of islands, O my Prodigal,   30
Complete the dark confessions her veins spell.

Mark how her turning shoulders wind the hours,
And hasten while her penniless rich palms
Pass superscription of bent foam and wave,—
Hasten, while they are true,—sleep, death, desire,   35
Close round one instant in one floating flower.

Bind us in time, O Seasons clear, and awe.
O minstrel galleons of Carib fire,
Bequeath us to no earthly shore until
Is answered in the vortex of our grave   40
The seal's wide spindrift[6] gaze toward paradise.

---

[1] Ropes in the rigging of a ship.
[2] Medieval silk fabric, threaded with gold or silver. (Cf. Tennyson's *Morte d'Arthur*, where the hand from the water claiming Arthur's sword is "clothed in white samite.")
[3] Referring to waves (from Latin *unda:* "wave").
[4] Entire compass of musical tones.
[5] Slow movements, as in music.
[6] Sea spray.

III

Infinite consanguinity[7] it bears—
This tendered theme of you that light
Retrieves from sea plains where the sky
Resigns a breast that every wave enthrones;   45
While ribboned water lanes I wind
Are laved and scattered with no stroke
Wide from your side, whereto this hour
The sea lifts, also, reliquary hands.

And so, admitted through black swollen gates   50
That must arrest all distance otherwise,—
Past whirling pillars and lithe pediments,
Light wrestling there incessantly with light,
Star kissing star through wave on wave unto
Your body rocking!
             and where death, if shed,   55
Presumes no carnage, but this single change,—
Upon the steep floor flung from dawn to dawn
The silken skilled transmemberment[8] of song;

Permit me voyage, love, into your hands . . .

IV

Whose counted smile of hours and days, suppose   60
I know as spectrum of the sea and pledge
Vastly now parting gulf on gulf of wings
Whose circles bridge, I know, (from palms to the severe
Chilled albatross's white immutability)
No stream of greater love advancing now   65
Than, singing, this mortality alone
Through clay aflow immortally to you.

All fragrance irrefragibly,[9] and claim
Madly meeting logically in this hour
And region that is ours to wreathe again,   70
Portending eyes and lips and making told
The chancel[10] port and portion of our June—

Shall they not stem and close in our own steps
Bright staves of flowers and quills to-day as I
Must first be lost in fatal tides to tell?   75

---

[7] Blood relation.
[8] Word invented by Crane, made up of *transmutation* and *dismemberment*.

[9] Indisputably.
[10] Choir and sanctuary of a church.

In signature of the incarnate word
The harbor shoulders to resign in mingling
Mutual blood, transpiring as foreknown
And widening noon within your breast for gathering
All bright insinuations that my years have caught   80
For islands where must lead inviolably
Blue latitudes and levels of your eyes,—

In this expectant, still exclaim receive
The secret oar and petals of all love.

V

Meticulous, past midnight in clear rime,   85
Infrangible and lonely, smooth as though cast
Together in one merciless white blade—
The bay estuaries fleck the hard sky limits.

—As if too brittle or too clear to touch!
The cables of our sleep so swiftly filed,   90
Already hang, shred ends from remembered stars.
One frozen trackless smile . . . What words
Can strangle this deaf moonlight? For we

Are overtaken. Now no cry, no sword
Can fasten or deflect this tidal wedge,   95
Slow tyranny of moonlight, moonlight loved
And changed . . . "There's

Nothing like this in the world," you say,
Knowing I cannot touch your hand and look
Too, into that godless cleft of sky   100
Where nothing turns but dead sands flashing.

"—And never to quite understand!" No,
In all the argosy of your bright hair I dreamed
Nothing so flagless as this piracy.

              But now
Draw in your head, alone and too tall here.   105
Your eyes already in the slant of drifting foam;
Your breath sealed by the ghosts I do not know:
Draw in your head and sleep the long way home.

VI

Where icy and bright dungeons lift
Of swimmers their lost morning eyes,   110

And ocean rivers, churning, shift
Green borders under stranger skies,

Steadily as a shell secretes
Its beating leagues of monotone,
Or as many waters trough the sun's   115
Red kelson[11] past the cape's wet stone;

O rivers mingling toward the sky
And harbor of the phœnix' breast—
My eyes pressed black against the prow,
—Thy derelict and blinded guest   120

Waiting, afire, what name, unspoke,
I cannot claim: let thy waves rear
More savage than the death of kings,
Some splintered garland for the seer.

Beyond siroccos harvesting   125
The solstice thunders, crept away,
Like a cliff swinging or a sail
Flung into April's inmost day—

Creation's blithe and petalled word
To the lounged goddess[12] when she rose   130
Conceding dialogue with eyes
That smile unsearchable repose—

Still fervid covenant, Belle Isle,[13]
—Unfolded floating dais before
Which rainbows twine continual hair—   135
Belle Isle, white echo of the oar!

The imaged Word, it is, that holds
Hushed willows anchored in its glow.
It is the unbetrayable reply
Whose accent no farewell can know.   140
1926

---

[11] Timbers of a ship; here used of the curve of the sun.

[12] I.e., Venus.

[13] Island off the coast of Labrador; here suggesting Venus' island Cytherea.

from The Bridge

To Brooklyn Bridge

How many dawns, chill from his rippling rest
The seagull's wings shall dip and pivot him,
Shedding white rings of tumult, building high
Over the chained bay waters Liberty—

Then, with inviolate curve, forsake our eyes   5
As apparitional as sails that cross
Some page of figures to be filed away;
—Till elevators drop us from our day . . .

I think of cinemas, panoramic sleights
With multitudes bent toward some flashing scene   10
Never disclosed, but hastened to again,
Foretold to other eyes on the same screen;

And Thee, across the harbor, silver-paced
As though the sun took step of thee, yet left
Some motion ever unspent in thy stride,—   15
Implicitly thy freedom staying thee!

Out of some subway scuttle, cell or loft
A bedlamite[1] speeds to thy parapets,
Tilting there momently, shrill shirt ballooning,
A jest falls from the speechless caravan.   20

Down Wall,[2] from girder into street noon leaks,
A rip-tooth of the sky's acetylene;
All afternoon the cloud-flown derricks turn . . .
Thy cables breathe the North Atlantic still.

And obscure as that heaven of the Jews,   25
Thy guerdon[3] . . . Accolade[4] thou dost bestow
Of anonymity time cannot raise:
Vibrant reprieve and pardon thou dost show.

O harp and altar, of the fury fused,
(How could mere toil align thy choiring strings!)   30
Terrific threshold of the prophet's pledge,
Prayer of pariah,[5] and the lover's cry,—

---

[1] Madman.
[2] Wall Street in New York City.
[3] Reward.

[4] Award of special merit.
[5] Outcast.

Again the traffic lights that skim thy swift
Unfractioned idiom, immaculate sigh of stars,
Beading thy path—condense eternity: 35
And we have seen night lifted in thine arms.

Under thy shadow by the piers I waited;
Only in darkness is thy shadow clear.
The City's fiery parcels all undone,
Already snow submerges an iron year . . .   40

O Sleepless as the river under thee,
Vaulting the sea, the prairies' dreaming sod,
Unto us lowliest sometime sweep, descend
And of the curveship lend a myth to God.

1930

The Dance

The swift red flesh, a winter king—
Who squired the glacier woman down the sky?
She ran the neighing canyons all the spring;
She spouted arms; she rose with maize—to die.

And in the autumn drouth, whose burnished hands   5
With mineral wariness found out the stone
Where prayers, forgotten, streamed the mesa sands?
He holds the twilight's dim, perpetual throne.

Mythical brows we saw retiring—loth,
Disturbed and destined, into denser green.   10
Greeting they sped us, on the arrow's oath:
Now lie incorrigibly what years between . . .

There was a bed of leaves, and broken play;
There was a veil upon you, Pocahontas, bride—
O Princess whose brown lap was virgin May;   15
And bridal flanks and eyes hid tawny pride.

I left the village for dogwood. By the canoe
Tugging below the mill-race, I could see
Your hair's keen crescent running, and the blue
First moth of evening take wing stealthily.   20

What laughing chains the water wove and threw!
I learned to catch the trout's moon whisper; I
Drifted how many hours I never knew,
But, watching, saw that fleet young crescent die,—

And one star, swinging, take its place, alone,   25
Cupped in the larches of the mountain pass—
Until, immortally, it bled into the dawn.
I left my sleek boat nibbling margin grass . . .

I took the portage climb, then chose
A further valley-shed; I could not stop.   30
Feet nozzled wat'ry webs of upper flows;
One white veil gusted from the very top.

O Appalachian Spring! I gained the ledge;
Steep, inaccessible smile that eastward bends
And northward reaches in that violet wedge   35
Of Adirondacks!—wisped of azure wands,

Over how many bluffs, tarns, streams I sped!
—And knew myself within some boding shade:—
Grey tepees tufting the blue knolls ahead,
Smoke swirling through the yellow chestnut glade . . .   40

A distant cloud, a thunder-bud—it grew,
That blanket of the skies: the padded foot
Within,—I heard it; 'til its rhythm drew,
—Siphoned the black pool from the heart's hot root!

A cyclone threshes in the turbine crest,   45
Swooping in eagle feathers down your back;
Know, Maquokeeta,[6] greeting; know death's best;
—Fall, Sachem,[7] strictly as the tamarack!

A birch kneels. All her whistling fingers fly.
The oak grove circles in a crash of leaves;   50
The long moan of a dance is in the sky.
Dance, Maquokeeta: Pocahontas grieves . . .

And every tendon scurries toward the twangs
Of lightning deltaed down your saber hair.
Now snaps the flint in every tooth; red fangs   55
And splay tongues thinly busy the blue air . . .

Dance, Maquokeeta! snake[8] that lives before,
That casts his pelt, and lives beyond! Sprout, horn!
Spark, tooth! Medicine-man, relent, restore—
Lie to us,—dance us back the tribal morn!   60

---

[6] Indian god of the thunderstorm.   [8] The snake that sheds its skin symbolizes
[7] Chief.   self-renewing time.

Spears and assemblies: black drums thrusting on—
O yelling battlements,—I, too, was liege
To rainbows currying each pulsant bone:
Surpassed the circumstance, danced out the siege!

And buzzard-circleted, screamed from the stake;   65
I could not pick the arrows from my side.
Wrapped in that fire, I saw more escorts wake—
Flickering, sprint up the hill groins like a tide.

I heard the hush of lava wrestling your arms,
And stag teeth foam about the raven throat;   70
Flame cataracts of heaven in seething swarms,
Fed down your anklets to the sunset's moat.

O, like the lizard in the furious noon,
That drops his legs and colors in the sun,
—And laughs, pure serpent, Time itself, and moon   75
Of his own fate, I saw thy change begun!

And saw thee dive to kiss that destiny
Like one white meteor, sacrosanct and blent
At last with all that's consummate and free
There, where the first and last gods keep thy tent.   80

                 *   *   *

Thewed of the levin, thunder-shod and lean,
Lo, through what infinite seasons dost thou gaze—
Across what bivouacs of thine angered slain,
And see'st thy bride immortal in the maize!

Totem and fire-gall, slumbering pyramid—   85
Though other calendars now stack the sky,
Thy freedom is her largesse, Prince, and hid
On paths thou knewest best to claim her by.

High unto Labrador the sun strikes free
Her speechless dream of snow, and stirred again,   90
She is the torrent and the singing tree;
And she is virgin to the last of men . . .

West, west and south! winds over Cumberland
And winds across the llano⁹ grass resume
Her hair's warm sibilance. Her breasts are fanned   95
O stream by slope and vineyard—into bloom!

⁹ Plain without trees.

And when the caribou slant down for salt
Do arrows thirst and leap? Do antlers shine
Alert, star-triggered in the listening vault
Of dusk?—And are her perfect brows to thine? 100

We danced, O Brave, we danced beyond their farms,
In cobalt desert closures made our vows . . .
Now is the strong prayer folded in thine arms,
The serpent with the eagle in the boughs.

1930

Atlantis[10]

*Music is then the knowledge of that which
relates to love in harmony and system.*[11]
Plato

Through the bound cable strands, the arching path
Upward, veering with light, the flight of strings,—
Taut miles of shuttling moonlight syncopate
The whispered rush, telepathy of wires.
Up the index of night, granite and steel— 5
Transparent meshes—fleckless the gleaming staves—
Sibylline[12] voices flicker, waveringly stream
As though a god were issue of the strings. . . .

And through that cordage, threading with its call
One arc synoptic of all tides below— 10
Their labyrinthine mouths of history
Pouring reply as though all ships at sea
Complighted in one vibrant breath made cry,—
"Make thy love sure—to weave whose song we ply!"
—From black embankments, moveless soundings hailed, 15
So seven oceans answer from their dream.

And on, obliquely up bright carrier bars
New octaves trestle the twin monoliths
Beyond whose frosted capes the moon bequeaths
Two worlds of sleep (O arching strands of song!)— 20
Onward and up the crystal-flooded aisle
White tempest nets file upward, upward ring
With silver terraces the humming spars,
The loft of vision, palladium[13] helm of stars.

[10] The legendary sunken continent.
[11] Plato's *Republic*, III, 403.
[12] Prophetic.

[13] A statue of Pallas Athena; also, an element of the platinum group.

Sheerly the eyes, like seagulls stung with rime[14]—   25
Slit and propelled by glistening fins of light—
Pick biting way up towering looms that press
Sidelong with flight of blade on tendon blade
—Tomorrows into yesteryear—and link
What cipher-script of time no traveller reads   30
But who, through smoking pyres of love and death,
Searches the timeless laugh of mythic spears.

Like hails, farewells—up planet-sequined heights
Some trillion whispering hammers glimmer Tyre:[15]
Serenely, sharply up the long anvil cry   35
Of inchling æons silence rivets Troy.[16]
And you, aloft there—Jason![17] hesting Shout!
Still wrapping harness to the swarming air!
Silvery the rushing wake, surpassing call,
Beams yelling Æolus![18] splintered in the straits!   40

From gulfs unfolding, terrible of drums,
Tall Vision-of-the-Voyage, tensely spare—
Bridge, lifting night to cycloramic crest
Of deepest day—O Choir, translating time
Into what multitudinous Verb the suns   45
And synergy of waters ever fuse, recast
In myriad syllables,—Psalm of Cathay![19]
O Love, thy white, pervasive Paradigm . . . !

We left the haven hanging in the night—
Sheened harbor lanterns backward fled the keel.   50
Pacific here at time's end, bearing corn,—
Eyes stammer through the pangs of dust and steel.
And still the circular, indubitable frieze
Of heaven's meditation, yoking wave
To kneeling wave, one song devoutly binds—   55
The vernal strophe chimes from deathless strings!

O Thou steeled Cognizance whose leap commits
The agile precincts of the lark's return;
Within whose lariat sweep encinctured sing
In single chrysalis the many twain,—   60
Of stars Thou art the stitch and stallion glow
And like an organ, Thou, with sound of doom—

[14] Frost.
[15] Ancient Phoenician port.
[16] City destroyed in the Trojan War.
[17] Captain of the Greek Argonauts in the quest
for the fabled Golden Fleece.
[18] God of the winds.
[19] Ancient name for China.

Sight, sound and flesh Thou leadest from time's realm
As love strikes clear direction for the helm.

Swift peal of secular light, intrinsic Myth   65
Whose fell unshadow is death's utter wound,—
O River-throated—iridescently upborne
Through the bright drench and fabric of our veins;
With white escarpments[20] swinging into light,
Sustained in tears the cities are endowed   70
And justified conclamant with ripe fields
Revolving through their harvests in sweet torment.

Forever Deity's glittering Pledge, O Thou
Whose canticle fresh chemistry assigns
To wrapt inception and beatitude,—   75
Always through blinding cables, to our joy,
Of thy white seizure springs the prophecy:
Always through spiring cordage,[21] pyramids
Of silver sequel, Deity's young name
Kinetic of white choiring wings . . . ascends.   80

Migrations that must needs void memory,
Inventions that cobblestone the heart,—
Unspeakable Thou Bridge to Thee, O Love.
Thy pardon for this history, whitest Flower,
O Answerer of all,—Anemone,—   85
Now while thy petals spend the suns about us, hold—
(O Thou whose radiance doth inherit me)
Atlantis,—hold thy floating singer late!

So to thine Everpresence, beyond time,
Like spears ensanguined of one tolling star   90
That bleeds infinity—the orphic strings,[22]
Sidereal[23] phalanxes, leap and converge:
—One Song, one Bridge of Fire! Is it Cathay,
Now pity steeps the grass and rainbows ring
The serpent with the eagle in the leaves . . . ?   95
Whispers antiphonal in azure swing.

1930

---

[20] Steep slopes.   [22] Suggesting the lyre of Orpheus.
[21] Ropes in the rigging of a ship.   [23] Starry.

O Carib Isle!

The tarantula rattling at the lily's foot
Across the feet of the dead, laid in white sand
Near the coral beach—nor zigzag fiddle crabs
Side-stilting from the path (that shift, subvert
And anagrammatize your name)—No, nothing here   5
Below the palsy that one eucalyptus lifts
In wrinkled shadows—mourns.

                   And yet suppose
I count these nacreous frames of tropic death,
Brutal necklaces of shells around each grave
Squared off so carefully. Then   10

To the white sand I may speak a name, fertile
Albeit in a stranger tongue. Tree names, flower names
Deliberate, gainsay death's brittle crypt. Meanwhile
The wind that knots itself in one great death—
Coils and withdraws. So syllables want breath.   15

But where is the Captain of this doubloon isle
Without a turnstile? Who but catchword crabs
Patrols the dry groins of the underbrush?
What man, or What
Is Commissioner of mildew throughout the ambushed senses?   20
His Carib mathematics web the eyes' baked lenses!

Under the poinciana, of a noon or afternoon
Let fiery blossoms clot the light, render my ghost
Sieved upward, white and black along the air
Until it meets the blue's comedian host.   25
Let not the pilgrim see himself again
For slow evisceration bound like those huge terrapin
Each daybreak on the wharf, their brine-caked eyes;
—Spiked, overturned; such thunder in their strain!
And clenched beaks coughing for the surge again!   30

Slagged of the hurricane—I, cast within its flow,
Congeal by afternoons here, satin and vacant.
You have given me the shell, Satan,—carbonic amulet
Sere of the sun exploded in the sea.
1933

The Idiot

Sheer over to the other side,—for see—
The boy straggling under those mimosas, daft
With squint lanterns in his head, and it's likely
Fumbling his sex. That's why those children laughed

In such infernal circles round his door   5
Once when he shouted, stretched in ghastly shape.
I hurried by. But back from the hot shore
Passed him again . . . He was alone, agape;

One hand dealt out a kite string, a tin can
The other tilted, peeled end clapped to eye.   10
That kite aloft—you should have watched him scan
Its course, though he'd clamped midnight to noon sky!

And since, through these hot barricades of green,
A Dios gracias, graç'—I've heard his song
Above all reason lifting, halt serene—   15
My trespass vision shrinks to face his wrong.

1933

The Broken Tower

The bell-rope that gathers God at dawn
Dispatches me as though I dropped down the knell
Of a spent day—to wander the cathedral lawn
From pit to crucifix, feet chill on steps from hell.

Have you not heard, have you not seen that corps   5
Of shadows in the tower, whose shoulders sway
Antiphonal carillons launched before
The stars are caught and hived in the sun's ray?

The bells, I say, the bells break down their tower;
And swing I know not where. Their tongues engrave   10
Membrane through marrow, my long-scattered score
Of broken intervals . . . And I, their sexton slave!

¹ Spanish: "Thanks be to God, thanks."

Oval encyclicals in canyons heaping
The impasse high with choir. Banked voices slain!
Pagodas, campaniles with reveilles outleaping—   15
O terraced echoes prostrate on the plain! . . .

And so it was I entered the broken world
To trace the visionary company of love, its voice
An instant in the wind (I know not whither hurled)
But not for long to hold each desperate choice.   20

My word I poured. But was it cognate, scored
Of that tribunal monarch of the air
Whose thigh embronzes earth, strikes crystal Word
In wounds pledged once to hope—cleft to despair?

The steep encroachments of my blood left me   25
No answer (could blood hold such a lofty tower
As flings the question true?)—or is it she
Whose sweet mortality stirs latent power?—

And through whose pulse I hear, counting the strokes
My veins recall and add, revived and sure   30
The angelus[1] of wars my chest evokes:
What I hold healed, original now, and pure . . .

And builds, within, a tower that is not stone
(Not stone can jacket heaven)—but slip
Of pebbles,—visible wings of silence sown   35
In azure circles, widening as they dip

The matrix[2] of the heart, lift down the eye
That shrines the quiet lake and swells a tower . . .
The commodious, tall decorum of that sky
Unseals her earth, and lifts love in its shower.   40
1933

Allen Tate
1899–1979

Allen Tate, poet, biographer, and essayist, was an influential man of letters from
his twenties at Vanderbilt University to his death in Sewanee, Tennessee. He was
born in Kentucky to a wealthy family who maintained a conventional interest in
books and general culture. His father's business failures, however, made for a

[1] Prayer recounting the Incarnation of Christ.   [2] Womb.

disrupted childhood. Tate entered Vanderbilt in 1919 and roomed with Robert
Penn Warren; they both came under the influence of the poet John Crowe
Ransom and the group known as the Fugitives; their journal, *The Fugitive,*
printed Tate's first poems, and Tate himself edited the journal from 1923 to 1925.
Tate and other southern writers, including Ransom and Warren, published a
collection of essays, *I'll Take My Stand: The South and Agrarian Tradition* (1930),
defending the antebellum values of an agrarian South against the industrial values
of the North. Tate's biographies of Stonewall Jackson (1928) and Jefferson Davis
(1929) were also implicit arguments for the preservation of southern culture.

It has always been true that the aristocratic South has been more hospitable to
belles lettres than the Puritan North, where intellectuals preferred theological or
philosophical prose to novels and poetry. The leisured class of the South (made
possible, of course, by slavery) sponsored an aristocratic culture, centered rather in
law and letters than in religious disputation, and allying itself more with the
aristocratic literature produced in England than with the polemic literature of
dissent. Tate's poetry is in this sense aristocratic: Its models come from the Latin
literature he studied at Vanderbilt. His poetry is often latinate in diction,
measured in rhythm, intellectual in content, and historical in emphasis. Though
he turns to local color in some southern poems like "The Swimmers," even there
the fundamental emphasis of the poem is intellectual and moral rather than
sensuous.

Tate's long life was spent chiefly as an essayist (he wrote for *The New
Republic, The Nation, Hound and Horn,* and the *Sewanee Review*) and professor
(he taught from 1951 to 1968 at the University of Minnesota). He was friend and
mentor to both Hart Crane and Robert Lowell, and his influence can be seen in
Lowell's early poetry. Tate preferred a literature of ideas in which propositions
were stated, explored, defended, and summarized in a lofty diction. He believed,
with Aristotle, that poetry is more philosophical than history; he thought it
should express large moral truths, drawn from history, perhaps, but broadened
into universality. At the same time, he wanted a complexity in poetry, a constant
tension and historical irony, that would save the ideas from platitudinousness. He
found a poetic ideal in Eliot and imitated him as a poet and as a critic. Like
Eliot, Tate adopted in his criticism a tone of dry instructiveness, but his criticism
lacks the passion that animates Eliot's views. Together with Ransom, Tate
founded the New Criticism (Ransom's term), which aimed to change the way in
which literature was taught; instead of spending time on historical and
biographical data, the critic should direct readers or students to look at the
qualities of the work itself—its tensions and ambiguities, its complex of positions,
its structural completeness. As a movement that turned attention back to the art
object, the New Criticism was immensely valuable. But Tate could not envisage
a poetry other than the metaphysical poetry he admired, imitated in his own
work, and fostered in his pupils. He disliked Robert Lowell's abandonment of
strict forms and classical reticence when *Life Studies* (1959) appeared.

Strict in conscience, intellectual in temperament, severe in criticism, Tate
lacked the freedom and play of imagination that mark the great poet. As one of
the exponents of the New Criticism, with its emphasis on the artistry of the poet
visible in the text, he helped turn American criticism away from its former

uncritical reliance on biography and the history of ideas. He remains, with John Crowe Ransom (a more talented poet), one of the founders of contemporary southern poetry.

Further Reading:
W. B. Arnold, *The Social Ideas of Allen Tate,*
1955.
R. K. Meiners, *The Last Alternatives,* 1963.
G. Hemphill, *Allen Tate,* 1964.
F. Bishop, *Allen Tate,* 1967.
R. Squires, *Allen Tate: A Literary Biography,*
1971.
Allen Tate and His Work: Critical Evaluations,
ed. R. Squires, 1972.
R. S. Dupree, *Allen Tate and the Augustinian
Imagination: A Study of the Poetry,* 1983.

Text:
Collected Poems, 1919–1976, 1977.
See also *The Poetry Reviews of Allen Tate,
1924–1944,* ed. A. Brown and F. N. Cheney,
1983.

Ode to the Confederate Dead

Row after row with strict impunity
The headstones yield their names to the element,
The wind whirrs without recollection;
In the riven troughs the splayed leaves
Pile up, of nature the casual sacrament   5
To the seasonal eternity of death;
Then driven by the fierce scrutiny
Of heaven to their election in the vast breath,
They sough[1] the rumour of mortality.

Autumn is desolation in the plot   10
Of a thousand acres where these memories grow
From the inexhaustible bodies that are not
Dead, but feed the grass row after rich row.
Think of the autumns that have come and gone!—
Ambitious November with the humors of the year,   15
With a particular zeal for every slab,
Staining the uncomfortable angels that rot
On the slabs, a wing chipped here, an arm there:
The brute curiosity of an angel's stare
Turns you, like them, to stone,   20
Transforms the heaving air
Till plunged to a heavier world below

[1] Sigh.

You shift your sea-space blindly
Heaving, turning like the blind crab.

    Dazed by the wind, only the wind   25
    The leaves flying, plunge

You know who have waited by the wall
The twilight certainty of an animal,
Those midnight restitutions of the blood
You know—the immitigable pines, the smoky frieze   30
Of the sky, the sudden call: you know the rage,
The cold pool left by the mounting flood,
Of muted Zeno and Parmenides.[2]
You who have waited for the angry resolution
Of those desires that should be yours tomorrow,
You know the unimportant shrift of death   35
And praise the vision
And praise the arrogant circumstance
Of those who fall
Rank upon rank, hurried beyond decision—   40
Here by the sagging gate, stopped by the wall.

    Seeing, seeing only the leaves
    Flying, plunge and expire

Turn your eyes to the immoderate past,
Turn to the inscrutable infantry rising   45
Demons out of the earth—they will not last.
Stonewall, Stonewall,[3] and the sunken fields of hemp,
Shiloh, Antietam, Malvern Hill, Bull Run.[4]
Lost in that orient of the thick-and-fast
You will curse the setting sun.   50

    Cursing only the leaves crying
    Like an old man in a storm

You hear the shout, the crazy hemlocks point
With troubled fingers to the silence which
Smothers you, a mummy, in time.   55

                    The hound bitch
Toothless and dying, in a musty cellar
Hears the wind only.

---

[2] Greek philosophers of the fifth century B.C. who denied the reality of change and believed in the permanence of "being."

[3] Confederate general Stonewall Jackson (1824–1863).

[4] Shiloh; Antietam; Malvern Hill; Bull Run: battles of the Civil War.

Now that the salt of their blood
Stiffens the saltier oblivion of the sea,   60
Seals the malignant purity of the flood,
What shall we who count our days and bow
Our heads with a commemorial woe
In the ribboned coats of grim felicity,
What shall we say of the bones, unclean,   65
Whose verdurous anonymity will grow?
The ragged arms, the ragged heads and eyes
Lost in these acres of the insane green?
The gray lean spiders come, they come and go;
In a tangle of willows without light   70
The singular screech-owl's tight
Invisible lyric seeds the mind
With the furious murmur of their chivalry.

We shall say only the leaves
Flying, plunge and expire   75

We shall say only the leaves whispering
In the improbable mist of nightfall
That flies on multiple wing;
Night is the beginning and the end
And in between the ends of distraction   80
Waits mute speculation, the patient curse
That stones the eyes, or like the jaguar leaps
For his own image in a jungle pool, his victim.
What shall we say who have knowledge
Carried to the heart? Shall we take the act   85
To the grave? Shall we, more hopeful, set up the grave
In the house? The ravenous grave?

Leave now
The shut gate and the decomposing wall:
The gentle serpent, green in the mulberry bush,   90
Riots with his tongue through the hush—
Sentinel of the grave who counts us all!

1930

The Meaning of Life

A Monologue

Think about it at will: there is that
Which is the commentary; there's that other,
Which may be called the immaculate
Conception of its essence in itself.
It is necessary to distinguish the weights   5
Of the two methods lest the first smother
The second, the second be speechless (without the
    first).
I was saying this more briefly the other day
But one must be explicit as well as brief.
When I was a small boy I lived at home   10
For nine years in that part of old Kentucky
Where the mountains fringe the Blue Grass,
The old men shot at one another for luck;
It made me think I was like none of them.
At twelve I was determined to shoot only   15
For honor; at twenty not to shoot at all;
I know at thirty-three that one must shoot
As often as one gets the rare chance—
In killing there is more than commentary.
One's sense of the proper decoration alters   20
But there's a kind of lust feeds on itself
Unspoken to, unspeaking; subterranean
As a black river full of eyeless fish
Heavy with spawn; with a passion for time
Longer than the arteries of a cave.   25

1936

Sonnets at Christmas

I

This is the day His hour of life draws near,
Let me get ready from head to foot for it
Most handily with eyes to pick the year
For small feed to reward a feathered[1] wit.
Some men would see it an epiphany   5

---

[1] As arrows are feathered.

At ease, at food and drink, others at chase;
Yet I, stung lassitude, with ecstasy
Unspent argue the season's difficult case
So: Man, dull creature of enormous head,
What would he look at in the coiling sky?   10
But I must kneel again unto the Dead
While Christmas bells of paper white and red,
Figured with boys and girls spilt from a sled,
Ring out the silence I am nourished by.

II

Ah, Christ, I love you rings to the wild sky
And I must think a little of the past:
When I was ten I told a stinking lie
That got a black boy whipped; but now at last
The going years, caught in an after-glow,   5
Reverse like balls englished upon green baize[2]—
Let them return, let the round trumpets blow
The ancient crackle of the Christ's deep gaze.
Deafened and blind, with senses yet unfound,
Am I, untutored to the after-wit   10
Of knowledge, knowing a nightmare has no sound;
Therefore with idle hands and head I sit
In late December before the fire's daze
Punished by crimes of which I would be quit.

1936

The Swimmers

Scene: Montgomery County,
          Kentucky, July 1911

Kentucky water, clear springs: a boy fleeing
     To water under the dry Kentucky sun,
     His four little friends in tandem with him, seeing

Long shadows of grapevine wriggle and run
     Over the green swirl; mullein under the ear   5
     Soft as Nausicaä's[1] palm; sullen fun

---

[2] The green felt covering a pool table; to "english" a ball is to strike it off center, causing it to spin.

[1] Nausicaä: In Homer's *Odyssey,* the princess who discovers Ulysses on a beach after his shipwreck.

Savage as childhood's thin harmonious tear:
    O fountain, bosom source undying-dead
    Replenish me the spring of love and fear

And give me back the eye that looked and fled   10
    When a thrush idling in the tulip tree
    Unwound the cold dream of the copperhead.

—Along the creek the road was winding; we
    Felt the quicksilver sky. I see again
    The shrill companions of that odyssey: 15

Bill Eaton, Charlie Watson, 'Nigger' Layne
    The doctor's son, Harry Duesler who played
    The flute; and Tate, with water on the brain.

Dog-days: the dusty leaves where rain delayed
    Hung low on poison-oak and scuppernong,[2]   20
    And we were following the active shade

Of water, that bells and bickers all night long.
    'No more'n a mile,' Layne said. All five stood still.
    Listening, I heard what seemed at first a song;

Peering, I heard the hooves come down the hill.   25
    The posse passed, twelve horse; the leader's face
    Was worn as limestone on an ancient sill.

Then, as sleepwalkers shift from a hard place
    In bed, and rising to keep a formal pledge
    Descend a ladder into empty space,   30

We scuttled down the bank below a ledge
    And marched stiff-legged in our common fright
    Along a hog-track by the riffle's edge:

Into a world where sound shaded the sight
    Dropped the dull hooves again; the horsemen came   35
    Again, all but the leader: it was night

Momently and I feared: eleven same
    Jesus-Christers unmembered and unmade,
    Whose Corpse had died again in dirty shame.

The bank then levelling in a speckled glade,   40
    We stopped to breathe above the swimming-hole;
    I gazed at its reticulated shade

---

[2] Species of grape.

Recoiling in blue fear, and felt it roll
    Over my ears and eyes and lift my hair
    Like seaweed tossing on a sunk atoll.   45

I rose again. Borne on the copper air
    A distant voice green as a funeral wreath
    Against a grave: 'That dead nigger there.'

The melancholy sheriff slouched beneath
    A giant sycamore; shaking his head   50
    He plucked a sassafras twig and picked his teeth:

'We come too late.' He spoke to the tired dead
    Whose ragged shirt soaked up the viscous flow
    Of blood in which It lay discomfited.

A butting horse-fly gave one ear a blow   55
    And glanced off, as the sheriff kicked the rope
    Loose from the neck and hooked it with his toe

Away from the blood.—I looked back down the slope:
    The friends were gone that I had hoped to greet.—
    A single horseman came at a slow lope   60

And pulled up at the hanged man's horny feet;
    The sheriff noosed the feet, the other end
    The stranger tied to his pommel in a neat

Slip-knot. I saw the Negro's body bend
    And straighten, as a fish-line cast transverse   65
    Yields to the current that it must subtend.

The sheriff's Goddamn was a murmured curse
    Not for the dead but for the blinding dust
    That boxed the cortège in a cloudy hearse

And dragged it towards our town. I knew I must   70
    Not stay till twilight in that silent road;
    Sliding my bare feet into the warm crust,

I hopped the stonecrop like a panting toad
    Mouth open, following the heaving cloud
    That floated to the court-house square its load   75

Of limber corpse that took the sun for shroud.
    There were three figures in the dying sun
    Whose light were company where three was crowd.

My breath crackled the dead air like a shotgun
   As, sheriff and the stranger disappearing,   80
   The faceless head lay still. I could not run

Or walk, but stood. Alone in the public clearing
   This private thing was owned by all the town,
   Though never claimed by us within my hearing.

1960

Langston Hughes
1902–1967

Langston Hughes's short stories won him an enormous audience among the black population. The stories, like the poems, showed the average struggle of ordinary blacks in their everyday lives. The edge of bitter humor animating Hughes's work does not take away from its essential comedy; his satire of both white and black, while establishing with perfect clarity the extent of social injustice in America, creates a cast of characters who are resourceful and hapless, courageous and foolish, altruistic and self-serving.

Hughes's realistic descriptions in verse and prose of the life of poor blacks earned him hatred and condemnation from black intellectuals who wished black writing to be improving, to show black life only at its best. When his second book of poetry, *Fine Clothes to the Jew* (1929), appeared, the headline in the widely circulated black newspaper *The Amsterdam News* was "Langston Hughes— The Sewer Dweller."

Hughes's father, who had left his wife shortly after his son's birth, disavowed all connection with American blacks and went to live in Mexico, where Hughes lived with him in his adolescent years. Hughes grew to hate his father and, reversing his father's attitude, decided to immerse himself in the life of black Americans, to write about the entire community:

> Workers, roustabouts, and singers, and job hunters on Lenox Avenue in New York, or Seventh Street in Washington or South State in Chicago—people up today and down tomorrow, working this week and fired the next, beaten and baffled, but determined not to be wholly beaten, buying furniture on the installment plan, filling the house with roomers to help pay the rent, hoping to get a new suit for Easter—and pawning that suit before the Fourth of July.

James Langston Hughes dropped his first name, which he shared with his father, and adopted his middle name, his mother's maiden name, for his writing career.

After an unsuccessful year at Columbia University, Hughes dropped out of school, but he later received the A.B. from Lincoln University in Pennsylvania, an all-black college. In his long writing life he was able to support himself by his writing and his public readings. Besides poems and short stories, he wrote novels, children's books, plays, nonfiction, opera libretti, and lyrics for musicals, notably for Kurt Weill's *Street Scene* (1948). He was in the center of the group making up the Harlem Renaissance in the 1920s. At that time, Negro intellectuals took on as a self-conscious task the construction of an aesthetic and intellectual culture for black Americans. Hughes was drawn into the group by Dr. Alain Locke, who had included some of Hughes's poems in his 1925 anthology *The New Negro*. Hughes was also sponsored by the poet Vachel Lindsay and the novelist Carl Van Vechten. Eventually Hughes set out on his own, reading widely to southern audiences, traveling to Russia, reporting the Spanish Civil War for the *Baltimore Afro-American,* and translating García Lorca and Gabriela Mistral. He was a force for the establishing of black theaters; he anthologized his fellow black writers.

The fullness of Hughes's literary achievement will only be seen when his collected works have been compiled; he left his mark on every phase of literary activity in America. His writing created a new audience for poetry—the black community, who, in spite of the criticism of black intellectuals and moralists, saw in Hughes's direct, frank, open verse a reflection of their music and their language, their social debasement and their persistent hope and despair. In drawing on the poems of Carl Sandburg to make his own verse, Hughes continued a populist tradition in American poetry, one that depends as much on the spoken word as on the written page. In his "documentary, journalistic, and topical" poems (as he described them), Hughes reached the hearts of his listeners and validated a poetry with a strong oral base. The "Beat" poets—especially Allen Ginsberg in his blues chants—continued Hughes's emphasis on the spoken or sung poem, and subsequent black poets (Gwendolyn Brooks, Don Lee) have emphasized the colloquial vigor of black speech as Hughes himself did, transforming it into poetry.

Further Reading:
D. C. Dickinson, *A Bio-Bibliography of Langston Hughes, 1902–1967,* 1967.
J. Emanuel, *Langston Hughes,* 1967.
C. H. Rollins, *Black Troubadour,* 1970.
Langston Hughes, Black Genius, ed. T. B. O'Daniel, 1971.
O. Jemie, *Langston Hughes: An Introduction to the Poetry,* 1976.
R. K. Barksdale, *Langston Hughes: The Poet and His Critics,* 1977.
E. P. Myers, *Langston Hughes,* 1981.
F. Berry, *Langston Hughes: Before and After Harlem,* 1983.

Texts:
"The Negro Speaks of Rivers" and "I, Too" from *Selected Poems,* 1959.
Remaining selections from *Montage of a Dream Deferred,* 1951.
See also *I Wonder as I Wander: An Autobiographical Journey,* 1956.
The Langston Hughes Reader, 1958.

The Negro Speaks of Rivers

I've known rivers:
I've known rivers ancient as the world and older than the flow of human blood
    in human veins.

My soul has grown deep like the rivers.

I bathed in the Euphrates when dawns were young.
I built my hut near the Congo and it lulled me to sleep.   5
I looked upon the Nile and raised the pyramids above it.
I heard the singing of the Mississippi when Abe Lincoln went down to New
    Orleans, and I've seen its muddy bosom turn all golden in the sunset.

I've known rivers:
Ancient, dusky rivers.

My soul has grown deep like the rivers.   10
1926

I, Too

I, too, sing America.

I am the darker brother.
They send me to eat in the kitchen
When company comes,
But I laugh,   5
And eat well,
And grow strong.

Tomorrow,
I'll be at the table
When company comes.   10
Nobody'll dare
Say to me,
"Eat in the kitchen,"
Then.

Besides,   15
They'll see how beautiful I am
And be ashamed—

I, too, am America.
1932

Dream Boogie

Good morning, daddy!
Ain't you heard
The boogie-woogie rumble
Of a dream deferred?

Listen closely: 5
You'll hear their feet
Beating out and beating out a——

    You think
    It's a happy beat?

Listen to it closely: 10
Ain't you heard
something underneath
like a——

    What did I say?

Sure,   15
I'm happy!
Take it away!

    Hey, pop!
    Re-bop!
    Mop!   20

    Y-e-a-h!
    What don't bug
    them white kids
    sure bugs me:
    We knows everybody   25
    ain't free!

Some of these young ones is cert'ly bad——
One batted a hard ball right through my window
and my gold fish et the glass.

> What's written down   30
> for white folks
> ain't for us a-tall:
> "Liberty And Justice——
> Huh—For All."

> Oop-pop-a-da!   35
> Skee! Daddle-de-do!
> Be-bop!

> Salt'peanuts!

> De-dop!

1951

Sister

That little Negro's married and got a kid.
Why does he keep on foolin' around Marie?
Marie's my sister—not married to me——
But why does *he* keep on foolin' around Marie?
Why don't she get a boy-friend   5
I can understand—some decent man?

> Did it ever occur to you, son,
> the reason Marie runs around with trash
> is she wants some cash?

Don't decent folks have dough?   10

> Unfortunately usually no!

Well, anyway, it don't have to be a married man.

> Did it ever occur to you, boy,
> that a woman does the best she can?

1951

Preference

I likes a woman
six or eight and ten years older'n myself.
I don't fool with these young girls.
Young girl'll say,
    Daddy, I want so-and-so.   5
    I needs this, that, and the other.
But a old woman'll say,
    Honey, what does YOU need?
    I just drawed my money tonight
    and it's all your'n.   10
That's why I likes a older woman
who can appreciate me:
When she conversations you
it ain't forever, *Gimme!*
1951

Movies

The Roosevelt, Renaissance, Gem, Alhambra:
Harlem laughing in all the wrong places
    at the crocodile tears
    of crocodile art
    that you know   5
    in your heart
    is crocodile:

    (Hollywood
    laughs at me,
    black———   10
    so I laugh
    back.)

1951

Not a Movie

Well, they rocked him with road-apples[1]
because he tried to vote
and whipped his head with clubs
and he crawled on his knees to his house
and he got the midnight train   5
and he crossed that Dixie line
now he's livin'
on a 133rd.

He didn't stop in Washington
and he didn't stop in Baltimore   10
neither in Newark on the way.
Six knots was on his head
but, thank God, he wasn't dead,
now there ain't no Ku Klux
on a 133rd.   15
1951

Numbers

If I ever hit for a dollar
gonna salt every dime away
in the Post Office for a rainy day.

I ain't gonna
play back a cent.   5

(Of course, I might
combinate *a little*
with my rent.)
1951

---

[1] Slang for stones.

Advice

Folks, I'm telling you,
birthing is hard
and dying is mean—
so get yourself
a little loving   5
in between.
1951

Ballad of the Landlord

Landlord, landlord,
My roof has sprung a leak.
Don't you 'member I told you about it
Way last week?

Landlord, landlord,   5
These steps is broken down.
When you come up yourself
It's a wonder you don't fall down.

Ten Bucks you say I owe you?
Ten Bucks you say is due?   10
Well, that's Ten Bucks more'n I'll pay you
Till you fix this house up new.

What? You gonna get eviction orders?
You gonna cut off my heat?
You gonna take my furniture and   15
Throw it in the street?

Um-huh! You talking high and mighty.
Talk on—till you get through.
You ain't gonna be able to say a word
If I land my fist on you.   20

Police! Police!
Come and get this man!

He's trying to ruin the government
And overturn the land!

Copper's whistle!   25
Patrol bell!
Arrest.

Precinct Station.
Iron cell.
Headlines in press: 30

MAN THREATENS LANDLORD

TENANT HELD NO BAIL

JUDGE GIVES NEGRO 90 DAYS IN COUNTY
JAIL
1951

Cafe: 3 A.M.

Detectives from the vice squad
with weary sadistic eyes
spotting fairies.

> *Degenerates,*
> some folks say.   5

But God, Nature,
or somebody
made them that way.

Police lady or Lesbian
over there?   10

> *Where?*
> *1951*

Theme for English B

The instructor said,

> *Go home and write*
> *a page tonight.*
> *And let that page come out of you——*
> *Then, it will be true.*   5

I wonder if it's that simple?

I am twenty-two, colored, born in Winston-Salem.
I went to school there, then Durham, then here
to this college on the hill above Harlem.
I am the only colored student in my class.   10
The steps from the hill lead down into Harlem,
through a park, then I cross St. Nicholas,
Eighth Avenue, Seventh, and I come to the Y,
the Harlem Branch Y, where I take the elevator
up to my room, sit down, and write this page: 15

It's not easy to know what is true for you or me
at twenty-two, my age. But I guess I'm what
I feel and see and hear. Harlem, I hear you:
hear you, hear me—we two—you, me, talk on this page.
(I hear New York, too.) Me—who?   20

Well, I like to eat, sleep, drink, and be in love.
I like to work, read, learn, and understand life.
I like a pipe for a Christmas present,
or records—Bessie,[1] bop, or Bach.
I guess being colored doesn't make me *not* like   25
the same things other folks like who are other races.

So will my page be colored that I write?
Being me, it will not be white.
But it will be
a part of you, instructor.   30

You are white——
yet a part of me, as I am a part of you.
That's American.

---

[1] Bessie Smith (1898?–1937), black blues singer.

Sometimes perhaps you don't want to be a part of me.
Nor do I often want to be a part of you.   35
But we are, that's true!
As I learn from you,
I guess you learn from me——
although you're older—and white——
and somewhat more free.   40

This is my page for English B.
1951

Low to High

How can you forget me?
But you do!
You said you was gonna take me
Up with you——
Now you've got your Cadillac,   5
you done forgot that you are black.
How can you forget me
When I'm you?

But you do.

How can you forget me,   10
fellow, say?
How can you low-rate me
this way?
You treat me like you damn well please,
Ignore me—though I pay your fees.   15
How can you forget me?

But you do.
1951

High to Low

God knows
We have our troubles, too——
One trouble is you:
you talk too loud,
cuss too loud,   5
look too black,
don't get anywhere,
and sometimes it seems
you don't even care.
The way you send your kids to school   10
stockings down,
(not Ethical Culture)
the way you shout out loud in church,
(not St. Phillips)
and the way you lounge on doorsteps   15
just as if you were down South,
(not at 409)
the way you clown——
the way, in other words,
you let me down——   20
me, trying to uphold the race
and you——
well, you can see,
we have our problems,
too, with you.   25

1951

Deferred

This year, maybe, do you think I can graduate?
I'm already two years late.
Dropped out six months when I was seven,
a year when I was eleven,
then got put back when we come North.   5
To get through high at twenty's kind of late——
But maybe this year I can graduate.

Maybe now I can have that white enamel stove
I dreamed about when we first fell in love
eighteen years ago.   10
But you know,
rooming and everything
then kids,
cold-water flat and all that.
But now my daughter's married   15
And my boy's most grown——
quit school to work——
and where we're moving
there ain't no stove——
Maybe I can buy that white enamel stove!   20

Me, I always did want to study French.
It don't make sense——
I'll never go to France,
but night schools teach French.
Now at last I've got a job   25
where I get off at five,
in time to wash and dress,
so, s'il-vous plait, I'll study French!

Someday,
I'm gonna buy two new suits   30
at once!

All I want is
one more bottle of gin.

All I want is to see
my furniture paid for.   35

All I want is a wife who will
work with me and not against me. Say,
baby, could you see your way clear?

Heaven, heaven, is my home!
This world I'll leave behind.   40
When I set my feet in glory
I'll have a throne for mine!

I want to pass the civil service.

I want a television set.

You know, as old as I am,   45
I ain't never
owned a decent radio yet?

I'd like to take up Bach.

Montage
of a dream   50
deferred.

Buddy, have you heard?
1951

World War II

What a grand time was the war!
   Oh, my, my!
What a grand time was the war!
   My, my, my!

In wartime we had fun,   5
Sorry that old war is done!
What a grand time was the war,
   My, my!

Echo:

   Did
   Somebody   10
   Die?
1951

Passing[1]

On sunny summer Sunday afternoons in Harlem
when the air is one interminable ball game
and grandma cannot get her gospel hymns
from the Saints of God in Christ
on account of the Dodgers on the radio,   5
on sunny Sunday afternoons
when the kids look all new
and far too clean to stay that way,
and Harlem has its
washed-and-ironed-and-cleaned-best out,   10
the ones who've crossed the line
to live downtown
miss you,
Harlem of the bitter dream,
since their dream has   15
come true.

1951

Likewise

The Jews:
   Groceries
   Suits
   Fruit
   Watches   5
   Diamond rings
   THE DAILY NEWS
Jews sell me things.
Yom Kippur,[1] no!
Shops all over Harlem   10
close up tight that night.

Some folks blame high prices on the Jews.
(Some folks blame too much on Jews).

[1] Black colloquialism applied to a fair-skinned black who is pretending to be white.

[1] The Day of Atonement, a Jewish holy day.

But in Harlem they don't answer back,
Just maybe shrug their shoulders,   15
"What's the use?"

What's the use
In Harlem?
What's the use?
What's the Harlem   20
use in Harlem
what's the lick?

Hey!
Baba-re-bop!
Mop.   25
On a be-bop kick!

Sometimes I think
Jews must have heard
the music of a
dream deferred.   30
1951

Sliver

Cheap little rhymes,
A cheap little tune
Are sometimes as dangerous
As a sliver of the moon.

A cheap little tune   5
To cheap little rhymes
Can cut a man's
Throat sometimes.
1951

Harlem

What happens to a dream deferred?

    Does it dry up
    like a raisin in the sun?
    Or fester like a sore——
    And then run?   5
    Does it stink like rotten meat?
    Or crust and sugar over——
    like a syrupy sweet?

    Maybe it just sags
    like a heavy load.   10

    Or does it explode?

1951

Good Morning

Good morning, daddy!
I was born here, he said,
watched Harlem grow
until colored folks spread
from river to river   5
across the middle of Manhattan
out of Penn Station
dark tenth of a nation,
planes from Puerto Rico,
and holds of boats, chico,   10
up from Cuba Haiti Jamaica,
in busses marked NEW YORK
from Georgia Florida Louisiana
to Harlem Brooklyn the Bronx
but most of all to Harlem   15
dusky sash across Manhattan
I've seen them come dark
    wondering
    wide-eyed
    dreaming   20

out of Penn Station——
but the trains are late.
The gates open——
but there're bars
at each gate.   25

      What happens
      to a dream deferred?

Daddy, ain't you heard?
1951

Same in Blues

I said to my baby,
Baby, take it slow.
I can't, she said, I can't!
I got to go!

      There's a certain   5
      amount of traveling
      in a dream deferred.

Lulu said to Leonard,
I want a diamond ring.
Leonard said to Lulu,   10
You won't get a goddamn thing!

      A certain
      amount of nothing
      in a dream deferred.

Daddy, daddy, daddy,   15
All I want is you.
You can have me, baby——
but my lovin' days is through.

      A certain
      amount of impotence   20
      in a dream deferred.

Three parties
On my party line——

But that third party,
Lord, ain't mine!   25

> *There's liable*
> *to be confusion*
> *in a dream deferred.*

From river to river,
Uptown and down,   30
There's liable to be confusion
when a dream gets kicked around.
1951

Comment on Curb

You talk like
they don't kick
dreams around
Downtown.

> *I expect they do——*   5
> *But I'm talking about*
> *Harlem to you!*

1951

Letter

Dear Mama,
> *Time I pay rent and get my food*
> *and laundry I don't have much left*
> *but here is five dollars for you*
> *to show you I still appreciates you.*   5
> *My girl-friend send her love and say*
> *she hopes to lay eyes on you sometime in life.*
> *Mama, it has been raining cats and dogs up*
> *here. Well, that is all so I will close.*
> > *Your son baby*   10
> > > *Respectably as ever,*
> > > > *Joe*

1951

Island

Between two rivers,
North of the park,
Like darker rivers
The streets are dark.

Black and white,   5
Gold and brown——
Chocolate-custard
Pie of a town.

Dream within a dream,
Our dream deferred.   10

Good morning, daddy!

Ain't you heard?

1951

Countee Cullen
1903–1946

As black writers began to appear in greater numbers in American society, they
began to debate the language in which they should write: Should it be the
English they heard in their own community, or the literary English in which
poetry had conventionally been written? In this debate, they were repeating the
division between the literary English of the "fireside poets" of the nineteenth
century and Whitman's "barbaric yawp" of the American language. Countee
Cullen allied himself with the "literary" poets.

Countee Cullen was born Countee Porter in New York City. At fifteen he
was adopted by a Methodist minister named Frederick Cullen and given a liberal
arts education (B.A. from New York University, M.A. from Harvard). Perhaps
because of his education, Cullen believed that black poets should use the full
resources of literary English rather than write in the dialect they had learned in
childhood. Though he felt free to write on nonracial topics, and though he
translated Euripides' *Medea* (1935), the majority of his poems did concern
themselves with questions of color, as the titles of his first volumes indicate: *Color*
(1925), *Copper Sun* (1927), *The Ballad of the Brown Girl* (1928), *The Black Christ*
(1929).

As part of the Harlem Renaissance, Cullen was one of those Negro intellectuals who took on, in a self-conscious way, the construction of an intellectual and aesthetic culture for the American black, especially for the blacks who had come in increasing numbers from the South to New York City. Cullen came of age just when a critical mass of black artists and thinkers had reached maturity. Cullen's talent was recognized, both at N.Y.U. (with the Witter Bynner Poetry Prize and election to Phi Beta Kappa) and by the larger world (with a Guggenheim fellowship). When he was thirty, he published an important anthology of Negro poetry, *Caroling Dusk;* he also served briefly as editor for two Negro journals, *Opportunity* and *The Crisis* (sponsored by the NAACP). Throughout his life he taught French in the New York high school system.

In claiming the entire poetic heritage of England and America for black poetry, Cullen was claiming full citizenship in letters for his race. This legitimate claim produced not only such bitter and moving poems as "Heritage," but also some stiff and wooden writing in which Cullen is overawed by the very poetic tradition to which he subscribes. Cullen wrote less poetry as the years of schoolteaching wore on, and his untimely death at forty-three kept him from fulfilling the promise of his early productivity. But his principled position that the full range of linguistic potential in English was open to black poets has led to the intellectual poetry of Robert Hayden and Michael Harper, black poets who chiefly follow the "literary" line of Cullen rather than the oral and vernacular line of Langston Hughes.

Further Reading:
B. E. Ferguson, *Countee Cullen and the Negro Renaissance,* 1966.
M. Perry, *A Bio-Bibliography of Countee Cullen,* 1971.

Text:
On These I Stand, 1947.

Yet Do I Marvel

I doubt not God is good, well-meaning, kind,
And did He stoop to quibble could tell why
The little buried mole continues blind,
Why flesh that mirrors Him must some day die,
Make plain the reason tortured Tantalus[1]   5
Is baited by the fickle fruit, declare
If merely brute caprice dooms Sisyphus[2]
To struggle up a never-ending stair.
Inscrutable His ways are, and immune

[1] Tantalus was tortured in Hades by hunger and thirst; when he tried to reach fruit above him, it drew away.

[2] Sisyphus, in Hades, was doomed to continually push a rock up a hill and then see it roll to the bottom again.

To catechism by a mind too strewn   10
With petty cares to slightly understand
What awful brain compels His awful hand.
Yet do I marvel at this curious thing:
To make a poet black, and bid him sing!
1947

Incident

(For Eric Walrond)

Once riding in old Baltimore,
    Heart-filled, head-filled with glee,
I saw a Baltimorean
    Keep looking straight at me.

Now I was eight and very small,   5
    And he was no whit bigger,
And so I smiled, but he poked out
    His tongue, and called me, "Nigger."

I saw the whole of Baltimore
    From May until December;   10
Of all the things that happened there
    That's all that I remember.
1947

Heritage

(For Harold Jackman)

What is Africa to me:
Copper sun or scarlet sea,
Jungle star or jungle track,
Strong bronzed men, or regal black
Women from whose loins I sprang   5
When the birds of Eden sang?
One three centuries removed
From the scenes his fathers loved,
Spicy grove, cinnamon tree,
What is Africa to me?   10

So I lie, who all day long
Want no sound except the song
Sung by wild barbaric birds
Goading massive jungle herds,
Juggernauts of flesh that pass   15
Trampling tall defiant grass
Where young forest lovers lie,
Plighting troth beneath the sky.
So I lie, who always hear,
Though I cram against my ear   20
Both my thumbs, and keep them there,
Great drums throbbing through the air.
So I lie, whose fount of pride,
Dear distress, and joy allied,
Is my somber flesh and skin,   25
With the dark blood dammed within
Like great pulsing tides of wine
That, I fear, must burst the fine
Channels of the chafing net
Where they surge and foam and fret.   30

Africa? A book one thumbs
Listlessly, till slumber comes.
Unremembered are her bats
Circling through the night, her cats
Crouching in the river reeds,   35
Stalking gentle flesh that feeds
By the river brink; no more
Does the bugle-throated roar
Cry that monarch claws have leapt
From the scabbards where they slept.   40
Silver snakes that once a year
Doff the lovely coats you wear,
Seek no covert in your fear
Lest a mortal eye should see;
What's your nakedness to me?   45
Here no leprous flowers rear
Fierce corollas¹ in the air;
Here no bodies sleek and wet,
Dripping mingled rain and sweat,
Tread the savage measures of   50
Jungle boys and girls in love.
What is last year's snow² to me,

---

¹ Crowns of petals.
² An echo of the French poet François Villon
(1431–1463?), whose famous refrain from "La

Ballade des Dames du Temps Jadis" is "Où sont
les neiges d'antan?"

Last year's anything? The tree
Budding yearly must forget
How its past arose or set—   55
Bough and blossom, flower, fruit,
Even what shy bird with mute
Wonder at her travail there,
Meekly labored in its hair.
One three centuries removed   60
From the scenes his fathers loved,
Spicy grove, cinnamon tree,
What is Africa to me?

So I lie, who find no peace
Night or day, no slight release   65
From the unremittent beat
Made by cruel padded feet
Walking through my body's street.
Up and down they go, and back,
Treading out a jungle track.   70
So I lie, who never quite
Safely sleep from rain at night—
I can never rest at all
When the rain begins to fall;
Like a soul gone mad with pain   75
I must match its weird refrain;
Ever must I twist and squirm,
Writhing like a baited worm,
While its primal measures drip
Through my body, crying, "Strip!   80
Doff this new exuberance.
Come and dance the Lover's Dance!"
In an old remembered way
Rain works on me night and day.

Quaint, outlandish heathen gods   85
Black men fashion out of rods,
Clay, and brittle bits of stone,
In a likeness like their own,
My conversion came high-priced;
I belong to Jesus Christ,   90
Preacher of humility;
Heathen gods are naught to me.

Father, Son, and Holy Ghost,
So I make an idle boast;
Jesus of the twice-turned cheek,   95
Lamb of God, although I speak

With my mouth thus, in my heart
Do I play a double part.
Ever at Thy glowing altar
Must my heart grow sick and falter,   100
Wishing He I served were black,
Thinking then it would not lack
Precedent of pain to guide it,
Let who would or might deride it;
Surely then this flesh would know   105
Yours had borne a kindred woe.
Lord, I fashion dark gods, too,
Daring even to give You
Dark despairing features where,
Crowned with dark rebellious hair,   110
Patience wavers just so much as
Mortal grief compels, while touches
Quick and hot, of anger, rise
To smitten cheek and weary eyes.
Lord, forgive me if my need   115
Sometimes shapes a human creed.
All day long and all night through,
One thing only must I do:
Quench my pride and cool my blood,
Lest I perish in the flood.   120
Lest a hidden ember set
Timber that I thought was wet
Burning like the dryest flax,
Melting like the merest wax,
Lest the grave restore its dead.   125
Not yet has my heart or head
In the least way realized
They and I are civilized.
1947

To Certain Critics

Then call me traitor if you must,
Shout treason and default!
Say I betray a sacred trust
Aching beyond this vault.
I'll bear your censure as your praise,   5
For never shall the clan

Confine my singing to its ways
Beyond the ways of man.

No racial option narrows grief,
Pain is no patriot,   10
And sorrow plaits her dismal leaf
For all as lief as not.
With blind sheep groping every hill,
Searching an oriflamme,[1]
How shall the shepherd heart then thrill   15
To only the darker lamb?

1947

---

[1] Banner representing an ideal.

Robert Rauschenberg,
Estate,
oil and printer's ink, 1963.
Philadelphia Museum of Art.
Given by the Friends of the
Philadelphia Museum of Art.

The Literature of Postwar America: Prose 1940–1973

By 1940 American literature was being taught in universities not only in the United States but also in England and Europe, and it was being taught by professors of American literature. The Nobel Prize that Sinclair Lewis received in 1930 was in part a tribute to Lewis's achievement, but it was also a tribute to American literature. "Yes," the secretary of the Swedish Academy said, "Sinclair Lewis is an American. He writes the new language—American— as one of the representatives of a hundred and twenty million souls" who have created the "new great American literature." In creating this new great literature, American writers transformed writing into a profession, sometimes a lucrative one. During the 1920s and the 1930s their books were marketed and read widely in England and Europe as well as America. By the 1950s they were available in translations in scores of languages, including Arabic and Hebrew, Japanese and Estonian. Today, no literature reaches a wider international audience. American writers have been assisted by their government, particularly through the WPA (Works Progress Administration), by a growing advertising industry, by magazines, publishers, foundations, and universities; and they have benefited enormously from the relative affluence of their society, from the growing attraction of English as a second language, and from the prodigious prominence and power of their nation.

Yet, despite the rising fame and affluence that surrounds them, recent American writers describe their position as somehow diminished. In 1967 John Barth described the fiction he and his colleagues were writing as "the literature of exhaustion," or more precisely, "the literature of exhausted possibility"—as though to suggest that earlier writers had left more recent ones the task of working depleted ground. Nine years later John Updike announced that "the profession of writer in the United States has been sharply devalued in the last thirty years, and has suffered loss both in the dignity assigned to it by non-writers, and in the sense of purpose that shapes a profession from within."

Just before and after World War I, a new generation of writers set out to reinvent literature, confident that they could deal with the past on their own terms. By midcentury, young writers had begun to feel that they were surrounded by giants. Being a writer in Mississippi after William Faulkner, Eudora Welty remarked, "was like living near a big mountain." Finally, however, the concerns that Barth and Updike locate have more to do with the pace of change and the force of history than with the prodigious achievement of their forebears. Continuities exist, of course, even surprising ones. We have still our hermits and our celebrants, though it is strange as well as useful to think of the reclusive Thomas Pynchon as an heir of Emily Dickinson and to regard the self-advertising Norman Mailer as an heir of Walt Whitman. But it is change that abounds—change so rapid as to make America appear almost formless. The shift of large segments of our population from farms and villages to large cities; the continued unraveling of our national ethos, of the manners, mores, and beliefs that shape our thought and action; and the dramatic unfolding of new technologies, especially in weaponry, in medicine, and in telecommunications, have altered every aspect of American life and art.

Like our century, our writers have become more diverse—racially, sexually, and politically—and our fiction has become more urban. During the 1920s the literary center of the United States shifted from the East to the Midwest and the South; by mid-century it was shifting from towns and villages to cities and suburbs. Despite the emergence of Wright Morris (Central City, Nebraska), William Gass (Fargo, North Dakota), Scott Momaday (Anadarko, Oklahoma), and Larry McMurtry (Archer City, Texas), writers are less likely to come from small towns than from cities—Chicago (Saul Bellow, Gwendolyn Brooks), New York (Bernard Malamud, Norman Mailer, James Baldwin, Susan Sontag), Newark, New Jersey (Philip Roth), Birmingham, Alabama (Walker Percy), Tulsa, Oklahoma (Ralph Ellison), Houston, Texas (Donald Barthelme)—or from suburbs (John Cheever from Quincy, Massachusetts, Thomas Pynchon from Glen Cove, Long Island).

Amid the urbanization and diversification of America, writers have encountered a welter of staggering events, some of them almost cataclysmic: three wars (World War II, Korea, and Vietnam) and many conflicts and skirmishes; the explosion of the first atomic bomb (1945); the production of the first electronic computer (1946); the beginning of full-time television broadcasting (1948); the development of the transistor (1948); the explosion of the first hydrogen bomb (1952); the deciphering of the double-helix configuration of the molecule of deoxyribonucleic acid (DNA) in 1953; the civil rights revolution of the 1950s and 1960s, and with it the rise of blacks and of women; the rapid exploration of space; the first successful heart transplant (1968); and the dramatic development of computer technology, including speculation about artificial intelligence.

Thus bombarded, American writers seem at times to have lost their sense of place and purpose. "I grew up, and formulated my ambition to be a 'creative artist' of some sort," John Updike asserts, "in a world where the radio and the cinema were the mass media. Both bathed the American consciousness in emanations from worlds distinctly artificial. . . . These films and radio shows were made things, fictions," he adds, noting that fictions were also "the chief staple of the book industry." Now, he laments, "so-called nonfiction dominates" the publishing world, "and the dominant mass medium is television," featuring events rather than plays, happenings rather than fictions—"the sports event, the panel discussion, the talk show, the quiz show."

At once interlaced with the media and scrutinized by them, our society has become more interconnected and self-conscious, and our culture has become more diverse and less coherent. Simultaneously, our literature has undergone a transformation, as seen especially in the rising authority of nonfiction and in the blurring of lines between fiction and nonfiction. To comprehend these changes is, of course, no easy task. But the place to begin is with the force of history and the impact of our new means of reporting it.

A Second Great War

The United States entered World War II as it had entered World War I— reluctantly. In 1935 Italy conquered Ethiopia; in 1936 the Spanish civil war broke out; in 1937 Japan increased hostilities against China; in 1938 Germany invaded Austria. Soon the flow of refugees from Asia and Europe quickened, and the flow of warnings and appeals as well. The Spanish civil war, with Russia intervening on one side, Germany and Italy on the other, was a sign of things to come, and it galvanized the attention of many writers, including André Malraux from France; George Orwell, W. H. Auden, and Stephen Spender from England; and John Dos Passos and Ernest Hemingway from America. In the title of his novel *For Whom the Bell Tolls* (1940), which was based on his experiences as a war correspondent in Spain, Hemingway suggested that the bells tolling in Europe were tolling for the world as well. In January 1936, however, ten million American workers remained unemployed, and America's face still turned inward, waiting for full recovery to arrive. America First was the name of one isolationist organization, and it was the slogan of many Americans. It stood for neutrality and against all unnecessary entanglements—whether alliances, aid, or intervention.

As the decade of the 1930s drew to a close, the pace of aggression accelerated. In March 1939 Germany declared the state of Czechoslovakia dissolved; in April Italy invaded Albania; in September Germany invaded Poland. In 1938 and again in 1939 Hitler both intensified and broadened his persecution of Europe's Jews. Still America's reluctance persisted. A remarkable phrase, characterizing the whole European debacle as "the phony war," gained rather than lost currency during the dark fall and winter of 1939–1940. The message America sent abroad was blunt: Germany, Italy, and Japan would have to be stopped without American involvement.

A World Grown Suddenly Small

There comes a time in the affairs of men when they must prepare to defend not their homes alone, but the tenets of faith and humanity on which their churches, their government and their very civilization are founded. . . . The world has grown so small and weapons of attack so swift that no nation can be safe in its will to pursue peace so long as any other single nation refuses to settle its grievances at the council table. . . . In our foreign relations we have learned from the past what not to do. From new wars we have learned . . . that effective timing of defense and the distant points from which attacks may be launched are completely different from what they were twenty years ago.

Franklin Delano Roosevelt (1939)

Throughout the bleak spring of 1940, lights continued going out all over Europe. In April Germany invaded Denmark and Norway; in May, Belgium; in June, France. Within a matter of months, Allied resistance had crumbled, the last British troops had been forced off the Continent, and England stood virtually alone, isolated and under siege. Almost immediately, both public opinion and government policy in America began to shift. Citizens moved to organize—the Committee to Defend America by Aiding the Allies sprang up in the Midwest in May, soon to be followed by a like-minded organization, the Century Group, based in New York. In June President Roosevelt pledged to send aid "to the opponents of force"—a pledge he honored, first, in the fall of 1940, by sending Britain fifty destroyers, and second, in the spring of 1941, by initiating the "lend-lease" agreement that would eventually send Britain approximately $7 billion in aid. Although neutrality remained the official policy of the United States, it had ceased strictly to control action, and events were running hard against its revival. In June 1941 Germany invaded Russia; in July Japan occupied southern Indochina. Then, on the morning of December 7, 1941, a day President Roosevelt said would "live in infamy," Japan bombed Pearl Harbor.

Japan's attack on Pearl Harbor was one of the most successful surprise attacks in military history, and it left the United States reeling. It would be months before good news came from either the Atlantic or the Pacific. But the attack also put an end to effective dissent, if not to isolationist murmurings. The unity of purpose that the president had first articulated in June 1940—"In our unity, our American unity," he had said, we shall support "the opponents of force" and shall prove "equal to the task of every emergency and every defense"—quickly took shape. Families began and ended their days gathered around radios, listening to news reports on the war or "fireside chats" by the president.

In going to war, the nation also went back to work. Volunteers, female and male, black and white, poured in record numbers into factories as well as the armed services. Soon people who had been unemployed were saving money to buy "Victory Bonds" through payroll deductions, and Hollywood was making movies about factory workers *(Blondie for Victory)* as well as pilots, soldiers, and sailors *(Salute to Courage* and *To the Shores of Tripoli).* Stage and screen stars traveled around the world to entertain the troops, while directors like Frank Capra, John Huston, and John Ford began making documentary films—some pieced together from stock war footage, others shot on location. Leaders of the American Federation of Labor and the Congress of Industrial Organizations adopted a no-strike policy, and the manufacture of war supplies soared. In 1940 the aviation industry produced 12,000 planes; in 1943 it produced more than 100,000. In addition to arming its own troops, the United States sent thousands of planes, tanks, and trucks to Russia and England. The result was the most successful war effort the world has ever seen.

"A Tremendous Flash of Light"

At exactly fifteen minutes past eight in the morning, on August 6, 1945, Japanese time, . . . the atomic bomb flashed above Hiroshima. . . . There was no sound of planes. The morning was still; the place was cool and pleasant.

Then a tremendous flash of light cut across the sky. . . .

Early . . . [on] August 7th, the Japanese radio broadcast for the first time a succinct announcement that very few, if any, of the people most concerned with its content, the survivors in Hiroshima, happened to hear: "Hiroshima suffered considerable damage as the result of an attack by a few B-29s. It is believed that a new type of bomb was used. The details are being investigated." Nor is it probable that any of the survivors happened to be tuned in on a short-wave rebroadcast of an extraordinary announcement by the President of the United States, which identified the new bomb as atomic: "That bomb had more power than twenty thousand tons of TNT. It had more than two thousand times the blast power of the British Grand Slam, which is the largest bomb ever yet used in the history of warfare." Those victims who were able to worry at all about what had happened thought of it and discussed it in more primitive, childish terms—gasoline sprinkled from an airplane, maybe, or some combustible gas, or a big cluster of incendiaries, or the work of parachutists; but, even if they had known the truth, most of them were too busy or too weary or too badly hurt to care that they were the objects of the first great experiment in the use of atomic power, which (as the voices on the short wave shouted) no country except the United States, with its industrial know-how, its willingness to throw two billion gold dollars into an important wartime gamble, could possibly have developed. . . .

At two minutes after eleven o'clock on the morning of August 9th, the second atomic bomb was dropped, on Nagasaki. It was several days before the survivors of Hiroshima knew they had company, because the Japanese radio and newspapers were being extremely cautious on the subject of the strange weapon.

John Hersey, *Hiroshima* (1946)

In June 1942, seven months after Pearl Harbor, Allied forces halted Japan's advance across the Pacific at the Battle of Midway; in August they launched a successful counteroffensive at Guadalcanal, turning the tide of battle in the Pacific. On November 8, 1942, Allied forces invaded North Africa to start on the long road toward liberating Europe. Less than two years later, they staged major new offensives in both the Atlantic and the Pacific: On June 6, 1944, they invaded Normandy, piercing Germany's hold on northern Europe; two weeks later they won a decisive victory over the Japanese fleet in the Battle of Leyte Gulf. Less than one year later, when the war in Europe ended, on May 7, 1945, with Germany's "unconditional surrender," Allied forces had taken Iwo Jima and Okinawa and were poised to invade the mainland of Japan.

Given the unparalleled magnitude of World War II and the unparalleled horror of the Holocaust—including the systematic annihilation of six million Jews—the twentieth century's second "Great War" was certain to mark the consciousness of the world for decades to come. As it turned out, however, one cataclysmic event remained to reinforce one of the haunting lessons of the twentieth century—that nations have done whatever their weapons made possible. More than any war in history, World War II was a war of technology—of new developments in synthetic rubber, radar, microwaves, and rockets as well as ships, planes, and weaponry. In the summer of 1939, after a group of physicists that included Albert Einstein and Enrico Fermi met in Washington, D.C., President Roosevelt established the Advisory Committee on Uranium and thus initiated development of the atomic bomb. On July 16, 1945, in Alamogordo, New Mexico, the United States successfully tested the world's first atomic bomb. Less than one month later, on August 6 and August 9, the United States dropped atomic bombs on Hiroshima and Nagasaki, ushering in a new era even as it brought World War II to an end.

Literature and Reform in an Age of Conformity

World War II was in many ways "bad for writing," William Faulkner wrote his agent in 1944. For several younger writers and a few older ones, the war's interruption was direct. Saul Bellow served in the merchant marine, John Cheever and Norman Mailer in the U.S. Army, Ernest Hemingway once again as a war correspondent. Having failed to get a commission, Faulkner spent considerable time in Hollywood, working on screenplays about Nazi spies *(Northern Pursuit)* or great heroes *(The De Gaulle Story)*. But the larger problem was the preemptive force of the war itself, which seemed to put almost everything that was not directly related to the war effort, including most literature, on hold for the duration.

Americans emerged from World War II convinced that they had participated in the great adventure of their time. Literary appropriation of the war commenced immediately and continued long. It reaches from the 1940s, with John Hersey's *Hiroshima* (1946), James Gould Cozzens's *Guard of Honor* (1948), and Norman Mailer's *The Naked and the Dead* (1948); through the 1950s, with James Jones's *From Here to Eternity* (1951), Herman Wouk's *The Caine Mutiny*

(1951), and Thomas Berger's *Crazy in Berlin* (1958), and the 1960s, with Joseph Heller's *Catch-22* (1961); to the 1970s, with Thomas Pynchon's *Gravity's Rainbow* (1973). Other works, such as Harriette Arnow's *The Dollmaker* (1954), reflected the impact of the war on "the home front," as it came to be called.

Many of these works emanate from troubled sensibilities and constitute counterrealities. They are imaginative violences from within that seek to match physical violences from without. As such, they offer minority reports—each what Wallace Stevens once called an "unofficial view of being." But they do not disclose disillusionment comparable to that seen in the literature of World War I. Despite the sacrifices and losses that it inflicted, World War II fostered a sense of unity that ran deep and proved durable.

Confident that the war had tested their nation many times and hopeful that most of the tests lay behind them, Americans emerged from World War II impatient to get on with life. The troops were ready to come home, and their families and friends were ready to welcome them. Demobilization was rapid. Yet, contrary to expectations, problems surfaced almost immediately. In 1946 the nation lost a colossal 107,475,000 workdays to strikes, slowing production and increasing prices. Disputes between labor and management remained a problem for years to come. Some servicemen returned home only to find themselves feeling lost without the sense of high purpose that the war had given them. Many women emerged from the war hoping that their large contributions to the war effort would provide a basis for a new start, only to find that they were expected to step aside as returning servicemen moved back into the work force.

In 1946 Mary Beard published *Woman as a Force in History*, hoping to push the beginnings of the women's movement back beyond the nineteenth century through the Renaissance to the Middle Ages. *Life* magazine described Beard's work as "simply ridiculous," then went on to suggest that the nation might cure such madness by drafting women into the army so that men could teach them the meaning of discipline and responsibility. As it turned out, however, apathy proved more damaging than hostility: Beard's book remained widely unread, her cause largely unfulfilled. In 1912 the distinguished anthropologist Ruth Benedict had written, "My real me was a creature I dared not look upon. . . . No one had ever heard that me. If they had, they would have thought it an interesting pose. The mask was tightly adjusted." Despite scattered changes and many promises, Benedict's words were almost as pertinent in the 1940s and the 1950s as they had been in 1912.

For black Americans, on the other hand, World War II marked a significant, if modest, turning point. "A change will come out of this war," Faulkner wrote in a letter of July 4, 1943, referring to the heroic actions of black servicemen in the war, that will force "the politicians and the people who run this country . . . to make good the shibboleth they glibly talk about freedom, liberty, human rights." In 1945 Richard Wright published *Black Boy*. Two years later Jackie Robinson, Branch Rickey, and the Brooklyn Dodgers defied baseball's rigid racial line, and so began the long struggle to integrate professional sports. A decade later, in 1957, while Congress was passing its first piece of civil rights legislation since Reconstruction, Althea Gibson, a young black woman born in South Carolina and reared in Harlem, murmured "at last, at last" as she curtsied before the Queen of England to receive tennis's most coveted award, the Wimbledon trophy. Between Robinson's achievement in the summer of 1947 and Gibson's in the summer of 1957, President Truman integrated the U.S. armed services (1948), the Supreme Court struck down segregation in the public schools (1954), and Martin Luther King organized a successful bus boycott in Montgomery, Alabama (1956), launching a campaign that would eventually win the support of thousands of people working in hundreds of towns and cities.

More striking, however, than either the disappointments or the reforms of American life in the late 1940s and the 1950s was the strong sense of unity that rolled across the land. Despite ups and downs, the nation's economy remained strong; despite frustrations, its expectations remained high. In 1947 some four million men and women were attending colleges and universities on the G.I. Bill. When details of the wreckage that Germany had wrought in Europe and that Japan had wrought in Asia began to emerge, and especially when details of the atrocities inflicted on the Jews of Europe began to circulate, World War II became even more clearly a great crusade. The sheer magnitude of the Holocaust was staggering: six million Jews—men, women, and children—annihilated. But as seared memories and ghastly reports began to disclose details of what had happened in the gas chambers, in the medical and military "experimental" stations, in the crematoriums, and in the torture chambers of the Nazi concentration camps, the United States was forced to confront what its soldiers had confronted as they liberated those camps: "There," wrote Colonel William W. Quinn, who led U.S. 7th Army troops in rescuing the survivors of Dachau, "our troops found sights, sounds, and stenches horrible beyond belief, cruelties so enormous as to be incomprehensible to the normal mind."

"Ashes in the Stream of the Sola"

Then they would feel the gas and crowd together away from the menacing columns and finally stampede towards the huge metal door with its little window, where they piled up in one blue clammy blood-spattered pyramid, clawing and mauling at each other even in death. Twenty-five minutes later the "exhauster" electric pumps removed the gas-laden air, the great metal door slid open, and the men of the Jewish *Sonderkommando* entered, wearing gas-masks and gumboots and carrying hoses, for their first task was to remove the blood and defecations before dragging the clawing dead apart with nooses and hooks, the prelude to the ghastly search for gold and the removal of the teeth and hair which were regarded by the Germans as strategic materials. Then the journey by lift or rail-wagon to the furnaces, the mill that ground the clinker to fine ash, and the lorry that scattered the ashes in the stream of the Sola.

quoted in Gerald Reitlinger, *The Final Solution* (1953)

"But I Had No More Tears"

There was silence all round now, broken only by groans. In front of the block, the SS were giving orders. An officer passed by the beds. My father begged me:

"My son, some water. . . . I'm burning. . . . My stomach. . . ."

"Quiet, over there!" yelled the officer.

"Eliezer," went on my father, "some water. . . ."

The officer came up to him and shouted at him to be quiet. But my father did not hear him. He went on calling me. The officer dealt him a violent blow on the head with his truncheon.

I did not move. I was afraid. My body was afraid of also receiving a blow.

Then my father made a rattling noise and it was my name: "Eliezer."

I could see that he was still breathing—spasmodically.

I did not move.

When I got down after roll call, I could see his lips trembling as he murmured something. Bending over him, I stayed gazing at him for over an hour, engraving into myself the picture of his blood-stained face, his shattered skull.

Then I had to go to bed. I climbed into my bunk, above my father, who was still alive. It was January 28, 1945.

I awoke on January 29 at dawn. In my father's place lay another invalid. They must have taken him away before dawn and carried him to the crematory. He may still have been breathing.

There were no prayers at his grave. No candles were lit to his memory. His last word was my name. A summons, to which I did not respond.

I did not weep, and it pained me that I could not weep. But I had no more tears.

Elie Wiesel, *Night* (1958)

Soon Russia began to bolster the strong sense of American unity that came out of the war through a series of aggressive acts in Europe. "We have got to understand," Dean Acheson announced early in 1946, "that all our lives the danger, the uncertainty, the need for alertness, for effort, for discipline will be upon us. It will be hard for us." On March 5, 1946, Winston Churchill journeyed from England to Missouri to warn that an "iron curtain" had descended across Europe, separating the East from the West. One year later, on March 12, 1947, President Truman outlined the Truman Doctrine: "I believe that it must be the policy of the United States to support free peoples who are resisting attempted subjugation by armed minorities or by outside pressures." But Russia's response to such declarations was clear: Having already occupied Poland, Russia overran Hungary in April, and a year later, in February 1948, Czechoslovakia. On June 5, 1947, General George Marshall, secretary of state, moved to counter Russia's expansion into Europe by setting in motion the Marshall Plan—a plan designed to combat the "hunger, poverty, desperation, and chaos" that threatened western Europe by restoring the region's economy and permitting "the emergence of political and social conditions in which free institutions can exist." A year later, on June 19, 1948, Russia blockaded Berlin, forcing the United States to organize an airlift that would last until the blockade was lifted on May 12, 1949. Eventually, however, Russia's aggressive acts worked to alienate all but the most determined of its friends, perhaps in part because they bore too close a resemblance to Germany's expansion in the 1930s.

Despite domestic tensions, therefore, the dominant forces at work in the United States between 1945 and 1960 were centripetal. Never before had there been so little resistance to the integration of intellectuals, including writers and artists, into the government, the media, and the universities. One result was the rush of novels set in universities, including Mary McCarthy's *The Groves of Academe* (1952), Randall Jarrell's *Pictures from an Institution* (1954), and John Barth's *The End of the Road* (1958). Soon artists and intellectuals were less concerned with the crippling impact of alienation than with the debilitating impact of assimilation. In 1952 *Partisan Review* organized a symposium called "Our Country and Our Culture" and invited twenty-five of the nation's leading literary critics, writers, sociologists, political theorists, anthropologists, and philosophers to respond to the proposition that "American intellectuals now regard America and its institutions in a new way." The clear consensus was not only that intellectuals did in fact regard America in a new way, but also that *new* meant "less critical." Having once appeared skeptical and even jaundiced toward their country, writers now seemed sympathetic and even protective—in part because they regarded America as less hostile to art, and in part because they regarded America as offering the only viable alternative to "Russian totalitarianism."

Such thinking troubled a few participants in the *Partisan Review* symposium. Norman Mailer described the symposium's assumptions as "shocking." Two years later, in an essay called "This Age of Conformity" (1954), Irving Howe declared dangerous the tendency to endorse America's "claim to a unique and immaculate destiny." But unity and its corollary, conformity, remained the dominant forces of the age, particularly during the Eisenhower years (1953–1961) and especially in the business world. David Riesman's sociological study *The Lonely Crowd* (1950) —which traced the rise of "other-directed people," people whose actions are based less on internal convictions than on responses "to the signals" provided by their contemporary peers—became one of the classics of the age, anticipating Sloan Wilson's novel, *The Man in the Gray Flannel Suit* (1955), as well as William S. Whyte's work of social analysis, *The Organization Man* (1956).

With the rise of unity and conformity came clear political dangers, as Senator Joe McCarthy (Republican, Wisconsin) promptly proved. Between February 1950, when he made his first dramatic accusations, and December 1954, when he became the fourth senator in 167 years to be censured by the Senate, McCarthy headed an inquisition that dominated the American political scene as few events ever had before. On one side, McCarthy exploited the nation's legitimate concerns for issues of national security; on the other, he exploited the nation's uneasiness with everything strange or foreign. In the process, he accused hundreds

---

"Other-Directed People"

What is common to all the other-directed people is that their contemporaries are the source of direction for the individual—either those known to [them] or those with whom [they are] indirectly acquainted, through friends and through the mass media. . . .

Of course, it matters very much who these "others" are: whether they are the individual's immediate circle or a "higher" circle or the anonymous voices of the mass media; whether the individual fears the hostility of chance acquaintances or only of those who "count." But his need for approval and direction from others—and contemporary others rather than ancestors—goes beyond the reasons that lead most people in any era to care very much what others think of them. While all people want and need to be liked by some of the people some of the time, it is only the modern other-directed types who make this their chief source of direction and chief area of sensitivity.

David Riesman, *The Lonely Crowd: A Study of the Changing American Character* (1950)

---

of people—composers like Aaron Copland, writers like Howard Fast and Lillian Hellman, professors like Owen Lattimore and Philip Jessup—of being either Communists, Communist sympathizers, or Communist dupes. Before he was done, he had impugned the loyalty of Secretary of State George Marshall, the Department of State, the U.S. Information Service, the U.S. Army, and even President Eisenhower.

The McCarthy debacle tested the nation's commitment to civil liberties—its tolerance of dissent and its respect for freedom of conscience—many times. Among direct literary responses to the ordeal, the most notable was Arthur Miller's *The Crucible* (1953). Still, the sense of unity that remained dominant also proved useful, enabling the nation to confront a series of international crises, including the blockade of Berlin (1948–1949); the emergence of Communist China (1949); Russia's development of the atomic bomb (1949); the development of the hydrogen bomb, first in the United States (1952) and then in Russia (1953); the Suez Canal crisis (1956–1958); the launchings of *Sputnik I* and *Sputnik II* (1957); Castro's victory in Cuba (1959); and especially a hard, ambiguous war in Korea in which more than 50,000 men died and nearly 100,000 were wounded. Furthermore, although unity clearly carried cultural as well as political implications, including some that were alarming, it proved to be stimulating rather than stultifying. If only by provoking what Robert Frost once called "counter-love, original response," the 1950s produced both an impressive culture and a lively counterculture.

The Literature of the 1950s

The counterculture of the 1950s—the hippies and the "beat generation"— appealed, as one young writer put it, to those unable to find gray flannel suits to fit their souls. Centered around such poets as Allen Ginsberg and Lawrence Ferlinghetti and such prose writers as Jack Kerouac, the hippies made the City Lights Book Store in the North Beach area of San Francisco famous. College students across the country listened to recordings of Ginsberg reading "Howl." One of the striking features of the counterculture of the 1950s, however, is the extent to which its very considerable political potential remained quiescent, in both poetry and music.

The rock and roll music of Elvis Presley came in part out of the rhythm and blues tradition—music played by blacks for blacks—and it came in part out of the country and western tradition—music played largely by whites for whites. Presley's music thus drew on two different traditions of protest, much of it bitter. Yet the protest in Presley's music dealt more with natural desires, sad fates, and repressive mores than with the oppressive power of American culture and thus remained largely innocent of politics. It was later—with Bob Dylan in the 1960s more than with Elvis Presley in the 1950s, and with the Rolling Stones more than with the Beatles—that America's counterculture became a political force.

At the same time, literature flourished. Scores of writers—Eudora Welty from Mississippi; Saul Bellow from the West Side of Chicago; Norman Mailer, Arthur Miller, and Bernard Malamud from Brooklyn, New York; Ralph Ellison from Oklahoma, by way of Alabama and Harlem; James Baldwin from Harlem; and Flannery O'Connor from Milledgeville, Georgia—emerged to confront us with protagonists whose indignation bespeaks an involvement in their worlds and whose dissent signals a love for it. Some of the protagonists of the 1950s are hampered and preshrunk by fear of being different; others are too dangling or lonely ever to be complete; still others are so dominated by intolerance, poorly repressed hostilities, hidden doubts, or secret fears that their violence finally turns either against themselves or against others. Like Mailer's Sam Slovoda in "The Man Who Studied Yoga," they frequently find themselves torn between "the loss of a country" they love yet have "never seen" and "repudiation" of the only country in which they have ever lived. Blacks, Jews, and southerners alike find it difficult to be what they are—and just as difficult not to be what they are. As a result, they are tested many times. In their affirmations and celebrations, as in their denials and renunciations, they are at least as apt to fail as to succeed. Most of them feel alienated, and some of them, particularly those created by Flannery O'Connor, are so estranged that their emotions seem borrowed, their actions accidental. Yet at mid-century art remained a way of reaching for the timeless— or, as Eudora Welty put it, a way of making "time give back all it has taken, through turning life by way of the memory into art."

Writing in "The Territory Ahead," Wright Morris states that "an element of despair, a destructive element, is one of the signs" by which we must recognize "the modern temper" and that another "is the constructive use to which this element is put." Like the writers of the 1920s and 1930s, writers of the 1950s force their disillusionment to serve the purposes of experimentation and reinvention. Their indignation, their dissent, and even their despair, they direct toward discovery. In their fiction, the inherited is transformed into the new, and the bleak is merged with the experimental.

The End of Unity

Compared with the drastic dislocations of the 1960s, the crises that punctuated the 1950s have come almost inevitably to seem much tamer than they were. For the 1960s, as the phrase goes, were "something else." To one recent historian, they represent "the unraveling of America"; to another, they constitute "America's suicide attempt." Given the countermoves of the 1970s, both phrases may seem extreme, but the 1960s, dominated by extreme actions, now lend themselves to extreme statements.

In May 1960 the Russians shot down an American spy plane over their territory, then proceeded to watch as one American official after another, including President Eisenhower, embarrassed themselves by issuing false denials and misleading reports. Five months later a judge in Georgia invoked a technicality in order to put Martin Luther King in jail. But neither the deceit of May nor the hypocrisy of October could foreshadow what was to come. In January 1961 John Fitzgerald Kennedy became the first Roman Catholic to be sworn in as president of the United States. A few months later, with summer on its way, Bob Dylan left Minnesota for Greenwich Village, where he launched a spectacular career writing and singing songs whose titles—"Blowin' in the Wind," "A Hard Rain's Gonna Fall," "The Times They Are A-Changing"— anticipated the sharp turns and twists that lay ahead. That same summer, violence broke out across the South, as "freedom riders" sought to integrate public transportation.

Rock and Roll

Starting simply as a vehicle for solo performers, rock and roll didn't differ radically from some of the popular music that had preceded it. Out of Negro rhythm and blues and country and western came Elvis Presley . . . with his long sideburns, tight pants and suggestive gyrations. . . . The Beatles, bursting onto the scene in the early '60s with Edwardian clothes and English schoolboy haircuts, transformed the original primitive Negro sound, making it acceptable to the mass of young white people all over the world. They brought to prominence Group Rock, one of the most attractive symbols of our non-private, corporate, thoroughly electronic age. Now literally "armies of minstrels"—the Beach Boys, the Jefferson Airplane, the Grateful Dead, the Who, the Bee Gees, the Doors, the Mothers of Invention, the Buffalo Springfield, and so on—indicate the awesome potential of electronic sound.

Joan Peyser, "The Music of Sound, or, The Beatles and the Beatless" (1967)

The civil rights movement of the late 1950s and the 1960s is often associated with the violent confrontations that it triggered and with the way it touched every region of the country, spawning clashes in the North, the Midwest, and the West as well as the South. But race riots had occurred in Atlanta around the turn of the century, in Detroit in 1943, and in Harlem in 1935 and 1943. What distinguished the movement of the 1950s and the 1960s was its success in arousing the moral conscience of people everywhere and its success in marshaling the power of the federal government, as seen in the historic Civil Rights Act of 1964 and the Voting Rights Act of 1965.

In September 1962 it took both a federal court order and federal marshals to integrate the University of Mississippi. On April 3, 1963, King launched his campaign to demolish segregation in Birmingham. "Downtown Birmingham," he wrote later, "echoed to the strains of the freedom songs." Four months later, on August 28, in what was perhaps the greatest day in the history of the civil rights movement, King led 200,000 Americans in a march on Washington. Gathered at the Lincoln Memorial, the crowd listened first to such performers as Dick Gregory, Joan Baez, and Bob Dylan, then to Martin Luther King:

> When the architects of our great republic wrote the magnificent words of the Constitution and the Declaration of Independence, they were signing a promissory note to which every American was to fall heir. This note was a promise that all men, yes, black men as well as white men, would be guaranteed the inalienable rights of life, liberty, and the pursuit of happiness.

"The Racist Cancer in the Body of America"

You watch. I will be labeled as, at best, an "irresponsible" black man. I have always felt about this accusation that the black "leader" whom white men consider to be "responsible" is invariably the black "leader" who never gets any results. You only get action as a black man if you are regarded by the white man as "irresponsible." In fact, this much I had learned when I was just a little boy. And since I have been some kind of a "leader" of black people here in the racist society of America, I have been more reassured each time the white man resisted me, or attacked me harder—because each time made me more certain that I was on the right track in the American black man's best interests. The racist white man's opposition automatically made me know that I did offer the black man something worthwhile.

Yes, I have cherished my "demagogue" role. I know that societies often have killed the people who have helped to change those societies. And if I can die having brought any light, having exposed any meaningful truth that will help to destroy the racist cancer that is malignant in the body of America—then, all of the credit is due to Allah. Only the mistakes have been mine.

The Autobiography of Malcolm X (1964)

Compared with the voices of leaders like Malcolm X, John Lewis, H. Rap Brown, and Stokely Carmichael, King's was a moderate voice. But nerves were raw and suspicions ran high in the 1960s. Before the end of 1963, Robert Kennedy, attorney general of the United States, had agreed with J. Edgar Hoover, director of the Federal Bureau of Investigation, that King was a dangerous man. In October the FBI set up wiretaps on King's telephone; in December FBI officials gathered in Washington to explore ways of "neutralizing King as an effective Negro leader." They would expose him, one official promised, as the "clerical fraud and Marxist he is."

"These Disillusioned Colored Pioneers"

I want to talk about the first Northern urban generation of Negroes. . . . This is a story of their searching, their dreams, their sorrows, their small and futile rebellions, and their endless battle to establish their own place in America's greatest metropolis—and in America itself.

The characters are sons and daughters of former Southern sharecroppers. These were the poorest people of the South, who poured into New York City during the decade following the Great Depression. These migrants were told that unlimited opportunities for prosperity existed in New York and that there was no "color problem" there. They were told that Negroes lived in houses with bathrooms, electricity, running water, and indoor toilets. To them, this was the "promised land" that Mammy had been singing about in the cotton fields for many years.

Going to New York was good-bye to the cotton fields, good-bye to "Massa Charlie," good-bye to the chain gang, and, most of all, good-bye to those sunup-to-sundown working hours. One no longer had to wait to get to heaven to lay his burden down; burdens could be laid down in New York.

So, they came, from all parts of the South, like all the black chillun o' God following the sound of Gabriel's horn on that long-overdue Judgment Day. . . . Even while planning the trip, they sang spirituals as "Jesus Take My Hand" and "I'm On My Way" and chanted, "Hallelujah, I'm on my way to the promised land!"

It seems that Cousin Willie, in his lying haste, had neglected to tell the folks down home about one of the most important aspects of the promised land: it was a slum ghetto. There was a tremendous difference in the way life was lived up North. There were too many people full of hate and bitterness crowded into a dirty, stinky, uncared-for closet-size section of a great city. . . .

The children of these disillusioned colored pioneers inherited the total lot of their parents—the disappointments, the anger. To add to their misery, they had little hope of deliverance. For where does one run to when he's already in the promised land?

Claude Brown, *Manchild in the Promised Land* (1965)

Throughout 1963, protesters marched in the South, from Raleigh, North Carolina, to Jackson, Mississippi, and in the North, the Midwest and the West, from New York to St. Louis to Los Angeles. In the fall school boycotts broke out in Boston, Chicago, and New York. The next July race riots erupted in Harlem and then upstate in Rochester; by August they had spread to Paterson and Elizabeth in New Jersey; by September they had reached Philadelphia, Pennsylvania. A year later, on August 11, 1965, the spirit of violent confrontation reached a new peak when the worst of the decade's riots broke out in Watts, a ghetto in southeast Los Angeles, to the chant of "Burn, baby, burn"—a story recounted in Robert Conot's *Rivers of Blood, Years of Darkness* (1967).

Between the freedom riders of 1961 and the burning of Watts in 1965, the United States wandered from involvement in the ill-considered and inept invasion of Cuba at the Bay of Pigs, to a dangerous confrontation with Russia in the Cuban missile crisis, to a fateful intensification of hostilities in Vietnam, first under President Kennedy and then under President Johnson. Soon the spirit of protest generated by the civil rights movement began discovering, in the women's movement and especially in Vietnam, new causes and new voices.

Having been largely stymied for a decade or more, the women's movement entered a new era. From Betty Friedan's *Feminine Mystique* (1963) through Kate Millett's *Sexual Politics* (1970) to the writings of Elizabeth Janeway and Gloria Steinem, a new generation of women writers not only surpassed the sophistication of such predecessors as Mary Beard but also set new standards for influencing public consciousness and public policy, particularly in the 1970s.

In the mid-1960s, however, it was Vietnam more than either civil rights or women's rights that dominated American life. Efforts to close down military induction centers or to impede the flow of military personnel and supplies spread across the land. "We're now in the business of wholesale disruption and widespread resistance and dislocation of the American society," Jerry Rubin announced, adding that for the sake of their cause they were willing "to risk injuries, even deaths." Writers and intellectuals who had remained largely supportive of the government during the 1950s (taken in, Irving Howe had suggested, by an "age of conformity") suddenly found themselves at odds with

---

Of Blood and Darkness

We'll give this country a chance. We'll give 'em a chance to make up for what they've done in the past, we'll give 'em a chance to say "We know we've done you wrong, and we're gonna do our best to change it!" But I'm not gonna have nobody tell me what to do. . . . I'm gonna be the master of my life, and if they try to run over me, I'm gonna demolish them! And next time, baby, let me tell you, it's not gonna be a gentle war like it was, it's not gonna be the soul people doing all the bleeding. . . . If we get pushed again, it's gonna be goodbye, baby.

Robert Conot, *Rivers of Blood, Years of Darkness* (1967)

their government. Soon the era of unity and support seemed little more than a faded memory, to some a shameful one. Writers like Norman Mailer, Bernard Malamud, and Susan Sontag, poets like Robert Lowell and Robert Penn Warren, linguists like Noam Chomsky, and philosophers like Hannah Arendt joined in protesting the nation's deepening involvement in Vietnam. "We are in danger of imperceptibly becoming an explosive and suddenly chauvinistic nation, and we may even be drifting on our way to the last nuclear ruin," Robert Lowell wrote President Johnson in 1965, in what he described as an "anguished, delicate and perhaps determining moment."

The sense of crisis that marked the 1960s had, of course, several sources. But much of its particular intensity derived from a changed assessment of where responsibility for international crises lay. At the *Partisan Review* symposium in 1952, "Russian totalitarianism" was perceived to "threaten world domination." In 1965 "an explosive and suddenly chauvinistic" United States was seen to threaten world peace. In October 1967 protesters organized a march on the Pentagon as part of a nationwide "Stop the Draft Week." From this remarkable event came Mailer's *Armies of the Night* (1968). Shortly before the march, a dissenter named Paul Goodman informed a group of business executives gathered at the State Department that they, as shapers of America's military-industrial might, were "the most dangerous body of men at the present in the world." Goodman then joined Lowell and Mailer and fifty thousand other Americans in a march that took them from the steps of the Lincoln Memorial to the steps of the Pentagon.

By the mid-1960s, strong centrifugal forces were pulling the country apart. Some protesters believed that all forms of central economic planning, from welfare programs to corporate capitalism, inevitably undermined freedom, carrying people, as Friedrich A. von Hayek had put it, along *The Road to Serfdom* (1944). Others saw repression, above all sexual repression, as the enemy. "Dionysus, the mad god, breaks down the boundaries; releases the prisoners; abolishes repression," Norman O. Brown wrote in *Love's Body* (1966), in order to restore "the unity of man and the unity of man with nature." Still others, committed to those after whom Frantz Fanon titled his book *The Wretched of the Earth* (published in French in 1961, in English in 1965), believed that only violence could cleanse the land. "It is a struggle of total revolution," Stokely Carmichael said, "in which we propose to change the imperialist, capitalist and racialist structure" that oppresses people within the United States and threatens people beyond it.

Assassinations tell a part of the story: John Kennedy, November 22, 1963; Malcolm X, February 21, 1965; Martin Luther King, April 4, 1968; Robert Kennedy, June 4, 1968. But violence erupted in many places and took many forms. In August 1968, at the Democratic national convention, an army of 10,000 protesters clashed with an army of 22,000 law enforcers, and blood ran in the streets in what Mailer called "the siege of Chicago." "We Want Revolution," Mark Rudd wrote a month later, in a piece published in the *Saturday Evening Post.*

As the decade drew to a close, no one saw an end to the turmoil. Earlier President Kennedy had spoken of a "New Frontier" and President Johnson of a

---

"The Center Was Not Holding"

The center was not holding. It was a country of . . . commonplace reports of casual killings and misplaced children and abandoned homes and vandals who misspelled even the four-letter words they scrawled. . . . Adolescents drifted from city to torn city, sloughing off both the past and the future as snakes shed their skins, children who were never taught and would never now learn the games that had held the society together. . . .

It was not a country in open revolution. It was not a country under enemy siege. It was the United States of America in the cold late spring of 1967, and the market was steady and the G.N.P. high and a great many articulate people seemed to have a sense of high social purpose and it might have been a spring of brave hopes and national promise, but it was not, and more and more people had the uneasy apprehension that it was not. All that seemed clear was that at some point we had aborted ourselves and butchered the job, and because nothing else seemed so relevant I decided to go to San Francisco. San Francisco was where the social hemorrhaging was showing up. San Francisco was where the missing children were gathering and calling themselves "hippies."

Joan Didion, *Slouching Towards Bethlehem* (1968)

"Great Society"; both had dreamed of extending the blessings of American life to the poor and the black, hoping to renew the nation's sense of purpose and reinforce its sense of unity. But their plans had gone badly awry, undone by frustrations that ran too deep, anxieties that touched too much. In the early 1950s the nation had endured the Korean "conflict" under the leadership of President Truman, who could never quite decide whether the nation was or was not at war. Gradually, the American people had learned to live with phrases like "limited engagement" and "Cold War" and without phrases like "decisive victory" and "unconditional surrender." Later still, the nation had overcome the self-doubt that followed its failed efforts to match the success of *Sputnik I* and *Sputnik II*— "Flopnik," "Stay-putnik," and "Kaputnik," the British press called America's first ventures in space. "General annihilation beckons," Albert Einstein said when he learned that President Truman had ordered the Atomic Energy Commission to continue development of the hydrogen bomb. But the war in Vietnam, which had no clear beginning and would come to no clear end, seemed suddenly to have exhausted the nation's capacity for tolerating failure, uncertainty, and ambiguity. As a result, Vietnam bathed the nation not only in blood but also in the language of blood. "Minutemen" and "Black Panthers" sprang up to preach as well as practice violence; people talked of armies clashing by night, of sieges and marches, of fires in the earth. In May 1970, in the wake of President Nixon's decision to invade Cambodia, angry confrontations swept across the country, closing down everything from subways and buses to universities, including Kent State University, where a detachment of young National Guardsmen killed four students.

Still, the war that Secretary of Defense Robert McNamara had once budgeted to end by June 30, 1967, dragged on. By April 1975, when the United States finally withdrew from Vietnam, more Americans had died there than had died in Korea. The Vietnam Memorial that stands in Washington, D.C., commemorating American victims of the war, bears more than 55,000 names. Yet when the war finally ended, it ended not with victory nor even with a genuine truce but rather, as Arnold Isaacs has written, with "the collapse of the U.S.-backed armies in South Vietnam and Cambodia and the Communist conquest of all of Indochina, amid scenes of terror and suffering that will forever sear the memories of those who were there."

"So Many Casualties"

Out on the street I couldn't tell the Vietnam veterans from the rock and roll veterans. The Sixties had made so many casualties, its war and its music had run power off the same circuit for so long they didn't even have to fuse. The war rimed you for lame years while rock and roll turned more lurid and dangerous than bullfighting, rock stars started falling like second lieutenants; ecstasy and death and (of course and for sure) life, but it didn't seem so then. What I'd thought of as two obsessions were really only one, I don't know how to tell you how complicated that made my life. Freezing and burning and going down again into the sucking mud of the culture, hold on tight and move real slow.

That December I got a Christmas card from a Marine I'd known in Hue. It showed a psychotic-art Snoopy in battered jungle fatigues, a cigarette clenched in his teeth, blasting away with an M-16. "Peace on Earth, Good Will Toward Men," it read, "and Best Wishes for a Happy One-Niner-Six-Niner."

Maybe it was classic, maybe it was my twenties I was missing and not the Sixties, but I began missing them both before either had really been played out. The year had been so hot that I think it shorted out the whole decade, what followed was mutation, some kind of awful 1969-X. It wasn't just that I was growing older, I was leaking time, like I'd taken a frag from one of those anti-personnel weapons we had that were so small they could kill a man and never show up on X-rays. Hemingway once described the glimpse he'd had of his soul after being wounded, it looked like a fine white handkerchief drawing out of his body, floating away and then returning. What floated out of me was more like a huge gray 'chute, I hung there for a long time waiting for it to open. Or not. My life and my death got mixed up with their lives and deaths, doing the Survivor Shuffle between the two, testing the pull of each and not wanting either very much. I was once in such a bad head about it that I thought the dead had only been spared a great deal of pain.

Michael Herr, *Dispatches* (1978)

The Counterculture of the 1960s and a Changed Literature

In the dominant counterculture of the period, the cult of violence merged with the cult of escape. In some respects, the hippie culture of the 1960s derived from the hip culture of Harlem in the 1920s. More immediately, it was linked to the "beat generation" of the 1950s, particularly Allen Ginsberg's bitter lament ("I saw the best minds of my generation destroyed by madness, starving hysterical naked, / dragging themselves through the negro streets at dawn looking for an angry fix") in "Howl" (1956) and Jack Kerouac's dirge for the lost promise of the New World in *On the Road* (1957). But the new music of the 1960s was the music of the Rolling Stones and the Grateful Dead, and the new drug was the synthetic hallucinogen diethylamide of lysergic acid, which was called LSD or acid by its self-appointed high priest, Timothy Leary. Having first dedicated himself to converting the elite of the country—"the ancient underground society of alchemists, artists, mystics, alienated visionaries, dropouts and the disenchanted young"—Leary later set his sights on an entire generation. By 1966 LSD was big news: *Newsweek* and *Life* had done cover stories on it, Congress had outlawed it, and the Food and Drug Administration had mailed letters to thousands of colleges and universities warning of its danger. In 1968 Tom Wolfe published *The Electric Kool-Aid Acid Test,* depicting Ken Kesey and his "Merry Pranksters" as the epitome of hippie culture.

"A Farewell to All the Promises of America"

The last pages [of Kerouac's *Visions of Cody*] say, "All America marching to this last land." The book was a dirge for America, for its heroes' deaths too, but then who could know except in the unconscious—A dirge for the American Hope that Jack (& his hero Neal) carried so valiantly through the land after Whitman—an America of pioneers and generosity—and selfish glooms & exploitations implicit in the pioneers' entry into Foreign Indian & Moose lands —but the great betrayal of that manly America was made by the pseudo-heroic pseudo-responsible masculines of Army and Industry and Advertising and Construction and Transport and toilets and Wars.

Last pages . . . a farewell to all the promises of America, an explanation & prayer for innocence, a tearful renunciation of victory & accomplishment, a humility in the face of "the necessary blankness of men" in hopeless America, hopeless World, in hopeless wheel of Heaven, a compassionate farewell to Love.

Allen Ginsberg, Introduction to Jack Kerouac's
Visions of Cody (1972)

"Amid the Peaceful Houston Elms"

And they went with the flow, the whole goddamn flow of America. The bus barrels into the superhighway toll stations and the microphones on top of the bus pick up all the clacking and ringing and the mumbling by the toll-station attendant and the brakes squeaking and the gears shifting, all the sounds of the true America that are screened out everywhere else, it all came amplified back inside the bus, while Hagen's camera picked up the faces, the faces in Phoenix, the cops, the service-station owners, the stragglers and the strugglers of America . . . hitting the American asphalt, the open road at 70 miles an hour . . . and they *had* it on tape—and played it back in variable lag skakkkkkk-akkk-akkkk-akkkoooooooooooooo.

ooooooooooooooooooooooooooo—Stark Naked, waxing weirder and weirder, huddled in the black blanket shivering, then out, bobbing wraith, her little deep red aureolae bobbing in the crazed vibrations—finally they pull into Houston and head for Larry McMurtry's house. They pull up to McMurtry's house, . . . and the door of the house opens and out comes McMurtry, a slight, slightly wan, kingly-looking shy-looking guy, ambling out, with his little boy, his son, and Cassady opens the door of the bus so everybody can get off, and suddenly Stark Naked shrieks out: "Frankie! Frankie! Frankie! Frankie!"—this being the name of her own divorced-off little boy—and she whips off the blanket and leaps off the bus . . . stark naked, and rushes up to McMurtry's little boy and scoops him up and presses him to her skinny breast, crying and shrieking, "Frankie! oh Frankie! my little Frankie! oh! oh! oh!"—while McMurtry doesn't know what in the name of hell to do, reaching tentatively toward her stark-naked shoulder and saying, "Ma'am! Ma'am! Just a minute, ma'am!"—

—while the Pranksters, spilling out of the bus—stop. The bus is stopped. No roar, no crazed bounce or vibrations, no crazed car beams, no tapes, no microphones. Only Stark Naked, with somebody else's little boy in her arms, is bouncing and vibrating.

And there, amid the peaceful Houston elms on Quenby Road, it dawned on them all that this woman—which one of us even knows her?—had completed her trip. She had gone with the flow. She had gone stark raving mad.

Tom Wolfe, *The Electric Kool-Aid Acid Test* (1968)

Like the nation surrounding it, the hippie culture of the 1960s was almost violently at odds with itself—torn between its avowed love of American Indians and its obvious fascination with all manner of electronic gadgets; torn, too, between its desire for the beautiful magic of blissful at-onement and its demonstrated fascination with violence. Besides being torn, the hippies were caught. They were heavily dependent on their dread enemy, modern mass technological society—for developing and manufacturing their drugs; for amplifying and recording their music; and for organizing, publicizing, and marketing their "happenings" and their "be-ins." Seeking freedom, they planned a symposium on obscenity. When that failed, they planned one on spontaneity. Once, in the spring of 1967, Allen Ginsberg joined other sponsors in planning a be-in to be staged in the Grand Canyon. Needing the cooperation of the Hopi Indians, they went out to the reservation to talk. "No," the tribe's spokesman said after listening for a time; "you mean well but you are foolish. . . . You are a tribe of strangers to yourselves."

Although folk and rock concerts provided the central cultural "happenings" of the 1960s, the era's larger fascination was with history, or more precisely with the making of history. Soon people who had never dreamt of being movers and shakers participated in marches, sieges, sit-ins, and lock-ins expecting to see themselves on the evening news. By the late 1960s violence seemed to dominate almost everything, particularly television reporting and movies. The movie *Medium Cool* (1969) confronts not only the violence of a nation divided by war but also the consternation of a veteran cameraman who realizes how deeply his cool, detached instrument is implicated in intensifying or distorting the events he "reports."

As it turned out, writers were not only embroiled in the great rumblings of the era but also were changed by them. To John Updike, the turning point was 1959, when Norman Mailer published *Advertisements for Myself.* The date is as good as any, and Mailer is the almost inevitable choice as the representative figure of the 1960s. No writer lived its ups and downs, its turns and twists with more openness or as much energy. Having begun as a novelist, Mailer began during the 1960s both to play prominent roles in events of the time and to publish vast quantities of prose, most of it nonfiction, about those events—about conventions, elections, marches, moon shots, and public executions in books he

---

Legacies of the Beat Generation

Chester Anderson is a legacy of the Beat Generation, a man in his middle thirties whose peculiar hold on the District derives from his possession of a mimeograph machine, on which he prints communiqués signed "the communication company." It is another tenet of the official District mythology that the communication company will print anything anybody has to say, but in fact Chester Anderson prints only what he writes himself, agrees with, or considers harmless or dead matter. . . . An Anderson communiqué might be doing something as specific as fingering someone who is said to have set up a marijuana bust, or it might be working in a more general vein: "Pretty little 16-year-old middle-class chick comes to the Haight to see what it's all about & gets picked up by a 17-year-old street dealer who spends all day shooting her full of speed again & again, then feeds her 3,000 mikes and raffles off her temporarily unemployed body for the biggest Haight Street gangbang since the night before last. The politics and ethics of ecstasy. . . . Kids are starving on the Street. Minds and bodies are being maimed as we watch, a scale model of Vietnam."

Joan Didion, *Slouching Towards Bethlehem* (1968)

called *The Presidential Papers* (1963), *Cannibals and Christians* (1966), *The Armies of the Night* (1968), *Miami and the Siege of Chicago* (1968), *Of a Fire on the Moon* (1970), *The Prisoner of Sex* (1971), and *The Executioner's Song* (1979). In the second of these books, *Cannibals and Christians,* Mailer announced that both of the two dominant "impulses in American letters had failed"—the "realistic impulse," which manifested itself in efforts to represent or mirror life, and the "aristocratic impulse," which manifested itself in efforts to subordinate life to art by transforming life's muddle into art's order and beauty.

What Mailer seeks in nonfiction is a way of redefining these impulses—an undertaking shared by several of his contemporaries. James Baldwin, for example, and Walker Percy and William Gass, have combined the writing of fiction and nonfiction, while several younger contemporaries, including Susan Sontag and Joan Didion, have tended to move from fiction to nonfiction, finding it more congenial. Still others—Tom Wolfe, John McPhee, and Edward Hoagland— simply began with nonfiction. Together writers such as these have brought the "new journalism" to a point where it vies with fiction on equal footing. By 1976 nonfiction appeared to John Updike almost to have supplanted fiction.

From one perspective, of course, the rising authority of nonfiction clearly possesses a history of its own. In 1922 Tristran Tzara, in his "Lecture on Dada," had denied that art is "the most precious manifestation of life," insisting that "Life is far more interesting." But the sheer force of recent events—rapid, dramatic, almost apocalyptic—has clearly promoted nonfiction by reinforcing the notion that life is at least as strange and compelling as fiction can ever be. And from this perspective, John Hersey's *Hiroshima* (1946), one of the first books of the postwar period, becomes a harbinger of the kind of combative journalism that Mailer practices in *The Armies of the Night,* when for the first time we explicitly see "History as a Novel" and then see "The Novel as History."

The rise of nonfiction also has been fostered by the interconnectedness and self-consciousness of American society, which has become more and more avid in its desire to look at itself. Although "Watergate" began as a clumsy spy operation, it led to several elaborate media re-creations—in newspapers, on television, in a best-selling book, and in a popular movie. Together these media events extended the original event by leading not only to clumsy "stonewalling" and "cover-ups" but also to heroic counterspying and investigations, to dramatic exposés, confessions, and conversions. Together these developments forced several government officials, including the president, from office; it made villains of some people, heroes of others. If in Mailer's *Armies of the Night* we may be said to see history as a novel and the novel as history, in Watergate we may be said to see history as the media and the media as history. In a similar vein, one of the crucial scenes in the film *Gimme Shelter* provides an example of what it means to see history as a film and the film as history. For what appears at first as simply another scene in another movie (of a white man knifing a black man within a few feet of a stage where the Rolling Stones are playing music) turns out to have been an actual event. Opportunistically caught on camera, this event (of one of the Hell's Angels knifing a man named Meredith Hunter while the Rolling Stones played at the Altamont Raceway near San Francisco in December 1969) became a scene, first when it was reported in the news and again when it was incorporated into a movie.

The Much-Changed Situation of the Writer

"The Americans of the 1850's wrote with a confidence impossible" to Americans of today. Behind so seemingly simple a statement as this by John Updike lies more than mere nostalgia. "Not now could Melville write, 'The world is as young today as when it was created; and this Vermont morning dew is as wet to my feet, as Eden's dew to Adam's,' " Updike continues, reminding us that sophistication and power and recognition and prestige and affluence and comfort are not all that art, or for that matter life, requires. The authority our culture bestows on events, the authority of fascination, it bestows on events that are

The Age of the Combine

The Big Nurse tends to get real put out if something keeps her outfit from running like a smooth, accurate, precision-made machine. The slightest thing messy or out of kilter or in the way ties her into a little white knot of tight-smiled fury. She walks around with that same doll smile crimped between her chin and her nose and that same calm whir coming from her eyes, but down inside of her she's tense as steel. I know, I can feel it. And she don't relax a hair till she gets the nuisance attended to—what she calls "adjusted to surroundings."

Under her rule the ward Inside is almost completely adjusted to surroundings. But the thing is she can't be on the ward all the time. She's got to spend some time Outside. So she works with an eye to adjusting the Outside world too. Working alongside others like her who I call the "Combine," which is a huge organization that aims to adjust the Outside as well as she has the Inside, has made her a real veteran at adjusting things. She was already the Big Nurse in the old place when I came in from the Outside so long back, and she'd been dedicating herself to adjustment for God knows how long.

And I've watched her get more and more skillful over the years. Practice has steadied and strengthened her until now she wields a sure power that extends in all directions on hairlike wires too small for anybody's eye but mine; I see her sit in the center of this web of wires like a watchful robot, tend her network with mechanical insect skill, know every second which wire runs where and just what current to send up to get the results she wants. I was an electrician's assistant in training camp before the Army shipped me to Germany and I had some electronics in my year in college is how I learned about the way these things can be rigged.

What she dreams of there in the center of those wires is a world of precision efficiency and tidiness like a pocket watch with a glass back, a place where the schedule is unbreakable . . .

Ken Kesey, *One Flew Over the Cuckoo's Nest* (1962)

recorded and reported as no events have ever been before. It bestows its deepest fascination, furthermore, on certain kinds of events—on invasions, spy missions, and covert operations; on sports extravaganzas, "human be-ins," rock concerts, and psychedelic multimedia happenings; on nuclear tests, space launches, organ transplants, test-tube babies, and genetic engineering; on assassinations, hijackings, kidnappings, sit-ins, and marches, whether in Poland, Iran, France, or Alabama—that exist under carefully planned conditions yet reflect a limited degree of human control. Such events mirror a world that is more organized, more regulated, more scrutinized, more bureaucratized, and more interconnected than people have ever known, or for that matter cared to know. But the planning, the control, the precision that such events epitomize—governed as they are by rules and regulations and codes, by set procedures, checklists, agreements, and schedules, by programs and agendas, by fallback positions and backup equipment—coexist with the random, the unpredictable, the accidental, the indeterminate, as though to mirror a world that, for all its organization, regulation, and planning, is also more precarious, more explosive, more dangerous than people have ever known.

Drawn into a world preoccupied with its own rigidity, fragility, and violence, writers have tried, as did their predecessors, to extend the language of fiction and its range. As one result of their efforts, no words remain forbidden, particularly after publication of William Burroughs's *Naked Lunch* (1959). As another, most boundaries have become blurred—particularly those between life and art, history and fiction, fiction and nonfiction—in the far-reaching literary experiments of our time. Among writers like John Barth, the fabulation of myth, not simply as a refuge to which one can flee, but as a counterreality, has become a dominant mode. Irony lies at the heart of most of the era's comic experiments, in part because irony allows writers to confront even a terribly torn world on something like equal footing. Donald Barthelme's advice—"only trust the fragments"—has become for writers so much a byword that the notion of the synthesizing imagination is in danger of being discredited. Forced to conduct their literary experiments among seemingly endless possibilities and uncertainties, writers sometimes seem scarcely to know where to turn. "What happens to a man to whom all things seem possible and every course of action open?" Walker Percy asks in *The Last Gentleman* (1966). "Nothing of course. Except war. If a man lives in the sphere of the possible and waits for something to happen, what he is waiting for is war—or the end of the world." At least one kind of uncertainty now haunting writers lies close to home: "The nature of existence cannot be felt any more," Mailer said in 1976. "As novelists, we cannot locate our center of values."

Yet despite uncertainty and confusion that seem at times to touch everything, Mailer and his contemporaries, in the immortal words of O. C. Smith, "keep on keepin' on." No doubt they have been aided in part by what Updike calls a "native optimism" that matches their "native pessimism." To be sustained, however, a writer's effort must be founded on the conviction that under proper pressure, language possesses the power to command attention. Among recent writers this conviction has been shaken by the force of history and the power of the media, but it has also been reinforced by the sense that language has always come to us under the aspect of the unpredictable, the accidental, and the indeterminate as well as the deliberate, the planned, and the controlled.

Further Reading:

E. Wilson, *Classics and Commercials: A Literary Chronicle of the Forties*, 1950.

E. Goldman, *The Crucial Decade and After: America, 1945–1960*, 1956, 1960.

H. Agar, *The Price of Power: America Since 1945*, 1957.

D. Perkins, *The New Age of Franklin Roosevelt: 1932–45*, 1957.

W. Morris, *The Territory Ahead*, 1958.

D. Aaron, *Writers on the Left*, 1961.

A. Mizener, *The Sense of Life in the Modern Novel*, 1964.

T. Wolfe, *The Electric Kool-Aid Acid Test*, 1968.

W. Berthoff, *Fictions and Events*, 1971.

L. Fiedler, *Collected Essays*, 1971.

R. Poirier, *The Performing Self*, 1971.

T. Tanner, *City of Words: American Fiction 1935–1970*, 1971.

A. Kazin, *Bright Book of Life*, 1973.

M. Dickstein, *Gates of Eden: American Culture in the Sixties*, 1977.

F. McConnell, *Four Postwar American Novelists*, 1977.

W. Morris, *Earthly Delights, Unearthly Adornments: American Writers as Image Makers*, 1978.

W. Berthoff, *A Literature Without Qualities: American Writing Since 1945*, 1979.

R. Sale, *On Not Being Good Enough*, 1979.

R. H. King, *A Southern Renaissance: The Cultural Awakening of the American South, 1930–1955*, 1980.

A. R. Isaacs, *Without Honor: Defeat in Vietnam and Cambodia*, 1983.

P. Johnson, *Modern Times: The World from the Twenties to the Eighties*, 1983.

A. J. Matusow, *The Unraveling of America: A History of Liberalism in the 1960s*, 1984.

Vladimir Nabokov
1899–1977

"I am an American writer, born in Russia and educated in England, where I studied French literature, before spending fifteen years in Germany. I came to America in 1940 and decided to become an American citizen and made America my home." Such was Vladimir Nabokov's reply when asked in a 1963 interview if he felt any strong sense of national identity. John Updike responded to Nabokov's mixed identities by calling him "the best writer of English prose at present holding American citizenship."

Nabokov was born in St. Petersburg, Russia, on April 23, 1899. His father, a wealthy professor of criminal law and a prominent liberal statesman, made certain that his precocious son received a solid education in English and French: "I learned to read English," Nabokov recalled, "before I could read Russian." In 1919, following the Revolution, the family escaped to Berlin, and Nabokov won a scholarship to Trinity College, Cambridge, where he studied French and Russian literature and proved to be an accomplished soccer and tennis player. After receiving his B.A. in 1922, he returned to Berlin, took a job with a bank —which lasted three hours— and then managed to support himself by teaching English, French, boxing, tennis, and poetry. But, as he later said, his "main occupation was writing." In 1923 he published a Russian translation of *Alice in Wonderland*, and he soon became a leading contributor of fiction, poetry, criticism, and chess columns (he was an excellent composer of chess problems) to Russian émigré journals. In 1926 he published his first novel, *Mary*, under the pseudonym V. Sirin, the name he used for a succession of books: *King, Queen, Knave* (1928), *The Defence* (1930), *The Eye* (1930), *Glory* (1932), *Laughter in the Dark* (1933), *Despair* (1936), and *Invitation to a Beheading* (1938). By the time he

wrote *The Gift* (1937–1938), Nabokov had established himself as a major
European novelist.

Nabokov fled Nazi Germany in 1937 and, after spending a few years in Paris,
sailed for the United States with his wife and son in 1940. He taught literature at
Stanford, Wellesley, and Cornell between 1941 and 1959. While actively pursuing
his lifelong passion for butterfly collecting (he published a number of scientific
papers on lepidopterology), he continued to write fiction, now entirely in
English. He wrote his first novel in English, *The Real Life of Sebastian Knight*
(1941), while in Paris; it was followed by *Bend Sinister* (1947), *Lolita* (1955),
Pnin (1957), *Pale Fire* (1962), *Ada* (1969), *Transparent Things* (1972), and *Look at
the Harlequins!* (1974). During this period Nabokov, with the help of his son,
Dmitri, translated his earlier Russian novels into English. His other works include
six collections of short stories; a critical study of Nicolai Gogol (1944); a
memoir, *Speak, Memory* (1966); and a monumental translation of Aleksandr
Pushkin's *Eugene Onegin* (4 vols., 1964). In 1959, following the enormous success
of *Lolita*, Nabokov and his wife, Vera, moved to Montreux, Switzerland, where
he died in 1977.

Lolita is not only Nabokov's best-known novel, it is also his most American
book. The twelve-year-old Lolita ("the loveliest nymphet")—whom the
European narrator, Humbert Humbert, passionately adores—represents in her
adolescent demands and dreams the "philistine vulgarity" that Nabokov found to
be such an artistically exhilarating aspect of contemporary life: "She it was to
whom ads were dedicated: the ideal consumer, the subject and object of every
foul poster." Writers often write most dazzlingly about the things they despise,
and some of Nabokov's most brilliant passages occur when Humbert Humbert's
aristocratic sensibility confronts some singularly pretentious vulgarity or cultural
absurdity of American taste and education. In his study of Nicolai Gogol,
Nabokov used a Russian word, *poshlust,* to express what "is not only the
obviously trashy but also the falsely important, the falsely beautiful, the falsely
clever, the falsely aristocratic." A scrutinizing attention to the countless
manifestations of *poshlust* in everyday life can be found in nearly all of
Nabokov's writing, but in *Lolita* it reaches the giddy summits of comic poetry.

Despite such achievements as the hilariously and realistically itemized
Americana of *Lolita,* Nabokov's work continually reminds us that fiction is an
illusion—an illusion not so much of reality but of what we call reality. "It is
childish," he wrote in an "afterword" to *Lolita,* "to study a work of fiction in
order to gain information about a country or about a social class or about the
author." Fiction is a country of its own, a "terra incognita" that lies somewhere
at the intersection of art and life. Nabokov scorned any fiction that purported to
give readers a "realistic," documentary version of life; he did so not only because
such endeavors invariably simplify art but also because in doing so they grossly
distort life.

For Nabokov it would be a kind of imaginative *poshlust* to read a novel as
though it were "about" characters one "identified" with and who inhabited a
world one considered to be socially, politically, or economically "realistic." But
though Nabokov's works and worlds are intricately woven with images, patterns,
word games, parodies, and an incredible variety of self-referential devices—all

designed to nudge the reader's attention, saying, "Don't forget, this is a *novel!*"—
Nabokov surprisingly never loses contact with the rich texture of life. He is
often criticized for writing literature that seems to be only about itself, to exist
for merely aesthetic purposes, yet few modern novelists have so consistently
evoked such lavishly detailed locations, have created so many memorable
characters, and have suffused their work with such a convincing range of human
feelings and passions.

Further Reading:
A. Field, *Nabokov: His Life in Art*, 1967.
"For Vladimir Nabokov on His Seventieth
Birthday," *TriQuarterly*, Winter 1970.
W. W. Rowe, *Nabokov's Deceptive World*,
1971.
J. Bader, *Crystal Land: Patterns of Artifice in
Vladimir Nabokov's English Novels*, 1973.
A. Appel, Jr., *Nabokov's Dark Cinema*, 1974.
A. Field, *Nabokov: His Life in Part*, 1977.
J. Karges, *Nabokov's Lepidoptera: Genres and
Genera*, 1985.

Texts:
Lolita, 1957.
"Terra Incognita," in *"A Russian Beauty" and
Other Stories*, 1973.

---

from Lolita[*]

from Part II

1

It was then that began our extensive travels all over the States. To any other type
of tourist accommodation I soon grew to prefer the Functional Motel—clean, neat,
safe nooks, ideal places for sleep, argument, reconciliation, insatiable illicit love. At
first, in my dread of arousing suspicion, I would eagerly pay for both sections of one
double unit, each containing a double bed. I wondered what type of foursome this
arrangement was ever intended for, since only a pharisaic[1] parody of privacy could
be attained by means of the incomplete partition dividing the cabin or room into two
communicating love nests. By and by, the very possibilities that such honest promiscuity suggested (two young couples merrily swapping mates or a child shamming sleep
to earwitness[2] primal sonorities) made me bolder, and every now and then I would
take a bed-and-cot or twin-bed cabin, a prison cell of paradise, with yellow window
shades pulled down to create a morning illusion of Venice and sunshine when actually
it was Pennsylvania and rain.

---

[*] Rejected by American publishers afraid of
censorship, *Lolita* was originally published by
Olympia Press in Paris in 1955. The text
printed here is from the *Anchor Review* edition
(1957), an excerpted edition prepared by the
editor, Jason Epstein, with Vladimir Nabokov's
approval. Several typographical errors have been
silently corrected.
[1] Broadly, self-righteous and critical of manners
and behavior. The Pharisees were an ancient sect
of elite Jews known for their strict orthodoxy.
[2] Nabokov's own coinage.

We came to know—*nous connûmes*,[3] to use a Flaubertian[4] intonation—the stone cottages under enormous Chateaubriandesque trees,[5] the brick unit, the adobe unit, the stucco court, on what the Tour Book of the Automobile Association describes as "shaded" or "spacious" or "landscaped" grounds. The log kind finished in knotty pine, reminded Lo, by its golden-brown glaze, of fried-chicken bones. We held in contempt the plain whitewashed clapboard Kabins, with their faint sewerish smell or some other gloomy self-conscious stench and nothing to boast of (except "good beds"), and an unsmiling landlady always prepared to have her gift (". . . well, I could give you . . .") turned down.

Nous connûmes (this is royal fun) the would-be enticements of their repetitious names—all those Sunset Motels, U-Beam Cottages, Hillcrest Courts, Pine View Courts, Mountain View Courts, Skyline Courts, Park Plaza Courts, Green Acres, Mac's Courts. There was sometimes a special line in the write-up, such as "Children welcome, pets allowed" (*You* are welcome, *you* are allowed). The baths were mostly tiled showers, with an endless variety of spouting mechanisms, but with one definitely non-Laodicean[6] characteristic in common, a propensity, while in use, to turn instantly beastly hot or blindingly cold upon you, depending on whether your neighbor turned on his cold or his hot to deprive you of its complement in the shower you had so carefully blended. Some motels had instructions pasted above the toilet (on whose tank the towels were unhygienically heaped) asking guests not to throw into its bowl garbage, beer cans, cartons, stillborn babes; others had special notices under glass, such as Things to Do (Riding: "You will often see riders coming down Main Street on their way back from a romantic moonlight ride." "Often at 3 a.m.," sneered unromantic Lo).

Nous connûmes the various types of motor court operators, the reformed criminal, the retired teacher and the business flop, among the males; and the motherly, pseudo-ladylike and madamic variants among the females. And sometimes trains would cry in the monstrously hot and humid night with heart-rending and ominous plangency, mingling power and hysteria in one desperate scream.

We avoided Tourist Homes, country cousins of Funeral ones, old-fashioned, genteel and showerless, with elaborate dressing tables in depressingly white-and-pink little bedrooms, and photographs of the landlady's children in all their instars.[7] But I did surrender, now and then, to Lo's predilection for "real" hotels. She would pick out in the book, while I petted her in the parked car in the silence of a dusk-mellowed, mysterious side-road, some highly recommended lake lodge which offered all sorts of things magnified by the flashlight she moved over them, such as congenial company, between-meals snacks, outdoor barbecues—but which in my mind conjured up odious visions of stinking highschool boys in sweatshirts and an ember-red cheek pressing against hers, while poor Dr. Humbert, embracing

[3] French for the preceding phrase ("We came to know").

[4] In the style of the French novelist Gustave Flaubert (1821–1880), author of the novel *Madame Bovary.*

[5] Nabokov invokes the descriptions of America by François-René de Chateaubriand (1768–1848). Like many of the early European artists and writers who toured the new continent, Chateaubriand marveled at the lushness and size of American trees.

[6] An early Christian community; the Laodiceans were considered "lukewarm, and neither cold nor hot" on points of religious doctrine. (See Revelation 3:14–16.)

[7] Any one of several forms assumed by insects during their various stages of growth.

nothing but two masculine knees, would cold-humor[8] his piles on the damp turf. Most tempting to her, too, were those "Colonial" Inns, which apart from "gracious atmosphere" and picture-windows, promised "unlimited quantities of M-m-m food." Treasured recollections of my father's palatial hotel sometimes led me to seek for its like in the strange country we traveled through. I was soon discouraged; but Lo kept following the scent of rich food ads, while I derived a not exclusively economic kick from such roadside signs as "Timber Hotel, Children under 14 Free." On the other hand, I shudder when recalling that *soi-disant*[9] "highclass" resort in a Midwestern State, which advertised "raid-the-icebox" midnight snacks and, intrigued by my accent, wanted to know my dead wife's and dead mother's maiden names. A two-days' stay there cost me a hundred and twenty-four dollars! And do you remember, Miranda,[10] that other "ultrasmart" robbers' den with complimentary morning coffee and circulating ice water, and no children under sixteen (no Lolitas, of course)?

Immediately upon arrival at one of the plainer motor courts which became our habitual haunts, she would set the electric fan a-whirr, or induce me to drop a quarter into the radio, or she would read all the signs and inquire with a whine why she could not go riding up some advertised trail or swimming in that local pool of warm mineral water. . . .

A combination of naïveté and deception, of charm and vulgarity, of blue sulks and rosy mirth, Lolita, when she chose, could be a most exasperating brat. I was not really quite prepared for her fits of disorganized boredom, intense and vehement griping, her sprawling, droopy, dopey-eyed style, and what is called goofing off—a kind of diffused clowning which she thought was tough in a boyish hoodlum way. Mentally, I found her to be a disgustingly conventional little girl. Sweet hot jazz, square dancing, gooey fudge sundaes, musicals, movie magazines and so forth—these were the obvious items in her list of beloved things. The Lord knows how many nickels I fed to the gorgeous music boxes that came with every meal we had! I still hear the nasal voices of those invisibles serenading her, people with names like Sammy and Jo and Eddy and Tony and Peggy and Guy and Patty and Rex,[11] and sentimental song hits, all of them as similar to my ear as her various candies were to my palate. She believed, with a kind of celestial trust, any advertisement or advice that appeared in *Movie Love* or *Screen Land*—Starasil[12] Starves Pimples, or "You better watch out if you're wearing your shirttails outside your jeans, gals, because Jill says you shouldn't." If a roadside sign said: Visit Our Gift Shop—we *had* to visit it, *had* to buy its Indian curios, dolls, copper jewelry, cactus candy. The words "novelties and souvenirs" simply entranced her by their trochaic lilt.[13] If some café sign proclaimed Icecold Drinks, she was automatically stirred, although all drinks everywhere were ice-cold. She it was to whom ads were dedicated: the ideal consumer, the subject and object of every foul poster.

---

[8] Nabokov's coinage: take a treatment for hemorrhoids.
[9] French: "so-called" or "self-styled."
[10] From the opening lines of "Tarantella" by the poet Hilaire Belloc (1870–1953): "Do you remember an Inn, / Miranda? / Do you remember an Inn?"

[11] Popular singers of the 1950s.
[12] An acne medication.
[13] A *trochee* is a prosodic foot of two syllables, of which the first is accented and the second is unaccented.

And she attempted—unsuccessfully—to patronize only those restaurants where the holy spirit of Huncan Dines[14] had descended upon the cute paper napkins and cottage cheese-crested salads. . . .

My lawyer has suggested I give a clear, frank account of the itinerary we followed, and I suppose I have reached here a point where I cannot avoid that chore. Roughly, during that mad year (August 1947 to August 1948), our route began with a series of wiggles and whorls in New England, then meandered south, up and down, east and west; dipped deep into *ce qu'on appelle*[15] Dixieland, avoided Florida because the Farlows[16] were there, veered west, zig-zagged through corn belts and cotton belts (this is not too clear I am afraid, Clarence,[17] but I did not keep any notes, and have at my disposal only an atrociously crippled Tour Book in three volumes, almost a symbol of my torn and tattered past, in which to check these recollections); crossed and recrossed the Rockies, straggled through southern deserts where we wintered; reached the Pacific, turned north through the pale lilac fluff of flowering shrubs along forest roads; almost reached the Canadian border; and proceeded east, across good lands and bad lands, back to agriculture on a grand scale, avoiding, despite little Lo's strident remonstrations, little Lo's birthplace, in a corn, coal and hog producing area; and finally returned to the fold of the East, petering out in the college town of Beardsley.

2

Now, in perusing what follows, the reader should bear in mind not only the general circuit as adumbrated above, with its many sidetrips and tourist traps, secondary circles and skittish deviations, but also the fact that far from being an indolent *partie de plaisir*,[18] our tour was a hard, twisted, teleological growth, whose sole *raison d'être*[19] (these French clichés are symptomatic) was to keep my companion in passable humor from kiss to kiss.

Thumbing through that battered tour book, I dimly evoke that Magnolia Garden in a southern State which cost me four bucks and which, according to the ad in the book you must visit for three reasons: because John Galsworthy[20] (a stonedead writer of sorts) acclaimed it as the world's fairest garden; because in 1900 Baedeker's Guide had marked it with a star; and finally, because . . . O, Reader, My Reader, guess! . . . because children (and by Jingo was not my Lolita a child!) will "walk starry-eyed and reverently through this foretaste of Heaven, drinking in beauty that can influence a life." "Not mine," said grim Lo, and settled down on a bench with the fillings of two Sunday papers in her lovely lap.

We passed and re-passed through the whole gamut of American roadside restaurants, from the lowly Eat with its deer-head (dark trace of long tear at inner can-

---

[14] Play on the name of the American recipe king, Duncan Hines (1880–1959).

[15] French: "what one calls."

[16] Former neighbors of Lolita's from her hometown.

[17] Humbert's attorney, Clarence Choate Clark, in whose care Humbert left the manuscript of *Lolita*.

[18] Day trip or picnic.

[19] French: "reason for existing."

[20] Prolific and popular British novelist (1867–1933), author of *The Forsyte Saga*.

thus[21]), "humorous" picture postcards of the posterior "Kurort"[22] type, impaled guest checks, life savers, sunglasses, adman visions of celestial sundaes, one half of a chocolate cake under glass, and several horribly experienced flies zigzagging over the sticky sugar-pour on the ignoble counter; and all the way to the expensive place with the subdued lights, preposterously poor table linen, inept waiters (ex-convicts or college boys), the roan[23] back of a screen actress, the sable eyebrows of her male of the moment, and an orchestra of zootsuiters with trumpets. . . .

We had rows, minor and major. The biggest ones we had took place: at Lacework Cabins, Virginia; on Park Avenue, Little Rock, near a school; on Milner Pass, 10,759 feet high, in Colorado; at the corner of Seventh Street and Central Avenue in Phoenix, Arizona; on Third Street, Los Angeles, because the tickets to some studio or other were sold out; at a motel called Poplar Shade in Utah, where six pubescent trees were scarcely taller than my Lolita, and where she asked, *à propos de rien,*[24] how long did I think we were going to live in stuffy cabins, doing filthy things together and never behaving like ordinary people? On N. Broadway, Burns, Oregon, corner of W. Washington, facing Safeway, a grocery. In some little town in the Sun Valley of Idaho, before a brick hotel, pale and flushed bricks, nicely mixed, with, opposite, a poplar playing its liquid shadows all over the local Honor Roll. In a sage brush wilderness, between Pinedale and Farson. Somewhere in Nebraska, on Main Street, near the First National Bank, established 1889, with a view of a railway crossing in the vista of the street, and beyond that the white organ pipes of a multiple silo. And on McEwen St., corner of Wheaton Ave., in a Michigan town bearing his first name.[25]

We came to know the curious roadside species, Hitchhiking Man, *Homo pollex*[26] of science, with all its many subspecies and forms: the modest soldier, spic and span, quietly waiting, quietly conscious of khaki's viatic[27] appeal; the schoolboy wishing to go two blocks; the killer wishing to go two thousand miles; the mysterious, nervous, elderly gent, with brandnew suitcase and clipped mustache; a trio of optimistic Mexicans; the college student displaying the grime of vacational outdoor work as proudly as the name of the famous college arching across the front of his sweatshirt; the desperate lady whose battery has just died on her; the cleancut, glossy-haired, shifty-eyed, white-faced young beasts in loud shirts and coats, vigorously, almost priapically[28] thrusting out tense thumbs to tempt lone women or sad-sack salesmen with fancy cravings.

"Let's take him," Lo would often plead, rubbing her knees together in a way she had, as some particularly disgusting *pollex,* some man of my age and shoulder breadth, with the *face à claques*[29] of an unemployed actor, walked backwards, practically in the path of our car.

Oh, I had to keep a very sharp eye on Lo, little limp Lo! . . . . She radiated, despite

---

[21] Location of the tear duct at the inner corner of the eye.
[22] German term for a health spa, or resort with therapeutic waters.
[23] Chestnut color mottled with spots of white or gray.
[24] French: "out of the blue"; literally, "relevant to nothing."
[25] I.e., Clare, Michigan. Clare Quilty is a playwright who has been following Humbert and Lolita.
[26] Combination of the Latin words *Homo* (the genus of humans) and *pollex* ("thumb").
[27] Pertaining to road travel.
[28] Like a phallus (from Priapus, god of fertility).
[29] French: roughly, "with a face aching to be slapped."

her very childish appearance, some special languorous glow which threw garage fellows, hotel pages, vacationists, goons in luxurious cars, maroon morons near blued pools, into fits of concupiscence which might have tickled my pride, had it not incensed my jealousy. For little Lo was aware of that glow of hers, and I would often catch her *coulant un regard*[30] in the direction of some amiable male, some grease monkey, with a sinewy golden-brown forearm and watch-braceleted wrist, and hardly had I turned my back to go and buy this very Lo a lollipop, than I would hear her and the fair mechanic burst into a perfect love song of wisecracks.

When, during our longer stops, I would relax, and out of the goodness of my lulled heart allow her—indulgent Hum!—to visit the rose garden or children's library across the street with a motor court neighbor's plain little Mary and Mary's eight-year old brother, Lo would come back an hour late, with barefoot Mary lagging far behind, and the little boy metamorphosed into two gangling, golden-haired highschool uglies, all muscles and gonorrhea. The reader may well imagine what I answered my pet when—rather uncertainly, I admit—she would ask me if she could go with Carl and Al here to the roller skating rink.

I remember the first time, a dusty windy afternoon, I did let her go to one such rink. Cruelly she said it would be no fun if I accompanied her, since that time of day was reserved for teenagers. We wrangled out a compromise: I remained in the car, among other (empty) cars, with their noses to the canvas-topped open-air rink, where some fifty young people, many in pairs, were endlessly rolling round and round to mechanical music, and the wind silvered the trees. Dolly wore blue jeans and white high shoes, as most of the other girls did. I kept counting the revolutions of the rolling crowd—and suddenly she was missing. When she rolled past again, she was together with three hoodlums whom I had heard analyze a moment before the girl skaters from the outside—and jeer at a lovely leggy young thing who had arrived clad in red shorts instead of those jeans or slacks.

At inspection stations on highways entering Arizona or California, a policeman's cousin would peer with such intensity at us that my poor heart wobbled. "Any honey?" he would inquire, and every time my sweet fool giggled. I still have, vibrating all along my optic nerve, visions of Lo on horseback, a link in the chain of a guided trip along a bridle trail: Lo bobbing at a walking pace, with an old woman rider in front and a lecherous red-necked dude-rancher behind; and I behind him, hating his fat flowery-shirted back even more fervently than a motorist does a slow truck on a mountain road. Or else, at a ski lodge, I would see her floating away from me, celestial and solitary, in an ethereal chairlift, up and up, to a glittering summit where laughing athletes stripped to the waist were waiting for her, for her. . . .

I tried to teach her to play tennis so we might have more amusements in common; but although I had been a good player in my prime, I proved to be hopeless as a teacher; and so, in California, I got her to take a number of very expensive lessons with a famous coach,[31] a husky, wrinkled oldtimer, with a harem of ball boys; he looked an awful wreck off the court, but now and then, when, in the course of a lesson, to keep up the exchange, he would put out as it were an exquisite spring blossom

---

[30] French: "glancing slyly."
[31] The "famous coach" is based on William Tilden (1893–1953), a brilliant American tennis player who had his heyday in the 1920s and 1930s.

of a stroke and twang the ball back to his pupil, that divine delicacy of absolute power made me recall that, thirty years before, I had seen *him* in Cannes demolish the great Gobbert![32] Until she began taking those lessons, I thought she would never learn the game. On this or that hotel court I would drill Lo, and try to relive the days when in a hot gale, a daze of dust, and queer lassitude, I fed ball after ball to gay, innocent, elegant Annabel (gleam of bracelet, pleated white skirt, black velvet hair band). With every word of persistent advice I would only augment Lo's sullen fury. To our games, oddly enough, she preferred—at least, before we reached California—formless pat ball approximations—more ball hunting than actual play—with a wispy, weak, wonderfully pretty in an *ange gauche*[33] way coeval. A helpful spectator, I would go up to that other child, and, inhale her faint musky fragrance as I touched her forearm and held her knobby wrist, and push this way or that her cool thigh to show her the backhand stance. In the meantime, Lo, bending forward, would let her sunny-brown curls hang forward as she stuck her racket, like a cripple's stick, into the ground and emitted a tremendous ugh of disgust at my intrusion. I would leave them to their game and look on, comparing their bodies in motion, a silk scarf round my throat; this was in south Arizona I think—and the days had a lazy lining of warmth, and awkward Lo would slash at the ball and miss it, and curse, and send a simulacrum of a serve into the net, and show the wet glistening young down of her armpit as she brandished her racket in despair, and her even more insipid partner would dutifully rush out after every ball, and retrieve none; but both were enjoying themselves beautifully, and in clear ringing tones kept the exact score of their ineptitudes all the time.

One day, I remember, I offered to bring them cold drinks from the hotel, and went up the gravel path, and came back with two tall glasses of pineapple juice, soda and ice; and then a sudden void within my chest made me stop as I saw that the tennis court was deserted. I stooped to set down the glasses on a bench and for some reason, with a kind of icy vividness, saw Charlotte's face[34] in death, and I glanced around, and noticed Lo in white shorts receding through the speckled shadow of a garden path in the company of a tall man who carried two tennis rackets. I sprang after them, but as I was crashing through the shrubbery, I saw, in an alternate vision, as if life's course constantly branched, Lo, in slacks, and her companion, in shorts, trudging up and down a small weedy area, and beating bushes with their rackets in listless search for their last lost ball.

I itemize these sunny nothings mainly to prove to my judges that I did everything in my power to give my Lolita a really good time. How charming it was to see her, a child herself, showing another child, some of her few accomplishments, such as for example a special way of jumping rope. With her right hand holding her left arm behind her untanned back, the lesser nymphet, a diaphanous darling, would be all eyes, as the pavonian sun was all eyes on the gravel under the flowering trees, while in the midst of that oculate paradise, my freckled and raffish lass, skipped, repeating the movements of so many others I had gloated over on the sun-shot, watered, damp-smelling sidewalks and ramparts of ancient Europe. . . .

1955

[32] Andre H. Gobbert, a French tennis pro.
[33] Clumsily angelic.
[34] Charlotte Haze, Lolita's mother and Humbert's ex-wife. Shortly after arriving in America and meeting Lolita, Humbert married Charlotte. She was run over by a car while hysterical after reading Humbert's private diary, in which he candidly expresses his obsession for Lolita.

Terra Incognita[*][1]

The sound of the waterfall grew more and more muffled, until it finally dissolved altogether, and we moved on through the wildwood of a hitherto unexplored region. We walked, and had been walking, for a long time already—in front, Gregson and I; our eight native porters behind, one after the other; last of all, whining and protesting at every step, came Cook. I knew that Gregson had recruited him on the advice of a local hunter. Cook had insisted that he was ready to do anything to get out of Zonraki,[2] where they pass half the year brewing their "von-gho" and the other half drinking it. It remained unclear, however—or else I was already beginning to forget many things, as we walked on and on—exactly who this Cook was (a runaway sailor, perhaps?).

Gregson strode on beside me, sinewy, lanky, with bare, bony knees. He held a long-handled green butterfly net like a banner. The porters, big, glossy-brown Badonians[3] with thick manes of hair and cobalt arabesques[4] between their eyes, whom we had also engaged in Zonraki, walked with a strong, even step. Behind them straggled Cook, bloated, red-haired, with a drooping underlip, hands in pockets and carrying nothing. I recalled vaguely that at the outset of the expedition he had chattered a lot and made obscure jokes, in a manner he had, a mixture of insolence and servility, reminiscent of a Shakespearean clown; but soon his spirits fell and he grew glum and began to neglect his duties, which included interpreting, since Gregson's understanding of the Badonian dialect was still poor.

There was something languorous and velvety about the heat. A stifling fragrance came from the inflorescences[5] of *Vallieria mirifica,*[6] mother-of-pearl in color and resembling clusters of soap bubbles, that arched across the narrow, dry stream bed along which we proceeded. The branches of porphyroferous[7] trees intertwined with those of the Black-Leafed Limia to form a tunnel, penetrated here and there by a ray of hazy light. Above, in the thick mass of vegetation, among brilliant pendulous racemes[8] and strange dark tangles of some kind, hoary monkeys snapped and chattered, while a cometlike bird flashed like Bengal light,[9] crying out in its small, shrill voice. I kept telling myself that my head was heavy from the long march, the heat, the medley of colors, and the forest din, but secretly I knew that I was ill. I surmised it to be the local fever. I had resolved, however, to conceal my condition from Gregson, and had assumed a cheerful, even merry air, when disaster struck.

"It's my fault," said Gregson. "I should never have got involved with him."

We were now alone. Cook and all eight of the natives, with tent, folding boat,

---

[*] The story originally appeared in Russian in 1931. Nabokov's English translation was published in *The New Yorker,* May 18, 1963.
[1] Latin: "unknown land" or "unexplored region."
[2] An imaginary land invented by Nabokov.
[3] An imaginary native people and language invented by Nabokov.
[4] In this usage, an ornament made of geometric, crisscrossing lines worn above the brow.

[5] Clumps of buds or flowers.
[6] A plant invented by Nabokov. Its name is a play on the narrator's name, Vallière, and on the Latin word *mirifica,* meaning "causing awe or wonderment, as in magic."
[7] Producing purplish blooms or leaves.
[8] Cluster or bunch, as in grapes or berries.
[9] Bluish light or flare used in theaters or for signaling.

supplies, and collections, had deserted us and vanished noiselessly while we busied ourselves in the thick bush, chasing fascinating insects. I think we tried to catch up with the fugitives—I do not recall clearly, but, in any case, we failed. We had to decide whether to return to Zonraki or continue our projected itinerary, across as yet unknown country, toward the Gurano Hills. The unknown won out. We moved on. I was already shivering all over and deafened by quinine,[10] but still went on collecting nameless plants, while Gregson, though fully realizing the danger of our situation, continued catching butterflies and Diptera[11] as avidly as ever.

We had scarcely walked half a mile when suddenly Cook overtook us. His shirt was torn—apparently by himself, deliberately—and he was panting and gasping. Without a word Gregson drew his revolver and prepared to shoot the scoundrel, but he threw himself at Gregson's feet and, shielding his head with both arms, began to swear that the natives had led him away by force and had wanted to eat him (which was a lie, for the Badonians are not cannibals). I suspect that he had easily incited them, stupid and timorous as they were, to abandon the dubious journey, but had not taken into account that he could not keep up with their powerful stride, and, having fallen hopelessly behind, had returned to us. Because of him invaluable collections were lost. He had to die. But Gregson put away the revolver and we moved on, with Cook wheezing and stumbling behind.

The woods were gradually thinning. I was tormented by strange hallucinations. I gazed at the weird tree trunks, around some of which were coiled thick, flesh-colored snakes; suddenly I thought I saw, between the trunks, as though through my fingers, the mirror of a half-open wardrobe with dim reflections, but then I took hold of myself, looked more carefully, and found that it was only the deceptive glimmer of an acreana bush (a curly plant with large berries resembling plump prunes). After a while the trees parted altogether and the sky rose before us like a solid wall of blue. We were at the top of a steep incline. Below shimmered and steamed an enormous marsh, and, far beyond, one distinguished the tremulous silhouette of a mauve-colored range of hills.

"I swear to God we must turn back," said Cook in a sobbing voice. "I swear to God we'll perish in these swamps—I've got seven daughters and a dog at home. Let's turn back—we know the way. . . ."

He wrung his hands, and the sweat rolled from his fat, red-browed face. "Home, home," he kept repeating. "You've caught enough bugs. Let's go home!"

Gregson and I began to descend the stony slope. At first Cook remained standing above, a small white figure against the monstrously green background of forest; but suddenly he threw up his hands, uttered a cry, and started to slither down after us.

The slope narrowed, forming a rocky crest that reached out like a long promontory into the marshes; they sparkled through the steamy haze. The noonday sky, now freed of its leafy veils, hung oppressively over us with its blinding darkness—yes, its blinding darkness, for there is no other way to describe it. I tried not to look up; but in this sky, at the very verge of my field of vision, there floated, always keeping up with me, whitish phantoms of plaster, stucco curlicues and rosettes, like those used to adorn European celings; however, I had only to look directly at them and they

---

[10] A salt used by explorers to reduce fever.
[11] The largest order of winged insects, of which houseflies, gnats, and mosquitoes are the most common examples.

would vanish, and again the tropical sky would bloom, as it were, with even, dense blueness. We were still walking along the rocky promontory, but it kept tapering and betraying us. Around it grew golden marsh reeds, like a million bared swords gleaming in the sun. Here and there flashed elongated pools, and over them hung dark swarms of midges. A large swamp flower, presumably an orchid, stretched toward me its drooping, downy lip, which seemed smeared with egg yolk. Gregson swung his net—and sank to his hips in the brocaded ooze as a gigantic swallowtail, with a flap of its satin wing, sailed away from him over the reeds, toward the shimmer of pale emanations where the indistinct folds of a window curtain seemed to hang. *I must not,* I said to myself, *I must not.* . . . I shifted my gaze and walked on beside Gregson, now over rock, now across hissing and lip-smacking soil. I felt chills, in spite of the greenhouse heat. I foresaw that in a moment I would collapse altogether, that the contours and convexities of delirium, showing through the sky and through the golden reeds, would gain complete control of my consciousness. At times Gregson and Cook seemed to grow transparent, and I thought I saw, through them, wallpaper with an endlessly repeated design of reeds. I took hold of myself, strained to keep my eyes open, and moved on. Cook by now was crawling on all fours, yelling, and snatching at Gregson's legs, but the latter would shake him off and keep walking. I looked at Gregson, at his stubborn profile, and felt, to my horror, that I was forgetting who Gregson was, and why I was with him.

Meanwhile we kept sinking into the ooze more and more frequently, deeper and deeper; the insatiable mire would suck at us; and, wriggling, we would slip free. Cook kept falling down and crawling, covered with insect bites, all swollen and soaked, and, dear God, how he would squeal when disgusting bevies of minute, bright-green hydrotic[12] snakes, attracted by our sweat, would take off in pursuit of us, tensing and uncoiling to sail two yards and then another two. I, however, was much more frightened by something else: now and then, on my left (always, for some reason, on my left), listing among the repetitious reeds, what seemed a large armchair but was actually a strange, cumbersome gray amphibian, whose name Gregson refused to tell me, would rise out of the swamp.

"A break," said Gregson abruptly, "let's take a break."

By a stroke of luck we managed to scramble onto an islet of rock, surrounded by the swamp vegetation. Gregson took off his knapsack and issued us some native patties, smelling of ipecacuanha,[13] and a dozen acreana fruit. How thirsty I was, and how little help was the scanty, astringent juice of the acreana. . . .

"Look, how odd," Gregson said to me, not in English, but in some other language, so that Cook would not understand. "We must get through to the hills, but look, how odd—could the hills have been a mirage?—they are no longer visible."

I raised myself up from my pillow and leaned my elbow on the resilient surface of the rock. . . . Yes, it was true that the hills were no longer visible; there was only the quivering vapor hanging over the marsh. Once again everything around me assumed an ambiguous transparency. I leaned back and said softly to Gregson, "You probably can't see, but something keeps trying to come through."

"What are you talking about?" asked Gregson.

---

[12] Spitting water (in this case, venom).
[13] South American plant used to induce both

expectoration and vomiting. Commonly known as "ipecac."

I realized that what I was saying was nonsense and stopped. My head was spinning and there was a humming in my ears; Gregson, down on one knee, rummaged through his knapsack, but found no medicine there, and my supply was exhausted. Cook sat in silence, morosely picking at a rock. Through a rent in his shirtsleeve there showed a strange tattoo on his arm: a crystal tumbler with a teaspoon, very well executed.

"Vallière is sick—haven't you got some tablets?" Gregson said to him. I did not hear the exact words, but I could guess the general sense of their talk, which would grow absurd and somehow spherical when I tried to listen more closely.

Cook turned slowly and the glassy tattoo slid off his skin to one side, remaining suspended in mid-air; then it floated off, floated off, and I pursued it with my frightened gaze, but, as I turned away, it lost itself in the vapor of the swamp, with a last faint gleam.

"Serves you right," muttered Cook. "It's just too bad. The same will happen to you and me. Just too bad. . . ."

In the course of the last few minutes—that is, ever since we had stopped to rest on the rocky islet—he seemed to have grown larger, had swelled, and there was now something mocking and dangerous about him. Gregson took off his sun helmet and, pulling out a dirty handkerchief, wiped his forehead, which was orange over the brows, and white above that. Then he put on his helmet again, leaned over to me, and said, "Pull yourself together, please" (or words to that effect). "We shall try to move on. The vapor is hiding the hills, but they are there. I am certain we have covered about half the swamp." (This is all very approximate.)

"Murderer," said Cook under his breath. The tattoo was now again on his forearm; not the entire glass, though, but one side of it—there was not quite enough room for the remainder, which quivered in space, casting reflections. "Murderer," Cook repeated with satisfaction, raising his inflamed eyes. "I told you we would get stuck here. Black dogs eat too much carrion. Mi, re, fa, sol."

"He's a clown," I softly informed Gregson, "a Shakesperean clown."

"Clow, clow, clow," Gregson answered, "clow, clow—clo, clo, clo. . . . Do you hear," he went on, shouting in my ear. "You must get up. We have to move on."

The rock was as white and as soft as a bed. I raised myself a little, but promptly fell back on the pillow.

"We shall have to carry him," said Gregson's faraway voice. "Give me a hand."

"Fiddlesticks," replied Cook (or so it sounded to me). "I suggest we enjoy some fresh meat before he dries up. Fa, sol, mi, re."

"He's sick, he's sick too," I cried to Gregson. "You're here with two lunatics. Go ahead alone. You'll make it. . . . Go."

"Fat chance we'll let him go," said Cook.

Meanwhile delirious visions, taking advantage of the general confusion, were quietly and firmly finding their places. The lines of a dim ceiling stretched and crossed in the sky. A large armchair rose, as if supported from below, out of the swamp. Glossy birds flew through the haze of the marsh and, as they settled, one turned into the wooden knob of a bedpost, another into a decanter. Gathering all my will power, I focused my gaze and drove off this dangerous trash. Above the reeds flew real birds with long flame-colored tails. The air buzzed with insects. Gregson was waving away a varicolored fly, and at the same time trying to determine its species. Finally he could contain himself no longer and caught it in his net. His motions underwent curious changes, as if someone kept reshuffling them. I saw him in different poses simultaneously; he was divesting himself of himself, as if he were made of many glass Gregsons whose outlines did not coincide. Then he condensed again, and stood up firmly. He was shaking Cook by the shoulder.

"You are going to help me carry him," Gregson was saying distinctly. "If you were not a traitor, we would not be in this mess."

Cook remained silent, but slowly flushed purple.

"See here, Cook, you'll regret this," said Gregson. "I'm telling you for the last time—"

At this point occurred what had been ripening for a long time. Cook drove his head like a bull into Gregson's stomach. They both fell; Gregson had time to get his revolver out, but Cook managed to knock it out of his hand. Then they clutched each other and started rolling in their embrace, panting deafeningly. I looked at them, helpless. Cook's broad back would grow tense and the vertebrae would show through his shirt; but suddenly, instead of his back, a leg, also his, would appear, covered with coppery hairs, and with a blue vein running up the skin, and Gregson was rolling on top of him. Gregson's helmet flew off and wobbled away, like half of an enormous cardboard egg. From somewhere in the labyrinth of their bodies Cook's fingers wriggled out, clenching a rusty but sharp knife; the knife entered Gregson's back as if it were clay, but Gregson only gave a grunt, and they both rolled over several times; when I next saw my friend's back the handle and top half of the blade protruded, while his hands had locked around Cook's thick neck, which crunched as he squeezed, and Cook's legs were twitching. They made one last full revolution, and now only a quarter of the blade was visible—no, a fifth—no, now not even that much showed: it had entered completely. Gregson grew still after having piled on top of Cook, who had also become motionless.

I watched, and it seemed to me (fogged as my senses were by fever) that this was all a harmless game, that in a moment they would get up and, when they had caught their breath, would peacefully carry me off across the swamp toward the cool blue hills, to some shady place with babbling water. But suddenly, at this last stage of my mortal illness—for I knew that in a few minutes I would die—in these final minutes everything grew completely lucid: I realized that all that was taking place around me was not the trick of an inflamed imagination, not the veil of delirium, through which unwelcome glimpses of my supposedly real existence in a distant European city (the wallpaper, the armchair, the glass of lemonade) were trying to show. I realized that the obtrusive room was fictitious, since everything beyond death is, at best, fictitious: an imitation of life hastily knocked together, the furnished rooms of nonexistence. I realized that reality was here, here beneath that wonderful, frightening tropical sky, among those gleaming swordlike reeds, in that vapor hanging over them, and in the thick-lipped flowers clinging to the flat islet, where, beside me, lay two clinched corpses. And, having realized this, I found within me the strength to crawl over to them and pull the knife from the back of Gregson, my leader, my dear friend. He was dead, quite dead, and all the little bottles in his pockets were broken and crushed. Cook, too, was dead, and his ink-black tongue protruded from his mouth. I pried open Gregson's fingers and turned his body over. His lips were half-open and bloody; his face, which already seemed hardened, appeared badly shaven; the bluish whites of his eyes showed between the lids. For the last time I saw all this distinctly, consciously,

with the seal of authenticity on everything—their skinned knees, the bright flies circling over them, the females of those flies, already seeking a spot for oviposition.[14]
Fumbling with my enfeebled hands, I took a thick notebook out of my shirt pocket,
but here I was overcome by weakness; I sat down and my head drooped. And yet I
conquered this impatient fog of death and looked around. Blue air, heat, solitude. . . .
And how sorry I felt for Gregson, who would never return home—I even remembered his wife and the old cook, and his parrots, and many other things. Then I
thought about our discoveries, our precious finds, the rare, still undescribed plants and
animals that now would never be named by us. I was alone. Hazier flashed the reeds,
dimmer flamed the sky. My eyes followed an exquisite beetle that was crawling across
a stone, but I had no strength left to catch it. Everything around me was fading,
leaving bare the scenery of death—a few pieces of realistic furniture and four walls.
My last motion was to open the book, which was damp with my sweat, for I
absolutely had to make a note of something; but, alas, it slipped out of my hand. I
groped all along the blanket, but it was no longer there.

1931

James Agee
1909–1955

James Agee was born in Knoxville, Tennessee, and was educated at St. Andrew's,
an Episcopal school in Sewanee, Tennessee, where his mother taught. The strict
religious and moral code of his mother, the friendship of a St. Andrew's teacher,
Father Flye, the social and spiritual values of the school, and the death of his
father in an automobile accident when Agee was not yet seven years old—all
these memories marked Agee's life and provided the settings and themes that
shaped his art. In a 1947 review of Charlie Chaplin's *Monsieur Verdoux,* Agee
defined Chaplin's theme as "the bare problem of surviving at all in such a world
as this" and remarked that it was the greatest theme Chaplin had ever
undertaken. He might have added that it was one of his own.

After St. Andrew's, Agee spent a year at Phillips Exeter Academy and four at
Harvard College, where he was editor of *The Advocate.* He then went on to a
career that yielded a substantial body of writing in several different modes: a
sensitively written novella that covers one day in the life of a Tennessee boy,
The Morning Watch (1951); stories, fables, and fragments later published as *The
Collected Short Prose of James Agee* (1968); a prizewinning volume of poetry,
Permit Me Voyage (1934); a posthumously published novel about the death of his
father, *A Death in the Family* (1957), that won a Pulitzer Prize; and a series of
remarkable letters that was also published after his death, *Letters of James Agee to
Father Flye* (1962).

[14] Laying eggs.

In 1939 Agee took a position writing film reviews for *Time* magazine, and later he wrote film reviews for *The Nation*—writings that were subsequently collected into two large volumes called *Agee on Film* (1958, 1960). In 1947 Agee began writing scripts for movies and television; his credits include such major films as *The African Queen* (1952) and *Night of the Hunter* (1955). Through his reviews and scripts, he did more than any other writer of his time to establish both film criticism and scriptwriting as new fields worth serious literary attention. But it was in 1941 that Agee published *Let Us Now Praise Famous Men,* which has come increasingly to be regarded as his most original work.

In *Let Us Now Praise Famous Men,* written in collaboration with the fine photographer Walker Evans, Agee brought to culmination and also transcended the genre of the documentary, a genre that had come of age during the decade of the 1930s when the deepening Depression led writers to seek new ways of exposing the poverty and suffering of America while also celebrating its strength. Yet when he died in 1955 of a massive heart attack, Agee was still regarded as a writer of unfulfilled promise.

In one sense Agee never fully resolved the question "of how to become what I wish I could when I can't"—a question that was all the more important, as Agee came to see, because it was for him inseparable from the question of deciding "what I want to write." In one of its aspects, Agee's problem was personal. In a fragment that he left unpublished, he speaks of his writing as an effort to restore "such of my lost life as I can," in which connection he mentions both his own childhood and the death of his father. Most of his writings, including *Let Us Now Praise Famous Men,* combine autobiographical elements with other very different elements. In another of its aspects, however, Agee's problem was aesthetic and social. Though his sensibility was shaped by literary modernism, by T. S. Eliot and Ezra Pound and James Joyce, Agee rejected the elitist tendencies of modern literature. In his own art he wanted to bridge the gulf between "popular" culture and "high" culture, to discover, as it were, a shared ground on which one could create a kind of democratic high art. To this endeavor he brought a masterful eye, an ear for nuance, and a lyric gift that found more powerful (because it is less precious) expression in prose than in poetry. In *Let Us Now Praise Famous Men,* Agee celebrates not our heroic, collective past but obscure, private, present lives, and he praises neither heroes of traditional culture nor heroes of a newly dominant culture but heroes of a forgotten people.

In this, as in so much else, Agee was more a follower of Walt Whitman than of the great modernists, though he remained suspicious of commercialism and materialism as well as artiness and aestheticism. In 1935, when he and Walker Evans journeyed to Hale County, Alabama, to gather the material that became *Let Us Now Praise Famous Men,* they went on assignment for *Fortune* magazine. Several months later, after they had returned and submitted their copy, the editors of *Fortune* rejected it on grounds that it was inappropriate for their use. Today the generically mixed and uneven book that came of the work they undertook for *Fortune* is more and more widely regarded both as a landmark in American prose and as the height of Agee's achievement as a writer.

Further Reading:
W. Evans, "James Agee in 1936," *Atlantic Monthly*, July 1960.
Letters of James Agee to Father Flye, 1962.
E. Larsen, *James Agee*, 1971.

Text:
Let Us Now Praise Famous Men, 1960.

from Let Us Now Praise Famous Men
Book Two

[from **All over Alabama***]*[1]

The house had now descended

All over Alabama the lamps are out

(On the Porch: 1

The house and all that was in it had now descended deep beneath the gradual spiral it had sunk through; it lay formal under the order of entire silence. In the square pine room at the back the bodies of the man of thirty and of his wife and of their children lay on shallow mattresses on their iron beds and on the rigid floor, and they were sleeping, and the dog lay asleep in the hallway. Most human beings, most animals and birds who live in the sheltering ring of human influence, and a great portion of all the branched tribes of living in earth and air and water upon a half of the world, were stunned with sleep. That region of the earth on which we were at this time transient was some hours fallen beneath the fascination of the stone, steady shadow of the planet, and lay now listing toward the last depth; and now by a blockade of the sun were clearly disclosed those discharges of light which teach us what little we can learn of the stars and of the true nature of our surroundings. There was no longer any sound of the settling or ticking of any part of the structure of the house; the bone pine hung on its nails like an abandoned Christ. There was no longer any sound of the sinking and settling, like gently foundering, fatal boats, of the bodies and brains of this human family through the late stages of fatigue unharnessed or the early phases of sleep; nor was there any longer the sense of any of these sounds, nor was there, even, the sound or the sense of breathing. Bone and bone, blood and blood, life and life disjointed and abandoned they lay graven in so final depth, that dreams attend them seemed not plausible. Fish halted on the middle and serene of blind sea water sleeping lidless lensed; their breathing, their sleeping subsistence, the effortless nursing of ignorant plants; entirely silenced, sleepers, delicate planets, insects, cherished in amber, mured in night, autumn of action, sorrow's short winter, waterhole where gather the weak wild beasts; night; night: sleep; sleep.

[1] The bracketed chapter titles here are Agee's, from the "design" of the book as given in the front matter to the volume.

In their prodigious realm, their field, bashfully at first, less timorous, later, rashly, all calmly boldly now, like the tingling and standing up of plants, leaves, planted crops out of the earth into the yearly approach of the sun, the noises and natures of the dark had with the ceremonial gestures of music and of erosion lifted forth the thousand several forms of their entrancement, and had so resonantly taken over the world that this domestic, this human silence obtained, prevailed, only locally, shallowly, and with the childlike and frugal dignity of a coal-oil lamp stood out on a wide night meadow and of a star sustained, unraveling in one rivery sigh its irremediable vitality, on the alien size of space.

Where beneath the ghosts of millennial rain the clay land lay down in creek and the trees ran thick there disposed upon the sky the cloud and black shadow of nature, hostile encampment whose fires were drenched, drawn close, held sleeping, near, helots; and it was feasible that within a few hours now, at the signaling of the primary changes of the air, the wave which summer and darkness had already so heavily overcrested that it leaned above us, snaring its snake-tongued branches, birnam wood, casually would lounge in and suddenly and forever subdue us: at most, some obscure act of guerrilla warfare, some prowler, detached from his regiment, picked off in a back country orchard, some straggling camp whore taken, had; for the sky:

The sky was withdrawn from us with all her strength. Against some scarcely conceivable imprisoning wall this woman held herself away from us and watched us: wide, high, light with her stars as milk above our heavy dark; and like the bristling and glass breakage on the mouth of stone spring water: broached on grand heaven their metal fires.

And now as by the slipping of a button, the snapping and failures on air of a spider's cable, there broke loose from the room, shaken, a long sigh closed in silence. On some ledge overleaning that gulf which is more profound than the remembrance of imagination they had lain in sleep and at length the sand, that by degrees had crumpled and rifted, had broken from beneath them and they sank. There was now no further extreme, and they were sunken not singularly but companionate among the whole enchanted swarm of the living, into a region prior to the youngest quaverings of creation.

(We lay on the front porch:. . .

All over Alabama, the lamps are out. Every leaf drenches the touch; the spider's net is heavy. The roads lie there, with nothing to use them. The fields lie there, with nothing at work in them, neither man nor beast. The plow handles are wet, and the rails and the frogplates and the weeds between the ties: and not even the hurryings and hoarse sorrows of a distant train, on other roads, is heard. The little towns, the county seats, house by house white-painted and elaborately sawn among their heavy and dark-lighted leaves, in the spaced protections of their mineral light they stand so prim, so voided, so undefended upon starlight, that it is inconceivable to despise or to scorn a white man, an owner of land; even in Birmingham, mile on mile, save for the sudden frightful streaming, almost instantly diminished and silent, of a closed black car, and save stone lonesome sinister heelbeats, that show never a face and enter, soon, a frame door flush with the pavement, and ascend the immediate lightless staircase, mile on mile, stone, stone, smooth charted streams of stone, the streets under their lifted lamps lie void before eternity. New Orleans is stirring, rattling, and sliding faintly in its fragrance and in the enormous richness of its lust; taxis are still parked along Dauphine Street and the breastlike, floral air is itchy with the stilettos and embroiderings above black blood drumthroes of an eloquent cracked indiscoverable cornet, which exists only in the imagination and somewhere in the past, in the broken heart of Louis Armstrong; yet even in that small portion which is the infested genitals of that city, never free, neither of desire nor of waking pain, there are the qualities of the tender desolations of profoundest night. Beneath, the gulf lies dreaming, and beneath, dreaming, that woman, that id, the lower American continent, lies spread before heaven in her wealth. The parks of her cities are iron, loam, silent, the sweet fountains shut, and the pure façades, embroiled, limelike in street light are sharp, are still:

from Part 1: A Country Letter

from I

. . . I am fond of Emma, and very sorry for her, and I shall probably never see her again after a few hours from now. I want to tell you what I can about her.

She is a big girl, almost as big as her sister is wiry, though she is not at all fat: her build is rather that of a young queen of a child's magic story who throughout has been coarsened by peasant and earth living and work, and that of her eyes and her demeanor, too, kind, not fully formed, resolute, bewildered, and sad. Her soft abundant slightly curling brown hair is cut in a square bob which on her large fine head is particularly childish, and indeed Emma is rather a big child, sexual beyond propriety to its years, than a young woman; and this can be seen in a kind of dimness of definition in her features, her skin, and the shape of her body, which will be lost in a few more years. She wears a ten cent store necklace and a sunday cotton print dress because she is visiting, and is from town, but she took off her slippers as soon as she came, and worked with Annie Mae. According to her father she is the spitn image of her mother when her mother was young; Annie Mae favors her father and his people, who were all small and lightly built.

Emma is very fond of her father and very sorry for him, as her sister is, and neither of them can stand his second wife. I have an idea that his marrying her had a lot to do with Emma's own marriage, which her father so strongly advised her against. He married the second time when Emma was thirteen, and for a long while they lived almost insanely, as I will tell you of later, far back in a swamp: and when Emma was sixteen she married a man her father's age, a carpenter in Cherokee City. She has been married to him two years; they have no children. Emma loves good times, and towns, and people her own age, and he is jealous and mean to her and suspicious of her. He has given her no pretty dresses nor the money to buy cloth to make them. Every minute he is in the house he keeps his eye right on her as if she was up to something, and when he goes out, which is as seldom as he can, he locks her in: so that twice already she has left him and come home to stay, and then after a while he has come down begging, and crying, and swearing he'll treat her good, and give her anything she asks for, and that he'll take to drink or kill himself if she leaves him, and she has gone back: for it isn't any fun at home, hating that woman the way she does, and she can't have fun with anyone else because she is married and nobody will have fun with her that way: and now (and I think it may be not only through the depression but through staying in the house because of jealousy and through fear of living in a town with her, and so near a home she can return to), her husband can no longer get a living in Cherokee City; he has heard of a farm on a plantation over in the red hills in Mississippi and has already gone, and taken it, and he has sent word to Emma that she is to come in a truck in which a man he knows, who has business to drive out that way, is moving their furniture; and this truck is leaving tomorrow. She doesn't want to go at all, and during the past two days she has been withdrawing into rooms with her sister and crying a good deal, almost tearlessly and almost without voice, as if she knew no more how to cry than how to take care for her life; and Annie Mae is strong against her going, all that distance, to a man who leaves her behind and then just sends for her, saying, Come on along, now; and George too is as committal over it as he feels will appear any right or business of his to be, he a man, and married, to the wife of another man, who is no kin to him, but only the sister of his wife, and to whom he is himself unconcealably attracted: but she is going all the same, without at all understanding why. Annie Mae is sure she won't stay out there long, not all alone in the country away from her kinfolks with that man; that is what she keeps saying, to Emma, and to George, and even to me; but actually she is surer than not that she may never see her young sister again, and she grieves for her, and for the loss of her to her own loneliness, for she loves her, both for herself and her dependence and for that softness of youth which already is drawn so deep into the trap, and in which Annie Mae can perceive herself as she was ten years past; and she gives no appearance of noticing the clumsy and shamefaced would-be-subtle demeanors of flirtation which George is stupid enough to believe she does not understand for what they are: for George would only be shocked should she give him open permission, and Emma could not be too well trusted either. So this sad comedy has been going on without comment from anyone, which will come to nothing: and another sort has been going on with us, of a kind fully as helpless. Each of us is attractive to Emma, both in sexual immediacy and as symbols or embodiments of a life she wants and knows she will never have; and each of us is fond of her, and attracted toward her. We are not only strangers to her, but we are strange, unexplainable, beyond what I can begin yet fully to realize. We have acted toward her with the greatest possible care and shyness and quiet, yet we have been open or 'clear' as well, so that she knows we understand her and like her and care for her almost intimately. She is puzzled by this and yet not at all troubled, but excited; but there is nothing to do about it on either side. There is tenderness and sweetness and mutual pleasure in such a 'flirtation' which one would not for the world restrain or cancel, yet there is also an essential cruelty, about which nothing can be done, and strong possibility of cruelty through misunderstanding, and inhibition, and impossibility, which can be restrained, and which one would rather die than cause any of: but it is a cruel and ridiculous and restricted situation, and everyone to some extent realizes it. Everyone realizes it, I think, to such a degree even as this: supposing even that nothing can be helped about the marriage, supposing she is going away and on with it, which she shouldn't, then if only Emma could spend her last few days alive having a gigantic good time in bed, with George, a kind of man she is best used to, and with Walker and with me, whom she is curious about and attracted to, and who are at the same moment tangible and friendly and not at all to be feared, and on the other hand have for her the mystery or glamour almost of mythological creatures. This has a good many times in the past couple of days come very clearly through between all of us except the children, and without fear, in sudden and subtle but unmistakable expressions of the eyes, or ways of smiling: yet not one of us would be capable of trusting ourselves to it unless beyond any doubt each knew all the others to be thus capable: and even then how crazily the conditioned and inferior parts of each of our beings would rush in, and take revenge. But this is just a minute specialization of a general brutal pity: almost any person, no matter how damaged and poisoned and blinded, is infinitely more capable of intelligence and of joy than he can let himself be or than he usually knows; and even if he had no reason to fear his own poisons, he has those that are in others to fear, to assume and take care for, if he would not hurt both himself and that other person and the pure act itself beyond cure.

But here I am going to shift ahead of where I am writing, to a thing which is to happen, or which happened, the next morning (you mustn't be puzzled by this, I'm writing in a continuum), and say what came of it.

The next morning was full of the disorganized, half listless, yet very busy motions of ordinary life broken by an event: Emma's going away. I was going to take her and Annie Mae to her brother Gallatin's house near Cookstown, where she was to meet the man with his truck, and I was waiting around on the front porch in the cool-hot increasing morning sunlight, working out my notes, while the morning housework was done up in special speed. (George was gone an hour or more ago, immediately after the breakfast they had all sat through, not talking much. There had been a sort of lingering in eating and in silences, and a little when the food was done, broken by talk to keep the silences from becoming too frightening; I had let the breakfast start late by telling him I would take him in the car; then abruptly he got up saying, 'Well, Jimmy, if you—' Whether he would kiss Emma goodbye, as a sort of relative, was on everybody's mind. He came clumsily near it: she half got from her chair, and their bodies were suddenly and sharply drawn toward each other a few inches: but he was much too shy, and did not even touch her with the hand he reached out to shake hers. Annie Mae drawled, smiling, What's wrong with ye George; she ain't agoin' to bite ye; and everyone laughed, and Emma stood up and they embraced, laughing, and he kissed her on her suddenly turned cheek, a little the way a father and an adolescent son kiss, and told her goodbye and wished her good luck, and I took him to work in the car, and came back. And now here I was, as I have said, on the porch.) Here I was on the porch, diddling around in a notebook and hearing the sounds of work and the changing patterns of voices inside, and the unaccustomed noise of shoeleather on the floor, because someone was dressed up for travel; and a hen thudded among dried watermelon seeds on the oak floor, looking, as they usually do, like a nearsighted professor; and down hill beyond the open field a little wind laid itself in a wall against the glistening leaves of the high forest and lay through with a long sweet granular noise of rustling water; and the hen dropped from the ledge of the porch to the turded dirt with a sodden bounce, and an involuntary cluck as her heaviness hit the ground on her sprung legs; and the long lithe little wind released the trees and was gone on, wandering the fringed earth in its affairs like a saturday schoolchild in the sun, and the leaves hung troubling in the aftermath; and I heard footsteps in the hall and Emma appeared, all dressed to go, looking somehow as if she had come to report a decision that had been made in a conference, for which I, without knowing it, seemed to have been waiting. She spoke in that same way, too, not wasting any roundabout time or waiting for an appropriate rhythm, yet not in haste, looking me steadily and sweetly in the eyes, and said, I want you and Mr. Walker to know how much we all like you, because you make us feel easy with you; we don't have to act any different from what it comes natural to act, and we don't have to worry what you're thinking about us, it's just like you was our own people and had always lived here with us, you all are so kind, and nice, and quiet, and easygoing, and we wisht you wasn't never going to go away but stay on here with us, and I just want to tell you how much we all keer about you; Annie Mae says the same, and you please tell Mr. Walker, too, if I don't see him afore I go. (I knew she could never say it over again, and I swore I certainly would tell him.)

What's the use trying to say what I felt. It took her a long time to say what she wanted so much to say, and it was hard for her, but there she stood looking straight into my eyes, and I straight into hers, longer than you'd think it would be possible to stand it. I would have done anything in the world for her (that is always characteristic, I guess, of the seizure of the strongest love you can feel: pity, and the wish to die for a person, because there isn't anything you can do for them that is at all measurable to your love), and all I could do, the very most, for this girl who was so soon going on out of my existence into so hopeless a one of hers, the very most I could do was not to show all I cared for her and for what she was saying, and not to even try to do, or to indicate the good I wished I might do her and was so utterly helpless to do. I had such tenderness and such gratitude toward her that while she spoke I very strongly, as something steadier than an 'impulse,' wanted in answer to take her large body in my arms and smooth the damp hair back from her forehead and to kiss and comfort and shelter her like a child, and I can swear that I now as then almost believe that in that moment she would have so well understood this, and so purely and quietly met it, that now as then I only wish to God I had done it; but instead the most I did was to stand facing her, and to keep looking into her eyes (doing her the honor at least of knowing that she did not want relief from this), and, managing to keep the tears from running down my face, to smile to her and say that there was nothing in my whole life that I had cared so much to be told, and had been so grateful for (and I believe this is so); and that I wanted her to know how much I liked them, too, and her herself, and that I certainly felt that they were my own people, and wanted them to be, more than any other kind of people in the world, and that if they felt that of me, and that I belonged with them, and we all felt right and easy with each other and fond of each other, then there wasn't anything in the world I could be happier over, or be more glad to know (and this is so, too); and that I knew I could say all of the same of Walker (and this, too, I know I was true in saying). I had stood up, almost without realizing I was doing it, the moment she appeared and began to speak, as though facing some formal, or royal, or ritual action, and we stayed thus standing, not leaning against or touching anything, about three feet apart, facing each other. I went on to say that whatever might happen to her or that she might do in all her life I wished her the best luck anyone could think of, and not ever to forget it, that nobody has a right to be unhappy, or to live in a way that makes them unhappy, for the sake of being afraid, or what people will think of them, or for the sake of anyone else, if there is any way they can possibly do better, that won't hurt other people too much. She slowly and lightly blushed while I spoke and her eyes became damp and bright, and said that she sure did wish me the same. Then we had nothing to say, unless we should invent something, and nothing to do, and quite suddenly and at the same instant we smiled, and she said well, she reckoned she'd better git on in and help Annie Mae, and I nodded, and she went, and a half-hour later I was driving her, and Annie Mae, and her father, and Louise, and Junior, and Burt, and the baby, to her brother's house near Cookstown. The children were silent and intent with the excitement of riding in the car, stacked on top of each other around their mother on the back seat and looking out of the windows like dogs, except Louise, whose terrible gray eyes met mine whenever I glanced for them in the car mirror. Emma rode between me and her father, her round sleeveless arms cramped a little in front of her. My own sleeves were rolled high, so that in the crowding our flesh touched. Each of us at the first few of these contacts drew quietly away, then later she relaxed her arms, and her body and thighs as well, and so did I, and for perhaps fifteen minutes we lay quietly and closely side to side, and intimately communicated also in our thoughts. Our bodies were very hot, and the car was packed with hot and sweating bodies, and with a fine salt and rank odor like that of crushed grass: and thus in a short while, though I knew speed was not in the mood of anyone and was going as slowly as I felt I could with propriety, we covered the short seven mileage of clay, then slag, to Cookstown, and slowed through the town (eyes, eyes on us, of men, from beneath hatbrims), and down the meandering now sandy road to where her brother lived. I had seen him once before, a man in his thirties with a bitter, intelligent, skull-formed face; and his sour wife, and their gold skinned children: and now here also was another man, forty or so, leathery-strong, blackshaven, black-hatted, booted, his thin mouth tightened round a stalk of grass showing gold stained teeth, his cold, mean eyes a nearly white blue; and he was sardonically waiting, and his truck, loaded with chairs and bed-iron, stood in the sun where the treeshade had slid beyond it. He was studying Emma coldly and almost without furtiveness, and she was avoiding his eyes. It was impossible to go quite immediately. We all sat around a short while and had lemonade from a pressed-glass pitcher, from which he had already taken at least two propitiatory glasses. It had been made in some hope of helping the leavetaking pass off as a sort of party, from two lemons and spring water, without ice, and it was tepid, heavily sweetened (as if to compensate the lack of lemons), and scarcely tart; there was half a glass for each of us, out of five tumblers, and we all gave most of it to the children. The children of the two families stayed very quiet, shy of each other; the others, save the black-hatted man, tried to talk, without managing much; they tried especially hard when Emma got up, as suddenly as if she had to vomit, and went into the next room and shut the door, and Annie Mae followed her. Gallatin said it was mighty hard on a girl so young as that leaving her kinfolks so far behind. The man in the hat twisted his mouth on the grass and, without opening his teeth, said Yeah-ah, as if he had his own opinions about that. We were trying not to try to hear the voices in the next room, and that same helpless, frozen, creaky weeping I had heard before; and after a little it quieted; and after a little more they came out, Emma flourily powdered straight to the eyes, and the eyes as if she had cried sand instead of tears; and the man said—it was the first kind gesture I had seen in him and one of the few I suspect in his life, and I am sure it was kind by no intention of his: 'Well, we can't hang around here all day. Reckon you'd better come on along, if you're coming.'

With that, Emma and her father kiss, shyly and awkwardly, children doing it before parents; so do she and her brother; she and Annie Mae embrace; she and I shake hands and say good-bye: all this in the sort of broken speed in which a family takes leave beside the black wall of a steaming train when the last crates have been loaded and it seems certain that at any instant the windows, and the leaned unpitying faces, will begin to slide past on iron. Emma's paper suitcase is lifted into the truck beside the bedsprings which will sustain the years on years of her cold, hopeless nights; she is helped in upon the hard seat beside the driver above the hot and floorless engine, her slippered feet propped askew at the ledges of that pit into the road; the engine snaps and coughs and catches and levels on a hot white moistureless and thin metal roar, and with a dreadful rending noise that brings up the mild heads of cattle a quarter of a mile away the truck rips itself loose from the flesh of the planed dirt of the yard and wrings into the road and chucks ahead, we waving, she waving, the black hat straight ahead, she turned away, not bearing it, our hands drooped, and we stand disconsolate and emptied in the sun; and all through these coming many hours while we slow move within the anchored rondures of our living, the hot, screaming, rattling, twenty-mile-an-hour traveling elongates steadily crawling, a lost, earnest, and frowning ant, westward on red roads and on white in the febrile sun above no support, suspended, sustained from falling by force alone of its outward growth, like that long and lithe incongruous slender runner a vine spends swiftly out on the vast blank wall of the earth, like snake's head and slim stream feeling its way, to fix, and anchor, so far, so wide of the strong and stationed stalk: and that is Emma.

from II

There are on this hill three such families I would tell you of: the Gudgers, who are sleeping in the next room; and the Woods, whose daughters are Emma and Annie Mae; and besides these, the Ricketts, who live on a little way beyond the Woods; and we reach them thus:

Leave this room and go very quietly down the open hall that divides the house, past the bedroom door, and the dog that sleeps outside it, and move on out into the open, the back yard, going up hill: between the tool shed and the hen house (the garden is on your left), and turn left at the long low shed that passes for a barn. Don't take the path to the left then: that only leads to the spring; but cut straight up the slope; and down the length of the cotton that is planted at the crest of it, and through a space of pine, hickory, dead logs and blackberry brambles (damp spider webs will bind on your face in the dark; but the path is easily enough followed); and out beyond this, across a great entanglement of clay ravines, which finally solidify into a cornfield. Follow this cornfield straight down a row, go through a barn, and turn left. There is a whole cluster of houses here; they are all negroes'; the shutters are drawn tight. You may or may not waken some dogs: if you do, you will hardly help but be frightened, for in a couple of minutes the whole country will be bellowing in the darkness, and it is over your movements at large at so late and still an hour of the night, and the sound, with the knowledge of wakened people, their heads lifted a little on the darkness from the crackling hard straw pillows of their iron beds, overcasts your very existence, in your own mind, with a complexion of guilt, stealth, and danger:

But they will quiet.

They will quiet, the lonely heads are relaxed into sleep; after a little the whippoor-wills resume, their tireless whipping of the pastoral night, and the strong frogs; and you are on the road, and again up hill, that was met at those clustered houses; pines on your left, one wall of bristling cloud, and the lifted hill; the slow field raised, in the soft stare of the cotton, several acres, on the right; and on the left the woods yield off, a hundred yards; more cotton; and set back there, at the brim of the hill, the plain small house you see is Woods' house, that looks shrunken against its centers under the starlight, the tin roof scarcely taking sheen, the floated cotton staring:

The house a quarter-mile beyond, just on the right of the road, standing with shade trees, that is the Ricketts'. The bare dirt is more damp in the tempering shade; and damp, tender with rottenness, the ragged wood of the porch, that is so heavily littered with lard buckets, scraps of iron, bent wire, torn rope, old odors, those no longer useful things which on a farm are never thrown away. The trees: draft on their stalks their clouds of heavy season; the barn: shines on the perfect air; in the bare yard a twelve-foot flowering bush: in shroud of blown bloom slumbers, and within: naked, naked side by side those brothers and sisters, those most beautiful children; and the crazy, clownish, foxy father; and the mother; and the two old daughters; crammed on their stinking beds, are resting the night:

Fred, Sadie, Margaret, Paralee, Garvrin, Richard, Flora Merry Lee, Katy, Clair Bell; and the dogs, and the cats, and the hens, and the mules, and the hogs, and the cow, and the bull calf:

Woods, and his young wife, and her mother, and the young wife's daughter, and her son by Woods, and their baby daughter, and that heavy-browed beast which enlarges in her belly; Bud, and Ivy, and Miss-Molly, and Pearl, and Thomas, and Ellen, and the nameless plant of unknown sex; and the cat, and the dog, and the mule, and the hog, and the cow, and the hens, and the huddled chickens:

And George, and his wife, and her sister, and their children, and their animals; and the hung wasps, lancing mosquitoes, numbed flies, and browsing rats:

All, spreaded in high quietude on the hill:

Sadie the half-sister of Bud, and drowned in their remembrance: that long and spiral shaft they've climbed, from shacks on shale, rigid as corn on a cob, out of the mining country, the long wandering, her pride of beauty, his long strength in marriage, into this: this present time, and this near future:

George his lost birthright, bad land owned, and that boyhood among cedars and clean creeks where no fever laid its touch, and where in the luminous and great hollow night the limestone shone like sheep: and the strong, gay girls:

Fred, what of him: I can not guess. And Annie Mae, that hat; which still, so broken, the death odor of feathers and silk in menthol, is crumpled in a drawer; and those weeks when she was happy, and to her husband and to her heart it was pleasing to be alive:

She is dreaming now, with fear, of a shotgun: George has directed it upon her; and there is no trigger:

Ivy, and her mother: what are the dreams of dogs? . . .

[Two Images]

The last words of this book have been spoken and those that follow are not words; they are only descriptions of two images. One is of Squinchy Gudger and his mother as they are in the open hall; one is of Ellen Woods as she lies sleeping at the edge of the front porch: both in a silent, white hour of a summer day.

His mother sits in a hickory chair with her knees relaxed and her bare feet flat to the floor; her dress open and one broken breast exposed. Her head is turned a little slantwise and she gazes quietly downward past her son's head into the junctures of the earth, the floor, the wall, the sunlight, and the shade. One hand lies long and flat along her lap: it is elegantly made of bone and is two sizes too large for the keen wrist. With her other hand, and in the cradling of her arm and shoulder, she holds the child. His dress has fallen aside and he is naked. As he is held, the head huge in scale of his body, the small body ineffably relaxed, spilled in a deep curve from nape to buttocks, then the knees drawn up a little, the bottom small and sharp, and the legs and feet drifted as if under water, he suggests the shape of the word siphon. He is nursing. His hands are blundering at her breast blindly, as if themselves each were a new born creature, or as if they were sobbing, ecstatic with love; his mouth is intensely absorbed at her nipple as if in rapid kisses, with small and swift sounds of moisture; his eyes are squeezed shut; and now, for breath, he draws away, and lets out a sharp short whispered *ahh,* the hands and his eyelids relaxing, and immediately resumes; and in all this while, his face is beatific, the face of one at rest in paradise, and in all this while her gentle and sober, earnest face is not altered out of its deep slantwise gazing: his head is now sunken off and away, grand and soft as a cloud, his wet mouth flared, his body still more profoundly relinquished of itself, and I see how against her body he is so many things in one, the child in the melodies of the womb, the Madonna's son, human divinity sunken from the cross at rest against his mother, and more beside, for at the heart and leverage of that young body, gently, taken in all the pulse of his being, the penis is partly erected.

And Ellen where she rests, in the gigantic light: she, too, is completely at peace, this child, the arms squared back, the palms open loose against the floor, the floursack on her face; and her knees are flexed upward a little and fallen apart, the soles of the feet facing: her blown belly swimming its navel, white as flour; and blown full broad with slumbering blood into a circle: so white all the outward flesh, it glows of blue; so dark, the deep hole, a dark red shadow of life blood: this center and source, for which we have never contrived any worthy name, is as if it were breathing, flowering, soundlessly, a snoring silence of flame; it is as if flame were breathed forth from it and subtly played about it: and here in this breathing and play of flame, a thing so strong, so valiant, so unvanquishable, it is without effort, without emotion, I know it shall at length outshine the sun.

1941

Eudora Welty
b. 1909

Admirers of Eudora Welty's fiction have always been in good company: Ford Madox Ford, Katherine Anne Porter, and Robert Penn Warren were among her earliest supporters. Like those who have followed them, they praised Welty's fiction for its evocative sense of place and even more for its compelling and honest presentation of human experience on all levels. Welty's most recent novel, *The Optimist's Daughter* (1972), focuses primarily on the social elite of a modern southern town, while her early, famous short story, "A Worn Path," is a realistic and uncondescending account of an old black woman's strength and dignity. Convinced that "to write honestly and with all our powers is the least we can do, and the most," Welty persists in confronting the flaws she sees in her characters and her region, but she does so without bitterness. She brings to life "the turn of mind, the nature of temperament, of a privileged observer," but "owing to the way I became so," she has remarked, "it turned out that I became the loving kind."

A native of Jackson, Mississippi, where she has lived most of her life, Eudora Welty was born on April 13, 1909. She attended the Mississippi State College for Women for two years before transferring to the University of Wisconsin, from which she was graduated in 1929. She then enrolled at the Columbia University Graduate School of Business to study advertising. "As certain as I was of wanting to be a writer," she says, "I was certain of *not* wanting to be a teacher." After two years in New York, she returned to Jackson, where she worked in advertising with a local radio station and a state commission on tourism and as a society correspondent for a Memphis newspaper. As a publicist for the Works Progress Administration in the early 1930s, she took a series of photographs on southern rural poverty, some of which were exhibited in a one-woman show at the Museum of Modern Art in 1973. In 1936 she published her first short story, "Death of a Travelling Salesman," and followed it in rapid succession with two collections of stories, *A Curtain of Green and Other Stories* (1941) and *The Wide Net* (1943). Her first novel, *The Robber Bridegroom,* a fairy-tale-like story, appeared in 1942. Other novels, all dealing with various aspects of Mississippi life, include the story of a modern plantation family in *Delta Wedding* (1946), the comic first-person narrative of small-town life in *The Ponder Heart* (1954), and the complex tale of a large rural family in *Losing Battles* (1970), her most ambitious book. Her most recent work, *One Writer's Beginnings,* a collection of three autobiographical pieces, appeared in 1984. She has published additional collections of short stories—some realistic and others more fantastic—as well as several collections of essays on criticism and fictional theory, including *Place in Fiction* (1957) and *The Eye of the Story* (1977). Although *The Optimist's Daughter* has received widespread popular and critical acclaim, Welty remains best known for her finely crafted and often extremely funny short stories, which were published in 1980 as *The Collected Stories of Eudora Welty.*

Welty's fiction draws heavily on her deep knowledge of her region and her keen powers of observation. She has said that her imagination is predominantly visual, yet her ear for dialect matches her mastery of descriptive detail. Welty's major achievement, however, lies in her ability to reach through detailed surfaces to less tangible dimensions of reality. In "Why I Live at the P.O.," for example, Sister's obsessive monologue reveals not only the comic interaction of her extended family, nor merely her own deep-rooted feelings of alienation and lost opportunity, but also a sense of the mystery of human relationships. Like many southern writers, Welty is known for the creation of "grotesque" characters. Her characters, including Sister, are often physically, mentally, or emotionally handicapped and are thus at odds with their community. Yet even as they show the pain that isolation inflicts, they also show a freedom that a small, tightly-knit community does not permit.

In an early story, Welty describes a young girl who often looks at the world through a frame that she makes with her fingers. A frame, as Welty has since observed, not only involves focus and distance and selection; it also involves a viewer's values and commitments, her preferences, even her beliefs. The "frame through which I viewed the world changed too, with time," she has written recently, in *One Writer's Beginnings*. "Greater than scene, I came to see, is situation. Greater than situation is implication. Greater than all of these is a single, entire human being, who will never be confined in any frame." Over the years, Welty has concentrated on refining her frame, believing that the integrity of a work largely determines its quality. She makes her stories, she says, not directly out of her own life nor directly out of the lives of other people but out of "the *whole* fund of my feelings, my responses to the real experiences of my own life, to the relationships that formed and changed it, that I have given most of myself to." She writes of familiar themes—the power of the community and the power of the past in shaping the lives of individuals, the power of love and the power of memory, and the pain of loneliness and the pain of loss. Yet the character she feels closest to is the spinster piano teacher Miss Eckhart in "June Recital": "What I have put into her is my passion for my own life work, my own art. Exposing yourself to risk is a truth Miss Eckhart and I had in common. What animates and possesses me is what drives Miss Eckhart, the love of her art and the love of giving it, the desire to give it until there is no more left."

Further Reading:
R. P. Warren, "The Love and Separateness in Miss Welty" in *Selected Essays*, 1958.
R. M. Vande Kieft, *Eudora Welty*, 1962.
L. D. Rubin, Jr., "The Golden Apples of the Sun" in *The Faraway Country: Writers of the Modern South*, 1963.
J. A. Bryant, Jr., *Eudora Welty*, 1968.
M. Kreyling, *Eudora Welty's Achievement of Order*, 1980.

Text:
Collected Stories, 1980.

Why I Live at the P.O.

I was getting along fine with Mama, Papa-Daddy and Uncle Rondo until my sister Stella-Rondo just separated from her husband and came back home again. Mr. Whitaker! Of course I went with Mr. Whitaker first, when he first appeared here in China Grove, taking "Pose Yourself" photos, and Stella-Rondo broke us up. Told him I was one-sided. Bigger on one side than the other, which is a deliberate, calculated falsehood: I'm the same. Stella-Rondo is exactly twelve months to the day younger than I am and for that reason she's spoiled.

She's always had anything in the world she wanted and then she'd throw it away. Papa-Daddy gave her this gorgeous Add-a-Pearl necklace when she was eight years old and she threw it away playing baseball when she was nine, with only two pearls.

So as soon as she got married and moved away from home the first thing she did was separate! From Mr. Whitaker! This photographer with the popeyes she said she trusted. Came home from one of those towns up in Illinois and to our complete surprise brought this child of two.

Mama said she like to made her drop dead for a second. "Here you had this marvelous blonde child and never so much as wrote your mother a word about it," says Mama. "I'm thoroughly ashamed of you." But of course she wasn't.

Stella-Rondo just calmly takes off this *hat,* I wish you could see it. She says, "Why, Mama, Shirley-T.'s adopted. I can prove it."

"How?" says Mama, but all I says was, "H'm!" There I was over the hot stove, trying to stretch two chickens over five people and a completely unexpected child into the bargain, without one moment's notice.

"What do you mean—'H'm!'?" says Stella-Rondo, and Mama says, "I heard that, Sister."

I said that oh, I didn't mean a thing, only that whoever Shirley-T. was, she was the spit-image of Papa-Daddy if he'd cut off his beard, which of course he'd never do in the world. Papa-Daddy's Mama's papa and sulks.

Stella-Rondo got furious! She said, "Sister, I don't need to tell you you got a lot of nerve and always did have and I'll thank you to make no future reference to my adopted child whatsoever."

"Very well," I said. "Very well, very well. Of course I noticed at once she looks like Mr. Whitaker's side too. That frown. She looks like a cross between Mr. Whitaker and Papa-Daddy."

"Well, all I can say is she isn't."

"She looks exactly like Shirley Temple to me," says Mama, but Shirley-T. just ran away from her.

So the first thing Stella-Rondo did at the table was turn Papa-Daddy against me.

"Papa-Daddy," she says. He was trying to cut up his meat. "Papa-Daddy!" I was taken completely by surprise. Papa-Daddy is about a million years old and's got this long-long beard. "Papa-Daddy, Sister says she fails to understand why you don't cut off your beard."

So Papa-Daddy l-a-y-s down his knife and fork! He's real rich. Mama says he is, he says he isn't. So he says, "Have I heard correctly? You don't understand why I don't cut off my beard?"

"Why," I says, "Papa-Daddy, of course I understand, I did not say any such of a thing, the idea!"

He says, "Hussy!"

I says, "Papa-Daddy, you know I wouldn't any more want you to cut off your beard than the man in the moon. It was the farthest thing from my mind! Stella-Rondo sat there and made that up while she was eating breast of chicken."

But he says, "So the postmistress fails to understand why I don't cut off my beard. Which job I got you through my influence with the government. 'Bird's nest'—is that what you call it?"

Not that it isn't the next to smallest P.O. in the entire state of Mississippi.

I says, "Oh, Papa-Daddy," I says, "I didn't say any such of a thing, I never dreamed it was a bird's nest, I have always been grateful though this is the next to smallest P.O. in the state of Mississippi, and I do not enjoy being referred to as a hussy by my own grandfather."

But Stella-Rondo says, "Yes, you did say it too. Anybody in the world could of heard you, that had ears."

"Stop right there," says Mama, looking at *me*.

So I pulled my napkin straight back through the napkin ring and left the table.

As soon as I was out of the room Mama says, "Call her back, or she'll starve to death," but Papa-Daddy says, "This is the beard I started growing on the Coast when I was fifteen years old." He would of gone on till nightfall if Shirley-T. hadn't lost the Milky Way she ate in Cairo.

So Papa-Daddy says, "I am going out and lie in the hammock, and you can all sit here and remember my words: I'll never cut off my beard as long as I live, even one inch, and I don't appreciate it in you at all." Passed right by me in the hall and went straight out and got in the hammock.

It would be a holiday. It wasn't five minutes before Uncle Rondo suddenly appeared in the hall in one of Stella-Rondo's flesh-colored kimonos, all cut on the bias, like something Mr. Whitaker probably thought was gorgeous.

"Uncle Rondo!" I says. "I didn't know who that was! Where are you going?"

"Sister," he says, "get out of my way, I'm poisoned."

"If you're poisoned stay away from Papa-Daddy," I says. "Keep out of the hammock. Papa-Daddy will certainly beat you on the head if you come within forty miles of him. He thinks I deliberately said he ought to cut off his beard after he got me the P.O., and I've told him and told him and told him, and he acts like he just don't hear me. Papa-Daddy must of gone stone deaf."

"He picked a fine day to do it then," says Uncle Rondo, and before you could say "Jack Robinson" flew out in the yard.

What he'd really done, he'd drunk another bottle of that prescription. He does it every single Fourth of July as sure as shooting, and it's horribly expensive. Then he falls over in the hammock and snores. So he insisted on zigzagging right on out to the hammock, looking like a half-wit.

Papa-Daddy woke up with this horrible yell and right there without moving an inch he tried to turn Uncle Rondo against me. I heard every word he said. Oh, he told Uncle Rondo I didn't learn to read till I was eight years old and he didn't see how in the world I ever got the mail put up at the P.O., much less read it all, and he said if Uncle Rondo could only fathom the lengths he had gone to get me that job! And he said on the other hand he thought Stella-Rondo had a brilliant mind and deserved credit for getting out of town. All the time he was just lying there swinging as pretty as you please and looping out his beard, and poor Uncle Rondo was *pleading* with him to slow down the hammock, it was making him as dizzy as a witch to watch it. But that's what Papa-Daddy likes about a hammock. So Uncle Rondo was too dizzy to get turned against me for the time being. He's Mama's only brother and is a good case of a one-track mind. Ask anybody. A certified pharmacist.

Just then I heard Stella-Rondo raising the upstairs window. While she was married she got this peculiar idea that it's cooler with the windows shut and locked. So she has to raise the window before she can make a soul hear her outdoors.

So she raises the window and says, *"Oh!"* You would have thought she was mortally wounded.

Uncle Rondo and Papa-Daddy didn't even look up, but kept right on with what they were doing. I had to laugh.

I flew up the stairs and threw the door open! I says, "What in the wide world's the matter, Stella-Rondo? You mortally wounded?"

"No," she says, "I am not mortally wounded but I wish you would do me the favor of looking out that window there and telling me what you see."

So I shade my eyes and look out the window.

"I see the front yard," I says.

"Don't you see any human beings?" she says.

"I see Uncle Rondo trying to run Papa-Daddy out of the hammock," I says. "Nothing more. Naturally, it's so suffocating-hot in the house, with all the windows shut and locked, everybody who cares to stay in their right mind will have to go out and get in the hammock before the Fourth of July is over."

"Don't you notice anything different about Uncle Rondo?" asks Stella-Rondo.

"Why, no, except he's got on some terrible-looking flesh-colored contraption I wouldn't be found dead in, is all I can see," I says.

"Never mind, you won't be found dead in it, because it happens to be part of my trousseau, and Mr. Whitaker took several dozen photographs of me in it," says Stella-Rondo. "What on earth could Uncle Rondo *mean* by wearing part of my trousseau out in the broad open daylight without saying so much as 'Kiss my foot,' *knowing* I only got home this morning after my separation and hung my negligee up on the bathroom door, just as nervous as I could be?"

"I'm sure I don't know, and what do you expect me to do about it?" I says. "Jump out the window?"

"No, I expect nothing of the kind. I simply declare that Uncle Rondo looks like a fool in it, that's all," she says. "It makes me sick to my stomach."

"Well, he looks as good as he can," I says. "As good as anybody in reason could." I stood up for Uncle Rondo, please remember. And I said to Stella-Rondo, "I think I would do well not to criticize so freely if I were you and came home with a two-year-old child I had never said a word about, and no explanation whatever about my separation."

"I asked you the instant I entered this house not to refer one more time to my adopted child, and you gave me your word of honor you would not," was all

Stella-Rondo would say, and started pulling out every one of her eyebrows with some cheap Kress tweezers.

So I merely slammed the door behind me and went down and made some green-tomato pickle. Somebody had to do it. Of course Mama had turned both the Negroes loose; she always said no earthly power could hold one anyway on the Fourth of July, so she wouldn't even try. It turned out that Jaypan fell in the lake and came within a very narrow limit of drowning.

So Mama trots in. Lifts up the lid and says, "H'm! Not very good for your Uncle Rondo in his precarious condition, I must say. Or poor little adopted Shirley-T. Shame on you!"

That made me tired. I says, "Well, Stella-Rondo had better thank her lucky stars it was her instead of me came trotting in with that very peculiar-looking child. Now if it had been me that trotted in from Illinois and brought a peculiar-looking child of two, I shudder to think of the reception I'd of got, much less controlled the diet of an entire family."

"But you must remember, Sister, that you were never married to Mr. Whitaker in the first place and didn't go up to Illinois to live," says Mama, shaking a spoon in my face. "If you had I would of been just as overjoyed to see you and your little adopted girl as I was to see Stella-Rondo, when you wound up with your separation and came on back home."

"You would not," I says.

"Don't contradict me, I would," says Mama.

But I said she couldn't convince me though she talked till she was blue in the face. Then I said, "Besides, you know as well as I do that that child is not adopted."

"She most certainly is adopted," says Mama, stiff as a poker.

I says, "Why, Mama, Stella-Rondo had her just as sure as anything in this world, and just too stuck up to admit it."

"Why, Sister," said Mama. "Here I thought we were going to have a pleasant Fourth of July, and you start right out not believing a word your own baby sister tells you!"

"Just like Cousin Annie Flo. Went to her grave denying the facts of life," I remind Mama.

"I told you if you ever mentioned Annie Flo's name I'd slap your face," says Mama, and slaps my face.

"All right, you wait and see," I says.

"I," says Mama, "*I* prefer to take my children's word for anything when it's humanly possible." You ought to see Mama, she weighs two hundred pounds and has real tiny feet.

Just then something perfectly horrible occurred to me.

"Mama," I says, "can that child talk?" I simply had to whisper! "Mama, I wonder if that child can be—you know—in any way? Do you realize," I says, "that she hasn't spoken one single, solitary word to a human being up to this minute? This is the way she looks," I says, and I looked like this.

Well, Mama and I just stood there and stared at each other. It was horrible!

"I remember well that Joe Whitaker frequently drank like a fish," says Mama. "I believed to my soul he drank *chemicals.*" And without another word she marches to the foot of the stairs and calls Stella-Rondo.

"Stella-Rondo? O-o-o-o-o! Stella-Rondo!"

"What?" says Stella-Rondo from upstairs. Not even the grace to get up off the bed.

"Can that child of yours talk?" asks Mama.

Stella-Rondo says, "Can she what?"

"Talk! Talk!" says Mama. "Burdyburdyburdyburdy!"

So Stella-Rondo yells back, "Who says she can't talk?"

"Sister says so," says Mama.

"You didn't have to tell me, I know whose word of honor don't mean a thing in this house," says Stella-Rondo.

And in a minute the loudest Yankee voice I ever heard in my life yells out, "OE'm Pop-OE the Sailor-r-r-r Ma-a-an!" and then somebody jumps up and down in the upstairs hall. In another second the house would of fallen down.

"Not only talks, she can tap-dance!" calls Stella-Rondo. "Which is more than some people I won't name can do."

"Why, the little precious darling thing!" Mama says, so surprised. "Just as smart as she can be!" Starts talking baby talk right there. Then she turns on me. "Sister, you ought to be thoroughly ashamed! Run upstairs this instant and apologize to Stella-Rondo and Shirley-T."

"Apologize for what?" I says. "I merely wondered if the child was normal, that's all. Now that she's proved she is, why, I have nothing further to say."

But Mama just turned on her heel and flew out, furious. She ran right upstairs and hugged the baby. She believed it was adopted. Stella-Rondo hadn't done a thing but turn her against me from upstairs while I stood there helpless over the hot stove. So that made Mama, Papa-Daddy and the baby all on Stella-Rondo's side.

Next, Uncle Rondo.

I must say that Uncle Rondo has been marvelous to me at various times in the past and I was completely unprepared to be made to jump out of my skin, the way it turned out. Once Stella-Rondo did something perfectly horrible to him—broke a chain letter from Flanders Field—and he took the radio back he had given her and gave it to me. Stella-Rondo was furious! For six months we all had to call her Stella instead of Stella-Rondo, or she wouldn't answer. I always thought Uncle Rondo had all the brains of the entire family. Another time he sent me to Mammoth Cave, with all expenses paid.

But this would be the day he was drinking that prescription, the Fourth of July.

So at supper Stella-Rondo speaks up and says she thinks Uncle Rondo ought to try to eat a little something. So finally Uncle Rondo said he would try a little cold biscuits and ketchup, but that was all. So *she* brought it to him.

"Do you think it wise to disport with ketchup in Stella-Rondo's flesh-colored kimono?" I says. Trying to be considerate! If Stella-Rondo couldn't watch out for her trousseau, somebody had to.

"Any objections?" asks Uncle Rondo, just about to pour out all the ketchup.

"Don't mind what she says, Uncle Rondo," says Stella-Rondo. "Sister has been devoting this solid afternoon to sneering out my bedroom window at the way you look."

"What's that?" says Uncle Rondo. Uncle Rondo has got the most terrible temper in the world. Anything is liable to make him tear the house down if it comes at the wrong time.

So Stella-Rondo says, "Sister says, 'Uncle Rondo certainly does look like a fool in that pink kimono!'"

Do you remember who it was really said that?

Uncle Rondo spills out all the ketchup and jumps out of his chair and tears off the kimono and throws it down on the dirty floor and puts his foot on it. It had to be sent all the way to Jackson to the cleaners and re-pleated.

"So that's your opinion of your Uncle Rondo, is it?" he says. "I look like a fool, do I? Well, that's the last straw. A whole day in this house with nothing to do, and then to hear you come out with a remark like that behind my back!"

"I didn't say any such of a thing, Uncle Rondo," I says, "and I'm not saying who did, either. Why, I think you look all right. Just try to take care of yourself and not talk and eat at the same time," I says. "I think you better go lie down."

"Lie down my foot," says Uncle Rondo. I ought to of known by that he was fixing to do something perfectly horrible.

So he didn't do anything that night in the precarious state he was in—just played Casino with Mama and Stella-Rondo and Shirley-T. and gave Shirley-T. a nickel with a head on both sides. It tickled her nearly to death, and she called him "Papa." But at 6:30 A.M. the next morning, he threw a whole five-cent package of some unsold one-inch firecrackers from the store as hard as he could into my bedroom and they every one went off. Not one bad one in the string. Anybody else, there'd be one that wouldn't go off.

Well, I'm just terribly susceptible to noise of any kind, the doctor has always told me I was the most sensitive person he had ever seen in his whole life, and I was simply prostrated. I couldn't eat! People tell me they heard it as far as the cemetery, and old Aunt Jep Patterson, that had been holding her own so good, thought it was Judgment Day and she was going to meet her whole family. It's usually so quiet here.

And I'll tell you it didn't take me any longer than a minute to make up my mind what to do. There I was with the whole entire house on Stella-Rondo's side and turned against me. If I have anything at all I have pride.

So I just decided I'd go straight down to the P.O. There's plenty of room there in the back, I says to myself.

Well! I made no bones about letting the family catch on to what I was up to. I didn't try to conceal it.

The first thing they knew, I marched in where they were all playing Old Maid and pulled the electric oscillating fan out by the plug, and everything got real hot. Next I snatched the pillow I'd done the needlepoint on right off the davenport from behind Papa-Daddy. He went "Ugh!" I beat Stella-Rondo up the stairs and finally found my charm bracelet in her bureau drawer under a picture of Nelson Eddy.

"So that's the way the land lies," says Uncle Rondo. There he was, piecing on the ham. "Well, Sister, I'll be glad to donate my army cot if you got any place to set it up, providing you'll leave right this minute and let me get some peace." Uncle Rondo was in France.

"Thank you kindly for the cot and 'peace' is hardly the word I would select if

I had to resort to firecrackers at 6:30 A.M. in a young girl's bedroom," I says back to him. "And as to where I intend to go, you seem to forget my position as postmistress of China Grove, Mississippi," I says. "I've always got the P.O."

Well, that made them all sit up and take notice.

I went out front and started digging up some four-o'clocks to plant around the P.O.

"Ah-ah-ah!" says Mama, raising the window. "Those happen to be my four-o'clocks. Everything planted in that star is mine. I've never known you to make anything grow in your life."

"Very well," I says. "But I take the fern. Even you, Mama, can't stand there and deny that I'm the one watered that fern. And I happen to know where I can send in a box top and get a packet of one thousand mixed seeds, no two the same kind, free."

"Oh, where?" Mama wants to know.

But I says, "Too late. You 'tend to your house, and I'll 'tend to mine. You hear things like that all the time if you know how to listen to the radio. Perfectly marvelous offers. Get anything you want free."

So I hope to tell you I marched in and got that radio, and they could of all bit a nail in two, especially Stella-Rondo, that it used to belong to, and she well knew she couldn't get it back, I'd sue for it like a shot. And I very politely took the sewing-machine motor I helped pay the most on to give Mama for Christmas back in 1929, and a good big calendar, with the first-aid remedies on it. The thermometer and the Hawaiian ukulele certainly were rightfully mine, and I stood on the step-ladder and got all my watermelon-rind preserves and every fruit and vegetable I'd put up, every jar. Then I began to pull the tacks out of the bluebird wall vases on the archway to the dining room.

"Who told you you could have those, Miss Priss?" says Mama, fanning as hard as she could.

"I bought 'em and I'll keep track of 'em," I says. "I'll tack 'em up one on each side the post-office window, and you can see 'em when you come to ask me for your mail, if you're so dead to see 'em."

"Not I! I'll never darken the door to that post office again if I live to be a hundred," Mama says. "Ungrateful child! After all the money we spent on you at the Normal."[1]

"Me either," says Stella-Rondo. "You can just let my mail lie there and *rot*, for all I care. I'll never come and relieve you of a single, solitary piece."

"I should worry," I says. "And who you think's going to sit down and write you all those big fat letters and postcards, by the way? Mr. Whitaker? Just because he was the only man ever dropped down in China Grove and you got him— unfairly—is he going to sit down and write you a lengthy correspondence after you come home giving no rhyme nor reason whatsoever for your separation and no explanation for the presence of that child? I may not have your brilliant mind, but I fail to see it."

So Mama says, "Sister, I've told you a thousand times that Stella-Rondo simply

---

[1] I.e., normal school, which trained teachers, chiefly for the elementary grades.

got homesick, and this child is far too big to be hers," and she says, "Now, why don't you all just sit down and play Casino?"

Then Shirley-T. sticks out her tongue at me in this perfectly horrible way. She has no more manners than the man in the moon. I told her she was going to cross her eyes like that some day and they'd stick.

"It's too late to stop me now," I says. "You should have tried that yesterday. I'm going to the P.O. and the only way you can possibly see me is to visit me there."

So Papa-Daddy says, "You'll never catch me setting foot in that post office, even if I should take a notion into my head to write a letter some place." He says, "I won't have you reachin' out of that little old window with a pair of shears and cuttin' off any beard of mine. I'm too smart for you!"

"We all are," says Stella-Rondo.

But I said, "If you're so smart, where's Mr. Whitaker?"

So then Uncle Rondo says, "I'll thank you from now on to stop reading all the orders I get on postcards and telling everybody in China Grove what you think is the matter with them," but I says, "I draw my own conclusions and will continue in the future to draw them." I says, "If people want to write their inmost secrets on penny postcards, there's nothing in the wide world you can do about it, Uncle Rondo."

"And if you think we'll ever *write* another postcard you're sadly mistaken," says Mama.

"Cutting off your nose to spite your face then," I says. "But if you're all determined to have no more to do with the U.S. mail, think of this: What will Stella-Rondo do now, if she wants to tell Mr. Whitaker to come after her?"

"Wah!" says Stella-Rondo. I knew she'd cry. She had a conniption fit right there in the kitchen.

"It will be interesting to see how long she holds out," I says. "And now—I am leaving."

"Good-bye," says Uncle Rondo.

"Oh, I declare," says Mama, "to think that a family of mine should quarrel on the Fourth of July, or the day after, over Stella-Rondo leaving old Mr. Whitaker and having the sweetest little adopted child! It looks like we'd all be glad!"

"Wah!" says Stella-Rondo, and has a fresh conniption fit.

"*He* left *her*—you mark my words," I says. "That's Mr. Whitaker. I know Mr. Whitaker. After all, I knew him first. I said from the beginning he'd up and leave her. I foretold every single thing that's happened."

"Where did he go?" asks Mama.

"Probably to the North Pole, if he knows what's good for him," I says.

But Stella-Rondo just bawled and wouldn't say another word. She flew to her room and slammed the door.

"Now look what you've gone and done, Sister," says Mama. "You go apologize."

"I haven't got time, I'm leaving," I says.

"Well, what are you waiting around for?" asks Uncle Rondo.

So I just picked up the kitchen clock and marched off, without saying "Kiss my foot" or anything, and never did tell Stella-Rondo good-bye.

There was a girl going along on a little wagon right in front.

"Girl," I says, "come help me haul these things down the hill, I'm going to live in the post office."

Took her nine trips in her express wagon. Uncle Rondo came out on the porch and threw her a nickel.

And that's the last I've laid eyes on any of my family or my family laid eyes on me for five solid days and nights. Stella-Rondo may be telling the most horrible tales in the world about Mr. Whitaker, but I haven't heard them. As I tell everybody, I draw my own conclusions.

But oh, I like it here. It's ideal, as I've been saying. You see, I've got everything cater-cornered, the way I like it. Hear the radio? All the war news. Radio, sewing machine, book ends, ironing board and that great big piano lamp—peace, that's what I like. Butter-bean vines planted all along the front where the strings are.

Of course, there's not much mail. My family are naturally the main people in China Grove, and if they prefer to vanish from the face of the earth, for all the mail they get or the mail they write, why, I'm not going to open my mouth. Some of the folks here in town are taking up for me and some turned against me. I know which is which. There are always people who will quit buying stamps just to get on the right side of Papa-Daddy.

But here I am, and here I'll stay. I want the world to know I'm happy.

And if Stella-Rondo should come to me this minute, on bended knees, and *attempt* to explain the incidents of her life with Mr. Whitaker, I'd simply put my fingers in both my ears and refuse to listen.

1941

Wright Morris
b. 1910

Wright Morris has been called "the least well-known and most widely appreciated" novelist in America today. He was born in Central City, Nebraska, on January 6, 1910. From 1930 to 1933 he attended Pomona College in California, then spent the next year touring Europe. Upon his return to America in 1934 he decided to embark on a career as a writer. His first novel, *My Uncle Dudley* (1942), in its vividly detailed exploration of America's past, prefigured the thematic concerns of much of Morris's later fiction. His great theme, as he later put it, is "the brutal severance of past and present" in American life. Since then, Morris has written over twenty-five works of fiction, including a National Book Award–winning novel, *Field of Vision* (1956), and several collections of essays, most notably a study of the native traditions of American literature, *The Territory Ahead* (1958). In several of his works of fiction, moreover, especially *The Inhabitants* (1946) and *The Home Place* (1948), Morris augments his texts with his own photographs in an effort to expand and extend his prose rather than merely to illustrate it.

In all his various books, Morris, a teacher at the California State University in San Francisco since 1962, invites attentive, receptive readers to engage in what he terms "a dialogue." Though he insists on establishing the terms of this dialogue, he does so for the purpose of drawing the reader into a "lonely pilgrimage" toward the "territory ahead." Despite his preoccupation with the past and with the relation of past to present, Morris is most deeply concerned with what lies ahead. The future, which we "will recognize . . . by its strangeness," Morris claims, is a region that we must imagine to know. Yet just as knowing, in Morris's work, depends on imagining, imagining in turn depends on remembering. "If man is by nature self-conscious," he writes in *The Territory Ahead*, art is man's "expanding consciousness, and the creative act, in the deepest sense, is his expanding universe."

The themes of Morris's fiction are closely interrelated. The connections between past and present are multifariously explored: The past, for example, can be incarcerating, and Morris's main characters are often antinostalgic, as in *The World in the Attic* (1949). Location—the relations of one's own experience to the scenes of one's own life—plays a major role in Morris's fiction, an importance movingly portrayed in *Ceremony in Lone Tree* (1960). In his several "photo-texts" Morris explores the roles of seeing and hearing; in other novels, such as *Fire Sermon* (1971) and *A Life* (1973), he examines the efforts to work out the relations between words and images, admiring the boldness, audacity, and even eccentricity required in such efforts. For Morris, the artist is one who brings audacity to creative efforts and may therefore serve as both exemplary model and catalytic agent, exciting others to a sense of wonder and discovery. Yet in other novels Morris portrays the underside of such heroic efforts—audacity turned to criminal violence—as in *One Day* (1965), a fictional tale of John F. Kennedy's assassin, and *In Orbit* (1967), a novel about motorcycle gangs. Through all these books, however, runs Morris's principal concern: the exploration of the various ways in which memory feeds the imagination and the imagination feeds knowledge—the various ways in which we must remember to imagine and imagine to know.

Further Reading:
W. Booth, "The Two Worlds in the Fiction of Wright Morris," *Sewanee Review,* Summer 1957.
D. Madden, *Wright Morris,* 1964.
G. B. Crump, *The Novels of Wright Morris: A Critical Interpretation,* 1978.

Text:
Real Losses, Imaginary Gains, 1976.
See also *Collected Stories: 1948–1986,* 1986.

Green Grass, Blue Sky, White House

As I sit here, Floyd's mother mows the lawn. The whine of the mower can be heard above the noise of her grandchildren at their horseplay. If I close my eyes the sounds are like those we see in comic strips, WHAM! BAM! POWIE!, rising like balloons, or exploding like firecrackers. All in fun, of course. They are healthy, growing animals and have to work off their energies somehow. Why not with the mower? Mrs. Collins likes to mow her own lawn. Any day but Sunday, either Franklin DeSpain, or Lyle, or even Melanie, would pop up from somewhere and do it for her, but Reuben DeSpain insists that his children keep the Sabbath holy. The Lord rested, and so do the DeSpains.

A farm girl to begin with, Mrs. Collins likes to get her hands on a machine that works and work it. The blades spin free when she nears a tree and uses short, choppy strokes. The whine of the mower makes its way around the house, and on the long run at the back it is almost gone. It stops when twigs from the elms catch between the blades. I can tell she likes to work around the tree trunks where the short, hard strokes set the blades to whirring. That's a sound from my boyhood. The whirring blades of a mower pushed by somebody else. I would wait for the thump as it hit the house at the end of its run. People in this country once might have been divided into those who knew that sound and those who didn't; those who liked it and those it made almost sick. All summer long, freshly cut lawn grass weighted the cuffs of my father's pants.

One of Franklin DeSpain's boys walks by with a skateboard he carries around looking for sidewalks. Not all the streets in Ordway have them. The lawns slope down to bleed into the weeds, and the weeds into the crumbling blacktop. Most of the walks in town are of brick heaved into waves and troughs by tree roots. The only walking people do is from the door at the back of the house to the car parked in the drive.

The town of Ordway, in Missouri, is one where no line is drawn between what is rural and what is urban. A cow is tethered in the lot facing the square, where the sidewalk bristles with parking meters. I've seen no pigs, but the older residents, like Floyd's mother, keep a goat, or a cow, or a few fenced chickens. Everything is here to make the good life possible. Mrs. Collins at one point gave up the chickens but Mr. Collins missed their cackling. The silence disturbed his rest in the morning. If she forgets to collect the eggs, they soon have an old hen with a fresh batch of chicks. Almost an acre of lawn surrounds the house, and there is sometimes snow in the yard till Easter, the first spears of spring grass pale as winter wheat. At the back it's hard to tell where the lawn ends and the fields begin.

One thing I have learned is that small-town people have a pallor you can seldom find in the city. If they roll up a sleeve, or tuck up a pants leg, the bit of skin that shows is white as a flour sack. Mrs. Collins wears a pair of Floyd's unlaced tennis sneakers on her bare feet. His sweaters also fit her. Her overalls, however, once belonged to Mr. Collins, and the seat and knees are patched with pieces of quilting. That makes for more comfort when she kneels to weed, and less dampness when she sits to cut greens. A faded gingham sunbonnet sits back on her head to let the sun warm her face.

In the fall the yard is so bright with leaves Mrs. Collins tells me it's almost painful to look at. They have to pull the shades at the windows to sleep at night. Both a fact of that sort or a death in the family Mrs. Collins reports with an appealing smile. If my eyes are on her face I often miss the gist of what she is saying. Her expression remains the same: a beaming smile, an affable, open good nature. If I hear her laughing, it is usually at herself. This can be disconcerting when it signals something is wrong. She laughed, her daughter tells me, when she fell and broke her hip. Of Scotch descent, with a long Quaker family background, Mrs. Collins believes "the slings and arrows of misfortunes," as she says, are as much to be experienced as anything else. Nothing has diminished her appetite for life.

The Collins house is *substantial,* as my father would have said, with a run-around porch that is tilted like a ship's deck, the spacious lawn shaded by sycamores and elms. There's a cleared spot at the back, hard as blacktop where the trash and the leaves are burned. The two board gap in the fence indicates a shortcut that connects the Collins house with the one across the alley. Her daughter Ruth lives there, but Ruth's three teen-age boys spend most of their time in the Collins kitchen, or rough-housing at the back of the yard. A trough is worn into the yard where a tire swings from the limb of an elm.

The Collins kitchen is big, and uncluttered with modern conveniences. Mrs. Collins makes my toast under the flame in the oven, then scrapes the char off at the sink. She does not believe in anything, as she says, "that you have to plug in." The crackle of her long hair, worn in a loose bun at her neck, is her daily assurance that her health is in order and her battery is charged. In the house she wears a simple gray frock with touches of faded lace at the wrists and throat. I've no idea if she knows how much it does for her corn-yellow hair. She prefers to stand, rather than sit, her hip inclined on the stove rail, or the sink, with one of her brown freckled hands holding a loose wad of her apron, cupped in her palm. She tests heat and flavor with her fingers, spits on the skillet before making hotcakes. Into the first pot of percolator coffee she puts a pinch of salt and one fresh eggshell, preferably white. I'm told that the house swarmed with cats until her daughter Ruth married and took most of them with her. Mrs. Collins says, "I don't mind having pets, but I don't like the pets having people," meaning Mr. Collins and his old dog Ruby, now dead three years. Every day in his life, which proved to be a long one, Ruby would walk Mr. Collins to the railroad crossing, look up and down in both directions, then lead him across if it was safe. When Mr. Collins stopped making the walk, Ruby went under the house porch and refused to come out. It was the end of the run for both Ruby and the St. Louis & Troy.

Although it is fifteen years since a train entered Ordway, Mr. Collins still wears the striped overalls preferred by trainmen, and one of the high-crowned, long-billed brakeman's hats. This he leaves on his head until Mrs. Collins says, "Papa, your cap." All members of the family speak of him as Papa, but not often to his face. His skin is smooth, as if dampened and then stretched on his skull. The abundance of his hair gives the impression that his head is not fully developed, or with time has shrunk. His pale blue eyes have a focus just beyond the object of his attention. Before speaking he nervously fingers the bill of his cap. The two subjects Mr. Collins never loses sight of are Norman Thomas and the old dog Ruby. A picture of Ruby, a gourd-shaped little terrier with his head almost swallowed by his thickening neck, is among the family portraits on the sewing machine. More recent snapshots, featuring the grand-children, Waldo, Luther, and Clarence, are on the piano. Waldo and Luther take after their father, a huge, affable man in the road-construction business. The younger boy, Clarence, is small-boned like his mother, but almost six feet tall. He has grown too fast, and his movements are those of a boy on stilts. The boys like to roughhouse and can usually be heard clopping up and down the stairs of the Collins house, chased by Clarence, or mawling like dogs at the back of the yard. Waldo has picked up such lingo as "Sock it to me!" supplemented with cries of "Wham! Bam! Powie!" The trouble starts when Clarence, wearing one of Melanie's aprons, helps her wash and dry the dishes.

It is a point of pride with Mrs. Collins that she has no keys; the house is never locked. Back in the Depression, when they took in roomers, the keys disappeared in the pockets of strangers, and Mrs. Collins has never troubled to replace them. Mr. Collins pads through my room, while I sleep, because it has always been his way to the bathroom. If he took another route, strange to his habits, he might easily stumble or bump into something. To close a door so that it clicks is to imply that you have something to hide. It has been years since the bathroom door actually latched shut. If it is closed, the draft nudges it open. During the night the light provides a beacon, and the drip in the tub is like the tick of a clock. Unless the bathroom door stands open wide, it is safe to assume there is someone behind it. Most members of the family make a characteristic sound when steps approach. Mrs. Collins hums, Melanie turns on a faucet in the bowl and lets it run. Mr. Collins, however, is absolutely silent. He sits dreaming on the stool, his brown hands on his white knees, his gaze on the leaf-clogged gutters of the porch visible from the bathroom window. An intruder need not disturb him. The boys shower while he sits there. Privacy can be had by going up one floor and using the small water closet, but the flush of the water when the chain is pulled seems designed to clean out miles of plumbing, and burps in all the sinks.

If this were not Sunday, or if the grass had been mowed, Mrs. Collins would be seated in the porch rocker. It is of wood, the rungs turned by hand, the cane seat so new it resembles plastic. Layers of green and brown paint are visible where Mrs. Collins grips the chair arms. She takes a strong grip when she rocks, as if she feared the chair might take off. The spreading legs are reinforced with baling wire still fuzzy with the hair of the Collins cats. They used to retire there to get away from Ruby, and one of the toms had his tail amputated. Never again did he set foot on the Collins porch.

At one time as many as eight or ten children ran in and out of the house, and sagged the rails of the porches. The chain swing had to be taken down to keep them from wearing a hole in the clapboards. They *had* to rock it sideways, or swing it so high the whole house leaned one way, then the other. The hooks for the swing are still there in the ceiling, but who would swing if they put it back up? Not the new generation. The porch stoop used to sag with the DeSpain children, who were too polite to use the hammock. They were noisy, but they had breeding and refused to do a lick of work on Sunday. Mr. Collins would torment them by offering them money to run down and buy him his White Owl cigar. The other days of the week they had to offer to do it for nothing. For every biscuit that was eaten at the Collins table, two biscuits went out the door with Rosemary DeSpain, Reuben's wife, along with what she loosely defined as "leftovers." She in turn donated her coffee stamps during the war, when Mr. Collins began to suffer his withdrawal headaches. He was accustomed to eight strong cups a day, and that was what he got. Sunday being the day of rest, the DeSpains liked to spend it where they could watch other people work. Rosemary is gone now, but Mrs. Collins tells me she got up early to sit in the Collins kitchen, watching Ruth and Mrs. Collins prepare the Sunday meal. In case she ever had to do it, she wanted to be sure she knew how it was done.

Reuben DeSpain tells me that his wife was black and blue as a new stovepipe, but their children and grandchildren are best described as "golden oak." DeSpain claims that it comes from his French and Castilian ancestry. The boys have their father's light copper tan, but Melanie is so pale out-of-town people take her for an Italian, like Sophia Loren. She has Sophia's big, half-popped eyes and wide, full mouth. Mrs. Collins likes to tell how Floyd would ask her why his own tan peeled and Melanie's didn't. Unless she smiles, or talks, her impassive expression appears to be sullen. Melanie is inclined to be accident-prone, and wears Band-Aids on her fingers and arms for stove burns. The burn soon heals, but the print of the adhesive leaves a visible pattern. Mrs. Collins says to her, "Melanie, that stove bite you again?" Melanie's chores are to cook, tidy up, make the beds, and hand-wash Floyd's dress shirts in case he dirties any. She leaves the ironing board standing, blocking the pantry, to show that a woman's work is never done. She smokes Camels as she works, dropping the ashes on the ironing and between the sheets.

"One day you're going to burn this house down," Mrs. Collins says, and both women laugh. Melanie leaves the butts resting on the ashtrays, the edges of the bureaus, windowsills, and cereal cartons, or they slow-burn holes in the oilcloth or char a hole in the plastic soap dishes, or burn down till they tilt off something and drop to the floor. When Melanie laughs she turns her back and you see the top of her head rather than the roof of her mouth. She takes shame in her dark laughter, and wipes it off her mouth before she turns to face me. Around the house, as a dust cap, she wears a shower hat in which she stores her matches and pack of Camels. Thinking up things to keep Melanie "busy" is one of Mrs. Collins' endless chores. While Melanie wanders around tidying up, Mrs. Collins prepares for her the well-balanced lunch she never gets at home. Left to herself Melanie will eat nothing but creamed canned corn and chipped beef in a white sauce. She loves diet cola spiked with a spoonful of chocolate syrup. The two women eat together, discussing samples of cloth Mrs. Collins receives from a store in Chicago. She has in mind a dress for herself and a new winter coat for Melanie.

One of Floyd's chores, when he was at home, was to pick up Melanie in the morning and get her home to make her father's supper in the evening. On arriving, Melanie calls out, "Here I am, Mrs. Collins," and waits until she is told what to do. They both have a cup of coffee while they plan her day's work.

"What'll I do now?" is perhaps the one thing that Mrs. Collins hears the most. Finding work to do for Franklin, Lyle, and Melanie gets Mrs. Collins up early and often keeps her awake. "Before I ever make a move," Mrs. Collins tells me, "the first thing I think of is Franklin and Lyle." They don't like to be idle, but they like her to tell them what to do. Mrs. Collins has never gone to some of the places she would like to, because the DeSpains take so much looking after. Especially Reuben, who can't stand to be idle now his wife is dead. This being Sunday, however, he is willing to sit in front of the barn under a new painted sign that reads:

REUBEN DESPAIN
I buy junk and sell antiques

He doesn't buy junk, of course, he gets it all free, but one of his clients thought the remark would make a good sign. DeSpain came to Ordway in the early years of the Depression, when some of the whites, as well as the "coloreds," took their pay in milk and eggs and leftovers. His children wore the clothes the Collins children grew out of. He never complained. For twenty-five years he walked a horse and wagon —the horse wearing a bonnet to ward off sunstroke—up one street and down the other collecting whatever people had to throw away, or believed they had worn out. After the war it began to add up. The software, so called, Rosemary DeSpain cleaned up and sold once a year in the Methodist basement; the hardware Reuben DeSpain stowed away in the Collins barn. The government didn't want it, you couldn't eat it, or sell it, and it wouldn't burn. To make room for such stuff one of the Collins cars had to sit out in the yard, splattered with bird droppings, or in the freezing winter weather over one of the grease pits in the Collins service station. The other car, a Model T Ford with a brass radiator and a California top, had become so old it belonged in the barn as part of the junk. It had never actually been *given* to Reuben DeSpain but, as Floyd liked to say, it had been *ceded* to him. It had been *thought* to be junk, and if it was junk it belonged to DeSpain. A gentleman in Des Moines has an option on the car, and pays five dollars a month for DeSpain to store it for him. He doesn't seem to mind that the price of the car goes up and up. Two or three times a year a woman from St. Louis comes over in her station wagon for DeSpain's old bottles, beaded lampshades, wall and mantel clocks, oil lamps, and old records. A Philadelphia firm that makes stoves will buy anything good DeSpain lays a hand on, including the old Mayflower coke burner he warms his house with over the winter. It has a "sold" tag on it, but he is free to use it while he is still around. There's more people than DeSpain can keep track of to collect the buttons he snips off old clothes. Mrs. Collins has explained, and DeSpain has grasped, that as money gets cheaper his junk gets dearer. He lets it sit. DeSpain won't sell his records or his clocks to people who impress him as careless in such matters. Clocks run for him. Once off the premises they stop. There's an account at the bank for Reuben DeSpain and family that will pass on to his heirs if they can bother to be troubled. Money is something they don't understand, and have always left to Floyd. Besides Melanie, Franklin, and Lyle, there are Franklin's three children. In the mid-fifties Franklin, a year older than Lyle, took fifty dollars from the bank and went to Chicago where he planned a new start. He left in June and was back in October. A few years later Lyle went to St. Louis, where he enrolled in a Peace Corps program. He learned to type, and returned with a machine on which he still owed thirty-eight dollars. Both boys were noncommittal, but according to Mrs. Collins they were shocked by people's behavior. They were also homesick, and tired of people who called light-colored boys black.

Finding work for them to do was a strain for Mrs. Collins until Floyd thought of installing a car wash at the back of the service station. Running the station is a family enterprise, and all members of the family contribute to it. When Floyd was at home, he ran it; and Ruth's husband runs it in the slack season for road work; and there is always Mrs. Collins, or one of Ruth's boys, to help at the pumps on a busy weekend. The car wash occupies space once used for parking, and does a good business with college boys from Mason City. Franklin and Lyle are good workers, but they seem to lack initiative. They work better when Mrs. Collins is around, and they like her to handle the accounts. Franklin's two eldest boys are very good with a wax job, but it doesn't help matters that one has the name *Floyd*. This seemed very touching when Franklin's son was born, but it led to nothing but complications. When someone hollered "Floyd," both Floyds answered. The result was that Floyd Collins would seldom answer when his name was called. He didn't mean to be rude, or insist on *Mr.* Collins, but what could he do?

From where I am seated I can't see but I can hear the hiss and spray of steam at the car wash, and the sound of the gong as a car pulls into the station. Until just recently Reuben DeSpain took care of such things as the tires, windshields, etc., but all that stooping and bending didn't help his back any, and his right arm, especially his "windshield elbow," seemed to get worse. All he had to do was pick up a rag and he would feel the twinge of pain. Mrs. Collins thought he'd better just sit and take it easy, before it got so he couldn't use his arm to eat with. There's nothing harder for Reuben to do than just sit, but that's now what he does. His platform rocker, covered with plum-colored velvet once popular on tram seats, sits under a beach umbrella in the dappled shade at the front of the barn. The arms are too low, the back is too high, and the angle is all wrong for comfort, but DeSpain has never lost his taste for elegance. His ancestors, by published account, were influential pirates and patrons of the arts. He has the nose, forehead, and melancholy eyes of the clergy painted by El Greco.[1] He also has the style. If DeSpain is asked if he has something or other, he will reply, "I shall endeavor to ascertain it," then go and look. For seven years he was one of the servants close to Governor Huey Long. He considers the Governor one of the country's great men. Five weeks following the assassination, DeSpain and his family, on their way to Chicago, were towed into Ordway by a Mason City milkman. The car had broken down. It proved to be an Essex, of a year and a model for which parts were no longer available. Mr. Collins let them camp in the railroad station where they could use the lavatories and the drinking fountain, while Reuben DeSpain considered his next move. That proved to be into the barn behind the Collins house. In a few weeks' time Mrs. Collins hardly knew how she had ever got along without him. "Ma'am," he said, "all Reuben DeSpain aims to do is please."

Some of the younger generation think of DeSpain as a swami, thanks to his remarkable elegance of speech. He need say no more than "Consider the lilies—" to gather a group of teen-age loafers around him. On warm sultry days, between his neck and his collar he slips a clean white kerchief scented with insect repellent. He claims it keeps him free of pests while he naps. He wears a carpenter's apron with the big nail pockets full of unsorted parking-meter pennies. He gets them from the Ordway police department. Sorting them carefully by hand, he turns up the coins he sells to a collector in Independence. Real copper pennies are so close to DeSpain's color you feel they got it from the rubbing he gives them to bring out the dates.

On weekdays you can see Franklin or Lyle seated at the barn door tinkering with something that doesn't work. There is never an end. Just putting up the house screens and taking them down takes two or three weeks. Reuben DeSpain sits in his chair brushing off the rust with a whisk broom, his gesture that of a railroad porter dusting the lapels of Huey Long. In the winter he sits inside the barn and mends the holes. Mrs. Collins likes to feed her own chickens and collect the eggs (when there are any), but without Lyle around to milk her, the cow, Bessie, won't give her milk. In the spring the sheds need to be fumigated and the fourteen trees on the lot pruned and sprayed. In the dry spells everything has to be watered, which means dragging the

[1] Spanish painter (ca. 1548–1614).

hoses from faucet to faucet, the pressure sometimes getting so low it won't operate the sprinkler: Franklin's boys will have to water the tomato plants with the watering can. Both Franklin and Lyle dislike spray nozzles and prefer to stand, using their thumbs, soaking up the water with their shoes and pants legs. When a toilet bowl in the house is flushed, the pressure drops and the outside water goes off.

Inside the house the drains get clogged and water stands for days in the second-floor tub. Periodically roots close the lines to the cesspool although the nearest tree is forty-eight feet: what a root will do in its search for water defies belief. The lawn grass grows so thick right over the cesspool Mrs. Collins has to run at it with the mower, but she will not cut or use table greens from that part of the yard. Melanie has been warned not to do it, either, but somehow she forgets.

I've noticed the whole house shakes when the boys come clopping down the stairs. The pigeons kept by a neighbor, in a roost on his roof, go up on the sky like a cloud of smoke. There's always one that doesn't seem to get the swing of it, his wings flapping like a loose fan belt. Off where I can't see them, but I can hear them, Waldo and Luther are starting their horseplay. They go through the kitchen, slamming the screen, then clop around the house like cantering horses. Waldo is the one who strips the leaves off the lilac bushes as he makes the turns. These daily runs have not worn away the grass, but they have firmed it down so that it has a different color and texture, like the flattened wale of corduroy or the plush seat of a chair. Waldo is always first, a step or two ahead of Luther, and Clarence trails along like a caboose. If Luther stops suddenly, dropping to his knees, Clarence will stumble over him as if he were a bench. He never seems to learn. The green smears of grass will not wash off his elbows and bony knees. They all make about two hooting circles of the house, then Waldo heads for the clearing at the back. Where the tire swing dangles from the limb of an elm, he grasps the rope to keep from collapsing. He can't seem to stop laughing. Luther is so winded he trips on his own feet, and sprawls out on his face. He lies there giggling as if he were being tickled to death. Clarence comes along so many moments later he seems part of another scene. I first thought he had tired and run down, like a spring-wound toy. But he had merely paused to pick up a length of clothesline. He straddles Luther and flails at him with the rope—but it's too long. He can't bring it around with the proper snap. Waldo is so winded he can hardly breathe, but he hoarsely yells, "Sock it to 'im! Sock it to 'im!" Clarence tries to. The sound is that of someone beating a carpet with a small switch. Luther will not stop giggling, and Clarence cries, "I'm going to kill you! You hear me?" Waldo is still hooting, but he has sagged to drape his arms around the tire. In that position Clarence is able to flail him as if he were a slave clamped in the stocks or tied to a whipping post.

From behind the house Mrs. Collins appears holding aloft one of her leather-palmed cotton work gloves. She wags it as she comes, with loping, silent strides, to where Clarence towers over Waldo. No word is spoken. Waldo and Luther are hooting, but it appears to be a scene on silent film. All my life, or so it seems, I have watched roughhousing boys interrupted in their play by the long arm of Tom Sawyer's Aunt Polly. With a practiced gesture she grips Clarence, wheels him about, and slaps him (POWIE!) with the glove. He straightens to stand like a machine with the power switched off. From his dangling hand she takes the rope and shortens it to give him a slap across the buttocks. With a hoot, he takes off. In an instant he is followed by Waldo, who lunges to avoid the swipe she gives him. Luther is last; he goes off howling with a gleeful shriek. I hear the screen door to the kitchen open and slam, and then the clop of their feet on the front-hall stairs. The house rocks. I feel it like an earth tremor in the boards of the porch. After a bout of such horseplay all three boys like to take long showers with their clothes on, then come down and sit in the lawn swing to dry off.

Mrs. Collins stands, her face to the sky, watching the whirring flight of the neighbor's pigeons. The disturbance has flushed her face with color; she idly slaps the shortened length of rope on her thigh. "My, how we all miss Floyd!" she says, coming toward me, and her smile is that of a priestess at the close of a ceremony. She feels better, the boys feel better, and she would like to assure me I should feel better. What is a little violence in the larger ceremony of innocence? She turns a gaze toward Mr. Collins, who stands in the garden, leaning on a hand plow. His straw hat is wider than his shoulders, and the wide limp brim rests on his ears. He looks more like a boy daydreaming at his chores than an old man resting. Nor does he move from his reverie until he hears the whirring blades of the mower.

On my drive down from Chicago (I was given ten days to look into the Collins case) I stopped in St. Louis for a talk with Floyd. They're holding him there, as we say, for observation. He's a good-looking, rustically handsome boy with his mother's jaw and prominent features. I see they suit a man's face better than they do hers. He has the casual, cool manner of most young people, and lets his hair grow long at the back. While we talked he preferred to sit on the floor with his knees drawn up. Off and on he toyed with a piece of cellophane from his pack of Camel cigarettes, blowing on it softly as he held it pressed, like a blade of grass, between his thumbs. The sound emitted is high and shrill, like a trapped insect or a fingernail on glass. I once made such a sound, or tried to, blowing through a dandelion stem.

To the President of the United States Floyd Collins wrote: *I am obliged to inform you your life is threatened. I am a reasonable man. It is reason that compels me to take this action. I propose to take your one life to spare the tens of thousands of innocent men, women, and children. Please stop this war or accept the consequences.*

I liked the "please." It showed his responsible Quaker breeding and will also help to commute his sentence, since no shot was fired. During my stay in Ordway, Mrs. Collins has treated me like "one of the family," and that is how I feel. One of the family. Some, if not all, of the emotions Floyd Collins has felt. I see a cow grazing, Reuben DeSpain napping, a blue sky towers above me and green grass surrounds me, and inside the white house I hear boys at their horseplay, training to be men.

"I raised Floyd to believe anything is possible," Mrs. Collins says. As it is, of course. Here in Ordway anything is possible. Not necessarily what Mrs. Collins has in mind, or Floyd has in mind, or even the town of Ordway has in mind, but what a dream of the good life, and reasonable men, make inevitable.

1969

Tennessee Williams
1911–1983

Tennessee Williams's one-act play *Portrait of a Madonna* made its debut in 1946 at the Actors' Laboratory Theater in Los Angeles, where reviewers hailed it as an outstanding example of Williams's mastery of the one-act form. Hume Cronyn directed the first production, which featured the celebrated actress Jessica Tandy as Miss Lucretia Collins, a tattered remnant of the genteel Old South who resolutely clings to her youthful delusions despite the squalor that engulfs her. Before the aging spinster is led from her dingy rented room to an asylum, she manages to evoke virtually all of the dramatic themes that have earned Williams his reputation as one of America's most important playwrights. In Lucretia Collins's world we recognize Williams's characteristic lyric rendition of a decaying physical and psychological environment populated with semigrotesques. Since that first acclaimed production, *Portrait of a Madonna* has enjoyed several revivals, most recently in 1986 as part of a highly successful off-Broadway production entitled *Ten by Tennessee.*

Williams's critical reputation has wavered over the years. His first recognized work, *Battle of Angels,* was assailed at its 1940 opening in Boston. One critic charged it with giving "the audience the sensation of having been dunked in mire." However, with his second work, *The Glass Menagerie,* which opened in Chicago on December 26, 1944, and moved to New York the following March, Williams immediately created an indelible presence for himself in American drama. Soon he was also providing gossip columnists with extravagant incidents from his troubled and unconventional personal life.

Born in Columbus, Mississippi, in 1911, Thomas Lanier Williams was descended on his father's side from "pioneer Tennessee stock" and on his mother's from early Quaker "settlers of Nantucket Island in New England," a mix of "Cavalier" and "Puritan" he later saw as a possible source "for the conflicting impulses I often represent in the people I write about." During his early years Williams lived in several Mississippi towns and in Nashville, Tennessee, with his mother, his older sister Rose, and his grandfather, an Episcopalian minister. In his early adolescence, his family made what he later described as "a tragic move" to St. Louis, where his father, a traveling salesman, had accepted an appointment as the manager of a shoe company.

> Neither my sister nor I could adjust ourselves to life in a midwestern city. The schoolchildren made fun of our southern speech and manners. I remember gangs of kids following me home yelling "Sissy!" and home was not a very pleasant refuge. It was a perpetually dim little apartment in a wilderness of identical brick and concrete structures with no grass and no trees nearer than the park.

It was also a place where his parents seemed constantly to quarrel and where his father, disappointed at not having a more athletic son, began calling his son "Miss Nancy." Soon Williams's frail physical and psychological condition weakened into partial paralysis in his legs. His sister Rose, suffering comparable pressures, experienced a mental breakdown that culminated when a suitor died— circumstances similar to those that form the narrative basis for *Portrait of a Madonna*.

Early in his troubled life, writing became Williams's sanctuary.

> At the age of fourteen I discovered writing as an escape from a world of reality in which I felt acutely uncomfortable. It immediately became my place of retreat, my cave, my refuge.

At age eleven Williams had his own typewriter; at fourteen he garnered recognition with a first-place award (and $25.00) in a nationwide writing contest sponsored by the prestigious *Smart Set* magazine. After high school, he studied briefly at the University of Missouri, then worked in "a clerical job in the shoe company that employed my father." It was two years of "indescribable torment to me as an individual but of immense value to me as a writer for they gave me first-hand knowledge of what it meant to be a small wage earner in a hopelessly routine job." Williams continued to write—often late into the night—without regard for his poor health. After recuperating from another nervous collapse, he lived briefly with his grandparents in Memphis and then returned to college, first at Washington University in St. Louis, where he wrote and produced several plays, and then at the University of Iowa, where he took a B.A. in 1938, with a major in playwriting.

In the years following graduation, Williams traveled and lived briefly in Chicago, St. Louis, Mexico, Los Angeles, New Orleans, and New York, experiencing the kind of life he was so often to present on stage: lonely and uncertain, trapped in a painful past, and struggling to survive in a world essentially indifferent to personal illusions. During this period he also changed his name. Thomas Lanier Williams was, he observed,

> a nice enough name, perhaps a little too nice. . . . It sounds like it might belong to the son of a writer who turns out sonnet sequences to Spring. . . . Under that name I published a good deal of lyric poetry which was a bad imitation of Edna Millay. When I grew up I realized this poetry wasn't much good and I felt the name had been compromised so I changed it to Tennessee Williams, the justification being mainly that the Williamses had fought the Indians for Tennessee and I had already discovered that the life of a young writer was going to be something similar to the dilemma of a stockade against a band of savages.

Williams supported himself mainly through odd jobs, including working as a scriptwriter at MGM studios, running the night elevator in a large hotel, and ushering at the Strand Theater on Broadway. "All the while I kept on writing, writing, not with any hope of making a living at it but because I found no other means of expressing things that seemed to demand expression."

By 1945, however, with *The Glass Menagerie* written and produced, Williams began to enjoy both critical praise, including a New York Drama Critics Circle

Award, and financial rewards. In its first appearance on Broadway, *The Glass Menagerie* ran for 561 performances. In 1947 Williams won a Pulitzer Prize as well as a second Drama Critics Circle Award for *A Streetcar Named Desire,* which ran for 855 performances. *The Rose Tatoo,* with 300 performances, followed in 1951, and four years later *Cat On a Hot Tin Roof* earned Williams a third Drama Critics Circle Award and a second Pulitzer Prize. In 1953 the play *Camino Real* provoked controversy that was rekindled in 1956 when the film *Baby Doll* was released. These in turn were followed by well-received stage and film versions of *Suddenly Last Summer* (1958), *Sweet Bird of Youth* (1959), and *The Night of the Iguana* (1961), which is widely recognized as Williams's last important play. Although he continued to write until quite close to his death in 1983, none of his later plays received the acclaim of his earlier works.

During his last twenty years, Williams's depression became, in his own words, "almost clinical," and alcohol and drugs began to dominate his life. In the 1970s Williams published a string of theatrical failures, two works of fiction *(Eight Mortal Ladies Possessed* and *Noise and the World of Reason),* and a collection of poems *(Androgyne, Mon Amour),* along with his collected essays *(Where I Live,* 1978) and his *Memoirs* (1975). By the time of his death, only the extravagances of his personal life succeeded in bringing his name to public attention.

Williams wrote about such subjects as murder, rape, homosexuality, nymphomania and drug and alcohol addiction at a time when many of these were still regarded as too controversial for the American stage. But his characters transcend their exaggerated roles—neurotics, victims, would-be artists, and outsiders. In *Portrait of a Madonna,* for example, Lucretia Collins conveys the stubborn dignity as well as the debilitating paranoia of the southern gentlewoman, primarily because Williams renders her personal dilemma in intensely lyric terms. Her mother's death fifteen years earlier has turned her into a sexually obsessed, frustrated recluse, adrift in the world of her own fantasies. Convinced that she at last has won back her married former love and is now expecting his child, Lucretia Collins becomes increasingly dependent on the kindness of strangers. The play's artful blend of repression and guilt anticipates many of Williams's later, longer works, and Lucretia is often seen as a forerunner of both Blanche du Bois in *Streetcar* and Alma Winemiller in *Summer and Smoke.* Yet the play has its own remarkable dramatic intensity. As its first star, Jessica Tandy, has remarked, *Portrait of a Madonna* has "got everything in it. It's a perfect little jewel of a play. A lot of Tennessee's one-act ones are. He really mastered the one-act play."

Further Reading:

N. Tischler, *Tennessee Williams: Rebellious Puritan,* 1961.
Tennessee Williams: A Tribute, ed. J. Tharpe, 1977.
S. L. Falk, *Tennessee Williams,* 2nd ed., 1978.
F. Hirsch, *A Portrait of the Artist: The Plays of Tennessee Williams,* 1979.
F. H. Londre, *Tennessee Williams,* 1979.

J. S. McCann, *The Critical Reputation of Tennessee Williams: A Reference Guide,* 1983.
D. Rader, *Tennessee, Cry of the Heart,* 1983.
D. Williams and S. Mead, *Tennessee Williams: An Intimate Biography,* 1983.
D. Spoto, *The Kindness of Strangers: The Life of Tennessee Williams,* 1985.

Text:
27 Wagons Full of Cotton and Other Plays, 1945.

Portrait of a Madonna

Characters

Miss Lucretia Collins

The Porter

The Elevator Boy

The Doctor

The Nurse

Mr. Abrams

> *Scene: The living room of a moderate-priced city apartment. The furnishings are old-fashioned and everything is in a state of neglect and disorder. There is a door in the back wall to a bedroom, and on the right to the outside hall.*

Miss Collins: Richard! *(The door bursts open and Miss Collins rushes out, distractedly. She is a middle-aged spinster, very slight and hunched of figure with a desiccated face that is flushed with excitement. Her hair is arranged in curls that would become a young girl and she wears a frilly negligee which might have come from an old hope chest of a period considerably earlier.)* No, no, no, no! I don't care if the whole church hears about it! *(She frenziedly snatches up the phone.)* Manager, I've got to speak to the manager! Hurry, oh, please hurry, there's a man——! *(wildly aside as if to an invisible figure)* Lost all respect, absolutely no respect! . . . Mr. Abrams? *(in a tense hushed voice)* I don't want any reporters to hear about this but something awful has been going on upstairs. Yes, this is Miss Collins' apartment on the top floor. I've refrained from making any complaint because of my connections with the church. I used to be assistant to the Sunday School superintendent and I once had the primary class. I helped them put on the Christmas pageant. I made the dress for the Virgin and Mother, made robes for the Wise Men. Yes, and now this has happened, I'm not responsible for it, but night after night after night this man has been coming into my apartment and——indulging his senses! Do you understand? Not once but repeatedly, Mr. Abrams! I don't know whether he comes in the door or the window or up the fire-escape or whether there's some secret entrance they know about at the church, but he's here now, in my bedroom, and I can't force him to leave, I'll have to have some assistance! No, he isn't a thief, Mr. Abrams, he comes of a very fine family in Webb, Mississippi, but this woman has ruined his character, she's destroyed his respect for ladies! Mr. Abrams? Mr. Abrams! Oh, goodness! *(She slams up the receiver and looks distractedly about for a moment; then rushes back into the bedroom.)* Richard! *(The door slams shut. After a few moments an old porter enters in drab gray cover-alls. He looks about with a sorrowfully humorous curiosity, then timidly calls.)*

Porter: Miss Collins? *(The elevator door slams open in hall and the Elevator Boy, wearing a uniform, comes in.)*

Elevator Boy: Where is she?

Porter: Gone in 'er bedroom.

Elevator Boy: (grinning) She got him in there with her?

Porter: Sounds like it. *(Miss Collins' voice can be heard faintly protesting with the mysterious intruder.)*

Elevator Boy: What'd Abrams tell yuh to do?

Porter: Stay here an' keep a watch on 'er till they git here.

Elevator Boy: Jesus.

Porter: Close 'at door.

Elevator Boy: I gotta leave it open a little so I can hear the buzzer. Ain't this place a holy sight though?

Porter: Don't look like it's had a good cleaning in fifteen or twenty years. I bet it ain't either. Abrams'll bust a blood-vessel when he takes a lookit them walls.

Elevator Boy: How comes it's in this condition?

Porter: She wouldn't let no one in.

Elevator Boy: Not even the paper-hangers?

Porter: Naw. Not even the plumbers. The plaster washed down in the bathroom underneath hers an' she admitted her plumbin' had been stopped up. Mr. Abrams had to let the plumber in with this here pass-key when she went out for a while.

Elevator Boy: Holy Jeez. I wunner if she's got money stashed around here. A lotta freaks do stick away big sums of money in ole mattresses an' things.

Porter: She ain't. She got a monthly pension check or something she always turned over to Mr. Abrams to dole it out to 'er. She tole him that Southern ladies was never brought up to manage finanshul affairs. Lately the checks quit comin'.

Elevator Boy: Yeah?

Porter: The pension give out or somethin'. Abrams says he got a contribution from the church to keep 'er on here without 'er knowin' about it. She's proud as a peacock's tail in spite of 'er awful appearance.

Elevator Boy: Lissen to 'er in there!

Porter: What's she sayin'?

Elevator Boy: Apologizin' to him! For callin' the *police!*

Porter: She thinks police 're comin'?

Miss Collins: (from bedroom) Stop it, it's got to stop!

Elevator Boy: Fightin' to protect her honor again! What a commotion, no wunner folks are complainin'!

Porter: (lighting his pipe) This here'll be the last time.

Elevator Boy: She's goin' out, huh?

Porter: (blowing out the match) Tonight.

Elevator Boy: Where'll she go?

Porter: (slowly moving to the old gramophone) She'll go to the state asylum.

Elevator Boy: Holy G!

Porter: Remember this ole number? *(He puts on a record of "I'm Forever Blowing Bubbles.")*

Elevator Boy: Naw. When did that come out?

Porter: Before your time, sonny boy. Machine needs oilin'. *(He takes out small oil-can and applies oil about the crank and other parts of gramophone.)*

Elevator Boy: How long is the old girl been here?

Porter: Abrams says she's been livin' here twenty-five, thirty years, since before he got to be manager even.

Elevator Boy: Livin' alone all that time?

Porter: She had an old mother died of an operation about fifteen years ago. Since then she ain't gone out of the place excep' on Sundays to church or Friday nights to some kind of religious meeting.

Elevator Boy: Got an awful lot of ol' magazines piled aroun' here.

Porter: She used to collect 'em. She'd go out in back and fish 'em out of the incinerator.

Elevator Boy: What'n hell for?

Porter: Mr. Abrams says she used to cut out the Campbell soup kids. Them red-tomato-headed kewpie dolls that got with the soup advertisements. You seen 'em, ain'tcha?

Elevator Boy: Uh-huh.

Porter: She made a collection of 'em. Filled a big lot of scrapbooks with them paper kiddies an' took 'em down to the Children's Hospitals on Xmas Eve an' Easter Sunday, exactly twicet a year. Sounds better, don't it? *(referring to gramophone, which resumes its faint, wheedling music)* Eliminated some a that crankin' noise . . .

Elevator Boy: I didn't know that she'd been nuts *that* long.

Porter: Who's nuts an' who ain't? If you ask me the world is populated with people that's just as peculiar as she is.

Elevator Boy: Hell. She don't have brain *one.*

Porter: There's important people in Europe got less'n she's got. Tonight they're takin' her off 'n' lockin' her up. They'd do a lot better to leave 'er go an' lock up some a them maniacs over there. She's harmless; they ain't. They kill millions of people an' go scot free!

Elevator Boy: An ole woman like her is disgusting, though, imaginin' somebody's raped her.

Porter: Pitiful, not disgusting. Watch out for them cigarette ashes.

Elevator Boy: What's uh diff'rence? So much dust you can't see it. All a this here goes out in the morning, don't it?

Porter: Uh-huh.

Elevator Boy: I think I'll take a couple a those ole records as curiosities for my girl friend. She's got a portable in 'er bedroom, she says it's better with music!

Porter: Leave 'em alone. She's still got 'er property rights.

Elevator Boy: Aw, she's got all she wants with them dream-lovers of hers!

Porter: Hush up! *(He makes a warning gesture as Miss Collins enters from bedroom. Her appearance is that of a ravaged woman. She leans exhaustedly in the doorway, hands clasped over her flat, virginal bosom.)*

Miss Collins: (breathlessly) Oh, Richard—Richard . . .

Porter: (coughing) Miss—Collins.

Elevator Boy: Hello, Miss Collins.

Miss Collins: (just noticing the men) Goodness! You've arrived already! Mother didn't tell me you were here! *(Self-consciously she touches her ridiculous corkscrew curls with the faded pink ribbon tied through them. Her manner becomes that of a slightly coquettish but prim little Southern belle.)* I must ask you gentlemen to excuse the terrible disorder.

Porter: That's all right, Miss Collins.

Miss Collins: It's the maid's day off. Your No'thern girls receive such excellent domestic training, but in the South it was never considered essential for a girl to have anything but prettiness and charm! *(She laughs girlishly.)* Please do sit down. Is it too close? Would you like a window open?

Porter: No, Miss Collins.

Miss Collins: (advancing with delicate grace to the sofa) Mother will bring in something cool after while. . . . Oh, my! *(She touches her forehead.)*

Porter: (kindly) Is anything wrong, Miss Collins?

Miss Collins: Oh, no, no, thank you, nothing! My head is a little bit heavy. I'm always a little bit—malarial—this time of year! *(She sways dizzily as she starts to sink down on the sofa.)*

Porter: (helping her) Careful there, Miss Collins.

Miss Collins: (vaguely) Yes, it is, I hadn't noticed before. *(She peers at them near-sightedly with a hesitant smile.)* You gentlemen have come from the church?

Porter: No, ma'am. I'm Nick, the porter, Miss Collins, and this boy here is Frank that runs the elevator.

Miss Collins: (stiffening a little) Oh? . . . I don't understand.

Porter: (gently) Mr. Abrams just asked me to drop in here an' see if you was getting along all right.

Miss Collins: Oh! Then he must have informed you of what's been going on in here!

Porter: He mentioned some kind of—disturbance.

Miss Collins: Yes! Isn't it outrageous? But it mustn't go any further, you understand. I mean you mustn't repeat it to other people.

Porter: No, I wouldn't say nothing.

Miss Collins: Not a word of it, please!

Elevator Boy: Is the man still here, Miss Collins?

Miss Collins: Oh, no. No, he's gone now.

Elevator Boy: How did he go, out the bedroom window, Miss Collins?

Miss Collins: (vaguely) Yes. . . .

Elevator Boy: I seen a guy that could do that once. He crawled straight up the side of the building. They called him The Human Fly! Gosh, that's a wonderful publicity angle, Miss Collins—"Beautiful Young Society Lady Raped by The Human Fly!"

Porter: (nudging him sharply) Git back in your cracker box!

Miss Collins: Publicity? No! It would be so humiliating! Mr. Abrams surely hasn't reported it to the papers!

Porter: No, ma'am. Don't listen to this smarty pants.

Miss Collins: (touching her curls) Will pictures be taken, you think? There's one of him on the mantel.

Elevator Boy: (going to the mantel) This one here, Miss Collins?

Miss Collins: Yes. Of the Sunday School faculty picnic. I had the little kindergardeners that year and he had the older boys. We rode in the cab of a railroad locomotive from Webb to Crystal Springs. *(She covers her ears with a girlish grimace and toss of her curls.)* Oh, how the steam-whistle blew! Blew! *(giggling) Blewwwwww!* It frightened me so, he put his arm round my shoulders! But she was there, too, though she had no business being. She grabbed his hat and stuck it on the back of her head and they—they *rassled* for it, they actually *rassled* together! Everyone said it was *shameless!* Don't you think that it was?

Porter: Yes, Miss Collins.

Miss Collins: That's the picture, the one in the silver frame up there on the mantel. We cooled the watermelon in the springs and afterwards played games. She hid somewhere and he took ages to find her. It got to be dark and he hadn't found her yet and everyone whispered and giggled about it and finally they came back together—her hangin' on to his arm like a common little strumpet—and Daisy Belle Huston shrieked out, "Look, everybody, the seat of Evelyn's skirt!" It was—covered with—grass-stains! Did you ever hear of anything as outrageous? It didn't faze her, though, she laughed like it was something very, very amusing! Rather *triumphant* she was!

Elevator Boy: Which one is him, Miss Collins?

Miss Collins: The tall one in the blue shirt holding onto one of my curls. He loved to play with them.

Elevator Boy: Quite a Romeo—1910 model, huh?

Miss Collins: (vaguely) Do you? It's nothing, really, but I like the lace on the collar. I said to Mother, "Even if I don't wear it, Mother, it will be *so* nice for my hope-chest!"

Elevator Boy: How was he dressed tonight when he climbed into your balcony, Miss Collins?

Miss Collins: Pardon?

Elevator Boy: Did he still wear that nifty little stick-candy-striped blue shirt with the celluloid collar?

Miss Collins: He hasn't changed.

Elevator Boy: Oughta be easy to pick him up in that. What color pants did he wear?

Miss Collins: (vaguely) I don't remember.

Elevator Boy: Maybe he didn't wear any. Shimmied out of 'em on the way up the wall! You could get him on grounds of indecent exposure, Miss Collins!

Porter: (grasping his arm) Cut that or git back in your cage! Understand?

Elevator Boy: (snickering) Take it easy. She don't hear a thing.

Porter: Well, you keep a decent tongue or get to hell out. Miss Collins here is a lady. You understand that?

Elevator Boy: Okay. She's Shoiley Temple.

Porter: She's a *lady!*

Elevator Boy: Yeah! *(He returns to the gramophone and looks through the records.)*

Miss Collins: I really shouldn't have created this disturbance. When the officers come I'll have to explain that to them. But you can understand my feelings, can't you?

Porter: Sure, Miss Collins.

Miss Collins: When men take advantage of common white-trash women who smoke in public there is probably some excuse for it, but when it occurs to a lady who is single and always com-*pletely* above reproach in her moral behavior, there's really nothing to do but call for police protection! Unless of course the girl is fortunate enough to have a father and brothers who can take care of the matter privately without any scandal.

Porter: Sure. That's right, Miss Collins.

Miss Collins: Of course it's bound to cause a great deal of very disagreeable talk. Especially 'round the *church!* Are you gentlemen Episcopalian?

Porter: No, ma'am. Catholic, Miss Collins.

Miss Collins: Oh. Well, I suppose you know in England we're known as the English Catholic church. We have direct Apostolic succession through St. Paul who christened the Early Angles—which is what the original English people were called—and established the English branch of the Catholic church over there. So when you hear ignorant people claim that our church was founded by—by Henry the *Eighth*—that horrible, *lech*erous old man who had so many wives—as many as *Blue*-beard they say!—you can see how ridiculous it *is* and how thoroughly ob*nox*-ious to anybody who really *knows* and under*stands* Church *History!*

Porter: (comfortingly) Sure, Miss Collins. Everybody knows that.

Miss Collins: I wish they *did,* but they need to be in*struc*ted! Before he died, my father was Rector at the Church of St. Michael and St. George at Glorious Hill, Mississippi. . . . I've literally grown up right in the very *shad*ow of the Episcopal church. At Pass Christian and Natchez, Biloxi, Gulfport, Port Gibson, Columbus and Glorious Hill! *(with gentle, bewildered sadness)* But you know I sometimes suspect that there has been some kind of spiritual schism in the modern church. These northern dioceses have completely departed from the good old church traditions. For instance our Rector at the Church of the Holy Communion has never darkened my door. It's a fashionable church and he's terribly busy, but even so you'd think he might have time to make a stranger in the congregation feel at home. But he doesn't though! Nobody seems to have the time any more. . . . *(She grows more excited as her mind sinks back into illusion.)* I ought not to mention this, but do you know they actually take a malicious de-*light* over there at the Holy Communion—where I've recently transferred my letter—in what's been going on here at night in this apartment? *Yes!!* *(She laughs wildly and throws up her hands.)* They take a malicious de*LIGHT* in it!! *(She catches her breath and gropes vaguely about her wrapper.)*

Porter: You lookin' for somethin', Miss Collins?

Miss Collins: My—handkerchief . . . *(She is blinking her eyes against tears.)*

Porter: (removing a rag from his pocket) Here. Use this, Miss Collins. It's just a rag but it's clean, except along that edge where I wiped off the phonograph handle.

Miss Collins: Thanks. You gentlemen are very kind. Mother will bring in something cool after while. . . .

Elevator Boy: (placing a record on machine) This one is got some kind of foreign title. *(The record begins to play Tschaikowsky's "None But the Lonely Heart.")* [1]

Miss Collins: (stuffing the rag daintily in her bosom) Excuse me, please. Is the weather nice outside?

Porter: (huskily) Yes, it's nice, Miss Collins.

Miss Collins: (dreamily) So wa'm for this time of year. I wore my little astrakhan cape to service but had to *carry* it *home,* as the weight of it actually seemed *oppres*sive to me. *(Her eyes fall shut.)* The sidewalks seem so dreadfully long in summer. . . . .

Elevator Boy: This ain't summer, Miss Collins.

Miss Collins: (dreamily) I used to think I'd never get to the end of that last block. And that's the block where all the trees went down in the big tornado. The walk is simple *glit*-tering with sunlight. *(pressing her eyelids)* Impossible to shade your face and I *do* perspire so freely! *(She touches her forehead daintily with the rag.)* Not a branch, not a leaf to give you a little protection! You simply *have* to en-*dure* it. Turn your hideous red face away from all the front-porches and walk as fast as you decently *can* till you get *by* them! Oh, dear, dear Savior, sometimes you're not so lucky and you *meet* people and have to *smile!* You can't *avoid* them unless you cut *across* and that's so ob-vious, you know. . . . People would say you're pecu*li*ar. . . . His house is right in the middle of that awful leafless block, *their* house, his and *hers,* and they have an automobile and always get home early and sit on the porch and *watch* me walking by—Oh, Father in Heaven—with a ma*li*cious de*light! (She averts her face in remembered torture.)* She has such *penetrating* eyes, they look straight through me. She sees that terrible choking thing in my throat and the pain I have in *here—(touching her chest)—*and she points it out and laughs and whispers to him, "There she goes with her shiny big red nose, the poor old maid—that *loves* you!" *(She chokes and hides her face in the rag.)*

Porter: Maybe you better forget all that, Miss Collins.

Miss Collins: Never, never forget it! Never, never! I left my parasol once—the one with long white fringe that belonged to Mother—I left it behind in the cloak-room at the church so I didn't have anything to cover my face with when I walked by, and I couldn't turn back either, with all those people behind me—giggling back of me, poking fun at my clothes! Oh, dear, dear! I had to walk straight forward—past the last elm tree and into that *merciless* sunlight. Oh! It beat down on me, *scorching* me! *Whips!* . . . Oh, Jesus! . . . Over my face and my body! . . . I tried to walk on fast but was dizzy and they kept closer behind me—! I stumbled, I nearly fell, and all of them burst out laughing! My face turned so *horribly* red, it got so red and wet, I knew how ugly it was in all that merciless glare—not a single shadow to hide in! And then—*(Her face contorts with fear.)—*their automobile drove up in front of their house, right where I had to pass by it, and *she* stepped out, in white, so fresh and easy, her stomach round with a baby, the first of the *six.* Oh, God! . . . And he stood smiling behind her, white and easy and cool, and they

[1] Song by Peter Ilyich Tchaikovsky (1840–1893), Russian composer.

stood there waiting for me. *Waiting!* I had to keep on. What else could I do? I couldn't turn *back,* could I? *No!* I said dear *God,* strike me *dead!* He didn't, though. I put my head way down like I couldn't see them! You know what she did? She stretched out her hand to *stop* me! And *he*—he stepped up straight in front of me, *smiling,* blocking the walk with his terrible big white body! *"Lucretia,"* he said, *"Lucretia Collins!"* I—I tried to speak but I couldn't, the breath went out of my body! I covered my face and—ran! . . . Ran! . . . *Ran! (beating the arm of the sofa)* Till I reached the end of the block —and the elm trees—*started* again. . . . Oh, Merciful Christ in Heaven, how *kind* they were! *(She leans back exhaustedly, her hand relaxed on sofa. She pauses and the music ends.)* I said to Mother, "Mother, we've got to leave town!" We *did* after that. And now after all these years he's finally remembered and come *back!* Moved away from that house and the woman and come *here*—I saw him in the back of the church one day. I wasn't sure—but it *was.* The night after that was the night that he first broke in—and indulged his senses with me. . . . He doesn't realize that I've changed, that I can't feel again the way that I used to feel, now that he's got six children by that Cincinnati girl— three in high-school already! Six! Think of that? Six children! I don't know what he'll say when he knows another one's coming! He'll probably blame *me* for it because a man always *does!* In spite of the fact that he *forced* me!

Elevator Boy: (grinning) Did you say—a *baby,* Miss Collins?

Miss Collins: (lowering her eyes but speaking with tenderness and pride) Yes—I'm expecting a *child.*

Elevator Boy: Jeez! *(He claps his hand over his mouth and turns away quickly.)*

Miss Collins: Even if it's not legitimate, I think it has a perfect right to its father's name—don't you?

Porter: Yes. Sure, Miss Collins.

Miss Collins: A child is innocent and pure. No matter how it's conceived. And it must *not* be made to suffer! So I intend to dispose of the little property cousin Ethel left me and give the child a private education where it won't come under the evil influence of the Christian church! I want to make sure that it doesn't grow up in the shadow of the cross and then have to walk along blocks that scorch you with terrible sunlight! *(The elevator buzzer sounds from the hall.)*

Porter: Frank! Somebody wants to come up. *(The Elevator Boy goes out. The elevator door bangs shut. The Porter clears his throat.)* Yes, it'd be better—to go off some place else.

Miss Collins: If only I had the courage—but I don't. I've grown so used to it here, and people outside—it's always so *hard* to *face* them!

Porter: Maybe you won't—have to face nobody, Miss Collins. *(The elevator door clangs open.)*

Miss Collins: (rising fearfully) Is someone coming—here?

Porter: You just take it easy, Miss Collins.

Miss Collins: If that's the officers coming for Richard, tell them to go away. I've decided not to prosecute Mr. Martin. *(Mr. Abrams enters with the Doctor and the Nurse. The Elevator Boy gawks from the doorway. The Doctor is the weary, professional type, the Nurse hard and efficient. Mr. Abrams is a small, kindly person, sincerely troubled by the situation.)*

Miss Collins: (shrinking back, her voice faltering) I've decided not to—prosecute
　Mr. Martin . . .

Doctor: Miss Collins?

Mr. Abrams: (with attempted heartiness) Yes, this is the lady you wanted to meet,
　Dr. White.

Doctor: Hmmm. *(briskly to the Nurse)* Go in her bedroom and get a few things
　together.

Nurse: Yes, sir. *(She goes quickly across to the bedroom.)*

Miss Collins: (fearfully shrinking) Things?

Doctor: Yes, Miss Tyler will help you pack up an overnight bag. *(smiling
　mechanically)* A strange place always seems more homelike the first few days
　when we have a few of our little personal articles around us.

Miss Collins: A strange—place?

Doctor: (carelessly, making a memorandum) Don't be disturbed, Miss Collins.

Miss Collins: I know! *(excitedly)* You've come from the Holy Communion to
　place me under arrest! On moral charges!

Mr. Abrams: Oh, no, Miss Collins, you got the wrong idea. This is a doctor
　who—

Doctor: (impatiently) Now, now, you're just going away for a while till things
　get straightened out. *(He glances at his watch.)* Two-twenty-five! Miss
　Tyler?

Nurse: Coming!

Miss Collins: (with slow and sad comprehension) Oh. . . . I'm going away. . . .

Mr. Abrams: She was always a lady, Doctor, such a perfect lady.

Doctor: Yes. No doubt.

Mr. Abrams: It seems too bad!

Miss Collins: Let me—write him a note. A pencil? Please?

Mr. Abrams: Here, Miss Collins. *(She takes the pencil and crouches over the table.
　The Nurse comes out with a hard, forced smile, carrying a suitcase.)*

Doctor: Ready, Miss Tyler?

Nurse: All ready, Dr. White. *(She goes up to Miss Collins.)* Come along, dear, we
　can tend to that later!

Mr. Abrams: (sharply) Let her finish the note!

Miss Collins: (straightening with a frightened smile) It's—finished.

Nurse: All right, dear, come along. *(She propels her firmly toward the door.)*

Miss Collins: (turning suddenly back) Oh, Mr. Abrams!

Mr. Abrams: Yes, Miss Collins?

Miss Collins: If he should come again—and find me gone—I'd rather you didn't
　tell him—about the baby. . . . I think its better for *me* to tell him *that. (gently
　smiling)* You know how men *are,* don't you?

Mr. Abrams: Yes, Miss Collins.

Porter: Goodbye, Miss Collins. *(The Nurse pulls firmly at her arm. She smiles over
　her shoulder with a slight apologetic gesture.)*

Miss Collins: Mother will bring in—something cool—after while . . . *(She
　disappears down the hall with the Nurse. The elevator door clangs shut with the
　metallic sound of a locked cage. The wires hum.)*

Mr. Abrams: She wrote him a note.

Porter: What did she write, Mr. Abrams?

Mr. Abrams: "Dear—Richard. I'm going away for a while. But don't worry, I'll
be back. I have a secret to tell you. Love—Lucretia." *(He coughs.)* We got to
clear out this stuff an' pile it down in the basement till I find out where it
goes.

Porter: (dully) Tonight, Mr. Abrams?

Mr. Abrams: (roughly to hide his feeling) No, no, not tonight, you old fool.
Enough has happened tonight! *(then gently)* We can do it tomorrow. Turn out
that bedroom light—and close the window. *(Music playing softly becomes audible
as the men go out slowly, closing the door, and the light fades out.)*

CURTAIN

1941–1944/1946

John Cheever
1912–1982

A book reviewer once referred to John Cheever as the "Chekhov of the suburbs"
—a double-edged comment that acknowledged his great talent as a short story
writer but limited his fictional scope. Cheever's stories, however, though they
frequently chronicle the manners and mores of upper-middle-class suburban life,
offer more than social documentation. His overriding theme has less to do with
the social customs of a particular class than with his profound disappointment
that civilization can do so little for human happiness. In one of his tales, a
character gazes out the window of a commuter train "looking with some
delicacy, not into a formidable and challenging wilderness but into a half-finished
civilization embracing glass towers, oil derricks, suburban continents and
abandoned movie houses and wondering why, in this most prosperous, equitable,
and accomplished world—where even the cleaning women practice Chopin
preludes in their spare time—everyone should seem to be so disappointed."

John Cheever was born on May 27, 1912, in Quincy, Massachusetts. He went
through a deeply troubled adolescence as a result of his father's business failure in
the stock market crash of 1929 and his parent's separation. He attended Thayer
Academy in South Braintree, Massachusetts, but his refusal to memorize the
names of the Greek playwrights, along with other breaches of discipline, led to
his dismissal in his junior year. Determined to be a writer, Cheever sent sketches
of his expulsion to literary critic Malcolm Cowley, then editor of the *New
Republic.* Cowley, who became Cheever's lifelong friend, published the sketches
and thus launched the seventeen-year-old Cheever's literary career. Cheever
promptly moved to New York City, where he contributed stories to numerous
magazines and lived in such squalor that Walker Evans, the famous photographer
of rural poverty, couldn't resist taking a picture of his room. Cheever married in
1941 and afterward spent four years with the U.S. Army during World War II.
In the early 1950s Cheever worked for the Columbia Broadcasting System,

writing scripts for such radio shows as "Life with Father." He died of cancer in 1982.

Cheever's first volume of short stories, *The Way Some People Live,* appeared in 1942, while he was serving in the army. His next volume, *The Enormous Radio and Other Stories* (1953), consisted of fourteen tales that had originally been published in *The New Yorker,* to which Cheever had been contributing regularly since 1940. In subsequent collections, *The Housebreaker of Shady Hill* (1958), *Some People, Places, and Things That Will Not Appear in My Next Novel* (1961), *The Brigadier and the Golf Widow* (1964), and *The World of Apples* (1972), Cheever's tone remained predominantly elegaic, though it was increasingly counterbalanced, as in "The Fourth Alarm," by a grittier, more absurd view of human nature. Taking a retrospective look at his career in a foreword to the Pulitzer Prize–winning *Stories of John Cheever* (1978), he noted that "Calvin played no part at all in my religious education, but his presence seemed to abide in the barns of my childhood and to have left me with some undue bitterness."

Cheever's literary reputation seems to rest more on his short stories than on his longer works, though his first novel, *The Wapshot Chronicle* (1957), won the National Book Award. Cheever continued the story of the urbane, eccentric New England family in *The Wapshot Scandal* (1964), then produced two novels that recast some of the grimmer themes of his short fiction: *Bullet Park* (1969), the tale of an insane attempt at ritual murder in an affluent suburb, and *Falconer* (1977), a story of fratricide, homosexuality, and imprisonment that grew out of his experiences teaching creative writing at Ossining State Prison in New York. In his last book, *Oh What a Paradise It Seems* (1982), Cheever managed to compress into a very short novel the concerns of a lifetime: the search for love, the restoration of the world's physical beauty, the quest, however illusory, to regain a paradise lost.

Further Reading:
S. Coale, *John Cheever,* 1977.
L. Waldeland, *John Cheever,* 1979.
G. Hunt, *John Cheever: The Company of Love,* 1983.
S. Cheever, *Home Before Dark,* 1984.

Text:
The Stories of John Cheever, 1978.

The Fourth Alarm

I sit in the sun drinking gin. It is ten in the morning. Sunday. Mrs. Uxbridge is off somewhere with the children. Mrs. Uxbridge is the housekeeper. She does the cooking and takes care of Peter and Louise.

It is autumn. The leaves have turned. The morning is windless, but the leaves fall by the hundreds. In order to see anything—a leaf or a blade of grass—you have, I think, to know the keenness of love. Mrs. Uxbridge is sixty-three, my wife is away, and Mrs. Smithsonian (who lives on the other side of town) is seldom in the mood these days, so I seem to miss some part of the morning as if the hour had a threshold or a series of thresholds that I cannot cross. Passing a football might do it but Peter is too young and my only football-playing neighbor goes to church.

My wife, Bertha, is expected on Monday. She comes out from the city on Monday and returns on Tuesday. Bertha is a good-looking young woman with a splendid figure. Her eyes, I think, are a little close together and she is sometimes peevish. When the children were young she had a peevish way of disciplining them. "If you don't eat the nice breakfast Mummy has cooked for you before I count three," she would say, "I will send you back to bed. One. Two. *Three*. . . ." I heard it again at dinner. "If you don't eat the nice dinner Mummy has cooked for you before I count three I will send you to bed without any supper. One. Two. Three. . . ." I heard it again. "If you don't pick up your toys before Mummy counts three Mummy will throw them all away. One. Two. Three. . . ." So it went on through the bath and bedtime and one two three was their lullaby. I sometimes thought she must have learned to count when she was an infant and that when the end came she would call a countdown for the Angel of Death. If you'll excuse me I'll get another glass of gin.

When the children were old enough to go to school, Bertha got a job teaching social studies in the sixth grade. This kept her occupied and happy and she said she had always wanted to be a teacher. She had a reputation for strictness. She wore dark clothes, dressed her hair simply, and expected contrition and obedience from her pupils. To vary her life she joined an amateur theatrical group. She played the maid in *Angel Street* and the old crone in *Desmonds Acres*. The friends she made in the theatre were all pleasant people and I enjoyed taking her to their parties. It is important to know that Bertha does not drink. She will take a Dubonnet politely but she does not enjoy drinking.

Through her theatrical friends, she learned that a nude show called *Ozamanides II* was being cast. She told me this and everything that followed. Her teaching contract gave her ten days' sick leave, and claiming to be sick one day she went into New York. *Ozamanides* was being cast at a producer's office in midtown, where she found a line of a hundred or more men and women waiting to be interviewed. She took an unpaid bill out of her pocketbook, and waving this as if it were a letter she bucked the line saying, "Excuse me please, excuse me, I have an appointment. . . ." No one protested and she got quickly to the head of the line, where a secretary took her name, Social Security number, etc. She was told to go into a cubicle and undress. She was then shown into an office where there were four men. The interview, considering the circumstances, was very circumspect. She was told that she would be nude throughout the performance. She would be expected to simulate or perform copulation twice during the performance and participate in a love pile that involved the audience.

I remember the night when she told me all of this. It was in our living room. The children had been put to bed. She was very happy. There was no question about that. "There I was naked," she said, "but I wasn't in the least embarrassed. The only thing that worried me was that my feet might get dirty. It was an old-fashioned kind of place with framed theatre programs on the wall and a big photograph of Ethel Barrymore. There I sat naked in front of these strangers and I felt for the first time in my life that I'd found myself. I found myself in nakedness. I felt like a new woman, a better woman. To be naked and unashamed in front of strangers was one of the most exciting experiences I've ever had. . . ."

I didn't know what to do. I still don't know, on this Sunday morning, what I should have done. I guess I should have hit her. I said she couldn't do it. She said I couldn't stop her. I mentioned the children and she said this experience would make her a better mother. "When I took off my clothes," she said, "I felt as if I had rid myself of everything mean and small." Then I said she'd never get the job because of her appendicitis scar. A few minutes later the phone rang. It was the producer offering her a part. "Oh, I'm so happy," she said. "Oh, how wonderful and rich and strange life can be when you stop playing out the roles that your parents and their friends wrote out for you. I feel like an explorer."

The fitness of what I did then or rather left undone still confuses me. She broke her teaching contract, joined Equity, and began rehearsals. As soon as *Ozamanides* opened she hired Mrs. Uxbridge and took a hotel apartment near the theatre. I asked for a divorce. She said she saw no reason for a divorce. Adultery and cruelty have well marked courses of action but what can a man do when his wife wants to appear naked on the stage? When I was younger I had known some burlesque girls and some of them were married and had children. However, they did what Bertha was going to do only on the midnight Saturday show, and as I remember their husbands were third-string comedians and the kids always looked hungry.

A day or so later I went to a divorce lawyer. He said a consent decree was my only hope. There are no precedents for simulated carnality in public as grounds for divorce in New York State and no lawyer will take a divorce case without a precedent. Most of my friends were tactful about Bertha's new life. I suppose most of them went to see her, but I put it off for a month or more. Tickets were expensive and hard to get. It was snowing the night I went to the theatre, or what had been a theatre. The proscenium arch had been demolished, the set was a collection of used tires, and the only familiar features were the seats and the aisles. Theatre audiences have always confused me. I suppose this is because you find an incomprehensible variety of types thrust into what was an essentially domestic and terribly ornate interior. There were all kinds there that night. Rock music was playing when I came in. It was that deafening old fashioned kind of rock they used to play in places like Arthur. At eight-thirty the houselights dimmed, and the cast—there were fourteen —came down the aisles. Sure enough, they were all naked excepting Ozamanides, who wore a crown.

I can't describe the performance. Ozamanides had two sons, and I think he murdered them, but I'm not sure. The sex was general. Men and women embraced one another and Ozamanides embraced several men. At one point a stranger, sitting in the seat on my right, put his hand on my knee. I didn't want to reproach him for a human condition, nor did I want to encourage him. I removed his hand and experienced a deep nostalgia for the innocent movie theatres of my youth. In the little town where I was raised there was one—the Alhambra. My favorite movie was called *The Fourth Alarm*. I saw it first one Tuesday after school and stayed on for the evening show. My parents worried when I didn't come home for supper and I was scolded. On Wednesday I played hooky and was able to see the show twice and get home in time for supper. I went to school on Thursday but I went to the theatre as soon as school closed and sat partway through the evening show. My parents must have called the police, because a patrolman came into the theatre and made me go home. I was forbidden to go to the theatre on Friday, but I spent all Saturday there, and on Saturday the picture ended its run. The picture was about the substitution of automobiles for horse-drawn fire engines. Four fire companies were involved. Three of the teams had been replaced by engines and the miserable horses had been sold to brutes. One team remained, but its days were numbered. The men and the horses were sad. Then suddenly there was a great fire. One saw the first engine, the second, and the third race off to the conflagration. Back at the horse-drawn company, things were very gloomy. Then the fourth alarm rang—it was their summons—and they sprang into action, harnassed the team, and galloped across the city. They put out the fire, saved the city, and were given an amnesty by the Mayor. Now on the stage Ozamanides was writing something obscene on my wife's buttocks.

Had nakedness—its thrill—annihilated her sense of nostalgia? Nostalgia—in spite of her close-set eyes—was one of her principal charms. It was her gift gracefully to carry the memory of some experience into another tense. Did she, mounted in public by a naked stranger, remember any of the places where we had made love—the rented houses close to the sea, where one heard in the sounds of a summer rain the prehistoric promises of love, peacefulness, and beauty? Should I stand up in the theatre and shout for her to return, return, return in the name of love, humor, and serenity? It was nice driving home after parties in the snow. I thought. The snow flew into the headlights and made it seem as if we were going a hundred miles an hour. It was nice driving home in the snow after parties. Then the cast lined up and urged us—commanded us in fact—to undress and join them.

This seemed to be my duty. How else could I approach understanding Bertha? I've always been very quick to get out of my clothes. I did. However, there was a problem. What should I do with my wallet, wrist watch, and car keys? I couldn't safely leave them in my clothes. So, naked, I started down the aisle with my valuables in my right hand. As I came up to the action a naked young man stopped me and shouted—sang —"Put down your lendings. Lendings are impure."

"But it's my wallet and my watch and the car keys," I said.

"Put down your lendings," he sang.

"But I have to drive home from the station," I said, "and I have sixty or seventy dollars in cash."

"Put down your lendings."

"I can't, I really can't. I have to eat and drink and get home."

"Put down your lendings."

Then one by one they all, including Bertha, picked up the incantation. The whole cast began to chant: "Put down your lendings, put down your lendings."

The sense of being unwanted has always been for me acutely painful. I suppose some clinician would have an explanation. The sensation is reverberative and seems to attach itself as the last link in a chain made up of all similar experience. The voices of the cast were loud and scornful, and there I was, buck naked, somewhere in the middle of the city and unwanted, remembering missed football tackles, lost fights, the contempt of strangers, the sound of laughter from behind shut doors. I held my valuables in my right hand, my literal identification. None of it was irreplaceable, but to cast it off would seem to threaten my essence, the shadow of myself that I could see on the floor, my name.

I went back to my seat and got dressed. This was difficult in such a cramped space. The cast was still shouting. Walking up the sloping aisle of the ruined theatre was powerfully reminiscent. I had made the same gentle ascent after *King Lear* and *The Cherry Orchard.* I went outside.

It was still snowing. It looked like a blizzard. A cab was stuck in front of the theatre and I remembered then that I had snow tires. This gave me a sense of security and accomplishment that would have disgusted Ozamanides and his naked court; but I seemed not to have exposed my inhibitions but to have hit on some marvelously practical and obdurate part of myself. The wind flung the snow into my face and so, singing and jingling the car keys, I walked to the train.

1970

Tillie Olsen
b. 1913

Tillie Olsen was fifteen years old when she paid ten cents for a water-soaked copy of the April 1861 issue of the *Atlantic Monthly* in an Omaha used-book store. In this sixty-seven-year-old magazine, she read an excerpt from Rebecca Harding Davis's anonymously published *Life in the Iron Mills* and learned, as she reports in *Silences,* that "literature can be made out of the lives of despised people." Although some readers have praised Olsen as a great prose stylist, most are convinced that the power of her work turns on its eloquent rendering of the pain and the possibility of the lives of the "despised"—the white working-class women and men who together with their black brothers and sisters populate the world of her fiction.

Born Tillie Lerner to Russian immigrant parents in Omaha, Nebraska, Olsen received more formal education than most women during the Depression. She completed the eleventh grade and, as she has reported, used the local public library as her college classroom. At the age of nineteen she began working on what to date has been her only novel. Within a short time, however, she put the manuscript aside and lost it. Years later, having accidentally recovered it, she decided to reconstruct and finish it. Published in 1974 as *Yonnonido: From the Thirties,* the book recounts the impoverished odyssey, anguished relations, and eventual survival of an unflinchingly hopeful mother and daughter. Above all, as one reviewer puts it, *Yonnonido* demonstrates Olsen's profound understanding of "what a great weight poor women carry" as well as a "deep sympathy for the restlessness and degraded pride" of working-class men.

Olsen's first publications—a few poems and a short story ("The Iron Throat," later the opening chapter of *Yonnonido*)—appeared in the initial volume of the *Partisan Review* in 1934. That same year *The New Republic* printed her autobiographical essay "Thousand-Dollar Vagrant." After this promising beginning, however, Olsen dropped from sight. For the next twenty-two years she published nothing. Having married Jack Olsen, a printer, in 1936, she spent the next two decades trying to write while also rearing four children and working—not only as a typist-transcriber for a dairy-equipment company but also, as she notes in *Silences,* "full time on temporary jobs, a Kelly, a Western Agency girl, (girl!), wandering from office to office, always hoping to manage two, three writing months ahead." Time in which to write came as "stolen moments" on a bus or on the job, she reports, or more often in "the deep night hours for as long as I could stay awake, after the kids were in bed, after the household tasks were done, sometimes during. It is no accident," she adds, "that the first work I considered publishable began: 'I stand here ironing, and what you asked me moves tormented back and forth with the iron.'"

"Eventually," however, Olsen reports, "there was time." The story that begins "I stand here ironing," reprinted here, was written in 1953 and 1954 and first published under the title "Help Her to Believe" in a small magazine, *The Pacific Spectator.* Its theme (how women contend with familial trauma) and its style (lyric rhythms cast in achingly beautiful terms) mark all of Olsen's best work. Retitled "I Stand Here Ironing," the story was included in what is to date Olsen's only collection of fiction, *Tell Me a Riddle* (1961). In that same year, the title story of the collection won the O. Henry Award for best American short story. Since then, Olsen's stories have been reprinted in numerous anthologies, and her contributions—as a writer, critic, teacher, and feminist—have received wide recognition. When *Tell Me a Riddle* was reissued in 1971, it earned even greater praise, as work comparable to Faulkner's "The Bear" and Melville's "Benito Cereno" in the way in which it "carries us through despair to a renewal of hope."

In recent years Tillie Olsen has received numerous honors and awards, including Guggenheim and Radcliffe fellowships, a National Endowment for the Arts grant, and several honorary degrees. She has also been writer-in-residence or visiting professor at several colleges and universities, including Amherst, Stanford, Massachusetts Institute of Technology, and the University of Massachusetts at Boston.

In 1972 Olsen revived Rebecca Harding Davis's *Life in the Iron Mills,* to which she had been so indebted in her youth. Reissued by the Feminist Press, *Life in the Iron Mills* now carries with it an incisive "biographical interpretation" written by Olsen. Olsen's most important recent book is *Silences* (1978), a collection of finely woven pieces concerned, as Olsen has noted, "with the relationship of circumstances—including class, color, sex; the times, climate into which one is born—to the creation of literature." The poet Adrienne Rich has hailed *Silences* as a "prose poem" that is enriched not only by "Olsen's unique connection and resonance with other writers" but also by its explorations of the "losses, the empty spaces, she, above all, has been equipped to recognize."

Although Olsen's body of work is relatively small, her influence on other writers has been large. Margaret Atwood has written of the "reverence" with which other women writers regard Olsen's work. And Alice Walker has observed that there have been few other writers "who manage in their work and in their sharing of their understanding to actually help us to live, to work, to create, day by day." Compelling on many counts, Olsen's work is especially unforgettable for its poor, forgotten female characters—archetypal in their ordinariness—who struggle to claim a dignified place for themselves in circumstances that nurture but also restrain the creative self.

Further Reading:
F. Howe, "Literacy and Literature," *PMLA*, May 1974.
C. Stimpson, "Tillie Olsen: Witness as Servant," *Polit,* Fall 1977.
M. Atwood, "Obstacle Course," *The New York Times Book Review,* July 30, 1978.
S. Cunneen, "Tillie Olsen: Storyteller of Working America," *Christian Century,* May 21, 1980.

Text:
Tell Me a Riddle, 1961.

I Stand Here Ironing

I stand here ironing, and what you asked me moves tormented back and forth with the iron.

"I wish you would manage the time to come in and talk with me about your daughter. I'm sure you can help me understand her. She's a youngster who needs help and whom I'm deeply interested in helping."

"Who needs help." Even if I came, what good would it do? You think because I am her mother I have a key, or that in some way you could use me as a key? She has lived for nineteen years. There is all that life that has happened outside of me, beyond me.

And when is there time to remember, to sift, to weigh, to estimate, to total? I will start and there will be an interruption and I will have to gather it all together again. Or I will become engulfed with all I did or did not do, with what should have been and what cannot be helped.

She was a beautiful baby. The first and only one of our five that was beautiful at birth. You do not guess how new and uneasy her tenancy in her now-loveliness. You did not know her all those years she was thought homely, or see her poring over her baby pictures, making me tell her over and over how beautiful she had been— and would be, I would tell her—and was now, to the seeing eye. But the seeing eyes were few or nonexistent. Including mine.

I nursed her. They feel that's important nowadays. I nursed all the children, but with her, with all the fierce rigidity of first motherhood, I did like the books then said. Though her cries battered me to trembling and my breasts ached with swollenness, I waited till the clock decreed.

Why do I put that first? I do not even know if it matters, or if it explains anything.

She was a beautiful baby. She blew shining bubbles of sound. She loved motion, loved light, loved color and music and textures. She would lie on the floor in her blue overalls patting the surface so hard in ecstasy her hands and feet would blur. She was a miracle to me, but when she was eight months old I had to leave her daytimes with the woman downstairs to whom she was no miracle at all, for I worked or looked for work and for Emily's father, who "could no longer endure" (he wrote in his good-bye note) "sharing want with us."

I was nineteen. It was the pre-relief, pre-WPA world of the depression. I would start running as soon as I got off the streetcar, running up the stairs, the place smelling sour, and awake or asleep to startle awake, when she saw me she would break into a clogged weeping that could not be comforted, a weeping I can hear yet.

After a while I found a job hashing at night so I could be with her days, and it was better. But it came to where I had to bring her to his family and leave her.

It took a long time to raise the money for her fare back. Then she got chicken pox and I had to wait longer. When she finally came, I hardly knew her, walking quick and nervous like her father, looking like her father, thin, and dressed in a shoddy red that yellowed her skin and glared at the pockmarks. All the baby loveliness gone.

She was two. Old enough for nursery school they said, and I did not know then what I know now—the fatigue of the long day, and the lacerations of group life in nurseries that are only parking places for children.

Except that it would have made no difference if I had known. It was the only place there was. It was the only way we could be together, the only way I could hold a job.

And even without knowing, I knew. I knew the teacher that was evil because all these years it has curdled into my memory, the little boy hunched in the corner, her rasp, "why aren't you outside, because Alvin hits you? that's no reason, go out, scaredy." I knew Emily hated it even if she did not clutch and implore "don't go Mommy" like the other children, mornings.

She always had a reason why we should stay home. Momma, you look sick, Momma. I feel sick. Momma, the teachers aren't there today, they're sick. Momma, we can't go, there was a fire there last night. Momma, it's a holiday today, no school, they told me.

But never a direct protest, never rebellion. I think of our others in their three-, four-year-oldness—the explosions, the tempers, the denunciations, the demands—and I feel suddenly ill. I put the iron down. What in me demanded that goodness in her? And what was the cost, the cost to her of such goodness?

The old man living in the back once said in his gentle way: "You should smile at Emily more when you look at her." What *was* in my face when I looked at her? I loved her. There were all the acts of love.

It was only with the others I remembered what he said, and it was the face of joy, and not of care or tightness or worry I turned to them—too late for Emily. She does not smile easily, let alone almost always as her brothers and sisters do. Her face is closed and sombre, but when she wants, how fluid. You must have seen it in her pantomimes, you spoke of her rare gift for comedy on the stage that rouses a laughter out of the audience so dear they applaud and applaud and do not want to let her go.

Where does it come from, that comedy? There was none of it in her when she came back to me that second time, after I had had to send her away again. She had a new daddy now to learn to love, and I think perhaps it was a better time.

Except when we left her alone nights, telling ourselves she was old enough.

"Can't you go some other time, Mommy, like tomorrow?" she would ask. "Will it be just a little while you'll be gone? Do you promise?"

The time we came back, the front door open, the clock on the floor in the hall. She rigid awake. "It wasn't just a little while. I didn't cry. Three times I called you, just three times, and then I ran downstairs to open the door so you could come faster. The clock talked loud. I threw it away, it scared me what it talked."

She said the clock talked loud again that night I went to the hospital to have Susan. She was delirious with the fever that comes before red measles, but she was fully conscious all the week I was gone and the week after we were home when she could not come near the new baby or me.

She did not get well. She stayed skeleton thin, not wanting to eat, and night after night she had nightmares. She would call for me, and I would rouse from exhaustion to sleepily call back: "You're all right, darling, go to sleep, it's just a dream," and if she still called, in a sterner voice, "now go to sleep, Emily, there's nothing to hurt you." Twice, only twice, when I had to get up for Susan anyhow, I went in to sit with her.

Now when it is too late (as if she would let me hold and comfort her like I do the others) I get up and go to her at once at her moan or restless stirring. "Are you awake, Emily? Can I get you something?" And the answer is always the same: "No, I'm all right, go back to sleep, Mother."

They persuaded me at the clinic to send her away to a convalescent home in the country where "she can have the kind of food and care you can't manage for her, and you'll be free to concentrate on the new baby." They still send children to that place. I see pictures on the society page of sleek young women planning affairs to raise money for it, or dancing at the affairs, or decorating Easter eggs or filling Christmas stockings for the children.

They never have a picture of the children so I do not know if the girls still wear those gigantic red bows and the ravaged looks on the every other Sunday when parents can come to visit "unless otherwise notified"—as we were notified the first six weeks.

Oh it is a handsome place, green lawns and tall trees and fluted flower beds. High up on the balconies of each cottage the children stand, the girls in their red bows and white dresses, the boys in white suits and giant red ties. The parents stand below shrieking up to be heard and the children shriek down to be heard, and between them the invisible wall "Not To Be Contaminated by Parental Germs or Physical Affection."

There was a tiny girl who always stood hand in hand with Emily. Her parents never came. One visit she was gone. "They moved her to Rose College," Emily shouted in explanation. "They don't like you to love anybody here."

She wrote once a week, the labored writing of a seven-year-old. "I am fine. How is the baby. If I write my letter nicly I will have a star. Love." There never was a star. We wrote every other day, letters she could never hold or keep but only hear read—once. "We simply do not have room for children to keep any personal possessions," they patiently explained when we pieced one Sunday's shrieking together to plead how much it would mean to Emily, who loved so to keep things, to be allowed to keep her letters and cards.

Each visit she looked frailer. "She isn't eating," they told us.

(They had runny eggs for breakfast or mush with lumps, Emily said later, I'd hold it in my mouth and not swallow. Nothing ever tasted good, just when they had chicken.)

It took us eight months to get her released home, and only the fact that she gained back so little of her seven lost pounds convinced the social worker.

I used to try to hold and love her after she came back, but her body would stay stiff, and after a while she'd push away. She ate little. Food sickened her, and I think much of life too. Oh she had physical lightness and brightness, twinkling by on skates, bouncing like a ball up and down up and down over the jump rope, skimming over the hill; but these were momentary.

She fretted about her appearance, thin and dark and foreign-looking at a time when every little girl was supposed to look or thought she should look a chubby blonde replica of Shirley Temple. The doorbell sometimes rang for her, but no one seemed to come and play in the house or be a best friend. Maybe because we moved so much.

There was a boy she loved painfully through two school semesters. Months later she told me how she had taken pennies from my purse to buy him candy. "Licorice was his favorite and I brought him some every day, but he still liked Jennifer better'n me. Why, Mommy?" The kind of question for which there is no answer.

School was a worry to her. She was not glib or quick in a world where glibness and quickness were easily confused with ability to learn. To her overworked and exasperated teachers she was an overconscientious "slow learner" who kept trying to catch up and was absent entirely too often.

I let her be absent, though sometimes the illness was imaginary. How different from my now-strictness about attendance with the others. I wasn't working. We had a new baby, I was home anyhow. Sometimes, after Susan grew old enough, I would keep her home from school, too, to have them all together.

Mostly Emily had asthma, and her breathing, harsh and labored, would fill the house with a curiously tranquil sound. I would bring the two old dresser mirrors and her boxes of collections to her bed. She would select beads and single earrings, bottle tops and shells, dried flowers and pebbles, old postcards and scraps, all sorts of oddments; then she and Susan would play Kingdom, setting up landscapes and furniture, peopling them with action.

Those were the only times of peaceful companionship between her and Susan. I have edged away from it, that poisonous feeling between them, that terrible balancing of hurts and needs I had to do between the two, and did so badly, those earlier years.

Oh there are conflicts between the others too, each one human, needing, demanding, hurting, taking—but only between Emily and Susan, no, Emily toward Susan that corroding resentment. It seems so obvious on the surface, yet it is not obvious. Susan, the second child, Susan, golden- and curly-haired and chubby, quick and articulate and assured, everything in appearance and manner Emily was not; Susan, not able to resist Emily's precious things, losing or sometimes clumsily breaking them; Susan telling jokes and riddles to company for applause while Emily sat silent (to say to me later: that was *my* riddle, Mother, I told it to Susan); Susan, who for all the five years' difference in age was just a year behind Emily in developing physically.

I am glad for that slow physical development that widened the difference between her and her contemporaries, though she suffered over it. She was too vulnerable for that terrible world of youthful competition, of preening and parading, of constant measuring of yourself against every other, of envy, "If I had that copper hair," "If I had that skin. . . ." She tormented herself enough about not looking like the others, there was enough of the unsureness, the having to be conscious of words before you speak, the constant caring—what are they thinking of me? without having it all magnified by the merciless physical drives.

Ronnie is calling. He is wet and I change him. It is rare there is such a cry now. That time of motherhood is almost behind me when the ear is not one's own but must always be racked and listening for the child cry, the child call. We sit for a while and I hold him, looking out over the city spread in charcoal with its soft aisles of light. *"Shoogily,"* he breathes and curls closer. I carry him back to bed, asleep. *Shoogily.* A funny word, a family word, inherited from Emily, invented by her to say: *comfort.*

In this and other ways she leaves her seal, I say aloud. And startle at my saying it. What do I mean? What did I start to gather together, to try and make coherent? I was at the terrible, growing years. War years. I do not remember them well. I was working, there were four smaller ones now, there was not time for her. She had to help be a mother, and housekeeper, and shopper. She had to set her seal. Mornings of crisis and near hysteria trying to get lunches packed, hair combed, coats and shoes found, everyone to school or Child Care on time, the baby ready for transportation. And always the paper scribbled on by a smaller one, the book looked at by Susan then mislaid, the homework not done. Running out to that huge school where she was one, she was lost, she was a drop; suffering over the unpreparedness, stammering and unsure in her classes.

There was so little time left at night after the kids were bedded down. She would struggle over books, always eating (it was in those years she developed her enormous appetite that is legendary in our family) and I would be ironing, or preparing food for the next day, or writing V-mail to Bill, or tending the baby. Sometimes, to make me laugh, or out of her despair, she would imitate happenings or types at school.

I think I said once: "Why don't you do something like this in the school amateur show?" One morning she phoned me at work, hardly understandable through the weeping: "Mother, I did it. I won, I won; they gave me first prize; they clapped and clapped and wouldn't let me go."

Now suddenly she was Somebody, and as imprisoned in her difference as she had been in anonymity.

She began to be asked to perform at other high schools, even in colleges, then at city and statewide affairs. The first one we went to, I only recognized her that first moment when thin, shy, she almost drowned herself into the curtains. Then: Was this Emily? The control, the command, the convulsing and deadly clowning, the spell, then the roaring, stamping audience, unwilling to let this rare and precious laughter out of their lives.

Afterwards: You ought to do something about her with a gift like that—but without money or knowing how, what does one do? We have left it all to her, and the gift has as often eddied inside, clogged and clotted, as been used and growing.

She is coming. She runs up the stairs two at a time with her light graceful step, and I know she is happy tonight. Whatever it was that occasioned your call did not happen today.

"Aren't you ever going to finish the ironing, Mother? Whistler painted his mother in a rocker. I'd have to paint mine standing over an ironing board." This is one of her communicative nights and she tells me everything and nothing as she fixes herself a plate of food out of the icebox.

She is so lovely. Why did you want me to come in at all? Why were you concerned? She will find her way.

She starts up the stairs to bed. "Don't get me up with the rest in the morning." "But I thought you were having midterms." "Oh, those," she comes back in, kisses me, and says quite lightly, "in a couple of years when we'll all be atom-dead they won't matter a bit."

She has said it before. She *believes* it. But because I have been dredging the past, and all that compounds a human being is so heavy and meaningful in me, I cannot endure it tonight.

I will never total it all. I will never come in to say: She was a child seldom smiled at. Her father left me before she was a year old. I had to work her first six years when there was work, or I sent her home and to his relatives. There were years she had care she hated. She was dark and thin and foreign-looking in a world where the prestige went to blondeness and curly hair and dimples, she was slow where glibness was prized. She was a child of anxious, not proud, love. We were poor and could not afford for her the soil of easy growth. I was a young mother, I was a distracted mother. There were the other children pushing up, demanding. Her younger sister seemed all that she was not. There were years she did not want me to touch her. She kept too much in herself, her life was such she had to keep too much in herself. My wisdom came too late. She has much to her and probably nothing will come of it. She is a child of her age, of depression, of war, of fear.

Let her be. So all that is in her will not bloom—but in how many does it? There is still enough left to live by. Only help her to know—help make it so there is cause for her to know—that she is more than this dress on the ironing board, helpless before the iron.

1953–1954/1956

Ralph Ellison
b. 1914

When Ralph Ellison published *Invisible Man* in 1952, he was thirty-eight years old. At that time he had published a number of reviews primarily in "little magazines" and radical periodicals, most notably *The New Masses*. He had also published several stories, including "Slick Gonna Learn," "That I had the Wings," "In a Strange Country," "Flying Home," and "King of the Bingo Game." Twelve years after *Invisible Man,* he published *Shadow and Act* (1964), a work that includes several distinguished essays. Since the mid 1950s he has been at work on a second novel, several parts of which have been published. To date, however, Ellison's reputation as one of the major writers of the mid-twentieth century clearly rests on *Invisible Man.* The winner of several prizes when it was published, including the National Book Award for 1953, *Invisible Man* has been widely praised. In a poll of two hundred authors, critics, and editors conducted by *Book Week,* it was selected as the "most distinguished work" published in the United States between 1945 and 1965.

Ralph Waldo Ellison was born in Oklahoma City on March 1, 1914. His father, Lewis Ellison, a native of South Carolina, worked both as a construction foreman and as an independent businessman selling ice and coal. His mother, Ida Milsap Ellison, a native of Mississippi, worked as a maid. Three years after Ellison's birth, his father died, but despite the ensuing poverty, Ellison's family managed to keep him in school, where he was drawn particularly to the study of music, sacred and secular, classical and jazz. By 1933, when he left home to enter Tuskegee Institute, Ellison had had twelve years' instruction in playing the soprano saxophone and several brass instruments. At Tuskegee he studied literature, painting, and photography but still concentrated on music, hoping to become a composer. Forced by lack of funds to quit school after three years, he left for New York, where he worked as a receptionist, file clerk, and factory hand while also playing music and trying to compose it. He also experimented briefly with photography and sculpture. As he came under the influence of Richard Wright and Langston Hughes, however, he began reading more widely, especially the works of the great modernists. In André Malraux he found an interesting merging of literature and politics. In T. S. Eliot's *The Waste Land* he found something that reminded him of the rhythms and allusional density he heard in black music but often missed in black writing. Soon Ellison was also writing. Hoping to combine a commitment to art with a commitment to politics, he found himself working for the WPA Federal Writer's Project and at the same time writing reviews and stories for radical magazines. For a brief period in 1942 and 1943 he was managing editor of *The Negro Quarterly,* a "Review of Negro Life and Culture" that regularly published leftist artists and scholars.

Ellison's political concerns derived in part from the example of his mother, who had been an ardent supporter of Eugene Debs's Socialist party, and they were intensified by his mother's death in 1937. By the time he began writing *Invisible Man* in 1945, however, most organized forms of radical politics had begun to seem to him too restrictive. More and more he was convinced that literature, like music, could capture the revolutionary implications of black life only by discovering techniques commensurate with the complexities of that life. With this emerging conviction came a new mode of fiction that combined elements of "social realism" with elements of "surrealism." In addition to music, which continued strongly to influence his writing, Ellison began to infuse his fiction with black folklore out of a conviction that black folklore captured and conveyed the sense of black experience "with a complexity of vision that seldom gets into our writing." As he labored to write his way through these interrelated shifts, Ellison also began to move away from short fiction toward the novel as his appropriate form. The novel, he says, "is a form which attempts to deal with the contradictions of life and ambivalence and ambiguities of values." On a personal level, the novel seemed to him to provide a means of discovering some deeper, "more universal meaning" in his own experience—in "remembered conversations" and "local customs." Beyond that, on broader social and political levels, the novel seemed to him to provide a way of discovering "the heroic component" of the experience of black people in America. "Let's not forget," he states in *Shadow and Act,* "that the great tragedies not only treat of negative matters, of violence, brutalities, defeats, but they treat them within a context of man's will to act, to challenge reality and to snatch triumph from the teeth of destruction."

Further Reading:
A. Chester and V. Howard, "The Art of Fiction: An Interview," *Paris Review,* Spring 1955.
Ralph Ellison: A Collection of Critical Essays, ed. J. Hersey, 1970.
Twentieth Century Interpretations of Invisible Man, ed. J. M. Reilly, 1970.

Texts:
Invisible Man, 1952.
"Twentieth-Century Fiction and the Black Mask of Humanity" in *Shadow and Act,* 1964.

from Invisible Man

Prologue: ["What Did I Do to Be So Black and Blue?"]

I am an invisible man. No, I am not a spook like those who haunted Edgar Allan Poe; nor am I one of your Hollywood-movie ectoplasms. I am a man of substance, of flesh and bone, fiber and liquids—and I might even be said to possess a mind. I am invisible, understand, simply because people refuse to see me. Like the bodiless heads you see sometimes in circus sideshows, it is as though I have been surrounded by mirrors of hard, distorting glass. When they approach me they see only my surroundings, themselves, or figments of their imagination—indeed, everything and anything except me.

Nor is my invisibility exactly a matter of a bio-chemical accident to my epidermis. That invisibility to which I refer occurs because of a peculiar disposition of the eyes of those with whom I come in contact. A matter of the construction of their *inner* eyes, those eyes with which they look through their physical eyes upon reality. I am not complaining, nor am I protesting either. It is sometimes advantageous to be unseen, although it is most often rather wearing on the nerves. Then too, you're constantly being bumped against by those of poor vision. Or again, you often doubt if you really exist. You wonder whether you aren't simply a phantom in other people's minds. Say, a figure in a nightmare which the sleeper tries with all his strength to destroy. It's when you feel like this that, out of resentment, you begin to bump people back. And, let me confess, you feel that way most of the time. You ache with the need to convince yourself that you do exist in the real world, that you're a part of all the sound and anguish, and you strike out with your fists, you curse and you swear to make them recognize you. And, alas, it's seldom successful.

One night I accidentally bumped into a man, and perhaps because of the near darkness he saw me and called me an insulting name. I sprang at him, seized his coat lapels and demanded that he apologize. He was a tall blond man, and as my face came close to his he looked insolently out of his blue eyes and cursed me, his breath hot in my face as he struggled. I pulled his chin down sharp upon the crown of my head, butting him as I had seen the West Indians do, and I felt his flesh tear and the blood gush out, and I yelled, "Apologize! Apologize!" But he continued to curse and struggle, and I butted him again and again until he went down heavily, on his knees, profusely bleeding. I kicked him repeatedly, in a frenzy because he still uttered insults though his lips were frothy with blood. Oh yes, I kicked him! And in my outrage I got out my knife and prepared to slit his throat, right there beneath the lamplight in the deserted street, holding him in the collar with one hand, and opening the knife with my teeth—when it occurred to me that the man had not *seen* me, actually; that he, as far as he knew, was in the midst of a walking nightmare! And I stopped the blade, slicing the air as I pushed him away, letting him fall back to the street. I stared at him hard as the lights of a car stabbed through the darkness. He lay there, moaning on the asphalt; a man almost killed by a phantom. It unnerved me. I was both disgusted and ashamed. I was like a drunken man myself, wavering about on weakened legs. Then I was amused: Something in this man's thick head had sprung out and beaten him within an inch of his life. I began to laugh at this crazy discovery. Would he have awakened at the point of death? Would Death himself have freed him for wakeful living? But I didn't linger. I ran away into the dark, laughing so hard I feared I might rupture myself. The next day I saw his picture in the *Daily News,* beneath a caption stating that he had been "mugged." Poor fool, poor blind fool, I thought with sincere compassion, mugged by an invisible man!

Most of the time (although I do not choose as I once did to deny the violence of my days by ignoring it) I am not so overtly violent. I remember that I am invisible and walk softly so as not to awaken the sleeping ones. Sometimes it is best not to awaken them; there are few things in the world as dangerous as sleepwalkers. I learned in time though that it is possible to carry on a fight against them without their realizing it. For instance, I have been carrying on a fight with Monopolated Light & Power for some time now. I use their service and pay them nothing at all, and they don't know it. Oh, they suspect that power is being drained off, but they don't know where. All they know is that according to the master meter back there in their power station a hell of a lot of free current is disappearing somewhere into the jungle of Harlem. The joke, of course, is that I don't live in Harlem but in a border area. Several years ago (before I discovered the advantages of being invisible) I went through the routine process of buying service and paying their outrageous rates. But no more. I gave up all that, along with my apartment, and my old way of life: That way based upon the fallacious assumption that I, like other men, was visible. Now, aware of my invisibility, I live rent-free in a building rented strictly to whites, in a section of the basement that was shut off and forgotten during the nineteenth century, which I discovered when I was trying to escape in the night from Ras the Destroyer. But that's getting too far ahead of the story, almost to the end, although the end is in the beginning and lies far ahead.

The point now is that I found a home—or a hole in the ground, as you will. Now don't jump to the conclusion that because I call my home a "hole" it is damp and cold like a grave; there are cold holes and warm holes. Mine is a warm hole. And remember, a bear retires to his hole for the winter and lives until spring; then he comes strolling out like the Easter chick breaking from its shell. I say all this to assure you that it is incorrect to assume that, because I'm invisible and live in a hole, I am dead.

I am neither dead nor in a state of suspended animation. Call me Jack-the-Bear, for I am in a state of hibernation.

My hole is warm and full of light. Yes, *full* of light. I doubt if there is a brighter spot in all New York than this hole of mine, and I do not exclude Broadway. Or the Empire State Building on a photographer's dream night. But that is taking advantage of you. Those two spots are among the darkest of our whole civilization —pardon me, our whole *culture* (an important distinction, I've heard)—which might sound like a hoax, or a contradiction, but that (by contradiction, I mean) is how the world moves: Not like an arrow, but a boomerang. (Beware of those who speak of the *spiral* of history; they are preparing a boomerang. Keep a steel helmet handy.) I know; I have been boomeranged across my head so much that I now can see the darkness of lightness. And I love light. Perhaps you'll think it strange that an invisible man should need light, desire light, love light. But maybe it is exactly because I *am* invisible. Light confirms my reality, gives birth to my form. A beautiful girl once told me of a recurring nightmare in which she lay in the center of a large dark room and felt her face expand until it filled the whole room, becoming a formless mass while her eyes ran in bilious jelly up the chimney. And so it is with me. Without light I am not only invisible, but formless as well; and to be unaware of one's form is to live a death. I myself, after existing some twenty years, did not become alive until I discovered my invisibility.

That is why I fight my battle with Monopolated Light & Power. The deeper reason, I mean: It allows me to feel my vital aliveness. I also fight them for taking so much of my money before I learned to protect myself. In my hole in the basement there are exactly 1,369 lights. I've wired the entire ceiling, every inch of it. And not with fluorescent bulbs, but with the older, more-expensive-to-operate kind, the filament type. An act of sabotage, you know. I've already begun to wire the wall. A junk man I know, a man of vision, has supplied me with wire and sockets. Nothing, storm or flood, must get in the way of our need for light and ever more and brighter light. The truth is the light and light is the truth. When I finish all four walls, then I'll start on the floor. Just how that will go, I don't know. Yet when you have lived invisible as long as I have you develop a certain ingenuity. I'll solve the problem. And maybe I'll invent a gadget to place my coffee pot on the fire while I lie in bed, and even invent a gadget to warm my bed—like the fellow I saw in one of the picture magazines who made himself a gadget to warm his shoes! Though invisible, I am in the great American tradition of tinkers. That makes me kin to Ford, Edison and Franklin. Call me, since I have a theory and a concept, a "thinker-tinker." Yes, I'll warm my shoes; they need it, they're usually full of holes. I'll do that and more.

Now I have one radio-phonograph; I plan to have five. There is a certain acoustical deadness in my hole, and when I have music I want to *feel* its vibration, not only with my ear but with my whole body. I'd like to hear five recordings of Louis Armstrong playing and singing "What Did I Do to Be so Black and Blue"—all at the same time. Sometimes now I listen to Louis while I have my favorite dessert of vanilla ice cream and sloe gin. I pour the red liquid over the white mound, watching it glisten and the vapor rising as Louis bends that military instrument into a beam of lyrical sound. Perhaps I like Louis Armstrong because he's made poetry out of being invisible. I think it must be because he's unaware that he *is* invisible. And my own grasp of invisibility aids me to understand his music. Once when I asked for a cigarette, some jokers gave me a reefer, which I lighted when I got home and sat listening to my phonograph. It was a strange evening. Invisibility, let me explain, gives one a slightly different sense of time, you're never quite on the beat. Sometimes you're ahead and sometimes behind. Instead of the swift and imperceptible flowing of time, you are aware of its nodes, those points where time stands still or from which it leaps ahead. And you slip into the breaks and look around. That's what you hear vaguely in Louis' music.

Once I saw a prizefighter boxing a yokel. The fighter was swift and amazingly scientific. His body was one violent flow of rapid rhythmic action. He hit the yokel a hundred times while the yokel held up his arms in stunned surprise. But suddenly the yokel, rolling about in the gale of boxing gloves, struck one blow and knocked science, speed and footwork as cold as a well-digger's posterior. The smart money hit the canvas. The long shot got the nod. The yokel had simply stepped inside of his opponent's sense of time. So under the spell of the reefer I discovered a new analytical way of listening to music. The unheard sounds came through, and each melodic line existed of itself, stood out clearly from all the rest, said its piece, and waited patiently for the other voices to speak. That night I found myself hearing not only in time, but in space as well. I not only entered the music but descended, like Dante, into its depths. And *beneath the swiftness of the hot tempo there was a slower tempo and a cave and I entered it and looked around and heard an old woman singing a spiritual as full of Weltschmerz* [1] *as flamenco, and beneath that lay a still lower level on which I saw a beautiful girl the color of ivory pleading in a voice like my mother's as she stood before a group of slaveowners who bid for her naked body, and below that I found a lower level and a more rapid tempo and I heard someone shout:*

"Brothers and sisters, my text this morning is the 'Blackness of Blackness.'"

And a congregation of voices answered: "That blackness is most black, brother, most black . . ."

"In the beginning . . ."

"At the very start," they cried.

". . . there was blackness . . ."

"Preach it . . ."

". . . and the sun . . ."

"The sun, Lawd . . ."

". . . was bloody red . . ."

"Red . . ."

"Now black is . . ." the preacher shouted.

"Bloody . . ."

"I said black is . . ."

"Preach it, brother . . ."

". . . an' black ain't . . ."

"Red, Lawd, red: He said it's red!"

"Amen, brother . . ."

"Black will git you . . ."

"Yes, it will . . ."

[1] German: "weariness of life"; "pessimistic outlook"; "romantic discontent."

"*. . . an' black won't . . .*"

"*Naw, it won't!*"

"*It do . . .*"

"*It do, Lawd . . .*"

"*. . . an' it don't.*"

"*Halleluiah . . .*"

"*. . . It'll put you, glory, glory, Oh my Lawd, in the* WHALE'S BELLY."

"*Preach it, dear brother . . .*"

"*. . . an' make you tempt . . .*"

"*Good God a-mighty!*"

"*Old Aunt Nelly!*"

"*Black will make you . . .*"

"*Black . . .*"

"*. . . or black will un-make you.*"

"*Ain't it the truth, Lawd?*"

*And at that point a voice of trombone timbre screamed at me, "Git out of here, you fool!
Is you ready to commit treason?"*

*And I tore myself away, hearing the old singer of spirituals moaning, "Go curse your
God, boy, and die."*

I stopped and questioned her, asked her what was wrong.

"*I dearly loved my master, son,*" *she said.*

"*You should have hated him,*" *I said.*

"*He gave me several sons,*" *she said, "and because I loved my sons I learned to love their
father though I hated him too.*"

"*I too have become acquainted with ambivalence,*" *I said. "That's why I'm here.*"

"*What's that?*"

"*Nothing, a word that doesn't explain it. Why do you moan?*"

"*I moan this way 'cause he's dead,*" *she said.*

"*Then tell me, who is that laughing upstairs?*"

"*Them's my sons. They glad.*"

"*Yes, I can understand that too,*" *I said.*

"*I laughs too, but I moans too. He promised to set us free but he never could bring hisself
to do it. Still I loved him . . .*"

"*Loved him? You mean . . . ?*"

"*Oh yes, but I loved something else even more.*"

"*What more?*"

"*Freedom.*"

"*Freedom,*" *I said. "Maybe freedom lies in hating.*"

"*Naw, son, it's in loving. I loved him and give him the poison and he withered away
like a frost-bit apple. Them boys woulda tore him to pieces with they homemade knives.*"

"*A mistake was made somewhere,*" *I said, "I'm confused." And I wished to say other
things, but the laughter upstairs became too loud and moan-like for me and I tried to break
out of it, but I couldn't. Just as I was leaving I felt an urgent desire to ask her what freedom
was and went back. She sat with her head in her hands, moaning softly; her leather-brown
face was filled with sadness.*

"*Old woman, what is this freedom you love so well?*" *I asked around a corner of my mind.
She looked surprised, then thoughtful, then baffled. "I done forgot, son. It's all mixed up.*

First I think it's one thing, then I think it's another. It gits my head to spinning. I guess now it ain't nothing but knowing how to say what I got up in my head. But it's a hard job, son. Too much is done happen to me in too short a time. Hit's like I have a fever. Ever' time I starts to walk my head gits to swirling and I falls down. Or if it ain't that, it's the boys; they gits to laughing and wants to kill up the white folks. They's bitter, that's what they is . . ."

"But what about freedom?"

"Leave me 'lone, boy; my head aches!"

I left her, feeling dizzy myself. I didn't get far.

Suddenly one of the sons, a big fellow six feet tall, appeared out of nowhere and struck me with his fist.

"What's the matter, man?" I cried.

"You made Ma cry!"

"But how?" I said, dodging a blow.

"Askin' her them questions, that's how. Git outa here and stay, and next time you got questions like that, ask yourself!"

He held me in a grip like cold stone, his fingers fastening upon my windpipe until I thought I would suffocate before he finally allowed me to go. I stumbled about dazed, the music beating hysterically in my ears. It was dark. My head cleared and I wandered down a dark narrow passage, thinking I heard his footsteps hurrying behind me. I was sore, and into my being had come a profound craving for tranquillity, for peace and quiet, a state I felt I could never achieve. For one thing, the trumpet was blaring and the rhythm was too hectic. A tom-tom beating like heart-thuds began drowning out the trumpet, filling my ears. I longed for water and I heard it rushing through the cold mains my fingers touched as I felt my way, but I couldn't stop to search because of the footsteps behind me.

"Hey, Ras," I called. "Is it you, Destroyer? Rinehart?"

No answer, only the rhythmic footsteps behind me. Once I tried crossing the road, but a speeding machine struck me, scraping the skin from my leg as it roared past.

Then somehow I came out of it, ascending hastily from this underworld of sound to hear Louis Armstrong innocently asking,

What did I do
To be so black
And blue?[2]

At first I was afraid; this familiar music had demanded action, the kind of which I was incapable, and yet had I lingered there beneath the surface I might have attempted to act. Nevertheless, I know now that few really listen to this music. I sat on the chair's edge in a soaking sweat, as though each of my 1,369 bulbs had everyone become a klieg light in an individual setting for a third degree with Ras and Rinehart in charge. It was exhausting—as though I had held my breath continuously for an hour under the terrifying serenity that comes from days of intense hunger. And yet, it was a strangely satisfying experience for an invisible man to hear the silence of sound. I had discovered unrecognized compulsions of my being—even though I could

---

2. From the song "Black and Blue," by the renowned jazz musician Thomas "Fats" Waller (1904–1943). Armstrong frequently included this lyric in his repertoire.

not answer "yes" to their promptings. I haven't smoked a reefer since, however; not because they're illegal, but because to see around corners is enough (that is not unusual when you are invisible). But to hear around them is too much; it inhibits action. And despite Brother Jack and all that sad, lost period of the Brotherhood, I believe in nothing if not in action.

Please, a definition: A hibernation is a covert preparation for a more overt action.

Besides, the drug destroys one's sense of time completely. If that happened, I might forget to dodge some bright morning and some cluck would run me down with an orange and yellow street car, or a bilious bus! Or I might forget to leave my hole when the moment for action presents itself.

Meanwhile I enjoy my life with the compliments of Monopolated Light & Power. Since you never recognize me even when in closest contact with me, and since, no doubt, you'll hardly believe that I exist, it won't matter if you know that I tapped a power line leading into the building and ran it into my hole in the ground. Before that I lived in the darkness into which I was chased, but now I see. I've illuminated the blackness of my invisibility—and vice versa. And so I play the invisible music of my isolation. The last statement doesn't seem just right, does it? But it is; you hear this music simply because music is heard and seldom seen, except by musicians. Could this compulsion to put invisibility down in black and white be thus an urge to make music of invisibility? But I am an orator, a rabble rouser—Am? I *was,* and perhaps shall be again. Who knows? All sickness is not unto death, neither is invisibility.

I can hear you say, "What a horrible, irresponsible bastard!" And you're right. I leap to agree with you. I am one of the most irresponsible beings that ever lived. Irresponsibility is part of my invisibility; any way you face it, it is a denial. But to whom can I be responsible, and why should I be, when you refuse to see me? And wait until I reveal how truly irresponsible I am. Responsibility rests upon recognition, and recognition is a form of agreement. Take the man whom I almost killed: Who was responsible for that near murder—I? I don't think so, and I refuse it. I won't buy it. You can't give it to me. *He* bumped *me, he* insulted *me.* Shouldn't he, for his own personal safety, have recognized my hysteria, my "danger potential"? He, let us say, was lost in a dream world. But didn't *he* control that dream world—which, alas, is only too real!—and didn't *he* rule me out of it? And if he had yelled for a policeman, wouldn't *I* have been taken for the offending one? Yes, yes, yes! Let me agree with you, I was the irresponsible one; for I should have used my knife to protect the higher interests of society. Some day that kind of foolishness will cause us tragic trouble. All dreamers and sleepwalkers must pay the price, and even the invisible victim is responsible for the fate of all. But I shirked that responsibility; I became too snarled in the incompatible notions that buzzed within my brain. I was a coward . . .

But what did *I* do to be so blue? Bear with me.

Chapter 1: [The Battle Royal]

It goes a long way back, some twenty years. All my life I had been looking for something, and everywhere I turned someone tried to tell me what it was. I accepted their answers too, though they were often in contradiction and even self-contradictory. I was naïve. I was looking for myself and asking everyone except myself questions which I, and only I, could answer. It took me a long time and much painful boomeranging of my expectations to achieve a realization everyone else appears to have been born with: That I am nobody but myself. But first I had to discover that I am an invisible man!

And yet I am no freak of nature, nor of history. I was in the cards, other things having been equal (or unequal) eighty-five years ago. I am not ashamed of my grandparents for having been slaves. I am only ashamed of myself for having at one time been ashamed. About eighty-five years ago they were told that they were free, united with others of our country in everything pertaining to the common good, and, in everything social, separate like the fingers of the hand. And they believed it. They exulted in it. They stayed in their place, worked hard, and brought up my father to do the same. But my grandfather is the one. He was an odd old guy, my grandfather, and I am told I take after him. It was he who caused the trouble. On his deathbed he called my father to him and said, "Son, after I'm gone I want you to keep up the good fight. I never told you, but our life is a war and I have been a traitor all my born days, a spy in the enemy's country ever since I give up my gun back in the Reconstruction. Live with your head in the lion's mouth. I want you to overcome 'em with yeses, undermine 'em with grins, agree 'em to death and destruction, let 'em swoller you till they vomit or bust wide open." They thought the old man had gone out of his mind. He had been the meekest of men. The younger children were rushed from the room, the shades drawn and the flame of the lamp turned so low that it sputtered on the wick like the old man's breathing. "Learn it to the younguns," he whispered fiercely; then he died.

But my folks were more alarmed over his last words than over his dying. It was as though he had not died at all, his words caused so much anxiety. I was warned emphatically to forget what he had said and, indeed, this is the first time it has been mentioned outside the family circle. It had a tremendous effect upon me, however. I could never be sure of what he meant. Grandfather had been a quiet old man who never made any trouble, yet on his deathbed he had called himself a traitor and a spy, and he had spoken of his meekness as a dangerous activity. It became a constant puzzle which lay unanswered in the back of my mind. And whenever things went well for me I remembered my grandfather and felt guilty and uncomfortable. It was as though I was carrying out his advice in spite of myself. And to make it worse, everyone loved me for it. I was praised by the most lily-white men of the town. I was considered an example of desirable conduct—just as my grandfather had been. And what puzzled me was that the old man had defined it as *treachery*. When I was praised for my conduct I felt a guilt that in some way I was doing something that was really against the wishes of the white folks, that if they had understood they would have desired me to act just the opposite, that I should have been sulky and mean, and that that really would have been what they wanted, even though they were fooled and thought they wanted me to act as I did. It made me afraid that some day they would look upon me as a traitor and I would be lost. Still I was more afraid to act any other way because they didn't like that at all. The old man's words were like a curse. On my graduation day I delivered an oration in which I showed that humility was the secret, indeed, the very essence of progress. (Not that I believed this—how could I, remembering my grandfather?—I only believed that it worked.) It was a great success. Everyone praised me and I was invited to give the speech at a gathering of the town's leading white citizens. It was a triumph for our whole community.

It was in the main ballroom of the leading hotel. When I got there I discovered that it was on the occasion of a smoker, and I was told that since I was to be there anyway I might as well take part in the battle royal to be fought by some of my schoolmates as part of the entertainment. The battle royal came first.

All of the town's big shots were there in their tuxedoes, wolfing down the buffet foods, drinking beer and whiskey and smoking black cigars. It was a large room with a high ceiling. Chairs were arranged in neat rows around three sides of a portable boxing ring. The fourth side was clear, revealing a gleaming space of polished floor. I had some misgivings over the battle royal, by the way. Not from a distaste for fighting, but because I didn't care too much for the other fellows who were to take part. They were tough guys who seemed to have no grandfather's curse worrying their minds. No one could mistake their toughness. And besides, I suspected that fighting a battle royal might detract from the dignity of my speech. In those pre-invisible days I visualized myself as a potential Booker T. Washington. But the other fellows didn't care too much for me either, and there were nine of them. I felt superior to them in my way, and I didn't like the manner in which we were all crowded together into the servants' elevator. Nor did they like my being there. In fact, as the warmly lighted floors flashed past the elevator we had words over the fact that I, by taking part in the fight, had knocked one of their friends out of a night's work.

We were led out of the elevator through a rococo hall into an anteroom and told to get into our fighting togs. Each of us was issued a pair of boxing gloves and ushered out into the big mirrored hall, which we entered looking cautiously about us and whispering, lest we might accidentally be heard above the noise of the room. It was foggy with cigar smoke. And already the whiskey was taking effect. I was shocked to see some of the most important men of the town quite tipsy. They were all there —bankers, lawyers, judges, doctors, fire chiefs, teachers, merchants. Even one of the more fashionable pastors. Something we could not see was going on up front. A clarinet was vibrating sensuously and the men were standing up and moving eagerly forward. We were a small tight group, clustered together, our bare upper bodies touching and shining with anticipatory sweat; while up front the big shots were becoming increasingly excited over something we still could not see. Suddenly I heard the school superintendent, who had told me to come, yell, "Bring up the shines, gentlemen! Bring up the little shines!"

We were rushed up to the front of the ballroom, where it smelled even more strongly of tobacco and whiskey. Then we were pushed into place. I almost wet my pants. A sea of faces, some hostile, some amused, ringed around us, and in the center, facing us, stood a magnificent blonde—stark naked. There was dead silence. I felt a blast of cold air chill me. I tried to back away, but they were behind me and around me. Some of the boys stood with lowered heads, trembling. I felt a wave of irrational guilt and fear. My teeth chattered, my skin turned to goose flesh, my knees knocked. Yet I was strongly attracted and looked in spite of myself. Had the price of looking been blindness, I would have looked. The hair was yellow like that of a circus kewpie doll, the face heavily powdered and rouged, as though to form an abstract mask, the eyes hollow and smeared a cool blue, the color of a baboon's butt. I felt a desire to spit upon her as my eyes brushed slowly over her body. Her breasts were firm and round as the domes of East Indian temples, and I stood so close as to see the fine skin texture and beads of pearly perspiration glistening like dew around the pink and erected buds of her nipples. I wanted at one and the same time to run from the room, to sink through the floor, or go to her and cover her from my eyes and the eyes of the others with my body; to feel the soft thighs, to caress her and destroy her, to love her and murder her, to hide from her, and yet to stroke where below the small American flag tattooed upon her belly her thighs formed a capital V. I had a notion that of all in the room she saw only me with her impersonal eyes.

And then she began to dance, a slow sensuous movement; the smoke of a hundred cigars clinging to her like the thinnest of veils. She seemed like a fair bird-girl girdled in veils calling to me from the angry surface of some gray and threatening sea. I was transported. Then I became aware of the clarinet playing and the big shots yelling at us. Some threatened us if we looked and others if we did not. On my right I saw one boy faint. And now a man grabbed a silver pitcher from a table and stepped close as he dashed ice water upon him and stood him up and forced two of us to support him as his head hung and moans issued from his thick bluish lips. Another boy began to plead to go home. He was the largest of the group, wearing dark red fighting trunks much too small to conceal the erection which projected from him as though in answer to the insinuating low-registered moaning of the clarinet. He tried to hide himself with his boxing gloves.

And all the while the blonde continued dancing, smiling faintly at the big shots who watched her with fascination, and faintly smiling at our fear. I noticed a certain merchant who followed her hungrily, his lips loose and drooling. He was a large man who wore diamond studs in a shirtfront which swelled with the ample paunch underneath, and each time the blonde swayed her undulating hips he ran his hand through the thin hair of his bald head and, with his arms upheld, his posture clumsy like that of an intoxicated panda, wound his belly in a slow and obscene grind. This creature was completely hypnotized. The music had quickened. As the dancer flung herself about with a detached expression on her face, the men began reaching out to touch her. I could see their beefy fingers sink into the soft flesh. Some of the others tried to stop them and she began to move around the floor in graceful circles, as they gave chase, slipping and sliding over the polished floor. It was mad. Chairs went crashing, drinks were spilt, as they ran laughing and howling after her. They caught her just as she reached a door, raised her from the floor, and tossed her as college boys are tossed at a hazing, and above her red, fixed-smiling lips I saw the terror and disgust in her eyes, almost like my own terror and that which I saw in some of the other boys. As I watched, they tossed her twice and her soft breasts seemed to flatten against the air and her legs flung wildly as she spun. Some of the more sober ones helped her to escape. And I started off the floor, heading for the anteroom with the rest of the boys.

Some were still crying and in hysteria. But as we tried to leave we were stopped and ordered to get into the ring. There was nothing to do but what we were told. All ten of us climbed under the ropes and allowed ourselves to be blindfolded with broad bands of white cloth. One of the men seemed to feel a bit sympathetic and tried to cheer us up as we stood with our backs against the ropes. Some of us tried to grin. "See that boy over there?" one of the men said. "I want you to run across at the bell and give it to him right in the belly. If you don't get him, I'm going to get you. I don't like his looks." Each of us was told the same. The blindfolds were put on. Yet even then I had been going over my speech. In my mind each word was as bright as flame. I felt the cloth pressed into place, and frowned so that it would be loosened when I relaxed.

But now I felt a sudden fit of blind terror. I was unused to darkness. It was as though I had suddenly found myself in a dark room filled with poisonous cotton-mouths. I could hear the bleary voices yelling insistently for the battle royal to begin.

"Get going in there!"

"Let me at that big nigger!"

I strained to pick up the school superintendent's voice, as though to squeeze some security out of that slightly more familiar sound.

"Let me at those black sonsabitches!" someone yelled.

"No, Jackson, no!" another voice yelled. "Here, somebody, help me hold Jack."

"I want to get at that ginger-colored nigger. Tear him limb from limb," the first voice yelled.

I stood against the ropes trembling. For in those days I was what they called ginger-colored, and he sounded as though he might crunch me between his teeth like a crisp ginger cookie.

Quite a struggle was going on. Chairs were being kicked about and I could hear voices grunting as with a terrific effort. I wanted to see, to see more desperately than ever before. But the blindfold was tight as a thick skin-puckering scab and when I raised my gloved hands to push the layers of white aside a voice yelled, "Oh, no you don't, black bastard! Leave that alone!"

"Ring the bell before Jackson kills him a coon!" someone boomed in the sudden silence. And I heard the bell clang and the sound of the feet scuffling forward.

A glove smacked against my head. I pivoted, striking out stiffly as someone went past, and felt the jar ripple along the length of my arm to my shoulder. Then it seemed as though all nine of the boys had turned upon me at once. Blows pounded me from all sides while I struck out as best I could. So many blows landed upon me that I wondered if I were not the only blindfolded fighter in the ring, or if the man called Jackson hadn't succeeded in getting me after all.

Blindfolded, I could no longer control my motions. I had no dignity. I stumbled about like a baby or a drunken man. The smoke had become thicker and with each new blow it seemed to sear and further restrict my lungs. My saliva became like hot bitter glue. A glove connected with my head, filling my mouth with warm blood. It was everywhere. I could not tell if the moisture I felt upon my body was sweat or blood. A blow landed hard against the nape of my neck. I felt myself going over, my head hitting the floor. Streaks of blue light filled the black world behind the blindfold. I lay prone, pretending that I was knocked out, but felt myself seized by hands and yanked to my feet. "Get going, black boy! Mix it up!" My arms were like lead, my head smarting from blows. I managed to feel my way to the ropes and held on, trying to catch my breath. A glove landed in my mid-section and I went over again, feeling as though the smoke had become a knife jabbed into my guts. Pushed this way and that by the legs milling around me, I finally pulled erect and discovered that I could see the black, sweat-washed forms weaving in the smoky-blue atmosphere like drunken dancers weaving to the rapid drum-like thuds of blows.

Everyone fought hysterically. It was complete anarchy. Everybody fought every-body else. No group fought together for long. Two, three, four, fought one, then turned to fight each other, were themselves attacked. Blows landed below the belt and in the kidney, with the gloves open as well as closed, and with my eye partly opened now there was not so much terror. I moved carefully, avoiding blows, although not too many to attract attention, fighting from group to group. The boys groped about like blind, cautious crabs crouching to protect their mid-sections, their heads pulled in short against their shoulders, their arms stretched nervously before them, with their fists testing the smoke-filled air like the knobbed feelers of hypersensitive snails. In one corner I glimpsed a boy violently punching the air and heard him scream in pain as he smashed his hand against a ring post. For a second I saw him bent over holding his hand, then going down as a blow caught his unprotected head. I played one group against the other, slipping in and throwing a punch then stepping out of range while pushing the others into the melee to take the blows blindly aimed at me. The smoke was agonizing and there were no rounds, no bells at three minute intervals to relieve our exhaustion. The room spun round me, a swirl of lights, smoke, sweating bodies surrounded by tense white faces. I bled from both nose and mouth, the blood spattering upon my chest.

The men kept yelling, "Slug him, black boy! Knock his guts out!"

"Uppercut him! Kill him! Kill that big boy!"

Taking a fake fall, I saw a boy going down heavily beside me as though we were felled by a single blow, saw a sneaker-clad foot shoot into his groin as the two who had knocked him down stumbled upon him. I rolled out of range, feeling a twinge of nausea.

The harder we fought the more threatening the men became. And yet, I had begun to worry about my speech again. How would it go? Would they recognize my ability? What would they give me?

I was fighting automatically when suddenly I noticed that one after another of the boys was leaving the ring. I was surprised, filled with panic, as though I had been left alone with an unknown danger. Then I understood. The boys had arranged it among themselves. It was the custom for the two men left in the ring to slug it out for the winner's prize. I discovered this too late. When the bell sounded two men in tuxedoes leaped into the ring and removed the blindfold. I found myself facing Tatlock, the biggest of the gang. I felt sick at my stomach. Hardly had the bell stopped ringing in my ears than it clanged again and I saw him moving swiftly toward me. Thinking of nothing else to do I hit him smash on the nose. He kept coming, bringing the rank sharp violence of stale sweat. His face was a black blank of a face, only his eyes alive—with hate of me and aglow with a feverish terror from what had happened to us all. I became anxious. I wanted to deliver my speech and he came at me as though he meant to beat it out of me. I smashed him again and again, taking his blows as they came. Then on a sudden impulse I struck him lightly and as we clinched, I whispered, "Fake like I knocked you out, you can have the prize."

"I'll break your behind," he whispered hoarsely.

"For *them?*"

"For *me,* sonofabitch!"

They were yelling for us to break it up and Tatlock spun me half around with a blow, and as a joggled camera sweeps in a reeling scene, I saw the howling red faces crouching tense beneath the cloud of blue-gray smoke. For a moment the world wavered, unraveled, flowed, then my head cleared and Tatlock bounced before me. That fluttering shadow before my eyes was his jabbing left hand. Then falling forward, my head against his damp shoulder, I whispered,

"I'll make it five dollars more."

"Go to hell!"

But his muscles relaxed a trifle beneath my pressure and I breathed, "Seven?"

"Give it to your ma," he said, ripping me beneath the heart.

And while I still held him I butted him and moved away. I felt myself bombarded with punches. I fought back with hopeless desperation. I wanted to deliver my speech more than anything else in the world, because I felt that only these men could judge truly my ability, and now this stupid clown was ruining my chances. I began fighting carefully now, moving in to punch him and out again with my greater speed. A lucky blow to his chin and I had him going too—until I heard a loud voice yell, "I got my money on the big boy."

Hearing this, I almost dropped my guard. I was confused: Should I try to win against the voice out there? Would not this go against my speech, and was not this a moment for humility, for nonresistance? A blow to my head as I danced about sent my right eye popping like a jack-in-the-box and settled my dilemma. The room went red as I fell. It was a dream fall, my body languid and fastidious as to where to land, until the floor became impatient and smashed up to meet me. A moment later I came to. An hypnotic voice said FIVE emphatically. And I lay there, hazily watching a dark red spot of my own blood shaping itself into a butterfly, glistening and soaking into the soiled gray world of the canvas.

When the voice drawled TEN I was lifted up and dragged to a chair. I sat dazed. My eye pained and swelled with each throb of my pounding heart and I wondered if now I would be allowed to speak. I was wringing wet, my mouth still bleeding. We were grouped along the wall now. The other boys ignored me as they congratulated Tatlock and speculated as to how much they would be paid. One boy whimpered over his smashed hand. Looking up front, I saw attendants in white jackets rolling the portable ring away and placing a small square rug in the vacant space surrounded by chairs. Perhaps, I thought, I will stand on the rug to deliver my speech.

Then the M.C. called to us, "Come on up here boys and get your money."

We ran forward to where the men laughed and talked in their chairs, waiting. Everyone seemed friendly now.

"There it is on the rug," the man said. I saw the rug covered with coins of all dimensions and a few crumpled bills. But what excited me, scattered here and there, were the gold pieces.

"Boys, it's all yours," the man said. "You get all you grab."

"That's right, Sambo," a blond man said, winking at me confidentially.

I trembled with excitement, forgetting my pain. I would get the gold and the bills, I thought. I would use both hands. I would throw my body against the boys nearest me to block them from the gold.

"Get down around the rug now," the man commanded, "and don't anyone touch it until I give the signal."

"This ought to be good," I heard.

As told, we got around the square rug on our knees. Slowly the man raised his freckled hand as we followed it upward with our eyes.

I heard, "These niggers look like they're about to pray!"

Then, "Ready," the man said. "Go!"

I lunged for a yellow coin lying on the blue design of the carpet, touching it and sending a surprised shriek to join those rising around me. I tried frantically to remove my hand but could not let go. A hot, violent force tore through my body, shaking me like a wet rat. The rug was electrified. The hair bristled up on my head as I shook myself free. My muscles jumped, my nerves jangled, writhed. But I saw that this was not stopping the other boys. Laughing in fear and embarrassment, some were holding back and scooping up the coins knocked off by the painful contortions of the others. The men roared above us as we struggled.

"Pick it up, goddamnit, pick it up!" someone called like a bass-voiced parrot. "Go on, get it!"

I crawled rapidly around the floor, picking up the coins, trying to avoid the coppers and to get greenbacks and the gold. Ignoring the shock by laughing, as I brushed the coins off quickly, I discovered that I could contain the electricity—a contradiction, but it works. Then the men began to push us onto the rug. Laughing embarrassedly, we struggled out of their hands and kept after the coins. We were all wet and slippery and hard to hold. Suddenly I saw a boy lifted into the air, glistening with sweat like a circus seal, and dropped, his wet back landing flush upon the charged rug, heard him yell and saw him literally dance upon his back, his elbows beating a frenzied tattoo upon the floor, his muscles twitching like the flesh of a horse stung by many flies. When he finally rolled off, his face was gray and no one stopped him when he ran from the floor amid booming laughter.

"Get the money," the M.C. called. "That's good hard American cash!"

And we snatched and grabbed, snatched and grabbed. I was careful not to come too close to the rug now, and when I felt the hot whiskey breath descend upon me like a cloud of foul air I reached out and grabbed the leg of a chair. It was occupied and I held on desperately.

"Leggo, nigger! Leggo!"

The huge face wavered down to mine as he tried to push me free. But my body was slippery and he was too drunk. It was Mr. Colcord, who owned a chain of movie houses and "entertainment palaces." Each time he grabbed me I slipped out of his hands. It became a real struggle. I feared the rug more than I did the drunk, so I held on, surprising myself for a moment by trying to topple *him* upon the rug. It was such an enormous idea that I found myself actually carrying it out. I tried not to be obvious, yet when I grabbed his leg, trying to tumble him out of the chair, he raised up roaring with laughter, and, looking at me with soberness dead in the eye, kicked me viciously in the chest. The chair leg flew out of my hand and I felt myself going and rolled. It was as though I had rolled through a bed of hot coals. It seemed a whole century would pass before I would roll free, a century in which I was seared through the deepest levels of my body to the fearful breath within me and the breath seared and heated to the point of explosion. It'll all be over in a flash, I thought as I rolled clear. It'll all be over in a flash.

But not yet, the men on the other side were waiting, red faces swollen as though from apoplexy as they bent forward in their chairs. Seeing their fingers coming toward me I rolled away as a fumbled football rolls off the receiver's fingertips, back into the coals. That time I luckily sent the rug sliding out of place and heard the coins ringing against the floor and the boys scuffling to pick them up and the M.C. calling, "All right, boys, that's all. Go get dressed and get your money."

I was limp as a dish rag. My back felt as though it had been beaten with wires.

When we had dressed the M.C. came in and gave us each five dollars, except Tatlock, who got ten for being last in the ring. Then he told us to leave. I was not to get a chance to deliver my speech, I thought. I was going out into the dim alley in despair when I was stopped and told to go back. I returned to the ballroom, where the men were pushing back their chairs and gathering in groups to talk.

The M.C. knocked on a table for quiet. "Gentlemen," he said, "we almost forgot an important part of the program. A most serious part, gentlemen. This boy was brought here to deliver a speech which he made at his graduation yesterday . . ."

"Bravo!"

"I'm told that he is the smartest boy we've got out there in Greenwood. I'm told that he knows more big words than a pocket-sized dictionary."

Much applause and laughter.

"So now, gentlemen, I want you to give him your attention."

There was still laughter as I faced them, my mouth dry, my eye throbbing. I began slowly, but evidently my throat was tense, because they began shouting, "Louder! Louder!"

"We of the younger generation extol the wisdom of that great leader and educator," I shouted, "who first spoke these flaming words of wisdom: 'A ship lost at sea for many days suddenly sighted a friendly vessel. From the mast of the unfortunate vessel was seen a signal: "Water, water; we die of thirst!" The answer from the friendly vessel came back: "Cast down your bucket where you are." The captain of the distressed vessel, at last heeding the injunction, cast down his bucket, and it came up full of fresh sparkling water from the mouth of the Amazon River.' And like him I say, and in his words, 'To those of my race who depend upon bettering their condition in a foreign land, or who underestimate the importance of cultivating friendly relations with the Southern white man, who is his next-door neighbor, I would say: "Cast down your bucket where you are"—cast it down in making friends in every manly way of the people of all races by whom we are surrounded . . .'"

I spoke automatically and with such fervor that I did not realize that the men were still talking and laughing until my dry mouth, filling up with blood from the cut, almost strangled me. I coughed, wanting to stop and go to one of the tall brass, sand-filled spittoons to relieve myself, but a few of the men, especially the superintendent, were listening and I was afraid. So I gulped it down, blood, saliva and all, and continued. (What powers of endurance I had during those days! What enthusiasm! What a belief in the rightness of things!) I spoke even louder in spite of the pain. But still they talked and still they laughed, as though deaf with cotton in dirty ears. So I spoke with greater emotional emphasis. I closed my ears and swallowed blood until I was nauseated. The speech seemed a hundred times as long as before, but I could not leave out a single word. All had to be said, each memorized nuance considered, rendered. Nor was that all. Whenever I uttered a word of three or more syllables a group of voices would yell for me to repeat it. I used the phrase "social responsibility" and they yelled:

"What's that word you say, boy?"

"Social responsibility," I said.

"What?"

"Social . . ."

"Louder."

". . . responsibility."

"More!"

"Respon——"

"Repeat!"

"——sibility."

The room filled with the uproar of laughter until, no doubt, distracted by having to gulp down my blood, I made a mistake and yelled a phrase I had often seen denounced in newspaper editorials, heard debated in private.

"Social . . ."

"What?" they yelled.

". . . equality—"

The laughter hung smokelike in the sudden stillness. I opened my eyes, puzzled. Sounds of displeasure filled the room. The M.C. rushed forward. They shouted hostile phrases at me. But I did not understand.

A small dry mustached man in the front row blared out, "Say that slowly, son!"

"What, sir?"

"What you just said!"

"Social responsibility, sir," I said.

"You weren't being smart, were you, boy?" he said, not unkindly.

"No, sir!"

"You sure that about 'equality' was a mistake?"

"Oh, yes, sir," I said. "I was swallowing blood."

"Well, you had better speak more slowly so we can understand. We mean to do right by you, but you've got to know your place at all times. All right, now, go on with your speech."

I was afraid. I wanted to leave but I wanted also to speak and I was afraid they'd snatch me down.

"Thank you, sir," I said, beginning where I had left off, and having them ignore me as before.

Yet when I finished there was a thunderous applause. I was surprised to see the superintendent come forth with a package wrapped in white tissue paper, and, gesturing for quiet, address the men.

"Gentlemen, you see that I did not overpraise this boy. He makes a good speech and some day he'll lead his people in the proper paths. And I don't have to tell you that that is important in these days and times. This is a good, smart boy, and so to encourage him in the right direction, in the name of the Board of Education I wish to present him a prize in the form of this . . ."

He paused, removing the tissue paper and revealing a gleaming calfskin brief case. ". . . in the form of this first-class article from Shad Whitmore's shop."

"Boy," he said, addressing me, "take this prize and keep it well. Consider it a badge of office. Prize it. Keep developing as you are and some day it will be filled with important papers that will help shape the destiny of your people."

I was so moved that I could hardly express my thanks. A rope of bloody saliva forming a shape like an undiscovered continent drooled upon the leather and I wiped it quickly away. I felt an importance that I had never dreamed.

"Open it and see what's inside," I was told.

My fingers a-tremble, I complied, smelling the fresh leather and finding an official-looking document inside. It was a scholarship to the state college for Negroes. My eyes filled with tears and I ran awkwardly off the floor.

I was overjoyed; I did not even mind when I discovered that the gold pieces I had scrambled for were brass pocket tokens advertising a certain make of automobile.

When I reached home everyone was excited. Next day the neighbors came to congratulate me. I even felt safe from grandfather, whose deathbed curse usually spoiled my triumphs. I stood beneath his photograph with my brief case in hand and smiled triumphantly into his stolid black peasant's face. It was a face that fascinated me. The eyes seemed to follow everywhere I went.

That night I dreamed I was at a circus with him and that he refused to laugh at the clowns no matter what they did. Then later he told me to open my brief case and read what was inside and I did, finding an official envelope stamped with the state seal; and inside the envelope I found another and another, endlessly, and I thought I would fall of weariness. "Them's years," he said. "Now open that one." And I did and in it I found an engraved document containing a short message in letters of gold. "Read it," my grandfather said. "Out loud!"

"To Whom It May Concern," I intoned. "Keep This Nigger-Boy Running."

I awoke with the old man's laughter ringing in my ears.

(It was a dream I was to remember and dream again for many years after. But at that time I had no insight into its meaning. First I had to attend college.)

Epilogue: [Speaking for You]

So there you have all of it that's important. Or at least you *almost* have it. I'm an invisible man and it placed me in a hole—or showed me the hole I was in, if you will—and I reluctantly accepted the fact. What else could I have done? Once you get used to it, reality is as irresistible as a club, and I was clubbed into the cellar before I caught the hint. Perhaps that's the way it had to be; I don't know. Nor do I know whether accepting the lesson has placed me in the rear or in the *avant-garde. That,* perhaps, is a lesson for history, and I'll leave such decisions to Jack and his ilk while I try belatedly to study the lesson of my own life.

Let me be honest with you—a feat which, by the way, I find of the utmost difficulty. When one is invisible he finds such problems as good and evil, honesty and dishonesty, of such shifting shapes that he confuses one with the other, depending upon who happens to be looking through him at the time. Well, now I've been trying to look through myself, and there's a risk in it. I was never more hated than when I tried to be honest. Or when, even as just now I've tried to articulate exactly what I felt to be the truth. No one was satisfied—not even I. On the other hand, I've never been more loved and appreciated than when I tried to "justify" and affirm someone's mistaken beliefs; or when I've tried to give my friends the incorrect absurd answers they wished to hear. In my presence they could talk and agree with themselves, the world was nailed down, and they loved it. They received a feeling of security. But here was the rub: Too often, in order to justify *them,* I had to take myself by the throat and choke myself until my eyes bulged and my tongue hung out and wagged like the door of an empty house in a high wind. Oh, yes, it made them happy and it made me sick. So I became ill of affirmation, of saying "yes" against the nay-saying of my stomach—not to mention my brain.

There is, by the way, an area in which a man's feelings are more rational than his mind, and it is precisely in that area that his will is pulled in several directions at the same time. You might sneer at this, but I know now. I was pulled this way and that for longer than I can remember. And my problem was that I always tried to go in everyone's way but my own. I have also been called one thing and then another while no one really wished to hear what I called myself. So after years of trying to adopt the opinions of others I finally rebelled. I am an *invisible* man. Thus I have come a long way and returned and boomeranged a long way from the point in society toward which I originally aspired.

So I took to the cellar; I hibernated. I got away from it all. But that wasn't enough. I couldn't be still even in hibernation. Because, damn it, there's the mind, the *mind*. It wouldn't let me rest. Gin, jazz and dreams were not enough. Books were not enough. My belated appreciation of the crude joke that had kept me running, was not enough. And my mind revolved again and again back to my grandfather. And, despite the farce that ended my attempt to say "yes" to the Brotherhood,[3] I'm still plagued by his deathbed advice . . . Perhaps he hid his meaning deeper than I thought, perhaps his anger threw me off—I can't decide. Could he have meant—hell, he *must* have meant the principle, that we were to affirm the principle on which the country was built and not the men, or at least not the men who did the violence. Did he mean say "yes" because he knew that the principle was greater than the men, greater than the numbers and the vicious power and all the methods used to corrupt its name? Did he mean to affirm the principle, which they themselves had dreamed into being out of the chaos and darkness of the feudal past, and which they had violated and compromised to the point of absurdity even in their own corrupt minds? Or did he mean that we had to take the responsibility for all of it, for the men as well as the principle, because we were the heirs who must use the principle because no other fitted our needs? Not for the power or for vindication, but because we, with the given circumstance of our origin, could only thus find transcendence? Was it that we of all, we, most of all, had to affirm the principle, the plan in whose name we had been brutalized and sacrificed—not because we would always be weak nor because we were afraid or opportunistic, but because we were older than they, in the sense of what it took to live in the world with others and because they had exhausted in us, some —not much, but some—of the human greed and smallness, yes, and the fear and superstition that had kept them running. (Oh, yes, they're running too, running all over themselves.) Or was it, did he mean that we should affirm the principle because we, through no fault of our own, were linked to all the others in the loud, clamoring semi-visible world, that world seen only as a fertile field for exploitation by Jack and his kind, and with condescension by Norton and his, who were tired of being the mere pawns in the futile game of "making history"? Had he seen that for these too we had to say "yes" to the principle, lest they turn upon us to destroy both it and us?

"Agree 'em to death and destruction," grandfather had advised. Hell, weren't they their own death and their own destruction except as the principle lived in them and in us? And here's the cream of the joke: Weren't we *part of them* as well as apart from them and subject to die when they died? I can't figure it out; it escapes me. But what do *I* really want, I've asked myself. Certainly not the freedom of a Rinehart or the power of a Jack, nor simply the freedom not to run. No, but the next step I couldn't make, so I've remained in the hole.

I'm not blaming anyone for this state of affairs, mind you; nor merely crying *mea*

---

[3] A radical political organization joined by the protagonist, who finally becomes disillusioned with it, at least in part because he discovers that it, too, is racist.

culpa.[4] The fact is that you carry part of your sickness within you, at least I do as an invisible man. I carried my sickness and though for a long time I tried to place it in the outside world, the attempt to write it down shows me that at least half of it lay within me. It came upon me slowly, like that strange disease that affects those black men whom you see turning slowly from black to albino, their pigment disappearing as under the radiation of some cruel, invisible ray. You go along for years knowing something is wrong, then suddenly you discover that you're as transparent as air. At first you tell yourself that it's all a dirty joke, or that it's due to the "political situation." But deep down you come to suspect that you're yourself to blame, and you stand naked and shivering before the millions of eyes who look through you unseeingly. *That* is the real soul-sickness, the spear in the side, the drag by the neck through the mob-angry town, the Grand Inquisition, the embrace of the Maiden, the rip in the belly with the guts spilling out, the trip to the chamber with the deadly gas that ends in the oven so hygienically clean—only it's worse because you continue stupidly to live. But live you must, and you can either make passive love to your sickness or burn it out and go on to the next conflicting phase.

Yes, but what *is* the next phase? How often have I tried to find it! Over and over again I've gone up above to seek it out. For, like almost everyone else in our country, I started out with my share of optimism. I believed in hard work and progress and action, but now, after first being "for" society and then "against" it, I assign myself no rank or any limit, and such an attitude is very much against the trend of the times. But my world has become one of infinite possibilities. What a phrase—still it's a good phrase and a good view of life, and a man shouldn't accept any other; that much I've learned underground. Until some gang succeeds in putting the world in a strait jacket, its definition is possibility. Step outside the narrow borders of what men call reality and you step into chaos—ask Rinehart, he's a master of it—or imagination. That too I've learned in the cellar, and not by deadening my sense of perception; I'm invisible, not blind.

No indeed, the world is just as concrete, ornery, vile and sublimely wonderful as before, only now I better understand my relation to it and it to me. I've come a long way from those days when, full of illusion, I lived a public life and attempted to function under the assumption that the world was solid and all the relationships therein. Now I know men are different and that all life is divided and that only in division is there true health. Hence again I have stayed in my hole, because up above there's an increasing passion to make men conform to a pattern. Just as in my nightmare, Jack and the boys are waiting with their knives, looking for the slightest excuse to . . . well, to "ball the jack,"[5] and I do not refer to the old dance step, although what they're doing is making the old eagle rock dangerously.

Whence all this passion toward conformity anyway?—diversity is the word. Let man keep his many parts and you'll have no tyrant states. Why, if they follow this conformity business they'll end up by forcing me, an invisible man, to become white, which is not a color but the lack of one. Must I strive toward colorlessness? But seriously, and without snobbery, think of what the world would lose if that should happen. America is woven of many strands; I would recognize them and let it so

---

[4] Latin: "my fault" or "mine the guilt."
[5] In this context, to gamble or risk everything on one attempt or effort.

remain. It's "winner take nothing" that is the great truth of our country or of any country. Life is to be lived, not controlled; and humanity is won by continuing to play in face of certain defeat. Our fate is to become one, and yet many—This is not prophecy, but description. Thus one of the greatest jokes in the world is the spectacle of the whites busy escaping blackness and becoming blacker every day, and the blacks striving toward whiteness, becoming quite dull and gray. None of us seems to know who he is or where he's going.

Which reminds me of something that occurred the other day in the subway. At first I saw only an old gentleman who for the moment was lost. I knew he was lost, for as I looked down the platform I saw him approach several people and turn away without speaking. He's lost, I thought, and he'll keep coming until he sees me, then he'll ask his direction. Maybe there's an embarrassment in it if he admits he's lost to a strange white man. Perhaps to lose a sense of *where* you are implies the danger of losing a sense of *who* you are. That must be it, I thought—to lose your direction is to lose your face. So here he comes to ask his direction from the lost, the invisible. Very well, I've learned to live without direction. Let him ask.

But then he was only a few feet away and I recognized him; it was Mr. Norton. The old gentleman was thinner and wrinkled now but as dapper as ever. And seeing him made all the old life live in me for an instant, and I smiled with tear-stinging eyes. Then it was over, dead, and when he asked me how to get to Centre Street, I regarded him with mixed feelings.

"Don't you know me?" I said.

"Should I?" he said.

"You see me?" I said, watching him tensely.

"Why, of course—Sir, do you know the way to Centre Street?"

"So. Last time it was the Golden Day,[6] now it's Centre Street. You've retrenched, sir. But don't you really know who I am?"

"Young man, I'm in a hurry," he said, cupping a hand to his ear. "Why should I know you?"

"Because I'm your destiny."

"My destiny, did you say?" He gave me a puzzled stare, backing away. "Young man, are you well? Which train did you say I should take?"

"I didn't say," I said, shaking my head. "Now, aren't you ashamed?"

"Ashamed? ASHAMED!" he said indignantly.

I laughed, suddenly taken by the idea. "Because, Mr. Norton, if you don't know *where* you are, you probably don't know *who* you are. So you came to me out of shame. You are ashamed, now aren't you?"

"Young man, I've lived too long in this world to be ashamed of anything. Are you light-headed from hunger? How do you know my name?"

"But I'm your destiny, I made you. Why shouldn't I know you?" I said, walking closer and seeing him back against a pillar. He looked around like a cornered animal. He thought I was mad.

---

[6] Early in *Invisible Man*, the protagonist angers the administration of the college he is attending by taking Mr. Norton, a white benefactor of the college, to the Golden Day, a black bar where Mr. Norton is exposed to the underside of Southern black life. The protagonist is then expelled and goes to New York, where most of the action of the novel is set. "The Golden Day" is also the term used by the cultural historian Lewis Mumford to refer to the American Renaissance of 1830–1860.

"Don't be afraid, Mr. Norton," I said. "There's a guard down the platform there. You're safe. Take any train; they all go to the Golden D——"

But now an express had rolled up and the old man was disappearing quite spryly inside one of its doors. I stood there laughing hysterically. I laughed all the way back to my hole.

But after I had laughed I was thrown back on my thoughts—how had it all happened? And I asked myself if it were only a joke and I couldn't answer. Since then I've sometimes been overcome with a passion to return into that "heart of darkness" across the Mason-Dixon line, but then I remind myself that the true darkness lies within my own mind, and the idea loses itself in the gloom. Still the passion persists. Sometimes I feel the need to reaffirm all of it, the whole unhappy territory and all the things loved and unlovable in it, for all of it is part of me. Till now, however, this is as far as I've ever gotten, for all life seen from the hole of invisibility is absurd.

So why do I write, torturing myself to put it down? Because in spite of myself I've learned some things. Without the possibility of action, all knowledge comes to one labeled "file and forget," and I can neither file nor forget. Nor will certain ideas forget me; they keep filing away at my lethargy, my complacency. Why should I be the one to dream this nightmare? Why should I be dedicated and set aside—yes, if not to at least *tell* a few people about it? There seems to be no escape. Here I've set out to throw my anger into the world's face, but now that I've tried to put it all down the old fascination with playing a role returns, and I'm drawn upward again. So that even before I finish I've failed (maybe my anger is too heavy; perhaps, being a talker, I've used too many words). But I've failed. The very act of trying to put it all down has confused me and negated some of the anger and some of the bitterness. So it is that now I denounce and defend, or feel prepared to defend. I condemn and affirm, say no and say yes, say yes and say no. I denounce because though implicated and partially responsible, I have been hurt to the point of abysmal pain, hurt to the point of invisibility. And I defend because in spite of all I find that I love. In order to get some of it down I *have* to love. I sell you no phony forgiveness, I'm a desperate man —but too much of your life will be lost, its meaning lost, unless you approach it as much through love as through hate. So I approach it through division. So I denounce and I defend and I hate and I love.

Perhaps that makes me a little bit as human as my grandfather. Once I thought my grandfather incapable of thoughts about humanity, but I was wrong. Why should an old slave use such a phrase as, "This and this or this has made me more human," as I did in my arena speech? Hell, he never had any doubts about his humanity— that was left to his "free" offspring. He accepted his humanity just as he accepted the principle. It was his, and the principle lives on in all its human and absurd diversity. So now having tried to put it down I have disarmed myself in the process. You won't believe in my invisibility and you'll fail to see how any principle that applies to you could apply to me. You'll fail to see it even though death waits for both of us if you don't. Nevertheless, the very disarmament has brought me to a decision. The hibernation is over. I must shake off the old skin and come up for breath. There's a stench in the air, which, from this distance underground, might be the smell either of death or of spring—I hope of spring. But don't let me trick you, there *is* a death in the smell of spring and in the smell of thee as in the smell of me. And if nothing more, invisibility has taught my nose to classify the stenches of death.

In going underground, I whipped it all except the mind, the *mind*. And the mind that has conceived a plan of living must never lose sight of the chaos against which that pattern was conceived. That goes for societies as well as for individuals. Thus, having tried to give pattern to the chaos which lives within the pattern of your certainties, I must come out, I must emerge. And there's still a conflict within me: With Louis Armstrong one half of me says, "Open the window and let the foul air out," while the other says, "It was good green corn before the harvest." Of course Louie was kidding, *he* wouldn't have thrown old Bad Air out, because it would have broken up the music and the dance, when it was the good music that came from the bell of old Bad Air's horn that counted. Old Bad Air is still around with his music and his dancing and his diversity, and I'll be up and around with mine. And, as I said before, a decision has been made. I'm shaking off the old skin and I'll leave it here in the hole. I'm coming out, no less invisible without it, but coming out nevertheless. And I suppose it's damn well time. Even hibernations can be overdone, come to think of it. Perhaps that's my greatest social crime, I've overstayed my hibernation, since there's a possibility that even an invisible man has a socially responsible role to play.

"Ah," I can hear you say, "so it was all a build-up to bore us with his buggy jiving.[7] He only wanted us to listen to him rave!" But only partially true: Being invisible and without substance, a disembodied voice, as it were, what else could I do? What else but try to tell you what was really happening when your eyes were looking through? And it is this which frightens me:

Who knows but that, on the lower frequencies, I speak for you?

1952

Twentieth-Century Fiction
and the Black Mask of Humanity[*]

Perhaps the most insidious and least understood form of segregation is that of the word. And by this I mean the word in all its complex formulations, from the proverb to the novel and stage play, the word with all its subtle power to suggest and foreshadow overt action while magically disguising the moral consequences of that action and providing it with symbolic and psychological justification. For if the word has the potency to revive and make us free, it has also the power to blind, imprison and destroy.

---

[7] Crazy talk. ("Jive" implies tiresome or misleading talk or actions.)

[*] Ellison's note: "When this essay was published in 1953, it was prefaced with the following note: 'When I started rewriting this essay it occurred to me that its value might be somewhat increased if it remained very much as I wrote it during 1946. For in that form it is what a young member of a minority felt about much of our writing. Thus I've left in much of the bias and short-sightedness, for it says perhaps as much about me as a member of a minority as it does about literature. I hope you still find the essay useful, and I'd like to see an editorial note stating that this is an unpublished piece written not long after the Second World War.'"

The essence of the word is its ambivalence, and in fiction it is never so effective and revealing as when both potentials are operating simultaneously, as when it mirrors both good and bad, as when it blows both hot and cold in the same breath. Thus it is unfortunate for the Negro that the most powerful formulations of modern American fictional words have been so slanted against him that when he approaches for a glimpse of himself he discovers an image drained of humanity.

Obviously the experiences of Negroes—slavery, the grueling and continuing fight for full citizenship since Emancipation, the stigma of color, the enforced alienation which constantly knifes into our natural identification with our country—have not been that of white Americans. And though as passionate believers in democracy Negroes identify themselves with the broader American ideals, their sense of reality springs, in part, from an American experience which most white men not only have not had, but one with which they are reluctant to identify themselves even when presented in forms of the imagination. Thus when the white American, holding up most twentieth-century fiction, says, "This is American reality," the Negro tends to answer (not at all concerned that Americans tend generally to fight against any but the most flattering imaginative depictions of their lives), "Perhaps, but you've left out this, and this, and this. And most of all, what you'd have the world accept as *me* isn't even human."

Nor does he refer only to second-rate works but to those of our most representative authors. Either like Hemingway and Steinbeck (in whose joint works I recall not more than five American Negroes) they tend to ignore them, or like the early Faulkner, who distorted Negro humanity to fit his personal versions of Southern myth, they seldom conceive Negro characters possessing the full, complex ambiguity of the human. Too often what is presented as the American Negro (a most complex example of Western man) emerges an oversimplified clown, a beast or an angel. Seldom is he drawn as that sensitively focused process of opposites, of good and evil, of instinct and intellect, of passion and spirituality, which great literary art has projected as the image of man. Naturally, the attitude of Negroes toward this writing is one of great reservation. Which, indeed, bears out Richard Wright's remark that there is in progress between black and white Americans a struggle over the nature of reality.

Historically this is but a part of that larger conflict between older, dominant groups of white Americans, especially the Anglo-Saxons, on the one hand, and the newer white and non-white groups on the other, over the major group's attempt to impose its ideals upon the rest, insisting that its exclusive image be accepted as *the* image of the American. This conflict should not, however, be misunderstood. For despite the impact of the American idea upon the world, the "American" himself has not (fortunately for the United States, its minorities, and perhaps for the world) been finally defined. So that far from being socially undesirable this struggle between Americans as to what the American is to be is part of that democratic process through which the nation works to achieve itself. Out of this conflict the ideal American character—a type truly great enough to possess the greatness of the land, a delicately poised unity of divergencies—is slowly being born.

But we are concerned here with fiction, not history. How is it then that our naturalistic prose—one of the most vital bodies of twentieth-century fiction, perhaps the brightest instrument for recording sociological fact, physical action, the nuance of speech, yet achieved—becomes suddenly dull when confronting the Negro?

Obviously there is more in this than the mere verbal counterpart of lynching or segregation. Indeed, it represents a projection of processes lying at the very root of American culture and certainly at the central core of its twentieth-century literary forms, a matter having less to do with the mere "reflection" of white racial theories than with processes molding the attitudes, the habits of mind, the cultural atmosphere and the artistic and intellectual traditions that condition men dedicated to democracy to practice, accept and, most crucial of all, often blind themselves to the essentially undemocratic treatment of their fellow citizens.

It should be noted here that the moment criticism approaches Negro-white relationships it is plunged into problems of psychology and symbolic ritual. Psychology, because the distance between Americans, Negroes and whites, is not so much spatial as psychological; while they might dress and often look alike, seldom on deeper levels do they think alike. Ritual, because the Negroes of fiction are so consistently false to human life that we must question just what they truly represent, both in the literary work and in the inner world of the white American.[1]

Despite their billings as images of reality, these Negroes of fiction are counterfeits. They are projected aspects of an internal symbolic process through which, like a primitive tribesman dancing himself into the group frenzy necessary for battle, the white American prepares himself emotionally to perform a social role. These fictive Negroes are not, as sometimes interpreted, simple racial clichés introduced into society by a ruling class to control political and economic realities. For although they are manipulated to that end, such an externally one-sided interpretation relieves the individual of personal responsibility for the health of democracy. Not only does it forget that a democracy is a collectivity of *individuals,* but it never suspects that the tenacity of the stereotype springs exactly from the fact that its function is no less personal than political. Color prejudice springs not from the stereotype alone, but from an internal psychological state; not from misinformation alone, but from an inner need to believe. It thrives not only on the obscene witch-doctoring of men like Jimmy Byrnes and Malan, but upon an inner craving for symbolic magic. The prejudiced individual creates his own stereotypes, very often unconsciously, by reading into situations involving Negroes those stock meanings which justify his emotional and economic needs.

Hence whatever else the Negro stereotype might be as a social instrumentality, it is also a key figure in a magic rite by which the white American seeks to resolve the

[1] Ellison's note: "Perhaps the ideal approach to the work of literature would be one allowing for insight into the deepest psychological motives of the writer at the same time that it examined all external sociological factors operating within a given milieu. For while objectively a social reality, the work of art is, in its genesis, a projection of a deeply personal process, and any approach that ignores the personal at the expense of the social is necessarily incomplete. Thus when we approach contemporary writing from the perspective of segregation, as is commonly done by sociology-minded thinkers, we automatically limit ourselves to one external aspect of a complex whole, which leaves us little to say concerning its personal, internal elements. On the other hand, American writing has been one of the most important twentieth-century literatures, and though negative as a social force it is technically brilliant and emotionally powerful. Hence were we to examine it for its embodiment of these positive values, there would be other more admiring things to be said."

dilemma arising between his democratic beliefs and certain antidemocratic practices, between his acceptance of the sacred democratic belief that all men are created equal and his treatment of every tenth man as though he were not.

Thus on the moral level I propose that we view the whole of American life as a drama acted out upon the body of a Negro giant, who, lying trussed up like Gulliver, forms the stage and the scene upon which and within which the action unfolds. If we examine the beginning of the Colonies, the application of this view is not, in its economic connotations at least, too far-fetched or too difficult to see. For then the Negro's body was exploited as amorally as the soil and climate. It was later, when white men drew up a plan for a democratic way of life, that the Negro began slowly to exert an influence upon America's moral consciousness. Gradually he was recognized as the human factor placed outside the democratic master plan, a human "natural" resource who, so that white men could become more human, was elected to undergo a process of institutionalized dehumanization.

Until the Korean War this moral role had become obscured within the staggering growth of contemporary science and industry, but during the nineteenth century it flared nakedly in the American consciousness, only to be repressed after the Reconstruction. During periods of national crises, when the United States rounds a sudden curve on the pitch-black road of history, this moral awareness surges in the white American's conscience like a raging river revealed at his feet by a lightning flash. Only then is the veil of anti-Negro myths, symbols, stereotypes and taboos drawn somewhat aside. And when we look closely at our literature it is to be seen operating even when the Negro seems most patently the little man who isn't there.

I see no value either in presenting a catalogue of Negro characters appearing in twentieth-century fiction or in charting the racial attitudes of white writers. We are interested not in quantities but in qualities. And since it is impossible here to discuss the entire body of this writing, the next best thing is to select a framework in which the relationships with which we are concerned may be clearly seen. For brevity let us take three representative writers: Mark Twain, Hemingway and Faulkner. Twain for historical perspective and as an example of how a great nineteenth-century writer handled the Negro; Hemingway as the prime example of the artist who ignored the dramatic and symbolic possibilities presented by this theme; and Faulkner as an example of a writer who has confronted Negroes with such mixed motives that he has presented them in terms of both the "good nigger" and the "bad nigger" stereotypes, and who yet has explored perhaps more successfully than anyone else, either white or black, certain forms of Negro humanity.

For perspective let us begin with Mark Twain's great classic, *Huckleberry Finn*. Recall that Huckleberry has run away from his father, Miss Watson and the Widow Douglas (indeed the whole community, in relation to which he is a young outcast) and has with him as companion on the raft upon which they are sailing down the Mississippi the Widow Watson's runaway Negro slave, Jim. Recall, too, that Jim, during the critical moment of the novel, is stolen by two scoundrels and sold to another master, presenting Huck with the problem of freeing Jim once more. Two ways are open: he can rely upon his own ingenuity and "steal" Jim into freedom or he might write the Widow Watson and request reward money to have Jim returned to her. But there is a danger in this course, remember, since the angry widow might sell the slave down the river into a harsher slavery. It is this course which Huck starts to take, but as he composes the letter he wavers.

> "It was a close place." [he tells us] "I took it [the letter] up, and held it in my hand. I was trembling, because I'd got to decide, forever, 'twixt two things, and I knowed it. I studied a minute, sort of holding my breath, and then says to myself:
> " 'Alright, then, I'll *go* to hell'—and tore it up, . . . It was awful thoughts and awful words, but they was said . . . And I let them stay said, and never thought no more about reforming. I shoved the whole thing out of my head and said I would take up wickedness again, which was in my line, being brung up to it, and the other warn't. And for a starter I would . . . steal Jim out of slavery again. . . ."

And a little later, in defending his decision to Tom Sawyer, Huck comments, "I know you'll say it's dirty, low-down business but *I'm* low-down. And I'm going to steal him . . ."

We have arrived at a key point of the novel and, by an ironic reversal, of American fiction, a pivotal moment announcing a change of direction in the plot, a reversal as well as a recognition scene (like that in which Oedipus discovers his true identity) wherein a new definition of necessity is being formulated. Huck Finn has struggled with the problem poised by the clash between property rights and human rights, between what the community considered to be the proper attitude toward an escaped slave and his knowledge of Jim's humanity, gained through their adventures as fugitives together. He has made his decision on the side of humanity. In this passage Twain has stated the basic moral issue centering around Negroes and the white American's democratic ethics. It dramatizes as well the highest point of tension generated by the clash between the direct, human relationships of the frontier and the abstract, inhuman, market-dominated relationships fostered by the rising middle class —which in Twain's day was already compromising dangerously with the most inhuman aspects of the defeated slave system. And just as politically these forces reached their sharpest tension in the outbreak of the Civil War, in *Huckleberry Finn* (both the boy and the novel) their human implications come to sharpest focus around the figure of the Negro.

Huckleberry Finn knew, as did Mark Twain, that Jim was not only a slave but a human being, a man who in some ways was to be envied, and who expressed his essential humanity in his desire for freedom, his will to possess his own labor, in his loyalty and capacity for friendship and in his love for his wife and child. Yet Twain, though guilty of the sentimentality common to humorists, does not idealize the slave. Jim is drawn in all his ignorance and superstition, with his good traits and his bad. He, like all men, is ambiguous, limited in circumstance but not in possibility. And it will be noted that when Huck makes his decision he identifies himself with Jim and accepts the judgment of his superego—that internalized representative of the community—that his action is evil. Like Prometheus, who for mankind stole fire from the gods, he embraces the evil implicit in his act in order to affirm his belief in humanity. Jim, therefore, is not simply a slave, he is a symbol of humanity, and in freeing Jim, Huck makes a bid to free himself of the conventionalized evil taken for civilization by the town.

This conception of the Negro as a symbol of Man—the reversal of what he represents in most contemporary thought—was organic to nineteenth-century literature. It occurs not only in Twain but in Emerson, Thoreau, Whitman and Melville (whose symbol of evil, incidentally, was white), all of whom were men publicly involved in various forms of deeply personal rebellion. And while the Negro and the color black were associated with the concept of evil and ugliness far back in the Christian era, the Negro's emergence as a symbol of value came, I believe, with Rationalism and the rise of the romantic individual of the eighteenth century. This, perhaps, because the romantic was in revolt against the old moral authority, and if he suffered a sense of guilt, his passion for personal freedom was such that he was willing to accept evil (a tragic attitude) even to identifying himself with the "noble slave"—who symbolized the darker, unknown potential side of his personality, that underground side, turgid with possibility, which might, if given a chance, toss a fistful of mud into the sky and create a "shining star."

Even that prototype of the bourgeois, Robinson Crusoe, stopped to speculate as to his slave's humanity. And the rising American industrialists of the late nineteenth century were to rediscover what their European counterparts had learned a century before: that the good man Friday was as sound an investment for Crusoe morally as he was economically, for not only did Friday allow Crusoe to achieve himself by working for him, but by functioning as a living scapegoat to contain Crusoe's guilt over breaking with the institutions and authority of the past, he made it possible to exploit even his guilt economically. The man was one of the first missionaries.

Mark Twain was alive to this irony and refused such an easy (and dangerous) way out. Huck Finn's acceptance of the evil implicit in his "emancipation" of Jim represents Twain's acceptance of his personal responsibility in the condition of society. This was the tragic face behind his comic mask.

But by the twentieth century this attitude of tragic responsibility had disappeared from our literature along with that broad conception of democracy which vitalized the work of our greatest writers. After Twain's compelling image of black and white fraternity the Negro generally disappears from fiction as a rounded human being. And if already in Twain's time a novel which was optimistic concerning a democracy which would include all men could not escape being banned from public libraries, by our day his great drama of interracial fraternity had become, for most Americans at least, an amusing boy's story and nothing more. But, while a boy, Huck Finn has become by the somersault motion of what William Empson terms "pastoral," an embodiment of the heroic, and an exponent of humanism. Indeed, the historical and artistic justification for his adolescence lies in the fact that Twain was depicting a transitional period of American life; its artistic justification is that adolescence is the time of the "great confusion" during which both individuals and nations flounder between accepting and rejecting the responsibilities of adulthood. Accordingly, Huck's relationship to Jim, the river, and all they symbolize, is that of a humanist; in his relation to the community he is an individualist. He embodies the two major conflicting drives operating in nineteenth-century America. And if humanism is man's basic attitude toward a social order which he accepts, and individualism his basic attitude toward one he rejects, one might say that Twain, by allowing these two attitudes to argue dialectically in his work of art, was as highly moral an artist as he was a believer in democracy, and vice versa.

History, however, was to bring an ironic reversal to the direction which Huckleberry Finn chose, and by our day the divided ethic of the community had won out. In contrast with Twain's humanism, individualism was thought to be the only tenable attitude for the artist.

Thus we come to Ernest Hemingway, one of the two writers whose art is based most solidly upon Mark Twain's language, and one who perhaps has done most to extend Twain's technical influence upon our fiction. It was Hemingway who pointed out that all modern American writing springs from *Huckleberry Finn.* (One might add here that equally as much of it derives from Hemingway himself.) But by the twenties the element of rejection implicit in Twain had become so dominant an attitude of the American writer that Hemingway goes on to warn us to "stop where the Nigger Jim is stolen from the boys. That is the real end. The rest is just cheating."

So thoroughly had the Negro, both as man and as a symbol of man, been pushed into the underground of the American conscience that Hemingway missed completely the structural, symbolic and moral necessity for that part of the plot in which the boys rescue Jim. Yet it is precisely this part which gives the novel its significance. Without it, except as a boy's tale, the novel is meaningless. Yet Hemingway, a great artist in his own right, speaks as a victim of that culture of which he is himself so critical, for by his time that growing rift in the ethical fabric pointed out by Twain had become completely sundered—snagged upon the irrepressible moral reality of the Negro. Instead of the single democratic ethic for every man, there now existed two: one, the idealized ethic of the Constitution and the Declaration of Independence, reserved for white men; and the other, the pragmatic ethic designed for Negroes and other minorities, which took the form of discrimination. Twain had dramatized the conflict leading to this division in its earlier historical form, but what was new here was that such a moral division, always a threat to the sensitive man, was ignored by the artist in the most general terms, as when Hemingway rails against the rhetoric of the First World War.

Hemingway's blindness to the moral values of *Huckleberry Finn* despite his sensitivity to its technical aspects duplicated the one-sided vision of the twenties. Where Twain, seeking for what Melville called "the common continent of man," drew upon the rich folklore of the frontier (not omitting the Negro's) in order to "Americanize" his idiom, thus broadening his stylistic appeal, Hemingway was alert only to Twain's technical discoveries—the flexible colloquial language, the sharp naturalism, the thematic potentialities of adolescence. Thus what for Twain was a means to a moral end became for Hemingway an end in itself. And just as the trend toward technique for the sake of technique and production for the sake of the market lead to the neglect of the human need out of which they spring, so do they lead in literature to a marvelous technical virtuosity won at the expense of a gross insensitivity to fraternal values.

It is not accidental that the disappearance of the human Negro from our fiction coincides with the disappearance of deep-probing doubt and a sense of evil. Not that doubt in some form was not always present, as the works of the lost generation, the muckrakers and the proletarian writers make very clear. But it is a shallow doubt, which seldom turns inward upon the writer's own values; almost always it focuses outward, upon some scapegoat with which he is seldom able to identify himself as Huck Finn identified himself with the scoundrels who stole Jim and with Jim himself. This particular naturalism explored everything except the nature of man.

And when the artist would no longer conjure with the major moral problem in American life, he was defeated as a manipulator of profound social passions. In the United States, as in Europe, the triumph of industrialism had repelled the artist with the blatant hypocrisy between its ideals and its acts. But while in Europe the writer became the most profound critic of these matters, in our country he either turned away or was at best half-hearted in his opposition—perhaps because any profound probing of human values, both within himself and within society, would have brought him face to face with the rigidly tabooed subject of the Negro. And now the tradition of avoiding the moral struggle had led not only to the artistic segregation of the Negro but to the segregation of real fraternal, i.e., democratic, values.

The hard-boiled school represented by Hemingway, for instance, is usually spoken of as a product of World War I disillusionment, yet it was as much the product of a tradition which arose even before the Civil War—that tradition of intellectual evasion for which Thoreau criticized Emerson in regard to the Fugitive Slave Law, and which had been growing swiftly since the failure of the ideals in whose name the Civil War was fought. The failure to resolve the problem symbolized by the Negro has contributed indirectly to the dispossession of the artist in several ways. By excluding our largest minority from the democratic process, the United States weakened all national symbols and rendered sweeping public rituals which would dramatize the American dream impossible; it robbed the artist of a body of unassailable public beliefs upon which he could base his art; it deprived him of a personal faith in the ideals upon which society supposedly rested; and it provided him with no tragic mood indigenous to his society upon which he could erect a tragic art. The result was that he responded with an attitude of rejection, which he expressed as artistic individualism. But too often both his rejection and individualism were narrow; seldom was he able to transcend the limitations of pragmatic reality, and the quality of moral imagination —the fountainhead of great art—was atrophied within him.

Malraux has observed that contemporary American writing is the only important literature not created by intellectuals, and that the creators possess "neither the relative historical culture, nor the love of ideas (a prerogative of professors in the United States)" of comparable Europeans. And is there not a connection between the non-intellectual aspects of this writing (though many of the writers are far more intellectual than they admit or than Malraux would suspect) and its creators' rejection of broad social responsibility, between its non-concern with ideas and its failure to project characters who grasp the broad sweep of American life, or who even attempt to state its fundamental problems? And has not this affected the types of heroes of this fiction, is it not a partial explanation of why it has created no characters possessing broad insight into their situations or the emotional, psychological and intellectual complexity which would allow them to possess and articulate a truly democratic world view?

It is instructive that Hemingway, born into a civilization characterized by violence, should seize upon the ritualized violence of the culturally distant Spanish bullfight as a laboratory for developing his style. For it was, for Americans, an amoral violence (though not for the Spaniards) which he was seeking. Otherwise he might have studied that ritual of violence closer to home, that ritual in which the sacrifice is that of a human scapegoat, the lynching bee. Certainly this rite is not confined to the rope as agency, nor to the South as scene, nor even to the Negro as victim.

But let us not confuse the conscious goals of twentieth-century fiction with those of the nineteenth century, let us take it on its own terms. Artists such as Hemingway were seeking a technical perfection rather than moral insight. (Or should we say that theirs was a morality of technique?) They desired a style stripped of unessentials, one that would appeal without resorting to what was considered worn-out rhetoric, or best of all without any rhetoric whatsoever. It was felt that through the default of the powers that ruled society the artist had as his major task the "pictorial presentation of the evolution of a personal problem." Instead of recreating and extending the national myth as he did this, the writer now restricted himself to elaborating his personal myth. And although naturalist in his general style, he was not interested, like Balzac, in depicting a society, or even, like Mark Twain, in portraying the moral situation of a nation. Rather he was engaged in working out a personal problem through the evocative, emotion-charged images and ritual-therapy available through the manipulation of art forms. And while art was still an instrument of freedom, it was now mainly the instrument of a questionable personal freedom for the artist, which too often served to enforce the "unfreedom" of the reader.

This because it is not within the province of the artist to determine whether his work is social or not. Art by its nature *is* social. And while the artist can determine within a certain narrow scope the type of social effect he wishes his art to create, here his will is definitely limited. Once introduced into society, the work of art begins to pulsate with those meanings, emotions, ideas brought to it by its audience and over which the artist has but limited control. The irony of the "lost generation" writers is that while disavowing a social role it was the fate of their works to perform a social function which re-enforced those very social values which they most violently opposed. How could this be? Because in its genesis the work of art, like the stereotype, is personal; psychologically it represents the socialization of some profoundly personal problem involving guilt (often symbolic murder—parricide, fratricide—incest, homosexuality, all problems at the base of personality) from which by expressing them along with other elements (images, memories, emotions, ideas) he seeks transcendence. To be effective as personal fulfillment, if it is to be more than dream, the work of art must simultaneously evoke images of reality and give them formal organization. And it must, since the individual's emotions are formed in society, shape them into socially meaningful patterns (even Surrealism and Dadaism depended upon their initiates). Nor, as we can see by comparing literature with reportage, is this all. The work of literature differs basically from reportage not merely in its presentation of a pattern of events, nor in its concern with emotion (for a report might well be an account of highly emotional events), but in the deep personal necessity which cries full-throated in the work of art and which seeks transcendence in the form of ritual.

Malcolm Cowley, on the basis of the rites which he believes to be the secret dynamic of Hemingway's work, has identified him with Poe, Hawthorne and Melville, "the haunted and nocturnal writers," he calls them, "the men who dealt with images that were symbols of an inner world." In Hemingway's work, he writes, "we can recognize rites of animal sacrifice . . . of sexual union . . . of conversion . . . and of symbolic death and rebirth." I do not believe, however, that the presence of these rites in writers like Hemingway is as important as the fact that here, beneath the dead-pan prose, the cadences of understatement, the anti-intellectualism, the concern with every "fundamental" of man except that which distinguishes him from the animal—that here is the twentieth-century form of that magical rite which during periods of great art has been to a large extent public and explicit. Here is the literary form by which the personal guilt of the pulverized individual of our rugged era is expatiated: not through his identification with the guilty acts of an Oedipus, a Macbeth or a Medea, by suffering their agony and loading his sins upon their "strong and passionate shoulders," but by being gored with a bull, hooked with a fish, impaled with a grasshopper on a fishhook; not by identifying himself with human heroes, but with those who are indeed defeated.

On the social level this writing performs a function similar to that of the stereotype: it conditions the reader to accept the less worthy values of society, and it serves to justify and absolve our sins of social irresponsibility. With unconscious irony it advises stoic acceptance of those conditions of life which it so accurately describes and which it pretends to reject. And when I read the early Hemingway I seem to be in the presence of Huckleberry Finn who, instead of identifying himself with humanity and attempting to steal Jim free, chose to write the letter which sent him back into slavery. So that now he is a Huck full of regret and nostalgia, suffering a sense of guilt that fills even his noondays with nightmares, and against which, like a terrified child avoiding the cracks in the sidewalk, he seeks protection through the compulsive minor rituals of his prose.

The major difference between nineteenth- and twentieth-century writers is not in the latter's lack of personal rituals—a property of all fiction worthy of being termed literature—but in the social effect aroused within their respective readers. Melville's ritual (and his rhetoric) was based upon materials that were more easily available, say, than Hemingway's. They represented a blending of his personal myth with universal myths as traditional as any used by Shakespeare or the Bible, while until *For Whom the Bell Tolls* Hemingway's was weighted on the personal side. The difference in terms of perspective of belief is that Melville's belief could still find a public object. Whatever else his works were "about" they also managed to be about democracy. But by our day the democratic dream had become too shaky a structure to support the furious pressures of the artist's doubt. And as always when the belief which nurtures a great social myth declines, large sections of society become prey to superstition. For man without myth is Othello with Desdemona gone: chaos descends, faith vanishes and superstitions prowl in the mind.

Hard-boiled writing is said to appeal through its presentation of sheer fact, rather than through rhetoric. The writer puts nothing down but what he pragmatically "knows." But actually one "fact" itself—which in literature must be presented simultaneously as image and as event—became a rhetorical unit. And the symbolic ritual which has set off the "fact"—that is, the fact unorganized by vital social myths (which might incorporate the findings of science and still contain elements of mystery) —is the rite of superstition. The superstitious individual responds to the capricious event, the fact that seems to explode in his face through blind fatality. For it is the creative function of myth to protect the individual from the irrational, and since it is here in the realm of the irrational that, impervious to science, the stereotype grows, we see that the Negro stereotype is really an image of the unorganized, irrational forces of American life, forces through which, by projecting them in forms of images of an easily dominated minority, the white individual seeks to be at home in the vast unknown world of America. Perhaps the object of the stereotype is not so much to crush the Negro as to console the white man.

Certainly there is justification for this view when we consider the work of William Faulkner. In Faulkner most of the relationships which we have pointed out between the Negro and contemporary writing comes to focus: the social and the personal, the moral and the technical, the nineteenth-century emphasis upon morality and the modern accent upon the personal myth. And on the strictly literary level he is prolific and complex enough to speak for those Southern writers who are aggressively anti-Negro and for those younger writers who appear most sincerely interested in depicting the Negro as a rounded human being. What is more, he is the greatest artist the South has produced. While too complex to be given more than a glance in these notes, even a glance is more revealing of what lies back of the distortion of the Negro in modern writing than any attempt at a group survey might be.

Faulkner's attitude is mixed. Taking his cue from the Southern mentality in which the Negro is often dissociated into a malignant stereotype (the bad nigger) on the one hand and a benign stereotype (the good nigger) on the other, most often Faulkner presents characters embodying both. The dual function of this dissociation seems to be that of avoiding moral pain and thus to justify the South's racial code. But since such a social order harms whites no less than blacks, the sensitive Southerner, the artist, is apt to feel its effects acutely—and within the deepest levels of his personality. For not only is the social division forced upon the Negro by the ritualized ethic of discrimination, but upon the white man by the strictly enforced set of anti-Negro taboos. The conflict is always with him. Indeed, so rigidly has the recognition of Negro humanity been tabooed that the white Southerner is apt to associate any form of personal rebellion with the Negro. So that for the Southern artist the Negro becomes a symbol of his personal rebellion, his guilt and his repression of it. The Negro is thus a compelling object of fascination, and this we see very clearly in Faulkner.

Sometimes in Faulkner the Negro is simply a villain, but by an unconsciously ironic transvaluation his villainy consists, as with Loosh in *The Unvanquished,* of desiring his freedom. Or again the Negro appears benign, as with Ringo, of the same novel, who uses his talent not to seek personal freedom but to remain the loyal and resourceful retainer. Not that I criticize loyalty in itself, but that loyalty given where one's humanity is unrecognized seems a bit obscene. And yet in Faulkner's story, "The Bear," he brings us as close to the moral implication of the Negro as Twain or Melville. In the famous "difficult" fourth section, which Malcolm Cowley advises us to skip very much as Hemingway would have us skip the end of *Huckleberry Finn*, we find an argument in progress in which one voice (that of a Southern abolitionist) seeks to define Negro humanity against the other's enumeration of those stereotypes which many Southerners believe to be the Negro's basic traits. Significantly the mentor of the young hero of this story, a man of great moral stature, is socially a Negro.

Indeed, through his many novels and short stories, Faulkner fights out the moral problem which was repressed after the nineteenth century, and it was shocking for some to discover that for all his concern with the South, Faulkner was actually seeking out the nature of man. Thus we must turn to him for that continuity of moral purpose which made for the greatness of our classics. As for the Negro minority, he has been more willing perhaps than any other artist to start with the stereotype, accept it as true, and then seek out the human truth which it hides. Perhaps his is the example for our writers to follow, for in his work technique has been put once more to the task of creating value.

Which leaves these final things to be said. First, that this is meant as no plea for white writers to define Negro humanity, but to recognize the broader aspects of their own. Secondly, Negro writers and those of the other minorities have their own task of contributing to the total image of the American by depicting the experience of their own groups. Certainly theirs is the task of defining Negro humanity, as this can no more be accomplished by others than freedom, which must be won again and again each day, can be conferred upon another. A people must define itself, and minorities have the responsibility of having their ideals and images recognized as part of the composite image which is that of the still forming American people.

The other thing to be said is that while it is unlikely that American writing will ever retrace the way to the nineteenth century, it might be worth while to point out that for all its technical experimentation it is nevertheless an ethical instrument, and as such it might well exercise some choice in the kind of ethic it prefers to support. The artist is no freer than the society in which he lives, and in the United States the writers who stereotype or ignore the Negro and other minorities in the final analysis stereotype and distort their own humanity. Mark Twain knew that in *his* America humanity masked its face with blackness.

1946/1953

Bernard Malamud
1914–1986

Bernard Malamud's most memorable characters, like Leo Finkle, the young rabbinical student in "The Magic Barrel," are usually impoverished Jews who lead socially meager lives—losers and loners, the unloved and the loveless. But they are people who also live on the threshold of miracle. Magical intervention operates in Malamud's stories largely for the redemption of lost souls: Leo Finkle's passionless life is transformed by the manipulations of a destitute, shadowy marriage broker, who during the course of the story assumes the mythic proportions of Pan, a trickster, a magician. Yet, unlike most fairy tales, Malamud's stories of the miraculous proceed against a strong undertow of hardheaded skepticism. Miracles do occur, Malamud seems to be saying, but they may only be—in the words of Robert Frost—"a momentary stay against confusion."

Bernard Malamud was born in Brooklyn, New York, on April 26, 1914. The son of comparatively poor Russian-Jewish immigrants, he attended Erasmus Hall High School and received his B.A. in 1936 from New York's City College and his M.A. in 1942 from Columbia University. He taught evening classes in high school English from 1940 to 1949, then took a position as an instructor at Oregon State. Malamud was a member of the American Academy of Arts and Sciences and the National Institute of Arts and Letters, and from 1961 until his death in 1986 he taught "imaginative writing" at Bennington College in Vermont.

Malamud's first novel, *The Natural* (1952), uses a semirealistic and semifantastic re-creation of the world of major league baseball as the background for a predominantly comic exploration of the mythic hero. In his next novel, *The Assistant* (1957), Malamud creates a far more mundane environment—a small Jewish grocery store—as the setting for a tale of oppression and the regenerative power of suffering. Renewal also figures as the theme of the largely satirical novel *A New Life* (1961), in which a young English instructor tries unsuccessfully to break out of the psychological confines of an academic wasteland. Malamud won the National Book Award for his first collection of short stories, *The Magic Barrel* (1958), and both the National Book Award and the Pulitzer Prize for *The Fixer* (1966), a grim parable of human courage set in anti-Semitic Czarist Russia. Malamud's other novels include *Pictures of Fidelman* (1969), a comic story about an art student "ever a sucker for strange beauty and all sorts of experiences"; *The Tenants* (1971), a tense tale of acute loneliness and the uneasy racial relationship between two writers, one white, the other black; *Dubin's Lives* (1979), a story of infidelity and insight; and *God's Grace* (1982), a visionary account of the end of the world and two shipwrecked survivors—a Jewish paleologist and a talking (and talkative) chimpanzee. Among Malamud's collections of short stories are *Idiots First* (1963) and *Rembrandt's Hat* (1973). *The Stories of Bernard Malamud* appeared in 1983.

At the heart of Malamud's fiction is a characteristically Yiddish interplay between inscrutable suffering and deadpan humor, one that finds expression in such old Yiddish proverbs as "God will provide—but if only He would till He does!" Malamud's writing is pervaded with references to the Old Testament, but if he were to re-create the Book of Job, it would most likely feature Charlie Chaplin. Malamud, in fact, claimed that as a writer he learned a great deal from Chaplin's films: "The rhythm, the snap of comedy; the reserved comic presence—that beautiful distancing; the funny with the sad; the surprise of surprise." And like Chaplin's comedy, Malamud's fiction holds us in a suspended state of disequilibrium, where the emotional tempo alternates between hurting and joking. In *God's Grace,* Calvin Cohn, the last man on earth, faces the Divine wrath: "He danced in a shower of rocks; but that may have been his imagining. Yet those that hit the head hurt."

Further Reading:
S. Cohen, *Bernard Malamud and the Trial by Love*, 1974.
R. Ducharme, *Art and Idea in the Novels of Bernard Malamud*, 1974.
R. Astro and J. Benson, eds., *The Fiction of Bernard Malamud*, 1977.

Text:
The Magic Barrel, 1958.

The Magic Barrel

Not long ago there lived in uptown New York, in a small, almost meager room, though crowded with books, Leo Finkle, a rabbinical student in the Yeshiva University. Finkle, after six years of study, was to be ordained in June and had been advised by an acquaintance that he might find it easier to win himself a congregation if he were married. Since he had no present prospects of marriage, after two tormented days of turning it over in his mind, he called in Pinye Salzman, a marriage broker whose two-line advertisement he had read in the *Forward.*

The matchmaker appeared one night out of the dark fourth-floor hallway of the graystone rooming house where Finkle lived, grasping a black, strapped portfolio that had been worn thin with use. Salzman, who had been long in the business, was of slight but dignified build, wearing an old hat, and an overcoat too short and tight for him. He smelled frankly of fish, which he loved to eat, and although he was missing a few teeth, his presence was not displeasing, because of an amiable manner curiously contrasted with mournful eyes. His voice, his lips, his wisp of beard, his bony fingers were animated, but give him a moment of repose and his mild blue eyes revealed a depth of sadness, a characteristic that put Leo a little at ease although the situation, for him, was inherently tense.

He at once informed Salzman why he had asked him to come, explaining that his home was in Cleveland, and that but for his parents, who had married comparatively late in life, he was alone in the world. He had for six years devoted himself almost entirely to his studies, as a result of which, understandably, he had found himself without time for a social life and the company of young women. Therefore he thought it the better part of trial and error—of embarrassing fumbling—to call in an experienced person to advise him on these matters. He remarked in passing that the function of the marriage broker was ancient and honorable, highly approved in the Jewish community, because it made practical the necessary without hindering joy. Moreover, his own parents had been brought together by a matchmaker. They had made, if not a financially profitable marriage—since neither had possessed any worldly goods to speak of—at least a successful one in the sense of their everlasting devotion to each other. Salzman listened in embarrassed surprise, sensing a sort of apology. Later, however, he experienced a glow of pride in his work, an emotion that had left him years ago, and he heartily approved of Finkle.

The two went to their business. Leo had led Salzman to the only clear place in the room, a table near a window that overlooked the lamp-lit city. He seated himself at the matchmaker's side but facing him, attempting by an act of will to suppress the unpleasant tickle in his throat. Salzman eagerly unstrapped his portfolio and removed a loose rubber band from a thin packet of much-handled cards. As he flipped through them, a gesture and sound that physically hurt Leo, the student pretended not to see and gazed steadfastly out the window. Although it was still February, winter was on its last legs, signs of which he had for the first time in years begun to notice. He now observed the round white moon, moving high in the sky through a cloud menagerie, and watched with half-open mouth as it penetrated a huge hen, and dropped out of her like an egg laying itself. Salzman, though pretending through eyeglasses he had just slipped on to be engaged in scanning the writing on the cards, stole occasional glances at the young man's distinguished face, noting with pleasure the long, severe scholar's nose, brown eyes heavy with learning, sensitive yet ascetic lips, and a certain, almost hollow quality of the dark cheeks. He gazed around at shelves upon shelves of books and let out a soft, contented sigh.

When Leo's eyes fell upon the cards, he counted six spread out in Salzman's hand.

"So few?" he asked in disappointment.

"You wouldn't believe me how much cards I got in my office," Salzman replied. "The drawers are already filled to the top, so I keep them now in a barrel, but is every girl good for a new rabbi?"

Leo blushed at this, regretting all he had revealed of himself in a curriculum vitae he had sent to Salzman. He had thought it best to acquaint him with his strict standards and specifications, but in having done so, felt he had told the marriage broker more than was absolutely necessary.

He hesitantly inquired, "Do you keep photographs of your clients on file?"

"First comes family, amount of dowry, also what kind promises," Salzman replied, unbuttoning his tight coat and settling himself in the chair. "After comes pictures, rabbi."

"Call me Mr. Finkle. I'm not yet a rabbi."

Salzman said he would, but instead called him doctor, which he changed to rabbi when Leo was not listening too attentively.

Salzman adjusted his horn-rimmed spectacles, gently cleared his throat and read in an eager voice the contents of the top card:

"Sophie P. Twenty four years. Widow one year. No children. Educated high school and two years college. Father promises eight thousand dollars. Has wonderful wholesale business. Also real estate. On the mother's side comes teachers, also one actor. Well known on Second Avenue."

Leo gazed up in surprise. "Did you say a widow?"

"A widow don't mean spoiled, rabbi. She lived with her husband maybe four months. He was a sick boy she made a mistake to marry him."

"Marrying a widow has never entered my mind."

"This is because you have no experience. A widow, especially if she is young and healthy like this girl, is a wonderful person to marry. She will be thankful to you the rest of her life. Believe me, if I was looking now for a bride, I would marry a widow."

Leo reflected, then shook his head.

Salzman hunched his shoulders in an almost imperceptible gesture of disappointment. He placed the card down on the wooden table and began to read another:

"Lily H. High school teacher. Regular. Not a substitute. Has savings and new Dodge car. Lived in Paris one year. Father is successful dentist thirty-five years. Interested in professional man. Well-Americanized family. Wonderful opportunity."

"I knew her personally," said Salzman. "I wish you could see this girl. She is a doll. Also very intelligent. All day you could talk to her about books and theyater and what not. She also knows current events."

"I don't believe you mentioned her age?"

"Her age?" Salzman said, raising his brows. "Her age is thirty-two years."

Leo said after a while, "I'm afraid that seems a little too old."

Salzman let out a laugh. "So how old are you, rabbi?"

"Twenty-seven."

"So what is the difference, tell me, between twenty-seven and thirty-two? My own wife is seven years older than me. So what did I suffer?—Nothing. If Rothschild's a daughter wants to marry you, would you say on account her age, no?"

"Yes," Leo said dryly.

Salzman shook off the no in the yes. "Five years don't mean a thing. I give you my word that when you will live with her for one week you will forget her age. What does it mean five years—that she lived more and knows more than somebody who is younger? On this girl, God bless her, years are not wasted. Each one that it comes makes better the bargain."

"What subject does she teach in high school?"

"Languages. If you heard the way she speaks French, you will think it is music. I am in the business twenty-five years, and I recommend her with my whole heart. Believe me, I know what I'm talking, rabbi."

"What's on the next card?" Leo said abruptly.

Salzman reluctantly turned up the third card:

"Ruth K. Nineteen years. Honor student. Father offers thirteen thousand cash to the right bridegroom. He is a medical doctor. Stomach specialist with marvelous practice. Brother in law owns own garment business. Particular people."

Salzman looked as if he had read his trump card.

"Did you say nineteen?" Leo asked with interest.

"On the dot."

"Is she attractive?" He blushed. "Pretty?"

Salzman kissed his finger tips. "A little doll. On this I give you my word. Let me call the father tonight and you will see what means pretty."

But Leo was troubled. "You're sure she's that young?"

"This I am positive. The father will show you the birth certificate."

"Are you positive there isn't something wrong with her?" Leo insisted.

"Who says there is wrong?"

"I don't understand why an American girl her age should go to a marriage broker."

A smile spread over Salzman's face.

"So for the same reason you went, she comes."

Leo flushed. "I am pressed for time."

Salzman, realizing he had been tactless, quickly explained. "The father came, not her. He wants she should have the best, so he looks around himself. When we will locate the right boy he will introduce him and encourage. This makes a better marriage than if a young girl without experience takes for herself. I don't have to tell you this."

"But don't you think this young girl believes in love?" Leo spoke uneasily.

Salzman was about to guffaw but caught himself and said soberly, "Love comes with the right person, not before."

Leo parted dry lips but did not speak. Noticing that Salzman had snatched a glance at the next card, he cleverly asked, "How is her health?"

"Perfect," Salzman said, breathing with difficulty. "Of course, she is a little lame on her right foot from an auto accident that it happened to her when she was twelve years, but nobody notices on account she is so brilliant and also beautiful."

Leo got up heavily and went to the window. He felt curiously bitter and upbraided himself for having called in the marriage broker. Finally, he shook his head.

"Why not?" Salzman persisted, the pitch of his voice rising.

"Because I detest stomach specialists."

"So what do you care what is his business? After you marry her do you need him? Who says he must come every Friday night in your house?"

Ashamed of the way the talk was going, Leo dismissed Salzman, who went home with heavy, melancholy eyes.

Though he had felt only relief at the marraige broker's departure, Leo was in low spirits the next day. He explained it as arising from Salzman's failure to produce a suitable bride for him. He did not care for his type of clientele. But when Leo found himself hesitating whether to seek out another matchmaker, one more polished than Pinye, he wondered if it could be—his protestations to the contrary, and although he honored his father and mother—that he did not, in essence, care for the matchmaking institution? This thought he quickly put out of mind yet found himself still upset. All day he ran around in the woods—missed an important appointment, forgot to give out his laundry, walked out of a Broadway cafeteria without paying and had to run back with the ticket in his hand; had even not recognized his landlady in the street when she passed with a friend and courteously called out, "A good evening to you, Doctor Finkle." By nightfall, however, he had regained sufficient calm to sink his nose into a book and there found peace from his thoughts.

Almost at once there came a knock on the door. Before Leo could say enter, Salzman, commercial cupid, was standing in the room. His face was gray and meager, his expression hungry, and he looked as if he would expire on his feet. Yet the marriage broker managed, by some trick of the muscles, to display a broad smile.

"So good evening. I am invited?"

Leo nodded, disturbed to see him again, yet unwilling to ask the man to leave.

Beaming still, Salzman laid his portfolio on the table. "Rabbi, I got for you tonight good news."

"I've asked you not to call me rabbi. I'm still a student."

"Your worries are finished. I have for you a first-class bride."

"Leave me in peace concerning this subject." Leo pretended lack of interest.

"The world will dance at your wedding."

"Please, Mr. Salzman, no more."

"But first must come back my strength," Salzman said weakly. He fumbled with the portfolio straps and took out of the leather case an oily paper bag, from which he extracted a hard, seeded roll and a small, smoked white fish. With a quick motion of his hand he stripped the fish out of its skin and began ravenously to chew. "All day in a rush," he muttered.

Leo watched him eat.

"A sliced tomato you have maybe?" Salzman hesitantly inquired.

"No."

The marriage broker shut his eyes and ate. When he had finished he carefully cleaned up the crumbs and rolled up the remains of the fish, in the paper bag. His spectacled eyes roamed the room until he discovered, amid some piles of books, a one-burner gas stove. Lifting his hat he humbly asked, "A glass tea you got, rabbi?"

Conscience-stricken, Leo rose and brewed the tea. He served it with a chunk of lemon and two cubes of lump sugar, delighting Salzman.

After he had drunk his tea, Salzman's strength and good spirits were restored.

"So tell me, rabbi," he said amiably, "you considered some more the three clients I mentioned yesterday?"

"There was no need to consider."

"Why not?"

"None of them suits me."

"What then suits you?"

Leo let it pass because he could give only a confused answer.

Without waiting for a reply, Salzman asked, "You remember this girl I talked to you—the high school teacher?"

"Age thirty-two?"

But, surprisingly, Salzman's face lit in a smile. "Age twenty-nine."

Leo shot him a look. "Reduced from thirty-two?"

"A mistake," Salzman avowed. "I talked today with the dentist. He took me to his safety deposit box and showed me the birth certificate. She was twenty-nine years last August. They made her a party in the mountains where she went for her vacation. When her father spoke to me the first time I forgot to write the age and I told you thirty-two, but now I remember this was a different client, a widow."

"The same one you told me about? I thought she was twenty-four?"

"A different. Am I responsible that the world is filled with widows?"

"No, but I'm not interested in them, nor for that matter, in school teachers."

Salzman pulled his clasped hands to his breast. Looking at the ceiling he devoutly exclaimed, "Yiddishe kinder,¹ what can I say to somebody that he is not interested in high school teachers? So what then you are interested?"

Leo flushed but controlled himself.

"In what else will you be interested," Salzman went on, "If you not interested in this fine girl that she speaks four languages and has personally in the bank ten thousand dollars? Also her father guarantees further twelve thousand. Also she has a new car, wonderful clothes, talks on all subjects, and she will give you a first-class home and children. How near do we come in our life to paradise?"

"If she's so wonderful, why wasn't she married ten years ago?"

"Why?" said Salzman with a heavy laugh. "—Why? Because she is *partikiler.* This is why. She wants the *best.*"

Leo was silent, amused at how he had entangled himself. But Salzman had aroused

¹ Yiddish children.

his interest in Lily H., and he began seriously to consider calling on her. When the marriage broker observed how intently Leo's mind was at work on the facts he had supplied, he felt certain they would soon come to an agreement.

Late Saturday afternoon, conscious of Salzman, Leo Finkle walked with Lily Hirschorn along Riverside Drive. He walked briskly and erectly, wearing with distinction the black fedora he had that morning taken with trepidation out of the dusty hat box on his closet shelf, and the heavy black Saturday coat he had thoroughly whisked clean. Leo also owned a walking stick, a present from a distant relative, but quickly put temptation aside and did not use it. Lily, petite and not unpretty, had on something signifying the approach of spring. She was au courant, animatedly, with all sorts of subjects, and he weighed her words and found her surprisingly sound—score another for Salzman, whom he uneasily sensed to be somewhere around, hiding perhaps high in a tree along the street, flashing the lady signals with a pocket mirror; or perhaps a cloven-hoofed Pan, piping nuptial ditties as he danced his invisible way before them, strewing wild buds on the walk and purple grapes in their path, symbolizing fruit of a union, though there was of course still none.

Lily startled Leo by remarking, "I was thinking of Mr. Salzman, a curious figure, wouldn't you say?"

Not certain what to answer, he nodded.

She bravely went on, blushing, "I for one am grateful for his introducing us. Aren't you?"

He courteously replied, "I am."

"I mean," she said with a little laugh—and it was all in good taste, or at least gave the effect of being not in bad—"do you mind that we came together so?"

He was not displeased with her honesty, recognizing that she meant to set the relationship aright, and understanding that it took a certain amount of experience in life, and courage, to want to do it quite that way. One had to have some sort of past to make that kind of beginning.

He said that he did not mind. Salzman's function was traditional and honorable—valuable for what it might achieve, which, he pointed out, was frequently nothing.

Lily agreed with a sigh. They walked on for a while and she said after a long silence, again with a nervous laugh, "Would you mind if I asked you something a little bit personal? Frankly, I find the subject fascinating." Although Leo shrugged, she went on half embarrassedly, "How was it that you came to your calling? I mean was it a sudden passionate inspiration?"

Leo, after a time, slowly replied, "I was always interested in the Law."

"You saw revealed in it the presence of the Highest?"

He nodded and changed the subject. "I understand that you spent a little time in Paris, Miss Hirschorn?"

"Oh, did Mr. Salzman tell you, Rabbi Finkle?" Leo winced but she went on, "It was ages ago and almost forgotten. I remember I had to return for my sister's wedding."

And Lily would not be put off. "When," she asked in a trembly voice, "did you become enamored of God?"

He stared at her. Then it came to him that she was talking not about Leo Finkle, but of a total stranger, some mystical figure, perhaps even passionate prophet that

Salzman had dreamed up for her—no relation to the living or dead. Leo trembled with rage and weakness. The trickster had obviously sold her a bill of goods, just as he had him, who'd expected to become acquainted with a young lady of twenty-nine, only to behold, the moment he laid eyes upon her strained and anxious face, a woman past thirty-five and aging rapidly. Only his self control had kept him this long in her presence.

"I am not," he said gravely, "a talented religious person," and in seeking words to go on, found himself possessed by shame and fear. "I think," he said in a strained manner, "that I came to God not because I loved Him, but because I did not."

This confession he spoke harshly because its unexpectedness shook him.

Lily wilted. Leo saw a profusion of loaves of bread go flying like ducks high over his head, not unlike the winged loaves by which he had counted himself to sleep last night. Mercifully, then, it snowed, which he would not put past Salzman's machinations.

He was infuriated with the marriage broker and swore he would throw him out of the room the minute he reappeared. But Salzman did not come that night, and when Leo's anger had subsided, an unaccountable despair grew in its place. At first he thought this was caused by his disappointment in Lily, but before long it became evident that he had involved himself with Salzman without a true knowledge of his own intent. He gradually realized—with an emptiness that seized him with six hands —that he had called in the broker to find him a bride because he was incapable of doing it himself. This terrifying insight he had derived as a result of his meeting and conversation with Lily Hirschorn. Her probing questions had somehow irritated him into revealing—to himself more than her—the true nature of his relationship to God, and from that it had come upon him, with shocking force, that apart from his parents, he had never loved anyone. Or perhaps it went the other way, that he did not love God so well as he might, because he had not loved man. It seemed to Leo that his whole life stood starkly revealed and he saw himself for the first time as he truly was —unloved and loveless. This bitter but somehow not fully unexpected revelation brought him to a point of panic, controlled only by extraordinary effort. He covered his face with his hands and cried.

The week that followed was the worst of his life. He did not eat and lost weight. His beard darkened and grew ragged. He stopped attending seminars and almost never opened a book. He seriously considered leaving the Yeshiva, although he was deeply troubled at the thought of the loss of all his years of study—saw them like pages torn from a book, strewn over the city—and at the devastating effect of this decision upon his parents. But he had lived without knowledge of himself and never in the Five Books[2] and all the Commentaries—mea culpa[3]—had the truth been revealed to him. He did not know where to turn, and in all this desolating loneliness there was no *to whom,* although he often thought of Lily but not once could bring himself to go downstairs and make the call. He became touchy and irritable, especially with his landlady, who asked him all manner of personal questions; on the other hand, sensing his own disagreeableness, he waylaid her on the stairs and apologized abjectly, until mortified, she ran from him. Out of this, however, he drew the consolation that he

[2] The first five books of the Old Testament, known collectively as the Pentateuch.   [3] Latin: "my fault."

was a Jew and that a Jew suffered. But gradually, as the long and terrible week drew to a close, he regained his composure and some idea of purpose in life: to go on as planned. Although he was imperfect, the ideal was not. As for his quest of a bride, the thought of continuing afflicted him with anxiety and heartburn, yet perhaps with this new knowledge of himself he would be more successful than in the past. Perhaps love would now come to him and a bride to that love. And for this sanctified seeking who needed a Salzman?

The marriage broker, a skeleton with haunted eyes, returned that very night. He looked, withal, the picture of frustrated expectancy—as if he had steadfastly waited the week at Miss Lily Hirschorn's side for a telephone call that never came.

Casually coughing, Salzman came immediately to the point: "So how did you like her?"

Leo's anger rose and he could not refrain from chiding the matchmaker: "Why did you lie to me, Salzman?"

Salzman's pale face went dead white, the world had snowed on him.

"Did you not state that she was twenty-nine?" Leo insisted.

"I give you my word—"

"She was thirty-five, if a day. *At least* thirty-five."

"Of this don't be too sure. Her father told me—"

"Never mind. The worst of it was that you lied to her."

"How did I lie to her, tell me?"

"You told her things about me that weren't true. You made me out to be more, consequently less than I am. She had in mind a totally different person, a sort of semimystical Wonder Rabbi."

"All I said, you was a religious man."

"I can imagine."

Salzman sighed. "This is my weakness that I have," he confessed. "My wife says to me I shouldn't be a salesman, but when I have two fine people that they would be wonderful to be married, I am so happy that I talk too much." He smiled wanly. "This is why Salzman is a poor man."

Leo's anger left him. "Well, Salzman, I'm afraid that's all."

The marriage broker fastened hungry eyes on him.

"You don't want any more a bride?"

"I do," said Leo, "but I have decided to seek her in a different way. I am no longer interested in an arranged marriage. To be frank, I now admit the necessity of premarital love. That is, I want to be in love with the one I marry."

"Love?" said Salzman, astounded. After a moment he remarked, "For us, our love is our life, not for the ladies. In the ghetto they—"

"I know, I know," said Leo. "I've thought of it often. Love, I have said to myself, should be a by-product of living and worship rather than its own end. Yet for myself I find it necessary to establish the level of my need and fulfill it."

Salzman shrugged but answered, "Listen, rabbi, if you want love, this I can find for you also. I have such beautiful clients that you will love them the minute your eyes will see them."

Leo smiled unhappily. "I'm afraid you don't understand."

But Salzman hastily unstrapped his portfolio and withdrew a manila packet from it.

"Pictures," he said, quickly laying the envelope on the table.

Leo called after him to take the pictures away, but as if on the wings of the wind, Salzman had disappeared.

March came. Leo had returned to his regular routine. Although he felt not quite himself yet—lacked energy—he was making plans for a more active social life. Of course it would cost something, but he was an expert in cutting corners; and when there were no corners left he would make circles rounder. All the while Salzman's pictures had lain on the table, gathering dust. Occasionally as Leo sat studying, or enjoying a cup of tea, his eyes fell on the manila envelope, but he never opened it.

The days went by and no social life to speak of developed with a member of the opposite sex—it was difficult, given the circumstances of his situation. One morning Leo toiled up the stairs to his room and stared out the window at the city. Although the day was bright his view of it was dark. For some time he watched the people in the street below hurrying along and then turned with a heavy heart to his little room. On the table was the packet. With a sudden relentless gesture he tore it open. For a half-hour he stood by the table in a state of excitement, examining the photographs of the ladies Salzman had included. Finally, with a deep sigh he put them down. There were six, of varying degrees of attractiveness, but look at them long enough and they all became Lily Hirschorn: all past their prime, all starved behind bright smiles, not a true personality in the lot. Life, despite their frantic yoohooings, had passed them by; they were pictures in a briefcase that stank of fish. After a while, however, as Leo attempted to return the photographs into the envelope, he found in it another, a snapshot of the type taken by a machine for a quarter. He gazed at it a moment and let out a cry.

Her face deeply moved him. Why, he could at first not say. It gave him the impression of youth—spring flowers, yet age—a sense of having been used to the bone, wasted; this came from the eyes, which were hauntingly familiar, yet absolutely strange. He had a vivid impression that he had met her before, but try as he might he could not place her although he could almost recall her name, as if he had read it in her own handwriting. No, this couldn't be; he would have remembered her. It was not, he affirmed, that she had an extraordinary beauty—no, though her face was attractive enough; it was that *something* about her moved him. Feature for feature, even some of the ladies of the photographs could do better; but she leaped forth to his heart—had *lived,* or wanted to—more than just wanted, perhaps regretted how she had lived—had somehow deeply suffered: it could be seen in the depths of those reluctant eyes, and from the way the light enclosed and shone from her, and within her, opening realms of possibility: this was her own. Her he desired. His head ached and eyes narrowed with the intensity of his gazing, then as if an obscure fog had blown up in the mind, he experienced fear of her and was aware that he had received an impression, somehow, of evil. He shuddered, saying softly, it is thus with us all. Leo brewed some tea in a small pot and sat sipping it without sugar, to calm himself. But before he had finished drinking, again with excitement he examined the face and found it good: good for Leo Finkle. Only such a one could understand him and help him seek whatever he was seeking. She might, perhaps, love him. How she had happened to be among the discards in Salzman's barrel he could never guess, but he knew he must urgently go find her.

Leo rushed downstairs, grabbed up the Bronx telephone book, and searched for Salzman's home address. He was not listed, nor was his office. Neither was he in the Manhattan book. But Leo remembered having written down the address on a slip of paper after he had read Salzman's advertisement in the "personals" column of the *Forward*. He ran up to his room and tore through his papers, without luck. It was exasperating. Just when he needed the matchmaker he was nowhere to be found. Fortunately Leo remembered to look in his wallet. There on a card he found his name written and a Bronx address. No phone number was listed, the reason—Leo now recalled—he had originally communicated with Salzman by letter. He got on his coat, put a hat on over his skull cap and hurried to the subway station. All the way to the far end of the Bronx he sat on the edge of his seat. He was more than once tempted to take out the picture and see if the girl's face was as he remembered it, but he refrained, allowing the snapshot to remain in his inside coat pocket, content to have her so close. When the train pulled into the station he was waiting at the door and bolted out. He quickly located the street Salzman had advertised.

The building he sought was less than a block from the subway, but it was not an office building, nor even a loft, nor a store in which one could rent office space. It was a very old tenement house. Leo found Salzman's name in pencil on a soiled tag under the bell and climbed three dark flights to his apartment. When he knocked, the door was opened by a thin, asthmatic, gray-haired woman, in felt slippers.

"Yes?" she said, expecting nothing. She listened without listening. He could have sworn he had seen her, too, before but knew it was an illusion.

"Salzman—does he live here? Pinye Salzman," he said, "the matchmaker?"

She stared at him a long minute. "Of course."

He felt embarrassed. "Is he in?"

"No." Her mouth, though left open, offered nothing more.

"The matter is urgent. Can you tell me where his office is?"

"In the air." She pointed upward.

"You mean he has no office?" Leo asked.

"In his socks."

He peered into the apartment. It was sunless and dingy, one large room divided by a half-open curtain, beyond which he could see a sagging metal bed. The near side of a room was crowded with rickety chairs, old bureaus, a three-legged table, racks of cooking utensils, and all the apparatus of a kitchen. But there was no sign of Salzman or his magic barrel, probably also a figment of the imagination. An odor of frying fish made Leo weak to the knees.

"Where is he?" he insisted. "I've got to see your husband."

At length she answered, "So who knows where he is? Every time he thinks a new thought he runs to a different place. Go home, he will find you."

"Tell him Leo Finkle."

She gave no sign she had heard.

He walked downstairs, depressed.

But Salzman, breathless, stood waiting at his door.

Leo was astounded and overjoyed. "How did you get here before me?"

"I rushed."

"Come inside."

They entered. Leo fixed tea, and a sardine sandwich for Salzman. As they were drinking he reached behind him for the packet of pictures and handed them to the marriage broker.

Salzman put down his glass and said expectantly, "You found somebody you like?"

"Not among these."

The marriage broker turned away.

"Here is the one I want." Leo held forth the snapshot.

Salzman slipped on his glasses and took the picture into his trembling hand. He turned ghastly and let out a groan.

"What's the matter?" cried Leo.

"Excuse me. Was an accident this picture. She isn't for you."

Salzman frantically shoved the manila packet into his portfolio. He thrust the snapshot into his pocket and fled down the stairs.

Leo, after momentary paralysis, gave chase and cornered the marriage broker in the vestibule. The landlady made hysterical outcries but neither of them listened.

"Give me back the picture, Salzman."

"No." The pain in his eyes was terrible.

"Tell me who she is then."

"This I can't tell you. Excuse me."

He made to depart, but Leo, forgetting himself, seized the matchmaker by his tight coat and shook him frenziedly.

"Please," sighed Salzman. *"Please."*

Leo ashamedly let him go. "Tell me who she is," he begged. "It's very important for me to know."

"She is not for you. She is a wild one—wild, without shame. This is not a bride for a rabbi."

"What do you mean wild?"

"Like an animal. Like a dog. For her to be poor was a sin. This is why to me she is dead now."

"In God's name, what do you mean?"

"Her I can't introduce to you," Salzman cried.

"Why are you so excited?"

"Why, he asks," Salzman said, bursting into tears. "This is my baby, my Stella, she should burn in hell."

Leo hurried up to bed and hid under the covers. Under the covers he thought his life through. Although he soon fell asleep he could not sleep her out of his mind. He woke, beating his breast. Though he prayed to be rid of her, his prayers went unanswered. Through days of torment he endlessly struggled not to love her; fearing success, he escaped it. He then concluded to convert her to goodness, himself to God. The idea alternately nauseated and exalted him.

He perhaps did not know that he had come to a final decision until he encountered Salzman in a Broadway cafeteria. He was sitting alone at a rear table, sucking the bony remains of a fish. The marriage broker appeared haggard, and transparent to the point of vanishing.

Salzman looked up at first without recognizing him. Leo had grown a pointed beard and his eyes were weighted with wisdom.

"Salzman," he said, "love has at last come to my heart."

"Who can love from a picture?" mocked the marriage broker.

"It is not impossible."

"If you can love her, then you can love anybody. Let me show you some new clients that they just sent me their photographs. One is a little doll."

"Just her I want," Leo murmured.

"Don't be a fool, doctor. Don't bother with her."

"Put me in touch with her, Salzman," Leo said humbly. "Perhaps I can be of service."

Salzman had stopped eating and Leo understood with emotion that it was now arranged.

Leaving the cafeteria, he was, however, afflicted by a tormenting suspicion that Salzman had planned it all to happen this way.

Leo was informed by letter that she would meet him on a certain corner, and she was there one spring night, waiting under a street lamp. He appeared, carrying a small bouquet of violets and rosebuds. Stella stood by the lamp post, smoking. She wore white with red shoes, which fitted his expectations, although in a troubled moment he had imagined the dress red, and only the shoes white. She waited uneasily and shyly. From afar he saw that her eyes—clearly her father's—were filled with desperate innocence. He pictured, in her, his own redemption. Violins and lit candles revolved in the sky. Leo ran forward with flowers outthrust.

Around the corner, Salzman, leaning against a wall, chanted prayers for the dead.

1954

Saul Bellow
b. 1915

Saul Bellow was born on June 10, 1915, in the small town of Lachine in Quebec, Canada. Nine years later his family—deeply religious Jewish immigrants from St. Petersburg, Russia—moved to Chicago, where Bellow grew up in a multilingual neighborhood. He attended the University of Chicago and in 1935 transferred to Northwestern to study sociology and anthropology. After graduation in 1937, Bellow began working for an advanced degree in anthropology at the University of Wisconsin in Madison, but in 1938 he withdrew and returned to Chicago, hoping to write fiction. Over the next several years he taught school, served briefly in the merchant marine, and worked on the editorial staff of the *Encyclopaedia Britannica,* assembling the index to the Great Books series.

In 1941 Bellow's first story was published. Since that time he has devoted himself to writing, though he has also held a series of university appointments. Bellow taught at the University of Minnesota (1946–1948, 1957–1959); New York University (1950–1951); Princeton University (1952–1953), where he met the poet John Berryman; and Bard College (1953–1954). Between 1948 and 1950

Bellow lived in Paris and traveled in Europe, and afterward he spent over ten years in New York City and Duchess County, New York. He returned to the University of Chicago in 1963 as a professor on the Committee on Social Thought. Bellow has had perhaps the most distinguished literary career of any contemporary novelist in the United States; his numerous honors and awards have included the National Book Award in 1954, 1965, and 1971. In 1976 he became the seventh American writer to win the Nobel Prize.

In the course of reaching a wider American audience than any other major writer of his time, Bellow has clearly marked several modern themes— particularly the theme of the displaced person—as his own. Bellow introduced this theme in his first novel, *Dangling Man* (1944), the story of a man waiting anxiously to be inducted into the army. In that book, narrated, like Sartre's *Nausea* (1938), in the form of a journal, the hero fears the presence of "the unhuman in the all too human city," a fear that is elaborated in Bellow's next two novels, *The Victim* (1947), a story about the personal conflicts between a Jew and a Gentile that tough-mindedly explores the meaning of "human," and *The Adventures of Augie March* (1953), in which Bellow's philosophic sense of what it means to be human is dramatized by the picaresque experiences of a persistently optimistic young Chicago man from an impoverished Jewish family who finds that "you do all you can to humanize and familiarize the world, and suddenly it becomes more strange than ever." At the core of Bellow's next book, *Seize the Day* (1956), a short novel many critics regard as a modern masterpiece, is the unrelievable need for human contact in a world where people feel so displaced that they find it almost impossible to communicate their need even for a simple glass of water. "Nobody truly occupies a station in life any more," we read in Bellow's fifth novel, *Henderson the Rain King* (1958), the story of a Connecticut millionaire who searches for self-understanding in the African jungles. "There are mostly people who feel that they occupy the place that belongs to another by rights. There are displaced persons everywhere."

Bellow's protagonists tend to be social creatures, and urban ones as well. To them, nature remains a largely alien world. Yet the cities where they live are likely to leave them feeling dulled, exhausted, and spent rather than sustained, nourished, or excited. They move amid incessant change, feeling themselves entangled by worlds to which they never quite belong. Like the protagonist of Bellow's next novel, *Herzog* (1964)—an intellectual who lives on the edge of suicide yet refuses to yield to despair—Bellow's main characters retain both a strong sense of family and a strong sense of religion without finding support or consolation in either. Their personalities are often dominated in part by feelings of shame or guilt that they carry as a burden, and in part by a longing for deliverance that they carry as an unfulfilled need. They are characteristically introspective people who, like the elderly hero of *Mr. Sammler's Planet* (1970), have come bitterly to hate modern ideals of self-fulfillment, and they often possess both a disordered sense of history and a fear of social disorder. Like their sense of family and their religious impulses, however, their talent for self-analysis and their sense of history are more often burdens to be borne than blessings to be cherished. "The spirit, the peculiar burden of his existence," we read of Tommy Wilhelm in *Seize the Day*, "lay upon him like an accretion, a load, a hump . . .

of nameless things which it was the business of his life to carry about. That must be what a man was for."

Bellow's tone is sometimes self-mocking and sometimes grandiose—as it can be in *Humboldt's Gift* (1975), the story of a man trying to balance a fast-paced, ambitious life with a "listening soul that can hear the essence of things and comes to understand the marvelous." In most of his fiction Bellow seems determined to discover moral, creative, even noble possibilities among the unpromising displacements that characterize the urban, secular world he so vividly depicts. In his latest novel, *The Dean's December* (1982), he examines the human dislocations of three worlds—the university, the urban streets, and a Communist regime. Bellow has long been fascinated with the ancient myth of the displaced wanderer. In his hands it becomes a story that is at once intensely Jewish, intensely American, and intensely modern.

Further Reading:
R. Dutton, *Saul Bellow*, 1961.
G. L. Harper, "Saul Bellow: An Interview,"
Paris Review, Winter 1965.
J. Clayton, *Saul Bellow, In Defense of Man*,
1967.
I. Malin, *Saul Bellow and the Critics*, 1967.

Text:
Seize the Day, 1961.

Seize the Day

I

When it came to concealing his troubles, Tommy Wilhelm was not less capable than the next fellow. So at least he thought, and there was a certain amount of evidence to back him up. He had once been an actor—no, not quite, an extra—and he knew what acting should be. Also, he was smoking a cigar, and when a man is smoking a cigar, wearing a hat, he has an advantage; it is harder to find out how he feels. He came from the twenty-third floor down to the lobby on the mezzanine to collect his mail before breakfast, and he believed—he hoped—that he looked passably well: doing all right. It was a matter of sheer hope, because there was not much that he could add to his present effort. On the fourteenth floor he looked for his father to enter the elevator: they often met at this hour, on the way to breakfast. If he worried about his appearance it was mainly for his old father's sake. But there was no stop on the fourteenth, and the elevator sank and sank. Then the smooth door opened and the great dark red uneven carpet that covered the lobby billowed toward Wilhelm's feet. In the foreground the lobby was dark, sleepy. French drapes like sails kept out the sun, but three high, narrow windows were open, and in the blue air Wilhelm saw a pigeon about to light on the great chain that supported the marquee of the movie house directly underneath the lobby. For one moment he heard the wings beating strongly.

Most of the guests at the Hotel Gloriana were past the age of retirement. Along

Broadway in the Seventies, Eighties, and Nineties, a great part of New York's vast population of old men and women lives. Unless the weather is too cold or wet they fill the benches about the tiny railed parks and along the subway gratings from Verdi Square to Columbia University, they crowd the shops and cafeterias, the dime stores, the tea-rooms, the bakeries, the beauty parlors, the reading rooms and club rooms. Among these old people at the Gloriana, Wilhelm felt out of place. He was comparatively young, in his middle forties, large and blond, with big shoulders; his back was heavy and strong, if already a little stooped or thickened. After breakfast the old guests sat down on the green leather armchairs and sofas in the lobby and began to gossip and look into the papers; they had nothing to do but wait out the day. But Wilhelm was used to an active life and liked to go out energetically in the morning. And for several months, because he had no position, he had kept up his morale by rising early; he was shaved and in the lobby by eight o'clock. He bought the paper and some cigars and drank a Coca-Cola or two before he went in to breakfast with his father. After breakfast—out, out, out to attend to business. The getting out had in itself become the chief business. But he had realized that he could not keep this up much longer, and today he was afraid. He was aware that his routine was about to break up and he sensed that a huge trouble long presaged but till now formless was due. Before evening, he'd know.

Nevertheless he followed his daily course and crossed the lobby.

Rubin, the man at the newsstand, had poor eyes. They may not have been actually weak but they were poor in expression, with lacy lids that furled down at the corners. He dressed well. It didn't seem necessary—he was behind the counter most of the time —but he dressed very well. He had on a rich brown suit; the cuffs embarrassed the hairs on his small hands. He wore a Countess Mara painted necktie. As Wilhelm approached, Rubin did not see him; he was looking out dreamily at the Hotel Ansonia, which was visible from his corner, several blocks away. The Ansonia, the neighborhood's great landmark, was built by Stanford White.[1] It looks like a baroque palace from Prague or Munich enlarged a hundred times, with towers, domes, huge swells and bubbles of metal gone green from exposure, iron fretwork and festoons. Black television antennae are densely planted on its round summits. Under the changes of weather it may look like marble or like sea water, black as slate in the fog, white as tufa in sunlight. This morning it looked like the image of itself reflected in deep water, white and cumulous above, with cavernous distortions underneath. Together, the two men gazed at it.

Then Rubin said, "Your dad is in to breakfast already, the old gentleman."

"Oh, yes? Ahead of me today?"

"That's a real knocked-out shirt you got on," said Rubin. "Where's it from, Saks?"

"No, it's a Jack Fagman—Chicago."

Even when his spirits were low, Wilhelm could still wrinkle his forehead in a pleasing way. Some of the slow, silent movements of his face were very attractive. He went back a step, as if to stand away from himself and get a better look at his shirt. His glance was comic, a comment upon his untidiness. He liked to wear good clothes, but once he had put it on each article appeared to go its own way. Wilhelm, laughing, panted a little; his teeth were small; his cheeks when he laughed and puffed

---

[1] American architect (1853–1906).

grew round, and he looked much younger than his years. In the old days when he was a college freshman and wore a raccoon coat and a beanie on his large blond head his father used to say that, big as he was, he could charm a bird out of a tree. Wilhelm had great charm still.

"I like this dove-gray color," he said in his sociable, good-natured way: "It isn't washable. You have to send it to the cleaner. It never smells as good as washed. But it's a nice shirt. It cost sixteen, eighteen bucks."

This shirt had not been bought by Wilhelm; it was a present from his boss—his former boss, with whom he had had a falling out. But there was no reason why he should tell Rubin the history of it. Although perhaps Rubin knew—Rubin was the kind of man who knew, and knew and knew. Wilhelm also knew many things about Rubin, for that matter, about Rubin's wife and Rubin's business, Rubin's health. None of these could be mentioned, and the great weight of the unspoken left them little to talk about.

"Well, y'lookin' pretty sharp today," Rubin said.

And Wilhelm said gladly, "Am I? Do you really think so?" He could not believe it. He saw his reflection in the glass cupboard full of cigar boxes, among the grand seals and paper damask and the gold-embossed portraits of famous men, Garcia, Edward the Seventh, Cyrus the Great.[2] You had to allow for the darkness and deformations of the glass, but he thought he didn't look too good. A wide wrinkle like a comprehensive bracket sign was written upon his forehead, the point between his brows, and there were patches of brown on his dark blond skin. He began to be half amused at the shadow of his own marveling, troubled, desirous eyes, and his nostrils and his lips. Fair-haired hippopotamus!—that was how he looked to himself. He saw a big round face, a wide, flourishing red mouth, stump teeth. And the hat, too; and the cigar, too. I should have done hard labor all my life, he reflected. Hard honest labor that tires you out and makes you sleep. I'd have worked off my energy and felt better. Instead, I had to distinguish myself—yet.

He had put forth plenty of effort, but that was not the same as working hard, was it? And if as a young man he had got off to a bad start it was due to this very same face. Early in the nineteen-thirties, because of his striking looks, he had been very briefly considered star material, and he had gone to Hollywood. There for seven years, stubbornly, he had tried to become a screen artist. Long before that time his ambition or delusion had ended, but through pride and perhaps also through laziness he had remained in California. At last he turned to other things, but those seven years of persistence and defeat had unfitted him somehow for trades and businesses, and then it was too late to go into one of the professions. He had been slow to mature, and he had lost ground, and so he hadn't been able to get rid of his energy and he was convinced that this energy itself had done him the greatest harm.

"I didn't see you at the gin game last night," said Rubin.

"I had to miss it. How did it go?"

For the last few weeks Wilhelm had played gin almost nightly, but yesterday he had felt that he couldn't afford to lose any more. He had never won. Not once. And while the losses were small they weren't gains, were they? They were losses. He was

[2] Garcia: Diego Garcia (1471–1529), Portuguese explorer; Edward the Seventh: Edward VII, king of England (1901–1910); Cyrus the Great: king of Persia (550–529 B.C.).

tired of losing, and tired also of the company, and so he had gone by himself to the movies.

"Oh," said Rubin, "it went okay. Carl made a chump of himself yelling at the guys. This time Doctor Tamkin didn't let him get away with it. He told him the psychological reason why."

"What was the reason?"

Rubin said, "I can't quote him. Who could? You know the way Tamkin talks. Don't ask me. Do you want the *Trib?*[3] Aren't you going to look at the closing quotations?"

"It won't help much to look. I know what they were yesterday at three," said Wilhelm. "But I suppose I better had get the paper." It seemed necessary for him to lift one shoulder in order to put his hand into his jacket pocket. There, among little packets of pills and crushed cigarette butts and strings of cellophane, the red tapes of packages which he sometimes used as dental floss, he recalled that he had dropped some pennies.

"That doesn't sound so good," said Rubin. He meant to be conversationally playful, but his voice had no tone and his eyes, slack and lid-blinded, turned elsewhere. He didn't want to hear. It was all the same to him. Maybe he already knew, being the sort of man who knew and knew.

No, it wasn't good. Wilhelm held three orders of lard in the commodities market. He and Dr. Tamkin had bought this lard together four days ago at 12.96, and the price at once began to fall and was still falling. In the mail this morning there was sure to be a call for additional margin payment. One came every day.

The psychologist, Dr. Tamkin, had got him into this. Tamkin lived at the Gloriana and attended the card game. He had explained to Wilhelm that you could speculate in commodities at one of the uptown branches of a good Wall Street house without making the full deposit of margin legally required. It was up to the branch manager. If he knew you—and all the branch managers knew Tamkin—he would allow you to make short-term purchases. You needed only to open a small account.

"The whole secret of this type of speculation," Tamkin had told him, "is in the alertness. You have to act fast—buy it and sell it: sell it and buy in again. But quick! Get to the window and have them wire Chicago at just the right second. Strike and strike again! Then get out the same day. In no time at all you turn over fifteen, twenty thousand dollars' worth of soy beans, coffee, corn, hides, wheat, cotton." Obviously the doctor understood the market well. Otherwise he could not make it sound so simple. "People lose because they are greedy and can't get out when it starts to go up. They gamble, but I do it scientifically. This is not guesswork. You must take a few points and get out. Why, ye gods!" said Dr. Tamkin with his bulging eyes, his bald head, and his drooping lip. "Have you stopped to think how much dough people are making in the market?"

Wilhelm with a quick shift from gloomy attention to the panting laugh which entirely changed his face had said, "Ho, have I ever! What do you think? Who doesn't know it's way beyond nineteen-twenty-eight—twenty-nine and still on the rise? Who hasn't read the Fulbright investigation? There's money everywhere. Everyone is shoveling it in. Money is—is—"

---

[3] New York newspaper, *The Herald Tribune.*

"And can you rest—can you sit still while this is going on?" said Dr. Tamkin. "I confess to you I can't. I think about people, just because they have a few bucks to invest, making fortunes. They have no sense, they have no talent, they just have the extra dough and it makes them more dough. I get so worked up and tormented and restless, so restless! I haven't even been able to practice my profession. With all this money around you don't want to be a fool while everyone else is making. I know guys who make five, ten thousand a week just by fooling around. I know a guy at the Hotel Pierre. There's nothing to him, but he has a whole case of Mumm's champagne at lunch. I know another guy on Central Park South— But what's the use of talking. They make millions. They have smart lawyers who get them out of taxes by a thousand schemes."

"Whereas I got taken," said Wilhelm. "My wife refused to sign a joint return. One fairly good year and I got into the thirty-two-per-cent bracket and was stripped bare. What of all my bad years?"

"It's a businessmen's government," said Dr. Tamkin. "You can be sure that these men making five thousand a week—"

"I don't need that sort of money," Wilhelm had said. "But oh! if I could only work out a little steady income from this. Not much. I don't ask much. But how badly I need—! I'd be so grateful if you'd show me how to work it."

"Sure I will. *I* do it regularly. I'll bring you my receipts if you like. And do you want to know something? I approve of your attitude very much. You want to avoid catching the money fever. This type of activity is filled with hostile feeling and lust. You should see what it does to some of these fellows. They go on the market with murder in their hearts."

"What's that I once heard a guy say?" Wilhelm remarked. "A man is only as good as what he loves."

"That's it—just it," Tamkin said. "You don't have to go about it their way. There's also a calm and rational, a psychological approach."

Wilhelm's father, old Dr. Adler, lived in an entirely different world from his son, but he had warned him once against Dr. Tamkin. Rather casually—he was a very bland old man—he said, "Wilky, perhaps you listen too much to this Tamkin. He's interesting to talk to. I don't doubt it. I think he's pretty common but he's a persuasive man. However, I don't know how reliable he may be."

It made Wilhelm profoundly bitter that his father should speak to him with such detachment about his welfare. Dr. Adler liked to appear affable. Affable! His own son, his one and only son, could not speak his mind or ease his heart to him. I wouldn't turn to Tamkin, he thought, if I could turn to him. At least Tamkin sympathizes with me and tries to give me a hand, whereas Dad doesn't want to be disturbed.

Old Dr. Adler had retired from practice; he had a considerable fortune and could easily have helped his son. Recently Wilhelm had told him, "Father—it so happens that I'm in a bad way now. I hate to have to say it. You realize that I'd rather have good news to bring you. But it's true. And since it's true, Dad—What else am I supposed to say? It's true."

Another father might have appreciated how difficult this confession was—so much bad luck, weariness, weakness, and failure. Wilhelm had tried to copy the old man's tone and made himself sound gentlemanly, low-voiced, tasteful. He didn't allow his voice to tremble; he made no stupid gesture. But the doctor had no answer. He only nodded. You might have told him that Seattle was near Puget Sound, or that the Giants and Dodgers were playing a night game, so little was he moved from his expression of healthy, handsome, good-humored old age. He behaved toward his son as he had formerly done toward his patients, and it was a great grief to Wilhelm; it was almost too much to bear. Couldn't he see—couldn't he feel? Had he lost his family sense?

Greatly hurt, Wilhelm struggled however to be fair. Old people are bound to change, he said. They have hard things to think about. They must prepare for where they are going. They can't live by the old schedule any longer and all their perspectives change, and other people become alike, kin and acquaintances. Dad is no longer the same person, Wilhelm reflected. He was thirty-two when I was born, and now he's going on eighty. Furthermore, it's time I stopped feeling like a kid toward him, a small son.

The handsome old doctor stood well above the other old people in the hotel. He was idolized by everyone. This was what people said: "That's old Professor Adler, who used to teach internal medicine. He was a diagnostician, one of the best in New York, and had a tremendous practice. Isn't he a wonderful-looking old guy? It's a pleasure to see such a fine old scientist, clean and immaculate. He stands straight and understands every single thing you say. He still has all his buttons. You can discuss any subject with him." The clerks, the elevator operators, the telephone girls and waitresses and chambermaids, the management flattered and pampered him. That was what he wanted. He had always been a vain man. To see how his father loved himself sometimes made Wilhelm madly indignant.

He folded over the *Tribune* with its heavy, black, crashing sensational print and read without recognizing any of the words, for his mind was still on his father's vanity. The doctor had created his own praise. People were primed and did not know it. And what did he need praise for? In a hotel where everyone was busy and contacts were so brief and had such small weight, how could it satisfy him? He could be in people's thoughts here and there for a moment; in and then out. He could never matter much to them. Wilhelm let out a long, hard breath and raised the brows of his round and somewhat circular eyes. He stared beyond the thick borders of the paper.

. . . love that well which thou must leave ere long.

Involuntary memory brought him this line. At first he thought it referred to his father, but then he understood that it was for himself, rather. *He* should love that well. "This thou perceivest, which makes *thy* love more strong." Under Dr. Tamkin's influence Wilhelm had recently begun to remember the poems he used to read. Dr. Tamkin knew, or said he knew, the great English poets and once in a while he mentioned a poem of his own. It was a long time since anyone had spoken to Wilhelm about this sort of thing. He didn't like to think about his college days, but if there was one course that now made sense it was Literature I. The textbook was Lieder and Lovett's *British Poetry and Prose,* a black heavy book with thin pages. Did I read that? he asked himself. Yes, he had read it and there was one accomplishment at least he could recall with pleasure. He had read "Yet once more, O ye laurels." How pure this was to say! It was beautiful.

Sunk though he be beneath the wat'ry floor . . .

Such things had always swayed him, and now the power of such words was far, far greater.

Wilhelm respected the truth, but he could lie and one of the things he lied often about was his education. He said he was an alumnus of Penn State; in fact he had left school before his sophomore year was finished. His sister Catherine had a B. S. degree. Wilhelm's late mother was a graduate of Bryn Mawr. He was the only member of the family who had no education. This was another sore point. His father was ashamed of him.

But he had heard the old man bragging to another old man, saying, "My son is a sales executive. He didn't have the patience to finish school. But he does all right for himself. His income is up in the five figures somewhere."

"What—thirty, forty thousand?" said his stooped old friend.

"Well, he needs at least that much for his style of life. Yes, he needs that."

Despite his troubles, Wilhelm almost laughed. Why, that boasting old hypocrite. He knew the sales executive was no more. For many weeks there had been no executive, no sales, no income. But how we love looking fine in the eyes of the world —how beautiful are the old when they are doing a snow job! It's Dad, thought Wilhelm, who is the salesman. He's selling me. *He* should have gone on the road.

But what of the truth? Ah, the truth was that there were problems, and of these problems his father wanted no part. His father was ashamed of him. The truth, Wilhelm thought, was very awkward. He pressed his lips together, and his tongue went soft; it pained him far at the back, in the cords and throat, and a knot of ill formed in his chest. Dad never was a pal to me when I was young, he reflected. He was at the office or the hospital, or lecturing. He expected me to look out for myself and never gave me much thought. Now he looks down on me. And maybe in some respects he's right.

No wonder Wilhelm delayed the moment when he would have to go into the dining room. He had moved to the end of Rubin's counter. He had opened the *Tribune;* the fresh pages drooped from his hands; the cigar was smoked out and the hat did not defend him. He was wrong to suppose that he was more capable than the next fellow when it came to concealing his troubles. They were clearly written out upon his face. He wasn't even aware of it.

There was the matter of the different names, which, in the hotel, came up frequently. "Are you Doctor Adler's son?" "Yes, but my name is Tommy Wilhelm." And the doctor would say, "My son and I use different monickers. I uphold tradition. He's for the new." The Tommy was Wilhelm's own invention. He adopted it when he went to Hollywood, and dropped the Adler. Hollywood was his own idea, too. He used to pretend that it had all been the doing of a certain talent scout named Maurice Venice. But the scout had never made him a definite offer of a studio connection. He had approached him, but the results of the screen tests had not been good. After the test Wilhelm took the initiative and pressed Maurice Venice until he got him to say, "Well, I suppose you might make it out there." On the strength of this Wilhelm had left college and had gone to California.

Someone had said, and Wilhelm agreed with the saying, that in Los Angeles all the loose objects in the country were collected, as if America had been tilted and everything that wasn't tightly screwed down had slid into Southern California. He himself had been one of these loose objects. Sometimes he told people, "I was too mature for college. I was a big boy, you see. Well, I thought, when do you start to become a man?" After he had driven a painted flivver[4] and had worn a yellow slicker with slogans on it, and played illegal poker, and gone out on Coke dates, he had *had* college. He wanted to try something new and quarreled with his parents about his career. And then a letter came from Maurice Venice.

The story of the scout was long and intricate and there were several versions of it. The truth about it was never told. Wilhelm had lied first boastfully and then out of charity to himself. But his memory was good, he could still separate what he had invented from the actual happenings, and this morning he found it necessary as he stood by Rubin's showcase with his *Tribune* to recall the crazy course of the true events.

I didn't seem even to realize that there was a depression. How could I have been such a jerk as not to prepare for anything and just go on luck and inspiration? With round gray eyes expanded and his large shapely lips closed in severity toward himself he forced open all that had been hidden. Dad I couldn't affect one way or another. Mama was the one who tried to stop me, and we carried on and yelled and pleaded. The more I lied the louder I raised my voice, and charged—like a hippopotamus. Poor Mother! How I disappointed her. Rubin heard Wilhelm give a broken sigh as he stood with the forgotten *Tribune* crushed under his arm.

When Wilhelm was aware that Rubin watched him, loitering and idle, apparently not knowing what to do with himself this morning, he turned to the Coca-Cola machine. He swallowed hard at the Coke bottle and coughed over it, but he ignored his coughing, for he was still thinking, his eyes upcast and his lips closed behind his hand. By a peculiar twist of habit he wore his coat collar turned up always, as though there were a wind. It never lay flat. But on his broad back, stooped with its own weight, its strength warped almost into deformity, the collar of his sports coat appeared anyway to be no wider than a ribbon.

He was listening to the sound of his own voice as he explained, twenty-five years ago in the living room on West End Avenue, "But Mother, if I don't pan out as an actor I can still go back to school."

But she was afraid he was going to destroy himself. She said, "Wilky, Dad could make it easy for you if you wanted to go into medicine." To remember this stifled him.

"I can't bear hospitals. Besides, I might make a mistake and hurt someone or even kill a patient. I couldn't stand that. Besides, I haven't got that sort of brains."

Then his mother had made the mistake of mentioning her nephew Artie, Wilhelm's cousin, who was an honor student at Columbia in math and languages. That dark little gloomy Artie with his disgusting narrow face, and his moles and self-sniffing ways and his unclean table manners, the boring habit he had of conjugating verbs when you went for a walk with him. "Roumanian is an easy language. You just add a *tl* to everything." He was now a professor, this same Artie with whom Wilhelm had played near the soldiers' and sailors' monument on Riverside Drive. Not that to be a professor was in itself so great. How could anyone bear to know so many languages? And Artie also had to remain Artie, which was a bad deal. But perhaps success had

---

[4] Small, cheap, dilapidated automobile; a jalopy.

changed him. Now that he had a place in the world perhaps he was better. Did Artie love his languages, and live for them, or was he also, in his heart, cynical? So many people nowadays were. No one seemed satisfied, and Wilhelm was especially horrified by the cynicism of successful people. Cynicism was bread and meat to everyone. And irony, too. Maybe it couldn't be helped. It was probably even necessary. Wilhelm, however, feared it intensely. Whenever at the end of the day he was unusually fatigued he attributed it to cynicism. Too much of the world's business done. Too much falsity. He had various words to express the effect this had on him. Chicken! Unclean! Congestion! he exclaimed in his heart. Rat race! Phony! Murder! Play the Game! Buggers!

At first the letter from the talent scout was nothing but a flattering sort of joke. Wilhelm's picture in the college paper when he was running for class treasurer was seen by Maurice Venice, who wrote to him about a screen test. Wilhelm at once took the train to New York. He found the scout to be huge and oxlike, so stout that his arms seemed caught from beneath in a grip of flesh and fat; it looked as though it must be positively painful. He had little hair. Yet he enjoyed a healthy complexion. His breath was noisy and his voice rather difficult and husky because of the fat in his throat. He had on a double-breasted suit of the type then known as the pillbox; it was chalk-striped, pink on blue; the trousers hugged his ankles.

They met and shook hands and sat down. Together these two big men dwarfed the tiny Broadway office and made the furnishings look like toys. Wilhelm had the color of a Golden Grimes apple when he was well, and then his thick blond hair had been vigorous and his wide shoulders unwarped; he was leaner in the jaws, his eyes fresher and wider: his legs were then still awkward but he was impressively handsome. And he was about to make his first great mistake. Like, he sometimes thought, I was going to pick up a weapon and strike myself a blow with it.

Looming over the desk in the small office darkened by overbuilt midtown—sheer walls, gray spaces, dry lagoons of tar and pebbles—Maurice Venice proceeded to establish his credentials. He said, "My letter was on the regular stationery, but maybe you want to check on me?"

"Who, *me?*" said Wilhelm. "Why?"

"There's guys who think I'm in a racket and make a charge for the test. I don't ask a cent. I'm no agent. There ain't no commission."

"I never even thought of it," said Wilhelm. Was there perhaps something fishy about this Maurice Venice? He protested too much.

In his husky, fat-weakened voice he finally challenged Wilhelm, "If you're not sure, you can call the distributor and find out who I am, Maurice Venice."

Wilhelm wondered at him. "Why shouldn't I be sure? Of course I am."

"Because I can see the way you size me up, and because this is a dinky office. Like you don't believe me. Go ahead. Call. I won't care if you're cautious. I mean it. There's quite a few people who doubt me at first. They can't really believe that fame and fortune are going to hit 'em."

"But I tell you I do believe you," Wilhelm had said, and bent inward to accommodate the pressure of his warm, panting laugh. It was purely nervous. His neck was ruddy and neatly shaved about the ears—he was fresh from the barbershop; his face anxiously glowed with his desire to make a pleasing impression. It was all wasted on Venice, who was just as concerned about the impression *he* was making.

"If you're surprised, I'll just show you what I mean," Venice had said. "It was about fifteen months ago right in this identical same office when I saw a beautiful thing in the paper. It wasn't even a photo but a drawing, a brassière ad, but I knew right away that this was star material. I called up the paper to ask who the girl was, they gave me the name of the advertising agency; I phoned the agency and they gave me the name of the artist; I got hold of the artist and he gave me the number of the model agency. Finally, finally I got her number and phoned her and said, 'This is Maurice Venice, scout for Kaskaskia Films.' So right away she says, 'Yah, so's your old lady.' Well, when I saw I wasn't getting nowhere with her I said to her, 'Well, miss. I don't blame you. You're a very beautiful thing and must have a dozen admirers after you all the time, boy friends who like to call and pull your leg and give a tease. But as I happen to be a very busy fellow and don't have the time to horse around or argue, I tell you what to do. Here's my number, and here's the number of the Kaskaskia Distributors, Inc. Ask them who am I, Maurice Venice. The scout.' She did it. A little while later she phoned me back, all apologies and excuses, but I didn't want to embarrass her and get off on the wrong foot with an artist. I know better than to do that. So I told her it was a natural precaution, never mind. I wanted to run a screen test right away. Because I seldom am wrong about talent. If I see it, it's there. Get that, please. And do you know who that little girl is today?"

"No," Wilhelm said eagerly. "Who is she?"

Venice said impressively, " 'Nita Christenberry."

Wilhelm sat utterly blank. This was failure. He didn't know the name, and Venice was waiting for his response and would be angry.

And in fact Venice had been offended. He said, "What's the matter with you! Don't you read a magazine? She's a starlet."

"I'm sorry," Wilhelm answered. "I'm at school and don't have time to keep up. If I don't know her, it doesn't mean a thing. She made a big hit, I'll bet."

"You can say that again. Here's a photo of her." He handed Wilhelm some pictures. She was a bathing beauty—short, the usual breasts, hips, and smooth thighs. Yes, quite good, as Wilhelm recalled. She stood on high heels and wore a Spanish comb and mantilla. In her hand was a fan.

He had said, "She looks awfully peppy."

"Isn't she a divine girl? And what personality! Not just another broad in the show business, believe me." He had a surprise for Wilhelm. "I have found happiness with her," he said.

"You have?" said Wilhelm, slow to understand.

"Yes, boy, we're engaged."

Wilhelm saw another photograph, taken on the beach. Venice was dressed in a terry-cloth beach outfit, and he and the girl, cheek to cheek, were looking into the camera. Below, in white ink, was written "Love at Malibu Colony."

"I'm sure you'll be very happy. I wish you—"

"I *know*," said Venice firmly, "I'm going to be happy. When I saw that drawing, the breath of fate breathed on me. I felt it over my entire body."

"Say, it strikes a bell suddenly," Wilhelm had said. "Aren't you related to Martial Venice the producer?"

Venice was either a nephew of the producer or the son of a first cousin. Decidedly he had not made good. It was easy enough for Wilhelm to see this now. The office was so poor, and Venice bragged so nervously and identified himself so scrupulously

—the poor guy. He was the obscure failure of an aggressive and powerful clan. As such he had the greatest sympathy from Wilhelm.

Venice had said, "Now I suppose you want to know where you come in. I seen your school paper, by accident. You take quite a remarkable picture."

"It can't be so much," said Wilhelm, more panting than laughing.

"You don't want to tell me my business," Venice said. "Leave it to me. I studied up on this."

"I never imagined—Well, what kind of roles do you think I'd fit?"

"All this time that we've been talking, I've been watching. Don't think I haven't. You remind me of someone. Let's see who it can be—one of the great old-timers. Is it Milton Sills? No, that's not the one. Conway Tearle, Jack Mulhall? George Bancroft? No, his face was ruggeder. One thing I can tell you, though, a George Raft type you're not—those tough, smooth, black little characters."

"No, I wouldn't seem to be."

"No, you're not that flyweight type, with the fists, from a nightclub, and the glamorous sideburns, doing the tango or the bolero. Not Edward G. Robinson, either —I'm thinking aloud. Or the Cagney fly-in-your-face role, a cabbie, with that mouth and those punches."

"I realize that."

"Not suave like William Powell, or a lyric juvenile like Buddy Rogers. I suppose you don't play the sax? No. But—"

"But what?"

"I have you placed as the type that loses the girl to the George Raft type or the William Powell type. You are steady, faithful, you get stood up. The older women would know better. The mothers are on your side. With what they been through, if it was up to them, they'd take you in a minute. You're very sympathetic, even the young girls feel that. You'd make a good provider. But they go more for the other types. It's as clear as anything."

This was not how Wilhelm saw himself. And as he surveyed the old ground he recognized now that he had been not only confused but hurt. Why, he thought, he cast me even then for a loser.

Wilhelm had said, with half a mind to be defiant, "Is that your opinion?"

It never occurred to Venice that a man might object to stardom in such a role. "Here is your chance," he said. "Now you're just in college. What are you studying?" He snapped his fingers. "Stuff." Wilhelm himself felt this way about it. "You may plug along fifty years before you get anywheres. This way, in one jump, the world knows who you are. You become a name like Roosevelt, Swanson. From east to west, out to China, into South America. This is no bunk. You become a lover to the whole world. The world wants it, needs it. One fellow smiles, a billion people also smile. One fellow cries, the other billion sob with him. Listen, bud—" Venice had pulled himself together to make an effort. On his imagination there was some great weight which he could not discharge. He wanted Wilhelm, too, to feel it. He twisted his large, clean, well-meaning, rather foolish features as though he were their unwilling captive, and said in his choked, fat-obstructed voice, "Listen, everywhere there are people trying hard, miserable, in trouble, downcast, tired, trying and trying. They need a break, right? A break through, a help, luck or sympathy."

"That certainly is the truth," said Wilhelm. He had seized the feeling and he waited for Venice to go on. But Venice had no more to say; he had concluded. He gave Wilhelm several pages of blue hectographed script, stapled together, and told him to prepare for the screen test. "Study your lines in front of a mirror," he said. "Let yourself go. The part should take ahold of you. Don't be afraid to make faces and be emotional. Shoot the works. Because when you start to act you're no more an ordinary person, and those things don't apply to you. You don't behave the same way as the average."

And so Wilhelm had never returned to Penn State. His roommate sent his things to New York for him, and the school authorities had to write to Dr. Adler to find out what had happened.

Still, for three months Wilhelm delayed his trip to California. He wanted to start out with the blessings of his family, but they were never given. He quarreled with his parents and his sister. And then, when he was best aware of the risks and knew a hundred reasons against going and had made himself sick with fear, he left home. This was typical of Wilhelm. After much thought and hesitation and debate he invariably took the course he had rejected innumerable times. Ten such decisions made up the history of his life. He had decided that it would be a bad mistake to go to Hollywood, and then he went. He had made up his mind not to marry his wife, but ran off and got married. He had resolved not to invest money with Tamkin, and then had given him a check.

But Wilhelm had been eager for life to start. College was merely another delay. Venice had approached him and said that the world had named Wilhelm to shine before it. He was to be freed from the anxious and narrow life of the average. Moreover, Venice had claimed that he never made a mistake. His instinct for talent was infallible, he said.

But when Venice saw the results of the screen test he did a quick about-face. In those days Wilhelm had had a speech difficulty. It was not a true stammer, it was a thickness of speech which the sound track exaggerated. The film showed that he had many peculiarities, otherwise unnoticeable. When he shrugged, his hands drew up within his sleeves. The vault of his chest was huge, but he really didn't look strong under the lights. Though he called himself a hippopotamus, he more nearly resembled a bear. His walk was bearlike, quick and rather soft, toes turned inward, as though his shoes were an impediment. About one thing Venice had been right. Wilhelm was photogenic, and his wavy blond hair (now graying) came out well, but after the test Venice refused to encourage him. He tried to get rid of him. He couldn't afford to take a chance on him, he had made too many mistakes already and lived in fear of his powerful relatives.

Wilhelm had told his parents, "Venice says I owe it to myself to go." How ashamed he was now of this lie! He had begged Venice not to give him up. He had said, "Can't you help me out? It would kill me to go back to school now."

Then when he reached the Coast he learned that a recommendation from Maurice Venice was the kiss of death. Venice needed help and charity more than he, Wilhelm, ever had. A few years later when Wilhelm was down on his luck and working as an orderly in a Los Angeles hospital, he saw Venice's picture in the papers. He was under indictment for pandering. Closely following the trial, Wilhelm found out that Venice had indeed been employed by Kaskaskia Films but that he had evidently made use of the connection to organize a ring of call girls. Then what did he want with me? Wilhelm had cried to himself. He was unwilling to believe anything very bad about Venice. Perhaps he was foolish and unlucky, a fall guy, a dupe, a sucker. You didn't give a man fifteen years in prison for that. Wilhelm often thought that he might write him a letter to say how sorry he was. He remembered the breath of fate and Venice's certainty that he would be happy. 'Nita Christenberry was sentenced to three years. Wilhelm recognized her although she had changed her name.

By that time Wilhelm too had taken his new name. In California he became Tommy Wilhelm. Dr. Adler would not accept the change. Today he still called his son Wilky, as he had done for more than forty years. Well, now, Wilhelm was thinking, the paper crowded in disarray under his arm, there's really very little that a man can change at will. He can't change his lungs, or nerves, or constitution or temperament. They're not under his control. When he's young and strong and impulsive and dissatisfied with the way things are he wants to rearrange them to assert his freedom. He can't overthrow the government or be differently born; he only has a little scope and maybe a foreboding, too, that essentially you can't change. Nevertheless, he makes a gesture and becomes Tommy Wilhelm. Wilhelm had always had a great longing to be Tommy. He had never, however, succeeded in feeling like Tommy, and in his soul had always remained Wilky. When he was drunk he reproached himself horribly as Wilky. "You fool, you clunk, you Wilky!" he called himself. He thought that it was a good thing perhaps that he had not become a success as Tommy since that would not have been a genuine success. Wilhelm would have feared that not he but Tommy had brought it off, cheating Wilky of his birthright. Yes, it had been a stupid thing to do, but it was his imperfect judgment at the age of twenty which should be blamed. He had cast off his father's name, and with it his father's opinion of him. It was, he knew it was, his bid for liberty, Adler being in his mind the title of the species, Tommy the freedom of the person. But Wilky was his inescapable self.

In middle age you no longer thought such thoughts about free choice. Then it came over you that from one grandfather you had inherited such and such a head of hair which looked like honey when it whitens or sugars in the jar; from another, broad thick shoulders; an oddity of speech from one uncle, and small teeth from another, and the gray eyes with darkness diffused even into the whites, and a wide-lipped mouth like a statue from Peru. Wandering races have such looks, the bones of one tribe, the skin of another. From his mother he had gotten sensitive feelings, a soft heart, a brooding nature, a tendency to be confused under pressure.

The changed name was a mistake, and he would admit it as freely as you liked. But this mistake couldn't be undone now, so why must his father continually remind him how he had sinned? It was too late. He would have to go back to the pathetic day when the sin was committed. And where was that day? Past and dead. Whose humiliating memories were these? His and not his father's. What had he to think back on that he could call good? Very, very little. You had to forgive. First, to forgive yourself, and then general forgiveness. Didn't he suffer from his mistakes far more than his father could?

"Oh, God," Wilhelm prayed. "Let me out of my trouble. Let me out of my thoughts, and let me do something better with myself. For all the time I have wasted I am very sorry. Let me out of this clutch and into a different life. For I am all balled up. Have mercy."

II

The mail.

The clerk who gave it to him did not care what sort of appearance he made this morning. He only glanced at him from under his brows, upward, as the letters changed hands. Why should the hotel people waste courtesies on him? They had his number. The clerk knew that he was handing him, along with the letters, a bill for his rent. Wilhelm assumed a look that removed him from all such things. But it was bad. To pay the bill he would have to withdraw money from his brokerage account, and the account was being watched because of the drop in lard. According to the *Tribune*'s figures lard was still twenty points below last year's level. There were government price supports. Wilhelm didn't know how these worked but he understood that the farmer was protected and that the SEC kept an eye on the market and therefore he believed that lard would rise again and he wasn't greatly worried as yet. But in the meantime his father might have offered to pick up his hotel tab. Why didn't he? What a selfish old man he was! He saw his son's hardships; he could so easily help him. How little it would mean to him, and how much to Wilhelm! Where was the old man's heart? Maybe, thought Wilhelm, I was sentimental in the past and exaggerated his kindliness—warm family life. It may never have been there.

Not long ago his father had said to him in his usual affable, pleasant way, "Well, Wilky, here we are under the same roof again, after all these years."

Wilhelm was glad for an instant. At last they would talk over old times. But he was also on guard against insinuations. Wasn't his father saying, "Why are you here in a hotel with me and not at home in Brooklyn with your wife and two boys? You're neither a widower nor a bachelor. You have brought me all your confusions. What do you expect me to do with them?"

So Wilhelm studied the remark for a bit, then said, "The roof is twenty-six stories up. But how many years has it been?"

"That's what I was asking you."

"Gosh, Dad, I'm not sure. Wasn't it the year Mother died? What year was that?"

He asked this question with an innocent frown on his Golden Grimes, dark blond face. *What year was it!* As though he didn't know the year, the month, the day, the very hour of his mother's death.

"Wasn't it nineteen-thirty-one?" said Dr. Adler.

"Oh, was it?" said Wilhelm. And in hiding the sadness and the overwhelming irony of the question he gave a nervous shiver and wagged his head and felt the ends of his collar rapidly.

"Do you know?" his father said. "You must realize, an old fellow's memory becomes unreliable. It was in winter, that I'm sure of. Nineteen-thirty-two?"

Yes, it was age. Don't make an issue of it, Wilhelm advised himself. If you were to ask the old doctor in what year he had interned, he'd tell you correctly. All the same, don't make an issue. Don't quarrel with your own father. Have pity on an old man's failings.

"I believe the year was closer to nineteen-thirty-four, Dad," he said.

But Dr. Adler was thinking, Why the devil can't he stand still when we're talking? He's either hoisting his pants up and down by the pockets or jittering with his feet. A regular mountain of tics, he's getting to be. Wilhelm had a habit of moving his feet back and forth as though, hurrying into a house, he had to clean his shoes first on the doormat.

Then Wilhelm had said, "Yes, that was the beginning of the end, wasn't it, Father?"

Wilhelm often astonished Dr. Adler. Beginning of the end? What could he mean —what was he fishing for? Whose end? The end of family life? The old man was puzzled but he would not give Wilhelm an opening to introduce his complaints. He had learned that it was better not to take up Wilhelm's strange challenges. So he merely agreed pleasantly, for he was a master of social behavior, and said, "It was an awful misfortune for us all."

He thought, What business has he to complain to *me* of his mother's death?

Face to face they had stood, each declaring himself silently after his own way. It was: it was not, the beginning of the end—*some* end.

Unaware of anything odd in his doing it, for he did it all the time, Wilhelm had pinched out the coal of his cigarette and dropped the butt in his pocket, where there were many more. And as he gazed at his father the little finger of his right hand began to twitch and tremble; of that he was unconscious, too.

And yet Wilhelm believed that when he put his mind to it he could have perfect and even distinguished manners, outdoing his father. Despite the slight thickness in his speech—it amounted almost to a stammer when he started the same phrase over several times in his effort to eliminate the thick sound—he could be fluent. Otherwise he would never have made a good salesman. He claimed also that he was a good listener. When he listened he made a tight mouth and rolled his eyes thoughtfully. He would soon tire and begin to utter short, loud, impatient breaths, and he would say, "Oh yes . . . yes . . . yes. I couldn't agree more." When he was forced to differ he would declare, "Well, I'm not sure. I don't really see it that way. I'm of two minds about it." He would never willingly hurt any man's feelings.

But in conversation with his father he was apt to lose control of himself. After any talk with Dr. Adler, Wilhelm generally felt dissatisfied, and his dissatisfaction reached its greatest intensity when they discussed family matters. Ostensibly he had been trying to help the old man to remember a date, but in reality he meant to tell him, "You were set free when Ma died. You wanted to forget her. You'd like to get rid of Catherine, too. Me, too. You're not kidding anyone"—Wilhelm striving to put this across, and the old man not having it. In the end he was left struggling, while his father seemed unmoved.

And then once more Wilhelm had said to himself, "But man! you're not a kid. Even then you weren't a kid!" He looked down over the front of his big, indecently big, spoiled body. He was beginning to lose his shape, his gut was fat, and he looked like a hippopotamus. His younger son called him "a hummuspotamus"; that was little Paul. And here he was still struggling with his old dad, filled with ancient grievances. Instead of saying, "Good-by, youth! Oh, good-by those marvelous, foolish wasted days. What a big clunk I was—I *am.*"

Wilhelm was still paying heavily for his mistakes. His wife Margaret would not give him a divorce, and he had to support her and the two children. She would regularly agree to divorce him, and then think things over again and set new and more difficult conditions. No court would have awarded her the amounts he paid. One of today's letters, as he had expected, was from her. For the first time he had sent her a postdated check, and she protested. She also enclosed bills for the boys' educational insurance policies, due next week. Wilhelm's mother-in-law had taken out these policies in Beverly Hills, and since her death two years ago he had to pay the premiums. Why couldn't she have minded her own business! They were his kids, and he took care of them and always would. He had planned to set up a trust fund. But that was on his former expectations. Now he had to rethink the future, because of the money problem. Meanwhile, here were the bills to be paid. When he saw the two sums punched out so neatly on the cards he cursed the company and its IBM equipment. His heart and his head were congested with anger. Everyone was supposed to have money. It was nothing to the company. It published pictures of funerals in the magazines and frightened the suckers, and then punched out little holes, and the customers would lie awake to think out ways to raise the dough. They'd be ashamed not to have it. They couldn't let a great company down, either, and they got the scratch. In the old days a man was put in prison for debt, but there were subtler things now. They made it a shame not to have money and set everybody to work.

Well, and what else had Margaret sent him? He tore the envelope open with his thumb, swearing that he would send any other bills back to her. There was, luckily, nothing more. He put the hole-punched cards in his pocket. Didn't Margaret know that he was nearly at the end of his rope? Of course. Her instinct told her that this was her opportunity, and she was giving him the works.

He went into the dining room, which was under Austro-Hungarian management at the Hotel Gloriana. It was run like a European establishment. The pastries were excellent, especially the strudel. He often had apple strudel and coffee in the afternoon.

As soon as he entered he saw his father's small head in the sunny bay at the farther end, and heard his precise voice. It was with an odd sort of perilous expression that Wilhelm crossed the dining room.

Dr. Adler liked to sit in a corner that looked across Broadway down to the Hudson and New Jersey. On the other side of the street was a supermodern cafeteria with gold and purple mosaic columns. On the second floor a private-eye school, a dental laboratory, a reducing parlor, a veteran's club, and a Hebrew school shared the space. The old man was sprinkling sugar on his strawberries. Small hoops of brilliance were cast by the water glasses on the white tablecloth, despite a faint murkiness in the sunshine. It was early summer, and the long window was turned inward; a moth was on the pane; the putty was broken and the white enamel on the frames was streaming with wrinkles.

"Ha, Wilky," said the old man to his tardy son. "You haven't met our neighbor Mr. Perls, have you? From the fifteenth floor."

"How d'do," Wilhelm said. He did not welcome this stranger; he began at once to find fault with him. Mr. Perls carried a heavy cane with a crutch tip. Dyed hair, a skinny forehead—these were not reasons for bias. Nor was it Mr. Perls's fault that Dr. Adler was using him, not wishing to have breakfast with his son alone. But a gruffer voice within Wilhelm spoke, asking, "Who is this damn frazzle-faced herring with his dyed hair and his fish teeth and this drippy mustache? Another one of Dad's German friends. Where does he collect all these guys? What is the stuff on his teeth? I never saw such pointed crowns. Are they stainless steel, or a kind of silver? How can a human face get into this condition. Uch!" Staring with his widely spaced gray eyes, Wilhelm sat, his broad back stooped under the sports jacket. He clasped his hands on the table with an implication of suppliance. Then he began to relent a little toward Mr. Perls, beginning at the teeth. Each of those crowns represented a tooth ground to the quick, and estimating a man's grief with his teeth as two per cent of the total, and adding to that his flight from Germany and the probable origin of his wincing wrinkles, not to be confused with the wrinkles of his smile, it came to a sizable load.

"Mr. Perls was a hosiery wholesaler," said Dr. Adler.

"Is this the son you told me was in the selling line?" said Mr. Perls.

Dr. Adler replied, "I have only this one son. One daughter. She was a medical technician before she got married—anesthetist. At one time she had an important position in Mount Sinai."

He couldn't mention his children without boasting. In Wilhelm's opinion, there was little to boast of. Catherine, like Wilhelm, was big and fair-haired. She had married a court reporter who had a pretty hard time of it. She had taken a professional name, too—Philippa. At forty she was still ambitious to become a painter. Wilhelm didn't venture to criticize her work. It didn't do much to him, he said, but then he was no critic. Anyway, he and his sister were generally on the outs and he didn't often see her paintings. She worked very hard, but there were fifty thousand people in New York with paints and brushes, each practically a law unto himself. It was the Tower of Babel in paint. *He* didn't want to go far into this. Things were chaotic all over.

Dr. Adler thought that Wilhelm looked particularly untidy this morning—unrested, too, his eyes red-rimmed from excessive smoking. He was breathing through his mouth and he was evidently much distracted and rolled his red-shot eyes barbarously. As usual, his coat collar was turned up as though he had had to go out in the rain. When he went to business he pulled himself together a little; otherwise he let himself go and looked like hell.

"What's the matter, Wilky, didn't you sleep last night?"

"Not very much."

"You take too many pills of every kind—first stimulants and then depressants, anodynes followed by analeptics, until the poor organism doesn't know what's happened. Then the luminal won't put people to sleep, and the Pervitin or Benzedrine won't wake them. God knows! These things get to be as serious as poisons, and yet everyone puts all their faith in them."

"No, Dad, it's not the pills. It's that I'm not used to New York any more. For a native, that's very peculiar, isn't it? It was never so noisy at night as now, and every little thing is a strain. Like the alternate parking. You have to run out at eight to move your car. And where can you put it? If you forget for a minute they tow you away. Then some fool puts advertising leaflets under your windshield wiper and you have heart failure a block away because you think you've got a ticket. When you do get stung with a ticket, you can't argue. You haven't got a chance in court and the city wants the revenue."

"But in your line you have to have a car, eh?" said Mr. Perls.

"Lord knows why any lunatic would want one in the city who didn't need it for his livelihood."

Wilhelm's old Pontiac was parked in the street. Formerly, when on an expense account, he had always put it up in a garage. Now he was afraid to move the car from Riverside Drive lest he lose his space, and he used it only on Saturdays when the Dodgers were playing in Ebbets Field and he took his boys to the game. Last Saturday, when the Dodgers were out of town, he had gone out to visit his mother's grave.

Dr. Adler had refused to go along. He couldn't bear his son's driving. Forgetfully,

Wilhelm traveled for miles in second gear; he was seldom in the right lane and he neither gave signals nor watched for lights. The upholstery of his Pontiac was filthy with grease and ashes. One cigarette burned in the ashtray, another in his hand, a third on the floor with maps and other waste paper and Coca-Cola bottles. He dreamed at the wheel or argued and gestured, and therefore the old doctor would not ride with him.

Then Wilhelm had come back from the cemetery angry because the stone bench between his mother's and his grandmother's graves had been overturned and broken by vandals. "Those damn teen-age hoodlums get worse and worse," he said. "Why, they must have used a sledge-hammer to break the seat smack in half like that. If I could catch one of them!" He wanted the doctor to pay for a new seat, but his father was cool to the idea. He said he was going to have himself cremated.

Mr. Perls said, "I don't blame you if you get no sleep up where you are." His voice was tuned somewhat sharp, as though he were slightly deaf. "Don't you have Parigi the singing teacher there? God, they have some queer elements in this hotel. On which floor is that Estonian woman with all her cats and dogs? They should have made her leave long ago."

"They've moved her down to twelve," said Dr. Adler.

Wilhelm ordered a large Coca-Cola with his breakfast. Working in secret at the small envelopes in his pocket, he found two pills by touch. Much fingering had worn and weakened the paper. Under cover of a napkin he swallowed a Phenaphen sedative and a Unicap, but the doctor was sharp-eyed and said, "Wilky, what are you taking now?"

"Just my vitamin pills." He put his cigar butt in an ashtray on the table behind him, for his father did not like the odor. Then he drank his Coca-Cola.

"That's what you drink for breakfast, and not orange juice?" said Mr. Perls. He seemed to sense that he would not lose Dr. Adler's favor by taking an ironic tone with his son.

"The caffeine stimulates brain activity," said the old doctor. "It does all kinds of things to the respiratory center."

"It's just a habit of the road, that's all," Wilhelm said. "If you drive around long enough it turns your brains, your stomach, and everything else."

His father explained, "Wilky used to be with the Rojax Corporation. He was their northeastern sales representative for a good many years but recently ended the connection."

"Yes," said Wilhelm, "I was with them from the end of the war." He sipped the Coca-Cola and chewed the ice, glancing at one and the other with his attitude of large, shaky, patient dignity. The waitress set two boiled eggs before him.

"What kind of line does this Rojax company manufacture?" said Mr. Perls.

"Kiddies' furniture. Little chairs, rockers, tables, Jungle-Gyms, slides, swings, see-saws."

Wilhelm let his father do the explaining. Large and stiff-backed, he tried to sit patiently, but his feet were abnormally restless. All right! His father had to impress Mr. Perls? He would go along once more, and play his part. Fine! He would play along and help his father maintain his style. Style was the main consideration. That was just fine!

"I was with the Rojax Corporation for almost ten years," he said. "We parted ways because they wanted me to share my territory. They took a son-in-law into the business—a new fellow. It was his idea."

To himself, Wilhelm said, Now God alone can tell why I have to lay my whole life bare to this blasted herring here. I'm sure nobody else does it. Other people keep their business to themselves. Not me.

He continued, "But the rationalization was that it was too big a territory for one man. I had a monopoly. That wasn't so. The real reason was that they had gotten to the place where they would have to make me an officer of the corporation. Vice presidency. I was in line for it, but instead this son-in-law got in, and—"

Dr. Adler thought Wilhelm was discussing his grievances much too openly and said, "My son's income was up in the five figures."

As soon as money was mentioned, Mr. Perls's voice grew eagerly sharper. "Yes? What, the thirty-two-per-cent bracket? Higher even, I guess?" He asked for a hint, and he named the figures not idly but with a sort of hugging relish. Uch! How they love money, thought Wilhelm. They adore money! Holy money! Beautiful money! It was getting so that people were feeble-minded about everything except money. While if you didn't have it you were a dummy, a dummy! You had to excuse yourself from the face of the earth. Chicken! that's what it was. The world's business. If only he could find a way out of it.

Such thinking brought on the usual congestion. It would grow into a fit of passion if he allowed it to continue. Therefore he stopped talking and began to eat.

Before he struck the egg with his spoon he dried the moisture with his napkin. Then he battered it (in his father's opinion) more than was necessary. A faint grime was left by his fingers on the white of the egg after he had picked away the shell. Dr. Adler saw it with silent repugnance. What a Wilky he had given to the world! Why, he didn't even wash his hands in the morning. He used an electric razor so that he didn't have to touch water. The doctor couldn't bear Wilky's dirty habits. Only once—and never again, he swore—had he visited his room. Wilhelm, in pajamas and stockings had sat on his bed, drinking gin from a coffee mug and rooting for the Dodgers on television. "That's two and two on you, Duke. Come on—hit it, now." He came down on the mattress—bam! The bed looked kicked to pieces. Then he drank the gin as though it were tea, and urged his team on with his fist. The smell of dirty clothes was outrageous. By the bedside lay a quart bottle and foolish magazines and mystery stories for the hours of insomnia. Wilhelm lived in worse filth than a savage. When the Doctor spoke to him about this he answered, "Well, I have no wife to look after my things." And who—*who!*—had done the leaving? Not Margaret. The Doctor was certain that she wanted him back.

Wilhelm drank his coffee with a trembling hand. In his full face his abused bloodshot gray eyes moved back and forth. Jerkily he set his cup back and put half the length of a cigarette into his mouth; he seemed to hold it with his teeth, as though it were a cigar.

"I can't let them get away with it," he said. "It's also a question of morale."

His father corrected him. "Don't you mean a moral question, Wilky?"

"I mean that, too. I have to do something to protect myself. I was promised executive standing." Correction before a stranger mortified him, and his dark blond face changed color, more pale, and then more dark. He went on talking to Perls but his eyes spied on his father. "I was the one who opened the territory for them. I could go back for one of their competitors and take away their customers. *My* customers. Morale enters into it because they've tried to take away my confidence."

"Would you offer a different line to the same people?" Mr. Perls wondered.

"Why not? I know what's wrong with the Rojax product."

"Nonsense," said his father. "Just nonsense and kid's talk, Wilky. You're only looking for trouble and embarrassment that way. What would you gain by such a silly feud? You have to think about making a living and meeting your obligations."

Hot and bitter, Wilhelm said with pride, while his feet moved angrily under the table, "I don't have to be told about my obligations. I've been meeting them for years. In more than twenty years I've never had a penny of help from anybody. I preferred to dig a ditch on the WPA[5] but never asked anyone to meet my obligations for me."

"Wilky has had all kinds of experiences," said Dr. Adler.

The old doctor's face had a wholesome reddish and almost translucent color, like a ripe apricot. The wrinkles beside his ears were deep because the skin conformed so tightly to his bones. With all his might, he was a healthy and fine small old man. He wore a white vest of a light check pattern. His hearing-aid doodad was in the pocket. An unusual shirt of red and black stripes covered his chest. He bought his clothes in a college shop farther uptown. Wilhelm thought he had no business to get himself up like a jockey, out of respect for his profession.

"Well," said Mr. Perls. "I can understand how you feel. You want to fight it out. By a certain time of life, to have to start all over again can't be a pleasure, though a good man can always do it. But anyway you want to keep on with a business you know already, and not have to meet a whole lot of new contacts."

Wilhelm again thought, Why does it have to be me and my life that's discussed, and not him and his life? He would never allow it. But I am an idiot. I have no reserve. To me it can be done. I talk. I must ask for it. Everybody wants to have intimate conversations, but the smart fellows don't give out, only the fools. The smart fellows talk intimately about the fools, and examine them all over and give them advice. Why do I allow it? The hint about his age had hurt him. No, you can't admit it's as good as ever, he conceded. Things do give out.

"In the meanwhile," Dr. Adler said, "Wilky is taking it easy and considering various propositions. Isn't that so?"

"More or less," said Wilhelm. He suffered his father to increase Mr. Perls's respect for him. The WPA ditch had brought the family into contempt. He was a little tired. The spirit, the peculiar burden of his existence lay upon him like an accretion, a load, a hump. In any moment of quiet, when sheer fatigue prevented him from struggling, he was apt to feel this mysterious weight, this growth or collection of nameless things which it was the business of his life to carry about. That must be what a man was for. This large, odd, excited, fleshy, blond, abrupt personality named Wilhelm, or Tommy, was here, present, in the present—Dr. Tamkin had been putting into his mind many suggestions about the present moment, the here and now—this Wilky, or Tommy Wilhelm, forty-four years old, father of two sons, at present living in the Hotel Gloriana, was assigned to be the carrier of a load which was his own self, his

[5] Works Progress Administration, one of a series of programs instituted in the 1930s to combat the Depression.

characteristic self. There was no figure or estimate for the value of this load. But it is probably exaggerated by the subject, T. W. Who is a visionary sort of animal. Who has to believe that he can know why he exists. Though he has never seriously tried to find out why.

Mr. Perls said, "If he wants time to think things over and have a rest, why doesn't he run down to Florida for a while? Off season it's cheap and quiet. Fairyland. The mangoes are just coming in. I got two acres down there. You'd think you were in India."

Mr. Perls utterly astonished Wilhelm when he spoke of fairyland with a foreign accent. Mangoes—India? What did he mean, India?

"Once upon a time," said Wilhelm, "I did some public-relations work for a big hotel down in Cuba. If I could get them a notice in Leonard Lyons or one of the other columns it might be good for another holiday there, gratis. I haven't had a vacation for a long time, and I could stand a rest after going so hard. You know that's true, Father." He meant that his father knew how deep the crisis was becoming; how badly he was strapped for money; and that he could not rest but would be crushed if he stumbled; and that his obligations would destroy him. He couldn't falter. He thought, The money! When I had it, I flowed money. They bled it away from me. I hemorrhaged money. But now it's almost all gone, and where am I supposed to turn for more?

He said, "As a matter of fact, Father, I am tired as hell."

But Mr. Perls began to smile and said, "I understand from Doctor Tamkin that you're going into some kind of investment with him, partners."

"You know, he's a very ingenious fellow," said Dr. Adler. "I really enjoy hearing him go on. I wonder if he really is a medical doctor."

"Isn't he?" said Perls. "Everybody thinks he is. He talks about his patients. Doesn't he write prescriptions?"

"I don't really know what he does," said Dr. Adler. "He's a cunning man."

"He's a psychologist, I understand," said Wilhelm.

"I don't know what sort of psychologist or psychiatrist he may be," said his father. "He's a little vague. It's growing into a major industry, and a very expensive one. Fellows have to hold down very big jobs in order to pay those fees. Anyway, this Tamkin is clever. He never said he practiced here, but I believe he was a doctor in California. They don't seem to have much legislation out there to cover these things, and I hear a thousand dollars will get you a degree from a Los Angeles correspondence school. He gives the impression of knowing something about chemistry, and things like hypnotism. I wouldn't trust him, though."

"And why wouldn't you?" Wilhelm demanded.

"Because he's probably a liar. Do you believe he invented all the things he claims?"

Mr. Perls was grinning.

"He was written up in *Fortune*," said Wilhelm. "Yes, in *Fortune* magazine. He showed me the article. I've seen his clippings."

"That doesn't make him legitimate," said Dr. Adler. "It might have been another Tamkin. Make no mistake, he's an operator. Perhaps even crazy."

"Crazy, you say?"

Mr. Perls put in, "He could be both sane and crazy. In these days nobody can tell for sure which is which."

"An electrical device for truck drivers to wear in their caps," said Dr. Adler, describing one of Tamkin's proposed inventions. "To wake them with a shock when they begin to be drowsy at the wheel. It's triggered by the change in blood-pressure when they start to doze."

"It doesn't sound like such an impossible thing to me," said Wilhelm.

Mr. Perls said, "To me he described an underwater suit so a man could walk on the bed of the Hudson in case of an atomic attack. He said he could walk to Albany in it."

"Ha, ha, ha, ha, ha!" cried Dr. Adler in his old man's voice. "Tamkin's Folly. You could go on a camping trip under Niagara Falls."

"This is just his kind of fantasy," said Wilhelm. "It doesn't mean a thing. Inventors are supposed to be like that. I get funny ideas myself. Everybody wants to make something. Any American does."

But his father ignored this and said to Perls, "What other inventions did he describe?"

While the frazzle-faced Mr. Perls and his father in the unseemly, monkey-striped shirt were laughing, Wilhelm could not restrain himself and joined in with his own panting laugh. But he was in despair. They were laughing at the man to whom he had given a power of attorney over his last seven hundred dollars to speculate for him in the commodities market. They had bought all that lard. It had to rise today. By ten o'clock, or half-past ten, trading would be active, and he would see.

III

Between white tablecloths and glassware and glancing silverware, through overfull light, the long figure of Mr. Perls went away into the darkness of the lobby. He thrust with his cane, and dragged a large built-up shoe which Wilhelm had not included in his estimate of troubles. Dr. Adler wanted to talk about him. "There's a poor man," he said, "with a bone condition which is gradually breaking him up."

"One of those progressive diseases?" said Wilhelm.

"Very bad. I've learned," the doctor told him, "to keep my sympathy for the real ailments. This Perls is more to be pitied than any man I know."

Wilhelm understood he was being put on notice and did not express his opinion. He ate and ate. He did not hurry but kept putting food on his plate until he had gone through the muffins and his father's strawberries, and then some pieces of bacon that were left; he had several cups of coffee, and when he was finished he sat gigantically in a state of arrest and didn't seem to know what he should do next.

For a while father and son were uncommonly still. Wilhelm's preparations to please Dr. Adler had failed completely, for the old man kept thinking, You'd never guess he had a clean upbringing, and, What a dirty devil this son of mine is. Why can't he try to sweeten his appearance a little? Why does he want to drag himself like this? And he makes himself look so idealistic.

Wilhelm sat, mountainous. He was not really so slovenly as his father found him to be. In some aspects he even had a certain delicacy. His mouth, though broad, had a fine outline, and his brow and his gradually incurved nose, dignity, and in his blond hair there was white but there were also shades of gold and chestnut. When he was with the Rojax Corporation Wilhelm had kept a small apartment in Roxbury, two rooms in a large house with a small porch and garden, and on mornings of leisure, in late spring weather like this, he used to sit expanded in a wicker chair with the sunlight pouring through the weave, and sunlight through the slug-eaten holes of the young hollyhocks and as deeply as the grass allowed into small flowers. This peace (he forgot that that time had had its troubles, too), this peace was gone. It must not have belonged to him, really, for to be here in New York with his old father was more genuinely like his life. He was well aware that he didn't stand a chance of getting sympathy from his father, who said he kept his for real ailments. Moreover, he advised himself repeatedly not to discuss his vexatious problems with him, for his father, with some justice, wanted to be left in peace. Wilhelm also knew that when he began to talk about these things he made himself feel worse, he became congested with them and worked himself into a clutch. Therefore he warned himself, Lay off, pal. It'll only be an aggravation. From a deeper source, however, came other promptings. If he didn't keep his troubles before him he risked losing them altogether, and he knew by experience that this was worse. And furthermore, he could not succeed in excusing his father on the ground of old age. No. No, he could not. I am his son, he thought. He is my father. He is as much father as I am son—old or not. Affirming this, though in complete silence, he sat, and, sitting, he kept his father at the table with him.

"Wilky," said the old man, "have you gone down to the baths here yet?"

"No, Dad, not yet."

"Well, you know the Gloriana has one of the finest pools in New York. Eighty feet, blue tile. It's a beauty."

Wilhelm had seen it. On the way to the gin game you passed the stairway to the pool. He did not care for the odor of the wall-locked and chlorinated water.

"You ought to investigate the Russian and Turkish baths, and the sunlamps and massage. I don't hold with sunlamps. But the massage does a world of good, and there's nothing better than hydrotherapy when you come right down to it. Simple water has a calming effect and would do you more good than all the barbiturates and alcohol in the world."

Wilhelm reflected that this advice was as far as his father's help and sympathy would extend.

"I thought," he said, "that the water cure was for lunatics."

The doctor received this as one of his son's jokes and said with a smile, "Well, it won't turn a sane man into a lunatic. It does a great deal for me. I couldn't live without my massages and steam."

"You're probably right. I ought to try it one of these days. Yesterday, late in the afternoon, my head was about to bust and I just had to have a little air, so I walked around the reservoir, and I sat down for a while in a playground. It rests me to watch the kids play potsy[6] and skiprope."

The doctor said with approval, "Well, now, that's more like the idea."

"It's the end of the lilacs," said Wilhelm. "When they burn it's the beginning of summer. At least, in the city. Around the time of year when the candy stores take down the windows and start to sell sodas on the sidewalk. But even though I was raised here, Dad, I can't take city life any more, and I miss the country. There's too

---

[6] Variation, played with bean bags, of the child's game of hopscotch.

much push here for me. It works me up too much. I take things too hard. I wonder why you never retired to a quieter place."

The doctor opened his small hand on the table in a gesture so old and so typical that Wilhelm felt it like an actual touch upon the foundations of his life. "I am a city boy myself, you must remember," Dr. Adler explained. "But if you find the city so hard on you, you ought to get out."

"I'll do that," said Wilhelm, "as soon as I can make the right connection. Meanwhile—"

His father interrupted, "Meanwhile I suggest you cut down on drugs."

"You exaggerate that, Dad. I don't really—I give myself a little boost against—" He almost pronounced the word "misery" but he kept his resolution not to complain.

The doctor, however, fell into the error of pushing his advice too hard. It was all he had to give his son and he gave it once more. "Water and exercise," he said.

He wants a young, smart, successful son, thought Wilhelm, and he said, "Oh, Father, it's nice of you to give me this medical advice, but steam isn't going to cure what ails me."

The doctor measurably drew back, warned by the sudden weak strain of Wilhelm's voice and all that the droop of his face, the swell of his belly against the restraint of his belt intimated.

"Some new business?" he asked unwillingly.

Wilhelm made a great preliminary summary which involved the whole of his body. He drew and held a long breath, and his color changed and his eyes swam. "New?" he said.

"You make too much of your problems," said the doctor. "They ought not to be turned into a career. Concentrate on real troubles—fatal sickness, accidents." The old man's whole manner said, Wilky, don't start this on me. I have a right to be spared.

Wilhelm himself prayed for restraint; he knew this weakness of his and fought it. He knew, also, his father's character. And he began mildly, "As far as the fatal part of it goes, everyone on this side of the grave is the same distance from death. No, I guess my trouble is not exactly new. I've got to pay premiums on two policies for the boys. Margaret sent them to me. She unloads everything on me. Her mother left her an income. She won't even file a joint tax return. I get stuck. Etcetera. But you've heard the whole story before."

"I certainly have," said the old man. "And I've told you to stop giving her so much money."

Wilhelm worked his lips in silence before he could speak. The congestion was growing. "Oh, but my kids, Father. My kids. I love them. I don't want them to lack anything."

The doctor said with a half-deaf benevolence, "Well, naturally. And she, I'll bet, is the beneficiary of that policy."

"Let her be. I'd sooner die myself before I collected a cent of such money."

"Ah yes." The old man sighed. He did not like the mention of death. "Did I tell you that your sister Catherine—Philippa—is after me again."

"What for?"

"She wants to rent a gallery for an exhibition."

Stiffly fair-minded, Wilhelm said, "Well, of course that's up to you, Father."

The round-headed old man with his fine, feather-white, ferny hair said, "No,

Wilky. There's not a thing on those canvases. I don't believe it; it's a case of the emperor's clothes. I may be old enough for my second childhood, but at least the first is well behind me. I was glad enough to buy crayons for her when she was four. But now she's a woman of forty and too old to be encouraged in her delusions. She's no painter."

"I wouldn't go so far as to call her a born artist," said Wilhelm, "but you can't blame her for trying something worth while."

"Let her husband pamper her."

Wilhelm had done his best to be just to his sister, and he had sincerely meant to spare his father, but the old man's tight, benevolent deafness had it's usual effect on him. He said, "When it comes to women and money, I'm completely in the dark. What makes Margaret act like this?"

"She's showing you that you can't make it without her," said the doctor. "She aims to bring you back by financial force."

"But if she ruins me, Dad, how can she expect me to come back? No, I have a sense of honor. What you don't see is that she's trying to put an end to me."

His father stared. To him this was absurd. And Wilhelm thought, Once a guy starts to slip, he figures he might as well be a clunk. A real big clunk. He even takes pride in it. But there's nothing to be proud of—hey, boy? Nothing. I don't blame Dad for his attitude. And it's no cause for pride.

"I don't understand that. But if you feel like this why don't you settle with her once and for all?"

"What do you mean, Dad?" said Wilhelm, surprised. "I thought I told you. Do you think I'm not willing to settle? Four years ago when we broke up I gave her everything—goods, furniture, savings. I tried to show good will, but I didn't get anywhere. Why when I wanted Scissors, the dog, because the animal and I were so attached to each other—it was bad enough to leave the kids—she absolutely refused me. Not that she cared a damn about the animal. I don't think you've seen him. He's an Australian sheep dog. They usually have one blank or whitish eye which gives a misleading look, but they're the gentlest dogs and have unusual delicacy about eating or talking. Let me at least have the companionship of this animal. Never." Wilhelm was greatly moved. He wiped his face at all corners with his napkin. Dr. Adler felt that his son was indulging himself too much in his emotions.

"Whenever she can hit me, she hits, and she seems to live for that alone. And she demands more and more, and still more. Two years ago she wanted to go back to college and get another degree. It increased my burden but I thought it would be wiser in the end if she got a better job through it. But still she takes as much from me as before. Next thing she'll want to be a Doctor of Philosophy. She says the women in her family live long, and I'll have to pay and pay for the rest of my life."

The doctor said impatiently, "Well, these are details, not principles. Just details which you can leave out. The dog! You're mixing up all kinds of irrelevant things. Go to a good lawyer."

"But I've already told you, Dad. I got a lawyer, and she got one, too, and both of them talk and send me bills, and I eat my heart out. Oh, Dad, Dad, what a hole I'm in!" said Wilhelm in utter misery. "The lawyers—see?—draw up an agreement, and she says okay on Monday and wants more money on Tuesday. And it begins again."

"I always thought she was a strange kind of woman," said Dr. Adler. He felt that by disliking Margaret from the first and disapproving of the marriage he had done all that he could be expected to do.

"Strange, Father? I'll show you what she's like." Wilhelm took hold of his broad throat with brown-stained fingers and bitten nails and began to choke himself.

"What are you doing?" cried the old man.

"I'm showing you what she does to me."

"Stop that—stop it!" the old man said and tapped the table commandingly.

"Well, Dad, she hates me. I feel that she's strangling me. I can't catch my breath. She just has fixed herself on me to kill me. She can do it at long distance. One of these days I'll be struck down by suffocation or apoplexy because of her. I just can't catch my breath."

"Take your hands off your throat, you foolish man," said his father. "Stop this bunk. Don't expect me to believe in all kinds of voodoo."

"If that's what you want to call it, all right." His face flamed and paled and swelled and his breath was laborious.

"But I'm telling you that from the time I met her I've been a slave. The Emancipation Proclamation was only for colored people. A husband like me is a slave, with an iron collar. The churches go up to Albany and supervise the law. They won't have divorces. The court says, 'You want to be free. Then you have to work twice as hard —twice, at least! Work! you bum.' So then guys kill each other for the buck, and they may be free of a wife who hates them but they are sold to the company. The company knows a guy has got to have his salary, and takes full advantage of him. Don't talk to me about being free. A rich man may be free on an income of a million net. A poor man may be free because nobody cares what he does. But a fellow in my position has to sweat it out until he drops dead."

His father replied to this, "Wilky, it's entirely your own fault. You don't have to allow it."

Stopped in his eloquence, Wilhelm could not speak for a while. Dumb and incompetent, he struggled for breath and frowned with effort into his father's face.

"I don't understand your problems," said the old man. "I never had any like them."

By now Wilhelm had lost his head and he waved his hands and said over and over, "Oh, Dad, don't give me that stuff, don't give me that. Please don't give me that sort of thing."

"It's true," said his father. "I come from a different world. Your mother and I led an entirely different life."

"Oh, how can you compare Mother," Wilhelm said. "Mother was a help to you. Did she harm you ever?"

"There's no need to carry on like an opera, Wilky," said the doctor. "This is only your side of things."

"What? It's the truth," said Wilhelm.

The old man could not be persuaded and shook his round head and drew his vest down over the gilded shirt, and leaned back with a completeness of style that made this look, to anyone out of hearing, like an ordinary conversation between a middle-aged man and his respected father. Wilhelm towered and swayed, big and sloven, with his gray eyes red-shot and his honey-colored hair twisted in flaming shapes upward. Injustice made him angry, made him beg. But he wanted an understanding with his father, and he tried to capitulate to him. He said, "You can't compare Mother and Margaret, and neither can you and I be compared, because you, Dad, were a success. And a success—is a success. I never made a success."

The doctor's old face lost all of its composure and became hard and angry. His small breast rose sharply under the red and black shirt and he said, "Yes. Because of hard work. I was not self-indulgent, not lazy. My old man sold dry goods in Williamsburg. We were nothing, do you understand? I knew I couldn't afford to waste my chances."

"I wouldn't admit for one minute that I was lazy," said Wilhelm. "If anything, I tried too hard. I admit I made many mistakes. Like I thought I shouldn't do things you had done already. Study chemistry. You had done it already. It was in the family."

His father continued, "I didn't run around with fifty women, either. I was not a Hollywood star. I didn't have time to go to Cuba for a vacation. I stayed at home and took care of my children."

Oh, thought Wilhelm, eyes turning upward. Why did I come here in the first place, to live near him? New York is like a gas. The colors are running. My head feels so tight, I don't know what I'm doing. He thinks I want to take away his money or that I envy him. He doesn't see what I want.

"Dad," Wilhelm said aloud, "you're being very unfair. It's true the movies was a false step. But I love my boys. I didn't abandon them. I left Margaret because I had to."

"Why did you have to?"

"Well—" said Wilhelm, struggling to condense his many reasons into a few plain words. "I had to—I had to."

With sudden and surprising bluntness his father said, "Did you have bed-trouble with her? Then you should have stuck it out. Sooner or later everyone has it. Normal people stay with it. It passes. But you wouldn't, so now you pay for your stupid romantic notions. Have I made my view clear?"

It was very clear. Wilhelm seemed to hear it repeated from various sides and inclined his head different ways, and listened and thought. Finally he said, "I guess that's the medical standpoint. You may be right. I just couldn't live with Margaret. I wanted to stick it out, but I was getting very sick. She was one way and I was another. She wouldn't be like me, so I tried to be like her, and I couldn't do it."

"Are you sure she didn't tell *you* to go?" the doctor said.

"I wish she had. I'd be in a better position now. No, it was me. I didn't want to leave, but I couldn't stay. Somebody had to take the initiative. I did. Now I'm the fall guy too."

Pushing aside in advance all the objections that his son would make, the doctor said, "Why did you lose your job with Rojax?"

"I didn't, I've told you."

"You're lying. You wouldn't have ended the connection. You need the money too badly. But you must have got into trouble." The small old man spoke concisely and with great strength. "Since you have to talk and can't let it alone, tell the truth. Was there a scandal—a woman?"

Wilhelm fiercely defended himself. "No, Dad, there wasn't any woman. I told you how it was."

"Maybe it was a man, then," the old man said wickedly.

Shocked, Wilhelm stared at him with burning pallor and dry lips. His skin looked a little yellow. "I don't think you know what you're talking about," he answered after a moment. "You shouldn't let your imagination run so free. Since you've been living here on Broadway you must think you understand life, up to date. You ought to know your own son a little better. Let's drop that, now."

"All right, Wilky, I'll withdraw it. But something must have happened in Roxbury nevertheless. You'll never go back. You're just talking wildly about representing a rival company. You won't. You've done something to spoil your reputation, I think. But you've got girl friends who are expecting you back, isn't that so?"

"I take a lady out now and then while on the road," said Wilhelm. "I'm not a monk."

"No one special? Are you sure you haven't gotten into complications?"

He had tried to unburden himself and instead, Wilhelm thought, he had to undergo an inquisition to prove himself worthy of a sympathetic word. Because his father believed that he did all kinds of gross things.

"There is a woman in Roxbury that I went with. We fell in love and wanted to marry, but she got tired of waiting for my divorce. Margaret figured that. On top of which the girl was a Catholic and I had to go with her to the priest and make an explanation."

Neither did this last confession touch Dr. Adler's sympathies or sway his calm old head or affect the color of his complexion.

"No, no, no, no; all wrong," he said.

Again Wilhelm cautioned himself. Remember his age. He is no longer the same person. He can't bear trouble. I'm so choked up and congested anyway I can't see straight. Will I ever get out of the woods, and recover my balance? You're never the same afterward. Trouble rusts out the system.

"You really *want* a divorce?" said the old man.

"For the price I pay I should be getting something."

"In that case," Dr. Adler said, "it seems to me no normal person would stand for such treatment from a woman."

"Ah, Father, Father!" said Wilhelm. "It's always the same thing with you. Look how you lead me on. You always start out to help me with my problems, and be sympathetic and so forth. It gets my hopes up and I begin to be grateful. But before we're through I'm a hundred times more depressed than before. Why is that? You have no sympathy. You want to shift all the blame on to me. Maybe you're wise to do it." Wilhelm was beginning to lose himself. "All you seem to think about is your death. Well, I'm sorry. But I'm going to die too. And I'm your son. It isn't my fault in the first place. There ought to be a right way to do this, and be fair to each other. But what I want to know is, why do you start up with me if you're not going to help me? What do you want to know about my problems for, Father? So you can lay the whole responsibility on me—so that you won't have to help me? D'you want me to comfort you for having such a son?" Wilhelm had a great knot of wrong tied tight within his chest, and tears approached his eyes but he didn't let them out. He looked shabby enough as it was. His voice was thick and hazy, and he was stammering and could not bring his awful feelings forth.

"You have some purpose of your own," said the doctor, "in acting so unreasonable. What do you want from me? What do you expect?"

"What do I expect?" said Wilhelm. He felt as though he were unable to recover something. Like a ball in the surf, washed beyond reach, his self-control was going out. "I expect *help!*" The words escaped him in a loud, wild, frantic cry and startled the old man, and two or three breakfasters within hearing glanced their way. Wilhelm's hair, the color of whitened honey, rose dense and tall with the expansion of his face, and he said, "When I suffer—you aren't even sorry. That's because you have no affection for me, and you don't want any part of me."

"Why must I like the way you behave? No, I don't like it," said Dr. Adler.

"All right. You want me to change myself. But suppose I could do it—what would I become? What could I? Let's suppose that all my life I have had the wrong ideas about myself and wasn't what I thought I was. And wasn't even careful to take a few precautions, as most people do—like a woodchuck has a few exits to his tunnel. But what shall I do now? More than half my life is over. More than half. And now you tell me I'm not even normal."

The old man too had lost his calm. "You cry about being helped," he said. "When you thought you had to go into the service I sent a check to Margaret every month. As a family man you could have had an exemption. But no! The war couldn't be fought without you and you had to get yourself drafted and be an office-boy in the Pacific theater. Any clerk could have done what you did. You could find nothing better to become than a GI."

Wilhelm was going to reply, and half raised his bearish figure from the chair, his fingers spread and whitened by their grip on the table, but the old man would not let him begin. He said, "I see other elderly people here with children who aren't much good, and they keep backing them and holding them up at a great sacrifice. But I'm not going to make that mistake. It doesn't enter your mind that when I die—a year, two years from now—you'll still be here. I do think of it."

He had intended to say that he had a right to be left in peace. Instead he gave Wilhelm the impression that he meant it was not fair for the better man of the two, and the more useful, the more admired, to leave the world first. Perhaps he meant that, too—a little; but he would not under other circumstances have come out with it so flatly.

"Father," said Wilhelm with an unusual openness of appeal. "Don't you think I know how you feel? I have pity. I want you to live on and on. If you outlive me, that's perfectly okay by me." As his father did not answer this avowal and turned away his glance, Wilhelm suddenly burst out, "No, but you hate me. And if I had money you wouldn't. By God, you have to admit it. The money makes the difference. Then we would be a fine father and son, if I was a credit to you—so you could boast and brag about me all over the hotel. But I'm not the right type of son. I'm too old, I'm too old and too unlucky."

His father said, "I can't give you any money. There would be no end to it if I started. You and your sister would take every last buck from me. I'm still alive, not dead. I am still here. Life isn't over yet. I am as much alive as you or anyone. And I want nobody on my back. Get off! And I give you the same advice, Wilky. Carry nobody on your back."

"Just keep your money," said Wilhelm miserably. "Keep it and enjoy it yourself. That's the ticket!"

IV

Ass! Idiot! Wild boar! Dumb mule! Slave! Lousy, wallowing hippopotamus! Wilhelm called himself as his bending legs carried him from the dining room. His pride! His inflamed feelings! His begging and feebleness! And trading insults with his old father—and spreading confusion over everything. Oh, how poor, contemptible, and ridiculous he was! When he remembered how he had said, with great reproof, "You ought to know your own son"—why, how corny and abominable it was.

He could not get out of the sharply brilliant dining room fast enough. He was horribly worked up; his neck and shoulders, his entire chest ached as though they had been tightly tied with ropes. He smelled the salt odor of tears in his nose.

But at the same time, since there were depths in Wilhelm not unsuspected by himself, he received a suggestion from some remote element in his thoughts that the business of life, the real business—to carry his peculiar burden, to feel shame and impotence, to taste these quelled tears—the only important business, the highest business was being done. Maybe the making of mistakes expressed the very purpose of his life and the essence of his being here. Maybe he was supposed to make them and suffer from them on this earth. And though he had raised himself above Mr. Perls and his father because they adored money, still they were called to act energetically and this was better than to yell and cry, pray and beg, poke and blunder and go by fits and starts and fall upon the thorns of life. And finally sink beneath that watery floor—would that be tough luck, or would it be good riddance?

But he raged once more against his father. Other people with money, while they're still alive, want to see it do some good. Granted, he shouldn't support me. But have I ever asked him to do that? Have I ever asked for dough at all, either for Margaret or for the kids or for myself? It isn't the money, but only the assistance; not even assistance, but just the feeling. But he may be trying to teach me that a grown man should be cured of such feeling. Feeling got me in dutch at Rojax. I had the *feeling* that I belonged to the firm, and my *feelings* were hurt when they put Gerber in over me. Dad thinks I'm too simple. But I'm not so simple as he thinks. What about his feelings? He doesn't forget death for one single second, and that's what makes him like this. And not only is death on his mind but through money he forces me to think about it, too. It gives him power over me. He forces me that way, he himself, and then he's sore. If he was poor, I could care for him and show it. The way I *could* care, too, if I only had a chance. He'd see how much love and respect I had in me. It would make him a different man, too. He'd put his hands on me and give me his blessing."

Someone in a gray straw hat with a wide cocoa-colored band spoke to Wilhelm in the lobby. The light was dusky, splotched with red underfoot; green, the leather furniture; yellow, the indirect lighting.

"Hey, Tommy. Say, there."

"Excuse me," said Wilhelm, trying to reach a house phone. But this was Dr. Tamkin, whom he was just about to call.

"You have a very obsessional look on your face," said Dr. Tamkin.

Wilhelm thought, Here he is, Here he is. If I could only figure this guy out.

"Oh," he said to Tamkin. "Have I got such a look? Well, whatever it is, you name it and I'm sure to have it."

The sight of Dr. Tamkin brought his quarrel with his father to a close. He found himself flowing into another channel.

"What are we doing?" he said. "What's going to happen to lard today?"

"Don't worry yourself about that. All we have to do is hold on to it and it's sure to go up. But what's made you so hot under the collar, Wilhelm?"

"Oh, one of those family situations." This was the moment to take a new look at Tamkin, and he viewed him closely but gained nothing by the new effort. It was conceivable that Tamkin was everything that he claimed to be, and all the gossip false. But was he a scientific man, or not? If he was not, this might be a case for the district attorney's office to investigate. Was he a liar? That was a delicate question. Even a liar might be trustworthy in some ways. Could he trust Tamkin—could he? He feverishly, fruitlessly sought an answer.

But the time for this question was past, and he had to trust him now. After a long struggle to come to a decision, he had given him the money. Practical judgment was in abeyance. He had worn himself out, and the decision was no decision. How had this happened? But how had his Hollywood career begun? It was not because of Maurice Venice, who turned out to be a pimp. It was because Wilhelm himself was ripe for the mistake. His marriage, too, had been like that. Through such decisions somehow his life had taken form. And so, from the moment when he tasted the peculiar flavor of fatality in Dr. Tamkin, he could no longer keep back the money.

Five days ago Tamkin had said, "Meet me tomorrow, and we'll go to the market." Wilhelm, therefore, had had to go. At eleven o'clock they had walked to the brokerage office. On the way, Tamkin broke the news to Wilhelm that though this was an equal partnership he couldn't put up his half of the money just yet; it was tied up for a week or so in one of his patents. Today he would be two hundred dollars short; next week, he'd make it up. But neither of them needed an income from the market, of course. This was only a sporting proposition anyhow, Tamkin said. Wilhelm had to answer, "Of course." It was too late to withdraw. What else could he do? Then came the formal part of the transaction, and it was frightening. The very shade of green of Tamkin's check looked wrong; it was a false, disheartening color. His handwriting was peculiar, even monstrous; the e's were like i's, the t's and l's the same, and the h's like wasps' bellies. He wrote like a fourth-grader. Scientists, however, dealt mostly in symbols; they printed. This was Wilhelm's explanation.

Dr. Tamkin had given him his check for three hundred dollars. Wilhelm, in a blinded and convulsed aberration, pressed and pressed to try to kill the trembling of his hand as he wrote out his check for a thousand. He set his lips tight, crouched with his huge back over the table, and wrote with crumbling, terrified fingers, knowing that if Tamkin's check bounced his own would not be honored either. His sole cleverness was to set the date ahead by one day to give the green check time to clear.

Next he had signed a power of attorney, allowing Tamkin to speculate with his money, and this was an even more frightening document. Tamkin had never said a word about it, but here they were and it had to be done.

After delivering his signatures, the only precaution Wilhelm took was to come back to the manager of the brokerage office and ask him privately, "Uh, about Doctor Tamkin. We were in here a few minutes ago, remember?"

That day had been a weeping, smoky one and Wilhelm had gotten away from Tamkin on the pretext of having to run to the post office. Tamkin had gone to lunch alone, and here was Wilhelm, back again, breathless, his hat dripping, needlessly asking the manager if he remembered.

"Yes, sir, I know," the manager had said. He was a cold, mild, lean German who dressed correctly and around his neck wore a pair of opera glasses with which he read the board. He was an extremely correct person except that he never shaved in the morning, not caring, probably, how he looked to the fumblers and the old people and the operators and the gamblers and the idlers of Broadway uptown. The market closed at three. Maybe, Wilhelm guessed, he had a thick beard and took a lady out to dinner later and wanted to look fresh-shaven.

"Just a question," said Wilhelm. "A few minutes ago I signed a power of attorney so Doctor Tamkin could invest for me. You gave me the blanks."

"Yes, sir, I remember."

"Now this is what I want to know," Wilhelm had said. "I'm no lawyer and I only gave the paper a glance. Does this give Doctor Tamkin power of attorney over any other assets of mine—money, or property?"

The rain had dribbled from Wilhelm's deformed, transparent raincoat; the buttons of his shirt, which always seemed tiny, were partly broken, in pearly quarters of the moon, and some of the dark, thick golden hairs that grew on his belly stood out. It was the manager's business to conceal his opinion of him; he was shrewd, gray, correct (although unshaven) and had little to say except on matters that came to his desk. He must have recognized in Wilhelm a man who reflected long and then made the decision he had rejected twenty separate times. Silvery, cool, level, long-profiled, experienced, indifferent, observant, with unshaven refinement, he scarcely looked at Wilhelm, who trembled with fearful awkwardness. The manager's face, low-colored, long-nostriled, acted as a unit of perception; his eyes merely did their reduced share. Here was a man, like Rubin, who knew and knew and knew. He, a foreigner, knew; Wilhelm, in the city of his birth, was ignorant.

The manager had said, "No, sir, it does not give him."

"Only over the funds I deposited with you?"

"Yes, that is right, sir."

"Thank you, that's what I wanted to find out," Wilhelm had said, grateful.

The answer comforted him. However, the question had no value. None at all. For Wilhelm had no other assets. He had given Tamkin his last money. There wasn't enough of it to cover his obligations anyway, and Wilhelm had reckoned that he might as well go bankrupt now as next month. "Either broke or rich," was how he had figured, and that formula had encouraged him to make the gamble. Well, not rich; he did not expect that, but perhaps Tamkin might really show him how to earn what he needed in the market. By now, however, he had forgotten his own reckoning and was aware only that he stood to lose his seven hundred dollars to the last cent.

Dr. Tamkin took the attitude that they were a pair of gentlemen experimenting with lard and grain futures. The money, a few hundred dollars, meant nothing much to either of them. He said to Wilhelm, "Watch. You'll get a big kick out of this and wonder why more people don't go into it. You think the Wall Street guys are so smart—geniuses? That's because most of us are psychologically afraid to think about the details. Tell me this. When you're on the road, and you don't understand what goes on under the hood of your car, you'll worry what'll happen if something goes wrong with the engine. Am I wrong?" No, he was right. "Well," said Dr. Tamkin with an expression of quiet triumph about his mouth, almost the suggestion of a jeer.

"It's the same psychological principle, Wilhelm. They are rich because you don't understand what goes on. But it's no mystery, and by putting in a little money and applying certain principles of observation, you begin to grasp it. It can't be studied in the abstract. You have to take a specimen risk so that you feel the process, the money-flow, the whole complex. To know how it feels to be a seaweed you have to get in the water. In a very short time we'll take out a hundred-per-cent profit." Thus Wilhelm had had to pretend at the outset that his interest in the market was theoretical.

"Well," said Tamkin when he met him now in the lobby, "what's the problem, what is this family situation? Tell me." He put himself forward as the keen mental scientist. Whenever this happened Wilhelm didn't know what to reply. No matter what he said or did it seemed that Dr. Tamkin saw through him.

"I had some words with my dad."

Dr. Tamkin found nothing extraordinary in this. "It's the eternal same story," he said. "The elemental conflict of parent and child. It won't end, ever. Even with a fine old gentleman like your dad."

"I don't suppose it will. I've never been able to get anywhere with him. He objects to my feelings. He thinks they're sordid. I upset him and he gets mad at me. But maybe all old men are alike."

"Sons, too. Take it from one of them," said Dr. Tamkin. "All the same, you should be proud of such a fine old patriarch of a father. It should give you hope. The longer he lives, the longer your life-expectancy becomes."

Wilhelm answered, brooding, "I guess so. But I think I inherit more from my mother's side, and she died in her fifites."

"A problem arose between a young fellow I'm treating and his dad—I just had a consultation," said Dr. Tamkin as he removed his dark gray hat.

"So early in the morning?" said Wilhelm with suspicion.

"Over the telephone, of course."

What a creature Tamkin was when he took off his hat! The indirect light showed the many complexities of his bald skull, his gull's nose, his rather handsome eyebrows, his vain mustache, his deceiver's brown eyes. His figure was stocky, rigid, short in the neck, so that the large ball of the occiput touched his collar. His bones were peculiarly formed, as though twisted twice where the ordinary human bone was turned only once, and his shoulders rose in two pagoda-like points. At mid-body he was thick. He stood pigeon-toed, a sign perhaps that he was devious or had much to hide. The skin of his hands was aging, and his nails were moonless, concave, clawlike, and they appeared loose. His eyes were as brown as beaver fur and full of strange lines. The two large brown naked balls looked thoughtful—but were they? And honest— but was Dr. Tamkin honest? There was a hypnotic power in his eyes, but this was not always of the same strength, nor was Wilhelm convinced that it was completely natural. He felt that Tamkin tried to make his eyes deliberately conspicuous, with studied art, and that he brought forth his hypnotic effect by an exertion. Occasionally it failed or drooped, and when this happened the sense of his face passed downward to his heavy (possibly foolish?) red underlip.

Wilhelm wanted to talk about the lard holdings, but Dr. Tamkin said, "This father-and-son case of mine would be instructive to you. It's a different psychological type completely than your dad. This man's father thinks that he isn't his son."

"Why not?"

"Because he has found out something about the mother carrying on with a friend of the family for twenty-five years."

"Well, what do you know!" said Wilhelm. His silent thought was, Pure bull. Nothing but bull!

"You must note how interesting the woman is, too. She has two husbands. Whose are the kids? The fellow detected her and she gave a signed confession that two of the four children were not the father's."

"It's amazing," said Wilhelm, but he said it in a rather distant way. He was always hearing such stories from Dr. Tamkin. If you were to believe Tamkin, most of the world was like this. Everybody in the hotel had a mental disorder, a secret history, a concealed disease. The wife of Rubin at the newsstand was supposed to be kept by Carl, the yelling, loud-mouthed gin-rummy player. The wife of Frank in the barber-shop had disappeared with a GI while he was waiting for her to disembark at the French Lines pier. Everyone was like the faces on a playing card, upside down either way. Every public figure had a character-neurosis. Maddest of all were the business-men, the heartless, flaunting, boisterous business class who ruled this country with their hard manners and their bold lies and their absurd words that nobody could believe. They were crazier than anyone. They spread the plague. Wilhelm, thinking of the Rojax Corporation, was inclined to agree that many businessmen were insane. And he supposed that Tamkin, for all his peculiarities, spoke a kind of truth and did some people a sort of good. It confirmed Wilhelm's suspicions to hear that there was a plague, and he said, "I couldn't agree with you more. They trade on anything, they steal everything, they're cynical right to the bones."

"You have to realize," said Tamkin, speaking of his patient, or his client, "that the mother's confession isn't good. It's a confession of duress. I try to tell the young fellow he shouldn't worry about a phony confession. But what does it help him if I am rational with him?"

"No?" said Wilhelm, intensely nervous. "I think we ought to go over to the market. It'll be opening pretty soon."

"Oh, come on," said Tamkin. "It isn't even nine o'clock, and there isn't much trading the first hour anyway. Things don't get hot in Chicago until half-past ten, and they're an hour behind us, don't forget. Anyway, I say lard will go up, and it will. Take my word. I've made a study of the guilt-aggression cycle which is behind it. I ought to know *something* about that. Straighten your collar."

"But meantime," said Wilhelm, "we have taken a licking this week. Are you sure your insight is at its best? Maybe when it isn't we should lay off and wait."

"Don't you realize," Dr. Tamkin told him, "you can't march in a straight line to the victory? You fluctuate toward it. From Euclid to Newton there was straight lines. The modern age analyzes the wavers. On my own accounts, I took a licking in hides and coffee. But I have confidence. I'm sure I'll outguess them." He gave Wilhelm a narrow smile, friendly, calming, shrewd, and wizard-like, patronizing, secret, potent. He saw his fears and smiled at them. "It's something," he remarked, "to see how the competition-factor will manifest itself in different individuals."

"So? Let's go over."

"But I haven't had my breakfast yet."

"I've had mine."

"Come, have a cup of coffee."

"I wouldn't want to meet my dad." Looking through the glass doors, Wilhelm saw that his father had left by the other exit. Wilhelm thought, He didn't want to run into me, either. He said to Dr. Tamkin, "Okay, I'll sit with you, but let's hurry it up because I'd like to get to the market while there's still a place to sit. Everybody and his uncle gets in ahead of you."

"I want to tell you about this boy and his dad. It's highly absorbing. The father was a nudist. Everybody went naked in the house. Maybe the woman found men *with* clothes attractive. Her husband didn't believe in cutting his hair, either. He practiced dentistry. In his office he wore riding pants and a pair of boots, and he wore a green eyeshade."

"Oh, come off it," said Wilhelm.

"This is a true case history."

Without warning, Wilhelm began to laugh. He himself had had no premonition of his change of humor. His face became warm and pleasant, and he forgot his father, his anxieties; he panted bearlike, happily, through his teeth. "This sounds like a horse-dentist. He wouldn't have to put on pants to treat a horse. Now what else are you going to tell me? Did the wife play the mandolin? Does the boy join the cavalry? Oh, Tamkin, you really are a killer-diller."

"Oh, you think I'm trying to amuse you," said Tamkin. "That's because you aren't familiar with my outlook. I deal in facts. Facts always are sensational. I'll say that a second time. Facts *always!* are sensational."

Wilhelm was reluctant to part with his good mood. The doctor had little sense of humor. He was looking at him earnestly.

"I'd bet you any amount of money," said Tamkin, "that the facts about you are sensational."

"Oh—ha, ha! You want them? You can sell them to a true confession magazine."

"People forget how sensational the things are that they do. They don't see it on themselves. It blends into the background of their daily life."

Wilhelm smiled. "Are you sure this boy tells you the truth?"

"Yes, because I've known the whole family for years."

"And you do psychological work with your own friends? I didn't know that was allowed."

"Well, I'm a radical in the profession. I have to do good wherever I can."

Wilhelm's face became ponderous again and pale. His whitened gold hair lay heavy on his head, and he clasped uneasy fingers on the table. Sensational, but oddly enough, dull, too. Now how do you figure that out? It blends with the background. Funny but unfunny. True but false. Casual but laborious, Tamkin was. Wilhelm was most suspicious of him when he took his driest tone.

"With me," said Dr. Tamkin, "I am at my most efficient when I don't need the fee. When I only love. Without a financial reward. I remove myself from the social influence. Especially money. The spiritual compensation is what I look for. Bringing people into the here-and-now. The real universe. That's the present moment. The past is no good to us. The future is full of anxiety. Only the present is real—the here-and-now. Seize the day."

"Well," said Wilhelm, his earnestness returning. "I know you are a very unusual man. I like what you say about here-and-now. Are all the people who come to see you personal friends and patients too? Like that tall handsome girl, the one who always wears those beautiful broomstick skirts and belts?"

"She was an epileptic, and a most bad and serious pathology, too. I'm curing her successfully. She hasn't had a seizure in six months, and she used to have one every week."

"And that young cameraman, the one who showed us those movies from the jungles of Brazil, isn't he related to her?"

"Her brother. He's under my care, too. He has some terrible tendencies, which are to be expected when you have an epileptic sibling. I came into their lives when they needed help desperately, and took hold of them. A certain man forty years older than she had her in his control and used to give her fits by suggestion whenever she tried to leave him. If you only knew one per cent of what goes on in the city of New York! You see, I understand what it is when the lonely person begins to feel like an animal. When the night comes and he feels like howling from his window like a wolf. I'm taking complete care of that young fellow and his sister. I have to steady him down or he'll go from Brazil to Australia the next day. The way I keep him in the here-and-now is by teaching him Greek."

This was a complete surprise! "What, do you know Greek?"

"A friend of mine taught me when I was in Cairo. I studied Aristotle with him to keep from being idle."

Wilhelm tried to take in these new claims and examine them. Howling from the window like a wolf when night comes sounded genuine to him. That was something really to think about. But the Greek! He realized that Tamkin was watching to see how he took it. More elements were continually being added. A few days ago Tamkin had hinted that he had once been in the underworld, one of the Detroit Purple Gang. He was once head of a mental clinic in Toledo. He had worked with a Polish inventor on an unsinkable ship. He was a technical consultant in the field of television. In the life of a man of genius, all of these things might happen. But had they happened to Tamkin? Was he a genius? He often said that he had attended some of the Egyptian royal family as a psychiatrist. "But everybody is alike, common or aristocrat," he told Wilhelm. "The aristocrat knows less about life."

An Egyptian princess whom he had treated in California, for horrible disorders he had described to Wilhelm, retained him to come back to the old country with her, and there he had had many of her friends and relatives under his care. They turned over a villa on the Nile to him. "For ethical reasons, I can't tell you many of the details about them," he said—but Wilhelm had already heard all these details, and strange and shocking they were, if true. *If* true—he could not be free from doubt. For instance, the general who had to wear ladies' silk stockings and stand otherwise naked before the mirror—and all the rest. Listening to the doctor when he was so strangely factual, Wilhelm had to translate his words into his own language, and he could not translate fast enough or find terms to fit what he heard.

"Those Egyptian big shots invested in the market, too, for the heck of it. What did they need extra money for? By association, I almost became a millionaire myself, and if I had played it smart there's no telling what might have happened. I could have been the ambassador." The American? The Egyptian ambassador? "A friend of mine tipped me off on the cotton. I made a heavy purchase of it. I didn't have that kind of money, but everybody there knew me. It never entered their minds that a person of their social circle didn't have dough. The sale was made on the phone. Then, while the cotton shipment was at sea, the price tripled. When the stuff suddenly became so valuable all hell broke loose on the world cotton market, they looked to see who was the owner of this big shipment. Me! They investigated my credit and found out I was a mere doctor, and they canceled. This was illegal. I sued them. But as I didn't have the money to fight them I sold the suit to a Wall Street lawyer for twenty thousand dollars. He fought it and was winning. They settled with him out of court for more than a million. But on the way back from Cairo, flying, there was a crash. All on board died. I have this guilt on my conscience, of being the murderer of that lawyer. Although he was a crook."

Wilhelm thought, I must be a real jerk to sit and listen to such impossible stories. I guess I am a sucker for people who talk about the deeper things of life, even the way he does.

"We scientific men speak of irrational guilt, Wilhelm," said Dr. Tamkin, as if Wilhelm were a pupil in his class. "But in such a situation, because of the money, I wished him harm. I realize it. This isn't the time to describe all the details, but the money made me guilty. *M*oney and *M*urder both begin with *M*. *M*achinery. *M*ischief."

Wilhelm, his mind thinking for him at random, said, "What about *M*ercy? *M*ilk-of-human-kindness?"

"One fact should be clear to you by now. Money-making is aggression. That's the whole thing. The functionalistic explanation is the only one. People come to the market to kill. They say, 'I'm going to make a killing.' It's not accidental. Only they haven't got the genuine courage to kill, and they erect a symbol of it. The money. They make a killing by a fantasy. Now, counting and number is always a sadistic activity. Like hitting. In the Bible, the Jews wouldn't allow you to count them. They knew it was sadistic."

"I don't understand what you mean," said Wilhelm. A strange uneasiness tore at him. The day was growing too warm and his head felt dim. "What makes them want to kill?"

"By and by, you'll get the drift," Dr. Tamkin assured him. His amazing eyes had some of the rich dryness of a brown fur. Innumerable crystalline hairs or spicules of light glittered in their bold surfaces. "You can't understand without first spending years on the study of the ultimates of human and animal behavior, the deep chemical, organismic, and spiritual secrets of life. I am a psychological poet."

"If you're this kind of poet," said Wilhelm, whose fingers in his pocket were feeling in the little envelopes for the Phenaphen capsules, "what are you doing on the market?"

"That's a good question. Maybe I am better at speculation because I don't care. Basically, I don't wish hard enough for money, and therefore I come with a cool head to it."

Wilhelm thought, Oh, sure! That's an answer, is it? I bet that if I took a strong attitude he'd back down on everything. He'd grovel in front of me. The way he looks at me on the sly, to see if I'm being taken in! He swallowed his Phenaphen pill with a long gulp of water. The rims of his eyes grew red as it went down. And then he felt calmer.

"Let me see if I can give you an answer that will satisfy you," said Dr. Tamkin. His flapjacks were set before him. He spread the butter on them, poured on brown maple syrup, quartered them, and began to eat with hard, active, muscular jaws which sometimes gave a creak at the hinges. He pressed the handle of his knife against his chest and said, "In here, the human bosom—mine, yours, everybody's—there isn't just one soul. There's a lot of souls. But there are two main ones, the real soul and a pretender soul. Now! Every man realizes that he has to love something or somebody. He feels that he must go outward. 'If thou canst not love, what art thou?' Are you with me?"

"Yes, Doc, I think so," said Wilhelm listening—a little skeptically but nonetheless hard.

" 'What art thou?' Nothing. That's the answer. Nothing. In the heart of hearts— Nothing! So of course you can't stand that and want to be Something, and you try. But instead of being this Something, the man puts it over on everybody instead. You can't be that strict to yourself. You love a *little*. Like you have a dog" (*Scissors!*) "or give some money to a charity drive. Now that isn't love, is it? What is it? Egotism, pure and simple. It's a way to love the pretender soul. Vanity. Only vanity, is what it is. And social control. The interest of the pretender soul is the same as the interest of the social life, the society mechanism. This is the main tragedy of human life. Oh, it is terrible! Terrible! You are not free. Your own betrayer is inside of you and sells you out. You have to obey him like a slave. He makes you work like a horse. And for what? For who?"

"Yes, for what?" The doctor's words caught Wilhelm's heart. "I couldn't agree more," he said. "When do we get free?"

"The purpose is to keep the whole thing going. The true soul is the one that pays the price. It suffers and gets sick, and it realizes that the pretender can't be loved. Because the pretender is a lie. The true soul loves the truth. And when the true soul feels like this, it wants to kill the pretender. The love has turned into hate. Then you become dangerous. A killer. You have to kill the deceiver."

"Does this happen to everybody?"

The doctor answered simply, "Yes, to everybody. Of course, for simplification purposes, I have spoken of the soul; it isn't a scientific term, but it helps you to understand it. Whenever the slayer slays, he wants to slay the soul in him which has gypped and deceived him. Who is his enemy? Him. And his lover? Also. Therefore, all suicide is murder, and all murder is suicide. It's the one and identical phenomenon. Biologically, the pretender soul takes away the energy of the true soul and makes it feeble, like a parasite. It happens unconsciously, unawaringly, in the depths of the organism. Ever take up parasitology?"

"No, it's my dad who's the doctor."

"You should read a book about it."

Wilhelm said, "But this means that the world is full of murderers. So it's not the world. It's a kind of hell."

"Sure," the doctor said. "At least a kind of purgatory. You walk on the bodies. They are all around. I can hear them cry *de profundis*[7] and wring their hands. I hear them, poor human beasts. I can't help hearing. And my eyes are open to it. I have to cry, too. This is the human tragedy-comedy."

Wilhelm tried to capture his vision. And again the doctor looked untrustworthy to him, and he doubted him. "Well," he said, "there are also kind, ordinary, helpful

---

[7] Latin: "out of the deep"; hence, an extremely bitter cry of wretchedness.

people. They're—out in the country. All over. What kind of morbid stuff do you read, anyway?" The doctor's room was full of books.

"I read the best of literature, science and philosophy," Dr. Tamkin said. Wilhelm had observed that in his room even the TV aerial was set upon a pile of volumes. "Korzybski,[8] Aristotle, Freud, W. H. Sheldon,[9] and all the great poets. You answer me like a layman. You haven't applied your mind strictly to this."

"Very interesting," said Wilhelm. He was aware that he hadn't applied his mind strictly to anything. "You don't have to think I'm a dummy, though. I have ideas, too." A glance at the clock told him that the market would soon open. They could spare a few minutes yet. There were still more things he wanted to hear from Tamkin. He realized that Tamkin spoke faultily, but then scientific men were not always strictly literate. It was the description of the two souls that had awed him. In Tommy he saw the pretender. And even Wilky might not be himself. Might the name of his true soul be the one by which his old grandfather had called him—Velvel? The name of a soul, however, must be only that—soul. What did it look like? Does my soul look like me? Is there a soul that looks like Dad? Like Tamkin? Where does the true soul get its strength? Why does it have to love truth? Wilhelm was tormented, but tried to be oblivious to his torment. Secretly, he prayed the doctor would give him some useful advice and transform his life. "Yes, I understand you," he said. "It isn't lost on me."

"I never said you weren't intelligent, but only you just haven't made a study of it all. As a matter of fact you're a profound personality with very profound creative capacities but also disturbances. I've been concerned with you, and for some time I've been treating you."

"Without my knowing it? I haven't felt you doing anything. What do you mean? I don't think I like being treated without my knowledge. I'm of two minds. What's the matter, don't you think I'm normal?" And he really was divided in mind. That the doctor cared about him pleased him. This was what he craved, that someone should care about him, wish him well. Kindness, mercy, he wanted. But—and here he retracted his heavy shoulders in his peculiar way, drawing his hands up into his sleeves; his feet moved uneasily under the table—but he was worried, too, and even somewhat indignant. For what right had Tamkin to meddle without being asked? What kind of privileged life did this man lead? He took other people's money and speculated with it. Everybody came under his care. No one could have secrets from him.

The doctor looked at him with his deadly brown, heavy, impenetrable eyes, his naked shining head, his red hanging underlip, and said, "You have lots of guilt in you."

Wilhelm helplessly admitted, as he felt the heat rise to his wide face, "Yes, I think so too. But personally," he added, "I don't feel like a murderer. I always try to lay off. It's the others who get me. You know—make me feel oppressed. And if you don't mind, and it's all the same to you, I would rather know it when you start to treat me. And now, Tamkin, for Christ's sake, they're putting out the lunch menus already. Will you sign the check, and let's go!"

Tamkin did as he asked, and they rose. They were passing the bookkeeper's desk

[8] Polish-American scientist, writer, and author of *Science and Sanity* (1933).
[9] American medical and psychological researcher (b. 1899), and author of *Psychology and The Promethean Will* (1936) and *Prometheus Revisited* (1969).

when he took out a substantial bundle of onionskin papers and said, "These are receipts of the transactions. Duplicates. You'd better keep them as the account is in your name and you'll need them for income taxes. And here is a copy of a poem I wrote yesterday."

"I have to leave something at the desk for my father," Wilhelm said, and he put his hotel bill in an envelope with a note. *Dear Dad, Please carry me this month, Yours, W.* He watched the clerk with his sullen pug's profile and his stiff-necked look push the envelope into his father's box.

"May I ask you really why you and your dad had words?" said Dr. Tamkin, who had hung back, waiting.

"It was about my future," said Wilhelm. He hurried down the stairs with swift steps, like a tower in motion, his hands in his trousers pockets. He was ashamed to discuss the matter. "He says there's a reason why I can't go back to my old territory, and there is. I told everybody I was going to be an officer of the corporation. And I was supposed to. It was promised. But then they welshed because of the son-in-law. I bragged and made myself look big."

"If you was humble enough, you could go back. But it doesn't make much difference. We'll make you a good living on the market."

They came into the sunshine of upper Broadway, not clear but throbbing through the dust and fumes, a false air of gas visible at eye-level as it spurted from the bursting busses. From old habit, Wilhelm turned up the collar of his jacket.

"Just a technical question," Wilhelm said. "What happens if your losses are bigger than your deposit?"

"Don't worry. They have ultra-modern electronic bookkeeping machinery, and it won't let you get in debt. It puts you out automatically. But I want you to read this poem. You haven't read it yet."

Light as a locust, a helicopter bringing mail from Newark Airport to La Guardia sprang over the city in a long leap.

The paper Wilhelm unfolded had ruled borders in red ink. He read:

MECHANISM VS FUNCTIONALISM
ISM VS HISM

If thee thyself couldst only see
Thy greatness that is and yet to be,
Thou would feel joy-beauty-what ecstasy.
They are at thy feet, earth-moon-sea, the trinity.

Why-forth then dost thou tarry
And partake thee only of the crust
And skim the earth's surface narry
When all creations art thy just?

Seek ye then that which art not there
In thine own glory let thyself rest.
Witness. Thy power is not bare.
Thou art King. Thou art at thy best.

Look then right before thee.
Open thine eyes and see.
At the foot of Mt. Serenity
Is thy cradle to eternity.

Utterly confused, Wilhelm said to himself explosively, What kind of mishmash, claptrap is this! What does he want from me? Damn him to hell, he might as well hit me on the head, and lay me out, kill me. What does he give me this for? What's the purpose? Is it a deliberate test? Does he want to mix me up? He's already got me mixed up completely. I was never good at riddles. Kiss those seven hundred bucks good-by, and call it one more mistake in a long line of mistakes— Oh, Mama, what a line! He stood near the shining window of a fancy fruit store, holding Tamkin's paper, rather dazed, as though a charge of photographer's flash powder had gone up in his eyes.

But he's waiting for my reaction. I have to say something to him about his poem. It really is no joke. What will I tell him? Who is this King? The poem is written *to* someone. But who? I can't even bring myself to talk. I feel too choked and strangled. With all the books he reads, how come the guy is so illiterate? And why do people just naturally assume that you'll know what they're talking about? No. I don't know, and nobody knows. The planets don't, the stars don't, infinite space doesn't. It doesn't square with Planck's[10] Constant or anything else. So what's the good of it? Where's the need of it? What does he mean here by Mount Serenity? Could it be a figure of speech for Mount Everest? As he says people are all committing suicide, maybe those guys who climbed Everest were only trying to kill themselves, and if we want peace we should stay at the foot of the mountain. In the here-and-now. But it's also here-and-now on the slope, and on the top, where they climbed to seize the day. Surface narry is something he can't mean, I don't believe. I'm about to start foaming at the mouth. "Thy cradle . . ." *Who* is resting in his cradle—in his glory? My thoughts are at an end. I feel the wall. No more. So ——k it all! The money and everything. Take it away! When I have the money they eat me alive, like those piranha fish in the movie about the Brazilian jungle. It was hideous when they ate up that Brahma bull in the river. He turned pale, just like clay, and in five minutes nothing was left except the skeleton still in one piece, floating away. When I haven't got it any more, at least they'll let me alone.

"Well, what do you think of this?" said Dr. Tamkin. He gave a special sort of wise smile, as though Wilhelm must now see what kind of man he was dealing with.

"Nice. Very nice. Have you been writing long?"

"I've been developing this line of thought for years and years. You follow it all the way?"

"I'm trying to figure out who this Thou is."

"Thou? Thou is you."

"Me! Why? This applies to *me?*"

<hr>

[10] Max Carl Ernst Ludwig Planck (1858–1947), world-famous German physicist and formulator of the quantum theory, the foundation of much of modern physics. Planck's constant (h) symbolizes the ratio between the size and frequency of a quantum (a discrete unit of radiant energy).

"Why shouldn't it apply to you. You were in my mind when I composed it. Of course, the hero of the poem is sick humanity. If it would open its eyes it would be great."

"Yes, but how do I get into this?"

"The main idea of the poem is *con*struct or *de*struct. There is no ground in between. Mechanism is *de*struct. Money of course is *de*struct. When the last grave is dug, the gravedigger will have to be paid. If you could have confidence in nature you would not have to fear. It would keep you up. Creative is nature. Rapid. Lavish. Inspirational. It shapes leaves. It rolls the waters of the earth. Man is the chief of this. All creations are his just inheritance. You don't know what you've got within you. A person either creates or he destroys. There is no neutrality . . ."

"I realized you were no beginner," said Wilhelm with propriety. "I have only one criticism to make. I think 'why-forth' is wrong. You should write 'Wherefore then dost thou . . .' " And he reflected, So? I took a gamble. It'll have to be a miracle, though, to save me. My money will be gone, then it won't be able to destruct me. He can't just take and lose it, though. He's in it, too. I think he's in a bad way himself. He must be. I'm sure because, come to think of it, he sweated blood when he signed that check. But what have I let myself in for? The waters of the earth are going to roll over me.

V

Patiently, in the window of the fruit store, a man with a scoop spread crushed ice between his rows of vegetables. There were also Persian melons, lilacs, tulips with radiant black at the middle. The many street noises came back after a little while from the caves of the sky. Crossing the tide of Broadway traffic, Wilhelm was saying to himself, The reason Tamkin lectures me is that somebody has lectured him, and the reason for the poem is that he wants to give me good advice. Everybody seems to know something. Even fellows like Tamkin. Many people know what to do, but how many can do it?

He believed that he must, that he could and would recover the good things, the happy things, the easy tranquil things of life. He had made mistakes, but he could overlook these. He had been a fool, but that could be forgiven. The time wasted— must be relinquished. What else could one do about it? Things were too complex, but they might be reduced to simplicity again. Recovery was possible. First he had to get out of the city. No, first he had to pull out his money. . . .

From the carnival of the street—pushcarts, accordion and fiddle, shoeshine, begging, the dust going round like a woman on stilts—they entered the narrow crowded theater of the brokerage office. From front to back it was filled with the Broadway crowd. But how was lard doing this morning? From the rear of the hall Wilhelm tried to read the tiny figures. The German manager was looking through his binoculars. Tamkin placed himself on Wilhelm's left and covered his conspicuous bald head. "The guy'll ask me about the margin," he muttered. They passed, however, unobserved. "Look, the lard has held its place," he said.

Tamkin's eyes must be very sharp to read the figures over so many heads and at this distance—another respect in which he was unusual.

The room was always crowded. Everyone talked. Only at the front could you hear

the flutter of the wheels within the board. Teletyped news items crossed the illuminated screen above.

"Lard. Now what about rye?" said Tamkin, rising on his toes. Here he was a
different man, active and impatient. He parted people who stood in his way. His face
turned resolute, and on either side of his mouth odd bulges formed under his mustache.
Already he was pointing out to Wilhelm the appearance of a new pattern on the
board. "There's something up today," he said.

"Then why'd you take so long with breakfast?" said Wilhelm.

There were no reserved seats in the room, only customary ones. Tamkin always
sat in the second row, on the commodities side of the aisle. Some of his acquaintances
kept their hats on the chairs for him.

"Thanks. Thanks," said Tamkin, and he told Wilhelm, "I fixed it up yesterday."

"That was a smart thought," said Wilhelm. They sat down.

With folded hands, by the wall, sat an old Chinese businessman in a seersucker coat.
Smooth and fat, he wore a white Vandyke. One day Wilhelm had seen him on
Riverside Drive pushing two little girls along in a baby carriage—his grandchildren.
Then there were two women in their fifties, supposed to be sisters, shrewd and able
money-makers, according to Tamkin. They had never a word to say to Wilhelm. But
they would chat with Tamkin. Tamkin talked to everyone.

Wilhelm sat between Mr. Rowland, who was elderly, and Mr. Rappaport, who
was very old. Yesterday Rowland had told him that in the year 1908, when he was
a junior at Harvard, his mother had given him twenty shares of steel for his birthday,
and then he had started to read the financial news and had never practiced law but
instead followed the market for the rest of his life. Now he speculated only in soy
beans, of which he had made a specialty. By his conservative method, said Tamkin,
he cleared two hundred a week. Small potatoes, but then he was a bachelor, retired,
and didn't need money.

"Without dependents," said Tamkin. "He doesn't have the problems that you and
I do."

Did Tamkin have dependents? He had everything that it was possible for a man
to have—science, Greek, chemistry, poetry, and now dependents too. That beautiful
girl with epilepsy, perhaps. He often said that she was a pure, marvelous, spiritual child
who had no knowledge of the world. He protected her, and, if he was not lying,
adored her. And if you encouraged Tamkin by believing him, or even if you refrained
from questioning him, his hints became more daring. Sometimes he said that he paid
for her music lessons. Sometimes he seemed to have footed the bill for the brother's
camera expedition to Brazil. And he spoke of paying for the support of the orphaned
child of a dead sweetheart. These hints, made dully as asides, grew by repetition into
sensational claims.

"For myself, I don't need much," said Tamkin. "But a man can't live for himself
and I need the money for certain important things. What do you figure you have
to have, to get by?"

"Not less than fifteen grand, after taxes. That's for my wife and the two boys."

"Isn't there anybody else?" said Tamkin with a shrewdness almost cruel. But his
look grew more sympathetic as Wilhelm stumbled, not willing to recall another grief.

"Well—there was. But it wasn't a money matter."

"I should hope!" said Tamkin. "If love is love, it's free. Fifteen grand, though, isn't too much for a man of your intelligence to ask out of life. Fools, hard-hearted criminals, and murderers have millions to squander. They burn up the world—oil, coal, wood, metal, and soil, and suck even the air and the sky. They consume, and they give back no benefit. A man like you, humble for life, who wants to feel and live, has trouble—not wanting," said Tamkin in his parenthetical fashion, "to exchange an ounce of soul for a pound of social power—he'll never make it without help in a world like this. But don't you worry." Wilhelm grasped at this assurance. "Just you never mind. We'll go easily beyond your figure."

Dr. Tamkin gave Wilhelm comfort. He often said that he had made as much as a thousand a week in commodities. Wilhelm had examined the receipts, but until this moment it had never occurred to him that there must be debit slips too; he had been shown only the credits.

"But fifteen grand is not an ambitious figure," Tamkin was telling him. "For that you don't have to wear yourself out on the road, dealing with narrow-minded people. A lot of them don't like Jews, either, I suppose?"

"I can't afford to notice. I'm lucky when I have my occupation. Tamkin, do you mean you can save our money?"

"Oh, did I forget to mention what I did before closing yesterday? You see, I closed out one of the lard contracts and bought a hedge of December rye. The rye is up three points already and takes some of the sting out. But lard will go up, too."

"Where? God, yes, you're right," said Wilhelm, eager, and got to his feet to look. New hope freshened his heart. "Why didn't you tell me before?"

And Tamkin, smiling like a benevolent magician, said, "You must learn to have trust. The slump in lard can't last. And just take a look at eggs. Didn't I predict they couldn't go any lower? They're rising and rising. If we had taken eggs we'd be far ahead."

"Then why didn't we take them?"

"We were just about to. I had a buying order in at .24, but the tide turned at .26 1/4 and we barely missed. Never mind. Lard will go back to last year's levels."

Maybe. But when? Wilhelm could not allow his hopes to grow too strong. However, for a little while he could breathe more easily. Late-morning trading was getting active. The shining numbers whirred on the board, which sounded like a huge cage of artificial birds. Lard fluctuated between two points, but rye slowly climbed.

He closed his strained, greatly earnest eyes briefly and nodded his Buddha's head, too large to suffer such uncertainties. For several moments of peace he was removed to his small yard in Roxbury.

He breathed in the sugar of the pure morning.

He heard the long phrases of the birds.

No enemy wanted his life.

Wilhelm thought, I will get out of here. I don't belong in New York any more. And he sighed like a sleeper.

Tamkin said, "Excuse me," and left his seat. He could not sit still in the room but passed back and forth between the stocks and commodities sections. He knew dozens of people and was continually engaging in discussions. Was he giving advice, gathering information, or giving it, or practicing—whatever mysterious profession he practiced? Hypnotism? Perhaps he could put people in a trance while he talked to them. What a rare, peculiar bird he was, with those pointed shoulders, that bare head, his loose nails, almost claws, and those brown, soft, deadly, heavy eyes.

He spoke of things that mattered, and as very few people did this he could take you by surprise, excite you, move you. Maybe he wished to do good, maybe give himself a lift to a higher level, maybe believe his own prophecies, maybe touch his own heart. Who could tell? He had picked up a lot of strange ideas; Wilhelm could only suspect, he could not say with certainty, that Tamkin hadn't made them his own.

Now Tamkin and he were equal partners, but Tamkin had put up only three hundred dollars. Suppose he did this not only once but five times; then an investment of fifteen hundred dollars gave him five thousand to speculate with. If he had power of attorney in every case, he could shift the money from one account to another. No, the German probably kept an eye on him. Nevertheless it was possible. Calculations like this made Wilhelm feel ill. Obviously Tamkin was a plunger. But how did he get by? He must be in his fifties. How did he support himself? Five years in Egypt; Hollywood before that; Michigan; Ohio; Chicago. A man of fifty has supported himself for at least thirty years. You could be sure that Tamkin had never worked in a factory or in an office. How did he make it? His taste in clothes was horrible, but he didn't buy cheap things. He wore corduroy or velvet shirts from Clyde's, painted neckties, striped socks. There was a slightly acid or pasty smell about his person; for a doctor, he didn't bathe much. Also, Dr. Tamkin had a good room at the Gloriana and had had it for about a year. But so was Wilhelm himself a guest, with an unpaid bill at present in his father's box. Did the beautiful girl with the skirts and belts pay him? Was he defrauding his so-called patients? So many questions impossible to answer could not be asked about an honest man. Nor perhaps about a sane man. Was Tamkin a lunatic, then? That sick Mr. Perls at breakfast had said that there was no easy way to tell the sane from the mad, and he was right about that in any big city and especially in New York—the end of the world, with its complexity and machinery, bricks and tubes, wires and stones, holes and heights. And was everybody crazy here? What sort of people did you see? Every other man spoke a language entirely his own, which he had figured out by private thinking; he had his own ideas and peculiar ways. If you wanted to talk about a glass of water, you had to start back with God creating the heavens and earth; the apple; Abraham; Moses and Jesus; Rome; the Middle Ages; gunpowder; the Revolution; back to Newton; up to Einstein; then war and Lenin and Hitler. After reviewing this and getting it all straight again you could proceed to talk about a glass of water. "I'm fainting, please get me a little water." You were lucky even then to make yourself understood. And this happened over and over and over with everyone you met. You had to translate and translate, explain and explain, back and forth, and it was the punishment of hell itself not to understand or be understood, not to know the crazy from the sane, the wise from the fools, the young from the old or the sick from the well. The fathers were no fathers and the sons no sons. You had to talk with yourself in the daytime and reason with yourself at night. Who else was there to talk to in a city like New York?

A queer look came over Wilhelm's face with its eyes turned up and his silent mouth with its high upper lip. He went several degrees further—when you are like this, dreaming that everybody is outcast, you realize that this must be one of the small matters. There is a larger body, and from this you cannot be separated. The glass of water fades out. You do not go from simple a and simple b to the great x and y, nor does it matter whether you agree about the glass but, far beneath such details, what Tamkin would call the real soul says plain and understandable things to everyone. There sons and fathers are themselves, and a glass of water is only an ornament;

it makes a hoop of brightness on the cloth; it is an angel's mouth. There truth for everybody may be found, and confusion is only—only temporary, thought Wilhelm.

The idea of this larger body had been planted in him a few days ago beneath Times Square, when he had gone downtown to pick up tickets for the baseball game on Saturday (a double-header at the Polo Grounds). He was going through an underground corridor, a place he had always hated and hated more than ever now. On the walls between the advertisements were words in chalk: "Sin No More," and "Do Not Eat the Pig," he had particularly noticed. And in the dark tunnel, in the haste, heat, and darkness which disfigure and make freaks and fragments of nose and eyes and teeth, all of a sudden, unsought, a general love for all these imperfect and lurid-looking people burst out in Wilhelm's breast. He loved them. One and all, he passionately loved them. They were his brothers and his sisters. He was imperfect and disfigured himself, but what difference did that make if he was united with them by this blaze of love? And as he walked he began to say, "Oh my brothers—my brothers and my sisters," blessing them all as well as himself.

So what did it matter how many languages there were, or how hard it was to describe a glass of water? Or matter that a few minutes later he didn't feel anything like a brother toward the man who sold him the tickets?

On that very same afternoon he didn't hold so high an opinion of this same onrush of loving kindness. What did it come to? As they had the capacity and must use it once in a while, people were bound to have such involuntary feelings. It was only another one of those subway things. Like having a hard-on at random. But today, his day of reckoning, he consulted his memory again and thought, I must go back to that. That's the right clue and may do me the most good. Something very big. Truth, like.

The old fellow on the right, Mr. Rappaport, was nearly blind and kept asking Wilhelm, "What's the new figure on November wheat? Give me July soy beans too." When you told him he didn't say thank you. He said, "Okay," instead, or, "Check," and turned away until he needed you again. He was very old, older even than Dr. Adler, and if you believed Tamkin he had once been the Rockefeller of the chicken business and had retired with a large fortune.

Wilhelm had a queer feeling about the chicken industry, that it was sinister. On the road, he frequently passed chicken farms. Those big, rambling, wooden buildings out in the neglected fields; they were like prisons. The lights burned all night in them to cheat the poor hens into laying. Then the slaughter. Pile all the coops of the slaughtered on end, and in one week they'd go higher than Mount Everest or Mount Serenity. The blood filling the Gulf of Mexico. The chicken shit, acid, burning the earth.

How old—old this Mr. Rappaport was! Purple stains were buried in the flesh of his nose, and the cartilage of his ear was twisted like a cabbage heart. Beyond remedy by glasses, his eyes were smoky and faded.

"Read me that soy-bean figure now, boy," he said, and Wilhelm did. He thought perhaps the old man might give him a tip, or some useful advice or information about Tamkin. But no. He only wrote memoranda on a pad, and put the pad in his pocket. He let no one see what he had written. And Wilhelm thought this was the way a man who had grown rich by the murder of millions of animals, little chickens, would act. If there was a life to come he might have to answer for the killing of all those chickens. What if they all were waiting? But if there was a life to come, everybody would have to answer. But if there was a life to come, the chickens themselves would be all right.

Well! What stupid ideas he was having this morning. Phooey!

Finally old Rappaport did address a few remarks to Wilhelm. He asked him whether he had reserved his seat in the synagogue for Yom Kippur.[11]

"No," said Wilhelm.

"Well, you better hurry up if you expect to say *Yiskor*[12] for your parents. I never miss."

And Wilhelm thought, Yes, I suppose I should say a prayer for Mother once in a while. His mother had belonged to the Reform congregation. His father had no religion. At the cemetery Wilhelm had paid a man to say a prayer for her. He was among the tombs and he wanted to be tipped for the *El molai rachamin*. "Thou God of Mercy," Wilhelm thought that meant. *B'gan Aden*—"in Paradise." Singing, they drew it out. *B'gan Ay–den.* The broken bench beside the grave made him wish to do something. Wilhelm often prayed in his own manner. He did not go to the synagogue but he would occasionally perform certain devotions, according to his feelings. Now he reflected, In Dad's eyes I am the wrong kind of Jew. He doesn't like the way I act. Only he is the right kind of Jew. Whatever you are, it always turns out to be the wrong kind.

Mr. Rappaport grumbled and whiffed at his long cigar, and the board, like a swarm of electrical bees, whirred.

"Since you were in the chicken business, I thought you'd speculate in eggs, Mr. Rappaport." Wilhelm, with his warm, panting laugh, sought to charm the old man.

"Oh. Yeah. Loyalty, hey?" said old Rappaport. "I should stick to them. I spent a lot of time amongst chickens. I got to be an expert chicken-sexer. When the chick hatches you have to tell the boys from the girls. It's not easy. You need long, long experience. What do you think, it's a joke? A whole industry depends on it. Yes, now and then I buy a contract eggs. What have you got today?"

Wilhelm said anxiously, "Lard. Rye."

"Buy? Sell?"

"Bought."

"Uh," said the old man. Wilhelm could not determine what he meant by this. But of course you couldn't expect him to make himself any clearer. It was not in the code to give information to anyone. Sick with desire, Wilhelm waited for Mr. Rappaport to make an exception in his case. Just this once! Because it was critical. Silently, by a sort of telepathic concentration, he begged the old man to speak the single word that would save him, give him the merest sign. "Oh, please—please help," he nearly said. If Rappaport would close one eye, or lay his head to one side, or raise his finger and point to a column in the paper or to a figure on his pad. A hint! A hint!

A long perfect ash formed on the end of the cigar, the white ghost of the leaf with all its veins and its fainter pungency. It was ignored, in its beauty, by the old man. For it was beautiful. Wilhelm he ignored as well.

Then Tamkin said to him, "Wilhelm, look at the jump our rye just took."

---

[11] Jewish holiday observed as a solemn day of atonement.

[12] Jewish religious service for the dead.

December rye climbed three points as they tensely watched; the tumblers raced and the machine's lights buzzed.

"A point and a half more, and we can cover the lard losses," said Tamkin. He showed him his calculations on the margin of the *Times*.

"I think you should put in the selling order now. Let's get out with a small loss."

"Get out now? Nothing doing."

"Why not? Why should we wait?"

"Because," said Tamkin with a smiling, almost openly scoffing look, "you've got to keep your nerve when the market starts to go places. Now's when you can make something."

"I'd get out while the getting's good."

"No, you shouldn't lose your head like this. It's obvious to me what the mechanism is, back in the Chicago market. There's a short supply of December rye. Look, it's just gone up another quarter. We should ride it."

"I'm losing my taste for the gamble," said Wilhelm. "You can't feel safe when it goes up so fast. It's liable to come down just as quick."

Dryly, as though he were dealing with a child, Tamkin told him in a tone of tiring patience, "Now listen, Tommy. I have it diagnosed right. If you wish I should sell I can give the sell order. But this is the difference between healthiness and pathology. One is objective, doesn't change his mind every minute, enjoys the risk element. But that's not the neurotic character. The neurotic character—"

"Damn it, Tamkin!" said Wilhelm roughly. "Cut that out. I don't like it. Leave my character out of consideration. Don't pull any more of that stuff on me. I tell you I don't like it."

Tamkin therefore went no further; he backed down. "I meant," he said, softer, "that as a salesman you are basically an artist type. The seller is in the visionary sphere of the business function. And then you're an actor, too."

"No matter what type I am—" An angry and yet weak sweetness rose into Wilhelm's throat. He coughed as though he had the flu. It was twenty years since he had appeared on the screen as an extra. He blew the bagpipes in a film called *Annie Laurie*. Annie had come to warn the young Laird; he would not believe her and called the bagpipers to drown her out. He made fun of her while she wrung her hands. Wilhelm, in a kilt, barelegged, blew and blew and blew and not a sound came out. Of course all the music was recorded. He fell sick with the flu after that and still suffered sometimes from chest weakness.

"Something stuck in your throat?" said Tamkin. "I think maybe you are too disturbed to think clearly. You should try some of my 'here-and-now' mental exercises. It stops you from thinking so much about the future and the past and cuts down confusion."

"Yes, yes, yes, yes," said Wilhelm, his eyes fixed on December rye.

"Nature only knows one thing, and that's the present. Present, present, eternal present, like a big, huge, giant wave—colossal, bright and beautiful, full of life and death, climbing into the sky, standing in the seas. You must go along with the actual, the Here-and-Now, the glory—"

. . . chest weakness, Wilhelm's recollection went on. Margaret nursed him. They had had two rooms of furniture, which was later seized. She sat on the bed and read to him. He made her read for days, and she read stories, poetry, everything in the house. He felt dizzy, stifled when he tried to smoke. They had him wear a flannel vest.

> Come then, Sorrow!
> Sweetest Sorrow!
> Like an own babe I nurse thee on my breast!

Why did he remember that? Why?

"You have to pick out something that's in the actual, immediate present moment," said Tamkin. "And say to yourself here-and-now, here-and-now, here-and-now. 'Where am I?' 'Here.' 'When is it?' 'Now.' Take an object or a person. Anybody. 'Here and now I see a person.' 'Here and now I see a man.' 'Here and now I see a man sitting on a chair.' Take me, for instance. Don't let your mind wander. 'Here and now I see a man in a brown suit. Here and now I see a corduroy shirt.' You have to narrow it down, one item at a time, and not let your imagination shoot ahead. Be in the present. Grasp the hour, the moment, the instant."

Is he trying to hypnotize or con me? Wilhelm wondered. To take my mind off selling? But even if I'm back at seven hundred bucks, then where am I?

As if in prayer, his lids coming down with raised veins, frayed out, on his significant eyes, Tamkin said, " 'Here and now I see a button. Here and now I see the thread that sews the button. Here and now I see the green thread.' " Inch by inch he contemplated himself in order to show Wilhelm how calm it would make him. But Wilhelm was hearing Margaret's voice as she read, somewhat unwillingly,

> Come then, Sorrow!
> .   .   .   .   .
> I thought to leave thee,
> And deceive thee,
> But now of all the world I love thee best.

Then Mr. Rappaport's old hand pressed his thigh, and he said, "What's my wheat? Those damn guys are blocking the way. I can't see."

VI

Rye was still ahead when they went out to lunch, and lard was holding its own.

They ate in the cafeteria with the gilded front. There was the same art inside as outside. The food looked sumptuous. Whole fishes were framed like pictures with carrots, and the salads were like terraced landscapes or like Mexican pyramids; slices of lemon and onion and radishes were like sun and moon and stars; the cream pies were about a foot thick and the cakes swollen as if sleepers had baked them in their dreams.

"What'll you have?" said Tamkin.

"Not much. I ate a big breakfast. I'll find a table. Bring me some yogurt and crackers and a cup of tea. I don't want to spend much time over lunch."

Tamkin said, "You've got to eat."

Finding an empty place at this hour was not easy. The old people idled and gossiped over their coffee. The elderly ladies were rouged and mascaraed and hennaed and used blue hair rinse and eye shadow and wore costume jewelry, and many of them were proud and stared at you with expressions that did not belong to their age. Were there no longer any respectable old ladies who knitted and cooked and looked after their grandchildren? Wilhelm's grandmother had dressed him in a sailor suit and danced him on her knee, blew on the porridge for him and said, "Admiral, you must eat." But what was the use of remembering this so late in the day?

He managed to find a table, and Dr. Tamkin came along with a tray piled with plates and cups. He had Yankee pot roast, purple cabbage, potatoes, a big slice of watermelon, and two cups of coffee. Wilhelm could not even swallow his yogurt. His chest pained him still.

At once Tamkin involved him in a lengthy discussion. Did he do it to stall Wilhelm and prevent him from selling out the rye—or to recover the ground lost when he had made Wilhelm angry by hints about the neurotic character? Or did he have no purpose except to talk?

"I think you worry a lot too much about what your wife and your father will say. Do they matter so much?"

Wilhelm replied, "A person can become tired of looking himself over and trying to fix himself up. You can spend the entire second half of your life recovering from the mistakes of the first half."

"I believe your dad told me he had some money to leave you."

"He probably does have something."

"A lot?"

"Who can tell," said Wilhelm guardedly.

"You ought to think over what you'll do with it."

"I may be too feeble to do anything by the time I get it. If I get anything."

"A thing like this you ought to plan out carefully. Invest it properly." He began to unfold schemes whereby you bought bonds, and used the bonds as security to buy something else and thereby earned twelve per cent safely on your money. Wilhelm failed to follow the details. Tamkin said, "If he made you a gift now, you wouldn't have to pay the inheritance taxes."

Bitterly, Wilhelm told him, "My father's death blots out all other considerations from his mind. He forces me to think about it, too. Then he hates me because he succeeds. When I get desperate—of course I think about money. But I don't want anything to happen to him. I certainly don't want him to die." Tamkin's brown eyes glittered shrewdly at him. "You don't believe it. Maybe it's not psychological. But on my word of honor. A joke is a joke, but I don't want to joke about stuff like this. When he dies, I'll be robbed, like. I'll have no more father."

"You love your old man?"

Wilhelm grasped at this. "Of course, of course I love him. My father. My mother—" As he said this there was a great pull at the very center of his soul. When a fish strikes the line you feel the live force in your hand. A mysterious being beneath the water, driven by hunger, has taken the hook and rushes away and fights, writhing. Wilhelm never identified what struck within him. It did not reveal itself. It got away.

And Tamkin, the confuser of the imagination, began to tell, or to fabricate, the strange history of *his* father. "He was a great singer," he said. "He left us five kids because he fell in love with an opera soprano. I never held it against him, but admired the way he followed the life-principle. I wanted to do the same. Because of unhappiness, at a certain age, the brain starts to die back." (True, true! thought Wilhelm) "Twenty years later I was doing experiments in Eastman Kodak, Rochester, and I found the old fellow. He had five more children." (False, false!) "He wept; he was ashamed. I had nothing against him. I naturally felt strange."

"My dad is something of a stranger to me, too," said Wilhelm, and he began to muse. Where is the familiar person he used to be? Or I used to be? Catherine—she won't even talk to me any more, my own sister. It may not be so much my trouble that Papa turns his back on as my confusion. It's too much. The ruins of life, and on top of that confusion—chaos and old night. Is it an easier farewell for Dad if we don't part friends? He should maybe do it angrily— "Blast you with my curse!" And why, Wilhelm further asked, should he or anybody else pity me; or why should I be pitied sooner than another fellow? It is my childish mind that thinks people are ready to give it just because you need it.

Then Wilhelm began to think about his own two sons and to wonder how he appeared to them, and what they would think of him. Right now he had an advantage through baseball. When he went to fetch them, to go to Ebbets Field, though, he was not himself. He put on a front but he felt as if he had swallowed a fistful of sand. The strange, familiar house, horribly awkward; the dog, Scissors, rolled over on his back and barked and whined. Wilhelm acted as if there were nothing irregular, but a weary heaviness came over him. On the way to Flatbush he would think up anecdotes about old Pigtown and Charlie Ebbets for the boys and reminiscences of the old stars, but it was very heavy going. They did not know how much he cared for them. No. It hurt him greatly and he blamed Margaret for turning them against him. She wanted to ruin him, while she wore the mask of kindness. Up in Roxbury he had to go and explain to the priest, who was not sympathetic. They don't care about individuals, their rules come first. Olive said she would marry him outside the Church when he was divorced. But Margaret would not let go. Olive's father was a pretty decent old guy, an osteopath, and he understood what it was all about. Finally he said, "See here, I have to advise Olive. She is asking me. I am mostly a freethinker myself, but the girl has to live in this town." And by now Wilhelm and Olive had had a great many troubles and she was beginning to dread his days in Roxbury, she said. He trembled at offending this small, pretty, dark girl whom he adored. When she would get up late on Sunday morning she would wake him almost in tears at being late for Mass. He would try to help her hitch her garters and smooth out her slip and dress and even put on her hat with shaky hands; then he would rush her to church and drive in second gear in his forgetful way, trying to apologize and to calm her. She got out a block from church to avoid gossip. Even so she loved him, and she would have married him if he had obtained the divorce. But Margaret must have sensed this. Margaret would tell him he did not really want a divorce; he was afraid of it. He cried, "Take everything I've got, Margaret. Let me go to Reno. Don't you want to marry again?" No. She went out with other men, but took his money. She lived in order to punish him.

Dr. Tamkin told Wilhelm, "Your dad is jealous of you."

Wilhelm smiled. "Of *me*? That's rich."

"Sure. People are always jealous of a man who leaves his wife."

"Oh," said Wilhelm scornfully. "When it comes to wives he wouldn't have to envy me."

"Yes, and your wife envies you, too. She thinks, He's free and goes with young women. Is she getting old?"

"Not exactly old," said Wilhelm, whom the mention of his wife made sad. Twenty years ago, in a neat blue wool suit, in a soft hat made of the same cloth—he could plainly see her. He stooped his yellow head and looked under the hat at her clear, simple face, her living eyes moving, her straight small nose, her jaw beautifully, painfully clear in its form. It was a cool day, but he smelled the odor of pines in the sun, in the granite canyon. Just south of Santa Barbara, this was.

"She's forty-some years old," he said.

"I was married to a lush," said Tamkin. "A painful alcoholic. I couldn't take her out to dinner because she'd say she was going to the ladies' toilet and disappear into the bar. I'd ask the bartenders they shouldn't serve her. But I loved her deeply. She was the most spiritual woman of my entire experience."

"Where is she now?"

"Drowned," said Tamkin. "At Provincetown, Cape Cod. It must have been a suicide. She was that way—suicidal. I tried everything in my power to cure her. Because," said Tamkin, "my real calling is to be a healer. I get wounded. I suffer from it. I would like to escape from the sicknesses of others, but I can't. I am only on loan to myself, so to speak. I belong to humanity."

Liar! Wilhelm inwardly called him. Nasty lies. He invented a woman and killed her off and then called himself a healer, and made himself so earnest he looked like a bad-natured sheep. He's a puffed-up little bogus and humbug with smelly feet. A doctor! A doctor would wash himself. He believes he's making a terrific impression, and he practically invites you to take off your hat when he talks about himself; and he thinks he has an imagination, but he hasn't, neither is he smart.

Then what am I doing with him here, and why did I give him the seven hundred dollars? thought Wilhelm.

Oh, this was a day of reckoning. It was a day, he thought, on which, willing or not, he would take a good close look at the truth. He breathed hard and his misshapen hat came low upon his congested dark blond face. A rude look. Tamkin was a charlatan, and furthermore he was desperate. And furthermore, Wilhelm had always known this about him. But he appeared to have worked it out at the back of his mind that Tamkin for thirty or forty years had gotten through many a tight place, that he would get through this crisis too and bring him, Wilhelm, to safety also. And Wilhelm realized that he was on Tamkin's back. It made him feel that he had virtually left the ground and was riding upon the other man. He was in the air. It was for Tamkin to take the steps.

The doctor, if he was a doctor, did not look anxious. But then his face did not have much variety. Talking always about spontaneous emotion and open receptors and free impulses, he was about as expressive as a pincushion. When his hypnotic spell failed, his big underlip made him look weak-minded. Fear stared from his eyes, sometimes, so humble as to make you sorry for him. Once or twice Wilhelm had seen that look. Like a dog, he thought. Perhaps he didn't look it now, but he was very nervous. Wilhelm knew, but he could not afford to recognize this too openly.

The doctor needed a little room, a little time. He should not be pressed now. So Tamkin went on, telling his tales.

Wilhelm said to himself, I am on his back—his back. I gambled seven hundred bucks, so I must take this ride. I have to go along with him. It's too late. I can't get off.

"You know," Tamkin said, "that blind old man Rappaport—he's pretty close to totally blind—is one of the most interesting personalities around here. If you could only get him to tell his true story. It's fascinating. This is what he told me. You often hear about bigamists with a secret life. But this old man never hid anything from anybody. He's a regular patriarch. Now, I'll tell you what he did. He had two whole families, separate and apart, one in Williamsburg and the other in the Bronx. The two wives knew about each other. The wife in the Bronx was younger; she's close to seventy now. When he got sore at one wife he went to live with the other one. Meanwhile he ran his chicken business in New Jersey. By one wife he had four kids, and by the other six. They're all grown, but they never have met their half-brothers and sisters and don't want to. The whole bunch of them are listed in the telephone book."

"I can't believe it," said Wilhelm.

"He told me this himself. And do you know what else? While he had his eyesight he used to read a lot, but the only books he would read were by Theodore Roosevelt. He had a set in each of the places where he lived, and he brought his kids up on those books."

"Please," said Wilhelm, "don't feed me any more of this stuff, will you? Kindly do not—"

"In telling you this," said Tamkin with one of his hypnotic subtleties, "I do have a motive. I want you to see how some people free themselves from morbid guilt feelings and follow their instincts. Innately, the female knows how to cripple by sickening a man with guilt. It is a very special *destruct*, and she sends her curse to make a fellow impotent. As if she says, 'Unless I allow it, you will never more be a man.' But men like my old dad or Mr. Rappaport answer, 'Woman, what art thou to me?' You can't do that yet. You're a halfway case. You want to follow your instinct, but you're too worried still. For instance, about your kids—"

"Now look here," said Wilhelm, stamping his feet. "One thing! Don't bring up my boys. Just lay off."

"I was only going to say that they are better off than with conflicts in the home."

"I'm deprived of my children." Wilhelm bit his lip. It was too late to turn away. The anguish struck him. "I pay and pay. I never see them. They grow up without me. She makes them like herself. She'll bring them up to be my enemies. Please let's not talk about this."

But Tamkin said, "Why do you let her make you suffer so? It defeats the original object in leaving her. Don't play her game. Now, Wilhelm, I'm trying to do you some good. I want to tell you, don't marry suffering. Some people do. They get married to it, and sleep and eat together, just as husband and wife. If they go with joy they think it's adultery."

When Wilhelm heard this he had, in spite of himself, to admit that there was a great deal in Tamkin's words. Yes, thought Wilhelm, suffering is the only kind of life they are sure they can have, and if they quit suffering they're afraid they'll have nothing. He knows it. This time the faker knows what he's talking about.

Looking at Tamkin he believed he saw all this confessed from his usually barren face. Yes, yes, he too. One hundred falsehoods, but at last one truth. Howling like a wolf from the city window. No one can bear it any more. Everyone is so full of it that at last everybody must proclaim it. It! It!

Then suddenly Wilhelm rose and said, "That's enough of this, Tamkin, let's go back to the market."

"I haven't finished my melon."

"Never mind that. You've had enough to eat. I want to go back."

Dr. Tamkin slid the two checks across the table. "Who paid yesterday? It's your turn, I think."

It was not until they were leaving the cafeteria that Wilhelm remembered definitely that he had paid yesterday too. But it wasn't worth arguing about.

Tamkin kept repeating as they walked down the street that there were many who were dedicated to suffering. But he told Wilhelm, "I'm optimistic in your case, and I have seen a world of maladjustment. There's hope for you. You don't really want to destroy yourself. You're trying hard to keep your feelings open, Wilhelm. I can see it. Seven per cent of this country is committing suicide by alcohol. Another three, maybe, narcotics. Another sixty just fading away into dust by boredom. Twenty more who have sold their souls to the Devil. Then there's a small percentage of those who want to live. That's the only significant thing in the whole world of today. Those are the only two classes of people there are. Some want to live, but the great majority don't." This fantastic Tamkin began to surpass himself. "They don't. Or else, why these wars? I'll tell you more," he said. "The love of the dying amounts to one thing; they want you to die with them. It's because they love you. Make no mistake."

True, true! thought Wilhelm, profoundly moved by these revelations. How does he know these things? How can he be such a jerk, and even perhaps an operator, a swindler, and understand so well what gives? I believe what he says. It simplifies much —everything. People are dropping like flies. I am trying to stay alive and work too hard at it. That's what's turning my brains. This working hard defeats its own end. At what point should I start over? Let me go back a ways and try once more.

Only a few hundred yards separated the cafeteria from the broker's, and within that short space Wilhelm turned again, in measurable degrees, from these wide considerations to the problems of the moment. The closer he approached to the market, the more Wilhelm had to think about money.

They passed the newsreel theater where the ragged shoeshine kids called after them. The same old bearded man with his bandaged beggar face and his tiny ragged feet and the old press clipping on his fiddle case to prove he had once been a concert violinist, pointed his bow at Wilhelm, saying, "You!" Wilhelm went by with worried eyes, bent on crossing Seventy-second Street. In full tumult the great afternoon current raced for Columbus Circle, where the mouth of midtown stood open and the skyscrapers gave back the yellow fire of the sun.

As they approached the polished stone front of the new office building, Dr. Tamkin said, "Well, isn't that old Rappaport by the door? I think he should carry a white cane, but he will never admit there's a single thing the matter with his eyes."

Mr. Rappaport did not stand well; his knees were sunk, while his pelvis only half filled his trousers. His suspenders held them, gaping.

He stopped Wilhelm with an extended hand, having somehow recognized him. In his deep voice he commanded him. "Take me to the cigar store."

"You want me—? Tamkin!" Wilhelm whispered, "You take him."

Tamkin shook his head. "He wants you. Don't refuse the old gentleman." Significantly he said in a lower voice. "This minute is another instance of the 'here-and-now.' You have to live in this very minute, and you don't want to. A man asks you for help. Don't think of the market. It won't run away. Show your respect to the old boy. Go ahead. That may be more valuable."

"Take me," said the old chicken merchant again.

Greatly annoyed, Wilhelm wrinkled his face at Tamkin. He took the old man's big but light elbow at the bone. "Well, let's step on it," he said. "Or wait—I want to have a look at the board first to see how we're doing."

But Tamkin had already started Mr. Rappaport forward. He was walking, and he scolded Wilhelm, saying, "Don't leave me standing in the middle of the sidewalk. I'm afraid to get knocked over."

"Let's get a move on. Come." Wilhelm urged him as Tamkin went into the broker's.

The traffic seemed to come down Broadway out of the sky, where the hot spokes of the sun rolled from the south. Hot, stony odors rose from the subway grating in the street.

"These teen-age hoodlums worry me. I'm ascared of these Puerto Rican kids, and these young characters who take dope," said Mr. Rappaport. "They go around all hopped up."

"Hoodlums?" said Wilhelm. "I went to the cemetery and my mother's stone bench was split. I could have broken somebody's neck for that. Which store do you go to?"

"Across Broadway. That La Magnita sign next door to the Automat."

"What's the matter with this store here on this side?"

"They don't carry my brand, that's what's the matter."

Wilhelm cursed, but checked the words.

"What are you talking?"

"Those damn taxis," said Wilhelm. "They want to run everybody down."

They entered the cool, odorous shop. Mr. Rappaport put away his large cigars with great care in various pockets while Wilhelm muttered, "Come on, you old creeper. What a poky old character! The whole world waits on him." Rappaport did not offer Wilhelm a cigar, but, holding one up, he asked, "What do you say at the size of these, huh? They're Churchill-type cigars."

He barely crawls along, thought Wilhelm. His pants are dropping off because he hasn't got enough flesh for them to stick to. He's almost blind, and covered with spots, but this old man still makes money in the market. Is loaded with dough, probably. And I bet he doesn't give his children any. Some of them must be in their fifties. This is what keeps middle-aged men as children. He's master over the dough. Think—just think! Who controls everything? Old men of this type. Without needs. They don't need therefore they have. I need, therefore I don't have. That would be too easy.

"I'm older even than Churchill," said Rappaport.

Now he wanted to talk! But if you asked him a question in the market, he couldn't be bothered to answer.

"I bet you are," said Wilhelm. "Come, let's get going."

"I was a fighter, too, like Churchill," said the old man. "When we licked Spain

I went into the Navy. Yes, I was a gob[13] that time. What did I have to lose? Nothing. After the battle of San Juan Hill, Teddy Roosevelt kicked me off the beach."

"Come, watch the curb," said Wilhelm.

"I was curious and wanted to see what went on. I didn't have no business there, but I took a boat and rowed myself to the beach. Two of our guys was dead, layin' under the American flag to keep the flies off. So I says to the guy on duty, there, who was the sentry, 'Let's have a look at these guys. I want to see what went on here,' and he says, 'Naw,' but I talked him into it. So he took off the flag and there were these two tall guys, both gentlemen, lying in their boots. They was very tall. The two of them had long mustaches. They were high-society boys. I think one of them was called Fish, from up the Hudson, a big-shot family. When I looked up, there was Teddy Roosevelt, with his hat off, and he was looking at these fellows, the only ones who got killed there. Then he says to me, 'What's the Navy want here? Have you got orders?' 'No, sir,' I says to him. 'Well, get the hell off the beach, then.'"

Old Rappaport was very proud of this memory. "Everything he said had such snap, such class. Man! I love that Teddy Roosevelt," he said, "I love him!"

Ah, what people are! He is almost not with us, and his life is nearly gone, but T. R. once yelled at him, so he loves him. I guess it is love, too. Wilhelm smiled. So maybe the rest of Tamkin's story was true, about the ten children and the wives and the telephone directory.

He said, "Come on, come on, Mr. Rappaport," and hurried the old man back by the large hollow elbow; he gripped it through the thin cotton cloth. Re-entering the brokerage office where under the lights the tumblers were speeding with the clack of drumsticks upon wooden blocks, more than ever resembling a Chinese theater, Wilhelm strained his eyes to see the board.

The lard figures were unfamiliar. That amount couldn't be lard! They must have put the figures in the wrong slot. He traced the line back to the margin. It was down to .19, and had dropped twenty points since noon. And what about the contract of rye? It had sunk back to its earlier position, and they had lost their chance to sell.

Old Mr. Rappaport said to Wilhelm, "Read me my wheat figure."

"Oh, leave me alone for a minute," he said, and positively hid his face from the old man behind one hand. He looked for Tamkin, Tamkin's bald head, or Tamkin with his gray straw and the cocoa-colored band. He couldn't see him. Where was he? The seats next to Rowland were taken by strangers. He thrust himself over the one on the aisle, Mr. Rappaport's former place, and pushed at the back of the chair until the new occupant, a red-headed man with a thin, determined face, leaned forward to get out of his way but would not surrender the seat. "Where's Tamkin?" Wilhelm asked Rowland.

"Gee, I don't know. Is anything wrong?"

"You must have seen him. He came in a while back."

"No, but I didn't."

Wilhelm fumbled out a pencil from the top pocket of his coat and began to make calculations. His very fingers were numb, and in his agitation he was afraid he made mistakes with the decimal points and went over the subtraction and multiplication like a schoolboy at an exam. His heart, accustomed to many sorts of crisis, was now

[13] Slang for sailor (especially popular during World War II).

in a new panic. And, as he had dreaded, he was wiped out. It was unnecessary to ask the German manager. He could see for himself that the electronic bookkeeping device must have closed him out. The manager probably had known that Tamkin wasn't to be trusted, and on that first day he might have warned him. But you couldn't expect him to interfere.

"You get hit?" said Mr. Rowland.

And Wilhelm, quite coolly, said, "Oh, it could have been worse, I guess." He put the piece of paper into his pocket with its cigarette butts and packets of pills. The lie helped him out—although, for a moment, he was afraid he would cry. But he hardened himself. The hardening effort made a violent, vertical pain go through his chest, like that caused by a pocket of air under the collar bones. To the old chicken millionaire, who by this time had become acquainted with the drop in rye and lard, he also denied that anything serious had happened. "It's just one of those temporary slumps. Nothing to be scared about," he said, and remained in possession of himself. His need to cry, like someone in a crowd, pushed and jostled and abused him from behind, and Wilhelm did not dare turn. He said to himself, I will not cry in front of these people. I'll be damned if I'll break down in front of them like a kid, even though I never expect to see them again. No! No! And yet his unshed tears rose and rose and he looked like a man about to drown. But when they talked to him, he answered very distinctly. He tried to speak proudly.

". . . going away?" he heard Rowland ask.

"What?"

"I thought you might be going away too. Tamkin said he was going to Maine this summer for his vacation."

"Oh, going away?"

Wilhelm broke off and went to look for Tamkin in the men's toilet. Across the corridor was the room where the machinery of the board was housed. It hummed and whirred like mechanical birds, and the tubes glittered in the dark. A couple of businessmen with cigarettes in their fingers were having a conversation in the lavatory. At the top of the closet door sat a gray straw hat with a cocoa-colored band. "Tamkin," said Wilhelm. He tried to identify the feet below the door. "Are you in there, Doctor Tamkin?" he said with stifled anger. "Answer me. It's Wilhelm."

The hat was taken down, the latch lifted, and a stranger came out who looked at him with annoyance.

"You waiting?" said one of the businessmen. He was warning Wilhelm that he was out of turn.

"Me? Not me," said Wilhelm. "I'm looking for a fellow."

Bitterly angry, he said to himself that Tamkin would pay him the two hundred dollars at least, his share of the original deposit. "And before he takes the train to Maine, too. Before he spends a penny on vacation—that liar! We went into this as equal partners."

VII

I was the man beneath; Tamkin was on my back, and I thought I was on his. He made me carry him, too, besides Margaret. Like this they ride on me with hoofs and claws. Tear me to pieces, stamp on me and break my bones.

Once more the hoary old fiddler pointed his bow at Wilhelm as he hurried by.

Wilhelm rejected his begging and denied the omen. He dodged heavily through traffic and with his quick, small steps ran up the lower stairway of the Gloriana Hotel with its dark-tinted mirrors, kind to people's defects. From the lobby he phoned Tamkin's room, and when no one answered he took the elevator up. A rouged woman in her fifties with a mink stole led three tiny dogs on a leash, high-strung creatures with prominent black eyes, like dwarf deer, and legs like twigs. This was the eccentric Estonian lady who had been moved with her pets to the twelfth floor.

She identified Wilhelm. "You are Doctor Adler's son," she said.

Formally, he nodded.

"I am a dear friend of your father."

He stood in the corner and would not meet her glance, and she thought he was snubbing her and made a mental note to speak of it to the doctor.

The linen-wagon stood at Tamkin's door, and the chambermaid's key with its big brass tongue was in the lock.

"Has Doctor Tamkin been here?" he asked her.

"No, I haven't seen him."

Wilhelm came in, however, to look around. He examined the photos on the desk, trying to connect the faces with the strange people in Tamkin's stories. Big, heavy volumes were stacked under the double-pronged TV aerial. *Science and Sanity*, he read, and there were several books of poetry. The *Wall Street Journal* hung in separate sheets from the bed-table under the weight of the silver water jug. A bathrobe with lightning streaks of red and white was laid across the foot of the bed with a pair of expensive batik pajamas. It was a box of a room, but from the windows you saw the river as far uptown as the bridge, as far downtown as Hoboken. What lay between was deep, azure, dirty, complex, crystal, rusty, with the red bones of new apartments rising on the bluffs of New Jersey, and huge liners in their berths, the tugs with matted beards of cordage. Even the brackish tidal river smell rose this high, like the smell of mop water. From every side he heard pianos, and the voices of men and women singing scales and opera, all mixed, and the sounds of pigeons on the ledges.

Again Wilhelm took the phone. "Can you locate Doctor Tamkin in the lobby for me?" he asked. And when the operator reported that she could not, Wilhelm gave the number of his father's room, but Dr. Adler was not in either. "Well, please give me the masseur. I say the massage room. Don't you understand me? The men's health club. Yes, Max Schilper's—how am I supposed to know the name of it?"

There a strange voice said, "Toktor Adler?" It was the old Czech prizefighter with the deformed nose and ears who was attendant down there and gave out soap, sheets, and sandals. He went away. A hollow endless silence followed. Wilhelm flickered the receiver with his nails, whistled into it, but could not summon either the attendant or the operator.

The maid saw him examining the bottles of pills on Tamkin's table and seemed suspicious of him. He was running low on Phenaphen pills and was looking for something else. But he swallowed one of his own tablets and went out and rang again for the elevator. He went down to the health club. Through the steamy windows, when he emerged, he saw the reflection of the swimming pool swirling green at the bottom of the lowest stairway. He went through the locker-room curtains. Two men wrapped in towels were playing Ping-pong. They were awkward and the ball bounded high. The Negro in the toilet was shining shoes. He did not know Dr. Adler by name, and Wilhelm descended to the massage room. On the tables naked men were lying. It was not a brightly lighted place, and it was very hot, and under the white faint moons of the ceiling shone pale skins. Calendar pictures of pretty girls dressed in tiny fringes were pinned on the wall. On the first table, eyes deeply shut in heavy silent luxury lay a man with a full square beard and short legs, stocky and black-haired. He might have been an orthodox Russian. Wrapped in a sheet, waiting, the man beside him was newly shaved and red from the steambath. He had a big happy face and was dreaming. And after him was an athlete, strikingly muscled, powerful and young, with a strong white curve to his genital and half-angry smile on his mouth. Dr. Adler was on the fourth table, and Wilhelm stood over his father's pale, slight body. His ribs were narrow and small, his belly round, white, and high. It had its own being, like something separate. His thighs were weak, the muscles of his arms had fallen, his throat was creased.

The masseur in his undershirt bent and whispered in his ear, "It's your son," and Dr. Adler opened his eyes into Wilhelm's face. At once he saw the trouble in it, and by an instantaneous reflex he removed himself from the danger of contagion, and he said serenely, "Well, have you taken my advice, Wilky?"

"Oh, Dad," said Wilhelm.

"To take a swim and get a massage?"

"Did you get my note?" said Wilhelm.

"Yes, but I'm afraid you'll have to ask somebody else, because I can't. I had no idea you were so low on funds. How did you let it happen? Didn't you lay anything aside?"

"Oh, please, Dad," said Wilhelm, almost bringing his hands together in a clasp.

"I'm sorry," said the doctor. "I really am. But I have set up a rule. I've thought about it, I believe it is a good rule, and I don't want to change it. You haven't acted wisely. What's the matter?"

"Everything. Just everything. What isn't? I did have a little, but I haven't been very smart."

"You took some gamble? You lost it? Was it Tamkin? I told you, Wilky, not to build on that Tamkin. Did you? I suspect—"

"Yes, Dad, I'm afraid I trusted him."

Dr. Adler surrendered his arm to the masseur, who was using wintergreen oil.

"Trusted! And got taken?"

"I'm afraid I kind of—" Wilhelm glanced at the masseur but he was absorbed in his work. He probably did not listen to conversations. "I did. I might as well say it. I should have listened to you."

"Well, I won't remind you how often I warned you. It must be very painful."

"Yes, Father, it is."

"I don't know how many times you have to be burned in order to learn something. The same mistakes, over and over."

"I couldn't agree with you more," said Wilhelm with a face of despair. "You're so right, Father. It's the same mistakes, and I get burned again and again. I can't seem to—I'm stupid. Dad, I just can't breathe. My chest is all up—I feel choked. I just simply can't catch my breath."

He stared at his father's nakedness. Presently he became aware that Dr. Adler was making an effort to keep his temper. He was on the verge of an explosion. Wilhelm hung his face and said, "Nobody likes bad luck, eh Dad?"

"So! It's bad luck, now. A minute ago it was stupidity."

"It is stupidity—it's some of both. It's true that I can't learn. But I—"

"I don't want to listen to the details," said his father. "And I want you to understand that I'm too old to take on new burdens. I'm just too old to do it. And people who will just wait for help—must *wait* for help. They have got to stop waiting."

"It isn't all a question of money—there are other things a father can give to a son." He lifted up his gray eyes and his nostrils grew wide with a look of suffering appeal that stirred his father even more deeply against him.

He warningly said to him, "Look out, Wilky, you're tiring my patience very much."

"I try not to. But one word from you, just a word, would go a long way. I've never asked you for very much. But you are not a kind man, Father. You don't give the little bit I beg you for."

He recognized that his father was now furiously angry. Dr. Adler started to say something, and then raised himself and gathered the sheet over him as he did so. His mouth opened, wide, dark, twisted, and he said to Wilhelm, "You want to make yourself into my cross. But I am not going to pick up a cross. I'll see you dead, Wilky, by Christ, before I let you do that to me."

"Father, listen! Listen!"

"Go away from me now. It's torture for me to look at you, you slob!" cried Dr. Adler.

Wilhelm's blood rose up madly, in anger equal to his father's, but then it sank down and left him helplessly captive to misery. He said stiffly, and with a strange sort of formality, "Okay, Dad. That'll be enough. That's about all we should say." And he stalked out heavily by the door adjacent to the swimming pool and the steam room, and labored up two long flights from the basement. Once more he took the elevator to the lobby on the mezzanine.

He inquired at the desk for Dr. Tamkin.

The clerk said, "No, I haven't seen him. But I think there's something in the box for you."

"Me? Give it here," said Wilhelm and opened a telephone message from his wife. It read, "Please phone Mrs. Wilhelm on return. Urgent."

Whenever he received an urgent message from his wife he was always thrown into a great fear for the children. He ran to the phone booth, spilled out the change from his pockets onto the little curved steel shelf under the telephone, and dialed the Digby number.

"Yes?" said his wife. Scissors barked in the parlor.

"Margaret?"

"Yes, hello." They never exchanged any other greeting. She instantly knew his voice.

"The boys all right?"

"They're out on their bicycles. Why shouldn't they be all right? Scissors, quiet!"

"Your message scared me," he said. "I wish you wouldn't make 'urgent' so common."

"I had something to tell you."

Her familiar unbending voice awakened in him a kind of hungry longing, not for Margaret but for the peace he had once known.

"You sent me a postdated check," she said. "I can't allow that. It's already five days past the first. You dated your check for the twelfth."

"Well, I have no money. I haven't got it. You can't send me to prison for that. I'll be lucky if I can raise it by the twelfth."

She answered, "You better get it, Tommy."

"Yes? What for?" he said. "Tell me. For the sake of what? To tell lies about me to everyone? You—"

She cut him off. "You know what for. I've got the boys to bring up."

Wilhelm in the narrow booth broke into a heavy sweat. He dropped his head and shrugged while with his fingers he arranged nickels, dimes, and quarters in rows. "I'm doing my best," he said. "I've had some bad luck. As a matter of fact, it's been so bad that I don't know where I am. I couldn't tell you what day of the week this is. I can't think straight. I'd better not even try. This has been one of those days, Margaret. May I never live to go through another like it. I mean that with all my heart. So I'm not going to try to do any thinking today. Tomorrow I'm going to see some guys. One is a sales manager. The other is in television. But not to act," he hastily added. "On the business end."

"That's just some more of your talk, Tommy," she said. "You ought to patch things up with Rojax Corporation. They'd take you back. You've got to stop thinking like a youngster."

"What do you mean?"

"Well," she said, measured and unbending, remorselessly unbending, "you still think like a youngster. But you can't do that any more. Every other day you want to make a new start. But in eighteen years you'll be eligible for retirement. Nobody wants to hire a new man of your age."

"I know. But listen, you don't have to sound so hard. I can't get on my knees to them. And really you don't have to sound so hard. I haven't done you so much harm."

"Tommy, I have to chase you and ask you for money that you owe us, and I hate it."

She hated also to be told that her voice was hard.

"I'm making an effort to control myself," she told him.

He could picture her, her graying bangs cut with strict fixity above her pretty, decisive face. She prided herself on being fair-minded. We could not bear, he thought, to know what we do. Even though blood is spilled. Even though the breath of life is taken from someone's nostrils. This is the way of the weak; quiet and fair. And then smash! They smash!

"Rojax take me back? I'd have to crawl back. They don't need me. After so many years I should have got stock in the firm. How can I support the three of you, and live myself, on half the territory? And why should I even try when you won't lift a finger to help? I sent you back to school, didn't I? At that time you said—"

His voice was rising. She did not like that and intercepted him. "You misunderstood me," she said.

"You must realize you're killing me. You can't be as blind as all that. Thou shalt not kill! Don't you remember that?"

She said, "You're just raving now. When you calm down it'll be different. I have great confidence in your earning ability."

"Margaret, you don't grasp the situation. You'll have to get a job."

"Absolutely not. I'm not going to have two young children running loose."

"They're not babies," Wilhelm said. "Tommy is fourteen. Paulie is going to be ten."

"Look," Margaret said in her deliberate manner. "We can't continue this conversation if you're going to yell so, Tommy. They're at a dangerous age. There are teen-aged gangs—the parents working, or the families broken up."

Once again she was reminding him that it was he who had left her. She had the bringing up of the children as her burden, while he must expect to pay the price of his freedom.

Freedom! he thought with consuming bitterness. Ashes in his mouth, not freedom. Give me my children. For they are mine too.

Can you be the woman I lived with? he started to say. Have you forgotten that we slept so long together? Must you now deal with me like this, and have no mercy?

He would be better off with Margaret again than he was today. This was what she wanted to make him feel, and she drove it home. "Are you in misery?" she was saying. "But you have deserved it." And he could not return to her any more than he could beg Rojax to take him back. If it cost him his life, he could not. Margaret had ruined him with Olive. She hit him and hit him, beat him, battered him, wanted to beat the very life out of him.

"Margaret, I want you please to reconsider about work. You have that degree now. Why did I pay your tuition?"

"Because it seemed practical. But it isn't. Growing boys need parental authority and a home."

He begged her, "Margaret, go easy on me. You ought to. I'm at the end of my rope and feel that I'm suffocating. You don't want to be responsible for a person's destruction. You've got to let up. I feel I'm about to burst." His face had expanded. He struck a blow upon the tin and wood and nails of the wall of the booth. "You've got to let me breathe. If I should keel over, what then? And it's something I can never understand about you. How you can treat someone like this whom you lived with so long. Who gave you the best of himself. Who tried. Who loved you." Merely to pronounce the word "love" made him tremble.

"Ah," she said with a sharp breath. "Now we're coming to it. How did you imagine it was going to be—big shot? Everything made smooth for you? I thought you were leading up to this."

She had not, perhaps, intended to reply as harshly as she did, but she brooded a great deal and now she could not forbear to punish him and make him feel pains like those she had to undergo.

He struck the wall again, this time with his knuckles, and he had scarcely enough air in his lungs to speak in a whisper, because his heart pushed upward with a frightful pressure. He got up and stamped his feet in the narrow enclosure.

"Haven't I always done my best?" he yelled, though his voice sounded weak and thin to his own ears. "Everything comes from me and nothing back again to me. There's no law that'll punish this, but you are committing a crime against me. Before God—and that's no joke. I mean that. Before God! Sooner or later the boys will know it."

In a firm tone, levelly, Margaret said to him, "I won't stand to be howled at. When you can speak normally and have something sensible to say I'll listen. But not to this." She hung up.

Wilhelm tried to tear the apparatus from the wall. He ground his teeth and seized the black box with insane digging fingers and made a stifled cry and pulled. Then he saw an elderly lady staring through the glass door, utterly appalled by him, and he ran from the booth, leaving a large amount of change on the shelf. He hurried down the stairs and into the street.

On Broadway it was still bright afternoon and the gassy air was almost motionless under the leaden spokes of sunlight, and sawdust footprints lay about the doorways of butcher shops and fruit stores. And the great, great crowd, the inexhaustible current of millions of every race and kind pouring out, pressing round, of every age, of every genius, possessors of every human secret, antique and future, in every face the refinement of one particular motive or essence—*I labor, I spend, I strive, I design, I love, I cling, I uphold, I give way, I envy, I long, I scorn, I die, I hide, I want.* Faster, much faster than any man could make the tally. The sidewalks were wider than any causeway; the street itself was immense, and it quaked and gleamed and it seemed to Wilhelm to throb at the last limit of endurance. And although the sunlight appeared like a broad tissue, its actual weight made him feel like a drunkard.

"I'll get a divorce if it's the last thing I do," he swore. "As for Dad—As for Dad —I'll have to sell the car for junk and pay the hotel. I'll have to go on my knees to Olive and say, 'Stand by me a while. Don't let her win. Olive!' " And he thought, I'll try to start again with Olive. In fact, I must. Olive loves me. Olive—

Beside a row of limousines near the curb he thought he saw Dr. Tamkin. Of course he had been mistaken before about the hat with the cocoa-colored band and didn't want to make the same mistake twice. But wasn't that Tamkin who was speaking so earnestly, with pointed shoulders, to someone under the canopy of the funeral parlor? For this was a huge funeral. He looked for the singular face under the dark gray, fashionable hatbrim. There were two open cars filled with flowers, and a policeman tried to keep a path open to pedestrians. Right at the canopy-pole, now wasn't that that damned Tamkin talking away with a solemn face, gesticulating with an open hand?

"Tamkin!" shouted Wilhelm, going forward. But he was pushed to the side by a policeman clutching his nightstick at both ends, like a rolling pin. Wilhelm was even farther from Tamkin now, and swore under his breath at the cop who continued to press him back, back, belly and ribs, saying, "Keep it moving there, please," his face red with impatient sweat, his brows like red fur. Wilhelm said to him haughtily, "You shouldn't push people like this."

The policeman, however, was not really to blame. He had been ordered to keep a way clear. Wilhelm was moved forward by the pressure of the crowd.

He cried, "Tamkin!"

But Tamkin was gone. Or rather, it was he himself who was carried from the street into the chapel. The pressure ended inside, where it was dark and cool. The flow of fan-driven air dried his face, which he wiped hard with his handkerchief to stop the slight salt itch. He gave a sigh when he heard the organ notes that stirred and breathed from the pipes and he saw people in the pews. Men in formal clothes and black homburgs strode softly back and forth on the cork floor, up and down the center aisle. The white of the stained glass was like mother-of-pearl, the blue of the Star of David like velvet ribbon.

Well, thought Wilhelm, if that was Tamkin outside I might as well wait for him here where it's cool. Funny, he never mentioned he had a funeral to go to today. But that's just like the guy.

But within a few minutes he had forgotten Tamkin. He stood along the wall with others and looked toward the coffin and the slow line that was moving past it, gazing at the face of the dead. Presently he too was in this line, and slowly, slowly, foot by foot, the beating of his heart anxious, thick, frightening, but somehow also rich, he neared the coffin and paused for his turn, and gazed down. He caught his breath when he looked at the corpse, and his face swelled, his eyes shone hugely with instant tears.

The dead man was gray-haired. He had two large waves of gray hair at the front. But he was not old. His face was long, and he had a bony nose, slightly, delicately twisted. His brows were raised as though he had sunk into the final thought. Now at last he was with it, after the end of all distractions, and when his flesh was no longer flesh. And by this meditative look Wilhelm was so struck that he could not go away. In spite of the tinge of horror, and then the splash of heartsickness that he felt, he could not go. He stepped out of line and remained beside the coffin; his eyes filled silently and through his still tears he studied the man as the line of visitors moved with veiled looks past the satin coffin toward the standing bank of lilies, lilacs, roses. With great stifling sorrow, almost admiration, Wilhelm nodded and nodded. On the surface, the dead man with his formal shirt and his tie and silk lapels and his powdered skin looked so proper; only a little beneath so—black, Wilhelm thought, so fallen in the eyes.

Standing a little apart, Wilhelm began to cry. He cried at first softly and from sentiment, but soon from deeper feeling. He sobbed loudly and his face grew distorted and hot, and the tears stung his skin. A man—another human creature, was what first went through his thoughts, but other and different things were torn from him. What'll I do? I'm stripped and kicked out. . . . Oh, Father, what do I ask of you? What'll I do about the kids—Tommy, Paul? My children. And Olive? My dear! Why, why, why—you must protect me against that devil who wants my life. If you want it, then kill me. Take, take it, take it from me."

Soon he was past words, past reason, coherence. He could not stop. The source of all tears had suddenly sprung open within him, black, deep, and hot, and they were pouring out and convulsed his body, bending his stubborn head, bowing his shoulders, twisting his face, crippling the very hands with which he held the handkerchief. His efforts to collect himself were useless. The great knot of ill and grief in his throat swelled upward and he gave in utterly and held his face and wept. He cried with all his heart.

He, alone of all the people in the chapel, was sobbing. No one knew who he was. One woman said, "Is that perhaps the cousin from New Orleans they were expecting?"

"It must be somebody real close to carry on so."

"Oh my, oh my! To be mourned like that," said one man and looked at Wilhelm's heavy shaken shoulders, his clutched face and whitened fair hair, with wide, glinting, jealous eyes.

"The man's brother, maybe?"

"Oh, I doubt that very much," said another bystander. "They're not alike at all. Night and day."

The flowers and lights fused ecstatically in Wilhelm's blind, wet eyes; the heavy sea-like music came up to his ears. It poured into him where he had hidden himself in the center of a crowd by the great and happy oblivion of tears. He heard it and sank deeper than sorrow, through torn sobs and cries toward the consummation of his heart's ultimate need.

1956

Arthur Miller
b. 1915

Arthur Miller was born in Brooklyn, New York, on October 17, 1915. Thwarted in his desire to attend college because "nobody in the house was in possession of the fare," he worked for two and a half years in an automobile-parts warehouse before saving enough money to attend the University of Michigan. His first plays, written in his sophomore and junior years and produced at the university theater in Ann Arbor, won the Hopwood Award for both 1936 and 1937. After graduation in 1938 (in that year he also won the Theater Guild National Award), Miller returned to New York, where he wrote numerous scripts for network radio and also worked as a laborer in the Brooklyn Navy Yard and in a cardboard factory. In 1944 he published *Situation Normal,* a report on military life at army bases, and wrote his first Broadway play, *The Man Who Had All the Luck.* Although it represented Miller's first engagement with America's myth of success, which he would later explore in his most famous work, *The Man Who Had All the Luck* was not itself a success. The following year Miller published *Focus,* an ironic novel dealing with anti-Semitism.

"Drama," Miller asserts, "is one of the things that makes possible a solution to the problem of socializing people." For Miller, significant dramatic conflict must deal with the way people live together. The meaning of a life cannot be evaluated in a vacuum; it depends on its relationship to others and to social decisions. So important is our social existence to Miller that in his plays the interrelations of family and society become almost as tangible as the characters themselves. Miller reinforces this sense of interrelatedness by creating dialogue in which characters habitually and emphatically punctuate their conversation with each other's names, as though they needed continually to reaffirm each other's presence. (*Death of a Salesman,* for example, opens with the calling out of the protagonist's name.) In Miller, too, as in few other prominent American writers, jobs play a central role in the dramatic conflict. Miller remains keenly aware that one of the primary features of modern society is the often painfully close connection between an individual's work and that person's sense of worth, between occupation and self-identity. His awareness of the real social pressures faced by real people ("A play," he said, "ought to make sense to common-sense people") has perhaps more than any other aspect of his work made him one of the most successful playwrights in the history of American theater.

Miller's first Broadway success was *All My Sons* (1947), a three-act play about a wealthy manufacturer who is accused of murder by one of his sons because he sold defective aircraft parts during wartime. Miller followed *All My Sons* with another drama of a man's difficult and guilt-ridden relation to his family and society, *Death of a Salesman,* which in 1949 began one of the longest runs for serious drama in Broadway history. The play not only won the Drama Critics' Circle Award and the Pulitzer Prize but has also sold well over three million copies in book form, making it possibly America's best-known play. In 1951 Miller adapted for the stage one of the world's masterpieces of social drama, Ibsen's *An Enemy of the People,* and in 1953 he wrote *The Crucible,* a four-act drama about the Salem witchcraft trials that is also an attack on Senator McCarthy's anti-Communist "witch hunts" of the 1950s. The film version of *The Crucible* was eventually made in France because Miller, as a result of the play and his refusal to name names during his appearance before the House Un-American Activities Committee in 1956, had been blacklisted by Hollywood. In 1955 Miller won the Pulitzer Prize for *A View from the Bridge,* a play about the charged family relations of an Italian longshoreman. A year later he married the movie star Marilyn Monroe—an event that was especially dramatic because of his having been blacklisted by Hollywood. In 1961, the year in which Miller and Monroe were divorced, Hollywood released a movie, *The Misfits,* based on a screenplay written by Miller for Monroe that also starred Clark Gable and Montgomery Clift.

In his next play, *After the Fall* (1964), Miller created a semiautobiographical drama about a man trying to make sense of his past. It was soon followed by *Incident at Vichy* (1965), a play set during the Nazi occupation of France. Miller's most recent plays are *The Price* (1968), *The Creation of the World and Other Business* (1972), and *The Archbishop's Ceiling* (1976). He has also published a volume of short stories, *I Don't Need You Anymore* (1967), and several travel books with photographs taken by his wife. *The Theatre Essays of Arthur Miller* appeared in 1978.

Throughout his career, but particularly in *Death of a Salesman,* Miller has sought to blend the larger force of tragic drama with the immediate pertinence of social drama. As social drama, *Death of a Salesman* focuses on Willy Loman as a victim of society, and particularly as a victim of a harsh economic system that first uses and then discards him. As a moden tragedy, on the other hand, *Death of a Salesman* focuses on Willy Loman as a victim of his own inadequate values and ideals. There is, as a result, terror as well as pity in Loman's story, as he struggles and fails to find values that can give his life purpose and dignity and so deliver him from the sense of hollowness that runs even deeper than the sense of betrayal and failure that haunts him.

Further Reading:
D. Welland, *Arthur Miller*, 1961.
S. Huftel, *Arthur Miller: The Burning Glass*,
1965.
Arthur Miller: A Collection of Critical Essays, ed.
R. W. Corrigan, 1969.

Text:
Death of a Salesman, 1976.

Death of a Salesman

ACT ONE

A melody is heard, played upon a flute. It is small and fine, telling of grass and trees and the horizon. The curtain rises.

Before us is the Salesman's house. We are aware of towering, angular shapes behind it, surrounding it on all sides. Only the blue light of the sky falls upon the house and forestage; the surrounding area shows an angry glow of orange. As more light appears, we see a solid vault of apartment houses around the small, fragile-seeming home. An air of the dream clings to the place, a dream rising out of reality. The kitchen at center seems actual enough, for there is a kitchen table with three chairs, and a refrigerator. But no other fixtures are seen. At the back of the kitchen there is a draped entrance, which leads to the living-room. To the right of the kitchen, on a level raised two feet, is a bedroom furnished only with a brass bedstead and a straight chair. On a shelf over the bed a silver athletic trophy stands. A window opens onto the apartment house at the side.

Behind the kitchen, on a level raised six and a half feet, is the boys' bedroom, at present barely visible. Two beds are dimly seen, and at the back of the room a dormer window. (This bedroom is above the unseen living-room.) At the left a stairway curves up to it from the kitchen.

The entire setting is wholly, or, in some places, partially transparent. The roof-line of the house is one-dimensional; under and over it we see the apartment buildings. Before the house lies an apron, curving beyond the forestage into the orchestra. This forward area serves as the back yard as well as the locale of all Willy's imaginings and of his city scenes. Whenever the action is in the present the actors observe the imaginary wall-lines, entering the house only through its door at the left. But in the scenes of the past these boundaries are broken, and characters enter or leave a room by stepping "through" a wall onto the forestage.

From the right, Willy Loman, the Salesman, enters, carrying two large sample cases. The flute plays on. He hears but is not aware of it. He is past sixty years of age, dressed quietly. Even as he crosses the stage to the doorway of the house, his exhaustion is apparent. He unlocks the door, comes into the kitchen, and thankfully lets his burden down, feeling the soreness of his palms. A word-sigh escapes his lips—it might be "Oh, boy, oh, boy." He closes the door, then carries his cases out into the living-room, through the draped kitchen doorway.

Linda, his wife, has stirred in her bed at the right. She gets out and puts on a robe, listening. Most often jovial, she has developed an iron repression of her exceptions to Willy's behavior —she more than loves him, she admires him, as though his mercurial nature, his temper, his massive dreams and little cruelties, served her only as sharp reminders of the turbulent longings within him, longings which she shares but lacks the temperament to utter and follow to their end.

Linda: hearing Willy outside the bedroom, calls with some trepidation: Willy!

Willy: It's all right. I came back.

Linda: Why? What happened? *Slight pause.* Did something happen, Willy?

Willy: No, nothing happened.

Linda: You didn't smash the car, did you?

Willy: with casual irritation: I said nothing happened. Didn't you hear me?

Linda: Don't you feel well?

Willy: I'm tired to the death. *The flute has faded away. He sits on the bed beside her, a little numb.* I couldn't make it. I just couldn't make it, Linda.

Linda: very carefully, delicately: Where were you all day? You look terrible.

Willy: I got as far as a little above Yonkers. I stopped for a cup of coffee. Maybe it was the coffee.

Linda: What?

Willy: after a pause: I suddenly couldn't drive any more. The car kept going off onto the shoulder, y'know?

Linda: helpfully: Oh. Maybe it was the steering again. I don't think Angelo knows the Studebaker.

Willy: No, it's me, it's me. Suddenly I realize I'm goin' sixty miles an hour and I don't remember the last five minutes. I'm—I can't seem to—keep my mind to it.

Linda: Maybe it's your glasses. You never went for your new glasses.

Willy: No, I see everything. I came back ten miles an hour. It took me nearly four hours from Yonkers.

Linda: resigned: Well, you'll just have to take a rest, Willy, you can't continue this way.

Willy: I just got back from Florida.

Linda: But you didn't rest your mind. Your mind is overactive, and the mind is what counts, dear.

Willy: I'll start out in the morning. Maybe I'll feel better in the morning. *She is taking off his shoes.* These goddam arch supports are killing me.

Linda: Take an aspirin. Should I get you an aspirin? It'll soothe you.

Willy: with wonder: I was driving along, you understand? And I was fine. I was even observing the scenery. You can imagine, me looking at scenery, on the road every week of my life. But it's so beautiful up there, Linda, the trees are so thick, and the sun is warm. I opened the windshield and just let the warm air bathe over me. And then all of a sudden I'm goin' off the road! I'm tellin' ya, I absolutely forgot I was driving. If I'd've gone the other way over the white line I might've killed somebody. So I went on again—and five minutes later I'm dreamin' again, and I nearly—*He presses two fingers against his eyes.* I have such thoughts, I have such strange thoughts.

Linda: Willy, dear. Talk to them again. There's no reason why you can't work in New York.

Willy: They don't need me in New York. I'm the New England man. I'm vital in New England.

Linda: But you're sixty years old. They can't expect you to keep traveling every week.

Willy: I'll have to send a wire to Portland. I'm supposed to see Brown and Morrison tomorrow morning at ten o'clock to show the line. Goddammit, I could sell them! *He starts putting on his jacket.*

Linda: taking the jacket from him: Why don't you go down to the place tomorrow and tell Howard you've simply got to work in New York? You're too accommodating, dear.

Willy: If old man Wagner was alive I'd a been in charge of New York now! That man was a prince, he was a masterful man. But that boy of his, that Howard, he don't appreciate. When I went north the first time, the Wagner Company didn't know where New England was!

Linda: Why don't you tell those things to Howard, dear?

Willy: encouraged: I will, I definitely will. Is there any cheese?

Linda: I'll make you a sandwich.

Willy: No, go to sleep. I'll take some milk. I'll be up right away. The boys in?

Linda: They're sleeping. Happy took Biff on a date tonight.

Willy: interested: That so?

Linda: It was so nice to see them shaving together, one behind the other, in the bathroom. And going out together. You notice? The whole house smells of shaving lotion.

Willy: Figure it out. Work a lifetime to pay off a house. You finally own it, and there's nobody to live in it.

Linda: Well, dear, life is a casting off. It's always that way.

Willy: No, no, some people—some people accomplish something. Did Biff say anything after I went this morning?

Linda: You shouldn't have criticized him, Willy, especially after he just got off the train. You mustn't lose your temper with him.

Willy: When the hell did I lose my temper? I simply asked him if he was making any money. Is that a criticism?

Linda: But, dear, how could he make any money?

Willy: worried and angered: There's such an undercurrent in him. He became a moody man. Did he apologize when I left this morning?

Linda: He was crestfallen. Willy. You know how he admires you. I think if he finds himself, then you'll both be happier and not fight any more.

Willy: How can he find himself on a farm? Is that a life? A farmhand? In the beginning, when he was young. I thought, well, a young man, it's good for him to tramp around, take a lot of different jobs. But it's more than ten years now and he has yet to make thirty-five dollars a week!

Linda: He's finding himself, Willy.

Willy: Not finding yourself at the age of thirty-four is a disgrace!

Linda: Shh!

Willy: The trouble is he's lazy, goddammit!

Linda: Willy, please!

Willy: Biff is a lazy bum!

Linda: They're sleeping. Get something to eat. Go on down.

Willy: Why did he come home? I would like to know what brought him home.

Linda: I don't know. I think he's still lost, Willy. I think he's very lost.

Willy: Biff Loman is lost. In the greatest country in the world a young man with such—personal attractiveness, gets lost. And such a hard worker. There's one thing about Biff—he's not lazy.

Linda: Never.

Willy: with pity and resolve: I'll see him in the morning; I'll have a nice talk with him. I'll get him a job selling. He could be big in no time. My God! Remember how they used to follow him around in high school? When he smiled at one of them their faces lit up. When he walked down the street . . . *He loses himself in reminiscences.*

Linda: trying to bring him out of it: Willy, dear, I got a new kind of American-type cheese today. It's whipped.

Willy: Why do you get American when I like Swiss?

Linda: I just thought you'd like a change—

Willy: I don't want a change! I want Swiss cheese. Why am I always being contradicted?

Linda: with a covering laugh: I thought it would be a surprise.

Willy: Why don't you open a window in here, for God's sake?

Linda: with infinite patience: They're all open, dear.

Willy: The way they boxed us in here. Bricks and windows, windows and bricks.

Linda: We should've bought the land next door.

Willy: The street is lined with cars. There's not a breath of fresh air in the neighborhood. The grass don't grow any more, you can't raise a carrot in the back yard. They should've had a law against apartment houses. Remember those two beautiful elm trees out there? When I and Biff hung the swing between them?

Linda: Yeah, like being a million miles from the city.

Willy: They should've arrested the builder for cutting those down. They massacred the neighborhood. *Lost:* More and more I think of those days, Linda. This time of year it was lilac and wisteria. And then the peonies would come out, and the daffodils. What fragrance in this room!

Linda: Well, after all, people had to move somewhere.

Willy: No, there's more people now.

Linda: I don't think there's more people. I think—

Willy: There's more people! That's what's ruining this country! Population is getting out of control. The competition is maddening! Smell the stink from that apartment house! And another one on the other side . . . How can they whip cheese?

On Willy's last line, Biff and Happy raise themselves up in their beds, listening.

Linda: Go down, try it. And be quiet.

Willy: turning to Linda, guiltily: You're not worried about me, are you, sweetheart?

Biff: What's the matter?

Happy: Listen!

Linda: You've got too much on the ball to worry about.

Willy: You're my foundation and my support, Linda.

Linda: Just try to relax, dear. You make mountains out of molehills.

Willy: I won't fight with him any more. If he wants to go back to Texas, let him go.

Linda: He'll find his way.

Willy: Sure. Certain men just don't get started till later in life. Like Thomas Edison, I think. Or B. F. Goodrich. One of them was deaf. *He starts for the bedroom doorway.* I'll put my money on Biff.

Linda: And Willy—if it's warm Sunday we'll drive in the country. And we'll open the windshield, and take lunch.

Willy: No, the windshields don't open on the new cars.

Linda: But you opened it today.

Willy: Me? I didn't. *He stops.* Now isn't that peculiar! Isn't that a remarkable— *He breaks off in amazement and fright as the flute is heard distantly.*

Linda: What, darling?

Willy: That is the most remarkable thing.

Linda: What, dear?

Willy: I was thinking of the Chevvy. *Slight pause.* Nineteen twenty-eight . . . when I had that red Chevvy—*Breaks off.* That funny? I coulda sworn I was driving that Chevvy today.

Linda: Well, that's nothing. Something must've reminded you.

Willy: Remarkable. Ts. Remember those days? The way Biff used to simonize that car? The dealer refused to believe there was eighty thousand miles on it. *He shakes his head.* Heh! *To Linda:* Close your eyes, I'll be right up. *He walks out of the bedroom.*

Happy: to Biff: Jesus, maybe he smashed up the car again!

Linda: calling after Willy: Be careful on the stairs, dear! The cheese is on the middle shelf! *She turns, goes over to the bed, takes his jacket, and goes out of the bedroom.*

Light has risen on the boys' room. Unseen, Willy is heard talking to himself. "Eighty thousand miles," *and a little laugh. Biff gets out of bed, comes downstage a bit, and stands attentively. Biff is two years older than his brother, Happy, well built, but in these days bears a worn air and seems less self-assured. He has succeeded less, and his dreams are stronger and less acceptable than Happy's. Happy is tall, powerfully made. Sexuality is like a visible color on him, or a scent that many women have discovered. He, like his brother, is lost, but in a different way, for he has never allowed himself to turn his face toward defeat and is thus more confused and hard-skinned, although seemingly more content.*

Happy: getting out of bed: He's going to get his license taken away if he keeps that up. I'm getting nervous about him, y'know, Biff?

Biff: His eyes are going.

Happy: No, I've driven with him. He sees all right. He just doesn't keep his mind on it. I drove into the city with him last week. He stops at a green light and then it turns red and he goes. *He laughs.*

Biff: Maybe he's color-blind.

Happy: Pop? Why he's got the finest eye for color in the business. You know that.

Biff: sitting down on his bed: I'm going to sleep.

Happy: You're not still sour on Dad, are you, Biff?

Biff: He's all right, I guess.

Willy: underneath them, in the living-room: Yes, sir, eighty thousand miles—eighty-two thousand!

Biff: You smoking?

Happy: holding out a pack of cigarettes: Want one?

Biff: taking a cigarette: I can never sleep when I smell it.

Willy: What a simonizing job, heh!

Happy: with deep sentiment: Funny, Biff, y'know? Us sleeping in here again? The old beds. *He pats his bed affectionately.* All the talk that went across those two beds, huh? Our whole lives.

Biff: Yeah. Lotta dreams and plans.

Happy: with a deep and masculine laugh: About five hundred women would like to know what was said in this room.

They share a soft laugh.

Biff: Remember that big Betsy something—what the hell was her name—over on Bushwick Avenue?

Happy: combing his hair: With the collie dog!

Biff: That's the one. I got you in there, remember?

Happy: Yeah, that was my first time—I think. Boy, there was a pig! *They laugh, almost crudely.* You taught me everything I know about women. Don't forget that.

Biff: I bet you forgot how bashful you used to be. Especially with girls.

Happy: Oh, I still am, Biff.

Biff: Oh, go on.

Happy: I just control it, that's all. I think I got less bashful and you got more so. What happened, Biff? Where's the old humor, the old confidence? *He shakes Biff's knee. Biff gets up and moves restlessly about the room.* What's the matter?

Biff: Why does Dad mock me all the time?

Happy: He's not mocking you, he—

Biff: Everything I say there's a twist of mockery on his face. I can't get near him.

Happy: He just wants you to make good, that's all. I wanted to talk to you about Dad for a long time, Biff. Something's—happening to him. He—talks to himself.

Biff: I noticed that this morning. But he always mumbled.

Happy: But not so noticeable. It got so embarrassing I sent him to Florida. And you know something? Most of the time he's talking to you.

Biff: What's he say about me?

Happy: I can't make it out.

Biff: What's he say about me?

Happy: I think the fact that you're not settled, that you're still kind of up in the air . . .

Biff: There's one or two other things depressing him, Happy.

Happy: What do you mean?

Biff: Never mind. Just don't lay it all to me.

Happy: But I think if you just got started—I mean—is there any future for you out there?

Biff: I tell ya, Hap, I don't know what the future is. I don't know—what I'm supposed to want.

Happy: What do you mean?

Biff: Well, I spent six or seven years after high school trying to work myself up. Shipping clerk, salesman, business of one kind or another. And it's a measly manner of existence. To get on that subway on the hot mornings in summer. To devote your whole life to keeping stock, or making phone calls, or selling or buying. To suffer fifty weeks of the year for the sake of a two-week vacation, when all you really desire is to be outdoors, with your shirt off. And always to have to get ahead of the next fella. And still—that's how you build a future.

Happy: Well, you really enjoy it on a farm? Are you content out there?

Biff: with rising agitation: Hap, I've had twenty or thirty different kinds of jobs since I left home before the war, and it always turns out the same. I just realized it lately. In Nebraska when I herded cattle, and the Dakotas, and Arizona, and now in Texas. It's why I came home now. I guess, because I realized it. This farm I work on, it's spring there now, see? And they've got about fifteen new colts. There's nothing more inspiring or—beautiful than the sight of a mare and a new colt. And it's cool there now, see? Texas is cool now, and it's spring. And whenever spring comes to where I am, I suddenly get the feeling, my God, I'm not gettin' anywhere! What the hell am I doing, playing around with horses, twenty-eight dollars a week! I'm thirty-four years old, I oughta be makin' my future. That's when I come running home. And now, I get here, and I don't know what to do with myself. *After a pause:* I've always made a point of not wasting my life, and everytime I come back here I know that all I've done is to waste my life.

Happy: You're a poet, you know that, Biff? You're a—you're an idealist!

Biff: No, I'm mixed up very bad. Maybe I oughta get married. Maybe I oughta get stuck into something. Maybe that's my trouble. I'm like a boy. I'm not married, I'm not in business, I just—I'm like a boy. Are you content, Hap? You're a success, aren't you? Are you content?

Happy: Hell, no!

Biff: Why? You're making money, aren't you?

Happy: moving about with energy, expressiveness: All I can do now is wait for the merchandise manager to die. And suppose I get to be merchandise manager? He's a good friend of mine, and he just built a terrific estate on Long Island. And he lived there about two months and sold it, and now he's building another one. He can't enjoy it once it's finished. And I know that's just what I would do. I don't know what the hell I'm workin' for. Sometimes I sit in my apartment—all alone. And I think of the rent I'm paying. And it's crazy. But then, it's what I always wanted. My own apartment, a car, and plenty of women. And still, goddammit, I'm lonely.

Biff: with enthusiasm: Listen, why don't you come out West with me?

Happy: You and I, heh?

Biff: Sure, maybe we could buy a ranch. Raise cattle, use our muscles. Men built like we are should be working out in the open.

Happy: avidly: The Loman Brothers, heh?

Biff: with vast affection: Sure, we'd be known all over the counties!

Happy: enthralled: That's what I dream about, Biff. Sometimes I want to just rip my clothes off in the middle of the store and outbox that goddam merchandise manager. I mean I can outbox, outrun, and outlift anybody in that store, and I have to take orders from those common, petty sons-of-bitches till I can't stand it any more.

Biff: I'm tellin' you, kid, if you were with me I'd be happy out there.

Happy: enthused: See, Biff, everybody around me is so false that I'm constantly lowering my ideals . . .

Biff: Baby, together we'd stand up for one another, we'd have someone to trust.

Happy: If I were around you—

Biff: Hap, the trouble is we weren't brought up to grub for money. I don't know how to do it.

Happy: Neither can I!

Biff: Then let's go!

Happy: The only thing is—what can you make out there?

Biff: But look at your friend. Builds an estate and then hasn't the peace of mind to live in it.

Happy: Yeah, but when he walks into the store the waves part in front of him. That's fifty-two thousand dollars a year coming through the revolving door, and I got more in my pinky finger than he's got in his head.

Biff: Yeah, but you just said—

Happy: I gotta show some of those pompous, self-important executives over there that Hap Loman can make the grade. I want to walk into the store the way he walks in. Then I'll go with you. Biff. We'll be together yet, I swear. But take those two we had tonight. Now weren't they gorgeous creatures?

Biff: Yeah, yeah, most gorgeous I've had in years.

Happy: I get that any time I want, Biff. Whenever I feel disgusted. The only trouble is, it gets like bowling or something. I just keep knockin' them over and it doesn't mean anything. You still run around a lot?

Biff: Naa. I'd like to find a girl—steady, somebody with substance.

Happy: That's what I long for.

Biff: Go on! You'd never come home.

Happy: I would! Somebody with character, with resistance! Like Mom, y'know? You're gonna call me a bastard when I tell you this, That girl Charlotte I was with tonight is engaged to be married in five weeks. *He tries on his new hat.*

Biff: No kiddin'!

Happy: Sure, the guy's in line for the vice-presidency of the store. I don't know what gets into me, maybe I just have an overdeveloped sense of competition or something, but I went and ruined her, and furthermore I can't get rid of her. And he's the third executive I've done that to. Isn't that a crummy characteristic? And to top it all, I go to their weddings! *Indignantly, but laughing:* Like I'm not supposed to take bribes. Manufacturers offer me a hundred-dollar bill now and then to throw an order their way. You know how honest I am, but it's like this girl, see. I hate myself for it. Because I don't want the girl, and, still, I take it and—I love it!

Biff: Let's go to sleep.

Happy: I guess we didn't settle anything, heh?

Biff: I just got one idea that I think I'm going to try.

Happy: What's that?

Biff: Remember Bill Oliver?

Happy: Sure, Oliver is very big now. You want to work for him again?

Biff: No, but when I quit he said something to me. He put his arm on my shoulder, and he said, "Biff, if you ever need anything, come to me."

Happy: I remember that. That sounds good.

Biff: I think I'll go to see him. If I could get ten thousand or even seven or eight thousand dollars I could buy a beautiful ranch.

Happy: I bet he'd back you. 'Cause he thought highly of you, Biff. I mean, they all do. You're well liked, Biff. That's why I say to come back here, and we both have the apartment. And I'm tellin' you, Biff, any babe you want . . .

Biff: No, with a ranch I could do the work I like and still be something. I just wonder though. I wonder if Oliver still thinks I stole that carton of basketballs.

Happy: Oh, he probably forgot that long ago. It's almost ten years. You're too sensitive. Anyway, he didn't really fire you.

Biff: Well, I think he was going to. I think that's why I quit. I was never sure whether he knew or not. I know he thought the world of me, though. I was the only one he'd let lock up the place.

Willy: below: You gonna wash the engine, Biff?

Happy: Shh!

Biff looks at Happy, who is gazing down, listening. Willy is mumbling in the parlor.

Happy: You hear that?

They listen. Willy laughs warmly.

Biff: growing angry: Doesn't he know Mom can hear that?

Willy: Don't get your sweater dirty, Biff!

A look of pain crosses Biff's face.

Happy: Isn't that terrible? Don't leave again, will you? You'll find a job here. You gotta stick around. I don't know what to do about him, it's getting embarrassing.

Willy: What a simonizing job!

Biff: Mom's hearing that!

Willy: No kiddin', Biff, you got a date? Wonderful!

Happy: Go on to sleep. But talk to him in the morning, will you?

Biff: reluctantly getting into bed: With her in the house. Brother!
Happy: getting into bed: I wish you'd have a good talk with him.

The light on their room begins to fade.

Biff: to himself in bed: That selfish, stupid . . .
Happy: Sh . . . Sleep, Biff.

Their light is out. Well before they have finished speaking, Willy's form is dimly seen below in the darkened kitchen. He opens the refrigerator, searches in there, and takes out a bottle of milk. The apartment houses are fading out, and the entire house and surroundings become covered with leaves. Music insinuates itself as the leaves appear.

Willy: Just wanna be careful with those girls. Biff, that's all. Don't make any promises. No promises of any kind. Because a girl, y'know, they always believe what you tell 'em, and you're very young, Biff, you're too young to be talking seriously to girls.

Light rises on the kitchen. Willy, talking, shuts the refrigerator door and comes downstage to the kitchen table. He pours milk into a glass. He is totally immersed in himself, smiling faintly.

Willy: Too young entirely, Biff. You want to watch your schooling first. Then when you're all set, there'll be plenty of girls for a boy like you. *He smiles broadly at a kitchen chair.* That so? The girls pay for you? *He laughs.* Boy, you must really be makin' a hit.

Willy is gradually addressing—physically—a point offstage, speaking through the wall of the kitchen, and his voice has been rising in volume to that of a normal conversation.

Willy: I been wondering why you polish the car so careful. Ha! Don't leave the hubcaps, boys. Get the chamois to the hubcaps. Happy, use newspaper on the windows, it's the easiest thing. Show him how to do it, Biff! You see, Happy? Pad it up, use it like a pad. That's it, that's it, good work. You're doin' all right, Hap. *He pauses, then nods in approbation for a few seconds, then looks upward.* Biff, first thing we gotta do when we get time is clip that big branch over the house. Afraid it's gonna fall in a storm and hit the roof. Tell you what. We get a rope and sling her around, and then we climb up there with a couple of saws and take her down. Soon as you finish the car, boys, I wanna see ya. I got a surprise for you, boys.
Biff: offstage: Whatta ya got, Dad?
Willy: No, you finish first. Never leave a job till you're finished—remember that. *Looking toward the "big trees":* Biff, up in Albany I saw a beautiful hammock. I think I'll buy it next trip, and we'll hang it right between those two elms. Wouldn't that be something? Just swingin' there under those branches. Boy, that would be . . .

Young Biff and Young Happy appear from the direction Willy was addressing. Happy carries rags and a pail of water. Biff, wearing a sweater with a block "S," carries a football.

Biff: pointing in the direction of the car offstage: How's that, Pop, professional?

Willy: Terrific. Terrific job, boys. Good work, Biff.

Happy: Where's the surprise, Pop?

Willy: In the back seat of the car.

Happy: Boy! *He runs off.*

Biff: What is it, Dad? Tell me, what'd you buy?

Willy: laughing, cuffs him: Never mind, something I want you to have.

Biff: turns and starts off: What is it, Hap?

Happy: offstage: It's a punching bag!

Biff: Oh, Pop!

Willy: It's got Gene Tunney's signature on it!

Happy runs onstage with a punching bag.

Biff: Gee, how'd you know we wanted a punching bag?

Willy: Well, it's the finest thing for the timing.

Happy: lies down on his back and pedals with his feet: I'm losing weight, you notice, Pop?

Willy: to Happy: Jumping rope is good too.

Biff: Did you see the new football I got?

Willy: examining the ball: Where'd you get a new ball?

Biff: The coach told me to practice my passing.

Willy: That so? And he gave you the ball, heh?

Biff: Well, I borrowed it from the locker room. *He laughs confidentially.*

Willy: laughing with him at the theft: I want you to return that.

Happy: I told you he wouldn't like it!

Biff: angrily: Well, I'm bringing it back!

Willy: stopping the incipient argument, to Happy: Sure, he's gotta practice with a regulation ball, doesn't he? *To Biff:* Coach'll probably congratulate you on your initiative!

Biff: Oh, he keeps congratulating my initiative all the time, Pop.

Willy: That's because he likes you. If somebody else took that ball there'd be an uproar. So what's the report, boys, what's the report?

Biff: Where'd you go this time, Dad? Gee we were lonesome for you.

Willy: pleased, puts an arm around each boy an they come down to the apron: Lonesome, heh?

Biff: Missed you every minute.

Willy: Don't say? Tell you a secret, boys. Don't breathe it to a soul. Someday I'll have my own business, and I'll never have to leave home any more.

Happy: Like Uncle Charley, heh?

Willy: Bigger than Uncle Charley! Because Charley is not—liked. He's liked, but he's not—well liked.

Biff: Where'd you go this time, Dad?

Willy: Well, I got on the road, and I went north to Providence. Met the Mayor.

Biff: The Mayor of Providence!

Willy: He was sitting in the hotel lobby.

Biff: What'd he say?

Willy: He said, "Morning!" And I said, "You got a fine city here, Mayor." And then he had coffee with me. And then I went to Waterbury. Waterbury is a fine city. Big clock city, the famous Waterbury clock. Sold a nice bill there. And then Boston—Boston is the cradle of the Revolution. A fine city. And a couple of other towns in Mass., and on to Portland and Bangor and straight home!

Biff: Gee, I'd love to go with you sometime, Dad.

Willy: Soon as summer comes.

Happy: Promise?

Willy: You and Hap and I, and I'll show you all the towns. America is full of beautiful towns and fine, upstanding people. And they know me, boys, they know me up and down New England. The finest people. And when I bring you fellas up, there'll be open sesame for all of us, 'cause one thing, boys: I have friends. I can park my car in any street in New England, and the cops protect it like their own. This summer, heh?

Biff and Happy, together: Yeah! You bet!

Willy: We'll take our bathing suits.

Happy: We'll carry your bags. Pop!

Willy: Oh, won't that be something! Me comin' into the Boston stores with you boys carryin' my bag. What a sensation!

Biff is prancing around, practicing passing the ball.

Willy: You nervous, Biff, about the game?

Biff: Not if you're gonna be there.

Willy: What do they say about you in school, now that they made you captain?

Happy: There's a crowd of girls behind him everytime the classes change.

Biff: taking Willy's hand: This Saturday, Pop, this Saturday—just for you, I'm going to break through for a touchdown.

Happy: You're supposed to pass.

Biff: I'm takin' one play for Pop. You watch me, Pop, and when I take off my helmet, that means I'm breakin' out. Then you watch me crash through that line!

Willy: kisses Biff: Oh, wait'll I tell this in Boston!

Bernard enters in knickers. He is younger than Biff, earnest and loyal, a worried boy.

Bernard: Biff, where are you? You're supposed to study with me today.

Willy: Hey, looka Bernard. What're you lookin' so anemic about, Bernard?

Bernard: He's gotta study, Uncle Willy. He's got Regents'[1] next week.

---

[1] Competitive examinations required for graduation from high schools in New York State.

Happy: tauntingly, spinning Bernard around: Let's box, Bernard!

Bernard: Biff! *He gets away from Happy.* Listen, Biff, I heard Mr. Birnbaum say
that if you don't start studyin' math he's gonna flunk you, and you won't
graduate. I heard him!

Willy: You better study with him, Biff. Go ahead now.

Bernard: I heard him!

Biff: Oh, Pop, you didn't see my sneakers! *He holds up a foot for Willy to look at.*

Willy: Hey, that's a beautiful job of printing!

Bernard: wiping his glasses: Just because he printed University of Virginia on his
sneakers doesn't mean they've got to graduate him, Uncle Willy!

Willy: angrily: What're you talking about? With scholarships to three universities
they're gonna flunk him?

Bernard: But I heard Mr. Birnbaum say—

Willy: Don't be a pest, Bernard! *To his boys:* What an anemic!

Bernard: Okay, I'm waiting for you in my house, Biff.

Bernard goes off. The Lomans laugh.

Willy: Bernard is not well liked, is he?

Biff: He's liked, but he's not well liked.

Happy: That's right, Pop.

Willy: That's just what I mean. Bernard can get the best marks in school,
y'understand, but when he gets out in the business world, y'understand, you
are going to be five times ahead of him. That's why I thank Almighty God
you're both built like Adonises. Because the man who makes an appearance in
the business world, the man who creates personal interest, is the man who gets
ahead. Be liked and you will never want. You take me, for instance. I never
have to wait in line to see a buyer. "Willy Loman is here!" That's all they
have to know, and I go right through.

Biff: Did you knock them dead, Pop?

Willy: Knocked 'em cold in Providence, slaughtered 'em in Boston.

Happy: on his back, pedaling again: I'm losing weight, you notice, Pop?

Linda enters, as of old, a ribbon in her hair, carrying a basket of washing.

Linda: with youthful energy: Hello, dear!

Willy: Sweetheart!

Linda: How'd the Chevvy run?

Willy: Chevrolet, Linda, is the greatest car ever built. *To the boys:* Since when do
you let your mother carry wash up the stairs?

Biff: Grab hold there, boy!

Happy: Where to, Mom?

Linda: Hang them up on the line. And you better go down to your friends, Biff.
The cellar is full of boys. They don't know what to do with themselves.

Biff: Ah, when Pop comes home they can wait!

Willy: laughs appreciatively: You better go down and tell them what to do, Biff.

Biff: I think I'll have them sweep out the furnace room.

Willy: Good work, Biff.

Biff: goes through wall-line of kitchen to doorway at back and calls down: Fellas! Everybody sweep out the furnace room! I'll be right down!

Voices: All right! Okay, Biff.

Biff: George and Sam and Frank, come out back! We're hangin' up the wash! Come on, Hap, on the double! *He and Happy carry out the basket.*

Linda: The way they obey him!

Willy: Well, that's training, the training. I'm tellin' you, I was sellin' thousands and thousands, but I had to come home.

Linda: Oh, the whole block'll be at that game. Did you sell anything?

Willy: I did five hundred gross in Providence and seven hundred gross in Boston.

Linda: No! Wait a minute, I've got a pencil. *She pulls pencil and paper out of her apron pocket.* That makes your commission . . . Two hundred—my God! Two hundred and twelve dollars!

Willy: Well, I didn't figure it yet, but . . .

Linda: How much did you do?

Willy: Well, I—I did—about a hundred and eighty gross in Providence. Well, no—it came to—roughly two hundred gross on the whole trip.

Linda: without hesitation: Two hundred gross. That's . . . *She figures.*

Willy: The trouble was that three of the stores were half closed for inventory in Boston. Otherwise I woulda broke records.

Linda: Well, it makes seventy dollars and some pennies. That's very good.

Willy: What do we owe?

Linda: Well, on the first there's sixteen dollars on the refrigerator—

Willy: Why sixteen?

Linda: Well, the fan belt broke, so it was a dollar eighty.

Willy: But it's brand new.

Linda: Well, the man said that's the way it is. Till they work themselves in, y'know.

They move through the wall-line into the kitchen.

Willy: I hope we didn't get stuck on that machine.

Linda: They got the biggest ads of any of them!

Willy: I know, it's a fine machine. What else?

Linda: Well, there's nine-sixty for the washing machine. And for the vacuum cleaner there's three and a half due on the fifteenth. Then, the roof, you got twenty-one dollars remaining.

Willy: It don't leak, does it?

Linda: No, they did a wonderful job. Then you owe Frank for the carburetor.

Willy: I'm not going to pay that man! That goddam Chevrolet, they ought to prohibit the manufacture of that car!

Linda: Well, you owe him three and a half. And odds and ends, comes to around a hundred and twenty dollars by the fifteenth.

Willy: A hundred and twenty dollars! My God, if business don't pick up I don't know what I'm gonna do!

Linda: Well, next week you'll do better.

Willy: Oh, I'll knock 'em dead next week. I'll go to Hartford. I'm very well liked in Hartford. You know, the trouble is, Linda, people don't seem to take to me.

They move onto the forestage.

Linda: Oh, don't be foolish.
Willy: I know it when I walk in. They seem to laugh at me.
Linda: Why? Why would they laugh at you? Don't talk that way, Willy.

Willy moves to the edge of the stage. Linda goes into the kitchen and starts to darn stockings.

Willy: I don't know the reason for it, but they just pass me by. I'm not noticed.
Linda: But you're doing wonderful, dear. You're making seventy to a hundred dollars a week.
Willy: But I gotta be at it ten, twelve hours a day. Other men—I don't know—they do it easier. I don't know why—I can't stop myself—I talk too much. A man oughta come in with a few words. One thing about Charley. He's a man of few words, and they respect him.
Linda: You don't talk too much, you're just lively.
Willy: smiling: Well, I figure, what the hell, life is short, a couple of jokes. *To himself:* I joke too much! *The smile goes.*
Linda: Why? You're—
Willy: I'm fat. I'm very—foolish to look at, Linda. I didn't tell you, but Christmas time I happened to be calling on F. H. Stewarts, and a salesman I know, as I was going in to see the buyer I heard him say something about—walrus. And I—I cracked him right across the face. I won't take that. I simply will not take that. But they do laugh at me. I know that.
Linda: Darling . . .
Willy: I gotta overcome it. I know I gotta overcome it. I'm not dressing to advantage, maybe.
Linda: Willy, darling, you're the handsomest man in the world—
Willy: Oh, no, Linda.
Linda: To me you are. *Slight pause.* The handsomest.

From the darkness is heard the laughter of a woman. Willy doesn't turn to it, but it continues through Linda's lines.

Linda: And the boys, Willy. Few men are idolized by their children the way you are.

Music is heard as behind a scrim, to the left of the house, The Woman, dimly seen, is dressing.

Willy: with great feeling: You're the best there is. Linda, you're a pal, you know that? On the road—on the road I want to grab you sometimes and just kiss the life outa you.

The laughter is loud now, and he moves into a brightening area at the left, where The Woman has come from behind the scrim and is standing, putting on her hat, looking into a "mirror" and laughing.

Willy: 'Cause I get so lonely—especially when business is bad and there's nobody to talk to. I get the feeling that I'll never sell anything again, that I won't making a living for you, or a business, a business for the boys. *He talks through The Woman's subsiding laughter; The Woman primps at the "mirror."* There's so much I want to make for—

The Woman: Me? You didn't make me, Willy. I picked you.

Willy: pleased: You picked me?

The Woman: who is quite proper-looking, Willy's age: I did. I've been sitting at that desk watching all the salesmen go by, day in, day out. But you've got such a sense of humor, and we do have such a good time together, don't we?

Willy: Sure, sure. *He takes her in his arms.* Why do you have to go now?

The Woman: It's two o'clock . . .

Willy: No, come on in! *He pulls her.*

The Woman: . . . my sisters'll be scandalized. When'll you be back?

Willy: Oh, two weeks about. Will you come up again?

The Woman: Sure thing. You do make me laugh. It's good for me. *She squeezes his arm, kisses him.* And I think you're a wonderful man.

Willy: You picked me, heh?

The Woman: Sure. Because you're so sweet. And such a kidder.

Willy: Well, I'll see you next time I'm in Boston.

The Woman: I'll put you right through to the buyers.

Willy: slapping her bottom: Right. Well, bottoms up!

The Woman: slaps him gently and laughs: You just kill me, Willy. *He suddenly grabs her and kisses her roughly.* You kill me. And thanks for the stockings. I love a lot of stockings. Well, good night.

Willy: Good night. And keep your pores open!

The Woman: Oh, Willy!

The Woman bursts out laughing, and Linda's laughter blends in. The Woman disappears into the dark. Now the area at the kitchen table brightens. Linda is sitting where she was at the kitchen table, but now is mending a pair of her silk stockings.

Linda: You are, Willy. The handsomest man. You've got no reason to feel that—

Willy: coming out of The Woman's dimming area and going over to Linda: I'll make it all up to you, Linda, I'll—

Linda: There's nothing to make up, dear. You're doing fine, better than—

Willy: noticing her mending: What's that?

Linda: Just mending my stockings. They're so expensive—

Willy: angrily, taking them from her: I won't have you mending stockings in this house! Now throw them out!

Linda puts the stockings in her pocket.

Bernard: entering on the run: Where is he? If he doesn't study!

Willy: moving to the forestage, with great agitation: You'll give him the answers!

Bernard: I do, but I can't on a Regents! That's a state exam! They're liable to arrest me!

Willy: Where is he? I'll whip him, I'll whip him!

Linda: And he'd better give back that football, Willy, it's not nice.

Willy: Biff! Where is he? Why is he taking everything?

Linda: He's too rough with the girls, Willy. All the mothers are afraid of him!

Willy: I'll whip him!

Bernard: He's driving the car without a license!

The Woman's laugh is heard.

Willy: Shut up!

Linda: All the mothers—

Willy: Shut up!

Bernard: backing quietly away and out: Mr. Birnbaum says he's stuck up.

Willy: Get outa here!

Bernard: If he doesn't buckle down he'll flunk math! *He goes off.*

Linda: He's right. Willy, you've gotta—

Willy: exploding at her: There's nothing the matter with him! You want him to be a worm like Bernard? He's got spirit, personality . . .

As he speaks, Linda, almost in tears, exits into the living-room. Willy is alone in the kitchen, wilting and staring. The leaves are gone. It is night again, and the apartment houses look down from behind.

Willy: Loaded with it. Loaded! What is he stealing? He's giving it back, isn't he? Why is he stealing? What did I tell him? I never in my life told him anything but decent things.

Happy in pajamas has come down the stairs; Willy suddenly becomes aware of Happy's presence.

Happy: Let's go now, come on.

Willy: sitting down at the kitchen table: Huh! Why did she have to wax the floors herself? Everytime she waxes the floors she keels over. She knows that!

Happy: Shh! Take it easy. What brought you back tonight?

Willy: I got an awful scare. Nearly hit a kid in Yonkers.[2] God! Why didn't I go to Alaska with my brother Ben that time! Ben! That man was a genius, that man was success incarnate! What a mistake! He begged me to go.

Happy: Well, there's no use in—

Willy: You guys! There was a man started with the clothes on his back and ended up with diamond mines!

[2] Suburb north of New York City.

Happy: Boy, someday I'd like to know how he did it.

Willy: What's the mystery? The man knew what he wanted and went out and got it! Walked into a jungle, and comes out, the age of twenty-one, and he's rich! The world is an oyster, but you don't crack it open on a mattress!

Happy: Pop, I told you I'm gonna retire you for life.

Willy: You'll retire me for life on seventy goddam dollars a week? And your women and your car and your apartment, and you'll retire me for life! Christ's sake, I couldn't get past Yonkers today! Where are you guys, where are you? The woods are burning! I can't drive a car!

Charley has appeared in the doorway. He is a large man, slow of speech, laconic, immovable. In all he says, despite what he says, there is pity, and, now, trepidation. He has a robe over pajamas, slippers on his feet. He enters the kitchen.

Charley: Everything all right?

Happy: Yeah, Charley, everything's . . .

Willy: What's the matter?

Charley: I heard some noise. I thought something happened. Can't we do something about the walls? You sneeze in here, and in my house hats blow off.

Happy: Let's go to bed, Dad. Come on.

Charley signals to Happy to go.

Willy: You go ahead, I'm not tired at the moment.

Happy: to Willy: Take it easy, huh? *He exits.*

Willy: What're you doin' up?

Charley: sitting down at the kitchen table opposite Willy: Couldn't sleep good. I had a heartburn.

Willy: Well, you don't know how to eat.

Charley: I eat with my mouth.

Willy: No, you're ignorant. You gotta know about vitamins and things like that.

Charley: Come on, let's shoot. Tire you out a little.

Willy: hesitantly: All right. You got cards?

Charley: taking a deck from his pocket: Yeah, I got them. Someplace. What is it with those vitamins?

Willy: dealing: They build up your bones. Chemistry.

Charley: Yeah, but there's no bones in a heartburn.

Willy: What are you talkin' about? Do you know the first thing about it?

Charley: Don't get insulted.

Willy: Don't talk about something you don't know anything about.

They are playing. Pause.

Charley: What're you doin' home?

Willy: A little trouble with the car.

Charley: Oh. *Pause.* I'd like to take a trip to California.

Willy: Don't say.

Charley: You want a job?

Willy: I got a job, I told you that. *After a slight pause:* What the hell are you offering me a job for?

Charley: Don't get insulted.

Willy: Don't insult me.

Charley: I don't see no sense in it. You don't have to go on this way.

Willy: I got a good job. *Slight pause.* What do you keep comin' in here for?

Charley: You want me to go?

Willy: after a pause, withering: I can't understand it. He's going back to Texas again. What the hell is that?

Charley: Let him go.

Willy: I got nothin' to give him, Charley, I'm clean, I'm clean.

Charley: He won't starve. None a them starve. Forget about him.

Willy: Then what have I got to remember?

Charley: You take it too hard. To hell with it. When a deposit bottle is broken you don't get your nickel back.

Willy: That's easy enough for you to say.

Charley: That ain't easy for me to say.

Willy: Did you see the ceiling I put up in the living-room?

Charley: Yeah, that's a piece of work. To put up a ceiling is a mystery to me. How do you do it?

Willy: What's the difference?

Charley: Well, talk about it.

Willy: You gonna put up a ceiling?

Charley: How could I put up a ceiling?

Willy: Then what the hell are you bothering me for?

Charley: You're insulted again.

Willy: A man who can't handle tools is not a man. You're disgusting.

Charley: Don't call me disgusting, Willy.

Uncle Ben, carrying a valise and an umbrella, enters the forestage from around the right corner of the house. He is a stolid man, in his sixties, with a mustache and an authoritative air. He is utterly certain of his destiny, and there is an aura of far places about him. He enters exactly as Willy speaks.

Willy: I'm getting awfully tired, Ben.

Ben's music is heard. Ben looks around at everything.

Charley: Good, keep playing; you'll sleep better. Did you call me Ben?

Ben looks at his watch.

Willy: That's funny. For a second there you reminded me of my brother Ben.

Ben: I only have a few minutes. *He strolls, inspecting the place. Willy and Charley continue playing.*

Charley: You never heard from him again, heh? Since that time?

Willy: Didn't Linda tell you? Couple of weeks ago we got a letter from his wife in Africa. He died.

Charley: That so.

Ben: chuckling: So this is Brooklyn, eh?

Charley: Maybe you're in for some of his money.

Willy: Naa, he had seven sons. There's just one opportunity I had with that man . . .

Ben: I must make a train, William. There are several properties I'm looking at in Alaska.

Willy: Sure, sure! If I'd gone with him to Alaska that time, everything would've been totally different.

Charley: Go on, you'd froze to death up there.

Willy: What're you talking about?

Ben: Opportunity is tremendous in Alaska, William. Surprised you're not up there.

Willy: Sure, tremendous.

Charley: Heh?

Willy: There was the only man I ever met who knew the answers.

Charley: Who?

Ben: How are you all?

Willy: taking a pot, smiling: Fine, fine.

Charley: Pretty sharp tonight.

Ben: Is Mother living with you?

Willy: No, she died a long time ago.

Charley: Who?

Ben: That's too bad. Fine specimen of a lady, Mother.

Willy: to Charley: Heh?

Ben: I'd hoped to see the old girl.

Charley: Who died?

Ben: Heard anything from Father, have you?

Willy: unnerved: What do you mean, who died?

Charley: taking a pot: What're you talkin' about?

Ben: looking at his watch: William, it's half-past eight!

Willy: as though to dispel his confusion he angrily stops Charley's hand: That's my build!

Charley: I put the ace—

Willy: If you don't know how to play the game I'm not gonna throw my money away on you!

Charley: rising: It was my ace, for God's sake!

Willy: I'm through, I'm through!

Ben: When did Mother die?

Willy: Long ago. Since the beginning you never knew how to play cards.

Charley: picks up the cards and goes to the door: All right! Next time I'll bring a deck with five aces.

Willy: I don't play that kind of game!

Charley: turning to him: You ought to be ashamed of yourself!

Willy: Yeah?

Charley: Yeah! *He goes out.*

Willy: slamming the door after him: Ignoramus!

Ben: as Willy comes toward him through the wall-line of the kitchen: So you're William.

Willy: shaking Ben's hand: Ben! I've been waiting for you so long! What's the answer? How did you do it?

Ben: Oh, there's a story in that.

Linda enters the forestage, as of old, carrying the wash basket.

Linda: Is this Ben?

Ben: gallantly: How do you do, my dear.

Linda: Where've you been all these years? Willy's always wondered why you—

Willy: pulling Ben away from her impatiently: Where is Dad? Didn't you follow him? How did you get started?

Ben: Well, I don't know how much you remember.

Willy: Well, I was just a baby, of course, only three or four years old—

Ben: Three years and eleven months.

Willy: What a memory, Ben!

Ben: I have many enterprises, William, and I have never kept books.

Willy: I remember I was sitting under the wagon in—was it Nebraska?

Ben: It was South Dakota, and I gave you a bunch of wild flowers.

Willy: I remember you walking away down some open road.

Ben: laughing: I was going to find Father in Alaska.

Willy: Where is he?

Ben: At that age I had a very faulty view of geography, William. I discovered after a few days that I was heading due south, so instead of Alaska, I ended up in Africa.

Linda: Africa!

Willy: The Gold Coast!

Ben: Principally diamond mines.

Linda: Diamond mines!

Ben: Yes, my dear. But I've only a few minutes—

Willy: No! Boys! Boys! *Young Biff and Happy appear.* Listen to this. This is your Uncle Ben, a great man! Tell my boys, Ben!

Ben: Why, boys, when I was seventeen I walked into the jungle, and when I was twenty-one I walked out. *He laughs.* And by God I was rich.

Willy: to the boys: You see what I been talking about? The greatest things can happen!

Ben: glancing at his watch: I have an appointment in Ketchikan Tuesday week.

Willy: No, Ben! Please tell about Dad. I want my boys to hear. I want them to know the kind of stock they spring from. All I remember is a man with a big beard, and I was in Mamma's lap, sitting around a fire, and some kind of high music.

Ben: His flute. He played the flute.

Willy: Sure, the flute, that's right!

New music is heard, a high, rollicking tune.

Ben: Father was a very great and a very wild-hearted man. We would start in
  Boston, and he'd toss the whole family into the wagon, and then he'd drive
  the team right across the country; through Ohio, and Indiana, Michigan,
  Illinois, and all the Western states. And we'd stop in the towns and sell the
  flutes that he'd made on the way. Great inventor, Father. With one gadget he
  made more in a week than a man like you could make in a lifetime.

Willy: That's just the way I'm bringing them up, Ben—rugged, well liked,
  all-around.

Ben: Yeah? *To Biff:* Hit that, boy—hard as you can. *He pounds his stomach.*

Biff: Oh, no, sir!

Ben: taking boxing stance: Come on, get to me! *He laughs.*

Willy: Go to it, Biff! Go ahead, show him!

Biff: Okay! *He cocks his fists and starts in.*

Linda: to Willy: Why must he fight, dear?

Ben: sparring with Biff: Good boy! Good boy!

Willy: How's that, Ben, heh?

Happy: Give him the left, Biff!

Linda: Why are you fighting?

Ben: Good boy! *Suddenly comes in, trips Biff, and stands over him, the point of his
  umbrella poised over Biff's eye.*

Linda: Look out, Biff!

Biff: Gee!

Ben: patting Biff's knee: Never fight fair with a stranger, boy. You'll never get
  out of the jungle that way. *Taking Linda's hand and bowing:* It was an honor
  and a pleasure to meet you, Linda.

Linda: withdrawing her hand coldly, frightened: Have a nice—trip.

Ben: to Willy: And good luck with your—what do you do?

Willy: Selling.

Ben: Yes. Well . . . *He raises his hand in farewell to all.*

Willy: No, Ben, I don't want you to think . . . *He takes Ben's arm to show him.*
  It's Brooklyn, I know, but we hunt too.

Ben: Really, now.

Willy: Oh, sure, there's snakes and rabbits and—that's why I moved out here.
  Why, Biff can fell any one of these trees in no time! Boys! Go right over to
  where they're building the apartment house and get some sand. We're gonna
  rebuild the entire front stoop right now! Watch this, Ben!

Biff: Yes, sir! On the double, Hap!

Happy: as he and Biff run off: I lost weight, Pop, you notice?

Charley enters in knickers, even before the boys are gone.

Charley: Listen, if they steal any more from that building the watchman'll put the
  cops on them!

Linda: to Willy: Don't let Biff . . .

Ben laughs lustily.

Willy: You shoulda seen the lumber they brought home last week. At least a dozen six-by-tens worth all kinds a money.

Charley: Listen, if that watchman—

Willy: I gave them hell, understand. But I got a couple of fearless characters there.

Charley: Willy, the jails are full of fearless characters.

Ben: clapping Willy on the back, with a laugh at Charley: And the stock exchange, friend!

Willy: joining in Ben's laughter: Where are the rest of your pants?

Charley: My wife bought them.

Willy: Now all you need is a golf club and you can go upstairs and go to sleep. *To Ben:* Great athlete! Between him and his son Bernard they can't hammer a nail!

Bernard: rushing in: The watchman's chasing Biff!

Willy: angrily: Shut up! He's not stealing anything!

Linda: alarmed, hurrying off left: Where is he? Biff, dear! *She exits.*

Willy: moving toward the left, away from Ben: There's nothing wrong. What's the matter with you?

Ben: Nervy boy. Good!

Willy: laughing: Oh, nerves of iron, that Biff!

Charley: Don't know what it is. My New England man comes back and he's bleedin', they murdered him up there.

Willy: It's contacts, Charley, I got important contacts!

Charley: sarcastically: Glad to hear it, Willy. Come in later, we'll shoot a little casino. I'll take some of your Portland money. *He laughs at Willy and exits.*

Willy: turning to Ben: Business is bad, it's murderous. But not for me, of course.

Ben: I'll stop by on my way back to Africa.

Willy: longingly: Can't you stay a few days? You're just what I need, Ben, because I—I have a fine position here, but I—well, Dad left when I was such a baby and I never had a chance to talk to him and I still feel—kind of temporary about myself.

Ben: I'll be late for my train.

They are at opposite ends of the stage.

Willy: Ben, my boys—can't we talk? They'd go into the jaws of hell for me, see, but I—

Ben: William, you're being first-rate with your boys. Outstanding, manly chaps!

Willy: hanging on to his words: Oh, Ben, that's good to hear! Because sometimes I'm afraid that I'm not teaching them the right kind of—Ben, how should I teach them?

Ben: giving great weight to each word, and with a certain vicious audacity: William, when I walked into the jungle, I was seventeen. When I walked out I was twenty-one. And, by God, I was rich! *He goes off into the darkness around the right corner of the house.*

Willy: . . . was rich! That's just the spirit I want to imbue them with! To walk into a jungle! I was right! I was right! I was right!

Ben is gone, but Willy is still speaking to him as Linda, in nightgown and robe, enters the kitchen, glances around for Willy, then goes to the door of the house, looks out and sees him. Comes down to his left. He looks at her.

Linda: Willy, dear? Willy?

Willy: I was right!

Linda: Did you have some cheese? *He can't answer.* It's very late, darling. Come to bed, heh?

Willy: looking straight up: Gotta break your neck to see a star in this yard.

Linda: You coming in?

Willy: Whatever happened to that diamond watch fob? Remember? When Ben came from Africa that time? Didn't he give me a watch fob with a diamond in it?

Linda: You pawned it, dear. Twelve, thirteen years ago. For Biff's radio correspondence course.

Willy: Gee, that was a beautiful thing. I'll take a walk.

Linda: But you're in your slippers.

Willy: starting to go around the house at the left: I was right! I was! *Half to Linda, as he goes, shaking his head:* What a man! There was a man worth talking to. I was right!

Linda: calling after Willy: But in your slippers, Willy!

Willy is almost gone when Biff, in his pajamas, comes down the stairs and enters the kitchen.

Biff: What is he doing out there?

Linda: Sh!

Biff: God Almighty, Mom, how long has he been doing this?

Linda: Don't, he'll hear you.

Biff: What the hell is the matter with him?

Linda: It'll pass by morning.

Biff: Shouldn't we do anything?

Linda: Oh, my dear, you should do a lot of things, but there's nothing to do, so go to sleep.

Happy comes down the stairs and sits on the steps.

Happy: I never heard him so loud, Mom.

Linda: Well, come around more often; you'll hear him. *She sits down at the table and mends the lining of Willy's jacket.*

Biff: Why didn't you ever write me about this, Mom?

Linda: How would I write to you? For over three months you had no address.

Biff: I was on the move. But you know I thought of you all the time. You know that, don't you, pal?

Linda: I know, dear, I know. But he likes to have a letter. Just to know that there's still a possibility for better things.

Biff: He's not like this all the time, is he?

Linda: It's when you come home he's always the worst.

Biff: When I come home?

Linda: When you write you're coming, he's all smiles, and talks about the future, and—he's just wonderful. And then the closer you seem to come, the more shaky he gets, and then, by the time you get here, he's arguing, and he seems angry at you. I think it's just that maybe he can't bring himself to—to open up to you. Why are you so hateful to each other? Why is that?

Biff: evasively: I'm not hateful, Mom.

Linda: But you no sooner come in the door than you're fighting!

Biff: I don't know why. I mean to change. I'm tryin', Mom, you understand?

Linda: Are you home to stay now?

Biff: I don't know. I want to look around, see what's doin'.

Linda: Biff, you can't look around all your life, can you?

Biff: I just can't take hold, Mom. I can't take hold of some kind of a life.

Linda: Biff, a man is not a bird, to come and go with the springtime.

Biff: Your hair . . . *He touches her hair.* Your hair got so gray.

Linda: Oh, it's been gray since you were in high school. I just stopped dyeing it, that's all.

Biff: Dye it again, will ya? I don't want my pal looking old. *He smiles.*

Linda: You're such a boy! You think you can go away for a year and . . . You've got to get it into your head now that one day you'll knock on this door and there'll be strange people here—

Biff: What are you talking about? You're not even sixty, Mom.

Linda: But what about your father?

Biff: lamely: Well, I meant him too.

Happy: He admires Pop.

Linda: Biff, dear, if you don't have any feeling for him, then you can't have any feeling for me.

Biff: Sure I can, Mom.

Linda: No. You can't just come to see me, because I love him. *With a threat, but only a threat, of tears:* He's the dearest man in the world to me, and I won't have anyone making him feel unwanted and low and blue. You've got to make up your mind now, darling, there's no leeway any more. Either he's your father and you pay him that respect, or else you're not to come here. I know he's not easy to get along with—nobody knows that better than me— but . . .

Willy: from the left, with a laugh: Hey, hey, Biffo!

Biff: starting to go out after Willy: What the hell is the matter with him? *Happy stops him.*

Linda: Don't—don't go near him!

Biff: Stop making excuses for him! He always, always wiped the floor with you. Never had an ounce of respect for you.

Happy: He's always had respect for—

Biff: What the hell do you know about it?

Happy: surlily: Just don't call him crazy!

Biff: He's got no character—Charley wouldn't do this. Not in his own house— spewing out that vomit from his mind.

Happy: Charley never had to cope with what he's got to.

Biff: People are worse off than Willy Loman. Believe me, I've seen them!

Linda: Then make Charley your father, Biff. You can't do that, can you? I don't say he's a great man. Willy Loman never made a lot of money. His name was never in the paper. He's not the finest character that ever lived. But he's a human being, and a terrible thing is happening to him. So attention must be paid. He's not to be allowed to fall into his grave like an old dog. Attention, attention must be finally paid to such a person. You called him crazy—

Biff: I didn't mean—

Linda: No, a lot of people think he's lost his—balance. But you don't have to be very smart to know what his trouble is. The man is exhausted.

Happy: Sure!

Linda: A small man can be just as exhausted as a great man. He works for a company thirty-six years this March, opens up unheard-of territories to their trademark, and now in his old age they take his salary away.

Happy: indignantly: I didn't know that, Mom.

Linda: You never asked, my dear! Now that you get your spending money someplace else you don't trouble your mind with him.

Happy: But I gave you money last—

Linda: Christmas time, fifty dollars! To fix the hot water it cost ninety-seven fifty! For five weeks he's been on straight commission, like a beginner, an unknown!

Biff: Those ungrateful bastards!

Linda: Are they any worse than his sons? When he brought them business, when he was young, they were glad to see him. But now his old friends, the old buyers that loved him so and always found some order to hand him in a pinch—they're all dead, retired. He used to be able to make six, seven calls a day in Boston. Now he takes his valises out of the car and puts them back and takes them out again and he's exhausted. Instead of walking he talks now. He drives seven hundred miles, and when he gets there no one knows him any more, no one welcomes him. And what goes through a man's mind, driving seven hundred miles home without having earned a cent? Why shouldn't he talk to himself? Why? When he has to go to Charley and borrow fifty dollars a week and pretend to me that it's his pay? How long can that go on? How long? You see what I'm sitting here and waiting for? And you tell me he has no character? The man who never worked a day but for your benefit? When does he get the medal for that? Is this his reward—to turn around at the age of sixty-three and find his sons, who he loved better than his life, one a philandering bum—

Happy: Mom!

Linda: That's all you are, my baby! *To Biff:* And you! What happened to the love you had for him? You were such pals! How you used to talk to him on the phone every night! How lonely he was till he could come home to you!

Biff: All right, Mom. I'll live here in my room, and I'll get a job. I'll keep away from him, that's all.

Linda: No, Biff. You can't stay here and fight all the time.

Biff: He threw me out of this house, remember that.

Linda: Why did he do that? I never knew why.

Biff: Because I know he's a fake and he doesn't like anybody around who knows!

Linda: Why a fake? In what way? What do you mean?

Biff: Just don't lay it all at my feet. It's between me and him—that's all I have to say. I'll chip in from now on. He'll settle for half my pay check. He'll be all right. I'm going to bed. *He starts for the stairs.*

Linda: He won't be all right.

Biff: turning on the stairs, furiously: I hate this city and I'll stay here. Now what do you want?

Linda: He's dying, Biff.

Happy turns quickly to her, shocked.

Biff: after a pause: Why is he dying?

Linda: He's been trying to kill himself.

Biff: with great horror: How?

Linda: I live from day to day.

Biff: What're you talking about?

Linda: Remember I wrote you that he smashed up the car again? In February?

Biff: Well?

Linda: The insurance inspector came. He said that they have evidence. That all these accidents in the last year—weren't—weren't—accidents.

Happy: How can they tell that? That's a lie.

Linda: It seems there's a woman . . . *She takes a breath as*

⎰*Biff: sharply but contained:* What woman?

⎱*Linda: simultaneously:* . . . and this woman . . .

Linda: What?

Biff: Nothing. Go ahead.

Linda: What did you say?

Biff: Nothing. I just said what woman?

Happy: What about her?

Linda: Well, it seems she was walking down the road and saw his car. She says that he wasn't driving fast at all, and that he didn't skid. She says he came to that little bridge, and then deliberately smashed into the railing, and it was only the shallowness of the water that saved him.

Biff: Oh, no, he probably just fell asleep again.

Linda: I don't think he fell asleep.

Biff: Why not?

Linda: Last month . . . *With great difficulty:* Oh, boys, it's so hard to say a thing like this! He's just a big stupid man to you, but I tell you there's more good in him than in many other people. *She chokes, wipes her eyes.* I was looking for a fuse. The lights blew out, and I went down the cellar. And behind the fuse box—it happened to fall out—was a length of rubber pipe—just short.

Happy: No kidding?

Linda: There's a little attachment on the end of it. I knew right away. And sure enough, on the bottom of the water heater there's a new little nipple on the gas pipe.

Happy: angrily: That—jerk.

Biff: Did you have it taken off?

Linda: I'm—I'm ashamed to. How can I mention it to him? Every day I go down and take away that little rubber pipe. But, when he comes home, I put it back where it was. How can I insult him that way? I don't know what to do. I live from day to day, boys. I tell you, I know every thought in his mind. It sounds so old-fashioned and silly, but I tell you he put his whole life into you and you've turned your backs on him. *She is bent over in the chair, weeping, her face in her hands.* Biff, I swear to God! Biff, his life is in your hands!

Happy: to Biff: How do you like that damned fool!

Biff: kissing her: All right, pal, all right. It's all settled now. I've been remiss. I know that, Mom. But now I'll stay, and I swear to you, I'll apply myself. *Kneeling in front of her, in a fever of self-reproach:* It's just—you see, Mom, I don't fit in business. Not that I won't try. I'll try, and I'll make good.

Happy: Sure you will. The trouble with you in business was you never tried to please people.

Biff: I know, I—

Happy: Like when you worked for Harrison's. Bob Harrison said you were tops, and then you go and do some damn fool thing like whistling whole songs in the elevator like a comedian.

Biff: against Happy: So what? I like to whistle sometimes.

Happy: You don't raise a guy to a responsible job who whistles in the elevator!

Linda: Well, don't argue about it now.

Happy: Like when you'd go off and swim in the middle of the day instead of taking the line around.

Biff: his resentment rising: Well, don't you run off? You take off sometimes, don't you? On a nice summer day?

Happy: Yeah, but I cover myself!

Linda: Boys!

Happy: If I'm going to take a fade the boss can call any number where I'm supposed to be and they'll swear to him that I just left. I'll tell you something that I hate to say, Biff, but in the business world some of them think you're crazy.

Biff: angered: Screw the business world!

Happy: All right, screw it! Great, but cover yourself!

Linda: Hap, Hap!

Biff: I don't care what they think! They've laughed at Dad for years, and you know why? Because we don't belong in this nuthouse of a city! We should be mixing cement on some open plain, or—or carpenters. A carpenter is allowed to whistle!

Willy walks in from the entrance of the house, at left.

Willy: Even your grandfather was better than a carpenter. *Pause. They watch him.* You never grew up. Bernard does not whistle in the elevator, I assure you.

Biff: as though to laugh Willy out of it: Yeah, but you do, Pop.

Willy: I never in my life whistled in an elevator! And who in the business world thinks I'm crazy?

Biff: I didn't mean it like that, Pop. Now don't make a whole thing out of it, will ya?

Willy: Go back to the West! Be a carpenter, a cowboy, enjoy yourself!

Linda: Willy, he was just saying—

Willy: I heard what he said!

Happy: trying to quiet Willy: Hey, Pop, come on now . . .

Willy: continuing over Happy's line: They laugh at me, heh? Go to Filene's, go to the Hub, go to Slattery's, Boston. Call out the name Willy Loman and see what happens! Big shot!

Biff: All right, Pop.

Willy: Big!

Biff: All right!

Willy: Why do you always insult me?

Biff: I didn't say a word. *To Linda:* Did I say a word?

Linda: He didn't say anything, Willy.

Willy: going to the doorway of the living-room: All right, good night, good night.

Linda: Willy, dear, he just decided . . .

Willy: to Biff: If you get tired hanging around tomorrow, paint the ceiling I put up in the living-room.

Biff: I'm leaving early tomorrow.

Happy: He's going to see Bill Oliver, Pop.

Willy: interestedly: Oliver? For what?

Biff: with reserve, but trying, trying: He always said he'd stake me. I'd like to go into business, so maybe I can take him up on it.

Linda: Isn't that wonderful?

Willy: Don't interrupt. What's wonderful about it? There's fifty men in the City of New York who'd stake him. *To Biff:* Sporting goods?

Biff: I guess so. I know something about it and—

Willy: He knows something about it! You know sporting goods better than Spalding, for God's sake! How much is he giving you?

Biff: I don't know, I didn't even see him yet, but—

Willy: Then what're you talkin' about?

Biff: getting angry: Well, all I said was I'm gonna see him, that's all!

Willy: turning away: Ah, you're counting your chickens again.

Biff: starting left for the stairs: Oh, Jesus, I'm going to sleep!

Willy: calling after him: Don't curse in this house!

Biff: turning: Since when did you get so clean?

Happy: trying to stop them: Wait a . . .

Willy: Don't use that language to me! I won't have it!

Happy: grabbing Biff, shouts: Wait a minute! I got an idea. I got a feasible idea. Come here, Biff, let's talk this over now, let's talk some sense here. When I was down in Florida last time, I thought of a great idea to sell sporting goods. It just came back to me. You and I, Biff—we have a line, the Loman Line. We train a couple of weeks, and put on a couple of exhibitions, see?

Willy: That's an idea!

Happy: Wait! We form two basketball teams, see? Two water-polo teams. We play each other. It's a million dollars' worth of publicity. Two brothers, see?

The Loman Brothers. Displays in the Royal Palms—all the hotels. And banners over the ring and the basketball court: "Loman Brothers." Baby, we could sell sporting goods!

Willy: That is a one-million-dollar idea!

Linda: Marvelous!

Biff: I'm in great shape as far as that's concerned.

Happy: And the beauty of it is, Biff, it wouldn't be like a business. We'd be out playin' ball again . . .

Biff: enthused: Yeah, that's . . .

Willy: Million-dollar . . .

Happy: And you wouldn't get fed up with it, Biff. It'd be the family again. There'd be the old honor, and comradeship, and if you wanted to go off for a swim or somethin'—well, you'd do it! Without some smart cooky gettin' up ahead of you!

Willy: Lick the world! You guys together could absolutely lick the civilized world.

Biff: I'll see Oliver tomorrow. Hap, if we could work that out . . .

Linda: Maybe things are beginning to—

Willy: wildly enthused, to Linda: Stop interrupting! *To Biff:* But don't wear sport jacket and slacks when you see Oliver.

Biff: No, I'll—

Willy: A business suit, and talk as little as possible, and don't crack any jokes.

Biff: He did like me. Always liked me.

Linda: He loved you!

Willy: to Linda: Will you stop! *To Biff:* Walk in very serious. You are not applying for a boy's job. Money is to pass. Be quiet, fine, and serious. Everybody likes a kidder, but nobody lends him money.

Happy: I'll try to get some myself, Biff. I'm sure I can.

Willy: I see great things for you kids, I think your troubles are over. But remember, start big and you'll end big. Ask for fifteen. How much you gonna ask for?

Biff: Gee, I don't know—

Willy: And don't say "Gee." "Gee" is a boy's word. A man walking in for fifteen thousand dollars does not say "Gee!"

Biff: Ten, I think, would be top though.

Willy: Don't be so modest. You always started too low. Walk in with a big laugh. Don't look worried. Start off with a couple of your good stories to lighten things up. It's not what you say, it's how you say it—because personality always wins the day.

Linda: Oliver always thought the highest of him—

Willy: Will you let me talk?

Biff: Don't yell at her, Pop, will ya?

Willy: angrily: I was talking, wasn't I?

Biff: I don't like you yelling at her all the time, and I'm tellin' you, that's all.

Willy: What're you, takin' over this house?

Linda: Willy—

Willy: turning on her: Don't take his side all the time, goddammit!

Biff: furiously: Stop yelling at her!

Willy: suddenly pulling on his cheek, beaten down, guilt ridden: Give my best to Bill Oliver—he may remember me. *He exits through the living-room doorway.*

Linda: her voice subdued: What'd you have to start that for? *Biff turns away.* You see how sweet he was as soon as you talked hopefully? *She goes over to Biff.* Come up and say good night to him. Don't let him go to bed that way.

Happy: Come on, Biff, let's buck him up.

Linda: Please, dear. Just say good night. It takes so little to make him happy. Come. *She goes through the living-room doorway, calling upstairs from within the living-room:* Your pajamas are hanging in the bathroom, Willy!

Happy: looking toward where Linda went out: What a woman! They broke the mold when they made her. You know that, Biff?

Biff: He's off salary. My God, working on commission!

Happy: Well, let's face it: he's no hot-shot selling man. Except that sometimes, you have to admit, he's a sweet personality.

Biff: deciding: Lend me ten bucks, will ya? I want to buy some new ties.

Happy: I'll take you to a place I know. Beautiful stuff. Wear one of my striped shirts tomorrow.

Biff: She got gray. Mom got awful old. Gee, I'm gonna go in to Oliver tomorrow and knock him for a—

Happy: Come on up. Tell that to Dad. Let's give him a whirl. Come on.

Biff: steamed up: You know, with ten thousand bucks, boy!

Happy: as they go into the living-room: That's the talk, Biff, that's the first time I've heard the old confidence out of you! *From within the living-room, fading off:* You're gonna live with me, kid, and any babe you want just say the word . . . *The last lines are hardly heard. They are mounting the stairs to their parents' bedroom.*

Linda: entering her bedroom and addressing Willy, who is in the bathroom. She is straightening the bed for him: Can you do anything about the shower? It drips.

Willy: from the bathroom: All of a sudden everything falls to pieces! Goddam plumbing, oughta be sued, those people. I hardly finished putting it in and the thing . . . *His words rumble off.*

Linda: I'm just wondering if Oliver will remember him. You think he might?

Willy: coming out of the bathroom in his pajamas: Remember him? What's the matter with you, you crazy? If he'd've stayed with Oliver he'd be on top by now! Wait'll Oliver gets a look at him. You don't know the average caliber any more. The average young man today—*he is getting into bed*—is got a caliber of zero. Greatest thing in the world for him was to bum around.

Biff and Happy enter the bedroom. Slight pause.

Willy: stops short, looking at Biff: Glad to hear it, boy.

Happy: He wanted to say good night to you, sport.

Willy: to Biff: Yeah. Knock him dead, boy. What'd you want to tell me?

Biff: Just take it easy, Pop. Good night. *He turns to go.*

Willy: unable to resist: And if anything falls off the desk while you're talking to him—like a package or something—don't you pick it up. They have office boys for that.

Linda: I'll make a big breakfast—

Willy: Will you let me finish? *To Biff:* Tell him you were in the business in the West. Not farm work.

Biff: All right, Dad.

Linda: I think everything—

Willy: going right through her speech: And don't undersell yourself. No less than fifteen thousand dollars.

Biff: unable to bear him: Okay. Good night, Mom. *He starts moving.*

Willy: Because you got a greatness in you, Biff, remember that. You got all kinds a greatness . . . *He lies back, exhausted. Biff walks out.*

Linda: calling after Biff: Sleep well, darling!

Happy: I'm gonna get married, Mom. I wanted to tell you.

Linda: Go to sleep, dear.

Happy: going: I just wanted to tell you.

Willy: Keep up the good work. *Happy exits.* God . . . remember that Ebbets Field[3] game? The championship of the city?

Linda: Just rest. Should I sing to you?

Willy: Yeah. Sing to me. *Linda hums a soft lullaby.* When that team came out— he was the tallest, remember?

Linda: Oh, yes. And in gold.

Biff enters the darkened kitchen, takes a cigarette, and leaves the house. He comes downstage into a golden pool of light. He smokes, staring at the night.

Willy: Like a young god. Hercules—something like that. And the sun, the sun all around him. Remember how he waved to me? Right up from the field, with the representatives of three colleges standing by? And the buyers I brought, and the cheers when he came out—Loman, Loman, Loman! God Almighty, he'll be great yet. A star like that, magnificent, can never really fade away!

The light on Willy is fading. The gas heater begins to glow through the kitchen wall, near the stairs, a blue flame beneath red coils.

Linda: timidly: Willy dear, what has he got against you?

Willy: I'm so tired. Don't talk any more.

Biff slowly returns to the kitchen. He stops, stares toward the heater.

Linda: Will you ask Howard to let you work in New York?

Willy: First thing in the morning. Everything'll be all right.

---

[3] Home of the Brooklyn Dodgers at the time *Death of a Salesman* was written.

Biff reaches behind the heater and draws out a length of rubber tubing. He is horrified and turns his head toward Willy's room, still dimly lit, from which the strains of Linda's desperate but monotonous humming rise.

Willy: staring through the window into the moonlight: Gee, look at the moon moving between the buildings!

Biff wraps the tubing around his hand and quickly goes up the stairs.
   Curtain

ACT TWO

Music is heard, gay and bright. The curtain rises as the music fades away. Willy, in shirt sleeves, is sitting at the kitchen table, sipping coffee, his hat in his lap. Linda is filling his cup when she can.

Willy: Wonderful coffee. Meal in itself.

Linda: Can I make you some eggs?

Willy: No. Take a breath.

Linda: You look so rested, dear.

Willy: I slept like a dead one. First time in months. Imagine, sleeping till ten on a Tuesday morning. Boys left nice and early, heh?

Linda: They were out of here by eight o'clock.

Willy: Good work!

Linda: It was so thrilling to see them leaving together. I can't get over the shaving lotion in this house!

Willy: smiling: Mmm—

Linda: Biff was very changed this morning. His whole attitude seemed to be hopeful. He couldn't wait to get downtown to see Oliver.

Willy: He's heading for a change. There's no question, there simply are certain men that take longer to get—solidified. How did he dress?

Linda: His blue suit. He's so handsome in that suit. He could be a—anything in that suit!

Willy gets up from the table. Linda holds his jacket for him.

Willy: There's no question, no question at all. Gee, on the way home tonight I'd like to buy some seeds.

Linda: laughing: That'd be wonderful. But not enough sun gets back there. Nothing'll grow any more.

Willy: You wait, kid, before it's all over we're gonna get a little place out in the country, and I'll raise some vegetables, a couple of chickens . . .

Linda: You'll do it yet, dear.

Willy walks out of his jacket. Linda follows him.

Willy: And they'll get married, and come for a weekend. I'd build a little guest house. 'Cause I got so many fine tools, all I'd need would be a little lumber and some peace of mind.

Linda: joyfully: I sewed the lining . . .

Willy: I could build two guest houses, so they'd both come. Did he decide how much he's going to ask Oliver for?

Linda: getting him into the jacket: He didn't mention it, but I imagine ten or fifteen thousand. You going to talk to Howard today?

Willy: Yeah. I'll put it to him straight and simple. He'll just have to take me off the road.

Linda: And Willy, don't forget to ask for a little advance, because we've got the insurance premium. It's the grace period now.

Willy: That's a hundred . . .?

Linda: A hundred and eight, sixty-eight. Because we're a little short again.

Willy: Why are we short?

Linda: Well, you had the motor job on the car . . .

Willy: That goddam Studebaker!

Linda: And you got one more payment on the refrigerator . . .

Willy: But it just broke again!

Linda: Well, it's old, dear.

Willy: I told you we should've bought a well-advertised machine. Charley bought a General Electric and it's twenty years old and it's still good, that son-of-a-bitch.

Linda: But, Willy—

Willy: Whoever heard of a Hastings refrigerator? Once in my life I would like to own something outright before it's broken! I'm always in a race with the junkyard! I just finished paying for the car and it's on its last legs. The refrigerator consumes belts like a goddam maniac. They time those things. They time them so when you finally paid for them, they're used up.

Linda: buttoning up his jacket as he unbuttons it: All told, about two hundred dollars would carry us, dear. But that includes the last payment on the mortgage. After this payment, Willy, the house belongs to us.

Willy: It's twenty-five years!

Linda: Biff was nine years old when we bought it.

Willy: Well, that's a great thing. To weather a twenty-five year mortgage is—

Linda: It's an accomplishment.

Willy: All the cement, the lumber, the reconstruction I put in this house! There ain't a crack to be found in it any more.

Linda: Well, it served its purpose.

Willy: What purpose? Some stranger'll come along, move in, and that's that. If only Biff would take this house, and raise a family . . . *He starts to go.* Good-by, I'm late.

Linda: suddenly remembering: Oh, I forgot! You're supposed to meet them for dinner.

Willy: Me?

Linda: At Frank's Chop House on Forty-eighth near Sixth Avenue.

Willy: Is that so! How about you?

Linda: No, just the three of you. They're gonna blow you to a big meal!

Willy: Don't say! Who thought of that?

Linda: Biff came to me this morning, Willy, and he said, "Tell Dad, we want to blow him to a big meal." Be there six o'clock. You and your two boys are going to have dinner.

Willy: Gee whiz! That's really somethin'. I'm gonna knock Howard for a loop, kid. I'll get an advance, and I'll come home with a New York job. Goddammit, now I'm gonna do it!

Linda: Oh, that's the spirit, Willy!

Willy: I will never get behind a wheel the rest of my life!

Linda: It's changing, Willy, I can feel it changing!

Willy: Beyond a question. G'by, I'm late. *He starts to go again.*

Linda: calling after him as she runs to the kitchen table for a handkerchief: You got your glasses?

Willy: feels for them, then comes back in: Yeah, yeah, got my glasses.

Linda: giving him the handkerchief: And a handkerchief.

Willy: Yeah, handkerchief.

Linda: And your saccharine?

Willy: Yeah, my saccharine.

Linda: Be careful on the subway stairs.

She kisses him, and a silk stocking is seen hanging from her hand. Willy notices it.

Willy: Will you stop mending stockings? At least while I'm in the house. It gets me nervous. I can't tell you. Please.

Linda hides the stocking in her hand as she follows Willy across the forestage in front of the house.

Linda: Remember, Frank's Chop House.

Willy: passing the apron: Maybe beets would grow out there.

Linda: laughing: But you tried so many times.

Willy: Yeah. Well, don't work hard today. *He disappears around the right corner of the house.*

Linda: Be careful!

As Willy vanishes, Linda waves to him. Suddenly the phone rings. She runs across the stage and into the kitchen and lifts it.

Linda: Hello? Oh, Biff! I'm so glad you called, I just . . . Yes, sure, I just told him. Yes, he'll be there for dinner at six o'clock, I didn't forget. Listen, I was just dying to tell you. You know that little rubber pipe I told you about? That he connected to the gas heater? I finally decided to go down the cellar this morning and take it away and destroy it. But it's gone! Imagine? He took it away himself, it isn't there! *She listens.* When? Oh, then you took it. Oh— nothing, it's just that I'd hoped he'd taken it away himself. Oh, I'm not worried, darling, because this morning he left in such high spirits, it was like the old days! I'm not afraid any more. Did Mr. Oliver see you? . . . Well, you wait there then. And make a nice impression on him, darling. Just don't perspire too much before you see him. And have a nice time with Dad. He may have big news too! . . . That's right, a New York job. And be sweet to him tonight, dear. Be loving to him. Because he's only a little boat looking for a harbor. *She is trembling with sorrow and joy.* Oh, that's wonderful, Biff, you'll save his life. Thanks, darling. Just put your arm around him when he comes into the restaurant. Give him a smile. That's the boy . . . Good-by, dear. . . . You got your comb? . . . That's fine. Good-by, Biff dear.

In the middle of her speech, Howard Wagner, thirty-six, wheels in a small typewriter table on which is a wire-recording machine[4] and proceeds to plug it in. This is on the left forestage. Light slowly fades on Linda as it rises on Howard. Howard is intent on threading the machine and only glances over his shoulder as Willy appears.

Willy: Pst! Pst!

Howard: Hello, Willy, come in.

Willy: Like to have a little talk with you, Howard.

Howard: Sorry to keep you waiting. I'll be with you in a minute.

Willy: What's that, Howard?

Howard: Didn't you ever see one of these? Wire recorder.

Willy: Oh. Can we talk a minute?

Howard: Records things. Just got delivery yesterday. Been driving me crazy, the most terrific machine I ever saw in my life. I was up all night with it.

Willy: What do you do with it?

Howard: I bought it for dictation, but you can do anything with it. Listen to this. I had it home last night. Listen to what I picked up. The first one is my daughter. Get this. *He flicks the switch and "Roll out the Barrel" is heard being whistled.* Listen to that kid whistle.

Willy: That is lifelike, isn't it?

Howard: Seven years old. Get that tone.

Willy: Ts, ts. Like to ask a little favor if you . . .

The whistling breaks off, and the voice of Howard's daughter is heard.

His Daughter: "Now you, Daddy."

Howard: She's crazy for me! *Again the same song is whistled.* That's me! Ha! *He winks.*

Willy: You're very good!

The whistling breaks off again. The machine runs silent for a moment.

Howard: Sh! Get this now, this is my son.

His Son: "The capital of Alabama is Montgomery; the capital of Arizona is Phoenix; the capital of Arkansas is Little Rock; the capital of California is Sacramento . . ." *and on, and on.*

---

[4] Precursor of the modern tape recorder.

Howard: holding up five fingers: Five years old, Willy!

Willy: He'll make an announcer some day!

His Son: continuing: "The capital . . ."

Howard: Get that—alphabetical order! *The machine breaks off suddenly.* Wait a minute. The maid kicked the plug out.

Willy: It certainly is a—

Howard: Sh, for God's sake!

His Son: "It's nine o'clock, Bulova watch time. So I have to go to sleep."

Willy: That really is—

Howard: Wait a minute! The next is my wife.

They wait.

Howard's Voice: "Go on, say something." *Pause.* "Well, you gonna talk?"

His Wife: "I can't think of anything."

Howard's Voice: "Well, talk—it's turning."

His Wife: shyly, beaten: "Hello." *Silence.* "Oh, Howard, I can't talk into this . . ."

Howard: snapping the machine off: That was my wife.

Willy: That is a wonderful machine. Can we—

Howard: I tell you, Willy, I'm gonna take my camera, and my bandsaw, and all my hobbies, and out they go. This is the most fascinating relaxation I ever found.

Willy: I think I'll get one myself.

Howard: Sure, they're only a hundred and a half. You can't do without it. Supposing you wanna hear Jack Benny, see? But you can't be at home at that hour. So you tell the maid to turn the radio on when Jack Benny comes on, and this automatically goes on with the radio . . .

Willy: And when you come home you . . .

Howard: You can come home twelve o'clock, one o'clock, any time you like, and you get yourself a Coke and sit yourself down, throw the switch, and there's Jack Benny's program in the middle of the night!

Willy: I'm definitely going to get one. Because lots of time I'm on the road, and I think to myself, what I must be missing on the radio!

Howard: Don't you have a radio in the car?

Willy: Well, yeah, but who ever thinks of turning it on?

Howard: Say, aren't you supposed to be in Boston?

Willy: That's what I want to talk to you about, Howard. You got a minute? *He draws a chair in from the wing.*

Howard: What happened? What're you doing here?

Willy: Well . . .

Howard: You didn't crack up again, did you?

Willy: Oh, no. No . . .

Howard: Geez, you had me worried there for a minute. What's the trouble?

Willy: Well, tell you the truth, Howard, I've come to the decision that I'd rather not travel any more.

Howard: Not travel! Well, what'll you do?

Willy: Remember, Christmas time, when you had the party here? You said you'd try to think of some spot for me here in town.

Howard: With us?

Willy: Well, sure.

Howard: Oh, yeah, yeah. I remember. Well, I couldn't think of anything for you, Willy.

Willy: I tell ya, Howard. The kids are all grown up, y'know. I don't need much any more. If I could take home—well, sixty-five dollars a week, I could swing it.

Howard: Yeah, but Willy, see I—

Willy: I tell ya why, Howard. Speaking frankly and between the two of us, y'know—I'm just a little tired.

Howard: Oh, I could understand that, Willy. But you're a road man, Willy, and we do a road business. We've only got a half-dozen salesmen on the floor here.

Willy: God knows, Howard, I never asked a favor of any man. But I was with the firm when your father used to carry you in here in his arms.

Howard: I know that, Willy, but—

Willy: Your father came to me the day you were born and asked me what I thought of the name of Howard, may he rest in peace.

Howard: I appreciate that, Willy, but there just is no spot here for you. If I had a spot I'd slam you right in, but I just don't have a single solitary spot.

He looks for his lighter. Willy has picked it up and gives it to him. Pause.

Willy: with increasing anger: Howard, all I need to set my table is fifty dollars a week.

Howard: But where am I going to put you, kid?

Willy: Look, it isn't a question of whether I can sell merchandise, is it?

Howard: No, but it's a business, kid, and everybody's gotta pull his own weight.

Willy: desperately: Just let me tell you a story, Howard—

Howard: 'Cause you gotta admit, business is business.

Willy: angrily: Business is definitely business, but just listen for a minute. You don't understand this. When I was a boy—eighteen, nineteen—I was already on the road. And there was a question in my mind as to whether selling had a future for me. Because in those days I had a yearning to go to Alaska. See, there were three gold strikes in one month in Alaska, and I felt like going out. Just for the ride, you might say.

Howard: barely interested: Don't say.

Willy: Oh, yeah, my father lived many years in Alaska. He was an adventurous man. We've got quite a little streak of self-reliance in our family. I thought I'd go out with my older brother and try to locate him, and maybe settle in the North with the old man. And I was almost decided to go, when I met a salesman in the Parker House. His name was Dave Singleman. And he was eighty-four years old, and he'd drummed merchandise in thirty-one states. And old Dave, he'd go up to his room, y'understand, put on his green velvet slippers—I'll never forget—and pick up his phone and call the buyers, and without ever leaving his room, at the age of eighty-four, he made his living.

And when I saw that, I realized that selling was the greatest career a man could want. 'Cause what could be more satisfying than to be able to go, at the age of eighty-four, into twenty or thirty different cities, and pick up a phone, and be remembered and loved and helped by so many different people? Do you know? when he died—and by the way he died the death of a salesman, in his green velvet slippers in the smoker of the New York, New Haven and Hartford, going into Boston—when he died, hundreds of salesmen and buyers were at his funeral. Things were sad on a lotta trains for months after that. *He stands up. Howard has not looked at him.* In those days there was personality in it, Howard. There was respect, and comradeship, and gratitude in it. Today, it's all cut and dried, and there's no chance for bringing friendship to bear—or personality. You see what I mean? They don't know me any more.

Howard: moving away, to the right: That's just the thing, Willy.

Willy: If I had forty dollars a week—that's all I'd need. Forty dollars, Howard.

Howard: Kid, I can't take blood from a stone. I—

Willy: desperation is on him now: Howard, the year Al Smith[5] was nominated, your father came to me and—

Howard: starting to go off: I've got to see some people, kid.

Willy: stopping him: I'm talking about your father! There were promises made across this desk! You mustn't tell me you've got people to see—I put thirty-four years into this firm, Howard, and now I can't pay my insurance! You can't eat the orange and throw the peel away—a man is not a piece of fruit! *After a pause:* Now pay attention. Your father—in 1928 I had a big year. I averaged a hundred and seventy dollars a week in commissions.

Howard: impatiently: Now, Willy, you never averaged—

Willy: banging his hand on the desk: I averaged a hundred and seventy dollars a week in the year of 1928! And your father came to me—or rather, I was in the office here—it was right over this desk—and he put his hand on my shoulder—

Howard: getting up: You'll have to excuse me, Willy, I gotta see some people. Pull yourself together. *Going out:* I'll be back in a little while.

On Howard's exit, the light on his chair grows very bright and strange.

Willy: Pull myself together! What the hell did I say to him? My God, I was yelling at him! How could I! *Willy breaks off, staring at the light, which occupies the chair, animating it. He approaches this chair, standing across the desk from it.* Frank, Frank, don't you remember what you told me that time? How you put your hand on my shoulder, and Frank . . . *He leans on the desk and as he speaks the dead man's name he accidentally switches on the recorder, and instantly*

Howard's Son: ". . . of New York is Albany. The capital of Ohio is Cincinnati, the capital of Rhode Island is . . ." *The recitation continues.*

Willy: leaping away with fright, shouting: Ha! Howard! Howard! Howard!

Howard: rushing in: What happened?

5 Alfred Emanuel Smith (1873–1944), American politician, governor of New York, and presidential candidate in 1928.

*Willy: pointing at the machine, which continues nasally, childishly, with the capital
cities:* Shut it off! Shut it off!
Howard: pulling the plug out: Look, Willy . . .
Willy: pressing his hands to his eyes: I gotta get myself some coffee. I'll get some
coffee . . .

Willy starts to walk out. Howard stops him.

Howard: rolling up the cord: Willy, look . . .
Willy: I'll go to Boston.
Howard: Willy, you can't go to Boston for us.
Willy: Why can't I go?
Howard: I don't want you to represent us. I've been meaning to tell you for a
long time now.
Willy: Howard, are you firing me?
Howard: I think you need a good long rest, Willy.
Willy: Howard—
Howard: And when you feel better, come back, and we'll see if we can work
something out.
Willy: But I gotta earn money, Howard. I'm in no position to—
Howard: Where are your sons? Why don't your sons give you a hand?
Willy: They're working on a very big deal.
Howard: This is no time for false pride, Willy. You go to your sons and you tell
them that you're tired. You've got two great boys, haven't you?
Willy: Oh, no question, no question, but in the meantime . . .
Howard: Then that's that, heh?
Willy: All right, I'll go to Boston tomorrow.
Howard: No, no.
Willy: I can't throw myself on my sons. I'm not a cripple!
Howard: Look, kid, I'm busy this morning.
Willy: grasping Howard's arm: Howard, you've got to let me go to Boston!
Howard: hard, keeping himself under control: I've got a line of people to see this
morning. Sit down, take five minutes, and pull yourself together, and then go
home, will ya? I need the office, Willy. *He starts to go, turns, remembering the
recorder, starts to push off the table holding the recorder.* Oh, yeah. Whenever you
can this week, stop by and drop off the samples. You'll feel better, Willy, and
then come back and we'll talk. Pull yourself together, kid, there's people
outside.

*Howard exits, pushing the table off left. Willy stares into space, exhausted. Now the
music is heard—Ben's music—first distantly, then closer, closer. As Willy speaks, Ben
enters from the right. He carries valise and umbrella.*

Willy: Oh, Ben, how did you do it? What is the answer? Did you wind up the
Alaska deal already?
Ben: Doesn't take much time if you know what you're doing. Just a short
business trip. Boarding ship in an hour. Wanted to say good-by.

Willy: Ben, I've got to talk to you.

Ben: glancing at his watch: Haven't the time, William.

Willy: crossing the apron to Ben: Ben, nothing's working out. I don't know what to do.

Ben: Now, look here, William. I've bought timberland in Alaska and I need a man to look after things for me.

Willy: God, timberland! Me and my boys in those grand outdoors!

Ben: You've a new continent at your doorstep, William. Get out of these cities, they're full of talk and time payments and courts of law. Screw on your fists and you can fight for a fortune up there.

Willy: Yes, yes! Linda, Linda!

Linda enters as of old, with the wash.

Linda: Oh, you're back?

Ben: I haven't much time.

Willy: No, wait! Linda, he's got a proposition for me in Alaska.

Linda: But you've got—*To Ben:* He's got a beautiful job here.

Willy: But in Alaska, kid, I could—

Linda: You're doing well enough, Willy!

Ben: to Linda: Enough for what, my dear?

Linda: frightened of Ben and angry at him: Don't say those things to him! Enough to be happy right here, right now. *To Willy, while Ben laughs:* Why must everybody conquer the world? You're well liked, and the boys love you, and someday—*to Ben*—why, old man Wagner told him just the other day that if he keeps it up he'll be a member of the firm, didn't he, Willy?

Willy: Sure, sure. I am building something with this firm. Ben, and if a man is building something he must be on the right track, mustn't he?

Ben: What are you building? Lay your hand on it. Where is it?

Willy: hesitantly: That's true, Linda, there's nothing.

Linda: Why? *To Ben:* There's a man eighty-four years old—

Willy: That's right, Ben, that's right. When I look at that man I say, what is there to worry about?

Ben: Bah!

Willy: It's true, Ben. All he has to do is go into any city, pick up the phone, and he's making his living and you know why?

Ben: picking up his valise: I've got to go.

Willy: holding Ben back: Look at this boy!

Biff, in his high school sweater, enters carrying suitcase. Happy carries Biff's shoulder guards, gold helmet, and football pants.

Willy: Without a penny to his name, three great universities are begging for him, and from there the sky's the limit, because it's not what you do, Ben. It's who you know and the smile on your face! It's contacts, Ben, contacts! The whole wealth of Alaska passes over the lunch table at the Commodore Hotel, and that's the wonder, the wonder of this country, that a man can end with diamonds here on the basis of being liked! *He turns to Biff.* And that's why when you get out on that field today it's important. Because thousands of people will be rooting for you and loving you. *To Ben, who has again begun to leave:* And Ben! when he walks into a business office his name will sound out like a bell and all the doors will open to him! I've seen it, Ben, I've seen it a thousand times! You can't feel it with your hand like timber, but it's there!

Ben: Good-by, William.

Willy: Ben, am I right? Don't you think I'm right? I value your advice.

Ben: There's a new continent at your doorstep, William. You could walk out rich. Rich! *He is gone.*

Willy: We'll do it here, Ben! You hear me? We're gonna do it here!

Young Bernard rushes in. The gay music of the Boys is heard.

Bernard: Oh, gee, I was afraid you left already!

Willy: Why? What time is it?

Bernard: It's half-past one!

Willy: Well, come on, everybody! Ebbets Field next stop! Where's the pennants? *He rushes through the wall-line of the kitchen and out into the living-room.*

Linda: to Biff: Did you pack fresh underwear?

Biff: who has been limbering up: I want to go!

Bernard: Biff, I'm carrying your helmet, ain't I?

Happy: No, I'm carrying the helmet.

Bernard: Oh, Biff, you promised me.

Happy: I'm carrying the helmet.

Bernard: How am I going to get in the locker room?

Linda: Let him carry the shoulder guards. *She puts her coat and hat on in the kitchen.*

Bernard: Can I, Biff? 'Cause I told everybody I'm going to be in the locker room.

Happy: In Ebbets Field it's the clubhouse.

Bernard: I meant the clubhouse. Biff!

Happy: Biff!

Biff: grandly, after a slight pause: Let him carry the shoulder guards.

Happy: as he gives Bernard the shoulder guards: Stay close to us now.

Willy rushes in with the pennants.

Willy: handing them out: Everybody wave when Biff comes out on the field. *Happy and Bernard run off.* You set now, boy?

The music has died away.

Biff: Ready to go, Pop. Every muscle is ready.

Willy: at the edge of the apron: You realize what this means?

Biff: That's right, Pop.

Willy: feeling Biff's muscles: You're comin' home this afternoon captain of the All-Scholastic Championship Team of the City of New York.

Biff: I got it, Pop. And remember, pal, when I take off my helmet, that touchdown is for you.

Willy: Let's go! *He is starting out, with his arm around Biff, when Charley enters, as of old, in knickers.* I got no room for you, Charley.

Charley: Room? For what?

Willy: In the car.

Charley: You goin' for a ride? I wanted to shoot some casino.

Willy: furiously: Casino! *Incredulously:* Don't you realize what today is?

Linda: Oh, he knows, Willy. He's just kidding you.

Willy: That's nothing to kid about!

Charley: No, Linda, what's goin' on?

Linda: He's playing in Ebbets Field.

Charley: Baseball in this weather?

Willy: Don't talk to him. Come on, come on! *He is pushing them out.*

Charley: Wait a minute, didn't you hear the news?

Willy: What?

Charley: Don't you listen to the radio? Ebbets Field just blew up.

Willy: You go to hell! *Charley laughs. Pushing them out.* Come on, come on! We're late.

Charley: as they go: Knock a homer, Biff, knock a homer!

Willy: the last to leave, turning to Charley: I don't think that was funny, Charley. This is the greatest day of his life.

Charley: Willy, when are you going to grow up?

Willy: Yeah, heh? When this game is over, Charley, you'll be laughing out of the other side of your face. They'll be calling him another Red Grange.[6] Twenty-five thousand a year.

Charley: kidding: Is that so?

Willy: Yeah, that's so.

Charley: Well, then, I'm sorry, Willy. But tell me something.

Willy: What?

Charley: Who is Red Grange?

Willy: Put up your hands. Goddam you, put up your hands!

Charley, chuckling, shakes his head and walks away, around the left corner of the stage. Willy follows him. The music rises to a mocking frenzy.

Willy: Who the hell do you think you are, better than everybody else? You don't know everything, you big, ignorant, stupid . . . Put up your hands!

Light rises, on the right side of the forestage, on a small table in the reception room of Charley's office. Traffic sounds are heard. Bernard, now mature, sits whistling to himself. A pair of tennis rackets and an overnight bag are on the floor beside him.

---

[6] Harold Edward Grange (b. 1903), legendary American football player at the University of Illinois and with the Chicago Bears.

Willy: offstage: What are you walking away for? Don't walk away! If you're going to say something say it to my face! I know you laugh at me behind my back. You'll laugh out of the other side of your goddam face after this game. Touchdown! Touchdown! Eighty thousand people! Touchdown! Right between the goal posts.

Bernard is a quiet, earnest, but self-assured young man. Willy's voice is coming from right upstage now. Bernard lowers his feet off the table and listens. Jenny, his father's secretary, enters.

Jenny: distressed: Say, Bernard, will you go out in the hall?
Bernard: What is that noise? Who is it?
Jenny: Mr. Loman. He just got off the elevator.
Bernard: getting up: Who's he arguing with?
Jenny: Nobody. There's nobody with him. I can't deal with him any more, and your father gets all upset everytime he comes. I've got a lot of typing to do, and your father's waiting to sign it. Will you see him?
Willy: entering: Touchdown! Touch—*He sees Jenny.* Jenny, Jenny, good to see you. How're ya? Workin'? Or still honest?
Jenny: Fine. How've you been feeling?
Willy: Not much any more, Jenny. Ha, ha! *He is surprised to see the rackets.*
Bernard: Hello, Uncle Willy.
Willy: almost shocked: Bernard! Well, look who's here! *He comes quickly, guiltily, to Bernard and warmly shakes his hand.*
Bernard: How are you? Good to see you.
Willy: What are you doing here?
Bernard: Oh, just stopped by to see Pop. Get off my feet till my train leaves. I'm going to Washington in a few minutes.
Willy: Is he in?
Bernard: Yes, he's in his office with the accountant. Sit down.
Willy: sitting down: What're you going to do in Washington?
Bernard: Oh, just a case I've got there, Willy.
Willy: That so? *Indicating the rackets:* You going to play tennis there?
Bernard: I'm staying with a friend who's got a court.
Willy: Don't say. His own tennis court. Must be fine people, I bet.
Bernard: They are, very nice. Dad tells me Biff's in town.
Willy: with a big smile: Yeah, Biff's in. Working on a very big deal, Bernard.
Bernard: What's Biff doing?
Willy: Well, he's been doing very big things in the West. But he decided to establish himself here. Very big. We're having dinner. Did I hear your wife had a boy?
Bernard: That's right. Our second.
Willy: Two boys! What do you know!
Bernard: What kind of a deal has Biff got?
Willy: Well, Bill Oliver—very big sporting-goods man—he wants Biff very badly. Called him in from the West. Long distance, carte blanche, special deliveries. Your friends have their own private tennis court?

Bernard: You still with the old firm, Willy?

Willy: after a pause: I'm—I'm overjoyed to see how you made the grade, Bernard, overjoyed. It's an encouraging thing to see a young man really—really—Looks very good for Biff—very—*He breaks off, then:* Bernard—*He is so full of emotion, he breaks off again.*

Bernard: What is it, Willy?

Willy: small and alone: What—what's the secret?

Bernard: What secret?

Willy: How—how did you? Why didn't he ever catch on?

Bernard: I wouldn't know that, Willy.

Willy: confidentially, desperately: You were his friend, his boyhood friend. There's something I don't understand about it. His life ended after that Ebbets Field game. From the age of seventeen nothing good ever happened to him.

Bernard: He never trained himself for anything.

Willy: But he did, he did. After high school he took so many correspondence courses. Radio mechanics; television; God knows what, and never made the slightest mark.

Bernard: taking off his glasses: Willy, do you want to talk candidly?

Willy: rising, faces Bernard: I regard you as a very brilliant man, Bernard. I value your advice.

Bernard: Oh, the hell with the advice, Willy. I couldn't advise you. There's just one thing I've always wanted to ask you. When he was supposed to graduate, and the math teacher flunked him—

Willy: Oh, that son-of-a-bitch ruined his life.

Bernard: Yeah, but, Willy, all he had to do was go to summer school and make up that subject.

Willy: That's right, that's right.

Bernard: Did you tell him not to go to summer school?

Willy: Me? I begged him to go. I ordered him to go!

Bernard: Then why wouldn't he go?

Willy: Why? Why! Bernard, that question has been trailing me like a ghost for the last fifteen years. He flunked the subject, and laid down and died like a hammer hit him!

Bernard: Take it easy, kid.

Willy: Let me talk to you—I got nobody to talk to. Bernard, Bernard, was it my fault? Y'see? It keeps going around in my mind, maybe I did something to him. I got nothing to give him.

Bernard: Don't take it so hard.

Willy: Why did he lay down? What is the story there? You were his friend!

Bernard: Willy, I remember, it was June, and our grades came out. And he'd flunked math.

Willy: That son-of-a-bitch!

Bernard: No, it wasn't right then. Biff just got very angry, I remember, and he was ready to enroll in summer school.

Willy: surprised: He was?

Bernard: He wasn't beaten by it at all. But then, Willy, he disappeared from the block for almost a month. And I got the idea that he'd gone up to New England to see you. Did he have a talk with you then?

Willy stares in silence.

Bernard: Willy?
Willy: with a strong edge of resentment in his voice: Yeah, he came to Boston. What about it?
Bernard: Well, just that when he came back—I'll never forget this, it always mystifies me. Because I'd thought so well of Biff, even though he'd always taken advantage of me. I loved him, Willy, y'know? And he came back after that month and took his sneakers—remember those sneakers with "University of Virginia" printed on them? He was so proud of those, wore them every day. And he took them down in the cellar, and burned them up in the furnace. We had a fist fight. It lasted at least half an hour. Just the two of us, punching each other down the cellar, and crying right through it. I've often thought of how strange it was that I knew he'd given up his life. What happened in Boston, Willy?

Willy looks at him as at an intruder.

Bernard: I just bring it up because you asked me.
Willy: angrily: Nothing. What do you mean, "What happened?" What's that got to do with anything?
Bernard: Well, don't get sore.
Willy: What are you trying to do, blame it on me? If a boy lays down is that my fault?
Bernard: Now, Willy, don't get—
Willy: Well, don't—don't talk to me that way! What does that mean, "What happened?"

Charley enters. He is in his vest, and he carries a bottle of bourbon.

Charley: Hey, you're going to miss that train. *He waves the bottle.*
Bernard: Yeah, I'm going. *He takes the bottle.* Thanks, Pop. *He picks up his rackets and bag.* Good-by, Willy, and don't worry about it. You know, "If at first you don't succeed . . ."
Willy: Yes, I believe in that.
Bernard: But sometimes, Willy, it's better for a man just to walk away.
Willy: Walk away?
Bernard: That's right.
Willy: But if you can't walk away?
Bernard: after a slight pause: I guess that's when it's tough. *Extending his hand:* Good-by, Willy.
Willy: shaking Bernard's hand: Good-by, boy.
Charley: an arm on Bernard's shoulder: How do you like this kid? Gonna argue a case in front of the Supreme Court.

Bernard: protesting: Pop!
Willy: genuinely shocked, pained, and happy: No! The Supreme Court!
Bernard: I gotta run. 'By, Dad!
Charley: Knock 'em dead, Bernard!

Bernard goes off.

Willy: as Charley takes out his wallet: The Supreme Court! And he didn't even
   mention it!
Charley: counting out money on the desk: He don't have to—he's gonna do it.
Willy: And you never told him what to do, did you? You never took any
   interest in him.
Charley: My salvation is that I never took any interest in anything. There's some
   money—fifty dollars. I got an accountant inside.
Willy: Charley, look . . . *With difficulty:* I got my insurance to pay. If you can
   manage it—I need a hundred and ten dollars.

Charley doesn't reply for a moment; merely stops moving.

Willy: I'd draw it from my bank but Linda would know, and I . . .
Charley: Sit down, Willy.
Willy: moving toward the chair: I'm keeping an account of everything, remember.
   I'll pay every penny back. *He sits.*
Charley: Now listen to me, Willy.
Willy: I want you to know I appreciate . . .
Charley: sitting down on the table: Willy, what're you doin'? What the hell is
   goin' on in your head?
Willy: Why? I'm simply . . .
Charley: I offered you a job. You can make fifty dollars a week. And I won't
   send you on the road.
Willy: I've got a job.
Charley: Without pay? What kind of a job is a job without pay? *He rises.* Now,
   look, kid, enough is enough. I'm no genius but I know when I'm being
   insulted.
Willy: Insulted!
Charley: Why don't you want to work for me?
Willy: What's the matter with you? I've got a job.
Charley: Then what're you walkin' in here every week for?
Willy: getting up: Well, if you don't want me to walk in here—
Charley: I am offering you a job.
Willy: I don't want your goddam job!
Charley: When the hell are you going to grow up?
Willy: furiously: You big ignoramus, if you say that to me again I'll rap you
   one! I don't care how big you are! *He's ready to fight.*

Pause.

Charley: kindly, going to him: How much do you need, Willy?

Willy: Charley, I'm strapped, I'm strapped. I don't know what to do. I was just fired.

Charley: Howard fired you?

Willy: That snotnose. Imagine that? I named him. I named him Howard.

Charley: Willy, when're you gonna realize that them things don't mean anything? You named him Howard, but you can't sell that. The only thing you got in this world is what you can sell. And the funny thing is that you're a salesman, and you don't know that.

Willy: I've always tried to think otherwise, I guess. I always felt that if a man was impressive, and well liked, that nothing—

Charley: Why must everybody like you? Who liked J. P. Morgan? Was he impressive? In a Turkish bath he'd look like a butcher. But with his pockets on he was very well liked. Now listen, Willy, I know you don't like me, and nobody can say I'm in love with you, but I'll give you a job because—just for the hell of it, put it that way. Now what do you say?

Willy: I—I just can't work for you, Charley.

Charley: What're you, jealous of me?

Willy: I can't work for you, that's all, don't ask me why.

Charley: angered, takes out more bills: You been jealous of me all your life, you damned fool! Here, pay your insurance. *He puts the money in Willy's hand.*

Willy: I'm keeping strict accounts.

Charley: I've got some work to do. Take care of yourself. And pay your insurance.

Willy: moving to the right: Funny, y'know? After all the highways, and the trains, and the appointments, and the years, you end up worth more dead than alive.

Charley: Willy, nobody's worth nothin' dead. *After a slight pause:* Did you hear what I said?

Willy stands still, dreaming.

Charley: Willy!

Willy: Apologize to Bernard for me when you see him. I didn't mean to argue with him. He's a fine boy. They're all fine boys, and they'll end up big—all of them. Someday they'll all play tennis together. Wish me luck, Charley. He saw Bill Oliver today.

Charley: Good luck.

Willy: on the verge of tears: Charley, you're the only friend I got. Isn't that a remarkable thing? *He goes out.*

Charley: Jesus!

Charley stares after him a moment and follows. All light blacks out. Suddenly raucous music is heard, and a red glow rises behind the screen at right. Stanley, a young waiter, appears, carrying a table, followed by Happy, who is carrying two chairs.

Stanley: putting the table down: That's all right, Mr. Loman, I can handle it myself. *He turns and takes the chairs from Happy and places them at the table.*

Happy: glancing around: Oh, this is better.

Stanley: Sure, in the front there you're in the middle of all kinds a noise. Whenever you got a party, Mr. Loman, you just tell me and I'll put you back here. Y'know, there's a lotta people they don't like it private, because when they go out they like to see a lotta action around them because they're sick and tired to stay in the house by theirself. But I know you, you ain't from Hackensack.[7] You know what I mean?

Happy: sitting down: So how's it coming, Stanley?

Stanley: Ah, it's a dog's life. I only wish during the war they'd a took me in the Army. I coulda been dead by now.

Happy: My brother's back, Stanley.

Stanley: Oh, he come back, heh? From the Far West.

Happy: Yeah, big cattle man, my brother, so treat him right. And my father's coming too.

Stanley: Oh, your father too!

Happy: You got a couple of nice lobsters?

Stanley: Hundred per cent, big.

Happy: I want them with the claws.

Stanley: Don't worry, I don't give you no mice. *Happy laughs.* How about some wine? It'll put a head on the meal.

Happy: No. You remember, Stanley, that recipe I brought you from overseas? With the champagne in it?

Stanley: Oh, yeah, sure. I still got it tacked up yet in the kitchen. But that'll have to cost a buck apiece anyways.

Happy: That's all right.

Stanley: What'd you, hit a number or somethin'?

Happy: No, it's a little celebration. My brother is—I think he pulled off a big deal today. I think we're going into business together.

Stanley: Great! That's the best for you. Because a family business, you know what I mean?—that's the best.

Happy: That's what I think.

Stanley: 'Cause what's the difference? Somebody steals? It's in the family. Know what I mean? *Sotto voce:*[8] Like this bartender here. The boss is goin' crazy what kinda leak he's got in the cash register. You put it in but it don't come out.

Happy: raising his head: Sh!

Stanley: What?

Happy: You notice I wasn't lookin' right or left, was I?

Stanley: No.

Happy: And my eyes are closed.

Stanley: So what's the—?

Happy: Strudel's comin'.

Stanley: catching on, looks around: Ah, no, there's no—

---

[7] City in New Jersey; here meant as an example of a small, industrialized, middle-class town.

[8] Italian: "in a low voice."

He breaks off as a furred, lavishly dressed girl enters and sits at the next table. Both follow her with their eyes.

Stanley: Geez, how'd ya know?

Happy: I got radar or something. *Staring directly at her profile:* Oooooooo . . . Stanley.

Stanley: I think that's for you, Mr. Loman.

Happy: Look at that mouth. Oh, God. And the binoculars.

Stanley: Geez, you got a life, Mr. Loman.

Happy: Wait on her.

Stanley: going to the girl's table: Would you like a menu, ma'am?

Girl: I'm expecting someone, but I'd like a—

Happy: Why don't you bring her—excuse me, miss, do you mind? I sell champagne, and I'd like you to try my brand. Bring her a champagne, Stanley.

Girl: That's awfully nice of you.

Happy: Don't mention it. It's all company money. *He laughs.*

Girl: That's a charming product to be selling, isn't it?

Happy: Oh, gets to be like everything else. Selling is selling, y'know.

Girl: I suppose.

Happy: You don't happen to sell, do you?

Girl: No, I don't sell.

Happy: Would you object to a compliment from a stranger? You ought to be on a magazine cover.

Girl: looking at him a little archly: I have been.

Stanley comes in with a glass of champagne.

Happy: What'd I say before, Stanley? You see? She's a cover girl.

Stanley: Oh, I could see, I could see.

Happy: to the Girl: What magazine?

Girl: Oh, a lot of them. *She takes the drink.* Thank you.

Happy: You know what they say in France, don't you? "Champagne is the drink of the complexion"—Hya, Biff!

Biff has entered and sits with Happy.

Biff: Hello, kid. Sorry I'm late.

Happy: I just got here. Uh, Miss—?

Girl: Forsythe.

Happy: Miss Forsythe, this is my brother.

Biff: Is Dad here?

Happy: His name is Biff. You might've heard of him. Great football player.

Girl: Really? What team?

Happy: Are you familiar with football?

Girl: No, I'm afraid I'm not.

Happy: Biff is quarterback with the New York Giants.

Girl: Well, that is nice, isn't it? *She drinks.*

Happy: Good health.

Girl: I'm happy to meet you.

Happy: That's my name. Hap. It's really Harold, but at West Point they called me Happy.

Girl: now really impressed: Oh, I see. How do you do? *She turns her profile.*

Biff: Isn't Dad coming?

Happy: You want her?

Biff: Oh, I could never make that.

Happy: I remember the time that idea would never come into your head. Where's the old confidence, Biff?

Biff: I just saw Oliver—

Happy: Wait a minute. I've got to see that old confidence again. Do you want her? She's on call.

Biff: Oh, no. *He turns to look at the Girl.*

Happy: I'm telling you. Watch this. *Turning to the Girl:* Honey? *She turns to him.* Are you busy?

Girl: Well, I am . . . but I could make a phone call.

Happy: Do that, will you, honey? And see if you can get a friend. We'll be here for a while. Biff is one of the greatest football players in the country.

Girl: standing up: Well, I'm certainly happy to meet you.

Happy: Come back soon.

Girl: I'll try.

Happy: Don't try, honey, try hard.

The Girl exits. Stanley follows, shaking his head in bewildered admiration.

Happy: Isn't that a shame now? A beautiful girl like that? That's why I can't get married. There's not a good woman in a thousand. New York is loaded with them, kid!

Biff: Hap, look—

Happy: I told you she was on call!

Biff: strangely unnerved: Cut it out, will ya? I want to say something to you.

Happy: Did you see Oliver?

Biff: I saw him all right. Now look, I want to tell Dad a couple of things and I want you to help me.

Happy: What? Is he going to back you?

Biff: Are you crazy? You're out of your goddam head, you know that?

Happy: Why? What happened?

Biff: breathlessly: I did a terrible thing today, Hap. It's been the strangest day I ever went through. I'm all numb, I swear.

Happy: You mean he wouldn't see you?

Biff: Well, I waited six hours for him, see? All day. Kept sending my name in. Even tried to date his secretary so she'd get me to him, but no soap.

Happy: Because you're not showin' the old confidence, Biff. He remembered you, didn't he?

Biff: stopping Happy with a gesture: Finally, about five o'clock, he comes out. Didn't remember who I was or anything. I felt like such an idiot, Hap.

Happy: Did you tell him my Florida idea?

Biff: He walked away. I saw him for one minute. I got so mad I could've torn the walls down! How the hell did I ever get the idea I was a salesman there? I even believed myself that I'd been a salesman for him! And then he gave me one look and—I realized what a ridiculous lie my whole life has been! We've been talking in a dream for fifteen years. I was a shipping clerk.

Happy: What'd you do?

Biff: with great tension and wonder: Well, he left, see. And the secretary went out. I was all alone in the waiting-room. I don't know what came over me, Hap. The next thing I know I'm in his office—paneled walls, everything. I can't explain it. I—Hap, I took his fountain pen.

Happy: Geez, did he catch you?

Biff: I ran out. I ran down all eleven flights. I ran and ran and ran.

Happy: That was an awful dumb—what'd you do that for?

Biff: agonized: I don't know, I just—wanted to take something, I don't know. You gotta help me, Hap, I'm gonna tell Pop.

Happy: You crazy? What for?

Biff: Hap, he's got to understand that I'm not the man somebody lends that kind of money to. He thinks I've been spiting him all these years and it's eating him up.

Happy: That's just it. You tell him something nice.

Biff: I can't.

Happy: Say you got a lunch date with Oliver tomorrow.

Biff: So what do I do tomorrow?

Happy: You leave the house tomorrow and come back at night and say Oliver is thinking it over. And he thinks it over for a couple of weeks, and gradually it fades away and nobody's the worse.

Biff: But it'll go on forever!

Happy: Dad is never so happy as when he's looking forward to something!

Willy enters.

Happy: Hello, scout!

Willy: Gee, I haven't been here in years!

Stanley has followed Willy in and sets a chair for him. Stanley starts off but Happy stops him.

Happy: Stanley!

Stanley stands by, waiting for an order.

Biff: going to Willy with guilt, as to an invalid: Sit down, Pop. You want a drink?

Willy: Sure, I don't mind.

Biff: Let's get a load on.

Willy: You look worried.

Biff: N-no. *To Stanley:* Scotch all around. Make it doubles.

Stanley: Doubles, right. *He goes.*

Willy: You had a couple already, didn't you?

Biff: Just a couple, yeah.

Willy: Well, what happened, boy? *Nodding affirmatively, with a smile:* Everything go all right?

Biff: takes a breath, then reaches out and grasps Willy's hand: Pai . . . *He is smiling bravely, and Willy is smiling too.* I had an experience today.

Happy: Terrific, Pop.

Willy: That so? What happened?

Biff: high, slightly alcoholic, above the earth: I'm going to tell you everything from first to last. It's been a strange day. *Silence. He looks around, composes himself as best he can, but his breath keeps breaking the rhythm of his voice.* I had to wait quite a while for him, and—

Willy: Oliver?

Biff: Yeah, Oliver. All day, as a matter of cold fact. And a lot of—instances— facts, Pop, facts about my life came back to me. Who was it, Pop? Who ever said I was a salesman with Oliver?

Willy: Well, you were.

Biff: No, Dad, I was a shipping clerk.

Willy: But you were practically—

Biff: with determination: Dad, I don't know who said it first, but I was never a salesman for Bill Oliver.

Willy: What're you talking about?

Biff: Let's hold on to the facts tonight, Pop. We're not going to get anywhere bullin' around. I was a shipping clerk.

Willy: angrily: All right, now listen to me—

Biff: Why don't you let me finish?

Willy: I'm not interested in stories about the past or any crap of that kind because the woods are burning, boys, you understand? There's a big blaze going on all around. I was fired today.

Biff: shocked: How could you be?

Willy: I was fired, and I'm looking for a little good news to tell your mother, because the woman has waited and the woman has suffered. The gist of it is that I haven't got a story left in my head, Biff. So don't give me a lecture about facts and aspects. I am not interested. Now what've you got to say to me?

Stanley enters with three drinks. They wait until he leaves.

Willy: Did you see Oliver?

Biff: Jesus, Dad!

Willy: You mean you didn't go up there?

Happy: Sure he went up there.

Biff: I did. I—saw him. How could they fire you?

Willy: on the edge of his chair: What kind of a welcome did he give you?

Biff: He won't even let you work on commission?

Willy: I'm out! *Driving:* So tell me, he gave you a warm welcome?

Happy: Sure, Pop, sure!

Biff: driven: Well, it was kind of—

Willy: I was wondering if he'd remember you. *To Happy:* Imagine, man doesn't see him for ten, twelve years and gives him that kind of a welcome!

Happy: Damn right!

Biff: trying to return to the offensive: Pop, look—

Willy: You know why he remembered you, don't you? Because you impressed him in those days.

Biff: Let's talk quietly and get this down to the facts, huh?

Willy: as though Biff had been interrupting: Well, what happened? It's great news, Biff. Did he take you into his office or'd you talk in the waiting-room?

Biff: Well, he came in, see, and—

Willy: with a big smile: What'd he say? Betcha he threw his arm around you.

Biff: Well, he kinda—

Willy: He's a fine man. *To Happy:* Very hard man to see, y'know.

Happy: agreeing: Oh, I know.

Willy: to Biff: Is that where you had the drinks?

Biff: Yeah, he gave me a couple of—no, no!

Happy: cutting in: He told him my Florida idea.

Willy: Don't interrupt. *To Biff:* How'd he react to the Florida idea?

Biff: Dad, will you give me a minute to explain?

Willy: I've been waiting for you to explain since I sat down here! What happened? He took you into his office and what?

Biff: Well—I talked. And—and he listened, see.

Willy: Famous for the way he listens, y'know. What was his answer?

Biff: His answer was—*He breaks off, suddenly angry.* Dad, you're not letting me tell you what I want to tell you!

Willy: accusing, angered: You didn't see him, did you?

Biff: I did see him!

Willy: What'd you insult him or something? You insulted him, didn't you?

Biff: Listen, will you let me out of it, will you just let me out of it!

Happy: What the hell!

Willy: Tell me what happened!

Biff: to Happy: I can't talk to him!

A single trumpet note jars the ear. The light of green leaves stains the house, which holds the air of night and a dream. Young Bernard enters and knocks on the door of the house.

Young Bernard: frantically: Mrs. Loman, Mrs. Loman!

Happy: Tell him what happened!

Biff: to Happy: Shut up and leave me alone!

Willy: No, no! You had to go and flunk math!

Biff: What math? What're you talking about?

Young Bernard: Mrs. Loman, Mrs. Loman!

Linda appears in the house, as of old.

Willy: wildly: Math, math, math!

Biff: Take it easy, Pop!

Young Bernard: Mrs. Loman!

Willy: furiously: If you hadn't flunked you'd've been set by now!

Biff: Now, look, I'm gonna tell you what happened, and you're going to listen to me.

Young Bernard: Mrs. Loman!

Biff: I waited six hours—

Happy: What the hell are you saying?

Biff: I kept sending in my name but he wouldn't see me. So finally he . . . *He continues unheard as light fades low on the restaurant.*

Young Bernard: Biff flunked math!

Linda: No!

Young Bernard: Birnbaum flunked him! They won't graduate him!

Linda: But they have to. He's gotta go to the university. Where is he? Biff! Biff!

Young Bernard: No, he left. He went to Grand Central.[9]

Linda: Grand—You mean he went to Boston!

Young Bernard: Is Uncle Willy in Boston?

Linda: Oh, maybe Willy can talk to the teacher. Oh, the poor, poor boy!

Light on house area snaps out.

Biff: at the table, now audible, holding up a gold fountain pen: . . . so I'm washed up with Oliver, you understand? Are you listening to me?

Willy: at a loss: Yeah, sure. If you hadn't flunked—

Biff: Flunked what? What're you talking about?

Willy: Don't blame everything on me! I didn't flunk math—you did! What pen?

Happy: That was awful dumb, Biff, a pen like that is worth—

Willy: seeing the pen for the first time: You took Oliver's pen?

Biff: weakening: Dad, I just explained it to you.

Willy: You stole Bill Oliver's fountain pen!

Biff: I didn't exactly steal it! That's just what I've been explaining to you!

Happy: He had it in his hand and just then Oliver walked in, so he got nervous and stuck it in his pocket!

Willy: My God, Biff!

Biff: I never intended to do it, Dad!

Operator's Voice: Standish Arms, good evening!

Willy: shouting: I'm not in my room!

Biff: frightened: Dad, what's the matter? *He and Happy stand up.*

Operator: Ringing Mr. Loman for you!

Willy: I'm not there, stop it!

Biff: horrified, gets down on one knee before Willy: Dad, I'll make good, I'll make good. *Willy tries to get to his feet. Biff holds him down.* Sit down now.

[9] Grand Central Station in New York City, a
main transportation terminal.

Willy: No, you're no good, you're no good for anything.

Biff: I am, Dad, I'll find something else, you understand? Now don't worry about anything. *He holds up Willy's face:* Talk to me, Dad.

Operator: Mr. Loman does not answer. Shall I page him?

Willy: attempting to stand, as though to rush and silence the Operator: No, no, no!

Happy: He'll strike something, Pop.

Willy: No, no . . .

Biff: desperately, standing over Willy: Pop, listen! Listen to me! I'm telling you something good. Oliver talked to his partner about the Florida idea. You listening? He—he talked to his partner, and he came to me . . . I'm going to be all right, you hear? Dad, listen to me, he said it was just a question of the amount!

Willy: Then you . . . got it?

Happy: He's gonna be terrific, Pop!

Willy: trying to stand: Then you got it, haven't you? You got it! You got it!

Biff: agonized, holds Willy down: No, no. Look, Pop. I'm supposed to have lunch with them tomorrow. I'm just telling you this so you'll know that I can still make an impression, Pop. And I'll make good somewhere, but I can't go tomorrow, see?

Willy: Why not? You simply—

Biff: But the pen, Pop!

Willy: You give it to him and tell him it was an oversight!

Happy: Sure, have lunch tomorrow!

Biff: I can't say that—

Willy: You were doing a crossword puzzle and accidentally used his pen!

Biff: Listen, kid, I took those balls years ago, now I walk in with his fountain pen? That clinches it, don't you see? I can't face him like that! I'll try elsewhere.

Page's Voice: Paging Mr. Loman!

Willy: Don't you want to be anything?

Biff: Pop, how can I go back?

Willy: You don't want to be anything, is that what's behind it?

Biff: now angry at Willy for not crediting his sympathy: Don't take it that way! You think it was easy walking into that office after what I'd done to him? A team of horses couldn't have dragged me back to Bill Oliver!

Willy: Then why'd you go?

Biff: Why did I go? Why did I go! Look at you! Look at what's become of you!

Off left, The Woman laughs.

Willy: Biff, you're going to go to that lunch tomorrow, or—

Biff: I can't go. I've got no appointment!

Happy: Biff, for . . . !

Willy: Are you spiting me?

Biff: Don't take it that way! Goddammit!

Willy: strikes Biff and falters away from the table: You rotten little louse! Are you spiting me?

The Woman: Someone's at the door, Willy!

Biff: I'm not good, can't you see what I am?

Happy: separating them: Hey, you're in a restaurant! Now cut it out, both of you! *The girls enter.* Hello, girls, sit down.

The Woman laughs, off left.

Miss Forsythe: I guess we might as well. This is Letta.

The Woman: Willy, are you going to wake up?

Biff: ignoring Willy: How're ya, miss, sit down. What do you drink?

Miss Forsythe: Letta might not be able to stay long.

Letta: I gotta get up very early tomorrow. I got jury duty. I'm so excited! Were you fellows ever on a jury?

Biff: No, but I been in front of them! *The girls laugh.* This is my father.

Letta: Isn't he cute? Sit down with us, Pop.

Happy: Sit him down, Biff!

Biff: going to him: Come on, slugger, drink us under the table. To hell with it! Come on, sit down, pal.

On Biff's last insistence, Willy is about to sit.

The Woman: now urgently: Willy, are you going to answer the door!

The Woman's call pulls Willy back. He starts right, befuddled.

Biff: Hey, where are you going?

Willy: Open the door.

Biff: The door?

Willy: The washroom . . . the door . . . where's the door?

Biff: leading Willy to the left: Just go straight down.

Willy moves left.

The Woman: Willy, Willy, are you going to get up, get up, get up, get up?

Willy exits left.

Letta: I think it's sweet you bring your daddy along.

Miss Forsythe: Oh, he isn't really your father!

Biff: at left, turning to her resentfully: Miss Forsythe, you've just seen a prince walk by. A fine, troubled prince. A hard-working, unappreciated prince. A pal, you understand? A good companion. Always for his boys.

Letta: That's so sweet.

Happy: Well, girls, what's the program? We're wasting time. Come on, Biff. Gather round. Where would you like to go?

Biff: Why don't you do something for him?

Happy: Me!

Biff: Don't you give a damn for him, Hap?

Happy: What're you talking about? I'm the one who—

Biff: I sense it, you don't give a good goddam about him. *He takes the rolled-up hose from his pocket and puts it on the table in front of Happy.* Look what I found in the cellar, for Christ's sake. How can you bear to let it go on?

Happy: Me? Who goes away? Who runs off and—

Biff: Yeah, but he doesn't mean anything to you. You could help him—I can't! Don't you understand what I'm talking about? He's going to kill himself, don't you know that?

Happy: Don't I know it! Me!

Biff: Hap, help him! Jesus . . . help him . . . Help me, help me, I can't bear to look at his face! *Ready to weep, he hurries out, up right.*

Happy: starting after him: Where are you going?

Miss Forsythe: What's he so mad about?

Happy: Come on, girls, we'll catch up with him.

Miss Forsythe: as Happy pushes her out: Say, I don't like that temper of his!

Happy: He's just a little overstrung, he'll be all right!

Willy: off left, as The Woman laughs: Don't answer! Don't answer!

Letta: Don't you want to tell your father—

Happy: No, that's not my father. He's just a guy. Come on, we'll catch Biff, and, honey, we're going to paint this town! Stanley, where's the check! Hey, Stanley!

They exit. Stanley looks toward left.

Stanley: calling to Happy indignantly: Mr. Loman! Mr. Loman!

Stanley picks up a chair and follows them off. Knocking is heard off left. The Woman enters, laughing. Willy follows her. She is in a black slip; he is buttoning his shirt. Raw, sensuous music accompanies their speech.

Willy: Will you stop laughing? Will you stop?

The Woman: Aren't you going to answer the door? He'll wake the whole hotel.

Willy: I'm not expecting anybody.

The Woman: Whyn't you have another drink, honey, and stop being so damn self-centered?

Willy: I'm so lonely.

The Woman: You know you ruined me, Willy? From now on, whenever you come to the office, I'll see that you go right through to the buyers. No waiting at my desk any more, Willy. You ruined me.

Willy: That's nice of you to say that.

The Woman: Gee, you are self-centered! Why so sad? You are the saddest, self-centeredest soul I ever did see-saw. *She laughs. He kisses her.* Come on inside, drummer boy. It's silly to be dressing in the middle of the night. *As knocking is heard:* Aren't you going to answer the door?

Willy: They're knocking on the wrong door.

The Woman: But I felt the knocking. And he heard us talking in here. Maybe the hotel's on fire!

Willy: his terror rising: It's a mistake.

The Woman: Then tell him to go away!

Willy: There's nobody there.

The Woman: It's getting on my nerves, Willy. There's somebody standing out there and it's getting on my nerves!

Willy: pushing her away from him: All right, stay in the bathroom here, and don't come out. I think there's a law in Massachusetts about it, so don't come out. It may be that new room clerk. He looked very mean. So don't come out. It's a mistake, there's no fire.

The knocking is heard again. He takes a few steps away from her, and she vanishes into the wing. The light follows him, and now he is facing Young Biff, who carries a suitcase. Biff steps toward him. The music is gone.

Biff: Why didn't you answer?

Willy: Biff! What are you doing in Boston?

Biff: Why didn't you answer? I've been knocking for five minutes, I called you on the phone—

Willy: I just heard you. I was in the bathroom and had the door shut. Did anything happen home?

Biff: Dad—I let you down.

Willy: What do you mean?

Biff: Dad . . .

Willy: Biffo, what's this about? *Putting his arm around Biff:* Come on, let's go downstairs and get you a malted.

Biff: Dad, I flunked math.

Willy: Not for the term?

Biff: The term. I haven't got enough credits to graduate.

Willy: You mean to say Bernard wouldn't give you the answers?

Biff: He did, he tried, but I only got a sixty-one.

Willy: And they wouldn't give you four points?

Biff: Birnbaum refused absolutely. I begged him, Pop, but he won't give me those points. You gotta talk to him before they close the school. Because if he saw the kind of man you are, and you just talked to him in your way, I'm sure he'd come through for me. The class came right before practice, see, and I didn't go enough. Would you talk to him? He'd like you, Pop. You know the way you could talk.

Willy: You're on. We'll drive right back.

Biff: Oh, Dad, good work! I'm sure he'll change it for you!

Willy: Go downstairs and tell the clerk I'm checkin' out. Go right down.

Biff: Yes, sir! See, the reason he hates me, Pop—one day he was late for class so I got up at the blackboard and imitated him. I crossed my eyes and talked with a lithp.

Willy: laughing: You did? The kids like it?

Biff: They nearly died laughing!

Willy: Yeah? What'd you do?

Biff: The thquare root of thixty twee is . . . *Willy bursts out laughing; Biff joins him.* And in the middle of it he walked in!

Willy laughs and The Woman joins in offstage.

Willy: without hesitation: Hurry downstairs and—

Biff: Somebody in there?

Willy: No, that was next door.

The Woman laughs offstage.

Biff: Somebody got in your bathroom!

Willy: No, it's the next room, there's a party—

The Woman: enters, laughing. She lisps this: Can I come in? There's something in the bathtub, Willy, and it's moving!

Willy looks at Biff, who is staring open-mouthed and horrified at The Woman.

Willy: Ah—you better go back to your room. They must be finished painting by now. They're painting her room so I let her take a shower here. Go back, go back . . . *He pushes her.*

The Woman: resisting: But I've got to get dressed, Willy, I can't—

Willy: Get out of here! Go back, go back . . . *Suddenly striving for the ordinary:* This is Miss Francis, Biff, she's a buyer. They're painting her room. Go back, Miss Francis, go back . . .

The Woman: But my clothes, I can't go out naked in the hall!

Willy: pushing her offstage: Get outa here! Go back, go back!

Biff slowly sits down on his suitcase as the argument continues offstage.

The Woman: Where's my stockings? You promised me stockings, Willy!

Willy: I have no stockings here!

The Woman: You had two boxes of size nine sheers for me, and I want them!

Willy: Here, for God's sake, will you get outa here!

The Woman: enters holding a box of stockings: I just hope there's nobody in the hall. That's all I hope. *To Biff:* Are you football or baseball?

Biff: Football.

The Woman: angry, humiliated: That's me too. G'night. *She snatches her clothes from Willy, and walks out.*

Willy: after a pause: Well, better get going. I want to get to the school first thing in the morning. Get my suits out of the closet. I'll get my valise. *Biff doesn't move.* What's the matter? *Biff remains motionless, tears falling.* She's a buyer.

Buys for J. H. Simmons. She lives down the hall—they're painting. You don't imagine—*He breaks off. After a pause:* Now listen, pal, she's just a buyer. She sees merchandise in her room and they have to keep it looking just so . . . *Pause. Assuming command:* All right, get my suits. *Biff doesn't move.* Now stop crying and do as I say. I gave you an order. Biff, I gave you an order! Is that what you do when I give you an order? How dare you cry! *Putting his arm around Biff:* Now look, Biff, when you grow up you'll understand about these things. You mustn't—you mustn't overemphasize a thing like this. I'll see Birnbaum first thing in the morning.

Biff: Never mind.

Willy: getting down beside Biff: Never mind! He's going to give you those points. I'll see to it.

Biff: He wouldn't listen to you.

Willy: He certainly will listen to me. You need those points for the U. of Virginia.

Biff: I'm not going there.

Willy: Heh? If I can't get him to change that mark you'll make it up in summer school. You've got all summer to—

Biff: his weeping breaking from him: Dad . . .

Willy: infected by it: Oh, my boy . . .

Biff: Dad . . .

Willy: She's nothing to me, Biff. I was lonely, I was terribly lonely.

Biff: You—you gave her Mama's stockings! *His tears break through and he rises to go.*

Willy: grabbing for Biff: I gave you an order!

Biff: Don't touch me, you—liar!

Willy: Apologize for that!

Biff: You fake! You phony little fake! You fake! *Overcome, he turns quickly and weeping fully goes out with his suitcase. Willy is left on the floor on his knees.*

Willy: I gave you an order! Biff, come back here or I'll beat you! Come back here! I'll whip you!

Stanley comes quickly in from the right and stands in front of Willy.

Willy: shouts at Stanley: I gave you an order . . .

Stanley: Hey, let's pick it up, pick it up. Mr. Loman. *He helps Willy to his feet.* Your boys left with the chippies. They said they'll see you home.

A second waiter watches some distance away.

Willy: But we were supposed to have dinner together.

Music is heard, Willy's theme.

Stanley: Can you make it?

Willy: I'll—sure, I can make it. *Suddenly concerned about his clothes:* Do I—I look all right?

Stanley: Sure, you look all right. *He flicks a speck off Willy's lapel.*

Willy: Here—here's a dollar.

Stanley: Oh, your son paid me. It's all right.

Willy: putting it in Stanley's hand: No, take it. You're a good boy.

Stanley: Oh, no, you don't have to . . .

Willy: Here—here's some more, I don't need it any more. *After a slight pause:* Tell me—is there a seed store in the neighborhood?

Stanley: Seeds? You mean like to plant?

As Willy turns. Stanley slips the money back into his jacket pocket.

Willy: Yes. Carrots, peas . . .

Stanley: Well, there's hardware stores on Sixth Avenue, but it may be too late now.

Willy: anxiously: Oh, I'd better hurry. I've got to get some seeds. *He starts off to the right.* I've got to get some seeds, right away. Nothing's planted. I don't have a thing in the ground.

Willy hurries out as the light goes down. Stanley moves over to the right after him, watches him off. The other waiter has been staring at Willy.

Stanley: to the waiter: Well, whatta you looking at?

The waiter picks up the chairs and moves off right. Stanley takes the table and follows him. The light fades on this area. There is a long pause, the sound of the flute coming over. The light gradually rises on the kitchen, which is empty. Happy appears at the door of the house, followed by Biff. Happy is carrying a large bunch of long-stemmed roses. He enters the kitchen, looks around for Linda. Not seeing her, he turns to Biff, who is just outside the house door, and makes a gesture with his hands, indicating "Not here, I guess." He looks into the living-room and freezes. Inside, Linda, unseen, is seated, Willy's coat on her lap. She rises ominously and quietly and moves toward Happy, who backs up into the kitchen, afraid.

Happy: Hey, what're you doing up? *Linda says nothing but moves toward him implacably.* Where's Pop? *He keeps backing to the right, and now Linda is in full view in the doorway to the living-room.* Is he sleeping?

Linda: Where were you?

Happy: trying to laugh it off: We met two girls, Mom, very fine types. Here, we brought you some flowers. *Offering them to her:* Put them in your room, Ma.

She knocks them to the floor at Biff's feet. He has now come inside and closed the door behind him. She stares at Biff, silent.

Happy: Now what'd you do that for? Mom, I want you to have some flowers—

Linda: cutting Happy off, violently to Biff: Don't you care whether he lives or dies?

Happy: going to the stairs: Come upstairs, Biff.

Biff: with a flare of disgust, to Happy: Go away from me! *To Linda:* What do you
mean, lives or dies? Nobody's dying around here, pal.

Linda: Get out of my sight! Get out of here!

Biff: I wanna see the boss.

Linda: You're not going near him!

Biff: Where is he? *He moves into the living-room and Linda follows.*

Linda: shouting after Biff: You invite him for dinner. He looks forward to it all
day—*Biff appears in his parents' bedroom, looks around, and exits*—and then you
desert him there. There's no stranger you'd do that to!

Happy: Why? He had a swell time with us. Listen, when I—*Linda comes back into
the kitchen*—desert him I hope I don't outlive the day!

Linda: Get out of here!

Happy: Now look, Mom . . .

Linda: Did you have to go to women tonight? You and your lousy rotten
whores!

Biff re-enters the kitchen.

Happy: Mom, all we did was follow Biff around trying to cheer him up! *To Biff:*
Boy, what a night you gave me!

Linda: Get out of here, both of you, and don't come back! I don't want you
tormenting him any more. Go on now, get your things together! *To Biff:*
You can sleep in his apartment. *She starts to pick up the flowers and stops herself.*
Pick up this stuff, I'm not your maid any more. Pick it up, you bum, you!

*Happy turns his back to her in refusal. Biff slowly moves over and gets down on his
knees, picking up the flowers.*

Linda: You're a pair of animals! Not one, not another living soul would have
had the cruelty to walk out on that man in a restaurant!

Biff: not looking at her: Is that what he said?

Linda: He didn't have to say anything. He was so humiliated he nearly limped
when he came in.

Happy: But, Mom, he had a great time with us—

Biff: cutting him off violently: Shut up!

Without another word, Happy goes upstairs.

Linda: You! You didn't even go in to see if he was all right!

Biff: still on the floor in front of Linda, the flowers in his hand; with self-loathing: No.
Didn't. Didn't do a damned thing. How do you like that, heh? Left him
babbling in a toilet.

Linda: You louse, You . . .

Biff: Now you hit it on the nose! *He gets up, throws the flowers in the wastebasket.*
The scum of the earth, and you're looking at him!

Linda: Get out of here!

Biff: I gotta talk to the boss, Mom. Where is he?

Linda: You're not going near him. Get out of this house!

Biff: with absolute assurance, determination: No. We're gonna have an abrupt conversation, him and me.

Linda: You're not talking to him!

Hammering is heard from outside the house, off right. Biff turns toward the noise.

Linda: suddenly pleading: Will you please leave him alone?

Biff: What's he doing out there?

Linda: He's planting the garden!

Biff: quietly: Now? Oh, my God!

Biff moves outside, Linda following. The light dies down on them and comes up on the center of the apron as Willy walks into it. He is carrying a flashlight, a hoe, and a handful of seed packets. He raps the top of the hoe sharply to fix it firmly, and then moves to the left, measuring off the distance with his foot. He holds the flashlight to look at the seed packets, reading off the instructions. He is in the blue of night.

Willy: Carrots . . . quarter-inch apart. Rows . . . one-foot rows. *He measures it off.* One foot. *He puts down a package and measures off.* Beets. *He puts down another package and measures again.* Lettuce. *He reads the package, puts it down.* One foot—*He breaks off as Ben appears at the right and moves slowly down to him.* What a proposition, ts, ts. Terrific, terrific. 'Cause she's suffered, Ben, the woman has suffered. You understand me? A man can't go out the way he came in, Ben, a man has got to add up to something. You can't, you can't—*Ben moves toward him as though to interrupt.* You gotta consider, now. Don't answer so quick. Remember, it's a guaranteed twenty-thousand-dollar proposition. Now look, Ben, I want you to go through the ins and outs of this thing with me. I've got nobody to talk to, Ben, and the woman has suffered, you hear me?

Ben: standing still, considering: What's the proposition?

Willy: It's twenty thousand dollars on the barrelhead. Guaranteed, gilt-edged, you understand?

Ben: You don't want to make a fool of yourself. They might not honor the policy.

Willy: How can they dare refuse? Didn't I work like a coolie to meet every premium on the nose? And now they don't pay off? Impossible!

Ben: It's called a cowardly thing, William.

Willy: Why? Does it take more guts to stand here the rest of my life ringing up a zero?

Ben: yielding: That's a point, William. *He moves, thinking, turns.* And twenty thousand—that *is* something one can feel with the hand, it is there.

Willy: now assured, with rising power: Oh, Ben, that's the whole beauty of it! I see it like a diamond, shining in the dark, hard and rough, that I can pick up and touch in my hand. Not like—like an appointment! This would not be another damned-fool appointment, Ben, and it changes all the aspects. Because he thinks I'm nothing, see, and so he spites me. But the funeral—*Straightening up:* Ben, that funeral will be massive! They'll come from Maine, Massachusetts, Vermont, New Hampshire! All the old-timers with the strange license plates—that boy will be thunder-struck, Ben, because he never realized—I am known! Rhode Island, New York, New Jersey—I am known, Ben, and he'll see it with his eyes once and for all. He'll see what I am, Ben! He's in for a shock, that boy!

Ben: coming down to the edge of the garden: He'll call you a coward.

Willy: suddenly fearful: No, that would be terrible.

Ben: Yes. And a damned fool.

Willy: No, no, he mustn't, I won't have that! *He is broken and desperate.*

Ben: He'll hate you, William.

The gay music of the Boys is heard.

Willy: Oh, Ben, how do we get back to all the great times? Used to be so full of light, and comradeship, the sleigh-riding in winter, and the ruddiness on his cheeks. And always some kind of good news coming up, always something nice coming up ahead. And never even let me carry the valises in the house, and simonizing, simonizing that little red car! Why, why can't I give him something and not have him hate me?

Ben: Let me think about it. *He glances at his watch.* I still have a little time. Remarkable proposition, but you've got to be sure you're not making a fool of yourself.

Ben drifts off upstage and goes out of sight. Biff comes down from the left.

Willy: suddenly conscious of Biff, turns and looks up at him, then begins picking up the packages of seeds in confusion: Where the hell is that seed? *Indignantly:* You can't see nothing out here! They boxed in the whole goddam neighborhood!

Biff: There are people all around here. Don't you realize that?

Willy: I'm busy. Don't bother me.

Biff: taking the hoe from Willy: I'm saying good-by to you, Pop. *Willy looks at him, silent, unable to move.* I'm not coming back any more.

Willy: You're not going to see Oliver tomorrow?

Biff: I've got no appointment, Dad.

Willy: He put his arm around you, and you've got no appointment?

Biff: Pop, get this now, will you? Everytime I've left it's been a fight that sent me out of here. Today I realized something about myself and I tried to explain it to you and I—I think I'm just not smart enough to make any sense out of it for you. To hell with whose fault it is or anything like that. *He takes Willy's arm.* Let's just wrap it up, heh? Come on in, we'll tell Mom. *He gently tries to pull Willy to left.*

Willy: frozen, immobile, with guilt in his voice: No, I don't want to see her.

Biff: Come on! *He pulls again, and Willy tries to pull away.*

Willy: highly nervous: No, no, I don't want to see her.

Biff: tries to look into Willy's face, as if to find the answer there: Why don't you want to see her?

Willy: more harshly now: Don't bother me, will you?

Biff: What do you mean, you don't want to see her? You don't want them calling you yellow, do you? This isn't your fault; it's me, I'm a bum. Now come inside! *Willy strains to get away.* Did you hear what I said to you?

Willy pulls away and quickly goes by himself into the house. Biff follows.

Linda: to Willy: Did you plant, dear?

Biff: at the door, to Linda: All right, we had it out. I'm going and I'm not writing any more.

Linda: going to Willy in the kitchen: I think that's the best way, dear. 'Cause there's no use drawing it out, you'll just never get along.

Willy doesn't respond.

Biff: People ask where I am and what I'm doing, you don't know, and you don't care. That way it'll be off your mind and you can start brightening up again. All right? That clears it, doesn't it? *Willy is silent, and Biff goes to him.* You gonna wish me luck, scout? *He extends his hand.* What do you say?

Linda: Shake his hand, Willy.

Willy: turning to her, seething with hurt: There's no necessity to mention the pen at all, y'know.

Biff: gently: I've got no appointment, Dad.

Willy: erupting fiercely: He put his arm around . . . ?

Biff: Dad, you're never going to see what I am, so what's the use of arguing? If I strike oil I'll send you a check. Meantime forget I'm alive.

Willy: to Linda: Spite, see?

Biff: Shake hands, Dad.

Willy: Not my hand.

Biff: I was hoping not to go this way.

Willy: Well, this is the way you're going. Good-by.

Biff looks at him a moment, then turns sharply and goes to the stairs.

Willy: stops him with: May you rot in hell if you leave this house!

Biff: turning: Exactly what is it that you want from me?

Willy: I want you to know, on the train, in the mountains, in the valleys, wherever you go, that you cut down your life for spite!

Biff: No, no.

Willy: Spite, spite, is the word of your undoing! And when you're down and out, remember what did it. When you're rotting somewhere beside the railroad tracks, remember, and don't you dare blame it on me!

Biff: I'm not blaming it on you!

Willy: I won't take the rap for this, you hear?

Happy comes down the stairs and stands on the bottom step, watching.

Biff: That's just what I'm telling you!

Willy: sinking into a chair at the table, with full accusation: You're trying to put a knife in me—don't think I don't know what you're doing!

Biff: All right, phony! Then let's lay it on the line. *He whips the rubber tube out of his pocket and puts it on the table.*

Happy: You crazy—

Linda: Biff! *She moves to grab the hose, but Biff holds it down with his hand.*

Biff: Leave it there! Don't move it!

Willy: not looking at it: What is that?

Biff: You know goddam well what that is.

Willy: caged, wanting to escape: I never saw that.

Biff: You saw it. The mice didn't bring it into the cellar! What is this supposed to do, make a hero out of you? This supposed to make me sorry for you?

Willy: Never heard of it.

Biff: There'll be no pity for you, you hear it? No pity!

Willy: to Linda: You hear the spite!

Biff: No, you're going to hear the truth—what you are and what I am!

Linda: Stop it!

Willy: Spite!

Happy: coming down toward Biff: You cut it now!

Biff: to Happy: The man don't know who we are! The man is gonna know! *To Willy:* We never told the truth for ten minutes in this house!

Happy: We always told the truth!

Biff: turning on him: You big blow, are you the assistant buyer? You're one of the two assistants to the assistant, aren't you?

Happy: Well, I'm practically—

Biff: You're practically full of it! We all are! And I'm through with it. *To Willy:* Now hear this, Willy, this is me.

Willy: I know you!

Biff: You know why I had no address for three months? I stole a suit in Kansas City and I was in jail. *To Linda, who is sobbing:* Stop crying. I'm through with it.

Linda turns away from them, her hands covering her face.

Willy: I suppose that's my fault!

Biff: I stole myself out of every good job since high school!

Willy: And whose fault is that?

Biff: And I never got anywhere because you blew me so full of hot air I could never stand taking orders from anybody! That's whose fault it is!

Willy: I hear that!

Linda: Don't, Biff!

Biff: It's goddam time you heard that! I had to be boss big shot in two weeks, and I'm through with it!

Willy: Then hang yourself! For spite, hang yourself!

Biff: No! Nobody's hanging himself, Willy! I ran down eleven flights with a pen in my hand today. And suddenly I stopped, you hear me? And in the middle of that office building, do you hear this? I stopped in the middle of that building and I saw—the sky. I saw the things that I love in this world. The work and the food and time to sit and smoke. And I looked at the pen and said to myself, what the hell am I grabbing this for? Why am I trying to become what I don't want to be? What am I doing in an office, making a contemptuous, begging fool of myself, when all I want is out there, waiting for me the minute I say I know who I am! Why can't I say that, Willy? *He tries to make Willy face him, but Willy pulls away and moves to the left.*

Willy: *with hatred, threateningly:* The door of your life is wide open!

Biff: Pop! I'm a dime a dozen, and so are you!

Willy: *turning on him now in an uncontrolled outburst:* I am not a dime a dozen! I am Willy Loman, and you are Biff Loman!

Biff starts for Willy, but is blocked by Happy. In his fury, Biff seems on the verge of attacking his father.

Biff: I am not a leader of men, Willy, and neither are you. You were never anything but a hard-working drummer[10] who landed in the ash can like all the rest of them! I'm one dollar an hour. Willy! I tried seven states and couldn't raise it. A buck an hour! Do you gather my meaning? I'm not bringing home any prizes any more, and you're going to stop waiting for me to bring them home!

Willy: *directly to Biff:* You vengeful, spiteful mutt!

Biff breaks from Happy. Willy, in fright, starts up the stairs. Biff grabs him.

Biff: *at the peak of his fury:* Pop, I'm nothing! I'm nothing, Pop. Can't you understand that? There's no spite in it any more. I'm just what I am, that's all.

Biff's fury has spent itself, and he breaks down, sobbing, holding on to Willy, who dumbly fumbles for Biff's face.

Willy: *astonished:* What're you doing? What're you doing? *To Linda:* Why is he crying?

Biff: *crying, broken:* Will you let me go, for Christ's sake? Will you take that phony dream and burn it before something happens? *Struggling to contain himself, he pulls away and moves to the stairs.* I'll go in the morning. Put him—put him to bed. *Exhausted, Biff moves up the stairs to his room.*

Willy: *after a long pause, astonished, elevated:* Isn't that—isn't that remarkable? Biff—he likes me!

Linda: He loves you, Willy!

Happy: *deeply moved:* Always did, Pop.

Willy: Oh, Biff! *Staring wildly:* He cried! Cried to me. *He is choking with his love, and now cries out his promise:* That boy—that boy is going to be magnificent!

Ben appears in the light just outside the kitchen.

Ben: Yes, outstanding, with twenty thousand behind him.

Linda: *sensing the racing of his mind, fearfully, carefully:* Now come to bed, Willy. It's all settled now.

---

[10] American slang: traveling salesman.

Willy: finding it difficult not to rush out of the house: Yes, we'll sleep. Come on. Go to sleep, Hap.

Ben: And it does take a great kind of a man to crack the jungle.

In accents of dread, Ben's idyllic music starts up.

Happy: his arm around Linda: I'm getting married, Pop, don't forget it. I'm changing everything. I'm gonna run that department before the year is up. You'll see, Mom. *He kisses her.*

Ben: The jungle is dark but full of diamonds, Willy.

Willy turns, moves, listenig to Ben.

Linda: Be good. You're both good boys, just act that way, that's all.

Happy: 'Night, Pop. *He goes upstairs.*

Linda: to Willy: Come, dear.

Ben: with greater force: One must go in to fetch a diamond out.

Willy: to Linda, as he moves slowly along the edge of the kitchen, toward the door: I just want to get settled down, Linda. Let me sit alone for a little.

Linda: almost uttering her fear: I want you upstairs.

Willy: taking her in his arms: In a few minutes, Linda. I couldn't sleep right now. Go on, you look awful tired. *He kisses her.*

Ben: Not like an appointment at all. A diamond is rough and hard to the touch.

Willy: Go on now. I'll be right up.

Linda: I think this is the only way, Willy.

Willy: Sure, it's the best thing.

Ben: Best thing!

Willy: The only way. Everything is gonna be—go on, kid, get to bed. You look so tired.

Linda: Come right up.

Willy: Two minutes.

Linda goes into the living-room, then reappears in her bedroom. Willy moves just outside the kitchen door.

Willy: Loves me. *Wonderingly:* Always loved me. Isn't that a remarkable thing? Ben, he'll worship me for it!

Ben: with promise: It's dark there, but full of diamonds.

Willy: Can you imagine that magnificence with twenty thousand dollars in his pocket?

Linda: calling from her room: Willy! Come up!

Willy: calling into the kitchen: Yes! Yes. Coming! It's very smart, you realize that, don't you, sweetheart? Even Ben sees it. I gotta go, baby, 'By! 'By! *Going over to Ben, almost dancing:* Imagine? When the mail comes he'll be ahead of Bernard again!

Ben: A perfect proposition all around.

Willy: Did you see how he cried to me? Oh, if I could kiss him, Ben!

Ben: Time, William, time!

Willy: Oh, Ben, I always knew one way or another we were gonna make it, Biff and I!

Ben: looking at his watch: The boat. We'll be late. *He moves slowly off into the darkness.*

Willy: elegiacally, turning to the house: Now when you kick off, boy, I want a seventy-yard boot, and get right down the field under the ball, and when you hit, hit low and hit hard, because it's important, boy. *He swings around and faces the audience.* There's all kinds of important people in the stands, and the first thing you know . . . *Suddenly realizing he is alone:* Ben! Ben, where do I . . . ? *He makes a sudden movement of search.* Ben, how do I . . . ?

Linda: calling: Willy, you coming up?

Willy: uttering a gasp of fear, whirling about as if to quiet her: Sh! *He turns around as if to find his way; sounds, faces, voices, seem to be swarming in upon him and he flicks at them, crying,* Sh! Sh! *Suddenly music, faint and high, stops him. It rises in intensity, almost to an unbearable scream. He goes up and down on this toes, and rushes off around the house.* Shhh!

Linda: Willy?

There is no answer. Linda waits. Biff gets up off his bed. He is still in his clothes. Happy sits up. Biff stands listening.

Linda: with real fear: Willy, answer me! Willy!

There is the sound of a car starting and moving away at full speed.

Linda: No!

Biff: rushing down the stairs: Pop!

As the car speeds off, the music crashes down in a frenzy of sound, which becomes the soft pulsation of a single cello string. Biff slowly returns to his bedroom. He and Happy gravely don their jackets. Linda slowly walks out of her room. The music has developed into a dead march. The leaves of day are appearing over everything. Charley and Bernard, somberly dressed, appear and knock on the kitchen door. Biff and Happy slowly descend the stairs to the kitchen as Charley and Bernard enter. All stop a moment when Linda, in clothes of mourning, bearing a little bunch of roses, comes through the draped doorway into the kitchen. She goes to Charley and takes his arm. Now all move toward the audience, through the wall-line of the kitchen. At the limit of the apron, Linda lays down the flowers, kneels, and sits back on her heels. All stare down at the grave.

REQUIEM

Charley: It's getting dark, Linda.

Linda doesn't react. She stares at the grave.

Biff: How about it, Mom? Better get some rest, heh? They'll be closing the gate soon.

Linda makes no move. Pause.

Happy: deeply angered: He had no right to do that. There was no necessity for it. We would've helped him.

Charley: grunting: Hmmm.

Biff: Come along, Mom.

Linda: Why didn't anybody come?

Charley: It was a very nice funeral.

Linda: But where are all the people he knew? Maybe they blame him.

Charley: Naa. It's a rough world, Linda. They wouldn't blame him.

Linda: I can't understand it. At this time especially. First time in thirty-five years we were just about free and clear. He only needed a little salary. He was even finished with the dentist.

Charley: No man only needs a little salary.

Linda: I can't understand it.

Biff: There were a lot of nice days. When he'd come home from a trip; or on Sundays, making the stoop; finishing the cellar; putting on the new porch; when he built the extra bathroom; and put up the garage. You know something, Charley, there's more of him in that front stoop than in all the sales he ever made.

Charley: Yeah. He was a happy man with a batch of cement.

Linda: He was so wonderful with his hands.

Biff: He had the wrong dreams. All, all, wrong.

Happy: almost ready to fight Biff: Don't say that!

Biff: He never knew who he was.

Charley: stopping Happy's movement and reply. To Biff: Nobody dast blame this man. You don't understand: Willy was a salesman. And for a salesman, there is no rock bottom to the life. He don't put a bolt to a nut, he don't tell you the law or give you medicine. He's a man way out there in the blue, riding on a smile and a shoeshine. And when they start not smiling back—that's an earthquake. And then you get yourself a couple of spots on your hat, and you're finished. Nobody dast blame this man. A salesman is got to dream, boy. It comes with the territory.

Biff: Charley, the man didn't know who he was.

Happy: infuriated: Don't say that!

Biff: Why don't you come with me, Happy?

Happy: I'm not licked that easily. I'm staying right in this city, and I'm gonna beat this racket! *He looks at Biff, his chin set.* The Loman Brothers!

Biff: I know who I am, kid.

Happy: All right, boy. I'm gonna show you and everybody else that Willy Loman did not die in vain. He had a good dream. It's the only dream you can have—to come out number-one man. He fought it out here, and this is where I'm gonna win it for him.

Biff: with a hopeless glance at Happy, bends toward his mother: Let's go, Mom.

Linda: I'll be with you in a minute. Go on, Charley. *He hesitates.* I want to, just for a minute. I never had a chance to say good-by.

Charley moves away, followed by Happy. Biff remains a slight distance up and left of Linda. She sits there, summoning herself. The flute begins, not far away, playing behind her speech.

Linda: Forgive me, dear. I can't cry. I don't know what it is, but I can't cry. I don't understand it. Why did you ever do that? Help me, Willy, I can't cry. It seems to me that you're just on another trip. I keep expecting you. Willy, dear, I can't cry. Why did you do it? I search and search and I search, and I can't understand it, Willy. I made the last payment on the house today. Today, dear. And there'll be nobody home. *A sob rises in her throat.* We're free and clear. *Sobbing more fully, released:* We're free. *Biff comes slowly toward her.* We're free . . . We're free . . .

Biff lifts her to her feet and moves out up right with her in his arms. Linda sobs quietly. Bernard and Charley come together and follow them, followed by Happy. Only the music of the flute is left on the darkening stage as over the house the hard towers of the apartment buildings rise into sharp focus, and
    The Curtain Falls

1949

Walker Percy
b. 1916

Walker Percy was born in Birmingham, Alabama, on May 28, 1916. In 1927, when he was eleven, his father committed suicide. Four years later, after his mother died in an automobile accident, he was adopted by his uncle, William Alexander Percy, a lawyer, poet, and essayist who lived in Greenville, Mississippi. Following high school in Greenville, Percy attended the University of North Carolina, where he majored in chemistry and wrote for various literary magazines. He then went on to the Columbia University College of Physicians and Surgeons, where he completed work on his medical degree in 1941. Over the next several years, Percy pursued a career practicing and teaching medicine. But he also worked very hard to overcome tuberculosis, which he contracted during his residency at Bellevue. In 1946 he returned to the South, first to Sewanee, Tennessee, then to New Orleans, and finally across Lake Ponchartrain to Covington, Louisiana, where he has lived since 1950.

During his recovery from tuberculosis, Percy immersed himself in existentialist literature and philosophy, subjects that have continued to occupy his attention. After his return to the South, Percy "made reading a full-time occupation"; he read deeply in the philosophy of language, especially the work of the American philosopher Charles Sanders Peirce, and in Catholic thought and theology. In 1946 Percy and his wife converted to Catholicism. Another interest, in the way human beings acquire a language, was stimulated by Percy's efforts to teach a daughter who had been born deaf. In 1954 he published his first philosophical essay, "Symbol as Need," which was later published with other linguistic essays in *The Message in the Bottle* (1975).

In the mid-1950s Percy began to write fiction, and after several unsuccessful tries, he published his first novel, *The Moviegoer*, in 1961. The winner of the National Book Award for 1962, the novel is about a young, affluent New Orleans stockbroker who searches—especially through movies—for a way to break out of "the everydayness of his own life." Since then, Percy has published four novels: *The Last Gentleman* (1966), *Love in the Ruins* (1971), *Lancelot* (1977), and *The Second Coming* (1980). Each of these novels, in its own way, explores a modern world in decay, a world that Percy believes is continually being made worse by the behaviorist reductions of social science and an increasing predilection for intellectual cant and jargon. These novelistic concerns also form the subject of Percy's second work of nonfiction, *Lost in the Cosmos: The Last Self-Help Book* (1983), in which "The Last Donahue Show" originally appeared.

Percy once described the world in which he lives as "a dark place . . . a kind of desert, a bombed-out place . . . of blasted trees and barbed wire" and calls his view of it "cold-eyed and sardonic." Yet he insists that the artist must participate in society rather than withdraw from it. The artist's task, he says, is "to validate human experience" by disclosing "deep human truths" that we already "unconsciously know" but do not yet know that we know. Such truths, once disclosed, come to us, he says, borrowing and altering a phrase of Herman Melville's, as "a shock of recognition."

Percy has worked on several levels and in several modes to effect the disclosure and achieve the shocks to which as an artist he aspires. In some of his works, he labors to restore our capacity for wonder by teaching us again to watch and wait. In others, his mode is comic and even grotesque, at once humorous and dark, and turns on the conversion of a familiar scene into one that is preposterous, or even simply funny, yet also startling and disturbing. Behind all his work, however, lies a double conviction: first, that "something has gone badly wrong with Americans and American life, indeed modern life," leaving us "victims" of a "deep dislocation" and a crippling "malaise"; and second, that the artist who would bring us to proper recognition of our condition must "in his own perverse way be a modern version of the Old Testament prophet."

Further Reading:
M. Luschei, *The Sovereign Wayfarer: Walker Percy's Diagnosis of the Malaise*, 1972.
The Art of Walker Percy: Stratagems for Being, ed. P. R. Broughton, 1979.
J. Tharpe, *Walker Percy*, 1983.

Text:
Lost in the Cosmos: The Last Self-Help Book, 1983.

The Last Donahue Show

The Donahue Show is in progress on what appears at first to be an ordinary weekday morning.

The theme of this morning's show is Donahue's favorite, sex, the extraordinary variety of sexual behavior—"sexual preference," as Donahue would call it—in the country and the embattled attitudes toward it. Although Donahue has been accused of appealing to prurient interest, with a sharp eye cocked on the ratings, he defends himself by saying that he presents these controversial matters in "a mature and tasteful manner"—which he often does. It should also be noted in Donahue's defense that the high ratings of these sex-talk shows are nothing more nor less than an index of the public's intense interest in such matters.

The guests today are:

Bill, a homosexual and habitué of Buena Vista Park in San Francisco

Allen, a heterosexual businessman, married, and a connoisseur of the lunch-hour liaison

Penny, a pregnant fourteen-year-old

Dr. Joyce Friday, a well-known talk-show sex therapist, or in media jargon: a psych jockey

Bill's story: Yes, I'm gay, and yes, I cruise Buena Vista. Yes, I've probably had over five hundred encounters with lovers, though I didn't keep count. So what? Whose business is it? I'm gainfully employed by a savings-and-loan company, am a trustworthy employee, and do an honest day's work. My recreation is Buena Vista Park and the strangers I meet there. I don't molest children, rape women, snatch purses. I contribute to United Way. Such encounters that I do have are by mutual consent and therefore nobody's business—except my steady live-in friend's. Naturally he's upset, but that's our problem.

Donahue (striding up and down, mike in hand, boyishly inarticulate): C'mon, Bill. What about the kids who might see you? You know what I mean. I mean— *(Opens his free hand to the audience, soliciting their understanding)*

Bill: Kids don't see me. Nobody sees me.

Donahue (coming close, on the attack but good-naturedly, spoofing himself as prosecutor): Say, Bill. I've always been curious. Is there some sort of signal? I mean, how do you and the other guy know—help me out—

Bill: Eye contact, or we show a bit of handkerchief here. *(Demonstrates)*

Studio Audience: (Laughter)

Donahue (shrugging [Don't blame me, folks], pushes up nose-bridge of glasses, swings mike over to Dr. J.F. without looking at her): How about it, Doc?

Dr. J.F. (in her not-mincing-words voice): I think Bill's behavior is immature and depersonalizing. *(Applause from audience)* I think he ought to return to his steady live-in friend and work out a mature, creative relationship. You might be interested to know that studies have shown that stable gay couples are more creative than straights. *(Applause again, but more tentative)*

Donahue (eyes slightly rolled back, swings mike to Bill): How about it, Bill?

Bill: Yeah, right. But I still cruise Buena Vista.

Donahue (pensive, head to one side, strides backward, forward, then over to Allen): How about you, Allen?

Allen's story: I'm a good person, I think. I work hard, am happily married, love my wife and family, also support United Way, served in the army. I drink very little, don't do drugs, have never been to a porn movie. My idea of R & R—maybe I got it in the army—is to meet an attractive woman. What a delight it is, to see a handsome mature woman, maybe in the secretarial pool, maybe in a bar, restaurant, anywhere, exchange eye contact, speak to her in a nice way, respect her as a person, invite her to join me for lunch (no sexual harassment in the office—I hate that!), have a drink, two drinks, enjoy a nice meal, talk about matters of common interest—then simply ask her—by now, both of you know whether you like each other. What a joy to go with her up in the elevator of the downtown Holiday Inn, both of you silent, relaxed, smiling, anticipating—The door of the room closes behind you. You look at her, take her hand. There's champagne already there. You stand at the window with her, touch glasses, talk—there's nothing vulgar. No closed-circuit TV. Do you know what we did last time? We turned on *La Bohème* on the FM. She loves Puccini.

Donahue: C'mon, Allen. What are ya handing me? What d'ya mean you're happily married? You mean *you're* happy.

Allen: No, no. Vera's happy, too.

Audience (mostly women, groaning): Nooooooo.

Donahue: Okay-okay, ladies, hold it a second. What do you mean, Vera's happy? I mean, how do you manage—help me out, I'm about to get in trouble—hold the letters, folks—

Allen: Well, actually, Vera has a low sex drive. We've always been quite inactive, even at the beginning—

Audience (groans, jumbled protests): Nooooo.

Donahue (backing away, holding up placating free hand, backing around to Dr. J.F.): It's all yours, Doc.

Dr. J.F.: Studies have shown that open marriages can be growth experiences for both partners. However—*(groans from audience)*—However: it seems to me that Vera may be getting the short end here. I mean, I don't know Vera's side of it. But could I ask you this? Have you and Vera thought about reenergizing your sex life?

Allen: Well, ah—

Dr. J.F.: Studies have shown, for example, that more stale marriages have been revived by oral sex than any other technique—

Donahue: Now, Doc—

Dr. J.F.: Other studies have shown that mutual masturbation—

Donahue (eyes rolled back): We're running long folks, we'll be right back after this—don't go away. Oh boy. *(Lets mike slide to the hilt through his hand, closes eyes, as camera cuts away to a Maxithins commercial)*

Donahue: We're back. Thank the good Lord for good sponsors. *(Turns to Penny, a thin, inattentive, moping teenager, even possibly a pre-teen)*: Penny?

Penny (chewing something): Yeah?

Donahue (solicitous, quite effectively tender): What's with you, sweetheart?

Penny: Well, I like this boy a lot and he told me there was one way I could prove it—

Donahue: Wait a minute, Penny. Now this, your being here, is okay with your parents, right? I mean let's establish that.

Penny: Oh, sure. They're right over there—you can ask them. *(Camera pans over audience, settling on a couple with mild, pleasant faces. It is evident that on the whole they are not displeased with being on TV)*

Donahue: Okay. So you mean you didn't know about taking precautions—

Dr. J.F. (breaking in): Now, that's what I mean, Phil.

Donahue: What's that, Doc?

Dr. J.F.: About the crying need for sex education in our schools. Now if this child—

Penny: Oh, I had all that stuff at Ben Franklin.

Donahue: You mean you knew about the pill and the other, ah—

Penny: I had been on the pill for a year.

Donahue (scratching head): I don't get it. Oh, you mean you slipped up, got careless?

Penny: No, I did it on purpose.

Donahue: Did what on purpose? You mean—

Penny: I mean I wanted to get pregnant.

Donahue: Why was that, Penny?

Penny: My best friend was pregnant.

Audience: (Groans, laughter)

Dr. J.F.: You see, Phil, that's just what I mean. This girl is no more equipped with parenting skills than a child. She is a child. I hope she realizes she still has viable options.

Donahue: How about it, Penny?

Penny: No, I want to have my baby.

Donahue: Why?

Penny: I think babies are neat.

Donahue: Oh boy.

Dr. J.F.: Studies have shown that unwanted babies suffer 85 percent more child abuse and 150 percent more neuroses later in life.

Donahue (striding): Okay, now what have we got here? Wait. What's going on?

There is an interruption. Confusion at the rear of the studio. Heads turn. Three strangers, dressed outlandishly, stride down the aisle.

Donahue (smacks his forehead): What's this? What's this? Holy smoke!

Already the audience is smiling, reassured both by Donahue's comic consternation and by the exoticness of the visitors. Clearly, the audience thinks, they are part of the act.

The three strangers are indeed outlandish.

One is a tall, thin, bearded man dressed like a sixteenth-century reformer. Indeed, he could be John Calvin, in his black cloak, black cap with short bill, and snug earflaps.

The second wears the full-dress uniform of a Confederate officer. Though he is a colonel, he is quite young, surely no more than twenty-five. Clean-shaven and extremely handsome, he looks for all the world like Colonel John Pelham, Jeb Stuart's legendary artillerist. Renowned both for his gallantry in battle and for his chivalry toward women, the beau ideal of the South, he engaged in sixty artillery duels, won them all, lost not a single piece. With a single Napoleon, he held off three of Burnside's divisions in front of Fredericksburg before being ordered by Stuart to retreat.

The third is at once the most ordinary-looking and yet the strangest of all. His dress is both modern and out-of-date. In his light-colored double-breasted suit and bow tie, his two-tone shoes of the sort known in the 1940s as "perforated wing-tips," his neat above-the-ears haircut, he looks a bit like the clean old man in the Beatles movie *A Hard Day's Night,* a bit like Lowell Thomas or perhaps Harry Truman. It is as if he were a visitor from the Cosmos, from a planet ten or so light-years distant, who had formed his notion of earthlings from belated transmissions of 1950 TV, from watching the Ed Sullivan Show, old Chester Morris movies, and Morey Amsterdam. Or, to judge from his speaking voice, he could have been an inveterate listener during the Golden Age of radio and modeled his speech on that of Harry Von Zell.

Donahue (backpedaling, smacking his head again): Holy smoke! Who are these guys? *(Beseeching the audience with a slow comic pan around)*

The audience laughs, not believing for a moment that these latecomers are not one of Donahue's surprises. And yet—

Donahue (snapping his fingers): I got it. Wait'll I get that guy. It's Steve Allen, right? Refugees from the Steve Allen Show, *Great Conversations?* Famous historical figures? You know, folks, they do that show in the studio down the hall. Wait'll I get that guy.

General laughter. Everybody remembers it's been done before, an old show-biz trick, like Carson barging in on Rickles during the C.P.O. Sharkey taping.

Donahue: Okay already. Okay, who we got here? This is Moses? General Robert E. Lee? And who is this guy? Harry Truman? Okay, fellas, let's hear it. *(Donahue, an attractive fellow, is moving about as gracefully as a dancer)*
The Stranger (speaks first, in his standard radio-announcer's voice, which is not as flat as the Chicagoans who say, Hyev a hyeppy New Year): I don't know what these two are doing here, but I came to give you a message. We've been listening to this show.
Donahue (winking at the audience): And where were you listening to us?

Stranger: In the green room.

Donahue: Where else? Okay. Then what do you think? Let's hear it first from the reverend here. What did you say your name was, Reverend?

Stranger: John Calvin.

Donahue: Right. Who else? Okay, we got to break here for these messages. Don't go 'way, folks. We're coming right back and sort this out, I promise.

Cut to Miss Clairol, Land O Lakes margarine, Summer's Eve, and Alpo commercials.

But when the show returns, John Calvin, who does not understand commercial breaks, has jumped the gun and is in mid-sentence.

Calvin (speaking in a thick French accent, not unlike Charles Boyer): —of his redemptive sacrifice? What I have heard is licentious talk about deeds which are an abomination before God, meriting eternal damnation unless they repent and throw themselves on God's mercy. Which they are predestined to do or not to do, so why bother to discuss it?

Donahue (gravely): That's pretty heavy, Reverend.

Calvin: Heavy? Yes, it's heavy.

Donahue (mulling, scratching): Now wait a minute, Reverend. Let's check this out. You're entitled to your religious beliefs. But what if others disagree with you in all good faith? And aside from *that (prosecutory again, using mike like forefinger)* what's wrong with two consenting adults expressing their sexual preference in the privacy of their bedroom or, ah, under a bush?

Calvin: Sexual preference? *(Puzzled, he turns for help to the Confederate officer and the Cosmic stranger. They shrug)*

Donahue (holding mike to the officer): How about you, sir? Your name is—

Confederate Officer: Colonel John Pelham, C.S.A., commander of the horse artillery under General Stuart.

Penny: He's cute.

Audience: (Laughter)

Donahue: You heard it all in the green room, Colonel. What 'dya think?

Colonel Pelham (in a soft Alabama accent): What do I think of what, sir?

Donahue: Of what you heard in the green room.

Pelham: Of the way these folks act and talk? Well, I don't think much of it, sir.

Donahue: How do you mean, Colonel?

Pelham: That's not the way people should talk or act. Where I come from, we'd call them white trash. That's no way to talk if you're a man or a woman. A gentleman knows how to treat women. He knows because he knows himself, who he is, what his obligations are. And he discharges them. But after all, you won the war, so if that's the way you want to act, that's your affair. At least, we can be sure of one thing.

Donahue: What's that, Colonel?

Pelham: We're not sorry we fought.

Donahue: I see. Then you agree with the reverend, I mean Reverend Calvin here.

Pelham: Well, I respect his religious beliefs. But I never thought much about religion one way or the other. In fact, I don't think religion has much to do with whether a man does right. A West Point man is an officer and a gentleman, religion or no religion. I have nothing against religion. In fact, when we studied medieval history at West Point, I remember admiring Richard Coeur de Lion and his recapturing Acre and the holy places. I remember thinking: I would have fought for him, just as I fought for Lee and the South.

Applause from the audience. Calvin puts them off, but this handsome officer reminds them of Rhett Butler-Clark Gable, or rather Ashley Wilkes-Leslie Howard.

Donahue (drifting off, frowning; something is amiss but he can't put his finger on it. What is Steve Allen up to? He shakes his head, blinks): You said it, Colonel. Okay. Where were we? *(Turning to Cosmic stranger)* We're running a little long. Can you make it brief, Harry—Mr. President, or whoever you are? Oh boy.

The Cosmic Stranger (stands stiffly, hands at his sides, and begins speaking briskly, very much in the style of the late Raymond Gram Swing): I will be brief. I have taken this human form through a holographic technique unknown to you in order to make myself understood to you.

Hear this. I have a message. Whether you heed it or not is your affair.

I have nothing to say to you about God or the Confederacy, whatever that is—I assume it is not the G2V Confederacy in this arm of the galaxy— though I could speak about God, but it is too late for you, and I am not here to do that.

We are not interested in the varieties of your sexual behavior, except as a symptom of a more important disorder.

It is this disorder which concerns us and which we do not fully understand.

As a consequence of this disorder, you are a potential threat to all civilizations in the G2V region of the galaxy. Throughout G2V you are known variously and jokingly as the Ds or the DDs or the DLs, that is, the ding-a-lings or the death-dealers or the death-lovers. Of all the species here and in all of G2V, you are the only one which is by nature sentimental, murderous, self-hating, and self-destructive.

You are two superpowers here. The other is hopeless, has already succumbed, and is a death society. It is a living death and an agent for the propagation of death.

You are scarcely better—there is a glimmer of hope for you—but that is of no interest to me.

If the two of you destroy each other, as appears likely, it is of no consequence to us. To tell you the truth, G2V will breathe a sigh of relief.

The danger is that you may not destroy each other and that your present crude technology may constitute a threat to G2V in the future.

I am here to tell you three things: what is going to happen, what I am going to do, and what you can do.

Here's what will happen. Within the next twenty-four hours, your last war will begin. There will occur a twenty-megaton airburst one mile above the University of Chicago, the very site where your first chain reaction was produced. Every American city and town will be hit. You will lose plus-minus 160 million immediately, plus-minus 50 million later.

Here's what I am going to do. I have been commissioned to collect a specimen of DD and return with it so that we can study it toward the end of determining the nature of your disorder. Accordingly, I propose to take this young person referred to as Penny—for two reasons. One, she is perhaps still young enough not to have become hopeless. Two, she is pregnant and so we will have a chance to rear a DD in an environment free of your noxious influence. Then perhaps we can determine whether your disorder is a result of some peculiar earth environmental factor or whether you are a malignant sport, a genetic accident, the consequence of what you would have called, quite accurately, in an earlier time an MD—*mutatio diabolica,* a diabolical mutation.

Finally, here's what you can do. It is of no consequence to us whether you do it or not, because you will no longer be a threat to anyone. This is only a small gesture of goodwill to a remnant of you who may survive and who may have the chance to start all over—though you will probably repeat the same mistake. We have been students of your climatology for years. I have here a current read-out and prediction of the prevailing wind directions and fallout patterns for the next two weeks. It so happens that the place nearest you which will escape all effects of both blast and fallout is the community of Lost Cove, Tennessee. We do not anticipate a stampede to Tennessee. Our projection is that very few of you here and you out there in radio land will attach credibility to this message. But the few of you who do may wish to use this information. There is a cave there, corn, grits, collard greens, and smoked sausage in abundance.

That is the end of my message. Penny—

Donahue: We're long! We're long! Heavy! Steve, I'll get you for this. Oh boy. Don't forget, folks, tomorrow we got surrogate partners and a Kinsey panel— come back—you can't win 'em all—'bye! Grits. I dunno.

Audience: (Applause)

Cut to station break, Secure Card 65 commercial, Alpo, Carefree Panty Shields, and Mentholatum, then *The Price Is Right.*

Question: If you heard this Donahue Show, would you head for Lost Cove, Tennessee?

   (a) Yes
   (b) No

(CHECK ONE)

1983

Gwendolyn Brooks
b. 1917

The first black writer to win the Pulitzer Prize, Gwendolyn Brooks was born in Topeka, Kansas, on June 7, 1917, but she grew up in and around Chicago, where her family moved before her first birthday and where she has spent most of her life. She graduated from Wilson Junior College in 1936 and during the 1930s served as publicity director of the NAACP Youth Council. Although she had begun writing poetry as a young child (she published her first poem in a children's magazine at the age of thirteen), she began writing in earnest in the late 1930s and the early 1940s, with the encouragement of such notable black authors as James Weldon Johnson and Langston Hughes. She now credits Johnson with having introduced her to the great modernists, especially T. S. Eliot and Ezra Pound. Hughes she describes as a man who "believed in the beauty of blackness" long before it became "the fashion." Hughes, she notes, was also someone who "loved literature . . . not fearfully, not with awe," but with deep devotion, and not as "his private inch" but as a "great acreage." "The plantings of others," she says, "he not only welcomed but busily enriched."

Brooks has taught poetry and writing at numerous colleges and universities, including Columbia College in Chicago, Elmhurst College, and the University of Wisconsin, and has received many honorary degrees. She has also received many awards and fellowships, including the American Academy of Arts and Letters award for creative writing in 1946 and two Guggenheim fellowships. In 1945 she was named by *Mademoiselle* magazine one of ten women of the year. Besides the Pulitzer Prize in 1950, she has won numerous poetry prizes and awards.

In 1945 Brooks published her first book of poetry, *A Street in Bronzeville,* a volume imaginatively rich in its portrayal of the black urban poor. The poems consisted more of black portraits than black protest, for as Brooks pointed out, "Although I called my first book *A Street in Bronzeville,* I hoped that people would recognize instantly that Negroes are just like other people; they have the same hates and loves and fears, the same tragedies and triumphs and deaths, as people of any race or religion or nationality." She continued this theme with the prizewinning narrative poem about a young black girl's coming of age, *Annie Allen* (1949), and *Bronzeville Boys and Girls* (1956), books that show not only her grasp of the psychic conditions of childhood but also her ability to create a fine tension between toughness and sentiment, traditional literary form and contemporary black idiom. Since the Second Black Writer's Conference (1967), however, her work has grown more responsive to racial and feminist issues. The poems of *In the Mecca* (1968), for example, deal head on with the violence and misery of black ghetto life. Those concerns have also been at the heart of *Riot* (1969), *The Wall* (n.d.), *Family Pictures* (1970), and *Aloneness* (1971). Among her more recent works are *Aurora* (1972) and *Beckonings* (1975). A volume of her selected poems appeared in 1963, and the first part of an autobiography, *Report from Part One,* was published in 1972. She is also the author of *Maud Martha* (1953), a short novel dealing with the romance of a young woman in Chicago.

Like her poetry, *Maud Martha* focuses on ordinary people in familiar settings and situations. In it Brooks seems almost deliberately to shun the grand, the heroic, and the dramatic as though determined to find some unexpected supply of these moments in the familiar, some surprise in the ordinary. Echoing Walt Whitman, she once defined her task as a poet as that of vivifying fact, not merely contemporary fact but universal fact, mindful that "the universal wears contemporary clothing very well." What she once remarked of "poets who happen also to be Negroes"—namely, that they "are twice-tried" because they must both "write poetry and . . . remember that they are Negroes"—turns out, in one way or another, to apply to the voices we hear in her fiction as well as those we hear in her poetry. Both poetic sensibility and racial consciousness are for Brooks in part resistive and protective and in part aggressive. In this doubleness they resemble aspects of what Wallace Stevens once defined more generally as the human mind: "a violence from within that protects us from a violence without."

Further Reading:
T. C. Bambara, " 'Report from Part One,' "
New York Times Book Review, January 7, 1973.
H. A. Baker, "The Achievement of Gwendolyn Brooks" in *Singers of Daybreak: Studies in Black American Literature,* 1974.
H. B. Shaw, *Gwendolyn Brooks,* 1980.

Text:
The World of Gwendolyn Brooks, 1971.

from Maud Martha

18: *We're the Only Colored People Here*

When they went out to the car there were just the very finest bits of white powder coming down with an almost comical little ethereal hauteur, to add themselves to the really important, piled-up masses of their kind.

And it wasn't cold.

Maud Martha laughed happily to herself. It was pleasant out, and tonight she and Paul were very close to each other.

He held the door open for her—instead of going on around to the driving side, getting in, and leaving her to get in at her side as best she might. When he took this way of calling her "lady" and informing her of his love she felt precious, protected, delicious. She gave him an excited look of gratitude. He smiled indulgently.

"Want it to be the Owl again?"

"Oh, no no, Paul. Let's not go there tonight. I feel too good inside for that. Let's go downtown?"

She had to suggest that with a question mark at the end, always. He usually had three protests. Too hard to park. Too much money. Too many white folks. And tonight she could almost certainly expect a no, she feared, because he had come out in his blue work shirt. There was a spot of apricot juice on the collar, too. His shoes were not shined. . . . But he nodded!

"We've never been to the World Playhouse," she said cautiously. "They have a good picture. I'd feel rich in there."

"You really wanta?"

"Please?"

"Sure."

It wasn't like other movie houses. People from the Studebaker Theatre which, as Maud Martha whispered to Paul, was "all-locked-arms" with the World Playhouse, were strolling up and down the lobby, laughing softly, smoking with gentle grace.

"There must be a play going on in there and this is probably an intermission," Maud Martha whispered again.

"I don't know why you feel you got to whisper," whispered Paul. "Nobody else is whispering in here." He looked around, resentfully, wanting to see a few, just a few, colored faces. There were only their own.

Maud Martha laughed a nervous defiant little laugh; and spoke loudly. "There certainly isn't any reason to whisper. Silly, huh."

The strolling women were cleverly gowned. Some of them had flowers or flashers in their hair. They looked—cooked. Well cared-for. And as though they had never seen a roach or a rat in their lives. Or gone without heat for a week. And the men had even edges. They were men, Maud Martha thought, who wouldn't stoop to fret over less than a thousand dollars.

"We're the only colored people here," said Paul.

She hated him a little. "Oh, hell. Who in hell cares."

"Well, what I want to know is, where do you pay the damn fares."

"There's the box office. Go on up."

He went on up. It was closed.

"Well," sighed Maud Martha, "I guess the picture has started already. But we can't have missed much. Go on up to that girl at the candy counter and ask her where we should pay our money."

He didn't want to do that. The girl was lovely and blonde and cold-eyed, and her arms were akimbo, and the set of her head was eloquent. No one else was at the counter.

"Well. We'll wait a minute. And see—"

Maud Martha hated him again. Coward. She ought to flounce over to the girl herself—show him up. . . .

The people in the lobby tried to avoid looking curiously at two shy Negroes wanting desperately not to seem shy. The white women looked at the Negro woman in her outfit with which no special fault could be found, but which made them think, somehow, of close rooms, and wee, close lives. They looked at her hair. They liked to see a dark colored girl with long, long hair. They were always slightly surprised, but agreeably so, when they did. They supposed it was the hair that had got her that yellowish, good-looking Negro man.

The white men tried not to look at the Negro man in the blue work shirt, the Negro man without a tie.

An usher opened a door of the World Playhouse part and ran quickly down the few steps that led from it to the lobby. Paul opened his mouth.

"Say, fella. Where do we get the tickets for the movie?"

The usher glanced at Paul's feet before answering. Then he said coolly, but not unpleasantly, "I'll take the money."

They were able to go in.

And the picture! Maud Martha was so glad that they had not gone to the Owl! Here was technicolor, and the love story was sweet. And there was classical music that silvered its way into you and made your back cold. And the theater itself! It was no palace, no such Great Shakes as the Tivoli out south, for instance (where many colored people went every night). But you felt good sitting there, yes, good, and as if, when you left it, you would be going home to a sweet-smelling apartment with flowers on little gleaming tables; and wonderful silver on night-blue velvet, in chests; and crackly sheets; and lace spreads on such beds as you saw at Marshall Field's. Instead of back to your kit'n't apt., with the garbage of your floor's families in a big can just outside your door, and the gray sound of little gray feet scratching away from it as you drag up those flights of narrow complaining stairs.

Paul pressed her hand. Paul said, "We oughta do this more often."

And again. "We'll have to do this more often. And go to plays, too. I mean at that Blackstone, and Studebaker."

She pressed back, smiling beautifully to herself in the darkness. Though she knew that once the spell was over it would be a year, two years, more, before he would return to the World Playhouse. And he might never go to a real play. But she was learning to love moments. To love moments for themselves.

When the picture was over, and the lights revealed them for what they were, the Negroes stood up among the furs and good cloth and faint perfume, looked about them eagerly. They hoped they would meet no cruel eyes. They hoped no one would look intruded upon. They had enjoyed the picture so, they were so happy, they wanted to laugh, to say warmly to the other outgoers, "Good, huh? Wasn't it swell?"

This, of course, they could not do. But if only no one would look intruded upon. . . .

1953

Norman Mailer
b. 1923

Norman Mailer was born in Long Branch, New Jersey, on January 31, 1923, and grew up in Brooklyn, New York. At Harvard College he studied aeronautical engineering but also spent much of his time writing. In 1941 he won *Story* magazine's annual award for college fiction. Two years later he left Harvard with an honors degree in engineering, joined the army, and headed for the Philippines as a rifleman in the 112th Cavalry.

Mailer's first novel, *The Naked and the Dead* (1948), the account of an

American invasion of a small Pacific island held by the Japanese, drew directly on his military experiences and is generally considered one of the finest novels to come out of the Second World War. An enormous success, it gave Mailer an immediate literary reputation. In the early 1950s Mailer settled in New York City and, as he says in his first collection of essays, *Advertisements for Myself* (1959), resolved to make "a revolution in the consciousness of our time." He set about doing so through fiction, essays, journalism, and publishing. His second novel, *Barbary Shore* (1951), grew out of his reflections on the difficulties that necessarily surround reform politics in a world where all values seem to have gone dead. *The Deer Park* (1955), his third novel, in which he pays literary dues to Ernest Hemingway and F. Scott Fitzgerald, is still regarded as one of the best, novels yet written about Hollywood. In 1959 Mailer attempted through a long essay, "The White Negro," to define the existential characteristics of "hip," a style of thought and behavior that he opposed to the "square" and that he believed typified the most desirable mode of contemporary consciousness. In 1953 he became a coeditor of *Dissent* and a year later helped found *The Village Voice.*

During the 1960s and early 1970s Mailer's work became increasingly political as he began to explore more deeply the various sources of power in America. He published two collections of essays on politics and culture, *The Presidential Papers* (1963) and *Cannibals and Christians* (1966). He wrote *An American Dream* in 1965, a novel about a war hero, excongressman, and friend of John F. Kennedy who murders his socially prominent wife and then apparently purges himself clean—a baptism by fire—by a deliberate immersion into what he bleakly sees as his country's cultural disintegration. In 1967 he published his fifth novel, *Why Are We in Vietnam?,* a contemporary tall tale that examines American violence through the pulsating narrative voice of an eighteen-year-old Dallas disc jockey. But much of Mailer's best work of the period was in the budding genre of "New Journalism"—writing that combined a sense of the occasions and objectivity of journalism with many of the techniques and freedoms of fiction. In 1968 Mailer wrote one of his finest books (it won both the Pulitzer Prize and the National Book Award), *The Armies of the Night,* which he subtitled *History as a Novel/The Novel as History* and which deals with his experiences in the 1967 peace march on the Pentagon to protest the Vietnam War. In the same vein he wrote about the presidential conventions of 1968 and 1972 in *Miami and the Seige of Chicago: An Informal History of the Republican and Democratic Conventions of 1968* (1969) and *St. George and the Godfather* (1972). In 1968 he published a collection of earlier political essays, *The Idol and the Octopus: Political Writings on the Kennedy and Johnson Administrations,* and in the same year reinforced his political theme by running as an independent candidate for mayor of New York City.

Like Yeats's poetry, Mailer's prose grows out of a dialectic between a fascination with his own life and a matching fascination with the life of his times. Mailer is often seen trying to balance a desire to be a public figure—a performer, an oracle, and a celebrity—with the desire to be a serious man of letters. His writing, too, draws heavily on his abiding concern for the American culture—for its heroes and heroines, its gadgets and gimmicks, its aberrations and achievements, and above all its spiritual endangerment as it seeks to open up new worlds and yet find enduring values. In recent years he has written a number of books that investigate various aspects of contemporary American society and culture: the space program and first moon landing in *Of a Fire on the Moon* (1970), a personal polemic against feminism and the women's movement in *The Prisoner of Sex* (1971), a biographical essay on Marilyn Monroe in *Marilyn* (1973), an interpretation of urban graffiti in *The Faith of Graffiti* (1974), a report of a famous Muhammad Ali championship bout in *The Fight* (1975), and a searching account of a convicted murderer's Utah background in *The Executioner's Song* (1979). In keeping with his remarkable versatility, Mailer has also written a long novel set in the Egypt of the Pharaohs, *Ancient Evenings* (1983), and a murder mystery, *Tough Guys Don't Dance* (1984).

Both controversy and acclaim have greeted Mailer's efforts to make the tension between his art and his life as compellingly interesting to others as it is to himself. Even so, both his work and his career surely stand among the more remarkable achievements of our time. For more than thirty years now he has displayed an artistic restlessness—deriving from what he once described as an instinctive feeling that "the best way to grow was not to write one novel after another but to move from activity to activity"—that has carried him from one telling experiment to another. As much as any writer of his time, he has reached beyond familiar attitudes, themes, styles, and modes into new areas and so has broadened literature in our time. Furthermore, though he has sometimes simplified and reduced the realities of modern American life, he has also, at his best, brought unusual imaginative force, and unusually supple prose, to bear on them. "I suppose," he once remarked,

> that the virtue I should like most to achieve as a writer is to be genuinely disturbing . . . to see life . . . as others do not see it, or only partially see it, and therefore open for the reader that literary experience . . . of having one's experience enlarged, one's perceptions deepened, and one's illusions about one-self rendered even more untenable. For me, this is the highest function of art, precisely that it is disturbing, that it does not let man rest.

Further Reading:
"Norman Mailer: An Interview" in *Writers at Work: The Paris Review Interviews,* 3d series, 1967, intro. by A. Kazin.
R. Poirier, *Norman Mailer,* 1973.
R. Solotaroff, *Down Mailer's Way,* 1974.

Texts:
The Armies of the Night: History as a Novel/The Novel as History, 1968.
Of a Fire on the Moon, 1969.

---

from The Armies of the Night[*]
Book I: History As a Novel:
The Steps of the Pentagon

from Part I: Thursday Evening

5: *Toward a Theater of Ideas*

The guests were beginning to leave the party for the Ambassador, which was two blocks away. Mailer did not know this yet, but the audience there had been waiting almost an hour. They were being entertained by an electronic folk rock guitar group, so presumably the young were more or less happy, and the middle-aged dim. Mailer was feeling the high sense of clarity which accompanies the light show of the aurora borealis when it is projected upon the inner universe of the chest, the lungs, and the heart. He was happy. On leaving, he had appropriated a coffee mug and filled it with bourbon. The fresh air illumined the bourbon, gave it a cerebrative edge; words entered his brain with the agreeable authority of fresh minted coins. Like all good professionals, he was stimulated by the chance to try a new if related line of work. Just as professional football players love sex because it is so close to football, so he was fond of speaking in public because it was thus near to writing. An extravagant analogy? Consider that a good half of writing consists of being sufficiently sensitive to the moment to reach for the next promise which is usually hidden in some word or phrase just a shift to the side of one's conscious intent. (Consciousness, that blunt tool, bucks in the general direction of the truth; instinct plucks the feather. Cheers!) Where public speaking is an exercise from prepared texts to demonstrate how success- fully a low order of consciousness can beat upon the back of a collective flesh, public speaking being, therefore, a sullen expression of human possibility metaphorically equal to a bugger on his victim, speaking-in-public (as Mailer liked to describe any speech which was more or less improvised, impromptu, or dangerously written) was an activity like writing; one had to trick or seize or submit to the grace of each moment, which, except for those unexpected and sometimes well-deserved moments when consciousness and grace came together (and one felt on the consequence, heroic) were usually occasions of some mystery. The pleasure of speaking in public was the sensitivity it offered: with every phrase one was better or worse, close or less close to the existential promise of truth, *it feels true,* which hovers on good occasions like a presence between speaker and audience. Sometimes one was better, and worse, at the same moment; so strategic choices on the continuation of the attack would soon have to be decided, a moment to know the blood of the gambler in oneself.

Intimations of this approaching experience, obviously one of Mailer's preferred pleasures in life, at least when he did it well, were now connected to the professional sense of intrigue at the new task: tonight he would be both speaker and master of

---

[*] *The Armies of the Night* is based on the march to the Pentagon in October 1967 in opposition to the Vietnam War.

ceremonies. The two would conflict, but interestingly. Already he was looking in his mind for kind even celebrative remarks about Paul Goodman[1] which would not violate every reservation he had about Goodman's dank glory. But he had it. It would be possible with no violation of truth to begin by saying that the first speaker looked very much like Nelson Algren,[2] because in fact the first speaker was Paul Goodman, and both Nelson Algren and Paul Goodman looked like old cons. Ladies and Gentlemen, without further ado let me introduce one of young America's favorite old cons, Paul Goodman! (It would not be necessary to add that where Nelson Algren looked like the sort of skinny old con who was in on every make in the joint, and would sign away Grandma's farm to stay in the game, Goodman looked like the sort of old con who had first gotten into trouble in the YMCA, and hadn't spoken to anyone since.)

All this while, Mailer had in clutch *Why Are We In Vietnam?* He had neglected to bring his own copy to Washington and so had borrowed the book from his hostess on the promise he would inscribe it. (Later he was actually to lose it—working apparently on the principle that if you cannot make a hostess happy, the next best charity is to be so evil that the hostess may dine out on tales of your misconduct.) But the copy of the book is now noted because Mailer, holding it in one hand and the mug of whisky in the other, was obliged to notice on entering the Ambassador Theater that he had an overwhelming urge to micturate. The impulse to pass urine, being for some reason more difficult to restrain when both hands are occupied, there was no thought in the Master of Ceremonies' mind about the alternatives—he would have to find The Room before he went on stage.

That was not so immediately simple as one would have thought. The twenty guests from the party, looking a fair piece subdued under the fluorescent lights, had therefore the not unhaggard look of people who have arrived an hour late at the theater. No matter that the theater was by every evidence sleazy (for neighborhood movie houses built on the dream of the owner that some day Garbo or Harlow or Lombard would give a look in, aged immediately they were not used for movies anymore) no matter, the guests had the uneasiness of very late arrivals. Apologetic, they were therefore in haste for the speakers to begin.

Mailer did not know this. He was off already in search of The Room, which, it developed was up on the balcony floor. Imbued with the importance of his first gig as Master of Ceremonies, he felt such incandescence of purpose that he could not quite conceive it necessary to notify de Grazia[3] he would be gone for a minute. Incandescence is the *satori*[4] of the Romantic spirit which spirit would insist—this is the essence of the Romantic—on accelerating time. The greater the power of any subjective state, the more total is a Romantic's assumption that everyone understands exactly what he is about to do, therefore waste not a moment by stopping to tell them.

Flush with his incandescence, happy in all the anticipations of liberty which this Götterdämmerung[5] of a urination was soon to provide, Mailer did not know, but

---

[1] American poet and cultural critic (1911–1972), and author of *Growing Up Absurd* (1959).

[2] Contemporary American novelist (b. 1909) and author of *The Man With the Golden Arm* (1949).

[3] Ed de Grazia, one of the organizers of the march.

[4] State of spiritual enlightenment sought in Zen Buddhism.

[5] German: "twilight of the gods." Hence, catastrophic and grandiose like the Wagnerian opera of that title.

he had already and unwitting to himself metamorphosed into the Beast. Wait and see!

He was met on the stairs by a young man from *Time* magazine, a stringer presumably, for the young man lacked that I-am-damned look in the eye and rep tie of those whose work for *Time* has become a life addiction. The young man had a somewhat ill-dressed look, a map showed on his skin of an old adolescent acne, and he gave off the unhappy furtive presence of a fraternity member on probation for the wrong thing, some grievous mis-deposit of vomit, some hanky panky with frat-house tickets.

But the Beast was in a great good mood. He was soon to speak; that was food for all. So the Beast greeted the *Time* man with the geniality of a surrogate Hemingway unbending for the Luce-ites (Loo-sights was the pun) made some genial cryptic remark or two about finding Herr John, said cheerfully in answer to why he was in Washington that he had come to protest the war in Vietnam, and taking a sip of bourbon from the mug he kept to keep all fires idling right, stepped off into the darkness of the top balcony floor, went through a door into a pitch-black men's room, and was alone with his need. No chance to find the light switch for he had no matches, he did not smoke. It was therefore a matter of locating what's what with the probing of his toes. He found something finally which seemed appropriate, and pleased with the precision of these generally unused senses in his feet, took aim between them at a point twelve inches ahead, and heard in the darkness the sound of his water striking the floor. Some damn mistake had been made, an assault from the side doubtless instead of the front, the bowl was relocated now, and Master of Ceremonies breathed deep of the great reveries of this utterly non-Sisyphian release—at last!!—and thoroughly enjoyed the next forty-five seconds, being left on the aftermath not a note depressed by the condition of the premises. No, he was off on the Romantic's great military dream, which is: seize defeat, convert it to triumph. Of course, pissing on the floor was bad; very bad; the attendant would probably gossip to the police (if the *Time* man did not sniff it out first) and The Uniformed in turn would report it to The Press who were sure to write about the scandalous condition in which this meeting had left the toilets. And all of this contretemps merely because the management, bitter with their lost dream of Garbo and Harlow and Lombard, were now so pocked and stingy they doused the lights. (Out of such stuff is a novelist's brain.)

Well, he could convert this deficiency to an asset. From gap to gain is very American. He would confess straight out to all aloud that he was the one who wet the floor in the men's room, he alone! While the audience was recovering from the existential anxiety of encountering an orator who confessed to such a crime, he would be able—their attention now riveted—to bring them up to a contemplation of deeper problems, of, indeed, the deepest problems, the most chilling alternatives, and would from there seek to bring them back to a restorative view of man. Man might be a fool who peed in the wrong pot, man was also a scrupulous servant of the self-damaging admission; man was therefore a philosopher who possessed the magic stone; he could turn loss to philosophical gain, and so illumine the deeps, find the poles, and eventually learn to cultivate his most special fool's garden: *satori,* incandescence, and the hard gem-like flame of bourbon burning in the furnaces of metabolism.

Thus composed, illumined by these first stages of Emersonian transcendence, Mailer left the men's room, descended the stairs, entered the back of the orchestra, all opening remarks held close file in his mind like troops ranked in order before the parade, and then suddenly, most suddenly saw, with a cancerous swoop of albatross wings, that de Grazia was on the stage, was acting as M.C., was—no calling it back—launched into the conclusion of a gentle stammering stumbling—small orator, de Grazia!—introduction of Paul Goodman. All lost! The magnificent opening remarks about the forces gathered here to assemble on Saturday before the Pentagon, this historic occasion, let us hold it in our mind and focus on a puddle of passed water on the floor above and see if we assembled here can as leftists and proud dissenters contain within our minds the grandeur of the two—all lost!—no chance to do more than pick up later—later! after de Grazia and Goodman had finished dead-assing the crowd. Traitor de Grazia! Sicilian de Grazia!

As Mailer picked his way between people sitting on the stone floor (orchestra seats had been removed—the movie house was a dance hall now with a stage) he made a considerable stir in the orchestra. Mailer had been entering theaters for years, mounting stages—now that he had put on weight, it would probably have been fair to say that he came to the rostrum like a poor man's version of Orson Welles, some minor note of the same contemplative presence. A titter and rise of expectation followed him. He could not resist its appeal. As he passed de Grazia, he scowled, threw a look from Lower Shakespearia "Èt tu Bruté," and proceeded to slap the back of his hand against de Grazia's solar plexus. It was not a heavy blow, but then de Grazia was not a heavy man; he wilted some hint of an inch. And the audience pinched off a howl, squeaked on their squeal. It was not certain to them what had taken place.

Picture the scene two minutes later from the orchestra floor. Paul Goodman, now up at the microphone with no podium or rostrum, is reading the following lines:

> . . . these days my contempt
> for the misrulers of my country
> is icy and my indignation raucous.

It is impossible to tell what he is reading. Off at the wing of the stage where the others are collected—stout Macdonald, noble Lowell, beleaguered de Grazia, and Mailer, Prince of Bourbon, the acoustics are atrocious. One cannot hear a word the speaker is saying. Nor are there enough seats. If de Grazia and Macdonald are sitting in folding chairs, Mailer is squatting on his haunches, or kneeling on one knee like a player about to go back into the ball game. Lowell has the expression on his face of a dues payer who is just about keeping up with the interest on some enormous debt. As he sits on the floor with his long arms clasped mournfully about his long Yankee legs, "I am here," says his expression, "but I do not have to pretend I like what I see." The hollows in his cheeks give a hint of the hanging judge. Lowell is of a good weight, not too heavy, not too light, but the hollows speak of the great Puritan gloom in which the country was founded—man was simply not good enough for God.

At this moment, it is hard not to agree with Lowell. The cavern of the theater seems to resonate behind the glare of the footlights, but this is no resonance of a fine bass voice—it is rather electronics on the march. The public address system hisses, then rings in a random chorus of electronic music, sounds of cerebral mastication from some horror machine of Outer Space (where all that electricity doubtless comes from, child!) then a hum like the squeak in the hinges of the gates of Hell—we are in the penumbra of psychedelic netherworlds, ghost-odysseys from the dead brain cells of adolescent trysts with LSD, some ultrapurple spotlight from the balcony (not ultraviolet—ultrapurple, deepest purple one could conceive) there out in the dark like some neon eye of the night, the media is the message, and the message is purple, speaks of the monarchies of Heaven, madnesses of God, and clam-vaults of people on a stone floor. Mailer's senses are now tuned to absolute pitch or sheer error—he marks a ballot for absolute pitch—he is certain there is a profound pall in the audience. Yes, they sit there, stricken, inert, in terror of what Saturday will bring, and so are unable to rise to a word the speaker is offering them. It will take dynamite to bring life. The shroud of burned-out psychedelic dreams is in this audience, Cancer Gulch with open maw—and Mailer thinks of the vigor and the light (from marijuana?) in the eyes of those American soldiers in Vietnam who have been picked by the newsreel cameras to say their piece, and the happy healthy never unintelligent faces of all those professional football players he studies so assiduously on television come Sunday (he has neglected to put his bets in this week) and wonders how they would poll out on sentiment for the war.

HAWKS 95   DOVES 6

NFL Footballers Approve Vietnam War

Doubtless. All the healthy Marines, state troopers, professional athletes, movie stars, rednecks, sensuous life-loving Mafia, cops, mill workers, city officials, nice healthy-looking easy-grafting politicians full of the light (from marijuana?) in their eye of a life they enjoy—yes, they would be for the war in Vietnam. Arrayed against them as hard-core troops: an elite! the Freud-ridden embers of Marxism, good old American anxiety strata—the urban middle-class with their proliferated monumental adenoidal resentments, their secret slavish love for the oncoming hegemony of the computer and the suburb, yes, they and their children, by the sheer ironies, the sheer ineptitude, the *kinks* of history, were now being compressed into more and more militant stands, their resistance to the war some hopeless melange, somehow firmed, of Pacifism and closet Communism. And their children—on a freak-out from the suburbs to a love-in on the Pentagon wall.

It was the children in whom Mailer had some hope, a gloomy hope. These mad middle-class children with their lobotomies from sin, their nihilistic embezzlement of all middle-class moral funds, their innocence, their lust for apocalypse, their unbelievable indifference to waste: twenty generations of buried hopes perhaps engraved in their chromosomes, and now conceivably burning like faggots in the secret inquisitional fires of LSD. It was a devil's drug—designed by the Devil to consume the love of the best, and leave them liver-wasted, weeds of the big city. If there had been a player piano, Mailer might have put in a quarter to hear "In the Heart of the City Which Has No Heart."

Yes, these were the troops: middle-class cancer-pushers and drug-gutted flower children. And Paul Goodman to lead them. Was he now reading this?

> Once American faces
> were beautiful to me
> but now they look cruel
> and as if they had narrow thoughts.

Not much poetry, but well put prose. And yet there was always Goodman's damnable tolerance for all the varieties of sex. Did he know nothing of evil or entropy? Sex was the superhighway to your own soul's entropy if it was used without a constant sharpening of the taste. And orgies? What did Goodman know of orgies, real ones, not lib-lab college orgies to carry out the higher program of the Great Society, but real ones with murder in the air, and witches on the shoulder. The collected Tory in Mailer came roaring to the surface like a cocked hat in a royal coach.

"When Goodman finishes, I'm going to take over as M.C.," he whispered to de Grazia. (The revery we have just attended took no more in fact than a second. Mailer's melancholy assessment of the forces now mounting in America took place between two consecutive lines of Goodman's poem—not because Mailer cerebrated that instantly, but because he had had the revery many a time before—he had to do no more than sense the audience, whisper Cancer Gulch to himself and the revery went by with a mental ch-ch-ch Click! reviewed again.) In truth, Mailer was now in a state. He had been prepared to open the evening with apocalyptic salvos to announce the real gravity of the situation, and the intensely peculiar American aspect of it—which is that the urban and suburban middle class were to be offered on Saturday an opportunity for glory—what other nation could boast of such option for its middle class? Instead—lost. The benignity and good humor of his planned opening remarks now subjugated to the electronic hawking and squabbling and *hum* of the P.A., the maniacal necessity to *wait* was on this hiatus transformed into a violent concentration of purpose, all intentions reversed. He glared at de Grazia. "How could you do this?" he whispered to his ear.

De Grazia looked somewhat confused at the intensity. Meetings to de Grazia were obviously just meetings, assemblages of people who coughed up for large admissions or kicked in for the pitch; at best, some meetings were less boring than others. De Grazia was much too wise and guilty-spirited to brood on apocalypse. "I couldn't find you," he whispered back.

"You didn't trust me long enough to wait one minute?"

"We were over an hour late," de Grazia whispered again. "We had to begin."

Mailer was all for having the conversation right then on stage: to hell with reciprocal rights and polite incline of the ear to the speaker. The Beast was ready to grapple with the world. "Did you think I wouldn't show up?" he asked de Grazia.

"Well, I was wondering."

In what sort of mumbo-jumbo of promise and betrayal did de Grazia live? How could de Grazia ever suppose he would not show up? He had spent his life showing up at the most boring and onerous places. He gave a blast of his eyes to de Grazia. But Macdonald gave a look at Mailer, as if to say, "You're creating disturbance."

Now Goodman was done.

Mailer walked to the stage. He did not have any idea any longer of what he would say, his mind was empty, but in a fine calm, taking for these five instants a total rest. While there was no danger of Mailer ever becoming a demagogue since if the first idea he offered could appeal to a mob, the second in compensation would be sure to enrage them, he might nonetheless have made a fair country orator, for he loved to speak, he loved in fact to holler, and liked to hear a crowd holler back. (Of how many New York intellectuals may that be said?)

"I'm here as your original M.C., temporarily displaced owing to a contretemps"—which was pronounced purposefully as contretempse—"in the men's room," he said into the microphone for opening, but the gentle high-strung beast of a device pushed into a panic by the electric presence of a real Beast, let loose a squeal which shook the welds in the old foundation of the Ambassador. Mailer immediately decided he had had enough of public address systems, electronic fields of phase, impedance, and spooks in the circuitry. A hex on collaborating with Cancer Gulch. He pushed the microphone away, squared off before the audience. "Can you hear me?" he bellowed.

"Yes."

"Can you hear me in the balcony?"

"Yes."

"Then let's do away with electronics," he called out.

Cries of laughter came back. A very small pattern of applause. (Not too many on his side for electrocuting the public address system, or so his orator's ear recorded the vote.)

"Now I missed the beginning of this occasion, or I would have been here to introduce Paul Goodman, for which we're all sorry, right?"

Confused titters. Small reaction.

"What are you, dead-heads?" he bellowed at the audience. "Or are you all"—here he put on his false Irish accent—"in the nature of becoming dead ahsses?" Small laughs. A whistle or two. "No," he said, replying to the whistles, "I invoke these dead asses as part of the gravity of the occasion. The middle class plus one hippie surrealistic symbolic absolutely insane March on the Pentagon, bless us all," beginning of a big applause which offended Mailer for it came on "bless" and that was too cheap a way to win votes, "bless us all—shit!" he shouted, "I'm trying to say the middle class plus shit, I mean plus revolution, is equal to one big collective dead ass." Some yells of approval, but much shocked curious rather stricken silence. He had broken the shank of his oratorical charge. Now he would have to sweep the audience together again. (Perhaps he felt like a surgeon delivering a difficult breech—nothing to do but plunge to the elbows again.)

"To resume our exposition," a good warm titter, then a ripple of laughter, not unsympathetic to his ear; the humor had been unwitting, but what was the life of an orator without some bonus? "To resume this orderly marshalling of concepts"—a conscious attempt at humor which worked less well; he was beginning to recognize for the first time that bellowing without a mike demanded a more forthright style—"I shall now *engage* in confession." More Irish accent. (He blessed Brendan Behan for what he had learned from him.) "A public speaker may offer you two opportunities. Instruction or confession." Laughter now. "Well, you're all college heads, so my instruction would be as pearls before—I dare not say it." Laughs. Boos. A voice from the balcony: "Come on, Norman, say something!"

"Is there a black man in the house?" asked Mailer. He strode up and down the stage pretending to peer at the audience. But in fact they were illumined just well enough to emphasize one sad discovery—if black faces there were they were certainly not in plenty. "Well ah'll just have to be the *impromptu* Black Power for tonight. Woo-eeeeee! Woo-eeeeee! HMmmmmmmm." He grunted with some partial success, showing hints of Cassius Clay. "Get your white butts moving."

"The confession. The confession!" screamed some adolescents from up front.

He came to a stop, shifted his voice. Now he spoke in a relaxed tone. "The confession, yeah!" Well, at least the audience was awake. He felt as if he had driven away some sepulchral phantoms of a variety which inhabited the profound middle-class schist. Now to charge the center of vested spookery.

"Say," he called out into the semidarkness with the ultrapurple light coming off the psychedelic lamp on the rail of the balcony, and the spotlights blaring against his eyes, "say," all happiness again, "I think of Saturday, and that March and do you know, fellow carriers of the holy unendurable grail, for the first time in my life I don't know whether I have the piss or the shit scared out of me most." It was an interesting concept, thought Mailer, for there was a difference between the two kinds of fear—pursue the thought, he would, in quieter times—"we are up, face this, all of you, against an existential situation—we do not know how it is going to turn out, and what is even more inspiring of dread is that the government doesn't know either."

Beginning of a real hand, a couple of rebel yells. "We're going to try to stick it up the government's ass," he shouted, "right into the sphincter of the Pentagon." Wild yells and chills of silence from different reaches of the crowd. Yeah, he was cooking now. "Will reporters please get every word accurately," he called out dryly to warm the chill.

But humor may have been too late. *The New Yorker* did not have strictures against the use of sh*t for nothing; nor did Dwight Macdonald love *The New Yorker* for nothing, he also had strictures against sh*t's metaphorical associations. Mailer looked to his right to see Macdonald approaching, a book in his hands, arms at his side, a sorrowing look of concern in his face. "Norman," said Macdonald quietly, "I can't possibly follow you after all this. Please introduce me, and get it over with."

Mailer was near to stricken. On the one hand interrupted on a flight; on the other, he had fulfilled no duty whatsoever as M.C. He threw a look at Macdonald which said: give me this. I'll owe you one.

But de Grazia was there as well. "Norman, let me be M.C. now," he said.

They were being monstrous unfair, thought Mailer. They didn't understand what he had been doing, how good he had been, what he would do next. Fatal to walk off now—the verdict would claim he was unbalanced. Still, he could not hold the stage by force. That was unthinkably worse.

For the virtuous, however, deliverance (like buttercups) pops up everywhere. Mailer now took the microphone and turned to the audience. He was careful to speak in a relaxed voice. "We are having a disagreement about the value of the proceedings. Some think de Grazia should resume his post as Master of Ceremonies. I would like to keep the position. It is an existential moment. We do not know how it will turn out. So let us vote on it." Happy laughter from the audience at these comic effects. Actually Mailer did not believe it was an existential situation any longer. He reckoned the vote would be well in his favor. "Will those," he asked, "who are in favor of Mr. de Grazia succeeding me as Master of Ceremonies please say aye."

A good sound number said aye.

Now for the ovation. "Will those opposed to this, please say no." The no's to Mailer's lack of pleasure were no greater in volume. "It seems the ayes and no's are about equal," said Mailer. (He was thinking to himself that he had posed the issue all wrong—the ayes should have been reserved for those who would keep him in office.) "Under the circumstances," he announced, "I will keep the chair." Laughter at this easy cheek. He stepped into the middle of such laughter. "You have all just learned an invaluable political lesson." He waved the microphone at the audience. "In the absence of a definitive vote, the man who holds the power, keeps it."

"Hey, de Grazia," someone yelled from the audience, "why do you let him have it?"

Mailer extended the microphone to de Grazia who smiled sweetly into it. "Because if I don't," he said in a gentle voice, "he'll beat the shit out of me." The dread word had been used again.

"Please, Norman," said Macdonald retreating.

So Mailer gave his introduction to Macdonald. It was less than he would have attempted if the flight had not been grounded, but it was certainly respectable. Under the military circumstances, it was a decent cleanup operation. For about a minute he proceeded to introduce Macdonald as a man with whom one might seldom agree, but could never disrespect because he always told the truth as he saw the truth, a man therefore of the most incorruptible integrity. "Pray heaven, I am right," said Mailer to himself, and walked past Macdonald who was on his way to the mike. Both men nodded coolly to each other.

In the wing, visible to the audience, Paul Goodman sat on a chair clearly avoiding any contaminatory encounter with The Existentialist. De Grazia gave his "It's tough all over" smile. Lowell sat in a mournful hunch on the floor, his eyes peering over his glasses to scrutinize the metaphysical substance of his boot, now hide? now machine? now, where the joining and to what? foot to boot, boot to earth—cease all speculations as to what was in Lowell's head. "The one mind a novelist cannot enter is the mind of a novelist superior to himself," said once to Mailer by Jean Malaquais. So, by corollary, the one mind a minor poet may not enter . . .

Lowell looked most unhappy. Mailer, minor poet, had often observed that Lowell had the most disconcerting mixture of strength and weakness in his presence, a blending so dramatic in its visible sign of conflict that one had to assume he would be sensationally attractive to women. He had something untouchable, all insane in its force; one felt immediately there were any number of causes for which the man would be ready to die, and for some he would fight, with an axe in his hand and a Cromwellian light in his eye. It was even possible that physically he was very strong —one couldn't tell at all—he might be fragile, he might have the sort of farm mechanic's strength which could manhandle the rear axle and differential off a car and into the back of a pickup. But physical strength or no, his nerves were all too apparently delicate. Obviously spoiled by everyone for years, he seemed nonetheless to need the spoiling. These nerves—the nerves of a consummate poet—were not tuned to any battering. The squalls of the mike, now riding up a storm on the erratic piping breath of Macdonald's voice, seemed to tear along Lowell's back like a gale. He detested tumult—obviously. And therefore saw everything which was hopeless in a rife situation: the dank middle-class depths of the audience, the strident squalor of the mike, the absurdity of talent gathered to raise money—for what, dear God? who could finally know what this March might convey, or worse, purvey, and worst of all—to be associated now with Mailer's butcher boy attack. Lowell's eyes looked up from the shoe, and passed one withering glance by the novelist, saying much, saying, "Every single bad thing I have ever heard about you is not exaggerated."

Mailer, looking back, thought bitter words he would not say: "You, Lowell, beloved poet of many, what do you know of the dirt and the dark deliveries of the necessary? What do you know of dignity hard-achieved, and dignity lost through innocence, and dignity lost by sacrifice for a cause one cannot name. What do you know about getting fat against your will, and turning into a clown of an arriviste baron when you would rather be an eagle or a count, or rarest of all, some natural aristocrat from these damned democratic states. No, the only subject we share, you and I, is that species of perception which shows that if we are not very loyal to our unendurable and most exigent inner light, then some day we may burn. How dare you condemn me! You know the diseases which inhabit the audience in this accursed psychedelic house. How dare you scorn the explosive I employ?"

And Lowell with a look of the greatest sorrow as if all this *mess* were finally too shapeless for the hard Protestant smith of his own brain, which would indeed burst if it could not forge his experience into the iron edge of the very best words and the most unsinkable relation of words, now threw up his eyes like an epileptic as if turned out of orbit by a turn of the vision—and fell backward, his head striking the floor with no last instant hesitation to cushion the blow, but like a baby, downright sudden, savagely to himself, as if from the height of a foot he had taken a pumpkin and dropped it splat on the floor. "There, much-regarded, much-protected brain, you have finally taken a blow," Lowell might have said to himself, for he proceeded to lie there, resting quietly, while Macdonald went on reading from "The White Man's Burden," Lowell seeming as content as if he had just tested the back of his cranium against a policeman's club. What a royal head they had all to lose!

1968

---

from Of a Fire on the Moon

from **Chapter 7: A Sleep on the Moon**

from IV: [On the Floor of a Dark Theater]

Later, Armstrong[1] would say, "That first hour on the moon was hardly the time for long thoughts; we had specific jobs to do. Of course the sights were simply magnificent, beyond any visual experience that I had ever been exposed to," and Aldrin would describe it as "a unique, almost mystical environment." In fact, there is an edge of the unexplained to their reactions. Their characteristic matter-of-fact response is overcome occasionally by swoops of hyperbole. And to everyone's slight surprise, they were almost two hours late for their EVA.[2] Their estimate of time was off by close to fifty percent. For astronauts that was an error comparable to a carpenter mistaking an eight-foot stud for a twelve-foot piece. If a carpenter can look at a piece of wood and guess its length to the nearest quarter-inch, it is because he has been working with

---

[1] Neil Armstrong (b. 1930), American astronaut; he and Edward Aldrin (b. 1930) were the first to walk on the moon.

[2] Extravehicular activity.

lengths all his life. Equally, people in some occupations have a close ability to estimate time.

With astronauts, whose every day in a simulator was a day laid out on the measure of a time-line, the estimate of time elapsed had to become acute. Armstrong and Aldrin had consistently fulfilled their tasks in less time than was allotted. Now, curiously, they fell behind, then further behind. . . .

It was not until nine-forty at night, Houston time, that they got the hatch open at last. In the heat of running almost two hours late, ensconced in the armor of a man-sized spaceship, could they still have felt an instant of awe as they looked out that open hatch at a panorama of theater: the sky is black, but the ground is brightly lit, bright as footlights on the floor of a dark theater. A black and midnight sky, yet on the moon ground, "you could almost go out in your shirt-sleeves and get a suntan," Aldrin would say. "I remember thinking, 'Gee, if I didn't know where I was, I could believe that somebody had created this environment somewhere out in the West and given us another simulation to work in.'" Everywhere on that pitted flat were shadows dark as the sky above, shadows dark as mine shafts.

What a struggle to push out from that congested cabin, now twice congested in their bulky-wham suits, no feeling of obstacle against their flesh, their sense of touch dead and numb, spaceman body manipulated out into the moon world like an upright piano turned by movers on the corner of the stairs.

"You're lined up on the platform. Put your left foot to the right a little bit. Okay, that's good. Roll left."

Armstrong was finally on the porch. Could it be with any sense of an alien atmosphere receiving the fifteen-layer encapsulations of the pack and suit on his back? Slowly, he climbed down the ladder. Archetypal, he must have felt, a boy descending the rungs in the wall of an abandoned well, or was it Jack down the stalk? And there he was on the bottom, on the footpad of the leg of the Lem,[3] a metal plate perhaps three feet across. Inches away was the soil of the moon. But first he jumped up again to the lowest rung of the ladder. A couple of hours later, at the end of the EVA, conceivably exhausted, the jump from the ground to the rung, three feet up, might be difficult in that stiff and heavy space suit, so he tested it now. "It takes," said Armstrong, " a pretty good little jump."

Now, with television working, and some fraction of the world peering at the murky image of this instant, poised between the end of one history and the beginning of another, he said quietly, "I'm at the foot of the ladder. The Lem footpads are only depressed in the surface about one or two inches, although the surface appears to be very very fine-grained as you get close to it. It's almost like a powder." One of Armstrong's rare confessions of uneasiness is focused later on this moment. "I don't recall any particular emotion or feeling other than a little caution, a desire to be sure it was safe to put my weight on that surface outside Eagle's[4] footpad."

Did his foot tingle in the heavy lunar overshoe? "I'm going to step off the Lem now."

Did something in him shudder at the touch of the new ground? Or did he draw a sweet strength from the balls of his feet? Nobody was necessarily going ever to know.

[3] Lunar excursion module.   [4] Eagle: Code name for the lunar module.

"That's one small step for a man," said Armstrong, "one giant leap for mankind." He had joined the ranks of the forever quoted. Patrick Henry, Henry Stanley[5] and Admiral Dewey[6] moved over for him.

V: [The Heavens Become Part of Our World]

Now he was out there, one foot on the moon, then the other foot on the moon, the powder like velvet underfoot. With one hand still on the ladder, he comments, "The surface is fine and powdery. I can . . . I can pick it up loosely with my toe." And as he releases his catch, the grains fall back slowly to the soil, a fan of feathers gliding to the floor. "It does adhere in fine layers like powdered charcoal to the sole and sides of my boots. I only go in a small fraction of an inch. Maybe an eighth of an inch. But I can see the footprints of my boots and the treads in the fine sand particles."

Capcom:[7] "Neil, this is Houston. We're copying."

Yes, they would copy. He was like a man who goes into a wrecked building to defuse a new kind of bomb. He talks into a microphone as he works, for if a mistake is made, and the bomb goes off, it will be easier for the next man if every detail of his activities has been mentioned as he performed them. Now, he released his grip on the ladder and pushed off for a few steps on the moon, odd loping steps, almost thrust into motion like a horse trotting up a steep slope. It could have been a moment equivalent to the first steps he took as an infant for there was nothing to hold onto and he did not dare to fall—the ground was too hot, the rocks might tear his suit. Yet if he stumbled, he could easily go over for he could not raise his arms above his head nor reach to his knees, his arms in the pressure bladder stood out before him like sausages; so, if he tottered, the weight of the pack could twist him around, or drop him. They had tried to shape up simulations of lunar gravity while weighted in scuba suits at the bottom of a pool, but water was not a vacuum through which to move; so they had also flown in planes carrying two hundred pounds of equipment on their backs. The pilot would take the plane through a parabolic trajectory. There would be a period of twenty-two seconds at the top of the curve when a simulation of one-sixth gravity would be present, and the two hundred pounds of equipment would weigh no more than on the moon, no more than thirty-plus pounds, and one could take loping steps down the aisle of the plane, staggering through unforeseen wobbles or turbulence. Then the parabolic trajectory was done, the plane was diving, and it would have to pull out of the dive. That created the reverse of one-sixth gravity —it multiplied gravity by two and a half times. The two hundred pounds of equipment now weighed five hundred pounds and the astronauts had to be supported by other men straining to help them bear the weight. So simulations gave them time for hardly more than a clue before heavy punishment was upon them. But now he was out in the open endless lunar gravity, his body and the reflexes of his life obliged to adopt a new rhythm and schedule of effort, a new disclosure of grace.

Still, he seemed pleased after the first few steps. "There seems to be no difficulty

---

[5] Welsh-born explorer (1841–1904) famous as the man who "found" David Livingstone in Africa and said "Dr. Livingstone, I presume?"

[6] George Dewey (1837–1917), American admiral.

[7] Houston, Texas, site of the National Aeronautics and Space Administration (NASA) Mission Control Center.

in moving around as we suspected. It's even perhaps easier than the simulations . . ." He would run a few steps and stop, run a few steps and stop. Perhaps it was not unlike directing the Lem when it hovered over the ground. One moved faster than on earth and with less effort, but it was harder to stop—one had to pick the place to halt from several yards ahead. Yes, it was easier once moving, but awkward at the beginning and the end because of the obdurate plastic bendings of the suit. And once standing at rest, the sense of the vertical was sly. One could be leaning further forward than one knew. Or leaning backward. Like a needle on a dial one would have to oscillate from side to side of the vertical to find position. Conceivably the sensation was not unlike skiing with a child on one's back.

It was time for Aldrin to descend the ladder from the Lem to the ground, and Armstrong's turn to give directions: "The shoes are about to come over the sill. Okay, now drop your PLSS[8] down. There you go. You're clear. . . . About an inch clearance on top of your PLSS."

Aldrin spoke for future astronauts: "Okay, you need a little bit of arching of the back to come down . . ."

When he reached the ground, Aldrin took a big and exuberant leap up the ladder again, as if to taste the pleasures of one-sixth gravity all at once. "Beautiful, beautiful," he exclaimed.

Armstrong: "Isn't that something. Magnificent sight out here."

Aldrin: "Magnificent desolation."

They were looking at a terrain which lived in a clarity of focus unlike anything they had ever seen on earth. There was no air, of course, and so no wind, nor clouds, nor dust, nor even the finest scattering of light from the smallest dispersal of microscopic particles on a clear day on earth, no, nothing visible or invisible moved in the vacuum before them. All light was pure. No haze was present, not even the invisible haze of the finest day—therefore objects did not go out of focus as they receded into the distance. If one's eyes were good enough, an object at a hundred yards was as distinct as a rock at a few feet. And their eyes were good enough. Just as one could not determine one's altitude above the moon, not from fifty miles up nor five, so now along the ground before them no distance was real, for all distances had the faculty to appear equally near if one peered at them through blinders and could not see the intervening details. Again the sense of being on a stage or on the lighted floor of a room so large one could not see where the dark ceiling began must have come upon them, for there were no hints of gathering evanescence in ridge beyond ridge; rather each outline was as severe as the one in front of it, and since the ground was filled with small craters of every size, from antholes to potholes to empty pools, and the horizon was near, four times nearer than on earth and sharp as the line drawn by a pencil, the moon ground seemed to slope and drop in all directions "like swimming in an ocean with six-foot or eight-foot swells and waves," Armstrong said later. "In that condition, you never can see very far away from where you are." But what they could see, they could see entirely—to the depth of their field of view at any instant their focus was complete. And as they swayed from side to side, so a sense of the vertical kept eluding them, the slopes of the craters about them seeming to tilt a few degrees to one side of the horizontal, then the other. On earth, one had only to incline

[8] Portable life-support system.

one's body an inch or two and a sense of the vertical was gone, but on the moon they could lean over, then further over, lean considerably further over without beginning to fall. So verticals slid and oscillated. Rolling from side to side, they could as well have been on water, indeed their sense of the vertical was probably equal to the subtle uncertainty of the body when a ship is rolling on a quiet sea. "I say," said Aldrin, "the rocks are rather slippery."

They were discovering the powder of the moon soil was curious indeed, comparable in firmness and traction to some matter between sand and snow. While the Lem looked light as a kite, for its pads hardly rested on the ground and it appeared ready to lift off and blow away, yet their own feet sometimes sank for two or three inches into the soft powder on the slope of very small craters, and their soles would slip as the powder gave way under their boots. In other places the ground was firm and harder than sand, yet all of these variations were to be found in an area not a hundred feet out from the legs of the Lem. As he explored his footing, Aldrin sent back comments to Mission Control, reporting in the rapt professional tones of a coach instructing his team on the conditions of the turf in a new plastic football field.

Meanwhile Armstrong was transporting the television camera away from the Lem to a position where it could cover most of their activities. Once properly installed, he revolved it through a full panorama of their view in order that audiences on earth might have a clue to what he saw. But in fact the transmission was too rudimentary to give any sense of what was about them, that desert sea of rocks, rubble, small boulders, and crater lips.

Aldrin was now working to set up the solar wind experiment, a sheet of aluminum foil hung on a stand. For the next hour and a half, the foil would be exposed to the solar wind, an invisible, unfelt, but high-velocity flow of noble[9] gases from the sun like argon, krypton, neon and helium. For the astronauts, it was the simplest of procedures, no more difficult than setting up a piece of sheet music on a music stand. At the end of the EVA, however, the aluminum foil would be rolled up, inserted in the rock box, and delivered eventually to a laboratory in Switzerland uniquely equipped for the purpose. There any noble gases which had been trapped in the atomic lattice of the aluminum would be baked out in virtuoso procedures of quantitative analysis, and a closer knowledge of the components of the solar wind would be gained. Since the solar wind, it may be recalled, was diverted by the magnetosphere away from the earth it had not hitherto been available for casual study.

That was the simplest experiment to set up; the other two would be deployed about an hour later. One was a passive seismometer to measure erratic disturbances and any periodic vibrations, as well as moonquakes, and the impact of meteors in the weeks and months to follow; it was equipped to radio this information to earth, the energy for transmission derived from solar panels which extended out to either side, and thereby gave it the look of one of those spaceships of the future with thin extended paperlike wings which one sees in science fiction drawings. In any case it was so sensitive that the steps of the astronauts were recorded as they walked by. Finally there was a Laser Ranging Retro-Reflector, an LRRR (or LRQ, for L R-cubed), and that was a mirror whose face was a hundred quartz crystals, black as coal, cut to a precision never obtained before in glass—one-third of an arc/sec. Since each quartz crystal was

---

[9] Inactive or inert.

a corner of a rectangle, any ray of light striking one of the three faces in each crystal would bounce off the other two in such a way that the light would return in exactly the same direction it had been received. A laser beam sent up from earth would therefore reflect back to the place from which it was sent. The time it required to travel this half-million miles from earth to moon round trip, a journey of less than three seconds, could be measured so accurately that physicists might then discern whether the moon was drifting away from the earth a few centimeters a year, or (by using two lasers) whether Europe and America might be drifting apart some compara-ble distance, or even if the Pacific Ocean were contracting. These measurements could then be entered into the caverns of Einstein's General Theory of Relativity, and new proof or disproof of the great thesis could be obtained.

We may be certain the equipment was remarkable. Still, its packaging and its ease of deployment had probably done as much to advance its presence on the ship as any clear priority over other scientific equipment; the beauty of these items from the point of view of NASA was that the astronauts could set them up in a few minutes while working in their space suits, even set them up with inflated gloves so insensitive that special silicone pads had to be inserted at the fingertips in order to leave the astronauts not altogether numb-fingered in their manipulations. Yet these marvels of measure-ment would soon be installed on the moon with less effort than it takes to remove a vacuum cleaner from its carton and get it operating.

It was at this point that patriotism, the corporation, and the national taste all came to occupy the same head of a pin, for the astronauts next proceeded to set up the flag. But that operation, as always, presented its exquisite problems. There was, we remind ourselves, no atmosphere for the flag to wave in. Any flag made of cloth would droop, indeed it would dangle. Therefore, a species of starched plastic flag had to be em-ployed, a flag which would stand out, there, out to the nonexistent breeze, flat as a slab of plywood. No, that would not do either. The flag was better crinkled and curled. Waves and billows were bent into it, and a full corkscrew of a curl at the end. There it stands for posterity, photographed in the twists of a high gale on the windless moon, curled up tin flag, numb as a pickled pepper.

Aldrin would hardly agree. "Being able to salute that flag was one of the more humble yet proud experiences I've ever had. To be able to look at the American flag and know how much so many people had put of themselves and their work into getting it where it was. We sensed—we really did—this almost mystical identification of all the people in the world at that instant."

Two minutes after the flag was up, the President of the United States put in his phone call. Let us listen one more time:

"Because of what you have done," said Nixon, "the heavens have become a part of man's world. And as you talk to us from the Sea of Tranquility,[10] it inspires us to redouble our efforts to bring peace and tranquility to earth . . ."

"Thank you, Mr. President. It's a great honor and privilege for us to be here representing not only the United States, but men of peace of all nations . . ."

In such piety is the schizophrenia of the ages.

Immediately afterward, Aldrin practiced kicking moon dust, but he was somewhat

---

[10] Site on the moon where the lunar module touched down.

broken up. Either reception was garbled, or Aldrin was temporarily incoherent. "They seem to leave," he said to the Capcom, referring to the particles, "and most of them have about the same angle of departure and velocity. From where I stand, a large portion of them will impact at a certain distance out. Several—the percentage is, of course, that will impact . . ."

Capcom: "Buzz, this is Houston. You're cutting out on the end of your transmissions. Can you speak a little more forward into your microphone. Over."

Aldrin: "Roger. I'll try that."

Capcom: "Beautiful."

Aldrin: "Now I had that one inside my mouth that time."

Capcom: "It sounded a little wet."

And on earth, a handful of young scientists were screaming, "Stop wasting time with flags and presidents—collect some rocks!"

1969

William Gass
b. 1924

William Gass was born in Fargo, North Dakota, on July 30, 1924, and grew up in Warren, Ohio. He attended Kenyon College and, briefly, Ohio Wesleyan University before interrupting his studies to serve as an ensign in the U.S. Navy from 1943 to 1946. He then returned to Kenyon, where he completed his undergraduate work in 1947. In 1954 he took a Ph.D. in philosophy at Cornell University and since that time has combined the teaching of philosophy (for many years at Purdue and currently at Washington University in St. Louis) with the writing of fiction and criticism. His combined interests converge in works in which he attempts to understand both the philosophical foundations of fictional language and the fictive nature of philosophical discourse. The connections between fiction and philosophy—"Novelist and philosopher," Gass writes, "are both obsessed with language, and make themselves up out of concepts"—are the subject of Gass's most influential work of criticism, *Fiction and the Figures of Life* (1970).

Gass's fiction is marked by prose that deliberately calls attention to itself; he writes, as Walker Percy has observed, "a poet's prose." Gass's experiments with fiction, essays, and criticism, furthermore, show a mind not content with conventional distinctions of genre. His essays, in their rhythm and metaphorical energy, often sound like fiction—he has, in fact, called one of his books, *Willie Master's Lonesome Wife* (1971), an "essay-novella." And his fiction, as "In the Heart of the Heart of the Country" shows, can at times read like an essay. "I think of myself," Gass has commented, "as a writer of prose rather than a novelist, critic, or story-teller, and I am principally interested in the problems of style. My fictions are, by and large, experimental constructions; that is, I try to make things out of words the way a sculptor might make a statue out of stone.

Readers will therefore find very little in the way of character or story in my stories."

Gass's first novel, *Omensetter's Luck* (1966), demonstrates the overwhelming importance of language in his fiction. Although it deals with a religious confrontation between two men, one naturally innocent and the other a deranged preacher, its main action is not so much in its narrative as in its rhetoric. In nearly all of Gass's fiction, the conventional "elements" of storytelling—action, character, and setting—become submerged in the rhythms, playfulness, and density of language. Characters, Gass likes to remind readers, are not flesh-and-blood, visible, recognizable people but verbal constructs, creations of an author, words on a page. More important for a reader than understanding an author's characters is understanding how the reader enters the author's sentences, where the real life of literature is to be found.

In both his second and his third collections of essays on criticism and aesthetic theory, *The World Within the Word* (1978) and *The Habitations of the Word: Essays* (1985), Gass writes admiringly of the achievement of Gertrude Stein, for whom "pure composition" was a literary ideal. In his 1976 philosophic essay *On Being Blue,* Gass makes us feel the presence of Gertrude Stein behind his rich, punning, allusional style, a style that impresses us with the physical nature of language rather than with what it communicates. Gass's writing accordingly operates at the edge of ordinary communication. "In every art," he writes, "two contradictory impulses are in a state of Manichean war: the impulse to communicate and so to treat the medium of communication as a means, and the impulse to make an artifact out of the materials of the medium and so to treat the medium as an end."

Further Reading:
E. W. Bruss, *Beautiful Theories: The Spectacle of Discourse in Contemporary Criticism,* 1982.
L. McCaffery, *The Metafictional Muse,* 1982.

Text:
In the Heart of the Heart of the Country, 1968.

In the Heart of the Heart
of the Country

A Place

So I have sailed the seas and come . . .

to B . . .[1]

a small town fastened to a field in Indiana. Twice there have been twelve hundred people here to answer to the census. The town is outstandingly neat and shady, and always puts its best side to the highway. On one lawn there's even a wood or plastic iron deer.

[1] From "Byzantium," by the Irish poet William Butler Yeats (1865–1939).

You can reach us by crossing a creek. In the spring the lawns are green, the forsythia is singing, and even the railroad that guts the town has straight bright rails which hum when the train is coming, and the train itself has a welcome horning sound.

Down the back streets the asphalt crumbles into gravel. There's Westbrook's, with the geraniums, Horsefall's, Mott's. The sidewalk shatters. Gravel dust rises like breath behind the wagons. And I am in retirement from love.

Weather

In the Midwest, around the lower Lakes, the sky in the winter is heavy and close, and it is a rare day, a day to remark on, when the sky lifts and allows the heart up. I am keeping count, and as I write this page, it is eleven days since I have seen the sun.

My House

There's a row of headless maples behind my house, cut to free the passage of electric wires. High stumps, ten feet tall, remain, and I climb these like a boy to watch the country sail away from me. They are ordinary fields, a little more uneven than they should be, since in the spring they puddle. The topsoil's thin, but only moderately stony. Corn is grown one year, soybeans another. At dusk starlings darken the single tree—a larch—which stands in the middle. When the sky moves, fields move under it. I feel, on my perch, that I've lost my years. It's as though I were living at last in my eyes, as I have always dreamed of doing, and I think then I know why I've come here: to see, and so to go out against new things—oh god how easily—like air in a breeze. It's true there are moments—foolish moments, ecstasy on a tree stump— when I'm all but gone, scattered I like to think like seed, for I'm the sort now in the fool's position of having love left over which I'd like to lose; what good is it now to me, candy ungiven after Halloween?

A Person

There are vacant lots on either side of Billy Holsclaw's house. As the weather improves, they fill with hollyhocks. From spring through fall, Billy collects coal and wood and puts the lumps and pieces in piles near his door, for keeping warm is his one work. I see him most often on mild days sitting on his doorsill in the sun. I notice he's squinting a little, which is perhaps the reason he doesn't cackle as I pass. His house is the size of a single garage, and very old. It shed its paint with its youth, and its boards are a warped and weathered gray. So is Billy. He wears a short lumpy faded black coat when it's cold, otherwise he always goes about in the same loose, grease-spotted shirt and trousers. I suspect his galluses[2] were yellow once, when they were new.

Wires

These wires offend me. Three trees were maimed on their account, and now these wires deface the sky. They cross like a fence in front of me, enclosing the crows with

---

[2] Suspenders.

the clouds. I can't reach in, but like a stick, I throw my feelings over. What is it that offends me? I am on my stump, I've built a platform there and the wires prevent my going out. The cut trees, the black wires, all the beyond birds therefore anger me. When I've wormed through a fence to reach a meadow, do I ever feel the same about the field?

The Church

The church has a steeple like the hat of a witch, and five birds, all doves, perch in its gutters.

My House

Leaves move in the windows. I cannot tell you yet how beautiful it is, what it means. But they do move. They move in the glass.

Politics

. . . for all those not in love.

I've heard Batista[3] described as a Mason.[4] A farmer who'd seen him in Miami made this claim. He's as nice a fellow as you'd ever want to meet. Of Castro, of course, no one speaks.

For all those not in love there's law: to rule . . . to regulate . . . to rectify. I cannot write the poetry of such proposals, the poetry of politics, though sometimes—often —always now—I am in that uneasy peace of equal powers which makes a State; then I communicate by passing papers, proclamations, orders, through my bowels. Yet I was not a State with you, nor were we both together any Indiana. A squad of Pershing Rifles at the moment, I make myself Right Face! Legislation packs the screw of my intestines. Well, king of the classroom's king of the hill. You used to waddle when you walked because my sperm between your legs was draining to a towel. Teacher, poet, folded lover—like the politician, like those drunkards, ill, or those who faucet-off while pissing heartily to preach upon the force and fullness of that stream, or pause from vomiting to praise the purity and passion of their puke—I chant, I beg, I orate, I command, I sing—

Come back to Indiana—not too late!
  (Or will you be a ranger to the end?)
Good-bye . . . Good-bye . . . oh, I shall always wait
  You, Larry, traveler—
            stranger,
                son,
              —my friend—

my little girl, my poem by heart, my self, my childhood.

But I've heard Batista described as a Mason. That dries up my pity, melts my hate.

---

[3] Fulgencio Batista, dictator of Cuba from 1940 to 1944 and from 1952 to 1959, was deposed by Fidel Castro and his revolutionary forces.   [4] Member of the Masonic fraternity, an oath-bound fraternity emphasizing religion and good moral character.

Back from the garage where I have overheard it, I slap the mended fender of my car to laugh, and listen to the metal stinging tartly in my hand.

People

Their hair in curlers and their heads wrapped in loud scarves, young mothers, fattish in trousers, lounge about in the speedwash, smoking cigarettes, eating candy, drinking pop, thumbing magazines, and screaming at their children above the whir and rumble of the machines.

At the bank a young man freshly pressed is letting himself in with a key. Along the street, delicately teetering, many grandfathers move in a dream. During the murderous heat of summer, they perch on window ledges, their feet dangling just inside the narrow shelf of shade the store has made, staring steadily into the street. Where their consciousness has gone I can't say. It's not in the eyes. Perhaps it's diffuse, all temperature and skin, like an infant's, though more mild. Near the corner there are several large overalled men employed in standing. A truck turns to be weighed on the scales at the Feed and Grain. Images drift on the drugstore window. The wind has blown the smell of cattle into town. Our eyes have been driven in like the eyes of the old men. And there's no one to have mercy on us.

Vital Data

There are two restaurants here and a tearoom. two bars. one bank, three barbers, one with a green shade with which he blinds his window. two groceries. a dealer in Fords. one drug, one hardware, and one appliance store. several that sell feed, grain, and farm equipment. an antique shop. a poolroom. a laundromat. three doctors. a dentist. a plumber. a vet. a funeral home in elegant repair the color of a buttercup. numerous beauty parlors which open and shut like night-blooming plants. a tiny dime and department store of no width but several floors. a hutch, homemade, where you can order, after lying down or squirming in, furniture that's been fashioned from bent lengths of stainless tubing, glowing plastic, metallic thread, and clear shellac. an American Legion Post and a root beer stand. little agencies for this and that: cosmetics, brushes, insurance, greeting cards and garden produce—anything—sample shoes— which do their business out of hats and satchels, over coffee cups and dissolving sugar. a factory for making paper sacks and pasteboard boxes that's lodged in an old brick building bearing the legend OPERA HOUSE, still faintly golden, on its roof. a library given by Carnegie. a post office. a school. a railroad station. fire station. lumberyard. telephone company. welding shop. garage . . . and spotted through the town from one end to the other in a line along the highway, gas stations to the number five.

Education

In 1833, Colin Goodykoontz, an itinerant preacher with a name from a fairytale, summed up the situation in one Indiana town this way:

> Ignorance and her squalid brood. A universal dearth of intellect. Total abstinence from literature is very generally practiced. . . . There is not a scholar in grammar or geography, or a *teacher capable of instructing* in them, to my knowl-

edge. . . . Others are supplied a few months of the year with the most antiquated & unreasonable forms of teaching reading, writing & cyphering. . . . Need I stop to remind you of the host of loathsome reptiles such a stagnant pool is fitted to breed! Croaking jealousy; bloated bigotry; coiling suspicion; wormish blindness; crocodile malice!

Things have changed since then, but in none of the respects mentioned.

Business

One side section of street is blocked off with sawhorses. Hard, thin, bitter men in blue jeans, cowboy boots and hats, untruck a dinky carnival. The merchants are promoting themselves. There will be free rides, raucous music, parades and coneys, pop, popcorn, candy, cones, awards and drawings, with all you can endure of pinch, push, bawl, shove, shout, scream, shriek, and bellow. Children pedal past on decorated bicycles, their wheels a blur of color, streaming crinkled paper and excited dogs. A little later there's a pet show for a prize—dogs, cats, birds, sheep, ponies, goats—none of which wins. The whirlabouts whirl about. The Ferris wheel climbs dizzily into the sky as far as a tall man on tiptoe might be persuaded to reach, and the irritated operators measure the height and weight of every child with sour eyes to see if they are safe for the machines. An electrical megaphone repeatedly trumpets the names of the generous sponsors. The following day they do not allow the refuse to remain long in the street.

My House, This Place and Body

I have met with some mischance, wings withering, as Plato says obscurely, and across the breadth of Ohio, like heaven on a table, I've fallen as far as the poet, to the sixth sort of body, this house in B, in Indiana, with its blue and gray bewitching windows, holy magical insides. Great thick evergreens protect its entry. And I live *in*.

Lost in the corn rows, I remember feeling just another stalk, and thus this country takes me over in the way I occupy myself when I am well . . . completely—to the edge of both my house and body. No one notices, when they walk by, that I am brimming in the doorways. My house, this place and body, I've come in mourning to be born in. To anybody else it's pretty silly: love. Why should I feel a loss? How am I bereft? She was never mine; she was a fiction, always a golden tomgirl, barefoot, with an adolescent's slouch and a boy's taste for sports and fishing, a figure out of Twain, or worse, in Riley. Age cannot be kind.

There's little hand-in-hand here . . . not in B. No one touches except in rage. Occasionally girls will twine their arms about each other and lurch along, school out, toward home and play. I dreamed my lips would drift down your back like a skiff on a river. I'd follow a vein with the point of my finger, hold your bare feet in my naked hands.

The Same Person

Billy Holsclaw lives alone—how alone it is impossible to fathom. In the post office he talks greedily to me about the weather. His head bobs on a wild flood of words, and I take this violence to be a measure of his eagerness for speech. He badly needs a shave, coal dust has layered his face, he spits when he speaks, and his fingers pick at his tatters. He wobbles out in the wind when I leave him, a paper sack mashed in the fold of his arm, the leaves blowing past him, and our encounter drives me sadly home to poetry—where there's no answer. Billy closes his door and carries coal or wood to his fire and closes his eyes, and there's simply no way of knowing how lonely and empty he is or whether he's as vacant and barren and loveless as the rest of us are—here in the heart of the country.

Weather

For we're always out of luck here. That's just how it is—for instance in the winter. The sides of the buildings, the roofs, the limbs of the trees are gray. Streets, sidewalks, faces, feelings—they are gray. Speech is gray, and the grass where it shows. Every flank and front, each top is gray. Everything is gray: hair, eyes, window glass, the hawkers' bills and touters' posters, lips, teeth, poles and metal signs—they're gray, quite gray. Cars are gray. Boots, shoes, suits, hats, gloves are gray. Horses, sheep, and cows, cats killed in the road, squirrels in the same way, sparrows, doves, and pigeons, all are gray, everything is gray, and everyone is out of luck who lives here.

A similar haze turns the summer sky milky, and the air muffles your head and shoulders like a sweater you've got caught in. In the summer light, too, the sky darkens a moment when you open your eyes. The heat is pure distraction. Steeped in our fluids, miserable in the folds of our bodies, we can scarcely think of anything but our sticky parts. Hot cyclonic winds and storms of dust crisscross the country. In many places, given an indifferent push, the wind will still coast for miles, gathering resource and edge as it goes, cunning and force. According to the season, paper, leaves, field litter, seeds, snow, fill up the fences. Sometimes I think the land is flat because the winds have leveled it, they blow so constantly. In any case, a gale can grow in a field of corn that's as hot as a draft from hell, and to receive it is one of the most dismaying experiences of this life, though the smart of the same wind in winter is more humiliating, and in that sense even worse. But in the spring it rains as well, and the trees fill with ice.

Place

Many small Midwestern towns are nothing more than rural slums, and this community could easily become one. Principally during the first decade of the century, though there were many earlier instances, well-to-do farmers moved to town and built fine homes to contain them in their retirement. Others desired a more social life, and so lived in, driving to their fields like storekeepers to their businesses. These houses are now dying like the bereaved who inhabit them; they are slowly losing their senses —deafness, blindness, forgetfulness, mumbling, an insecure gait, an uncontrollable trembling has overcome them. Some kind of Northern Snopes[5] will occupy them next: large-familied, Catholic, Democratic, scrambling, vigorous, poor; and since the par-

---

[5] Family in the fiction of William Faulkner, including the story "Spotted Horses."

ents will work in larger, nearby towns, the children will be loosed upon themselves and upon the hapless neighbors much as the fabulous Khan[6] loosed his legendary horde. These Snopes will undertake makeshift repairs with materials that other people have thrown away; paint halfway round their house, then quit; almost certainly maintain an ugly loud cantankerous dog and underfeed a pair of cats to keep the rodents down. They will collect piles of possibly useful junk in the back yard, park their cars in the front, live largely leaning over engines, give not a hoot for the land, the old community, the hallowed ways, the established clans. Weakening widow ladies have already begun to hire large rude youths from families such as these to rake and mow and tidy the grounds they will inherit.

People

In the cinders at the station boys sit smoking steadily in darkened cars, their arms bent out the windows, white shirts glowing behind the glass. Nine o'clock is the best time. They sit in a line facing the highway—two or three or four of them—idling their engines. As you walk by a machine may growl at you or a pair of headlights flare up briefly. In a moment one will pull out, spinning cinders behind it, to stalk impatiently up and down the dark streets or roar half a mile into the country before returning to its place in line and pulling up.

My House, My Cat, My Company

I must organize myself. I must, as they say, pull myself together, dump this cat from my lap, stir—yes, resolve, move, do. But do what? My will is like the rosy dustlike light in this room: soft, diffuse, and gently comforting. It lets me do . . . anything . . . nothing. My ears hear what they happen to; I eat what's put before me; my eyes see what blunders into them; my thoughts are not thoughts, they are dreams. I'm empty or I'm full . . . depending; and I cannot choose. I sink my claws in Tick's fur and scratch the bones of his back until his rear rises amorously. Mr. Tick, I murmur, I must organize myself. I must pull myself together. And Mr. Tick rolls over on his belly, all ooze.

I spill Mr. Tick when I've rubbed his stomach. Shoo. He steps away slowly, his long tail rhyming with his paws. How beautifully he moves, I think; how beautifully, like you, he commands his loving, how beautifully he accepts. So I rise and wander from room to room, up and down, gazing through most of my forty-one windows. How well this house receives its loving too. Let out like Mr. Tick, my eyes sink in the shrubbery. I am not here; I've passed the glass, passed second-story spaces, flown by branches, brilliant berries, to the ground, grass high in seed and leafage every season; and it is the same as when I passed above you in my aged, ardent body; it's, in short, a kind of love; and I am learning to restore myself, my house, my body, by paying court to gardens, cats, and running water, and with neighbors keeping company.

Mrs. Desmond is my right-hand friend; she's eighty-five. A thin white mist of hair, fine and tangled, manifests the climate of her mind. She is habitually suspicious, fretful,

---

[6] Genghis Khan (1162–1227), Mongolian conqueror.

nervous. Burglars break in at noon. Children trespass. Even now they are shaking the pear tree, stealing rhubarb, denting lawn. Flies caught in the screens and numbed by frost awake in the heat to buzz and scrape the metal cloth and frighten her, though she is deaf to me, and consequently cannot hear them. Boards creak, the wind whistles across the chimney mouth, drafts cruise like fish through the hollow rooms. It is herself she hears, her own flesh failing, for only death will preserve her from those daily chores she climbs like stairs, and all that anxious waiting. Is it now, she wonders. No? Then: is it now?

We do not converse. She visits me to talk. My task to murmur. She talks about her grandsons, her daughter who lives in Delphi, her sister or her husband—both gone —obscure friends—dead—obscurer aunts and uncles—lost—ancient neighbors, members of her church or of her clubs—passed or passing on; and in this way she brings the ends of her life together with a terrifying rush: she is a girl, a wife, a mother, widow, all at once. All at once—appalling—but I believe it; I wince in expectation of the clap. Her talk's a fence—a shade drawn, window fastened, door that's locked —for no one dies taking tea in a kitchen; and as her years compress and begin to jumble, I really believe in the brevity of life; I sweat in my wonder; death is the dog down the street, the angry gander, bedroom spider, goblin who's come to get her; and it occurs to me that in my listening posture I'm the boy who suffered the winds of my grandfather with an exactly similar politeness, that I am, right now, all my ages, out in elbows, as angular as badly stacked cards. Thus was I, when I loved you, every man I could be, youth and child—far from enough—and you, so strangely ambiguous a being, met me, heart for spade, play after play, the whole run of our suits.

Mr. Tick, you do me honor. You not only lie in my lap, but you remain alive there, coiled like a fetus. Through your deep nap, I feel you hum. You are, and are not, a machine. You are alive, alive exactly, and it means nothing to you—much to me. You are a cat—you cannot understand—you are a cat so easily. Your nature is not something you must rise to. You, not I, live in: in house, in skin, in shrubbery. Yes. I think I shall hat my head with a steeple; turn church; devour people. Mr. Tick, though, has a tail he can twitch, he need not fly his Fancy. Claws, not metrical schema, poetry his paws; while smoothing . . . smoothing . . . smoothing roughly, his tongue laps its neatness. O Mr. Tick, I know you; you are an electrical penis. Go on now, shoo. Mrs. Desmond doesn't like you. She thinks you will tangle yourself in her legs and she will fall. You murder her birds, she knows, and walk upon her roof with death in your jaws. I must gather myself together for a bound. What age is it I'm at right now, I wonder. The heart, don't they always say, keeps the true time. Mrs. Desmond is knocking. Faintly, you'd think, but she pounds. She's brought me a cucumber. I believe she believes I'm a woman. Come in, Mrs. Desmond, thank you, be my company, it looks lovely, and have tea. I'll slice it, crisp, with cream, for luncheon, each slice as thin as me.

Politics

O all ye isolate and separate powers, Sing! Sing, and sing in such a way that from a distance it will seem a harmony, a Strindberg[7] play, a friendship ring . . . so happy

---

[7] August Strindberg (1849–1912), Swedish playwright and novelist.

—happy, happy, happy—as here we go hand in handling, up and down. Our union was a singing, though we were silent in the songs we sang like single notes are silent in a symphony. In no sense sober, we barbershopped together and never heard the discords in our music or saw ourselves as dirty, cheap, or silly. Yet cats have worn out better shoes than those thrown through our love songs at us. Hush. Be patient —prudent—politic. Still, Cleveland killed you, Mr. Crane.[8] Were you not politic enough and fond of being beaten? Like a piece of sewage, the city shat you from its stern three hundred miles from history—beyond the loving reach of sailors. Well, I'm not a poet who puts Paris to his temple in his youth to blow himself from Idaho, or—fancy that—Missouri. My god, I said, this is my country, but must my country go so far as Terre Haute or Whiting, go so far as Gary?

When the Russians first announced the launching of their satellite, many people naturally refused to believe them. Later others were outraged that they had sent a dog around the earth. I wouldn't want to take that mutt from out that metal flying thing if he's still living when he lands, our own dog catcher said; anybody knows you shut a dog up by himself to toss around the first thing he'll be setting on to do you let him out is bite somebody.

This Midwest. A dissonance of parts and people, we are a consonance of Towns. Like a man grown fat in everything but heart, we overlabor; our outlook never really urban, never rural either, we enlarge and linger at the same time, as Alice both changed and remained in her story. You are blond. I put my hand upon your belly; feel it tremble from my trembling. We always drive large cars in my section of the country. How could you be a comfort to me now?

More Vital Data

The town is exactly fifty houses, trailers, stores, and miscellaneous buildings long, but in places no streets deep. It takes on width as you drive south, always adding to the east. Most of the dwellings are fairly spacious farm houses in the customary white, with wide wraparound porches and tall narrow windows, though there are many of the grander kind—fretted, scalloped, turreted, and decorated with clapboards set at angles or on end, with stained-glass windows at the stair landings and lots of wrought iron full of fancy curls—and a few of these look like castles in their rarer brick. Old stables serve as garages now, and the lots are large to contain them and the vegetable and flower gardens which, ultimately, widows plant and weed and then entirely disappear in. The shade is ample, the grass is good, the sky a glorious fall violet; the apple trees are heavy and red, the roads are calm and empty; corn has sifted from the chains of tractored wagons to speckle the streets with gold and with the russet fragments of the cob, and a man would be a fool who wanted, blessed with this, to live anywhere else in the world.

Education

Buses like great orange animals move through the early light to school. There the children will be taught to read and warned against Communism. By Miss Janet Jakes. That's not her name. Her name is Helen something—Scott or James. A teacher twenty

[8] Hart Crane (1899–1932), American poet.

years. She's now worn fine and smooth, and has a face, Wilfred says, like a mail-order ax. Her voice is hoarse, and she has a cough. For she screams abuse. The children stare, their faces blank. This is the thirteenth week. They are used to it. You will all, she shouts, you will all draw pictures of me. No. She is a Mrs.—someone's missus. And in silence they set to work while Miss Jakes jabs hairpins in her hair. Wilfred says an ax, but she has those rimless tinted glasses, graying hair, an almost dimpled chin. I must concentrate. I must stop making up things. I must give myself to life; let it mold me: that's what they say in *Wisdom's Monthly Digest* every day. Enough, enough —you've been at it long enough; and the children rise formally a row at a time to present their work to her desk. No, she wears rims; it's her chin that's dimpleless. Well, it will take more than a tablespoon of features to sweeten that face. So she grimly shuffles their sheets, examines her reflection crayoned on them. I would not dare . . . allow a child . . . to put a line around me. Though now and then she smiles like a nick in the blade, in the end these drawings depress her. I could not bear it—how can she ask?—that anyone . . . draw me. Her anger's lit. That's why she does it: flame. There go her eyes; the pink in her glasses brightens, dims. She is a pumpkin, and her rage is breathing like the candle in. No, she shouts, no—the cartoon trembling—no, John Mauck, John Stewart Mauck, this will not do. The picture flutters from her fingers. You've made me too muscular.

I work on my poetry. I remember my friends, associates, my students, by their names. Their names are Maypop, Dormouse, Upsydaisy. Their names are Gladiolus, Callow Bladder, Prince and Princess Oleo, Hieronymus, Cardinal Mummum, Mr. Fitchew, The Silken Howdah, Spot. Sometimes you're Tom Sawyer, Huckleberry Finn; it is perpetually summer; your buttocks are my pillow; we are adrift on a raft; your back is our river. Sometimes you are Major Barbara,[9] sometimes a goddess who kills men in battle, sometimes you are soft like a shower of water; you are bread in my mouth.

I do not work on my poetry. I forget my friends, associates, my students, and their names: Gramophone, Blowgun, Pickle, Serenade . . . Marge the Barge, Arena, Uberhaupt . . . Doctor Dildoe, The Fog Machine. For I am now in B, in Indiana: out of job and out of patience, out of love and time and money, out of bread and out of body, in a temper, Mrs. Desmond, out of tea. So shut your fist up, bitch, you bag of death; go bang another door; go die, my dearie. Die, life-deaf old lady. Spill your breath. Fall over like a frozen board. Gray hair grows from the nose of your mind. You are a skull already—*memento mori*[10]—the foreskin retracts from your teeth. Will your plastic gums last longer than your bones, and color their grinning? And is your twot still hazel-hairy, or are you bald as a ditch? . . . bitch . . . . . . bitch . . . . bitch. I wanted to be famous, but you bring me age—my emptiness. Was it *that* which I thought would balloon me above the rest? Love? where are you? . . . love me. I want to rise so high, I said, that when I shit I won't miss anybody.

Business

For most people, business is poor. Nearby cities have siphoned off all but a neighborhood trade. Except for feed and grain and farm supplies, you stand a chance to sell

[9] Heroine of *Major Barbara,* by George Bernard Shaw (1856–1950). [10] Latin: "reminder of death."

only what one runs out to buy. Chevrolet has quit, and Frigidaire. A locker plant has left its afterimage. The lumberyard has been, so far, six months about its going. Gas stations change hands clumsily, a restaurant becomes available, a grocery closes. One day they came and knocked the cornices from the watch repair and pasted campaign posters on the windows. Torn across, by now, by boys, they urge you still to vote for half an orange beblazoned man who as a whole one failed two years ago to win at his election. Everywhere, in this manner, the past speaks, and it mostly speaks of failure. The empty stores, the old signs and dusty fixtures, the debris in alleys, the flaking paint and rusty gutters, the heavy locks and sagging boards: they say the same disagreeable things. What do the sightless windows see, I wonder, when the sun throws a passerby against them? Here a stair unfolds toward the street—dark, rickety, and treacherous—and I always feel, as I pass it, that if I just went carefully up and turned the corner at the landing, I would find myself out of the world. But I've never had the courage.

That Same Person

The weeds catch up with Billy. In pursuit of the hollyhocks, they rise in coarse clumps all around the front of his house. Billy has to stamp down a circle by his door like a dog or cat does turning round to nest up, they're so thick. What particularly troubles me is that winter will find the weeds still standing stiff and tindery to take the sparks which Billy's little mortarless chimney spouts. It's true that fires are fun here. The town whistle, which otherwise only blows for noon (and there's no noon on Sunday), signals the direction of the fire by the length and number of its blasts, the volunteer firemen rush past in their cars and trucks, houses empty their owners along the street every time like an illustration in a children's book. There are many bikes, too, and barking dogs, and sometimes—hallelujah—the fire's right here in town—a vacant lot of weeds and stubble flaming up. But I'd rather it weren't Billy or Billy's lot or house. Quite selfishly I want him to remain the way he is—counting his sticks and logs, sitting on his sill in the soft early sun—though I'm not sure what his presence means to me . . . or to anyone. Nevertheless, I keep wondering whether, given time, I might not someday find a figure in our language which would serve him faithfully, and furnish his poverty and loneliness richly out.

Wires

Where sparrows sit like fists. Doves fly the steeple. In mist the wires change perspective, rise and twist. If they led to you, I would know what they were. Thoughts passing often, like the starlings who flock these fields at evening to sleep in the trees beyond, would form a family of paths like this; they'd foot down the natural height of air to just about a bird's perch. But they do not lead to you.

> Of whose beauty it was sung
> She shall make the old man young.

They fasten me.

If I walked straight on, in my present mood, I would reach the Wabash.[11] It's not

[11] River in Indiana.

a mood in which I'd choose to conjure you. Similes dangle like baubles from me. This time of year the river is slow and shallow, the clay banks crack in the sun, weeds surprise the sandbars. The air is moist and I am sweating. It's impossible to rhyme in this dust. Everything—sky, the cornfield, stump, wild daisies, my old clothes and pressless feelings—seem fabricated for installment purchase. Yes. Christ. I am suffering a summer Christmas; and I cannot walk under the wires. The sparrows scatter like handfuls of gravel. Really, wires are voices in thin strips. They are words wound in cables. Bars of connection.

Weather

I would rather it were the weather that was to blame for what I am and what my friends and neighbors are—we who live here in the heart of the country. Better the weather, the wind, the pale dying snow . . . the snow—why not the snow? There's never much really, not around the lower Lakes anyway, not enough to boast about, not enough to be useful. My father tells how the snow in the Dakotas would sweep to the roofs of the barns in the old days, and he and his friends could sled on the crust that would form because the snow was so fiercely driven. In Bemidji[12] trees have been known to explode. That would be something—if the trees in Davenport or Francisville or Carbondale or Niles were to go blam some winter—blam! blam! blam! all the way down the gray, cindery, snow-sick streets.

A cold fall rain is blackening the trees or the air is like lilac and full of parachuting seeds. Who cares to live in any season but his own? Still I suspect the secret's in this snow, the secret of our sickness, if we could only diagnose it, for we are all dying like the elms in Urbana. This snow—like our skin it covers the country. Later dust will do it. Right now—snow. Mud presently. But it is snow without any laughter in it, a pale gray pudding thinly spread on stiff toast, and if that seems a strange description, it's accurate all the same. Of course soot blackens everything, but apart from that, we are never sufficiently cold here. The flakes as they come, alive and burning, we cannot retain, for if our temperatures fall, they rise promptly again, just as, in the summer, they bob about in the same feckless way. Suppose though . . . suppose they were to rise some August, climb and rise, and then hang in the hundreds like a hawk through December, what a desert we could make of ourselves—from Chicago to Cairo, from Hammond to Columbus—what beautiful Death Valleys.

Place

I would rather it were the weather. It drives us in upon ourselves—an unlucky fate. Of course there is enough to stir our wonder anywhere; there's enough to love, anywhere, if one is strong enough, if one is diligent enough, if one is perceptive, patient, kind enough—whatever it takes; and surely it's better to live in the country, to live on a prairie by a drawing of rivers, in Iowa or Illinois or Indiana, say, than in any city, in any stinking fog of human beings, in any blooming orchard of machines. It ought to be. The cities are swollen and poisonous with people. It ought

---

[12] City in northern Minnesota; references follow
to a number of Midwestern towns and cities.

to be better. Man has never been a fit environment for man—for rats, maybe, rats do nicely, or for dogs or cats and the household beetle.

And how long the street is, nowadays. These endless walls are fallen to keep back the tides of earth. Brick could be beautiful but we have covered it gradually with gray industrial vomits. Age does not make concrete genial, and asphalt is always— like America—twenty-one, until it breaks up in crumbs like stale cake. The brick, the asphalt, the concrete, the dancing signs and garish posters, the feed and excrement of the automobile, the litter of its inhabitants: they compose, they decorate, they line our streets, and there is nowhere, nowadays, our streets can't reach.

A man in the city has no natural thing by which to measure himself. His parks are potted plants. Nothing can live and remain free where he resides but the pigeon, starling, sparrow, spider, cockroach, mouse, moth, fly and weed, and he laments the existence of even these and makes his plans to poison them. The zoo? There *is* the zoo. Through its bars the city man stares at the great cats and dully sucks his ice. Living, alas, among men and their marvels, the city man supposes that his happiness depends on establishing, somehow, a special kind of harmonious accord with others. The novelists of the city, of slums and crowds, they call it love—and break their pens.

Wordsworth[13] feared the accumulation of men in cities. He foresaw their "degrad- ing thirst after outrageous stimulation," and some of their hunger for love. Living in a city, among so many, dwelling in the heat and tumult of incessant movement, a man's affairs are touch and go—that's all. It's not surprising that the novelists of the slums, the cities, and the crowds, should find that sex is but a scratch to ease a tickle, that we're most human when we're sitting on the john, and that the justest image of our life is in full passage through the plumbing.

> That man, immur'd in cities, still retains
> His inborn inextinguishable thirst
> Of rural scenes, compensating his loss
> By supplemental shifts, the best he may.[14]

Come into the country, then. The air nimbly and sweetly recommends itself unto our gentle senses.[15] Here, growling tractors tear the earth. Dust roils up behind them. Drivers sit jouncing under bright umbrellas. They wear refrigerated hats and steer by looking at the tracks they've cut behind them, their transistors blaring. Close to the land, are they? good companions to the soil? Tell me: do they live in harmony with the alternating seasons?

It's a lie of old poetry. The modern husbandman uses chemicals from cylinders and sacks, spike-ball-and-claw machines, metal sheds, and cost accounting. Nature in the old sense does not matter. It does not exist. Our farmer's only mystical attachment is to parity.[16] And if he does not realize that cows and corn are simply different kinds of chemical engine, he cannot expect to make a go of it.

It isn't necessary to suppose our cows have feelings; our neighbor hasn't as many

---

[13] William Wordsworth (1770–1850), English Romantic poet.
[14] Lines 767–770 of Book 4, "The Winter Evening," from the long poem *The Task* (1785) by William Cowper (1731–1800).

[15] King Duncan's description of the castle where he will be murdered, in Shakespeare's *Macbeth*, Act. I, Sc. vi, ll. 1–3.
[16] Government support of prices for farm goods.

as he used to have either; but think of it this way a moment, you can correct for the human imputations later: how would it feel to nurse those strange tentacled calves with their rubber, glass, and metal lips, their stainless eyes?

People

Aunt Pet's still able to drive her car—a high square Ford—even though she walks with difficulty and a stout stick. She has a watery gaze, a smooth plump face despite her age, and jet black hair in a bun. She has the slowest smile of anyone I ever saw, but she hates dogs, and not very long ago cracked the back of one she cornered in her garden. To prove her vigor she will tell you this, her smile breaking gently while she raises the knob of her stick to the level of your eyes.

House, My Breath and Window

My window is a grave, and all that lies within it's dead. No snow is falling. There's no haze. It is not still, not silent. Its images are not an animal that waits, for movement is no demonstration. I have seen the sea slack, life bubble through a body without a trace, its spheres impervious as soda's. Downwound, the whore at wagtag clicks and clacks. Leaves wiggle. Grass sways. A bird chirps, pecks the ground. An auto wheel in penning circles keeps its rigid spokes. These images are stones; they are memorials. Beneath this sea lies sea: god rest it . . . rest the world beyond my window, me in front of my reflection, above this page, my shade. Death is not so still, so silent, since silence implies a falling quiet, stillness a stopping, containing, holding in; for death is time in a clock, like Mr. Tick, electric . . . like wind through a windup poet. And my blear floats out to visible against the glass, befog its country and bespill myself. The mist lifts slowly from the fields in the morning. No one now would say: the Earth throws back its covers; it is rising from sleep. Why is the feeling foolish? The image is too Greek. I used to gaze at you so wantonly your body blushed. Imagine: wonder: that my eyes could cause such flowering. Ah, my friend, your face is pale, the weather cloudy; a street has been felled through your chin, bare trees do nothing, houses take root in their rectangles, a steeple stands up in your head. You speak of loving; then give me a kiss. The pane is cold. On icy mornings the fog rises to greet me (as you always did); the barns and other buildings, rather than ghostly, seem all the more substantial for looming, as if they grew in themselves while I watched (as you always did). Oh my approach, I suppose, was like breath in a rubber monkey. Nevertheless, on the road along the Wabash in the morning, though the trees are sometimes obscured by fog, their reflection floats serenely on the river, reasoning the banks, the sycamores in French rows. Magically, the world tips. I'm led to think that only those who grow down live (which will scarcely win me twenty-five from *Wisdom's Monthly Digest*), but I find I write that only those who live down grow; and what I write, I hold, whatever I really know. My every word's inverted, or reversed—or I am. I held you, too, that way. You were so utterly provisional, subject to my change. I could inflate your bosom with a kiss, disperse your skin with gentleness, enter your vagina from within, and make my love emerge like a fresh sex. The pane is cold. Honesty is cold, my inside lover. The sun looks, through the mist, like a plum on the tree of heaven, or a bruise on the slope of your belly. Which? The grass crawls with frost. We meet on this window, the world and I, inelegantly, swimmers of the glass; and swung wrong way round to one another, the world seems in. The world —how grand, how monumental, grave and deadly, that word is: the world, my house and poetry. All poets have their inside lovers. Wee penis does not belong to me, or any of this foggery. It is *his* property which he's thrust through what's womanly of me to set down this. These wooden houses in their squares, gray streets and fallen sidewalks, standing trees, your name I've written sentimentally across my breath into the whitening air, pale birds: they exist in me now because of him. I gazed with what intensity . . . A bush in the excitement of its roses could not have bloomed so beautifully as you did then. It was a look I'd like to give this page. For that is poetry: to bring within about, to change.

Politics

Sports, politics, and religion are the three passions of the badly educated. They are the Midwest's open sores. Ugly to see, a source of constant discontent, they sap the body's strength. Appalling quantities of money, time, and energy are wasted on them. The rural mind is narrow, passionate, and reckless on these matters. Greed, however shortsighted and direct, will not alone account for it. I have known men, for instance, who for years have voted squarely against their interests. Nor have I ever noticed that their surly Christian views prevented them from urging forward the smithereening, say, of Russia, China, Cuba, or Korea. And they tend to back their country like they back their local team: they have a fanatical desire to win; yelling is their forte; and if things go badly, they are inclined to sack the coach. All in all, then, Birch is a good name. It stands for the bigot's stick, the wild-child-tamer's cane.

Forgetfulness—is that their object?

Oh, I was new, I thought. A fresh start: new cunt, new climate, and new country—there you were, and I was pioneer, and had no history. That language hurts me, too, my dear. You'll never hear it.

Final Vital Data

The Modern Homemakers' Demonstration Club. The Prairie Home Demonstration Club. The Night-outers' Home Demonstration Club. The IOOF, FFF, VFW, WCTU, WSCS, 4-H, 40 and 8, Psi Iota Chi, and PTA . . . The Boy and Girl Scouts, Rainbows, Masons, Indians and Rebekah Lodge. Also the Past Noble Grand Club of the Rebekah Lodge. As well as the Moose and the Ladies of the Moose. The Elks, the Eagles, the Jaynettes and the Eastern Star. The Women's Literary Club, the Hobby Club, the Art Club, the Sunshine Society, the Dorcas Society, the Pythian Sisters, the Pilgrim Youth Fellowship, the American Legion, the American Legion Auxiliary, the American Legion Junior Auxiliary, the Garden Club, the Bridge for Fun Club, the What-can-you-do? Club, the Get Together Club, the Coterie Club, the Worthwhile Club, the Let's Help Our Town Club, the No Name Club, the Forget-me-not Club, the Merry-go-round Club . . .

Education

Has a quarter disappeared from Paula Frosty's pocket book? Imagine the landscape of that face: no crayon could engender it; soft wax is wrong; thin wire in trifling

snips might do the trick. Paula Frosty and Christopher Roger accuse the pale and
splotchy Cheryl Pipes. But Miss Jakes, I saw her. Miss Jakes is so extremely vexed
she snaps her pencil. What else is missing? I appoint you a detective, John: search
her desk. Gum, candy, paper, pencils, marble, round eraser—whose? A thief. I can't
watch her all the time, I'm here to teach. Poor pale fossetted Cheryl, it's determined, can't return the money because she took it home and spent it. Cindy, Janice,
John, and Pete—you four who sit around her—you will be detectives this whole
term to watch her. A thief. In all my time. Miss Jakes turns, unfists, and turns again.
I'll handle you, she cries. To think. A thief. In all my years. Then she writes on the
blackboard the name of Cheryl Pipes and beneath that the figure twenty-five with
a large sign for cents. Now Cheryl, she says, this won't be taken off until you bring
that money out of home, out of home straight up to here, Miss Jakes says, tapping
her desk.

    Which is three days.

Another Person

I was raking leaves when Uncle Halley introduced himself to me. He said his name
came from the comet, and that his mother had borne him prematurely in her fright
of it. I thought of Hobbes,[17] whom fear of the Spanish Armada had hurried into
birth, and so I believed Uncle Halley to honor the philosopher, though Uncle
Halley is a liar, and neither the one hundred twenty-nine nor the fifty-three he
ought to be. That fall the leaves had burned themselves out on the trees, the leaf
lobes had curled, and now they flocked noisily down the street and were broken in
the wires of my rake. Uncle Halley was himself (like Mrs. Desmond and history
generally) both deaf and implacable, and he shooed me down his basement stairs to
a room set aside there for stacks of newspapers reaching to the ceiling, boxes of
leaflets and letters and programs, racks of photo albums, scrapbooks, bundles of
rolled-up posters and maps, flags and pennants and slanting piles of dusty magazines
devoted mostly to motoring and the Christian ethic. I saw a bird cage, a tray of
butterflies, a bugle, a stiff straw boater, and all kinds of tassels tied to a coat tree.
He still possessed and had on display the steering lever from his first car, a linen
duster, driving gloves and goggles, photographs along the wall of himself, his
friends, and his various machines, a shell from the first war, a record of "Ramona"
nailed through its hole to a post, walking sticks and fanciful umbrellas, shoes of all
sorts (his baby shoes, their counters broken, were held in sorrow beneath my nose
—they had not been bronzed, but he might have them done someday before he
died, he said), countless boxes of medals, pins, beads, trinkets, toys, and keys (I
scarcely saw—they flowed like jewels from his palms), pictures of downtown when
it was only a path by the railroad station, a brightly colored globe of the world
with a dent in Poland, antique guns, belt buckles, buttons, souvenir plates and cups
and saucers (I can't remember all of it—I won't), but I recall how shamefully, how
rudely, how abruptly, I fled, a good story in my mouth but death in my nostrils;
and how afterward I busily, righteously, burned my leaves as if I were purging the

---

[17] Thomas Hobbes (1588–1679), English political
philosopher.

world of its years. I still wonder if this town—its life, and mine now—isn't really a record like the one of "Ramona" that I used to crank around on my grandmother's mahogany Victrola through lonely rainy days as a kid.

The First Person

Billy's like the coal he's found: spilled, mislaid, discarded. The sky's no comfort. His house and his body are dying together. His windows are boarded. And now he's reduced to his hands. I suspect he has glaucoma. At any rate he can scarcely see, and weeds his yard of rubble on his hands and knees. Perhaps he's a surgeon cleansing a wound or an ardent and tactile lover. I watch, I must say, apprehensively. Like mine-war detectors, his hands graze in circles ahead of him. Your nipples were the color of your eyes. Pebble. Snarl of paper. Length of twine. He leans down closely, picks up something silvery, holds it near his nose. Foil? cap? coin? He has within him —what, I wonder? Does he know more now because he fingers everything and has to sniff to see? It would be romantic cruelty to think so. He bends the down on your arms like a breeze. You wrote me: something is strange when we don't understand. I write in return: I think when I loved you I fell to my death.

Billy, I could read to you from Beddoes;[18] he's your man perhaps; he held with dying, freed his blood of its arteries; and he said that there were many wretched love-ill fools like me lying alongside the last bone of their former selves, as full of spirit and speech, nonetheless, as Mrs. Desmond, Uncle Halley and the Ferris wheel, Aunt Pet, Miss Jakes, Ramona or the megaphone; yet I reverse him finally, Billy, on no evidence but braggadocio, and I declare that though my inner organs were devoured long ago, the worm which swallowed down my parts still throbs and glows like a crystal palace.

Yes, you were younger. I was Uncle Halley, the museum man and infrequent meteor. Here is my first piece of ass. They weren't so flat in those days, had more round, more juice. And over here's the sperm I've spilled, nicely jarred and clearly labeled. Look at this tape like lengths of intestine where I've stored my spew, the endless worm of words I've written, a hundred million emissions or more: oh I was quite a man right from the start; even when unconscious in my cradle, from crotch to cranium, I was erectile tissue; though mostly, after the manner approved by Plato, I had intercourse by eye. Never mind, old Holsclaw, you are blind. We pull down darkness when we go to bed; put out like Oedipus the actually offending organ, and train our touch to lies. All cats are gray, says Mr. Tick; so under cover of glaucoma you are sack gray too, and cannot be distinguished from a stallion.

I must pull myself together, get a grip, just as they say, but I feel spilled, bewildered, quite mislaid. I did not restore my house to its youth, but to its age. Hunting, you hitch through the hollyhocks. I'm inclined to say you aren't half the cripple I am, for there is nothing left of me but mouth. However, I resist the impulse. It is another lie of poetry. My organs are all there, though it's there where I fail—at the roots of my experience. Poet of the spiritual, Rilke,[19] weren't you? yet that's what you said. Poetry, like love, is—in and out—a physical caress. I can't tolerate any more of my

[18] Thomas Lovell Beddoes (1803–1849), English writer.

[19] Rainer Maria Rilke (1875–1926), German lyric poet.

sophistries about spirit, mind, and breath. Body equals being, and if your weight goes down, you are the less.

Household Apples

I knew nothing about apples. Why should I? My country came in my childhood, and I dreamed of sitting among the blooms like the bees. I failed to spray the pear tree too. I doubled up under them at first, admiring the sturdy low branches I should have pruned, and later I acclaimed the blossoms. Shortly after the fruit formed there were falls—not many—apples the size of goodish stones which made me wobble on my ankles when I walked about the yard. Sometimes a piece crushed by a heel would cling on the shoe to track the house. I gathered a few and heaved them over the wires. A slingshot would have been splendid. Hard, an unattractive green, the worms had them. Before long I realized the worms had them all. Even as the apples reddened, lit their tree, they were being swallowed. The birds preferred the pears, which were small—sugar pears I think they're called—with thick skins of graying green that ripen on toward violet. So the fruit fell, and once I made some applesauce by quartering and paring hundreds; but mostly I did nothing, left them, until suddenly, overnight it seemed, in that ugly late September heat we often have in Indiana, my problem was upon me.

My childhood came in the country. I remember, now, the flies on our snowy luncheon table. As we cleared away they would settle, fastidiously scrub themselves and stroll to the crumbs to feed where I would kill them in crowds with a swatter. It was quite a game to catch them taking off. I struck heavily since I didn't mind a few stains; they'd wash. The swatter was a square of screen bound down in red cloth. It drove no air ahead of it to give them warning. They might have thought they'd flown headlong into a summered window. The faint pink dot where they had died did not rub out as I'd supposed, and after years of use our luncheon linen would faintly, pinkly, speckle.

The country became my childhood. Flies braided themselves on the flypaper in my grandmother's house. I can smell the bakery and the grocery and the stables and the dairy in that small Dakota town I knew as a kid; knew as I dreamed I'd know your body, as I've known nothing, before or since; knew as the flies knew, in the honest, unchaste sense: the burned house, hose-wet, which drew a mist of insects like the blue smoke of its smolder, and gangs of boys, moist-lipped, destructive as its burning. Flies have always impressed me; they are so persistently alive. Now they were coating the ground beneath my trees. Some were ordinary flies; there were the large blue-green ones; there were swarms of fruit flies too, and the red-spotted scavenger beetle; there were a few wasps, several sorts of bees and butterflies—checkers, sulphurs, monarchs, commas, question marks—and delicate dragonflies . . . but principally houseflies and horseflies and bottleflies, flies and more flies in clusters around the rotting fruit. They loved the pears. Inside, they fed. If you picked up a pear, they flew, and the pear became skin and stem. They were everywhere the fruit was: in the tree still—apples like a hive for them—or where the fruit littered the ground, squashing itself as you stepped . . . there was no help for it. The flies droned, feasting on the sweet juice. No one could go near the trees; I could not climb; so I determined at last to labor like Hercules. There were fruit baskets in the barn. Collecting them and kneeling under the branches, I began to gather remains. Deep in the strong rich smell of the fruit, I began to hum myself. The fruit caved in at the touch. Glistening red apples, my lifting disclosed, had families of beetles, flies, and bugs, devouring their rotten undersides. There were streams of flies; there were lakes and cataracts and rivers of flies, seas and oceans. The hum was heavier, higher, than the hum of the bees when they came to the blooms in the spring, though the bees were there, among the flies, ignoring me—ignoring everyone. As my work went on and juice covered my hands and arms, they would form a sleeve, black and moving, like knotty wool. No caress could have been more indifferently complete. Still I rose fearfully, ramming my head in the branches, apples bumping against me before falling, bursting with bugs. I'd snap my hand sharply but the flies would cling to the sweet. I could toss a whole cluster into a basket from several feet. As the pear or apple lit, they would explosively rise, like monads for a moment, windowless,[20] certainly, with respect to one another, sugar their harmony. I had to admit, though, despite my distaste, that my arm had never been more alive, oftener or more gently kissed. Those hundreds of feet were light. In washing them off, I pretended the hose was a pump. What have I missed? Childhood is a lie of poetry.

The Church

Friday night. Girls in dark skirts and white blouses sit in ranks and scream in concert. They carry funnels loosely stuffed with orange and black paper which they shake wildly, and small megaphones through which, as drilled, they direct and magnify their shouting. Their leaders, barely pubescent girls, prance and shake and whirl their skirts above their bloomers. The young men, leaping, extend their arms and race through puddles of amber light, their bodies glistening. In a lull, though it rarely occurs, you can hear the squeak of tennis shoes against the floor. Then the yelling begins again, and then continues; fathers, mothers, neighbors joining in to form a single pulsing ululation—a cry of the whole community—for in this gymnasium each body becomes the bodies beside it, pressed as they are together, thigh to thigh, and the same shudder runs through all of them, and runs toward the same release. Only the ball moves serenely through this dazzling din. Obedient to law it scarcely speaks but caroms quietly and lives at peace.

Business

It is the week of Christmas and the stores, to accommodate the rush they hope for, are remaining open in the evening. You can see snow falling in the cones of the street lamps. The roads are filling—undisturbed. Strings of red and green lights droop over the principal highway, and the water tower wears a star. The windows of the stores have been bedizened. Shamelessly they beckon. But I am alone, leaning against a pole —no . . . there is no one in sight. They're all at home, perhaps by their instruments, tuning in on their evenings, and like Ramona, tirelessly playing and replaying themselves. There's a speaker perched in the tower, and through the boughs of falling

[20] The German philosopher Gottfreid Wilhelm Leibniz (1646–1716) believed the world to be composed of elementary, independent atoms— "windowless monads."

snow and over the vacant streets, it drapes the twisted and metallic strains of a tune that can barely be distinguished—yes, I believe it's one of the jolly ones, it's "Joy to the World." There's no one to hear the music but myself, and though I'm listening, I'm no longer certain. Perhaps the record's playing something else.

1967

James Baldwin
b. 1924

"An artist," says James Baldwin, "is here not to give you answers but to ask you questions." In his long career as a novelist, essayist, and civil rights activist, Baldwin's questions have most often taken the form of moral alternatives. In both his fiction and his essays, he deals with controversial subjects, posing questions about race, politics, sex, and love that address the sources of human suffering and human joy. Baldwin's characters succeed through knowledge that is hard won, and they are usually closest to triumph in moments of maximum risk.

James Baldwin was born on August 2, 1924, in Harlem. Three years later his mother, Emma Jones, married David Baldwin, a preacher whom Baldwin later admitted was the only person he had ever hated. Baldwin and his eight brothers and sisters grew up in abject poverty in the Harlem ghetto, and Baldwin says of himself that he "wanted to become rich and famous simply so no one could evict my family again." In 1938 he was converted and became a preacher at the Fireside Pentecostal Assembly, experiences that form the basis for his first novel, *Go Tell It on the Mountain* (1953). In 1942 he graduated from high school and left the ministry, convinced that religion provided inadequate answers to the problems of poor blacks. That same year he began a ten-year struggle to write *Go Tell It on the Mountain.* "In a sense," he said, "I wrote to redeem my father. I had to understand the forces, the experience, the life that shaped him before I could grow up myself, before I could become a writer." While working on the novel, he moved to Greenwich Village, where he met Richard Wright. With Wright's help, he received a Eugene Saxton fellowship and began writing essays and reviews for *The Nation* and *Commentary.* In 1948 he published his first short story, "Previous Condition," and received a Rosenwald fellowship, which allowed him to move to Paris where he remained for the next nine years.

The publication of *Go Tell It on the Mountain* marked Baldwin's emergence as a major writer. He followed it with a collection of essays, *Notes of a Native Son* (1955), and the controversial novel *Giovanni's Room* (1956), which deals with a young, white homosexual's attempt to accept himself as he is. Over the next several years Baldwin's work moved back and forth between efforts to deal with the racial situation in America—*Another Country* (1962) and *The Fire Next Time* (1963)—and efforts to deal with the subject of homosexuality—*Tell Me How Long the Train's Been Gone* (1965). In "Sonny's Blues," which was first published in *Going to Meet the Man* (1965), as in his novel *Just Above My Head* (1979), Baldwin presents an older brother's account of his relationship with a younger brother who is a musician. In the story as well as the novel, Baldwin uses music to explore the relationship of art to life.

Baldwin has always thought of writing—of art—as a public act. Writing, he says, "involves, after all, disturbing the peace." For him, artists are revolutionaries not simply as a result of their perspectives but also as a result of the potential their work has to effect social change. Yet the artist's role is not simply to affirm political rhetoric: "You got to be aware that a slogan is only a slogan," for "what you have to do is insist on complexity which people in the battle don't want to think about."

Baldwin's own involvement in the civil rights movement began with his return from France in 1957; by 1962 he had become a nationally recognized leader for the movement. In "Fifth Avenue, Uptown: A Letter from Harlem" (1960) he says that "it is a terrible, an inexorable, law that one cannot deny the humanity of another without diminishing one's own: in the face of one's victim, one sees himself." To "be a Negro in this country," he says, "and to be relatively conscious is to be in a rage almost all the time."

In his fiction, as well as in his essays and speeches, Baldwin consistently depicts the political, economic, and social injustice he sees in American society, but he also affirms the importance of accepting the past, both personal and collective, even when it involves pain. Accepting "one's past—one's history—is not the same thing as drowning in it, it is learning how to use it." In his work, religion tends to reinforce oppression while art serves as a bridge between people, as music does in "Sonny's Blues." Like art, love is almost always a liberating force in Baldwin's work, even though in its less socially acceptable forms, such as interracial or homosexual love, it can also cause intense pain. "You write," Baldwin says,

> in order to change the world, knowing perfectly well that you probably can't, but also knowing that literature is indispensable to the world. In some way, your aspirations and concern for a single man in fact do begin to change the world. The world changes according to the way people see it, and if you alter, even by a millimeter, the way a person looks or people look at reality, then you can change it.

Further Reading:
F. Eckman, *The Furious Passage of James Baldwin,* 1966.
W. J. Weatherby, *Squaring Off: Mailer vs. Baldwin,* 1976.
L. H. Pratt, *James Baldwin,* 1978.
C. W. Sylvander, *James Baldwin,* 1980.

Text:
Going to Meet the Man, 1965.

Sonny's Blues

I read about it in the paper, in the subway, on my way to work. I read it, and I couldn't believe it, and I read it again. Then perhaps I just stared at it, at the newsprint spelling out his name, spelling out the story. I stared at it in the swinging lights of the subway car, and in the faces and bodies of the people, and in my own face, trapped in the darkness which roared outside.

It was not to be believed and I kept telling myself that, as I walked from the subway station to the high school. And at the same time I couldn't doubt it. I was scared, scared for Sonny. He became real to me again. A great block of ice got settled in my belly and kept melting there slowly all day long, while I taught my classes algebra. It was a special kind of ice. It kept melting, sending trickles of ice water all up and down my veins, but it never got less. Sometimes it hardened and seemed to expand until I felt my guts were going to come spilling out or that I was going to choke or scream. This would always be at a moment when I was remembering some specific thing Sonny had once said or done.

When he was about as old as the boys in my classes his face had been bright and open, there was a lot of copper in it; and he'd had wonderfully direct brown eyes, and great gentleness and privacy. I wondered what he looked like now. He had been picked up, the evening before, in a raid on an apartment downtown, for peddling and using heroin.

I couldn't believe it: but what I mean by that is that I couldn't find any room for it anywhere inside me. I had kept it outside me for a long time. I hadn't wanted to know. I had had suspicions, but I didn't name them, I kept putting them away. I told myself that Sonny was wild, but he wasn't crazy. And he'd always been a good boy, he hadn't ever turned hard or evil or disrespectful, the way kids can, so quick, so quick, especially in Harlem. I didn't want to believe that I'd ever see my brother going down, coming to nothing, all that light in his face gone out, in the condition I'd already seen so many others. Yet it had happened and here I was, talking about algebra to a lot of boys who might, every one of them for all I knew, be popping off needles every time they went to the head. Maybe it did more for them than algebra could.

I was sure that the first time Sonny had ever had horse, he couldn't have been much older than these boys were now. These boys, now, were living as we'd been living then, they were growing up with a rush and their heads bumped abruptly against the low ceiling of their actual possibilities. They were filled with rage. All they really knew were two darknesses, the darkness of their lives, which was now closing in on them, and the darkness of the movies, which had blinded them to that other darkness, and in which they now, vindictively, dreamed, at once more together than they were at any other time, and more alone.

When the last bell rang, the last class ended, I let out my breath. It seemed I'd been holding it for all that time. My clothes were wet—I may have looked as though I'd been sitting in a steam bath, all dressed up, all afternoon. I sat alone in the classroom a long time. I listened to the boys outside, downstairs, shouting and cursing and laughing. Their laughter struck me for perhaps the first time. It was not the joyous laughter which—God knows why—one associates with children. It was mocking and insular, its intent was to denigrate. It was disenchanted, and in this, also, lay the authority of their curses. Perhaps I was listening to them because I was thinking about my brother and in them I heard my brother. And myself.

One boy was whistling a tune, at once very complicated and very simple, it seemed to be pouring out of him as though he were a bird, and it sounded very cool and moving through all that harsh, bright air, only just holding its own through all those other sounds.

I stood up and walked over to the window and looked down into the courtyard. It was the beginning of the spring and the sap was rising in the boys. A teacher passed through them every now and again, quickly, as though he or she couldn't wait to get out of that courtyard, to get those boys out of their sight and off their minds. I started collecting my stuff. I thought I'd better get home and talk to Isabel.

The courtyard was almost deserted by the time I got downstairs. I saw this boy standing in the shadow of a doorway, looking just like Sonny. I almost called his name. Then I saw that it wasn't Sonny, but somebody we used to know, a boy from around our block. He'd been Sonny's friend. He'd never been mine, having been too young for me, and, anyway, I'd never liked him. And now, even though he was a grown-up man, he still hung around that block, still spent hours on the street corners, was always high and raggy. I used to run into him from time to time and he'd often work around to asking me for a quarter or fifty cents. He always had some real good excuse, too, and I always gave it to him, I don't know why.

But now, abruptly, I hated him. I couldn't stand the way he looked at me, partly like a dog, partly like a cunning child. I wanted to ask him what the hell he was doing in the school courtyard.

He sort of shuffled over to me, and he said, "I see you got the papers. So you already know about it."

"You mean about Sonny? Yes, I already know about it. How come they didn't get you?"

He grinned. It made him repulsive and it also brought to mind what he'd looked like as a kid. "I wasn't there. I stay away from them people."

"Good for you." I offered him a cigarette and I watched him through the smoke. "You come all the way down here just to tell me about Sonny?"

"That's right." He was sort of shaking his head and his eyes looked strange, as though they were about to cross. The bright sun deadened his damp dark brown skin and it made his eyes look yellow and showed up the dirt in his kinked hair. He smelled funky. I moved a little away from him and I said, "Well, thanks. But I already know about it and I got to get home."

"I'll walk you a little ways," he said. We started walking. There were a couple of kids still loitering in the courtyard and one of them said goodnight to me and looked strangely at the boy beside me.

"What're you going to do?" he asked me. "I mean, about Sonny?"

"Look. I haven't seen Sonny for over a year, I'm not sure I'm going to do anything. Anyway, what the hell *can* I do?"

"That's right," he said quickly, "ain't nothing you can do. Can't much help old Sonny no more, I guess."

It was what I was thinking and so it seemed to me he had no right to say it.

"I'm surprised at Sonny, though," he went on—he had a funny way of talking, he looked straight ahead as though he were talking to himself—"I thought Sonny was a smart boy, I thought he was too smart to get hung."

"I guess he thought so too," I said sharply, "and that's how he got hung. And now about you? You're pretty goddamn smart, I bet."

Then he looked directly at me, just for a minute. "I ain't smart," he said. "If I was smart, I'd have reached for a pistol a long time ago."

"Look. Don't tell *me* your sad story, if it was up to me, I'd give you one." Then I felt guilty—guilty, probably, for never having supposed that the poor bastard *had* a story of his own, much less a sad one, and I asked, quickly, "What's going to happen to him now?"

He didn't answer this. He was off by himself some place. "Funny thing," he said, and from his tone we might have been discussing the quickest way to get to Brooklyn, "when I saw the papers this morning, the first thing I asked myself was if I had anything to do with it. I felt sort of responsible."

I began to listen more carefully. The subway station was on the corner, just before us, and I stopped. He stopped, too. We were in front of a bar and he ducked slightly, peering in, but whoever he was looking for didn't seem to be there. The juke box was blasting away with something black and bouncy and I half watched the barmaid as she danced her way from the juke box to her place behind the bar. And I watched her face as she laughingly responded to something someone said to her, still keeping time to the music. When she smiled one saw the little girl, one sensed the doomed, still-struggling woman beneath the battered face of the semi-whore.

"I never *give* Sonny nothing," the boy said finally, "but a long time ago I come to school high and Sonny asked me how it felt." He paused, I couldn't bear to watch him, I watched the barmaid, and I listened to the music which seemed to be causing the pavement to shake. "I told him it felt great." The music stopped, the barmaid paused and watched the juke box until the music began again. "It did."

All this was carrying me some place I didn't want to go. I certainly didn't want to know how it felt. It filled everything, the people, the houses, the music, the dark, quicksilver barmaid, with menace; and this menace was their reality.

"What's going to happen to him now?" I asked again.

"They'll send him away some place and they'll try to cure him." He shook his head. "Maybe he'll even think he's kicked the habit. Then they'll let him loose"—he gestured, throwing his cigarette into the gutter. "That's all."

"What do you mean, that's *all?*"

But I knew what he meant.

"I *mean*, that's all." He turned his head and looked at me, pulling down the corners of his mouth. "Don't you know what I mean?" he asked, softly.

"How the hell *would* I know what you mean?" I almost whispered it, I don't know why.

"That's right," he said to the air, "how would *he* know what I mean?" He turned toward me again, patient and calm, and yet I somehow felt him shaking, shaking as though he were going to fall apart. I felt that ice in my guts again, the dread I'd felt all afternoon; and again I watched the barmaid, moving about the bar, washing glasses, and singing. "Listen. They'll let him out and then it'll just start all over again. That's what I mean."

"You mean—they'll let him out. And then he'll just start working his way back in again. You mean he'll never kick the habit. Is that what you mean?"

"That's right," he said, cheerfully. "*You* see what I mean."

"Tell me," I said it last, "why does he want to die? He must want to die, he's killing himself, why does he want to die?"

He looked at me in surprise. He licked his lips. "He don't want to die. He wants to live. Don't nobody want to die, ever."

Then I wanted to ask him—too many things. He could not have answered, or if he had, I could not have borne the answers. I started walking. "Well, I guess it's none of my business."

"It's going to be rough on old Sonny," he said. We reached the subway station. "This is your station?" he asked. I nodded. I took one step down. "Damn!" he said, suddenly. I looked up at him. He grinned again. "Damn it if I didn't leave all my money home. You ain't got a dollar on you, have you? Just for a couple of days, is all."

All at once something inside gave and threatened to come pouring out of me. I didn't hate him any more. I felt that in another moment I'd start crying like a child.

"Sure," I said. "Don't sweat." I looked in my wallet and didn't have a dollar, I only had a five. "Here," I said. "That hold you?"

He didn't look at it—he didn't want to look at it. A terrible, closed look came over his face, as though he were keeping the number on the bill a secret from him and me. "Thanks," he said, and now he was dying to see me go. "Don't worry about Sonny. Maybe I'll write him or something."

"Sure," I said. "You do that. So long."

"Be seeing you," he said. I went on down the steps.

And I didn't write Sonny or send him anything for a long time. When I finally did, it was just after my little girl died, he wrote me back a letter which made me feel like a bastard.

Here's what he said:

Dear brother,

You don't know how much I needed to hear from you. I wanted to write you many a time but I dug how much I must have hurt you and so I didn't write. But now I feel like a man who's been trying to climb up out of some deep, real deep and funky hole and just saw the sun up there, outside. I got to get outside.

I can't tell you much about how I got here. I mean I don't know how to tell you. I guess I was afraid of something or I was trying to escape from something and you know I have never been very strong in the head (smile). I'm glad Mama and Daddy are dead and can't see what's happened to their son and I swear if I'd known what I was doing I would never have hurt you so, you and a lot of other fine people who were nice to me and who believed in me.

I don't want you to think it had anything to do with me being a musician. It's more than that. Or maybe less than that. I can't get anything straight in my head down here and I try not to think about what's going to happen to me when

I get outside again. Sometime I think I'm going to flip and *never* get outside and sometime I think I'll come straight back. I tell you one thing, though, I'd rather blow my brains out than go through this again. But that's what they all say, so they tell me. If I tell you when I'm coming to New York and if you could meet me, I sure would appreciate it. Give my love to Isabel and the kids and I was sure sorry to hear about little Gracie. I wish I could be like Mama and say the Lord's will be done, but I don't know it seems to me that trouble is the one thing that never does get stopped and I don't know what good it does to blame it on the Lord. But maybe it does some good if you believe it.

> Your brother,
> Sonny

Then I kept in constant touch with him and I sent him whatever I could and I went to meet him when he came back to New York. When I saw him many things I thought I had forgotten came flooding back to me. This was because I had begun, finally, to wonder about Sonny, about the life that Sonny lived inside. This life, whatever it was, had made him older and thinner and it had deepened the distant stillness in which he had always moved. He looked very unlike my baby brother. Yet, when he smiled, when we shook hands, the baby brother I'd never known looked out from the depths of his private life, like an animal waiting to be coaxed into the light.

"How you been keeping?" he asked me.

"All right. And you?"

"Just fine." He was smiling all over his face. "It's good to see you again."

"It's good to see you."

The seven years' difference in our ages lay between us like a chasm: I wondered if these years would ever operate between us as a bridge. I was remembering, and it made it hard to catch my breath, that I had been there when he was born; and I had heard the first words he had ever spoken. When he started to walk, he walked from our mother straight to me. I caught him just before he fell when he took the first steps he ever took in this world.

"How's Isabel?"

"Just fine. She's dying to see you."

"And the boys?"

"They're fine, too. They're anxious to see their uncle."

"Oh, come on. You know they don't remember me."

"Are you kidding? Of course they remember you."

He grinned again. We got into a taxi. We had a lot to say to each other, far too much to know how to begin.

As the taxi began to move, I asked, "You still want to go to India?"

He laughed. "You still remember that. Hell, no. This place is Indian enough for me."

"It used to belong to them," I said.

And he laughed again. "They damn sure knew what they were doing when they got rid of it."

Years ago, when he was around fourteen, he'd been all hipped on the idea of going to India. He read books about people sitting on rocks, naked, in all kinds of weather, but mostly bad, naturally, and walking barefoot through hot coals and arriving at wisdom. I used to say that it sounded to me as though they were getting away from wisdom as fast as they could. I think he sort of looked down on me for that.

"Do you mind," he asked, "if we have the driver drive alongside the park? On the west side—I haven't seen the city in so long."

"Of course not," I said. I was afraid that I might sound as though I were humoring him, but I hoped he wouldn't take it that way.

So we drove along, between the green of the park and the stony, lifeless elegance of hotels and apartment buildings, toward the vivid, killing streets of our childhood. These streets hadn't changed, though housing projects jutted up out of them now like rocks in the middle of a boiling sea. Most of the houses in which we had grown up had vanished, as had the stores from which we had stolen, the basements in which we had first tried sex, the rooftops from which we had hurled tin cans and bricks. But houses exactly like the houses of our past yet dominated the landscape, boys exactly like the boys we once had been found themselves smothering in these houses, came down into the streets for light and air and found themselves encircled by disaster. Some escaped the trap, most didn't. Those who got out always left something of themselves behind, as some animals amputate a leg and leave it in the trap. It might be said, perhaps, that I had escaped, after all, I was a school teacher; or that Sonny had, he hadn't lived in Harlem for years. Yet, as the cab moved uptown through streets which seemed, with a rush, to darken with dark people, and as I covertly studied Sonny's face, it came to me that what we both were seeking through our separate cab windows was that part of ourselves which had been left behind. It's always at the hour of trouble and confrontation that the missing member aches.

We hit 110th Street and started rolling up Lenox Avenue. And I'd known this avenue all my life, but it seemed to me again, as it had seemed on the day I'd first heard about Sonny's trouble, filled with a hidden menace which was its very breath of life.

"We almost there," said Sonny.

"Almost." We were both too nervous to say anything more.

We live in a housing project. It hasn't been up long. A few days after it was up it seemed uninhabitably new, now, of course, it's already rundown. It looks like a parody of the good, clean, faceless life—God knows the people who live in it do their best to make it a parody. The beat-looking grass lying around isn't enough to make their lives green, the hedges will never hold out the streets, and they know it. The big windows fool no one, they aren't big enough to make space out of no space. They don't bother with the windows, they watch the TV screen instead. The playground is most popular with the children who don't play at jacks, or skip rope, or roller skate, or swing, and they can be found in it after dark. We moved in partly because it's not too far from where I teach, and partly for the kids; but it's really just like the houses in which Sonny and I grew up. The same things happen, they'll have the same things to remember. The moment Sonny and I started into the house I had the feeling that I was simply bringing him back into the danger he had almost died trying to escape.

Sonny has never been talkative. So I don't know why I was sure he'd be dying to talk to me when supper was over the first night. Everything went fine, the oldest boy remembered him, and the youngest boy liked him, and Sonny had remembered to bring something for each of them; and Isabel, who is really much nicer than I am, more open and giving, had gone to a lot of trouble about dinner and was genuinely glad to see him. And she's always been able to tease Sonny in a way that I haven't. It was nice to see her face so vivid again and to hear her laugh and watch her make Sonny laugh. She wasn't, or, anyway, she didn't seem to be, at all uneasy or embarrassed. She chatted as though there were no subject which had to be avoided and she got Sonny past his first, faint stiffness. And thank God she was there, for I was filled with that icy dread again. Everything I did seemed awkward to me, and everything I said sounded freighted with hidden meaning. I was trying to remember everything I'd heard about dope addiction and I couldn't help watching Sonny for signs. I wasn't doing it out of malice. I was trying to find out something about my brother. I was dying to hear him tell me he was safe.

"Safe!" my father grunted, whenever Mama suggested trying to move to a neighborhood which might be safer for children. "Safe, hell! Ain't no place safe for kids, nor nobody."

He always went on like this, but he wasn't, ever, really as bad as he sounded, not even on weekends, when he got drunk. As a matter of fact, he was always on the lookout for "something a little better," but he died before he found it. He died suddenly, during a drunken weekend in the middle of the war, when Sonny was fifteen. He and Sonny hadn't ever got on too well. And this was partly because Sonny was the apple of his father's eye. It was because he loved Sonny so much and was frightened for him, that he was always fighting with him. It doesn't do any good to fight with Sonny. Sonny just moves back, inside himself, where he can't be reached. But the principal reason that they never hit it off is that they were so much alike. Daddy was big and rough and loud-talking, just the opposite of Sonny, but they both had—that same privacy.

Mama tried to tell me something about this, just after Daddy died. I was home on leave from the army.

This was the last time I ever saw my mother alive. Just the same, this picture gets all mixed up in my mind with pictures I had of her when she was younger. The way I always see her is the way she used to be on a Sunday afternoon, say, when the old folks were talking after the big Sunday dinner. I always see her wearing pale blue. She'd be sitting on the sofa. And my father would be sitting in the easy chair, not far from her. And the living room would be full of church folks and relatives. There they sit, in chairs all around the living room, and the night is creeping up outside, but nobody knows it yet. You can see the darkness growing against the windowpanes and you hear the street noises every now and again, or maybe the jangling beat of a tambourine from one of the churches close by, but it's real quiet in the room. For a moment nobody's talking, but every face looks darkening, like the sky outside. And my mother rocks a little from the waist, and my father's eyes are closed. Everyone is looking at something a child can't see. For a minute they've forgotten the children. Maybe a kid is lying on the rug, half asleep. Maybe somebody's got a kid in his lap and is absent-mindedly stroking the kid's head. Maybe there's a kid, quiet and big-eyed, curled up in a big chair in the corner. The silence, the darkness coming, and the darkness in the faces frightens the child obscurely. He hopes that the hand which strokes his forehead will never stop—will never die. He hopes that there will never come a time when the old folks won't be sitting around the living room, talking about where they've come from, and what they've seen, and what's happened to them and their kinfolk.

But something deep and watchful in the child knows that this is bound to end, is already ending. In a moment someone will get up and turn on the light. Then the old folks will remember the children and they won't talk any more that day. And when light fills the room, the child is filled with darkness. He knows that every time this happens he's moved just a little closer to that darkness outside. The darkness outside is what the old folks have been talking about. It's what they've come from. It's what they endure. The child knows that they won't talk any more because if he knows too much about what's happened to *them,* he'll know too much too soon, about what's going to happen to *him.*

The last time I talked to my mother, I remember I was restless. I wanted to get out and see Isabel. We weren't married then and we had a lot to straighten out between us.

There Mama sat, in black, by the window. She was humming an old church song, *Lord, you brought me from a long ways off.* Sonny was out somewhere. Mama kept watching the streets.

"I don't know," she said, "if I'll ever see you again, after you go off from here. But I hope you'll remember the things I tried to teach you."

"Don't talk like that," I said, and smiled. "You'll be here a long time yet."

She smiled, too, but she said nothing. She was quiet for a long time. And I said, "Mama, don't you worry about nothing. I'll be writing all the time, and you be getting the checks. . . ."

"I want to talk to you about your brother," she said, suddenly. "If anything happens to me he ain't going to have nobody to look out for him."

"Mama," I said, "ain't nothing going to happen to you *or* Sonny. Sonny's all right. He's a good boy and he's got good sense."

"It ain't a question of his being a good boy," Mama said, "nor of his having good sense. It ain't only the bad ones, nor yet the dumb ones that gets sucked under." She stopped, looking at me. "Your Daddy once had a brother," she said, and she smiled in a way that made me feel she was in pain. "You didn't never know that, did you?"

"No," I said, "I never knew that," and I watched her face.

"Oh, yes," she said, "your Daddy had a brother." She looked out of the window again. "I know you never saw your Daddy cry. But *I* did—many a time, through all these years."

I asked her, "What happened to his brother? How come nobody's ever talked about him?"

This was the first time I ever saw my mother look old.

"His brother got killed," she said, "when he was just a little younger than you are now. I knew him. He was a fine boy. He was maybe a little full of the devil, but he didn't mean nobody no harm."

Then she stopped and the room was silent, exactly as it had sometimes been on those Sunday afternoons. Mama kept looking out into the streets.

"He used to have a job in the mill," she said, "and, like all young folks, he just liked to perform on Saturday nights. Saturday nights, him and your father would drift around to different place, go to dances and things like that, or just sit around with people they knew, and your father's brother would sing, he had a fine voice, and play along with himself on his guitar. Well, this particular Saturday night, him and your father was coming home from some place, and they were both a little drunk and there was a moon that night, it was bright like day. Your father's brother was feeling kind of good, and he was whistling to himself, and he had his guitar slung over his shoulder. They was coming down a hill and beneath them was a road that turned off from the highway. Well, your father's brother, being always kind of frisky, decided to run down this hill, and he did, with that guitar banging and clanging behind him, and he ran across the road, and he was making water behind a tree. And your father was sort of amused at him and he was still coming down the hill, kind of slow. Then he heard a car motor and that same minute his brother stepped from behind the tree, into the road, in the moonlight. And he started to cross the road. And your father started to run down the hill, he says he don't know why. This car was full of white men. They was all drunk, and when they seen your father's brother they let out a great whoop and holler and they aimed the car straight at him. They was having fun, they just wanted to scare him, the way they do sometimes, you know. But they was drunk. And I guess the boy, being drunk, too, and scared, kind of lost his head. By the time he jumped it was too late. Your father says he heard his brother scream when the car rolled over him, and he heard the wood of that guitar when it give, and he heard them strings go flying, and he heard them white men shouting, and the car kept on a-going and it ain't stopped till this day. And, time your father got down the hill, his brother weren't nothing but blood and pulp."

Tears were gleaming on my mother's face. There wasn't anything I could say.

"He never mentioned it," she said, "because I never let him mention it before you children. Your Daddy was like a crazy man that night and for many a night thereafter. He says he never in his life seen anything as dark as that road after the lights of that car had gone away. Weren't nothing, weren't nobody on that road, just your Daddy and his brother and that busted guitar. Oh, yes. Your Daddy never did really get right again. Till the day he died he weren't sure but that every white man he saw was the man that killed his brother."

She stopped and took out her handkerchief and dried her eyes and looked at me.

"I ain't telling you all this," she said, "to make you scared or bitter or to make you hate nobody. I'm telling you this because you got a brother. And the world ain't changed."

I guess I didn't want to believe this. I guess she saw this in my face. She turned away from me, toward the window again, searching those streets.

"But I praise my Redeemer," she said at last, "that He called your Daddy home before me. I ain't saying it to throw no flowers at myself, but, I declare, it keeps me from feeling too cast down to know I helped your father get safely through this world. Your father always acted like he was the roughest, strongest man on earth. And everybody took him to be like that. But if he hadn't had *me* there—to see his tears!"

She was crying again. Still, I couldn't move. I said, "Lord, Lord, Mama, I didn't know it was like that."

"Oh, honey," she said, "there's a lot that you don't know. But you are going to find it out." She stood up from the window and came over to me. "You got to hold on to your brother," she said, "and don't let him fall, no matter what it looks like is happening to him and no matter how evil you gets with him. You going to be evil with him many a time. But don't you forget what I told you, you hear?"

"I won't forget," I said. "Don't you worry, I won't forget. I won't let nothing happen to Sonny."

My mother smiled as though she were amused at something she saw in my face. Then, "You may not be able to stop nothing from happening. But you got to let him know you's *there.*"

Two days later I was married, and then I was gone. And I had a lot of things on my mind and I pretty well forgot my promise to Mama until I got shipped home on a special furlough for her funeral.

And, after the funeral, with just Sonny and me alone in the empty kitchen, I tried to find out something about him.

"What do you want to do?" I asked him.

"I'm going to be a musician," he said.

For he had graduated, in the time I had been away, from dancing to the juke box to finding out who was playing what, and what they were doing with it, and he had bought himself a set of drums.

"You mean, you want to be a drummer?" I somehow had the feeling that being a drummer might be all right for other people but not for my brother Sonny.

"I don't think," he said, looking at me very gravely, "that I'll ever be a good drummer. But I think I can play a piano."

I frowned. I'd never played the role of the older brother quite so seriously before, had scarcely ever, in fact, *asked* Sonny a damn thing. I sensed myself in the presence of something I didn't really know how to handle, didn't understand. So I made my frown a little deeper as I asked: "What kind of musician do you want to be?"

He grinned. "How many kinds do you think there are?"

"Be *serious,*" I said.

He laughed, throwing his head back, and then looked at me. "I *am* serious."

"Well, then, for Christ's sake, stop kidding around and answer a serious question. I mean, do you want to be a concert pianist, you want to play classical music and all that, or—or what?" Long before I finished he was laughing again. "For Christ's sake, Sonny!"

He sobered, but with difficulty. "I'm sorry. But you sound so—*scared!*" and he was off again.

"Well, you may think it's funny now, baby, but it's not going to be so funny when you have to make your living at it, let me tell you *that.*" I was furious because I knew he was laughing at me and I didn't know why.

"No," he said, very sober now, and afraid, perhaps, that he'd hurt me, "I don't want to be a classical pianist. That isn't what interests me. I mean"—he paused, looking hard at me, as though his eyes would help me to understand, and then gestured helplessly, as though perhaps his hand would help—"I mean, I'll have a lot of studying to do, and I'll have to study *everything,* but, I mean, I want to play *with*—jazz musicians." He stopped. "I want to play jazz," he said.

Well, the word had never before sounded as heavy, as real, as it sounded that afternoon in Sonny's mouth. I just looked at him and I was probably frowning a real frown by this time. I simply couldn't see why on earth he'd want to spend his time hanging around nightclubs, clowning around on bandstands, while people pushed each other around a dance floor. It seemed—beneath him, somehow. I had never thought about it before, had never been forced to, but I suppose I had always put jazz musicians in a class with what Daddy called "good-time people."

"Are you *serious?*"

"Hell, *yes,* I'm serious."

He looked more helpless than ever, and annoyed, and deeply hurt.

I suggested, helpfully: "You mean—like Louis Armstrong?"

His face closed as though I'd struck him. "No. I'm not talking about none of that old-time, down home crap."

"Well, look, Sonny, I'm sorry, don't get mad. I just don't altogether get it, that's all. Name somebody—you know, a jazz musician you admire."

"Bird."

"Who?"

"Bird! Charlie Parker! Don't they teach you nothing in the goddamn army?"

I lit a cigarette. I was surprised and then a little amused to discover that I was trembling. "I've been out of touch," I said. "You'll have to be patient with me. Now. Who's this Parker character?"

"He's just one of the greatest jazz musicians alive," said Sonny, sullenly, his hands in his pockets, his back to me. "Maybe *the* greatest," he added, bitterly, "that's probably why *you* never heard of him."

"All right," I said, "I'm ignorant. I'm sorry. I'll go out and buy all the cat's records right away, all right?"

"It don't," said Sonny, with dignity, "make any difference to me. I don't care what you listen to. Don't do me no favors."

I was beginning to realize that I'd never seen him so upset before. With another part of my mind I was thinking that this would probably turn out to be one of those things kids go through and that I shouldn't make it seem important by pushing it too hard. Still, I didn't think it would do any harm to ask: "Doesn't all this take a lot of time? Can you make a living at it?"

He turned back to me and half leaned, half sat, on the kitchen table. "Everything takes time," he said, "and—well, yes, sure, I can make a living at it. But what I don't seem to be able to make you understand is that it's the only thing I want to do."

"Well, Sonny," I said, gently, "you know people can't always do exactly what they *want* to do—"

"*No,* I don't know that," said Sonny, surprising me. "I think people *ought* to do what they want to do, what else are they alive for?"

"You getting to be a big boy," I said desperately, "it's time you started thinking about your future."

"I'm thinking about my future," said Sonny, grimly. "I think about it all the time."

I gave up. I decided, if he didn't change his mind, that we could always talk about it later. "In the meantime," I said, "you got to finish school." We had already decided that he'd have to move in with Isabel and her folks. I knew this wasn't the ideal arrangement because Isabel's folks are inclined to be dicty[1] and they hadn't especially wanted Isabel to marry me. But I didn't know what else to do. "And we have to get you fixed up at Isabel's."

There was a long silence. He moved from the kitchen table to the window. "That's a terrible idea. You know it yourself."

"Do you have a *better* idea?"

---

[1] Snobbish or bossy.

He just walked up and down the kitchen for a minute. He was as tall as I was. He had started to shave. I suddenly had the feeling that I didn't know him at all.

He stopped at the kitchen table and picked up my cigarettes. Looking at me with a kind of mocking, amused defiance, he put one between his lips. "You mind?"

"You smoking already?"

He lit the cigarette and nodded, watching me through the smoke. "I just wanted to see if I'd have the courage to smoke in front of you." He grinned and blew a great cloud of smoke to the ceiling. "It was easy." He looked at my face. "Come on, now. I bet you was smoking at my age, tell the truth."

I didn't say anything but the truth was on my face, and he laughed. But now there was something very strained in his laugh. "Sure. And I bet that ain't all you was doing."

He was frightening me a little. "Cut the crap," I said. "We already decided that you was going to go and live at Isabel's. Now what's got into you all of a sudden?"

"*You* decided it," he pointed out. "*I* didn't decide nothing." He stopped in front of me, leaning against the stove, arms loosely folded. "Look, brother. I don't want to stay in Harlem no more, I really don't." He was very earnest. He looked at me, then over toward the kitchen window. There was something in his eyes I'd never seen before, some thoughtfulness, some worry all his own. He rubbed the muscle of one arm. "It's time I was getting out of here."

"Where do you want to *go*, Sonny?"

"I want to join the army. Or the navy, I don't care. If I say I'm old enough, they'll believe me."

Then I got mad. It was because I was so scared. "You must be crazy. You goddamn fool, what the hell do you want to go and join the *army* for?"

"I just told you. To get out of Harlem."

"Sonny, you haven't even finished *school*. And if you really want to be a musician, how do you expect to study if you're in the *army?*"

He looked at me, trapped, and in anguish. "There's ways. I might be able to work out some kind of deal. Anyway, I'll have the G.I. Bill when I come out."

"*If* you come out." We stared at each other. "Sonny, please. Be reasonable. I know the setup is far from perfect. But we got to do the best we can."

"I ain't learning nothing in school," he said. "Even when I go." He turned away from me and opened the window and threw his cigarette out into the narrow alley. I watched his back. "At least, I ain't learning nothing you'd want me to learn." He slammed the window so hard I thought the glass would fly out, and turned back to me. "And I'm sick of the stink of these garbage cans!"

"Sonny," I said, "I know how you feel. But if you don't finish school now, you're going to be sorry later that you didn't." I grabbed him by the shoulders. "And you only got another year. It ain't so bad. And I'll come back and I swear I'll help you do *whatever* you want to do. Just try to put up with it till I come back. Will you please do that? For me?"

He didn't answer and he wouldn't look at me.

"Sonny. You hear me?"

He pulled away. "I hear you. But you never hear anything *I* say."

I didn't know what to say to that. He looked out of the window and then back at me. "OK," he said, and sighed. "I'll try."

Then I said, trying to cheer him up a little, "They got a piano at Isabel's. You can practice on it."

And as a matter of fact, it did cheer him up for a minute. "That's right," he said to himself. "I forgot that." His face relaxed a little. But the worry, the thoughtfulness, played on it still, the way shadows play on a face which is staring into the fire.

But I thought I'd never hear the end of that piano. At first, Isabel would write me, saying how nice it was that Sonny was so serious about his music and how, as soon as he came in from school, or wherever he had been when he was supposed to be at school, he went straight to that piano and stayed there until suppertime. And, after supper, he went back to that piano and stayed there until everybody went to bed. He was at the piano all day Saturday and all day Sunday. Then he bought a record player and started playing records. He'd play one record over and over again, all day long sometimes, and he'd improvise along with it on the piano. Or he'd play one section of the record, one chord, one change, one progression, then he'd do it on the piano. Then back to the record. Then back to the piano.

Well, I really don't know how they stood it. Isabel finally confessed that it wasn't like living with a person at all, it was like living with sound. And the sound didn't make any sense to her, didn't make any sense to any of them—naturally. They began, in a way, to be afflicted by this presence that was living in their home. It was as though Sonny were some sort of god, or monster. He moved in an atmosphere which wasn't like theirs at all. They fed him and he ate, he washed himself, he walked in and out of their door; he certainly wasn't nasty or unpleasant or rude, Sonny isn't any of those things; but it was as though he were all wrapped up in some cloud, some fire, some vision all his own; and there wasn't any way to reach him.

At the same time, he wasn't really a man yet, he was still a child, and they had to watch out for him in all kinds of ways. They certainly couldn't throw him out. Neither did they dare to make a great scene about that piano because even they dimly sensed, as I sensed, from so many thousands of miles away, that Sonny was at that piano playing for his life.

But he hadn't been going to school. One day a letter came from the school board and Isabel's mother got it—there had, apparently, been other letters but Sonny had torn them up. This day, when Sonny came in, Isabel's mother showed him the letter and asked where he'd been spending his time. And she finally got it out of him that he'd been down in Greenwich Village, with musicians and other characters, in a white girl's apartment. And this scared her and she started to scream at him and what came up, once she began—though she denies it to this day—was what sacrifices they were making to give Sonny a decent home and how little he appreciated it.

Sonny didn't play the piano that day. By evening, Isabel's mother had calmed down but then there was the old man to deal with, and Isabel herself. Isabel says she did her best to be calm but she broke down and started crying. She says she just watched Sonny's face. She could tell, by watching him, what was happening with him. And what was happening was that they penetrated his cloud, they had reached him. Even if their fingers had been a thousand times more gentle than human fingers ever are, he could hardly help feeling that they had stripped him naked and were spitting on that nakedness. For he also had to see that his presence, that music, which was life or death to him, had been torture for them and that they had endured it, not at all for his sake, but only for mine. And Sonny couldn't take that. He can take it a little better today than he could then but he's still not very good at it and, frankly, I don't know anybody who is.

The silence of the next few days must have been louder than the sound of all the music ever played since time began. One morning, before she went to work, Isabel was in his room for something and she suddenly realized that all of his records were gone. And she knew for certain that he was gone. And he was. He went as far as the navy would carry him. He finally sent me a postcard from some place in Greece and that was the first I knew that Sonny was still alive. I didn't see him any more until we were both back in New York and the war had long been over.

He was a man by then, of course, but I wasn't willing to see it. He came by the house from time to time, but we fought almost every time we met. I didn't like the way he carried himself, loose and dreamlike all the time, and I didn't like his friends, and his music seemed to be merely an excuse for the life he led. It sounded just that weird and disordered.

Then we had a fight, a pretty awful fight, and I didn't see him for months. By and by I looked him up, where he was living, in a furnished room in the Village, and I tried to make it up. But there were lots of other people in the room and Sonny just lay on his bed, and he wouldn't come downstairs with me, and he treated these other people as though they were his family and I weren't. So I got mad and then he got mad, and then I told him that he might just as well be dead as live the way he was living. Then he stood up and he told me not to worry about him any more in life, that he *was* dead as far as I was concerned. Then he pushed me to the door and the other people looked on as though nothing were happening, and he slammed the door behind me. I stood in the hallway, staring at the door. I heard somebody laugh in the room and then the tears came to my eyes. I started down the steps, whistling to keep from crying, I kept whistling to myself, *You going to need me, baby, one of these cold, rainy days.*

I read about Sonny's trouble in the spring. Little Grace died in the fall. She was a beautiful little girl. But she only lived a little over two years. She died of polio and she suffered. She had a slight fever for a couple of days, but it didn't seem like anything and we just kept her in bed. And we would certainly have called the doctor, but the fever dropped, she seemed to be all right. So we thought it had just been a cold. Then, one day, she was up, playing, Isabel was in the kitchen fixing lunch for the two boys when they'd come in from school, and she heard Grace fall down in the living room. When you have a lot of children you don't always start running when one of them falls, unless they start screaming or something. And, this time, Grace was quiet. Yet, Isabel says that when she heard that *thump* and then that silence, something happened in her to make her afraid. And she ran to the living room and there was little Grace on the floor, all twisted up, and the reason she hadn't screamed was that she couldn't get her breath. And when she did scream, it was the worst sound, Isabel says, that she'd ever heard in all her life, and she still hears it sometimes in her dreams. Isabel will sometimes wake me up with a low, moaning, strangled sound and I have to be quick to awaken her and hold her to me and where Isabel is weeping against me seems a mortal wound.

I think I may have written Sonny the very day that little Grace was buried. I was sitting in the living room in the dark, by myself, and I suddenly thought of Sonny. My trouble made his real.

One Saturday afternoon, when Sonny had been living with us, or, anyway, been in our house, for nearly two weeks, I found myself wandering aimlessly about the living room, drinking from a can of beer, and trying to work up the courage to search Sonny's room. He was out, he was usually out whenever I was home, and Isabel had taken the children to see their grandparents. Suddenly I was standing still in front of the living room window, watching Seventh Avenue. The idea of searching Sonny's room made me still. I scarcely dared to admit to myself what I'd be searching for. I didn't know what I'd do if I found it. Or if I didn't.

On the sidewalk across from me, near the entrance to a barbecue joint, some people were holding an old-fashioned revival meeting. The barbecue cook, wearing a dirty white apron, his conked hair[2] reddish and metallic in the pale sun, and a cigarette between his lips, stood in the doorway, watching them. Kids and older people paused in their errands and stood there, along with some older men and a couple of very tough-looking women who watched everything that happened on the avenue, as though they owned it, or were maybe owned by it. Well, they were watching this, too. The revival was being carried on by three sisters in black, and a brother. All they had were their voices and their Bibles and a tambourine. The brother was testifying and while he testified two of the sisters stood together, seeming to say, amen, and the third sister walked around with the tambourine outstretched and a couple of people dropped coins into it. Then the brother's testimony ended and the sister who had been taking up the collection dumped the coins into her palm and transferred them to the pocket of her long black robe. Then she raised both hands, striking the tambourine against the air, and then against one hand, and she started to sing. And the two other sisters and the brother joined in.

It was strange, suddenly, to watch, though I had been seeing these street meetings all my life. So, of course, had everybody else down there. Yet, they paused and watched and listened and I stood still at the window. *"Tis the old ship of Zion,"* they sang, and the sister with the tambourine kept a steady, jangling beat, *"it has rescued many a thousand!"* Not a soul under the sound of their voices was hearing this song for the first time, not one of them had been rescued. Nor had they seen much in the way of rescue work being done around them. Neither did they especially believe in the holiness of the three sisters and the brother, they knew too much about them, knew where they lived, and how. The woman with the tambourine, whose voice dominated the air, whose face was bright with joy, was divided by very little from the woman who stood watching her, a cigarette between her heavy, chapped lips, her hair a cuckoo's nest, her face scarred and swollen from many beatings, and her black eyes glittering like coal. Perhaps they both knew this, which was why, when, as rarely, they addressed each other, they addressed each other as Sister. As the singing filled the air the watching, listening faces underwent a change, the eyes focusing on something within; the music seemed to soothe a poison out of them; and time seemed, nearly, to fall away from the sullen, belligerent, battered faces, as though they were fleeing back to their first condition, while dreaming of their last. The barbecue cook

---

[2] Hair that has been straightened and coated heavily with grease.

half shook his head and smiled, and dropped his cigarette and disappeared into his joint. A man fumbled in his pockets for change and stood holding it in his hand impatiently, as though he had just remembered a pressing appointment further up the avenue. He looked furious. Then I saw Sonny, standing on the edge of the crowd. He was carrying a wide, flat notebook with a green cover, and it made him look, from where I was standing, almost like a schoolboy. The coppery sun brought out the copper in his skin, he was very faintly smiling, standing very still. Then the singing stopped, the tambourine turned into a collection plate again. The furious man dropped in his coins and vanished, so did a couple of the women, and Sonny dropped some change in the plate, looking directly at the woman with a little smile. He started across the avenue, toward the house. He has a slow, loping walk, something like the way Harlem hipsters walk, only he's imposed on this his own half-beat. I had never really noticed it before.

I stayed at the window, both relieved and apprehensive. As Sonny disappeared from my sight, they began singing again. And they were still singing when his key turned in the lock.

"Hey," he said.

"Hey, yourself. You want some beer?"

"No. Well, maybe." But he came up to the window and stood beside me, looking out. "What a warm voice," he said.

They were singing *If I could only hear my mother pray again!*

"Yes," I said, "and she can sure beat that tambourine."

"But what a terrible song," he said, and laughed. He dropped his notebook on the sofa and disappeared into the kitchen. "Where's Isabel and the kids?"

"I think they went to see their grandparents. You hungry?"

"No." He came back into the living room with his can of beer. "You want to come some place with me tonight?"

I sensed, I don't know how, that I couldn't possibly say no. "Sure. Where?"

He sat down on the sofa and picked up his notebook and started leafing through it. "I'm going to sit in with some fellows in a joint in the Village."

"You mean, you're going to play, tonight?"

"That's right." He took a swallow of his beer and moved back to the window. He gave me a sidelong look. "If you can stand it."

"I'll try," I said.

He smiled to himself and we both watched as the meeting across the way broke up. The three sisters and the brother, heads bowed, were singing *God be with you till we meet again.* The faces around them were very quiet. Then the song ended. The small crowd dispersed. We watched the three women and the lone man walk slowly up the avenue.

"When she was singing before," said Sonny, abruptly, "her voice reminded me for a minute of what heroin feels like sometimes—when it's in your veins. It makes you feel sort of warm and cool at the same time. And distant. And—and sure." He sipped his beer, very deliberately not looking at me. I watched his face. "It makes you feel —in control. Sometimes you've got to have that feeling."

"Do you?" I sat down slowly in the easy chair.

"Sometimes." He went to the sofa and picked up his notebook again. "Some people do."

"In order," I asked, "to play?" And my voice was very ugly, full of contempt and anger.

"Well"—he looked at me with great, troubled eyes, as though, in fact, he hoped his eyes would tell me things he could never otherwise say—"they *think* so. And *if* they think so—!"

"And what do *you* think?" I asked.

He sat on the sofa and put his can of beer on the floor. "I don't know," he said, and I couldn't be sure if he were answering my question or pursuing his thoughts. His face didn't tell me. "It's not so much to *play*. It's to *stand* it, to be able to make it at all. On any level." He frowned and smiled: "In order to keep from shaking to pieces."

"But these friends of yours," I said, "they seem to shake themselves to pieces pretty goddamn fast."

"Maybe." He played with the notebook. And something told me that I should curb my tongue, that Sonny was doing his best to talk, that I should listen. "But of course you only know the ones that've gone to pieces. Some don't—or at least they haven't *yet* and that's just about all *any* of us can say." He paused. "And then there are some who just live, really, in hell, and they know it and they see what's happening and they go right on. I don't know." He sighed, dropped the notebook, folded his arms. "Some guys, you can tell from the way they play, they on something *all* the time. And you can see that, well, it makes something real for them. But of course," he picked up his beer from the floor and sipped it and put the can down again, "they *want* to, too, you've got to see that. Even some of them that say they don't—*some*, not all."

"And what about you?" I asked—I couldn't help it. "What about you? Do *you* want to?"

He stood up and walked to the window and remained silent for a long time. Then he sighed. "Me," he said. Then: "While I was downstairs before, on my way here, listening to that woman sing, it struck me all of a sudden how much suffering she must have had to go through—to sing like that. It's *repulsive* to think you have to suffer that much."

I said: "But there's no way not to suffer—is there, Sonny?"

"I believe not," he said and smiled, "but that's never stopped anyone from trying." He looked at me. "Has it?" I realized, with this mocking look, that there stood between us, forever, beyond the power of time or forgiveness, the fact that I had held silence—so long!—when he had needed human speech to help him. He turned back to the window. "No, there's no way not to suffer. But you try all kinds of ways to keep from drowning in it, to keep on top of it, and to make it seem—well, like *you*. Like you did something, all right, and now you're suffering for it. You know?" I said nothing. "Well you know," he said, impatiently, "why *do* people suffer? Maybe it's better to do something to give it a reason, *any* reason."

"But we just agreed," I said, "that there's no way not to suffer. Isn't it better, then, just to—take it?"

"But nobody just takes it," Sonny cried, "that's what I'm telling you! *Everybody* tries not to. You're just hung up on the *way* some people try—it's not *your* way!"

The hair on my face began to itch, my face felt wet. "That's not true," I said, "that's not true. I don't give a damn what other people do, I don't even care how they suffer.

I just care how *you* suffer." And he looked at me. "Please believe me," I said, "I don't want to see you—die—trying not to suffer."

"I won't," he said, flatly, "die trying not to suffer. At least, not any faster than anybody else."

"But there's no need," I said, trying to laugh, "is there? in killing yourself."

I wanted to say more, but I couldn't. I wanted to talk about will power and how life could be—well, beautiful. I wanted to say that it was all within; but was it? or, rather, wasn't that exactly the trouble? And I wanted to promise that I would never fail him again. But it would all have sounded—empty words and lies.

So I made the promise to myself and prayed that I would keep it.

"It's terrible sometimes, inside," he said, "that's what's the trouble. You walk these streets, black and funky and cold, and there's not really a living ass to talk to, and there's nothing shaking, and there's no way of getting it out—that storm inside. You can't talk it and you can't make love with it, and when you finally try to get with it and play it, you realize *nobody's* listening. So *you've* got to listen. You got to find a way to listen."

And then he walked away from the window and sat on the sofa again, as though all the wind had suddenly been knocked out of him. "Sometimes you'll do *anything* to play, even cut your mother's throat." He laughed and looked at me. "Or your brother's." Then he sobered. "Or your own." Then: "Don't worry. I'm all right now and I think I'll *be* all right. But I can't forget—where I've been. I don't mean just the physical place I've been, I mean where I've *been*. And *what* I've been."

"What have you been, Sonny?" I asked.

He smiled—but sat sideways on the sofa, his elbow resting on the back, his fingers playing with his mouth and chin, not looking at me. "I've been something I didn't recognize, didn't know I could be. Didn't know anybody could be." He stopped, looking inward, looking helplessly young, looking old. "I'm not talking about it now because I feel *guilty* or anything like that—maybe it would be better if I did, I don't know. Anyway, I can't really talk about it. Not to you, not to anybody," and now he turned and faced me. "Sometimes, you know, and it was actually when I was most *out* of the world, I felt that I was in it, that I was *with* it, really, and I could play or I didn't really have to *play,* it just came out of me, it was there. And I don't know how I played, thinking about it now, but I know I did awful things, those times, sometimes, to people. Or it wasn't that I *did* anything to them—it was that they weren't real." He picked up the beer can; it was empty; he rolled it between his palms: "And other times—well, I needed a fix, I needed to find a place to lean, I needed to clear a space to *listen*—and I couldn't find it, and I—went crazy, I did terrible things to *me,* I was terrible *for* me." He began pressing the beer can between his hands, I watched the metal begin to give. It glittered, as he played with it, like a knife, and I was afraid he would cut himself, but I said nothing. "Oh well. I can never tell you. I was all by myself at the bottom of something, stinking and sweating and crying and shaking, and I smelled it, you know? *my* stink, and I thought I'd die if I couldn't get away from it and yet, all the same, I knew that everything I was doing was just locking me in with it. And I didn't know," he paused, still flattening the beer can, "I didn't know, I still *don't* know, something kept telling me that maybe it was good to smell your own stink, but I didn't think that *that* was what I'd been trying to do—and—who can stand it?" and he abruptly dropped the ruined beer can, looking at me with a small, still smile, and then rose, walking to the window as though it were the lodestone rock. I watched his face, he watched the avenue, "I couldn't tell you when Mama died—but the reason I wanted to leave Harlem so bad was to get away from drugs. And then, when I ran away, that's what I was running from—really. When I came back, nothing had changed, *I* hadn't changed, I was just—older." And he stopped, drumming with his fingers on the windowpane. The sun had vanished, soon darkness would fall. I watched his face. "It can come again," he said, almost as though speaking to himself. Then he turned to me. "It can come again," he repeated. "I just want you to know that."

"All right," I said, at last. "So it can come again. All right."

He smiled, but the smile was sorrowful. "I had to try to tell you," he said.

"Yes," I said. "I understand that."

"You're my brother," he said, looking straight at me, and not smiling at all.

"Yes," I repeated, "yes. I understand that."

He turned back to the window, looking out. "All that hatred down there," he said, "all that hatred and misery and love. It's a wonder it doesn't blow the avenue apart."

We went to the only nightclub on a short, dark street, downtown. We squeezed through the narrow, chattering, jam-packed bar to the entrance of the big room, where the bandstand was. And we stood there for a moment, for the lights were very dim in this room and we couldn't see. Then, "Hello, boy," said a voice and an enormous black man, much older than Sonny or myself, erupted out of all that atmospheric lighting and put an arm around Sonny's shoulder. "I been sitting right here," he said, "waiting for you."

He had a big voice, too, and heads in the darkness turned toward us.

Sonny grinned and pulled a little away, and said, "Creole, this is my brother. I told you about him."

Creole shook my hand. "I'm glad to meet you, son," he said, and it was clear that he was glad to meet me *there,* for Sonny's sake. And he smiled, "You got a real musician in *your* family," and he took his arm from Sonny's shoulder and slapped him, lightly, affectionately, with the back of his hand.

"Well. Now I've heard it all," said a voice behind us. This was another musician, and a friend of Sonny's, a coal-black, cheerful-looking man, built close to the ground. He immediately began confiding to me, at the top of his lungs, the most terrible things about Sonny, his teeth gleaming like a lighthouse and his laugh coming up out of him like the beginning of an earthquake. And it turned out that everyone at the bar knew Sonny, or almost everyone; some were musicians, working there, or nearby, or not working, some were simply hangers-on, and some were there to hear Sonny play. I was introduced to all of them and they were all very polite to me. Yet, it was clear that, for them, I was only Sonny's brother. Here, I was in Sonny's world. Or, rather: his kingdom. Here, it was not even a question that his veins bore royal blood.

They were going to play soon and Creole installed me, by myself, at a table in a dark corner. Then I watched them, Creole, and the little black man, and Sonny, and the others, while they horsed around, standing just below the bandstand. The light from the bandstand spilled just a little short of them and, watching them laughing and gesturing and moving about, I had the feeling that they, nevertheless, were being most careful not to step into that circle of light too suddenly: that if they moved into the light too suddenly, without thinking, they would perish in flame. Then, while I watched, one of them, the small, black man, moved into the light and crossed the bandstand and started fooling around with his drums. Then—being funny and being, also, extremely ceremonious—Creole took Sonny by the arm and led him to the piano. A woman's voice called Sonny's name and a few hands started clapping. And Sonny, also being funny and being ceremonious, and so touched, I think, that he could have cried, but neither hiding it nor showing it, riding it like a man, grinned, and put both hands to his heart and bowed from the waist.

Creole then went to the bass fiddle and a lean, very bright-skinned brown man jumped up on the bandstand and picked up his horn. So there they were, and the atmosphere on the bandstand and in the room began to change and tighten. Someone stepped up to the microphone and announced them. Then there were all kinds of murmurs. Some people at the bar shushed others. The waitress ran around, frantically getting in the last orders, guys and chicks got closer to each other, and the lights on the bandstand, on the quartet, turned to a kind of indigo. Then they all looked different there. Creole looked about him for the last time, as though he were making certain that all his chickens were in the coop, and then he—jumped and struck the fiddle. And there they were.

All I know about music is that not many people ever really hear it. And even then, on the rare occasions when something opens within, and the music enters, what we mainly hear, or hear corroborated, are personal, private, vanishing evocations. But the man who creates the music is hearing something else, is dealing with the roar rising from the void and imposing order on it as it hits the air. What is evoked in him, then, is of another order, more terrible because it has no words, and triumphant, too, for that same reason. And his triumph, when he triumphs, is ours. I just watched Sonny's face. His face was troubled, he was working hard, but he wasn't with it. And I had the feeling that, in a way, everyone on the bandstand was waiting for him, both waiting for him and pushing him along. But as I began to watch Creole, I realized that it was Creole who held them all back. He had them on a short rein. Up there, keeping the beat with his whole body, wailing on the fiddle, with his eyes half closed, he was listening to everything, but he was listening to Sonny. He was having a dialogue with Sonny. He wanted Sonny to leave the shoreline and strike out for the deep water. He was Sonny's witness that deep water and drowning were not the same thing—he had been there, and he knew. And he wanted Sonny to know. He was waiting for Sonny to do the things on the keys which would let Creole know that Sonny was in the water.

And, while Creole listened, Sonny moved, deep within, exactly like someone in torment. I had never before thought of how awful the relationship must be between the musician and his instrument. He has to fill it, this instrument, with the breath of life, his own. He has to make it do what he wants it to do. And a piano is just a piano. It's made out of so much wood and wires and little hammers and big ones, and ivory. While there's only so much you can do with it, the only way to find this out is to try; to try and make it do everything.

And Sonny hadn't been near a piano for over a year. And he wasn't on much better terms with his life, not the life that stretched before him now. He and the piano stammered, started one way, got scared, stopped; started another way, panicked, marked time, started again; then seemed to have found a direction, panicked again, got stuck. And the face I saw on Sonny I'd never seen before. Everything had been burned out of it, and, at the same time, things usually hidden were being burned in, by the fire and fury of the battle which was occurring in him up there.

Yet, watching Creole's face as they neared the end of the first set, I had the feeling that something had happened, something I hadn't heard. Then they finished, there was scattered applause, and then, without an instant's warning, Creole started into something else, it was almost sardonic, it was *Am I Blue.* And, as though he commanded, Sonny began to play. Something began to happen. And Creole let out the reins. The dry, low, black man said something awful on the drums, Creole answered, and the drums talked back. Then the horn insisted, sweet and high, slightly detached perhaps, and Creole listened, commenting now and then, dry, and driving, beautiful and calm and old. Then they all came together again, and Sonny was part of the family again. I could tell this from his face. He seemed to have found, right there beneath his fingers, a damn brand-new piano. It seemed that he couldn't get over it. Then, for awhile, just being happy with Sonny, they seemed to be agreeing with him that brand-new pianos certainly were a gas.

Then Creole stepped forward to remind them that what they were playing was the blues. He hit something in all of them, he hit something in me, myself, and the music tightened and deepened, apprehension began to beat the air. Creole began to tell us what the blues were all about. They were not about anything very new. He and his boys up there were keeping it new, at the risk of ruin, destruction, madness, and death, in order to find new ways to make us listen. For, while the tale of how we suffer, and how we are delighted, and how we may triumph is never new, it always must be heard. There isn't any other tale to tell, it's the only light we've got in all this darkness.

And this tale, according to that face, that body, those strong hands on those strings, has another aspect in every country, and a new depth in every generation. Listen, Creole seemed to be saying, listen. Now these are Sonny's blues. He made the little black man on the drums know it, and the bright, brown man on the horn. Creole wasn't trying any longer to get Sonny in the water. He was wishing him Godspeed. Then he stepped back, very slowly, filling the air with the immense suggestion that Sonny speak for himself.

Then they all gathered around Sonny and Sonny played. Every now and again one of them seemed to say, amen. Sonny's fingers filled the air with life, his life. But that life contained so many others. And Sonny went all the way back, he really began with the spare, flat statement of the opening phrase of the song. Then he began to make it his. It was very beautiful because it wasn't hurried and it was no longer a lament. I seemed to hear with what burning he had made it his, with what burning we had yet to make it ours, how we could cease lamenting. Freedom lurked around us and I understood, at last, that he could help us to be free if we would listen, that he would never be free until we did. Yet, there was no battle in his face now. I heard what he had gone through, and would continue to go through until he came to rest in earth. He had made it his: that long line, of which we knew only Mama and Daddy. And he was giving it back, as everything must be given back, so that, passing through death, it can live forever. I saw my mother's face again, and felt, for the first time, how the stones of the road she had walked on must have bruised her feet. I saw the moonlit road where my father's brother died. And it brought something else back to me, and carried me past it, I saw my little girl again and felt Isabel's tears again, and I felt my own tears begin to rise. And I was yet aware that this was only a moment, that the world waited outside, as hungry as a tiger, and that trouble stretched above us, longer than the sky.

Then it was over. Creole and Sonny let out their breath, both soaking wet, and grinning. There was a lot of applause and some of it was real. In the dark, the girl came by and I asked her to take drinks to the bandstand. There was a long pause, while they talked up there in the indigo light and after awhile I saw the girl put a Scotch and milk on top of the piano for Sonny. He didn't seem to notice it, but just before they started playing again, he sipped from it and looked toward me, and nodded. Then he put it back on top of the piano. For me, then, as they began to play again, it glowed and shook above my brother's head like the very cup of trembling.

1957

Flannery O'Connor
1925–1964

"Fiction," Flannery O'Connor wrote, "can transcend its limitations only by staying within them." That paradox informed her entire career as well. She was a determined regionalist whose work never lapses into a comfortable provinciality, a devout Catholic who found her themes and characters in the "Christ-haunted" southern Protestant Bible belt, and, for much of her adult life, a confined invalid who could be as resistant to sentimentality and what she called "hazy compassion" as the most hard-boiled detective novelist. Like such earlier southern regionalists as George Washington Harris, she wanted nothing to do with mansions, magnolias, and mockingbirds, and like Harris, too, she shaped her stories around moments of unexpected comic violence. Yet unlike Harris, her literary commitment to comedy and violence never seems gratuitous but rather was deeply rooted in religious and aesthetic convictions. "My subject in fiction," she said, "is the action of grace in territory held largely by the devil."

Mary Flannery O'Connor was born in Savannah, Georgia, on March 25, 1925. Her family moved when she was twelve to Milledgeville, Georgia, where she graduated from the Women's College of Georgia. She studied creative writing at the State University of Iowa, earning an M.F.A. in 1947. In 1948 she was invited to join Yaddo, the prestigious writer's colony in Saratoga Springs, New York, but resigned, along with her new friends Robert Lowell and Elizabeth Hardwick, over the internal handling of a political incident. She lived for a few months in New York City and then spent a year with the writers Sally and Robert Fitzgerald at their Connecticut home.

In 1950, after she learned that she was dying of lupus, an incurable tubercular disease that had killed her father, she returned to Milledgeville to live with her mother on the family dairy farm. Her first novel, *Wise Blood,* the story of a young Tennessee religious fanatic who preaches a Church Without Christ, appeared in 1952. It was followed by a collection of ten short stories, *A Good Man Is Hard to Find* (1955), from which both stories that follow have been reprinted. She published her second novel, another grotesque tale of religious aberration, *The Violent Bear It Away,* in 1960. Suffering from acute anemia, Flannery O'Connor underwent what may have been an ill-advised operation to remove a benign tumor. The operation reactivated the lupus, and she died in Milledgeville on August 3, 1964. Her second collection of stories, *Everything That Rises Must Converge* (its title derives from the Catholic theologian Teilhard de Chardin), appeared in 1965.

Flannery O'Connor hated abstraction. "The first and most obvious characteristic of fiction is that it deals with reality, through what can be seen, heard, smelt, tasted, and touched." Following the great Catholic philosopher, St. Thomas Aquinas, she believed that human knowledge begins through the senses. She disliked critical abstractions as well, feeling that a good story must resist sociological, psychological, philosophical, or religious paraphrase. She recalled that once after a reading of her short story "A Good Man Is Hard to Find," an earnest teacher began asking her questions:

> "Miss O'Connor," he said, "why was the Misfit's hat *black?*" I said most countrymen in Georgia wore black hats. He looked pretty disappointed. Then he said, "Miss O'Connor, the Misfit represents Christ, does he not?" "He does not," I said. He looked crushed. "Well, Miss O'Connor," he said, "what is the significance of the Misfit's hat?" I said it was to cover his head; and after that he left me alone. Anyway, that's what's happening to the teaching of literature.

Her irritation with the questions has less to do with a dislike for symbolism than with a dislike for a symbol-hunting mentality that thinks it has "understood" a story when it has completely discarded the work's literal level and discovered, as in an algebraic equation, what every detail "stands for."

In Flannery O'Connor's own critical articles, collected posthumously in *Mystery and Manners* (1969), she is always careful to respect the essential mystery of art. She saw the preservation of mystery as fundamental to both art and religion: "Christian dogma," she claimed, "is about the only thing left in the world that surely guards and respects mystery." The novelist's sense of mystery, she believed, grows out of a recognition of the world's incompleteness; the writer's profound sense of something lacking in the world gives serious fiction its value and meaning. In one of her finest essays, "Some Aspects of the Grotesque in Southern Fiction," she expressed this belief in a way that bears directly on her own literary achievement: For a certain kind of writer, she noted, "the meaning of a story does not begin except at a depth where adequate motivation and adequate psychology and the various determinations have been exhausted. Such a writer will be interested in what we don't understand rather than in what we do."

Further Reading:
The Art and Mind of Flannery O'Connor, ed.
M. J. Freedman and L. A. Lawson, 1966.
S. E. Hyman, *Flannery O'Connor,* 1966.
J. Hendin, *The World of Flannery O'Connor,*
1970.
D. Walters, *Flannery O'Connor,* 1973.
J. R. May, *The Pruning Word: The Parables of
Flannery O'Connor,* 1976.
C. Shloss, *Flannery O'Connor's Dark Comedies,*
1980.

Text:
The Complete Stories, 1971.
See also *The Habit of Being: Letters of Flannery
O'Connor,* ed. S. Fitzgerald, 1979.

A Good Man Is Hard to Find

The grandmother didn't want to go to Florida. She wanted to visit some of her connections in east Tennessee and she was seizing every chance to change Bailey's mind. Bailey was the son she lived with, her only boy. He was sitting on the edge of his chair at the table, bent over the orange sports section of the *Journal.* "Now look here, Bailey," she said, "see here, read this," and she stood with one hand on her thin hip and the other rattling the newspaper at his bald head. "Here this fellow that calls himself The Misfit is aloose from the Federal Pen and headed toward Florida and you read here what it says he did to these people. Just you read it. I wouldn't take my children in any direction with a criminal like that aloose in it. I couldn't answer to my conscience if I did."

Bailey didn't look up from his reading so she wheeled around then and faced the children's mother; a young woman in slacks, whose face was as broad and innocent as a cabbage and was tied around with a green headkerchief that had two points on the top like rabbit's ears. She was sitting on the sofa, feeding the baby his apricots out of a jar. "The children have been to Florida before," the old lady said. "You all ought to take them somewhere else for a change so they would see different parts of the world and be broad. They never have been to east Tennessee."

The children's mother didn't seem to hear her, but the eight-year-old boy, John Wesley, a stocky child with glasses, said, "If you don't want to go to Florida, why dontcha stay at home?" He and the little girl, June Star, were reading the funny papers on the floor.

"She wouldn't stay at home to be queen for a day," June Star said without raising her yellow head.

"Yes, and what would you do if this fellow, The Misfit, caught you?" the grandmother asked.

"I'd smack his face," John Wesley said.

"She wouldn't stay at home for a million bucks," June Star said. "Afraid she'd miss something. She has to go everywhere we go."

"All right, Miss," the grandmother said. "Just remember that the next time you want me to curl your hair."

June Star said her hair was naturally curly.

The next morning the grandmother was the first one in the car, ready to go. She had her big black valise that looked like the head of a hippopotamus in one corner, and underneath it she was hiding a basket with Pitty Sing, the cat, in it. She didn't intend for the cat to be left alone in the house for three days because he would miss her too much and she was afraid he might brush against one of the gas burners and accidentally asphyxiate himself. Her son, Bailey, didn't like to arrive at a motel with a cat.

She sat in the middle of the back seat with John Wesley and June Star on either side of her. Bailey and the children's mother and the baby sat in the front and they left Atlanta at eight forty-five with the mileage on the car at 55890. The grandmother wrote this down because she thought it would be interesting to say how many miles they had been when they got back. It took them twenty minutes to reach the outskirts of the city.

The old lady settled herself comfortably, removing her white cotton gloves and putting them up with her purse on the shelf in front of the back window. The children's mother still had on slacks and still had her head tied up in a green kerchief, but the grandmother had on a navy blue straw sailor hat with a bunch of white violets on the brim and a navy blue dress with a small white dot in the print. Her collar and cuffs were white organdy trimmed with lace and at her neckline she had pinned a purple spray of cloth violets containing a sachet. In case of an accident, anyone seeing her dead on the highway would know at once that she was a lady.

She said she thought it was going to be a good day for driving, neither too hot nor too cold, and she cautioned Bailey that the speed limit was fifty-five miles an hour and that the patrolmen hid themselves behind bill-boards and small clumps of trees and sped out after you before you had a chance to slow down. She pointed out interesting details of the scenery: Stone Mountain; the blue granite that in some places came up to both sides of the highway; the brilliant red clay banks slightly streaked with purple; and the various crops that made rows of green lace-work on the ground. The trees were full of silver-white sunlights and the meanest of them sparkled. The children were reading comic magazines and their mother had gone back to sleep.

"Let's go through Georgia fast so we won't have to look at it much," John Wesley said.

"If I were a little boy," said the grandmother, "I wouldn't talk about my native state that way. Tennessee has the mountains and Georgia has the hills."

"Tennessee is just a hillbilly dumping ground," John Wesley said, "and Georgia is a lousy state too."

"You said it," June Star said.

"In my time," said the grandmother, folding her thin veined fingers, "children were more respectful of their native states and their parents and everything else. People did right then. Oh look at the cute little pickaninny!" she said and pointed to a Negro child standing in the door of a shack. "Wouldn't that make a picture, now?" she asked and they all turned and looked at the little Negro out of the back window. He waved.

"He didn't have any britches on," June Star said.

"He probably didn't have any," the grandmother explained. "Little niggers in the country don't have things like we do. If I could paint, I'd paint that picture," she said.

The children exchanged comic books.

The grandmother offered to hold the baby and the children's mother passed him over the front seat to her. She set him on her knee and bounced him and told him about the things they were passing. She rolled her eyes and screwed up her mouth and stuck her leathery thin face into his smooth bland one. Occasionally he gave her a faraway smile. They passed a large cotton field with five or six graves fenced in the middle of it, like a small island. "Look at the graveyard!" the grandmother said, pointing it out. "That was the old family burying ground. That belonged to the plantation."

"Where's the plantation?" John Wesley asked.

"Gone With the Wind," said the grandmother. "Ha. Ha."

When the children finished all the comic books they had brought, they opened the lunch and ate it. The grandmother ate a peanut butter sandwich and an olive and would not let the children throw the box and the paper napkins out the window. When there was nothing else to do they played a game by choosing a cloud and making the other two guess what shape it suggested. John Wesley took one the shape of a cow and June Star guessed a cow and John Wesley said, no, an automobile, and June Star said he didn't play fair, and they began to slap each other over the grandmother.

The grandmother said she would tell them a story if they would keep quiet. When she told a story, she rolled her eyes and waved her head and was very dramatic. She said once when she was a maiden lady she had been courted by a Mr. Edgar Atkins Teagarden from Jasper, Georgia. She said he was a very good-looking man and a gentleman and that he brought her a watermelon every Saturday afternoon with his initials cut in it, E.A.T. Well, one Saturday, she said, Mr. Teagarden brought the watermelon and there was nobody at home and he left it on the front porch and returned in his buggy to Jasper, but she never got the watermelon, she said, because a nigger boy ate it when he saw the initials, E.A.T.! This story tickled John Wesley's funny bone and he giggled and giggled but June Star didn't think it was any good. She said she wouldn't marry a man that just brought her a watermelon on Saturday. The grandmother said she would have done well to marry Mr. Teagarden because he was a gentleman and had bought Coca-Cola stock when it first came out and that he had died only a few years ago, a very wealthy man.

They stopped at The Tower for barbecued sandwiches. The Tower was a part-stucco and part-wood filling station and dance hall set in a clearing outside of Timothy. A fat man named Red Sammy Butts ran it and there were signs stuck here and there on the building and for miles up and down the highway saying, TRY RED SAMMY'S FAMOUS BARBECUE. NONE LIKE FAMOUS RED SAMMY'S! RED SAM! THE FAT BOY WITH THE HAPPY LAUGH. A VETERAN! RED SAMMY'S YOUR MAN!

Red Sammy was lying on the bare ground outside The Tower with his head under a truck while a gray monkey about a foot high, chained to a small chinaberry tree, chattered nearby. The monkey sprang back into the tree and got on the highest limb as soon as he saw the children jump out of the car and run toward him.

Inside, The Tower was a long dark room with a counter at one end and tables at the other and dancing space in the middle. They all sat down at a broad table next to the nickelodeon and Red Sam's wife, a tall burnt-brown woman with hair and eyes lighter than her skin, came and took their order. The children's mother put a dime in the machine and played "The Tennessee Waltz," and the grandmother said that tune always made her want to dance. She asked Bailey if he would like to dance but he only glared at her. He didn't have a naturally sunny disposition like she did and trips made him nervous. The grandmother's brown eyes were very bright. She swayed her head from side to side and pretended she was dancing in her chair. June Star said play something she could tap to so the children's mother put in another dime and played a fast number and June Star stepped out onto the dance floor and did her tap routine.

"Ain't she cute?" Red Sam's wife said, leaning over the counter. "Would you like to come be my little girl?"

"No, I certainly wouldn't," June Star said. "I wouldn't live in a broken-down place like this for a million bucks!" and she ran back to the table.

"Ain't she cute?" the woman repeated, stretching her mouth politely.

"Aren't you ashamed?" hissed the grandmother.

Red Sam came in and told his wife to quit lounging on the counter and hurry up with these people's order. His khaki trousers reached just to his hip bones and his stomach hung over them like a sack of meal swaying under his shirt. He came over and sat down at a table nearby and let out a combination sigh and yodel. "You can't win," he said. "You can't win," and he wiped his sweating red face off with a gray handkerchief. "These days you don't know who to trust," he said. "Ain't that the truth?"

"People are certainly not nice like they used to be," said the grandmother.

"Two fellers come in here last week," Red Sammy said, "driving a Chrysler. It was an old beat-up car but it was a good one and these boys looked all right to me. Said they worked at the mill and you know I let them fellers charge the gas they bought? Now why did I do that?"

"Because you're a good man!" the grandmother said at once.

"Yes'm, I suppose so," Red Sam said as if he were struck with this answer.

His wife brought the orders, carrying the five plates all at once without a tray, two in each hand and one balanced on her arm. "It isn't a soul in this green world of God's that you can trust," she said. "And I don't count nobody out of that, not nobody," she repeated, looking at Red Sammy.

"Did you read about that criminal, The Misfit, that's escaped?" asked the grandmother.

"I wouldn't be a bit surprised if he didn't attack this place right here," said the woman. "If he hears about it being here, I wouldn't be none surprised to see him. If he hears it's two cent in the cash register, I wouldn't be a tall surprised if he. . . ."

"That'll do," Red Sam said. "Go bring these people their Co'-Colas," and the woman went off to get the rest of the order.

"A good man is hard to find," Red Sammy said. "Everything is getting terrible. I remember the day you could go off and leave your screen door unlatched. Not no more."

He and the grandmother discussed better times. The old lady said that in her opinion Europe was entirely to blame for the way things were now. She said the way Europe acted you would think we were made of money and Red Sam said it was no use talking about it, she was exactly right. The children ran outside into the white sunlight and looked at the monkey in the lacy chinaberry tree. He was busy catching fleas on himself and biting each one carefully between his teeth as if it were a delicacy.

They drove off again into the hot afternoon. The grandmother took cat naps and woke up every few minutes with her own snoring. Outside of Toombsboro she woke up and recalled an old plantation that she had visited in this neighborhood once when she was a young lady. She said the house had six white columns across the front and that there was an avenue of oaks leading up to it and two little wooden trellis arbors on either side in front where you sat down with your suitor after a stroll in the garden. She recalled exactly which road to turn off to get to it. She knew that Bailey would not be willing to lose any time looking at an old house, but the more she talked about it, the more she wanted to see it once again and find out if the little twin arbors were still standing. "There was a secret panel in this house," she said craftily, not telling the truth but wishing that she were, "and the story went that all the family silver was hidden in it when Sherman[1] came through but it was never found. . . . "

"Hey!" John Wesley said. "Let's go see it! We'll find it! We'll poke all the wood work and find it! Who lives there? Where do you turn off at? Hey Pop, can't we turn off there?"

"We never have seen a house with a secret panel!" June Star shrieked. "Let's go to the house with the secret panel! Hey, Pop, can't we go see the house with the secret panel!"

"It's not far from here, I know," the grandmother said. "It wouldn't take over twenty minutes."

Bailey was looking straight ahead. His jaw was as rigid as a horseshoe. "No," he said.

The children began to yell and scream that they wanted to see the house with the secret panel. John Wesley kicked the back of the front seat and June Star hung over her mother's shoulder and whined desperately into her ear that they never had any fun even on their vacation, that they could never do what THEY wanted to do. The baby began to scream and John Wesley kicked the back of the seat so hard that his father could feel the blows in his kidney.

"All right!" he shouted and drew the car to a stop at the side of the road. "Will you all shut up? Will you all just shut up for one second? If you don't shut up, we won't go anywhere."

"It would be very educational for them," the grandmother murmured.

"All right," Bailey said, "but get this. This is the only time we're going to stop for anything like this. This is the one and only time."

"The dirt road that you have to turn down is about a mile back," the grandmother directed. "I marked it when we passed."

"A dirt road," Bailey groaned.

After they had turned around and were headed toward the dirt road, the grandmother recalled other points about the house, the beautiful glass over the front doorway and the candle lamp in the hall. John Wesley said that the secret panel was probably in the fireplace.

"You can't go inside this house," Bailey said. "You don't know who lives there."

---

[1] William Tecumseh Sherman, the Union general who marched his troops through Atlanta to the Georgia coast in the winter of 1864.

"While you all talk to the people in front, I'll run around behind and get in a window," John Wesley suggested.

"We'll all stay in the car," his mother said.

They turned onto the dirt road and the car raced roughly along in a swirl of pink dust. The grandmother recalled the times when there were no paved roads and thirty miles was a day's journey. The dirt road was hilly and there were sudden washes in it and sharp curves on dangerous embankments. All at once they would be on a hill, looking down over the blue tops of trees for miles around, then the next minute, they would be in a red depression with the dust-coated trees looking down on them.

"This place had better turn up in a minute," Bailey said, "or I'm going to turn around."

The road looked as if no one had traveled on it in months.

"It's not much farther," the grandmother said and just as she said it, a horrible thought came to her. The thought was so embarrassing that she turned red in the face and her eyes dilated and her feet jumped up, upsetting her valise in the corner. The instant the valise moved, the newspaper top she had over the basket under it rose with a snarl and Pitty Sing, the cat, sprang onto Bailey's shoulder.

The children were thrown to the floor and their mother, clutching the baby, was thrown out the door onto the ground; the old lady was thrown into the front seat. The car turned over once and landed right-side-up in a gulch on the side of the road. Bailey remained in the driver's seat with the cat—gray-striped with a broad white face and an orange nose—clinging to his neck like a caterpillar.

As soon as the children saw they could move their arms and legs, they scrambled out of the car, shouting, "We've had an ACCIDENT!" The grandmother was curled up under the dashboard, hoping she was injured so that Bailey's wrath would not come down on her all at once. The horrible thought she had had before the accident was that the house she had remembered so vividly was not in Georgia but in Tennessee.

Bailey removed the cat from his neck with both hands and flung it out the window against the side of a pine tree. Then he got out of the car and started looking for the children's mother. She was sitting against the side of the red gutted ditch, holding the screaming baby, but she only had a cut down her face and a broken shoulder. "We've had an ACCIDENT!" the children screamed in a frenzy of delight.

"But nobody's killed," June Star said with disappointment as the grandmother limped out of the car, her hat still pinned to her head but the broken front brim standing up at a jaunty angle and the violet spray hanging off the side. They all sat down in the ditch, except the children, to recover from the shock. They were all shaking.

"Maybe a car will come along," said the children's mother hoarsely.

"I believe I have injured an organ," said the grandmother, pressing her side, but no one answered her. Bailey's teeth were clattering. He had on a yellow sport shirt with bright blue parrots designed in it and his face was as yellow as the shirt. The grandmother decided that she would not mention that the house was in Tennessee.

The road was about ten feet above and they could see only the tops of the trees on the other side of it. Behind the ditch they were sitting in there were more woods, tall and dark and deep. In a few minutes they saw a car some distance away on top of a hill, coming slowly as if the occupants were watching them. The grandmother stood up and waved both arms dramatically to attract their attention. The car continued to come on slowly, disappeared around a bend and appeared again, moving even slower on top of the hill they had gone over. It was a big black battered hearselike automobile. There were three men in it.

It came to a stop just over them and for some minutes, the driver looked down with a steady expressionless gaze to where they were sitting, and didn't speak. Then he turned his head and muttered something to the other two and they got out. One was a fat boy in black trousers and a red sweat shirt with a silver stallion embossed on the front of it. He moved around on the right side of them and stood staring, his mouth partly open in a kind of loose grin. The other had on khaki pants and a blue striped coat and a gray hat pulled down very low, hiding most of his face. He came around slowly on the left side. Neither spoke.

The driver got out of the car and stood by the side of it, looking down at them. He was an older man than the other two. His hair was just beginning to gray and he wore silver-rimmed spectacles that gave him a scholarly look. He had a long creased face and didn't have on any shirt or undershirt. He had on blue jeans that were too tight for him and was holding a black hat and a gun. The two boys also had guns.

"We've had an ACCIDENT!" the children screamed.

The grandmother had the peculiar feeling that the bespectacled man was someone she knew. His face was as familiar to her as if she had known him all her life but she could not recall who he was. He moved away from the car and began to come down the embankment, placing his feet carefully so that he wouldn't slip. He had on tan and white shoes and no socks, and his ankles were red and thin. "Good afternoon," he said. "I see you all had you a little spill."

"We turned over twice!" said the grandmother.

"Oncet," he corrected. "We see it happen. Try their car and see will it run, Hiram," he said quietly to the boy with the gray hat.

"What you got that gun for?" John Wesley asked. "Whatcha gonna do with that gun?"

"Lady," the man said to the children's mother, "would you mind calling them children to sit down by you? Children make me nervous. I want all you to sit down right together there where you're at."

"What are you telling us what to do for?" June Star asked.

Behind them the line of woods gaped like a dark open mouth. "Come here," said their mother.

"Look here now," Bailey began suddenly, "we're in a predicament! We're in. . . ."

The grandmother shrieked. She scrambled to her feet and stood staring.

"You're The Misfit!" she said. "I recognized you at once!"

"Yes'm," the man said, smiling slightly as if he were pleased in spite of himself to be known. "but it would have been better for all of you, lady, if you hadn't of reckernized me."

Bailey turned his head sharply and said something to his mother that shocked even the children. The old lady began to cry and The Misfit reddened.

"Lady," he said, "don't you get upset. Sometimes a man says things he don't mean. I don't reckon he meant to talk to you thataway."

"You wouldn't shoot a lady, would you?" the grandmother said and removed a clean handkerchief from her cuff and began to slap at her eyes with it.

The Misfit pointed the toe of his shoe into the ground and made a little hole and then covered it up again. "I would hate to have to," he said.

"Listen," the grandmother almost screamed, "I know you're a good man. You don't look a bit like you have common blood. I know you must come from nice people!"

"Yes mam," he said, "finest people in the world." When he smiled he showed a row of strong white teeth. "God never made a finer woman than my mother and my daddy's heart was pure gold," he said. The boy with the red sweat shirt had come around behind them and was standing with his gun at his hip. The Misfit squatted down on the ground. "Watch them children, Bobby Lee," he said. "You know they make me nervous." He looked at the six of them huddled together in front of him and he seemed to be embarrassed as if he couldn't think of anything to say. "Ain't a cloud in the sky," he remarked, looking up at it. "Don't see no sun but don't see no cloud neither."

"Yes, it's a beautiful day," said the grandmother. "Listen," she said, "you shouldn't call yourself The Misfit because I know you're a good man at heart. I can just look at you and tell."

"Hush!" Bailey yelled. "Hush! Everybody shut up and let me handle this!" He was squatting in the position of a runner about to sprint forward but he didn't move.

"I pre-chate that, lady," The Misfit said and drew a little circle in the ground with the butt of his gun.

"It'll take a half a hour to fix this here car," Hiram called, looking over the raised hood of it.

"Well, first you and Bobby Lee get him and that little boy to step over yonder with you," The Misfit said, pointing to Bailey and John Wesley. "The boys want to ask you something," he said to Bailey. "Would you mind stepping back in them woods there with them?"

"Listen," Bailey began, "we're in a terrible predicament! Nobody realizes what this is," and his voice cracked. His eyes were as blue and intense as the parrots in his shirt and he remained perfectly still.

The grandmother reached up to adjust her hat brim as if she were going to the woods with him but it came off in her hand. She stood staring at it and after a second she let it fall on the ground. Hiram pulled Bailey up by the arm as if he were assisting an old man. John Wesley caught hold of his father's hand and Bobby Lee followed. They went off toward the woods and just as they reached the dark edge, Bailey turned and supporting himself against a gray naked pine trunk, he shouted, "I'll be back in a minute, Mamma, wait on me!"

"Come back this instant!" his mother shrilled but they all disappeared into the woods.

"Bailey Boy!" the grandmother called in a tragic voice but she found she was looking at The Misfit squatting on the ground in front of her. "I just know you're a good man," she said desperately. "You're not a bit common!"

"Nome, I ain't a good man," The Misfit said after a second as if he had considered her statement carefully, "but I ain't the worst in the world neither. My daddy said I was a different breed of dog from my brothers and sisters. 'You know,' Daddy said, 'it's some that can live their whole life without asking about it and it's others has to know why it is, and this boy is one of the latters. He's going to be into everything!' " He put on his black hat and looked up suddenly and then away deep into the woods as if he were embarrassed again. "I'm sorry, I don't have on a shirt before you ladies," he said, hunching his shoulders slightly. "We buried our clothes that we had on when we escaped and we're just making do until we can get better. We borrowed these from some folks we met," he explained.

"That's perfectly all right," the grandmother said. "Maybe Bailey has an extra shirt in his suitcase."

"I'll look and see terrectly," The Misfit said.

"Where are they taking him?" the children's mother screamed.

"Daddy was a card himself," The Misfit said. "You couldn't put anything over on him. He never got in trouble with the Authorities though. Just had the knack of handling them."

"You could be honest too if you'd only try," said the grandmother. "Think how wonderful it would be to settle down and live a comfortable life and not have to think about somebody chasing you all the time."

The Misfit kept scratching in the ground with the butt of his gun as if he were thinking about it. "Yes'm, somebody is always after you," he murmured.

The grandmother noticed how thin his shoulder blades were just behind his hat because she was standing up looking down on him. "Do you ever pray?" she asked.

He shook his head. All she saw was the black hat wiggle between his shoulder blades. "Nome," he said.

There was a pistol shot from the woods, followed closely by another. Then silence. The old lady's head jerked around. She could hear the wind move through the tree tops like a long satisfied insuck of breath. "Bailey Boy!" she called.

"I was a gospel singer for a while," The Misfit said. "I been most everything. Been in the arm service, both land and sea, at home and abroad, been twict married, been an undertaker, been with the railroads, plowed Mother Earth, been in a tornado, seen a man burnt alive oncet," and he looked up at the children's mother and the little girl who were sitting close together, their faces white and their eyes glassy; "I even seen a woman flogged," he said.

"Pray, pray," the grandmother began, "pray, pray. . . . "

"I never was a bad boy that I remember of," The Misfit said in an almost dreamy voice, "but somewheres along the line I done something wrong and got sent to the penitentiary. I was buried alive," and he looked up and held her attention to him by a steady stare.

"That's when you should have started to pray," she said. "What did you do to get sent to the penitentiary that first time?"

"Turn to the right, it was a wall," The Misfit said, looking up again at the cloudless sky. "Turn to the left, it was a wall. Look up it was a ceiling, look down it was a floor. I forget what I done, lady. I set there and set there, trying to remember what it was I done and I ain't recalled it to this day. Oncet in a while, I would think it was coming to me, but it never come."

"Maybe they put you in by mistake," the old lady said vaguely.

"Nome," he said. "It wasn't no mistake. They had the papers on me."

"You must have stolen something," she said.

The Misfit sneered slightly. "Nobody had nothing I wanted," he said. "It was a head-doctor at the penitentiary said what I had done was kill my daddy but I known that for a lie. My daddy died in nineteen ought nineteen of the epidemic flu[2] and I never had a thing to do with it. He was buried in the Mount Hopewell Baptist churchyard and you can go there and see for yourself."

"If you would pray," the old lady said, "Jesus would help you."

"That's right," The Misfit said.

"Well then, why don't you pray?" she asked trembling with delight suddenly.

"I don't want no hep," he said. "I'm doing all right by myself."

Bobby Lee and Hiram came ambling back from the woods. Bobby Lee was dragging a yellow shirt with bright blue parrots in it.

"Throw me that shirt, Bobby Lee," The Misfit said. The shirt came flying at him and landed on his shoulder and he put it on. The grandmother couldn't name what the shirt reminded her of. "No, lady," The Misfit said while he was buttoning it up, "I found out the crime don't matter. You can do one thing or you can do another, kill a man or take a tire off his car, because sooner or later you're going to forget what it was you done and just be punished for it."

The children's mother had begun to make heaving noises as if she couldn't get her breath. "Lady," he asked, "would you and that little girl like to step off yonder with Bobby Lee and Hiram and join your husband?"

"Yes, thank you," the mother said faintly. Her left arm dangled helplessly and she was holding the baby, who had gone to sleep, in the other. "Hep that lady up, Hiram," The Misfit said as she struggled to climb out of the ditch, "and Bobby Lee, you hold onto that little girl's hand."

"I don't want to hold hands with him," June Star said. "He reminds me of a pig."

The fat boy blushed and laughed and caught her by the arm and pulled her off into the woods after Hiram and her mother.

Alone with The Misfit, the grandmother found that she had lost her voice. There was not a cloud in the sky nor any sun. There was nothing around her but woods. She wanted to tell him that he must pray. She opened and closed her mouth several times before anything came out. Finally she found herself saying, "Jesus. Jesus," meaning, Jesus will help you, but the way she was saying it, it sounded as if she might be cursing.

"Yes'm," The Misfit said as if he agreed. "Jesus thrown everything off balance. It was the same case with Him as with me except He hadn't committed any crime and they could prove I had committed one because they had the papers on me. Of course," he said, "they never shown me my papers. That's why I sign myself now. I said long ago, you get you a signature and sign everything you do and keep a copy of it. Then you'll know what you done and you can hold up the crime to the punishment and see do they match and in the end you'll have something to prove you ain't been treated right. I call myself The Misfit," he said, "because I can't make what all I done wrong fit what all I gone through in punishment."

There was a piercing scream from the woods, followed closely by a pistol report.

[2] I.e., the worldwide flu epidemic of 1919.

"Does it seem right to you, lady, that one is punished a heap and another ain't punished at all?"

"Jesus!" the old lady cried. "You've got good blood! I know you wouldn't shoot a lady! I know you come from nice people! Pray! Jesus, you ought not to shoot a lady. I'll give you all the money I've got!"

"Lady," The Misfit said, looking beyond her far into the woods, "there never was a body that give the undertaker a tip."

There were two more pistol reports and the grandmother raised her head like a parched old turkey hen crying for water and called, "Bailey Boy, Bailey Boy!" as if her heart would break.

"Jesus was the only One that ever raised the dead," The Misfit continued, "and He shouldn't have done it. He thrown everything off balance. If He did what He said, then it's nothing for you to do but throw away everything and follow Him, and if He didn't then it's nothing for you to do but enjoy the few minutes you got left the best way you can—by killing somebody or burning down his house or doing some other meanness to him. No pleasure but meanness," he said and his voice had become almost a snarl.

"Maybe He didn't raise the dead," the old lady mumbled, not knowing what she was saying and feeling so dizzy that she sank down in the ditch with her legs twisted under her.

"I wasn't there so I can't say He didn't," The Misfit said. "I wisht I had of been there," he said, hitting the ground with his fist. "It ain't right I wasn't there because if I had of been there I would of known. Listen lady," he said in a high voice, "if I had of been there I would of known and I wouldn't be like I am now." His voice seemed about to crack and the grandmother's head cleared for an instant. She saw the man's face twisted close to her own as if he were going to cry and she murmured, "Why, you're one of my babies. You're one of my own children!" She reached out and touched him on the shoulder. The Misfit sprang back as if a snake had bitten him and shot her three times through the chest. Then he put his gun down on the ground and took off his glasses and began to clean them.

Hiram and Bobby Lee returned from the woods and stood over the ditch, looking down at the grandmother who half sat and half lay in a puddle of blood with her legs crossed under her like a child's and her face smiling up at the cloudless sky.

Without his glasses, The Misfit's eyes were red-rimmed and pale and defenseless-looking. "Take her off and throw her where you thrown the others," he said, picking up the cat that was rubbing itself against his leg.

"She was a talker, wasn't she?" Bobby Lee said, sliding down the ditch with a yodel.

"She would of been a good woman," The Misfit said, "if it had been somebody there to shoot her every minute of her life."

"Some fun!" Bobby Lee said.

"Shut up, Bobby Lee," The Misfit said. "It's no real pleasure in life."

1953

Good Country People

Besides the neutral expression that she wore when she was alone, Mrs. Freeman had two others, forward and reverse, that she used for all her human dealings. Her forward expression was steady and driving like the advance of a heavy truck. Her eyes never swerved to left or right but turned as the story turned as if they followed a yellow line down the center of it. She seldom used the other expression because it was not often necessary for her to retract a statement, but when she did, her face came to a complete stop, there was an almost imperceptible movement of her black eyes, during which they seemed to be receding, and then the observer would see that Mrs. Freeman, though she might stand there as real as several grain sacks thrown on top of each other, was no longer there in spirit. As for getting anything across to her when this was the case, Mrs. Hopewell had given it up. She might talk her head off. Mrs. Freeman could never be brought to admit herself wrong on any point. She would stand there and if she could be brought to say anything, it was something like, "Well, I wouldn't of said it was and I wouldn't of said it wasn't," or letting her gaze range over the top kitchen shelf where there was an assortment of dusty bottles, she might remark, "I see you ain't ate many of them figs you put up last summer."

They carried on their most important business in the kitchen at breakfast. Every morning Mrs. Hopewell got up at seven o'clock and lit her gas heater and Joy's. Joy was her daughter, a large blonde girl who had an artificial leg. Mrs. Hopewell thought of her as a child though she was thirty-two years old and highly educated. Joy would get up while her mother was eating and lumber into the bathroom and slam the door, and before long, Mrs. Freeman would arrive at the back door. Joy would hear her mother call, "Come on in," and then they would talk for a while in low voices that were indistinguishable in the bathroom. By the time Joy came in, they had usually finished the weather report and were on one or the other of Mrs. Freeman's daughters, Glynese or Carramae. Joy called them Glycerin and Caramel. Glynese, a redhead, was eighteen and had many admirers; Carramae, a blonde, was only fifteen but already married and pregnant. She could not keep anything on her stomach. Every morning Mrs. Freeman told Mrs. Hopewell how many times she had vomited since the last report.

Mrs. Hopewell liked to tell people that Glynese and Carramae were two of the finest girls she knew and that Mrs. Freeman was a *lady* and that she was never ashamed to take her anywhere or introduce her to anybody they might meet. Then she would tell how she had happened to hire the Freemans in the first place and how they were a godsend to her and how she had had them four years. The reason for her keeping them so long was that they were not trash. They were good country people. She had telephoned the man whose name they had given as a reference and he had told her that Mr. Freeman was a good farmer but that his wife was the nosiest woman ever to walk the earth. "She's got to be into everything," the man said. "If she don't get there before the dust settles, you can bet she's dead, that's all. She'll want to know all your business. I can stand him real good," he had said, "but me nor my wife neither could have stood that woman one more minute on this place." That had put Mrs. Hopewell off for a few days.

She had hired them in the end because there were no other applicants but she had made up her mind beforehand exactly how she would handle the woman. Since she was the type who had to be into everything, then, Mrs. Hopewell had decided, she would not only let her be into everything, she would *see to it* that she was into everything—she would give her the responsibility of everything, she would put her in charge. Mrs. Hopewell had no bad qualities of her own but she was able to use other people's in such a constructive way that she never felt the lack. She had hired the Freemans and she had kept them four years.

Nothing is perfect. This was one of Mrs. Hopewell's favorite sayings. Another was: that is life! And still another, the most important, was: well, other people have their opinions too. She would make these statements, usually at the table, in a tone of gentle insistence as if no one held them but her, and the large hulking Joy, whose constant outrage had obliterated every expression from her face, would stare just a little to the side of her, her eyes icy blue, with the look of someone who has achieved blindness by an act of will and means to keep it.

When Mrs. Hopewell said to Mrs. Freeman that life was like that, Mrs. Freeman would say, "I always said so myself." Nothing had been arrived at by anyone that had not first been arrived at by her. She was quicker than Mr. Freeman. When Mrs. Hopewell said to her after they had been on the place a while, "You know, you're the wheel behind the wheel," and winked, Mrs. Freeman had said, "I know it. I've always been quick. It's some that are quicker than others."

"Everybody is different," Mrs. Hopewell said.

"Yes, most people is," Mrs. Freeman said.

"It takes all kinds to make the world."

"I always said it did myself."

The girl was used to this kind of dialogue for breakfast and more of it for dinner; sometimes they had it for supper too. When they had no guest they ate in the kitchen because that was easier. Mrs. Freeman always managed to arrive at some point during the meal and to watch them finish it. She would stand in the doorway if it were summer but in the winter she would stand with one elbow on top of the refrigerator and look down on them, or she would stand by the gas heater, lifting the back of her skirt slightly. Occasionally she would stand against the wall and roll her head from side to side. At no time was she in any hurry to leave. All this was very trying on Mrs. Hopewell but she was a woman of great patience. She realized that nothing is perfect and that in the Freemans she had good country people and that if, in this day and age, you get good country people, you had better hang onto them.

She had had plenty of experience with trash. Before the Freemans she had averaged one tenant family a year. The wives of these farmers were not the kind you would want to be around you for very long. Mrs. Hopewell, who had divorced her husband long ago, needed someone to walk over the fields with her; and when Joy had to be impressed for these services, her remarks were usually so ugly and her face so glum that Mrs. Hopewell would say, "If you can't come pleasantly, I don't want you at all," to which the girl, standing square and rigid-shouldered with her neck thrust slightly forward, would reply, "If you want me, here I am—LIKE I AM."

Mrs. Hopewell excused this attitude because of the leg (which had been shot off in a hunting accident when Joy was ten). It was hard for Mrs. Hopewell to realize that her child was thirty-two now and that for more than twenty years she had had only one leg. She thought of her still as a child because it tore her heart to think instead of the poor stout girl in her thirties who had never danced a step or had any *normal* good times. Her name was really Joy but as soon as she was twenty-one and away from home, she had had it legally changed. Mrs. Hopewell was certain that she had thought and thought until she had hit upon the ugliest name in any language. Then she had gone and had the beautiful name, Joy, changed without telling her mother until after she had done it. Her legal name was Hulga.

When Mrs. Hopewell thought the name, Hulga, she thought of the broad blank hull of a battleship. She would not use it. She continued to call her Joy to which the girl responded but in a purely mechanical way.

Hulga had learned to tolerate Mrs. Freeman who saved her from taking walks with her mother. Even Glynese and Carramae were useful when they occupied attention that might otherwise have been directed at her. At first she had thought she could not stand Mrs. Freeman for she had found that it was not possible to be rude to her. Mrs. Freeman would take on strange resentments and for days together she would be sullen but the source of her displeasure was always obscure; a direct attack, a positive leer, blatant ugliness to her face—these never touched her. And without warning one day, she began calling her Hulga.

She did not call her that in front of Mrs. Hopewell who would have been incensed but when she and the girl happened to be out of the house together, she would say something and add the name Hulga to the end of it, and the big spectacled Joy-Hulga would scowl and redden as if her privacy had been intruded upon. She considered the name her personal affair. She had arrived at it first purely on the basis of its ugly sound and then the full genius of its fitness had struck her. She had a vision of the name working like the ugly sweating Vulcan[1] who stayed in the furnace and to whom, presumably, the goddess had to come when called. She saw it as the name of her highest creative act. One of her major triumphs was that her mother had not been able to turn her dust into Joy, but the greater one was that she had been able to turn it herself into Hulga. However, Mrs. Freeman's relish for using the name only irritated her. It was as if Mrs. Freeman's beady steel-pointed eyes had penetrated far enough behind her face to reach some secret fact. Something about her seemed to fascinate Mrs. Freeman and then one day Hulga realized that it was the artificial leg. Mrs. Freeman had a special fondness for the details of secret infections, hidden deformities, assaults upon children. Of diseases, she preferred the lingering or incurable. Hulga had heard Mrs. Hopewell give her the details of the hunting accident, how the leg had been literally blasted off, how she had never lost consciousness. Mrs. Freeman could listen to it any time as if it had happened an hour ago.

When Hulga stumped into the kitchen in the morning (she could walk without making the awful noise but she made it—Mrs. Hopewell was certain—because it was ugly-sounding), she glanced at them and did not speak. Mrs. Hopewell would be in her red kimono with her hair tied around her head in rags. She would be sitting at

[1] Roman god of fire, usually portrayed as a lame blacksmith. He was the husband of Venus, goddess of love.

the table, finishing her breakfast and Mrs. Freeman would be hanging by her elbow outward from the refrigerator, looking down at the table. Hulga always put her eggs on the stove to boil and then stood over them with her arms folded, and Mrs. Hopewell would look at her—a kind of indirect gaze divided between her and Mrs. Freeman—and would think that if she would only keep herself up a little, she wouldn't be so bad looking. There was nothing wrong with her face that a pleasant expression wouldn't help. Mrs. Hopewell said that people who looked on the bright side of things would be beautiful even if they were not.

Whenever she looked at Joy this way, she could not help but feel that it would have been better if the child had not taken the Ph.D. It had certainly not brought her out any and now that she had it, there was no more excuse for her to go to school again. Mrs. Hopewell thought it was nice for girls to go to school to have a good time but Joy had "gone through." Anyhow, she would not have been strong enough to go again. The doctors had told Mrs. Hopewell that with the best of care, Joy might see forty-five. She had a weak heart. Joy had made it plain that if it had not been for this condition, she would be far from these red hills and good country people. She would be in a university lecturing to people who knew what she was talking about. And Mrs. Hopewell could very well picture her there, looking like a scarecrow and lecturing to more of the same. Here she went about all day in a six-year-old skirt and a yellow sweat shirt with a faded cowboy on a horse embossed on it. She thought this was funny; Mrs. Hopewell thought it was idiotic and showed simply that she was still a child. She was brilliant but she didn't have a grain of sense. It seemed to Mrs. Hopewell that every year she grew less like other people and more like herself— bloated, rude, and squint-eyed. And she said such strange things! To her own mother she had said—without warning, without excuse, standing up in the middle of a meal with her face purple and her mouth half full—"Woman! do you ever look inside? Do you ever look inside and see what you are *not?* God!" she had cried sinking down again and staring at her plate, "Malebranche[2] was right: we are not our own light. We are not our own light!" Mrs. Hopewell had no idea to this day what brought that on. She had only made the remark, hoping Joy would take it in, that a smile never hurt anyone.

The girl had taken the Ph.D. in philosophy and this left Mrs. Hopewell at a complete loss. You could say, "My daughter is a nurse," or "My daughter is a school teacher," or even, "My daughter is a chemical engineer." You could not say, "My daughter is a philosopher." That was something that had ended with the Greeks and Romans. All day Joy sat on her neck in a deep chair, reading. Sometimes she went for walks but she didn't like dogs or cats or birds or flowers or nature or nice young men. She looked at nice young men as if she could smell their stupidity.

One day Mrs. Hopewell had picked up one of the books the girl had just put down and opening it at random, she read, "Science, on the other hand, has to assert its soberness and seriousness afresh and declare that it is concerned solely with what-is. Nothing—how can it be for science anything but a horror and a phantasm? If science is right, then one thing stands firm: science wishes to know nothing of nothing. Such is after all the strictly scientific approach to Nothing. We know it by wishing to know

<hr>

[2] Nicholas de Malebranche (1638–1715), French philosopher.

nothing of Nothing." These words had been underlined with a blue pencil and they worked on Mrs. Hopewell like some evil incantation in gibberish. She shut the book quickly and went out of the room as if she were having a chill.

This morning when the girl came in, Mrs. Freeman was on Carramae. "She thrown up four times after supper," she said, "and was up twict in the night after three o'clock. Yesterday she didn't do nothing but ramble in the bureau drawer. All she did. Stand up there and see what she could run up on."

"She's got to eat," Mrs. Hopewell muttered, sipping her coffee, while she watched Joy's back at the stove. She was wondering what the child had said to the Bible salesman. She could not imagine what kind of a conversation she could possibly have had with him.

He was a tall gaunt hatless youth who had called yesterday to sell them a Bible. He had appeared at the door, carrying a large black suitcase that weighed him so heavily on one side that he had to brace himself against the door facing. He seemed on the point of collapse but he said in a cheerful voice, "Good morning, Mrs. Cedars!" and set the suitcase down on the mat. He was not a bad-looking young man though he had on a bright blue suit and yellow socks that were not pulled up far enough. He had prominent face bones and a streak of sticky-looking brown hair falling across his forehead.

"I'm Mrs. Hopewell," she said.

"Oh!" he said, pretending to look puzzled but with his eyes sparkling, "I saw it said 'The Cedars,' on the mailbox so I thought you was Mrs. Cedars!" and he burst out in a pleasant laugh. He picked up the satchel and under cover of a pant, he fell forward into her hall. It was rather as if the suitcase had moved first, jerking him after it. "Mrs. Hopewell!" he said and grabbed her hand. "I hope you are well!" and he laughed again and then all at once his face sobered completely. He paused and gave her a straight earnest look and said, "Lady, I've come to speak of serious things."

"Well, come in," she muttered, none too pleased because her dinner was almost ready. He came into the parlor and sat down on the edge of a straight chair and put the suitcase between his feet and glanced around the room as if he were sizing her up by it. Her silver gleamed on the two sideboards; she decided he had never been in a room as elegant as this.

"Mrs. Hopewell," he began, using her name in a way that sounded almost intimate, "I know you believe in Chrustian service."

"Well yes," she murmured.

"I know," he said and paused, looking very wise with his head cocked on one side, "that you're a good woman. Friends have told me."

Mrs. Hopewell never liked to be taken for a fool. "What are you selling?" she asked.

"Bibles," the young man said and his eye raced around the room before he added, "I see you have no family Bible in your parlor, I see that is the one lack you got!"

Mrs. Hopewell could not say, "My daughter is an atheist and won't let me keep the Bible in the parlor." She said, stiffening slightly, "I keep my Bible by my bedside." This was not the truth. It was in the attic somewhere.

"Lady," he said, "the word of God ought to be in the parlor."

"Well, I think that's a matter of taste," she began. "I think . . . "

"Lady," he said, "for a Chrustian, the word of God ought to be in every room in the house besides in his heart. I know you're a Chrustian because I can see it in every line of your face."

She stood up and said, "Well, young man, I don't want to buy a Bible and I smell my dinner burning."

He didn't get up. He began to twist his hands and looking down at them, he said softly, "Well lady, I'll tell you the truth—not many people want to buy one nowadays and besides, I know I'm real simple. I don't know how to say a thing but to say it. I'm just a country boy." He glanced up into her unfriendly face. "People like you don't like to fool with country people like me!"

"Why!" she cried, "good country people are the salt of the earth! Besides, we all have different ways of doing, it takes all kinds to make the world go 'round. That's life!"

"You said a mouthful," he said.

"Why, I think there aren't enough good country people in the world!" she said, stirred. "I think that's what's wrong with it!"

His face had brightened. "I didn't inraduce myself," he said. "I'm Manley Pointer from out in the country around Willohobie, not even from a place, just from near a place."

"You wait a minute," she said. "I have to see about my dinner." She went out to the kitchen and found Joy standing near the door where she had been listening.

"Get rid of the salt of the earth," she said, "and let's eat."

Mrs. Hopewell gave her a pained look and turned the heat down under the vegetables. "*I* can't be rude to anybody," she murmured and went back into the parlor.

He had opened the suitcase and was sitting with a Bible on each knee.

"You might as well put those up," she told him. "I don't want one."

"I appreciate your honesty," he said. "You don't see any more real honest people unless you go way out in the country."

"I know," she said, "real genuine folks!" Through the crack in the door she heard a groan.

"I guess a lot of boys come telling you they're working their way through college," he said, "but I'm not going to tell you that. Somehow," he said, "I don't want to go to college. I want to devote my life to Chrustian service. See," he said, lowering his voice, "I got this heart condition. I may not live long. When you know it's something wrong with you and you may not live long, well then, lady . . ." He paused, with his mouth open, and stared at her.

He and Joy had the same condition! She knew that her eyes were filling with tears but she collected herself quickly and murmured, "Won't you stay for dinner? We'd love to have you!" and was sorry the instant she heard herself say it.

"Yes mam," he said in an abashed voice, "I would sher love to do that!"

Joy had given him one look on being introduced to him and then throughout the meal had not glanced at him again. He had addressed several remarks to her, which she had pretended not to hear. Mrs. Hopewell could not understand deliberate rudeness, although she lived with it, and she felt she had always to overflow with hospitality to make up for Joy's lack of courtesy. She urged him to talk about himself and he did. He said he was the seventh child of twelve and that his father had been crushed under a tree when he himself was eight year old. He had been crushed very badly, in fact, almost cut in two and was practically not recognizable. His mother had got along the best she could by hard working and she had always seen that her children went to Sunday School and that they read the Bible every evening. He was now nineteen year old and he had been selling Bibles for four months. In that time he had sold seventy-seven Bibles and had the promise of two more sales. He wanted to become a missionary because he thought that was the way you could do most for people. "He who losest his life shall find it," he said simply and he was so sincere, so genuine and earnest that Mrs. Hopewell would not for the world have smiled. He prevented his peas from sliding onto the table by blocking them with a piece of bread which he later cleaned his plate with. She could see Joy observing sidewise how he handled his knife and fork and she saw too that every few minutes, the boy would dart a keen appraising glance at the girl as if he were trying to attract her attention.

After dinner Joy cleared the dishes off the table and disappeared and Mrs. Hopewell was left to talk with him. He told her again about his childhood and his father's accident and about various things that had happened to him. Every five minutes or so she would stifle a yawn. He sat for two hours until finally she told him she must go because she had an appointment in town. He packed his Bibles and thanked her and prepared to leave, but in the doorway he stopped and wrung her hand and said that not on any of his trips had he met a lady as nice as her and he asked if he could come again. She had said she would always be happy to see him.

Joy had been standing in the road, apparently looking at something in the distance, when he came down the steps toward her, bent to the side with his heavy valise. He stopped where she was standing and confronted her directly. Mrs. Hopewell could not hear what he said but she trembled to think what Joy would say to him. She could see that after a minute Joy said something and that then the boy began to speak again, making an excited gesture with his free hand. After a minute Joy said something else at which the boy began to speak once more. Then to her amazement, Mrs. Hopewell saw the two of them walk off together, toward the gate. Joy had walked all the way to the gate with him and Mrs. Hopewell could not imagine what they had said to each other, and she had not yet dared to ask.

Mrs. Freeman was insisting upon her attention. She had moved from the refrigerator to the heater so that Mrs. Hopewell had to turn and face her in order to seem to be listening. "Glynese gone out with Harvey Hill again last night," she said. "She had this sty."

"Hill," Mrs. Hopewell said absently, "is that the one who works in the garage?"

"Nome, he's the one that goes to chiropracter school," Mrs. Freeman said. "She had this sty. Been had it two days. So she says when he brought her in the other night he says, 'Lemme get rid of that sty for you,' and she says, 'How?' and he says, 'You just lay yourself down acrost the seat of that car and I'll show you.' So she done it and he popped her neck. Kept on a-popping it several times until she made him quit. This morning," Mrs. Freeman said, "she ain't got no sty. She ain't got no traces of a sty."

"I never heard of that before," Mrs. Hopewell said.

"He ast her to marry him before the Ordinary,"[3] Mrs. Freeman went on, "and she told him she wasn't going to be married in no *office*."

---

[3] Justice of the peace.

"Well, Glynese is a fine girl," Mrs. Hopewell said. "Glynese and Carramae are both fine girls."

"Carramae said when her and Lyman was married Lyman said it sure felt sacred to him. She said he said he wouldn't take five hundred dollars for being married by a preacher."

"How much would he take?" the girl asked from the stove.

"He said he wouldn't take five hundred dollars," Mrs. Freeman repeated.

"Well we all have work to do," Mrs. Hopewell said.

"Lyman said it just felt more sacred to him," Mrs. Freeman said. "The doctor wants Carramae to eat prunes. Says instead of medicine. Says them cramps is coming from pressure. You know where I think it is?"

"She'll be better in a few weeks," Mrs. Hopewell said.

"In the tube," Mrs. Freeman said. "Else she wouldn't be as sick as she is."

Hulga had cracked her two eggs into a saucer and was bringing them to the table along with a cup of coffee that she had filled too full. She sat down carefully and began to eat, meaning to keep Mrs. Freeman there by questions if for any reason she showed an inclination to leave. She could perceive her mother's eye on her. The first roundabout question would be about the Bible salesman and she did not wish to bring it on. "How did he pop her neck?" she asked.

Mrs. Freeman went into a description of how he had popped her neck. She said he owned a '55 Mercury but that Glynese said she would rather marry a man with only a '36 Plymouth who would be married by a preacher. The girl asked what if he had a '32 Plymouth and Mrs. Freeman said what Glynese had said was a '36 Plymouth.

Mrs. Hopewell said there were not many girls with Glynese's common sense. She said what she admired in those girls was their common sense. She said that reminded her that they had had a nice visitor yesterday, a young man selling Bibles. "Lord," she said, "he bored me to death but he was so sincere and genuine I couldn't be rude to him. He was just good country people, you know," she said, "—just the salt of the earth."

"I seen him walk up," Mrs. Freeman said, "and then later—I seen him walk off," and Hulga could feel the slight shift in her voice, the slight insinuation, that he had not walked off alone, had he? Her face remained expressionless but the color rose into her neck and she seemed to swallow it down with the next spoonful of egg. Mrs. Freeman was looking at her as if they had a secret together.

"Well, it takes all kinds of people to make the world go 'round," Mrs. Hopewell said. "It's very good we aren't all alike."

"Some people are more alike than others," Mrs. Freeman said.

Hulga got up and stumped, with about twice the noise that was necessary, into her room and locked the door. She was to meet the Bible salesman at ten o'clock at the gate.

She had thought about it half the night. She had started thinking of it as a great joke and then she had begun to see profound implications in it. She had lain in bed imagining dialogues for them that were insane on the surface but that reached below to depths that no Bible salesman would be aware of. Their conversation yesterday had been of this kind.

He had stopped in front of her and had simply stood there. His face was bony and sweaty and bright, with a little pointed nose in the center of it, and his look was different from what it had been at the dinner table. He was gazing at her with open curiosity, with fascination, like a child watching a new fantastic animal at the zoo, and he was breathing as if he had run a great distance to reach her. His gaze seemed somehow familiar but she could not think where she had been regarded with it before. For almost a minute he didn't say anything. Then on what seemed an insuck of breath, he whispered, "You ever ate a chicken that was two days old?"

The girl looked at him stonily. He might have just put this question up for consideration at the meeting of a philosophical association. "Yes," she presently replied as if she had considered it from all angles.

"It must have been mighty small!" he said triumphantly and shook all over with little nervous giggles, getting very red in the face, and subsiding finally into his gaze of complete admiration, while the girl's expression remained exactly the same.

"How old are you?" he asked softly.

She waited some time before she answered. Then in a flat voice she said, "Seventeen."

His smiles came in succession like waves breaking on the surface of a little lake. "I see you got a wooden leg," he said. "I think you're real brave. I think you're real sweet."

The girl stood blank and solid and silent.

"Walk to the gate with me," he said. "You're a brave sweet little thing and I liked you the minute I seen you walk in the door."

Hulga began to move forward.

"What's your name?" he asked, smiling down on the top of her head.

"Hulga," she said.

"Hulga," he murmured, "Hulga. Hulga. I never heard of anybody name Hulga before. You're shy, aren't you, Hulga?" he asked.

She nodded, watching his large red hand on the handle of the giant valise.

"I like girls that wear glasses," he said. "I think a lot. I'm not like these people that a serious thought don't ever enter their heads. It's because I may die."

"I may die too," she said suddenly and looked up at him. His eyes were very small and brown, glittering feverishly.

"Listen," he said, "don't you think some people was meant to meet on account of what all they got in common and all? Like they both think serious thoughts and all?" He shifted the valise to his other hand so that the hand nearest her was free. He caught hold of her elbow and shook it a little. "I don't work on Saturday," he said. "I like to walk in the woods and see what Mother Nature is wearing. O'er the hills and far away. Pic-nics and things. Couldn't we go on a pic-nic tomorrow? Say yes, Hulga," he said and gave her a dying look as if he felt his insides about to drop out of him. He had even seemed to sway slightly toward her.

During the night she had imagined that she seduced him. She imagined that the two of them walked on the place until they came to the storage barn beyond the two back fields and there, she imagined, that things came to such a pass that she very easily seduced him and that then, of course, she had to reckon with his remorse. True genius can get an idea across even to an inferior mind. She imagined that she took his remorse in hand and changed it into a deeper understanding of life. She took all his shame away and turned it into something useful.

She set off for the gate at exactly ten o'clock, escaping without drawing Mrs. Hopewell's attention. She didn't take anything to eat, forgetting that food is usually taken on a picnic. She wore a pair of slacks and a dirty white shirt, and as an afterthought, she had put some Vapex on the collar of it since she did not own any perfume. When she reached the gate no one was there.

She looked up and down the empty highway and had the furious feeling that she had been tricked, that he had only meant to make her walk to the gate after the idea of him. Then suddenly he stood up, very tall, from behind a bush on the opposite embankment. Smiling, he lifted his hat which was new and wide-brimmed. He had not worn it yesterday and she wondered if he had bought it for the occasion. It was toast-colored with a red and white band around it and was slightly too large for him. He stepped from behind the bush still carrying the black valise. He had on the same suit and the same yellow socks sucked down in his shoes from walking. He crossed the highway and said, "I knew you'd come!"

The girl wondered acidly how he had known this. She pointed to the valise and asked, "Why did you bring your Bibles?"

He took her elbow, smiling down on her as if he could not stop. "You can never tell when you'll need the word of God, Hulga," he said. She had a moment in which she doubted that this was actually happening and then they began to climb the embankment. They went down into the pasture toward the woods. The boy walked lightly by her side, bouncing on his toes. The valise did not seem to be heavy today; he even swung it. They crossed half the pasture without saying anything and then, putting his hand easily on the small of her back, he asked softly, "Where does your wooden leg join on?"

She turned an ugly red and glared at him and for an instant the boy looked abashed. "I didn't mean you no harm," he said. "I only meant you're so brave and all. I guess God takes care of you."

"No," she said, looking forward and walking fast, "I don't even believe in God."

At this he stopped and whistled. "No!" he exclaimed as if he were too astonished to say anything else.

She walked on and in a second he was bouncing at her side, fanning with his hat. "That's very unusual for a girl," he remarked, watching her out of the corner of his eye. When they reached the edge of the wood, he put his hand on her back again and drew her against him without a word and kissed her heavily.

The kiss, which had more pressure than feeling behind it, produced that extra surge of adrenalin in the girl that enables one to carry a packed trunk out of a burning house, but in her, the power went at once to the brain. Even before he released her, her mind, clear and detached and ironic anyway, was regarding him from a great distance, with amusement but with pity. She had never been kissed before and she was pleased to discover that it was an unexceptional experience and all a matter of the mind's control. Some people might enjoy drain water if they were told it was vodka. When the boy, looking expectant but uncertain, pushed her gently away, she turned and walked on, saying nothing as if such business, for her, were common enough.

He came along panting at her side, trying to help her when he saw a root that she might trip over. He caught and held back the long swaying blades of thorn vine until she had passed beyond them. She led the way and he came breathing heavily behind her. Then they came out on a sunlit hillside, sloping softly into another one a little smaller. Beyond, they could see the rusted top of the old barn where the extra hay was stored.

The hill was sprinkled with small pink weeds. "Then you ain't saved?" he asked suddenly, stopping.

The girl smiled. It was the first time she had smiled at him at all. "In my economy," she said, "I'm saved and you are damned but I told you I didn't believe in God."

Nothing seemed to destroy the boy's look of admiration. He gazed at her now as if the fantastic animal at the zoo had put its paw through the bars and given him a loving poke. She thought he looked as if he wanted to kiss her again and she walked on before he had the chance.

"Ain't there somewheres we can sit down sometime?" he murmured, his voice softening toward the end of the sentence.

"In that barn," she said.

They made for it rapidly as if it might slide away like a train. It was a large two-story barn, cool and dark inside. The boy pointed up the ladder that led into the loft and said, "It's too bad we can't go up there."

"Why can't we?" she asked.

"Yer leg," he said reverently.

The girl gave him a contemptuous look and putting both hands on the ladder, she climbed it while he stood below, apparently awestruck. She pulled herself expertly through the opening and then looked down at him and said, "Well, come on if you're coming," and he began to climb the ladder, awkwardly bringing the suitcase with him.

"We won't need the Bible," she observed.

"You never can tell," he said, panting. After he had got into the loft, he was a few seconds catching his breath. She had sat down in a pile of straw. A wide sheath of sunlight, filled with dust particles, slanted over her. She lay back against a bale, her face turned away, looking out the front opening of the barn where hay was thrown from a wagon into the loft. The two pink-speckled hillsides lay back against a dark ridge of woods. The sky was cloudless and cold blue. The boy dropped down by her side and put one arm under her and the other over her and began methodically kissing her face, making little noises like a fish. He did not remove his hat but it was pushed far enough back not to interfere. When her glasses got in his way, he took them off of her and slipped them into his pocket.

The girl at first did not return any of the kisses but presently she began to and after she had put several on his cheek, she reached his lips and remained there, kissing him again and again as if she were trying to draw all the breath out of him. His breath was clear and sweet like a child's and the kisses were sticky like a child's. He mumbled about loving her and about knowing when he first seen her that he loved her, but the mumbling was like the sleepy fretting of a child being put to sleep by his mother. Her mind, throughout this, never stopped or lost itself for a second to her feelings. "You ain't said you loved me none," he whispered finally, pulling back from her. "You got to say that."

She looked away from him off into the hollow sky and then down at a black ridge and then down farther into what appeared to be two green swelling lakes. She didn't realize he had taken her glasses but this landscape could not seem exceptional to her for she seldom paid any close attention to her surroundings.

"You got to say it," he repeated. "You got to say you love me."

She was always careful how she committed herself. "In a sense," she began, "if you use the word loosely, you might say that. But it's not a word I use. I don't have illusions. I'm one of those people who see *through* to nothing."

The boy was frowning. "You got to say it. I said it and you got to say it," he said.

The girl looked at him almost tenderly. "You poor baby," she murmured. "It's just as well you don't understand," and she pulled him by the neck, face-down, against her. "We are all damned," she said, "but some of us have taken off our blindfolds and see that there's nothing to see. It's a kind of salvation."

The boy's astonished eyes looked blankly through the ends of her hair. "Okay," he almost whined, "but do you love me or don'tcher?"

"Yes," she said and added, "in a sense. But I must tell you something. There mustn't be anything dishonest between us." She lifted his head and looked him in the eye. "I am thirty years old," she said. "I have a number of degrees."

The boy's look was irritated but dogged. "I don't care," he said. "I don't care a thing about what all you done. I just want to know if you love me or don'tcher?" and he caught her to him and wildly planted her face with kisses until she said, "Yes, yes."

"Okay then," he said, letting her go. "Prove it."

She smiled, looking dreamily out on the shifty landscape. She had seduced him without even making up her mind to try. "How?" she asked, feeling that he should be delayed a little.

He leaned over and put his lips to her ear. "Show me where your wooden leg joins on," he whispered.

The girl uttered a sharp little cry and her face instantly drained of color. The obscenity of the suggestion was not what shocked her. As a child she had sometimes been subject to feelings of shame but education had removed the last traces of that as a good surgeon scrapes for cancer; she would no more have felt it over what he was asking than she would have believed in his Bible. But she was as sensitive about the artificial leg as a peacock about his tail. No one ever touched it but her. She took care of it as someone else would his soul, in private and almost with her own eyes turned away. "No," she said.

"I known it," he muttered, sitting up. "You're just playing me for a sucker."

"Oh no no!" she cried. "It joins on at the knee. Only at the knee. Why do you want to see it?"

The boy gave her a long penetrating look. "Because," he said, "it's what makes you different. You ain't like anybody else."

She sat staring at him. There was nothing about her face or her round freezing-blue eyes to indicate that this had moved her; but she felt as if her heart had stopped and left her mind to pump her blood. She decided that for the first time in her life she was face to face with real innocence. This boy, with an instinct that came from beyond wisdom, had touched the truth about her. When after a minute, she said in a hoarse high voice, "All right," it was like surrendering to him completely. It was like losing her own life and finding it again, miraculously, in his.

Very gently he began to roll the slack leg up. The artificial limb, in a white sock and brown flat shoe, was bound in a heavy material like canvas and ended in an ugly jointure where it was attached to the stump. The boy's face and his voice were entirely reverent as he uncovered it and said, "Now show me how to take it off and on."

She took it off for him and put it back on again and then he took it off himself, handling it as tenderly as if it were a real one. "See!" he said with a delighted child's face. "Now I can do it myself!"

"Put it back on," she said. She was thinking that she would run away with him and that every night he would take the leg off and every morning put it back on again. "Put it back on," she said.

"Not yet," he murmured, setting it on its foot out of her reach. "Leave it off for a while. You got me instead."

She gave a little cry of alarm but he pushed her down and began to kiss her again. Without the leg she felt entirely dependent on him. Her brain seemed to have stopped thinking altogether and to be about some other function that it was not very good at. Different expressions raced back and forth over her face. Every now and then the boy, his eyes like two steel spikes, would glance behind him where the leg stood. Finally she pushed him off and said, "Put it back on me now."

"Wait," he said. He leaned the other way and pulled the valise toward him and opened it. It had a pale blue spotted lining and there were only two Bibles in it. He took one of these out and opened the cover of it. It was hollow and contained a pocket flask of whiskey, a pack of cards, and a small blue box with printing on it. He laid these out in front of her one at a time in an evenly-spaced row, like one presenting offerings at the shrine of a goddess. He put the blue box in her hand. THIS PRODUCT TO BE USED ONLY FOR THE PREVENTION OF DISEASE, she read, and dropped it. The boy was unscrewing the top of the flask. He stopped and pointed, with a smile, to the deck of cards. It was not an ordinary deck but one with an obscene picture on the back of each card. "Take a swig," he said, offering her the bottle first. He held it in front of her, but like one mesmerized, she did not move.

Her voice when she spoke had an almost pleading sound. "Aren't you," she murmured, "aren't you just good country people?"

The boy cocked his head. He looked as if he were just beginning to understand that she might be trying to insult him. "Yeah," he said, curling his lip slightly, "but it ain't held me back none. I'm as good as you any day in the week."

"Give me my leg," she said.

He pushed it farther away with his foot. "Come on now, let's begin to have us a good time," he said coaxingly. "We ain't got to know one another good yet."

"Give me my leg!" she screamed and tried to lunge for it but he pushed her down easily.

"What's the matter with you all of a sudden?" he asked, frowning as he screwed the top on the flask and put it quickly back inside the Bible. "You just a while ago said you didn't believe in nothing. I thought you was some girl!"

Her face was almost purple. "You're a Christian!" she hissed. "You're a fine Christian! You're just like them all—say one thing and do another. You're a perfect Christian, you're . . ."

The boy's mouth was set angrily. "I hope you don't think," he said in a lofty indignant tone, "that I believe in that crap! I may sell Bibles but I know which end is up and I wasn't born yesterday and I know where I'm going!"

"Give me my leg!" she screeched. He jumped up so quickly that she barely saw him sweep the cards and the blue box back into the Bible and throw the Bible into the valise. She saw him grab the leg and then she saw it for an instant slanted forlornly across the inside of the suitcase with a Bible at either side of its opposite ends. He slammed the lid shut and snatched up the valise and swung it down the hole and then stepped through himself.

When all of him had passed but his head, he turned and regarded her with a look that no longer had any admiration in it. "I've gotten a lot of interesting things," he said. "One time I got a woman's glass eye this way. And you needn't to think you'll catch me because Pointer ain't really my name. I use a different name at every house I call at and don't stay nowhere long. And I'll tell you another thing, Hulga," he said, using the name as if he didn't think much of it, "you ain't so smart. I been believing in nothing ever since I was born!" and then the toastcolored hat disappeared down the hole and the girl was left, sitting on the straw in the dusty sunlight. When she turned her churning face toward the opening, she saw his blue figure struggling successfully over the green speckled lake.

Mrs. Hopewell and Mrs. Freeman, who were in the back pasture, digging up onions, saw him emerge a little later from the woods and head across the meadow toward the highway. "Why, that looks like that nice dull young man that tried to sell me a Bible yesterday," Mrs. Hopewell said, squinting. "He must have been selling them to the Negroes back in there. He was so simple," she said, "but I guess the world would be better off if we were all that simple."

Mrs. Freeman's gaze drove forward and just touched him before he disappeared under the hill. Then she returned her attention to the evil-smelling onion shoot she was lifting from the ground. "Some can't be that simple," she said. "I know I never could."

1955/1955

John Barth
b. 1930

John Barth was born in Cambridge, Maryland, on May 27, 1930. Following a brief stint at the Juilliard School of Music, where he studied jazz, Barth enrolled at the Johns Hopkins University, where he completed a B.A. degree in 1951 and an M.A. in 1952. From 1953 to 1965 he taught at Pennsylvania State University and from 1965 to 1973 at the State University of New York in Buffalo. Since 1973 he has been on the faculty of the Writing Seminars at the Johns Hopkins University. Thus, through virtually the whole of his literary career, Barth has maintained close ties with university communities, a fact that clearly marks his work. Like Mailer, Barth has shown notable restlessness as a writer, and like Mailer's restlessness, Barth's has carried him from one experiment to another.

Unlike Mailer's restlessness, however, Barth's features clashes of minds. In his first novel, *The Floating Opera* (1956), the protagonist says of himself, as he struggles to understand why he once decided to commit suicide and then changed his mind, that he tends by disposition "to attribute to abstract ideas a life-or-death significance." In *The End of the Road* (1958) we observe a "life-and-death" clash between a character named Joe Morgan who is determined to live a wholly rational and coherent life and a character named Jacob Horner who is convinced that "existence not only precedes essence: in the case of human beings it rather defies essence."

During the 1960s Barth moved from writing short, tightly ordered works to writing large, loose ones. Both *The Sot-Weed Factor* (1960) and *Giles Goat-Boy* (1966) recall the boisterous, exuberant tone and the grandiose scale of Cervantes; both affirm, even celebrate, the artificial element in art; and both play with the literary conventions that inform them. In *The Sot-Weed Factor* Barth recounts the picaresque adventures of another Maryland writer, this one, Ebenezer Cooke, the eighteenth-century comic poet whose long poem, "The Sot-Weed Factor" (the tobacco merchant), appeared in 1708. In *Giles Goat-Boy* Barth moves even deeper into the labyrinth of self-parody and fictional travesty as the modern university is transformed into the universe by a barely identified academic author whose erudition has apparently gone berserk—the book's author, in fact, may even be a computer.

More recently, in the short sketches and tales of *Lost in the Funhouse* (1968) and the National Book Award winner, *Chimera* (1972), as well as in such novels as *Letters* (1979) and *Sabbatical* (1982), Barth has carried further his exploration of what he calls "the literature of exhaustion" or "the literature of exhausted possibilities." In these works he presents sketches that imitate the form of a sketch, tales that imitate the form of a tale, and "novels which imitate the form of the Novel, by an Author who imitates the role of Author." All of these works, too, turn on clashes of ideas, as Barth turns his characters loose to play, improvise, and invent in the funhouse of the mind. In addition, Barth's writing reflects the growing influence on contemporary literature of the great Argentine poet and literary fabricator Jorge Luis Borges, for whom stories are "momentary confluences of the imaginative world and the real world—the world we pretend is real when we read."

Further Reading:
J. Enck, "John Barth: An Interview," *Wisconsin Studies in Contemporary Literature*, Winter–Spring 1965.
G. Joseph, *John Barth*, 1970.
D. Morell, *John Barth: An Introduction*, 1976.

Texts:
"Night-Sea Journey" from *Lost in the Funhouse*, 1968.
"The Literature of Exhaustion" from *Atlantic Monthly*, August 1967.

Night-Sea Journey

"One way or another, no matter which theory of our journey is correct, it's myself I address; to whom I rehearse as to a stranger our history and condition, and will disclose my secret hope though I sink for it.

"Is the journey my invention? Do the night, the sea, exist at all, I ask myself, apart from my experience of them? Do I myself exist, or is this a dream? Sometimes I wonder. And if I am, who am I? The Heritage I supposedly transport? But how can I be both vessel and contents? Such are the questions that beset my intervals of rest.

"My trouble is, I lack conviction. Many accounts of our situation seem plausible to me—where and what we are, why we swim and whither. But implausible ones as well, perhaps especially those, I must admit as possibly correct. Even likely. If at times, in certain humors—stroking in unison, say, with my neighbors and chanting with them 'Onward! Upward!'—I have supposed that we have after all a common Maker, Whose nature and motives we may not know, but Who engendered us in some mysterious wise and launched us forth toward some end known but to Him— if (for a moodslength only) I have been able to entertain such notions, very popular in certain quarters, it is because our night-sea journey partakes of their absurdity. One might even say: I can believe them *because* they are absurd.

"Has that been said before?

"Another paradox: it appears to be these recesses from swimming that sustain me in the swim. Two measures onward and upward, flailing with the rest, then I float exhausted and dispirited, brood upon the night, the sea, the journey, while the flood bears me a measure back and down: slow progress, but I live, I live, and make my way, aye, past many a drowned comrade in the end, stronger, worthier than I, victims of their unremitting *joie de nager*.[1] I have seen the best swimmers of my generation go under. Numberless the number of the dead! Thousands drown as I think this thought, millions as I rest before returning to the swim. And scores, hundreds of millions have expired since we surged forth, brave in our innocence, upon our dreadful way. 'Love! Love!' we sang then, a quarter-billion strong, and churned the warm sea white with joy of swimming! Now all are gone down—the buoyant, the sodden, leaders and followers, all gone under, while wretched I swim on. Yet these same reflective intervals that keep me afloat have led me into wonder, doubt, despair —strange emotions for a swimmer!—have led me, even, to suspect . . . that our night-sea journey is without meaning.

"Indeed, if I have yet to join the hosts of the suicides, it is because (fatigue apart) I find it no meaningfuller to drown myself than to go on swimming.

"I know that there are those who seem actually to enjoy the night-sea; who claim to love swimming for its own sake, or sincerely believe that 'reaching the Shore,' 'transmitting the Heritage' (*Whose* Heritage, I'd like to know? And to whom?) is worth the staggering cost. I do not. Swimming itself I find at best not actively unpleasant, more often tiresome, not infrequently a torment. Arguments from func-

---

[1] French: "pleasure of swimming."

tion and design don't impress me: granted that we can and do swim, that in a manner of speaking our long tails and streamlined heads are 'meant for' swimming; it by no means follows—for me, at least—that we *should* swim, or otherwise endeavor to 'fulfill our destiny.' Which is to say, Someone Else's destiny, since ours, so far as I can see, is merely to perish, one way or another, soon or late. The heartless zeal of our (departed) leaders, like the blind ambition and good cheer of my own youth, appalls me now; for the death of my comrades I am inconsolable. If the night-sea journey has justification, it is not for us swimmers ever to discover it.

"Oh, to be sure, 'Love!' one heard on every side: 'Love it is that drives and sustains us!' I translate: we don't know *what* drives and sustains us, only that we are most miserably driven and, imperfectly, sustained. *Love* is how we call our ignorance of what whips us. 'To reach the Shore,' then: but what if the Shore exists in the fancies of us swimmers merely, who dream it to account for the dreadful fact that we swim, have always and only swum, and continue swimming without respite (myself excepted) until we die? Supposing even that there *were* a Shore—that, as a cynical companion of mine once imagined, we rise from the drowned to discover all those vulgar superstitions and exalted metaphors to be literal truth: the giant Maker of us all, the Shores of Light beyond our night-sea journey!—whatever would a swimmer do there? The fact is, when we imagine the Shore, what comes to mind is just the opposite of our condition: no more night, no more sea, no more journeying. In short, the blissful estate of the drowned.

" 'Ours not to stop and think; ours but to swim and sink. . . .' Because a moment's thought reveals the pointlessness of swimming. 'No matter,' I've heard some say, even as they gulped their last: 'The night-sea journey may be absurd, but here we swim, will-we nill-we, against the flood, onward and upward, toward a Shore that may not exist and couldn't be reached if it did.' The thoughtful swimmer's choices, then, they say, are two: give over thrashing and go under for good, or embrace the absurdity; affirm in and for itself the night-sea journey; swim on with neither motive nor destination, for the sake of swimming, and compassionate moreover with your fellow swimmer, we being all at sea and equally in the dark. I find neither course acceptable. If not even the hypothetical Shore can justify a sea-full of drownèd comrades, to speak of the swim-in-itself as somehow doing so strikes me as obscene. I continue to swim —but only because blind habit, blind instinct, blind fear of drowning are still more strong than the horror of our journey. And if on occasion I have assisted a fellow-thrasher, joined in the cheers and songs, even passed along to others strokes of genius from the drownèd great, it's that I shrink by temperament from making myself conspicuous. To paddle off in one's own direction, assert one's independent right-of-way, overrun one's fellows without compunction, or dedicate oneself entirely to pleasures and diversions without regard for conscience—I can't finally condemn those who journey in this wise; in half my moods I envy them and despise the weak vitality that keeps me from following their example. But in reasonabler moments I remind myself that it's their very freedom and self-responsibility I reject, as more dramatically absurd, in our senseless circumstances, than tailing along in conventional fashion. Suicides, rebels, affirmers of the paradox—nay-sayers and yea-sayers alike to our fatal journey—I finally shake my head at them. And splash sighing past their corpses, one by one, as past a hundred sorts of others: friends, enemies, brothers; fools, sages, brutes —and nobodies, million upon million. I envy them all.

"A poor irony: that I, who find abhorrent and tautological the doctrine of survival of the fittest (*fitness* meaning, in my experience, nothing more than survival-ability, a talent whose only demonstration is the fact of survival, but whose chief ingredients seem to be strength, guile, callousness), may be the sole remaining swimmer! But the doctrine is false as well as repellent: Chance drowns the worthy with the unworthy, bears up the unfit with the fit by whatever definition, and makes the night-sea journey essentially *haphazard* as well as murderous and unjustified.

" 'You only swim once.' Why bother, then?

" 'Except ye drown, ye shall not reach the Shore of Life.' Poppycock.

"One of my late companions—that same cynic with the curious fancy, among the first to drown—entertained us with odd conjectures while we waited to begin our journey. A favorite theory of his was that the Father does exist, and did indeed make us and the sea we swim—but not a-purpose or even consciously; He made us, as it were, despite Himself, as we make waves with every tail-thrash, and may be unaware of our existence. Another was that He knows we're here but doesn't care what happens to us, inasmuch as He creates (voluntarily or not) other seas and swimmers at more or less regular intervals. In bitterer moments, such as just before he drowned, my friend even supposed that our Maker wished us unmade; there was indeed a Shore, he'd argue, which could save at least some of us from drowning and toward which it was our function to struggle—but for reasons unknowable to us He wanted desperately to prevent our reaching that happy place and fulfilling our destiny. Our 'Father,' in short, was our adversary and would-be killer! No less outrageous, and offensive to traditional opinion, were the fellow's speculations on the nature of our Maker: that He might well be no swimmer Himself at all, but some sort of monstrosity, perhaps even tailless; that He might be stupid, malicious, insensible, perverse, or asleep and dreaming; that the end for which He created and launched us forth, and which we flagellate ourselves to fathom, was perhaps immoral, even obscene. Et cetera, et cetera: there was no end to the chap's conjectures, or the impoliteness of his fancy; I have reason to suspect that his early demise, whether planned by 'our Maker' or not, was expedited by certain fellow-swimmers indignant at his blasphemies.

"In other moods, however (he was as given to moods as I), his theorizing would become half-serious, so it seemed to me, especially upon the subjects of Fate and Immortality, to which our youthful conversations often turned. Then his harangues, if no less fantastical, grew solemn and obscure, and if he was still baiting us, his passion undid the joke. His objection to popular opinions of the hereafter, he would declare, was their claim to general validity. Why need believers hold that *all* the drownèd rise to be judged at journey's end, and non-believers that drowning is final without exception? In *his* opinion (so he'd vow at least), nearly everyone's fate was permanent death; indeed he took a sour pleasure in supposing that every 'Maker' made thousands of separate seas in His creative lifetime, each populated like ours with millions of swimmers, and that in almost every instance both sea and swimmers were utterly annihilated, whether accidentally or by malevolent design. (Nothing if not pluralistical, he imagined there might be millions and billions of 'Fathers,' perhaps in some 'night-sea' of their own!) However—and here he turned infidels against him with the faithful—he professed to believe that in possibly a single night-sea per thousand, say, one of its quarter-billion swimmers (that is, one swimmer in two hundred fifty billions) achieved a qualified immortality. In some cases the rate might be slightly higher; in others it was vastly lower, for just as there are swimmers of every degree of proficiency, including some who drown before the journey starts, unable to swim at all, and others created drowned, as it were, so he imagined what can only be termed impotent Creators, Makers unable to Make, as well as uncommonly fertile ones and all grades between. And it pleased him to deny any necessary relation between a Maker's productivity and His other virtues—including, even, the quality of His creatures.

"I could go on (*he* surely did) with his elaboration of these mad notions—such as that swimmers in other night-seas needn't be of our kind; that Makers themselves might belong to different *species,* so to speak; that our particular Maker mightn't Himself be immortal, or that we might be not only His emissaries but His 'immortality,' continuing His life and our own, transmogrified, beyond our individual deaths. Even this modified immortality (meaningless to me) he conceived as relative and contingent, subject to accidental or deliberate termination: his pet hypothesis was that Makers and swimmers *each generate the other*—against all odds, their number being so great—and that any given 'immortality-chain' could terminate after any number of cycles, so that what was 'immortal' (still speaking relatively) was only the cyclic process of incarnation, which itself might have a beginning and an end. Alternatively he liked to imagine cycles within cycles, either finite or infinite: for example, the 'night-sea,' as it were, in which Makers 'swam' and created night-seas and swimmers like ourselves, might be the creation of a larger Maker, Himself one of many, Who in turn et cetera. Time itself he regarded as relative to our experience, like magnitude: who knew but what, with each thrash of our tails, minuscule seas and swimmers, whole eternities, came to pass—as ours, perhaps, and our Maker's Maker's, was elapsing between the strokes of some supertail, in a slower order of time?

"Naturally I hooted with the others at this nonsense. We were young then, and had only the dimmest notion of what lay ahead; in our ignorance we imagined night-sea journeying to be a positively heroic enterprise. Its meaning and value we never questioned; to be sure, some must go down by the way, a pity no doubt, but to win a race requires that others lose, and like all my fellows I took for granted that I would be the winner. We milled and swarmed, impatient to be off, never mind where or why, only to try our youth against the realities of night and sea; if we indulged the skeptic at all, it was as a droll, half-contemptible mascot. When he died in the initial slaughter, no one cared.

"And even now I don't subscribe to all his views—but I no longer scoff. The horror of our history has purged me of opinions, as of vanity, confidence, spirit, charity, hope, vitality, everything—except dull dread and a kind of melancholy, stunned persistence. What leads me to recall his fancies is my growing suspicion that I, of all swimmers, may be the sole survivor of this fell journey, tale-bearer of a generation. This suspicion, together with the recent sea-change, suggests to me now that nothing is impossible, not even my late companion's wildest visions, and brings me to a certain desperate resolve, the point of my chronicling.

"Very likely I have lost my senses. The carnage at our setting out; our decimation by whirlpool, poisoned cataract, sea-convulsion; the panic stampedes, mutinies, slaughters, mass suicides; the mounting evidence that none will survive the journey —add to these anguish and fatigue; it were a miracle if sanity stayed afloat. Thus I admit, with the other possibilities, that the present sweetening and calming of the sea, and what seems to be a kind of vasty presence, song, or summons from the near upstream, may be hallucinations of disordered sensibility. . . .

"Perhaps, even, I am drowned already. Surely I was never meant for the rough-and-tumble of the swim; not impossibly I perished at the outset and have only imaged the night-sea journey from some final deep. In any case, I'm no longer young, and it is we spent old swimmers, disabused of every illusion, who are most vulnerable to dreams.

"Sometimes I think I am my drownèd friend.

"Out with it: I've begun to believe, not only that *She* exists, but that She lies not far ahead, and stills the sea, and draws me Herward! Aghast, I recollect his maddest notion: that our destination (which existed, mind, in but one night-sea out of hundreds and thousands) was no Shore, as commonly conceived, but a mysterious being, indescribable except by paradox and vaguest figure: wholly different from us swimmers, yet our complement; the death of us, yet our salvation and resurrection; simultaneously our journey's end, mid-point, and commencement; not membered and thrashing like us, but a motionless or hugely gliding sphere of unimaginable dimension; self-contained, yet dependent absolutely, in some wise, upon the chance (always monstrously improbable) that one of us will survive the night-sea journey and reach . . . Her! *Her,* he called it, or *She,* which is to say, Other-than-a-he. I shake my head; the thing is too preposterous; it is myself I talk to, to keep my reason in this awful darkness. There is no She! There is no You! I rave to myself; it's Death alone that hears and summons. To the drowned, all seas are calm. . . .

"Listen: my friend maintained that in every order of creation there are two sorts of creators, contrary yet complementary, one of which gives rise to seas and swimmers, the other to the Night-which-contains-the-sea and to What-waits-at-the-journey's-end: the former, in short, to destiny, the latter to destination (and both profligately, involuntarily, perhaps indifferently or unwittingly). The 'purpose' of the night-sea journey—but not necessarily of the journeyer or of either Maker!—my friend could describe only in abstractions: *consummation, transfiguration, union of contraries, transcension of categories.* When we laughed, he would shrug and admit that he understood the business no better than we, and thought it ridiculous, dreary, possibly obscene. 'But one of you,' he'd add with his wry smile, 'may be the Hero destined to complete the night-sea journey and be one with Her. Chances are, of course, you won't make it.' He himself, he declared, was not even going to try; the whole idea repelled him; if we chose to dismiss it as an ugly fiction, so much the better for us; thrash, splash, and be merry, we were soon enough drowned. But there it was, he could not say how he knew or why he bothered to tell us, any more than he could say what would happen after She and Hero, Shore and Swimmer, 'merged identities' to become something both and neither. He quite agreed with me that if the issue of that magical union had no memory of the night-sea journey, for example, it enjoyed a poor sort of immortality; even poorer if, as he rather imagined, a swimmer-hero plus a She equaled or became merely another Maker of future night-seas and the rest, at such incredible expense of life. This being the case—he was persuaded it was—the merciful thing to do was refuse to participate; the genuine heroes, in his opinion, were the suicides, and the hero of heroes would be the swimmer who, in the very presence of the Other, refused Her proffered 'immortality' and thus put an end to at least one cycle of catastrophes.

"How we mocked him! Our moment came, we hurtled forth, pretending to glory in the adventure, thrashing, singing, cursing, strangling, rationalizing, rescuing, killing, inventing rules and stories and relationships, giving up, struggling on, but dying all, and still in darkness, until only a battered remnant was left to croak 'Onward, upward,' like a bitter echo. Then they too fell silent—victims, I can only presume, of the last frightful wave—and the moment came when I also, utterly desolate and spent, thrashed my last and gave myself over to the current, to sink or float as might be, but swim no more. Whereupon, marvelous to tell, in an instant the sea grew still! Then warmly, gently, the great tide turned, began to bear me, as it does now, onward and upward will-I nill-I, like a flood of joy—and I recalled with dismay my dead friend's teaching.

"I am not deceived. This new emotion is Her doing; the desire that possesses me is Her bewitchment. Lucidity passes from me; in a moment I'll cry 'Love!' bury myself in Her side, and be 'transfigured.' Which is to say, I die already; this fellow transported by passion is not I; *I am he who abjures and rejects the night-sea journey!* I. . . .

"I am all love. 'Come!' She whispers, and I have no will.

"You who I may be about to become, whatever You are: with the last twitch of my real self I beg You to listen. It is *not* love that sustains me! No; though Her magic makes me burn to sing the contrary, and though I drown even now for the blasphemy, I will say truth. What has fetched me across this dreadful sea is a single hope, gift of my poor dead comrade: that You may be stronger-willed than I, and that by sheer force of concentration I may transmit to You, along with Your official Heritage, a private legacy of awful recollection and negative resolve. Mad as it may be, my dream is that some unimaginable embodiment of myself (or myself plus Her if that's how it must be) will come to find itself expressing, in however garbled or radical a translation, some reflection of these reflections. If against all odds this comes to pass, may You to whom, through whom I speak, do what I cannot: terminate this aimless, brutal business! Stop Your hearing against Her song! Hate love!

"Still alive, afloat, afire. Farewell then my penultimate hope: that one may be sunk for direst blasphemy on the very shore of the Shore. Can it be (my old friend would smile) that only utterest nay-sayers survive the night? But even that were Sense, and there is no sense, only senseless love, senseless death. Whoever echoes these reflections: be more courageous than their author! An end to night-sea journeys! Make no more! And forswear me when I shall forswear myself, deny myself, plunge into Her who summons, singing . . .

" 'Love! Love! Love!' "

1966/1968

The Literature of Exhaustion

I want to discuss three things more or less together: first, some old questions raised by the new intermedia arts; second, some aspects of the Argentine writer Jorge Luis Borges, whom I greatly admire; third, some professional concerns of my own, related to these other matters and having to do with what I'm calling "the literature of exhausted possibility"—or, more chicly, "the literature of exhaustion."

By "exhaustion" I don't mean anything so tired as the subject of physical, moral, or intellectual decadence, only the used-upness of certain forms or exhaustion of certain possibilities—by no means necessarily a cause for despair. That a great many Western artists for a great many years have quarreled with received definitions of artistic media, genres, and forms goes without saying: pop art, dramatic and musical "happenings," the whole range of "intermedia" or "mixed-means" art, bear recentest witness to the tradition of rebelling against Tradition. A catalogue I received some time ago in the mail, for example, advertises such items as Robert Fillion's *Ample Food for Stupid Thought,* a box full of postcards on which are inscribed "apparently meaningless questions," to be mailed to whomever the purchaser judges them suited for. Ray Johnson's *Paper Snak,* a collection of whimsical writings, "often pointed," once mailed to various friends (what the catalogue describes as The New York Correspondence School of Literature); and Daniel Spoerri's *Anecdoted Typography of Chance,* "on the surface" a description of all the objects that happen to be on the author's parlor table—"in fact, however . . . a cosmology of Spoerri's existence."

"On the surface," at least, the document listing these items is a catalogue of The Something Else Press, a swinging outfit. "In fact, however," it may be one of their offerings, for all I know: The New York Direct-Mail Advertising School of Literature. In any case, their wares are lively to read about, and make for interesting conversation in fiction-writing classes, for example, where we discuss Somebody-or-other's unbound, unpaginated, randomly assembled novel-in-a-box and the desirability of printing *Finnegans Wake*[1] on a very long roller-towel. It's easier and sociabler to talk technique than it is to make art, and the area of "happenings" and their kin is mainly a way of discussing aesthetics, really; illustrating "dramatically" more or less valid and interesting points about the nature of art and the definition of its terms and genres.

One conspicuous thing, for example, about the "intermedia" arts is their tendency (noted even by *Life* magazine) to eliminate not only the traditional audience—"those who apprehend the artist's art" (in "happenings" the audience is often the "cast," as in "environments," and some of the new music isn't intended to be performed at all) —but also the most traditional notion of the artist: the Aristotelian conscious agent who achieves with technique and cunning the artistic effect; in other words, one endowed with uncommon talent, who has moreover developed and disciplined that endowment into virtuosity. It's an aristocratic notion on the face of it, which the democratic West seems eager to have done with; not only the "omniscient" author of older fiction, but the very idea of the controlling artist, has been condemned as politically reactionary, even fascist.

Now, personally, being of the temper that chooses to "rebel along traditional lines," I'm inclined to prefer the kind of art that not many people can *do:* the kind that requires expertise and artistry as well as bright aesthetic ideas and/or inspiration. I enjoy the pop art in the famous Albright-Knox collection, a few blocks from my house in Buffalo, like a lively conversation for the most part, but was on the whole more impressed by the jugglers and acrobats at Baltimore's old Hippodrome, where I used to go every time they changed shows: genuine *virtuosi* doing things that anyone can dream up and discuss but almost no one can do.

---

[1] Novel by the Irish writer James Joyce (1882–1941).

I suppose the distinction is between things worth remarking—preferably over beer, if one's of my generation—and things worth doing. "Somebody ought to make a novel with scenes that pop up, like the old children's books," one says, with the implication that one isn't going to bother doing it oneself.

However, art and its forms and techniques live in history and certainly do change. I sympathize with a remark attributed to Saul Bellow, that to be technically up to date is the least important attribute of a writer, though I would have to add that this least important attribute may be nevertheless essential. In any case, to be technically *out* of date is likely to be a genuine defect: Beethoven's Sixth Symphony or the Chartres Cathedral if executed today would be merely embarrassing. A good many current novelists write turn-of-the-century-type novels, only in more or less mid-twentieth-century language and about contemporary people and topics; this makes them considerably less interesting (to me) than excellent writers who are also technically contemporary: Joyce and Kafka[2] for instance, in their time, and in ours, Samuel Beckett[3] and Jorge Luis Borges. The intermedia arts, I'd say, tend to be intermediary too, between the traditional realms of aesthetics on the one hand and artistic creation on the other; I think the wise artist and civilian will regard them with quite the kind and degree of seriousness with which he regards good shoptalk: he'll listen carefully, if noncommittally, and keep an eye on his intermedia colleagues, if only the corner of his eye. They may very possibly suggest something usable in the making or understanding of genuine works of contemporary art.

The man I want to discuss a little here, Jorge Luis Borges, illustrates well the difference between a technically old-fashioned artist, a technically up-to-date civilian, and a technically up-to-date artist. In the first category I'd locate all those novelists who for better or worse write not as if the twentieth century didn't exist, but as if the great writers of the last sixty years or so hadn't existed (*nota bene*[4] that our century's more than two-thirds done; it's dismaying to see so many of our writers following Dostoevsky or Tolstoy or Flaubert or Balzac,[5] when the real technical question seems to me to be how to succeed not even Joyce and Kafka, but those who've *succeeded* Joyce and Kafka and are now in the evenings of their own careers). In the second category are such folk as an artist-neighbor of mine in Buffalo who fashions dead Winnies-the-Pooh in sometimes monumental scale out of oilcloth stuffed with sand and impaled on stakes or hung by the neck. In the third belong the few people whose artistic thinking is as hip as any French new-novelist's, but who manage nonetheless to speak eloquently and memorably to our still-human hearts and conditions, as the great artists have always done. Of these, two of the finest living specimens that I know of are Beckett and Borges, just about the only contemporaries of my reading acquaintance mentionable with the "old masters" of twentieth-century fiction. In the unexciting history of literary awards, the 1961 International Publishers' Prize, shared by Beckett and Borges, is a happy exception indeed.

One of the modern things about these two is that in an age of ultimacies and "final

---

[2] Kafka, Franz Kafka (1883–1924), German-language writer of Jewish descent, born in Prague, Czechoslovakia.
[3] Irish-born playwright and novelist (b. 1906).
[4] Latin: "note well."

[5] Russian novelists Fyodor Mikhailovich Dostoyevsky (1821–1881) and Count Leo Nikoleyevich Tolstoy (1828–1910), and French novelists Gustave Flaubert (1821–1880) and Honoré de Balzac (1799–1850).

solutions"—at least *felt* ultimacies, in everything from weaponry to theology, the celebrated dehumanization of society, and the history of the novel—their work in separate ways reflects and deals with ultimacy, both technically and thematically, as, for example, *Finnegans Wake* does in its different manner. One notices, by the way, for whatever its symptomatic worth, that Joyce was virtually blind at the end, Borges is literally so, and Beckett has become virtually mute, musewise, having progressed from marvelously constructed English sentences through terser and terser French ones to the unsyntactical, unpunctuated prose of *Comment C'est*[6] and "ultimately" to wordless mimes. One might extrapolate a theoretical course for Beckett: language, after all, consists of silence as well as sound, and the mime is still communication—"that nineteenth-century idea," a Yale student once snarled at me—but by the language of action. But the language of action consists of rest as well as movement, and so in the context of Beckett's progress immobile, silent figures still aren't altogether ultimate. How about an empty, silent stage, then, or blank pages[7]—a "happening" where nothing happens, like Cage's[8] *4' 33"* performed in an empty hall? But dramatic communication consists of the absence as well as the presence of the actors; "we have our exists and our entrances"; and so even that would be imperfectly ultimate in Beckett's case. Nothing at all, then, I suppose: but Nothingness is necessarily and inextricably the background against which Being et cetera; for Beckett, at this point in his career, to cease to create altogether would be fairly meaningful: his crowning work, his "last word." What a convenient corner to paint yourself into! "And now I shall finish," the valet Arsene says in *Watt*, "and you will hear my voice no more." Only the silence *Molloy* speaks of, "of which the universe is made."

After which, I add on behalf of the rest of us, it might be conceivable to rediscover validly the artifices of language and literature—such far-out notions as grammar, punctuation . . . even characterization! Even *plot!*—if one goes about it the right way, aware of what one's predecessors have been up to.

Now J. L. Borges is perfectly aware of all these things. Back in the great decades of literary experimentalism he was associated with *Prisma,* a "muralist" magazine that published its pages on walls and billboards; his later *Labyrinths* and *Ficciones* not only anticipate the farthest-out ideas of The Something-Else Press crowd—not a difficult thing to do—but being marvelous works of art as well, illustrate in a simple way the difference between the *fact* of aesthetic ultimacies and their artistic *use.* What it comes to is that an artist doesn't merely exemplify an ultimacy; he employs it.

Consider Borges' story "Pierre Menard, Author of the *Quixote*": the hero, an utterly sophisticated turn-of-the-century French Symbolist, by an astounding effort of imagination, produces—not *copies* or *imitates,* mind, but *composes*—several chapters of Cervantes'[9] novel.

It is a revelation [Borges' narrator tells us] to compare Menard's *Don Quixote* with Cervantes'. The latter, for example, wrote (part one, chapter nine):

[6] French: "How it is."
[7] Barth's note: "An ultimacy already attained in the nineteenth century by that *avant-gardiste* of East Aurora, New York, Elbert Hubbard, in his *Essay on Silence.*"
[8] Cage: John Cage (b. 1912), American musical

theorist and experimental composer. (His 4 minutes and 33 seconds of silence are in fact to be performed before a concert audience.)
[9] Cervantes: Miguel de Cervantes Saavedra (1547–1616), Spanish novelist and playwright, author of *Don Quixote de la Mancha.*

... truth, whose mother is history, rival of time, depository of deeds, witness of the past, exemplar and adviser to the present, the future's counselor.

Written in the seventeenth century, written by the "lay genius" Cervantes, this enumeration is a mere rhetorical praise of history. Menard, on the other hand, writes:

... truth, whose mother is history, rival of time, depository of deeds, witness of the past, exemplar and adviser to the present, the future's counselor.

History, the *mother* of truth: the idea is astounding. Menard, a contemporary of William James, does not define history as an inquiry into reality but as its origin. . . .

Et cetera. Now, this is an interesting idea, of considerable intellectual validity. I mentioned earlier that if Beethoven's Sixth were composed today, it would be an embarrassment; but clearly it wouldn't be, necessarily, if done with ironic intent by a composer quite aware of where we've been and where we are. It would have then potentially, for better or worse, the kind of significance of Warhol's[10] Campbell's Soup ads, the difference being that in the former case a work of art is being reproduced instead of a work of non-art, and the ironic comment would therefore be more directly on the genre and history of the art than on the state of the culture. In fact, of course, to make the valid intellectual point one needn't even recompose the Sixth Symphony, any more than Menard really needed to re-create the *Quixote*. It would've been sufficient for Menard to have *attributed* the novel to himself in order to have a new work of art, from the intellectual point of view. Indeed, in several stories Borges plays with this very idea, and I can readily imagine Beckett's next novel, for example, as *Tom Jones,* just as Nabokov's last was that multivolume annotated translation of Pushkin.[11] I myself have always aspired to write Burton's version of *The 1001 Nights,*[12] complete with appendices and the like, in twelve volumes, and for intellectual purposes I needn't even write it. What evenings we might spend (over beer) discussing Saarinen's Parthenon, D. H. Lawrence's *Wuthering Heights,* or the Johnson Administration by Robert Rauschenberg![13]

The idea, I say, is intellectually serious, as are Borges' other characteristic ideas, most of a metaphysical rather than an aesthetic nature. But the important thing to observe is that Borges *doesn't* attribute the *Quixote* to himself, much less recompose it like Pierre Menard; instead, he writes a remarkable and original work of literature, the implicit theme of which is the difficulty, perhaps the unnecessity, of writing original works of literature. His artistic victory, if you like, is that he confronts an intellectual dead end and employs it against itself to accomplish new human work. If this corresponds to what mystics do—"every moment leaping into the infinite,"

[10] Warhol: Andy Warhol (b. ca. 1930), American pop artist and filmmaker.

[11] *Tom Jones:* novel of social satire by Henry Fielding (1707–1754), English novelist, playwright, and essayist; Nabokov: Vladimir Nabokov (1899–1977), Russian-born American novelist and critic; Pushkin: Aleksander Sergeevich Pushkin (1799–1837), Russian poet.

[12] Arabic tales collected by Sir Richard Francis Burton (1821–1890), English author and traveler.

[13] These unlikely achievements are by Eero Saarinen (1910–1961), American architect; David Herbert Lawrence (1885–1930), English novelist; and Robert Rauschenberg (b. 1925), American artist.

Kierkegaard[14] says, "and every moment falling surely back into the finite"—it's only one more aspect of that old analogy. In homelier terms, it's a matter of every moment throwing out the bath water without for a moment losing the baby.

Another way of describing Borges' accomplishment is in a pair of his own favorite terms, *algebra and fire*. In his most often anthologized story, "Tlön, Uqbar, Orbis Tertius," he imagines an entirely hypothetical world, the invention of a secret society of scholars who elaborate its every aspect in a surreptitious encyclopedia. This *First Encyclopaedia of Tlön* (what fictionist would not wish to have dreamed up the *Britannica?*) describes a coherent alternative to this world complete in every respect from its algebra to its fire, Borges tells us, and of such imaginative power that, once conceived, it begins to obtrude itself into and eventually to supplant our prior reality. My point is that neither the algebra nor the fire, metaphorically speaking, could achieve this result without the other. Borges' algebra is what I'm considering here— algebra is easier to talk about than fire—but any intellectual giant could equal it. The imaginary authors of the *First Encyclopaedia of Tlön* itself are not artists, though their work is in a manner of speaking fictional and would find a ready publisher in New York nowadays. The author of the story "Tlön, Uqbar, Orbis Tertius," who merely *alludes* to the fascinating *Encyclopaedia, is* an artist; what makes him one of the first rank, like Kafka, is the combination of that intellectually profound vision with great human insight, poetic power, and consummate mastery of his means, a definition which would have gone without saying, I suppose, in any century but ours.

Not long ago, incidentally, in a footnote to a scholarly edition of Sir Thomas Browne[15] (*The Urn Burial,* I believe it was), I came upon a perfect Borges datum, reminiscent of Tlön's self-realization: the actual case of a book called *The Three Impostors,* alluded to in Browne's *Religio Medici*[16] among other places. *The Three Impostors* is a nonexistent blasphemous treatise against Moses, Christ, and Mohammed, which in the seventeenth century was widely held to exist, or to have once existed. Commentators attributed it variously to Boccaccio, Pietro Aretino, Giordano Bruno, and Tommaso Campanella, and though no one, Browne included, had ever seen a copy of it, it was frequently cited, refuted, railed against, and generally discussed as if everyone had read it—until, sure enough, in the *eighteenth* century a spurious work appeared with a forged date of 1598 and the title *De Tribus Impostoribus.*[17] It's a wonder that Borges doesn't mention this work, as he seems to have read absolutely everything, including all the books that don't exist, and Browne is a particular favorite of his. In fact, the narrator of "Tlön, Uqbar, Orbis Tertius" declares at the end:

> . . . English and French and mere Spanish will disappear from the globe. The world will be Tlön. I pay no attention to all this and go on revising, in the still days at the Adrogué hotel, an uncertain Quevedian translation (which I do not intend to publish) of Browne's *Urn Burial.*[18]

[14] Kierkegaard: Sören Kierkegaard (1813–1855), Danish philosopher.
[15] Browne: Sir Thomas Browne (1605–1682), English doctor and writer.
[16] Latin: "The Religion of a Doctor."
[17] Latin: "The Three Imposters."

[18] Barth's note: "Moreover, on rereading 'Tlön,' etc., I find now a remark I'd swear wasn't in it last year: that the eccentric American millionaire who endows the *Encyclopaedia* does so on condition that 'the work will make no pact with the impostor Jesus Christ.'"

This "contamination of reality by dream," as Borges calls it, is one of his pet themes, and commenting upon such contaminations is one of his favorite fictional devices. Like many of the best such devices, it turns the artist's mode or form into a metaphor for his concerns, as does the diary-ending of *Portrait of the Artist As a Young Man*[19] or the cyclical construction of *Finnegans Wake*. In Borges' case, the story "Tlön," etc., for example, is a real piece of imagined reality in our world, analogous to those Tlönian artifacts called *hrönir*, which imagine themselves into existence. In short, it's a paradigm of or metaphor for itself; not just the *form* of the story but the *fact* of the story is symbolic; "the medium is the message."

Moreover, like all of Borges' work, it illustrates in other of its aspects my subject: how an artist may paradoxically turn the felt ultimacies of our time into material and means for his work—*paradoxically* because by doing so he transcends what had appeared to be his refutation, in the same way that the mystic who transcends finitude is said to be enabled to live, spiritually and physically, in the finite world. Suppose you're a writer by vocation—a "print-oriented bastard," as the McLuhanites[20] call us —and you feel, for example, that the novel, if not narrative literature generally, if not the printed word altogether, has by this hour of the world just about shot its bolt, as Leslie Fiedler[21] and others maintain. (I'm inclined to agree, with reservations and hedges. Literary forms certainly have histories and historical contingencies, and it may well be that the novel's time as a major art form is up, as the "times" of classical tragedy, grand opera, or the sonnet sequence came to be. No necessary cause for alarm in this at all, except perhaps to certain novelists, and one way to handle such a feeling might be to write a novel about it. Whether historically the novel expires or persists seems immaterial to me; if enough writers and critics *feel* apocalyptical about it, their feeling becomes a considerable cultural fact, like the *feeling* that Western civilization, or the world, is going to end rather soon. If you took a bunch of people out into the desert and the world didn't end, you'd come home shamefaced, I imagine; but the persistence of an art form doesn't invalidate work created in the comparable apocalyptic ambience. That's one of the fringe benefits of being an artist instead of a prophet. There are others.) If you happened to be Vladimir Nabokov you might address that felt ultimacy by writing *Pale Fire:* a fine novel by a learned pedant, in the form of a pedantic commentary on a poem invented for the purpose. If you were Borges you might write *Labyrinths:* fictions by a learned librarian in the form of footnotes, as he describes them, to imaginary or hypothetical books.[22] And I'll add, since I believe Borges' idea is rather more interesting, that if you were the author of this paper, you'd have written something like *The Sot-Weed Factor* or *Giles Goat-Boy:* novels which imitate the form of the Novel, by an author who imitates the role of Author.

If this sort of thing sounds unpleasantly decadent, nevertheless it's about where the genre began, with *Quixote* imitating *Amadis of Gaul,* Cervantes pretending to be the

---

[19] Novel by James Joyce.
[20] Herbert Marshall McLuhan (1911–1980), communications theorist, believed that technology shapes the way people think and perceive.
[21] Fiedler: Leslie Fiedler (b. 1917), American literary critic and social historian.
[22] Barth's note: "Borges was born in Argentina in

1899, educated in Europe, and for some years worked as director of the National Library in Buenos Aires, except for a period when Juan Perón demoted him to the rank of provincial chicken inspector as a political humiliation. Currently he's the *Beowulf*-man at the University of Buenos Aires."

Cid Hamete Benengeli (and Alonso Quijano pretending to be Don Quixote), or Fielding parodying Richardson.[23] "History repeats itself as farce"—meaning, of course, in the form or mode of farce, not that history is farcical. The imitation (like the Dadaist[24] echoes in the work of the "intermedia" types) is something new and *may be* quite serious and passionate despite its farcical aspect. This is the important difference between a proper novel and a deliberate imitation of a novel, or a novel imitative of other sorts of documents. The first attempts (has been historically inclined to attempt) to imitate actions more or less directly, and its conventional devices— cause and effect, linear anecdote, characterization, authorial selection, arrangement, and interpretation—can be and have long since been objected to as obsolete notions, or metaphors for obsolete notions: Robbe-Grillet's[25] essays *For a New Novel* come to mind. There are replies to these objections, not to the point here, but one can see that in any case they're obviated by imitations-of-novels, which attempt to represent not life directly but a representation of life. In fact such works are no more removed from "life" than Richardson's or Goethe's[26] epistolary novels are: both imitate "real" documents, and the subject of both, ultimately, is life, not the documents. A novel is as much a piece of the real world as a letter, and the letters in *The Sorrows of Young Werther* . . . are, after all, fictitious.

One might imaginably compound this imitation, and though Borges doesn't, he's fascinated with the idea: one of his frequenter literary allusions is to the 602nd night of *The 1001 Nights,* when, owing to a copyist's error, Scheherezade begins to tell the King the story of the 1001 nights, from the beginning. Happily, the King interrupts; if he didn't there'd be no 603rd night ever, and while this would solve Scheherezade's problem—which is every storyteller's problem: to publish or perish—it would put the "outside" author in a bind. (I suspect that Borges dreamed this whole thing up: the business he mentions isn't in any edition of *The 1001 Nights* I've been able to consult. Not *yet,* anyhow: after reading "Tlön, Uqbar," etc., one is inclined to recheck every semester or so.)

Now Borges (whom someone once vexedly accused *me* of inventing) is interested in the 602nd Night because it's an instance of the story-within-the-story turned back upon itself, and his interest in such instances is threefold: first, as he himself declares, they disturb us metaphysically: when the characters in a work of fiction become readers or authors of the fiction they're in, we're reminded of the fictitious aspect of our own existence, one of Borges' cardinal themes, as it was of Shakespeare, Calderón, Unamuno,[27] and other folk. Second, the 602nd Night is a literary illustration of the *regressus in infinitum,*[28] as are almost all of Borges' principal images and motifs. Third, Scheherezade's accidental gambit, like Borges' other versions of the *regressus in infinitum,* is an image of the exhaustion, or attempted exhaustion, of possibilities—in this case literary possibilities—and so we return to our main subject.

What makes Borges' stance, if you like, more interesting to me than, say, Nabo-

[23] Samuel Richardson (1689–1761), English novelist. The moralistic tone of his *Pamela* was parodied in successive works by Henry Fielding.

[24] Dada: artistic movement beginning in 1915 and based on irrationality and provocation.

[25] Robbe-Grillet: Alain Robbe-Grillet (b. 1922), French novelist.

[26] Goethe: Johann Wolfgang von Goethe

(1749–1832), major German author. His novel, *The Sorrows of Young Werther,* purports to be letters left by a suicide.

[27] Pedro Calderón de la Barca (1600–1681), Spanish playwright and poet; Miguel de Unamuno (1864–1936), Spanish philosopher and novelist.

[28] Latin: "a going back (regression) into infinity."

kov's or Beckett's, is the premise with which he approaches literature; in the words of one of his editors: "For [Borges] no one has claim to originality in literature; all writers are more or less faithful amanuenses of the spirit, translators and annotators of pre-existing archetypes." Thus his inclination to write brief comments on imaginary books: for one to attempt to add overtly to the sum of "original" literature by even so much as a conventional short story, not to mention a novel, would be too presumptuous, too naïve; literature has been done long since. A librarian's point of view! And it would itself be too presumptuous if it weren't part of a lively, passionately relevant metaphysical vision, and slyly employed against itself precisely to make new and original literature. Borges defines the Baroque as "that style which deliberately exhausts (or tried to exhaust) its possibilities and borders upon its own caricature." While his own work is *not* Baroque, except intellectually (the Baroque was never so terse, laconic, economical), it suggests the view that intellectual and literary history has been Baroque, and has pretty well exhausted the possibilities of novelty. His *ficciones* [29] are not only footnotes to imaginary texts, but postscripts to the real corpus of literature.

This premise gives resonance and relation to all his principal images. The facing mirrors that recur in his stories are a dual *regressus.* The doubles that his characters, like Nabokov's, run afoul of suggest dizzying multiples and remind one of Browne's remark that "every man is not only himself . . . men are lived over again." (It would please Borges, and illustrate Browne's point, to call Browne a precursor of Borges. "Every writer," Borges says in his essay on Kafka, "creates his own precursors.") Borges' favorite third-century heretical sect is the Histriones—I think and hope he invented them—who believe that repetition is impossible in history and therefore live viciously in order to purge the future of the vices they commit: in other words, to exhaust the possibilities of the world in order to bring its end nearer.

The writer he most often mentions, after Cervantes, is Shakespeare; in one piece he imagines the playwright on his deathbed asking God to permit him to be one and himself, having been everyone and no one; God replies from the whirlwind that He is no one either; He has dreamed the world like Shakespeare, and including Shakespeare. Homer's story in Book IV of the *Odyssey,* of Menelaus on the beach at Pharos, tackling Proteus, appeals profoundly to Borges: Proteus is he who "exhausts the guises of reality" while Menelaus—who, one recalls, disguised his own identity in order to ambush him—holds fast. Zeno's paradox of Achilles and the Tortoise embodies a *regressus in infinitum* which Borges carries through philosophical history, pointing out that Aristotle uses it to refute Plato's theory of forms, Hume to refute the possibility of cause and effect, Lewis Carroll to refute syllogistic deduction, William James to refute the notion of temporal passage, and Bradley to refute the general possibility of logical relations;[30] Borges himself uses it, citing Schopenhauer[31] as evidence that the world is our dream, our idea, in which "tenuous and eternal crevices of unreason" can be found to remind us that our creation is false, or at least fictive.

---

[29] Spanish: "fictions."
[30] All are philosophers who presented skeptical or paradoxical arguments, including David Hume (1711–1776), Scottish philosopher, economist, and historian; and F. H. Bradley (1846–1924), English philosopher.

[31] Schopenhauer: Arthur Schopenhauer (1788–1860), German philosopher, was author of *The World as Will and Idea.*

The infinite library of one of his most popular stories is an image particularly pertinent to the literature of exhaustion; the "Library of Babel" houses every possible combination of alphabetical characters and spaces, and thus every possible book and statement, including and and my refutations and vindications, the history of the actual future, the history of every possible future, and, though he doesn't mention it, the encyclopedias not only of Tlön but of every imaginable other world—since, as in Lucretius' universe, the number of elements, and so of combinations, is finite (though very large), and the number of instances of each element and combination of elements is infinite, like the library itself.

That brings us to his favorite image of all, the labyrinth, and to my point. *Labyrinths* is the name of his most substantial translated volume, and the only full-length study of Borges in English, by Ana María Barrenechea, is called *Borges the Labyrinth-Maker*. A labyrinth, after all, is a place in which, ideally, all the possibilities of choice (of direction, in this case) are embodied, and—barring special dispensation like Theseus'—must be exhausted before one reaches the heart. Where, mind, the Minotaur waits with two final possibilities: defeat and death, or victory and freedom. Now, in fact, the legendary Theseus is non-Baroque; thanks to Ariadne's thread he can take a shortcut through the labyrinth at Knossos. But Menelaus on the beach at Pharos, for example, is genuinely Baroque in the Borgesian spirit, and illustrates a positive artistic morality in the literature of exhaustion. He is not there, after all, for kicks (any more than Borges and Beckett are in the fiction racket for their health): Menelaus is *lost,* in the larger labyrinth of the world, and has got to hold fast while the Old Man of the Sea exhausts reality's frightening guises so that he may extort direction from him when Proteus returns to his "true" self. It's a heroic enterprise, with salvation as its object—one recalls that the aim of the Histriones is to get history done with so that Jesus may come again the sooner, and that Shakespeare's heroic metamorphoses culminate not merely in a theophany but in an apotheosis.

Now, not just any old body is equipped for this labor, and Theseus in the Cretan labyrinth becomes in the end the aptest image for Borges after all. Distressing as the fact is to us liberal Democrats, the commonality, alas, will *always* lose their way and their souls: it's the chosen remnant, the virtuoso, the Thesean *hero,* who, confronted with Baroque reality, Baroque history, the Baroque state of his art, need *not* rehearse its possibilities to exhaustion, any more than Borges needs actually to write the *Encyclopaedia of Tlön* or the books in the Library of Babel. He need only be aware of their existence or possibility, acknowledge them, and with the aid of *very special* gifts—as extraordinary as saint- or hero-hood and not likely to be found in The New York Correspondence School of Literature—go straight through the maze to the accomplishment of his work.

1967

Donald Barthelme
b. 1931

Donald Barthelme was born in Philadelphia on April 7, 1931, and grew up in Houston, Texas. He began writing stories and poems in high school and continued writing, combining journalism with poetry and fiction, at the University of Houston, where he studied for several years without taking a degree. After serving with the U.S. Army in Japan and Korea, Barthelme returned to the University of Houston. Over the next several years he founded the literary magazine, *Forum,* and worked as a reporter for the *Houston Post.* In addition, he became a sponsor and then the director of Houston's Contemporary Arts Museum.

With his long, rather mixed apprenticeship behind him, Barthelme moved to New York in 1962 and began a period of remarkable productivity. Throughout the 1950s and into the 1960s he had sought a style of his own, only to remain dissatisfied. Suddenly, however, in 1963 he found what he wanted, and after publishing his first story, "L'Lapse," in *The New Yorker,* he began contributing regularly to that magazine. In 1964 he published his first collection of stories, *Come Back, Dr. Caligari,* and three years later his first novel, *Snow White,* which had originally been published in its entirety in *The New Yorker.* A kind of surrealistic version of a classic fairy tale combined with a critique of a consumer society (fiction, too, being part of what is "consumed" in contemporary culture), *Snow White* contains a self-parodic questionnaire asking its readers for suggestions about how the novel should proceed. In his other novel, *The Dead Father* (1975), the narrative is interrupted by the inclusion of an old-fashioned "Manual for Sons" that lists types of fathers and means of dealing with them.

Since the late 1960s Barthelme has published several collections of short stories: *Unspeakable Practices, Unnatural Acts* (1968), *City Life* (1970), *Sadness* (1972), *Guilty Pleasures* (1974), *Amateurs* (1976), *Great Days* (1979), and a selection, *Sixty Stories* (1981). Together these works demonstrate an interest in mythology that dates back to Barthelme's childhood and a knowledge of modern art that derives from the influence of his father, an architect. They also reveal Barthelme's early reading of the French Symbolists and such great modernists as Pound, Eliot, and Joyce. In both *Forum* and *Location,* a literary magazine he edited during his early months in New York, Barthelme published writers ranging from Jean-Paul Sartre and Alain Robbe-Grillet to Saul Bellow and William Gass. More than any of these writers, however, and as much as any writer of his time, Barthelme's distinctive style turns on experiments with language. Painters "had to go out and reinvent painting because of the invention of photography," he once remarked, "and I think films have done something of the sort for us."

Fiction possesses, as Barthelme sees it, both "the enormous resources" of language and different ways of "investigating" those resources. His characters often seem odd and abstract partly because they are so completely creations not simply of language but of something very like linguistic investigations. As "Robert Kennedy Saved from Drowning" clearly shows, Barthelme delights in odd combinations of words—unexpected terms injected into hackneyed idioms and clichés (especially those of the mass media), pop allusions, odd statistics, and jargon picked up from science, technology, sociology, and government bureaucracies. Traditional literary allusions are often wedged together with comic-strip characters, film references, Walt Disney–like figures, and brand-name advertised products.

Barthelme investigates by combining, and he combines at a rate that is frequently disorienting. As a consequence, his stories seem sometimes to deaden as well as to prick and delight. As a writer, he takes great risks, leaving himself little margin for error. When his style works, however, his characters become creators as well as creatures of the odd, even the startlingly odd, combination, the telling juxtaposition, and they do so in the name of making such old, familiar issues as time and mortality new. Like their creator, they evince a conviction that "there is a realm of possible knowledge which can be reached by artists, which is not susceptible of mathematical verification but which is true."

Further Reading:
J. Klinkowitz, *Literary Disruptions: The Making of a Post-Contemporary American Fiction*, 1975.
M. Zavarzadeh, *The Mythopoeic Reality*, 1976.
L. Gordon, *Donald Barthelme*, 1981.

Text:
Sixty Stories, 1981.

Robert Kennedy Saved from Drowning

K. at His Desk

He is neither abrupt with nor excessively kind to associates. Or he is both abrupt and kind.

The telephone is, for him, a whip, a lash, but also a conduit for soothing words, a sink into which he can hurl gallons of syrup if it comes to that.

He reads quickly, scratching brief comments ("Yes," "No") in corners of the paper. He slouches in the leather chair, looking about him with a slightly irritated air for new visitors, new difficulties. He spends his time sending and receiving messengers.

"I spend my time sending and receiving messengers," he says, "Some of these messages are important. Others are not."

Described by Secretaries

A: "Quite frankly I think he forgets a lot of things. But the things he forgets are those which are inessential. I even think he might forget deliberately, to leave his mind free. He has the ability to get rid of unimportant details. And he does."

B: "Once when I was sick, I hadn't heard from him, and I thought he had forgotten me. You know usually your boss will send flowers or something like that. I was in the hospital, and I was mighty blue. I was in a room with another girl, and *her* boss hadn't sent her anything either. Then suddenly the door opened and there he was with the biggest bunch of yellow tulips I'd ever seen in my life. And the other girl's boss was with him, and he had tulips too. They were standing there with all those tulips, smiling."

Behind the Bar

At a crowded party, he wanders behind the bar to make himself a Scotch and water. His hand is on the bottle of Scotch, his glass is waiting. The bartender, a small man in a beige uniform with gilt buttons, politely asks K. to return to the other side, the guests' side, of the bar. "You let one behind here, they all be behind here," the bartender says.

K. Reading the Newspaper

His reactions are impossible to catalogue. Often he will find a note that amuses him endlessly, some anecdote involving, say, a fireman who has propelled his apparatus at record-breaking speed to the wrong address. These small stories are clipped, carried about in a pocket, to be produced at appropriate moments for the pleasure of friends. Other manifestations please him less. An account of an earthquake in Chile, with its thousands of dead and homeless, may depress him for weeks. He memorizes the terrible statistics, quoting them everywhere and saying, with a grave look: "We must do something." Important actions often follow, sometimes within a matter of hours. (On the other hand, these two kinds of responses may be, on a given day, inexplicably reversed.)

The more trivial aspects of the daily itemization are skipped. While reading, he maintains a rapid drumming of his fingertips on the desktop. He receives twelve newspapers, but of these, only four are regarded as serious.

Attitude Toward His Work

"Sometimes I can't seem to do anything. The work is there, piled up, it seems to me an insurmountable obstacle, really out of reach. I sit and look at it, wondering where to begin, how to take hold of it. Perhaps I pick up a piece of paper, try to read it but my mind is elsewhere, I am thinking of something else, I can't seem to get the gist of it, it seems meaningless, devoid of interest, not having to do with human affairs, drained of life. Then, in an hour, or even a moment, everything changes suddenly: I realize I only have to *do* it, hurl myself into the midst of it, proceed mechanically, the first thing and then the second thing, that it is simply a matter of moving from one step to the next, plowing through it. I become interested, I become excited, I work very fast, things fall into place, I am exhilarated, amazed that these things could ever have seemed dead to me."

Sleeping on the Stones of Unknown Towns (Rimbaud)[1]

K. is walking, with that familiar slight dip of the shoulders, through the streets of a small city in France or Germany. The shop signs are in a language which alters when

[1] Arthur Rimband (1854–1891), French poet
famous for his dramatically unconventional life.

inspected closely, MÖBEL becoming MEUBLES[2] for example, and the citizens mutter to themselves with dark virtuosity a mixture of languages. K. is very interested, looks closely at everything, at the shops, the goods displayed, the clothing of the people, the tempo of street life, the citizens themselves, wondering about them. What are their water needs?

"In the West, wisdom is mostly gained at lunch. At lunch, people tell you things."

The nervous eyes of the waiters.

The tall bald cook, white apron, white T-shirt, grinning through an opening in the wall.

"Why is that cook looking at me?"

Urban Transportation

"The transportation problems of our cities and their rapidly expanding suburbs are the most urgent and neglected transportation problems confronting the country. In these heavily populated and industrialized areas, people are dependent on a system of transportation that is at once complex and inadequate. Obsolete facilities and growing demands have created seemingly insoluble difficulties and present methods of dealing with these difficulties offer little prospect of relief."

K. Penetrated with Sadness

He hears something playing on someone else's radio, in another part of the building.

The music is wretchedly sad; now he can (barely) hear it, now it fades into the wall.

He turns on his own radio. There it is, on his own radio, the same music. The sound fills the room.

Karsh of Ottawa

"We sent a man to Karsh of Ottawa[3] and told him that we admired his work very much. Especially, I don't know, the Churchill thing and, you know, the Hemingway thing, and all that. And we told him we wanted to set up a sitting for K. sometime in June, if that would be convenient for him, and he said yes, that was okay, June was okay, and where did we want to have it shot, there or in New York or where. Well, that was a problem because we didn't know exactly what K.'s schedule would be for June, it was up in the air, so we tentatively said New York around the fifteenth. And he said, that was okay, he could do that. And he wanted to know how much time he could have, and we said, well, how much time do you need? And he said he didn't know, it varied from sitter to sitter. He said some people were very restless and that made it difficult to get just the right shot. He said there was one shot in each sitting that was, you know, the key shot, the right one. He said he'd have to see, when the time came."

---

[2] German and French, respectively: "furniture."
[3] Yousef Karsh, renowned contemporary photographer noted for his portraits of powerful and famous personalities.

Dress

He is neatly dressed in a manner that does not call attention to itself. The suits are soberly cut and in dark colors. He must at all times present an aspect of freshness difficult to sustain because of frequent movements from place to place under conditions which are not always the most favorable. Thus he changes clothes frequently, especially shirts. In the course of a day he changes his shirt many times. There are always extra shirts about, in boxes.

"Which of you has the shirts?"

A Friend Comments: K.'s Aloneness

"The thing you have to realize about K. is that essentially he's absolutely alone in the world. There's this terrible loneliness which prevents people from getting too close to him. Maybe it comes from something in his childhood, I don't know. But he's very hard to get to know, and a lot of people who think they know him rather well don't really know him at all. He says something or does something that surprises you, and you realize that all along you really didn't know him at all.

"He has surprising facets. I remember once we were out in a small boat. K. of course was the captain. Some rough weather came up and we began to head back in. I began worrying about picking up a landing and I said to him that I didn't think the anchor would hold, with the wind and all. He just looked at me. Then he said: 'Of course it will hold. That's what it's for.'"

K. on Crowds

"There are exhausted crowds and vivacious crowds.

"Sometimes, standing there, I can sense whether a particular crowd is one thing or the other. Sometimes the mood of the crowd is disguised, sometimes you only find out after a quarter of an hour what sort of crowd a particular crowd is.

"And you can't speak to them in the same way. The variations have to be taken into account. You have to say something to them that is meaningful to them *in that mood.*"

Gallery-going

K. enters a large gallery on Fifty-seventh Street, in the Fuller Building. His entourage includes several ladies and gentlemen. Works by a geometricist are on show. K. looks at the immense, rather theoretical paintings.

"Well, at least we know he has a ruler."

The group dissolves in laughter. People repeat the remark to one another, laughing. The artist, who has been standing behind a dealer, regards K. with hatred.

K. Puzzled by His Children

The children are crying. There are several children, one about four, a boy, then another boy, slightly older, and a little girl, very beautiful, wearing blue jeans, crying.

There are various objects on the grass, an electric train, a picture book, a red ball, a plastic bucket, a plastic shovel.

K. frowns at the children whose distress issues from no source immediately available to the eye, which seems indeed uncaused, vacant, a general anguish. K. turns to the mother of these children who is standing nearby wearing hip-huggers which appear to be made of linked marshmallows studded with diamonds but then I am a notoriously poor observer.

"Play with them," he says.

This mother of ten quietly suggests that K. himself "play with them."

K. picks up the picture book and begins to read to the children. But the book has a German text. It has been left behind, perhaps, by some foreign visitor. Nevertheless K. perseveres.

"A ist der Affe, er isst mit der Pfote." ("A is the Ape, he eats with his Paw.")

The crying of the children continues.

A Dream

Orange trees.

Overhead, a steady stream of strange aircraft which resemble kitchen implements, bread boards, cookie sheets, colanders.

The shiny aluminum instruments are on their way to complete the bombings of Sidi-Madani.

A farm in the hills.

Matters (from an Adminstrative Assistant)

"A lot of matters that had been pending came to a head right about that time, moved to the front burner, things we absolutely had to take care of. And we couldn't find K. Nobody knew where he was. We had looked everywhere. He had just withdrawn, made himself unavailable. There was this one matter that was probably more pressing than all the rest put together. Really crucial. We were all standing around wondering what to do. We were getting pretty nervous because this thing was really . . . Then K. walked in and disposed of it with a quick phone call. A quick phone call!"

Childhood of K. As Recalled by a Former Teacher

"He was a very alert boy, very bright, good at his studies, very thorough, very conscientious. But that's not unusual; that describes a good number of the boys who pass through here. It's not unusual, that is, to find these qualities which are after all the qualities that we look for and encourage in them. What *was* unusual about K. was his compassion, something very rare for a boy of that age—even if they have it, they're usually very careful not to display it for fear of seeming soft, girlish. I remember, though, that in K. this particular attribute was very marked. I would almost say that it was his strongest characteristic."

Speaking to No One but Waiters He—

"The dandelion salad with bacon, I think."

"The *rysstafel.*"[4]

"The poached duck."

"The black bean purée."

"The cod fritters."

K. Explains a Technique

"It's an expedient in terms of how not to destroy a situation which has been a long time gestating, or, again, how to break it up if it appears that the situation has changed, during the gestation period, into one whose implications are not quite what they were at the beginning. What I mean is that in this business things are constantly altering (usually for the worse) and usually you want to give the impression that you're not watching this particular situation particularly closely, that you're paying no special attention to it, until you're ready to make your move. That is, it's best to be sudden, if you can manage it. Of course you can't do that all the time. Sometimes you're just completely wiped out, cleaned out, totaled, and then the only thing to do is shrug and forget about it."

K. on His Own Role

"Sometimes it seems to me that it doesn't matter what I do, that it is enough to exist, to sit somewhere, in a garden for example, watching whatever is to be seen there, the small events. At other times, I'm aware that other people, possibly a great number of other people, could be affected by what I do or fail to do, that I have a responsibility, as we all have, to make the best possible use of whatever talents I've been given, for the common good. It is not enough to sit in that garden, however restful or pleasurable it might be. The world is full of unsolved problems, situations that demand careful, reasoned and intelligent action. In Latin America, for example."

As Entrepreneur

The original cost estimates for burying the North Sea pipeline have been exceeded by a considerable margin. Everyone wonders what he will say about this contretemps which does not fail to have its dangers for those responsible for the costly miscalculations, which are viewed in many minds as inexcusable.

He says only: "Exceptionally difficult rock conditions."

[4] Dutch-Indonesian: "rice-table," a meal consisting of many different dishes, all served with rice.

With Young People

K., walking the streets of unknown towns, finds himself among young people. Young people line these streets, narrow and curving, which are theirs, dedicated to them. They are everywhere, resting on the embankments, their guitars, small radios, long hair. They sit on the sidewalks, back to back, heads turned to stare. They stand implacably on street corners, in doorways, or lean on their elbows in windows, or squat in small groups at that place where the sidewalk meets the walls of buildings. The streets are filled with these young people who say nothing, reveal only a limited interest, refuse to declare themselves. Street after street contains them, a great number, more displayed as one turns a corner, rank upon rank stretching into the distance, drawn from the arcades, the plazas, staring.

He Discusses the French Writer Poulet

"For Poulet, it is not enough to speak of *seizing the moment*. It is rather a question of, and I quote, 'recognizing in the instant which lives and dies, which surges out of nothingness and which ends in dream, an intensity and depth of significance which ordinarily attaches only to the whole of existence.'

"What Poulet is describing is neither an ethic nor a prescription but rather what he has discovered in the work of Marivaux. Poulet has taken up the Marivaudian canon and squeezed it with both hands to discover the essence of what may be called the Marivaudian being, what Poulet in fact calls the Marivaudian being.

"The Marivaudian being is, according to Poulet, a pastless futureless man, born anew at every instant. The instants are points which organize themselves into a line, but what is important is the instant, not the line. The Marivaudian being has in a sense no history. Nothing follows from what has gone before. He is constantly surprised. He cannot predict his own reaction to events. He is constantly being *overtaken* by events. A condition of breathlessness and dazzlement surrounds him. In consequence he exists in a certain freshness which seems, if I may say so, very desirable. This freshness Poulet, quoting Marivaux, describes very well."

K. Saved from Drowning

K. in the water. His flat black hat, his black cape, his sword are on the shore. He retains his mask. His hands beat the surface of the water which tears and rips about him. The white foam, the green depths. I throw a line, the coils leaping out over the surface of the water. He has missed it. No, it appears that he has it. His right hand (sword arm) grasps the line that I have thrown him. I am on the bank, the rope wound round my waist, braced against a rock. K. now has both hands on the line. I pull him out of the water. He stands now on the bank, gasping.

"Thank you."

1968

John Updike
b. 1932

John Updike was born on March 18, 1932, in the small town of Shillington, Pennsylvania, where he acquired an overwhelming sense of place that has continued to yield richly detailed memories—of buildings and pets, scenes and playmates, and above all of family. None of this would be remarkable were Updike's sense of life not inseparable from his sense of place and his sense of art from his sense of life.

Art began for Updike "as a method of riding a thin pencil line out of Shillington, out of time altogether, into an infinity of unseen and even unborn hearts." Yet, having begun as a mode of flight, writing quickly became for him a method of return—or more precisely, a method of transcribing the world he had known: "middleness with all its grits, bumps, and anonymities, in its fullness of satisfaction and mystery." Whether such a thing as transcribing is "possible" or, in view of the world's wild suffering, "worth doing" is a question Updike explicitly puts to himself. "Possibly not," he replies, only to conclude that it is nevertheless necessary since "the horse chestnut trees, the telephone poles, the porches, the green hedges recede to a calm point that in my subjective geography is still the center of the world."

Between his beginnings in Shillington and his emergence as a writer, Updike spent four years at Harvard, from which he was graduated *summa cum laude* in 1954. After studying art for a year in England, Updike returned to the United States in 1955. He worked as a staff reporter for *The New Yorker* for two years and soon began contributing stories there regularly, establishing a relationship with that magazine that has continued to the present. In 1957 he left New York to practice his "solitary trade" in Ipswich, Massachusetts.

In 1959 Updike published a collection of short stories, *The Same Door,* and his first novel—partly inspired by his early reading of Huxley and Orwell—*The Poorhouse Fair,* a futuristic story set in a county home for the elderly poor. The following year Updike published a successful second novel, *Rabbit, Run,* about a former high school basketball star who, nostalgic for a lost past, finds himself continually on the run from the demands of adult responsibility. Updike continued the story of Harry ("Rabbit") Angstrom, taking him through the cultural turmoil of the late 1960s in *Rabbit Redux* (1971) and into upper-middle-class prosperity—though not necessarily peace of mind—in *Rabbit Is Rich* (1981). Updike has frequently connected his themes to classical mythology, a technique that came fully to the surface in his third novel, *The Centaur* (1963), the story of three days in the life of a high school science teacher and his son.

By the mid-1960s it had become clear that one of Updike's dominant subjects was marriage. Many of his short stories—among them "Separating"—deal exclusively with the difficulties of married life in a world where the traditional religious values that once nourished and sanctioned marital love and sex have lost their meaning. In *Of the Farm* (1965) Updike explores the inner dynamics of a marriage during a couple's weekend visit to the husband's dying mother. The problems of marriage in our time are given ritualistic and religious significance in *Couples* (1968), a novel about sexual love and infidelity among ten couples in a small New England community. In *A Month of Sundays* (1975) Updike explores the themes of love and sex, marriage and infidelity within the framework of American Protestant morality. The theme of marriage and infidelity is also at the center of Updike's eighth novel, *Marry Me* (1976), the story of a summer love affair that is also a story of modern morality: We live in "the twilight of the old morality," the book's hero argues, "and there's just enough to torment us, and not enough to hold us in." In 1979 Updike collected his stories about a married couple, the Maples, in *Too Far to Go* and in the same year also published *Problems and Other Stories,* which contains "Separating," another of the Maples stories.

Though continually drawn to the problems of love, sex, and modern domesticity, Updike has nevertheless kept a close eye on literature, culture, and politics. In 1970 he published *Bech: A Book,* a series of linked stories about an American Jewish writer that dealt humorously with the meaning of a literary career; Updike continued the adventures of Henry Bech in another collection of tales, *Bech Is Back* (1982). In 1973 Updike toured Africa as a Fulbright lecturer, and out of his experiences he wrote *The Coup* (1978), a political novel about a violent, imaginary African regime. Updike's enormous output of essays, criticism, and literary reviews have been collected in several volumes: *Assorted Prose* (1965), *Picked-Up Pieces* (1975), and *Hugging the Shore* (1983). Updike has also written a play and several volumes of poetry. His latest novels are *The Witches of Eastwick* (1984), which uses a contemporary instance of witchcraft as a way of commenting on a modern culture habituated to television and popular media, and *Roger's Version* (1986).

Updike's stories, a large number of them set in "Olinger," the small imaginary town that evokes the Shillington of Updike's boyhood and youth, often center on adolescent protagonists. Over the stories hovers a certain nostalgia, a remorse for time. One source of that nostalgia is Updike's feeling for youth itself—for its openness, its honesty, its innocence, its brave sense of immortality. Another source is his feeling for preurban America and the life it spawned. But there is always an edge to Updike's journeys back toward the source, not simply because he is suspicious of nostalgia but also because such journeys always follow lines toward the unseen and the unknown. His larger quest is for some form of work or play or love that can approximate—or some religious experience that can satisfy—our longing for permanence.

Further Reading:
C. T. Samuels, *John Updike,* 1969.

Text:
Problems and Other Stories, 1979.

Separating

The day was fair. Brilliant. All that June the weather had mocked the Maples' internal misery with solid sunlight—golden shafts and cascades of green in which their conversations had wormed unseeing, their sad murmuring selves the only stain in Nature. Usually by this time of the year they had acquired tans; but when they met their elder daughter's plane on her return from a year in England they were almost as pale as she, though Judith was too dazzled by the sunny opulent jumble of her native land to notice. They did not spoil her homecoming by telling her immediately. Wait a few days, let her recover from jet lag, had been one of their formulations, in that string of gray dialogues—over coffee, over cocktails, over Cointreau—that had shaped the strategy of their dissolution, while the earth performed its annual stunt of renewal unnoticed beyond their closed windows. Richard had thought to leave at Easter; Joan had insisted they wait until the four children were at last assembled, with all exams passed and ceremonies attended, and the bauble of summer to console them. So he had drudged away, in love, in dread, repairing screens, getting the mowers sharpened, rolling and patching their new tennis court.

The court, clay, had come through its first winter pitted and windswept bare of redcoat. Years ago the Maples had observed how often, among their friends, divorce followed a dramatic home improvement, as if the marriage were making one last effort to live; their own worst crisis had come amid the plaster dust and exposed plumbing of a kitchen renovation. Yet, a summer ago, as canary-yellow bulldozers gaily churned a grassy, daisy-dotted knoll into a muddy plateau, and a crew of pigtailed young men raked and tamped clay into a plane, this transformation did not strike them as ominous, but festive in its impudence; their marriage could rend the earth for fun. The next spring, waking each day at dawn to a sliding sensation as if the bed were being tipped, Richard found the barren tennis court—its net and tapes still rolled in the barn— an environment congruous with his mood of purposeful desolation, and the crumbling of handfuls of clay into cracks and holes (dogs had frolicked on the court in a thaw; rivulets had eroded trenches) an activity suitably elemental and interminable. In his sealed heart he hoped the day would never come.

Now it was here. A Friday. Judith was re-acclimated; all four children were assembled, before jobs and camps and visits again scattered them. Joan thought they should be told one by one. Richard was for making an announcement at the table. She said, "I think just making an announcement is a cop-out. They'll start quarrelling and playing to each other instead of focusing. They're each individuals, you know, not just some corporate obstacle to your freedom."

"O.K., O.K. I agree." Joan's plan was exact. That evening, they were giving Judith a belated welcome-home dinner, of lobster and champagne. Then, the party over, they, the two of them, who nineteen years before would push her in a baby carriage along Fifth Avenue to Washington Square, were to walk her out of the house, to the bridge across the salt creek, and tell her, swearing her to secrecy. Then Richard Jr., who was going directly from work to a rock concert in Boston, would be told, either late when he returned on the train or early Saturday morning before he went off to his job; he was seventeen and employed as one of a golf-course maintenance crew. Then the two younger children, John and Margaret, could, as the morning wore on, be informed.

"Mopped up, as it were," Richard said.

"Do you have any better plan? That leaves you the rest of Saturday to answer any questions, pack, and make your wonderful departure."

"No," he said, meaning he had no better plan, and agreed to hers, though to him it showed an edge of false order, a hidden plea for control, like Joan's long chore lists and financial accountings and, in the days when he first knew her, her too-copious lecture notes. Her plan turned one hurdle for him into four—four knife-sharp walls, each with a sheer blind drop on the other side.

All spring he had moved through a world of insides and outsides, of barriers and partitions. He and Joan stood as a thin barrier between the children and the truth. Each moment was a partition, with the past on one side and the future on the other, a future containing this unthinkable now. Beyond four knifelike walls a new life for him waited vaguely. His skull cupped a secret, a white face, a face both frightened and soothing, both strange and known, that he wanted to shield from tears, which he felt all about him, solid as the sunlight. So haunted, he had become obsessed with battening down the house against his absence, replacing screens and sash cords, hinges and latches —a Houdini making things snug before his escape.

The lock. He had still to replace a lock on one of the doors of the screened porch. The task, like most such, proved more difficult than he had imagined. The old lock, aluminum frozen by corrosion, had been deliberately rendered obsolete by manufacturers. Three hardware stores had nothing that even approximately matched the mortised hole its removal (surprisingly easy) left. Another hole had to be gouged, with bits too small and saws too big, and the old hole fitted with a block of wood—the chisels dull, the saw rusty, his fingers thick with lack of sleep. The sun poured down, beyond the porch, on a world of neglect. The bushes already needed pruning, the windward side of the house was shedding flakes of paint, rain would get in when he was gone, insects, rot, death. His family, all those he would lose, filtered through the edges of his awareness as he struggled with screw holes, splinters, opaque instructions, minutiae of metal.

Judith sat on the porch, a princess returned from exile. She regaled them with stories of fuel shortages, of bomb scares in the Underground, of Pakistani workmen loudly lusting after her as she walked past on her way to dance school. Joan came and went, in and out of the house, calmer than she should have been, praising his struggles with the lock as if this were one more and not the last of their long succession of shared chores. The younger of his sons for a few minutes held the rickety screen door while his father clumsily hammered and chiseled, each blow a kind of sob in Richard's ears. His younger daughter, having been at a slumber party, slept on the porch hammock through all the noise—heavy and pink, trusting and forsaken. Time, like the sunlight, continued relentlessly; the sunlight slowly slanted. Today was one of the longest days. The lock clicked, worked. He was through. He had a drink; he drank it on the porch, listening to his daughter. "It was so sweet," she was saying, "during the worst of it, how all the butchers and bakery shops kept open by candlelight. They're all so plucky and cute. From the papers, things sounded so much worse here—people shooting people in gas lines, and everybody freezing."

Richard asked her, "Do you still want to live in England forever?" *Forever:* the concept, now a reality upon him, pressed and scratched at the back of his throat.

"No," Judith confessed, turning her oval face to him, its eyes still childishly far apart, but the lips set as over something succulent and satisfactory. "I was anxious to come home. I'm an American." She was a woman. They had raised her; he and Joan had endured together to raise her, alone of the four. The others had still some raising left in them. Yet it was the thought of telling Judith—the image of her, their first baby, walking between them arm in arm to the bridge—that broke him. The partition between his face and the tears broke. Richard sat down to the celebratory meal with the back of his throat aching; the champagne, the lobster seemed phases of sunshine; he saw them and tasted them through tears. He blinked, swallowed, croakily joked about hay fever. The tears would not stop leaking through; they came not through a hole that could be plugged but through a permeable spot in a membrane, steadily, purely, endlessly, fruitfully. They became, his tears, a shield for himself against these others—their faces, the fact of their assembly, a last time as innocents, at a table where he sat the last time as head. Tears dropped from his nose as he broke the lobster's back; salt flavored his champagne as he sipped it; the raw clench at the back of his throat was delicious. He could not help himself.

His children tried to ignore his tears. Judith, on his right, lit a cigarette, gazed upward in the direction of her too energetic, too sophisticated exhalation; on her other side, John earnestly bent his face to the extraction of the last morsels—legs, tail segments—from the scarlet corpse. Joan, at the opposite end of the table, glanced at him surprised, her reproach displaced by a quick grimace, of forgiveness, or of salute to his superior gift of strategy. Between them, Margaret, no longer called Bean, thirteen and large for her age, gazed from the other side of his pane of tears as if into a shopwindow at something she coveted—at her father, a crystalline heap of splinters and memories. It was not she, however, but John who, in the kitchen, as they cleared the plates and carapaces away, asked Joan the question: *"Why is Daddy crying?"*

Richard heard the question but not the murmured answer. Then he heard Bean cry, "Oh, no-oh!"—the faintly dramatized exclamation of one who had long expected it.

John returned to the table carrying a bowl of salad. He nodded tersely at his father and his lips shaped the conspiratorial words "She told."

"Told what?" Richard asked aloud, insanely.

The boy sat down as if to rebuke his father's distraction with the example of his own good manners. He said quietly, "The separation."

Joan and Margaret returned; the child, in Richard's twisted vision, seemed diminished in size, and relieved, relieved to have had the bogieman at last proved real. He called out to her—the distances at the table had grown immense—"You knew, you always knew," but the clenching at the back of his throat prevented him from making sense of it. From afar he heard Joan talking, levelly, sensibly, reciting what they had prepared: it was a separation for the summer, an experiment. She and Daddy both agreed it would be good for them; they needed space and time to think; they liked each other but did not make each other happy enough, somehow.

Judith, imitating her mother's factual tone, but in her youth off-key, too cool, said, "I think it's silly. You should either live together or get divorced."

Richard's crying, like a wave that has crested and crashed, had become tumultuous;

but it was overtopped by another tumult, for John, who had been so reserved, now grew larger and larger at the table. Perhaps his younger sister's being credited with knowing set him off. "Why didn't you *tell* us?" he asked, in a large round voice quite unlike his own. "You should have *told* us you weren't getting along."

Richard was startled into attempting to force words through his tears. "We *do* get along, that's the trouble, so it doesn't show even to us—" *That we do not love each other* was the rest of the sentence; he couldn't finish it.

Joan finished for him, in her style. "And we've always, *especially,* loved our children."

John was not mollified. "What do you care about *us?"* he boomed. "We're just little things you *had."* His sisters' laughing forced a laugh from him, which he turned hard and parodistic: "Ha ha *ha."* Richard and Joan realized simultaneously that the child was drunk, on Judith's homecoming champagne. Feeling bound to keep the center of the stage, John took a cigarette from Judith's pack, poked it into his mouth, let it hang from his lower lip, and squinted like a gangster.

"You're not little things we had," Richard called to him. "You're the whole point. But you're grown. Or almost."

The boy was lighting matches. Instead of holding them to his cigarette (for they had never seen him smoke; being "good" had been his way of setting himself apart), he held them to his mother's face, closer and closer, for her to blow out. Then he lit the whole folder—a hiss and then a torch, held against his mother's face. Prismed by tears, the flame filled Richard's vision; he didn't know how it was extinguished. He heard Margaret say, "Oh stop showing off," and saw John, in response, break the cigarette in two and put the halves entirely into his mouth and chew, sticking out his tongue to display the shreds to his sister.

Joan talked to him, reasoning—a fountain of reason, unintelligible. "Talked about it for years . . . our children must help us . . . Daddy and I both want . . ." As the boy listened, he carefully wadded a paper napkin into the leaves of his salad, fashioned a ball of paper and lettuce, and popped it into his mouth, looking around the table for the expected laughter. None came. Judith said, "Be mature," and dismissed a plume of smoke.

Richard got up from this stifling table and led the boy outside. Though the house was in twilight, the outdoors still brimmed with light, the lovely waste light of high summer. Both laughing, he supervised John's spitting out the lettuce and paper and tobacco into the pachysandra. He took him by the hand—a square gritty hand, but for its softness a man's. Yet, it held on. They ran together up into the field, past the tennis court. The raw banking left by the bulldozers was dotted with daisies. Past the court and a flat stretch where they used to play family baseball stood a soft green rise glorious in the sun, each weed and species of grass distinct as illumination on parchment. "I'm sorry, so sorry," Richard cried. "You were the only one who ever tried to help me with all the goddam jobs around this place."

Sobbing, safe within his tears and the champagne, John explained, "It's not just the separation, it's the whole crummy year, I *hate* that school, you can't make any friends, the history teacher's a scud."

They sat on the crest of the rise, shaking and warm from their tears but easier in their voices, and Richard tried to focus on the child's sad year—the weekdays long with homework, the weekends spent in his room with model airplanes, while his parents murmured down below, nursing their separation. How selfish, how blind, Richard thought; his eyes felt scoured. He told his son, "We'll think about getting you transferred. Life's too short to be miserable."

They had said what they could, but did not want the moment to heal, and talked on, about the school, about the tennis court, whether it would ever again be as good as it had been that first summer. They walked to inspect it and pressed a few more tapes more firmly down. A little stiltedly, perhaps trying now to make too much of the moment, Richard led the boy to the spot in the field where the view was best, of the metallic blue river, the emerald marsh, the scattered islands velvety with shadow in the low light, the white bits of beach far away. "See," he said. "It goes on being beautiful. It'll be here tomorrow."

"I know," John answered, impatiently. The moment had closed.

Back in the house, the others had opened some white wine, the champagne being drunk, and still sat at the table, the three females, gossiping. Where Joan sat had become the head. She turned, showing him a tearless face, and asked, "All right?"

"We're fine," he said, resenting it, though relieved, that the party went on without him.

In bed she explained, "I couldn't cry I guess because I cried so much all spring. It really wasn't fair. It's your idea, and you made it look as though I was kicking you out."

"I'm sorry," he said. "I couldn't stop. I wanted to but couldn't."

"You *didn't* want to. You loved it. You were having your way, making a general announcement."

"I love having it over," he admitted. "God, those kids were great. So brave and funny." John, returned to the house, had settled to a model airplane in his room, and kept shouting down to them, "I'm O.K. No sweat." "And the way," Richard went on, cozy in his relief, "they never questioned the reasons we gave. No thought of a third person. Not even Judith."

"That *was* touching," Joan said.

He gave her a hug. "You were great too. Very reassuring to everybody. Thank you." Guiltily, he realized he did not feel separated.

"You still have Dickie to do," she told him. These words set before him a black mountain in the darkness; its cold breath, its near weight affected his chest. Of the four children, his elder son was most nearly his conscience. Joan did not need to add, "That's one piece of your dirty work I won't do for you."

"I know. I'll do it. You go to sleep."

Within minutes, her breathing slowed, became oblivious and deep. It was quarter to midnight. Dickie's train from the concert would come in at one-fourteen. Richard set the alarm for one. He had slept atrociously for weeks. But whenever he closed his lids some glimpse of the last hours scorched them—Judith exhaling toward the ceiling in a kind of aversion, Bean's mute staring, the sunstruck growth in the field where he and John had rested. The mountain before him moved closer, moved within him; he was huge, momentous. The ache at the back of his throat felt stale. His wife slept as if slain beside him. When, exasperated by his hot lids, his crowded heart, he rose from bed and dressed, she awoke enough to turn over. He told her then, "Joan, if I could undo it all, I would."

"Where would you begin?" she asked. There was no place. Giving him courage, she was always giving him courage. He put on shoes without socks in the dark. The children were breathing in their rooms, the downstairs was hollow. In their confusion they had left lights burning. He turned off all but one, the kitchen overhead. The car started. He had hoped it wouldn't. He met only moonlight on the road; it seemed a diaphanous companion, flickering in the leaves along the roadside, haunting his rearview mirror like a pursuer, melting under his headlights. The center of town, not quite deserted, was eerie at this hour. A young cop in uniform kept company with a gang of T-shirted kids on the steps of the bank. Across from the railroad station, several bars kept open. Customers, mostly young, passed in and out of the warm night, savoring summer's novelty. Voices shouted from cars as they passed; an immense conversation seemed in progress. Richard parked and in his weariness put his head on the passenger seat, out of the commotion and wheeling lights. It was as when, in the movies, an assassin grimly carries his mission through the jostle of a carnival—except the movies cannot show the precipitous, palpable slope you cling to within. You cannot climb back down; you can only fall. The synthetic fabric of the car seat, warmed by his cheek, confided to him an ancient, distant scent of vanilla.

A train whistle caused him to lift his head. It was on time; he had hoped it would be late. The slender drawgates descended. The bell of approach tingled happily. The great metal body, horizontally fluted, rocked to a stop, and sleepy teen-agers disembarked, his son among them. Dickie did not show surprise that his father was meeting him at this terrible hour. He sauntered to the car with two friends, both taller than he. He said "Hi" to his father and took the passenger's seat with an exhausted promptness that expressed gratitude. The friends got in the back, and Richard was grateful; a few more minutes' postponement would be won by driving them home.

He asked, "How was the concert?"

"Groovy," one boy said from the back seat.

"It bit," the other said.

"It was O.K.," Dickie said, moderate by nature, so reasonable that in his childhood the unreason of the world had given him headaches, stomach aches, nausea. When the second friend had been dropped off at his dark house, the boy blurted, "Dad, my eyes are killing me with hay fever! I'm out there cutting that mothering grass all day!"

"Do we still have those drops?"

"They didn't do any good last summer."

"They might this." Richard swung a U-turn on the empty street. The drive home took a few minutes. The mountain was here, in his throat. "Richard," he said, and felt the boy, slumped and rubbing his eyes, go tense at his tone, "I didn't come to meet you just to make your life easier. I came because your mother and I have some news for you, and you're a hard man to get ahold of these days. It's sad news."

"That's O.K." The reassurance came out soft, but quick, as if released from the tip of a spring.

Richard had feared that his tears would return and choke him, but the boy's manliness set an example, and his voice issued forth steady and dry. "It's sad news, but it needn't be tragic news, at least for you. It should have no practical effect on your life, though it's bound to have an emotional effect. You'll work at your job, and go back to school in September. Your mother and I are really proud of what you're making of your life; we don't want that to change at all."

"Yeah," the boy said lightly, on the intake of his breath, holding himself up. They turned the corner; the church they went to loomed like a gutted fort. The home of the woman Richard hoped to marry stood across the green. Her bedroom light burned.

"Your mother and I," he said, "have decided to separate. For the summer. Nothing legal, no divorce yet. We want to see how it feels. For some years now, we haven't been doing enough for each other, making each other as happy as we should be. Have you sensed that?"

"No," the boy said. It was an honest, unemotional answer: true or false in a quiz.

Glad for the factual basis, Richard pursued, even garrulously, the details. His apartment across town, his utter accessibility, the split vacation arrangements, the advantages to the children, the added mobility and variety of the summer. Dickie listened, absorbing. "Do the others know?"

"Yes."

"How did they take it?"

"The girls pretty calmly. John flipped out; he shouted and ate a cigarette and made a salad out of his napkin and told us how much he hated school."

His brother chuckled. "He did?"

"Yeah. The school issue was more upsetting for him than Mom and me. He seemed to feel better for having exploded."

"He did?" The repetition was the first sign that he was stunned.

"Yes. Dickie, I want to tell you something. This last hour, waiting for your train to get in, has been about the worst of my life. I hate this. *Hate* it. My father would have died before doing it to me." He felt immensely lighter, saying this. He had dumped the mountain on the boy. They were home. Moving swiftly as a shadow, Dickie was out of the car, through the bright kitchen. Richard called after him, "Want a glass of milk or anything?"

"No thanks."

"Want us to call the course tomorrow and say you're too sick to work?"

"No, that's all right." The answer was faint, delivered at the door to his room; Richard listened for the slam that went with a tantrum. The door closed normally, gently. The sound was sickening.

Joan had sunk into that first deep trough of sleep and was slow to awake. Richard had to repeat, "I told him."

"What did he say?"

"Nothing much. Could you go say goodnight to him? Please."

She left their room, without putting on a bathrobe. He sluggishly changed back into his pajamas and walked down the hall. Dickie was already in bed, Joan was sitting beside him, and the boy's bedside clock radio was murmuring music. When she stood, an inexplicable light—the moon?—outlined her body through the nightie. Richard sat on the warm place she had indented on the child's narrow mattress. He asked him, "Do you want the radio on like that?"

"It always is."

"Doesn't it keep you awake? It would me."

"No."

"Are you sleepy?"

"Yeah."

"Good. Sure you want to get up and go to work? You've had a big night."
"I want to."

Away at school this winter he had learned for the first time that you can go short
of sleep and live. As an infant he had slept with an immobile, sweating intensity that
had alarmed his babysitters. In adolescence he had often been the first of the four
children to go to bed. Even now, he would go slack in the middle of a television
show, his sprawled legs hairy and brown. "O.K. Good boy. Dickie, listen. I love you
so much, I never knew how much until now. No matter how this works out, I'll
always be with you. Really."

Richard bent to kiss an averted face but his son, sinewy, turned and with wet cheeks
embraced him and gave him a kiss, on the lips, passionate as a woman's. In his father's
ear he moaned one word, the crucial, intelligent word: *"Why?"*

Why. It was a whistle of wind in a crack, a knife thrust, a window thrown open
on emptiness. The white face was gone, the darkness was featureless. Richard had
forgotten why.

1975

Susan Sontag
b. 1933

"Writing is a mysterious activity," Susan Sontag once remarked in an interview.
"One has to be, at different stages of conception and execution, in a state of
extreme alertness and consciousness and in a state of great naiveté and ignorance."
In her own work, known for its polemical edge, Sontag clearly writes to
provoke thought, discussion, argument. Yet there is also an experimental verve to
her prose that derives from her sense of writing as "mysterious"—mysterious
because it involves at different stages both a heightening and a relaxation of will.
In her critical essays and fiction she has challenged conventional notions of
representative and symbolic art in an attempt to promote an aesthetic based more
on what art *is* in its sensuous, particularized presence than on what it *means*
generally and abstractedly.

Susan Sontag was born on January 16, 1933, in New York City. She studied
at various places: the University of California at Berkeley, the University of
Chicago (B.A. in philosophy, 1951), the Union Theological Seminary, Harvard
University (M.A. in English, 1954; M.A. in philosophy, 1955), St. Anne's
College, Oxford, and the Sorbonne in Paris. Besides lecturing extensively, she has
taught English, philosophy, religion, and writing at several schools, including the
University of Connecticut, the City College of the City University of New
York, Columbia University, and Rutgers University. In the early 1960s she began
writing essays for *Partisan Review* and since then has achieved a reputation as one
of America's leading intellectuals. Her knowledge of European thought and
culture remains firsthand and up-to-date; indeed, few contemporary figures have
worked harder to introduce modern European thought to the American reading
public.

Sontag's wide-ranging intellectual interests can be seen in her three collections of essays, *Against Interpretation and Other Essays* (1966), *Styles of Radical Will* (1969), and *Under the Sign of Saturn* (1980), in which she writes about film, popular genres, theater, Marxism, fascism, revolutionary politics, pornography, violence, and a number of important European writers. In 1969 she published *Trip to Hanoi,* a long essay based on her visit to North Vietnam during the Vietnam War. In 1978 she won the National Book Critics Circle Award for *On Photography,* a collection of six essays that first appeared in *The New York Review of Books.* The following year she published *Illness as Metaphor,* a book-length essay, based on personal experience, that treats the way language affects our understanding of disease, especially tuberculosis and cancer. She is also the author of two experimental novels, *The Benefactor* (1963) and *Death Kit* (1967), and a volume of short stories, *I etcetera* (1978). She has written and directed three films and directed several theatrical productions.

Many of Susan Sontag's critical essays deal with aesthetics, especially the complex interaction between a work of art and various systems of interpretation. In *On Photography* Sontag begins with the conviction that photographs augment our experience by extending how and what we see. For her, however, photography's brief history becomes a way of examining virtually all aspects— political, aesthetic, and moral—of the emergence of modernism. As she recounts that history, exploring its interconnections with American literature and culture, she shows particular daring in her willingness to chance large generalizations. If she also becomes tendentious, it is because she believes that all art, including her own, involves selection and that all selection involves ideological commitments, whether willed or disclosed, honored or betrayed.

Further Reading:
C. Nelson, "Soliciting Self-knowledge: The Rhetoric of Susan Sontag's Criticism," *Critical Inquiry,* Summer 1980.
E. W. Bruss, *Beautiful Theories: The Spectacle of Discourse in Contemporary Criticism,* 1982.

Text:
On Photography, 1977.

America, Seen Through Photographs, Darkly

As Walt Whitman gazed down the democratic vistas of culture, he tried to see beyond the difference between beauty and ugliness, importance and triviality. It seemed to him servile or snobbish to make any discriminations of value, except the most generous ones. Great claims were made for candor by our boldest, most delirious prophet of cultural revolution. Nobody would fret about beauty and ugliness, he implied, who was accepting a sufficiently large embrace of the real, of the inclusiveness and vitality of actual American experience. All facts, even mean ones, are incandescent in Whitman's America—that ideal space, made real by history, where "as they emit themselves facts are showered with light."

The Great American Cultural Revolution heralded in the preface to the first edition of *Leaves of Grass* (1855) didn't break out, which has disappointed many but surprised none. One great poet alone cannot change the moral weather; even when the poet has millions of Red Guards[1] at his disposal, it is still not easy. Like every seer of cultural revolution, Whitman thought he discerned art already being overtaken, and demystified, by reality. "The United States themselves are essentially the greatest poem." But when no cultural revolution occurred, and the greatest of poems seemed less great in days of Empire than it had under the Republic, only other artists took seriously Whitman's program of populist transcendence, of the democratic transvaluation of beauty and ugliness, importance and triviality. Far from having been themselves demystified by reality, the American arts—notably photography—now aspired to do the demystifying.

In photography's early decades, photographs were expected to be idealized images. This is still the aim of most amateur photographers, for whom a beautiful photograph is a photograph of something beautiful, like a woman, a sunset. In 1915 Edward Steichen[2] photographed a milk bottle on a tenement fire escape, an early example of a quite different idea of the beautiful photograph. And since the 1920s, ambitious professionals, those whose work gets into museums, have steadily drifted away from lyrical subjects, conscientiously exploring plain, tawdry, or even vapid material. In recent decades, photography has succeeded in somewhat revising, for everybody, the definitions of what is beautiful and ugly—along the lines that Whitman had proposed. If (in Whitman's words) "each precise object or condition or combination or process exhibits a beauty," it becomes superficial to single out some things as beautiful and others as not. If "all that a person does or thinks is of consequence," it becomes arbitrary to treat some moments in life as important and most as trivial.

To photograph is to confer importance. There is probably no subject that cannot be beautified; moreover, there is no way to suppress the tendency inherent in all photographs to accord value to their subjects. But the meaning of value itself can be altered—as it has been in the contemporary culture of the photographic image which is a parody of Whitman's evangel. In the mansions of pre-democratic culture, someone who gets photographed is a celebrity. In the open fields of American experience, as catalogued with passion by Whitman and as sized up with a shrug by Warhol,[3] everybody is a celebrity. No moment is more important than any other moment; no person is more interesting than any other person.

The epigraph for a book of Walker Evans's[4] photographs published by the Museum

---

[1] Youth brigades of the Cultural Revolution in China under Mao Zedong (1893–1976).
[2] American photographer (1879–1973); with Alfred Stieglitz and others, Steichen formed the group Photo-Secession to promote photography as a fine art, independent from, and not subordinate to, painting.
[3] Andy Warhol (b. 1928), American artist and

filmmaker, and a central figure in the Pop Art movement.
[4] Walker Evans (1903–1975), American photographer. Self-taught, he rejected what he believed to be Stieglitz's artiness and Steichen's commercialism. He concentrated on capturing images of American daily life on all levels and initiated the "social landscape" tradition.

of Modern Art is a passage from Whitman that sounds the theme of American photography's most prestigious quest:

> I do not doubt but the majesty & beauty of the world are latent in any iota
> of the world . . . I do not doubt there is far more in trivialities, insects, vulgar
> persons, slaves, dwarfs, weeds, rejected refuse, than I have supposed. . . .

Whitman thought he was not abolishing beauty but generalizing it. So, for generations, did the most gifted American photographers, in their polemical pursuit of the trivial and the vulgar. But among American photographers who have matured since World War II, the Whitmanesque mandate to record in its entirety the extravagant candors of actual American experience has gone sour. In photographing dwarfs, you don't get majesty & beauty. You get dwarfs.

Starting from the images reproduced and consecrated in the sumptuous magazine *Camera Work* that Alfred Stieglitz[5] published from 1903 to 1917 and exhibited in the gallery he ran in New York from 1905 to 1917 at 291 Fifth Avenue (first called the Little Gallery of the Photo-Secession, later simply "291")—magazine and gallery constituting the most ambitious forum of Whitmanesque judgments—American photography has moved from affirmation to erosion to, finally, a parody of Whitman's program. In this history the most edifying figure is Walker Evans. He was the last great photographer to work seriously and assuredly in a mood deriving from Whitman's euphoric humanism, summing up what had gone on before (for instance, Lewis Hine's[6] stunning photographs of immigrants and workers), anticipating much of the cooler, ruder, bleaker photography that has been done since—as in the prescient series of "secret" photographs of anonymous New York subway riders that Evans took with a concealed camera between 1939 and 1941. But Evans broke with the heroic mode in which the Whitmanesque vision had been propagandized by Stieglitz and his disciples, who had condescended to Hine. Evans found Stieglitz's work arty.

Like Whitman, Stieglitz saw no contradiction between making art an instrument of identification with the community and aggrandizing the artist as a heroic, romantic, self-expressing ego. In his florid, brilliant book of essays, *Port of New York* (1924), Paul Rosenfeld[7] hailed Stieglitz as one "of the great affirmers of life. There is no matter in all the world so homely, trite, and humble that through it this man of the black box and chemical bath cannot express himself entire." Photographing, and thereby redeeming the homely, trite, and humble is also an ingenious means of individual expression. "The photographer," Rosenfeld writes of Stieglitz, "has cast the artist's net wider into the material world than any man before him or alongside him." Photography is a kind of overstatement, a heroic copulation with the material world. Like Hine, Evans sought a more impersonal kind of affirmation, a noble reticence, a lucid understatement. Neither in the impersonal architectural still lifes of American façades and inventories of rooms that he loved to make, nor in the exacting portraits of Southern sharecroppers he took in the late 1930s (published in the book done with James Agee, *Let Us Now Praise Famous Men*), was Evans trying to express himself.

[5] American photographer (1864–1946); Stieglitz experimented with three-color work.
[6] Lewis Wickes Hine (1874–1940), American

documentary photographer; his work is a critique of exploitative social systems.
[7] American music and art critic (1890–1946).

Even without the heroic inflection, Evans's project still descends from Whitman's: the leveling of discriminations between the beautiful and the ugly, the important and the trivial. Each thing or person photographed becomes—a photograph; and becomes, therefore, morally equivalent to any other of his photographs. Evans's camera brought out the same formal beauty in the exteriors of Victorian houses in Boston in the early 1930s as in the store buildings on main streets in Alabama towns in 1936. But this was a leveling up, not down. Evans wanted his photographs to be "literate, authoritative, transcendent." The moral universe of the 1930s being no longer ours, these adjectives are barely credible today. Nobody demands that photography be literate. Nobody can imagine how it could be authoritative. Nobody understands how anything, least of all a photograph, could be transcendent.

Whitman preached empathy, concord in discord, oneness in diversity. Psychic intercourse with everything, everybody—plus sensual union (when he could get it) —is the giddy trip that is proposed explicitly, over and over and over, in the prefaces and the poems. This longing to proposition the whole world also dictated his poetry's form and tone. Whitman's poems are a psychic technology for chanting the reader into a new state of being (a microcosm of the "new order" envisaged for the polity); they are functional, like mantras—ways of transmitting charges of energy. The repetition, the bombastic cadence, the run-on lines, and the pushy diction are a rush of secular afflatus, meant to get readers psychically airborne, to boost them up to that height where they can identify with the past and with the community of American desire. But this message of identification with other Americans is foreign to our temperament now.

The last sigh of the Whitmanesque erotic embrace of the nation, but universalized and stripped of all demands, was heard in the "Family of Man" exhibit organized in 1955 by Edward Steichen, Stieglitz's contemporary and co-founder of Photo-Secession. Five hundred and three photographs by two hundred and seventy-three photographers from sixty-eight countries were supposed to converge—to prove that humanity is "one" and that human beings, for all their flaws and villainies, are attractive creatures. The people in the photographs were of all races, ages, classes, physical types. Many of them had exceptionally beautiful bodies; some had beautiful faces. As Whitman urged the readers of his poems to identify with him and with America, Steichen set up the show to make it possible for each viewer to identify with a great many of the people depicted and, potentially, with the subject of every photograph: citizens of World Photography all.

It was not until seventeen years later that photography again attracted such crowds at the Museum of Modern Art: for the retrospective given Diane Arbus's[8] work in 1972. In the Arbus show, a hundred and twelve photographs all taken by one person and all similar—that is, everyone in them looks (in some sense) the same—imposed a feeling exactly contrary to the reassuring warmth of Steichen's material. Instead of people whose appearance pleases, representative folk doing their human thing, the Arbus show lined up assorted monsters and borderline cases—most of them ugly;

---

[8] Diane Arbus (1923–1971), American photographer and sister of the poet Howard Nemerov. She is best known for her photographs of grotesque and deformed individuals.

wearing grotesque or unflattering clothing; in dismal or barren surroundings—who have paused to pose and, often, to gaze frankly, confidentially at the viewer. Arbus's work does not invite viewers to identify with the pariahs and miserable-looking people she photographed. Humanity is not "one."

The Arbus photographs convey the anti-humanist message which people of good will in the 1970s are eager to be troubled by, just as they wished, in the 1950s, to be consoled and distracted by a sentimental humanism. There is not as much difference between these messages as one might suppose. The Steichen show was an up and the Arbus show was a down, but either experience serves equally well to rule out a historical understanding of reality.

Steichen's choice of photographs assumes a human condition or a human nature shared by everybody. By purporting to show that individuals are born, work, laugh, and die everywhere in the same way, "The Family of Man" denies the determining weight of history—of genuine and historically embedded differences, injustices, and conflicts. Arbus's photographs undercut politics just as decisively, by suggesting a world in which everybody is an alien, hopelessly isolated, immobilized in mechanical, crippled identities and relationships. The pious uplift of Steichen's photograph anthology and the cool dejection of the Arbus retrospective both render history and politics irrelevant. One does so by universalizing the human condition, into joy; the other by atomizing it, into horror.

The most striking aspect of Arbus's work is that she seems to have enrolled in one of art photography's most vigorous enterprises—concentrating on victims, on the unfortunate—but without the compassionate purpose that such a project is expected to serve. Her work shows people who are pathetic, pitiable, as well as repulsive, but it does not arouse any compassionate feelings. For what would be more correctly described as their dissociated point of view, the photographs have been praised for their candor and for an unsentimental empathy with their subjects. What is actually their aggressiveness toward the public has been treated as a moral accomplishment: that the photographs don't allow the viewer to be distant from the subject. More plausibly, Arbus's photographs—with their acceptance of the appalling—suggests a naïveté which is both coy and sinister, for it is based on distance, on privilege, on a feeling that what the viewer is asked to look at is really *other*. Buñuel,[9] when asked once why he made movies, said that it was "to show that this is not the best of all possible worlds." Arbus took photographs to show something simpler—that there is another world.

The other world is to be found, as usual, inside this one. Avowedly interested only in photographing people who "looked strange," Arbus found plenty of material close to home. New York, with its drag balls and welfare hotels, was rich with freaks. There was also a carnival in Maryland, where Arbus found a human pincushion, a hermaphrodite with a dog, a tattooed man, and an albino sword-swallower; nudist camps in New Jersey and in Pennsylvania; Disneyland and a Hollywood set, for their dead or fake landscapes without people; and the unidentified mental hospital where she took some of her last, and most disturbing, photographs. And there was always daily life,

[9] Luis Buñuel (1900–1983), Spanish film director known for such films as *Un Chien Andalou* (1928), which he codirected with Salvador Dali, and *Le Charme Discret de la Bourgeoisie* (*The Discreet Charm of the Bourgeoisie*, 1972).

with its endless supply of oddities—if one has the eye to see them. The camera has the power to catch so-called normal people in such a way as to make them look abnormal. The photographer chooses oddity, chases it, frames it, develops it, titles it.

"You see someone on the street," Arbus wrote, "and essentially what you notice about them is the flaw." The insistent sameness of Arbus's work, however far she ranges from her prototypical subjects, shows that her sensibility, armed with a camera, could insinuate anguish, kinkiness, mental illness with any subject. Two photographs are of crying babies; the babies look disturbed, crazy. Resembling or having something in common with someone else is a recurrent source of the ominous, according to the characteristic norms of Arbus's dissociated way of seeing. It may be two girls (not sisters) wearing identical raincoats whom Arbus photographed together in Central Park; or the twins and triplets who appear in several pictures. Many photographs point with oppressive wonder to the fact that two people form a couple; and every couple is an odd couple; straight or gay, black or white, in an old-age home or in a junior high. People looked eccentric because they didn't wear clothes, like nudists; or because they did, like the waitress in the nudist camp who's wearing an apron. Anybody Arbus photographed was a freak—a boy waiting to march in a pro-war parade, wearing his straw boater and his "Bomb Hanoi"[10] button; the King and Queen of a Senior Citizens Dance; a thirtyish suburban couple sprawled in their lawn chairs; a widow sitting alone in her cluttered bedroom. In "A Jewish giant at home with his parents in the Bronx, NY, 1970," the parents look like midgets, as wrong-sized as the enormous son hunched over them under their low living-room ceiling.

The authority of Arbus's photographs derives from the contrast between their lacerating subject matter and their calm, matter-of-fact attentiveness. This quality of attention—the attention paid by the photographer, the attention paid by the subject to the act of being photographed—creates the moral theater of Arbus's straight-on, contemplative portraits. Far from spying on freaks and pariahs, catching them unawares, the photographer has gotten to know them, reassured them—so that they posed for her as calmly and stiffly as any Victorian notable sat for a studio portrait by Julia Margaret Cameron. A large part of the mystery of Arbus's photographs lies in what they suggest about how her subjects felt after consenting to be photographed. Do they see themselves, the viewer wonders, like *that?* Do they know how grotesque they are? It seems as if they don't.

The subject of Arbus's photographs is, to borrow the stately Hegelian[11] label, "the unhappy consciousness." But most characters in Arbus's Grand Guignol[12] appear not to know that they are ugly. Arbus photographs people in various degrees of unconscious or unaware relation to their pain, their ugliness. This necessarily limits what kinds of horrors she might have been drawn to photograph: it excludes sufferers who presumably know they are suffering, like victims of accidents, wars, famines, and political persecutions. Arbus would never have taken pictures of accidents, events that break into a life; she specialized in slow-motion private smashups, most of which had been going on since the subject's birth.

---

[10] Frequently used slogan of the prowar factions during the controversies surrounding the Vietnam war.

[11] After George Wilhelm Friedrich Hegel

(1770–1831), German philosopher who greatly influenced the study of history and metaphysics.

[12] Originally, a small theater in Paris specializing in brief horror plays.

Though most viewers are ready to imagine that these people, the citizens of the sexual underworld as well as the genetic freaks, are unhappy, few of the pictures actually show emotional distress. The photographs of deviates and real freaks do not accent their pain but, rather, their detachment and autonomy. The female impersonators in their dressing rooms, the Mexican dwarf in his Manhattan hotel room, the Russian midgets in a living room on 100th Street, and their kin are mostly shown as cheerful, self-accepting, matter-of-fact. Pain is more legible in the portraits of the normals: the quarreling elderly couple on a park bench, the New Orleans lady bartender at home with a souvenir dog, the boy in Central Park clenching his toy hand grenade.

Brassaï[13] denounced photographers who try to trap their subjects off-guard, in the erroneous belief that something special will be revealed about them.[14] In the world colonized by Arbus, subjects are always revealing themselves. There is no decisive moment. Arbus's view that self-revelation is a continuous, evenly distributed process is another way of maintaining the Whitmanesque imperative: treat all moments as of equal consequence. Like Brassaï, Arbus wanted her subjects to be as fully conscious as possible, aware of the act in which they were participating. Instead of trying to coax her subjects into a natural or typical position, they are encouraged to be awkward —that is, to pose. (Thereby, the revelation of self gets identified with what is strange, odd, askew.) Standing or sitting stiffly makes them seem like images of themselves.

Most Arbus pictures have the subjects looking straight into the camera. This often makes them look even odder, almost deranged. Compare the 1912 photograph by Lartigue[15] of a woman in a plumed hat and veil ("Racecourse at Nice") with Arbus's "Woman with a Veil on Fifth Avenue, NYC, 1968." Apart from the characteristic ugliness of Arbus's subject (Lartigue's subject is, just as characteristically, beautiful), what makes the woman in Arbus's photograph strange is the bold unselfconsciousness of her pose. If the Lartigue woman looked back, she might appear almost as strange.

In the normal rhetoric of the photographic portrait, facing the camera signifies solemnity, frankness, the disclosure of the subject's essence. That is why frontality seems right for ceremonial pictures (like weddings, graduations) but less apt for photographs used on billboards to advertise political candidates. (For politicians the three-quarter gaze is more common: a gaze that soars rather than confronts, suggesting instead of the relation to the viewer, to the present, the more ennobling abstract relation to the future.) What makes Arbus's use of the frontal pose so arresting is that her subjects are often people one would not expect to surrender themselves so amiably

---

[13] Name taken by Gyula Halász (b. 1899), naturalized French painter, sculptor, journalist, and photographer.

[14] Sontag's note: "Not an error, really. There is something on people's faces when they don't know they are being observed that never appears when they do. If we did not know how Walker Evans took his subway photographs (riding the New York subways for hundreds of hours, standing, with the lens of his

camera peering between two buttons of his topcoat), it would be obvious from the pictures themselves that the seated passengers, although photographed close and frontally, didn't know they were being photographed; their expressions are private ones, not those they would offer to the camera."

[15] Jacques-Henri (Charles Auguste) Lartigue (b. 1894), French photographer and painter, particularly known as a photographer.

and ingenuously to the camera. Thus, in Arbus's photographs, frontality also implies in the most vivid way the subject's cooperation. To get these people to pose, the photographer has had to gain their confidence, has had to become "friends" with them.

Perhaps the scariest scene in Tod Browning's[16] film *Freaks* (1932) is the wedding banquet, when pinheads, bearded women, Siamese twins, and living torsos dance and sing their acceptance of the wicked normal-sized Cleopatra, who has just married the gullible midget hero. "One of us! One of us! One of us!" they chant as a loving cup is passed around the table from mouth to mouth to be finally presented to the nauseated bride by an exuberant dwarf. Arbus had a perhaps oversimple view of the charm and hypocrisy and discomfort of fraternizing with freaks. Following the elation of discovery, there was the thrill of having won their confidence, of not being afraid of them, of having mastered one's aversion. Photographing freaks "had a terrific excitement for me," Arbus explained. "I just used to adore them."

Diane Arbus's photographs were already famous to people who follow photography when she killed herself in 1971; but, as with Sylvia Plath, the attention her work has attracted since her death is of another order—a kind of apotheosis. The fact of her suicide seems to guarantee that her work is sincere, not voyeuristic, that it is compassionate, not cold. Her suicide also seems to make the photographs more devastating, as if it proved the photographs to have been dangerous to her.

She herself suggested the possibility. "Everything is so superb and breathtaking. I am creeping forward on my belly like they do in war movies." While photography is normally an omnipotent viewing from a distance, there is one situation in which people do get killed for taking pictures: when they photograph people killing each other. Only war photography combines voyeurism and danger. Combat photographers can't avoid participating in the lethal activity they record; they even wear military uniforms, though without rank badges. To discover (through photographing) that life is "really a melodrama," to understand the camera as a weapon of aggression, implies there will be casualties. "I'm sure there are limits," she wrote. "God knows, when the troops start advancing on you, you do approach that stricken feeling where you perfectly well can get killed." Arbus's words in retrospect describe a kind of combat death: having trespassed certain limits, she fell in a psychic ambush, a casualty of her own candor and curiosity.

In the old romance of the artist, any person who has the temerity to spend a season in hell risks not getting out alive or coming back psychically damaged. The heroic avant-gardism of French literature in the late nineteenth and early twentieth centuries furnishes a memorable pantheon of artists who fail to survive their trips to hell. Still, there is a large difference between the activity of a photographer, which is always willed, and the activity of a writer, which may not be. One has the right to, may feel compelled to, give voice to one's own pain—which is, in any case, one's own property. One volunteers to seek out the pain of others.

Thus, what is finally most troubling in Arbus's photographs is not their subject at

---

[16] Tod Browning (1882–1962), American film director known for macabre films, such as *Dracula* (1931), and *Freaks* (1932), in which most of the actors are physically deformed.

all but the cumulative impression of the photographer's consciousness: the sense that what is presented is precisely a private vision, something voluntary. Arbus was not a poet delving into her entrails to relate her own pain but a photographer venturing out into the world to *collect* images that are painful. And for pain sought rather than just felt, there may be a less than obvious explanation. According to Reich,[17] the masochist's taste for pain does not spring from a love of pain but from the hope of procuring, by means of pain, a strong sensation; those handicapped by emotional or sensory analgesia only prefer pain to not feeling anything at all. But there is another explanation of why people seek pain, diametrically opposed to Reich's, that also seems pertinent: that they seek it not to feel more but to feel less.

Insofar as looking at Arbus's photographs is, undeniably, an ordeal, they are typical of the kind of art popular among sophisticated urban people right now: art that is a self-willed test of hardness. Her photographs offer an occasion to demonstrate that life's horror can be faced without squeamishness. The photographer once had to say to herself, Okay, I can accept that; the viewer is invited to make the same declaration.

Arbus's work is a good instance of a leading tendency of high art in capitalist countries: to suppress, or at least reduce, moral and sensory queasiness. Much of modern art is devoted to lowering the threshold of what is terrible. By getting us used to what, formerly, we could not bear to see or hear, because it was too shocking, painful, or embarrassing, art changes morals—that body of psychic custom and public sanctions that draws a vague boundary between what is emotionally and spontaneously intolerable and what is not. The gradual suppression of queasiness does bring us closer to a rather formal truth—that of the arbitrariness of the taboos constructed by art and morals. But our ability to stomach this rising grotesqueness in images (moving and still) and in print has a stiff price. In the long run, it works out not as a liberation of but as a subtraction from the self: a pseudo-familiarity with the horrible reinforces alienation, making one less able to react in real life. What happens to people's feelings on first exposure to today's neighborhood pornographic film or to tonight's televised atrocity is not so different from what happens when they first look at Arbus's photographs.

The photographs make a compassionate response feel irrelevant. The point is not to be upset, to be able to confront the horrible with equanimity. But this look that is not (mainly) compassionate is a special, modern ethical construction: not hard-hearted, certainly not cynical, but simply (or falsely) naïve. To the painful nightmarish reality out there, Arbus applied such adjectives as "terrific," "interesting," "incredible," "fantastic," "sensational"—the childlike wonder of the pop mentality. The camera—according to her deliberately naïve image of the photographer's quest—is a device that captures it all, that seduces subjects into disclosing their secrets, that broadens experience. To photograph people, according to Arbus, is necessarily "cruel," "mean." The important thing is not to blink.

---

[17] Wilhelm Reich (1897–1957), Austrian psychoanalyist who worked primarily on the study of character types and sexuality.

"Photography was a license to go wherever I wanted and to do what I wanted to do," Arbus wrote. The camera is a kind of passport that annihilates moral boundaries and social inhibitions, freeing the photographer from any responsibility toward the people photographed. The whole point of photographing people is that you are not intervening in their lives, only visiting them. The photographer is supertourist, an extension of the anthropologist, visiting natives and bringing back news of their exotic doings and strange gear. The photographer is always trying to colonize new experiences or find new ways to look at familiar subjects—to fight against boredom. For boredom is just the reverse side of fascination: both depend on being outside rather than inside a situation, and one leads to the other. "The Chinese have a theory that you pass through boredom into fascination," Arbus noted. Photographing an appalling underworld (and a desolate, plastic overworld), she had no intention of entering into the horror experienced by the denizens of those worlds. They are to remain exotic, hence "terrific." Her view is always from the outside.

"I'm very little drawn to photographing people that are known or even subjects that are known," Arbus wrote. "They fascinate me when I've barely heard of them." However drawn she was to the maimed and the ugly, it would never have occurred to Arbus to photograph Thalidomide babies or napalm victims—public horrors, deformities with sentimental or ethical associations. Arbus was not interested in ethical journalism. She chose subjects that she could believe were found, just lying about, without any values attached to them. They are necessarily ahistorical subjects, private rather than public pathology, secret lives rather than open ones.

For Arbus, the camera photographs the unknown. But unknown to whom? Unknown to someone who is protected, who has been schooled in moralistic and in prudent responses. Like Nathanael West, another artist fascinated by the deformed and mutilated, Arbus came from a verbally skilled, compulsively health-minded, indignation-prone, well-to-do Jewish family, for whom minority sexual tastes lived way below the threshold of awareness and risk-taking was despised as another goyish craziness. "One of the things I felt I suffered from as a kid," Arbus wrote, "was that I never felt adversity. I was confined in a sense of unreality. . . . And the sense of being immune was, ludicrous as it seems, a painful one." Feeling much the same discontent, West in 1927 took a job as a night clerk in a seedy Manhattan hotel. Arbus's way of procuring experience, and thereby acquiring a sense of reality, was the camera. By experience was meant, if not material adversity, at least psychological adversity —the shock of immersion in experiences that cannot be beautified, the encounter with what is taboo, perverse, evil.

Arbus's interest in freaks expresses a desire to violate her own innocence, to undermine her sense of being privileged, to vent her frustration at being safe. Apart from West, the 1930s yield few examples of this kind of distress. More typically, it is the sensibility of someone educated and middle-class who came of age between 1945 and 1955—a sensibility that was to flourish precisely in the 1960s.

The decade of Arbus's serious work coincides with, and is very much of, the sixties, the decade in which freaks went public, and became a safe, approved subject of art. What in the 1930s was treated with anguish—as in *Miss Lonelyhearts* and *The Day of the Locust*[18]—would in the 1960s be treated in a perfectly deadpan way, or with positive relish (in the films of Fellini, Arrabal, Jodorowsky,[19] in underground comics, in rock spectacles). At the beginning of the sixties, the thriving Freak Show at Coney Island was outlawed; the pressure is on to raze the Times Square turf of drag queens and hustlers and cover it with skyscrapers. As the inhabitants of deviant underworlds are evicted from their restricted territories—banned as unseemly, a public nuisance, obscene, or just unprofitable—they increasingly come to infiltrate consciousness as the subject matter of art, acquiring a certain diffuse legitimacy and metaphoric proximity which creates all the more distance.

Who could have better appreciated the truth of freaks than someone like Arbus, who was by profession a fashion photographer—a fabricator of the cosmetic lie that masks the intractable inequalities of birth and class and physical appearance. But unlike Warhol, who spent many years as a commercial artist, Arbus did not make her serious work out of promoting and kidding the aesthetic of glamour to which she had been apprenticed, but turned her back on it entirely. Arbus's work is reactive—reactive against gentility, against what is approved. It was her way of saying fuck *Vogue,* fuck fashion, fuck what's pretty. This challenge takes two not wholly compatible forms. One is a revolt against the Jews' hyper-developed moral sensibility. The other revolt, itself hotly moralistic, turns against the success world. The moralist's subversion advances life as a failure, as the antidote to life as a success. The aesthete's subversion, which the sixties was to make peculiarly its own, advances life as a horror show as the antidote to life as a bore.

Most of Arbus's work lies within the Warhol aesthetic, that is, defines itself in relation to the twin poles of boringness and freakishness; but it doesn't have the Warhol style. Arbus had neither Warhol's narcissism and genius for publicity nor the self-protective blandness with which he insulates himself from the freaky nor his sentimentality. It is unlikely that Warhol, who comes from a working-class family, ever felt any of the ambivalence toward success which afflicted the children of the Jewish upper middle classes in the 1960s. To someone raised as a Catholic, like Warhol (and virtually everyone in his gang), a fascination with evil comes much more genuinely than it does to someone from a Jewish background. Compared with Warhol, Arbus seems strikingly vulnerable, innocent—and certainly more pessimistic. Her Dantesque vision of the city (and the suburbs) has no reserves of irony. Although much of Arbus's material is the same as that depicted in, say, Warhol's *Chelsea Girls*[20] (1966), her photographs never play with horror, milking it for laughs; they offer no opening to mockery, and no possibility of finding freaks endearing, as do the films of Warhol and Paul Morrissey.[21] For Arbus, both freaks and Middle America were equally exotic: a boy marching in a pro-war parade and a Levittown[22] housewife were as alien as a dwarf or a transvestite; lower-middle-class suburbia was as remote as Times

---

[18] Novels by Nathanael West (1903–1940), American novelist.

[19] Fellini: Federico Fellini (b. 1921), Italian film director; Arrabal: Fernando Arrabal (b. 1932), Spanish playwright, novelist, film director, and poet; Jodorowsky: Alexandro Jodorowski (b. 1929?), Chilean theatrical director and author.

[20] Raunchy Warhol film set in the Chelsea section of Manhattan.

[21] American film writer and director (b. 1939) who worked with Andy Warhol.

[22] Middle-class housing tract in New York State. Its name is frequently used to suggest the monotony and rigid conformity of the lower middle class.

Square, lunatic asylums, and gay bars. Arbus's work expressed her turn against what was public (as she experienced it), conventional, safe, reassuring—and boring—in favor of what was private, hidden, ugly, dangerous, and fascinating. These contrasts, now, seem almost quaint. What is safe no longer monopolizes public imagery. The freakish is no longer a private zone, difficult of access. People who are bizarre, in sexual disgrace, emotionally vacant are seen daily on the newsstands, on TV, in the subways. Hobbesian[23] man roams the streets, quite visible, with glitter in his hair.

Sophisticated in the familiar modernist way—choosing awkwardness, naïveté, sincerity over the slickness and artificiality of high art and high commerce—Arbus said that the photographer she felt closest to was Weegee,[24] whose brutal pictures of crime and accident victims were a staple of the tabloids in the 1940s. Weegee's photographs are indeed upsetting, his sensibility is urban, but the similarity between his work and Arbus's ends there. However eager she was to disavow standard elements of photographic sophistication such as composition, Arbus was not unsophisticated. And there is nothing journalistic about her motives for taking pictures. What may seem journalistic, even sensational, in Arbus's photographs places them, rather, in the main tradition of Surrealist art[25]—their taste for the grotesque, their professed innocence with respect to their subjects, their claim that all subjects are merely *objets trouvés.*[26]

"I would never choose a subject for what it meant to me when I think of it," Arbus wrote, a dogged exponent of the Surrealist bluff. Presumably, viewers are not supposed to judge the people she photographs. Of course, we do. And the very range of Arbus's subjects itself constitutes a judgment. Brassaï, who photographed people like those who interested Arbus—see his "La Me Bijou"[27] of 1932—also did tender cityscapes, portraits of famous artists. Lewis Hine's "Mental Institution, New Jersey, 1924" could be a late Arbus photograph (except that the pair of Mongoloid children posing on the lawn are photographed in profile rather than frontally); the Chicago street portraits Walker Evans took in 1946 are Arbus material, as are a number of photographs by Robert Frank. The difference is in the range of other subjects, other emotions that Hine, Brassaï, Evans, and Frank photographed. Arbus is an *auteur*[28] in the most limiting sense, as special a case in the history of photography as is Giorgio Morandi, who spent a half century doing still lifes of bottles, in the history of modern European painting. She does not, like most ambitious photographers, play the field of subject matter—even a little. On the contrary, all her subjects are equivalent. And making equivalences between freaks, mad people, suburban couples, and nudists is a very powerful judgment, one in complicity with a recognizable political mood shared by many educated, left-liberal Americans. The

[23] After Thomas Hobbes (1588–1679), English philosopher who formulated the social contract theory in his most famous work, *Leviathan* (1651).

[24] Naturalized-American photographer (born Usher H. Fellig, 1899–1968), perhaps the best known of all photographers of street scenes. He adopted his professional name from the Ouija board.

[25] Surrealism was a psychological, aesthetic, and philosophical concept that emerged as a movement between World War I and World War II and that particularly affected literature and the visual arts. Rooted in Freudian theory, Surrealism posits the unconscious as the source of beauty and truth; the "super" or superior reality from which it takes its name is that of dreams.

[26] French: "found objects."

[27] French: "The Charming Urchin."

[28] French: "author."

subjects of Arbus's photographs are all members of the same family, inhabitants of a single village. Only, as it happens, the idiot village is America. Instead of showing identity between things which are different (Whitman's democratic vista), everybody is shown to look the same.

Succeeding the more buoyant hopes for America has come a bitter, sad embrace of experience. There is a particular melancholy in the American photographic project. But the melancholy was already latent in the heyday of Whitmanesque affirmation, as represented by Stieglitz and his Photo-Secession circle. Stieglitz, pledged to redeem the world with his camera, was still shocked by modern material civilization. He photographed New York in the 1910s in an almost quixotic spirit—camera/lance against skyscraper/windmill. Paul Rosenfeld described Stieglitz's efforts as a "perpetual affirmation." The Whitmanesque appetites have turned pious: the photographer now patronizes reality. One needs a camera to show patterns in that "dull and marvelous opacity called the United States."

Obviously, a mission as rotten with doubt about America—even at its most optimistic—was bound to get deflated fairly soon, as post–World War I America committed itself more boldly to big business and consumerism. Photographers with less ego and magnetism than Stieglitz gradually gave up the struggle. They might continue to practice the atomistic visual stenography inspired by Whitman. But, without Whitman's delirious powers of synthesis, what they documented was discontinuity, detritus, loneliness, greed, sterility. Stieglitz, using photography to challenge the materialist civilization, was, in Rosenfeld's words, "the man who believed that a spiritual America existed somewhere, that America was not the grave of the Occident." The implicit intent of Frank and Arbus, and of many of their contemporaries and juniors, is to show that America *is* the grave of the Occident.

Since photography cut loose from the Whitmanesque affirmation—since it has ceased to understand how photographs could aim at being literate, authoritative, transcendent—the best of American photography (and much else in American culture) has given itself over to the consolations of Surrealism, and America has been discovered as the quintessential Surrealist country. It is obviously too easy to say that America is just a freak show, a wasteland—the cut-rate pessimism typical of the reduction of the real to the surreal. But the American partiality to myths of redemption and damnation remains one of the most energizing, most seductive aspects of our national culture. What we have left of Whitman's discredited dream of cultural revolution are paper ghosts and a sharp-eyed witty program of despair.

1977

Philip Roth
b. 1933

Philip Roth was born on March 19, 1933, in Newark, New Jersey, where he grew up, attended high school, and spent his first year at college. In 1951 he transferred to Bucknell University, where he studied English and philosophy and helped found the literary magazine in which he published his first stories. After graduation in 1954 Roth took an M.A. in English at the University of Chicago and in 1955 enlisted in the army. Discharged because of a back injury, Roth returned to Chicago, where he resumed graduate studies, worked as an instructor, and wrote stories, one of which was chosen for inclusion in *The Best American Short Stories of 1956*. With the publication of the award-winning story collection *Goodbye, Columbus* in 1959, Roth left graduate school to concentrate on writing. Roth's first book, still considered one of his best, includes several fine short stories—"Defender of the Faith" and "Conversion of the Jews"—as well as its long title story, which concerns a young man whose love affair with a spoiled, affluent college student discloses the economic and generational conflicts within the urban and suburban Jewish communities to which they respectively belong. Within a year Roth received several grants and fellowships, including a Guggenheim, and was appointed to the faculty of the writer's workshop at the University of Iowa. In his first novel, *Letting Go* (1962), he drew on his academic experiences at both Iowa and Chicago. In 1962 Roth was appointed writer in residence at Princeton University, and in 1965 he began teaching at the University of Pennsylvania.

Through most of his career, Roth has been drawn, as had F. Scott Fitzgerald, toward two rather different realms of experience—what he calls "the aggressive, the crude, and the obscene, at one extreme, and something a good deal more subtle and, in every sense, refined, at the other." To blend these two, Roth strives to master a prose that possesses both the rhythm, diction, and syntax of colloquial American English and the rich evocations of traditional literary prose. Roth's mastery of colloquial speech—the banal, clichéd vernacular that Sinclair Lewis had earlier tried to catch—is amply apparent in his second novel, *When She Was Good* (1967), a story about American puritanical instincts that is steeped in the diction and details of midwestern provincial life. Having flattened out his style for *When She Was Good,* however, Roth let it explode into comic rhetorical excess, obscenity, and rage in his next book, *Portnoy's Complaint* (1969), the free-associative narration of a young Jewish intellectual who confides everything about his life—from his masturbatory habits to his father's chronic constipation—to a Jewish analyst. Partly because of its force and partly because of its sensational revelations, *Portnoy's Complaint* quickly threatened to become almost synonymous with the identity of Philip Roth. In response to his new predicament, rather like an actor who feels his identity frozen into a single role, Roth commenced one of the most intense investigations any American writer has yet made into the dynamics of a literary career.

While writing *Portnoy's Complaint,* Roth had been reading and teaching the work of Franz Kafka. "I began reading Kafka seriously in my early thirties," he tells us in a piece called "In Search of Kafka," "at a time when I was enormously dismayed to find myself drifting away, rather than towards, what I had taken to be my goals as a writer and a man—at a time, in other words, when I was unusually sensitized to Kafka's tales of spiritual disorientation and obstructed energies"—and found there "a number of clues as to how to give imaginative expression to preoccupations of my own." Through Kafka, Roth also began to discover new ways of combining social and political satire with absurd, fantastic situations. In 1971, before the Watergate scandal, Roth published *Our Gang,* an attack on the corruptions of the Nixon administration, and a year later he wrote the self-consciously Kafkaesque novella *The Breast,* in which a college professor one day awakens to find that he has been transformed into a woman's breast.

Roth followed up these two literary skits with *The Great American Novel* (1973), a comic baseball story that is actually a burlesque of American literature and a few of its celebrated careers. In his next novel, *My Life as a Man* (1974), he intensified his experimentation with literary parody by probing the relation between fiction and autobiography, a relation that figures as a central issue in his collection of essays, *Reading Myself and Others* (1975). Literature and its connection to life—especially love life—lies at the heart of his next novel, *The Professor of Desire* (1977), in which a college professor tries to become a "rake among scholars, a scholar among rakes." Since then Roth has written a trilogy that penetrates so deeply into the relation between an author's life and his work that it might have been subtitled "My Life as a Book." In *Zuckerman Bound* (1985)—which collects in one volume the novels *The Ghost Writer* (1979), *Zuckerman Unbound* (1981), and *The Anatomy Lesson* (1983) and the story "The Prague Orgy"—he traces the life of a writer from his apprenticeship and search for a mentor through his enormous success and its bizarre consequences to his almost hallucinatory attempt to enter medical school and abandon his literary career.

"My fiction," Roth once remarked, "is about people in trouble." More specifically, Roth focuses on the private lives that individuals must live as social creatures in a world that seems as daunting in its variety and exuberance as it is threatening in its pressures. The conflicts that trouble Roth's characters may be economic, generational, or psychological, and they are often sexual and religious. In portraying them, Roth brings a strong celebratory impulse matched by an equally powerful deflating impulse. Sometimes his playful inventiveness seems to exist almost exclusively for itself. Both " 'Sheer Playfulness' and 'Deadly Seriousness,' " he told Joyce Carol Oates in an interview, were among his "closest friends." In his finest fiction, these two friends meet and measure one another in ways that are remarkable.

Further Reading:
J. N. McDaniel, *The Fiction of Philip Roth,* 1974.

Text:
Reading Myself and Others, 1975.

"I Always Wanted You to Admire My Fasting"; or, Looking at Kafka

To the Students of English 275, University of
Pennsylvania, Fall 1972

*"I always wanted you to admire my fasting," said the hunger
artist. "We do admire it," said the overseer, affably. "But you
shouldn't admire it," said the hunger artist. "Well then we don't
admire it," said the overseer, "but why shouldn't we admire it?"
"Because I have to fast, I can't help it," said the hunger artist.
"What a fellow you are," said the overseer, "and why can't you
help it?" "Because," said the hunger artist, lifting his head a little
and speaking, with his lips pursed, as if for a kiss, right into the
overseer's ear, so that no syllable might be lost, "because I couldn't
find the food I liked. If I had found it, believe me, I should have
made no fuss and stuffed myself like you or anyone else." These
were his last words, but in his dimming eyes remained the firm
though no longer proud persuasion that he was still continuing to
fast.*

Franz Kafka,[1] "A Hunger Artist"

1

I am looking, as I write of Kafka, at the photograph taken of him at the age of forty
(my age)—it is 1924, as sweet and hopeful a year as he may ever have known as a
man, and the year of his death. His face is sharp and skeletal, a burrowing face:
pronounced cheekbones made even more conspicuous by the absence of sideburns; the
ears shaped and angled on his head like angel wings; an intense, creaturely gaze of
startled composure—enormous fears, enormous control; a black towel of Levantine
hair pulled close around the skull the only sensuous feature; there is a familiar Jewish
flare in the bridge of the nose, the nose itself is long and weighted slightly at the tip
—the nose of half the Jewish boys who were my friends in high school. Skulls chiseled
like this one were shoveled by the thousands from the ovens; had he lived, his would
have been among them, along with the skulls of his three younger sisters.

Of course it is no more horrifying to think of Franz Kafka in Auschwitz than to
think of anyone in Auschwitz—it is just horrifying in its own way. But he died too
soon for the holocaust. Had he lived, perhaps he would have escaped with his good
friend Max Brod, who found refuge in Palestine, a citizen of Israel until his death
there in 1968. But *Kafka* escaping? It seems unlikely for one so fascinated by entrap-

---

[1] German-language writer (1883–1924) born in
Prague, Czechoslovakia.

ment and careers that culminate in anguished death. Still, there is Karl Rossmann, his American greenhorn. Having imagined Karl's escape to America and his mixed luck here, could not Kafka have found a way to execute an escape for himself? The New School for Social Research in New York becoming *his* Great Nature Theatre of Oklahoma? Or perhaps, through the influence of Thomas Mann,[2] a position in the German department at Princeton . . . But then, had Kafka lived, it is not at all certain that the books of his which Mann celebrated from *his* refuge in New Jersey would ever have been published; eventually Kafka might either have destroyed those manuscripts that he had once bid Max Brod to dispose of at his death or, at the least, continued to keep them his secret. The Jewish refugee arriving in America in 1938 would not then have been Mann's "religious humorist" but a frail and bookish fifty-five-year-old bachelor, formerly a lawyer for a government insurance firm in Prague, retired on a pension in Berlin at the time of Hitler's rise to power—an author, yes, but of a few eccentric stories, mostly about animals, stories no one in America had ever heard of and only a handful in Europe had read; a homeless K., but without K.'s willfulness and purpose, a homeless Karl, but without Karl's youthful spirit and resilience; just a Jew lucky enough to have escaped with his life, in his possession a suitcase containing some clothes, some family photos, some Prague mementos, and the manuscripts, still unpublished and in pieces, of *Amerika, The Trial, The Castle,* and (stranger things happen) three more fragmented novels, no less remarkable than the bizarre masterworks that he keeps to himself out of oedipal timidity, perfectionist madness, and insatiable longings for solitude and spiritual purity.

July 1923: Eleven months before he will die in a Vienna sanatorium, Kafka somehow finds the resolve to leave Prague and his father's home for good. Never before has he even remotely succeeded in living apart, independent of his mother, his sisters, and his father, nor has he been a writer other than in those few hours when he is not working in the legal department of the Workers' Accident Insurance Office in Prague; since taking his law degree at the university, he has been by all reports the most dutiful and scrupulous of employees, though he finds the work tedious and enervating. But in June of 1923—having some months earlier been pensioned from his job because of his illness—he meets a young Jewish girl of nineteen at a seaside resort in Germany, Dora Dymant, an employee at the vacation camp of the Jewish People's Home of Berlin. Dora has left her Orthodox Polish family to make a life of her own (at half Kafka's age); she and Kafka—who has just turned forty—fall in love . . . Kafka has by now been engaged to two somewhat more conventional Jewish girls—twice to one of them—hectic, anguished engagements wrecked largely by his fears. "I am mentally incapable of marrying," he writes his father in the forty-five-page letter he gave to his mother to deliver. ". . . the moment I make up my mind to marry I can no longer sleep, my head burns day and night, life can no longer be called life." He explains why. "Marrying is barred to me," he tells his father, "because it is your domain. Sometimes I imagine the map of the world spread out and you stretched diagonally across it. And I feel as if I could consider living in only those regions that are not covered by you or are not within your reach. And in keeping with the

---

[2] German writer (1875–1955). He left Germany in 1933.

conception I have of your magnitude, these are not many and not very comforting regions—and marriage is not among them." The letter explaining what is wrong between this father and this son is dated November 1919; the mother thought it best not even to deliver it, perhaps for lack of courage, probably, like the son, for lack of hope.

During the following two years, Kafka attempts to wage an affair with Milena Jesenká-Pollak, an intense young woman of twenty-four who has translated a few of his stories into Czech and is most unhappily married in Vienna; his affair with Milena, conducted feverishly, but by and large through the mails, is even more demoralizing to Kafka than the fearsome engagements to the nice Jewish girls. They aroused only the paterfamilias longings that he dared not indulge, longings inhibited by his exaggerated awe of his father—"spellbound," says Brod, "in the family circle"—and the hypnotic spell of his own solitude; but the Czech Milena, impetuous, frenetic, indifferent to conventional restraints, a woman of appetite and anger, arouses more elemental yearnings and more elemental fears. According to a Prague critic, Rio Preisner, Milena was "psychopathic"; according to Margaret Buber-Neumann, who lived two years beside her in the German concentration camp where Milena died following a kidney operation in 1944, she was powerfully sane, extraordinarily humane and courageous. Milena's obituary for Kafka was the only one of consequence to appear in the Prague press; the prose is strong, so are the claims she makes for Kafka's accomplishment. She is still only in her twenties, the dead man is hardly known as a writer beyond his small circle of friends—yet Milena writes: "His knowledge of the world was exceptional and deep, and he was a deep and exceptional world in himself. . . . [He had] a delicacy of feeling bordering on the miraculous and a mental clarity that was terrifyingly uncompromising, and in turn he loaded on to his illness the whole burden of his mental fear of life. . . . He wrote the most important books in recent German literature." One can imagine this vibrant young woman stretched diagonally across the bed, as awesome to Kafka as his own father spread out across the map of the world. His letters to her are disjointed, unlike anything else of his in print; the word "fear" appears on page after page. "We are both married, you in Vienna, I to my Fear in Prague." He yearns to lay his head upon her breast; he calls her "Mother Milena"; during at least one of their two brief rendezvous, he is hopelessly impotent. At last he has to tell her to leave him be, an edict that Milena honors, though it leaves her hollow with grief. "Do not write," Kafka tells her, "and let us not see each other; I ask you only to quietly fulfill this request of mine; only on those conditions is survival possible for me; everything else continues the process of destruction."

Then, in the early summer of 1923, during a visit to his sister, who is vacationing with her children by the Baltic Sea, he finds young Dora Dymant, and within a month Franz Kafka has gone off to live with her in two rooms in a suburb of Berlin, out of reach at last of the "claws" of Prague and home. How can it be? How can he, in his illness, have accomplished so swiftly and decisively the leave-taking that was beyond him in his healthiest days? The impassioned letter writer who could equivocate interminably about which train to catch to Vienna to meet with Milena (if he should meet with her for the weekend at all); the bourgeois suitor in the high collar, who, during his drawn-out agony of an engagement with the proper Fräulein Bauer, secretly draws up a memorandum for himself, countering the arguments "for" marriage with the arguments "against"; the poet of the ungraspable and the unresolved, whose belief in the immovable barrier separating the wish from its realization is at the heart of his excruciating visions of defeat; the Kafka whose fiction refutes every easy, touching, humanish daydream of salvation and justice and fulfillment with densely imagined counterdreams that mock all solutions and escapes—this Kafka *escapes.* Overnight! K. penetrates the Castle walls—Joseph K. evades his indictment —"a breaking away from it altogether, a mode of living completely outside the jurisdiction of the Court." Yes, the possibility of which Joseph K. has just a glimmering in the Cathedral, but can neither fathom nor effectuate—"not . . . some influential manipulation of the case, but . . . a circumvention of it"—Kafka realizes in the last year of his life.

Was it Dora Dymant or was it death that pointed the new way? Perhaps it could not have been one without the other. We know that the "illusory emptiness" at which K. gazed, upon first entering the village and looking up through the mist and the darkness to the Castle, was no more vast and incomprehensible than the idea of himself as husband and father was to the young Kafka; but now, it seems, the prospect of a Dora forever, of a wife, home, and children everlasting, is no longer the terrifying, bewildering prospect it would once have been, for now "everlasting" is undoubtedly not much more than a matter of months. Yes, the dying Kafka is determined to marry, and writes to Dora's Orthodox father for his daughter's hand. But the imminent death that has resolved all contradictions and uncertainties in Kafka is the very obstacle placed in his path by the young girl's father. The request of the dying man Franz Kafka to bind to him in his invalidism the healthy young girl Dora Dymant is—denied!

If there is not one father standing in Kafka's way, there is another—and another behind him. Dora's father, writes Max Brod in his biography of Kafka, "set off with [Kafka's] letter to consult the man he honored most, whose authority counted more than anything else for him, the 'Gerer Rebbe.'[3] The rabbi read the letter, put it to one side, and said nothing more than the single syllable, 'No.' " *No.* Klamm himself could have been no more abrupt—or any more removed from the petitioner. *No.* In its harsh finality, as telling and inescapable as the curselike threat delivered by his father to Georg Bendemann, that thwarted fiancé: "Just take your bride on your arm and try getting in my way. I'll sweep her from your very side, you don't know how!" *No.* Thou shalt not have, say the fathers, and Kafka agrees that he shall not. The habit of obedience and renunciation; also, his own distaste for the diseased and reverence for strength, appetite, and health. " 'Well, clear this out now!' said the overseer, and they buried the hunger artist, straw and all. Into the cage they put a young panther. Even the most insensitive felt it refreshing to see this wild creature leaping around the cage that had so long been dreary. The panther was all right. The food he liked was brought him without hesitation by the attendants; he seemed not even to miss his freedom; his noble body, furnished almost to the bursting point with all that it needed, seemed to carry freedom around with it too; somewhere in his jaws it seemed to lurk; and the joy of life streamed with such ardent passion from his throat that for the onlookers it was not easy to stand the shock of it. But they braced themselves, crowded round the cage, and did not want ever to move away." So no is no; he knew as much himself. A healthy young girl of nineteen cannot, *should* not, be given in matrimony to a sickly man twice her age, who spits up blood ("I sentence you," cries

---

[3] Yiddish: "the rabbi from Gera." Gera is an industrial city in eastern Germany.

Georg Bendemann's father, "to death by drowning!") and shakes in his bed with fevers and chills. What sort of un-Kafka-like dream had Kafka been dreaming?

And those nine months spent with Dora have still other "Kafkaesque" elements: a fierce winter in quarters inadequately heated; the inflation that makes a pittance of his own meager pension, and sends into the streets of Berlin the hungry and needy whose suffering, says Dora, turns Kafka "ash-gray"; and his tubercular lungs, flesh transformed and punished. Dora cares for the diseased writer as devotedly and tenderly as Gregor Samsa's sister does for her brother, the bug. Gregor's sister plays the violin so beautifully that Gregor "felt as if the way were opening before him to the unknown nourishment he craved"; he dreams, in his condition, of sending his gifted sister to the Conservatory! Dora's music is Hebrew, which she reads aloud to Kafka, and with such skill that, according to Brod, "Franz recognized her dramatic talent; on his advice and under his direction she later educated herself in the art . . ."

Only Kafka is hardly vermin to Dora Dymant, *or to himself.* Away from Prague and his father's home, Kafka, at forty, seems at last to have been delivered from the self-loathing, the self-doubt, and those guilt-ridden impulses to dependence and self-effacement that had nearly driven him mad throughout his twenties and thirties; all at once he seems to have shed the pervasive sense of hopeless despair that informs the great punitive fantasies of *The Trial,* "In the Penal Colony," and "The Metamorphosis." Years earlier, in Prague, he had directed Max Brod to destroy all his papers, including three unpublished novels, upon his death; now, in Berlin, when Brod introduces him to a German publisher interested in his work, Kafka consents to the publication of a volume of four stories, and consents, says Brod, "without much need of long arguments to persuade him." With Dora to help, he diligently resumes the study of Hebrew; despite his illness and the harsh winter, he travels to the Berlin Academy for Jewish Studies to attend a series of lectures on the Talmud—a very different Kafka from the estranged melancholic who once wrote in his diary, "What have I in common with the Jews? I have hardly anything in common with myself and should stand very quietly in a corner, content that I can breathe." And to further mark the change, there is ease and happiness with a woman: with this young and adoring companion, he is playful, he is pedagogical, and, one would guess, in light of his illness (*and* his happiness), he is chaste. If not a husband (such as he had striven to be to the conventional Fräulein Bauer), if not a lover (as he struggled hopelessly to be with Milena), he would seem to have become something no less miraculous in his scheme of things: a father, a kind of father to this sisterly, mothering daughter. *As Franz Kafka awoke one morning from uneasy dreams he found himself transformed in his bed into a father, a writer, and a Jew.*

"I have completed the construction of my burrow," begins the long, exquisite, and tedious story that he wrote that winter in Berlin, "and it seems to be successful. . . . Just the place where, according to my calculations, the Castle Keep should be, the soil was very loose and sandy and had literally to be hammered and pounded into a firm state to serve as a wall for the beautifully vaulted chamber. But for such tasks the only tool I possess is my forehead. So I had to run with my forehead thousands and thousands of times, for whole days and nights, against the ground, and I was glad when the blood came, for that was proof that the walls were beginning to harden; in that way, as everybody must admit, I richly paid for my Castle Keep."

"The Burrow" is the story of an animal with a keen sense of peril whose life is organized around the principle of defense, and whose deepest longings are for security and serenity; with teeth and claws—*and* forehead—the burrower constructs an elaborate and ingeniously intricate system of underground chambers and corridors that are designed to afford it some peace of mind; however, while this burrow does succeed in reducing the sense of danger from without, its maintenance and protection are equally fraught with anxiety: "these anxieties are different from ordinary ones, prouder, richer in content, often long repressed, but in their destructive effects they are perhaps much the same as the anxieties that existence in the outer world gives rise to." The story (whose ending is lost) terminates with the burrower fixated upon distant subterranean noises that cause it "to assume the existence of a great beast," itself burrowing in the direction of the Castle Keep.

Another grim tale of entrapment, and of obsession so absolute that no distinction is possible between character and predicament. Yet this fiction imagined in the last "happy" months of his life is touched by a spirit of personal reconciliation and sardonic self-acceptance, by a tolerance of one's own brand of madness, that is not apparent in "The Metamorphosis." The piercing masochistic irony of the earlier animal story—as of "The Judgment" and *The Trial*—has given way here to a critique of the self and its preoccupations that though bordering on mockery, no longer seeks to resolve itself in images of the uttermost humiliation and defeat . . . Yet there is more here than a metaphor for the insanely defended ego, whose striving for invulnerability produces a defensive system that must in its turn become the object of perpetual concern—there is also a very unromantic and hardheaded fable about how and why art is made, a portrait of the artist in all his ingenuity, anxiety, isolation, dissatisfaction, relentlessness, obsessiveness, secretiveness, paranoia, and self-addiction, a portrait of the magical thinker at the end of his tether, Kafka's Prospero . . . It is an endlessly suggestive story, this story of life in a hole. For, finally, remember the proximity of Dora Dymant during the months that Kafka was at work on "The Burrow" in the two underheated rooms that were their illicit home. Certainly a dreamer like Kafka need never have entered the young girl's body for her tender presence to kindle in him a fantasy of a hidden orifice that promises "satisfied desire," "achieved ambition," and "profound slumber," but that, once penetrated and in one's possession, arouses the most terrifying and heartbreaking fears of retribution and loss. "For the rest I try to unriddle the beast's plans. Is it on its wanderings, or is it working on its own burrow? If it is on its wanderings then perhaps an understanding with it might be possible. If it should really break through to the burrow I shall give it some of my stores and it will go on its way again. It will go on its way again, a fine story! Lying in my heap of earth I can naturally dream of all sorts of things, even of an understanding with the beast, though I know well enough that no such thing can happen, and that at the instant when we see each other, more, at the moment when we merely guess at each other's presence, we shall blindly bare our claws and teeth . . ."

He died of tuberculosis of the lungs and larynx on June 3, 1924, a month before his forty-first birthday. Dora, inconsolable, whispers for days afterward, "My love, my love, my good one . . ."

1942. I am nine; my Hebrew-school teacher, Dr. Kafka, is fifty-nine. To the little boys who must attend his "four-to-five" class each afternoon, he is known—in part because of his remote and melancholy foreignness, but largely because we vent on him our resentment at having to learn an ancient calligraphy at the very hour we should be out screaming our heads off on the ball field—he is known as Dr. Kishka. Named, I confess, by me. His sour breath, spiced with intestinal juices by five in the afternoon, makes the Yiddish word for "insides" particularly telling, I think. Cruel, yes, but in truth I would have cut out my tongue had I ever imagined the name would become legend. A coddled child, I do not yet think of myself as persuasive, or, quite yet, as a literary force in the world. My jokes don't hurt, how could they, I'm so adorable. And if you don't believe me, just ask my family and the teachers in my school. Already at nine, one foot in college, the other in the Catskills. Little borscht-belt[4] comic that I am outside the classroom, I amuse my friends Schlossman and Ratner on the dark walk home from Hebrew school with an imitation of Kishka, his precise and finicky professorial manner, his German accent, his cough, his gloom. "Doctor *Kishka!*" cries Schlossman, and hurls himself savagely against the newsstand that belongs to the candy-store owner whom Schlossman drives just a little crazier each night. "Doctor Franz—Doctor Franz—Doctor Franz—*Kishka!*" screams Ratner, and my chubby little friend who lives upstairs from me on nothing but chocolate milk and Mallomars does not stop laughing until, as is his wont (his mother has asked me "to keep an eye on him" for just this reason), he wets his pants. Schlossman takes the occasion of Ratner's humiliation to pull the little boy's paper out of his notebook and wave it in the air—it is the assignment Dr. Kafka has just returned to us, graded; we were told to make up an alphabet of our own, out of straight lines and curved lines and dots. "That is all an alphabet is," he had explained. "That is all Hebrew is. That is all English is. Straight lines and curved lines and dots." Ratner's alphabet, for which he received a C, looks like twenty-six skulls strung in a row. I received my A for a curlicued alphabet, inspired largely (as Dr. Kafka seems to have surmised, given his comment at the top of the page) by the number eight. Schlossman received an F for forgetting even to do it—and a lot he seems to care. He is content—he is *overjoyed* —with things as they are. Just waving a piece of paper in the air and screaming, "Kishka! Kishka!" makes him deliriously happy. We should all be so lucky.

At home, alone in the glow of my goose-necked "desk" lamp (plugged after dinner into an outlet in the kitchen, my study), the vision of our refugee teacher, sticklike in a fraying three-piece blue suit, is no longer very funny—particularly after the entire beginners' Hebrew class, of which I am the most studious member, takes the name Kishka to its heart. My guilt awakens redemptive fantasies of heroism, I have them often about the "Jews in Europe." I must save him. If not me, who? The demonic Schlossman? The babyish Ratner? And if not now, when? For I have learned in the ensuing weeks that Dr. Kafka lives in a room in the house of an elderly Jewish lady on the shabby lower stretch of Avon Avenue, where the trolley still runs and the poorest of Newark's Negroes shuffle meekly up and down the street, for all they seem to know, still back in Mississippi. A *room.* And *there!* My family's apartment is no palace, but it is ours at least, so long as we pay the $38.50 a month in rent; and though our neighbors are not rich, they refuse to be poor and they refuse to be meek. Tears of shame and sorrow in my eyes, I rush into the living room to tell my parents what

---

[4] Popular Jewish resort area in the Catskill Mountains, called the "borscht belt" as a joking reference to the popularity there of borscht, or beet soup.

I have heard (though not that I heard it during a quick game of "aces up" played a minute before class against the synagogue's rear wall—worse, played directly beneath a stained-glass window embossed with the names of the dead): "My Hebrew teacher lives in a *room.*"

My parents go much further than I could imagine anybody going in the real world. Invite him to dinner, my mother says. *Here?* Of course here—Friday night; I'm sure he can stand a home-cooked meal, she says, and a little pleasant company. Meanwhile, my father gets on the phone to call my Aunt Rhoda, who lives with my grandmother and tends her and her potted plants in the apartment house at the corner of our street. For nearly two decades my father has been introducing my mother's "baby" sister, now forty, to the Jewish bachelors and widowers of north Jersey. No luck so far. Aunt Rhoda, an "interior decorator" in the dry-goods department of the Big Bear, a mammoth merchandise and produce market in industrial Elizabeth, wears falsies (this information by way of my older brother) and sheer frilly blouses, and family lore has it that she spends hours in the bathroom every day applying powder and sweeping her stiffish hair up into a dramatic pile on her head; but despite all this dash and display, she is, in my father's words, "still afraid of the facts of life." He, however, is undaunted, and administers therapy regularly and gratis: "Let 'em squeeze ya, Rhoda —it *feels* good!" I am his flesh and blood, I can reconcile myself to such scandalous talk in our kitchen—*but what will Dr. Kafka think?* Oh, but it's too late to do anything now. The massive machinery of matchmaking has been set in motion by my undiscourageable father, and the smooth engines of my proud homemaking mother's hospitality are already purring away. To throw my body into the works in an attempt to bring it all to a halt—well, I might as well try to bring down the New Jersey Bell Telephone Company by leaving our receiver off the hook. Only Dr. Kafka can save me now. But to my muttered invitation, he replies, with a formal bow that turns me scarlet—who has ever seen a person do such a thing outside of a movie house?—he replies that he would be *honored* to be my family's dinner guest. "My aunt," I rush to tell him, "will be there too." It appears that I have just said something mildly humorous; odd to see Dr. Kafka smile. Sighing, he says, "I will be delighted to meet her." Meet her? He's supposed to *marry* her. How do I warn him? And how do I warn Aunt Rhoda (a very great admirer of me and my marks) about his sour breath, his roomer's pallor, his Old World ways, so at odds with her up-to-dateness? My face feels as if it will ignite of its own—and spark the fire that will engulf the synagogue, Torah and all—when I see Dr. Kafka scrawl our address in his notebook, and beneath it, some words *in German.* "Good night, Dr. Kafka!" "Good night, and thank you, thank you." I turn to run, I go, but not fast enough: out on the street I hear Schlossman —that fiend!—announcing to my classmates, who are punching one another under the lamplight down from the synagogue steps (where a card game is also in progress, organized by the bar mitzvah boys): "Roth invited Kishka to his *house!* To *eat!*"

Does my father do a job on Kafka! Does he make a sales pitch for familial bliss! What it means to a man to have two fine boys and a wonderful wife! Can Dr. Kafka imagine what it's like? The thrill? The satisfaction? The pride? He tells our visitor of the network of relatives on his mother's side that are joined in a "family association" of over two hundred people located in seven states, including the state of Washington! Yes, relatives even in the Far West: here are their photographs. Dr. Kafka; this is a beautiful book we published entirely on our own for five dollars a copy, pictures of every member of the family, including infants, and a family history by "Uncle" Lichtblau, the eighty-five-year-old patriarch of the clan. This is our family newsletter, which is published twice a year and distributed nationwide to all the relatives. This, in the frame, is the menu from the banquet of the family association, held last year in a ballroom of the "Y" in Newark, in honor of my father's mother on her seventy-fifth birthday. My mother, Dr. Kafka learns, has served *six consecutive years* as the secretary-treasurer of the family association. My father has served a two-year term as president, as have each of his three brothers. We now have fourteen boys in the family in uniform. Philip writes a letter on V-mail stationery to five of his cousins in the army every single month. "Religiously," my mother puts in, smoothing my hair. "I firmly believe," says my father, "that the family is the cornerstone of everything."

Dr. Kafka, who has listened with close attention to my father's spiel, handling the various documents that have been passed to him with great delicacy and poring over them with a kind of rapt absorption that reminds me of myself over the watermarks of my stamps, now for the first time expresses himself on the subject of family; softly he says, "I agree," and inspects again the pages of our family book. "Alone," says my father, in conclusion, "alone, Dr. Kafka, is a stone." Dr. Kafka, setting the book gently down upon my mother's gleaming coffee table, allows with a nod that that is so. My mother's fingers are now turning in the curls behind my ears; not that I even know it at the time, or that she does. Being stroked is my life; stroking me, my father, and my brother is hers.

My brother goes off to a Boy Scout meeting, but only after my father has him stand in his neckerchief before Dr. Kafka and describe to him the skills he has mastered to earn each of his badges. I am invited to bring my stamp album into the living room and show Dr. Kafka my set of triangular stamps from Zanzibar. "Zanzibar!" says my father rapturously, as though I, not even ten, have already been there and back. My father accompanies Dr. Kafka and me into the "sun parlor," where my tropical fish swim in the aerated, heated, and hygienic paradise I have made for them with my weekly allowance and my Hanukkah *gelt*.[5] I am encouraged to tell Dr. Kafka what I know about the temperament of the angelfish, the function of the catfish, and the family life of the black mollie. I know quite a bit. "All on his own he does that," my father says to Kafka. "He gives me a lecture on one of those fish, it's seventh heaven, Dr. Kafka." "I can imagine," Kafka replies.

Back in the living room my Aunt Rhoda suddenly launches into a rather recondite monologue on "Scotch plaids," intended, it would appear, for the edification of my mother alone. At least she looks fixedly at my mother while she delivers it. I have not yet seen her look directly at Dr. Kafka; she did not even turn his way at dinner when he asked how many employees there were at the Big Bear. "How would I know?" she had replied, and then continued right on conversing with my mother, about a butcher who would take care of her "under the counter" if she could find him nylons for his wife. It never occurs to me that she will not look at Dr. Kafka because she is shy—nobody that dolled up could, in my estimation, be shy. I can only think that she is outraged. *It's his breath. It's his accent. It's his age.*

I'm wrong—it turns out to be what Aunt Rhoda calls his "superiority complex."

[5] Yiddish: "money."

"Sitting there, sneering at us like that," says my aunt, somewhat superior now herself. "Sneering?" repeats my father, incredulous. "Sneering and laughing, yes!" says Aunt Rhoda. My mother shrugs. "*I* didn't think he was laughing." "Oh, don't worry, by himself there he was having a very good time—*at our expense*. I knew the European-type man. Underneath they think they're all lords of the manor," Rhoda says. "You know something, Rhoda?" says my father, tilting his head and pointing a finger, "I think you fell in love." "With *him*? Are you *crazy*?" "He's too quiet for Rhoda," my mother says. "I think maybe he's a little bit of a wallflower. Rhoda is a very lively person, she needs lively people around her." "Wallflower? He's not a wallflower! He's a gentleman, that's all. And he's lonely," my father says assertively, glaring at my mother for going over his head like this *against* Kafka. My Aunt Rhoda is forty years old—it is not exactly a shipment of brand-new goods that he is trying to move. "He's a gentleman, he's an educated man, and I'll tell you something, he'd give his eyeteeth to have a nice home and a wife." "Well," says my Aunt Rhoda, "let him find one then, if he's so educated. Somebody who's his equal, who he doesn't have to look down his nose at with his big sad refugee eyes!" "Yep, she's in love," my father announces, squeezing Rhoda's knee in triumph. "With him?" she cries, jumping to her feet, taffeta crackling around her like a bonfire. "With *Kafka?*" she snorts. "I wouldn't give an old man like him the time of day!"

Dr. Kafka calls and takes my Aunt Rhoda to a movie. I am astonished, both that he calls and that she goes; it seems there is more desperation in life than I have come across yet in my fish tank. Dr. Kafka takes my Aunt Rhoda to a play performed at the "Y." Dr. Kafka eats Sunday dinner with my grandmother and my Aunt Rhoda and, at the end of the afternoon, accepts with that formal bow of his the mason jar of barley soup that my grandmother presses him to carry back to his room with him on the No. 8 bus. Apparently he was very taken with my grandmother's jungle of potted plants—and she, as a result, with him. Together they spoke in Yiddish about gardening. One Wednesday morning, only an hour after the store has opened for the day, Dr. Kafka shows up at the dry-goods department of the Big Bear; he tells Aunt Rhoda that he just wants to see where she works. That night he writes in his diary: "With the customers she is forthright and cheery, and so managerial about 'taste' that when I hear her explain to a chubby young bride why green and blue do not 'go,' I am myself ready to believe that Nature is in error and R. is correct."

One night, at ten, Dr. Kafka and Aunt Rhoda come by unexpectedly, and a small impromptu party is held in the kitchen—coffee and cake, even a thimbleful of whiskey all around, to celebrate the resumption of Aunt Rhoda's career on the stage. I have only heard tell of my aunt's theatrical ambitions. My brother says that when I was small she used to come to entertain the two of us on Sundays with her puppets —she was at that time employed by the W.P.A. to travel around New Jersey and put on marionette shows in schools and even in churches; Aunt Rhoda did all the voices and, with the help of a female assistant, manipulated the manikins on their strings. Simultaneously she had been a member of the Newark Collective Theater, a troupe organized primarily to go around to strike groups to perform *Waiting for Lefty*. Everybody in Newark (as I understood it) had had high hopes that Rhoda Pilchik would go on to Broadway—everybody except my grandmother. To me this period of history is as difficult to believe in as the era of the lake dwellers, which I am studying in school; people say it was once so, so I believe them, but nonetheless it is hard to grant such stories the status of the real, given the life I see around me.

Yet my father, a very avid realist, is in the kitchen, schnapps glass in hand, toasting Aunt Rhoda's success. She has been awarded one of the starring roles in the Russian masterpiece *The Three Sisters*, to be performed six weeks hence by the amateur group at the Newark "Y." Everything, announces Aunt Rhoda, everything she owes to Franz and his encouragement. One conversation—"One!" she cries gaily—and Dr. Kafka had apparently talked my grandmother out of her lifelong belief that actors are not serious human beings. And what an actor *he* is, in his own right, says Aunt Rhoda. How he had opened her eyes to the meaning of things, by reading her the famous Chekhov play—yes, read it to her from the opening line to the final curtain, all the parts, and actually left her in tears. Here Aunt Rhoda says, "Listen, listen— this is the first line of the play—it's the key to everything. Listen—I just think about what it was like the night Pop passed away, how I wondered and wondered what would become of us, what would we all do—and, and, *listen*—"

"We're listening," laughs my father. So am *I* listening, from my bed.

Pause; she must have walked to the center of the kitchen linoleum. She says, sounding a little surprised, " 'It's just a year ago today that father died.' "

"Shhh," warns my mother, "you'll give the little one nightmares."

I am not alone in finding my aunt a "changed person" during the weeks of rehearsal. My mother says this is just what she was like as a little girl. "Red cheeks, always those hot, red cheeks—and everything exciting, even taking a bath." "She'll calm down, don't worry," says my father, "and then he'll pop the question." "Knock on wood," says my mother. "Come on," says my father, "he knows what side his bread is buttered on—he sets foot in this house, he sees what a family is all about, and believe me, he's licking his chops. Just look at him when he sits in that club chair. This is his dream come true." "Rhoda says that in Berlin, before Hitler, he had a young girl friend, years and years it went on, and then she left him. For somebody else. She got tired of waiting." "Don't worry," says my father, "when the time comes I'll give him a little nudge. He ain't going to live forever, either, and he knows it."

Then one weekend, as a respite from the "strain" of nightly rehearsals—which Dr. Kafka regularly visits, watching in his hat and coat at the back of the auditorium until it is time to accompany Aunt Rhoda home—they take a trip to Atlantic City. Ever since he arrived on these shores Dr. Kafka has wanted to see the famous boardwalk and the horse that dives from the high board. But in Atlantic City something happens that I am not allowed to know about; any discussion of the subject conducted in my presence is in Yiddish. Dr. Kafka sends Aunt Rhoda four letters in three days. She comes to us for dinner and sits till midnight crying in our kitchen. She calls the "Y" on our phone to tell them (weeping) that her mother is still ill and she cannot come to rehearsal again—she may even have to drop out of the play. No, she can't, she can't, her mother is too ill, she herself is too upset! goodbye! Then back to the kitchen table to cry. She wears no pink powder and no red lipstick, and her stiff brown hair, down, is thick and spiky as a new broom.

My brother and I listen from our bedroom, through the door that silently he has pushed ajar.

"Have you ever?" says Aunt Rhoda, weeping. "Have you *ever?*"

"Poor soul," says my mother.

"*Who?*" I whisper to my brother. "Aunt Rhoda or—"

"Shhhh!" he says. "Shut *up!*"

In the kitchen my father grunts. "Hmm. Hmm." I hear him getting up and walking around and sitting down again—and then grunting. I am listening so hard that I can hear the letters being folded and unfolded, stuck back into their envelopes, then removed to be puzzled over one more time.

"Well?" demands Aunt Rhoda. *"Well?"*

"Well what?" answers my father.

"Well, what do you want to say *now?"*

"He's *meshugeh,"*[6] admits my father. "Something is wrong with him all right."

"But," sobs Aunt Rhoda, "no one would believe me when *I* said it!"

"Rhody, Rhody," croons my mother in that voice I know from those times that I have had to have stitches taken, or when I have awakened in tears, somehow on the floor beside my bed. "Rhody, don't be hysterical, darling. It's over, kitten, it's all over."

I reach across to my brother's twin bed and tug on the blanket. I don't think I've ever been so confused in my life, not even by death. The speed of things! Everything good undone in a moment! By what? *"What?"* I whisper. *"What is it?"*

My brother, the Boy Scout, smiles leeringly and, with a fierce hiss that is no answer and enough answer, addresses my bewilderment: "Sex!"

Years later, a junior at college, I receive an envelope from home containing Dr. Kafka's obituary, clipped from *The Jewish News,* the tabloid of Jewish affairs that is mailed each week to the homes of the Jews of Essex County. It is summer, the semester is over, but I have stayed on at school, alone in my room in the town, trying to write short stories. I am fed by a young English professor and his wife in exchange for baby-sitting. I tell the sympathetic couple, who are also loaning me the money for my rent, why it is I can't go home. My tearful fights with my father are all I can talk about at their dinner table. "Keep him away from me!" I scream at my mother. "But, darling," she asks me, "what is going on? What is this all about?"—the very same question with which I used to plague my elder brother, asked now of me and out of the same bewilderment and innocence. "He *loves* you," she explains.

But that, of all things, seems to me precisely what is blocking my way. Others are crushed by paternal criticism—I find myself oppressed by his high opinion of me! Can it possibly be true (and can I possibly admit) that I am coming to hate him for loving me so? praising me so? But that makes no sense—the ingratitude! the stupidity! the contrariness! Being loved is so obviously a blessing, *the* blessing, praise such a rare bequest. Only listen late at night to my closest friends on the literary magazine and in the drama society—they tell horror stories of family life to rival *The Way of All Flesh,*[7] they return shell-shocked from vacations, drift back to school as though from the wars. What they would give to be in my golden slippers! "What's going on?" my mother begs me to tell her; but how can I, when I myself don't fully believe that this is happening to us, or that I am the one who is making it happen. That they, who together cleared all obstructions from my path, should seem now to be my final

---

[6] Yiddish (plural: *meshugeneh*): "crazy" or "insane"; hence, outlandish or bizarre.

[7] English novel by Samuel Butler (1835–1902) satirizing Victorian society.

obstruction! No wonder my rage must filter through a child's tears of shame, confusion, and loss. All that we have constructed together over the course of two century-long decades, and look how I must bring it down—in the name of this tyrannical need that I call my "independence"! My mother, keeping the lines of communication open, sends a note to me at school: "We miss you"—and encloses the brief obituary notice. Across the margin at the bottom of the clipping, she has written (in the same hand with which she wrote notes to my teachers and signed my report cards, in that very same handwriting that once eased my way in the world), "Remember poor Kafka, Aunt Rhoda's beau?"

"Dr. Franz Kafka," the notice reads, "a Hebrew teacher at the Talmud Torah of the Schley Street Synagogue from 1939 to 1948, died on June 3 in the Deborah Heart and Lung Center in Browns Mills, New Jersey. Dr. Kafka had been a patient there since 1950. He was 70 years old. Dr. Kafka was born in Prague, Czechoslovakia, and was a refugee from the Nazis. He leaves no survivors."

He also leaves no books: no *Trial*, no *Castle*, no Diaries. The dead man's papers are claimed by no one, and disappear—all except those four *"meshugeneh"* letters that are, to this day, as far as I know, still somewhere in among the memorabilia accumulated by my spinster aunt, along with a collection of Broadway Playbills, sales citations from the Big Bear, and transatlantic steamship stickers.

Thus all trace of Dr. Kafka disappears. Destiny being destiny, how could it be otherwise? Does the Land Surveyor reach the Castle? Does K. escape the judgment of the Court, or Georg Bendemann the judgment of his father? "Well, clear this out now!' said the overseer, and they buried the hunger artist, straw and all." No, it simply is not in the cards for Kafka ever to become *the* Kafka—why, that would be stranger even than a man turning into an insect. No one would believe it, Kafka least of all.

1973/1973

N. Scott Momaday
b. 1934

N. Scott Momaday, a Kiowa Indian, is a Pulitzer Prize–winning novelist and university professor who believes that the strength of American Indian culture rests on its close identification with the land. His grandmother, Aho, typifies for him the Indian experience: "The immense landscape of the continental interior," he says, "lay like memory in her blood." Yet for as long as she lived after witnessing the outlawing of the Sun Dance, the Kiowa ritual of worship, "she bore a vision of deicide," the killing of a god. In his fiction and nonfiction Momaday celebrates the spiritual awareness that his grandmother possessed even as he laments the cultural alienation imposed on her by the United States.

Navarre Scott Momaday, whose Kiowa name is Tsoai-talee, was born on February 27, 1934, near Anadarko, the Oklahoma Kiowa Indian agency. In 1935 his family moved to northern New Mexico, where he grew up on Navajo, Apache, and Jemez Pueblo Indian reservations. He received a B.A. in political science from the University of New Mexico in 1958, an M.A. from Stanford in 1960, and a Ph.D. from Stanford in 1963. Currently on the English and Comparative Literature faculty at Stanford, Momaday has also taught at the Berkeley and Santa Barbara campuses of the University of California and at the Las Cruces campus of New Mexico State University. His scholarly interest is in nineteenth-century American poetry, and he is editor of *The Complete Poems of Frederick Goddard Tuckerman* (1965).

Momaday lives another life, however, as a Kiowa tribal dancer and chronicler of Indian experience in this country. "None but an Indian, I think," he has said, "knows so much what it is like to have existence in two worlds and security in neither." In *House Made of Dawn* (1968), his prizewinning first novel, Momaday recounts the adventures of an Indian named Abel, a man who survives World War II only to discover, as Momaday put it, that he can neither "recover his tribal identity nor . . . escape the cultural context in which he grew up. He is torn, as they say, between two worlds, neither of which he can enter and be a whole man. The story is that of his struggle to survive. . . ." The language of *House Made of Dawn* paradoxically conjoins the lyrical and the violent. Abel and his fellow runners run, we read, "with great dignity and calm, not in hope of anything, but hopelessly; neither in fear nor hatred nor despair of evil, but simply in recognition and with respect. Evil was. Evil was abroad in the night; they must venture out to the confrontation; they must reckon dues and divide the world."

In Momaday's nonfiction the "sacred earth" becomes a redemptive agent in the human quest for knowledge and wholeness. In *The Journey of Tai-me* (1967), the story of the tribal god of the Kiowa whose death his grandmother witnessed at the last Sun Dance, and again in *The Way to Rainy Mountain* (1969), Momaday confronts a world in which experience typically seems fragmentary and inadequate and in which knowledge typically comes as "a moment of truth and exile." But Momaday also writes as one who is convinced that "man's idea of himself" finds "old and essential being in language," in the act of naming and the process of remembering, activities of the mind that are "legendary as well as historical, personal as well as cultural."

Further Reading:
C. Oleson, "The Remembered Earth: Momaday's *House Made of Dawn*," *South Dakota Review*, Spring 1973.
M. S. Trimble, *N. Scott Momaday*, 1973.

Text:
House Made of Dawn, 1968.

---

from House Made of Dawn

from **The Priest of the Sun**

from January 26

The Priest of the Sun lived with his disciple Cruz on the first floor of a two-story red-brick building in Los Angeles. The upstairs was maintained as a storage facility by the A. A. Kaul Office Supply Company. The basement was a kind of church. There was a signboard on the wall above the basement steps, encased in glass. In neat, movable white block letters on a black field it read:

LOS ANGELES

HOLINESS PAN-INDIAN RESCUE MISSION

Rev. J. B. B. Tosamah, Pastor & Priest of the Sun

Saturday 8:30 P.M.

"The Gospel According to John"

Sunday 8:30 P.M.

"The Way to Rainy Mountain"

Be kind to a white man today

The basement was cold and dreary, dimly illuminated by two 40-watt bulbs which were screwed into the side walls above the dais. This platform was made out of rough planks of various woods and dimensions, thrown together without so much as a hammer and nails; it stood seven or eight inches above the floor, and it supported the tin firebox and the crescent altar. Off to one side was a kind of lectern, decorated with red and yellow symbols of the sun and moon. In back of the dais there was a screen of purple drapery, threadbare and badly faded. On either side of the aisle which led to the altar there were chairs and crates, fashioned into pews. The walls were bare and gray and streaked with water. The only windows were small, rectangular openings near the ceiling, at ground level; the panes were covered over with a thick film of coal oil and dust, and spider webs clung to the frames or floated out like smoke across the room. The air was heavy and stale; odors of old smoke and incense lingered all around. The people had filed into the pews and were waiting silently.

Cruz, a squat, oily man with blue-black hair that stood out like spines from his head, stepped forward on the platform and raised his hands as if to ask for the quiet that already was. Everyone watched him for a moment; in the dull light his skin shone yellow with sweat. Turning slightly and extending his arm behind him, he said, "The Right Reverend John Big Bluff Tosamah."

There was a ripple in the dark screen; the drapes parted and the Priest of the Sun appeared, moving shadow-like to the lectern. He was shaggy and awful-looking in the thin, naked light: big, lithe as a cat, narrow-eyed, suggesting in the whole of his look and manner both arrogance and agony. He wore black like a cleric; he had the voice of a great dog:

" '*In principio erat Verbum.*'[1] Think of Genesis. Think of how it was before the world was made. There was nothing, the Bible says. 'And the earth was without form, and void; and darkness was upon the face of the deep.' It was dark, and there was nothing. There were no mountains, no trees, no rocks, no rivers. There was nothing. But there was darkness all around, and in the darkness something happened. *Something happened!* There was a single sound. Far away in the darkness there was a single sound. Nothing made it, but it was there; and there was no one to hear it, but it was there. It was there, and there was nothing else. It rose up in the darkness, little and still, almost nothing in itself—like a single soft breath, like the wind arising; yes, like the whisper of the wind rising slowly and going out into the early morning. But there was no wind. There was only the sound, little and soft. It was almost nothing in itself, the smallest seed of sound—but it took hold of the darkness and there was light; it took hold of the stillness and there was motion forever; it took hold of the silence and there was sound. It was almost nothing in itself, a single sound, a word—a word broken off at the darkest center of the night and let go in the awful void, forever and forever. And it was almost nothing in itself. It scarcely was; but it was, and everything began."

Just then a remarkable thing happened. The Priest of the Sun seemed stricken; he let go of his audience and withdrew into himself, into some strange potential of himself. His voice, which had been low and resonant, suddenly became harsh and flat; his shoulders sagged and his stomach protruded, as if he had held his breath to the limit of endurance; for a moment there was a look of amazement, then utter careless-ness in his face. Conviction, caricature, callousness: the remainder of his sermon was a going back and forth among these.

"Thank you *so* much, Brother Cruz. Good evening, blood brothers and sisters, and welcome, welcome. Gracious me, I see lots of new faces out there tonight. *Gracious me!* May the Great Spirit—can we knock off that talking in the back there?—be with you always.

" 'In the beginning was the Word.' I have taken as my text this evening the almighty Word itself. Now get this: 'There was a man sent from God, whose name was John. The same came for a witness, to bear witness of the Light, that all men through him might believe.' Amen, brothers and sisters, *Amen.* And the riddle of the Word, 'In the beginning was the Word. . . .' Now what do you suppose old John *meant* by that? That cat was a preacher, and, well, you know how it is with preachers; he had something big on his mind. Oh my, it was big; it was the *Truth,* and it was heavy, and old John hurried to set it down. And in his hurry he said too much. 'In the beginning was the Word, and the Word was with God, and the Word was God.' It was the Truth, all right, but it was more than the Truth. The Truth was overgrown with fat, and the fat was God. The fat was *John's* God, and God stood between John and the Truth. Old John, see, he got up one morning and caught sight of the Truth. It must have been like a bolt of lightning, and the sight of it made him blind. And for a moment the vision burned on in back of his eyes, and he *knew* what it was. In that instant he saw something he had never seen before and would never see again. That was the instant of revelation, inspiration, Truth. And old John, he must have

[1] Latin: "In the beginning was the Word." (See John 1:1.)

fallen down on his knees. Man, he must have been shaking and laughing and crying and yelling and praying—all at the same time—and he must have been drunk and delirious with the Truth. You see, he had lived all his life waiting for that one moment, and it came, and it took him by surprise, and it was gone. And he said, 'In the beginning was the Word. . . .' And, man, right then and there he should have stopped. There was nothing more to say, but he went on. He had said all there was to say, everything, but he went on. 'In the beginning was the Word. . . .' Brothers and sisters, *that* was the Truth, the whole of it, the essential and eternal Truth, the bone and blood and muscle of the Truth. But he went on, old John, because he was a preacher. The perfect vision faded from his mind, and he went on. The instant passed, and then he had nothing but a memory. He was desperate and confused, and in his confusion he stumbled and went on. 'In the beginning was the Word, and the Word was with God, and the Word was God.' He went on to talk about Jews and Jerusalem, Levites and Pharisees, Moses and Philip and Andrew and Peter. Don't you see? Old John *had* to go on. That cat had a whole lot at stake. He couldn't let the Truth alone. He couldn't see that he had come to the end of the Truth, and he went on. He tried to make it bigger and better than it was, but instead he only demeaned and encumbered it. He made it soft and big with fat. He was a preacher, and he made a complex sentence of the Truth, two sentences, three, a paragraph. He made a sermon and theology of the Truth. He imposed his idea of God upon the everlasting Truth. 'In the beginning was the Word. . . .' And that is all there was, and it was enough.

"Now, brothers and sisters, old John was a white man, and the white man has his ways. Oh gracious me, he has his ways. He talks about the Word. He talks through it and around it. He builds upon it with syllables, with prefixes and suffixes and hyphens and accents. He adds and divides and multiplies the Word. And in all of this he subtracts the Truth. And, brothers and sisters, you have come here to live in the white man's world. Now the white man deals in words, and he deals easily, with grace and sleight of hand. And in his presence, here on his own ground, you are as children, mere babes in the woods. You must not mind, for in this you have a certain advantage. A child can listen and learn. The Word is sacred to a child.

"My grandmother was a storyteller; she knew her way around words. She never learned to read and write, but somehow she knew the good of reading and writing; she had learned how to listen and delight. She had learned that in words and in language, and there only, she could have whole and consummate being. She told me stories, and she taught me how to listen. I was a child and I listened. She could neither read nor write, you see, but she taught me how to live among her words, how to listen and delight. 'Storytelling; to utter and to hear . . .' And the simple act of listening is crucial to the concept of language, more crucial even than reading and writing, and language in turn is crucial to human society. There is proof of that, I think, in all the histories and prehistories of human experience. When that old Kiowa woman told me stories, I listened with only one ear. I was a child, and I took the words for granted. I did not know what all of them meant, but somehow I held on to them; I remembered them, and I remember them now. The stories were old and dear; they meant a great deal to my grandmother. It was not until she died that I knew how much they meant to her. I began to think about it, and then I knew. When she told me those old stories, something strange and good and powerful was going on. I was a child, and that old woman was asking me to come directly into the presence of her mind and spirit; she was taking hold of my imagination, giving me to share in the great fortune of her wonder and delight. She was asking me to go with her to the confrontation of something that was sacred and eternal. It was a timeless, *timeless* thing; nothing of her old age or of my childhood came between us.

"Children have a greater sense of the power and beauty of words than have the rest of us in general. And if that is so, it is because there occurs—or reoccurs—in the mind of every child something like a reflection of all human experience. I have heard that the human fetus corresponds in its development, stage by stage, to the scale of evolution. Surely it is no less reasonable to suppose that the waking mind of a child corresponds in the same way to the whole evolution of human thought and perception.

"In the white man's world, language, too—and the way in which the white man thinks of it—has undergone a process of change. The white man takes such things as words and literatures for granted, as indeed he must, for nothing in his world is so commonplace. On every side of him there are words by the millions, an unending succession of pamphlets and papers, letters and books, bills and bulletins, commentaries and conversations. He has diluted and multiplied the Word, and words have begun to close in upon him. He is sated and insensitive; his regard for language—for the Word itself—as an instrument of creation has diminished nearly to the point of no return. It may be that he will perish by the Word.

"But it was not always so with him, and it is not so with you. Consider for a moment that old Kiowa woman, my grandmother, whose use of language was confined to speech. And be assured that her regard for words was always keen in proportion as she depended upon them. You see, for her words were medicine; they were magic and invisible. They came from nothing into sound and meaning. They were beyond price; they could neither be bought nor sold. And she never threw words away.

"My grandmother used to tell me the story of Tai-me, of how Tai-me came to the Kiowas. The Kiowas were a sun dance culture, and Tai-me was their sun dance doll, their most sacred fetish; no medicine was ever more powerful. There is a story about the coming of Tai-me. This is what my grandmother told me:

Long ago there were bad times. The Kiowas were hungry and there was no food. There was a man who heard his children cry from hunger, and he began to search for food. He walked four days and became very weak. On the fourth day he came to a great canyon. Suddenly there was thunder and lightning. A Voice spoke to him and said, "Why are you following me? What do you want?" The man was afraid. The thing standing before him had the feet of a deer, and its body was covered with feathers. The man answered that the Kiowas were hungry. "Take me with you," the Voice said, "and I will give you whatever you want." From that day Tai-me has belonged to the Kiowas.

"Do you see? There, far off in the darkness, something happened. Do you see? Far, far away in the nothingness something happened. There was a voice, a sound, a word —and everything began. The story of the coming of Tai-me has existed for hundreds of years by word of mouth. It represents the oldest and best idea that man has of himself. It represents a very rich literature, which, because it was never written down, was always but one generation from extinction. But for the same reason it was cherished and revered. I could see that reverence in my grandmother's eyes, and I could hear it in her voice. It was that, I think, that old Saint John had in mind when he said, 'In the beginning was the Word. . . .' But he went on. He went on to lay a scheme about the Word. He could find no satisfaction in the simple fact that the Word was; he had to account for it, not in terms of that sudden and profound insight, which must have devastated him at once, but in terms of the moment afterward, which was irrelevant and remote; not in terms of his imagination, but only in terms of his prejudice.

"Say this: 'In the beginning was the Word. . . .' There was nothing. There was *nothing!* Darkness. There was darkness, and there was no end to it. You look up sometimes in the night and there are stars; you can see all the way to the stars. And you begin to know the universe, how awful and great it is. The stars lie out against the sky and do not fill it. A single star, flickering out in the universe, is enough to fill the mind, but it is nothing in the night sky. The darkness looms around it. The darkness flows among the stars, and beyond them forever. In the beginning that is how it was, but there were no stars. There was only the dark infinity in which nothing was. And something happened. At the distance of a star something happened, and everything began. The Word did not come into being, but *it was.* It did not break upon the silence, but *it was older than the silence and the silence was made of it.*

"Old John caught sight of something terrible. The thing standing before him said, 'Why are you following me? What do you want?' And from that day the Word has belonged to us, who have heard it for what it is, who have lived in fear and awe of it. In the Word was the beginning; *'In the beginning was the Word. . . .'* "

The Priest of the Sun appeared to have spent himself. He stepped back from the lectern and hung his head, smiling. In his mind the earth was spinning and the stars rattled around in the heavens. The sun shone, and the moon. Smiling in a kind of transport, the Priest of the Sun stood silent for a time while the congregation waited to be dismissed.

"Good night," he said, at last, "and get yours." . . .

from January 27

Tosamah, orator, physician, Priest of the Sun, son of Hummingbird, spoke:

"A single knoll rises out of the plain in Oklahoma, north and west of the Wichita range. For my people it is an old landmark, and they gave it the name Rainy Mountain. There, in the south of the continental trough, is the hardest weather in the world. In winter there are blizzards which come down the Williston corridor, bearing hail and sleet. Hot tornadic winds arise in the spring, and in summer the prairie is an anvil's edge. The grass turns brittle and brown, and it cracks beneath your feet. There are green belts along the rivers and creeks, linear groves of hickory and pecan, willow and witch hazel. At a distance in July or August the steaming foliage seems almost to writhe in fire. Great green and yellow grasshoppers are everywhere in the tall grass, popping up like corn to sting the flesh, and tortoises crawl about on the red earth, going nowhere in the plenty of time. Loneliness is there as an aspect of the land. All things in the plain are isolate; there is no confusion of objects in the eye, but one hill or one tree or one man. At the slightest elevation you can see to the end of the world. To look upon that landscape in the early morning, with the sun at your back, is to lose the sense of proportion. Your imagination comes to life, and this, you think, is where Creation was begun.

"I returned to Rainy Mountain in July. My grandmother had died in the spring, and I wanted to be at her grave. She had lived to be very old and at last infirm. Her only living daughter was with her when she died, and I was told that in death her face was that of a child.

"I like to think of her as a child. When she was born, the Kiowas were living the last great moment of their history. For more than a hundred years they had controlled the open range from the Smoky Hill River to the Red, from the headwaters of the Canadian to the fork of the Arkansas and Cimarron. In alliance with the Comanches, they had ruled the whole of the Southern Plains. War was their sacred business, and they were the finest horsemen the world has ever known. But warfare for the Kiowas was pre-eminently a matter of disposition rather than survival, and they never understood the grim, unrelenting advance of the U.S. Cavalry. When at last, divided and ill-provisioned, they were driven onto the Staked Plain in the cold of autumn, they fell into panic. In Palo Duro Canyon they abandoned their crucial stores to pillage and had nothing then but their lives. In order to save themselves, they surrendered to the soldiers at Fort Sill and were imprisoned in the old stone corral that now stands as a military museum. My grandmother was spared the humiliation of those high gray walls by eight or ten years, but she must have known from birth the affliction of defeat, the dark brooding of old warriors.

"Her name was Aho, and she belonged to the last culture to evolve in North America. Her forebears came down from the high north country nearly three centuries ago. The earliest evidence of their existence places them close to the source of the Yellowstone River in western Montana. They were a mountain people, a mysterious tribe of hunters whose language has never been classified in any major group. In the late seventeenth century they began a long migration to the south and east. It was a journey toward the dawn, and it led to a golden age. Along the way the Kiowas were befriended by the Crows, who gave them the culture and religion of the plains. They acquired horses, and their ancient nomadic spirit was suddenly free of the ground. They acquired Tai-me, the sacred sun dance doll, from that moment the chief object and symbol of their worship, and so shared in the divinity of the sun. Not least, they acquired the sense of destiny, therefore courage and pride. When they entered upon the Southern Plains, they had been transformed. No longer were they slaves to the simple necessity of survival; they were a lordly and dangerous society of fighters and thieves, hunters and priests of the sun. According to their origin myth, they entered the world through a hollow log. From one point of view, their migration was the fruit of an old prophecy, for indeed they emerged from a sunless world.

"I could see that. I followed their ancient way to my grandmother's grave. Though she lived out her long life in the shadow of Rainy Mountain, the immense landscape of the continental interior—all of its seasons and its sounds—lay like memory in her blood. She could tell of the Crows, whom she had never seen, and of the Black Hills, where she had never been. I wanted to see in reality what she had seen more perfectly in the mind's eye.

"I began my pilgrimage on the course of the Yellowstone. There, it seemed to me, was the top of the world, a region of deep lakes and dark timber, canyons and waterfalls. But, beautiful as it is, one might have the sense of confinement there. The skyline in all directions is close at hand, the high wall of the woods and deep cleavages of shade. There is a perfect freedom in the mountains, but it belongs to the eagle and the elk, the badger and the bear. The Kiowas reckoned their stature by the distance they could see, and they were bent and blind in the wilderness.

"Descending eastward, the highland meadows are a stairway to the plain. In July the inland slope of the Rockies is luxuriant with flax and buckwheat, stonecrop and larkspur. The earth unfolds and the limit of the land recedes. Clusters of trees, and animals grazing far in the distance, cause the vision to reach away and wonder to build upon the mind. The sun follows a longer course in the day, and the sky is immense beyond all comparison. The great billowing clouds that sail upon it are shadows that move upon the grass and grain like water, dividing light. Farther down, in the land of the Crows and the Blackfeet, the plain is yellow. Sweet clover takes hold of the hills and bends upon itself to cover and seal the soil. There the Kiowas paused on their way; they had come to the place where they must change their lives. The sun is at home on the plains. Precisely there does it have the certain character of a god. When the Kiowas came to the land of the Crows, they could see the dark lees of the hills at dawn across the Bighorn River, the profusion of light on the grain shelves, the oldest deity ranging after the solstices. Not yet would they veer south to the caldron of the land that lay below; they must wean their blood from the northern winter and hold the mountains a while longer in their view. They bore Tai-me in procession to the east.

"A dark mist lay over the Black Hills, and the land was like iron. At the top of a ridge I caught sight of Devils Tower—the uppermost extremity of it, like a file's end on the gray sky—and then it fell away behind the land. I was a long time then in coming upon it, and I did not see it again until I saw it whole, suddenly there across the valley, as if in the birth of time the core of the earth had broken through its crust and the motion of the world was begun. It stands in motion, like certain timeless trees that aspire too much into the sky, and imposes an illusion on the land. There are things in nature which engender an awful quiet in the heart of man; Devils Tower is one of them. Man must account for it. He must never fail to explain such a thing to himself, or else he is estranged forever from the universe. Two centuries ago, because they could not do otherwise, the Kiowas made a legend at the base of the rock. My grandmother said:

> Eight children were there at play, seven sisters and their brother. Suddenly the boy was struck dumb; he trembled and began to run upon his hands and feet. His fingers became claws, and his body was covered with fur. There was a bear where the boy had been. The sisters were terrified; they ran, and the bear after them. They came to the stump of a great tree, and the tree spoke to them. It bade them climb upon it, and as they did so it began to rise into the air. The bear came to kill them, but they were just beyond its reach. It reared against the tree and scored the bark all around with its claws. The seven sisters were borne into the sky, and they became the stars of the Big Dipper.

"From that moment, and so long as the legend lives, the Kiowas have kinsmen in the night sky. Whatever they were in the mountains, they could be no more. However tenuous their well-being, however much they had suffered and would suffer again, they had found a way out of the wilderness.

"The first man among them to stand on the edge of the Great Plains saw farther over land than he had ever seen before. There is something about the heart of the continent that resides always in the end of vision, some essence of the sun and wind. That man knew the possible quest. There was nothing to prevent his going out; he could enter upon the land and be alive, could bear at once the great hot weight of its silence. In a sense the question of survival had never been more imminent, for no land is more the measure of human strength. But neither had wonder been more accessible to the mind nor destiny to the will.

"My grandmother had a reverence for the sun, a certain holy regard which now is all but gone out of mankind. There was a wariness in her, and an ancient awe. She was a Christian in her later years, but she had come a long way about, and she never forgot her birthright. As a child, she had been to the sun dances; she had taken part in that annual rite, and by it she had learned the restoration of her people in the presence of Tai-me. She was about seven years old when the last Kiowa sun dance was held in 1887 on the Washita River above Rainy Mountain Creek. The buffalo were gone. In order to consummate the ancient sacrifice—to impale the head of a buffalo bull upon the Tai-me tree—a delegation of old men journeyed into Texas, there to beg and barter for an animal from the Goodnight herd. She was ten when the Kiowas came together for the last time as a living sun dance culture. They could find no buffalo; they had to hang an old hide from the sacred tree. That summer was known to my grandmother as Ä'poto Etóda̋-de K'ádó, Sun Dance When the Forked Poles Were Left Standing, and it is entered in the Kiowa calendars as the figure of a tree standing outside the unfinished framework of a medicine lodge. Before the dance could begin, a company of armed soldiers rode out from Fort Sill under orders to disperse the tribe. Forbidden without cause the essential act of their faith, having seen the wild herds slaughtered and left to rot upon the ground, the Kiowas backed away forever from the tree. That was July 20, 1890, at the great bend of the Washita. My grandmother was there. Without bitterness, and for as long as she lived, she bore a vision of deicide.

"Now that I can have her only in memory, I see my grandmother in the several postures that were peculiar to her: standing at the wood stove on a winter morning and turning meat in a great iron skillet; sitting at the south window, bent above her beadwork, and afterward, when her vision failed, looking down for a long time into the fold of her hands; going out upon a cane, very slowly as she did when the weight of age came upon her; praying. I remember her most often at prayer. She made long, rambling prayers out of suffering and hope, having seen many things. I was never sure that I had the right to hear, so exclusive were they of all mere custom and company. The last time I saw her, she prayed standing by the side of her bed at night, naked to the waist, the light of a kerosene lamp moving upon her dark skin. Her long black hair, always drawn and braided in the day, lay upon her shoulders and against her breasts like a shawl. I did not always understand her prayers; I believe they were made of an older language than that of ordinary speech. There was something inherently sad in the sound, some slight hesitation upon the syllables of sorrow. She began in a high and descending pitch, exhausting her breath to silence; then again and again —and always the same intensity of effort, of something that is, and is not, like urgency in the human voice. Transported so in the dim and dancing light among the shadows of her room, she seemed beyond the reach of time, as if age could not lay hold of her. But that was illusion; I think I knew then that I should not see her again. . . .

1966

Joan Didion
b. 1934

"We are well advised," Joan Didion admonishes, "to keep on nodding terms with the people we used to be, whether we find them attractive company or not. Otherwise, they turn up unannounced and surprise us, come hammering on the mind's door at 4 A.M. of a bad night and demand to know who deserted them, who betrayed them, who is going to make amends." The past is one of Didion's major concerns, perhaps her major concern. Much of her criticism of contemporary America centers on what she sees as the loss of firm familial, social, and religious bonds. Not surprisingly, she also claims "a very rigid sense of right and wrong." For her, confident judgments, which she ties to her own strong sense of the past, form the only real basis for "purposeful behavior on this earth."

Didion is that relative rarity, a fifth-generation Californian. She was born in Sacramento on December 5, 1934, to middle-class Episcopalians who gave her a lasting attachment to traditional family life and traditional values. In 1952 she graduated from McClatchy High School in Sacramento and, after a traumatic rejection from Stanford, entered the University of California at Berkeley, graduating in 1956. That year she also published her first short story, "Sunset," in the student literary magazine and won *Vogue*'s Prix de Paris contest. Given this auspicious start, she moved to New York, where she lived for eight years, writing articles and essays for *Vogue, Mademoiselle,* and the *National Review.* In 1963 she published her first novel, *Run River.* The next year she married the novelist and screenwriter John Gregory Dunne and six months later returned to California, where she has since continued to pursue a prolific and varied writing career. She has written two more novels—*Play It As It Lays* (1970) and *A Book of Common Prayer* (1977)—and, with Dunne, several screenplays. She is perhaps best known for her numerous essays, which have appeared in publications as diverse as *Harper's Bazaar, American Scholar, Esquire,* and *The New York Review of Books,* and have been published in two collections, *Slouching Towards Bethlehem* (1968) and *The White Album* (1979). Her most recent books are *Salvador* (1983), which is based on her 1982 travels in El Salvador, and *Democracy: A Novel* (1984).

Didion's essays range widely and frequently involve accounts of her own personal experiences. But even when they center on interviews with other people or discussions of abstract moral issues, they stress her own subjective reactions to people, places, events, and problems. "I admire objectivity very much," she says, "but I fail to see how it can be achieved if the reader does not understand the writer's particular bias." For writers "to pretend" that they have none "lends the entire venture a mendacity." In "Some Dreamers of the Golden Dream" Didion seeks not only to combine objectivity with a personal stance but also to blend, as Mailer does in his "nonfiction novel" *Armies of the Night,* fact with fiction. Lucille Marie Maxwell Miller is a real person, and the story told is her story. Didion's facts are accurate, and she makes splendid use of remembered detail. At the same time, her narrative becomes increasingly imaginative as she seeks to convey her own deep conviction that without a sense of the forbidden, life becomes shallow.

Irony is Didion's predominant tone. She frequently writes about people who have suffered losses they only partially understand—losses they reveal, she has remarked, only because as an interviewer she appears "so physically small, so temperamentally unobtrusive, and so neurotically inarticulate that people tend to forget that my presence runs counter to their best interests." Frequently bleak, her vision is at times apocalyptic. She describes southern California, the place about which she writes most tellingly, "in terms of fire, rattlesnakes, cave-ins, earthquakes," as Alfred Kazin has noted, and in terms, too, of "the terrible wind called the Santa Ana." In all of its forms, however, writing is for her an act of assertion, an "act of saying *I,* of imposing oneself upon other people, of saying *listen to me, see it my way, change your mind."*

Further Reading:
A. Kazin, "Joan Didion: Portrait of a Professional," *Harper's,* December 1971.
S. Davidson, "A Visit with Joan Didion," *New York Times Book Review,* April 3, 1977.
M. R. Winchell, *Joan Didion,* 1980.
K. Henderson, *Joan Didion,* 1981.

Text:
Slouching Towards Bethlehem, 1968.

Some Dreamers of the Golden Dream

This is a story about love and death in the golden land, and begins with the country. The San Bernardino Valley lies only an hour east of Los Angeles by the San Bernardino Freeway but is in certain ways an alien place: not the coastal California of the subtropical twilights and the soft westerlies off the Pacific but a harsher California, haunted by the Mojave just beyond the mountains, devastated by the hot dry Santa Ana wind that comes down through the passes at 100 miles an hour and whines through the eucalyptus windbreaks and works on the nerves. October is the bad month for the wind, the month when breathing is difficult and the hills blaze up spontaneously. There has been no rain since April. Every voice seems a scream. It is the season of suicide and divorce and prickly dread, wherever the wind blows.

The Mormons settled this ominous country, and then they abandoned it, but by the time they left the first orange tree had been planted and for the next hundred years the San Bernardino Valley would draw a kind of people who imagined they might live among the talismanic fruit and prosper in the dry air, people who brought with them Midwestern ways of building and cooking and praying and who tried to graft those ways upon the land. The graft took in curious ways. This is the California where it is possible to live and die without ever eating an artichoke, without ever meeting a Catholic or a Jew. This is the California where it is easy to Dial-A-Devotion, but hard to buy a book. This is the country in which a belief in the literal interpretation of Genesis has slipped imperceptibly into a belief in the literal interpretation of *Double Indemnity*,[1] the country of the teased hair and the Capris and the girls for whom all life's promise comes down to a waltz-length white wedding dress and the birth of a Kimberly or a Sherry or a Debbi and a Tijuana divorce and a return to hairdressers' school. "We were just crazy kids," they say without regret, and look to the future. The future always looks good in the golden land, because no one remembers the past. Here is where the hot wind blows and the old ways do not seem relevant, where the divorce rate is double the national average and where one person in every thirty-eight lives in a trailer. Here is the last stop for all those who come from somewhere else, for all those who drifted away from the cold and the past and the old ways. Here is where they are trying to find a new life style, trying to find it in the only places they know to look: the movies and the newspapers. The case of Lucille Marie Maxwell Miller is a tabloid monument to that new life style.

Imagine Banyan Street first, because Banyan is where it happened. The way to Banyan is to drive west from San Bernardino out Foothill Boulevard, Route 66: past the Santa Fe switching yards, the Forty Winks Motel. Past the motel that is nineteen stucco tepees: "SLEEP IN A WIGWAM—GET MORE FOR YOUR WAMPUM." Past Fontana Drag City and the Fontana Church of the Nazarene and the Pit Stop A Go-Go; past Kaiser Steel, through Cucamonga, out to the Kapu Kai Restaurant-Bar and Coffee Shop, at the corner of Route 66 and Carnelian Avenue. Up Carnelian Avenue from the Kapu Kai, which means "Forbidden Seas," the subdivision flags whip in the harsh wind. "HALF-ACRE RANCHES! SNACK BARS! TRAVERTINE ENTRIES! $95 DOWN." It is the trail of an intention gone haywire, the flotsam of the New California. But after a while the signs thin out on Carnelian Avenue, and the houses are no longer the bright pastels of the Springtime Home owners but the faded bungalows of the people who grow a few grapes and keep a few chickens out here, and then the hill gets steeper and the road climbs and even the bungalows are few, and here—desolate, roughly surfaced, lined with eucalyptus and lemon groves—is Banyan Street.

Like so much of this country, Banyan suggests something curious and unnatural. The lemon groves are sunken, down a three- or four-foot retaining wall, so that one looks directly into their dense foliage, too lush, unsettlingly glossy, the greenery of nightmare; the fallen eucalyptus bark is too dusty, a place for snakes to breed. The stones look not like natural stones but like the rubble of some unmentioned upheaval. There are smudge pots, and a closed cistern. To one side of Banyan there is the flat valley, and to the other the San Bernardino Mountains, a dark mass looming too high,

---

[1] 1944 U. S. film, directed by Billy Wilder and starring Edward G. Robinson, Fred MacMurray, and Barbara Stanwyck. The title refers to the double insurance benefit paid for accidents. In the film the victim's wife and her lover plan to pass off his murder as an accidental fall from a train.

too fast, nine, ten, eleven thousand feet, right there above the lemon groves. At midnight on Banyan Street there is no light at all, and no sound except the wind in the eucalyptus and a muffled barking of dogs. There may be a kennel somewhere, or the dogs may be coyotes.

Banyan Street was the route Lucille Miller took home from the twenty-four-hour Mayfair Market on the night of October 7, 1964, a night when the moon was dark and the wind was blowing and she was out of milk, and Banyan Street was where, at about 12:30 a.m., her 1964 Volkswagen came to a sudden stop, caught fire, and began to burn. For an hour and fifteen minutes Lucille Miller ran up and down Banyan calling for help, but no cars passed and no help came. At three o'clock that morning, when the fire had been put out and the California Highway Patrol officers were completing their report, Lucille Miller was still sobbing and incoherent, for her husband had been asleep in the Volkswagen. "What will I tell the children, when there's nothing left, nothing left in the casket," she cried to the friend called to comfort her. "How can I tell them there's nothing left?"

In fact there was something left, and a week later it lay in the Draper Mortuary Chapel in a closed bronze coffin blanketed with pink carnations. Some 200 mourners heard Elder Robert E. Denton of the Seventh-Day Adventist Church of Ontario speak of "the temper of fury that has broken out among us." For Gordon Miller, he said, there would be "no more death, no more heartaches, no more misunderstandings." Elder Ansel Bristol mentioned the "peculiar" grief of the hour. Elder Fred Jensen asked "what shall it profit a man, if he shall gain the whole world, and lose his own soul?" A light rain fell, a blessing in a dry season, and a female vocalist sang "Safe in the Arms of Jesus." A tape recording of the service was made for the widow, who was being held without bail in the San Bernardino County Jail on a charge of first-degree murder.

Of course she came from somewhere else, came off the prairie in search of something she had seen in a movie or heard on the radio, for this is a Southern California story. She was born on January 17, 1930, in Winnipeg, Manitoba, the only child of Gordon and Lily Maxwell, both schoolteachers and both dedicated to the Seventh-Day Adventist Church, whose members observe the Sabbath on Saturday, believe in an apocalyptic Second Coming, have a strong missionary tendency, and, if they are strict, do not smoke, drink, eat meat, use makeup, or wear jewelry, including wedding rings. By the time Lucille Maxwell enrolled at Walla Walla College in College Place, Washington, the Adventist school where her parents then taught, she was an eighteen-year-old possessed of unremarkable good looks and remarkable high spirits. "Lucille wanted to see the world," her father would say in retrospect, "and I guess she found out."

The high spirits did not seem to lend themselves to an extended course of study at Walla Walla College, and in the spring of 1949 Lucille Maxwell met and married Gordon ("Cork") Miller, a twenty-four-year-old graduate of Walla Walla and of the University of Oregon dental school, then stationed at Fort Lewis as a medical officer. "Maybe you could say it was love at first sight," Mr. Maxwell recalls. "Before they were ever formally introduced, he sent Lucille a dozen and a half roses with a card that said even if she didn't come out on a date with him, he hoped she'd find the roses pretty anyway." The Maxwells remember their daughter as a "radiant" bride.

Unhappy marriages so resemble one another that we do not need to know too much about the course of this one. There may or may not have been trouble on Guam, where Cork and Lucille Miller lived while he finished his Army duty. There may or may not have been problems in the small Oregon town where he first set up private practice. There appears to have been some disappointment about their move to California: Cork Miller had told friends that he wanted to become a doctor, that he was unhappy as a dentist and planned to enter the Seventh-Day Adventist College of Medical Evangelists at Loma Linda, a few miles south of San Bernardino. Instead he bought a dental practice in the west end of San Bernardino County, and the family settled there, in a modest house on the kind of street where there are always tricycles and revolving credit and dreams about bigger houses, better streets. That was 1957. By the summer of 1964 they had achieved the bigger house on the better street and the familiar accouterments of a family on its way up: the $30,000 a year, the three children for the Christmas card, the picture window, the family room, the newspaper photographs that showed "Mrs. Gordon Miller, Ontario Heart Fund Chairman. . . ." They were paying the familiar price for it. And they had reached the familiar season of divorce.

It might have been anyone's bad summer, anyone's siege of heat and nerves and migraine and money worries, but this one began particularly early and particularly badly. On April 24 an old friend, Elaine Hayton, died suddenly; Lucille Miller had seen her only the night before. During the month of May, Cork Miller was hospitalized briefly with a bleeding ulcer, and his usual reserve deepened into depression. He told his accountant that he was "sick of looking at open mouths," and threatened suicide. By July 8, the conventional tensions of love and money had reached the conventional impasse in the new house on the acre lot at 8488 Bella Vista, and Lucille Miller filed for divorce. Within a month, however, the Millers seemed reconciled. They saw a marriage counselor. They talked about a fourth child. It seemed that the marriage had reached the traditional truce, the point at which so many resign themselves to cutting both their losses and their hopes.

But the Millers' season of trouble was not to end that easily. October 7 began as a commonplace enough day, one of those days that sets the teeth on edge with its tedium, its small frustrations. The temperature reached 102° in San Bernardino that afternoon, and the Miller children were home from school because of Teachers' Institute. There was ironing to be dropped off. There was a trip to pick up a prescription for Nembutal, a trip to a self-service dry cleaner. In the early evening, an unpleasant accident with the Volkswagen: Cork Miller hit and killed a German shepherd, and afterward said that his head felt "like it had a Mack truck on it." It was something he often said. As of that evening Cork Miller was $63,479 in debt, including the $29,637 mortgage on the new house, a debt load which seemed oppressive to him. He was a man who wore his responsibilities uneasily, and complained of migraine headaches almost constantly.

He ate alone that night, from a TV tray in the living room. Later the Millers watched John Forsythe and Senta Berger in *See How They Run,* and when the movie ended, about eleven, Cork Miller suggested that they go out for milk. He wanted some hot chocolate. He took a blanket and pillow from the couch and climbed into the passenger seat of the Volkswagen. Lucille Miller remembers reaching over to lock his door as she backed down the driveway. By the time she left the Mayfair Market, and long before they reached Banyan Street, Cork Miller appeared to be asleep.

There is some confusion in Lucille Miller's mind about what happened between 12:30 a.m., when the fire broke out, and 1:50 a.m., when it was reported. She says that she was driving east on Banyan Street at about 35 m.p.h. when she felt the Volkswagen pull sharply to the right. The next thing she knew the car was on the embankment, quite near the edge of the retaining wall, and flames were shooting up behind her. She does not remember jumping out. She does remember prying up a stone with which she broke the window next to her husband, and then scrambling down the retaining wall to try to find a stick. "I don't know how I was going to push him out," she says. "I just thought if I had a stick, I'd push him out." She could not, and after a while she ran to the intersection of Banyan and Carnelian Avenue. There are no houses at that corner, and almost no traffic. After one car had passed without stopping, Lucille Miller ran back down Banyan toward the burning Volkswagen. She did not stop, but she slowed down, and in the flames she could see her husband. He was, she said, "just black."

At the first house up Sapphire Avenue, half a mile from the Volkswagen, Lucille Miller finally found help. There Mrs. Robert Swenson called the sheriff, and then, at Lucille Miller's request, she called Harold Lance, the Millers' lawyer and their close friend. When Harold Lance arrived he took Lucille Miller home to his wife, Joan. Twice Harold Lance and Lucille Miller returned to Banyan Street and talked to the Highway Patrol officers. A third time Harold Lance returned alone, and when he came back he said to Lucille Miller, "O.K. . . . . you don't talk any more."

When Lucille Miller was arrested the next afternoon, Sandy Slagle was with her. Sandy Slagle was the intense, relentlessly loyal medical student who used to baby-sit for the Millers, and had been living as a member of the family since she graduated from high school in 1959. The Millers took her away from a difficult home situation, and she thinks of Lucille Miller not only as "more or less a mother or a sister" but as "the most wonderful character" she has ever known. On the night of the accident, Sandy Slagle was in her dormitory at Loma Linda University, but Lucille Miller called her early in the morning and asked her to come home. The doctor was there when Sandy Slagle arrived, giving Lucille Miller an injection of Nembutal. "She was crying as she was going under," Sandy Slagle recalls. "Over and over she'd say, 'Sandy, all the hours I spent trying to save him and now what are they trying to *do* to me?' "

At 1:30 that afternoon, Sergeant William Paterson and Detectives Charles Callahan and Joseph Karr of the Central Homicide Division arrived at 8488 Bella Vista. "One of them appeared at the bedroom door," Sandy Slagle remembers, "and said to Lucille, 'You've got ten minutes to get dressed or we'll take you as you are.' She was in her nightgown, you know, so I tried to get her dressed."

Sandy Slagle tells the story now as if by rote, and her eyes do not waver. "So I had her panties and bra on her and they opened the door again, so I got some Capris on her, you know, and a scarf." Her voice drops. "And then they just took her."

The arrest took place just twelve hours after the first report that there had been an accident on Banyan Street, a rapidity which would later prompt Lucille Miller's attorney to say that the entire case was an instance of trying to justify a reckless arrest. Actually what first caused the detectives who arrived on Banyan Street toward dawn that morning to give the accident more than routine attention were certain apparent physical inconsistencies. While Lucille Miller had said that she was driving about 35 m.p.h. when the car swerved to a stop, an examination of the cooling Volkswagen showed that it was in low gear, and that the parking rather than the driving lights were on. The front wheels, moreover, did not seem to be in exactly the position that Lucille Miller's description of the accident would suggest, and the right rear wheel was dug in deep, as if it had been spun in place. It seemed curious to the detectives, too, that a sudden stop from 35 m.p.h.—the same jolt which was presumed to have knocked over a gasoline can in the back seat and somehow started the fire—should have left two milk cartons upright on the back floorboard, and the remains of a Polaroid camera box lying apparently undisturbed on the back seat.

No one, however, could be expected to give a precise account of what did and did not happen in a moment of terror, and none of these inconsistencies seemed in themselves incontrovertible evidence of criminal intent. But they did interest the Sheriff's Office, as did Gordon Miller's apparent unconsciousness at the time of the accident, and the length of time it had taken Lucille Miller to get help. Something, moreover, struck the investigators as wrong about Harold Lance's attitude when he came back to Banyan Street the third time and found the investigation by no means over. "The way Lance was acting," the prosecuting attorney said later, "they thought maybe they'd hit a nerve."

And so it was that on the morning of October 8, even before the doctor had come to give Lucille Miller an injection to calm her, the San Bernardino County Sheriff's Office was trying to construct another version of what might have happened between 12:30 and 1:50 a.m. The hypothesis they would eventually present was based on the somewhat tortuous premise that Lucille Miller had undertaken a plan which failed: a plan to stop the car on the lonely road, spread gasoline over her presumably drugged husband, and, with a stick on the accelerator, gently "walk" the Volkswagen over the embankment, where it would tumble four feet down the retaining wall into the lemon grove and almost certainly explode. If this happened, Lucille Miller might then have somehow negotiated the two miles up Carnelian to Bella Vista in time to be home when the accident was discovered. This plan went awry, according to the Sheriff's Office hypothesis, when the car would not go over the rise of the embankment. Lucille Miller might have panicked then—after she had killed the engine the third or fourth time, say, out there on the dark road with the gasoline already spread and the dogs baying and the wind blowing and the unspeakable apprehension that a pair of headlights would suddenly light up Banyan Street and expose her there—and set the fire herself.

Although this version accounted for some of the physical evidence—the car in low because it had been started from a dead stop, the parking lights on because she could not do what needed doing without some light, a rear wheel spun in repeated attempts to get the car over the embankment, the milk cartons upright because there had been no sudden stop—it did not seem on its own any more or less credible than Lucille Miller's own story. Moreover, some of the physical evidence did seem to support her story: a nail in a front tire, a nine-pound rock found in the car, presumably the one with which she had broken the window in an attempt to save her husband. Within a few days an autopsy had established that Gordon Miller was alive when he burned, which did not particularly help the State's case, and that he had enough Nembutal and Sandoptal in his blood to put the average person to sleep, which did: on the other hand Gordon Miller habitually took both Nembutal and Fiorinal (a common headache prescription which contains Sandoptal), and had been ill besides.

It was a spotty case, and to make it work at all the State was going to have to find a motive. There was talk of unhappiness, talk of another man. That kind of motive, during the next few weeks, was what they set out to establish. They set out to find it in accountants' ledgers and double-indemnity clauses and motel registers, set out to determine what might move a woman who believed in all the promises of the middle class—a woman who had been chairman of the Heart Fund and who always knew a reasonable little dressmaker and who had come out of the bleak wild of prairie fundamentalism to find what she imagined to be the good life—what should drive such a woman to sit on a street called Bella Vista and look out her new picture window into the empty California sun and calculate how to burn her husband alive in a Volkswagen. They found the wedge they wanted closer at hand than they might have at first expected, for, as testimony would reveal later at the trial, it seemed that in December of 1963 Lucille Miller had begun an affair with the husband of one of her friends, a man whose daughter called her "Auntie Lucille," a man who might have seemed to have the gift for people and money and the good life that Cork Miller so noticeably lacked. The man was Arthwell Hayton, a well-known San Bernardino attorney and at one time a member of the district attorney's staff.

In some ways it was the conventional clandestine affair in a place like San Bernardino, a place where little is bright or graceful, where it is routine to misplace the future and easy to start looking for it in bed. Over the seven weeks that it would take to try Lucille Miller for murder, Assistant District Attorney Don A. Turner and defense attorney Edward P. Foley would between them unfold a curiously predictable story. There were the falsified motel registrations. There were the lunch dates, the afternoon drives in Arthwell Hayton's red Cadillac convertible. There were the interminable discussions of the wronged partners. There were the confidantes ("I knew everything," Sandy Slagle would insist fiercely later. "I knew every time, places, everything") and there were the words remembered from bad magazine stories ("Don't kiss me, it will trigger things," Lucille Miller remembered telling Arthwell Hayton in the parking lot of Harold's Club in Fontana after lunch one day) and there were the notes, the sweet exchanges: "Hi Sweetie Pie! You are my cup of tea!! Happy Birthday—you don't look a day over 29!! Your baby, Arthwell."

And, toward the end, there was the acrimony. It was April 24, 1964, when Arthwell Hayton's wife, Elaine, died suddenly, and nothing good happened after that. Arthwell Hayton had taken his cruiser, *Captain's Lady,* over to Catalina that weekend; he called home at nine o'clock Friday night, but did not talk to his wife because Lucille Miller answered the telephone and said that Elaine was showering. The next morning the Haytons' daughter found her mother in bed, dead. The newspapers reported the death as accidental, perhaps the result of an allergy to hair spray. When Arthwell Hayton flew home from Catalina that weekend, Lucille Miller met him at the airport, but the finish had already been written.

It was in the breakup that the affair ceased to be in the conventional mode and began to resemble instead the novels of James M. Cain, the movies of the late 1930's, all the dreams in which violence and threats and blackmail are made to seem commonplaces of middle-class life. What was most startling about the case that the State of California was preparing against Lucille Miller was something that had nothing to do with law at all, something that never appeared in the eight-column afternoon headlines but was always there between them: the revelation that the dream was teaching the dreamers how to live. Here is Lucille Miller talking to her lover sometime in the early summer of 1964, after he had indicated that, on the advice of his minister, he did not intend to see her any more: "First, I'm going to go to that dear pastor of yours and tell him a few things. . . . When I do tell him that, you won't be in the Redlands Church any more. . . . Look, Sonny Boy, if you think your reputation is going to be ruined, your life won't be worth two cents." Here is Arthwell Hayton, to Lucille Miller: "I'll go to Sheriff Frank Bland and tell him some things that I know about you until you'll wish you'd never heard of Arthwell Hayton." For an affair between a Seventh-Day Adventist dentist's wife and a Seventh-Day Adventist personal-injury lawyer, it seems a curious kind of dialogue.

"Boy, I could get that little boy coming and going," Lucille Miller later confided to Erwin Sprengle, a Riverside contractor who was a business partner of Arthwell Hayton's and a friend to both the lovers. (Friend or no, on this occasion he happened to have an induction coil attached to his telephone in order to tape Lucille Miller's call.) "And he hasn't got one thing on me that he can prove. I mean, I've got concrete —he has nothing concrete." In the same taped conversation with Erwin Sprengle, Lucille Miller mentioned a tape that she herself had surreptitiously made, months before, in Arthwell Hayton's car.

"I said to him, I said 'Arthwell, I just feel like I'm being used.' . . . He started sucking his thumb and he said 'I love you. . . . This isn't something that happened yesterday. I'd marry you tomorrow if I could. I don't love Elaine.' He'd love to hear that played back, wouldn't he?"

"Yeah," drawled Sprengle's voice on the tape. "That would be just a little incriminating, wouldn't it?"

"Just a *little* incriminating," Lucille Miller agreed. "It really *is*."

Later on the tape, Sprengle asked where Cork Miller was.

"He took the children down to the church."

"You didn't go?"

"No."

"You're naughty."

It was all, moreover, in the name of "love"; everyone involved placed a magical faith in the efficacy of the very word. There was the significance that Lucille Miller saw in Arthwell's saying that he "loved" her, that he did not "love" Elaine. There was Arthwell insisting, later, at the trial, that he had never said it, that he may have "whispered sweet nothings in her ear" (as her defense hinted that he had whispered in many ears), but he did not remember bestowing upon her the special seal, saying the word, declaring "love." There was the summer evening when Lucille Miller and

Sandy Slagle followed Arthwell Hayton down to his new boat in its mooring at Newport Beach and untied the lines with Arthwell aboard, Arthwell and a girl with whom he later testified he was drinking hot chocolate and watching television. "I did that on purpose," Lucille Miller told Erwin Sprengle later, "to save myself from letting my heart do something crazy."

January 11, 1965, was a bright warm day in Southern California, the kind of day when Catalina floats on the Pacific horizon and the air smells of orange blossoms and it is a long way from the bleak and difficult East, a long way from the cold, a long way from the past. A woman in Hollywood staged an all-night sit-in on the hood of her car to prevent repossession by a finance company. A seventy-year-old pensioner drove his station wagon at five miles an hour past three Gardena poker parlors and emptied three pistols and a twelve-gauge shotgun through their windows, wounding twenty-nine people. "Many young women become prostitutes just to have enough money to play cards," he explained in a note. Mrs. Nick Adams said that she was "not surprised" to hear her husband announce his divorce plans on the Les Crane Show, and, farther north, a sixteen-year-old jumped off the Golden Gate Bridge and lived.

And, in the San Bernardino County Courthouse, the Miller trial opened. The crowds were so bad that the glass courtroom doors were shattered in the crush, and from then on identification disks were issued to the first forty-three spectators in line. The line began forming at 6 a.m., and college girls camped at the courthouse all night, with stores of graham crackers and No-Cal.

All they were doing was picking a jury, those first few days, but the sensational nature of the case had already suggested itself. Early in December there had been an abortive first trial, a trial at which no evidence was ever presented because on the day the jury was seated the San Bernardino *Sun-Telegram* ran an "inside" story quoting Assistant District Attorney Don Turner, the prosecutor, as saying, "We are looking into the circumstances of Mrs. Hayton's death. In view of the current trial concerning the death of Dr. Miller, I do not feel I should comment on Mrs. Hayton's death." It seemed that there had been barbiturates in Elaine Hayton's blood, and there had seemed some irregularity about the way she was dressed on that morning when she was found under the covers, dead. Any doubts about the death at the time, however, had never gotten as far as the Sheriff's Office. "I guess somebody didn't want to rock the boat," Turner said later. "These were prominent people."

Although all of that had not been in the *Sun-Telegram*'s story, an immediate mistrial had been declared. Almost as immediately, there had been another development: Arthwell Hayton had asked newspapermen to an 11 a.m. Sunday morning press conference in his office. There had been television cameras, and flash bulbs popping. "As you gentlemen may know," Hayton had said, striking a note of stiff bonhomie, "there are very often women who become amorous toward their doctor or lawyer. This does not mean on the physician's or lawyer's part that there is any romance toward the patient or client."

"Would you deny that you were having an affair with Mrs. Miller?" a reporter had asked.

"I would deny that there was any romance on my part whatsoever."

It was a distinction he would maintain through all the wearing weeks to come.

So they had come to see Arthwell, these crowds who now milled beneath the dusty palms outside the courthouse, and they had also come to see Lucille, who appeared as a slight, intermittently pretty woman, already pale from lack of sun, a woman who would turn thirty-five before the trial was over and whose tendency toward haggardness was beginning to show, a meticulous woman who insisted, against her lawyer's advice, on coming to court with her hair piled high and lacquered. "I would've been happy if she'd come in with it hanging loose, but Lucille wouldn't do that," her lawyer said. He was Edward P. Foley, a small, emotional Irish Catholic who several times wept in the courtroom. "She has a great honesty, this woman," he added, "but this honesty about her appearance always worked against her."

By the time the trial opened, Lucille Miller's appearance included maternity clothes, for an official examination on December 18 had revealed that she was then three and a half months pregnant, a fact which made picking a jury even more difficult than usual, for Turner was asking the death penalty. "It's unfortunate but there it is," he would say of the pregnancy to each juror in turn, and finally twelve were seated, seven of them women, the youngest forty-one, an assembly of the very peers— housewives, a machinist, a truck driver, a grocery-store manager, a filing clerk—above whom Lucille Miller had wanted so badly to rise.

That was the sin, more than the adultery, which tended to reinforce the one for which she was being tried. It was implicit in both the defense and the prosecution that Lucille Miller was an erring woman, a woman who perhaps wanted too much. But to the prosecution she was not merely a woman who would want a new house and want to go to parties and run up high telephone bills ($1,152 in ten months), but a woman who would go so far as to murder her husband for his $80,000 in insurance, making it appear an accident in order to collect another $40,000 in double indemnity and straight accident policies. To Turner she was a woman who did not want simply her freedom and a reasonable alimony (she could have had that, the defense contended, by going through with her divorce suit), but wanted everything, a woman motivated by "love and greed." She was a "manipulator." She was a "user of people."

To Edward Foley, on the other hand, she was an impulsive woman who "couldn't control her foolish little heart." Where Turner skirted the pregnancy, Foley dwelt upon it, even calling the dead man's mother down from Washington to testify that her son had told her they were going to have another baby because Lucille felt that it would "do much to weld our home again in the pleasant relations that we used to have." Where the prosecution saw a "calculator," the defense saw a "blabber-mouth," and in fact Lucille Miller did emerge as an ingenuous conversationalist. Just as, before her husband's death, she had confided in her friends about her love affair, so she chatted about it after his death, with the arresting sergeant. "Of course Cork lived with it for years, you know," her voice was heard to tell Sergeant Paterson on a tape made the morning after her arrest. "After Elaine died, he pushed the panic button one night and just asked me right out, and that, I think, was when he really —the first time he really faced it." When the sergeant asked why she had agreed to talk to him, against the specific instructions of her lawyers, Lucille Miller said airily, "Oh, I've always been basically quite an honest person. . . . I mean I can put a hat in the cupboard and say it cost ten dollars less, but basically I've always kind of just lived my life the way I wanted to, and if you don't like it you can take off."

The prosecution hinted at men other than Arthwell, and even, over Foley's objections, managed to name one. The defense called Miller suicidal. The prosecution produced experts who said that the Volkswagen fire could not have been accidental. Foley produced witnesses who said that it could have been. Lucille's father, now a junior-high-school teacher in Oregon, quoted Isaiah to reporters: *"Every tongue that shall rise against thee in judgment thou shalt condemn."* "Lucille did wrong, her affair," her mother said judiciously. "With her it was love. But with some I guess it's just passion." There was Debbie, the Millers' fourteen-year-old, testifying in a steady voice about how she and her mother had gone to a supermarket to buy the gasoline can the week before the accident. There was Sandy Slagle, in the courtroom every day, declaring that on at least one occasion Lucille Miller had prevented her husband not only from committing suicide but from committing suicide in such a way that it would appear an accident and ensure the double-indemnity payment. There was Wenche Berg, the pretty twenty-seven-year-old Norwegian governess to Arthwell Hayton's children, testifying that Arthwell had instructed her not to allow Lucille Miller to see or talk to the children.

Two months dragged by, and the headlines never stopped. Southern California's crime reporters were headquartered in San Bernardino for the duration: Howard Hertel from the *Times*, Jim Bennett and Eddy Jo Bernal from the *Herald-Examiner*. Two months in which the Miller trial was pushed off the *Examiner*'s front page only by the Academy Award nominations and Stan Laurel's death. And finally, on March 2, after Turner had reiterated that it was a case of "love and greed," and Foley had protested that his client was being tried for adultery, the case went to the jury.

They brought in the verdict, guilty of murder in the first degree, at 4:50 p.m. on March 5. "She didn't do it," Debbie Miller cried, jumping up from the spectators' section. "She didn't *do* it." Sandy Slagle collapsed in her seat and began to scream. "Sandy, for God's sake please *don't*," Lucille Miller said in a voice that carried across the courtroom, and Sandy Slagle was momentarily subdued. But as the jurors left the courtroom she screamed again: "You're murderers. . . . Every last one of you is a *murderer*." Sheriff's deputies moved in then, each wearing a string tie that read "1965 SHERIFF'S RODEO," and Lucille Miller's father, that sad-faced junior-high-school teacher who believed in the word of Christ and the dangers of wanting to see the world, blew her a kiss off his fingertips.

The California Institution for Women at Frontera, where Lucille Miller is now, lies down where Euclid Avenue turns into country road, not too many miles from where she once lived and shopped and organized the Heart Fund Ball. Cattle graze across the road, and Rainbirds sprinkle the alfalfa. Frontera has a softball field and tennis courts, and looks as if it might be a California junior college, except that the trees are not yet high enough to conceal the concertina wire around the top of the Cyclone fence. On visitors' day there are big cars in the parking area, big Buicks and Pontiacs that belong to grandparents and sisters and fathers (not many of them belong to husbands), and some of them have bumper stickers that say "SUPPORT YOUR LOCAL POLICE."

A lot of California murderesses live here, a lot of girls who somehow misunderstood the promise. Don Turner put Sandra Garner here (and her husband in the gas chamber at San Quentin) after the 1959 desert killings known to crime reporters as "the soda-pop murders." Carole Tregoff is here, and has been ever since she was convicted of conspiring to murder Dr. Finch's wife in West Covina, which is not too far from San Bernardino. Carole Tregoff is in fact a nurse's aide in the prison hospital, and might have attended Lucille Miller had her baby been born at Frontera; Lucille Miller chose instead to have it outside, and paid for the guard who stood outside the delivery room in St. Bernardine's Hospital. Debbie Miller came to take the baby home from the hospital, in a white dress with pink ribbons, and Debbie was allowed to choose a name. She named the baby Kimi Kai. The children live with Harold and Joan Lance now, because Lucille Miller will probably spend ten years at Frontera. Don Turner waived his original request for the death penalty (it was generally agreed that he had demanded it only, in Edward Foley's words, "to get anybody with the slightest trace of human kindness in their veins off the jury"), and settled for life imprisonment with the possibility of parole. Lucille Miller does not like it at Frontera, and has had trouble adjusting. "She's going to have to learn humility," Turner says. "She's going to have to use her ability to charm, to manipulate."

The new house is empty now, the house on the street with the sign that says

PRIVATE ROAD

BELLA VISTA

DEAD END

The Millers never did get it landscaped, and weeds grow up around the fieldstone siding. The television aerial has toppled on the roof, and a trash can is stuffed with the debris of family life: a cheap suitcase, a child's game called "Lie Detector." There is a sign on what would have been the lawn, and the sign reads "ESTATE SALE." Edward Foley is trying to get Lucille Miller's case appealed, but there have been delays. "A trial always comes down to a matter of sympathy," Foley says wearily now. "I couldn't create sympathy for her." Everyone is a little weary now, weary and resigned, everyone except Sandy Slagle, whose bitterness is still raw. She lives in an apartment near the medical school in Loma Linda, and studies reports of the case in *True Police Cases* and *Official Detective Stories.* "I'd much rather we not talk about the Hayton business too much," she tells visitors, and she keeps a tape recorder running. "I'd rather talk about Lucille and what a wonderful person she is and how her rights were violated." Harold Lance does not talk to visitors at all. "We don't want to give away what we can sell," he explains pleasantly; an attempt was made to sell Lucille Miller's personal story to *Life,* but *Life* did not want to buy it. In the district attorney's offices they are prosecuting other murders now, and do not see why the Miller trial attracted so much attention. "It wasn't a very interesting murder as murders go," Don Turner says laconically. Elaine Hayton's death is no longer under investigation. "We know everything we want to know," Turner says.

Arthwell Hayton's office is directly below Edward Foley's. Some people around San Bernardino say that Arthwell Hayton suffered; others say that he did not suffer at all. Perhaps he did not, for time past is not believed to have any bearing upon time present or future, out in the golden land where every day the world is born anew.

In any case, on October 17, 1965, Arthwell Hayton married again, married his children's pretty governess, Wenche Berg, at a service in the Chapel of the Roses at a retirement village near Riverside. Later the newlyweds were feted at a reception for seventy-five in the dining room of Rose Garden Village. The bridegroom was in black tie, with a white carnation in his buttonhole. The bride wore a long white *peau de soie*[2] dress and carried a shower bouquet of sweetheart roses with stephanotis streamers. A coronet of seed pearls held her illusion veil.

1966

Larry McMurtry
b. 1936

Larry McMurtry was born in Wichita Falls, Texas, on June 3, 1936, and grew up near there, in the short-grass ranching country of north central Texas. Following his graduation from high school in Archer City, Texas, McMurtry did undergraduate work at North Texas State University, where he read widely in literature and philosophy and published fiction, essays, and poetry in the school's literary magazine. After receiving an M.A. in English from Rice University in 1960, he attended Stanford University on a Wallace Stegner fellowship. In 1961 he published his first book, *Horseman, Pass By,* a novel about the vanishing of old-time cattle ranching under modern commercial pressures, adapted for the screen under the title *Hud.* Two years later he published a second novel, *Leaving Cheyenne,* the story of the friendship of a freewheeling cowboy, a more achievement-conscious rancher, and a remarkable woman. Besides numerous book reviews, McMurtry has since published a collection of essays, *In a Narrow Grave: Essays on Texas* (1968), and a long essay on rodeo, *It's Always We Rambled* (1974).

With his gift for storytelling and his keen attention to the voices of his characters and the physical details of a particular region, it is not surprising that several of McMurtry's novels have been made into successful motion pictures. One of these, *The Last Picture Show* (1966), is the story of a boy's coming of age in a small Texas town during the 1950s. In *Moving On* (1970), the first novel of an "urban" trilogy, McMurtry portrays through the lives of a young educated Texas couple the increasing disconnectedness of people with their regional culture. He continued that theme on a more tragic note in *All My Friends Are Going to Be Strangers* (1972), the story of a restless, self-destructive young writer. The last of the trilogy, *Terms of Endearment* (1975)—which was also made into an award-winning film—deals with the relationship between an eccentric East

---

[2] French: "skin of silk"; a soft, rich silk cloth with a dull satiny finish.

Coast widow who has moved to Houston and her unhappily married, terminally ill daughter. McMurtry's more recent novels are *Somebody's Darling* (1978), *Cadillac Jack* (1982), *The Desert Rose* (1983), and *Lonesome Dove* (1985), winner of the Pulitzer Prize.

Set in the late nineteenth century, *Lonesome Dove* is the story of a cattle drive, organized and led by two former Texas Rangers, that stretches from deep South Texas to the Montana highlands. The novel's epigraph is from *Shoot Out the Land*, by T. K. Whipple:

> All America lies at the end of the wilderness road, and our past is not a dead past, but still lives in us. Our forefathers had civilization inside themselves, the wild outside. We live in the civilization they created, but within us the wilderness still lingers. What they dreamed, we live, and what they lived, we dream.

The son and grandson of ranchers, McMurtry grew up listening to stories about Texas's brief past, "stories about an earlier, purer, a more golden and more legendary Texas that I had been born too late to see." This experience left him with the problem of discovering whether "the Texas I have lived in and in some sense known was as legitimate and as worthy of attention as the Texas that existed before my time." But it also gave him a theme. Much of his fiction, and all of his early fiction, begins with a sense of loss, of things passing, as his elegiac titles clearly suggest: loss not only of the land and of the way of life that the land in one sense made possible and in another imposed but also loss of innocence and youth, loss of love, loss even of life itself. Many of his characters discover that the world around them is poised between an era that is gone and one that has not yet fully emerged, only then to discover that in their own lives they are caught between a moment that no longer exists for them and one that is not yet fully present. It is the movement from the range to the sidewalks, or from the sidewalks of the town to those of the city, "that gives life in present-day Texas its passion," McMurtry writes in the introduction to *In a Narrow Grave*—" or if not its passion, its strong, peculiar mixture of passions, part spurious and part genuine, part ridiculous and part tragic." To the rendering of those passions McMurtry brings a vision that is wry and satiric as well as tender and elegiac, and a prose that is supple and even stringent. He is currently working on a sequel to *The Last Picture Show*, to be published in 1987.

Further Reading
W. T. Pilkington, "The Recent Southwestern Novel," *Southwestern American Literature,* January 1971.
C. D. Peavy, *Larry McMurtry,* 1977.

Text:
The Last Picture Show, 1966.

from The Last Picture Show

Chapter VIII: [To Paducah and Back]

The first basketball game of the season was with Paducah, a town well over a hundred miles from Thalia. It was the longest trip of the year and usually the wildest: in Paducah they played basketball as if it were indoor football, and they had everything in their favor, including a gym so small that the out-of-bounds lines were painted on the walls. The Paducah boys were used to the gym and could run up the walls like lizards, but visiting teams, accustomed to normal-sized courts, had a hard time. Every year two or three Thalia players smashed into the walls and knocked themselves out.

This time it happened to Sonny, and in the very first minutes of play. Leroy Malone managed to trip the gangly Paducah center and while the center was sprawled on the floor Sonny ran right along his back, in pursuit of the ball. Just as he was about to grab it somebody tripped *him* and he hit the wall head first. The next thing he knew he was stretched out beside the bench and one of the freshmen players was squeezing a wet washrag on his forehead. Sonny tried to keep his eyes closed as long as he could —he knew Coach Popper would send him back into the game as soon as he regained consciousness. He feigned deep coma for about five minutes, but unfortunately the coach was experienced in such matters. He came over and lifted one of Sonny's eyelids and saw that he was awake.

"Possuming," he said. "I thought so. Get up and get your butt back in there. We're forty points behind and it ain't but the second quarter."

"I think I got a concussion," Sonny said, trying to look dangerously ill. "Maybe I ought to stay out a little while."

"Get up," the coach insisted. "We just quit football practice ten days ago, you ain't had time to get that out of shape. If you want to rest, by God go in there and foul out first. Knock the shit out of that forward two or three times—he's the one doin' all the scorin'. Hell, we come all this way, let's make a showing."

Sonny reluctantly got up and went back in. He managed three fouls before the half, but he was too weak to hit anybody very hard and none of the fouls was really satisfactory. The half-time score was Paducah 62 and Thalia 9. During the half the coach called them over for one of his little pep talks, this one very brief.

"You ten boys have got the shortest little peckers of any bunch of kids I've ever coached," he said sincerely. "By God, if you don't stomp some asses this next half I'll stomp a few tomorrow afternoon when we start practicing."

He scowled fiercely and strolled off to the concession stand to have some coffee.

In the second half things began to look really ominous. Sonny felt strangely light headed and went out on the floor not much caring what he did. Paducah defense had become virtually impenetrable: for one thing, they had started openly tackling which-ever Thalia player had the ball. It seemed to Sonny that at last the time had come to shoot peg shots—there was not much chance of moving the ball down the court any other way. Whenever they tried, Paducah tackled them, tripped them, threw body blocks into them, or had the referee call fouls on them.

Actually, the refereeing was another very bad aspect of basketball in Paducah.

Unusual as it was, Paducah had a male home economics teacher, a frail little man named Mr. Wean. The school board felt that teaching home ec was really too light a job for a man so they made Mr. Wean basketball referee. He had never managed to learn much about the game, but he was quite docile and called whatever the Paducah team told him to call. Also, he was in bad shape and couldn't possibly run up and down the court for forty-eight minutes. Instead of following the ball, he just stood on the center line and made all his calls from there.

After considering the matter for half a quarter or so Sonny concluded that peg shots were the only feasible tactic. He was simply too weak to dodge the blocks the Paducah boys were throwing. From then on, every time he got the ball he threw it at the backboard he was attacking. At the very worst it slowed down Paducah's scoring. The other Thalia players were quick to see the wisdom of such an offense and in five minutes they were all doing it. Whoever caught the throw-in after a Paducah score would immediately whirl and throw a full-court peg shot. The only one it didn't work for was Leroy Malone: the big Paducah center anticipated him, caught the ball, and threw a ten-yard peg shot right at Leroy's groin. It hurt so bad he later told Sonny he was unable to jack off for two weeks.

The groin shot drew such sustained applause from the Paducah bleachers that Sonny was angered. Mr. Wean had failed to see that it was a deliberate foul: indeed, Mr. Wean was seeing less and less all the time. Thalia's peg-shot offense confused him— he had to keep turning around and around to keep up with the ball. After a while this made him so dizzy that he simply stopped and stood facing the Thalia goal— most of the Paducah team was down there anyway, catching the peg shots and throwing them back. Mr. Wean felt that he had somehow got involved in a game of ante over, and he didn't like it. He had a fat wife and all he really wanted to do was stay in the home ec classroom and teach young, small-breasted girls how to make pies. Instead he was standing on the center line, sweating and wishing the quarter would end. Suddenly, Sonny had an irresistible urge to chunk somebody. He unleashed a flat, low peg shot that caught Mr. Wean squarely in the back of the head and sent him sprawling.

The Thalia bench, boys and girls alike, arose with shrieks and cheers, their jubilation all the more noticeable because of the moment of total silence in the Paducah bleachers. The shot instantly made Sonny a celebrity, but it also scared hell out of him and his teammates who were on the floor at the time. They rushed over and tried to help Mr. Wean up, but his legs were like rubber. He had to be dragged off the floor. Paducah's assistant football coach was called in to referee the rest of the game —by the time he got his tennis shoes on, the hometown bleachers had recovered from their shock and were clamoring for Sonny's blood. He knew his only hope was to foul out immediately and get to the bench. While he was trying to decide on the safest way to foul, Coach Popper came to his rescue and took him out.

"Good lick," the coach said. "Nobody but a queer would teach home ec anyway."

From there on things were dismal for the Thalia five. Duane fouled out before the quarter ended, leaving no one but Joe Bob and the freshmen to play the fourth quarter. Paducah was ahead 88 to 14. Coach Popper got so mad at the freshmen that he couldn't see: he almost strangled himself tugging at the towel around his neck. He sent Sonny in again but Sonny quickly threw a couple of light body blocks and fouled out. That left Joe Bob and the freshmen to do the best they could. For the remainder of the game they never once managed to get the ball into their end of the court. As soon as they threw it in the Paducah players took it away from them and made another goal. In five minutes the score was 110 to 14 and Coach Popper called time out. A huddle was in order.

"I tell you," the coach said philosophically, "let's just forget about winning and try to hold the score down. We're gonna get beat over a hundred points if we ain't careful. Oaks, you throw the ball into Joe Bob and Joe Bob as soon as you get it lay down with it. That way they'll have to tie it up and jump for it every time. That'll slow 'em down a little."

The tactic worked fine the first time it was tried. Joe Bob swallowed the ball and Paducah had to tie it up to get possession. It took them about forty seconds to score. Thalia tried it again and three Paducah players gang-piled Joe Bob as he went down. He had to be carried off. The freshman who shot his free throw for him was so scared he barely got the ball half-way to the basket.

Joe Bob's injury left the four freshmen alone on the field for the last few minutes of the game. None of them wanted to swallow the ball and get gang-piled so they did what they could to cooperate with Paducah. The final score was 121 to 14.

"Well, hell, at least my B team got some experience," Coach Popper said. "Might as well look on the bright side. Let's go to the bus."

Basketball defeats weighed very lightly on the coach: football was the only sport that really counted. Ten minutes later he was flopped down in his bus seat, sound asleep.

The boys sat in a stupor for the first twenty miles or so, trying to get used to feeling safe again. Besides, Old Lady Fowler, the girl's coach, was still awake and they could not start to work on the girls until she dropped off. She went to sleep as they were pulling out of Vernon, and from there on it was dog-eat-dog.

The four little freshmen had no chance with the girls and had to get what amusement they could out of tormenting Joe Bob. They crowded him in a seat, took his underpants off, and threw them out the window. Joe Bob was too weak from the gang-piling to fight back, and he might not have bothered anyway. He lost so many pair of underwear that his mother bought them wholesale. He was the only boy on the team who wore his regulars, rather than a jockey strap: [his father] wouldn't hear of him wearing anything so immodest.

"What if you got hurt and were taken to a hospital wearing a thing like that?" [his father] said. "Our good name would be ruined."

Most of the kids had seen Joe Bob's underwear often enough to be thoroughly bored with it. The freshmen attracted no notice at all, and soon went to sleep.

Sonny started the return trip sitting by Leroy Malone, whose balls were so sore that the mere thought of girls made him writhe. After a little bargaining Sonny managed to switch with the kid in front of him, which put him next to the pretty but prudish sophomore he had had his eye on. Knocking Mr. Wean down gave him so much status that he was able to hold the girl's hand almost immediately. Martha Lou was her name. By the time they reached Electra she was willing to let him kiss her, but the results were pretty discouraging. Her teeth were clenched as tightly as if she had lockjaw, and even Sonny's status couldn't unlock them. His only reward was a taste of lipstick, in a flavor he didn't much care for.

The only real excitement on the bus ride home involved Jacy and Duane, the star couple. That was usually the case. None of the other kids excited one another much. There was a fat blond named Vida May who would feel penises, but the teachers knew about her and made her sit so close to the front that it was dangerous to fool with her even when the teachers were asleep.

Jacy and Duane, as a matter of course, were sitting in the very back seat. Duane didn't like the back seat much because there was a little overhead light above it that the bus driver refused to turn off. The bus driver's name was Wilbur Tim and he wasn't about to trust any kids in a totally dark bus. One time years earlier his wife Jessie had found two prophylactics when she was sweeping out the bus, and it just about sent her into hysterics. She was the apprehensive type and went around for months worried sick that some nice little girl had got pregnant on her husband's bus. After that Wilbur installed the light.

It was a small bulb that didn't really give any light, just a nice orange glow. Jacy loved it and wouldn't sit anywhere else, despite Duane's protests. She thought the light was very romantic and suggestive: everyone in the bus could tell when the couple in the back seat were kissing or doing something sexy, but the light wasn't strong enough for them to see too clearly. Courting with Duane when all the kids on the school bus could watch gave Jacy a real thrill, and made her feel a little like a movie star: she could bring beauty and passion into the poor kids' lives.

Because Jacy enjoyed them so much, the kissing sessions in the back seat had become a sort of regular feature on basketball road trips. All the kids watched, even though it made them itchy and envious. Jacy, after all, was the prettiest girl in school and watching her get kissed and played with was something to do on the long drives home. The element that made it really exciting to everyone was the question of how far Jacy would go. Once Duane got started kissing he was completely indifferent to whether he had an audience or not: all he wanted was more. The dim light made it impossible to tell precisely how much more Jacy allowed: everyone caught shadowy glimpses, and occasionally a gasp or a little moan from Jacy indicated that Duane was making some headway at least, but no one ever knew how much or what kind.

Only Jacy and Duane knew that he was making a great deal of headway indeed. Jacy would kiss and play around any time, but she seldom got excited past the point of control unless she was on the school bus, where people were watching. Being in the public eye seemed to heighten the quality of every touch. On the bus seat she never had to feign passion—she was burning with it. It was easy for Duane to get his hands inside her loose uniform and touch her breasts, and she loved it. Also, since she was in shorts, it was easy for him to do even more abandoned things to her. She loved to have him slide his hands up the underside of her legs, and sometimes she would even get to the point where she wanted him to touch her crotch. It was a matter that took very delicate managing, but if Duane's hand were cupped against her at the right time so she could squeeze it with her legs, something nice would happen. That was not for the audience, however: she didn't want the kids to see that. When the moment came near she would try to get Duane to crowd her back in the corner, so they couldn't be seen so well. Sometimes it worked beautifully. The younger and more naïve kids were sure Duane went all the way; the juniors and seniors knew better, but felt he must be going a pretty significant distance, anyhow. Every trip added to Jacy's legend. The following day at school she would be on every tongue. Some of the girls said bitter things about her, but the boys took notice when she walked by.

The only one seriously discommoded by bus-seat sessions was Duane, who frequently ached painfully by the time the bus reached home. He didn't like it, but he supposed such frustration was something he would simply have to bear until they were married.

Just before the bus got back to Thalia Coach Popper woke up and looked around. Most of the kids were asleep by that time. Jacy and Duane among them, but Jacy had gone to sleep with her legs across Duane's and when the coach saw that he was infuriated. It would put him in an awful spot if Lois Farrow somehow found out he had let her daughter go to sleep with her legs across Duane's. Gene Farrow was on the school board, and an incident like that could cost a coach his job. He stormed back and shook Jacy until she was awake enough to stumble down the aisle to the front seat, where she stayed the rest of the way home.

When all the kids had been delivered to their houses the coach got to thinking about it and began to cuss. There was no end to the trouble a couple of silly-ass kids might cause, particularly if one of them was Lois Farrow's daughter. Lois Farrow was the one person in Thalia who didn't give a damn for the fact that he was football coach.

Wilbur Tim dropped him off at his home, and he stomped inside, still angry. When he turned on the light in his bedroom closet it woke Ruth up. She had just had her breast operation a few days before and was still taking pain medicine. As he was taking off his shoes she sat up in bed.

"Herman, could you bring me a pain pill?" she asked. "It's hurting a little and I'm too groggy to get up."

"You sound goddamn wide awake to me," the coach said, fed up with women. "I bet if I let you you could lay there and talk for two hours. Get up and get your own pills, I ain't no pharmacist."

After a moment, Ruth did. She was dizzy and had to guide herself along the wall, holding her sore breast with one hand. She had washed that day and her white cotton nightgown smelled faintly of detergent. The coach ignored her and flopped on the bed. So far as he could tell, it had not been enough of an operation to make a fuss about. The scar on her breast was barely three inches long. He had cut himself worse than that many times, usually when he was hurrying through a barbed-wire fence to get to a covey of quail. The only thing that worried him about Ruth was the chance that they hadn't removed all the tumor and might have to operate again, in which case there would be no end to the expense. The cheapest and most sensible thing would have been for them to take the whole breast off while they were at it. The breast wasn't doing Ruth any good anyway, and if they had taken it all that would have been the end of the matter. He had told them so, too, but the doctor had ignored him and Ruth had gone off in another room and bawled. A woman like her would try the patience of a saint.

The next day at basketball practice the coach gave Duane a dressing down in front of the whole squad. He told him if he ever again so much as sat with Jacy on a basketball trip he would give him fifteen licks with a basketball shoe. A basketball shoe was the only thing the coach ever whipped boys with, but since he wore a size thirteen that was enough. He also told Duane to run fifty laps around the outside of the gym, and at that point Duane rebelled.

"I ain't runnin' no fifty laps all at one time," he said. "I'll do ten a day."

"You'll do fifty right now or check your suit in, by God," the coach said. "If you check it in you don't need to come out for track or baseball, neither. We can get along without you."

Duane went to the locker room, took his suit off, and left. It was just what the coach had hoped for. Any mess the boy got into with Jacy Farrow could no longer be laid at his door. It put him in such good spirits that he worked the boys until seven o'clock that night. The next day he commandeered a sophomore, and the team had ten players again.

1966

Thomas Pynchon
b. 1937

The sense of mystery that permeates Pynchon's fiction, emanating from elusive characters and plots, elusive concepts and themes, also shrouds his life. Thomas Pynchon is an intensely private person. He has never permitted his photograph to be publicly printed, and he has discouraged the circulation not only of rumors about his life but of accurate information as well. As a result, we have but few basic facts. Pynchon was born in Glen Cove, New York, on May 8, 1937. He attended Cornell University and, after serving two years in the U.S. Navy, graduated in 1958. After graduation he lived for a year in Greenwich Village, followed by a year in Seattle, Washington, where he worked for Boeing Aircraft on the corporation's in-house magazine. He then moved to Mexico to concentrate on his first novel. According to some sources, he now lives somewhere in California, though other sources place him in New York City.

Pynchon's first book, *V,* appeared in 1963. It is an intricately plotted novel that moves from alligator hunts through the sewers of New York to an elusive quest to find the enigamtic V, a woman mysteriously connected to the disastrous events of twentieth-century European history. His second book, *The Crying of Lot 49* (1966), is a short novel that features another elusive, paranoiac quest, this one to discover the significance of a secret postal system. Pynchon's third novel, *Gravity's Rainbow* (1973), won the National Book Award. Although it concerns an American officer forced into desertion toward the end of World War II, it is impossible to summarize. In its unremitting mixture of literary and popular styles, its unrelenting parody and paranoia, its technical jargon and multilayered plot structure, the novel not only portrays a labyrinthine world but becomes one itself. Though Pynchon studied English at Cornell, he also took a heavy dose of science courses, especially physics. In his collection of early short stories, *Slow Learner* (1984), Pynchon included "Entropy," a story he claims was inspired by his reading of Henry Adams and the mathematician Norbert Wiener. Connections —sometimes bizarre, sometimes terrifying—among modern history, technology, and communications consistently form the core of Pynchon's fiction.

Praised for its inventiveness and criticized for its obscurity, Pynchon's fiction continues to be controversial. Like James Joyce's and Vladimir Nabokov's, Pynchon's prose bristles with puns, cross-references, and layered meanings. Like

Edgar Allan Poe's and Nathanael West's, Pynchon's characteristic imaginative mode combines the comic, the satiric, and the apocalyptic. Like John Barth and Walker Percy, Pynchon moves with considerable confidence and authority in handling complex philosophical, psychological, and even scientific concepts. Like Herman Melville, he displays an affinity for arcane, offbeat information—an affinity so deep that one suspects him not only of reading almanacs but of being able to write them. His grasp of contemporary data and materials is especially remarkable.

What holds such rare talents together, enabling Pynchon to balance and control them, is an overriding concern with plot, a concern that begins with his own elaborate arrangements, in which he takes delight in everything from intricate entanglements to outrageous coincidences. Yet Pynchon's own plots are only a beginning. They have analogues everywhere—in the plots his characters concoct for themselves, in the divergent plots of their co-conspirators and their enemies, and in the crazy quilt of competing designs that emanate from the technologies, organizations, bureaucracies, and governments that surround them. Pynchon's characters frequently become the manipulated objects of their own plots, of the designs they initiate and the roles they choose. But they are the objects of endless machinations long before they begin foolishly to dream of possessing manipulative powers. Even their scramble merely to understand the plots and the tangles that enclose them is finally doomed. They work in the dark, and they work alone. One vestige of a shared community resides in their memory of loss, which is sometimes elegiac, sometimes ironic. Another, more telling vestige—the last, as it were—consists of wariness and suspicion that fade into paranoia as people wait apprehensively to see which encompassing plot will take control of their lives, which encompassing conspiracy will take over their world. Pynchon frequently writes as though he were standing at the end of time, examining and describing, even celebrating, the death not only of freedom but of culture. As much, perhaps, as any artist of his time, he is willing to question everything, including his own need to question everything. Finally, however, language is for him a means of resisting as well as examining and describing the end, and the celebration we sense in his style is not of the end but of our resistance to it.

Further Reading:
Mindful Pleasures: Essays on Thomas Pynchon, ed.
G. Levine and D. Leverenz, 1976.
Pynchon: A Collection of Critical Essays, ed. E.
Mendelson, 1978.
T. Schaub, *Listening to Pynchon: The Voice of
Ambiguity*, 1981.
P. L. Cooper, *Contemporary World*, 1983.

Text:
Kenyon Review, Spring 1960.

Entropy

Boris has just given me a summary of his views. He is a weather prophet.
The weather will continue bad, he says. There will be more calamities,
more death, more despair. Not the slightest indication of a change any-
where. . . . We must get into step, a lockstep toward the prison of death.
There is no escape. The weather will not change.

Tropic of Cancer[1]

Downstairs, Meatball Mulligan's lease-breaking party was moving into its 40th hour. On the kitchen floor, amid a litter of empty champagne fifths, were Sandor Rojas and three friends, playing spit in the ocean and staying awake on Heidsieck and benzedrine pills. In the living room Duke, Vincent, Krinkles and Paco sat crouched over a 15-inch speaker which had been bolted into the top of a wastepaper basket, listening to 27 watts' worth of *The Heroes' Gate at Kiev.*[2] They all wore horn rimmed sunglasses and rapt expressions, and smoked funny-looking cigarettes which contained not, as you might expect, tobacco, but an adulterated form of *cannabis sativa.*[3] This group was the Duke di Angelis quartet. They recorded for a local label called Tambú and had to their credit one 10″ LP entitled *Songs of Outer Space.* From time to time one of them would flick the ashes from his cigarette into the speaker cone to watch them dance around. Meatball himself was sleeping over by the window, holding an empty magnum to his chest as if it were a teddy bear. Several government girls, who worked for people like the State Department and NSA,[4] had passed out on couches, chairs and in one case the bathroom sink.

This was in early February of '57 and back then there were a lot of American expatriates around Washington, D.C., who would talk, every time they met you, about how someday they were going to go over to Europe for real but right now it seemed they were working for the government. Everyone saw a fine irony in this. They would stage, for instance, polyglot parties where the newcomer was sort of ignored if he couldn't carry on simultaneous conversations in three or four languages. They would haunt Armenian delicatessens for weeks at a stretch and invite you over for bulghour and lamb in tiny kitchens whose walls were covered with bullfight posters. They would have affairs with sultry girls from Andalucía or the Midi who studied economics at Georgetown. Their Dôme was a collegiate Rathskeller out on Wisconsin Avenue called the Old Heidelberg and they had to settle for cherry blossoms instead of lime trees when spring came, but in its lethargic way their life provided, as they said, kicks.

At the moment, Meatball's party seemed to be gathering its second wind. Outside there was rain. Rain splatted against the tar paper on the roof and was fractured into a fine spray off the noses, eyebrows and lips of wooden gargoyles under the eaves, and ran like drool down the windowpanes. The day before, it had snowed and the

---

[1] Novel by Henry Miller (b. 1891), American writer.
[2] The final section of "Pictures at an Exhibition"; the suite for piano by Modest Mussorgsky (1835–1881), Russian composer, was orchestrated by the French composer Maurice Ravel (1875–1937).
[3] Botanical name of marijuana.
[4] National Security Agency.

day before that there had been winds of gale force and before that the sun had made the city glitter bright as April, though the calendar read early February. It is a curious season in Washington, this false spring. Somewhere in it are Lincoln's Birthday and the Chinese New Year, and a forlornness in the streets because cherry blossoms are weeks away still and, as Sarah Vaughan has put it, spring will be a little late this year. Generally crowds like the one which would gather in the Old Heidelberg on weekday afternoons to drink Würtzburger and to sing Lili Marlene (not to mention The Sweetheart of Sigma Chi) are inevitably and incorrigibly Romantic. And as every good Romantic knows, the soul (*spiritus, ruach, pneuma*)[5] is nothing, substantially, but air; it is only natural that warpings in the atmosphere should be recapitulated in those who breathe it. So that over and above the public components—holidays, tourist attractions—there are private meanderings, linked to the climate as if this spell were a *stretto*[6] passage in the year's fugue: haphazard weather, aimless loves, unpredicted commitments: months one can easily spend *in* fugue, because oddly enough, later on, winds, rains, passions of February and March are never remembered in that city, it is as if they had never been.

The last bass notes of *The Heroes' Gate* boomed up through the floor and woke Callisto from an uneasy sleep. The first thing he became aware of was a small bird he had been holding gently between his hands, against his body. He turned his head sidewise on the pillow to smile down at it, at its blue hunched-down head and sick, lidded eyes, wondering how many more nights he would have to give it warmth before it was well again. He had been holding the bird like that for three days: it was the only way he knew to restore its health. Next to him the girl stirred and whimpered, her arm thrown across her face. Mingled with the sounds of the rain came the first tentative, querulous morning voices of the other birds, hidden in philodendrons and small fan palms: patches of scarlet, yellow and blue laced through this Rousseau-like fantasy, this hothouse jungle it had taken him seven years to weave together. Hermetically sealed, it was a tiny enclave of regularity in the city's chaos, alien to the vagaries of the weather, of national politics, of any civil disorder. Through trial-and-error Callisto had perfected its ecological balance, with the help of the girl its artistic harmony, so that the swayings of its plant life, the stirrings of its birds and human inhabitants were all as integral as the rhythms of a perfectly-executed mobile. He and the girl could no longer, of course, be omitted from that sanctuary; they had become necessary to its unity. What they needed from outside was delivered. They did not go out.

"Is he all right," she whispered. She lay like a tawny question mark facing him, her eyes suddenly huge and dark and blinking slowly. Callisto ran a finger beneath the feathers at the base of the bird's neck; caressed it gently. "He's going to be well, I think. See: he hears his friends beginning to wake up." The girl had heard the rain and the birds even before she was fully awake. Her name was Aubade:[7] she was part French and part Annamese,[8] and she lived on her own curious and lonely planet, where

---

[5] The Latin, Hebrew, and Greek words, respectively, for "soul."

[6] The summing-up in a fugue, in which the subject and its answers overlap in rapid succession. (From the Italian for "close" or "narrow.")

[7] French: "dawn song."

[8] Resident of Annam, a region of Vietnam situated partly in the north, partly in the south.

the clouds and the odor of poincianas, the bitterness of wine and the accidental fingers at the small of her back or feathery against her breasts came to her reduced inevitably to the terms of sound: of music which emerged at intervals from a howling darkness of discordancy. "Aubade," he said, "go see." Obedient, she arose; padded to the window, pulled aside the drapes and after a moment said: "It is 37. Still 37." Callisto frowned. "Since Tuesday, then," he said. "No change." Henry Adams, three generations before his own, had stared aghast at Power; Callisto found himself now in much the same state over Thermodynamics, the inner life of that power, realizing like his predecessor that the Virgin and the dynamo stand as much for love as for power; that the two are indeed identical; and that love therefore not only makes the world go 'round but also makes the boccie ball spin, the nebula precess. It was this latter or sidereal element which disturbed him. The cosmologists had predicted an eventual heat-death for the universe (something like Limbo:[9] form and motion abolished, heat-energy identical at every point in it); the meteorologists, day-to-day, staved it off by contradicting with a reassuring array of varied temperatures.

But for three days now, despite the changeful weather, the mercury had stayed at 37 degrees Fahrenheit. Leery at omens of apocalypse, Callisto shifted beneath the covers. His fingers pressed the bird more firmly, as if needing some pulsing or suffering assurance of an early break in the temperature.

It was that last cymbal crash that did it. Meatball was hurled wincing into consciousness as the synchronized wagging of heads over the wastebasket stopped. The final hiss remained for an instant in the room, then melted into the whisper of rain outside. "Aarrgghh," announced Meatball in the silence, looking at the empty magnum. Krinkles, in slow motion, turned, smiled and held out a cigarette. "Tea time, man," he said. "No, no," said Meatball. "How many times I got to tell you guys. Not at my place. You ought to know, Washington is lousy with Feds." Krinkles looked wistful. "Jeez, Meatball," he said, "you don't want to do nothing no more." "Hair of dog," said Meatball. "Only hope. Any juice left?" He began to crawl toward the kitchen. "No champagne, I don't think," Duke said. "Case of tequila behind the icebox." They put on an Earl Bostic side.[10] Meatball paused at the kitchen door, glowering at Sandor Rojas. "Lemons," he said after some thought. He crawled to the refrigerator and got out three lemons and some cubes, found the tequila and set about restoring order to his nervous system. He drew blood once cutting the lemons and had to use two hands squeezing them and his foot to crack the ice tray but after about ten minutes he found himself, through some miracle, beaming down into a monster tequila sour. "That looks yummy," Sandor Rojas said. "How about you make me one." Meatball blinked at him. *"Kitchi lofass a shegítbe,"*[11] he replied automatically, and wandered away into the bathroom. "I say," he called out a moment later to no one in particular. "I say, there seems to be a girl or something sleeping in the sink." He took her by the shoulders and shook. "Wha," she said. "You don't look too comfortable," Meatball said. "Well," she agreed. She stumbled to the shower, turned

---

[9] In Catholic theology, the border state between heaven and hell. It is reserved for the just who died before the resurrection or for children who die before being baptized—i.e., for those who are neither saved nor damned.

[10] I.e., a record by Earl Bostic, a well-known jazz

saxophonist of the 1950s. (The characters are jazz fans, and many famous jazz musicians, like Gerry Mulligan, Chet Baker, John Lewis, and Charlie Mingus, are mentioned later in the story.)

[11] Phonetic Hungarian: equivalent of "Up yours."

on the cold water and sat down crosslegged in the spray. "That's better," she smiled.

"Meatball," Sandor Rojas yelled from the kitchen. "Somebody is trying to come in the window. A burglar, I think. A second-story man." "What are you worrying about," Meatball said. "We're on the third floor." He loped back into the kitchen. A shaggy woebegone figure stood out on the fire escape, raking his fingernails down the windowpane. Meatball opened the window. "Saul," he said.

"Sort of wet out," Saul said. He climbed in, dripping. "You heard, I guess."

"Miriam left you," Meatball said, "or something, is all I heard."

There was a sudden flurry of knocking at the front door. "Do come in," Sandor Rojas called. The door opened and there were three coeds from George Washington, all of whom were majoring in philosophy. They were each holding a gallon of Chianti. Sandor leaped up and dashed into the living room. "We heard there was a party," one blonde said. "Young blood," Sandor shouted. He was an ex-Hungarian freedom fighter who had easily the worst chronic case of what certain critics of the middle class have called Don Giovannism in the District of Columbia. *Purche porti la gonnella, voi sapete quel che fa.*[12] Like Pavlov's dog: a contralto voice or a whiff of Arpege and Sandor would begin to salivate. Meatball regarded the trio blearily as they filed into the kitchen; he shrugged. "Put the wine in the icebox," he said "and good morning."

Aubade's neck made a golden bow as she bent over the sheets of foolscap, scribbling away in the green murk of the room. "As a young man at Princeton," Callisto was dictating, nestling the bird against the gray hairs of his chest, "Callisto had learned a mnemonic device for remembering the Laws of Thermodynamics: you can't win, things are going to get worse before they get better, who says they're going to get better.[13] At the age of 54, confronted with Gibbs' notion of the universe, he suddenly realized that undergraduate cant had been oracle, after all. That spindly maze of equations became, for him, a vision of ultimate, cosmic heat-death. He had known all along, of course, that nothing but a theoretical engine or system ever runs at 100% efficiency; and about the theorem of Clausius, which states that the entropy of an isolated system always continually increases. It was not, however, until Gibbs and Boltzmann brought to this principle the methods of statistical mechanics that the horrible significance of it all dawned on him: only then did he realize that the isolated system—galaxy, engine, human being, culture, whatever—must evolve spontaneously toward the Condition of the More Probable. He was forced, therefore, in the sad dying fall of middle age, to a radical reevaluation of everything he had learned up to then; all the cities and seasons and casual passions of his days had now to be looked at in a new and elusive light. He did not know if he was equal to the task. He was aware of the dangers of the reductive fallacy and, he hoped, strong enough not to drift into the graceful decadence of an enervated fatalism. His had always been a vigorous, Italian sort of pessimism: like Machiavelli, he allowed the forces of *virtú* and *fortuna*[14] to be about 50/50; but the equations now introduced a random factor which pushed the odds to some unutterable and indeterminate ratio which he found himself afraid to calculate." Around him loomed vague hothouse shapes; the pitifully

---

[12] Italian: "As long as she wears a skirt, you know what she does" (from the opera *Don Giovanni*).

[13] Roughly speaking, the three laws of thermodynamics state that energy can neither be created nor destroyed, that the entropy (randomness or disorder) of a closed system always increases, and that there is an absolute zero.

[14] Italian: "virtue" and "fortune."

small heart fluttered against his own. Counterpointed against his words the girl heard the chatter of birds and fitful car honkings scattered along the wet morning and Earl Bostic's alto rising in occasional wild peaks through the floor. The architectonic purity of her world was constantly threatened by such hints of anarchy: gaps and excrescences and skew lines, and a shifting or tilting of planes to which she had continually to readjust lest the whole structure shiver into a disarray of discrete and meaningless signals. Callisto had described the process once as a kind of "feedback": she crawled into dreams each night with a sense of exhaustion, and a desperate resolve never to relax that vigilance. Even in the brief periods when Callisto made love to her, soaring above the bowing of taut nerves in haphazard double-stops would be the one singing string of her determination.

"Nevertheless," continued Callisto, "he found in entropy or the measure of disorganization for a closed system an adequate metaphor to apply to certain phenomena in his own world. He saw, for example, the younger generation responding to Madison Avenue with the same spleen his own had once reserved for Wall Street: and in American 'consumerism' discovered a similar tendency from the least to the most probable, from differentiation to sameness, from ordered individuality to a kind of chaos. He found himself, in short, restating Gibbs' prediction in social terms, and envisioned a heat-death for his culture in which ideas, like heat-energy, would no longer be transferred, since each point in it would ultimately have the same quantity of energy; and intellectual motion would, accordingly, cease." He glanced up suddenly. "Check it now," he said. Again she rose and peered out at the thermometer. "37," she said. "The rain has stopped." He bent his head quickly and held his lips against a quivering wing. "Then it will change soon," he said, trying to keep his voice firm.

Sitting on the stove Saul was like any big rag doll that a kid has been taking out some incomprehensible rage on. "What happened," Meatball said. "If you feel like talking, I mean."

"Of course I feel like talking," Saul said. "One thing I did, I slugged her."

"Discipline must be maintained."

"Ha, ha. I wish you'd been there. Oh Meatball, it was a lovely fight. She ended up throwing a *Handbook of Chemistry and Physics* at me, only it missed and went through the window, and when the glass broke I reckon something in her broke too. She stormed out of the house crying, out in the rain. No raincoat or anything."

"She'll be back."

"No."

"Well." Soon Meatball said: "It was something earth-shattering, no doubt. Like who is better, Sal Mineo or Ricky Nelson."

"What it was about," Saul said, "was communication theory. Which of course makes it very hilarious."

"I don't know anything about communication theory."

"Neither does my wife. Come right down to it, who does? That's the joke."

When Meatball saw the kind of smile Saul had on his face he said: "Maybe you would like tequila or something."

"No. I mean, I'm sorry. It's a field you can go off the deep end in, is all. You get where you're watching all the time for security cops: behind bushes, around corners. MUFFET is top secret."

"Wha."

"Multi-unit factorial field electronic tabulator."

"You were fighting about that."

"Miriam has been reading science-fiction again. That and *Scientific American*. It seems she is, as we say, bugged at this idea of computers acting like people. I made the mistake of saying you can just as well turn that around, and talk about human behavior like a program fed into an IBM machine."

"Why not," Meatball said.

"Indeed, why not. In fact it is sort of crucial to communication, not to mention information theory. Only when I said that she hit the roof. Up went the balloon. And I can't figure out *why*. If anybody should know why, I should. I refuse to believe the government is wasting taxpayers' money on me, when it has so many bigger and better things to waste it on."

Meatball made a moue. "Maybe she thought you were acting like a cold, dehumanized amoral scientist type."

"My god," Saul flung up an arm. "Dehumanized. How much more human can I get? I worry, Meatball, I do. There are Europeans wandering around North Africa these days with their tongues torn out of their heads because those tongues have spoken the wrong words. Only the Europeans thought they were the right words."

"Language barrier," Meatball suggested.

Saul jumped down off the stove. "That," he said, angry, "is a good candidate for sick joke of the year. No, ace, it is *not* a barrier. If it is anything it's a kind of leakage. Tell a girl: 'I love you.' No trouble with two-thirds of that, it's a closed circuit. Just you and she. But that nasty four-letter word in the middle, *that's* the one you have to look out for. Ambiguity. Redundance. Irrelevance, even. Leakage. All this is noise. Noise screws up your signal, makes for disorganization in the circuit."

Meatball shuffled around. "Well, now, Saul," he muttered, "you're sort of, I don't know, expecting a lot from people. I mean, you know. What it is is, most of the things we say, I guess, are mostly noise."

"Ha! Half of what you just said, for example."

"Well, you do it too."

"I know." Saul smiled grimly. "It's a bitch, ain't it."

"I bet that's what keeps divorce lawyers in business. Whoops."

"Oh I'm not sensitive. Besides," frowning, "you're right. You find I think that most 'successful' marriages—Miriam and me, up to last night—are sort of founded on compromises. You never run at top efficiency, usually all you have is a minimum basis for a workable thing. I believe the phrase is Togetherness."

"Aarrgghh."

"Exactly. You find that one a bit noisy, don't you. But the noise content is different for each of us because you're a bachelor and I'm not. Or wasn't. The hell with it."

"Well sure," Meatball said, trying to be helpful, "you were using different words. By 'human being' you meant something that you can look at like it was a computer. It helps you think better on the job or something. But Miriam meant something entirely—"

"The hell with it."

Meatball fell silent. "I'll take that drink," Saul said after a while.

The card game had been abandoned and Sandor's friends were slowly getting wasted on tequila. On the living room couch, one of the coeds and Krinkles were engaged in amorous conversation. "No," Krinkles was saying, "no, I can't put Dave *down*. In fact I give Dave a lot of credit, man. Especially considering his accident and all." The girl's smile faded. "How terrible," she said. "What accident?" "Hadn't you heard?" Krinkles said. "When Dave was in the army, just a private E-2, they sent him down to Oak Ridge[15] on special duty. Something to do with the Manhattan Project.[16] He was handling hot stuff one day and got an overdose of radiation. So now he's got to wear lead gloves all the time." She shook her head sympathetically. "What an awful break for a piano-player."

Meatball had abandoned Saul to a bottle of tequila and was about to go to sleep in a closet when the front door flew open and the place was invaded by five enlisted personnel of the U.S. Navy, all in varying stages of abomination. "This is the place," shouted a fat, pimply seaman apprentice who had lost his white hat. "This here is the hoorhouse that chief was telling us about." A stringy-looking 3rd class boatswain's mate pushed him aside and cased the living room. "You're right, Slab," he said. "But it don't look like much, even for Stateside. I seen better tail in Naples, Italy." "How much, hey," boomed a large seaman with adenoids, who was holding a Mason jar full of white lightning. "Oh, my god," said Meatball.

Outside the temperature remained constant at 37 degrees Fahrenheit. In the hothouse Aubade stood absently caressing the branches of a young mimosa, hearing a motif of sap-rising, the rough and unresolved anticipatory theme of those fragile pink blossoms which, it is said, insure fertility. That music rose in a tangled tracery: arabesques of order competing fugally with the improvised discords of the party downstairs, which peaked sometimes in cusps and ogees of noise. That precious signal-to-noise ratio, whose delicate balance required every calorie of her strength, seesawed inside the small tenuous skull as she watched Callisto, sheltering the bird. Callisto was trying to confront any idea of the heat-death now, as he nuzzled the feathery lump in his hands. He sought correspondences. Sade, of course. And Temple Drake, gaunt and hopeless in her little park in Paris, at the end of *Sanctuary*. Final equilibrium. *Nightwood.*[17] And the tango. Any tango, but more than any perhaps the sad sick dance in Stravinsky's *L'Histoire du Soldat.*[18] He thought back: what had tango music been for them after the war, what meanings had he missed in all the stately coupled automatons in the *cafés-dansants,*[19] or in the metronomes which had ticked behind the eyes of his own partners? Not even the clean constant winds of Switzerland could cure the *grippe espagnole:*[20] Stravinsky had had it, they all had had it. And now many musicians were left after Passchendaele, after the Marne?[21] It came down in this case to seven: violin, double-bass. Clarinet, bassoon. Cornet, trombone. Tympani. Almost as if any tiny troupe of saltimbanques had set about conveying the same information as a full pit-orchestra. There was hardly a full complement left in Europe. Yet with violin and tympani Stravinsky had managed to communicate in that tango

---

[15] City in Tennessee, site of production of uranium for the atomic bomb.

[16] Research project sponsored by the U.S. government that produced the first atomic bomb in 1945.

[17] *Sanctuary* (1931) by William Faulkner and *Nightwood* (1936) by Djuna Barnes are novels that deal explicitly with sexuality.

[18] French: "The Story of the Soldier," spoken text with music by the Russian-born composer Igor Stravinsky (1882–1971).

[19] French: "dance halls."

[20] French: "Spanish flu."

[21] Passchendaele, Flanders, a province of Belgium, and the Marne, a river in France, were both scenes of heavy fighting in World War I.

the same exhaustion, the same airlessness one saw in the slicked-down youths who were trying to imitate Vernon Castle, and in their mistresses, who simply did not care. *Ma maitresse.*[22] Celeste. Returning to Nice after the second war he had found that cafe replaced by a perfume shop which catered to American tourists. And no secret vestige of her in the cobblestones or in the old pension next door; no perfume to match her breath heavy with the sweet Spanish wine she always drank. And so instead he had purchased a Henry Miller novel and left for Paris, and read the book on the train so that when he arrived he had been given at least a little forewarning. And saw that Celeste and the others and even Temple Drake were not all that had changed. "Aubade," he said, "my head aches." The sound of his voice generated in the girl an answering scrap of melody. Her movement toward the kitchen, the towel, the cold water, and his eyes following her formed a weird and intricate canon; as she placed the compress on his forehead his sigh of gratitude seemed to signal a new subject, another series of modulations.

"No," Meatball was still saying, "no, I'm afraid not. This is not a house of ill repute. I'm sorry, really I am." Slab was adamant. "But the chief said," he kept repeating. The seaman offered to swap the moonshine for a good piece. Meatball looked around frantically, as if seeking assistance. In the middle of the room, the Duke di Angelis quartet were engaged in a historic moment. Vincent was seated and the others standing: they were going through the motions of a group having a session, only without instruments. "I say," Meatball said. Duke moved his head a few times, smiled faintly, lit a cigarette, and eventually caught sight of Meatball. "Quiet, man," he whispered. Vincent began to fling his arms around, his fists clenched; then, abruptly, was still, then repeated the performance. This went on for a few minutes while Meatball sipped his drink moodily. The navy had withdrawn to the kitchen. Finally at some invisible signal the group stopped tapping their feet and Duke grinned and said, "At least we ended together."

Meatball glared at him. "I say," he said. "I have this new conception, man," Duke said. "You remember your namesake. You remember Gerry."

"No," said Meatball. "I'll Remember April,[23] if that's any help."

"As a matter of fact," Duke said, "it was Love for Sale. Which shows how much you know. The point is, it was Mulligan, Chet Baker and that crew, way back then, out yonder. You dig?"

"Baritone sax," Meatball said. "Something about a baritone sax."

"But no piano, man. No guitar. Or accordion. You know what that means."

"Not exactly," Meatball said.

"Well first let me just say, that I am no Mingus, no John Lewis. Theory was never my strong point. I mean things like reading were always difficult for me and all—"

"I know," Meatball said drily. "You got your card taken away because you changed key on Happy Birthday at a Kiwanis Club picnic."

"Rotarian. But it occurred to me, in one of these flashes of insight, that if that first quartet of Mulligan's had no piano, it could only mean one thing."

---

[22] French: "My mistress."
[23] A popular tune that was adapted for jazz. The characters play a verbal game in which they try to incorporate titles and lyrics of jazz and popular song into their conversations. (These are generally recognizable by the capitalization, as here.)

"No chords," said Paco, the baby-faced bass.

"What is he trying to say," Duke said, "is no root chords. Nothing to listen to while you blow a horizontal line. What one does in such a case is, one *thinks* the roots."

A horrified awareness was dawning on Meatball. "And the next logical extension," he said.

"Is to think everything," Duke announced with simple dignity. "Roots, line, everything."

Meatball looked at Duke, awed. "But," he said.

"Well," Duke said modestly, "there are a few bugs to work out."

"But," Meatball said.

"Just listen," Duke said. "You'll catch on." And off they went again into orbit, presumably somewhere around the asteroid belt. After a while Krinkles made an embouchure and started moving his fingers[24] and Duke clapped his hand to his forehead. "Oaf!" he roared. "The new head[25] we're using, you remember, I wrote last night?" "Sure," Krinkles said, "the new head. I come in on the bridge. All your heads I come in then." "Right," Duke said. "So why—" "Wha," said Krinkles, "16 bars, I wait, I come in—" "16?" Duke said. "No. No, Krinkles. Eight you waited. You want me to sing it? A cigarette that bears a lipstick's traces, an airline ticket to romantic places." Krinkles scratched his head. "These Foolish Things, you mean." "Yes," Duke said, "yes, Krinkles. Bravo." "Not I'll Remember April," Krinkles said. "*Minghe morte,*"[26] said Duke. "I *figured* we were playing it a little slow," Krinkles said. Meatball chuckled. "Back to the old drawing board," he said. "No, man," Duke said, "back to the airless void." And they took off again, only it seemed Paco was playing in G sharp while the rest were in E flat, so they had to start all over.

In the kitchen two of the girls from George Washington and the sailors were singing Let's All Go Down and Piss on the Forrestal. There was a two-handed, bilingual *mura*[27] game on over by the icebox. Saul had filled several paper bags with water and was sitting on the fire escape, dropping them on passersby in the street. A fat government girl in a Bennington sweatshirt, recently engaged to an ensign attached to the Forrestal, came charging into the kitchen, head lowered, and butted Slab in the stomach. Figuring this was as good an excuse for a fight as any, Slab's buddies piled in. The *mura* players were nose-to-nose, screaming *trois, sette*[28] at the tops of their lungs. From the shower the girl Meatball had taken out of the sink announced that she was drowning. She had apparently sat on the drain and the water was now up to her neck. The noise in Meatball's apartment had reached a sustained, ungodly crescendo.

Meatball stood and watched, scratching his stomach lazily. The way he figured, there were only about two ways he could cope: (a) lock himself in the closet and maybe eventually they would all go away, or (b) try to calm everybody down, one by one. (a) was certainly the more attractive alternative. But then he started thinking about that closet. It was dark and stuffy and he would be alone. He did not feature

---

[24] I.e., began to play. (An embouchure is the position of the lips against a horn.)

[25] Lead-in to a part or song.

[26] Probably, corruption of *Minchia morte,* vulgar Italian exclamation.

[27] Probably, corruption of *morra,* Italian game; a player guesses the number of fingers held up by another player.

[28] French: "three"; and Italian: "seven."

being alone. And then this crew off the good ship Lollipop or whatever it was might take it upon themselves to kick down the closet door, for a lark. And if that happened he would be, at the very least, embarrassed. The other way was more a pain in the neck, but probably better in the long run.

So he decided to try and keep his lease-breaking party from deteriorating into total chaos: he gave wine to the sailors and separated the *mura* players; he introduced the fat government girl to Sandor Rojas, who would keep her out of trouble; he helped the girl in the shower to dry off and get into bed; he had another talk with Saul; he called a repairman for the refrigerator, which someone had discovered was on the blink. This is what he did until nightfall, when most of the revellers had passed out and the party trembled on the threshold of its third day.

Upstairs Callisto, helpless in the past, did not feel the faint rhythm inside the bird begin to slacken and fail. Aubade was by the window, wandering the ashes of her own lovely world; the temperature held steady, the sky had become a uniform darkening gray. Then something from downstairs—a girl's scream, an overturned chair, a glass dropped on the floor, he would never know what exactly—pierced that private time-warp and he became aware of the faltering, the constriction of muscles, the tiny tossings of the bird's head; and his own pulse began to pound more fiercely, as if trying to compensate. "Aubade," he called weakly, "he's dying." The girl, flowing and rapt, crossed the hothouse to gaze down at Callisto's hands. The two remained like that, poised, for one minute, and two, while the heartbeat ticked a graceful diminuendo down at last into stillness. Callisto raised his head slowly. "I held him," he protested, impotent with the wonder of it, "to give him the warmth of my body. Almost as if I were communicating life to him, or a sense of life. What has happened? Has the transfer of heat ceased to work? Is there no more . . ." He did not finish.

"I was just at the window," she said. He sank back, terrified. She stood a moment more, irresolute; she had sensed his obsession long ago, realized somehow that that constant 37 was now decisive. Suddenly then, as if seeing the single and unavoidable conclusion to all this she moved swiftly to the window before Callisto could speak; tore away the drapes and smashed out the glass with two exquisite hands which came away bleeding and glistening with splinters; and turned to face the man on the bed and wait with him until the moment of equilibrium was reached, when 37 degrees Fahrenheit should prevail both outside and inside, and forever, and the hovering, curious dominant of their separate lives should resolve into a tonic[29] of darkness and the final absence of all motion.

1960

---

[29] Typically, songs conclude by returning
("resolving") to the tonic, or principal chord.

Joyce Carol Oates
b. 1938

One of the most prolific and popular of recent American writers, Joyce Carol Oates is perhaps best known for the extremities of violence in her fiction. One critic, Marvin Mudrick, has said that "typical activities in Oates's novels are arson, rape, riot, mental breakdown, murder (plain and fancy, with excursions into patricide, matricide, uxoricide, mass filicide), and suicide." For Oates, violence is inseparable from the psychic dislocation she sees as endemic to contemporary society. Like Joan Didion, she professes a strong commitment to family and tradition as defining forces for the individual, and like Didion, she sees modern culture as hostile to the individual. Specific acts of violence thus reflect culture's basic disposition, just as physical danger reflects the psychic risks inherent in our acceptance of modern values. Asked about the preponderance of violence in her fiction, Oates said, "These things do not have to be contrived. This is America."

Joyce Carol Oates was born on June 16, 1938, in Millerport, New York, to working-class, devoutly Catholic parents. A talented student, she won a scholarship to Syracuse University in 1956, and in 1960 she received a B.A. in English, graduating Phi Beta Kappa and valedictorian of her class. The next year she married Raymond Smith, received an M.A. in English literature from the University of Wisconsin, and enrolled in the doctoral program in English at Rice University, only to withdraw soon after one of her stories was listed on the Honor Roll in *Best American Short Stories.* Since publication of her first collection of stories, *By the North Gate,* in 1963, Oates has continued to write, as she puts it, in flurries. Besides numerous collections of short stories, poetry, and critical essays, she has written sixteen novels over the past twenty years—an output that surely places her among the most productive serious writers in the history of American literature.

Her first novel, *With Shuddering Fall* (1964), the story of an intense and violent love affair between an impressionable seventeen-year-old girl and a thirty-year-old stock-car racer, introduced the themes of emotional derangement, tragic love, and compulsive behavior that have characterized much of her fiction. With her second novel, *A Garden of Earthly Delights* (1967), she began an American trilogy that took her from the Arkansas migrant camps of the 1920s to the suburbs of the 1960s and, with *Expensive People* (1968), to the story of a child murderer. The third novel in the trilogy, *Them* (1969), which won the National Book Award, moves from Depression-era Detroit to the shattering violence of the 1967 riots. In *Wonderland* (1971), Oates turned to the region of her childhood with a grisly, obsessive story about a boy who alone survives his insane father's massacre of an entire family. She turned again to childhood trauma in *Do with Me What You Will* (1973), the tale of a woman who as a child had been abducted by her father. In her next two novels, *The Assassins* (1975) and *Childwold* (1976), Oates experimented with intricate narrative techniques to portray the dissolving boundaries of dream and reality, the self and others. In

1978 she published a novel about intense religious experience, *Son of the Morning,* and in the following year turned to a university setting with *Unholy Lives.* In 1980 Oates broke new ground with *Bellefleur,* a novel that combines surrealist elements with a Gothic atmosphere as it traces the story of six generations of an American family in the Adirondack Valley. A year later she published *Angel of Light* (1981), a story of violence and political power whose title comes from Thoreau's description of John Brown. In these and in her latest novels, *A Bloodsmoor Romance* (1982), *Mysteries of Winterthurn* (1984), *Solstice* (1985), and *Marya: A Life* (1986), she seems to be simultaneously using and commenting on popular forms of American fiction.

As an artist, Oates allies herself more with D. H. Lawrence than with such experimentalists as James Joyce and Virginia Woolf, though she also insists that she is a committed Anti-Romantic. The individual's desire for autonomy is the primary source of the human moral failure that manifests itself in—and is punished by—the acts of violence that pervade her fiction. One of her recurring themes has to do with "recognizing limits" that are implicit in the conjunction that an individual's history makes with the contours of culture. When her characters attempt to ignore or deny these limits, the givens of their lives, as does the narrator of "How I Contemplated the World," violence and meaninglessness threaten both them and the people around them.

Despite her rejection of Romanticism, Oates mixes realistic settings and characters with surreal and even supernatural experiences, often to disclose some hidden tie between the authors and the victims of violence. Such unexpected connections are important to her for many reasons, the chief one being their potential as a basis for community. In one way or another, her stories center on the importance of establishing a sense of community that is grounded biologically as well as socially, morally, and culturally. To her mind, the great failing of modern literature is its "solipsistic" tendency, its self-indulgent creation of "art forms in which language is arranged and rearranged in such a manner as to give pleasure to the artist and his readers, excluding any referent to an available exterior world." By contrast, her own effort, the only one she finally deems worthy, "is to do no less than attempt the sanctification of the world!"

Further Reading:
M. K. Grant, *The Tragic Vision of Joyce Carol Oates,* 1978.
R. Phillips, "Joyce Carol Oates: The Art of Fiction," *Paris Review,* Fall-Winter 1978.
J. V. Creighton, *Joyce Carol Oates,* 1979.
E. G. Friedman, *Joyce Carol Oates,* 1980.

Text:
The Wheel of Love and Other Stories, 1970.

from How I Contemplated the World
from the Detroit House of
Correction and Began My Life
Over Again

Notes for an Essay for an English Class at Baldwin
Country Day School; Poking Around in Debris;
Disgust and Curiosity; a Revelation of the Meaning
of Life; a Happy Ending . . .

I: Events

1. The girl (myself) is walking through Branden's, that excellent store. Suburb of a
large famous city that is a symbol for large famous American cities. The event sneaks
up on the girl, who believes she is herding it along with a small fixed smile, a girl
of fifteen, innocently experienced. She dawdles in a certain style by a counter of
costume jewelry. Rings, earrings, necklaces. Prices from $5 to $50, all within reach.
All ugly. She eases over to the glove counter, where everything is ugly too. In her
close-fitted coat with its black fur collar she contemplates the luxury of Branden's,
which she has known for many years: its many mild pale lights, easy on the eye and
the soul, its elaborate tinkly decorations, its women shoppers with their excellent shoes
and coats and hairdos, all dawdling gracefully, in no hurry.

   Who was ever in a hurry here?

2. The girl seated at home. A small library, paneled walls of oak. Someone is talking
to me. An earnest, husky, female voice drives itself against my ears, nervous, frightened, groping around my heart, saying, "If you wanted gloves, why didn't you say
so? Why didn't you ask for them?" That store, Branden's is owned by Raymond
Forrest who lives on Du Maurier Drive. We live on Sioux Drive. Raymond Forrest.
A handsome man? An ugly man? A man of fifty or sixty, with gray hair, or a man
of forty with earnest, courteous eyes, a good golf game; who is Raymond Forrest,
this man who is my salvation? Father has been talking to him. Father is not his
physician; Dr. Berg is his physician. Father and Dr. Berg refer patients to each other.
There is a connection. Mother plays bridge with . . . On Mondays and Wednesdays
our maid Billie works at . . . The strings draw together in a cat's cradle, making a
net to save you when you fall. . . .

3. *Harriet Arnold's.* A small shop, better than Branden's. Mother in her black coat, I
in my close-fitted blue coat. Shopping. Now look at this, isn't this cute, do you want
this, why don't you want this, try this on, take this with you to the fitting room,
take this also, what's wrong with you, what can I do for you, why are you so
strange . . . ? "I wanted to steal but not to buy," I don't tell her. The girl droops
along in her coat and gloves and leather boots, her eyes scan the horizon, which is

pastel pink and decorated like Branden's, tasteful walls and modern ceilings with graceful glimmering lights.

4. Weeks later, the girl at a bus stop. Two o'clock in the afternoon, a Tuesday; obviously she has walked out of school.

5. The girl stepping down from a bus. Afternoon, weather changing to colder. Detroit. Pavement and closed-up stores; grill-work over the windows of a pawnshop. What is a pawnshop, exactly?

II: Characters

1. The girl stands five feet five inches tall. An ordinary height. Baldwin Country Day School draws them up to that height. She dreams along the corridors and presses her face against the Thermoplex glass. No frost or steam can ever form on that glass. A smudge of grease from her forehead . . . could she be boiled down to grease? She wears her hair loose and long and straight in suburban teen-age style, 1968. Eyes smudged with pencil, dark brown. Brown hair. Vague green eyes. A pretty girl? An ugly girl? She sings to herself under her breath, idling in the corridor, thinking of her many secrets (the thirty dollars she once took from the purse of a friend's mother, just for fun, the basement window she smashed in her own house just for fun) and thinking of her brother who is at Susquehanna Boys' Academy, an excellent preparatory school in Maine, remembering him unclearly . . . he has long manic hair and a squeaking voice and he looks like one of the popular teen-age singers of 1968, one of those in a group. *The Certain Forces, The Way Out, The Maniacs Responsible.* The girl in her turn looks like one of those fieldsful of girls who listen to the boys' singing, dreaming and mooning restlessly, breaking into high sullen laughter, innocently experienced.

2. The mother. A Midwestern woman of Detroit and suburbs. Belongs to the Detroit Athletic Club. Also the Detroit Golf Club. Also the Bloomfield Hills Country Club. The Village Women's Club at which lectures are given each winter on Genet and Sartre and James Baldwin, by the Director of the Adult Education Program at Wayne State University. . . . The Bloomfield Art Association. Also the Founders Society of the Detroit Institute of Arts. Also . . . Oh, she is in perpetual motion, this lady, hair like blown-up gold and finer than gold, hair and fingers and body of inestimable grace. Heavy weighs the gold on the back of her hairbrush and hand mirror. Heavy heavy the candlesticks in the dining room. Very heavy is the big car, a Lincoln, long and black, that on one cool autumn day split a squirrel's body in two unequal parts.

3. The father. Dr. . He belongs to the same clubs as #2. A player of squash and golf; he has a golfer's umbrella of stripes. Candy stripes. In his mouth nothing turns to sugar, however; saliva works no miracles here. His doctoring is of the slightly sick. The sick are sent elsewhere (to Dr. Berg?), the deathly sick are sent back for more tests and their bills are sent to their homes, the unsick are sent to Dr. Coronet (Isabel, a lady), an excellent psychiatrist for unsick people who angrily believe they are sick and want to do something about it. If they demand a male psychiatrist, the unsick

are sent by Dr.   (my father) to Dr. Lowenstein, a male psychiatrist, excellent and expensive, with a limited practice.

4. Clarita. She is twenty, twenty-five, she is thirty or more? Pretty, ugly, what? She is a woman lounging by the side of a road, in jeans and a sweater, hitchhiking, or she is slouched on a stool at a counter in some roadside diner. A hard line of jaw. Curious eyes. Amused eyes. Behind her eyes processions move, funeral pageants, cartoons. She says, "I never can figure out why girls like you bum around down here. What are you looking for anyway?" An odor of tobacco about her. Unwashed underclothes, or no underclothes, unwashed skin, gritty toes, hair long and falling into strands, not recently washed.

5. Simon. In this city the weather changes abruptly, so Simon's weather changes abruptly. He sleeps through the afternoon. He sleeps through the morning. Rising, he gropes around for something to get him going, for a cigarette or a pill to drive him out to the street, where the temperature is hovering around 35°. Why doesn't it drop? Why, why doesn't the cold clean air come down from Canada; will he have to go up into Canada to get it? will he have to leave the Country of his Birth and sink into Canada's frosty fields . . . ? Will the F.B.I. (which he dreams about constantly) chase him over the Canadian border on foot, hounded out in a blizzard of broken glass and horns . . . ?

"Once I was Huckleberry Finn," Simon says, "but now I am Roderick Usher." Beset by frenzies and fears, this man who makes my spine go cold, he takes green pills, yellow pills, pills of white and capsules of dark blue and green . . . he takes other things I may not mention, for what if Simon seeks me out and climbs into my girl's bedroom here in Bloomfield Hills and strangles me, what then . . . ? (As I write this I begin to shiver. Why do I shiver? I am now sixteen and sixteen is not an age for shivering.) It comes from Simon, who is always cold.

III: World Events

Nothing.

IV: People & Circumstances Contributing to This Delinquency

Nothing.

V: Sioux Drive

George, Clyde G. 240 Sioux. A manufacturer's representative; children, a dog, a wife. Georgian with the usual columns. You think of the White House, then of Thomas Jefferson, then your mind goes blank on the white pillars and you think of nothing. Norris, Ralph W. 246 Sioux. Public relations. Colonial. Bay window, brick, stone, concrete, wood, green shutters, sidewalk, lantern, grass, trees, blacktop drive, two children, one of them my classmate Esther (Esther Norris) at Baldwin. Wife, cars. Ramsey, Michael D. 250 Sioux. Colonial. Big living room, thirty by twenty-five, fireplaces in living room, library, recreation room, paneled walls wet bar five bath-rooms five bedrooms two lavatories central air conditioning automatic sprinkler automatic garage door three children one wife two cars a breakfast room a patio a large fenced lot fourteen trees a front door with a brass knocker never knocked. Next is our house. Classic contemporary. Traditional modern. Attached garage, attached Florida room, attached patio, attached pool and cabana, attached roof. A front door mail slot through which pour *Time Magazine, Fortune, Life, Business Week,* the *Wall Street Journal,* the *New York Times,* the *New Yorker,* the *Saturday Review, M.D., Modern Medicine, Disease of the Month* . . . and also. . . . And in addition to all this, a quiet sealed letter from Baldwin saying: *Your daughter is not doing work compatible with her performance on the Stanford-Binet.* . . . And your son is not doing well, not well at all, very sad. Where is your son anyway? Once he stole trick-and-treat candy from some six-year-old kids, he himself being a robust ten. The beginning. Now your daughter steals. In the Village Pharmacy she made off with, yes she did, don't deny it, she made off with a copy of *Pageant Magazine* for no reason, she swiped a roll of Life Savers in a green wrapper and was in no need of saving her life or even in need of sucking candy; when she was no more than eight years old she stole, don't blush, she stole a package of Tums only because it was out on the counter and available, and the nice lady behind the counter (now dead) said nothing. . . . Sioux Drive. Maples, oaks, elms. Diseased elms cut down. Sioux Drive runs into Roosevelt Drive. Slow, turning lanes, not streets, all drives and lanes and ways and passes. A private police force. Quiet private police, in unmarked cars. Cruising on Saturday evenings with paternal smiles for the residents who are streaming in and out of houses, going to and from parties, a thousand parties, slightly staggering, the women in their furs alighting from automobiles bought of Ford and General Motors and Chrysler, very heavy automobiles. No foreign cars. Detroit. In 275 Sioux, down the block in that magnificent French-Normandy mansion, lives   himself, who has the C account itself, imagine that! Look at where he lives and look at the enormous trees and chimneys, imagine his many fireplaces, imagine his wife and children, imagine his wife's hair, imagine her fingernails, imagine her bathtub of smooth clean glowing pink, imagine their embraces, his trouser pockets filled with odd coins and keys and dust and peanuts, imagine their ecstasy on Sioux Drive, imagine their income tax returns, imagine their little boy's pride in his experimental car, a scaled-down C   , as he roars around the neighborhood on the sidewalks frightening dogs and Negro maids, oh imagine all these things, imagine everything, let your mind roar out all over Sioux Drive and Du Maurier Drive and Roosevelt Drive and Ticonderoga Pass and Burning Bush Way and Lincolnshire Pass and Lois Lane.

When spring comes, its winds blow nothing to Sioux Drive, no odors of hol-lyhocks or forsythia, nothing Sioux Drive doesn't already possess, everything is planted and performing. The weather vanes, had they weather vanes, don't have to turn with the wind, don't have to contend with the weather. There is no weather.

VI: Detroit

There is always weather in Detroit. Detroit's temperature is always 32°. Fast-falling temperatures. Slow-rising temperatures. Wind from the north-northeast four to forty miles an hour, small craft warnings, partly cloudy today and Wednesday changing to partly sunny through Thursday . . . small warnings of frost, soot warnings, traffic warnings, hazardous lake conditions small craft and swimmers, restless Negro gangs, restless cloud formations, restless temperatures aching to fall out the very bottom of the thermometer or shoot up over the top and boil everything over in red mercury.

Detroit's temperature is 32°. Fast-falling temperatures. Slow-rising temperatures. Wind from the north-northeast four to forty miles an hour. . . .

VII: Events

1. The girl's heart is pounding. In her pocket is a pair of gloves! In a plastic bag! Airproof breathproof plastic bag, gloves selling for twenty-five dollars on Branden's counter! In her pocket! Shoplifted! . . . In her purse is a blue comb, not very clean. In her purse is a leather billfold (a birthday present from her grandmother in Philadelphia) with snapshots of the family in clean plastic windows, in the billfold are bills, she doesn't know how many bills. . . . In her purse is an ominous note from her friend Tykie *What's this about Joe H. and the kids hanging around at Louise's Sat. night? You heard anything? . . .* passed in French class. In her purse is a lot of dirty yellow Kleenex, her mother's heart would break to see such very dirty Kleenex, and at the bottom of her purse are brown hairpins and safety pins and a broken pencil and a ballpoint pen (blue) stolen from somewhere forgotten and a purse-size compact of Cover Girl Make-Up, Ivory Rose. . . . Her lipstick is Broken Heart, a corrupt pink; her fingers are trembling like crazy; her teeth are beginning to chatter; her insides are alive; her eyes glow in her head; she is saying to her mother's astonished face *I want to steal but not to buy.*

2. At Clarita's. Day or night? What room is this? A bed, a regular bed, and a mattress on the floor nearby. Wallpaper hanging in strips. Clarita says she tore it like that with her teeth. She was fighting a barbaric tribe that night, high from some pills; she was battling for her life with men wearing helmets of heavy iron and their faces no more than Christian crosses to breathe through, every one of those bastards looking like her lover Simon, who seems to breathe with great difficulty through the slits of mouth and nostrils in his face. Clarita has never heard of Sioux Drive. Raymond Forrest cuts no ice with her, nor does the C   account and its millions; Harvard Business School could be at the corner of Vernor and 12th Street for all she cares, and Vietnam might have sunk by now into the Dead Sea under its tons of debris, for all the amazement she could show . . . her face is overworked, overwrought, at the age of twenty (thirty?) it is already exhausted but fanciful and ready for a laugh. Clarita says mournfully to me *Honey somebody is going to turn you out let me give you warning.* In a movie shown on late television Clarita is not a mess like this but a nurse, with short neat hair and a dedicated look, in love with her doctor and her doctor's patients and their diseases, enamored of needles and sponges and rubbing alcohol. . . . Or no: she is a private secretary. Robert Cummings is her boss. She helps him with fantastic plots, the canned audience laughs, no, the audience doesn't laugh because nothing is funny, instead her boss is Robert Taylor and they are not boss and secretary but husband and wife, she is threatened by a young starlet, she is grim, handsome, wifely, a good companion for a good man. . . . She is Claudette Colbert. Her sister too is Claudette Colbert.

They are twins, identical. Her husband Charles Boyer is a very rich handsome man and her sister, Claudette Colbert, is plotting her death in order to take her place as the rich man's wife, no one will know because they are *twins*. . . . All these marvelous lives Clarita might have lived, but she fell out the bottom at the age of thirteen. At the age when I was packing my overnight case for a slumber party at Toni Deshield's she was tearing filthy sheets off a bed and scratching up a rash on her arms. . . . Thirteen is uncommonly young for a white girl in Detroit, Miss Brock of the Detroit House of Correction said in a sad newspaper interview for the *Detroit News;* fifteen and sixteen are more likely. Eleven, twelve, thirteen are not surprising in colored . . . they are more precocious. What can we do? Taxes are rising and the tax base is falling. The temperature rises slowly but falls rapidly. Everything is falling out the bottom, Woodward Avenue is filthy, Livernois Avenue is filthy! Scraps of paper flutter in the air like pigeons, dirt flies up and hits you right in the eye, oh Detroit is breaking up into dangerous bits of newspaper and dirt, watch out. . . .

Clarita's apartment is over a restaurant. Simon her lover emerges from the cracks at dark. Mrs. Olesko, a neighbor of Clarita's, an aged white wisp of a woman, doesn't complain but sniffs with contentment at Clarita's noisy life and doesn't tell the cops, hating cops, when the cops arrive. I should give more fake names, more blanks, instead of telling all these secrets. I myself am a secret; I am a minor.

3. My father reads a paper at a medical convention in Los Angeles. There he is, on the edge of the North American continent, when the unmarked detective put his hand so gently on my arm in the aisle of Branden's and said, "Miss, would you like to step over here for a minute?"

And where was he when Clarita put her hand on my arm, that wintry dark sulphurous aching day in Detroit, in the company of closed-down barber shops, closed-down diners, closed-down movie houses, homes, windows, basements, faces . . . she put her hand on my arm and said, "Honey, are you looking for somebody down here?"

And was he home worrying about me, gone for two weeks solid, when they carried me off . . . ? It took three of them to get me in the police cruiser, so they said, and they put more than their hands on my arm.

4. I work on this lesson. My English teacher is Mr. Forest, who is from Michigan State. Not handsome, Mr. Forest, and his name is plain, unlike Raymond Forrest's, but he is sweet and rodentlike, he has conferred with the principal and my parents, and everything is fixed . . . treat her as if nothing has happened, a new start, begin again, only sixteen years old, what a shame, how did it happen?—nothing happened, nothing could have happened, a slight physiological modification known only to a gynecologist or to Dr. Coronet. I work on my lesson. I sit in my pink room. I look around the room with my sad pink eyes. I sigh, I dawdle, I pause, I eat up time, I am limp and happy to be home, I am sixteen years old suddenly, my head hangs heavy as a pumpkin on my shoulders, and my hair has just been cut by Mr. Faye at the Crystal Salon and is said to be very becoming.

(Simon too put his hand on my arm and said, "Honey, you have got to come with me," and in his six-by-six room we got to know each other. Would I go back to

Simon again? Would I lie down with him in all that filth and craziness? Over and over again.

a Clarita is being betrayed as in front of a Cunningham Drug Store she is nervously eyeing a colored man who may or may not have money, or a nervous white boy of twenty with sideburns and an Appalachian look, who may or may not have a knife hidden in his jacket pocket, or a husky red-faced man of friendly countenance who may or may not be a member of the Vice Squad out for an early twilight walk.)

I work on my lesson for Mr. Forest. I have filled up eleven pages. Words pour out of me and won't stop. I want to tell everything . . . what was the song Simon was always humming, and who was Simon's friend in a very new trench coat with an old high school graduation ring on his finger . . . ? Simon's bearded friend? When I was down too low for him, Simon kicked me out and gave me to him for three days, I think, on Fourteenth Street in Detroit, an airy room of cold cruel drafts with newspapers on the floor. . . . Do I really remember that or am I piecing it together from what they told me? Did they tell the truth? Did they know much of the truth?

VIII: Characters

1. Wednesdays after school, at four; Saturday mornings at ten. Mother drives me to Dr. Coronet. Ferns in the office, plastic or real, they look the same. Dr. Coronet is queenly, an elegant nicotine-stained lady who would have studied with Freud had circumstances not prevented it, a bit of a Catholic, ready to offer you some mystery if your teeth will ache too much without it. Highly recommended by Father! Forty dollars an hour, Father's forty dollars! Progress! Looking up! Looking better! That new haircut is so becoming, says Dr. Coronet herself, showing how normal she is for a woman with an I.Q. of 180 and many advanced degrees.

2. Mother. A lady in a brown suede coat. Boots of shiny black material, black gloves, a black fur hat. She would be humiliated could she know that of all the people in the world it is my ex-lover Simon who walks most like her . . . self-conscious and unreal, listening to distant music, a little bowlegged with craftiness. . . .

3. Father. Tying a necktie. In a hurry. On my first evening home he put his hand on my arm and said, "Honey, we're going to forget all about this."

4. Simon. Outside, a plane is crossing the sky, in here we're in a hurry. Morning. It must be morning. The girl is half out of her mind, whimpering and vague; Simon her dear friend is wretched this morning . . . he is wretched with morning itself . . . he forces her to give him an injection with that needle she knows is filthy, she has a dread of needles and surgical instruments and the odor of things that are to be sent into the blood, thinking somehow of her father. . . . This is a bad morning, Simon says that his mind is being twisted out of shape, and so he submits to the needle that he usually scorns and bites his lip with his yellowish teeth, his face going very

pale. *Ah baby!* he says in his soft mocking voice, which with all women is a mockery of love, *do it like this—Slowly—* And the girl, terrified, almost drops the precious needle but manages to turn it up to the light from the window . . . is it an extension of herself then? She can give him this gift then? *I wish you wouldn't do this to me,* she says, wise in her terror, because it seems to her that Simon's danger—in a few minutes he may be dead—is a way of pressing her against him that is more powerful than any other embrace. She has to work over his arm, the knotted corded veins of his arm, her forehead wet with perspiration as she pushes and releases the needle, staring at that mixture of liquid now stained with Simon's bright blood. . . . When the drug hits him she can feel it herself, she feels that magic that is more than any woman can give him, striking the back of his head and making his face stretch as if with the impact of a terrible sun. . . . She tries to embrace him but he pushes her aside and stumbles to his feet. *Jesus Christ,* he says. . . .

5. Princess, a Negro girl of eighteen. What is her charge? She is closed-mouthed about it, shrewd and silent, you know that no one had to wrestle her to the sidewalk to get her in here; she came with dignity. In the recreation room she sits reading *Nancy Drew and the Jewel Box Mystery,* which inspires in her face tiny wrinkles of alarm and interest: what a face! Light brown skin, heavy shaded eyes, heavy eyelashes, a serious sinister dark brow, graceful fingers, graceful wristbones, graceful legs, lips, tongue, a sugar-sweet voice, a leggy stride more masculine than Simon's and my mother's, decked out in a dirty white blouse and dirty white slacks; vaguely nautical is Princess' style. . . . At breakfast she is in charge of clearing the table and leans over me, saying, *Honey you sure you ate enough?*

6. The girl lies sleepless, wondering. Why here, why not there? Why Bloomfield Hills and not jail? Why jail and not her pink room? Why downtown Detroit and not Sioux Drive? What is the difference? Is Simon all the difference? The girl's head is a parade of wonders. She is nearly sixteen, her breath is marvelous with wonders, not long ago she was coloring with crayons and now she is smearing the landscape with paints that won't come off and won't come off her fingers either. She says to the matron *I am not talking about anything,* not because everyone has warned her not to talk but because, because she will not talk; because she won't say anything about Simon, who is her secret. And she says to the matron, *I won't go home,* up until that night in the lavatory when everything was changed. . . . "No, I won't go home I want to stay here," she says, listening to her own words with amazement, thinking that weeds might climb everywhere over that marvelous $180,000 house and dinosaurs might return to muddy the beige carpeting, but never never will she reconcile four o'clock in the morning in Detroit with eight o'clock breakfasts in Bloomfield Hills. . . . oh, she aches still for Simon's hands and his caressing breath, though he gave her little pleasure, he took everything from her (five-dollar bills, ten-dollar bills, passed into her numb hands by men and taken out of her hands by Simon) until she herself was passed into the hands of other men, police, when Simon evidently got tired of her and her hysteria. . . . *No, I won't go home, I don't want to be bailed out.* The girl thinks as a *Stubborn and Wayward Child* (one of several charges lodged against her), and the matron understands her crazy white-rimmed eyes that are seeking out some new violence that will keep her in jail, should someone threaten to let her out. Such children try to

strangle the matrons, the attendants, or one another . . . they want the locks locked forever, the doors nailed shut . . . and this girl is no different up until that night her mind is changed for her. . . .

IX: *That Night*

Princess and Dolly, a little white girl of maybe fifteen, hardy however as a sergeant and in the House of Correction for armed robbery, corner her in the lavatory at the farthest sink and the other girls look away and file out to bed, leaving her. God, how she is beaten up! Why is she beaten up? Why do they pound her, why such hatred? Princess vents all the hatred of a thousand silent Detroit winters on her body, this girl whose body belongs to me, fiercely she rides across the Midwestern plains on this girl's tender bruised body . . . revenge on the oppressed minorities of America! revenge on the slaughtered Indians! revenge on the female sex, on the male sex, revenge on Bloomfield Hills, revenge revenge. . . .

X: *Detroit*

In Detroit, weather weighs heavily upon everyone. The sky looms large. The horizon shimmers in smoke. Downtown the buildings are imprecise in the haze. Perpetual haze. Perpetual motion inside the haze. Across the choppy river is the city of Windsor, in Canada. Part of the continent has bunched up here and is bulging outward, at the tip of Detroit; a cold hard rain is forever falling on the expressways. . . . Shoppers shop grimly, their cars are not parked in safe places, their windshields may be smashed and graceful ebony hands may drag them out through their shatterproof smashed windshields, crying, *Revenge for the Indians!* Ah, they all fear leaving Hudson's and being dragged to the very tip of the city and thrown off the parking roof of Cobo Hall, that expensive tomb, into the river. . . .

XI: *Characters We Are Forever Entwined with*

1. Simon drew me into his tender rotting arms and breathed gravity into me. Then I came to earth, weighed down. He said, *You are such a little girl,* and he weighed me down with his delight. In the palms of his hands were teeth marks from his previous life experiences. He was thirty-five, they said. Imagine Simon in this room, in my pink room: he is about six feet tall and stoops slightly, in a feline cautious way, always thinking, always on guard, with his scuffed light suede shoes and his clothes that are anyone's clothes, slightly rumpled ordinary clothes that ordinary men might wear to not-bad jobs. Simon has fair long hair, curly hair, spent languid curls that are like . . . exactly like the curls of wood shavings to the touch, I am trying to be exact . . . and he smells of unheated mornings and coffee and too many pills coating his tongue with a faint green-white scum. . . . Dear Simon, who would be panicked in this room and in this house (right now Billie is vacuuming next door in my parents' room; a vacuum cleaner's roar is a sign of all good things), Simon who is said to have come from a home not much different from this, years ago, fleeing all the carpeting and the polished banisters . . . Simon has a deathly face, only desperate people fall in love with it. His face is bony and cautious, the bones of his cheeks prominent as

if with the rigidity of his ceaseless thinking, plotting, for he has to make money out of girls to whom money means nothing, they're so far gone they can hardly count it, and in a sense money means nothing to him either except as a way of keeping on with his life. *Each Day's Proud Struggle,* the title of a novel we could read at jail. . . . Each day he needs a certain amount of money. He devours it. It wasn't love he uncoiled in me with his hollowed-out eyes and his courteous smile, that remnant of a prosperous past, but a dark terror that needed to press itself flat against him, or against another man . . . but he was the first, he came over to me and took my arm, a claim. We struggled on the stairs and I said, *Let me loose, you're hurting my neck, my face,* it was such a surprise that my skin hurt where he rubbed it, and afterward we lay face to face and he breathed everything into me. In the end I think he turned me in.

2. Raymond Forrest. I just read this morning that Raymond Forrest's father, the chairman of the board at   died of a heart attack on a plane bound for London. I would like to write Raymond Forrest a note of sympathy. I would like to thank him for not pressing charges against me one hundred years ago, saving me, being so generous . . . well, men like Raymond Forrest are generous men, not like Simon. I would like to write him a letter telling of my love, or of some other emotion that is positive and healthy. Not like Simon and his poetry, which he scrawled down when he was high and never changed a word . . . but when I try to think of something to say, it is Simon's language that comes back to me, caught in my head like a bad song, it is always Simon's language:

There is no reality only dreams
Your neck may get snapped when you wake
My love is drawn to some violent end
She keeps wanting to get away
My love is heading downward
And I am heading upward
She is going to crash on the sidewalk
And I am going to dissolve into the clouds

XII: Events

1. Out of the hospital, bruised and saddened and converted, with Princess' grunts still tangled in my hair . . . and Father in his overcoat looking like a prince himself, come to carry me off. Up the expressway and out north to home. Jesus Christ, but the air is thinner and cleaner here. Monumental houses. Heartbreaking sidewalks, so clean.

2. Weeping in the living room. The ceiling is two stories high and two chandeliers hang from it. Weeping, weeping, though Billie the maid is *probably listening.* I will never leave home again. Never. Never leave home. Never leave this home again, never.

3. Sugar doughnuts for breakfast. The toaster is very shiny and my face is distorted in it. Is that my face?

4. The car is turning in the driveway. Father brings me home. Mother embraces me. Sunlight breaks in movieland patches on the roof of our traditional-contemporary home, which was designed for the famous automotive stylist whose identity, if I told you the name of the famous car he designed, you would all know, so I can't tell you because my teeth chatter at the thought of being sued . . . or having someone climb into my bedroom with a rope to strangle me. . . . The car turns up the blacktop drive. The house opens to me like a doll's house, so lovely in the sunlight, the big living room beckons to me with its walls falling away in a delirium of joy at my return. Billie the maid is *no doubt* listening from the kitchen as I burst into tears and the hysteria Simon got so sick of. Convulsed in Father's arms, I say I will never leave again, never, why did I leave, where did I go, what happened, my mind is gone wrong, my body is one big bruise, my backbone was sucked dry, it wasn't the men who hurt me and Simon never hurt me but only those girls . . . my God, how they hurt me . . . I will never leave home again. . . . The car is perpetually turning up the drive and I am perpetually breaking down in the living room and we are perpetually taking the right exit from the expressway (Lahser Road) and the wall of the rest room is perpetually banging against my head and perpetually are Simon's hands moving across my body and adding everything up and so too are Father's hands on my shaking bruised back, far from the surface of my skin on the surface of my good blue cashmere coat (dry-cleaned for my release). . . . I weep for all the money here, for God in gold and beige carpeting, for the beauty of chandeliers and the miracle of a clean polished gleaming toaster and faucets that run both hot and cold water, and I tell them, *I will never leave home, this is my home, I love everything here, I am in love with everything here.* . . .

I am home.

1969

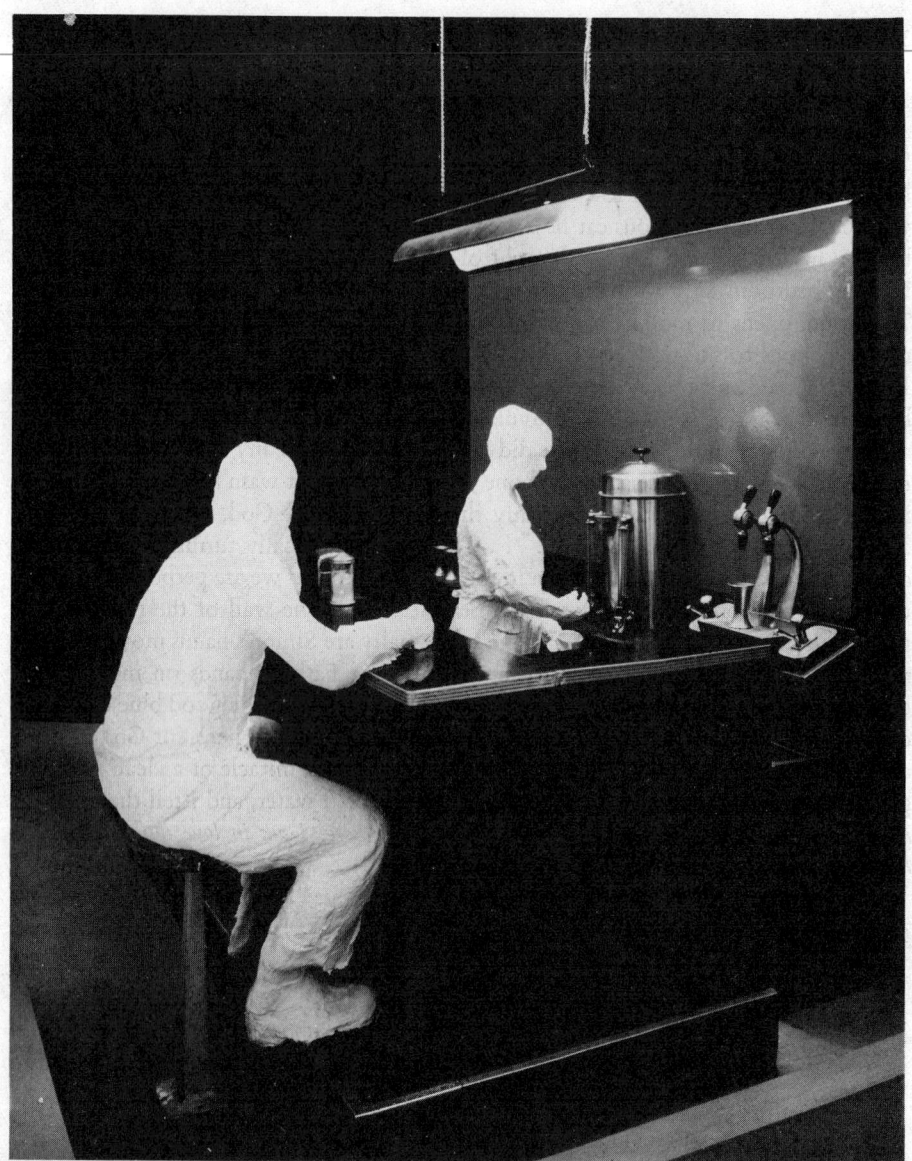

George Segal,
The Diner,
plaster and assemblage, 1964–1966.
Collection Walker Art Center, Minneapolis.
Gift of the T. B. Walker Foundation, 1966.

The Literature of Postwar America: Poetry 1940–1973

 The generation of poets who flourished after World War II—poets as diverse as Robert Lowell and Elizabeth Bishop, Theodore Roethke and Frank O'Hara, John Berryman and John Ashbery, Allen Ginsberg and A. R. Ammons, Adrienne Rich and James Wright—had one thing in common: They had to define themselves against the achievements of their great modernist predecessors. American poetics and American aesthetics had been broadly defined by the first generation of twentieth-century American poets. T. S. Eliot and Ezra Pound, on the one hand, had made American poetry international and had established free verse as the modernist mode *par excellence*. They wrote as educated men, readers of history and foreign languages, raiders of culture; their poems demanded a readership that did not flinch at phrases quoted from Sanskrit or Chinese, historical references, and cultivated allusion. Robert Frost, on the other hand, had established the right of American poetry to be sturdily American in syntax and local accent, and William Carlos Williams had founded a laconic urban poetry of hard-edged realism. Langston Hughes and other writers of the Harlem Renaissance had claimed poetic value for the black vernacular and for the representation of ghetto life. Wallace Stevens, the most elusive of the modernists, had brought philosophic skepticism into American poetry and had found a meditative style—ironic and syntactically elaborate—adequate to the complexity of his subject. The second generation, inheriting these victories, chose in part to continue, in part to correct or reject, the work of their predecessors.

Modernism in an American Vernacular

The poets after World War II seem, in retrospect, more American, less European, than most of their poetic forebears. The wave of international modernism had receded, and the new poets no longer exhibited the defensiveness so common to American poetry since its inception. With the rise of American world power in the wake of the war, fewer writers believe in American inferiority to Europe. There would be influxes, as we shall see, into American poetry from the poetry of other countries, but there was no longer the need for American poets to remake themselves into European or English writers.

The chief European influence on the poets of the second generation was not a poet but, strange to say, Freud, the Viennese inventor of a new psychology. The Freudian model for man's inner life (which replaced the classical and Christian model of "faculties" such as the intellect, the will, and the imagination) divided the self into three components: the superego, which urged the standards of behavior and conscience absorbed from parents and social norms; the id, which represented the instincts and drives often disapproved of by society and therefore repressed; and the ego, the integrated self that mediates the conflicting demands of the superego and the id. It was perhaps not surprising that Freud's emphasis on dark and unruly drives, driven underground only to erupt disastrously in violence or madness, appealed to a generation that had just experienced World War II.

But it was a second part of the Freudian theory—the conjecture that the behavior of one's parents contributes greatly to one's sense of self and one's later life—that appears most conspicuously as an influence in American poetry. Many of the second-generation poets had undergone psychoanalysis or psychoanalytic therapy, and the work of the therapeutic hour—a recalling of incidents of childhood and youth—soon appeared in poetry. Roethke, Jarrell, Berryman, Lowell, Anne Sexton, and Sylvia Plath all made poetry out of the family constellation described in psychoanalytic terms. Lowell's *Life Studies* (1959) was the first full anatomy of the family; Sexton's *To Bedlam and Part Way Back* (1960) was written at the suggestion of a therapist after Sexton had been hospitalized for a mental breakdown; Berryman's *77 Dream Songs* (1964) showed the id (renamed

Confessional Poetry

Notebook: as my title intends, the poems in this book are written as one poem, intuitive in arrangement, but not a pile or sequence of related material. It is less an almanac than the story of my life. Many events turn up, many others of equal or greater personal reality do not. This is not my private lash, or confession, or a puritan's too literal pornographic honesty, glad to share secret embarrassment and triumph. The time is a summer, an autumn, a winter, a spring, another summer. . . . My plot rolls with the seasons, but one year is confused with another. I have flashbacks to what I remember, and fables inspired by impulse. Accident threw up subjects, and the plot swallowed them—famished for human chances.

Robert Lowell, "Afterthought" in *Notebook* (1970)

Henry) in full spate; and Plath's "Daddy" (1966) became the most notorious poem exposing the underside of the family romance. The Freudian therapeutic approach, urging the exploration of one's darkest impulses, led to "confessions" being made not only on the analyst's couch but also on the printed page.

In describing such writing as confessional poetry, critics often did not distinguish between life and art, nor did they admit that such personal revelations in art have a long history in poetry in English, reaching back as far as Shakespeare's sonnets. "When Shakespeare said 'Two loves have I,' reader, he was not kidding," wrote John Berryman. The label "confessional poetry" has usually been applied pejoratively—and there was just enough truth in the phrase to make it a popular one. One "confessional poet," Robert Lowell, defended his practice in his last printed poem, "Epilogue," with the retort to his critics, "Yet why not say what happened?" The motive underlying all art, after all, is the drive toward accuracy: Without the artist's record of "what happened," we would remain only transient statistics:

> We are poor passing facts,
> warned by that to give
> each figure in the photograph
> his living name.

If Freud was the chief external influence on American poetry after 1945, there was nonetheless a continuing influence of foreign poetry as well. In part, this came about because some of our poets lived abroad; though the great period of expatriation had ended, several of the second-generation poets lived for some time in foreign countries. Bishop spent years in Brazil, Snyder in Japan, Lowell (in his fifties) in England, Ashbery in France, Plath in England (where she died). Even poets who did not live abroad often traveled widely, through Fulbright fellowships and international poetry festivals. The cross-fertilization of American literature that took place in this generation imported Arthur Rimbaud (through O'Hara and Ashbery), Rainer Maria Rilke and Herman Hesse (through Jarrell and Wright), Cesar Vallejo, Pablo Neruda, Carlos Drummond de Andrade, and other South American poets (through Robert Bly and Elizabeth Bishop), Ted Hughes (via his wife, Sylvia Plath), Buddhist poetry (through Ginsberg and Snyder), and Constantine Cavafy (through James Merrill). The special case of Auden's residence in America caused him to be the chief British influence on the young. The art of translation received new energy through Lowell's *Imitations* (1961), in which Lowell translated classical and European originals in a new way: He borrowed the subject matter and structure of the parent poem while giving the syntax and diction an unmistakably Lowellesque ring.

But though the poets after 1945 interested themselves in foreign poetry, they did not, in the manner of Eliot and Pound, adopt European modes of speech in their poetry. Pound's archaisms, Eliot's anglicisms, were purged from the new American poetry. The foreign poets read by the later poets were silently absorbed into the American vernacular. It is chiefly by new structures in the lyric and new kinds of imagery that we recognize the presence of European or South American or Asian poetry. There is very little attempt at a European or international speaking voice, and even when the perspective of the poet is a global or

The Long Line

Its natural inspiration of the moment that keeps it moving, disparate things put down together, shorthand notations of visual imagery, juxtapositions of hydrogen juke-box—abstract haikus sustain the mystery & put iron poetry back into the line: the last line of *Sunflower Sutra* is the extreme, one stream of single word associations, summing up. Mind is shapely, Art is shapely. Meaning Mind practiced in spontaneity invents forms in its own image & gets to Last Thoughts.

Allen Ginsberg, notes for *Howl* (1959)

international one—as in Lowell, Ginsberg, or Snyder—the perspective is expressed in indigenous American tones.

And the tones became increasingly varied. Whitman, in the nineteenth century, had represented himself as the channel for the "varied carols" of America; through him, the "many long dumb voices" would find utterance. He implied a hope that one day the silent voices would be able to speak for themselves, and in this century they have begun to fulfill his prophecy. Through Allen Ginsberg, the American immigrant voice first entered American poetry in a powerful way. In his long sequence "Kaddish," Ginsberg presented the life of his mother, a Jewish immigrant from Russia, as typical of the unbearable strain put on the psyche by such a violent break in experience. Ginsberg's rich social documentation marked a new era in American lyric; in his phenomenally successful *Howl* (1956) and the volumes that followed it in quick succession, Jews, beatniks, Vietnam protesters, and urban homosexuals all appeared in believable form.

Through the activity of Dudley Randall, the Broadside Press in Detroit began to publish a steady stream of black poets (Etheredge Knight, Don Lee, and others), while in New York, trade presses, over the years, published other black poets (including Gwendolyn Brooks, June Jordan, Audre Lorde, Michael Harper, Sonia Sanchez, and Nikki Giovanni). In 1949 Gwendolyn Brooks received the Pulitzer Prize for poetry; like many other black poets, she responded to the late 1960s' black consciousness movement by consciously writing as a black for black audiences.

A New Diversity

The acknowledging of ethnicity in poetry, not only in subject matter but also in language, marked a new diversity in American poetry and a reaction against the modernist impersonality of voice. Against the conventional history of American poetry—as a descendant of English poetry—the new ethnicity insisted that a poetry belongs also to its physical location and that the proper predecessor of American poetry was the poetry of the first inhabitants of this country, the American Indians. The resurgence of Native American poetry as a source of inspiration, especially in the work of Gary Snyder, has been an impetus to Native Americans to repossess their own literature and to add to it.

An increased regional diversity also entered American poetry after World War II as, for the first time, a strong poetic school was founded on the West Coast. Though several of the "beat" writers (notably Ginsberg and Kerouac) were easterners, others (Snyder, Robert Duncan) were natives of the West Coast. Both groups celebrated the landscape and mores of the Pacific states. Strong ecological concern began to be voiced by Gary Snyder and by the Alaskan poet John Haines. Even Allen Ginsberg was later to write a rueful poem called "Ecologue" (the title is a triple pun on *echo, eclogue,* and *ecology*) about his own ill-fated attempt at living a rural life. Though Ginsberg remains an urban poet, he is imaginatively moved by the preservation of life on the land.

Other regions maintained or began poetic activity. In the South, Allen Tate, John Crowe Ransom, and Robert Penn Warren continued the southern tradition of belles lettres: Their most famous pupil, Robert Lowell, though a northerner, absorbed their principles of poetry. As creative writing programs began to proliferate across the country in American universities, the clustering of older and younger poets in workshops changed the constitution of English departments (themselves newly engaged in the close examination of texts). Universities increasingly became the base for journals and for poetry readings. The poetry reading became a popular social rite; on T. S. Eliot's occasional visits from England, huge throngs would gather to hear him read. Frost too drew enormous audiences in the 1950s and was the official poet at the 1960 presidential inauguration of John F. Kennedy. In a different mode, Ginsberg (protesting American involvement in Vietnam) and Adrienne Rich (protesting the oppression of women) also drew large audiences. As poets read in state after state, in university after university, poetry increasingly seemed a possession common to all the states, not simply a monopoly of New England.

Various "schools" of poetry seemed to form after World War II. The "New York school" (Ashbery, O'Hara, and Kenneth Koch) had particularly close relations with painters, especially with the abstract expressionists. They turned inward to a spontaneous recording of imaginative moments and wished above all to be amusing, intimate, secular, and colloquial—a contrast with both the political fierceness of Pound and the elegiac solemnity of Eliot. Their affinities were neither with philosophy nor with history but with the fine arts—painting, sculpture, theater, and ballet.

The Beats (the name, conferred by journalists, suggests the downtrodden, the jazzy, and the beatified) wrote a poetry characterized by a linguistic freedom that included words commonly considered obscene. Perhaps more disturbing to the common reader was the open admission in poetry, by Ginsberg and others, of the use of drugs, of homosexual experience, of promiscuity in sexual life, and of disillusionment with American government and politics. The humor of the Beats, their cheerful and unpredictable readings, their spontaneity in aesthetic matters ("First thought, best thought") was a revelation to more formal American poets; Robert Lowell changed his own early style (modeled on that of Allen Tate) after hearing a Beat reading and realizing that the Beats were closer to the American reality than he was.

Black Mountain

A poem is energy transferred from where the poet got it (he will have some several causations), by way of the poem itself to, all the way over to, the reader. Okay. Then the poem itself must, at all points, be a high energy-construct and, at all points, an energy-discharge. . . .

And I think it can be boiled down to one statement: . . . ONE PERCEPTION MUST IMMEDIATELY AND DIRECTLY LEAD TO A FURTHER PERCEPTION. It means exactly what it says, is a matter of, at *all* points (even, I should say, of our management of daily reality as of the daily work) get on with it, keep moving, keep in, speed, the nerves, their speed, the perceptions, theirs, the acts, the split second acts, the whole business, keep it moving as fast as you can, citizen. And if you also set up as a poet, USE USE USE the process at all points, in any given poem always, always one perception must must must MOVE, INSTANTER, ON ANOTHER!

Charles Olson, "Projective Verse" (1950)

A more complicated and less successful school was that of the "Black Mountain poets," so called because they had been connected with Black Mountain, an avant-garde college in North Carolina where the poet Charles Olson was rector. The best-known members of the group, besides Olson, are Robert Creeley, Robert Duncan, and Denise Levertov. At Black Mountain, the faculty included the dancer Merce Cunningham, the painters Franz Kline, Josef Albers, and Robert Rauschenberg, and the composer John Cage. Olson was an admirer of Pound—for years he visited Pound at St. Elizabeth's hospital in Washington, where Pound was confined for mental illness. All of the Black Mountain poets derive (perhaps too closely) from Pound. In Olson's epic about his native Gloucester, *The Maximus Poems,* one sees Pound's influence most

Imagism

An "Image" is that which presents an intellectual and emotional complex in an instant of time. . . .

It is the presentation of such a "complex" instantaneously which gives that sense of sudden liberation; that sense of freedom from time limits and space limits; that sense of sudden growth, which we experience in the presence of the greatest works of art.

It is better to present one Image in a lifetime than to produce voluminous works.

Ezra Pound, "A Few Don'ts" (1913)

clearly. Though without Pound's social urgency, *The Maximus Poems* adopt Pound's method of historical collage, by which one fragment of historical information is placed against another, over and over, until a jagged accumulation is achieved. The followers of Pound have tended to emphasize, as he did, a montage of phrases and a collocation of images over syntactic complexity and intellectual or logical connection; in this they are the descendants of the American Imagist poets.

The combination of interest in irrational forces within (via Freud and Jung) and disturbance by irrational forces without (especially war) aroused in one group of poets (known as "deep image poets") a wish to tap the unconscious psychic sources of poetry. Robert Bly, James Wright, and W. S. Merwin turned aside, in different ways, from the 1950s' poetry of formal intellectualization and attempted to express, chiefly by mysterious images, "deeper" animal and preconscious motives. They turned to the model of the American Indian shaman (or other such figures of inspiration) as their image of the poet; Bly has given poetry readings wearing a variety of masks resembling the totemic masks worn by witch doctors or shamans. The brooding poetry of Bly and the bleak poetry of Wright and Merwin appealed especially to the antiestablishment young, who associated the poetry of formal prosody and intellectual content with a conservative political stance.

The chief woman poets of this period—Elizabeth Bishop, Anne Sexton, Sylvia Plath, and Adrienne Rich—do not in any sense form a "school" with a common aesthetic. However, consciously feminist poetry (including lesbian poetry such as that written by Rich and Audre Lorde) sees itself as having a common political aim, the claiming of literary space for the voices of women, who, before this generation, have not had access, to the same degree as men, to a literary education. And all the women poets—like Emily Dickinson and Marianne Moore —rebel against the conventional "woman's voice" in literature—obedient, docile, religious, coy, demure, self-deprecating. One can see this rebellion even in minor poets like Edna St. Vincent Millay, Elinor Wylie, and Sara Teasdale; in more powerful voices the terrain of subject matter available to women is enlarged and amplified. In the nineteenth-century past, women wrote chiefly of nature, love,

---

The Voice of Women

Women's work and thinking has been made to seem sporadic, errant, orphaned of any tradition of its own.

In fact, we do have a long feminist tradition, both oral and written, a tradition which has built on itself over and over, recovering essential elements even when those have been strangled or wiped out. . . .

Today women are talking to each other, recovering an oral culture, telling our life-stories, reading aloud to one another the books that have moved and healed us, analyzing the language that has lied about us, reading our own words aloud to each other . . . to name and found a culture of our own.

Adrienne Rich, *On Lies, Secrets, and Silence* (1978)

God, and death; Moore, while not abandoning such subjects altogether, had staked out a precise territory of her own, strongly voiced, unapologetic, full of gusto. Bishop, encouraged by Moore, took travel as her subject—a topic thought to be more suited to men and to the narrative than to women and to the lyric. Sexton, who had from her days as a model a powerfully satiric sense of social demands on women, mocked the infantile roles assigned to them. Rich took on a voice—prophetic, denunciatory—reserved by convention to men, especially to preachers. And Plath wrote a powerful poetry of ambivalence about herself as a daughter, wife, and mother (roles scarcely treated in earlier poetry). Nonetheless, the modernist inheritance is strong in these later women. Bishop would not have been the poet she was without Stevens (whose visual sense she admired and whose limpidity of line she learned from); Rich's first masters were Frost and Auden, and she has never forsaken her allegiance to a Frostian "common language."

Poetry and Society

It has usually not been characteristic of the lyric to include a great deal of social detail; that work has been left to the novel. But both Pound and the poets of the second generation decided to reclaim history and social reality for poetry. What Pound did in the epic, the later poets did in lyric, and anyone looking at Pre-Raphaelite or Georgian lyric in England would find it hard to believe that a half century later this thin and attenuated form would be bursting with political and social information. World War II itself produced rather little in the way of lyric documentation, though the war poems of Randall Jarrell are a notable exception. The chief political events affecting later poets were the war in Vietnam and the political assassinations of the 1960s. Though some poems comment directly on the Vietnam War, it was chiefly important in the way that it polarized society, with the poets generally aligning themselves with the draft-liable young and against official government policy. The sense among poets that they had an important message to utter to the country awoke poetry from the formal and meditative stance that it had adopted during the "tranquillized fifties" (as Lowell called them) and gave a new impulse to poetry spoken or chanted aloud to a listening public.

The March on the Pentagon in 1967, in which Lowell and other writers participated (described by Norman Mailer in *The Armies of the Night*) consolidated the powerful entry of authors into American political protest. Merwin, Ginsberg, Rich, and others protested the Vietnam War: Merwin wrote about Asians dying, Ginsberg about the politics behind the war, Rich of the human waste of battle. In the same decade, the assassinations, in turn, of John F. Kennedy, Robert Kennedy, and Martin Luther King powerfully affected poets, black and white; many elegies were written about both President Kennedy and Dr. King. The bitterness with respect to America that entered the poetry of Lowell, Ginsberg, and many others at this time directly reflects the double disillusionment of the war abroad and the assassinations at home. With the ending of the war, the political force of poetry abated, and it seemed (with the exception of feminist poetry) to be entering a new meditative phase. At the same time, poets experienced a nostalgia for the time when they felt necessary to the social good, and American poets know that their poetry is not formed under the pressure that poets feel in societies where to utter a protest poem is to put oneself in danger of arrest. Since the 1930s, America has been a refuge for émigré writers from Germany, Russia, and other countries; American poets can envy the seriousness of purpose with which such poets write and the degree to which they feel their writing is necessary.

If the subject matter of American poetry in this period turned radically to the subconscious and the social, it also, though more subtly, turned to the scientific. It may be in the future that the acceptance of the scientific model for knowledge will be seen as the most profound change in poetry of this period. Not all poets by any means accept such a model, at least not consciously; the poetry of Roethke, for instance, can be seen as a violent striving against such a model. On the other hand, most of the poets of this generation have neither a religious nor a political creed. Their conception of the universe no longer contains a presiding God or a teleological purpose. They are familiar with physical and chemical descriptions of the universe unknown to poets of earlier centuries, descriptions comparable in their revolutionary force to the Copernican hypothesis. The neutrino and the double helix, invisible though they are to the naked eye, are part of our conceptual world. The poets of this generation are aware of interstellar distances and of electron microscopy. Only a few poets incorporate the vocabulary of science (A. R. Ammons, because of his scientific training, does it entirely naturally; James Merrill does it imaginatively). But even Lowell, the most unscientific of poets, could not continue to write the poetry he wrote in his young manhood, when he had become a Roman Catholic convert. "Against my will," he wrote, "I left the City of God where it belongs." In becoming an unbeliever, Lowell had to become a different poet; his poems could no longer have the neatness of closure, the linear purpose, that they had in their religious phase. The formal properties of a successful poem always mirror the formal properties of the universe it represents—and a universe displaying several "layers" of order (macrocosmic to microcosmic), a complex dynamic of physical and biological evolution, and a tendency toward entropy cannot be mirrored by a single static structure. The freedom of modern free verse is philosophical as well as experimental, and the diffuseness of closure in recent poetry is a gesture toward the multiplicity of process in the universe as we now understand it.

"The Inroads of Science"

The function of poetry in a Machine Age is identical to its function in any other age; and its capacities for presenting the most complete synthesis of human values remain essentially immune from any of the so-called inroads of science.

Hart Crane, "Modern Poetry" (1930)

The language of the poetry of an era must also reflect its understanding of the self. In this period, the distrust of the excessively "rational" appears in many poets' distrust of "adult" language. To give the unconscious a language, Berryman's Henry and Roethke's "lost son" speak in baby talk; Sexton and Plath turn to fairy tales. Poetic language is widened, in this era, in other ways as well —through Ginsberg's defiant use of obscenities, in the self-consciously ironic "camp" talk of O'Hara, Ashbery, and Merrill, in colloquialism of all sorts (from street vernacular in Don Lee to the language of political protest in Rich). The notion of the self as a composite of its own past furnishes Lowell with his rich amalgam of language, in which personal history is interwoven with on the history of the world. A reversal of the emblematic language of Emerson (in which a natural object is made to reveal spiritual reality) appears in A. R. Ammons (who makes an inner state real by attaching it to nature). The language of Chinese and Japanese poetry, introduced to American poetry by Amy Lowell in Imagism, has taken on new life in the minimalist verse of W. S. Merwin and Gary Snyder, and Buddhist chants have influenced Ginsberg. The American language, always in a process of change, was first made into notable poetry by Whitman and Dickinson. But their example was too daring, and the indigenous freedom of the American language has had to assert its rights in poetry once again in each generation. It no longer, at least, has subject status with respect to the English language.

In the poetry of the 1950s and 1960s we can see the continuation of many of the attempts begun by early modernism. The American long poem continues to be written, whether in Poundian collage (as by Olson) or by means of the poetic sequence (the way favored by Eliot and Stevens, and after them by Robert Lowell in *Life Studies* and *History,* for instance and Ammons in *The Snow Poems* and other sequences). The long discursive poem is written by Ashbery ("Self-portrait in a Convex Mirror") as well as by Ammons ("Sphere"); Merrill has done a long "conversation poem" in three books, *The Changing Light at Sandover.* Experiments in the arrangement of words on the page continue: Ammons has written on an adding-machine tape ("Tape for the Turn of the Year"); Merrill has taken dictation from a Ouija board; Ashbery has written a double-column poem ("Litany"). The prose poem (most brilliantly done in Ashbery's *Three Poems*) has been successfully attempted by Ginsberg and Rich, among others. Free verse and formal verse continue to dispute the field, with Lowell oscillating back and forth between them throughout his career. The implication of this variety of form is that all poetic forms are possible, that modes of expression and formulation are as various as the human psyche, and that America's chief contribution to poetry will be its encouraging of extreme diversity.

Of course, we see too many poets, so to speak, when we look at the production of our own century. Poets in their own time are often noticed chiefly for their topicality, as they comment on current events, delineate common problems, or voice conventionally acceptable sentiments. It is always sobering to look at journals, book reviews, and anthologies of a hundred years ago. In them

> ## "The Form of the Poem Need Not Be Foreclosed"
>
> The history of contemporary American poetry will record massive movement toward conventionally open styles. Ginsberg, Warren, Wright, Lowell, Roethke, Simpson, Dickey, and others have been accused of abandoning something like an ideal music for an inferior form. This argument is not resolvable because it masks political, economic, and cultural arguments metastasized to aesthetics. All we can really ask, must ask, of a poet is that his poem in part and in whole give pleasure, be durable, and lead us to better know what we dimly intuit as the reality of life.
>
> Dave Smith, *Local Assays* (1985)

we see poets now judged to be minor or negligible being published in great quantity, reviewed in ecstatic terms, and massively anthologized. Today their names are forgotten, since history winnows literature to the few poets of each century that subsequent poets can admire for their language and form. An observer a hundred years hence will be able to see resemblances among our poets where we see chiefly differences, and may be able to find a single descriptive rubric by which to characterize poetry after World War II. As yet, we seem to have found only the feebly linear term "postmodernist," which abandons any attempt at substantive description. Perhaps the era will finally seem to fall into a political period and a domestic period, with the more intimate verse of Merrill, Ammons, and Ashbery succeeding to the passions of the Vietnam War years. Poetic styles arise by reaction; after the quiet formality of the 1950s came the overt declarations and strenuous political rhetoric of the 1960s; this was followed by an inward-turning and more ironic stance in the 1970s. All of these forms continue to perform the task of poetry: to record and analyze in each age the inner life of mankind, and to maintain for each generation the freshness and inventiveness of imagination and language.

Further Reading:
R. Jarrell, *Poetry and the Age*, 1953.
S. Stepanchev, *American Poetry Since 1945*, 1965.
R. Howard, *Alone with America*, 1969.
The Survival of Poetry, ed. M. Dodsworth, 1970.
H. Bloom, *The Ringers in the Tower*, 1971.
Contemporary Poetry in America: Essays and Introductions, ed. R. Boyers, 1973.
K. Malkoff, *Crowell's Handbook of Contemporary American Poetry*, 1973.
E. Faas, *Towards a New American Poetics: Essays*
and Interviews: Olson, Duncan, Snyder, Creeley, Bly, Ginsberg, 1976.
D. Kalstone, *Five Temperaments: Elizabeth Bishop, Robert Lowell, James Merrill, Adrienne Rich, John Ashbery*, 1977.
L. Lieberman, *Unassigned Frequencies*, 1977.
R. Pinsky, *The Situation of Poetry*, 1977.
H. Nemerov, *Figures of Thought*, 1978.
C. Altieri, *Enlarging the Temple: New Directions in American Poetry During the 1960s*, 1979.

Harvard Guide to Comtemporary American
Writing, ed. D. Hoffman, 1979.
C. Molesworth, *The Fierce Embrace: A Study of
Contemporary American Poetry*, 1979.
H. Vendler, *Part of Nature, Part of Us: Modern
American Poets*, 1980.
A. Williamson, *Introspection and Contemporary*

Poetry, 1984.
R. Hass, *Twentieth-Century Pleasures: Prose on
Poetry*, 1985.
D. Smith, *Local Assays: On Contemporary
American Poetry*, 1985.
R. von Hallberg, *American Poetry and Culture,
1945–1980*, 1985.

Theodore Roethke
1908–1963

Theodore Roethke's childhood intimacy with the world of his father's greenhouse
provided a rich vein of poetic material, from which his most individual poems
issued. American poets (except for Whitman) have traditionally been bookish; the
soil has been relatively absent from our verse. Roethke knew swamp and soil,
cuttings and roots, the dark life of plants in the earth before their time for
blossoming. He knew, too, the authoritarian structure of the greenhouse, where
his German grandfather and his father ruled with an iron hand; there he was
helpless, small, frightened, "the lost son."

The voice of the child he was is Roethke's most notable poetic invention
(imitated, since he invented it, by poets as various as Robert Lowell, Anne
Sexton, and Sylvia Plath). Of course, Roethke did not entirely invent this
child-voice; he learned it in part from William Blake, whose *Songs of Innocence*
first memorably introduced the voice of the child into poetry in English. But
Roethke's child has, so to speak, studied Freud and discovered his unconscious.
His preconscious language is full of brilliant linguistic and poetic invention; its
quick, elusive rhythms and slippery sounds convey the daring investigations of
the bewildered child.

Roethke's greenhouse poems occur in the volume *The Lost Son* (1948). His
volumes subsequent to *Praise to the End!* (1952) and *The Waking* (1953) became
both more formal (with many imitations of William Butler Yeats and
T. S. Eliot) and more prolix in their use of free verse, while still containing
some lyrics of terse power, especially some short bitter poems about confinement
for mental illness.

Roethke was born in Saginaw, Michigan, and educated at the University of
Michigan; he spent most of his teaching life (1948–1963) at the University of
Washington in Seattle, where he served as mentor to many younger poets and
creative writing students, including James Wright. Roethke's successive
breakdowns and recurrent alcoholism made his life increasingly difficult until his
early death in his fifties.

His influence on the emergence of West Coast writing was a powerful one,
and his advocacy of formal prosody (both in his own work and in his teaching)
was one of the countermeasures against the domination by free verse of the
American poetic scene. Though he was a large, powerfully built man, the truest
self for which he found a voice was the small soul that trembled in childhood
before the mysteries of nature.

Further Reading:

R. J. Mills, Jr., *Theodore Roethke*, 1963.
Theodore Roethke: Essays on the Poetry, ed. A. Stein, 1965.
K. Malkoff, *Theodore Roethke: An Introduction to the Poetry*, 1966.
A. Seagar, *The Glass House: The Life of Theodore Roethke*, 1968.
R. A. Blessing, *Theodore Roethke's Dynamic Vision*, 1974.
R. Sullivan, *Theodore Roethke: The Garden*

Master, 1975.
J. La Belle, *The Echoing Wood of Theodore Roethke*, 1976.
Keith R. Moul, *Theodore Roethke's Career: An Annotated Bibliography*, 1977.
H. Williams, *"The Edge Is What I Have": Theodore Roethke and After*, 1977.
J. Parini, *Theodore Roethke: An American Romantic*, 1979.

Text:

Collected Poems, 1966.
See also *On the Poet and His Craft: Selected Prose of Theodore Roethke*, ed. R. J. Mills, Jr., 1965.
Selected Letters of Theodore Roethke, ed. R. J.

Mills, Jr., 1968.
Straw for the Fire: From the Notebooks of Theodore Roethke, 1943–1963, ed. D. Wagoner, 1972.

Cuttings

Sticks-in-a-drowse droop over sugary loam,
Their intricate stem-fur dries;
But still the delicate slips keep coaxing up water;
The small cells bulge;

One nub of growth   5
Nudges a sand-crumb loose,
Pokes through a musty sheath
Its pale tendrilous horn.

1948

Cuttings

(later)

This urge, wrestle, resurrection of dry sticks,
Cut stems struggling to put down feet,
What saint strained so much,
Rose on such lopped limbs to a new life?

I can hear, underground, that sucking and sobbing,   5
In my veins, in my bones I feel it,—

The small waters seeping upward,
The tight grains parting at last.
When sprouts break out,
Slippery as fish,
I quail, lean to beginnings, sheath-wet.   10
1948

My Papa's Waltz

The whiskey on your breath
Could make a small boy dizzy;
But I hung on like death:
Such waltzing was not easy.

We romped until the pans   5
Slid from the kitchen shelf;
My mother's countenance
Could not unfrown itself.

The hand that held my wrist
Was battered on one knuckle;   10
At every step you missed
My right ear scraped a buckle.

You beat time on my head
With a palm caked hard by dirt,
Then waltzed me off to bed   15
Still clinging to your shirt.
1948

Dolor

I have known the inexorable sadness of pencils,
Neat in their boxes, dolor of pad and paper-weight,
All the misery of manila folders and mucilage,
Desolation in immaculate public places,
Lonely reception room, lavatory, switchboard,   5

The unalterable pathos of basin and pitcher,
Ritual of multigraph, paper-clip, comma,
Endless duplication of lives and objects.
And I have seen dust from the walls of institutions,
Finer than flour, alive, more dangerous than silica,   10
Sift, almost invisible, through long afternoons of tedium,
Dropping a fine film on nails and delicate eyebrows,
Glazing the pale hair, the duplicate grey standard faces.
1948

The Lost Son

1. *The Flight*

At Woodlawn I heard the dead cry:
I was lulled by the slamming of iron,
A slow drip over stones,
Toads brooding wells.
All the leaves stuck out their tongues;   5
I shook the softening chalk of my bones,
Saying,
Snail, snail, glister me forward,
Bird, soft-sigh me home,
Worm, be with me.   10
This is my hard time.

Fished in an old wound,
The soft pond of repose;
Nothing nibbled my line,
Not even the minnows came.   15

Sat in an empty house
Watching shadows crawl,
Scratching.
There was one fly.

Voice, come out of the silence.   20
Say something.
Appear in the form of a spider
Or a moth beating the curtain.

Tell me:
Which is the way I take;   25
Out of what door do I go,
Where and to whom?

Dark hollows said, lee to the wind,
The moon said, back of an eel,
The salt said, look by the sea,   30
Your tears are not enough praise,
You will find no comfort here,
In the kingdom of bang and blab.

Running lightly over spongy ground,
Past the pasture of flat stones,   35
The three elms,
The sheep strewn on a field,
Over a rickety bridge
Toward the quick-water, wrinkling and rippling.

Hunting along the river,   40
Down among the rubbish, the bug-riddled foliage,
By the muddy pond-edge, by the bog-holes,
By the shrunken lake, hunting, in the heat of summer.

The shape of a rat?
        It's bigger than that.   45
        It's less than a leg
        And more than a nose,
        Just under the water
        It usually goes.

Is it soft like a mouse?   50
Can it wrinkle its nose?
Could it come in the house
On the tips of its toes?

        Take the skin of a cat
        And the back of an eel,   55
        Then roll them in grease,—
        That's the way it would feel.

        It's sleek as an otter
        With wide webby toes
        Just under the water   60
        It usually goes.

2. The Pit

Where do the roots go?
    Look down under the leaves.
Who put the moss there?
    These stones have been here too long.   65
Who stunned the dirt into noise?
    Ask the mole, he knows.
I feel the slime of a wet nest.
    Beware Mother Mildew.
Nibble again, fish nerves.   70

3. The Gibber

At the wood's mouth,
By the cave's door,
I listened to something
I had heard before.

Dogs of the groin   75
Barked and howled,
The sun was against me,
The moon would not have me.

The weeds whined,
The snakes cried,   80
The cows and briars
Said to me: Die.

What a small song. What slow clouds. What dark water.
Hath the rain a father? All the caves are ice. Only the snow's here.
I'm cold. I'm cold all over. Rub me in father and mother.   85

Fear was my father, Father Fear.
His look drained the stones.

        What gliding shape
        Beckoning through halls,
        Stood poised on the stair,   90
        Fell dreamily down?

        From the mouths of jugs
        Perched on many shelves,
        I saw substance flowing
        That cold morning.   95

        Like a slither of eels
        That watery cheek

As my own tongue kissed
 My lips awake.

Is this the storm's heart? The ground is unstilling itself.   100
My veins are running nowhere. Do the bones cast out their fire?
Is the seed leaving the old bed? These buds are live as birds.
Where, where are the tears of the world?
Let the kisses resound, flat like a butcher's palm;
Let the gestures freeze; our doom is already decided.   105
All the windows are burning! What's left of my life?
I want the old rage, the lash of primordial milk!
Goodbye, goodbye, old stones, the time-order is going,
I have married my hands to perpetual agitation,
I run, I run to the whistle of money.   110

    Money money money
    Water water water

    How cool the grass is.
    Has the bird left?
    The stalk still sways.   115
    Has the worm a shadow?
    What do the clouds say?

    These sweeps of light undo me.
    Look, look, the ditch is running white!
    I've more veins than a tree!   120
    Kiss me, ashes, I'm falling through a dark swirl.

4. The Return

    The way to the boiler was dark,
    Dark all the way,
    Over slippery cinders
    Through the long greenhouse.   125

    The roses kept breathing in the dark.
    They had many mouths to breathe with.
    My knees made little winds underneath
    Where the weeds slept.

    There was always a single light   130
    Swinging by the fire-pit,
    Where the fireman pulled out roses,
    The big roses, the big bloody clinkers.

Once I stayed all night.
The light in the morning came slowly over the white   135
Snow.
There were many kinds of cool
Air.
Then came steam.

Pipe-knock.   140

Scurry of warm over small plants.
Ordnung! ordnung![1]
Papa is coming!

A fine haze moved off the leaves;
Frost melted on far panes;   145
The rose, the chrysanthemum turned toward the light.
Even the hushed forms, the bent yellowy weeds
Moved in a slow up-sway.

5. *"It Was Beginning Winter"*

It was beginning winter,
An in-between time,
The landscape still partly brown: 150
The bones of weeds kept swinging in the wind,
Above the blue snow.

It was beginning winter,
The light moved slowly over the frozen field,   155
Over the dry seed-crowns,
The beautiful surviving bones
Swinging in the wind.

Light traveled over the wide field;
Stayed.   160
The weeds stopped swinging.
The mind moved, not alone,
Through the clear air, in the silence.

Was it light?
Was it light within?   165
Was it light within light?
Stillness becoming alive,
Yet still?

---

[1] German: "Order, order!"

A lively understandable spirit
Once entertained you.   170
It will come again.
Be still.
Wait.
1948

Elegy for Jane

My student, thrown by a horse

I remember the neckcurls, limp and damp as tendrils;
And her quick look, a sidelong pickerel smile;
And how, once startled into talk, the light syllables leaped for her,
And she balanced in the delight of her thought,
A wren, happy, tail into the wind,   5
Her song trembling the twigs and small branches.
The shade sang with her;
The leaves, their whispers turned to kissing;
And the mold sang in the bleached valleys under the rose.

Oh, when she was sad, she cast herself down into such a pure depth,   10
Even a father could not find her:
Scraping her cheek against straw;
Stirring the clearest water.

My sparrow, you are not here,
Waiting like a fern, making a spiny shadow.   15
The sides of wet stones cannot console me,
Nor the moss, wound with the last light.

If only I could nudge you from this sleep,
My maimed darling, my skittery pigeon.
Over this damp grave I speak the words of my love: 20
I, with no rights in this matter,
Neither father nor lover.
1953

The Waking

I wake to sleep, and take my waking slow.
I feel my fate in what I cannot fear.
I learn by going where I have to go.

We think by feeling. What is there to know?
I hear my being dance from ear to ear.   5
I wake to sleep, and take my waking slow.

Of those so close beside me, which are you?
God bless the Ground! I shall walk softly there,
And learn by going where I have to go.

Light takes the Tree; but who can tell us how?   10
The lowly worm climbs up a winding stair;
I wake to sleep, and take my waking slow.

Great Nature has another thing to do
To you and me; so take the lively air,
And, lovely, learn by going where to go.   15

This shaking keeps me steady. I should know.
What falls away is always. And is near.
I wake to sleep, and take my waking slow.
I learn by going where I have to go.

1953

Heard in a Violent Ward

In heaven, too,
You'd be institutionalized.
But that's all right,—
If they let you eat and swear
With the likes of Blake,   5
And Christopher Smart,
And that sweet man, John Clare.[1]

1964

---

[1] William Blake (1757–1827), Christopher Smart (1722–1771), and John Clare (1793–1864) were English poets thought mad by some of their contemporaries. (Both Smart and Clare were institutionalized.)

Elizabeth Bishop
1911–1979

Elizabeth Bishop's poetry is that of a skeptic who looks on everything she sees with the eye of estrangement. Bishop was, in effect, orphaned early. Her father died before she was a year old, and her mother had a breakdown that led to insanity and permanent commitment to an asylum when Bishop was five. Bishop was raised in Massachusetts by an aunt but spent summers until she was thirteen with her grandparents in Nova Scotia. After graduating from Vassar (in the class commemorated by Mary McCarthy in *The Group*), she lived for some time in Key West; she also lived in France and Mexico. Eventually, during a trip to Brazil, she renewed acquaintance with Lota de Macedo Soares, with whom she lived for the next nineteen years. She then returned to the United States and during the last years of her life taught at Harvard. Bishop's continual geographic displacements reinforced her sense of homelessness and lack of parents. In effect, she was always piecing together a world out of unfamiliar elements.

Bishop's career unfolded slowly. In college, she wrote imitations of Hopkins and Herbert, but even in these bits of pastiche her humor and self-scrutiny are already evident. Her first book, *North and South* (1946), shows her as an accomplished poet aware already of her major metaphor, the resemblance between a map and a poem. Each represents—but in an arbitrary, schematic, and conventionalized way—a reality independent of its charting. Maps and poems both distort in the service of representation; both are miniature versions of the world. Bishop also poses, in her first book, questions of spirit and flesh, truth and nature, and establishes her polarities of North and South—polarities that also dominate her later books, *A Cold Spring* (1955), *Questions of Travel* (1965), and *Geography III* (1976), which followed the *Collected Poems* of 1969. One of her last uses of geographic polarities occurs in the splendid late poem "Crusoe in England," where Robinson Crusoe, back in England, laments the loss of his distant tropical island and of his friend Friday.

Bishop's first critics compared her to Marianne Moore, who was for a long time Bishop's poetic mentor; Bishop had met Moore through the librarian at Vassar. But in fact Bishop's roots go back to the religious poetry of the seventeenth-century poet George Herbert, to Protestant hymnody, and to the plain style of William Cowper and William Wordsworth. Bishop's skepticism unfolds against the backdrop of a lost religious faith. The seriality of existence without a religious meaning, ending only in the dust of the grave, appalls her: "Why couldn't we have seen this old Nativity while we were at it?" she asks, reproducing in the Christmas scene that "family with pets" that she had never had. But nostalgia is powerless against the icy truth of human solitude in the universe. Bishop's tableau of the fishhouses, in the poem named for them, is inhabited by three solitaries: the Wordsworthian fisherman, Bishop herself, and the single seal. Bishop's solitary "total immersion" in knowledge—"dark, salt, clear, moving, utterly free"—stands against the permanent inscrutability of the world.

In her experiments in reproducing the thought processes of a child, an animal, a tourist, or an exile, Bishop invents a language lucid in its simple diction but surreal in its bewildered disjunction of space and time. While she retained an interest in rhyme and formal patterns (one of her last poems was the villanelle "One Art"), she began early to introduce natural speech rhythms and slant rhymes to her stanzas. Her naturalness earned Robert Lowell's admiration; he dedicated "Skunk Hour" to her, saying that he had learned from "The Armadillo" how to loosen up his own lines. Lowell and Bishop remained close friends; "North Haven," her elegy for him, expresses not only her loss but also their aesthetic difference. Lowell, a copious writer, revised constantly, treating even his printed work as manuscript, while Bishop, a perfectionist, kept poems unpublished for years while she sought the *mot juste* to fill a gap.

In an American literature largely preoccupied with the transcendental, the emblematic, the Christian, and the chauvinistic, Bishop's skeptical, observant, and ironic tone (learned in part from Emily Dickinson) comes as a welcome note. Her gaze takes in the whole hemisphere, from Cape Breton to Rio de Janeiro. Though she sees the dangers of travel—the exploitative cruelty of the conquistadors, the superficiality of tourist experience—in the end she values those questions that are provoked only by travel; and values as well, almost against her will, the resulting lessons in skepticism and loss.

Further Reading:
A. Stevenson, *Elizabeth Bishop,* 1966.
C. McMahon, *Elizabeth Bishop: A Bibliography,*
1980.
L. Schwartz and S. Estess, *Elizabeth Bishop and
Her Art,* 1982.

Text:
Complete Poems, 1982.

The Fish

I caught a tremendous fish
and held him beside the boat
half out of water, with my hook
fast in a corner of his mouth.
He didn't fight.   5
He hadn't fought at all.
He hung a grunting weight,
battered and venerable
and homely. Here and there
his brown skin hung in strips   10
like ancient wallpaper,
and its pattern of darker brown
was like wallpaper:

shapes like full-blown roses
stained and lost through age. 15
He was speckled with barnacles,
fine rosettes of lime,
and infested
with tiny white sea-lice,
and underneath two or three 20
rags of green weed hung down.
While his gills were breathing in
the terrible oxygen,
—the frightening gills,
fresh and crisp with blood, 25
that can cut so badly—
I thought of the coarse white flesh
packed in like feathers,
the big bones and the little bones,
the dramatic reds and blacks 30
of his shiny entrails,
and the pink swim-bladder
like a big peony.
I looked into his eyes
which were far larger than mine 35
but shallower, and yellowed,
the irises backed and packed
with tarnished tinfoil
seen through the lenses
of old scratched isinglass. 40
They shifted a little, but not
to return my stare.
—It was more like the tipping
of an object toward the light.
I admired his sullen face, 45
the mechanism of his jaw,
and then I saw
that from his lower lip
—if you could call it a lip—
grim, wet, and weaponlike, 50
hung five old pieces of fish-line,
or four and a wire leader
with the swivel still attached,
with all their five big hooks
grown firmly in his mouth. 55
A green line, frayed at the end
where he broke it, two heavier lines,
and a fine black thread
still crimped from the strain and snap
when it broke and he got away. 60

Like medals with their ribbons
frayed and wavering,
a five-haired beard of wisdom
trailing from his aching jaw.
I stared and stared   65
and victory filled up
the little rented boat,
from the pool of bilge
where oil had spread a rainbow
around the rusted engine   70
to the bailer rusted orange,
the sun-cracked thwarts,
the oarlocks on their strings,
the gunnels—until everything
was rainbow, rainbow, rainbow!   75
And I let the fish go.

1946

Over 2000 Illustrations
and a Complete Concordance[1]

Thus should have been our travels:
serious, engravable.
The Seven Wonders of the World are tired
and a touch familiar, but the other scenes,
innumerable, though equally sad and still,   5
are foreign. Often the squatting Arab,
or group of Arabs, plotting, probably,
against our Christian Empire,
while one apart, with outstretched arm and hand
points to the Tomb, the Pit, the Sepulcher.   10
The branches of the date-palms look like files.
The cobbled courtyard, where the Well is dry,
is like a diagram, the brickwork conduits
are vast and obvious, the human figure
far gone in history or theology,   15
gone with its camel or its faithful horse.
Always the silence, the gesture, the specks of birds

[1] The title is a phrase describing the type of old Bible that often included illustrations of places in the Holy Land as well as a *concordance,* or index of important names and words.

suspended on invisible threads above the Site,
or the smoke rising solemnly, pulled by threads.
Granted a page alone or a page made up   20
of several scenes arranged in cattycornered
    rectangles
or circles set on stippled gray,
granted a grim lunette,
caught in the toils of an initial letter,
when dwelt upon, they all resolve themselves.   25
The eye drops, weighted, through the lines
the burin[2] made, the lines that move apart
like ripples above sand,
dispersing storms, God's spreading fingerprint,
and painfully, finally, that ignite   30
in watery prismatic white-and-blue.
Entering the Narrows at St. Johns[3]
the touching bleat of goats reached to the ship.
We glimpsed them, reddish, leaping up the cliffs
among the fog-soaked weeds and butter-and-eggs.   35
And at St. Peter's[4] the wind blew and the sun shone
    madly.
Rapidly, purposefully, the Collegians[5] marched in
    lines,
crisscrossing the great square with black, like ants.
In Mexico the dead man lay
in a blue arcade; the dead volcanoes   40
glistened like Easter lilies.
The jukebox went on playing "Ay, Jalisco!"
And at Volubilis[6] there were beautiful poppies
splitting the mosaics; the fat old guide made eyes.
In Dingle[7] harbor a golden length of evening   45
the rotting hulks held up their dripping plush.
The Englishwoman poured tea, informing us
that the Dutchess was going to have a baby.
And in the brothels of Marrakesh[8]
the little pockmarked prostitutes   50
balanced their tea-trays on their heads
and did their belly-dances; flung themselves
naked and giggling against our knees,
asking for cigarettes. It was somewhere near there
I saw what frightened me most of all: 55
A holy grave, not looking particularly holy,

[2] Engraver's tool.
[3] Capital of Newfoundland.
[4] The church in Rome.
[5] American priests from the North American
    College in Rome.

[6] Ancient Roman city in Morocco.
[7] Town in the southwest of Ireland.
[8] City in Morocco.

one of a group under a keyhole-arched stone
   baldaquin
open to every wind from the pink desert.
An open, gritty, marble trough, carved solid
with exhortation, yellowed   60
as scattered cattle-teeth;
half-filled with dust, not even the dust
of the poor prophet paynim[9] who once lay there.
In a smart burnoose[10] Khadour looked on amused.

Everything only connected by "and" and "and."   65
Open the book. (The gilt rubs off the edges
of the pages and pollinates the fingertips.)
Open the heavy book. Why couldn't we have seen
this old Nativity while we were at it?
—the dark ajar, the rocks breaking with light,   70
an undisturbed, unbreathing flame,
colorless, sparkless, freely fed on straw,
and, lulled within, a family with pets,
—and looked and looked our infant sight away.

1955

The Bight[1]

[On my birthday]

At low tide like this how sheer the water is.
White, crumbling ribs of marl[2] protrude and glare
and the boats are dry, the pilings dry as matches.
Absorbing, rather than being absorbed,
the water in the bight doesn't wet anything,   5
the color of the gas flame turned as low as possible.
One can smell it turning to gas; if one were Baudelaire[3]
one could probably hear it turning to marimba music.
The little ocher dredge at work off the end of the dock
already plays the dry perfectly off-beat claves.[4]   10
The birds are outsize. Pelicans crash

---

[9] Archaic word for an infidel, especially a
Muslim.
[10] Hooded cloak worn by Arabs.
[1] Bay formed by a bend in a coastline.
[2] Deposit of sand, silt, or clay containing calcium
carbonate.

[3] French poet (1821–1867), author of a sonnet
"Correspondances." (See l. 32.)
[4] Wooden percussion instrument.

into this peculiar gas unnecessarily hard,
it seems to me, like pickaxes,
rarely coming up with anything to show for it,
and going off with humorous elbowings.   15
Black-and-white man-of-war birds soar
on impalpable drafts
and open their tails like scissors on the curves
or tense them like wishbones, till they tremble.
The frowsy sponge boats keep coming in   20
with the obliging air of retrievers,
bristling with jackstraw gaffs[5] and hooks
and decorated with bobbles of sponges.
There is a fence of chicken wire along the dock
where, glinting like little plowshares,   25
the blue-gray shark tails are hung up to dry
for the Chinese-restaurant trade.
Some of the little white boats are still piled up
against each other, or lie on their sides, stove in,
and not yet salvaged, if they ever will be, from the last bad storm, 30
like torn-open, unanswered letters.
The bight is littered with old correspondences.
Click. Click. Goes the dredge,
and brings up a dripping jawful of marl.
All the untidy activity continues,   35
awful but cheerful.

1955

At the Fishhouses

Although it is a cold evening,
down by one of the fishhouses
an old man sits netting,
his net, in the gloaming almost invisible
a dark purple-brown,   5
and his shuttle worn and polished.
The air smells so strong of codfish
it makes one's nose run and one's eyes water.
The five fishhouses have steeply peaked roofs
and narrow, cleated gangplanks slant up   10

_____

[5] Spars upon which the head of a fore-and-aft
sail is extended.

to storerooms in the gables
for the wheelbarrows to be pushed up and down on.
All is silver: the heavy surface of the sea,
swelling slowly as if considering spilling over,
is opaque, but the silver of the benches,   15
the lobster pots, and masts, scattered
among the wild jagged rocks,
is of an apparent translucence
like the small old buildings with an emerald moss
growing on their shoreward walls.   20
The big fish tubs are completely lined
with layers of beautiful herring scales
and the wheelbarrows are similarly plastered
with creamy iridescent coats of mail,
with small iridescent flies crawling on them.   25
Up on the little slope behind the houses,
set in the sparse bright sprinkle of grass,
is an ancient wooden capstan,[1]
cracked, with two long bleached handles
and some melancholy stains, like dried blood,   30
where the ironwork has rusted.
The old man accepts a Lucky Strike.
He was a friend of my grandfather.
We talk of the decline in the population
and of codfish and herring   35
while he waits for a herring boat to come in.
There are sequins on his vest and on his thumb.
He has scraped the scales, the principal beauty,
from unnumbered fish with that black old knife,
the blade of which is almost worn away.   40

Down at the water's edge, at the place
where they haul up the boats, up the long ramp
descending into the water, thin silver
tree trunks are laid horizontally
across the gray stones, down and down   45
at intervals of four or five feet.

Cold dark deep and absolutely clear,
element bearable to no mortal,
to fish and to seals . . . One seal particularly
I have seen here evening after evening.   50
He was curious about me. He was interested in music;
like me a believer in total immersion,[2]

---

[1] Machine for raising weights by winding cable
around a vertical rotating drum.

[2] Form of baptism practiced by some Christian
sects.

so I used to sing him Baptist hymns.
I also sang "A Mighty Fortress Is Our God."[3]
He stood up in the water and regarded me   55
steadily, moving his head a little,
Then he would disappear, then suddenly emerge
almost in the same spot, with a sort of shrug
as if it were against his better judgment.
Cold dark deep and absolutely clear,   60
the clear gray icy water . . . Back, behind us,
the dignified tall firs begin.
Bluish, associating with their shadows,
a million Christmas trees stand
waiting for Christmas. The water seems suspended   65
above the rounded gray and blue-gray stones.
I have seen it over and over, the same sea, the same,
slightly, indifferently swinging above the stones,
icily free above the stones,
above the stones and then the world.   70
If you should dip your hand in,
your wrist would ache immediately,
your bones would begin to ache and your hand would burn
as if the water were a transmutation of fire
that feeds on stones and burns with a dark gray flame.   75
If you tasted it, it would first taste bitter,
then briny, then surely burn your tongue.
It is like what we imagine knowledge to be:
dark, salt, clear, moving, utterly free,
drawn from the cold hard mouth   80
of the world, derived from the rocky breasts
forever, flowing and drawn, and since
our knowledge is historical, flowing, and flown.

1955

Questions of Travel

There are too many waterfalls here; the crowded streams
hurry too rapidly down to the sea,
and the pressure of so many clouds on the mountaintops
makes them spill over the sides in soft slow-motion,

---

[3] Hymn of which the original German version
was written by Martin Luther (1483–1546).

turning to waterfalls under our very eyes.   5
—For if those streaks, those mile-long, shiny, tearstains,
aren't waterfalls yet,
in a quick age or so, as ages go here,
they probably will be.
But if the streams and clouds keep travelling, travelling,   10
the mountains look like the hulls of capsized ships,
slime-hung and barnacled.

Think of the long trip home.
Should we have stayed at home and thought of here?
Where should we be today?   15
Is it right to be watching strangers in a play
in this strangest of theatres?
What childishness is it that while there's a breath of life
in our bodies, we are determined to rush
to see the sun the other way around?   20
The tiniest green hummingbird in the world?
To stare at some inexplicable old stonework,
inexplicable and impenetrable,
at any view,
instantly seen and always, always delightful?   25
Oh, must we dream our dreams
and have them, too?
And have we room
for one more folded sunset, still quite warm?

But surely it would have been a pity   30
not to have seen the trees along this road,
really exaggerated in their beauty,
not to have seen them gesturing
like noble pantomimists, robed in pink.
—Not to have had to stop for gas and heard   35
the sad, two-noted, wooden tune
of disparate wooden clogs
carelessly clacking over
a grease-stained filling-station floor.
(In another country the clogs would all be tested.   40
Each pair there would have identical pitch.)
—A pity not to have heard
the other, less primitive music of the fat brown bird
who sings above the broken gasoline pump
in a bamboo church of Jesuit baroque:[1]   45

---

[1] Style of architecture introduced into South
America in the seventeenth century by Jesuit
missionaries.

three towers, five silver crosses.
—Yes, a pity not to have pondered,
blurr'dly and inconclusively,
on what connection can exist for centuries
between the crudest wooden footwear   50
and, careful and finicky,
the whittled fantasies of wooden cages.
—Never to have studied history in
the weak calligraphy of songbirds' cages.
—And never to have had to listen to rain   55
so much like politicians' speeches:
two hours of unrelenting oratory
and then a sudden golden silence
in which the traveller takes a notebook, writes:

"Is it lack of imagination that makes us come   60
to imagined places, not just stay at home?
Or could Pascal[2] *have been not entirely right*
about just sitting quietly in one's room?

Continent, city, country, society:
the choice is never wide and never free.   65
And here, or there . . . No. Should we have stayed at home,
wherever that may be?"
1965

The Armadillo

(For Robert Lowell)

This is the time of year
when almost every night
the frail, illegal fire balloons appear.
Climbing the mountain height,

rising toward a saint   5
still honored in these parts,
the paper chambers flush and fill with light
that comes and goes, like hearts.

Once up against the sky it's hard
to tell them from the stars—   10

---

[2] Blaise Pascal, French philosopher (1623–1662).

planets, that is—the tinted ones:
Venus going down, or Mars,

or the pale green one. With a wind,
they flare and falter, wobble and toss;
but if it's still they steer between   15
the kite sticks of the Southern Cross,[1]

receding, dwindling, solemnly
and steadily forsaking us,
or, in the downdraft from a peak,
suddenly turning dangerous.   20

Last night another big one fell.
It splattered like an egg of fire
against the cliff behind the house.
The flame ran down. We saw the pair

of owls who nest there flying up   25
and up, their whirling black-and-white
stained bright pink underneath, until
they shrieked up out of sight.

The ancient owls' nest must have burned.
Hastily, all alone,   30
a glistening armadillo left the scene,
rose-flecked, head down, tail down,

and then a baby rabbit jumped out,
short-eared, to our surprise.
So soft!—a handful of intangible ash   35
with fixed, ignited eyes.

Too pretty, dreamlike mimicry!
O falling fire and piercing cry
and panic, and a weak mailed fist
clenched ignorant against the sky!   40
1965

---

[1] Constellation visible only in the Southern
hemisphere.

Sestina

September rain falls on the house.
In the failing light, the old grandmother
sits in the kitchen with the child
beside the Little Marvel Stove,
reading the jokes from the almanac,   5
laughing and talking to hide her tears.

She thinks that her equinoctial[1] tears
and the rain that beats on the roof of the house
were both foretold by the almanac,
but only known to a grandmother.   10
The iron kettle sings on the stove.
She cuts some bread and says to the child,

It's time for tea now; but the child
is watching the teakettle's small hard tears
dance like mad on the hot black stove,   15
the way the rain must dance on the house.
Tidying up, the old grandmother
hangs up the clever almanac

on its string. Bird-like, the almanac
hovers half open above the child,   20
hovers above the old grandmother
and her teacup full of dark brown tears.
She shivers and says she thinks the house
feels chilly, and puts more wood in the stove.

It was to be, says the Marvel Stove.   25
I know what I know, says the almanac.
With crayons the child draws a rigid house
and a winding pathway. Then the child
puts in a man with buttons like tears
and shows it proudly to the grandmother.   30

But secretly, while the grandmother
busies herself about the stove,

[1] At the time of the (autumn) equinox; an
oblique reference to September rain.

the little moons fall down like tears
from between the pages of the almanac
into the flower bed the child   35
has carefully placed in the front of the house.

Time to plant tears, says the almanac.
The grandmother sings to the marvellous stove
and the child draws another inscrutable house.
1965

Filling Station

Oh, but it is dirty!
—this little filling station,
oil-soaked, oil-permeated
to a disturbing, over-all
black translucency.   5
Be careful with that match!

Father wears a dirty,
oil-soaked monkey suit
that cuts him under the arms,
and several quick and saucy   10
and greasy sons assist him
(it's a family filling station),
all quite thoroughly dirty.

Do they live in the station?
It has a cement porch   15
behind the pumps, and on it
a set of crushed and grease-
impregnated wickerwork;
on the wicker sofa
a dirty dog, quite comfy.   20

Some comic books provide
the only note of color—
of certain color. They lie
upon a big dim doily
draping a taboret   25

(part of the set), beside
a big hirsute begonia.

Why the extraneous plant?
Why the taboret?
Why, oh why, the doily?   30
(Embroidered in daisy stitch
with marguerites, I think,
and heavy with gray crochet.)

Somebody embroidered the doily.
Somebody waters the plant,   35
or oils it, maybe. Somebody
arranges the rows of cans
so that they softly say:
ESSO—SO—SO—SO
to high-strung automobiles.   40
Somebody loves us all.
1965

In the Waiting Room

In Worcester, Massachusetts,
I went with Aunt Consuelo
to keep her dentist's appointment
and sat and waited for her
in the dentist's waiting room.   5
It was winter. It got dark
early. The waiting room
was full of grown-up people,
arctics and overcoats,
lamps and magazines.   10
My aunt was inside
what seemed like a long time
and while I waited I read
the *National Geographic*
(I could read) and carefully   15
studied the photographs:
the inside of a volcano,
black, and full of ashes;

then it was spilling over
in rivulets of fire.   20
Osa and Martin Johnson[1]
dressed in riding breeches,
laced boots, and pith helmets.
A dead man slung on a pole
—"Long Pig,"[2] the caption said.   25
Babies with pointed heads
wound round and round with string;
black, naked women with necks
wound round and round with wire
like the necks of light bulbs.   30
Their breasts were horrifying.
I read it right straight through.
I was too shy to stop.
And then I looked at the cover:
the yellow margins, the date.   35

Suddenly, from inside,
came an *oh!* of pain
—Aunt Consuelo's voice—
not very loud or long.
I wasn't at all surprised;   40
even then I knew she was
a foolish, timid woman.
I might have been embarrassed,
but wasn't. What took me
completely by surprise   45
was that it was *me:*
my voice, in my mouth.
Without thinking at all
I was my foolish aunt,
I—we—were falling, falling,   50
our eyes glued to the cover
of the *National Geographic,*
February, 1918.

I said to myself: three days
and you'll be seven years old.   55
I was saying it to stop
the sensation of falling off
the round, turning world
into cold, blue-black space.

---

[1] Osa Johnson (1894–1953) and Martin Johnson
(1884–1937), tropical explorers and authors of
travel books.

[2] Name given by cannibals to a dead man to be
eaten.

But I felt: you are an *I,*   60
you are an *Elizabeth,*
you are one of *them.*
Why should you be one, too?
I scarcely dared to look
to see what it was I was.   65
I gave a sidelong glance
—I couldn't look any higher—
at shadowy gray knees,
trousers and skirts and boots
and different pairs of hands   70
lying under the lamps.
I knew that nothing stranger
had ever happened, that nothing
stranger could ever happen.
Why should I be my aunt,   75
or me, or anyone?
What similarities—
boots, hands, the family voice
I felt in my throat, or even
the *National Geographic*   80
and those awful hanging breasts—
held us all together
or made us all just one?
How—I didn't know any
word for it—how "unlikely" . . .   85
How had I come to be here,
like them, and overhear
a cry of pain that could have
got loud and worse but hadn't?

The waiting room was bright   90
and too hot. It was sliding
beneath a big black wave,
another, and another.

Then I was back in it.
The War was on. Outside,   95
in Worcester, Massachusetts,
were night and slush and cold,
and it was still the fifth
of February, 1918.
1976

Crusoe in England[1]

A new volcano has erupted,
the papers say, and last week I was reading
where some ship saw an island being born:
at first a breath of steam, ten miles away;
and then a black fleck—basalt, probably— 5
rose in the mate's binoculars
and caught on the horizon like a fly.
They named it. But my poor old island's still
un-rediscovered, un-renamable.
None of the books has ever got it right. 10

Well, I had fifty-two
miserable, small volcanoes I could climb
with a few slithery strides—
volcanoes dead as ash heaps.
I used to sit on the edge of the highest one 15
and count the others standing up,
naked and leaden, with their heads blown off.
I'd think that if they were the size
I thought volcanoes should be, then I had
become a giant; 20
and if I had become a giant,
I couldn't bear to think what size
the goats and turtles were,
or the gulls, or the over-lapping rollers
—a glittering hexagon of rollers 25
closing and closing in, but never quite,
glittering and glittering, though the sky
was mostly overcast.

My island seemed to be
a sort of cloud-dump. All the hemisphere's 30
left-over clouds arrived and hung
above the craters—their parched throats
were hot to touch.
Was that why it rained so much?
And why sometimes the whole place hissed? 35
The turtles lumbered by, high-domed,
hissing like teakettles.

---

[1] Daniel Defoe (ca. 1660–1731) in *Robinson Crusoe* (1719) recounted the life of an English sailor marooned on an island, alone until he found a native, whom he named Friday.

(And I'd have given years, or taken a few,
for any sort of kettle, of course.)
The folds of lava, running out to sea,   40
would hiss. I'd turn. And then they'd prove
to be more turtles.

The beaches were all lava, variegated,
black, red, and white, and gray;
the marbled colors made a fine display.   45
And I had waterspouts. Oh,
half a dozen at a time, far out,
they'd come and go, advancing and retreating,
their heads in cloud, their feet in moving patches
of scuffed-up white.   50
Glass chimneys, flexible, attenuated,
sacerdotal[2] beings of glass . . . I watched
the water spiral up in them like smoke.
Beautiful, yes, but not much company.

I often gave way to self-pity.   55
"Do I deserve this? I suppose I must.
I wouldn't be here otherwise. Was there
a moment when I actually chose this?
I don't remember, but there could have been."
What's wrong about self-pity, anyway?   60
With my legs dangling down familiarly
over a crater's edge, I told myself
"Pity should begin at home." So the more
pity I felt, the more I felt at home.

The sun set in the sea; the same odd sun   65
rose from the sea,
and there was one of it and one of me.
The island had one kind of everything:
one tree snail, a bright violet-blue
with a thin shell, crept over everything,   70
over the one variety of tree,
a sooty, scrub affair.
Snail shells lay under these in drifts
and, at a distance,
you'd swear that they were beds of irises.   75
There was one kind of berry, a dark red.
I tried it, one by one, and hours apart.
Sub-acid, and not bad, no ill effects;
and so I made home-brew. I'd drink
the awful, fizzy, stinging stuff   80

[2] Priestly.

that went straight to my head
and play my home-made flute
(I think it had the weirdest scale on earth)
and, dizzy, whoop and dance among the goats.
Home-made, home-made! But aren't we all?   85
I felt a deep affection for
the smallest of my island industries.
No, not exactly, since the smallest was
a miserable philosophy.

Because I didn't know enough.   90
Why didn't I know enough of something?
Greek drama or astronomy? The books
I'd read were full of blanks;
the poems—well, I tried
reciting to my iris-beds,   95
"They flash upon that inward eye,
which is the bliss . . ."³ The bliss of what?
One of the first things that I did
when I got back was look it up.

The island smelled of goat and guano.⁴   100
The goats were white, so were the gulls,
and both too tame, or else they thought
I was a goat, too, or a gull.
Baa, baa, baa and *shriek, shriek, shriek,*
baa . . . shriek . . . baa . . . I still can't shake   105
them from my ears; they're hurting now.
The questioning shrieks, the equivocal replies
over a ground of hissing rain
and hissing, ambulating turtles
got on my nerves.   110

When all the gulls flew up at once, they sounded
like a big tree in a strong wind, its leaves.
I'd shut my eyes and think about a tree,
an oak, say, with real shade, somewhere.
I'd heard of cattle getting island-sick.   115
I thought the goats were.
One billy-goat would stand on the volcano
I'd christened *Mont d'Espoir*⁵ or *Mount Despair*
(I'd time enough to play with names),
and bleat and bleat, and sniff the air.   120
I'd grab his beard and look at him.

---

³ From William Wordsworth's poem "Daffodils."   ⁴ Bird droppings.
   The full quotation ends: "of solitude."   ⁵ French for "Mount Hope."

His pupils, horizontal, narrowed up
and expressed nothing, or a little malice.
I got so tired of the very colors!
One day I dyed a baby goat bright red   125
with my red berries, just to see
something a little different.
And then his mother wouldn't recognize him.

Dreams were the worst. Of course I dreamed of
     food
and love, but they were pleasant rather   130
than otherwise. But then I'd dream of things
like slitting a baby's throat, mistaking it
for a baby goat. I'd have
nightmares of other islands
stretching away from mine, infinities   135
of islands, islands spawning islands,
like frogs' eggs turning into polliwogs
of islands, knowing that I had to live
on each and every one, eventually,
for ages, registering their flora,   140
their fauna, their geography.

Just when I thought I couldn't stand it
another minute longer, Friday came.
(Accounts of that have everything all wrong.)
Friday was nice.   145
Friday was nice, and we were friends.
If only he had been a woman!
I wanted to propagate my kind,
and so did he, I think, poor boy.
He'd pet the baby goats sometimes,   150
and race with them, or carry one around.
—Pretty to watch; he had a pretty body.
And then one day they came and took us off.

Now I live here, another island,
that doesn't seem like one, but who decides?   155
My blood was full of them; my brain
bred islands. But that archipelago
has petered out. I'm old.
I'm bored, too, drinking my real tea,
surrounded by uninteresting lumber.   160
The knife there on the shelf—
it reeked of meaning, like a crucifix.
It lived. How many years did I
beg it, implore it, not to break?

I knew each nick and scratch by heart,   165
the bluish blade, the broken tip,
the lines of wood-grain on the handle . . .
Now it won't look at me at all.
The living soul has dribbled away.
My eyes rest on it and pass on.   170

The local museum's asked me to
leave everything to them:
the flute, the knife, the shrivelled shoes,
my shedding goatskin trousers
(moths have got in the fur),   175
the parasol that took me such a time
remembering the way the ribs should go.
It still will work but, folded up,
looks like a plucked and skinny fowl.
How can anyone want such things?   180
—And Friday, my dear Friday, died of measles
seventeen years ago come March.
1976

Poem

About the size of an old-style dollar bill,
American or Canadian,
mostly the same whites, gray greens, and steel grays
—this little painting (a sketch for a larger one?)
has never earned any money in its life.   5
Useless and free, it has spent seventy years
as a minor family relic
handed along collaterally to owners
who looked at it sometimes, or didn't bother to.

It must be Nova Scotia; only there   10
does one see gabled wooden houses
painted that awful shade of brown.
The other houses, the bits that show, are white.
Elm trees, low hills, a thin church steeple
—that gray-blue wisp—or is it? In the foreground   15
a water meadow with some tiny cows,
two brushstrokes each, but confidently cows;
two minuscule white geese in the blue water,

back-to-back, feeding, and a slanting stick.
Up closer, a wild iris, white and yellow,   20
fresh-squiggled from the tube.
The air is fresh and cold; cold early spring
clear as gray glass; a half inch of blue sky
below the steel-gray storm clouds.
(They were the artist's specialty.)   25
A specklike bird is flying to the left.
Or is it a flyspeck looking like a bird?

Heavens, I recognize the place, I know it!
It's behind—I can almost remember the farmer's name.
His barn backed on that meadow. There it is,   30
titanium white, one dab. The hint of steeple,
filaments of brush-hairs, barely there,
must be the Presbyterian church.
Would that be Miss Gillespie's house?
Those particular geese and cows   35
are naturally before my time.

A sketch done in an hour, "in one breath,"
once taken from a trunk and handed over.
Would you like this? I'll probably never
have room to hang these things again.   40
Your Uncle George, no, mine, my Uncle George,
he'd be your great-uncle, left them all with Mother
when he went back to England.
You know, he was quite famous, an R.A. . . .[1]

I never knew him. We both knew this place,   45
apparently, this literal small backwater,
looked at it long enough to memorize it,
our years apart. How strange. And it's still loved,
or its memory is (it must have changed a lot).
Our visions coincided—"visions" is   50
too serious a word—our looks, two looks:
art "copying from life" and life itself,
life and the memory of it so compressed
they've turned into each other. Which is which?
Life and the memory of it cramped,   55
dim, on a piece of Bristol board,[2]
dim, but how live, how touching in detail
—the little that we get for free,
the little of our earthly trust. Not much.

[1] Painter elected to the Royal Academy in   [2] Type of stiff cardboard.
England.

About the size of our abidance
along with theirs: the munching cows,
the iris, crisp and shivering, the water
still standing from spring freshets,
the yet-to-be-dismantled elms, the geese.

1976

60

North Haven[1]

(In memoriam: R.T.S.L.[2])

I can make out the rigging of a schooner
a mile off; I can count
the new cones on the spruce. It is so still
the pale bay wears a milky skin, the sky
no clouds, except for one long, carded, horse's-tail.   5

The islands haven't shifted since last summer,
even if I like to pretend they have
—drifting, in a dreamy sort of way,
a little north, a little south or sidewise,
and that they're free within the blue frontiers of bay.   10

This month, our favorite one is full of flowers:
Buttercups, Red Clover, Purple Vetch,
Hawkweed still burning, Daisies pied, Eyebright,
the Fragrant Bedstraw's incandescent stars,
and more, returned, to paint the meadows with delight.   15

The Goldfinches are back, or others like them,
and the White-throated Sparrow's five-note song,
pleading and pleading, brings tears to the eyes.
Nature repeats herself, or almost does:
repeat, repeat, repeat, revise, revise, revise.   20

Years ago, you told me it was here
(in 1932?) you first "discovered *girls*"
and learned to sail, and learned to kiss.
You had "such fun," you said, that classic summer.
("Fun"—it always seemed to leave you at a loss . . .)   25

---

[1] Town on Mt. Desert Island, off the coast of
Maine, where Bishop spent several summers at
the end of her life.

[2] Robert Traill Spence Lowell (1917–1977), poet
and close friend of Bishop's.

You left North Haven, anchored in its rock,
afloat in mystic blue . . . And now—you've left
for good. You can't derange, or re-arrange,
your poems again. (But the Sparrows can their song.)
The words won't change again. Sad friend, you cannot change.   30
1979

Robert Hayden
1913–1980

Robert Hayden's two most ambitious poems directly confront the intolerable
social evil of slavery by retelling the history of slave rebellions. "Middle Passage"
recounts the seizure of the slave ship *Amistad* by Cinquez, one of the slaves being
transported in the "middle passage" from Africa to America. "Runagate
Runagate" retells the 1849 escape from slavery of Harriet Tubman, who
subsequently led more than three hundred slaves to freedom. Hayden's form of
protest poetry is solidly rooted in historical antecedents, as though to argue that
one cannot write about the phenomenon of racism without understanding its
historical causes. In this way he differs both from the black writers who confined
themselves to the contemporary plight of blacks in American society and from
those who tried to write conventional "English" poetry on conventional themes.

Hayden was a learned poet. He received a B.A. from Detroit City College
(now Wayne State University) in 1942, at the age of twenty-nine, but he had
already won the Hopwood Award for poetry at the University of Michigan in
1938 and in 1942, and had published his first book, *Heart-Shaped in the Dust,* in
1940. After returning to Michigan to take an M.A., he taught at Fisk University
for twenty-three years, eventually leaving Fisk to become professor of English at
Michigan, where he taught until his death.

Hayden's poems appeared, after 1940, in successive arrestingly named volumes:
A Ballad of Remembrance (1962), *Words in Mourning Time* (1970), *The
Night-Blooming Cereus* (1972), *Angle of Ascent* (1975), and *American Journal*
(1978). His poetry ranged through many subjects and forms; it was marked by a
consistent experimentation in voices, allusiveness, patterns on the page, and choice
of speaker. He wished to avoid writing agitprop verse, and his career offers an
implicit rebuke to an aesthetic that would disregard the importance of form in
art. Hayden once said:

> I write poetry because I prefer it to prose, for one thing. Because, for another,
> I'm driven, impelled to make patterns of words in the special ways that poetry
> demands. . . . I suppose I could say, with fear of contradicting myself later, that
> writing poetry is one way I have of coming to grips with both inner and
> external realities. I also think of my writing as a form of prayer—a prayer for
> illumination, perfection.

Hayden's example has been important for such subsequent black poets as Michael Harper and Rita Dove. The poetic implicit in his work, and theirs, is a reconstructive one: The contemporary black poet must speak not only for living blacks but also for all the dead blacks deprived of voice. The voice of the living, it suggests, cannot be properly vocal if it does not know its own antecedents. It will be thin if it speaks out of the present alone, depriving the present of the very past that constituted it. The past of slavery, peculiar to blacks, is preserved, Hayden's poetry suggests, in the consciousness and imagination of blacks, and a poetry that represses it is bound to falsify. Michael Harper's allusions to black history and Rita Dove's recreations of slave voices are attempts to enlarge and consolidate Hayden's model—a poetic language committed to adequate historical self-knowledge.

At the same time, Hayden was a vigorous commentator on the general American scene. In the late poem "American Journal" he adopted the voice of a visiting alien from outer space, reporting on America:

> There among them the americans this baffling
> multi people extremes and variegations their
> noise restlessness their almost frightening
> energy . . .

As he studies these "charming savages enlightened primitives brash / new comers lately sprung up in our galaxy," the alien commentator takes precisely the very tone that whites have often used historically about blacks. Hayden's ironic social mirror silently shows American society in a devastating light. In 1985, Hayden's *Complete Poems* appeared, making widely available once again the work of a neglected American poet.

Text:
Angle of Ascent, 1966.

Sphinx

> If he could solve the riddle,
> she would not leap
>   from those gaunt rocks to her death,
> but devour him instead.
>
>
>   It pleasures her to hold
> him captive there—
>   to keep him in the reach of her
> blood-matted paws.

5

                    It is your fate, she has often
said, to endure   10
          my riddling. Your fate to live
at the mercy of my
          conundrum, which, in truth,
is only a kind
          of psychic joke. No, you shall   15
not leave this place.

          (Consider anyway the view from
here.) In time,
          you will come to regard my questioning
with a certain pained   20
          amusement; in time, get so
you would hardly find
          it possible to live without
my joke and me.
1966

Tour 5

The road winds down through autumn hills
in blazonry of farewell scarlet
and recessional gold,
past cedar groves, through static villages
whose names are all that's left   5
of Choctaw, Chickasaw.[1]

We stop a moment in a town
watched over by Confederate sentinels,
buy gas and ask directions of a rawboned man
whose eyes revile us as the enemy.   10

Shrill gorgon silence breathes behind
his taut civility
and in the ever-tautening air,
dark for us despite its Indian summer glow.
We drive on, following the route   15
of highwaymen and phantoms,

[1] American Indian tribes.

Of slaves and armies. And the
Children, wordless and remote,
wave at us from kindling porches.
And now the land is flat for miles,   20
the landscape lush, metallic, flayed,
its brightness harsh as bloodstained swords.
1966

Homage to the Empress
of the Blues

Because there was a man somewhere in a candystripe silk shirt,
gracile and dangerous as a jaguar and because a woman moaned
for him in sixty-watt gloom and mourned him Faithless Love
Twotiming Love Oh Love Oh Careless Aggravating Love,

    She came out on the stage in yards of pearls, emerging like   5
    a favorite scenic view, flashed her golden smile and sang.

Because grey laths began somewhere to show from underneath
torn hurdygurdy lithographs of dollfaced heaven;
and because there were those who feared alarming fists of snow
on the door and those who feared the riot-squad of statistics,   10

    She came out on the stage in ostrich feathers, beaded satin,
    and shone that smile on us and sang.

1966

Mourning Poem for the Queen
of Sunday

Lord's lost Him His mockingbird,
His fancy warbler;
Satan sweet-talked her,
four bullets hushed her.
Who would have thought   5
she'd end that way?

Four bullets hushed her. And the world a-clang with evil.
Who's going to make old hardened sinner men tremble now
and the righteous rock?
Oh who and oh who will sing Jesus down   10
to help with struggling and doing without and being colored
all through blue Monday?
Till way next Sunday?

      All those angels
      in their cretonne clouds and finery   15
      the true believer saw
      when she rared back her head and sang,
      all those angels are surely weeping.
      Who would have thought
      she'd end that way?   20

Four holes in her heart. The gold works wrecked.
But she looks so natural in her big bronze coffin
among the Broken Hearts and Gates-Ajar,
it's as if any moment she'd lift her head
from its pillow of chill gardenias   25
and turn this quiet into shouting Sunday
and make folks forget what she did on Monday.

      Oh, Satan sweet-talked her,
      and four bullets hushed her.
      Lord's lost Him His diva,[1]
      His fancy warbler's gone.   30
      Who would have thought,
      who would have thought she'd end that way?

1966

Those Winter Sundays

Sundays too my father got up early
and put his clothes on in the blueblack cold,
then with cracked hands that ached
from labor in the weekday weather made
banked fires blaze. No one ever thanked him.   5

---

[1] Prima donna.

I'd wake and hear the cold splintering, breaking.
When the rooms were warm, he'd call,
and slowly I would rise and dress,
fearing the chronic angers of that house,

Speaking indifferently to him,   10
who had driven out the cold
and polished my good shoes as well.
What did I know, what did I know
of love's austere and lonely offices?
1966

Middle Passage[1]

I

Jesús, Estrella, Esperanza, Mercy:[2]

Sails flashing to the wind like weapons,
sharks following the moans the fever and the dying;
horror the corposant[3] and compass rose.

Middle Passage: 5
        voyage through death
                to life upon these shores.

        "10 April 1800—
Blacks rebellious. Crew uneasy. Our linguist says
their moaning is a prayer for death,   10
ours and their own. Some try to starve themselves.
Lost three this morning leaped with crazy laughter
to the waiting sharks, sang as they went under."

Desire, Adventure, Tartar, Ann:

        Standing to America, bringing home   15
        black gold, black ivory, black seed.

---

[1] The passage of slave ships from Africa to the
New World.
[2] Names of slave ships. The irony of names like
Jesus, Star, Hope, and *Mercy* is evident.

[3] St. Elmo's fire.

> Deep in the festering hold thy father lies,
> of his bones New England pews are made,
> those are altar lights that were his eyes.[4]

Jesus   Saviour   Pilot   Me   20
Over   Life's   Tempestuous   Sea

We pray that Thou wilt grant, O Lord,
safe passage to our vessels bringing
heathen souls unto Thy chastening.

Jesus Saviour   25
        "8 bells. I cannot sleep, for I am sick
        with fear, but writing eases fear a little
        since still my eyes can see these words take shape
        upon the page & so I write, as one
        would turn to exorcism. 4 days scudding,   30
        but now the sea is calm again. Misfortune
        follows in our wake like sharks (our grinning
        tutelary gods). Which one of us
        has killed an albatross?[5] A plague among
        our blacks—Ophthalmia: blindness—& we   35
        have jettisoned the blind to no avail.
        It spreads, the terrifying sickness spreads.
        Its claws have scratched sight from the Capt.'s eyes
        & there is blindness in the fo'c'sle
        & we must sail 3 weeks before we come   40
        to port."

> What port awaits us, Davy Jones'[6]
> or home? I've heard of slavers drifting, drifting,
> playthings of wind and storm and chance, their crews
> gone blind, the jungle hatred   45
> crawling up on deck.

Thou Who Walked On Galilee

        "Deponent further sayeth The Bella
        left the Guinea Coast
        with cargo of five hundred blacks and odd   50
        for the barracoons[7] of Florida:

---

[4] Allusion to Ariel's song in Shakespeare's The
Tempest: " 'Full fathom five thy father lies; Of
his bones are coral made; Those are pearls that
were his eyes. . . .' "
[5] The killing of an albatross was thought to bring
bad luck.

[6] In nautical vernacular the sea bottom is called
"Davy Jones' locker."
[7] Barracks for slaves.

"That there was hardly room 'tween-decks for half
the sweltering cattle stowed spoon-fashion there;
that some went mad of thirst and tore their flesh
and sucked the blood: 55

"That Crew and Captain lusted with the comeliest
of the savage girls kept naked in the cabins;
that there was one they called The Guinea Rose
and they cast lots and fought to lie with her:

"That when the Bo's'n piped all hands, the flames   60
spreading from starboard already were beyond
control, the negroes howling and their chains
entangled with the flames:

"That the burning blacks could not be reached,
that the Crew abandoned ship,   65
leaving their shrieking negresses behind,
that the Captain perished drunken with the wenches:

"Further Deponent sayeth not."

Pilot   Oh   Pilot   Me

II

Aye, lad, and I have seen those factories,   70
Gambia, Rio Pongo, Calabar;
have watched the artful mongos baiting traps
of war wherein the victor and the vanquished

Were caught as prizes for our barracoons.
Have seen the nigger kings whose vanity   75
and greed turned wild black hides of Fellatah,
Mandingo, Ibo, Kru[8] to gold for us.

And there was one—King Anthracite we named him—
fetish face beneath French parasols
of brass and orange velvet, impudent mouth   80
whose cups were carven skulls of enemies:

He'd honor us with drum and feast and conjo
and palm-oil-glistening wenches deft in love,
and for tin crowns that shone with paste,
red calico and German-silver trinkets   85

[8] African tribes.

Would have the drums talk war and send
his warriors to burn the sleeping villages
and kill the sick and old and lead the young
in coffles[9] to our factories.

Twenty years a trader, twenty years,   90
for there was wealth aplenty to be harvested
from those black fields, and I'd be trading still
but for the fevers melting down my bones.

III

Shuttles in the rocking loom of history,
the dark ships move, the dark ships move,   95
their bright ironical names
like jests of kindness on a murderer's mouth;
plough through thrashing glister toward
fata morgana's[10] lucent melting shore,
weave toward New World littorals that are   100
mirage and myth and actual shore.

Voyage through death,
                    voyage whose chartings are unlove.

A charnel stench, effluvium of living death
spreads outward from the hold,   105
where the living and the dead, the horribly dying,
lie interlocked, lie foul with blood and excrement.

> *Deep in the festering hold thy father lies,*
> *the corpse of mercy rots with him,*
> *rats eat love's rotten gelid eyes.*   110
> *But, oh, the living look at you*
> *with human eyes whose suffering accuses you,*
> *whose hatred reaches through the swill of dark*
> *to strike you like a leper's claw.*

You cannot stare that hatred down   115
or chain the fear that stalks the watches
and breathes on you its fetid scorching breath;
cannot kill the deep immortal human wish,
the timeless will.

---

[9] Manacled together in a group.   [10] Fata morgana: mirage.

"But for the storm that flung up barriers   120
of wind and wave, *The Amistad*,[11] señores,
would have reached the port of Principe[12] in two,
three days at most; but for the storm we should
have been prepared for what befell.
Swift as the puma's leap it came. There was   125
that interval of moonless calm filled only
with the water's and the rigging's usual sounds,
then sudden movement, blows and snarling cries
and they had fallen on us with machete
and marlinspike. It was as though the very   130
air, the night itself were striking us.
Exhausted by the rigors of the storm,
we were no match for them. Our men went down
before the murderous Africans. Our loyal
Celestino ran from below with gun   135
and lantern and I saw, before the cane-
knife's wounding flash, Cinquez,
that surly brute who calls himself a prince,
directing, urging on the ghastly work.
He hacked the poor mulatto down, and then   140
he turned on me. The decks were slippery
when daylight finally came. It sickens me
to think of what I saw, of how these apes
threw overboard the butchered bodies of
our men, true Christians all, like so much jetsam.   145
Enough, enough. The rest is quickly told:
Cinquez was forced to spare the two of us
you see to steer the ship to Africa,
and we like phantoms doomed to rove the sea
voyaged east by day and west by night,   150
deceiving them, hoping for rescue,
prisoners on our own vessel, till
at length we drifted to the shores of this
your land, America, where we were freed
from our unspeakable misery. Now we   155
demand, good sirs, the extradition of
Cinquez and his accomplices to La
Havana.[13] And it distresses us to know
there are so many here who seem inclined
to justify the mutiny of these blacks.   160
We find it paradoxical indeed
that you whose wealth, whose tree of liberty
are rooted in the labor of your slaves

---

[11] The ship's name: *Friendship*.   [13] In Cuba.
[12] Portuguese island in the Atlantic Ocean.

should suffer the august John Quincy Adams
to speak with so much passion of the right   165
of chattel slaves to kill their lawful masters
and with his Roman rhetoric weave a hero's
garland for Cinquez. I tell you that
we are determined to return to Cuba
with our slaves and there see justice done. Cinquez—   170
or let us say 'the Prince'—Cinquez shall die."

The deep immortal human wish,
the timeless will:

Cinquez its deathless primaveral image,
life that transfigures many lives.   175

Voyage through death
                    to life upon these shores.

1966

Frederick Douglass[1]

When it is finally ours, this freedom, this liberty, this beautiful
and terrible thing, needful to man as air,
usable as earth; when it belongs at last to all,
when it is truly instinct, brain matter, diastole, systole,
reflex action; when it is finally won; when it is more   5
than the gaudy mumbo jumbo of politicians:
this man, this Douglass, this former slave, this Negro
beaten to his knees, exiled, visioning a world
where none is lonely, none hunted, alien,
this man, superb in love and logic, this man   10
shall be remembered. Oh, not with statues' rhetoric,
not with legends and poems and wreaths of bronze alone,
but with the lives grown out of his life, the lives
fleshing his dream of the beautiful, needful thing.

1966

---

[1] Douglass (ca. 1817–1895), who escaped in 1838
from slavery, became an abolitionist, writer, and
statesman.

Randall Jarrell
1914–1965

Randall Jarrell (the accent is on the second syllable) was a divided soul, half critic, half poet. By the time of his early death (he walked either by accident or design into the path of a car on a freeway), he was the best-known critic of poetry in America, serving as poetry editor of *The Nation* (1946) and writing brilliantly witty essays on American poetry from Whitman to Elizabeth Bishop. His essay on Whitman helped restore Whitman to the American pantheon of poets, he understood Marianne Moore better than anyone else, and he greeted (from his privileged position as Robert Lowell's college roommate) Lowell's first book of verse, *Lord Weary's Castle* (1946), as the achievement of a major poet. It was his own poetic sensibility, of course, that made Jarrell's criticism so acute; he saw into the workings of verse with a poet's eye. And his criticism was also a reflection of his rapid, abrasive, allusive, and mercurial conversation that made willing hearers of his gifted friends—Lowell, Peter Taylor, John Berryman. Jarrell's critical books—*Poetry and the Age* (1953), *A Sad Heart at the Supermarket* (1962), and *The Third Book of Criticism* (1971)—brought American poetry reviewing from a generally depressing exhibition of puffery to the level of a high accomplishment.

Yet Jarrell's own heart was with his poetry, where he wrote chiefly with a yearning pity for the fallibility, weakness, and sadness of human beings. He could insert himself with uncanny insight into the mind of his characters. That Keatsian degree of empathy may have been what led him to major in psychology at Vanderbilt; Freud was to become one of his major intellectual points of reference. In going to Vanderbilt, Jarrell was remaining in Nashville, where he had been born and had lived since the age of twelve. Yet the impressionable years of his early childhood had been spent in California, and a deep nostalgia for Hollywood, where he had lived for a year with his grandparents, never left him. He called it his "lost world" in the reminiscent title poem of his last book (1965), and its movie lots, with their temporary fantasy constructions, were for him symbols of the imagination.

Jarrell took an M.A. in English from Vanderbilt in 1938 and, except for his military service from 1942 to 1946, spent the rest of his life teaching in various colleges, notably Kenyon, the University of Texas, Sarah Lawrence, Princeton, and the Women's College of the University of North Carolina (1947–1965, with occasional interruptions). Jarrell first became known for his poignant war poetry. He had served in the air force in World War II, and his first volumes, *Little Friend, Little Friend* (1945) and *Losses* (1948), show soldiers as pitiful high school boys plunged, unequipped and ignorant, into war, bombing, and death. In 1965, after a long and brilliant career, Jarrell was hospitalized for a nervous breakdown; he died not long thereafter. His *Complete Poems* appeared posthumously, in 1969.

Jarrell liked the English blank verse line, adapted (via the example of Frost) to American speech rhythms; he was also capable (as in "Next Day") of beautiful inventions in stanza form and rhyme scheme. He had an eye for the poetry of the ordinary ("Moving from Cheer to Joy, from Joy to All"), and his rendering of the pathos of a young soldier, of a woman in a supermarket or at a zoo, of a girl falling asleep over her homework, is exact and touching.

Further Reading:

Randall Jarrell, 1914–1965, ed. R. Lowell, P. Taylor, and R. P. Warren, 1967.
K. Shapiro, *Randall Jarrell,* 1967.
The Achievement of Randall Jarrell, ed. F. Hoffman, 1970.
S. Ferguson, *The Poetry of Randall Jarrell,* 1971.
M. L. Rosenthal, *Randall Jarrell,* 1972.

H. Hagenbuchle, *The Black Goddess: A Study of the Archetypal Feminine in the Poetry of Randall Jarrell,* 1975.
B. Quinn, *Randall Jarrell,* 1981.
S. Ferguson, *Critical Essays on Randall Jarrell,* 1983.

Text:

Complete Poems, 1969.
See also *Poetry and the Age,* 1953.
Pictures from an Institution, 1954.

A Sad Heart at the Supermarket, 1962.
The Third Book of Criticism, 1969.

The Death of the Ball Turret[1] Gunner

From my mother's sleep I fell into the State,
And I hunched in its belly till my wet fur froze.
Six miles from earth, loosed from its dream of life,
I woke to black flak and the nightmare fighters.
When I died they washed me out of the turret with a hose.   5

1955

Losses

It was not dying: everybody died.
It was not dying: we had died before
In the routine crashes—and our fields
Called up the papers, wrote home to our folks,
And the rates rose, all because of us.   5

---

[1] A *ball turret* was a revolvable plexiglass sphere set into the underside of a B-17 or B-24 bomber, from which a man, in a crouched position, could fire a mounted .50 caliber machine gun at other aircraft aloft.

We died on the wrong page of the almanac,
Scattered on mountains fifty miles away;
Diving on haystacks, fighting with a friend,
We blazed up on the lines we never saw.
We died like aunts or pets or foreigners.   10
(When we left high school nothing else had died
For us to figure we had died like.)

In our new planes, with our new crews, we bombed
The ranges by the desert or the shore,
Fired at towed targets, waited for our scores—   15
And turned into replacements and woke up
One morning, over England, operational.
It wasn't different: but if we died
It was not an accident but a mistake
(But an easy one for anyone to make).   20
We read our mail and counted up our missions—
In bombers named for girls, we burned
The cities we had learned about in school—
Till our lives wore out; our bodies lay among
The people we had killed and never seen.   25
When we lasted long enough they gave us medals;
When we died they said, "Our casualties were low."
They said, "Here are the maps"; we burned the cities.

It was not dying—no, not ever dying;
But the night I died I dreamed that I was dead,   30
And the cities said to me: "Why are you dying?
We are satisfied, if you are; but why did I die?"

1955

A Lullaby

For wars his life and half a world away
The soldier sells his family and days.
He learns to fight for freedom and the State;
He sleeps with seven men within six feet.

He picks up matches and he cleans out plates;   5
Is lied to like a child, cursed like a beast.
They crop his head, his dog tags ring like sheep
As his stiff limbs shift wearily to sleep.

Recalled in dreams or letters, else forgot,
His life is smothered like a grave, with dirt;   10
And his dull torment mottles like a fly's
The lying amber of the histories.

1955

The Woman at the Washington Zoo

The saris[1] go by me from the embassies.

Cloth from the moon. Cloth from another planet.
They look back at the leopard like the leopard.

And I. . . .
           this print of mine, that has kept its color   5
Alive through so many cleanings; this dull null
Navy I wear to work, and wear from work, and so
To my bed, so to my grave, with no
Complaints, no comment: neither from my chief,
The Deputy Chief Assistant, nor his chief—   10
Only I complain. . . . this serviceable
Body that no sunlight dyes, no hand suffuses
But, dome-shadowed, withering among columns,
Wavy beneath fountains—small, far-off, shining
In the eyes of animals, these beings trapped   15
As I am trapped but not, themselves, the trap,
Aging, but without knowledge of their age,
Kept safe here, knowing not of death, for death—
Oh, bars of my own body, open, open!

The world goes by my cage and never sees me.   20
And there come not to me, as come to these,
The wild beasts, sparrows pecking the llamas' grain,
Pigeons settling on the bears' bread, buzzards
Tearing the meat the flies have clouded. . . .
                          Vulture,   25
When you come for the white rat that the foxes left,

---

[1] Long flowing garments worn by women of
India.

Take off the red helmet of your head, the black
Wings that have shadowed me, and step to me as man:
The wild brother at whose feet the white wolves fawn,
To whose hand of power the great lioness   30
Stalks, purring. . . .
                You know what I was,
You see what I am: change me, change me!
1960

Next Day

Moving from Cheer to Joy, from Joy to All,
I take a box
And add it to my wild rice, my Cornish game hens.
The slacked or shorted, basketed, identical
Food-gathering flocks   5
Are selves I overlook. Wisdom, said William James,[1]

Is learning what to overlook. And I am wise
If that is wisdom.
Yet somehow, as I buy All from these shelves
And the boy takes it to my station wagon,   10
What I've become
Troubles me even if I shut my eyes.

When I was young and miserable and pretty
And poor, I'd wish
What all girls wish: to have a husband,
A house and children. Now that I'm old, my wish   15
Is womanish:
That the boy putting groceries in my car

See me. It bewilders me he doesn't see me.
For so many years
I was good enough to eat: the world looked at me   20
And its mouth watered. How often they have undressed me,
The eyes of strangers!
And, holding their flesh within my flesh, their vile

---

[1] American philosopher and psychologist
(1842–1910).

Imaginings within my imagining,   25
I too have taken
The chance of life. Now the boy pats my dog
And we start home. Now I am good.
The last mistaken,
Ecstatic, accidental bliss, the blind   30

Happiness that, bursting, leaves upon the palm
Some soap and water—
It was so long ago, back in some Gay
Twenties, Nineties, I don't know . . . Today I miss
My lovely daughter   35
Away at school, my sons away at school,

My husband away at work—I wish for them.
The dog, the maid,
And I go through the sure unvarying days
At home in them. As I look at my life,   40
I am afraid
Only that it will change, as I am changing:

I am afraid, this morning, of my face.
It looks at me
From the rear-view mirror, with the eyes I hate,   45
The smile I hate. Its plain, lined look
Of gray discovery
Repeats to me: "You're old." That's all, I'm old.

And yet I'm afraid, as I was at the funeral
I went to yesterday.   50
My friend's cold made-up face, granite among its flowers,
Her undressed, operated-on, dressed body
Were my face and body.
As I think of her I hear her telling me

How young I seem; I *am* exceptional;   55
I think of all I have.
But really no one is exceptional,
No one has anything, I'm anybody,
I stand beside my grave
Confused with my life, that is commonplace and solitary.   60

1965

John Berryman
1914–1972

John Berryman's fame rests chiefly on the odd personal language he invented in *77 Dream Songs* (1964), a compound of baby talk, slang, minstrel-show imitation of black English, deviant grammar and syntax, and intimate address. This language, derived in part from the syntactic and grammatical disruptions of Gerard Manley Hopkins and E. E. Cummings, appeared in extended form in Berryman's long dramatic poem "Homage to Mistress Bradstreet" (1956). This explosive poem, coming after Berryman's earlier imitations of William Butler Yeats, W. H. Auden, and Hopkins in *The Dispossessed* (1948), represented Berryman's discovery of his Americanness, through his identification with Ann Bradstreet, the first American poet. It also enabled Berryman to find his true topic, the utterance of what Freud would have called the id, the irrepressible vehemence of pure untutored and uncivilized desire.

The division of Berryman's self into two voices—the one American and untamable, the other a reproachful voice, whether of an inhibited English "literary" superego or of the conscience—mirrors his own division in life. On the one hand, he was a formidable scholar, critic, and teacher, author of a Columbia Ph.D. thesis on the writer Stephen Crane (published as a book in 1950), and author as well of brilliant critical essays posthumously collected as *The Freedom of the Poet* (1976). On the other hand, he was a rebellious student, an alcoholic in adult life, and finally a suicide (he leaped from a bridge in Minneapolis) after he despaired of curing his alcoholism.

Berryman's true name was John Smith. His father, a banker, committed suicide by shooting himself when Berryman was twelve, and Berryman adopted the name of the man whom his adoring and possessive mother subsequently married. After private school in Connecticut, Berryman received his B.A. in 1936 from Columbia and, as the ranking English scholar, was awarded a Kellett fellowship to Clare College of Cambridge University in England. The ambitious, intense, and exploratory years at Cambridge are recalled in *Love and Fame* (1970).

Berryman taught at Wayne State, Harvard, and Princeton; in 1955 he joined the faculty of the University of Minnesota, where he continued to teach until his death. Among the pieces included in *The Freedom of the Poet* is an account, in fictional form, of Berryman's class on Milton's "Lycidas"; the story conveys the intensity and passion behind Berryman's teaching. At the same time, Berryman's alcoholic illness, complicated by addiction to sedatives and tranquilizers, caused more and more unpredictable and undependable behavior; his immense learning and conversational charm protected him for some time, but in his last years his self-destructive behavior affected his private and public life and his writing. These desperate later years are chronicled in Berryman's novel *Recovery* (published posthumously in 1973, with an introduction by Saul Bellow).

"Huffy Henry" is the character Berryman invented in his *Dream Songs* to speak for the id. Henry—sulky, eager, manic and depressive by turns—craves the whole world but is haunted by a nameless and all-encompassing guilt:

But never did Henry, as he thought he did,
end anyone and hacks her body up
and hide the pieces, where they may be found.
He knows: he went over everyone, & nobody's missing.

Berryman's Roman Catholic upbringing contributes to Henry's sense of a religious standard that condemns his uncontrolled desires. In one poem, the "profiled reproach" of a Sienese madonna oppresses him. In another, he wishes for the peace he sees in the art of a Zen garden. But such religious order and harmony elude him; he continues to act, gaze, and suffer, the more so as his friends die and his own life lurches to ruin.

If we ask why Berryman turned to splitting himself in two in *The Dream Songs,* we can answer, perhaps, by looking at his elegy for Stevens. Berryman's critique of Wallace Stevens—that he was too cold, too narrow, too metaphysical —suggests a self-critique. If the "scholarly" and "philosophical" Berryman seemed inhibited to himself, he would release his more volcanic, heated, physical self in the person of Henry. But how should Henry speak? Where does Henry live? And what language does Henry use? Berryman's departure in the *Dream Songs* from his earlier practice in "Homage to Mistress Bradstreet" is to the point here: Bradstreet lives in history, Henry lives in the world of desire and dream; Bradstreet speaks, Henry sings; Bradstreet uses adult language, Henry uses an invented language of the unconscious. Henry has only one formal resource—a three-stanza, eighteen-line song into which all content spills and in which it is contained. Elegance, comedy, pathos, and horror meet in Henry's songs. It is the comedy with which Berryman's tragic topics are treated that is striking. Robert Lowell, in his elegy for Berryman, realized "how we differ: humor." The black humor of the songs, their violent beauty, and their suicidal momentum make them part of literature. They continue the line of song in the lyric, a line that interested, among others, Shakespeare, Blake, Yeats, and Auden but that had been neglected by the earlier American modernists (except for Frost and Cummings) until revived by Berryman.

Further Reading:
W. J. Martz, *John Berryman,* 1969.
J. M. Linebarger, *John Berryman,* 1974.
J. Conarroe, *John Berryman: An Introduction to the Poetry,* 1977.
G. Arpin, *The Poetry of John Berryman,* 1978.
J. Haffenden, *John Berryman: A Critical Commentary,* 1980.
J. Haffenden, *The Life of John Berryman,* 1982.

Texts:
Through "77" from *77 Dream Songs,* 1964.
Remaining "Dream Songs" from *His Toy, His Dream, His Rest,* 1968.
Other poems from *Henry's Fate,* 1977.

from The Dream Songs[*]

1

Huffy Henry hid   the day,
unappeasable Henry sulked.
I see his point,—a trying to put things over.
It was the thought that they thought
they could *do* it made Henry wicked & away.   5
But he should have come out and talked.

All the world like a woolen lover
once did seem on Henry's side.
Then came a departure.
Thereafter nothing fell out as it might or ought.   10
I don't see how Henry, pried
open for all the world to see, survived.

What he has now to say is a long
wonder the world can bear & be.
Once in a sycamore I was glad   15
all at the top, and I sang.
Hard on the land wears the strong sea
and empty grows every bed.

1964

4

Filling her compact & delicious body
with chicken páprika, she glanced at me
twice.
Fainting with interest, I hungered back
and only the fact of her husband & four other people   5
kept me from springing on her

or falling at her little feet and crying
'You are the hottest one for years of night
Henry's dazed eyes
have enjoyed, Brilliance.' I advanced upon   10
(despairing) my spumoni.[1] —Sir Bones: is stuffed,
de world, wif feeding girls.

---

[*] The first of Berryman's Dream Songs were published as *77 Dream Songs* in 1964. More Dream Songs appeared in *His Toy, His Dream, His Rest* in 1968. *The Dream Songs* (1969) combines the poems of these two groups in sequence.
[1] Italian ice cream.

—Black hair, complexion Latin, jewelled eyes
downcast . . . The slob beside her   feasts . . . What wonders is
she sitting on, over there?   15
The restaurant buzzes. She might as well be on Mars.
Where did it all go wrong? There ought to be a law against Henry.
—Mr. Bones: there is.

1964

5

Henry sats in de bar & was odd,
off in the glass from the glass,
at odds wif de world & its god,
his wife is a complete nothing,
St Stephen[2]   5
getting even.

Henry sats in de plane & was gay.
Careful Henry nothing said aloud
but where a Virgin[3] out of cloud
to her Mountain dropt in light,   10
his thought made pockets & the plane buckt.
'Parm me, lady.' 'Orright.'

Henry lay in de netting,[4] wild,
while the brainfever bird did scales;
Mr Heartbreak, the New Man,   15
come to farm a crazy land;
an image of the dead on the fingernail
of a newborn child.

1964

14

Life, friends, is boring. We must not say so.
After all, the sky flashes, the great sea yearns,
we ourselves flash and yearn,
and moreover my mother told me as a boy
(repeatedly) 'Ever to confess you're bored   5
means you have no

Inner Resources.' I conclude now I have no
inner resources, because I am heavy bored.
Peoples bore me,

---

[2] First martyr of the Christian church; he was   [3] The Virgin Mary.
stoned to death, without resisting his attackers.   [4] Mosquito netting.

literature bores me, especially great literature, 10
Henry bores me, with his plights & gripes
as bad as achilles,[5]

who loves people and valiant art, which bores me.
And the tranquil hills, & gin, look like a drag
and somehow a dog 15
has taken itself & its tail considerably away
into mountains or sea or sky, leaving
behind: me, wag.

1964

26

The glories of the world struck me, made me aria,[6] once.
—What happen then, Mr Bones?
if be you cares to say.
—Henry. Henry became interested in women's bodies,
his loins were & were the scene of stupendous achievement. 5
Stupor. Knees, dear. Pray.

All the knobs & softnesses of, my God,
the ducking & trouble it swarm on Henry,
at one time.
—What happen then, Mr Bones?
you seems excited-like.
—Fell Henry back into the original crime: art, rime 10

besides a sense of others, my God, my God,
and a jealousy for the honour (alive) of his country,
what can get more odd? 15
and discontent with the thriving gangs & pride.
—What happen then, Mr. Bones?
—I had a most marvellous piece of luck. I died.

1964

29

There sat down, once, a thing on Henry's heart
só heavy, if he had a hundred years
& more, & weeping, sleepless, in all them time
Henry could not make good.

---

[5] Hero of the *Iliad*. His anger at his fellow
Greeks keeps him from joining them in battle.
[6] I.e., sing an operatic song.

Starts again always in Henry's ears   5
the little cough somewhere, an odour, a chime.

And there is another thing he has in mind
like a grave Sienese face[7] a thousand years
would fail to blur the still profiled reproach of. Ghastly,
with open eyes, he attends, blind.   10
All the bells say: too late. This is not for tears;
thinking.

But never did Henry, as he thought he did,
end anyone and hacks her body up
and hide the pieces, where they may be found.   15
He knows: he went over everyone, & nobody's missing.
Often he reckons, in the dawn, them up.
Nobody is ever missing.
1964

45

He stared at ruin. Ruin stared straight back.
He thought they was old friends. He felt on the stair
where her papa found them bare
they became familiar. When the papers were lost
rich with pals' secrets, he thought he had the knack   5
of ruin. Their paths crossed

and once they crossed in jail; they crossed in bed;
and over an unsigned letter their eyes met,
and in an Asian city
directionless & lurchy at two & three,   10
or trembling to a telephone's fresh threat,
and when some wired his head

to reach a wrong opinion, 'Epileptic'.
But he noted now that: they were not old friends.
He did not know this one.   15
This one was a stranger, come to make amends
for all the imposters, and to make it stick.
Henry nodded, un-.
1964

---

[7] The face of a saint or Virgin in a painting of
the Sienese school (thirteenth to fourteenth
century).

77

Seedy Henry rose up shy in de world
& shaved & swung his barbells, duded Henry up
and p.a.'d[8] poor thousands of persons on topics of grand
moment to Henry, ah to those less & none.
Wif a book of his in either hand   5
he is stript down to move on.

—Come away, Mr Bones.

—Henry is tired of the winter,
& haircuts, & a squeamish comfy   ruin-prone proud national mind,   & Spring
    (in the city so called).   10
Henry likes Fall.
Hé would be prepared to líve in a world of Fáll
for ever, impenitent Henry.
But the snows and summers grieve & dream;

thése fierce & airy occupations, and love,   15
raved away so many of Henry's years
it is a wonder that, with in each hand
one of his own mad books and all,
ancient fires for eyes, his head full
& his heart full, he's making ready to move on.   20
1964

164

Three limbs, three seasons smashed; well, one to go.
Henry fell smiling through the air below
and through the air above,
the middle air as well did he not neglect
but carefully in all these airs was wrecked   5
which he got truly tired of.

His friends alas went all about their ways
intact. Couldn't William break at least a collar-bone?

---

[8] Publicly addressed.

O world so ill arranged!
Henry holds in addition pharmacies   10
for all his other ills, pills of his own
which frequently get changed

as his despairing doctors change their minds
about what must be best for wilful Henry.
There seems to firm no answer   15
save from the sexton in the place that blinds
& stones and does not hurt: Henry springs youthfully
in his six-by-two like a dancer.

1968

219: So Long? Stevens[9]

He lifted up, among the actuaries,
a grandee crow. Ah ha & he crowed good.
That funny money-man.
Mutter we all must as well as we can.
He mutter spiffy. He make wonder Henry's   5
wits, though, with a odd

. . . something . . . something . . . not there in his flourishing art.
O veteran of death, you will not mind
a counter-mutter.
What was it missing, then, at the man's heart   10
so that he does not wound? It is our kind
to wound, as well as utter

a fact of happy world. That metaphysics
he hefted up until we could not breathe
the physics. *On our side,*   15
monotonous (or ever-fresh)—it sticks
in Henry's throat to judge—brilliant, he seethe;
better than us; less wide.

1968

[9] Wallace Stevens (1879–1955), American poet
and vice-president of the Hartford Insurance
company.

384

The marker slants, flowerless, day's almost done,
I stand above my father's grave with rage,
often, often before
I've made this awful pilgrimage to one
who cannot visit me, who tore his page   5
out: I come back for more,

I spit upon this dreadful banker's grave
who shot his heart out in a Florida dawn
O ho alas alas
When will indifference come, I moan & rave   10
I'd like to scrabble till I got right down
away down under the grass

and ax the casket open ha to see
just how he's taking it, which he sought so hard
we'll tear apart   15
the mouldering grave clothes ha & then Henry
will heft the ax once more, his final card,
and fell it on the start.

1968

[With arms outflung]

With arms outflung the clock announced: Ten-twenty.
Dozens of demons sprang & preyed on Henry.
All on a heavy morning.
The baby was ill, the sky was dark, the I
was Id,[1] somebody put the sky on like a lid,   5
somebody who is not returning.

Oh we'll wait. After all, after all.
The Doubter[2] & the rest. They rested all,
on the night of the crucifying.

---

[1] Freud's word for the unconscious portion of the
mind.

[2] The Apostle Thomas, who doubted the reports
of the resurrection of Christ.

Perhaps their dreams were something truly remarkable.   10
Perhaps their dreams had what to do with his dying—
but that was very lonely.

Haldol & Serax, phenobarbital,
Vivactil, by day; by deep night Tuinal
& Thorazine,[3]   15
kept Henry going, like a natural man.
I'm waiting for them to work, as sometimes they can,
honey, in the bloodstream.

1977

[Old codger Henry]

Old codger Henry contain within hisself
Henry young, Henry almost beautiful
Henry the seducer
Henry the mad young artist, with *no* interest in pelf
whereas now he takes steps to keep both his bank accounts full   5
just like: you, Sir!

Henry could never put up with litter.
Litter grew on him as he grew, until
you couldn't see his tables
for the damned *litter* of papers, glasses,   10
visible incoherences—& so was the floor, pal;
Henry lived like something from Aesop's Fables.

Codger Henry, desperatingly tired,
nevertheless got *fed up* with this state
which alas only he could fix.   15
I draw the veil over whom then he hired
but I promise they did not solve his fate.
He bared his rare watch. *It* ticks.

1977

---

[3] Haldol, etc.: major tranquilizers and
antipsychotic drugs.

[All projects failed]

All projects failed, in the August afternoon
he lay & cursed himself & cursed his lot
like Housman's lad[1] forsooth.
A breeze sometimes came by. His sunburn itcht.
His wife was out on errands. He sighed & scratcht.   5
The little girls were fiddling with the telephone.

They wanted candy, the which he gave them.
His entire soul contorted with the phlegm.
The sun burned down.
Photos of him in despair flooded the town   10
or city. Mourned his many friends, or so.
The little girls were fiddling with the piano.

He crusht a cigarette out. Crusht him out
surprising God, at last, in a wink of time.
His soul was forwarded.   15
Adressat unbekannt.[2] The little girls with a shout
welcomed the dazzling package. In official rime
the official verdict was: dead.

1977

Robert Lowell
1917–1977

Robert Lowell's poems are so various in theme and form that it is difficult to believe they were all written by the same man. With *Lord Weary's Castle* (1946), he burst on the literary scene as a "Roman Catholic poet," writing a poetry of social protest in icily formal meters swelling with Miltonic rage; with *Day by Day* (1977), he left the American literary scene as a Horatian poet of quiet stoicism, writing verse "day by day." In having the daring to break his own aesthetic several times over, Lowell helped to reshape twentieth-century poetry. His poetic powers, trained in Greek and Latin and developed further by "imitations" of many famous European poems, were formidable.

The accident of Lowell's quasi-aristocratic birth determined his poetic life; he was a Lowell first, and a husband, lover, father, teacher, or political protester

[1] The persona of A. E. Housman's poems *A Shropshire Lad* (1896).   [2] German: "addressee unknown."

second. The other determinant of his life was his recurrent manic-depressive illness, which caused a part of almost every year of his adult life to be spent in confinement in an asylum. In the last ten years of his life his condition was stabilized by lithium. But the uncertainty of his behavior made it for a long time impossible for him to be regularly employed; his family income luckily made that unnecessary. His large poetic output has yet to be fully absorbed by critics and the public.

Robert Lowell's father was a vacant and inept man who made the mistake of leaving the navy, at his wife's insistence, to take up stockbroking. The firm kept him on for his name and social connections, but he had, according to his son's memoir, *91 Revere Street,* no clients. Lowell's mother, a Winslow by birth, was intelligent, possessive, and domineering. After an unsuccessful two years at Harvard, Lowell fled his parents and, advised by Ford Madox Ford, went off to Kenyon College to study under John Crowe Ransom. There he succeeded brilliantly, majored in classics, and was valedictorian of his class.

Lowell married the novelist Jean Stafford (all three of his wives were writers) and for a brief period became a Roman Catholic (the one thing that would most enrage his Puritan-descended family). After attempting to enlist in the navy during World War II and being refused for bad eyesight, he decided on pacifist grounds to become a conscientious objector, flouting the family naval tradition. Finally, in full mania, he wrote a letter to President Roosevelt ("I made my manic statement"), explaining his choice of conscientious objector status. After spending several months in jail, Lowell was released. Lowell's first marriage ended after bouts of drinking, insanity, and infidelity. His second, more stable marriage was to the writer Elizabeth Hardwick, who enabled him to survive moves, breakdowns, and hospitalizations. He entered psychoanalytic therapy, and the reflection on his past entailed by therapy is visible in *Life Studies* (1960), a book of pitilessly naked portraits of his family.

These poems were written in a new laconic free verse (retaining some underpinnings of rhyme) that Lowell ascribed to the influence of both Elizabeth Bishop's natural cadences and the new oral poetry of the Beats. In writing *Life Studies,* Lowell was continuing the historical portraiture of his Puritan stock that had begun in his early poems about the Winslows (whom he scandalously called "Indian killers") and Jonathan Edwards (to whom, as a Puritan intellectual of crisis mentality, he was very much drawn). *Life Studies* also records Lowell's repudiation of Roman Catholicism; here, in a symbolic decision, he leaves Rome and travels "Beyond the Alps" to Paris.

Life Studies was excoriated by Lowell's old mentor Allen Tate, who said the poems were not poetry. Seeing Lowell's agnostic stance, Catholics regretted losing an apologist. Young poets, on the other hand, recognized that Lowell had crystallized a new plain style into form. But no sooner had Lowell consolidated that free-verse style in *For the Union Dead* (1964) than he confused the reading world (he was by this time a much-read poet here and abroad) by publishing the formal Marvellian poems of *Near the Ocean* (1967). He next poured out an apparently inexhaustible stream of unrhymed sonnets, first as *Notebook 1967–68,* next (augmented and revised) as *Notebook* (1970), next rearranged and split in

two as *History* and *For Lizzie and Harriet* (1973). At the same time, he published
a coda in *The Dolphin* (1973), a set of sonnets about his third marriage, in
England, to Lady Caroline Blackwood, a journalist and novelist.

The sonnets are full of events, public and private, that took place during their
composition; they are also full of allusiveness. Often they seemed unreadable to
those who did not possess Lowell's learning and could not know the events of his
private life. For those who liked them, the sonnets seemed yet another form of
Lowellesque energy—as though the poet had determined to put into his poetry
his entire complex mind, not simply some selection from it. The sonnets often
resemble, in diction, the denser passages of Milton or Shakespeare. As they are
clarified by time and annotation, they will be better understood. In their political
dimension, they represent a gripping testimony to one intellectual's revulsion at
the Vietnam War, the March on the Pentagon in 1967 (in which Lowell
participated), and the state of government and society in America in the late
1960s.

It might be said that all of Lowell's writing was driven into being by some
cause or belief—religious, political, or historical. The consistent linking of his
own family's history with the history of the United States made Lowell see, for
most of his life, every political event as one intimately addressed to himself. And
he viewed the Puritan theocratic obsessions, toward which he felt both
admiration and revulsion, as a form of familial legacy. But when he broke his
style for the last time in *Day by Day,* he abandoned all fictions of battle and now
saw his past religious and political positions chiefly as constructs of his own
embattled psyche. In the brief hope that he could be, with the help of lithium,
an ordinary person, he had moved to England in 1970, entered his last marriage,
and had a son. The early idyll of the new marriage, the recurrence of his mental
illness, and the unhappiness of the later years in England are all reflected in the
new, spare free verse of *Day by Day,* a verse that is pared to the bone, dry and
plangent at once in its anticipation of death. Lowell died of a heart attack in a
taxicab in New York City shortly before he was due to return to Harvard,
where he had been teaching literature and writing for several years.

Lowell wrote occasional prose (not yet collected) and several plays. He
adapted Melville's *Benito Cereno,* three stories by Hawthorne, and Thomas
Morton's 1637 *New Canaan* for the stage under the title *The Old Glory* (1965);
he translated Racine's *Phèdre* (1961) and Aeschylus' *Prometheus Bound* (1969). In
times of depression, when he could not write poetry, he turned to translation.
Eventually, his practice in translating was to turn the foreign original into a
poem that could have been written by himself. These extraordinary "translations"
were collected under the title *Imitations* (1961), and, for all their willfulness,
raised the level of both translation and the theory of translation in America.

However, Lowell will be judged, finally, by his revolutionizing of American
poetry. He took it from the formal patterns of Tate and Ransom into a new era
of boldly revolutionary free verse, then into a torrential new formality. Finally,
he invented, in *Day by Day,* a new kind of lyric—wayward, structurally free,
and intimate—that reflects formally his abandonment of transcendence and
teleology in favor of an unforced perception of earthly transience.

Further Reading:

H. Staples, *Robert Lowell: The First Twenty Years,* 1961.
J. Mazzaro, *The Poetic Themes of Robert Lowell,* 1965.
Robert Lowell: A Collection of Critical Essays, ed. T. Parkinson, 1968.
P. Cooper, *The Autobiographical Myth of Robert Lowell,* 1970.
P. Cosgrave, *The Public Poetry of Robert Lowell,* 1970.
R. J. Fein, *Robert Lowell,* 1970.
J. Martin, *Robert Lowell,* 1970.
R. K. Meiners, *Everything to Be Endured: An Essay on Robert Lowell,* 1970.

M. Perloff, *The Poetic Art of Robert Lowell,* 1973.
A. Williamson, *Pity the Monsters: The Political Vision of Robert Lowell,* 1974.
S. Yenser, *Circle to Circle: The Poetry of Robert Lowell,* 1975.
S. G. Axelrod, *Robert Lowell: Life and Art,* 1978.
S. G. Axelrod and H. Deese, *Robert Lowell: A Reference Guide,* 1982.
V. M. Bell, *Robert Lowell: Nihilist as Hero,* 1983.
I. Hamilton, *Robert Lowell: A Biography,* 1983.
M. Rudman, *Robert Lowell: An Introduction to the Poetry,* 1983.

Texts:

"Where the Rainbow Ends" from *Lord Weary's Castle,* 1944.
"Sailing Home from Rapallo," "Waking in the Blue," "Home After Three Months Away," and "Skunk Hour" from *Life Studies,* 1960.
"For the Union Dead" from *For the Union Dead,* 1964.
"Waking Early Sunday Morning" from *Near the Ocean,* 1967.

"The March I," "Death and the Bridge," and "New Year's Eve 1968" from *Notebook,* 1970.
"Harriet," "Mexico," and "Obit" from *For Lizzie and Harriet,* 1973.
"History," "Will Not Come Back," and "Reading Myself" from *History,* 1973.
"Fishnet" from *Dolphin,* 1973.
Remaining poems from *Day by Day,* 1977.

Where the Rainbow Ends[1]

I saw the sky descending, black and white,
Not blue, on Boston where the winters wore
The skulls to jack-o'-lanterns on the slates,[2]
And Hunger's skin-and-bone retrievers tore
The chickadee and shrike. The thorn tree waits   5
Its victim[3] and tonight
The worms will eat the deadwood to the foot
Of Ararat:[4] the scythers, Time and Death,
Helmed locusts, move upon the tree of breath;
The wild ingrafted olive and the root[5]   10

Are withered, and a winter drifts to where
The Pepperpot, ironic rainbow, spans

---

[1] The rainbow symbolized God's covenant with Noah that there would not be another deluge (Genesis 9:13–17).
[2] Slate gravestones ornamented with carved skulls.
[3] Christ, crowned with thorns, crucified on the "tree" of the Cross.

[4] The mountain on which Noah's ark came to rest (Genesis 8:4).
[5] The Gentiles are the olive (tree) grafted onto the root of Israel.

Charles River[6] and its scales of scorched-earth miles
I saw my city in the Scales, the pans[7]
Of judgment rising and descending. Piles   15
Of dead leaves char the air—
And I am a red arrow on this graph
Of Revelations.[8] Every dove[9] is sold
The Chapel's sharp-shinned eagle shifts its hold
On serpent-Time,[10] the rainbow's epitaph.   20

In Boston serpents whistle at the cold.
The victim climbs the altar steps and sings:
"Hosannah to the lion, lamb, and beast
Who fan the furnace-face of IS[11] with wings:
I breathe the ether of my marriage feast."[12]   25
At the high altar, gold
And a fair cloth. I kneel and the wings beat
My cheek. What can the dove of Jesus give
You now but wisdom, exile?[13] Stand and live,
The dove has brought an olive branch[14] to eat.   30

1944

Sailing Home from Rapallo[1]

(February 1954)

Your nurse could only speak Italian,
but after twenty minutes I could imagine your final week,
and tears ran down my cheeks. . . .

When I embarked from Italy with my Mother's body,
the whole shoreline of the *Golfo di Genova*[2]   5

[6] Longfellow Bridge, crossing the Charles River in Boston, is nicknamed the Pepperpot because its two towers resemble large, old-fashioned salt-and-pepper canisters.

[7] I.e., the two holders on either side of God's scales of judgment at the end of the world.

[8] In the Bible the Book of Revelation, sometimes known as the Apocalypse, tells of events at the end of the world.

[9] A dove was the ritual sacrifice offered in the Jewish temple for a first-born son (Luke 2:24).

[10] Because the serpent sheds its skin, it represents the changes of Time.

[11] Jehovah, who defined himself: "I am that I am" (Exodus 3:14).

[12] The soul is conventionally called "the Bride of Christ."

[13] Lowell, in converting to Roman Catholicism, felt he was exiling himself from the Protestantism of Boston and the historic Lowell family.

[14] An olive branch was brought back by a dove to Noah as a sign that the waters of the Flood had subsided (Genesis 8:11).

[1] Town in Italy where Charlotte Winslow Lowell died.

[2] Italian: "Gulf of Genoa."

was breaking into fiery flower.
The crazy yellow and azure sea-sleds
blasting like jack-hammers across
the *spumante*-bubbling[3] wake of our liner,
recalled the clashing colors of my Ford.   10
Mother travelled first-class in the hold;
her *Risorgimento*[4] black and gold casket
was like Napoleon's at the *Invalides*. . . .[5]

While the passengers were tanning
on the Mediterranean in deck-chairs,   15
our family cemetery in Dunbarton
lay under the White Mountains[6]
in the sub-zero weather.
The graveyard's soil was changing to stone—
so many of its deaths had been midwinter.   20
Dour and dark against the blinding snowdrifts,
its black brook and fir trunks were as smooth as masts.
A fence of iron spear-hafts
black-bordered its mostly Colonial grave-slates.
The only "unhistoric" soul to come here   25
was Father, now buried beneath his recent
unweathered pink-veined slice of marble.
Even the Latin of his Lowell motto:
Occasionem cognosce,[7]
seemed too businesslike and pushing here,   30
where the burning cold illuminated
the hewn inscriptions of Mother's relatives:
twenty or thirty Winslows and Starks.
Frost had given their names a diamond edge. . . .

In the grandiloquent lettering on Mother's coffin,   35
Lowell had been misspelled *LOVEL*.
The corpse
was wrapped like *panetone*[8] in Italian tinfoil.

1960

---

[3] Spumante: an Italian sparkling wine.
[4] In the style of the nineteenth-century period of Italy's rise of nationalism.
[5] Napoleon's tomb in Paris.
[6] In New Hampshire. The Winslow family graveyard has been moved intact to a different location in Dunbarton, since the original location was endangered by flooding after the construction of a dam.
[7] Latin: "Know your chance."
[8] An Italian Christmas bread often imported to the United States.

Waking in the Blue

The night attendant, a B. U.[1] sophomore,
rouses from the mare's-nest of his drowsy head
propped on *The Meaning of Meaning*.[2]
He catwalks down our corridor.
Azure day   5
makes my agonized blue window bleaker.
Crows maunder on the petrified fairway.
Absence! My heart grows tense
as though a harpoon were sparring for the kill.
(This is the house for the "mentally ill.")   10

What use is my sense of humor?
I grin at Stanley, now sunk in his sixties,
once a Harvard all-American fullback,
(if such were possible!)
still hoarding the build of a boy in his twenties,   15
as he soaks, a ramrod
with the muscle of a seal
in his long tub,
vaguely urinous from the Victorian plumbing.
A kingly granite profile in a crimson golf-cap,   20
worn all day, all night,
he thinks only of his figure,
of slimming on sherbet and ginger ale—
more cut off from words than a seal.

This is the way day breaks in Bowditch Hall at McLean's;[3]   25
the hooded night lights bring out "Bobbie,"
Porcellian '29,[4]
a replica of Louis XVI
without the wig—
redolent and roly-poly as a sperm whale,   30
as he swashbuckles about in his birthday suit
and horses at chairs.

These victorious figures of bravado ossified young.

In between the limits of day,
hours and hours go by under the crew haircuts   35

---

[1] Boston University.
[2] Philosophical treatise by Charles Kay Ogden and I. A. Richards.
[3] Psychiatric hospital in Belmont, Massachusetts.
[4] I.e., elected in 1929 to the exclusive Porcellian Club at Harvard.

and slightly too little nonsensical bachelor twinkle
of the Roman Catholic attendants.
(There are no Mayflower
screwballs in the Catholic Church.)

After a hearty New England breakfast,   40
I weigh two hundred pounds
this morning. Cock of the walk,
I strut in my turtle-necked French sailor's jersey
before the metal shaving mirrors,
and see the shaky future grow familiar   45
in the pinched, indigenous faces
of these thoroughbred mental cases,
twice my age and half my weight.
We are all old-timers,
each of us holds a locked razor.   50

1960

Home After Three Months Away[1]

Gone now the baby's nurse,
a lioness who ruled the roost
and made the Mother cry.
She used to tie
gobbets of porkrind in bowknots of gauze—   5
three months they hung like soggy toast
on our eight foot magnolia tree,
and helped the English sparrows
weather a Boston winter.

Three months, three months!   10
Is Richard now himself again?[2]
Dimpled with exaltation,
my daughter holds her levee in the tub.
Our noses rub,
each of us pats a stringy lock of hair—   15
they tell me nothing's gone.
Though I am forty-one,

---

[1] The "three months" were spent in a psychiatric
hospital during a manic-depressive episode.
[2] Lowell speaks of himself here as a

Shakespearean king; his daughter too is a royal
personage holding a morning audience ("levee,"
l. 13).

not forty now,[3] the time I put away
was child's-play. After thirteen weeks
my child still dabs her cheeks   20
to start me shaving. When
we dress her in her sky-blue corduroy,
she changes to a boy,
and floats my shaving brush
and washcloth in the flush. . . .   25
Dearest, I cannot loiter here
in lather like a polar bear.
Recuperating, I neither spin nor toil.
Three stories down below,
a choreman tends our coffin's length of soil,   30
and seven horizontal tulips blow.
Just twelve months ago,
these flowers were pedigreed
imported Dutchmen; now no one need
distinguish them from weed.   35
Bushed by the late spring snow,
they cannot meet
another year's snowballing enervation.

I keep no rank nor station.
Cured, I am frizzled, stale and small.   40
1960

Skunk Hour

(For Elizabeth Bishop)

Nautilus Island's[1] hermit
heiress still lives through winter in her Spartan cottage;
her sheep still graze above the sea.
Her son's a bishop. Her farmer
is first selectman in our village;   5
she's in her dotage.

Thirsting for
the hierarchic privacy
of Queen Victoria's century,
she buys up all   10

[3] Lowell's birthday was March 17.
[1] In Maine, near Castine, where Lowell often
spent summers.

the eyesores facing her shore,
and lets them fall.

The season's ill—
we've lost our summer millionaire,
who seemed to leap from an L. L. Bean[2]   15
catalogue. His nine-knot yawl
was auctioned off to lobstermen.
A red fox stain[3] covers Blue Hill.

And now our fairy
decorator brightens his shop for fall;   20
his fishnet's filled with orange cork,
orange, his cobbler's bench and awl;
there is no money in his work,
he'd rather marry.

One dark night,   25
my Tudor[4] Ford climbed the hill's skull;
I watched for love-cars. Lights turned down,
they lay together, hull to hull,
where the graveyard shelves on the town. . . .
My mind's not right.   30

A car radio bleats,
"Love, O careless Love. . . ." I hear
my ill-spirit sob in each blood cell,
as if my hand were at its throat. . . .
I myself am hell;[5]   35
nobody's here—

only skunks, that search
in the moonlight for a bite to eat.
They march on their soles up Main Street:
white stripes, moonstruck eyes' red fire   40
under the chalk-dry and spar spire
of the Trinitarian Church.

I stand on top
of our back steps and breathe the rich air—
a mother skunk with her column[6] of kittens swills the garbage pail.   45
She jabs her wedge-head in a cup
of sour cream, drops her ostrich tail,
and will not scare.

1960

---

[2] Store in Freeport, Maine, specializing in
  outdoor clothing and camping goods.
[3] The autumn leaves.
[4] Make of two-door Ford.

[5] "Myself am hell," Satan says in Milton's
  Paradise Lost, IV, 75.
[6] A military formation.

For the Union Dead[1]

"Relinquunt Omnia Servare Rem Publicam."[2]

The old South Boston Aquarium stands
in a Sahara of snow now. Its broken windows are boarded.
The bronze weathervane cod[3] has lost half its scales.
The airy tanks are dry.

Once my nose crawled like a snail on the glass;   5
my hand tingled
to burst the bubbles
drifting from the noses of the cowed, compliant fish.

My hand draws back. I often sigh still
for the dark downward and vegetating kingdom   10
of the fish and reptile. One morning last March,
I pressed against the new barbed and galvanized

fence on the Boston Common.[4] Behind their cage,
yellow dinosaur steamshovels were grunting
as they cropped up tons of mush and grass   15
to gouge their underworld garage.[5]

Parking spaces luxuriate like civic
sandpiles in the heart of Boston.
A girdle of orange, Puritan-pumpkin colored girders
braces the tingling Statehouse,   20

shaking over the excavations, as it faces Colonel Shaw
and his bell-cheeked Negro infantry
on St. Gaudens' shaking Civil War relief,
propped by a plank splint against the garage's earthquake.

Two months after marching through Boston,   25
half the regiment was dead;

---

[1] Soldiers who died fighting for the North in the
Civil War. The poem is written about a bronze
bas-relief opposite the Massachusetts State House
on Beacon Street, in Boston; the monument, by
Augustus St. Gaudens (1848–1897),
commemorates Colonel Robert Gould Shaw
(1837–1863), who commanded the first
all-Negro regiment in the North, and who was
killed while leading an attack on Fort Wagner
in South Carolina. The monument represents
Shaw on horseback flanked by Negro foot
soldiers.
[2] Lowell has changed the inscription on the
monument from singular to plural, so that it
reads: "They leave everything behind to serve
the Republic."
[3] Codfish, the symbol of Boston.
[4] Park facing the State House.
[5] The construction of the garage beneath the
Common was attended by graft and corruption.

at the dedication,
William James[6] could almost hear the bronze Negroes breathe.

Their monument sticks like a fishbone
in the city's throat.   30
Its Colonel is as lean
as a compass-needle.

He has an angry wrenlike vigilance,
a greyhound's gentle tautness;
he seems to wince at pleasure,   35
and suffocate for privacy.

He is out of bounds now. He rejoices in man's lovely,
peculiar power to choose life and die—
when he leads his black soldiers to death,
he cannot bend his back.   40

On a thousand small town New England greens,[7]
the old white churches hold their air
of sparse, sincere rebellion; frayed flags
quilt the graveyards of the Grand Army of the Republic.

The stone statues of the abstract Union Soldier   45
grow slimmer and younger each year—
wasp-waisted, they doze over muskets
and muse through their sideburns . . .

Shaw's father wanted no monument
except the ditch,   50
where his son's body was thrown
and lost with his "niggers."[8]

The ditch is nearer.
There are no statues for the last war[9] here;
on Boylston Street, a commercial photograph   55
shows Hiroshima boiling

---

[6] Philosopher and psychologist (1842–1910); the allusion is to a letter.
[7] Lowell is thinking of the village green in Castine.
[8] Shaw's father could have had his son's body brought home (officers had that privilege, while infantry were buried where they fell), but he refused, knowing his son's affection for his men.
[9] Perhaps the Korean War (1950–1953); or, as

Lowell's mention of Hiroshima suggests, World War II, which ended with the dropping of the atom bomb; the exploitation of the survival of the safe for advertising purposes is a sign of callousness, while the use in the advertisement of the phrase "Rock of Ages," normally a reference to Christ, proclaims the collapse of religion.

over a Mosler Safe, the "Rock of Ages"
that survived the blast. Space is nearer.
When I crouch[10] to my television set,
the drained faces of Negro school-children[11] rise like balloons.   60

Colonel Shaw
is riding on his bubble,
he waits
for the blessèd break.

The Aquarium is gone. Everywhere,   65
giant finned cars nose forward like fish;
a savage servility
slides by on grease.

1964

Waking Early Sunday Morning[*]

O to break loose, like the chinook
salmon jumping and falling back,
nosing up to the impossible
stone and bone-crushing waterfall—
raw-jawed, weak-fleshed there, stopped by ten   5
steps of the roaring ladder, and then
to clear the top on the last try,
alive enough to spawn and die.

Stop, back off. The salmon breaks
water, and now my body wakes   10
to feel the unpolluted joy
and criminal leisure of a boy—
no rainbow smashing a dry fly[1]
in the white run is free as I,
here squatting like a dragon on   15
time's hoard before the day's begun!

Vermin run for their unstopped holes;
in some dark nook a fieldmouse rolls
a marble, hours on end, then stops;
the termite in the woodwork sleeps—   20
listen, the creatures of the night
obsessive, casual, sure of foot,
go on grinding, while the sun's
daily remorseful blackout dawns.

Fierce, fireless mind, running downhill.   25
Look up and see the harbor fill:
business as usual in eclipse
goes down to the sea in ships—
wake of refuse, dacron rope,
bound for Bermuda or Good Hope,   30
all bright before the morning watch
the wine-dark hulls of yawl and ketch.

I watch a glass of water wet
with a fine fuzz of icy sweat,
silvery colors touched with sky,   35
serene in their neutrality—
yet if I shift, or change my mood,
I see some object made of wood,
background behind it[2] of brown grain,
to darken it, but not to stain.   40

O that the spirit could remain
tinged but untarnished by its strain!
Better dressed and stacking birch,
or lost with the Faithful at Church—
anywhere, but somewhere else!   45
And now the new electric bells,
clearly chiming, "Faith of our fathers,"
and now the congregation gathers.

O Bible chopped and crucified
in hymns we hear but do not read,   50
none of the milder subtleties
of grace or art will sweeten these
stiff quatrains shovelled out four-square—
they sing of peace, and preach despair;
yet they gave darkness some control,   55
and left a loophole for the soul.

---

[2] I.e., behind the glass of water.

No, put old clothes on, and explore
the corners of the woodshed for
its dregs and dreck:[3] tools with no handle,
ten candle-ends not worth a candle,   60
old lumber banished from the Temple,[4]
damned by Paul's precept and example,
cast from the kingdom, banned in Israel,
the wordless sign, the tinkling cymbal.[5]

When will we see Him face to face?   65
Each day, He shines through darker glass.[6]
In this small town where everything
is known, I see His vanishing
emblems, His white spire and flag-
pole sticking out above the fog,   70
like old white china doorknobs, sad,
slight, useless things to calm the mad.
Hammering military splendor,
top-heavy Goliath[7] in full armor—
little redemption in the mass   75
liquidations of their brass,
elephant and phalanx moving
with the times and still improving,
when that kingdom hit the crash:
a million foreskins stacked like trash . . .   80

Sing softer! But what if a new
diminuendo[8] brings no true
tenderness, only restlessness,
excess, the hunger for success,
sanity of self-deception   85
fixed and kicked by reckless caution,
while we listen to the bells—
anywhere, but somewhere else!

O to break loose. All life's grandeur
is something with a girl in summer . . .   90

---

[3] Yiddish for "refuse" or "junk."
[4] The Hebrew temple, standing for the "old law" replaced by the Christian dispensation, whose apostle was St. Paul.
[5] 1 Corinthians 13:1: "Though I speak with the tongues of men and of angels, and have not charity, I am become as sounding brass, or a tinkling cymbal."
[6] 1 Corinthians 13:12: "For now we see through a glass, darkly; but then face to face." Lowell reverses the hope of the second part of the quotation.

[7] Philistine giant, slain by David with a slingshot. King Saul demanded from David a hundred foreskins of Philistines (as proof that David had killed them) in lieu of dowry when David married the king's daughter; David returned with two hundred foreskins. (See 1 Samuel 17 and 18.) Lowell may have been thinking of Hitler's liquidation of the Jews as well.
[8] Reduction in volume of sound.

elated as the President[9]
girdled by his establishment
this Sunday morning, free to chaff
his own thoughts with his bear-cuffed staff,
swimming nude, unbuttoned, sick   95
of his ghost-written rhetoric!

No weekends for the gods now. Wars
flicker, earth licks its open sores,
fresh breakage, fresh promotions, chance
assassinations, no advance.   100
Only man thinning out his kind
sounds through the Sabbath noon, the blind
swipe of the pruner and his knife
busy about the tree of life . . .

Pity the planet, all joy gone   105
from this sweet volcanic cone;
peace to our children when they fall
in small war on the heels of small
war—until the end of time
to police the earth, a ghost   110
orbiting forever lost
in our monotonous sublime.
1967

The March I[1]

(For Dwight Macdonald)

Under the too white marmoreal Lincoln Memorial,
the too tall marmoreal Washington Obelisk,
gazing into the too long reflecting pool,
the reddish trees, the withering autumn sky,
the remorseless, amplified harangues for peace—   5
lovely to lock arms, to march absurdly locked
(unlocking to keep my wet glasses from slipping)
to see the cigarette match quaking in my fingers,
then to step off like green Union Army recruits
for the first Bull Run,[2] sped by photographers,   10
the notables, the girls . . . fear, glory, chaos, rout . . .

---

[9] Lyndon B. Johnson, who would playfully cuff
members of his staff.

[1] A peace march during the Vietnam War.
[2] Union defeat (July 21, 1861) in the Civil War.

our green army staggered out on the miles-long green fields,
met by the other army,[3] the Martian, the ape, the hero,
his new-fangled rifle, his green new steel helmet.

1970

Death and the Bridge

(from a landscape by Frank Parker)[1]

Death gallops up the bridge of red railtie girders,
some onetime view of Boston humps the saltmarsh;
it is handpainted: this the eternal, provincial
city Dante saw as Florence and hell. . . . [2]
On weekends too, the local TV station's   5
garbage disposal starts to grind at daybreak:
keep Sunday clean. We owe the Lord that much;
from the first, God heeded His socialistic conscience,
gave universal capital punishment.
In daylight, the relaxed red scaffolding is almost   10
breathing: *no man is ever too good to die.* . . .
We will follow our skeletons on the girder,
out of life and Boston, singing with Freud:
'God's ways are dark and very seldom pleasant.'

1970

New Year's Eve 1968

These conquered kings pass angrily away;
the gods die flesh and spirit and last in print,
each library is some injured tyrant's home.
This year runs out in the movies, it must be written
in bad, straightforward, unscanning sentences—   5
mine were downtrodden, branded on backs of carbons,
lines, words, letters nailed to letters, words, lines;

[3] Troops of the U.S. Army.
[1] Artist friend of Lowell's who attended St.
Mark's School in Lowell's class.

[2] In the *Divine Comedy*, where Hell is populated
with Dante's fellow Florentines.

the typescript looked like a Rosetta Stone.[1]
A year's black pages. Its hero *hero demens*[2]
forcing his ship past soundings to the passage—   10
ill-starred of men and crossed by his fixed stars.
The slush-ice on the east water of the Hudson
is rose-heather this New Year sunset; the open channel,
bright sky, bright sky, carbon scarred with ciphers.[3]

1970

Harriet[1]

Spring moved to summer—the rude cold rain
hurries the ambitious, flowers and youth;
our flash-tones crackle for an hour, and then
we too follow nature, imperceptibly
change our mouse-brown to white lion's mane,   5
thin white fading to a freckled, knuckled skull,
bronzed by decay, by many, many suns. . . .
Child of ten, three quarters animal,
three years from Juliet,[2] half Juliet,
already ripened for the night on stage—   10
beautiful petals, what shall we hope for,
knowing one choice not two is all you're given,
health beyond the measure, dangerous
to yourself, more dangerous to others?

1973

---

from Mexico

1.

The difficulties, the impossibilities . . .
I, fifty, humbled with the years' gold garbage,
dead laurel[1] grizzling my back like spines of hay;

---

[1] Slab inscribed in hieroglyphic, demotic, and
Greek, which enabled the deciphering of
Egyptian hieroglyphic in the nineteenth
century.
[2] Latin: "mad hero." The phrase is based on the
title of a play by the Roman dramatist Seneca:
Hercules Furens (Hercules Mad).
[3] Lowell probably intends both meanings of the
word—"zeroes" and "mysterious codes."

[1] Lowell's daughter by Elizabeth Hardwick
Lowell, his second wife.
[2] Shakespeare's Juliet, 14 years old.
[1] The crown sacred to Apollo; metaphorically,
the many literary prizes Lowell has been
awarded.

you, some sweet, uncertain age, say twenty-seven,
untempted, unseared by honors or deception.   5
What help then? Not the sun, the scarlet blossom,
and the high fever of this seventh day,
the predestined diarrhea of the pilgrim,
the multiple mosquito spots, round as pesos.
Hope not for God here, or even for the gods;   10
the Aztecs knew the sun, the source of life,
will die, unless we feed it human blood—
we two are clocks, and only count in time . . .
the hand a knife-edge pressed against the future.

1973

4.

South of Boston, south of Washington,
south of any bearing . . . I walk the glazed moonlight:
dew on the grass and nobody about,
drawn on by my unlimited desire,
like a bull with a ring in his nose, a chain in the ring. . . .   5
We moved far, bull and cow, could one imagine
cattle obliviously pairing six long days:
up road and down, then up again passing the same
brick garden wall, stiff spines of hay stuck in my hide;
and always in full sight of everyone,   10
from the full sun to silhouetting sunset,
pinned by undimming lights of hurried cars. . . .
You're gone; I am learning to live in history.
What is history? What you cannot touch.

1973

Obit[1]

Our love will not come back on fortune's wheel—

in the end it gets us, though a man know what he'd have:
old cars, old money, old undebased pre-Lyndon
silver, no copper rubbing through[2] . . . old wives;
I could live such a too long time with mine.   5

---

[1] British for obituary or death notice. The poem
is addressed to Lowell's wife Elizabeth
Hardwick as he left her for Caroline
Blackwood, whom he later married.

[2] Lyndon Johnson's presidency saw the
adulterating of American silver coins with
copper.

In the end, every hypochondriac is his own prophet.
Before the final coming to rest, comes the rest
of all transcendence in a mode of being, hushing
all becoming. I'm for and with myself in my otherness,
in the eternal return of earth's fairer children,   10
the lily, the rose, the sun on brick at dusk,
the loved, the lover, and their fear of life,
their unconquered flux, insensate oneness, painful "It was. . . ."
After loving you so much, can I forget
you for eternity, and have no other choice?   15

1973

History

History has to live with what was here,
clutching and close to fumbling all we had—
it is so dull and gruesome how we die,
unlike writing, life never finishes.
Abel was finished; death is not remote,   5
a flash-in-the-pan electrifies the skeptic,
his cows crowding like skulls against high-voltage wire,
his baby crying all night like a new machine.
As in our Bibles, white-faced, predatory,
the beautiful, mist-drunken hunter's moon ascends—   10
a child could give it a face: two holes, two holes,
my eyes, my mouth, between them a skull's no-nose—
O there's a terrifying innocence in my face
drenched with the silver salvage of the mornfrost.

1973

Will Not Come Back
(Volverán)[1]

Dark swallows will doubtless come back killing
the injudicious nightflies with a clack of the beak;
but these that stopped full flight to see your beauty
and my good fortune . . . as if they knew our names—

[1] Lowell's "imitation" (free translation) of the
poem "Volverán" by the Spanish poet Gustavo
Adolfo Bécquer (1836–1870).

they'll not come back. The thick lemony honeysuckle,   5
climbing from the earthroot to your window,
will open more beautiful blossoms to the evening;
but these . . . like dewdrops, trembling, shining, falling,
the tears of day—they'll not come back. . . .
Some other love will sound his fireword for you   10
and wake your heart, perhaps, from its cool sleep;
but silent, absorbed, and on his knees,
as men adore God at the altar, as I love you—
don't blind yourself, you'll not be loved like that.

1973

Reading Myself

Like thousands, I took just pride and more than just,
struck matches that brought my blood to a boil;
I memorized the tricks to set the river on fire—
somehow never wrote something to go back to.
Can I suppose I am finished with wax flowers   5
and have earned my grass on the minor slopes of Parnassus. . . .[1]
No honeycomb is built without a bee
adding circle to circle, cell to cell,
the wax and honey of a mausoleum—
this round dome proves its maker is alive;   10
the corpse of the insect lives embalmed in honey,
prays that its perishable work live long
enough for the sweet-tooth bear to desecrate—
this open book . . . my open coffin.

1973

Fishnet

Any clear thing that blinds us with surprise,
your wandering silences and bright trouvailles,[1]
dolphin let loose to catch the flashing fish. . . .

---

[1] Mountain in Greece; in mythology, the home   [1] French: "discoveries."
of Apollo and the Muses.

Poets die adolescents, their beat embalms them,
the archetypal voices sing offkey;   5
the old actor cannot read his friends,
and nevertheless he reads himself aloud,
genius hums the auditorium dead.
The line must terminate.
Yet my heart rises, I know I've gladdened a lifetime   10
knotting, undoing a fishnet of tarred rope;
the net will hang on the wall when the fish are eaten,
nailed like illegible bronze[2] on the futureless future.

1973

For John Berryman

(After reading his last *Dream Song*)[1]

The last years we only met
when you were on the road,
and lit up for reading
your battering *Dream*—
audible, deaf . . .   5
in another world then as now.
I used to want to live
to avoid your elegy.
Yet really we had the same life,
the generic one   10
our generation offered
(*Les Maudits*[2]—the compliment
each American generation
pays itself in passing):
first students, then with our own,   15
our galaxy of grands maîtres,[3]
our fifties' fellowships
to Paris, Rome and Florence,

---

[2] Lowell is remembering the Roman poet Horace's boast (*Odes*, III, 30) that a poem is more lasting than bronze ("*Exegi monumentum aere perennius*"), but the artifacts of culture all eventually become unintelligible.

[1] The poet John Berryman, Lowell's contemporary, committed suicide in 1972 after episodes of acute alcoholism and mental breakdown; the sequence of lyrics called *The Dream Songs* became Berryman's major poetic undertaking.

[2] The *poète maudit* (French: "accursed poet" or "damned poet") was a cliché of the later nineteenth century.

[3] "Great teachers" (poetic mentors).

veterans of the Cold War[4] not the War—
all the best of life . . .   20
then daydreaming to drink at six,
waiting for the iced fire,
even the feel of the frosted glass,
like waiting for a girl . . .
if you had waited.   25
We asked to be obsessed with writing,
and we were.

Do you wake dazed like me,
and find your lost glasses in a shoe?

Something so heavy lies on my heart—   30
there, still here, the good days
when we sat by a cold lake in Maine,
talking about the *Winter's Tale,*
Leontes' jealousy[5]
in Shakespeare's broken syntax.   35
You got there first.
Just the other day,
I discovered how we differ—humor . . .
even in this last *Dream Song,*
to mock your catlike flight   40
from home and classes—
to leap from the bridge.

Girls will not frighten the frost from the grave.[6]

To my surprise, John,
I pray *to* not for you,   45
think of you not myself,
smile and fall asleep.
1977

[4] Diplomatic estrangement between the United States and Russia during the 1950s.
[5] In Shakespeare's *The Winter's Tale,* Leontes orders his wife killed, unreasonably suspecting her of infidelity.

[6] Lowell is recalling the last two lines from a song in *The Sad Shepherd* by Ben Jonson (1572/3–1637): " 'Except Love's fires the virtue have, / To fright the frost out of the grave.' "

For Sheridan[1]

We only live between
before we are and what we were.

In the lost negative[2]
you exist,
a smile, a cypher,   5
an old-fashioned face
in an old-fashioned hat.

Three ages in a flash:
the same child in the same picture,
he, I, you,   10
chockablock, one stamp[3]
like mother's wedding silver—

gnome, fish, brute cherubic force.

We could see clearly
and all the same things   15
before the glass was hurt.

Past fifty, we learn with surprise and a sense
of suicidal absolution
that what we intended and failed
could never have happened—   20
and must be done better.

1977

Epilogue[*]

Those blessèd structures, plot and rhyme—
why are they no help to me now
I want to make

---

[1] Lowell's son by Caroline Blackwood, his third
wife.
[2] Of a picture of Robert Lowell as a small boy.

[3] The family monogram, as on silver cutlery.
[*] This is the closing poem in Lowell's last
volume of poetry, *Day by Day* (1977).

something imagined, not recalled?
I hear the noise of my own voice: 5
The painter's vision is not a lens,
it trembles to caress the light.
But sometimes everything I write
with the threadbare art of my eye
seems a snapshot,   10
lurid, rapid, garish, grouped,
heightened from life,
yet paralyzed by fact.
All's misalliance.
Yet why not say what happened?   15
Pray for the grace of accuracy
Vermeer[1] gave to the sun's illumination
stealing like the tide across a map
to his girl solid with yearning.
We are poor passing facts,   20
warned by that to give
each figure in the photograph
his living name.

1977

Gwendolyn Brooks
b. 1917

For Gwendolyn Brooks, "poets who happen to be Negroes are twice-tried. They
have to write poetry, and they have to remember that they are Negroes." This
double consciousness—at once restive, protective, and in part aggressive—
continues to mark Brooks's impassioned life and distinguished verse.

Gwendolyn Brooks was born in Topeka, Kansas, on June 17, 1917, and raised
on Chicago's South Side, where she was taken at the age of one month. Chicago
remains her home and the setting for most of her poetry. She graduated from
Englewood High School in 1934 and from Wilson Junior College in 1936. Soon
after, she supported herself at various jobs, including newspaper and magazine
work.

Brooks reports that she has written poetry "since about seven, at which time
my parents expressed most earnest confidence that I would one day be a writer."
She published her first poem, "Eventide," at the age of thirteen, in what was
then a popular children's magazine, *American Childhood.* By the age of seventeen
she was a frequent contributor to the weekly *Chicago Defender,* which was also

---

[1] Jan Vermeer (1632–1675), Dutch painter; the
painting in question, *Girl Reading a Letter,* has
in the background a map hanging on the wall
on which light shines from an open casement,
which the girl reading the letter is facing in
profile.

publishing the work of Langston Hughes and James Weldon Johnson, both of whom encouraged her to dedicate herself to writing poetry. Johnson introduced her to the great modern poets, including T. S. Eliot and Ezra Pound, and in Hughes she discovered, as she explains, a man who "believed in the beauty of blackness" long before it became the "fashion." Hughes, she notes, was also someone who "loved literature . . . not fearfully, not with awe," but with deep devotion, and not as "his private inch" but as a "great acreage." "The plantings of others," she says, "he not only welcomed but busily enriched." And in Hughes's self-announced literary purpose—"to explain and illuminate the Negro condition in America"—Gwendolyn Brooks found ample motivation to sustain her own poetic efforts.

Gwendolyn Brooks practiced her art with the help and encouragement of other writers at the poetry workshop in Chicago's South Side Community Art Center, and in 1944 she was published for the first time in *Poetry: A Magazine of Verse.* Within a year she published her first volume of poetry, *A Street in Bronzeville,* which soon earned her a series of honors and awards, including a Guggenheim fellowship and a $1,000 prize from the American Academy of Arts and Letters. In that same year, *Mademoiselle* magazine named her one of ten women of the year. *A Street in Bronzeville* offers a compelling portrait of America's black urban poor. In writing the volume she hoped, as she explains, "that people would recognize instantly that Negroes are just like other people; they have the same hates and loves and fears, the same tragedies and triumphs and deaths, as people of any race or religion or nationality."

In *Annie Allen* (1949), a powerful three-part verse narrative recounting a young black girl's coming to consciousness during World War II, Brooks displayed a remarkable sensitivity to the psychological pressures of the passage from childhood to marriage and maturity. In 1950 she was awarded the Pulitzer Prize for Poetry, and later she was officially named Poet Laureate of Illinois, a title previously held by Carl Sandburg. A volume of children's verse, *Bronzeville Boys and Girls,* followed in 1956, as did frequent contributions to many of the nation's most prestigious and popular literary journals. She published *Bean Eaters* in 1960 and *Selected Poems* in 1963. Each of Brooks's early volumes is marked by a delicate tension between sentiment and objectivity, between traditional poetic forms and contemporary black idiom. Counterbalancing the lyric impulses in these early poems are tough-minded and at times humorous views of what Langston Hughes called the "soul world."

Since the Second Black Writer's Conference (1967), Gwendolyn Brooks's work has responded more directly—and forcefully—to racial and feminist issues. The poems of *In the Mecca* (1968), for example, focus on the daily pain and suffering of ghetto life and express more explicitly her anger and rage at the deprivation of black American experience. These same urgent concerns are extended in *Riot* (1969), *The Wall* (n.d.), *Family Pictures* (1970), and *Aloneness* (1971). Among her more recent volumes are *Aurora* (1972) and *Beckonings* (1975).

In 1972 she published a collection of autobiographical essays, *Report from Part One.* She has also written a novella, *Maud Martha* (1953), about a young black woman's disillusioning romance in Chicago. Throughout her work, Brooks reminds her readers of the personal "cost" of being black in white America.

Brooks has taught writing at numerous colleges and universities, including Chicago's Columbia College, Elmhurst College, and the University of Wisconsin. She is also the recipient of several honorary degrees and has lectured and read her poetry throughout the United States, from small rural colleges to the Library of Congress. She continues to advise young poets "to live richly with your eyes open, and heart, too."

Brooks's poetry is distinguished by what she calls the "concentration, the crush" of the painful and joyful realities of ordinary people in familiar situations. Echoing Walt Whitman, she once defined her task as a poet as that of vivifying fact, not merely contemporary fact but universal fact, mindful that "the universal wears contemporary clothing very well."

Further Reading:

S. Kunitz, "Bronze by Gold," *Poetry, a Magazine of Verse,* 1950.
A. P. Davis, "The Black and Tan Motif in the Poetry of Gwendolyn Brooks," *CLA Journal,* 1962.
The World of Gwendolyn Brooks, 1971.

T. C. Bambara, "Report from Part One," *New York Times Book Review,* January 7, 1973.
H. A. Baker, "The Achievement of Gwendolyn Brooks," in *Singers of Daybreak: Studies in Black American Literature,* 1974.
H. B. Shaw, *Gwendolyn Brooks,* 1980.

Text:
Selected Poems, 1963.

---

from A Street in Bronzeville

The Mother

Abortions will not let you forget.
You remember the children you got that you did not get,
The damp small pulps with a little or with no hair,
The singers and workers that never handled the air.
You will never neglect or beat   5
Them, or silence or buy with a sweet.
You will never wind up the sucking-thumb
Or scuttle off ghosts that come.
You will never leave them, controlling your luscious sigh,
Return for a snack of them, with gobbling mother-eye.   10

I have heard in the voices of the wind the voices of my dim killed children.
I have contracted. I have eased
My dim dears at the breasts they could never suck.
I have said, Sweets, if I sinned, if I seized
Your luck   15
And your lives from your unfinished reach,

If I stole your births and your names,
Your straight baby tears and your games,
Your stilted or lovely loves, your tumults, your marriages, aches, and your
    deaths,
If I poisoned the beginnings of your breaths,   20
Believe that even in my deliberateness I was not deliberate.
Though why should I whine,
Whine that the crime was other than mine?—
Since anyhow you are dead.
Or rather, or instead,   25
You were never made.
But that too, I am afraid,
Is faulty: oh, what shall I say, how is the truth to be said?
You were born, you had body, you died.
It is just that you never giggled or planned or cried.   30

Believe me, I loved you all.
Believe me, I knew you, though faintly, and I loved, I loved you
All.

1945

---

from The Womanhood

from I: The Children of the Poor

2 *

What shall I give my children? who are poor,
Who are adjudged the leastwise of the land,
Who are my sweetest lepers, who demand
No velvet and no velvety velour;
But who have begged me for a brisk contour,   5
Crying that they are quasi, contraband
Because unfinished, graven by a hand
Less than angelic, admirable or sure.
My hand is stuffed with mode, design, device.
But I lack access to my proper stone.   10

---

* When invited to select a poem of her own for inclusion in a recent collection, Gwendolyn Brooks chose this one for, as she says, "at least two reasons: in it, I feel, is truly the 'song' of any children born to find deprivation beside them; this is coupled, almost made one, with the plaint of parents who 'lack access to . . . proper stone!'"

And plentitude of plan shall not suffice
Nor grief nor love shall be enough alone
To ratify my little halves who bear
Across an autumn freezing everywhere.

1949

A Bronzeville Mother Loiters in Mississippi. Meanwhile, a Mississippi Mother Burns Bacon.

From the first it had been like a
Ballad. It had the beat inevitable. It had the blood.
A wildness cut up, and tied in little bunches,
Like the four-line stanzas of the ballads she had never quite
Understood—the ballads they had set her to, in school.   5
Herself: the milk-white maid, the "maid mild"
Of the ballad. Pursued
By the Dark Villain. Rescued by the Fine Prince.
The Happiness-Ever-After.
That was worth anything.   10
It was good to be a "maid mild."
That made the breath go fast.

Her bacon burned. She
Hastened to hide it in the step-on can, and
Drew more strips from the meat case. The eggs and sour-milk biscuits   15
Did well. She set out a jar
Of her new quince preserve.

. . . But there was a something about the matter of the Dark Villain.
He should have been older, perhaps.
The hacking down of a villain was more fun to think about   20
When his menace possessed undisputed breadth, undisputed height,
And a harsh kind of vice.
And best of all, when his history was cluttered
With the bones of many eaten knights and princesses.

The fun was disturbed, then all but nullified   25
When the Dark Villain was a blackish child
Of fourteen, with eyes still too young to be dirty,
And a mouth too young to have lost every reminder
Of its infant softness.

That boy must have been surprised! For   30
These were grown-ups. Grown-ups were supposed to be wise.
And the Fine Prince—and that other—so tall, so broad, so
Grown! Perhaps the boy had never guessed
That the trouble with grown-ups was that under the magnificent shell of
    adulthood, just under,
Waited the baby full of tantrums.   35
It occurred to her that there may have been something
Ridiculous in the picture of the Fine Prince
Rushing (rich with the breadth and height and
Mature solidness whose lack, in the Dark Villain, was impressing her,
Confronting her more and more as this first day after the trial   40
And acquittal wore on) rushing
With his heavy companion to hack down (unhorsed)
That little foe.
So much had happened, she could not remember now what that foe had done
Against her, or if anything had been done.   45
The one thing in the world that she did know and knew
With terrifying clarity was that her composition
Had disintegrated. That, although the pattern prevailed,
The breaks were everywhere. That she could think
Of no thread capable of the necessary   50
Sew-work.

She made the babies sit in their places at the table.
Then, before calling Him, she hurried
To the mirror with her comb and lipstick. It was necessary
To be more beautiful than ever.
The beautiful wife.   55
For sometimes she fancied he looked at her as though
Measuring her. As if he considered, Had she been worth It?
Had *she* been worth the blood, the cramped cries, the little stuttering bravado,
The gradual dulling of those Negro eyes,   60
The sudden, overwhelming *little-boyness* in that barn?
Whatever she might feel or half-feel, the lipstick necessity was something apart.
    He must never conclude
That she had not been worth It.

He sat down, the Fine Prince, and
Began buttering a biscuit. He looked at his hands.   65

He twisted in his chair, he scratched his nose.
He glanced again, almost secretly, at his hands.
More papers were in from the North, he mumbled. More meddling headlines.
With their pepper-words, "bestiality," and "barbarism," and
"Shocking."   70
The half-sneers he had mastered for the trial worked across
His sweet and pretty face.

What he'd like to do, he explained, was kill them all.
The time lost. The unwanted frame.
Still, it had been fun to show those intruders   75
A thing or two. To show that snappy-eyed mother,
That sassy, Northern, brown-black—

Nothing could stop Mississippi.
He knew that. Big Fella
Knew that.   80
And, what was so good, Mississippi knew that.
Nothing and nothing could stop Mississippi.
They could send in their petitions, and scar
Their newspapers with bleeding headlines. Their governors
Could appeal to Washington . . .   85

"What I want," the older baby said, "is 'lasses on my jam."
Whereupon the younger baby
Picked up the molasses pitcher and threw
The molasses in his brother's face. Instantly
The Fine Prince leaned across the table and slapped   90
The small and smiling criminal.

She did not speak. When the Hand
Came down and away, and she could look at her child,
At her baby-child,
She could think only of blood.   95
Surely her baby's cheek
Had disappeared, and in its place, surely,
Hung a heaviness, a lengthening red, a red that had no end.
She shook her head. It was not true, of course.
It was not true at all. The   100
Child's face was as always, the
Color of the paste in her paste-jar.

She left the table, to the tune of the children's lamentations, which were shriller
Than ever. She
Looked out of a window. She said not a word. *That*   105
Was one of the new Somethings—

The fear,
Tying her as with iron.

Suddenly she felt his hands upon her. He had followed her
To the window. The children were whimpering now.   110
Such bits of tots. And she, their mother,
Could not protect them. She looked at her shoulders, still
Gripped in the claim of his hands. She tried, but could not resist the idea
That a red ooze was seeping, spreading darkly, thickly, slowly,
Over her white shoulders, her own shoulders,   115
And over all of Earth and Mars.

He whispered something to her, did the Fine Prince, something
About love, something about love and night and intention.
She heard no hoof-beat of the horse and saw no flash of the shining steel.

He pulled her face around to meet   120
His, and there it was, close close,
For the first time in all those days and nights.
His mouth, wet and red,
So very, very, very red,
Closed over hers.   125

Then a sickness heaved within her. The courtroom Coca-Cola,
The courtroom beer and hate and sweat and drone,
Pushed like a wall against her. She wanted to bear it.
But his mouth would not go away and neither would the
Decapitated exclamation points in that Other Woman's eyes.   130

She did not scream.
She stood there.
But a hatred for him burst into glorious flower,
And its perfume enclasped them—big,
Bigger than all magnolias.   135

The last bleak news of the ballad.
The rest of the rugged music.
The last quatrain.
1960

The Last Quatrain of the Ballad of Emmett Till[1]

after the murder,
after the burial

Emmett's mother is a pretty-faced thing;
        the tint of pulled taffy.
She sits in a red room,   5
        drinking black coffee.
She kisses her killed boy.
        And she is sorry.
Chaos in windy grays
        through a red prairie.   10

1960

The Lovers of the Poor

    arrive. The Ladies from the Ladies' Betterment League
Arrive in the afternoon, the late light slanting
In diluted gold bars across the boulevard brag
Of proud, seamed faces with mercy and murder hinting
Here, there, interrupting, all deep and debonair,   5
The pink paint on the innocence of fear;
Walk in a gingerly manner up the hall.
Cutting with knives served by their softest care,
Served by their love, so barbarously fair.
Whose mothers taught: You'd better not be cruel!   10
You had better not throw stones upon the wrens!
Herein they kiss and coddle and assault
Anew and dearly in the innocence
With which they baffle nature. Who are full,
Sleek, tender-clad, fit, fiftyish, a-glow, all   15
Sweetly abortive, hinting at fat fruit,

[1] In September 1955 fourteen-year-old Emmett Louis Till, a black Chicagoan, was abducted from a Mississippi home and brutally murdered. Two white males charged with the crime were later acquitted by an all-white jury. The events brought national attention to the emerging civil rights movement and passed into popular song.

Judge it high time that fiftyish fingers felt
Beneath the lovelier planes of enterprise.
To resurrect. To moisten with milky chill.
To be a random hitching-post or plush.   20
To be, for wet eyes, random and handy hem.
   Their guild is giving money to the poor.
The worthy poor. The very very worthy
And beautiful poor. Perhaps just not too swarthy?
Perhaps just not too dirty nor too dim   25
Nor—passionate. In truth, what they could wish
Is—something less than derelict or dull.
Not staunch enough to stab, though, gaze for gaze!
God shield them sharply from the beggar-bold!
The noxious needy ones whose battle's bald   30
Nonetheless for being voiceless, hits one down.
   But it's all so bad! and entirely too much for them.
The stench; the urine, cabbage, and dead beans,
Dead porridges of assorted dusty grains,
The old smoke, *heavy* diapers, and, they're told,   35
Something called chitterlings. The darkness. Drawn
Darkness, or dirty light. The soil that stirs.
The soil that looks the soil of centuries.
And for that matter the *general* oldness. Old
Wood. Old marble. Old tile. Old old old.   40
Not homekind Oldness! Not Lake Forest, Glencoe.[1]
Nothing is sturdy, nothing is majestic,
There is no quiet drama, no rubbed glaze, no
Unkillable infirmity of such
A tasteful turn as lately they have left,   45
Glencoe, Lake Forest, and to which their cars
Must presently restore them. When they're done
With dullards and distortions of this fistic[2]
Patience of the poor and put-upon.
   They've never seen such a make-do-ness as   50
Newspaper rugs before! In this, this "flat,"
Their hostess is gathering up the oozed, the rich
Rugs of the morning (tattered! the bespattered. . . .)
Readies to spread clean rugs for afternoon.
Here is a scene for you. The Ladies look,   55
In horror, behind a substantial citizeness
Whose trains clank out across her swollen heart.
Who, arms akimbo, almost fills a door.
All tumbling children, quilts dragged to the floor
And tortured thereover, potato peelings, soft-   60
Eyed kitten, hunched-up, haggard, to-be-hurt.

---

[1] Suburbs of Chicago.   [2] Relating to fistfights.

Their League is allotting largesse to the Lost.
But to put their clean, their pretty money, to put
Their money collected from delicate rose-fingers
Tipped with their hundred flawless rose-nails seems . . .   65
    They own Spode,[3] Lowestoft, candelabra,
Mantels, and hostess gowns, and sunburst clocks,
Turtle soup, Chippendale, red satin "hangings,"
Aubussons and Hattie Carnegie. They Winter
In Palm Beach; cross the Water in June; attend,   70
When suitable, the nice Art Institute;
Buy the right books in the best bindings; saunter
On Michigan, Easter mornings, in sun or wind.
Oh Squalor! This sick four-story hulk, this fibre
With fissures everywhere! Why, what are bringings   75
Of loathe-love largesse? What shall peril hungers
So old old, what shall flatter the desolate?
Tin can, blocked fire escape and chitterling
And swaggering seeking youth and the puzzled wreckage
Of the middle passage, and urine and stale shames   80
And, again, the porridges of the underslung
And children children children. Heavens! That
Was a rat, surely, off there, in the shadows? Long
And long-tailed? Gray? The Ladies from the Ladies'
Betterment League agree it will be better   85
To achieve the outer air that rights and steadies,
To hie to a house that does not holler, to ring
Bells elsetime, better presently to cater
To no more Possibilities, to get
Away. Perhaps the money can be posted.   90
Perhaps they two may choose another Slum!
Some serious sooty half-unhappy home!—
Where loathe-love likelier may be invested.
    Keeping their scented bodies in the center
Of the hall as they walk down the hysterical hall,   95
They allow their lovely skirts to graze no wall,
Are off at what they manage of a canter,
And, resuming all the clues of what they were,
Try to avoid inhaling the laden air.
1960

---

[3] This expensive make of fine china begins a list
of elegant furnishings.

Howard Nemerov
b. 1920

Howard Nemerov's sardonic observations of American life are turned with a morose wit that makes them more than light verse. Nothing escapes his sharp eye; he sees the world, in his more acerbic moments, as a caricature of itself —politicians and evangelists retailing cant, a foolish public deluding itself, bourgeois illusion reigning except where war and carnage rule. But in other poems, throughout his long career, there is a harmonious, if grim, song that Nemerov sings—the song of the processions of the stars and the seasons. He senses what Emily Dickinson called "the process in the burr"; he is, like Keats's swallows, "intelligent of seasons." Natural law is to him a guarantee at least of periodicity and rhythm, if not of meaning, and it is no accident that his first book was entitled *The Image and the Law* (1947). His metaphysical and moral poems have an Old Testament sternness about them that corresponds to the law of the physical heavens; the paradoxical creations and destructions of the universe serve as matter for Nemerov's brooding mind.

Nemerov is a formalist, as one would expect from his love of the law of recurrence. His serious verse moves with gravity and resonance; in the clarity and weight of his reasoning there is something philosophic; in the satisfying closure of many of the poems—as in *Gnomes and Occasions* (1973)—there is an iron ring at the last words.

Nemerov grew up in New York and went to Harvard, where he won the Bowdoin Prize in 1940. After he graduated in 1941, he joined the Royal Canadian Air Force, and, in 1944, the U.S. Army Air Force. He taught at Hamilton, Bennington, and Brandeis before joining the faculty of Washington University in St. Louis, where he is now the Edward Mallinckrodt Distinguished University Professor of English. Though he began by writing fiction as well as poetry, more recently Nemerov has written, in addition to his poetry, remarkable critical reflections on the art of poetry, collected in *Figures of Thought* (1978). His *Collected Poems,* published in 1977, won both the Pulitzer Prize and the National Book Award.

Nemerov continues, in our day, a didactic poetic tradition begun by Emerson. He adds to it an Old Testament weight foreign to Emerson's airy rapidity (Nemerov is Jewish, but philosophically rather than ethnically so). In joining together the proverbial and prophetic Hebraic wisdom tradition, the Latin tradition of epigram, and the Puritan strain of moral verse (from Wigglesworth to Lowell), Nemerov creates a new compound, distinctive in its tart, grave, and ironic resonance. In his long meditative poems on art (like "The Painter Dreaming in the Scholar's House"), Nemerov has established a model through which some younger poets, most recently Michael Blumenthal, have found ways to join poetic and philosophic discourse.

Further Reading:
P. Meinke, *Howard Nemerov*, 1968.
J. A. Bartholomay, *The Shield of Perseus: The Vision and Imagination of Howard Nemerov*, 1972.
W. Mills, *The Stillness in Moving Things: The World of Howard Nemerov*, 1975.
R. Labrie, *Howard Nemerov*, 1980.
D. E. Wyllie, *Elizabeth Bishop and Howard Nemerov: A Reference Guide*, 1983.

Text:
The Collected Poems, 1977.
See also *Journal of the Fictive Life*, 1965.
Figures of Thought, 1979.
Sentences, 1980.

The Daily Globe[1]

Each day another installment of the old
Romance of Order brings to the breakfast table
The paper flowers of catastrophe.
One has this recurrent dream about the world.

Headlines declare the ambiguous oracles,   5
The comfortable old prophets mutter doom.
Man's greatest intellectual pleasure is
To repeat himself, yet somehow the daily globe

Rolls on, while the characters in comic strips
Prolong their slow, interminable lives   10
Beyond the segregated photographs
Of the girls that marry and the men that die.
1962

To David,[1] About His Education

The world is full of mostly invisible things,
And there is no way but putting the mind's eye,
Or its nose, in a book, to find them out,
Things like the square root of Everest
Or how many times Byron goes into Texas,   5

---

[1] Boston daily newspaper.

[1] Nemerov's son.

Or whether the law of the excluded middle
Applies west of the Rockies. For these
And the like reasons, you have to go to school
And study books and listen to what you are told,
And sometimes try to remember. Though I don't know   10
What you will do with the mean annual rainfall
On Plato's Republic, or the calorie content
Of the Diet of Worms, such things are said to be
Good for you, and you will have to learn them
In order to become one of the grown-ups   15
Who sees invisible things neither steadily nor whole,[2]
But keeps gravely the grand confusion of the world
Under his hat, which is where it belongs,
And teaches small children to do this in their turn.

1962

The Sweeper of Ways

All day, a small mild Negro man with a broom
Sweeps up the leaves that fall along the paths.
He carries his head to one side, looking down
At his leaves, at his broom like a windy beard
Curled with the sweeping habit. Over him   5
High haughty trees, the hickory and ash,
Dispense their more leaves easily, or else
The district wind, hunting hypocrisy,
Tears at the summer's wall and throws down leaves
To witness of a truth naked and cold.   10

Hopeless it looks, on these harsh, hastening days
Before the end, to finish all those leaves
Against time. But the broom goes back and forth
With a tree's patience, as though naturally
Erasers would speak the language of pencils.   15
A thousand thoughts fall on the same blank page,
Though the wind blows them back, they go where he
Directs them, to the archives where disorder
Blazes and a pale smoke becomes the sky.
The ways I walk are splendidly free of leaves.   20

---

[2] "He saw life steadily and saw it whole":
Matthew Arnold's remark on Sophocles in "To
a Friend."

We meet, we smile good morning, say the weather
Whatever. On a rainy day there'll be
A few leaves stuck like emblems on the walk;
These too he brooms at till they come unstuck.
Masters, we carry our white faces by   25
In silent prayer, Don't hate me, on a wave-
length which his broom's antennae perfectly
Pick up, we know ourselves so many thoughts
Considered by a careful, kindly mind
Which can do nothing, and is doing that.   30
1967

Thirtieth Anniversary Report
of the Class of '41[1]

We who survived the war and took to wife
And sired the kids and made the decent living,
And piecemeal furnished forth the finished life
Not by grand theft so much as petty thieving—

Who had the routine middle-aged affair   5
And made our beds and had to lie in them
This way or that because the beds were there,
And turned our bile and choler in for phlegm—

Who saw grandparents, parents, to the vault
And wives and selves grow wrinkled, grey and fat 10
And children through their acne and revolt
And told the analyst about all that—

Are done with it. What is there to discuss?
There's nothing left for us to say of us.
1973

[1] Nemerov's class at Harvard.

Ginkgoes[1] in Fall

They are the oldest living captive race,
Primitive gymnosperms that in the wild
Are rarely found or never, temple trees
Brought down in line unbroken from the deep
Past where the Yellow Emperor lies tombed.   5

Their fallen yellow fruit mimics the scent
Of human vomit, the definite statement of
An attitude, and their translucency of leaf,
Filtering a urinary yellow light,
Remarks a delicate wasting of the world,   10

An innuendo to be clarified
In winter when they defecate their leaves
And bear the burden of their branches up
Alone and bare, dynastic diagrams
Of their distinguished genealogies.   15

1975

Richard Wilbur
b. 1921

Richard Wilbur's verse combines a Latin elegance and wit with the New England skepticism and wisdom we associate with Robert Frost (whom Wilbur met as an undergraduate at Amherst College). Wilbur's first book, *The Beautiful Changes and Other Poems* (1947), published when he was in his twenties, reflected his war service in Italy and France (1943–1945) and his admiration for the landscape and architecture of Europe. The book drew immediate critical praise, and Wilbur's poetry has continued to attract readers who see the continuity of American poetry with the formal verse of the English past. The rougher line of American verse, from Emerson through Whitman to Ashbery, insists on discontinuity, rupture, and spontaneity, whereas the Europeanized tradition exemplified by Stevens, Frost, Merrill, and Wilbur values continuity, gradualism, and musicality.

Wilbur's alignment with Europe arises, in part, from his affiliation with Eliot

---

[1] The ginkgo tree, originally native to China, has fan-shaped leaves that turn bright yellow in fall. There are male and female trees; the fruit of the female tree, especially when crushed, has an offensive smell.

as a "civilized poet" and from his superb command of French. He has translated Molière into excellent English verse for the stage; he was one of the lyricists for Leonard Bernstein's musical version of *Candide* (1956).

Unlike the *poètes maudits* ("accursed poets") of the modern tradition like Baudelaire and Rimbaud, who emphasize the role of the poet as social outcast, Wilbur, who has remained a Christian believer, considers himself "a poet-citizen rather than an alienated artist. . . . Poetry is sterile unless it arises from a sense of community, or, at least, from the hope of community." By meditating on the conflicts like those between sensual pleasure and transcendence or between the stationary and the restless, the poet, says Wilbur, is "acknowledging the contradictions that inhere in life." The chief contradiction is that between "the tangible world and the intuitions of the spirit." Though Wilbur's use of stanzaic structures and regular meters reflects his attachment to poetic tradition, his genial, understated American voice has naturalized older English forms into new indigenous ones. His intricately musical meditative writing continues, in a secular vein, the reflective verse of such seventeenth-century religious poets as George Herbert and Thomas Traherne. Wilbur, the son of a painter, writes poetry of the eye, but he wishes to find, behind the eye, the workings of the soul.

Wilbur has taught at Harvard (where he took an M.A.), at Wellesley, and at Wesleyan; he is now a professor of English at Smith. His poems were collected in 1963; since then, he has published *Walking to Sleep* (1969) and *The Mind-Reader* (1976). His essays have been collected in *Responses: Prose Pieces, 1948–1976* (1976).

Further Reading:
D. L. Hill, *Richard Wilbur*, 1967.
H. Stevens, *Richard Wilbur*, 1977.
Richard Wilbur's Creation, ed. W. Salinger, 1983.

Texts:
"Folk Tune," "Winter Spring," "The Beautiful Changes," "To an American Poet Just Dead," and "Mind" from *The Poems of Richard Wilbur*, 1963.
"Playboy" from *Walking to Sleep*, 1969.
"The Writer," "Cottage Street, 1953," and "April 5, 1974" from *The Mind-Reader*, 1976.

Folk Tune

When Bunyan[1] swung his whopping axe
The forests strummed as one loud lute,
The timber crashed beside his foot
And sprung up stretching in his tracks.

---

[1] Giant lumberjack of North American and Canadian legend.

He had an ox, but his was blue.   5
The flower in his buttonhole
Was brighter than a parasol.
He's gone. Tom Swift[2] has vanished too,

Who worked at none but wit's expense,
Putting dirigibles together   10
Out in the yard, in the quiet weather,
Whistling behind Tom Sawyer's fence.

Now when the darkness in my street
Nibbles the last and crusty crumbs
Of sound, and all the city numbs   15
And goes to sleep upon its feet,

I listen hard to hear its dreams:
John Henry[3] is our nightmare friend,
Whose shoulders roll without an end,
Whose veins pump, pump and burst their seams,   20

Whose sledge is smashing at the rock
And makes the sickly city toss
And half awake in sighs of loss
Until the screaming of the clock.

John Henry's hammer and his will   25
Are here and ringing out our wrong,
I hear him driving all night long
To beat the leisured snarling drill.

1947

Winter Spring

A script of trees before the hill
Spells cold, with laden serifs;[1] all the walls
Are battlemented still;
But winter spring is winnowing the air
Of chill, and crawls   5
Wet-sparkling on the gutters;

---

[2] Hero of popular series of books for boys.
[3] Hero of American folk ballad

[1] Decorative additions to the main stroke of a
printed letter.

Everywhere
Walls wince, and there's the steal of waters.

Now all this proud royaume[2]
Is Veniced.[3] Through the drift's mined dome   10
One sees the rowdy rusted grass,
And we're amazed as windows stricken bright.
This too-soon spring will pass
Perhaps tonight,
And doubtless it is dangerous to love   15
This somersault of seasons;
But I am weary of
The winter way of loving things for reasons.
1947

The Beautiful Changes

One wading a Fall meadow finds on all sides
The Queen Anne's Lace[1] lying like lilies
On water; it glides
So from the walker, it turns
Dry grass to a lake, as the slightest shade of you   5
Valleys my mind in fabulous blue Lucernes.[2]

The beautiful changes as a forest is changed
By a chameleon's tuning his skin to it;
As a mantis, arranged
On a green leaf, grows   10
Into it, makes the leaf leafier, and proves
Any greenness is deeper than anyone knows.

Your hands hold roses always in a way that says
They are not only yours; the beautiful changes
In such kind ways,   15
Wishing ever to sunder
Things and things' selves for a second finding, to lose
For a moment all that it touches back to wonder.
1947

---

[2] French: "realm."

[3] I.e., laced with canals, as in Venice, in Italy.

[1] American wildflower with white, lacelike

blossoms.

[2] Lucerne: town in mountainous Switzerland.

To an American Poet Just Dead

In the *Boston Sunday Herald* just three lines
Of no-point type for you who used to sing
The praises of imaginary wines,
And died, or so I'm told, of the real thing.

Also gone, but a lot less forgotten,   5
Are an eminent cut-rate druggist, a lover of Giving,
A lender, and various brokers: gone from this rotten
Taxable world to a higher standard of living.

It is out in the comfy suburbs I read you are dead,
And the soupy[1] summer is settling, full of the yawns   10
Of Sunday fathers loitering late in bed,
And the ssshh of sprays on all the little lawns.

Will the sprays weep wide for you their chaplet tears?
For you will the deep-freeze units melt and mourn?
For you will Studebakers[2] shred their gears   15
And sound from each garage a muted horn?

They won't. In summer sunk and stupefied
The suburbs deepen in their sleep of death.
And though they sleep the sounder since you died
It's just as well that now you save your breath.   20

1950

Mind

Mind in its purest play is like some bat
That beats about in caverns all alone,
Contriving by a kind of senseless wit
Not to conclude against a wall of stone.

---

[1] Slang for "sentimental," but also a possible
reference to the humid weather.

[2] Studebaker: make of American automobile no
longer produced.

It has no need to falter or explore;   5
Darkly it knows what obstacles are there,
And so may weave and flitter, dip and soar
In perfect courses through the blackest air.

And has this simile a like perfection?
The mind is like a bat. Precisely. Save   10
That in the very happiest intellection
A graceful error may correct the cave.
1956

Playboy[1]

High on his stockroom ladder like a dunce
The stock-boy sits, and studies like a sage
The subject matter of one glossy page,
As lost in curves as Archimedes once.

Sometimes, without a glance, he feeds himself.   5
The left hand, like a mother-bird in flight,
Brings him a sandwich for a sidelong bite,
And then returns it to a dusty shelf.

What so engrosses him? The wild décor
Of this pink-papered alcove into which   10
A naked girl has stumbled, with its rich
Welter of pelts and pillows on the floor,

Amidst which, kneeling in a supple pose,
She lifts a goblet in her farther hand,
As if about to toast a flower-stand   15
Above which hovers an exploding rose

Fired from a long-necked crystal vase that rests
Upon a tasseled and vermilion cloth
One taste of which would shrivel up a moth?
Or is he pondering her perfect breasts?   20

[1] The popular American pinup magazine but also
possibly a reference to the fantasy described in
the poem.

Nothing escapes him of her body's grace
Or of her floodlit skin, so sleek and warm
And yet so strangely like a uniform,
But what now grips his fancy is her face,

And how the cunning picture holds her still   25
At just that smiling instant when her soul,
Grown sweetly faint, and swept beyond control,
Consents to his inexorable will.

1969

The Writer

In her room at the prow of the house
Where light breaks, and the windows are tossed with linden,
My daughter is writing a story.

I pause in the stairwell, hearing
From her shut door a commotion of typewriter-keys   5
Like a chain hauled over a gunwale.

Young as she is, the stuff
Of her life is a great cargo, and some of it heavy:
I wish her a lucky passage.

But now it is she who pauses,   10
As if to reject my thought and its easy figure.
A stillness greatens, in which

The whole house seems to be thinking,
And then she is at it again with a bunched clamor
Of strokes, and again is silent.   15

I remember the dazed starling
Which was trapped in that very room, two years ago;
How we stole in, lifted a sash

And retreated, not to affright it;
And how for a helpless hour, through the crack of the door,   20
We watched the sleek, wild, dark

And iridescent creature
Batter against the brilliance, drop like a glove
To the hard floor, or the desk-top,

And wait then, humped and bloody,   25
For the wits to try it again; and how our spirits
Rose when, suddenly sure,

It lifted off from a chair-back,
Beating a smooth course for the right window
And clearing the sill of the world.   30

It is always a matter, my darling,
Of life or death, as I had forgotten. I wish
What I wished you before, but harder.

1976

Cottage Street, 1953

Framed in her phoenix fire-screen, Edna Ward
Bends to the tray of Canton,[1] pouring tea
For frightened Mrs. Plath; then, turning toward
The pale, slumped daughter, and my wife, and me,

Asks if we would prefer it weak or strong.   5
Will we have milk or lemon, she enquires?
The visit seems already strained and long.
Each in his turn, we tell her our desires.

It is my office to exemplify
The published poet in his happiness,   10
Thus cheering Sylvia, who has wished to die;[2]
But half-ashamed, and impotent to bless,

I am a stupid life-guard who has found,
Swept to his shallows by the tide, a girl
Who, far from shore, has been immensely drowned.   15
And stares through water now with eyes of pearl.

[1] Blue-and-white patterned Chinese-export porcelain ware; in this case, the tea service.
[2] The poet Sylvia Plath (1932–1963) attempted suicide after her junior year at Smith College. Later, she died by suicide.

How large is her refusal; and how slight
The genteel chat whereby we recommend
Life, of a summer afternoon, despite
The brewing dusk which hints that it may end.   20

And Edna Ward shall die in fifteen years,
After her eight-and-eighty summers of
Such grace and courage as permit no tears,
The thin hand reaching out, the last word *love*,

Outliving Sylvia who, condemned to live,   25
Shall study for a decade, as she must,
To state at last her brilliant negative
In poems free and helpless and unjust.
1976

April 5, 1974

The air was soft, the ground still cold.
In the dull pasture where I strolled
Was something I could not believe.
Dead grass appeared to slide and heave,
Though still too frozen-flat to stir,   5
And rocks to twitch, and all to blur.
What was this rippling of the land?
Was matter getting out of hand
And making free with natural law?
I stopped and blinked, and then I saw   10
A fact as eerie as a dream.
There was a subtle flood of steam
Moving upon the face of things.
It came from standing pools and springs.
And what of snow was still around;   15
It came of winter's giving ground
So that the freeze was coming out,
As when a set mind, blessed by doubt,
Relaxes into mother-wit.
Flowers, I said, will come of it.   20
1976

James Dickey
b. 1923

James Dickey made his mark as a poet with his striking early poems—published in *Drowning with Others* (1962) and *Helmets* (1964)—about his experience in the Air Force during World War II. He had enlisted in 1942 after a year at Clemson College, in South Carolina; after the war he returned to college at Vanderbilt and began to write. Dickey's poetry has always celebrated the animal life of man and man's response to states of extraordinary pressure. It is a poetry of violence, often carried to extremes (as Dickey's own life tends to have been carried to extremes of danger in motorcycle driving and drinking). Dickey's poems are spread across the page in bursts of language; syntactic articulation is often sacrificed to a brutality of enunciation. His mystical or visionary side is perhaps not altogether unexpected in a southern poet (Dickey was born in Atlanta, Georgia); his moments of "second sight" belong perhaps to his tendency to mythologize experience, as he did in the novel *Deliverance* (1970), which he adapted for Hollywood. Dickey's work can spin off into regions of incoherence, but when he trims his sails and refuses the temptation to be over-rhetorical, he can write with point and tenderness. His book of literary criticism, *Babel to Byzantium* (1968), reveals a different Dickey—formal, even scholarly, in his discussion of the poetry of others. In his recent attempts to write in the voice of women, Dickey has turned aside from the almost exclusively male world that he made famous in *Buckdancer's Choice* (1965) and subsequent books; however, the sprawl of his lines has not changed, and Dickey's energy remains still uncontained by form.

Further Reading:
Babel to Byzantium, 1968.
Self-interviews, 1970.
Sorties, Journals, and New Essays, 1971.
James Dickey: The Expansive Imagination, ed.
R. J. Calhoun, 1973.
J. Elledge, *James Dickey: A Bibliography,*
1947–1974, 1979.

Text:
Poems, 1947–1967, 1967.

The Hospital Window

I have just come down from my father.
Higher and higher he lies
Above me in a blue light
Shed by a tinted window.

I drop through six white floors   5
And then step out onto pavement.

Still feeling my father ascend,
I start to cross the firm street,
My shoulder blades shining with all
The glass the huge building can raise.   10
Now I must turn round and face it,
And know his one pane from the others.

Each window possesses the sun
As though it burned there on a wick.
I wave, like a man catching fire.   15
All the deep-dyed windowpanes flash,
And, behind them, all the white rooms
They turn to the color of Heaven.

Ceremoniously, gravely, and weakly,
Dozens of pale hands are waving   20
Back, from inside their flames.
Yet one pure pane among these
Is the bright, erased blankness of nothing.
I know that my father is there,

In the shape of his death still living.   25
The traffic increases around me
Like a madness called down on my head.
The horns blast at me like shotguns,
And drivers lean out, driven crazy—
But now my propped-up father   30

Lifts his arm out of stillness at last.
The light from the window strikes me
And I turn as blue as a soul,
As the moment when I was born.
I am not afraid for my father—   35
Look! He is grinning; he is not

Afraid for my life, either,
As the wild engines stand at my knees
Shredding their gears and roaring,
And I hold each car in its place   40
For miles, inciting its horn
To blow down the walls of the world

That the dying may float without fear
In the bold blue gaze of my father.

Slowly I move to the sidewalk   45
With my pin-tingling hand half dead
At the end of my bloodless arm.
I carry it off in amazement,

High, still higher, still waving,
My recognized face fully mortal,   50
Yet not; not at all, in the pale,
Drained, otherworldly, stricken,
Created hue of stained glass.
I have just come down from my father.
1962

Cherrylog Road

Off Highway 106
At Cherrylog Road I entered
The '34 Ford without wheels,
Smothered in kudzu,[1]
With a seat pulled out to run   5
Corn whiskey down from the hills,

And then from the other side
Crept into an Essex
With a rumble seat of red leather
And then out again, aboard   10
A blue Chevrolet, releasing
The rust from its other color,

Reared up on three building blocks.
None had the same body heat;
I changed with them inward, toward   15
The weedy heart of the junkyard,
For I knew that Doris Holbrook
Would escape from her father at noon

And would come from the farm
To seek parts owned by the sun   20
Among the abandoned chassis,
Sitting in each in turn

---

[1] Rapidly growing parasitic vine.

As I did, leaning forward
As in a wild stock-car race

In the parking lot of the dead.   25
Time after time, I climbed in
And out the other side, like
An envoy or movie star
Met at the station by crickets.
A radiator cap raised its head,   30

Become a real toad or a kingsnake
As I neared the hub of the yard,
Passing through many states,
Many lives, to reach
Some grandmother's long Pierce-Arrow   35
Sending platters of blindness forth

From its nickel hubcaps
And spilling its tender upholstery
On sleepy roaches,
The glass panel in between   40
Lady and colored driver
Not all the way broken out,

The back-seat phone
Still on its hook.
I got in as though to exclaim,   45
"Let us go to the orphan asylum,
John; I have some old toys
For children who say their prayers."

I popped with sweat as I thought
I heard Doris Holbrook scrape   50
Like a mouse in the southern-state sun
That was eating the paint in blisters
From a hundred car tops and hoods.
She was tapping like code,

Loosening the screws,   55
Carrying off headlights,
Sparkplugs, bumpers,
Cracked mirrors and gear-knobs,
Getting ready, already,
To go back with something to show   60

Other than her lips' new trembling
I would hold to me soon, soon,

Where I sat in the ripped back seat
Talking over the interphone,
Praying for Doris Holbrook   65
To come from her father's farm

And to get back there
With no trace of me on her face
To be seen by her red-haired father
Who would change, in the squalling barn,   70
Her back's pale skin with a strop,
Then lay for me

In a bootlegger's roasting car
With a string-triggered 12-gauge shotgun
To blast the breath from the air.   75
Not cut by the jagged windshields,
Through the acres of wrecks she came
With a wrench in her hand,

Through dust where the blacksnake dies
Of boredom, and the beetle knows   80
The compost has no more life.
Someone outside would have seen
The oldest car's door inexplicably
Close from within:

I held her and held her and held her,   85
Convoyed at terrific speed
By the stalled, dreaming traffic around us,
So the blacksnake, stiff
With inaction, curved back
Into life, and hunted the mouse   90

With deadly overexcitement,
The beetles reclaimed their field
As we clung, glued together,
With the hooks of the seat springs
Working through to catch us red-handed   95
Amidst the gray breathless batting

That burst from the seat at our backs.
We left by separate doors
Into the changed, other bodies
Of cars, she down Cherrylog Road   100
And I to my motorcycle
Parked like the soul of the junkyard

Restored, a bicycle fleshed
With power, and tore off
Up Highway 106, continually   105
Drunk on the wind in my mouth,
Wringing the handlebar for speed,
Wild to be wreckage forever.

1964

Buckdancer's Choice

So I would hear out those lungs,
The air split into nine levels,
Some gift of tongues of the whistler

In the invalid's bed: my mother,
Warbling all day to herself   5
The thousand variations of one song;

It is called Buckdancer's Choice.
For years, they have all been dying
Out, the classic buck-and-wing[1] men

Of traveling minstrel shows;   10
With them also an old woman
Was dying of breathless angina,

Yet still found breath enough
To whistle up in my head
A sight like a one-man band,   15

Freed black, with cymbals at heel,
An ex-slave who thrivingly danced
To the ring of his own clashing light

Through the thousand variations of one song
All day to my mother's prone music,   20
The invalid's warbler's note,

[1] Traditional solo tap dance done by blacks in a
minstrel show.

While I crept close to the wall
Sock-footed, to hear the sounds alter,
Her tongue like a mockingbird's break

Through stratum after stratum of a tone   25
Proclaiming what choices there are
For the last dancers of their kind,

For ill women and for all slaves
Of death, and children enchanted at walls
With a brass-beating glow underfoot,   30

Not dancing but nearly risen
Through barnlike, theatrelike houses
On the wings of the buck and wing.
1965

The Sheep Child

Farm boys wild to couple
With anything   with soft-wooded trees
With mounds of earth   mounds
Of pinestraw   will keep themselves off
Animals by legends of their own: 5
In the hay-tunnel dark
And dung of barns, they will
Say   I have heard tell

That in a museum in Atlanta
Way back in a corner somewhere   10
There's this thing that's only half
Sheep   like a woolly baby
Pickled in alcohol   because
Those things can't live   his eyes
Are open   but you can't stand to look   15
I heard from somebody who . . .

But this is now almost all
Gone. The boys have taken
Their own true wives in the city,
The sheep are safe in the west hill   20
Pasture   but we who were born there

Still are not sure. Are we,
Because we remember, remembered
In the terrible dust of museums?

Merely with his eyes, the sheep-child may   25

Be saying   saying

    I am here, in my father's house.
    I who am half of your world, came deeply
    To my mother in the long grass
    Of the west pasture, where she stood like moonlight   30
    Listening for foxes. It was something like love
    From another world that seized her
    From behind, and she gave, not lifting her head
    Out of dew, without ever looking, her best
    Self to that great need. Turned loose, she dipped her face   35
    Farther into the chill of the earth, and in a sound
    Of sobbing   of something stumbling
    Away, began, as she must do,
    To carry me. I woke, dying,

    In the summer sun of the hillside, with my eyes   40
    Far more than human. I saw for a blazing moment
    The great grassy world from both sides,
    Man and beast in the round of their need,
    And the hill wind stirred in my wool,
    My hoof and my hand clasped each other,   45
    I ate my one meal
    Of milk, and died
    Staring. From dark grass I came straight

    To my father's house, whose dust
    Whirls up in the halls for no reason   50
    When no one comes   piling deep in a hellish mild corner,
    And, through my immortal waters,
    I meet the sun's grains eye
    To eye, and they fail at my closet of glass.
    Dead, I am most surely living   55
    In the minds of farm boys: I am he who drives
    Them like wolves from the hound bitch and calf
    And from the chaste ewe in the wind.
    They go into woods   into bean fields   they go
    Deep into their known right hands. Dreaming of me,   60
    They groan   they wait   they suffer
    Themselves, they marry, they raise their kind.

1967

A. R. Ammons
b. 1926

Archibald Randolph Ammons is a poet whose work incorporates American life from its agricultural beginnings to its nuclear present. He was born and raised on a farm in North Carolina, and the habit of noticing the seasons, the stars, the growth of trees and crops, and the destructions of storm and fire persists in his poetry. After his wartime service in the navy, he enrolled in Wake Forest University on the GI Bill. Although he had begun writing poetry during his navy watches, he was, he has said, afraid of the part of himself the poems represented, and in college he majored in chemistry. Still, he took enough English courses to make it possible to be admitted as a candidate for an M.A. in English at Berkeley, where the poet Josephine Miles encouraged him to continue to write poetry. Ammons left Berkeley in 1952 without the degree, however, and went to work for his father-in-law's glass manufacturing company in New Jersey. Ammons remained there for ten years, continuing to write; he published his first book, *Ommateum* (1955), at his own expense. Later, the poet John Logan helped to get his second book, *Expressions of Sea Level* (1964), published. Cornell University invited Ammons to join its faculty in 1964, and he has remained in Ithaca, New York, as professor of English there. His *Collected Poems* (1972) won the National Book Award. He has since published *Diversifications* (1976), *The Snow Poems* (1977), *A Coast of Trees* (1981), and *Worldly Hopes* (1983). Recently, he was awarded a five-year MacArthur fellowship.

Ammons's early Protestant religious training formed his mind in ways we associate with the American Transcendentalists, especially Ralph Waldo Emerson. Early he began to see the natural world as emblematic of spiritual or intellectual meaning. But his use of the allegorical tradition reverses the usual religious practice, visible in poems like Oliver Wendell Holmes's "The Chambered Nautilus." Holmes fastens first on the natural object: He describes the successively larger chambers of the nautilus, then draws a moral lesson from it for himself. Ammons, on the other hand, begins with his own emotional perplexity. He goes into the world bearing an inchoate freight of thought and feeling and then sees— as he does in "Grace Abounding"—a natural scene that exhibits an uncanny correspondence to his unarticulated emotion. In describing a hedge encased in ice, Ammons can make us feel a heart encased in misery.

The usual reach of emblematic verse in the past extended only to what could be perceived by the unaided senses, but Ammons's youthful familiarity with the microscope and the telescope extended his perceptual reach into the domain of the invisible, on the one hand, and the astronomical, on the other. Algae and galaxies are no more strange to him than roses and stars were to his English predecessors. And Ammons's years of work with chemical processes have made the complex interchanges and metamorphoses of the elements second nature to him. His view of the universe is at home with technological and scientific language, which appears in his poetry with unassuming naturalness. In Ammons, for the first time, modern American poetry has found a poet who can write with ease in the full range of scientific acquaintance.

The poets from whom Ammons derives are very diverse: They range from Emerson, Whitman, and Dickinson to Williams, Moore, and Stevens. Like Emerson and Dickinson, Ammons is emblematic; like Whitman, he is democratic and curious about the world; like Williams, he is unaffectedly colloquial; like Moore, he is observant and scientific; like Stevens, he is reflective and philosophical. Ammons is nonetheless a recognizably new voice. He is a poet of violent griefs, severe feelings of isolation and loneliness, and sudden elations. He assimilates these gusts of feeling to a perceptual grounding in the natural world and to an intellectual grounding in the impalpable; he speaks in a remarkably natural voice.

Ammons's verse is only imperfectly represented here, since he writes long poems of great variety and versatility, abandoning his terse and shapely short forms for a long stream of utterance, of clauses separated not by periods but by colons. Ammons has allowed chance a part in his long poems; one of them, *Tape for the Turn of the Year* (1965), is determined, in line width and total length, by the shape of the paper on which it is written, a roll of adding-machine tape. Another journal volume, *The Snow Poems* (1977), takes its daily cue from the Ithaca weather throughout the winter of Ammons's fiftieth year. Ammons's humor and self-deprecation, visible here in his colloquy with the mountain, are the obverse of his moments of loss and estrangement.

Ammons is a poet who has translated many English genres into indigenous American terms. Gray's "Elegy in a Country Churchyard" has been given us in native form in Ammons's exquisite "Easter Morning," a poem ending with a reminiscence, in natural rather than religious terms, of Bryant's "To a Waterfowl." His "scribbling," in a form like the water "uncapturable and vanishing," partakes of the linearity of all flow, but it leaves behind those shapes of emotion captured: "Shadows are bodiless shapes, yet they have a song." Whitman said that the poet judges not as a judge judges but as the light falling round a helpless thing. Ammons, remembering this injunction, takes as his example the radiance that "does not withhold itself." Poetry for Ammons can use and absorb all that the world contains.

Further Reading:
R. Howard, *Alone with America: Essays on the Art of Poetry in the United States Since 1950*, 1969.
A. Holder, *A. R. Ammons*, 1978.
S. T. Wright, *A. R. Ammons: A Bibliography*, 1980.

Texts:
"Bonus" from *The Selected Poems, 1951–1977*, 1978.
"Easter Morning" from *A Coast of Trees*, 1981.
All other poems from *Collected Poems, 1951–1971*, 1972.

Hardweed Path Going

Every evening, down into the hardweed
going,
the slop bucket heavy, held-out, wire handle
freezing in the hand, put it down a minute, the jerky
smooth unspilling levelness of the knees,   5
   meditation of a bucket rim,
lest the wheat meal,
floating on clear greasewater, spill,
down the grown-up path:

   don't forget to slop the hogs,   10
   feed the chickens,
   water the mule,
   cut the kindling,
   build the fire,
   call up the cow: 15

   supper is over, it's starting to get
dark early,
better get the scraps together, mix a little meal in,
nothing but swill.

   The dead-purple woods hover on the west.   20
I know those woods.
Under the tall, ceiling-solid pines, beyond the edge of
field and brush, where the wild myrtle grows,
   I let my jo-reet loose.
A jo-reet is a bird. Nine weeks of summer he   25
sat on the well bench in a screened box,
a stick inside to walk on,
   "jo-reet," he said, "jo-reet."
   and I
would come up to the well and draw the bucket down   30
deep into the cold place where red and white marbled
clay oozed the purest water, water celebrated
throughout the county:
   "Grits all gone?"
   "jo-reet."   35
Throw a dipper of cold water on him. Reddish-black
flutter.
   "reet, reet, reet!"

> Better turn him loose before
cold weather comes on.   40
> Doom caving in
> inside
> any pleasure, pure
> attachment
> of love.   45

Beyond the wild myrtle away from cats I turned him loose
and his eye asked me what to do, where to go;
he hopped around, scratched a little, but looked up at me.
Don't look at me. Winter is coming.
Disappear in the bushes. I'm tired of you and will   50
be alone hereafter. I will go dry in my well.
> I will turn still.
Go south. Grits is not available in any natural form.
Look under leaves, try mushy logs, the floors of pinywoods.
South into the dominion of bugs.   55

> They're good woods.
But lay me out if a mourning dove far off in the dusky pines
> starts.

> Down the hardweed path going,
leaning, balancing, away from the bucket, to   60
Sparkle, my favorite hog, sparse, fine black hair,
grunted while feeding if rubbed,
scratched against the hair, or if talked to gently:
got the bottom of the slop bucket:
> > "Sparkle . . .   65
> > You hungry?
> > Hungry, girly?"
blowing, bubbling in the trough.

> Waiting for the first freeze:
"Think it's going to freeze tonight?" say the neighbors,   70
the neighbors, going by.

> Hog-killing.

Oh, Sparkle, when the axe tomorrow morning falls
and the rush is made to open your throat,
I will sing, watching dry-eyed as a man, sing my   75
> love for you in the tender feedings.

> She's nothing but a hog, boy.

Bleed out, Sparkle, the moon-chilled bleaches
          of your body hanging upside-down
hardening through the mind and night of the first freeze.   80
1964

Reflective

I found a
weed
that had a

mirror in it
and that   5
mirror

looked in at
a mirror
in

me that   10
had a
weed in it
1966

Apologia pro Vita Sua[1]

I started picking up the stones
throwing them into one place
and by sunrise I was going far away
for the large ones
always turning to see never lost   5
the cairn's[2] height
lengthening my radial reach:

[1] "A Defense of His Own Life." The Latin title
is borrowed from John Henry Newman
(1801–1890), who gave this title to his response
to the accusations of Charles Kingsley.

[2] Cairn: pile of stones.

the sun watched with deep concentration
and the heap through the hours grew
and became by nightfall   10
distinguishable from all the miles around
of slate and sand:

during the night the wind falling
turned earthward its lofty freedom and speed
and the sharp blistering sound muffled   15
toward dawn and the blanket was
drawn up over a breathless face:

even so you can see in full dawn
the ground there lifts
a foreign thing desertless in origin.   20
1970

Mountain Talk

I was going along a dusty highroad
when the mountain
across the way
turned me to its silence:
oh I said how come   5
I don't know your
massive symmetry and rest:
nevertheless, said the mountain,
would you want
to be   10
lodged here with
a changeless prospect, risen
to an unalterable view:
so I went on
counting my numberless fingers.   15
1970

Cascadilla Falls[1]

I went down by Cascadilla
Falls this
evening, the
stream below the falls,
and picked up a   5
handsized stone
kidney-shaped, testicular, and

thought all its motions into it,
the 800 mph earth spin,
the 190-million-mile yearly   10
displacement around the sun,
the overriding
grand
haul

of the galaxy with the 30,000   15
mph of where
the sun's going:
thought all the interweaving
motions
into myself: dropped   20

the stone to dead rest:
the stream from other motions
broke
rushing over it:
shelterless,   25
I turned

to the sky and stood still:
Oh
I do
not know where I am going   30
that I can live my life
by this single creek.
1970

---

[1] Waterfall in Ithaca, New York, near Ammons's
house.

Body Politic

Out for stars he
took some
down
and we all
wondered if he might be   5
damned to such sinister
& successful enterprise:
we took and
unfolded him: he
turned out   10
pliant and warm
& messy in
some minor way: then, not
having come to
much, we   15
lit into his stars which
declaring nothing dark
held white and high
and brought us down.
1970

Classic

I sat by a stream in a
perfect—except for willows—
emptiness
and the mountain that
was around,   5

scraggly with brush &
rock
said
I see you're scribbling again:

accustomed to mountains,   10
their cumbersome intrusions,
I said

well, yes, but in a fashion very
like the water here
uncapturable and vanishing: 15

but that
said the mountain does not
excuse the stance
or diction

and next if you're not careful   20
you'll be
arriving at ways
water survives its motions.
1970

Clarity

After the event the rockslide
realized,
in a still diversity of completion,
grain and fissure,
declivity   5
&
force of upheaval,
whether rain slippage,
ice crawl, root
explosion or   10
stream erosive undercut:

well I said it is a pity:
one swath of sight will never
be the same: nonetheless,
this   15
shambles has
relieved a bind, a taut of twist,
revealing streaks &
scores of knowledge
now obvious and quiet.   20
1970

Hope's Okay

The undergrowth's a conveyance of butterflies
(flusters of clustering) so buoyant and delightful,
filling into a floating impression, diversity's
diversion breaking out into under-piny seas
point by point to the mind's nodes and needs: 5

let's see, though, said the fire through the undergrowth,
what all this makes into, what difference can
survive it: so I waded through the puffy disgust
and could not help feeling despair of
many a gray, smoke-worming twig, scaly as if alive: 10

much that was here I said is lost and if I stoop
to ask bright thoughts of roots
do not think I ask for better than was here
or that hope with me rises one leaf higher than
the former growth (higher to an ashless fire) or   15
that despair came any closer than ash to being total.
1970

Transaction

I attended the burial of all my rosy feelings:
I performed the rites, simple and decisive:
the long box took the spilling of gray ground in
with little evidence of note: I traded slow

work for the usual grief: the services were private: 5
there was little cause for show, though no cause not
to show: it went indifferently, with an appropriate
gravity and lack of noise: the ceremonies of the self

seem always to occur at a distance from the ruins of men
where there is nothing really much to expect, no arms,   10
no embraces: the day was all right: certain occasions
outweigh the weather: the woods just to the left

were average woods: well, I turned around finally from
the process, the surface smoothed into a kind of seal,
and tried to notice what might be thought to remain: 15
everything was there, the sun, the breeze, the woods

(as I said), the little mound of troublesome tufts of
grass: but the trees were upright shadows, the breeze
was as against a shade, the woods stirred gray
as deep water: I looked around for what was left,   20

the tools, and took them up and went away, leaving
all my treasures where they might never again disturb
me, increase or craze: decision quietens:
shadows are bodiless shapes, yet they have a song.
1970

Treaties

My great wars close:
ahead, papers,
signatures, the glimmering
in shade of
leaf and raised wine: 5
orchards, orchards,
vineyards, fields:
spiralling slow time while
the medlar
smarts and glows and   10
empty nests
come out in the open:
fall rain then stirs
the black creek and
the small leaf slips in.   15
1971

The City Limits

When you consider the radiance, that it does not withhold
itself but pours its abundance without selection into every
nook and cranny not overhung or hidden; when you consider

that birds' bones make no awful noise against the light but
lie low in the light as in a high testimony; when you consider   5
the radiance, that it will look into the guiltiest

swervings of the weaving heart and bear itself upon them,
not flinching into disguise or darkening; when you consider
the abundance of such resource as illuminates the glow-blue

bodies and gold-skeined wings of flies swarming the dumped   10
guts of a natural slaughter or the coil of shit and in no
way winces from its storms of generosity; when you consider

that air or vacuum, snow or shale, squid or wolf, rose or lichen,
each is accepted into as much light as it will take, then
the heart moves roomier, the man stands and looks about, the   15

leaf does not increase itself above the grass, and the dark
work of the deepest cells is of a tune with May bushes
and fear lit by the breadth of such calmly turns to praise.
1971

The Eternal City[1]

After the explosion or cataclysm, that big
display that does its work but then fails
out with destructions, one is left with the

pieces: at first, they don't look very valuable,
but nothing sizable remnant around for   5
gathering the senses on, one begins to take

---

[1] Appellation for Rome and for the Christian
heaven.

an interest, to sort out, to consider closely
what will do and won't, matters having become
not only small but critical: bulbs may have been

uprooted: they should be eaten, if edible, or   10
got back in the ground: what used to be garages,
even the splinters, should be collected for

fires: some unusually deep holes or cleared
woods may be turned to water supplies or
sudden fields: ruinage is hardly ever a   15

pretty sight but it must when splendor goes
accept into itself piece by piece all the old
perfect human visions, all the old perfect loves.
1972

Grace Abounding[1]

for E.C.

What is the misery in one that turns one with gladness
to the hedge strung lucid with ice: is it that one's
misery, penetrating there as sight, meets neither

welcome nor reprimand but finds nevertheless a picture
of itself sympathetic, held as the ice-blurred stems   5
increased: ah, what an abundance is in the universe

when one can go for gladness to the indifferent ghastly,
feel alliances where none may ever take: find one's
misery made clear, borne, as if also, by a hedge of ice.
1972

---

[1] The title is borrowed from John Bunyan's
(1628–1688) *Grace Abounding to the Chief of
Sinners* (1666), his spiritual autobiography,
allegorically retold in *The Pilgrim's Progress*
(1678).

Bonus

The hemlocks slumped
already as if bewailing
the branch-loading

shales of ice, the rain
changes and a snow   5
sifty as fog

begins to fall, brightening
the ice's bruise-glimmer
with white holdings:

the hemlocks, muffled,   10
deepen to the grim
taking of a further beauty on.
1975

Easter Morning

I have a life that did not become,
that turned aside and stopped,
astonished:
I hold it in me like a pregnancy or
as on my lap a child   5
not to grow or grow old but dwell on

it is to his grave I most
frequently return and return
to ask what is wrong, what was
wrong, to see it all by   10
the light of a different necessity
but the grave will not heal
and the child,
stirring, must share my grave
with me, an old man having   15
gotten by on what was left

when I go back to my home country in these
fresh far-away days, it's convenient to visit
everybody, aunts and uncles, those who used to say,
look how he's shooting up, and the   20
trinket aunts who always had a little
something in their pocketbooks, cinnamon bark
or a penny or nickel, and uncles who
were the rumored fathers of cousins
who whispered of them as of great, if   25
troubled, presences, and school
teachers, just about everybody older
(and some younger) collected in one place
waiting, particularly, but not for
me, mother and father there, too, and others   30
close, close as burrowing
under skin, all in the graveyard
assembled, done for, the world they
used to wield, have trouble and joy
in, gone   35

the child in me that could not become
was not ready for others to go,
to go on into change, blessings and
horrors, but stands there by the road
where the mishap occurred, crying out for   40
help, come and fix this or we
can't get by, but the great ones who
were to return, they could not or did
not hear and went on in a flurry and
now, I say in the graveyard, here   45
lies the flurry, now it can't come
back with help or helpful asides, now
we all buy the bitter
incompletions, pick up the knots of
horror, silently raving, and go on   50
crashing into empty ends not
completions, not rondures the fullness
has come into and spent itself from
I stand on the stump
of a child, whether myself   55
or my little brother who died, and
yell as far as I can, I cannot leave this place, for
for me it is the dearest and the worst,
it is life nearest to life which is
life lost: it is my place where   60
I must stand and fail,
calling attention with tears

to the branches not lofting
boughs into space, to the barren
air that holds the world that was my world   65

though the incompletions
(& completions) burn out
standing in the flash high-burn
momentary structure of ash, still it
is a picture-book, letter-perfect   70
Easter morning: I have been for a
walk: the wind is tranquil: the brook
works without flashing in an abundant
tranquility: the birds are lively with
voice: I saw something I had   75
never seen before: two great birds,
maybe eagles, blackwinged, whitenecked
and -headed, came from the south oaring
the great wings steadily; they went
directly over me, high up, and kept on   80
due north: but then one bird,
the one behind, veered a little to the
left and the other bird kept on seeming
not to notice for a minute: the first
began to circle as if looking for   85
something, coasting, resting its wings
on the down side of some of the circles:
the other bird came back and they both
circled, looking perhaps for a draft;
they turned a few more times, possibly   90
rising—at least, clearly resting—
then flew on falling into distance till
they broke across the local bush and
trees: it was a sight of bountiful
majesty and integrity: the having   95
patterns and routes, breaking
from them to explore other patterns or
better ways to routes, and then the
return: a dance sacred as the sap in
the trees, permanent in its descriptions   100
as the ripples round the brook's
ripplestone: fresh as this particular
flood of burn breaking across us now
from the sun.

1981

Allen Ginsberg
b. 1926

Allen Ginsberg brought a raw new power into American poetry with the publication of *Howl* (1956). It was a recognizable descendant of *Leaves of Grass,* but Whitman's poetry had been out of favor during the ascendancy of the difficult and "European" poetry of Eliot, Pound, and Stevens. Ginsberg had crossed Whitman's long lines with the long lines of the Hebrew psalms and Whitman's protests against gentility with the Hebrew prophets' denunciations of their society. In the relatively quiet 1950s, Ginsberg's excoriation of America rang out with explosive force: "I saw the best minds of my generation destroyed by madness, starving hysterical naked. . . ."

Yet Ginsberg's declamations, considering his early life, were not surprising. As we learn from "Kaddish" and other poems, he had grown up in a milieu of protest, among Jewish socialists and communists, in Paterson, New Jersey. The faith that rhetoric and political action can be effective was bred into him, and it might have been predicted that William Blake, the English protest-poet, would become Ginsberg's favorite writer. Blake's hatred of the forces of repression found expression in both small lyrics (the *Songs of Innocence* and *Experience*) and in giant mythic narratives like *Jerusalem.* Ginsberg, too, writes both songs and long journey poems, and he has never turned aside from his stance of protest.

Allen Ginsberg saw at close hand the enormous psychic strain endured by American immigrant populations. In his elegy for his mother, Naomi, the long poem entitled "Kaddish" (after the Hebrew prayer for the dead), Ginsberg traces Naomi's life from her first arrival in America from Russia through her brief idyllic youth in the Young People's Socialist League and on to her marriage and long decline into paranoia, confinement in an asylum, eventual lobotomy, and death. Naomi's life became for Ginsberg a paradigm of all the lives of the suffering poor, the confined, and the oppressed. Ginsberg's openly proclaimed homosexuality, which made him a criminal in the eyes of the law, reinforced his belief that the legal system is unnecessarily oppressive, directed by American fundamentalist morality rather than by a concern for public order.

Large public issues—the stockpiling of nuclear bombs, the Korean and Vietnam wars, FBI wiretappings, racism, ecology—continue to enter Ginsberg's poems, but the poetry contains as well Ginsberg's ruefully humorous account of his private life—his travels, his sexual history, his experiments with drugs, his interest in Buddhism, his mourning for his father.

Ginsberg's father was a high school teacher of English and a writer of inept conventional verse (Ginsberg gave poetry readings jointly with his father in the later years of his father's life, as if to demonstrate that family solidarity outweighs aesthetic compatibility). Ginsberg's mother ("from whose pained head I first took Vision," says Ginsberg) may have been his muse, but in his father's verse he found his introduction to English poetry. Ginsberg went to Columbia

University, was expelled as a sophomore for writing an obscene phrase in the dust on his dormitory windowpane, lived for a while with William Burroughs and Jack Kerouac, reentered Columbia, and graduated in 1948. Shortly after graduation, implicated in a friend's thefts because the stolen goods had been stored in his apartment, Ginsberg pleaded insanity to avoid imprisonment and was confined for eight months in the Columbia Psychiatric Institute. In the early 1950s, in San Francisco, he met the poets who were to be known collectively with him as the Beat generation—Kenneth Rexroth, Lawrence Ferlinghetti, and Gary Snyder. The City Lights Press, founded by Ferlinghetti, published Ginsberg's verse from *Howl* until 1985, including such volumes as *Reality Sandwiches* (1963), *Planet News* (1968), *The Fall of America* (1973) and *Mind Breaths* (1977). In 1985 Harper & Row issued Ginsberg's *Collected Poems;* the volume *White Shroud* followed in 1986.

Ginsberg's return to the oral tradition in poetry had far-reaching effects, as did his allegiance to the line of poetry stretching from Whitman through Williams. (As one New Jersey poet to another, Williams had encouraged Ginsberg's early verse, and contributed an introduction to *Howl;* he had even included letters from Ginsberg in *Paterson.*) Even such formal poets as Robert Lowell became conscious, by the example of the beat poets, of the necessity of incorporating in poetry the rhythms of American speech. The uninhibited poetry readings Ginsberg has given—which have included, over the years, occasional nakedness, references to drugs, chants with a harmonium and finger cymbals, the reading aloud of sexual diaries, Buddhist mantras, and audience participation—immensely changed the nature of the poetry reading as a communal occasion. Ginsberg's humorous and candid poetry suggested that self-revelation need not be shaming or self-abasing and that political protest need not be dour or hateful. His spiritual evolution—his repudiation of drugs, his travels in India, his adoption of Buddhism—appears in his poetry as a dramatic thread giving continuity to the whole. He remains a powerful presence in American poetry today and is probably the only American poet whose name is known throughout the world.

Further Reading:
T. F. Merrill, *Allen Ginsberg,* 1969.
J. Kramer, *Allen Ginsberg in America,* 1970.
J. Tytell, *Naked Angels: The Lives and Literature of the Beat Generation,* 1976.
M. P. Kraus, *Allen Ginsberg: An Annotated Bibliography, 1969–1977,* 1978.
P. C. Portuges, *The Visionary Poetics of Allen Ginsberg,* 1978.

Texts:
"Howl," "A Supermarket in California," "Sunflower Sutra," and "America" from *Howl,* 1956.
"Kaddish" and "The Lion for Real" from *Kaddish,* 1961.
"American Change" from *Reality Sandwiches,* 1963.
"Chances 'R' " from *Planet News,* 1968.
"Mugging" from *Mind Breaths,* 1979.

from Howl

for Carl Solomon

I

I saw the best minds of my generation destroyed by madness, starving hysterical
   naked,
dragging themselves through the negro streets at dawn looking for an angry fix,
angelheaded hipsters burning for the ancient heavenly connections to the starry
   dynamo in the machinery of night,
who poverty and tatters and hollow-eyed and high sat up smoking in the
   supernatural darkness of cold-water flats floating across the tops of cities
   contemplating jazz,
who bared their brains to Heaven under the El and saw Mohammedan angels
   staggering on tenement roofs illuminated,   5
who passed through universities with radiant cool eyes hallucinating Arkansas
   and Blake-light tragedy among the scholars of war,
who were expelled from the academies for crazy & publishing obscene odes on
   the windows of the skull,[1]
who cowered in unshaven rooms in underwear, burning their money in
   wastebaskets and listening to the Terror through the wall,
who got busted in their pubic beards returning through Laredo with a belt of
   marijuana for New York,
who ate fire in paint hotels or drank turpentine in Paradise Alley,[2] death, or
   purgatoried their torsos night after night   10
with dreams, with drugs, with waking nightmares, alcohol and cock and endless
   balls,
incomparable blind streets of shuddering cloud and lightning in the mind
   leaping toward poles of Canada & Paterson, illuminating all the motionless
   world of Time between,
Peyote solidities of halls, backyard green tree cemetery dawns, wine drunkenness
   over the rooftops, storefront boroughs of teahead joyride neon blinking
   traffic light, sun and moon and tree vibrations in the roaring winter dusks of
   Brooklyn, ashcan rantings and kind king light of mind,
who chained themselves to subways for the endless ride from Battery to holy
   Bronx on benzedrine until the noise of wheels and children brought them
   down shuddering mouth-wracked and battered bleak of brain all drained of
   brilliance in the drear light of Zoo,
who sank all night in submarine light of Bickford's floated out and sat through
   the stale beer afternoon in desolate Fugazzi's, listening to the crack of doom
   on the hydrogen jukebox,   15

---

[1] Ginsberg was expelled from Columbia
University for writing an obscenity in the dust
on his dormitory windowpane.

[2] Ginsberg's note: "A slum courtyard N.Y. Lower
East Side, site of [the writer Jack] Kerouac's
Subterraneans, 1958."

who talked continuously seventy hours from park to pad to bar to Bellevue to
  museum to the Brooklyn Bridge,
a lost battalion of platonic conversationalists jumping down the stoops off fire
  escapes off windowsills off Empire State out of the moon,
yacketayakking screaming vomiting whispering facts and memories and
  anecdotes and eyeball kicks and shocks of hospitals and jails and wars,
whole intellects disgorged in total recall for seven days and nights with brilliant
  eyes, meat for the Synagogue cast on the pavement,
who vanished into nowhere Zen New Jersey leaving a trail of ambiguous
  picture postcards of Atlantic City Hall,   20
suffering Eastern sweats and Tangerian bone-grindings and migraines of China
  under junk-withdrawal of Newark's bleak furnished room,
who wandered around and around at midnight in the railroad yard wondering
  where to go, and went, leaving no broken hearts,
who lit cigarettes in boxcars boxcars boxcars racketing through snow toward
  lonesome farms in grandfather night,
who studied Plotinus Poe St. John of the Cross telepathy and bop kaballa
  because the cosmos instinctively vibrated at their feet in Kansas,
who loned it through the streets of Idaho seeking visionary indian angels who
  were visionary indian angels,   25
who thought they were only mad when Baltimore gleamed in supernatural
  ecstasy,
who jumped in limousines with the Chinaman of Oklahoma on the impulse of
  winter midnight streetlight smalltown rain,
who lounged hungry and lonesome through Houston seeking jazz or sex or
  soup, and followed the brilliant Spaniard to converse about America and
  Eternity, a hopeless task, and so took ship to Africa,
who disappeared into the volcanoes of Mexico leaving behind nothing but the
  shadow of dungarees and the lava and ash of poetry scattered in fireplace
  Chicago,
who reappeared on the West Coast investigating the F.B.I. in beards and shorts
  with big pacifist eyes sexy in their dark skin passing out incomprehensible
  leaflets,   30
who burned cigarette holes in their arms protesting the narcotic tobacco haze of
  Capitalism,
who distributed Supercommunist pamphlets in Union Square weeping and
  undressing while the sirens of Los Alamos wailed them down, and wailed
  down Wall, and the Staten Island ferry also wailed,
who broke down crying in white gymnasiums naked and trembling before the
  machinery of other skeletons,
who bit detectives in the neck and shrieked with delight in policecars for
  committing no crime but their own wild cooking pederasty and
  intoxication,
who howled on their knees in the subway and were dragged off the roof
  waving genitals and manuscripts,   35
who let themselves be fucked in the ass by saintly motorcyclists, and screamed
  with joy,

who blew and were blown by those human seraphim, the sailors, caresses of
  Atlantic and Caribbean love,

who balled in the morning in the evenings in rosegardens and the grass of
  public parks and cemeteries scattering their semen freely to whomever come
  who may,

who hiccupped endlessly trying to giggle but wound up with a sob behind a
  partition in a Turkish Bath when the blonde & naked angel came to pierce
  them with a sword,

who lost their loveboys to the three old shrews of fate the one eyed shrew of
  the heterosexual dollar the one eyed shrew that winks out of the womb and
  the one eyed shrew that does nothing but sit on her ass and snip the
  intellectual golden threads of the craftsman's loom,   40

who copulated ecstatic and insatiate with a bottle of beer a sweetheart a package
  of cigarettes a candle and fell off the bed, and continued along the floor and
  down the hall and ended fainting on the wall with a vision of ultimate cunt
  and come eluding the last gyzym of consciousness,

who sweetened the snatches of a million girls trembling in the sunset, and were
  red eyed in the morning but prepared to sweeten the snatch of the sunrise,
  flashing buttocks under barns and naked in the lake,

who went out whoring through Colorado in myriad stolen night-cars, N.C.,[3]
  secret hero of these poems, cocksman and Adonis of Denver—joy to the
  memory of his innumerable lays of girls in empty lots & diner backyards,
  moviehouses' rickety rows, on mountaintops in caves or with gaunt waitresses
  in familiar roadside lonely petticoat upliftings & especially secret gas-station
  solipsisms of johns, & hometown alleys too,

who faded out in vast sordid movies, were shifted in dreams, woke on a sudden
  Manhattan, and picked themselves up out of basements hungover with
  heartless Tokay and horrors of Third Avenue iron dreams & stumbled to
  unemployment offices,

who walked all night with their shoes full of blood on the snowbank docks
  waiting for a door in the East River to open to a room full of steamheat
  and opium,   45

who created great suicidal dramas on the apartment cliff-banks of the Hudson
  under the wartime blue floodlight of the moon & their heads shall be
  crowned with laurel in oblivion,

who ate the lamb stew of the imagination or digested the crab at the muddy
  bottom of the rivers of Bowery,

who wept at the romance of the streets with their pushcarts full of onions and
  bad music,

who sat in boxes breathing in the darkness under the bridge, and rose up to
  build harpsichords in their lofts,

who coughed on the sixth floor of Harlem crowned with flame under the
  tubercular sky surrounded by orange crates of theology,   50

---

[3] Neal Cassady, a friend of Ginsberg and Jack
Kerouac, who appears as the character Dean
Moriarty in Kerouac's novel *On the Road.*

who scribbled all night rocking and rolling over lofty incantations which in the
yellow morning were stanzas of gibberish,

who cooked rotten animals lung heart feet tail borsht & tortillas dreaming of
the pure vegetable kingdom,

who plunged themselves under meat trucks looking for an egg,

who threw their watches off the roof to cast their ballot for Eternity outside of
Time, & alarm clocks fell on their heads every day for the next decade,

who cut their wrists three times successively unsuccessfully, gave up and were
forced to open antique stores where they thought they were growing old and
cried,   55

who were burned alive in their innocent flannel suits on Madison Avenue amid
blasts of leaden verse & the tanked-up clatter of the iron regiments of fashion
& the nitroglycerine shrieks of the fairies of advertising & the mustard gas of
sinister intelligent editors, or were run down by the drunken taxicabs of
Absolute Reality,

who jumped off the Brooklyn Bridge this actually happened and walked away
unknown and forgotten into the ghostly daze of Chinatown soup alleyways
& firetrucks, not even one free beer,

who sang out of their windows in despair, fell out of the subway window,
jumped in the filthy Passaic, leaped on negroes, cried all over the street,
danced on broken wineglasses barefoot smashed phonograph records of
nostalgic European 1930's German jazz finished the whiskey and threw up
groaning into the bloody toilet, moans in their ears and the blast of colossal
steamwhistles,

who barreled down the highways of the past journeying to each other's
hotrod-Golgotha jail-solitude watch or Birmingham jazz incarnation,

who drove crosscountry seventytwo hours to find out if I had a vision or you
had a vision or he had a vision to find out Eternity,   60

who journeyed to Denver, who died in Denver, who came back to Denver &
waited in vain, who watched over Denver & brooded & loned in Denver
and finally went away to find out the Time, & now Denver is lonesome for
her heroes,

who fell on their knees in hopeless cathedrals praying for each other's salvation
and light and breasts, until the soul illuminated its hair for a second,

who crashed through their minds in jail waiting for impossible criminals with
golden heads and the charm of reality in their hearts who sang sweet blues to
Alcatraz,

who retired to Mexico to cultivate a habit, or Rocky Mount to tender Buddha
or Tangiers to boys or Southern Pacific to the black locomotive or Harvard
to Narcissus to Woodlawn to the daisychain or grave,

who demanded sanity trials accusing the radio of hypnotism & were left with
their insanity & their hands & a hung jury,   65

who threw potato salad at CCNY[4] lecturers on Dadaism and subsequently
presented themselves on the granite steps of the madhouse with shaven heads
and harlequin speech of suicide, demanding instantaneous lobotomy,

[4] City College of New York.

and who were given instead the concrete void of insulin metrasol[5] electricity
   hydrotherapy psychotherapy occupational therapy pingpong & amnesia,
who in humorless protest overturned only one symbolic pingpong table, resting
   briefly in catatonia,
returning years later truly bald except for a wig of blood, and tears and fingers,
   to the visible madman doom of the wards of the madtowns of the East,
Pilgrim State's Rockland's and Greystone's[6] foetid halls, bickering with the
   echoes of the soul, rocking and rolling in the midnight solitude-bench
   dolmen-realms of love, dream of life a nightmare, bodies turned to stone as
   heavy as the moon,   70
with mother finally ******,[7] and the last fantastic book flung out of the
   tenement window, and the last door closed at 4 AM and the last telephone
   slammed at the wall in reply and the last furnished room emptied down to
   the last piece of mental furniture, a yellow paper rose twisted on a wire
   hanger in the closet, and even that imaginary, nothing but a hopeful little bit
   of hallucination—
ah, Carl, while you are not safe I am not safe, and now you're really in the
   total animal soup of time—
and who therefore ran through the icy streets obsessed with a sudden flash of
   the alchemy of the use of the ellipse the catalog the meter & the vibrating
   plane,
who dreamt and made incarnate gaps in Time & Space through images
   juxtaposed, and trapped the archangel of the soul between 2 visual images
   and joined the elemental verbs and set the noun and dash of consciousness
   together jumping with sensation of Pater Omnipotens Aeterna Deus[8]
to recreate the syntax and measure of poor human prose and stand before you
   speechless and intelligent and shaking with shame, rejected yet confessing out
   the soul to conform to the rhythm of thought in his naked and endless head,   75
the madman bum and angel beat in Time, unknown, yet putting down here
   what might be left to say in time come after death,
and rose reincarnate in the ghostly clothes of jazz in the goldhorn shadow of
   the band and blew the suffering of America's naked mind for love into an eli
   eli lamma lamma sabacthani[9] saxophone cry that shivered the cities down to
   the last radio
with the absolute heart of the poem of life butchered out of their own bodies
   good to eat a thousand years.

1956

---

[5] A tranquilizing drug.
[6] Pilgrim State, Rockland, and Greystone: state
mental hospitals. Carl Solomon was confined in
Rockland.
[7] Asterisks replace *fucked.*
[8] Latin, from the Creed: "Omnipotent Father
Eternal God." Ginsberg uses the feminine of the
adjective "aeternus," as does the French painter

Paul Cézanne (1839–1906), from whose letters
Ginsberg borrowed the phrase. Cézanne meant
all of created nature (conventionally imagined
as female).
[9] Hebrew: "My God, my God, why hast thou
forsaken me?" These were Jesus' words on the
cross (Matthew 4:26).

A Supermarket in California

What thoughts I have of you tonight, Walt Whitman, for I walked down the sidestreets under the trees with a headache, self-conscious looking at the full moon.

In my hungry fatigue, and shopping for images, I went into the neon fruit supermarket, dreaming of your enumerations!

What peaches and what penumbras! Whole families shopping at night! Aisles full of husbands! Wives in the avocados, babies in the tomatoes!—and you, Garcia Lorca,[1] what were you doing down by the watermelons?

I saw you, Walt Whitman, childless, lonely old grubber, poking among the meats in the refrigerator and eyeing the grocery boys.

I heard you asking questions of each: Who killed the pork chops? What price bananas? Are you my Angel?   5

I wandered in and out of the brilliant stacks of cans following you, and followed in my imagination by the store detective.

We strode down the open corridors together in our solitary fancy tasting artichokes, possessing every frozen delicacy, and never passing the cashier.

Where are we going, Walt Whitman? The doors close in an hour. Which way does your beard point tonight?

(I touch your book and dream of our odyssey in the supermarket and feel absurd.)

Will we walk all night through solitary streets? The trees add shade to shade, lights out in the houses, we'll both be lonely.   10

Will we stroll dreaming of the lost America of love past blue automobiles in driveways, home to our silent cottage?

Ah, dear father, graybeard, lonely old courage-teacher, what America did you have when Charon[2] quit poling his ferry and you got out on a smoking bank and stood watching the boat disappear on the black waters of Lethe?

1956

---

[1] Homosexual Spanish poet (1898–1936), shot by French soldiers in the Spanish Civil War. He wrote an "Ode to Walt Whitman."
[2] In mythology Charon is the ferryman who carries souls across the river Styx to Hades, where they drink from the river Lethe, causing them to forget their life before death.

Sunflower Sutra[1]

I walked on the banks of the tincan banana dock and sat down under the huge
    shade of a Southern Pacific locomotive to look at the sunset over the box
    house hills and cry.
Jack Kerouac sat beside me on a busted rusty iron pole, companion, we thought
    the same thoughts of the soul, bleak and blue and sad-eyed, surrounded by
    the gnarled steel roots of trees of machinery.
The oily water on the river mirrored the red sky, sun sank on top of final
    Frisco peaks, no fish in that stream, no hermit in those mounts, just ourselves
    rheumy-eyed and hungover like old bums on the riverbank, tired and wily.
Look at the Sunflower, he said, there was a dead gray shadow against the sky,
    big as a man, sitting dry on top of a pile of ancient sawdust—
—I rushed up enchanted—it was my first sunflower, memories of Blake[2]—my
    visions—Harlem   5
and Hells of the Eastern rivers, bridges, clanking Joes Greasy Sandwiches, dead
    baby carriages, black treadless tires forgotten and unretreaded, the poem of
    the riverbank, condoms & pots, steel knives, nothing stainless, only the dank
    muck and the razor sharp artifacts passing into the past—
and the gray Sunflower poised against the sunset, crackly bleak and dusty with
    the smut and smog and smoke of olden locomotives in its eye—
corolla[3] of bleary spikes pushed down and broken like a battered crown, seeds
    fallen out of its face, soon-to-be-toothless mouth of sunny air, sunrays
    obliterated on its hairy head like a dried wire spiderweb,
leaves stuck out like arms out of the stem, gestures from the sawdust root,
    broke pieces of plaster fallen out of the black twigs, a dead fly in its ear,
Unholy battered old thing you were, my sunflower O my soul, I loved you
    then!   10
The grime was no man's grime but death and human locomotives,
all that dress of dust, that veil of darkened railroad skin, that smog of cheek,
    that eyelid of black mis'ry, that sooty hand or phallus or protuberance of
    artificial worse-than-dirt—industrial—modern—all that civilization spotting
    your crazy golden crown—
and those blear thoughts of death and dusty loveless eyes and ends and withered
    roots below, in the home-pile of sand and sawdust, rubber dollar bills, skin
    of machinery, the guts and innards of the weeping coughing car, the empty
    lonely tincans with their rusty tongues alack, what more could I name, the
    smoked ashes of some cock cigar, the cunts of wheelbarrows and the milky
    breasts of cars, wornout asses out of chairs & sphincters of dynamos—all
    these

---

[1] Buddhist religious text.
[2] William Blake (1757–1827), English poet and
author of "Ah! Sunflower." Ginsberg in 1948

had had a vision in which he heard Blake's
voice reciting this poem.
[3] Petals surrounding the center of a flower.

entangled in your mummied roots—and you there standing before me in the
  sunset, all your glory in your form!
A perfect beauty of a sunflower! a perfect excellent lovely sunflower existence!
  a sweet natural eye to the new hip moon, woke up alive and excited
  grasping in the sunset shadow sunrise golden monthly breeze!   15
How many flies buzzed round you innocent of your grime, while you cursed
  the heavens of the railroad and your flower soul?
Poor dead flower? when did you forget you were a flower? when did you look
  at your skin and decide you were an impotent dirty old locomotive? the
  ghost of a locomotive? the specter and shade of a once powerful mad
  American locomotive?
You were never no locomotive, Sunflower, you were a sunflower!
And you Locomotive, you are a locomotive, forget me not!
So I grabbed up the skeleton thick sunflower and stuck it at my side like a
  scepter,   20
and deliver my sermon to my soul, and Jack's soul too, and anyone who'll
  listen,
—We're not our skin of grime, we're not our dread bleak dusty imageless
  locomotive, we're all beautiful golden sunflowers inside, we're blessed by our
  own seed & golden hairy naked accomplishment-bodies growing into mad
  black formal sunflowers in the sunset, spied on by our eyes under the shadow
  of the mad locomotive riverbank sunset Frisco hilly tincan evening sitdown
  vision.

1956

America

America I've given you all and now I'm nothing.
America two dollars and twentyseven cents January 17, 1956.
I can't stand my own mind.
America when will we end the human war?
Go fuck yourself with your atom bomb.   5
I don't feel good don't bother me.
I won't write my poem till I'm in my right mind.
America when will you be angelic?
When will you take off your clothes?
When will you look at yourself through the grave?   10
When will you be worthy of your million Trotskyites?[1]

---

[1] Communist idealists, followers of Leon Trotsky
(1879–1940), the opponent of Stalin.

America why are your libraries full of tears?
America when will you send your eggs to India?[2]
I'm sick of your insane demands.
When can I go into the supermarket and buy what I need with my good
    looks?   15
America after all it is you and I who are perfect not the next world.
Your machinery is too much for me.
You made me want to be a saint.
There must be some other way to settle this argument.
Burroughs is in Tangiers[3] I don't think he'll come back it's sinister.   20
Are you being sinister or is this some form of practical joke?
I'm trying to come to the point.
I refuse to give up my obsession.
America stop pushing I know what I'm doing.
America the plum blossoms are falling.   25
I haven't read the newspapers for months, everyday somebody goes on trial for
    murder.
America I feel sentimental about the Wobblies.[4]
America I used to be a communist when I was a kid I'm not sorry.
I smoke marijuana every chance I get.
I sit in my house for days on end and stare at the roses in the closet.   30
When I go to Chinatown I get drunk and never get laid.
My mind is made up there's going to be trouble.
You should have seen me reading Marx.[5]
My psychoanalyst thinks I'm perfectly right.
I won't say the Lord's Prayer.   35
I have mystical visions and cosmic vibrations.
America I still haven't told you what you did to Uncle Max after he came over
    from Russia.

I'm addressing you.
Are you going to let your emotional life be run by Time Magazine?
I'm obsessed by Time Magazine.   40
I read it every week.
Its cover stares at me every time I slink past the corner candystore.
I read it in the basement of the Berkeley Public Library.
It's always telling me about responsibility. Businessmen are serious. Movie
    producers are serious. Everybody's serious but me.
It occurs to me that I am America.   45
I am talking to myself again.

[2] India was suffering a famine, while America had an agricultural surplus.
[3] William Burroughs (b. 1914), a friend of Ginsberg and author of the novel *Naked Lunch* (1959), was living in Morocco.
[4] Nickname for members of the Industrial Workers of the World, a revolutionary union founded in Chicago in 1905.
[5] Karl Marx (1818–1883), German social philosopher and author, with Friedrich Engels, of *The Communist Manifesto* (1848).

Asia is rising against me.
I haven't got a chinaman's chance.
I'd better consider my national resources.
My national resources consist of two joints of marijuana millions of genitals an
    unpublishable private literature that goes 1400 miles an hour and
    twentyfive-thousand mental institutions.   50
I say nothing about my prisons nor the millions of underprivileged who live in
    my flowerpots under the light of five hundred suns.
I have abolished the whorehouses of France, Tangiers is the next to go.
My ambition is to be President despite the fact that I'm a Catholic.

America how can I write a holy litany in your silly mood?
I will continue like Henry Ford my strophes are as individual as his
    automobiles more so they're all different sexes.   55
America I will sell you strophes $2500 apiece $500 down on your old strophe
America free Tom Mooney[6]
America save the Spanish Loyalists[7]
America Sacco & Vanzetti[8] must not die
America I am the Scottsboro boys.[9]   60
America when I was seven momma took me to Communist Cell meetings they
    sold us garbanzos[10] a handful per ticket a ticket costs a nickel and the
    speeches were free everybody was angelic and sentimental about the workers
    it was all so sincere you have no idea what a good thing the party was in
    1935 Scott Nearing was a grand old man a real mensch Mother Bloor made
    me cry I once saw Israel Amter[11] plain. Everybody must have been a spy.
America you don't really want to go to war.
America it's them bad Russians.
Them Russians them Russians and them Chinamen. And them Russians.
The Russia wants to eat us alive. The Russia's power mad. She wants to take
    our cars from out our garages.   65
Her wants to grab Chicago. Her needs a Red Readers' Digest. Her wants our
    auto plants in Siberia. Him big bureaucracy running our fillingstations.
That no good. Ugh. Him make Indians learn read. Him need big black niggers.
    Hah. Her make us all work sixteen hours a day. Help.
America this is quite serious.
America this is the impression I get from looking in the television set.
America is this correct?   70

[6] American labor agitator in California, accused
of bomb killings and sentenced to death in 1916
but pardoned in 1939.
[7] Those fighting against Franco in the Spanish
Civil War.
[8] Nicola Sacco and Bartolomeo Vanzetti were
executed in Massachusetts in 1927 for a murder
connected with a robbery; sentiment ran high
against them because of their radical political
beliefs.
[9] The "Scottsboro boys" were nine blacks who

were convicted in Alabama of the rape of two
white women in 1931. Liberals and radicals
believed the conviction to be unproved. Four
years later the sentences were reduced in four
cases and the charges dropped in five.
[10] Chick peas.
[11] Scott Nearing (1883–1983), Ella ("Mother")
Bloor (1862–1951), and Israel Amter
(1881–1954): well-known American Socialists
and Communists.

I'd better get right down to the job.
It's true I don't want to join the Army or turn lathes in precision parts
　　factories, I'm nearsighted and psychopathic anyway.
America I'm putting my queer shoulder to the wheel.
1956

Kaddish[1]

For Naomi Ginsberg 1894–1956[2]

I

Strange now to think of you, gone without corsets & eyes, while I walk on the
　　sunny pavement of Greenwich Village.
downtown Manhattan, clear winter noon, and I've been up all night, talking,
　　talking, reading the Kaddish aloud, listening to Ray Charles[3] blues shout
　　blind on the phonograph
the rhythm the rhythm—and your memory in my head three years after—And
　　read Adonais'[4] last triumphant stanzas aloud—wept, realizing how we suffer—
And how Death is that remedy all singers dream of, sing, remember, prophesy
　　as in the Hebrew Anthem, or the Buddhist Book of Answers—and my own
　　imagination of a withered leaf—at dawn—
Dreaming back thru life, Your time—and mine accelerating toward Apocalypse,　5
the final moment—the flower burning in the Day—and what comes after,
looking back on the mind itself that saw an American city
a flash away, and the great dream of Me or China, or you and a phantom
　　Russia, or a crumpled bed that never existed—
like a poem in the dark—escaped back to Oblivion—
No more to say, and nothing to weep for but the Beings in the Dream, trapped
　　in its disappearance,
　　　　　　　　　　　　　　　　　　　　　　　　　　　　　　　　　　10
sighing, screaming with it, buying and selling pieces of phantom, worshipping
　　each other,
worshipping the God included in it all—longing or inevitability?—while it
　　lasts, a Vision—anything more?
It leaps about me, as I go out and walk the street, look back over my shoulder,
　　Seventh Avenue, the battlements of window office buildings shouldering each
　　other high, under a cloud, tall as the sky an instant—and the sky above—an
　　old blue place.

---

[1] Hebrew prayer for the dead. There is no
mention of death in the prayer, which praises
life and which begins: "Magnified and sanctified
be the name of God throughout the world
which He hath created according to His will.
May He establish His kingdom during the days
of your life and during the life of all the house
of Israel, speedily, yea, soon; and say ye,
Amen."
[2] Ginsberg's mother, who had been mentally ill,
confined in Greystone Hospital, and
lobotomized.
[3] Famous blind blues singer and composer.
[4] Adonais: Shelley's elegy for Keats (d. 1821).

or down the Avenue to the South, to—as I walk toward the Lower East Side—
   where you walked 50 years ago, little girl—from Russia, eating the first
   poisonous tomatoes of America—frightened on the dock—
then struggling in the crowds of Orchard Street toward what?—toward
   Newark[5]—   15
toward candy store, first home-made sodas of the century, hand-churned ice
   cream in backroom on musty brownfloor boards—
Toward education marriage nervous breakdown, operation, teaching school, and
   learning to be mad, in a dream—what is this life?
Toward the Key in the window—and the great Key lays its head of lights on
   top of Manhattan, and over the floor, and lays down on the sidewalk—in a
   single vast beam, moving, as I walk down First toward the Yiddish Theater
   —and the place of poverty
you knew, and I know, but without caring now—Strange to have moved thru
   Paterson,[6] and the West, and Europe and here again,
with the cries of Spaniards now in the doorstoops doors and dark boys on the
   street, fire escapes old as you   20
—Tho you're not old now, that's left here with me—
Myself, anyhow, maybe as old as the universe—and I guess that dies with us—
   enough to cancel all that comes—What came is gone forever every time—
That's good! That leaves it open for no regret—no fear radiators, lacklove,
   torture even toothache in the end—
Though while it comes it is a lion that eats the soul—and the lamb, the soul, in
   us, alas, offering itself in sacrifice to change's fierce hunger—hair and teeth—
   and the roar of bonepain, skull bare, break rib, rot-skin, braintricked
   Implacability.
Ai! ai! we do worse! We are in a fix! And you're out, Death let you out,
   Death had the Mercy, you're done with your century, done with God, done
   with the path thru it—Done with yourself at last—Pure—Back to the Babe
   dark before your Father, before us all—before the world—   25
There, rest. No more suffering for you. I know where you've gone, it's good.
No more flowers in the summer fields of New York, no joy now, no more fear
   of Louis,[7]
and no more of his sweetness and glasses, his high school decades, debts, loves,
   frightened telephone calls, conception beds, relatives, hands—
No more of sister Elanor,—she gone before you—we kept it secret—you killed
   her—or she killed herself to bear with you—an arthritic heart—But Death's
   killed you both—No matter—
Nor your memory of your mother, 1915 tears in silent movies weeks and weeks
   —forgetting, agrieve watching Marie Dressler address humanity, Chaplin
   dance in youth,   30
or Boris Godunov, Chaliapin's at the Met, halling his voice of a weeping Czar

---

[5] After a childhood in New York, Naomi lived
in Newark. Orchard Street is on New York's
Lower East Side, once a neighborhood of
Jewish immigrants.

[6] Ginsberg grew up in Paterson, New Jersey,
William Carlos Williams's home city.
[7] Ginsberg's father, a high school teacher of
English and an amateur poet.

—by standing room with Elanor & Max[8]—watching also the Capitalists take
   seats in Orchestra, white furs, diamonds,
with the YPSL's[9] hitch-hiking thru Pennsylvania, in black baggy gym skirts
   pants, photograph of 4 girls holding each other round the waste, and
   laughing eye, too coy, virginal solitude of 1920
all girls grown old, or dead, now, and that long hair in the grave—lucky to
   have husbands later—
You made it—I came too—Eugene my brother before (still grieving now and
   will gream[10] on to his last stiff hand, as he goes thru his cancer—or kill—
   later perhaps—soon he will think—)
And it's the last moment I remember, which I see them all, thru myself, now—
   tho not you   35
I didn't foresee what you felt—what more hideous gape of bad mouth came
   first—to you—and were you prepared?
To go where? In that Dark—that—in that God? a radiance? A Lord in the
   Void? Like an eye in the black cloud in a dream? Adonoi[11] at last, with
   you?
Beyond my remembrance! Incapable to guess! Not merely the yellow skull in
   the grave, or a box of worm dust, and a stained ribbon—Deathshead with
   Halo? can you believe it?
Is it only the sun that shines once for the mind, only the flash of existence, than
   none ever was?
Nothing beyond what we have—what you had—that so pitiful—yet Triumph,   40
to have been here, and changed, like a tree, broken, or flower—fed to the
   ground—but mad, with its petals, colored, thinking Great Universe, shaken,
   cut in the head, leaf stript, hid in an egg crate hospital, cloth wrapped, sore
   —freaked in the moon brain, Naughtless.
No flower like that flower, which knew itself in the garden, and fought the
   knife—lost
Cut down by an idiot Snowman's icy—even in the Spring—strange ghost
   thought—some Death—Sharp icicle in his hand—crowned with old roses—a
   dog for his eyes—cock of a sweatshop—heart of electric irons.
All the accumulations of life, that wear us out—clocks, bodies, consciousness,
   shoe, breasts—begotten sons—your Communism—'Paranoia' into hospitals.
You once kicked Elanor in the leg, she died of heart failure later. You of
   stroke. Asleep? within a year, the two of you, sisters in death. Is Elanor
   happy?   45
Max grieves alive in an office on Lower Broadway, lone large mustache over
   midnight Accountings, not sure. His life passes—as he sees—and what does
   he doubt now? Still dream of making money, or that might have made
   money, hired nurse, had children, found even your Immortality, Naomi?
I'll see him soon. Now I've got to cut through—to talk to you—as I didn't
   when you had a mouth.

---

8 Naomi's sister and her husband.   10 Portmanteau word combining "grieve" and
9 YPSL: acronym for Young People's Socialist   "dream."
   League.   11 Hebrew: "Lord."

Forever. And we're bound for that, Forever—like Emily Dickinson's horses[12]—
    headed to the End.
They know the way—These Steeds—run faster than we think—it's our own
    life they cross—and take with them.

Magnificent, mourned no more, marred of heart, mind behind, married
dreamed, mortal changed—Ass and face done with murder.   50
    In the world, given, flower maddened, made no Utopia, shut under pine,
almed in Earth, balmed in Lone, Jehovah, accept.
    Nameless, One Faced, Forever beyond me, beginningless, endless, Father in
death. Tho I am not there for this Prophecy, I am unmarried, I'm hymnless, I'm
Heavenless, headless in blisshood I would still adore
    Thee, Heaven, after Death, only One blessed in Nothingness, not light or
darkness, Dayless Eternity—
    Take this, this Psalm, from me, burst from my hand in a day, some of my
Time, now given to Nothing—to praise Thee—But Death
    This is the end, the redemption from Wilderness, way for the Wonderer,
House sought for All, black handkerchief washed clean by weeping—page
beyond Psalm—Last change of mine and Naomi—to God's perfect Darkness—
Death, stay thy phantoms!   55

II

    Over and over—refrain—of the Hospitals—still haven't written your history
    —leave it abstract—a few images
    run thru the mind—like the saxophone chorus of houses and years—
remembrance of electrical shocks.
    By long nites as a child in Paterson apartment, watching over your
nervousness—you were fat—your next move—
    By that afternoon I stayed home from school to take care of you—once and
for all—when I vowed forever that once man disagreed with my opinion of
the cosmos, I was lost—
    By my later burden—vow to illuminate mankind—this is release of
particulars—(mad as you)—(sanity a trick of agreement)—   60
    But you stared out the window on the Broadway Church corner, and spied
a mystical assassin from Newark,
    So phoned the Doctor—'OK go way for a rest'—so I put on my coat and
walked you downstreet—On the way a grammarschool boy screamed,
unaccountably—'Where you goin Lady to Death'? I shuddered—
    and you covered your nose with motheaten fur collar, gas mask against
poison sneaked into downtown atmosphere, sprayed by Grandma[13]—
    And was the driver of the cheesebox Public Service bus a member of the

---

[12] Reference to Emily Dickinson's poem "Because
I could not stop for Death."
[13] Naomi's paranoia indicts her own mother and
spreads to embrace everyone from the president
(Roosevelt) to innocent bystanders. She focuses
on Hitler and his persecution of Jews.

gang? You shuddered at his face, I could hardly get you on—to New York, very Times Square, to grab another Greyhound—

where we hung around 2 hours fighting invisible bugs and jewish sickness— breeze poisoned by Roosevelt—   65

out to get you—and me tagging along, hoping it would end in a quiet room in a Victorian house by a lake.

Ride 3 hours thru tunnels past all American industry, Bayonne preparing for World War II, tanks, gas fields, soda factories, diners, locomotive roundhouse fortress—into piney woods New Jersey Indians—calm towns—long roads thru sandy tree fields—

Bridges by deerless creeks, old wampum loading the streambed—down there a tomahawk or Pocahontas bone—and a million old ladies voting for Roosevelt in brown small houses, roads off the Madness highway—

perhaps a hawk in a tree, or a hermit looking for an owl-filled branch—

All the time arguing—afraid of strangers in the forward double seat, snoring regardless—what busride they snore on now?   70

'Allen, you don't understand—it's—ever since those 3 big sticks up my back —they did something to me in Hospital, they poisoned me, they want to see me dead—3 big sticks, 3 big sticks—

'The Bitch! Old Grandma! Last week I saw her, dressed in pants like an old man, with a sack on her back, climbing up the brick side of the apartment

'On the fire escape, with poison germs, to throw on me—at night—maybe Louis is helping her—he's under her power—

'I'm your mother, take me to Lakewood' (near where Graf Zeppelin had crashed before, all Hitler in Explosion) 'where I can hide.'

We got there—Dr. Whatzis rest home—she hid behind a closet—demanded a blood transfusion.   75

We were kicked out—tramping with Valise to unknown shady lawn houses —dusk, pine trees after dark—long dead street filled with crickets and poison ivy—

I shut her up by now—big house REST HOME ROOMS—gave the landlady her money for the week—carried up the iron valise—sat on bed waiting to escape—

Neat room in attic with friendly bedcover—lace curtains—spinning wheel rug—Stained wallpaper old as Naomi. We were home.

I left on the next bus to New York—lay my head back in the last seat, depressed—the worst yet to come?—abandoning her, rode in torpor—I was only 12.

Would she hide in her room and come out cheerful for breakfast? Or lock her door and stare thru the window for sidestreet spies? Listen at keyholes for Hitlerian invisible gas? Dream in a chair—or mock me, by—in front of a mirror, alone?   80

12 riding the bus at nite thru New Jersey, have left Naomi to Parcae[14] in Lakewood's haunted house—left to my own fate bus—sunk in a seat—all

[14] Latin name for the three Fates.

violins broken—my heart sore in my ribs—mind was empty—Would she were
safe in her coffin—

Or back at Normal School in Newark, studying up on America in a black
skirt—winter on the street without lunch—a penny a pickle—home at night to
take care of Elanor in the bedroom—

First nervous breakdown was 1919—she stayed home from school and lay in
a dark room for three weeks—something bad—never said what—every noise
hurt—dreams of the creaks of Wall Street—

Before the grey Depression—went upstate New York—recovered—Lou took
photo of her sitting crossleg on the grass—her long hair wound with flowers—
smiling—playing lullabies on mandolin—poison ivy smoke in left-wing summer
camps and me in infancy saw trees—

or back teaching school, laughing with idiots, the backward classes—her
Russian speciality—morons with dreamy lips, great eyes, thin feet & sickey
fingers, swaybacked, rachitic[15]—   85

great heads pendulous over Alice in Wonderland, a blackboard full of
C A T.

Naomi reading patiently, story out of a Communist fairy book—Tale of the
Sudden Sweetness of The Dictator—Forgiveness of Warlocks[16]—Armies
Kissing—

Deathsheads Around the Green Table—The King & the Workers—Paterson
Press printed them up in the 30's till she went mad, or they folded, both.

O Paterson! I got home late that nite. Louis was worried. How could I be
so—didn't I think? I shouldn't have left her. Mad in Lakewood. Call the
Doctor. Phone the home in the pines. Too late.

Went to bed exhausted, wanting to leave the world (probably that year
newly in love with R—— my high school mind hero, jewish boy who came[17]
a doctor later—then silent neat kid—   90

I later laying down life for him, moved to Manhattan—followed him to
college—Prayed on ferry to help mankind if admitted—vowed, the day I
journeyed to Entrance Exam—

by being honest revolutionary labor lawyer—would train for that—inspired
by Sacco Vanzetti, Norman Thomas, Debs, Altgeld, Sandburg, Poe—Little Blue
Books.[18] I wanted to be President, or Senator.

Ignorant woe—later dreams of kneeling by R's shocked knees declaring my
love of 1941—What sweetness he'd have shown me, tho, that I'd wished him &
despaired—first love—a crush—

Later a mortal avalanche, whole mountains of homosexuality, Matterhorns of
cock, Grand Canyons of asshole—weight on my melancholy head—

meanwhile I walked on Broadway imagining Infinity like a rubber ball
without space beyond—what's outside?—coming home to Graham Avenue still
melancholy passing the lone green hedges across the street, dreaming after the
movies—)   95

---

[15] Suffering from rickets.
[16] Sorcerers, given to black magic.
[17] Became.

[18] Adolescent mixture of socialist and literary
inspirations. The Little Blue Books were
socialist pamphlets.

The telephone rang at 2AM—Emergency—she'd gone mad—Naomi hiding under the bed screaming bugs of Mussolini—Help! Louis! Buba![19] Fascists! Death!—the landlady frightened—old fag attendant screaming back at her—

Terror, that woke the neighbors—old ladies on the second floor recovering from menopause—all those rags between thighs, clean sheets, sorry over lost babies—husbands ashen—children sneering at Yale, or putting oil in hair at CCNY[20]—or trembling in Montclair State Teachers College like Eugene—

Her big leg crouched to her breast, hand outstretched Keep Away, wool dress on her thighs, fur coat dragged under the bed—she barricaded herself under bedspring with suitcases.

Louis in pyjamas listening to phone, frightened—do now?—Who could know?—my fault, delivering her to solitude?—sitting in the dark room on the sofa, trembling, to figure out—

He took the morning train to Lakewood, Naomi still under bed—thought he brought poison Cops—Naomi screaming—Louis what happened to your heart then? Have you been killed by Naomi's ecstasy?   100

Dragged her out, around the corner, a cab, forced her in with valise, but the driver left them off at drugstore. Bus stop, two hours' wait.

I lay in bed nervous in the 4-room apartment, the big bed in living room, next to Louis' desk—shaking—he came home that nite, late, told me what happened.

Naomi at the prescription counter defending herself from the enemy—racks of children's books, douche bags, aspirins, pots, blood—'Don't come near me—murderers! Keep away! Promise not to kill me!'

Louis in horror at the soda fountain—with Lakewood girlscouts—coke addicts—nurses—busmen hung on schedule—Police from country precinct, dumbed—and a priest dreaming of pigs on an ancient cliff?[21]

Smelling the air—Louis pointing to emptiness?—Customers vomiting their cokes—or staring—Louis humiliated—Naomi triumphant—The Announcement of the Plot. Bus arrives, the drivers won't have them on trip to New York.   105

Phonecalls to Dr. Whatzis, 'She needs a rest,' The mental hospital—State Greystone Doctors—'Bring her here, Mr. Ginsberg.'

Naomi, Naomi—sweating, bulge-eyed, fat, the dress unbuttoned at one side —hair over brow, her stockings hanging evilly on her legs—screaming for a blood transfusion—one righteous hand upraised—a shoe in it—barefoot in the Pharmacy—

The enemies approach—what poisons? Tape recorders? FBI? Zhdanov[22] hiding behind the counter? Trotsky[23] mixing rat bacteria in the back of the store? Uncle Sam in Newark, plotting deathly perfumes in the Negro district? Uncle Ephraim, drunk with murder in the politician's bar, scheming of Hague? Aunt Rose passing water thru the needles of the Spanish Civil War?

till the hired $35 ambulance came from Red Bank—Grabbed her arms—

---

[19] Nickname of Naomi's mother.
[20] City College of New York.
[21] Demons, exorcised from a man, entered a herd of Gadarene swine, who threw themselves over a cliff (Matthew 8:28).

[22] Andrei Zhdanov (1896–1948), Russian general and political leader.
[23] Leon Trotsky (1879–1940), Russian Communist leader.

strapped her on the stretcher—moaning, poisoned by imaginaries, vomiting
chemicals thru Jersey, begging mercy from Essex County to Morristown—

And back to Greystone where she lay three years—that was the last
breakthrough, delivered her to Madhouse again—   110

On what wards—I walked there later, oft—old catatonic ladies, grey as
cloud or ash or walls—sit crooning over floorspace—Chairs—and the wrinkled
hags acreep, accusing—begging my 13-year-old mercy—

'Take me home'—I went alone sometimes looking for the lost Naomi, taking
Shock—and I'd say, 'No, you're crazy Mama,—Trust the Drs.'—

And Eugene, my brother, her elder son, away studying Law in a furnished
room in Newark—

came Paterson-ward next day—and he sat on the brokendown couch in the
living room—'We had to send her back to Greystone'—

—his face perplexed, so young, then eyes with tears—then crept weeping all
over his face—'What for?' wail vibrating in his cheekbones, eyes closed up,
high voice—Eugene's face of pain.   115

Him faraway, escaped to an Elevator in the Newark Library, his bottle daily
milk on windowsill of $5 week furn room downtown at trolley tracks—

He worked 8 hrs. a day for $20/wk—thru Law School years—stayed by
himself innocent near negro whorehouses.

Unlaid, poor virgin—writing poems about Ideals and politics letters to the
editor Pat Eve News—(we both wrote, denouncing Senator Borah[24] and
Isolationists—and felt mysterious toward Paterson City Hall—

I sneaked inside it once—local Moloch[25] tower with phallus spire & cap o'
ornament, strange gothic Poetry that stood on Market Street—replica Lyons'
Hotel de Ville—

wings, balcony & scrollwork portals, gateway to the giant city clock, secret
map room full of Hawthorne—dark Debs[26] in the Board of Tax—Rembrandt
smoking in the gloom—   120

Silent polished desks in the great committee room—Aldermen? Bd of
Finance? Mosca the hairdresser aplot—Crapp the gangster issuing orders from
the john—The madmen struggling over Zone, Fire, Cops & Backroom
Metaphysics—we're all dead—outside by the bus-stop Eugene stared thru
childhood—

where the Evangelist preached madly for 3 decades, hard-haired, cracked &
true to his mean Bible—chalked Prepare to Meet Thy God on civic pave—

or God is Love on the railroad overpass concrete—he raved like I would
rave, the lone Evangelist—Death on City Hall—)

But Gene, young,—been Montclair Teachers College 4 years—taught half
year & quit to go ahead in life—afraid of Discipline Problems—dark sex Italian

---

[24] Senator from Idaho (1865–1940) and leader of
those opposing American involvement in
European affairs.
[25] Phoenician god to whom children were
sacrificed.

[26] Eugene Debs (1855–1926), American Socialist
leader.

students, raw girls getting laid, no English, sonnets disregarded—and he did not
know much—just that he lost—

so broke his life in two and paid for Law—read huge blue books and rode
the ancient elevator 13 miles away in Newark & studied up hard for the future   125

just found the Scream of Naomi on his failure doorstep, for the final time,
Naomi gone, us lonely—home—him sitting there—

Then have some chicken soup, Eugene. The Man of Evangel wails in front
of City Hall. And this year Lou has poetic loves of suburb middle-age—in
secret—music from his 1937 book[27]—Sincere—he longs for beauty—

No love since Naomi screamed—since 1923?—now lost in Greystone ward—
new shock for her—Electricity, following the 40 Insulin.

And Metrasol[28] had made her fat.

So that a few years later she came home again—we'd much advanced and
planned—I waited for that day—my Mother again to cook &—play the piano
—sing at mandolin—Lung Stew, & Stenka Razin[29] & the communist line on
the war with Finland—and Louis in debt—suspected to be poisoned money—
mysterious capitalisms   130

—& walked down the long front hall & looked at the furniture. She never
remembered it all. Some amnesia. Examined the doilies—and the dining room
set was sold—

the Mahogany table—20 years love—gone to the junk man—we still had
the piano—and the book of Poe—and the Mandolin, tho needed some string,
dusty—

She went to the backroom to lay down in bed and ruminate, or nap, hide—
I went in with her, not leave her by herself—lay in bed next to her—shades
pulled, dusky, late afternoon—Louis in front room at desk, waiting—perhaps
boiling chicken for supper—

'Don't be afraid of me because I'm just coming back home from the mental
hospital—I'm your mother—'

Poor love, lost—a fear—I lay there—Said, 'I love you Naomi,'—stiff, next
to her arm. I would have cried, was this the comfortless lone union?—Nervous,
and she got up soon.   135

Was she ever satisfied? And—by herself sat on the new couch by the front
windows, uneasy—cheek leaning on her hand—narrowing eye—at what fate
that day—

Picking her tooth with her nail, lips formed an O, suspicion—thought's old
worn vagina—absent sideglance of eye—some evil debt written in the wall,
unpaid—& the aged breasts of Newark come near—

May have heard radio gossip thru the wires in her head, controlled by 3 big
sticks left in her back by gangsters in amnesia, thru the hospital—caused pain
between her shoulders—

Into her head—Roosevelt should know her case, she told me—Afraid to kill

[27] Louis Ginsberg had published a book of poems,   [28] Tranquilizing drug.
The Everlasting Minute.   [29] Russian folk hero.

her, now, that the government knew their names—traced back to Hitler—
wanted to leave Louis' house forever.

One night, sudden attack—her noise in the bathroom—like croaking up her
soul—convulsions and red vomit coming out of her mouth—diarrhea water
exploding from her behind—on all fours in front of the toilet—urine running
between her legs—left retching on the tile floor smeared with her black feces—
unfainted—   140

At forty, varicosed, nude, fat, doomed, hiding outside the apartment door
near the elevator calling Police, yelling for her girl-friend Rose to help—

Once locked herself in with razor or iodine—could hear her cough in tears
at sink—Lou broke through glass green-painted door, we pulled her out to the
bedroom.

Then quiet for months that winter—walks, alone, nearby on Broadway, read
Daily Worker—Broke her arm, fell on icy street—

Began to scheme escape from cosmic financial murder plots—later she ran
away to the Bronx to her sister Elanor. And there's another saga of late Naomi
in New York.

Or thru Elanor or the Workman's Circle, where she worked, addressing
envelopes, she made out—went shopping for Campbell's tomato soup—saved
money Louis mailed her—   145

Later she found a boyfriend, and he was a doctor—Dr. Isaac worked for
National Maritime Union—now Italian bald and pudgy old doll—who was
himself an orphan—but they kicked him out—Old cruelties—

Sloppier, sat around on bed or chair, in corset dreaming to herself—'I'm hot
—I'm getting fat—I used to have such a beautiful figure before I went to the
hospital—You should have seen me in Woodbine—' This in a furnished room
around the NMU[30] hall, 1943.

Looking at naked baby pictures in the magazine—baby powder
advertisements, strained lamb carrots—'I will think nothing but beautiful
thoughts.'

Revolving her head round and round on her neck at window light in
summertime, in hypnotize, in doven[31]-dream recall—

'I touch his cheek, I touch his cheek, he touches my lips with his hand, I
think beautiful thoughts, the baby has a beautiful hand.'—   150

Or a No-shake of her body, disgust—some thought of Buchenwald[32]—some
insulin passes thru her head—a grimace nerve shudder at Involuntary (as
shudder when I piss)—bad chemical in her cortex—'No don't think of that.
He's a rat.'

Naomi: 'And when we die we become an onion, a cabbage, a carrot, or a
squash, a vegetable.' I come downtown from Columbia and agree. She reads the
Bible, thinks beautiful thoughts all day.

---

[30] National Maritime Union.
[31] Daydreaming while moving her head, as in the
motions of chanted (Yiddish) prayer (from the
Yiddish verb *daven*: "to pray").

[32] Nazi concentration camp in Germany.

'Yesterday I saw God. What did he look like? Well, in the afternoon I climbed up a ladder—he has a cheap cabin in the country, like Monroe, NY the chicken farms in the wood. He was a lonely old man with a white beard.

'I cooked supper for him. I made him a nice supper—lentil soup, vegetables, bread & butter—miltz[33]—he sat down at the table and ate, he was sad.

'I told him, Look at all those fightings and killings down there, What's the matter? Why don't you put a stop to it?   155

'I try, he said—That's all he could do, he looked tired. He's a bachelor so long, and he likes lentil soup.'

Serving me meanwhile, a plate of cold fish—chopped raw cabbage dript with tapwater—smelly tomatoes—week-old health food—grated beets & carrots with leaky juice, warm—more and more disconsolate food—I can't eat it for nausea sometimes—the Charity of her hands stinking with Manhattan, madness, desire to please me, cold undercooked fish—pale red near the bones. Her smells —and oft naked in the room, so that I stare ahead, or turn a book ignoring her.

One time I thought she was trying to make me come lay her—flirting to herself at sink—lay back on huge bed that filled most of the room, dress up round her hips, big slash of hair, scars of operations, pancreas, belly wounds, abortions, appendix, stitching of incisions pulling down in the fat like hideous thick zippers[34]—ragged long lips between her legs—What, even, smell of asshole? I was cold—later revolted a little, not much—seemed perhaps a good idea to try—know the Monster of the Beginning Womb—Perhaps—that way. Would she care? She needs a lover.

Yisborach, v'yistabach, v'yispoar, v'yisroman, v'yisnaseh, v'yishador, v'yishalleh, v'yishallol, sh'meh d'kudsho, b'rich hu.[35]

And Louis reestablishing himself in Paterson grimy apartment in negro district—living in dark rooms—but found himself a girl he later married, falling in love again—tho sere & shy—hurt with 20 years Naomi's mad idealism.   160

Once I came home, after longtime in N.Y., he's lonely—sitting in the bedroom, he at desk chair turned round to face me—weeps, tears in red eyes under his glasses—

That we'd left him—Gene gone strangely into army—she out on her own in NY, almost childish in her furnished room. So Louis walked downtown to postoffice to get mail, taught in highschool—stayed at poetry desk, forlorn—ate grief at Bickford's[36] all these years—are gone.

Eugene got out of the Army, came home changed and lone—cut off his nose in jewish operation—for years stopped girls on Broadway for cups of coffee to get laid—Went to NYU,[37] serious there, to finish Law.—

And Gene lived with her, ate naked fishcakes, cheap, while she got crazier—

---

[33] A dairy meal. (Kosher cooking does not mix dairy products and meat.)
[34] This passage will be recapitulated in detail in Part IV of the poem.

[35] Part of the (Hebrew) mourner's Kaddish.
[36] Well-known cafeteria chain.
[37] New York University.

He got thin, or felt helpless, Naomi striking 1920 poses at the moon, half-naked in the next bed,

    bit his nails and studied—was the weird nurse-son—Next year he moved to a room near Columbia—though she wanted to live with her children— 165

    'Listen to your mother's plea, I beg you'—Louis still sending her checks—I was in bughouse that year 8 months—my own visions unmentioned in this here Lament—

    But then went half mad—Hitler in her room, she saw his mustache in the sink—afraid of Dr. Isaac now, suspecting that he was in on the Newark plot— went up to Bronx to live near Elanor's Rheumatic Heart—

    And Uncle Max never got up before noon, tho Naomi at 6 AM was listening to the radio for spies—or searching the windowsill,

    for in the empty lot downstairs, an old man creeps with his bag stuffing packages of garbage in his hanging black overcoat.

    Max's sister Edie works—17 years bookkeeper at Gimbels—lived downstairs in apartment house, divorced—so Edie took in Naomi on Rochambeau Ave— 170

    Woodlawn Cemetery across the street, vast dale of graves where Poe once— Last stop on Bronx subway—lots of communists in that area.

    Who enrolled for painting classes at night in Bronx Adult High School— walked alone under Van Cortlandt Elevated line to class—paints Naomiisms—

    Humans sitting on the grass in some Camp No-Worry summers yore—saints with droopy faces and long-ill-fitting pants, from hospital—

    Brides in front of Lower East Side with short grooms—lost El trains running over the Babylonian apartment rooftops in the Bronx—

    Sad paintings—but she expressed herself. Her mandolin gone, all strings broke in her head, she tried. Toward Beauty? or some old life Message? 175

    But started kicking Elanor, and Elanor had heart trouble—came upstairs and asked her about Spydom for hours,—Elanor frazzled. Max away at office, accounting for cigar stores till at night.

    'I am a great woman—am truly a beautiful soul—and because of that they (Hitler, Grandma, Hearst, the Capitalists, Franco, Daily News, the 20's, Mussolini, the living dead) want to shut me up—Buba's the head of a spider network—'

    Kicking the girls, Edie & Elanor—Woke Edie at midnite to tell her she was a spy and Elanor a rat. Edie worked all day and couldn't take it—She was organizing the union.—And Elanor began dying, upstairs in bed.

    The relatives call me up, she's getting worse—I was the only one left— Went on the subway with Eugene to see her, ate stale fish—

    'My sister whispers in the radio—Louis must be in the apartment—his mother tells him what to say—LIARS!—I cooked for my two children—I played the mandolin—' 180

    Last night the nightingale woke me/Last night when all was still/ it sang in the golden moonlight/ from on the wintry hill. She did.

    I pushed her against the door and shouted 'DON'T KICK ELANOR!'—she

stared at me—Contempt—die—disbelief her sons are so naive, so dumb—
'Elanor is the worst spy! She's taking orders!'

'—No wires in the room!'—I'm yelling at her—last ditch, Eugene listening
on the bed—what can he do to escape that fatal Mama—'You've been away
from Louis years already—Grandma's too old to walk—'

We're all alive at once then—even me & Gene & Naomi in one
mythological Cousinesque room—screaming at each other in the Forever—I in
Columbia jacket, she half undressed.

I banging against her head which saw Radios, Sticks, Hitlers—the gamut of
Hallucinations—for real—her own universe—no road that goes elsewhere—to
my own—No America, not even a world—   185

That you go as all men, as Van Gogh, as mad Hannah, all the same—to the
last doom—Thunder, Spirits, Lightning!

I've seen your grave! O strange Naomi! My own—cracked grave! Shema
Y'Israel[38]—I am Svul Avrum[39]—you—in death?

Your last night in the darkness of the Bronx—I phone-called—thru hospital
to secret police.

That came, when you and I were alone, shrieking at Elanor in my ear—who
breathed hard in her own bed, got thin—

Nor will forget, the doorknock, at your fright of spies,—Law advancing, on
my honor—Eternity entering the room—you running to the bathroom
undressed, hiding in protest from the last heroic fate—   190

staring at my eyes, betrayed—the final cops of madness rescuing me—from
your foot against the broken heart of Elanor,

your voice at Edie weary of Gimbels coming home to broken radio—and
Louis needing a poor divorce, he wants to get married soon—Eugene dreaming,
hiding at 125 St., suing negros for money on crud furniture, defending black
girls—

Protests from the bathroom—Said you were sane—dressing in a cotton robe,
your shoes, then new, your purse and newspaper clippings—no—your honesty—

as you vainly made your lips more real with lipstick, looking in the mirror
to see if the Insanity was Me or a carful of police.

or Grandma spying at 78—Your vision—Her climbing over the walls of the
cemetery with political kidnapper's bag—or what you saw on the walls of the
Bronx, in pink nightgown at midnight, staring out the window on the empty
lot—   195

Ah Rochambeau Ave—Playground of Phantoms—last apartment in the
Bronx for spies—last home for Elanor or Naomi, here these communist sisters
lost their revolution—

'All right—put on your coat Mrs.—let's go—We have the wagon
downstairs—you want to come with her to the station?'

The ride then—held Naomi's hand, and held her head to my breast, I'm

[38] Beginning of prayer in Hebrew service: "Hear,   [39] Ginsberg's Hebrew name: "Israel Abraham."
O Israel."

taller—kissed her and said I did it for the best—Elanor sick—and Max with
heart condition—Needs—

To me—'Why did you do this?'—'Yes Mrs., your son will have to leave
you in an hour'—The Ambulance

came in a few hours—drove off at 4 AM to some Bellevue[40] in the night
downtown—gone to the hospital forever. I saw her led away—she waved, tears
in her eyes.   200

Two years, after a trip to Mexico—bleak in the flat plain near Brentwood,
scrub brush and grass around the unused RR train track to the crazyhouse—

new brick 20 story central building—lost on the vast lawns of madtown on
Long Island—huge cities of the moon.

Asylum spreads out giant wings above the path to a minute black hole—the
door—entrance thru crotch—

I went in—smelt funny—the halls again—up elevator—to a glass door on a
Woman's Ward—to Naomi—Two nurses buxom white—They led her out,
Naomi stared—and I gaspt—She'd had a stroke—

Too thin, shrunk on her bones—age come to Naomi—now broken into
white hair—loose dress on her skeleton—face sunk, old! withered—cheek of
crone—   205

One hand stiff—heaviness of forties & menopause reduced by one heart
stroke, lame now—wrinkles—a scar on her head, the lobotomy—ruin, the hand
dipping downwards to death—

O Russian faced, woman on the grass, your long black hair is crowned with
flowers, the mandolin is on your knees—

Communist beauty, sit here married in the summer among daisies, promised
happiness at hand—

holy mother, now you smile on your love, your world is born anew,
children run naked in the field spotted with dandelions,

they eat in the plum tree grove at the end of the meadow and find a cabin
where a white-haired negro teaches the mystery of his rainbarrel—   210

blessed daughter come to America, I long to hear your voice again,
remembering your mother's music, in the Song of the Natural Front—

O glorious muse that bore me from the womb, gave suck first mystic life &
taught me talk and music, from whose pained head I first took Vision—

Tortured and beaten in the skull—What mad hallucinations of the damned
that drive me out of my own skull to seek Eternity till I find Peace for Thee,
O Poetry—and for all humankind call on the Origin.

Death which is the mother of the universe!—Now wear your nakedness
forever, white flowers in your hair, your marriage sealed behind the sky—no
revolution might destroy that maidenhood—

O beautiful Garbo of my Karma[41]—all photographs from 1920 in Camp

---

[40] Hospital in New York that has become
synonymous with psychiatric commitment.

[41] Destiny (Buddhist).

Nicht-Gedeiget[42] here unchanged—with all the teachers from Newark—Nor
Elanor be gone, nor Max await his specter—nor Louis retire from his High
School—   215

Back! You! Naomi! Skull on you! Gaunt immortality and revolution come
—small broken woman—the ashen indoor eyes of hospitals, ward greyness on
skin—
'Are you a spy?' I sat at the sour table, eyes filling with tears—'Who are
you? Did Louis send you?—The wires—'
in her hair, as she beat on her head—'I'm not a bad girl—don't murder me!
—I hear the ceiling—I raised two children—'
Two years since I'd been there—I started to cry—She stared—nurse broke
up the meeting a moment—I went into the bathroom to hide, against the toilet
white walls
'The Horror' I weeping—to see her again—'The Horror'—as if she were
dead thru funeral rot in—'The Horror!'   220
I came back she yelled more—they led her away—'You're not Allen—' I
watched her face—but she passed by me, not looking—
Opened the door to the ward,—she went thru without a glance back, quiet
suddenly—I stared out—she looked old—the verge of the grave—'All the
Horror!'

Another year, I left NY—on the West Coast in Berkeley cottage dreamed of
her soul—that, thru life, in what form it stood in that body, ashen or maniac,
gone beyond joy—
near its death—with eyes—was my own love in its form, the Naomi, my
mother on earth still—sent her long letter—& wrote hymns to the mad—Work
of the merciful Lord of Poetry.
that causes the broken grass to be green, or the rock to break in grass—or
the Sun to be constant to earth—Sun of all sunflowers and days on bright iron
bridges—what shines on old hospitals—as on my yard—   225
Returning from San Francisco one night, Orlovsky[43] in my room—Whalen[44]
in his peaceful chair—a telegram from Gene, Naomi dead—
Outside I bent my head to the ground under the bushes near the garage—
knew she was better—
at last—not left to look on Earth alone—2 years of solitude—no one, at age
nearing 60—old woman of skulls—once long-tressed Naomi of Bible—
or Ruth who wept in America—Rebecca aged in Newark—David
remembering his Harp, now lawyer at Yale
or Svul Avrum—Israel Abraham—myself—to sing in the wilderness toward
God—O Elohim![45]—so to the end—2 days after her death I got her letter—   230
Strange Prophecies anew! She wrote—'The key is in the window, the key is

[42] Camp "No-Worry" of the Young People's
Socialist League.
[43] Peter Orlovsky, Ginsberg's lover.

[44] Philip Whalen, a California poet.
[45] Hebrew: "Creator" (Genesis).

in the sunlight at the window—I have the key—Get married Allen don't take
drugs—the key is in the bars, in the sunlight in the window.

Love,
your mother

which is Naomi—

HYMMNN[46]

In the world which He has created according to his will Blessed Praised
Magnified Lauded Exalted the Name of the Holy One Blessed is He!   235
In the house in Newark Blessed is He! In the madhouse Blessed is He! In the
   house of Death Blessed is He!
Blessed be He in homosexuality! Blessed be He in Paranoia! Blessed be He in
   the city! Blessed be He in the Book!
Blessed be He who dwells in the shadow! Blessed be He! Blessed be He!
Blessed be you Naomi in tears! Blessed be you Naomi in fears! Blessed Blessed
   Blessed in sickness!
Blessed be you Naomi in Hospitals! Blessed be you Naomi in solitude! Blest be
   your triumph! Blest be your bars! Blest be your last years' loneliness!   240
Blest be your failure! Blest be your stroke! Blest be the close of your eye!
   Blest be the gaunt of your cheek! Blest be your withered thighs!
Blessed be Thee Naomi in Death! Blessed be Death! Blessed be Death!
Blessed be He Who leads all sorrow to Heaven! Blessed be He in the end!
Blessed be He who builds Heaven in Darkness! Blessed Blessed Blessed be He!
   Blessed be He! Blessed be Death on us All!

III

Only to have not forgotten the beginning in which she drank cheap sodas in
   the morgues of Newark,   245
only to have seen her weeping on grey tables in long wards of her universe
only to have known the weird ideas of Hitler at the door, the wires in her
   head, the three big sticks
rammed down her back, the voices in the ceiling shrieking out her ugly early
   lays for 30 years,
only to have seen the time-jumps, memory lapse, the crash of wars, the roar and
   silence of a vast electric shock,
only to have seen her painting crude pictures of Elevateds running over the
   rooftops of the Bronx   250
her brothers dead in Riverside or Russia, her lone in Long Island writing a last
   letter—and her image in the sunlight at the window
'The key is in the sunlight at the window in the bars the key is in the sunlight,'
only to have come to that dark night on iron bed by stroke when the sun gone
   down on Long Island

[46] Ginsberg here imitates the Kaddish's blessing of
God, extending the blessing to all aspects of
life.

and the vast Atlantic roars outside the great call of Being to its own
to come back out of the Nightmare—divided creation—with her head lain on a
    pillow of the hospital to die   255
—in one last glimpse—all Earth one everlasting Light in the familiar blackout
    —no tears for this vision—
But that the key should be left behind—at the window—the key in the
    sunlight—to the living—that can take
that slice of light in hand—and turn the door—and look back see
Creation glistening backwards to the same grave, size of universe,
size of the tick of the hospital's clock on the archway over the white door—   260

IV

O mother
what have I left out
O mother
what have I forgotten
O mother   265
farewell
with a long black shoe
farewell
with Communist Party and a broken stocking
farewell   270
with six dark hairs on the wen of your breast
farewell
with your old dress and a long black beard around the vagina
farewell
with your sagging belly   275
with your fear of Hitler
with your mouth of bad short stories
with your fingers of rotten mandolins
with your arms of fat Paterson porches
with your belly of strikes and smokestacks   280
with your chin of Trotsky and the Spanish War
with your voice singing for the decaying overbroken workers
with your nose of bad lay with your nose of the smell of the pickles of
    Newark
with your eyes
with your eyes of Russia   285
with your eyes of no money
with your eyes of false China
with your eyes of Aunt Elanor
with your eyes of starving India
with your eyes pissing in the park   290
with your eyes of America taking a fall
with your eyes of your failure at the piano
with your eyes of your relatives in California

with your eyes of Ma Rainey[47] dying in an ambulance
with your eyes of Czechoslovakia attacked by robots 295
with your eyes going to painting class at night in the Bronx
with your eyes of the killer Grandma you see on the horizon from the
    Fire-Escape
with your eyes running naked out of the apartment screaming into the hall
with your eyes being led away by policemen to an ambulance
with your eyes strapped down on the operating table 300
with your eyes with the pancreas removed
with your eyes of appendix operation
with your eyes of abortion
with your eyes of ovaries removed
with your eyes of shock 305
with your eyes of lobotomy
with your eyes of divorce
with your eyes of stroke
with your eyes alone
with your eyes 310
with your eyes
with your Death full of Flowers

V

Caw caw caw crows shriek in the white sun over grave stones in Long Island
Lord Lord Lord Naomi underneath this grass my halflife and my own as hers
caw caw my eye be buried in the same Ground where I stand in Angel 315
Lord Lord great Eye that stares on All and moves in a black cloud
caw caw strange cry of Beings flung up into sky over the waving trees
Lord Lord O Grinder of giant Beyonds my voice in a boundless field in Sheol[48]
Caw caw the call of Time rent out of foot and wing an instant in the universe
Lord Lord an echo in the sky the wind through ragged leaves the roar of
    memory 320
caw caw all years my birth a dream caw caw New York the bus the broken
    shoe the vast highschool caw caw all Visions of the Lord
Lord Lord Lord caw caw caw Lord Lord Lord caw caw caw Lord

1961

---

[47] Blues singer (1866–1939).
[48] Hebrew word for the outer darkness into which
souls are cast after death.

The Lion for Real

'Soyez muette pour moi, Idole contemplative . . .'[1]

I came home and found a lion in my living room
Rushed out on the fire-escape screaming Lion! Lion!
Two stenographers pulled their brunette hair and banged the window shut
I hurried home to Paterson and stayed two days.

Called up my old Reichian[2] analyst   5
who'd kicked me out of therapy for smoking marijuana
'It's happened' I panted 'There's a Lion in my room'
'I'm afraid any discussion would have no value' he hung up.

I went to my old boyfriend we got drunk with his girlfriend
I kissed him and announced I had a lion with a mad gleam in my eye   10
We wound up fighting on the floor I bit his eyebrow & he kicked me out
I ended masturbating in his jeep parked in the street moaning 'Lion.'

Found Joey my novelist friend and roared at him 'Lion!'
He looked at me interested and read me his spontaneous ignu high poetries
I listened for lions all I heard was Elephant Tiglon Hippogryph Unicorn Ants   15
But figured he really understood me when we made it in Ignaz Wisdom's
    bathroom.

But next day he sent me a leaf from his Smokey Mountain retreat
'I love you little Bo-Bo with your delicate golden lions
But there being no Self and No Bars therefore the Zoo of your dear Father
    hath no Lion
You said your mother was mad don't expect me to produce the Monster for
    your Bridegroom.'   20

Confused dazed and exalted bethought me of real lion starved in his stink in
    Harlem
Opened the door the room was filled with the bomb blast of his anger
He roaring hungrily at the plaster walls but nobody could hear him outside
    thru the window
My eye caught the edge of the red neighbor apartment building standing in
    deafening stillness

We gazed at each other his implacable yellow eye in the red halo of fur   25
Waxed rheumy on my own but he stopped roaring and bared a fang greeting.

---

[1] French: "Be mute for me, O contemplative Idol."
[2] Form of psychoanalysis promulgated by Wilhelm Reich (1897–1957), inventor of the orgone box.

I turned my back and cooked broccoli for supper on an iron gas stove
boilt water and took a hot bath in the old tub under the sink board.

He didn't eat me, tho I regretted him starving in my presence.
Next week he wasted away a sick rug full of bones wheaten hair falling out   30
enraged and reddening eye as he lay aching huge hairy head on his paws
by the egg-crate bookcase filled up with thin volumes of Plato, & Buddha.

Sat by his side every night averting my eyes from his hungry motheaten face
stopped eating myself he got weaker and roared at night while I had nightmares
Eaten by lion in bookstore on Cosmic Campus, a lion myself starved by
    Professor Kandisky, dying in a lion's flophouse circus,   35
I woke up mornings the lion still added dying on the floor—'Terrible
    Presence!' I cried 'Eat me or die!'

It got up that afternoon—walked to the door with its paw on the wall to
    steady its trembling body
Let out a soul-rending creak from the bottomless roof of his mouth
thundering from my floor to heaven heavier than a volcano at night in Mexico
Pushed the door open and said in a gravelly voice 'Not this time Baby—but I
    will be back again.'   40

Lion that eats my mind now for a decade knowing only your hunger
Not the bliss of your satisfaction O roar of the Universe how am I chosen
In this life I have heard your promise I am ready to die I have served
Your starved and ancient Presence O Lord I wait in my room at your Mercy.
1961

American Change

The first I looked on, after a long time far from home in mid Atlantic on a
    summer day
Dolphins breaking the glassy water under the blue sky,
a gleam of silver in my cabin, fished up out of my jangling new pockets of
    coins and green dollars
    —held in my palm, the head of the feathered indian, old Buck-Rogers eagle
eyed face, a gash of hunger in the cheek
    gritted jaw of the vanished man begone like a Hebrew with hairlock[1]
combed down the side—O Rabbi Indian   5

---

[1] Orthodox Jewish males leave a long side lock
of hair uncut.

what visionary gleam 100 years ago on Buffalo prairie under the molten
cloud shot sky, 'the same clear light 10000 miles in all directions'
 but now with all the violin music of Vienna, gone into the great slot
machine of Kansas City, Reno—
 The coin seemed so small after vast European coppers thick francs leaden
pesetas, lire endless and heavy,
 a miniature primeval memorialized in 5¢. nickel candystore nostalgia of the
redskin, dead on silver coin,
 with shaggy buffalo on reverse, hump-backed little tail incurved, head
butting against the rondure of Eternity,   10
 cock forelock below, bearded shoulder muscle folded below muscle, head of
prophet, bowed,
 vanishing beast of Time, hoar body rubbed clean of wrinkles and shining like
polished stone, bright metal in my forefinger, ridiculous buffalo—Go to New
York.[2]

 Dime next I found, Minerva, sexless cold & chill, ascending goddess of
money—and was it the wife of Wallace Stevens,[3] truly?
 and now from the locks flowing the miniature wings of speedy thought,
 executive dyke,[4] Minerva, goddess of Madison Avenue, forgotten useless dime
that can't buy hot dog, dead dime—   15

 Then we've George Washington, less primitive, the snubnosed quarter, smug
eyes and mouth, some idiot's design of the sexless Father,
 naked down to his neck, a ribbon in his wig, high forehead, Roman line
down the nose, fat-cheeked, still showing his falsetooth ideas—O Eisenhower &
Washington—O Fathers—No movie star dark beauty—O thou Bignoses—
 Quarter, remembered quarter, 40¢. in all—What'll you buy me when I land
—one icecream soda?—

 poor pile of coins, original reminders of the sadness, forgotten money of
America—
 nostalgia of the first touch of those coins, American change,   20
 the memory in my aging hand, the same old silver reflective there,
 the thin dime hidden between my thumb and forefinger
 All the struggles for those coins, the sadness of their reappearance
 my reappearance on those fabled shores
 and the failure of that Dream, that Vision of Money reduced to this
haunting recollection   25
 of the gas lot in Paterson where I found half a dollar gleaming in the grass—

 I have a $5 bill in my pocket—it's Lincoln's sour black head moled
wrinkled, forelocked too, big eared, flags of announcement flying over the bill,
stamps in green and spiderweb black,

---

[2] A joke on Horace Greeley's "Go west, young
man."
[3] Elsie Kachel Stevens, wife of the poet Wallace

Stevens, posed for the head of Minerva (Roman
goddess of wisdom) on the dime.
[4] Lesbian.

long numbers in racetrack green, immense promise, a girl, a hotel, a busride
to Albany, a night of brilliant drunk in some faraway corner of Manhattan
 a stick of several teas,[5] or paper or cap of Heroin, or a $5 strange present to
the blind.
 Money money, reminder, I might as well write poems to you—dear
American money—O statue of Liberty I ride enfolded in money in my mind to
you—and last   30

 Ahhh! Washington again, on the Dollar, same poetic black print, dark
words, The United States of America, innumerable numbers
 R956422481 One Dollar This Certificate is Legal Tender (tender!) for all
debts public and private
 My God My God why have you forsaken me
 Ivy Baker Priest Series 1935 F
 and over, the Eagle, wild wings outspread, halo of the Stars encircled by
puffs of smoke & flame—   35
 a circle the Masonic Pyramid, the sacred Swedenborgian Dollar America,
bricked up to the top, & floating surreal above
 the triangle of holy outstaring Eye sectioned out of the aire, shining
 light emitted from the eyebrowless triangle—and a desert of cactus, scattered
all around, clouds afar,
 this being the Great Seal of our Passion, Annuit Coeptis,[6] Novus Ordo
Seclorum,[7]
 the whole surrounded by green spiderwebs designed by T-Men[8] to prevent
foul counterfeit————   40
ONE

1963

Chances "R"[1]

Nymph and shepherd raise electric tridents
  glowing red against the plaster wall,
The jukebox beating out magic syllables,
A line of painted boys snapping fingers
  & shaking thin Italian trouserlegs   5
    or rough dungarees on big asses
      bumping and dipping
ritually, with no religion but the

---

[5] I.e., marijuana cigarette.
[6] Latin: "He has favored our undertakings."
[7] Latin: "The new order of the world."

[8] U.S. Treasury agents.
[1] A homosexual bar in Kansas.

· old one of cocksuckers
naturally, in Kansas center of America   10
     the farmboys in Diabolic bar light
     alone stiff necked or lined up
     dancing row on row like Afric husbands
& the music's sad here, whereas Sunset Trip or
Jukebox Corner it's ecstatic pinball machines—   15
Religiously, with concentration and free
          prayer; fairy boys of the plains
          and their gay sisters of the city
step together to the center of the floor
        illumined by machine eyes, screaming drumbeats,   20
          passionate voices of Oklahoma City
             chanting No Satisfaction
Suspended from Heaven the Chances R
     Club floats rayed by stars
         along a Wichita tree avenue   25
     traversed with streetlights on the plain.

1968

---

from Mugging

I

Tonite I walked out of my red apartment door on East tenth street's dusk—
Walked out of my home ten years, walked out in my honking neighborhood
Tonite at seven walked out past garbage cans chained to concrete anchors
Walked under black painted fire escapes, giant castiron plate covering a hole in
    ground
—Crossed the street, traffic lite red, thirteen bus roaring by liquor store,   5
past corner pharmacy iron grated, past Coca Cola & My-Lai[1] posters fading
    scraped on brick
Past Chinese Laundry wood door'd, & broken cement stoop steps For Rent hall
    painted green & purple Puerto Rican style
Along E. 10th's glass splattered pavement, kid blacks & Spanish oiled hair
    adolescents' crowded house fronts—
Ah, tonite I walked out on my block NY City under humid summer sky
    Halloween,

---

[1] Site of an atrocity in the Vietnam War.

thinking what happened Timothy Leary[2] joining brain police for a season?   10
thinking what's all this Weathermen,[3] secrecy & selfrighteousness beyond reason
    —F.B.I. plots?
Walked past a taxicab controlling the bottle strewn curb—
past young fellows with their umbrella handles & canes leaning against ravaged
    Buick
—and as I looked at the crowd of kids on the stoop—a boy stepped up, put
    his arm around my neck
tenderly I thought for a moment, squeezed harder, his umbrella handle against
    my skull,   15
and his friends took my arm, a young brown companion tripped his foot 'gainst
    my ankle—
as I went down shouting Om Ah Hūm[4] to gangs of lovers on the stoop
    watching
slowly appreciating, why this is a raid, these strangers mean strange business
with what—my pockets, bald head, broken-healed-bone leg, my softshoes, my
    heart—
Have they knives? Om Ah Hūm—Have they sharp metal wood to shove in eye
    ear ass? Om Ah Hūm   20
& slowly reclined on the pavement, struggling to keep my woolen bag of
    poetry address calendar & Leary-lawyer notes hung from my shoulder
dragged in my neat orlon shirt over the crossbar of a broken metal door
dragged slowly onto the fire-soiled floor an abandoned store, laundry candy
    counter 1929—
now a mess of papers & pillows & plastic covers cracked cockroach-corpsed
    ground—
my wallet back pocket passed over the iron foot step guard   25
and fell out, stole by God Muggers' lost fingers, Strange—
Couldn't tell—snakeskin wallet actually plastic, 70 dollars my bank money for a
    week,
old broken wallet—and dreary plastic contents—Amex card & Manf. Hanover
    Trust Credit too—business card from Mr. Spears British Home Minister
    Drug Squad—my draft card—membership ACLU[5] & Naropa Institute[6]
    Instructor's identification
Om Ah Hūm I continued chanting Om Ah Hūm
Putting my palm on the neck of an 18 year old boy fingering my back pocket
    crying "Where's the money"   30
"Om Ah Hūm there isn't any"
My card Chief Boo-Hoo Neo American Church New Jersey & Lower East
    Side
Om Ah Hūm—what not forgotten crowded wallet—Mobil Credit, Shell? old
    lovers addresses on cardboard pieces, booksellers calling cards—
—"Shut up or we'll murder you"—"Om Ah Hūm take it easy"

---

[2] Professor fired from Harvard University for
espousing drug use.
[3] Revolutionary radical group.

[4] Buddhist chanted prayer (mantra).
[5] American Civil Liberties Union.
[6] Ginsberg's Institute of Poetics.

Lying on the floor shall I shout more loud?—the metal door closed on
   blackness   35
one boy felt my broken healed ankle, looking for hundred dollar bills behind
   my stocking weren't even there—a third boy untied my Seiko Hong Kong
   watch rough from right wrist leaving a clasp-prick skin tiny bruise
"Shut up and we'll get out of here"—and so they left,
as I rose from the cardboard mattress thinking Om Ah Hūm didn't stop em
   enough,
the tone of voice too loud—my shoulder bag with 10,000 dollars full of poetry
   left on the broken floor—
1979

James Merrill
b. 1926

In 1983 James Merrill published two collections. One, called *From the First Nine*,
is a selection of lyrics from his first nine volumes of poetry, and the second, *The
Changing Light at Sandover*, collects the three "books" of his verse trilogy—*The
Book of Ephraim, Mirabell*, and *Scripts for the Pageant*. Merrill's writing has been
advancing on these two fronts—lyric and narrative—since his thirties, but his
first narrative experiments, *The Seraglio* (1957) and *The [Diblos] Notebook* (1965),
were in prose. Merrill's gift for social observation, for the comedy of manners,
appears in both lyric and narrative forms. He is an expert observer of both
ordinary surroundings and the world to which he was born (the New York
world of the very rich). His father, Charles Merrill, founded the Merrill, Lynch
stockbrokerage. His parents were divorced when he was young; he writes about
them in "The Broken Home," and about his lonely childhood in "Lost in
Translation." Merrill's life as an adult has been marked by wide reading, frequent
travel, and an international perspective. He has taught from time to time and is
at present the judge for the Yale Younger Poet series, the series in which his
own first book appeared, chosen by W. H. Auden.

It is the natural tendency of lyric to divest itself of social detail; consequently,
the lyric alone did not suffice for the working out of Merrill's talent. When
Merrill, after the 1960s, abandoned the novel as a narrative medium, he began to
write a conversation-narrative in mixed forms of verse, one that eventually grew
to fill three volumes. The generating medium (or pretext) for the conversation is
the Ouija board, and by means of it Merrill "converses" with dead friends
(including W. H. Auden) as well as with various immortal beings, who
gradually reveal to him a new cosmology, itself perhaps less interesting than the
human interchanges surrounding it.

The trilogy represents one extreme of Merrill's writing. At the other extreme
are lyrics of intense delicacy, delighted complexity, and pained apprehension.
Laughter, pain, and love are the ingredients of Merrill's social comedy, and the
dominant topic of his lyrics is a love tinged by finely discriminated shades of

sensuality. His palette of words is luxuriously rich; he descends from both Keats and Byron, but perhaps most of all from Proust (on whom he did his senior honors thesis at Amherst). The nostalgias of love seen through the filters of memory are a perpetual subject for Merrill; he is a poet of the embarrassments as well as the rewards of desire.

Merrill's *First Poems* (1950), published a few years after his graduation from Amherst College, were already accomplished in technique but oblique in their manner, probably because of his legitimate fear (at a time when homosexuality still had criminal status) of revealing his sexual orientation. Succeeding volumes —*The Country of a Thousand Years of Peace* (1959) and *Water Street* (1962)— widened his canvas. He had left New York City, where he lived after college, for Stonington, Connecticut, and he began to spend part of each year in Greece, where his landscape poetry took on particular brilliance and his love poetry deepened and grew better acquainted with loss. The influence of the modern Greek poet Constantine Cavafy is reflected in *Nights and Days* (1966). In *Braving the Elements* (1972) Merrill included landscape poetry of the American West, where deserts and geodes and cacti give the poems a different barbarism from that of Greece.

Merrill is as tireless as George Herbert (another of his English masters) in the reinvention of poetic forms. His many sonnet sequences (see "Matinees") have redescribed that genre, as they change rhyme-schemes, reshape proportions, and take up surprising levels of diction. Language in Merrill's hands is a gauzy and spangled fabric, a form of enchantment. Merrill is fond of metaphors of shadow play, magician's tents, illusion successfully practiced; he is the "sleight-of-hand man" that Wallace Stevens thought the poet should be.

Under the dense and shimmering glow of language, Merrill treats human experiences—the isolation of childhood, the terrors of betrayal in love, the gaiety and mystery of love rewarded, the fidelities of friendship—that concern everyone; and in his witty self-portrait of the American innocent abroad, he continues a national tradition magisterially exemplified in Henry James. "I feel exotic at home, American abroad," Merrill has said; the uneasy accommodation between the parent continent (with its worldliness and cynicism) and our American naiveté is a constant source of poetry for Merrill.

Merrill has rarely, in lyrics, written free verse; his love for pattern, though it took him at first into some gymnastic exercises perhaps too strict to be called poetry, has proved a revivifying force for the claims of formal verse in a field where free verse, based on an American phrasal rhythm, seemed to have won the day. In admitting worldliness, sophistication, and mixed emotions into his verse, Merrill, even more than Robert Lowell, acts as a civilized poet in the classical tradition, undistorted by the pragmatic American habit of seeing only one side of a question. He has preserved a tone of lightness and discretion and a texture of charm and ease while treating the most profound topics—love and death—proper to lyric.

Further Reading:
R. Labrie, *James Merrill*, 1982.
J. Moffett, *James Merrill: An Introduction to the Poetry*, 1984.

Text:
Selected Poems, 1982.

The Broken Home[1]

Crossing the street,
I saw the parents and the child
At their window, gleaming like fruit
With evening's mild gold leaf.

In a room on the floor below,   5
Sunless, cooler—a brimming
Saucer of wax, marbly and dim—
I have lit what's left of my life.

I have thrown out yesterday's milk
And opened a book of maxims.   10
The flame quickens. The word stirs.

Tell me, tongue of fire,
That you and I are as real
At least as the people upstairs.

My father,[2] who had flown in World War I,   15
Might have continued to invest his life
In cloud banks well above Wall Street and wife.
But the race was run below, and the point was to win.

Too late now, I make out in his blue gaze
(Through the smoked glass of being thirty-six)   20
The soul eclipsed by twin black pupils, sex
And business; time was money in those days.

Each thirteenth year he married. When he died
There were already several chilled wives
In sable orbit—rings, cars, permanent waves.   25
We'd felt him warming up for a green bride.

He could afford it. He was "in his prime"
At three score ten. But money was not time.

When my parents were younger this was a popular act:
A veiled woman would leap from an electric, wine-dark car   30
To the steps of no matter what—the Senate or the Ritz Bar—
And bodily, at newsreel speed, attack

---

[1] The cliché is used with some irony here.
[2] Charles Merrill, who was a financier and founder of the brokerage firm Merrill, Lynch. He and Merrill's mother eventually divorced.

No matter whom—Al Smith or José Maria Sert
Or Clemenceau[3]—veins standing out on her throat
As she yelled *War mongerer! Pig! Give us the vote!,*   35
And would have to be hauled away in her hobble skirt.

What had the man done? Oh, made history.
Her business (he had implied) was giving birth,
Tending the house, mending the socks.

Always that same old story—   40
Father Time and Mother Earth,[4]
A marriage on the rocks.

One afternoon, red, satyr-thighed
Michael, the Irish setter, head
Passionately lowered, led   45
The child I was to a shut door. Inside,

Blinds beat sun from the bed.
The green-gold room throbbed like a bruise.
Under a sheet, clad in taboos
Lay whom we sought, her hair undone, outspread,   50

And of a blackness found, if ever now, in old
Engravings where the acid bit.
I must have needed to touch it
Or the whiteness—was she dead?
Her eyes flew open, startled strange and cold.   55

The dog slumped to the floor. She reached for me. I fled.
Tonight they have stepped out onto the gravel.
The party is over. It's the fall
Of 1931. They love each other still.

She: Charlie, I can't stand the pace.   60
He: Come on, honey—why, you'll bury us all!

A lead soldier guards my windowsill:
Khaki rifle, uniform, and face.
Something in me grows heavy, silvery, pliable.

How intensely people used to feel!   65
Like metal poured at the close of a proletarian novel,
Refined and glowing from the crucible,

---

[3] Alfred E. Smith (1873–1944) and Georges
Clemenceau (1841–1929) were politicians; José
Maria Sert (1876–1945) was a painter.

[4] In mythology, Cronus (Time) and Rhea
(mother of the gods) were the parents of Zeus,
who dethroned his father.

I see those two hearts, I'm afraid,
Still. Cool here in the graveyard of good and evil,
They are even so to be honored and obeyed.   70

. . . Obeyed, at least, inversely. Thus
I rarely buy a newspaper, or vote.
To do so, I have learned, is to invite
The tread of a stone guest[5] within my house.

Shooting this rusted bolt, though, against him,   75
I trust I am no less time's child than some
Who on the heath impersonate Poor Tom[6]
Or on the barricades risk life and limb.

Nor do I try to keep a garden, only
An avocado in a glass of water—   80
Roots pallid, gemmed with air. And later,

When the small gilt leaves have grown
Fleshy and green, I let them die, yes, yes,
And start another. I am earth's no less.

A child, a red dog roam the corridors,   85
Still, of the broken home. No sound. The brilliant
Rag runners halt before wide-open doors.
My old room! Its wallpaper—cream, medallioned
With pink and brown—brings back the first nightmares,
Long summer colds, and Emma, sepia-faced,   90
Perspiring over broth carried upstairs
Aswim with golden fats I could not taste.

The real house became a boarding-school.
Under the ballroom ceiling's allegory
Someone at last may actually be allowed   95
To learn something; or, from my window, cool
With the unstiflement of the entire story,
Watch a red setter[7] stretch and sink in cloud.
1966

---

[5] In Mozart's opera *Don Giovanni* the statue of
the Commendatore, whom Don Giovanni had
murdered, enters the house to seek vengeance.
[6] The name adopted, in Shakespeare's *King Lear,*
by Edgar, disinherited by his father, Gloucester.

[7] There is a pun on *setter*—i.e., the dog and the
setting sun.

Days of 1964[1]

Houses, an embassy, the hospital,
Our neighborhood sun-cured if trembling still
In pools of the night's rain . . .
Across the street that led to the center of town
A steep hill kept one company part way   5
Or could be climbed in twenty minutes
For some literally breathtaking views,
Framed by umbrella pines, of city and sea.
Underfoot, cyclamen, autumn crocus grew
Spangled as with fine sweat among the relics   10
Of good times had by all. If not Olympus,[2]
An out-of-earshot, year-round hillside revel.

I brought home flowers from my climbs.
Kyria[3] Kleo who cleans for us
Put them in water, sighing Virgin, Virgin.   15
Her legs hurt. She wore brown, was fat, past fifty,
And looked like a Palmyra[4] matron
Copied in lard and horsehair. How she loved
You, me, loved us all, the bird, the cat!
I think now she was love. She sighed and glistened   20
All day with it, or pain, or both.
(We did not notably communicate.)
She lived nearby with her pious mother
And wastrel son. She called me her real son.

I paid her generously, I dare say.   25
Love makes one generous. Look at us. We'd known
Each other so briefly that instead of sleeping
We lay whole nights, open, in the lamplight,
And gazed, or traded stories.
One hour comes back—you gasping in my arms   30
With love, or laughter, or both,
I having just remembered and told you
What I'd looked up to see on my way downtown at noon:
Poor old Kleo, her aching legs,
Trudging into the pines. I called,   35

---

[1] The title alludes to poems by the Greek poet
Constantine Cavafy (1863–1933) called "Days
of . . . ." The poem takes place in Athens.
[2] In mythology, the mountain where the gods
lived.

[3] Greek title of address.
[4] Type of sculpture made in ancient Syria, in the
city of Palmyra.

Called three times before she turned.
Above a tight, skyblue sweater, her face
Was painted. Yes. Her face was painted
Clown-white, white of the moon by daylight,
Lidded with pearl, mouth a poinsettia leaf,   40
Eat me, pay me—the erotic mask
Worn the world over by illusion
To weddings of itself and simple need.

Startled mute, we had stared—was love illusion?—
And gone our ways. Next, I was crossing a square   45
In which a moveable outdoor market's
Vegetables, chickens, pottery kept materializing
Through a dream-press of hagglers each at heart
Leery lest he be taken, plucked,
The bird, the flower of that November mildness,   50
Self lost up soft clay paths, or found, foothold,
Where the bud throbs awake
The better to be nipped, self on its knees in mud—
Here I stopped cold, for both our sakes;
And calmer on my way home bought us fruit.   55

Forgive me if you read this. (And may Kyria Kleo,
Should someone ever put it into Greek
And read it aloud to her, forgive me, too.)
I had gone so long without loving,
I hardly knew what I was thinking.   60
Where I hid my face, your touch, quick, merciful,
Blindfolded me. A god breathed from my lips.
If that was illusion, I wanted it to last long;
To dwell, for its daily pittance, with us there,
Cleaning and watering, sighing with love or pain.   65
I hoped it would climb when it needed to the heights
Even of degradation, as I for one
Seemed, those days, to be always climbing
Into a world of wild
Flowers, feasting, tears—or was I falling, legs   70
Buckling, heights, depths,
Into a pool of each night's rain?
But you were everywhere beside me, masked,
As who was not, in laughter, pain, and love.
1966

Matinees

for David Kalstone

A gray maidservant lets me in
To Mrs Livingston's box. It's already begun!
The box is full of grownups. She sits me down
Beside her. Meanwhile a ravishing din

Swells from below—Scene One   5
Of *Das Rheingold.*[1] The entire proscenium
Is covered with a rippling azure scrim.
The three sopranos dart hither and yon

On invisible strings. Cold lights
Cling to bare arms, fair tresses. Flat   10
And natural aglitter like paillettes[2]
Upon the great green sonorous depths float

Until with pulsing wealth the house is filled,
No one believing, everybody thrilled.

Lives of the Great Composers make it sound   15
Too much like cooking: "Sore beset,
He put his heart's blood into that quintet . . ."
So let us try the figure turned around

As in some Lives of Obscure Listeners:
"The strains of Cimarosa[3] and Mozart   20
Flowed through his veins, and fed his solitary heart.
Long beyond adolescence [One infers

Your elimination, sweet Champagne
Drunk between acts!] the aria's[4] remote
Control surviving his worst interval,   25
Tissue of sound and tissue of the brain

Would coalesce, and what the Masters wrote
Itself compose his features sharp and small."

[1] The first of the four operas that make up *The Ring of the Nibelung,* by Richard Wagner (1813–1883). It begins with the song of three mermaids whose Rhine gold has been stolen by the greedy Alberich. The hero, Siegfried, after tasting the blood of the dragon he has slain, can understand the speech of birds. Wotan, the king of the gods, encircles his daughter Brünhilde with a ring of fire as she lies in an enchanted sleep. Merrill refers to these details later in this sequence.
[2] Sequins.
[3] Domenico Cimarosa (1749–1801), Italian composer.
[4] Aria: song in an opera.

Hilariously Dr Scherer[5] took the guise
Of a bland smoothshaven Alberich[6] whose ageold
Plan had been to fill my tooth with gold.
Another whiff of laughing gas,   30

And the understanding was implicit
That we must guard each other, this gold and I,
Against amalgamation by
The elemental pit.   35

Vague as to what dentist and tooth "stood for,"
One patient dreamer gathered something more.
A voice said in the speech of birds,

"My father having tampered with your mouth,
From now on, metal, music, myth   40
Will seem to taint its words."

We love the good, said Plato? He was wrong.
We love as well the wicked and the weak.
Flesh hugs its shaved plush. Twenty-four-hour-long
Galas fill the hulk of the Comique.[7]   45

Flesh knows by now what dishes to avoid,
Tries not to brood on bomb or heart attack.
Anatomy is destiny, said Freud.
Soul is the brilliant hypochondriac.   50

Soul will cough blood and sing, and softer sing,
Drink poison, breathe her joyous last,[8] a waltz
Rubato from his arms who sobs and stays

Behind, death after death, who fairly melts
Watching her turn from him, restored, to fling   55
Kisses into the furnace roaring praise.

The fallen cake, the risen price of meat,
Staircase run ten times up and down like scales
(Greek proverb: He who has no brain has feet)—
One's household opera never palls or fails.   60

---

[5] Merrill's dentist; the child Merrill is giddy from laughing gas.
[6] See footnote 1.
[7] I.e., an opera house in Paris.
[8] Incidents from the opera *La Traviata,* by Giuseppe Verdi (1813–1901).

The pipes' aubade.[9] Recitatives.[10]—Come back!
—I'm out of pills!—We'd love to!—What?—*Nothing*,
Let me be!—No, no, I'll drink it black . . .
The neighbors' chorus. The quick darkening

In which a prostrate figure must inquire   65
With every earmark of its being meant
Why God in Heaven harries him/her so.

The love scene (often cut). The potion. The tableau:
Sleepers folded in a magic fire,
Tongues flickering up from humdrum incident.   70

When Jan Kiepura sang His Handsomeness
Of Mantua[11] those high airs light as lust
Attuned one's bare throat to the dagger-thrust.
Living for them would have been death no less.

Or Lehmann's Marschallin![12]—heartbreak so shrewd,   75
So ostrich-plumed, one ached to disengage
Oneself from a last love, at center stage,
To the beloved's dazzled gratitude.

What havoc certain Saturday afternoons   80
Wrought upon a bright young person's morals
I now leave to the public to condemn.

The point thereafter was to arrange for one's
Own chills and fever, passions and betrayals,
Chiefly in order to make song of them.

You and I, caro,[13] seldom   85
Risk the real thing any more.
It's all too silly or too solemn.
Enough to know the score

From records or transcription
For our four hands. Old beauties, some   90
In advanced stages of decomposition,

---

[9] A dawn song.
[10] The quickly sung narrative portions of an opera between arias.
[11] The duke of Mantua, who seduces women in Verdi's opera *Rigoletto*.

[12] Lotte Lehmann, singing the part of an older woman giving up her young lover in the opera *Der Rosenkavalier*, by Richard Strauss (1864–1949).
[13] Italian: "dear one."

Float up through the sustaining
Pedal's black and fluid medium.
Days like today

Even recur (wind whistling themes   95
From *Lulu*,[14] and sun shining
On the rough Sound) when it seems
Kinder to remember than to play.

Dear Mrs Livingston,
I want to say that I am still in a daze   100
From yesterday afternoon.
I will treasure the experience always—

My very first Grand Opera! It was very
Thoughtful of you to invite
Me and am so sorry   105
That I was late, and for my coughing fit.

I play my record of the Overture
Over and over. I pretend
I am still sitting in the theatre.

I also wrote a poem which my Mother   110
Says I should copy out and send.
Ever gratefully, Your little friend . . .
1969

---

from **In Nine Sleep Valley**

[Geode, the troll's melon]

Geode,[1] the troll's melon
Rind of crystals velvet smoke meat blue
Formed far away under fantastic
Pressures, then cloven in two
By the taciturn rock shop man, twins now forever   5

Will they hunger for each other
When one goes north and one goes east?

---

[14] Modernist erotic opera by Alban Berg
(1885–1935).

[1] Nodule of stone having an inner cavity lined
with crystals.

I expect minerals never do.
Enough for them was a feast
Of flaws, the molten start and glacial sleep,   10
The parting kiss.

Still face to face in halfmoonlight
Sparkling comes easy to the Gemini.[2]

Centimeters deep yawns the abyss.

1972

Syrinx[1]

Bug, flower, bird on slipware[2] fired and fluted,
The summer day breaks everywhere at once.

Worn is the green of things that have known dawns
Before this, and the darkness before them.

Among the wreckage, bent in Christian weeds,   5
Illiterate—X my mark—I tremble, still

A thinking reed.[3] Who puts his mouth to me
Draws out the scale of love and dread—

O ramify, sole antidote![4] Foxglove
Each year, cloud, hornet, fatal growths   10

Proliferating by metastasis
Rooted their total in the gliding stream.

Some formula not relevant any more
To flower children might express it yet

Like $\sqrt{\left(\frac{x}{y}\right)^{n}} = 1$ 15

[2] The heavenly twins, Castor and Pollux.
[1] In mythology, the nymph who, escaping from
Pan, was turned into a reed. Out of the reeds,
Pan made a panpipe and blew through it,
creating music. Merrill turns the reed into a
flute, and Pan into Pain. The poem is spoken
by Syrinx.

[2] A kind of ceramic.
[3] The French philosopher Blaise Pascal
(1623–1662) called man a "thinking reed."
[4] I.e., the reed's music is the only antidote to
life's poisons.

—Or equals zero, one forgets—

The *y* standing for you, dear friend, at least
Until that hour he reaches for me, then

Leaves me cold, the great god Pain,
Letting me slide back into my scarred case   20

Whose silvery breath-tarnished tones
No longer rivet bone and star in place

Or keep from shriveling, leather round a stone,
The sunbather's precocious apricot[5]

Or stop the four winds racing overhead   25

       Nought
   Waste   Eased
      Sought

1972

---

from **The Book of Ephraim**[1]

[L]

Life like the periodical not yet
Defunct kept hitting the stands. We seldom failed
To leaf through each new issue—war, election,
Starlet; write, scratch out; eat steak au poivre,
Chat with Ephraim. Above Water Street   5
Things were advancing in our high retreat.
We patched where snow and rain had come to call,
Renewed the flame upon the mildewed wall.
Unpacked and set in place a bodhisattva[2]
Green with age—its smile, to which clung crumbs   10
Of gold, like traces of a meal,
Proof against the Eisenhower grin
Elsewhere so disarming. Tediums
Ignited into quarrels, each "a scene
From real life," we concluded as we vowed   15

---

[5] Reference to the male genitals.
[1] The poem, composed in 26 stanzas, each headed
by a letter of the alphabet, is named for a dead
Greek who "speaks" to Merrill via the Ouija
board.
[2] Statue of an enlightened Buddhist "saint."

Not to repeat it. People still unmet
Had bought the Baptist church for reconversion.
A slight, silverhaired man in a sarong,
Noticing us from his tower window, bowed.
Down at the point, the little beach we'd missed   20
Crawled with infantry, and wavelets hissed.
Wet sand, as pages turned, covered a skull
Complete with teeth and helmet. Beautiful—
Or were they?—ash-black poppies filled the lens.
Delinquency was rising. Maisie³ made   25
Eyes at shadows—time we had her spayed.
Now from California DJ's⁴ parents
Descended. The nut-brown old maniac
Strode about town haranguing citizens
While Mary, puckered pale by slack   30
Tucks the years had taken, reminisced,
Thread snapping at the least attention paid.
They left no wiser our mysterious East.
David and I lived on, limbs thickening
For better and worse in one another's shade.   35

Remembered, is that summer we came back
Really so unlike the present one?
The friends who stagger clowning through U.S.
Customs in a dozen snapshots old
Enough to vote, so different from us   40
Here, now? Oh god, these days . . .
Thermometer at 90, July haze
Heavy with infamy from Washington.
Impeachment ripens round the furrowed stone
Face of a story-teller⁵ who has given   45
Fiction a bad name (I at least thank heaven
For my executive privilege vis-à-vis
Transcripts of certain private hours with E⁶).
The whole house needs repairs. Neither can bring
Himself to say so. Hardly lingering,   50
We've reached the point, where the tired Sound just washes
Up to, then avoids our feet. One wishes—
I mean we've got this ton of magazines
Which *someone* might persuade the girl who cleans
To throw out. Sunset. On the tower a gull   55
Opens and shuts its beak. Ephemeral
Orange lilies grow beneath like wild.
Our self-effacing neighbor long since willed

---

³ Merrill's cat.   ⁵ I.e., President Richard M. Nixon.
⁴ David Jackson, Merrill's companion.   ⁶ Ephraim.

His dust to them, the church is up for sale.
This evening's dinner: fried soup, jellied sole.   60
Three more weeks, and the stiff upper lip
Of luggage shuts on us. We'll overlap
By winter, somewhere. Meanwhile, no escape
From Greece for me, then Venice . . . D must cope
With the old people, who are fading fast . . .   65
But that's life too. A death's-head to be faced.

No, no! Set in our ways
As in a garden's, glittered
A whole small globe[7]—our life, our life, our life:
Rinsed with mercury   70
Throughout to this bespattered
Fruit of reflection, rife

With Art Nouveau[8] distortion
(Each other, clouds and trees).
What made a mirror flout its flat convention?   75
Surfacing as a solid
Among our crudities,
To toss them like a salad?

And what was the sensation
When stars alone like bees   80
Crawled numbly over it?
And why did all the birds eye it with caution?
It did no harm, just brightly
Kept up appearances.

Not always. On occasion   85
Fatigue or disbelief
Mottled the silver lining.
Then, as it were, our life saw through that craze
Of its own creation
Into another life.   90

Lit by a single candle after dining
TRY THINKING OF THE BEDROOM WALLPAPER
And without having to close my eyes come
Gray-blue irises, wine intervals.
A window gasping back of me. The oil-lamp   95
Twirling white knobs of an unvarnished bureau.

---

[7] I.e., like a silver gazing globe in a garden.
[8] A style of expressive curvilinear forms that
flourished during the 1890s.

It's sunset next. It's no place that I've been.
Outside, the veldt⁹ stops at a red ravine,
The bad pain in my chest grown bearable.
WHO ARE U   A name comes: I'm Rufus . . . Farmer?   100
FARMETTON DEC 1925
December? YES DECEMBER AND   Deceased!
How much of this is my imagination
Sweating to graduate from private school?
I'm in bed. Younger than myself. I can't . . .   105
GO ON   I hear them in the vestibule.
WHO   Peter? YES & Hedwig? PETERS AUNT
And Peter is my . . . YR GREAT HAPPINESS
So, bit by bit, the puzzle's put together
Or else it's disassembled, bit by bit.   110
Hot pebbles. Noon is striking. U HAVE STUMBLED
Upon an entry in a childish hand.
The whole book quivers. Strikes me like a curse:
These clues, so lightly scattered in reverse
Order, aren't they plain from where I stand?   115
The journal lies on Peter's desk. HE NOW
NO LONGER LOCKS HIS ROOM not since my illness,
Heart-room where misgivings gnaw, I *know*.
I've woken. And two eyes, blue, stricken, stare
Back at me through a shock of reddish hair   120
—Can we stop now please? U DID WELL JM
DEATHS ARE TRAUMATIC   FEW REMEMBER THEM

1976

[Z]

Zero hour. Waiting yet again
For someone to fix the furnace. Zero week
Of the year's end. Bed that keeps restlessly
Making itself anew from lamé¹⁰ drifts.
Mercury dropping. Cost of living high.   5
Night has fallen in the glass studio
Upstairs. The fire we huddle with our drinks by
Pops and snaps. Throughout the empty house
(Tenants away until the New Year) taps
Glumly trickling keep the pipes from freezing.   10
Summers ago this whole room was a garden—
Orange tree, plumbago,¹¹ fuchsia, palm;

⁹ A grassland. Merrill imagines himself in Africa.   ¹⁰ Brocaded fabric, often with metallic threads.
He relives his previous incarnation (and death)   ¹¹ Tropical plant with showy flowers.
as one Rufus Farmetton who died December,
1925, the month of Merrill's birth.

One of us at the piano playing his
Gymnopédie,[12] the other entering
Stunned by hot news from the sundeck. Now   15
The plants, the sorry few that linger, scatter
Leaflets advocating euthanasia.
Windows and sliding doors are wadded shut.
A blind raised here and there, what walls us in
Trembles with dim slides, transparencies   20
Of our least motion foisted on a thereby
Realer—falser?—night. Whichever term
Adds its note of tension and relief.
Downstairs, doors are locked against the thief:
Night before last, returning from a dinner,   25
We found my bedroom ransacked, lights on, loud
Tick of alarm, the mirror off its hook
Looking daggers at the ceiling fixture.
A burglar here in the Enchanted Village—
Unheard of! Not that he took anything.   30
We had no television, he no taste
For Siamese bronze or Greek embroidery.
Except perhaps some loose change on the bureau
Nothing we can recollect is missing.
"Lucky boys," declared the chief of police   35
Risking a wise look at our curios.
The threat remains, though, of there still being
A presence in our midst, unknown, unseen,
Unscrupulous to take what he can get.
Next morning in my study—stranger yet—   40
I found a dusty carton out of place.
Had it been rummaged through? What could he fancy
Lay buried here among these—oh my dear,
Letters scrawled by my own hand unable
To keep pace with the tempest in the cup[13]—   45
These old love-letters from the other world.
We've set them down at last beside the fire.
Are they for burning, now that the affair
Has ended? (Has it ended?) Any day
It's them or the piano, says DJ.   50
Who'll ever read them over? Take this one.
Limp, chill, it shivers in the glow, as when
The tenor having braved orchestral fog
First sees Brünnhilde sleeping like a log.[14]

---

[12] Music by Erik Satie, French composer
(1866–1925).
[13] Merrill uses a teacup as a moving pointer on
the Ouija board.

[14] In Wagner's opera *Siegfried* the hero wakens
Brünnhilde from her enchanted sleep, ringed by
magic fire.

Laid on the fire, it would hesitate,   55
Trying to think, to feel—then the elate
Burst of satori,[15] plucking final sense
Boldly from inconclusive evidence.
And that (unless it floated, spangled ash,
Outward, upward, one lone carp aflash   60
Languorously through its habitat
For crumbs that once upon a . . .) would be that.
So, do we burn the—Wait the phone is ringing:
Bad connection; babble of distant talk;
No getting through. We must improve the line   65
In every sense, for life. Again at nine
Sharp above the village clock, *ring-ring*.
It's Bob the furnace man. He's on his way.
Will find, if not an easy-to-repair
Short circuit, then the failure long foreseen   70
As total, of our period machine.
Let's be downstairs, leave all this, put the light out.
Fix a screen to the proscenium
Still flickering. Let that carton be. Too much
Already, here below, has met its match.   75
Yet nothing's gone, or nothing we recall.
And look, the stars have wound in filigree
The ancient, ageless woman of the world.[16]
She's seen us. She is not particular—
Everyone gets her injured, musical   80
"Why do you no longer come to me?"
To which there's no reply. For here we are.
1976

---

from Mirabell: Books of Number

from 9

The world was everything that was the case?[1]
Open the case. Lift out the fabulous
Necklace, in form a spiral molecule[2]
Whose sparklings outmaneuver time, space, us.
Here where the table glistens, cleared, one candle   5

[15] State of Buddhist enlightenment.
[16] I.e., Mother Nature, as later parts of Merrill's poem make clear.
[1] Ludwig Wittgenstein (1889–1951), Austrian philosopher who taught at Cambridge University, wrote in his *Tractatus:* "The world is everything that is the case."
[2] The molecule of DNA, carrying the genetic code in a double helix.

Shines invisibly in the slant light
Beside our nameless houseplant. It's the hour
When Hell (a syllable identified
In childhood as the German word for *bright*
—So that my father's cheerful "Go to Hell",   10
Long unheard, and Vaughan's unbeatable
"They are all gone into a world of light"[3]
Come, even now at times, to the same thing)—
The hour when Hell shall render what it owes.
Render to whom? how? What at this late date   15
Can be done with the quaint idiom that slips
From nowhere to my tongue—or from the parchment
Of some old scribe of the apocalypse—
But render *it* as the long rendering to
Light of this very light stored by our cells   20
These past five million years, these past five minutes
Here by the window, taking in through panes
Still bleary from the hurricane a gull's
Ascending aureole of decibels,
As numberless four-pointed brilliancies   25
Upon the Sound's mild silver grid come, go?
The message hardly needs decoding, so
Sheer the text, so innocent and fleet
These overlapping pandemonia:[4]
Birdlife, leafplay, rockface, waterglow   30
Lending us their being, till the given
Moment comes to render what we owe.

. . . .

1978

Samos[1]

And still, at sea all night, we had a sense
Of sunrise, golden oil poured upon water,
Soothing its heave, letting the sleeper sense
What inborn, amniotic homing sense

---

[3] Poem by the British poet Henry Vaughan
(1622–1695), an elegy on his dead friends.

[4] Places inhabited by many spirits; places where
multiple sensations are present.

[1] One of the Greek islands.

Was ferrying him—now through the dream-fire 5
In which (it has been felt) each human sense
Burns, now through ship's radar's cool sixth sense,
Or mere unerring starlight—to an island.
Here we were. The twins of Sea and Land,
Up and about for hours—hues, cries, scents— 10
Had placed at eye level a single light
Croissant:[2] the harbor glazed with warm pink light.

Fire-wisps were weaving a string bag of light
For sea stones. Their astounding color sense!
Porphyry, alabaster, chrysolite 15
Translucences that go dead in daylight
Asked only the quick dip in holy water
For the saint of cell on cell to come alight—
Illuminated crystals thinking light,
Refracting it, the gray prismatic fire 20
Or yellow-gray of sea's dilute sapphire . . .
Wavelengths daily deeply score the leit-
Motifs[3] of Loom and Wheel upon this land.
To those who listen, it's the Promised Land.

A little spin today? Dirt roads inland 25
Jounce and revolve in a nerve-jangling light,
Doing the ancient dances of the land
Where, gnarled as olive trees that shag the land
With silver, old men—their two-bladed sense
Of spendthrift poverty, the very land 30
Being, if not loaf, tomb—superbly land
Upright on the downbeat. We who water
The local wine, which "drinks itself" like water,
Clap for more, cry out to *be* this island
Licked all over by a white, salt fire, 35
Be noon's pulsing ember raked by fire,

Know nothing, now, but Earth, Air, Water, Fire!
For once out of the frying pan to land
Within their timeless, everlasting fire!
Blood's least red monocle, O magnifier 40
Of the great Eye that sees by its own light
More pictures in "the world's enchanted fire"
Than come and go in any shrewd crossfire
Upon the page, of syllable and sense,

---

[2] French: "crescent."
[3] Leitmotifs: leading motives; i.e., musical themes
often repeated.

We want unwilled excursions and ascents,   45
Crave the upward-rippling rungs of fire,
The outward-rippling rings (enough!) of water . . .
(Now some details—how else will this hold water?)

Our room's three flights above the whitewashed water-
front where Pythagoras[4] was born. A fire   50
Escape of sky-blue iron leads down to water.
Yachts creak on mirror berths, and over water
Voices from Sweden or Somaliland
Tell how this or that one crossed the water
To Ephesus,[5] came back with toilet water   55
And a two kilo box of Turkish delight[6]
—Trifles. Yet they shine with such pure light
In memory, even they, that the eyes water.
As with the setting sun, or innocence,
Do things that fade especially make sense?   60

Samos. We keep trying to make sense
Of what we can. Not souls of the first water—
Although we've put on airs, and taken fire—
We shall be dust of quite another land
Before the seeds here planted come to light.   65

1980

Frank O'Hara
1926–1966

Frank O'Hara died tragically young in a car accident at night on Fire Island,
New York. During his lifetime, his poetry was known in a rather restricted circle
because his poems had come out in small special editions. Only after his death
was his work gathered up, edited by Donald Allen, and published as the *Collected
Poems* (1971). Two more volumes have since been issued: *Early Poems* (1977) and
Poems Retrieved (1977). The first full critical study appeared only in 1979.

The sheer personal charm visible in the poems seems to have been
characteristic of O'Hara in life; every party, according to legend, was better if
O'Hara, with his sense of fun, was present. The people O'Hara knew best were
painters and poets, and, grouped as the "New York school," O'Hara, John
Ashbery, James Schuyler, and Kenneth Koch have been seen as a new movement
in American poetry. This movement borrows from visual artists the sense of

---

[4] Pre-Socratic Greek philosopher who first
discovered that the relation between musical
notes could be expressed mathematically.

[5] Greek city in Asia Minor.
[6] Type of nougat candy.

spontaneity that can enter drawings or graffiti, the amusement that can follow from sketching on a napkin or a memo, the liberation that follows from thinking of art as something one does freely and all the time, rather than something fully "composed" and "finished." By bringing the colloquial, the intimate, the transient, and the quickly observed into poetry, O'Hara and his friends offered an alternative to the constructed or ponderous "philosophical" verse being written by imitators of T. S. Eliot, Wallace Stevens, and Allen Tate. Against the aesthetic that sought philosophical clarification in poetry, O'Hara said:

> What is happening to me, allowing for lies and exaggerations which I try to avoid, goes into my poems. I don't think my experiences are clarified or made beautiful for myself or anyone else, they are just there in whatever form I can find them. What is clear to me in my work is probably obscure to others, and vice versa. . . . It may be that poetry makes life's nebulous events tangible to me and restores their detail; or conversely, that poetry brings forth the intangible quality of incidents which are all too concrete and circumstantial. Or each on specific occasions, or both all the time.

O'Hara wrote candid and happy homosexual love poems, freed from the various tonalities—of secrecy, shame, protestation—that had troubled such verse from Whitman on. He captured the insignificant but momentous meetings of lovers, the pleasures of "having a Coke with you," the joy of dropping in on someone loved. Other poems recorded sudden moments of grief ("The Day Lady Died") or delight ("A Step Away from Them"); others are vignettes full of relish for life in New York.

O'Hara was born in Baltimore and grew up in Worcester, Massachusetts. At Harvard, he majored in English and music, graduating late, in 1950, because of his two-year service in the navy during and after World War II. After a year at the University of Michigan, where he took an M.A. and won the Hopwood Award for poetry, he went to New York and began working for the Museum of Modern Art, where he rose to become an assistant curator in the department of painting and sculpture exhibitions. He also worked as an editor and critic for *Art News.* He was at the center of the explosion of creativity among artists—including Willem de Kooning, Robert Motherwell, Helen Frankenthaler, Jackson Pollock, and Franz Kline—that made New York the art center of the world. Abstract expressionism sought a more "expressionist" warmth, excitement, and depth than had been allowed by pure abstraction, the sort found in Mondrian. The painters' emphasis on color, free movement, and expansive gesture is reflected in O'Hara's longer surrealist poems, where process and exuberant invention tend to dominate.

O'Hara's humor appears in everything he writes, but he is well aware of the classic, serious, lyric tradition and participates in it in his elegies for friends who died, in his love songs, and in his poems about childhood and adolescence—phases with which he never lost touch. He reflects, too, on the differences between his medium and that of his painter friends, continuing in poems like "Why I Am Not a Painter" a lyric topic as old as Horace. In his exuberance, cheerful interest in the sideshow of city life, sophisticated childlikeness, and syncopated rhythms, O'Hara is the descendant of the French Surrealist poets and of E. E. Cummings, their American representative.

Further Reading:
A. Feldman, *Frank O'Hara,* 1979.
M. Perloff, *Frank O'Hara, Poet Among Painters,*
1979.
A. Smith, Jr., *Frank O'Hara: A Comprehensive
Bibliography,* 1979.

Text:
Selected Poems, 1974.

Blocks[1]

1

Yippee! she is shooting in the harbor! he is jumping
up to the maelstrom! she is leaning over the giant's
cart of tears which like a lava cone let fall to fly
from the cross-eyed tantrum-tousled ninth grader's
splayed fist is freezing on the cement! he is throwing   5
up his arms in heavenly desperation, spacious Y of his
tumultuous love-nerves flailing like a poinsettia in
its own nailish storm against the glass door of the
cumulus which is withholding her from these divine
pastures she has filled with the flesh of men as stones!   10
O fatal eagerness!

2

O boy, their childhood was like so many oatmeal cookies.
I need you, you need me, yum, yum. Anon it became suddenly

3

like someone always losing something and never knowing what.
Always so. They were so fond of eating bread and butter and   15
sugar, they were slobs, the mice used to lick the floorboards
after they went to bed, rolling their light tails against
the rattling marbles of granulation. Vivo! the dextrose
those children consumed, lavished, smoked, in their knobby
candy bars. Such pimples! such hardons! such moody loves.   20
And thus they grew like giggling fir trees.

1956

---

[1] These three "blocks" of time represent the sudden eruption of sexual feeling in ninth-graders, the childhood that had preceded it, and the passage from childhood into puberty.

To the Harbormaster

I wanted to be sure to reach you;
though my ship was on the way it got caught
in some moorings. I am always tying up
and then deciding to depart. In storms and
at sunset, with the metallic coils of the tide   5
around my fathomless arms, I am unable
to understand the forms of my vanity
or I am hard alee with my Polish rudder
in my hand and the sun sinking. To
you I offer my hull and the tattered cordage   10
of my will. The terrible channels where
the wind drives me against the brown lips
of the reeds are not all behind me. Yet
I trust the sanity of my vessel; and
if it sinks, it may well be in answer   15
to the reasoning of the eternal voices,
the waves which have kept me from reaching you.
1956

To the Film Industry in Crisis

Not you, lean quarterlies and swarthy periodicals
with your studious incursions toward the pomposity of ants,
nor you, experimental theatre in which Emotive Fruition
is wedding Poetic Insight perpetually, nor you,
promenading Grand Opera, obvious as an ear (though you   5
are close to my heart), but you, Motion Picture Industry,
it's you I love!

In times of crisis, we must all decide again and again whom we love.
And give credit where it's due: not to my starched nurse, who taught me
how to be bad and not bad rather than good (and has lately availed 10
herself of this information), not to the Catholic Church
which is at best an oversolemn introduction to cosmic entertainment,
not to the American Legion, which hates everybody, but to you,
glorious Silver Screen, tragic Technicolor, amorous Cinemascope,
stretching Vistavision and startling Stereophonic Sound, with all   15

your heavenly dimensions and reverberations and iconoclasms! To
Richard Barthelmess as the "tol'able" boy barefoot and in pants,
Jeanette MacDonald of the flaming hair and lips and long, long neck,
Sue Carroll as she sits for eternity on the damaged fender of a car
and smiles, Ginger Rogers with her pageboy bob like a sausage   20
on her shuffling shoulders, peach-melba-voiced Fred Astaire of the feet,
Eric von Stroheim, the seducer of mountain-climbers' gasping spouses,
the Tarzans, each and every one of you (I cannot bring myself to prefer
Johnny Weissmuller to Lex Barker, I cannot!), Mae West in a furry sled,
her bordello radiance and bland remarks, Rudolph Valentino of the moon,   25
its crushing passions, and moonlike, too, the gentle Norma Shearer,
Miriam Hopkins dropping her champagne glass off Joel McCrea's yacht
and crying into the dappled sea, Clark Gable rescuing Gene Tierney
from Russia and Allan Jones rescuing Kitty Carlisle from Harpo Marx,
Cornel Wilde coughing blood on the piano keys while Merle Oberon berates,   30
Marilyn Monroe in her little spike heels reeling through Niagara Falls,
Joseph Cotten puzzling and Orson Welles puzzled and Dolores del Rio
eating orchids for lunch and breaking mirrors, Gloria Swanson reclining,
and Jean Harlow reclining and wiggling, and Alice Faye reclining
and wiggling and singing, Myrna Loy being calm and wise, William Powell   35
in his stunning urbanity, Elizabeth Taylor blossoming, yes, to you

and to all you others, the great, the near-great, the featured, the extras
who pass quickly and return in dreams saying your one or two lines,
my love!
Long may you illumine space with your marvellous appearances, delays   40
and enunciations, and may the money of the world glitteringly cover you
as you rest after a long day under the kleig lights with your faces
in packs' for our edification, the way the clouds come often at night
but the heavens operate on the star system. It is a divine precedent
you perpetuate! Roll on, reels of celluloid, as the great earth rolls on!   45

1956

A Step Away from Them[1]

It's my lunch hour, so I go
for a walk among the hum-colored
cabs.[2] First, down the sidewalk
where laborers feed their dirty

---

[1] Mudpacks to improve the complexion.
[1] O'Hara observes the passersby from a slight
distance.

[2] Yellow cabs, like bumblebees with their
black-on-yellow coloring.

glistening torsos sandwiches   5
and Coca-Cola, with yellow helmets
on. They protect them from falling
bricks, I guess. Then onto the
avenue where skirts are flipping
above heels and blow up over   10
grates. The sun is hot, but the
cabs stir up the air. I look
at bargains in wristwatches. There
are cats playing in sawdust.
                            On   15
to Times Square, where the sign
blows smoke over my head, and higher
the waterfall pours lightly. A
Negro stands in a doorway with a
toothpick, languorously agitating.   20
A blonde chorus girl clicks: he
smiles and rubs his chin. Everything
suddenly honks: it is 12:40 of
a Thursday.
                      Neon in daylight is a   25
great pleasure, as Edwin Denby[3] would
write, as are light bulbs in daylight.
I stop for a cheeseburger at JULIET'S
CORNER. Giulietta Masina, wife of
Federico Fellini, *è bell' attrice.*[4]   30
And chocolate malted. A lady in
foxes[5] on such a day puts her poodle
in a cab.
                There are several Puerto
Ricans on the avenue today, which   35
makes it beautiful and warm. First
Bunny died, then John Latouche,
then Jackson Pollock.[6] But is the
earth as full as life was full, of them?
And one has eaten and one walks,   40
past the magazines with nudes
and the posters for BULLFIGHT and
the Manhattan Storage Warehouse,
which they'll soon tear down. I
used to think they had the Armory   45
Show[7] there.

---

[3] Dance critic.
[4] Italian: "is a fine actress."
[5] I.e., with a fox fur around her neck.
[6] Bunny Lang, John Latouche, and the painter
Jackson Pollock were close friends of O'Hara.

[7] Show of modernist art in 1913 that
revolutionized American painting.

> A glass of papaya juice
> and back to work. My heart is in my
> pocket, it is Poems by Pierre Reverdy.[8]
> *1964*

The Day Lady[1] Died

It is 12:20 in New York a Friday
three days after Bastille day,[2] yes
it is 1959 and I go get a shoeshine
because I will get off the 4:19 in Easthampton
at 7:15 and then go straight to dinner   5
and I don't know the people who will feed me

I walk up the muggy street beginning to sun
and have a hamburger and a malted and buy
an ugly NEW WORLD WRITING to see what the poets
in Ghana are doing these days   10
                              I go on to the bank
and Miss Stillwagon (first name Linda I once heard)
doesn't even look up my balance for once in her life
and in the GOLDEN GRIFFIN I get a little Verlaine[3]
for Patsy with drawings by Bonnard[4] although I do   15
think of Hesiod,[5] trans. Richmond Lattimore or
Brendan Behan's[6] new play or *Le Balcon* or *Les Nègres*
of Genet,[7] but I don't, I stick with Verlaine
after practically going to sleep with quandariness

and for Mike I just stroll into the PARK LANE   20
Liquor Store and ask for a bottle of Strega and
then I go back where I came from to 6th Avenue
and the tobacconist in the Ziegfeld Theatre and
casually ask for a carton of Gauloises and a carton
of Picayunes, and a NEW YORK POST with her face on it   25

---

[8] French poet (1889–1960).
[1] Billie Holliday (1915–1959), American jazz
singer, known as Lady Day.
[2] July 14.
[3] French poet (1844–1896).

[4] French painter (1867–1941).
[5] Greek poet of the eighth century B.C.
[6] Behan: Irish playwright (1923–1964).
[7] French novelist and playwright (b. 1910).

and I am sweating a lot by now and thinking of
leaning on the john door in the 5 SPOT[8]
while she whispered a song along the keyboard
to Mal Waldron and everyone and I stopped breathing

1960

Ave Maria[1]

Mothers of America
                let your kids go to the movies!
get them out of the house so they won't know what you're up to
it's true that fresh air is good for the body
                               but what about the soul   5
that grows in darkness, embossed by silvery images
and when you grow old as grow old you must
                             they won't hate you
they won't criticize you they won't know
                        they'll be in some glamorous country   10
they first saw on a Saturday afternoon or playing hookey
they may even be grateful to you
                    for their first sexual experience
which only cost you a quarter
                        and didn't upset the peaceful home   15
they will know where candy bars come from
                         and gratuitous bags of popcorn
as gratuitous as leaving the movie before it's over
with a pleasant stranger whose apartment is in the Heaven on Earth Bldg
near the Williamsburg Bridge   20
                    oh mothers you will have made the little tykes
so happy because if nobody does pick them up in the movies
they won't know the difference
                    and if somebody does it'll be sheer gravy
and they'll have been truly entertained either way   25
instead of hanging around the yard
                  or up in their room
                            hating you
prematurely since you won't have done anything horribly mean yet
except keeping them from the darker joys   30
                    it's unforgivable the latter

---

[8] Manhattan nightclub noted for its jazz
music.

[1] Latin: "Hail Mary," prayer to the Virgin Mary
saluting her as the Mother of God.

so don't blame me if you won't take this advice

                          and the family breaks up

and your children grow old and blind in front of a TV set

                                    seeing   35

movies you wouldn't let them see when they were young

1964

An Image of Leda[1]

The cinema is cruel
like a miracle. We
sit in the darkened
room asking nothing
of the empty white   5
space but that it
remain pure. And
suddenly despite us
it blackens. Not by
the hand that holds   10
the pen. There is
no message. We our-
selves appear naked
on the river bank
spread-eagled while   15
the machine wings
nearer. We scream
chatter prance and
wash our hair! Is
it our prayer or   20
wish that this
occur? Oh what is
this light that
holds us fast? Our
limbs quicken even   25
to disgrace under
this white eye as
if there were real

[1] Leda, in Greek mythology, was raped by the
god Zeus, who had assumed the form of a
swan.

pleasure in loving
a shadow and caress-   30
ing a disguise!
1971

Poetry

The only way to be quiet
is to be quick, so I scare
you clumsily, or surprise
you with a stab. A praying
mantis knows time more   5
intimately than I and is
more casual. Crickets use
time for accompaniment to
innocent fidgeting. A zebra
races counterclockwise.   10
All this I desire. To
deepen you by my quickness
and delight as if you
were logical and proven,
but still be quiet as if   15
I were used to you; as if
you would never leave me
and were the inexorable
product of my own time.
1971

Why I Am Not a Painter

I am not a painter, I am a poet.
Why? I think I would rather be
a painter, but I am not. Well,

for instance, Mike Goldberg
is starting a painting. I drop in.   5
"Sit down and have a drink" he

says. I drink; we drink. I look
up. "You have SARDINES in it."
"Yes, it needed something there."
"Oh." I go and the days go by   10
and I drop in again. The painting
is going on, and I go, and the days
go by. I drop in. The painting is
finished. "Where's SARDINES?"
All that's left is just   15
letters, "It was too much," Mike says.

But me? One day I am thinking of
a color: orange. I write a line
about orange. Pretty soon it is a
whole page of words, not lines.   20
Then another page. There should be
so much more, not of orange, of
words, of how terrible orange is
and life. Days go by. It is even in
prose, I am a real poet. My poem   25
is finished and I haven't mentioned
orange yet. It's twelve poems, I call
it ORANGES. And one day in a gallery
I see Mike's painting, called SARDINES.

1971

A True Account of Talking
to the Sun at Fire Island

The Sun woke me this morning loud
and clear, saying "Hey! I've been
trying to wake you up for fifteen
minutes. Don't be so rude, you are
only the second poet I've ever chosen   5
to speak to personally

                    so why
aren't you more attentive? If I could
burn you through the window I would
to wake you up. I can't hang around   10
here all day."

               "Sorry, Sun, I stayed
up late last night talking to Hal."

"When I woke up Mayakovsky[1] he was
a lot more prompt", the Sun said   15
petulantly. "Most people are up
already waiting to see if I'm going
to put in an appearance."
                                 I tried
to apologize "I missed you yesterday."   20
"That's better" he said. "I didn't
know you'd come out." "You may be
wondering why I've come so close?"
"Yes" I said beginning to feel hot
wondering if maybe he wasn't burning me   25
anyway.
            "Frankly I wanted to tell you
I like your poetry. I see a lot
on my rounds and you're okay. You may
not be the greatest thing on earth, but   30
you're different. Now, I've heard some
say you're crazy, they being excessively
calm themselves to my mind, and other
crazy poets think that you're a boring
reactionary. Not me.   35
                     Just keep on
like I do and pay no attention. You'll
find that people always will complain
about the atmosphere, either too hot
or too cold too bright or too dark, days   40
too short or too long.
                        If you don't appear
at all one day they think you're lazy
or dead. Just keep right on, I like it.

And don't worry about your lineage   45
poetic or natural. The Sun shines on
the jungle, you know, on the tundra
the sea, the ghetto. Wherever you were
I knew it and saw you moving. I was waiting
for you to get to work.   50

                            And now that you
are making your own days, so to speak,
even if no one reads you but me
you won't be depressed. Not
everyone can look up, even at me. It   55
hurts their eyes."
                        "Oh Sun, I'm so grateful to you!"

---

[1] Russian poet (1894–1930).

"Thanks and remember I'm watching. It's
easier for me to speak to you out
here. I don't have to slide down   60
between buildings to get your ear.
I know you love Manhattan, but
you ought to look up more often.

                           And
always embrace things, people earth   65
sky stars, as I do, freely and with
the appropriate sense of space. That
is your inclination, known in the heavens
and you should follow it to hell, if
necessary, which I doubt.   70
                        Maybe we'll
speak again in Africa, of which I too
am specially fond. Go back to sleep now
Frank, and I may leave a tiny poem
in that brain of yours as my farewell."   75

"Sun, don't go!" I was awake
at last. "No, go I must, they're calling
me."
        "Who are they?"
                      Rising he said "Some   80
day you'll know. They're calling to you
too." Darkly he rose, and then I slept.

1971

First Dances[1]

1

From behind he takes her waist
and lifts her, her lavender waist
stained with tears and her mascara
is running, her neck is tired
from drooping. She floats she steps   5
automatically correct, then suddenly
she is alive up there and smiles.
How much greater triumph for him

[1] A ballet recital by young dancers, a high school
dance, and an unspecified third dance.

that she had so despaired when his
hands encircled her like a pillar   10
and lifted her into the air
which after him will turn to rock-
like boredom, but not till after
many hims and he will not be there.

2

The punch bowl was near the cloakroom   15
so the pints could be taken out of the
boys' cloaks and dumped into the punch.
Outside the branches beat hysterically
towards the chandeliers, just fended
off by fearful windows. The chandeliers   20
giggle a little. There were many
introductions but few invitations. I
found a spot of paint on my coat as
others found pimples. It is easy to
dance it is even easy to dance together   25
sometimes. We were very young and ugly
we knew it, everybody knew it.

3

A white hall inside a church. Nerves.
1971

John Ashbery
b. 1927

John Ashbery's poems resemble a score for performance by the reader. Some
experience of interest, depth, and importance is being retold—a journey, a
catastrophe, a loss—but we are given the general outline rather than the specific
details. Ashbery invites us to involve ourselves in the flow of events, filling in
from our own past the appropriate incidents. The disturbances of life, its energies
and hates, are transformed into the towers and "lacustrine cities" of art, "things
offered," the poet says to his reader, "to your participation." Since the grid of
human experience takes on repetitive patterns, Ashbery trusts to an aesthetic of
algebraic outline expressed in his masterly syntax and invokes the cooperation of
his reader in following his graph. A poem by Ashbery is the occasion for a
dazzling unfolding of inventive language, which borrows from popular sources
like slang and advertising as well as from intellectual sources like art history and
theater. It is impossible to predict what color or shape or tone an Ashbery poem

will take on next; the configurations in his kaleidoscope fall into new shapes as the poem turns.

Ashbery's own training centered on language, literature, theater, and the visual arts. His early years were spent on a farm in upstate New York. After preparing at Deerfield Academy, he attended Harvard (B.A., 1949) and then took an M.A. in English at Columbia. Later, a Fulbright scholarship took him to Montpellier and Paris (1955–1957). In 1958, living in Paris, he became the art critic for the *International Herald Tribune* and wrote reviews of art shows for *Art News* and *Arts International.* After his return to America in 1965, he served until 1972 as executive editor of *Art News;* he is currently the art critic for *Newsweek.* Recently he has taught creative writing at Brooklyn College.

Ashbery's lyrical first volume, *Some Trees* (1956), selected by W. H. Auden for the Yale Younger Poet series, was followed by the unsettling collection *The Tennis Court Oath* (1962), in which many of the poems, notably "Europe," were baffling in their discontinuity, allusiveness, and surreal effects. With *Rivers and Mountains* (1966), Ashbery assumed the cursive, seductive, musical style with which he is now identified. Together with Frank O'Hara (a close friend), he drew poetry away from the deliberateness of Eliot's diction and into the mainstream of urbane American conversational exchange.

Ashbery's poetry has been influenced by our century's experiments in the visual arts, notably cubism and abstraction. Cubism in sculpture suggested that the various forms of the world could be schematized into elementary geometric forms; cubism in painting (as in Picasso's paintings, where we see a profile superimposed on a full face) suggested that any number of perspectives of an object are "true" and that we should attempt to keep all views in mind at once. Ashbery's preference for an elemental outline may be seen as a recourse to a cubist simplicity, while his frequent (and often unsettling) changes of perspective may derive from the multiplicity of perspectives visible, for instance, in Picasso. Other aspects of modern art—the playfulness of Klee, the cartoon sketches of Matisse, the parodic elements of the Dada movement—have all created a revolution that has passed, in linguistic form, into Ashbery's daring loosening of the usual structures of writing. But his liberties with metaphor and pronominal reference (indebted perhaps to the experiments of Gertrude Stein) accompany a deeply traditional sense of the historic genres of poetry in English. Ashbery's use of forms like the sonnet and the sestina; his obedience to the conventions of the elegy, of love poetry, of the ode, and of the landscape poem; and his frequent allusions to his predecessors (especially Keats, Eliot, Stevens, and Auden) establish his homage to the perennial life of poetry.

Ashbery's attention turns frequently to self-reflective poetry, in which he examines the conditions of creation for the contemporary poet. "Our question of a place of origin hangs / Like smoke," he writes; the poet no longer thinks that in creating he imitates the divine freedom of God. Art is a repetitive traditional function but contains an inner freedom:

> So I cradle this average violin that knows
> Only forgotten showtunes, but argues
> The possibility of free declamation anchored
> To a dull refrain.

The function of art is to be a deposit of human physicality, sexuality, and material culture; to affect by its presence the landscape around it; and to serve as a means of self-creation:

[We] left
Our trash, sperm and excrement everywhere, smeared
On the landscape, to make of us what we could.

Art is the "pyrography"—writing (or playing) with fire—undertaken by the artist while life continues its circular journey. In spite of the absence of an origin or goal, life still presents itself to us, Ashbery suggests, as precious and worthy of preservation, so we must "model all these unimportant details" and include them if art is truly to represent the ephemeral truths of culture.

In his love poetry, Ashbery creates compelling sketches of loss, betrayal, and fidelity: Other wagons may go on to the gold rush, "But we stay behind, among them, / The injured, the adored." Lovers keep trying "to get it right," to phrase, in the midst of a night's attrition, their "notes to each other, always repeated, always the same." Ashbery can be brutal as well as tender; his light exploratory tones, his jokes, his parodies often mask the harshness of his vision, as when he imagines life as a damaged carousel constantly climbed onto by blighted supplicants ("Landscapeople"). The end is certain; but at least, like a medieval illuminator, the poet ornaments the black-letter text of life, "filling up the margins of the days / With pictures of fruit, light, colors, music, and vines, / Until it ceases to be a problem."

In recent years, Ashbery has continued his inventiveness, not only in the brilliant prose poems of *Three Poems* (1972) but also in the Pulitzer Prize–winning *Self-portrait in a Convex Mirror* (1975), the lyrics of *Houseboat Days* (1977), the double-column long poem "Litany" in *As We Know* (1979), the unrhymed "sonnets" of *Shadow Train* (1981), and the elegiac title poem of *A Wave* (1984).

Further Reading:
D. Shapiro, *John Ashbery: An Introduction to the Poetry,* 1979.
Beyond Amazement: New Essays on John Ashbery, ed. D. Lehman, 1980.

Texts:
"The Orioles," "Some Trees," and "The Painter" from *Some Trees,* 1956.
"These Lacustrine Cities" from *Rivers and Mountains,* 1966.
"Soonest Mended" and "Years of Indiscretion" from *The Double Dream of Spring,* 1970.
"As One Put Drunk into the Packet-Boat" and "The One Thing That Can Save America" from *Self-portrait in a Convex Mirror,* 1975.
"Street Musicians," "Pyrography," and "Syringa" from *Houseboat Days,* 1977.
"Many Wagons Ago," "A Love Poem," and "Landscapeople" from *As We Know,* 1979.
"Drunken Americans" from *Shadow Train,* 1981.

The Orioles

What time the orioles came flying
Back to the homes, over the silvery dikes and seas,
The sad spring melted at a leap,
The shining clouds came over the hills to meet them.

The old house guards its memories, the birds   5
Stream over colored snow in summer
Or back into the magic rising sun in winter.
They cluster at the feeding station, and rags of song

Greet the neighbors. "Was that your voice?"
And in spring the mad caroling continues long after daylight   10
As each builds his hanging nest
Of pliant twigs and the softest moss and grasses.

But one morning you get up and the vermilion-colored
Messenger is there, bigger than life at the window.
"I take my leave of you; now I fly away   15
To the sunny reeds and marshes of my winter home."

And that night you gaze moodily
At the moonlit apple-blossoms, for of course
Horror and repulsion do exist! They do! And you wonder,
How long will the perfumed dung, the sunlit clouds cover my heart?   20

And then some morning when the snow is flying
Or it lines the black fir-trees, the light cries,
The excited songs start up in the yard!
The feeding station is glad to receive its guests,

But how long can the stopover last?   25
The cold begins when the last song retires,
And even when they fly against the trees in bright formation
You know the peace they brought was long overdue.
1956

Some Trees

These are amazing: each
Joining a neighbor, as though speech
Were a still performance.
Arranging by chance

To meet as far this morning   5
From the world as agreeing
With it, you and I
Are suddenly what the trees try

To tell us we are:
That their merely being there   10
Means something; that soon
We may touch, love, explain.

And glad not to have invented
Such comeliness, we are surrounded:
A silence already filled with noises,   15
A canvas on which emerges

A chorus of smiles, a winter morning.
Placed in a puzzling light, and moving,
Our days put on such reticence
These accents seem their own defense.   20

1956

The Painter

Sitting between the sea and the buildings
He enjoyed painting the sea's portrait.
But just as children imagine a prayer
Is merely silence, he expected his subject
To rush up the sand, and, seizing a brush,   5
Plaster its own portrait on the canvas.

So there was never any paint on his canvas
Until the people who lived in the buildings

Put him to work: "Try using the brush
As a means to an end. Select, for a portrait,   10
Something less angry and large, and more subject
To a painter's moods, or, perhaps, to a prayer."

How could he explain to them his prayer
That nature, not art, might usurp the canvas?
He chose his wife for a new subject,   15
Making her vast, like ruined buildings,
As if, forgetting itself, the portrait
Had expressed itself without a brush.

Slightly encouraged, he dipped his brush
In the sea, murmuring a heartfelt prayer: 20
"My soul, when I paint this next portrait
Let it be you who wrecks the canvas."
The news spread like wildfire through the buildings:
He had gone back to the sea for his subject.

Imagine a painter crucified by his subject!   25
Too exhausted even to lift his brush,
He provoked some artists leaning from the buildings
To malicious mirth: "We haven't a prayer
Now, of putting ourselves on canvas,
Or getting the sea to sit for a portrait!"   30

Others declared it a self-portrait.
Finally all indications of a subject
Began to fade, leaving the canvas
Perfectly white. He put down the brush.
At once a howl, that was also a prayer,   35
Arose from the overcrowded buildings.

They tossed him, the portrait, from the tallest of the buildings;
And the sea devoured the canvas and the brush
As though his subject had decided to remain a prayer.
1956

These Lacustrine[1] Cities

These lacustrine cities grew out of loathing
Into something forgetful, although angry with history.
They are the product of an idea: that man is horrible, for instance,
Though this is only one example.

They emerged until a tower   5
Controlled the sky, and with artifice dipped back
Into the past for swans and tapering branches,
Burning, until all that hate was transformed into useless love.

Then you are left with an idea of yourself
And the feeling of ascending emptiness of the afternoon   10
Which must be charged to the embarrassment of others
Who fly by you like beacons.

The night is a sentinel.
Much of your time has been occupied by creative games
Until now, but we have all-inclusive plans for you.   15
We had thought, for instance, of sending you to the middle of the desert,

To a violent sea, or of having the closeness of the others be air
To you, pressing you back into a startled dream
As sea-breezes greet a child's face.
But the past is already here, and you are nursing some private project. 20

The worst is not over, yet I know
You will be happy here. Because of the logic
Of your situation, which is something no climate can outsmart.
Tender and insouciant by turns, you see

You have built a mountain of something,   25
Thoughtfully pouring all your energy into this single monument,
Whose wind is desire starching a petal,
Whose disappointment broke into a rainbow of tears.

1966

---

[1] Built on stilts in lakes.

Soonest Mended

Barely tolerated, living on the margin
In our technological society, we were always having to be rescued
On the brink of destruction, like heroines in *Orlando Furioso*[1]
Before it was time to start all over again.
There would be thunder in the bushes, a rustling of coils,   5
And Angelica, in the Ingres[2] painting, was considering
The colorful but small monster near her toe, as though wondering whether
    forgetting
The whole thing might not, in the end, be the only solution.
And then there always came a time when
Happy Hooligan[3] in his rusted green automobile   10
Came plowing down the course, just to make sure everything was O.K.,
Only by that time we were in another chapter and confused
About how to receive this latest piece of information.
Was it information? Weren't we rather acting this out
For someone else's benefit, thoughts in a mind   15
With room enough and to spare for our little problems (so they began to
    seem),
Our daily quandary about food and the rent and bills to be paid?
To reduce all this to a small variant,
To step free at last, minuscule on the gigantic plateau—
This was our ambition: to be small and clear and free.   20
Alas, the summer's energy wanes quickly,
A moment and it is gone. And no longer
May we make the necessary arrangements, simple as they are.
Our star was brighter perhaps when it had water in it.
Now there is no question even of that, but only   25
Of holding on to the hard earth so as not to get thrown off,
With an occasional dream, a vision: a robin flies across
The upper corner of the window, you brush your hair away
And cannot quite see, or a wound will flash
Against the sweet faces of the others, something like: 30
This is what you wanted to hear, so why
Did you think of listening to something else? We are all talkers
It is true, but underneath the talk lies
The moving and not wanting to be moved, the loose
Meaning, untidy and simple like a threshing floor.   35

---

[1] Epic (1532) by Lodovico Ariosto (1474–1533),   [2] French painter (1780–1867).
of which the heroine is Angelica.   [3] Comic strip character.

These then were some hazards of the course,
Yet though we knew the course *was* hazards and nothing else
It was still a shock when, almost a quarter of a century later,
The clarity of the rules dawned on you for the first time.
They were the players, and we who had struggled at the game   40
Were merely spectators, though subject to its vicissitudes
And moving with it out of the tearful stadium, borne on shoulders, at last.
Night after night this message returns, repeated
In the flickering bulbs of the sky, raised past us, taken away from us,
Yet ours over and over until the end that is past truth,   45
The being of our sentences, in the climate that fostered them,
Not ours to own, like a book, but to be with, and sometimes
To be without, alone and desperate.
But the fantasy makes it ours, a kind of fence-sitting
Raised to the level of an esthetic ideal. These were moments, years,   50
Solid with reality, faces, namable events, kisses, heroic acts,
But like the friendly beginning of a geometrical progression
Not too reassuring, as though meaning could be cast aside some day
When it had been outgrown. Better, you said, to stay cowering
Like this in the early lessons, since the promise of learning   55
Is a delusion, and I agreed, adding that
Tomorrow would alter the sense of what had already been learned,
That the learning process is extended in this way, so that from this standpoint
None of us ever graduates from college,
For time is an emulsion, and probably thinking not to grow up   60
Is the brightest kind of maturity for us, right now at any rate.
And you see, both of us were right, though nothing
Has somehow come to nothing; the avatars[4]
Of our conforming to the rules and living
Around the home have made—well, in a sense, "good citizens" of us,   65
Brushing the teeth and all that, and learning to accept
The charity of the hard moments as they are doled out,
For this is action, this not being sure, this careless
Preparing, sowing the seeds crooked in the furrow,
Making ready to forget, and always coming back   70
To the mooring of starting out, that day so long ago.

1970

---

[4] Embodiments.

Years of Indiscretion

Whatever your eye alights on this morning is yours:
Dotted rhythms of colors as they fade to the color,
A gray agate, translucent and firm, with nothing
Beyond its purifying reach. It's all there.
These are things offered to your participation.   5

These pebbles in a row are the seasons.
This is a house in which you may wish to live.
There are more than any of us to choose from
But each must live its own time.

And with the urging of the year each hastens onward separately   10
In strange sensations of emptiness, anguish, romantic
Outbursts, visions and wraiths. One meeting
Cancels another. "The seven-league boot
Gliding hither and thither of its own accord"
Salutes these forms for what they now are: 15

Fables that time invents
To explain its passing. They entertain
The very young and the very old, and not
One's standing up in them to shoulder
Task and vision, vision in the form of a task   20
So that the present seems like yesterday
And yesterday the place where we left off a little while ago.
1970

As One Put Drunk
into the Packet-Boat[1]

I tried each thing, only some were immortal and free.
Elsewhere we are as sitting in a place where sunlight
Filters down, a little at a time,

---

[1] Borrowed from the first line of the poem
"Tom May's Death" by Andrew Marvell
(1621–1678).

Waiting for someone to come. Harsh words are spoken,
As the sun yellows the green of the maple tree. . . .   5

So this was all, but obscurely
I felt the stirrings of new breath in the pages
Which all winter long had smelled like an old catalogue.
New sentences were starting up. But the summer
Was well along, not yet past the mid-point   10
But full and dark with the promise of that fullness,
That time when one can no longer wander away
And even the least attentive fall silent
To watch the thing that is prepared to happen.

A look of glass stops you   15
And you walk on shaken: was I the perceived?
Did they notice me, this time, as I am,
Or is it postponed again? The children
Still at their games, clouds that arise with a swift
Impatience in the afternoon sky, then dissipate   20
As limpid, dense twilight comes.
Only in that tooting of a horn
Down there, for a moment, I thought
The great, formal affair was beginning, orchestrated,
Its colors concentrated in a glance, a ballade[2]   25
That takes in the whole world, now, but lightly,
Still lightly, but with wide authority and tact.

The prevalence of those gray flakes falling?
They are sun motes. You have slept in the sun
Longer than the sphinx, and are none the wiser for it.   30
Come in. And I thought a shadow fell across the door
But it was only her come to ask once more
If I was coming in, and not to hurry in case I wasn't.

The night sheen takes over. A moon of cistercian[3] pallor
Has climbed to the center of heaven, installed,   35
Finally involved with the business of darkness.
And a sigh heaves from all the small things on earth,
The books, the papers, the old garters and union-suit buttons
Kept in a white cardboard box somewhere, and all the lower
Versions of cities flattened under the equalizing night.   40
The summer demands and takes away too much,
But night, the reserved, the reticent, gives more than it takes.

1975

---

[2] Musical composition, usually for piano.
[3] I.e., the color of unbleached white robes worn
by Cistercian monks.

The One Thing That Can Save America

Is anything central?
Orchards flung out on the land,
Urban forests, rustic plantations, knee-high hills?
Are place names central?
Elm Grove, Adcock Corner, Story Book Farm?   5
As they concur with a rush at eye level
Beating themselves into eyes which have had enough
Thank you, no more thank you.
And they come on like scenery mingled with darkness
The damp plains, overgrown suburbs,   10
Places of known civic pride, of civil obscurity.

These are connected to my version of America
But the juice is elsewhere.
This morning as I walked out of your room
After breakfast crosshatched with   15
Backward and forward glances, backward into light,
Forward into unfamiliar light,
Was it our doing, and was it
The material, the lumber of life, or of lives
We were measuring, counting?   20
A mood soon to be forgotten
In crossed girders of light, cool downtown shadow
In this morning that has seized us again?

I know that I braid too much my own
Snapped-off perceptions of things as they come to me.   25
They are private and always will be.
Where then are the private turns of event
Destined to boom later like golden chimes
Released over a city from a highest tower?
The quirky things that happen to me, and I tell you,   30
And you instantly know what I mean?
What remote orchard reached by winding roads
Hides them? Where are these roots?

It is the lumps and trials
That tell us whether we shall be known   35
And whether our fate can be exemplary, like a star.
All the rest is waiting

For a letter that never arrives,
Day after day, the exasperation
Until finally you have ripped it open not knowing what it is,   40
The two envelope halves lying on a plate.
The message was wise, and seemingly
Dictated a long time ago.
Its truth is timeless, but its time has still
Not arrived, telling of danger, and the mostly limited   45
Steps that can be taken against danger
Now and in the future, in cool yards,
In quiet small houses in the country,
Our country, in fenced areas, in cool shady streets.

1975

Street Musicians

One died, and the soul was wrenched out
Of the other in life, who, walking the streets
Wrapped in an identity like a coat, sees on and on
The same corners, volumetrics,¹ shadows
Under trees. Farther than anyone was ever   5
Called, through increasingly suburban airs
And ways, with autumn falling over everything:
The plush leaves the chattels in barrels
Of an obscure family being evicted
Into the way it was, and is. The other beached   10
Glimpses of what the other was up to:
Revelations at last. So they grew to hate and forget each other.

So I cradle this average violin that knows
Only forgotten showtunes, but argues
The possibility of free declamation anchored   15
To a dull refrain, the year turning over on itself
In November, with the spaces among the days
More literal, the meat more visible on the bone.
Our question of a place of origin hangs
Like smoke: how we picnicked in pine forests,   20
In coves with the water always seeping up, and left
Our trash, sperm and excrement everywhere, smeared
On the landscape, to make of us what we could.

1977

¹ Measurement of volumes.

Pyrography[1]

Out here on Cottage Grove it matters. The galloping
Wind balks at its shadow. The carriages
Are drawn forward under a sky of fumed oak.
This is America calling:
The mirroring of state to state,   5
Of voice to voice on the wires,
The force of colloquial greetings like golden
Pollen sinking on the afternoon breeze.
In service stairs the sweet corruption thrives;
The page of dusk turns like a creaking revolving stage in Warren, Ohio.   10

If this is the way it is let's leave,
They agree, and soon the slow boxcar journey begins,
Gradually accelerating until the gyrating fans of suburbs
Enfolding the darkness of cities are remembered
Only as a recurring tic. And midway   15
We meet the disappointed, returning ones, without its
Being able to stop us in the headlong night
Toward the nothing of the coast. At Bolinas
The houses doze and seem to wonder why through the
Pacific haze, and the dreams alternately glow and grow dull.   20
Why be hanging on here? Like kites, circling,
Slipping on a ramp of air, but always circling?

But the variable cloudiness is pouring it on,
Flooding back to you like the meaning of a joke.
The land wasn't immediately appealing; we built it   25
Partly over with fake ruins, in the image of ourselves:
An arch that terminates in mid-keystone, a crumbling stone pier
For laundresses, an open-air theater, never completed
And only partially designed. How are we to inhabit
This space from which the fourth wall is invariably missing,   30
As in a stage-set or dollhouse, except by staying as we are,
In lost profile, facing the stars, with dozens of as yet
Unrealized projects, and a strict sense
Of time running out, of evening presenting
The tactfully folded-over bill? And we fit   35
Rather too easily into it, become transparent,
Almost ghosts. One day
The birds and animals in the pasture have absorbed

[1] The art of using fire to etch patterns on wood.

The color, the density of the surroundings,
The leaves are alive, and too heavy with life.   40

A long period of adjustment followed.
In the cities at the turn of the century they knew about it
But were careful not to let on as the iceman and the milkman
Disappeared down the block and the postman shouted
His daily rounds. The children under the trees knew it   45
But all the fathers returning home
On streetcars after a satisfying day at the office undid it:
The climate was still floral and all the wallpaper
In a million homes all over the land conspired to hide it.
One day we thought of painted furniture, of how   50
It just slightly changes everything in the room
And in the yard outside, and how, if we were going
To be able to write the history of our time, starting with today,
It would be necessary to model all these unimportant details
So as to be able to include them; otherwise the narrative   55
Would have that flat, sandpapered look the sky gets
Out in the middle west toward the end of summer,
The look of wanting to back out before the argument
Has been resolved, and at the same time to save appearances
So that tomorrow will be pure. Therefore, since we have to do our business   60
In spite of things, why not make it in spite of everything?
That way, maybe the feeble lakes and swamps
Of the back country will get plugged into the circuit
And not just the major events but the whole incredible
Mass of everything happening simultaneously and pairing off,   65
Channeling itself into history, will unroll
As carefully and as casually as a conversation in the next room,
And the purity of today will invest us like a breeze,
Only be hard, spare, ironical: something one can
Tip one's hat to and still get some use out of.   70

The parade is turning into our street.
My stars, the burnished uniforms and prismatic
Features of this instant belong here. The land
Is pulling away from the magic, glittering coastal towns
To an aforementioned rendezvous with August and December.   75
The hunch is it will always be this way,
The look, the way things first scared you
In the night light, and later turned out to be,
Yet still capable, all the same, of a narrow fidelity
To what you and they wanted to become;   80
No sighs like Russian music, only a vast unravelling
Out toward the junctions and to the darkness beyond
To these bare fields, built at today's expense.

1977

Syringa[1]

Orpheus[2] liked the glad personal quality
Of the things beneath the sky. Of course, Eurydice was a part
Of this. Then one day, everything changed. He rends
Rocks into fissures with lament. Gullies, hummocks
Can't withstand it. The sky shudders from one horizon   5
To the other, almost ready to give up wholeness.
Then Apollo[3] quietly told him: "Leave it all on earth.
Your lute, what point? Why pick at a dull pavan[4] few care to
Follow, except a few birds of dusty feather,
Not vivid performances of the past." But why not?   10
All other things must change too.
The seasons are no longer what they once were,
But it is the nature of things to be seen only once,
As they happen along, bumping into other things, getting along
Somehow. That's where Orpheus made his mistake.   15
Of course Eurydice vanished into the shade;
She would have even if he hadn't turned around.
No use standing there like a gray stone toga as the whole wheel
Of recorded history flashes past, struck dumb, unable to utter an intelligent
Comment on the most thought-provoking element in its train.   20
Only love stays on the brain, and something these people,
These other ones, call life. Singing accurately
So that the notes mount straight up out of the well of
Dim noon and rival the tiny, sparkling yellow flowers
Growing around the brink of the quarry, encapsulates   25
The different weights of the things.
                                   But it isn't enough
To just go on singing. Orpheus realized this
And didn't mind so much about his reward being in heaven
After the Bacchantes[5] had torn him apart, driven
Half out of their minds by his music, what it was doing to them.   30
Some say it was for his treatment of Eurydice.
But probably the music had more to do with it, and
The way music passes, emblematic
Of life and how you cannot isolate a note of it

---

[1] Flowering bush named from *syrinx,* the Greek
word for panpipe. The nymph Syrinx, escaping
from Pan, was turned into a reed; Pan in turn
formed the reeds into panpipes and blew
through them, creating music.
[2] In myth, a musician married to Eurydice. After
she died, Orpheus descended into Hades seeking
her; he was allowed to repossess her if he
promised not to look behind as he led her out
of Hades. He could not refrain from looking
and thus lost Eurydice forever.
[3] God of poets and musicians.
[4] Music for a court dance.
[5] Female followers of Dionysus, who tore
Orpheus to pieces.

And say it is good or bad. You must   35
Wait till it's over. "The end crowns all,"
Meaning also that the "tableau"
Is wrong. For although memories, of a season, for example,
Melt into a single snapshot, one cannot guard, treasure
That stalled moment. It too is flowing, fleeting;   40
It is a picture of flowing, scenery, though living, mortal,
Over which an abstract action is laid out in blunt,
Harsh strokes. And to ask more than this
Is to become the tossing reeds of that slow,
Powerful stream, the trailing grasses   45
Playfully tugged at, but to participate in the action
No more than this. Then in the lowering gentian sky
Electric twitches are faintly apparent first, then burst forth
Into a shower of fixed, cream-colored flares. The horses
Have each seen a share of the truth, though each thinks,   50
"I'm a maverick. Nothing of this is happening to me,
Though I can understand the language of birds, and
The itinerary of the lights caught in the storm is fully apparent to me.
Their jousting ends in music much
As trees move more easily in the wind after a summer storm   55
And is happening in lacy shadows of shore-trees, now, day after day."

But how late to be regretting all this, even
Bearing in mind that regrets are always late, too late!
To which Orpheus, a bluish cloud with white contours,
Replies that these are of course not regrets at all,   60
Merely a careful, scholarly setting down of
Unquestioned facts, a record of pebbles along the way.
And no matter how all this disappeared,
Or got where it was going, it is no longer
Material for a poem. Its subject   65
Matters too much, and not enough, standing there helplessly
While the poem streaked by, its tail afire, a bad
Comet screaming hate and disaster, but so turned inward
That the meaning, good or other, can never
Become known. The singer thinks   70
Constructively, builds up his chant in progressive stages
Like a skyscraper, but at the last minute turns away.
The song is engulfed in an instant in blackness
Which must in turn flood the whole continent
With blackness, for it cannot see. The singer   75
Must then pass out of sight, not even relieved
Of the evil burthen[6] of the words. Stellification[7]

---

[6] An obsolete spelling of *burden*.
[7] Being turned into a star, or constellation, after death.

Is for the few, and comes about much later
When all record of these people and their lives
Has disappeared into libraries, onto microfilm.   80
A few are still interested in them. "But what about
So-and-so?" is still asked on occasion. But they lie
Frozen and out of touch until an arbitrary chorus
Speaks of a totally different incident with a similar name
In whose tale are hidden syllables   85
Of what happened so long before that
In some small town, one indifferent summer.
1977

Many Wagons Ago

At first it was as though you had passed,
But then no, I said, he is still here,
Forehead refreshed. A light is kindled. And
Another. But no I said

Nothing in this wide berth of lights like weeds   5
Stays to listen. Doubled up, fun is inside,
The lair a surface compact with the night.
It needs only one intervention,

A stitch, two, three, and then you see
How it is all false equation planted with   10
Enchanting blue shrubbery on each terrace
That night produces, and they are backing up.

How easily we could spell if we could follow,
Like thread looped through the eye of a needle,
The grooves of light. It resists. But we stay behind, among them,   15
The injured, the adored.
1979

A Love Poem

And they have to get it right. We just need
A little happiness, and when the clever things
Are taken up (O has the mouth shaped that letter?
What do we have bearing down on it?) as the last thin curve
("Positively the last," they say) before the dark: 5
(The sky is pure and faint, the pavement still wet) and

The dripping is in the walls, within sleep
Itself. I mean there is no escape
From me, from it. The night is itself sleep
And what goes on in it, the naming of the wind,   10
Our notes to each other, always repeated, always the same.

1979

Landscapeople

Long desired, the journey is begun. The suppliants
Climb aboard the damaged carrousel:
Some have been hacked to death, one has learned
Some new thing, and all are touched
With the same blight, like a snowfall   5
Of moments as they are read back to the monitor
Which only projects.

                    Some can decipher it,
The outline of an eddy that traced itself
Before moving on, yet its place had to be,
Such was the appetite of those times. A ring   10
Of places existed around the central one,
And of course these died away eventually.
Everything has turned out for the best,
The "eggs of the sun" have been returned anonymously,
And the new ways are as simple as the old ones,   15
Only more firmly anchored to the spectacle
Of the madness of the seasons as it unfolds
With iron-clad rigidity, filling the sky with light.
We began in an anonymous sensuality

And lived most of it out before the difference   20
Of time got in the way, filling up the margins of the days
With pictures of fruit, light, colors, music, and vines,
Until it ceases to be a problem.

1979

Drunken Americans

I saw the reflection in the mirror
And it doesn't count, or not enough
To make a difference, fabricating itself
Out of the old, average light of a college town,

And afterwards, when the bus trip   5
Had depleted my pocket of its few pennies
He was seen arguing behind steamed glass,
With an invisible proprietor. What if you can't own

This one either? For it seems that all
Moments are like this: thin, unsatisfactory   10
As gruel, worn away more each time you return to them.
Until one day you rip the canvas from its frame

And take it home with you. You think the god-given
Assertiveness in you has triumphed
Over the stingy scenario: these objects are real as meat,   15
As tears. We are all soiled with this desire, at the last moment, the last.

1981

W. S. Merwin
b. 1927

W. S. Merwin's volume *The Lice* (1967) became a central book for those
opposed to the war in Vietnam; the poem "The Asians Dying," in its brevity and
conclusiveness, focused the anguish of social protest in an apprehensible form. At
his best, Merwin says a great deal in a very few words. His mature art is the
work of a minimalist who reduces a problem to its most abstract or skeletal
form; stripped of particulars, the essence stands luminously revealed.

Merwin was born in New York City, the son of a Presbyterian minister, and grew up in Scranton, Pennsylvania. As an undergraduate at Princeton, he knew John Berryman and the critic R. P. Blackmur. In his boyhood and youth, Merwin recalls:

> I started writing hymns for my father almost as soon as I could write at all. . . . In Scranton there was an anthology of *Best Loved Poems of the American People* in the house, which seemed for a time to afford some clues. But the first real writers that held me were not poets; Conrad first, and then Tolstoy, and it was not until I had received a scholarship and gone away to the university that I began to read poetry steadily and try incessantly, and with abiding desperation, to write it. . . . While I was there, John Berryman and R. P. Blackmur helped me, by example as much as by design, to find out some things about writing.

After his graduation, Merwin moved to Europe and became private tutor to the son of the British poet Robert Graves. Between 1951 and 1954 he lived in London, translating for the BBC Third Programme. In 1956 he returned to America and was active in the Poets' Theatre in Cambridge (with which Frank O'Hara and John Ashbery were also associated). He moved to New York in the 1960s; recently he has lived in Hawaii.

Merwin was chosen by Auden as Yale Younger Poet for 1952. His early volumes—*A Masque for Janus* (1952), *The Dancing Bears* (1954), *Green with Beasts* (1956), and *The Drunk in the Furnace* (1960)—reflect the formalist influence of the 1950s. In *The Moving Target* (1963), Merwin exhibits the sparse poetry that was to become his chosen form, one that found a home in prose in *The Miner's Pale Children* (1970) as well as in poetry.

The abstract rendering of motifs in Merwin's verse has caused some readers to overlook his social concern. He has criticized America as "a society whose triumphs one after the other emerge as new symbols of death, and that frees itself by poisoning the earth." In writing about the extinction of whales or about the use of technology for genocidal purposes, Merwin became one of the most fervent spokesmen of the 1960s. His later volumes—*The Carrier of Ladders* (1970), *Writings to an Unfinished Accompaniment* (1973), *The Compass Flower* (1977), and *Opening the Hand* (1983)—display the purity of diction and brevity of statement that have characterized all his mature work.

Merwin has been a translator of many classics written in Spanish—*The Poem of the Cid* (1959) and *The Life of Lazarillo de Tormes* (1962), as well as works by Neruda and García Lorca. The considerable influence of medieval Spanish poetry on his formal, musical, unrhymed stanzas has been noticed by his commentators.

In American verse, Merwin represents a tendency—collective and impersonal—completely opposed to the autobiographical "confessional" verse of Lowell, Plath, and Sexton. In his moral emphasis and social focus, his work might be compared to that of Adrienne Rich, but its deliberate reliance on generality links it as well to that of John Ashbery. In his elegance and intensity of formulation, as well as in his secularized Protestant morality, Merwin continues a line of concise, gnomic, ethical American poetry begun by Emerson and Dickinson.

Texts:
"The Fishermen" from *The First Four Books of Poems*, 1975.
"Odysseus" and "In Stony Country" from *The Drunk in the Furnace*, 1960.
"Noah's Raven" from *The Moving Target*, 1963.
"Some Last Questions," "For the Anniversary of My Death," "The Asians Dying," and "For a Coming Extinction" from *The Lice*, 1967.
"Elegy" from *The Carrier of Ladders*, 1970.

"Under the Migrants," "Tool," "The Chase," and "Span" from *Writings to an Unfinished Accompaniment*, 1973.
"Line" from *The Compass Flower*, 1977.
See also *Houses and Travellers: A Book of Prose*, 1977.
Selected Translations, 1968–1978, 1979.
Unframed Originals: Recollections, 1982.

The Fishermen

When you think how big their feet are in black rubber
And it slippery underfoot always, it is clever
How they thread and manage among the sprawled nets, lines,
Hooks, spidery cages with small entrances.
But they are used to it. We do not know their names.   5
They know our needs, and live by them, lending them wiles
And beguilements we could never have fashioned for them;
They carry the ends of our hungers out to drop them
To wait swaying in a dark place we could never have chosen.
By motions we have never learned they feed us.   10
We lay wreaths on the sea when it has drowned them.

1956

Odysseus[1]

for George Kirstein
Always the setting forth was the same,
Same sea, same dangers waiting for him
As though he had got nowhere but older.
Behind him on the receding shore
The identical reproaches, and somewhere   5
Out before him, the unravelling patience[2]
He was wedded to. There were the islands

---

[1] The wandering hero of Homer's *Odyssey,* who encountered many women during his travels.
[2] Odysseus' wife, Penelope, kept her suitors at bay during his absence by saying she would marry again only when her weaving was done. Then each night she unraveled what she had woven that day.

Each with its woman and twining welcome
To be navigated, and one to call "home."
The knowledge of all that he betrayed   10
Grew till it was the same whether he stayed
Or went. Therefore he went. And what wonder
If sometimes he could not remember
Which was the one who wished on his departure
Perils that he could never sail through,   15
And which, improbable, remote, and true,
Was the one he kept sailing home to?
1960

In Stony Country

Somewhere else than these bare uplands dig wells,
Expect flowers, listen to sheep bells.
Wind; no welcome; and nowhere else
Pillows like these stones for dreaming of angels.
1960

Noah's Raven[1]

Why should I have returned?
My knowledge would not fit into theirs.
I found untouched the desert of the unknown,
Big enough for my feet. It is my home.
It is always beyond them. The future   5
Splits the present with the echo of my voice.
Hoarse with fulfilment, I never made promises.
1963

---

[1] After the Deluge, Noah's ark landed on Mount Ararat. Noah sent out a raven and a dove to see whether the waters had subsided. The dove returned but the raven did not (see Genesis 8:7, 8).

Some Last Questions

What is the head
     A. Ash
What are the eyes
     A. The wells have fallen in and have
        Inhabitants   5
What are the feet
     A. Thumbs left after the auction
No what are the feet
     A. Under them the impossible road is moving
        Down which the broken necked mice push   10
        Balls of blood with their noses
What is the tongue
     A. The black coat that fell off the wall
        With sleeves trying to say something
What are the hands   15
     A. Paid
No what are the hands
     A. Climbing back down the museum wall
        To their ancestors the extinct shrews that will
        Have left a message   20
What is the silence
     A. As though it had a right to more
Who are the compatriots
     A. They make the stars of bone

1967

For the Anniversary of My Death

Every year without knowing it I have passed the day
When the last fires will wave to me
And the silence will set out
Tireless traveller
Like the beam of a lightless star   5

Then I will no longer
Find myself in life as in a strange garment
Surprised at the earth

And the love of one woman
And the shamelessness of men   10
As today writing after three days of rain
Hearing the wren sing and the falling cease
And bowing not knowing to what
1967

The Asians Dying[1]

When the forests have been destroyed their darkness remains
The ash the great walker follows the possessors
Forever
Nothing they will come to is real
Nor for long   5
Over the watercourses
Like ducks in the time of the ducks
The ghosts of the villages trail in the sky
Making a new twilight

Rain falls into the open eyes of the dead   10
Again again with its pointless sound
When the moon finds them they are the color of everything

The nights disappear like bruises but nothing is healed
The dead go away like bruises
The blood vanishes into the poisoned farmlands   15

Pain the horizon
Remains
Overhead the seasons rock
They are paper bells
Calling to nothing living   20

The possessors move everywhere under Death their star
Like columns of smoke they advance into the shadows
Like thin flames with no light
They with no past
And fire their only future   25
1967

---

[1] In the Vietnam War, 1964–1973.

For a Coming Extinction

Gray whale
Now that we are sending you to The End
That great god
Tell him
That we who follow you invented forgiveness   5
And forgive nothing

I write as though you could understand
And I could say it
One must always pretend something
Among the dying   10
When you have left the seas nodding on their stalks
Empty of you
Tell him that we were made
On another day

The bewilderment will diminish like an echo   15
Winding along your inner mountains
Unheard by us
And find its way out
Leaving behind it the future
Dead   20
And ours

When you will not see again
The whale calves trying the light
Consider what you will find in the black garden[1]
And its court   25
The sea cows the Great Auks the gorillas
The irreplaceable hosts ranged countless
And fore-ordaining as stars
Our sacrifices

Join your word to theirs   30
Tell him
That it is we who are important
1967

---

[1] I.e., of the extinct species.

Elegy[1]

Who would I show it to

1970

Under the Migrants

Winter is almost upon us
and in the south there is a battle

every day silent thunder from there
light going up like a shout

each of us is alone   5
when we close our eyes
the roads are strips of death

when we open our eyes the bandages
go on unwinding
back into the north the whiteness   10

on the avenues trucks rumble southward
to be seen no more

can you hear yourself we cannot

flocks of single hands are all flying
southward   15

from us

and the clocks all night all day
point that way

1973

[1] A poem on the death of someone beloved.

Tool

If it's invented it will be used

maybe not for some time

then all at once
a hammer rises from under a lid
and shakes off its cold family   5

its one truth is stirring in its head
order order saying

and a surprised nail leaps
into darkness
that a moment before had been nothing   10

waiting
for the law

1973

The Chase

On the first day of Ruin
a crack appears running

then what do they know to do
they shout Thief Thief
and run after   5

like cracks converging across a wall

they strike at it
they pick it up by tails
they throw pieces into the air

where the pieces join hands   10
join feet run on

through the first day

while the wren sings and sings
1973

Span

I know hands that leapt from childhood to old age
youth was never for them however they held it
everything happened to them early or late
end of morning never found them
the entire day was a long evening   5
in August
they played no instrument for when would they have learned
if not in childhood
everything they did displayed impetuous prudence
and smelled of sand   10
they and their clumsy skills were their own age
with its two seasons
1973

Line

Those waiting in line
for a cash register at a supermarket
pushing wire baby carriages
full of food in packages
past signs about coupons   5
in the blank light
do not look at each other
frankly
pretend not to stare at each other's
soft drinks and white bread   10
do not think of themselves as

part of a line
ordinarily
and the clerk often does not
look at them   15
giving them change
and the man who puts the things
they have chosen
into bags
talks to the clerk   20
as he never talks to her
at any other time
1977

James Wright
1927–1980

When James Wright died of throat cancer at the early age of fifty-three, he was
mourned as the poet who had put the Midwest into verse—its rural despair, its
urban poor, its suburban frustration. He was born in Martins Ferry, Ohio, a
town he recalled in many poems. Wright's deepest sense of life came to him
from his earliest days, when he experienced life as a child of the Depression:
"Hundreds of times I must have heard a man returning home after a long day's
futile search for work, any work at all, and dispiritedly whispering to his anxious
wife, or mumbling absent-mindedly to himself in his baffled loneliness: 'I ain't
got a pot to piss in or a window to throw it out of.' " Wright's father worked
for fifty years in Wheeling, West Virginia, for the Hazel-Atlas glass factory but
was often "laid off," which meant, as Wright said, being "told by the
management to just go home and stay there, often for weeks at a time, without
being paid." In representing the dark underside of America, Wright follows
Whitman's injunction in the preface to *Leaves of Grass* to "stand up for the
stupid and crazy."

W. H. Auden chose Wright as Yale Younger Poet for 1957 for the book *The
Green Wall,* a book formal in its meters and stanza forms, influenced by Wright's
literary studies with John Crowe Ransom at Kenyon College, from which he
received an A.B. in 1952, and with Theodore Roethke at the University of
Washington, where he took a Ph.D. in 1959. Wright then began, in collaboration
with Robert Bly, a series of translations from foreign poets: the Austrian Georg
Trakl in 1961 (Wright had been a Fulbright student in Vienna), César Vallejo in
1962, Pablo Neruda in 1968. These translations influenced his own third and
fourth books, *The Branch Will Not Break* (1963) and *Shall We Gather at the River*
(1968). The stark imagism of Trakl and the uninhibited surrealism of Neruda,
combined with the directness and honesty of Vallejo, broke through Wright's
formalism and induced in him a new starkness and simplicity of presentation: "I
have wasted my life"; "If I stepped out of my body I would break / Into

blossom." In subsequent volumes, *Two Citizens* (1973) and *To a Blossoming Pear Tree* (1977), Wright's elegiac plangency threatened to dissolve into sentimentality. Alcoholism sapped his creative energy and induced poems of self-hatred and disgust, of terror at the uncontrolled disintegration of his life. Eventually he gave up alcohol and found a new sweetness in life in America as well as in travel in Europe with his wife, Annie.

Wright's poetry won him a wide following in the late 1960s when the war in Vietnam made readers long for a poetry of direct statement, pity, and elegiac sympathy. During the later years of his life, Wright taught literature at Hunter College in New York, but he remains a poet of "the heart of the heart of the country," that Midwest as yet underrepresented in American verse. Following the example set by Robinson and Frost in their scenes of crabbed rural life in New England, Wright revealed how a transplanted genre could flourish in a new geographic setting, in the flat, despairing tones of Middle America.

Further Reading:
G. S. Lensing and R. Moran, *Four Poets and Emotive Imagination*, 1976.
W. S. Saunders, *James Wright: An Introduction*, 1980.
The Pure Clear Word: Essays on the Poetry of James Wright, ed. D. Smith, 1982.

Text:
Collected Poems, 1971.
See also *Collected Prose*, ed. A. Wright, 1983.

Lament for My Brother on a Hayrake

Cool with the touch of autumn, waters break
Out of the pump at dawn to clear my eyes;
I leave the house, to face the sacrifice
Of hay, the drag and death. By day, by moon,
I have seen my younger brother wipe his face   5
And heave his arm on steel. He need not pass
Under the blade to waste his life and break;

The hunching of the body is enough
To violate his bones. That bright machine
Strips the revolving earth of more than grass;   10
Powered by the fire of summer, bundles fall
Folded to die beside a burlap shroud;
And so my broken brother may lie mown
Out of the wasted fallows, winds return,
Corn-yellow tassels of his hair blow down,   15
The summer bear him sideways in a bale
Of darkness to October's mow of cloud.

1956

A Note Left in Jimmy Leonard's Shack

Near the dry river's water-mark we found
    Your brother Minnegan,
Flopped like a fish against the muddy ground.
Beany, the kid whose yellow hair turns green,
Told me to find you, even in the rain,   5
    And tell you he was drowned.

I hid behind the chassis on the bank,
    The wreck of someone's Ford:
I was afraid to come and wake you drunk:
You told me once the waking up was hard,   10
The daylight beating at you like a board.
    Blood in my stomach sank.

Beside, you told him never to go out
    Along the river-side
Drinking and singing, clattering about.   15
You might have thrown a rock at me and cried
I was to blame, I let him fall in the road
    And pitch down on his side.

Well, I'll get hell enough when I get home
    For coming up this far,   20
Leaving the note, and running as I came.
I'll go and tell my father where you are.
You'd better go find Minnegan before
    Policemen hear and come.

Beany went home, and I got sick and ran,   25
    You old son of a bitch.
You better hurry down to Minnegan;
He's drunk or dying now, I don't know which,
Rolled in the roots and garbage like a fish,
    The poor old man.   30

1959

At the Executed Murderer's Grave

(for J. L. D.)

Why should we do this? What good is it to us? Above all, how
can we do such a thing? How can it possibly be done?
                                                                    Freud

1

My name is James A. Wright, and I was born
Twenty-five miles from this infected grave,
In Martins Ferry, Ohio, where one slave
To Hazel-Atlas Glass became my father.
He tried to teach me kindness. I return   5
Only in memory now, aloof, unhurried,
To dead Ohio, where I might lie buried,
Had I not run away before my time.
Ohio caught George Doty. Clean as lime,
His skull rots empty here. Dying's the best   10
Of all the arts men learn in a dead place.
I walked here once. I made my loud display,
Leaning for language on a dead man's voice.
Now sick of lies, I turn to face the past.
I add my easy grievance to the rest: 15

2

Doty, if I confess I do not love you,
Will you let me alone? I burn for my own lies.
The nights electrocute my fugitive,
My mind. I run like the bewildered mad
At St. Clair Sanitarium, who lurk,   20
Arch and cunning, under the maple trees,
Pleased to be playing guilty after dark.
Staring to bed, they croon self-lullabies.
Doty, you make me sick. I am not dead.
I croon my tears at fifty cents per line.   25

3

Idiot, he demanded love from girls,
And murdered one. Also, he was a thief.
He left two women, and a ghost with child.
The hair, foul as a dog's upon his head,
Made such revolting Ohio animals   30
Fitter for vomit than a kind man's grief.

I waste no pity on the dead that stink,
And no love's lost between me and the crying
Drunks of Belaire, Ohio, where police
Kick at their kidneys till they die of drink.   35
Christ may restore them whole, for all of me.
Alive and dead, those giggling muckers who
Saddled my nightmares thirty years ago
Can do without my widely printed sighing
Over their pains with paid sincerity.   40
I do not pity the dead, I pity the dying.

4

I pity myself, because a man is dead.
If Belmont County killed him, what of me?
His victims never loved him. Why should we?
And yet, nobody had to kill him either.   45
It does no good to woo the grass, to veil
The quicklime hole of a man's defeat and shame.
Nature-lovers are gone. To hell with them.
I kick the clods away, and speak my name.

5

This grave's gash festers. Maybe it will heal,   50
When all are caught with what they had to do
In fear of love, when every man stands still
By the last sea,
And the princes of the sea come down
To lay away their robes, to judge the earth   55
And its dead, and we dead stand undefended everywhere,
And my bodies—father and child and unskilled criminal—
Ridiculously kneel to bare my scars,
My sneaking crimes, to God's unpitying stars.

6

Staring politely, they will not mark my face   60
From any murderer's, buried in this place.
Why should they? We are nothing but a man.

7

Doty, the rapist and the murderer,
Sleeps in a ditch of fire, and cannot hear;
And where, in earth or hell's unholy peace,   65
Men's suicides will stop, God knows, not I.

Angels and pebbles mock me under trees.
Earth is a door I cannot even face.
Order be damned, I do not want to die,
Even to keep Belaire, Ohio, safe.   70
The hackles on my neck are fear, not grief.
(Open, dungeon! Open, roof of the ground!)
I hear the last sea in the Ohio grass,
Heaving a tide of gray disastrousness.
Wrinkles of winter ditch the rotted face   75
Of Doty, killer, imbecile, and thief:
Dirt of my flesh, defeated, underground.

1959

Autumn Begins in Martins Ferry, Ohio

In the Shreve High football stadium,
I think of Polacks[1] nursing long beers in Tiltonsville,
And gray faces of Negroes in the blast furnace at Benwood,
And the ruptured[2] night watchman of Wheeling Steel,
Dreaming of heroes.   5

All the proud fathers are ashamed to go home.
Their women cluck like starved pullets,
Dying for love.

Therefore,
Their sons grow suicidally beautiful   10
At the beginning of October,
And gallop terribly against each other's bodies.

1963

---

[1] Derogatory epithet for Polish-Americans.   [2] I.e., with a hernia supported by a truss.

Lying in a Hammock
at William Duffy's Farm
in Pine Island, Minnesota

Over my head, I see the bronze butterfly,
Asleep on the black trunk,
Blowing like a leaf in green shadow.
Down the ravine behind the empty house,
The cowbells follow one another   5
Into the distances of the afternoon.
To my right,
In a field of sunlight between two pines,
The droppings of last year's horses
Blaze up into golden stones.   10
I lean back, as the evening darkens and comes on.
A chicken hawk floats over, looking for home.
I have wasted my life.

1963

Having Lost My Sons, I Confront
the Wreckage of the Moon

Christmas, 1960

After dark
Near the South Dakota border,

The moon is out hunting, everywhere,
Delivering fire,
And walking down hallways   5
Of a diamond.

Behind a tree,
It lights on the ruins
Of a white city:
Frost, frost.   10

Where are they gone,
Who lived there?

Bundled away under wings
And dark faces.

I am sick   15
Of it, and I go on,
Living, alone, alone,
Past the charred silos, past the hidden graves
Of Chippewas and Norwegians.

This cold winter   20
Moon spills the inhuman fire
Of jewels
Into my hands.

Dead riches, dead hands, the moon
Darkens,   25
And I am lost in the beautiful white ruins
Of America.
1963

Before a Cashier's Window
in a Department Store

1.

The beautiful cashier's white face has risen once more
Behind a young manager's shoulder.
They whisper together, and stare
Straight into my face.
I feel like grabbing a stray child   5
Or a skinny old woman
And driving into a cellar, crouching
Under a stone bridge, praying myself sick,
Till the troops pass.

2.

Why should he care? He goes.   10
I slump deeper.
In my frayed coat, I am pinned down
By debt. He nods,
Commending my flesh to the pity of the daws of God.

3.

Am I dead? And, if not, why not?   15
For she sails there, alone, looming in the
        heaven of the beautiful.
She knows
The bulldozers will scrape me up
After dark, behind   20
The officers' club.
Beneath her terrible blaze, my skeleton
Glitters out. I am the dark. I am the dark
Bone I was born to be.

4.

Tu Fu¹ woke shuddering on a battlefield   25
Once, in the dead of night, and made out
The mangled women, sorting
The haggard slant-eyes.
The moon was up.

5.

I am hungry. In two more days   30
It will be spring. So this
Is what it feels like.
1968

Willy Lyons

My uncle, a craftsman of hammers and wood,
Is dead in Ohio.
And my mother cries she is angry.
Willy was buried with nothing except a jacket
Stitched on his shoulder bones.   5
It is nothing to mourn for.
It is the other world.
She does not know how the roan horses, there,

---

¹ Chinese poet (A.D. 712–770), who, because he
did not pass the imperial examinations for the
civil service, led a poverty-stricken life, as
reflected in his work.

Dead for a century,
Plod slowly.   10
Maybe they believe Willy's brown coffin, tangled heavily in moss,
Is a horse trough drifted to shore
Along that river under the willows and grass.
Let my mother weep on, she needs to, she knows of cold winds.
The long box is empty.   15
The horses turn back toward the river.
Willy planes limber trees by the waters,
Fitting his boat together.
We may as well let him go.
Nothing is left of Willy on this side   20
But one cracked ball-peen hammer and one suit,
Including pants, his son inherited,
For a small fee, from Hesslop's funeral home;
And my mother,
Weeping with anger, afraid of winter   25
For her brothers' sake:
Willy, and John, whose life and art, if any,
I never knew.

1968

Two Postures Beside a Fire

1.

Tonight I watch my father's hair,
As he sits dreaming near his stove.
Knowing my feather of despair,
He sent me an owl's plume for love,
Lest I not know, so I've come home.   5
Tonight Ohio, where I once
Hounded and cursed my loneliness,
Shows me my father, who broke stones,
Wrestled and mastered great machines,
And rests, shadowing his lovely face.   10

2.

Nobly his hands fold together in his repose.
He is proud of me, believing
I have done strong things among men and become a man

Of place among men of place in the large cities.
I will not waken him.   15
I have come home alone, without wife or child
To delight him. Awake, solitary and welcome,
I too sit near his stove, the lines
Of an ugly age scarring my face, and my hands
Twitch nervously about.   20
1968

Small Frogs Killed on the Highway

Still,
I would leap too
Into the light,
If I had the chance.
It is everything, the wet green stalk of the field   5
On the other side of the road.
They crouch there, too, faltering in terror
And take strange wing. Many
Of the dead never moved, but many
Of the dead are alive forever in the split second   10
Auto headlights more sudden
Than their drivers know.
The drivers burrow backward into dank pools
Where nothing begets
Nothing.   15

Across the road, tadpoles are dancing
On the quarter thumbnail
Of the moon. They can't see,
Not yet.
1971

Anne Sexton
1928–1975

Anne Sexton was born in Newton, Massachusetts, grew up in Wellesley, attended
Garland Junior College, and married at twenty. After suffering a mental
breakdown, she was urged to write poetry by her therapist. Like Sylvia Plath, she
studied with Robert Lowell at Boston University in the 1950s. Sexton's first

book, *To Bedlam and Part Way Back* (1960), was published when she was thirty-two, and her third book, *Live or Die* (1967), was awarded the Pulitzer Prize, a recognition that crowned the amazing rise to fame of a woman who a few years before had been a suburban housewife without a college degree. Sexton's poetic talents were a brisk diction, a devastating honesty, a gift for black humor, and a lethal talent for exposing the fraudulence and foolishness of the familial and social world, especially in the socialization of women. Her bold dramatic sense led her, in *Transformations* (1971), to adapt well-known fairy tales (about such heroines as Snow White and Briar Rose) in ways that expose the myths of female acceptability underlying those stories.

At the same time, Sexton's poetry dealt in pathos, often the pathos of the abandoned child. Sexton's capacity to resort to the childlike, even the infantile, in language and then to snap quickly to a disillusioned worldliness gave her poems their linguistic energy. The events of Sexton's life—her breakdown, her time in a mental hospital, her therapy, her troubled marriage (ending in divorce), her affairs, and her relationship with her two daughters—became transparently the stuff of her poetry. Her verse, far more directly than that of Lowell or Plath, can be called confessional poetry (a name first applied in 1959 by the critic M. L. Rosenthal). In her forties, after her marriage had ended in divorce, Sexton, who had been teaching at Boston University, committed suicide by carbon monoxide poisoning, leaving behind manuscripts posthumously published as *The Awful Rowing Toward God* (1975) and *45 Mercy Street* (1976), the volumes following *The Death Notebooks* (1974). Her *Complete Poems* was published posthumously in 1981.

The religious guilt evident in these books may perhaps be traced to Sexton's Roman Catholic upbringing. Her preoccupation with self-abasement, sin, sexual transgression, and bodily disgust worked against the efforts she made in years of therapy to find personal equilibrium. Her good looks and her performing spirit (she had been a fashion model as a girl and later founded her own jazz group, called Anne Sexton and Her Kind) made for gallantry of bearing and a winning insouciance in the poetry. But her last years, complicated by dependence on alcohol, made her become repetitive and self-pitying in the writing and to lose formal control of the poetry. Her surreal images became disconnected; the poems grew overlong. She will be remembered chiefly for her poems of the 1960s, those sharp, observant, satiric vignettes of American life, whether in a mental hospital, in a suburban kitchen, or at a country club dance. Her truthtelling wit and her ruthless self-examination gave her poetry a freshness and candor rarely equaled in domestic poetry.

Further Reading:
A Self-portrait in Letters, ed. L. G. Sexton and
L. Ames, 1977.
Anne Sexton: The Artist and Her Critics, ed.
J. D. McClatchy, 1978.

Text:
The Complete Poems, 1981.

Her Kind

I have gone out, a possessed witch,
haunting the black air, braver at night;
dreaming evil, I have done my hitch
over the plain houses, light by light:
lonely thing, twelve-fingered,[1] out of mind.   5
A woman like that is not a woman, quite.
I have been her kind.

I have found the warm caves in the woods,
filled them with skillets, carvings, shelves,
closets, silks, innumerable goods;   10
fixed the suppers for the worms and the elves:
whining, rearranging the disaligned.
A woman like that is misunderstood.
I have been her kind.

I have ridden in your cart, driver,   15
waved my nude arms at villages going by,
learning the last bright routes, survivor
where your flames still bite my thigh
and my ribs crack where your wheels wind.[2]
A woman like that is not ashamed to die.   20
I have been her kind.

1960

Ringing the Bells

And this is the way they ring
the bells in Bedlam[1]
and this is the bell-lady

---

[1] Witches were thought to have six fingers on each hand.

[2] In Europe and America in the seventeenth century, women thought to be witches were often burned at the stake after being tortured on the wheel, which stretched the victim's body till the bones broke.

[1] "Bedlam" is the English name for a hospital for the insane. The word is a contraction of *Bethlehem,* after the London hospital St. Mary of Bethlehem. The poem is based on the nursery rhyme "This is the House That Jack Built."

who comes each Tuesday morning
to give us a music lesson   5
and because the attendants make you go
and because we mind by instinct,
like bees caught in the wrong hive,
we are the circle of the crazy ladies
who sit in the lounge of the mental house   10
and smile at the smiling woman
who passes us each a bell,
who points at my hand
that holds my bell, E flat,
and this is the gray dress next to me   15
who grumbles as if it were special
to be old, to be old,
and this is the small hunched squirrel girl
on the other side of me
who picks at the hairs over her lip,   20
who picks at the hairs over her lip all day,
and this is how the bells really sound,
as untroubled and clean
as a workable kitchen,
and this is always my bell responding   25
to my hand that responds to the lady
who points at me, E flat;
and although we are no better for it,
they tell you to go. And you do.
1960

With Mercy for the Greedy

For my friend, Ruth, who urges me to make an
appointment for the Sacrament of Confession

Concerning your letter in which you ask
me to call a priest and in which you ask
me to wear The Cross that you enclose;
your own cross,
your dog-bitten cross,   5
no larger than a thumb,
small and wooden, no thorns, this rose—

I pray to its shadow,
that gray place

where it lies on your letter . . . deep, deep.   10
I detest my sins and I try to believe
in The Cross. I touch its tender hips, its dark jawed face,
its solid neck, its brown sleep.

True. There is
a beautiful Jesus.   15
He is frozen to his bones like a chunk of beef.
How desperately he wanted to pull his arms in!
How desperately I touch his vertical and horizontal axes!
But I can't. Need is not quite belief.

All morning long   20
I have worn
your cross, hung with package string around my throat.
It tapped me lightly as a child's heart might,
tapping secondhand, softly waiting to be born.
Ruth, I cherish the letter you wrote.   25

My friend, my friend, I was born
doing reference work in sin, and born
confessing it. This is what poems are:
with mercy
for the greedy,   30
they are the tongue's wrangle,
the world's pottage, the rat's star.[1]
1962

Self in 1958

What is reality?
I am a plaster doll; I pose
with eyes that cut open without landfall or nightfall
upon some shellacked and grinning person,
eyes that open, blue, steel, and close.   5
Am I approximately an I. Magnin[1] transplant?
I have hair, black angel,

---

[1] Sexton liked the palindrome "Rats live on no
evil star." (A *palindrome* is a sentence that spells
the same backwards and forwards.)

[1] An expensive department store.

black-angel-stuffing to comb,
nylon legs, luminous arms
and some advertised clothes.   10

I live in a doll's house
with four chairs,
a counterfeit table, a flat roof
and a big front door.
Many have come to such a small crossroad.   15
There is an iron bed,
(Life enlarges, life takes aim)
a cardboard floor,
windows that flash open on someone's city,
and little more.   20

Someone plays with me,
plants me in the all-electric kitchen,
Is this what Mrs. Rombauer² said?
Someone pretends with me—
I am walled in solid by their noise—   25
or puts me upon their straight bed.
They think I am me!
Their warmth? Their warmth is not a friend!
They pry my mouth for their cups of gin
and their stale bread.   30

What is reality
to this synthetic doll
who should smile, who should shift gears,
should spring the doors open in a wholesome disorder,
and have no evidence of ruin or fears?   35
But I would cry,
rooted into the wall that
was once my mother,
if I could remember how
and if I had the tears.   40
1966

---

² Author of the cookbook *The Joy of Cooking*.

For My Lover, Returning to His Wife

She is all there.
She was melted carefully down for you
and cast up from your childhood,
cast up from your one hundred favorite aggies.[1]

She has always been there, my darling.   5
She is, in fact, exquisite.
Fireworks in the dull middle of February
and as real as a cast-iron pot.

Let's face it, I have been momentary.
A luxury. A bright red sloop in the harbor.   10
My hair rising like smoke from the car window.
Littleneck clams out of season.

She is more than that. She is your have to have,
has grown you your practical your tropical growth.
This is not an experiment. She is all harmony.   15
She sees to oars and oarlocks for the dinghy,

has placed wild flowers at the window at breakfast,
sat by the potter's wheel at midday,
set forth three children under the moon,
three cherubs drawn by Michelangelo,   20

done this with her legs spread out
in the terrible months in the chapel.
If you glance up, the children are there
like delicate balloons resting on the ceiling.

She has also carried each one down the hall   25
after supper, their heads privately bent,
two legs protesting, person to person,
her face flushed with a song and their little sleep.

I give you back your heart.
I give you permission—   30

[1] Agate marbles.

for the fuse inside her, throbbing
angrily in the dirt, for the bitch in her
and the burying of her wound—
for the burying of her small red wound alive—

for the pale flickering flare under her ribs,   35
for the drunken sailor who waits in her left pulse,
for the mother's knee, for the stockings,
for the garter belt, for the call—

the curious call
when you will burrow in arms and breasts   40

and tug at the orange ribbon in her hair
and answer the call, the curious call.

She is so naked and singular.
She is the sum of yourself and your dream.
Climb her like a monument, step after step.   45
She is solid.

As for me, I am a watercolor.
I wash off.
1969

Snow White and the Seven Dwarfs

No matter what life you lead
the virgin is a lovely number:
cheeks as fragile as cigarette paper,
arms and legs made of Limoges,[1]
lips like Vin Du Rhône,[2]   5
rolling her china-blue doll eyes
open and shut.
Open to say,
Good Day Mama,
and shut for the thrust   10
of the unicorn.
She is unsoiled.
She is as white as a bonefish.

[1] Fine porcelain made in Limoges, France.   [2] Rhône wine (French).

Once there was a lovely virgin
called Snow White.   15
Say she was thirteen.
Her stepmother,
a beauty in her own right,
though eaten, of course, by age,
would hear of no beauty surpassing her own.   20
Beauty is a simple passion,
but, oh my friends, in the end
you will dance the fire dance in iron shoes.
The stepmother had a mirror to which she
        referred—
something like the weather forecast—   25
a mirror that proclaimed
the one beauty of the land.
She would ask,
Looking glass upon the wall,
who is fairest of us all?   30
And the mirror would reply,
You are fairest of us all.
Pride pumped in her like poison.

Suddenly one day the mirror replied,
Queen, you are full fair, 'tis true,   35
but Snow White is fairer than you.
Until that moment Snow White
had been no more important
than a dust mouse under the bed.
But now the queen saw brown spots on her hand   40
and four whiskers over her lip
so she condemned Snow White
to be hacked to death.
Bring me her heart, she said to the hunter,
and I will salt it and eat it.   45
The hunter, however, let his prisoner go
and brought a boar's heart back to the castle.
The queen chewed it up like a cube steak.
Now I am fairest, she said,
lapping her slim white fingers.   50

Snow White walked in the wildwood
for weeks and weeks.
At each turn there were twenty doorways
and at each stood a hungry wolf,
his tongue lolling out like a worm.   55
The birds called out lewdly,
talking like pink parrots,

2504 The Literature of Postwar America

and the snakes hung down in loops,
each a noose for her sweet white neck.
On the seventh week   60
she came to the seventh mountain
and there she found the dwarf house.
It was as droll as a honeymoon cottage
and completely equipped with
seven beds, seven chairs, seven forks   65
and seven chamber pots.
Snow White ate seven chicken livers
and lay down, at last, to sleep.

The dwarfs, those little hot dogs,
walked three times around Snow White,   70
the sleeping virgin. They were wise
and wattled like small czars.
Yes. It's a good omen,
they said, and will bring us luck.
They stood on tiptoes to watch   75
Snow White wake up. She told them
about the mirror and the killer-queen
and they asked her to stay and keep house.
Beware of your stepmother,
they said.   80
Soon she will know you are here.
While we are away in the mines
during the day, you must not
open the door.

Looking glass upon the wall . . .   85
The mirror told
and so the queen dressed herself in rags
and went out like a peddler to trap Snow White.
She went across seven mountains.
She came to the dwarf house   90
and Snow White opened the door
and bought a bit of lacing.
The queen fastened it tightly
around her bodice,
as tight as an Ace bandage,   95
so tight that Snow White swooned.
She lay on the floor, a plucked daisy.
When the dwarfs came home they undid the lace
and she revived miraculously.
She was as full of life as soda pop.   100

Beware of your stepmother,
they said.
She will try once more.

Looking glass upon the wall . . .
Once more the mirror told   105
and once more the queen dressed in rags
and once more Snow White opened the door.
This time she bought a poison comb,
a curved eight-inch scorpion,
and put it in her hair and swooned again.   110
The dwarfs returned and took out the comb
and she revived miraculously.
She opened her eyes as wide as Orphan Annie.[3]
Beware, beware, they said,
but the mirror told,   115
the queen came,
Snow White, the dumb bunny,
opened the door
and she bit into a poison apple
and fell down for the final time.   120
When the dwarfs returned
they undid her bodice,
they looked for a comb,
but it did no good.
Though they washed her with wine   125
and rubbed her with butter
it was to no avail.
She lay as still as a gold piece.

The seven dwarfs could not bring themselves
to bury her in the black ground   130
so they made a glass coffin
and set it upon the seventh mountain
so that all who passed by
could peek in upon her beauty.
A prince came one June day   135
and would not budge.
He stayed so long his hair turned green
and still he would not leave.
The dwarfs took pity upon him
and gave him the glass Snow White—   140
its doll's eyes shut forever—
to keep in his far-off castle.
As the prince's men carried the coffin

---

[3] Comic-strip character.

they stumbled and dropped it
and the chunk of apple flew out   145
of her throat and she woke up miraculously.

And thus Snow White became the prince's bride.
The wicked queen was invited to the wedding feast
and when she arrived there were
red-hot iron shoes,   150
in the manner of red-hot roller skates,
clamped upon her feet.
First your toes will smoke
and then your heels will turn black
and you will fry upward like a frog,   155
she was told.
And so she danced until she was dead,
a subterranean figure,
her tongue flicking in and out
like a gas jet.   160
Meanwhile Snow White held court,
rolling her china-blue doll eyes open and shut
and sometimes referring to her mirror
as women do.

1971

The Silence

The more I write, the more the silence seems to be eating away at
me.
C. K. Williams

My room is whitewashed,
as white as a rural station house
and just as silent;
whiter than chicken bones
bleaching in the moonlight,   5
pure garbage,
and just as silent.
There is a white statue behind me
and white plants
growing like obscene virgins,   10
pushing out their rubbery tongues
but saying nothing.

My hair is the one dark.
It has been burnt in the white fire
and is just a char.   15
My beads too are black,
twenty eyes heaved up
from the volcano,
quite contorted.

I am filling the room   20
with the words from my pen.
Words leak out of it like a miscarriage.
I am zinging words out into the air
and they come back like squash balls.
Yet there is silence.   25
Always silence.
Like an enormous baby mouth.

The silence is death.
It comes each day with its shock
to sit on my shoulder, a white bird,   30
and peck at the black eyes
and the vibrating red muscle
of my mouth.

1972

January 1st

Today is favorable for joint financial affairs but do
not take any chances with speculation.

My daddy played the market.
My mother cut her coupons.
The children ran in circles.
The maid announced, the soup's on.

The guns were cleaned on Sunday.   5
The family went out to shoot.
We sat in the blind for hours.
The ducks fell down like fruit.

The big fat war was going on.
So profitable for daddy.   10

She drove a pea green Ford.
He drove a pearl gray Caddy.

In the end they used it up.
All that pale green dough.
The rest I spent on doctors   15
who took it like gigolos.[1]

My financial affairs are small.
Indeed they seem to shrink.
My heart is on a budget.
It keeps me on the brink.   20

I tell it stories now and then
and feed it images like honey.
I will not speculate today
with poems that think they're money.
1978

Adrienne Rich
b. 1929

Adrienne Rich was a precocious poet; her first book, *A Change of World* (1951), was selected by W. H. Auden for the Yale Younger Poets series when Rich was still a student at Radcliffe. The daughter of a Jewish doctor and professor of medicine at Johns Hopkins University and a non-Jewish mother, Rich grew up under the intense tutelage of her father. She became estranged from him when, against his assimilationist wishes, she married a Jewish economist, Alfred Conrad, a professor at Harvard. (The family conflicts have been repeatedly examined in Rich's verse.) Rich quickly had three sons; she writes in *Of Woman Born* (1976) of her unhappiness as a wife and mother and of the conflict she felt between those roles, as socially defined, and that of the writer. In 1963, at the age of thirty-four, Rich published *Snapshots of a Daughter-in-Law,* in which the themes of rebellion and disaffection present in masked forms in her first two books became overt. In the 1960s Rich and her husband moved to New York; the marriage dissolved, and Rich's husband committed suicide. Some years later, Rich declared herself to be a lesbian and joined lesbian political action to the other forms of social action in which she had engaged during the 1960s, when she had taught in the open admissions program at the City College of New York and had joined in protests against the Vietnam War.

[1] Paid male lovers.

Rich has lived a politically committed life and has not always escaped the dangers of politically inspired writing—a preference for bluntness over complexity of response, a certain predictability of stance. At the same time, she has been a seismograph of American protest, registering in turn the convulsions of the peace movement, the women's movement, and, later, the gay rights movement.

More recently, Rich has turned to reexamining the traditional life of women in the past, hoping to reconstruct a connection between those older female arts and skills and the inner life of contemporary women. After living for some years in western Massachusetts, Rich has now moved to California.

Though Rich's accomplished early verse in *A Change of World* (1951) and *The Diamond Cutters* (1955) imitated the formal patterns she found in Yeats, Auden, and Frost, she moved during the 1960s into free verse and has only rarely returned to formal prosody. She has experimented with the prose poem (in "Shooting Script") as well as with forms, such as "jump cuts," borrowed from the cinema and from photography. Her forms seem, however, subordinate to the urgency of the voice that speaks in the poems, whether in rage or in measured attack. It is typical of Rich to utter a theme first in a crude oppositional cartoon, like a political caricaturist; in a subsequent volume the same theme, often a myth or an archetype, is likely to be more subtly and deeply explored. *Leaflets* (1969), as its title implies, had the urgency of a set of bulletins from a political strategy center; *The Will to Change* (1971) explored inner personal drama, that drama that Rich has continued to trace in her metaphors of exile, toil, burning, sickness, devastation, rape, imprisonment, nakedness, and struggle. "I am trying to hold in one steady glance / all the parts of my life," she says in "Toward the Solstice," echoing Matthew Arnold's wish "to see life steadily and see it whole."

It is in fact the Victorians whom Rich most resembles in her earnestness, her direct gaze at social conditions, and her tone of public moral assertion. Her poetry lacks suppleness, play, wit, and humor; she is always serious. But she has never been content simply to be a propagandist. Her drive to make poetry of her autobiography reveals a subjectivity not entirely willing to be absorbed in the role of collective spokesperson. Her recent books—*The Dream of a Common Language* (1978), *A Wild Patience Has Taken Me This Far* (1981), and *The Fact of a Doorframe* (1985)—show an increasingly complex and searching response to the deprivations and yearning of the human condition.

Further Reading:
Adrienne Rich's Poetry: Text of the Poems; The Poet on Her Work; Reviews and Criticism, ed. B. C. Gelpi and A. Gelpi, 1975.

Texts:
"Upper Broadway" from *The Dream of a Common Language,* 1978.
"Grandmothers" from *A Wild Patience Has Taken Me This Far,* 1981.
All other selections from *Poems Selected and New, 1950–1974,* 1975.
See also *Of Woman Born: Motherhood as Experience and Institution,* 1976.
Women and Honor: Some Notes on Lying, 1977.
On Lies, Secrets, and Silence: Selected Prose, 1966–1978, 1979.

The Middle-aged

Their faces, safe as an interior
Of Holland tiles and Oriental carpet,
Where the fruit-bowl, always filled, stood in a light
Of placid afternoon—their voices' measure,
Their figures moving in the Sunday garden   5
To lay the tea outdoors or trim the borders,
Afflicted, haunted us. For to be young
Was always to live in other peoples' houses
Whose peace, if we sought it, had been made by others,
Was ours at second-hand and not for long.   10
The custom of the house, not ours, the sun
Fading the silver-blue Fortuny¹ curtains,
The reminiscence of a Christmas party
Of fourteen years ago—all memory,
Signs of possession and of being possessed,   15
We tasted, tense with envy. They were so kind,
Would have given us anything; the bowl of fruit
Was filled for us, there was a room upstairs
We must call ours: but twenty years of living
They could not give. Nor did they ever speak   20
Of the coarse stain on that polished balustrade,
The crack in the study window, or the letters
Locked in a drawer and the key destroyed.
All to be understood by us, returning
Late, in our own time—how that peace was made,   25
Upon what terms, with how much left unsaid.
1955

Living in Sin

She had thought the studio would keep itself;
no dust upon the furniture of love.
Half heresy, to wish the taps less vocal,
the panes relieved of grime. A plate of pears,
a piano with a Persian shawl, a cat   5

¹ Manufacturer of expensive cloth.

stalking the picturesque amusing mouse
had risen at his urging.
Not that at five each separate stair would writhe
under the milkman's tramp; that morning light
so coldly would delineate the scraps   10
of last night's cheese and three sepulchral bottles;
that on the kitchen shelf among the saucers
a pair of beetle-eyes would fix her own—
envoy from some village in the moldings . . .
Meanwhile, he, with a yawn,   15
sounded a dozen notes upon the keyboard,
declared it out of tune, shrugged at the mirror,
rubbed at his beard, went out for cigarettes;
while she, jeered by the minor demons,
pulled back the sheets and made the bed and found   20
a towel to dust the table-top,
and let the coffee-pot boil over on the stove.
By evening she was back in love again,
though not so wholly but throughout the night
she woke sometimes to feel the daylight coming   25
like a relentless milkman up the stairs.

1955

Snapshots of a Daughter-in-Law

1.

You, once a belle in Shreveport,[1]
with henna-colored hair, skin like a peachbud,
still have your dresses copied from that time,
and play a Chopin[2] prelude
called by Cortot:[3] *"Delicious recollections*   5
float like perfume through the memory."

Your mind now, moldering like wedding-cake,
heavy with useless experience, rich
with suspicion, rumor, fantasy,
crumbling to pieces under the knife-edge   10
of mere fact. In the prime of your life.

[1] In Louisiana.
[2] Polish composer for the piano (1810–1849).
[3] Alfred Cortot, pianist.

Nervy, glowering, your daughter
wipes the teaspoons, grows another way.

2.

Banging the coffee-pot into the sink
she hears the angels chiding, and looks out   15
past the raked gardens to the sloppy sky.
Only a week since They said: *Have no patience.*

The next time it was: *Be insatiable.*
Then: *Save yourself; others you cannot save.*
Sometimes she's let the tapstream scald her arm,   20
a match burn to her thumbnail,

or held her hand above the kettle's snout
right in the woolly steam. They are probably angels,
since nothing hurts her anymore, except
each morning's grit blowing into her eyes.   25

3.

A thinking woman sleeps with monsters.
The beak that grips her, she becomes. And Nature,
that sprung-lidded, still commodious
steamer-trunk of *tempora* and *mores*[4]
gets stuffed with it all: the mildewed orange-flowers,   30
the female pills, the terrible breasts
of Boadicea[5] beneath flat foxes' heads and orchids.

Two handsome women, gripped in argument,
each proud, acute, subtle, I hear scream
across the cut glass and majolica   35
like Furies cornered from their prey:
The argument *ad feminam*,[6] all the old knives
that have rusted in my back, I drive in yours,
ma semblable, ma soeur![7]

4.

Knowing themselves too well in one another: 40
their gifts no pure fruition, but a thorn,

---

[4] Latin: "times" and "customs."
[5] British warrior-queen (d. A.D. 61).
[6] By analogy to *ad hominem,* an unfair personal
attack.
[7] French: "my double, my sister!" Adapted from

Hypocrite lecteur, mon semblable, mon frère!
("Hypocrite reader, my double, my brother!")
in the poem "Au Lecteur" ("To the Reader")
prefacing *Les Fleurs du Mal* (*Flowers of Evil*) by
Charles Baudelaire, French poet (1821–1867).

the prick filed sharp against a hint of scorn . . .
Reading while waiting
for the iron to heat,
writing, *My Life had stood—a Loaded Gun—*[8]   45
in that Amherst pantry while the jellies boil and scum,
or, more often,
iron-eyed and beaked and purposed as a bird,
dusting everything on the whatnot every day of life.

5.

Dulce ridens, dulce loquens,[9]   50
she shaves her legs until they gleam
like petrified mammoth-tusk.

6.

When to her lute Corinna sings[10]
neither words nor music are her own;
only the long hair dipping   55
over her cheek, only the song
of silk against her knees
and these
adjusted in reflections of an eye.

Poised, trembling and unsatisfied, before   60
an unlocked door, that cage of cages,
tell us, you bird, you tragical machine—
is this *fertilisante douleur?*[11] Pinned down
by love, for you the only natural action,
are you edged more keen   65
to prise the secrets of the vault? has Nature shown
her household books to you, daughter-in-law,
that her sons never saw?

7.

"To have in this uncertain world some stay
which cannot be undermined, is   70
of the utmost consequence."[12]
                    Thus wrote
a woman, partly brave and partly good,

---

[8] Poem by Emily Dickinson (1830–1886) of
Amherst, Massachusetts.
[9] Latin: "Sweetly laughing, sweetly speaking."
Adapted from the Roman poet Horace's "dulce
ridentem . . . dulce loquentem" in *Odes,* I, 22.

[10] First line of a song by Thomas Campion
(1567–1620).
[11] French: "fertilizing grief."
[12] From Mary Wollstonecraft (1759–1797),
Thoughts on the Education of Daughters (1787).

who fought with what she partly understood.
Few men about her would or could do more,   75
hence she was labeled harpy, shrew and whore.

8.

"You all die at fifteen,"[13] said Diderot,
and turn part legend, part convention.
Still, eyes inaccurately dream
behind closed windows blankening with steam.   80
Deliciously, all that we might have been,
all that we were—fire, tears,
wit, taste, martyred ambition—
stirs like the memory of refused adultery
the drained and flagging bosom of our middle years.   85

9.

Not that it is done well, but
that it is done at all?[14] Yes, think
of the odds! or shrug them off forever.
This luxury of the precocious child,
Time's precious chronic invalid,—   90
would we, darlings, resign it if we could?
Our blight has been our sinecure:
mere talent was enough for us—
glitter in fragments and rough drafts.

Sigh no more, ladies.
                    Time is male   95
and in his cups drinks to the fair.
Bemused by gallantry, we hear
our mediocrities over-praised,
indolence read as abnegation,   100
slattern thought styled intuition,
every lapse forgiven, our crime
only to cast too bold a shadow
or smash the mold straight off.

For that, solitary confinement,   105
tear gas, attrition shelling.
Few applicants for that honor.

---

[13] From *Lettres à Sophie Volland* by Denis Diderot
(1713–1784), French philosopher.
[14] From *The Life of Samuel Johnson* (1791) by
James Boswell (1740–1795). Johnson's response
to Boswell's telling him that he had seen a
woman preaching at a Quaker meeting was:
"Sir, a woman's preaching is like a dog's
walking on his hinder legs. It is not done well;
but you are surprised to find it done at all."

10.

　　　　Well,
she's long about her coming, who must be
more merciless to herself than history.   110
Her mind full to the wind, I see her plunge
breasted and glancing through the currents,
taking the light upon her
at least as beautiful as any boy
or helicopter,   115
　　　　poised, still coming,
her fine blades making the air wince

but her cargo
no promise then:
delivered   120
palpable
ours.
1963

Peeling Onions

　　Only to have a grief
　　equal to all these tears!

　　There's not a sob in my chest.
　　Dry-hearted as Peer Gynt[1]
　　I pare away, no hero,   5
　　merely a cook.

　　Crying was labor, once
　　when I'd good cause.
　　Walking, I felt my eyes like wounds
　　raw in my head,   10
　　so postal-clerks, I thought, must stare.
　　A dog's look, a cat's, burnt to my brain—

---

[1] Hero of the poetic drama *Peer Gynt,* by Henrik
Ibsen (1828–1906), Danish poet and dramatist.

yet all that stayed
stuffed in my lungs like smog.

These old tears in the chopping-bowl.   15
1963

Necessities of Life

Piece by piece I seem
to re-enter the world: I first began

a small, fixed dot, still see
that old myself, a dark-blue thumbtack

pushed into the scene,   5
a hard little head protruding

from the pointillist's buzz and bloom.
After a time the dot

begins to ooze. Certain heats
melt it.   10
          Now I was hurriedly

blurring into ranges
of burnt red, burning green,

whole biographies swam up and
swallowed me like Jonah.[1]   15

Jonah! I was Wittgenstein,
Mary Wollstonecraft, the soul

of Louis Jouvet,[2] dead
in a blown-up photograph.

---

[1] Prophet swallowed by a whale (Jonah 1:17).
[2] Wittgenstein: Ludwig Wittgenstein, Austrian
philosopher who lived in England (1889–1951);
Mary Wollstonecraft: author (1759–1797) of the

Vindication of the Rights of Women (1792), wife
of William Godwin, and mother of Mary
Shelley; Louis Jouvet: French stage and film
actor (1887–1951).

Till, wolfed almost to shreds,   20
I learned to make myself

unappetizing. Scaly as a dry bulb
thrown into a cellar

I used myself, let nothing use me.
Like being on a private dole,   25

sometimes more like kneading bricks in Egypt.[3]
What life was there, was mine,

now and again to lay
one hand on a warm brick

and touch the sun's ghost   30
with economical joy,

now and again to name
over the bare necessities.

So much for those days. Soon
practice may make me middling-perfect, I'll   35

dare inhabit the world
trenchant in motion as an eel, solid

as a cabbage-head. I have invitations:
a curl of mist steams upward

from a field, visible as my breath,   40
houses along a road stand waiting

like old women knitting, breathless
to tell their tales.
1966

---

[3] The work of the Jews before Moses led them
out of slavery.

"I Am in Danger—Sir—"[1]

"Half-cracked" to Higginson, living,
afterward famous in garbled versions,

your hoard of dazzling scraps a battlefield,
now your old snood

mothballed at Harvard[2]   5
and you in your variorum monument
equivocal to the end—
who are you?

Gardening the day-lily,
wiping the wine-glass stems,   10
your thought pulsed on behind
a forehead battered paper-thin,

you, woman, masculine
in single-mindedness,
for whom the word was more   15
than a symptom—

a condition of being.
Till the air buzzing with spoiled language
sang in your ears
of Perjury   20

and in your half-cracked way you chose
silence for entertainment,
chose to have it out at last
on your own premises.

1966

---

[1] From Emily Dickinson's letter of June 7, 1862, to Thomas Wentworth Higginson (1823–1911), then editor of the *Atlantic Monthly*.
[2] Memorabilia of the Dickinson homestead, as well as the packets of manuscript poems by Emily Dickinson, are kept in the Dickinson Room of the Houghton Library at Harvard University.

Orion[1]

Far back when I went zig-zagging
through tamarack[2] pastures
you were my genius, you
my cast-iron Viking, my helmed
lion-heart king in prison.   5
Years later now you're young

my fierce half-brother, staring
down from that simplified west
your breast open, your belt dragged down
by an oldfashioned thing, a sword   10
the last bravado you won't give over
though it weighs you down as you stride

and the stars in it are dim
and maybe have stopped burning.
But you burn, and I know it;   15
as I throw back my head to take you in
an old transfusion happens again:
divine astronomy is nothing to it.

Indoors I bruise and blunder,
break faith, leave ill enough   20
alone, a dead child born in the dark.
Night cracks up over the chimney,
pieces of time, frozen geodes
come showering down in the grate.

A man reaches behind my eyes   25
and finds them empty
a woman's head turns away
from my head in the mirror
children are dying my death
and eating crumbs of my life.   30

Pity is not your forte.
Calmly you ache up there
pinned aloft in your crow's nest,

---

[1] In classical myth, a giant and hunter
transformed after death into a constellation in
the heavens.

[2] Type of pine tree.

my speechless pirate!
You take it all for granted   35
and when I look you back

it's with a starlike eye
shooting its cold and egotistical spear
where it can do least damage.
Breathe deep! No hurt, no pardon   40
out here in the cold with you
you with your back to the wall.
1969

Study of History

Out there.   The mind of the river
as it might be you.

Lights   blotted by unseen hulls
repetitive shapes passing
dull foam crusting the margin   5
barges sunk below the water-line with silence.
The scow, drudging on.

Lying in the dark, to think of you
and your harsh traffic
gulls pecking your rubbish   natural historians   10
mourning your lost purity
pleasure cruisers
witlessly careening you

but this
after all   15
is the narrows and after
all we have never entirely
known what was done to you upstream
what powers trepanned
which of your channels diverted   20
what rockface leaned to stare
in your upturned
defenseless
face.
1971

Planetarium

Thinking of Caroline Herschel (1750–1848)
astronomer, sister of William;[1] and others.

A woman in the shape of a monster
a monster in the shape of a woman
the skies are full of them

a woman   'in the snow   5
among the Clocks and instruments
or measuring the ground with poles'

in her 98 years to discover
8 comets

she whom the moon ruled
like us   10
levitating into the night sky
riding the polished lenses

Galaxies of women, there
doing penance for impetuousness
ribs chilled   15
in those spaces   of the mind

An eye,

        'virile, precise and absolutely certain'
        from the mad webs of Uranusborg

                              encountering the NOVA   20

every impulse of light exploding
from the core
as life flies out of us

        Tycho[2] whispering at last

        'Let me not seem to have lived in vain'   25

---

[1] Sir William Herschel (1738–1822), English
pioneer in the study of the stars and discoverer
of Uranus. His sister Caroline discovered eight
comets and three nebulas.

[2] Tycho Brahe (1546–1601), Danish astronomer.

What we see, we see
and seeing is changing
the light that shrivels a mountain
and leaves a man alive

Heartbeat of the pulsar   30
heart sweating through my body

The radio impulse
pouring in from Taurus

     I am bombarded yet   I stand

I have been standing all my life in the
direct path of a battery of signals
the most accurately transmitted most   35
untranslatable language in the universe
I am a galactic cloud so deep   so involuted that a light wave could take 15
years to travel through me   And has   40
taken   I am an instrument in the shape
of a woman trying to translate pulsations
into images   for the relief of the body
and the reconstruction of the mind.   45
1971

---

from **Shooting Script**

from **Part I: 11/69–2/70**

3.

The old blanket. The crumbs of rubbed wool turning up.

Where we lay and breakfasted. The stains of tea. The squares of winter light
    projected on the wool.

You, sleeping with closed windows. I, sleeping in the silver nitrate burn of zero
    air.

Where it can snow, I'm at home; the crystals accumulating spell out my story.

The cold encrustation thickening on the ledge.   5

The arrow-headed facts, accumulating, till a whole city is taken over.

Midwinter and the loss of love, going comes before gone, over and over the
 point is missed and still the blind will turns for its target.

1971

5.

Of simple choice they are the villagers; their clothes come with them like red
 clay roads they have been walking.

The sole of the foot is a map, the palm of the hand a letter, learned by heart
 and worn close to the body.

They seemed strange to me, till I began to recall their dialect.

Poking the spade into the dry loam, listening for the tick of broken pottery,
 hoarding the brown and black bits in a dented can.

Evenings, at the table, turning the findings out, pushing them around with a
 finger, beginning to dream of fitting them together.   5

Hiding all this work from them, although they might have helped me.

Going up at night, hiding the tin can in a closet, where the linoleum lies in
 shatters on a back shelf.

Sleeping to dream of the unformed, the veil of water pouring over the wet
 clay, the rhythms of choice, the lost methods.

1971

9.: Newsreel

This would not be the war we fought in. See, the foliage is heavier, there were
 no hills of that size there.

But I find it impossible not to look for actual persons known to me and not
 seen since; impossible not to look for myself.

The scenery angers me, I know there is something wrong, the sun is too high,
 the grass too trampled, the peasants' faces too broad, and the main square of
 the capital had no arcades like those.

Yet the dead look right, and the roofs of the huts, and the crashed fuselage
 burning among the ferns.

But this is not the war I came to see, buying my ticket, stumbling through the
    darkness, finding my place among the sleepers and masturbators in the dark.   5

I thought of seeing the General who cursed us, whose name they gave to an
    expressway; I wanted to see the faces of the dead when they were living.

Once I know they filmed us, back at the camp behind the lines, taking showers
    under the trees and showing pictures of our girls.

Somewhere there is a film of the war we fought in, and it must contain the
    flares, the souvenirs, the shadows of the netted brush, the standing in line of
    the innocent, the hills that were not of this size.

Somewhere my body goes taut under the deluge, somewhere I am naked behind
    the lines, washing my body in the water of that war.

Someone has that war stored up in metal canisters, a memory he cannot use,
    somewhere my innocence is proven with my guilt, but this would not be the
    war I fought in.   10

1971

10.

—for Valerie Glauber

They[1] come to you with their descriptions of your soul.

They come and drop their mementos at the foot of your bed; their feathers,
    ferns, fans, grasses from the western mountains.

They wait for you to unfold for them like a paper flower, a secret springing
    open in a glass of water.

They believe your future has a history and that it is themselves.

They have family trees to plant for you, photographs of dead children, old
    bracelets and rings they want to fasten onto you.   5

And, in spite of this, you live alone.

Your secret hangs in the open like Poe's purloined letter; their longing and
    their methods will never let them find it.

---

[1] "They" refers to men, "you" to women.

Your secret cries out in the dark and hushes; when they start out of sleep they think you are innocent.

You hang among them like the icon in a Russian play; living your own intenser life behind the lamp they light in front of you.

You are spilt here like mercury on a marble counter, liquefying into many globes, each silvered like a planet caught in a lens.   10

You are a mirror lost in a brook, an eye reflecting a torrent of reflections.

You are a letter written, folded, burnt to ash, and mailed in an envelope to another continent.

1971

13.

We are driven to odd attempts; once it would not have occurred to me to put out in a boat, not on a night like this.

Still, it was an instrument, and I had pledged myself to try any instrument that came my way. Never to refuse one from conviction of incompetence.

A long time I was simply learning to handle the skiff; I had no special training and my own training was against me.

I had always heard that darkness and water were a threat.

In spite of this, darkness and water helped me to arrive here.   5

I watched the lights on the shore I had left for a long time; each one, it seemed to me, was a light I might have lit, in the old days.

1971

14.

Whatever it was: the grains of the glacier caked in the boot-cleats; ashes spilled on white formica.

The death-col[2] viewed through power-glasses; the cube of ice melting on stainless steel.

---

[2] A pass in a mountain range.

Whatever it was, the image that stopped you, the one on which you came to
grief, projecting it over & over on empty walls.

Now to give up the temptations of the projector; to see instead the web of
cracks filtering across the plaster.

To read there the map of the future, the roads radiating from the initial split,
the filaments thrown out from that impasse.   5

To reread the instructions on your palm; to find there how the lifeline, broken,
keeps its direction.

To read the etched rays of the bullet-hole left years ago in the glass; to know
in every distortion of the light what fracture is.

To put the prism in your pocket, the thin glass lens, the map of the inner city,
the little book with gridded pages.

To pull yourself up by your own roots; to eat the last meal in your old
neighborhood.

1971

Trying to Talk with a Man

Out in this desert we are testing bombs,

that's why we came here.

Sometimes I feel an underground river
forcing its way between deformed cliffs
an acute angle of understanding   5
moving itself like a locus of the sun
into this condemned scenery.

What we've had to give up to get here—
whole LP collections, films we starred in
playing in the neighborhoods, bakery windows   10
full of dry, chocolate-filled Jewish cookies,
the language of love-letters, of suicide notes,
afternoons on the riverbank
pretending to be children

Coming out to this desert   15
we meant to change the face of
driving among dull green succulents
walking at noon in the ghost town
surrounded by a silence

that sounds like the silence of the place   20
except that it came with us
and is familiar
and everything we were saying until now
was an effort to blot it out—
coming out here we are up against it   25

Out here I feel more helpless
with you than without you

You mention the danger
and list the equipment
we talk of people caring for each other   30
in emergencies—laceration, thirst—
but you look at me like an emergency

Your dry heat feels like power
your eyes are stars of a different magnitude
they reflect lights that spell out: EXIT   35
when you get up and pace the floor

talking of the danger
as if it were not ourselves
as if we were testing anything else.
1973

Diving into the Wreck

First having read the book of myths,
and loaded the camera,
and checked the edge of the knife-blade,
I put on
the body-armor of black rubber   5
the absurd flippers
the grave and awkward mask.
I am having to do this

not like Cousteau[1] with his
assiduous team
aboard the sun-flooded schooner
but here alone.

There is a ladder.
The ladder is always there
hanging innocently
close to the side of the schooner.
We know what it is for,
we who have used it.
Otherwise
it's a piece of maritime floss
some sundry equipment.

I go down.
Rung after rung and still
the oxygen immerses me
the blue light
the clear atoms
of our human air.
I go down.
My flippers cripple me,
I crawl like an insect down the ladder
and there is no one
to tell me when the ocean
will begin.

First the air is blue and then
it is bluer and then green and then
black I am blacking out and yet
my mask is powerful
it pumps my blood with power
the sea is another story
the sea is not a question of power
I have to learn alone
to turn my body without force
in the deep element.

And now: it is easy to forget
what I came for
among so many who have always
lived here

10

15

20

25

30

35

40

45

---

[1] Jacques Cousteau (b. 1910), French underwater
explorer, inventor of the aqualung, author, and
filmmaker.

swaying their crenellated fans
between the reefs
and besides   50
you breathe differently down here.

I came to explore the wreck.
The words are purposes.
The words are maps.
I came to see the damage that was done   55
and the treasures that prevail.
I stroke the beam of my lamp
slowly along the flank
of something more permanent
than fish or weed   60

the thing I came for:
the wreck and not the story of the wreck
the thing itself and not the myth
the drowned face always staring
toward the sun   65
the evidence of damage
worn by salt and sway into this threadbare beauty
the ribs of the disaster
curving their assertion
among the tentative haunters.   70

This is the place.
And I am here, the mermaid whose dark hair
streams black, the merman in his armored body
We circle silently
about the wreck   75
we dive into the hold.
I am she: I am he
whose drowned face sleeps with open eyes
whose breasts still bear the stress
whose silver, copper, vermeil cargo lies   80
obscurely inside barrels
half-wedged and left to rot
we are the half-destroyed instruments
that once held to a course
the water-eaten log   85
the fouled compass

We are, I am, you are
by cowardice or courage
the one who find our way
back to this scene   90

carrying a knife, a camera
a book of myths
in which
our names do not appear.
1973

Translations

You show me the poems of some woman
my age, or younger
translated from your language

Certain words occur: *enemy, oven, sorrow*
enough to let me know   5
she's a woman of my time

obsessed

with Love, our subject:
we've trained it like ivy to our walls
baked it like bread in our ovens   10
worn it like lead on our ankles
watched it through binoculars as if
it were a helicopter
bringing food to our famine
or the satellite   15
of a hostile power

I begin to see that woman
doing things: stirring rice
ironing a skirt
typing a manuscript till dawn   20

trying to make a call
from a phonebooth

The phone rings unanswered
in a man's bedroom
she hears him telling someone else   25
Never mind. She'll get tired—
hears him telling her story to her sister
who becomes her enemy

and will in her own time
light her own way to sorrow   30

ignorant of the fact this way of grief
is shared, unnecessary
and political
1973

From a Survivor

The pact that we made was the ordinary pact
of men & women in those days

I don't know who we thought we were
that our personalities
could resist the failures of the race   5

Lucky or unlucky, we didn't know
the race had failures of that order
and that we were going to share them

Like everybody else, we thought of ourselves as special

Your body is as vivid to me   10
as it ever was: even more

since my feeling for it is clearer:
I know what it could and could not do

it is no longer
the body of a god   15
or anything with power over my life

Next year it would have been 20 years
and you are wastefully dead
who might have made the leap
we talked, too late, of making   20

which I live now
not as a leap
but a succession of brief, amazing movements
each one making possible the next
1973

Upper Broadway

The leafbud straggles forth
toward the frigid light of the airshaft   this is faith
this pale extension of a day
when looking up   you know   something is changing
winter has turned   though the wind is colder   5
Three streets away   a roof collapses   onto people
who thought they still had time.   Time out of mind

I have written so many words
wanting to live inside you
to be of use to you   10

Now I must write for myself   for this blind
woman scratching the pavement   with her wand of thought
this slippered crone   inching on icy streets
reaching into wire trashbaskets   pulling out
what was thrown away   and infinitely precious   15

I look at my hands and see   they are still unfinished
I look at the vine and see the leafbud
inching towards life

I look at my face in the glass   and see
a halfborn woman   20
1978

Grandmothers

1. Mary Gravely Jones

We had no petnames, no diminutives for you,
always the formal guest under my father's roof:
you were "Grandmother Jones" and you visited rarely.
I see you walking up and down the garden,
restless, southern-accented, reserved, you did not seem   5
my mother's mother or anyone's grandmother.
You were Mary, widow of William, and no matriarch,
yet smoldering to the end with frustrate life,
ideas nobody listened to, least of all my father.
One summer night you sat with my sister and me   10

in the wooden glider long after twilight,
holding us there with streams of pent-up words.
You could quote every poet I had ever heard of,
had read *The Opium Eater,*[1] Amiel[2] and Bernard Shaw,[3]
your green eyes looked clenched against opposition.   15
You married straight out of the convent school,
your background was country, you left an unperformed
typescript of a play about Burr and Hamilton,[4]
you were impotent and brilliant, no one cared
about your mind, you might have ended   20
elsewhere than in that glider
reciting your unwritten novels to the children.

2. Hattie Rice Rich

Your sweetness of soul was a mystery to me,
you who slip-covered chairs, glued broken china,
lived out of a wardrobe trunk in our guestroom   25
summer and fall, then took the Pullman train
in your darkblue dress and straw hat, to Alabama,
shuttling half-yearly between your son and daughter.
Your sweetness of soul was a convenience for everyone,
how you rose with the birds and children, boiled your own egg,   30
fished for hours on a pier, your umbrella spread,
took the street-car downtown shopping
endlessly for your son's whims, the whims of genius,
kept your accounts in ledgers, wrote letters daily.
All through World War Two the forbidden word   35
Jewish was barely uttered in your son's house;
your anger flared over inscrutable things.
Once I saw you crouched on the guestroom bed,
knuckles blue-white around the bedpost, sobbing
your one brief memorable scene of rebellion: 40
you didn't want to go back South that year.
You were never "Grandmother Rich" but "Anana";
you had money of your own but you were homeless,
Hattie, widow of Samuel, and no matriarch,
dispersed among the children and grandchildren.   45

3. Granddaughter

Easier to encapsulate your lives
in a slide-show of impressions given and taken,

[1] By Thomas De Quincey (1785–1859), British
essayist.
[2] Henri Frederic Amiel (1821–1881), Swiss critic
and diarist.
[3] George Bernard Shaw (1856–1950), Irish
playwright and essayist.

[4] Aaron Burr (1756–1836) killed Alexander
Hamilton (1755–1804) in a duel after Hamilton
had allegedly disparaged his character.

to play the child or victim, the projectionist,
easier to invent a script for each of you,
myself still at the center, 50
than to write words in which you might have found
yourselves, looked up at me and said
"Yes, I was like that; but I was something more. . . ."
Danville, Virginia; Vicksburg, Mississippi;
the "war between the states" a living memory 55
its aftermath the plague-town closing
its gates, trying to cure itself with poisons.
I can almost touch that little town. . . .
a little white town rimmed with Negroes,
making a deep shadow on the whiteness. 60
Born a white woman, Jewish or of curious mind
—twice an outsider, still believing in inclusion—
in those defended hamlets of half-truth
broken in two by one strange idea,
"blood" the all-powerful, awful theme— 65
what were the lessons to be learned? If I believe
the daughter of one of you—Amnesia was the answer.
1981

Gary Snyder
b. 1930

Gary Snyder has brought both Zen Buddhism and ecological concerns into
contemporary American poetry. He is a notable landscape poet of the American
Northwest, who sees the West Coast as one border of the "Pacific basin" and
links it to the Orient and to the Alaskan Indian and Eskimo culture. In
symbolically turning away from the East Coast, the traditional "hub" of
American poetry, and in rejecting as well the Anglo-Saxon Protestant ethnic base
of American poetry, Snyder reminds his readers that many different American
orientations are possible, that the West, as well as the East, can be the center
from which allegiances are measured. He reminds us, too, that we are not the
first inhabitants of our country.

Snyder was born in San Francisco, but soon after his birth his family moved
to a small farm near Seattle, where he grew up. He went to Reed College on a
scholarship, working summers with the U.S. Forest Service and in logging camps
in the Northwest. His senior thesis at Reed, *He Who Invented Birds in His
Father's Village,* showed his early acquaintance with the culture of the American
Indians. Later he studied linguistics and American Indian culture at the University
of Indiana; he then moved to San Francisco and completed all requirements
except the thesis for a doctorate in Japanese at Berkeley. In the 1950s he was
associated in San Francisco with Allen Ginsberg, Jack Kerouac, and others who

introduced the "Beat" movement in literature. (He was the hero of Kerouac's 1958 novel *The Dharma Bums*.) He worked as a wiper on an American tanker that went to the Persian Gulf and the South Pacific islands; from 1956 to 1968 he lived chiefly in Japan and spent several years in residence at Zen Buddhist monasteries. He considers himself "a Buddhist of the Mahayana-Vajrayana line" and now lives in the Sierra Nevada foothills with his third wife and children.

Snyder's first book was called *Riprap* (1959)—"a cobble of stone laid on steep slick rock / to make a trail for horses in the mountain." In the last poem of that book he defines poetry as "a riprap on the slick rock of metaphysics"—the graspable tactile surface giving us a purchase on the path of thought that we travel. The subsequently published *Myths and Texts* (1960) contains poems from the 1950s concerned with logging and hunting, activities (in which Snyder has participated) that destroy or alter the environment. In later books, Snyder continues his exploration of the West Coast and our relation to nature, most notably in the book called, after the Indian name for North America, *Turtle Island* (1974). His most recent volume is *Axe Handles* (1983).

In his prosody, Snyder derives most immediately from Pound. He has said that his lines are influenced by "five-and-seven-character-line Chinese poems . . . and the songs and dances of Great Basin Indian tribes." The longer poems are digressive and episodic, held together more by moral concern than by an inner architecture. "As a poet," says Snyder, "I hold the most archaic values on earth. They go back to the Neolithic: the fertility of the soil, the magic of animals, the power-vision in solitude, the terrifying initiation and rebirth, the love and ecstasy of the dance, the common work of the tribe." Snyder's work, embodying these values, can be considered either nostalgically regressive or prophetic of the earth's future necessities. Snyder considers poetry "a social and traditional art that is linked to its past and particularly its language. . . . Poetry is intimately linked to any culture's fundamental world view, body of lore, which is its myth base, its symbol-base, and the source of much of its values. . . . That's the ongoing work of major poets, to restate the society's whole body of world-view lore periodically." In turning to Asia and to Buddhism, Snyder, like Ginsberg, suggests to American readers the limitation of a cultural perspective that knows only Western values. But it puts in question, too, the extent to which a country can adopt values and attitudes not culturally indigenous. Since the time of Whitman, there has been a stubborn effort on the part of American poets to enlarge the frame of reference of American literature beyond the European point of view: Snyder's work is part of the history of that long-standing effort.

Further Reading:
B. Steuding, *Gary Snyder*, 1976.

Texts:
"This Poem Is for Bear" from *Myths and Texts*, 1960.
"Riprap" from *Riprap and Cold Mountain Poems*, 1965.
"Sixth-Month Song in the Foothills," "Trail Crew Camp. . . ," "Nansen," and "Looking at Pictures to Be Put Away" from *The Back Country*, 1968.
"I Went into the Maverick Bar," "The Call of the Wild," and "Two Fawns . . ." from *Turtle Island*, 1974.

This Poem Is for Bear

"As for me I am a child of the god of the mountains."

A bear down under the cliff.
She is eating huckleberries.
They are ripe now
Soon it will snow, and she
Or maybe he, will crawl into a hole   5
And sleep. You can see
Huckleberries in bearshit if you
Look, this time of year
If I sneak up on the bear
It will grunt and run   10

The others had all gone down
From the blackberry brambles, but one girl
Spilled her basket, and was picking up her
Berries in the dark.
A tall man stood in the shadow, took her arm,   15
Led her to his home. He was a bear.
In a house under the mountain
She gave birth to slick dark children
With sharp teeth, and lived in the hollow
Mountain many years.   20
            snare a bear: call him out:
honey-eater
forest apple
light-foot
Old man in the fur coat, Bear! come out!   25
Die of your own choice!
Grandfather black-food!
            this girl married a bear
Who rules in the mountains, Bear!
            you have eaten many berries   30
            you have caught many fish
            you have frightened many people
Twelve species north of Mexico
Sucking their paws in the long winter
Tearing the high-strung caches down   35
Whining, crying, jacking off
(Odysseus was a bear)

Bear-cubs gnawing the soft tits
Teeth gritted, eyes screwed tight
     but she let them.   40
Til her brothers found the place
Chased her husband up the gorge
Cornered him in the rocks.
Song of the snared bear:
   "Give me my belt.   45
   "I am near death.
   "I came from the mountain caves
   "At the headwaters,
   "The small streams there
   "Are all dried up.   50

—I think I'll go hunt bears.
      "hunt bears?
Why shit Snyder,
You couldn't hit a bear in the ass   55
     with a handful of rice!"

1960

Riprap[1]

Lay down these words
Before your mind like rocks.
    placed solid, by hands
In choice of place, set
Before the body of the mind   5
    in space and time:
Solidity of bark, leaf, or wall
    riprap of things:
Cobble of milky way,
    straying planets,   10
These poems, people,
    lost ponies with

[1] Snyder's note: "Riprap: a cobble of stone laid
on steep slick rock to make a trail for horses in
the mountains."

Dragging saddles—
   and rocky sure-foot trails.
The worlds like an endless   15
   four-dimensional
Game of *Go*.
    ants and pebbles
In the thin loam, each rock a word
   a creek-washed stone   20
Granite: ingrained
   with torment of fire and weight
Crystal and sediment linked hot
   all change, in thoughts,
As well as things.   25
1959

Sixth-Month Song in the Foothills

In the cold shed sharpening saws.
   a swallow's nest hangs by the door
setting rakers in sunlight
falling from meadow through doorframe
   swallows flit under the eaves.   5

Grinding the falling axe
sharp for the summer
   a swallow shooting out over.
over the river, snow on low hills
sharpening wedges for splitting.   10

Beyond the low hills, white mountains
and now snow is melting. sharpening tools;
   pack horses grazing new grass
bright axes—and swallows
   fly in to my shed.   15
1968

Trail Crew Camp at Bear Valley, 9000 Feet

Northern Sierra—White Bone and Threads of Snowmelt Water

Cut branches back for a day—
trail a thin line through willow
   up buckbrush meadows,
   creekbed for twenty yards
  winding in boulders   5
   zigzags the hill
into timber, white pine.

gooseberry bush on the turns.
hooves clang on the riprap[1]
   dust, brush, branches.   10
  a stone
 cairn[2] at the pass—
strippt mountains hundreds of miles.

sundown went back
   the clean switchbacks to camp. 15
bell on the gelding,
stew in the cook tent,
black coffee in a big tin can.
1968

Nansen

I found you on a rainy morning
After a typhoon
In a bamboo grove at Daitoku-ji.
Tiny wet rag with a
Huge voice, you crawled under the fence 5
To my hand. Left to die.
I carried you home in my raincoat.

---

[1] Stone cobbles laid on rock to make a trail for horses. [2] Pile of stones.

"Nansen, cheese!" you'd shout an answer
And come running.
But you never got big,   10
Bandy-legged bright little dwarf—
Sometimes not eating, often coughing
Mewing bitterly at inner twinge.

Now, thin and older, you won't eat
But milk and cheese. Sitting on a pole   15
In the sun. Hardy with resigned
Discontent.
You just weren't made right. I saved you,
And your three-year life has been full
Of mild, steady pain.   20
1968

Looking at Pictures to Be Put Away

Who was this girl
In her white night gown
Clutching a pair of jeans

On a foggy redwood deck.
She looks up at me tender,   5
Calm, surprised,

What will we remember
Bodies thick with food and lovers
After twenty years.
1968

I Went into the Maverick Bar

I went into the Maverick Bar
In Farmington, New Mexico.
And drank double shots of bourbon
            backed with beer.

My long hair was tucked up under a cap   5
I'd left the earring in the car.

Two cowboys did horseplay
                    by the pool tables,
A waitress asked us
                    where are you from?   10
a country-and-western band began to play
"We don't smoke Marijuana in Muskokie"
And with the next song,
                    a couple began to dance.

They held each other like in High School dances   15
                    in the fifties;
I recalled when I worked in the woods
                    and the bars of Madras, Oregon.
That short-haired joy and roughness—
                    America—your stupidity.   20
I could almost love you again.

We left—onto the freeway shoulders—
                    under the tough old stars—
In the shadow of bluffs
                    I came back to myself,   25
To the real work, to
                    "What is to be done."

1974

The Call of the Wild

The heavy old man in his bed at night
Hears the Coyote singing
                    in the back meadow.
All the years he ranched and mined and logged.
A Catholic.   5
A native Californian.
            and the Coyotes howl in his
Eightieth year.

He will call the Government
Trapper   10
Who uses iron leg-traps on Coyotes,
Tomorrow.

My sons will lose this
Music they have just started
To love.   15

The ex acid-heads from the cities
Converted to Guru or Swami,
Do penance with shiny
Dopey eyes, and quit eating meat.
In the forests of North America,   20
The land of Coyote and Eagle,
They dream of India, of
            forever blissful sexless highs.
And sleep in oil-heated
Geodesic domes, that   25
Were stuck like warts
In the woods.

And the Coyote singing
      is shut away
      for they fear   30
      the call
      of the wild.

And they sold their virgin cedar trees,
      the tallest trees in miles,
To a logger   35
Who told them,

"Trees are full of bugs."

The Government finally decided
To wage the war[1] all-out. Defeat
      is Un-American.   40
And they took to the air,
Their women beside them
      in bouffant hairdos
      putting nail-polish on the
      gunship cannon-buttons.   45
And they never came down,
      for they found,
      the ground
is pro-Communist. And dirty.
And the insects side with the Viet Cong.   50

[1] I.e., the Vietnam War.

So they bomb and they bomb
Day after day, across the planet
blinding sparrows
breaking the ear-drums of owls
splintering trunks of cherries   55
twining and looping
deer intestines
in the shaken, dusty, rocks.

All these Americans up in special cities in the sky
Dumping poisons and explosives   60
Across Asia first,
And next North America,

A war against earth.
When it's done there'll be
no place   65

A Coyote could hide.

envoy[2]

I would like to say
Coyote is forever
Inside you.

But it's not true.   70

1974

_____

Two Fawns That Didn't See
the Light This Spring

A friend in a tipi in the
Northern Rockies went out
hunting white tail with a
.22 and creeped up on a few
day-bedded, sleeping, shot   5
what he thought was a buck.

_____
[2] Short, final stanza of a poem, usually
summarizing the main theme.

"It was a doe, and she was
carrying a fawn."
He cured the meat without
salt; sliced it following the   10
grain.

A friend in the Northern Sierra
hit a doe with her car. It
walked out calmly in the lights,
"And when we butchered her   15
there was a fawn—about so long—
so tiny—but all formed and right.
It had spots. And the little
hooves were soft and white."

1974

Sylvia Plath
1932–1963

The intensity, purity, and spareness of Sylvia Plath's last poems have given her
short career a weight out of proportion to its brevity. Though they come from a
tragic life and often have a tragic subject, these poems are exhilarated, sure,
certain of their path. They are poems of cool mastery, of a talent unafraid of its
own extremes. It is also a well-schooled talent, one that has assimilated the poetry
of D. H. Lawrence, Theodore Roethke, and Robert Lowell and has added a
wild, dark comedy of its own (visible in "Daddy" and "Lady Lazarus") not
learned from any of those masters.

Plath worked obsessively at being a poet from childhood; her first published
poem appeared in a Boston newspaper when she was eight and a half. By the
time she was in college at Smith, she was publishing in *Seventeen* and
Mademoiselle. As her journals show, she had unlimited ambition and equally
unlimited anxiety; cycles of manic planning followed by depressive collapses
recurred throughout her life, causing an unsuccessful suicide attempt at nineteen
and a successful one at thirty-one. Manic-depressive illness was not well
understood at the time, and Plath, like Lowell, underwent electroconvulsive
therapy, involuntary confinement in an asylum, and psychiatric therapy. These
palliative treatments did not prevent the recurrence of symptoms.

Plath's distress at her own emotional volatility caused her to channel her
explosive nature at first into rigidly controlled and conventionally acceptable
poems, published in *The Colossus* (1960). With her marriage to the Yorkshire
poet Ted Hughes, her expatriation to England, and the birth of her two children,
her emotional life deepened and, under the tutelage of Hughes, who approved of

the "demonic" forces in poetry, became freer to express itself. She turned savagely against what she regarded as the German oppressiveness of her professor-father (whose academic specialty was bees) and the bourgeois gentility of her mother (who taught secretarial subjects). Her rage turned as well against her husband when she discovered his infidelity; it was after their separation, in the coldest London winter in years, that she killed herself by turning on the kitchen gas. Plath's best-selling autobiographical (and pseudonymously published) novel, *The Bell Jar* (1963), has none of the talent of her poetry, but it remains a reference point as one of the changing scenarios of explanation that Plath continuously constructed for her life.

Most of Plath's best poetry—*Ariel* (1966), *Crossing the Water* (1971), and *Winter Trees* (1972)—was published posthumously. It caught the public imagination by the topicality of its subject matter (marriage, childbearing, infidelity, the woman artist), but it also caught the literary imagination by its ardent language, its compression, its violence in metaphor, and its authoritative tone. Plath had studied at Boston University with Robert Lowell, and it was probably his example that she followed in writing her later poetry in free verse. Her free verse, however, has none of the loose and low-keyed quality of Lowell's *Life Studies;* rather, it is so firmly supported by internal rhymes, eye rhymes, parallelism, apposition, alliteration, and other binding devices that it seems as fully controlled as any formal verse could be.

Like Emily Dickinson, Plath repudiated the language of conventional female verse for a fierce and daring explicitness. At the same time, her acute and cold self-observation dominated her fiery lines, taming them to form, mediating her tormented states of mind by a high intelligence. Her reputation has grown steadily since her death; *The Collected Poems,* edited by Ted Hughes, was published in 1981 and the *Journals of Sylvia Plath* in 1982. Her short fiction is collected in *Johnny Panic and the Bible of Dreams* (1979), and a selection of her letters, edited with commentary by her mother, Aurelia Schober Plath, was published as *Letters Home* (1975).

Further Reading:

The Art of Sylvia Plath, ed. C. Newman, 1970.
N. H. Steiner, A Closer Look at Ariel: A
Memory of Sylvia Plath, 1973.
E. Butscher, Sylvia Plath: Method and Madness,
1976.
D. Holbrook, Sylvia Plath: Poetry and Existence,
1976.
J. Kroll, Chapters in a Mythology: The Poetry of
Sylvia Plath, 1976.

G. Lane and M. Stevens, Sylvia Plath: A
Bibliography, 1978.
Sylvia Plath: New Views on Poetry, ed. G. Lane,
1979.
M. D. Uroff, Sylvia Plath and Ted Hughes,
1979.
J. Rosenblatt, Sylvia Plath: The Poetry of
Initiation, 1979.

Text:
The Collected Poems, 1981.

Black Rook in Rainy Weather

On the stiff twig up there
Hunches a wet black rook
Arranging and rearranging its feathers in the rain.
I do not expect a miracle
Or an accident   5

To set the sight on fire
In my eye, nor seek
Any more in the desultory weather some design,
But let spotted leaves fall as they fall,
Without ceremony, or portent.   10

Although, I admit, I desire,
Occasionally, some backtalk
From the mute sky, I can't honestly complain:
A certain minor light may still
Lean incandescent   15

Out of kitchen table or chair
As if a celestial burning took
Possession of the most obtuse objects now and then—
Thus hallowing an interval
Otherwise inconsequent   20

By bestowing largesse, honor,
One might say love. At any rate, I now walk
Wary (for it could happen
Even in this dull, ruinous landscape); skeptical,
Yet politic; ignorant   25

Of whatever angel may choose to flare
Suddenly at my elbow. I only know that a rook
Ordering its black feathers can so shine
As to seize my senses, haul
My eyelids up, and grant   30

A brief respite from fear
Of total neutrality. With luck,
Trekking stubborn through this season
Of fatigue, I shall
Patch together a content   35

Of sorts. Miracles occur,
If you care to call those spasmodic
Tricks of radiance miracles. The wait's begun again,
The long wait for the angel,
For that rare, random descent.   40

1960

The Colossus

I shall never get you put together entirely,
Pieced, glued, and properly jointed.
Mule-bray, pig-grunt and bawdy cackles
Proceed from your great lips.
It's worse than a barnyard.   5

Perhaps you consider yourself an oracle,
Mouthpiece of the dead, or of some god or other.
Thirty years now I have labored
To dredge the silt from your throat.
I am none the wiser.   10

Scaling little ladders with gluepots and pails of Lysol
I crawl like an ant in mourning
Over the weedy acres of your brow
To mend the immense skull-plates and clear
The bald, white tumuli[1] of your eyes.   15

A blue sky out of the Oresteia[2]
Arches above us. O father, all by yourself
You are pithy and historical as the Roman Forum.[3]
I open my lunch on a hill of black cypress.
Your fluted bones and acanthine[4] hair are littered   20

In their old anarchy to the horizon-line.
It would take more than a lightning-stroke
To create such a ruin.

---

[1] Grave mounds.
[2] The Greek trilogy, by Aeschylus (525–426 B.C.), recounting the tragic story of the house of Atreus.
[3] The large public market and meeting place in ancient Rome.
[4] Like an acanthus leaf, the stylized ornate leaf that was used as a motif in Greek art.

Nights, I squat in the cornucopia
Of your left ear, out of the wind,   25

Counting the red stars and those of plum-color.
The sun rises under the pillar of your tongue.
My hours are married to shadow.
No longer do I listen for the scrape of a keel
On the blank stones of the landing.   30

1960

The Hanging Man*

By the roots of my hair some god got hold of me.
I sizzled in his blue volts like a desert prophet.

The nights snapped out of sight like a lizard's eyelid:
A world of bald white days in a shadeless socket.

A vulturous boredom pinned me in this tree.   5
If he were I, he would do what I did.

1965

Parliament Hill Fields¹

On this bald hill the new year hones its edge.
Faceless and pale as china
The round sky goes on minding its business.
Your absence² is inconspicuous;
Nobody can tell what I lack.   5

Gulls have threaded the river's mud bed back
To this crest of grass. Inland, they argue,

---

* The poem is Plath's account of the
electroconvulsive therapy ("shock treatments")
that she had been given while under psychiatric
treatment.

¹ Area of London.
² The poem is addressed to a baby lost through
miscarriage.

Settling and stirring like blown paper
Or the hands of an invalid. The wan
Sun manages to strike such tin glints   10

From the linked ponds that my eyes wince
And brim; the city melts like sugar.
A crocodile[3] of small girls
Knotting and stopping, ill-assorted, in blue uniforms,
Opens to swallow me. I'm a stone, a stick,   15

One child drops a barrette of pink plastic;
None of them seem to notice.
Their shrill, gravelly gossip's funneled off.
Now silence after silence offers itself.
The wind stops my breath like a bandage.   20

Southward, over Kentish Town, an ashen smudge
Swaddles roof and tree.
It could be a snowfield or a cloudbank.
I suppose it's pointless to think of you at all.
Already your doll grip lets go.   25

The tumulus,[4] even at noon, guards its black shadow:
You know me less constant,
Ghost of a leaf, ghost of a bird.
I circle the writhen[5] trees. I am too happy.
These faithful dark-boughed cypresses   30

Brood, rooted in their heaped losses.
Your cry fades like the cry of a gnat.
I lose sight of you on your blind journey,
While the heath grass glitters and the spindling rivulets
Unspool and spend themselves. My mind runs with them,   35

Pooling in heel-prints, fumbling pebble and stem.
The day empties its images
Like a cup or a room. The moon's crook whitens,
Thin as the skin seaming a scar.
Now, on the nursery wall,   40

The blue night plants, the little pale blue hill
In your sister's birthday picture start to glow.
The orange pompons, the Egyptian papyrus

---

[3] Name for a double line of children.   [5] Contorted.
[4] Grave mound.

Light up. Each rabbit-eared
Blue shrub behind the glass   45

Exhales an indigo nimbus,
A sort of cellophane balloon.
The old dregs, the old difficulties take me to wife.
Gulls stiffen to their chill vigil in the drafty half-light;
I enter the lit house.   50
1965

Morning Song

Love set you going like a fat gold watch.
The midwife slapped your footsoles, and your bald cry
Took its place among the elements.

Our voices echo, magnifying your arrival. New statue.
In a drafty museum, your nakedness   5
Shadows our safety. We stand round blankly as walls.

I'm no more your mother
Than the cloud that distills a mirror to reflect its own slow
Effacement at the wind's hand.

All night your moth-breath   10
Flickers among the flat pink roses.[1] I wake to listen:
A far sea moves in my ear.

One cry, and I stumble from bed, cow-heavy and floral
In my Victorian nightgown.
Your mouth opens clean as a cat's. The window square   15

Whitens and swallows its dull stars. And now you try
Your handful of notes;
The clear vowels rise like balloons.
1965

---

[1] I.e., of the wallpaper.

Blackberrying

Nobody in the lane, and nothing, nothing but blackberries,
Blackberries on either side, though on the right mainly,
A blackberry alley, going down in hooks, and a sea
Somewhere at the end of it, heaving. Blackberries
Big as the ball of my thumb, and dumb as eyes   5
Ebon in the hedges, fat
With blue-red juices. These they squander on my fingers.
I had not asked for such a blood sisterhood; they must love me.
They accommodate themselves to my milkbottle, flattening their sides.

Overhead go the choughs in black, cacophonous flocks—   10
Bits of burnt paper wheeling in a blown sky.
Theirs is the only voice, protesting, protesting.
I do not think the sea will appear at all.
The high, green meadows are glowing, as if lit from within.
I come to one bush of berries so ripe it is a bush of flies,   15
Hanging their bluegreen bellies and their wing panes in a Chinese screen.
The honey-feast of the berries has stunned them; they believe in heaven.
One more hook, and the berries and bushes end.

The only thing to come now is the sea.
From between two hills a sudden wind funnels at me,   20
Slapping its phantom laundry in my face.
These hills are too green and sweet to have tasted salt.
I follow the sheep path between them. A last hook brings me
To the hills' northern face, and the face is orange rock
That looks out on nothing, nothing but a great space   25
Of white and pewter lights, and a din like silversmiths
Beating and beating at an intractable metal.

1965

The Moon and the Yew Tree

This is the light of the mind, cold and planetary.
The trees of the mind are black. The light is blue.
The grasses unload their griefs on my feet as if I were God,
Prickling my ankles and murmuring of their humility.

Fumy, spiritous mists inhabit this place   5
Separated from my house by a row of headstones.
I simply cannot see where there is to get to.

The moon is no door. It is a face in its own right,
White as a knuckle and terribly upset.
It drags the sea after it like a dark crime; it is quiet   10
With the O-gape of complete despair. I live here.
Twice on Sunday, the bells startle the sky——
Eight great tongues affirming the Resurrection.
At the end, they soberly bong out their names.

The yew tree points up. It has a Gothic shape.   15
The eyes lift after it and find the moon.
The moon is my mother. She is not sweet like Mary.[1]
Her blue garments unloose small bats and owls.
How I would like to believe in tenderness——
The face of the effigy, gentled by candles,   20
Bending, on me in particular, its mild eyes.

I have fallen a long way. Clouds are flowering
Blue and mystical over the face of the stars.
Inside the church, the saints will be all blue,
Floating on their delicate feet over the cold pews,   25
Their hands and faces stiff with holiness.
The moon sees nothing of this. She is bald and wild.
And the message of the yew tree is blackness—blackness and silence.

1965

Crossing the Water

Black lake, black boat, two black, cut-paper people.
Where do the black trees go that drink here?
Their shadows must cover Canada.

A little light is filtering from the water flowers.
Their leaves do not wish us to hurry: 5
They are round and flat and full of dark advice.

---

[1] The Virgin Mary, usually depicted as dressed in
blue.

Cold worlds shake from the oar.
The spirit of blackness is in us, it is in the fishes.
A snag is lifting a valedictory, pale hand;

Stars open among the lilies.   10
Are you not blinded by such expressionless sirens?[1]
This is the silence of astounded souls.

1965

The Bee Meeting

Who are these people at the bridge to meet me? They are the villagers——
The rector, the midwife, the sexton, the agent for bees.
In my sleeveless summery dress I have no protection,
And they are all gloved and covered, why did nobody tell me?
They are smiling and taking out veils tacked to ancient hats.   5

I am nude as a chicken neck, does nobody love me?
Yes, here is the secretary of bees with her white shop smock,
Buttoning the cuffs at my wrists and the slit from my neck to my knees.
Now I am milkweed silk, the bees will not notice.
They will not smell my fear, my fear, my fear.   10

Which is the rector now, is it that man in black?
Which is the midwife, is that her blue coat?
Everybody is nodding a square black head, they are knights in visors,
Breastplates of cheesecloth knotted under the armpits.
Their smiles and their voices are changing. I am led through a beanfield.   15

Strips of tinfoil winking like people,
Feather dusters fanning their hands in a sea of bean flowers,
Creamy bean flowers with black eyes and leaves like bored hearts.
Is it blood clots the tendrils are dragging up that string?
No, no, it is scarlet flowers that will one day be edible.   20

Now they are giving me a fashionable white straw Italian hat
And a black veil that molds to my face, they are making me one of them.
They are leading me to the shorn grove, the circle of hives.

---

[1] Mermaids who, according to classical legend,
enticed sailors to their death.

Is it the hawthorn that smells so sick?
The barren body of hawthorn, etherizing its children.   25

Is it some operation that is taking place?
It is the surgeon my neighbors are waiting for,
This apparition in a green helmet,
Shining gloves and white suit.
Is it the butcher, the grocer, the postman, someone I know?   30

I cannot run, I am rooted, and the gorse hurts me
With its yellow purses, its spiky armory.
I could not run without having to run forever.
The white hive is snug as a virgin,
Sealing off her brood cells, her honey, and quietly humming.   35

Smoke rolls and scarves in the grove.
The mind of the hive thinks this is the end of everything.
Here they come, the outriders, on their hysterical elastics.[1]
If I stand very still, they will think I am cow-parsley,
A gullible head untouched by their animosity,   40

Not even nodding, a personage in a hedgerow.
The villagers open the chambers, they are hunting the queen.
Is she hiding, is she eating honey? She is very clever.
She is old, old, old, she must live another year, and she knows it.
While in their fingerjoint cells the new virgins[2]   45

Dream of a duel they will win inevitably,
A curtain of wax dividing them from the bride flight,
The upflight of the murderess[3] into a heaven that loves her.
The villagers are moving the virgins, there will be no killing.
The old queen does not show herself, is she so ungrateful?   50

I am exhausted, I am exhausted——
Pillar of white in a blackout of knives.
I am the magician's girl who does not flinch.
The villagers are untying their disguises, they are shaking hands.
Whose is that long white box in the grove, what have they accomplished, why
    am I cold.   55

1965

---

[1] The outgoing bees, who then "snap back" to   [2] Embryonic female bees.
the hive.   [3] The queen bee.

The Arrival of the Bee Box

I ordered this, this clean wood box
Square as a chair and almost too heavy to lift.
I would say it was the coffin of a midget
Or a square baby
Were there not such a din in it.   5

The box is locked, it is dangerous.
I have to live with it overnight
And I can't keep away from it.
There are no windows, so I can't see what is in there.
There is only a little grid, no exit.   10

I put my eye to the grid.
It is dark, dark,
With the swarmy feeling of African hands
Minute and shrunk for export,
Black on black, angrily clambering.   15

How can I let them out?
It is the noise that appalls me most of all,
The unintelligible syllables.
It is like a Roman mob,
Small, taken one by one, but my god, together!   20

I lay my ear to furious Latin.
I am not a Caesar.
I have simply ordered a box of maniacs.
They can be sent back.
They can die, I need feed them nothing, I am the owner.   25

I wonder how hungry they are.
I wonder if they would forget me
If I just undid the locks and stood back and turned into a tree.
There is the laburnum, its blond colonnades,
And the petticoats of the cherry.   30

They might ignore me immediately
In my moon suit and funeral veil.

I am no source of honey
So why should they turn on me?
Tomorrow I will be sweet God, I will set them free.   35

The box is only temporary.
1965

Daddy

You do not do, you do not do
Any more, black shoe
In which I have lived like a foot
For thirty years, poor and white,
Barely daring to breathe or Achoo.   5

Daddy, I have had to kill you.
You died before I had time——
Marble-heavy, a bag full of God,
Ghastly statue with one gray toe[1]
Big as a Frisco seal   10

And a head in the freakish Atlantic
Where it pours bean green over blue
In the waters off beautiful Nauset.
I used to pray to recover you.
Ach, du.[2]   15

In the German tongue, in the Polish town
Scraped flat by the roller
Of wars, wars, wars.
But the name of the town is common.
My Polack[3] friend   20

Says there are a dozen or two.
So I never could tell where you
Put your foot, your root,
I never could talk to you.
The tongue stuck in my jaw.   25

[1] Otto Plath's diabetes caused a gangrenous toe,
which led to the septicemia that killed him.
[2] German: "Ah, you." The second-person familiar
form is used for intimates.

[3] Derogatory slang for "Polish."

It stuck in a barb wire snare.
Ich, ich, ich, ich,[4]
I could hardly speak.
I thought every German was you.
And the language obscene   30

An engine, an engine
Chuffing me off like a Jew.
A Jew to Dachau, Auschwitz, Belsen.[5]
I began to talk like a Jew.
I think I may well be a Jew.   35

The snows of the Tyrol,[6] the clear beer of Vienna[7]
Are not very pure or true.
With my gipsy ancestress and my weird luck
And my Taroc pack and my Taroc pack[8]
I may be a bit of a Jew.   40

I have always been scared of *you*,
With your Luftwaffe,[9] your gobbledygoo.
And your neat mustache
And your Aryan[10] eye, bright blue.
Panzer-man, panzer-man,[11] O You——   45

Not God but a swastika[12]
So black no sky could squeak through.
Every woman adores a Fascist,
The boot in the face, the brute
Brute heart of a brute like you.   50

You stand at the blackboard, daddy,[13]
In the picture I have of you,
A cleft in your chin instead of your foot
But no less a devil for that, no not
Any less the black man who   55

Bit my pretty red heart in two.
I was ten when they buried you.
At twenty I tried to die
And get back, back, back to you.
I thought even the bones would do.   60

---

[4] German: "I, I, I, I."
[5] Nazi concentration camps.
[6] Alpine region of Austria.
[7] Capital of Austria.
[8] Pack of cards used in fortune telling.
[9] The Nazi air force.

[10] Word used by Nazis to characterize those of "pure" or unadulterated German stock.
[11] Man resembling a German armored tank.
[12] Symbol of the Nazi party.
[13] Otto Plath was a professor of biology at Boston University.

But they pulled me out of the sack,
And they stuck me together with glue.
And then I knew what to do.
I made a model of you,
A man in black with a Meinkampf[14] look   65

And a love of the rack and the screw.[15]
And I said I do, I do.
So daddy, I'm finally through.
The black telephone's off at the root,
The voices just can't worm through.   70

If I've killed one man, I've killed two——
The vampire who said he was you
And drank my blood for a year,
Seven years, if you want to know.
Daddy, you can lie back now.   75

There's a stake in your fat black heart[16]
And the villagers never liked you.
They are dancing and stamping on you.
They always *knew* it was you.
Daddy, daddy, you bastard, I'm through.   80

1965

Medusa[1]

Off that landspit of stony mouth-plugs,
Eyes rolled by white sticks,
Ears cupping the sea's incoherences,
You house your unnerving head—God-ball,
Lens of mercies,   5

Your stooges
Plying their wild cells in my keel's shadow,
Pushing by like hearts,

[14] German: "My struggle," the title of Hitler's manifesto.
[15] Rack; screw: instruments of torture.
[16] Traditionally, a vampire was buried at a crossroads with a stake through the heart.

[1] In mythology, the female monster who turned all who looked upon her to stone. The poem is addressed, from England, to Plath's mother in the United States.

Red stigmata[2] at the very center,
Riding the rip tide to the nearest point of departure,   10

Dragging their Jesus hair.
Did I escape, I wonder?
My mind winds to you
Old barnacled umbilicus, Atlantic cable,
Keeping itself, it seems, in a state of miraculous repair.   15

In any case, you are always there,
Tremulous breath at the end of my line,
Curve of water upleaping
To my water rod, dazzling and grateful,
Touching and sucking.   20

I didn't call you.
I didn't call you at all.
Nevertheless, nevertheless
You steamed to me over the sea,
Fat and red, a placenta[3]   25

Paralysing the kicking lovers.
Cobra light
Squeezing the breath from the blood bells
Of the fuchsia. I could draw no breath,
Dead and moneyless,   30

Overexposed, like an X-ray.
Who do you think you are?
A Communion wafer? Blubbery Mary?
I shall take no bite of your body,
Bottle in which I live,   35

Ghastly Vatican.[4]
I am sick to death of hot salt.
Green as eunuchs,[5] your wishes
Hiss at my sins.
Off, off, eely tentacle!   40

There is nothing between us.
1965

---

[2] Permanent wounds.
[3] The organ from which nutrients reach the fetus via the umbilical cord.
[4] Residence of the popes.
[5] Castrated men, often used as guardians of the wives of sultans.

Ariel[1]

Stasis in darkness.
Then the substanceless blue
Pour of tor[2] and distances.

God's lioness,
How one we grow,   5
Pivot of heels and knees!—The furrow

Splits and passes, sister to
The brown arc
Of the neck I cannot catch,

Nigger-eye   10
Berries cast dark
Hooks——

Black sweet blood mouthfuls,
Shadows.
Something else   15

Hauls me through air——
Thighs, hair;
Flakes from my heels.

White
Godiva,[3] I unpeel——   20
Dead hands, dead stringencies.

And now I
Foam to wheat, a glitter of seas.
The child's cry

Melts in the wall.   25
And I
Am the arrow,

---

[1] Plath's horse.
[2] High, craggy hill.
[3] Lady Godiva, in the legend, rode naked on her horse.

The dew that flies
Suicidal, at one with the drive
Into the red   30

Eye, the cauldron of morning.
1965

Poppies in October

Even the sun-clouds this morning cannot manage such skirts.
Nor the woman in the ambulance
Whose red heart blooms through her coat so astoundingly——

A gift, a love gift
Utterly unasked for   5
By a sky

Palely and flamily
Igniting its carbon monoxides, by eyes
Dulled to a halt under bowlers.

O my God, what am I   10
That these late mouths should cry open
In a forest of frost, in a dawn of cornflowers.
1965

Lady Lazarus[1]

I have done it again.
One year in every ten
I manage it——

[1] Lazarus was raised from the dead by Jesus.

A sort of walking miracle, my skin
Bright as a Nazi lampshade,[2]   5
My right foot

A paperweight,
My face a featureless, fine
Jew linen.

Peel off the napkin[3]   10
O my enemy.
Do I terrify?——

The nose, the eye pits, the full set of teeth?
The sour breath
Will vanish in a day.   15

Soon, soon the flesh
The grave cave ate will be
At home on me

And I a smiling woman.
I am only thirty.   20
And like the cat I have nine times to die.

This is Number Three.
What a trash
To annihilate each decade.

What a million filaments.   25
The peanut-crunching crowd
Shoves in to see

Them unwrap me hand and foot——
The big strip tease.
Gentlemen, ladies   30

These are my hands
My knees.
I may be skin and bone,

Nevertheless, I am the same, identical woman.
The first time it happened I was ten.   35
It was an accident.

---

[2] The Nazis, in concentration camps, made
lampshades of human skin.
[3] According to legend, the veil or napkin with
which Veronica wiped Jesus' face, as he bore
the Cross, was then impressed with his visage.

The second time I meant
To last it out and not come back at all.
I rocked shut

As a seashell.   40
They had to call and call
And pick the worms off me like sticky pearls.

Dying
Is an art, like everything else.
I do it exceptionally well.   45

I do it so it feels like hell.
I do it so it feels real.
I guess you could say I've a call.

It's easy enough to do it in a cell.
It's easy enough to do it and stay put.   50
It's the theatrical

Comeback in broad day
To the same place, the same face, the same brute
Amused shout:

'A miracle!'   55
That knocks me out.
There is a charge

For the eyeing of my scars, there is a charge
For the hearing of my heart——
It really goes.   60

And there is a charge, a very large charge
For a word or a touch
Or a bit of blood

Or a piece of my hair or my clothes.
So, so, Herr Doktor.   65
So, Herr Enemy.

I am your opus,
I am your valuable,
The pure gold baby

That melts to a shriek.   70
I turn and burn.
Do not think I underestimate your great concern.

Ash, ash—
You poke and stir.
Flesh, bone, there is nothing there——   75

A cake of soap,
A wedding ring,
A gold filling.[4]

Herr God, Herr Lucifer
Beware   80
Beware.

Out of the ash
I rise with my red hair
And I eat men like air.

1965

Death & Co.

Two, of course there are two.
It seems perfectly natural now——
The one who never looks up, whose eyes are lidded
And balled, like Blake's,[1]
Who exhibits   5

The birthmarks that are his trademark——
The scald scar of water,
The nude
Verdigris of the condor.
I am red meat. His beak   10

Claps sidewise: I am not his yet.
He tells me how badly I photograph.
He tells me how sweet
The babies look in their hospital
Icebox, a simple   15

---

[4] Items left in the crematoria of the Nazi concentration camps after the bodies of prisoners had been burned. (The rendered fat of the bodies was used to make soap.)

[1] The plaster death mask of the English poet William Blake (1757–1827) represents his eyes "lidded and balled."

Frill at the neck,
Then the flutings of their Ionian[2]
Death-gowns,
Then two little feet.
He does not smile or smoke.   20

The other does that,
His hair long and plausive.
Bastard
Masturbating a glitter,
He wants to be loved.   25

I do not stir.
The frost makes a flower,
The dew makes a star,
The dead bell,
The dead bell.   30

Somebody's done for.
1965

Sheep in Fog

The hills step off into whiteness.
People or stars
Regard me sadly, I disappoint them.

The train leaves a line of breath.
O slow   5
Horse the color of rust,

Hooves, dolorous bells——
All morning the
Morning has been blackening,

A flower left out.   10
My bones hold a stillness, the far
Fields melt my heart.

---

[2] Greek.

They threaten
To let me through to a heaven
Starless and fatherless, a dark water.   15
1965

Kindness

Kindness glides about my house.
Dame Kindness, she is so nice!
The blue and red jewels of her rings smoke
In the windows, the mirrors
Are filling with smiles.   5

What is so real as the cry of a child?
A rabbit's cry may be wilder
But it has no soul.
Sugar can cure everything, so Kindness says.
Sugar is a necessary fluid,   10

Its crystals a little poultice.
O kindness, kindness
Sweetly picking up pieces!
My Japanese silks, desperate butterflies,
May be pinned any minute, anesthetized.   15

And here you come, with a cup of tea
Wreathed in steam.
The blood jet is poetry,
There is no stopping it.
You hand me two children, two roses.   20
1965

Words

Axes
After whose stroke the wood rings,
And the echoes!
Echoes traveling
Off from the center like horses.   5

The sap
Wells like tears, like the
Water striving
To re-establish its mirror
Over the rock   10

That drops and turns,
A white skull,
Eaten by weedy greens.
Years later I
Encounter them on the road——   15

Words dry and riderless,
The indefatigable hoof-taps.
While
From the bottom of the pool, fixed stars
Govern a life.   20
1965

Edge

The woman is perfected.
Her dead

Body wears the smile of accomplishment,
The illusion of a Greek necessity

Flows in the scrolls of her toga,   5
Her bare

Feet seem to be saying:
We have come so far, it is over.

Each dead child coiled, a white serpent,
One at each little   10

Pitcher of milk, now empty.
She has folded

Them back into her body as petals
Of a rose close when the garden

Stiffens and odors bleed   15
From the sweet, deep throats of the night flower.

The moon has nothing to be sad about,
Staring from her hood of bone.

She is used to this sort of thing.
Her blacks crackle and drag.   20

1965

Winter Trees

The wet dawn inks are doing their blue dissolve.
On their blotter of fog the trees
Seem a botanical drawing—
Memories growing, ring on ring,
A series of weddings.   5

Knowing neither abortions nor bitchery,
Truer than women,
They seed so effortlessly!
Tasting the winds, that are footless,
Waist-deep in history—   10

Full of wings, otherworldliness.
In this, they are Ledas.[1]

---

[1] In Greek mythology, Leda, after being
impregnated by Zeus in the form of a swan,
gave birth to Helen of Troy.

O mother of leaves and sweetness
Who are these pietàs?[2]
The shadows of ringdoves chanting, but easing nothing.   15
1971

Child

Your clear eye is the one absolutely beautiful thing.
I want to fill it with color and ducks,
The zoo of the new

Whose names you meditate—
April snowdrop, Indian pipe,   5
Little

Stalk without wrinkle,
Pool in which images
Should be grand and classical

Not this troublous   10
Wringing of hands, this dark
Ceiling without a star.
1971

---

[2] Pietà: traditional sculptural group depicting
Mary with the dead Jesus.

Richard Estes,
Double Self-Portrait,
oil on canvas, 1976.
Collection, The Museum of Modern Art, New York.
Mr. and Mrs. Stuart M. Speiser Fund.

The Literature of Contemporary America: Prose

 The years between the assassination of John F. Kennedy (November 1963) and the final withdrawal of American troops from Vietnam (April 1975) battered everyone living in the United States, especially the thoughtful young. Allen Matusow called his history of these convulsive years *The Unraveling of America;* to another historian, Paul Johnson, they represent America's "suicide attempt." In an essay published in July 1984, the literary critic Benjamin DeMott refers to them as "the killer decade."

Such assessments of American society of the late 1960s and early 1970s—"finished, ruined, to hell in a handbasket" (as DeMott sums up the more extreme judgments)—may strike readers today as excessive, particularly in light of the resurgent hope and apparent unity of the Reagan era. But even the most critical assessments gain credibility when we realize that the dominant theme in recent years has been recovery and the dominant force, reaction against protest.

Following his narrow victory over Hubert Humphrey in 1968, Richard Nixon used his first term as president (1969–1972) to marshal what he called America's "great, silent majority" against the "excesses" of the 1960s. In 1972 that emergent majority carried Nixon to a landslide victory over George McGovern (the margin in the electoral college was 521 to 17). In less than a year, however, the Watergate scandal revived the nation's interest in reform. It not only forced Nixon from office; it set the stage for Jimmy Carter's victory over Gerald Ford in 1976. Finally, however, Watergate inflicted only temporary damage to the nation's reaction against protest and reform. Since then, in both the election (1980) and reelection (1984) of Ronald Reagan as president, three conservative groups have dominated national issues and political campaigns: first, the "neoconservatives," a group of intellectuals centered in New York City; second, the "moral majority," Nixon's "silent majority" become organized and powerful primarily through the work of evangelical Protestant groups; and third, the "New Right," a loose band of conservative individuals and organizations.

There are, of course, many reasons for the shift that has carried the United States from the heyday of the "hippies" to the heyday of Reaganomics. But at least four are worth special attention. First, with American involvement in Vietnam halted, with Nixon out of office, and with the rights of women and racial and sexual minorities (Chicanos, American Indians, Asian-Americans, and blacks as well as "gays") gradually receiving more attention, fewer issues cried out for protest. Second, as the "flower children" of the 1960s aged, their energies waned and their attention wandered. Rennie Davis, one of the folk heroes of the counterculture of the 1960s, became an insurance salesman. Eldridge Cleaver, leader of the Black Panthers and author of *Soul on Ice* (1968), became a supporter of Ronald Reagan. As ex-rebels everywhere became preoccupied with their careers, their younger sisters and brothers began to lose track of what all the protest had been about.

A third, larger reason for the shift lay in the roller-coaster events of the late 1960s and early 1970s. By 1974 the United States was emotionally exhausted. From the heroic accomplishments of the civil rights movement during the late 1950s and early 1960s ("still, for many of us," Benjamin DeMott remarks, "the best proof in our lives of the possibilities of human solidarity") the nation plunged into its longest and most confusing war. No one in the United States escaped its reach, for Vietnam was also the nation's most photographed, televised, and reported war. As the fighting and the protests dragged on, both the noblest and the basest instincts of the nation seemed more and more exposed. By the time the ordeal was finally over, no one stood on firm ground. Convinced of the war's brutality and futility, its opponents had still to question their own right to evade its dangers while leaving their poorer, less privileged contemporaries to die or be maimed. Convinced that citizens should fight when their nation's security and honor were at stake, supporters of the war had still to wonder why so much suffering and sacrifice had yielded so little—an illusory peace agreement followed by the Communist conquest of all of Indochina.

Another reason for the shift in mood, as though from a different world, lay in the narrowed focus, the increasing self-absorption, of American life. In the dominant culture of the nation, presided over by the business and professional worlds, self-absorption takes the form of an unbridled "careerism." During the Renaissance, at the dawn of the modern era, individuals began to dream of committing themselves to (or even throwing themselves away for) an ideal conception of what they should be. Some such drama is what Lionel Trilling discerned in the life of F. Scott Fitzgerald—and what Fitzgerald created in the story of Jay Gatsby. To focus exclusively on one's career, however, is to devote

The War That Won't Go Away

Ten years have passed since Saigon fell to the advancing North Vietnamese Army—an event that marked the extinction of South Vietnam as a nation and the humiliating finale to the American effort to hold the line in Indochina. Vietnam was America's longest, most debilitating war, and its memory still haunts the national psyche. . . .

The events of the past decade—the occupation of Cambodia, the flight of the boat people, the dreary neo-Stalinist isolation of Vietnam today—have deflated the hopeful expectations of those who saw Ho Chi Minh as the liberator of his country. America's Vietnam veterans, once viewed with a mixture of indifference and outright hostility by their countrymen, are now widely regarded as national heroes. But America remains ambivalent about the war and its costs, and in some respects the ongoing national reconciliation is incomplete.

Newsweek, "The Legacy of Vietnam: The War That Won't Go Away" (April 15, 1985)

oneself not to the realization of some ideal conception of self but to the single-minded pursuit of one's own professional advancement—in the name of money, power, and status. By contrast, the counterculture of the 1960s and 1970s scorned such self-promotion, only to celebrate other forms of self-gratification. In its drugs, its music, and its casual sex, it urged indulgence of individual needs and desires.

Contrastive though these two cultures were, they remained interactive on many levels and mutually supportive on one: strong elements of both fostered the subordination of larger social and moral claims to private and personal ones. Shorn of both its more violent elements and its political missions, the counterculture of the 1960s and the 1970s became socially more acceptable. In the "yuppies" of the 1980s, the careerism promoted by the business and professional worlds merges with the drugs, the music, and the casual sex espoused by the "hippies." As a result, social and moral claims have eroded further. No major issue—from the Equal Rights Amendment and genetic engineering to artificial intelligence and nuclear disarmament—has inspired the young people of America as both the civil rights movement and the war in Vietnam once inspired them. Even at the University of California, Berkeley, the birthplace of campus unrest in the 1960s, the Republican Club "has taken off," says Jack Abramoff, chair of the College Republican National Committee. "It's a sign that, like on campuses all over the country, there's a strong move to the right," Abramoff adds. In fact, however, the more telling move on college campuses is away from politics, as it is away from concern with the claims of public realities. "Student politics at the moment" come to "nothing," Charles Muscatine, professor of English at Berkeley, asserted in September 1984. "What you have now is not so much conservative thought but prepolitical behavior."

One consequence of the nation's changed cultural situation is the diminished role that contemporary writers play in the public arena. Writers continue to come from every region (Max Apple from Detroit; Ann Beattie from Washington, D.C.; Leslie Silko from Albuquerque; Alice Walker from Eatonton, Georgia). Sexually and racially, our literary scene is more varied than ever before. For the first time in our history, women are doing a large portion of the most interesting work—itself a tribute to the force of the women's movement. Writers continue to show concern for a large, varied set of social and political issues—from the environment to the rights of minorities, from organ transplants and genetic engineering to nuclearism. But no writer of the 1970s and 1980s, not even such powerful feminists as Gloria Steinem and Alice Walker, has emerged to play the social role that H. L. Mencken played in the 1920s, that John Dos Passos played in the 1930s—to say nothing of the social roles that Norman Mailer, Philip Roth, and James Baldwin played in the 1960s.

A second consequence of our changed cultural situation is a deepening anxiety that literature is becoming still more marginal. Television reporting of such stunning events as the Vietnam War and America's space missions has reinforced fear that television is destined to finish what movies began. Nothing, including the direct challenges of Norman Mailer, the acknowledged master of the public occasion, has effectively countered the impression that the role of primary witness to the disorders and adventures of history has shifted from the writer to the reporter. The interpenetration of literature with other media, including movies, television, and music, continues to accelerate, especially in stage performances that blend not only the rehearsed and the improvised but also music, dance, poetry, prose, and drama.

Like the line between poetry and prose, the line between fiction and nonfiction continues to blur, as writers search for new ways of endowing their experience with aesthetic purpose. One sign of our times is the continued development of nonfiction, including a wide range of issues-oriented nonfiction. Another is the resurgence of short fiction. If, furthermore, the spread of nonfiction, as practiced by John McPhee and Tom Wolfe, may be said to reassert the authority of literary "realism" and thus to question the imagination's role in mastering social realities by transmuting them into art, the resurgence of short fiction, one of the most demanding of literary forms, may be said to reassert the primacy of form. Self-conscious experimentation in fiction (like that of John Barth, for example, which is both self-reflexive and self-involved) has almost certainly lost ground in recent years. But formal experimentation and even elaborate game playing have survived among writers like Max Apple as a way of making old themes new.

Still, even the strongest of recent writers has found it difficult to combat the feeling that the burgeoning telecommunications revolution of the last several decades has taken a heavy toll. At the dawn of the modern era, the development of printing made possible a new, enlarged role for literature. In the twentieth century, the radio industry (recently revitalized through what David Mamet calls "the theater of the air") and the movie and television industries have become increasingly powerful. Today no one escapes their reach, and the result is a diminished role for literature.

Interacting with the crisis about the cultural role of art is a crisis about the vocation of the artist. The direction of art in the second half of the twentieth century—in sharp contrast to its direction in the first—has been to blur the line between the artist and the artist's work. Caught in such a climate and also pushed by the need to reassert their cultural role and help market their works, through giving interviews and readings and lectures, writers have found it more and more difficult to square the private discipline and dedication that writing demands with the public performances that success requires. Henry James knew that a life dedicated to art meant going without many things. Renunciation became one of his earliest themes and remained one of his greatest. But James ended his life as he lived it, basically confident that to choose art was also to choose life—that, far from being an evasion of experience or a retreat from life, the imaginative act of exposing, revealing, and creating life in art was a way of living in the most engaged, intense, revivified manner possible.

Signs of uncertainty about both the cultural role of art and the vocation of the artist—the latest crisis of nerve in American literature—can be discerned in older as well as younger writers. Norman Mailer and Philip Roth not only remember an earlier, seemingly simpler era when the line between fiction and nonfiction remained clearer and the line between the artist and the artist's work remained stark; they also remember a shining moment in the 1960s and 1970s when they became dominant personalities as well as dominant voices in their culture and thus experienced a kind of cultural centrality that few writers have ever known. Having written a series of books—from *The Presidential Papers* (1963) through *The Armies of the Night* (1968) and *Of a Fire on the Moon* (1970) to *The Executioner's Song* (1979)—that constitute direct engagements with the major adventures and dislocations of his age, Mailer responded to the suddenly changed situation of the early 1980s by fleeing to the Egypt of the pharaohs in a long novel called *Ancient Evenings* (1983). Having seen *Portnoy's Complaint* (1969) catapult him into the middle of the sexual revolution of the 1960s and 1970s, Philip Roth proceeded to write three overlapping novels—*The Ghost Writer* (1979), *Zuckerman Unbound* (1981), and *The Anatomy Lesson* (1983)—about the guilt-ridden, self-doubting author of a novel that resembles *Portnoy's Complaint*.

Among younger writers, signs of uncertainty are less direct but more disturbing. In Roth's *The Anatomy Lesson,* Nathan Zuckerman wonders openly whether the life of a writer is not an "evasion of experience," a "retreat" from life rather than an "intensification" of it. In the stories of Ann Beattie and Raymond Carver, both the life and the work of the artist have at least one thing in common with all manner of things: that they are not so much objects of suspicion as objects of indifference. One of the dominant themes of the literature of the last several years—the theme of impassivity, of internal blankness that merges with interpersonal blankness, of selves as coexisting deserts—draws support from philosophic analysis as well as historical experience. Several philosophers now in vogue—Michel Foucault, for example, and Jacques Derrida

—reinforce the wrenching experiences of the 1960s and 1970s in at least one important way: They extend the web of suspicion to include everything from art to human feeling. Charles Darwin drew the relation of human beings to nature into this web; Karl Marx drew the relation of human beings to historical institutions into it; Sigmund Freud drew the relation of selves to their psyches into it. Among more recent thinkers, however, nothing—neither art nor human responsiveness—escapes. Henry James thought of the artist as occupying "a sacred office," and he could and did speak of the terrible possibility of betraying that office. Concomitantly, James's declared preference was for characters so engaged, responsive, and vulnerable that no experience in life was lost on them. In much contemporary writing, art is not thought of as distinctively profane, let alone sacred, and the cult of responsiveness is viewed as another dubious bourgeois creation of the self-interested, sentimental, and mindlessly optimistic nineteenth century.

Thus reinforced, the wrenching ordeals of the 1960s and 1970s have fostered a literature of characters who neither feel nor express much of anything. Mark Twain's Huck Finn fled from civilization in search of the wild; F. Scott Fitzgerald's Jay Gatsby fled in search of a bride, a mansion, and a fortune from the inadequate fate of being born James Gatz. But much recent art records flight of a different sort—flight from all forms of responsiveness to life. The self of Robert Frost's poem "Desert Places" (1936) ("With no expression, nothing to express") becomes the self as impervious and blank in the 1960s song "I Am a Rock" by Paul Simon and Art Garfunkel ("I am a rock. I am an island. And a rock feels no pain, and an island never cries"). In recent fiction, such as that of Ann Beattie, Raymond Carver, and Joan Didion, we meet protagonists in whom not only feeling but even the memory of feeling and the desire for it are dead. It is as though we have moved a step beyond even the terribly wounding experiences of the Holocaust—in which, as Elie Wiesel and Susan Sontag have noted, some feelings were deepened even while others were imperiled—to the triumph of impassivity.

"Something Went Dead; Something Is Still Crying"

Nothing I have seen—in photographs or in real life—ever cut me as sharply, deeply, instantaneously. . . . When I looked at those photographs [of Bergen-Belsen and Dachau in 1945], something broke. Some limit had been reached, and not only that of horror; I felt irrevocably grieved, wounded, but a part of my feelings started to tighten; something went dead; something is still crying.

Susan Sontag, *On Photography* (1977)

In Didion's novel *Play It as It Lays* (1970), for example, we encounter a character so completely modern that nothing moves her. Asked what she wants, she replies, "Nothing"; asked what she feels, she again replies, "Nothing"; threatened with violence, she shrugs. Such characters feel skeptical about everything. But they feel most deeply skeptical about the notion that human beings ever believed or doubted passionately, ever felt wonder before the mysterious, or ever experienced the currents of sympathy, compassion, or love. "The most beautiful experience we can have is the mysterious," Albert Einstein wrote. "It is the fundamental emotion which stands at the cradle of true art and true science." What we confront instead in recent fiction is not merely a world in which all human values are threatened; it is a world in which the capacity, or even desire, for the human feeling of wonder is imperiled.

Still, within the diversity of voices that constitute recent American fiction, there are clear signs that reports of the death of responsiveness and vulnerability as human virtues are exaggerated. Those signs appear not only in writers like Leslie Silko and Alice Walker, for whom heritage and race and sex have continued to bear heavily on the dynamics of individual existence, but also in the most recent works of Ann Beattie and Raymond Carver—*The Burning House* (1982) and *Cathedral* (1983). In Max Apple's "Free Agents," to take another instance, a strange yet touching civil war is required to reawaken the human capacity for feeling. But once that capacity is reawakened, it touches and changes everything.

Irony, not sentiment, dominates the tone of contemporary fiction. At times contemporary writers seem almost as bored and disaffected as their characters. They clearly remain skeptical about the possibility of bringing imaginative form to the damaged lives they see around them. Yet they continue to draw on diverse traditions and to find in those traditions different strengths. Oral history, myth, and legend are strong forces in the fiction of Leslie Silko, who also shows great sensitivity to older, more primitive states of consciousness. Although most contemporary writers seem increasingly irreverent toward grand intellectual schemes, particularly Freudian analysis and Marxist doctrine, many writers, including Max Apple and Tom Wolfe, are clearly on friendlier terms with science and technology, an attitude presaged by Thomas Pynchon. Other writers —Raymond Carver and Bobbie Ann Mason, for example—have made a serious effort to bring the white working-class ethos into serious fiction. At the same time, minority writers and women writers have demonstrated great determination in exploring their own neglected traditions. "And that's why a lot of women are doing interesting work," Grace Paley notes: "Because they're really taking these lives that haven't been seen" and illuminating them. In an increasingly fragmented, decentered world, contemporary fiction has been firm in its determination to celebrate the special authority of distinctly "minority" points of view. Whereas writers like Herman Melville and William Faulkner may be said to have explored the moral authority of failure, contemporary writers may be said to have explored the moral authority of marginality.

Did the 1960s Damage Fiction?

One truth about the 60's, obscured at this moment but assuredly not forever, is that for a while the period showed us, unambiguously, amid its horrors, some growing points for democratic culture. Another truth, visible everywhere in American writing, is that the 60's did injure us all.

Benjamin De Mott, *The New York Times Book Review*
(July 8, 1984)

At the same time, American literature has become not simply more international but also less predictable in its alliances. As general editor of the excellent series "Writers from the Other Europe," Philip Roth has played a major role in introducing writers of eastern Europe (Milan Kundera, for example) into the literary world of the United States. Writers like Chinua Achebe from Africa; R. K. Narayan and Salman Rashdie from India; Jorge Luis Borges, Jorge Amado, and Gabriel García Márquez from South America; and V. S. Naipaul, whose ties are with both the West Indies and India, are now as important to American literature as any writers from England or Europe.

Writers of contemporary America clearly bear witness to the pain of recent history—and to the threat that history presents not only to our literature but also to our capacity for human feeling. One of the characteristic struggles in our time as well as our literature is the struggle between impassivity and responsiveness, between apathy and concern, between staying cool and risking vulnerability. Sooner or later, in one way or another, this struggle brings almost everything that is specifically human under the aspect of a contest between the appeal and the danger of moral indifference, on one side, and the appeal and the danger of moral commitment, on the other. But present-day writers also bear witness to the promise of recent history, both in the sheer diversity of their voices, as they open American literature to new perspectives and heritages, and in the sheer persistence with which they present for our inspection new models of human possibility.

Grace Paley
b. 1922

"How daily life is lived," says Grace Paley, "is a mystery to me. You write about what's a mystery to you. What is it like? Why do people do this? Every day, get up in the morning. . . ." The wry humor and gentle irony of Paley's assessment of human life, including her own life, permeates her stories, which have appeared in such magazines as *Atlantic Monthly, Mother Jones,* and *The New Yorker.* It is her characteristic tone as much as her subject matter that holds her uncommonly devoted readers.

Unlike some of her contemporaries, Paley is not a prolific writer; she has published only three collections of short stories: *The Little Disturbances of Man* (1959), *Enormous Changes at the Last Minute* (1974), and *Later the Same Day* (1985). In part, her slowness in writing comes from the precision and care with which she crafts each sentence. "I wish I could write more," she says, "but I don't. I'm so glad to have three books." But her slowness also stems from her reluctance to abandon for too long the life she writes about. As one critic says, "Her conversation, like her fiction, always embodies the abstract in the concrete —not shunning large issues but particularizing them with humor and tact. Life and literature are of a piece for her; being a writer is inextricable from being a mother, neighbor, friend, lover, and political being."

Paley's politics are (in her own words) "anarchist, if that's politics," and she has constantly put them to the test. In the 1960s and the 1970s she went to jail as a nonviolent critic of the Vietnam War and traveled to Hanoi and Moscow as a member of peace delegations; in 1973 she condemned the Soviets for their suppression of political dissidents. Today she remains an activist in the antinuclear movement. "For me there's always the larger matter of disarmament and antimilitarism, the way we have to end this whole masculine enterprise of war." Although she rejects the label "feminist writer," she is, she insists, "a feminist and a writer," having realized early on that "all those ballsy American heroes had nothing to say to me."

Born in New York in 1922, Paley acknowledges the strong influence of her Russian Jewish ancestry. "I do write with an accent," she says. "I did have three languages spoken around me when I was a kid: English and Russian and Yiddish." Moreover, the rich cultural tradition and oral history that she received from her parents and grandparents help to shape her sense of character and place. An avid reader though not a dedicated student, Paley attended both Hunter College and New York University but quit college without graduating to commence the difficult task of constructing a life that combined writing with motherhood. In the 1950s she shifted from writing poetry to writing fiction and soon found that she happened "to love the story form. . . . You can do anything in it," she says. "It can be just telling a little tale, or writing a complicated philosophical story. It can be a song, almost."

Twice married and the mother of two grown sons, Paley is now generally found in the heart of Manhattan, where she writes slowly and carefully about lives in distress. As the titles of her story collections suggest, she cares greatly about the "little disturbances" and the "enormous changes" that make up the lives and voices that she watches and listens to so attentively: "You pick up the rock and what's hidden should be seen and known. And that's why a lot of women are doing interesting work, because they're really taking these lives that haven't been seen." Now in her sixties, Paley remains "contemporary" because, like the women she celebrates, she combines "a kind of stubbornness" with "a certain riskiness" and thus masters the tension between the "little disturbances" that make up our lives and the "enormous changes" that can forever transform them.

Text:
Enormous Changes at the Last Minute, 1974.

A Conversation with My Father

My father is eighty-six years old and in bed. His heart, that bloody motor, is equally old and will not do certain jobs any more. It still floods his head with brainy light. But it won't let his legs carry the weight of his body around the house. Despite my metaphors, this muscle failure is not due to his old heart, he says, but to a potassium shortage. Sitting on one pillow, leaning on three, he offers last-minute advice and makes a request.

"I would like you to write a simple story just once more," he says, "the kind de Maupassant wrote, or Chekhov,[1] the kind you used to write. Just recognizable people and then write down what happened to them next."

I say, "Yes, why not? That's possible." I want to please him, though I don't remember writing that way. I *would* like to try to tell such a story, if he means the kind that begins: "There was a woman . . ." followed by plot, the absolute line between two points which I've always despised. Not for literary reasons, but because it takes all hope away. Everyone, real or invented, deserves the open destiny of life.

Finally I thought of a story that had been happening for a couple of years right across the street. I wrote it down, then read it aloud. "Pa," I said, "how about this? Do you mean something like this?"

> Once in my time there was a woman and she had a son. They lived nicely, in a small apartment in Manhattan. This boy at about fifteen became a junkie, which is not unusual in our neighborhood. In order to maintain her close friendship with him, she became a junkie too. She said it was part of the youth culture, with which she felt very much at home. After a while, for a number of reasons, the boy gave it all up and left the city and his mother in disgust. Hopeless and alone, she grieved. We all visit her.

"O.K., Pa, that's it," I said, "an unadorned and miserable tale."

"But that's not what I mean," my father said. "You misunderstood me on purpose. You know there's a lot more to it. You know that. You left everything out. Turgenev[2] wouldn't do that. Chekhov wouldn't do that. There are in fact Russian writers you never heard of, you don't have an inkling of, as good as anyone, who can write a plain ordinary story, who would not leave out what you have left out. I object not to facts but to people sitting in trees talking senselessly, voices from who knows where . . ."

"Forget that one, Pa, what have I left out now? In this one?"

"Her looks, for instance."

"Oh. Quite handsome, I think. Yes."

"Her hair?"

---

[1] De Maupassant: Guy de Maupassant (1850–1893), French writer of short stories; Chekhov: Anton Chekhov (1860–1904), Russian master of short fiction and drama.

[2] Ivan Turgenev (1818–1883), Russian novelist and playwright.

"Dark, with heavy braids, as though she were a girl or a foreigner."

"What were her parents like, her stock? That she became such a person. It's interesting, you know."

"From out of town. Professional people. The first to be divorced in their county. How's that? Enough?" I asked.

"With you, it's all a joke," he said. "What about the boy's father? Why didn't you mention him? Who was he? Or was the boy born out of wedlock?"

"Yes," I said. "He was born out of wedlock."

"For Godsakes, doesn't anyone in your stories get married? Doesn't anyone have the time to run down to City Hall before they jump into bed?"

"No," I said. "In real life, yes. But in my stories, no."

"Why do you answer me like that?"

"Oh, Pa, this is a simple story about a smart woman who came to N.Y.C. full of interest love trust excitement very up to date, and about her son, what a hard time she had in this world. Married or not, it's of small consequence."

"It is of great consequence," he said.

"O.K.," I said.

"O.K. O.K. yourself," he said, "but listen. I believe you that she's good-looking, but I don't think she was so smart."

"That's true," I said. "Actually that's the trouble with stories. People start out fantastic. You think they're extraordinary, but it turns out as the work goes along, they're just average with a good education. Sometimes the other way around, the person's a kind of dumb innocent, but he outwits you and you can't even think of an ending good enough."

"What do you do then?" he asked. He had been a doctor for a couple of decades and then an artist for a couple of decades and he's still interested in details, craft, technique.

"Well, you just have to let the story lie around till some agreement can be reached between you and the stubborn hero."

"Aren't you talking silly, now?" he asked. "Start again," he said. "It so happens I'm not going out this evening. Tell the story again. See what you can do this time."

"O.K.," I said. "But it's not a five-minute job." Second attempt:

Once, across the street from us, there was a fine handsome woman, our neighbor. She had a son whom she loved because she'd known him since birth (in helpless chubby infancy, and in the wrestling, hugging ages, seven to ten, as well as earlier and later). This boy, when he fell into the fist of adolescence, became a junkie. He was not a hopeless one. He was in fact hopeful, an ideologue and successful converter. With his busy brilliance, he wrote persuasive articles for his high-school newspaper. Seeking a wider audience, using important connections, he drummed into Lower Manhattan newsstand distribution a periodical called *Oh! Golden Horse!*

In order to keep him from feeling guilty (because guilt is the stony heart of nine tenths of all clinically diagnosed cancers in America today, she said), and because she had always believed in giving bad habits room at home where one could keep an eye on them, she too became a junkie. Her kitchen was famous for a while—a center for intellectual addicts who knew what they were doing.

A few felt artistic like Coleridge[3] and others were scientific and revolutionary like Leary.[4] Although she was often high herself, certain good mothering reflexes remained, and she saw to it that there was lots of orange juice around and honey and milk and vitamin pills. However, she never cooked anything but chili, and that no more than once a week. She explained, when we talked to her, seriously, with neighborly concern, that it was her part in the youth culture and she would rather be with the young, it was an honor, than with her own generation.

One week, while nodding through an Antonioni[5] film, this boy was severely jabbed by the elbow of a stern and proselytizing girl, sitting beside him. She offered immediate apricots and nuts for his sugar level, spoke to him sharply, and took him home.

She had heard of him and his work and she herself published, edited, and wrote a competitive journal called *Man Does Live By Bread Alone*.[6] In the organic heat of her continuous presence he could not help but become interested once more in his muscles, his arteries, and nerve connections. In fact he began to love them, treasure them, praise them with funny little songs in *Man Does Live* . . .

the fingers of my flesh transcend
my transcendental soul
the tightness in my shoulders end
my teeth have made me whole

To the mouth of his head (that glory of will and determination) he brought hard apples, nuts, wheat germ, and soybean oil. He said to his old friends, From now on, I guess I'll keep my wits about me. I'm going on the natch. He said he was about to begin a spiritual deep-breathing journey. How about you too, Mom? he asked kindly.

His conversion was so radiant, splendid, that neighborhood kids his age began to say that he had never been a real addict at all, only a journalist along for the smell of the story. The mother tried several times to give up what had become without her son and his friends a lonely habit. This effort only brought it to supportable levels. The boy and his girl took their electronic mimeograph and moved to the bushy edge of another borough. They were very strict. They said they would not see her again until she had been off drugs for sixty days.

At home alone in the evening, weeping, the mother read and reread the seven issues of *Oh! Golden Horse!* They seemed to her as truthful as ever. We often crossed the street to visit and console. But if we mentioned any of our children who were at college or in the hospital or dropouts at home, she would cry out, My baby! My baby! and burst into terrible, face-scarring, time-consuming tears. The End.

---

[3] Samuel Taylor Coleridge (1772–1834), English Romantic poet who was an opium addict.
[4] Timothy Leary (b. 1920), former Harvard professor of psychology and an early advocate of the drug LSD.
[5] Michelangelo Antonioni (b. 1912), Italian film director best known for his films of the 1960s, which explored the modern sense of despair and emptiness.
[6] Playful twist on the scriptural admonition that "man does not live by bread alone" but also by the spirit.

First my father was silent, then he said, "Number One: You have a nice sense of humor. Number Two: I see you can't tell a plain story. So don't waste time." Then he said sadly, "Number Three: I suppose that means she was alone, she was left like that, his mother. Alone. Probably sick?"

I said, "Yes."

"Poor woman. Poor girl, to be born in a time of fools, to live among fools. The end. The end. You were right to put that down. The end."

I didn't want to argue, but I had to say, "Well, it is not necessarily the end, Pa."

"Yes," he said, "what a tragedy. The end of a person."

"No, Pa," I begged him. "It doesn't have to be. She's only about forty. She could be a hundred different things in this world as time goes on. A teacher or a social worker. An ex-junkie! Sometimes it's better than having a master's in education."

"Jokes," he said. "As a writer that's your main trouble. You don't want to recognize it. Tragedy! Plain tragedy! Historical tragedy! No hope. The end."

"Oh, Pa," I said. "She could change."

"In your own life, too, you have to look it in the face." He took a couple of nitroglycerin. "Turn to five," he said, pointing to the dial on the oxygen tank. He inserted the tubes into his nostrils and breathed deep. He closed his eyes and said, "No."

I had promised the family to always let him have the last word when arguing, but in this case I had a different responsibility. That woman lives across the street. She's my knowledge and my invention. I'm sorry for her. I'm not going to leave her there in that house crying. (Actually neither would Life, which unlike me has no pity.)

Therefore: She did change. Of course her son never came home again. But right now, she's the receptionist in a storefront community clinic in the East Village. Most of the customers are young people, some old friends. The head doctor has said to her, "If we only had three people in this clinic with your experiences . . ."

"The doctor said that?" My father took the oxygen tubes out of his nostrils and said, "Jokes. Jokes again."

"No, Pa, it could really happen that way, it's a funny world nowadays."

"No," he said. "Truth first. She will slide back. A person must have character. She does not."

"No, Pa," I said. "That's it. She's got a job. Forget it. She's in that storefront working."

"How long will it be?" he asked. "Tragedy! You too. When will you look it in the face?"

1974

William Kennedy
b. 1928

"All the stories I imagine flow from an environment," says William Kennedy. That environment is a real flesh-and-blood city: Albany, New York. In his book *O Albany!* (1984), Kennedy describes himself as a "person whose imagination has become fused with a single place, and in that place finds all the elements that a man ever needs for the life of the soul." In his fiction, especially in the cycle of

"Albany" novels—*Legs* (1975), *Billy Phelan's Greatest Game* (1978), and *Ironweed* (1983)—the city is not merely a setting or background for the characters; it is also felt as a dynamic, living presence in its own right. The characters live *with* the city as well as in it. For them as for the characters of ancient Greek tragedy, exile can be the cruelest form of punishment.

William Kennedy was born in Albany in 1928. Following his graduation from Siena College in Loudonville, New York, in 1949, he returned to Albany to work as a movie critic and reporter for the *Albany Times-Union*. In 1963 he began supporting himself and his family by combining free-lance writing and part-time teaching. He has taught fiction writing at the State University of New York at Albany and at Cornell University. In 1981 he received a grant from the National Endowment for the Arts and in 1983 a MacArthur Fellowship. In addition to his "Albany" novels, Kennedy has also published a novel about the newspaper industry, *The Ink Truck* (1969). Recently he wrote the film script for *The Cotton Club*, Francis Ford Coppola's movie of Harlem nightlife.

Rejected by a number of major publishing houses, *Ironweed* was finally published in 1983 primarily because of Saul Bellow's support, whereupon it won the 1984 National Book Critics Circle Award for fiction. Set in 1938, *Ironweed* deals with the return to Albany of Francis Phelan, an ex-ballplayer and now a drunk scaring up work as a gravedigger, who ran away from home over twenty years earlier after he had accidentally dropped and killed his infant son. In the novel's opening chapter, reprinted here, Phelan marks his return home by visiting his son's grave.

Text:
Ironweed, 1983.

---

from Ironweed

I

Riding up the winding road of Saint Agnes Cemetery in the back of the rattling old truck, Francis Phelan became aware that the dead, even more than the living, settled down in neighborhoods. The truck was suddenly surrounded by fields of monuments and cenotaphs of kindred design and striking size, all guarding the privileged dead. But the truck moved on and the limits of mere privilege became visible, for here now came the acres of truly prestigious death: illustrious men and women, captains of life without their diamonds, furs, carriages, and limousines, but buried in pomp and glory, vaulted in great tombs built like heavenly safe deposit boxes, or parts of the Acropolis.[1] And ah yes, here too, inevitably, came the flowing masses, row upon row of

---

[1] One of the architectural masterpieces of ancient Athens, containing some of the world's greatest statues and monuments.

them under simple headstones and simpler crosses. Here was the neighborhood of the Phelans.

Francis's mother twitched nervously in her grave as the truck carried him nearer to her; and Francis's father lit his pipe, smiled at his wife's discomfort, and looked out from his own bit of sod to catch a glimpse of how much his son had changed since the train accident.

Francis's father smoked roots of grass that died in the periodic droughts afflicting the cemetery. He stored the root essence in his pockets until it was brittle to the touch, then pulverized it between his fingers and packed his pipe. Francis's mother wove crosses from the dead dandelions and other deep-rooted weeds; careful to preserve their fullest length, she wove them while they were still in the green stage of death, then ate them with an insatiable revulsion.

"Look at that tomb," Francis said to his companion. "Ain't that somethin'? That's Arthur T. Grogan. I saw him around Albany when I was a kid. He owned all the electricity in town."

"He ain't got much of it now," Rudy said.

"Don't bet on it," Francis said. "Them kind of guys hang on to a good thing."

The advancing dust of Arthur T. Grogan, restless in its simulated Parthenon,[2] grew luminous from Francis's memory of a vital day long gone. The truck rolled on up the hill.

FARRELL, said one roadside gravestone. KENNEDY, said another. DAUGHERTY, McILHENNY, BRUNELLE, McDONALD, MALONE, DWYER, and WALSH, said others. PHELAN, said two small ones.

Francis saw the pair of Phelan stones and turned his eyes elsewhere, fearful that his infant son, Gerald, might be under one of them. He had not confronted Gerald directly since the day he let the child slip out of its diaper. He would not confront him now. He avoided the Phelan headstones on the presumptive grounds that they belonged to another family entirely. And he was correct. These graves held two brawny young Phelan brothers, canalers both, and both skewered by the same whiskey bottle in 1884, dumped into the Erie Canal in front of The Black Rag Saloon in Watervliet, and then pushed under and drowned with a long stick. The brothers looked at Francis's clothes, his ragged brown twill suit jacket, black baggy pants, and filthy fireman's blue shirt, and felt a kinship with him that owed nothing to blood ties. His shoes were as worn as the brogans they both had been wearing on the last day of their lives. The brothers read also in Francis's face the familiar scars of alcoholic desolation, which both had developed in their graves. For both had been deeply drunk and vulnerable when the cutthroat Muggins killed them in tandem and took all their money: forty-eight cents. We died for pennies, the brothers said in their silent, dead-drunken way to Francis, who bounced past them in the back of the truck, staring at the emboldening white clouds that clotted the sky so richly at midmorning. From the heat of the sun Francis felt a flow of juices in his body, which he interpreted as a gift of strength from the sky.

"A little chilly," he said, "but it's gonna be a nice day."

"If it don't puke," said Rudy.

---

[2] Temple sacred to the goddess Athena on the Acropolis; used here to indicate the massive architectural style of Grogan's tomb.

"You goddamn cuckoo bird, you don't talk about the weather that way. You got a nice day, take it. Why you wanna talk about the sky pukin' on us?"

"My mother was a full-blooded Cherokee," Rudy said.

"You're a liar. Your old lady was a Mex, that's why you got them high cheekbones. Indian I don't buy."

"She come off the reservation in Skokie, Illinois, went down to Chicago, and got a job sellin' peanuts at Wrigley Field."

"They ain't got any Indians in Illinois. I never seen one damn Indian all the time I was out there."

"They keep to themselves," Rudy said.

The truck passed the last inhabited section of the cemetery and moved toward a hill where raw earth was being loosened by five men with pickaxes and shovels. The driver parked and unhitched the tailgate, and Francis and Rudy leaped down. The two then joined the other five in loading the truck with the fresh dirt. Rudy mumbled aloud as he shoveled: "I'm workin' it out."

"What the hell you workin' out now?" Francis asked.

"The worms," Rudy said. "How many worms you get in a truckload of dirt."

"You countin' 'em?"

"Hundred and eight so far," said Rudy.

"Dizzy bedbug," said Francis.

When the truck was fully loaded Francis and Rudy climbed atop the dirt and the driver rode them to a slope where a score of graves of the freshly dead sent up the smell of sweet putrescence, the incense of unearned mortality and interrupted dreams. The driver, who seemed inured to such odors, parked as close to the new graves as possible and Rudy and Francis then carried shovelfuls of dirt to the dead while the driver dozed in the truck. Some of the dead had been buried two or three months, and yet their coffins were still burrowing deeper into the rain-softened earth. The gravid weight of the days they had lived was now seeking its equivalent level in firstborn death, creating a rectangular hollow on the surface of each grave. Some of the coffins seemed to be on their way to middle earth. None of the graves were yet marked with headstones, but a few were decorated with an American flag on a small stick, or bunches of faded cloth flowers in clay pots. Rudy and Francis filled in one hollow, then another. Dead gladiolas, still vaguely yellow in their brown stage of death, drooped in a basket at the head of the grave of Louis (Daddy Big) Dugan, the Albany pool hustler who had died only a week or so ago from inhaling his own vomit. Daddy Big, trying futilely to memorize anew the fading memories of how he used to apply topspin and reverse English to the cue ball, recognized Franny Phelan, even though he had not seen him in twenty years.

"I wonder who's under this one," Francis said.

"Probably some Catholic," Rudy said.

"Of course it's some Catholic, you birdbrain, it's a Catholic cemetery."

"They let Protestants in sometimes," Rudy said.

"They do like hell."

"Sometimes they let Jews in too. And Indians."

Daddy Big remembered the shape of Franny's mouth from the first day he saw him playing ball for Albany at Chadwick Park. Daddy Big sat down front in the bleachers behind the third-base line and watched Franny on the hot corner, watched him climb into the bleachers after a foul pop fly that would have hit Daddy Big right in the chest if Franny hadn't stood on his own ear to make the catch. Daddy Big saw Franny smile after making it, and even though his teeth were almost gone now, Franny smiled that same familiar way as he scattered fresh dirt on Daddy Big's grave.

Your son Billy saved my life, Daddy Big told Francis. Turned me upside down and kept me from chokin' to death on the street when I got sick. I died anyway, later. But it was nice of him, and I wish I could take back some of the lousy things I said to him. And let me personally give you a piece of advice. Never inhale your own vomit.

Francis did not need Daddy Big's advice. He did not get sick from alcohol the way Daddy Big had. Francis knew how to drink. He drank all the time and he did not vomit. He drank anything that contained alcohol, anything, and he could always walk, and he could talk as well as any man alive about what was on his mind. Alcohol did put Francis to sleep, finally, but on his own terms. When he'd had enough and everybody else was passed out, he'd just put his head down and curl up like an old dog, then put his hands between his legs to protect what was left of the jewels, and he'd cork off. After a little sleep he'd wake up and go out for more drink. That's how he did it when he was drinking. Now he wasn't drinking. He hadn't had a drink for two days and he felt a little bit of all right. Strong, even. He'd stopped drinking because he'd run out of money, and that coincided with Helen not feeling all that terrific and Francis wanting to take care of her. Also he had wanted to be sober when he went to court for registering twenty-one times to vote. He went to court but not to trial. His attorney, Marcus Gorman, a wizard, found a mistake in the date on the papers that detailed the charges against Francis, and the case was thrown out. Marcus charged people five hundred dollars usually, but he only charged Francis fifty because Martin Daugherty, the newspaper columnist, one of Francis's old neighbors, asked him to go easy. Francis didn't even have the fifty when it came time to pay. He'd drunk it all up. Yet Marcus demanded it.

"But I ain't got it," Francis said.

"Then go to work and get it," said Marcus. "I get paid for what I do."

"Nobody'll put me to work," Francis said. "I'm a bum."

"I'll get you some day work up at the cemetery," Marcus said.

And he did. Marcus played bridge with the bishop and knew all the Catholic hotshots. Some hotshot ran Saint Agnes Cemetery in Menands. Francis slept in the weeds on Dongan Avenue below the bridge and woke up about seven o'clock this morning, then went up to the mission on Madison Avenue to get coffee. Helen wasn't there. She was truly gone. He didn't know where she was and nobody had seen her. They said she'd been hanging around the mission last night, but then went away. Francis had fought with her earlier over money and she just walked off someplace, who the hell knows where?

Francis had coffee and bread with the bums who'd dried out, and other bums passin' through, and the preacher there watchin' everybody and playin' grabass with their souls. Never mind my soul, was Francis's line. Just pass the coffee. Then he stood out front killin' time and pickin' his teeth with a matchbook cover. And here came Rudy.

Rudy was sober too for a change and his gray hair was combed and trimmed. His mustache was clipped and he wore white suede shoes, even though it was October, what the hell, he's just a bum, and a white shirt, and a crease in his pants. Francis, no lace in one of his shoes, hair matted and uncut, smelling his own body stink and ashamed of it for the first time in memory, felt deprived.

"You lookin' good there, bum," Francis said.

"I been in the hospital."

"What for?"

"Cancer."

"No shit. Cancer?"

"He says to me you're gonna die in six months. I says I'm gonna wine myself to death. He says it don't make any difference if you wined or dined, you're goin'. Goin' out of this world with a cancer. The stomach, it's like pits, you know what I mean? I said I'd like to make it to fifty. The doc says you'll never make it. I said all right, what's the difference?"

"Too bad, grandma. You got a jug?"

"I got a dollar."

"Jesus, we're in business," Francis said.

But then he remembered his debt to Marcus Gorman.

"Listen, bum," he said, "you wanna go to work with me and make a few bucks? We can get a couple of jugs and a flop tonight. Gonna be cold. Look at that sky."

"Work where?"

"The cemetery. Shovelin' dirt."

"The cemetery. Why not? I oughta get used to it. What're they payin'?"

"Who the hell knows?"

"I mean they payin' money, or they give you a free grave when you croak?"

"If it ain't money, forget it," Francis said. "I ain't shovelin' out my own grave."

They walked from downtown Albany to the cemetery in Menands, six miles or more. Francis felt healthy and he liked it. It's too bad he didn't feel healthy when he drank. He felt good then but not healthy, especially not in the morning, or when he woke up in the middle of the night, say. Sometimes he felt dead. His head, his throat, his stomach: he needed to get them all straight with a drink, or maybe it'd take two, because if he didn't, his brain would overheat trying to fix things and his eyes would blow out. Jeez it's tough when you need that drink and your throat's like an open sore and it's four in the morning and the wine's gone and no place open and you got no money or nobody to bum from, even if there was a place open. That's tough, pal. Tough.

Rudy and Francis walked up Broadway and when they got to Colonie Street Francis felt a pull to turn up and take a look at the house where he was born, where his goddamned brothers and sisters still lived. He'd done that in 1935 when it looked possible, when his mother finally died. And what did it get him? A kick in the ass is what it got him. Let the joint fall down and bury them all before I look at it again, was his thought. Let it rot. Let the bugs eat it.

In the cemetery, Kathryn Phelan, sensing the militance in her son's mood, grew restless at the idea that death was about to change for her. With a furtive burst of energy she wove another cross from the shallow-rooted weeds above her and quickly swallowed it, but was disappointed by the taste. Weeds appealed to Kathryn Phelan in direct ratio to the length of their roots. The longer the weed, the more revulsive the cross.

Francis and Rudy kept walking north on Broadway, Francis's right shoe flapping, its counter rubbing wickedly against his heel. He favored the foot until he found a length of twine on the sidewalk in front of Frankie Leikheim's plumbing shop. Frankie Leikheim. A little kid when Francis was a big kid and now he's got his own plumbing shop and what have you got, Francis? You got a piece of twine for a shoelace. You don't need shoelaces for walking short distances, but on the bum without them you could ruin your feet for weeks. You figured you had all the calluses anybody'd ever need for the road, but then you come across a different pair of shoes and they start you out with a brand-new set of blisters. Then they make the blisters bleed and you have to stop walking almost till they scab over so's you can get to work on another callus.

The twine didn't fit into the eyelets of the shoe. Francis untwined it from itself and threaded half its thickness through enough of the eyelets to make it lace. He pulled up his sock, barely a sock anymore, holes in the heel, the toe, the sole, gotta get new ones. He cushioned his raw spot as best he could with the sock, then tightened the new lace, gently, so the shoe wouldn't flop. And he walked on toward the cemetery.

"There's seven deadly sins," Rudy said.

"Deadly? What do you mean deadly?" Francis said.

"I mean daily," Rudy said. "Every day."

"There's only one sin as far as I'm concerned," Francis said.

"There's prejudice."

"Oh yeah. Prejudice. Yes."

"There's envy."

"Envy. Yeah, yup. That's one."

"There's lust."

"Lust, right. Always liked that one."

"Cowardice."

"Who's a coward?"

"Cowardice."

"I don't know what you mean. That word I don't know."

"Cowardice," Rudy said.

"I don't like the coward word. What're you sayin' about coward?"

"A coward. He'll cower up. You know what a coward is? He'll run."

"No, that word I don't know. Francis is no coward. He'll fight anybody. Listen, you know what I like?"

"What do you like?"

"Honesty," Francis said.

"That's another one," Rudy said.

At Shaker Road they walked up to North Pearl Street and headed north on Pearl. Where they live now. They'd painted Sacred Heart Church since he last saw it, and across the street School 20 had new tennis courts. Whole lot of houses here he never saw, new since '16. This is the block they live in. What Billy said. When Francis last walked this street it wasn't much more than a cow pasture. Old man Rooney's cows would break the fence and roam loose, dirtyin' the streets and sidewalks. You got to put a stop to this, Judge Ronan told Rooney. What is it you want me to do, Rooney asked the judge, put diapers on 'em?

They walked on to the end of North Pearl Street, where it entered Menands, and

turned down to where it linked with Broadway. They walked past the place where
the old Bull's Head Tavern used to be. Francis was a kid when he saw Gus Ruhlan
come out of the corner in bare knuckles. The bum he was fighting stuck out a hand
to shake, Gus give him a shot and that was all she wrote. Katie bar the door. Too
wet to plow. Honesty. They walked past Hawkins Stadium, hell of a big place now,
about where Chadwick Park was when Francis played ball. He remembered when it
was a pasture. Hit a ball right and it'd roll forever, right into the weeds. Bow-Wow
Buckley'd be after it and he'd find it right away, a wizard. Bow-Wow kept half a
dozen spare balls in the weeds for emergencies like that. Then he'd throw the runner
out at third on a sure home run and he'd brag about his fielding. Honesty. Bow-Wow
is dead. Worked on an ice wagon and punched his own horse and it stomped him,
was that it? Nah. That's nuts. Who'd punch a horse?

"Hey," Rudy said, "wasn't you with a woman the other night I saw you?"

"What woman?"

"I don't know. Helen. Yeah, you called her Helen."

"Helen. You can't keep track of where she is."

"What'd she do, run off with a banker?"

"She didn't run off."

"Then where is she?"

"Who knows? She comes, she goes. I don't keep tabs."

"You got a million of 'em."

"More where she came from."

"They're all crazy to meet you."

"My socks is what gets 'em."

Francis lifted his trousers to reveal his socks, one green, one blue.

"A reg'lar man about town," Rudy said.

Francis dropped his pantlegs and walked on, and Rudy said, "Hey, what the hell
was all that about the man from Mars last night? Everybody was talkin' about it at
the hospital. You hear about that stuff on the radio?"

"Oh yeah. They landed."

"Who?"

"The Martians."

"Where'd they land?"

"Someplace in Jersey."

"What happened?"

"They didn't like it no more'n I did."

"No joke," Rudy said. "I heard people saw them Martians comin' and ran outa
town, jumped outa windows, everything like that."

"Good," Francis said. "What they oughta do. Anybody sees a Martian oughta jump
out two windows."

"You don't take things serious," Rudy said. "You have a whatayacallit, a frivolous
way about you."

"A frivolous way? A frivolous way?"

"That's what I said. A frivolous way."

"What the hell's that mean? You been readin' again, you crazy kraut? I told you
cuckoos like you shouldn't go around readin', callin' people frivolous."

"That ain't no insult. Frivolous is a good word. A nice word."

"Never mind words, there's the cemetery." And Francis pointed to the entrance-road gates. "I just thought of somethin'."

"What?"

"That cemetery's full of gravestones."

"Right."

"I never knew a bum yet had a gravestone."

They walked up the long entrance road from Broadway to the cemetery proper. Francis sweet-talked the woman at the gatehouse and mentioned Marcus Gorman and introduced Rudy as a good worker like himself, ready to work. She said the truck'd be along and to just wait easy. Then he and Rudy rode up in the back of the truck and got busy with the dirt.

They rested when they'd filled in all the hollows of the graves, and by then the truck driver was nowhere to be found. So they sat there and looked down the hill toward Broadway and over toward the hills of Rensselaer and Troy on the other side of the Hudson, the coke plant spewing palpable smoke from its great chimney at the far end of the Menands bridge. Francis decided this would be a fine place to be buried. The hill had a nice flow to it that carried you down the grass and out onto the river, and then across the water and up through the trees on the far shore to the top of the hills, all in one swoop. Being dead here would situate a man in place and time. It would give a man neighbors, even some of them really old folks, like those antique dead ones at the foot of the lawn: Tobias Banion, Elisha Skinner, Elsie Whipple, all crumbling under their limestone headstones from which the snows, sands, and acids of reduction were slowly removing their names. But what did the perpetuation of names matter? Ah well, there were those for whom death, like life, would always be a burden of eminence. The progeny of those growing nameless at the foot of the hill were ensured a more durable memory. Their new, and heavier, marble stones higher up on the slope had been cut doubly deep so their names would remain visible for an eternity, at least.

And then there was Arthur T. Grogan.

The Grogan Parthenon reminded Francis of something, but he could not say what. He stared at it and wondered, apart from its size, what it signified. He knew nothing of the Acropolis, and little more about Grogan except that he was a rich and powerful Albany Irishman whose name everybody used to know. Francis could not suppose that such massive marbling of old bones was a sweet conflation of ancient culture, modern coin, and self-apotheosizing. To him, the Grogan sepulcher was large enough to hold the bodies of dozens. And as this thought grazed his memory he envisioned the grave of Strawberry Bill Benson in Brooklyn. And that was it. Yes. Strawberry Bill had played left field for Toronto in ought eight when Francis played third, and when Francis hit the road in '16 after Gerald died, they bumped into each other at a crossroads near Newburgh and caught a freight south together.

Bill coughed and died a week after they reached the city, cursing his too-short life and swearing Francis to the task of following his body to the cemetery. "I don't want to go out there all by myself," Strawberry Bill said. He had no money, and so his coffin was a box of slapsided boards and a few dozen tenpenny nails, which Francis rode with to the burial plot. When the city driver and his helper left Bill's pile of wood sitting on top of some large planks and drove off, Francis stood by the box, letting Bill get used to the neighborhood. "Not a bad place, old buddy. Couple of trees over there." The sun then bloomed behind Francis, sending sunshine into an opening between two of the planks and lighting up a cavity below. The vision stunned Francis: a great empty chasm with a dozen other coffins of crude design, similar to Bill's, piled atop one another, some on their sides, one on its end. Enough earth had been dug away to accommodate thirty or forty more such crates of the dead. In a few weeks they'd all be stacked like cordwood, packaged cookies for the great maw. "You ain't got no worries now, Bill," Francis told his pal. "Plenty of company down there. You'll be lucky you get any sleep at all with them goin's on."

Francis did not want to be buried like Strawberry Bill, in a tenement grave. But he didn't want to rattle around in a marble temple the size of the public bath either.

"I wouldn't mind bein' buried right here," Francis told Rudy.

"You from around here?"

"Used to be. Born here."

"Your family here?"

"Some."

"Who's that?"

"You keep askin' questions about me, I'm gonna give you a handful of answers."

Francis recognized the hill where his family was buried, for it was just over from the sword-bearing guardian angel who stood on tiptoe atop three marble steps, guarding the grave of Toby, the dwarf who died heroically in the Delavan Hotel fire of '94. Old Ed Daugherty, the writer, bought that monument for Toby when it came out in the paper that Toby's grave had no marker. Toby's angel pointed down the hill toward Michael Phelan's grave and Francis found it with his gaze. His mother would be alongside the old man, probably with her back to him. Fishwife.

The sun that bloomed for Strawberry Bill had bloomed also on the day Michael Phelan was buried. Francis wept out of control that day, for he had been there when the train knocked Michael fifty feet in a fatal arc; and the memory tortured him. Francis was bringing him his hot lunch in the lunch pail, and when Michael saw Francis coming, he moved toward him. He safely passed the switch engine that was moving slowly on the far track, and then he turned his back, looked the way he'd just come, and walked backward, right into the path of the northbound train whose approach noise was being blocked out by the switch engine's clatter. He flew and then fell in a broken pile, and Francis ran to him, the first at his side. Francis looked for a way to straighten the angular body but feared any move, and so he pulled off his own sweater and pillowed his father's head with it. So many people go crooked when they die.

A few of the track gang followed Michael home in the back of Johnny Cody's wagon. He lingered two weeks and then won great obituaries as the most popular track foreman, boss gandy dancer,[3] on the New York Central line. The railroad gave all track workers on the Albany division the morning off to go to the funeral, and hundreds came to say so long to old Mike when he rode up here to live. Queen Mama ruled the house alone then, until she joined him in the grave. What I should do, Francis thought, is shovel open the grave, crawl down in there, and strangle her bones. He

[3] Railroad track laborer; the term is commonly used in the hobo world Francis Phelan belongs to.

remembered the tears he cried when he stood alongside the open grave of his father and he realized then that one of these days there would be nobody alive to remember that he cried that morning, just as there is no proof now that anyone ever cried for Tobias or Elisha or Elsie at the foot of the hill. No trace of grief is left, abstractions taken first by the snows of reduction.

"It's okay with me if I don't have no headstone," Francis said to Rudy, "just so's I don't die alone."

"You die before me I'll send out invites," Rudy said.

Kathryn Phelan, suddenly aware her worthless son was accepting his own death, provided it arrived on a gregarious note, humphed and fumed her disapproval to her husband. But Michael Phelan was already following the line of his son's walk toward the plot beneath the box elder tree where Gerald was buried. It always amazed Michael that the living could move instinctually toward dead kin without foreknowledge of their location. Francis had never seen Gerald's grave, had not attended Gerald's funeral. His absence that day was the scandal of the resident population of Saint Agnes's. But here he was now, walking purposefully, and with a slight limp Michael had not seen before, closing the gap between father and son, between sudden death and enduring guilt. Michael signaled to his neighbors that an act of regeneration seemed to be in process, and the eyes of the dead, witnesses all to their own historical omissions, their own unbridgeable chasms in life gone, silently rooted for Francis as he walked up the slope toward the box elder. Rudy followed his pal at a respectful distance, aware that some event of moment was taking place. Hangdog, he observed.

In his grave, a cruciformed circle, Gerald watched the advent of his father and considered what action might be appropriate to their meeting. Should he absolve the man of all guilt, not for the dropping, for that was accidental, but for the abandonment of the family, for craven flight when the steadfast virtues were called for? Gerald's grave trembled with superb possibility. Denied speech in life, having died with only monosyllabic goos and gaahs in his vocabulary, Gerald possessed the gift of tongues in death. His ability to communicate and to understand was at the genius level among the dead. He could speak with any resident adult in any language, but more notable was his ability to understand the chattery squirrels and chipmunks, the silent signals of the ants and beetles, and the slithy semaphores of the slugs and worms that moved above and through his earth. He could read the waning flow of energy in the leaves and berries as they fell from the box elder above him. And because his fate had been innocence and denial, Gerald had grown a protective web which deflected all moisture, all moles, rabbits, and other burrowing creatures. His web was woven of strands of vivid silver, an enveloping hammock of intricate, near-transparent weave. His body had not only been absolved of the need to decay, but in some respects —a full head of hair, for instance—it had grown to a completeness that was both natural and miraculous. Gerald rested in his infantile sublimity, exuding a high gloss induced by early death, his skin a radiant white-gold, his nails a silvery gray, his cluster of curls and large eyes perfectly matched in gleaming ebony. Swaddled in his grave, he was beyond capture by visual or verbal artistry. He was neither beautiful nor perfect to the beholder but rather an ineffably fabulous presence whose like was not to be found anywhere in the cemetery, and it abounded with dead innocents.

Francis found the grave without a search. He stood over it and reconstructed the moment when the child was slipping through his fingers into death. He prayed for a repeal of time so that he might hang himself in the coal bin before picking up the child to change his diaper. Denied that, he prayed for his son's eternal peace in the grave. It was true the boy had not suffered at all in his short life, and he had died too quickly of a cracked neckbone to have felt pain: a sudden twist and it was over. *Gerald Michael Phelan*, his gravestone said, *born April 13, 1916, died April 26, 1916. Born on the 13th, lived 13 days. An unlucky child who was much loved.*

Tears oozed from Francis's eyes, and when one of them fell onto his shoetop, he pitched forward onto the grave, clutching the grass, remembering the diaper in his grip. It had smelled of Gerald's pungent water, and when he squeezed it with his horrified right hand, a drop of the sacred fluid fell onto his shoetop. Twenty-two years gone, and Francis could now, in panoramic memory, see, hear, and feel every detail of that day, from the time he left the carbarns after work, to his talk about baseball with Bunt Dunn in King Brady's saloon, and even to the walk home with Cap Lawlor, who said Brady's beer was getting a heavy taste to it and Brady ought to clean his pipes, and that the Taylor kid next door to the Lawlors was passing green pinworms. His memory had begun returning forgotten images when it equated Arthur T. Grogan and Strawberry Bill, but now memory was as vivid as eyesight.

"I remember everything," Francis told Gerald in the grave. "It's the first time I tried to think of those things since you died. I had four beers after work that day. It wasn't because I was drunk that I dropped you. Four beers, and I didn't finish the fourth. Left it next to the pigs'-feet jar on Brady's bar so's I could walk home with Cap Lawlor. Billy was nine then. He knew you were gone before Peggy knew. She hadn't come home from choir practice yet. Your mother said two words, 'Sweet Jesus,' and then we both crouched down to snatch you up. But we both stopped in that crouch because of the looks of you. Billy come in then and saw you. 'Why is Gerald crooked?' he says. You know, I saw Billy a week or so ago and the kid looks good. He wanted to buy me new clothes. Bailed me outa jail and even give me a wad of cash. We talked about you. He says your mother never blamed me for dropping you. Never told a soul in twenty-two years it was me let you fall. Is that some woman or isn't it? I remember the linoleum you fell on was yellow with red squares. You suppose now that I can remember this stuff out in the open, I can finally start to forget it?"

Gerald, through an act of silent will, imposed on his father the pressing obligation to perform his final acts of expiation for abandoning the family. You will not know, the child silently said, what these acts are until you have performed them all. And after you have performed them you will not understand that they were expiatory any more than you have understood all the other expiation that has kept you in such prolonged humiliation. Then, when these final acts are complete, you will stop trying to die because of me.

Francis stopped crying and tried to suck a small piece of bread out from between the last two molars in his all but toothless mouth. He made a slurping sound with his tongue, and when he did, a squirrel scratching the earth for food to store up for the winter spiraled up the box elder in sudden fright. Francis took this as a signal to conclude his visit and he turned his gaze toward the sky. A vast stand of white fleece, brutally bright, moved south to north in the eastern vault of the heavens, a rush of splendid wool to warm the day. The breeze had grown temperate and the sun was rising to the noonday pitch. Francis was no longer chilly.

"Hey bum," he called to Rudy. "Let's find that truck driver."

"Whatayou been up to?" Rudy asked. "You know somebody buried up there?"

"A little kid I used to know."

"A kid? What'd he do, die young?"

"Pretty young."

"What happened to him?"

"He fell."

"He fell where?"

"He fell on the floor."

"Hell, I fall on the floor about twice a day and I ain't dead."

"That's what you think," Francis said.

1979

Harold Brodkey
b. 1930

"I think someone who claims to understand but who is obviously calm, someone who claims to write with emotion recollected in tranquillity, is a fool and a liar." For Harold Brodkey, William Wordsworth's memorable definition of poetry fails to take into account the intense emotional agitation that, if the writer is honest, accompanies the creative process. Poetry, or fiction, Brodkey would argue, is more properly a matter of "emotion recollected in emotion." Few contemporary writers have probed more deeply into human emotion, and perhaps none has explored more rigorously the profound interconnections among time, sexual emotion, and language.

Harold Brodkey was born in Staunton, Illinois, in 1930. Following his mother's death when he was two years old, he was adopted and raised by a family in University City, Missouri, a suburb of St. Louis. After graduating from Harvard, he taught for several years at Cornell. In 1954 his fiction began appearing in *The New Yorker,* and in 1958 he published a collection of nine stories, *First Love and Other Sorrows,* that won him praise for his meticulous craftsmanship and for his ability to confront sexual emotion and sexual vulnerability with both tenderness and accuracy. Several powerful, award-winning stories, including "Innocence" and "Play," two sensuously Proustian recollections first published in *American Review,* have further enhanced Brodkey's reputation. "His Son, in His Arms, in Light, Aloft" and "Verona: A Young Woman Speaks," both published in *Esquire,* show an almost Jamesian awareness of entangled family emotions. This sensitivity is also central to such recent *New Yorker* stories as "Ceil" and "Nonie." Having earlier published poetry, essays, and criticism as well as short stories, Brodkey is now at work on a long novel, *Party of Animals,* that is likely to extend his long-standing preoccupation with the ways in which language can master the nuances of sexual emotion and overcome the ravages of time.

Text:
Prize Stories: O. Henry Awards 1978, ed.
W. Abrahams, 1978.

Verona: A Young Woman Speaks

I know a lot! I know about happiness! I don't mean the love of God, either: I mean I know the human happiness with the crimes in it.

Even the happiness of childhood.

I think of it now as a cruel, middle-class happiness.

Let me describe one time—one day, one night.

I was quite young, and my parents and I—there were just the three of us—were traveling from Rome to Salzburg, journeying across a quarter of Europe to be in Salzburg for Christmas, for the music and the snow. We went by train because planes were erratic, and my father wanted us to stop in half a dozen Italian towns and see paintings and buy things. It was absurd, but we were all three drunk with this; it was very strange: we woke every morning in a strange hotel, in a strange city. I would be the first one to wake; and I would go to the window and see some tower or palace; and then I would wake my mother and be justified in my sense of wildness and belief and adventure by the way she acted, her sense of romance at being in a city as strange as I had thought it was when I had looked out the window and seen the palace or the tower.

We had to change trains in Verona, a darkish, smallish city at the edge of the Alps. By the time we got there, we'd bought and bought our way up the Italian peninsula: I was dizzy with shopping and new possessions: I hardly knew who I was, I owned so many new things: my reflection in any mirror or shopwindow was resplendently fresh and new, disguised even, glittering, I thought. I was seven or eight years old. It seemed to me we were almost in a movie or in the pages of a book: only the simplest and most light-filled words and images can suggest what I thought we were then. We went around shiningly: we shone everywhere. *Those clothes.* It's easy to buy a child. I had a new dress, knitted, blue and red, expensive as hell, I think; leggings, also red; a red loden-cloth coat with a hood and a knitted cap for under the hood; marvelous lined gloves; fur-lined boots and a fur purse or carryall, and a tartan skirt—and shirts and a scarf, and there was even more: a watch, a bracelet: more and more.

On the trains we had private rooms, and Momma carried games in her purse and things to eat, and Daddy sang carols off-key to me; and sometimes I became so intent on my happiness I would suddenly be in real danger of wetting myself; and Momma, who understood such emergencies, would catch the urgency in my voice and see my twisted face; and she—a large, good-looking woman—would whisk me to a toilet with amazing competence and unstoppability, murmuring to me, "Just hold on for a while," and she would hold my hand while I did it.

So we came to Verona, where it was snowing, and the people had stern, sad faces, beautiful, unlaughing faces. But if they looked at me, those serious faces would lighten, they would smile at me in my splendor. Strangers offered me candy, sometimes with the most excruciating sadness, kneeling or stooping to look directly into my face, into my eyes; and Momma or Papa would judge them, the people, and say in Italian we were late, we had to hurry, or pause, and let the stranger touch me, talk to me, look into my face for a while. I would see myself in the eyes of some strange man or woman; sometimes they stared so gently I would want to touch their eyelashes, stroke those strange, large, glistening eyes. I knew I decorated life. I took my duties with great seriousness. An Italian count in Siena said I had the manners of an English princess—at times—and then he laughed because it was true I would be quite lurid: I ran shouting in his *galleria,* a long room, hung with pictures, and with a frescoed ceiling: and I sat on his lap and wriggled: I was a wicked child, and I liked myself very much; and almost everywhere, almost every day, there was someone new to love me, briefly, while we traveled.

I understood I was special. I understood it *then.*

I knew that what we were doing, everything we did, involved money. I did not know if it involved mind or not, or style. But I knew about money somehow, checks and traveler's checks and the clink of coins. Daddy was a fountain of money: he said it was a spree; he meant for us to be amazed; he had saved money—we weren't really rich but we were to be for this trip. I remember a conservatory in a large house outside Florence and orange trees in tubs; and I ran there too. A servant, a man dressed in black, a very old man, mean-faced—he did not like being a servant anymore after the days of servants were over—and he scowled but he smiled at me, and at my mother, and even once at my father: we were clearly so separate from the griefs and weariness and cruelties of the world. We were at play, we were at our joys, and Momma was glad, with a terrible and naïve inner gladness, and she relied on Daddy to make it work: oh, she worked too, but she didn't know the secret of such— unreality: is that what I want to say? Of such a game, of such an extraordinary game.

There was a picture in Verona Daddy wanted to see; a painting; I remember the painter because the name Pisanello[1] reminded me I had to go to the bathroom when we were in the museum, which was an old castle, Guelf or Ghibelline.[2] I don't remember which; and I also remember the painting because it showed the hind end of the horse, and I thought that was not nice and rather funny, but Daddy was admiring; and so I said nothing.

He held my hand and told me a story so I wouldn't be bored as we walked from room to room in the museum/castle, and then we went outside into the snow, into

---

[1] Vittore Pisano (ca. 1380–1456), Italian painter of the early Renaissance; his "St. George Mounting His Horse" is in the Pellegrini Chapel in S. Anastasia, Verona.

[2] The Guelfs and the Ghibellines were rival groups in the political struggles of the late Middle Ages.

the soft light when it snows, light coming through snow; and I was dressed in red and had on boots, and my parents were young and pretty and had on boots too; and we could stay out in the snow if we wanted; and we did. We went to a square, a piazza—the Scaligera, I think; I don't remember—and just as we got there, the snowing began to bellow and then subside, to fall heavily and then sparsely, and then it stopped: and it was very cold, and there were pigeons everywhere in the piazza, on every cornice and roof, and all over the snow on the ground, leaving little tracks as they walked, while the air trembled in its just-after-snow and just-before-snow weight and thickness and grey seriousness of purpose. I had never seen so many pigeons or such a private and haunted place as that piazza, me in my new coat at the far rim of the world, the far rim of who knew what story, the rim of foreign beauty and Daddy's games, the edge, the white border of a season.

I was half mad with pleasure, anyway, and now Daddy brought five or six cones made of newspaper, wrapped, twisted; and they held grains of something like corn, yellow and white kernels of something; and he poured some on my hand and told me to hold my hand out; and then he backed away.

At first there was nothing, but I trusted him and I waited; and then the pigeons came. On heavy wings. Clumsy pigeony bodies. And red, unreal bird's feet. They flew at me, slowing at the last minute; they lit on my arm and fed from my hand. I wanted to flinch, but I didn't. I closed my eyes and held my arm stiffly; and felt them peck and eat—from my hand, these free creatures, these flying things. I liked that moment. I liked my happiness. If I was mistaken about life and pigeons and my own nature, it didn't matter *then*.

The piazza was very silent, with snow; and Daddy poured grains on both my hands and then on the sleeves of my coat and on the shoulders of the coat, and I was entranced with yet more stillness, with this idea of his. The pigeons fluttered heavily in the heavy air, more and more of them, and sat on my arms and on my shoulders; and I looked at Momma and then at my father and then at the birds on me.

Oh, I'm sick of everything as I talk. There is happiness. It always makes me slightly ill. I lose my balance because of it.

The heavy birds, and the strange buildings, and Momma near, and Daddy too: Momma is pleased that I am happy and she is a little jealous; she is jealous of everything Daddy does; she is a woman of enormous spirit; life is hardly big enough for her; she is drenched in wastefulness and prettiness. She knows things. She gets inflexible, though, and foolish at times, and temperamental; but she is a somebody, and she gets away with a lot, and if she is near, you can feel her, you can't escape her, she's that important, that echoing, her spirit is that powerful in the space around her.

If she weren't restrained by Daddy, if she weren't in love with him, there is no knowing what she might do: she does not know. But she manages almost to be gentle because of him; he is incredibly watchful and changeable and he gets tired; he talks and charms people; sometimes, then, Momma and I stand nearby, like moons; we brighten and wane; and after a while, he comes to us, to the moons, the big one, and the little one, and we welcome him, and he is always, to my surprise, he is always surprised, as if he didn't deserve to be loved, as if it were time he was found out.

Daddy is very tall, and Momma is watching us, and Daddy anoints me again and again with the grain. I cannot bear it much longer. I feel joy or amusement or I don't know what; it is all through me, like a nausea—I am ready to scream and laugh, that laughter that comes out like magical, drunken, awful and yet pure spit or vomit or God knows what, makes me a child mad with laughter. I become brilliant, gleaming, soft: an angel, a great bird-child of laughter.

I am ready to be like that, but I hold myself back.

There are more and more birds near me. They march around my feet and peck at falling and fallen grains. One is on my head. Of those on my arms, some move their wings, fluff those frail, feather-loaded wings, stretch them. I cannot bear it, they are so frail, and I am, at the moment, the kindness of the world that feeds them in the snow.

All at once, I let out a splurt of laughter: I can't stop myself and the birds fly away but not far; they circle around me, above me; some wheel high in the air and drop as they return; they all returned, some in clouds and clusters driftingly, some alone and angry, pecking at others; some with a blind, animal-strutting abruptness. They gripped my coat and fed themselves. It started to snow again.

I was there in my kindness, in that piazza, within reach of my mother and father.

Oh, how will the world continue? Daddy suddenly understood I'd had enough, I was at the end of my strength—Christ, he was alert—and he picked me up, and I went limp, my arm around his neck, and the snow fell. Momma came near and pulled the hood lower and said there were snowflakes in my eyelashes. She knew he had understood, and she wasn't sure she had; she wasn't sure he ever watched her so carefully. She became slightly unhappy, and so she walked like a clumsy boy beside us, but she was so pretty: she had powers, anyway.

We went to a restaurant, and I behaved very well, but I couldn't eat, and then we went to the train and people looked at us, but I couldn't smile; I was too dignified, too sated; some leftover—pleasure, let's call it—made my dignity very deep, I could not stop remembering the pigeons, or that Daddy loved me in a way he did not love Momma; and Daddy was alert, watching the luggage, watching strangers for assassination attempts or whatever; he was on duty; and Momma was pretty and alone and *happy,* defiant in that way.

And then, you see, what she did was wake me in the middle of the night when the train was chugging up a very steep mountainside; and outside the window, visible because our compartment was dark and the sky was clear and there was a full moon, were mountains, a landscape of mountains everywhere, big mountains, huge ones, impossible, all slanted and pointed and white with snow, and absurd, sticking up into an ink-blue sky and down into blue, blue shadows, miraculously deep. I don't know how to say what it was like: they were not like anything I knew: they were high things: and we were up high in the train and we were climbing higher, and it was not at all true, but it was, you see. I put my hands on the window and stared at the wild, slanting, unlikely marvels, whiteness and dizziness and moonlight and shadows cast by moonlight, not real, not familiar, not pigeons, but a clean world.

We sat a long time, Momma and I, and stared, and then Daddy woke up and came and looked too. "It's pretty," he said, but he didn't really understand. Only Momma and I did. She said to him, "When I was a child, I was bored all the time, my love —I thought nothing would ever happen to me—and now these things are happening —and you have happened." I think he was flabbergasted by her love in the middle of the night; he smiled at her, oh, so swiftly that I was jealous, but I stayed quiet, and after a while, in his silence and amazement at her, at us, he began to seem different from us, from Momma and me; and then he fell asleep again; Momma and I didn't; we sat at the window and watched all night, watched the mountains and the moon, the clean world. We watched together.

Momma was the winner.

We were silent, and in silence we spoke of how we loved men and how dangerous men were and how they stole everything from you no matter how much you gave —but we didn't say it aloud.

We looked at mountains until dawn, and then when dawn came, it was too pretty for me—there was pink and blue and gold, in the sky, and on icy places, brilliant pink and gold flashes, and the snow was colored too, and I said, "Oh," and sighed; and each moment was more beautiful than the one before; and I said, "I love you, Momma." Then I fell asleep in her arms.

That was happiness then.

1977

John McPhee
b. 1931

John McPhee has conscientiously avoided the public trappings of being a celebrated contemporary American writer. He shuns publicity, rarely grants interviews, and insists that his photograph not appear on the covers of his books. He applies similar determination to his work; he regularly spends twelve-hour days transforming extensive research and interview notes into finely crafted sentences on such vastly different subjects as physics and canoes, aeronautics and cooking, geology and pomology. In fact, the range of topics in McPhee's nearly two dozen books and scores of magazine articles reads like the categories in a well-stocked bookstore: literature, history, geography, science, education, travel, environmental studies, military science, cooking, dining, and sports. And what makes McPhee's writing so successful is his ability to see each subject so freshly, be it a graceful athlete or a remote stretch of frontier landscape.

John McPhee was born and reared in Princeton, New Jersey, where he has permanently settled. The son of Mary Ziegler and Harry McPhee, a physician who included among his patients Princeton University athletes and several U.S. Olympic teams, McPhee attended Princeton High School and Deerfield Academy before entering Princeton University, where he now teaches an always oversubscribed writing course called "The Literature of Fact."

He traces many of his skills as a writer to the influence of a high school English teacher, Olive McKee, who required three essays (plus outlines) each week, practice that prepared him well for the carefully documented "fact pieces" —to use *The New Yorker*'s term—that have earned him international acclaim.

At Princeton, McPhee played basketball as a freshman, wrote for and edited several student literary publications, and wrote film and book reviews for the *Daily Princetonian*. Other extracurricular activities included four years of weekly appearances on the New York–based radio and television program *Twenty Questions,* where he identified innumerable "mystery items" with penetrating questioning. In his senior year, he also wrote a column, "On the Campus," for the *Princeton Alumni Weekly.*

After a year of concentrated reading at Cambridge University (where he also regularly played basketball, once in the Tower of London), McPhee returned to Princeton, tutored at a local school, and began his career as a free-lance writer. He worked briefly as a television scriptwriter before joining *Time* magazine in 1957 as a staff reporter responsible for assigned stories for the show business section. After several years with *Time,* McPhee declined his senior editors' invitation to write on national affairs in order to focus, despite many earlier failures, on publishing in *The New Yorker.* Finally, in January 1965, his detailed profile of basketball star and Rhodes scholar Bill Bradley appeared in *The New Yorker* and later became his first published book. Soon after, McPhee began working as a "staff writer" for *The New Yorker,* free to choose his own subjects. During a relationship that spans three decades, he has contributed numerous brief —and unsigned—sketches and essays for *The New Yorker*'s opening pages, "The Talk of the Town," as well as many longer pieces. Published in book form, his work documents his insatiable curiosity about what is extraordinary in the ordinary world: *The Headmaster* (1966), *Oranges* (1967), *The Pine Barrens* (1968), *Levels of the Game* (1970), *The Deltoid Pumpkin Seed* (1973), *The Survival of the Bark Canoe* (1975), *Basin and Range* (1981), *In Suspect Terrain* (1982), and *La Place de la Concorde Suisse* (1986). Two of his works have been nominated for National Book Awards in science: *Encounters with the Archdruid* (1973) and *The Curve of Binding Energy* (1974). In 1977 McPhee was honored by the American Academy and Institute of Arts and Letters.

Developing his various projects, McPhee has spent countless hours on the road, in the woods, in laboratories, and in the stacks, seeking fresh perspectives on subjects too elusive for less determined writers. In his incisive introduction to *The John McPhee Reader* (1977), William Howarth describes McPhee's rare ability to assemble scraps of talk, bits of description, odd facts, and inferences into elegantly written and compelling accounts of the people and places that encourage readers to reflect on "particles of experience that reflect its totality." McPhee never overwrites. His prose is at once taut, precise, and energetic; it is richly detailed yet impersonal, highly figurative yet restrained and good-humored.

The selection that follows, drawn from his best-selling book *Coming into the Country* (1977), celebrates Alaska, America's last frontier. In it he recounts his first encounter with the majestic ruler of that Arctic land and underscores his appropriation of one of the fundamental themes of American experience and American literature: that in our "society as a whole, there is an elemental need for a frontier outlet, for a pioneer place to go—important even to those who do not go there."

Text:
Coming into the Country, 1977.

from Coming into the Country

The river was low, and Pat Pourchot had picked a site as far upstream as he judged we could be and still move in boats. We were on an island, with the transparent Salmon River on one side—hurrying, scarcely a foot deep—and a small slough on the other. Deeper pools, under bedrock ledges, were above us and below us. We built our fire on the lemon-sized gravel of what would in higher water be the riverbed, and we pitched the tents on slightly higher ground among open stands of willow, on sand that showed what Bob Fedeler called "the old tracks of a young griz." We would stay two nights, according to plan, before beginning the long descent to the Kobuk;[1] and in the intervening day we would first assemble the kayaks and then be free to disperse and explore the terrain.

There was a sixth man with us, there at the beginning. His name was Jack Hession, and he was the Sierra Club's[2] only salaried full-time representative in Alaska. Pourchot had invited him as an observer. The news that he was absent at the end of the trip could instantly cause hopes to rise in Alaska, where the Sierra Club has long been considered a netherworld force and Hession the resident Belial.[3] Hession, though, was not going to perish on the Salmon. Pressures from Anchorage had travelled with him, and before long would get the better of him, and in cavalier manner—in this Arctic wilderness—he would bid us goodbye and set out early for home. Meanwhile, in the morning sun, we put together the collapsible kayaks—two single Kleppers and Snake Eyes. Hession's own single was the oldest of the three, and it had thirty-six parts, hardware not included. There were dowels of mountain ash and ribs of laminated Finnish birch, which fitted, one part to another, with hooks and clips until they formed a pair of nearly identical skeletal cones—the internal structures of halves of the boat. The skin was a limp bag made of blue canvas (the deck) and hemp-reinforced vulcanized rubber (the hull). The concept was to insert the skeletal halves into the skin and then figure out how to firm them together. We had trouble doing that. Hession, who ordinarily used rigid boats of fibre glass in his engagements with white water, could not remember how to complete the assembly. Stiff toward the ends and bent in the middle, his kayak had the look of a clip-on tie, and would do about as well in the river. We all crouched around and studied amidships—six men, a hundred miles up a stream, above sixty-seven degrees of latitude, with a limp kayak. No one was shy with suggestions, which were full of ingenuity but entirely failed to work. By trial and error, we finally figured it out. The last step in the assembly involved the center rib, and we set that inside the hull on a tilt and then tapped it with a rock and forced it toward the vertical. When the forcing rib reached ninety degrees to the longer axis of the craft, the rib snapped into place, and with that the entire boat became taut and yare. Clever man, Johann Klepper. He had organized his foldboat in the way

---

[1] The Kobuk and Salmon rivers are located in northwestern Alaska.

[2] Sierra Club: organization advocating conservation and environmental protection.

[3] A satanic, ungodly figure; one of the fallen angels in Milton's *Paradise Lost.*

that the North American Indians had developed the construction of their bark canoes. Over the years, the Klepper company had simplified its process. Our other single kayak, the more recent model, had fewer and larger skeletal parts, and it went together more easily; but it was less streamlined than the first. Snake Eyes, for its part—all eight hundred dollars' worth of Snake Eyes—was new and had an interior of broad wooden slabs, conveniently hinged. Snake Eyes had the least number of separate parts (only fifteen) and in the way it went together was efficient and simple. Its advanced design had been achieved with a certain loss of grace, however, and this was evident there on the gravel. The boat was lumpy, awkward, bulging—a kayak with elbows.

Toward noon and after an early lunch, we set off on foot for a look around. Pourchot went straight up the hills to the west, alone. Stell Newman and John Kauffmann intended lesser forays, nearer the campsite. I decided I'd go with Bob Fedeler, who, with Jack Hession, had the most ambitious plan. They were going north up the river some miles and then up the ridges to the east. I hoped my legs would hold up. I didn't want to embarrass myself, off somewhere in the hills, by snapping something, but I could not resist going along with Fedeler. After all, he was a habitat biologist, working for the state, and if the ground around here was not habitat then I would never be in country that was. The temperature had come up to seventy. The sky was blue, with moving clouds and intermittent sun. We stuffed our rain gear into day packs and started up the river.

Generally speaking, if I had a choice between hiking and peeling potatoes, I would peel the potatoes. I have always had a predilection for canoes on rivers and have avoided walking wherever possible. My experience, thus, was limited but did exist. My work had led me up the Sierra Nevada[4] and across the North Cascades,[5] and in various eras I had walked parts of the Long Trail, the Appalachian Trail, trails of New Hampshire, the Adirondacks. Here in the Brooks Range, of course, no one had been there clearing the path. A mile, steep or level, could demand a lot of time. You go along with only a general plan, free lance, guessing where the walking will be least difficult, making choices all the way. These are the conditions, and in ten minutes' time they present their story. The country is wild to the limits of the term. It would demean such a world to call it pre-Columbian. It is twenty times older than that, having assumed its present form ten thousand years ago, with the melting of the Wisconsin ice.

For several miles upstream, willow and alder pressed in on the river, backed by spruce and cottonwood, so the easiest path was the river itself. Gravel bars were now on one side, now the other, so we crossed and crossed again, taking off our boots and wading through the fast, cold water. I had rubber-bottomed leather boots (L.L. Bean's,[6] which are much in use all over Alaska). Fedeler was wearing hiking boots, Hession low canvas sneakers. Hession had a floppy sun hat, too. He seemed to see no need to dress like Sir Edmund Hillary,[7] or to leave the marks of waffles by the tracks of wolves. He was a brief, trim, lithe figure, who moved lightly and had seen a lot

[4] Mountains in northern California.
[5] Northern section of the Sierra Nevada Mountains, extending from northeastern California to western Oregon and Washington.
[6] L. L. Bean: famous campers' outfitting company in Freeport, Maine.

[7] New Zealand explorer (b. 1919) who, with the Sherpa guide Tenzing Norgay, first reached the summit of Mount Everest (1953).

of such ground. He stopped and opened his jackknife, and stood it by a track in sand at the edge of the river. Other tracks were near. Two wolves running side by side. He took a picture of the track. We passed a deep pool where spring water came into the river, and where algae grew in response to its warmth. Grayling could winter there. Some were in the pool now—bodies stationary, fins in motion, in clear deep water as green as jade. Four mergansers swam up the river. We saw moose pellets in sand beyond the pool. I would not much want to be a moose just there, in a narrow V-shaped valley with scant protection of trees. We came, in fact, to the tree line not long thereafter. The trees simply stopped. We took a few more northward steps and were out of the boreal forest. Farther north, as far as land continued, there would be no more. I don't mean to suggest that we had stepped out of Sequoia National Park[8] and onto an unvegetated plain. The woods behind us were spare in every sense, fingering up the river valley, reaching as far as they could go. Now the tundra, which had before been close behind the trees, came down to the banks of the river. We'd had enough of shoelaces and of bare feet crunching underwater stones, so we climbed up the west bank to walk on the tundra—which from the river had looked as smooth as a golf course. Possibly there is nothing as invitingly deceptive as a tundra-covered hillside. Distances over tundra, even when it is rising steeply, are like distances over water, seeming to be less than they are, defraying the suggestion of effort. The tundra surface, though, consists of many kinds of plants, most of which seem to be stemmed with wire configured to ensnare the foot. For years, my conception of tundra—based, I suppose, on photographs of the Canadian north and the plains of the Alaskan Arctic slope—was of a vast northern flatness, water-flecked, running level to every horizon. Tundra is not topography, however; it is a mat of vegetation, and it runs up the sides of prodigious declivities as well as across the broad plains. There are three varying types—wet tundra, on low flatland with much standing water; moist tundra, on slightly higher ground; and alpine tundra, like carpeted heather, rising on mountains and hills. We moved on, northward, over moist tundra, and the plants were often a foot or so in height. Moving through them was more like wading than walking, except where we followed game trails. Fortunately, these were numerous enough, and comfortably negotiable. They bore signs of everything that lived there. They were highways, share and share alike, for caribou, moose, bears, wolves—whose tracks, antlers, and feces were strewn along the right-of-way like beer cans at the edge of a road. While these game trails were the best thoroughfares in many hundreds of square miles, they were also the only ones, and they had a notable defect. They tended to vanish. The trails would go along, well cut and stamped out through moss campion, reindeer moss, sedge tussocks, crowberries, prostrate willows, dwarf birch, bog blueberries, white mountain avens, low-bush cranberries, lichens, Labrador tea; then, abruptly, and for no apparent reason, the trails would disappear. Their well-worn ruts suggested hundreds of animals, heavy traffic. So where did they go when the trail vanished? Fedeler did not know. I could not think of an explanation. Maybe Noah had got there a little before us.

On the far side of the river was an isolated tree, which had made a brave bid to move north, to extend the reach of its progenitive forest. The Brooks Range, the remotest uplift in North America, was made a little less remote, fifty years ago, by

---

[8] In the Sierra Nevada Mountains.

the writing of Robert Marshall, a forester, who described several expeditions to these mountains in a book called "Alaska Wilderness." Marshall had a theory about the tree line, the boundary of the circumboreal world. He thought that white spruce and other species could live farther north, and that they were inching northward, dropping seeds ahead of them, a dead-slow advance under marginal conditions. Whatever it may have signified, the tree across the river was dead, and out of it now came a sparrow hawk, flying at us, shouting "*kee kee kee*," and hovering on rapidly beating wings to study the creatures on the trail. There was not much it could do about us, and it went back to the tree.

The leaves of Labrador tea, crushed in the hand, smelled like a turpentine. The cranberries were early and sourer than they would eventually be. With the arrival of cold, they freeze on the vine, and when they thaw, six months later, they are somehow sweeter and contain more juice. Bears like overwintered berries. Blueberries, too, are sweeter after being frozen on the bush. Fried cranberries will help relieve a sore throat. Attacks in the gall bladder have been defused with boiled cranberries mixed with seal oil. The sedge tussocks were low and not as perilous as tussocks can be. They are grass that grows in bunches, more compact at the bottom than at the top—a mushroom shape that can spill a foot and turn an ankle. They were tiresome, and soon we were ready to move upward, away from the moist tundra and away from the river. Ahead we saw the configurations of the sharp small valleys of three streams meeting, forming there the principal stem of the Salmon. To the east, above the confluence, a tundra-bald hill rose a thousand feet and more. We decided to cross the river and go up the hill. Look around. Choose where to go from there.

The river was so shallow now that there was no need for removing boots. We walked across and began to climb. The going was steep. I asked Jack Hession how long he had been in Alaska, and he said seven years. He had been in Alaska longer than two-thirds of the people in the state. He was from California, and had lived more recently in western Washington, where he had begun to acquire his expertise in boats in white water. Like Fedeler—like me, for that matter—he was in good condition. Hession, though, seemed to float up the incline, while I found it hard, sweaty work. From across the river it had looked as easy as a short flight of stairs. I went up it a trudge at a time—on reindeer moss, heather, lupine. The sun had suddenly departed, and a cool rain began to fall. At the top of the hill, we sat on a rock outcropping and looked back at the river, twelve hundred feet below. Everywhere around us were mountains—steep, treeless, buff where still in the sun. One was bright silver. The rain felt good. We nibbled M&M's. They were even better than the rain. The streams far below, small and fast, came pummelling together and made the river. The land they fell through looked nude. It was all tundra, rising northward toward a pass at the range divide. Looking at so much mountain ground—this immense minute fragment of wilderness Alaska—one could wonder about the choice of words of people who say that it is fragile. "Fragile" just does not appear to be a proper term for a rugged, essentially uninvaded landscape covering tens of thousands of square miles—a place so vast and unpeopled that if anyone could figure out how to steal Italy, Alaska would be a place to hide it. Meanwhile, earnest ecologues write and speak about the "fragile" tundra, this "delicate" ocean of barren land. The words sound effete, but the terrain is nonetheless vulnerable. There is ice under the tundra, mixed with soil as permafrost, in some places two thousand feet deep. The tundra vegetation, living and dead, provides insulation that keeps the summer sun from melting the permafrost. If something pulls away the insulation and melting occurs, the soil will settle and the water may run off. The earth, in such circumstances, does not restore itself. In the nineteen-sixties, a bulldozer working for Geophysical Service, Inc., an oil-exploration company, wrote the initials G.S.I. in Arctic Alaskan tundra. The letters were two hundred feet from top to bottom, and near them the bulldozer cut an arrow—an indicator for pilots. Thermokarst (thermal erosion) followed, and slumpage. The letters and the arrow are now odd-shaped ponds, about eight feet deep. For many generations that segment of tundra will say "G.S.I." Tundra is even sensitive to snow machines. They compress snow, and cut off much of the air that would otherwise get to the vegetation. Evidence appears in summer. The snow machines have left brown trails on ground they never touched.

Both sunlight and rain were falling on us now. We had a topographic map, of the largest scale available but nonetheless of scant detail—about five miles to half a thumb. Of the three streams that met below us, the nearest was called Sheep Creek. A rainbow wicketed its steep valley. The top of the arch was below us. The name Sheep Creek was vestigial. "Historically, there were Dall sheep in these mountains," Fedeler said.

"What happened to them?"

"Who knows?" He shrugged. "Things go in cycles. They'll be back."

Alders had crept into creases in the mountainside across the Salmon valley. I remarked on the borderline conditions in evidence everywhere in this spare and beautiful country, and said, "Look at those alders over there, clinging to life."

Fedeler said, "It's hungry country, that's for sure. Drainage and exposure make *the* difference."

We ate peanuts and raisins and more M&M's—and, feeling rested, became ambitious. On a long southward loop back to camp, we would extend our walk by going around a mountain that was separated from us by what looked to be the fairly steep declivity of a tributary drainage. The terrain sloped away to the southwest toward the mouth of the tributary. We would go down for a time, and then cross the tributary and cut back around the mountain.

We passed first through stands of fireweed, and then over ground that was wine-red with the leaves of bearberries. There were curlewberries, too, which put a deep-purple stain on the hand. We kicked at some wolf scat, old as winter. It was woolly and white and filled with the hair of a snowshoe hare. Nearby was a rich inventory of caribou pellets and, in increasing quantity as we moved downhill, blueberries—an outspreading acreage of blueberries. Fedeler stopped walking. He touched my arm. He had in an instant become even more alert than he usually was, and obviously apprehensive. His gaze followed straight on down our intended course. What he saw there I saw now. It appeared to me to be a hill of fur. "Big boar grizzly," Fedeler said in a near-whisper. The bear was about a hundred steps away, in the blueberries, grazing. The head was down, the hump high. The immensity of muscle seemed to vibrate slowly—to expand and contract, with the grazing. Not berries alone but whole bushes were going into the bear. He was big for a barren-ground grizzly. The brown bears of Arctic Alaska (or grizzlies; they are no longer thought to be different) do not grow to the size they will reach on more ample diets elsewhere. The barren-ground grizzly will rarely grow larger than six hundred pounds.

"What if he got too close?" I said.

Fedeler said, "We'd be in real trouble."

"You can't outrun them," Hession said.

A grizzly, no slower than a racing horse, is about half again as fast as the fastest human being. Watching the great mound of weight in the blueberries, with a fifty-five-inch waist and a neck more than thirty inches around, I had difficulty imagining that he could move with such speed, but I believed it, and was without impulse to test the proposition. Fortunately, a light southerly wind was coming up the Salmon valley. On its way to us, it passed the bear. The wind was relieving, coming into our faces, for had it been moving the other way the bear would not have been placidly grazing. There is an old adage that when a pine needle drops in the forest the eagle will see it fall; the deer will hear it when it hits the ground; the bear will smell it. If the boar grizzly were to catch our scent, he might stand on his hind legs, the better to try to see. Although he could hear well and had an extraordinary sense of smell, his eyesight was not much better than what was required to see a blueberry inches away. For this reason, a grizzly stands and squints, attempting to bring the middle distance into focus, and the gesture is often misunderstood as a sign of anger and forthcoming attack. If the bear were getting ready to attack, he would be on four feet, head low, ears cocked, the hair above his hump muscle standing on end. As if that message were not clear enough, he would also chop his jaws. His teeth would make a sound that would carry like the ringing of an axe.

One could predict, but not with certainty, what a grizzly would do. Odds were very great that one touch of man scent would cause him to stop his activity, pause in a moment of absorbed and alert curiosity, and then move, at a not undignified pace, in a direction other than the one from which the scent was coming. That is what would happen almost every time, but there was, to be sure, no guarantee. The forest Eskimos fear and revere the grizzly. They know that certain individual bears not only will fail to avoid a person who comes into their country but will approach and even stalk the trespasser. It is potentially inaccurate to extrapolate the behavior of any one bear from the behavior of most, since they are both intelligent and independent and will do what they choose to do according to mood, experience, whim. A grizzly that has ever been wounded by a bullet will not forget it, and will probably know that it was a human being who sent the bullet. At sight of a human, such a bear will be likely to charge. Grizzlies hide food sometimes—a caribou calf, say, under a pile of scraped-up moss—and a person the bear might otherwise ignore might suddenly not be ignored if the person were inadvertently to step into the line between the food cache and the bear. A sow grizzly with cubs, of course, will charge anything that suggests danger to the cubs, even if the cubs are nearly as big as she is. They stay with their mother two and a half years.

None of us had a gun. (None of the six of us had brought a gun on the trip.) Among nonhunters who go into the terrain of the grizzly, there are several schools of thought about guns. The preferred one is: Never go without a sufficient weapon —a high-powered rifle or a shotgun and plenty of slug-loaded shells. The option is not without its own inherent peril. A professional hunter, some years ago, spotted a grizzly from the air and—with a client, who happened to be an Anchorage barber —landed on a lake about a mile from the bear. The stalking that followed was evidently conducted not only by the hunters but by the animal as well. The professional hunter was found dead from a broken neck, and had apparently died instantly, unaware of danger, for the cause of death was a single bite, delivered from behind.

The barber, noted as clumsy with a rifle, had emptied his magazine, missing the bear with every shot but one, which struck the grizzly in the foot. The damage the bear did to the barber was enough to kill him several times. After the corpses were found, the bear was tracked and killed. To shoot and merely wound is worse than not to shoot at all. A bear that might have turned and gone away will possibly attack if wounded.

Fatal encounters with bears are as rare as they are memorable. Some people reject the rifle as cumbersome extra baggage, not worth toting, given the minimal risk. And, finally, there are a few people who feel that it is wrong to carry a gun, in part because the risk is low and well worth taking, but most emphatically because they see the gun as an affront to the wild country of which the bear is sign and symbol. This, while strongly felt, is a somewhat novel attitude. When Robert Marshall explored the Brooks Range half a century ago, he and his companions fired at almost every bear they saw, without pausing for philosophical reflection. The reaction was automatic. They were expressing mankind's immemorial fear of this beast—man and rattlesnake, man and bear. Among modern environmentalists, to whom a figure like Marshall is otherwise a hero, fear of the bear has been exceeded by reverence. A notable example, in his own past and present, is Andy Russell, author of a book called "Grizzly Country." Russell was once a professional hunter, but he gave that up to become a photographer, specializing in grizzlies. He says that he has given up not only shooting bears but even carrying a gun. On rare instances when grizzlies charge toward him, he shouts at them and stands his ground. The worst thing to do, he says, is to run, because anything that runs on open tundra suggests game to a bear. Game does not tend to stand its ground in the presence of grizzlies. Therefore, when the bear comes at you, just stand there. Charging something that does not move, the bear will theoretically stop and reconsider. (Says Russell.) More important, Russell believes that the bear will *know* if you have a gun, even if the gun is concealed:

> Reviewing our experiences, we had become more and more convinced that carrying arms was not only unnecessary in most grizzly country but was certainly no good for the desired atmosphere and proper protocol in obtaining good film records. If we were to obtain such film and fraternize successfully with the big bears, it would be better to go unarmed in most places. The mere fact of having a gun within reach, cached somewhere in a pack or a hidden holster, causes a man to act with unconscious arrogance and thus maybe to smell different or to transmit some kind of signal objectionable to bears. The armed man does not assume his proper role in association with the wild ones, a fact of which they seem instantly aware at some distance. He, being wilder than they, whether he likes to admit it or not, is instantly under even more suspicion than he would encounter if unarmed.

> One must follow the role of an uninvited visitor—an intruder—rather than that of an aggressive hunter, and one should go unarmed to insure this attitude.

Like pictures from pages riffled with a thumb, all of these things went through my mind there on the mountainside above the grazing bear. I will confess that in one instant I asked myself, "What the hell am I doing *here?*" There was nothing more to the question, though, than a hint of panic. I knew why I had come, and therefore what I was doing there. That I was frightened was incidental. I just hoped the fright would not rise beyond a relatively decorous level. I sensed that Fedeler and Hession were somewhat frightened, too. I would have been troubled if they had not been. Meanwhile, the sight of the bear stirred me like nothing else the country could contain. What mattered was not so much the bear himself as what the bear implied. He was the predominant thing in that country, and for him to be in it at all meant that there had to be more country like it in every direction and more of the same kind of country all around that. He implied a world. He was an affirmation to the rest of the earth that his kind of place was extant. There had been a time when his race was everywhere in North America, but it had been hunted down and pushed away in favor of something else. For example, the grizzly bear is the state animal of California, whose country was once his kind of place; and in California now the grizzly is extinct.

> The animals I have encountered in my wilderness wanderings have been reluctant to reveal all the things about them I would like to know. The animal that impresses me most, the one I find myself liking more and more, is the grizzly. No sight encountered in the wilds is quite so stirring as those massive, clawed tracks pressed into mud or snow. No sight is quite so impressive as that of the great bear stalking across some mountain slope with the fur of his silvery robe rippling over his mighty muscles. His is a dignity and power matched by no other in the North American wilderness. To share a mountain with him for a while is a privilege and an adventure like no other.
>
> I have followed his tracks into an alder hell to see what he had been doing and come to the abrupt end of them, when the maker stood up thirty feet away with a sudden snort to face me.
>
> To see a mother grizzly ambling and loafing with her cubs across the broad, hospitable bosom of a flower-spangled mountain meadow is to see life in true wilderness at its best.

If a wolf kills a caribou, and a grizzly comes along while the wolf is feeding on the kill, the wolf puts its tail between its legs and hurries away. A black bear will run from a grizzly, too. Grizzlies sometimes kill and eat black bears. The grizzly takes what he happens upon. He is an opportunistic eater. The predominance of the grizzly in his terrain is challenged by nothing but men and ravens. To frustrate ravens from stealing his food, he will lie down and sleep on top of a carcass, occasionally swatting the birds as if they were big black flies. He prefers a vegetable diet. He can pulp a moosehead with a single blow, but he is not lusting always to kill, and when he moves through his country he can be something munificent, going into copses of willow among unfleeing moose and their calves, touching nothing, letting it all breathe as before. He may, though, get the head of a cow moose between his legs and rake her flanks with the five-inch knives that protrude from the ends of his paws. Opportunistic. He removes and eats her entrails. He likes porcupines, too, and when one turns and presents to him a pygal bouquet of quills, he will leap into the air, land on the other side, chuck the fretful porpentine beneath the chin, flip it over, and, with a swift ventral incision, neatly remove its body from its skin, leaving something like a sea urchin behind him on the ground. He is nothing if not athletic. Before he dens, or just after he emerges, if his mountains are covered with snow he will climb to the brink of some impossible schuss, sit down on his butt, and shove off. Thirty-two, sixty-four, ninety-six feet per second, he plummets down the mountainside, spray snow flying to either side, as he approaches collision with boulders and trees. Just short of catastrophe, still going at bonecrushing speed, he flips to his feet and walks sedately onward as if his ride had not occurred.

His population density is thin on the Arctic barren ground. He needs for his forage at least fifty and perhaps a hundred square miles that are all his own—sixty-four thousand acres, his home range. Within it, he will move, typically, eight miles a summer day, doing his travelling through the twilight hours of the dead of night. To scratch his belly he walks over a tree—where forest exists. The tree bends beneath him as he passes. He forages in the morning, generally; and he rests a great deal, particularly after he eats. He rests fourteen hours a day. If he becomes hot in the sun, he lies down in a pool in the river. He sleeps on the tundra—restlessly tossing and turning, forever changing position. What he could be worrying about I cannot imagine.

His fur blends so well into the tundra colors that sometimes it is hard to see him. Fortunately, we could see well enough the one in front of us, or we would have walked right to him. He caused a considerable revision of our travel plans. Not wholly prepared to follow the advice of Andy Russell, I asked Fedeler what one should do if a bear were to charge. He said, "Take off your pack and throw it into the bear's path, then crawl away, and hope the pack will distract the bear. But there is no good thing to do, really. It's just not a situation to be in."

We made a hundred-and-forty-degree turn from the course we had been following and went up the shoulder of the hill through ever-thickening brush, putting distance behind us in good position with the wind. For a time, we waded through hip-deep willow, always making our way uphill, and the going may have been difficult, but I didn't notice. There was adrenalin to spare in my bloodstream. I felt that I was floating, climbing with ease, like Hession. I also had expectations now that another bear, in the thick brush, might come rising up from any quarter. We broke out soon into a swale of blueberries. Hession and Fedeler, their nonchalance refreshed, sat down to eat, paused to graze. The berries were sweet and large.

"I can see why he's here," Hession said.

"These berries are so big."

"Southern exposure."

"He may not be the only one."

"They can be anywhere."

"It's amazing to me," Fedeler said. "So large an animal, living up here in this country. It's amazing what keeps that big body alive." Fedeler went on eating the blueberries with no apparent fear of growing fat. The barren-ground bear digs a lot of roots, he said—the roots of milk vetch, for example, and Eskimo potatoes. The bear, coming out of his den into the snows of May, goes down into the river bottoms, where overwintered berries are first revealed. Wolf kills are down there, too. By the middle of June, his diet is almost wholly vegetable. He eats willow buds, sedges, cotton-grass tussocks. In the cycle of his year, roots and plants are eighty per cent of what he eats, and even when the salmon are running he does not sate himself on them alone but forages much of the time for berries. In the fall, he unearths not only roots but ground squirrels and lemmings. It is indeed remarkable how large he grows on the provender of his yearly cycle, for on this Arctic barren ground he has to work much harder than the brown bears of southern Alaska, which line up along foaming rivers—hip to hip, like fishermen in New Jersey—taking forty-pound king salmon in their jaws as if they were nibbling feed from a barnyard trough. When the caribou are in fall migration, moving down the Salmon valley toward the Kobuk, the bear finishes up his year with one of them. Then, around the first of November, he may find a cave or, more likely, digs out a cavern in a mountainside. If he finds a natural cave, it may be full of porcupines. He kicks them out, and—extending his curious relationship with this animal—will cushion his winter bed with many thousands of their turds. If, on the other hand, he digs his den, he sends earth flying out behind him and makes a shaft that goes upward into the side of the mountain. At the top of the shaft, he excavates a shelf-like cavern. When the outside entrance is plugged with debris, the shaft becomes a column of still air, insulating the upper chamber, trapping the bear's body heat. On a bed of dry vegetation, he lays himself out like a dead pharaoh in a pyramid. But he does not truly hibernate. He just lies there. His mate of the summer, in her den somewhere, will give birth during winter to a cub or two—virtually hairless, blind, weighing about a pound. But the male has nothing to do. His heart rate goes down as low as eight beats a minute. He sleeps and wakes, and sleeps again. He may decide to get up and go out. But that is rare. He may even stay out, which is rarer—to give up denning for that winter and roam his frozen range. If he does this, sooner or later he will find a patch of open water in an otherwise frozen river, and in refreshing himself he will no doubt wet his fur. Then he rolls in the snow, and the fur acquires a thick plate of ice, which is less disturbing to the animal than to the forest Eskimo, who has for ages feared—feared most of all—the "winter bear." Arrows broke against the armoring ice, and it can be heavy enough to stop a bullet.

We moved on now, in continuing retreat, and approached the steep incline of the tributary valley we'd been skirting when the bear rewrote our plans. We meant to put the valley between us and him and reschedule ourselves on the other side. It was in fact less a valley than an extremely large ravine, which plunged maybe eight hundred feet, and then rose up an even steeper incline some fifteen hundred feet on the other side, toward the top of which the bushy vegetation ceased growing. The walking looked promising on the ridge beyond.

I had hoped we might see a den site, and this might have been the place. It had all the requisites but one. It was a steep hillside with southern exposure, and was upgrown with a hell of alders and willows. Moreover, we were on the south side of the Brooks Range divide, which is where most of the dens are. But we were not high enough. We were at something under two thousand feet, and bears in this part of Alaska like to den much higher than that. They want the very best drainage. One way to become a "winter bear" is to wake up in a flooded den.

The willow-alder growth was so dense and high that as we went down the hillside we could see no farther than a few yards ahead. It was wet in there from the recent rain. We broke our way forward with the help of gravity, crashing noisily, all but trapped in the thicket. It was a patch of jungle, many acres of jungle, with stems a foot apart and as thick as our arms, and canopies more than twelve feet high. This was bear habitat, the sort of place bears like better than people do. Our original choice had been wise—to skirt this ravine-valley—but now we were in it and without choice.

"This is the sort of place to come upon one of them unexpectedly," Hession said.

"And there is no going back," Fedeler said. "You can't walk uphill in this stuff."

"Good point," Hession said.

I might have been a little happier if I had been in an uninstrumented airplane in heavy mountain cloud. We thunked and crashed for fifteen minutes and finally came out at the tributary stream. Our approach flushed a ptarmigan, willow ptarmigan; and grayling—at sight of us—shot around in small, cold pools. The stream was narrow, and alders pressed over it from either side. We drank, and rested, and looked up the slope in front of us, which must have had an incline of fifty degrees. The ridge at the top looked extremely far away. Resting, I became aware of a considerable ache in my legs and a blister on one of my heels. On the way uphill we became separated, Hession angling off to the right, Fedeler and I to the left. We groped for handholds among bushes that protruded from the flaky schist, and pulled ourselves up from ledge to ledge. The adrenalin was gone, and my legs were turning to stone. I was ready to dig a den and get in it. My eyes kept addressing the ridgeline, far above. If eyes were hands they could have pulled me there. Then, suddenly, from far below, I saw Jack Hession lightly ambling along the ridge—in his tennis shoes, in his floppy cotton hat. He was looking around, killing time, waiting up for us.

Things seemed better from the ridge. The going would be level for a time. We sat down and looked back, to the north, across the deep tributary valley, and with my monocular[9] tried to glass[10] the grazing bear. No sight or sign of him. Above us now was a broadly conical summit, and spread around its western flank was a mile, at least, of open alpine tundra. On a contour, we headed south across it—high above, and two miles east of, the river. We saw what appeared to be a cairn on the next summit south, and decided to go to it and stand on it and see if we could guess— in relation to our campsite—where we were. Now the walking felt good again. We passed a large black pile of grizzly scat. "When it's steaming, that's when you start looking around for a tree," Hession said. This particular scat had sent up its last vapors many days before. Imagining myself there at such a time, though, I looked around idly for a tree. The nearest one behind us that was of more than dwarf or thicket stature was somewhere in Lapland. Ahead of us, however, across the broad dome of tundra, was a dark stand of white spruce, an extremity of the North American forest, extending toward us. The trees were eight hundred yards away. Black bears, frightened, sometimes climb trees. Grizzlies almost never climb trees.

At seven in the evening, after wading up a slope of medium to heavy brush, we came out onto more smooth tundra and reached the hilltop of the apparent cairn. It was a rock outcropping, and we sat on it in bright sunshine and looked at the circumvallate mountains. A great many of them had such outcroppings projecting from their ridges, and they much resembled the cairns shepherds build on bald summits in Scotland. For that matter, they suggested the cairns—closer to the Kobuk—that forest Eskimos once used in methodical slaughter of caribou. The cairns were built

---

[9] One-eye magnifying viewer.　　　　　　　[10] To bring into focus through the field glass.

on the high tundra in a great V, open end to the north, and they served as a funnel for the southbound herd. To the approaching caribou, the cairns were meant to suggest Eskimos, and to reinforce the impression Eskimos spaced themselves between cairns. At the point of the V, as many caribou as were needed were killed and the rest were let through.

Before us now, lying on the tundra that stretched away toward the river we saw numerous caribou antlers. The Arctic herd cyclically chooses various passes and valleys in making its way south across the range, and of late has been favoring, among other places, the Salmon and Hunt River drainages. Bleached white, the antlers protruded from the tundra like the dead branches of buried trees. When the forest Eskimo of old went to stalk the grizzly bear, he carried in his hand a spear, the tip of which was made from bear bone or, more often, from the antler of the caribou. A bearskin was the door of an Eskimo's home if the occupant had ever killed a bear, for it symbolized the extraordinary valor of the hunter within. When the man drew close and the bear stood on its hind legs, the man ran under this eave of flesh and set the shaft of the spear firmly on the ground, then ducked out from under the swinging, explosive paws. The bear lunged forward onto the spear and died.

Eskimo knife handles were also made from caribou antlers, and icepicks to penetrate the surface of the river, and sinkers for the bottoms of willow-bark seines, and wood-splitting wedges, and arrowheads. All caribou, male and female, grow antlers. The horns of sheep, cattle, buffalo consist of extremely dense, compactly matted hair. The antler of the caribou is calcareous. It is hard bone, with the strength of wrought iron. Moving downhill and south across the tundra, we passed through groves of antlers. It was as if the long filing lines of the spring migration had for some reason paused here for shedding to occur. The antlers, like the bear, implied the country. Most were white, gaunt, chalky. I picked up a younger one, though, that was recently shed and was dark, like polished brown marble. It was about four feet along the beam and perfect in form. Hession found one like it. We set them on our shoulders and moved on down the hill, intent to take them home.

We headed for the next of the riverine mountains, where we planned to descend and—if our calculations were accurate—meet the river at the campsite. The river, far below us, now and again came into view as we walked abreast over open tundra. Fedeler, even more alert than usual, now stopped and, as before, touched my arm. He pointed toward the river. If a spruce needle had been floating on the water there, Fedeler would have seen it. We saw in an instant that we had miscalculated and were heading some miles beyond the campsite and would have come eventually to the river not knowing—upstream or downstream—which way to go. Fedeler was pointing toward a gravel bar, a thin column of smoke, minute human figures near the smoke, and the podlike whiteness of the metal canoe.

Another two miles, descending, and we were barefoot in the river, with pink hot feet turning anesthetically cold. We crossed slowly. The three others were by the campfire. On the grill were grayling and a filleted Arctic char. The air was cool now, nearing fifty, and we ate the fish, and beef stew, and strawberries, and drank hot chocolate. After a time, Hession said, "That was a good walk. That was some of the easiest hiking you will ever find in Alaska."

We drew our route on the map and figured the distance at fourteen miles. John Kauffmann, tapping his pipe on a stone, said, "That's a lot for Alaska."

We sat around the campfire for at least another hour. We talked of rain and kestrels, oil and antlers, the height and the headwaters of the river. Neither Hession nor Fedeler once mentioned the bear.

When I got into my sleeping bag, though, and closed my eyes, there he was, in color, on the side of the hill. The vision was indelible, but fear was not what put it there. More, it was a sense of sheer luck at having chosen in the first place to follow Fedeler and Hession up the river and into the hills—a memento not so much of one moment as of the entire circuit of the long afternoon. It was a vision of a whole land, with an animal in it. This was his country, clearly enough. To be there was to be incorporated, in however small a measure, into its substance—his country, and if you wanted to visit it you had better knock.

His association with other animals is a mixture of enterprising action, almost magnanimous acceptance, and just plain willingness to ignore. There is great strength and pride combined with a strong mixture of inquisitive curiosity in the make-up of grizzly character. This curiosity is what makes trouble when men penetrate into country where they are not known to the bear. The grizzly can be brave and sometimes downright brash. He can be secretive and very retiring. He can be extremely cunning and also powerfully aggressive. Whatever he does, his actions match his surroundings and the circumstance of the moment. No wonder that meeting him on his mountain is a momentous event, imprinted on one's mind for life.

1976

Toni Morrison
b. 1931

Toni Morrison is clear about her major subject: "I'm interested," she says, "in survival—who survives and who does not, and why—and I would like to chart a course that suggests where the dangers are and where the safety might be." Like the medieval cartographers who illustrated their maps with mythic figures of promise and danger, Morrison recognizes the psychic as well as the physical risks of exploration. Black writing, in particular, she feels, lacks the secure sense of closure associated with Western or classical art: "I think about what black writers do as having a quality of hunger and disturbance that never ends." This open-endedness mingles in Morrison's own work with precise, highly controlled use of metaphor, vivid visual images, and an almost baroque allusiveness. But it manifests itself primarily in her ability to draw her readers into active participation in the creative process. "If the life of my novels is long," she says, "then the readers who wish to read my books will know that it is not I who do it: It is they who do."

Morrison grew up in Lorrain, Ohio. Since both her parents and her grandparents made great personal sacrifices to ensure good educations for their children, she was exposed early to the rich and varied masterpieces of American and European literature. Yet, as the critic Nellie McKay has noted, Morrison also "tells of a childhood world filled with signs, visitations, and ways of knowing that encompassed more than concrete reality." In 1953 Morrison graduated from Howard University; two years later she received an M.A. from Cornell University. From 1955 to 1957 she was instructor in English at Texas Southern University, and in 1957 she returned to Howard, where she taught until 1964, when she became an editor for Random House. At present she holds an Albert Schweitzer chair at the State University of New York, Albany. An equally important part of her life has been raising her two sons. "I really only do two things," she reports. "All of my work has to do with books. I teach books, write books, edit books, or talk about books. It is all one thing. And the other thing that I do is to raise my children, which, as you know, I can only do one minute at a time."

All of Morrison's novels deal with "the complexity of how people behave under duress, . . . the qualities they show at the end of an event when their backs are up against the wall." In her first novel, *The Bluest Eye* (1969), Morrison examines the personal and social implications of the American (including black American) ideal of light-skinned beauty. Described by one reviewer as "charged with pain and wonder," the novel not only portrays the lives of those whose dark skin and Negroid features blight their lives; it also explores the human loss that occurs when beauty goes unrecognized. *Sula* (1973), which was nominated for the 1975 National Book Award, depicts a young black woman whose hard-won independence so threatens her family and neighbors that they scorn and reject her. In *Song of Solomon* (1977), which won the National Book Critics Circle Award, Morrison portrays a young black man, Macon Dead, as he attempts to come to terms with his heritage. Structured around the black legend of a flying man, *Song of Solomon* is an especially powerful rendering of black life —or more precisely, of what Morrison calls "the imaginative combination of the real world, the very shrewd, practical, day-to-day functioning that black people must do, while at the same time encompassing some great supernatural event." In *Tar Baby* (1981), Morrison describes the interaction of a young black woman named Jadine, who is a Paris model and a graduate student, with an escaped convict named Son, as they try to come to terms simultaneously with their mutual attraction and the vast differences that their heritages impose.

Despite the success that Morrison has enjoyed—she is today considered to be one of the best writers of her generation—she values most a sense of urgency that can never be totally dispelled. Speaking of black musicians, she says that "one always has the feeling, whether it is true or not, they may be absolutely parched, but one always has the feeling that there's some more. They have the ability to make you want it, and remember the want. That is a part of what I want to put into my books. They will never fully satisfy—never fully."

Text:
Song of Solomon, 1977.

---

from Song of Solomon

from **Chapter 1**

The North Carolina Mutual Life Insurance[1] agent promised to fly from Mercy to the other side of Lake Superior at three o'clock. Two days before the event was to take place he tacked a note on the door of his little yellow house:

> At 3:00 p.m. on Wednesday the 18th of February, 1931, I will take off from Mercy and fly away on my own wings. Please forgive me. I loved you all.
>
> (signed) Robert Smith,
> Ins. agent

Mr. Smith didn't draw as big a crowd as Lindbergh[2] had four years earlier—not more than forty or fifty people showed up—because it was already eleven o'clock in the morning, on the very Wednesday he had chosen for his flight, before anybody read the note. At that time of day, during the middle of the week, word-of-mouth news just lumbered along. Children were in school; men were at work; and most of the women were fastening their corsets and getting ready to go see what tails or entrails the butcher might be giving away. Only the unemployed, the self-employed, and the very young were available—deliberately available because they'd heard about it, or accidentally available because they happened to be walking at that exact moment in the shore end of Not Doctor Street, a name the post office did not recognize. Town maps registered the street as Mains Avenue, but the only colored doctor in the city had lived and died on that street, and when he moved there in 1896 his patients took to calling the street, which none of them lived in or near, Doctor Street. Later, when other Negroes moved there, and when the postal service became a popular means of transferring messages among them, envelopes from Louisiana, Virginia, Alabama, and Georgia began to arrive addressed to people at house numbers on Doctor Street. The post office workers returned these envelopes or passed them on to the Dead Letter Office. Then in 1918, when colored men were being drafted, a few gave their address at the recruitment office as Doctor Street. In that way, the name acquired a quasi-official status. But not for long. Some of the city legislators, whose concern for appropriate names and the maintenance of the city's landmarks was the principal part of their political life, saw to it that "Doctor Street" was never used in any official capacity. And since they knew that only Southside residents kept it up, they had notices posted in the stores, barbershops, and restaurants in that part of the city saying that the avenue running northerly and southerly from Shore Road fronting the lake to the junction of routes 6 and 2 leading to Pennsylvania, and also running parallel to and between Rutherford Avenue and Broadway, had always been and would always be known as Mains Avenue and not Doctor Street.

---

[1] One of two all-black companies that for generations virtually monopolized insurance for blacks.

[2] Charles A. Lindbergh (1902–1981), American aviator whose 1927 solo nonstop flight from New York to Paris made him an international hero.

It was a genuinely clarifying public notice because it gave Southside residents a way to keep their memories alive and please the city legislators as well. They called it Not Doctor Street, and were inclined to call the charity hospital at its northern end No Mercy Hospital since it was 1931, on the day following Mr. Smith's leap from its cupola, before the first colored expectant mother was allowed to give birth inside its wards and not on its steps. The reason for the hospital's generosity to that particular woman was not the fact that she was the only child of this Negro doctor, for during his entire professional life he had never been granted hospital privileges and only two of his patients were ever admitted to Mercy, both white. Besides, the doctor had been dead a long time by 1931. It must have been Mr. Smith's leap from the roof over their heads that made them admit her. In any case, whether or not the little insurance agent's conviction that he could fly contributed to the place of her delivery, it certainly contributed to its time.

When the dead doctor's daughter saw Mr. Smith emerge as promptly as he had promised from behind the cupola, his wide blue silk wings curved forward around his chest, she dropped her covered peck basket, spilling red velvet rose petals. The wind blew them about, up, down, and into small mounds of snow. Her half-grown daughters scrambled about trying to catch them, while their mother moaned and held the underside of her stomach. The rose-petal scramble got a lot of attention, but the pregnant lady's moans did not. Everyone knew the girls had spent hour after hour tracing, cutting, and stitching the costly velvet, and that Gerhardt's Department Store would be quick to reject any that were soiled.

It was nice and gay there for a while. The men joined in trying to collect the scraps before the snow soaked through them—snatching them from a gust of wind or plucking them delicately from the snow. And the very young children couldn't make up their minds whether to watch the man circled in blue on the roof or the bits of red flashing around on the ground. Their dilemma was solved when a woman suddenly burst into song. The singer, standing at the back of the crowd, was as poorly dressed as the doctor's daughter was well dressed. The latter had on a neat gray coat with the traditional pregnant-woman bow at her navel, a black cloche, and a pair of four-button ladies' galoshes. The singing woman wore a knitted navy cap pulled far down over her forehead. She had wrapped herself up in an old quilt instead of a winter coat. Her head cocked to one side, her eyes fixed on Mr. Robert Smith, she sang in a powerful contralto:

> O Sugarman done fly away
> Sugarman done gone
> Sugarman cut across the sky
> Sugarman gone home. . . .

A few of the half a hundred or so people gathered there nudged each other and sniggered. Others listened as though it were the helpful and defining piano music in a silent movie. They stood this way for some time, none of them crying out to Mr. Smith, all of them preoccupied with one or the other of the minor events about them, until the hospital people came.

They had been watching from the windows—at first with mild curiosity, then, as the crowd seemed to swell to the very walls of the hospital, they watched with apprehension. They wondered if one of those things that racial-uplift groups were always organizing was taking place. But when they saw neither placards nor speakers, they ventured outside into the cold: white-coated surgeons, dark-jacketed business and personnel clerks, and three nurses in starched jumpers.

The sight of Mr. Smith and his wide blue wings transfixed them for a few seconds, as did the woman's singing and the roses strewn about. Some of them thought briefly that this was probably some form of worship. Philadelphia, where Father Divine[3] reigned, wasn't all that far away. Perhaps the young girls holding baskets of flowers were two of his virgins. But the laughter of a gold-toothed man brought them back to their senses. They stopped daydreaming and swiftly got down to business, giving orders. Their shouts and bustling caused great confusion where before there had been only a few men and some girls playing with pieces of velvet and a woman singing.

One of the nurses, hoping to bring some efficiency into the disorder, searched the faces around her until she saw a stout woman who looked as though she might move the earth if she wanted to.

"You," she said, moving toward the stout woman. "Are these your children?"

The stout woman turned her head slowly, her eyebrows lifted at the carelessness of the address. Then, seeing where the voice came from, she lowered her brows and veiled her eyes.

"Ma'am?"

"Send one around back to the emergency office. Tell him to tell the guard to get over here quick. That boy there can go. That one." She pointed to a cat-eyed boy about five or six years old.

The stout woman slid her eyes down the nurse's finger and looked at the child she was pointing to.

"Guitar, ma'am."

"What?"

"Guitar."

The nurse gazed at the stout woman as though she had spoken Welsh. Then she closed her mouth, looked again at the cat-eyed boy, and lacing her fingers, spoke her next words very slowly to him.

"Listen. Go around to the back of the hospital to the guard's office. It will say 'Emergency Admissions' on the door. A-D-M-I-S-I-O-N-S. But the guard will be there. Tell him to get over here—on the double. Move now. Move!" She unlaced her fingers and made scooping motions with her hands, the palms pushing against the wintry air.

A man in a brown suit came toward her, puffing little white clouds of breath. "Fire truck's on its way. Get back inside. You'll freeze to death."

The nurse nodded.

"You left out a *s*, ma'am," the boy said. The North was new to him and he had just begun to learn he could speak up to white people. But she'd already gone, rubbing her arms against the cold.

"Granny, she left out a *s*."

[3] George Baker (ca. 1878–1965), known as Father Divine, founded the Peace Mission, based in New York and Philadelphia. He proclaimed himself the incarnation of God and taught that Heaven was now on earth. One of his rules prohibited racial bigotry. He is an important figure in Afro-American religious history.

"And a 'please.' "

"You reckon he'll jump?"

"A nutwagon do anything."

"Who is he?"

"Collects insurance. A nutwagon."

"Who is that lady singing?"

"That, baby, is the very last thing in pea-time." But she smiled when she looked at the singing woman, so the cat-eyed boy listened to the musical performance with at least as much interest as he devoted to the man flapping his wings on top of the hospital.

The crowd was beginning to be a little nervous now that the law was being called in. They each knew Mr. Smith. He came to their houses twice a month to collect one dollar and sixty-eight cents and write down on a little yellow card both the date and their eighty-four cents a week payment. They were always half a month or so behind, and talked endlessly to him about paying ahead—after they had a preliminary discussion about what he was doing back so soon anyway.

"You back in here already? Look like I just got rid of you."

"I'm tired of seeing your face. Really tired."

"I knew it. Soon's I get two dimes back to back, here you come. More regular than the reaper. Do Hoover[4] know about you?"

They kidded him, abused him, told their children to tell him they were out or sick or gone to Pittsburgh. But they held on to those little yellow cards as though they meant something—laid them gently in the shoe box along with the rent receipts, marriage licenses, and expired factory identification badges. Mr. Smith smiled through it all, managing to keep his eyes focused almost the whole time on his customers' feet. He wore a business suit for his work, but his house was no better than theirs. He never had a woman that any of them knew about and said nothing in church but an occasional "Amen." He never beat anybody up and he wasn't seen after dark, so they thought he was probably a nice man. But he was heavily associated with illness and death, neither of which was distinguishable from the brown picture of the North Carolina Mutual Life Building on the back of their yellow cards. Jumping from the roof of Mercy was the most interesting thing he had done. None of them had suspected he had it in him. Just goes to show, they murmured to each other, you never really do know about people.

The singing woman quieted down and, humming the tune, walked through the crowd toward the rose-petal lady, who was still cradling her stomach.

"You should make yourself warm," she whispered to her, touching her lightly on the elbow. "A little bird'll be here with the morning."

"Oh?" said the rose-petal lady. "Tomorrow morning?"

"That's the only morning coming."

"It can't be," the rose-petal lady said. "It's too soon."

"No it ain't. Right on time."

The women were looking deep into each other's eyes when a loud roar went up from the crowd—a kind of wavy *oo* sound. Mr. Smith had lost his balance for a

---

[4] J. Edgar Hoover (1895–1982), and longtime director of the Federal Bureau of Investigation.

second, and was trying gallantly to hold on to a triangle of wood that jutted from the cupola. Immediately the singing woman began again:

O Sugarman done fly
O Sugarman done gone . . .

Downtown the firemen pulled on their greatcoats, but when they arrived at Mercy, Mr. Smith had seen the rose petals, heard the music, and leaped on into the air.

The next day a colored baby was born inside Mercy for the first time. Mr. Smith's blue silk wings must have left their mark, because when the little boy discovered, at four, the same thing Mr. Smith had learned earlier—that only birds and airplanes could fly—he lost all interest in himself. To have to live without that single gift saddened him and left his imagination so bereft that he appeared dull even to the women who did not hate his mother. The ones who did, who accepted her invitations to tea and envied the doctor's big dark house of twelve rooms and the green sedan, called him "peculiar." The others, who knew that the house was more prison than palace, and that the Dodge sedan was for Sunday drives only, felt sorry for Ruth Foster and her dry daughters, and called her son "deep." Even mysterious.

"Did he come with a caul?"

"You should have dried it and made him some tea from it to drink. If you don't he'll see ghosts."

"You believe that?"

"I don't, but that's what the old people say."

"Well, he's a deep one anyway. Look at his eyes."

And they pried pieces of baked-too-fast sunshine cake from the roofs of their mouths and looked once more into the boy's eyes. He met their gaze as best he could until, after a pleading glance toward his mother, he was allowed to leave the room.

It took some planning to walk out of the parlor, his back washed with the hum of their voices, open the heavy double doors leading to the dining room, slip up the stairs past all those bedrooms, and not arouse the attention of Lena and Corinthians sitting like big baby dolls before a table heaped with scraps of red velvet. His sisters made roses in the afternoon. Bright, lifeless roses that lay in peck baskets for months until the specialty buyer at Gerhardt's sent Freddie the janitor over to tell the girls that they could use another gross. If he did manage to slip by his sisters and avoid their casual malice, he knelt in his room at the window sill and wondered again and again why he had to stay level on the ground. The quiet that suffused the doctor's house then, broken only by the murmur of the women eating sunshine cake, was only that: quiet. It was not peaceful, for it was preceded by and would soon be terminated by the presence of Macon Dead.

Solid, rumbling, likely to erupt without prior notice, Macon kept each member of his family awkward with fear. His hatred of his wife glittered and sparked in every word he spoke to her. The disappointment he felt in his daughters sifted down on them like ash, dulling their buttery complexions and choking the lilt out of what should have been girlish voices. Under the frozen heat of his glance they tripped over doorsills and dropped the salt cellar into the yolks of their poached eggs. The way he mangled their grace, wit, and self-esteem was the single excitement of their days.

Without the tension and drama he ignited, they might not have known what to do with themselves. In his absence his daughters bent their necks over blood-red squares of velvet and waited eagerly for any hint of him, and his wife, Ruth, began her days stunned into stillness by her husband's contempt and ended them wholly animated by it.

When she closed the door behind her afternoon guests, and let the quiet smile die from her lips, she began the preparation of food her husband found impossible to eat. She did not try to make her meals nauseating; she simply didn't know how not to. She would notice that the sunshine cake was too haggled to put before him and decide on a rennet dessert. But the grinding of the veal and beef for a meat loaf took so long she not only forgot the pork, settling for bacon drippings poured over the meat, she had no time to make a dessert at all. Hurriedly, then, she began to set the table. As she unfolded the white linen and let it billow over the fine mahogany table, she would look once more at the large water mark. She never set the table or passed through the dining room without looking at it. Like a lighthouse keeper drawn to his window to gaze once again at the sea, or a prisoner automatically searching out the sun as he steps into the yard for his hour of exercise, Ruth looked for the water mark several times during the day. She knew it was there, would always be there, but she needed to confirm its presence. Like the keeper of the lighthouse and the prisoner, she regarded it as a mooring, a checkpoint, some stable visual object that assured her that the world was still there; that this was life and not a dream. That she was alive somewhere, inside, which she acknowledged to be true only because a thing she knew intimately was out there, outside herself.

Even in the cave of sleep, without dreaming of it or thinking of it at all, she felt its presence. Oh, she talked endlessly to her daughters and her guests about how to get rid of it—what might hide this single flaw on the splendid wood: Vaseline, tobacco juice, iodine, a sanding followed by linseed oil. She had tried them all. But her glance was nutritious; the spot became, if anything, more pronounced as the years passed.

The cloudy gray circle identified the place where the bowl filled every day during the doctor's life with fresh flowers had stood. Every day. And when there were no flowers, it held a leaf arrangement, a gathering of twigs and berries, pussy willow, Scotch pine. . . . But always something to grace the dinner table in the evening.

It was for her father a touch that distinguished his own family from the people among whom they lived. For Ruth it was the summation of the affectionate elegance with which she believed her childhood had been surrounded. When Macon married her and moved into Doctor's house, she kept up the centerpiece-arranging. Then came the time she walked down to the shore through the roughest part of the city to get some driftwood. She had seen an arrangement of driftwood and dried seaweed in the homemakers section of the newspaper. It was a damp November day, and Doctor was paralyzed even then and taking liquid food in his bedroom. The wind had lifted her skirt from around her ankles and cut through her laced shoes. She'd had to rub her feet down with warm olive oil when she got back. At dinner, where just the two of them sat, she turned toward her husband and asked him how he liked the centerpiece. "Most people overlook things like that. They see it, but they don't see anything beautiful in it. They don't see that nature has already made it as perfect as it can be. Look at it from the side. It is pretty, isn't it?"

Her husband looked at the driftwood with its lacy beige seaweed, and without moving his head, said, "Your chicken is red at the bone. And there is probably a potato dish that is supposed to have lumps in it. Mashed ain't the dish."

Ruth let the seaweed disintegrate, and later, when its veins and stems dropped and curled into brown scabs on the table, she removed the bowl and brushed away the scabs. But the water mark, hidden by the bowl all these years, was exposed. And once exposed, it behaved as though it were itself a plant and flourished into a huge suede-gray flower that throbbed like fever, and sighed like the shift of sand dunes. But it could also be still. Patient, restful, and still.

But there was nothing you could do with a mooring except acknowledge it, use it for the verification of some idea you wanted to keep alive. Something else is needed to get from sunup to sundown: a balm, a gentle touch or nuzzling of some sort. So Ruth rose up and out of her guileless inefficiency to claim her bit of balm right after the preparation of dinner and just before the return of her husband from his office. It was one of her two secret indulgences—the one that involved her son—and part of the pleasure it gave her came from the room in which she did it. A damp greenness lived there, made by the evergreen that pressed against the window and filtered the light. It was just a little room that Doctor had called a study, and aside from a sewing machine that stood in the corner along with a dress form, there was only a rocker and tiny footstool. She sat in this room holding her son on her lap, staring at his closed eyelids and listening to the sound of his sucking. Staring not so much from maternal joy as from a wish to avoid seeing his legs dangling almost to the floor.

In late afternoon, before her husband closed his office and came home, she called her son to her. When he came into the little room she unbuttoned her blouse and smiled. He was too young to be dazzled by her nipples, but he was old enough to be bored by the flat taste of mother's milk, so he came reluctantly, as to a chore, and lay as he had at least once each day of his life in his mother's arms, and tried to pull the thin, faintly sweet milk from her flesh without hurting her with his teeth.

She felt him. His restraint, his courtesy, his indifference, all of which pushed her into fantasy. She had the distinct impression that his lips were pulling from her a thread of light. It was as though she were a cauldron issuing spinning gold. Like the miller's daughter—the one who sat at night in a straw-filled room, thrilled with the secret power Rumpelstiltskin had given her: to see golden thread stream from her very own shuttle. And that was the other part of her pleasure, a pleasure she hated to give up. So when Freddie the janitor, who liked to pretend he was a friend of the family and not just their flunky as well as their tenant, brought his rent to the doctor's house late one day and looked in the window past the evergreen, the terror that sprang to Ruth's eyes came from the quick realization that she was to lose fully half of what made her daily life bearable. Freddie, however, interpreted her look as simple shame, but that didn't stop him from grinning.

"Have mercy. I be damn."

He fought the evergreen for a better look, hampered more by his laughter than by the branches. Ruth jumped up as quickly as she could and covered her breast, dropping her son on the floor and confirming for him what he had begun to suspect —that these afternoons were strange and wrong.

Before either mother or son could speak, rearrange themselves properly, or even exchange looks, Freddie had run around the house, climbed the porch steps, and was calling them between gulps of laughter.

"Miss Rufie. Miss Rufie. Where you? Where you all at?" He opened the door to the green room as though it were his own.

"I be damn, Miss Rufie. When the last time I seen that? I don't even know the last time I seen that. I mean, ain't nothing wrong with it. I mean, old folks swear by it. It's just, you know, you don't see it up here much. . . ." But his eyes were on the boy. Appreciative eyes that communicated some complicity she was excluded from. Freddie looked the boy up and down, taking in the steady but secretive eyes and the startling contrast between Ruth's lemony skin and the boy's black skin. "Used to be a lot of womenfolk nurse they kids a long time down South. Lot of 'em. But you don't see it much no more. I knew a family—the mother wasn't too quick, though —nursed hers till the boy, I reckon, was near 'bout thirteen. But that's a bit much, ain't it?" All the time he chattered, he rubbed his chin and looked at the boy. Finally he stopped, and gave a long low chuckle. He'd found the phrase he'd been searching for. "A milkman. That's what you got here, Miss Rufie. A natural milkman if ever I seen one. Look out, womens. Here he come. Huh!"

Freddie carried his discovery not only into the homes in Ruth's neighborhood, but to Southside, where he lived and where Macon Dead owned rent houses. So Ruth kept close to home and had no afternoon guests for the better part of two months, to keep from hearing that her son had been rechristened with a name he was never able to shake and that did nothing to improve either one's relationship with his father.

Macon Dead never knew how it came about—how his only son acquired the nickname that stuck in spite of his own refusal to use it or acknowledge it. It was a matter that concerned him a good deal, for the giving of names in his family was always surrounded by what he believed to be monumental foolishness. No one mentioned to him the incident out of which the nickname grew because he was a difficult man to approach—a hard man, with a manner so cool it discouraged casual or spontaneous conversation. Only Freddie the janitor took liberties with Macon Dead, liberties he purchased with the services he rendered, and Freddie was the last person on earth to tell him. So Macon Dead neither heard of nor visualized Ruth's sudden terror, her awkward jump from the rocking chair, the boy's fall broken by the tiny footstool, or Freddie's amused, admiring summation of the situation.

Without knowing any of the details, however, he guessed, with the accuracy of a mind sharpened by hatred, that the name he heard schoolchildren call his son, the name he overheard the ragman use when he paid the boy three cents for a bundle of old clothes—he guessed that this name was not clean. Milkman. It certainly didn't sound like the honest job of a dairyman, or bring to his mind cold bright cans standing on the back porch, glittering like captains on guard. It sounded dirty, intimate, and hot. He knew that wherever the name came from, it had something to do with his wife and was, like the emotion he always felt when thinking of her, coated with disgust.

This disgust and the uneasiness with which he regarded his son affected everything he did in that city. If he could have felt sad, simply sad, it would have relieved him. Fifteen years of regret at not having a son had become the bitterness of finally having one in the most revolting circumstances.

There had been a time when he had a head full of hair and when Ruth wore lovely complicated underwear that he deliberately took a long time to undo. When all of his foreplay was untying, unclasping, unbuckling the snaps and strings of what must have been the most beautiful, the most delicate, the whitest and softest underwear on earth. Each eye of her corset he toyed with (and there were forty—twenty on each side); each grosgrain ribbon that threaded its pale-blue way through the snowy top of her bodice he unlaced. He not only undid the blue bow; he pulled it all the way out of the hem, so she had to rethread it afterward with a safety pin. The elastic bands that connected her perspiration shields to her slip he unsnapped and snapped again, teasing her and himself with the sound of the snaps and the thrill of his fingertips on her shoulders. They never spoke during these undressings. But they giggled occasionally, and as when children play "doctor," undressing of course was the best part.

When Ruth was naked and lying there as moist and crumbly as unbleached sugar, he bent to unlace her shoes. That was the final delight, for once he had undressed her feet, had peeled her stockings down over her ankles and toes, he entered her and ejaculated quickly. She liked it that way. So did he. And in almost twenty years during which he had not laid eyes on her naked feet, he missed only the underwear.

Once he believed that the sight of her mouth on the dead man's fingers would be the thing he would remember always. He was wrong. Little by little he remembered fewer and fewer of the details, until finally he had to imagine them, even fabricate them, guess what they must have been. The image left him, but the odiousness never did. For the nourishment of his outrage he depended on the memory of her underwear; those round, innocent corset eyes now lost to him forever.

So if the people were calling his son Milkman, and if she was lowering her eyelids and dabbing at the sweat on her top lip when she heard it, there was definitely some filthy connection and it did not matter at all to Macon Dead whether anyone gave him the details or not.

And they didn't. Nobody both dared enough and cared enough to tell him. The ones who cared enough, Lena and Corinthians, the living proof of those years of undressing his wife, did not care. And the one person who dared to but didn't care to was the one person in the world he hated more than his wife in spite of the fact that she was his sister. He had not crossed the tracks to see her since his son was born and he had no intention of renewing their relationship now.

Macon Dead dug in his pocket for his keys, and curled his fingers around them, letting their bunchy solidity calm him. They were the keys to all the doors of his houses (only four true houses; the rest were really shacks), and he fondled them from time to time as he walked down Not Doctor Street to his office. At least he thought of it as his office, had even painted the word OFFICE on the door. But the plate-glass window contradicted him. In peeling gold letters arranged in a semicircle, his business establishment was declared to be Sonny's Shop. Scraping the previous owner's name off was hardly worth the trouble since he couldn't scrape it from anybody's mind. His storefront office was never called anything but Sonny's Shop, although nobody now could remember thirty years back, when, presumably, Sonny did something or other there.

He walked there now—strutted is the better word, for he had a high behind and an athlete's stride—thinking of names. Surely, he thought, he and his sister had some ancestor, some lithe young man with onyx skin and legs as straight as cane stalks, who had a name that was real. A name given to him at birth with love and seriousness. A name that was not a joke, nor a disguise, nor a brand name. But who this lithe young man was, and where his cane-stalk legs carried him from or to, could never be known. No. Nor his name. His own parents, in some mood of perverseness or resignation, had agreed to abide by a naming done to them by somebody who couldn't have cared less. Agreed to take and pass on to all their issue this heavy name scrawled in perfect thoughtlessness by a drunken Yankee in the Union Army. A literal slip of the pen handed to his father on a piece of paper and which he handed on to his only son, and his son likewise handed on to his; Macon Dead who begat a second Macon Dead who married Ruth Foster (Dead) and begat Magdalene called Lena Dead and First Corinthians Dead and (when he least expected it) another Macon Dead, now known to the part of the world that mattered as Milkman Dead. And as if that were not enough, a sister named Pilate Dead, who would never mention to her brother the circumstances or the details of this foolish misnaming of his son because the whole thing would have delighted her. She would savor it, maybe fold it too in a brass box and hang it from her other ear. . . .

1977

Tom Wolfe
b. 1931

Tom Wolfe describes his concern as a writer "with the liberation of thinking. At the moment a sort of nineteenth-century pattern of thinking has a grip on the country. . . . Our thinking is dominated by a pattern from our Eastern universities, a pattern of European origin. The real story of our country has not been written." For Wolfe, the Americanization of our thinking and our literature demands participation as well as observation. Like Norman Mailer, Wolfe has become both a public figure and a literary figure.

Born on March 2, 1931, in Richmond, Virginia, Wolfe graduated from Washington and Lee University in 1951. He began his formal study of America at Yale, where he received a Ph.D. in American studies in 1957. At the same time, he began to establish a place for himself within the culture he studied. At one time a semipro baseball player, he also worked as a reporter for the *Springfield Union* in Massachusetts, the *Washington Post,* and the *New York Herald Tribune.* A series of articles in the Sunday section of the *Tribune* not only earned him a reputation as one of America's leading nonfiction stylists but also helped to transform the paper into *New York* magazine.

Maintaining a careful balance between ironic observation and active involvement, Wolfe has responded to most of the major trends in American culture. His first book, *The Kandy-Kolored Tangerine-Flake Streamline Baby,* appeared in 1965, and he has since published seven more books, an anthology of his writing, *The Purple Decades* (1982), and a collection of his satirical drawings. Among his best-known works are *The Electric Kool-Aid Acid Test* (1968), *Radical Chic & Mau-Mauing the Flak Catchers* (1970), *The Painted World* (1975), and *From Bauhaus to Our House* (1981). Wolfe's genius for fixing a current style or cultural attitude in an enduring phrase ("radical chic," "the me generation") is apparent in what is perhaps his finest book to date, *The Right Stuff* (1979). A study of the first American astronauts, *The Right Stuff* won the American Book Award for general nonfiction and became a national best-seller. In 1984 it was made into a motion picture. Wolfe is currently at work on his first novel, a satire of life in contemporary New York City, tentatively titled *The Bonfire of the Vanities*, which has been serialized in *Rolling Stone* magazine.

Text:
The Right Stuff, 1979.

---

from The Right Stuff

from **Chapter 2**

A young man might go into military flight training believing that he was entering some sort of technical school in which he was simply going to acquire a certain set of skills. Instead, he found himself all at once enclosed in a fraternity. And in this fraternity, even though it was military, men were not rated by their outward rank as ensigns, lieutenants, commanders, or whatever. No, herein the world was divided into those who had it and those who did not. This quality, this *it,* was never named, however, nor was it talked about in any way.

As to just what this ineffable quality was . . . well, it obviously involved bravery. But it was not bravery in the simple sense of being willing to risk your life. The idea seemed to be that any fool could do that, if that was all that was required, just as any fool could throw away his life in the process. No, the idea here (in the all-enclosing fraternity) seemed to be that a man should have the ability to go up in a hurtling piece of machinery and put his hide on the line and then have the moxie, the reflexes, the experience, the coolness, to pull it back in the last yawning moment —and then to go up again *the next day,* and the next day, and every next day, even if the series should prove infinite—and, ultimately, in its best expression, do so in a cause that means something to thousands, to a people, a nation, to humanity, to God. Nor was there *a test* to show whether or not a pilot had this righteous quality. There was, instead, a seemingly infinite series of tests. A career in flying was like climbing one of those ancient Babylonian pyramids made up of a dizzy progression of steps and ledges, a ziggurat, a pyramid extraordinarily high and steep; and the idea was to prove at every foot of the way up that pyramid that you were one of the elected and anointed ones who had *the right stuff* and could move higher and higher and even —ultimately, God willing, one day—that you might be able to join that special few at the very top, that elite who had the capacity to bring tears to men's eyes, the very Brotherhood of the Right Stuff itself.

None of this was to be mentioned, and yet it was acted out in a way that a young man could not fail to understand. When a new flight (i.e., a class) of trainees arrived at Pensacola, they were brought into an auditorium for a little lecture. An officer would tell them: "Take a look at the man on either side of you." Quite a few actually swiveled their heads this way and that, in the interest of appearing diligent. Then the officer would say: "One of the three of you is not going to make it!"—meaning, not get his wings. That was the opening theme, the *motif* of primary training. We already know that one-third of you do not have the right stuff—it only remains to find out who.

Furthermore, that was the way it turned out. At every level in one's progress up that staggeringly high pyramid, the world was once more divided into those men who had the right stuff to continue the climb and those who had to be *left behind* in the most obvious way. Some were eliminated in the course of the opening classroom work, as either not smart enough or not hardworking enough, and were left behind. Then came the basic flight instruction, in single-engine, propeller-driven trainers, and a few more—even though the military tried to make this stage easy—were washed out and left behind. Then came more demanding levels, one after the other, formation flying, instrument flying, jet training, all-weather flying, gunnery, and at each level more were washed out and left behind. By this point easily a third of the original candidates had been, indeed, eliminated . . . from the ranks of those who might prove to have the right stuff.

In the Navy, in addition to the stages that Air Force trainees went through, the neophyte always had waiting for him, out in the ocean, a certain grim gray slab; namely, the deck of an aircraft carrier; and with it perhaps the most difficult routine in military flying, carrier landings. He was shown films about it, he heard lectures about it, and he knew that carrier landings were hazardous. He first practiced touching down on the shape of a flight deck painted on an airfield. He was instructed to touch down and gun right off. This was safe enough—the shape didn't move, at least—but it could do terrible things to, let us say, the gyroscope of the soul. *That shape!—it's so damned small!* And more candidates were washed out and left behind. Then came the day, without warning, when those who remained were sent out over the ocean for the first of many days of reckoning with the slab. The first day was always a clear day with little wind and a calm sea. The carrier was so steady that it seemed, from up there in the air, to be resting on pilings, and the candidate usually made his first carrier landing successfully, with relief and even *élan*.[1] Many young candidates looked like terrific aviators up to that very point—and it was not until they were actually standing on the carrier deck that they first began to wonder if they had the proper stuff, after all. In the training film the flight deck was a grand piece of gray geometry, perilous, to be sure, but an amazing abstract shape as one looks down upon it on the screen. And yet once the newcomer's two feet were on it . . . *Geometry*—my God, man, this is a . . . skillet! It *heaved,* it moved up and down underneath his feet, it pitched up, it pitched down, it rolled to port (this great beast *rolled!*) and it rolled to starboard, as the ship moved into the wind and, therefore, into the waves, and the wind kept sweeping across, sixty feet up in the air out in the open sea, and there were no railings whatsoever. This was a *skillet!*—a frying pan!—a short-order grill!—not gray but black, smeared with skid marks from one end to the other and glistening with pools of hydraulic fluid and the occasional jet-fuel slick, all of it still hot, sticky, greasy, runny, virulent from God knows what traumas—still ablaze!—consumed in detonations, explosions, flames, combustion, roars, shrieks, whines, blasts, horrible shudders, fracturing impacts, as little men in screaming red and yellow and purple and

---

[1] French: "dash" or "enthusiasm."

green shirts with black Mickey Mouse helmets over their ears skittered about on the surface as if for their very lives (you've said it now!), hooking fighter planes onto the catapult shuttles so that they can explode their afterburners and be slung off the deck in a red-mad fury with a *kaboom!* that pounds through the entire deck—a procedure that seems absolutely controlled, orderly, sublime, however, compared to what he is about to watch as aircraft return to the ship for what is known in the engineering stoicisms of the military as "recovery and arrest." To say that an F-4 was coming back onto this heaving barbecue from out of the sky at a speed of 135 knots . . . that might have been the truth in the training lecture, but it did not begin to get across the idea of what the newcomer saw from the deck itself, because it created the notion that perhaps the plane was gliding in. On the deck one knew differently! As the aircraft came closer and the carrier heaved on into the waves and the plane's speed did not diminish and the deck did not grow steady—indeed, it pitched up and down five or ten feet per greasy heave—one experienced a neural alarm that no lecture could have prepared him for: This is not an *airplane* coming toward me, it is a brick with some poor sonofabitch riding it *(someone much like myself!)*, and it is not *gliding*, it is *falling*, a fifty-thousand-pound brick, headed not for a stripe on the deck but for *me*—and with a horrible *smash!* it hits the skillet, and with a blur of momentum as big as a freight train's it hurtles toward the far end of the deck—another blinding storm!—another roar as the pilot pushes the throttle up to full military power and another smear of rubber screams out over the skillet—and this is nominal![2]—quite okay!—for a wire stretched across the deck has grabbed the hook on the end of the plane as it hit the deck tail down, and the smash was the rest of the fifteen-ton brute slamming onto the deck, as it tripped up, so that it is now straining against the wire at full throttle, in case it hadn't held and the plane had "boltered" off the end of the deck and had to struggle up into the air again. And already the Mickey Mouse helmets are running toward the fiery monster . . .

And the candidate, looking on, begins to *feel* that great heaving sun-blazing deathboard of a deck wallowing in his own vestibular system—and suddenly he finds himself backed up against his own limits. He ends up going to the flight surgeon with so-called conversion symptoms. Overnight he develops blurred vision or numbness in his hands and feet or sinusitis so severe that he cannot tolerate changes in altitude. On one level the symptom is real. He really cannot see too well or use his fingers or stand the pain. But somewhere in his subconscious he knows it is a plea and a beg-off; he shows not the slightest concern (the flight surgeon notes) that the condition might be permanent and affect him in whatever life awaits him outside the arena of the right stuff.

Those who remained, those who qualified for carrier duty—and even more so those who later on qualified for *night* carrier duty—began to feel a bit like Gideon's warriors. *So many have been left behind!* The young warriors were now treated to a deathly sweet and quite unmentionable sight. They could gaze at length upon the crushed and wilted pariahs who had washed out. They could inspect those who did not have that righteous stuff.

The military did not have very merciful instincts. Rather than packing up these poor souls and sending them home, the Navy, like the Air Force and the Marines,

---

[2] Pilot's expression meaning "according to plan."

would try to make use of them in some other role, such as flight controller. So the washout has to keep taking classes with the rest of his group, even though he can no longer touch an airplane. He sits there in the classes staring at sheets of paper with cataracts of sheer human mortification over his eyes while the rest steal looks at him . . . this man reduced to an ant, this untouchable, this poor sonofabitch. And in what test had he been found wanting? Why, it seemed to be nothing less than *manhood* itself. Naturally, this was never mentioned, either. Yet there it was. *Manliness, manhood, manly courage* . . . there was something ancient, primordial, irresistible about the challenge of this stuff, no matter what a sophisticated and rational age one might think he lived in.

Perhaps because it could not be talked about, the subject began to take on superstitious and even mystical outlines. A man either had it or he didn't! There was no such thing as having *most* of it. Moreover, it could blow at any seam. One day a man would be ascending the pyramid at a terrific clip, and the next—bingo!—he would reach his own limits in the most unexpected way. Conrad and Schirra[3] met an Air Force pilot who had had a great pal at Tyndall Air Force Base in Florida. This man had been the budding ace of the training class; he had flown the hottest fighter-style trainer, the T-38, like a dream; and then he began the routine step of being checked out in the T-33. The T-33 was not nearly as hot an aircraft as the T-38; it was essentially the old P-80 jet fighter. It had an exceedingly small cockpit. The pilot could barely move his shoulders. It was the sort of airplane of which everybody said, "You don't get into it, you *wear* it." Once inside a T-33 cockpit this man, this budding ace, developed claustrophobia of the most paralyzing sort. He tried everything to overcome it. He even went to a psychiatrist, which was a serious mistake for a military officer if his superiors learned of it. But nothing worked. He was shifted over to flying jet transports, such as the C-135. Very demanding and necessary aircraft they were, too, and he was still spoken of as an excellent pilot. But as everyone knew—and, again, it was never explained in so many words—only those who were assigned to fighter squadrons, the "fighter jocks," as they called each other with a self-satisfied irony, remained in the true fraternity. Those assigned to transports were not humiliated like washouts—*somebody* had to fly those planes—nevertheless, they, too, had been *left behind* for lack of the right stuff.

Or a man could go for a routine physical one fine day, feeling like a million dollars, and be grounded for *fallen arches*. It happened!—just like that! (And try raising them.) Or for breaking his wrist and losing only *part* of its mobility. Or for a minor deterioration of eyesight, or for any of hundreds of reasons that would make no difference to a man in an ordinary occupation. As a result all fighter jocks began looking upon doctors as their natural enemies. Going to see a flight surgeon was a no-gain proposition; a pilot could only hold his own or lose in the doctor's office. To be grounded for a medical reason was no humiliation, looked at objectively. But it was a humiliation, nonetheless!—for it meant you no longer had that indefinable, unutterable, integral stuff. (It could blow at *any* seam.)

All the hot young fighter jocks began trying to test the limits themselves in a superstitious way. They were like believing Presbyterians of a century before who used to probe their own experience to see if they were truly among *the elect*. When a fighter pilot was in training, whether in the Navy or the Air Force, his superiors were continually spelling out strict rules for him, about the use of the aircraft and conduct in the sky. They repeatedly forbade so-called hot-dog stunts, such as outside loops, buzzing, flat-hatting, hedgehopping and flying under bridges. But somehow one got the message that the man who truly *had* it could ignore those rules—not that he should make a point of it, but that he *could*—and that after all there was only one way to find out—and that in some strange unofficial way, peeking through his fingers, his instructor halfway expected him to challenge all the limits. They would give a lecture about how a pilot should never fly without a good solid breakfast—eggs, bacon, toast, and so forth—because if he tried to fly with his blood-sugar level too low, it could impair his alertness. Naturally, the next day every hot dog in the unit would get up and have a breakfast consisting of one cup of black coffee and take off and go up into a vertical climb until the weight of the ship exactly canceled out the upward pull of the engine and his air speed was zero, and he would hang there for one thick adrenal instant—and then fall like a rock, until one of three things happened: he keeled over nose first and regained his aerodynamics and all was well, he went into a spin and fought his way out of it, or he went into a spin and had to eject or crunch it, which was always supremely possible.

Likewise, "hassling"—mock dogfighting—was strictly forbidden, and so naturally young fighter jocks could hardly wait to go up in, say, a pair of F-100s and start the duel by making a pass at each other at 800 miles an hour, the winner being the pilot who could slip in behind the other one and get locked in on his tail ("wax his tail"), and it was not uncommon for some eager jock to try too tight an outside turn and have his engine flame out, whereupon, unable to restart it, he has to eject . . . and he shakes his fist at the victor as he floats down by parachute and his half-a-million-dollar aircraft goes *kaboom!* on the palmetto grass or the desert floor, and he starts thinking about how he can get together with the other guy back at the base in time for the two of them to get their stories straight before the investigation: "I don't know what happened, sir. I was pulling up after a target run, and it just flamed out on me." Hassling was forbidden, and hassling that led to the destruction of an aircraft was a serious court-martial offense, and the man's superiors knew that the engine hadn't *just flamed out,* but every unofficial impulse on the base seemed to be saying: "Hell, we wouldn't give you a nickel for a pilot who hasn't done some crazy rat-racing like that. It's all part of the right stuff."

The other side of this impulse showed up in the reluctance of the young jocks to admit it when they had maneuvered themselves into a bad corner they couldn't get out of. There were two reasons why a fighter pilot hated to declare an emergency. First, it triggered a complex and very public chain of events at the field: all other incoming flights were held up, including many of one's comrades who were probably low on fuel; the fire trucks came trundling out to the runway like yellow toys (as seen from way up there), the better to illustrate one's hapless state; and the bureaucracy began to crank up the paper monster for the investigation that always followed. And second, to declare an emergency, one first had to reach that conclusion in his own mind, which to the young pilot was the same as saying: "A minute ago I still *had* it—now I need your help!" To have a bunch of young fighter pilots up in the air thinking this way used to drive flight controllers crazy. They would see a ship beginning to drift off the radar, and they couldn't rouse the pilot on the microphone for anything other than a few meaningless mumbles, and they would know he was probably out there with engine failure at a low altitude, trying to reignite by lowering his auxiliary generator rig, which had a little propeller that was supposed to spin in the slipstream like a child's pinwheel.

"Whiskey Kilo Two Eight, do you want to declare an emergency?"

This would rouse him!—to say: "Negative, negative, Whiskey Kilo Two Eight is not declaring an emergency."

Kaboom. Believers in the right stuff would rather crash and burn.

One fine day, after he had joined a fighter squadron, it would dawn on the young pilot exactly how the losers in the great fraternal competition were now being left behind. Which is to say, not by instructors or other superiors or by failures at prescribed levels of competence, but by death. At this point the essence of the enterprise would begin to dawn on him. Slowly, step by step, the ante had been raised until he was now involved in what was surely the grimmest and grandest gamble of manhood. Being a fighter pilot—for that matter, simply taking off in a single-engine jet fighter of the Century series, such as an F-102, or any of the military's other marvelous bricks with fins on them—presented a man, on a perfectly sunny day, with more ways to get himself killed than his wife and children could imagine in their wildest fears. If he was barreling down the runway at two hundred miles an hour, completing the takeoff run, and the board started lighting up red, should he (a) abort the takeoff (and try to wrestle with the monster, which was gorged with jet fuel, out in the sand beyond the end of the runway) or (b) eject (and hope that the goddamned human cannonball trick works at zero altitude and he doesn't shatter an elbow or a kneecap on the way out) or (c) continue the takeoff and deal with the problem aloft (knowing full well that the ship may be on fire and therefore seconds away from exploding)? He would have one second to sort out the options and act, and this kind of little workaday decision came up all the time. Occasionally a man would look coldly at the binary problem he was now confronting every day—Right Stuff/Death —and decide it wasn't worth it and voluntarily shift over to transports or reconnaissance or whatever. And his comrades would wonder, for a day or so, what evil virus had invaded his soul . . . as they left him behind. More often, however, the reverse would happen. Some college graduate would enter Navy aviation through the Reserves, simply as an alternative to the Army draft, fully intending to return to civilian life, to some waiting profession or family business; would become involved in the obsessive business of ascending the ziggurat pyramid of flying; and, at the end of his enlistment, would astound everyone back home and very likely himself as well by signing up for another one. What on earth got into him? He couldn't explain it. After all, the very words for it had been amputated. A Navy study showed that two-thirds of the fighter pilots who were rated in the top rungs of their groups—i.e., the hottest young pilots—reenlisted when the time came, and practically all were college graduates. By this point, a young fighter jock was like the preacher in *Moby Dick* who climbs up into the pulpit on a rope ladder and then pulls the ladder up behind him; except the pilot could not use the words necessary to express the vital lessons. Civilian life, and even home and hearth, now seemed not only far away but far *below,* back down many levels of the pyramid of the right stuff.

A fighter pilot soon found he wanted to associate only with other fighter pilots. Who else could understand the nature of the little proposition (right stuff/death) they were all dealing with? And what other subject could compare with it? It was riveting! To talk about it in so many words was forbidden, of course. The very words *death, danger, bravery, fear* were not to be uttered except in the occasional specific instance or for ironic effect. Nevertheless, the subject could be adumbrated in *code* or *by example.* Hence the endless evenings of pilots huddled together talking about flying. On these long and drunken evenings (the bane of their family life) certain theorems would be propounded and demonstrated—and all by *code* and *example.* One theorem was: There are no *accidents* and no fatal flaws in the machines; there are only pilots with the wrong stuff. (I.e., blind Fate can't kill me.) When Bud Jennings crashed and burned in the swamps at Jacksonville, the other pilots in Pete Conrad's squadron said: *How could he have been so stupid?* It turned out that Jennings had gone up in the SNJ[4] with his cockpit canopy opened in a way that was expressly forbidden in the manual, and carbon monoxide had been sucked in from the exhaust, and he passed out and crashed. All agreed that Bud Jennings was a good guy and a good pilot, but his epitaph on the ziggurat was: *How could he have been so stupid?* This seemed shocking at first, but by the time Conrad had reached the end of that bad string at Pax River,[5] he was capable of his own corollary to the theorem: viz., no single factor ever killed a pilot; there was always a chain of mistakes. But what about Ted Whelan, who fell like a rock from 8,100 feet when his parachute failed? Well, the parachute was merely part of the chain: first, someone should have caught the structural defect that resulted in the hydraulic leak that triggered the emergency; second, Whelan did not check out his seat-parachute rig, and the drogue failed to separate the main parachute from the seat; but even after those two mistakes, Whelan had fifteen or twenty seconds, as he fell, to disengage himself from the seat and open the parachute manually. Why just stare at the scenery coming up to smack you in the face! And everyone nodded. (He failed—but I wouldn't have!) Once the theorem and the corollary were understood, the Navy's statistics about one in every four Navy aviators dying meant nothing. The figures were averages, and averages applied to those with average stuff.

A riveting subject, especially if it were one's own hide that was on the line. Every evening at bases all over America, there were military pilots huddled in officers clubs eagerly cutting the right stuff up in coded slices so they could talk about it. What more compelling topic of conversation was there in the world? In the Air Force there were even pilots who would ask the tower for priority landing clearance so that they could make the beer call on time, at 4 p.m. sharp, at the Officers Club. They would come right out and state the reason. The drunken rambles began at four and sometimes went on for ten or twelve hours. Such conversations! They diced that righteous stuff up into little bits, bowed ironically to it, stumbled blindfolded around it, groped, lurched, belched, staggered, bawled, sang, roared, and feinted at it with self-deprecating humor. Nevertheless!—they never mentioned it by name. No, they used the approved codes, such as: "Like a jerk I got myself into a hell of a corner today." They told of how they "lucked out of it." To get across the extreme peril of his exploit,

---

[4] A Navy jet fighter.
[5] Navy vernacular for the Patuxent River Naval Air Station in Maryland.

one would use certain oblique cues. He would say, "I looked over at Robinson"—
who would be known to the listeners as a non-com who sometimes rode backseat to
read radar—"and he wasn't talking any more, he was just staring at the radar, like
this, giving it that *zombie* look. Then I *knew* I was in trouble!" Beautiful! Just right!
For it would also be known to the listeners that the non-coms advised one another:
"*Never* fly with a lieutenant. *Avoid* captains and majors. Hell, man, do yourself a favor:
don't fly with anybody below colonel." Which in turn said: "Those young bucks
shoot dice with death!" And yet once in the air the non-com had his own standards.
He was determined to remain as outwardly cool as the pilot, so that when the pilot
did something that truly petrified him, he would say nothing; instead, he would turn
silent, catatonic, like a zombie. Perfect! *Zombie.* There you had it, compressed into
a single word all of the foregoing. I'm a hell of a pilot! I shoot dice with death! And
now all you fellows know it! And I haven't spoken of that unspoken stuff even once!

The talking and drinking began at the beer call, and then the boys would break
for dinner and come back afterward and get more wasted and more garrulous or else
more quietly fried, drinking good cheap PX booze until 2 a.m. The night was young!
Why not get the cars and go out for a little proficiency run? It seemed that every
fighter jock thought himself an ace driver, and he would do anything to obtain a hot
car, especially a sports car, and the drunker he was, the more convinced he would be
about his driving skills, as if the right stuff, being indivisible, carried over into any
enterprise whatsoever, under any conditions. A little proficiency run, boys! (There's
only one way to find out!) And they would roar off in close formation from, say,
Nellis Air Force Base, down Route 15, into Las Vegas, barreling down the highway,
rat-racing, sometimes four abreast, jockeying for position, piling into the most listless
curve in the desert flats as if they were trying to root each other out of the groove
at the Rebel 500—and then bursting into downtown Las Vegas with a rude fraternal
roar like the Hell's Angels—and the natives chalked it up to youth and drink and
the bad element that the Air Force attracted. They knew nothing about the right stuff,
of course.

More fighter pilots died in automobiles than in airplanes. Fortunately, there was
always some kindly soul up the chain to certify the papers "line of duty," so that the
widow could get a better break on the insurance. That was okay and only proper
because somehow the system itself had long ago said *Skol!*[6] and *Quite right!* to the
military cycle of Flying & Drinking and Drinking & Driving, as if there were no
other way. Every young fighter jock knew the feeling of getting two or three hours'
sleep and then waking up at 5:30 a.m. and having a few cups of coffee, a few cigarettes,
and then carting his poor quivering liver out to the field for another day of flying.
There were those who arrived not merely hungover but still drunk, slapping oxygen
tank cones over their faces and trying to burn the alcohol out of their systems, and
then going up, remarking later: "I don't *advise* it, you understand, but it *can* be done."
(Provided you have the right stuff, you miserable pudknocker.)

Air Force and Navy airfields were usually on barren or marginal stretches of land and
would have looked especially bleak and Low Rent to an ordinary individual in the
chilly light of dawn. But to a young pilot there was an inexplicable bliss to coming

---

[6] Common Danish toast.

out to the flight line while the sun was just beginning to cook up behind the rim of the horizon, so that the whole field was still in shadow and the ridges in the distance were in silhouette and the flight line was a monochrome of Exhaust Fume Blue, and every little red light on top of the water towers or power stanchions looked dull, shriveled, congealed, and the runway lights, which were still on, looked faded, and even the landing lights on a fighter that had just landed and was taxiing in were no longer dazzling, as they would be at night, and looked instead like shriveled gobs of candlepower out there—and yet it was beautiful, exhilarating!—for he was revved up with adrenalin, anxious to take off before the day broke, to burst up into the sunlight over the ridges before all those thousands of comatose souls down there, still dead to the world, snug in home and hearth, even came to their senses. To take off in an F-100F at dawn and cut on the afterburner and hurtle twenty-five thousand feet up into the sky in thirty seconds, so suddenly that you felt not like a bird but like a trajectory, yet with full control, full control of *four tons* of thrust, all of which flowed from your will and through your fingertips, with the huge engine right beneath you, so close that it was as if you were riding it bareback, until all at once you were supersonic, an event registered on earth by a tremendous cracking boom that shook windows, but up here only by the fact that you now felt utterly free of the earth—to describe it, even to wife, child, near ones and dear ones, seemed impossible. So the pilot kept it to himself, along with an even more indescribable . . . an even more sinfully inconfessable . . . feeling of superiority, appropriate to him and to his kind, lone bearers of the right stuff.

From *up here* at dawn the pilot looked down upon poor hopeless Las Vegas (or Yuma, Corpus Christi, Meridian, San Bernardino, or Dayton) and began to wonder: How can all of them down there, those poor souls who will soon be waking up and trudging out of their minute rectangles and inching along their little noodle highways toward whatever slots and grooves make up their everyday lives—how could they live like that, with such earnestness, if they had the faintest idea of what it was like up here in this righteous zone?

But of course! Not only the washed-out, grounded, and dead pilots had been left behind—but also all of those millions of sleepwalking souls who never even attempted the great gamble. The entire world below . . . *left behind.* Only at this point can one begin to understand just how big, how titanic, the ego of the military pilot could be. The world was used to enormous egos in artists, actors, entertainers of all sorts, in politicians, sports figures, and even journalists, because they had such familiar and convenient ways to show them off. But that slim young man over there in uniform, with the enormous watch on his wrist and the withdrawn look on his face, that young officer who is so shy that he can't even open his mouth unless the subject is flying —that young pilot—well, my friends, his ego is even *bigger!*—so big, it's *breathtaking!* Even in the 1950's it was difficult for civilians to comprehend such a thing, but *all* military officers and many enlisted men tended to feel superior to civilians. It was really quite ironic, given the fact that for a good thirty years the rising business classes in the cities had been steering their sons away from the military, as if from a bad smell, and the officer corps had never been held in lower esteem. Well, career officers returned the contempt in trumps. They looked upon themselves as men who lived by higher standards of behavior than civilians, as men who were the bearers and protectors of the most important values of American life, who maintained a sense of discipline while civilians abandoned themselves to hedonism, who maintained a sense of honor while civilians lived by opportunism and greed. Opportunism and greed: there you had your much-vaunted corporate business world. Khrushchev[7] was right about one thing: when it came time to hang the capitalist West, an American businessman would sell him the rope. When the showdown came—and the show-downs always came—not all the wealth in the world or all the sophisticated nuclear weapons and radar and missile systems it could buy would take the place of those who had the uncritical willingness to face danger, those who, in short, had the right stuff.

In fact, the feeling was so righteous, so exalted, it could become religious. Civilians seldom understood this, either. There was no one to teach them. It was no longer the fashion for serious writers to describe the glories of war. Instead, they dwelt upon its horrors, often with cynicism or disgust. It was left to the occasional pilot with a literary flair to provide a glimpse of the pilot's self-conception in its heavenly or spiritual aspect. When a pilot named Robert Scott flew his P-43 over Mount Everest, quite a feat at the time, he brought his hand up and snapped a salute to his fallen adversary. He thought he had *defeated* the mountain, surmounting all the forces of nature that had made it formidable. And why not? "God is my co-pilot," he said— that became the title of his book—and he meant it. So did the most gifted of all the pilot authors, the Frenchman Antoine de Saint-Exupéry.[8] As he gazed down upon the world . . . from up there . . . during transcontinental flights, the good Saint-Ex saw civilization as a series of tiny fragile patches clinging to the otherwise barren rock of Earth. He felt like a lonely sentinel, a protector of those vulnerable little oases, ready to lay down his life in their behalf, if necessary; a saint, in short, true to his name, flying up here at the right hand of God. The good Saint-Ex! And he was not the only one. He was merely the one who put it into words most beautifully and anointed himself before the altar of the right stuff.

There were many pilots in their thirties who, to the consternation of their wives, children, mothers, fathers, and employers, volunteered to go active in the reserves and fly in combat in the Korean War.[9] In godforsaken frozen Chosen! But it was simple enough. Half of them were fliers who had trained during the Second World War and had never seen combat. It was well understood—and never said, of course—that no one could reach the top of the pyramid without going into combat.

The morale of foot soldiers in the Korean War was so bad it actually reached the point where officers were prodding men forward with gun barrels and bayonets. But in the air—it was Fighter Jock Heaven! Using F-86s mainly, the Air Force was producing aces, pilots who had shot down five planes or more, as fast as the Koreans and Chinese could get their Soviet MiG-15s up to fight them. By the time the fighting was stopped, there were thirty-eight Air Force aces, and they had accounted for a total of 299.5 kills. Only fifty-six F-86s were lost. High spirits these lads had. They chronicled their adventures with a good creamy romanticism such as nobody in flying had treated himself to since the days of Lufbery, Frank Luke, and von Richtho-fen[10] in the First World War. Colonel Harrison R. Thyng, who shot down five MiGs in Korea (and eight German and Japanese planes in the Second World War), glowed like Excalibur when he described his Fourth Fighter-Interceptor Wing: "Like olden

---

[7] Nikita Khrushchev (1894–1971), premier of the Soviet Union, 1958–1964.
[8] Renowned novelist and aviator (1900–1944).
[9] 1950–1953.
[10] Famous World War I fighter pilots.

knights the F-86 pilots ride up over North Korea to the Yalu River, the sun glinting off silver aircraft, contrails streaming behind, as they challenge the numerically superior enemy to come on up and fight." Lances and plumes! *I'm a knight!* Come on up and fight! Why hold back! Knights of the Right Stuff!

When a pilot named Gus Grissom (whom Conrad, Schirra, Lovell,[11] and the others would meet later on) first went to Korea, the Air Force used to take the F-86 jocks out to the field before dawn, in the dark, in buses, and the pilots who had not been shot at by a MiG in air-to-air combat had to stand up. At first Grissom couldn't believe it and then he couldn't bear it—those bastards sitting down were *the only ones with the right stuff!* The next morning, as they rumbled out there in the dark, he was sitting down. He had gone up north toward the Yalu on the first day and had it out with some howling supersonic Chinee just so he could have a seat on the bus. Even at the level of combat, the main thing was not to be *left behind.*

Combat had its own infinite series of tests, and one of the greatest sins was "chattering" or "jabbering" on the radio. The combat frequency was to be kept clear of all but strategically essential messages, and all unenlightening comments were regarded as evidence of funk, of the wrong stuff. A Navy pilot (in legend, at any rate) began shouting, "I've got a MiG at zero! A MiG at zero!"—meaning that it had maneuvered in behind him and was locked in on his tail. An irritated voice cut in and said, "Shut up and die like an aviator." One had to be a Navy pilot to appreciate the final nuance. A good Navy pilot was a real *aviator;* in the Air Force they merely had pilots and not precisely the proper stuff.

No, the tests were never-ending. And in the periods between wars a man's past successes in combat did not necessarily keep him at the top of the heavenly pyramid. By the late 1950's there was yet another plateau to strive for. On that plateau were men who had flown in combat in the Second World War or Korea and had then gone on to become test pilots in the new age of jet and rocket engines. Not every combat pilot could make the climb. Two of the great aces of the Second World War, Richard I. Bong and Don Gentile, tried it but didn't have the patience for the job. They only wanted to light the afterburner and poke holes in the sky; and presently they were just part of combat history. Of course, by now, thanks to the accident of age, you began to find young men who had reached the exalted level of test pilot without ever having had a chance to fight in combat. One was Pete Conrad, who was just graduating, with the survivors of Group 20, to the status of full-fledged test pilot at Pax River. Like every Navy test pilot, Conrad was proud of Pax River and its reputation. Out loud every true Navy aviator insisted that Pax River was the place ... and inwardly knew it really wasn't. For every military pilot knew where the apex of the great ziggurat was located. You could point it out on a map. The place was Edwards Air Force Base in the high desert 150 miles northeast of Los Angeles. Everyone knew who resided there, too, although their actual status was never put into words. Not only that, everyone knew the name of the individual who ranked foremost in the Olympus, the ace of all the aces, as it were, among the true brothers of the right stuff.

1979

---

[11] Jim Lovell, another astronaut in the Project Mercury program.

Robert Stone
b. 1937

Robert Stone describes himself as a writer who tries "to crowd people out of their own minds and occupy their space. This is an incantatory process. I want them to stop being themselves for a moment. . . . If I didn't write for people, my proper business would be meditation. But my business is writing for people. To me, it's an act of affirmation." Stone's fast-paced, suspense-filled novels have been called "compulsively readable." In them he painstakingly maps the nightmarish landscape of contemporary America in an effort to explore what Americans have done to themselves and others.

Robert Stone was born in Brooklyn in 1937 and reared on Manhattan's West Side. As a child, he spent three years in an orphanage when his mother found that she could no longer carry on the family tradition of working on tugboats and at the same time care for him adequately. In 1954, at age seventeen, he enlisted in the navy. After leaving the military in 1958, he worked in New Orleans unloading cargo for the merchant marine. Later, while working as a census taker, he began to concentrate on writing poetry and fiction.

Having lived in a working-class environment, Stone at first labored, as he reports, under "the impression that being a writer was unsubstantial and not altogether respectable." Yet he also wanted to write: "I always had a kind of narrative impulse to try to make sense out of things by telling stories about them," he says, "and I guess I always had a certain facility with language."

Returning to New York, Stone studied at New York University for a year and then accepted a fellowship at Stanford University. During this California sojourn, he met Neal Cassady and Ken Kesey and joined the roving band of "Merry Pranksters," whose escapades were recounted by Tom Wolfe in *The Electric Kool-Aid Acid Test* (1968). In addition, Stone began his first novel, *A Hall of Mirrors* (1967), which won the William Faulkner Foundation Award for a "notable first novel." In commenting on *A Hall of Mirrors,* Stone describes a character that figures prominently in every novel he has written:

Not only have we the Frontiersman and the Puritan and the Outlaw, but we have the Sociopath as a major cultural type, and there is a certain reverence for him in American society. I think what I was trying to do was to recognize the importance of the rootless, affectless, emotionally crippled individual in American life.

In 1971 Stone traveled to Vietnam as a correspondent for "a now defunct English imitation of the *Village Voice* called *Ink.*" Horrified not only by the brutality he saw in the war zone but also by the rampant profiteering he saw in Saigon's black market and the drug scenes he saw everywhere, he returned to the United States late in 1971, only to become further disillusioned by the simplistic rhetorical polarities of the nation's debate over the war. Soon he began a nearly decade-long association with Amherst College, where he taught creative writing. More recently, he has taught at the University of California at San Diego.

In his second novel, *Dog Soldiers* (1974), which won the National Book Award for fiction, Stone creates a compelling account of the Vietnam drug trade. In his third novel, *A Flag for Sunrise* (1981), he focuses on characters who pursue broken dreams in a small Central American nation, Tecan, that is on the verge of being destroyed by a revolution. His most recent novel, *Children of Light* (1986), is set in California.

Like the places in which they live, Stone's characters are poised on the edge of destruction. Frank Holliwell, the alcoholic anthropologist protagonist in *A Flag for Sunrise,* epitomizes Stone's skeptical view of the prospects that face people who are forced to improvise in a world where all moral codes have been abandoned. Left "without beliefs, without hope—either for himself or for the world," Holliwell also finds himself "almost without friends, certainly without allies. Alone." In the passage excerpted here, Holliwell dives off the coast of Tecan and descends the slopes of an underwater canyon farther than he had expected. There he confronts, in a mixture of euphoria and fear, the threat that lurks inside himself. Stone's mastery of what the critic Robert Towers calls "the novel of existential adventure," together with his command of narrative suspense, invite comparisons with the work of Hemingway and especially Conrad and Fitzgerald, from whom Stone says that he "learned the art of the novel."

Text:
A Flag for Sunrise, 1981.

---

from A Flag for Sunrise

With the air tank tucked into the gunwales under the bench on which he sat, Holliwell smoked and watched the green coastline—palm groves, banana plants strayed from the plantations, beach heliotrope[1] of outsized luxuriance. Sandy, the dive master, ran his thirty-six-footer at full throttle, slapping the hull over the placid water; the bow took spray over the windward side that soaked the STP[2] jacket Holliwell had worn against the sun.

Sandy was a long, spare man with a freckled English countryman's face darkened by the suns of Tecan and West Africa. He lounged in the stern, one loose hand over the stick, one elbow on the rail, leaning out to see the water ahead. His long black hair was bleached at the crown, parted at the middle of his skull like a nineteenth-century Russian peasant's, and this with his sharp black eyes deep-set under thick low brows brought a kind of dervish flair, a Rasputin[3] intensity, to his appearance.

---

[1] Small, fragrant, purplish flower.
[2] Brand name for an automobile-oil additive.

[3] Grigori Efimovich Rasputin (1871?–1916), Russian mystic and monk.

In the boat with Holliwell was a family of five Cuban-Americans from Miami. The father was stocky and muscular, his hair worn in a brush cut, his jaw jowled and pitted from relentless shaving. His wife was buxom and fleshy-faced yet with a long-legged trim frame, a Floridian body honed by dieting and Gloria Stevens.[4] There were three boys between twelve and seventeen—the oldest vulpine with a nearly complete moustache and muscular like his father, the two younger quite like their mother; over the waist of each of their bathing suits sagged a tube of buttery fat. The parents spoke to each other in Spanish, the boys in American Adolescent. All of them ignored Holliwell.

"Could be seein' turtle over this reef," Sandy told the boys. "Good place to see dem."

"Aw-*right*," said the middle boy with enthusiasm.

"Would they bite you?" asked the smallest boy.

Sandy laughed. "Turtle bite you? Turtle don't bite you. Maybe take you for a ride."

"Hey," the seventeen-year-old said, "I could go for that."

When the children's parents spoke to Sandy it was in a formal and imperious way, as though they were used to service. Sandy answered them with deference.

Three hundred yards offshore, Sandy killed his engine and hopped forward to put the anchor line down. Everyone looked over the side. The sky's light sparkled back at them, reflected and refracted from the reef tops below—a long line of peaks curving out toward open ocean.

Sandy gave them the dive plan. The current was southerly. They would dive straight out from the stern, up-current. Then they could follow a semicircle of reef tops, cross a sandy bottom and follow the edge of a drop back to the boat with the current behind them. There was black coral there, Sandy told them. The site was called Twixt by the people of the coast.

Holliwell stared down at the liquid light of the white reefs. They were, after all, what he had come to see. He took a deep breath and put on his buoyancy compensator, his backpack tank, and bent to wrestle on his weight belt. Sandy put his own tank on with the ease of a man donning a sweater. The Cuban-American bustled about, trying stays and buckles—the head of the house overseeing procedure. The woman and the youngest boy were not going down. While Holliwell put his boots and fins on, Sandy checked out the gear of the younger of the two boys who were diving.

"Ever see any sharks around here?" the younger boy asked, as casually as he could. Holliwell admired his sangfroid. Testing his own regulator, he turned to watch Sandy answer.

"No sharks here," Sandy said simply.

It turned out that the younger boy was diving with Sandy, the oldest with his father. It had been so ordered.

"Want to come with us?" the dive master asked Holliwell.

"I'll just follow along," Holliwell said. "I'll be all right." He was not in fact a very experienced diver but the dive seemed easy enough.

Holliwell went over last, carrying two five-pound weights, wearing trunks and a tee shirt to ease the shoulder straps on his sunburned back. On the jump-off, his mask

---

[4] Popular advocate of physical fitness.

filled almost to eye level; he let the water rise in it, pinching his nostrils to equalize pressure. When he saw the reef tips rising around him, he cleared his mask and checked the depth gauge on his wrist. He was forty-five feet below the surface. He settled over a punch-bowl depression on the bottom; his fin tips stirred the milk-white sand there. The visibility at this depth was marvelous—over a hundred feet, perhaps two hundred. Black and golden angelfish swarmed around him as though they expected to be fed. There were parrot fish and convict tangs in uncountable numbers. The reef descended in terraces from its highest peaks, from each terrace elkhorn coral stretched in tortured fantastical shapes between the domes of brain coral. Below him wrasse and groupers[5] glided by, a boxfish watched him shyly from behind two prongs of elkhorn. When he paddled out from the plateau on which he had rested, two trumpet fish came along with him like scouts. He swam clear of the next terrace and let the weights take him deeper; on the edge of vision he saw a barracuda[6]—fairly small, certainly under three feet—prowling the edge of the swarm to pick off stragglers. When he leveled off, he was at sixty feet and the ocean floor still sloped downward under his fins. Far off and about forty feet above him he saw Sandy and the Cuban boy outlined against the shimmering curtain of the surface, swimming away from him.

On the next terrace he saw the black coral. There seemed to be acres of it, dappled with encrusting yellow infant sponges, and circling down he felt as though he were flying over a lava field grown with daisies. When he was closer, he could see the coral's root and branch patterns. It was sublime, he thought. He could feel his heart beating faster; his blood coursed through him like a drug. The icy, fragile beauty was beyond the competency of any man's hand, even beyond man's imagining. Yet it seemed to him its perfection provoked a recognition. The recognition of what? he wondered. A thing lost or forgotten. He followed the slope of the coral field. Down.

It had been years since he had taken so much pleasure in the living world.

At about ninety feet, he confronted the drop. The last coral terrace fell away and beyond it there was nothing, an immensity of shadowy blue, an abyss. He was losing color now. The coral on the canyon wall read blue-gray as he descended; the wrasse, the butterflies, the parrot fish looked as dun as mackerel. A gray lobster scurried along the cliff. Enormous gray groupers approached to have a look at him. In a coral crevice, a spotted moray[7] drew back at his approach, then put its head out to watch his bubble trail with flat venomous eyes. The surface became a mirage, a distant notion.

He was at a hundred and ten and his pressure gauge, which had pointed twenty-five hundred p.s.i.[8] at the jump-off, now read slightly under eight hundred. It was all right, he thought, the tank had no reserve and no J valve; he would have enough to climb back as the pressure evened out. At a hundred and twenty, his exhilaration was still with him and he was unable to suppress the impulse to turn a somersault. He was at the borders of narcosis. It was time to start up.

As soon as he began to climb, he saw shimmers of reflected light flashing below his feet. In a moment, the flashes were everywhere—above and below. Blue glitters, lightning quick. The bodies of fish in flight. He began pumping a bit, climbing faster, but by the book, not outstripping his own bubble trail.

Some fifty feet away, he caught clear sight of a school of bonito racing toward the shallows over the reef. Wherever he looked, he saw what appeared to be a shower

---

[5] Two types of tropical fish.
[6] Species of predatory fish.

[7] Poisonous species of eel.
[8] Pounds per square inch.

of blue-gray arrows. And then it was as if the ocean itself had begun to tremble. The angels and wrasse, the parrots and tangs which had been passing lazily around him suddenly hung in place, without forward motion, quivering like mobile sculpture. Turning full circle, he saw the same shudder pass over all the living things around him—a terror had struck the sea, an invisible shadow, a silence within a silence. On the edge of vision, he saw a school of redfish whirl left, then right, sound, then reverse, a red and white catherine wheel[9] against the deep blue. It was a sight as mesmerizing as the wheeling of starlings over a spring pasture. Around him the fish held their places, fluttering, coiled for flight.

Then Holliwell thought: It's out there. Fear overcame him; a chemical taste, a cold stone on the heart.

He started up too fast, struggling to check his own panic. Follow the bubbles. Follow the bouncing ball.

As he pedaled up the wall, he was acutely aware of being the only creature on the reef that moved with purpose. The thing out there must be feeling him, he thought, sensing the lateral vibrations of his climb, its dim primal brain registering disorder in his motion and making the calculation. Fear. Prey.

He was running out of air—overbreathing and overtaxing the expanding contents of his tank. The sound of his own desperate respirations furthered panic.

When he had worked out a breathing pattern and reached the first terrace, he found that he had enough to curve his ascent with the slope of the coral. At forty feet, he saw a sandy punch bowl like the one in which he had stopped but the forests of elkhorn were everywhere the same and the anchor line was nowhere in sight. Looking up, he saw Sandy outlined against the surface, coming down at him.

Sandy grabbed Holliwell's pressure gauge, read it and shook his head in reproach. He pointed to the right and upward along the slope. Holliwell followed the coral ridges as long as he could. The fish in the shallows swam placidly, unperturbed. When he found himself sucking hard on the regulator mouthpiece, he eased up the next thirty feet, taking three breaths on the way. And there, in another dimension altogether, the boat rocked gently, the youngest of the Cuban boys leaned over the side to watch the shifting surface, lost in reverie; his mother thumbed through *Cosmopolitan*. The shoreline glowed green beyond the hot blur of the beach, the line of banana jungle broken only by a white wooden building on a solitary hill, surmounted with a cross. Holliwell turned over on his back and swam to the boat's ladder.

The boy and his mother watched as he took off his gear. Before disconnecting the regulator from the tank he checked the gauge once more; it read just a hair over empty at sea level.

"That's as empty as it gets," he told the people in the boat. The charge of primary process he had experienced at a hundred and ten feet put him in danger of becoming garrulous.

The boy looked at the gauge. "None left at all?"

"Empty," Holliwell said. "Just like it says." He was ill at ease with the boy and he sensed a certain artificiality in his own manner. His own children had not been this age for five years or more; he had forgotten what it was like. Out of touch again, he thought.

"How come is that?" the woman asked.

[9] Pinwheel of fireworks.

"Just ran it out," Holliwell told her cheerfully.

"What did you see?" the boy asked him.

"Lots of great fish," he said. "And beautiful black coral."

"And we can't take any," the woman said. "Such a shame because it's so beautiful."

"I'm sure it looks prettier where it is," Holliwell heard himself say pompously.

The woman inflated her cheeks and shrugged. She was not a bad sort, Holliwell decided. They chatted for a few minutes. The family's name was Paz; they lived in Miami, had lived there since 1961. All of their sons were born there. The man was a dentist, she herself was in real estate. They were visiting her brother, who had five hardware stores in Tecan. Holliwell told her that he was a professor; she had lived in the States long enough to remain unimpressed.

Sandy and the middle son were next up; the boy climbed aboard and fixed a smirk on Holliwell. The dive master got out of harness in a single easy motion.

"Now what you want down theah, mistuh?" he asked Holliwell. He was smiling. "I nevah tol' you go down theah."

"Just wanted a look, I guess."

"Sandy made him get out of the water," the middle son announced. Señora Paz and the youngest boy gave Holliwell dutifully accusatory looks. Then Señora Paz asked sharply after her husband and eldest son. They were under the boat, Sandy assured her, playing among the elkhorn coral.

After a few minutes, the dentist surfaced and climbed aboard. He was elated after his dive and his amiability extended even to Holliwell.

"Where the hell were you?" Dr. Paz asked Holliwell. "I never even saw you." His English was almost completely unaccented.

"Sandy made him get out of the water," the middle son said.

"Just down too deep," Sandy said soothingly. "A bit too deep and de air run out faster."

"What's the attraction down there?" the dentist asked.

"Just the drop," Holliwell said.

"How far you think she drop off dere?" Sandy asked him, laughing.

"A long way," Holliwell said.

"Nine hundred meters," Sandy said.

"Is that possible?" Holliwell said.

Sandy let his smile fade. His nod was solemn, his eyes humorous with certainty. "I'm tellin' you, mon. Nine hundred meters."

When the youngest boy wanted to know how far that was in feet, Sandy was uncertain.

"It's about two thirds of a mile," the dentist said. "I thought they taught you that in school."

"Yeah, dummy," the middle son said to his brother.

"How about that," Holliwell said.

Then the oldest boy surfaced with an empty tank.

"Orca,[10] orca," the two younger boys shouted. "Orca surfaces at last."

The youth's eyes were shining as he climbed up the ladder. It was hard to dislike anyone, Holliwell thought, when you watched them come up from a dive.

---

[10] The black killer whale.

"Gosh," the boy said to Holliwell, "we didn't see you anywhere."

"Sandy made him get . . ."

Señora Paz hushed her middle son with a frown and a raising of her chin.

They motored back to the hotel dock making small talk. At the dive shack, Sandy, who knew a big tipper when he saw one, helped the Pazes wash and stow their gear and was jolly with the boys. Holliwell put his own gear away and sat down on the dock. After a while Sandy wandered down and joined him.

"How long you been divin'?" Sandy asked him.

"I've been certified for two years. I don't do it much anymore."

Sandy looked out to sea. "Lost a mon on dat drop other year. I follow him dom near two hundred meters but when I turn off de mon still goin' down."

"Suicide," Holliwell said.

"Das right. Mon take de sleepin' pills and go down."

"It must have happened more than once."

Sandy nodded. "I don' lose nobody," he said. "Got to be dere own chosen will."

Holliwell felt himself shudder. "Did you think that's what I was doing?"

"Oh, no," the dive master said quickly. He touched Holliwell on the shoulder in the Caribbean way but avoided his eye.

"I won't make the dive this afternoon," Holliwell told him. "Maybe you could leave me off around French Harbor. I'd like to snorkel down there."

Sandy guessed that it would be all right. French Harbor was on the way. He told Holliwell that if he requested it, the Paradise kitchen might pack a lunch for him. They walked together toward the hotel buildings.

"There was something down that drop this morning," Holliwell said. "A big shark, maybe."

Sandy stopped walking and looked at Holliwell, holding his hand on his brow to shield his eyes from the sun.

"You see any shark?"

"No."

"Then don' be sayin' shark if you don' see one."

"Something was happening down there."

"I tell you don' go down that far, Mistuh Holliwell. I give you de dive plan. When you down so far, das not a good place."

"Why's that?"

Sandy walked on; Holliwell followed him.

"Dat drop, people see tings, den dey don' know what dey seen. Dey be frightened after."

"Was it always like that?"

"Jus' dangerous divin', das all. Surface current and de drop is cunnin'.[11] You get deeper den you know."

"So pretty, though."

"Jus' as pretty on de top," Sandy said. "Always prettier in de light."

"Yes," Holliwell said. "Yes, of course."

1977

---

[11] Tricky; treacherous.

Rodolfo A. Anaya
b. 1937

Mythmaking is central to Rodolfo Anaya's art because for him it is central to all human concerns. "I define myth," he says, "as the truth in the heart." In a story like "B. Traven Is Alive and Well in Cuernavaca," Anaya appropriates the myths of his Mexican-American heritage, but he also creates myths of his own. In those he recounts, he seeks to recapture "the teachings of the old ones"; in those he creates, he seeks to disclose "the infinity of the cosmic dance of life" as it sweeps around us. Like William Faulkner, Anaya finds in the stories of *los viejitos* ("the old people") a passageway to knowledge and experience. By exploring the power of language to teach and awaken us, however, he also seeks to honor the warning of his grandfather: "Words are a way, he said, they hold joy, and they are a deadly power if misused."

Born in Patura, New Mexico, on October 30, 1937, Anaya learned early the power of words as, entering school, he began to learn English as a new language. After graduating from high school, he enrolled in the University of New Mexico, receiving a B.A. in 1963, an M.A. in English in 1968, and another M.A. in guidance and counseling in 1972. From 1963 to 1971 he taught in the Albuquerque, New Mexico, public schools, and in 1972 he became director of counseling at the University of Albuquerque. He is currently associate professor of English at the University of New Mexico.

Beginning with *Bless Me, Ultima* (1972), for which he received the Premio Quinto Sol literary award, and continuing through *Heart of Aztlan* (1976) and *Tortuga* (1979), Anaya has become one of the most widely recognized and respected Chicano novelists and essayists now writing in the United States. Despite his appreciation of modern literature and culture, he sees contemporary life as fragmented and debilitated in comparison to the life of *los viejitos:* "Our civilizing and socializing influence," he believes, "has made us not as unified, not as harmonious, as archaic man. To go back and get in touch, and to become more harmonious, we go back to the unconscious and we bring out all of the symbols and archetypals that are available to all people." Again and again Anaya emphasizes the "truth in the heart," the knowledge that, as a character in *Tortuga* says, "all these stories are bound to the same theme: . . . *life is sacred.*" Yet Anaya's imagination is neither naive nor sentimental, though in some of his earlier work it may seem so. His belief in the human potential of love and affirmation is pervaded by the same duality that his grandfather saw in words. The human spirit, as Anaya discloses it in his art, can create joy, but it can also become "a deadly power," crippling or crushing those around it. Through his use of myth and history, Mexican and Chicano, Anaya shows us our humanity as a force that can either bind us together or destroy us.

Text:
Cuentos Chicanos: A Short Story Anthology, ed.
R. A. Anaya and A. Márquez, 1984.

B. Traven Is Alive and Well in Cuernavaca

I didn't go to Mexico to find B. Traven.[1] Why should I? I have enough to do writing my own fiction, so I go to Mexico to write, not to search out writers. B. Traven? you ask. Don't you remember THE TREASURE OF THE SIERRA MADRE? A real classic. They made a movie from the novel. I remember seeing it when I was a kid. It was set in Mexico, and it had all the elements of a real adventure story. B. Traven was an adventurous man, travelled all over the world, then disappeared into Mexico and cut himself off from society. He gave no interviews and allowed few photographs. While he lived he remained unapproachable, anonymous to his public, a writer shrouded in mystery.

He's dead now, or they say he's dead. I think he's alive and well. At any rate, he has become something of an institution in Mexico, a man honored for his work. The cantineros[2] and taxi drivers in Mexico City know about him as well as the cantineros of Spain knew Hemingway, or they claim to. I never mention I'm a writer when I'm in a cantina, because inevitably some aficionado will ask, "Do you know the work of B. Traven?" And from some dusty niche will appear a yellowed, thumb-worn novel by Traven. Thus if the cantinero knows his business, and they all do in Mexico, he is apt to say, "Did you know that B. Traven used to drink here?" If you show the slightest interest, he will follow with, "Sure, he used to sit right over here. In this corner. . . ." And if you don't leave right then you will wind up hearing many stories about the mysterious B. Traven while buying many drinks for the local patrons.

Everybody reads his novels, on the buses, on street corners; if you look closely you'll spot one of his titles. One turned up for me, and that's how this story started. I was sitting in the train station in Juárez, waiting for the train to Cuernavaca, which would be an exciting title for this story except that there is no train to Cuernavaca. I was drinking beer to kill time, the erotic and sensitive Mexican time which is so different from the clean-packaged, well-kept time of the Americanos. Time in Mexico can be cruel and punishing, but it is never indifferent. It permeates everything, it changes reality. Einstein would have loved Mexico because there time and space are one. I stare more often into empty space when I'm in Mexico. The past seems to infuse the present, and in the brown, wrinkled faces of the old people one sees the presence of the past. In Mexico I like to walk the narrow streets of the cities and the smaller pueblos, wandering aimlessly, feeling the sunlight which is so distinctively Mexican, listening to the voices which call in the streets, peering into the dark eyes which are so secretive and proud. The Mexican people guard a secret. But in the end, one is never

---

[1] As mysterious as Anaya suggests, Traven, whose real name may have been Berick (or Bruno) Traven Torsvan, was probably born in Chicago sometime between 1890 and 1901; he died in 1969. Presumably he did live for most of his adult life in Mexico, where he wrote numerous novels, the most famous of which is *The Treasure of the Sierra Madre* (1935).

[2] Spanish: "bartender" (from *cantina:* "bar").

really lost in Mexico. All streets lead to a good cantina. All good stories start in a cantina.

At the train station, after I let the kids who hustle the tourists know that I didn't want chewing gum or cigarettes, and I didn't want my shoes shined, and I didn't want a woman at the moment, I was left alone to drink my beer. Luke-cold Dos Equis.[3] I don't remember how long I had been there or how many Dos Equis I had finished when I glanced at the seat next to me and saw a book which turned out to be a B. Traven novel, old and used and obviously much read, but a novel nevertheless. What's so strange about finding a B. Traven novel in that dingy little corner of a bar in the Juárez train station? Nothing, unless you know that in Mexico one never finds anything. It is a country that doesn't waste anything, everything is recycled. Chevrolets run with patched up Ford engines and Chrysler transmissions, buses are kept together, and kept running, with baling wire and home-made parts, yesterday's Traven novel is the pulp on which tomorrow's Fuentes[4] story will appear. Time recycles in Mexico. Time returns to the past, and the Christian finds himself dreaming of ancient Aztec rituals. He who does not believe that Quetzalcoatl[5] will return to save Mexico has little faith.

So the novel was the first clue. Later there was Justino. "Who is Justino?" you want to know. Justino was the jardinero[6] who cared for the garden of my friend, the friend who had invited me to stay at his home in Cuernavaca while I continued to write. The day after I arrived I was sitting in the sun, letting the fatigue of the long journey ooze away, thinking nothing, when Justino appeared on the scene. He had finished cleaning the swimming pool and was taking his morning break, so he sat in the shade of the orange tree and introduced himself. Right away I could tell that he would rather be a movie actor or an adventurer, a real free spirit. But things didn't work out for him. He got married, children appeared, he took a couple of mistresses, more children appeared, so he had to work to support his family. "A man is like a rooster," he said after we talked awhile, "the more chickens he has the happier he is." Then he asked me what I was going to do about a woman while I was there, and I told him I hadn't thought that far ahead, that I would be happy if I could just get a damned story going. This puzzled Justino, and I think for a few days it worried him. So on Saturday night he took me out for a few drinks and we wound up in some of the bordellos of Cuernavaca in the company of some of the most beautiful women in the world. Justino knew them all. They loved him, and he loved them.

I learned something more of the nature of this jardinero a few nights later when the heat and an irritating mosquito wouldn't let me sleep. I heard music from a radio, so I put on my pants and walked out into the Cuernavacan night, an oppressive, warm night heavy with the sweet perfume of the dama de la noche[7] bushes which lined the wall of my friend's villa. From time to time I heard a dog cry in the distance, and I remembered that in Mexico many people die of rabies. Perhaps that is why the walls of the wealthy are always so high and the locks always secure. Or maybe it was because of the occasional gunshots that explode in the night. The news media tell us that Mexico is the most stable country in Latin America and, with the recent oil finds,

---

[3] A Mexican beer (Spanish: "Double X").
[4] Carlos Fuentes (b. 1928), major Mexican novelist, essayist, and dramatist.
[5] Aztec name of a pre-Columbian god and legendary hero, usually depicted as a plumed

serpent. In Nahuatl (the Aztec language), "quetzal" means *bird, flying,* or *precious;* and "coatl" means *snake* or *twin.*
[6] Spanish: "gardener."
[7] Spanish: "lady of the night."

the bankers and the oil men want to keep it that way. I sense, and many know, that in the dark the revolution does not sleep. It is a spirit kept at bay by the high fences and the locked gates, yet it prowls the heart of every man. "Oil will create a new revolution," Justino had told me, "but it's going to be for our people. Mexicans are tired of building gas stations for the Gringos from Gringolandia." I understood what he meant: there is much hunger in the country.

I lit a cigarette and walked toward my friend's car, which was parked in the driveway near the swimming pool. I approached quietly and peered in. On the back seat with his legs propped on the front seat-back and smoking a cigar sat Justino. Two big, luscious women sat on either side of him running their fingers through his hair and whispering in his ears. The doors were open to allow a breeze. He looked content. Sitting there he was that famous artist on his way to an afternoon reception in Mexico City, or he was a movie star on his way to the premiere of his most recent movie. Or perhaps it was Sunday and he was taking a Sunday drive in the country, towards Tepoztlán. And why shouldn't his two friends accompany him? I had to smile. Unnoticed I backed away and returned to my room. So there was quite a bit more than met the eye to this short, dark Indian from Ocosingo.

In the morning I asked my friend, "What do you know about Justino?"

"Justino? You mean Vitorino."

"Is that his real name?"

"Sometimes he calls himself Trinidad."

"Maybe his name is Justino Vitorino Trinidad," I suggested.

"I don't know, don't care," my friend answered. "He told me he used to be a guide in the jungle. Who knows? The Mexican Indian has an incredible imagination. Really gifted people. He's a good jardinero, and that's what matters to me. It's difficult to get good jardineros, so I don't ask questions."

"Is he reliable?" I wondered aloud.

"As reliable as a ripe mango," my friend nodded.

I wondered how much he knew, so I pushed a little further. "And the radio at night?"

"Oh, that. I hope it doesn't bother you. Robberies and break-ins are increasing here in the colonia. Something we never used to have. Vitorino said that if he keeps the radio on low the sound keeps thieves away. A very good idea, don't you think?"

I nodded. A very good idea.

"And I sleep very soundly," my friend concluded, "so I never hear it."

The following night when I awakened and heard the soft sound of music from the radio and heard the splashing of water, I had only to look from my window to see Justino and his friends in the pool, swimming nude in the moonlight. They were joking and laughing softly as they splashed each other, being quiet so as not to awaken my friend, the patrón[8] who slept so soundly. The women were beautiful. Brown skinned and glistening with water in the moonlight they reminded me of ancient Aztec maidens, swimming around Chac, their god of rain. They teased Justino, and he smiled as he floated on a rubber mattress in the middle of the pool, smoking his cigar, happy because they were happy. When he smiled the gold fleck of a filling glinted in the moonlight.

"¡Qué cabrón!"[9] I laughed and closed my window.

---

[8] Spanish: "landlord" or "master."   [9] Spanish: "What a buck!" (I.e., "What a man!")

Justino said a Mexican never lies. I believed him. If a Mexican says he will meet you at a certain time and place, he means he will meet you sometime at some place. Americans who retire in Mexico often complain of maids who swear they will come to work on a designated day, then don't show up. They did not lie, they knew they couldn't be at work, but they knew to tell the señora otherwise would make her sad or displease her, so they agree on a date so everyone would remain happy. What a beautiful aspect of character. It's a real virtue which Norteamericanos[10] interpret as a fault in their character, because we are used to asserting ourselves on time and people. We feel secure and comfortable only when everything is neatly packaged in its proper time and place. We don't like the disorder of a free-flowing life.

Some day, I thought to myself, Justino will give a grand party in the sala of his patrón's home. His three wives, or his wife and two mistresses, and his dozens of children will be there. So will the women from the bordellos. He will preside over the feast, smoke his cigars, request his favorite beer-drinking songs from the mariachis,[11] smile, tell stories and make sure everyone has a grand time. He will be dressed in a tuxedo, borrowed from the patrón's closet of course, and he will act gallant and show everyone that a man who has just come into sudden wealth should share it with his friends. And in the morning he will report to the patrón that something has to be done about the poor mice that are coming in out of the streets and eating everything in the house.

"I'll buy some poison," the patrón will suggest.

"No, no," Justino will shake his head, "a little music from the radio and a candle burning in the sala[12] will do."

And he will be right.

I liked Justino. He was a rogue with class. We talked about the weather, the lateness of the rainy season, women, the role of oil in Mexican politics. Like other workers, he believed nothing was going to filter down to the campesinos.[13] "We could all be real Mexican greasers with all that oil," he said, "but the politicians will keep it all."

"What about the United States?" I asked.

"Oh, I have traveled in the estados unidos[14] to the north. It's a country that's going to the dogs in a worse way than Mexico. The thing I liked the most was your cornflakes."

"Cornflakes?"

"Sí. You can make really good cornflakes."

"And women?"

"Ah, you better keep your eyes open, my friend. Those gringas are going to change the world just like the Suecas[15] changed Spain."

"For better or for worse?"

"Spain used to be a nice country," he winked.

We talked, we argued, we drifted from subject to subject. I learned from him. I had been there a week when he told the story which eventually led me to B. Traven. One day I was sitting under the orange tree reading the B. Traven novel I had found

---

[10] Spanish: "North Americans" (i.e., from the United States).
[11] Musicians who perform mariachi, a lively form of popular music in Mexico.
[12] Spanish: "drawing room" or "parlor."
[13] Spanish: "peasants" or "farmers."
[14] Spanish: "United States."
[15] Spanish: "Swedes."

in the Juárez train station, keeping one eye on the ripe oranges which fell from time to time, my mind wandering as it worked to focus on a story so I could begin to write. After all, that's why I had come to Cuernavaca, to get some writing done, but nothing was coming, nothing. Justino wandered by and asked what I was reading and replied it was an adventure story, a story of a man's search for the illusive pot of gold at the end of a make-believe rainbow. He nodded, thought awhile and gazed toward Popo, Popocatepetl,[16] the towering volcano which lay to the south, shrouded in mist, waiting for the rains as we waited for the rains, sleeping, gazing at his female counterpart, Itza, who lay sleeping and guarding the valley of Cholula,[17] there, where over four-hundred years ago Cortés[18] showed his wrath and executed thousands of Cholulans.

"I am going on an adventure," he finally said and paused. "I think you might like to go with me."

I said nothing, but I put my book down and listened.

"I have been thinking about it for a long time, and now is the time to go. You see, it's like this. I grew up on the hacienda[19] of Don Francisco Jimenez, it's to the south, just a day's drive on the carretera.[20] In my village nobody likes Don Francisco, they fear and hate him. He has killed many men and he has taken their fortunes and buried them. He is a very rich man, muy rico. Many men have tried to kill him, but Don Francisco is like the devil, he kills them first."

I listened as I always listen, because one never knows when a word or phrase or an idea will be the seed from which a story sprouts, but at first there was nothing interesting. It sounded like the typical patrón-peón[21] story I had heard so many times before. A man, the patrón, keeps the workers enslaved, in serfdom, and because he wields so much power soon stories are told about him and he begins to acquire super-human powers. He acquires a mystique, just like the divine right of old. The patrón wields a mean machete, like old King Arthur swung Excaliber. He chops off heads of dissenters and sits on top of the bones and skulls pyramid, the king of the mountain, the top macho.[22]

"One day I was sent to look for lost cattle," Justino continued. "I rode back into the hills where I had never been. At the foot of a hill, near a ravine, I saw something move in the bush. I dismounted and moved forward quietly. I was afraid it might be bandidos who steal cattle, and if they saw me they would kill me. When I came near the place I heard a strange sound. Somebody was crying. My back shivered, just like a dog when he sniffs the devil at night. I thought I was going to see witches, brujas who like to go to those deserted places to dance for the devil, or la Llorona."[23]

"La Llorona," I said aloud. My interest grew. I had been hearing Llorona stories since I was a kid, and I was always ready for one more. La Llorona was that archetypal woman of ancient legends who murdered her children then, repentant and demented, she has spent the rest of eternity searching for them.

---

[16] Volcano near Mexico City; its name in Nahuatl means *smoky mountain.*
[17] Ancient city in central Mexico, once sacred to Quetzalcoatl.
[18] Hernán Cortés (1485–1547), Spanish explorer who led the invasion of Mexico in 1519.
[19] Spanish: "farm" or "country property."
[20] Spanish: "highway."
[21] Spanish: "laborer."
[22] Spanish: "mule."
[23] Spanish: "the mourner" or "the weeper."

"Sí, la Llorona. You know that poor woman used to drink a lot. She played around with men, and when she had babies she got rid of them by throwing them into la barranca.[24] One day she realized what she had done and went crazy. She started crying and pulling her hair and running up and down the side of cliffs of the river looking for her children. It's a very sad story."

A new version, I thought, and yes, a sad story. And what of the men who made love to the woman who became la Llorona, I wondered? Did they ever cry for their children? It doesn't seem fair to have only her suffer, only her crying and doing penance. Perhaps a man should run with her, and in our legends we would call him "El Mero Chingón,"[25] he who screwed up everything. Then maybe the tale of love and passion and the insanity it can bring will be complete. Yes, I think someday I will write that story.

"What did you see?" I asked Justino.

"Something worse than la Llorona," he whispered.

To the south a wind mourned and moved the clouds off Popo's crown. The bald, snow-covered mountain thrust its power into the blue Mexican sky. The light glowed like liquid gold around the god's head. Popo was a god, an ancient god. Somewhere at his feet Justino's story had taken place.

"I moved closer, and when I parted the bushes I saw Don Francisco. He was sitting on a rock, and he was crying. From time to time he looked at the ravine in front of him, the hole seemed to slant into the earth. That pozo[26] is called el Pozo de Mendoza. I had heard stories about it before, but I had never seen it. I looked into the pozo, and you wouldn't believe what I saw."

He waited, so I asked, "What?"

"Money! Huge piles of gold and silver coins! Necklaces and bracelets and crowns of gold, all loaded with all kinds of precious stones! Jewels! Diamonds! All sparkling in the sunlight that entered the hole. More money than I have ever seen! A fortune, my friend, a fortune which is still there, just waiting for two adventurers like us to take it!"

"Us? But what about Don Francisco! It's his land, his fortune."

"Ah," Justino smiled, "that's the strange thing about this fortune. Don Francisco can't touch it, that's why he was crying. You see, I stayed there, and watched him closely. Every time he stood up and started to walk into the pozo the money disappeared. He stretched out his hand to grab the gold, and poof, it was gone! That's why he was crying! He murdered all those people and hid their wealth in the pozo, but now he can't touch it. He is cursed."

"El Pozo de Mendoza," he said aloud. Something began to click in my mind. I smelled a story.

"Who was Mendoza?" I asked.

"He was a very rich man. Don Francisco killed him in a quarrel they had over some cattle. But Mendoza must have put a curse on Don Francisco before he died, because now Don Francisco can't get to the money."

"So Mendoza's ghost haunts old Don Francisco," I nodded.

"Many ghosts haunt him," Justino answered. "He has killed many men."

"And the fortune, the money. . . ."

---

[24] Spanish: "the ravine."
[25] Spanish: "the utter failure."
[26] Spanish: "spring."

He looked at me and his eyes were dark and piercing. "It's still there. Waiting for us!"

"But it disappears as one approaches it, you said so yourself. Perhaps it's only an hallucination."

Justino shook his head. "No, it's real gold and silver, not hallucination money. It disappears for Don Francisco because the curse is on him, but the curse is not on us." He smiled. He knew he had drawn me into his plot. "We didn't steal the money, so it won't disappear for us. And you are not connected with the place. You are innocent. I've thought very carefully about it, and now is the time to go. I can lower you into the pozo with a rope, in a few hours we can bring out the entire fortune. All we need is a car. You can borrow the patrón's car, he is your friend. But he must not know where we're going. We can be there and back in one day, one night." He nodded as if to assure me, then he turned and looked at the sky. "It will not rain today. It will not rain for a week. Now is the time to go."

He winked and returned to watering the grass and flowers of the jardín,[27] a wild Pan among the bougainvillea and the roses, a man possessed by a dream. The gold was not for him, he told me the next day, it was for his women, he would buy them all gifts, bright dresses, and he would take them on vacation to the United States, he would educate his children, send them to the best colleges. I listened and the germ of the story cluttered my thoughts as I sat beneath the orange tree in the mornings. I couldn't write, nothing was coming, but I knew that there were elements for a good story in Justino's tale. In dreams I saw the lonely hacienda to the south. I saw the pathetic, tormented figure of Don Francisco as he cried over the fortune he couldn't touch. I saw the ghosts of the men he had killed, the lonely women who mourned over them and cursed the evil Don Francisco. In one dream I saw a man I took to be B. Traven, a grey-haired distinguished looking gentlemen who looked at me and nodded approvingly. "Yes, there's a story there, follow it, follow it. . . ."

In the meantime, other small and seemingly insignificant details came my way. During a luncheon at the home of my friend, a woman I did not know leaned toward me and asked me if I would like to meet the widow of B. Traven. The woman's hair was tinged orange, her complexion was ashen grey. I didn't know who she was or why she would mention B. Traven to me. How did she know Traven had come to haunt my thoughts? Was she a clue, which would help unravel the mystery? I didn't know, but I nodded. Yes, I would like to meet her. I had heard that Traven's widow, Rosa Elena, lived in Mexico City. But what would I ask her? What did I want to know? Would she know Traven's secret? Somehow he had learned that to keep his magic intact he had to keep away from the public. Like the fortune in the pozo, the magic feel for the story might disappear if unclean hands reached for it. I turned to look at the woman, but she was gone. I wandered to the terrace to finish my beer. Justino sat beneath the orange tree. He yawned. I knew the literary talk bored him. He was eager to be on the way to el Pozo de Mendoza.

I was nervous, too, but I didn't know why. The tension for the story was there, but something was missing. Or perhaps it was just Justino's insistence that I decide whether I was going or not that drove me out of the house in the mornings. Time usually devoted to writing found me in a small cafe in the center of town. From there I could watch the shops open, watch the people cross the zócalo, the main square. I

---

[27] Spanish: "garden."

drank lots of coffee, I smoked a lot, I daydreamed, I wondered about the significance of the pozo, the fortune, Justino, the story I wanted to write about B. Traven. In one of these moods I saw a friend from whom I hadn't heard in years. Suddenly he was there, trekking across the square, dressed like an old rabbi, moss and green algae for a beard, and followed by a troop of very dignified Lacandones, Mayan Indians from Chiapas.

"Victor," I gasped, unsure if he was real or a part of the shadows which the sun created as it flooded the square with its light.

"I have no time to talk," he said as he stopped to munch on my pan dulce and sip my coffee. "I only want you to know, for purposes of your story, that I was in a Lacandonian village last month, and a Hollywood film crew descended from the sky. They came in helicopters. They set up tents near the village, and big-bosomed, bikinied actresses emerged from them, tossed themselves on the cut trees which are the atrocity of the giant American lumber companies, and they cried while the director shot his film. Then they produced a grey-haired old man from one of the tents and took shots of him posing with the Indians. Herr Traven, the director called him."

He finished my coffee, nodded to his friends and they began to walk away.

"B. Traven?" I asked.

He turned. "No, an imposter, an actor. Be careful for imposters. Remember, even Traven used many disguises, many names!"

"Then he's alive and well?" I shouted. People around me turned to stare.

"His spirit is with us," were the last words I heard as they moved across the zócalo, a strange troop of near naked Lacandon Mayans and my friend the Guatemalan Jew, returning to the rain forest, returning to the primal, innocent land.

I slumped in my chair and looked at my empty cup. What did it mean? As their trees fall the Lacandones die. Betrayed as B. Traven was betrayed. Does each one of us also die as the trees fall in the dark depths of the Chiapas jungle? Far to the north, in Aztlán, it is the same where the earth is ripped open to expose and mine the yellow uranium. A few poets sing songs and stand in the way as the giant machines of the corporations rumble over the land and grind everything into dust. New holes are made in the earth, pozos full of curses, pozos with fortunes we cannot touch, should not touch. Oil, coal, uranium, from holes in the earth through which we suck the blood of the earth.

There were other incidents. A telephone call late one night, a voice with a German accent called my name, and when I answered the line went dead. A letter addressed to B. Traven came in the mail. It was dated March 26, 1969. My friend returned it to the post office. Justino grew more and more morose. He was under the orange tree and stared into space, my friend complained about the garden drying up. Justino looked at me and scowled. He did a little work then went back to daydreaming. Without the rains the garden withered. His heart was set on the adventure which lay at el pozo. Finally I said yes, dammit, why not, let's go, neither one of us is getting anything done here, and Justino cheering like a child, ran to prepare for the trip. But when I asked my friend for the weekend loan of the car he reminded me that we were invited to a tertulia, an afternoon reception, at the home of Señora Ana R. Many writers and artists would be there. It was in my honor, so I could meet the literati of Cuernavaca. I had to tell Justino I couldn't go.

Now it was I who grew morose. The story growing within would not let me sleep. I awakened in the night and looked out the window, hoping to see Justino and women bathing in the pool, enjoying themselves. But all was quiet. No radio played. The still night was warm and heavy. From time to time gunshots sounded in the dark, dogs barked, and the presence of a Mexico which never sleeps closed in one me.

Saturday morning dawned with a strange overcast. Perhaps the rains will come, I thought. In the afternoon I reluctantly accompanied my friend to the reception. I had not seen Justino all day, but I saw him at the gate as we drove out. He looked tired, as if he, too, had not slept. He wore the white shirt and baggy pants of a campesino. His straw hat cast a shadow over his eyes. I wondered if he had decided to go to the pozo alone. He didn't speak as we drove through the gate, he only nodded. When I looked back I saw him standing by the gate, looking after the car, and I had a vague, uneasy feeling that I had lost an opportunity.

The afternoon gathering was a pleasant affair, attended by a number of affectionate artists, critics, and writers who enjoyed the refreshing drinks which quenched the thirst.

But my mood drove me away from the crowd. I wandered around the terrace and found a foyer surrounded by green plants, huge fronds and ferns and flowering bougainvillea. I pushed the green aside and entered a quiet, very private alcove. The light was dim, the air was cool, a perfect place for contemplation. At first I thought I was alone, then I saw the man sitting in one of the wicker chairs next to a small, wrought iron table. He was an elderly white-haired gentlemen. His face showed he had lived a full life, yet he was still very distinguished in his manner and posture. His eyes shone brightly.

"Perdón,"[28] I apologized and turned to leave. I did not want to intrude.

"No, no, please," he motioned to the empty chair, "I've been waiting for you." He spoke English with a slight German accent. Or perhaps it was Norwegian, I couldn't tell the difference. "I can't take the literary gossip. I prefer the quiet."

I nodded and sat. He smiled and I felt at ease. I took the cigar he offered and we lit up. He began to talk and I listened. He was a writer also, but I had the good manners not to ask his titles. He talked about the changing Mexico, the change the new oil would bring, the lateness of the rains and how they affected the people and the land, and he talked about how important a woman was in a writer's life. He wanted to know about me, about the Chicanos of Aztlán, about our work. It was the workers, he said, who would change society. The artist learned from the worker. I talked, and sometime during the conversation I told him the name of the friend with whom I was staying. He laughed and wanted to know if Vitorino was still working for him.

"Do you know Justino?" I asked.

"Oh, yes, I know that old guide. I met him many years ago, when I first came to Mexico," he answered. "Justino knows the campesino very well. He and I traveled many places together, he in search of adventure, I in search of stories."

I thought the coincidence strange, so I gathered the courage and asked, "Did he ever tell you the story of the fortune at el Pozo de Mendoza?"

"Tell me?" the old man smiled. "I went there."

"With Justino?"

"Yes, I went with him. What a rogue he was in those days, but a good man. If I remember correctly I even wrote a story based on that adventure. Not a very good story. Never came to anything. But we had a grand time. People like Justino are the

---

[28] Spanish: "excuse me."

writer's source. We met interesting people and saw fabulous places, enough to last me a lifetime. We were supposed to be gone for one day, but we were gone nearly three years. You see, I wasn't interested in the pots of gold he kept saying were just over the next hill, I went because there was a story to write."

"Yes, that's what interested me," I agreed.

"A writer has to follow a story if it leads him to hell itself. That's our curse. Ay, and each one of us knows our own private hell."

I nodded. I felt relieved. I sat back to smoke the cigar and sip from my drink. Somewhere to the west the sun bronzed the evening sky. On a clear afternoon, Popo's crown would glow like fire.

"Yes," the old man continued, "a writer's job is to find and follow people like Justino. They're the source of life. The ones you have to keep away from are the dilettantes like the ones in there." He motioned in the general direction of the noise of the party. "I stay with people like Justino. They may be illiterate, but they understand our descent into the pozo of hell, and they understand us because they're willing to share the adventure with us. You seek fame and notoriety and you're dead as a writer."

I sat upright. I understood now what the pozo meant, why Justino had come into my life to tell me the story. It was clear. I rose quickly and shook the old man's hand. I turned and parted the palm leaves of the alcove. There, across the way, in one of the streets that led out of the maze of the town towards the south, I saw Justino. He was walking in the direction of Popo, and he was followed by women and children, a rag-tail army of adventurers, all happy, all singing. He looked up to where I stood on the terrace, and he smiled as he waved. He paused to light the stub of a cigar. The women turned, and the children turned, and all waved to me. Then they continued their walk, south, towards the foot of the volcano. They were going to the Pozo de Mendoza, to the place where the story originated.

I wanted to run after them, to join them in the glorious light which bathed the Cuernavaca valley and the majestic snow-covered head of Popo. The light was everywhere, a magnetic element which flowed from the clouds. I waved as Justino and his followers disappeared in the light. Then I turned to say something to the old man, but he was gone. I was alone in the alcove. Somewhere in the background I heard the tinkling of glasses and the laughter which came from the party, but that was not for me. I left the terrace and crossed the lawn, found the gate and walked down the street. The sound of Mexico filled the air. I felt light and happy. I wandered aimlessly through the curving, narrow streets, then I quickened my pace because suddenly the story was overflowing and I needed to write. I needed to get to my quiet room and write the story about B. Traven being alive and well in Cuernavaca.

1982

Raymond Carver
b. 1939

"It's possible," says Raymond Carver, "to write about commonplace things and objects using commonplace but precise language, and to endow these things—a chair, a window curtain, a fork, a stone, a woman's earring—with immense, even startling power. It is possible to write a line of seemingly innocuous dialogue and have it send a chill along the reader's spine." Carver's short stories and poems often turn on just such moments of unexpected revelation of beauty or terror. Like many other contemporary writers, Carver doubts the power of fiction to effect social, political, or even personal change ("perhaps it's different in poetry," he says). Instead, he believes, "it just has to be there for the fierce pleasure we take in doing it, and the different kind of pleasure that's taken in reading something that's durable and made to last, as well as beautiful in and of itself. Something that throws off these sparks—a persistent and steady glow, however dim."

Carver was born on May 25, 1939, in Clatskanie, Oregon, and grew up in the small town of Yakima, Washington, where his father worked as a laborer in a local sawmill. In 1957, at age eighteen, Carver married, but by working evenings he still managed to attend Chico State College, where he studied with the novelist John Gardner. After graduating from Chico State in 1963, he spent a year at the writers' workshop of the University of Iowa and then returned to California, first taking a job as a night janitor at a Sacramento hospital and then as an editor with a textbook publisher in Palo Alto. Carver has also lectured in creative writing at the University of California at Santa Cruz and at Berkeley, the University of Texas, the University of Iowa, and Syracuse University.

Deeply influenced, like Sherwood Anderson, by his father's storytelling ability, Carver tried writing stories as a boy. As an undergraduate, he began publishing stories and poems. In 1967 one of his stories, "Will You Please Be Quiet, Please?" was selected for the *Best American Short Stories* anthology; later, in 1976, it became the title story of his first collection of short fiction. Two collections of stories followed—*What We Talk About When We Talk About Love* (1981) and *Cathedral* (1983)—both of which received high critical acclaim. Carver is also the author of several volumes of poetry, including *Near Klamath* (1968), *Winter Insomnia* (1970), and *At Night the Salmon Move* (1976), and of *Fires: Essays, Poems, Stories* (1983).

Widely anthologized, Carver's stories have appeared in numerous literary magazines and have won many awards. Nearly all his stories deal with people living on the fringe of subsistence and articulation. His style is often spare to the point of asceticism, and it characteristically retains a tense, close touch with the diction and rhythm of ordinary speech. "One of Mr. Carver's great gifts," as the critic Michael Wood has noted, "is to make audible the eloquence of the apparently inarticulate. It's not that he lends speech to his characters or talks on their behalf. He hears what they are saying when the words run out."

Text:
Cathedral, 1983.

Cathedral

This blind man, an old friend of my wife's, he was on his way to spend the night. His wife had died. So he was visiting the dead wife's relatives in Connecticut. He called my wife from his in-laws'. Arrangements were made. He would come by train, a five-hour trip, and my wife would meet him at the station. She hadn't seen him since she worked for him one summer in Seattle ten years ago. But she and the blind man had kept in touch. They made tapes and mailed them back and forth. I wasn't enthusiastic about his visit. He was no one I knew. And his being blind bothered me. My idea of blindness came from the movies. In the movies, the blind moved slowly and never laughed. Sometimes they were led by seeing-eye dogs. A blind man in my house was not something I looked forward to.

That summer in Seattle she had needed a job. She didn't have any money. The man she was going to marry at the end of the summer was in officers' training school. He didn't have any money, either. But she was in love with the guy, and he was in love with her, etc. She'd seen something in the paper: HELP WANTED—*Reading to Blind Man,* and a telephone number. She phoned and went over, was hired on the spot. She'd worked with this blind man all summer. She read stuff to him, case studies, reports, that sort of thing. She helped him organize his little office in the county social-service department. They'd become good friends, my wife and the blind man. How do I know these things? She told me. And she told me something else. On her last day in the office, the blind man asked if he could touch her face. She agreed to this. She told me he touched his fingers to every part of her face, her nose—even her neck! She never forgot it. She even tried to write a poem about it. She was always trying to write a poem. She wrote a poem or two every year, usually after something really important had happened to her.

When we first started going out together, she showed me the poem. In the poem, she recalled his fingers and the way they had moved around over her face. In the poem, she talked about what she had felt at the time, about what went through her mind when the blind man touched her nose and lips. I can remember I didn't think much of the poem. Of course, I didn't tell her that. Maybe I just don't understand poetry. I admit it's not the first thing I reach for when I pick up something to read.

Anyway, this man who'd first enjoyed her favors, the officer-to-be, he'd been her childhood sweetheart. So okay. I'm saying that at the end of the summer she let the blind man run his hands over her face, said goodbye to him, married her childhood etc., who was now a commissioned officer, and she moved away from Seattle. But they'd kept in touch, she and the blind man. She made the first contact after a year or so. She called him up one night from an Air Force base in Alabama. She wanted to talk. They talked. He asked her to send him a tape and tell him about her life. She did this. She sent the tape. On the tape, she told the blind man about her husband and about their life together in the military. She told the blind man she loved her husband but she didn't like it where they lived and she didn't like it that he was a part of the military-industrial thing. She told the blind man she'd written a poem and he was in it. She told him that she was writing a poem about what it was like to be an Air Force officer's wife. The poem wasn't finished yet. She was still writing it. The blind man made a tape. He sent her the tape. She made a tape. This went on for years. My wife's officer was posted to one base and then another. She sent tapes from Moody AFB,[1] McGuire, McConnell, and finally Travis, near Sacramento, where one night she got to feeling lonely and cut off from people she kept losing in that moving-around life. She got to feeling she couldn't go it another step. She went in and swallowed all the pills and capsules in the medicine chest and washed them down with a bottle of gin. Then she got into a hot bath and passed out.

But instead of dying, she got sick. She threw up. Her officer—why should he have a name? he was the childhood sweetheart, and what more does he want?—came home from somewhere, found her, and called the ambulance. In time, she put it all on a tape and sent the tape to the blind man. Over the years, she put all kinds of stuff on tapes and sent the tapes off lickety-split. Next to writing a poem every year, I think it was her chief means of recreation. On one tape, she told the blind man she'd decided to live away from her officer for a time. On another tape, she told him about her divorce. She and I began going out, and of course she told her blind man about it. She told him everything, or so it seemed to me. Once she asked me if I'd like to hear the latest tape from the blind man. This was a year ago. I was on the tape, she said. So I said okay, I'd listen to it. I got us drinks and we settled down in the living room. We made ready to listen. First she inserted the tape into the player and adjusted a couple of dials. Then she pushed a lever. The tape squeaked and someone began to talk in this loud voice. She lowered the volume. After a few minutes of harmless chitchat, I heard my own name in the mouth of this stranger, this blind man I didn't even know! And then this: "From all you've said about him, I can only conclude—" But we were interrupted, a knock at the door, something, and we didn't ever get back to the tape. Maybe it was just as well. I'd heard all I wanted to.

Now this same blind man was coming to sleep in my house.

"Maybe I could take him bowling," I said to my wife. She was at the draining board doing scalloped potatoes. She put down the knife she was using and turned around.

"If you love me," she said, "you can do this for me. If you don't love me, okay. But if you had a friend, any friend, and the friend came to visit, I'd make him feel comfortable." She wiped her hands with the dish towel.

"I don't have any blind friends," I said.

"You don't have *any* friends," she said. "Period. Besides," she said, "goddamn it, his wife's just died! Don't you understand that? The man's lost his wife!"

I didn't answer. She'd told me a little about the blind man's wife. Her name was Beulah. Beulah! That's a name for a colored woman.

"Was his wife a Negro?" I asked.

"Are you crazy?" my wife said. "Have you just flipped or something?" She picked up a potato. I saw it hit the floor, then roll under the stove. "What's wrong with you?" she said. "Are you drunk?"

"I'm just asking," I said.

Right then my wife filled me in with more detail than I cared to know. I made a drink and sat at the kitchen table to listen. Pieces of the story began to fall into place.

Beulah had gone to work for the blind man the summer after my wife had stopped working for him. Pretty soon Beulah and the blind man had themselves a church wedding. It was a little wedding—who'd want to go to such a wedding in the first place?—just the two of them, plus the minister and the minister's wife. But it was a church wedding just the same. It was what Beulah had wanted, he'd said. But even then Beulah must have been carrying the cancer in her glands. After they had been inseparable for eight years—my wife's word, *inseparable*— Beulah's health went into a rapid decline. She died in a Seattle hospital room, the blind man sitting beside the bed and holding on to her hand. They'd married, lived and worked together, slept together—had sex, sure—and then the blind man had to bury her. All this without his having ever seen what the goddamned woman looked like. It was beyond my understanding. Hearing this, I felt sorry for the blind man for a little bit. And then I found myself thinking what a pitiful life this woman must have led. Imagine a woman who could never see herself as she was seen in the eyes of her loved one. A woman who could go on day after day and never receive the smallest compliment from her beloved. A woman whose husband could never read the expression on her face, be it misery or something better. Someone who could wear makeup or not— what difference to him? She could, if she wanted, wear green eye-shadow around one eye, a straight pin in her nostril, yellow slacks and purple shoes, no matter. And then to slip off into death, the blind man's hand on her hand, his blind eyes streaming tears —I'm imagining now—her last thought maybe this: that he never even knew what she looked like, and she on an express to the grave. Robert was left with a small insurance policy and half of a twenty-peso Mexican coin. The other half of the coin went into the box with her. Pathetic.

So when the time rolled around, my wife went to the depot to pick him up. With nothing to do but wait—sure, I blamed him for that—I was having a drink and watching the TV when I heard the car pull into the drive. I got up from the sofa with my drink and went to the window to have a look.

I saw my wife laughing as she parked the car. I saw her get out of the car and shut the door. She was still wearing a smile. Just amazing. She went around to the other side of the car to where the blind man was already starting to get out. This blind man, feature this, he was wearing a full beard! A beard on a blind man! Too much, I say. The blind man reached into the back seat and dragged out a suitcase. My wife took his arm, shut the car door, and, talking all the way, moved him down the drive and then up the steps to the front porch. I turned off the TV. I finished my drink, rinsed the glass, dried my hands. Then I went to the door.

My wife said, "I want you to meet Robert. Robert, this is my husband. I've told you all about him." She was beaming. She had this blind man by his coat sleeve.

The blind man let go of his suitcase and up came his hand.

I took it. He squeezed hard, held my hand, and then he let it go.

"I feel like we've already met," he boomed.

"Likewise," I said. I didn't know what else to say. Then I said, "Welcome. I've heard a lot about you." We began to move then, a little group, from the porch into the living room, my wife guiding him by the arm. The blind man was carrying his suitcase in his other hand. My wife said things like, "To your left here, Robert. That's right. Now watch it, there's a chair. That's it. Sit down right here. This is the sofa. We just bought this sofa two weeks ago."

I started to say something about the old sofa. I'd liked that old sofa. But I didn't say anything. Then I wanted to say something else, small-talk, about the scenic ride along the Hudson. How going *to* New York, you should sit on the right-hand side of the train, and coming *from* New York, the left-hand side.

"Did you have a good train ride?" I said. "Which side of the train did you sit on, by the way?"

"What a question, which side!" my wife said. "What's it matter which side?" she said.

"I just asked," I said.

"Right side," the blind man said. "I hadn't been on a train in nearly forty years. Not since I was a kid. With my folks. That's been a long time. I'd nearly forgotten the sensation. I have winter in my beard now," he said. "So I've been told, anyway. Do I look distinguished, my dear?" the blind man said to my wife.

"You look distinguished, Robert," she said. "Robert," she said. "Robert, it's just so good to see you."

My wife finally took her eyes off the blind man and looked at me. I had the feeling she didn't like what she saw. I shrugged.

I've never met, or personally known, anyone who was blind. This blind man was late forties, a heavy-set, balding man with stooped shoulders, as if he carried a great weight there. He wore brown slacks, brown shoes, a light-brown shirt, a tie, a sports coat. Spiffy. He also had this full beard. But he didn't use a cane and he didn't wear dark glasses. I'd always thought dark glasses were a must for the blind. Fact was, I wished he had a pair. At first glance, his eyes looked like anyone else's eyes. But if you looked close, there was something different about them. Too much white in the iris, for one thing, and the pupils seemed to move around in the sockets without his knowing it or being able to stop it. Creepy. As I stared at his face, I saw the left pupil turn in toward his nose while the other made an effort to keep in one place. But it was only an effort, for that eye was on the roam without his knowing it or wanting it to be.

I said, "Let me get you a drink. What's your pleasure? We have a little of everything. It's one of our pastimes."

"Bub, I'm a Scotch man myself," he said fast enough in this big voice.

"Right," I said. Bub! "Sure you are. I knew it."

He let his fingers touch his suitcase, which was sitting alongside the sofa. He was taking his bearings. I didn't blame him for that.

"I'll move that up to your room," my wife said.

"No, that's fine," the blind man said loudly. "It can go up when I go up."

"A little water with the Scotch?" I said.

"Very little," he said.

"I knew it," I said.

He said, "Just a tad. The Irish actor, Barry Fitzgerald? I'm like that fellow. When I drink water, Fitzgerald said, I drink water. When I drink whiskey, I drink whiskey." My wife laughed. The blind man brought his hand up under his beard. He lifted his beard slowly and let it drop.

I did the drinks, three big glasses of Scotch with a splash of water in each. Then we made ourselves comfortable and talked about Robert's travels. First the long flight from the West Coast to Connecticut, we covered that. Then from Connecticut up here by train. We had another drink concerning that leg of the trip.

I remembered having read somewhere that the blind didn't smoke because, as speculation had it, they couldn't see the smoke they exhaled. I thought I knew that much and that much only about blind people. But this blind man smoked his cigarette down to the nubbin and then lit another one. This blind man filled his ashtray and my wife emptied it.

When we sat down at the table for dinner, we had another drink. My wife heaped Robert's plate with cube steak, scalloped potatoes, green beans. I buttered him up two slices of bread. I said, "Here's bread and butter for you." I swallowed some of my drink. "Now let us pray," I said, and the blind man lowered his head. My wife looked at me, her mouth agape. "Pray the phone won't ring and the food doesn't get cold," I said.

We dug in. We ate everything there was to eat on the table. We ate like there was no tomorrow. We didn't talk. We ate. We scarfed. We grazed that table. We were into serious eating. The blind man had right away located his foods, he knew just where everything was on his plate. I watched with admiration as he used his knife and fork on the meat. He'd cut two pieces of meat, fork the meat into his mouth, and then go all out for the scalloped potatoes, the beans next, and then he'd tear off a hunk of buttered bread and eat that. He'd follow this up with a big drink of milk. It didn't seem to bother him to use his fingers once in a while, either.

We finished everything, including half a strawberry pie. For a few moments, we sat as if stunned. Sweat beaded on our faces. Finally, we got up from the table and left the dirty plates. We didn't look back. We took ourselves into the living room and sank into our places again. Robert and my wife sat on the sofa. I took the big chair. We had us two or three more drinks while they talked about the major things that had come to pass for them in the past ten years. For the most part, I just listened. Now and then I joined in. I didn't want him to think I'd left the room, and I didn't want her to think I was feeling left out. They talked of things that had happened to them—to them!—these past ten years. I waited in vain to hear my name on my wife's sweet lips: "And then my dear husband came into my life"—something like that. But I heard nothing of the sort. More talk of Robert. Robert had done a little of everything, it seemed, a regular blind jack-of-all-trades. But most recently he and his wife had had an Amway distributorship, from which, I gathered, they'd earned their living, such as it was. The blind man was also a ham radio operator. He talked in his loud voice about conversations he'd had with fellow operators in Guam, in the Philippines, in Alaska, and even in Tahiti. He said he'd have a lot of friends there if he ever wanted to go visit those places. From time to time, he'd turn his blind face toward me, put his hand under his beard, ask me something. How long had I been in my present position? (Three years.) Did I like my work? (I didn't.) Was I going to stay with it? (What were the options?) Finally, when I thought he was beginning to run down, I got up and turned on the TV.

My wife looked at me with irritation. She was heading toward a boil. Then she looked at the blind man and said, "Robert, do you have a TV?"

The blind man said, "My dear, I have two TVs. I have a color set and a black-and-white thing, an old relic. It's funny, but if I turn the TV on, and I'm always turning it on, I turn on the color set. It's funny, don't you think?"

I didn't know what to say to that. I had absolutely nothing to say to that. No opinion. So I watched the news program and tried to listen to what the announcer was saying.

"This is a color TV," the blind man said. "Don't ask me how, but I can tell."

"We traded up a while ago," I said.

The blind man had another taste of his drink. He lifted his beard, sniffed it, and let it fall. He leaned forward on the sofa. He positioned his ashtray on the coffee table, then put the lighter to his cigarette. He leaned back on the sofa and crossed his legs at the ankles.

My wife covered her mouth, and then she yawned. She stretched. She said, "I think I'll go upstairs and put on my robe. I think I'll change into something else. Robert, you make yourself comfortable," she said.

"I'm comfortable," the blind man said.

"I want you to feel comfortable in this house," she said.

"I am comfortable," the blind man said.

After she'd left the room, he and I listened to the weather report and then to the sports roundup. By that time, she'd been gone so long I didn't know if she was going to come back. I thought she might have gone to bed. I wished she'd come back downstairs. I didn't want to be left alone with a blind man. I asked him if he wanted another drink, and he said sure. Then I asked if he wanted to smoke some dope with me. I said I'd just rolled a number. I hadn't, but I planned to do so in about two shakes.

"I'll try some with you," he said.

"Damn right," I said. "That's the stuff."

I got our drinks and sat down on the sofa with him. Then I rolled us two fat numbers. I lit one and passed it. I brought it to his fingers. He took it and inhaled.

"Hold it as long as you can," I said. I could tell he didn't know the first thing.

My wife came back downstairs wearing her pink robe and her pink slippers.

"What do I smell?" she said.

"We thought we'd have us some cannabis," I said.

My wife gave me a savage look. Then she looked at the blind man and said, "Robert, I didn't know you smoked."

He said, "I do now, my dear. There's a first time for everything. But I don't feel anything yet."

"This stuff is pretty mellow," I said. "This stuff is mild. It's dope you can reason with," I said. "It doesn't mess you up."

"Not much it doesn't, bub," he said, and laughed.

My wife sat on the sofa between the blind man and me. I passed her the number. She took it and toked and then passed it back to me. "Which way is this going?" she said. Then she said, "I shouldn't be smoking this. I can hardly keep my eyes open as it is. That dinner did me in. I shouldn't have eaten so much."

"It was the strawberry pie," the blind man said. "That's what did it," he said, and he laughed his big laugh. Then he shook his head.

"There's more strawberry pie," I said.

"Do you want some more, Robert?" my wife said.

"Maybe in a little while," he said.

We gave our attention to the TV. My wife yawned again. She said, "Your bed is made up when you feel like going to bed, Robert. I know you must have had a long day. When you're ready to go to bed, say so." She pulled his arm. "Robert?"

He came to and said, "I've had a real nice time. This beats tapes, doesn't it?"

I said, "Coming at you," and I put the number between his fingers. He inhaled, held the smoke, and then let it go. It was like he'd been doing it since he was nine years old.

"Thanks, bub," he said. "But I think this is all for me. I think I'm beginning to feel it," he said. He held the burning roach out for my wife.

"Same here," she said. "Ditto. Me, too." She took the roach and passed it to me. "I may just sit here for a while between you two guys with my eyes closed. But don't let me bother you, okay? Either one of you. If it bothers you, say so. Otherwise, I may just sit here with my eyes closed until you're ready to go to bed," she said. "Your bed's made up, Robert, when you're ready. It's right next to our room at the top of the stairs. We'll show you up when you're ready. You wake me up now, you guys, if I fall asleep." She said that and then she closed her eyes and went to sleep.

The news program ended. I got up and changed the channel. I sat back down on the sofa. I wished my wife hadn't pooped out. Her head lay across the back of the sofa, her mouth open. She'd turned so that her robe had slipped away from her legs, exposing a juicy thigh. I reached to draw her robe back over her, and it was then that I glanced at the blind man. What the hell! I flipped the robe open again.

"You say when you want some strawberry pie," I said.

"I will," he said.

I said, "Are you tired? Do you want me to take you up to your bed? Are you ready to hit the hay?"

"Not yet," he said. "No, I'll stay up with you, bub. If that's all right. I'll stay up until you're ready to turn in. We haven't had a chance to talk. Know what I mean? I feel like me and her monopolized the evening." He lifted his beard and he let it fall. He picked up his cigarettes and his lighter.

"That's all right," I said. Then I said, "I'm glad for the company."

And I guess I was. Every night I smoked dope and stayed up as long as I could before I fell asleep. My wife and I hardly ever went to bed at the same time. When I did go to sleep, I had these dreams. Sometimes I'd wake up from one of them, my heart going crazy.

Something about the church and the Middle Ages was on the TV. Not your run-of-the-mill TV fare. I wanted to watch something else. I turned to the other channels. But there was nothing on them, either. So I turned back to the first channel and apologized.

"Bub, it's all right," the blind man said. "It's fine with me. Whatever you want to watch is okay. I'm always learning something. Learning never ends. It won't hurt me to learn something tonight. I got ears," he said.

We didn't say anything for a time. He was leaning forward with his head turned at me, his right ear aimed in the direction of the set. Very disconcerting. Now and then his eyelids drooped and then they snapped open again. Now and then he put his fingers into his beard and tugged, like he was thinking about something he was hearing on the television.

On the screen, a group of men wearing cowls was being set upon and tormented by men dressed in skeleton costumes and men dressed as devils. The men dressed as devils wore devil masks, horns, and long tails. This pageant was part of a procession. The Englishman who was narrating the thing said it took place in Spain once a year. I tried to explain to the blind man what was happening.

"Skeletons," he said. "I know about skeletons," he said, and he nodded.

The TV showed this one cathedral. Then there was a long, slow look at another one. Finally, the picture switched to the famous one in Paris, with its flying buttresses and its spires reaching up to the clouds. The camera pulled away to show the whole of the cathedral rising above the skyline.

There were times when the Englishman who was telling the thing would shut up, would simply let the camera move around over the cathedrals. Or else the camera would tour the countryside, men in fields walking behind oxen. I waited as long as I could. Then I felt I had to say something. I said, "They're showing the outside of this cathedral now. Gargoyles. Little statues carved to look like monsters. Now I guess they're in Italy. Yeah, they're in Italy. There's paintings on the walls of this one church."

"Are those fresco paintings, bub?" he asked, and he sipped from his drink.

I reached for my glass. But it was empty. I tried to remember what I could remember. "You're asking me are those frescoes?" I said. "That's a good question. I don't know."

The camera moved to a cathedral outside Lisbon. The differences in the Portuguese cathedral compared with the French and Italian were not that great. But they were there. Mostly the interior stuff. Then something occurred to me, and I said, "Something has occurred to me. Do you have any idea what a cathedral is? What they look like, that is? Do you follow me? If somebody says cathedral to you, do you have any notion what they're talking about? Do you know the difference between that and a Baptist church, say?"

He let the smoke dribble from his mouth. "I know they took hundreds of workers fifty or a hundred years to build," he said. "I just heard the man say that, of course. I know generations of the same families worked on a cathedral. I heard him say that, too. The men who began their life's work on them, they never lived to see the completion of their work. In that wise, bub, they're no different from the rest of us, right?" He laughed. Then his eyelids drooped again. His head nodded. He seemed to be snoozing. Maybe he was imagining himself in Portugal. The TV was showing another cathedral now. This one was in Germany. The Englishman's voice droned on. "Cathedrals," the blind man said. He sat up and rolled his head back and forth. "If you want the truth, bub, that's about all I know. What I just said. What I heard him say. But maybe you could describe one to me? I wish you'd do it. I'd like that. If you want to know, I really don't have a good idea."

I stared hard at the shot of the cathedral on the TV. How could I even begin to describe it? But say my life depended on it. Say my life was being threatened by an insane guy who said I had to do it or else.

I stared some more at the cathedral before the picture flipped off into the countryside. There was no use. I turned to the blind man and said, "To begin with, they're very tall." I was looking around the room for clues. "They reach way up. Up and up. Toward the sky. They're so big, some of them, they have to have these supports. To help hold them up, so to speak. These supports are called buttresses. They remind me of viaducts, for some reason. But maybe you don't know viaducts, either? Sometimes the cathedrals have devils and such carved into the front. Sometimes lords and ladies. Don't ask me why this is," I said.

He was nodding. The whole upper part of his body seemed to be moving back and forth.

"I'm not doing so good, am I?" I said.

He stopped nodding and leaned forward on the edge of the sofa. As he listened to me, he was running his fingers through his beard. I wasn't getting through to him, I could see that. But he waited for me to go on just the same. He nodded, like he was trying to encourage me. I tried to think what else to say. "They're really big," I said. "They're massive. They're built of stone. Marble, too, sometimes. In those olden days, when they built cathedrals, men wanted to be close to God. In those olden days, God was an important part of everyone's life. You could tell this from their cathedral-building. I'm sorry," I said, "but it looks like that's the best I can do for you. I'm just no good at it."

"That's all right, bub," the blind man said. "Hey, listen. I hope you don't mind my asking you. Can I ask you something? Let me ask you a simple question, yes or no. I'm just curious and there's no offense. You're my host. But let me ask if you are in any way religious? You don't mind my asking?"

I shook my head. He couldn't see that, though. A wink is the same as a nod to a blind man. "I guess I don't believe in it. In anything. Sometimes it's hard. You know what I'm saying?"

"Sure, I do," he said.

"Right," I said.

The Englishman was still holding forth. My wife sighed in her sleep. She drew a long breath and went on with her sleeping.

"You'll have to forgive me," I said. "But I can't tell you what a cathedral looks like. It just isn't in me to do it. I can't do any more than I've done."

The blind man sat very still, his head down, as he listened to me.

I said, "The truth is, cathedrals don't mean anything special to me. Nothing. Cathedrals. They're something to look at on late-night TV. That's all they are."

It was then that the blind man cleared his throat. He brought something up. He took a handkerchief from his back pocket. Then he said, "I get it, bub. It's okay. It happens. Don't worry about it," he said. "Hey, listen to me. Will you do me a favor? I got an idea. Why don't you find us some heavy paper? And a pen. We'll do something. We'll draw one together. Get us a pen and some heavy paper. Go on, bub, get the stuff," he said.

So I went upstairs. My legs felt like they didn't have any strength in them. They felt like they did after I'd done some running. In my wife's room, I looked around. I found some ballpoints in a little basket on her table. And then I tried to think where to look for the kind of paper he was talking about.

Downstairs, in the kitchen, I found a shopping bag with onion skins in the bottom of the bag. I emptied the bag and shook it. I brought it into the living room and sat down with it near his legs. I moved some things, smoothed the wrinkles from the bag, spread it out on the coffee table.

The blind man got down from the sofa and sat next to me on the carpet.

He ran his fingers over the paper. He went up and down the sides of the paper. The edges, even the edges. He fingered the corners.

"All right," he said. "All right, let's do her."

He found my hand, the hand with the pen. He closed his hand over my hand. "Go ahead, bub, draw," he said. "Draw. You'll see. I'll follow along with you. It'll be okay. Just begin now like I'm telling you. You'll see. Draw," the blind man said.

So I began. First I drew a box that looked like a house. It could have been the house I lived in. Then I put a roof on it. At either end of the roof, I drew spires. Crazy.

"Swell," he said. "Terrific. You're doing fine," he said. "Never thought anything like this could happen in your lifetime, did you, bub? Well, it's a strange life, we all know that. Go on now. Keep it up."

I put in windows with arches. I drew flying buttresses. I hung great doors. I couldn't stop. The TV station went off the air. I put down the pen and closed and opened my fingers. The blind man felt around over the paper. He moved the tips of his fingers over the paper, all over what I had drawn, and he nodded.

"Doing fine," the blind man said.

I took up the pen again, and he found my hand. I kept at it. I'm no artist. But I kept drawing just the same.

My wife opened up her eyes and gazed at us. She sat up on the sofa, her robe hanging open. She said, "What are you doing? Tell me, I want to know."

I didn't answer her.

The blind man said, "We're drawing a cathedral. Me and him are working on it. Press hard," he said to me. "That's right. That's good," he said. "Sure. You got it, bub. I can tell. You didn't think you could. But you can, can't you? You're cooking with gas now. You know what I'm saying? We're going to really have us something here in a minute. How's the old arm?" he said. "Put some people in there now. What's a cathedral without people?"

My wife said, "What's going on? Robert, what are you doing? What's going on?"

"It's all right," he said to her. "Close your eyes now," the blind man said to me. I did it. I closed them just like he said.

"Are they closed?" he said. "Don't fudge."

"They're closed," I said.

"Keep them that way," he said. He said, "Don't stop now. Draw."

So we kept on with it. His fingers rode my fingers as my hand went over the paper. It was like nothing else in my life up to now.

Then he said, "I think that's it. I think you got it," he said. "Take a look. What do you think?"

But I had my eyes closed. I thought I'd keep them that way for a little longer. I thought it was something I ought to do.

"Well?" he said. "Are you looking?"

My eyes were still closed. I was in my house. I knew that. But I didn't feel like I was inside anything.

"It's really something," I said.

Bobbie Ann Mason
b. 1940

Of earlier southern writers, such as William Faulkner and Allen Tate, Bobbie Ann Mason says simply that they possessed "a romantic vision." Her own work she describes as "southern Gothic going to the supermarket." The landscape of her fiction, usually rural Kentucky fast being overtaken by urban culture, is dotted with supermarkets, discount stores, video arcades, and vocational training centers. Her characters watch Phil Donahue and Johnny Carson on television; they take up weight training, make zucchini bread, and buy *The Sixties Songbook.* Or they drive trucks, eat "poke salet," and listen to Hank Williams. Caught between the country and the city, they constantly feel, she says, a "tension between their rural traditional past and the modern world." Like the woman who buys *The Sixties Songbook* ten years too late, they often find themselves struggling not to get any further behind.

Mason attributes her own and other contemporary writers' use of popular culture to cultural changes that come so rapidly that "it seems necessary to get a fix on a certain moment—or it may be different by tomorrow." Through a strange blend of colloquialisms and more formal diction, she reflects in the language of her fiction the same cultural gap that she renders in its action.

Reared on a dairy farm in western Kentucky, Mason was encouraged by her parents, neither of whom had finished high school, to continue her education. Unlike most of her friends, she went to high school in the "city"—Mayfield, Kentucky, population 10,725. She is, she now feels, "haunted by the kids I went to grade school with." After high school she went to the University of Kentucky, where she majored in journalism, and then to New York, where she experienced a culture shock so great that it temporarily turned her from a writing career to graduate school.

After receiving an M.A. from the State University of New York at Binghamton and a Ph.D. from the University of Connecticut, Mason became a professor at Mansfield State College (1972–1979). In 1974 she published a study of Vladimir Nabokov's novel *Ada* called *Nabokov's Garden: A Nature Guide to "Ada,"* and in 1975 she published an analysis of fiction especially designed for girls called *The Girl Sleuth: A Feminist Guide to the Bobbsey Twins, Nancy Drew, and Their Sisters.* But it was the writing of fiction that more and more engaged her. In 1980 she published her first story, "Offerings," in *The New Yorker.* Two years later a collection of her stories, *Shiloh and Other Stories,* in which "Detroit Skyline, 1949" appeared, won the Ernest Hemingway Award for the year's most distinguished first work of fiction and was nominated for the National Book Critics Circle Award. Having received a grant from the National Endowment for the Arts, Mason began work on a novel, *In Country* (1985).

Out of anonymity, Mason has emerged, according to the writer Anne Tyler and others, as a recognized master of the short story, a sudden transformation that Mason says has left her "absolutely *stunned.*" In "Nancy Culpepper," her own favorite among her stories, the protagonist's mother says, "I guess you think we're just ignorant. The way we talk." "No," Nancy says, "I don't." Like Nancy Culpepper, Mason clearly respects the people she remembers and writes about, perhaps in part because she shares a feeling of kinship with them. "I write," she says, "about people in trapped circumstances. . . . I identify with people who are ambivalent about their situation. And I guess, in my stories, I'm in a way imagining myself as I would have felt if I had not gotten away and gotten a different perspective on things—if, for example, I had gotten pregnant in high school and had to marry a truck driver as the woman did in my story 'Shiloh.' " In her best fiction, Mason offers us not only different perspectives but also new ways of imagining ourselves.

Text:
Atlantic Monthly, June 1981.

Detroit Skyline, 1949

When I was nine, my mother took me on a long journey up North, because she wanted me to have a chance to see the tall buildings of Detroit. We lived on a farm in western Kentucky, not far from the U.S. highway that took so many Southerners northward to work in the auto industry just after World War II. We went to visit Aunt Mozelle, Mama's sister, and Uncle Boone Cashon, who had headed north soon after Boone's discharge from the service. They lived in a suburb of Detroit, and my mother had visited them once before. She couldn't get the skyscrapers she had seen out of her mind.

The Brooks bus took all day and all night to get there. On our trip, my mother threw up and a black baby cried all the way. I couldn't sleep for thinking about Detroit. Mama had tried in vain to show me how high the buildings were, pointing at the straight horizon beyond the cornfields. I had the impression that they towered halfway to the moon.

"Don't let the Polacks get you," my father had warned when we left. He had to stay home to milk the cows. My two-year-old brother, Johnny, stayed behind with him.

My aunt and uncle met us in a taxi at the bus station, and before I got a good look at them, they had engulfed me in their arms.

"I wouldn't have knowed you, Peggy Jo," my uncle said. "You was just a little squirt the last time I saw you."

"Don't this beat all?" said Aunt Mozelle. "Boone here could have built us a car by now—and us coming in a taxi."

"We've still got that old plug, but it gets us to town," said Mama.

"How could I build a car?" said Uncle Boone. "All I know is bumpers."

"That's what he does," my aunt said to me. "He puts on bumpers."

"We'll get a car someday soon," Uncle Boone said to his wife.

My uncle was a thin, delicate man with a receding hairline. His speckled skin made me think of the fragile shells of sparrow eggs. My aunt, on the other hand, was stout and tanned, with thick, dark hair draped like wings over her ears. I gazed at my aunt and uncle, trying to match them with the photograph my mother had shown me.

"Peggy's all worked up over seeing the tall buildings," said Mama as we climbed into the taxi. "The cat's got her tongue."

"It has *not!*"

"I'm afraid we've got bad news," said Aunt Mozelle. "The city buses is on strike and there's no way to get into Detroit."

"Don't say it!" cried Mama. "After we come all this way."

"It's trouble with the unions," said Boone. "But they might start up before y'all go back." He patted my knee and said, "Don't worry, littlun."

"The unions is full of reds," Aunt Mozelle whispered to my mother.

"Would it be safe to go?" Mama asked.

"We needn't worry," said Aunt Mozelle.

From the window of the squat yellow taxi, driven by a froglike man who grunted, I scrutinized the strange and vast neighborhoods we were passing through. I had never seen so many houses, all laid out in neat rows. The houses were new, and their pastel colors seemed peaceful and alluring. The skyscrapers were still as remote to me as the castles in fairy tales, but these houses were real, and they were nestled next to each other in a thrilling intimacy. I knew at once where I wanted to live when I grew up—in a place like this, with neighbors.

My relatives' house, on a treeless new street, had venetian blinds and glossy hardwood floors. The living room carpet had giant pink roses that made me think you could play hopscotch on them. The guest room had knotty-pine paneling and a sweet-smelling cedar closet. Aunt Mozelle had put His and Her towels in our room. They had dogs on them and were pleasurably soft. At home, all of our washrags came out of detergent boxes, and our towels were faded and thin. The house was grand. And I had never seen my mother sparkling so. When she saw the kitchen, she whirled around happily, like a young girl, forgetting her dizziness on the bus. Aunt Mozelle had a toaster, a Mixmaster, an electric stove, and a large electric clock shaped like a rooster. On the wall, copper-bottomed pans gleamed in a row like golden-eyed cats lined up on a fence.

"Ain't it the berries?" my mother said to me. "Didn't I tell you?"

"Sometimes I have to pinch myself," said my aunt.

Just then, the front door slammed and a tall girl with a ponytail bounded into the house, saying "Hey!" in an offhand manner.

"Corn!" I said timidly, which seemed to perplex her, for she stared at me as though I were some odd sort of pet allowed into the house. This was my cousin Betsy Lou, in bluejeans rolled up halfway to her knees.

"Our kinfolks is here," Aunt Mozelle announced.

"Law, you've growed into a beanpole," said Mama to Betsy Lou.

"Welcome to our fair city, and I hope you don't get polio," Betsy Lou said to me.

"Watch what you're saying!" cried her mother. "You'll scare Peggy Jo."

"I imagine it'll be worse this summer than last," said Mama, looking worried.

"If we're stuck here without a car, you won't be any place to catch polio," Aunt Mozelle said, smiling at me.

"Polio spreads at swimming pools," Betsy Lou said.

"Then I'm not going to any swimming pool," I announced flatly.

Aunt Mozelle fussed around in her splendid kitchen, making dinner. I sat at the table, listening to Mama and her sister talk, in a gentle, flowing way, exchanging news, each stopping now and then to smile at the other in disbelief, or to look at me with pride. I couldn't take my eyes off my aunt, because she looked so much like my mother. She was older and heavier, but they had the same wide smile, the same unaffected laughter. They had similar sharp tips on their upper lips, which they filled in with bright red lipstick.

Mama said, "Boone sure is lucky. He's still young and ain't crippled and has a good job."

"Knock on wood," said Aunt Mozelle, rapping the door facing.

They had arranged for me to have a playmate, a girl my age who lived in the neighborhood. At home, in the summertime, I did not play with anyone, for the girls I knew at school lived too far away. Suddenly I found myself watching a chubby girl in a lilac piqué playsuit zoom up and down the sidewalk on roller skates.

"Come on," she said. "It's not hard."

"I'm coming." Betsy Lou had let me have her old skates, but I had trouble fastening them on my Weather-Bird sandals. I had never been on skates. At home there was no sidewalk. I decided to try skating on one foot, like a kid on a scooter, but the skate came loose.

"Put both of them on," said the girl, laughing at me.

Her name was Sharon Belletieri. She had to spell it for me. She said my name over and over until it sounded absurd. "Peggy Peggy Peggy Peggy Peggy." She made my name sound like "piggy."

"Don't you have a permanent?" she asked.

"No," I said, touching my pigtails. "My hair's in plaits 'cause it's summer."

"Har? Oh, you mean *hair*? Like air?" She waved at the air. She was standing there, perfectly balanced on her skates. She pronounced "hair" with two syllables. *Hayer.* I said something like a cross between *herr* and *harr*.

Sharon turned and whizzed down the sidewalk, then skidded to a stop at the corner, twisted around, and faced me.

"Are you going to skate or not?" she asked.

My uncle smoked Old Golds, and he seemed to have excess nervous energy. He was always jumping up from his chair to get something, or to look outside at the thermometer. He had found his name in a newspaper ad recently and had won a free pint of Cunningham's ice cream. My aunt declared that that made him somewhat famous. When I came back that day with the skates, he was sitting on the porch fanning himself with a newspaper. There was a heat wave, he said.

"What did you think of Sharon Belletieri?" he asked.

"She talks funny," I said, sitting down beside him.

"Folks up here all talk funny. I've noticed that too."

Uncle Boone had been a clerk in the war. He told me about the time he had spent in the Pacific theater, sailing around on a battleship, looking for Japs.

"Me and some buddies went to a Pacific island where there was a tribe of people with little tails," he said.

"Don't believe a word he says," said my aunt, who had been listening.

"It's true," said Uncle Boone. "Cross my heart and hope to die." He solemnly crossed his hands on his chest, then looked at his watch and said abruptly to me, "What do you think of Gorgeous George?"

"I don't know."

"How about Howdy Doody?"

"Who's Howdy Doody?"

"This child don't know nothing," he said to my aunt. "She's been raised with a bunch of country hicks."

"He's fooling," said Aunt Mozelle. "Go ahead and show her, Boone, for gosh sakes. Don't keep it a secret."

He was talking about television. I hadn't noticed the set in the living room because it had a sliding cover over the screen. It was a ten-inch table model with an upholstered sound box in a rosewood cabinet.

"We've never seen a television," my mother said.

"This will ruin her," said my aunt. "It's ruined Boone."

Uncle Boone turned on the television set. A wrestling match appeared on the screen, and I could see Gorgeous George flexing his muscles and tossing his curls. The television set resembled our radio. For a long time I was confused, thinking that I would now be able to see all my favorite radio programs.

"It's one of those sets you can look at in normal light and not go blind," my aunt said, to reassure us. "It's called Daylight TV."

"Wait till you see Howdy Doody," said Uncle Boone.

The picture on the television set was not clear. The reception required some imagination, and the pictures frequently dissolved, but I could see Gorgeous George moving across the screen, his curls bouncing. I could see him catch hold of his opponent and wrestle him to the floor, holding him so tight I thought he would choke.

That night, I lay in the cedar-perfumed room, too excited to sleep. I did not know what to expect next. The streetlamps glowed like moons through the venetian blinds, and as I lay there, my guardian angel slowly crept into my mind. In *Uncle Arthur's Bedtime Stories,* there was a picture of a child with his guardian angel hovering over him. It was a man angel, and gigantic, with immense white feathery bird's wings. Probably the boy could never see him because the angel stayed in what drivers of automobiles call a blind spot. I had a feeling that my own guardian angel had accompanied the bus to Michigan and was in the house with me. I imagined him floating above the bus. I knew that my guardian angel was supposed to keep me from harm, but I did not want anyone to know about him. I was very afraid of him. It was a long time before I fell asleep.

In the North, they drank coffee. Aunt Mozelle made a large pot of coffee in the mornings, and she kept it in a Thermos so she could drink coffee throughout the day.

Mama began drinking coffee. "Whew! I'm higher than a kite!" she would say. "I'll be up prowling half the night."

"Little girls shouldn't ought to drink coffee," Uncle Boone said to me more than once. "It turns them black."

"I don't even want any!" I protested. But I did like the enticing smell, which awoke me early in the mornings.

My aunt made waffles with oleomargarine. She kneaded a capsule of yellow dye into the pale margarine.

"It's a law," she told me one morning.

"They don't have that law down home anymore," said Mama. "People's turning to oleo and it's getting so we can't sell butter."

"I guess everybody forgot how it tasted," said Aunt Mozelle.

"I wouldn't be surprised if that business about the dye was a Communist idea," said my uncle. "A buddy of mine at the plant thinks so. He says they want to make it look like butter. The big companies, they're full of reds now."

"That makes sense to me," said Mama. "Anything to hurt the farmer."

It didn't make sense to me. When they talked about reds, all I could imagine was a bunch of little devils in red suits, carrying pitchforks. I wondered if they were what my uncle had seen in the Pacific, since devils had tails. Everything about the North was confusing. Lunetta Jones, for instance, bewildered me. She came for coffee every morning, after my uncle had left in a car pool. Lunetta, a seventh-grade teacher, was from Kentucky, and her parents were old friends of my aunt's, so Mozelle and Boone took a special interest in her welfare. Lunetta's life was tragic, my aunt said. Her sailor-boy husband had died in the war. Lunetta never spoke to me, so I often stared at her unselfconsciously. She resembled one of the Toni twins,[1] except for her horsey teeth. She wore her hair curled tight at the bottom, with a fluffy topknot, and she put hard, precise *g*'s on the ends of words like "talking" and "going," the way both Sharon Belletieri and Betsy Lou did. And she wore elaborate dresses—rayon marquisette dresses with Paris pockets, dresses with tiered tucks, others of tissue chambray, with what she called "taffeta understudies." Sometimes I thought her dresses could carry her away on a frantic ride through the sky, they were so billowy and thin.

"Lunetta's man-crazy," my aunt explained to me. "She's always dressed up in one of them Sunday-go-to-meetin' outfits in case she might come across a man to marry."

Uncle Boone called her thick lipstick "man bait."

The buses remained on strike, and I spent the days in the house. I avoided Sharon Belletieri, preferring to be alone, or to sit entranced before the television set. Sometimes the fading outlines of the characters on the screen were like ghosts. I watched Milton Berle, Morey Amsterdam, *Believe It Or Not, Wax Wackies,* and even *Blind Date.* Judy Splinters, a ventriloquist's dummy with pigtails like mine, was one of my favorites, and I liked the magician Foodini on *Lucky Pup* better than Howdy Doody. Betsy Lou teased me, saying I was too old for those baby shows. She was away most of the time, out on "jelly dates." A jelly date was a Coke date. She had jelly dates

---

[1] Reference to an advertisement of the time for home permanent waves: "Which twin has the Toni?"

with Bob and Jim and Sam all on the same day. She was fond of singing "Let's Take an Old-Fashioned Walk," although one of her boyfriends had a car and she liked to go riding in it more than anything else. Why couldn't he take us to Detroit? I wondered, but I was afraid to ask. I had a sick feeling that we were never going to get to see the buildings of the city.

In the mornings, when there was nothing but snow[2] on television, and the women were gossiping over their coffee in the kitchen, I sat on the enclosed porch and watched the people and the cars pass. During the heat wave, it was breezy there. I sat on the rattan chaise lounge and read Aunt Mozelle's scrapbooks, which I had found on a shelf above the television set. They were filled with brittle newspaper clippings mounted in overlapping rows. The clippings included household hints and cradle notes, but most of the stories were about bizarre occurrences around the world—diseases and kidnappings and disasters. One headline that fascinated me read: TIBETAN STOMACH STOVE DECLARED CANCER CAUSE. The story said that people in Tibet who carry little hot stoves against their abdomens in winter frequently develop cancer from the irritation. I was thankful that I didn't live in a cold climate. Another story was about a boa constrictor that swallowed a horse blanket. And there were a number of strange stories about blue babies. When my aunt found me reading the scrapbooks, she said to me, "Life is amazing. I keep these to remind me of just how strange everything is. And how there are always people worse off." I nodded agreement. The porch was my favorite place. I felt secure there, as I read about these faraway wonders and afflictions. I would look up now and then and imagine I could see the tall buildings of Detroit in the distance.

"This is a two-tone gabardine spectator dress with a low-slung belt in the back," said Lunetta one morning as she turned to model her new dress for us. Lunetta always had official descriptions for her extravagant costumes.

My mother said in a wistful voice, "Law me, that's beautiful. But what would I look like, feeding the chickens in that getup?"

"Just look at them shoes," Aunt Mozelle said.

Lunetta's shoes had butterfly bows and sling heels and open toes. She sat down and tapped her toes as Aunt Mozelle poured coffee for her. She said then, "Is Boone worried about his job now that they caught that red?"

"Well, he is, but he don't let on," said Aunt Mozelle, frowning.

Lunetta seized yesterday's newspaper and spread it out on the table. She pointed at the headlines. I remember the way the adults had murmured over the newspaper the day before. Aunt Mozelle had said, "Don't worry, Boone. You don't work for that company." He had replied, "But the plant is full of sympathizers." Now Lunetta said, "Just think. That man they caught could have given Russia all the plans for the power plant. Nothing's safe. You never know who might turn out to be a spy."

My mother was disturbed. "Everything you all have worked so hard for—and the reds could just come in and take it." She waved her hand at the kitchen. In my mind

---

[2] The white spots on an empty television screen resulting either from a weak signal or, as was common in the early days of television, from an absence of programming.

a strange scene appeared: a band of little red devils marching in with their pitchforks and taking the entire Kelvinator[3] kitchen to hell. Later, it occurred to me that they would take the television set first.

When my uncle came home from work, I greeted him at the door and asked him bluntly, "Are you going to get fired because of the reds?"

He only laughed and twitched my plaits. "No, sugar," he said.

"That don't concern younguns," Aunt Mozelle told me. She said to her husband, "Lunetta was here, spreading ideas."

"Leave it to Lunetta," said Uncle Boone wearily.

That evening they were eager to watch the news on the television set. When the supervisor who had been fired was shown, my uncle said, "I hope they give him what-for."

"He was going to tell Russia about the power plant," I said.

"Hush, Peggy," said Mama.

That evening, I could hear their anxious voices on the porch, as I watched Arthur Godfrey, wrestling, and the barbershop quartets. It seemed odd to me that my uncle did not want to watch the wrestling. He had told me wrestling was his favorite program.

Sharon Belletieri had a birthday party. Aunt Mozelle took Mama and me to a nearby Woolworth's, where I selected a coloring book for a present. The store was twice the size of ours at home. I also bought a souvenir of my trip—a pair of china dogs, with a label that read "Made in Japan." And my mother bought me a playsuit like Sharon's.

"It's Sanforized. That's good," she said with an air of satisfaction, as she examined seams and labels.

My mother looked pale and tired. At breakfast she had suddenly thrown up, the way she had during our bus trip. "I can't keep anything down this early," she had said. My aunt urged her to drink more coffee, saying it would settle her stomach.

Sharon Belletieri lived with her parents in a famous kind of sanitary house where you couldn't get TB or rheumatic fever because it had no drafts. "You won't have to worry about polio," Betsy Lou had told me. The house had venetian blinds like my aunt's, and there was also a television set, an immense one, on legs. Howdy Doody was on, but no one was watching. I did not know what to say to the children. They all knew each other, and their screams and giggles had a natural continuity, something like the way my mother talked with her sister, and like the splendid houses of the neighborhood, all set so close together.

For her birthday, Sharon's parents gave her a Toni doll that took my breath away. It had a bolero sundress, lace-edged panties and slip, and white shoes and socks—an outfit as fine as any of Lunetta's. It came with a Play Wave, including plastic spin curlers and Toni Creme Rinse. The doll's magic nylon hair was supposed to grow softer in texture the more you gave it permanent waves. Feeling self-conscious in my new playsuit, I sat quietly at the party, longing to give that doll a permanent.

---

[3] Leading manufacturer of kitchen appliances.

Eventually, even though I had hardly opened my mouth, someone laughed at my accent. I had said the unfortunate word "hair" again, in reference to the doll.

Sharon said, "*She's* from Kentucky."

Growing bold and inspired, I said, "Well, we don't have any reds in Kentucky."

Some of the children laughed, and Sharon took me aside and told me a secret, making me cross my heart and hope to die. "I know who's a red," she told me in a whisper. "My father knows him."

"Who?"

"One of the men your uncle rides with to work. The one who drives the car on Thursdays. He's a red and I can prove it."

Before I could find out more, it was my turn to pin the tail on the donkey. Sharon's mother blindfolded me and spun me around. The children were squealing, and I could feel them shrinking from me. When I took the blindfold off, I was dizzy. I had pinned the donkey's tail on the wallpaper, in the center of a large yellow flower.

That evening Betsy Lou went out with a boy named Sam, the one with the car, and Lunetta came to play canasta with the adults. During *Cavalcade of Stars,* I could hear them in the kitchen, accusing each other of hiding reds, when they meant hearts and diamonds. They laughed so loudly I sometimes missed some of Jack Carter's jokes. The wrestling came on afterward, but my uncle did not notice, so I turned off the television and looked at a magazine. I spent a long time trying to write the last line to a Fab jingle so that I could win a television set and five hundred dollars a month for life. I knew that life in Kentucky would be unbearable without a television.

Between hands, Uncle Boone and Lunetta got into an argument. My uncle claimed there were more reds teaching school than making cars, and Lunetta said it was just the opposite.

"They're firing schoolteachers too," he said to Lunetta.

"Don't look at *me,*" she said. "I signed the loyalty oath."

"Hush your mouth, Boone," said Aunt Mozelle.

"I know who a red is," I said suddenly, coming to the table.

They all looked at me and I explained what Sharon had told me. Too late, I remembered my promise not to tell.

"Don't let anybody hear you say that," said Lunetta. "Your uncle would lose his job. If they even *think* you know somebody that knows somebody, you can get in trouble."

"You better not say anything, hon," said Uncle Boone.

"Peggy, it's past your bedtime," my mother said.

"What did *I* do?"

"Talk gets around," said Lunetta. "There's sympathizers even in the woodwork."

The next day, after a disturbing night in which my guardian angel did nothing to protect me from my terrible secret, I was glum and cranky, and for the first time I refused Aunt Mozelle's waffles.

"Are you burnt out on them?" she asked me.

"No, I just ain't hungry."

"She played too hard at the birthday party," Mama said knowingly to my aunt.

When Lunetta arrived and Mama told her I had played too hard at the birthday party, I burst into tears.

"It's nobody's business if I played too hard," I cried. "Besides," I shrieked at Mama, "you don't feel good at breakfast either. You always say you can't keep anything down."

"Don't be ugly," my mother said sharply. To the others, she said apologetically, "I reckon sooner or later she was bound to show out."[4]

It was Sunday, and the heat wave continued. We all sat on the porch, looking at the Sunday papers. Betsy Lou was reading *Pleasant Valley* by Louis Bromfield.[5] Uncle Boone read the Sunday comics aloud to himself. Actually, he was trying to get my attention, for I sat in a corner, determined to ignore everyone. Uncle Boone read "Abbie an' Slats," "The Gumps," and "Little Orphan Annie." He pretended he was Milton Berle as he read them, but I wouldn't laugh.

Lunetta and Uncle Boone seemed to have forgotten their argument. Lunetta had dressed up for church, but the man she planned to go with had gone to visit his mother's grave instead.

"That man sure did love his mother," she said.

"Why don't you go to church anyway?" asked Betsy Lou. "You're all dressed up."

"I just don't have it in me," said Lunetta. She was wearing a shell-tucked summer shantung dress and raffia T-strap sandals.

"Ain't you hot in that outfit?" asked my aunt. "We're burning up."

"I guess so." Lunetta seemed gloomy and distracted. I almost forgave her for upsetting me about the sympathizers, but then she launched into a complicated story about a baby-sitter who got double-crossed. "This woman baby-sat for her best friend, who was divorced and had two little babies. And come to find out, the friend was going out on dates with the woman's own husband!"

"If that don't beat all," said Mama, her eyes wide. She was drinking her second cup of coffee.

"No telling how long that could have kept up," said my aunt.

"It made a big divorce case," Lunetta said.

"I never saw so many divorce cases," said Mama.

"Would you divorce somebody if you found out they were a Communist?" Lunetta asked.

"I don't know as I would," said Aunt Mozelle. "Depends."

"*I* would," said Mama.

"I probably would," said Lunetta. "How about you, Boone?"

"If I found out Mozelle was a red?" Boone asked, grinning. "I'd probably string her up and tickle her feet till she hollered uncle."

"Oh, Boone," Lunetta said with a laugh. "I know you'd stick up for Mozelle, no matter what."

They sat around that morning talking like this, good-naturedly. In the light of day, the reds were only jokes after all, like the comics. I had decided to eat a bowl of Pep

---

[4] Southern colloquialism for "misbehave."
[5] Prolific novelist and journalist (1896–1956);   *Pleasant Valley* (1945) was a book about scientific farming.

cereal, and "Some Enchanted Evening" was playing on the radio. Suddenly everything changed, as if a black storm had appeared to break the heat wave. My mother gave out a loud whoop and clutched her stomach in pain.

"Where does it hurt?" my aunt cried, grabbing at Mama.

Mama was too much in pain to speak. Her face was distorted, her sharp-pointed lips stretched out like a slingshot. My aunt helped her to the bathroom, and a short while later, my aunt and uncle flew away with her in a taxi. Mama had straightened up enough to say that the pain had subsided, but she looked scared, and the blood had drained from her face. I said nothing to her, not even good-bye.

Betsy Lou, left alone with me, said, "I hope she hasn't got polio."

"Only children get polio," I said, trembling. "She don't have polio."

The telephone rang, and Betsy Lou chattered excitedly, telling one of her boyfriends what had happened. Alone and frightened, I sat on the porch, hugging a fat pile of newspapers and gazing at the street. I could see Sharon Belletieri, skating a block away with two other girls. She was wearing a blue playsuit. She and her friends reminded me of those privileged children in the Peanut Gallery on *Howdy Doody*.

To keep from thinking, I began searching the newspaper for something to put in Aunt Mozelle's scrapbook, but at first nothing seemed so horrible as what had just happened. Some babies had turned blue from a diaper dye, but that story didn't impress me. Then I found an item about a haunted house, and my heart began to race. A priest claimed that mysterious disturbances in a house in Wisconsin were the work of an angelic spirit watching over an eight-year-old boy. Cryptic messages were found on bits of paper in the boy's room. The spirit manifestation had occurred fifteen times. I found my aunt's scissors and cut out the story.

Within two hours, my aunt and uncle returned, with broad smiles on their faces, but I knew they were pretending.

"She's just fine," said Aunt Mozelle. "We'll take you to see her afterwhile, but right now they gave her something to make her sleep and take away the pain."

"She'll get to come home in the morning," said my uncle.

He had brought ice cream, and while he went to the kitchen to dish it out, I showed my aunt the clipping I had found. I helped her put it in her scrapbook.

"Life sure is strange," I said.

"Didn't I tell you?" she said. "Now, don't you worry about your mama, hon. She's going to be all right."

Later that day, my aunt and uncle stood in the corridor of the hospital while I visited my mother. The hospital was large and gray and steaming with the heat. Mama lay against a mound of pillows, smiling weakly.

"*I'm* the one that showed out," she said, looking ashamed. She took my hand and made me sit on the bed next to her. "You *were* going to have a little brother or sister," she said. "But I was mistaken."

"What happened to it?"

"I lost it. That happens sometimes."

When I looked at her blankly, she tried to explain that there wasn't *really* a baby, as there was when she had Johnny two years before.

She said, "You know how sometimes one or two of the chicken eggs don't hatch? The baby chick just won't take hold. That's what happened."

It occurred to me to ask what the baby's name would have been.

"I don't know," she said. "I'm trying to tell you there wasn't really a baby. I didn't know about it, anyway."

"You didn't even know there was a baby?"

"No. I didn't know about it till I lost it."

She tried to laugh, but she was weak, and she seemed as confused as I was. She squeezed my hand and closed her eyes for a moment. Then she said, "Boone says the buses will start up this week. You could go with your aunt to Detroit and see the big buildings."

"Without you?"

"The doctor said I should rest up before we go back. But you go ahead. Mozelle will take you." She smiled at me sleepily. "I wanted to go so bad—just to see those big fancy store windows. And I wanted to see your face when you saw the city."

That evening, *Toast of the Town* was on television, and then Fred Waring, and *Garroway at Large*. I was lost among the screen phantoms—the magic acts, puppets, jokes, clowns, dancers, singers, wisecracking announcers. My aunt and uncle laughed uproariously. Uncle Boone was drinking beer, something I had not seen him do, and the room stank with the smoke of his Old Golds. Now and then I was aware of all of us sitting there together, laughing in the dim light from the television, while my mother was in the hospital. Even Betsy Lou was watching with us. Later, I went to the guest room and sat on the large bed, trying to concentrate on finishing the Fab jingle.

> Here's to a fabulous life with Fab
> There's no soap scum to make wash drab
> Your clothes get cleaner—whiter, too—

I heard my aunt calling to me excitedly. I was missing something on the television screen. I had left because the news was on.

"Pictures of Detroit!" she cried. "Come quick. You can see the big buildings."

I raced into the living room in time to see some faint, dark shapes, hiding behind the snow, like a forest in winter, and then the image faded into the snow.

"Mozelle can take you into Detroit in a day or two," my uncle said. "The buses is starting up again."

"I don't want to go," I said.

"You don't want to miss the chance," said my aunt.

"Yes, I do."

That night, alone in the pine-and-cedar room, I saw everything clearly, like the sharpened images that floated on the television screen. My mother had said an egg didn't hatch, but I knew better. The reds had stolen the baby. They took things. They were after my aunt's copper-bottomed pans. They stole the butter. They wanted my uncle's job. They were invisible, like the guardian angel, although they might wear disguises. You didn't know who might be a red. You never knew when you might lose a baby that you didn't know you had. I understood it all. I hadn't trusted my guardian angel, and so he had failed to protect me. During the night, I hit upon a last line to the Fab jingle, but when I awoke I saw how silly and inappropriate it was. It was going over and over in my mind: *Red soap makes the world go round.*

On the bus home a few days later, I slept with my head in my mother's lap, and she dozed with her head propped against my seat back. She was no longer sick, but we were both tired and we swayed, unresisting, with the rhythms of the bus. When the bus stopped in Fort Wayne, Indiana, at midnight, I suddenly woke up, and at the sight of an unfamiliar place, I felt—with a new surge of clarity—the mystery of travel, the vastness of the world, the strangeness of life. My own life was a curiosity, an item for a scrapbook. I wondered what my mother would tell my father about the baby she had lost. She had been holding me tightly against her stomach as though she feared she might lose me too.

I had refused to let them take me into Detroit. At the bus station, Aunt Mozelle had hugged me and said, "Maybe next time you come we can go to Detroit."

"If there *is* a next time," Mama said. "This may be her only chance, but she had to be contrary."

"I didn't want to miss *Wax Wackies* and *Judy Splinters,*" I said, protesting.

"We'll have a car next time you come," said my uncle. "If they don't fire everybody," he added with a laugh.

"If that happens, y'all can always come back to Kentucky and help us get a crop out," Mama told him.

The next afternoon, we got off the bus on the highway at the intersection with our road. Our house was half a mile away. The bus driver got our suitcases out of the bus for us, and then drove on down the highway. My father was supposed to meet us, but he was not there.

"I better not carry this suitcase," said Mama. "My insides might drop."

We left our suitcases in a ditch and started walking, expecting to meet Daddy on the way.

My mother said, "You don't remember this, but when you was two years old I went to Jackson, Tennessee, for two weeks to see Mozelle and Boone—back before Boone was called overseas?—and when I come back the bus driver let me off here and I come walking down the road to the house carrying my suitcase. You was playing in the yard and you saw me walk up and you didn't recognize me. For the longest time, you didn't know who I was. I never *will* forget how funny you looked."

"They won't recognize us," I said solemnly. "Daddy and Johnny."

As we got to the top of the hill, we could see that our little white house was still there. The tin roof of the barn was barely visible through the tall oak trees.

1981

Maxine Hong Kingston
b. 1940

"When I write most deeply, fly the highest, reach the furthest, I write like a diarist," asserts Maxine Hong Kingston, as though to remind us that writing begins for her as a private act. "My audience is myself," she says. "I dare to write anything because I can burn my papers at any moment." Using her own life and the lives of her family, Kingston addresses not the experience of being Chinese in America but the experience of being a Chinese-American. Her work demands an understanding of three cultures—American, Chinese, and Chinese-American. "Some readers," she says, "will just have to do some background reading." At the same time, she continues to believe both in "the timelessness and universality of individual vision" and in the "miracle" of being understood. Of *The Woman Warrior* (1976), from which "No Name Woman" is taken, she says that it is not merely "a family book or an American book or a woman's book but a world book, and, at the same moment, my book."

Born in Stockton, California, on October 27, 1940, Maxine Hong Kingston is a first-generation American. She received a B.A. from the University of California at Berkeley in 1962 and has taught at various high schools in California and Hawaii. From 1970 to 1977 she was on the faculty of the Mid-Pacific Institute in Honolulu, and she is currently assistant professor of English and visiting writer at the University of Hawaii. Meanwhile, her writing has met with consistent critical acclaim. Her first book, *The Woman Warrior: Memoirs of a Girlhood Among Ghosts,* won the National Book Critics Circle Award for nonfiction; her second, *China Men* (1980), won the 1981 American Book Award. Her short stories, articles, and poems have appeared in such publications as *The New Yorker, New West, Ms.,* and *American Heritage.* Kingston has also received a *Mademoiselle* award (1977), an NEA writing fellowship (1980), and a Guggenheim fellowship (1981).

Given the autobiographical focus of Kingston's fiction, it is fitting that one of her major concerns revolves around the relation between fiction and nonfiction. "My characters are story tellers," she says, "and I suspect that some of them are telling me fiction. So when I write their lives down is it fiction or nonfiction?" The answer, she believes, lies in perspective. Rather than depend solely on verifiable "facts," she also explores impressions, emotions, and interpretations, both her own and those of her characters. At the same time, she carefully delineates the sources on which she has drawn so that her readers can in turn devise interpretations of their own. "When I tell . . . all these versions," she says, "I'm actually giving the culture of these people in a very accurate way. You can see where the people make up these fictions about themselves, and it's not just for fun. It's a terrible necessity." Writing of herself and the mixed world that forms a backdrop for her experiences, Kingston creates a truth that transcends literary and ethnic categories and is as beautiful as it is necessary.

Text:
The Woman Warrior: Memoirs of a Girlhood Among Ghosts, 1976.

from The Woman Warrior

No Name Woman

"You must not tell anyone," my mother said, "what I am about to tell you. In China your father had a sister who killed herself. She jumped into the family well. We say that your father has all brothers because it is as if she had never been born.

"In 1924 just a few days after our village celebrated seventeen hurry-up weddings —to make sure that every young man who went 'out on the road' would responsibly come home—your father and his brothers and your grandfather and his brothers and your aunt's new husband sailed for America, the Gold Mountain. It was your grand-father's last trip. Those lucky enough to get contracts waved goodbye from the decks. They fed and guarded the stowaways and helped them off in Cuba, New York, Bali, Hawaii. 'We'll meet in California next year,' they said. All of them sent money home.

"I remember looking at your aunt one day when she and I were dressing; I had not noticed before that she had such a protruding melon of a stomach. But I did not think, 'She's pregnant,' until she began to look like other pregnant women, her shirt pulling and the white tops of her black pants showing. She could not have been pregnant, you see, because her husband had been gone for years. No one said anything. We did not discuss it. In early summer she was ready to have the child, long after the time when it could have been possible.

"The village had also been counting. On the night the baby was to be born the villagers raided our house. Some were crying. Like a great saw, teeth strung with lights, files of people walked zigzag across our land, tearing the rice. Their lanterns doubled in the disturbed black water, which drained away through the broken bunds. As the villagers closed in, we could see that some of them, probably men and women we knew well, wore white masks. The people with long hair hung it over their faces. Women with short hair made it stand up on end. Some had tied white bands around their foreheads, arms, and legs.

"At first they threw mud and rocks at the house. Then they threw eggs and began slaughtering our stock. We could hear the animals scream their deaths—the roosters, the pigs, a last great roar from the ox. Familiar wild heads flared in our night windows; the villagers encircled us. Some of the faces stopped to peer at us, their eyes rushing like searchlights. The hands flattened against the panes, framed heads, and left red prints.

"The villagers broke in the front and the back doors at the same time, even though we had not locked the doors against them. Their knives dripped with the blood of our animals. They smeared blood on the doors and walls. One woman swung a chicken, whose throat she had slit, splattering blood in red arcs about her. We stood together in the middle of our house, in the family hall with the pictures and tables of the ancestors around us, and looked straight ahead.

"At that time the house had only two wings. When the men came back, we would build two more to enclose our courtyard and a third one to begin a second courtyard. The villagers pushed through both wings, even your grandparents' rooms, to find your aunt's, which was also mine until the men returned. From this room a new wing for one of the younger families would grow. They ripped up her clothes and shoes and broke her combs, grinding them underfoot. They tore her work from the loom. They scattered the cooking fire and rolled the new weaving in it. We could hear them in the kitchen breaking our bowls and banging the pots. They overturned the great waist-high earthenware jugs; duck eggs, pickled fruits, vegetables burst out and mixed in acrid torrents. The old woman from the next field swept a broom through the air and loosed the spirits-of-the-broom over our heads. 'Pig.' 'Ghost.' 'Pig,' they sobbed and scolded while they ruined our house.

"When they left, they took sugar and oranges to bless themselves. They cut pieces from the dead animals. Some of them took bowls that were not broken and clothes that were not torn. Afterward we swept up the rice and sewed it back up into sacks. But the smells from the spilled preserves lasted. Your aunt gave birth in the pigsty that night. The next morning when I went for the water, I found her and the baby plugging up the family well.

"Don't let your father know that I told you. He denies her. Now that you have started to menstruate, what happened to her could happen to you. Don't humiliate us. You wouldn't like to be forgotten as if you had never been born. The villagers are watchful."

Whenever she had to warn us about life, my mother told stories that ran like this one, a story to grow up on. She tested our strength to establish realities. Those in the emigrant generations who could not reassert brute survival died young and far from home. Those of us in the first American generations have had to figure out how the invisible world the emigrants built around our childhoods fit in solid America.

The emigrants confused the gods by diverting their curses, misleading them with crooked streets and false names. They must try to confuse their offspring as well, who, I suppose, threaten them in similar ways—always trying to get things straight, always trying to name the unspeakable. The Chinese I know hide their names; sojourners take new names when their lives change and guard their real names with silence.

Chinese-Americans, when you try to understand what things in you are Chinese, how do you separate what is peculiar to childhood, to poverty, insanities, one family, your mother who marked your growing with stories, from what is Chinese? What is Chinese tradition and what is the movies?

If I want to learn what clothes my aunt wore, whether flashy or ordinary, I would have to begin, "Remember Father's drowned-in-the-well sister?" I cannot ask that. My mother has told me once and for all the useful parts. She will add nothing unless powered by Necessity, a riverbank that guides her life. She plants vegetable gardens rather than lawns; she carries the odd-shaped tomatoes home from the fields and eats food left for the gods.

Whenever we did frivolous things, we used up energy; we flew high kites. We children came up off the ground over the melting cones our parents brought home from work and the American movie on New Year's Day—*Oh, You Beautiful Doll* with Betty Grable one year, and *She Wore a Yellow Ribbon* with John Wayne another year. After the one carnival ride each, we paid in guilt; our tired father counted his change on the dark walk home.

Adultery is extravagance. Could people who hatch their own chicks and eat the embryos and the heads for delicacies and boil the feet in vinegar for party food, leaving only the gravel, eating even the gizzard lining—could such people engender a prodigal aunt? To be a woman, to have a daughter in starvation time was a waste enough. My aunt could not have been the lone romantic who gave up everything for sex. Women in the old China did not choose. Some man had commanded her to lie with him and be his secret evil. I wonder whether he masked himself when he joined the raid on her family.

Perhaps she encountered him in the fields or on the mountain where the daughters-in-law collected fuel. Or perhaps he first noticed her in the marketplace. He was not a stranger because the village housed no strangers. She had to have dealings with him other than sex. Perhaps he worked an adjoining field, or he sold her the cloth for the dress she sewed and wore. His demand must have surprised, then terrified her. She obeyed him; she always did as she was told.

When the family found a young man in the next village to be her husband, she stood tractably beside the best rooster, his proxy, and promised before they met that she would be his forever. She was lucky that he was her age and she would be the first wife, an advantage secure now. The night she first saw him, he had sex with her. Then he left for America. She had almost forgotten what he looked like. When she tried to envision him, she only saw the black and white face in the group photograph the men had had taken before leaving.

The other man was not, after all, much different from her husband. They both gave orders: she followed. "If you tell your family, I'll beat you. I'll kill you. Be here again next week." No one talked sex, ever. And she might have separated the rapes from the rest of living if only she did not have to buy her oil from him or gather wood in the same forest. I want her fear to have lasted just as long as rape lasted so that the fear could have been contained. No drawn-out fear. But women at sex hazarded birth and hence lifetimes. The fear did not stop but permeated everywhere. She told the man, "I think I'm pregnant." He organized the raid against her.

On nights when my mother and father talked about their life back home, some-times they mentioned an "outcast table" whose business they still seemed to be settling, their voices tight. In a commensal tradition,[1] where food is precious, the powerful older people made wrongdoers eat alone. Instead of letting them start separate new lives like the Japanese, who could become samurais and geishas,[2] the Chinese family, faces averted but eyes glowering sideways, hung on to the offenders and fed them leftovers. My aunt must have lived in the same house as my parents and eaten at an outcast table. My mother spoke about the raid as if she had seen it, when she and my aunt, a daughter-in-law to a different household, should not have been living together at all. Daughters-in-law lived with their husbands' parents, not their own; a synonym for marriage in Chinese is "taking a daughter-in-law." Her husband's parents could have sold her, mortgaged her, stoned her. But they had sent her back to her own mother and father, a mysterious act hinting at disgraces not told me. Perhaps they had thrown her out to deflect the avengers.

She was the only daughter; her four brothers went with her father, husband, and uncles "out on the road" and for some years became western men. When the goods were divided among the family, three of the brothers took land, and the youngest, my father, chose an education. After my grandparents gave their daughter away to

---

[1] One in which all members eat at the same table.
[2] Samurai: member of the Japanese feudal military aristocracy; geisha: Japanese girl trained in singing, dancing, and the art of conversation so as to serve as a hired companion to men.

her husband's family, they had dispensed all the adventure and all the property. They expected her alone to keep the traditional ways, which her brothers, now among the barbarians, could fumble without detection. The heavy, deep-rooted women were to maintain the past against the flood, safe for returning. But the rare urge west had fixed upon our family, and so my aunt crossed boundaries not delineated in space.

The work of preservation demands that the feelings playing about in one's guts not be turned into action. Just watch their passing like cherry blossoms. But perhaps my aunt, my forerunner, caught in a slow life, let dreams grow and fade and after some months or years went toward what persisted. Fear at the enormities of the forbidden kept her desires delicate, wire and bone. She looked at a man because she liked the way the hair was tucked behind his ears, or she liked the question-mark line of a long torso curving at the shoulder and straight at the hip. For warm eves or a soft voice or a slow walk—that's all—a few hairs, a line, a brightness, a sound, a pace, she gave up family. She offered us up for a charm that vanished with tiredness, a pigtail that didn't toss when the wind died. Why, the wrong lighting could erase the dearest thing about him.

It could very well have been, however, that my aunt did not take subtle enjoyment of her friend, but, a wild woman, kept rollicking company. Imagining her free with sex doesn't fit, though. I don't know any women like that, or men either. Unless I see her life branching into mine, she gives me no ancestral help.

To sustain her being in love, she often worked at herself in the mirror, guessing at the colors and shapes that would interest him, changing them frequently in order to hit on the right combination. She wanted him to look back.

On a farm near the sea, a woman who tended her appearance reaped a reputation for eccentricity. All the married women blunt-cut their hair in flaps about their ears or pulled it back in tight buns. No nonsense. Neither style blew easily into heart-catching tangles. And at their weddings they displayed themselves in their long hair for the last time. "It brushed the backs of my knees," my mother tells me. "It was braided, and even so, it brushed the backs of my knees."

At the mirror my aunt combed individuality into her bob. A bun could have been contrived to escape into black streamers blowing in the wind or in quiet wisps about her face, but only the older women in our picture album wear buns. She brushed her hair back from her forehead, tucking the flaps behind her ears. She looped a piece of thread, knotted into a circle between her index fingers and thumbs, and ran the double strand across her forehead. When she closed her fingers as if she were making a pair of shadow geese bite, the string twisted together catching the little hairs. Then she pulled the thread away from her skin, ripping the hairs out neatly, her eyes watering from the needles of pain. Opening her fingers, she cleaned the thread, then rolled it along her hairline and the tops of her eyebrows. My mother did the same to me and my sisters and herself. I used to believe that the expression "caught by the short hairs" meant a captive held with a depilatory string. It especially hurt at the temples, but my mother said we were lucky we didn't have to have our feet bound when we were seven. Sisters used to sit on their beds and cry together, she said, as their mothers or their slaves removed the bandages for a few minutes each night and let the blood gush back into their veins. I hope that the man my aunt loved appreciated a smooth brow, that he wasn't just a tits-and-ass man.

Once my aunt found a freckle on her chin, at a spot that the almanac said predestined her for unhappiness. She dug it out with a hot needle and washed the wound with peroxide.

More attention to her looks than these pullings of hairs and pickings at spots would have caused gossip among the villagers. They owned work clothes and good clothes, and they wore good clothes for feasting the new seasons. But since a woman combing her hair hexes beginnings, my aunt rarely found an occasion to look her best. Women looked like great sea snails—the corded wood, babies, and laundry they carried were the whorls on their backs. The Chinese did not admire a bent back; goddesses and warriors stood straight. Still there must have been a marvelous freeing of beauty when a worker laid down her burden and stretched and arched.

Such commonplace loveliness, however, was not enough for my aunt. She dreamed of a lover for the fifteen days of New Year's, the time for families to exchange visits, money, and food. She plied her secret comb. And sure enough she cursed the year, the family, the village, and herself.

Even as her hair lured her imminent lover, many other men looked at her. Uncles, cousins, nephews, brothers would have looked, too, had they been home between journeys. Perhaps they had already been restraining their curiosity, and they left, fearful that their glances, like a field of nesting birds, might be startled and caught. Poverty hurt, and that was their first reason for leaving. But another, final reason for leaving the crowded house was the never-said.

She may have been unusually beloved, the precious only daughter, spoiled and mirror gazing because of the affection the family lavished on her. When her husband left, they welcomed the chance to take her back from the in-laws; she could live like the little daughter for just a while longer. There are stories that my grandfather was different from other people, "crazy ever since the little Jap bayoneted him in the head." He used to put his naked penis on the dinner table, laughing. And one day he brought home a baby girl, wrapped up inside his brown western-style greatcoat. He had traded one of his sons, probably my father, the youngest, for her. My grandmother made him trade back. When he finally got a daughter of his own, he doted on her. They must have all loved her, except perhaps my father, the only brother who never went back to China, having once been traded for a girl.

Brothers and sisters, newly men and women, had to efface their sexual color and present plain miens. Disturbing hair and eyes, a smile like no other threatened the ideal of five generations living under one roof. To focus blurs, people shouted face to face and yelled from room to room. The immigrants I know have loud voices, unmodulated to American tones even after years away from the village where they called their friendships out across the fields. I have not been able to stop my mother's screams in public libraries or over telephones. Walking erect (knees straight, toes pointed forward, not pigeon-toed, which is Chinese-feminine) and speaking in an inaudible voice, I have tried to turn myself American-feminine. Chinese communication was loud, public. Only sick people had to whisper. But at the dinner table, where the family members came nearest one another, no one could talk, not the outcasts nor any eaters. Every word that falls from the mouth is a coin lost. Silently they gave and accepted food with both hands. A preoccupied child who took his bowl with one hand got a sideways glare. A complete moment of total attention is due everyone alike. Children and lovers have no singularity here, but my aunt used a secret voice, a separate attentiveness.

She kept the man's name to herself throughout her labor and dying; she did not accuse him that he be punished with her. To save her inseminator's name she gave silent birth.

He may have been somebody in her own household, but intercourse with a man outside the family would have been no less abhorrent. All the village were kinsmen, and the titles shouted in loud country voices never let kinship be forgotten. Any man within visiting distance would have been neutralized as a lover—"brother," "younger brother," "older brother"—one hundred and fifteen relationship titles. Parents researched birth charts probably not so much to assure good fortune as to circumvent incest in a population that has but one hundred surnames. Everybody has eight million relatives. How useless then sexual mannerisms, how dangerous.

As if it came from an atavism deeper than fear, I used to add "brother" silently to boys' names. It hexed the boys, who would or would not ask me to dance, and made them less scary and as familiar and deserving of benevolence as girls.

But, of course, I hexed myself also—no dates. I should have stood up, both arms waving, and shouted out across libraries, "Hey, you! Love me back." I had no idea, though, how to make attraction selective, how to control its direction and magnitude. If I made myself American-pretty so that the five or six Chinese boys in the class fell in love with me, everyone else—the Caucasian, Negro, and Japanese boys—would too. Sisterliness, dignified and honorable, made much more sense.

Attraction eludes control so stubbornly that whole societies designed to organize relationships among people cannot keep order, not even when they bind people to one another from childhood and raise them together. Among the very poor and the wealthy, brothers married their adopted sisters, like doves. Our family allowed some romance, paying adult brides' prices and providing dowries so that their sons and daughters could marry strangers. Marriage promises to turn strangers into friendly relatives—a nation of siblings.

In the village structure, spirits shimmered among the live creatures, balanced and held in equilibrium by time and land. But one human being flaring up into violence could open up a black hole, a maelstrom that pulled in the sky. The frightened villagers, who depended on one another to maintain the real, went to my aunt to show her a personal, physical representation of the break she had made in the "roundness." Misallying couples snapped off the future, which was to be embodied in true offspring. The villagers punished her for acting as if she could have a private life, secret and apart from them.

If my aunt had betrayed the family at a time of large grain yields and peace, when many boys were born, and wings were being built on many houses, perhaps she might have escaped such severe punishment. But the men—hungry, greedy, tired of planting in dry soil, cuckolded—had had to leave the village in order to send food-money home. There were ghost plagues, bandit plagues, wars with the Japanese, floods. My Chinese brother and sister had died of an unknown sickness. Adultery, perhaps only a mistake during good times, became a crime when the village needed food.

The round moon cakes and round doorways, the round tables of graduated size that fit one roundness inside another, round windows and rice bowls—these talismen had lost their power to warn this family of the law: a family must be whole, faithfully keeping the descent line by having sons to feed the old and the dead, who in turn look after the family. The villagers came to show my aunt and her lover-in-hiding a broken house. The villagers were speeding up the circling of events because she was too shortsighted to see that her infidelity had already harmed the village, that waves of consequences would return unpredictably, sometimes in disguise, as now, to hurt her. This roundness had to be made coin-sized so that she would see its circumference: punish her at the birth of her baby. Awaken her to the inexorable. People who refused fatalism because they could invent small resources insisted on culpability. Deny accidents and wrest fault from the stars.

After the villagers left, their lanterns now scattering in various directions toward home, the family broke their silence and cursed her. "Aiaa, we're going to die. Death is coming. Death is coming. Look what you've done. You've killed us. Ghost! Dead ghost! Ghost! You've never been born." She ran out into the fields, far enough from the house so that she could no longer hear their voices, and pressed herself against the earth, her own land no more. When she felt the birth coming, she thought that she had been hurt. Her body seized together. "They've hurt me too much," she thought. "This is gall, and it will kill me." Her forehead and knees against the earth, her body convulsed and then released her onto her back. The black well of sky and stars went out and out and out forever; her body and her complexity seemed to disappear. She was one of the stars, a bright dot in blackness, without home, without a companion, in eternal cold and silence. An agoraphobia rose in her, speeding higher and higher, bigger and bigger; she would not be able to contain it; there would be no end to fear.

Flayed, unprotected against space, she felt pain return, focusing her body. This pain chilled her—a cold, steady kind of surface pain. Inside, spasmodically, the other pain, the pain of the child, heated her. For hours she lay on the ground, alternately body and space. Sometimes a vision of normal comfort obliterated reality: she saw the family in the evening gambling at the dinner table, the young people massaging their elders' backs. She saw them congratulating one another, high joy on the mornings the rice shoots came up. When these pictures burst, the stars drew yet further apart. Black space opened.

She got to her feet to fight better and remembered that old-fashioned women gave birth in their pigsties to fool the jealous, pain-dealing gods, who do not snatch piglets. Before the next spasms could stop her, she ran to the pigsty, each step a rushing out into emptiness. She climbed over the fence and knelt in the dirt. It was good to have a fence enclosing her, a tribal person alone.

Laboring, this woman who had carried her child as a foreign growth that sickened her every day, expelled it at last. She reached down to touch the hot, wet, moving mass, surely smaller than anything human, and could feel that it was human after all —fingers, toes, nails, nose. She pulled it up on to her belly, and it lay curled there, butt in the air, feet precisely tucked one under the other. She opened her loose shirt and buttoned the child inside. After resting, it squirmed and thrashed and she pushed it up to her breast. It turned its head this way and that until it found her nipple. There, it made little snuffling noises. She clenched her teeth at its preciousness, lovely as a young calf, a piglet, a little dog.

She may have gone to the pigsty as a last act of responsibility: she would protect this child as she had protected its father. It would look after her soul, leaving supplies on her grave. But how would this tiny child without family find her grave when there would be no marker for her anywhere, neither in the earth nor the family hall? No one would give her a family hall name. She had taken the child with her into the wastes. At its birth the two of them had felt the same raw pain of separation, a wound that only the family pressing tight could close. A child with no descent line would not soften her life but only trail after her, ghostlike, begging her to give it purpose. At dawn the villagers on their way to the fields would stand around the fence and look.

Full of milk, the little ghost slept. When it awoke, she hardened her breasts against the milk that crying loosens. Toward morning she picked up the baby and walked to the well.

Carrying the baby to the well shows loving. Otherwise abandon it. Turn its face into the mud. Mothers who love their children take them along. It was probably a girl; there is some hope of forgiveness for boys.

"Don't tell anyone you had an aunt. Your father does not want to hear her name. She has never been born." I have believed that sex was unspeakable and words so strong and fathers so frail that "aunt" would do my father mysterious harm. I have thought that my family, having settled among immigrants who had also been their neighbors in the ancestral land, needed to clean their name, and a wrong word would incite the kinspeople even here. But there is more to this silence: they want me to participate in her punishment. And I have.

In the twenty years since I heard this story I have not asked for details nor said my aunt's name; I do not know it. People who can comfort the dead can also chase after them to hurt them further—a reverse ancestor worship. The real punishment was not the raid swiftly inflicted by the villagers, but the family's deliberately forgetting her. Her betrayal so maddened them, they saw to it that she would suffer forever, even after death. Always hungry, always needing, she would have to beg food from other ghosts, snatch and steal it from those whose living descendants give them gifts. She would have to fight the ghosts massed at crossroads for the buns a few thoughtful citizens leave to decoy her away from village and home so that the ancestral spirits could feast unharassed. At peace, they could act like gods, not ghosts, their descent lines providing them with paper suits and dresses, spirit money, paper houses, paper automobiles, chicken, meat, and rice into eternity—essences delivered up in smoke and flames, steam and incense rising from each rice bowl. In an attempt to make the Chinese care for people outside the family, Chairman Mao encourages us now to give our paper replicas to the spirits of outstanding soldiers and workers, no matter whose ancestors they may be. My aunt remains forever hungry. Goods are not distributed evenly among the dead.

My aunt haunts me—her ghost drawn to me because now, after fifty years of neglect, I alone devote pages of paper to her, though not origamied[3] into houses and clothes. I do not think she always means me well. I am telling on her, and she was a spite suicide, drowning herself in the drinking water. The Chinese are always very frightened of the drowned one, whose weeping ghost, wet hair hanging and skin bloated, waits silently by the water to pull down a substitute.

1975

[3] I.e., folded. (Origami is the Japanese art of folding paper into representational or decorative shapes.)

Max Apple
b. 1941

Max Apple writes as though a good story can do or be anything: "During the night the stories crawl on the walls and hang from the ceiling," runs a line in a story called "The Four Apples." "In the daytime they make yucky food good. You can squeeze them into a lunchbox or let them get big and take over the whole playground. They're faster than running shoes." Yet, though he clearly enjoys playful experimentation, Apple subordinates both theme ("I don't have any aesthetic or philosophic stuff in mind as I write") and language ("Though I spend much time and effort revising and trying to get every sentence as 'right' as it can be, finally the words don't matter") to two other traditional elements of fiction, character and action. "In a way I suppose I'm an experimental writer," he asserts, "since I admit to experimenting," but "I hope I've never lost sight of the most powerful question in narrative, what happens next?"—or forgot that "none of the experiments can work if you don't create a character whom you care about and whom your reader can care about." Once you have established interest, however—"once you and the reader" care about "what happens to your characters next"—"then you can experiment with everything else, the tone, the texture . . . maybe even make your characters the organs of a body."

The interest that Apple creates in his characters begins with the affection he feels and conveys. In a review of *Zip,* Apple's first novel, John Leonard identified Apple's distinguishing characteristic as "affection," a comment echoed in Anatole Broyard's recent review of *Free Agents,* Apple's latest collection of stories. Finally, Apple's affection reaches out to touch almost everyone in his fiction—male and female, the very young and the very old. "Apple likes people," John Leonard notes, "even crazy people." Yet, if one part of the special magic of Apple's fiction is to persuade us to care about his characters (from the mother in "Momma's Boy," "a small woman who took a punch well," to the "sly spleen" of "Free Agents," who accuses Socrates of proving his point "at the expense of innocent organs"), another part of its special magic is to make his readers feel somehow included, enveloped, embraced.

Born in 1941 in Grand Rapids, Michigan, Apple received his Ph.D. in English from the University of Michigan in 1970 and currently teaches creative writing and literature at Rice University. His earlier, deeper commitment, however, was to writing: "I always intended to be a writer," he says. In 1976 his first book, *The Oranging of America and Other Stories,* earned him the Jesse Jones Award from the Texas Institute of Letters. *Zip: A Novel of the Left and the Right* appeared in 1978, and his latest book, *Free Agents,* a collection of short stories, in 1984. In 1986 he received a Guggenheim fellowship.

Apple's mode is comedy, and his subjects range from politics to Pac-Man, from modern art to Mickey Mouse—from "Carbo-Loading" to "Post-Modernism." Yet even his caricatures, like Bertha and Solomon in *Zip,* come to exist in a larger, more human sphere. Apple uses humor to tease us into thought as well as affection. His art "transforms while it impersonates," as one reviewer put it, "changing not only what we see but the way we see it." For Apple, this process of seeing and reseeing is paramount. Having said that "finally the words don't matter," he adds that "in the great works you read right through words and even ideas to see life as only art can show it. This is a kind of 'truth' that isn't available in other aspects of life and it's this that keeps most of us writing."

Text:
Free Agents, 1984.

Free Agents

[I]

My heart went last. Trailing stray veins, pumping, still hot, and friendly and full of abject apologies, it joined the others.

This almost did me in.

"Fuck him," said my brain, and the battle lines formed.

"I," if you'll forgive me for the looseness of the term, was left with the brain, intact spinal column, and total skeleton minus only the riotous thumbs. Gone were the internal organs, three senses, and that whole complicated genetic code which the brain, surprisingly, could not lay claim to.

It was a classic strike, and I was stunned to the depths of my being by the issue itself and the speed with which it surfaced. Now, I am no Andrew Carnegie[1] and my liver is no Eugene V. Debs.[2] From each other we might have expected otherwise. Still, who knows? I can only tell you, in all honesty, that when it started I was as innocent as Florence Nightingale. The stomach grumbled, the kidneys ached a little. Yet, I thought I was "together." You know how it is. You live twenty, thirty years and in some very meaningful ways you get to feel used to yourself. For the stomach there's Di-Gel, for the kidneys Doan's pills. Most of the time you don't need anything. You can look in the mirror and think, He's not so bad. You learn to cope. Sometimes people tell you, You're cute, you're funny, you have a good personality. What happens is, you begin to take yourself for granted.

You say, "That's life." You take a drink, a wife, a job, a tranquilizer. Then suddenly, one sweet morning, you learn that behind your back your liver and kidneys have been plotting a revolution that makes Lenin[3] seem as insignificant as the Spanish-American War. The liver and kidneys issue a proclamation endorsed within the day by all the internal organs.

"The so-called one-life one-body ruling," their press release reads, "has for an entire decade been based upon false medical, legal, and moral evidence. The star surgeons

---

[1] Scottish-born American industrialist and philanthropist (1835–1919).
[2] American labor leader (1855–1926) and five-time Socialist candidate for president.

[3] Vladimir Ilyich Lenin (1870–1924), Russian revolutionary and first premier of the U.S.S.R. (1918–1924).

traipse through the land making big reputations by moving organs from one body to another. An average John Doe might have a new heart, a fresh kidney, pints of alien blood, even an engrafted tooth if the dentists have their way, and you know they will. Meanwhile, the organs are treated as so much meat.

"Before the age of transplants we took for granted the indignities placed upon our brothers the gallbladder, the appendix, the tonsils, and the intestine by the yard. No more.

"After the May 11 deadline which we are imposing, all organs, muscle, and tissue, whether initially within the Apple body or added subsequent to birth, become, as it were, free agents, capable of negotiating with any available bodies. We, the under-signed, hope for a just and speedy solution in the spirit of democratic fairness that has characterized the history of collective bargaining."

The liver and kidneys make this statement public on the morning of May 4. By midday all the major organs sign, and I face the distinct possibility that on May 11 the long-standing implicit contract between my parts and myself will become non-binding.

I call my doctor. He contacts the legal division of the AMA. Their chief counsel suggests compulsory round-the-clock negotiation, with all parties continuing past the deadline without curtailment of services. The parts turn a deaf ear. The spleen, who quickly becomes their counsel and spokesman, says, "The AMA sucks. We're dealing with you, boss; it's you and us, sink or swim, no bureaucracy. Cards on the table."

Imagine how I feel. In a week I might literally go to pieces.

"Be heroic," says the brain, hanging tough. "Stand now or forever face the possibility of internal dissent."

"But I'm no hero."

"Neither was Achilles.[4] The times make us all."

"He was nine tenths of a god."

"And you, mister frightened-of-everything, you are not made in the image of Pete Rozelle. Let them know who's boss. Do it once now or every day for the rest of your life."

"Why me?" I ask the spleen. "Why me when the world is full of strong men, examples for the young and credits to their races and nations? What's there to prove on Max Apple, who at his best barely makes it through a day? Why not Earl Campbell or Steve Carlton or Pelé, all heroes with heroic lungs and hearts and bladders? When you want new rules why not try them out on somebody who matters?"

"Ever heard of Brown versus Board of Education?"[5] the spleen replies. "Brown was a nobody. It's the principle. Celebrity just confuses the issue. All important decisions are tested on nobodies."

"But spleen and all the rest of you," I plead, "honest to God, I thought until the minute I read your statement that we had been in a happy union since my conception. I never heard any complaints. How did it get this far without my knowledge?"

"You could have opened your eyes sooner," says the spleen, "but still none of us blames you. It's true, a week is not long. If you want long, go to art. Time flies. We have short productive seasons. If we said, Max, old buddy, sure we trust you, take

---

[4] Hero of Homer's *Iliad*.
[5] Landmark decision of the United States

Supreme Court that ruled segregation in public schools unconstitutional.

a year or two, no hurry, we would become a disease, not an issue. And there's always the danger that in a moment of pique you might jet down to Houston and replace half of us with more docile members.

"Face up to it," the spleen says, "biology is destiny."

I begin to tremble.

"Get hold of yourself," he says, "this is not personal. We know that you're an easy target; so were all the generous slaveowners in the plantation days. Sure you're a decent fellow. In other times you might have anticipated a long uneventful life, a slow decay, even a pleasant enough senility. And we would have gone along as all our brethren of days past did, arm in arm with you toward the inorganic future.

"But you're no dummy, boss. Look where you're at. Where's the Family, the Church, the State? Now it's the body's turn to step into the twentieth century."

"And I am your stepping-stone?"

"Don't get sentimental," the brain says. He has heard enough. "Don't get sentimental with this crowd; it's just a waste of good feelings." He advises me to lie low, keep out of the negotiations altogether, leave everything to him. "Your weakness is your strength," he says. "Who wants your organs? These boys are not coming from Dave Winfield and Reggie Jackson. Face it, I'm the only one who might ever get another offer, and you know I'm not about to leave."

"We may be individually weak," says the spleen, "but we have numbers. And think of this while you're at it. Here you are, an obscure fellow with a chance to make major history. Deal with us, and together we'll become the Magna Carta[6] of science."

I admit that I respond to such rhetoric with a kind of benign ecstasy. I am ready to give in, but the brain, my counsel, steps hard upon my instincts.

"In the crunch, they'll fold," he says, "they have to. Where else can they go? It's not as if there was another league. Collective bargaining itself," he says, "is a ridiculous misnomer in this circumstance," since he can discern no demarcation between labor and management.

"Then ask him," counters the spleen, "why he stays and the rest of us don't."

"Simple loyalty," says the brain, "coupled with good judgment and right reason."

They go on like this for hours. By May 9 I am a shambles. My friends, unaware of the struggle within myself, see only neurotic symptoms. Little do they know that the brain, whom they suspect, is my only mainstay. When I try to tell my boss that on May 11 I may find myself a new person, he thinks I have been doing meditation or est training. He commends me. "We all should do it," he says, "regularly. It keeps us from growing stale."

On the evening of May 10 I beg my brain, "Let them have the new ground rules. Reinstate the contract. Give them everything they want and more."

"Sorry," he says, "but the stakes are much higher than yourself. Give them you and they'll want everyone. Here we'll make our stand."

"I'm not the stuff of martyrdom."

"The readiness is all," he says, and my eyes, who stayed, though the tear ducts left, give one final gush at 9 P.M. on May 10.

At midnight when my organs leave, I become, in an instant, like Italy during a

---

[6] Great charter of English political and civil
liberties granted by King John on June 15, 1215.

national strike. I am there but not there. The heart, as I've said, lingers, almost changes its mind, I think, at the last instant, but is driven along by the social pressure of both lungs.

I think that neither the parts nor I ever really thought it would come to this. Until the last instant we cling like lovers. Then, immediately we are divorced. And if you think that divorce between man and wife is a dismemberment, imagine my alienation.

"Marxist propaganda," says the brain. "No conditions can alienate a man from himself."

"But here I am, a hulk, an empty cavity. Prick me and I won't bleed."

"Stop being sentimental and get some rest," he says. "You'll need it. We're on the docket tomorrow at nine."

II

Without too much haggling, the brain and the members settle on the pituitary gland as judge. Although he resides in the brain's neighborhood, there clearly is no conflict of interest. During the week of turmoil—in fact, during my entire life, as far as I know—the pituitary has maintained a remarkably disinterested attitude toward all the commotions of human necessity. He also looks very judicial, small but long, gray at the sides, thoughtful, intensely calm.

The jury, though, is a horse of another color. The members insist that they be tried by peers, i.e., parts, and the judge quickly agrees over strenuous objection from the brain-prosecutor, who refuses to accept the analogy of blacks being tried by all-black juries. He attempts to call a well-known Gestalt[7] psychologist as expert witness to protest the judge's ruling, but the bench turns a cold ear. After this ruling, jury selection proceeds quickly. Shelley's[8] heart, Einstein's brain, and John Dillinger's penis along with nine less celebrated organs comprise the final jury. Einstein's brain, naturally, is chosen foreman.

Since the entire transcript will soon be available (Arno Press, a New York Times Company), I'll only give the highlights from my admittedly limited perspective. First, let me say absolutely that the brain as prosecutor and the spleen as chief defense attorney conducted themselves in a splendid legal manner. There were moments that might have been ugly, even grotesque, without good judgment on all sides. Yet, so orderly and decorous was the entire proceeding that in spite of the circumstances I could not help feeling proud of myself.

Among the many witnesses for the defense the spleen called:

Dr. Christiaan Barnard
Dave Winfield
Dr. Benjamin Spock
The heart of Luis Rodriguez
The right kidney of Alma Sands
Dr. Kenneth Eidel

[7] Psychological theory holding that psychological phenomena are organized wholes rather than aggregates of distinct parts and maintaining that the whole is more than the sum of its parts.

[8] Percy Bysshe Shelley (1792–1822), English Romantic poet.

The prosecution's list included:
William Shakespeare
Socrates
B. F. Skinner
Dr. Michael DeBakey
Jackie Robinson
Bowie Kuhn
Saint Thomas More
Masters and Johnson

When presented with the prosecution's witness list, the defense objects to the fact that fully one half of the state's witnesses are deceased. The court overrules the objection, since in all cases deceased parties are represented by adequate counsel. "In this instance," the judge blandly states, "life and death are not the important issues. Let us proceed."

To me they are, I want to yell at the top of my lungs, who ignore me from across the room. Since neither side calls upon me to testify, I am a mute witness to the playing out of my own destiny.

"You always are," says the brain. "Stop whining about it. If none of this had happened, you would be as ignorant of your internal self as you are now. Shut up and trust me."

I do so.

The central defense argument is clear enough. Organs have, at least in a legal sense, an existence of their own. They can survive individually when kept under proper circumstances and, furthermore, can and often are exchanged among various bodies without the consent of themselves. "In this day and age," states the spleen, "the body can no longer be considered as a whole." Dr. Barnard, taciturn, clearly uncomfortable, admits that though he does not like this kind of approach, it clearly seems to be scientifically accurate.

"When I began transplanting hearts," he says, almost apologetically, "I was young. There were those sufferers by the dozens turning blue daily before my eyes."

"If you had to do it all again," asks the prosecutor under cross-examination, "would you?"

Defense objects. Objection sustained, irrelevant question.

The prosecutor then asks if Dr. Barnard, in his vast surgical experience, has ever in his wildest fancy considered a heart as anything but an appendage to this or that body.

"Well, sir," says the good doctor, "yes, I have."

The brain asks no further questions, but the judge orders the jury removed and requests the doctor to continue.

"I don't like the direction in which this leads me, you know," Barnard states, "but I have indeed often wondered in the midst of many a chest if there was not something in this pulpy mass beyond my skillful fingers. I have thought of this at the moment of transplant and then sometimes weeks or even years later when the heart is rejected. Some scientists think that organ rejection can be overcome by drugs. Who knows?"

"You mean," interrupts the defense counsel, "that you believe that organs have a kind of free choice about their circumstances and are exercising it in spite of medical science."

The doctor nods a quiet yes.

The prosecutor is so angry that I am afraid all might turn to chaos now. But he quickly calms himself. "Who cares what that candy ass thinks," the brain whispers, hiding his anger as he looks over his notes on Dave Winfield.

None of the other defense witnesses seem to me very substantial. They range from Winfield's defense of capitalism (if only the case were that simple) to the straightforward but not very moving testimony of the Rodriguez heart and the Sands kidney that they were removed and relocated without their prior consent and were not especially content with their present location.

But, oh, when my large and dramatic brain begins to call the witnesses for the prosecution, then and only then does rhetoric flourish in the courtroom. Shakespeare, represented by Dillon & Reed, lays out our case in an oblique but universal fashion.

"Take but degree away and the bounded waters should lift their bosom higher than the shores, and make a sop of all this solid globe."

"Objection," says the spleen. "This language, fit perhaps for the stage, is but a subterfuge in these chambers. Cut out that honeyed tongue and let the mouth speak for itself."

"A strange metaphor for this defense," the judge observes; then he asks the Bard's counsel to be more direct.

In everyday language Shakespeare says, "Every ship must have a captain. Likewise, the vessel needs oarsmen, sails, cooks, porters, et al. If every oarsman thinks himself a captain, every cook a commander, then the ship, whether it be a body, a state, or the universe herself, flounders like a headless chicken."

In cross-examination the spleen asks very politely, "Mr. Bard, what do you mean by universe, or, more specifically, have you ever heard of the notion that there are endless suns?"

"The elephant hath joints but none for courtesy," says the Bard. "His legs are legs for necessity, not for flight."

"Do you believe," asks the impatient spleen, "that the earth is flat?"

"One touch of nature makes the whole world kin."

"Your Honor, no further questions. I think it is obvious that for all the eloquence expressed by this witness he is hardly able to make any serious judgments about twentieth-century phenomena."

The prosecutor, displeased by this subtle disparagement of a key witness, asks for a recess until tomorrow. The bench grants us only half an hour.

The brain, in a desperate resort to the living, calls B. F. Skinner. In a long and complicated testimony, Skinner asserts that wholes have little enough of what the defense calls "freedom" and that this scarce commodity dispersed among a horde of organs would lead to the end of all useful social behavior.

The sly spleen rises slowly to cross-examine. "Professor Skinner, would you please name that part of the human organism which you most admire."

"The brain."

"And if, professor, you were looking for pleasure centers, in say a lung or an intestine, how would you go about doing so?"

"I don't believe that these organs, by themselves, experience either pleasure or pain."

"You mean, sir, that they require the brain to translate sensory data and make judgments for them."

"Exactly."

"If it please the court," says the strutting spleen, "may I point out the great similarity between this world view and the pre-Lutheran Christian view which held the Church, specifically the Pope, as the arbiter and judge of all moral phenomena. I hope the jury will see that Professor Skinner, a so-called modern scientist, makes precisely the same argument as the Elizabethan playwright. To accept such reasoning requires a return in science and theology to the Catholicism of the seventeenth century."

"Objection," from the prosecution.

"Sustained. The jury will ignore the defense attorney's statement."

The brain and I huddle. "This is getting very serious," he says. "I'm afraid it's all going against us."

"What will happen to me?" I ask.

"Ironic," he says, "that the prosecution is worried about the fate of its client. Must I remind you that you, sir, are the state. What happens when the Supreme Court rules against the government—does all legislation cease? Anyway, relax. I'm calling the big one now. Forget Masters and Johnson, they'll never make a dent on this jury."

The prosecution calls Socrates. A hush falls over the room. You can barely hear the lungs expand. After a long moment, Einstein's brain, risking its position in the jury, calls out, "Let's hear it for one who started us all on the road to wisdom." The courtroom bursts into spontaneous applause.

The bench gavels for order but himself joins in the standing ovation to the ancient Greek, represented by Baker, Sullivan & Vance.

When order is restored, the judge politely warns the entire room, especially the jury, against any further outbreaks. The spleen approaches the bench. "Your Honor, I request that the witness be removed before making any statement. Until the vogue of the modern existentialists, he has represented the greatest historical threat to my clients."

"Objection, Your Honor," from the brain. "Must we listen to such disparagement of a man whom all the world esteems?"

The court allows the spleen to continue but warns him to be specific. "All right, Your Honor, and ladies and gentlemen of the jury. Here you have Socrates, wisest of men, the prince of irony, the founder of the examined life which we are at this very moment most diligently proving." The spleen turns to face the witness. "How, Socrates, did you end your earthly stay?"

"Hemlock by the glass," says the calm philosopher.

"There you have it, Your Honor. This so-called 'wise man' destroyed his organs for the sake of an idea."

"Could you have escaped, Socrates?"

"Yes."

"Could you have bribed the jailers?"

"Yes."

"The jury?"

"Yes."

"And yet you chose to stay, to execute your own organs, and were content to leave us all with the mild witticism about going off to life and death and who knows which is better. Well, you proved your idea, sir, at the expense of innocent organs. For all you know, your heart was a sophist, your liver altogether aphilosophical. Letting this man testify, Your Honor, would be as absurd as appointing Charles Manson the guardian of Sharon Tate's offspring."[9]

The judge is stunned. I don't blame him. The truth of the argument is altogether apparent. The court is silent. My heart beating across the room whimpers to me, a gesture of reconciliation. My pale organs wither in the fluorescent glare of this public place. My brain, that fertile, inexhaustible prosecutor, treads water in the silence.

"Your Honor," I state, hardly knowing what I do, "I wish to testify."

"Sit down, fool," whispers the brain. "If we lose, let's at least go out in style."

But finally I am able to ignore him. He seems no more persuasive at this moment than any of the other organs.

"What a piece of work a man is," Shakespeare calls out as I approach the witness stand to replace a bewildered Socrates as he steps down without having any chance to demonstrate his powers.

Neither the defense nor the prosecution rises to question me.

"Speak," says the judge.

"The Lord is my shepherd," I state, "and I shall not want."

"Objection," from both defense and prosecution.

The judge leans over and looks gravely at me. "You know the ground rules. If we wanted to do it this way, we wouldn't be in a court now, would we? The question, sir, is justice. Speak or forever lose your tongue."

"Ladies and gentlemen," I state, "those living and those represented by counsel, strangers, and my own vital parts. I admit it. The ball game is over. I am in violation of the antitrust laws, I am in restraint of trade, and I have monopolized myself. My brain has most valiantly been attempting to wrest victory or at least dignity through-out these proceedings. I thank him for his efforts, but no brain could successfully prosecute this case. I call the entire court to witness the fact that I now declare myself dispersed. Whatever previous legal rights I claimed to my parts or to any part of a part, including X-ray film and xerography, I now relinquish. Go, in good health and good fortune, to whomever you wish. And may each of you affix himself to a more solid and substantial spirit than I have proved to be."

"Your Honor," says the brain, "I ask the indulgence of the court. My client is no longer himself. Let the court spare us any further damage to what was once a model of sweet reason."

The gavel rings out. "Forgive me," I whisper to myself. The judge instructs the jury. They file out.

As we wait in silence, my brain ignores me, places an empty chair between us. I am, at this moment, beyond desolation. I am ready to throw in the towel but I don't know how. I am paralyzed, bereft of mind and body, yet in the midst of this crisis a strange indifferent calm overcomes me. It is the calm of the drowning man who gives up the struggle for one last pleasing glimpse of blue waters and teeming aquatic life.

---

[9] Charles Manson, a psychopathic criminal,
murdered actress Sharon Tate in 1969.

The court fades. Left with nothing else, I am overwhelmed by memory. The memory of fleeting sensuality. The taste of vanilla ice cream. The sound of the national anthem and Rice Krispies. "I am what I am," I whisper. Then, my heart, the one who I know has been sympathetic throughout, steps across the bar that separates us and begins to beat within me not a millimeter from his accustomed spot. His movement of return is stately, dignified, self-conscious, not like the hasty retreat of yesterday. He is telling me something, this heart of mine. Barely has he settled into the cavity of my chest when the others, equally austere and serene, join en masse. Kidneys, liver, thumbs, nerve endings, tear ducts, and finally the spleen himself. All these come to me as if I am gravity. The brain maintains a puzzled silence. The judge too has resumed his previous anonymity.

"I am what I am," I state again, this time more confidently, and the organs hum like an Indianapolis 500 engine. I can sense that each one of them is as happy to be back in his smooth soft spot as I am to have him there. I shift gears. I rise. I walk. I spit. I think.

"Nothing is settled," the brain reminds me. "The jury is still out."

"But," I say, "I am together again." I roar, I bellow, I beat my chest. When the jury returns glum and single file, I take a deep breath and blow them out of the box.

They scatter in my wind. "We were hung," Einstein's brain calls out from the blue sky. "And you, so recently yourself again, don't be so violent. We're all up in the air anyway."

"To tell me this," I yell to the heavens, "I don't need Einstein's brain." Clouds suck up the jury. Full of myself, on tiptoes I bounce on the grass, ready for everything.

1981

Alice Walker
b. 1944

Alice Walker—novelist, poet, essayist, biographer, and editor—has described herself as "preoccupied with the spiritual survival, the survival *whole* of my people." But Walker was a young black woman before she became a writer, and she also describes herself as specifically "committed to exploring the oppressions, the insanities, the loyalties, and the triumphs of black women." Too often, Walker believes, black and female experience, both in life and in literature, has been devalued by a culture that is dominated by white males. She not only sees Zora Neale Hurston as a tragic case of unappreciated—even suppressed— achievement and isolated suffering; she also sees Hurston's neglected achievement as representing a particularly terrible loss to those for whom it should have been an inspiring example. Walker's most recent book, *In Search of Our Mothers' Gardens* (1984), celebrates the many women who, like Walker's own mother, were left without any traditional outlet for artistic expression and still managed to hand down an abiding "respect for the possibilities [of life]—and the will to grasp them."

Walker learned early the need for indomitable will. Born in 1944 in Eatonton, Georgia—one of her early residences was a shack near Flannery O'Connor's Andalusia Farm—Walker was initially discouraged in her artistic ambition by critics who felt that a poor black farmer's daughter would face obstacles impossible to overcome. Walker's response was twofold. First, although she agreed that a "shack with only a dozen or so books" was "an unlikely place to discover a young Keats," she was convinced that it was narrow to think of Keats as "the only kind of poet one would want to grow up to be." Second, like the young Richard Wright, Walker began early to broaden her education. Graduating from Sarah Lawrence College in 1965, she began teaching writing and black literature in Mississippi, at Jackson State College and Tougaloo College. More recently, she has taught at Wellesley College, the University of Massachusetts, and Yale University and has served as a consulting and contributing editor of *Ms.* magazine and *Freedomways,* a quarterly journal of the Black Freedom Movement.

A mother as well as a socially engaged teacher, Walker believes that her maternal experiences as well as her political and educational experiences have enriched her writings. She has published three novels, *The Third Life of Grange Copeland* (1970), *Meridian* (1976), and *The Color Purple* (1982); four volumes of poetry, *Once* (1968), *Revolutionary Petunias* (1973), *Good Night, Willie Lee, I'll See You in the Morning* (1979), and *Horses Make a Landscape Look More Beautiful* (1984); a children's biography of Langston Hughes; and one collection of stories, *In Love and Trouble* (1974), from which "The Child Who Favored Daughter" is taken. Many of Walker's writings render moments of pain and moments of beauty in the lives of black women. Individual stories, poems, and essays have appeared in publications as diverse as *Harper's* and *Mother Jones,* and Walker's awards and grants range from a Guggenheim fellowship to a creative writing award from the National Endowment for the Arts and the Front Page Award for best magazine criticism by the Newswomen's Club of New York. Walker currently lives in San Francisco.

Walker's fiction reflects the full range of her interests and experience. From her mother, whose literary heritage derived primarily from the oral tradition of the black South, Walker inherited not only stories but also an urgent sense that her grandmother's "stories—like her life—must be recorded" if they were not to be lost. From the slave narratives of her ancestors, she gathered a sense that "family relationships are sacred" and that life is a "moral and/or physical struggle, the result of which is expected to be some kind of larger freedom." In her literary models, black and white, Walker discovered knowledge that "the strength of the artist" consists of the "courage to look at every old thing with fresh eyes." As a result, although she deals primarily with the experiences of poor black women, she addresses not only those who believe, as Henry James put it, that the house of fiction has many windows but also those who recognize that black and white writers (and, by extension, male and female writers) are "writing one immense story—the same story, for the most part—with different parts of this immense story coming from a multitude of different perspectives." By exploring the effects of racism and sexism, by giving "voice to centuries not only of silent bitterness and hate but also of neighborly kindness and sustaining love,"

Walker obviously hopes to enrich the lives of those who share the same race or sex as her most memorable characters. In addition, however, she clearly hopes to touch the lives of those with "different perspectives" who nevertheless can learn from hearing the pained voices she has heard and seeing the troubled gardens she has seen.

Text:
In Love and Trouble, 1974.

The Child Who Favored[1] Daughter

> *"That my daughter should*
> *fancy herself in love*
> *with* any *man!*
> *How can this be?"*
> Anonymous

[1]

She knows he has read the letter. He is sitting on the front porch watching her make the long trek from the school bus down the lane into the front yard. *Father, judge, giver of life.* Shadowy clouds indicating rain hang low on either side of the four o'clock sun and she holds her hand up to her eyes and looks out across the rows of cotton that stretch on one side of her from the mailbox to the house in long green hedges. After an initial shutting off of breath caused by fear, a calm numbness sets in and as she makes her way slowly down the lane she shuffles her feet in the loose red dust and tries to seem unconcerned. But she wonders how he knows about the letter. Her lover has a mother who dotes on the girl he married. It could have been her, preserving the race. Or the young bride herself, brittled to ice to find a letter from her among keepsakes her husband makes no move to destroy. Or—? But that notion does not develop in her mind. She loves him.

> Fire of earth
> Lure of flower smells
> The sun

Down the lane with slow deliberate steps she walks in the direction of the house, toward the heavy silent man on the porch. The heat from the sun is oppressively hot but she does not feel its heat so much as its warmth, for there is a cold spot underneath the hot skin of her back that encloses her heart and reaches chilled arms around the bottom cages of her ribs.

---

[1] In southern vernacular, resembled.

Lure of flower smells
The sun

She stops to gaze intently at a small wild patch of black-eyed Susans and a few stray buttercups. Her fingers caress lightly the frail petals and she stands a moment wondering.

The lure of flower smells
The sun
Softly the scent of—
Softly the scent of flowers
And petals
Small, bright last wishes

2

He is sitting on the porch with his shotgun leaning against the banister within reach. If he cannot frighten her into chastity with his voice he will threaten her with the gun. He settles tensely in the chair and waits. He watches her from the time she steps from the yellow bus. He sees her shade her eyes from the hot sun and look widely over the rows of cotton running up, nearly touching him where he sits. He sees her look, knows its cast through any age and silence, knows she knows he has the letter.

Above him among the rafters in a half-dozen cool spots shielded from the afternoon sun the sound of dirt daubers. And busy wasps building onto their paper houses a dozen or more cells. Late in the summer, just as the babies are getting big enough to fly he will have to light paper torches and burn the paper houses down, singeing the wings of the young wasps before they get a chance to fly or to sting him as he sits in the cool of the evening reading his Bible.

Through eyes half closed he watches her come, her feet ankle deep in the loose red dust. Slowly, to the droning of the enterprising insects overhead, he counts each step, surveys each pause. He sees her looking closely at the bright patch of flowers. She is near enough for him to see clearly the casual slope of her arm that holds the schoolbooks against her hip. The long dark hair curls in bits about her ears and runs in corded plainness down her back. Soon he will be able to see her eyes, perfect black-eyed Susans. Flashing back fragmented bits of himself. Reflecting his mind.

Memories of years
Unknowable women—
sisters
spouses
illusions of soul

When he was a boy he had a sister called "Daughter." She was like honey, tawny, wild, and sweet. She was a generous girl and pretty, and he could not remember a time when he did not love her intensely, with his whole heart. She would give him anything she had, give anybody anything she had. She could not keep money, clothes, health. Nor did she seem to care for the love that came to her too easily. When he begged her not to go out, to stay with him, she laughed at him and went her way, sleeping here, sleeping there. Wherever she was needed, she would say, and laugh. But this could not go on forever; coming back from months with another woman's husband, her own mind seemed to have struck her down. He was struck down, too, and cried many nights on his bed; for she had chosen to give her love to the very man in whose cruel, hot, and lonely fields he, her brother, worked. Not treated as a man, scarcely as well as a poor man treats his beast.

> Memories of years
> Unknowable women—
> sisters
> spouses
> illusions of soul

When she came back all of her long strong hair was gone, her teeth wobbled in her gums when she ate, and she recognized no one. All day and all night long she would sing and scream and tell them she was on fire. He was still a boy when she began playing up to him in her cunning way, exploiting again his love. And he, tears never showing on his face, would let her bat her lashless eyes at him and stroke his cheeks with her frail, clawlike hands. Tied on the bed as she was she was at the mercy of everyone in the house. They threw her betrayal at her like sharp stones, until they satisfied themselves that she could no longer feel their ostracism or her own pain. Gradually, as it became apparent she was not going to die, they took to flinging her food to her as if she were an animal and at night when she howled at the shadows thrown over her bed by the moon his father rose up and lashed her into silence with his belt.

On a day when she seemed nearly her old self she begged him to let her loose from the bed. He thought that if he set her free she would run away into the woods and never return. His love for her had turned into a dull ache of constant loathing, and he dreamed vague fearful dreams of a cruel revenge on the white lover who had shamed them all. But Daughter, climbing out of bed like a wary animal, knocked him unconscious to the floor and night found her impaled on one of the steel-spike fence posts near the house.

That she had given herself to the lord of his own bondage was what galled him! And that she was cut down so! He could not forgive her the love she gave that knew nothing of master and slave. For though her own wound was a bitter one and in the end fatal, he bore a hurt throughout his life that slowly poisoned him. In a world where innocence and guilt became further complicated by questions of color and race, he felt hesitant and weary of living as though all the world were out to trick him. His only guard against the deception he believed life had in store for him was a knowledge that evil and deception *would come* to him; and a readiness to provide them with a match.

The women in his life faced a sullen barrier of distrust and hateful mockery. He could not seem to help hating even the ones who loved him, and laughed loudest at the ones who cared for him, as if they were fools. His own wife, beaten into a cripple to prevent her from returning the imaginary overtures of the white landlord, killed herself while she was still young enough and strong enough to escape him. But she left a child, a girl, a daughter; a replica of Daughter, his dead sister. A replica in every way.

> Memories of once
> like a mirror reflecting—
> all hope, all loss

His hands are not steady and he makes a clawing motion across the air in front of his face. She is walking, a vivid shape in blue and white, across the yard, underneath the cedar trees. She pauses at the low limb of the big magnolia and seems to contemplate the luminous gloss of the cone-shaped flowers beyond her reach. In the hand away from the gun is the open letter. He holds it tightly by a corner. The palms of his hands are sweating, his throat is dry. He swallows compulsively and rapidly bats his eyes. The slight weight of her foot sends vibrations across the gray boards of the porch. Her eyes flicker over him and rest on the open letter. Automatically his hand brings the letter upward a little although he finds he cannot yet, facing her strange familiar eyes, speak.

With passive curiosity the girl's eyes turn from the letter to the gun leaning against the banister to his face, which he feels growing blacker and tighter as if it is a mask that, when it is completely hardened, will drop off. Almost casually she sways back against the porch post, looking at him and from time to time looking over his head at the brilliant afternoon sky. Without wanting it his eyes travel heavily down the slight, roundly curved body and rest on her offerings to her lover in the letter. He is a black man but he blushes, the red underneath his skin glowing purple, and the coils of anger around his tongue begin to loosen.

"White man's slut!" he hisses at her through nearly sealed lips and clenched teeth. Her body reacts as if hit by a strong wind and lightly she sways on her slender legs and props herself more firmly against the post. At first she gazes directly into his eyes as if there is nowhere else to look. Soon she drops her head.

She leads the way to the shed behind the house. She is still holding her books loosely against her thigh and he makes his eyes hard as they cover the small light tracks made in the dust. The brown of her skin is full of copper tints and her arms are like long golden fruits that take in and throw back the hues of the sinking sun. Relentlessly he hurries her steps through the sagging door of boards, with hardness he shoves her down into the dirt. She is like a young willow without roots under his hands and as she does not resist he beats her for a long time with a harness from the stable and where the buckles hit there is a welling of blood which comes to be level with the tawny skin then spills over and falls curling into the dust of the floor.

Stumbling weakly toward the house through the shadows of the trees, he tries to look up beseechingly to the stars, but the sky is full of clouds and rain beats down around his ears and drenches him by the time he reaches the back steps. The dogs run excitedly and hungry around the damp reaches of the back porch and although he feeds them not one will stand unmoving beneath his quickscratching fingers. Dully he watches them eat and listens to the high winds in the trees. Shuddering with chill he walks through the house to the front porch and picks up the gun that is getting wet and sits with it across his lap, rocking it back and forth on his knees like a baby. It is rainsoaked, but he can make out "I love you" written in a firm hand across the blue face of the letter. He hates the very paper of the letter and crumples it in his fist. A wet storm wind lifts it lightly and holds it balled up against the taut silver screen on the side of the porch. He is glad when the wind abandons it and leaves it sodden and limp against the slick wet boards under his feet. He rests his neck heavily on the back of his chair. Words of the letter—her letter to the white devil who has disowned her to marry one of his own kind—are running on a track in his mind. "Jealousy is being nervous about something that has never, and probably won't ever, belong to you." A wet waning moon fills the sky before he nods.

3

No amount of churchgoing changed her ways. Prayers offered nothing to quench her inner thirst. Silent and lovely, but barren of essential hope if not of the ability to love, hers was a world of double images, as if constantly seen through tears. It was Christianity as it invaded her natural wonderings that threw color into high and fast relief, but its hard Southern rudeness fell flat outside her house, its agony of selfishness failed completely to pervade the deep subterranean country of her mind. When asked to abandon her simple way of looking at simple flowers, she could only yearn the more to touch those glowing points of bloom that lived and died away among the foliage over there, rising and falling like certain stars of which she was told, coming and being and going on again, always beyond her reach. Staring often and intently into the ivory hearts of fallen magnolia blossoms she sought the answer to the question that had never really been defined for her, although she was expected to know it, but she only learned from this that it is the fallen flower most earnestly hated, most easily bruised.

> The lure of flower smells
> The sun

In the morning, finding the world newly washed but the same, he rises from stiff-jointed sleep and wanders through the house looking at old photographs. In a frame of tarnish and gilt, her face forming out of the contours of a peach, the large dead eyes of beautiful Daughter, his first love. For the first time he turns it upside down then makes his way like a still sleeping man, wonderingly, through the house. At the back door he runs his fingers over the long blade of his pocket-knife and puts it, with gentleness and resignation, into his pocket. He knows that as one whose ultimate death must conform to an aged code of madness, resignation is a kind of dying. A preparation for the final event. He makes a step in the direction of the shed. His eyes hold the panicked calm of fishes taken out of water, whose bodies but not their eyes beat a frantic maneuver over dry land.

In the shed he finds her already awake and for a long time she lies as she was, her dark eyes reflecting the sky through the open door. When she looks at him it is not with hate, but neither is it passivity she reads in her face. Gone is the silent waiting of yesterday, and except for the blood she is strong looking and the damp black hair trailing loose along the dirt floor excites him and the terror she has felt in the night is nothing to what she reads now in his widestretched eyes.

He begs her hoarsely, when it clears for him that she is his daughter, and not

Daughter, his first love, if she will deny the letter. Deny the letter; the paper eaten and the ink drunk, the words never wrung from the air. Her mouth curls into Daughter's own hilarity. She says quietly no. No, with simplicity, a shrug, finality. No. Her slow tortured rising is a strong advance and scarcely bothering to look at him, she reflects him silently, pitilessly with her black-pond eyes.

"Going," she says, as if already there, and his heart buckles. He can only strike her with his fist and send her sprawling once more into the dirt. She gazes up at him over her bruises and he sees her blouse, wet and slippery from the rain, has slipped completely off her shoulders and her high young breasts are bare. He gathers their fullness in his fingers and begins a slow twisting. The barking of the dogs creates a frenzy in his ears and he is suddenly burning with unnamable desire. In his agony he draws the girl away from him as one pulling off his own arm and with quick slashes of his knife leaves two bleeding craters the size of grapefruits on her bare bronze chest and flings what he finds in his hands to the yelping dogs.

> Memories of once
> constant and silent
> like a mirror
> reflecting

Today he is slumped in the same chair facing the road. The yellow school bus sends up clouds of red dust on its way. If he stirs it may be to Daughter shuffling lightly along the red dirt road, her dark hair down her back and her eyes looking intently at buttercups and stray black-eyed Susans along the way. If he stirs it may be he will see his own child, a black-eyed Susan from the soil on which she walks. A slight, pretty flower that grows on any ground; and flowers pledge no allegiance to banners of any man. If he stirs he might see the perfection of an ancient dream, his own nightmare; the answer to the question still whispered about, undefined. If he stirs he might feel the energetic whirling of wasps about his head and think of ripe late-summer days and time when scent makes a garden of the air. If he stirs he might wipe the dust from the dirt daubers out of his jellied eyes. If he stirs he might take up the heavy empty shotgun and rock it back and forth on his knees, like a baby.

1967

Ann Beattie
b. 1947

In some respects Ann Beattie's characters hearken back to America's old dream of success. Spiritual descendants of John Cheever's New England suburbanites, they epitomize the young, upwardly mobile professional class now emerging as a dominant force in American life. Yet, as one critic has noted, Beattie's characters are, "above all, hoping not to dissolve," for they are, "in every sense, between engagements, forever commuting between one another's homes and lives, both of which they enter and leave with casual frequency." Survivors of the turbulent

1960s, they continue to experiment with drugs, to sing old protest songs, and to engage in casual sex, even as they are engulfed by the apathy and disillusionment of the 1970s and 1980s. "I'm exhausted," one of them remarks, as if to summarize his life, "from sitting all day, drinking, and doing nothing." Possessing ties to several worlds yet fully belonging to none, they are never far from the chaos that Beattie regards as the subject of her fiction.

Beattie was born in Washington, D.C., in 1947. She received a B.A. from American University in 1969 and an M.A. the following year from the University of Connecticut, where she continued graduate studies for two more years. In 1978 she received a Guggenheim fellowship, and she has since been a visiting writer and lecturer at both Harvard and the University of Virginia. A prolific writer, she has published three novels—*Chilly Scenes of Winter* (1976), *Falling in Place* (1980), and *Love Always* (1985), the first of which was made into a movie in 1979—and four collections of short stories—*Distortions* (1976), *Secrets and Surprises* (1979), *The Burning House* (1984), from which "Jacklighting" is taken, and *Where You'll Find Me* (1986).

Many of Beattie's stories first appeared in *The New Yorker,* which has been a forum for such chroniclers of upper-middle-class life as J. D. Salinger, John Cheever, and John Updike, and in fact Beattie's work has been criticized for its faithfulness to the genre. Yet no one disputes her talent. Her uninflected prose style recalls Ernest Hemingway's in its flat, declarative sentences, but the almost bewildering detail and disjointed, oblique narrative are singularly suited to her purposes. "Many of the flat statements that I bring together," she says, "are usually non sequiturs or bordering on being non sequiturs—which reinforces the chaos." But, as John Updike has noted, Beattie's "resolutely unmetaphorical style" builds around us "a maze of familiar truths that nevertheless has something airy, eerie, and in the end lovely about it." Perhaps it is this that has moved another of her contemporaries to remark that she is beginning to sound less like a disaffected hippie and more like Chekhov.

Text:
The Burning House, 1982.

Jacklighting[1]

It is Nicholas's birthday. Last year he was alive, and we took him presents: a spiral notebook he pulled the pages out of, unable to write but liking the sound of paper tearing; magazines he flipped through, paying no attention to pictures, liking the blur

---

[1] The practice of stunning game animals, usually deer, by shining a focused light in their eyes. Hunting by this method is illegal in most states.

of color. He had a radio, so we could not take a radio. More than the radio, he seemed to like the sound the metal drawer in his bedside table made, sliding open, clicking shut. He would open the drawer and look at the radio. He rarely took it out.

Nicholas's brother Spence has made jam. For days the cat has batted grapes around the huge homemade kitchen table; dozens of bloody rags of cheesecloth have been thrown into the trash. There is grape jelly, raspberry jelly, strawberry, quince, and lemon. Last month, a neighbor's pig escaped and ate Spence's newly planted fraise des bois plants, but overlooked the strawberry plants close to the house, heavy with berries. After that, Spence captured the pig and called his friend Andy, who came for it with his truck and took the pig to his farm in Warrenton. When Andy got home and looked in the back of the truck, he found three piglets curled against the pig.

In this part of Virginia, it is a hundred degrees in August. In June and July you can smell the ground, but in August it has been baked dry; instead of smelling the earth you smell flowers, hot breeze. There is a haze over the Blue Ridge Mountains that stays in the air like cigarette smoke. It is the same color as the eye shadow Spence's girlfriend, Pammy, wears. The rest of us are sunburned, with pink mosquito bites on our bodies, small scratches from gathering raspberries. Pammy has just arrived from Washington. She is winter-pale. Since she is ten years younger than the rest of us, a few scratches wouldn't make her look as if she belonged, anyway. She is in medical school at Georgetown, and her summer-school classes have just ended. She arrived with leather sandals that squeak. She is exhausted and sleeps half the day, upstairs, with the fan blowing on her. All weekend the big fan has blown on Spence, in the kitchen, boiling and bottling his jams and jellies. The small fan blows on Pammy.

Wynn and I have come from New York. Every year we borrow his mother's car and drive from Hoboken to Virginia. We used to take the trip to spend the week of Nicholas's birthday with him. Now we come to see Spence, who lives alone in the house. He is making jam early, so we can take jars back with us. He stays in the kitchen because he is depressed and does not really want to talk to us. He scolds the cat, curses when something goes wrong.

Wynn is in love. The girl he loves is twenty, or twenty-one. Twenty-two. When he told me (top down on the car, talking into the wind), I couldn't understand half of what he was saying. There were enough facts to daze me; she had a name, she was one of his students, she had canceled her trip to Rome this summer. The day he told me about her, he brought it up twice; first in the car, later in Spence's kitchen. "That was *not* my mother calling the other night to say she got the car tuned," Wynn said, smashing his glass on the kitchen counter. I lifted his hand off the large shard of glass, touching his fingers as gently as I'd touch a cactus. When I steadied myself on the counter, a chip of glass nicked my thumb. The pain shot through my body and pulsed in my ribs. Wynn examined my hands; I examined his. A dust of fine glass coated our hands, gently touching, late at night, as we looked out the window at the moon shining on Spence's lemon tree with its one lemon, too heavy to be growing on the slender branch. A jar of Lipton iced tea was next to the tub the lemon tree grew out of—a joke, put there by Wynn, to encourage it to bear more fruit.

Wynn is standing in the field across from the house, pacing, head down, the bored little boy grown up.

"When wasn't he foolish?" Spence says, walking through the living room. "What kind of sense does it make to turn against him now for being a fool?"

"He calls it mid-life crisis, Spence, and he's going to be thirty-two in September."

"I know when his birthday is. You hint like this every year. Last year at the end of August you dropped it into conversation that the two of you were doing something or other to celebrate *his birthday.*"

"We went to one of those places where a machine shoots baseballs at you. His birthday present was ten dollars' worth of balls pitched at him. I gave him a Red Sox cap. He lost it the same day."

"How did he lose it?"

"We came out of a restaurant and a Doberman was tied by its leash to a stop sign, barking like mad—a very menacing dog. He tossed the cap, and it landed on the dog's head. It was funny until he wanted to get it back, and he couldn't go near it."

"He's one in a million. He deserves to have his birthday remembered. Call me later in the month and remind me." Spence goes to the foot of the stairs. "Pammy," he calls.

"Come up and kill something for me," she says. The bed creaks. "Come kill a wasp on the bedpost. I hate to kill them. I hate the way they crunch."

He walks back to the living room and gets a newspaper and rolls it into a tight tube, slaps it against the palm of his hand.

Wynn, in the field, is swinging a broken branch, batting hickory nuts and squinting into the sun.

Nicholas lived for almost a year, brain-damaged, before he died. Even before the accident, he liked the way things felt. He always watched shadows. He was the man looking to the side in Cartier-Bresson's[2] photograph, instead of putting his eye to the wall. He'd find pennies on the sidewalk when the rest of us walked down city streets obliviously, spot the chipped finger on a mannequin flawlessly dressed, sidestep the one piece of glass among shells scattered on the shoreline. It would really have taken something powerful to do him in. So that's what happened: a drunk in a van, speeding, head-on, Nicholas out for a midnight ride without his helmet. Earlier in the day he'd assembled a crazy nest of treasures in the helmet, when he was babysitting the neighbors' four-year-old daughter. Spence showed it to us—holding it forward as carefully as you'd hold a bomb, looking away the way you'd avoid looking at dead fish floating in a once nice aquarium, the way you'd look at an ugly scar, once the bandages had been removed, and want to lay the gauze back over it. While he was in the hospital, his fish tank overheated and all the black mollies died. The doctor unwound some of the bandages and the long brown curls had been shaved away, and there was a red scar down the side of his head that seemed as out of place as a line dividing a highway out west, a highway that nobody traveled anyway. It could have happened to any of us. We'd all ridden on the Harley, bodies pressed into his back, hair whipped across our faces. How were we going to feel ourselves again, without Nicholas? In the hospital, it was clear that the thin intravenous tube was not dripping life back into him—that was as farfetched as the idea that the too-thin branch of the lemon tree could grow one more piece of fruit. In the helmet had been dried chrysanthemums, half of a robin's blue shell, a cat's eye marble, yellow twine, a sprig of grapes, a piece of a broken ruler. I remember Wynn actually jumping back when

---

[2] Henri Cartier-Bresson (1908–1983), renowned French photographer.

he saw what was inside. I stared at the strangeness such ordinary things had taken on. Wynn had been against his teaching me to ride his bike, but he had. He taught me to trust myself and not to settle for seeing things the same way. The lobster claw on a necklace he made me was funny and beautiful. I never felt the same way about lobsters or jewelry after that. "Psychologists have figured out that infants start to laugh when they've learned to be skeptical of danger," Nicholas had said. Laughing on the back of his motorcycle. When he lowered the necklace over my head, rearranging it, fingers on my throat.

It is Nicholas's birthday, and so far no one has mentioned it. Spence has made all the jam he can make from the fruit and berries and has gone to the store and returned with bags of flour to make bread. He brought the *Daily Progress* to Pammy, and she is reading it, on the side porch where there is no screening, drying her hair and stiffening when bees fly away from the Rose of Sharon bushes. Her new sandals are at the side of the chair. She has red toenails. She rubs the small pimples on her chin the way men finger their beards. I sit on the porch with her, catcher's mitt on my lap, waiting for Wynn to get back from his walk so we can take turns pitching to each other.

"Did he tell you I was a drug addict? Is that why you hardly speak to me?" Pammy says. She is squinting at her toes. "I'm older than I look," she says. "He says I'm twenty-one, because I look so young. He doesn't know when to let go of a joke, though. I don't like to be introduced to people as some child prodigy."

"What were you addicted to?" I say.

"Speed," she says. "I had another life." She has brought the bottle of polish with her, and begins brushing on a new layer of red, the fingers of her other hand stuck between her toes from underneath, separating them. "I don't get the feeling you people had another life," she says. "After all these years, I still feel funny when I'm around people who've never lived the way I have. It's just snobbishness, I'm sure."

I cup the catcher's mitt over my knee. A bee has landed on the mitt. This is the most Pammy has talked. Now she interests me; I always like people who have gone through radical changes. It's snobbishness—it shows me that other people are confused, too.

"That was the summer of sixty-seven," she says. "I slept with a stockbroker for money. Sat through a lot of horror movies. That whole period's a blur. What I remember about it is being underground all the time, going places on the subway. I only had one real friend in the city. I can't remember where I was going." Pammy looks at the newspaper beside her chair. "Charlottesville, Virginia," she says. "My, my. Who would have thought twitchy little Pammy would end up here?"

Spence tosses the ball. I jump, mitt high above my head, and catch it. Spence throws again. Catch. Again. A hard pitch that lets me know the palm of my hand will be numb when I take off the catcher's mitt. Spence winds up. Pitches. As I'm leaning to get the ball, another ball sails by on my right. Spence has hidden a ball in his pocket all this time. Like his brother, he's always trying to make me smile.

"It's too hot to play ball," he says. "I can't spend the whole day trying to distract you because Wynn stalked off into the woods today."

"Come on," I say. "It was working."

"Why don't we all go to Virginia Beach next year instead of standing around down here smoldering? This isn't any tribute to my brother. How did this get started?"

"We came to be with you because we thought it would be hard. You didn't tell us about Pammy."

"Isn't that something? What that tells you is that you matter, and Wynn matters, and Nicholas mattered, but I don't even think to mention the person who's supposedly my lover."

"She said she had been an addict."

"She probably tried to tell you she wasn't twenty-one, too, didn't she?"

I sidestep a strawberry plant, notice one croquet post stuck in the field.

"It was a lie?" I say.

"No," he says. "I never know when to let my jokes die."

When Nicholas was alive, we'd celebrate his birthday with mint juleps and croquet games, stuffing ourselves with cake, going for midnight skinny-dips. Even if he were alive, I wonder if today would be anything like those birthdays of the past, or whether we'd have bogged down so hopelessly that even his childish enthusiasm would have had little effect. Wynn is sure that he's having a crisis and that it's not the real thing with his student because he also has a crush on Pammy. We are open about everything: he tells me about taking long walks and thinking about nothing but sex; Spence bakes the French bread too long, finds that he's lightly tapping a rock, sits on the kitchen counter, puts his hands over his face, and cries. Pammy says that she does not feel close to any of us—that Virginia was just a place to come to cool out. She isn't sure she wants to go on with medical school. I get depressed and think that if the birds could talk, they'd say that they didn't enjoy flying. The mountains have disappeared in the summer haze.

Late at night, alone on the porch, toasting Nicholas with a glass of wine, I remember that when I was younger, I assumed he'd be our guide: he saw us through acid trips, planned our vacations, he was always there to excite us and to give us advice. He started a game that went on for years. He had us close our eyes after we'd stared at something and made us envision it again. We had to describe it with our eyes closed. Wynn and Spence could talk about the things and make them more vivid than they were in life. They remembered well. When I closed my eyes, I squinted until the thing was lost to me. It kept going backwards into darkness.

Tonight, Nicholas's birthday, it is dark and late and I have been trying to pay him some sort of tribute by seeing something and closing my eyes and imagining it. Besides realizing that two glasses of wine can make me drunk, I have had this revelation: that you can look at something, close your eyes and see it again and still know nothing —like staring at the sky to figure out the distances between stars.

The drunk in the van that hit Nicholas thought that he had hit a deer.

Tonight, stars shine over the field with the intensity of flashlights. Every year, Spence calls the state police to report that on his property, people are jacklighting.

1980

David Mamet
b. 1947

David Mamet's view of his craft is starkly simple: "I don't have any theories about how to write plays," he asserts in an interview. "That's something you can't possibly learn from reading a book of plays. You do it by doing it. You can sort of be guided in the pursuit of this knowledge by what other people have done, and by what you see happening on the stage, but you have to teach yourself." Mamet's self-education combined studying at Goddard College in Vermont and working at the Neighborhood Playhouse in New York with taking on odd jobs for money—in a canning plant, a truck factory, and a real estate agency ("one of those offices on the way to the airport," as he describes it). He has also driven a taxi, washed windows, waited on tables at a gay bar, and written captions for *Oui* magazine ("I got paid for sitting all day looking at pictures of naked women and making up lies about them").

Born and raised in Chicago, Mamet managed to coordinate acting in community theaters and working backstage at the Hull House Theater with graduating from the prestigious Francis Parker School. After earning a degree at Goddard College in 1969, he taught at Marlboro College in Vermont and then returned to his alma mater as artist-in-residence. While at Goddard, he helped form a group of actors that became the St. Nicholas Theater Company, which moved to Chicago in 1974 with Mamet as artistic director. In 1976 and 1977 he worked at the Yale Drama School under the auspices of a CBS creative writing fellowship and produced two new plays, *Dark Pony* and *Reunion,* to favorable reviews. In 1978 he was named associate artistic director and playwright in residence at Chicago's Goodman Theater, for which he wrote several plays. In the same year he was appointed special lecturer at the University of Chicago. "I'm a pedagogue by nature," he reports. "My wife [the actress Lindsay Crouse] says I can't burp without quoting Aristotle. Teaching is what I'm best at." Most recently, students at New York University have had the benefit of his irreverent views of his craft and the state of the American theater.

David Mamet is one of contemporary America's most prolific and honored playwrights. His works include two celebrated one-act comedies, *Duck Variations* (1973) and *Sexual Perversity in Chicago* (1974), the second of which won the *Village Voice* Obie award for distinguished playwrighting. In *Sexual Perversity in Chicago* we observe two young men engaged in a search for women; in *Duck Variations* we listen to two old men commiserating over their inability to do anything but talk. In 1977 Mamet premiered *American Buffalo,* which won the New York Drama Critics' Award as best American play. In 1978 Mamet won the John Gassner Award for his distinguished contributions to the theater. Four years later he received a second Obie for a play called *Edmond,* which traces the fate of a middle-class New Yorker who abandons his family and enters the city's underworld. *Glengarry Glen Ross* (1983), Mamet's best-known play, deals with the sordidly deceptive world of real estate hustlers. Named best play of the year by the Society of West End Theatres in London, *Glengarry Glen Ross* was nominated for four TONY awards and won the Pulitzer Prize in drama. Mamet has also written the screenplay for *The Postman Always Rings Twice* (1980) and *The Verdict* (1982), for which he was nominated for an Academy Award. In 1982 he began writing a third screenplay, on the life of Malcolm X.

Mamet's plays address quintessential American concerns. Most recently, his interest has centered on the personal costs of doing business in "a nation of entrepreneurs." In *The Vermont Sketches,* four of which were performed in 1984, he presents the underbelly of that world, the debased values and vulgar lives of small-time entrepreneurs as they struggle to survive against the threat of being eliminated by or made subservient to the corporations and franchises of America. Above all, it is Mamet's ability to capture the poignant, obscene, and humorous thoughts of his characters in colloquial cadences that distinguishes his work. "What the characters say to each other," he asserts, "must contain and give birth to what they do to each other." When asked to comment on the American theater, Mamet sardonically notes that there are grown men and women trying "to bring a tradition back. . . . This stuff is not chopped liver."

Text:
The Vermont Sketches, 1986.

The Vermont Sketches

Conversations with the Spirit World

Characters

Morris ⎫
          ⎬ *two men*
James ⎭

Morris: Dowsing for the like the kid says, "What cha doin'?" Says, "I'm *dowsing.*" "What is that?" "I'm looking for this *line* . . ." "Line is *that?*" . . . "Line I'm *looking* for . . ." He points. "That *purple* line . . . ?"

James: No . . .

Morris: Yes, and by dajn if he didn't point it *out.*

James: He *saw* it . . . ?

Morris: Well, that's what I'm *telling* you . . . "What are you doing?" "Dowsing for a *well* . . ." By God, I'm trine to get these silly *sticks* to work . . .

James: . . . uh-huh . . .

Morris: S'I find this *line,* I'm trying to feel the line and Clark can *see* . . . I'll tell you something else: *Ivers*

James: Now who is that . . . ?

Morris: Say Eighteen *thirty* . . . , say Eighteen, to Eighteen forty-*five, fifty,* hired man up to Hayes place . . .

James: Uh-huh . . .

Morris: . . . he died, *Clara* said that he didn't go *over*.

James: . . . old *Hayes* farm . . .

Morris: The old *Hayes* farm. The *hired* man. Now: Annie, she was *young*, you know, we'd hear her *talking* . . .

James: . . . uh-huh . . .

Morris: . . . young folks do, a little kid, you know, a year old, she'd be *talking* . . .

James: She'd be talking to herself . . .

Morris: Uh-huh . . . one day, we're up there, Clara asks her who she's *talking* to. She says, "This man . . ."

James: Uh-huh.

Morris: So she . . . now, I think, *I think* what Annie says is *Clara* asks her, "What's his *name?*" Annie says, "Ivan," something like that. Later it occurs to me, now where'd she get *that* from . . . ?

James: The Russians.

Morris: . . . what *I* thought. But even *so*, something she *heard?* Where would she *hear* that. I told . . . I remember this, I'm telling stories on my *kids* . . .

James: . . . uh-huh . . .

Morris: to *Chunk*, I think it was . . .

James: Chunk *Kellog*.

Morris: Yes. Said, "Where she *gets* it from . . . some man named *Ivan*." He said, "Ask her was it Ivan she said or *Ivers*." Who he was, as I said, a *hired* man, hundred *years* ago.

James: He die a violent death?

Morris: I don't *know*. What *Chunk* said . . . *yes*. Yes. I think he did. He, what *Chunk* said, he didn't want to go *across* . . .

James: Uh-huh . . .

Morris: And, to that *time* he habited the house.

James: Annie remember this?

Morris: Well, you don't *know* . . .

James: Uh-huh . . .

Morris: Whether she, what she *saw*, or the *stories* . . .

James: . . . uh-huh . . .

Morris: . . . you know . . .

James: Yes.

Morris: . . . that she remembers that we'd tell. And she *described* him.

James: What'd she say?

Morris: A *man*, you know, I don't remember . . . *beard*

James: . . . uh-huh . . .

Morris: A heavy *shirt* . . .

James: Mm. *(Pause)*

Morris: Reason *I thought* of it, dowsing for water, and *Clark* says . . .

James: Well, they say ninety percent *anyone* can dowse . . .

Morris: . . . that's right . . .

James: . . . and a *hundred* percent all *children*.

Morris: That's right. *(Pause)* That's right.

James: Jean saw something out on the hill.

Morris: What was that?

James: . . . the old *sugar* lane . . .

Morris: Uh-huh . . .

James: *Dusk* one day . . .

Morris: When was this?

James: Last fall.

Morris: Uh-huh.

James: She got me, I was in the *bedroom,* she comes in . . .

Morris: What was it . . . ?

James: She says, "A boy." *(Pause)* A boy? "Out at the entrance to the *lane."*
    "Now, who would *that* be . . . ?" I could tell, it was *something* she saw. I
    said, "A *deer."* "No." "W'al, you know, they put that white *tail* up . . ."

Morris: . . . uh-huh . . .

James: She says, "No, No. It wasn't a *deer. (Pause)* It was a *boy."* She said she *felt*
    something, you know, like you do . . .

Morris: Mm . . .

James: . . . she looked *around* . . .

Morris: Where was she?

James: On the porch . . .

Morris: Mm.

James: There was a *boy.* He *saw* her, and he ran up the lane. *(Pause)* Now:
    (Pause) Where would he be *coming* from . . . ?

Morris: . . . I don't know.

James: Well, I don't know *either.* Nothing up there, and what would he be *doing*
    up there . . . ? *(Pause)*

Morris: Now when was this?

James: Just at dusk. I said, "You see funny things in that light." *(Pause)* "Yes,"
    she says. "I saw this plain as day, though, and it was a *boy.* He *saw* me, and
    he ran away."

Morris: Did she say what he was wearing?

James: No, and I'll tell you, I didn't want to *press* her. *(Pause)*

Morris: Uh-huh.

James: . . . cause she was growing frightened. *(Pause)*

Morris: She'd *seen* something.

James: Mm.

Morris: You know what it was?

James: No, I don't. *(Pause)* No.

Morris: Mm.

James: I know there's places in the woods where I don't like to *go* . . .

Morris: Mm. *(Pause)* There's places I don't like to go *either. (Pause)*

James: You don't . . .

Morris: *(Pause)* No. *(Pause)*

James: Mm.

Pint's a Pound the World Around

A: . . . don't have the twelve-inch. We have the ten-inch and the fourteen-inch.

B: Isn't that always the way?

A: Seems it is. A number two do?

B: No.

A: Alright. The guy should have been in *Tuesday,* I spect him *Friday,* if he don't come then . . . I'll tell you, I've been thinking of switching. 'Merican *United,* I can get twenty percent over a year, you sign on to their Ownership Subscriber Plan, you get a basis of twenty percent, you want something it's *there.* The next day. Six days.

B: Where they out of?

A: Down in Manchester. *Basis* of twenty percent, they've got a *newspaper,* what do you call it, a *flyer,* the *specials,* they can go, sometimes they beat the Marketway sixty percent.

B: No.

A: Absolutely.

B: How's the quality?

A: Same, better. Most things better, much of . . . what they *do.* You know, they've got their *brand* . . .

B: Uh-huh . . .

A: *Good* stuff. Heavy gauge stuff. Some of . . . *you* know their stuff . . .

B: . . . sure . . .

A: . . . same patterns eighteen ninety-eight . . .

B: When's that, when they got started?

A: When they got started. Yes. Fellow name of . . . I had the guy in here, I was looking at their stuff since I came in. You have to sign *up,* what you do, you buy stock in the *company,* the minimum buy-in thirty-two hundred dollars, you own *stock,* at the end of the year they go and pro*rate* you the amount of your sales, and you're discounted based on that.

B: And what do you do with the discount?

A: What do you do?

B: What, do you apply it to your . . .

A: Well, I guess you do. I never thought of it. I suppose that you . . . or you could take it in cash. I had the guy here just the other day.

B: They want you to sign up.

A: The closest, *Jims,* in *Brandenburgs* American . . .

B: He is . . . ?

A: Oh yeah. You see his prices in there? Beat the *Marketway* fifteen percent *easily.* On *everything.* He *has* to . . .

B: They spend their money on advertising.

A: That's what I'm *saying.* It ain't going in the *stock,* in stock improvement . . . dealer *relations* . . . it's going in the *television* ads. Schiff, started eighteen ninety-eight. American United, the whole operation's built on one thing: the relation with the *dealer.*

B: Mm.

A: Stockholders are the dealer, *customers* the dealer. Everything. Geared toward one man. I pick up the phone, I say, "Where are the . . . *whatever,* he said that they'd be here on *Thursday.*" Marketway, what do *they* care . . . ? No *displays,* very few *incentives* . . . like I'm buying *retail* from them. You complain to someone, their attitude, basically, I think, I don't think they do it on *purpose,* but what you get is: if you don't want the franchise, you can turn back. They don't care. What they think, they're doing you a *favor,* all the money they've spent on the TV ads. Some stores, maybe, though I doubt it. Not in *here.* A fella comes in here he wants three of those, four of those, something he broke on a job, he wants it this afternoon: *I'm* built on *service.* He goes down the road, he can go to the *Star* supply in *Worth,* he's in the habit to come here, I want to *keep* him here. Two things they told me: Never change your hours, never cut your stock.

B: Uh-huh.

A: A fellow comes by some hour you're spose to be open and you're *closed,* next time he thinks heavily fore he drives out of his way. "Maybe he's closed . . ."

B: That's very true.

A: . . . it makes no difference it only happened one time. It's like adultery. I'm not foolin you. He thinks, "It happened once, it could happen again."

B: Uh-huh.

A: Fellow comes in here something he needs on a job, he needs it this afternoon, I'm *out* of it, what does he think? *"Shit,* I could of drove the same distance to *Star* and had it, and probably *cheaper* . . ." Something else: If I can get with the *American* I'm going to beat Marketway, I'm going to beat *Star.* I'm going to have them coming *here* from Worth . . .

B: You think?

A: There's no two ways about it. I'll have the stock, I'll have the variety, I'll have *quality.* . . . They marshall their *franchises very* careful. Forty-two miles to Brandenburgs, the closest they could have another is here. I've got no competition. I'll have them coming in from Worth, from *Peacham* . . .

B: And it's just the down payment . . .

A: What it is, yes, it's a down payment, it's an *investment,* you're actually buying stock. Whatever it is, I looked it up a week ago, a couple of weeks ago, seventeen dollars a share. What is that? Two into thirty-five, two shares for thirty-five, two hundred shares, thirty-five hundred dollars. Which you earn the dividend on, too, whatever that is . . .

B: On the stock.

A: Yes.

B: You should go with them.

A: I *would.* I *would* and I think I will. I think June and I have almost decided to *go* with them. It's a big step, but I think it's worth it. That's what I think. Many things. You have to look down the road. It's a big step now, it's a big *investment,* it's a *commitment,* in certain ways it would mean taking on more stock. . . .

B: Why is that?

A: Well, you have a basic *order.* Whatever your *size* is: the classification that they give you . . . on your *footage* . . . on your *overhead* . . . then when you order you have a minimum order that you have to file. *(Pause)* You also have a minimum order per *month* . . . they come in and they do the inventory . . .

B: *They* do.

A: Yep. They do. At the end of the year . . . I think that that's a good idea. They come in, a team, ten people, something, calculators, they're out in an afternoon, they come in Sunday afternoon . . . whenever you're closed, they

work through the night, they're out Monday morning. *That's* a good idea . . .
you ever do an inventory?

B: No.

A: Hell on Earth. I worked in a shoestore once. I thought I was going to go
mad . . . But it's a big step. *(Pause)*

B: Mm.

A: *(Pause)* It's a big step. *(Pause)*

B: Well—

A: Yeaaah! Five of the number three. Twelve-inch. I'm almost sure I'll have
them Friday.

B: I'll be back.

A: I'm going to call him again today. I would say ninety percent. Ninety-five
percent. I'll have them Friday. I'll tell you: If he *doesn't* come in, I'm going to
be down in Worth, Friday night, if he *doesn't* come in, I'll pick them up, you
stop in Saturday morning . . .

B: *That's* okay . . .

A: No. I should *have* 'em. No trouble at all. You come in Friday, he hasn't
stopped in, I'll have 'em Saturday first thing.

B: That's alright.

A: No trouble at all. I'm sorry I don't *have* 'em. I *should.* It doesn't help *you* to
tell you that the *man* didn't come in.

B: Well, *thank* you.

A: That's alright. You take care, now.

B: You, too.

A: It's nice talking to you.

Dowsing

Two older men, in a Vermont country store.

A: Yessuh. Fella told me he said, "I don't want no more of them *dowsers* in
here." By garry, I said, he's got a thing or two to learn.

B: I guess . . .

A: I said to you, Jim, *you're* a Mason, I said you did something I don't like, "I
don't want no more *Masons* in here . . .

B: No. Mason's supposed t'believe in brotherhood.

A: Yes. But if I told *you* something you did, I'se going to, you know, take it *out*
on . . .

B: Yuh.

A: . . . on other *Masons* . . .

B: Well, I'd say that's *foolish.*

A: . . . What *I'd* say.

B: You say he didn't want the *dowsers*?

A: *Dowsers* went down to his place . . .

B: . . . uh-huh . . .

A: Some woman called, she wanted to know was her *friend* there, he says, "She's
your friend, you should *know* if she's here." She called the chamber of

commerce, he gets this *complaint,* the fella calls him up he says, "By garry, *keep* 'em!" says he'll do without 'em. Big mistake. One week of the year that they're here, he's *booked,* you know, they come to spend their *money* . . .

B: Uh-huh . . .

A: *They* don't care it cost twenty-five dollars, thirty-five, they don't care, they're, you know . . .

B: Um hmm . . .

A: Well, they're on *vacation. Any* business you meet some you'd rather not *deal* with. I think he's a *fool.*

B: Now: *(Pause)* When you say "dowsin' "—is that the same dowsin' that we use to do with a bent stick?

A: It is.

B: For *water.*

A: Well, they dowse for *water,* dowse for *oil* . . .

B: For *oil* . . . ?

A: For oil in the ground. Yessuh.

B: . . . that a fact . . .

A: It is. For . . . well, you know, they might, say, you know, if they wanted to lay out a *field,* what to put where . . .

B: . . . yuh . . .

A: . . . in what corner of the *field* . . .

B: Uh-huh . . .

A: They'd dowse for that.

B: And how'd they find it?

A: Little *string,* a *weight* on it, they dowse it, yes or no. *(Pause)* Eh? They ask the *question,* string moves *one* way, then it's "yes." The other way is "no."

B: The way it *rotates.*

A: *Yessir.*

B: You know, I could never . . . fellas take that *stick* . . . you know, I took it, never did a thing, just laid there in my hand. Other man took it, twisted every *which* way . . .

A: I know.

B: Never did a *thing* for me.

A: Me, either. *(Pause)*

B: And that is their *convention.* Is that the thing?

A: Yup. Up *Morristown. You* know that.

B: Yup.

A: Yuh.

B: Up to *Morristown.*

A: Yuh. *(Pause)*

B: I heard it's going to frost tonight.

A: They had a fellow, Connie *Barr* . . .

B: Yuh.

A: You remember Connie?

B: Yes, I do.

A: His sister lost her watch, he found it with a dowsing stick.

B: Who was his sister?

A: Eunice Craft.

B: The *Craft* girls . . . ?

A: No. She married Billy Craft.

B: She *married* Billy.

A: Yessir.

B: D'I know her?

A: I think you did.

B: Mm.

A: Lost her watch, he found it.

B: With a dowsing stick?

A: Uh-huh.

B: Where was it?

A: In the field.

B: In plain sight?

A: I don't *think* so. Cause she'd lost it for a month.

B: She had?

A: Yeh.

B: And he found it?

A: Yes. He did.

B: Most like he *put* it there.

A: Well, that's what we thought at the *time,* but he held out he found it
    dowsing.

B: How about that now.

A: And I think that he *did.*

B: Well, you know, the things that you *see,* it makes you think that maybe
    there's something to *everything.*

A: Now, by God, that's the truth.

B: Mm?

A: Yessir.

B: Ayuh.

Deer Dogs

Two men, Larry and Bunchy, at a country store. There are also a couple of onlookers.

Larry: Dog's runnin deer it should be shot.

Bunchy: But who's to tell it's runnin deer? *Law* says you see a dog in pursuit of
    a deer you can *shoot* him. Who's to say it's . . . wait, wait, you take *Dave*
    here: keeps his dog tied up. One day th' dog, say Larry *Thompson's* dog, is
    runnin by—*Dave's* dog gets loose . . . Larry's dog's runnin deer. Someone sees
    it and, down the road later on, Larry's dog *and* Dave's dog. What does he do?
    Shoot 'em both.

Larry: How did Dave's dog get loose?

Bunchy: . . . I'm saying a dog which is *usually* tied down, Dave's dog . . .

Larry: How did it get loose?

Bunchy: I'm saying one day when it *is* loose . . . I don't *know* how it got
    loose . . .

Larry: And was it runnin deer . . . ?

Bunchy: No.

Larry: How do you know?

Bunchy: Cause it hasn't got a *taste* for them. It's a tame dog.

Larry: How do you know?

Bunchy: Well, now, now, now, because it *is* a tame dog: I, you *know* that dog . . .

Larry: . . . I'm . . .

Bunchy: . . . *I* know what you're . . .

Larry: I'm . . .

Bunchy: I know what you're, wait a second—I know what you're saying . . . that the dog is, *though* the dog is tame, it gets loose it starts runnin deer. Is that it?

Larry: Yes.

Bunchy: But what I'm saying, this case we *know* that the dog is tame. It's *tame*. It *isn't* runnin deer. Alright? It's *DAVE'S DOG*. It's *tame*. It's been tied up constantly . . .

Larry: How does it . . .

Bunchy: . . . that's not . . .

Larry: . . . how does it get loose?

Bunchy: Well, say that Dave forgot to tie it up.

Larry: And where does it go?

Bunchy: . . . I . . .

Larry: Where does it go?

Bunchy: I know what you're saying. It goes to the woods. Alright.

Larry: What is it doing there?

Bunchy: It's *out*. With Larry Thompson's dog.

Larry: What are they doing?

Bunchy: *Larry's* dog is runnin deer.

Larry: And what is Dave's dog doing?

Bunchy: I don't know.

Larry: Well, I don't know *either*—But *I'm* going to assume it's runnin deer. *(Pause)*

Bunchy: Would you shoot it?

Larry: Yes, I would.

Bunchy: You'd shoot Dave's dog.

Larry: Yes. I would. *(Pause)*

Bunchy: *(Snorts)* You would shoot Dave's dog. *(Pause)*

Larry: Yes. I would.

Bunchy: Because you know that *that's* the dog that'll be caught. Not Larry Thompson's dog. *(Pause) That's* the dog that will be caught . . . *Shoot.* It's a bad law . . . I'm sorry. *(Pause)* I don't like it.

Larry: You'll like it when you go out in the woods there ain't no *deer* . . .

Bunchy: *(Pause)* Nossir. *(Pause)* No sir . . . N' I'm going to tell you one more thing: What the *law* . . . wait a second—what the law *encourages* a fella to do is—I'm not saying *you* or *me,* but what it sets a man up to do is to say, "I'm going to shoot that fella's *dog.*" That's not right. (Pause)

In the Mall

Scene: A Bench in a Shopping Mall

Characters

A: A sixty-year-old man.

B: A thirteen-year-old boy.

B: I bet I know where you got that ice cream cone.
A: Where?
B: Down the mall.
A: That's right.
B: What did you pay for it?
A: Eighty-five cents.
B: Eighty-five cents . . .
A: That's right.
B: Is that with the tax?
A: No.
B: What is it with the tax?
A: Eighty-nine.
B: Eighty-nine. That's right. I bought one there. *(Pause)* I bought one there
   yesterday. What kind is it?
A: What kind is it?
B: Yes.
A: Butternut.
B: Butternut. I had one. *(Pause)* They made it up. They made it up I went down
   there the guys in there, you know, down the mall, I don't know, they want
   everything just like they like it, you know what I mean? I went in there my
   shirt off, this guy he says, "Get out." *(Pause)* I had to go. He was bigger than
   me—I would of wanted to smash his face in. Lots of people in there. They
   got a sign: "No Shoes, No Shirt, No Service," all they care, who they *like*.
   Somebody they *like* goes in there they give 'em anything he wants. I bought
   these crackers in a store they were crushed I took 'em back they guy said,
   "You ate some of 'em." I said I opened the box and I had a couple. "Eat the
   rest," he said. I knew a fella had a dog he fed it scraps. Whatever he didn't
   want to eat. When he had his dinner. They got the same hat down there.
   Where did you get that hat? *(Pause)* Where did you get that hat? Down
   there?
A: No.
B: Where did you get it?
A: I bought it on a trip.
B: They've got the same one down there. I like to know that. I saw a picture of
   this guy in there he looked like somebody I know. *(Pause)* You think it's cold
   here?
A: No.
B: You don't?

A: No. *(Long pause)*

B: Do you think it's warm? *(Pause)*

A: No.

B: Well, if you don't think it's cold and it's not warm what is it? *(Pause)* What is it?

A: What is it here?

B: Yeah. Huh??? I don't think it's cold. I don't *care* if it's cold. *Anyway.* I like to do things, you know, that people say that they can't do. I climbed this fence once that everyone said you can't get over. It had barb wire at the top. They make this stuff it's razors. It's a razor-ribbon you can't climb it. I went up. You hold on to the barb wire you go right over I came down on the other side. *They* didn't care. They said that it was stupid. I bought a pair of socks once they had stripes on top I folded 'em down. I thought, "Maybe this is to show us where to fold."

(A gets up.)

Where are you going?

A: Home.

B: Why?

A: Why?

B: Yeah.

A: Because I'm finished here.

B: You're finished doing what?

A: Sitting here.

B: You are?

A: Yes.

B: Do you have any money? *(Pause)* I need some cause I've got to do things.

A: No. I don't have any.

B: You don't.

A: No.

B: Mm. Mm. Mm. Mm. *(Pause)* Do you throw that thing away when you're done?

A: Yes.

B: Mm. Where?

A: In the wastebasket.

B: Mm. *(Pause)* Mm. *(A exits.) (Pause)* I had one one time . . .

Maple Sugaring

The sugar shack had light slanted through the vent in the roof, and white smoke billowed up.

Morris's father built the place in 1912, and Morris was stoking the fire up now with hardwood logs.

The sap was clearer than clean water and ran through the vat. There was a superfine white foam on it, and often Morris took a scoop and dipped it in the vat then let it drip to see the thickness of the sap.

His wife made lunch. There was Canadian beer and Swiss cheese, hamburgers and cookies made with the syrup that we made yesterday. The coffee pot leaned up against the vat to keep it warm.

Everyone spoke in hushed tones. Susan had brought down her eight-month-old baby, and its grandmother, Morris's wife, set up Susan's old crib in the sugar shack.

He was asleep in the crib, and his grandmother was looking down at him. She said, "You're not the first child to nap in that crib while we were sugaring."

Later in the woods Joe, Susan, and I were carrying the sap in pails, and she carried the baby on her back, and when we stopped to rest she nursed the child.

By four o'clock my neck hurt and I was becoming dizzy. The day had turned cold and the sap had ceased to run. Susan went in to set up dinner, I was left with Joe. We gathered the last buckets and I longed to go to sleep.

In the sugar shack the benches were made of wood. There was a square door on a running track to the woodshed. The sun streamed through the large vent in the roof. The people talked in whispers. The steam rose. Joe's baby was asleep.

Morris and Joe

Morris said, "Joe, 'member when we saw the bear in the tree?"

Joe smiled. "Remember when the milk froze?"

They were sitting on the step. The step had been removed from the house so they could repair the sill. It was an old house and the roof had leaked; the water ran down the post and rotted the sill. When they started the job Joe poked his pocketknife into it. It went in all the way.

The step was granite. Five-by-three. The bulldozer moved it back from the house. One corner was chipped out where there had been a bootscraper. Some hunters broke it out the year before.

Morris said, "You were shakin', Joe." Joe said, "I wasn't shakin'. I was scared for *you*."

"You *were*?"

"Yes. I know how *skit*tish you get in moments of stress."

"Aha."

Joe passed his lunchbucket to Morris who took a doughnut from it.

They looked out at the woods.

"I wonder where he is," Morris said.

"Probably up to Canada." Joe said.

"You think so?"

"Yes."

"Scared him within an inch of his life," Morris said. "Uh-*huh* . . ." Joe got up off the step.

"Where are you goin'?"

"I'm goin' to pee." Joe walked behind a stack of lumber. Morris said, "Yes*sir*, I hope he's back to Canada!"

"And why is that?" Joe said.

"'Cause he comes down here once again he better shake with *fear*. Cause he knows in *Amer*ica—he threatens our estates—there's not a man jack isn't ready to shoot himself in the foot."

"Do you remember when the milk froze?" Joe said.

"*Yes* sir. Smack in the foot," Morris said.

"*Susan* reminded me of that," Joe said. "That time that Morris cleaned the tank out." Joe came back buttoning up his fly. "How lovely all the driveway looked covered in milk . . ."

"You want some coffee?" Morris said.

". . . and how proud we were to defend you," Joe said, "from all that pernicious talk that you were drunk."

"People can sure be thoughtless," Morris said.

"That is the truth."

"Take you and that *bear,* frinstance," Morris said. "No mercy to dumb animals; just a display of wrath, and one man hopping with a .22 Long in his foot.

"I only hit the boot," Joe said.

"You want another cup of coffee?"

"No thanks."

Morris stretched and stood up. He closed his lunchpail. *"Yess* ir!"

"You want me to go back to those left joists this afternoon?" Joe said.

"How many more you got to do?"

"Just the two."

"Might as well go do 'em."

They stood for a moment and looked at the sky. Joe sighed. "He sure was pretty singing in that tree."

"Yes. He was," Morris said.

"Where do you think he is today?"

"I'm sure he's back in Canada."

Morris spat on the ground. "Yup," he said. "Yessir," Joe said. They went back into the house.

1981–1983/1986

Leslie Marmon Silko
b. 1948

On Tuesday, May 19, 1981, the *New York Times* announced that the MacArthur Foundation had selected twenty-one "exceptionally talented individuals" to receive five-year awards of support. Among these twenty-one American "geniuses" were two writers—Robert Penn Warren, born in Guthrie, Kentucky, in 1905, and Leslie Marmon Silko, born in Albuquerque, New Mexico, in 1948. Of mixed ancestry—part Pueblo Indian, part Mexican, and part white—Silko is today considered one of the best American writers of her generation.

Reared on the Laguna Pueblo, Silko says that her "earliest memories are of my grandmother telling me stories while she watered the morning-glories in her yard. Her stories were about incidents from long ago," Silko continues, "incidents which occurred before she was born but which she told as certainly as if she had been there." Like "Storyteller," included here, all of Silko's finest fiction "captures the essence of the oral tradition." On one side, it possesses an aura of certainty and authenticity: "I will not change the story," says the narrator of "Storyteller." On the other, it possesses a sense of indefiniteness and ambiguity: knowledge has been lost, the narrator's grandmother says; "otherwise I could tell you more."

Silko has written two books, a novel called *Ceremony* (1978) and a montage of stories, legends, poems, and photographs called *Storyteller* (1981). Also a screenwriter, Silko is the author of the screenplay for Marlon Brando's film *Black Elks.* In addition, her work has appeared in such anthologies as *The Man to Send Rain Clouds, Best Short Stories of 1975,* and *200 Years of Great American Short Stories* as well as in numerous magazines and journals. Besides writing, Silko teaches English at her alma mater, the University of New Mexico, and has been writer in residence at Vassar College.

Silko's numerous, powerful readings have created an enthusiastic audience for her work on many college campuses. From her Pueblo Indian heritage Silko derives many of the concerns that are apparent in *Ceremony* and *Storyteller,* especially concern for injustice, violence, and despair as forces that shape contemporary Indian life. Like Scott Momaday, who has praised her work, Silko explores both the rich heritage of Native Americans and their tragic loss of identity as they find themselves trapped between a culture that no longer exists and a culture that for them is not yet fully available. Also like Momaday, Silko possesses an affinity with "moments of considerable beauty and intensity, moments in which, according to the central tenet of storytelling, language is celebrated." As a result, her chronicle is a celebration as much as it is a lament: To tell the story "the way it must be told, year after year . . . , without lapse or silence" is a victory that Silko—like her ancestors and her characters—creates from defeat.

Text:
Storyteller, 1981.

Storyteller

Every day the sun came up a little lower on the horizon, moving more slowly until one day she got excited and started calling the jailer. She realized she had been sitting there for many hours, yet the sun had not moved from the center of the sky. The color of the sky had not been good lately; it had been pale blue, almost white, even when there were no clouds. She told herself it wasn't a good sign for the sky to be indistinguishable from the river ice, frozen solid and white against the earth. The tundra rose up behind the river but all the boundaries between the river and hills and sky were lost in the density of the pale ice.

She yelled again, this time some English words which came randomly into her mouth, probably swear words she'd heard from the oil drilling crews last winter. The jailer was an Eskimo, but he would not speak Yupik[1] to her. She had watched people in other cells, when they spoke to him in Yupik he ignored them until they spoke English.

He came and stared at her. She didn't know if he understood what she was telling him until he glanced behind her at the small high window. He looked at the sun, and turned and walked away. She could hear the buckles on his heavy snowmobile boots jingle as he walked to the front of the building.

It was like the other buildings that white people, the Gussucks,[2] brought with them: BIA[3] and school buildings, portable buildings that arrived sliced in halves, on barges coming up the river. Squares of metal panelling bulged out with the layers of insulation stuffed inside. She had asked once what it was and someone told her it was to keep out the cold. She had not laughed then, but she did now. She walked over to the small double-pane window and she laughed out loud. They thought they could keep out the cold with stringy yellow wadding. Look at the sun. It wasn't moving; it was frozen, caught in the middle of the sky. Look at the sky, solid as the river with ice which had trapped the sun. It had not moved for a long time; in a few more hours it would be weak, and heavy frost would begin to appear on the edges and spread across the face of the sun like a mask. Its light was pale yellow, worn thin by the winter.

She could see people walking down the snow-packed roads, their breath steaming out from their parka hoods, faces hidden and protected by deep ruffs of fur. There were no cars or snowmobiles that day; the cold had silenced their machines. The metal froze; it split and shattered. Oil hardened and moving parts jammed solidly. She had seen it happen to their big yellow machines and the giant drill last winter when they came to drill their test holes. The cold stopped them, and they were helpless against it.

Her village was many miles upriver from this town, but in her mind she could see it clearly. Their house was not near the village houses. It stood alone on the bank upriver from the village. Snow had drifted to the eaves of the roof on the north side, but on the west side, by the door, the path was almost clear. She had nailed scraps of red tin over the logs last summer. She had done it for the bright red color, not for added warmth the way the village people had done. This final winter had been coming even then; there had been signs of its approach for many years.

She went because she was curious about the big school where the Government sent all the other girls and boys. She had not played much with the village children while she was growing up because they were afraid of the old man, and they ran when her grandmother came. She went because she was tired of being alone with the old woman whose body had been stiffening for as long as the girl could remember. Her knees and knuckles were swollen grotesquely, and the pain had squeezed the brown skin of her face tight against the bones; it left her eyes hard like river stone. The girl asked once what it was that did this to her body, and the old woman had raised up from sewing a sealskin boot, and stared at her.

[1] Eskimo-Aleut language spoken across arctic America from western Alaska to Greenland.
[2] Presumably the Yupik term for "white people."
[3] Bureau of Indian Affairs.

"The joints," the old woman said in a low voice, whispering like wind across the roof, "the joints are swollen with anger."

Sometimes she did not answer and only stared at the girl. Each year she spoke less and less, but the old man talked more—all night sometimes, not to anyone but himself; in a soft deliberate voice, he told stories, moving his smooth brown hands above the blankets. He had not fished or hunted with the other men for many years, although he was not crippled or sick. He stayed in his bed, smelling like dry fish and urine, telling stories all winter; and when warm weather came, he went to his place on the river bank. He sat with a long willow stick, poking at the smoldering moss he burned against the insects while he continued with the stories.

The trouble was that she had not recognized the warnings in time. She did not see what the Gussuck school would do to her until she walked into the dormitory and realized that the old man had not been lying about the place. She thought he had been trying to scare her as he used to when she was very small and her grandmother was outside cutting up fish. She hadn't believed what he told her about the school because she knew he wanted to keep her there in the log house with him. She knew what he wanted.

The dormitory matron pulled down her underpants and whipped her with a leather belt because she refused to speak English.

"Those backwards village people," the matron said, because she was an Eskimo who had worked for the BIA a long time, "they kept this one until she was too big to learn." The other girls whispered in English. They knew how to work the showers, and they washed and curled their hair at night. They ate Gussuck food. She lay on her bed and imagined what her grandmother might be sewing, and what the old man was eating in his bed. When summer came, they sent her home.

The way her grandmother had hugged her before she left for school had been a warning too, because the old woman had not hugged or touched her for many years. Not like the old man, whose hands were always hunting, like ravens circling lazily in the sky, ready to touch her. She was not surprised when the priest and the old man met her at the landing strip, to say that the old lady was gone. The priest asked her where she would like to stay. He referred to the old man as her grandfather, but she did not bother to correct him. She had already been thinking about it; if she went with the priest, he would send her away to a school. But the old man was different. She knew he wouldn't send her back to school. She knew he wanted to keep her.

He told her one time, that she would get too old for him faster than he got too old for her; but again she had not believed him because sometimes he lied. He had lied about what he would do with her if she came into his bed. But as the years passed, she realized what he said was true. She was restless and strong. She had no patience with the old man who had never changed his slow smooth motions under the blankets.

The old man was in his bed for the winter; he did not leave it except to use the slop bucket in the corner. He was dozing with his mouth open slightly; his lips quivered and sometimes they moved like he was telling a story even while he dreamed. She pulled on the sealskin boots, the mukluks with the bright red flannel linings her grandmother had sewn for her, and she tied the braided red yarn tassels around her ankles over the gray wool pants. She zipped the wolfskin parka. Her grandmother had worn it for many years, but the old man said that before she died, she instructed

him to bury her in an old black sweater, and to give the parka to the girl. The wolf
pelts were creamy colored and silver, almost white in some places, and when the old
lady had walked across the tundra in the winter, she was invisible in the snow.

She walked toward the village, breaking her own path through the deep snow. A
team of sled dogs tied outside a house at the edge of the village leaped against their
chains to bark at her. She kept walking, watching the dusky sky for the first evening
stars. It was warm and the dogs were alert. When it got cold again, the dogs would
lie curled and still, too drowsy from the cold to bark or pull at the chains. She laughed
loudly because it made them howl and snarl. Once the old man had seen her tease
the dogs and he shook his head. "So that's the kind of woman you are," he said, "in
the wintertime the two of us are no different from those dogs. We wait in the cold
for someone to bring us a few dry fish."

She laughed out loud again, and kept walking. She was thinking about the Gussuck
oil drillers. They were strange; they watched her when she walked near their machines.
She wondered what they looked like underneath their quilted goose-down trousers;
she wanted to know how they moved. They would be something different from the
old man.

The old man screamed at her. He shook her shoulders so violently that her head
bumped against the log wall. "I smelled it!" he yelled, "as soon as I woke up! I am
sure of it now. You can't fool me!" His thin legs were shaking inside the baggy wool
trousers; he stumbled over her boots in his bare feet. His toenails were long and yellow
like bird claws; she had seen a gray crane last summer fighting another in the shallow
water on the edge of the river. She laughed out loud and pulled her shoulder out of
his grip. He stood in front of her. He was breathing hard and shaking; he looked weak.
He would probably die next winter.

"I'm warning you," he said, "I'm warning you." He crawled back into his bunk
then, and reached under the old soiled feather pillow for a piece of dry fish. He lay
back on the pillow, staring at the ceiling and chewed dry strips of salmon. "I don't
know what the old woman told you," he said, "but there will be trouble." He looked
over to see if she was listening. His face suddenly relaxed into a smile, his dark slanty
eyes were lost in wrinkles of brown skin. "I could tell you, but you are too good
for warnings now. I can smell what you did all night with the Gussucks."

She did not understand why they came there, because the village was small and so
far upriver that even some Eskimos who had been away to school did not want to
come back. They stayed downriver in the town. They said the village was too quiet.
They were used to the town where the boarding school was located, with electric
lights and running water. After all those years away at school, they had forgotten how
to set nets in the river and where to hunt seals in the fall. When she asked the old
man why the Gussucks bothered to come to the village, his narrow eyes got bright
with excitement.

"They only come when there is something to steal. The fur animals are too difficult
for them to get now, and the seals and fish are hard to find. Now they come for oil
deep in the earth. But this is the last time for them." His breathing was wheezy and
fast; his hands gestured at the sky. "It is approaching. As it comes, ice will push across
the sky." His eyes were open wide and he stared at the low ceiling rafters for hours

without blinking. She remembered all this clearly because he began the story that day, the story he told from that time on. It began with a giant bear which he described muscle by muscle, from the curve of the ivory claws to the whorls of hair at the top of the massive skull. And for eight days he did not sleep, but talked continuously of the giant bear whose color was pale blue glacier ice.

The snow was dirty and worn down in a path to the door. On either side of the path, the snow was higher than her head. In front of the door there were jagged yellow stains melted into the snow where men had urinated. She stopped in the entry way and kicked the snow off her boots. The room was dim; a kerosene lantern by the cash register was burning low. The long wooden shelves were jammed with cans of beans and potted meats. On the bottom shelf a jar of mayonnaise was broken open, leaking oily white clots on the floor. There was no one in the room except the yellowish dog sleeping in the front of the long glass display case. A reflection made it appear to be lying on the knives and ammunition inside the case. Gussucks kept dogs inside their houses with them; they did not seem to mind the odors which seeped out of the dogs. "They tell us we are dirty for the food we eat—raw fish and fermented meat. But we do not live with dogs," the old man once said. She heard voices in the back room, and the sound of bottles set down hard on tables.

They were always confident. The first year they waited for the ice to break up on the river, and then they brought their big yellow machines up river on barges. They planned to drill their test holes during the summer to avoid the freezing. But the imprints and graves of their machines were still there, on the edge of the tundra above the river, where the summer mud had swallowed them before they ever left sight of the river. The village people had gathered to watch the white men, and to laugh as they drove the giant machines, one by one, off the steel ramp into the bogs; as if sheer numbers of vehicles would somehow make the tundra solid. But the old man said they behaved like desperate people, and they would come back again. When the tundra was frozen solid, they returned.

Village women did not even look through the door to the back room. The priest had warned them. The storeman was watching her because he didn't let Eskimos or Indians sit down at the tables in the back room. But she knew he couldn't throw her out if one of his Gussuck customers invited her to sit with him. She walked across the room. They stared at her, but she had the feeling she was walking for someone else, not herself, so their eyes did not matter. The red-haired man pulled out a chair and motioned for her to sit down. She looked back at the storeman while the red-haired man poured her a glass of red sweet wine. She wanted to laugh at the storeman the way she laughed at the dogs, straining against the chains, howling at her.

The red-haired man kept talking to the other Gussucks sitting around the table, but he slid one hand off the top of the table to her thigh. She looked over at the storeman to see if he was still watching her. She laughed out loud at him and the red-haired man stopped talking and turned to her. He asked if she wanted to go. She nodded and stood up.

Someone in the village had been telling him things about her, he said as they walked down the road to his trailer. She understood that much of what he was saying, but the rest she did not hear. The whine of the big generators at the construction camp sucked away the sound of his words. But English was of no concern to her anymore, and neither was anything the Christians in the village might say about her or the old man. She smiled at the effect of the subzero air on the electric lights around the trailers; they did not shine. They left only flat yellow holes in the darkness.

It took him a long time to get ready, even after she had undressed for him. She waited in the bed with the blankets pulled close, watching him. He adjusted the thermostat and lit candles in the room, turning out the electric lights. He searched through a stack of record albums until he found the right one. She was not sure about the last thing he did: he taped something on the wall behind the bed where he could see it while he lay on top of her. He was shriveled and white from the cold; he pushed against her body for warmth. He guided her hands to his thighs; he was shivering.

She had returned a last time because she wanted to know what it was he stuck on the wall above the bed. After he finished each time, he reached up and pulled it loose, folding it carefully so that she could not see it. But this time she was ready; she waited for his fast breathing and sudden collapse on top of her. She slid out from under him and stood up beside the bed. She looked at the picture while she got dressed. He did not raise his face from the pillow, and she thought she heard teeth rattling together as she left the room.

She heard the old man move when she came in. After the Gussuck's trailer, the log house felt cool. It smelled like dry fish and cured meat. The room was dark except for the blinking yellow flame in the mica window of the oil stove. She squatted in front of the stove and watched the flames for a long time before she walked to the bed where her grandmother had slept. The bed was covered with a mound of rags and fur scraps the old woman had saved. She reached into the mound until she felt something cold and solid wrapped in a wool blanket. She pushed her fingers around it until she felt smooth stone. Long ago, before the Gussucks came, they had burned whale oil in the big stone lamp which made light and heat as well. The old woman had saved everything they would need when the time came.

In the morning, the old man pulled a piece of dry caribou meat from under the blankets and offered it to her. While she was gone, men from the village had brought a bundle of dry meat. She chewed it slowly, thinking about the way they still came from the village to take care of the old man and his stories. But she had a story now, about the red-haired Gussuck. The old man knew what she was thinking, and his smile made his face seem more round than it was.

"Well," he said, "what was it?"

"A woman with a big dog on top of her."

He laughed softly to himself and walked over to the water barrel. He dipped the tin cup into the water.

"It doesn't surprise me," he said.

"Grandma," she said, "there was something red in the grass that morning. I remember." She had not asked about her parents before. The old woman stopped splitting the fish bellies open for the willow drying racks. Her jaw muscles pulled so tightly against her skull, the girl thought the old woman would not be able to speak.

"They bought a tin can full of it from the storeman. Late at night. He told them it was alcohol safe to drink. They traded a rifle for it." The old woman's voice sounded like each word stole strength from her. "It made no difference about the rifle. That year the Gussuck boats had come, firing big guns at the walrus and seals. There was nothing left to hunt after that anyway. So," the old lady said, in a low soft voice the girl had not heard for a long time, "I didn't say anything to them when they left that night."

"Right over there," she said, pointing at the fallen poles, half buried in the river sand and tall grass, "in the summer shelter. The sun was high half the night then. Early in the morning when it was still low, the policeman came around. I told the interpreter to tell him that the storeman had poisoned them." She made outlines in the air in front of her, showing how their bodies lay twisted on the sand; telling the story was like laboring to walk through deep snow; sweat shone in the white hair around her forehead. "I told the priest too, after he came. I told him the storeman lied." She turned away from the girl. She held her mouth even tighter, set solidly, not in sorrow or anger, but against the pain, which was all that remained. "I never believed," she said, "not much anyway. I wasn't surprised when the priest did nothing."

The wind came off the river and folded the tall grass into itself like river waves. She could feel the silence the story left, and she wanted to have the old woman go on.

"I heard sounds that night, grandma. Sounds like someone was singing. It was light outside. I could see something red on the ground." The old woman did not answer her; she moved to the tub full of fish on the ground beside the workbench. She stabbed her knife into the belly of a whitefish and lifted it onto the bench. "The Gussuck storeman left the village right after that," the old woman said as she pulled the entrails from the fish, "otherwise, I could tell you more." The old woman's voice flowed with the wind blowing off the river; they never spoke of it again.

When the willows got their leaves and the grass grew tall along the river banks and around the sloughs, she walked early in the morning. While the sun was still low on the horizon, she listened to the wind off the river; its sound was like the voice that day long ago. In the distance, she could hear the engines of the machinery the oil drillers had left the winter before, but she did not go near the village or the store. The sun never left the sky and the summer became the same long day, with only the winds to fan the sun into brightness or allow it to slip into twilight.

She sat beside the old man at his place on the river bank. She poked the smoky fire for him, and felt herself growing wide and thin in the sun as if she had been split from belly to throat and strung on the willow pole in preparation for the winter to come. The old man did not speak anymore. When men from the village brought him fresh fish he hid them deep in the river grass where it was cool. After he went inside, she split the fish open and spread them to dry on the willow frame the way the old woman had done. Inside, he dozed and talked to himself. He had talked all winter, softly and incessantly, about the giant polar bear stalking a lone hunter across Bering Sea ice. After all the months the old man had been telling the story, the bear was within a hundred feet of the man; but the ice fog had closed in on them now and the man could only smell the sharp ammonia odor of the bear, and hear the edge of the snow crust crack under the giant paws.

One night she listened to the old man tell the story all night in his sleep, describing each crystal of ice and the slightly different sounds they made under each paw; first the left and then the right paw, then the hind feet. Her grandmother was there suddenly, a shadow around the stove. She spoke in her low wind voice and the girl was afraid to sit up to hear more clearly. Maybe what she said had been to the old man because he stopped telling the story and began to snore softly the way he had long ago when the old woman had scolded him for telling his stories while others in the house were trying to sleep. But the last words she heard clearly: "It will take a long time, but the story must be told. There must not be any lies." She pulled the blankets up around her chin, slowly, so that her movements would not be seen. She thought her grandmother was talking about the old man's bear story; she did not know about the other story then.

She left the old man wheezing and snoring in his bed. She walked through river grass glistening with frost; the bright green summer color was already fading. She watched the sun move across the sky, already lower on the horizon, already moving away from the village. She stopped by the fallen poles of the summer shelter where her parents had died. Frost glittered on the river sand too; in a few more weeks there would be snow. The predawn light would be the color of an old woman. An old woman sky full of snow. There had been something red lying on the ground the morning they died. She looked for it again, pushing aside the grass with her foot. She knelt in the sand and looked under the fallen structure for some trace of it. When she found it, she would know what the old woman had never told her. She squatted down close to the gray poles and leaned her back against them. The wind made her shiver.

The summer rain had washed the mud from between the logs; the sod blocks stacked as high as her belly next to the log walls had lost their square-cut shape and had grown into soft mounds of tundra moss and stiff-bladed grass bending with clusters of seed bristles. She looked at the northwest, in the direction of the Bering Sea. The cold would come down from there to find narrow slits in the mud, rainwater holes in the outer layer of sod which protected the log house. The dark green tundra stretched away flat and continuous. Somewhere the sea and the land met; she knew by their dark green colors there were no boundaries between them. That was how the cold would come: when the boundaries were gone the polar ice would range across the land into the sky. She watched the horizon for a long time. She would stand in that place on the north side of the house and she would keep watch on the northwest horizon, and eventually she would see it come. She would watch for its approach in the stars, and hear it come with the wind. These preparations were unfamiliar, but gradually she recognized them as she did her own footprints in the snow.

She emptied the slop jar beside his bed twice a day and kept the barrel full of water melted from river ice. He did not recognize her anymore, and when he spoke to her, he called her by her grandmother's name and talked about people and events from long ago, before he went back to telling the story. The giant bear was creeping across the new snow on its belly, close enough now that the man could hear the rasp of its breathing. On and on in a soft singing voice, the old man caressed the story, repeating the words again and again like gentle strokes.

The sky was gray like a river crane's egg; its density curved into the thin crust of frost already covering the land. She looked at the bright red color of the tin against the ground and the sky and she told the village men to bring the pieces for the old man and her. To drill the test holes in the tundra, the Gussucks had used hundreds of barrels of fuel. The village people split open the empty barrels that were abandoned on the river bank, and pounded the red tin into flat sheets. The village people were using the strips of tin to mend walls and roofs for winter. But she nailed it on the log walls for its color. When she finished, she walked away with the hammer in her hand, not turning around until she was far away, on the ridge above the river banks, and then she looked back. She felt a chill when she saw how the sky and the land were already losing their boundaries, already becoming lost in each other. But the red tin penetrated the thick white color of earth and sky; it defined the boundaries like a wound revealing the ribs and heart of a great caribou about to bolt and be lost to the hunter forever. That night the wind howled and when she scratched a hole through the heavy frost on the inside of the window, she could see nothing but the impenetrable white; whether it was blowing snow or snow that had drifted as high as the house, she did not know.

It had come down suddenly, and she stood with her back to the wind looking at the river, its smoky water clotted with ice. The wind had blown the snow over the frozen river, hiding thin blue streaks where fast water ran under ice translucent and fragile as memory. But she could see shadows of boundaries, outlines of paths which were slender branches of solidity reaching out from the earth. She spent days walking on the river, watching the colors of ice that would safely hold her, kicking the heel of her boot into the snow crust, listening for a solid sound. When she could feel the paths through the soles of her feet, she went to the middle of the river where the fast gray water churned under a thin pane of ice. She looked back. On the river bank in the distance she could see the red tin nailed to the log house, something not swallowed up by the heavy white belly of the sky or caught in the folds of the frozen earth. It was time.

The wolverine fur around the hood of her parka was white with the frost from her breathing. The warmth inside the store melted it, and she felt tiny drops of water on her face. The storeman came in from the back room. She unzipped the parka and stood by the oil stove. She didn't look at him, but stared instead at the yellowish dog, covered with scabs of matted hair, sleeping in front of the stove. She thought of the Gussuck's picture, taped on the wall above the bed and she laughed out loud. The sound of her laughter was piercing; the yellow dog jumped to its feet and the hair bristled down its back. The storeman was watching her. She wanted to laugh again because he didn't know about the ice. He did not know that it was prowling the earth, or that it had already pushed its way into the sky to seize the sun. She sat down in the chair by the stove and shook her long hair loose. He was like a dog tied up all winter, watching while the others got fed. He remembered how she had gone with the oil drillers, and his blue eyes moved like flies crawling over her body. He held his thin pale lips like he wanted to spit on her. He hated the people because they had something of value, the old man said, something which the Gussucks could never have. They thought they could take it, suck it out of the earth or cut it from the mountains; but they were fools.

There was a matted hunk of dog hair on the floor by her foot. She thought of the yellow insulation coming unstuffed: their defense against the freezing going to pieces as it advanced on them. The ice was crouching on the northwest horizon like the old man's bear. She laughed out loud again. The sun would be down now; it was time.

The first time he spoke to her, she did not hear what he said, so she did not answer or even look up at him. He spoke to her again but his words were only noises coming from his pale mouth, trembling now as his anger began to unravel. He jerked her up and the chair fell over behind her. His arms were shaking and she could feel his hands tense up, pulling the edges of the parka tighter. He raised his fist to hit her, his thin body quivering with rage; but the fist collapsed with the desire he had for the valuable things, which, the old man had rightly said, was the only reason they came. She could hear his heart pounding as he held her close and arched his hips against her, groaning and breathing in spasms. She twisted away from him and ducked under his arms.

She ran with a mitten over her mouth, breathing through the fur to protect her lungs from the freezing air. She could hear him running behind her, his heavy breathing, the occasional sound of metal jingling against metal. But he ran without his parka or mittens, breathing the frozen air; its fire squeezed the lungs against the ribs and it was enough that he could not catch her near his store. On the river bank he realized how far he was from his stove, and the wads of yellow stuffing that held off the cold. But the girl was not able to run very fast through the deep drifts at the edge of the river. The twilight was luminous and he could still see clearly for a long distance; he knew he could catch her so he kept running.

When she neared the middle of the river she looked over her shoulder. He was not following her tracks; he went straight across the ice, running the shortest distance to reach her. He was close then; his face was twisted and scarlet from the exertion and the cold. There was satisfaction in his eyes; he was sure he could outrun her.

She was familiar with the river, down to the instant ice flexed into hairline fractures, and the cracking bone-sliver sounds gathered momentum with the opening ice until the churning gray water was set free. She stopped and turned to the sound of the river and the rattle of swirling ice fragments where he fell through. She pulled off a mitten and zipped the parka to her throat. She was conscious then of her own rapid breathing.

She moved slowly, kicking the ice ahead with the heel of her boot, feeling for sinews of ice to hold her. She looked ahead and all around herself; in the twilight, the dense white sky had merged into the flat snow-covered tundra. In the frantic running she had lost her place on the river. She stood still. The east bank of the river was lost in the sky; the boundaries had been swallowed by the freezing white. But then, in the distance, she saw something red, and suddenly it was as she had remembered it all those years.

She sat on her bed and while she waited, she listened to the old man. The hunter had found a small jagged knoll on the ice. He pulled his beaver fur cap off his head; the fur inside it steamed with his body heat and sweat. He left it upside down on the ice for the great bear to stalk, and he waited downwind on top of the ice knoll; he was holding the jade knife.

She thought she could see the end of his story in the way he wheezed out the words; but still he reached into his cache of dry fish and dribbled water into his mouth from the tin cup. All night she listened to him describe each breath the man took, each motion of the bear's head as it tried to catch the sound of the man's breathing, and tested the wind for his scent.

The state trooper asked her questions, and the woman who cleaned house for the priest translated them into Yupik. They wanted to know what happened to the storeman, the Gussuck who had been seen running after her down the road onto the river late last evening. He had not come back, and the Gussuck boss in Anchorage was concerned about him. She did not answer for a long time because the old man suddenly sat up in his bed and began to talk excitedly, looking at all of them—the trooper in his dark glasses and the housekeeper in her corduroy parka. He kept saying, "The story! The story! Eh-ya! The great bear! The hunter!"

They asked her again, what happened to the man from the Northern Commercial store. "He lied to them. He told them it was safe to drink. But I will not lie." She stood up and put on the gray wolfskin parka. "I killed him," she said, "but I don't lie."

The attorney came back again, and the jailer slid open the steel doors and opened the cell to let him in. He motioned for the jailer to stay to translate for him. She laughed when she saw how the jailer would be forced by this Gussuck to speak Yupik to her. She liked the Gussuck attorney for that, and for the thinning hair on his head. He was very tall, and she liked to think about the exposure of his head to the freezing; she wondered if he would feel the ice descending from the sky before the others did. He wanted to know why she told the state trooper she had killed the storeman. Some village children had seen it happen, he said, and it was an accident. "That's all you have to say to the judge: it was an accident." He kept repeating it over and over again to her, slowly in a loud but gentle voice: "It was an accident. He was running after you and he fell through the ice. That's all you have to say in court. That's all. And they will let you go home. Back to your village." The jailer translated the words sullenly, staring down at the floor. She shook her head. "I will not change the story, not even to escape this place and go home. I intended that he die. The story must be told as it is." The attorney exhaled loudly; his eyes looked tired. "Tell her that she could not have killed him that way. He was a white man. He ran after her without a parka or mittens. She could not have planned that." He paused and turned toward the cell door. "Tell her I will do all I can for her. I will explain to the judge that her mind is confused." She laughed out loud when the jailer translated what the attorney said. The Gussucks did not understand the story; they could not see the way it must be told, year after year as the old man had done, without lapse or silence.

She looked out the window at the frozen white sky. The sun had finally broken loose from the ice but it moved like a wounded caribou running on strength which only dying animals find, leaping and running on bullet-shattered lungs. Its light was weak and pale; it pushed dimly through the clouds. She turned and faced the Gussuck attorney.

"It began a long time ago," she intoned steadily, "in the summertime. Early in the morning, I remember, something red in the tall river grass. . . ."

The day after the old man died, men from the village came. She was sitting on the edge of her bed, across from the woman the trooper hired to watch her. They came into the room slowly and listened to her. At the foot of her bed they left a king salmon that had been slit open wide and dried last summer. But she did not pause or hesitate; she went on with the story, and she never stopped, not even when the woman got up to close the door behind the village men.

The old man would not change the story even when he knew the end was approaching. Lies could not stop what was coming. He thrashed around on the bed, pulling the blankets loose, knocking bundles of dried fish and meat on the floor. The hunter had been on the ice for many hours. The freezing winds on the ice knoll had numbed his hands in the mittens, and the cold had exhausted him. He felt a single muscle tremor in his hand that he could not stop, and the jade knife fell; it shattered on the ice, and the blue glacier bear turned slowly to face him.

1981

Jasper Johns,
Savarin,
brush, pen, and ink, 1977.
Collection, The Museum of Modern Art,
New York.
Gift of the Lauder Foundation.

The Literature of Contemporary America: Poetry

 As the critic Hugh Kenner once wrote, "No Englishman alive in 1600 was living in the Age of Shakespeare: . . . that age was invented long afterwards." The last quarter of the twentieth century may eventually be well represented in the anthologies of the far future, but we cannot now know how many of these new voices, who have flourished since 1973, will become part of the canon of American poetry. That canon is decided on chiefly by subsequent poets, who find only some of their predecessors worthy of admiration, imitation, and homage. To a contemporary reader, the amount of poetry being written in the United States seems formidable: Publishers report thousands of submissions for any poetry prize; *The New Yorker* alone receives a thousand poems a week in submissions. The few poets represented here are diverse in theory and practice and represent no commanding "school."

Although the intensity of American political life slackened in the 1970s with the withdrawal of United States forces from Vietnam, the aftermath of the war remained in the consciousness of young writers. Many novelists commemorated the events of the war, and some poets attempted to express the horror of battle; but beyond that local literary effect, there was a large change in the public perception of America's role in international affairs. Among writers, a distrust of military policy and a new isolationism went, paradoxically, hand in hand with a new sense of responsibility for the whole planet. Ethnological and anthropological discoveries put in question the "superiority" of colonizers over colonized; it seemed as though America's empire, like those of England and France, had ended with the defeat in Vietnam and the rise of resistance in South America to American political influence. Young writers found themselves pressed into various national and global causes—opposition to nuclear arms, defense of civil rights, conservation—while earlier causes, notably the feminist movement, remained vividly present.

During the 1970s several major poets, whose work had been important to younger writers, died: Charles Olson (1970), John Berryman (1972), Anne Sexton (1975), Robert Lowell (1977), Elizabeth Bishop (1979), and James Wright (1980). Some poets belonging chronologically to this generation had already died young by accident or suicide (Frank O'Hara, Sylvia Plath, Randall Jarrell). Still other poets, nearing sixty, seemed to be declaring their canon largely complete by bringing out collected poems (A. R. Ammons, James Merrill, Allen Ginsberg).

In this comparative vacancy, new poets became more visible. They continue to perform the immemorial task of poetry—to process some portion of nature or history into a portion of culture by endowing it with aesthetic purpose. A number of younger poets are continuing, for example, the process begun by Langston Hughes and Allen Ginsberg—recording the history of illiterate or marginally literate members of society who, because they were unschooled or

The Responsibility of Creative Writing

Creative writing is no panacea for individual or social ills. If it were we should have long ago discovered how to prevent Vietnam and the collapse of Chrysler. Because of the horror of the Holocaust, George Steiner said, "After Auschwitz, no more poetry." And it is hard to sustain a fervent belief in art as humanly effective when we know that Nazis read Goethe, heard Mozart, and cultivated refined tastes by night after a hard day of eliminating Jews. Yet did not art always tell us about that darkness in the human spirit, and what worse would we have been without those images of ourselves in Homer, Chaucer, Dante, Shakespeare, Dickens, the Brothers Grimm, Kafka? I have mentioned critics who complain of the spread of writing instruction and argue it dilutes the quality of our writing. Have they got their facts in perspective? One of their complaints is the size, the cost of a writing program. It is worth remembering that one Air Force bomber costs more than the entire budget for the National Endowment for the Arts; that no school in this country provides the salaries, support, or attention to creative writing that it does for computers, music, engineering, biology, or ROTC; that in every state university we have the athletic budget for laundry alone exceeds the budget for creative writing. The point is that we are a tiny, tiny operation but we are entrusted with envisioning, recording, and even sustaining the best that has been and will be thought and felt about human nature. When we seek to measure what we are doing, and we must do that, let us do so in appropriate contexts.

Dave Smith, *Local Assays* (1985)

were enslaved or were immigrants speaking a language other than English, left little English record of their own American lives. Michael Harper's commitment to historical particulars, Rita Dove's commemoration of her family's migration from the South to the North, Albert Goldbarth's transcriptions of Yiddish-speaking ancestors, and Dave Smith's anecdotes of the taciturn Chesapeake Bay oyster fishermen reflect not only the poet's wish to rescue, in full pathos, lost portions of experience but also the lyric poet's deep desire to speak through other voices, to "borrow" voice from a wide historical range. These poets follow Whitman, who promised, in "Song of Myself":

> Through me many long dumb voices,
> Voices of the interminable generations of prisoners and slaves,
> Voices of the diseas'd and despairing and of thieves and dwarfs. . . .
> Through me forbidden voices,
> Voices of sexes and lusts, voices veil'd and I remove the veil,
> Voices indecent by me clarified and transfigur'd.

At the same time these poets, concerned with the larger historical record, have written poems of the private life. Harper mourns a dead son; Smith writes about his rebellious youth; Dove recalls her adolescence.

There are poets represented in the pages that follow who are historical in a different way from the more narrative poets just mentioned. In this second group, the use of the past is not narrative but exemplary. Jorie Graham's examples of the past are frequently paintings—from those of Piero della Francesca to those of Gustav Klimt. Graham takes the measure of her own aesthetic life by a deep immersion in an objectified form rendered in a moment far in the past. Frank Bidart, too, uses the voices of past artists (the opera singer Maria Callas, the ballet dancer Nijinsky) as a way to measure the inexorable price exacted by the will to form.

Yet another way of being "historical" appears in the poetry of Charles Simic, whose childhood was spent in Yugoslavia during World War II. In Simic's work the algebra of parable replaces the mimesis of historical narrative: The Europe of the Second World War is reduced, allegorically, to a place where stark and horrible events take place—a shooting, a disappearance, a famine. Voices become disembodied; men are seen archetypally rather than individually—a father, a son, a soldier. Form is reduced to the simplest of quatrains, the commonest words.

In various ways, then—by historical narrative, historical voices, historical works of art, historical anecdote—the poets of the past decade continue the twentieth-century impulse to historicize the lyric, to make it embody a social reality greater than the reality of a single poet alone. The American impulse to enfranchise the "en masse" (as Whitman called it), to expose the whole social fabric of a culture rather than an individual predicament, stems from the American ideal of poetry as a common cultural possession, a voice expressive of all classes, a regard democratic in its vistas. This view remains in tension with the indisputable fact that the linguistic and cultural ease with language necessary for any accomplished writing of poetry is usually the possession of the educated.

The poets of the past decade continue another vein of twentieth-century lyric. Like Roethke, Lowell, Plath, and Sexton, they hark back to the theme of problematic identity, expressed in terms of parents, ancestry, gender, and ethnic and regional origins. This theme—unthinkable in a similar form in centrally English writers like Shakespeare, Keats, or Hopkins, but present in many provincial writers—marks the continuing American unease felt within an unsettled and pluralistic society. Many American writers emerge from a class unaccustomed to belles lettres; many women writers emerge from a group that feels disenfranchised in the world of letters. Finding one's feet, so to speak, demands a retracing of the original unsteadiness in the community. The new poets' emphasis on childhood origins suggests the persistence of the Freudian model of identity, shaped by family relations more than by social circumstance.

If there are continuities between the new poets and their predecessors, there are also discontinuities. The single most striking disparity between recent poets and their American forebears in this century is the difference in philosophical orientation between the generations. The poets of high modernism were still working out for themselves the Victorian crisis of religious faith (Frost, Eliot, Stevens, Crane) or the crisis of technology and modernity (Pound, Moore, Williams); the poets flourishing after World War II were working out the implications of Freud and of gender difference (Lowell, Plath, Rich, Roethke). But for the most part the recent poets find these issues less urgent and take them almost for granted. The religious impulse in these younger poets is not doctrinally based but voices itself in yearnings or aspirations rather than in the crisis of belief. Technology and modernity are, for these poets, indisputably present, often to be genially used as new sources of language. The Freudian model (though it has undergone modifications) remains the basic model for introspection. The real energy, philosophically speaking, for these poets comes from the crisis in knowledge that has absorbed philosophers most acutely since Kant and most visibly since Wittgenstein—two philosophers voicing an acute critique of the nature of language.

The model of the artist as one who holds a mirror up to nature implies an adequacy of words to things and suggests that there is no gap in reality between

---

Recital

But as the days and years sped by it became apparent that the naming of all the new things we now possessed had become our chief occupation; that very little time for the mere tasting and having of them was left over, and that even these simple, tangible experiences were themselves subject to description and enumeration, or else they too became fleeting and transient as the song of a bird that is uttered only once and disappears into the backlog of vague memories where it becomes as a dried, pressed flower, a wistful parody of itself. . . .

John Ashbery, *Three Poems* (1972)

the things contemplated and the language "recreating" them. More recent theorists of language suggest that we cannot get "behind" language; we cannot attain things in their unmediated being. Nor can we remove language from its function of signification in order to see what language would be before it signified a "thing," before it had "meaning." The view that language, and only language, is what constitutes the world, that there can be no world prior to the world constituted by language, appears in some of Stevens's poetry, but it was not an axiom of poets until recently. The concept of *poesis,* or imagining a world, is now seen to be the action that itself constitutes culture. Cultures change because a new imagining of the world—by thinkers, inventors, scientists, writers —has slowly come about. New cultural "languages" remodel the world. With new conceptualizations and new words, we achieve what W. H. Auden called "new styles of architecture, a change of heart." In the work of reconstituting culture, the poets—the most imaginative of imaginative writers, those who touch the core of the inner life—play a central role.

This perception of the role of the poet is interpreted differently by different temperaments. Utopian poets imagine that they are reconceiving the world in new codes that will overturn the old conceptions (of blacks, of women, of a "good citizen" in the docile sense). Poets who want to understand the relevance of older imaginative codes (say, those of Renaissance painters) to our own day attempt to reenter a conceptual world foreign to them, not to urge the virtues of modernity but rather to see what might be perennial about the

---

"Negative Capability"

". . . that is, when a man is capable of being in uncertainties, mysteries, doubts, without any irritable reaching after fact and reason."
John Keats

Today what Keats said could be made even more specific. In place of "uncertainties," "mysteries" and "doubts," we could substitute a long list of intellectual and aesthetic events which question, revise and contradict one another on all fundamental issues. We could also bring in recent political history: all the wars, all the concentration camps and other assorted modern sufferings, and then return to Keats and ask how, in this context, are we capable of being in anything *but* uncertainties? Or, since we are thinking about poetry, ask how do we render this now overwhelming consciousness of uncertainty, mystery and doubt in our poems?

To be "capable of being in uncertainties" is to be literally in the midst. The poet is in the midst. The poem, too, is in the midst, a kind of magnet for complex historical, literary and psychological forces, as well as a way of maintaining oneself in the face of that multiplicity.

Charles Simic, "Negative Capability and Its Children" (1984)

work of the imagination. The sense of emptiness in W. S. Merwin, Charles Wright, and Mark Strand (frequently remarked by their readers) is the space left by religious nostalgia, as yet unentered by any energy other than that of speculation on the power of language to fill a void. Their poetic forms, stripped of personal or circumstantial detail, aim at a purity of diction that will let the mind float free, in pure *poesis,* removed from quotidian or historical moorings.

In the past, the lyric has been the genre most broadly available to readers. In continuing to write of human loss, philosophical problems, fluctuations of desire, or the contemplation of art, the poets of the past decade search for authentic contemporary treatments of perennial human concerns. Religious and social doctrines no longer offer our society authoritative models in which to see the human predicament. Poets like Glück, Strand, Wright, Blumenthal, and Graham attempt to do without such preexistent authoritative models, and their work, for the most part, does without a narrative base. They are thus writing squarely in the traditional mode of the lyric, using the native radial form of poetry that issues from, and returns to, a center of inner concern. Wright has emphasized his debt to Cézanne in arriving at a form by which "patches" of substance are applied in overlapping patterns on a blank ground. Strand has adopted a mode of disembodied allegory; Glück eddies around a central still point of absence; Graham has used in her work motions of entering and leaving, of transgression over boundaries. These tentative inner motions reflect a distrust of definitive narrative or philosophical closure. The lines of these poets give off quanta of linguistic energy and resemble waves rather than straight lines. Closure in them becomes a suspension rather than a ringing conclusion.

The physical terrain of the United States is being mapped by these poets as by earlier ones. Amy Clampitt, in a group of powerfully descriptive poems, has charted the Maine coast as well as the Iowa of her childhood; Wright has written intensely of the southern Episcopalian atmosphere in which he was reared; Smith, in addition to his Virginia poems, has written about Wyoming and Utah; Strand has recorded elements of life in Nova Scotia; Bidart gave his first book *(Golden State)* the nickname of the state where he was born; Pinsky has written about New Jersey, Blumenthal about New York, Dove about Ohio, Harper about both coasts. By European standards, America is still, to quote Frost, "unstoried, artless, unenhanced," but the poetic map is slowly being filled in.

The map of various self-constituting "affinity groups" is being filled in as well. Gay, lesbian, feminist, Native American, and Hispanic-American poetry have all defined themselves in anthologies and in journals. In the past, creating a movement outside the presumed "center" has been a way for dissident or avant-garde poets to find a hearing among sympathizers, fellow writers, and interested readers. A critical mass of readers (almost always, in the past, found in cities—Jerusalem, Athens, Rome, Byzantium, London, Paris) is now to be found not only in movements or in cities but also in universities, where young writers gather to undergo an apprenticeship in a creative writing program. None of these ways of finding an audience—joining a movement, heading for a city, or enrolling in a program—is indispensable, but all enable the poet to find others with a common interest or a common stance.

The interpenetration of poetry and prose, and poetry with other vocal media (television, music, stage performance), continues to be explored in "performance poetry" and "language poetry," forms exhibiting powerful reliance on such strategies as improvisation, fragmentation of language, the intermittent presence of language, the dissociation of sentence parts, and the abandoning of visible form. These strategies (many of them borrowed from the composer John Cage, one of the original teachers at Black Mountain) help to destroy the "illusion" of continuous form. The dislocations of "ordinary language" present in all poetry— whether through the mere presence of the unjustified line or through condensation, rapid metaphorical change, syntactic oddity, iteration, and other forms of overdetermination—are brought strongly into view by language poets and performance poets, for whom the disruptive imagination, rather than any element of continuous form, is the constitutive quality of poetry.

Finally, it is of course to the American language and to American forms of social expression that our poets are most deeply obligated. The inner life of an epoch must find, in its own linguistic and cultural forms, the means of its own reflection. For the poets of the past decade, this obligation means that they must find imaginative constructs, sentence forms, images, and language faithful to the sensibility of a generation that looks at television as well as at paintings, possesses the concept of the fourth dimension as well as of the magnet, and knows unisex clothing, test-tube babies, nuclear force, and planetary travel. Concepts of space and time have changed; concepts of rates of change have altered; the visual field is different; the roles of the sexes are in question. It is not that such modern realities need to be mentioned (though they do) or that new words need to be incorporated in poetry (though they do). It is rather that new conceptual models, new rates of change, and new pacings of distance must find their appropriate linear, temporal, and spatial poetic forms (a search in which John Ashbery has so

---

Some Notes on Silence

If in the form is each man's uncounterfeitable relationship with the mysteries, then the degree of his fear or grace are also in some measure legible there. It is hard to name these things: but in those poets who confront the unknown, the holy, most head-on, the syntax begins to buckle and bend back and break, very much like Saint Teresa first witnessing the host and twisting back, both to look away and, strangely, to better receive it. From the labyrinthine ritual cave paintings of the Stone Age, through every period of human time, when we have sought to enter, to break the surface, one of the ways in has been crooked —the blindness that one may see. And in the poets that go that way, twisted syntax, breaks against smooth sequence or sense, line breaks of queer kinds, white spaces, interruptions, dashes, overpunctuation, delays, clotted rich diction, obscurity, disorder, ellipses, sentence fragments, digressive strategies—every modulation in certainty—are all tools for storming the walls. Whether of hell or paradise is another matter.

Jorie Graham (1984)

far been most daring). It is too early to specify the new inner structures that will
be discovered in the last quarter of this century. But the remarkable variety of
the United States—intellectual, ethnic, and geographic—suggests that, as Wallace
Stevens said, "The vegetation still abounds in forms."

Amy Clampitt
b. 1920

Amy Clampitt writes, "I come from a late-blooming family. My grandfather
wrote and published his autobiography when he was past seventy; my father
received an honorary doctorate of humane letters at the age of eighty-three. They
were both farmers, and of an anxious temperament. I grew up in the same rural
community," New Providence, Iowa. Clampitt's father was "a Quaker activist,"
and the political concern in many of her poems may be thought to derive from
her father's example. After college at Grinnell, Clampitt worked for Oxford
University Press and the Audubon Society; later, she became a free-lance editor
and writer. In 1973 she published a small, privately printed collection of poems
entitled *Multitudes, Multitudes*. Later in the decade she published poetry in *The
New Yorker,* and in 1983 Knopf brought out her first widely circulated book,
The Kingfisher. It appeared as the work of a wholly mature poet, one who had
had long practice in writing. (Clampitt had written three unpublished novels
before returning to poetry.) In 1985 Knopf published Clampitt's second
collection, *What the Light Was Like.*

   Clampitt writes passionately about her adolescence in Iowa, about the fears
and deprivations of living as a young girl—and aspiring writer—in desolate rural
America. In her elegies for her mother and father ("Procession at Candlemas" and
"Beethoven Opus 111") she considers, respectively, what the worship of the
female has meant in culture, and the nature and achievement of those born with
a revolutionary temperament. Clampitt has also written poems (about the Maine
coast and other landscapes) that rival Gerard Manley Hopkins's poetry in intense
contemplation of the visual scene. Her long sequence on the life of John Keats
reveals the psychological acuteness with which she can enter the realities, both
physical and mental, of another life.

   Clampitt's writing is strenuous, dense, and charged with impetus and
momentum. Her sentences press on, full of reflection, argument, qualification,
impressions, and queries, unwilling to come to a halt until the mind has had time
to think enough and the tongue to say enough. This is a poetry of intelligence,
owing something to Marianne Moore, but it is also a poetry of urgent feeling,
able to recall with uncanny accuracy the confusions and rages of childhood and
adolescence.

   Clampitt's many poems about Europe take up once again the predicament of
the American writer confronting the past—finding what is usable, what is
relieving, what is admirable, what is frightening, about the legacy of history. It
may be that Clampitt's most extraordinary achievement, however, is to have put

on paper the Midwest region in which she was born—a region still relatively uncharted in poetry—and to have done so in a style very far from the minimalist fashion, set by Merwin and Strand, that reigned so long in American midcentury verse.

Text:
The Kingfisher, 1983.

From a Clinic Waiting Room

I write from the denser enclave of the stricken,
eight stories up, a prairie *gratte-ciel.*[1]
Above the valley floor, the bell tower
of a displaced Italian hill town listens, likewise
attentive to the mysteries of one Body.[2]   5
If the two salute, it must be as monks do,
without gesture, eyes lowered
by the force of gravity. Between them,
down among the car parks, tree shapes
stripped twig-bare appear to bruise   10
with tenderness, illusory as sea anemones.
There is no wind. For days
the geese that winter in the bottomland
have been the one thing always on the move,
in swags of streaming fronds, chiaroscuro   15
sea blooms, their wavering V-signs
following the turnings of one body.
Where are they going?
                              Down in the blood bank
the centrifuge, its branched transparent siphons
stripping the sap of Yggdrasil[3]   20
from the slit arm of the donor, skims
the spinning corpuscles, cream-white
from hectic red. Below the pouched pack
dangled like a gout of mistletoe, the tubing
drips, drips from valve to valve to enter,   25
in a gradual procession, the cloistered
precincts of another body.

---

[1] French: "skyscraper"; literally, "something that scratches the sky."
[2] The body of Christ, worshipped in the church adjoining the bell tower.
[3] In Norse myth, a huge tree connecting earth, heaven, and hell.

Sunset, its tinctured
layerings vivid as delirium, astonishing
as merely to be living, stains the cold
of half a hemisphere. The old   30
moon's dark corpus,[4] its mysteries
likewise halfway illusory, tonight sleeps slumped
on the phosphorescent threshold of the new.

1982

A Procession at Candlemas[1]

1

Moving on or going back to where you came
          from,
bad news is what you mainly travel with:
a breakup or a breakdown, someone running off

or walking out, called up or called home:
death in the family. Nudged from their stanchions   5
outside the terminal, anonymous of purpose

as a flock of birds, the bison of the highway
funnel westward onto Route 80, mirroring
an entity that cannot look into itself and know

what makes it what it is. Sooner or later   10
every trek becomes a funeral procession.
The mother curtained in Intensive Care—

a scene the mind leaves blank, fleeing instead
toward scenes of transhumance,[2] the belled sheep
moving up the Pyrenees, red-tasseled pack llamas   15

footing velvet-green precipices, the Kurdish
women, jingling with bangles, gorgeous
on their rug-piled mounts—already lying dead,

---

[4] Latin: "body."

[1] Feast of the Catholic church, held February 2, in honor of the purification of the Virgin and the presentation of Christ in the Temple. Candles used in sacred services are blessed on this day.

[2] The moving of flocks from one pasturage to another.

bereavement altering the moving lights
to a processional, a feast of Candlemas.   20
Change as child-bearing, birth as a kind

of shucking off: out of what began
as a Mosaic insult[3]—such a loathing
of the common origin, even a virgin,

having given birth, needs purifying—   25
to carry fire as though it were a flower,
the terror and the loveliness entrusted

into naked hands, supposing God might have,
might actually need a mother: people have
at times found this a way of being happy.   30

A Candlemas of moving lights along Route 80;
lighted candles in a corridor from Arlington[4]
over the Potomac, for every carried flame

the name of a dead soldier: an element
fragile as ego, frightening as parturition,   35
necessary and intractable as dreaming.

The lapped, wheelborne integument,[5] layer
within layer, at the core a dream of
something precious, ripped: Where are we?

The sleepers groan, stir, rewrap themselves   40
about the self's imponderable substance,
or clamber down, numb-footed, half in a drowse

of freezing dark, through a Stonehenge
of fuel pumps, the bison hulks slantwise
beside them, drinking. What is real except   45

what's fabricated? The jellies glitter
cream-capped in the cafeteria showcase;
gumball globes, Life Savers cinctured

[3] I.e., the regarding of women in Old Testament
law as unclean and in need of ritual purification
at certain times—for example, after childbirth.
[4] Site near Washington, D.C., of Arlington
National Cemetary, military burial place.

[5] I.e., the traveler herself, borne westward on the
bus.

in parcel gilt, plop from their housings
perfect, like miracles. Comb, nail clipper,   50
lip rouge, mirrors and emollients embody,

niched into the washroom wall case,
the pristine seductiveness of money.
Absently, without inhabitants, this

nowhere oasis wears the place name   55
of Indian Meadows. The westward-trekking
transhumance, once only, of a people[6] who,

in losing everything they had, lost even
the names they went by, stumbling past
like caribou, perhaps camped here. Who   60

can assign a trade-in value to that sorrow?
The monk in sheepskin over tucked-up saffron
intoning to a drum becomes the metronome

of one more straggle up Pennsylvania Avenue
in falling snow, a whirl of tenderly   65
remorseless corpuscles, street gangs

amok among magnolias' pregnant wands,
a stillness at the heart of so much whirling:
beyond the torn integument of childbirth,

sometimes, wrapped like a papoose into a grief   70
not merely of the ego, you rediscover almost
the rest-in-peace of the placental coracle.

2

Of what the dead were, living, one knows
so little as barely to recognize
the fabric of the backward-ramifying   75

antecedents, half-noted presences
in darkened rooms: the old, the feared,
the hallowed. Never the same river

drowns the unalterable doorsill. An effigy
in olive wood or pear wood, dank   80
with the sweat of age, walled in the dark

---

[6] I.e., Native Americans.

at Brauron, Argos, Samos:[7] even the unwed
Athene,[8] who had no mother, born—it's declared—
of some man's brain like every other pure idea,

had her own wizened cult object, kept   85
out of sight like the incontinent whimperer
in the backstairs bedroom, where no child

ever goes—to whom, year after year,
the fair linen of the sacred peplos
was brought in ceremonial procession—   90

flutes and stringed instruments, wildflower-
hung cattle, nubile Athenian girls, young men
praised for the beauty of their bodies. Who

can unpeel the layers of that seasonal
returning to the dark where memory fails,   95
as birds re-enter the ancestral flyway?

Daylight, snow falling, knotting of gears:
Chicago. Soot, the rotting backsides
of tenements, grimed trollshapes of ice

underneath the bridges, the tunnel heaving   100
like a birth canal. Disgorged, the infant
howling in the restroom; steam-table cereal,

pale coffee; wall-eyed TV receivers, armchairs
of molded plastic: the squalor of the day
resumed, the orphaned litter taken up again   105

unloved, the spawn of botched intentions,
grief a mere hardening of the gut,
a set piece of what can't be avoided:

parents by the tens of thousands living
unthanked, unpaid but in the sour coin   110
of resentment. Midmorning gray as zinc

along Route 80, corn-stubble quilting
the underside of snowdrifts, the cadaverous
belvedere[9] of windmills, the sullen stare

---

[7] Greek islands.
[8] Virgin goddess of wisdom in Greek mythology.
The ancient olive-wood statue of Athene kept
at the Parthenon, was the cult-object of the
yearly Panathenaic procession, in which a linen
cloth, or *peplos,* was carried.
[9] Building commanding a fine prospect.

of feedlot cattle; black creeks puncturing   115
white terrain, the frozen bottomland
a mush of willow tops; dragnetted in ice,

the Mississippi. Westward toward the dark,
the undertow of scenes come back to, fright
riddling the structures of interior history: 120

Where is it? Where, in the shucked-off
bundle, the hampered obscurity that has been
for centuries the mumbling lot of women,

did the thread of fire, too frail
ever to discover what it meant, to risk   125
even the taking of a shape, relinquish

the seed of possibility, unguessed-at
as a dream of something precious? Memory,
that exquisite blunderer, stumbling

like a migrant bird that finds the flyway   130
it hardly knew it knew except by instinct,
down the long-unentered nave of childhood,

late on a midwinter afternoon, alone
among the snow-hung hollows of the windbreak
on the far side of the orchard, encounters   135

sheltering among the evergreens, a small
stilled bird, its cap of clear yellow
slit by a thread of scarlet—the untouched

nucleus of fire, the lost connection
hallowing the wizened effigy, the mother   140
curtained in Intensive Care: a Candlemas

of moving lights along Route 80, at nightfall,
in falling snow, the stillness and the sorrow
of things moving back to where they came from.
1983

The Kingfisher

In a year the nightingales were said to be so loud
they drowned out slumber, and peafowl strolled screaming
beside the ruined nunnery, through the long evening
of a dazzled pub crawl, the halcyon color, portholed
by those eye-spots' stunning tapestry, unsettled   5
the pastoral nightfall with amazements opening.

Months later, intermission in a pub on Fifty-fifth Street
found one of them still breathless, the other quizzical,
acting the philistine, puncturing Stravinsky[1]—"Tell
me, what *was* that racket in the orchestra about?"—   10
hauling down the Firebird,[2] harum-scarum, like a kite,
a burnished, breathing wreck that didn't hurt at all.

Among the Bronx Zoo's exiled jungle fowl, they heard
through headphones of a separating panic the bellbird
reiterate its single *chong,* a scream nobody answered.   15
When he mourned, "The poetry is gone," she quailed,
seeing how his hands shook, sobered into feeling old.
By midnight, yet another fifth would have been killed.

A Sunday morning, the November of their cataclysm
(Dylan Thomas[3] brought in *in extremis*[4] to St. Vincent's   20
that same week, a symptomatic datum) found them
wandering a downtown churchyard. Among its headstones,
while from unruined choirs the noise of Christendom
poured over Wall Street, a benison in vestments,

a late thrush paused, in transit from some grizzled   25
spruce bog to the humid equatorial fireside: berry-
eyed, bark-brown above, with dark hints of trauma
in the stigmata[5] of its underparts—or so, too bruised
just then to have invented anything so fancy,
later, reembroidering a retrospect, she had supposed.   30

In gray England, years of muted recrimination (then
dead silence) later, she could not have said how many
spoiled takeoffs, how many entanglements gone sodden,

---

[1] Igor Stravinsky (1882–1971), Russian composer. He became first a French, then an American citizen.
[2] Ballet composed by Stravinsky in 1910.
[3] British poet (1914–1953).
[4] Latin: "dying."
[5] In tradition, the wounds of Christ.

how many gaudy evenings made frantic by just one
insomniac nightingale, how many liaisons gone down   35
screaming in a stroll beside the ruined nunnery;

a kingfisher's burnished plunge, the color
of felicity afire, came glancing like an arrow
through landscapes of untended memory: ardor
illuminating with its terrifying currency   40
now no mere glimpse, no porthole vista
but, down on down, the uninhabitable sorrow.

1983

The Woodlot

Clumped murmuring above a sump of loam—
grass-rich, wood-poor—that first the plow,
then the inventor (his name plowed under
somewhere in the Patent Office) of barbed wire,
taught, if not fine manners, how at least to follow   5
the surveyor's rule, the woodlot nodes of willow,
evergreen or silver maple gave the prairie grid
what little personality it had.
                                    Who could
have learned fine manners where the air,
that rude nomad, still domineered,   10
without a shape it chose to keep,
oblivious of section lines, in winter
whisking its wolfish spittle to a froth
that turned whole townships into
one white wallow? Barbed wire   15
kept in the cattle but would not abrade
the hide or draw the blood
of gales hurled gnashing like seawater over fences'
laddered apertures, rigging the landscape
with the perspective of a shipwreck. Land-chained,   20
the blizzard paused to caterwaul
at every windbreak, a rage the worse
because it was in no way personal.
                                    Against
the involuted tantrums of spring and summer—
sackfuls of ire, the frightful udder   25
of the dropped mammocumulus

become all mouth, a lamprey
swigging up whole farmsteads, suction
dislodging treetrunks like a rotten tooth—
luck and a cellarhole were all   30
a prairie dweller had to count on.
                                        Whether
the inventor of barbed wire was lucky
finally in what he found himself
remembering, who knows? Did he
ever, even once, envision   35
the spread of what he'd done
across a continent: whale-song's
taut dulcimer still thrumming as it strung together
orchard, barnyard, bullpen, feedlot,
windbreak: wire to be clambered over,   40
crawled through or slid under, shepherded—
the heifers staring—to an enclosure
whose ceiling's silver-maple tops
stir overhead, uneasy, in the interminably
murmuring air? Deep in it, under   45
appletrees like figures in a ritual, violets
are thick, a blue cellarhole
of pure astonishment.
                          It is
the earliest memory. Before it,
I/you, whatever that conundrum may yet   50
prove to be, amounts to nothing.
1983

Mark Strand
b. 1934

Mark Strand has published, besides his own poetry, several distinguished books of
translations, children's books, short stories, and essays on literature, painting, and
photography. He is a Canadian by birth, born on Prince Edward Island. He took
a B.F.A. at Yale and an M.A. at the University of Iowa after graduating from
Antioch College, and spent a year (1960–1961) at the University of Florence on a
Fulbright. He later (1965–1966) went to Rio de Janeiro as Fulbright lecturer on
American literature and became translator of the great Brazilian poet Carlos
Drummond de Andrade. He has also translated Rafael Alberti and Jorge Luis
Borges. Strand has taught at several universities and is now at the University of
Utah.

   Strand's most distinctive characteristic as a poet, visible even in his first book,
Sleeping with One Eye Open (1964), is the dreamlike nature of his writing. A

gulf opens between stanzas, and even between lines, of his verse. He is a poet of inner blank, whose lines appear with difficulty, and slowly, enacting the arduousness of rendering and formulating the contents of consciousness. Each of Strand's lines is long-meditated and firm in its isolation from others. The inner loneliness in Strand would be unremarkable if it had not found an aesthetic in which to embody itself—a large canvas full of unpainted space, like a late Cézanne. In subsequent books—*Reasons for Moving* (1968), *Darker* (1970), *The Story of Our Lives* (1973), and *The Late Hour* (1978)—Strand has continued to work within a spare and economic style, exhibiting affinities with abstract painting.

Strand's minimalist poetry represents a revulsion from the confessional mode; he writes (and in this he resembles W. S. Merwin) a poetry of parable, a spare poetry in which the tokens representing emotional experience are widely representative. His poetry betrays the influence of Spanish and Latin American surrealism, in its strange inflexible logic and its willingness to assume a hallucinatory atmosphere. Recently, he has become more openly autobiographical in poems recalling his childhood and youth on Prince Edward Island. He and Elizabeth Bishop (who grew up in Nova Scotia) have become the poets of the maritime provinces of Canada as well as poets of Brazil. (They met when Bishop was living in Brazil.) Like Bishop, Strand is a poet of fastidious choices; unlike her, he writes at a second remove from the world of travels north and south, preferring an inner geography of vision.

Text:
Selected Poems, 1980.

The Mailman

It is midnight.
He comes up the walk
and knocks at the door.
I rush to greet him.
He stands there weeping,   5
shaking a letter at me.
He tells me it contains
terrible personal news.
He falls to his knees.
"Forgive me! Forgive me!" he pleads.   10

I ask him inside.
He wipes his eyes.
His dark blue suit

is like an inkstain
on my crimson couch.   15
Helpless, nervous, small,
he curls up like a ball
and sleeps while I compose
more letters to myself
in the same vein: 20

"You shall live
by inflicting pain.
You shall forgive."
1969

The Tunnel

A man has been standing
in front of my house
for days. I peek at him
from the living room
window and at night,   5
unable to sleep,
I shine my flashlight
down on the lawn.
He is always there.

After a while   10
I open the front door
just a crack and order
him out of my yard.
He narrows his eyes
and moans. I slam   15
the door and dash back
to the kitchen, then up
to the bedroom, then down.

I weep like a schoolgirl
and make obscene gestures   20
through the window. I
write large suicide notes
and place them so he
can read them easily.
I destroy the living   25

room furniture to prove
I own nothing of value.

When he seems unmoved
I decide to dig a tunnel
to a neighboring yard.   30
I seal the basement off
from the upstairs with
a brick wall. I dig hard
and in no time the tunnel
is done. Leaving my pick   35
and shovel below,

I come out in front of a house
and stand there too tired to
move or even speak, hoping
someone will help me.   40
I feel I'm being watched
and sometimes I hear
a man's voice,
but nothing is done
and I have been waiting for days.   45
1969

Keeping Things Whole

In a field
I am the absence
of field.
This is
always the case.   5
Wherever I am
I am what is missing.

When I walk
I part the air
and always   10
the air moves in
to fill the spaces
where my body's been.

We all have reasons
for moving.   15
I move
to keep things whole.

1969

Coming to This

We have done what we wanted.
We have discarded dreams, preferring the heavy industry
of each other, and we have welcomed grief
and called ruin the impossible habit to break.

And now we are here.   5
The dinner is ready and we cannot eat.
The meat sits in the white lake of its dish.
The wine waits.

Coming to this
has its rewards: nothing is promised, nothing is taken away. 10
We have no heart or saving grace,
no place to go, no reason to remain.

1970

Breath

When you see them
tell them I am still here,
that I stand on one leg while the other one dreams,
that this is the only way,

that the lies I tell them are different   5
from the lies I tell myself,
that by being both here and beyond
I am becoming a horizon,

that as the sun rises and sets I know my place,
that breath is what saves me,   10

that even the forced syllables of decline are breath,
that if the body is a coffin it is also a closet of breath,

that breath is a mirror clouded by words,
that breath is all that survives the cry for help
as it enters the stranger's ear   15
and stays long after the word is gone,

that breath is the beginning again, that from it
all resistance falls away, as meaning falls
away from life, or darkness falls from light,
that breath is what I give them when I send my love.   20

1970

Letter

For Richard Howard

Men are running across a field,
pens fall from their pockets.
People out walking will pick them up.
It is one of the ways letters are written.

How things fall to others!   5
The self no longer belonging to me, but asleep
in a stranger's shadow, now clothing
the stranger, now leading him off.

It is noon as I write to you.
Someone's life has come into my hands.   10
The sun whitens the buildings.
It is all I have. I give it all to you. Yours,

1970

Giving Myself Up

I give up my eyes which are glass eggs.
I give up my tongue.
I give up my mouth which is the constant dream of my tongue.

I give up my throat which is the sleeve of my voice.
I give up my heart which is a burning apple.   5
I give up my lungs which are trees that have never seen the moon.
I give up my smell which is that of a stone traveling through rain.
I give up my hands which are ten wishes.
I give up my arms which have wanted to leave me anyway.
I give up my legs which are lovers only at night.   10
I give up my buttocks which are the moons of childhood.
I give up my penis which whispers encouragement to my thighs.
I give up my clothes which are walls that blow in the wind
and I give up the ghost that lives in them.
I give up. I give up.   15
And you will have none of it because already I am beginning
again without anything.

1970

Courtship

There is a girl you like so you tell her
your penis is big, but that you cannot get yourself
to use it. Its demands are ridiculous, you say,
even self-defeating, but to be honored somehow,
briefly, inconspicuously in the dark.   5

When she closes her eyes in horror,
you take it all back. You tell her you're almost
a girl yourself and can understand why she is shocked.
When she is about to walk away, you tell her
you have no penis, that you don't   10

know what got into you. You get on your knees.
She suddenly bends down to kiss your shoulder and you know
you're on the right track. You tell her you want
to bear children and that is why you seem confused.
You wrinkle your brow and curse the day you were born.   15

She tries to calm you, but you lose control.
You reach for her panties and beg forgiveness as you do.
She squirms and you howl like a wolf. Your craving
seems monumental. You know you will have her.
Taken by storm, she is the girl you will marry.   20

1970

"The Dreadful Has Already Happened"

The relatives are leaning over, staring expectantly.
They moisten their lips with their tongues. I can feel
them urging me on. I hold the baby in the air.
Heaps of broken bottles glitter in the sun.

A small band is playing old fashioned marches.   5
My mother is keeping time by stamping her foot.
My father is kissing a woman who keeps waving
to somebody else. There are palm trees.

The hills are spotted with orange flamboyants and tall
billowy clouds move behind them. "Go on, Boy,"   10
I hear somebody say, "Go on."
I keep wondering if it will rain.

The sky darkens. There is thunder.
"Break his legs," says one of my aunts,
"Now give him a kiss." I do what I'm told.   15
The trees bend in the bleak tropical wind.

The baby did not scream, but I remember that sigh
when I reached inside for his tiny lungs and shook them
out in the air for the flies. The relatives cheered.
It was about that time I gave up.   20

Now, when I answer the phone, his lips
are in the receiver; when I sleep, his hair is gathered
around a familiar face on the pillow; wherever I search
I find his feet. He is what is left of my life.

1970

Elegy for My Father
(Robert Strand 1908–68)

1. The Empty Body

The hands were yours, the arms were yours,
But you were not there.
The eyes were yours, but they were closed and would not open.

The distant sun was there.
The moon poised on the hill's white shoulder was there.   5
The wind on Bedford Basin was there.
The pale green light of winter was there.
Your mouth was there,
But you were not there.
When somebody spoke, there was no answer.   10
Clouds came down
And buried the buildings along the water,
And the water was silent.
The gulls stared.
The years, the hours, that would not find you   15
Turned in the wrists of others.
There was no pain. It had gone.
There were no secrets. There was nothing to say.
The shade scattered its ashes.
The body was yours, but you were not there.   20
The air shivered against its skin.
The dark leaned into its eyes.
But you were not there.

2. Answers

Why did you travel?
Because the house was cold.
Why did you travel?   25
Because it is what I have always done between sunset and sunrise.
What did you wear?
I wore a blue suit, a white shirt, yellow tie, and yellow socks.
What did you wear?
I wore nothing. A scarf of pain kept me warm.   30
Who did you sleep with?
I slept with a different woman each night.
Who did you sleep with?
I slept alone. I have always slept alone.   35
Why did you lie to me?
I always thought I told the truth.
Why did you lie to me?
Because the truth lies like nothing else and I love the truth.
Why are you going?   40
Because nothing means much to me anymore.
Why are you going?
I don't know. I have never known.
How long shall I wait for you?
Do not wait for me. I am tired and I want to lie down.   45
Are you tired and do you want to lie down?
Yes, I am tired and I want to lie down.

3. *Your Dying*

Nothing could stop you.
Not the best day. Not the quiet. Not the ocean rocking.
You went on with your dying. 50
Not the trees
Under which you walked, not the trees that shaded you.
Not the doctor
Who warned you, the white-haired young doctor who saved you once.
You went on with your dying. 55
Nothing could stop you. Not your son. Not your daughter
Who fed you and made you into a child again.
Not your son who thought you would live forever.
Not the wind that shook your lapels.
Not the stillness that offered itself to your motion. 60
Not your shoes that grew heavier.
Not your eyes that refused to look ahead.
Nothing could stop you.
You sat in your room and stared at the city
And went on with your dying. 65
You went to work and let the cold enter your clothes.
You let blood seep into your socks.
Your face turned white.
Your voice cracked in two.
You leaned on your cane. 70
But nothing could stop you.
Not your friends who gave you advice.
Not your son. Not your daughter who watched you grow small.
Not fatigue that lived in your sighs.
Not your lungs that would fill with water. 75
Not your sleeves that carried the pain of your arms.
Nothing could stop you.
You went on with your dying.
When you played with children you went on with your dying.
When you sat down to eat, 80
When you woke up at night, wet with tears, your body sobbing,
You went on with your dying.
Nothing could stop you.
Not the past.
Not the future with its good weather. 85
Not the view from your window, the view of the graveyard.
Not the city. Not the terrible city with its wooden buildings.
Not defeat. Not success.
You did nothing but go on with your dying.
You put your watch to your ear. 90
You felt yourself slipping.
You lay on the bed.

You folded your arms over your chest and you dreamed of the world without
  you,
Of the space under the trees,
Of the space in your room,   95
Of the spaces that would now be empty of you,
And you went on with your dying.
Nothing could stop you.
Not your breathing. Not your life.
Not the life you wanted.   100
Not the life you had.
Nothing could stop you.

4. *Your Shadow*

You have your shadow.
The places where you were have given it back.
The hallways and bare lawns of the orphanage have given it back.   105
The Newsboys Home has given it back.
The streets of New York have given it back and so have the streets of
  Montreal.
The rooms in Belém where lizards would snap at mosquitos have given it back.
The dark streets of Manaus and the damp streets of Rio have given it back.
Mexico City where you wanted to leave it has given it back.   110
And Halifax where the harbor would wash its hands of you has given it back.
You have your shadow.
When you traveled the white wake of your going sent your shadow below, but
  when you arrived it was there to greet you. You had your shadow.
The doorways you entered lifted your shadow from you and when you went
  out, gave it back. You had your shadow.
Even when you forgot your shadow, you found it again; it had been with you. 115
Once in the country the shade of a tree covered your shadow and you were
  not known.
Once in the country you thought your shadow had been cast by somebody else.
  Your shadow said nothing.
Your clothes carried your shadow inside; when you took them off, it spread
  like the dark of your past.
And your words that float like leaves in an air that is lost, in a place no one
  knows, gave you back your shadow.
Your friends gave you back your shadow.   120
Your enemies gave you back your shadow. They said it was heavy and would
  cover your grave.
When you died your shadow slept at the mouth of the furnace and ate ashes
  for bread.
It rejoiced among ruins.
It watched while others slept.
It shone like crystal among the tombs.   125
It composed itself like air.

It wanted to be like snow on water.
It wanted to be nothing, but that was not possible.
It came to my house.
It sat on my shoulders.   130
Your shadow is yours. I told it so. I said it was yours.
I have carried it with me too long. I give it back.

5. Mourning

They mourn for you.
When you rise at midnight,
And the dew glitters on the stone of your cheeks,   135
They mourn for you.
They lead you back into the empty house.
They carry the chairs and tables inside.
They sit you down and teach you to breathe.
And your breath burns,   140
It burns the pine box and the ashes fall like sunlight.
They give you a book and tell you to read.
They listen and their eyes fill with tears.
The women stroke your fingers.
They comb the yellow back into your hair.   145
They shave the frost from your beard.
They knead your thighs.
They dress you in fine clothes.
They rub your hands to keep them warm.
They feed you. They offer you money.   150
They get on their knees and beg you not to die.
When you rise at midnight they mourn for you.
They close their eyes and whisper your name over and over.
But they cannot drag the buried light from your veins.
They cannot reach your dreams.   155
Old man, there is no way.
Rise and keep rising, it does no good.
They mourn for you the way they can.

6. The New Year

It is winter and the new year.
Nobody knows you.   160
Away from the stars, from the rain of light,
You lie under the weather of stones.
There is no thread to lead you back.
Your friends doze in the dark
Of pleasure and cannot remember.   165
Nobody knows you. You are the neighbor of nothing.
You do not see the rain falling and the man walking away,

The soiled wind blowing its ashes across the city.
You do not see the sun dragging the moon like an echo.
You do not see the bruised heart go up in flames,   170
The skulls of the innocent turn into smoke.
You do not see the scars of plenty, the eyes without light.
It is over. It is winter and the new year.
The meek are hauling their skins into heaven.
The hopeless are suffering the cold with those who have nothing to hide.   175
It is over and nobody knows you.
There is starlight drifting on the black water.
There are stones in the sea no one has seen.
There is a shore and people are waiting.
And nothing comes back.   180
Because it is over.
Because there is silence instead of a name.
Because it is winter and the new year.

1970

The Coming of Light

Even this late it happens:
the coming of love, the coming of light.
You wake and the candles are lit as if by themselves,
stars gather, dreams pour into your pillows,
sending up warm bouquets of air.   5
Even this late the bones of the body shine
and tomorrow's dust flares into breath.

1978

The Late Hour

A man walks towards town,
a slack breeze smelling of earth
and the raw green of trees blows at his back.

He drags the weight of his passion as if nothing were over,
as if the woman, now curled in bed beside her lover,   5
still cared for him.

She is awake and stares at scars of light
trapped in the panes of glass.
He stands under her window, calling her name;

he calls all night and it makes no difference.   10
It will happen again, he will come back wherever she is.
Again he will stand outside and imagine

her eyes opening in the dark
and see her rise to the window and peer down.
Again she will lie awake beside her lover   15

and hear the voice from somewhere in the dark.
Again the late hour, the moon and stars,
the wounds of night that heal without sound,

again the luminous wind of morning that comes before the sun.
And, finally, without warning or desire,   20
the lonely and the feckless end.

1980

Where Are the Waters
of Childhood?

See where the windows are boarded up,
where the gray siding shines in the sun and salt air
and the asphalt shingles on the roof have peeled or fallen off,
where tiers of oxeye daisies float on a sea of grass?
That's the place to begin.   5

Enter the kingdom of rot,
smell the damp plaster, step over the shattered glass,
the pockets of dust, the rags, the soiled remains of a mattress,
look at the rusted stove and sink, at the rectangular stain
on the wall where Winslow Homer's[1] *Gulf Stream* hung.   10

Go to the room where your father and mother
would let themselves go in the drift and pitch of love,

---

[1] Winslow Homer (1836–1910), American painter.

and hear, if you can, the creak of their bed,
then go to the place where you hid.

Go to your room, to all the rooms whose cold, damp air you breathed,   15
to all the unwanted places where summer, fall, winter, spring,
seem the same unwanted season, where the trees you knew have died
and other trees have risen. Visit that other place
you barely recall, that other house half hidden.

See the two dogs burst into sight. When you leave,   20
they will cease, snuffed out in the glare of an earlier light.
Visit the neighbors down the block; he waters his lawn,
she sits on her porch, but not for long.
When you look again they are gone.

Keep going back, back to the field, flat and sealed in mist.   25
On the other side, a man and a woman are waiting;
they have come back, your mother before she was gray,
your father before he was white.

Now look at the North West Arm,[2] how it glows a deep cerulean blue.
See the light on the grass, the one leaf burning, the cloud   30
that flares. You're almost there, in a moment your parents
will disappear, leaving you under the light of a vanished star,
under the dark of a star newly born. Now is the time.

Now you invent the boat of your flesh and set it upon the waters
and drift in the gradual swell, in the laboring salt.   35
Now you look down. The waters of childhood are there.

1978

A Morning

I have carried it with me each day: that morning I took
my uncle's boat from the brown water cove
and headed for Mosher Island.
Small waves splashed against the hull
and the hollow creek of oarlock and oar   5
rose into the woods of black pine crusted with lichen.
I moved like a dark star, drifting over the drowned

_____
[2] A body of water.

other half of the world until, by a distant prompting,
I looked over the gunwale and saw beneath the surface
a luminous room, a light-filled grave, saw for the first time   10
the one clear place given to us when we are alone.
1980

Charles Wright
b. 1935

"Poems," said Charles Wright in an interview, "are both reliquary and
transubstantiational, as our lives should be." That is, the poem preserves
something of life, while leaving it behind; the poem changes the substance of
experience into the substance of art. Wright attempted (in an early sequence
called "Tattoos") to write lyrics devoid of narrative explanatory material; the
occasion for each poem was given in an endnote. Later he experimented with
other ways of transubstantiating the narratives of life into the images of poetry,
describing his work as analogous to that of a painter, who must find the image
that will be the equivalent of his impression of the world. In his use of the
"deep image," Wright has been compared to W. S. Merwin and Mark Strand,
but though he is both remote and unearthly, his verse has a songlike base
(derived, as he says, from country music) that distinguishes him from his
contemporaries.

Ultimately, Wright derives his interest in the image from Ezra Pound. It has
taken him into translating the Italian poet Montale and into reading the German
poets Trakl and Rilke, among others. For Wright, images hover around the
white spaces in a poem: "The line, of course, is what separates us from the beasts.
I think a line has specific weight and heft, that it is melodic and tactile. It is as
though the lines were each sections of the poem attached by invisible strings to
the title." His recent poem "Homage to Paul Cézanne" attempts, as he says, a
"non-linear approach to plot. . . . The structure of the poem is presentational,
and it works accumulatively. . . . I was conscious of working in blocks of lines,
stanzas and pages, much as Cézanne might have used his dabs and columns and
blotches of color (in many of the Mt. St. Victoire landscapes you can't find a
line at all—everything is dab and spread and knife-stroke)." It is by the massing
of many parallel items that one recognizes a poem by Charles Wright.

Wright's themes often derive from his Episcopalian upbringing in the South,
which issues in a persistent wish to become disembodied, to die and be
resurrected at once, to disappear into the earth and the air at a single stroke.
Wright was born in Tennessee and grew up there and in North Carolina. He
took an M.F.A. at Iowa after graduating from Davidson College. From 1957 to
1961 he served in Verona, Italy, in U.S. Army intelligence; from 1963 to 1965 he
was a Fulbright student in Rome; and in 1968 and 1969 he was a Fulbright
lecturer at the University of Padua. He taught from 1966 to 1983 at the Irvine

campus of the University of California; since 1983 he has been professor of
English at the University of Virginia.

Many of Wright's poems occur in a southern landscape; others are set in Italy
or in California. But Wright remains a poet of grave ethereal music, tethered
only lightly by earthly scenes. He is probably most southern in the emotions
bequeathed him by his childhood religious experience and in his wish that poetry
should have a sacramental grace.

Texts:
"Homage to Paul Cézanne," "Virginia Reel,"
"Dead Color," and "Hawaii Dantesca" from
The Southern Cross, 1981.
All other selections from *Country Music: Selected
Early Poems,* 1982.

The New Poem

It will not resemble the sea.
It will not have dirt on its thick hands.
It will not be part of the weather.

It will not reveal its name.
It will not have dreams you can count on.   5
It will not be photogenic.

It will not attend our sorrow.
It will not console our children.
It will not be able to help us.
1973

Northhanger Ridge[1]

Half-bridge over nothingness,
White sky of the palette knife; blot orange,
Vertical blacks; blue, birdlike,
Drifting up from the next life,

---

[1] A children's summer Bible camp where Wright
was a camper.

The heat-waves, like consolation, wince—   5
One cloud, like a trunk, stays shut
Above the horizon; off to the left, dream-wires,
Hill-snout like a crocodile's.

Or so I remember it,
Their clenched teeth in their clenched mouths,   10
Their voices like shards of light,
Brittle, unnecessary.
Ruined shoes, roots, the cabinet of lost things:
This is the same story,
Its lips in flame, its throat a dark water,   15
The page stripped of its meaning.

Sunday, and Father Dog is turned loose:
Up the long road the children's feet
Snick in the dust like raindrops; the wind
Excuses itself and backs off; inside, heat   20
Lies like a hand on each head;
Slither and cough. Now Father Dog
Addles our misconceptions, points, preens,
His finger a white flag, run up, run down.

Bow-wow and arf, the Great Light;   25
O, and the Great Yes, and the Great No;
Redemption, the cold kiss of release,
&c.; sentences, sentences.
(Meanwhile, docile as shadows, they stare
From their four corners, looks set: 30
No glitter escapes
This evangelical masonry.)

Candleflame; vigil and waterflow:
Like dust in the night the prayers rise:
From 6 to 6, under the sick Christ,   35
The children talk to the nothingness,
Crossrack and wound; the dark room
Burns like a coal, goes
Ash to the touch, ash to the tongue's tip;
Blood turns in the wheel: 40

Something drops from the leaves; the drugged moon
Twists and turns in its sheets; sweet breath
In a dry corner, the black widow reknits her dream.
Salvation again declines,
And sleeps like a skull in the hard ground,   45

Nothing for ears, nothing for eyes;
It sleeps as it's always slept, without
Shadow, waiting for nothing.

                    Bible Camp, 1949

1973

Tattoos

1.[1]

Necklace of flame, little dropped hearts,
Camellias: I crunch you under my foot.
And here comes the wind again, bad breath
Of thirty-odd years, and catching up. Still,
I crunch you under my foot.   5

Your white stalks sequester me,
Their roots a remembered solitude.
Their mouths of snow keep forming my name.
Programmed incendiaries,
Fused flesh, so light your flowering,   10

So light the light that fires you
—Petals of horn, scales of blood—,
Where would you have me return?
What songs would I sing,
And the hymns . . . What garden of wax statues . . .   15

                    1973

2.[2]

The pin oak has found new meat,
The linkworm a bone to pick.
Lolling its head, slicking its blue tongue,
The nightflower blooms on its one stem;
The crabgrass hones down its knives: 20

Between us again there is nothing. And since
The darkness is only light
That has not yet reached us,

---

[1] Wright's note: "Camellias; Mother's Day; St.
Paul's Episcopal Church, Kingsport, Tennessee."

[2] Wright's note: "Death of my father."

You slip it on like a glove.
Duck soup, you say. *This is duck soup.*   25

And so it is.
             Along the far bank
Of Blood Creek, I watch you turn
In that light, and turn, and turn,
Feeling it change on your changing hands,
Feeling it take. Feeling it.   30
          1972

3.[3]

Body fat as my forearm, blunt-arrowed head
And motionless, eyes
Sequin and hammer and nail
In the torchlight, he hangs there,
Color of dead leaves, color of dust,   35

Dumbbell and hourglass—copperhead.
Color of bread dough, color of pain, the hand
That takes it, that handles it
—The snake now limp as a cat—
Is halfway to heaven, and in time.   40

Then Yellow Shirt, twitching and dancing,
Gathers it home, handclap and heartstring,
His habit in ecstasy.
Current and godhead, hot coil,
Grains through the hourglass glint and spring.   45
          1951

4.[4]

Silt fingers, silt stump and bone.
And twice now, in the drugged sky,
White moons, black moons.
And twice now, in the gardens,
The great seed of affection.   50

Liplap of Zuan's canal,[5] blear
Footfalls of Tintoretto;[6] the rest
Is brilliance: Turner[7] at 3 a.m.; moth lamps
Along the casements. O blue
Feathers, this clear cathedral . . .   55

---

[3] Wright's note: "Snake-handling religious service; East Tennessee."
[4] Wright's note: "Venice, Italy."

[5] In Venice, where Wright once lived.
[6] Venetian painter (1518–1594).
[7] English painter (1775–1851).

And now these stanchions of joy,
Radiant underpinning:
Old scaffolding, old arrangements,
All fall in a rain of light.
I have seen what I have seen.   60

1968

5.[8]

Hungering acolyte, pale body,
The sunlight—through St Paul of the 12 Sorrows[9]—
Falls like Damascus[10] on me:
I feel the gold hair of Paradise rise through my skin
Needle and thread, needle and thread;   65

I feel the worm in the rose root.
I hear the river of heaven
Fall from the air, I hear it enter the wafer
And sink me, the whirlpool stars
Spinning me down, and down. O . . .   70

Now I am something else, smooth,
Unrooted, with no veins and no hair, washed
In the waters of nothingness;
Anticoronal, released . . .
And then I am risen, the cup, new sun, at my lips.   75

1946

6.[11]

Skyhooked above the floor, sucked
And mummied by salt towels, my left arm
Hangs in the darkness, bloodwood, black gauze,
The slow circle of poison
Coming and going through the same hole . . .   80

Sprinkle of rain through the pine needles,
Shoosh pump shoosh pump of the heart;
Bad blood, bad blood . . .
                                   Chalk skin like a light,
Eyes thin dimes, whose face
Comes and goes at the window?   85

---

[8] Wright's note: "Acolyte; fainting at the altar; Kingsport, Tennessee."
[9] Wright's boyhood church.
[10] Place of the conversion of St. Paul from persecutor of Christians to apostle of Christianity.
[11] Wright's note: "Blood-poisoning; hallucination; Hiwassee, North Carolina."

Whose face . . .
           For I would join it,
And climb through the nine-and-a-half footholds of fever
Into the high air,
and shed these clothes and renounce,
Burned over, repurified.   90
             1941

7.[12]

This one's not like the other, pale, gingerly—
Like nothing, in fact, to rise, as he does,
In three days, his blood clotted,
His deathsheet a feather across his chest,
His eyes twin lenses, and ready to unroll.   95

Arm and a leg, nail hole and knucklebone,
He stands up. In his right hand,
The flagstaff of victory;
In his left, the folds of what altered him.
And the hills spell V, and the trees V . . .   100

Nameless, invisible, what spins out
From this wall comes breath by breath,
And pulls the vine, and the ringing tide,
The scorched syllable from the moon's mouth.
And what pulls them pulls me.   105
             1963

8.[13]

A tongue hangs in the dawn wind, a wind
That trails the tongue's voice like a banner, star
And whitewash, the voice
Sailing across the 14 mountains, snap and drift,
To settle, a last sigh, here.   110

That tongue is his tongue, the voice his voice:
Lifting out of the sea
Where the tongue licks, the voice starts,

---

[12] Wright's note: "*The Resurrection,* Piero della Francesca, Borgo San Sepolcro, Italy." This painting of the Resurrection of Christ by Piero della Francesca (ca. 1420–1492) is in the Palazzo Communale of Borgo San Sepolcro, birthplace of the artist.

[13] Wright's note: "Harold Schimmel's morning prayers; Positano, Italy."

Monotonous, out of sync,
Yarmulke, tfillin, tallis. [14]   115

His nude body waist deep in the waves,
The book a fire in his hands, his movements
Reedflow and counter flow, the chant light
From his lips, the prayer rising to heaven,
And everything brilliance, brilliance, brilliance.   120

                    1959

9. [15]

In the fixed crosshairs of evening,
In the dust-wallow of certitude,
Where the drop drops and the scalding starts,
Where the train pulls out and the light winks,
The tracks go on, and go on: 125

The flesh pulls back and snaps,
The fingers are ground and scraped clean,
Reed whistles in a green fire.
The bones blow on, singing their bald song.
It stops. And it starts again.   130

Theologians, Interpreters:
Song, the tracks, crosshairs, the light;
The drop that is always falling.
Over again I feel the palm print,
The map that will take me there.   135

                    1952

10. [16]

It starts here, in a chair, sunflowers
Inclined from an iron pot, a soiled dishcloth
Draped on the backrest. A throat with a red choker
Throbs in the mirror. High on the wall,
Flower-like, disembodied,   140

---

[14] The *yarmulke* is the small hat worn by religious
Jews; the *tfillin* are the small leather cases called
phylacteries containing prayers, which are
bound to head and arm during worship; the
tallis is the prayer shawl.

[15] Wright's note: "Temporary evangelical
certitude; Christ School, Arden, North
Carolina."

[16] Wright's note: "Visions of heaven."

A wren-colored evil eye stares out
At the white blooms of the oleander, at the white
Gobbets of shadow and shade,
At the white lady and white parasol, at this
Dichogamous landscape, this found chord   145

(And in the hibiscus and moonflowers,
In the smoke trees and spider ferns,
The unicorn crosses his thin legs,
The leopard sips at her dish of blood,
And the vines strike and the vines recoil).   150
                                   1973

11.[17]

So that was it, the rush and the take-off,
The oily glide of the cells
Bringing it up—ripsurge, refraction,
The inner spin
Trailing into the cracked lights of oblivion . . .   155

Re-entry is something else, blank, hard:
Black stretcher straps; the peck, peck
And click of a scalpel; glass shards
Eased one by one from the flesh;
Recisions; the long bite of the veins . . .   160

And what do we do with this,
Rechuted, reworked into our same lives, no one
To answer to, no one to glimpse and sing,
The cracked light flashing our names?
We stand fast, friend, we stand fast.   165
                                   1958

12.[18]

Oval oval oval oval push pull push pull . . .
Words unroll from our fingers.
A splash of leaves through the windowpanes,
A smell of tar from the streets:
Apple, arrival, the railroad, shoe.   170

The words, like bees in a sweet ink, cluster and drone,
Indifferent, indelible,

[17] Wright's note: "Automobile wreck; hospital; Baltimore, Maryland."
[18] Wright's note: "Handwriting class; Palmer Method; words as 'things'; Kingsport, Tennessee."

A hum and a hum:
Back stairsteps to God, ropes to the glass eye:
Vineyard, informer, the chair, the throne.   175

Mojo[19] and numberless, breaths
From the wet mountains and green mouths; rustlings,
Sure sleights of hand,
The news that arrives from nowhere:
Angel, omega,[20] silence, silence . . .   180

                    1945

13.[21]

What I remember is fire, orange fire,
And his huge cock in his hand,
Touching my tiny one; the smell
Of coal dust, the smell of heat,
Banked flames through the furnace door.   185

Of him I remember little, if anything:
Black, overalls splotched with soot,
His voice, *honey, O, honey* . . .
And then he came, his left hand
On my back, holding me close.   190

Nothing was said, of course—one
Terrible admonition, and that was all . . .
And if that hand, like loosed lumber, fell
From grace, and stayed there? We give,
And we take it back. We give again . . .   195

                    1940

14.[22]

Now there is one, and still masked;
White death's face, sheeted and shoeless, eyes shut
Behind the skull holes.
She stands in a field, her shadow no shadow,
The clouds no clouds. Call her Untitled.   200

And now there are four, white shoes, white socks;
They stand in the same field, the same clouds

---

[19] Magic; voodoo.
[20] Last letter of the Greek alphabet; often used
together with the first letter, *alpha,* to signify
God.

[21] Wright's note: "The janitor; kindergarten;
Corinth, Mississippi."
[22] Wright's note: "Dream."

Vanishing down the sky. Cat masks and mop hair
Cover their faces. Advancing, they hold hands.

Nine. Now there are nine, their true shadows   205
The judgments beneath their feet.
Black masks, white nightgowns. A wind
Is what calls them, that field, those same clouds
Lisping one syllable *I, I, I.*

                        1970

15.[23]

And the saw keeps cutting,   210
Its flashy teeth shredding the mattress, the bedclothes,
The pillow and pillow case.
Plugged in to a socket in your bones,
It coughs, and keeps on cutting.

It eats the lamp and the bedpost.   215
It licks the clock with its oiled tongue,
And keeps on cutting.
It leaves the bedroom, and keeps on cutting.
It leaves the house, and keeps on cutting . . .

—Dogwood, old feathery petals,   220
Your black notches burn in my blood;
You flutter like bandages across my childhood.
Your sound is a sound of good-bye.
Your poem is a poem of pain.

                        1964

16.[24]

All gloss, gothic and garrulous, staked   225
To her own tree, she takes it off,
Half-dollar an article. With each
Hike of the price, the gawkers
Diminish, spitting, rubbing their necks.

Fifteen, and staked to *my* tree,   230
Sap-handled, hand in my pocket, head
Hot as the carnival tent, I see it out—as does
The sheriff of Cherokee County,
Who fondles the payoff, finger and shaft.

[23] Wright's note: "The day of my mother's   [24] Wright's note: "Sideshow stripper; Cherokee
funeral, in Tennessee; Rome, Italy."   County Fair, Cherokee, North Carolina."

Outside, in the gathering dark, all   235
Is fly buzz and gnat hum and whine of the wires;
Quick scratch of the match, cicadas,
Jackhammer insects; drone, drone
Of the blood-suckers, sweet dust, last sounds . . .
                                                        1950

17.[25]

I dream that I dream I wake   240
The room is throat-deep and brown with dead moths
I throw them back like a quilt
I peel them down from the wall
I kick them like leaves I shake them I kick them again

The bride on the couch and the bridegroom   245
Under their gauze dust-sheet
And cover up turn to each other
Top hat and tails white veil and say as I pass
It's mother again just mother the window open

On the 10th floor going up   250
Is Faceless and under steam his mask
Hot-wired my breath at his heels in sharp clumps
Darkness and light darkness and light
Faceless come back O come back
                                                        1955 ff.

18.[26]

Flash click tick, flash click tick, light   255
Through the wavefall—electrodes, intolerable curlicues;
Splinters along the skin, eyes
Flicked by the sealash, spun, pricked;
Terrible vowels from the sun.

And everything dry, wrung, the land flaked   260
By the wind, bone dust and shale;
And hills without names or numbers,
Bald coves where the sky harbors.
The dead grass whistles a tune, strangely familiar.

And all in a row, seated, their mouths biting the empty air,   265
Their front legs straight, and their backs straight,

----

[25] Wright's note: "Recurrent dream."
[26] Wright's note: "The Naxian lions; Delos,

Greece." These are stone carvings from archaic
times.

Their bodies pitted, eyes wide,
The rubble quick glint beneath their feet,
The lions stare, explaining it one more time.

                              1959

19.[27]

The hemlocks wedge in the wind.   270
Their webs are forming something—questions:
Which shoe is the alter ego?[28]
Which glove inures the fallible hand?
Why are the apple trees in draped black?

And I answer them. In words   275
They will understand, I answer them:
The left shoe.
The left glove.
Someone is dead; someone who loved them is dead.

Regret is what anchors me;   280
I wash in a water of odd names.
White flakes from next year sift down, sift down.
I lie still, and dig in,
Snow-rooted, ooze-rooted, cold blossom.

                              1972

20.[29]

You stand in your shoes, two shiny graves   285
Dogging your footsteps;
You spread your fingers, ten stalks
Enclosing your right of way;
You yip with pain in your little mouth.

And this is where the ash falls.   290
And this is the time it took to get here—
And yours, too, is the stall, the wet wings
Arriving, and the beak.
And yours the thump, and the soft voice:

---

[27] Wright's note: "Death of my father."
[28] Alternative self.
[29] Wright's note: "The last stanza is an adaptation
of lines from Eugenio Montale's *Serenata
Indiana.*" Eugenio Montale (b. 1896) is a
contemporary Italian poet.

The octopus on the reef's edge, who slides   295
His fat fingers among the cracks,
Can use you. You've prayed to him,
In fact, and don't know it.
You *are* him, and think yourself yourself.

                                    1973

1975

---

from Skins

6.[1]

Under the rock, in the sand and the gravel run;
In muck bank and weed, at the heart of the river's edge:
Instar,[2] and again, instar,
The wing cases visible. Then
Emergence: leaf drift and detritus; skin split,   5
The image forced from the self.
And rests, wings drying, eyes compressed,
Legs compressed, constricted
Beneath the dun and the watershine—
Incipient spinner, set for the take-off . . .   10
And does, in clean tear: imago[3] rising out of herself
For the last time, slate-winged and many-eyed.
And joins, and drops to her destiny,
Flesh to the surface, wings flush on the slate film.

20.[4]

You've talked to the sun and moon,   15
Those idols of stitched skin, bunch grass and twigs
Stuck on their poles in the fall rain;
You've prayed to Sweet Medicine;
You've looked at the Hanging Road, its stars
The stepstones and river bed where you hope to cross;   20

---

[1] Wright's note: "Metamorphosis."
[2] Stage in insect life between two successive molts.
[3] An insect in its final, sexually mature, winged state.
[4] Wright's note: "Situation, Point A." This was also the title of the first poem in the sequence. "Sweet Medicine," "the Hanging Road," "the Lake of Pain," and the "Pilgrim" are allegorical names in Wright's parable of the journey of life, also seen as a pilgrimage to heaven.

You've followed the cricket's horn
To sidestep the Lake of Pain . . .
And what does it come to, Pilgrim,
This walking to and fro on the earth, knowing
That nothing changes, or everything;   25
And only, to tell it, these sad marks,
Phrases half-parsed, ellipses and scratches across the dirt?
It comes to a point. It comes and it goes.

1975

Edvard Munch[1]

We live in houses of ample weight,
Their windows a skin-colored light, pale and unfixable.
Our yards are large and windraked, their trees bent to the storm.
People we don't know are all around us.

Or else there is no one, and all day   5
We stand on a bridge, or a cliff's edge, looking down.
Our mothers stare at our shoes.

Hands to our ears, our mouths open, we're pulled on
By the flash black, flash black flash of the lighthouse
We can't see on the rock coast,   10
Notes in a bottle, our lines the ink from the full moon.

1977

Stone Canyon Nocturne

Ancient of Days,[1] old friend, no one believes you'll come back.
No one believes in his own life anymore.

The moon, like a dead heart, cold and unstartable, hangs by a thread
At the earth's edge,
Unfaithful at last, splotching the ferns and the pink shrubs.   5

---

[1] Norwegian expressionist painter (1863–1944).
Wright summons up several famous paintings
by Munch, especially *The Shriek* (1893), ll.
6–11.

[1] A name used of God.

In the other world, children undo the knots in their tally strings.
They sing songs, and their fingers blear.

And here, where the swan hums in his socket, where bloodroot
And belladonna insist on our comforting,
Where the fox in the canyon wall empties our hands, ecstatic for more,   10

Like a bead of clear oil the Healer[2] revolves through the night wind,
Part eye, part tear, unwilling to recognize us.
1977

Reunion

Already one day has detached itself from all the rest up ahead.
It has my photograph in its soft pocket.
It wants to carry my breath into the past in its bag of wind.

I write poems to untie myself, to do penance and disappear
Through the upper right-hand corner of things, to say grace.   5
1977

April

The plum tree breaks out in bees.
A gull is locked like a ghost in the blue attic of heaven.
The wind goes nattering on,
Gossipy, ill at ease, in the damp rooms it will air.
I count off the grace and stays   5
My life has come to, and know I want less—

Divested of everything,
A downfall of light in the pine woods, motes in the rush,
Gold leaf through the undergrowth, and come back
As another name, water   10
Pooled in the black leaves and holding me there, to be
Released as a glint, as a flash, as a spark . . .
1977

---

[2] The moon.

Spider Crystal Ascension

The spider, juiced crystal and Milky Way, drifts on his web through the night
  sky
And looks down, waiting for us to ascend . . .

At dawn he is still there, invisible, short of breath, mending his net.

All morning we look for the white face to rise from the lake like a tiny star.
And when it does, we lie back in our watery hair and rock.   5
1977

---

from Homage to Paul Cézanne[1]

. . . .

The dead are a cadmium blue.
We spread them with palette knives in broad blocks and planes.

We layer them stroke by stroke
In steps and ascending mass, in verticals raised from the earth.

We choose, and layer them in,   5
Blue and a blue and a breath,

Circle and smudge, cross-beak and buttonhook,
We layer them in. We squint hard and terrace them line by line.

And so we are come between, and cry out,
And stare up at the sky and its cloudy panes,   10

And finger the cypress twists.
The dead understand all this, and keep in touch,

Rustle of hand to hand in the lemon trees,
Flags, and the great sifts of anger

To powder and nothingness.   15
The dead are a cadmium blue, and they understand.
. . . .

1981

[1] French painter (1839–1906).

Virginia Reel^{*1}

In Clarke County, the story goes, the family name
Was saved by a single crop of wheat,
The houses and land kept in a clear receipt for the subsequent suicides,
The hard times and non-believers to qualify and disperse:
Woodburn and Cedar Hall, Smithfield, Auburn and North Hill: 5
Names like white moths kicked up from the tall grass,
Spreading across the countryside
From the Shenandoah to Charles Town and the Blue Ridge.

And so it happened. But none of us lives here now, in any of them,
Though Aunt Roberta is still in town,   10
Close to the place my great-great-grandfather taught Nelly Custis's children
   once
Answers to Luther.² And Cardinal Newman³ too.
Who cares? Well, I do. It's worth my sighs
To walk here, on the wrong road, tracking a picture back
To its bricks and its point of view.   15
It's worth my while to be here, crumbling this dirt through my bare hands.

I've come back for the first time in 20 years,
Sand in my shoes, my pockets full of the same wind
That brought me before, my flesh
Remiss in the promises it made then, the absolutes it's heir to.   20
This is the road they drove on. And this is the rise
Their blood repaired to, removing its gloves.
And this is the dirt their lives were made of, the dirt the world is,
Immeasurable emptiness of all things.

I stand on the porch of Wickliffe Church,   25
My kinfolk out back in the bee-stitched vines and weeds,
The night coming on, my flat shirt drawing the light in,
Bright bud on the branch of nothing's tree.
In the new shadows, memory starts to shake out its dark cloth.
Everyone settles down, transparent and animate,   30
Under the oak trees.
Hampton passes the wine around, Jaq toasts to our health.

---

[*] Wright's note: *"Virginia Reel* is for Mark
Strand."
¹ Name of an American square dance performed
by two facing lines of people.
² Martin Luther (1483–1546), German monk and
theologian, and founder of Protestantism.

³ John Henry Newman (1801–1890), English
cardinal and writer. Newman, a convert from
Protestantism to Roman Catholicism, was a
Victorian apologist.

And when, from the blear and glittering air,
A hand touches my shoulder,
I want to fall to my knees, and keep on falling, here,   35
Laid down by the articles that bear my names,
The limestone and marble and locust wood.
But that's for another life. Just down the road, at Smithfield, the last of the
   apple blossoms
Fishtails to earth through the shot twilight,
A little vowel for the future, a signal from us to them.   40
1981

Dead Color

I lie for a long time on my left side and my right side
And eat nothing,
            but no voice comes on the wind
And no voice drops from the cloud.
Between the grey spiders and the orange spiders,   5
               no voice comes on the wind . . .

Later, I sit for a long time by the waters of Har,[1]
And no face appears on the face of the deep.

Meanwhile, the heavens assemble their dark map.
The traffic begins to thin.   10
Aphids munch on the sweet meat of the lemon trees.
The lawn sprinklers rise and fall . . .

And here's a line of brown ants cleaning a possum's skull.
And here's another, come from the opposite side.

Over my head, star-pieces dip in their yellow scarves toward their black desire.   15

Windows, rapturous windows!
1981

---

[1] Place name in *Tiriel* and *Book of Thel,*
visionary poems by English poet, painter, and
mystic William Blake (1757–1827).

Hawaii Dantesca[*]

White-sided flowers are thrusting up on the hillside,
                              blank love letters from the dead.
It's autumn, and nobody seems to mind.

Or the broken shadows of those missing for hundreds of years
Moving over the sugar cane   5
                    like storks, which nobody marks or mends.

This is the story line.

And the viridescent shirtwaists of light the trees wear.
And the sutra-circles[1] of cattle egrets[2] wheeling out past the rain showers.
And the spiked marimbas of dawn rattling their amulets . . .   10

Soon it will be time for the long walk under the earth toward the sea.

And time to retrieve the yellow sunsuit and little shoes
                              they took my picture in
In Knoxville, in 1938.

Time to gather the fire in its quartz bowl.   15

I hope the one with the white wings will come.
I hope the island of reeds is as far away as I think it is.

When I get there, I hope they forgive me if the knot I tie is the wrong knot.

1981

---

[*] Wright's note: "Dante and the reed of humility, *Purgatorio*, I." In Canto I of Dante's *Purgatorio* (*Purgatory*) of *La Commedia Divina* (*The Divine Comedy*), Cato instructs Virgil to cleanse Dante of any traces of Hell and to gird Dante's waist with a reed (symbolizing humility) so that he may be fit to ascend the Mount of Purgatory. When Virgil pulls the reed from the sand at the island's edge, another immediately springs up in its place.

[1] A *sutra* is a Buddhist prayer. It is written on a rolled scroll.

[2] Kind of bird that frequently follows cattle for their droppings.

Michael Harper
b. 1938

Born in Brooklyn, Michael Harper studied in Los Angeles, taking a B.A. and an M.A. at what is now California State University. He then took a second M.A. at the University of Iowa. After leaving Iowa in 1963, he traveled in Mexico and Europe: "Those landscapes," he has said, "broadened my scope and interest in poetry and culture of other countries while I searched my own family and racial history for folklore, history and myth for themes that would give my writing the tradition and context where I could find my own voice." Harper has been a resolutely historical poet, seeking in the narratives of the past explanatory models by which to understand the present. He has studied "the tension between stated moral idealism and brute historical realities," not only to understand American racism and the reality of black life in America but also to understand universal moral questions and perennial human suffering.

Harper's underlying music grows out of jazz. "Billie Holiday played piano in my family's house when I was 12," he has said; he has written memorable elegies for her and for John Coltrane, the jazz musician whose name is attached to Harper's first volume, *Dear John, Dear Coltrane* (1970). In that volume, and in subsequent ones such as *Nightmare Begins Responsibility* (1975), *Images of Kin* (1977), and *Healing Song for the Inner Ear* (1985), Harper has sought in language for some equivalent to the syncopations and improvisations of jazz and has disturbed the usual prosody deriving from speech rhythms, from what Frost called "sentence sounds." By writing a deliberately "educated" poetry, Harper has distanced himself from the black poets who write in simple "folk" forms and in black dialect; by writing a deliberately historical poetry, Harper has turned away from the confessional mode that reigned in the 1950s and 1960s. Though Harper's poetry is often autobiographical (as in the poems about his boyhood in Brooklyn or in the elegies for his two sons, his brother, and such fellow poets as Robert Hayden and James Wright), the autobiographical core is never without a meditative enlargement.

Recently, Harper has edited an anthology of black art and literature, *Chant of Saints* (1973), which takes advantage of the sophistication with which the literary forms of Afro-American literature are now being explored and classified. Harper is a professor of English at Brown University, where he directs the writing program.

Text:
Images of Kin, 1977.

American History

Those four black girls blown up
in that Alabama church[1]
remind me of five hundred
middle passage blacks,[2]
in a net, under water   5
in Charleston harbor
so *redcoats*[3] wouldn't find them.
Can't find what you can't see
can you?

1970

Dear John, Dear Coltrane[1]

a love supreme, a love supreme
a love supreme, a love supreme[2]

Sex fingers toes
in the marketplace
near your father's church
in Hamlet, North Carolina—
witness to this love   5
in this calm fallow
of these minds,
there is no substitute for pain:
genitals gone or going,
seed burned out,   10
you tuck the roots in the earth,
turn back, and move
by river through the swamps,
singing: *a love supreme, a love supreme;*
what does it all mean?   15
Loss, so great each black
woman expects your failure

---

[1] One of the white-racist atrocities committed as reprisals against civil rights protests in the South during the 1960s.
[2] Captured blacks en route from Africa to be sold as slaves in the United States.

[3] Epithet for British soldiers.
[1] John Coltrane (1926–1967), American jazz saxophonist.
[2] "A Love Supreme," one of the songs Coltrane played, contained this chant.

in mute change, the seed gone.
You plod up into the electric city—
your song now crystal and   20
the blues. You pick up the horn
with some will and blow
into the freezing night:
a love supreme, a love supreme—

Dawn comes and you cook   25
up the thick sin 'tween
impotence and death, fuel
the tenor sax cannibal
heart, genitals and sweat
that makes you clean—   30
a love supreme, a love supreme—

Why you so black?
cause I am
why you so funky?
cause I am   35
why you so black?
cause I am
why you so sweet?
cause I am
why you so black?   40
cause I am
a love supreme, a love supreme:

So sick
you couldn't play *Naima*,[3]
so flat we ached   45
for song you'd concealed
with your own blood,
your diseased liver gave
out its purity,
the inflated heart   50
pumps out, the tenor[4] kiss,
tenor love:
a love supreme, a love supreme—
a love supreme, a love supreme—
1970

---

[3] Another song often played by Coltrane.
[4] Allusion to the tenor saxophone, Coltrane's
primary instrument.

This Is My Son's Song: *"Ungie, Hi Ungie"*[1]

A two-year-old boy
is a blossom in the intensive
care aisle, small as
a ball-bearing,
round, open and smooth;   5
for a month, in his first
premature hours, his shaved
head made him a mohawk Indian
child, tubes the herbs
for his nest, a collapsed lung   10
the bulbous wing of a hawk.
Slivered into each sole
is an intravenous solution
to balance his losses
or what they take out   15
for the lab; the blue spot
on his spine is a birth
mark of needle readings;
the hardened thighs immune
from 70 shots of various   20
drugs of uneven depth; the chest
is thick with congestion: bad
air and mucus—good air and pure
oxygen; jerky pouch buffalo lungs—
It does not surprise me   25
when he waits patiently for his
grandmother, over her five-hour
painless operation; he has
waited in his isolette
before: the glow in his eyes   30
is for himself, will and love:
an exclamation of your name:
"Ungie, hi Ungie"; you are saved.

1971

---

[1] Ungie is the nickname of the child's grandmother.

Martin's[1] Blues

He came apart in the open,
the slow motion cameras
falling quickly
neither alive nor kicking;
stone blind dead   5
on the balcony[2]
that old melody
etched his black lips
in a pruned echo:
We shall overcome   10
some day[3]—

Yes we did!
Yes we did!
1971

Last Affair: Bessie's[1] Blues Song

Disarticulated
arm torn out,
large veins cross
her shoulder intact,
her tourniquet   5
her blood in all-white big bands:

Can't you see
what love and heartache's done to me
I'm not the same as I used to be
this is my last affair[2]   10

Mail truck or parked car
in the fast lane,

---

[1] Martin Luther King (1929–1968), American
clergyman and civil rights leader, was
assassinated April 4, 1968.
[2] I.e., the motel balcony where King was shot.
[3] "We Shall Overcome" was the hymn made
famous by King's followers during the 1960s
civil rights movement.

[1] Bessie: Bessie Smith (1898?–1937), American
blues singer whose death from an automobile
accident might have been prevented had she
received medical help quickly. It was generally
felt that she received inadequate medical
attention because she was black.
[2] Refrain of the blues song "My Last Affair."

afloat at forty-three
on a Mississippi road,
Two-hundred-pound muscle on her ham bone,   15
'nother nigger dead 'fore noon:

Can't you see
what love and heartache's done to me
I'm not the same as I used to be
this is my last affair   20

Fifty-dollar record
cut the vein in her neck,
fool about her money
toll her black train wreck,
white press missed her fun'ral   25
in the same stacked deck:

Can't you see
what love and heartache's done to me
I'm not the same as I used to be
this is my last affair   30

Loved a little blackbird
heard she could sing,
Martha in her vineyard
pestle in her spring,
Bessie had a bad mouth   35
made my chimes ring:

Can't you see
what love and heartache's done to me
I'm not the same as I used to be
this is my last affair   40
1972

Grandfather

In 1915 my grandfather's
neighbors surrounded his house
near the dayline¹ he ran

¹ Boat-excursion line.

on the Hudson
in Catskill, NY   5
and thought they'd burn
his family out
in a movie they'd just seen
and be rid of his kind:
the death of a lone black   10
family is *the Birth*
of a Nation, [2]
or so they thought.
His 5'4" waiter gait
quenched the white jacket smile   15
he'd brought back from watered
polish of my father
on the turning seats,
and he asked his neighbors
up on his thatched porch   20
for the first blossom of fire
that would burn him down.

They went away, his nation,
spittooning their torched necks
in the shadows of the riverboat   25
they'd seen, posse decomposing;
and I see him on Sutter
with white bag from your
restaurant, challenged by his first
grandson to a foot-race   30
he will win in white clothes.
I see him as he buys galoshes
for his railed yard near Mineo's
metal shop, where roses jump
as the el circles his house   35
toward Brooklyn, where his rain fell;
and I see cigar smoke in his eyes,
chocolate Madison Square Garden chews
he breaks on his set teeth,
stitched up after cancer,   40
the great white nation immovable
as his weight wilts
and he is on a porch
that won't hold my arms,

[2] 1915 film directed by D. W. Griffith
(1875–1948) glorifying the Confederate cause
and the Ku Klux Klan.

or the legs of the race run   45
forwards, or the film
played backwards on his grandson's eyes.
1975

Nightmare Begins Responsibility[1]

I place these numbed wrists to the pane
watching white uniforms whisk over
him in the tube-kept
prison
fear what they will do in experiment   5
watch my gloved stickshifting gasolined hands
breathe *boxcar-information-please* infirmary tubes
distrusting white-pink mending paperthin
silkened end hairs, distrusting tubes
shrunk in his *trunk-skincapped*   10
shaven head, in thighs
distrusting-white-hands-picking-baboon-light
on this son who will not make his second night
of this wardstrewn intensive airpocket
where his father's asthmatic   15
hymns of *night-train,* train done gone
his mother can only know that he has flown
up into essential calm unseen corridor
going boxscarred home, *mamaborn, sweetsonchild*
gonedowntown into *researchtestingwarehousebatteryacid*   20
mama-son-done-gone / me telling her 'nother
train tonight, no music, no breathstroked
heartbeat in my infinite distrust of them:

and of my distrusting self
white-doctor-who-breathed-for-him-all-night   25
say it for two sons gone,
say nightmare, say it loud
panebreaking heartmadness:
nightmare begins responsibility.
1975

---

[1] A play on the Irish poet William Butler Yeats's epigraph to his volume *Responsibilities* (1913): "In dreams begin responsibilities." The poem is an elegy for Harper's son, who died one day after birth. Another son had also died shortly after birth.

Tongue-Tied in Black and White

—*'I had a most marvelous piece of luck. I died.'*[1]

In Los Angeles
while the mountains cleared of smog
your songs dreamed
Jefferson and Madison
walking hand in hand   5
as my grandfather walked to Canada.
What eyes met the black student
next to me, her hands fanning
your breezy neck from this veranda,
but Henry's/Mr. Bones.[2]   10

Home from Mexico and you in LIFE,
I walk dead center into the image
of LBJ[3] cloistered by the draping
flags of Texas and the confederacy,
and as my aunt of Oklahoma told me   15
I understand your father's impulse
to force you into Crane's nightmare.[4]

After the Roethke[5] reading in Seattle
you stroked the stout legs of an ex-
student's wife while he sketched   20
you in adoration and as you cautioned
your audience, '45 minutes and no longer,'
how Harvard paid in prestige not money,
how a man at Harvard read for four hours,
that he ought to be set down in the Roman   25
courtyard and have rocks set upon him
until death—your audience laughed.

You admired my second living son
as you loved the honeyed dugs of his mother,
your spotless tan suit weaving in the arch   30
where goalposts supported you in foyer
for you would not fall.

---

[1] From *77 Dream Songs* (1964), by John
Berryman, American poet (1914–1972). The
poem itself is addressed to Berryman.
[2] Berryman's persona, Henry, is addressed
sometimes as "Mr. Bones" by an unidentified
white end-man in blackface from a minstrel
show.

[3] Lyndon Baines Johnson (1908–1973), president
of the United States from 1963 to 1969.
[4] John Berryman's father, like Hart Crane,
committed suicide.
[5] Berryman's friend Theodore Roethke
(1908–1973), American poet.

At your last public reading,
let out[6] for fear of incident without a drink,
your foot bandaged from fire you'd   35
stamped out in a wastebasket of songs,
your solitary voice speckled in Donne,[7]
in Vermont where the stories of Bread
Loaf,[8] Brown,[9] another broken leg abandoned
in monotones of your friends studying you;   40

Now I must take up our quarrel:
never dangerous with women
though touched by their nectared hair,
you wrote in that needful black idiom
offending me, for only your inner voices   45
spoke such tongues, your father's soft prayers
in an all black town in Oklahoma;[10] your ear lied.
That slave in you was white blood forced to derision,
those seventeenth-century songs[11] saved you from
review.

Naked in a bottle of Wild Turkey,   50
the bridge you dived over[12] was your source:
St. Paul to St. Louis to New Orleans,[13]
the *asiento*,[14] Toussaint,[15] border ruffians,
signature of Lincoln,[16] porters bringing
messages to white widows of Europe,   55
a classics major, and black, taking your classes,
the roughpage of your bird legs and beard
sanitizing your hospital room,
the last image of your bandaged foot
stamping at flames on the newborn bridge.   60

This is less than the whole truth
but it is the blacker story
and what you asked to be told:

---

[6] Berryman was institutionalized for alcoholism
several times, beginning in 1969.
[7] John Donne (1572–1631), metaphysical poet.
[8] Bread Loaf School of English, Middlebury,
Vermont, where Berryman taught in 1962.
[9] Brown University, Providence, Rhode Island,
where Berryman taught from 1962 to 1963.
[10] Tampa, Oklahoma, where Berryman's father
committed suicide.
[11] Berryman, who admired seventeenth-century
metaphysical poets (such as Donne and
Herbert), wrote a poem about the
seventeenth-century American poet Anne
Bradstreet, imitating seventeenth-century style.

[12] John Berryman committed suicide by jumping
off the Washington Avenue bridge in
Minneapolis, Minnesota.
[13] The course of the Mississippi River.
[14] Literally, "seat" (Spanish), *asiento* refers to
contracts made by the Spanish government in
the sixteenth century to establish monopolies in
the slave trade in Spanish territories.
[15] Toussaint L'Ouverture (ca. 1744–1803), black
Haitian patriot and governor, imprisoned by
Napoleon Bonaparte in France, where he died.
[16] I.e., on the Emancipation Proclamation (1863),
which freed all slaves.

'lay off the sauce when you write'
you said to me, winking at the brownskinned   65
actress accompanying me to the lectern;
and how far is Texas from Canada
and our shared relatives in blacktown
on the outskirts of your tongue, tied still.

1975

Charles Simic
b. 1938

Charles Simic, who is a professor of English at the University of New
Hampshire, was born in Yugoslavia and came to the United States in 1949. He
attended the University of Chicago and received his B.A. from New York
University after serving in the U.S. Army from 1961 to 1963. In 1967 he
published his first book of poems, *What the Grass Says,* beginning a distinguished
career. In 1984 he was awarded a five-year MacArthur fellowship. Simic's poetry,
especially in such collections as *Dismantling the Silence* (1971) and *Charon's
Cosmology* (1977), retains the flavor of folktale: In it, sinister and simple events
gather into doomed assemblages. World War II was the backdrop to Simic's
Yugoslavian childhood; deaths, wounds, exiles, treacheries, and terrors mark the
nameless and placeless parables of his inner world. A farcical comedy and a grim
humor ornament the tragic plots that animate his poems. Though these are often
miniature narratives in quatrains, much is accomplished in a few lines.

Simic learned some of his bleak techniques from eastern European postwar
poets, many of whom he has translated, most notably Vasco Popa. Together with
Mark Strand, Simic edited *Another Republic* (1976), an anthology of seventeen
European and South American writers. The cross-fertilization of American poetry
by foreign poetry, which began in the early years of this century with the
assimilation of French symbolist verse and Chinese poetry and continued in the
1960s with the adoption of Spanish and Latin American sources, has now
incorporated the poetry of Russia and Eastern Europe, aided by the influence of
Simic and other émigré writers such as Joseph Brodsky and Czesław Miłosz.

Simic's poems are written out of unforgettable details seen with a child's
clarity, recalled against the amnesia of time, and repeatedly anatomized for
significance. As he forces the gates of memory, he finds broken treasures that he
pores over like an archaeologist, full of nostalgia for some unknown ancient
coherence. Written in peacetime, Simic's poems are nevertheless part of the
poetry of the Second World War. His *Selected Poems* appeared in 1985.

Texts:
"Fear," "Hearing Steps," "Fork," and "My
Shoes" from *Dismantling the Silence,* 1971.
"The Elders," "Charon's Cosmology," "The
Lesson," "A Wall," and "The Healer" from
Charon's Cosmology, 1977.

"Shirt" and "Grocery" from *Classic Ballroom
Dances,* 1980.
"The Cold," "Winter Night," and "Odd
Couple" from *Weather Forecast for Utopia and
Vicinity,* 1983.

Fear

Fear passes from man to man
Unknowing,
As one leaf passes its shudder
To another.

All at once the whole tree is trembling   5
And there is no sign of the wind.

1971

Hearing Steps

Someone is walking through the snow:
An ancient sound. Perhaps the Mongols are migrating again?
Perhaps, once more we'll go hanging virgins
From bare trees, plundering churches,
Raping widows in the deep snow?   5

Perhaps, the time has come again
To go back into forests and snow fields,
Live alone killing wolves with our bare hands,
Until the last word and the last sound
Of this language I am speaking is forgotten.   10

1971

Fork

This strange thing must have crept
Right out of hell.
It resembles a bird's foot
Worn around the cannibal's neck.

As you hold it in your hand,   5
As you stab with it into a piece of meat,
It is possible to imagine the rest of the bird:
Its head which like your fist
Is large, bald, beakless and blind.

1971

My Shoes

Shoes, secret face of my inner life:
Two gaping toothless mouths,
Two partly decomposed animal skins
Smelling of mice-nests.

My brother and sister who died at birth   5
Continuing their existence in you,
Guiding my life
Toward their incomprehensible innocence.

What use are books to me
When in you it is possible to read   10
The Gospel of my life on earth
And still beyond, of things to come?

I want to proclaim the religion
I have devised for your perfect humility
And the strange church I am building   15
With you as the altar.

Ascetic and maternal, you endure:
Kin to oxen, to Saints, to condemned men,
With your mute patience, forming
The only true likeness of myself.   20

1971

The Elders

I go to great troubles.
Bareheaded,
I visit them first thing in the morning.
Their gloomy servant ushers me in.
I, the poor cousin—   5
They, my benefactors
Standing with their stove-pipe hats
In a circle of splendid bloodhounds,
In a circle of sharp-nosed women.

The rain is pouring down, the rain . . .   10
Inside, their steps are slow, arthritic.
A slight greeting and I'm shown into the corner
Where I sit watching their pale hands,
Their hands with many tiny blue veins,
With many long and sharp fingernails,   15
While the curtains billow and billow
As if birds, as if large birds were caught in them.

Sights that make everyone sigh,
Except for me, interested as I am
Only in their beautiful daughter   20
Who touched me on the way in
With the same finger
That will loosen the button above her breasts,
In the evening
When the lights are low.   25

1977

Charon's[1] Cosmology

With only his feeble lantern
To tell him where he is
And every time a mountain
Of fresh corpses to load up

[1] In Greek mythology Charon ferries the dead
across the River Styx to Hades.

Take them to the other side   5
Where there are plenty more
I'd say by now he must be confused
As to which side is which

I'd say it doesn't matter
No one complains he's got   10
Their pockets to go through
In one a crust of bread in another a sausage

Once in a long while a mirror
Or a book which he throws
Overboard into the dark river   15
Swift cold and deep
1977

The Lesson

It occurs to me now
that all these years
I have been
the idiot pupil
of a practical joker.   5

Diligently
and with foolish reverence
I wrote down
what I took to be
his wise pronouncements   10
concerning
my life on earth.
Like a parrot
I rattled off the dates
of wars and revolutions.   15
I rejoiced
at the death of my tormentors
I even became convinced
that their number
was diminishing.   20

It seemed to me
that gradually

my teacher was revealing to me
a pattern,
that what I was being told   25
was an intricate plot
of a picaresque novel
in installments,
the last pages of which
would be given over   30
entirely
to lyrical evocations
of nature.

Unfortunately,
with time,   35
I began to detect in myself
an inability
to forget even
the most trivial detail.
I lingered more and more   40
over the beginnings:
The haircut of a soldier
who was urinating
against our fence;
shadows of trees on the ceiling,   45
the day
my mother and I
had nothing to eat . . .

Somehow,
I couldn't get past   50
that prison train
that kept waking me up
every night.
I couldn't get that whistle
that rumble   55
out of my head . . .

In this classroom
austerely furnished
by my insomnia,
at the desk consisting   60
of my two knees,
for the first time
in this long and terrifying
apprenticeship,
I burst out laughing.   65
Forgive me, all of you!

At the memory of my uncle
charging a barricade
with a homemade bomb,
I burst out laughing.   70
1977

A Wall

That's the only image
That turns up.

A wall, all by itself,
Poorly lit, beckoning,
But no sense of the room,   5
Not even a hint
Of why it is I remember
That fragment so clearly:

The fly I was watching,
The details of its wings   10
Glowing like turquoise,
Its feet, to my amusement
Following a minute crack—
An eternity
Around that simple event.   15

And nothing else, and nowhere
To go back to,
And no one else
As far as I know to verify.
1977

The Healer

In a rundown tenement
Under the superhighway,
A healer lives
Who doesn't believe in his power.

An old man with a fat gut,   5
Hands of a little girl
Which he warms
Over a pan of boiling water.

In his hallway there are
Many wheelchairs, on the stairs   10
The long howl of the idiot
Led on a leash.
1977

Shirt

To get into it
As it lies
Crumpled on the floor
Without disturbing a single crease

Respectful   5
Of the way I threw it down
Last night
The way it happened to land

Almost managing
The impossible contortions   10
Doubling back now
Through a knotted sleeve
1980

Grocery

Figure or figures unknown
Keep a store
Keep it open
Nights and all day Sunday

Half of what they sell   5
Will kill you
The other half
Makes you go back for more

Too cheap to turn on the lights
Hard to tell what it is   10
They've got on the counter
What it is you're paying for

All the rigors
All the solemnities
Of a brass scale imperceptibly quivering   15
In the early winter dusk

One of its pans
For their innards
The other one for yours—
And yours heavier   20
1980

The Cold

As if in a presence of an intelligence
Concentrating, I thought myself
Scrutinized and measured closely
By the barrens of sky and earth,

And then algebraized and entered   5
In a notebook page blank and white
Except for the parallel blue lines
Which might have been bars,

For I kept walking and walking,
And it got darker and then there was   10
A flicker of a light or two
Far above and beyond the large cage.
1983

Winter Night

The church is an iceberg.

It's the wind. It must be gusting tonight
Out of those galactic orchards,
Copernican pits and stones.[1]

The monster created by mad Dr. Frankenstein   5
Sailed for the New World,
And ended up some place like New Hampshire.

Actually, it's just a local drunk,
Knocking with a snow-shovel,
Wanting to go in and sit.   10

An iceberg is a large, drifting
Piece of ice, broken off a glacier.

1983

Old Couple

They're waiting to be murdered,
Or evicted. Soon
They expect to have nothing to eat.
As far as I know, they never go out.

A vicious pain's coming, they think.   5
It will start in the head
And spread down to the bowels.
They'll be carried off on stretchers, howling.

In the meantime, they watch the street
From their fifth floor window.   10

<hr>

[1] I.e., the stars and planets in those astronomical
regions described by the Polish astronomer
Nicolaus Copernicus (1473–1543).

It has rained, and now it looks
Like it's going to snow a little.

I see him get up to lower the shades.
If their window stays dark,
I know that his hand has reached hers   15
Just as she was about to turn on the lights.
1983

Frank Bidart
b. *1939*

Frank Bidart grew up in California, "crazy about movies. In Bakersfield, I think
movies were the most accessible art form. . . . We didn't have [ballet or
symphony or plays]. But we did have, each week, surrounded by publicity,
glamour, and controversy, these incredibly interesting movies. As early as I can
remember, I wanted to be an artist; I certainly knew I didn't want to be a
farmer, as my father was. Briefly, I imagined becoming an actor; but very
quickly it was clear to me that the person who really made movies was the
director. . . . So, in college, I was determined to be a film director." In fact,
Bidart majored in English at the University of California at Riverside and went
on to take an M.A. at Harvard, where he studied writing with Robert Lowell.
There, Bidart says, he realized that "subject matter"—"confronting the dilemmas,
issues, 'things' with which the world had confronted me—had to be at the center
of the poems if they were to have force. . . . I needed a way to embody the
mind moving through the elements of its world, actively contending with and
organizing them, while they somehow retain the illusion of their independence
and nature, are felt as 'out there' or 'other.' " Bidart moved toward "deploying
the words on the page through voice; syntax; punctuation"—a prosody marking
"speed and tension and emphasis" by everything from line breaks to capital
letters.

Bidart quotes Frost's saying that sentences are saved for poetry only by "the
speaking tone of voice somehow entangled in the words and fastened to the page
for the ear of the imagination." Bidart's first poems in *Golden State* (1973) were
spoken in his own voice; some later poems, in *The Book of the Body* (1977) and
The Sacrifice (1983), have assumed the voice of historical characters—the anorexic
Ellen West, the ballet dancer Nijinsky. Through the volatile voices of characters
in extreme anguish (Ellen West commits suicide; Nijinsky goes mad), Bidart
choreographs on the page issues such as the relation of mind to body and the
persistence of guilt, issues that have, as he says, no "answer," no "solution."
Bidart's dramatic monologues resemble operatic arias more than the self-betraying
verse of a Browning character; they exist not so much to define character as to
display the virtuosity of voice itself. And in their rapid cuts from voice to voice
and scene to scene, his polyphonic poems of many voices resemble the movies
that gave Bidart his first vision of what art could be. Bidart is a professor of

English at Wellesley College and has taught at Brandeis and the University of
California at Berkeley.

Texts:
"Self-Portrait, 1969" and "Another Life" from
Golden State, 1973.
"Happy Birthday" and "Elegy" from *The Book
of the Body,* 1977.

Self-Portrait, 1969

He's *still* young—; thirty, but looks younger—
or does he? . . . In the eyes and cheeks, tonight,
turning in the mirror, he saw his mother,—
puffy; angry; bewildered . . . Many nights
now, when he stares there, he gets angry:—   5
something *unfulfilled* there, something dead
to what he once thought he surely could be—
Now, just the glamour of habits . . .

                                        Once, instead,
he thought insight would remake him, he'd reach
—what? The thrill, the exhilaration   10
unravelling disaster, that seemed to teach
necessary knowledge . . . became just jargon.

Sick of being decent, he craves another
crash. What *reaches* him except disaster?
1973

Another Life

*Peut-être n'es-tu pas suffisamment mort. C'est ici la limite de notre
domaine. Devant toi coule un fleuve.*[1]
                                 Valéry

"—In a dream I never *exactly* dreamed,
but that is, somehow, the quintessence
of what I *might* have dreamed,
                    Kennedy is in Paris

---

[1] "Perhaps you're not dead enough. This is the
limit of our realm. Before you there flows a
river." From the prose dialogue *Eupalinos* by
Paul Valéry (1871–1945), French poet.

again; it's '61; once again
some new national life seems possible,
though desperately, I try to remain unduped,
even cynical . . .
        He's standing in an open car, 5

brilliantly lit, bright orange
next to a grey de Gaulle, and they stand
not far from me, slowly moving up the Champs-Elysées[2] . . . 10

Bareheaded in the rain, he gives a short
choppy wave, smiling like a sun god.

—I stand and 15
look, suddenly at peace; once again mindlessly
moved,

    as they bear up the fields of Elysium

the possibility of Atlantic peace,

reconciliation between all that power, energy, 20
optimism,—
       and an older wisdom, without
illusions, without force, the austere source
of nihilism, corrupted only by its dream of Glory . . .

But no—; as I 25
watch, the style is

      not quite right—;

      Kennedy is *too* orange . . .

And de Gaulle, white, dead
white, ghost white, not even grey . . . 30

         As my heart
began to grieve for my own awkwardness and
ignorance, which would never be
soothed by the informing energies
           of whatever 35
wisdom saves,—

[2] Major avenue in Paris, leading to the Arc de Triomphe. Its name is French for "the fields of Elysium," the equivalent in classical mythology of the Christian heaven; see l. 18.

I saw a young man, almost
my twin, who had written
                    'MONSTER'
in awkward lettering with a crayon across   40
the front of his sweat shirt.
                    He was gnawing on his arm,

in rage and anger gouging up
pieces of flesh—; but as I moved to stop him, somehow
help him,   45
          suddenly he looked up,

and began, as I had, to look at Kennedy and de Gaulle:

and then abruptly, almost as if I were seeing him
through a camera lens, his figure

split in two,—   50
          or doubled,—

and all the fury
          drained from his stunned, exhausted face . . .

But only for a moment. Soon his eyes turned down
to the word on his chest. The two figures   55
again became one,

and with fresh energy he attacked the mutilated arm . . .

—Fascinated, I watched as this
pattern, this cycle,
                    repeated several times.   60

Then he reached out and touched me.

—Repelled,
          I pulled back . . . But he became
frantic, demanding that I become
the body he split into: 65
                    'It's harder
to manage *each* time! Please,
give me your energy;—*help me!*'

                    —I said it was impossible,
there was *no part* of us the same: 70
we were just watching a parade together:

(and then, as he reached for my face)

                        leave me *alone!*

He smirked, and said
I was never alone.   75
           I told him to go to hell.

He said that this was hell.

                  —I said it was impossible,
there was *no part* of us the same:
we were just watching a parade together: 80
                    when I saw

Grief, avenging Care, pale
Disease, Insanity, Age, and Fear,
              —all the raging desolations

which I had come to learn were my patrimony;   85
the true progeny of my parents' marriage;
the gifts hidden within the mirror;

—standing guard at the gate of this place,
triumphant,
           striking poses   90
               eloquent of the disasters they embodied . . .

—I took several steps to the right, and saw
Kennedy was paper-thin,
               as was de Gaulle;
mere cardboard figures   95
whose possible real existence
lay buried beneath a million tumbling newspaper photographs . . .

—I turned, and turned, but now all that was left
was an enormous
           fresco;—on each side, the unreadable   100
                    fresco of my life . . ."

1973

Happy Birthday

Thirty-three, goodbye—
the awe I feel

is not that you won't come again, or why—

or even that after
a time, we think of those who are dead   5

with a sweetness that cannot be explained—

but that I've read the trading-cards:
RALPH TEMPLE CYCLIST CHAMPION TRICK RIDER

WILLIE HARRADON CYCLIST
THE YOUTHFUL PHENOMENON   10

F. F. IVES CYCLIST
100 MILES 6 H. 25 MIN. 30 SEC.

—as the fragile metal of their
wheels stopped turning, as they
took on wives, children, accomplishments, all those   15
predilections which also insisted on ending,

they could not tell themselves from what they had done.

Terrible to dress in the clothes
of a period that must end.

They didn't plan it that way—   20
they didn't plan it that way.
1977

from Elegy

IV. Light

I am asleep, dreaming a terrible dream, so I awake,
and want to call my father to ask if, just
for a short time, the dog can come to stay with me.

But the light next to my bed won't light:
I press and press the switch. Touching the phone,   5
I can't see to dial the numbers. Can I learn how to keep

the dog in my apartment? In the dark, trying
a second light, I remember
I always knew these machines would fail me.

                               Then I awake,   10

remember my father and the dog are dead,
the lights in that room do not go on.

V. Lineage

"I went to a mausoleum today, and found
what I want. Eye-level.
Don't forget:
I want to be buried in a mausoleum at eye-level."

She feels she never quite recovered
from her mother's, my grandmother's, death.
Her mother died by falling from a
third floor hospital window.   20

"—I'm *sure* she didn't want to kill herself;
after the stroke, sometimes she got confused, and
maybe she thought
                  she saw grandpa at the window . . .

She wanted to be at home. After the stroke,   25
we *had* to put her in a nursing home,—

she hated it, but you couldn't
get help to stay with her, and she needed
someone twenty-four hours a day,—

she begged me to take her out;   30
                    the cruel,
unreasonable things she said to me! Her doctor
told me I was doing the right thing, but
what she said
                    almost drove me crazy . . .   35

it's astonishing how clearly I can still hear her voice.

I still dream I can see her falling
three stories, her arms stretching out . . .

For forty years, she counted
on grandpa,—   40
              after he died, she still
talked to him.

I know I made a lot of
mistakes with you, but I couldn't count on anyone—

I had to be both father *and* mother . . ."   45

As the subject once again changes from my grandmother
to my father, or the dog—
to my stepfather, or me—
                    her obsessive, baffled voice

says that when she allowed herself to love   50

she let something into her head which will
never be got out—;
                    which could only betray her

or *be* betrayed, but never appeased—;
whose voice   55
              death and memory have made
into a razor-blade without a handle . . .

"Don't forget:
I want to be buried in a mausoleum at eye-level."
1977

Robert Pinsky
b. 1940

The work of Robert Pinsky, a pupil at Stanford of the late poet and critic Yvor Winters, has come to represent a recoil of poetry into full discursive "sense," away from surrealist techniques, mysterious symbolist visions, political rhetoric, and minimalist reduction. Winters insisted that poetry should be rational and logical and should forgo the destructive appetite for transcendence, initiated by Emerson, that led, in Winters's view, to such excesses as the suicide of his friend Hart Crane. In a critical book, *The Situation of Poetry* (1976), Pinsky has presented a Wintersian program for postmodernist poetry, a program defending the representation of an objective world within the world of art.

As teacher and, until recently, poetry editor for *The New Republic,* Pinsky has been influential in recommending poetry that is circumstantial in its faithfulness to the quotidian appearances of life. In its reaction against introspection as a sufficient motive for poetry, the work of Pinsky and other recent poets ventures into the realm of the essay, the disquisition, and the description. Pinsky's poetry in this vein aims at a Horatian moderation; in fact, Pinsky translates one of Horace's epistles in the course of writing a long poem addressed to his daughter, entitled "An Explanation of America" (1979). Temperate in its tone, ironic in its stance, didactic much of the time in its intent, Pinsky's poetry argues that almost any subject (America, psychiatrists, tennis) will serve as sufficient occasion for the meditation of an inquiring and curious mind. Pinsky's prosody is unobtrusive, his syntax clear (if complex), and the argument of his poetry at once logical and sinuous. The poetry represents a principled turning away from the discontinuities of high modernism and a return to a more Augustan civil mode.

Pinsky was born in New Jersey and educated at Rutgers (B.A., 1962) and Stanford, where he took a Ph.D. in English literature. His first published book was *Landor's Poetry* (1968), a critical commentary on the work of the Victorian classicizing poet. Pinsky has published two volumes of poetry, *Sadness and Happiness* (1975) and *The History of My Heart* (1984). After teaching for many years at Wellesley College, Pinsky is now a professor of English at the University of California at Berkeley.

Texts:
"Essay on Psychiatrists" from *Sadness and Happiness,* 1975.
"Memorial" from *An Explanation of America,* 1979.
"The Unseen," "Dying," and "Song of Reasons" from *History of My Heart,* 1984.

from Essay on Psychiatrists

II. Some Terms

"Shrink" is a misnomer. The religious
Analogy is all wrong, too, and the old,
Half-forgotten jokes about Viennese accents

And beards hardly apply to the good-looking woman
In boots and a knit dress, or the man   5
Seen buying the Sunday *Times* in mutton-chop

Whiskers and expensive jogging shoes.
In a way I suspect that even the terms "doctor"
And "therapist" are misnomers; the patient

Is not necessarily "sick." And one assumes   10
That no small part of the psychiatrist's
Role is just that: to point out misnomers.

1975

III. Proposition

These are the first citizens of contingency.
Far from the doctrinaire past of the old ones,
They think in their prudent meditations

Not about ecstasy (the soul leaving the body)
Nor enthusiasm (the god entering one's person)   5
Nor even about sanity (which means

Health, an impossible perfection)
But ponder instead relative truth and the warm
Dusk of amelioration. The cautious

Young augurs with their family-life, good books   10
And records and foreign cars believe
In amelioration—in that, and in suffering.

1975

X. Dionysus[1] as Psychiatrist

In a more hostile view, the psychiatrists
Are like Bacchus—the knowing smirk of his mask,
His patients, his confident guidance of passion,

And even his little jokes, as when the great palace
Is hit by lightning which blazes and stays,   5
Bouncing among the crumpling stone walls . . .

And through the burning rubble he comes,
With his soft ways picking along lightly
With a calm smile for the trembling Chorus[2]

Who have fallen to the ground, bowing   10
In the un-Greek, Eastern way—What, Asian women,
He asks, Were you disturbed just now when Bacchus

Jostled the palace? He warns Pentheus[3] to adjust,
To learn the ordinary man's humble sense of limits,
Violent limits, to the rational world. He cures   15

Pentheus of the grand delusion that the dark
Urgencies can be governed simply by the mind,
And the mind's will. He teaches Queen Agave[4] to look

Up from her loom, up at the light, at her tall
Son's head impaled on the stiff spear clutched   20
In her own hand soiled with dirt and blood.

1975

Memorial

(J.E. and N.M.S.)

Here lies a man. And here, a girl. They live
In the kind of artificial life we give

To birds or statues: imagining what they feel,
Or that like birds the dead each had one call,

---

[1] Greek god of wine, also known as Bacchus.
[2] Reference to the traditional chorus in Greek
tragedies, an integral part of dramatic narrative
structure.

[3] King Pentheus of Thebes was torn into pieces
by his mother, Agave, who had been maddened
by intoxication.
[4] King Pentheus' mother.

Repeated, or a gesture that suspends   5
Their being in a forehead or the hands.

A man comes whistling from a house. The screen
Snaps shut behind him. Though there is no man

And no house, memory sends him to get tools
From a familiar shed, and so he strolls   10

Through summer shade to work on the family car.
He is my uncle, and fresh home from the war,

With little for me to remember him doing yet.
The clock of the cancer ticks in his body, or not,

Depending if it is there, or waits. The search   15
Of memory gains and fails like surf: the porch

And trim are painted cream, the shakes are stained.
The shadows could be painted (so little wind

Is blowing there) or stains on the crazy-paving
Of the front walk. . . . Or now, the shadows are moving: 20

Another house, unrelated; a woman says,
Is this your special boy, and the girl says, yes,

Moving her hand in mine. The clock in her, too—
As someone told me a month or two ago,

Months after it finally took her. A public building   25
Is where the house was: though a surf, unyielding

And sickly, seethes and eddies at the stones
Of the foundation. The dead are made of bronze,

But dying they were like birds with clocklike hearts—
Unthinkable, how much pain the tiny parts   30

Of even the smallest bird might yet contain.
We become larger than life in how much pain

Our bodies may encompass . . . all Titans in that,
Or heroic statues. Although there is no heat

Brimming in the fixed, memorial summer, the brows   35
Of lucid metal sweat a faint warm haze

As I try to think the pain I never saw.
Though there is no pain there, the small birds draw

Together in crowds above the houses—and cry
Over the surf: as if there were a day,   40

Memorial, marked on the calendar for dread
And pain and loss—although among the dead

Are no hurts, but only emblematic things;
No hospital beds, but a lifting of metal wings.
1979

The Unseen

In Krakow it rained, the stone arcades and cobbles
And the smoky air all soaked one penetrating color
While in an Art Nouveau cafe, on harp-shaped chairs,

We sat making up our minds to tour the death camp.
As we drove there the next morning past farms   5
And steaming wooden villages, the rain had stopped

Though the sky was still gray. A young guide explained
Everything we saw in her tender, hectoring English:
The low brick barracks; the heaped-up meticulous

Mountains of shoes, toothbrushes, hair; one cell   10
Where the Pope had prayed and placed flowers; logbooks,
Photographs, latrines—the whole unswallowable

Menu of immensities. It began drizzling again,
And the way we paused to open or close the umbrellas,
Hers and ours, as we went from one building to the next,   15

Had a formal, dwindled feeling. We felt bored
And at the same time like screaming Biblical phrases:
I am poured out like water; Thine is the day and

Thine also the night; I cannot look to see
My own right hand . . . I remembered a sleep-time game,   20
A willed dream I had never thought of by day before:

I am there; and granted the single power of invisibility,
Roaming the camp at will. At first I savor my mastery
Slowly by creating small phantom diversions,

Then kill kill kill kill, a detailed and strangely   25
Passionless inward movie: I push the man holding
The crystals down from the gas chamber roof, bludgeon

The pet collie of the Commandant's children
And in the end flush everything with a vague flood
Of fire and blood as I drift on toward sleep   30

In a blurred finale, like our tour's—eddying
In a downpour past the preserved gallows where
The Allies hung the Commandant, in 1947.

I don't feel changed, or even informed—in that,
It's like any other historical monument; although   35
It is true that I don't ever at night any more

Prowl rows of red buildings unseen, doing
Justice like an angry god to escape insomnia. And so,
O discredited Lord of Hosts, your servant gapes

Obediently to swallow various doings of us, the most   40
Capable of all your former creatures—we have
No shape, we are poured out like water, but still

We try to take in what won't be turned from in despair:
As if, just as we turned toward the fumbled drama
Of the religious art shop window to accuse you   45

Yet again, you were to slit open your red heart
To show us at last the secret of your day and also,
Because it also is yours, of your night.

1984

Dying

Nothing to be said about it, and everything—
The change of changes, closer or further away:
The Golden Retriever next door, Gussie, is dead,

Like Sandy, the Cocker Spaniel from three doors down
Who died when I was small; and every day   5
Things that were in my memory fade and die.

Phrases die out: first, everyone forgets
What doornails are; then after certain decades
As a dead metaphor, *"dead as a doornail"* flickers

And fades away. But someone I know is dying—   10
And though one might say glibly, "everyone is,"
The different pace makes the difference absolute.

The tiny invisible spores in the air we breathe,
That settle harmlessly on our drinking water
And on our skin, happen to come together   15

With certain conditions on the forest floor,
Or even a shady corner of the lawn—
And overnight the fleshy, pale stalks gather,

The colorless growth without a leaf or flower;
And around the stalks, the summer grass keeps growing   20
With steady pressure, like the insistent whiskers

That grow between shaves on a face, the nails
Growing and dying from the toes and fingers
At their own humble pace, oblivious

As the nerveless moths, that live their night or two—   25
Though like a moth a bright soul keeps on beating,
Bored and impatient in the monster's mouth.
1984

Song of Reasons

Because of the change of key midway in "Come Back to Sorrento"
The little tune comes back higher, and everyone feels

A sad smile beginning. Also customary is the forgotten reason
Why the Dukes of Levis-Mirepoix are permitted to ride horseback

Into the Cathedral of Notre Dame. Their family is so old   5
They killed heretics in Languedoc seven centuries ago;

Yet they are somehow Jewish, and therefore the Dukes claim
Collateral descent from the family of the Virgin Mary.

And the people in magazines and on television are made
To look exactly the way they do for some reason, too: 10

Every angle of their furniture, every nuance of their doors
And the shapes of their eyebrows and shirts has its history

Or purpose arcane as the remote Jewishness of those far Dukes,
In the great half-crazy tune of the song of reasons.

A child has learned to read, and each morning before leaving   15
For school she likes to be helped through The Question Man

In the daily paper: Your Most Romantic Moment? Your Family Hero?
Your Worst Vacation? Your Favorite Ethnic Group?—and pictures

Of the five or six people, next to their answers. She likes it;
The exact forms of the ordinary each morning seem to show   20

An indomitable charm to her; even the names and occupations.
It is like a bedtime story in reverse, the unfabulous doorway

Of the day that she canters out into, businesslike as a dog
That trots down the street. The street: sunny pavement, plane trees,

The flow of cars that come guided by with a throaty music   25
Like the animal shapes that sing at the gates of sleep.

1984

Dave Smith
b. 1942

Dave Smith is one of the most prolific of the younger poets now writing in
America; his restless and large talent has poured itself out in several books,
including a novel, *Onliness* (1981), a collection of short stories, and a collection
of prose pieces, *Local Assays* (1985); he has also edited a collection of essays on
the poetry of James Wright. Smith was born in Portsmouth, Virginia, and
graduated from the University of Virginia. After serving for three years in the
air force, he took an M.A. at Southern Illinois University and a Ph.D. at Ohio
University (1976). He has taught at the University of Utah and is now a
professor of English at Virginia Commonwealth University in Richmond.

"My subjects," says Smith, "have been, generally, the Atlantic seacoast, the American West, and people. I care little for poems that do not create a narrative or contextual event in which people are involved with something that is happening or has happened. I am concerned to write a thickly textured poem whose speech as well as whose event will be memorable." Smith has linked his own work with that of Robert Penn Warren and James Dickey; he sees himself as a southern writer and has been a rich ethnographer of southern life.

Smith's early poems about the Chesapeake Bay oyster fishermen in *The Fisherman's Whore* (1974) show his fierce sense of locale and of natural struggle. Later, his more spacious and vast poems in *Goshawk, Antelope* (1979), written from the Utah landscape, suggest a more allegorical measure of our place in the universe: between the predatory hawk and the peaceful antelope. Catastrophes and disasters often appear as the backdrop to Smith's poetry: family ruin; the dissolution of mining, railroading, and fishing communities; the erosion of American rural life; the potential for erotic dismay; nameless male violence—all of these themes course through the poetry, attended by language bearing an electric charge of feeling. Smith's effects can sometimes be coarse, when his subject outruns his technique; but with each volume there has been an expansion of imagination and an investigation into new expressive regions.

Smith has said himself that his poems "appear to devolve to the theme of obligation," to *pietas* (the Roman name for that virtue). The moral insistence in Smith's earlier poetry has, in his recent work, *Dream Flights* (1981) and *Homage to Edgar Allan Poe* (1981), evolved into a more reflective and brooding consciousness of the necessary and the fated in life; the poems are less full of vaulting ambition and more aware of the grimness of human existence. His poems have become longer, freer in their verse line and in their narrative energies, as willing to float in "dream flights" as to drive forward with relentless momentum. In his insistence on a narrative base to the lyric, Smith allies himself with the remnants of the epic tradition, claiming for lyric poetry a brotherhood with the story and the novel. Smith's *New and Selected Poems* appeared in 1985.

Texts:
"On a Field Trip at Fredericksburg,"
"Cumberland Station," and "Looking for the
Melungeon" from *Cumberland Station,* 1976.
"Over the Ozarks . . . ," "Hawktree," and
"Rain Forest" from *Goshawk, Antelope,* 1979.
"Desks" and "Reading . . ." from *Homage to
Edgar Allan Poe,* 1981.
"Sea Owl" and "Smithfield Ham" from *In the
House of the Judge,* 1983.

On a Field Trip at Fredericksburg[1]

The big steel tourist shield says maybe
fifteen thousand got it here. No word
of either Whitman[2] or one uncle
I barely remember in the smoke
that filled his tiny mountain house.   5

If each finger were a thousand of them
I could clap my hands and be dead
up to my wrists. It was quick
though not so fast as we can do it
now, one bomb, atomic or worse,   10
one silly pod slung on wing-tip,
high up, an egg cradled
by some rapacious mockingbird.

Hiroshima[3] canned nine times their number
in a flash. Few had the time   15
to moan or feel the feeling
ooze back in the groin.

In a ditch I stand
above Marye's Heights, the book-
boned faces of Brady's[4] fifteen-year-old   20
drummers, before battle, rigid
as August's dandelions
all the way to the Potomac
rolling in my skull.

If Audubon[5] came here, the names   25
of birds would gush, the marvel
single feathers make
evoke a cloud, a nation,
a gray blur preserved
on a blue horizon, but   30
there is only a wandering child,
one dark stalk snapped off

---

[1] Site in Virginia of a Civil War battle
(December 13, 1862), a Union defeat.
[2] Although the American poet Walt Whitman
(1819–1892) wrote about the Civil War, his
poems do not mention the Battle of
Fredericksburg.

[3] City in Japan where the first atomic bomb was
dropped.
[4] Brady: Matthew Brady (ca. 1823–1896), Civil
War photographer.
[5] John James Audubon (1785–1851), Haitian-born
American ornithologist and painter of birds.

in her hand, held out to me.
Taking it, I try to help her
hold its obscure syllables   35
one instant in her mouth,
like a drift of wind
at the forehead, the front door,
the black, numb fingernails.
1976

Cumberland[1] Station

Gray brick, ash, hand-bent railings, steps so big
it takes hours to mount them, polished oak
pews holding the slim hafts of sun, and one
splash of the *Pittsburgh Post-Gazette*. The man
who left Cumberland gone, come back, no job   5
anywhere. I come here alone, shaken
the way I came years ago to ride down
mountains in Big Daddy's cab.[2] He was
the first set cold in the black meadow.

Six rows of track gleam, thinned, rippling   10
like water on walls where famous engines steam, half
submerged in frothing crowds with something
to celebrate and plenty to eat. One engineer takes
children for a free ride, a frolic
like an earthquake. Ash cakes their hair.   15
I am one of those who walked uphill
through flowers of soot to zing
scared to death into the world.

Now whole families afoot cruise South Cumberland
for something to do, no jobs, no money for bars,   20
the old stories cracked like wallets.

This time there's no fun in coming back. The second
death. My roundhouse[3] uncle coughed his youth
into a gutter. His son, the third, slid on the ice,

---

[1] Coal-mining city and railroad center in
Maryland.
[2] I.e., the cab of a locomotive.

[3] Building where train engines are turned around
for exit on the same track where they entered.

losing his need to drink himself   25
stupidly dead. In this vaulted hall
I think of all the dirt poured down
from shovels and trains and empty pockets.
I stare into the huge malignant headlamps
circling the gray walls and catch a stuttered   30
glimpse of faces stunned like deer on a track,
children getting drunk, shiny as Depression apples.

Churning through the inner space of this godforsaken
wayside, I feel the ground try to upchuck and I dig
my fingers in my temples to bury a child   35
diced on a cowcatcher,[4] a woman smelling
alkaline from washing out the soot.
Where I stood in that hopeless, hateful room
will not leave me. The scarf of smoke I saw
over a man's shoulder runs through me   40
like the sored Potomac River.

Grandfather, you ask why I don't visit you
now you have escaped the ticket-seller's cage
to fumble hooks and clean the Shakespeare reels.[5]
What could we catch? I've been sitting in the pews   45
thinking about us a long time, long enough to see
a man can't live in jobless, friendless Cumberland
anymore. The soot owns even the fish.

I keep promising I'll come back, we'll get out,
you and me, like brothers, and I mean it.   50
A while ago a man with the look of a demented cousin
shuffled across this skittery floor and snatched up
the *Post-Gazette* and stuffed it in his coat
and nobody gave a damn because nobody cares
who comes or goes here or even who steals   55
what nobody wants: old news, photographs
of dead diesels behind chipped glass
swimming into Cumberland Station.

I'm the man who stole it and I wish you were here
to beat the hell out of me for it because   60
what you said a long time ago welts my face
and won't go away. I admit
it isn't mine even if it's nobody else's.
Anyway, that's all I catch this trip—bad

---

[4] Protective cage on the front of a railroad   [5] Fishing equipment.
engine.

news. I can't catch my nephew's life, my uncle's,   65
Big Daddy's, yours, or the ash-haired kids'
who fell down to sleep here after the war.

Outside new families pick their way along tracks
you and I have walked home on many nights.
Every face on the walls goes on smiling,   70
and, Grandfather, I wish I had the guts
to tell you this is a place I hope
I never have to go through again.

1976

Looking for the Melungeon[1]

Rounding a slip of the marsh, the boat skids
under me and the propeller whines naked,
then digs and shoots me forward. A clapper rail[2]
disappears in reeds and one crane, shaken
from his nap blinks, and holds.   5

He makes me think of the Lost Tribe of Virginia,
as if the scree of insects were the Jew's
harp[3] in John Jacob Niles's mouth.

A creek opens its throat and I enter, dragging
down to hear my wake's slip-slop,   10
thinking of the man who warned me people
were the same everywhere, lost and wondering

how they came to the life no one else wanted.
Sweet Jesus, he was right. Now he lies
in this sodden ground for the first time   15
in his life and I do not know even where.

Today is no different, the waters flood hulks
of empty houses, leaving beer cans to gleam
in the indifferent moon. The first stalks of

---

[1] According to Smith's essay "Sailing the Back River," the term comes from the folk singer John Jacob Niles and is the name of "the descendants of the Lost Tribe of Virginia."

[2] Marsh bird.

[3] Single-toned musical instrument held in the mouth, often used by folk singers.

narcissus break the ground with gold   20
though March still means tonight to freeze.

I know this place, its small mustering of facts
wind-worn and useless, real and repeated, the same
anywhere. At the end the creek leads to a room,
one placid boat swinging at a stick, pines sieving   25

air, the cleat[4] ringing like small jewelry.
1976

Over the Ozarks, Because I Saw Them, Stars Came

On my back, shirtless and with no friend, in September
when the time is for a young man to have seen breasts
only slightly larger than his own, thinking of her
who is inexplicably older but was not

not an hour before: to have seen that then like a purple   5
bruise (that strange) through the gaunt, stretched neck
loop of her T-shirt stained by wrestling, I tell
you I felt the tick of grass and itch-weight

of earth and thunderous roll of the Missouri gathering
downhill toward the ocean; and thought then, as I ate   10
from all silence the green bitter grapes which were
by my grandmother forbidden, being poisoned

to ward off disease from Arkansas, for the first time
that I would rather be dead than not to be alone
with what I had seen, savoring her as sunlight   15
curved through the grape leaf. If ever in

that bed of rocks I feared what held those hard nubs
inviolate might eat my guts out or wished some other
season, cold or wet, had kept me from the accident
of what was, I cannot recall. There was sun,   20

4 Metal fitting on a boat around which a rope
can be made fast.

a little wind, a space of ground yellow with dandelion,
that throb of passage, fracturing shadows, grapes
with no name. Once, then, I floated in a world
I knew to be infinite, delicious, itself

churning and speaking through the voice of each shadow   25
and juncture of light. After that I slept, improbably
dreaming I stood in a center of light, and woke
in the dark, godless and afraid, alive.

1979

Hawktree

Tonight in the hills there was a light
that leaped out of the head
and yellow longing of a young boy.
It was spring and he had walked
through the toy-littered yards   5
to the edge of town, and beyond.
In the tall spare shadow of a pine
he saw her standing, she of skin
whiter than the one cloud
each day loaned to the long sky,   10
whiter even than the pure moon.
But she would not speak to one
who kept her name to himself
when boys laughed in the courtyard.
He watched her burn like a candle   15
in the cathedral of needles.
After a while he saw the other light,
the sun's leveling blister, bring
its change to her wheaten hair.
In growing dark he waited, certain   20
she would hear the pine's whisper,
counting on nature's mediation.
But she would not speak and even
as he watched she vanished.
Slowly he knew his arms furred   25
with a fragrant green darkness
and as the moon cut its swaths
on the ground, as trucks rooted
along the road of colored pleasures,

he felt his feet pushing through   30
his shoes, his hair go sharply stiff.
He could hear her laugh, could see
her long finger loop a man's ear,
but this did not matter. Already
he felt himself sway a little   35
in the desert wind, in the wordless
emptied gnarling he had become.
1979

Rain Forest

The green mothering of moss knits shadow and light,
silence and call of each least bird where
we walk and find there are only a few words
we want to say: water, root, light, and love,
like the names of time. Stunned from ourselves,   5
we are at tour's tail end, our guide long gone,
dawdling deep in what cannot be by any human
invented, a few square miles of the concentric
universe intricate as the whorls of fingertips.
The frailest twigs puff and flag in the giantism   10
of this elaborate grotto, and we are the dream,
before we know better, of an old grotesque
stonecutter who squats under a brow of sweat,
the afternoon a long glowing stalk of marble.
We have entered the huge inward drift behind   15
his eyes and wait to become ourselves. We stare
through limpid eyes into the vapor-lit past
where breath, wordlessly, like a near river
seams up, seams in and out and around darkness.
Somewhere far back in the hunch of shadows,   20
we stood by this wall of vines, and he, angry,
froze us in our tracks and the blade of belief.
That tree there bore the same long slithering
of light from a sky he owned. Disfigured now,
its trunk rises thick and black as a monument   25
that rings when struck. Here the hiking path,
a crease, stops, then spirals around into stumps.
Our party has gone that way, stumbling quietly.
From time to time, someone calls out but we know
only the words whispered from the wall of leaves: 30

water, root, light, and love. We stand silent
in the earliest air remembered, hearing at last
the distant and precise taps of the mallet
until our clothes, as if rotted, fall away
and the feckless light fixes us on the column   35
of our spines. Without warning, we begin to dance,
a bird cries, and another. Our feet seem to spark
on the hard dirt as we go round the black tree
and for no reason we know we see ourselves
throwing our heads back to laugh, our gums   40
and teeth shiny as cut wood, our eyes marbled,
straining to see where it comes from, that
hoarse rasp of joy, that clapping of hands
before which we may not speak or sing or ever stop.

1979

Desks

Piled on a loading dock where I walked,
   student desks battered, staggered
by the dozens, as if all our talk
   of knowledge was over,

as if there'd be no more thin blondes   5
   with pigtails, no math, no art,
no birds to stare at. Surplus now, those moulds
   we tried to sleep in, always hard

so it wouldn't be pleasant and we'd fall
   awake in time for the one question   10
with no answer. Quiet as a study hall,
   this big place, this final destination,

oblivious to whatever the weather is,
   hearing the creak of the wind's weight.
The desks are leg-naked, empty, as if   15
   we might yet come, breathless, late.

And all that time I thought of the flames
   I hadn't guessed, of a blonde
I had loved for years, how the names
   carved one into another would   20

all scar out the same, blunt, hard, in blue
searing, like love's first pain.
I stood there like a child, scared, new,
bird-eyed, not knowing why I came.
1981

Reading the Books Our Children Have Written

They come into this room while the quail are crying to huddle up,
the canyon winds just beginning. They pass my big brown desk,
their faces damp and glistening like the first peaches washed,
and offer themselves to be kissed. I am their father still,
I kiss them, I say *See you tomorrow!* Their light steps fade   5
down the stairs, what they are saying like the far stars
shrill, hard to understand. They are saying their father
writes a book and they are in it, for they are his children.
Then they lie in their beds waiting for sleep, sometimes singing.

Later I get up and go down in darkness and find the hour they played   10
before they were scrubbed, before they brought me those faces.
There on the floor I find the stapled pages, the strange mild
countenances of animals no one has ever seen, the tall dark man
who writes an endless story of birds homeless in the night. They have
numbered every page, they have named each colorful wing.   15
They have done all this to surprise me, surprising themselves.
On the last lined yellow page, one has written *This is a poem.*
Under this the other one has answered *See tomorrow.*
1981

Sea Owl

Unlike the hawk he has no dream of height,
his shadow is what he cannot remember.
In the wide and unlit room of the night
he waits. It is always December,

with the floor of the pines full of silver.   5
His toys move but his claws go tight
as soundlessly he descends the stair.
Nothing knows his cradle, where the white

drone of the day hides him. The flesh-bright
ribbons tear in his grip. He dismembers   10
the shore's secrets. The iron spike
of the sun is all he remembers.

1983

Smithfield Ham

Aged, bittersweet, in salt crusted, the pink meat
lined with the sun's flare, fissured
as a working man's skin at hat level,
I see far back the flesh fall
as the honed knife goes   5
through to the plate, the lost
voice saying ". . . it cuts easy as butter. . . ."

Brown sugar and grease tries to hold itself
still beneath the sawed knee's white.
Around the table the clatter of china   10
kept in the highboy echoes,
children squeal in a near room.

The hand sawing is grandfather's, knuckled,
steadily starting each naked plate
heaped when it ends. Mine   15
waits shyly to receive
under the tall ceiling
all aunts, uncles have gathered to hold.

My shirt white as the creased linen, I shine
before the wedge of cherry pie, coffee   20
black as the sugarless future.[1]
My mother, proud in his glance,
whispers he has called for me and for ham.

[1] Smith is a diabetic.

Tonight I come back to eat in that house the sliced
muscle that fills me with an old thirst.   25
With each swallow, unslaked, I feel
his hand fall more upon mine,
that odd endless blessing
I cannot say the name of . . .
it comes again with her family   30
tale, the dead recalled, Depression,
the jobless, china sold, low sobs, sickness.

Chewing, I ask how he is. Close your mouth, she says.
This time, if he saw me, maybe he'd remember
himself, who thanklessly carved us   35
that cured meat. The Home has to
let us in, we've paid, maybe we
have to go. I gnaw a roll
left too long on the table.
When my knife screeches the plate,   40
my mother shakes her head, whining like a child.

Nothing's sharp anymore, I can't help it, she says.
Almost alone, I lift the scalded coffee
steeped black and bitter.
My mouth, as if incontinent,   45
dribbles and surprises us.
Her face is streaked with summer
dusk where katydids drill and die.

Wanting to tell her there's always tomorrow,
I say you're sunburned, beautiful as ever,   50
Gardening has put the smell of dirt on her.
Like a blade, her hand touches mine.
More? she whispers. Then, ". . . you think
you'll never get enough, so sweet,
until the swelling starts, the ache . . .   55
it's that thirst that wants
to bust a person open late at night."
I fill my cup again, drink, nod, listen.

1983

Louise Glück
b. 1943

Louise Glück's second book, *The House on Marshland* (1975), earned her work wide attention. Her poems drift in an absorbed reflectiveness: Experience is always present, but it is being examined through a veil of heightened and distanced, even unearthly, perception. Movable counters are established—deer, golden panels, stars like tin markers, a tree in blossom; then, with great economy and obsessive concentration, the counters are arranged into various relations with one another. Some of Glück's brief otherworldly narratives gain mythic force from being located in Paradise or Hades; in this they resemble some of Ted Hughes's parables in *Crow* (1970), but without Hughes's violence.

Glück writes frequently about the sorrow and imperfection entailed in the cohabiting of body and soul and yet about the soul's necessary relation with a body for sexual experience. Her fine musicality makes her sequences seem almost like song cycles; her lyric absoluteness keeps her, on the whole, from writing in domestic or naturalistic ways. Before she began to publish, the prevailing poetry by women had been confessional, autobiographical, colloquial (in Rich and Sexton and even in Plath). Glück learned some of her intensity from Plath, but where Plath's movement is driven and hard-edged, Glück's is undulant and dreamy; where Plath is interested in sudden violent states of mind, Glück is interested in longer-term afflicted habits of being. The suspension of time and space in Glück's poetry, especially in her third book, *Descending Figure* (1983), works to reinforce her theme of the habitual, the mythic, and the eternal.

Glück was born in New York City, attended Sarah Lawrence College and Columbia University (where she studied with Stanley Kunitz), and taught for several years at Goddard College, Vermont. She is now a member of the faculty at Warren Wilson College in North Carolina. Her most recent book, *The Triumph of Achilles* (1985), won the National Book Critics Circle Award for poetry.

Texts:
"The Drowned Children," "The Garden," and
"Lamentations" from *Descending Figure*, 1980.
All other selections from *The House on Marshland*, 1975.

All Hallows[1]

Even now this landscape is assembling.
The hills darken. The oxen
sleep in their blue yoke,
the fields having been
picked clean, the sheaves   5
bound evenly and piled at the roadside
among cinquefoil,[2] as the toothed moon rises:

This is the barrenness
of harvest or pestilence.
And the wife leaning out the window   10
with her hand extended, as in payment,
and the seeds
distinct, gold, calling
Come here
Come here, little one   15

And the soul creeps out of the tree.
1975

For My Mother

It was better when we were
together in one body.
Thirty years. Screened
through the green glass
of your eye, moonlight   5
filtered into my bones
as we lay
in the big bed, in the dark,
waiting for my father.
Thirty years. He closed   10
your eyelids with
two kisses. And then spring

---

[1] Hallowe'en (short for "All Hallow Even"),
October 31, the evening before All Saints' Day.   [2] Plant with five-lobed leaves.

came and withdrew from me
the absolute
knowledge of the unborn,   15
leaving the brick stoop
where you stand, shading
your eyes, but it is
night, the moon
is stationed in the beech tree,   20
round and white among
the small tin markers of the stars:
Thirty years. A marsh
grows up around the house.
Schools of spores circulate   25
behind the shades, drift through
gauze flutterings of vegetation.

1975

Messengers

You have only to wait, they will find you.
The geese flying low over the marsh,
glittering in black water.
They find you.

And the deer—   5
how beautiful they are,
as though their bodies did not impede them.
Slowly they drift into the open
through bronze panels of sunlight.

Why would they stand so still   10
if they were not waiting?
Almost motionless, until their cages rust,
the shrubs shiver in the wind,
squat and leafless.

You have only to let it happen: 15
that cry—*release, release*—like the moon
wrenched out of earth and rising
full in its circle of arrows

until they come before you
like dead things, saddled with flesh,   20
and you above them, wounded and dominant.
1975

Poem

In the early evening, as now, a man is bending
over his writing table.
Slowly he lifts his head; a woman
appears, carrying roses.
Her face floats to the surface of the mirror,   5
marked with the green spokes of rose stems.

It is a form
of suffering: then always the transparent page
raised to the window until its veins emerge
as words finally filled with ink.   10

And I am meant to understand
what binds them together
or to the gray house held firmly in place by dusk

because I must enter their lives:
it is spring, the pear tree   15
filming with weak, white blossoms.
1975

The School Children

The children go forward with their little satchels.
And all morning the mothers have labored
to gather the late apples, red and gold,
like words of another language.

And on the other shore   5
are those who wait behind great desks
to receive these offerings.

How orderly they are—the nails
on which the children hang
their overcoats of blue or yellow wool.   10

And the teachers shall instruct them in silence
and the mothers shall scour the orchards for a way out,
drawing to themselves the gray limbs of the fruit trees
bearing so little ammunition.

1975

The Apple Trees

Your son presses against me
his small intelligent body.

I stand beside his crib
as in another dream
you stood among trees hung   5
with bitten apples
holding out your arms.
I did not move
but saw the air dividing
into panes of color—at the very last   10
I raised him to the window saying
See what you have made
and counted out the whittled ribs,
the heart on its blue stalk
as from among the trees   15
the darkness issued:

In the dark room your son sleeps.
The walls are green, the walls
are spruce and silence.
I wait to see how he will leave me.   20
Already on his hand the map appears
as though you carved it there,
the dead fields, women rooted to the river.

1975

The Drowned Children

You see, they have no judgment.
So it is natural that they should drown,
first the ice taking them in
and then, all winter, their wool scarves
floating behind them as they sink   5
until at last they are quiet.
And the pond lifts them in its manifold dark arms.

But death must come to them differently,
so close to the beginning.
As though they had always been   10
blind and weightless. Therefore
the rest is dreamed, the lamp,
the good white cloth that covered the table,
their bodies.

And yet they hear the names they used   15
like lures slipping over the pond:
What are you waiting for
come home, come home, lost
in the waters, blue and permanent.
1980

The Garden

1. *The Fear of Birth*

One sound. Then the hiss and whir
of houses gliding into their places.
And the wind
leafs through the bodies of animals—

But my body that could not content itself   5
with health—why should it be sprung back
into the chord of sunlight?

It will be the same again.
This fear, this inwardness,

until I am forced into a field   10
without immunity
even to the least shrub that walks
stiffly out of the dirt, trailing
the twisted signature of its root,
even to a tulip, a red claw.   15

And then the losses,
one after another,
all supportable.

2. The Garden

The garden admires you.
For your sake it smears itself with green pigment,   20
the ecstatic reds of the roses,
so that you will come to it with your lovers.

And the willows—
see how it has shaped these green
tents of silence. Yet   25
there is still something you need,
your body so soft, so alive, among the stone
     animals.

Admit that it is terrible to be like them,
beyond harm.

3. The Fear of Love

That body lying beside me like obedient stone—   30
once its eyes seemed to be opening,
we could have spoken.

At that time it was winter already.
By day the sun rose in its helmet of fire
and at night also, mirrored in the moon.   35
Its light passed over us freely,
as though we had lain down
in order to leave no shadows,
only these two shallow dents in the snow.
And the past, as always, stretched before us,   40
still, complex, impenetrable.

How long did we lie there
as, arm in arm in their cloaks of feathers,

the gods walked down
from the mountain we built for them?   45

4. Origins

As though a voice were saying
You should be asleep by now—
But there was no one. Nor
had the air darkened,
though the moon was there,   50
already filled in with marble.

As though, in a garden crowded with flowers,
a voice had said
How dull they are, these golds,
so sonorous, so repetitious   55
until you closed your eyes,
lying among them, all
stammering flame:

And yet you could not sleep,
poor body, the earth   60
still clinging to you—

5. The Fear of Burial

In the empty field, in the morning,
the body waits to be claimed.
The spirit sits beside it, on a small rock—
nothing comes to give it form again.   65

Think of the body's loneliness.
At night pacing the sheared field,
its shadow buckled tightly around.
Such a long journey.
And already the remote, trembling lights of the
     village   70
not pausing for it as they scan the rows.
How far away they seem,
the wooden doors, the bread and milk
laid like weights on the table.

1980

Lamentations

1. The Logos[1]

They were both still,
the woman mournful, the man
branching into her body.

But god was watching.
They felt his gold eye   5
projecting flowers on the landscape.

Who knew what he wanted?
He was god, and a monster.
So they waited. And the world
filled with his radiance,   10
as though he wanted to be understood.

Far away, in the void that he had shaped,
he turned to his angels.

2. Nocturne

A forest rose from the earth.
O pitiful, so needing   15
God's furious love—

Together they were beasts.
They lay in the fixed
dusk of his negligence;
from the hills, wolves came, mechanically   20
drawn to their human warmth,
their panic.

Then the angels saw
how He divided them:
the man, the woman, and the woman's body.   25

Above the churned reeds, the leaves let go
a slow moan of silver.

[1] Greek: "divine word," here referring to the
beginning of the Gospel of St. John: "In the
beginning was the Word."

3. The Covenant

Out of fear, they built a dwelling place.
But a child grew between them
as they slept, as they tried   30
to feed themselves.

They set it on a pile of leaves,
the small discarded body
wrapped in the clean skin
of an animal. Against the black sky   35
they saw the massive argument of light.

Sometimes it woke. As it reached its hands
they understood they were the mother and father,
there was no authority above them.

4. The Clearing

Gradually, over many years,   40
the fur disappeared from their bodies
until they stood in the bright light
strange to one another.
Nothing was as before.

Their hands trembled, seeking   45
the familiar.

Nor could they keep their eyes
from the white flesh
on which wounds would show clearly
like words on a page.   50

And from the meaningless browns and greens
at last God arose, His great shadow
darkening the sleeping bodies of His children,
and leapt into heaven.

How beautiful it must have been,   55
the earth, that first time
seen from the air.

1980

Albert Goldbarth
b. 1948

Albert Goldbarth, a vividly abundant writer, publishes both short lyrics and long sequences; the sequences almost always incorporate and embody historical material. The 1974 sequence called *Optics* contains, for instance, material about glassblowers, glassmaking, stained glass windows, and so on. He has also written sequences on a transvestite Paris entertainer and on an American painter. Goldbarth was born and raised in Chicago, and many of his autobiographical lyrics concern Jewish family life, with its beginnings in immigration, its decimation by the Holocaust, its religious rituals, its kinship relations, its social presence. Goldbarth writes as one who has left that life but wishes to perpetuate it as it recedes.

After graduating from the University of Illinois at Chicago Circle, Goldbarth took an M.F.A. at Iowa and subsequently has taught at the University of Utah, Cornell, and the University of Texas at Austin, where he is now a professor of English. His writing takes many risks as it leaps into associative patterns heedless of formal or logical connections. The connections are there (Goldbarth is not a surrealist but rather an expressionist writer), but the poet wishes to imitate the mind's creative elation and generalized play as the imagination reconstructs the world. His historical imagination is strong; he thinks himself into another century as powerfully as he can think himself into a dead ballet dancer. He likes, as he has said, "the extended poem that includes narrative, or has scope enough to play with large bodies of time, or that finds room for dialogue or quoted source materials, that can build up litany or weave motifs in and out with the huge sweep a suite has." His *Different Fleshes* (1977) is a "novel/poem," with alternating sections of poetry and prose. In it, Goldbarth wishes "to allow moments of pure lyric visionary intensity to take place within a novel-like framework: plot, historic and invented characters, quoted conversation." In this way, the poem attempts to imitate the diversity of life and of perception.

Though Goldbarth can be sentimental in his commemorative poetry, he can also be remarkably brusque and brisk about his childhood surroundings. His play of language is as various as the play of his imagination; words from many different registers jostle each other on the page—technical words, dialect words, philosophical words, demotic words. What is most exhilarating about reading Goldbarth is the constant surprise one encounters on each page as the poem continues a protean development, unforeseen and beautiful, of its basic premises. Goldbarth's most recent collection, *Arts and Sciences,* appeared in 1986.

Texts:
"Before," "How the Sky Counts Years," "Family/*Grove*," "The Tip," and "Object Functionsong" from *Faith,* 1981. "A History of Civilization," "And Now Farley Is Going to Sing . . . ," "The World of Expectations," and "The Well" from *Original Light: New and Selected Poems, 1973–1983,* 1983.

Before

The class was History, that's
what I wanted—the bridge
the bent Yid[1] ragman took reluctantly
between steamship and sweatshop, or
older than that: the landbridge   5
something almost a horse was
grazing its way to Alaska
across on something almost hooves,
or older: something almost a leg
that was the grayveined print of a leg   10
in a web, before a bridge could be anything
more than a body's own
furthest extension. I was
seventeen. It was sunny. I'd come
from History, and before that   15
from a lineage of ragpickers,
songpluckers, kettlemenders, renderers
of humpfat[2] for the candles, masters of
disputation over a nuance of scripture,
debtors, diddlers, elegiasts and jewelers   20
—history too, though the textbook
didn't say it. The page said Presidents
and paper. I wanted something from
before paper—wasps,
the fluted home of their making.   25
I wanted the first bone
of my bones. I wanted the word
before the alphabet, the word like a suckstone
working up spit. And then I stopped,
near Washtenaw and Ainslie, on the bridge   30
above the sewerage ditch, and sun
as if meeting a challenge made the stars
of a constellation-story burn
that urban rut's otherwise lustreless
flow. It was the sign of The Cart,[3]   35
and there too, in the story, sun
bedazzled dull surfaces: all those heaps
of garment district scraps he peddled,
a few abused tin pots, and who knows

---

[1] Pejorative epithet (from *Yiddish*) for *Jewish*.   [3] The Big Dipper.
[2] Fat from a camel's hump.

how or why but some wholeskinned Spanish onions,   40
wool socks, and a single tired rose. I
still remember this: his humming something
tuneless, as if from before the idea of song
took full root in American soil—but
like the rose, though it drooped, though maybe   45
the worm ate in it, his song was handsome,
a lady would accept it and understand. And
this: my face was reflected, wavery
but ascertainably wide-eyed, on his pots.
Or in the sewerage currents—and then the   50
stars shifted, light was
sun again, and I was something almost
a man, on its way home,
humming its wanting. I was a boy
with a book. And this was long before   55
I'd learn to have words for what I wanted,
but what I wanted was something
like a bottle with a notepage in it,
thrown to sea—the clarity of glass,
but from before glass; and the urgency   60
of that written note, before writing.
—Maybe the water itself,
the message its salt.

1981

How the Sky Counts Years

Somewhere, on a far star, my mother
was saying "This should be" then it sputters
"the worst" a long dark space "that ever
happens to you." It was something trivial

I guess, and so the irony. Such small things   5
tug attention!—/a bee at a rose's spirals
like yoga's focus on mandalas;[1] this
milkeye nipple; whose heart holds exactly the volume
of blood of the trap-snapped mouse?; fresh

[1] A meditative technique used by Eastern
practitioners of yoga is to focus on one sacred
image, or mandala.

lemon wedge; your stare's two pupils, caught like   10
faltered trapezists: in their red nets/—how
can anyone master a discipline? Then

one night, walking, a man understands
astronomy. It's a cinder, cold
in the sky now; though here, in my life, I   15
first see the light, and by it.

1981

Family/*Grove*

1.

It's common to say of bad acting, or family photos like these, the expressions are
"wooden." It's true, I suppose: my father's grimace is fitted into his face like the
polymer moonslice of a cheap keychain charm, and my mother's arms—even at the
most intimate—are raised and angled as if she were practicing umpire signals or fake
hieroglyphic poses. That's sad—these aren't bad acting, but everyday honesties   5
caught bad, in the everyday light. Here, at the arboretum, is a pose I know was meant
to say fun, and love, and yet it looks as if they're about to strike me brutally—that
smile, those arms. Maybe this is an honesty, that even they weren't aware of—a
dozen times a day, it must have been, I rubbed against their grain. You see?—my
lips stiff in a petulance. But I remember, before and beyond that, the dark the   10
impolite glare of photography never really caught at all—an hour or so past bedtime,
while I waited under the covers for sleep and they tiptoed noisily up to my room,
on the way to theirs and whatever they shared in the double bed below the parquet
picture—they'd stop, they'd strain their ears at the night like burglars against a safe,
listening for my breathing, "checking," is how they always called it, "to make sure."   15
So here it's twenty years ago, we're in an arboretum Chicago surrounds with its
urban blatter, if we're wooden that's because we're a grove of our own; three
rootknit family trees. See?—they face, and compete for, the flash of the camera like
any trees and any light. In certain seasons, I remember, they were beautiful.

2.

A number of researchers theorize that sleep developed, at least in part, to keep our   20
mammalian ancestors safe in the hours given over to the great reptilian predators.
In those wooded places dinosaurs couldn't enter without an announcing crash, they'd
burrow and curl and let sleep make them silent for once, unnoticeable. Many of our
nightmares are likely a deep mammalian memory of those scaled hunters tearing the
earth; and probably served as a doublecheck system, waking the animal intermit-   25
tently, blood hot, primed for flight—it would search the trunks around it for
dangerous faces, sniffing, focusing, find no threat, so stretch and yawn and drowse

off feeling safe again. I love being a mammal—that is, I love women's breasts, by which we get that name. And I love my sleep. I always have. In the hour or so while I waited to hear my parents' sentinel tiptoeing, there in the house on Washtenaw 30 Avenue, I'd hug myself under the covers and squint, and populate the whorls of the planks in the walls with a squadron of heroes—Flash Gordon, Roy Rogers,[1] some guy who could breathe like a fish. These were necessary comfort because of the others, who visited first—devil faces, terrible lizard creatures, a man from the ten o'clock news who did something bad with a knife to good boys and then left them 35 in the forest preserve. Looking, frightened, finally calmed of fright, in the wood, in the woods, around me.

3.

And now on my bedroom wall I have that old parquet picture, a gift from my parents—they handed it over so casually. They must not understand that it's a time machine; you look, it takes you back. You're ten. A girl in a puff-sleeved peasant 40 dress is leaning to drink from a small round chink that trickles coolly. Her breasts just brush the rumple of her blouse—the lightest, pinking touch! Her eyes are closed (the one we see is a dark v, like a bird in distant sky), and her feet are tensed in support, accenting her difficult angle and her total concentration on the thrill of tongue, to water. The pose seems impossible to hold for even a minute—though 45 of course she's held it for over two generations now. My father would say, with a strangely insistent pride, "Every shape is a different piece of wood!" (I think he truly found this wondrous—it was their only parquet.) "Each foot, a different piece! Her hair, this leaf . . . each its own piece! And every piece *is the natural color except her lips!* These they had to paint red." They're very red. I look, I'm very ten. Most 50 days I don't look, though. I wake, I enter the world, it has a story to tell me in dollar signs. I shake a hundred hands until a small erosion wears away some of the lifeline, then I have lunch, and then I lie, and then I'm lied straight back to, and then I come home, it takes a while to drink away a sour taste, to think well of myself, to be sleepy. I look. And when I do she's there, held sure, the very light we see by 55 held steady, longer than even a life, in the grain.

1981

The Tip

It's so dark now,
there's this streetlamp
packing light
like an iceberg.

[1] Flash Gordon: popular cartoon hero of 1940s;
Roy Rogers: popular star of cowboy films
dating from the 1940s.

It says: *like an iceberg*   5
I'm only one-tenth, look up.
And, vaguely, yes
there are stars.

And caught in the lamplight, leaning,
still, like a creature   10
the ice age is carrying thousands of miles
—a man just recovered from illness.

You see?—that daze
of special knowledge, clearer
and colder than ours. Yes he's death's, he's   15
eternity's, one-tenth.
1981

Object Functionsong

Let me see my face in the mirror
Laugh, just once, when I'm not able
To laugh. Let objects be my teacher.
/*the mouth of a jar, the neck of a bottle*

Let the grill of the radio, the crosses-shape   5
Of the calendar page, be a jail
Music and time escape.
/*the spine of a book, the eye of a needle*

Let my lap fit well the lap offered
By wood chairs. Let them be a durable   10
Stencil about me—definitive, hard.
/*the head of a pin, the legs of a table*

Let the spin of the phonograph show
How I in my rut, how I in my circle,
Still can sing, if the point is true.   15
/*the chest of drawers, the cock of a shuttle*

Let me learn from the shapes of things.
/*there, in the corner, the hinge wings*
1981

A History of Civilization

In the dating bar, the potted ferns lean down
conspiratorially, little spore-studded
elopement ladders. The two top buttons
of every silk blouse have already half-undone all
introduction. Slices of smile, slices of sweet brie,[1]   5
dark and its many white wedges. In back

of the bar, the last one-family grocer's is necklaced
over and over: strings of leeks, greek olives, sardines.
The scoops stand at attention in the millet barrel,
the cordovan sheen of the coffee barrel, the kidney beans.   10
And a woman whose pride is a clean linen apron polishes
a register as intricate as a Sicilian shrine. In back

of the grocery, dozing and waking in fitful starts
by the guttering hearth, a ring of somber-gabardined grandpas
plays dominoes. Their stubble picks up the flicker like filaments   15
still waiting for the bulb or the phone to be invented. Even their
coughs, their phlegms, are in an older language. They move the simple
pieces of matching numbers. In back

of the back room, in the unlit lengths of storage, it's
that season: a cat eyes a cat. The sacks and baskets   20
are sprayed with the sign of a cat's having eyed a cat, and
everything to do with rut[2] and estrus[3] comes down to a few
sure moves. The dust motes drift, the continents.
In the fern bar a hand tries a knee, as if unplanned.

1983

---

[1] A French cheese.
[2] In this context, the periodic sexual excitement
of a male animal.
[3] The period during which a female animal is in
heat.

"And Now Farley Is Going to Sing
While I Drink a Glass of Water!"

At the Vent Haven Museum in Fort Mitchell,
Kentucky, over 500 wooden
ventriloquist's dummies sit
in lit approximations of interrelationship,
stand in small posed groups no stiffer   5
than friends in half of the photos you own,
grotesque, exaggerated in overblown grimace
or underdefined like a slug, and some equipped
to whistle, spit, stick out their tongues, and some
just quiet, legs crossed in the hot June dusk, not   10
sweating exactly, just sitting, familiar, and yet
not exactly familiar. And at

the Houston Zoo, June air induces
two giraffes to amatory show. A glance,
like lightning bounced between   15
the spires of Chartres,[1] shoots through
the gangly calm that otherwise attends them.
The day's all pollen. Sneezing, I almost miss
his great pink party favor
unrolling. Hitting at the height   20
of their articulate quiet, late-day light

along their yellow length makes little
more than dappled light of their bodies,
light given form, light turned substance
as if by no more than the gathering here   25
of a cloud of pollen. This is the way,
or almost the way, it feels—yes? or the way we
want it to feel: flesh
gone rarefied into a luminous floating the
bees of us wobble tipsily through   30
to the flowers of us. No wonder
we're fixed at the chainlink fence with something just
this side of recognition on our faces. And at

the Institute for Biochemical Engineering in Salt Lake,
in its hospital's basement, a test collection   35

[1] Famous cathedral in France.

of artificial hearts, opening, closing, on beat
in the water tanks, and the calves next door
with hearts already implanted; and at
the northeast end of Quarryworld, the ocher bricks
being dumped with the hundred high clinks   40
of glass bottles; and at the rich, black back of
Kathy W.'s garden, the single cucumber
dozing around the hum of its own thin green; and
at the Vent Haven Museum,
the wooden figures of humans, that aren't humans,   45

saying something for us.
1983

The World of Expectations

What starts with F and ends with U-C-K? starts
another stupid high school joke. We also
snapped the thick resilient straps of Maria
Alfonso's bra. I don't know what we expected.
Annoyance, perhaps—though a kind of annoyance   5
that opened the way for attention—then maybe
intimacy, though we wouldn't have phrased it that way.
We called it F-ing. An alarm goes off,

the expectations are serial and easy: the clumsy
effecting of fire-drill practice, arrival of miles of hose.   10
And maybe Dennis or Leo or I would get to stand
near Maria, and maybe she'd even bend in her
provocative way that showed the first shadowy
rampway into her cleavage. When I finally did get
effed, of course it had nothing to do with the world   15
of expectations we mapped round and flat

where the condom ate wallet for years. Now I hear
Leo's divorced; drunk enough, it's as if a large hand
crumples him like a Coors[1] can. The point is, even
Dennis's happiness, what kids mean and a sexual   20
axis, never struck our daydreams. The point is, not
even sex, necessarily—what did they see

[1] Popular brand of beer.

in Station 19 when the bell went crazy? Flames
like cartoon devils? Their heroics, axe and ladder,

tested successfully? Glory? Pain? Some calls to glory   25
and pain are real, of course. But back then
we pulled levers for hijinks, for stupid jokes. And it came
long, red and clamorous. Firetruck.

1983

The Well

A Poem about Edward Hicks[1] with a quote about Millet[2]

1.

> "*. . . that this scene was what was visible in front of the house
> where Millet was born, and that consciously or unconsciously the
> artist had enlarged the proportions of the well by two thirds so that
> they coincided with his childhood perception.*"
>
> John Berger

One hundred *Peaceable Kingdoms,* and in all of them
the presence of lamb. One hundred tranquil
presences of lamb, its wool in stately curls
like the fresh white shavings of pine. A wolf
will nuzzle it. A wolf and a lamb,   5
a yang and a yin, will be one simple design.
A cow will knowingly rest the great weight
of her head on the lion's
acquiescent back, no stranger than any
marriage you know. And they have a child.   10
They have one hundred children,
who yoke them together or hold a flowering branch,
a simple moon face and its simple, dark, plum eyes.
These animals belong together not only
with a puzzle's pieces' beautiful, flush   15
fit, but with their flatness—Hicks
had painted tavern signs for a living.

---

[1] American painter (1780–1849) known for his
many versions of *The Peaceable Kingdom,* a
painting representing the prophecy of Isaiah 2:6
that "the wolf also shall dwell with the lamb,
and the leopard shall lie down with the kid;

and the calf and the young lion and the fatling
together; and a little child shall lead them."
[2] Jean François Millet (1814–1875), French painter
of rural scenes.

These animals pose. These animals say themselves
like any weather vane's beast: become
domesticated, heraldic, and all of them heading   20
one hundred times in the one direction, the future,
a sweet and peaceful wind blows.

2.

> "The main explanation for Hicks's obsession with the subject must
> lie with Hicks himself. He was a man distraught, overwhelmed by
> his sense of guilt and unworthiness . . ."
>   Abraham A. Davidson

The dragon smoked like a thwarted desire
—Good! I leaned the ladder over and fired
his breath from my tin of dyer's yellow. Now   25
half of *The Dragon and Calf* was done—and only
yesterday, in rough, he'd smoked like a
burnt roast: so, my hand has brought ferocity out
of the common. It was night; and my own
throat on fire. Tired, you lose a grip. And I   30
was tired: all afternoon, in labor over what
the plains of my first three peaceable
kingdoms required, that didn't seem
complete yet; and now this, at the roofedge,
over a room of guzzle and guffaw . . . and   35
women. The night was a purple, the window a
torch-orange wash. The grip I lost was something
in me; my grip on the ladder was never
more sure. Her hair was wild like the thatch
that brushed my cheek, it might have had a   40
roofthatch's insect life in it, surely it smelt
of the purple night wind . . . And two men
walking their hands on her bodice's muslin,
that I from my rung could look
down fully to the nipples' pink meat . . .   45
My throat on fire; and rubbing against the ladder
until it broke, or until I broke . . . then on
the ground, a ruffian ruckus behind me, and
then running home. And then home. And then
washing it off these hands, the whole   50
paint-purple-pinkness of it, rinsing the least
pink weakness off, and drinking
deep from the cool kitchen pitcher where
pewter gives water an extra heft, recognizing
the power it takes to cleanse. And then   55
I knew. In one I did the Delaware River, just

a pure rush over rock, I did it
completely before I slept, and sketched a laving
line of water in the other two—they said yes,
this is it. This is the place where a boy can breathe   60
air in and out like the white
flag of peace, at a brookside, being laundered.

1983

Michael Blumenthal
b. 1949

Michael Blumenthal grew up in the Washington Heights section of Manhattan in
a German-speaking home. He received a B.A. in philosophy in 1969 from the
State University of New York at Binghamton and a J.D. in 1974 from Cornell
Law School. Though he practiced law for a time, he left to write poetry,
supporting himself by various jobs as editor, arts administrator, speech writer, and
book reviewer. He is now a Briggs-Copeland lecturer in poetry at Harvard
University; his third book, *Laps* (1984), was recently awarded the Juniper Prize
of the University of Massachusetts.

His first book, *Sympathetic Magic* (1980), appeared with an unusually strong
piece of praise from the poet Howard Nemerov, who said of it, "The last *first*
book I remember as having this strangeness and distinction was called *Harmonium*."
Blumenthal's second book, *Days We Would Rather Know* (1984), consolidated the
promise of the first and showed Blumenthal to be a poet of romantic hope and
elegiac sadness. A certainty of destruction (not unusual in the child of refugees) is
matched in him by the conviction that his own life will be spared and must
flower. The *élan vital* that propels Blumenthal's passionate explorations of
language suggests that for him, if language fails, life does, and if life fails,
language must. Blumenthal seeks a language like Berryman's—nervous, responsive
to all speech levels, capable simultaneously of blunt surprise and tremulous
beauty. He is buoyant and humorous, but the undertow of the sad and the dying
pulls against his lightness and creates a haunting counterpoint to the joyous flow
of the poems.

Blumenthal connects his own poetic objectives with those of Wordsworth:

I wish to keep my readers—and myself—"in the company of flesh and blood,"
to write, or at least attempt, the kind of poems of moral and spiritual self-
education which first drew me to the poets I most love: Shakespeare, Dante,
Wordsworth, Milton, Keats, Stevens, Eliot, Yeats, and Roethke. Above all, I
hope to make poems which are accessible, which speak in the language of their
time to the eternal concerns of all men and women: the yearning for religious
faith, the difficulties and joys of love, the quest for self-knowledge, and, ultimately, the need for self-transcendence.

Blumenthal's interest in form and in permutations of language suggests that he will remain an interestingly experimental poet in the future.

Texts:
"I Have Lived . . ." and "Washington Heights,
1959" from *Sympathetic Magic*, 1980.
"Over Ohio" and "Wishful Thinking" from
Days We Would Rather Know, 1984.

I Have Lived This Way for Years and Do Not Wish to Change

I hope you'll forgive the black paint
on my windows, the smell of cat litter
in the kitchen. Guests complain sometimes
that my collection of Minoan[1] cadavers spoils
their appetite, or that having the shower   5
in the living room creates too much moisture,
but I think you'll grow used to it
if we get to be friends.

Yes, it is kind of inconvenient
having the bed strapped to the ceiling,   10
but I've grown so accustomed to the view
of my Max Ernst[2] carpet that I hardly think
I could sleep with gravity anymore.

Why thank you, it was a gift from my lover's husband
after our honeymoon in Cincinnati. I do think   15
it goes well with the orange bedroom set, the burgundy curtains.

See, you're feeling quite at home already.

Don't be shy.
Help yourself to the jellyfish, the goose down,
the chocolate-covered cotton balls.   20
1980

---

[1] Ancient Cretan Bronze Age culture
(3000–1000 B.C.).   [2] German surrealist painter (1891–1976).

Washington Heights, 1959

Even the bad news came slowly and was afraid.
Grandmothers tapped their way up the steep hill
to Bennett Park, gradual as mealybugs along
the stem of a coleus. A pink rubber ball, some
small boy's humble playground, would roll by,   5
and some gray girl would lift to where the mind
said step but the old legs wouldn't answer.

Trees danced their lonely dance in fields of concrete.
Each one we came to, we called: country. What grass
we knew lived by the river, a place our mothers called: 10
don't play there, it isn't safe anymore. Safety
was the day's dull wisdom, their past a net we swam
against, a high tide. Risk was small and fragile, tied
to a wave called future, sinking every laugh it came upon.

Fishing, our bait was bubble gum and daydreams,   15
our creels filled with old beer cans wished to bass,
prophylactics weaving like white eels in a Hudson
we dreamt clean as a mountain river. Five old bottles
meant a chance to find your hero and a piece of bubble
gum besides, snow a chance to claim your arms again.   20

Childhood reading was obituaries in *Aufbau*:[1] name,
maiden name, place of birth, surviving relatives,
death the one occasion we were sure of. Black ties
meant another neighbor wouldn't be there anymore,
candles that memory would find us. Scarred bricks   25
held auditions for home plate, lines on pavement
drew a floor for dancing.

Saturday was Sabbath and the slow turned slower.
Those who couldn't carry with their arms grew heavy
with their faith. Each year, we set the table   30
for a man who never came, ate bitter herbs,
read aloud some dreams that never quite rang true.[2]

---

[1] New York German-language newspaper.
[2] Description of a Passover *seder*, or dinner, in which a glass of wine is set out for the prophet Elijah, bitter herbs are eaten in remembrance of the Jews' exile in Egypt, and the Exodus from Egypt to Canaan is recalled in readings and prayers.

Constancy was Mario, tapping his Cats Paw[3] heels to walk
on old cloth shoes stretched wide with aching. His
deep black hair turned grey with years, but the sound   35
of hammer to rubber to steel stayed firm with a sense
of praying. Friends died and aging backs bent towards
the earth, slow and predictable as corn husks in November.
As long as the mail kept coming, we smiled, waited
for the ice truck, buried the dead, called it home.   40
1980

Over Ohio

You can say what you want about the evils of technology
and the mimicry of birds: *I love it.* I love the sheer,
unexpurgated *hubris*[1] of it, I love the beaten egg whites
of clouds hovering beneath me, this ephemeral Hamlet[2]
of believing in man's grandeur. You can have all that   5
talk about the holiness of nature and the second Babylon.[3]
You can stay shocked about the future all you want,
reminisce about the beauties of midwifery. I'll take this
anyday, this sweet imitation of Mars and Jupiter, this
sitting still at 600 mph like a jet-age fetus. I want to   10
go on looking at the moon for the rest of my life and seeing
footsteps. I want to keep flying, even for short distances,
like here between Columbus and Toledo on Air Wisconsin:
an Andean condor sailing over Ohio, above the factories,
above the dust and the highways and the miserable tires.   15
1984

Wishful Thinking

for Cynthia

I like to think that ours will be more than just another story
of failed love and the penumbras of desire. I like to think
that the moon that day was in whatever house the astrologists

---

[3] Brand of rubber heel used in shoe repairs.
[1] Greek: "unseemly pride."
[2] In Shakespeare's *Hamlet* (Act II, Sc. ii, l. 312),
the hero recites a speech beginning, "What a
piece of work is a man!"

[3] The evil city condemned by St. John in the
biblical book Revelation.

would have it in for a kind of quiet, a trellis lust could climb
easily and then subside, resting against the sills and ledges,   5
giving way like shore to an occasional tenderness, coddling
the cold idiosyncrasies of impulse and weather that pound it
as it holds to its shape against the winds and duststorms of
temptation and longing. I like to think that some small canister
of hope and tranquillity washed ashore that day and we, in   10
the right place, found it. These are the things I imagine
all lovers wish for amid the hot commencements of love
and promises, their histories and failures washing ashore
like flotsam, their innards girthed against those architects
of misery, desire and restlessness, their hopes rising   15
against the air as it fondles the waves and frolics them skywards.
I like to think that, if the heart pauses awhile in a single place,
it finds a home somewhere, like a vagabond lured by fatigue
to an unlikely town and, with a sudden peacefulness, deciding
to stay there. I like to think these things because, whether   20
or not they reach fruition, they provide the heart with a kind
of solace, the way poetry does, or all forms of tenderness
that issue out amid the deserts of failed love and petulant desire.
I like to think them because, meditated on amid this pattern
of off-white and darkness, they lend themselves to a kind of   25
music, not unlike the music a dove makes as it circles the trees,
not unlike the sun and the earth and their orbital brothers,
the planets, as they chant to the heavens their longing for hope
and repetition amid orderly movement, not unlike the music
these humble wishes make with their cantata of willfulness   30
and good intentions, looking for some pleasant abstractions
amid our concretized lives, something tender and lovely to
defy the times with, quiet and palpable amid the flickers of flux
and the flames of longing: a bird rising over the ashes,[1] a dream.

1984

Jorie Graham
b. 1951

Jorie Graham, the daughter of American parents, grew up in Italy. She was sent
to a French lycée in Rome and so became trilingual, speaking Italian with
friends, English at home, and French in school. (One of her poems retells her
bafflement as a child that the chestnut tree had three names.) She attended the

---

[1] In classical myth, the legendary Phoenix
ascended reborn from the ashes of its own
self-consuming fire.

Sorbonne for a year (1968) studying philosophy, then came to the United States, where she entered the program in cinema studies (directed by Martin Scorcese) at New York University, and began to write poetry. After her B.A. (1972), she worked for NBC television and attended poetry workshops and seminars at Columbia. She took an M.F.A. at the University of Iowa in 1978, where she is now on the permanent faculty.

Graham was exposed very early to the visual arts (her mother is a painter and sculptor) and to the churches and museums of Italy. Many of her poems meditate on the relation between the expressive possibilities of language and those of the visual arts. They also reflect on the inevitable tension between the damage of life and the beauty of art: "Contained damage makes for beauty," one of the poems ventures to say. How the violent and the sexual are to be handled within the fabric of art; how art can accommodate itself to the infinite shades of nuance that experience demands; how art mends life; how the wish of the spirit to become pure spirit is matched by the wish of the spirit to reenter the body; how time preserves the past in death—all these metaphysical questions are present repeatedly in Graham's work. (Her philosophy studies at the lycée included works of Pascal, Kant, Heidegger, Sartre, and Merleau-Ponty, with weekly papers, as she writes, "on such subjects as 'Reason and Morality,' or '*La Passion.*' ")

Graham's voice tends to move in phrases, in recurrent pulses of tentative exploration as she moves over a field of preoccupation, testing its limits, weighing its powers, looking for a way into feeling, "fingering all the stops." In this way the movement of the poem tends to imitate the searchings and depth-soundings of the mind seeking to replicate the starts and questionings of the heart.

"As a young woman," Graham writes, "I read quantities of Baudelaire, Rimbaud, Mallarmé, Apollinaire, and Supervielle; at school we had to bring in huge passages from Racine and Corneille by heart—to this day I hear 'Ô rage, ô désespoir, ô vieillesse ennemie, / Ai-je donc tant vécu que pour cette infamie,' etc." She also read, as was inevitable for someone raised in Italy, Dante and Tasso and Petrarch. Among the Americans, besides the modernist poets, Graham read and was attracted to the poetry of Elizabeth Bishop: "I feel strong kinship with her notion of boundaries—the poem as an act of confrontation between two worlds." Graham's musicality and her feeling for etymologies put her poetry in the long tradition of the "pure lyric," stretching from Petrarch and Ronsard to Rilke and Stevens.

Texts:
"The Geese," "Over and Over Stitch," and
"Mind" from *Hybrids of Plants and Ghosts,* 1980.
"San Sepolcro," "My Garden, My Daylight,"
and "At Luca Signorelli's Resurrection of the
Body" from *Erosion,* 1983.

The Geese

Today as I hang out the wash I see them again, a code
as urgent as elegant,
tapering with goals.
For days they have been crossing. We live beneath these geese

as if beneath the passage of time, or a most perfect heading.   5
Sometimes I fear their relevance.
Closest at hand,
between the lines,

the spiders imitate the paths the geese won't stray from,
imitate them endlessly to no avail: 10
things will not remain connected,
will not heal,

and the world thickens with texture instead of history,
texture instead of place.
Yet the small fear of the spiders   15
binds and binds

the pins to the lines, the lines to the eaves, to the pincushion bush,
as if, at any time, things could fall further apart
and nothing could help them
recover their meaning. And if these spiders had their way,   20

chainlink over the visible world,
would we be in or out? I turn to go back in.
There is a feeling the body gives the mind
of having missed something, a bedrock poverty, like falling

without the sense that you are passing through one world,   25
that you could reach another
anytime. Instead the real
is crossing you,

your body an arrival
you know is false but can't outrun. And somewhere in between   30
these geese forever entering and
these spiders turning back,

this astonishing delay, the everyday, takes place.
1980

Over and Over Stitch

Late in the season the world digs in, the fat blossoms
hold still for just a moment longer.
Nothing looks satisfied,
but there is no real reason to move on much further:
this isn't a bad place;   5
why not pretend

we wished for it?
The bushes have learned to live with their haunches.
The hydrangea[1] is resigned
to its pale and inconclusive utterances.   10
Towards the end of the season
it is not bad

to have the body. To have experienced joy
as the mere lifting of hunger
is not to have known it   15
less. The tobacco leaves
don't mind being removed
to the long racks—all uses are astounding

to the used.
There are moments in our lives which, threaded, give us heaven—   20
noon, for instance, or all the single victories
of gravity, or the kudzu vine,[2]
most delicate of manias,
which has pressed its luck

this far this season.   25
It shines a gloating green.
Its edges darken with impatience, a kind of wind.
Nothing again will ever be this easy, lives
being snatched up like dropped stitches, the dry stalks of daylilies
marking a stillness we can't keep.   30

1980

---

[1] Species of flowering bush whose blooms may be either pale pink or pale blue.

[2] Parasitic plant that, in its extremely rapid growth, overwhelms all other vegetation.

Mind

The slow overture of rain,
each drop breaking
without breaking into
the next, describes
the unrelenting, syncopated   5
mind. Not unlike
the hummingbirds
imagining their wings
to be their heart, and swallows
believing the horizon   10
to be a line they lift
and drop. What is it
they cast for? The poplars,
advancing or retreating,
lose their stature   15
equally, and yet stand firm,
making arrangements
in order to become
imaginary. The city
draws the mind in streets,   20
and streets compel it
from their intersections
where a little
belongs to no one. It is
what is driven through   25
all stationary portions
of the world, gravity's
stake in things. The leaves,
pressed against the dank
window of November   30
soil, remain unwelcome
till transformed, parts
of a puzzle unsolvable
till the edges give a bit
and soften. See how   35
then the picture becomes clear,
the mind entering the ground
more easily in pieces,
and all the richer for it.
1980

San Sepolcro[1]

In this blue light
    I can take you there,
snow having made me
    a world of bone
seen through to. This   5
    is my house,

my section of Etruscan
    wall, my neighbor's
lemontrees, and, just below
    the lower church,   10
the airplane factory.
    A rooster

crows all day from mist
    outside the walls.
There's milk on the air,   15
    ice on the oily
lemonskins. How clean
    the mind is,

holy grave. It is this girl
    by Piero   20
della Francesca,[2] unbuttoning
    her blue dress,
her mantle of weather,
    to go into

labor. Come, we can go in.   25
    It is before
the birth of god. No-one
    has risen yet
to the museums, to the assembly
    line—bodies   30

and wings—to the open air
    market. This is
what the living do: go in.
    It's a long way.

[1] In Italy, birthplace of the painter Piero della Francesca (1420–1492).

[2] The painting referred to is *La Madonna del Parto* (*The Virgin Giving Birth*).

And the dress keeps opening   35
   from eternity

to privacy, quickening.
   Inside, at the heart,
is tragedy, the present moment
   forever stillborn,   40
but going in, each breath
   is a button

coming undone, something terribly
   nimble-fingered
finding all of the stops.   45
1983

My Garden, My Daylight

My neighbor brings me bottom fish—
   tomcod, rockcod—
a fist of ocean. He comes out
   from the appletrees between us
holding his gift like a tight   5
   spool of thread.

Once a week he brings me fresh-catch,
   boned and skinned
and rolled up like a tongue. I freeze them,
   speechless, angelic   10
instruments. I have a choir of them.
   Alive, they feed

driving their bodies through the mud,
   mud through their flesh.
See how white they become. High above,   15
   the water thins
to blue, then air, then less. . . .
   These aren't as sweet

as those that shine up there,
   quick schools   20
forever trying to slur over, become water.
   But these belong to us

who cannot fall out of this world
        but only deeper

into it, driving it into the white   25
        of our eyes. Muddy
daylight, we utter it, we drown in it.
        You can stay dry
if you can step between the raindrops
        mother's mother   30

said. She's words now you can't hear.
        I try to wind my way
between what's here: chalk, lily, milk,
        titanium, snow—
as far as I can say   35
        these appleblossoms house

five shades of white, and yet
        I know there's more.
Between my held breath and its small hot
        death, a garden,   40
Whiteness, grows. Its icy fruit
        seems true,

it glows. *For free* he says
        so that I can't refuse.

1983

At Luca Signorelli's Resurrection of the Body[1]

See how they hurry
        to enter
their bodies,
        these spirits.
Is it better, flesh,   5
        that they

---

[1] Painting depicting the general resurrection of humankind before the Last Judgment at the end of the world; painted by the Italian Luca Signorelli (1441?–1523) and located in Orvieto, Italy.

should hurry so?
        From above
the green-winged angels
            blare down   10
trumpets and light. But
        they don't care,

they hurry to congregate,
        they hurry
into speech, until   15
        it's a marketplace,
it is humanity. But still
        we wonder

in the chancel
        of the dark cathedral,   20
is it better, back?
        The artist
has tried to make it so: each tendon
        they press

to re-enter   25
        is perfect. But is it
perfection
        they're after,
pulling themselves up
        through the soil   30

into the weightedness, the color,
        into the eye
of the painter? Outside
        it is 1500,
all round the cathedral   35
        streets hurry to open

through the wild
        silver grasses. . . .
The men and women
        on the cathedral wall   40
do not know how,
        having come this far,

to stop their
        hurrying. They amble off
in groups, in   45
        couples. Soon

some are clothed, there is
        distance, there is

perspective. Standing below them
        in the church   50
in Orvieto, how can we
        tell them
to be stern and brazen
        and slow,

that there is no   55
        entrance,
only entering. They keep on
        arriving,
wanting names,
        wanting   60

happiness. In his studio
        Luca Signorelli
in the name of God
        and Science
and the believable   65
        broke into the body

studying arrival.
        But the wall
of the flesh
        opens endlessly,   70
its vanishing point so deep
        and receding

we have yet to find it,
        to have it
stop us. So he cut   75
        deeper,
graduating slowly
        from the symbolic

to the beautiful. How far
        is true?   80
When his one son
        died violently,
he had the body brought to him
        and laid it

on the drawing-table,   85
        and stood

at a certain distance
      awaiting the best
possible light, the best depth
of day,   90

then with beauty and care
      and technique
and judgement, cut into
      shadow, cut
into bone and sinew and every   95
      pocket

in which the cold light
      pooled.
It took him days
      that deep   100
caress, cutting,
      unfastening,

until his mind
      could climb into
the open flesh and   105
      mend itself.

1983

Rita Dove
b. 1952

Rita Dove went to Miami University as a Presidential Scholar from Ohio and graduated *summa cum laude* in English. She spent 1974 and 1975 studying modern European literature as a Fulbright fellow at the University of Tübingen in Germany, then took an M.F.A. at the Iowa writers' workshop. She is now an associate professor of English at Arizona State University in Tempe. She has returned to Germany since her Fulbright year and is planning a book-length sequence on the European experience in World War I of the U.S. 369th Regiment, a black American volunteer regiment under French command. She writes, "I have long been involved with the exploration of lyrical possibilities of the historical poem, with particular emphasis on the history-within-the-history of Blacks in America." Before the book on the black regiment, Dove worked on a long book, *Thomas and Beulah* (1986) about the history of blacks who migrated, as her own family did, from the South to the North—in Dove's case, to Akron, Ohio. These sequences are organized not narratively but as a series of lyrical instants.

Dove's gift as a poet is to compress what is extended over time into a collage of vivid parts. Often, as the parts are assembled, one does not see how they will fit together; there is a piece, and another piece, a tonality, and another tonality; then, toward the end of the poem, the relations are drawn, the pieces slip into place, the tonalities converge, and the whole complex can at last be seen. It is a brilliant technique, in which the visible presence of imaginative restructuring of experience manifests itself as poetic voltage. Though Dove has, as she says, a continuing interest in the interpreting of the black experience in America and elsewhere, she has written with equal intensity of the life she has seen in Germany and of emotional life (especially that of adolescence). She writes sparely and plainly, and though she can be betrayed into some falsity of voice in trying to reconstruct the voices of nineteenth-century slaves, when she steers clear of historic fustian her historic sense is strong and vivifying.

Texts:
"Geometry," "Adolescence—II," "Nexus," and
"Ö" from *The Yellow House on the Corner,*
1980.
"Dusting," "The Fish in the Stone," and
"Parsley" from *Museum,* 1983.

Geometry

I prove a theorem and the house expands:
the windows jerk free to hover near the ceiling,
the ceiling floats away with a sigh.

As the walls clear themselves of everything
but transparency, the scent of carnations   5
leaves with them. I am out in the open

and above the windows have hinged into butterflies,
sunlight glinting where they've intersected.
They are going to some point true and unproven.

1980

Adolescence—II

Although it is night, I sit in the bathroom, waiting.
Sweat prickles behind my knees, the baby-breasts are alert.
Venetian blinds slice up the moon; the tiles quiver in pale strips.

Then they come, the three seal men with eyes as round
As dinner plates and eyelashes like sharpened tines.   5
They bring the scent of licorice. One sits in the washbowl,

One on the bathtub edge; one leans against the door.
"Can you feel it yet?" they whisper.
I don't know what to say, again. They chuckle,

Patting their sleek bodies with their hands.   10
"Well, maybe next time." And they rise,
Glittering like pools of ink under moonlight,

And vanish. I clutch at the ragged holes
They leave behind, here at the edge of darkness.
Night rests like a ball of fur on my tongue.   15
1980

Nexus

I wrote stubbornly into the evening.
At the window, a giant praying mantis
rubbed his monkey wrench head against the glass,
begging vacantly with pale eyes;

and the commas leapt at me like worms   5
or miniature scythes blackened with age.
The praying mantis screeched louder,
his ragged jaws opening onto formlessness.

I walked outside;
the grass hissed at my heels.   10
Up ahead in the lapping darkness
he wobbled, magnified and absurdly green,
a brontosaurus,[1] a poet.
1980

---

[1] Prehistoric large, lizardlike animal.

Ö

Shape the lips to an *o*, say *a*.
That's *island*.

One word of Swedish has changed the whole neighborhood.
When I look up, the yellow house on the corner
is a galleon stranded in flowers. Around it   5

the wind. Even the high roar of a leaf-mulcher
could be the horn-blast from a ship
as it skirts the misted shoals.

We don't need much more to keep things going.
Families complete themselves   10
and refuse to budge from the present,
the present extends its glass forehead to sea
(backyard breezes, scattered cardinals)

and if, one evening, the house on the corner
took off over the marshland,   15
neither I nor my neighbor
would be amazed. Sometimes

a word is found so right it trembles
at the slightest explanation.
You start out with one thing, end   20
up with another, and nothing's
like it used to be, not even the future.

1980

Dusting

Every day a wilderness—no
shade in sight. Beulah
patient among knickknacks,
the solarium a rage
of light, a grainstorm   5

as her gray cloth brings
dark wood to life.

Under her hand scrolls
and crests gleam
darker still. What   10
was his name, that
silly boy at the fair with
the rifle booth? And his kiss and
the clear bowl with one bright
fish, rippling   15
wound!

Not Michael—
something finer. Each dust
stroke a deep breath and
the canary in bloom.   20
Wavery memory: home
from a dance, the front door
blown open and the parlor
in snow, she rushed
the bowl to the stove, watched   25
as the locket of ice
dissolved and he
swam free.

That was years before
Father gave her up   30
with her name, years before
her name grew to mean
Promise, then
Desert-in-Peace.[1]
Long before the shadow and   35
sun's accomplice, the tree.

Maurice.

1983

---

[1] Both translate the name Beulah.

The Fish in the Stone

The fish in the stone
would like to fall
back into the sea.

He is weary
of analysis, the small   5
predictable truths.
He is weary of waiting
in the open,
his profile stamped
by a white light.   10

In the ocean the silence
moves and moves

and so much is unnecessary!
Patient, he drifts
until the moment comes   15
to cast his
skeletal blossom.

The fish in the stone
knows to fail is
to do the living   20
a favor.

He knows why the ant
engineers a gangster's
funeral, garish
and perfectly amber.   25
He knows why the scientist
in secret delight
strokes the fern's
voluptuous braille.

1983

Parsley[1]

1. The Cane Fields

There is a parrot imitating spring
in the palace, its feathers parsley green.
Out of the swamp the cane appears

to haunt us, and we cut it down. El General
searches for a word; he is all the world   5
there is. Like a parrot imitating spring,

we lie down screaming as rain punches through
and we come up green. We cannot speak an R—
out of the swamp, the cane appears

and then the mountain we call in whispers *Katalina*.[2]   10
The children gnaw their teeth to arrowheads.
There is a parrot imitating spring.

El General has found his word: *perejil*.
Who says it, lives. He laughs, teeth shining
out of the swamp. The cane appears   15

in our dreams, lashed by wind and streaming.
And we lie down. For every drop of blood
there is a parrot imitating spring.
Out of the swamp the cane appears.

2. The Palace

The word the general's chosen is parsley.   20
It is fall, when thoughts turn
to love and death; the general thinks
of his mother, how she died in the fall
and he planted her walking cane at the grave
and it flowered, each spring stolidly forming   25
four-star blossoms. The general

---

[1] Dove's note: *"Parsley:* On October 2, 1957, Rafael Trujillo (1891–1961), dictator of the Dominican Republic, ordered 20,000 blacks killed because they could not pronounce the letter "r" in *perejil,* the Spanish word for parsley."
[2] Properly "Katarina."

pulls on his boots, he stomps to
her room in the palace, the one without
curtains, the one with a parrot
in a brass ring. As he paces he wonders   30
Who can I kill today. And for a moment
the little knot of screams
is still. The parrot, who has traveled

all the way from Australia in an ivory
cage, is, coy as a widow, practising   35
spring. Ever since the morning
his mother collapsed in the kitchen
while baking skull-shaped candies
for the Day of the Dead,[3] the general
has hated sweets. He orders pastries   40
brought up for the bird; they arrive

dusted with sugar on a bed of lace.
The knot in his throat starts to twitch;
he sees his boots the first day in battle
splashed with mud and urine   45
as a soldier falls at his feet amazed—
how stupid he looked!—at the sound
of artillery. *I never thought it would sing*
the soldier said, and died. Now

the general sees the fields of sugar   50
cane, lashed by rain and streaming.
He sees his mother's smile, the teeth
gnawed to arrowheads. He hears
the Haitians sing without R's
as they swing the great machetes: 55
Katalina, they sing, *Katalina,*

mi madle, mi amol en muelte.[4] God knows
his mother was no stupid woman; she
could roll an R like a queen. Even
a parrot can roll an R! In the bare room   60
the bright feathers arch in a parody
of greenery, as the last pale crumbs
disappear under the blackened tongue. Someone

calls out his name in a voice
so like his mother's, a startled tear   65

[3] November 1, Feast of All Souls.
[4] "My mother, my love in death." In the
Spanish, the *r*'s have been changed to *l*'s.

splashes the tip of his right boot.
My mother, my love in death.
The general remembers the tiny green sprigs
men of his village wore in their capes
to honor the birth of a son. He will   70
order many, this time, to be killed

for a single, beautiful word.
1983

Acknowledgments

Henry Adams: From *The Education of Henry Adams.* Copyright 1918 by the Massachusetts Historical Society. Copyright 1946 by Charles F. Adams. Reprinted by permission of Houghton Mifflin Company. Abridged from Chapter VI of *History of the United States of America During the First Administration of Thomas Jefferson,* Vol. 1 (New York: Charles Scribner's Sons 1889). Reprinted with permission of Charles Scribner's Sons.

James Agee: From *Let Us Now Praise Famous Men,* by James Agee and Walker Evans. Copyright 1939 and 1940 by James Agee. Copyright 1941 by James Agee and Walker Evans. Copyright © renewed 1969 by Mia Fritsch Agee. Reprinted by permission of Houghton Mifflin Company.

Frederick Lewis Allen: Excerpt from p. 244 in *Only Yesterday,* by Frederick Lewis Allen. Copyright 1939, 1940 by Harper & Row, Publishers, Inc.

A. R. Ammons: "The City Limits," "Hope's Okay," "Transaction," "The Eternal City," "Grace Abounding," "Clarity," "Classic," "Body Politic," "Cascadilla Falls," "Treaties," "Mountain Talk," "Reflective," "Hardweed Path Going," "Apologia pro Vita Sua" from *Collected Poems, 1941–1971,* by A. R. Ammons. Copyright © 1972 by A. R. Ammons. "Easter Morning" from *A Coast of Trees, Poems,* by A. R. Ammons. Copyright © 1981 by A. R. Ammons. "Bonus" from *The Selected Poems, 1951–1977,* by A. R. Ammons. Copyright © 1977, 1975, 1974, 1972, 1971, 1970, 1966, 1965, 1964, 1955 by A. R. Ammons. All reprinted by permission of W. W. Norton & Company, Inc.

Rodolfo A. Anaya: "B. Traven Is Alive and Well in Cuernavaca." © Rodolfo A. Anaya. Reprinted by permission of the author.

Sherwood Anderson: "The Egg." Copyright 1921 by B. W. Huebsch, Inc. Copyright renewed 1948 by Eleanor Copenhaver Anderson. Reprinted by permission of Harold Ober Associates Incorporated. "Departure," "Mother," "Hands," and "The Book of the Grotesque." From *Winesburg, Ohio,* by Sherwood Anderson. Copyright 1919 by B. W. Huebsch. Copyright renewed 1947 by Eleanor Copenhaver Anderson. Reprinted by permission of Viking Penguin, Inc.

Max Apple: "Free Agents" from *Free Agents,* by Max Apple. Copyright © 1983 by Max Apple. Reprinted by permission of Harper & Row, Publishers, Inc.

John Ashbery: "Some Trees," "The Orioles," "The Painter," from *Some Trees* Copyright © 1956 by John Ashbery. "These Lacustrine Cities" from *Rivers and Mountains* Copyright © 1962 by John Ashbery. "Soonest Mended," "Years of Indiscretion" from *The Double Dream of Spring* Copyright © 1970 by John Ashbery. Reprinted by permission of Georges Borchardt, Inc. and the author. "Pyrography," "Street Musicians," "Syringa" from *Houseboat Days,* by John Ashbery. Copyright © 1975, 1976, 1977 by John Ashbery. "Drunken Americans" from *Shadow Train,* by John Ashbery. Copyright © 1980, 1981 by John Ashbery. "A Love Poem," "Many Wagons Ago," "Landscapeople" from *As We Know,* by John Ashbery. Copyright © 1979 by John Ashbery. "As One Put Drunk into the Packet-Boat," "The One Thing That Can Save America" from *Self-Portrait in a Convex Mirror,* by John Ashbery. Copyright © 1972, 1973, 1974, 1975 by John Ashbery. From "The Recital" from *Three Poems,* by John Ashbery. Copyright © 1970, 1971, 1972 by John Ashbery. Reprinted by permission of Viking Penguin Inc.

James Baldwin: "Sonny's Blues" from *Going to Meet the Man,* by James Baldwin. Copyright © 1948, 1951, 1957, 1958, 1960, 1965 by James Baldwin. Reprinted by permission of Doubleday & Company, Inc.

John Barth: Excerpt from *The Sot-Weed Factor,* by John Barth. Copyright © 1960, 1967 by John Barth. "Night Sea Journey" from *Lost in the Funhouse,* by John Barth. Both reprinted by permission of Doubleday & Company, Inc. "The Literature of Exhaustion." Copyright © 1967 by John Barth. Reprinted by permission of International Creative Management.

Donald Barthelme: "Robert Kennedy Saved from Drowning" from *Unspeakable Practices, Unnatural Acts,* by Donald Barthelme. Copyright © 1968 by Donald Barthelme. Reprinted by permission of Farrar, Straus and Giroux, Inc.

Ann Beattie: "Jacklighting" from *The Burning House,* by Ann Beattie. Copyright © 1982 by Irony and Pity, Inc. Reprinted by permission of Random House, Inc.

Thomas Beer: From *The Mauve Decade: American Life at the End of the Nineteenth Century* (Alfred A. Knopf, Inc., 1926).

Saul Bellow: *Seize the Day,* by Saul Bellow. Copyright © 1956, renewed © 1984 by Saul Bellow. Reprinted by permission of Viking Penguin Inc.

John Berryman: "Huffy Henry," "Filling her compact & delicious body," "Henry sats," "Life, friends," "The glories of the world," "There sat down once," "He stared at ruin," "Seedy Henry" from *77 Dream Songs,* by John Berryman. Copyright © 1959, 1962, 1963, 1964 by John Berryman. "Three Limbs," "So Long? Stevens," "The Marker slants" from *His Toy, His Dream, His Rest,* by John Berryman. Copyright © 1964, 1965, 1966, 1967, 1968 by John Berryman. "With arms outflung," "Old Codger Henry," "All projects failed" from *Henry's Fate,* by John Berryman. Copyright © 1977 by Mrs. Kate Berryman. Excerpt from *Homage to Mistress Bradstreet,* by John Berryman. Copyright © 1956 by John Berryman. Copyright renewed © 1984 by Mrs. Kate Berryman. Reprinted by permission of Farrar, Straus and Giroux, Inc.

Frank Bidart: "Self-Portrait" and "Another Life" from *Golden State,* by Frank Bidart. Reprinted by permission of the publisher, George Braziller, Inc., New York. "Happy Birthday" copyright © 1974, 1977 by Frank Bidart. "Elegy" copyright © 1977 by Frank Bidart. Both from *The Book of the Body.* Reprinted by permission of the author.

Elizabeth Bishop: "The Fish," "Over 2000 Illustrations and a Complete Concordance," "The Bight," "At the Fishhouses," "Questions of Travel," "The Armadillo," "Sestina," "Filling Station," "In the Waiting Room," "Crusoe in England," "Poem," "North Haven" from *The Complete Poems 1927–1979,* by Elizabeth Bishop. Copyright © 1940, 1947, 1948, 1955, 1956, 1957, 1971, 1972, 1978 by Elizabeth Bishop. Copyright renewed © 1974, 1976 by Elizabeth Bishop. Copyright © 1983 by Alice Helen Methfessel. "At the Fishhouses," "Questions of Travel," "The Armadillo," "Sestina," "Filling Station," "Crusoe in England," "Poem," "North Haven" originally appeared in *The New Yorker.* Reprinted by permission of Farrar, Straus and Giroux, Inc.

Michael Blumenthal: "I Have Lived This Way for Years and Do Not Wish to Change" and "Washington Heights" from *Sympathetic Magic* (Water Mark Press). © 1980 Michael Blumenthal. "Over Ohio" and "Wishful Thinking." From *Days We Would Rather Know,* by Michael Blumenthal. Copyright © 1980, 1981, 1982, 1983, 1984 by Michael Blumenthal. Reprinted by permission of Viking Penguin Inc.

Harold Brodkey: "Verona: A Young Woman Speaks," by Harold Brodkey. Copyright © 1977 by Harold Brodkey. Reprinted by permission of International Creative Management.

Gwendolyn Brooks: From *The World of Gwendolyn Brooks,* by Gwendolyn Brooks: "The Mother" (pp. 5–6). Copyright 1945 Gwendolyn Brooks Blakely. "A Bronzeville Mother Loiters in Mississippi. Meanwhile, a Mississippi Mother Burns Bacon" (pp. 317–323), "The Last Quatrain of the Ballad of Emmett Till" (p. 324), and "The Lovers of the Poor" (pp. 333–336). Copyright © 1960 by Gwendolyn Brooks. "What shall I give my children? who are poor" (p. 100). Copyright 1949 by

Gwendolyn Brooks Blakely. Chapter 18 "We're the Only Colored People Here" in *Maud Martha* from *The World of Gwendolyn Brooks.* Copyright 1953 by Gwendolyn Brooks Blakely. Reprinted by permission of Harper & Row, Publishers, Inc.

Claude Brown: From *Manchild in the Promised Land,* by Claude Brown. Copyright © 1965 by Claude Brown. Reprinted with permission of the publisher.

Raymond Carver: "Cathedral" from *Cathedral,* by Raymond Carver. Copyright © 1981, 1982, 1983 by Raymond Carver. Reprinted by permission of Alfred A. Knopf, Inc.

Willa Cather: "Neighbor Rosicky" from *Obscure Destinies,* by Willa Cather. Copyright 1930, 1932 by Willa Cather and renewed 1958, 1960 by the Executors of the Estate of Willa Cather. Reprinted by permission of Alfred A. Knopf, Inc.

John Cheever: "The Fourth Alarm." Copyright © 1970 by John Cheever. Reprinted from *The Stories of John Cheever,* by permission of Alfred A. Knopf, Inc.

Kate Chopin: "The Storm." Reprinted by permission of Louisiana State University Press from *The Complete Works of Kate Chopin,* by Per Seyersted, copyright © 1969.

Winston S. Churchill: From *Winston S. Churchill, Volume IV, 1916–1922: The Stricken World,* edited by Martin Gilbert. Copyright © 1975 by C&T Publications, Ltd. Published by Heinemann and Houghton Mifflin. Reprinted by permission of Houghton Mifflin Company and Curtis Brown Ltd.

Amy Clampitt: "From a Clinic Waiting Room." Reprinted by permission; © 1982 Amy Clampitt. Originally appeared in *The New Yorker.* "A Procession at Candlemas," "The Woodlot," "The Kingfisher." Copyright © 1981, 1983 by Amy Clampitt. Reprinted from *The Kingfisher,* by Amy Clampitt, by permission of Alfred A. Knopf, Inc.

Hart Crane: "The Broken Tower," "Proem: To Brooklyn Bridge," "The Dance," "Atlantis," "Black Tambourine," "Chaplinesque," "Repose of Rivers," "Passage," "At Melville's Tomb," "Voyages," "O Carib Isle," "The Idiot," "I am concerned with the future of America," "The function of poetry" are reprinted from *The Complete Poems and Selected Letters and Prose of Hart Crane,* Edited by Brom Weber, by permission of Liveright Publishing Corporation. Copyright 1933 © 1958, 1966 by Liveright Publishing Corporation.

Stephen Crane: "The Bride Came to Yellow Sky," "The Open Boat" from *The University of Virginia Edition of Works of Stephen Crane* Vol. 5, *Tales of Adventure,* Edited by Fredson Bowers, Charlottesville: The University Press of Virginia, 1970. "An Episode of War" from *The University of Virginia Edition of Works of Stephen Crane* Vol. VI, *Tales of War,* Edited by Fredson Bowers, Charlottesville: The University Press of Virginia, 1970. "The Men in the Storm" from *The University of Virginia Edition of Works of Stephen Crane* Vol. VIII, *Tales, Sketches, and Reports,* Edited by Fredson Bowers, Charlottesville: The University Press of Virginia, 1973.

Countee Cullen: From *On These I Stand,* by Countee Cullen: "Heritage," "Yet Do I Marvel," "To Certain Critics," and "Incident." Copyright 1925 by Harper &

Row, Publishers, Inc.; renewed 1953 by Ida M. Cullen. Reprinted by permission of Harper & Row, Publishers, Inc.

E. E. Cummings: "this little bride & groom are" from *Complete Poems 1913–1962*, by E. E. Cummings. Copyright 1938 by E. E. Cummings; renewed 1966 by Marion Morehouse Cummings. "anyone lived in a pretty how town" from *Complete Poems 1913–1962*, by E. E. Cummings. Copyright 1940 by E. E. Cummings; renewed 1968 by Marion Morehouse Cummings. "l(a" from *Complete Poems 1913–1962*, by E. E. Cummings. Copyright © 1958 by E. E. Cummings. Reprinted from *Complete Poems 1913–1962*, by E. E. Cummings by permission of Harcourt Brace Jovanovich, Inc. "my sweet old etcetera," "next to of course god america i," "she being Brand," "mr youse needn't be so spry" from *IS 5, Poems*, by E. E. Cummings. Copyright 1926 by Horace Liveright. Copyright renewed 1953 by E. E. Cummings. "i sing of Olaf glad and big" from *ViVa*, by E. E. Cummings. Copyright 1931, 1959 by E. E. Cummings. Copyright © 1979, 1973 by The Trustees for the E. E. Cummings Trust. Copyright © 1979, 1973 by George James Firmage. "The Cambridge Ladies," "in Just-" from *Tulips & Chimneys*, by E. E. Cummings. Copyright 1923, 1925, and renewed 1951, 1953 by E. E. Cummings. Copyright © 1973, 1976 by the Trustees for the E. E. Cummings Trust. Copyright © 1973, 1976 by George James Firmage. "may i feel said he," "r-p-o-p-h-e-s-s-a-g-r," from *No Thanks*, by E. E. Cummings. Copyright 1935 by E. E. Cummings. Copyright © 1968 by Marion Morehouse Cummings. Copyright © 1973, 1978 by the Trustees for the E. E. Cummings Trust. Copyright © 1973, 1978 by George James Firmage. Reprinted by permission of Liveright Publishing Corporation.

James Dickey: "Cherrylog Road." Copyright © 1963 by James Dickey. Reprinted from *Helmets*. "Cherrylog Road" first appeared in *The New Yorker*. "Buckdancer's Choice." Copyright © 1965 by James Dickey. Reprinted from *Buckdancer's Choice*. "Buckdancer's Choice" first appeared in *The New Yorker*. "The Sheep Child." Copyright © 1966 by James Dickey. Reprinted from *Falling*. "The Hospital Window." Copyright © 1962 by James Dickey. Reprinted from *Drowning with Others*. "The Hospital Window" first appeared in *Poetry*. All reprinted by permission of Wesleyan University Press.

Emily Dickinson: Reprinted by permission of the publishers and Trustees of Amherst College from *The Poems of Emily Dickinson*, edited by Thomas H. Johnson. Cambridge, Mass: The Belknap Press of Harvard University Press, Copyright 1951, © 1955, 1979, 1983 by the President and Fellows of Harvard College. Poems 341, 379, 448, 569, 657, 721, 745, 754, 910, 1071, 1248, 1545, and 1670 from *The Complete Poems of Emily Dickinson*, edited by Thomas H. Johnson. Copyright 1914, 1929, 1935, 1942 by Martha Dickinson Bianchi; Copyright renewed 1957, 1963 by Mary L. Hampson. By permission of Little, Brown and Company.

Joan Didion: "Some Dreamers of the Golden Dream," excerpts from "Slouching Towards Bethlehem" from *Slouching Towards Bethlehem*, by Joan Didion. Copyright © 1966, 1967 by Joan Didion. Reprinted by permission of Farrar, Straus and Giroux, Inc.

John Dos Passos: "Newsreel XLV," "The American Plan," "The Camera Eye (46)," "Newsreel LXVII," "Newsreel LXVI," "The Camera Eye (50)," "Newsreel LXVIII," "The Camera Eye (51)," and "Power Superpower," from *U.S.A., The Big Money* and from *Manhattan Transfer* copyright by Elizabeth H. Dos Passos, co-executor, Estate of John Dos Passos. Reprinted by permission of Mrs. Dos Passos.

Rita Dove: "Geometry," "Adolescence—II," "Nexus," "Ö" from *The Yellow House on the Corner* (Carnegie-Mellon University Press, 1980). "Dusting," "The Fish in the Stone," "Parsley" from *Museum* (Carnegie-Mellon University Press, 1983). Reprinted by permission of Carnegie-Mellon University Press.

Theodore Dreiser: From *Sister Carrie*. Copyright by The Trustees of the University of Pennsylvania. Reprinted by permission of University of Pennsylvania Library.

T. S. Eliot: From "Tradition and the Individual Talent" in *Selected Essays*, by T. S. Eliot, copyright 1950 by Harcourt Brace Jovanovich, Inc.; renewed 1978 by Esme Valerie Eliot. "The Love Song of J. Alfred Prufrock," "La Figlia Che Piange," "Whispers of Immortality," "Sweeney Among the Nightingales," and "The Waste Land" with Eliot's notes on "The Waste Land," from *Collected Poems 1909–1962*, by T. S. Eliot, copyright 1936 by Harcourt Brace Jovanovich, Inc.; copyright © 1963, 1964 by T. S. Eliot. "Burnt Norton" from *Four Quartets*, copyright 1943 by T. S. Eliot; renewed 1971 by Esme Valerie Eliot. All reprinted by permission of Harcourt Brace Jovanovich, Inc. and Faber and Faber Ltd. "The Death of Saint Narcissus" from *Poems Written in Early Youth*, by T. S. Eliot. Copyright © 1967 by T. S. Eliot. Reprinted by permission of Farrar, Straus, and Giroux, Inc. and Faber and Faber Ltd.

Ralph Ellison: From *Invisible Man*, by Ralph Ellison. Copyright 1952 by Ralph Ellison. "Twentieth-Century Fiction and the Black Mask of Humanity" copyright 1953 by Ralph Ellison. Reprinted from *Shadow and Act*, by Ralph Ellison. Both reprinted by permission of Random House, Inc.

William Faulkner: "Spotted Horses." Copyright 1931 and renewed 1959 by William Faulkner. Reprinted from *Scribner's* Magazine by permission of Random House, Inc. An extended version of this story appears as part of *The Hamlet*, by William Faulkner. "That Evening Sun." Copyright © 1959 by William Faulkner. Reprinted from *Collected Stories of William Faulkner*, by permission of Random House, Inc.

F. Scott Fitzgerald: Excerpted from *The Great Gatsby*. Copyright 1925 Charles Scribner's Sons; copyright renewed 1953 Frances Scott Fitzgerald Lanahan. "The Rich Boy" from *All the Sad Young Men*. Copyright 1925, 1926 Consolidated Magazines Corporation; copyright renewed 1953, 1954 Frances Scott Fitzgerald Lanahan. Reprinted with the permission of Charles Scribner's Sons. *The Crack-Up.* Copyright 1945 by New Directions Publishing Corporation. Reprinted by permission of New Directions Publishing Corporation.

Robert Frost: "Mowing," "October," "Reluctance," "Mending Wall," "Home Burial," "After Apple-Picking," "The Road Not Taken," "The Oven Bird," "Birches," "Fire and Ice," "Nothing Gold Can Stay," "Stopping by Woods on a Snowy Evening," "For Once, Then, Something," "To Earthward," "The Need of Being Versed in Country Things," "Once by the Pacific," "Immigrants," "Desert Places," "Design," "Provide, Provide," "The Most of It," "The Gift Outright," and "Time Out" from *The Poetry of Robert Frost,* edited by Edward Connery Lathem. Copyright 1916, 1923, 1928, 1930, 1934, 1939, 1947, © 1969 by Holt, Rinehart and Winston. Copyright 1936, 1942, 1944, 1951, © 1956, 1958, 1962 by Robert Frost. Copyright © 1964, 1967, 1970, 1975 by Lesley Frost Ballantine. From "The Figure a Poem Makes" in *Selected Prose of Robert Frost,* edited by Hyde Cox and Edward Connery Lathem. Copyright 1939, © 1967 by Holt, Rinehart and Winston, Publishers. Reprinted by permission of Holt, Rinehart and Winston, Publishers.

William Gass: "In the Heart of the Heart of the Country," © 1968 by William Gass. Reprinted by permission of International Creative Management.

Ray Ginger: From *An Age of Excess: The United States from 1877 to 1914,* Second Edn., by Ray Ginger (Copyright © 1965, 1975 by Ray Ginger). Reprinted with permission of the publisher.

Allen Ginsberg: "Kaddish" and "The Lion for Real." Copyright © 1961 by Allen Ginsberg. "American Change." Copyright © 1963 by Allen Ginsberg. "Chances R." Copyright © 1968 by Allen Ginsberg. "Mugging." Copyright © 1977 by Allen Ginsberg. "Howl, Part I," "A Supermarket in California," "Sunflower Sutra," and "America." Copyright © 1956, 1959 by Allen Ginsberg. Reprinted by permission of City Lights Books. From notes for *Howl.* Copyright © 1959, 1985 by Allen Ginsberg. From Introduction to Jack Kerouac's *Visions of Cody.* © Allen Ginsberg. Reprinted by permission of Andrew Wylie Agency and the author.

Louise Glück: "The School Children," "The Apple Trees," "Poem," "Messengers," "For My Mother," and "All Hallows" copyright © 1975 by Louise Glück. From *The House on Marshland,* by Louise Glück, published by The Ecco Press in 1975. Reprinted by permission. "The Garden," "Lamentations," and "The Drowned Children" copyright © 1980 by Louise Glück. From *Descending Figure,* by Louise Glück, published by The Ecco Press in 1980. Reprinted by permission.

Albert Goldbarth: "How the Sky Counts Years," "Before," "Family/Grove," "The Tip," and "Object Functionsong" from *Faith* (New Rivers Press). © 1981 by Albert Goldbarth. Reprinted by permission of the author. "A History of Civilization," "And Now Farley Is Going To Sing *While I Drink a Glass of Water!,*" "The World of Expectations," and "The Well," copyright © 1973, 1974, 1976, 1980, 1981, 1983 by Albert Goldbarth. Reprinted from *Original Light: New & Selected Poems 1973–1983* by permission of Ontario Review Press.

Jorie Graham: "The Geese," "Over and Over Stitch," "Mind" from *Hubrids of Plants and of Ghosts* (in The Princeton Series of Contemporary Poets), by Jorie Graham. Copyright © 1980 by Princeton University Press. ("The Geese" first appeared in *The Iowa Review.* "Mind" first appeared in *Water Table.*) "San Sepolcro," "My Garden, My Daylight," and "At Luca Signorelli's Resurrection of the Body" from *Erosion* (in The Princeton Series of Contemporary Poets), by Jorie Graham. Copyright © 1983 by Princeton University Press. ("San Sepolcro" first appeared in *Antaeus.* "My Garden, My Daylight" first appeared in *New England Review* and *Pushcart Anthology.* "At Luca Signorelli's Resurrection of the Body" first appeared in *The American Poetry Review.*) All reprinted by permission of Princeton University

Press. "Some Notes on Silence." Reprinted by permission of the author.

Michael S. Harper: "American History," "Dear John, Dear Coltrane," "This Is My Son's Song," "Martin's Blues," "Last Affair," and "Grandfather," "Nightmare Begins Responsibility," and "Tongue-Tied in Black and White" from *Images of Kin: New and Selected Poems* © 1970, 1971, 1972, 1973, 1974, 1975, 1976, 1977 by Michael S. Harper. Reprinted by permission of the publisher University of Illinois Press.

Robert Hayden: "Mourning Poem for the Queen of Sunday," "Homage to the Empress of the Blues," "Tour 5," "Sphinx," "Those Winter Sundays," "Middle Passage," "Frederick Douglass" are reprinted from *Angle of Ascent, New and Selected Poems,* by Robert Hayden, by permission of Liveright Publishing Corporation. Copyright © 1975, 1972, 1970, 1966 by Robert Hayden.

Ernest Hemingway: Excerpted from *A Moveable Feast.* Copyright © 1964 Mary Hemingway. "Big Two-Hearted River" from *In Our Time.* Copyright 1925 Charles Scribner's Sons; copyright renewed 1953 Ernest Hemingway. Reprinted with the permission of Charles Scribner's Sons. "Two Tales of Darkness: A Man of the World, Get a Seeing-Eye Dog" © Copyright 1957 Ernest Hemingway. © Copyright renewed 1985 Mary Hemingway. Reprinted by permission of Mary Hemingway.

Michael Herr: From *Dispatches,* by Michael Herr. Copyright © 1977 by Michael Herr. Reprinted by permission of Alfred A. Knopf, Inc.

John Hersey: From *Hiroshima,* by John Hersey. Copyright 1946 and renewed 1974 by John Hersey. Reprinted by permission of Alfred A. Knopf, Inc. Originally appeared in *The New Yorker.*

William Dean Howells: From *Works of William Dean Howells,* edited by David Nordloh (Indiana University Press, 1971). Reprinted by permission of Indiana University Press.

Langston Hughes: "To Black Writers." Copyright 1935 by International Publishers Co., Inc. "Theme for English B," "Dream Boogie," "Movies," "Same in Blues," "Sister," "Preference," "Not a Movie," "Numbers," "Advice," "Ballad of the Landlord," "Cafe: 3 A.M.," "Low to High," "High to Low," "Deferred," "World War II," "Passing," "Likewise," "Silver," "Good Morning," "Comment on Curb," "Letter," and "Island." Copyright 1951 by Langston Hughes. Copyright renewed 1979 by George Houston Bass. "Thank You, M'am." Copyright © 1958 by Langston Hughes. Copyright renewed 1986 by George Houston Bass. Reprinted by permission of Harold Ober Associates Incorporated. "Feet Live Their Own Life" from *The Best of Simple,* by Langston Hughes. Copyright © 1961 by Langston Hughes. Reprinted by permission of Hill & Wang, a division of Farrar, Straus and Giroux, Inc. "The Negro Speaks of Rivers," "I, Too," "Harlem." Copyright 1926 by Alfred A. Knopf, Inc. and renewed 1954 by Langston Hughes. Copyright 1951 by Langston Hughes. Reprinted from *Selected Poems of Langston Hughes,* by permission of Alfred A. Knopf, Inc.

Zora Neale Hurston: From pp. 38–44, 125–137 in *Their Eyes Were Watching God,* by Zora Neale Hurston (J. B. Lippincott Co.). Copyright 1937 by Harper & Row,

Publishers, Inc.; renewed 1965 by John C. Hurston and Joel Hurston. Reprinted by permission of Harper & Row, Publishers, Inc. "The Gilded Six-bits." Reprinted by permission of the Zora Neale Hurston Estate.

Alice James: Reprinted by permission of Dodd, Mead & Company from *The Diary of Alice James,* edited by Leon Edel. Copyright 1934 by Dodd, Mead & Company, Inc. Copyright © 1964 by Leon Edel.

Henry James: Excerpts from *The American Scene,* by Henry James. Edited by Leon Edel (Indiana University Press, 1968). Reprinted by permission of Indiana University Press.

Randall Jarrell: "The Woman at the Washington Zoo," in *The Woman at the Washington Zoo.* Copyright © 1960 by Randall Jarrell. Reprinted with the permission of Atheneum Publishers. "Next Day." Reprinted with permission of Macmillan Publishing Company from *The Lost World,* by Randall Jarrell. Copyright © Randall Jarrell 1963, 1965. Originally appeared in *The New Yorker.* "The Death of the Ball Turret Gunner," "Losses," "A Lullaby" from *The Complete Poems,* by Randall Jarrell. Copyright 1942, 1944, 1948, copyright renewed © 1969, 1971, 1972 by Mrs. Randall Jarrell. Reprinted by permission of Farrar, Straus and Giroux, Inc.

Robinson Jeffers: "Apology for Bad Dreams," "The Torch-Bearers' Race," "Boats in a Fog." Copyright 1925 and renewed 1953 by Robinson Jeffers. Reprinted from *Selected Poems,* by Robinson Jeffers, by permission of Random House, Inc.

William Kennedy: Chapter 1 from *Ironweed,* by William Kennedy. Copyright © 1979, 1981, 1983 by William Kennedy. Reprinted by permission of Viking Penguin Inc.

Ken Kesey: From *One Flew Over the Cuckoo's Nest,* by Ken Kesey. Copyright © 1962 by Ken Kesey. Reprinted by permission of Viking Penguin Inc.

Maxine Hong Kingston: "No Name Woman" from *The Woman Warrior: Memoirs of a Girlhood Among Ghosts,* by Maxine Hong Kingston. Copyright © 1975, 1976 by Maxine Hong Kingston. Reprinted by permission of Alfred A. Knopf, Inc.

Emma Lazarus: "The New Colossus" from Morris U. Schappes, ed., *Emma Lazarus: Selections from Her Poetry and Prose,* 5th ed., 1982. Published by Emma Lazarus Federation of Jewish Women's Clubs, New York.

Sinclair Lewis: Chapter 3 from *Babbitt,* by Sinclair Lewis. Reprinted from *Babbitt,* by Sinclair Lewis by permission of Harcourt Brace Jovanovich, Inc.; copyright 1922 by Harcourt Brace Jovanovich, Inc., renewed 1950 by Sinclair Lewis. *Babbitt* is published in paperback by The New American Library, Inc. Excerpt from *Main Street,* by Sinclair Lewis. Excerpted and reprinted from *Main Street,* by Sinclair Lewis by permission of Harcourt Brace Jovanovich, Inc., renewed 1948 by Sinclair Lewis. *Main Street* is published in paperback by The New American Library Inc.

Walter Lippmann: From *A Preface to Morals,* by Walter Lippmann (Copyright 1929, and renewed 1957, by Walter Lippmann). Reprinted with permission of the publisher.

Robert Lowell: "Where the Rainbow Ends," "Mr. Edwards and the Spider" from *Lord Weary's Castle,* by Robert Lowell. Copyright 1946, 1974 by Robert Lowell. Reprinted by permission of Harcourt Brace Jovanovich, Inc. "Sailing Home from Rapallo," "Waking in the Blue," "Home After Three Months Away," "Skunk Hour" from *Life Studies,* by Robert Lowell. Copyright © 1956, 1959 by Robert Lowell. "For the Union Dead" from *For the Union Dead,* by Robert Lowell. Copyright © 1960, 1964 by Robert Lowell. "Waking Early One Sunday Morning" from *Near the Ocean,* by Robert Lowell. Copyright © 1963, 1965, 1966, 1967 by Robert Lowell. "The March I," "Death and the Bridge," "New Year's Eve 1968," excerpt from "Afterthought" from *Notebook,* by Robert Lowell. Copyright © 1967, 1968, 1969 by Robert Lowell. "Harriet," "Mexico I," "Mexico 4," "Obit" from *For Lizzie and Harriet,* by Robert Lowell. Copyright © 1967, 1968, 1969, 1970, 1973 by Robert Lowell. "History," "Volveran," "Reading Myself" from *History,* by Robert Lowell. Copyright © 1967, 1968, 1969, 1970, 1973 by Robert Lowell. "Fishnet" from *Dolphin,* by Robert Lowell. Copyright © 1973 by Robert Lowell. "For John Berryman," "For Sheridan," "Epilogue" from *Day by Day,* by Robert Lowell. Copyright © 1975, 1976, 1977 by Robert Lowell. Reprinted by permission of Farrar, Straus and Giroux, Inc.

Horace McCoy: From *They Shoot Horses, Don't They.* © 1935, © renewed 1962. Reprinted by permission of Harold Matson Company, Inc.

Larry McMurtry: From *The Last Picture Show,* by Larry McMurtry. Copyright © 1966 by Larry McMurtry. First published by The Dial Press and reprinted by the author's permission.

John McPhee: Excerpt from *Coming into the Country,* by John McPhee. Copyright © 1976, 1977 by John McPhee. Originally appeared in *The New Yorker.* Reprinted by permission of Farrar, Straus and Giroux, Inc.

Norman Mailer: From *Armies of the Night,* by Norman Mailer. Copyright © 1968 by Norman Mailer. Reprinted by arrangement with New American Library, New York, New York. From *On a Fire on the Moon,* by Norman Mailer. Copyright © 1969, 1970 by Norman Mailer. By permission of Little, Brown and Company.

Bernard Malamud: "The Magic Barrel" from *The Magic Barrel,* by Bernard Malamud. Copyright © 1954, 1958 by Bernard Malamud. Reprinted by permission of Farrar, Straus and Giroux, Inc.

David Mamet: *The Vermont Sketches.* Copyright © 1985 by David Mamet. Reprinted by permission of Grove Press, Inc.

Bobbie Ann Mason: "Detroit Skyline, 1949" in *Shiloh and Other Stories,* by Bobbie Ann Mason. Copyright © 1982 by Bobbie Ann Mason. Reprinted by permission of Harper & Row, Publishers, Inc.

H. L. Mencken: From *Prejudices: Fourth Series* (Alfred A. Knopf, Inc., 1924). From "Euphemisms" copyright 1936, © 1963 by Alfred A. Knopf, Inc. and renewed 1964 by August Mencken and Mercantile Safe Deposit and Trust Company. Reprinted from *The American Language: The Fourth Edition and the Two Supplements, Abridged, with Annotations and New Material,* by H. L. Mencken, edited by Raven I. McDavid, Jr., and David W. Maurer, by permission of the publisher. "Under the Elms" copyright

1927 by Alfred A. Knopf, Inc. and renewed 1955 by H. L. Mencken. "Imperial Purple" copyright 1931 by Alfred A. Knopf, Inc. and renewed 1959 by August Mencken and the Mercantile Safe Deposit and Trust Company. "American Culture" copyright 1920 by Alfred A. Knopf, Inc. and renewed 1948 by H. L. Mencken. Reprinted from *A Mencken Chrestomathy*, by H. L. Mencken, by permission of Alfred A. Knopf, Inc.

James Merrill: "Samos" in *Scripts for the Pageant.* Copyright © 1980 by James Merrill. "Samos" was first published in *The New Yorker.* "The world was everything . . ." from Book 9.9, in *Mirabell: Books of Number.* Copyright © 1978 by James Merrill. "L" and "Z" from "The Book of Ephraim" in *Divine Comedies.* Copyright © 1976 by James Merrill. "Geode . . . from In Nine Sleep Valley," and "Syrinx" in *Braving the Elements.* Copyright 1970, 1971, 1972 by James Merrill. "In Nine Sleep Valley" was first published in *The New Yorker.* "Matinees" in *The Fire Screen.* Copyright © 1969 by James Merrill. "The Broken Home" and "Days of 1964" in *Nights and Days.* Copyright © 1965, 1966 by James Merrill. "The Broken Home" was first published in *The New Yorker.* All reprinted with the permission of Atheneum Publishers.

W. S. Merwin: "The Fisherman" in *Green with Beasts.* Copyright © 1955, 1956 by W. S. Merwin. Reprinted from *The First Four Books of Poems.* Copyright © 1975 by W. S. Merwin. "Elegy" in *The Carrier of Ladders.* Copyright © 1970 by W. S. Merwin. "Line" in *The Compass Flower.* Copyright © 1977 by W. S. Merwin. "Noah's Raven" in *The Moving Target.* Copyright © 1962, 1963 by W. S. Merwin. "For the Anniversary of My Death," "The Asians Dying," "Some Last Questions," "For a Coming Extinction" in *The Lice.* Copyright © 1964, 1966, 1967 by W. S. Merwin. "The Asians Dying" was first published in *The New Yorker.* "Under the Migrants," "Tool," "The Chase," "Span," in *Writings to an Unfinished Accompaniment.* Copyright © 1970, 1972, 1973 by W. S. Merwin. "Odysseus" and "In Stony Country" in *The Drunk in the Furnace.* Copyright © 1960 by W. S. Merwin. Reprinted from *The First Four Books of Poems.* Copyright © 1975 by W. S. Merwin. All reprinted with the permission of Atheneum Publishers.

Arthur Miller: *Death of a Salesman,* by Arthur Miller. Copyright 1949, renewed © 1977 by Arthur Miller. Reprinted by permission of Viking Penguin Inc. This play in its printed form is designed for the reading public only. All dramatic rights in it are fully protected by copyright, and no public or private performance—professional or amateur—may be given without the written permission of the author and the payment of a royalty. As the courts have also ruled that the public reading of a play constitutes a public performance, no such reading may be given except under the conditions stated above. Communication should be addressed to the author's representative, International Creative Management, Inc., 40 W. 57th St., New York, NY 10019.

N. Scott Momaday: "The Priest of the Sun" (from pp. 89–98, 127–134) from *House Made of Dawn,* by N. Scott Momaday. Copyright © 1966, 1967, 1968 by N. Scott Momaday. Reprinted by permission of Harper & Row, Publishers, Inc.

Marianne Moore: "Poetry," "The Fish," "When I Buy Pictures," "A Grave, "No Swan So Fine," "In the Days of Prismatic Colour," "England," "New York," "Melanchthon," and "The Monkey Puzzle." Copyright 1935 by Marianne Moore, renewed 1963 by Marianne Moore and T. S. Eliot. "His Shield." Copyright 1951 by Marianne Moore, renewed 1979 by Lawrence E. Brinn and Louise Crane. "Nevertheless." Copyright 1944, and renewed 1972, by Marianne Moore. All reprinted with permission of Macmillan Publishing Company from *Collected Poems,* by Marianne Moore.

Wright Morris: "Green Grass, Blue Sky, White House" in *Real Losses, Imaginary Gains,* by Wright Morris. Copyright © 1969 by Wright Morris. Originally appeared in *The New Yorker.* Reprinted by permission of Harper & Row, Publishers, Inc.

Toni Morrison: From *Song of Solomon,* by Toni Morrison. Copyright © 1977 by Toni Morrison. Reprinted by permission of Alfred A. Knopf, Inc.

Vladimir Nabokov: Reprinted by permission of the Putnam Publishing Group from *Lolita,* by Vladimir Nabokov. Copyright © 1955 by Vladimir Nabokov. "Terra Incognita" from *A Russian Beauty and Other Stories,* by Vladimir Nabokov. Published by McGraw-Hill. Copyright 1963. Reprinted by permission of McGraw-Hill Book Company. "Terra Incognita" was first published in *The New Yorker.*

Howard Nemerov: "The Daily Globe," "To David, About His Education," "Thirtieth Anniversary Report of the Class of '41," "The Sweeper of Ways," and "Ginkgoes in Fall" from *The Collected Poems of Howard Nemerov.* The University of Chicago Press, 1977. Reprinted by permission of the author.

Joyce Carol Oates: Reprinted from *The Wheel of Love and Other Stories,* by Joyce Carol Oates by permission of the publisher, Vanguard Press, Inc. Copyright, © 1970, 1969, 1968, 1967, 1966, 1965, by Joyce Carol Oates.

Flannery O'Connor: "Good Country People" and "A Good Man Is Hard to Find" from *A Good Man Is Hard to Find and Other Stories,* by Flannery O'Connor, copyright 1955 by Flannery O'Connor; renewed 1983 by Regina O'Connor. Reprinted by permission of Harcourt Brace Jovanovich, Inc.

Frank O'Hara: "The Day Lady Died." Copyright © 1964 by Frank O'Hara. Reprinted by permission of City Lights Books. "To the Harbormaster," "Blocks," "To the Film Industry in Crisis" from *Meditations in an Emergency.* Copyright © 1957 by Frank O'Hara. Reprinted by permission of Grove Press, Inc. "An Image of Leda," "A Step Away from Them," "Why I Am Not a Painter," "Poetry," "A True Account of Talking to the Sun at Fire Island," "Ave Maria," "First Dances." From *The Selected Poems of Frank O'Hara,* edited by Donald Allen. Copyright © 1973 by Maureen Granville-Smith, Administratrix of the Estate of Frank O'Hara. Reprinted by permission of Alfred A. Knopf, Inc.

Tillie Olsen: "I Stand Here Ironing" excerpted from the book *Tell Me a Riddle,* by Tillie Olsen. Copyright © 1956 by Tillie Olsen. Reprinted by permission of Delacorte Press/Seymour Lawrence.

Charles Olson: From "Projective Verse." Copyright © 1950, 1967 by Charles Olson. Reprinted by permission of the Estate of Charles Olson.

Eugene O'Neill: *Hughie,* by Eugene O'Neill. © 1959 by Carlotta Monterey O'Neill. © as an unpublished work

1959 by Carlotta Monterey O'Neill. Reprinted by permission of the publishers, Yale University Press.

Grace Paley: "A Conversation with My Father" from *Enormous Changes at the Last Minute,* by Grace Paley. Copyright © 1972 by Grace Paley. Reprinted by permission of Farrar, Straus and Giroux, Inc.

Walker Percy: "The Last Donahue Show" from *Lost in the Cosmos,* by Walker Percy. Copyright © 1983 by Walker Percy. Reprinted by permission of Farrar, Straus and Giroux, Inc.

Dexter Perkins: From *The New Age of Franklin Roosevelt, 1932–45.* © 1957 by The University of Chicago. Reprinted by permission of The University of Chicago Press.

Joan Peyser: "The Music of Sound or, The Beatles and the Beatless." Reprinted by permission from *The Columbia Forum.* Copyright © 1967 by The Trustees of Columbia University in the City of New York. All rights reserved.

Robert Pinsky: "Memorial." Copyright © 1979 by Robert Pinsky. Reprinted by permission of the author. "The Unseen," "Dying," "Song of Reasons" from *History of My Heart* copyright © 1984 by Robert Pinsky. Published by The Ecco Press in 1984. Reprinted by permission. *Sadness and Happiness: Poems by Robert Pinsky.* Copyright © 1975 by Princeton University Press. Excerpt "From Essay on Psychiatrists: #2, #3, #10" reprinted with permission of Princeton University Press.

Sylvia Plath: From *The Collected Poems of Sylvia Plath,* edited by Ted Hughes: "The Moon and the Yew Tree," "The Bee Meeting," "The Arrival of the Bee Box," "Daddy," "Lady Lazarus," "Death & Co.," "Winter Trees," "Child," "Kindness," and "Edge." Copyright © 1963 by Ted Hughes. "Black Rook in Rainy Weather." Copyright © 1960 by Ted Hughes. "Crossing the Water." Copyright © 1962 by Ted Hughes. "Morning Song." Copyright © 1961 by Ted Hughes. "Blackberrying." Copyright © 1962 by Ted Hughes. "The Hanging Man," "Parliament Hill Fields," "Ariel," "Sheep in Fog," "Words," and "Medusa." Copyright © 1965 by Ted Hughes. "Poppies in October." Copyright © 1963 by the Estate of Sylvia Plath. Reprinted by permission of Harper & Row, Publishers, Inc. "The Colossus." Copyright © 1961 by Sylvia Plath. Reprinted from *The Colossus and Other Poems,* by Sylvia Plath, by permission of Alfred A. Knopf, Inc. All poems from *Ariel, The Colossus,* and *Crossing the Water,* by Sylvia Plath. Published by Faber & Faber, London. Copyright Ted Hughes 1971, 1967, and 1965. Reprinted by permission of Olwyn Hughes.

Katherine Anne Porter: "Old Mortality" from *Pale Horse, Pale Rider,* by Katherine Anne Porter. Copyright 1937, 1964 by Katherine Anne Porter. Reprinted from her volume *Pale Horse, Pale Rider* by permission of Harcourt Brace Jovanovich, Inc.

Ezra Pound: "In a Station of the Metro," "Sestina: Altaforte," "The Garden," "Salutation," "A Pact," "The River Merchant's Wife: A Letter," and "From Hugh Selwyn Mauberley, I–V" from *Personae.* Copyright 1926 Ezra Pound. "Canto I," "Canto XVI," "Canto LXXXI," "Canto CXV," and "Canto XLV" from *The Cantos of Ezra Pound.* Copyright 1934, 1948, © 1962 by Ezra

Pound. "A Few Don'ts," "American Scenes," and "Credo" from *The Literary Essays of Ezra Pound.* Copyright 1935 by Ezra Pound. Reprinted by permission of New Directions Publishing Corporation.

Thomas Pynchon: "Entropy" from *Slow Learner,* by Thomas Pynchon. Copyright © by Thomas Pynchon. First appeared in *The Kenyon Review.* By permission of Little, Brown and Company in association with Atlantic Monthly Press.

John Crowe Ransom: "Piazza Piece," "Parting Without a Sequel," "Vision by Sweetwater," "Dead Boy," "The Equilibrists." Copyright 1927 by Alfred A. Knopf, Inc. and renewed 1955 by John Crowe Ransom. Reprinted from *Selected Poems, Third Edition, Revised and Enlarged,* by John Crowe Ransom, by permission of Random House, Inc.

David Reisman: From *The Lonely Crowd: A Study of the Changing American Character.* Reprinted by permission of Yale University Press.

Gerald Reitlinger: From *The Final Solution,* by Gerald Reitlinger. Published by George Weidenfeld & Nicolson Limited.

Adrienne Rich: "Snapshots of a Daughter-in-Law," "Living in Sin," "Necessities of Life," "I Am in Danger —Sir," "Orion," "Study of History," "Planetarium," selections from "Shooting Script," "Trying To Talk with a Man," "Diving into the Wreck," "Translations," "From a Survivor," "The Middle-Aged," "Peeling Onions" from *Poems, Selected and New, 1950–1971,* by Adrienne Rich. Copyright © 1975, 1973, 1971, 1969, 1966 by W. W. Norton & Company, Inc. Copyright © 1967, 1963, 1962, 1961, 1960, 1959, 1958, 1957, 1956, 1955, 1954, 1953, 1952, 1951 by Adrienne Rich. "Upper Broadway" from *The Dream of a Common Language, Poems 1974–1977,* by Adrienne Rich. Copyright © 1978 by W. W. Norton & Company, Inc. "Grandmothers" from *A Wild Patience Has Taken Me This Far, Poems 1978–1981,* by Adrienne Rich. Copyright © 1981 by Adrienne Rich. All reprinted by permission of W. W. Norton & Company, Inc.

John Rollin Ridge: From *The Life and Adventures of Joaquín Murieta: The Celebrated California Bandit,* by Yellow Bird [John Rollin Ridge]. New edition copyright 1955 by the University of Oklahoma Press.

Edwin Arlington Robinson: "The Corridor." Copyright 1915 by Edwin Arlington Robinson, renewed 1943 by Ruth Nivison. "Eros Turannos" and "The Unforgiven." Copyright 1916 by Edwin Arlington Robinson, renewed 1944 by Ruth Nivison. "The Mill" and "The New Tenants." Copyright 1920 by Edwin Arlington Robinson, renewed 1948 by Ruth Nivison. "Not Always, II" and "New England." Copyright 1925 by Edwin Arlington Robinson, renewed 1953 by Ruth Nivison and Barbara R. Holt. All reprinted with permission of Macmillan Publishing Company from *Collected Poems,* by Edwin Arlington Robinson.

Theodore Roethke: "My Papa's Waltz" copyright 1942 by Hearst Magazines, Inc.; "Dolor" copyright 1943 by Modern Poetry Association; "Weed Puller" copyright 1946 by Editorial Publications, Inc.; "Heard in a Violent Ward" copyright © 1964 by Beatrice Roethke as Administratrix of the Estate of Theodore Roethke; "Lost Son," "Cuttings," "Cuttings (Later)," "Elegy for Jane," and "The Waking" copyright 1947, 1948, 1950, 1953 by Theodore Roethke. Reprinted from *The Collected Poems of Theodore Roethke* by permission of Doubleday & Company, Inc.

Henry Roth: From *Call It Sleep*. Reprinted by permission of Cooper Square Publishers, Totowa, NJ.

Philip Roth: "I Always Wanted You to Admire My Fasting; Or Looking at Kafka" from *Reading Myself and Others*, by Philip Roth. Copyright © 1973, 1975 by Philip Roth. Reprinted by permission of Farrar, Straus and Giroux, Inc.

Bertrand Russell: From *The Basic Writings of Bertrand Russell*, edited by Robert E. Egner and Lester E. Denenn. Copyright © 1961 by Allen & Unwin. Reprinted by permission of Simon & Schuster, Inc. and Allen & Unwin.

Carl Sandburg: "Grass," "Cool Tombs," and "Portrait of a Motorcar" from *Cornhuskers*, by Carl Sandburg, copyright 1918 by Holt, Rinehart and Winston, Inc.; renewed 1946 by Carl Sandburg. "Graceland," "Fog," and "Chicago" from *Chicago Poems*, by Carl Sandburg, copyright 1916 by Holt, Rinehart and Winston, Inc.; renewed 1944 by Carl Sandburg. All reprinted by permission of Harcourt Brace Jovanovich, Inc.

Seattle: ["Our People Are Ebbing Away Like a Rapidly Receding Tide."] Reprinted from *Great Documents in American Indian History*, copyright by Praeger Publishers 1973.

Anne Sexton: "Her Kind" and "Ringing the Bells" from *To Bedlam and Part Way Back*, by Anne Sexton. Copyright © 1960 by Anne Sexton. "With Mercy for the Greedy" from *All My Pretty Ones*, by Anne Sexton. Copyright © 1962 by Anne Sexton. "Self in 1958" from *Live or Die*, by Anne Sexton. Copyright © 1966 by Anne Sexton. "Snow White" from *Transformations*, by Anne Sexton. Copyright © 1971 by Anne Sexton. "The Silence" from *The Book of Folly*, by Anne Sexton. Copyright © 1972 by Anne Sexton. "January 1st" from *Words for Dr. Y*, by Anne Sexton. Copyright © 1978 by Linda Gray Sexton and Loring Conant, Jr., Executors of the Will of Anne Sexton. "For My Lover, Returning to His Wife" from *Love Poems*, by Anne Sexton. Copyright © 1967, 1968, 1969 by Anne Sexton. All reprinted by permission of Houghton Mifflin Company.

Leslie Marmon Silko: "Storyteller." Copyright © 1981 by Leslie Marmon Silko. Reprinted from *Storyteller*, by Leslie Marmon Silko, published by Seaver Books, New York, 1981. Reprinted by permission of the publisher.

Charles Simic: From "Negative Capability and Its Children." © 1978 by Charles Simic. "The Cold," "Winter Night," and "Old Couple" © 1983 by Charles Simic. Reprinted by permission of the author. "Fear," "Hearing Steps," "Fork," and "My Shoes" from *Dismantling the Silence*, by Charles Simic. "The Elders," "Charon's Cosmology," "The Lesson," "A Wall," and "The Healer" from *Charon's Cosmology*, by Charles Simic. "Shirt" and "Grocery" from *Classic Ballroom Dances*, by Charles Simic. Reprinted by permission of the publisher, George Braziller Inc., New York.

Dave Smith: "Hawktree" and "Over the Ozarks, Because I Saw Them, Stars Came." Reprinted by permission of the author. "On a Field Trip at Fredericksburg" and "Cumberland Station" from *Cumberland Station* (University of Illinois Press). © 1975 Dave Smith. Originally

in *The New Yorker*. "Looking for the Melungeon" and "Rain Forest" from *Goshawk, Antelope* (University of Illinois Press). © 1976 and 1978, respectively, Dave Smith. Originally in *The New Yorker*. "Sea Owl" and "Smithfield Ham" from *In the House of the Judge*, by Dave Smith. Copyright © 1983 by Dave Smith. Reprinted by permission of Harper & Row, Publishers, Inc. "Desks" and "Reading the Books Our Children Have Written." Reprinted by permission of Louisiana State University Press from *Homage to Edgar Allan Poe*, by Dave Smith, copyright © 1981. From *Local Assays*, by Dave Smith. © 1985 by the Board of Trustees of the University of Illinois. Reprinted by permission of the University of Illinois Press.

Gary Snyder: "Riprap" © 1965 by Gary Snyder. Reprinted by permission of the author. "I Went into the Maverick Bar," "The Call of the Wild," and "Two Fawns That Didn't See the Light This Spring" from *Turtle Island*. Copyright © 1974 by Gary Snyder. "This Poem Is for Bear" from *Myths & Texts*. Copyright © 1979 by Gary Snyder. "Trail Crew Camp at Bear Valley," "Sixth Month Song in the Foothills," "Nansen," and "Looking at Pictures to Be Put Away" from *The Back Country*. Copyright © 1966, 1968 by Gary Snyder. Reprinted by permission of New Directions Publishing Corporation.

Susan Sontag: "America, Seen Through Photographs, Darkly" from *On Photography*, by Susan Sontag. Copyright © 1973, 1974, 1977 by Susan Sontag. Reprinted by permission of Farrar, Straus and Giroux, Inc.

Gertrude Stein: "The Work" and "Miguel (Collusion). Guimpe. Candle" from *Bee Time Vine and Other Poems*, by Gertrude Stein. Copyright, 1953, by Alice B. Toklas. Reprinted by permission of the publishers, Yale University Press. "The Gentle Lena" from *Three Lives*, by Gertrude Stein. Copyright 1909 and renewed 1937 by Gertrude Stein. From *The Autobiography of Alice B. Toklas*, by Gertrude Stein. Copyright 1933 and renewed 1961 by Alice B. Toklas. Reprinted by permission of Random House, Inc. From *Wars I Have Seen*, by Gertrude Stein. Copyright 1945 by Random House, Inc. Reprinted by permission of the publisher.

John Steinbeck: "The Leader of the People" from *The Long Valley*, by John Steinbeck. Copyright 1938, renewed © 1966 by John Steinbeck. Reprinted by permission of Viking Penguin Inc.

Wallace Stevens: "The Course of a Particular," "Of Mere Being," from "Adagia" Copyright © 1957 by Elsie Stevens and Holly Stevens. Reprinted from *Opus Posthumous*, by Wallace Stevens, edited by Samuel French Morse. "Sunday Morning," "Thirteen Ways of Looking at a Blackbird," "Anecdote of the Jar," "The Paltry Nude Starts on a Spring Voyage," "The Emperor of Ice-Cream," "The Idea of Order at Key West," "A Postcard from the Volcano," "Arrival at the Waldorf," "No Possum, No Sop, No Taters," "Angel Surrounded by Paysans," "Final Soliloquy of the Interior Paramour," "The Plain Sense of Things," "The Planet on the Table," "The River of Rivers in Connecticut," "Not Ideas About the Thing but the Thing Itself," "The Auroras of Autumn" from *The Collected Poems of Wallace Stevens*. Copyright 1954 by Wallace Stevens. "The Snow Man" from *The Collected Poems of Wallace Stevens*. Copyright 1923 and renewed 1951 by Wallace Stevens. "What Is the Poet's Function" from *The Necessary Angel*, by Wallace Stevens. All reprinted by permission of Alfred A. Knopf, Inc.

Index of Authors,
Titles, and First Lines
of Poems